THE COLUMBIA
GRANGER'S®

INDEX TO POETRY
in Collected and Selected Works

OTHER COLUMBIA UNIVERSITY PRESS PUBLICATIONS

The Columbia Granger's® World of Poetry Online at www.columbiagrangers.org

The Columbia Granger's® Index to Poetry in Anthologies, Twelfth Edition (2001)

The Columbia Granger's® Index to African-American Poetry (1999)

THE COLUMBIA
GRANGER'S®
INDEX TO POETRY
in Collected and Selected Works

SECOND EDITION, COMPLETELY REVISED
INDEXING WORKS
PUBLISHED THROUGH MARCH 31, 2003

EDITED BY

KEITH NEWTON

COLUMBIA UNIVERSITY PRESS
NEW YORK

LIBRARY OF CONGRESS CATALOGING-IN-PUBLICATION DATA

Newton, Keith.
The Columbia Granger's Index to Poetry in collected and selected
works / edited by Keith Newton. — 2nd ed., completely rev.
p.   cm.
ISBN 0–231–12528–3
1. Poetry—Indexes. 2. English poetry—Indexes.
I. Newton, Keith, 1974–
PN1022.C63   2004
016.80881—dc21   2003051469
CIP

Casebound Editions of Columbia University Press Books
are printed on permanent and durable acid-free paper.

Printed in the United States of America
c   10 9 8 7 6 5 4 3 2 1

CONTENTS

The Columbia Granger's® Index to Poetry in Collected and Selected Works

SECOND EDITION

DIRECTOR OF DESIGN AND PRODUCTION
Linda Secondari

EDITORIAL MANAGER, GRANGER'S
Tessa Kale

EDITOR
Keith Newton

EDITOR, ELECTRONIC REFERENCE
Stephen Sterns

STAFF

Amy Carothers	Eugene Lim
Colin Enriquez	Kiva Offenholley
Haesun Kim	Joanna Sondheim

PREFACE

The second edition of *The Columbia Granger's® Index to Poetry in Collected and Selected Works* greatly expands the range of one of the oldest continuously published reference works in the United States. With the publication of the first edition in 1996, Granger's effectively became a two-volume work, indexing the two types of poetry books most frequently shelved by libraries—anthologies and collections of the work of individual authors. The companion volume, *The Columbia Granger's® Index to Poetry in Anthologies*, has been published by Columbia University Press since the fourth edition in 1953 and is now in its twelfth edition.

The works in this volume were chosen by the editorial staff of Granger's, together with our consultants, Richard Howard and William Harmon, with many considerations in mind. The most important—whether the work is likely to be found on the shelves of libraries—guided our selections, yet other considerations were also instrumental, such as the importance and reputation of the poet and the editorial and design standards of the book.

Included in this edition are the works of many of the major American and British poets of the last thirty years, such as Robert Pinsky, Seamus Heaney, and Paul Muldoon; important twentieth-century American poets, such as Langston Hughes, Kenneth Rexroth, Lorine Niedecker, George Oppen, Stanley Kunitz, Denise Levertov, Dorothy Parker, and Robert Penn Warren; twentieth-century foreign-language poets in new translations, such as Eugenio Montale, Federico García Lorca, Constantine Cavafy, Czeslaw Milosz, Paul Celan, Wisława Szymborska, Yehuda Amichai, and Joseph Brodsky; and poets from all times and places, collected in new editions, such as Guido Cavalcanti, Cold Mountain, Jelaluddin Rumi, Jones Very, Dante Gabriel Rossetti, and G. K. Chesterton.

In total, the second edition includes 315 works, by 266 different poets, locating more than 65,000 poems by title, first line, author, and subject. In addition to works that have been previously indexed, we've added revised and varied editions of the collected and selected works of poets such as Robert Browning, T. S. Eliot, and Adrienne Rich, in order to keep the index current with library collections.

This edition also includes an expanded subject index. There are now more than 4,400 subjects, including many new subjects relating to specific people, places, or events from the history and culture of the twentieth century. Langston Hughes's poems on the Scottsboro case and the Spanish Civil War, Ai's poems on Robert Oppenheimer and J. Edgar Hoover, and Octavio Paz's poems on Marcel Duchamp and Robert Rauschenberg are as easy to find as Wallace Stevens's poems about perception and Yusef Komunyakaa's poems about jazz. The poems in the Subject Index are arranged alphabetically by authors' names, allowing for quick identification.

HOW TO USE THE INDEXES

This volume is divided into three sections:
- —Title and First Line Index
- —Author Index
- —Subject Index

Each section is arranged alphabetically.

Every poem covered here is cited at least once in each of the three sections (except for those that are too abstract to be assigned to any heading in the Subject Index). Every poem cited here appears in at least one volume of the collected and selected works listed on pages xiii–xxii.

See also the explanatory notes at the beginning of each of the three sections, pages 1, 1049, and 1309.

Title and First Line Index

The clearest way to explain the Title and First Line Index is to begin by showing how it answers specific questions brought to it.

Where can I find a poem called "Electric Elegy"*?* Go to the Title and First Line Index. The citation for "Electric Elegy" is followed by the name of the poem's author, Adam Zagajewski, and by the letter code SP-ZagaA. Look up SP-ZagaA in the List of Collected and Selected Works, where the codes, not the titles of the works, are arranged alphabetically. The prefixes "CP-," "SP-," and "MW-" were ignored in the alphabetization of this list. Therefore, SP-ZagaA can be found between CP-YeatW and SP-ZatuM. Here you learn that you can read "Electric Elegy" in *Without End: New and Selected Poems* by Adam Zagajewski, published by Farrar, Straus and Giroux in 2002.

What is the title of the poem that begins "Well they are gone, and here must I remain"*?* The first-line citation is followed by the title, "This Lime-Tree Bower My Prison," and then by the author, Samuel Taylor Coleridge, and two letter codes, CP-ColeS and MW-ColeS. The List of Collected and Selected Works shows that the codes stand for two collected works of Coleridge's poetry: *Poems*, edited by John Beer and published by Everyman in 1993, and *The Major Works*, edited by H. J. Jackson and published by Oxford University Press in 2000.

Titles. Initial capitals in important words usually indicate that the citation is the title of the poem. For example, "Oregon Landscape with Lost Lover," by Olga Broumas, is a title.

First Lines. First-line citations are followed by the title, except where the poem has no title. You know, for example, that "Oh! kangaroos, sequins, chocolate sodas!" is not a title because the title, "Today," follows it, and because the initial letters of all the words (except the first one) are lowercase.

Brackets. Brackets usually show variant spellings. For example, see the first-line citation "Earth has not anything to show [*or* shew] more fair." In the different works in which that first line appears, the spelling may vary as indicated in brackets.

Capitalization. The first letter of the first word in every citation is capitalized, even when in its published form it appears as lowercase.

Initial Articles. An article—"a," "an," or "the"—that begins a title or a line is transposed to the end of the citation. "The Return" by Ezra Pound, for example, is listed as "Return, The."

Parentheses. When an entire citation is enclosed by parentheses, it usually means that it is a variant title or variant first line. Parentheses are used instead of brackets when it is necessary to indicate a version that varies widely from the standard version, with the result that, in this alphabetized index, it can also be found in a place that may be far from where the standard version is listed.

See, for example, "Elegy upon the Untimely Death of the Incomparable Prince Henry" by John Donne:

> Elegy upon the Untimely Death of the Incomparable Prince Henry. John Donne. CP-DonnJ
> (Elegy on Prince Henry.) MW-DonnJ

In the work indicated by the code CP-DonnJ, *The Complete English Poems*, the poem can be found under the title, "Elegy upon the Untimely Death of the Incomparable Prince Henry." But in the work indicated by the code MW-DonnJ, *The Major Works*, the same poem can be found under a different title, "Elegy on Prince Henry." This information is especially useful when looking for a poem in the table of contents or the title or first line index of the indicated work.

Indentation. Indentation of a citation indicates that it is a selection. See, for example, "Treatise on Poetry, A," by Czeslaw Milosz:

> Treatise on Poetry, A. Czeslaw Milosz. CP-MiloCN, *tr. by* Robert Hass
>   Preface. CP-MiloC, *tr. by* Robert Hass
>   Beautiful Times.
>   Cabbies dozed under St. Mary's Tower. CP-MiloC, *tr. by* Robert Hass
>   Spirit of History, The.
>   Under a linden tree, as before, daylight. CP-MiloC, *tr. by* Robert Hass

"Preface," "Beautiful Times," and "Spirit of History, The" are indented because they are selections from "Treatise on Poetry, A." "Cabbies dozed under St. Mary's Tower" and "Under a linden tree, as before, daylight" are further indented because they are selections from "Beautiful Times" and "Spirit of History, The," respectively. The complete poem, "Treatise on Poetry, A," can be found in the work to which the code CP-MiloCN refers, *New and Collected Poems (1931–2001)*, while only the selections "Preface," "Cabbies dozed under St. Mary's Tower," and "Under a linden tree, as before, daylight" can be found in the work to which the code CP-MiloC refers, *The Collected Poems*.

Author Index

Under each author's name, poems are listed alphabetically by title or, where the poem has no title, by first line.
What poems can I find by Denise Levertov? The Author Index lists 431 poems.

Subject Index

Under each subject heading, poems are listed alphabetically by author's name.

What poems can I find about marriage? The subject index shows that there are 507 poems about marriage, by 140 different poets. Citations for all these poems can be found in the Title and First Line Index, where the letter codes, which refer to the List of Collected and Selected Works, indicate in which books the poems are published.

Did Stephen Crane write poems about religion? Go to the heading for "Religion" and locate "Crane, S." in the list of poems alphabetized by author.

LIST OF COLLECTED AND SELECTED WORKS

The collected and selected works in this list are arranged alphabetically by their codes, not by their titles. The prefixes "CP-," "SP-," and "MW-" were ignored in the alphabetization of this list, so that works can be found solely by the author's last name, which is abbreviated in the code directly after the prefix.

SP-Ai   Vice; New and Selected Poems [Ai]. (1999) W.W. Norton. 256p.

SP-AmicY   The Selected Poetry of Yehuda Amichai. *Chana Bloch and Stephen Mitchell, ed.* (2nd ed., 1996) University of California Press. 194p.

SP-AmicYL   Yehuda Amichai: A Life of Poetry 1948–1994. *Benjamin and Barbara Harshav, ed.* (1994) HarperCollins. 477p.

CP-AmmoA   Collected Poems 1951–1971 [A. R. Ammons]. (2001) W. W. Norton. 396p.

SP-AngeM   Maya Angelou; Poems. (1986) Bantam Books / Random House. 209p., pap.

SP-ArmaA   Veil; New and Selected Poems [Rae Armantrout]. (2001) Wesleyan University Press. 147p., pap.

SP-ArnoM   Selected Poems and Prose [Matthew Arnold]. *Allott, Miriam, ed.* (1993) J. M. Dent. 293p., pap.

SP-AshbJ   Selected Poems [John Ashbery]. (1986) Penguin Books. 348p., pap.

SP-AtwM1   Selected Poems, 1965–1975 [Margaret Atwood]. (1976) Houghton Mifflin. 240p., pap.

SP-AtwM2   Selected Poems II; Poems Selected and New, 1976–1986 [Margaret Atwood]. (1987) Houghton Mifflin. 147p., pap.

CP-AudeW   Collected Poems [W. H. Auden]. *Mendelson, Edward, ed.* (1991) Vintage. 926p., pap.

CP-AustJ   The Poetry of Jane Austen and the Austen Family. *David Selwyn, ed.* (1997) University of Iowa Press. 106p.

CP-BaudC   Complete Poems [Charles Baudelaire]. *Walter Martin, ed.* (1997) Carcanet. 447p.

CP-BeckS   Collected Poems 1930–1978 [Samuel Beckett]. (1984) John Calder. 179p.

CP-BerrJ   Collected Poems, 1937–1971 [John Berryman]. (1989) Farrar, Straus and Giroux. 348p., pap.

SP-BerrT   Selected Poems [Ted Berrigan]. *Saroyan, Aram, ed.* (1994) Penguin Books. 142p., pap.

CP-BerrW   Collected Poems, 1957–1982 [Wendell Berry]. (1984) Farrar, Straus and Giroux. 268p.

SP-BierA   Poems of Ambrose Bierce. *M. E. Grenander, ed.* (1995) University of Nebraska Press. 202p.

CP-BishE   The Complete Poems, 1927–1979 [Elizabeth Bishop]. (1983) Farrar, Straus and Giroux. 287p., pap.

CP-BlakW   The Complete Poems [William Blake]. *Ostriker, Alicia, ed.* (1977) Penguin Books. 1,071p., pap.

SP-BlokA   Selected Poems of Aleksandr Blok. (2nd ed., 2000) Carcanet. 123p., pap.

SP-BlueP   Clans of Many Nations; Selected Poems 1969–1994 [Peter Blue Cloud]. (1995) White Pine Press. 166p., pap.

SP-BlyR   Selected Poems of Robert Bly. (1986) HarperCollins. 211p., pap.

CP-BogaL   The Blue Estuaries; Poems 1923–1968 [Louise Bogan]. (1968; repr. 1988) Ecco Press. 136p., pap.

SP-BorgJ   Selected Poems [Jorge Luis Borges]. *Alexander Coleman, ed.* (2000) Penguin. 483p., pap.

CP-BradA   The Poems of Mrs. Anne Bradstreet. (1897) The De Vinne Press. 347p.

CP-BroEB   The Complete Poetical Works of Mrs. Browning [Elizabeth Barrett Browning]. *Harriet Waters Preston, ed.* (1900) Houghton Mifflin. 548p.

SP-BroR   Selected Poems [Robert Browning]. *Daniel Karlin, ed.* (1989) Penguin. 340p., pap.

CP-BroR1   The Poems; Vol. 1 [Robert Browning]. *John Pettigrew, ed.* (1981) Penguin. 1,191p., pap.

CP-BroR2   The Poems; Vol. 2 [Robert Browning]. *John Pettigrew, ed.* (1981) Penguin. 1,167p., pap.

CP-BrodJ   Collected Poems in English [Joseph Brodsky]. *Ann Kjellberg, ed.* (2000) Farrar, Straus and Giroux. 540p.

CP-BronE   The Complete Poems of Emily Jane Brontë. (1941) Columbia University Press. 262p.

SP-BrooG   Selected Poems by Gwendolyn Brooks. (1963) Harper & Row. 127p., pap.

SP-BrouO   Rave; Poems 1975–1999 [Olga Broumas]. (1999) Copper Canyon. 363p., pap.

SP-BukC1   Love Is a Dog from Hell; Poems 1974–1977 [Charles Bukowski].   (1993)   Black Sparrow Press. 307p., pap.

SP-BukC2   The Roominghouse Madrigals; Early Selected Poems 1946–1966 [Charles Bukowski].   (1988) Black Sparrow Press. 256p., pap.

SP-BukC3   War All the Time; Poems 1981–1984 [Charles Bukowski].   (1984)   Black Sparrow Press. 280p.

CP-BurnR   Burns; Complete Poems and Songs.   *James Kinsley, ed.*   (1969)   Oxford University Press. 786p., pap.

CP-Byron   The Poems of Byron.   *Paul E. More, ed.*   (1933)   Houghton Mifflin. 1,055p.

CP-CampT   The Works of Thomas Campion.   *Walter R. Davis, ed.*   (1969)   W. W. Norton. 521p., pap.

CP-CarHL   Collected Longer Poems [Hayden Carruth].   (1994)   Copper Canyon Press. 205p., pap.

CP-CarHS   Collected Shorter Poems, 1946–1991 [Hayden Carruth].   (1992)   Copper Canyon Press. 417p., pap.

CP-CareT   Poems of Thomas Carew.   *Arthur Vincent, ed.*   (1899; reprinted 1972)   Books for Libraries Press. 264p.

CP-CarvR   All of Us; The Collected Poems [Raymond Carver].   *William A. Stull, ed.*   (1996)   Alfred A. Knopf. 386p.

CP-Catul   The Poems of Catullus.   *Peter Whigham, ed.*   (1966)   Penguin Books. 246p., pap.

CP-CavaC   Before Time Could Change Them; The Complete Poems of Constantine P. Cavafy.   *Theoharis C. Theoharis, ed.*   (2001)   Harcourt. 354p.

CP-CavaG   The Complete Poems [Guido Cavalcanti].   *Marc A. Cirigliano, ed.*   (1992)   Italica Press. 156p.

SP-CelaP   Selected Poems and Prose of Paul Celan.   *John Felstiner, ed.*   (2001)   W.W. Norton. 426p.

CP-ChauG   The Riverside Chaucer.   *F. N. Robinson, ed.*   (3rd ed., 1987)   Houghton Mifflin. 1,327p.

CP-ChesG   Collected Works [G. K. Chesterton]; Vol. 10: Collected Poetry, Part 1.   *Aidan Mackey, ed.*   (1994) Ignatius. 595p.

CP-CiarJ   The Collected Poems of John Ciardi.   *Edward M. Cifelli, ed.*   (1997)   University of Arkansas Press. 618p.

CP-ClamA   The Collected Poems of Amy Clampitt.   (1st ed., 1997)   Knopf. 471p.

SP-ClarJ   Selected Poems [John Clare].   *Elaine Feinstein, ed.*   (1968)   University Tutorial Press. 152p.

SP-ClifL   Blessing the Boats; New and Selected Poems 1988–2000 [Lucille Clifton].   (2000)   BOA Editions. 132p., pap.

SP-ClouA   Selected Poems [Arthur Hugh Clough].   *Jim McCue, ed.*   (1991)   Penguin Books. 252p., pap.

SP-CodrA   Alien Candor; Selected Poems 1970–1995 [Andrei Codrescu].   (1996)   Black Sparrow. 303p., pap.

CP-ColdM   The Collected Songs of Cold Mountain.   *Red Pine, ed.*   (2000)   Copper Canyon Press. 309p.

CP-ColeS   Poems [Samuel Taylor Coleridge].   *John Beer, ed.*   (1993)   Everyman. 535p., pap.

MW-ColeS   The Major Works [Samuel Taylor Coleridge].   *H. J. Jackson, ed.*   (2000)   Oxford University Press. 733p.

SP-CollB   Sailing Alone Around the Room; New and Selected Poems [Billy Collins].   (2001)   Random House. 172p., pap.

CP-CoopJ   The Flashboat: Poems Collected and Reclaimed [Jane Cooper].   (2000)   W.W. Norton. 263p.

SP-CorbW   New & Selected Poems [William Corbett].   (1995)   Zoland Books. 246p.

CP-CowpW   The Poetical Works of William Cowper.   *H. S. Milford, ed.*   (1926, 3rd ed.)   Oxford University Press. 677p.

SP-CrabG   Selections from the Poems of George Crabbe.   *Anthony C. Deane, ed.*   (1903, repr. 1932)   Methuen. 251p., pap.

CP-CranH   Complete Poems of Hart Crane.   (1986)   Liveright. 269p., pap.

CP-CranS   The Complete Poems of Stephen Crane.   *Joseph Katz, ed.*   (1972)   Cornell University Press. 154p.

CP-CrasR   The Complete Poetry of Richard Crashaw.   *Williams, George Walton, ed.*   (1972)   New York University Press. 707p.

CP-CreeR   The Collected Poems of Robert Creeley, 1945–1975.   (1982)   University of California Press. 671p., pap.

SP-CreeR   So There; Poems 1976–83 [Robert Creeley].   (1998)   New Directions. 248p., pap.

CP-CullC   My Soul's High Song; the Collected Writings of Countee Cullen, Voice of the Harlem Renaissance. *Gerald Early, ed.*   (1991)   Doubleday. 618p., pap.

SP-CummE   100 Selected Poems by E. E. Cummings.   (1959; repr. 1988)   Grove Press. 121p., pap.

CP-CummE   Complete Poems, 1904–1962 [E. E. Cummings]. *George J. Firmage, ed.* (1991) Liveright. 1,102p.

CP-CunnJ   The Poems of J. V. Cunningham. *Timothy Steele, ed.* (1997) Swallow Press/Ohio Univ. Press. 215p.

SP-DariR   Selected Poems of Rubén Darío. *Alberto Acereda and Will Derusha, ed.* (2001) Bucknell University Press. 268p.

CP-DaviDC   Collected Poems [Donald Davie]. *Neil Powell, ed.* (2002) Carcanet. 634p.

CP-DeLaW   Collected Poems [Walter De La Mare]. (1941) Henry Holt. 327p.

CP-DickE   The Complete Poems of Emily Dickinson. *Thomas H. Johnson, ed.* (1960) Little, Brown. 770p., pap.

SP-DickE   New Poems of Emily Dickinson. *William H. Shurr and Anna Dunlap and Emily Grey S, ed.* (1993) University of North Carolina Press. 125p.

CP-DickJ   The Whole Motion; Collected Poems, 1945–1992 [James Dickey]. (1992) Wesleyan University Press / University Press of New England. 475p., pap.

SP-DickW   In the Dreaming; Selected Poems [William Dickey]. (1994) University of Arkansas Press. 106p.

CP-DonnJ   The Complete English Poems [John Donne]. *A. J. Smith, ed.* (1971) Penguin Books. 677p., pap.

MW-DonnJ   The Major Works [John Donne]. *John Carey, ed.* (2000) Oxford University Press. 488p.

CP-DoolH   Collected Poems, 1912–1944 [H.D. (Hilda Doolittle)]. *Louis L. Martz, ed.* (1983) New Directions. 629p., pap.

SP-DoveR   Selected Poems [Rita Dove]. (1993) Vintage Books. 207p., pap.

CP-DryJ2   The Poems of John Dryden. Vol. 2, 1682–1685. *Paul Hammond, ed.* (1995) Longman. 447p.

SP-DrydJ   Dryden; Poems and Prose. *Douglas Grant, ed.* (1955; repr. 1985) Penguin Books. 357p., pap.

CP-DubiN   The Mercy Seat; Collected & New Poems 1967–2001 [Norman Dubie]. (2001) Copper Canyon. 409p.

CP-DugaA   Poems Seven; New and Complete Poetry [Alan Dugan]. (2001) Seven Stories Press. 422p.

CP-DunbP   The Collected Poetry of Paul Laurence Dunbar. *Joanne M. Braxton, ed.* (1993) University Press of Virginia. 396p., pap.

CP-DunbW   The Poems of William Dunbar. 2 Vols. *Priscilla Bawcutt, ed.* (1998) Assoc for Scottish Lit Studies. 621p.

SP-DuncR   Selected Poems [Robert Duncan]. *Robert J. Bertholf, ed.* (1993) New Directions. 147p., pap.

CP-EberR   Collected Poems, 1930–1986 [Richard Eberhart]. (1988) Oxford University Press. 444p.

CP-ElioT   Collected Poems 1909–1962 [T. S. Eliot]. (1963; repr. 1991) Harcourt Brace. 221p.

SP-ElioT   Inventions of the March Hare; Poems 1909–1917 [T. S. Eliot]. *Christopher Ricks, ed.* (1996) Faber and Faber. 428p.

CP-EmerR   Ralph Waldo Emerson; Collected Poems and Translations. *Harold Bloom and Paul Kane, ed.* (1994) The Library of America. 637p.

SP-EnzeH   Selected Poems [Hans Magnus Enzensberger]. (1999) Sheep Meadow Press. 261p., pap.

SP-FentJ   Children in Exile; Poems, 1968–1984 [James Fenton]. (1994) Farrar, Straus and Giroux. 110p., pap.

SP-FerlL   These Are My Rivers; New & Selected Poems [Lawrence Ferlinghetti]. (1993) New Directions. 308p.

CP-FrosR   The Poetry of Robert Frost. *Edward Connery Lathem, ed.* (1979) Henry Holt. 607p., pap.

SP-GallT   Amplitude; New and Selected Poems [Tess Gallagher]. (1987) Graywolf Press. 199p., pap.

SP-GarcF   The Selected Poems of Federico García Lorca. *Francisco García Lorca and Donald M. Allen, ed.* (1955) New Directions. 180p., pap.

CP-GarcF   Collected Poems [Federico García Lorca]. *Christopher Maurer, ed.* (Rev. ed., 2002) Farrar, Straus and Giroux. 990p.

CP-GinsA   Collected Poems 1947–1980 [Allen Ginsberg]. (1984) Harper & Row. 837p., pap.

SP-GinsA   Selected Poems 1947–1995 [Allen Ginsberg]. (1996) HarperCollins. 442p.

SP-GlucL   The First Four Books of Poems [Louise Glück]. (1995) The Ecco Press. 216p.

CP-GravR   Collected Poems, 1975 [Robert Graves]. (1988) Oxford University Press. 592p.

CP-GrayT   Gray's English Poems; Original and Translated from the Norse and the Welsh [Thomas Gray]. *D. C. Tovey, ed.* (1922) Reprint Services. 293p.

CP-GunnT   Collected Poems [Thom Gunn]. (1994) Faber and Faber. 495p.

SP-GurnI   Selected Poems [Ivor Gurney]. *P. J. Kavanagh, ed.* (1990) Oxford University Press. 149p., pap.

SP-HaNaS   Selected Poems of Shmuel HaNagid. *Peter Cole, ed.* (1996) Princeton University Press. 236p., pap.

SP-HackM   Selected Poems 1965–1990 [Marilyn Hacker]. (1994) W. W. Norton. 250p.

CP-HallD   Old and New Poems [Donald Hall]. (1990) Ticknor & Fields. 244p.

SP-HamiS   Destination Zero; Poems 1970–1995 [Sam Hamill]. (1995) White Pine Press. 235p., pap.

CP-HardT   The Complete Poems of Thomas Hardy. *James Gibson, ed.* (1978) Macmillan. 1,002p.

CP-HaydR   Collected Poems [Robert Hayden]. *Frederick Glaysher, ed.* (1985) Liveright. 205p., pap.

SP-HeanSO   Opened Ground; Selected Poems 1966–1996 [Seamus Heaney]. (1998) Farrar, Straus and Giroux. 444p.

CP-HerbG   The Complete English Poems [George Herbert]. *John Tobin, ed.* (1991) Penguin Books. 460p. pap.

CP-HerrR   The Poems of Robert Herrick. *L. C. Martin, ed.* (1965) Oxford University Press. 478p.

CP-HillG   New & Collected Poems, 1952–1992 [Geoffrey Hill]. (1994) Houghton Mifflin. 228p.

CP-HopkG   Gerard Manley Hopkins. *Catherine Phillips, ed.* (1986) Oxford University Press. 429p.

CP-HousA   The Collected Poems of A. E. Housman. (1965) Henry Holt. 254p., pap.

SP-HoweF   Selected Poems [Fanny Howe]. (2000) University of California Press. 213p., pap.

SP-HoweS   The Europe of Trusts [Susan Howe]. (1990) New Directions. 218p., pap.

SP-HoweSE   Frame Structures; Early Poems 1974–1979 [Susan Howe]. (1996) New Directions. 122p., pap.

CP-HughL   The Collected Poems of Langston Hughes. *Arnold Rampersad and David Roessel, ed.* (1995) Vintage Books. 717p.

CP-HughL1   The Collected Works of Langston Hughes; Vol. 1, The Poems: 1921–1940. *Arnold Rampersad, ed.* (2001) University of Missouri Press. 276p.

CP-HughL2   The Collected Works of Langston Hughes; Vol. 2, The Poems: 1941–1950. *Arnold Rampersad, ed.* (2001) University of Missouri Press. 292p.

CP-HughL3   The Collected Works of Langston Hughes; Vol. 3, The Poems: 1951–1967. *Arnold Rampersad, ed.* (2001) University of Missouri Press. 329p.

SP-HughTN   New Selected Poems 1957–1994 [Ted Hughes]. (1995) Faber and Faber. 332p.

SP-IgnaD   Against the Evidence; Selected Poems 1934–1994 [David Ignatow]. (1993) Wesleyan University Press. 178p., pap.

CP-JacoJ   In the Crevice of Time; New and Collected Poems [Josephine Jacobsen]. (1995) Johns Hopkins University Press. 258p.

CP-JarrR   The Complete Poems [Randall Jarrell]. (1969; repr. 1989) Farrar, Straus and Giroux. 507p., pap.

CP-JefR1   The Collected Poetry of Robinson Jeffers; Vol. 1. *Tim Hunt, ed.* (1988) Stanford University Press. 521p.

CP-JefR2   The Collected Poetry of Robinson Jeffers; Vol. 2. *Tim Hunt, ed.* (1989) Stanford University Press. 610p.

CP-JefR3   The Collected Poetry of Robinson Jeffers; Vol. 3. *Tim Hunt, ed.* (1991) Stanford University Press. 485p.

CP-JohnS   The Complete English Poems [Samuel Johnson]. *J. D. Fleeman, ed.* (1971) Penguin Books. 260p., pap.

CP-JonsB   The Complete Poems [Ben Jonson]. *George Parfitt, ed.* (1988) Penguin. 634p., pap.

SP-JonsB   Selected Poems [Ben Jonson]. *Ian Donaldson, ed.* (1995) Oxford University Press. 224p., pap.

CP-KeatJ   The Complete Poems [John Keats]. *John Barnard, ed.* (3d ed., 1988) Penguin. 754p., pap.

SP-KinnGN   New Selected Poems (Galway Kinnell). (1st ed., 2000) Houghton Mifflin. 171p.

CP-KinsT   Collected Poems 1956–1994 [Thomas Kinsella]. (1996) Oxford University Press. 339p.

CP-KiplR   Rudyard Kipling; Complete Verse; Definitive Edition. (1989) Doubleday. 850p., pap.

CP-KizeC   Cool, Calm and Collected; Poems, 1960–2000 [Carolyn Kizer]. (2001) Copper Canyon Press. 509p.

SP-KochK   Selected Poems, 1950–1982 [Kenneth Koch]. (1985) Random House. 239p.

CP-KomuY   Pleasure Dome; New and Collected Poems [Yusef Komunyakaa]. (2001) Wesleyan University Press. 445p.

SP-KumiM   Selected Poems 1960–1990 [Maxine Kumin]. (1997) W.W. Norton. 294p., pap.

CP-KunSC   The Collected Poems [Stanley Kunitz]. (2000) W.W. Norton. 285p.

CP-LarkP   Collected Poems of Philip Larkin. *Anthony Thwaite, ed.* (1988) Farrar, Straus and Giroux. 330p.

CP-LaugJ   The Collected Poems of James Laughlin.   (1994)   Moyer Bell. 574p.

CP-LawrD   The Complete Poems [D. H. Lawrence].   *Vivian de Sola Pinto and Warren Roberts, ed.*   (1993)   Penguin Books. 1,079p., pap.

SP-LeveDL   Poems 1972–1982 [Denise Levertov].   (2001)   New Directions. 280p., pap.

SP-LeveDP   Poems 1960–1967 [Denise Levertov].   (1983)   New Directions. 247p., pap.

SP-LeveDS   Selected Poems [Denise Levertov].   *Paul A. Lacey, ed.*   (2002)   New Directions. 220p., pap.

SP-LeviP   New Selected Poems [Philip Levine].   (1991)   Alfred A. Knopf. 292p.

CP-LeviP   Collected Poems [Primo Levi].   *Ruth Feldman and Brian Swann, ed.*   (1988)   Faber and Faber. 104p.

CP-LincA   The Poems of Abraham Lincoln.   (1991)   Applewood Books. 28p.

CP-LindV   Collected Poems of Vachel Lindsay.   (1925)   Macmillan. 464p.

CP-LogaJ   John Logan: The Collected Poems.   *Jerome Mazzaro and A. Poulin, Jr., ed.*   (1989)   BOA Editions. 499p.

SP-LoguC   Selected Poems [Christopher Logue].   *Christopher Reid, ed.*   (1996)   Faber and Faber. 145p., pap.

SP-LongH   Selected Poems [Henry Wadsworth Longfellow].   *Lawrence Buell, ed.*   (1988)   Penguin. 389p., pap.

SP-LordA   Undersong; Chosen Poems, Old and New [Audre Lord].   (1992)   W. W. Norton. 206p., pap.

SP-LoweR   Selected Poems [Robert Lowell].   (Rev. ed. 1977; repr. 1993)   Farrar, Straus and Giroux. 256p., pap.

SP-LuxT   New and Selected Poems 1975–1995 [Thomas Lux].   (1997)   Houghton Mifflin. 177p.

SP-LyndD   Selected Poems [Sir David Lyndsay].   *Janet Hadley Williams, ed.*   (2000)   Assoc for Scottish Literary Studies. 348p.

SP-MacDH   Selected Poetry [Hugh MacDiarmid].   *Alan Riach and Michael Grieve, ed.*   (1992)   New Directions. 289p.

CP-MacLA   New & Collected Poems, 1917–1976 [Archibald MacLeish].   (1976)   Houghton Mifflin. 493p.

CP-MacNL   The Collected Poems of Louis MacNeice.   *Dodds, E. R., ed.*   (1966)   Faber and Faber. 575p.

CP-MahoD   Collected Poems [Derek Mahon].   (1999)   The Gallery Press. 288p.

SP-MajoC   Configurations; New & Selected Poems 1958–1998 [Clarence Major].   (1998)   Copper Canyon. 323p., pap.

CP-MallS   Collected Poems [Stéphane Mallarmé].   *Henry Weinfield, ed.*   (1994)   University of California Press. 282p.

CP-MarlC   The Complete Poems and Translations [Christopher Marlowe].   *Stephen Orgel, ed.*   (1971)   Penguin Books. 282p., pap.

CP-MarvA   The Complete Poems [Andrew Marvell].   *Elizabeth Story Donno, ed.*   (1972, repr. 1985)   Penguin. 314p., pap.

SP-McGrT   Selected Poems, 1938–1988 [Thomas McGrath].   *Thomas McGrath, ed.*   (1988)   Copper Canyon Press. 180p., pap.

SP-McHuH   Hinge & Sign; Poems 1968–1993 [Heather McHugh].   (1994)   Wesleyan University Press. 219p., pap.

SP-McMiJ   The World at Large; New and Selected Poems, 1971–1996 [James McMichael].   (1996)   University of Chicago Press. 203p., pap.

SP-MelvH   Selected Poems of Herman Melville.   *Hennig Cohen, ed.*   (1991)   Fordham University Press. 259p., pap.

CP-MerG1   The Poems of George Meredith. Vol. 1.   *Phyllis B. Bartlett, ed.*   (1978)   Yale University Press. 707p.

CP-MerG2   The Poems of George Meredith. Vol. 2.   *Phyllis B. Bartlett, ed.*   (1978)   Yale University Press. 542p.

SP-MereW   Effort at Speech; New and Selected Poems [William Meredith].   (1997)   Northwestern University Press. 231p., pap.

SP-MerrJ   Selected Poems [James Merrill].   (1992)   Alfred A. Knopf. 340p., pap.

CP-MertT   The Collected Poems of Thomas Merton.   (1977)   New Directions. 1,048p., pap.

SP-MerwW   The Second Four Books of Poems [W. S. Merwin].   (1993)   Copper Canyon. 308p., pap.

SP-MerwWF   Flower & Hand: Poems 1977–1983 [W. S. Merwin].   (1997)   Copper Canyon. 172p., pap.

CP-Miche   The Complete Poems of Michelangelo.   *John Frederick Nims, ed.*   (1998)   University of Chicago Press. 185p.

CP-MillE   Collected Poems [Edna St. Vincent Millay]. *Norma Millay, ed.* (1956) Harper and Row. 738p., pap.

CP-MiloC   The Collected Poems 1931–1987 [Czeslaw Milosz]. (1988) Ecco. 511p.

CP-MiloCN   New and Collected Poems: 1931–2001 [Czeslaw Milosz]. (2001) HarperCollins. 776p.

CP-MiltJ   The Complete Poetry of John Milton. *John T. Shawcross, ed.* (1963, rev. ed. 1971) Doubleday. 654p., pap.

SP-MistG   A Gabriela Mistral Reader. *Marjorie Agosin, ed.* (1993) White Pine Press. 227p., pap.

CP-MontE   Collected Poems 1920–1954 [Eugenio Montale]. *Jonathan Galassi, ed.* (1998) Farrar, Straus and Giroux. 626p.

CP-MoorM   The Complete Poems of Marianne Moore. (1981) Penguin Books. 305p.

CP-MuldP   Poems, 1968–1998 [Paul Muldoon]. (2001) Farrar, Straus and Giroux. 479p.

CP-NashO   Verses from 1929 On [Ogden Nash]. (1959) Random House. 522p.

CP-NemeH   The Collected Poems of Howard Nemerov. (1981) University of Chicago Press. 516p., pap.

SP-NeruP   Late and Posthumous Poems 1968–1974 [Pablo Neruda]. *Ben Belitt, ed.* (1988) Grove Press. 239p., pap.

CP-NiedL   Collected Works [Lorine Niedecker]. *Jenny Penberthy, ed.* (2002) University of California Press. 471p.

SP-OharF   The Selected Poems of Frank O'Hara. *Donald Allen, ed.* (1974) Vintage Books / Random House. 233p., pap.

SP-OlivM   New and Selected Poems [Mary Oliver]. (1992) Beacon Press. 255p., pap.

SP-OlsoC   Selected Poems [Charles Olson]. *Robert Creeley, ed.* (1993) University of California Press. 225p.

CP-OlsoC   The Collected Poems of Charles Olson. *George F. Butterick, ed.* (1987) University of California Press. 675p.

CP-OppGN   New Collected Poems [George Oppen]. *Michael Davidson, ed.* (2002) New Directions. 433p.

SP-OrrG   The Caged Owl; New and Selected Poems [Gregory Orr]. (2002) Copper Canyon. 235p., pap.

CP-OwenW   The Collected Poems of Wilfred Owen. *C. Day Lewis, ed.* (1963) New Directions. 191p., pap.

SP-PagiD   The Selected Poetry of Dan Pagis. *Stephen Mitchell, ed.* (1989) University of California Press. 153p., pap.

CP-PalGC   Begin Again; Collected Poems [Grace Paley]. (2000) Farrar, Straus and Giroux. 178p.

SP-PalmM   Codes Appearing; Poems 1979–1988 [Michael Palmer]. (2001) New Directions. 245p., pap.

CP-ParkD   Complete Poems [Dorothy Parker]. *Colleen Breese, ed.* (1999) Penguin. 408p.

SP-PasoP   Pier Paolo Pasolini: Poems. *Norman MacAfee, ed.* (1996) Farrar, Straus and Giroux. 231p., pap.

CP-PatcK   Collected Poems [Kenneth Patchen]. (1982) New Directions. 504p., pap.

SP-PessF   Poems of Fernando Pessoa. *Edwin Honig and Susan M. Brown, ed.* (1998) City Lights. 240p., pap.

CP-Petra   Canzoniere [Petrarch]. *J. G. Nichols, ed.* (2000) Carcanet. 309p.

SP-PierM   Circles on the Water; Selected Poems of Marge Piercy. (1982) Alfred A. Knopf. 299p., pap.

CP-PinkH   Taken in Faith; Poems [Helen Pinkerton]. (2002) Swallow Press. 129p.

CP-PinsR   The Figured Wheel; New and Collected Poems 1966–1996 [Robert Pinsky]. (1996) Farrar, Straus and Giroux. 304p.

CP-PlatS   The Collected Poems [Sylvia Plath]. *Hughes, Ted, ed.* (1981) HarperCollins. 351p., pap.

CP-PoCan   The Cantos of Ezra Pound. (1970, repr. 1991) New Directions. 818p.

CP-PoEar   Collected Early Poems of Ezra Pound. *Michael John King, ed.* (1976) New Directions. 330p.

CP-PoeEd   Complete Poems and Selected Essays [Edgar Allan Poe]. *Richard Gray, ed.* (1993) Everyman. 306p., pap.

CP-PopeA   Poetical Works [Alexander Pope]. *Herbert Davis, ed.* (1978; repr. 1990) Oxford University Press. 754p.

SP-PounE   The Selected Poems of Ezra Pound. (1957) New Directions. 184p., pap.

SP-PrunW   Unarmed and Dangerous; New and Selected Poems [Wyatt Prunty]. (2000) Johns Hopkins Univ. Press. 179p., pap.

SP-RainK   Selected Poems [Kathleen Raine]. (1988) Lindisfarne Press. 157p., pap.

CP-RaleW   The Poems of Sir Walter Ralegh. *Agnes M. C. Latham, ed.* (1929) Constable. 200p.

CP-RamaA   The Collected Poems of A. K. Ramanujan. (1995) Oxford University Press. 289p.

SP-RansJ   Selected Poems of John Crowe Ransom.   (1969)   Alfred A. Knopf. 159p.

CP-RexrK   The Complete Poems of Kenneth Rexroth.   *Sam Hamill and Bradford Morrow, ed.*   (2003)   Copper Canyon. 764p.

SP-RicA1   Adrienne Rich's Poetry and Prose.   *Barbara Charlesworth Gelpi and Albert Gelpi, ed.*   (1975, repr. 1993)   W. W. Norton. 434p. pap.

SP-RicA2   The Fact of a Doorframe; Poems Selected and New 1950–1984 [Adrienne Rich].   (1984)   W. W. Norton. 341p., pap.

CP-RicAE   Collected Early Poems 1950–1970 [Adrienne Rich].   (1993)   W. W. Norton. 435p.

CP-RidiL   The Poems of Laura Riding.   (Rev. ed., 2001)   Persea Books. 498p.

CP-RileJ   The Complete Poetical Works of James Whitcomb Riley.   (1993)   Indiana University Press. 886p.

CP-RilkFr   The Complete French Poems of Rainer Maria Rilke.   *A. Poulin, Jr., ed.*   (1986)   Graywolf Press. 383p.

CP-RimbA   Collected Poems [Arthur Rimbaud].   *Martin Sorrell, ed.*   (2001)   Oxford University Press. 337p.

SP-RitsY   Yannis Ritsos: Selected Poems 1938–1988.   *Kimon Friar and Kostas Myrsiades, ed.*   (1989)   BOA Editions. 486p.

CP-RobiE   Collected Poems [Edward Arlington Robinson].   (1922)   Macmillan. 591p.

CP-RoetT   The Collected Poems of Theodore Roethke.   (1975)   Doubleday / Anchor Books. 272p

CP-RosC1   The Complete Poems of Christina Rossetti. Vol. 1.   *R. W. Crump, ed.*   (1979)   Louisiana State University Press. 332p.

CP-RosC2   The Complete Poems of Christina Rossetti. Vol. 2.   *R. W. Crump, ed.*   (1986)   Louisiana State University Press. 525p.

CP-RosC3   The Complete Poems of Christina Rossetti. Vol. 3.   *R. W. Crump, ed.*   (1990)   Louisiana State University Press. 601p.

CW-RossD   Collected Writings [Dante Gabriel Rossetti].   *Jan Marsh, ed.*   (2000)   New Amsterdam Books. 531p.

CP-RukeM   The Collected Poems of Muriel Rukeyser.   (1978)   McGraw-Hill. 588p.

SP-Rumi   The Essential Rumi.   *Coleman Barks, ed.*   (1995)   HarperCollins. 310p., pap.

CP-SandC   The Complete Poems of Carl Sandburg.   (1970)   Harcourt Brace Jovanovich. 707p.

SP-SartM   Selected Poems of May Sarton.   *Serena Sue Hilsinger and Lois Brynes, ed.*   (1978)   W. W. Norton. 206p., pap.

CP-SchuJ   Collected Poems [James Schuyler].   *Tom Carey and Raymond Foye and Darragh Park, ed.*   (1993)   Farrar, Straus and Giroux. 429p.

SP-ScotW   Selections from the Poems of Sir Walter Scott.   *Thompson, A. Hamilton, ed.*   (1921)   Reprint Services. 196p.

SP-SeifJ   The Poetry of Jaroslav Seifert.   *George Gibian, ed.*   (1998)   Catbird Press. 255p., pap.

CP-SextA   The Complete Poems [Anne Sexton].   (1981)   Houghton Mifflin. 622p., pap.

SP-SextA   Selected Poems of Anne Sexton.   *Diane Wood Middlebrook and Diana Hume George, ed.*   (2000)   Mariner Books. 266p., pap.

SP-ShapK   New & Selected Poems, 1940–1986 [Karl Shapiro].   (1987)   University of Chicago Press. 103p., pap.

CP-ShelP   The Complete Poems of Percy Bysshe Shelley.   *Mary Shelley, ed.*   (1994)   The Modern Library / Random House. 914p.

CP-SherT   The Poems of Thomas Sheridan.   *Robert Hogan, ed.*   (1994)   Associated University Presses. 431p.

SP-SidnP   Selected Poems [Sir Philip Sidney].   *Catherine Bates, ed.*   (1994)   Penguin Books. 219p., pap.

SP-SimiC   Selected Poems, 1963–1983—Revised and Expanded [Charles Simic].   (1990)   George Braziller. 229p., pap.

SP-SimiCE   Selected Early Poems [Charles Simic].   (3rd ed. Rev. and exp. ed., 1999)   George Braziller. 245p., pap.

SP-SmarC   Christopher Smart; Selected Poems.   *Karina Williamson and Marcus Walsh, ed.*   (1990)   Penguin Books. 390p., pap.

CP-SmitS   Collected Poems [Stevie Smith].   *James MacGibbon, ed.*   (1976)   New Directions. 591p., pap.

CP-SnydG   No Nature; New and Selected Poems [Gary Snyder].   (1992)   Pantheon Books. 390p., pap.

CP-SpenS   Collected Poems [Stephen Spender].   (1985)   Faber and Faber. 204p.

CP-Spens   The Complete Poetical Works of Spenser.   *R. E. Neil Dodge, ed.*   (1936)   Houghton Mifflin. 851p.

SP-StafW   The Darkness around Us Is Deep; Selected Poems of William Stafford.   *Robert Bly, ed.*   (1993) HarperCollins. 138p., pap.

SP-StafWW   The Way It Is; New and Selected Poems [William Stafford].   *Robert Bly, Naomi Shihab Nye and Kim Stafford, ed.*   (1998)   Graywolf Press. 268p.

CP-SteiG   The Yale Gertrude Stein.   *Richard Kostelanetz, ed.*   (1980)   Yale University Press. 464p., pap.

CP-StevW   The Collected Poems of Wallace Stevens.   (1954, repr. 1990)   Vintage. 534p., pap.

CP-StevWP   Collected Poetry and Prose [Wallace Stevens].   *Frank Kermode and Joan Richardson, ed.*   (1997) The Library of America. 1032p.

CP-StocA   Only for the Eye of a Friend; The Poems of Annis Boudinot Stockton.   *Carla Mulford, ed.*   (1995) University Press of Virginia. 336p.

SP-StocR   Selected Poems 1947–1980 [Robert Stock].   *David Galler and Harriette Stock, ed.*   (1994)   Crane & Hopper. 1994p.

CP-SuckJ   The Works of Sir John Suckling in Prose and Verse.   *A. Hamilton Thompson, ed.*   (1910; repr. by Reprint Services)   Reprint Services. 424p.

SP-SwenM   Nature; Poems Old and New [May Swenson].   (1994)   Houghton Mifflin. 240p., pap.

CP-SwifJ   The Complete Poems [Jonathan Swift].   *Pat Rogers, ed.*   (1983)   Penguin Books. 956p., pap.

SP-SwinA   A Choice of Swinburne's Verse.   *Robert Nye, ed.*   (1973)   Faber and Faber. 169p.

SP-SzeA   The Redshifting Web; Poems 1970–1998 [Arthur Sze].   (1998)   Copper Canyon. 267p., pap.

SP-SzymW   View with a Grain of Sand; Selected Poems [Wisława Szymborska].   (1995)   Harcourt Brace. 214p.

SP-SzymWM   Miracle Fair; Selected Poems of Wisława Szymborska.   (1st ed., 2001)   W.W. Norton. 159p.

CP-TateA   Collected Poems, 1919–1976 [Allen Tate].   (1989)   Louisiana State University Press. 218p., pap.

SP-TateJ   Selected Poems [James Tate].   (1991)   Wesleyan University Press. 239p., pap.

CP-TennA   Tennyson; a Selected Edition.   *Christopher Ricks, ed.*   (1989)   University of California Press. 1,032p., pap.

CP-ThomD   The Collected Poems of Dylan Thomas, 1934–1952.   (1953, rev. ed. 1956)   New Directions. 203p., pap.

CP-ThorH   Collected Essays and Poems [Henry David Thoreau].   *Elizabeth Hall Witherell, ed.*   (2001)   The Library of America. 703p.

CP-TomlC   Collected Poems [Charles Tomlinson].   (1985)   Oxford University Press. 388p.

SP-TomlC   Selected Poems 1955–1997 (Charles Tomlinson).   (1st ed., 1997) New Directions. 226p., pap.

CP-UpdiJ   Collected Poems, 1953–1993 [John Updike].   (1993)   Alfred A. Knopf. 387p.

SP-VanDM   If It Be Not I; Poems, 1959–1982 [Mona Van Duyn].   (1993)   Alfred A. Knopf. 305p.

CP-VeryJ   The Complete Poems [Jones Very].   *Helen R. Deese, ed.*   (1993)   University of Georgia Press. 896p.

CP-WalcD   Collected Poems, 1948–1984 [Derek Walcott].   (1986)   Farrar, Straus and Giroux. 516p., pap.

CP-WalkA   Her Blue Body Everything We Know; Earthling Poems, 1965–1990 Complete [Alice Walker].   (1991)   Harcourt Brace. 459p., pap.

CP-WarrR   The Collected Poems of Robert Penn Warren.   *John Burt, ed.*   (1998)   Louisiana State University Press. 830p.

SP-WeisT   Selected Poems [Theodore Weiss].   (1995)   Northwestern University Press. 330p., pap.

SP-WhalP   Overtime; Selected Poems [Philip Whalen].   *Michael Rothenberg, ed.*   (1999)   Penguin. 309p., pap.

CP-WheaP   Complete Writings [Phillis Wheatley].   *Vincent Carretta, ed.*   (1st ed., 2001)   Penguin. 224p.

CP-WhitJ   The Complete Poetical Works of John Greenleaf Whittier.   (1904)   Houghton, Mifflin; repr. by Reprint Services. 656p.

CP-WhitW   The Complete Poems [Walt Whitman].   *Francis Murphy, ed.*   (1975; repr. 1986)   Penguin Books. 892p., pap.

CP-WilW1   The Collected Poems of William Carlos Williams; Vol. 1, 1909–1939.   *A. Walton Litz and Christopher MacGowan, ed.*   (1986)   New Directions. 579p., pap.

CP-WilW2   The Collected Poems of William Carlos Williams; Vol. 2, 1939–1962.   *Christopher MacGowan, ed.*   (1988)   New Directions. 553p., pap.

CP-WilbR   New and Collected Poems [Richard Wilbur].   (1988)   Harcourt Brace Jovanovich. 393p.

CP-WildO   Complete Poetry [Oscar Wilde].   *Isobel Murray, ed.*   (1997)   Oxford University Press. 212p.

SP-WillC   Selected Poems [C. K. Williams].   (1994)   Farrar, Straus and Giroux. 289p.

CP-WillC   Poems; 1963–1983 [C. K. Williams].   (1988)   Farrar, Straus and Giroux. 244p., pap.

CP-WillM   Some Jazz a While; Collected Poems [Miller Williams].   (1999)   University of Illinois Press. 279p.

CP-WillT   The Collected Poems of Tennessee Williams.   *David Roessel and Nicholas Moschovakis, ed.*
                  (2002)   New Directions. 304p.

SP-WilnE   Reversing the Spell; New & Selected Poems [Eleanor Wilner].   (1998)   Copper Canyon. 341p.,
                  pap.

MW-WorW   The Major Works [William Wordsworth].   *Stephen Gill, ed.*   (2000)   Oxford University Press.
                  752p.

CP-WorW1   The Poems; Vol. 1 [William Wordsworth].   *John O. Hayden, ed.*   (1977, repr. 1990)   Penguin
                  Books. 1,066p., pap.

CP-WorW2   The Poems; Vol. 2 [William Wordsworth].   *John O. Hayden, ed.*   (1977, repr. 1989)   Penguin
                  Books. 1,104p., pap.

CP-WorW3   The Prelude; a Parallel Text [William Wordsworth].   *J. C. Maxwell, ed.*   (1971; repr. 1972, 1986)
                  Penguin. 573p., pap.

SP-WrigC   The World of the Ten Thousand Things; Poems 1980–1990 [Charles Wright].   (1990)   Farrar,
                  Straus and Giroux. 231p., pap.

SP-WrigCN   Negative Blue; Selected Later Poems [Charles Wright].   (2000)   Farrar, Straus and Giroux. 206p.

CP-WrigJ   Collected Poems [James Wright].   (1972)   Wesleyan University Press. 215p.

SP-WrigJ   Selected Poems of Jay Wright.   *Robert B. Stepto, ed.*   (1987)   Princeton University Press. 197p.,
                  pap.

CP-WrotM   The Poems of Lady Mary Wroth.   *Josephine A. Roberts, ed.*   (1983)   Louisiana State University
                  Press. 251p., pap.

CP-WyatT   Complete Poems [Sir Thomas Wyatt].   *R. A. Rebholz, ed.*   (1978)   Penguin Books. 558p., pap.

CP-YeatW   The Collected Poems of W. B. Yeats.   *Richard J. Finneran, ed.*   (1989)   Macmillan. 544p., pap.

SP-ZagaA   Without End; New and Selected Poems [Adam Zagajewski].   (2002)   Farrar, Straus and Giroux.
                  285p., pap.

SP-ZatuM   New Selected Poems of Marya Zaturenska.   *Robert Phillips, ed.*   (2002)   Syracuse University
                  Press. 169p.

CP-ZukLS   Complete Short Poetry [Louis Zukofsky].   (1991)   The Johns Hopkins University Press. 365p.

ABBREVIATIONS

abr.	abridged	*mod.*	modernized or modern
ad.	adapted	*N.T.*	New Testament
add.	additional	*O.T.*	Old Testament
arr.	arranged	*orig.*	original
at.	attributed	*par.*	paraphrase or paraphrased
Bk.	book	*pr.*	prose
br.	brief	*Pt.*	part
ch.	chapter	*rev.*	revised
comp.	compiled or compiler	*sc.*	scene
comps.	compilers	*Sec.*	section
cond.	condensed	*sel.*	selection
diff.	different	*sels.*	selections
fr.	from	*sl.*	slightly
frag.	fragment	*st.*	stanza
incl.	included or including	*sts.*	stanzas
introd.	introduction or introductory	*tr.*	translator, translation, or translated
ll.	lines	*trs.*	translators or translations
LL.	last line	*var.*	various
med.	medieval	*vers.*	version or versions
misc.	miscellaneous	*wr.*	wrong or wrongly

TITLE AND FIRST LINE INDEX

Titles and first lines are arranged in one alphabetical listing in the Title and First Line Index. Titles are distinguished by initial capital letters on the important words. All first-line entries are followed by the title of the poem, if there is a title.

Letter codes for volumes of collected and selected works are listed after titles and first lines.

An indented citation indicates that the poem is a selection from the work listed one level above. A citation indented and inside parentheses indicates a variant title or variant first line as used in the collected or selected works that follow.

Generic title entries, such as "Ode," "Song," and "Sonnet," are followed by the first line in quotation marks for easy identification. Such entries, of course, may also be located by the listing for the poem's first line.

Titles and first lines beginning with "O" and "Oh" are filed separately.

$$$$$$. Charles Bukowski. SP-BukC1
"?!" "Shu Ting." CP-KizeC, *tr. by* Carolyn Kizer *and* Y. H. Zhao

A

A. Robert Creeley. CP-CreeR
A. Heather McHugh. SP-McHuH
A.A.A. Emily Jane Brontë. *See* Sleep not, dream not; this bright day
A, B & C of It, The. William Carlos Williams. CP-WilW2
A B Cs. Charles Olson. CP-OlsoC
A B Cs (2). Charles Olson. CP-OlsoC
A B Cs (3—for Rimbaud). Charles Olson. CP-OlsoC
A black, E white, I red, U green, O blue: vowels. Vowels. Arthur Rimbaud. CP-RimbA, *tr. by* Martin Sorrell
A Calais / Trop de frais. French Distichs. Samuel Johnson. CP-JohnS
À Constance, This Day. Charles Olson. CP-OlsoC
A. E. and R. C. Emily Jane Brontë. *See* Two Children, The
A. E. F. Carl Sandburg. CP-SandC
A. E. Housman. W. H. Auden. CP-AudeW
À elle l'acte calme. Samuel Beckett. CP-BeckS
À Face. Andrei Codrescu. SP-CodrA
A- / float on some. E. E. Cummings. CP-CummE
À Francis Ponge. Andrei Codrescu. SP-CodrA
A. G. A. to A. E. Emily Jane Brontë. CP-BronE
A. G. A. to A. S. Emily Jane Brontë. CP-BronE
A. H., 1855–1912. Thomas Hardy. CP-HardT
A is for ANT. John Ciardi. CP-CiarJ
A is the Alphabet, A at its head. Alphabet, An. Christina Georgina Rossetti. CP-RosC3
A. J. J. A. E. Housman. CP-HousA
A l f a l f a l f a l f a l f a. Plot, The. Paul Muldoon. CP-MuldP
À La Maniere De D. H. Lawrence. D. H. Lawrence. CP-LawrD
A la Mystérieuse. Gregory Orr. SP-OrrG
À l'École Berlitz. John Updike. CP-UpdiJ
À l'instant de s'entendre dire. Samuel Beckett. CP-BeckS
A. Love's very fleas are mine. Enter. A, B & C of It, The. William Carlos Williams. CP-WilW2
À mi-hauteur. Rue de Vaugirard. Samuel Beckett. CP-BeckS
A / mong crum / bling people(a). E. E. Cummings. CP-CummE
A peels an apple, while B kneels to God. Primer of the Daily Round, A. Howard Nemerov. CP-NemeH
À peine à bien mené. Samuel Beckett. CP-BeckS
A quoy servent tant d'artifices. Desdain. Sir John Suckling. CP-SuckJ
A.S. to G.S. Emily Jane Brontë. CP-BronE
A Terre. Wilfred Owen. CP-OwenW
A' the lads o' Thornie-bank. Lady Onlie. Robert Burns. CP-BurnR
À travers la mince cloison. Ascension. Samuel Beckett. CP-BeckS

A was an elegant Ape. Billy's Alphabetical Animal Show. James Whitcomb Riley. CP-RileJ
A-Wishing Well. Robert Frost. CP-FrosR
A' ye wha live by sowps o' drink. On a Scotch Bard Gone to the West Indies. Robert Burns. CP-BurnR
Aardvark, The. Christopher Logue. SP-LoguC
Aaron. George Herbert. CP-HerbG
Aaron Stark. Edwin Arlington Robinson. CP-RobiE
Ab lo dolchor qu'al cor mi vai. Canto 91: "Ab lo dolchor qu'al cor mi vai." Ezra Pound. SP-PounE *Fr.* Cantos.
Ab Ovo. Joseph Brodsky. CP-BrodJ
Ab Urbe Condita. Michael Palmer. SP-PalmM
Abalone. Peter Blue Cloud. SP-BlueP
Aban Kavost and Ivar Oakeson. Robert Bly. SP-BlyR
Abandon for a moment, friends. Electra Becomes Morbid. Ogden Nash. CP-NashO
Abandon surrounds abandon. Rainer Maria Rilke. CP-RilkFr, *tr. by* A. Poulin, Jr. *Fr.* Roses, The.
Abandoned. Federico García Lorca. CP-GarcF, *tr. by* Christopher Maurer
Abandoned Church. Federico García Lorca. CP-GarcF, *tr. by* Greg Simon *and* Steven F. White
Abandoned Church, An. Walter De la Mare. CP-DeLaW
Abandoned Ranch, Big Bend. Hayden Carruth. CP-CarHS
Abandoned tractor sinking in the mud, An. Evidence. Yehuda Amichai. SP-AmicYL, *tr. by* Benjamin Harshav *and* Barbara Harshav
Abandoned tractor stuck in the mud, An. Evidence. Yehuda Amichai. SP-AmicY, *tr. by* Chana Bloch
Abature: I think you'd all be better off. "I'd Understand Yer Poemes Better," Writes the Lady Editor from San Francisco, "If I Knowed What the Words Mean." Robert Stock. SP-StocR
Abbé Voltaire, alias Arouet, The. Caraway Seed, The. Ogden Nash. CP-NashO
Abbey Mason, The. Thomas Hardy. CP-HardT
Abbeyforde. Donald Davie. CP-DaviDC
Abbot is painting me so true. On His Portrait. William Cowper. CP-CowpW
Abt Vogler. Robert Browning. CP-BroR1
ABC, An. Geoffrey Chaucer. CP-ChauG
Abdhur Rahman, the Durani Chief, of him is the story told. Ballad of the King's Mercy, The. Rudyard Kipling. CP-KiplR
Abdolonymus—The Sidonian. Jones Very. CP-VeryJ
Abduction, The. Rita Dove. SP-DoveR
Abduction, The. Stanley Kunitz. CP-KunSC
Abduction of Saints, The. Alice Walker. CP-WalkA
Abe Lincoln. Langston Hughes. CP-HughL; CP-HughL3
Abe Martin!—dad-burn his old picture! James Whitcomb Riley. CP-RileJ
Abel and Cain. Charles Baudelaire. CP-BaudC, *tr. by* Walter Martin
Abel was blond and woolly. Brothers. Dan Pagis. SP-PagiD, *tr. by* Stephen Mitchell
Abels Bloud. Robert Herrick. CP-HerrR

Abel's Bride. Denise Levertov. SP-LeveDP

Aberdeen. Thomas Hardy. CP-HardT

Abiquiu. Charles Tomlinson. CP-TomlC

Abishag. Louise Glück. SP-GlucL

Ablaze / with candles sconced. Dawnbreaker. Robert Earl Hayden. CP-HaydR

Able, just, or maybe not quite so. Interpretation of High Finance. Robert Stock. SP-StocR

Abnegation. Adrienne Rich. CP-RicAE; SP-RicA2

Aboard at a Ship's Helm. Walt Whitman. CP-WhitW

Aboard this boat of rotten wood. Han-shan. CP-ColdM, tr. by Red Pine

Abode. Czeslaw Milosz. CP-MiloCN, tr. by Robert Hass

Abode of the nightingale is bare, The. Alone. Walter De la Mare. CP-DeLaW

Abolished, and her frightful wing in the tears. Hérodiade. Stéphane Mallarmé. CP-MallS, tr. by Henry Weinfield

Abolition of Serfdom in Russia, The. Jones Very. CP-VeryJ

Abominable Lake, The. Stevie Smith. CP-SmitS

Abortion. Ai. SP-Ai

Abortion, The. Anne Sexton. CP-SextA; SP-SextA

Abou Ben Adhem (may his tribe decrease). Philanthropist, The. G. K. Chesterton. CP-ChesG

About. Rae Armantrout. SP-ArmaA

About a year has passed. I've returned to the place of battle. Elegy. Joseph Brodsky. CP-BrodJ, tr. by Joseph Brodsky

About blood, he said, be. Concerning Exaggeration, or How, Properly, to Heap Up. Charles Olson. CP-OlsoC

About Cranes. Charles Bukowski. SP-BukC1

About Her whom I have not yet met. Madonna Mia. G. K. Chesterton. CP-ChesG

About Infinity. Norman Dubie. CP-DubiN

About Marriage. Denise Levertov. SP-LeveDP; SP-LeveDS

About Money. David Ignatow. SP-IgnaD

About my being a poet, the trees certainly haven't expressed an interest. Talking to Myself. David Ignatow. SP-IgnaD

About my brow bind the black crow's wings. Earth's Champion. G. K. Chesterton. CP-ChesG

About my temples go, triumphant bays! Elegy 2.12. Ovid. CP-MarlC Fr. Elegies.

About My Very Tortured Friend, Peter. Charles Bukowski. SP-BukC2

About Opera. William Meredith. SP-MereW

About Pain. Charles Bukowski. SP-BukC3

About Photography. Andrei Codrescu. SP-CodrA

About Poetry. William Meredith. SP-MereW

About Political Action in Which Each Individual Acts from the Heart. Denise Levertov. SP-LeveDL

About suffering, about adoration, the old masters. Old and the New Masters, The. Randall Jarrell. CP-JarrR

About suffering they were never wrong. Musée des Beaux Arts. W. H. Auden. CP-AudeW

About ten days or so. Reassurance, The. Thom Gunn. CP-GunnT

About the Phoenix. James Merrill. SP-MerrJ

About the Pseudo St. Dionysius. Alan Dugan. CP-DugaA

About the Shark, phlegmatical one. Maldive Shark, The. Herman Melville. SP-MelvH

About the size of an old-style dollar bill. Poem. Elizabeth Bishop. CP-BishE

About the skull of the beloved, filled. Presentation Piece. Marilyn Hacker. SP-HackM

About the sweet bag of a bee. Bag of the Bee, The. Robert Herrick. CP-HerrR

About the time I got my first baseman's mitt. Baseball. Wyatt Prunty. SP-PrunW

About the time that taverns shut. Ballad of Minepit Shaw, The. Rudyard Kipling. CP-KiplR

About their chances for divorce. Actuarial Wife, The. Wyatt Prunty. SP-PrunW

About twenty years ago. Wild Oats. Philip Larkin. CP-LarkP

About what sort of thing. Arthur Hugh Clough. SP-ClouA

Above. Howard Nemerov. CP-NemeH

Above a between-the-acts prattling of. E. E. Cummings. CP-CummE

Above a stretch of still unravaged weald. Garden Party, The. Donald Davie. CP-DaviDC

Above all, I curse and strive to combat. My Songs Are Kandym in the Waste Land. Hugh MacDiarmid. SP-MacDH

Above all, not by violence—. Bacterial War, The. Howard Nemerov. CP-NemeH

Above Ashleworth. Ivor Gurney. SP-GurnI

Above Bear Lake. May Swenson. SP-SwenM

Above, below, in sky and sod. Over-Heart, The. John Greenleaf Whittier. CP-WhitJ

Above Carrara. Charles Tomlinson. CP-TomlC; SP-TomlC

Above Cold Mountain the moon shines alone. Han-shan. CP-ColdM, tr. by Red Pine

Above Druida, below Druida. Druida. Laura Riding Jackson. CP-RidiL

Above Everything. David Ignatow. SP-IgnaD

Above Manhattan. Charles Tomlinson. CP-TomlC; SP-TomlC

Above my desk / the Rabbi of Auschwitz. On a Drawing by Flavio. Philip Levine. SP-LeviP

Above my desk, whirring and self-important. Angel. James Merrill. SP-MerrJ

Above my face is a map. Cloud-Mobile, The. May Swenson. SP-SwenM

Above Oblivion's Tide there is a Pier. Emily Dickinson. CP-DickE

Above Pate Valley. Gary Snyder. CP-SnydG

Above Taos now / I peer through the crack. Man Who Rode Away, The. Lawrence Ferlinghetti. SP-FerlL

Above the ancient Burying place. Lines on the Old Danvers Burying Ground. Jones Very. CP-VeryJ

Above the Arno. May Swenson. SP-SwenM

Above the Battle's Front. Nicholas Vachel Lindsay. CP-LindV

Above the Cave. Denise Levertov. SP-LeveDP

Above the City. James Laughlin. CP-LaugJ

Above the closed day only this star remained. End of a Day, The. Yannis Ritsos. SP-RitsY, tr. by Kimon Friar

Above the cold. William Corbett. SP-CorbW

Above the crystal vase. Because of the Influence of Spring. "Rubén Dario." SP-DariR, tr. by Alberto Acereda and Will Derusha

Above / the darkness of a river upon. Marriage Ritual, A. William Carlos Williams. CP-WilW1

Above the Edge of Doom. Robert Graves. CP-GravR

Above the elephantine blankets of flower-beds. Prague. Jaroslav Seifert. SP-SeifJ, tr. by Ewald Osers

Above the forest of the parakeets. Bird with the Coppery, Keen Claws, The. Wallace Stevens. CP-StevW; CP-StevWP

Above the fresh ruffles of the surf. Voyages. Hart Crane. CP-CranH

Above the lakes and woods and valley floors. Transcendence. Charles Baudelaire. CP-BaudC, tr. by Walter Martin

Above the Oxbow. Sylvia Plath. CP-PlatS

Above the Rio Grande. Charles Tomlinson. SP-TomlC

Above the scribbled wall. Eugenio Montale. CP-MontE, tr. by Jonathan Galassi

Above the waters in their toil. Randall Jarrell. CP-JarrR

Above—the well-know lips, delicately downed. Fragment of an Ancient Tablet. Ted Hughes. SP-HughTN

Above the whispering sea. Air Raid Across the Bay at Plymouth. Stephen Spender. CP-SpenS

Above These Cares. Edna St. Vincent Millay. CP-MillE

Above trees and rooftops. Below. Wendell Berry. CP-BerrW

Above white paths a bugle. Prints, The. W. S. Merwin. SP-MerwW

Above whorled, spindling gorse. Two Views of Withens. Sylvia Plath. CP-PlatS

Abracadabra. Ambrose Bierce. SP-BierA

Abracadabra boys—have they been in the stacks and cloisters? Have, The. Abracadabra Boys, The. Carl Sandburg. CP-SandC

Abracadabra Boys, The. Carl Sandburg. CP-SandC

Abragrammatica / He she will or did. Notes for Echo Lake 8. Michael Palmer. SP-PalmM

Abraham Davenport. John Greenleaf Whittier. CP-WhitJ

Abraham Lincoln. Robert Lowell. SP-LoweR

Abraham Lincoln, Born Feb. 12, 1809. Walt Whitman. CP-WhitW

Abraham Lincoln Walks at Midnight. Nicholas Vachel Lindsay. CP-LindV

Abraham Lincoln was giggling uncontrollably. Every few minutes he. Presentiad, The. Donald Hall. CP-HallD

Abraham to kill him. Emily Dickinson. CP-DickE

Abrahamic River, The. Muster, The. Herman Melville. SP-MelvH

Abram Morrison. John Greenleaf Whittier. CP-WhitJ

Abroad. Joseph Brodsky. CP-BrodJ Fr. Shorts.

Abroad Thoughts from Home. Donald Hall. CP-HallD

Abrupt tempter; close enough to survive. Little Apocalypse; Hölderlin: 1770–1843. Geoffrey Hill. CP-HillG

Abrupt the supernatural Cross. Apparition, The. Herman Melville. SP-MelvH

Abrupt, unexpected movement; his hand, An. Audible and the Inaudible, The. Yannis Ritsos. SP-RitsY, tr. by Kimon Friar

Abruptly paused the strife;—the field throughout. Germans on the Heights of Hochheim, The. William Wordsworth. CP-WorW2

Absalom. Walter De la Mare. CP-DeLaW

Absalom. Muriel Rukeyser. CP-RukeM

Absalom and Achitophel. John Dryden. SP-DrydJ

Absalom and Achitophel, Part 2. Nahum Tate. CP-DryJ2
  "Doeg, though without knowing how or why." SP-DrydJ

Absence. Samuel Taylor Coleridge. CP-ColeS

Absence. Paul Laurence Dunbar. CP-DunbP

Absence. Dorothy Parker. CP-ParkD

Absence. Yannis Ritsos. SP-RitsY, tr. by Athan Anagnostopoulos

Absence. Stephen Spender. CP-SpenS

Absence! Absenting causeth me to complain. Sir Thomas Wyatt. CP-WyatT

Absence, alas, / Causeth me pass. Sir Thomas Wyatt. CP-WyatT

Absence disembodies—so does Death. Emily Dickinson. CP-DickE

Absence Inside an Absence. Charles Wright. SP-WrigCN

Absence Makes the Heart Grow Heart Trouble. Ogden Nash. CP-NashO

Absence, my angel, presence at my side. James Vincent Cunningham. CP-CunnJ

Absence of a Noble Presence, The. John Ashbery. SP-AshbJ

Absence of heart—as in public buildings. Chimaeras, The. W. H. Auden. CP-AudeW

Absence of Little Wesley, The. James Whitcomb Riley. CP-RileJ

Absence of Noise Presence of Sound. Olga Broumas. SP-BrouO

Absence of Slaves, An. Josephine Jacobsen. CP-JacoJ

Absences. Philip Larkin. CP-LarkP

Absences. James Tate. SP-TateJ

Absent, The. Jones Very. CP-VeryJ

Absent Crusader. Robert Graves. CP-GravR

Absent Friends. G. K. Chesterton. CP-ChesG

Absent Good Girl, Life of My Mind. Alan Dugan. CP-DugaA

Absent-Minded Are Always to Blame, The. Adrienne Rich. CP-RicAE

Absent-Minded Beggar, The. Rudyard Kipling. CP-KiplR

Absent or present, still to thee. Lines Written on a Blank Leaf of the "Pleasures of Memory." Lord Byron. CP-Byron

Absent Place—an April Day. Emily Dickinson. CP-DickE

Absent, this morning. Aube Provençale. Marilyn Hacker. SP-HackM

Absent with Official Leave. Randall Jarrell. CP-JarrR

Absentees, The. Ogden Nash. CP-NashO

Absinthe, datura, and vigna. Bouquets. Constantine P. Cavafy. CP-CavaC, tr. by Theoharis Constantine Theoharis

Absolute Explains, The. Thomas Hardy. CP-HardT

Absolute / patience, An. Breathing, The. Denise Levertov. SP-LeveDP

Absolute Reverence. D. H. Lawrence. CP-LawrD

Absolutely. Making a Love Poem. James Laughlin. CP-LaugJ

Absolutely Vernal. Charles Olson. CP-OlsoC

Abstinence. Robert Herrick. CP-HerrR

Abstinence from Melody. Emily Dickinson. SP-DickE

Abstract. Sam Hamill. SP-HamiS

Abstract Greek absurdity has crazed the man, An. Ribh Denounces Patrick. William Butler Yeats. CP-YeatW

Abstract Love Poem. John Logan. CP-LogaJ

Abstract #1, Yucatan. Charles Olson. CP-OlsoC

Abstract of Knowledge, The / The First Test. Jay Wright. SP-WrigJ

Abstracted Painter. Yannis Ritsos. SP-RitsY, tr. by Kimon Friar

Abstracted, sour, as he reaches across a dish. Scylla and Charybdis. Thomas Kinsella. CP-KinsT

Abstraction. Eleanor Wilner. SP-WilnE

Abstracts hover like dull angels, The. Magi. Sylvia Plath. CP-PlatS

Absurd Hour. Fernando Pessoa.
  "Someone's about to enter the doorway . . . One feels the air smiling." SP-PessF
  "To be and not to be again! . . . Oh, lions born in cages!" SP-PessF
  "Today the sky is heavy like the thought of never making port." SP-PessF
  "Your silence a ship, each sail taut in the wind." SP-PessF

Abt the dead he sd. Charles Olson. CP-OlsoC

Abundance. John Ciardi. CP-CiarJ

Abundant bores afflict this world, and some. King of Bores, The. Ambrose Bierce. SP-BierA

Abundant plagues I late have had. Patience, or Comforts in Crosses. Robert Herrick. CP-HerrR

Abusing its otherness, its soul and wit. Literary Theorist. Helen Pinkerton. CP-PinkH

Abysmal Abyssinia, iridescent irate Ireland. First Atlas, The. Primo Levi. CP-LeviP, tr. by Ruth Feldman

Abysmal Immortality. D. H. Lawrence. CP-LawrD

Abyss, The. Charles Baudelaire. CP-BaudC, tr. by Walter Martin

Abyss, The. Theodore Roethke. CP-RoetT

Acacia. Federico García Lorca. CP-GarcF, tr. by Jerome Rothenberg Fr.

Acacia. Federico García Lorca. CP-GarcF, tr. by Jerome Rothenberg Fr. Garden in Umber; or The Garden of the Brownhaired Girls.

Acacia. Federico García Lorca. CP-GarcF, tr. by Jerome Rothenberg Fr. Water Suite.

Acacia Tree. Kathleen Jessie Raine. SP-RainK

Academic. Theodore Roethke. CP-RoetT

Academic Discourse at Havana. Wallace Stevens. CP-StevW; CP-StevWP

Academic Graffiti. W. H. Auden. CP-AudeW

Academy. John Updike. CP-UpdiJ

Academy of Sincerity. Robert Stock. SP-StocR

Academy of the future is opening its doors, The. Ted Berrigan. SP-BerrT Fr. Sonnets, The.

Acapulco. George Oppen. CP-OppGN

Acapulco Canyon: Two Kodachromes. John Logan. CP-LogaJ

Accented Colors. Yannis Ritsos. SP-RitsY, tr. by Athan Anagnostopoulos

Accept my dear the chearful lay. To Mrs Rush, on Her Birth Day. Annis Boudinot Stockton. CP-StocA

Accept my timid happiness. Emily Dickinson. SP-DickE

Accept these records of pure love. Records. Robert Graves. CP-GravR

Acceptance. Robert Frost. CP FrosR

Acceptance. Langston Hughes. CP-HughL; CP-HughL3

Acceptances. Jane Cooper. CP-CoopJ

Acceptum pro me perhibes te, Castrice, ludis. Ad Castricum. Thomas Campion. CP-CampT

Accident. Maya Angelou. SP-AngeM

Accident. Norman Dubie. CP-DubiN

Accident: A Short Story. Miller Williams. CP WillM

Accident could be a god to little boys. Train, The. Norman Dubie. CP-DubiN

Accidentally on Purpose. Robert Frost. CP-FrosR

Accidents of Birth. William Meredith. SP-MereW

Acclimatization. W. S. Merwin. SP-MerwW

Accolade of the Animals, The. Maxine W. Kumin. SP-KumiM

Accommodation to Detroit. Alan Dugan. CP-DugaA

Accomplice, The. Jorge Luis Borges. SP-BorgJ, tr. by Hoyt Rogers

Accomplice, The. Robert Graves. CP-GravR

Accomplished Facts. Carl Sandburg. CP-SandC

Accomplished hetaira toys for this Knave of Hearts, The. Knave of Hearts, The. Donald Davie. CP-DaviDC

Accomplishment. Tess Gallagher. SP-GallT

Accordeon, accordeon! Aleksandr Aleksandrovich Blok. SP-BlokA, tr. by Peter France and Jon Stallworthy

According to His Seasons. Howard Nemerov. CP-NemeH

According to the helicopter pilot. Survivor, The. Miller Williams. CP-WillM

According to the Mighty Working. Thomas Hardy. CP-HardT

According to their need. Host, The. William Carlos Williams. CP-WilW2

According to Thy will: That this day only. Usual Prayer, A. John Berryman. CP-BerrJ

According to Webster's, "the condition" Neotony. John Updike. CP-UpdiJ

Account. Czeslaw Milosz. CP-MiloC; CP-MiloCN, tr. by Robert Pinsky

Account, An. Raymond Carver. CP-CarvR

Account, The. A. R. Ammons. CP-AmmoA

Account in the Present Tense of How It all Happened, An. David Ignatow. SP-IgnaD

Account of a Visit to Hawaii, An. William Meredith. SP-MereW

Account of your what critics call Prose Style. On the Platform. Howard Nemerov. CP-NemeH

Accountability. Gerrit Achterberg. CP-RicAE

Accountability. Paul Laurence Dunbar. CP-DunbP

Accountability. William Stafford. SP-StafWW

Accumulation. John Updike. CP-UpdiJ

Accurate knowledge was prerequisite. In a Copy of Yeats' Poems. William Meredith. SP-MereW

Accursed from their birth they be. Reuben's Children. Dorothy Parker. CP-ParkD

Accursed, The. Dorothy Parker. CP-ParkD

Accusation. Robert Herrick. CP-HerrR

Accusation, The. James Wright. CP-WrigJ

Accused though I be without desert. Sir Thomas Wyatt. CP-WyatT

Ach, mein Kurt, when we were young we sang. Tanck's Song About Youth and Age. Hayden Carruth. CP-CarHS Fr. Songs About What Comes Down: The Complete Works of Mr. Septic Tank.

Ach, Mutter, / This old, black dress. Explanation. Wallace Stevens. CP-StevW; CP-StevWP

Ache, The. Andromeda Chained to Her Rock the Great Nebula in Her Heart. Kenneth Rexroth. CP-RexrK

Ache of Marriage, The. Denise Levertov. SP-LeveDP; SP-LeveDS

Ache's End. Marge Piercy. SP-PierM

Achill. Derek Mahon. CP-MahoD

Achilles after Death. Yannis Ritsos. SP-RitsY, *tr.* by N. C. Germanacos

Achilles and Hector and Homer and all. On Hayley's Portrait. William Cowper. CP-CowpW

Achilles and the King: A Verse Re-telling. John Logan. CP-LogaJ

Achilles over the Trench. Homer. CP-MerG2 *Fr.* Iliad, The.

Achilles. Penthesilea. Zbigniew Herbert. CP-BrodJ, *tr.* by Joseph Brodsky

Achilles' Song. Robert Duncan. SP-DuncR

Aching bones of lovers, The. Yehuda Amichai. SP-AmicYL, *tr.* by Benjamin Harshav *and* Barbara Harshav

Aching sense. Window. Robert Creeley. SP-CreeR

Acid. Mary Oliver. SP-OlivM

Acids. C. K. Williams. CP-WillC

Acknowledge last this human peace. Nocturne for the Heirs of Light. Kenneth Patchen. CP-PatcK

Acknowledgement. James Vincent Cunningham. CP-CunnJ

Acknowledgement. Archibald MacLeish. CP-MacLA

Acme. Christina Georgina Rossetti. CP-RosC3

Acme, Septimius, sighs so amorous. Catullus. *See* Phyllis Corydon clutched to him

Acolyte, The. Denise Levertov. SP-LeveDL

Acon. "H. D." CP-DoolH

Acorn, The. Jones Very. CP-VeryJ

Acorns. Donald Hall. CP-HallD

Acqua alta, high water. Venexia 2. Charles Wright. SP-WrigCN

Acquaintance; companion. Results of Thought, The. William Butler Yeats. CP-YeatW

Acquaintance with Death, Sir. Carl Sandburg. CP-SandC

Acquaintance with Time in Early Autumn. Robert Penn Warren. CP-WarrR

Acquainted with the Night. Robert Frost. CP-FrosR

Acquiescence of Pure Love, The. Jeanne Marie Bouvier de la Motte- Guyon. CP-CowpW

Acquit of evil intention. Canto 62. Ezra Pound. SP-PounE *Fr.* Cantos.

Acre of Grass, An. William Butler Yeats. CP-YeatW

Acre of music, An. L. Z. Lorine Niedecker. CP-NiedL

Acrid scents of autumn, The. Dolour of Autumn. D. H. Lawrence. CP-LawrD

Acrobat, An. Yannis Ritsos. SP-RitsY, *tr.* by Kostas Myrsiades

Acrobat, The. Wisława Szymborska. SP-SzymW, *tr.* by Stanisław Barańczak *and* Clare Cavanagh

Acrobat on the border of the sea, An. Woman That Had More Babies than That, The. Wallace Stevens. CP-StevWP

Acrobatics. Dan Pagis. SP-PagiD, *tr.* by Stephen Mitchell

Acrobatics. Yannis Ritsos. SP-RitsY, *tr.* by Kostas Myrsiades

Acrobats. Robert Graves. CP-GravR

Across a continent imaginary. Yes And No. Laura Riding Jackson. CP-RidiL

Across a world where all men grieve. Justice. Rudyard Kipling. CP-KiplR

Across bay's loop. Beach. Robert Creeley. SP-CreeR

Across from me the whole ride. Chicago Train, The. Louise Glück. SP-GlucL

Across his eyes the mourners lay. Enigma of a Final Scene. Robert Stock. SP-StocR

Across Kansas. William Stafford. SP-StafWW

Across Lamarck Col. Gary Snyder. CP-SnydG

Across lunar wastes of wind and snow. Robert Earl Hayden. CP-HaydR *Fr.* Snow Lamp, The.

Across Nevada and Utah. March of the Hungry Mountains. Carl Sandburg. CP-SandC

Across salt marshes north of. Little Songs for Gaia. Gary Snyder. CP-SnydG

Across Space and Time. Charles Olson. CP-OlsoC

Across the Bay. Donald Davie. CP-DaviDC

Across the bridge across the dyke. Fugitive's Ride, The. Stevie Smith. CP-SmitS

Across the cages of the keyless aviaries. Aubade—Harlem. Thomas Merton. CP-MertT

Across the floor flits the mechanical toy. Cirque d'Hiver. Elizabeth Bishop. CP-BishE

Across the frontiers of the helpless world. Nineteen Thirty-Eight. John Berryman. CP-BerrJ

Across the frozen marshes. Conquest of Finland, The. John Greenleaf Whittier. CP-WhitJ

Across the Great Schism, through our whole landscape. Old Man's Road, The. W. H. Auden. CP-AudeW

Across the hills and down the narrow ways. Winter's Day, A. Paul Laurence Dunbar. CP-DunbP

Across the millstream below the bridge. Blue Swallows, The. Howard

Nemerov. CP-NemeH

Across the mud flats and the wide roads, over rivers and borders. Marilyn Hacker. SP-HackM *Fr.* Navigators, The.

Across the open countryside. Unsettled Motorcyclist's Vision of His Death, The. Thom Gunn. CP-GunnT

Across the painted colonnades. Suite Clownesque. T. S. Eliot. SP-ElioT

Across the Room. David Ignatow. SP-IgnaD

Across the room the shifting smoke. Interlude: in a Bar. T. S. Eliot. SP-ElioT

Across the sea I heard the groans. Italy. John Greenleaf Whittier. CP-WhitJ

Across the snowy pastures of the estate. Fox Who Watched for the Midnight Sun, The. Norman Dubie. CP-DubiN

Across the space between. Tennessee Williams. CP-WillT

Across the Stony Mountains, o'er the desert's drouth and sand. Crisis, The. John Greenleaf Whittier. CP-WhitJ

Across the thin / façade, the galleried. To Be Engraved on the Skull of a Cormorant. Charles Tomlinson. CP-TomlC; SP-TomlC

Across the tracks in Cheyenne, behind the biggest billboard. Long Way Outside Yellowstone, A. Thomas McGrath. SP-McGrT

Across the trampled, program-littered grass. After Commencement. Howard Nemerov. CP-NemeH

Across the way hands / move nervously on curtains. Other Side, The. C. K. Williams. CP-WillC

Across the wide waters / something comes. Swan, The. Mary Oliver. SP-OlivM

Across the world / in the high mountains of the West. Philip Levine. SP-LeviP *Fr.* Poem with No Ending, A.

Acrostic. John Keats. CP-KeatJ

Acrostic for Abby Stockton. Annis Boudinot Stockton. CP-StocA

Acrostic for Georgeana Cuthbert. Annis Boudinot Stockton. CP-StocA

Act, The. Heather McHugh. SP-McHuH

Act, The. William Carlos Williams. CP-WilW2

Act of building Progress is immense—everyone, The. Builders. Constantine P. Cavafy. CP-CavaC, *tr.* by Theoharis Constantine Theoharis

Act of love seemed a dead metaphor, The. Metaphor, The. Robert Graves. CP-GravR

Act of Love, The. Robert Creeley. CP-CreeR

Act of seeing a tree is the act of pressing, The. Spell of Conjunctivitis: A. Mona Van Duyn. SP-VanDM

Act of Union. Seamus Heaney. SP-HeanSO

Act Sederunt of the Session—A Scots Ballad. Robert Burns. CP-BurnR

Actfive. Archibald MacLeish. CP-MacLA

Acting younger than I am and thinking older. To Hedli. Louis MacNeice. CP-MacNL

Action. Denise Levertov. SP-LeveDS

Action and Non-Action. Chuang Tzu. CP-MertT

Action is a pain of being. Autumnal. Richard Eberhart. CP-EberR

Action of Therapy, The. May Sarton. SP-SartM

Active Life. Chuang Tzu. CP-MertT

Actor they'd brought in to entertain them, The. Young Men of Sidon (400 A.D.). Constantine P. Cavafy. CP-CavaC, *tr.* by Theoharis Constantine Theoharis

Actors; A Hate Song. Dorothy Parker. CP-ParkD

Actors with their variety of voices. Mexican Guitar, A. Frank O'Hara. SP-OharF

Actress, The. Stevie Smith. CP-SmitS

Actresses; A Hate Song. Dorothy Parker. CP-ParkD

Acts 8; On the Baptized Æthiopian. Richard Crashaw. *See* On the Baptized Ethiopian

Acts 21; I Am Ready Not Onely To Be Bound but To Dye. Richard Crashaw. CP-CrasR

Acts of God. Heather McHugh. SP-McHuH

Acts of Helplessness. Jelaluddin Rumi. SP-Rumi, *tr.* by Coleman Barks

Acts of Light which beautified, The. Emily Dickinson. SP-DickE

Acts Passed Beyond. Stephen Spender. CP-SpenS

Actual Cause, The. Yannis Ritsos. SP-RitsY, *tr.* by Kostas Myrsiades

Actual Vision of Morning's Extrusion. Alan Dugan. CP-DugaA

Actually there isn't a thing. Feng-kan. CP-ColdM, *tr.* by Red Pine

Actuarial Wife, The. Wyatt Prunty. SP-PrunW

Ad Amicos. G. K. Chesterton. CP-ChesG

Ad Amicum Eruditum Thomam Sheridan [To My Learned Friend, Thomas Sheridan]. Jonathan Swift. CP-SherT, *tr.* by Robert Hogan

Ad Amorem. Thomas Campion. CP-CampT

Ad ampliss. totius Angliae Cancellarium, Fr. Ba. Thomas Campion. CP-CampT

Ad Cambricum. Thomas Campion. CP-CampT

Ad Carolum Fitz Geofridum. Thomas Campion. CP-CampT

Ad Caspiam. Thomas Campion. CP-CampT

Ad Castitatem. Louise Bogan. CP-BogaL

Ad Castricum. Thomas Campion. CP-CampT

Ad Chloen. Thomas Campion. CP-CampT

Ad Ed. Mychelburnum. Thomas Campion. CP-CampT

Ad Ed. Spencerum. Thomas Campion. CP-CampT

Ad Episcopum Salopiensem. Gerard Manley Hopkins. CP-HopkG

Ad Ge. Chapmannum. Thomas Campion. CP-CampT

Ad Graios. Thomas Campion. CP-CampT

Ad Guil. Camdenum. Thomas Campion. CP-CampT

Ad Infinitum. William Carlos Williams. CP-WilW1

Ad Io. Davisium. Thomas Campion. CP-CampT

Ad Io. Dolundum. Thomas Campion. CP-CampT

Ad Leam. Thomas Campion. CP-CampT

Ad Librum. Thomas Campion. CP-CampT

Ad Lucium. Thomas Campion. CP-CampT

Ad Lyram. Samuel Taylor Coleridge. CP-ColeS

Ad Mariam. Gerard Manley Hopkins. CP-HopkG

Ad Matrem Virginem. Gerard Manley Hopkins. CP HopkG

Ad Melleam. Thomas Campion. CP-CampT

Ad Nashum. Thomas Campion. CP-CampT

Ad nobiliss. virum Gul. Percium. Thomas Campion. CP-CampT

Ad Pisonem. Lucan.
  "Unlike the ribald, whose licentious jest." CP-JohnS

Ad Regem Carolum Parodia [A Parody: To King Charles]. Andrew Marvell. CP-MarvA

Ad Reinhardt's black, in *Abstract Painting 33*. Gradations of Black. John Updike. CP-UpdiJ

Ad Reverendum Patrem Fratrem Thomam Burke O.P. Collegium S. Beunonis Invisentem. Gerard Manley Hopkins. CP-HopkG

Ad Rob. Caraeum Equitem Auratum Nobilissimum. Thomas Campion. CP-CampT

Ad Rusticum. Thomas Campion. CP-CampT

Ad Te, Doctissime Delany. Thomas Sheridan. CP-SherT, *tr. by* Robert Hogan

Ad Thamesin. Thomas Campion. CP-CampT

Ad Tho. Munsonium, equitem Auratum et Baronetum. Thomas Campion. CP-CampT

Ad Venetos venit corio Coryatus ab uno. *Incipit Thomas Campianus Medicinae Doctor.* In Peragrantissimi, Itinerosissimi, *Montiscandentissimique Peditis, Thomae Coryati,* viginti-hebdomadarium *Diarium, sex pedibus gradiens,* partim vero claudicans, Encomiasticon. Thomas Campion. CP-CampT

Ad Vilmum Axiologum. Samuel Taylor Coleridge. CP-ColeS

Adagio. Wallace Stevens. CP-StevWP

Adam. Federico García Lorca. SP-GarcF, *tr. by* Roy Campbell

Adam. Federico García Lorca. CP-GarcF, *tr. by* Christopher Maurer

Adam. Stephen Spender. CP-SpenS

Adam. Charles Tomlinson. CP-TomlC; SP-TomlC

Adam. William Carlos Williams CP-WilW1

Adam and Eve. Karl Shapiro. SP-ShapK

Adam and Eve. Arthur Hugh Clough. SP-ClouA

Adam and Eve sat in their garden. Throwing the Apple. Richard Eberhart. CP-EberR

Adam & Eve. / The serpent cracked. Initium. Federico García Lorca. CP-GarcF, *tr. by* Jerome Rothenberg *Fr.* Mirror Suite.

Adam and Eve were created for another purpose. Gardener. Czeslaw Milosz. CP-MiloCN, *tr. by* Brian Glazer *and* Martin Sabiniewicz

Adam and Eve were reading about a monkey in a bath. Czeslaw Milosz. CP-MiloCN, *tr. by* Robert Hass

Adam A———'s Prayer. Robert Burns. CP-BurnR

Adam ate an apple. Reply. Federico García Lorca. CP-GarcF, *tr. by* Jerome Rothenberg *Fr.* Newton.

Adam Cast Forth. Jorge Luis Borges. SP-BorgJ, *tr. by* Alastair Reid

Adam Cast Forth. Richard Eberhart. CP-EberR

Adam had found what was not his to seek. Eden. Donald Davie. CP-DaviDC

Adam in Extremis. Robert Stock. SP-StocR

Adam in Winter. James Dickey. CP-DickJ

Adam Is Your Ashes. Jorge Luis Borges. SP-BorgJ, *tr. by* Eric McHenry

Adam Lay Ibounden. Robert Stock. SP-StocR

Adam, Lilith, and Eve. Robert Browning. CP-BroR2

Adam made the world. Continuous Is Broken, and Resumes, The. Eleanor Wilner. SP-WilnE

Adam, on such a morning, named the beasts. Adam. Charles Tomlinson. CP-TomlC; SP-TomlC

Adam scriveyn [*or* scrivain *or* scrivein], if ever it thee bifalle. Chaucer's Wordes unto Adam, his Owne Scriveyn. Geoffrey Chaucer. CP-ChauG

Adam Thinking. Lucille Clifton. SP-ClifL

Adamant, The. Theodore Roethke. CP-RoetT

Adamo Me. Charles Olson. CP-OlsoC

Adam's Curse. William Butler Yeats. CP-YeatW

Adam's Song. Derek Walcott. CP-WalcD

Adaption of a Theme from Catullus. Catullus. *See* Carmina

Add This to Rhetoric. Wallace Stevens. CP-StevW; CP-StevWP

Add to your show, before you close it, France. Bravo, Paris Exposition! Walt Whitman. CP-WhitW

Added to / making a Republic. Charles Olson. SP-OlsoC *Fr.* Maximus Poems, The.

Addenda Quaedam. Jonathan Swift. CP-SwifJ

Addendum. Yusef Komunyakaa. CP-KomuY

Addict, The. Anne Sexton. CP-SextA; SP-SextA

Addio. John Ciardi. CP-CiarJ

Addition. Constantine P. Cavafy. CP-CavaC, *tr. by* Theoharis Constantine Theoharis

Addition ("Put 5 and 5 together"). Langston Hughes. CP-HughL; CP-HughL3

Addition ("7 x 7 + love ="). Langston Hughes. CP-HughL; CP-HughL2

Additional Poem, An. John Ashbery. SP-AshbJ

Address. Lord Byron. CP Byron

Address. William Carlos Williams. CP-WilW2

Address, An. William Carlos Williams. CP-WilW2

Address Intended to be Recited at the Caledonian Meeting. Lord Byron. CP-Byron

Address of Beelzebub. Robert Burns. CP-BurnR

Address to a Bird on a Visit Home. Alan Dugan. CP-DugaA

Address to Edinburgh. Robert Burns. CP-BurnR

Address to General Dumourier. Robert Burns. CP-BurnR

Address to Kilchurn Castle, upon Loch Awe. William Wordsworth. CP-WorW1

Address to Miss Phillis Wheatl[e]y, An. Jupiter Hammon. CP-WheaP

Address to My Infant Daughter, Dora on Being Reminded That She Was a Month Old That Day, September 16. William Wordsworth. CP-WorW1

Address to Silence. William Wordsworth. CP-WorW1

Address to the Angels. Maxine W. Kumin. SP-KumiM

Address to the Atheist, by P. Wheatley at the Age of 14 Years—1767, An. Phillis Wheatley. CP-WheaP

Address to the Beasts. W. H. Auden. CP-AudeW

Address to the Boobus. Philip Whalen. SP-WhalP

Address to the Deil. Robert Burns. CP-BurnR

Address to the Deist—1767, An. Phillis Wheatley. CP-WheaP

Address to the Mob, An. William Cowper. CP-CowpW

Address to the Ocean. William Wordsworth. CP-WorW1

Address to the Scholars of New England. John Crowe Ransom. SP-RansJ (To the Scholars of Harvard.) SP-RansJ

Address to the Scholars of the Village School of—1798. William Wordsworth. CP-WorW1

Address to the Senior Class. William Stafford. SP-StafWW

Address, to the Shade of Thomson, on Crowning His Bust, at *Ednam, Roxburgh-shire,* with Bays. Robert Burns. CP-BurnR

Address to the Sons of Burns, after Visiting Their Father's Grave (August 14th, 1803). William Wordsworth. MW-WorW

Address to the Tooth-Ache. Robert Burns. CP-BurnR

Address to the Unco Guid, or the Rigidly Righteous. Robert Burns. CP-BurnR

Address to the Woodlark. Robert Burns. CP-BurnR

Address to Tyger. James Austen. CP-AustJ

Addressed to a Student of Divinity. Annis Boudinot Stockton. CP-StocA

Addressed to a Young Man of Fortune. Samuel Taylor Coleridge. CP-ColeS

Addressed to General Washington, in the Year 1777, after the Battles of Trenton and Princeton. Annis Boudinot Stockton. CP-StocA

Addressed to Haydon. John Keats. CP-KeatJ

Addressing reason, yet above it still. Revelation. Jones Very. CP-VeryJ

Adela is such a silly woman. V. Stevie Smith. CP-SmitS

Adelaide Abner. Stevie Smith. CP-SmitS

Adelaide Crapsey. Carl Sandburg. CP-SandC

Adelina Out Walking. Federico García Lorca. CP-GarcF, *tr. by* Alan S. Trueblood *Fr.* Andalusian Songs.

Adept, too late, at art of tears he stands. Aged Man Surveys the Past. Robert Penn Warren. CP-WarrR

Adequacy. Elizabeth Barrett Browning. CP-BroEB

Adhuc sub Judice Lis. E. E. Cummings. CP-CummE

Adieu. Walter De la Mare. CP-DeLaW

Adieu. Dante Gabriel Rossetti. CW-RossD

Adieu, The. Lord Byron. CP-Byron

Adieu À Charlot. Lawrence Ferlinghetti. SP-FerlL

Adieu! a heart-warm, fond adieu! Farewell. To the Brethren of St. James' Lodge, Tarbolton, The. Robert Burns. CP-BurnR

Adieu, adieu, my Friar, he cried. George Meredith. CP-MerG2

Adieu, New-England's smiling meads.   Farewel[l] to America, A. To Mrs. S. W.   Phillis Wheatley.   CP-WheaP

Adieu O soldier.   Adieu to a Soldier.   Walt Whitman.   CP-WhitW

Adieu to a Soldier.   Walt Whitman.   CP-WhitW

Adieu to Norman, Bon Jour to Joan and Jean-Paul.   Frank O'Hara.   SP-OharF

Adieu, ye joys of La Valette!   Farewell to Malta.   Lord Byron.   CP-Byron

Adirondack Summer.   Lorine Niedecker.   CP-NiedL

Adirondacs, The.   Ralph Waldo Emerson.   CP-EmerR

Adjustable Lunatic, An.   James Whitcomb Riley.
   Dream of Death, The.   CP-RileJ
   Fantasy.   CP-RileJ

Adjusting to the Light.   Miller Williams.   CP-WillM

Adjustment.   John Greenleaf Whittier.   CP-WhitJ

Admetus, from my marrow's core I do.   Edna St. Vincent Millay.   CP-MillE

Administration.   Philip Larkin.   CP-LarkP

Administrator.   Thomas Kinsella.   CP-KinsT

Administrators of minutes into hours.   Elegy for G. B. Shaw.   John Ciardi.   CP-CiarJ

Admirable number pi, The.   Pi.   Wisława Szymborska.   SP-SzymW, tr. by Stanislaw Barańczak and Clare Cavanagh

Admirable number pi, The.   Pi.   Wisława Szymborska.   SP-SzymWM, tr. by Joanna Trzeciak

Admiral Fan, The.   C. K. Williams.   CP-WillC

Admiral to His Lady, The.   Donald Davie.   CP-DaviDC

Admirals Curse-You and No-More.   Little Daughters of America, The.   Stevie Smith.   CP-SmitS

Admirations—and Contempts—of time, The.   Emily Dickinson.   CP-DickE

Admire Cranmer!   Stevie Smith.   CP-SmitS

Admire the old man, admire him, admire him.   Admire Cranmer!   Stevie Smith.   CP-SmitS

Admiring Nature in her wildest grace.   Written with a Pencil over the Chimney-Piece, in the Parlour of the Inn at Kenmore, Taymouth.   Robert Burns.   CP-BurnR

Admission.   A. R. Ammons.   CP-AmmoA

Admission.   Rae Armantrout.   SP-ArmaA

Admit the ruse to fix and name her chaste.   Romantic, The.   Louise Bogan.   CP-BogaL

Admit the sky carries no threatening message.   To Oneself.   David Ignatow.   SP-IgnaD

Admit, thou darling of mine eyes.   To His Jealous Mistress.   Thomas Carew.   CP-CareT

Admonition.   James Laughlin.   CP-LaugJ

Admonition.   Eleanor Wilner.   SP-WilnE

Admonition.   William Wordsworth.   CP-WorW1

Admonition, An.   Joseph Brodsky.   CP-BrodJ, tr. by George L. Kline

Admonition to the Dead.   Robert Penn Warren.   CP-WarrR

Admonition to Those Who Mourn.   Robert Penn Warren.   CP-WarrR

Admonitions.   Sylvia Plath.   CP-PlatS

Admonitions to a Special Person.   Anne Sexton.   CP-SextA

Admonitor: A Pearl for Arrogance.   Alan Dugan.   CP-DugaA

Adolescence.   W. H. Auden.   CP-AudeW

Adolescence.   Thom Gunn.   CP-GunnT

Adolescence.   David Ignatow.   SP-IgnaD

Adolescence.   Gregory Orr.   SP-OrrG

Adolescence—I.   Rita Dove.   SP-DoveR

Adolescence—II.   Rita Dove.   SP-DoveR

Adolescence—III.   Rita Dove.   SP-DoveR

Adolescent.   Yannis Ritsos.   SP-RitsY, tr. by Athan Anagnostopoulos

Adolescent Franz Schubert, The.   Seventeen.   Adam Zagajewski.   SP-ZagaA, tr. by Renata Gorczynski, Benjamin Ivry and C. K. Williams

Adolescent stone hand on the chair, The.   Memorial Services.   Yannis Ritsos.   SP-RitsY, tr. by N. C. Germanacos

Adolf Eichmann.   Hayden Carruth.   CP-CarHS

Adonais; An Elegy on the Death of John Keats.   Percy Bysshe Shelley.   CP-ShelP

Adonis.   "H. D."   CP-DoolH

Adonis.   David Ignatow.   SP-IgnaD

Adonis in Summer.   Kenneth Rexroth.   CP-RexrK

Adonis in Winter.   Kenneth Rexroth.   CP-RexrK

Adorable images.   To the Mannequins.   Howard Nemerov.   CP-NemeH

Adorable is an adjective and womankind is a noun.   Allow Me, Madam, But It Won't Help.   Ogden Nash.   CP-NashO

Adoration of the Virgin, The.   Robert Duncan.   SP-DuncR

Adore the Roses; nor delay.   Rosary Beads.   Herman Melville.   SP-MelvH

Adoro Te. The Hymn of Saint Thomas in Adoration of the Blessed Sacrament.   Richard Crashaw.   CP-CrasR

Adown the west a golden glow.   At Sunset Time.   Paul Laurence Dunbar.   CP-DunbP

Adown winding Nith I did wander.   Song: "Adown winding Nith I did wander."   Robert Burns.   CP-BurnR

Adriano in Syria.   Pietro Metastasio.
   Translations from Metastasio.   CP-JohnS

Adrian's Address to His Soul When Dying.   Emperor Hadrian.   CP-Byron   Fr. Hadrian's Address to His Soul When Dying.

Adrift! A little boat adrift!   Emily Dickinson.   CP-DickE

Adrift, / distracted.   Theodore Weiss.   SP-WeisT   Fr. Storeroom, The.

Adrogué.   Jorge Luis Borges.   SP-BorgJ, tr. by Alastair Reid

Adulation is inexpensive.   Emily Dickinson.   SP-DickE

Adult Bookstore.   Karl Shapiro.   SP-ShapK

Adult Entertainment.   Marilyn Hacker.   SP-HackM

Adult Epigram.   Wallace Stevens.   CP-StevW; CP-StevWP

Adult Grief.   Louise Glück.   SP-GlucL

Adulteress stoned to death, The.   Adam's Song.   Derek Walcott.   CP-WalcD

Adultery.   Raymond Carver.   CP-CarvR

Adultery.   James Dickey.   CP-DickJ

Adultery.   Alan Dugan.   CP-DugaA

Adultery.   Thom Gunn.   CP-GunnT

Adultery At Forty.   Donald Hall.   CP-HallD

Adults Only.   William Stafford.   SP-StafW; SP-StafWW

Advance and take your place.   Greeting for Old Age.   William Carlos Williams.   CP-WilW2

Advance—come forth from the Tyrolean ground.   William Wordsworth.   CP-WorW1

Advance is Life's condition.   Emily Dickinson.   CP-DickE

Advance your choral [or chorall] motions now.   Stars Dance, The.   Thomas Campion.   CP-CampT   Fr. Lords Mask[e], The.

Advanced out toward the external from.   Celestial Evening, October 1967.   Charles Olson.   SP-OlsoC   Fr. Maximus Poems, The.

Advancing with a self-denying gaze, he.   Mechanist, The.   Richard Wilbur.   CP-WilbR

Advantage, The.   Charles Olson.   CP-OlsoC

Advantages of Learning, The.   Kenneth Rexroth.   CP-RexrK

Adveniat Regnum Tuum.   G. K. Chesterton.   CP-ChesG

Advent.   Donald Davie.   CP-DaviDC

Advent.   Thomas Merton.   CP-MertT

Advent.   Kenneth Rexroth.   CP-RexrK

Advent.   Christina Georgina Rossetti.   CP-RosC2

Advent.   Christina Georgina Rossetti.   CP-RosC1

Advent.   Christina Georgina Rossetti.   CP-RosC3

Advent.   James Schuyler.   CP-SchuJ

Advent 1966.   Denise Levertov.   SP-LeveDS

Advent of Summer.   Robert Graves.   CP-GravR

Advent of Today.   William Carlos Williams.   CP-WilW1

Advent Sunday.   Christina Georgina Rossetti.   CP-RosC2

Adverse and prosperous Fortunes both work on.   All Things Run Well for the Righteous.   Robert Herrick.   CP-HerrR

Adversity.   Robert Herrick.   CP-HerrR

Adversity.   Robert Herrick.   CP-HerrR

Advertisement.   Laura Riding Jackson.   CP-RidiL

Advertisement.   Wisława Szymborska.   SP-SzymW, tr. by Stanislaw Barańczak and Clare Cavanagh

Advertisement, The.   Rudyard Kipling.   CP-KiplR   Fr. Muse among the Motors, The.

Advertisement for a Reader.   John Ciardi.   CP-CiarJ

Advertisement for the Waldorf-Astoria.   Langston Hughes.   CP-HughL; CP-HughL1

Advertising in Paris.   Alan Dugan.   CP-DugaA

Adverts.   James Schuyler.   CP-SchuJ

Advice.   Paul Laurence Dunbar.   CP-DunbP

Advice.   Ivor Gurney.   SP-GurnI

Advice.   Langston Hughes.   CP-HughL; CP-HughL3

Advice.   Fernando Pessoa.   SP-PessF, tr. by Susan M. Brown and Edwin Honig

Advice doesn't help lovers!   Each Note.   Jelaluddin Rumi.   SP-Rumi, tr. by Coleman Barks

Advice for good love: don't love a woman.   Yehuda Amichai.   SP-AmicY, tr. by Chana Bloch

Advice from a Mother.   Robert Graves.   CP-GravR

Advice from the Holy Tomb.   Howard Nemerov.   CP-NemeH

Advice from the Muse.   Richard Wilbur.   CP-WilbR

Advice of good love: do not love.   Yehuda Amichai.   SP-AmicYL, tr. by Benjamin Harshav and Barbara Harshav

Advice of the Popes Who Succeeded the Age of Rafael.   William Blake.   CP-BlakW

Advice outside a Church.   Ogden Nash.   CP-NashO

Advice, The. Sir Walter Ralegh. CP-RaleW

Advice the Best Actor. Robert Herrick. CP-HerrR

Advice to a Beauty. Countee Cullen. CP-CullC

Advice to a Girl. Thomas Campion. CP-CampT

Advice to a God. Mona Van Duyn. SP-VanDM

Advice to a Maid. Robert Herrick. CP-HerrR

Advice to a Parson. Jonathan Swift. CP-SwifJ

Advice to a Prophet. Richard Wilbur. CP-WilbR

Advice to a Young Prophet. Thomas Merton. CP-MertT

Advice to Aurelius. James Laughlin. CP-LaugJ

Advice to Pilgrims. Robinson Jeffers. CP-JefR3

Advice to the Grub Street Verse-Writers. Jonathan Swift. CP-SwifJ

Advice to Writers. Billy Collins. SP-CollB

Advice to Young Children. Stevie Smith. CP-SmitS

Adviser to the Court. Tu Fu. CP-KizeC, tr. by Carolyn Kizer

Advising the Prince. Chuang Tzu. CP-MertT

Advocates. Robert Graves. CP-GravR

Adze, The. Wendell Berry. CP-BerrW

Ae day, as Death, that grusome carl. Lines Addressed to Mr. John Ranken. Robert Burns. CP-BurnR

Ae weet forenicht i' the yow-trummle. Watergaw, The. Hugh MacDiarmid. SP-MacDH

Aegeus in Prison. Alfonso Cortes. CP-MertT

Aegle, beauty and poet, has two little crimes. From the French. Lord Byron CP-Byron

Aegupton. Ezra Pound. CP-PoEar

Aeneas at New York. Allen Tate. CP-TateA

Aeneas at Washington. Allen Tate. CP-TateA

Aeneas: *Then I will found a temple of solid marble to.* On Lines 69–70, Book 4, of Virgil's *Aeneid.* Alan Dugan. CP-DugaA

Aeneas Underground. Robert Stock. SP-StocR

Aeneas was praying and holding on the altar. Golden Bough, The. Virgil. SP-HeanSO *Fr. Aeneid [or Eneados or Aeneis], The.*

Aeneid. Virgil.

  Book 5.

    Nisus and Euryalus ("From thence his way the Trojan hero bent"). CP-DryJ2, tr. by John Dryden

  Book 8.

    Speech of Venus to Vulcan, The. CP-DryJ2, tr. by John Dryden

  Book 9.

    Nisus and Euryalus ("Trojan camp the common danger shared, The"). CP-DryJ2, tr. by John Dryden

  Book 10.

    Mezentius and Lausus. CP-DryJ2, tr. by John Dryden

Aeneid [or Eneados or Aeneis], The. Virgil.

  "All breathed in silence, and intensely gazed." CP-WorW2, tr. by William Wordsworth

  "Amazons with Crescent-formed shield, The." CP-RaleW, tr. by Walter Ralegh

  Anchises to Aeneas. CP-RaleW, tr. by Walter Ralegh

  "Arms, and the Man I sing, the first who bore." CP-WorW2, tr. by William Wordsworth

  "Ev'n yet his voice from Hell's dread shades we hear." CP-JohnS, tr. by Samuel Johnson

  "For healthful indigence in vain they pray." CP-JohnS, tr. by Samuel Johnson

  Golden Bough, The. SP-HeanSO, tr. by Seamus Heaney

  "Hesperia the Gr[a]ecians call the place." CP-RaleW, tr. by Walter Ralegh

  "In the main[e] sea the i[s]le of Cre[e]te doth lie." CP-RaleW, tr. by Walter Ralegh

  "Now when the Gods had crushed the Asian State." CP-WorW2, tr. by William Wordsworth

  "Of mortal Justice if thou scorn the rod." CP-JohnS, tr. by Samuel Johnson

  "Queene anone commands the waightie bowle, The." CP-RaleW, tr. by Walter Ralegh

  "Saturne descending from the heavens high." CP-RaleW, tr. by Walter Ralegh

  "She who to lift her heavy eyes had tried." CP-WorW2, tr. by William Wordsworth

  "Some old Auruncans, I remember well." CP-RaleW, tr. by Walter Ralegh

  "There is a Land which Greekes Hesperia name." CP-RaleW, tr. by Walter Ralegh

  "This scarcely uttered they advance, and straight." CP-WorW2, tr. by William Wordsworth

  "Thus was Italy mov'd—nor did the chief." CP-CowpW, tr. by William Cowper

Ænigma, An. Vincent Bourne. CP-CowpW

Æolian. Hayden Carruth. CP-CarHS

Aeolian Harp, The. Herman Melville. SP-MelvH

Aërial Rock—Whose Solitary Brow. William Wordsworth. CP-WorW2

Aerialist. Sylvia Plath. CP-PlatS

Aerie. John Updike. CP-UpdiJ

Aerolite, The. Thomas Hardy. CP-HardT

Aeschylus' Soliloquy. Robert Browning. CP-BroR2

Aesthete [or Esthete] in Harlem. Langston Hughes. CP-HughL; CP-HughL1

Aesthetic. Charles Tomlinson. CP-TomlC; SP-TomlC

Aesthetic Distance. Miller Williams. CP-WillM

Aesthetics after War. Richard Eberhart. CP-EberR

Aetatis suae fifty-two. Progress of Marriage, The. Jonathan Swift. CP-SwifJ

Aeterna Poetae Memoria. Archibald MacLeish. CP-MacLA

Æternall love! what 'tis to love thee well. In Amorem Divinum. Richard Crashaw. CP-CrasR

Aeterne Rerum Conditor. Saint Ambrose. CP-CunnJ, tr. by James Vincent Cunningham

Aether. Allen Ginsberg. CP-GinsA

Ævo diversi tres et regione poetae. Milton. John Dryden. CP-HopkG

Afar away the light that brings cold cheer. Proserpina. Dante Gabriel Rossetti. CW-RossD

Afar th' illustrious Exile roams. Birth-Day Ode. December 31st 1787, A. Robert Burns. CP-BurnR

Affable, bibulous, / corpulent, dull. Capacity. John Updike. CP-UpdiJ

Affable Irregular, An Road at My Door, The. William Butler Yeats. CP-YeatW *Fr. Meditations in Time of Civil War.*

Affair, The. Miller Williams. CP-WillM

Affair was badly flawed, The. Georgy Vladimirovich Ivanov. SP-WeisT

Affection is a noble quality. Reflection on Caution. Ogden Nash. CP-NashO

Affection is like bread. Emily Dickinson. SP-DickE

Affection wants you to know it is here. Emily Dickinson. SP-DickE

Affectionate Taxes to France. Rainer Maria Rilke.

  Grave. CP-RilkFr, tr. by A. Poulin, Jr.

  "Let's stay by the lamp and say little." CP-RilkFr, tr. by A. Poulin, Jr.

  L'Indifférent. CP-RilkFr, tr. by A. Poulin, Jr.

  "Of what anticipation." CP-RilkFr, tr. by A. Poulin, Jr.

  Pegasus. CP-RilkFr, tr. by A. Poulin, Jr.

  Prayer of One Not Indifferent Enough. CP-RilkFr, tr. by A. Poulin, Jr.

  Sleeper, The. CP-RilkFr, tr. by A. Poulin, Jr.

  "Sometimes lovers or writers." CP-RilkFr, tr. by A. Poulin, Jr.

  "Stay still, if the angel." CP-RilkFr, tr. by A. Poulin, Jr.

  To a Friend. CP-RilkFr, tr. by A. Poulin, Jr.

  "We must believe that all is well." CP-RilkFr, tr. by A. Poulin, Jr.

  "What could those Three." CP-RilkFr, tr. by A. Poulin, Jr.

  "Will I have expressed it before I leave." CP-RilkFr, tr. by A. Poulin, Jr.

Affections lose their object; Time brings forth. Sonnet (To an Octogenarian). William Wordsworth. CP-WorW2

Affirmed. Pent by power that holds it fast. Like a Bulwark. Marianne Craig Moore. CP-MoorM

Affliction. Robert Herrick. CP-HerrR

Affliction: "Kill me not every [or ev'ry] day." George Herbert. CP-HerbG (Affliction (2).) CP-HerbG

Affliction (1). George Herbert. CP-HerbG

Affliction (2). George Herbert. *See* Affliction: "Kill me not every [or ev'ry] day"

Affliction (3). George Herbert. CP-HerbG

Affliction (4). George Herbert. CP-HerbG

Afflction (5). George Herbert. CP-HerbG

Affliction of Margaret, The. William Wordsworth. CP-WorW1

Affliction of William Cowper, The. Marya Alexandrovna Zaturenska. SP-ZatuM

Affliction sore long time he bore. Henry Hardiman. Christina Georgina Rossetti. CP-RosC3

Afflictions bring us joy in times to come. Pain[e] Ends in Pleasure. Robert Herrick. CP-HerrR

Afflictions they most profitable are. Persecutions Profitable. Robert Herrick. CP-HerrR

Affronted Moon, The. Charles Baudelaire. CP-BaudC, tr. by Walter Martin

Afghanistan. Raymond Carver. CP-CarvR

Afica. Charles Olson. CP-OlsoC

Afield. Wallace Stevens. CP-StevWP

Afoot and light-hearted I take to the open road. Song of the Open Road. Walt Whitman. CP-WhitW

Afoot, on horseback, with bugles and baying hounds. Idea. Czeslaw Milosz. CP-MiloC; CP-MiloCN, tr. by Robert Hass

Afraid. Langston Hughes. CP-HughL; CP-HughL1

Afraid of the table, afraid of the alcove. Sleep. Rainer Maria Rilke. CP-RilkFr, tr. by A. Poulin, Jr.

Afraid! Of whom am I afraid? Emily Dickinson. CP-DickE

Africa. Maya Angelou. SP-AngeM

Africa. G. K. Chesterton. CP-ChesG

Africa. Langston Hughes. CP-HughL; CP-HughL3

Africa. William Carlos Williams. CP-WilW1

African Images, Glimpses from a Tiger's Back. Alice Walker. CP-WalkA

African Violet. Louis Zukofsky. CP-ZukLS

African's First Sight of the Ocean, The. Jones Very. CP-VeryJ

Afro-American Fragment. Langston Hughes. CP-HughL; CP-HughL1

Aften hae I played at the cards and the dice. Rantin Laddie, The. Robert Burns. CP-BurnR

After. Maya Angelou. SP-AngeM

After. Robert Browning. CP-BroR1

After. Robert Creeley. SP-CreeR

After. Czeslaw Milosz. CP-MiloCN, *tr. by* Robert Hass

After, a bloodstain appeared in the asphalt. Blood. Yannis Ritsos. SP-RitsY, *tr. by* Christian McEwen *and* Nikos Tsingos

After a brief unconsciousness. Emily Dickinson. SP-DickE

After a Brubeck Concert. Miller Williams. CP-WillM

After a Change of Régime. Donald Davie. CP-DaviDC

After a day of practical rain. Rainer Maria Rilke. CP-RilkFr, *tr. by* A. Poulin, Jr. *Fr.* Fragments.

After a day of wind. Rainer Maria Rilke. CP-RilkFr, *tr. by* A. Poulin, Jr. *Fr.* Valaisian Quatrains, The.

After a Death. Gregory Orr. SP-OrrG

After a Death. Charles Tomlinson. CP-TomlC; SP-TomlC

After a Few Whiffs of Another World. Thomas Lux. SP-LuxT

After a good beating on a cold day. Fanny Howe. SP-HoweF *Fr.* Q.

After a hundred years. Emily Dickinson. CP-DickE

After a Journey. Thomas Hardy. CP-HardT

After a little I could not have told—. Song of the Tortured Girl, The. John Berryman. CP-BerrJ

After a Long Illness. Robert Duncan. SP-DuncR

After a long journey we awoke. Place of Pilgrimage. Jaroslav Seifert. SP-SeifJ, *tr. by* Ewald Osers

After a long, long course, hundreds of years, denials. Long, Long Hence. Walt Whitman. CP-WhitW

After a long walk in the woods clear cut for lumber. Fifty Males Sitting Together. Robert Bly. SP-BlyR

After a month and a half without rain. August Rain. Robert Bly. SP-BlyR

After a night of opium and alcohol, Edgar Poe. Jeremiad. Norman Dubie. CP-DubiN

After a Night of Perplexing Dreams. Annis Boudinot Stockton. CP-StocA

After a night of rage. Love Poem for a Wife, 2. A. K. Ramanujan. CP-RamaA

After a Poem by Carlos Drummond de Andrade Translated by Elizabeth Bishop as *Don't Kill Yourself.* Alan Dugan. CP-DugaA

After a Romantic Day. Thomas Hardy. CP-HardT

After a Sentence in "Malte Laurids Brigge" Adrienne Rich. CP-RicAE

After a Settlement of Debts. Yannis Ritsos. SP-RitsY, *tr. by* Kimon Friar *and* Kostas Myrsiades

After a Spanish Proverb. Dorothy Parker. CP-ParkD

After a Storm. W. S. Merwin. SP-MerwWF

After a string of failed romances and intensely remarked sexual adventures she'd finally married. Experience. C. K. Williams. SP-WillC

After a thoughtful, almost painful pause. Christmas Afterthought. James Whitcomb Riley. CP-RileJ

After a Visit. Countee Cullen. CP-CullC

After a Visit. Paul Laurence Dunbar. CP-DunbP

After a Visit. Tennessee Williams. CP-WillT

After a Walk. Federico García Lorca. CP-GarcF, *tr. by* Greg Simon *and* Steven F. White

After a war come the memorials. Men. William Stafford. SP-StafWW

After a week of physical anguish. Evening Lull, An. Walt Whitman. CP-WhitW

After a winter of seclusion. Spring Was Begging to Be Born. James Tate. SP-TateJ

After Adam broke his rib in two. Rats Live on No Evil Star. Anne Sexton. CP-SextA

After all Birds have been investigated and laid aside. Emily Dickinson. CP-DickE

After All Saints' Day. D. H. Lawrence. CP-LawrD

After all that. At Songfall. Federico García Lorca. CP-GarcF, *tr. by* Jerome Rothenberg *Fr.* Moments of Song.

After All the Tragedies Are Over. D. H. Lawrence. CP-LawrD

After all, there's no need. Flirtation. Rita Dove. SP-DoveR

After all these years of hating. Winter Garden. Eleanor Wilner. SP-WilnE

After all those swerving arcs in air. Literal = The Abstract, The: A

Demonstration. Eleanor Wilner. SP-WilnE

After all, we also stand on a height. Our blood and culture have. Decaying Lambskins. Robinson Jeffers. CP-JefR2

After All, What Else Is There to Say? Allen Ginsberg. CP-GinsA

After all white horses are in bed. E. E. Cummings. CP-CummE

After all you are quite. Margaret Atwood. SP-AtwM1

After an Accident. Donald Davie. CP-DaviDC

After an Interval. Walt Whitman. CP-WhitW

After an Old Song. Kenneth Patchen. CP-PatcK

After Apple-Picking. Robert Frost. CP-FrosR

After Arguing against the Contention That Art Must Come from Discontent. William Stafford. SP-StafWW

After Auschwitz. Anne Sexton. CP-SextA

After Autumne, Winter. Robert Herrick. CP-HerrR

After Basho. Carolyn Kizer. CP-KizeC

After Botticelli's *Birth of Venus.* Gregory Orr. SP-OrrG

After Charles Sedley. Louis Zukofsky. CP-ZukLS

After close, unembittered meditation. Deed of Gift. Robert Graves. CP-GravR

After Commencement. Howard Nemerov. CP-NemeH

After Communion. Christina Georgina Rossetti. CP-RosC1

After comparing lives with you for years. Letter to a Friend about Girls. Philip Larkin. CP-LarkP

After counting all the sheep in the world. Insomnia. Billy Collins. SP-CollB

After Cumae. Geoffrey Hill. CP-HillG

After Dark. D. H. Lawrence. CP-LawrD

After Dark. Adrienne Rich. CP-RicAE; SP-RicA1; SP-RicA2

After dark / Near the South Dakota border. Having Lost My Sons, I Confront the Wreckage of the Moon: Christmas, 1960. James Wright. CP-WrigJ

After Dark Vapours Have Oppressed Our Plains. John Keats. CP-KeatJ

After Dawn. Dorothy Parker. CP-ParkD

After Dead Souls. Allen Ginsberg. CP-GinsA

After Death. James Whitcomb Riley. CP-RileJ

After Death. Yannis Ritsos. SP-RitsY, *tr. by* Kimon Friar

After Death. Christina Georgina Rossetti. CP-RosC1

After Death. Algernon Charles Swinburne. SP-SwinA

After-Dinner Remarks. Philip Larkin. CP-LarkP

After Drinking All Night with a Friend, We Go Out in a Boat at Dawn to See Who Can Write the Best Poem. Robert Bly. SP-BlyR

After dying, now alone, torn apart, and rejected by his body, he fell asleep. His End and His Beginning. Jorge Luis Borges. SP-BorgJ, *tr. by* Alexander Coleman

After each war. End and Beginning. Wisława Szymborska. CP-BrodJ, *tr. by* Joseph Brodsky

After Election. John Greenleaf Whittier. CP-WhitJ

After Eli Whitney's gin. Southeast Arkanasia. Maya Angelou. SP-AngeM

After Enduring. Czeslaw Milosz. CP-MiloCN, *tr. by* Robert Hass

After every war. End and the Beginning, The. Wisława Szymborska. SP-SzymWM, *tr. by* Joanna Trzeciak

After every war. End and the Beginning, The. Wisława Szymborska. SP-SzymW, *tr. by* Stanislaw Barańczak *and* Clare Cavanagh

After everything I do, they march. As at Funerals. Yehuda Amichai. SP-AmicYL, *tr. by* Benjamin Harshav *and* Barbara Harshav

After fifty years Amelia Earhart's Lockheed fretted with rust. Persistence of 1937. Donald Hall. CP-HallD

After fifty years, the hawthorn hedge. Hawthorn in Trent Vale, The. Charles Tomlinson. CP-TomlC

After Fifty-five Years. Kathleen Jessie Raine. SP-RainK

After 53 years. Some Love. Allen Ginsberg. CP-GinsA

After five / times the poem. E. E. Cummings. CP-CummE

After Five Years. Theodore Weiss. SP-WeisT

After-Flight. Rainer Maria Rilke. CP-RilkFr, *tr. by* A. Poulin, Jr.

After ghosts & goblins. Halloween, the Late Fifties. Yusef Komunyakaa. CP-KomuY

After-Glow. E. E. Cummings. CP-CummE

After God's house burned down, they found the shirt. Notre Dame de Chartres. William Meredith. SP-MereW

After great pain a formal feeling comes. Emily Dickinson. CP-DickE

After great storms the calm returns. Sir Thomas Wyatt. CP-WyatT

After Greece. James Merrill. SP-MerrJ

After hard rain the eaves repeat their beads. Walk, The. Derek Walcott. CP-WalcD

After he died. Photograph. W. S. Merwin. SP-MerwWF

After he retired, for something to do. Obit. John Ciardi. CP-CiarJ

After Heraclitus. Margaret Atwood. SP-AtwM2

After His Realms and States were moved. King and the Sea, The. Rudyard Kipling. CP-KiplR

After hours of small talk and music. Body of Summer, The. Sam Hamill.

SP-HamiS

After hundreds of years of common sense. Holiday. Alan Dugan. CP-DugaA

After I am dead, darling. What They Said. Muriel Rukeyser. CP-RukeM

After I fled the place where many years. Petrarch. CP-Petra, *tr. by* J. G. Nichols

After I forgot about the horses. Marching. Charles Simic. SP-SimiC; SP-SimiCE

After it was over, though still gusting balefully. Eternity. Hart Crane. CP-CranH

After its capture, the animal. Cage, The. Gregory Orr. SP-OrrG

After Joe Was at the Island. James Schuyler. CP-SchuJ

After Jonah. Hart Crane. CP-CranH

After Lake Leman. Robinson Jeffers. CP-JefR3

After Lalon. Allen Ginsberg.
"It's true I got caught in / the world." SP-GinsA

After Long Busyness. Robert Bly. SP-BlyR

After Long Silence. William Butler Yeats. CP-YeatW

After long wars when comes release. Herba Santa. Herman Melville. SP-MelvH

After Lorca. Robert Creeley. CP-CreeR

After Love. Maxine W. Kumin. SP-KumiM

After Lunch. Olga Broumas. SP-BrouO

After making love, we are like. Mountains and Rivers without End. Sam Hamill. SP-HamiS

After Making Love We Hear Footsteps. Galway Kinnell. SP-KinnGN

After Mallarmé. Robert Creeley. CP-CreeR

After many battles / The good angel killed the bad one. Song of Purification. Carlos Drummond de Andrade. CP-MertT

After Many Days. Paul Laurence Dunbar. CP-DunbP

After Many Days. D. H. Lawrence. CP-LawrD

After Many Springs. Langston Hughes. CP-HughL; CP-HughL1

After many strange thoughts, thoughts. After Working. Robert Bly. SP-BlyR

After many winters the moss. Tale. W. S. Merwin. SP-MerwW

After many years, the sick woman got up. In the Old Garden. Yannis Ritsos. SP-RitsY, *tr. by* N. C. Germanacos

After Margrave died, nothing. History of a Literary Movement. Howard Nemerov. CP-NemeH

After Martial. James Laughlin. CP-LaugJ

After Melville. Muriel Rukeyser. CP-RukeM

After midnight, and my sister Lizzie. Mona Van Duyn. SP-VanDM

After midnight, in the dark / The clock strikes one. Praying Always. Christina Georgina Rossetti. CP-RosC2

After Midnight Mass. Phaedo. Kenneth Rexroth. CP-RexrK

After midnight they load up. Boat People. Yusef Komunyakaa. CP-KomuY

After Music. Wallace Stevens. CP-StevWP

After my father died fighting at. On a Benign Bureaucratization of Death. Alan Dugan. CP-DugaA

After my marriage, I found myself in constant. 1930's. Robert Lowell. SP-LoweR

After Nam he lost himself. Losses. Yusef Komunyakaa. CP-KomuY

After our Aesop's fable shown today. Epilogue. John Dryden. CP-DryJ2 *Fr.* Albion and Albanius.

After our death, when scholars try. Complaint and Reply. Robert Graves. CP-GravR

After our industrial civilisation has broken, and the civilisation of touch has begun. Future War. D. H. Lawrence. CP-LawrD

After our march from the Hudson to the top. Memorial Day. Gregory Orr. SP-OrrG

After overwhelming filth and amazing betrayals Odd Nansen looked at. Shoes of Travel. Carl Sandburg. CP-SandC

After Paradise. Czeslaw Milosz. CP-MiloC; CP-MiloCN, *tr. by* Robert Hass

After Peire Vidal, & Myself. Ted Berrigan. SP-BerrT

After Piero di Cosimo's *Venus, Mars, and Amor*. Gregory Orr. SP-OrrG

After Portsmouth. Ambrose Bierce. SP-BierA

After R.M. Rilke. Primo Levi. CP-LeviP, *tr. by* Ruth Feldman *and* Brian Swann

After rainy days and the same serious doubts. Raymond Carver. CP-CarvR

After ranging at large in a region. Another. Pablo Neruda. SP-NeruP

After reading. Louis Zukofsky. CP-ZukLS

After Reading a Book of Modern Verse. G. K. Chesterton. CP-ChesG

After Reading a Child's Guide to Modern Physics. W. H. Auden. CP-AudeW

After Reading H.D.'s *Hermetic Definitions*. Robert Duncan. SP-DuncR

After Reading Psalms XXXIX, XL, etc. Thomas Hardy. CP-HardT

After Reading T'ao Ch'ing, I Wander Untethered through the Short Grass. Charles Wright. SP-WrigCN

After Reading the Sad Story of the Fall of Babylon. Nicholas Vachel Lindsay. CP-LindV

After Reading Tu Fu, I Go Outside to the Dwarf Orchard. Charles Wright. SP-WrigCN

After Reading *Two Towns in Provence*. Raymond Carver. CP-CarvR

After Reading Wang Wei, I Go Outside to the Full Moon. Charles Wright. SP-WrigCN

After Rereading Robert Graves, I Go Outside to Get My Head Together. Charles Wright. SP-WrigCN

After Restless Night. Robert Penn Warren. CP-WarrR

After Rilke. Heather McHugh. SP-McHuH

After Rishikesh / the Ganges is still green. Key of Water, The. Octavio Paz. CP-BishE, *tr. by* Elizabeth Bishop

After Rochester (or somebody). James Laughlin. CP-LaugJ

After scanning its face again and again. John Muir on Mt. Ritter. Gary Snyder. CP-SnydG *Fr.* Myths and Texts.

After Schiller. Thomas Hardy. CP-HardT

After School. D. H. Lawrence. CP-LawrD

After screamgroa / ning.ish:ly. E. E. Cummings. CP-CummE

After Seeing French Funeral. E. E. Cummings. CP-CummE

After Sky X. Norman Dubie. CP-DubiN

After Smiling. Laura Riding Jackson. CP-RidiL

After so long a race as I have run. Sonnet 80. Edmund Spenser. CP-Spens *Fr.* Amoretti.

After so many deaths to breathe again. Variations on a Theme by George Herbert. Marya Alexandrovna Zaturenska. SP-ZatuM

After so many decades of , , , of what? To Whom It May Concern. James Vincent Cunningham. CP-CunnJ

After so many years, I come walking to you. Conversation with a Holy Woman Not Seen for Many Years. Robert Bly. SP-BlyR

After so much battering of fire and steel. Butchers and Tombs. Ivor Gurney. SP-GurnI

After So Much Loss. Laura Riding Jackson. CP-RidiL

After some fifty generations. Embarking on the Study of Anglo-Saxon Grammer. Jorge Luis Borges. SP-BorgJ, *tr. by* Alastair Reid

After some miserable disaffection. On a Photograph by Aaron Siskind. John Logan. CP-LogaJ

After Song, An. William Carlos Williams. CP-WilW1

After Spring Snow, What They Saw. Norman Dubie. CP-DubiN

After such a day, too cluttered. Working Day, A. Theodore Weiss. SP-WeisT

After Summer Fell Apart. Yusef Komunyakaa. CP-KomuY

After Sunday Dinner We Uncles Snooze. John Ciardi. CP-CiarJ

After sundown yellow sky beyond shadow mountains. Remembering a Boatman. W. S. Merwin. SP-MerwWF

After surmounting three-score and ten. My 71st Year. Walt Whitman. CP-WhitW

After Teacups. Robert Penn Warren. CP-WarrR

After That. C. K. Williams. CP-WillC

After that hot gospeller had levelled all but the churched sky. City's Death by Fire, A. Derek Walcott. CP-WalcD

After that knifeblade, we breathed. Retirement. William Stafford. SP-StafWW

After the agony in the guest / bedroom, you lying by the. Margaret Atwood. SP-AtwM1

After the Anthology. Kenneth Rexroth. CP-RexrK

After the Argument. Walt Whitman. CP-WhitW

After the argument—argument? battle, war, harrowing; you need shrieks, moans from the pit. Toil. C. K. Williams. CP-WillC; SP-WillC

After the autumn storms, we chose a night. Night Fishers. Charles Tomlinson. CP-TomlC; SP-TomlC

After the ball. James Merrill. SP-MerrJ

After the Big Parade. Allen Ginsberg. SP-GinsA

After the Blackout (1965). Jane Cooper. CP-CoopJ

After the blast of lightning from the east. End, The. Wilfred Owen. CP-OwenW

After the blood wedding. General George Armstrong Custer: My Life in the Theater. Ai. SP-Ai

After the Bomb Tests. Jane Cooper. CP-CoopJ

After the Breakdown of the Treaty between the Lacedaemonians and the Athenians. Yannis Ritsos. SP-RitsY, *tr. by* Kimon Friar *and* Karelisa Hartigan

After the bronzed, heroic traveller. Mapmaker on His Art, The. Howard Nemerov. CP-NemeH

After the Burial. Thomas Hardy. CP-HardT

After the burial-parties leave. Hyænas [*or* Hyenas], The. Rudyard Kipling. CP-KiplR

After the Calamitous Convoy (July 1942). Donald Davie. CP-DaviDC

After the cancer, the kidneys. Dialysis. Lucille Clifton. SP-ClifL

After the centers' naked files, the basic line. Lines, The. Randall Jarrell. CP-JarrR

After the Ceremony.   Yannis Ritsos.   SP-RitsY, *tr. by* Kimon Friar

After the chores are done, I tune.   Friends, Farewell.   William Stafford.   SP-StafWW

After the Christening.   Ogden Nash.   CP-NashO

After the Crash.   Louis MacNeice.   CP-MacNL

After the days of walking alone in mountains.   Pause by the Water.   W. S. Merwin.   SP-MerwWF

After the Dazzle of Day.   Walt Whitman.   CP-WhitW

After the Death of a Friend.   Thomas Hardy.   CP-HardT

After the Defeat.   Yannis Ritsos.   SP-RitsY, *tr. by* Kimon Friar *and* Karelisa Hartigan

After the Dinner Party.   Robert Penn Warren.   CP-WarrR

After the door shuts and the footsteps die.   Hunt in the Black Forest, A.   Randall Jarrell.   CP-JarrR

After the door shuts, and the footsteps die.   Prince, The.   Randall Jarrell.   CP-JarrR

After the dread tales and red yarns of the Line.   First Time In.   Ivor Gurney.   SP-GurnI

After the engagement they stacked their arms.   Brutalization under the Heart of Peace.   Alan Dugan.   CP-DugaA

After the event the rockslide.   Clarity.   A. R. Ammons.   CP-AmmoA

After the explosion or cataclysm, that big.   Eternal City, The.   A. R. Ammons.   CP-AmmoA

After the Fall [of Saigon].   Yusef Komunyakaa.   CP-KomuY

After the feast, my Shapcott, see.   Oberon's Palace.   Robert Herrick.   CP-HerrR

After the fiesta, the beauty-contests, the drunken wrestling.   Apple Dumps.   Ted Hughes.   SP-HughTN

After the fight at Otterburn.   English Way, The.   Rudyard Kipling.   CP-KiplR

After the final no there comes a yes.   Well Dressed Man with a Beard, The.   Wallace Stevens.   CP-StevW; CP-StevWP

After the Fire.   Raymond Carver.   CP-CarvR

After the Fire.   James Merrill.   SP-MerrJ

After the Fire.   Yannis Ritsos.   SP-RitsY, *tr. by* Minas Savvas

After the first powerful plain manifesto.   Express, The.   Stephen Spender.   CP-SpenS

After the first terror.   Nuclear Winter.   Thomas McGrath.   SP-McGrT

After the five-month draught.   Rain-charm for the Duchy.   Ted Hughes.   SP-HughTN

After the Flight of Ranger 7.   May Swenson.   SP-SwenM

After the flight, the tired body.   Elegy for Henry Street.   Charles Tomlinson.   CP-TomlC

After the Flood.   Robert Graves.   CP-GravR

After the Flood.   Arthur Rimbaud.   CP-RimbA, *tr. by* Martin Sorrell

After the Flood, We.   Margaret Atwood.   SP-AtwM1

After the French Liberation of Italy.   Dante Gabriel Rossetti.   CW-RossD

After the frost! O the rose is dead.   James Whitcomb Riley.   CP-RileJ

After the Funeral.   Dylan Thomas.   CP-ThomD

After the German Subjugation of France, 1871.   Dante Gabriel Rossetti.   CW-RossD

After the great intrusion of Death.   Emily Dickinson.   SP-DickE

After the Guest.   Gregory Orr.   SP-OrrG

After the Harvest.   Maxine W. Kumin.   SP-KumiM

After the Harvests.   W. S. Merwin.   SP-MerwW

After the hay was baled and stacked in henges.   Harvest.   Charles Tomlinson.   SP-TomlC

After the Heart's Interrogation.   Yusef Komunyakaa.   CP-KomuY

After the history has been made.   Adolescence.   Thom Gunn.   CP-GunnT

After the hour of illumination, when the tottering mind.   Gold and Malachite.   Robert Graves.   CP-GravR

After the interminable play.   Introduction, The.   Andrei Codrescu.   SP-CodrA

After the laboring birth, the clean stripped hull.   My Father's Death.   May Sarton.   SP-SartM

After the Last Breath.   Thomas Hardy.   CP-HardT

After the Last Bulletins.   Richard Wilbur.   CP-WilbR

After the last cold mountain.   Outpost.   Muriel Rukeyser.   CP-RukeM

After the Last Dynasty.   Stanley Kunitz.   CP-KunSC

After the last freeze, in easy air.   Fighting for Roses.   Muriel Rukeyser.   CP-RukeM

After the last red sunset glimmer.   Plowboy.   Carl Sandburg.   CP-SandC

After the lean road looping the narrow river.   Up the Dark Valley.   Thomas McGrath.   SP-McGrT

After the leaves have fallen, the sky turns blue again.   Autumn's Sidereal, November's a Ball and Chain.   Charles Wright.   SP-WrigCN

After the leaves have fallen, we return.   Plain Sense of Things, The.   Wallace Stevens.   CP-StevW; CP-StevWP

After the lights and after the rumba and after the bourbon.   Charm for Cantinflas, A.   Muriel Rukeyser.   CP-RukeM

After *The Little Mariner*.   Olga Broumas.   SP-BrouO

After the living, the attic. Then the rain.   Thursday.   John Ciardi.   CP-CiarJ

After the long strike.   Triumphal March.   Thomas McGrath.   SP-McGrT

After the many courses, hot bowls of rice.   Photographs of China.   Donald Hall.   CP-HallD

After the Match.   Donald Davie.   CP-DaviDC

After the Meditation.   Jelaluddin Rumi.   SP-Rumi, *tr. by* Coleman Barks

After the morning of amazing rain.   First Point of Aries, The.   Howard Nemerov.   CP-NemeH

After the murder.   Last Quatrain of the Ballad of Emmett Till, The.   Gwendolyn Brooks.   SP-BrooG

After the Night Office—Gethsemani Abbey.   Thomas Merton.   CP-MertT

After the Opera.   D. H. Lawrence.   CP-LawrD

After the Party.   Meng Hao Jan.   SP-WilW2

After the picture show, the explanation is usually found in.   New Year's Eve, 1979.   Charles Wright.   SP-WrigC

After the Pleasure Party.   Herman Melville.   SP-MelvH

After the promise has been kept, or.   Afterward.   Robert Penn Warren.   CP-WarrR

After the Puritans landed at Provincetown.   Significance of Corn in American History, The.   Alan Dugan.   CP-DugaA

After the Quarrel.   Paul Laurence Dunbar.   CP-DunbP

After the quarrel in the house I walked the grasses of the field.   After Their Quarrel.   Muriel Rukeyser.   CP-RukeM

After the rainfall, a little Buddha in each water drop.   Spring Storm.   Charles Wright.   SP-WrigCN

After the rapture comes, and everyone goes away.   March Journal.   Charles Wright.   SP-WrigC

After the rare arch-poet Jonson died.   Upon M. Ben Jo[h]nson: Epigram.   Robert Herrick.   CP-HerrR

After the Reading.   Charles Bukowski.   SP-BukC1

After the red leaf and the gold have gone.   Spell before Winter, A.   Howard Nemerov.   CP-NemeH

After the Revolution.   Marilyn Hacker.   SP-HackM

After the revolution came the Fuehrer.   Traditional Tune.   Muriel Rukeyser.   CP-RukeM

After the Revolution for Jesus a Secular Man [or the Associate Professor] Prepares His Final Remarks.   Miller Williams.   CP-WillM

After the sack of the City when Rome was sunk to a name.   King's Task, The.   Rudyard Kipling.   CP-KiplR

After the satyr's twilight in the park.   Homecoming—Massachusetts.   John Ciardi.   CP-CiarJ

After the Sea-Ship.   Walt Whitman.   CP-WhitW

After the shifts and dis.   Prodigal.   A. R. Ammons.   CP-AmmoA

After the Shrink.   Alice Walker.   CP-WalkA

After the sleekness of moleskin trews.   Big Liz.   Paul Muldoon.   CP-MuldP

After the sleeper has burst his night pod.   Dreamer, the Dream, The.   Maxine W. Kumin.   SP-KumiM

After the Solstice.   W. S. Merwin.   SP-MerwW

After the songless rose of evening.   Unchanging, The.   Walter De la Mare.   CP-DeLaW

After the Storm.   Charles Tomlinson.   CP-TomlC

After the stormy night: / the crack of lightning and.   Cornflowers.   James Schuyler.   CP-SchuJ

After the Sun comes out.   Emily Dickinson.   CP-DickE

After the sunlight and the fiery vision.   From a Chapter on Literature.   Adrienne Rich.   CP-RicAE

After the sun's eclipse.   Teresa.   Richard Wilbur.   CP-WilbR

After the sunset in the mountains.   Flat Waters of the West in Kansas.   Carl Sandburg.   CP-SandC

After the Supper and Talk.   Walt Whitman.   CP-WhitW

After the Surprising Conversions.   Robert Lowell.   SP-LoweR

After the sweet promise.   Operation, The.   Anne Sexton.   CP-SextA; SP-SextA

After the swirling snowfall, days of whole.   Homage to the North.   Richard Eberhart.   CP-EberR

After the test they sent an expert.   School Days.   William Stafford.   SP-StafWW

After the thorns I came to the first page.   Sleeping Beauty: Variation of the Prince, The.   Randall Jarrell.   CP-JarrR

After the Titanic.   Derek Mahon.   CP-MahoD

After the treetop-filtered.   Tidewater Winter.   Amy Clampitt.   CP-ClamA

After the victory he loped.   On Breeding, from Plutarch.   Alan Dugan.   CP-DugaA

After the Visit.   Thomas Hardy.   CP-HardT

After the War.   Thomas Hardy.   CP-HardT

After the weeks of unrelenting heat.   Ending, An.   Howard Nemerov.   CP-NemeH

After the welfare hotel.   News Items.   Denise Levertov.   SP-LeveDL

After the whirlwind when all things. Action of Therapy, The. May Sarton. SP-SartM

After the winter, grieving and dull. Sweet Light. Raymond Carver. CP-CarvR

After the winter thawed away, I rose. Assignation, The. James Wright. CP-WrigJ

After Their Quarrel. Muriel Rukeyser. CP-RukeM

After these years of lectures heard. To a Friend, on Her Examination for the Doctorate in English. James Vincent Cunningham. CP-CunnJ

After they had been in the woods. Of a Sun She Can Remember. Eleanor Wilner. SP-WilnE

After this girl was grown. Fanny Howe. SP-HoweF *Fr.* O'Clock.

After this life, the wages shall. Wages. Robert Herrick. CP-HerrR

After this much time, it's still impossible. The SS man with his stiff hair and his uniform. Spit. C. K. Williams. CP-WillC; SP-WillC

After this oracle there will be no more oracles. Last Statement for a Last Oracle. Alan Dugan. CP-DugaA

After This the Judgement. Christina Georgina Rossetti. CP-RosC1

After those reverend papers, whose soul is. To Sir Henry Wotton, at His Going Ambassador to Venice. John Donne. CP-DonnJ; MW-DonnJ

After-Thought. William Wordsworth. CP-WorW2 *Fr.* River Duddon [A Series of Sonnets], The.

After-Thought, The. Stevie Smith. CP-SmitS

After Thoughts. Allen Ginsberg. CP-GinsA

After thrashing in the water of the reservoir. Merlin and the Deer. Thomas Merton. CP-MertT

After three days of steady rain. November. Billy Collins. SP-CollB

After Three Photographs of Brassaï. Norman Dubie. CP-DubiN

After three years—a 3-decker novel. Writing to Aaron. Denise Levertov. SP-LeveDL

After three years of constant courtship. Gateway, The. Robert Graves. CP-GravR

After thy labour take thine ease. Mount of the Muses, The. Robert Herrick. CP-HerrR

After Traveling. Czeslaw Milosz. CP-MiloCN, *tr. by* Robert Hass

After Troy. "H. D." CP-DoolH

After true sorrow for our sinnes, our strife. Sin and Strife. Robert Herrick. CP-HerrR

After Twenty Years. Adrienne Rich. SP-RicA2

After two gray sunless days of warm. Batsto. A. R. Ammons. CP-AmmoA

After two months, already. Humanly Speaking. Donald Davie. CP-DaviDC

After two rainy days, a sunny one. Evenings in Vermont. James Schuyler. CP-SchuJ

After two sittings, now our Lady State. Last Instructions to a Painter, The. Andrew Marvell. CP-MarvA

After two years. Island. W. S. Merwin. SP-MerwWF

After us, it is certainly not the flood. Joseph Brodsky. CP-BrodJ, *tr. by* Jonathan Aaron

After venting all my spite. To a Lady. Jonathan Swift. CP-SwifJ

After War. Ivor Gurney. SP-GurnI

After we had crossed the long illness. Further Arrivals. Margaret Atwood. SP-AtwM1

After we had loved each other intently. Listening to the Köln Concert. Robert Bly. SP-BlyR

After we have made love. Two Spoons. James Laughlin. CP-LaugJ

After we saw the wild ducks. To Gary Snyder. Wendell Berry. CP-BerrW

After we talked, after the moon. In Hurricane Canyon. William Stafford. SP-StafWW

After we / were all. Here Again ("After we / were all"). Robert Creeley. CP-CreeR

After we / were all. Days and Days. Robert Creeley. CP-CreeR

After While. Paul Laurence Dunbar. CP-DunbP

After Whitman & Reznikoff. Allen Ginsberg. CP-GinsA Lower East Side. SP-GinsA

After Work. Gary Snyder. CP-SnydG

After work, a walk. Lake Road. William Corbett. SP-CorbW

After Working. Robert Bly. SP-BlyR

After years of bickering. Spite Fence. Richard Eberhart. CP-EberR

After years smuggling poems. Poem in Translation, A. Tess Gallagher. SP-GallT

After Yeats. Allen Ginsberg. CP-GinsA

After Yesterday. A. R. Ammons. CP-AmmoA

After You Die You Don't Give a Piddling Damn. Miller Williams. CP-WillM

After you finish your work. Ballad of Orange and Grape. Muriel Rukeyser. CP-RukeM

After you have spent all the money modistes and manicures and mannikins. Proud and Beautiful. Carl Sandburg. CP-SandC

After you left me. Dog After Love, A. Yehuda Amichai. SP-AmicY, *tr. by* Chana Bloch

After you left me forever. Semele Recycled. Carolyn Kizer. CP-KizeC

After your first poetry reading. Poem: "After your first poetry reading." Alan Dugan. CP-DugaA

After your pleasant morning travel. Day's Journey, A. John Greenleaf Whittier. CP-WhitJ

After your poppied hair inaugurates. E. E. Cummings. CP-CummE

After your thankless flight. After-Flight. Rainer Maria Rilke. CP-RilkFr, *tr. by* A. Poulin, Jr.

After you've been to bed together for the first time. Life Story. Tennessee Williams. CP-WillT

After you've hit the bars a while. Walls, The. Charles Bukowski. SP-BukC3

Afterflakes. Robert Frost. CP-FrosR

Afterglow. Raymond Carver. CP-CarvR

Afterglow goldens the. Mountain Afterglow, The. James Laughlin. CP-LaugJ

Afterimages. Audre Lorde. SP-LordA

Afterlives. Derek Mahon. CP-MahoD

Aftermath. Henry Wadsworth Longfellow. SP-LongH

Aftermath. Louis MacNeice. CP-MacNL

Aftermath. Paul Muldoon. CP-MuldP

Aftermath. Howard Nemerov. CP-NemeH

Aftermath. Sylvia Plath. CP-PlatS

Aftermath, The. William Carlos Williams. CP-WilW2

Afternoon. T. S. Eliot. SP-ElioT

Afternoon. Laura Riding Jackson. CP-RidiL

Afternoon. Charles Olson. CP-OlsoC

Afternoon. Dorothy Parker. CP-ParkD

Afternoon. Yannis Ritsos. SP-RitsY, *tr. by* Kimon Friar

Afternoon, An. Raymond Carver. CP-CarvR

Afternoon, The. Jorge Luis Borges. SP-BorgJ, *tr. by* W. S. Merwin

Afternoon as ripe with heat, An. At Utter Loaf. James Whitcomb Riley. CP-RileJ

Afternoon breaks from a pale, The. Art of a Novel, The. Marilyn Hacker. SP-HackM

Afternoon Call, An. G. K. Chesterton. CP-ChesG

Afternoon ends with red, The. Mirror. Kenneth Rexroth. CP-RexrK

Afternoon Evening and Night in the Courtyard of the Museum of Modern Art. William Dickey. SP-DickW

Afternoon Happiness. Carolyn Kizer. CP-KizeC

Afternoon in my brother's backyard, The. Going. Miller Williams. CP-WillM

Afternoon in the Park, An. John Ciardi. CP-CiarJ

Afternoon in the Stacks, An. William Stafford. SP-StafWW

Afternoon is full of fallen plaster, black stones, dry thorns, The. Afternoon. Yannis Ritsos. SP-RitsY, *tr. by* Kimon Friar

Afternoon lengthens like sunlight. Wall, A. Robert Creeley. CP-CreeR

Afternoon lies glazed upon the wall, The. Glass Poem. Karl Shapiro. SP-ShapK

Afternoon light like pollen. In Berkeley. Robert Pinsky. CP-PinsR

Afternoon of a Doll. Marya Alexandrovna Zaturenska. SP-ZatuM

Afternoon of a Faun. Stéphane Mallarmé. CP-CarHS

Afternoon of a Faun, The. Stéphane Mallarmé. CP-MallS, *tr. by* Henry Weinfield

Afternoon of a McGrath. Thomas McGrath. SP-McGrT

Afternoon of summer folds, The. Fruit-Piece, A. James Whitcomb Riley. CP-RileJ

Afternoon on a Hill. Edna St. Vincent Millay. CP-MillE

Afternoon overcast the color of water. Tennessee Line. Charles Wright. SP-WrigCN

Afternoon says: / "I'm thirsty for shadow!", The. New Songs. Federico García Lorca. CP-GarcF, *tr. by* Catherine Brown

Afternoon Seattle. Allen Ginsberg. CP-GinsA

Afternoon Service at Mellstock. Thomas Hardy. CP-HardT

Afternoon storm has hit, An. After the Fall [of Saigon]. Yusef Komunyakaa. CP-KomuY

Afternoon sun on her back. Sonnet: "Afternoon sun on her back." Robert Pinsky. CP-PinsR

Afternoon Sun, The. Constantine P. Cavafy. CP-CavaC, *tr. by* Theoharis Constantine Theoharis

Afternoon sunlight plays. Kathleen Jessie Raine. SP-RainK

Afternoon was already dark and unnatural, The. House behind This One, The. Raymond Carver. CP-CarvR

Afternoon with Circus and Citadel. Paul Celan. SP-CelaP, *tr. by* John Felstiner

Afternoon with heavy hours, The. Traveller, The. Allen Tate. CP-TateA

Afternoon with Irish Cows. Billy Collins. SP-CollB

Afternoons. Philip Larkin. CP-LarkP

Afternoons in the backyard, our lives like photographs. Silent Generation, The.

Charles Wright. SP-WrigCN

Afternoons to come and those that have been, The. Afternoon, The. Jorge Luis Borges. SP-BorgJ, tr. by W. S. Merwin

Afterschool Lessons from a Hitman. Ai. SP-Ai

Afterthought, An. Christina Georgina Rossetti. CP-RosC3

Afterthoughts. Edwin Arlington Robinson. CP-RobiE

Afterthoughts of Donna Elvira. Carolyn Kizer. CP-KizeC

Afterwake, The. Adrienne Rich. CP-RicAE; SP-RicA2

Afterward. Adrienne Rich. CP-RicAE; SP-RicA1; SP-RicA2

Afterward. James Schuyler. CP-SchuJ

Afterward. Robert Penn Warren. CP-WarrR

Afterward He Repented, and Went. Christina Georgina Rossetti. CP-RosC2

Afterward they will get up. Resurrection. Yehuda Amichai. SP-AmicY, tr. by Stephen Mitchell

Afterwards. Thomas Hardy. CP-HardT

Afterwards. Randall Jarrell. CP-JarrR

Afterwards. Muriel Rukeyser. CP-RukeM

Afterwards. William Stafford. SP-StafWW

Afterwards, An. Seamus Heaney. SP-HeanSO

Afterwards ("I've pulled up to the doorway / of *Then*"). Federico García Lorca. CP-GarcF, tr. by Jerome Rothenberg

Afterwards, the compromise. After Love. Maxine W. Kumin. SP-KumiM

Afterwhiles. James Whitcomb Riley. CP-RileJ

Afterword. Joseph Brodsky. CP-BrodJ, tr. by Jamey Gambrell

Afton Water. Robert Burns. *See* Flow Gently, Sweet Afton

Again. Robert Creeley. CP-CreeR

Again. Robert Herrick. CP-HerrR

Again. Howard Nemerov. CP-NemeH

Again? Carl Sandburg. CP-SandC

Again a love is finished, like a successful citrus season. Yehuda Amichai. SP-AmicYL, tr. by Benjamin Harshav *and* Barbara Harshav

Again a verse for sake of you. Ashes of Soldiers: Epigraph. Walt Whitman. CP-WhitW

Again, again, I see this form repeated. In Attica. Stephen Spender. CP-SpenS

Again and again. Again lips, again breast, again hand, thigh, loin and bed and bed. With Ignorance. C. K. Williams. CP-WillC; SP-WillC

Again and Again and Again. Anne Sexton. CP-SextA

Again and again I make the intolerable journey. Repeated Journey, The. Thomas McGrath. SP-McGrT

Again and again, when it came to her turn. Green Gown. Paul Muldoon. CP-MuldP

Again, as in the golden age. Russia ("Again, as in the golden age"). Aleksandr Aleksandrovich Blok. SP-BlokA, tr. by Peter France *and* Jon Stallworthy

Again, at evening, the winter walks. Coleorton. Amy Clampitt. CP-ClamA

Again at Waldheim. Kenneth Rexroth. CP-RexrK

Again—but other faces bend with mine. At Chinese Checkers. John Berryman. CP-BerrJ

Again doth France, unhappy France, behold. Lessons of History Unlearned, The. Jones Very. CP-VeryJ

Again doth lust of Power lift up its head. Political Ambition. Jones Very. CP-VeryJ

Again, from the goblet, your presence. Snow Wine. Aleksandr Aleksandrovich Blok. SP-BlokA, tr. by Peter France *and* Jon Stallworthy

Again, great season, sing it through again. Again. Howard Nemerov. CP-NemeH

Again he fac'd the battle-field. Death of Argentine, The. Sir Walter Scott. SP-ScotW *Fr.* Lord of the Isles, The.

Again heavy rain drives him home. Stepfather: A Girl's Song. Yusef Komunyakaa. CP-KomuY

Again, here it comes, the nothing. Salamanders. A. K. Ramanujan. CP-RamaA

Again—his voice is at the door. Emily Dickinson. CP-DickE

Again I come to buy the image fated. Fitting of the Mask, The. Stanley Kunitz. CP-KunSC

Again I reply to the triple winds. January. William Carlos Williams. CP-WilW1

Again I see my bliss at hand. Lake, The. Matthew Arnold. SP-ArnoM *Fr.* Switzerland.

Again I see those who leave home. Han-shan. CP-ColdM, tr. by Red Pine

Again I'm Torched and Wonder What We've Wrought. Robert Stock. SP-StocR

Again I'm torched in one of those grandiose. Again I'm Torched and Wonder What We've Wrought. Robert Stock. SP-StocR

Again in conversations. Never Stronger. W. H. Auden. CP-AudeW

Again in space, / elsewhere. Smoke. Robert Creeley. CP-CreeR

Again last night I dreamed the dream called Laundry. Mad Scene, The. James Merrill. SP-MerrJ

Again? new Tumults in my breast? First Ode of the Fourth Book of Horace Imitated, The. Alexander Pope. CP-PopeA

Again on dark looms. Hayden Carruth. CP-CarHS *Fr.* Clay Hill Anthology, The.

Again rejoicing Nature sees. Song: "Again rejoicing Nature sees." Robert Burns. CP-BurnR

Again so I subside / nudged by the softening. Pre-Amphibian. Margaret Atwood. SP-AtwM1

Again / the bare brush of. Tree and Sky. William Carlos Williams. CP-WilW1

Again the cry that it's late. Letter to the Heart. W. S. Merwin. SP-MerwW

Again the flying horses, the strange voice of drunken Nicanor. Two Carriages. Raymond Carver. CP-CarvR

Again the last ebb. Samuel Beckett. CP-BeckS

Again, the sea, the singing and eternally unrestrained sea. Sea, The. Gabriela Mistral. SP-MistG, tr. by Maria Giachetti [*or* Jacketti]

Again the silent wheels of time. To Miss L———. Robert Burns. CP-BurnR

Again, the violet bows to the lily. Spring. Jelaluddin Rumi. SP-Rumi, tr. by Coleman Barks

Again this morning trembles on the swift stream the image of the sun. Images. Kathleen Jessie Raine. SP-RainK

Again this procession of the speechless. Daybreak. W. S. Merwin. SP-MerwW

Again this spring the birds returned too early. Birds Returning. Wisława Szymborska. SP-SzymWM, tr. by Joanna Trzeciak

Again to measure with the foe. Red Coats & the Blue, The. George Meredith. CP-MerG2

Again tonight I read "Before Disaster" Letter to Yvor Winters, A. Kenneth Rexroth. CP-RexrK

Again, traveller, you have come a long way led by that star. Epitaph: "Again, traveller, you have come a long way led by that star." Thomas McGrath. SP-McGrT

Again you / feel the air. Fall. Robert Creeley. CP-CreeR

Againe. Robert Herrick. CP-HerrR

Against a Dark Field. Heather McHugh. SP-McHuH

Against a gun-metal sky. Sycamore, The. Marianne Craig Moore. CP-MoorM

Against a Sickness: To the Female Double Principle God. Alan Dugan. CP-DugaA

Against a sunset gold and red. Resurrection. G. K. Chesterton. CP-ChesG

Against a thunderhead's / Blue marble, the eagle. Violent Pastoral. James Merrill. SP-MerrJ

Against Absence. Sir John Suckling. CP-SuckJ

Against Confidences. Donald Davie. CP-DaviDC

Against / darkness. Fund Appeal. Grace Paley. CP-PalGC

Against Disaster. Theodore Roethke. CP-RoetT

Against diseases here the strongest fence. Abstinence. Robert Herrick. CP-HerrR

Against Eutropius. Claudian.
  "Over the Medes and light Sabaeans reigns [*or* raignes]." CP-RaleW

Against Extremity. Charles Tomlinson. CP-TomlC; SP-TomlC

Against France: On the Algerian Pleasures of Entity. Alan Dugan. CP-DugaA

Against Fruition. Sir John Suckling. CP-SuckJ

Against Hope. Abraham Cowley. CP-CrasR *Fr.* Mistress, The.

Against Illuminations. Archibald MacLeish. CP-MacLA

Against Interested Love. William Cowper. CP-CowpW

Against Jealousy [*or* Jealousie]. Ben Jonson. CP-JonsB

Against Love. Robert Herrick. CP-HerrR

Against Meaning. Andrei Codrescu. SP-CodrA

Against my will. Footprints. Dan Pagis. SP-PagiD, tr. by Stephen Mitchell

Against our puny sound and sight. For Helen Keller. Countee Cullen. CP-CullC

Against Portraits. Charles Tomlinson. CP-TomlC

Against Silence. Marilyn Hacker. SP-HackM

Against snow a tall Being of Beauty. Hisses of death and circles of muted music. Being Beauteous. Arthur Rimbaud. CP-RimbA, tr. by Martin Sorrell

Against Still Life. Margaret Atwood. SP-AtwM1

Against the Bermudas we foundered, whereby. Coiner, The. Rudyard Kipling. CP-KiplR

Against the bright / grass the white-knickered. Baseball Players, The. Donald Hall. CP-HallD

Against the burly air I strode. Genesis. Geoffrey Hill. CP-HillG

Against the clapboards and the window panes. Elegy for Wesley Wells. Donald Hall. CP-HallD

Against the Evidence. David Ignatow. SP-IgnaD

Against the False Magicians. Thomas McGrath. SP-McGrT

Against the Fear of Death. Lucretius. CP-DryJ2, tr. by John Dryden *Fr.* De Rerum Natura (On the Nature of Things).

Against the glass. Antique. George Oppen. CP-OppGN

Against the green sky. Federico García Lorca. CP-GarcF, *tr. by* Alan S. Trueblood　*Fr.* Love.

Against the low, New York State. Lines on Locks (or Jail and the Erie Canal). John Logan. CP-LogaJ

Against the meadow's transparency, / a black bell tower. Bell Tower of Authenay, The. Pablo Neruda. SP-NeruP

Against the outcrop boulders of a raised beach. Last Conservative, The. Robinson Jeffers. CP-JefR3

Against the Poetry of Philip Larkin. Czeslaw Milosz. CP-MiloCN, *tr. by* Robert Hass

Against the rock I climb, both high and hard. Sir Thomas Wyatt. CP-WyatT

Against the rubber tongues of cows and the hoeing hands of men. Thistles. Ted Hughes. SP-HughTN

Against the south wall of a monastery. Fig Tree, The. W. S. Merwin. SP-MerwWF

Against the stone breakwater. Storm, The. Theodore Roethke. CP-RoetT

Against the sunset's glowing wall. Wife of Manoah to Her Husband, The. John Greenleaf Whittier. CP-WhitJ

Against the Text "Art Is Immortal." Alan Dugan. CP-DugaA

Against the wall he / gropes like ivy, you pray, I. Hayden Carruth. CP-CarHS　*Fr.* Clay Hill Anthology, The.

Against the War in Vietnam. Wendell Berry. CP-BerrW

Against the wooded hills it stands. Homestead, The. John Greenleaf Whittier. CP-WhitJ

Against Travel. Charles Tomlinson. SP-TomlC

Against Unworthy Praise. William Butler Yeats. CP-YeatW

Against Veils on Exodus 33:23 and 34:33. Alan Dugan. CP-DugaA

Against weather, and the random. Ceremony for Any Beginning. Robert Pinsky. CP-PinsR

Against what, then, do we measure. Silent Whole, The. Rainer Maria Rilke. CP-RilkFr, *tr. by* A. Poulin, Jr.

Against Witchcraft. Robert Graves. CP-GravR

Against Women Unconstant [*or* A Ballade against Woman Inconstant]. Geoffrey Chaucer. CP-ChauG

Agamemnon. Aeschylus.
　"O well for him who lives at ease." CP-WildO
　"Thy prophecies are but a lying tale." CP-WildO

Agamemnon. Yannis Ritsos. SP-RitsY, *tr. by* Philip Pastras *and* George Pilitsis

Agamemnon in the Fight. Homer. CP-MerG1　*Fr.* Iliad, The. *tr. by* George Meredith

Agatha Christie and Beatrix Potter. John Updike. CP-UpdiJ

Agave. Primo Levi. CP-LeviP, *tr. by* Ruth Feldman

Agave in the West. Donald Davie. CP-DaviDC

Agave on the Reef, The. Eugenio Montale. CP-MontE, *tr. by* Jonathan Galassi

Age ("He is thinking of everyone"). Robert Creeley. SP-CreeR

Age. Walter De la Mare. CP-DeLaW

Age. Philip Larkin. CP-LarkP

Age. W. S. Merwin. SP-MerwW

Age. Grace Paley. CP-PalGC

Age, and the deaths, and the ghosts. He Resigns. John Berryman. CP-BerrJ

Age Changeful and Worldly, The. Jones Very. CP-VeryJ

Age Gap. Robert Graves. CP-GravR

Age hath been when Earth was proud, An. Ode to Lycoris; May, 1817. William Wordsworth. CP-WorW2

Age in Prospect. Robinson Jeffers. CP-JefR1

Age is a pale bird, film of ice on the sea. Vindication of Jovan Babič, The. Donald Davie. CP-DaviDC

Age is dull and mean, The. Men creep. For Righteousness' Sake. John Greenleaf Whittier. CP-WhitJ

Age is when to a man. Song: "Age is when to a man." Samuel Beckett. CP-BeckS　*Fr.* Words and Music.

Age of Anxiety, The. W. H. Auden. CP-AudeW

Age of Bronze, The. Lord Byron. CP-Byron

Age of Pericles, The. Kenneth Patchen. CP-PatcK

Age of petty tit-for-tat, An. George Meredith. CP-MerG2

Age of Reason, The. G. K. Chesterton. CP-ChesG

Age of Terror. Denise Levertov. SP-LeveDL

Age of the Antonines, The. Herman Melville. SP-MelvH

Age saw two quiet children. Carpe Diem. Robert Frost. CP-FrosR

Age shall not daunt me, nor sorrow for youth that is gone. Strange Spirit, The. Walter De la Mare. CP-DeLaW

Age! twine thy brows with fresh spring flowers. Matron of Jedborough and Her Husband, The. William Wordsworth. CP-WorW1; MW-WorW

Age Unfit for Love. Robert Herrick. CP-HerrR

Aged Lover Discourses in the Flat Style, The. James Vincent Cunningham. CP-CunnJ

Aged Man Surveys the Past. Robert Penn Warren. CP-WarrR

Aged Newspaper Soliloquizes, The. Thomas Hardy. CP-HardT

Aged Parents, The. Yehuda Amichai. SP-AmicYL, *tr. by* Benjamin Harshav *and* Barbara Harshav

Aged parents visited their aging son, The. Aged Parents, The. Yehuda Amichai. SP-AmicYL, *tr. by* Benjamin Harshav *and* Barbara Harshav

Aged Tamba Temple Plum Tree Song. Gary Snyder. CP-SnydG

Ageing House, The. Thomas Hardy. CP-HardT

Ageless again, / I stand on this bridge of railroad ties. Baptism in the Lead Avenue Ditch. Jay Wright. SP-WrigJ

Ageless Brow, An. Laura Riding Jackson. CP-RidiL

Ageless Reason. Robert Graves. CP-GravR

Agenda. Wallace Stevens. CP-StevWP

Agent death assails me now, The. Life and Death. Richard Eberhart. CP-EberR

Agent, The. Richard Wilbur. CP-WilbR

Ages and Ages Returning at Intervals. Walt Whitman. CP-WhitW

Ages blaspheme, The. Breughel. Stevie Smith. CP-SmitS

Ages of Oath, The. Robert Graves. CP-GravR

Ages pass;—yet still delayed, The. Hymn: The Cause of Peace. Jones Very. CP-VeryJ

Agh—man / thinks. Robert Creeley. CP-CreeR

Aging. Randall Jarrell. CP-JarrR

Aging Actress Sees Herself a Starlet on the Late Show, The. Miller Williams. CP-WillM

Aging Female Poet on Laundry Day. Margaret Atwood. SP-AtwM2

Aging Female Poet Reads Little Magazines. Margaret Atwood. SP-AtwM2

Aging Female Poet Sits on the Balcony. Margaret Atwood. SP-AtwM2

Aging, forsaken, passionate, and unloved. Marya Alexandrovna Zaturenska. SP-ZatuM　*Fr.* Madness of Jean-Jacques Rousseau, The.

Aging Lovers, The. John Ciardi. CP-CiarJ

Aging Man at Noon in Timeless Noon of Summer. Robert Penn Warren. CP-WarrR

Aging of my body and my features, The. Melancholy of Jason Kleander; Poet in Kommagini; 595 A.D. Constantine P. Cavafy. CP-CavaC, *tr. by* Theoharis Constantine Theoharis

Aging Painter Sits Where the Great Tower Heaves Down Midnight. Robert Penn Warren. CP-WarrR

Aging pilgrim on a, An. On Flower Wreath Hill. Kenneth Rexroth. CP-RexrK

Aging Together. Clarence Major. SP-MajoC

Aginst the Head which Innocence secures. Samuel Johnson. CP-JohnS　*Fr.* Irene.

Aginst the Sky. William Carlos Williams. CP-WilW2

Agitation of the air, An. End of Summer. Stanley Kunitz. CP-KunSC

Agitations of April in the sky, The. Spring 1967. Hayden Carruth. CP-CarHS

Aglaura. Sir John Suckling. CP-SuckJ

Agnellina orfanellina. Christina Georgina Rossetti. CP-RosC3

Agnosco Veteris Vestigia Flammae. James Vincent Cunningham. CP-CunnJ

Agnostic, An. Stevie Smith. CP-SmitS

Agnostic, The. Edna St. Vincent Millay. CP-MillE

Agnostic Speaks to Her Horse's Hoof, The. Maxine W. Kumin. SP-KumiM

Agnosto Theo [To an Unknown God]. Thomas Hardy. CP-HardT

Agonies confirm His hour. Bahá'u'lláh in the Garden of Ridwan. Robert Earl Hayden. CP-HaydR

Agonized Spires, The. William Carlos Williams. CP-WilW1

Agony Among the Crowd, The. Nicolas Calas. CP-WilW2

Agony in the Garret, An. T. S. Eliot.
　Little Passion, The ("Of those ideas in his head"). SP-ElioT
　Little Passion, The ("Upon those stifling August nights"). · SP-ElioT

Agony [*or* Agonie], The. George Herbert. CP-HerbG

Agosta the Winged Man and Rasha the Black Dove. Rita Dove. SP-DoveR

Agree we call the place. She-Bear (II), The. Charles Olson. CP-OlsoC

Agreed: Familiarity breeds. Adult Entertainment. Marilyn Hacker. SP-HackM

Agreed that all these birds. All These Birds. Richard Wilbur. CP-WilbR

Agreeing. Miller Williams. CP-WillM

"Agriculture the Source of Individual and of National Prosperity."—Anne Pratt. Jones Very. CP-VeryJ

Agrigentum Road, The. Salvatore Quasimodo. CP-WilbR

Agrippina. Thomas Gray. CP-GrayT

Ah. Charles Bukowski. SP-BukC1

Ah, Anima! Robert Penn Warren. CP-WarrR

Ah, Are You Digging on My Grave? Thomas Hardy. CP-HardT

Ah! at last alone, love! In the Corridor. James Whitcomb Riley. CP-RileJ

Ah Ben! / Say how, or when. Ode for Him [*or* Ben Jonson], An. Robert

Herrick.   CP-HerrR

Ah Biancha! now I see.   To Biancha.   Robert Herrick.   CP-HerrR

Ah, bird, / our love is never spent.   Cuckoo Song.   "H. D."   CP-DoolH

Ah, blaze of vision in the dark hour! Once.   Twice Born.   Robert Penn Warren.   CP-WarrR

Ah, broken garden, frost on the melons and on the beans!   Thanksgiving Dinner.   Edna St. Vincent Millay.   CP-MillE

Ah, broken is the golden bowl!—the spirit flown forever!   Lenore.   Edgar Allan Poe.   CP-PoeEd

Ah, Brother, good-day.   Tartuffe.   Molière.   CP-WilbR

Ah brother Poet! send me of your shade.   William Cowper.   CP-CowpW

Ah, but a good wife!   Late Abed.   Archibald MacLeish.   CP-MacLA

Ah, but—because you were struck blind, could bless.   With Gerard de Lairesse.   Robert Browning.   CP-BroR2

Ah, but how each loved each, Marquis!   Cristina and Monaldeschi.   Robert Browning.   CP-BroR2

Ah, cannot the curled shoots of the larkspur that you loved so.   Spring in the Garden.   Edna St. Vincent Millay.   CP-MillE

Ah! cease thy tears and sobs, my little Life!   To an Infant.   Samuel Taylor Coleridge.   MW-ColeS   Fr. Effusions.

Ah! changed and cold, how changed and very cold!   Dead before Death.   Christina Georgina Rossetti.   CP-RosC1

Ah child, no Persian—perfect art.   Horace.   See Boy, I hate their empty shows

Ah, child, thou art but half thy darling mother's.   To a Motherless Child.   Thomas Hardy.   CP-HardT

Ah, Chloris, since it may not be.   To Chloris.   Robert Burns.   CP-BurnR

Ah, Christ, what a CREW.   O, We Are the Outcasts.   Charles Bukowski.   SP-BukC2

Ah cock, cock of treachery.   Yannis Ritsos.   SP-RitsY   Fr. Paper Poems 2.

Ah, come with me.   To an Usherette.   John Updike.   CP-UpdiJ

Ah come ye gay nymphs of the plain.   Elegy on the Death of Miss Chandler, as if Written in Her Fathers Church Yard.   Annis Boudinot Stockton.   CP-StocA

Ah, could I hide me in my song.   Hafiz.   CP-EmerR   Fr. Odes.

Ah, could I lay me down in this long grass.   Journey.   Edna St. Vincent Millay.   CP-MillE

Ah could we wake in mercy's name.   Song for an Allegorical Play.   John Ciardi.   CP-CiarJ

Ah! County Guy, the hour is nigh.   Serenade, A: "Ah! County Guy, the hour is nigh."   Sir Walter Scott.   SP-ScotW   Fr. Quentin Durward.

Ah, cruell Love! must I endure.   To Pansies.   Robert Herrick.   CP-HerrR

Ah! dainty—dainty Death!   Emily Dickinson.   SP-DickE

Ah! dear one, we were young so long.   Alas, So Long!   Dante Gabriel Rossetti.   CW-RossD

Ah, did you once see Shelley plain.   Memorabilia.   Robert Browning.   CP-BroR1; SP-BroR

Ah! Do not damp those cruel coals.   Pagan's Prayer, The.   Charles Baudelaire.   CP-BaudC, tr. by Walter Martin

Ah, Douglass, we have fall'n on evil days.   Douglass.   Paul Laurence Dunbar.   CP-DunbP

Ah downward through the dark coulisse.   Orfeo.   James Merrill.   SP-MerrJ

Ah, drink again.   Lethe.   Edna St. Vincent Millay.   CP-MillE

Ah fading joy, how quickly art thou past!   John Dryden.   SP-DrydJ   Fr. Indian Emperor, The.

Ah, Fate! cannot a man.   Fame.   Ralph Waldo Emerson.   CP-EmerR

Ah for that time when open daylight pours.   George Meredith.   CP-MerG2

Ah, friend of mine, how goes it.   My Jolly Friend's Secret.   James Whitcomb Riley.   CP-RileJ

Ah friend! 'tis true—this truth you lovers know—.   To Mr. Gay, Congratulating Pope on Finishing His House and Gardens.   Alexander Pope.   CP-PopeA

Ah! gentle, fleeting, wav'ring sprite.   Adrian's Address to His Soul When Dying.   Emperor Hadrian.   CP-Byron   Fr. Hadrian's Address to His Soul When Dying.

Ah gentle Shade the muse of pity pours.   Lines on a Young Gentleman Who Died of the Yellow Fever at Princeton a Day or Two after He Fled from the City for Fear of It.   Annis Boudinot Stockton.   CP-StocA

Ah, George Bubb Dodington Lord Melcombe,—no.   With George Bubb Dodington.   Robert Browning.   CP-BroR2

Ah, God, dear Brother, the mild and frowning rose.   Kenneth Patchen.   CP-PatcK

Ah God, life, law, so many names you keep.   Martyr à la Mode.   D. H. Lawrence.   CP-LawrD

Ah, God, the way your little finger moved.   Stephen Crane.   CP-CranS

Ah, green Elysia.   Drama.   Howard Nemerov.   CP-NemeH

Ah, grief, I should not treat you.   Talking to Grief.   Denise Levertov.   SP-LeveDL; SP-LeveDS

Ah, haggard purse, why ope thy mouth.   Stephen Crane.   CP-CranS

Ah! have you seen a bird of sweetest tone.   On the Death of an Unfortunate Lady.   William Wordsworth.   CP-WorW1

Ah heaven, send.   No News.   D. H. Lawrence.   CP-LawrD

Ah, heedless girl! why thus disclose.   To a Vain Lady.   Lord Byron.   CP-Byron

Ah how could love so well disguise.   Ode—Written 1756, An.   Annis Boudinot Stockton.   CP-StocA

Ah, how delightful.   Liberty.   Fernando Pessoa.   SP-PessF, tr. by Susan M. Brown and Edwin Honig

Ah, how the human mind wearies her self.   John Milton.   See Alas how the wandering mind of man grows weak, driven

Ah, I have changed, I do not know.   Lost Dream, A.   Paul Laurence Dunbar.   CP-DunbP

Ah I know how you have sought me.   Separated.   D. H. Lawrence.   CP-LawrD

Ah, in the night, all music haunts me here.   Amaranth, The.   Nicholas Vachel Lindsay.   CP-LindV

Ah, in the past, towards rare individuals.   Desire.   D. H. Lawrence.   CP-LawrD

Ah in the thunder air.   Trees in the Garden.   D. H. Lawrence.   CP-LawrD

Ah, it's a damn pity that you were put to all the trouble.   Portrait of the Artist as an Interior Decorator.   Kenneth Patchen.   CP-PatcK

Ah—it's the skeleton of a lady's sunshade.   Sunshade, The.   Thomas Hardy.   CP-HardT

Ah Jean Dubuffet.   Naphtha.   Frank O'Hara.   SP-OharF

Ah, Joyce, this is our task.   Hugh MacDiarmid.   SP-MacDH   Fr. World of Words, The.

Ah! Ken Ye What I Met the Day.   John Keats.   CP-KeatJ

Ah, Lenin, you were richt. But I'm a poet.   Hugh MacDiarmid.   Fr. Second Hymn to Lenin.

Ah! little Angel, child of bliss!   George Meredith.   CP-MerG2

Ah little cloud that in Love's shadow lief.   La Nuvoletta.   Dante Alighieri.   CP-PoeEar, tr. by Ezra Pound

Ah little recks the laborer.   Song of the Exposition.   Walt Whitman.   CP-WhitW

Ah Lord, Lord, if my heart were right with Thine.   Christina Georgina Rossetti.   CP-RosC2

Ah, Lord, we all have pierced Thee: wilt Thou be.   One of the Soldiers with a Spear Pierced His Side.   Christina Georgina Rossetti.   CP-RosC2

Ah, Love, but a day.   James Lee's Wife.   Robert Browning.   CP-BroR1; SP-BroR

Ah, love, my love is like a cry in the night.   Love Song, A: "Ah, love, my love is like a cry in the night."   Paul Laurence Dunbar.   CP-DunbP

Ah, luxury! Beyond the heat.   At Broad Ripple.   James Whitcomb Riley.   CP-RileJ

Ah! Lycidas, come tell me why.   Eclogue, or Pastorall between Endimion Porter and Lycidas Herrick, An.   Robert Herrick.   CP-HerrR

Ah, Madam; you've indeed come back here?   Woman's Fancy, A.   Thomas Hardy.   CP-HardT

Ah, many, many are the dead.   Kathleen Jessie Raine.   SP-RainK

Ah me, it is cold and chill.   Wraith, The.   Paul Laurence Dunbar.   CP-DunbP

Ah me, that I should be / Exposed and open evermore to Thee!   Thou, God, Seest Me.   Christina Georgina Rossetti.   CP-RosC2

Ah me! the lowliest children of the spring.   In Part from Moschus's Lament for Bion.   William Wordsworth.   CP-WorW1

Ah, Memory—that strange deceiver.   Memory.   Walter De la Mare.   CP-DeLaW

Ah, money, you colorless flat shit growing.   Looks from Money.   Andrei Codrescu.   SP-CodrA

Ah, Moon—and Star!   Emily Dickinson.   CP-DickE

Ah, Muriel!   D. H. Lawrence.   CP-LawrD

Ah my Anthea! must my heart still break?   To Anthea.   Robert Herrick.   CP-HerrR

Ah, / My black one.   Poem: "Ah, / My black one."   Langston Hughes.   CP-HughL; CP-HughL1

Ah, my darling, when over the purple horizon shall loom.   Prophet.   D. H. Lawrence.   CP-LawrD

Ah my dear[e] angry [or angrie] Lord.   Bitter-Sweet.   George Herbert.   CP-HerbG

Ah, my heart, ah, what aileth thee.   Sir Thomas Wyatt.   CP-WyatT

Ah my Perilla! do'st thou grieve to see.   To Perilla.   Robert Herrick.   CP-HerrR

Ah, Necromancy Sweet!   Emily Dickinson.   CP-DickE

Ah, no, I dare not lose myself in dreams.   Rosemary ("Ah, no, I dare not lose myself in dreams").   Dorothy Parker.   CP-ParkD

Ah non chiamarlo pena.   Pitia a Damone.   Christina Georgina Rossetti.   CP-RosC3

Ah, Nora, my Nora, the light fades away.   Nora: A Serenade.   Paul Laurence Dunbar.   CP-DunbP

Ah! not by Cam or Isis, famous streams.   To a Lady.   Samuel Taylor Coleridge.   CP-ColeS

Ah, not this marble, dead and cold.   Washington's Monument, February, 1885.

Walt Whitman. CP-WhitW

Ah! not to me these dreams belong. Ralph Waldo Emerson. CP-EmerR

Ah now great brothers, you two centuries past. Sonnet: The Recollected Actual Voices of Romanticism. Hayden Carruth. CP-CarHS *Fr.* Sonnets.

Ah nuts! It's boring reading French newspapers. Les Luths. Frank O'Hara. SP-OharF

Ah! / Our floating and inconstant life. Phoenix Undying, *sel.* Kuo Mo-jo. CP-WilW2, *tr. by* William Wordsworth

Ah, pink tip of sixth sense. Passions. Yusef Komunyakaa. CP-KomuY

Ah Posthumus! our year[e]s hence fly[e]. His Age, Dedicated to His Peculiar Friend, Master John Wickes, under the Name of Posthumus. Robert Herrick. CP-HerrR

Ah! Posthumus, the years, the years. Horace. *See* Ah, Postumus, fleet-footed are the years!

Ah, Postumus, fleet-footed are the years! Ode 2.14: "Ah, Postumus, fleet-footed are the years!" Horace. CP-CummE *Fr.* Odes.

Ah Poverties, Wincings, and Sulky Retreats. Walt Whitman. CP-WhitW

Ah! red-leafed time hath driven out the rose. Canzon: The Yearly Slain. Ezra Pound. CP-PoEar

Ah! reign, wherever Man is found. Triumph of Heavenly Love Desired, The. Jeanne Marie Bouvier de la Motte- Guyon. CP-CowpW

Ah, Robin, / Jolly Robin. Sir Thomas Wyatt. CP-WyatT

Ah said Sipsop, I only wish Jack [*Hunter*] Tearguts had. William Blake. CP-BlakW *Fr.* Island in the Moon, An.

Ah! See them weep—the gaurdians of the trees. Elegy on the Destruction of the Trees by the Icicles Sunday and Monday of Feb, the 17th and 18th, 1788. Annis Boudinot Stockton. CP-StocA

Ah *Serenissa*, from our arms. Of Her Sickness. Alexander Pope. CP-PopeA

Ah, she was music in herself. How a Little Girl Sang. Nicholas Vachel Lindsay. CP-LindV

Ah, Silence! It is certain that stretched out beside me. Declaration at a Fair, The. Stéphane Mallarmé. CP-MallS, *tr. by* Henry Weinfield

Ah, so our first load of honey heavy Christmas trees. Monologues of the Son of Saul. John Logan. CP-LogaJ

Ah! so very slowly. Away. John Berryman. CP-BerrJ

Ah spring, when with a thaw of blue. Louis Zukofsky. CP-ZukLS

Ah, stern, cold man. Man Who Died, A. D. H. Lawrence. CP-LawrD

Ah, still Lord, ah sweet Divinity. Psalm II: "Ah, still Lord, ah sweet Divinity" Allen Ginsberg. CP-GinsA

Ah strange strange strange. Ralph Waldo Emerson. CP-EmerR

Ah, sudden lover, we have simply. Rainer Maria Rilke. CP-RilkFr, *tr. by* A. Poulin, Jr. *Fr.* Fragments.

Ah, summer clouds / of the Baltic! I swear. Clouds. Joseph Brodsky. CP-BrodJ

Ah, Sun-Flower [*or* Ah! Sun-Flower]. William Blake. CP-BlakW *Fr.* Songs of Experience.

Ah, sweetheart, what a pool! Broad, deep, strong, silent, and sedate! Hugh MacDiarmid. SP MacDII *Fr.* Kind of Poetry I Want, The.

Ah talk to me not of the charms of the mind. Doubt, a Pastoral Ballad—1762. Annis Boudinot Stockton. CP-StocA

Ah, Teneriffe! Emily Dickinson. CP-DickE

Ah! that life of my childhood, the high road in all weathers. Impossible, The. Arthur Rimbaud. CP-RimbA, *tr. by* Martin Sorrell

Ah that the world could use a dream or a flaming truth. Red Wine and Yellow Hair. Kenneth Patchen. CP-PatcK

Ah, that Time could touch a form. Peace. William Butler Yeats. CP-YeatW

Ah, the bird-like fluting. Flute-Music, with an Accompaniment. Robert Browning. CP-BroR2

Ah, the doe: what lovely hearts. Doe, The. Rainer Maria Rilke. CP-RilkFr, *tr. by* A. Poulin, Jr. *Fr.* Orchards.

Ah the great / the venerable. Furniture Mover. Charles Simic. SP-SimiC; SP-SimiCE

Ah the people, the people! People, The. D. H. Lawrence. CP-LawrD

Ah these are the poor. Street. George Oppen. CP-OppGN

Ah these sweet Roman mornings. Roman Morn. Lawrence Ferlinghetti. SP-FerlL

Ah, they are passing, passing by. In Praise of Songs That Die. Nicholas Vachel Lindsay. CP-LindV

Ah! this delights me more than words could tell. After Death. James Whitcomb Riley. CP-RileJ

Ah this January's nights. January 1904. Constantine P. Cavafy. CP-CavaC, *tr. by* Theoharis Constantine Theoharis

Ah this night, this night mortality wails out. Mercy. James Dickey. CP-DickJ

Ah, through the open door. Spring Morning. D. H. Lawrence. CP-LawrD

Ah, 'tis in vain the peaceful din. Henry David Thoreau. CP-ThorH

Ah to be alive. For All. Gary Snyder. CP-SnydG

Ah to be alone and uninhibited! American against Solitude. Alan Dugan. CP-DugaA

Ah, to be set and printed in. Tune, in American Type. John Updike. CP-UpdiJ

Ah . . . to the Villages! Thomas McGrath. SP-McGrT

Ah well! ah well! maybe. Maybe. D. H. Lawrence. CP-LawrD

Ah, well, I abandon you, cherrywood smokestack. Artist, The. Kenneth Koch. SP-KochK

Ah welladay and wherefore am I here? Christina Georgina Rossetti. CP-RosC3

Ah, what a dawn of splendour, when her sowers. George Meredith. CP-MerG1 *Fr.* France.

Ah, what a long and loitering way. Loveliness, The. James Whitcomb Riley. CP-RileJ

Ah! What avails the classic bent. Benfactors, The. Rudyard Kipling. CP-KiplR

Ah what bastards they all were, and are. On Shields. Against World War 3. Alan Dugan. CP-DugaA

Ah, what is love, our love, she said. Arthur Hugh Clough. SP-ClouA

Ah! where is Palafox? Nor tongue nor pen. 1810. William Wordsworth. CP-WorW1

Ah! wherefore should my weeping maid suppress. On Her Endeavoring to Conceal Her Grief at Parting. William Cowper. CP-CowpW

Ah, whispering, something again, unseen. To the Sun-set Breeze. Walt Whitman. CP-WhitW

Ah why deceive ourselves! by no mere fit. At Bologna, in Remembrance of the Late Insurrections, 1837. William Wordsworth. CP-WorW2

Ah! why Friend Frank. To F.S., who accused the Author of partiality in writing verses for F C Fowle, & not for him. Mrs. Austen. CP-AustJ

Ah! why hath Nature to so hard a hart. Sonnet 31. Edmund Spenser. CP-Spens *Fr.* Amoretti.

Ah, Will the Saviour . . . ? Stevie Smith. CP-SmitS

Ah, with His Blessing Bright on Thy Mouth and Thy Brow. D. H. Lawrence. CP-LawrD

Ah woe is me for pleasure that is vain. Vanity of Vanities. Christina Georgina Rossetti. CP-RosC1

Ah, woe is me, my Mother dear! Jeremiah 15th Ch. 10 V. Robert Burns. CP-BurnR

Ah! woe is me! poor silver-wing! Faery Song. John Keats. CP-KeatJ

Ah, woe, woe, woe, man was created to live by the sweat of his brow. Grasshoppers Are Very Intelligent. Ogden Nash. CP-NashO

Ah would you turn me back now from the flowers. Victorian Eclogues. Ezra Pound. CP-PoEar

Ah wretched they that worship vanities. Sir Walter Ralegh. CP-RaleW

Ah yes! beyond these barren walls. Song: "Ah yes! beyond these barren walls." Wallace Stevens. CP-StevWP

Ah yes, I know you well, a sojourner. Lady Wife. D. H. Lawrence. CP-LawrD

Ah yes, men must learn to serve. Service. D. H. Lawrence. CP-LawrD

Ah, yes, 't is sweet still to remember. Ione. Paul Laurence Dunbar. CP-DunbP

Ah, yes, the chapter ends to-day. End of the Chapter, The. Paul Laurence Dunbar. CP-DunbP

Ah, you stack of white lilies, all white and gold! Lilies in the Fire. D. H. Lawrence. CP-LawrD

Ah your face. Lorine Niedecker. CP-NiedL

Ahasuerus. Howard Nemerov. CP-NemeH

Ahasuerus Jenkins of the "Operatic Own" Army Headquarters. Rudyard Kipling. CP-KiplR

Ahead, starting from the far north, it wanders. Flowering Death. John Ashbery. SP-AshbJ

Ahi culla vuota! ed ahi sepolcro pieno. Christina Georgina Rossetti. CP-RosC3

Ai me! I love, give him your hand to kisse. To Mistresse Amie Potter. Robert Herrick. CP-HerrR

Ai, they all pass in front of me those girls! Song of the Young Hawaiian, The. John Berryman. CP-BerrJ

Aigeltinger. William Carlos Williams. CP-WilW2

Aiie for the toad flute. Three Disillusioning Witches, The. Federico García Lorca. CP-GarcF, *tr. by* Jerome Rothenberg *Fr.* In the Forest of the Lunar Grapefruits.

Ailanthus, goldenrod, scrapiron, what makes you flower? Open-Air Museum. Adrienne Rich. CP-RicAE; SP-RicA2

Aim Was Song, The. Robert Frost. CP-FrosR

Aimée. George Meredith. CP-MerG2

Aimilianos Monai, Alexandrian, 628–655 A.D. Constantine P. Cavafy. CP-CavaC, *tr. by* Theoharis Constantine Theoharis

Aimless / Wet finger no foresight. Bead. Philip Whalen. SP-WhalP

Ain' committed no federal crime. Canto 80: "Ain' committed no federal crime." Ezra Pound. SP-PounE *Fr.* Cantos.

Ainsi a-t-on beau. Samuel Beckett. CP-BeckS

Ain't got a reason. Slave's Critique of Practical Reason, The. Rita Dove.

SP-DoveR

Ain't it nice to have a mammy. Scamp. Paul Laurence Dunbar. CP-DunbP

Ain't nobody better's my Daddy. Little Girl Speakings. Maya Angelou. SP-AngeM

Ain't nobody nevah tol' you not a wo'd a-tall. Critters' Dance, De. Paul Laurence Dunbar. CP-DunbP

Ain't That Bad. Maya Angelou. SP-AngeM

Air. Alfonso Cortes. CP-MertT

Air: "Cat Bird Singing." Robert Creeley. CP-CreeR

Air: "The Love of a Woman." Robert Creeley. CP-CreeR

Air ("Air / pregnant with rainbows, The"). Federico García Lorca. CP-GarcF, *tr. by* Jerome Rothenberg *Fr.* Mirror Suite.

Air ("Full of scars / & fast asleep"). Federico García Lorca. CP-GarcF, *tr. by* Jerome Rothenberg *Fr.* Palimpsests.

Air. Christopher Logue. SP-LoguC

Air: "Naturally it is night." W. S. Merwin. SP-MerwW

Air. Muriel Rukeyser. CP-RukeM

Air. Derek Walcott. CP-WalcD

Air. Louis Zukofsky. CP-ZukLS

Air, The. Gabriela Mistral. SP-MistG, *tr. by* Maria Giachetti [*or* Jacketti]

Air a-gittin' cool an' coolah. Signs of the Times. Paul Laurence Dunbar. CP-DunbP

Air above Jerusalem is filled with prayers and dreams, The. Jerusalem Ecology. Yehuda Amichai. SP-AmicYL, *tr. by* Benjamin Harshav *and* Barbara Harshav

Air—air! I can barely breathe . . . aah! Adjusting to the Light. Miller Williams. CP-WillM

Air and Angels. Kenneth Rexroth. CP-RexrK

Air and Fire. Wendell Berry. CP-BerrW

Air and Light, The. William Corbett. SP-CorbW

Air at evening thickens with a scent, The. Hay. Charles Tomlinson. CP-TomlC; SP-TomlC

Air, / be / comes / or. E. E. Cummings. CP-CummE

Air Circus. Carl Sandburg. CP-SandC

Air crowds into my cell so considerately. Grace Abounding. William Stafford. SP-StafWW

Air darkened toward morning, The. Letters for the Dead. Philip Levine. SP-LeviP

Air deals blows, The: surely too hard, too often? Autumn. Philip Larkin. CP-LarkP

Air falls chill, The. September Dark. James Whitcomb Riley. CP-RileJ

Air Flower, The. Gabriela Mistral. SP-MistG, *tr. by* Maria Giachetti [*or* Jacketti]

Air for the Witness of a Departure. Christopher Logue. SP-LoguC

Air from the west, The. 3:00 p.m. Federico García Lorca. CP-GarcF, *tr. by* Jerome Rothenberg

Air grew dark with anger, The. At the Head Table. Thomas Kinsella. CP-KinsT

Air has no Residence, no Neighbor. Emily Dickinson. CP-DickE

Air has the late summer, The. Star and Crescent. Kenneth Rexroth. CP-RexrK

Air is a mill of hooks, The. Mystic. Sylvia Plath. CP-PlatS

Air is dark, the night is sad, The. Refrain. Allen Ginsberg. CP-GinsA

Air is dark, the sky is gray, The. Drowsy Day, A. Paul Laurence Dunbar. CP-DunbP

Air is full of a farewell—, The. On Leaving Ullswater. Kathleen Jessie Raine. SP-RainK

Air is grey-white as a pigeon-feather, The. Foggy Street. Andrey Andreievich Voznesensky. CP-WilbR

Air is soft as Italy, The. Emily Dickinson. SP-DickE

Air is sweetest that a thistle guards, The. Variations: The Air Is Sweetest That a Thistle Guards. James Merrill. SP-MerrJ

Air is the first international. General Prothalamion in Populous Times. Alan Dugan. CP-DugaA

Air lay softly on the green fur, The. Told. Philip Levine. SP-LeviP

Air of heaven sings. For Allen. Robert Creeley. CP-CreeR

Air of lateness blows through the redone bedroom, An. Late Summer at *Milgate*. Robert Lowell. SP-LoweR

Air of November. Denise Levertov. SP-LeveDP

Air one breathes with Smith may be the sharper, The. Couplet for Furnivall on Two Publishers. Robert Browning. CP-BroR2

Air over Jerusalem is saturated with prayers and dreams, The. Ecology of Jerusalem. Yehuda Amichai. SP-AmicY, *tr. by* Chana Bloch

Air Plant, The. Hart Crane. CP-CranH

Air / pregnant with rainbows, The. Air ("Air / pregnant with rainbows, The"). Federico García Lorca. CP-GarcF, *tr. by* Jerome Rothenberg *Fr.* Mirror Suite.

Air Raid Across the Bay at Plymouth. Stephen Spender. CP-SpenS

Air Raid: Barcelona. Langston Hughes. CP-HughL; CP-HughL1

Air Raid over Harlem. Langston Hughes. CP-HughL; CP-HughL1

Air-Raid Rehearsals. Robinson Jeffers. CP-JefR2

Air Show. John Updike. CP-UpdiJ

Air staggers under the sun, and heat-morasses, The. Sun and Air. Richard Wilbur. CP-WilbR

Air stiffens to a crust, The. Wound, The. Louise Glück. SP-GlucL

Air swarms with piranhas, The. Bronchitis on the 14th Floor. Marge Piercy. SP-PierM

Air / through which invisible birds are flying. Grace. Olga Broumas. SP-BrouO

Air was soft, the ground still cold, The. April 5, 1974. Richard Wilbur. CP-WilbR

Air weighed down, and the oppressive cloud, The. Petrarch. CP-Petra, *tr. by* J. G. Nichols

Air without Incense. Adrienne Rich. CP-RicAE

Aircraft. Rita Dove. SP-DoveR

Air[e] and Angels. John Donne. CP-DonnJ; MW-DonnJ

Airey-Force Valley. William Wordsworth. CP-WorW2; MW-WorW

Airily ice congeals on high. Melting. John Updike. CP-UpdiJ

Airman. Stephen Spender. *See* Icarus

Airman Considers His Power, An. Richard Eberhart. CP-EberR

Airman's Virtue. William Meredith. SP-MereW

Airplane Blues. Allen Ginsberg. SP-GinsA

Airplane flies through the storm, a mobile, The. Over America. Adam Zagajewski. SP-ZagaA, *tr. by* Renata Gorczynski

Airplane passes over the fig tree, An. I Want to Confuse the Bible. Yehuda Amichai. SP-AmicYL, *tr. by* Benjamin Harshav *and* Barbara Harshav

Airport. Ruth Feldman. CP-LeviP

Airport. John Updike. CP-UpdiJ

Airport bus from JFK. Queens Cemetery, Setting Sun. Lawrence Ferlinghetti. SP-FerlL

Airport coffee tastes less of America, The. Gulf, The. Derek Walcott. CP-WalcD

Airport in Amsterdam. Adam Zagajewski. SP-ZagaA, *tr. by* Clare Cavanagh

Airs of Palestine, No. 2. T. S. Eliot. SP-ElioT

Airstrip in Essex, 1960, An. Donald Hall. CP-HallD

Airy Christ, The. Stevie Smith. CP-SmitS

Airy del Castro was as bold a knight. Anti-Thelyphthora. William Cowper. CP-CowpW

Aisling. Paul Muldoon. CP-MuldP

Aix-en-Provence. Kenneth Rexroth. CP-RexrK

Ajaccio Violets. James Schuyler. CP-SchuJ

Ajanta. Muriel Rukeyser. CP-RukeM

Akbar's Bridge. Rudyard Kipling. CP-KiplR

Akhziv. Yehuda Amichai. SP-AmicYL, *tr. by* Benjamin Harshav *and* Barbara Harshav

Akiba. Muriel Rukeyser. CP-RukeM

Al Aaraaf. Edgar Allan Poe. CP-PoeEd

Alabama Earth. Langston Hughes. CP-HughL; CP-HughL1

Alabama 9/15/63. Lucille Clifton. SP-ClifL

Alabaster. Gary Snyder. CP-SnydG

Aladdin and the Jinn. Nicholas Vachel Lindsay. CP-LindV

'Alamein to Zem-Zem'—have you read it? Another Old Bolshevik. Donald Davie. CP-DaviDC

Alarm, The. Thomas Hardy. CP-HardT

Alarm, The. James Wright. CP-WrigJ

Alas, alas! for the self-destroyed / Vanish as images from a glass. Christina Georgina Rossetti. CP-RosC2

Alas! Alas! for the way I've been betrayed. Michelangelo Buonarroti. CP-Miche, *tr. by* John Frederick Nims

Alas, Alas, that I am betrayed. Michelangelo Buonarroti. CP-EmerR

Alas, dear heart! what hap [*or* hope] had I. Sir Thomas Wyatt. CP-WyatT

Alas, dear mother, fairest queen and best. Dialogue between Old England and New, A. Anne Bradstreet. CP-BradA

Alas, dear Tadeusz. Unde Malum. Czeslaw Milosz. CP-MiloCN, *tr. by* Robert Hass

Alas for obstinate doubt: the dread. Restless Ghost, A. Robert Graves. CP-GravR

Alas, Fortune, what aileth thee. Sir Thomas Wyatt. CP-WyatT

Alas, good friend, what profit can you see. Lines to a Reviewer. Percy Bysshe Shelley. CP-ShelP

Alas her sweet expression, pleasure-filled. Petrarch. CP-Petra, *tr. by* J. G. Nichols

Alas, how pleasant are their days. Unfortunate Lover, The. Andrew Marvell. CP-MarvA

Alas how the wandering mind of man grows weak, driven. Nature Does Not Suffer Decay. John Milton. CP-MiltJ

Alas how unprepared I was at first. Petrarch. CP-Petra, *tr. by* J. G. Nichols

Alas, I burn, and no one will believe it. Petrarch. CP-Petra, *tr. by* J. G. Nichols

Alas I can't, for tell me how. To his Girles who Would Have Him Sportfull. Robert Herrick. CP-HerrR

Alas, it is too late! I can no more. Perjury Excused. Sir John Suckling. CP-SuckJ

Alas, madam[e], for stealing [*or* stelying] of a kiss [*or* kysse]. Sir Thomas Wyatt. CP-WyatT

Alas! my dear, the word thou spakest. Sir Thomas Wyatt. CP-WyatT

Alas my Lord, / How should I wrestle all the livelong night. Christina Georgina Rossetti. CP-RosC3

Alas, my poor young men. Vitality. D. H. Lawrence. CP-LawrD

Alas, my spirits, when you see me. Guido Cavalcanti. CP-CavaG, *tr. by* Marc Cirigliano

Alas, O Lovely One, / Imprisoned here. Monologue, The. Walter De la Mare. CP-DeLaW

Alas! poor Brag, thou boastful Game!—What now avails thine empty name? Jane Austen. CP-AustJ

Alas, poor Death, where is thy glory? Dialogue-Anthem, A. George Herbert. CP-HerbG

Alas, poor man, what hap have I. Sir Thomas Wyatt. CP-WyatT

Alas, poor muse! What's wrong with you today? Sick Muse, The. Charles Baudelaire. CP-BaudC, *tr. by* Walter Martin

Alas, slain is the head of Israel. David's Lamentation for Saul and Jonathan. Anne Bradstreet. CP-BradA

Alas, So Long! Dante Gabriel Rossetti. CW-RossD

Alas, that faith is wanting now. Hymn: Nevertheless, when the Son of Man cometh, shall he find faith on the earth? Luke 18:8. Jones Very. CP-VeryJ

Alas, that memory at its height. Near Siena. Eugenio Montale. CP-MontE, *tr. by* Jonathan Galassi

Alas, that time has now passed over when. Petrarch. CP-Petra, *tr. by* J. G. Nichols

Alas, the grief and deadly wo[e]ful smart[!]. Sir Thomas Wyatt. CP-WyatT

Alas, the last of days when I was glad. Petrarch. CP-Petra, *tr. by* J. G. Nichols

Alas! this is not what I thought life was. Fragment: "Alas! this is not what I thought life was." Percy Bysshe Shelley. CP-ShelP

Alas, this Rembrandtesque design. Apology ("Alas, this Rembrandtesque design"). G. K. Chesterton. CP-ChesG

Alas! till now I had not known. Hafiz. CP-EmerR *Fr.* Odes.

Alas! what boots the long laborious quest. William Wordsworth. CP-WorW1

Alas, when he laughs, it is not he. Helmut. Stephen Spender. CP-SpenS

Alas! ye Bards, the Elegies you've made. Poem on Tom Pun——bi on Occasion of His Late Death, and in Vindication of Some Verses Written, Entitled "Sheridan's Resurrection," A. *Unknown.* CP-SherT

Alaska oil spill, I edit you out. Suppressing the Evidence. Carolyn Kizer. CP-KizeC

Alass, dear Friend, the fleeting years. Ode 2.14: Translation of Horace *Odes* 2.14 ("Eheu Fugaces"). Horace. CP-JohnS *Fr.* Odes.

Alastor; or, The Spirit of Solitude. Percy Bysshe Shelley. CP-ShelP

Alatus. Richard Wilbur. CP-WilbR

Alba. Samuel Beckett. CP-BeckS

Alba. Robert Creeley. CP-CreeR

Alba. James Laughlin. CP-LaugJ

Alba. Ezra Pound. SP-PounE

Alba. Arthur Sze. SP-SzeA

Alba, The. Charles Olson. CP-OlsoC

Alba Belingalis. Ezra Pound. CP-PoEar

Alba Innominata. *Unknown.* CP-PoEar, *tr. by* Ezra Pound

Alba (1952). Louis Zukofsky. CP-ZukLS

Albany throned in snow! It's winter, Poe. To Poe: Over the Planet, Air Albany–Baltimore. Allen Ginsberg. CP-GinsA

Albatross, The. Charles Baudelaire. CP-BaudC, *tr. by* Walter Martin

Albeit my prayers have not so long delay'd. Canzone: On the Death of Beatrice Portinari. Cino da Pistoia. CW-RossD, *tr. by* Dante Gabriel Rossetti

Albeit nurtured in democracy. Libertatis Sacra Fames. Oscar Wilde. CP-WildO

Albert! / Hey, Albert! Baby. Langston Hughes. CP-HughL; CP-HughL1

Alberta. Andrei Codrescu. SP-CodrA

Albi. Adam Zagajewski. SP-ZagaA, *tr. by* Clare Cavanagh

Albigenses, The. Robert Duncan. SP-DuncR

Albino. Yusef Komunyakaa. CP-KomuY

Albino-pale, half-blind, his orbit revolved. So You Agree with What I Say? Well, What Did I Say? Robert Penn Warren. CP-WarrR

Albion and Albanius. John Dryden.
Epilogue: "After our Aesop's fable shown today." CP-DryJ2
Prologue: "Full twenty years and more our labouring stage." CP-DryJ2

Song: "Albion, hail; the gods present thee." CP-DryJ2
Song: "Albion, loved of gods and men." CP-DryJ2
Song: "All hail, ye royal pair!" CP-DryJ2
Song: "From the low palace of old father Ocean." CP-DryJ2
Song: "Old father Ocean calls my tide." CP-DryJ2; SP-DrydJ
Song: "Then Zeal and Commonwealth infest." CP-DryJ2
Song: "Ye nymphs, the charge is royal." CP-DryJ2

Albion, hail; the gods present thee. Song: "Albion, hail; the gods present thee." John Dryden. CP-DryJ2 *Fr.* Albion and Albanius.

Albion, loved of gods and men. Song: "Albion, loved of gods and men." John Dryden. CP-DryJ2 *Fr.* Albion and Albanius.

Album. Lucille Clifton. SP-ClifL

Album Leaf. Stéphane Mallarmé. CP-MallS, *tr. by* Henry Weinfield

Album of Dreams. Czeslaw Milosz. CP-MiloCN, *tr. by* Lawrence Davis

Album Verses. John Greenleaf Whittier. CP-WhitJ

Albumania. James Whitcomb Riley. CP-RileJ

Albuquerque. Charles Tomlinson. CP-TomlC

Albuquerque Graveyard, The. Jay Wright. SP-WrigJ

Alcaeus to Sappho. William Wordsworth. CP-WorW1

Alcaics. Arthur Hugh Clough. SP-ClouA

Alcatraz. Peter Blue Cloud. SP-BlueP

Alcestis. Euripides.
Strength of Fate, The. CP-HousA, *tr. by* A. E. Housman

Alchemist, The. Louise Bogan. CP-BogaL

Alchemist, The. Jorge Luis Borges. SP-BorgJ, *tr. by* Alastair Reid

Alchemist, The. Ezra Pound. CP-PoEar

Alchemist, The. Ezra Pound. CP-PoEar

Alchemist in the City, The. Gerard Manley Hopkins. CP-HopkG

Alchemist of Sorrows, The. Charles Baudelaire. CP-BaudC, *tr. by* Walter Martin

Alcméne. Yannis Ritsos. SP-RitsY, *tr. by* N. C. Germanacos

Alcohol. Raymond Carver. CP-CarvR

Alcohol. Louis MacNeice. CP-MacNL

Alcoholic dream. Lorine Niedecker. CP-NiedL

Alcoholic Enters the Gates of Heaven, An. Czeslaw Milosz. CP-MiloCN, *tr. by* Robert Hass

Alcona, in its changing mood. Emily Jane Brontë. CP-BronE

Alders. Amy Clampitt. CP-ClamA

Alec. John Ciardi. CP-CiarJ

Aleksander Wat's Tie. Czeslaw Milosz. CP-MiloCN, *tr. by* Robert Hass

Alert Pillow, The. Hart Crane. CP-CranH

Alex. Mary Oliver. SP-OlivM

Alexander. Robert Lowell. SP-LoweR

Alexander. Walter de la Mare. CP-DeLaW

Alexander, before the sepulchre. Petrarch. CP-Petra, *tr. by* J. G. Nichols

Alexander Campbell. Nicholas Vachel Lindsay. CP-LindV

Alexander Crummel—Dead. Paul Laurence Dunbar. CP-DunbP

Alexander Selkirk. Jorge Luis Borges. SP-BorgJ, *tr. by* Stephen Kessler

Alexander Selkirk. William Cowper. CP-CowpW

Alexander, son of Philip, and the Greeks except the Lacedaimonians. In the Year 200 B.C. Constantine P. Cavafy. CP-CavaC, *tr. by* Theoharis Constantine Theoharis

Alexander's Feast; or, The Power of Music [*or* Musique]. John Dryden. SP-DrydJ

Alexandria, A.D. 641. Jorge Luis Borges. SP-BorgJ, *tr. by* Stephen Kessler

Alexandrian Kings. Constantine P. Cavafy. CP-CavaC, *tr. by* Theoharis Constantine Theoharis

Alexandrian Merchant. Constantine P. Cavafy. CP-CavaC, *tr. by* Theoharis Constantine Theoharis

Alexandrians flocked, The. Alexandrian Kings. Constantine P. Cavafy. CP-CavaC, *tr. by* Theoharis Constantine Theoharis

Alexandros Iannaios, and Alexandra. Constantine P. Cavafy. CP-CavaC, *tr. by* Theoharis Constantine Theoharis

Alexias. Richard Crashaw. CP-CrasR

Alf Burt, Tenant Farmer. Robert Penn Warren. CP-WarrR

Alfenus from Cremona / forsakes the friendship of friends. Carmen 30. Catullus. CP-ZukLS *Fr.* Carmina.

Alfenus, remember *kind intimacies*? false? They elated us. Catullus. *See* Alfenus from Cremona / forsakes the friendship of friends

Alfenus Varus / buttonholes me. Carmen 10. Catullus. CP-ZukLS *Fr.* Carmina.

Alfonso Lacklustre. James Tate. SP-TateJ

Alfred Corning Clark. Robert Lowell. SP-LoweR

Alfred the Great. Stevie Smith. CP-SmitS

Alfred, this couple here. Liverpool Epistle, A. Donald Davie. CP-DaviDC

Algeria. Hayden Carruth. CP-CarHS

Algernon Sydney. G. K. Chesterton. CP-ChesG

Algol, Mizar: / I wanted to become pure like the Arabic. Forget Fez. Arthur Sze. SP-SzeA

Alhambra. Jorge Luis Borges. SP-BorgJ, *tr. by* Hoyt Rogers

Alhough from then / Steep stands of beech and sugar-maple stem. Fern-Beds in Hampshire County. Richard Wilbur. CP-WilbR

Ali. W. S. Merwin. SP-MerwWF

Ali in Battle. Jelaluddin Rumi. SP-Rumi, *tr. by* Coleman Barks

Alias to a wand the height lowered. Atque in Perpetuum A.W. Louis Zukofsky. CP-ZukLS

Alicante Lullaby. Sylvia Plath. CP-PlatS

Alice. Amy Clampitt. CP-ClamA

Alice. Robert Creeley. CP-CreeR

Alice. Paul Laurence Dunbar. CP-DunbP

Alice. Robert Graves. CP-GravR

Alice Corbin Is Gone. Carl Sandburg. CP-SandC

Alice, dear, what ails you. Frosty Night, A. Robert Graves. CP-GravR

Alice Du Clos. Samuel Taylor Coleridge. CP-ColeS; MW-ColeS

Alice Faye at Ruby Foo's. James Schuyler. CP-SchuJ

Alice Fell; or, Poverty. William Wordsworth. CP-WorW1; MW-WorW

Alice grown lazy, mammoth but not fat. Last Days of Alice. Allen Tate. CP-TateA

Alice's Brilliance. Andrei Codrescu. SP-CodrA

Alien. A. K. Ramanujan. CP-RamaA

Alien wind that blew and blew, An. Sleeping Beauty, A. James Whitcomb Riley. CP-RileJ

Aliens, The. W. H. Auden. CP-AudeW

Alighting from my horse to drink with you. William Carlos Williams. CP-WilW2

Alike and Unlike. Thomas Hardy. CP-HardT

Alike and Yet Unlike: General Richard Taylor Writes to Henry Adams. Helen Pinkerton. CP-PinkH

Alison's Letter Used as a Bookmark for Ungaretti's Poems. William Corbett. SP-CorbW

Alive. Hayden Carruth. CP-CarHS

Alive. Grace Paley.

"Alive?"—And I leapt in my wonder. My Cicely. Thomas Hardy. CP-HardT

Alive for an Instant. Kenneth Koch. SP-KochK

Alivia sus fatigas. Translations from the Spanish. William Carlos Williams. CP-WilW1

Alix. Carl Sandburg. CP-SandC

All after pleasures as I rid one day. Christmas. George Herbert. CP-HerbG

All Afternoon. Charles Tomlinson. CP-TomlC; SP-TomlC

All afternoon cutting bramble blackberries off a tottering brown fence. Strange New Cottage in Berkeley, A. Allen Ginsberg. CP-GinsA; SP-GinsA

All afternoon it rained, then. Rain. Mary Oliver. SP-OlivM

All afternoon the gramophone [*or* gramaphone]. Search for Sound Free from Motion, The. Wallace Stevens. CP-StevW; CP-StevWP

All afternoon / the tree shadows, accelerating. Recovery. A. R. Ammons. CP-AmmoA

All All and All the Dry Worlds Lever. Dylan Thomas. CP-ThomD

All, All Are Gone, the Old Familiar Quotations. Ogden Nash. CP-NashO

All alone from his dark sanctum the lingam fronts, affronts the sea. Mahabalipuram. Louis MacNeice. CP-MacNL

All alone, O abundant flower. Rainer Maria Rilke. CP-RilkFr, *tr. by* A. Poulin, Jr. *Fr.* Roses, The.

All along certainly it's been there, waiting before us, waiting to receive us, not to waver. Past, The. C. K. Williams. SP-WillC

All along the valley, stream that flashest white. In the Valley of Cauteretz. Alfred Tennyson. CP-TennA

All are indebted much to thee. Gratitude and Love to God. Jeanne Marie Bouvier de la Motte Guyon. CP-CowpW, *tr. by* William Cowper

All are limitory, but each has her own. Old People's Home. W. H. Auden. CP-AudeW

All are not ill Plots, that doe sometimes faile. Plots Not Still Prosperous. Robert Herrick. CP-HerrR

All are not taken; there are left behind. Consolation. Elizabeth Barrett Browning. CP-BroEB

All around the altar, huge lianas. Reading the Bible Backwards. Eleanor Wilner. SP-WilnE

All around the apt. swimming pool. Swimming Pool, The. Thomas Lux. SP-LuxT

All around / the snow / don't fall. Xmas Poem: Bolinas. Robert Creeley. CP-CreeR

All around / the town. Robert Creeley. CP-CreeR

All art is temporal. All art is lost. Against the Text "Art Is Immortal." Alan Dugan. CP-DugaA

All as that moth call'd Underwing, alighted. Gerard Manley Hopkins. CP-HopkG

All 'at I ever want to be. His Pa's Romance. James Whitcomb Riley. CP-

RileJ

All beauty, resonance, integrity. Le Livre Est sur la Table. John Ashbery. SP-AshbJ

All beneath the sun hasteth, / All that hath begun wasteth. Christina Georgina Rossetti. CP-RosC2

All blood and body for the sun's delight. Roundel for Arms. Ezra Pound. CP-PoEar

All blue and bright, in glorious light. On the Fall of Zalona. Emily Jane Brontë. CP-BronE

All bodies have their yearnings for true evil. True Evil. Robert Graves. CP-GravR

All Bread. Margaret Atwood. SP-AtwM2

All breathed in silence, and intensely gazed. Virgil. CP-WorW2 *Fr.* Aeneid [*or* Eneados *or* Aeneis], The.

All bubbles travelling. Spring-Shock. James Dickey. CP-DickJ

All but Death can be Adjusted. Emily Dickinson. CP-DickE

All but / for me and Paul. Places ("All but / for me and Paul"). Robert Creeley. SP-CreeR

All but the future is Antiquity. Few Words, and Some His, In Memory of Clayton Stafford, A. James Vincent Cunningham. CP-CunnJ

All Catches Alight. Philip Larkin. CP-LarkP

All changed now through neglect. The steps dismantled. House at the Cascades, The. Adrienne Rich. CP-RicAE; SP-RicA2

All Choice Is Error. James Vincent Cunningham. CP-CunnJ

All Circumstances are the Frame. Emily Dickinson. CP-DickE

All cities are open in the hot season. Topography of History, The. Thomas McGrath. SP-McGrT

All Clear. Marge Piercy. SP-PierM

All condemns us to be part. Rainer Maria Rilke. CP-RilkFr, *tr. by* A. Poulin, Jr. *Fr.* Fragments.

All connections / are made by energy. *Petite Histoire* of Red Fascism, A. Andrei Codrescu. SP-CodrA

All-conquering Death! by thy resistless pow'r. To His Honour the Lieutenant-Governor, on the Death of His Lady. *March* 24, 1773. Phillis Wheatley. CP-WheaP

All cries rise, & the three of us. Ode on Nativity, An. Charles Olson. CP-OlsoC; SP-OlsoC

All crying, "We will go with you, O Wind!" Misgiving. Robert Frost. CP-FrosR

All dark is now no more. Sleeping Out at Easter. James Dickey. CP-DickJ

All darkness comes together, rounding an egg. Flayed Crow in the Hall of Judgement, A. Ted Hughes. SP-HughTN

All day, a small mild Negro man with a broom. Sweeper of Ways, The. Howard Nemerov. CP-NemeH

All day all over the city every person. City Elegies. Robert Pinsky. CP-PinsR

All day, amidst the forests' splendor bright. October ("All day, amidst the forests' splendor bright"). Jones Very. CP-VeryJ

All day an odor of damp, rotting floorboards. Invalid's Day, An. Yannis Ritsos. SP-RitsY, *tr. by* Kimon Friar

All day and night, music. Jelaluddin Rumi. SP-Rumi, *tr. by* Coleman Barks

All day / and sometimes in the hollow evening. Interrogation. Josephine Jacobsen. CP-JacoJ

All day at the window seat. Three Poems for the New Year [3]. Charles Wright. SP-WrigC *Fr.* Three Poems for the New Year.

All-Day Bird, the artist, The. Claritas. Denise Levertov. SP-LeveDP; SP-LeveDS

All day he'd been working like a locomotive. Painter & the Fish, The. Raymond Carver. CP-CarvR

All day I bang and bang at you in thought. Abraham Lincoln. Robert Lowell. SP-LoweR

All day I have been thinking about girls. Thinking about Girls. John Ciardi. CP-CiarJ

All day I loved you in a fever, holding on to the tail of the horse. At Midocean. Robert Bly. SP-BlyR

All day I think about it, then at night I say it. Who Says Words with My Mouth. Jelaluddin Rumi. SP-Rumi, *tr. by* Coleman Barks *and* John Moyne

All day I tried to distinguish. Elms. Louise Glück. SP-GlucL

All day I wandered the difficult reverie of the sea. Requiem. Sam Hamill. SP-HamiS

All day—I'm. Communication. A. R. Ammons. CP-AmmoA

All day in the sun. Consumptive, The. Langston Hughes. CP-HughL; CP-HughL1

All day I've toiled, but not with pain. Emily Jane Brontë. CP-BronE

All Day Long. Carl Sandburg. CP-SandC

All day long in fog and wind. All Day Long. Carl Sandburg. CP-SandC

All day long to the judgement-seat. Gallio's Song. Rudyard Kipling. CP-KiplR

All day my husband pounds on the upstairs porch. Time of Bees, A. Mona

Van Duyn. SP-VanDM

All day our eyes could find no resting place. Elegy: "All day our eyes could find no resting place." Wendell Berry. CP-BerrW

All day she plays at chess with the bones of the world. Female Author. Sylvia Plath. CP-PlatS

All day subdued, polite. Negro Servant. Langston Hughes. CP-HughL; CP-HughL2

All day the children await the coming. Coming, The. Josephine Jacobsen. CP-JacoJ

All day the darkness and the cold. On Receiving an Eagle's Quill from Lake Superior. John Greenleaf Whittier. CP-WhitJ

All day the fitful rain. Vermont Ballad: Change of Season. Robert Penn Warren. CP-WarrR

All Day the Light Is Clear. Tess Gallagher. SP-GallT

All day the nations climb and crawl and pray. Man and His Image, A. G. K. Chesterton. CP-ChesG

All day the opposite house. Opposite House, The. Robert Lowell. SP-LoweR

All day the rain. Hafiz. CP-EmerR Fr. Odes.

All day the snow festered. Meister Eckhart. Norman Dubie. CP-DubiN

All day the sun and rain have been as friends. Sun and Rain. James Whitcomb Riley. CP-RileJ

All day the waves assailed the rock. Nahant. Ralph Waldo Emerson. CP-EmerR

All day the yellow elevator cage. Cathedral Bells, The. Karl Shapiro. SP-ShapK

All day under acrobat. Ruins under the Stars. Galway Kinnell. SP-KinnGN

All day we watched the gulls. Torn Down from Glory Daily. Anne Sexton. CP-SextA

All de night long twell de moon goes down. Twell de Night Is Pas'. Paul Laurence Dunbar. CP-DunbP

All devil as I am, a damned wretch. Penitential Thought, in the Hour of Remorse—Intended for a Tragedy, A. Robert Burns. CP-BurnR

All Do Not All Things Well. Thom Gunn. CP-GunnT

All does draw back. Disposition, The. Charles Olson. CP-OlsoC

All dreams of "imperialism" must be exorcised. Hugh MacDiarmid. SP-MacDH Fr. In Memoriam James Joyce.

All dripping in tangles green. Tuft of Kelp, The. Herman Melville. SP-MelvH

All ends as all must end. As All Must End. Robert Graves. CP-GravR

All evening, daisies outside the window. Daisies, The. Charles Tomlinson. CP-TomlC

All Except Hannibal. Robert Graves. CP-GravR

All eyes were open. November. Federico García Lorca. CP-GarcF, tr. by Catherine Brown

All fables of adventure stress. History of Science, The. W. H. Auden. CP-AudeW

All fears, all doubts and even dreams. To Jane; and in Imitation of Coleridge. Frank O'Hara. SP-OharF

All-feeling God, hear in the war-night. Stephen Crane. CP-CranS

All feeling hearts must feel for him. Coming Storm, The. Herman Melville. SP-MelvH

All fine lads in jest upon the yellow world. It Was a Bomby Evening. Kenneth Patchen. CP-PatcK

All five shades of chameleon. April's Anarchy. Yusef Komunyakaa. CP-KomuY

All Flesh Is Grass. Christina Georgina Rossetti. CP-RosC2

All folks who pretend to religion and grace. Place of the Damned [or Damn'd], The. Jonathan Swift. CP-SwifJ

All forgot for recollecting. Emily Dickinson. CP-DickE

All from the light of the sweet moon. Night. Walter De la Mare. CP-DeLaW

All Gentle Folks Who Owe a Grudge. John Keats. CP-KeatJ

All girls grown old. On Phrase from Ginsberg's Kaddish. Robert Creeley. SP-CreeR

All glass may yet be whole. Scarred Girl, The. James Dickey. CP-DickJ

All goes back to the earth. Want of Peace, The. Wendell Berry. CP-BerrW

All-Golden, The. James Whitcomb Riley. CP-RileJ

All gone into the world of light? Perhaps. Seamus Heaney. SP-HeanSO Fr. Squarings.

All good men believe that women would rather get rid of a piece. Don't Even Tell Your Wife, Particularly. Ogden Nash. CP-NashO

All good things / eggs & hashish. Inner Source, The. Andrei Codrescu. SP-CodrA

All Greece hates. Helen. "H. D." CP-DoolH

All grim and soiled and brown with tan. Reformer, The. John Greenleaf Whittier. CP-WhitJ

All hail! inexorable lord! To Ruin. Robert Burns. CP-BurnR

All hail my friend on whom kind heaven bestows. To Mr Lewis Pintard on His

Retirement at New Rochelle. Annis Boudinot Stockton. CP-StocA

All hail new year! though clad in storms thou com'st. New Year, The. Jones Very. CP-VeryJ

All hail, sweet poet, more full of more strong fire. To Mr T. W. ("All hail, sweet poet, more full of more strong fire"). John Donne. CP-DonnJ; MW-DonnJ

"All hail!" the bells of Christmas rang. Mystic's Christmas, The. John Greenleaf Whittier. CP-WhitJ

All hail to him, the Protean! A tough old chap is he. Our Old Friend Dualism. Thomas Hardy. CP-HardT

All hail to you, two thousand years too late. Bust of Tiberius, The. Joseph Brodsky. CP-BrodJ, tr. by Alan Myers

All hail, ye royal pair! Song: "All hail, ye royal pair!" John Dryden. CP-DryJ2 Fr. Albion and Albanius.

All Hallows. Louise Glück. SP-GlucL

All Hallows' Eve. Czeslaw Milosz. CP-MiloC; CP-MiloCN, tr. by Leonard Nathan

All has been plundered from me, but my wit. His Losse. Robert Herrick. CP-HerrR

All Havens Astern. Charles Olson. CP-OlsoC

All health to thee lov'd nymph I send. Wish to Miss Hannah Stockton, The. Annis Boudinot Stockton. CP-StocA

All hearts should beat when Cho Fu's orchestra plays "Love." Our Hearts. Kenneth Koch. SP-KochK

All heaven is blazing yet / With the meridian sun. Christina Georgina Rossetti. CP-RosC3

All heavy minds. Sir Thomas Wyatt. CP-WyatT

All her charms. Lovely Ad. William Carlos Williams. CP-WilW1

All her hours were yellow sands. Epitaph for a Darling Lady. Dorothy Parker. CP-ParkD

All her kamikaze friends admired my aunt. Family Turn, A. William Stafford. SP-StafW; SP-StafWW

All Her Life. Raymond Carver. CP-CarvR

All hills and all interesting—in one field. Country Was, The. Randall Jarrell. CP-JarrR

All his eighth spring he watched. Ditch, The. Gregory Orr. SP-OrrG

All his life he was building something, inventing something. Daedalus in Sicily. Joseph Brodsky. CP-BrodJ

All holy souls / pray for us fellows. Litany: "All holy souls / pray for us fellows." Thomas Merton. CP-MertT

All hope of rest withdrawn me! Curse of the Wandering Foot, The. James Whitcomb Riley. CP-RileJ

All horns should honk like anything. Iva's Birthday Poem. Marilyn Hacker. SP-HackM

All hot and grimy from the road. Fount of Tears, The. Paul Laurence Dunbar. CP-DunbP

All human race would fain be wits. On Poetry: a Rhapsody. Jonathan Swift. CP-SwifJ

All human things are subject to decay. Mac Flecknoe [or, A Satire upon the True-Blue Protestant Poet T. S.]. John Dryden. SP-DrydJ

All hushed and still within the house. Emily Jane Brontë. CP-BronE

All Hybla's honey, all that sweetnesse can. John 15; Upon Our Lords Last Comfortable Discourse with His Disciples. Bible, N.T. CP-CrasR Fr. St. John.

All I Ask. D. H. Lawrence. CP-LawrD

All I believed is true! Mesmerism. Robert Browning. CP-BroR1; SP-BroR

All I can dream tonight is an autumn sunset. Boyhood in Tobacco Country. Robert Penn Warren. CP-WarrR

All I can give you is broken-face gargoyles. Broken-Face Gargoyles. Carl Sandburg. CP-SandC

All I can say is—I saw it! Natural Magic. Robert Browning. CP-BroR2

All I care about in a man. Man, A. D. H. Lawrence. CP-LawrD

All I could see from where I stood. Renascence. Edna St. Vincent Millay. CP-MillE

All I have is the moment of my life. You. Offense, The. James Wright. CP-WrigJ

All I have lost, that co'd be rapt from me. Recompence, The. Robert Herrick. CP-HerrR

All I Know. Charles Bukowski. SP-BukC2

All I know about medicine I picked up. Medicine. Raymond Carver. CP-CarvR

All I know is a door into the dark. Forge, The. Seamus Heaney. SP-HeanSO

All I may, if small. Emily Dickinson. CP-DickE

All I met were two birds and the wind. Notes of a Parachute Jumper. Jorge Carrera Andrade. CP-MertT

All I planted came up. Annuals. Denise Levertov. SP-LeveDP; SP-LeveDS

All I remember is. Nursery Tale. Philip Larkin. CP-LarkP

All I remember of the long lecture. Direction. W. S. Merwin. SP-MerwWF

All I see are fools. Han-shan. CP-ColdM, *tr. by* Red Pine

All I Tell You From My Heart. Robert Graves. CP-GravR

All I want today is to keep an eye on these birds. What I Can Do. Raymond Carver. CP-CarvR

All I Wanted to Say. Robert Stock. SP-StocR

All ignorance toboggans into know. E. E. Cummings. CP-CummE; SP-CummE

All in a dream of the time it was. Memory of the Sad Chair, A. John Ciardi. CP-CiarJ

All in Due Time: love will emerge from hate. James Vincent Cunningham. CP-CunnJ

All in green went my love riding. E. E. Cummings. CP-CummE; SP-CummE

All in green went my love riding. All in green went my love riding. E. E. Cummings. CP-CummE; SP-CummE

All in that day that I was born. Last Song. Adrienne Rich. CP-RicAE

All in thy sight my life doth whole depend. Sir Thomas Wyatt. CP-WyatT

All infatuated with the future, I contemplate the skies. Rainer Maria Rilke. CP-RilkFr, *tr. by* A. Poulin, Jr. *Fr.* Fragments.

All is a kind of toys, all is a kind of play. Time Passes. Richard Eberhart. CP-EberR

All is Emptiness, And I Must Spin. Thomas Kinsella. CP-KinsT

All is far. Lament: "All is far." Randall Jarrell. CP-JarrR

All is in perfect harmony. Saint Sulpice. Rainer Maria Rilke. CP-RilkFr, *tr. by* A. Poulin, Jr.

All Is Safe. Kenneth Patchen. CP-PatcK

All Is Truth. Walt Whitman. CP-WhitW

'All Is Vanity, Saith the Preacher.' Lord Byron. CP-Byron

All Is Well with the Child. Marya Alexandrovna Zaturenska. SP-ZatuM

All it takes is one to throw a room. Bonsai. Billy Collins. SP-CollB

All I've ever known are whores, ex-prostitutes. Quiet Clean Girls in Gingham Dresses. Charles Bukowski. SP-BukC1

All June I bound the rose in sheaves. One Way of Love. Robert Browning. CP-BroR1

All-kind Mother, The. James Whitcomb Riley. CP-RileJ

All kinds of people exist under Heaven. Han-shan. CP-ColdM, *tr. by* Red Pine

All kings, and all their favourites [*or* favorites]. Anniversary [*or* Anniversarie], The. John Donne. CP-DonnJ; MW-DonnJ

All-Knowing. D. H. Lawrence. CP-LawrD

All Landscape Is Abstract, and Tends to Repeat Itself. Charles Wright. SP-WrigCN

All life is but the climbing of a hill. Search. Langston Hughes. CP-HughL; CP-HughL1

All life's million conflicting interests and relationships. Hugh MacDiarmid. SP-MacDH *Fr.* Plaited Like the Generations of Men.

All listlessly we float. Where Shall We Land? James Whitcomb Riley. CP-RileJ

All living things. Will To, The. Charles Olson. CP-OlsoC

All look or [*or* and] likeness caught from earth. Phantom. Samuel Taylor Coleridge. CP-ColeS

All looks be pale, hearts [*or* harts] cold as stone. Lamentation, A. Thomas Campion. CP-CampT

All lovers war, and Cupid hath his tent. Elegy 1.9: "All lovers war, and Cupid hath his tent." Ovid. CP-MarlC *Fr.* Elegies.

All men are lonely now. Dawn. Edna St. Vincent Millay. CP-MillE

All men are worms [*or* wormes]: but this no man. In silk[e]. On Court-Worm[e]. Ben Jonson. CP-JonsB; SP-JonsB

All men are worshippers. Worship. D. H. Lawrence. CP-LawrD

All men around me running to and fro. Prisoner, The. Jones Very. CP-VeryJ

All men for Honor hardest work. Emily Dickinson. CP-DickE

All men of mirth and sense admire and love. Lucretius. CP-SherT *Fr.* De Rerum Natura (On the Nature of Things).

All Men throughout the peopled Earth. Book III. Metre 6. Boethius. CP-JohnS *Fr.* Consolation of Philosophy, The ("De Consolacione Philosophie").

All month eating the heart out. Break, The. Adrienne Rich. CP-RicAE

All Morning. Theodore Roethke. CP-RoetT

All morning I have been reading poems. Lament: "All morning I have been reading poems." Eleanor Wilner. SP-WilnE

All morning I've walked about. Cicada. Charles Wright. SP-WrigCN

All morning / rain slowly filled. Making It New. Philip Levine. SP-LeviP

All morning the tree men have been taking down the stricken elms skirting the broad sidewalks. Elms. C. K. Williams. SP-WillC

All morning with dry instruments. Provision. W. S. Merwin. SP-MerwW

All morning with gloved. Work Gloves. Gregory Orr. SP-OrrG

All Mountains. "H. D." CP-DoolH

All must be used. Barracks Apt. 14. Theodore Weiss. SP-WeisT

All my dark thoughts. Euclid Avenue. Charles Simic. SP-SimiC; SP-SimiCE

All my feelin's in the Spring. Me and Mary. James Whitcomb Riley. CP-

All my goodbyes are said. Many separations. Rainer Maria Rilke. CP-RilkFr, *tr. by* A. Poulin, Jr. *Fr.* Orchards.

All my life I have been a witness of things. Two Goes into Two Once, If You Can Get It There. Ogden Nash. CP-NashO

All my life I have wondered. 140 Syllables. Kenneth Rexroth. CP-RexrK

All my life, / so far, / I have loved. Moccasin Flowers. Mary Oliver. SP-OlivM

All my life that's been / the watchword: Resist! Resist! Hayden Carruth. CP-CarHS *Fr.* Clay Hill Anthology, The.

All my life too lazy to work. Han-shan. CP-ColdM, *tr. by* Red Pine

All my miserable secrets. My Secrets. Czeslaw Milosz. CP-MiloCN, *tr. by* Robert Hass

All My Pretty Ones. Anne Sexton. CP-SextA; SP-SextA

All my woods are / tangle. Ancient. Line, The. Hayden Carruth. CP-CarHS

All my words and deeds were lost between the writing and the reading. Yehuda Amichai. SP-AmicYL *Fr.* At Right Angles.

All Nature dies! wide over hill and plain. Death of Man, The. Jones Very. CP-VeryJ

All Nature is a temple where the alive. Correspondences. Charles Baudelaire. CP-TateA, *tr. by* Allen Tate

All Nature seems at work. Slugs leave their lair. Work without Hope. Samuel Taylor Coleridge. CP-ColeS; MW-ColeS

All nearness pauses, while a star can grow. E. E. Cummings. CP-CummE

All night above their rocky bed. Pass of the Sierra, The. John Greenleaf Whittier. CP-WhitJ

All night and all day the wind roared in the trees. Mid-Country Blow. Theodore Roethke. CP-RoetT

All night, and as the wind lieth among. Speech for Psyche in the Golden Book of Apuleius. Ezra Pound. CP-PoEar

All Night Fair. Federico García Lorca. CP-GarcF, *tr. by* Jerome Rothenberg *Fr.* Fairs.

All night / he is thinking of it. Fetish. Hans Magnus Enzensberger. SP-EnzeH

All night he ran, his body air. Transformations. Stanley Kunitz. CP-KunSC

All night his window / shines in the woods. Poet, The. Hayden Carruth. CP-CarHS

All night I drank love's wine. Love. Nothing's Left. Rainer Maria Rilke. CP-RilkFr, *tr. by* A. Poulin, Jr.

All night i dream of lips. Lumpectomy Eve. Lucille Clifton. SP-ClifL

All night I dream of that which cannot be. Hopeless Case, A. Christina Georgina Rossetti. CP-RosC3

All night I dream you love me well. Christina Georgina Rossetti. CP-RosC3

All night I dreamed of heaven. Nantucket Morning / This World. Gregory Orr. SP-OrrG

All night / I float / in the shallow ponds. White Night. Mary Oliver. SP-OlivM

All night I hear the hammers. Students of Justice, The. W. S. Merwin. SP-MerwW

All night I lay awake beside you. She Is Away [*or* Marthe Away (She Is Away)]. Kenneth Rexroth. CP-RexrK

All night I sat reading a book. Reader, The. Wallace Stevens. CP-StevW; CP-StevWP

All night in a thoughtful / mood, she. For Somebody's Marriage. Robert Creeley. CP-CreeR

All night / in and out the slippery shadows. Nature. Mary Oliver. SP-OlivM

All night, in May, dogs barked in the hollow woods. Eidolon. Robert Penn Warren. CP-WarrR

All night in the flue like a trapped thing. January 25th. Maxine W. Kumin. SP-KumiM *Fr.* Joppa Diary.

All night in the womb I heard the stories. Little Poem, A. Randall Jarrell. CP-JarrR

All Night, Legs Pointed East. Thom Gunn. CP-GunnT

All night long I hear the sleepers toss. Such Simple Love. Thomas McGrath. SP-McGrT

All night long the darling daughter squirms. Flapper, The. Allen Tate. CP-TateA

All night long the rush and trampling of water. Robinson Jeffers. CP-JefR3

All night long they talked, raged, wrangled. Honest Confrontation. Yannis Ritsos. SP-RitsY, *tr. by* Kimon Friar

All night, over roof, over forest, you hear. Wind and Gibbon. Robert Penn Warren. CP-WarrR

All night rain falls through fog. Northampton, 1922–San Francisco, 1939. Kenneth Rexroth. CP-RexrK

All night rain lashed the windows. Fragment of a Letter. Jaroslav Seifert. SP-SeifJ, *tr. by* Ewald Osers

All night, snow, then, near dawn, freezing rain, so that by morning the whole city glistens. Snow: I. C. K. Williams. SP-WillC

All night summer wind, hot, An. Gentle Earthquake, A. Peter Blue Cloud. SP-BlueP

All night the army came up from Gilgal.　I Want to Die in My Own Bed.　Yehuda Amichai.　SP-AmicYL, *tr. by* Benjamin Harshav *and* Barbara Harshav

All night the cocks crew, under a moon like day.　Tears in Sleep.　Louise Bogan.　CP-BogaL

All night the crib creaks.　During Fever.　Robert Lowell.　SP-LoweR

All night the *douanier* in his sentry box.　Grandchild.　Maxine W. Kumin.　SP-KumiM

All night the loose shutter bangs. This way it won't last.　Loose Shutter, The.　Robert Penn Warren.　CP-WarrR

All night the nurses let me listen.　Family Portrait for Our Daughter, A.　Wyatt Prunty.　SP-PrunW

All night the rain.　Fanny Howe.　SP-HoweF　*Fr.* Vineyard, The.

All night the sound had.　Rain, The.　Robert Creeley.　CP-CreeR

All night the wind.　History.　Thomas McGrath.　SP-McGrT

All night the wind sings like a surf.　Storm at Night, The.　Thomas Merton.　CP-MertT

All night, this headland.　Sleepless at Crown Point.　Richard Wilbur.　CP-WilbR

All Nothing, Nothing.　Laura Riding Jackson.　CP-RidiL

All nouns in *a* make Feminine.　Declension 1.　Thomas Sheridan.　CP-SherT　*Fr.* Of Knowing the Gender of Nouns by Termination.

All of a sudden I'm a painter.　Artist.　Charles Bukowski.　SP-BukC1

All of December Toward New Year's.　Louis Zukofsky.　CP-ZukLS

All of it went on the wrong page.　Philip Whalen.　SP-WhalP

All of our ancestors' pleasures.　Rainer Maria Rilke.　CP-RilkFr, *tr. by* A. Poulin, Jr.　*Fr.* Orchards.

All of Roses.　D. H. Lawrence.　CP-LawrD

All of the branches / None of the roots.　Thomas Merton.　CP-MertT

All of them are sitting.　Screened Porch in the Country, A.　James Dickey.　CP-DickJ

All of us believe.　Question, The: "All of us believe."　W. H. Auden.　CP-AudeW

All of us on the sofa in a line, kneeling.　Sofa in the Forties, A.　Seamus Heaney.　SP-HeanSO

All of you are priceless gems.　Han-shan.　CP-ColdM, *tr. by* Red Pine

All on the mountains, as on tapestries.　For Robert Frost, in the Autumn, in Vermont.　Howard Nemerov.　CP-NemeH

All one knows, and knows / upon the possibility of knowing.　For Lewis, to Say It.　Robert Creeley.　CP-CreeR

All one winter, in every crowded hall.　Fragment: "All one winter, in every crowded hall."　Denise Levertov.　SP-LeveDL

All or None.　Randall Jarrell.　CP-JarrR

All others talked as if.　Caedmon.　Denise Levertov.　SP-LeveDS

"All our French poets can turn an inspired line."　Nihilist as Hero, The.　Robert Lowell.　SP-LoweR

All our lives we've looked.　Jelaluddin Rumi.　SP-Rumi, *tr. by* Coleman Barks

All out of doors [*or* out-of-doors] looked darkly in at him.　Old Man's Winter Night, An.　Robert Frost.　CP-FrosR

All Over Again.　Louis MacNeice.　CP-MacNL

All over America tonight.　In Warm Rooms, Before a Blue Light.　Maxine W. Kumin.　SP-KumiM

All over America women are burning dinners.　What's That Smell in the Kitchen?　Marge Piercy.　SP-PierM

All over Minnesota, / Cerise sopranos.　Primordia.　Wallace Stevens.　CP-StevWP

All over the world.　Shall the Good Go Down?　Langston Hughes.　CP-HughL; CP-HughL2

All overgrown by cunning moss.　Emily Dickinson.　CP-DickE

All Pictures thats Panted with sense & with Thought.　William Blake.　CP-BlakW

All Pink from the Bath She Slept.　Charles Olson.　CP-OlsoC

All plants grow here; the most minute.　Garden of the Gods, The.　Thom Gunn.　CP-GunnT

All poems can be represented by.　Still Lifes.　William Carlos Williams.　CP-WilW2

All poetry up to the present time.　Poetry.　John Ciardi.　CP-CiarJ

All power is saved, having no end. Rises.　Dam, The.　Muriel Rukeyser.　CP-RukeM

All praise the Likeness by thy skill portrayed.　To a Painter.　William Wordsworth.　CP-WorW2

All praise to him who hath now turned.　On My Son's Return Out of England.　Anne Bradstreet.　CP-BradA

All profits disappear: the gain.　Reckoning, The.　Theodore Roethke.　CP-RoetT

All Quiet.　David Ignatow.　SP-IgnaD

All rage, all misery, all show of strength.　Michelangelo Buonarroti.　CP-Miche, *tr. by* John Frederick Nims

"All ready?" cried the captain.　Slave-Ships, The.　John Greenleaf Whittier.　CP-WhitJ

All Religions Are One.　William Blake.　CP-BlakW

All Revelation.　Robert Frost.　CP-FrosR

All revolutions in modern times have led.　Sonnet: "All revolutions in modern times have led."　Hayden Carruth.　CP-CarHS　*Fr.* Sonnets.

All right, gentlemen who cry blue murder as always.　Draft of a Reparations Agreement.　Dan Pagis.　SP-PagiD, *tr. by* Stephen Mitchell

All right, let's say you could take a skull and break it.　Sonnet: To Eva.　Sylvia Plath.　CP-PlatS

All right, they're playing Beethoven again; when I was.　Sardines in Striped Dresses.　Charles Bukowski.　SP-BukC3

All right. Try this.　Northern Pike.　James Wright.　CP-WrigJ

All Rivers at Once.　Jelaluddin Rumi.　SP-Rumi, *tr. by* Coleman Barks

All roses are enchantment to the wise.　Of Roses.　Tennessee Williams.　CP-WillT

All round about, the clouds encompassed me.　To Dr. James Newton Matthews, Mason, Ill.　Paul Laurence Dunbar.　CP-DunbP

All round they murmur, 'O profane.'　Vulgarised.　G. K. Chesterton.　CP-ChesG

All Saints.　Christina Georgina Rossetti.　CP-RosC2

All Saints: Martyrs.　Christina Georgina Rossetti.　CP-RosC2

All saints revile her, and all sober men.　White Goddess, The.　Robert Graves.　CP-GravR

All Seated.　Pablo Neruda.　SP-NeruP

All seemed delighted, though the elders more.　Floretty's Musical Contribution.　James Whitcomb Riley.　CP-RileJ　*Fr.* Child-World, A.

All shivers, / Dear friends.　Peaceful Trees.　Charles Simic.　SP-SimiC; SP-SimiCE

All slumbered whom our rud red tiles.　Elopement, The.　Gerard Manley Hopkins.　CP-HopkG

All Sorts of Gods.　D. H. Lawrence.　CP-LawrD

All sorts of singers have this common vice.　On Singers.　Robert Browning.　CP-BroR2

All Souls.　D. H. Lawrence.　CP-LawrD

All Souls.　Muriel Rukeyser.　CP-RukeM

All Souls.　May Sarton.　SP-SartM

All Soul's Day.　D. H. Lawrence.　CP-LawrD

All Souls' Night.　William Butler Yeats.　CP-YeatW　*Fr.* Vision, A.

All sound is religion.　Sunday Sermon.　Andrei Codrescu.　SP-CodrA

All Sounds Have Been As Music.　Wilfred Owen.　CP-OwenW

All spring the birds walked on this wormy world.　Elementary Attitudes.　Mona Van Duyn.　SP-VanDM

All stars are(and not one star only)love.　E. E. Cummings.　CP-CummE

All submit to them where they sit, inner, secure, unaproachable to analysis in the soul.　Tests.　Walt Whitman.　CP-WhitW

All such proclivities are tabulated.　Quiet Glades of Eden, The.　Robert Graves.　CP-GravR

All sudden she hath ceased to sing.　Silent Singer, The.　James Whitcomb Riley.　CP-RileJ

All sullen blares the wintry blast.　Song of a Contented Heart.　Dorothy Parker.　CP-ParkD

All summer I heard them.　Snakes of September, The.　Stanley Kunitz.　CP-KunSC

All summer in power, outroaring the bull fiend.　On the Orthodoxy and Creed of My Power Mower.　John Ciardi.　CP-CiarJ

All summer / they grew unseen.　Shelling Jacobs Cattle Beans.　Maxine W. Kumin.　SP-KumiM

All summer we moved in a villa brimful of echoes.　Other Two, The.　Sylvia Plath.　CP-PlatS

All summer's warmth was stored there in the hay.　At the Back of the North Wind.　Thom Gunn.　CP-GunnT

All tears done away with the bitter unquiet sea.　Churchyard Song of Patient Hope, A.　Christina Georgina Rossetti.　CP-RosC2

All that blesses the step of the antelope.　Else a great Prince in prison lies.　Denise Levertov.　SP-LeveDP

All that could change: never again.　But It Is Purer to Die.　Rainer Maria Rilke.　CP-RilkFr, *tr. by* A. Poulin, Jr.

All that day we banged at geese.　Limits.　Raymond Carver.　CP-CarvR

All that I do.　Emily Dickinson.　CP-DickE

All that I know / Of a certain star.　My Star.　Robert Browning.　CP-BroR1

All that I serve will die, all my delights.　Wish to Be Generous, The.　Wendell Berry.　CP-BerrW

All That Is.　Richard Wilbur.　CP-WilbR

All that is is a harmony.　They Say This Isn't a Poem.　Kenneth Rexroth.　CP-RexrK

All That Is Lovely in Men.　Robert Creeley.　CP-CreeR

All That is Perfect in Woman.　William Carlos Williams.　CP-WilW2

All that is: / The unbroken surface of the sea.　Kathleen Jessie Raine.　SP-RainK

All that is unnatural violates the atrocious gestures of Hortense. H. Arthur Rimbaud. CP-RimbA, *tr.* by Martin Sorrell

All that matters is to be at one with the living God. Pax. D. H. Lawrence. CP-LawrD

All that morning in the strawberry field. Bitter Strawberries. Sylvia Plath. CP-PlatS

All that night / I prayed for eyes to see again. South: The Name of Home. Alice Walker. CP-WalkA

All That Night Lights Were Seen Moving in Every Direction. Kenneth Patchen. CP-PatcK

All that passes, all that perishes. Ravenna. Aleksandr Aleksandrovich Blok. SP-BlokA, *tr.* by Peter France *and* Jon Stallworthy

All that passes descends. Gift of Gravity, The. Wendell Berry. CP-BerrW

All that she did she did not aim to do. Lay of the Badde Wyf. Miller Williams. CP-WillM

All that spinning on your stem. Rainer Maria Rilke. CP-RilkFr, *tr.* by A. Poulin, Jr. *Fr.* Roses, The.

All that the thin Knight's thinner shadow here. Inscribed in a Copy of "The Return of Don Quixote" G. K. Chesterton. CP-ChesG

All that thy virgin soul can ask be thine. Ralph Waldo Emerson. CP-EmerR

All That Time. May Swenson. SP-SwenM

All that was divine remains divine. Rainer Maria Rilke. CP-RilkFr, *tr.* by A. Poulin, Jr. *Fr.* Fragments.

All That We Have Is Life. D. H. Lawrence. CP-LawrD

All that we know is nothing, we are merely crammed waste-paper baskets. All-Knowing. D. H. Lawrence. CP-LawrD

All that we see is penetrated by it. As We Know. John Ashbery. SP-AshbJ

All that we see rejoices in the sunshine. Let Everything That Hath Breath Praise the Lord. Christina Georgina Rossetti. CP-RosC2

All that which lies outside our sort of why. Objects. W. H. Auden. CP-AudeW

All That's Past. Walter De la Mare. CP-DeLaW

All the angels are here this morning, in the striped light. Angels at "Unsubdued." May Swenson. SP-SwenM

All the bad Bauhaus comes to a head. Humanities Building, The. Karl Shapiro. SP-ShapK

All the Beautiful are Blameless. James Wright. CP-WrigJ

All the beer was poisoned and the capt. went down. Love Is a Piece of Paper Torn to Bits. Charles Bukowski. SP-BukC2

All the bells were ringing / And all the birds were singing. Christina Georgina Rossetti. CP-RosC2

All the boys are gathered there. On Vulture Peak. Gary Snyder. CP-SnydG

All the breath and the bloom of the year in the bag of one bee. Summum Bonum. Robert Browning. CP-BroR2

All the Bright Foam of Talk. Kenneth Patchen. CP-PatcK

All the buildings in Glasgow are grey. John Maclean (1879–1923). Hugh MacDiarmid. SP-MacDH

All the Casualties. Charles Bukowski. SP-BukC3

All the complicated details. Winter Trees. William Carlos Williams. CP-WilW1

All the craziness. Dixie South Africa. Langston Hughes. CP-HughL; CP-HughL3

All the dark hours everywhere repair. Night. Gary Snyder. CP-SnydG

All the Day. Kenneth Patchen. CP-PatcK

All the dead are eating little yellow peas. For Randall Jarrell, 1914–1965. Norman Dubie. CP-DubiN

All the Dead Dears. Sylvia Plath. CP-PlatS

All the Dead Soldiers. Thomas McGrath. SP-McGrT

All the Earth, All the Air. Theodore Roethke. CP-RoetT

All the Fancy Things. William Carlos Williams. CP-WilW1

All the fantasies that. Robert Creeley. CP-CreeR

All the Flowery. Kenneth Patchen. CP-PatcK

All the generations before me contributed me. Yehuda Amichai. SP-AmicYL, *tr.* by Benjamin Harshav *and* Barbara Harshav

All the gold that exists was transmuted once. History of Alchemy. W. S. Merwin. SP-MerwW

All the grass / dies. Night Sky, A. Robert Creeley. CP-CreeR

All the great & good. Ralph Waldo Emerson. CP-EmerR

All the grievous wounds the murderers. Dragon of Revolutionary Love. Denise Levertov. SP-LeveDL

All the heaven and earth. João Cabral de Melo Neto. CP-BishE, *tr.* by Elizabeth Bishop. *Fr.* Death and Life of a Severino, The.

All the heavy. Abstract Love Poem. John Logan. CP-LogaJ

All the heavy days are over. Countess Cathleen in Paradise, The. William Butler Yeats. CP-YeatW

All the here and all the there. Our Two Worthies. John Crowe Ransom. SP-RansJ

All the huskies are eaten. There is no space. Polar Explorer, A. Joseph Brodsky. CP-BrodJ

All the Leaves Were Green. Jane Cooper. CP-CoopJ

All the letters I can write. Emily Dickinson. CP-DickE

All the Little Animals. Muriel Rukeyser. CP-RukeM

All the Little Hoof-Prints. Robinson Jeffers. CP-JefR2

All the livelong way this day of sweet showers from Portrane on the seashore. Sanies I. Samuel Beckett. CP-BeckS

All the long school-hours, round the irregular hum of the class. Snowy Day in School, A. D. H. Lawrence. CP-LawrD

All the lost interpretations. Return, The. Louis MacNeice. CP-MacNL

All the more reason, then, that men and women. Ovid. CP-MuldP *Fr.* Metamorphoses.

All the night in woe. Little Girl Found, The. William Blake. CP-BlakW *Fr.* Songs of Experience.

All the night in woe. Little Girl Found, The. William Blake. CP-BlakW *Fr.* Songs of Innocence.

All the night sleep came not upon my eyelids. Sapphics. Sappho. SP-SwinA, *tr.* by Algernon Charles Swinburne

All the others translate: the painter sketches. Composer, The. W. H. Auden. CP-AudeW

All the people I see. Han-shan. CP-ColdM, *tr.* by Red Pine

All the people of the play were there. Landscape with Wave Approaching. Muriel Rukeyser. CP-RukeM

All the policemen, saloonkeepers and efficiency experts in Toledo knew. Potomac River Mist. Carl Sandburg. CP-SandC

All the quiet afternoons splitting wood. Old Bones. Sam Hamill. SP-HamiS

All the Robin Redbreasts. 1885. St. Valentine's Day. Christina Georgina Rossetti. CP-RosC3

All the Roses of the World. Kenneth Patchen. CP-PatcK

All the sexually active people in Westport. Chaste Stranger, The. James Tate. SP-TateJ

All the Sioux were defeated. Our clan. Report to Crazy Horse. William Stafford. SP-StafW; SP-StafWW

All the Slaves [within me]. Thomas Lux. SP-LuxT

All the soft runs of it, the tin-white gashes. Bougainville. Donald Davie. CP-DaviDC

All the stones have been us. Eyes of Summer. W. S. Merwin. SP-MerwW

All the stream that's roaring by. Needle's Eye, A. William Butler Yeats. CP-YeatW

All The Time. Laura Riding Jackson. CP-RidiL

All the tom-toms of the jungles beat in my blood. Poem: "All the tom-toms of the jungles beat in my blood." Langston Hughes. CP-HughL; CP-HughL1

All the toothy Fräuleins are left behind. Son, The. Rita Dove. SP-DoveR

All the trees all their boughs all their leaves. Out of Sight in the Direction of My Body. Paul Éluard. CP-BeckS

All the voices of the sea called *Muriel!* Calling, The. Jane Cooper. CP-CoopJ

All the voices of the wood called "Muriel!" Then I Saw What the Calling Was. Muriel Rukeyser. CP-RukeM

All the waters of the river Deben. River Deben, The. Stevie Smith. CP-SmitS

All the Way. Robert Creeley. SP-CreeR

All the way across the Bay Bridge I sang. Buying and Selling. Philip Levine. SP-LeviP

All the Way Down. Thomas Merton. CP-MertT

All the way from Mexico. Art, An. Charles Bukowski. SP-BukC1

All the way / on the road to Gary. Helmet, The. Philip Levine. SP-LeviP

All the way through the forest, a sound of birdsong. Muriel Rukeyser. CP-RukeM

All the way to my station I was trying to make out who was the guy responsible. Puzzle, The. David Ignatow. SP-IgnaD

All the way to the city a crying in the air. Grand Central Station. Muriel Rukeyser. CP-RukeM

All the while among. Fragrance of Life, Odor of Death. Denise Levertov. SP-LeveDL

All the while they were talking the new morality. Encounter, The. Ezra Pound. SP-PounE

All the Wide Grin of Him. Eleanor Wilner. SP-WilnE

All the wolves of the forest. Lyceia. Robert Graves. CP-GravR

All the women / all their kisses the. Love Poem, A. Charles Bukowski. SP-BukC3

All the world is so sweet, dear. To Alice Dunbar. Paul Laurence Dunbar. CP-DunbP

All the world is walking on the Gran Via. Madrid, 1974. Mona Van Duyn. SP-VanDM

All the world over, nursing their scars. Rudyard Kipling. CP-KiplR

All their lives out here some people know. Is This Feeling about the West Real? William Stafford. SP-StafWW

All there's to say of him, no way of saying. Michelangelo Buonarroti. CP-

Miche, *tr. by* John Frederick Nims

All These Birds. Richard Wilbur. CP-WilbR

All these dreams: the dream of the mountain cabin. Jane Cooper. CP-CoopJ

All these illegitimate babies. Valuable. Stevie Smith. CP-SmitS

All these love-poems . . .! Love-Poems: for Mairi MacInnes. Donald Davie. CP-DaviDC

All These Make a Dance Rhythm. Yehuda Amichai. SP-AmicY, *tr. by* Chana Bloch

All these my banners be. Emily Dickinson. CP-DickE

All these stones, all this sorrow, all this. Yehuda Amichai. SP-AmicY, *tr. by* Chana Bloch *Fr.* Songs of Zion the Beautiful.

All these years behind windows. Animals, The. W. S. Merwin. SP-MerwW

All Things. Hayden Carruth. CP-CarHS

All Things. Laura Riding Jackson. CP-RidiL

All things are current found. Henry David Thoreau. CP-ThorH

All things are fair, if we had eyes to see. Behold, It Was Very Good. Christina Georgina Rossetti. CP-RosC2

All things are open to these two events Rewards and Punishments. Robert Herrick. CP-HerrR

All things are real. Letter to a Friend: Who Is Nancy Daum? James Schuyler. CP-SchuJ

All things are Thine: no gift have we. Hymn for the Opening of Plymouth Church. John Greenleaf Whittier. CP-WhitJ

All things are words of some strange tongue, in thrall. Compass. Jorge Luis Borges. CP-WilbR

All things aspire to weightlessness. Poem Half in the Manner of Li Ho. Charles Wright. SP WrigCN

"All things become thee, being thine," I think sometimes. Woman. Randall Jarrell. CP-JarrR

All Things Can Tempt Me. William Butler Yeats. CP-YeatW

All things confirm me in the thought that dust. In Spite of Death. Countee Cullen. CP-CullC

All things decay. Henry David Thoreau. CP-ThorH

All Things Decay and Die. Robert Herrick. CP-HerrR

All things decay with Time: The Forrest sees. All Things Decay and Die. Robert Herrick. CP-HerrR

All things grew upwards, foul and fair. Fairy Tale, A. G. K. Chesterton. CP-ChesG

All things imagined are of earth compact. Wallace Stevens. CP-StevWP

All things lean at you, and some are. Trying to Tell You Something. Robert Penn Warren. CP-WarrR

All things new / But I: no shadow. Kathleen Jessie Raine. SP-RainK

All things o'r-rul'd are here by Chance. Large Bounds Doe but Bury Us. Robert Herrick. CP-HerrR

All Things Pass. Stevie Smith. CP-SmitS

All things rehearse. Ralph Waldo Emerson. CP-EmerR

All Things Run Well for the Righteous. Robert Herrick. CP-HerrR

All things seem mention of themselves. Grand Galop. John Ashbery. SP-AshbJ

All things stand out against the sky. Charles Olson. CP-OlsoC

All things subjected are to Fate. Change Common to All. Robert Herrick. CP-HerrR

All things swept sole away. Emily Dickinson. CP-DickE

All things that go deep enough. Ice Skin, The. James Dickey. CP-DickJ

All things that pass / Are woman's looking-glass. Passing and Glassing. Christina Georgina Rossetti. CP-RosC2

All things uncomely and broken, all things worn out and old. Lover Tells of the Rose in His Heart, The. William Butler Yeats. CP-YeatW

All Things Wait upon Thee. Christina Georgina Rossetti. CP-RosC2

(These All Wait upon Thee.) CP-RosC2

All things with you it seems to me smile affable. Epic in the Heart. Constantine P. Cavafy. CP-CavaC, *tr. by* Theoharis Constantine Theoharis

All things within this fading world hath [*or* have] end. Before the Birth of One of Her Children. Anne Bradstreet. CP-BradA

All This. Hart Crane. CP-CranH

All this and more, though is there more? Emily Dickinson. SP-DickE

All this flesh, meat. Robert Creeley. CP-CreeR

All this for me, he asked. Moral Tale, A. David Ignatow. SP-IgnaD

All this light stuff falling down. Towards Eternal Peace. Hans Magnus Enzensberger. SP-EnzeH

All this quiet sweeping round us on the earth's edge. Small but Brilliant Fire Blazed in the Grate, A. Kenneth Patchen. CP-PatcK

All this stood on her and was the world. Grown-Up, The. Randall Jarrell. CP-JarrR

All This Strangeness. George Oppen. CP-OppGN

All this talk of equality between the sexes is merely an expression of sex-hate. Men and Women. D. H. Lawrence. CP-LawrD

All this time / You were dead and I did not know. One Month. Muriel Rukeyser. CP-RukeM

All those flourishes and curlicues were his. Literal. Heather McHugh. SP-McHuH

All those he never ate. Accolade of the Animals, The. Maxine W. Kumin. SP-KumiM

All those treasures that lie in the little bolted box whose tiny space is. Slow Movement. William Carlos Williams. CP-WilW1

All those who have not died have married. End, The. Charles Tomlinson. CP-TomlC

All those words we once used for things but have now discarded in order to come to know things. Michael Palmer. SP-PalmM

All those years, alone. You Taught Me. Thomas McGrath. SP-McGrT

All those years that you ate and changed. Peasant. W. S. Merwin. SP-MerwW

All thoughts, all passions, all delights. Love. Samuel Taylor Coleridge. CP-ColeS; MW-ColeS

All three are bare. Three. Thom Gunn. CP-GunnT

All thro' the livelong night I lay awake. Sonnet from the Psalms. Christina Georgina Rossetti. CP-RosC3

All through that Sunday afternoon. Kite for Michael and Christopher, A. Seamus Heaney. SP-HeanSO

All through the blazing afternoon. Ariadne. Thomas Merton. CP-MertT

All through the damp morning he works, he reads. His Rooms in College. Thom Gunn. CP-GunnT

All through the dark the wind looks. Night Wind. W. S. Merwin. SP-MerwW

All through the Rains. Gary Snyder. CP-SnydG

"All Thy Works Praise Thee, O Lord": A Processional of Creation. Christina Georgina Rossetti. CP-RosC2

All today I lie in the bottom of the wardrobe. Yoko. Thom Gunn. CP-GunnT

All too often now your voice is too bright. Christmas. Robert Lowell. SP-LoweR

All Trees, all leavy Groves confesse the Spring. Out of Virgil, in the Praise of the Spring. Virgil. CP-CrasR *Fr.* Georgics.

All trucks were from Hell and deserved my bite. Coach. Wyatt Prunty. SP-PrunW

All up and down the avenues. Condition, The. Charles Bukowski. SP-BukC3

All up and down the street they came back. Conversation on Morality, Eternity and Copulation, A. Charles Bukowski. SP-BukC2

All Wars Are Holy. Andrei Codrescu. SP-CodrA

All was taken away from you: white dresses. On Angels. Czeslaw Milosz. CP-MiloC; CP-MiloCN

All we can dream of loveliness within. Conclusion of a Sonnet on "Keely's Discovery." Robert Browning. CP-BroR2

All we do—how old are we? I must be twelve, she a little older; thirteen, fourteen—is hold hands. Still Life. C. K. Williams. CP-WillC

All we have is God's, and yet. Mark 12; (Give to Cæsar———) (And to God———). Bible, *N.T.* CP-CrasR *Fr.* St. Mark.

All we need is fourteen lines, well, thirteen now. Sonnet: "All we need is fourteen lines, well, thirteen now." Billy Collins. SP-CollB

All we secure of Beauty. Emily Dickinson. SP-DickE

All weareth, all wasteth, / All flitteth, all hasteth. Vigil of the Annunciation. Christina Georgina Rossetti. CP-RosC2

All week the rain holds off. We sweat. July, Against Hunger. Maxine W. Kumin. SP-KumiM

All were quite gracious in their plaudits of. Delicious Interruption, A. James Whitcomb Riley. CP-RileJ *Fr.* Child-World, A.

All what you are still one, his own to find. Sir Philip Sidney. SP-SidnP *Fr.* Arcadia.

All wheels; a man breathed fire. Celebration, The. James Dickey. CP-DickJ

All which, because it was. Once Only. Denise Levertov. SP-LeveDS

All which isn't singing is mere talking. E. E. Cummings. CP-CummE

All who'd live by risk. Three Things. Shmuel HaNagid. SP-HaNaS, *tr. by* Peter Cole

All whom I love, all neighbors. Ultima Thule. Thomas Lux. SP-LuxT

All will be in vain unless—unless what? Unless. Unless. Robert Penn Warren. CP-WarrR

All winter long. Confession. Alice Walker. CP-WalkA

All winter long the huge sad lady. Duet, The. W. H. Auden. CP-AudeW

All winter through I bow my head. Scarecrow, The. Walter De la Mare. CP-DeLaW

All winter your brute shoulders strained against collars, padding. Names of Horses. Donald Hall. CP-HallD

All Wise. Louis Zukofsky. CP-ZukLS

All women are pets. Thoughts Thought after a Bridge Party. Ogden Nash. CP-NashO

All worlds have halfsight,seeing either with. E. E. Cummings. CP-CummE

All-worshipp'd Gold! thou mighty mystery! R.S.S. William Cowper. CP-CowpW

All ye that know of care and heaviness. Sir Thomas Wyatt. CP-WyatT

All ye who list a ballad sad. High Master and the Abbot of Fulham, The. G. K. Chesterton. CP-ChesG

All year round the whin. Whinlands. Seamus Heaney. SP-HeanSO

All year the flax-dam festered in the heart. Death of a Naturalist. Seamus Heaney. SP-HeanSO

All you are doing and saying is to America dangled mirages. To a President. Walt Whitman. CP-WhitW

All you can about animals as persons. What You Should Know to Be a Poet. Gary Snyder. CP-SnydG

All You Can Do. Charles Olson. CP-OlsoC

All you have to do is listen to the way a man. Man in Space. Billy Collins. SP-CollB

All you need to do is wait, fountain pen ready. Profession, A. Primo Levi. CP-LeviP, tr. by Ruth Feldman

All you senseless buried heads. Han-shan. CP-ColdM, tr. by Red Pine

All you that are enamored of my name. Demos. Edwin Arlington Robinson. CP-RobiE

All you that view this humble stone. Epitaph by a Young Lady, Design'd by Herself, An. Annis Boudinot Stockton. CP-StocA

All you that would refine your blood. Ballyspellin. Thomas Sheridan. CP-SherT

All you who read my poems. Han-shan.

All Your Seals Broken? Never. Paul Celan. SP-CelaP, tr. by John Felstiner

Alla Sua Amica. Samuel Taylor Coleridge. CP-ColeS

Allan-Bane's Lament. Sir Walter Scott. SP-ScotW Fr. Lady of the Lake, The.

Allan Water. Robert Burns. CP-BurnR

Allbutnotquitemost. E. E. Cummings. CP-CummE

Allegiance. René Char. CP-MertT

Allegiance is assigned. Choice. James Vincent Cunningham. CP-CunnJ

Allegiances. William Stafford. SP-StafW; SP-StafWW

Allegorical Painting: Capitalist Society Destroyed by the Contradiction Within Itself. (Second Five-Year Plan). Philip Whalen. SP-WhalP

Allegorical Seduction. Yusef Komunyakaa. CP-KomuY

Allegory. Charles Baudelaire. CP-BaudC, tr. by Walter Martin

Allegory, An. Percy Bysshe Shelley. CP-ShelP

Allegory of the Wolf Boy, The. Thom Gunn. CP-GunnT

Allegory of Wealth, The. Charles Olson. CP-OlsoC

Allegro Ma Non Troppo. Wisława Szymborska. SP-SzymW, tr. by Stanisław Barańczak and Clare Cavanagh

Alleluia! or Alas! my heart is crying. Christina Georgina Rossetti. CP-RosC2

Allen, you good man, great poet of the murderous century, who persisting in folly attained wisdom. To Allen Ginsberg. Czeslaw Milosz. CP-MiloCN, tr. by Robert Hass

Allenby Road. Joseph Brodsky. CP-BrodJ

Alley, The. Alexander Pope. CP-PopeA

Alley between the elm trees ends, The. Some Aspects of Immortality. Archibald MacLeish. CP-MacLA

Alley Rats. Carl Sandburg. CP-SandC

Alleyway. Philip Whalen. SP-WhalP

Allhallows Party. Josephine Jacobsen. CP-JacoJ

Alliance. Lorine Niedecker. CP-NiedL

Alliance, The. Consider. Lorine Niedecker. CP-NiedL

Alliance of Education and Government, The. Thomas Gray. CP-GrayT

Allie. Robert Graves. CP-GravR

Allie, call the birds in. Allie. Robert Graves. CP-GravR

Allied Convoy / Reaches Russia. Lorine Niedecker. CP-NiedL

Allies: According to Herodotus. C. K. Williams. SP-WillC

Alligator Bride, The. Donald Hall. CP-HallD

Alligator Poem. Mary Oliver. SP-OlivM

Alligator steal your blanket off. Catfish River Lullaby. Kenneth Patchen. CP-PatcK

Alligators and Paris and North America. William Dickey. SP-DickW

Allow Me, Madam, But It Won't Help. Ogden Nash. CP-NashO

Alloy. Muriel Rukeyser. CP-RukeM

All's Brillig in Tin Pan Alley. Ogden Nash. CP-NashO

All's over, then: does truth sound bitter. Lost Mistress, The. Robert Browning. CP-BroR1

All's Well. John Greenleaf Whittier. CP-WhitJ

Allus when our Pa he's away. Defective Santa Claus, A. James Whitcomb Riley. CP-RileJ

Alma. Frank O'Hara. SP-OharF

Alma Mater. Edwin Arlington Robinson. CP-RobiE

Alma Sol Veneziae. Ezra Pound. CP-PoEar

Almanac. Primo Levi. CP-LeviP, tr. by Ruth Feldman

Almanac. Carl Sandburg. CP-SandC

Almanac. May Swenson. SP-SwenM

Almanac, An. James Schuyler. CP-SchuJ

Almanach du Printemps Vivarois. Hayden Carruth. CP-CarHS

Almes. Robert Herrick. CP-HerrR

Almighty and al merciable queene. ABC, An. Geoffrey Chaucer. CP-ChauG

Almighty crowd, thou shorten'st all dispute. John Dryden. SP-DrydJ Fr. Medal [or Medall], The.

Almighty Lord, who from thy glorious throne. Church Militant, The. George Herbert. CP-HerbG

Almighty Mammon, make me rich! Modern Prayer. D. H. Lawrence. CP-LawrD

Almighty [or Almightie] Judge, how shall poor[e] wretches brook. Judgement. George Herbert. CP-HerbG

Almira to Celadon, Founded on a Story in a Magazine. Annis Boudinot Stockton. CP-StocA

Almond Blossom. D. H. Lawrence. CP-LawrD

Almonding one, you half-spoke only. Paul Celan. SP-CelaP, tr. by John Felstiner

Almost a Conjuror. Yannis Ritsos. SP-RitsY, tr. by Kimon Friar

Almost a Love Poem. Yehuda Amichai. SP-AmicY, tr. by Chana Bloch

Almost a Love Poem. Yehuda Amichai. SP-AmicYL, tr. by Benjamin Harshav and Barbara Harshav

Almost at the equator. Once Only. Gary Snyder. CP-SnydG

Almost awake? Why, what is this, and whence. Parliamentary Oscillators. Samuel Taylor Coleridge. CP-ColeS

Almost beyond Endurance. James Whitcomb Riley. CP-RileJ

Almost Complete. Yannis Ritsos. SP-RitsY, tr. by Kostas Myrsiades

Almost happy now, he looked at his estate. Voltaire at Ferney. W. H. Auden. CP-AudeW

Almost I am tempted to essay. Elizabeth Hoar. Ralph Waldo Emerson. CP-EmerR

Almost I could prefer. Patience. Robert Graves. CP-GravR

Almost I welcome the dirty subterfuges. In Disguise. Robert Graves. CP-GravR

Almost Made Up Poem, An. Charles Bukowski. SP-BukC1

Almost nothing concerns me but communication. Instances of Communication. Josephine Jacobsen. CP-JacoJ

Almost yesterday, those gentle ladies stole. Lost Ingredient, The. Anne Sexton. CP-SextA; SP-SextA

Alms. Stéphane Mallarmé. CP-MallS, tr. by Henry Weinfield

Alms. Edna St. Vincent Millay. CP-MillE

Alms-House and Trustees, The. George Crabbe. SP-CrabG Fr. Borough, The.

Alnaschar and the Oxen. Rudyard Kipling. CP-KiplR Fr. Debits and Credits.

Aloe. Louis Zukofsky. CP-ZukLS

Aloft, / In the loft. Croft. Stevie Smith. CP-SmitS

Alogon. Michael Palmer. SP-PalmM

Alone. Maya Angelou. SP-AngeM

Alone. W. H. Auden. CP-AudeW

Alone. G. K. Chesterton. CP-ChesG

Alone. Walter De la Mare. CP-DeLaW

Alone / a still state hard. Lorine Niedecker. CP-NiedL

Alone, alone, I lie. The canoe. Antinomy: Time and Identity. Robert Penn Warren. CP-WarrR

Alone among the many new ones, an old keel. Laid Up. Primo Levi. CP-LeviP, tr. by Ruth Feldman

Alone and in a Circumstance. Emily Dickinson. CP-DickE

Alone and Not Alone. Carl Sandburg. CP-SandC

Alone and silent there he sat. Solitary Worshipper, The. Jones Very. CP-VeryJ

Alone at night. 1951. Frank O'Hara. SP-OharF

Alone at night, she rose noiselessly. Deadly Victory. Yannis Ritsos. SP-RitsY, tr. by Minas Savvas

Alone at the end of green allées alone. Statues in the Public Gardens, The. Howard Nemerov. CP-NemeH

Alone here. Beach, drum out. Two Women. James Dickey. CP-DickJ

Alone, I cannot be. Emily Dickinson. CP-DickE

Alone I sat; the summer day. Emily Jane Brontë. CP-BronE

Alone, I went into that special. Clarence Major. SP-MajoC

Alone in Rome! Why Rome is lonely too. Ralph Waldo Emerson. CP-EmerR

Alone / in that same self where I always was. Nov. 23, 1963: Alone. Allen Ginsberg. CP-GinsA

Alone in the darkling apartment the boy. Messias. Karl Shapiro. SP-ShapK

Alone in the Wind, on the Prairie. Nicholas Vachel Lindsay. CP-LindV

Alone in the Woods. Stevie Smith. CP-SmitS

Alone Lord God, in Whom our trust and peace. Christina Georgina Rossetti. CP-RosC2

Alone musing, / Remembering. Sir Thomas Wyatt. CP-WyatT

Alone, on the deserted dock, this Summer morning. Maritime Ode. Fernando Pessoa. SP-PessF, *tr. by* Susan M. Brown *and* Edwin Honig

Alone on the jagged rock. November Day at McClure's Beach. Robert Bly. SP-BlyR

Alone on the railroad track. Chemin de Fer. Elizabeth Bishop. CP-BishE

Alone, one can but toy with imagery. Hourglass. James Merrill. SP-MerrJ

Alone, remote, nor witting where I went. Altar, The. Edwin Arlington Robinson. CP-RobiE

Alone that afternoon also. O red cloud—he said. Hues of a Cloud. Yannis Ritsos. SP-RitsY, *tr. by* Kimon Friar *and* Kostas Myrsiades

Alone they walked—their fingers knit together. Lost Path, The. James Whitcomb Riley. CP-RileJ

Alone today I mounted that steep hill. Martin and Katherine. William Carlos Williams. CP-WilW1

Alone upon the housetops to the North. Love Song of Har Dyal, The. Rudyard Kipling. CP-KiplR *Fr.* Plain Tales from the Hills.

Alone we make symbols of love. Echoes. Thomas Kinsella. CP-KinsT

Alone with Everybody. Charles Bukowski. SP-BukC1

Alone / With nothing to say / Which is better? Reduced to This. Thomas Merton. CP-MertT

Alone with our madness and favorite flower. Late Echo. John Ashbery. SP-AshbJ

Alone, you are no more than many another. Son Altesse. Robert Graves. CP-GravR

Along a precipice they wound their way. Fragment of a "Gothic" Tale. William Wordsworth. CP-WorW1

Along a trail / Don Pedro came. Joke about Don Pedro on Horseback. Federico García Lorca. CP-GarcF, *tr. by* Will Kirkland

Along an avenue of almond-trees. Mercutio. Walter De la Mare. CP-DeLaW

Along and back the creamed arcade. Return to Lahore. Louis MacNeice. CP-MacNL

Along by the river of ruin. River of Ruin, The. Paul Laurence Dunbar. CP-DunbP

Along by the shacks at the edge of town. Sun, The. Charles Baudelaire. CP-BaudC, *tr. by* Walter Martin

Along, come along. Tinkers Song, The. Robert Herrick. CP-HerrR

Along Crane River's sunny slopes. Witch of Wenham, The. John Greenleaf Whittier. CP-WhitJ

Along Galeana Street. Octavio Paz. CP-BishE, *tr. by* Elizabeth Bishop

Along History. Muriel Rukeyser. CP-RukeM

Along Route Two I saw a sign. Route Two. Howard Nemerov. CP-NemeH

Along the aisle where prayer was made. Prayer-Seeker, The. John Greenleaf Whittier. CP-WhitJ

Along the Appian Way / children are playing. Lawrence Ferlinghetti. SP-FerlL *Fr.* Canti Romani.

Along the avenue of cypresses. Giorno dei Morti. D. H. Lawrence. CP-LawrD

Along the back farm road the. Return to the Island. John Logan. CP-LogaJ

Along the back street, on the other side, on the iron stairs. Inevitably. Yannis Ritsos. SP-RitsY, *tr. by* N. C. Germanacos

Along the base of Norman's Rocks. Norman's Rocks. Jones Very. CP-VeryJ

Along the beach beyond La Boca the Luquillo River. Bridges. Grace Paley. CP-PalGC

Along the brittle treacherous bright streets. E. E. Cummings. CP-CummE

Along the city streets. Silence. T. S. Eliot. SP-ElioT

Along the coastal waters, signals run. Eastport to Block Island. Adrienne Rich. CP-RicAE

Along the dark, and silent night. Bell-Man, The. Robert Herrick. CP-HerrR

Along the East River and the Bronx. Ode to Walt Whitman. Federico García Lorca. SP-GarcF, *tr. by* J. L. Gili *and* Stephen Spender

Along the field as we came by. A. E. Housman. CP-HousA

Along the grass sweet airs are blown. New Year's Burden, A. Dante Gabriel Rossetti. CW-RossD

Along the groves of the Tamarit. Casida of the Branches. Federico García Lorca. SP-GarcF, *tr. by* J. L. Gili *and* Stephen Spender

Along the highroad the way is too long. Christina Georgina Rossetti. CP-RosC3

Along the Hudson trade roads. Poems along the Hudson River. Yehuda Amichai. SP-AmicYL, *tr. by* Benjamin Harshav *and* Barbara Harshav

Along the justexisting road to Roupy. E. E. Cummings. CP-CummE

Along the lake, like seals, like seals. August Holidays. D. H. Lawrence. CP-LawrD

Along the mazes of this song I go. William Wordsworth. CP-WorW1

Along the red ledge I. All the Flowery. Kenneth Patchen. CP-PatcK

Along the river / wild sunflowers. Lorine Niedecker. CP-NiedL

Along the Road. Mona Van Duyn. SP-VanDM

Along the sculptures of the western wall. Cathedral Façade at Midnight, A. Thomas Hardy. CP-HardT

Along the sprawled body of the derailed. Outside Fargo, North Dakota. James Wright. CP-WrigJ

Along the summer, along the sandy shoreline. Yehuda Amichai. SP-AmicY *Fr.* In a Right Angle: A Cycle of Quatrains.

Along the way / He walked that day. Self-Unconscious. Thomas Hardy. CP-HardT

Along the west of the woods is a row of tall pines. Line of Trees. W. S. Merwin. SP-MerwWF

Alongside. Denise Levertov. SP-LeveDL

Alongside the train I labor. Snow on a Southern State. James Dickey. CP-DickJ

Aloof. Carl Sandburg. CP-SandC

Aloof, as if a thing of mood and whim. Schreckhorn, The. Thomas Hardy. CP-HardT

Aloof in Gaiety. D. H. Lawrence. CP-LawrD

Aloof they crown the foreland lone. Off Cape Colona. Herman Melville. SP-MelvH

Aloud, I said, with a slight stir of heart. Far West Once. Robert Penn Warren. CP-WarrR

Álow álow loo no words. Aloe. Louis Zukofsky. CP-ZukLS

Alpaca, The. Gabriela Mistral. SP-MistG, *tr. by* Maria Giachetti [*or* Jacketti]

Alphabet, An. Christina Georgina Rossetti. CP-RosC3

Alphabet, The. Karl Shapiro. SP-ShapK

Alphabet of, The. Botticellian Trees, The. William Carlos Williams. CP-WilW1

Alphabets. Seamus Heaney. SP-HeanSU

Alphonso of Castile. Ralph Waldo Emerson. CP-EmerR

Alpine. George Oppen. CP-OppGN

Alpine Rosy Bells. Louis Zukofsky. CP-ZukLS

Already. Dan Pagis. SP-PagiD, *tr. by* Stephen Mitchell

Already Ben Abbas and all of his friends. Dream, The. Shmuel HaNagid. SP-HaNaS, *tr. by* Peter Cole

Already blushes on thy cheek. Nemesis. Ralph Waldo Emerson. CP-EmerR

Already burdened with a heavy heart. Michelangelo Buonarroti. CP-Miche, *tr. by* John Frederick Nims

Already fall's harsher. September Song. William Corbett. SP-CorbW

Already, here and there in the meadow. Autumn Hammer. Rainer Maria Rilke. CP-RilkFr, *tr. by* A. Poulin, Jr.

Already I am no longer looked at with lechery or love. Sunset of the City, A. Gwendolyn Brooks. SP-BrooG

Already I begin, at morning. New Place, The. William Dickey. SP-DickW

Already I was before I am. Already. Dan Pagis. SP-PagiD, *tr. by* Stephen Mitchell

Already in midsummer / I miss your feet and fur. To a Butterfly. James Merrill. SP-MerrJ

Already running, sprang from the womb; met. Pacer in the Fresco, The. John the Baptist. Donald Davie. CP-DaviDC

Already she seems bone thin. Poem about Breasts, A. James Wright. CP-WrigJ

Already the father has sent enough of plague. Ad Regem Carolum Parodia [A Parody: To King Charles]. Andrew Marvell. CP-MarvA

Already you can see the tragic setting. To One No Longer Young. Jorge Luis Borges. SP-BorgJ, *tr. by* Alastair Reid

Already you have done, remorseless Death. Petrarch. CP-Petra, *tr. by* J. G. Nichols

Alright make it a series and call it Marry Nettie. Marry Nettie. Gertrude Stein. CP-SteiG

Alsace-Lorraine. George Meredith. CP-MerG1

Also in death we are going to live. Without End. Adam Zagajewski. SP-ZagaA, *tr. by* Renata Gorczynski

Also shines. "Sun Rises and Sets in That Child," So My Grandmother Used to Say, The. Philip Whalen. SP-WhalP

Also the headache of / to do right by feeling. Eros. Robert Creeley. CP-CreeR

Also your / wound, Rosa. Coagula. Paul Celan. SP-CelaP, *tr. by* John Felstiner

Altar, The. George Herbert. CP-HerbG

Altar, The. Edwin Arlington Robinson. CP-RobiE

Altar, The. Jones Very. CP-VeryJ

Altars in the Street, The. Denise Levertov. SP-LeveDP

Altarwise by Owl-Light. Dylan Thomas. CP-ThomD

Alter! When the Hills do—. Emily Dickinson. CP-DickE

Alteram Partem. Arthur Hugh Clough. SP-ClouA

Alterations. Yannis Ritsos. SP-RitsY, *tr. by* Kostas Myrsiades

Altercation. D. H. Lawrence. CP-LawrD

Altered body, The. τροπη. Michael Palmer. SP-PalmM

Altered from an Old English Song. Robert Burns. CP-BurnR

Altered look about the hills, An. Emily Dickinson. CP-DickE

Alternate Hosts. May Swenson. SP-SwenM

Alternate Thoughts from Underground. Margaret Atwood. SP-AtwM1

Alternation. George Meredith. CP-MerG1

Alternative Song for the Severed Head in "The King of the Great Clock Tower." William Butler Yeats. CP-YeatW

Alternative to flying is cowardice, The. Notes for an Elegy. William Meredith. SP-MereW

Alternatives. A. R. Ammons. CP-AmmoA

Alternatives. James Tate. SP-TateJ

Altgeld. Carl Sandburg. CP-SandC

Altham says / they were in a pinnance. Gulf of Maine, The. Charles Olson. SP-OlsoC *Fr.* Maximus Poems, The.

Altho' my bed were in yon muir. Fragment: "Altho' my bed were in yon muir." Robert Burns. CP-BurnR

Although another's fault takes from me what. Petrarch. CP-Petra, *tr. by* J. G. Nichols

Although constructed of the most up-to-date, technically advanced elements of woven glass. Work. C. K. Williams. SP-WillC

Although crowds gathered once if she but showed her face. Fallen Majesty. William Butler Yeats. CP-YeatW

Although entangled in prolonged grief. Carmen 65. Catullus. CP-ZukLS *Fr.* Carmina.

Although, great Queen, thou now in silence lie. In Honour of that High and Mighty Princess Queen Elizabeth of Happy Memory. Anne Bradstreet. CP-BradA

Although he's apparently the youngest (his little rasta-beard is barely down and feathers). Instinct. C. K. Williams. SP-WillC

Although I can see him still. Fisherman, The. William Butler Yeats. CP-YeatW

Although I have never learned to mow. Coney, The. Paul Muldoon. CP-MuldP

Although I mean it, and project the meaning. Ice-Cream Wars, The. John Ashbery. SP-AshbJ

Although I put away his life. Emily Dickinson. CP-DickE

Although I saw before me there the face. Inferential. Edwin Arlington Robinson. CP-RobiE

Although I shelter from the rain. Lamentation of the Old Pensioner, The. William Butler Yeats. CP-YeatW

Although I'd lie lapped up in linen. Under the Round Tower. William Butler Yeats. CP-YeatW

Although I'm apparently alone, with a pleasant but unextraordinary feeling of self-sufficiency. Solid, The. C. K. Williams. SP-WillC

Although it is a cold evening. At the Fishhouses. Elizabeth Bishop. CP-BishE

Although it is midsummer, the great blue heron. Black Marsh Eclogue. Sam Hamill. SP-HamiS

Although it is night, I sit in the bathroom, waiting. Adolescence—II. Rita Dove. SP-DoveR

Although it never rivaled wheat, soybean. Commercial Leech Farming Today. Thomas Lux. SP-LuxT

Although it was not my home. Bread and Butter Letter, A. Kenneth Rexroth. CP-RexrK

Although it's amply true your human face. Michelangelo Buonarroti. CP-Miche, *tr. by* John Frederick Nims

Although my heart had often been aflame. Michelangelo Buonarroti. CP-Miche, *tr. by* John Frederick Nims

Although [*or* Altho'] I be the basest of mankind. St. Simeon Stylites. Alfred Tennyson. CP-TennA

Although [*or* Altho'] my back be at the wa'. Here's His Health in Water. Robert Burns. CP-BurnR

Although our suffering meet with no reliefe. Sauce for Sorrowes. Robert Herrick. CP-HerrR

Although the aepyornis. He "Digesteth Harde Yron." Marianne Craig Moore. CP-MoorM

Although the car radio warned that. Tomorrow. Donald Hall. CP-HallD

Although the lamp is out, and although it's dusk, late, dull, stifling summer dusk. Color of Time, The. C. K. Williams. CP-WillC

Although the letter said. New Readings. Gerard Manley Hopkins. CP-HopkG

Although the relatives in the summer house. Poem for Bhain, A. John Berryman. CP-BerrJ

Although thou maun never be mine. Here's a Health to Ane I Lo'e Dear. Robert Burns. CP-BurnR

Although thou see th'outrageous climb aloft. Bible, *O.T. See* Fret not thyself because of evildoers

Although thy hand and faith, and good work[e]s too. Change. John Donne. MW-DonnJ *Fr.* Elegies.

Although time presses hard and prods us on. Michelangelo Buonarroti. CP-Miche, *tr. by* John Frederick Nims

Although we cannot turne the fervent fit. Will To Be Working, A. Robert Herrick. CP-HerrR

Although we say we disbelieve. Louis MacNeice. CP-MacNL *Fr.* Jigsaws.

Although you hide in the ebb and flow. Fish, The. William Butler Yeats. CP-YeatW

Although you sit in a room that is gray. Gray Room. Wallace Stevens. CP-StevWP

Altitudes. Richard Wilbur. CP-WilbR

Alto Minho. Charles Tomlinson. SP-TomlC *Fr.* Portugeuse Pieces.

Always. Robert Graves. CP-GravR

Always an angel rises from the figure. Masseuse, The. Olga Broumas. SP-BrouO

Always Another Viewpoint. Kenneth Patchen. CP-PatcK

Always as it holds us in one place, the earth. Immortals. James Dickey. CP-DickJ

Always at the end of the week my father and I would go to the sauna on Tartar Street. Plato's Dialogues. Czeslaw Milosz. CP-MiloCN, *tr. by* Robert Hass

Always before your voice my soul. E. E. Cummings. CP-CummE

Always begins. Emily Dickinson. SP-DickE

Always between his eyes and objects stood. His Glasses. Yannis Ritsos. SP-RitsY, *tr. by* Kimon Friar

Always caught up in what they called. My Aunts. Adam Zagajewski. SP-ZagaA, *tr. by* Clare Cavanagh

Always day & night. Ralph Waldo Emerson. CP-EmerR

Always Ether Comes. Pertussin. Allen Ginsberg. CP-GinsA

Always for thirty years now. Fish Peddler and Cobbler. Kenneth Rexroth. CP-RexrK

Always getting ready to go out. On Voyage. Alan Dugan. CP-DugaA

Always I have to resist. Like. Heather McHugh. SP-McHuH

Always I knew that it could not last. Nocturne: "Always I knew that it could not last." Dorothy Parker. CP-ParkD

Always I see her in a saintly guise. Dead Wife, The. James Whitcomb Riley. CP-RileJ

Always I travelled farther. This House, This Country. Muriel Rukeyser. CP-RukeM

Always / wanted to do it myself. Self-Service. John Updike. CP-UpdiJ

Always / I'm the one slightly slighted, he said. No Time for Self-Pity. Clarence Major. SP-MajoC

Always / in the middle. Love, Maybe. Audre Lorde. SP-LordA

Always in the middle of a kiss. Dirge for a Joker. Sylvia Plath. CP-PlatS

Always it happens when we are not there. Metamorphosis. May Sarton. SP-SartM

Always Marry an April Girl. Ogden Nash. CP-NashO

Always Mine! Emily Dickinson. CP-DickE

Always north of him. Florida. Lorine Niedecker. CP-NiedL

Always, on their generation's breaking wave. Farmer, Speaking of Monuments, The. Wendell Berry. CP-BerrW

Always our old feuillage! Our Old Feuillage. Walt Whitman. CP-WhitW

Always prudent but unprepared. Poem: "Always prudent but unprepared." Alan Dugan. CP-DugaA

Always pyrotechnics. Leda 3. Lucille Clifton. SP-ClifL

Always So. Yannis Ritsos. SP-RitsY, *tr. by* Minas Savvas

Always suddenly they are gone. Three Dead Friends. James Whitcomb Riley. CP-RileJ

Always, sweetheart / Carry into your room the blossoming boughs of cherry. Disagreeable Advice. D. H. Lawrence. CP-LawrD

Always the August evenings come. Goldfish (Essence of Summer Magazines). T. S. Eliot. SP-ElioT

Always the fair extensions of his will. Lament of the Valkyrie, The. Eleanor Wilner. SP-WilnE

Always the fox gets caught, yet not by skill. How They Hunt the Quick Red Fox. Robert Stock. SP-StocR

Always the Mob. Carl Sandburg. CP-SandC

Always the Same. Langston Hughes. CP-HughL; CP-HughL1

Always the Same. Adrienne Rich. CP-RicAE

Always the same, when on a fated night. Onset, The. Robert Frost. CP-FrosR

Always the solemnest moment of the year. First Snow. Howard Nemerov. CP-NemeH

Always, the world we invent or build. Elegy: "Always, the world we invent or build." Sam Hamill. SP-HamiS

Always there would be stories of lights. Fireside. Seamus Heaney. SP-HeanSO

Always This Paying. D. H. Lawrence. CP-LawrD

Always this special / secret feeling, the failure. Hayden Carruth. CP-CarHS *Fr.* Clay Hill Anthology, The.

Always this waking dream of palmtrees. Islands, The. Robert Earl Hayden. CP-HaydR

Always to see the world made whole. Yes. Wyatt Prunty. SP-PrunW

Always too eager for the future, we. Next, Please. Philip Larkin. CP-LarkP

Always, whatever the title. Newspaper Vendor, The. Stéphane Mallarmé. CP-MallS *Fr.* Street Songs.

Always, you lie. Yehuda Amichai. SP-AmicYL *Fr.* Six Poems for Tamar.

Alyscamps at Arles, The. May Swenson. SP-SwenM

Alzheimer's Disease. Donald Davie. CP-DaviDC

Alzheimer's: The Husband. C. K. Williams. SP-WillC

Alzheimer's: The Wife. C. K. Williams. SP-WillC

Am I a fanatic? The opposite. Enough. Marianne Craig Moore. CP-MoorM

Am I a stone and not a sheep. Good Friday. Christina Georgina Rossetti. CP-RosC1

Am I blind alas. Fragment 41: "Am I blind alas." "H. D." CP-DoolH

Am I despised because you say. To a Gentlewoman Objecting to Him His Grey Hairs. Robert Herrick. CP-HerrR

Am I detached enough. Prothalamion. Heather McHugh. SP-McHuH

Am I in your light? / No, go on reading. Three Sides of a Coin. Muriel Rukeyser. CP-RukeM

Am I kin to Sorrow. Kin to Sorrow. Edna St. Vincent Millay. CP-MillE

Am I My Neighbor's Keeper. Richard Eberhart. CP-EberR

Am I obsessed by stone? Life has worn thin here. Almanach du Printemps Vivarois. Hayden Carruth. CP-CarHS

Am I real way out in space. Lorine Niedecker. CP-NiedL.

Am I sitting on your wrist, someone immense? Alternate Hosts. May Swenson. SP-SwenM

Am I the river your white birds fly over? They Ask Each Other Where They Came From. Carl Sandburg. CP-SandC

Am I to be cursed forever with becoming. Change of Season. Audre Lorde. SP-LordA

Am I to become profligate as if I were a blonde? Meditations in an Emergency. Frank O'Hara. SP-OharF

Am I wrong? The roads. Hayden Carruth. CP-CarHS *Fr.* Clay Hill Anthology, The.

Am told that fasting gives to food. Emily Dickinson. SP-DickE

Am was. Are Leaves Few this. Is these a or. E. E. Cummings. CP-CummE

Amabel. Thomas Hardy. CP-HardT

Amalgamated, The. George Oppen. CP-OppGN

Amalgams are abundant. Emily Dickinson. SP-DickE

Amami, t'amo / Figliolin mio. Christina Georgina Rossetti. CP-RosC3

Amanda Dreams She Has Died and Gone to the Elysian Fields. Maxine W. Kumin. SP-KumiM

Amanda Is Shod. Maxine W. Kumin. SP-KumiM

Amanda, you'll be going. Thinking of Death and Dogfood. Maxine W. Kumin. SP-KumiM

Amang the trees, where humming bees. Robert Burns. CP-BurnR

Amang thir freiris within ane cloister. Ballat of the Passioun, Ane. William Dunbar. CP-DunbW

Amant in bed. Very Rich Hours, The. James McMichael. SP-McMiJ

Amaranth, The. Nicholas Vachel Lindsay. CP-LindV

Amaranth and Moly. Amy Clampitt. CP-ClamA

Amargo. / The oleanders of my courtyard. Dialogue of Amargo. Federico García Lorca. CP-GarcF, *tr. by* Christopher Maurer

Amaryllis. Edwin Arlington Robinson. CP-RobiE

Amatory Lines. Thomas Gray. CP-GrayT

Amazement. Czeslaw Milosz. CP-MiloC; CP-MiloCN, *tr. by* Lillian Vallee

Amazing creatues, I was delighted. Giant Sequoias. Philip Whalen. SP-WhalP

Amazing Grace in the Back Country. Robert Penn Warren. CP-WarrR

Amazing human [*or* Human] heart [*or* Heart]. Emily Dickinson. SP-DickE

Amazing Potato Peeler, The. Charles Simic. SP-SimiCE

Amazingly active a toothless old man. Going to Horse Flats. Robinson Jeffers. CP-JefR2

Amazingly young beautiful woman poets. Aging Female Poet Reads Little Magazines. Margaret Atwood. SP-AtwM2

Amazon Twins. Olga Broumas. SP-BrouO

Amazonian. Donald Davie. CP-DaviDC

Amazons. Lucille Clifton. SP-ClifL

Amazons with Crescent-formed shield, The. Virgil. CP-RaleW *Fr.* Aeneid [*or* Eneados *or* Aeneis], The.

Ambassador, The. Pablo Neruda. SP-NeruP

Ambassador, The. Stevie Smith. CP-SmitS

Ambassador From India. Robert Stock. SP-StocR

Ambassador Puser the ambassador. Memorial Rain. Archibald MacLeish. CP-MacLA

Ambassadors of Grief. Carl Sandburg. CP-SandC

Amber Bead, The. Robert Herrick. CP-HerrR

Amber husk / fluted with gold. Sea Poppies. "H. D." CP-DoolH

Amber is a fossilized resin, yellow. Fanny Howe. SP-HoweF *Fr.* Lines Out to Silence.

Amber spray of trees feather-brushed with the dusk, The. Watteau. Derek

Walcott. CP-WalcD *Fr.* Midsummer.

Ambergris. Stanley Kunitz. CP-KunSC

Amberose Triste. Olga Broumas. SP-BrouO

Ambience. Robert Graves. CP-GravR

Ambition. Robert Creeley. SP-CreeR

Ambition. Robert Herrick. CP-HerrR

Ambition. George Meredith. CP-MerG2

Ambition. Walt Whitman. CP-WhitW

Ambition. Eleanor Wilner. SP-WilnE

Ambition Bird, The. Anne Sexton. CP-SextA

Ambition cannot find him. Emily Dickinson. CP-DickE

Ambition is the Stamp impress'd by Heav'n. Samuel Johnson. CP-JohnS *Fr.* Irene.

Ambitione inani pectus caret. Jones Very. CP-VeryJ

Ambrosia of Dionysus and Semele, The. Robert Graves. CP-GravR

Ambulances. Philip Larkin. CP-LarkP

Ambuscade, The. Sir Walter Scott. SP-ScotW *Fr.* Lady of the Lake, The.

Ambush. Yusef Komunyakaa. CP-KomuY

Ameana pulling, a foot touted high. Catullus. *See* Formianus's whore, / long-nosed

Amelia. Eleanor Wilner. SP-WilnE

Amen. Norman Dubie. CP-DubiN

Amen. Christina Georgina Rossetti. CP-RosC1

Amen. The casket like a spaceship bears her. Annie Hill's Grave. James Merrill. SP-MerrJ

Amendis [*or* Amends] to the Telyouris [*or* Tailors] and Sowtaris [*or* Soutaris *or* Soutars *or* Shoemakers]. William Dunbar. CP-DunbW

Amenities, The. Heather McHugh. SP-McHuH

America. Maya Angelou. SP-AngeM

America. Langston Hughes. CP-HughL; CP-HughL1

America. Herman Melville. SP-MelvH

America. Czeslaw Milosz. CP-MiloCN, *tr. by* Robert Hass

America. James Whitcomb Riley. CP-RileJ

America. Phillis Wheatley. CP-WheaP

America. Walt Whitman. CP-WhitW

America! Philip Whalen. SP-WhalP

America: A Prophecy. William Blake. CP-BlakW

America, America. Generation of Drivers. George Oppen. CP-OppGN

America I Love You. James Laughlin.

"First thing he said, The." CP-LaugJ

"He was talking so fast I." CP-LaugJ

"Man from Jehovah's, A." CP-LaugJ

"There was a little black." CP-LaugJ

"Well here's a salute to." CP-LaugJ

"When questioned by re-." CP-LaugJ

America Inside & Outside Bill Brown's House in Bolinas. Philip Whalen. SP-WhalP

America Is Hard to See. Robert Frost. CP-FrosR

America is healthy. i am healthy. Gist. Andrei Codrescu. SP-CodrA

America is like Russia. Poem on America, A. Allen Ginsberg. CP-GinsA

America I've given you all and now I'm nothing. Allen Ginsberg. CP-GinsA; SP-GinsA

America rhymes with Australia. Under the Harbour Bridge. Yusef Komunyakaa. CP-KomuY

America was ablaze with lights. Atlantic Tunnel, The. Louis MacNeice. CP-MacNL

America Was Promises. Archibald MacLeish. CP-MacLA

America, when you were born, and when the plains. Letter to America, A. Thomas Merton. CP-MertT

aMERICA, you caTNip bIN. Hymn to These Newly Abbreviated States. John Updike. CP-UpdiJ

America, you ode for reality! Robert Creeley. CP-CreeR

American against Solitude. Alan Dugan. CP-DugaA

American Aloe on Exhibition, The. Herman Melville. SP-MelvH

American, An. Rudyard Kipling. CP-KiplR

American Archangel you are going. Moose. Anne Sexton. CP-SextA

American Beauty, An. Carolyn Kizer. CP-KizeC

American Cancer Society Or There Is More Than One Way to Skin a Coon. Audre Lorde. SP-LordA

American Century, The. Kenneth Rexroth. CP-RexrK

American Change. Allen Ginsberg. CP-GinsA

American critic ad 1935. E. E. Cummings. CP-CummE

American Eagle, The. D. H. Lawrence. CP-LawrD

American Express. Ted Berrigan. SP-BerrT

. . . American Express, Athens, Greece. Charles Bukowski. SP-BukC2

American Gothic. William Stafford. SP-StafWW

American Hakluyt. Richard Eberhart. CP-EberR

American Heartbreak. Langston Hughes. CP-HughL; CP-HughL3

American hero must triumph over, The. Eisenhower's Visit to Franco, 1959. James Wright. CP-WrigJ

[American Journal]. Robert Earl Hayden. CP-HaydR

American Letter. Archibald MacLeish. CP-MacLA

American Lights, Seen from Off Abroad. John Berryman. CP-BerrJ

American Living Room, The: A Tract. William Meredith. SP-MereW

American Love. Robert Creeley. SP-CreeR

American Painting, with Rain. Eleanor Wilner. SP-WilnE

American papermatch packet, An. Simplex Sigilum Veri: A Catalogue. William Carlos Williams. CP-WilW1

American Portrait: Old Style. Robert Penn Warren. CP-WarrR

American Rebellion, The. Rudyard Kipling. CP-KiplR

American Scene, An. Norman Dubie. CP-DubiN

American Sentences. Allen Ginsberg. SP-GinsA

American Sonnet. Billy Collins. SP-CollB

American Sublime, The. Wallace Stevens. CP-StevW; CP-StevWP

American Sublime, The: Robert Penn Warren. Eleanor Wilner. SP-WilnE

American Tourist to a Guatemalan Tarantula. Alan Dugan. CP-DugaA

American Tradition. William Wordsworth. CP-WorW2 *Fr.* River Duddon [A Series of Sonnets], The.

American Twilight. Charles Wright. SP-WrigCN

American Twilights, 1957. James Wright. CP-WrigJ

American Variation on How Rilke Loved a Princess and Got to Stay in Her Castle. Alan Dugan. CP-DugaA

American Wedding. James Wright. CP-WrigJ

Americana. Wallace Stevens. CP-StevWP

Americans, The. Charles Olson. CP-OlsoC

American's a hustler, for he says so, The. Ballad of Abbreviations, A. G. K. Chesterton. CP-ChesG

Americans are innocents abroad. Mr Sharp in Florence. Donald Davie. CP-DaviDC

Americans attend to Freedom's cry! Voice of Freedom, The. Phillis Wheatley. CP-WheaP

Americans! / The word stands for something. O! Americans. D. H. Lawrence. CP-LawrD

America's Plutonic Ecstasies. Hart Crane. CP-CranH

America's Thanksgiving. James Whitcomb Riley. CP-RileJ

America's Young Black Joe! Langston Hughes. CP-HughL; CP-HughL3

Ametas and Thestylis Making Hay-Ropes. Andrew Marvell. CP-MarvA

Amherst. Amy Clampitt. CP-ClamA

Amherst Heart is plain and whole, The. Emily Dickinson. SP-DickE

Amherst to Easthampton. James Tate. SP-TateJ

Amiable putrescence carpenters, An. E. E. Cummings. CP-CummE

Amico pesce, poiver vorrà. Christina Georgina Rossetti. CP-RosC3

Amid a fertile region green with wood. Picture of Daniel in the Lions' Den, at Hamilton Palace. William Wordsworth. CP-WorW2

Amid a thousand clouds and streams. Han-shan. CP-ColdM, *tr. by* Red Pine

Amid fear and suspicions. Things Run Out. Constantine P. Cavafy. CP-CavaC, *tr. by* Theoharis Constantine Theoharis

Amid his foes that slumbered round. Arab Steed, The. Jones Very. CP-VeryJ

Amid that Platonic statuary, of athletes. Class Will Come to Order, The. Stanley Kunitz. CP-KunSC

Amid the blending. Bagni di Lucca. Eugenio Montale. CP-MontE, *tr. by* Jonathan Galassi

Amid the dark control of lawless sway. Sonnet on Milton. William Wordsworth. CP-WorW1

Amid the desolation of a city. Tower of Famine, The. Percy Bysshe Shelley. CP-ShelP

Amid the doctors in the Temple at twelve, between. Prayer of the Middle-Aged Man, The. John Berryman. CP-BerrJ

Amid the gray trunks of ancient trees we found. Lilies, The. Wendell Berry. CP-BerrW

Amid the indecision of the brocade. Empty Drawing Room. Jorge Luis Borges. SP-BorgJ, *tr. by* W. S. Merwin

Amid the luxuries, the plush divans. Martyr, A. Charles Baudelaire. CP-BaudC, *tr. by* Walter Martin

Amid the shade of a deserted hall. Ruin. Christina Georgina Rossetti. CP-RosC3

Amid the smoke of cities did you pass. To Joanna. William Wordsworth. CP-WorW1; MW-WorW

Amid the storms of war, with curious eyes. Lucan. CP-JohnS, *tr. by* Samuel Johnson *Fr.* Civil War [Bellum Civile] *or* Pharsalia.

Amid the swift onrushing years. Hymn, Sung at the Fiftieth Anniversary of the Essex Historical Society, Salem. April 21, 1871. Jones Very. CP-VeryJ

Amid these crowded pews must I sit and seem to pray. O Qui Me—! Arthur Hugh Clough. SP-ClouA

Amid these days of order, ease, prosperity. Dying Veteran, The. Walt Whitman. CP-WhitW

Amidst a band of worthies bold and true. Endecott. Jones Very. CP-VeryJ

Amidst a changeful, worldly age like ours. Age Changeful and Worldly, The. Jones Very. CP-VeryJ

Amidst great clamor. Hearing. Yannis Ritsos. SP-RitsY, *tr. by* Kostas Myrsiades

Amidst the ample field of things. Reason and Imagination. Christopher Smart. SP-SmarC

Amidst the dwellings of a distant age. Pompeii. Jones Very. CP-VeryJ

Amidst the memories of the past. Hymn: Sung at the Unitarian Festival, in Faneuil Hall, May 26th 1863. Jones Very. CP-VeryJ

Amidst the pastures green. Hymn: "Amidst the pastures green." Jones Very. CP-VeryJ

Amidst the sick and dying, falling round. To the Memory of the Rev. James Chisholm. Jones Very. CP-VeryJ

Amidst these glorious works of Thine. Hymn for the Opening of Thomas Starr King's House of Worship. John Greenleaf Whittier. CP-WhitJ

Amidst those scenes of wonder do I stand. On Viewing the Falls of Niagara, as Photographed by George Barker. Jones Very. CP-VeryJ

Amidst Thuringia's wooded hills she dwelt. Two Elizabeths, The. John Greenleaf Whittier. CP-WhitJ

Amidst thy sacred effigies. Emancipation Group, The. John Greenleaf Whittier. CP-WhitJ

Amiel's Leg. Thomas Lux. SP-LuxT

Amish, The. John Updike. CP-UpdiJ

Amitabha's Vow. Gary Snyder. CP-SnydG *Fr.* Myths and Texts.

Amities of morning, The. Sum of Destructions, A. Theodore Weiss. SP-WeisT

Amitites. Ezra Pound. SP-PounE

Amnesia. Adrienne Rich. SP-RicA2

Amnesia People. James Tate. SP-TateJ

Amnesiac. Sylvia Plath. CP-PlatS

Amnesic goatherds tromboning. Tragedy Comes to the Bad Lands. James Tate. SP-TateJ

Amnesty. Howard Nemerov. CP-NemeH

Amo Amas Amat. James Laughlin. CP-LaugJ

Amo Ergo Sum. Kathleen Jessie Raine. SP-RainK

Amo Sacrum Vulgus. D. H. Lawrence. CP-LawrD

Amoeba. John Updike. CP-UpdiJ

Amoebaean for Daddy. Maya Angelou. SP-AngeM

Among a grave fraternity of Monks. Foregoing Subject Resumed, The. William Wordsworth. CP-WorW2

Among a hundred windows shining. Window, A. Denise Levertov. SP-LeveDP

Among all lovely things my Love had been. William Wordsworth. CP-WorW1; MW-WorW

Among all objects. Dead Sparrow. Adam Zagajewski. SP-ZagaA, *tr. by* Clare Cavanagh

Among all the losses, this was immense. Dream of Fifty, A. Gregory Orr. SP-OrrG

Among Artisans' Houses. Donald Davie. CP-DaviDC

Among brick pots, buckets and rakes. Fanny Howe. SP-HoweF *Fr.* Sea-Garden, The.

Among cocoa-nut palms of a far oasis. Moth That Made God Blind, The. Hart Crane. CP-CranH

Among / fucks / directly. Poemless Rhymes for the Times. Charles Olson. CP-OlsoC

Among Grass. Muriel Rukeyser. CP-RukeM

Among high cliffs. Han-shan. CP-ColdM, *tr. by* Red Pine

Among leaf-green / this morning, they. Delta Poems. Muriel Rukeyser. CP-RukeM

Among My Friends. Robert Duncan. SP-DuncR

Among my friends could I find. Shmuel HaNagid. SP-HaNaS, *tr. by* Peter Cole

Among my friends love is a great sorrow. Among My Friends. Robert Duncan. SP-DuncR

Among my marionettes I find. Convictions (Curtain Raiser). T. S. Eliot. SP-ElioT

Among / of / green. Locust Tree in Flower, The. William Carlos Williams. CP-WilW1

Among orange-tile rooftops. Prospect. Sylvia Plath. CP-PlatS

Among our good deeds of this date. Behavior. Howard Nemerov. CP-NemeH

Among [*or* Amang] our young lass[i]es there's [*or* is] Muirland Meg. Muirland Meg. Robert Burns. CP-BurnR

Among Ourselves and with All Nations. Kenneth Patchen. CP-PatcK

Among ourselves like this, we are elaborate. William Meredith. SP-MereW

Among pelagian travellers. On the Circuit. W. H. Auden. CP-AudeW

Among School Children. William Butler Yeats. CP-YeatW

Among the admirers of Carmen, all. Aleksandr Aleksandrovich Blok. SP-BlokA, *tr. by* Peter France *and* Jon Stallworthy

Among the anthropophagi. Funebrial Reflection. Ogden Nash. CP-NashO

Among the Brobdingnagians Gulliver. Shaving Mirror. John Updike. CP-UpdiJ

Among the bumblebees in red-top hay, a freckled field of brown-eyed. Adelaide Crapsey. Carl Sandburg. CP-SandC

Among the Cypresses at the End of the Way of the Cross. Kenneth Rexroth. CP-RexrK

Among the disasters that discention brings. Blame the Reward of Princes. Robert Herrick. CP-HerrR

Among the dwellers in the silent fields. Grace Darling. William Wordsworth. CP-WorW2

Among the dwellings framed by birds. Wren's Nest, A. William Wordsworth. CP-WorW2

Among the fast machines. Funeral. Rainer Maria Rilke. CP-RilkFr, *tr. by* A. Poulin, Jr.

Among the forests of the North. Caribou, The. Ogden Nash. CP-NashO

Among the Gods. Stanley Kunitz. CP-KunSC

Among the grassroots. Dogheads. Carl Sandburg. CP-SandC

Among the happy wits this age hath shown. In Honor of Du Bartas, 1641. Anne Bradstreet. CP-BradA

Among the heathy hills and ragged woods. Written with a Pencil, Standing by the Fall of Fyers, near Loch-Ness. Robert Burns. CP-BurnR

Among the hieroglyphs, the masks, the unfinished poems. Artaud. Raymond Carver. CP-CarvR

Among the high-branching, leafless boughs. View from an Attic Window, The. Howard Nemerov. CP-NemeH

Among the Hills. John Greenleaf Whittier. CP-WhitJ

Among the holy Mountains high. Bible, *O.T. See* His foundation is in the holy mountains

Among the iodoform, in twilight-sleep. Leg, The. Karl Shapiro. SP-ShapK

Among / the leaves. William Carlos Williams. *See* Among / of / green

Among the legends sung or said. Wishing Bridge, The. John Greenleaf Whittier. CP-WhitJ

Among the memory of all lovely things. Michelangelo Buonarroti. CP-Miche, *tr. by* John Frederick Nims

Among the men and women the multitude. Among the Multitude. Walt Whitman. CP-WhitW

Among the *Mirtles*, as I walkt. Mrs. Eliz. Wheeler, Under the Name of the Lost Shepardesse. Robert Herrick. CP-HerrR

Among the more irritating minor ideas. Looking across the Fields and Watching the Birds Fly. Wallace Stevens. CP-StevW; CP-StevWP

Among the mountains I wandered and saw blue haze and red crag and. Masses. Carl Sandburg. CP-SandC

Among the Multitude. Walt Whitman. CP-WhitW

Among the Narcissi. Sylvia Plath. CP-PlatS

Among the numbers who employ. To Lord Harley, since Earl of Oxford, on His Marriage. Jonathan Swift. CP-SwifJ

Among the old men that you know. Child Asleep in Its Own Life, A. Wallace Stevens. CP-StevWP

Among the pines we ran and called. Monologue at Midnight. Robert Penn Warren. CP-WarrR

Among the rain. Great Figure, The. William Carlos Williams. CP-WilW1

Among the Red Guns. Carl Sandburg. CP-SandC

Among the Roses. James Laughlin. CP-LaugJ

Among the sages of the past. Han-shan. CP-ColdM, *tr. by* Red Pine

Among the second selves, sailor, observe. Desire to Make Love in a Pagoda, The. Wallace Stevens. CP-StevWP

Among the serviceable mills and. Feeders, The. Donald Davie. CP-DaviDC

Among the shades and cries of the night. Indian, The. Randall Jarrell. CP-JarrR

Among the shadows where two streets cross. Trafficker. Carl Sandburg. CP-SandC

Among the signs of autumn I perceive. Tall Ambrosia. Henry David Thoreau. CP-ThorH

Among the silvery, the dulled sparkling mica lights of tar roofs. East Window on Elizabeth Street, An. James Schuyler. CP-SchuJ

Among the smoke and fog [*or* fog and smoke] of a December afternoon. Portrait of a Lady. T. S. Eliot. CP-ElioT; SP-ElioT

Among the Stars You May Be right. Yehuda Amichai. SP-AmicYL, *tr. by* Benjamin Harshav *and* Barbara Harshav

Among the thousands who with hail and cheer. To Oliver Wendell Holmes. John Greenleaf Whittier. CP-WhitJ

Among the worst of men that ever lived. Henry David Thoreau. CP-ThorH

Among their graven shapes to whom. Fitz-Greene Halleck. John Greenleaf Whittier. CP-WhitJ

Among these latter busts we count by scores. Protus. Robert Browning. CP-BroR1

Among these North Shore tennis tans I sit. Commencement, Pingree School. John Updike. CP-UpdiJ

Among / these / red pieces of. E. E. Cummings. CP-CummE

Among these tempests great and manifold. His Hope or Sheet-Anchor. Robert Herrick. CP-HerrR

Among These Turf-Stacks. Louis MacNeice. CP-MacNL (Turf-Stacks.) CP-MacNL

Among Those Killed in the Dawn Raid Was a Man Aged a Hundred. Dylan Thomas. CP-ThomD

Among thy fancies, tell me this. Kisse, The. Robert Herrick. CP-HerrR

Among twenty snowy mountains. Thirteen Ways of Looking at a Blackbird. Wallace Stevens. ·CP-StevW; CP-StevWP

Among white lilac trusses, green-gold spaces of sunlit grass. May 24th or So. James Schuyler. CP-SchuJ

Amor Intellectualis. Oscar Wilde. CP-WildO

Amor Loci. W. H. Auden. CP-AudeW

Amor Mundi. Christina Georgina Rossetti. CP-RosC1

Amore E Dispetto. Christina Georgina Rossetti. CP-RosC3

Amore E Dovere. Christina Georgina Rossetti. CP-RosC3

Amore Fuggitivo. Torquato Tasso. CP-SherT, *tr. by* Thomas Sheridan

Amores. Ovid.
  "Bleat was my reign, retiring Cynthia cry'd." CP-JohnS, *tr. by* Samuel Johnson
  "Here Tantalus in water seek[e]s for water, and doth miss[e]." CP-RaleW, *tr. by* Walter Ralegh
  Ovid in Love. CP-MahoD, *tr. by* Derek Mahon

Amoretti. Edmund Spenser. CP-Spens

Amorous Debate, An. Thom Gunn. CP-GunnT

Amorphous is the mind; its quality. Edna St. Vincent Millay. CP-MillE

Amos. John Berryman. CP-BerrJ

Amour. D. H. Lawrence. CP-LawrD (Early Spring.) CP-LawrD

Amours de Voyage. Arthur Hugh Clough. SP-ClouA

Amphibian. Robert Browning. CP-BroR2

Amphibious Crocodile. John Crowe Ransom. SP-RansJ (Crocodile.) SP-RansJ

Amphion the Theban and Arion the Methymnian were both mythical and both singers. New Song, The. Clement of Alexandria. CP-MertT

Ample Garden, The. Robert Graves. CP-GravR

Ample make this Bed. Emily Dickinson. CP-DickE

Amplitude. Tess Gallagher. SP-GallT

Amplitude,—voltage,—the one friend calls for the one. Message. John Berryman. CP-BerrJ

Amsterdam. James Merrill. SP-MerrJ

Amtrak left the Bridgeport platform. Bridgeport Station. William Corbett. SP-CorbW

Amulet, The. Norman Dubie. CP-DubiN

Amulet, The. Ralph Waldo Emerson. CP-EmerR

Amusing Our Daughters. Carolyn Kizer. CP-KizeC

Amy Lowell Thoughts. James Schuyler. CP-SchuJ

Amy Wentworth. John Greenleaf Whittier. CP-WhitJ

Amy's Cruelty. Elizabeth Barrett Browning. CP-BroEB

An' O, for ane-and-twenty, Tam! O, for Ane-and-Twenty Tam. Robert Burns. CP-BurnR

An somebodie were come again. Carl an the King Come. Robert Burns. CP-BurnR

An' that year Metevsky went over to America del Sud. Canto 38: "An' that year Metevsky went over to America del Sud." Ezra Pound. SP-PounE *Fr.* Cantos.

Anabasis, The. Allen Tate. CP-TateA

Anacreon. William Wordsworth. CP-WorW1

Anacreon's Dove. Samuel Johnson. CP-JohnS (Translation of Anacreon's *Dove* (Ode ix).) CP-JohnS

Anacreon's Grave. Johann Wolfgang von Goethe. CP-WrigJ

Anacreontic. Robert Herrick. CP-HerrR (Anacreontike.) CP-HerrR

Anacreontic for a Chinese Scholar. Robert Stock. SP-StocR

Anacreontic[k] Verse. Robert Herrick. CP-HerrR (Anacrontik Verse.) CP-HerrR

Anacreontike. Robert Herrick. CP-HerrR

Anactoria. Algernon Charles Swinburne. SP-SwinA

Anaemia, dyspepsia and ulcer / affect the chambermaid. Below the Stairs. James Schuyler. CP-SchuJ

Anagke. "Rubén Dario." SP-DariR, *tr. by* Alberto Acereda *and* Will Derusha

Anagram. George Herbert. CP-HerbG

Anagram, An. *Unknown.* CP-BradA

Anagram, The. John Donne. MW-DonnJ *Fr.* Elegies.

Anagram Born of Madness at Czernowitz, 23 November 1920.   Norman Dubie.   CP-DubiN

Anahorish.   Seamus Heaney.   SP-HeanSO

Analogue.   Howard Nemerov.   CP-NemeH

Analogue of Unity in Multeity.   Richard Eberhart.   CP-EberR

Analysand.   Stevie Smith.   CP-SmitS

Analysis.   Fernando Pessoa.   SP-PessF, *tr. by* Susan M. Brown *and* Edwin Honig

Analysis of a Theme.   Wallace Stevens.   CP-StevW; CP-StevWP

Anansi, black busybody of the folktales.   Spider.   Sylvia Plath.   CP-PlatS

Anaphora.   Elizabeth Bishop.   CP-BishE

Anaphylactic shock, they talk about.   And Is Silent.   Howard Nemerov.   CP-NemeH

Anarchic anger came to beat us down.   Storm of Angels, A.   May Sarton.   SP-SartM

Anasazi.   Gary Snyder.   CP-SnydG

Anashuya and Vijaya.   William Butler Yeats.   CP-YeatW

Anat and Acbat.   Loves of Anat, I, The.   Charles Olson.   CP-OlsoC

Anathema.   Raymond Carver.   CP-CarvR

Anatomical dishabille.   Emily Dickinson.   SP-DickE

Anatomize their work.   Novices.   Marianne Craig Moore.   CP-MoorM

Anatomy.   Walter De la Mare.   CP-DeLaW

Anatomy Lab.   John Ciardi.   CP-CiarJ

Anatomy of Melancholy, The.   Thomas Merton.   CP-MertT

Anatomy of Migraine, An.   Amy Clampitt.   CP-ClamA

Anatomy of Monotony.   Wallace Stevens.   CP-StevW; CP-StevWP

Anatomy [*or* Anatomie] of the World, An: The First Anniversary.   John Donne.   CP-DonnJ; MW-DonnJ

Anaxagoras.   D. H. Lawrence.   CP-LawrD

Ance mair I hail thee, thou gloomy December!   Gloomy December.   Robert Burns.   CP-BurnR

Ance)dance / -ing millions all.   E. E. Cummings.   CP-CummE

Ancestor.   John Berryman.   CP-BerrJ

Ancestor.   Thomas Kinsella.   CP-KinsT

Ancestors.   Robert Graves.   CP-GravR

Ancestors, The.   Allen Tate.   CP-TateA

Ancestors give them aristocratic tastes.   Army Ants.   A. K. Ramanujan.   CP-RamaA

Ancestral.   Archibald MacLeish.   CP-MacLA

Ancestral Houses.   William Butler Yeats.   CP-YeatW   *Fr.* Meditations in Time of Civil War.

Ancestral voices bicker; ghosts.   Northern Star.   Derek Mahon.   CP-MahoD

Anchises to Aeneas.   Virgil.   CP-RaleW   *Fr.* Aeneid [*or* Eneados *or* Aeneis], The.

Anchor Song.   Rudyard Kipling.   CP-KiplR

Anchorage.   Margaret Atwood.   SP-AtwM2

Anchored.   Paul Laurence Dunbar.   CP-DunbP

Anchored a ways off Buoy Rocks the sailboat.   Smalley Bar.   Marge Piercy.   SP-PierM

A(ncient)a / weigh / tless.   E. E. Cummings.   CP-CummE

Ancient Amphitheater.   Yannis Ritsos.   SP-RitsY, *tr. by* Kimon Friar

Ancient Ballet, An.   Thomas Kinsella.   CP-KinsT

Ancient bridge, and a more ancient tower, An.   My House.   William Butler Yeats.   CP-YeatW   *Fr.* Meditations in Time of Civil War.

Ancient Burial Places in Peabody, The.   Jones Very.   CP-VeryJ

Ancient clay lamps lay beside the grave.   One-Armed Man, The.   Yannis Ritsos.   SP-RitsY, *tr. by* Kostas Myrsiades

Ancient Comedy follows its conventions and shares out its idylls, The.   Scenes.   Arthur Rimbaud.   CP-RimbA, *tr. by* Martin Sorrell

Ancient Complaint, An.   Dan Pagis.   SP-PagiD, *tr. by* Stephen Mitchell

Ancient country with towers insisting.   Rainer Maria Rilke.   CP-RilkFr, *tr. by* A. Poulin, Jr.   *Fr.* Valaisian Quatrains, The.

Ancient dame, how wide and vast.   Ode on the Death of a Lady.   Vincent Bourne.   CP-CowpW

Ancient drop of feudal blood, An.   Ralph Waldo Emerson.   CP-EmerR

Ancient forests of China logged, The.   Gary Snyder.   CP-SnydG   *Fr.* Myths and Texts.

Ancient Gesture, An.   Edna St. Vincent Millay.   CP-MillE

Ancient Greeks a fable had, that he, The.   Cadmus.   Jones Very.   CP-VeryJ

Ancient History.   Adam Zagajewski.   SP-ZagaA, *tr. by* Clare Cavanagh

Ancient lady who dwelt in Rome, An.   Ralph Waldo Emerson.   CP-EmerR

Ancient Mansion, The.   George Crabbe.   SP-CrabG   *Fr.* Posthumous Tales.

Ancient of Days, The.   G. K. Chesterton.   CP-ChesG

Ancient poets and their learned rhymes [*or* rimes], The.   Answer to Some Verses Made in His Praise, An.   Sir John Suckling.   CP-SuckJ

Ancient Printerman, The.   James Whitcomb Riley.   CP-RileJ

Ancient Proverb, An.   William Blake.   CP-BlakW

Ancient rule prescribed for true knights, An.   Absent Crusader.   Robert Graves.   CP-GravR

Ancient song, reciting, ending, An.   Old Chants.   Walt Whitman.   CP-WhitW

Ancient to Ancients, An.   Thomas Hardy.   CP-HardT

Ancient tragedy, ancient tragedy.   Constantine P. Cavafy.   CP-CavaC, *tr. by* Theoharis Constantine Theoharis

Ancient Tree, An.   Denise Levertov.   SP-LeveDL

Ancient Wisdom Speaks.   "H. D."   CP-DoolH

Ancient, world-old Elk paths.   Elk Trails.   Gary Snyder.   CP-SnydG

Ancients called me Chaos: my great yeares.   Sir Walter Ralegh.   CP-RaleW

Ancients said that poetry, The.   Syria.   Eugenio Montale.   CP-MontE, *tr. by* Jonathan Galassi

Ancients thought, The.   Some Monarchs and a Wish.   A. K. Ramanujan.   CP-RamaA

Ancre ridgedge et poissoble gongpoint.   Sufficient The.   Kenneth Rexroth.   CP-RexrK

&.   Andrei Codrescu.   SP-CodrA

And.   Robert Creeley.   CP-CreeR

&.   Richard Wilbur.   CP-WilbR

And a Day.   Laura Riding Jackson.   CP-RidiL

And a girl singing in the symbol air, crossing of gold, a.   Muriel Rukeyser.   CP-RukeM

And a little child shall lead them. Isaiah 11.6.   Jones Very.   CP-VeryJ

And a man is waiting in the streets and meets a woman.   Ballad in the Streets of Buenos Aires.   Yehuda Amichai.   SP-AmicYL, *tr. by* Benjamin Harshav *and* Barbara Harshav

And a man waits in the street and meets a woman.   Ballad in the Streets of Buenos Aires.   Yehuda Amichai.   SP-AmicY, *tr. by* Chana Bloch

And a Man Went Out Alone.   Kenneth Patchen.   CP-PatcK

And a poetry in which as in a film.   Hugh MacDiarmid.   SP-MacDH   *Fr.* Kind of Poetry I Want, The.

And a small.   To a Mexican Pig-Bank.   William Carlos Williams.   CP-WilW1

And a voice like a voice in dreams cried out in the stone wilderness.   Incident in the Life of a Prophet, An.   Thomas McGrath.   SP-McGrT

And adam rose.   Birth of Language, The.   Lucille Clifton.   SP-ClifL

And After All That—the Rain.   Yehuda Amichai.   SP-AmicYL, *tr. by* Benjamin Harshav *and* Barbara Harshav

And afterward? I don't know.   Twenty Years in the Valley.   Dan Pagis.   SP-PagiD, *tr. by* Stephen Mitchell

And again the screech of the scaffold.   Window Washer.   Charles Simic.   SP-SimiC; SP-SimiCE

And Aged Tiriel. stood before the Gates of his beautiful palace.   Tiriel.   William Blake.   CP-BlakW

&(all during the / dropsin).   E. E. Cummings.   CP-CummE

And all hours long, the town.   Noise of Battle.   D. H. Lawrence.   CP-LawrD

And all of the time you are seeing these things she.   Purples of Barley.   Michael Palmer.   SP-PalmM

And all that is this day.   Hangman's Great Hands, The.   Kenneth Patchen.   CP-PatcK

And all this here, everything I write, of course.   Hugh MacDiarmid.   SP-MacDH   *Fr.* In Memoriam James Joyce.

And all who read these lines shall love her then.   To La Contessa Bianzafior (Cent. XIV).   Ezra Pound.   CP-PoEar

And another regrettable thing about death.   Perfection Wasted.   John Updike.   CP-UpdiJ

And arise whatever for? / SUGAR FREE! SUGAR FREE? TAB.   I Sit Down to Type.   James Schuyler.   CP-SchuJ

And art thou born, brave babe? Blessed be thy birth!   Epigram on the Prince's Birth. 1630, An.   Ben Jonson.   CP-JonsB

And art thou cold and lowly laid.   Allan-Bane's Lament.   Sir Walter Scott.   SP-ScotW   *Fr.* Lady of the Lake, The.

And art thou grieved, sweet and sacred Dove.   Grieve Not the Holy Spirit, etc.   George Herbert.   CP-HerbG

And as far as Abu Ghosh we were silent.   Yehuda Amichai.   SP-AmicY, *tr. by* Stephen Mitchell

And as the light divided the dark.   Ralph Waldo Emerson.   CP-EmerR

And as the memory of each.   Clarence Major.   SP-MajoC

And as the war in its fifth spring.   Legend of the Dead Soldier, The.   Bertolt Brecht.   CP-MacNL

And as time past when Cato the Severe.   Ultimus Heroum: or, To the Most Learned, and to the Right Honourable, Henry, Marquesse of Dorchester.   Robert Herrick.   CP-HerrR

And ate so much the bill was five dollars.   Two Boys Went Into a Dream Diner.   Allen Ginsberg.   CP-GinsA

And beauty becomes ever more difficult.   Rainer Maria Rilke.   CP-RilkFr, *tr. by* A. Poulin, Jr.   *Fr.* Fragments.

And because you love me.   Both Sides of the Medal.   D. H. Lawrence.   CP-LawrD

And Bees of Paradise.   Hart Crane.   CP-CranH

And beneath the star.   Fragments from the Alfoxden Note-Book (III).   William

the Land of Zion and Jerusalem.

And in that shrill antithesis of calm. Throe of Apocalypse. Laura Riding Jackson. CP-RidiL

And is he gone, whom these armes held but now? Luke 2; Quærit Jesum Suum Maria. Bible, *N.T.* CP-CrasR *Fr.* St. Luke.

And is indeed truth beauty?—at the cost. Edna St. Vincent Millay. CP-MillE

And is it among rude untutored Dales. William Wordsworth. CP-WorW1

And is it stamina / that unseasonably freaks. Bluet, The. James Schuyler. CP-SchuJ

And is it thus the dear Illusive dream. Lines on the Death of Mrs Hill Suppos'd to Be Spoken by Her Sister Mrs Clymer. Annis Boudinot Stockton. CP-StocA

And is it thus, ye base and blind. Address to the Mob, An. William Cowper. CP-CowpW

And Is Silent. Howard Nemerov. CP-NemeH

And is the water come? Sure't cannot be. Upon Sir John Lawrence's Bringing Water over the Hills [to My L. Middlesex His House at Witten]. Sir John Suckling. CP-SuckJ

And is there care in heaven? and is there love. Book 2, Canto 8. Edmund Spenser. CP-Spens *Fr.* Faerie Queene, The.

And is this all? Can reason do no more. Reflection on the Foregoing Ode. William Cowper. CP-CowpW

And is this August weather? nay not so. Christina Georgina Rossetti. CP-RosC3

And is this—Yarrow?—*This* the Stream. Yarrow Visited [September, 1814]. William Wordsworth. CP-WorW2; MW-WorW

And is thy soul so wrapt in sleep? World of Dreams, The. George Crabbe. SP-CrabG

And it was almost a boy who undid. First Kiss. Rita Dove. SP-DoveR

And its eyes as deep. Federico García Lorca. CP-GarcF, *tr. by* Jerome Rothenberg *Fr.* Epitaph for a Bird.

And Jove's right hand approached the ambrosial bowl. Marriage of Psyche and Cupid. Elizabeth Barrett Browning. CP-BroEB

And Jude the Obscure and His Beloved. D. H. Lawrence. CP-LawrD

And learn O voyager to walk. Seafarer. Archibald MacLeish. CP-MacLA

And let her loves, when she is dead. For a Sad Lady. Dorothy Parker. CP-ParkD

And lifting belly fond of a fond a sweet. Portrait of Gertrude Stein. Robert Stock. SP-StocR

And lightening? One meaning of that. Seamus Heaney. SP-HeanSO *Fr.* Squarings.

And like a boyscout is prepared. She Is So Practical. James Laughlin. CP-LaugJ

And like a dying lady, lean and pale. Waning Moon, The. Percy Bysshe Shelley. CP-ShelP

And like myself lone, wholly lone. Emily Jane Brontë. CP-BronE

And listening to its. Poet Li Po Admiring a Waterfall, The. Denise Levertov. SP-LeveDL

And live I still to see relations gone? To the Memory of My Dear Daughter in Law, Mrs. Mercy Bradstreet. Anne Bradstreet. CP-BradA

And long ago, the almond was the symbol of resurrection. Flowers. D. H. Lawrence. CP-LawrD

And love is then no more than a compromise? To His Cynical Mistress. Thom Gunn. CP-GunnT

And man of wit & mark. Ralph Waldo Emerson. CP-EmerR

And many there were hurt by that strong boy. Love, Hope, Desire and Fear. Percy Bysshe Shelley. CP-ShelP

And Max's queer crystalline sense. Beerbohm and Belloc. G. K. Chesterton. CP-ChesG

&-moon-He-be-hind-a-mills. E. E. Cummings. CP-CummE

And must I sing? What subject shall I choose? Ben Jonson. CP-JonsB; SP-JonsB

And must I then, indeed, Pain, live with you. Edna St. Vincent Millay. CP-MillE

And must the loveliest youth depart. To Mr Stockton on His Departure from America to England, 1769. Annis Boudinot Stockton. CP-StocA

And must we part, because some say. Suspition upon His Over-much Familiarity with a Gentlewoman, The. Robert Herrick. CP-HerrR

And ninety-nine soldiers piled on the train at Amarillo. Allen Ginsberg. SP-GinsA *Fr.* Iron Horse.

And now as the iron rinds over. Skunk Cabbage. Mary Oliver. SP-OlivM

And now creeps down. Imber Nocturnus. Elizabeth Bishop. CP-BishE

And now gentlemen. Base of All Metaphysics, The. Walt Whitman. CP-WhitW

And Now Goodbye. Jaroslav Seifert. SP-SeifJ, *tr. by* Ewald Osers

And now I have another lad! Danger of Writing Defiant Verse, The. Dorothy Parker. CP-ParkD

And now I wish to pray and perform. In the Garden. David Ignatow. SP-IgnaD

And now in turn see Swinburne bent. Lines on Swinburne. Robert Browning.

CP-BroR2

And now let all the ships come in. Charles Olson. SP-OlsoC *Fr.* Maximus Poems, The.

And now Love sang: but his was such a song. Willowwood ("And now Love sang: but his was such a song"). Dante Gabriel Rossetti. CW-RossD *Fr.* House of Life, The.

And now old mammal, gall. Phronesis. Kenneth Rexroth. CP-RexrK

And now, outside, the walls. Night Watch. Adrienne Rich. CP-RicAE; SP-RicA2

And now September burns the careful tree. September Ode. Donald Hall. CP-HallD

And now th'art set wide ope, the Speare's sad art. I Am the Door [*or* Doore]. Richard Crashaw. CP-CrasR

And now / the best of all. Image-Making Love. D. H. Lawrence. CP-LawrD

And now the green household is dark. In the Tree House at Night. James Dickey. CP-DickJ

And now the house-dog stretched once more. Emily Jane Brontë. CP-BronE

And Now the Leaves Suddenly Lose Strength. Philip Larkin. CP-LarkP

And now the season climbs in conflagration. Blaubeuren. Charles Tomlinson. SP-TomlC

And now the splendor of your work is here. To Frank O'Hara. James Schuyler. CP-SchuJ

And now the vessel skirts the strand. Lords Strand of Northumberland, The. Sir Walter Scott. SP-ScotW *Fr.* Marmion.

And Now, the Weather. Karl Shapiro. SP-ShapK

And now the winds return. Blue Monody. Sam Hamill. SP-HamiS

And now, *Vexilla regis produent*. Dante Alighieri. CP-PinsR *Fr.* Divina Commedia.

And now when the branches were beginning to be heavy. Bird Talk. Carl Sandburg. CP-SandC

And now / When the rumble of death. Sunday Morning Prophecy. Langston Hughes. CP-HughL; CP-HughL2

And Now Why Tarriest Thou? Christina Georgina Rossetti. CP-RosC2

And now you be my guest. Mysteries, The. John Berryman. CP-BerrJ

And, O beloved voices, upon which. Futurity. Elizabeth Barrett Browning. CP-BroEB

And Oblige. Dorothy Parker. CP-ParkD

And of course I cried. Grass Widow. Paul Muldoon. CP-MuldP

And Oh—That the Man I Am Might Cease to Be. D. H. Lawrence. CP-LawrD

And Ole Ez said that the. James Laughlin. CP-LaugJ

And once again. Henry David Thoreau. CP-ThorH

And One for My Dame. Anne Sexton. CP-SextA; SP-SextA

And one / who a hundred years ago. Failure. Dan Pagis. SP-PagiD, *tr. by* Stephen Mitchell

And others cry for you. Epilogue. John Logan. CP-LogaJ *Fr.* Epilogue, Songs of the Spouses, Complaint of Love.

And Others, Vaguer Presences. John Ashbery. SP-AshbJ

And Our Eternal Home. Donald Davie. CP-DaviDC

And people who talk about faith. Talk of Faith. D. H. Lawrence. CP-LawrD

And Pergamos, / City of the Phrygians. Euripides. CP-DoolH *Fr.* Iphigenia [*or* Iphigeneia] in Aulis.

And Pound in his despair in the Army prison camp at Pisa. La Tristesse. James Laughlin. CP-LaugJ

& Power. Andrei Codrescu. SP-CodrA

And Psyche brought to Venus what was sent. Psyche and Venus. Elizabeth Barrett Browning. CP-BroEB

And Rest. David Ignatow. SP-IgnaD

—And Return. Dorothy Parker. CP-ParkD

And rival Coxcombs with enamored stare. Ralph Waldo Emerson. CP-EmerR

And said the dove. Anagke. "Rubén Dario." SP-DariR, *tr. by* Alberto Acereda *and* Will Derusha

And search. Striders, The. A. K. Ramanujan. CP-RamaA

And shall Love cease? Ask thine own heart, O Woman. Praise of Love. Christina Georgina Rossetti. CP-RosC3

And shall we build a little nest. Song: "And shall we build a little nest." Dorothy Parker. CP-ParkD

And she 'like a young year.' Lawrence Ferlinghetti. SP-FerlL

And since round lines are drawn. Hafiz. CP-EmerR *Fr.* Odes.

And slowly, in the middle, I close the book and lay aside. Getting It Wrong Again. Sam Hamill. SP-HamiS

And so an easier life our Cyclops drew. Cyclops, The. Theocritus. CP-BroEB *Fr.* Idylls.

And so, Ernie, your laughing head floats along. Deceased Writer, The: Photograph in the Rain. Dan Pagis. SP-PagiD, *tr. by* Stephen Mitchell

And so for nights. Night-Blooming Cereus, The. Robert Earl Hayden. CP-HaydR

And So Goodbye to Cities. Thomas Merton. CP-MertT

And so, here happily we meet, fair friend! Red Cotton Night-Cap Country.

Robert Browning. CP-BroR2

And so I am getting old! Don't Think You Know My Name! Thomas McGrath. SP-McGrT

And so I cross into another world. New Heaven and Earth. D. H. Lawrence. CP-LawrD

And so I went, hands thrust in torn pockets. My Bohemia (Fantasy). Arthur Rimbaud. CP-RimbA, *tr. by* Martin Sorrell

And so the days pass. Harmonica Humdrums. Carl Sandburg. CP-SandC

And so the official archangels. Old Archangels. D. H. Lawrence. CP-LawrD

And so, the retraction. Penelope. Donald Davie. CP-DaviDC

And so the river moves. Lost Children, The. Richard Eberhart. CP-EberR

And so the seed / Becomes a flower. For Russell and Rowena Jelliffe. Langston Hughes. CP-HughL; CP-HughL3

And so these daughters fair of Pandarus. Daughters of Pandarus, The. Homer. CP-BroEB *Fr.* Odyssey.

And so / they go back: violin. Da Capo. Charles Tomlinson. CP-TomlC

And so till we have died. Louis Zukofsky. CP-ZukLS

And So Today. Carl Sandburg. CP-SandC

And so today—they lay him away. And So Today. Carl Sandburg. CP-SandC

And so / we lick our chops at Birmingham. Northern Liberal. Langston Hughes. CP-HughL; CP-HughL3

And so we live here. Like the sea. Yehuda Amichai. SP-AmicYL *Fr.* Poems on the Shore of Caesarea.

And so you are returning, livid flush of early dusk The chalk. In England. Joseph Brodsky. CP-BrodJ, *tr. by* Alan Myers

And so you found that poor room dull. Appearances. Robert Browning. CP-BroR2

And so you might have been. I Have Said, Ye Are Gods. Donald Davie. CP-DaviDC

And so you're dead. And you're not underground yet. Isaac Leybush Peretz. Moyshe-Leyb Halpern. CP-PinsR, *tr. by* Robert Pinsky

And some are sulky, while some will plunge. Rudyard Kipling. CP-KiplR *Fr.* Plain Tales from the Hills.

And some time make the time to drive out west. Postscript. Seamus Heaney. SP-HeanSO

And something that . . . that is theirs—no longer ours. Dispossessed, The. John Berryman. CP-BerrJ

And sometimes there's this parlor trick. Thaumatrope. Wyatt Prunty. SP-PrunW

And Step. David Ignatow. SP-IgnaD

And still at dawn the fire is lit. Mornings in a New House. James Merrill. SP-MerrJ

And still I lie here. Song of the Invisible Corpse in the Field. Gregory Orr. SP-OrrG

And still I look for the men who will dare to be. Rose and Cabbage. D. H. Lawrence. CP-LawrD

And still, in spite of all they do, I love the rose of England. Rose Is Not a Cabbage, A. D. H. Lawrence. CP-LawrD

And Still It Comes. Thomas Lux. SP-LuxT

And still we wear our uniforms, follow. Progress, The. Gwendolyn Brooks. SP-BrooG

And strike this scene in gold too, in relief. Seamus Heaney. SP-HeanSO *Fr.* Squarings.

And suddenly the giants tired of play. Thunder. Elizabeth Bishop. CP-BishE

And Summer mornings the mute child, rebellious. Eleven. Archibald MacLeish. CP-MacLA

And summer turns her head with its dark tangle. Ralegh's Prizes. Robert Pinsky. CP-PinsR

& sun & / sil / e / nce. E. E. Cummings. CP-CummE

And suppose the darlings get to Mantua. Purgatory. Maxine W. Kumin. SP-KumiM

And sweet it is to see in summer time. Michelangelo Buonarroti. CP-WorW1

And tallness stood upon the sky like a sparkling mane. O She Is as Lovely-Often as Every Day. Kenneth Patchen. CP-PatcK

And that I walk thus proudly crowned withal. Fragment: "And that I walk thus proudly crowned withal." Percy Bysshe Shelley. CP-ShelP

And that inevitable accident. Next Time, The. Robert Graves. CP-GravR

And That Is Your Glory. Yehuda Amichai. SP-AmicY, *tr. by* Stephen Mitchell

And That Night. David Ignatow. SP-IgnaD

And that was all his life. Kathleen Jessie Raine. SP-RainK

And that woman. Still Another for Mother. A. K. Ramanujan. CP-RamaA

And that's how I found him. Capture. Ai. SP-Ai

And the afternoon, the evening, sleeps so peacefully! Love Song of J. Alfred Prufrock, Resumed, The. T. S. Eliot. SP-ElioT *Fr.* Love Song of J. Alfred Prufrock, The.

And the / best. To Friends, for Good Health. Louis Zukofsky. CP-ZukLS

And the best gift of God. Ralph Waldo Emerson. CP-EmerR

And the Bordeaux plum / from Marmande (France) in parenthesis with.

Camellia Sabina. Marianne Craig Moore. CP-MoorM

And the child sitting alone planning her hope. Fourth Elegy. The Refugees. Muriel Rukeyser. CP-RukeM

And the Children of Birmingham. Thomas Merton. CP-MertT

And the city stood in its brightness when years later I returned. Czeslaw Milosz. CP-MiloC; CP-MiloCN, *tr. by* Peter Dale Scott

And the Clouds Return after the Rain. Stevie Smith. CP-SmitS

And the cloven waters like a chasm of mountains. Virgil. CP-ShelP, *tr. by* Percy Bysshe Shelley *Fr.* Georgics.

And the Communists have nothing to offer but fat cheeks and eyeglasses and lying policemen. Kral Majales. Allen Ginsberg. CP-GinsA; SP-GinsA

And the corn singing Millennium! Background with Revolutionaries. Archibald MacLeish. CP-MacLA

And the curtain rose in that theatre so long ago. Mood Indigo. James Schuyler. CP-SchuJ

And the day so mild. Misfortune Is on the Way. Charles Simic. SP-SimiCE

And 'the earth under our feet.' At Kenneth Burke's Place. William Carlos Williams. CP-WilW2

And the first with his hands folded and a money belt for a truss. Vision of Three Angels Viewing the Progress of Socialism. Thomas McGrath. SP-McGrT

And the gutter I dream of. I Float Between the Spheres. James Laughlin. CP-LaugJ

And the hedges wet in the rain, flaking in a sheet of wind. Anthony. Charles Bukowski. SP-BukC2

And the keen hound overcomes fortune. Note in Honor of Machiavelli, A. Thomas Merton. CP-MertT

And the land is divided into districts of memory and provinces of hope. Love of the Land. Yehuda Amichai. SP-AmicYL, *tr. by* Benjamin Harshav *and* Barbara Harshav

And the light without: the shade. Light Within, The. James Schuyler. CP-SchuJ

And the magic law governing our lives. Singleness in Love. Robert Graves. CP-GravR

And the Migration of My Parents. Yehuda Amichai. SP-AmicYL, *tr. by* Benjamin Harshav *and* Barbara Harshav

And the mist rising. Water Lace and White Eyes. Eleanor Wilner. SP-WilnE

And the Mother, shutting his homework. Seven-year-old Poets. Arthur Rimbaud. CP-RimbA, *tr. by* Martin Sorrell

And the mountain: each day. Cézanne at Aix. Charles Tomlinson. CP-TomlC; SP-TomlC

And the next I remembered I'm on a table. Loser, The. Charles Bukowski. SP-BukC2

And the poor stars. At the Poorhouse. Federico García Lorca. CP-GarcF, *tr. by* Jerome Rothenberg *Fr.* Night (Suite for Piano and Poet's Voice).

And the Same Words. David Ignatow. SP-IgnaD

And the sap is running in. It's March. James Laughlin. CP-LaugJ

And the secret names. I Learned That Her Name Was Proverb. Denise Levertov. SP-LeveDS

And the single reality. Clarence Major. SP-MajoC

And the song of water. Morning. Federico García Lorca. CP-GarcF, *tr. by* Catherine Brown

And the Spirit said. Clock of the Years, The. Thomas Hardy. CP-HardT

And the streams here, ledge to ledge. Lights among Redwood. Thom Gunn. CP-GunnT

And the subnormal. Insane Always Loved Me, The. Charles Bukowski. SP-BukC1

And the sun high over horizon hidden in cloud bank. Canto 76: "And the sun high over horizon hidden in cloud bank." Ezra Pound. SP-PounE *Fr.* Cantos.

And the sun wields mercy. Sun Wields Mercy, The. Charles Bukowski. SP-BukC2

And the Trains Go On. Philip Levine. SP-LeviP

And the walker sees the sunlit battlefield. Spring Warning. Philip Larkin. CP-LarkP

And the Wave Sings Because It Is Moving. Philip Larkin. CP-LarkP

And the waves / gush pearls. Winter. Mary Oliver. SP-OlivM

And the Woods, with gnarled and cruel. Fragment, A: "And the Woods, with gnarled and cruel." G. K. Chesterton. CP-ChesG

And the world changed. Survival: Infantry. George Oppen. CP-OppGN

And the youth free stripling bounding along the Hills of Color. Contest of Bards. Allen Ginsberg. CP-GinsA

And their murder towns me sick O it red-streets. Blind Maidens of Our Homelessness, The. Kenneth Patchen. CP-PatcK

And Then. Miller Williams. CP-WillM

And Then I Headed on Back Home. Miller Williams. CP-WillM

And then i see the cattle of my own town. My Dream About the Cows. Lucille Clifton. SP-ClifL

And then once more. Antiphon, The: "And then once more." Denise Levertov. SP-LeveDS

And then one sometimes sees waterfalls. Waterfalls in a Bank. A. K. Ramanujan. CP-RamaA

And then the cow did write. Another Day (And then the cow). Muriel Rukeyser. CP-RukeM

And then there was Myrtle's Cousin. Myrtle's Cousin. Theodore Roethke. CP-RoetT

And then there was St Kevin and the blackbird. St Kevin and the Blackbird. Seamus Heaney. SP-HeanSO

And then they pressed the melon. Happy End. Charles Simic. SP-SimiC; SP-SimiCE

And then went down to the ship. Canto 1: "And then went down to the ship." Ezra Pound. SP-PounE *Fr.* Cantos.

And there are poets who are artists. Fernando Pessoa. SP-PessF *Fr.* Keeper of Sheep, The.

And there, in that ripe Summer night, once more. Little Jack Janitor. James Whitcomb Riley. CP-RileJ *Fr.* Child-World, A.

And there, sir, comes a rehearsal of history. I Visit Brooklyn with a Queen in Mind. Andrei Codrescu. SP-CodrA

And There Was a Great Calm. Thomas Hardy. CP-HardT

And There Was No More Sea. Christina Georgina Rossetti. CP-RosC2

And there we were together again. Return of Morgan and Fingal, The. Edwin Arlington Robinson. CP-RobiE

And there you are again, now as you are. Rembrandt to Rembrandt. Edwin Arlington Robinson. CP-RobiE

And there's Petrarch, our first. Western Invention of Lyrical Nature, The. Gregory Orr. SP-OrrG

And these about me die. Sandalphon. Ezra Pound. CP-PoEar

And these / these are scavengers birds. In the Zoo. A. K. Ramanujan. CP-RamaA

And they have to get it right. We just need. Love Poem, A. John Ashbery. SP-AshbJ

And They Obey. Carl Sandburg. CP-SandC

And they took Abu and stoked the fire with him. In Ancient Times. David Ignatow. SP-IgnaD

And they were stronger hands than mine. Dedication, A: "And they were stronger hands than mine." Rudyard Kipling. CP-KiplR

And think how the nightingale, who is so shy. Paltry-Looking People. D. H. Lawrence. CP-LawrD

And this day it was Spring . . . .us. E. E. Cummings. CP-CummE

And this hard jealousy against me. Laura Riding Jackson. CP-RidiL

And this is the way the baby woke. Way the Baby Woke, The. James Whitcomb Riley. CP-RileJ

And this is the way they ring. Ringing the Bells. Anne Sexton. CP-SextA; SP-SextA

And This Is Your Glory. Yehuda Amichai. SP-AmicYL, *tr. by* Benjamin Harshav *and* Barbara Harshav

And this, ladies and gentlemen, whom I am not in fact. Suicide, The. Louis MacNeice. CP-MacNL

And this of all my Hopes. Emily Dickinson. CP-DickE

And this place our forefathers made for man! Dungeon, The. Samuel Taylor Coleridge. CP-ColeS

And This Will Be All? Carl Sandburg. CP-SandC

And tho' my friar's mandate is severe. George Meredith. CP-MerG2

And Thou Art Dead, as Young and Fair. Lord Byron. CP-Byron

And Thou hast placed me on a lofty hill. City, The. Jones Very. CP-VeryJ

And thou, O Life, the lady of all bliss. Newborn Death ("And thou, O Life, the lady of all bliss"). Dante Gabriel Rossetti. CW-RossD *Fr.* House of Life, The.

And thou wast out on yesternight. Wounded Pigeon, The. Jones Very. CP-VeryJ

And thou wert sad—yet I was not with thee. Lines on Hearing That Lady Byron Was Ill. Lord Byron. CP-Byron

And though he dearly prized the bards of fame. Ralph Waldo Emerson. CP-EmerR

And though the walls have ears. To One "Investigated" by the Last Senate Committee, or the Next. John Ciardi. CP-CiarJ

And Three Hundred and Sixty-Six in Leap Year. Ogden Nash. CP-NashO

And thus a poetry which fully understands. Hugh MacDiarmid. SP-MacDH *Fr.* Kind of Poetry I Want, The.

And thus declared that Arab lady. Solomon and the Witch. William Butler Yeats. CP-YeatW

And Thus in Nineveh. Ezra Pound. CP-PoEar

And thus the people every year. Attack of the Squash People. Marge Piercy. SP-PierM

And Thus with All Praise. William Carlos Williams. CP-WilW1

And Thy Mother. John Ciardi. CP-CiarJ

And "thy true faith can alter never?" On the Quotation "And My True Faith Can Alter Never, Though Thou Art Gone Perhaps Forever." Lord Byron. CP-Byron

And to begin again, the night was dark and dreary, and. Sister Water. Robert Penn Warren. CP-WarrR

And to dissolve the heaps. Afternoon lumber water filling. Darjeeling. Thomas Merton. CP-MertT

And to Her-Without-Bounds I send. Tribal Memories. Robert Duncan. SP-DuncR *Fr.* Passages.

And to the kings of the world. Mohammed. Kenneth Patchen. CP-PatcK

And to these Rhodians She, the Sharp-eyed One. Translation from Pindar's Seventh Olympian, Epode III. Robert Browning. CP-BroR2

And tomorrow morning at 8 o'clock in Springfield, Massachusetts. Poem: "And tomorrow morning at 8 o'clock in Springfield, Massachusetts." Frank O'Hara. SP-OharF

And / Unto thine eyes my heart. Xenia ("And / Unto thine eyes my heart"). Ezra Pound. CP-PoEar

And "Ut Pictura Poesis" Is Her Name. John Ashbery. SP-AshbJ

And was it along this torpid muddy river. Mythical Founding of Buenos Aires, The. Jorge Luis Borges. SP-BorgJ, *tr. by* Alastair Reid

And watching Hoppy curled up. Pleasure, Pleasure. Theodore Weiss. SP-WeisT

And we came near Corofin through a narrow gate. Wild Swans of Inverane, The. Richard Eberhart. CP-EberR

And we kept going. Poem on My Birthday, July 2. Raymond Carver. CP-CarvR

And we read in the books of the ancients. I Love Therefore I Am I Suffer But I'm Alive. James Laughlin. CP-LaugJ

And we shall not get excited. Because a translator. Yehuda Amichai. SP-AmicYL, *tr. by* Benjamin Harshav *and* Barbara Harshav

And we were speaking easily and all the light stayed low. In Judgment of the Leaf. Kenneth Patchen. CP-PatcK

And What About the Children. Audre Lorde. SP-LordA (We've made a child.) SP-LordA

And what are you that, wanting you. Philosopher, The. Edna St. Vincent Millay. CP-MillE

And what can you appeal to. Cure, The. Theodore Weiss. SP-WeisT

And what do I care. What Do I Care? D. H. Lawrence. CP-LawrD

And what ever happened. Song of the Dead Girls. Gabriela Mistral. SP-MistG, *tr. by* Maria Giachetti [*or* Jacketti]

And what if Heraclitus and Parmenides. Lava. Adam Zagajewski. SP-ZagaA, *tr. by* Renata Gorczynski, Benjamin Ivry *and* C. K. Williams

And what if the stream. Part 2—February. Denise Levertov. SP-LeveDL *Fr.* Metamorphic Journal.

And What Is Love? It Is a Doll Dressed Up. John Keats. CP-KeatJ

And what is love? Misunderstanding, pain. Epigram: "And what is love? Misunderstanding, pain." James Vincent Cunningham. CP-CunnJ

"And what is love?" said Pilate. Dragon and the Unicorn, The. Kenneth Rexroth. CP-RexrK

And what might that bold man's announcement be. Sun, The. Robert Browning. CP-BroR2

And what. One must groan and stretch in order to break. October First. Philip Whalen. SP-WhalP

And what were roses. Perfume?for i do. E. E. Cummings. CP-CummE

And What with the Blunders. Kenneth Patchen. CP-PatcK

And what would I do in heaven, pray. She of the Dancing Feet Sings. Countee Cullen. CP-CullC

And what you liked. Lorine Niedecker. CP-NiedL

And what's new on the beach? A twisted path. Information. Dan Pagis. SP-PagiD, *tr. by* Stephen Mitchell

And what's the snow that melts the soonest? Boon. Paul Muldoon. CP-MuldP

And When Freedom Is Achieved. Kenneth Patchen. CP-PatcK

And when I am entombed in my place. Ralph Waldo Emerson. CP-EmerR

And when I see the heavy red fleece. Erotic. D. H. Lawrence. CP-LawrD

And when I thought, "Our love might end." Daylight. James Schuyler. CP-SchuJ

And When in Scenes of Glory. Miller Williams. CP-WillM

And when on earth thy voice again is heard. La Pia. Dante Alighieri. CW-RossD *Fr.* Divina Commedia.

And when on the dark steel came the roads. We Have Gone Through Great Rooms Together. Carl Sandburg. CP-SandC

And when that ballad lady went. Road in Kentucky, A. Robert Earl Hayden. CP-HaydR

And when the sun puts out his lamp. To the Mountains. Henry David Thoreau. CP-ThorH

And when was dust a thing so rash? He Remembereth That We Are Dust. Adrienne Rich. CP-RicAE

And whence and why come you? Lingering Last Drops. Walt Whitman. CP-WhitW

And where is truth? On tombs? for such to thee. Fragment: The Sepulchre of Memory. Percy Bysshe Shelley. CP-ShelP

And where it falls, a quality. Fire in a Dark Landscape. Charles Tomlinson. CP-TomlC

And where now, Bayard, will thy footsteps tend?   Bayard Taylor.   John Greenleaf Whittier.   CP-WhitJ

And where's the Land of Used-to-be, does little baby wonder?   Land of Used-to-Be, The.   James Whitcomb Riley.   CP-RileJ

And while for the sake of sanity.   Love Poem: "And while for the sake of sanity."   Andrei Codrescu.   SP-CodrA

And who art thou? said I to the soft-falling shower.   Voice of the Rain, The.   Walt Whitman.   CP-WhitW

And Who Do You Think "They" Are?   William Carlos Williams.   CP-WilW2

And who feels discord now or sorrow?   Fragment: Love the Universe To-day.   Percy Bysshe Shelley.   CP-ShelP

And who has seen the moon, who has not seen.   Moonrise.   D. H. Lawrence.   CP-LawrD

And who hath known her—like as I.   Flying Islands of the Night, The.   James Whitcomb Riley.   CP-RileJ

And who is He that, sculptured in huge stone.   "Moses" of Michael Angelo, The.   Robert Browning.   CP-BroR2

And who is this lies prostrate at thy feet?   Will These Hands Ne'er Be Clean?   Christina Georgina Rossetti.   CP-RosC3

And who must remain.   Clarence Major.   SP-MajoC

And who will speak of the worst.   Suspicion.   Constantine P. Cavafy.   CP-CavaC, tr. by Theoharis Constantine Theoharis

And whoever forces himself to love anybody.   Retort to Jesus.   D. H. Lawrence.   CP-LawrD

And whoever walks a mile full of false sympathy.   Retort to Whitman.   D. H. Lawrence.   CP-LawrD

And who's this little fellow in his itty-bitty robe?   Hitler's First Photograph.   Wisława Szymborska.   SP-SzymW, tr. by Stanisław Barańczak and Clare Cavanagh

And why is the sun such a poor friend.   Pablo Neruda.   SP-NeruP   Fr. Question Book.

And why to me this, thou lame lord of fire.   Execration upon Vulcan, An.   Ben Jonson.   CP-JonsB; SP-JonsB

And will Cleander's sympathizing heart.   To Doctor Rush Enclosing the Foregoing Ode of 1782.   Annis Boudinot Stockton.   CP-StocA

And Will That Magic World.   James Laughlin.   CP-LaugJ

And will you leave me thus alone.   Ballad, A: "And will you leave me thus alone."   William Wordsworth.   CP-WorW1

And wilt [or wylt] thou le[a]ve me thus?   Lover's Appeal, The.   Sir Thomas Wyatt.   CP-WyatT

And Wilt Thou Weep When I Am Low?   Lord Byron.   CP-Byron

And with what body do they come?   Emily Dickinson.   CP-DickE

And Without.   Louis Zukofsky.   CP-ZukLS

And women with small heads.   Men With Small Heads.   Thomas Lux.   SP-LuxT

And would you faine the reason know.   Thomas Campion and Philip Rosseter.   CP-CampT

And would you gather turds.   History of Love, A.   William Carlos Williams.   CP-WilW2

And Would You See My Mistress' Face?   Thomas Campion and Philip Rosseter.   CP-CampT

And wouldst thou hasten, in another soul.   Christian Influence.   Jones Very.   CP-VeryJ

And yes, my friend, we too walked through a valley.   Seamus Heaney.   SP-HeanSO   Fr. Squarings.

And yet can she.   Theodore Weiss.   SP-WeisT   Fr. Storeroom, The.

And yet how many ports, and in those ports.   Rainer Maria Rilke.   CP-RilkFr, tr. by A. Poulin, Jr.   Fr. Orchards.

And yet how speak of her as one distracted?   Theodore Weiss.   SP-WeisT   Fr. Storeroom, The.

And yet I have seen thee happy with me.   Stephen Crane.   CP-CranS

And yet it's Alexandria. Should you walk a little.   Exiles.   Constantine P. Cavafy.   CP-CavaC, tr. by Theoharis Constantine Theoharis

And yet I've lived like this for years.   Game, The.   Louise Glück.   SP-GlucL

And yet life's secret is in us.   Rainer Maria Rilke.   CP-RilkFr, tr. by A. Poulin, Jr.   Fr. Fragments.

And yet more should be loved.   Imenos.   Constantine P. Cavafy.   CP-CavaC, tr. by Theoharis Constantine Theoharis

And yet not everyone is given a true old age.   Submerged.   Czeslaw Milosz.   CP-MiloCN, tr. by Robert Hass

And yet one arrives somehow.   Arrival.   William Carlos Williams.   CP-WilW1

And yet the books will be there on the shelves, separate beings.   Czeslaw Milosz.   CP-MiloC; CP-MiloCN, tr. by Robert Hass

And yet we were so like one another.   Czeslaw Milosz.   CP-MiloCN, tr. by Robert Hass

And yet you experienced the flames of Hell.   Proof.   Czeslaw Milosz.   CP-MiloC; CP-MiloCN, tr. by Lillian Vallee

And "Yonder look! yoho! yoho!"   Doe: A Fragment, The.   George Meredith.   CP-MerG1

And you are startled when your reflected face.   Golden Mirror, The.   Marya Alexandrovna Zaturenska.   SP-ZatuM

And you as well must die, belovèd dust.   Edna St. Vincent Millay.   CP-MillE

And you came when I / feared that everything.   You Are My Future.   James Laughlin.   CP-LaugJ

And you Diotima who walk humbly among the living.   Friedrich Hölderlin.   SP-ZatuM, tr. by Marya Alexandrovna Zaturenska

And you have come.   Year of the Child, The.   Robert Earl Hayden.   CP-HaydR

And You Know.   John Ashbery.   SP-AshbJ

And you love me?   Stephen Crane.   CP-CranS

And you may lead a thousand men.   Rudyard Kipling.   CP-KiplR   Fr. Light That Failed, The.

And you my cone.   Dry Cup.   James Tate.   SP-TateJ

And you never liked parties.   Table, The.   Carlos Drummond de Andrade.   CP-BishE

And you, old woman, are carrying scrub buckets tonight.   Heavy and Light.   Carl Sandburg.   CP-SandC

And you remember, in the afternoon.   Coldness in Love.   D. H. Lawrence.   CP-LawrD

And you sang eloquently.   For Sappho/After Sappho.   Carolyn Kizer.   CP-KizeC

And You, Too, Brutus.   Robert Stock.   SP-StocR

And you too, old man, so we have heard.   Eros.   George Oppen.   CP-OppGN

And you're the poet of this concern?   Wash Lowry's Reminiscence.   James Whitcomb Riley.   CP-RileJ

Andalusian Songs.   Federico García Lorca.
  Adelina Out Walking.   CP-GarcF, tr. by Alan S. Trueblood
  "Bramble gray of stalk."   CP-GarcF, tr. by Alan S. Trueblood
  Evening ("Three looming poplars").   CP-GarcF, tr. by Alan S. Trueblood
  It's True.   CP-GarcF, tr. by Alan S. Trueblood
  "My girl went down to the sea."   CP-GarcF, tr. by Alan S. Trueblood
  Rider's Song.   CP-GarcF, tr. by Alan S. Trueblood
  Rider's Song (1860).   CP-GarcF, tr. by Alan S. Trueblood
  "Suitor, / suitor of mine."   CP-GarcF, tr. by Alan S. Trueblood
  "Tree, lifeless tree, / tree live green."   CP-GarcF, tr. by Alan S. Trueblood

Andean Flute, The.   Derek Mahon.   CP-MahoD

Anderson, I thought of you when I loitered.   Harley's Swans.   Raymond Carver.   CP-CarvR

Andraitx—Pomegranate Flowers.   D. H. Lawrence.   CP-LawrD

Andrea del Sarto.   Robert Browning.   CP-BroR1; SP-BroR

Andrée Rexroth ("Now once more gray mottled buckeye branches").   Kenneth Rexroth.   CP-RexrK

Andrée Rexroth ("Purple and green, blue and white").   Kenneth Rexroth.   CP-RexrK

Andrée Rexroth ("Years have gone, The. It is spring").   Kenneth Rexroth.   CP-RexrK

Andrew Jackson was eight feet tall.   Statue of Old Andrew Jackson, The.   Nicholas Vachel Lindsay.   CP-LindV

Andrew Jones.   William Wordsworth.   CP-WorW1

Andrew Lord Poems.   James Schuyler.   CP-SchuJ

Andrew Rykman's dead and gone.   Andrew Rykman's Prayer.   John Greenleaf Whittier.   CP-WhitJ

Andrew Rykman's Prayer.   John Greenleaf Whittier.   CP-WhitJ

Androcles from his injur'd lord, in dread.   Reciprocal Kindness the Primary Law of Nature.   Vincent Bourne.   CP-CowpW

Androgyne, Mon Amour.   Tennessee Williams.   CP-WillT

Androids.   William Dickey.   SP-DickW

Andromeda.   Gerard Manley Hopkins.   CP-HopkG

Andromeda, by Perseus saved and wed.   Aspecta Medusa.   Dante Gabriel Rossetti.   CW-RossD

Andromeda Chained to Her Rock the Great Nebula in Her Heart.   Kenneth Rexroth.   CP-RexrK

Anecdote.   Dorothy Parker.   CP-ParkD

Anecdote.   Charles Tomlinson.   CP-TomlC

Anecdote for Fathers.   William Wordsworth.   CP-WorW1; MW-WorW

Anecdote of Canna.   Wallace Stevens.   SP-StevW; CP-StevWP

Anecdote of Hemlock for Two Athenians.   Carl Sandburg.   CP-SandC

Anecdote of Men by the Thousand.   Wallace Stevens.   CP-StevW; CP-StevWP

Anecdote of Rain.   Adam Zagajewski.   SP-ZagaA, tr. by Renata Gorczynski, Benjamin Ivry and C. K. Williams

Anecdote of the Abnormal.   Wallace Stevens.   CP-StevWP

Anecdote of the Jar.   Wallace Stevens.   CP-StevW; CP-StevWP

Anecdote of the Prince of Peacocks ("In the land of the peacocks, the prince thereof").   Wallace Stevens.   CP-StevWP

Anecdote of the Prince of Peacocks ("In the moonlight / I met Berserk").   Wallace Stevens.   CP-StevW; CP-StevWP

Anecdotes of the Late War.   Charles Olson.   CP-OlsoC

Anelida and Arcite. Geoffrey Chaucer. CP-ChauG

Anemone. Muriel Rukeyser. CP-RukeM

Anent Socrates, or Somebody. Hayden Carruth. CP-CarHS

Aneurin's Harp. George Meredith. CP-MerG1

Anew, sun, to fire summer. Louis Zukofsky. CP-ZukLS

An(fragrance)Of / (Begins) / millions. E. E. Cummings. CP-CummE

Angel. Joseph Brodsky. CP-BrodJ

Angel. James Merrill. SP-MerrJ

Angel, The. William Blake. CP-BlakW *Fr.* Songs of Experience.

Angel, The. James Wright. CP-WrigJ

Angel and Stone. Howard Nemerov. CP-NemeH

Angel and the Clown, The. Nicholas Vachel Lindsay. CP-LindV

Angel, be ye ne'er in doubt, An. George Meredith. CP-MerG2

Angel begins in the morning, The. Emily Dickinson. SP-DickE

Angel Boley. Stevie Smith. CP-SmitS

Angel Butcher. Philip Levine. SP-LeviP

Angel Face. Stevie Smith. CP-SmitS

Angel Food Dogs, The. Anne Sexton. CP-SextA

Angel from his Paradise drove Adam, An. Variation on Lines of Landor, A. Robert Browning. CP-BroR2

Angel most cynical. Violent Hand, The. Stevie Smith. CP-SmitS

Angel of fire and genitals, do you know slime. Angels of the Love Affair. Anne Sexton. CP-SextA; SP-SextA

Angel of Grace. Stevie Smith. CP-SmitS

Angel of Mercy's, The. Red Cross. Langston Hughes. CP-HughL; CP-HughL2

Angel of Patience, The. John Greenleaf Whittier. CP-WhitJ

Angel of the Maze, The. James Dickey. CP-DickJ

Angel of Tones / flame of accord. Ritornelli. Geoffrey Hill. CP-HillG

Angel of Words, in vain I have striven with thee. Child Asleep, A. Walter De la Mare. CP-DeLaW

Angel, robed in spotless white, An. Dawn. Paul Laurence Dunbar. CP-DunbP

Angel Surrounded by Paysans. Wallace Stevens. CP-StevW; CP-StevWP

Angel Syphilis in the circle of Signators, The. In Blood's Domaine. Robert Duncan. SP-DuncR *Fr.* Passages.

Angel that rebellion raised, The. Fallen, Fallen. Stevie Smith. CP-SmitS

Angel Visitant, An. Samuel Taylor Coleridge. CP-ColeS

Angela Burdett-Coutts. George Meredith. CP-MerG2

Angeli al capo, al piede. Christina Georgina Rossetti. CP-RosC3

Angelic, lonely, autochthonous, one white. Timeless, Twinned. Robert Penn Warren. CP-WarrR

Angelic Love. George Meredith. CP-MerG1

Angelina. Paul Laurence Dunbar. CP-DunbP

Angells. Robert Herrick. CP-HerrR

Angels, The. Richard Eberhart. CP-EberR

Angels, The. John Updike. CP-UpdiJ

Angels and the souls of the elect, The. Petrarch. CP-Petra, *tr.* by J. G. Nichols

Angels are bright still, though the brightest fell. Lucifer. D. H. Lawrence. CP-LawrD

Angels are gaurds to innocence so pure. Acrostic for Abby Stockton. Annis Boudinot Stockton. CP-StocA

Angels are stooping, The. Cradle Song, A: "Angels are stooping, The." William Butler Yeats. CP-YeatW

Angels at Hamburg, The. Randall Jarrell. CP-JarrR

Angels at the foot, / And Angels at the head. Christina Georgina Rossetti. CP-RosC2

Angels at "Unsubdued." May Swenson. SP-SwenM

Angels coming down the aisles, The. Ascending over Ohio. Lawrence Ferlinghetti. SP-FerlL

Angels gather. / The rush of mad air. Arrival. Maya Angelou. SP-AngeM

Angels guide him now, The. In Memory of a Child. Nicholas Vachel Lindsay. CP-LindV

Angels have somewhere fought and lost, The. Hymn to Nothingness. D. H. Lawrence. CP-LawrD

Angels, in the early morning. Emily Dickinson. CP-DickE

Angels is a-mindin' you, my baby. Jack Frost at Bedtime. Paul Laurence Dunbar. CP-DunbP

Angels of Buena Vista, The. John Greenleaf Whittier. CP-WhitJ

Angels of Fructification, The. Tennessee Williams. CP-WillT

Angels of the Love Affair. Anne Sexton. CP-SextA; SP-SextA

Angels rejoice in, The. Their Rectitude Their Beauty. Donald Davie. CP-DaviDC

Angels' Surprise. Rainer Maria Rilke. CP-RilkFr, *tr.* by A. Poulin, Jr.

Angels' view: perhaps the tips of trees, The. Rainer Maria Rilke. CP-RilkFr, *tr.* by A. Poulin, Jr. *Fr.* Orchards.

Angels wept to see poor Tolly dead, The. Toll of the Roads, The. Stevie Smith. CP-SmitS

Angels wings is white as snow, The [*or* De]. Langston Hughes. CP-HughL; CP HughL1

Angelus. Kathleen Jessie Raine. SP-RainK

Angelus Ad Virginem. Gerard Manley Hopkins. CP-HopkG

Anger. Robert Creeley. CP-CreeR

Anger. Robert Herrick. CP-HerrR

Anger. César Vallejo. CP-MertT, *tr.* by Thomas Merton

Anger against Beasts. Wendell Berry. CP-BerrW

Anger, / as black as a hook. After Auschwitz. Anne Sexton. CP-SextA

Anger can be transformed. New Mexico. William Carlos Williams. CP-WilW2

"Anger? Do you wish to see anger?" I. Backward Dancer. Peter Blue Cloud. SP-BlueP

Anger does this. Changing the Children. Maxine W. Kumin. SP-KumiM

Anger is a fire in the mind. Han-shan. CP-ColdM, *tr.* by Red Pine

Anger reduced Alexander the Great. Petrarch. CP-Petra, *tr.* by J. G. Nichols

Anger shines through me. Just Anger, A. Marge Piercy. SP-PierM

Anger violent distraction. Mosaic. Olga Broumas. SP-BrouO

Anger which breaks a man into children. Anger. César Vallejo. CP-MertT, *tr.* by Thomas Merton

Anger & Wrath my bosom rends. William Blake. CP-BlakW

Anger, yes. But God is God. Being Angry with God. Donald Davie. CP-DaviDC

Anger's Freeing Power. Stevie Smith. CP-SmitS

Angina. James Dickey. CP-DickJ

Anginal Equivalent, An. James Laughlin. CP-LaugJ

Angkor—on top of the terrace. Angkor Wat. Allen Ginsberg. CP-GinsA

Angkor Wat. Allen Ginsberg. CP-GinsA

Anglais Mort à Florence. Wallace Stevens. CP-StevW; CP-StevWP

Angle of a Landscape, The. Emily Dickinson. CP-DickE

Angler's coat and trowsers should be of cloth, The. What You Need to Know for Fishing. Raymond Carver. CP-CarvR

Anglican Lady, An. Donald Davie. CP-DaviDC

Angling. Robert Lowell. SP-LoweR

Angling shadows of itself are what. Poet's Chair. Seamus Heaney. SP-HeanSO

Anglo-Latin Verses. Jonathan Swift. CP-SwifJ

Angola Question Mark. Langston Hughes. CP-HughL; CP-HughL3

Angry and ashamed at. Revulsion. Donald Davie. CP-DaviDC

Angry Angel, like a bird of prey, An. Rebel, The. Charles Baudelaire. CP-BaudC, *tr.* by Walter Martin

Angry, I speak, and pass the hurt to you. Marilyn Hacker. SP-HackM *Fr.* Taking Notice.

Angry if Irene be. Upon Irene. Robert Herrick. CP-HerrR

Angry men and furious machines. Dutch Graves in Bucks County. Wallace Stevens. CP-StevW; CP-StevWP

Angry nettle and the mild, The. Plum Gatherer, The. Edna St. Vincent Millay. CP-MillE

Angry Samson. Robert Graves. CP-GravR

Angst, / ennui & angst. Carmen 38. Catullus. CP-ZukLS *Fr.* Carmina.

Anguilla, Adina. Sea-Chantey, A. Derek Walcott. CP-WalcD

Anguish. Stéphane Mallarmé. CP-MallS, *tr.* by Henry Weinfield

Anguish. Arthur Rimbaud. CP-RimbA, *tr.* by Martin Sorrell

Anguish, The. Edna St. Vincent Millay. CP-MillE

Anguish and revenge made visible, her serpents lifted. Medea. Kathleen Jessie Raine. SP-RainK

Anguish of a naked body is more terrible, The. Prayer to the Lord Ramakrishna, A. James Wright. CP-WrigJ

Anguish sometimes gives a cause. Emily Dickinson. SP-DickE

Angular picture of suffering, An. Opening Poem. Jaroslav Seifert. SP-SeifJ, *tr.* by Ewald Osers

Angutivaun Taina. Rudyard Kipling. CP-KiplR *Fr.* Second Jungle Book, The.

Anima. Hayden Carruth. CP-CarHS

Anima. Richard Eberhart. CP-EberR

Anima Poeta: A Christmas Entry for the Suicide, Mayakovsky. Norman Dubie. CP-DubiN

Anima quodammodo omnia. Translation. Howard Nemerov. CP-NemeH

Anima Sola. Ezra Pound. CP-PoEar

Animal, The. Robert Creeley. CP-CreeR

Animal Acts. Charles Simic. SP-SimiC; SP-SimiCE

Animal Ball, The. Edna St. Vincent Millay. CP-MillE

Animal dwelt, An. Fable for Slumber. Charles Olson. CP-OlsoC

Animal I wanted, The. Kenneth Patchen. CP-PatcK

Animal Inside the Animal, The. Josephine Jacobsen. CP-JacoJ

Animal *is* the act, the keeper says, The. Bear in English. Heather McHugh. SP-McHuH

Animal is the comforter and the betrayer, The. Comforter and the Betrayer,

The.   Tennessee Williams.   CP-WillT

Animal Song.   Heather McHugh.   SP-McHuH

Animal That Drank up Sound, The.   William Stafford.   SP-StafWW

Animal Trainer, The.   John Berryman.   CP-BerrJ

Animal Tranquillity and Decay.   William Wordsworth.   CP-WorW1

Animal, Vegetable and Mineral.   Louise Bogan.   CP-BogaL

Animal willows of November.   Willows of Massachusetts, The.   Denise Levertov.   SP-LeveDP

Animals.   Robinson Jeffers.   CP-JefR3

Animals.   Frank O'Hara.   SP-OharF

Animals.   Miller Williams.   CP-WillM

Animals, The.   Josephine Jacobsen.   CP-JacoJ

Animals, The.   W. S. Merwin.   SP-MerwW

Animals and Birds.   Charles Simic.   SP-SimiCE

Animals Are Passing from Our Lives.   Philip Levine.   SP-LeviP

Animals bring us tranquillity. Cats.   On Not Learning from Animals.   A. K. Ramanujan.   CP-RamaA

Animals from Mountains.   W. S. Merwin.   SP-MerwW

Animals full of light.   Meditation.   William Stafford.   SP-StafW; SP-StafWW

Animals, hanging around in forms, The.   On Visiting Central Park Zoo.   Alan Dugan.   CP-DugaA

Animals in That Country, The.   Margaret Atwood.   SP-AtwM1

Animals own a fur world.   Adults Only   William Stafford.   SP-StafW; SP-StafWW

Animals seem so sad to be themselves.   Topsfield Fair.   John Updike.   CP-UpdiJ

Animals Sick of the Plague, The.   Marianne Craig Moore.   CP-MoorM   *Fr.* Fables of La Fontaine.

Animuccia, vagantucccia, morbiduccia.   Christina Georgina Rossetti.   CP-RosC3

Animula.   T. S. Eliot.   CP-ElioT

Animula.   Robinson Jeffers.   CP-JefR3

Animula.   W. S. Merwin.   SP-MerwW

Animula.   George Oppen.   CP-OppGN

Animula, Vagula, Blandula.   Stevie Smith.   CP-SmitS

Animus Mundi.   Sam Hamill.   SP-HamiS

Anka.   Czeslaw Milosz.   CP-MiloC; CP-MiloCN, *tr. by* Robert Hass

Ann Arbor Song.   Ted Berrigan.   SP-BerrT

Ann Arbor Variations.   Frank O'Hara.   SP-OharF

Ann Burlak.   Muriel Rukeyser.   CP-RukeM

Anna.   Robert Burns.   CP-BurnR
   (Song.) CP-BurnR

Anna Dalassini.   Constantine P. Cavafy.   CP-CavaC, *tr. by* Theoharis Constantine Theoharis

Anna Imroth.   Carl Sandburg.   CP-SandC

Anna Karenina and the Love-sick River.   Kenneth Patchen.   CP-PatcK

Anna Komnina.   Constantine P. Cavafy.   CP-CavaC, *tr. by* Theoharis Constantine Theoharis

Anna, my daughter.   Easter.   Derek Walcott.   CP-WalcD

Anna, thy charms my bosom fire.   Song: "Anna, thy charms my bosom fire."   Robert Burns.   CP-BurnR

Anna Who Was Mad.   Anne Sexton.   CP-SextA

Annabel Lee.   Edgar Allan Poe.   CP-PoeEd

Annabelle.   Yusef Komunyakaa.   CP-KomuY

Annalena.   Czeslaw Milosz.   CP-MiloC; CP-MiloCN, *tr. by* Robert Hass

Annals.   John Ciardi.   CP-CiarJ

Annals of Jack.   Wyatt Prunty.   SP-PrunW

Annals of *Tai Chi*: "Push Hands."   William Stafford.   SP-StafWW

Annals of Volusius, cock at his offal.   Catullus.   *See* Volusian sheets / shit-shotten Annals

Annals say: when the monks of Clonmacnoise, The.   Seamus Heaney.   SP-HeanSO   *Fr.* Squarings.

Anne.   Mary Oliver.   SP-OlivM

Anne, Anne, my hunger.   Festivals of Hunger.   Arthur Rimbaud.   CP-RimbA, *tr. by* Martin Sorrell

Anne Dick 1. 1936.   Robert Lowell.   SP-LoweR

Anne Dick 2. 1936.   Robert Lowell.   SP-LoweR

Anne Spencer's Table.   Langston Hughes.   CP-HughL; CP-HughL1

Anne's Eye is liken'd to the *Sun*.   On the Eyes of Miss A———— H————.   Lord Byron.   CP-Byron

Anniad, The.   Gwendolyn Brooks.   SP-BrooG

Annie.   Guillaume Apollinaire.   SP-MereW, *tr. by* William Meredith

Annie.   Christina Georgina Rossetti.   CP-RosC3

Annie.   Christina Georgina Rossetti.   CP-RosC3

Annie and Rhoda, sisters twain.   Sisters, The.   John Greenleaf Whittier.   CP-WhitJ

Annie died the other day.   E. E. Cummings.   CP-CummE

Annie Hill's Grave.   James Merrill.   SP-MerrJ

Annie, your face is in fashion this year and so are your legs.   To an Ex-Student.   Alan Dugan.   CP-DugaA

Annihilation of Nothing, The.   Thom Gunn.   CP-GunnT

Annisquam / Atlantic / river, sea.   New England March.   Charles Olson.   CP-OlsoC

Anniversaries.   Thomas Kinsella.   CP-KinsT

Anniversaries.   Thomas McGrath.   SP-McGrT

Anniversaries: Claremont Avenue, from 1945.   Carolyn Kizer.   CP-KizeC

Anniversaries of Love.   Yehuda Amichai.   SP-AmicYL, *tr. by* Benjamin Harshav *and* Barbara Harshav

Anniversaries of War.   Yehuda Amichai.   SP-AmicYL, *tr. by* Benjamin Harshav *and* Barbara Harshav

Anniversary.   Rita Dove.   SP-DoveR

Anniversary.   Ted Hughes.   SP-HughTN

Anniversary.   Eugenio Montale.   CP-MontE, *tr. by* Jonathan Galassi

Anniversary.   Howard Nemerov.   CP-NemeH

Anniversary.   Charles Olson.   CP-OlsoC

Anniversary, An.   Wendell Berry.   CP-BerrW

Anniversary, An.   Thomas Hardy.   CP-HardT

Anniversary, The.   Amy Clampitt.   CP-ClamA

Anniversary, The.   William Dickey.   SP-DickW

Anniversary, The.   Ogden Nash.   CP-NashO

Anniversary Elegy on the Death of Mr Stockton the 28th of Feb 1783.   Annis Boudinot Stockton.   CP-StocA

Anniversary of love. A hymn from the forties.   Anniversaries of Love.   Yehuda Amichai.   SP-AmicYL, *tr. by* Benjamin Harshav *and* Barbara Harshav

Anniversary of My Father's Death, The.   Yehuda Amichai.   SP-AmicYL, *tr. by* Benjamin Harshav *and* Barbara Harshav

Anniversary [*or* Anniversarie], The.   John Donne.   CP-DonnJ; MW-DonnJ

Anniversary Poem.   John Greenleaf Whittier.   CP-WhitJ

Anno Domini.   Joseph Brodsky.   CP-BrodJ, *tr. by* Daniel Weissbort

Annos tres vesperi, passer venit, sub tecto.   De Fera Dormita.   Kenneth Rexroth.   CP-RexrK

Annotation for an Epitaph.   Adrienne Rich.   CP-RicAE

Annotations in Verse.   Robert Burns.   CP-BurnR

Announced by all the trumpets of the sky.   Snow-Storm [*or* Snowstorm], The.   Ralph Waldo Emerson.   CP-EmerR

Announcement.   Langston Hughes.   CP-HughL; CP-HughL2

Announcement, The.   Thomas Hardy.   CP-HardT

Annual and Perennial Problem, An.   Mona Van Duyn.   SP-VanDM

Annual Gaiety.   Wallace Stevens.   CP-StevWP

Annual of the Dark Physics, An.   Norman Dubie.   CP-DubiN

Annuals.   Denise Levertov.   SP-LeveDP; SP-LeveDS

Annuities of peat moss.   Easedale Tarn.   Amy Clampitt.   CP-ClamA

Annunciation.   Denise Levertov.   SP-LeveDS

Annunciation.   Primo Levi.   CP-LeviP, *tr. by* Ruth Feldman

Annunciation.   May Sarton.   SP-SartM

Annunciation.   Charles Tomlinson.   SP-TomlC

Annunciation, The.   Thomas Merton.   CP-MertT

Annunciations.   Hart Crane.   CP-CranH

Annunciations.   Geoffrey Hill.   CP-HillG

Annus Memorabilis, 1789.   William Cowper.   CP-CowpW

Annus Mirabilis.   John Dryden.
   "Cheerful soldiers, with new stores supplied, The."   SP-DrydJ

Annus Mirabilis.   Philip Larkin.   CP-LarkP

Ano Prinios.   Amy Clampitt.   CP-ClamA

Anodyne.   Yusef Komunyakaa.   CP-KomuY

Anointed stone, the coruscated crown, The.   Circumstance, The.   Hart Crane.   CP-CranH

Anon with gaping fearlessness they quaff.   My Boots.   Henry David Thoreau.   CP-ThorH

Anong the grackles in a half circle on the grass.   Seven Eleven.   Carl Sandburg.   CP-SandC

Anonymity has a name.   Parable.   Thomas McGrath.   SP-McGrT

Anonymous as cherubs.   Two Voices in a Meadow.   Richard Wilbur.   CP-WilbR

Anonymous captive of the pensive habit.   Jangling Yarn, A.   James Tate.   SP-TateJ

Anonymous Secrets.   Robert Stock.   SP-StocR

Another.   Anne Bradstreet.   CP-BradA

Another.   William Cowper.   CP-CowpW

Another.   Robert Herrick.   CP-HerrR

Another.   Pablo Neruda.   SP-NeruP

Another.   *Unknown.*   CP-BradA

Another ["Art thou some individual of a kind"].   *Unknown.*   CP-CowpW

Another ["At three-score winters' end I died"].   *Unknown.*   CP-CowpW

Another ["Miser, traversing his house, A"].   *Unknown*.   CP-CowpW

Another ["Painter, this likeness is too strong"].   *Unknown*.   CP-CowpW

Another ["Take to thy bosom, gentle earth, a swain"].   *Unknown*.   CP-CowpW

Another [Addressed to a Young Lady].   William Cowper.   *See* To a Young Lady

Another All-Night Party.   Thom Gunn.   CP-GunnT

Another and Another and.   Theodore Weiss.   SP-WeisT

Another and still another.   Nurse's Song, The.   G. K. Chesterton.   CP-ChesG

Another armored animal—scale.   Pangolin, The.   Marianne Craig Moore.   CP-MoorM

Another Ashtray.   Louis Zukofsky.   CP-ZukLS

Another August.   James Merrill.   SP-MerrJ

Another Bed.   Charles Bukowski.   SP-BukC1

Another body inside his body, large, inscrutable.   Silence.   Yannis Ritsos.   SP-RitsY, *tr.* by N. C. Germanacos

Another bull! Another bull!   Exploit in the Bullring.   "Rubén Dario."   SP-DariR, *tr.* by Alberto Acereda *and* Will Derusha

Another Cat Poem: A Cat Is Not a Dancer but a Hunter.   Alan Dugan.   CP-DugaA

Another Cat Poem. To a Cat Person.   Alan Dugan.   CP-DugaA

Another Chain Letter.   John Ashbery.   SP-AshbJ

Another Charme for Stables.   Robert Herrick.   CP-HerrR

Another Cold May.   Louis MacNeice.   CP-MacNL

Another Comedy.   John Ciardi.   CP-CiarJ

Another cove of shale.   On the Marginal Way.   Richard Wilbur.   CP-WilbR

Another curious thing about the English middle classes.   Middle-Class Children.   D. H. Lawrence.   CP-LawrD

Another Dark Lady.   Edwin Arlington Robinson.   CP-RobiE

Another dawn, leaden.   Words.   Philip Levine.   SP-LeviP

Another Day. A Game of Toys. Paul, Telling the Game.   Muriel Rukeyser.   CP-RukeM

Another Day (And then the cow).   Muriel Rukeyser.   CP-RukeM

Another Day (Child among his powers).   Muriel Rukeyser.   CP-RukeM

Another Day (Day Lilies, Yellow Daisies).   Muriel Rukeyser.   CP-RukeM

Another day, deep in the stacks.   Under Soracte.   Kenneth Rexroth.   CP-RexrK

Another Day. For a Moment Slipping Back, Again the Unreal King.   Muriel Rukeyser.   CP-RukeM

Another day gone, and still.   Little Vesper, A.   Jane Cooper.   CP-CoopJ

Another Day (I will now sing).   Muriel Rukeyser.   CP-RukeM

Another Day. In a Field of Peace the Child, Playing. The Child Preparing for Daytime Sleep.   Muriel Rukeyser.   CP-RukeM

Another Day (Miss Lorence).   Muriel Rukeyser.   CP-RukeM

Another Day. Paul in the Mountains of Fantasy. Paul Tells His Adventure.   Muriel Rukeyser.   CP-RukeM

Another Day. The Children Are All Eating.   Muriel Rukeyser.   CP-RukeM

Another Day (You can't come).   Muriel Rukeyser.   CP-RukeM

Another Day (You sit there).   Muriel Rukeyser.   CP-RukeM

Another Descent.   Wendell Berry.   CP-BerrW

Another Dimension.   Robert Penn Warren.   CP-WarrR

Another Dog's Death.   John Updike.   CP-UpdiJ

Another Dollar.   C. K. Williams.   CP-WillC

Another Duffer.   Sam Hamill.   SP-HamiS

Another Early Morning Exercise.   Kenneth Rexroth.   CP-RexrK

Another Elegy.   Margaret Atwood.   SP-AtwM2

Another [Epigram].   Alexander Pope.   CP-PopeA

Another [Epigram on Said Occasion].   Robert Burns.   CP-BurnR

Another Epilogue: "Two houses joined, two poets to a play?"   Nathaniel Lee.   CP-DryJ2   *Fr.* Duke of Guise, The.

Another [Epitaph].   William Blake.   *See* Epitaph, An: "I was buried near this dyke [*or* Dike]"

Another [Epitaph]: "Here lies John Trot, the Friend of all mankind."   William Blake.   CP-BlakW

Another Epitaph on an Army of Mercenaries.   Hugh MacDiarmid.   SP-MacDH

Another [Epitaph on the Lady Mary Villiers].   Thomas Carew.   CP-CareT

Another evening in another park.   Owl's Clover.   Wallace Stevens.   CP-StevWP

Another evening we sprawled about discussing.   Charles on Fire.   James Merrill.   SP-MerrJ

Another Fan; of Mademoiselle Mallarmé.   Stéphane Mallarmé.   CP-MallS, *tr.* by Henry Weinfield

Another four I've left yet to bring on.   Four Seasons of the Year, The.   Anne Bradstreet.   CP-BradA

Another Fragment to Music.   Percy Bysshe Shelley.   CP-ShelP

Another front, sleet, snow, and the feeder.   Cold.   Wyatt Prunty.   SP-PrunW

Another Grace for a Child.   Robert Herrick.   *See* Grace for a Child

Another hand is beckoning us.   Gone.   John Greenleaf Whittier.   CP-WhitJ

Another. In Defense of Their Inconstancy [*or* Inconstancie]. A Song.   Ben Jonson.   CP-JonsB

Another Irish landlord gone to grass.   Fair Division, A.   Ambrose Bierce.   SP-BierA

Another kind of Quantity.   Of Quantity Which Depends upon the Authority of the Poets.   Thomas Sheridan.   CP-SherT

Another land, another age, another self.   Covered Bridge.   Robert Penn Warren.   CP-WarrR

Another Leonora captured the poet Torquato.   To the Same ["Another Leonora captured the poet Torquato"].   John Milton.   CP-MiltJ

Another Leonora once inspir'd.   John Milton.   *See* Another Leonora captured the poet Torquato

Another Life.   Derek Walcott.   CP-WalcD

Another Man's Wife.   Ezra Pound.   CP-PoEar

Another misty one. These opaline.   Last Mornings in California.   James Merrill.   SP-MerrJ

Another Monday.   Primo Levi.   CP-LeviP, *tr.* by Ruth Feldman *and* Brian Swann

Another Moon Effect.   Eugenio Montale.   CP-MontE, *tr.* by Jonathan Galassi

Another Mystery.   Raymond Carver.   CP-CarvR

Another New-Yeeres Gift, or Song for the Circumcision.   Robert Herrick.   CP-HerrR

Another Night in the Ruins.   Galway Kinnell.   SP-KinnGN

Another novel, and the prostitute.   James Vincent Cunningham.   CP-CunnJ

Another of God.   Robert Herrick.   CP-HerrR

Another of the Same.   Sir Walter Ralegh.   CP-RaleW   *Fr.* Commendatory Verses to Edmund Spenser's Fairy Queen.

Another of the Same Nature, Made Since.   *Unknown*.   CP-MarlC

Another Old Bolshevik.   Donald Davie.   CP-DaviDC

Another old friend, long afterward.   Views of Myself.   John Berryman.   CP-BerrJ

Another Old Woman.   William Carlos Williams.   CP-WilW2

Another on Her.   Robert Herrick.   CP-HerrR

Another on Love.   Robert Herrick.   CP-HerrR

Another on [Mr. Herrys].   Richard Crashaw.   CP-CrasR

Another [On the Duke of Buckingham].   Thomas Carew.   CP-CareT

Another on the Same.   Robert Herrick.   CP-HerrR

Another on the Same.   John Milton.   CP-MiltJ

Another One.   Pablo Neruda.   SP-NeruP

Another One.   Kenneth Rexroth.   CP-RexrK

Another Ophelia.   D. H. Lawrence.   CP-LawrD

Another Picture of Dan.   Thomas Sheridan.   CP-SherT

Another Reason Why I Don't Keep a Gun in the House.   Billy Collins.   SP-CollB

Another Reply by the Dean.   Jonathan Swift.   CP-SwifJ

Another ribald tale of the good times at Madame Lipsky's.   Pleasures of Peace, The.   Kenneth Koch.   SP-KochK

Another Ride from Ghent to Aix.   James Whitcomb Riley.   CP-RileJ

Another Season.   Thomas McGrath.   SP-McGrT

Another season, proposing a name and a distant resolution.   Ivory Tower, The.   John Ashbery.   SP-AshbJ

Another September.   Thomas Kinsella.   CP-KinsT

Another Simple Ballat.   Lord Byron.   CP-Byron

Another Snowstorm.   Marya Alexandrovna Zaturenska.   SP-ZatuM

Another Song of a Fool.   William Butler Yeats.   CP-YeatW

Another Spring.   Denise Levertov.   SP-LeveDP

Another Spring.   Kenneth Rexroth.   CP-RexrK

Another Spring.   Christina Georgina Rossetti.   CP-RosC1

Another spring dries in the wild-oat grasses.   Celebration.   Helen Pinkerton.   CP-PinkH

Another Spring Uncovered.   May Swenson.   SP-SwenM

Another story still: a porch with trees.   Peterborough.   Marilyn Hacker.   SP-HackM

Another strom, another blizzard.   Third Snowfall.   Marilyn Hacker.   SP-HackM

Another summer! Our Independence.   Fourth of July in Maine.   Robert Lowell.   SP-LoweR

Another sunlight might make another world.   As at a Theatre.   Wallace Stevens.   CP-StevWP

Another Time.   W. H. Auden.   CP-AudeW

Another to Bring in the Witch.   Robert Herrick.   CP-HerrR

Another, to God.   Robert Herrick.   CP-HerrR

Another to Him.   Ben Jonson.   CP-JonsB

Another [To His Booke].   Robert Herrick.   *See* To His Book[e]

Another [To His Booke].   Martial.

Another, to His Saviour.   Robert Herrick.   CP-HerrR

Another to Mrs. Anne Bradstreet, Author of this Poem.   *Unknown*.   CP-BradA

Another to Neptune.   Robert Herrick.   CP-HerrR

Another to the Maids.   Robert Herrick.   CP-HerrR

Another Translation of the Same Ode. Horace. *See* Odes
Another type that England has produced. Little-Boy Brilliant. D. H. Lawrence. CP-LawrD
Another Upon Her. Robert Herrick. CP-HerrR
Another upon Her Weeping. Robert Herrick. CP-HerrR
Another Version. William Cowper. CP-CowpW
Another Version of the Same. Percy Bysshe Shelley. CP-ShelP
Another Voice. Richard Wilbur. CP-WilbR
Another Way. Ambrose Bierce. SP-BierA
Another Way of Love. Robert Browning. CP-BroR1
Another Weeping Woman. Wallace Stevens. CP-StevW; CP-StevWP
Another Year. William Carlos Williams. CP-WilW2
Another year! another deadly blow! November, 1806. William Wordsworth. CP-WorW1; MW-WorW
Another Year Come. W. S. Merwin. SP-MerwW
Another year of joy & grief. 1884. Christina Georgina Rossetti. CP-RosC3
Ansel Adams Card, The. Arthur Sze. SP-SzeA
Anselmo. James Whitcomb Riley. CP-RileJ
Anseo. Paul Muldoon. CP-MuldP
Anson Dart pierced the forest. Pioneers. Lorine Niedecker. CP-NiedL
Answer, George Rochfort. CP-SherT
Answer, An. Robert Frost. CP-FrosR
Answer, An. Christina Georgina Rossetti. CP-RosC3
Answer, An. Jonathan Swift. *See* Answer to a Scandalous Poem, An
Answer, The. Robert Creeley. CP-CreeR
Answer, The. George Herbert. CP-HerbG
Answer, The. Robinson Jeffers. CP-JefR2
Answer, The. Rudyard Kipling. CP-KiplR
Answer, The. Carl Sandburg. CP-SandC
Answer, The. John Greenleaf Whittier. CP-WhitJ
Answer, The. Sir Thomas Wyatt. CP-WyatT
Answer, The [By the Gentleman of the Navy]. *Unknown*. CP-WheaP
Answer, The [To the Guidwife of Wauchope-House]. Robert Burns. CP-BurnR
Answer: how old / is the wind, shakes the trees & moves with the movement of. Hart Crane 2. Robert Creeley. CP-CreeR
Answer July. Emily Dickinson. CP-DickE
Answer me when I call / God of my righteousness. Bible, *O.T.* *See* Hear me when I call, O God of my righteousness
Answer that ye made to me, my dear, The [*or* Th']. Sir Thomas Wyatt. CP-WyatT
Answer to a Beautiful Poem, Entitled "The Common Lot" Lord Byron. CP-Byron
Answer to a Child's Question. Samuel Taylor Coleridge. CP-ColeS; MW-ColeS
Answer to a Scandalous Poem, An. Jonathan Swift. CP-SwifJ (Answer, An.) CP-SwifJ
Answer to an Invitation. Robert Burns. CP-BurnR
Answer to Delany's Riddle, The. Jonathan Swift. CP-SwifJ
Answer to Dr. Delany, The. Jonathan Swift. CP-SwifJ
Answer to Dr. Delany's Fable of the Pheasant and the Lark, An. Jonathan Swift. CP-SwifJ
Answer to "Paulus," The. Jonathan Swift. CP-SwifJ
Answer to Prayer. Robert Penn Warren. CP-WarrR
Answer to ——'s Professions of Affection. Lord Byron. CP-Byron
Answer to Some Elegant Verses. Lord Byron. CP-Byron
Answer to Some Verses Made in His Praise, An. Sir John Suckling. CP-SuckJ
Answer to Stanzas Addressed to Lady Hesketh. William Cowper. CP-CowpW
Answer to the Ballyspellin Ballad, An. Jonathan Swift. CP-SwifJ
Answer to the Christmas-Box, An. *Unknown, sometimes at. to* Thomas Sheridan. CP-SherT
Answer to the Following Question of Mrs. Howe. Alexander Pope. CP-PopeA
Answer to the Foregoing, Addressed to Miss———. Lord Byron. CP-Byron
Answer to the Foregoing—Extempore [Clarinda]. Robert Burns. CP-BurnR
Answer to the Kingis Flyting, The. Sir David Lyndsay. SP-LyndD
Answer to the Parson, An. William Blake. CP-BlakW
Answer to the *Rebus*, by the Author of These Poems, An. Phillis Wheatley. CP-WheaP
Answer to the Rilke Question. Alan Dugan. CP-DugaA
Answer to Vanessa's Rebus, The. Jonathan Swift. CP-SwifJ
Answer to Voznesensky and Evtushenko. Frank O'Hara. SP-OharF
Answered when you appeared at the gate. Not always, or even. It Was Being. Kenneth Patchen. CP-PatcK
Answering a letter to somebody in Alaska. Love. Charles Bukowski. SP-BukC3

Answers. Mary Oliver. SP-OlivM
Ant, The. Samuel Johnson. *See* Paraphrase
Ant, The. Ogden Nash. CP-NashO
Ant! / lugging half an ounce, an. Grace Paley. CP-PalGC
Ant Mansion, The. Robert Bly. SP-BlyR
Ant on the tablecloth, An. Departmental. Robert Frost. CP-FrosR
Ant-sting's prickly at first, An. Dante Gabriel Rossetti. CW-RossD
Antaeus. Seamus Heaney. SP-HeanSO
Antaeus. Robert Stock. SP-StocR
Antaeus: A Fragment. Wilfred Owen. CP-OwenW
Antarctica. Derek Mahon. CP-MahoD
Antarctica is no place for the eye. Preferences. Heather McHugh. SP-McHuH
Antares. Arthur Sze. SP-SzeA
Ante-Bellum Sermon, An. Paul Laurence Dunbar. CP-DunbP
Ante Mortem. Robinson Jeffers. CP-JefR1
Ante mortem qui defletus. Sit Mihi Terra Levis. Robert Graves. CP-GravR
Antecedents. Charles Tomlinson. CP-TomlC
    Something: a Direction. SP-TomlC
Antennae of the race. Somerset. Donald Davie. CP-DaviDC
Antéros. Gérard de Nerval. CP-WilbR
Anthea bade me tic [*or* tye] her sho[o]e. Sho[o]e Tying, The. Robert Herrick. CP-HerrR
Anthea I am going hence. To Anthea. Robert Herrick. CP-HerrR
Anthea laught, and fearing lest excess[e]. Anthea's Retractation. Robert Herrick. CP-HerrR
Anthea, your shy flanks in starlight. Nuda Natens. John Updike. CP-UpdiJ
Anthea's Retractation. Robert Herrick. CP-HerrR
Anthem: "Let us praise our Maker, with true passion extol Him." W. H. Auden. CP-AudeW
Anthem: "Milton Avery Altmar." William Corbett. SP-CorbW
Anthem: "Praised be the climate." Joseph Brodsky. CP-BrodJ
Anthem for Doomed Youth. Wilfred Owen. CP-OwenW
Anthem for St. Cecilia's Day. W. H. Auden. CP-AudeW
Anthem for the Children of Christ's Hospital. Samuel Taylor Coleridge. CP-ColeS
Anthony. Charles Bukowski. SP-BukC2
Anthropos apteros for days. Maze, The. W. H. Auden. CP-AudeW
Anti-aircraft seen from a certain distance. Dam Neck, Virginia. Richard Eberhart. CP-EberR
Anti-Father. Rita Dove. SP-DoveR
Anti-Love Poem, An. James Laughlin. CP-LaugJ
Anti-master-man, floribund ascetic, an. Landscape with Boat. Wallace Stevens. SP-StevW; CP-StevWP
Anti-Shenandoah: Two Skits and a Chorus. Joseph Brodsky. CP-BrodJ
Anti-Short Story. Rae Armantrout. SP-ArmaA
Anti-Thelyphthora. William Cowper. CP-CowpW
Anti-Vietnam War Peace Mobilization. Allen Ginsberg. CP-GinsA
Antichrist, playing his lissome flute and merry. Armageddon. John Crowe Ransom. SP-RansJ
Anticipation. Emily Jane Brontë. CP-BronE
Anticipation. October, 1803. William Wordsworth. CP-WorW1; MW-WorW
Anticipation of Love. Jorge Luis Borges. SP-BorgJ, *tr. by* Robert Fitzgerald
Antigone. Sophocles.
    Chorus from *Antigone*, A. SP-LoguC
    From the 'Antigone.' CP-YeatW
    "Happy are those who have never tasted evil." CP-SpenS
Antigone. George Meredith. CP-MerG1
Antigone. Howard Nemerov. CP-NemeH
Antigone Riddle, The. Derek Mahon. CP-MahoD
Antigua. John Updike. CP-UpdiJ
Antihero, The. Ai. SP-Ai
Antinomy: Time and Identity. Robert Penn Warren. CP-WarrR
Antinoüs: The Diaries. Adrienne Rich. CP-RicAE; SP-RicA1; SP-RicA2
Antioch boasts of its splendid buildings. Greek from Ancient Times. Constantine P. Cavafy. CP-CavaC, *tr. by* Theoharis Constantine Theoharis
Antipas. Christina Georgina Rossetti. CP-RosC2
Antipater of Sidon. "H. D." CP-DoolH
Antiphilus. James Laughlin. CP-LaugJ
Antiphon: "Let all the world in ev'ry corner sing / *My God and King*." George Herbert. CP-HerbG
Antiphon (2): "Praised be the God of love." George Herbert. CP-HerbG
Antiphon, The: "And then once more." Denise Levertov. SP-LeveDS
Antiphonal. Amy Clampitt. CP-ClamA
Antipoem 1. Thomas Merton. CP-MertT

Antipoetic is the thing. Entity, The. William Carlos Williams. CP-WilW1

Antipolis. James Dickey. CP-DickJ

Antiquary. John Donne. CP-DonnJ; MW-DonnJ

Antiquated Grace, An. Emily Dickinson. CP-DickE

Antiquated Tree, An. Emily Dickinson. CP-DickE

Antique. George Oppen. CP-OppGN

Antique. Arthur Rimbaud. CP-RimbA, *tr. by* Martin Sorrell

Antique Father. Carolyn Kizer. `CP-KizeC

Antique Harvesters. John Crowe Ransom. SP-RansJ

Antique story comes to me, An. Die Lorelei. Stevie Smith. CP-SmitS

Antiquity in blindness praised the son of Iapetus. On the Inventor of Gunpowder. John Milton. CP-MiltJ

Antitheses. John Berryman. CP-BerrJ

Antiworlds. Andrey Andreievich Voznesensky. CP-WilbR

Anton Bruckner. Adam Zagajewski. SP-ZagaA, *tr. by* Renata Gorczynski, Benjamin Ivry *and* C. K. Williams

Antonio Torres Heredia. Taking of Little Tony Camborio on the Seville Highway, The. Federico García Lorca. CP-GarcF, *tr. by* Will Kirkland

Antorcha Y Corona, 1968. Robert Graves. CP-GravR

Antrim. Robinson Jeffers. CP-JefR2

Ants. Robert Bly. SP-BlyR

Ants, The. Charles Bukowski. SP-BukC2

Ants crawl upon paper flowers with all the insect color. Soirée. Charles Bukowski. SP-BukC2

Ants of Argos, The. Rita Dove. SP-DoveR

Ants, or wise bees, or a gang of wolves. Faith. Robinson Jeffers. CP-JefR3

Ants, when they meet each other. Things I Learned Last Week. William Stafford. SP-StafW; SP-StafWW

Anubis, jackal-headed god. Average Egyptian Faces Death, The. John Updike. CP-UpdiJ

Anubis will stare. Charles Olson. CP-OlsoC

Anvil, The. Rudyard Kipling. CP-KiplR

Anxia dum natura nimis tibi, Mellea, formam. In Melleam. Thomas Campion. CP-CampT

Anxiety. A. R. Ammons. CP-AmmoA

Anxiety. Frank O'Hara. SP-OharF

Anxiety. A. K. Ramanujan. CP-RamaA

Anxiety I Felt in Guanajuato, The. Richard Eberhart. CP-EberR

Anxiety thou canker of the heart. Soliliguy in a Sleepless Night. Annis Boudinot Stockton. CP-StocA

Anxious milk-blood in the veins of the earth, The. Annunciations. Hart Crane. CP-CranH

Anxious Parent, I guess you have just never been around. "My Child Is Phlegmatic . . ."—Anxious Parent. Ogden Nash. CP-NashO

Anxious to publicise and pay our dues. Last Will and Testament. Philip Larkin. CP-LarkP

Anxious View of a Tree. Hayden Carruth. CP-CarHS

Any cassandra with some e s p. One More after Reading Homer. A. K. Ramanujan. CP-RamaA

Any clear thing that blinds us with surprise. Fishnet. Robert Lowell. SP-LoweR

Any Cow's Horn Can Do It. A. K. Ramanujan. CP-RamaA

Any day now he's going. Figlio Mio. James Laughlin. CP-LaugJ

Any entangling however. Clearing the Dark Symbiosis. A. R. Ammons. CP-AmmoA

Any fool can make a rule. Henry David Thoreau. CP-ThorH

Any Honest Housewife. Robert Graves. CP-GravR

Any hound a porcupine nudges. Porcupine, The. Ogden Nash. CP-NashO

Any Human to Another. Countee Cullen. CP-CullC

Any Husband to Any Wife. Adrienne Rich. CP-RicAE

Any lady desiring fame and honour. Petrarch. CP-Petra, *tr. by* J. G. Nichols

Any little mirror holds. For a Good Man. Heather McHugh. SP-McHuH

Any Little Old Song. Thomas Hardy. CP-HardT

Any man—God, if he had the money. Praise of Good Poets in a Bad Age, A. John Ciardi. CP-CiarJ

Any man is wonderful. E. E. Cummings. CP-CummE

Any Millenniums Today, Lady? Ogden Nash. CP-NashO

Any Object before the Eye. May Swenson. SP-SwenM

Any plant that makes its own spring. Spring Song for *Symplocarpus Fœtida* and Me. Alan Dugan. CP-DugaA

Any point in that wood. Plantation, The. Seamus Heaney. SP-HeanSO

Any Porch. Dorothy Parker. CP-ParkD

Any Size We Please. Robert Frost. CP-FrosR

Any Time. William Stafford. SP-StafW; SP-StafWW

Any Way But Back. George Oppen. CP-OppGN

Any Way for Wealth. Robert Herrick. CP-HerrR

Any way you can work now, brain. Young Man, a Writer—in His 24th Year, A. Constantine P. Cavafy. CP-CavaC, *tr. by* Theoharis Constantine Theoharis

Any way you walk. You Have Pissed Your Life. William Carlos Williams. CP-WilW1

Any Wife to Any Husband. Robert Browning. CP-BroR1

Any woman who says to me. Can't Be Borne. D. H. Lawrence. CP-LawrD

Anybody / Better than. Desert. Langston Hughes. CP-HughL; CP-HughL2

Anybody Else Hate Nicknames? Ogden Nash. CP-NashO

Anybody for Money? or, Just Bring Your Own Basket. Ogden Nash. CP-NashO

Anyhow, once full Dervish, youngsters came. Shah Abbas. Robert Browning. CP-BroR2

Anyone Lived in a Pretty How Town. E. E. Cummings. CP-CummE; SP-CummE

Anyone watching you in the water would think: 'A siren!'. Siren, A. Umberto Saba. CP-MahoD, *tr. by* Derek Mahon

Anyone with quiet pace who. Walking West. William Stafford. SP-StafWW

Anyone would love to paint from memory. On the Ramblas A Tree A Girl. Grace Paley. CP-PalGC

Anything Is Beautiful If You Say It Is. Wallace Stevens. CP-StevW; SP-StevWP

Anything is possible. Summer Poem. Hans Magnus Enzensberger. SP-EnzeH, *tr. by* Michael Hamburger

Anything to have done! Solomon's Mines. Geoffrey Hill. CP-HillG

Anywhere. Robert Creeley. CP-CreeR

Anywhere and Everywhere People. Carl Sandburg. CP-SandC

AP: Who would prefer a brothel to a school? Preguntas sin respuestas for Nicanor Parra. James Laughlin. CP-LaugJ

Apache Plume. Arthur Sze. SP-SzeA

Apache word for love twists, The. In the Night Desert. William Stafford. SP-StafW; SP-StafWW

Apart. James Whitcomb Riley. CP-RileJ

Apart from my sisters, estranged. Cinderella. Olga Broumas. SP-BrouO

Apartment Cats. Thom Gunn. CP-GunnT

Apartment for Scholars. Adam Zagajewski. SP-ZagaA, *tr. by* Clare Cavanagh

Apartment for visiting scholars holds, The. Apartment for Scholars. Adam Zagajewski. SP-ZagaA, *tr. by* Clare Cavanagh

Apartment with a View, An. John Ciardi. CP-CiarJ

Apathy and Enthusiasm. Herman Melville. SP-MelvH

Ape Experiment Room. Philip Larkin. CP-LarkP

Ape-handed, too bungle-knuckled. Done for the Doing. John Ciardi. CP-CiarJ

Apelles hearing that his boy. Tears of a Painter, The. Vincent Bourne. CP-CowpW

Apeneck Sweeney spreads his knees. Sweeney among the Nightingales. T. S. Eliot. CP-ElioT; SP-ElioT

Apes. Adam Zagajewski. SP-ZagaA, *tr. by* Renata Gorczynski, Benjamin Ivry *and* C. K. Williams

Apes, may I speak to you a moment? Is Wisdom a Lot of Language? Carl Sandburg. CP-SandC

Apes, yawn and adore their fleas in the sun, The. Jaguar, The. Ted Hughes. SP-HughTN

Apex, triangle . . . a dead child. Palimpsest. Yusef Komunyakaa. CP-KomuY

Aphrodisiac, The. Arthur Sze. SP-SzeA

Aphrodite. Olga Broumas. SP-BrouO

Aphrodite. Louise Glück. SP-GlucL

Aphrodite, foam-born, blown. After Botticelli's *Birth of Venus*. Gregory Orr. SP-OrrG

Aphrodite, / my Cape Town lady. To Like, to Love. Anne Sexton. CP-SextA

Aphrodite phoned. Could I come over? Interruption, An. John Ciardi. CP-CiarJ

Apocalypse ("First of the seals was opened; the gold of the dawn unsealed, The"). G. K. Chesterton. CP-ChesG

Apocalypse ("In seas and stones and painful lore of weeds"). G. K. Chesterton. CP-ChesG

Apocalypse Now. Robert Creeley. SP-CreeR

Apocalypse. Umbrian Master, about 1490. Hans Magnus Enzensberger. SP-EnzeH

Apocrypha. David Ignatow. SP-IgnaD

Apocrypha of Jacques Derrida, The. Norman Dubie. CP-DubiN

Apollo. James Dickey. CP-DickJ

Apollo. Alan Dugan. CP-DugaA

Apollo. Jonathan Swift. CP-SwifJ

Apollo and Daphne. Christopher Smart. SP-SmarC

Apollo and the Fates. Robert Browning. CP-BroR2

Apollo, god of light and wit. Apollo. Jonathan Swift. CP-SwifJ

Apollo Great. Sir Philip Sidney. SP-SidnP *Fr.* Arcadia.

Apollo great, whose beams the greater world do light. Apollo Great. Sir Philip Sidney. SP-SidnP *Fr.* Arcadia.

Apollo—if you nourish still desires. Petrarch. CP-Petra, *tr.* by J. G. Nichols

Apollo of the Physiologists. Robert Graves. CP-GravR

Apollo Outwitted. Jonathan Swift. CP-SwifJ

Apollo sings, his harpe resounds; give roome. Upon Master Fletchers Incomparable Playes. Robert Herrick. CP-HerrR

Apollo to the Dean. Jonathan Swift. CP-SwifJ

Apollo to the Graces. John Keats. CP-KeatJ

Apollonios of Tyana in Rhodes. Constantine P. Cavafy. CP-CavaC, *tr.* by Theoharis Constantine Theoharis

Apollonios was speaking. Apollonios of Tyana in Rhodes. Constantine P. Cavafy. CP-CavaC, *tr.* by Theoharis Constantine Theoharis

Apollo's Edict. Jonathan Swift. CP-SwifJ

Apollo's wrath to man the dreadful spring. Niobe in Distress for Her Children Slain by Apollo, from *Ovid's* Metamorphoses, Book 6. And from a View of the Painting of Mr. *Richard Wilson.* Phillis Wheatley. CP-WheaP

Apologia. Oscar Wilde. CP-WildO

Apologia for Grief. Robert Penn Warren. CP-WarrR

Apologia Pro Poemate Meo. Wilfred Owen. CP-OwenW

Apologia Pro Vita Sua. Charles Wright. SP-WrigCN

Apologia pro Vita Sua. A. R. Ammons. CP-AmmoA

Apologia pro Vita Sua. Samuel Taylor Coleridge. CP-ColeS

Apologies. Marge Piercy. SP-PierM

Apologies. Chuang Tzu. CP-MertT

Apologies to Harvard. John Updike. CP-UpdiJ

Apology ("Alas, this Rembrandtesque design"). G. K. Chesterton. CP-ChesG

Apology ("Forgive us you, whose pageant flames"). G. K. Chesterton. CP-ChesG

Apology. Adrienne Rich. CP-RicAE

Apology. Richard Wilbur. CP-WilbR

Apology. William Carlos Williams. CP-WilW1

Apology. William Wordsworth. CP-WorW2

Apology, An. G. K. Chesterton. CP-ChesG

Apology, An. William Cowper. CP-CowpW

Apology, The. Robert Creeley. CP-CreeR

Apology, The. Ralph Waldo Emerson. CP-EmerR

Apology for a Letter Unposted, An. G. K. Chesterton. CP-ChesG

Apology for a Lost Classicism, An. John Ciardi. CP-CiarJ

Apology for Bad Dreams. Robinson Jeffers. CP-JefR1

Apology for Clowns, An. G. K. Chesterton. CP-ChesG

Apology for Her. Emily Dickinson. CP-DickE

Apology for Not Invoking the Muse, An. John Ciardi. CP-CiarJ

Apology for the Bottle Volcanic, An. Nicholas Vachel Lindsay. CP-LindV

Apology for the Revival of Christian Architecture in England, An. Geoffrey Hill. CP-HillG

Apology for Using the Word "Heart" in Too Many Poems, An. Hayden Carruth. CP-CarHS

Apology of Bottom the Weaver, The. G. K. Chesterton. CP-ChesG

Apology [*or* Apologie] for the Foregoing Hymn[e], An. Richard Crashaw. CP-CrasR

Apology to the Lady Carteret, An. Jonathan Swift. CP-SwifJ

Apology (to the Muse). Alan Dugan. CP-DugaA

Apon the Midsummer Ewin [*or* evin], mirriest of nichtis. Tretis [*or* Book] of the Tua Mariit Wemen [*or* Two Married Women] and the Wedo[w] [*or* Widow], The. William Dunbar. CP-DunbW

Apostate, The. Carolyn Kizer. CP-KizeC *Fr.* Heine Journal, A.

Apostle, The. Jones Very. CP-VeryJ

Apostle of Hope. Thomas Kinsella. CP-KinsT

Apostles, The. Jones Very. CP-VeryJ

Apostroph. Walt Whitman. CP-WhitW

Apostrophe to a Buddhist Monk. D. H. Lawrence. CP-LawrD

Apostrophe to a Dead Friend. Maxine W. Kumin. SP-KumiM

Apostrophe to an Old Psalm Tune. Thomas Hardy. CP-HardT

Apostrophe to Man. Edna St. Vincent Millay. CP-MillE

Apostrophe to the Land. Countee Cullen. CP-CullC

Apostrophe to Vincentine, The. Wallace Stevens. CP-StevW; CP-StevWP

Apothecary. Federico García Lorca. CP-GarcF, *tr.* by Jerome Rothenberg *Fr.* Secrets.

Apotheosis of Tins, The. Derek Mahon. CP-MahoD

Apotropaic Decision, An. James Laughlin. CP-LaugJ

Appalachian Book of the Dead, The. Charles Wright. SP-WrigCN

Appalachian Book of the Dead 2, The. Charles Wright. SP-WrigCN

Appalachian Book of the Dead 3, The. Charles Wright. SP-WrigCN

Appalachian Book of the Dead 4, The. Charles Wright. SP-WrigCN

Appalachian Book of the Dead 5, The. Charles Wright. SP-WrigCN

Appalachian Book of the Dead 6, The. Charles Wright. SP-WrigCN

Appalled heart at goosegray dawn, The. Mr. Tantripp's Day. Josephine Jacobsen. CP-JacoJ

Apparent Failure. Robert Browning. CP-BroR1; SP-BroR

Apparently with no surprise. Emily Dickinson. CP-DickE

Apparition. Stéphane Mallarmé. CP-MallS, *tr.* by Henry Weinfield

Apparition. W. S. Merwin. SP-MerwW

Apparition. Tennessee Williams. CP-WillT

Apparition, An. Donald Davie. CP-DaviDC

Apparition, The. John Berryman. CP-BerrJ

Apparition, The. John Donne. CP-DonnJ; MW-DonnJ

Apparition, The. Herman Melville. SP-MelvH

Apparition, The. Theodore Roethke. CP-RoetT

Apparition, The. Charles Tomlinson. CP-TomlC

Apparition, The. William Carlos Williams. CP-WilW2

Apparition of Splendor. Marianne Craig Moore. CP-MoorM

Apparition of these faces in the crowd, The. In a Station of the Metro. Ezra Pound. SP-PounE

Apparition, The—A Retrospect. Herman Melville. SP-MelvH

Apparitions. W. S. Merwin. SP-MerwWF

Apparitions. Walt Whitman. CP-WhitW

Apparitions, The. William Butler Yeats. CP-YeatW

Apparuit. Ezra Pound. CP-PoEar; SP-PounE

Appeal. Jones Very. CP-VeryJ

Appeal. William Carlos Williams. CP-WilW1

Appeal, An. Czeslaw Milosz. CP-MiloC; CP-MiloCN, *tr.* by Robert Hass

Appeal, The. Rudyard Kipling. CP-KiplR

Appeal, The. D. H. Lawrence. CP-LawrD

Appeal for Death, An. Ivor Gurney. SP-GurnI

Appeal of the Peers, The. G. K. Chesterton. CP-ChesG

Appeal to America on Behalf of the Belgian Destitute, An. Thomas Hardy. CP-HardT

Appear far up the cove at low tide. Clam Diggers and Diggers of Sea Worms, The. Richard Eberhart. CP-EberR

Appearance. Charles Tomlinson. CP-TomlC

Appearance, An. Sylvia Plath. CP-PlatS

Appearances. Robert Browning. CP-BroR2

Appearances. Hans Magnus Enzensberger. SP-EnzeH, *tr.* by Michael Hamburger

Appearing unannounced, the moon. Nocturne: "Appearing unannounced, the moon." W. H. Auden. CP-AudeW

Appeasement of Demeter, The. George Meredith. CP-MerG1

Appendicitis is his worst. Hypochondriac Logic. Donald Davie. CP-DaviDC

Appendix to the Anniad. Gwendolyn Brooks. SP-BrooG

Appendix to the "Religion": A Light. Pier Paolo Pasolini. SP-PasoP, *tr.* by Norman MacAfee *and* Luciano Martinengo

Appetite. Maxine W. Kumin. SP-KumiM

Appetite. Stevie Smith. CP-SmitS

Appian Way, The. Kenneth Patchen. CP-PatcK

Applause. Charles Olson. CP-OlsoC

Applause is a shower. Increment. A. R. Ammons. CP-AmmoA

Applaws) / "fell / ow." E. E. Cummings. CP-CummE

Apple, The. Shmuel HaNagid. SP-HaNaS, *tr.* by Peter Cole

Apple Blossom. Louis MacNeice. CP-MacNL

Apple blossom and / squirrel. What We Think We Know. Thomas McGrath. SP-McGrT

Apple blossoms falling o'er thee. Come and Kiss Me Sweet and Twenty. Paul Laurence Dunbar. CP-DunbP

Apple Buds. Richard Eberhart. CP-EberR

Apple Core. Clarence Major. SP-MajoC

Apple Dumps. Ted Hughes. SP-HughTN

Apple Garths of Avalon, The. Kenneth Rexroth. CP-RexrK

Apple Gathering, An. Christina Georgina Rossetti. CP-RosC1

Apple green chasuble, so, The. Argonauts, The. Frank O'Hara. SP-OharF

Apple in, The. Alice. Robert Creeley. CP-CreeR

Apple Island. Robert Graves. CP-GravR

Apple-Maggot Fly, The. Clarence Major. SP-MajoC

Apple on its bough is her desire, The. Garden Abstract. Hart Crane. CP-CranH

Apple orchards, the trees all cover'd with blossoms. Out of May's Shows Selected. Walt Whitman. CP-WhitW

Apple Slump. Paul Muldoon. CP-MuldP

Apple Tragedy. Ted Hughes. SP-HughTN

Apple-tree, a cedar and an oak, An. Man's Work, A. Archibald MacLeish. CP-MacLA

Apple Tree in May. May Sarton. SP-SartM

Apple Tree, The. Dorothy Parker. CP-ParkD

Apple Tree with Cobweb Strings. Jaroslav Seifert. SP-SeifJ, tr. by Ewald Osers

Apple trees are hung with gold, The. Endymion. Oscar Wilde. CP-WildO

Apple-trees bud, but I do not, The. Edna St. Vincent Millay. CP-MillE

Apple Trees, The. Louise Glück. SP-GlucL

Apple Uppfle. Robert Creeley. CP-CreeR

Apples. Donald Hall. CP-HallD

Apples. W. S. Merwin. SP-MerwWF

Apples and Water. Robert Graves. CP-GravR

Apples barely grazed. Cry to Rome. Federico García Lorca. CP-GarcF, tr. by Greg Simon and Steven F. White

Apples hung until a wind at the equinox, The. Give Your Heart to the Hawks. Robinson Jeffers. CP-JefR2

Apples of the Hesperides 1, The. Yannis Ritsos. SP-RitsY, tr. by Gwendolyn MacEwen and Nikos Tsingos

Apples of the Hesperides 2, The. Yannis Ritsos. SP-RitsY, tr. by Gwendolyn MacEwen and Nikos Tsingos

Applicant for post as literary critic: Here are my credentials, Sir! Editorial Office. D. H. Lawrence. CP-LawrD

Applicant, The. Sylvia Plath. CP-PlatS

Apply for the position (I've forgotten now for what) I had to. In Order to. Kenneth Patchen. CP-PatcK

Appointed winners in a long-stretch'd game, The. To-day and Thee. Walt Whitman. CP-WhitW

Appointment, An. William Butler Yeats. CP-YeatW

Appointment, The. Maxine W. Kumin. SP-KumiM

Appreciation. Paul Laurence Dunbar. CP-DunbP

Appreciation. George Meredith. CP-MerG1

Apprehendee Then Exited Vee-hicle. John Ciardi. CP-CiarJ

Apprehension, An. Elizabeth Barrett Browning. CP-BroEB

Apprehensions. Sylvia Plath. CP-PlatS

Apprenticeship. Yusef Komunyakaa. CP-KomuY

Approach—Calcutta, The. May Sarton. SP-SartM

Approach of Autumn. Stanley Kunitz. CP-KunSC

Approach of Winter. William Carlos Williams. CP-WilW1

Approach to a City. William Carlos Williams. CP-WilW2

Approach to Thebes, The. Stanley Kunitz. CP-KunSC

Approaches, The. W. S. Merwin. SP-MerwW

Approaching Hour, The. William Carlos Williams. CP-WilW2

Approaching, nearing, curious. Queries to My Seventieth Year. Walt Whitman. CP-WhitW

Approaching ninety, and still with a hope. Prayer: "Approaching ninety, and still with a hope." Czeslaw Milosz. CP-MiloCN, tr. by Robert Hass

Approaching Prayer. James Dickey. CP-DickJ

Approximations. Robert Earl Hayden. CP-HaydR

Après la Politique, la Haine des Bourbons. Stevie Smith. CP-SmitS

Après le Bain. William Carlos Williams. CP-WilW2

Apricot blossom opens to five petals, An. String Diamond, The. Arthur Sze. SP-SzeA

April. Ralph Waldo Emerson. CP-EmerR

April. A. R. Ammons. CP-AmmoA

April. Walter De la Mare. CP-DeLaW

April. Thomas Merton. CP-MertT

April. W. S. Merwin. SP-MerwW

April. Dan Pagis. SP-PagiD, tr. by Stephen Mitchell

April. Ezra Pound. SP-PounE

April. John Greenleaf Whittier. CP-WhitJ

April. William Carlos Williams. CP-WilW1

April abomination, that's what I call. Essay on Stone. Hayden Carruth. CP-CarHS

April again. Aries comes forth. Journal of One Significant Landscape, A. Charles Wright. SP-WrigC

April again in Avrillé. Road to Avrillé, The. Edna St. Vincent Millay. CP-MillE

April and Its Forsythia. James Schuyler. CP-SchuJ

April, and the last of the plum blossoms. Sleepless Night, A. Philip Levine. SP-LeviP

April Asylum. Josephine Jacobsen. CP-JacoJ

April Aubade. Sylvia Plath. CP-PlatS

April—Dull Afternoon. Ivor Gurney. SP-GurnI

April 18. Sylvia Plath. CP-PlatS

April 5, 1974. Richard Wilbur. CP-WilbR

April Fool. Louis MacNeice. CP-MacNL

April Fools' Day. Yusef Komunyakaa. CP-KomuY

April 4th 1968. Thomas Merton. CP-MertT

April Gale. Ivor Gurney. SP-GurnI

April he'd invoked from the despond, The. He Dreams of Being Warm. Amy Clampitt. CP-ClamA

April, in another fortnight, metropolitan April. Piano Practice. Derek Walcott. CP-WalcD

April in November. Archibald MacLeish. CP-MacLA

April in Ohio. Denise Levertov. SP-LeveDL

April Interval. Marilyn Hacker. SP-HackM

April is over. May moon. Still Life with Stick and Word. Charles Wright. SP-WrigCN

April is the cruellest month, breeding. Waste Land, The. T. S. Eliot. CP-ElioT

April is the Saddest Month. William Carlos Williams. CP-WilW2

April Light. May Swenson. SP-SwenM

April, like a leopard in the windy woods. April. Thomas Merton. CP-MertT

April Manifesto, An. Louis MacNeice. CP-MacNL

April Moon. Walter De la Mare. CP-DeLaW

April Rain Song. Langston Hughes. CP-HughL

April Showers Bring Rain? Philip Whalen. SP-WhalP

April Snow, The. Jones Very. CP-VeryJ

April Sunday Brings the Snow, An. Philip Larkin. CP-LarkP

"April" / this letter's dated. E. E. Cummings. CP-CummE

April this year, not otherwise. Song of a Second April. Edna St. Vincent Millay. CP-MillE

April Today Main Street. Charles Olson. SP-OlsoC Fr. Maximus Poems, The.

April Treason. John Crowe Ransom. SP-RansJ

April what an ice-cold promise. Hudson Ferry. James Schuyler. CP-SchuJ

April winds are magical, The. April. Ralph Waldo Emerson. CP-EmerR

April Woods: Morning. Wendell Berry. CP-BerrW

April Yule, Daddy! Ogden Nash. CP-NashO

April's Anarchy. Yusef Komunyakaa. CP-KomuY

April's new apple buds on an old lichened tree. Kathleen Jessie Raine. SP-RainK

Apri's sweet hand in the margins betrayed. Fifth Sunday after Easter. Thomas Kinsella. CP-KinsT

Apron of Flowers, The. Robert Herrick. CP-HerrR

Aprons of Silence. Carl Sandburg. CP-SandC

Apsarases. James Laughlin. CP-LaugJ

Aquae Sulis. Thomas Hardy. CP-HardT

Aquarium. John Ciardi. CP-CiarJ

Aquatic Nocturne. Sylvia Plath. CP-PlatS

Aqueduct. Thom Gunn. CP-GunnT

Aqueduct. Charles Tomlinson. CP-TomlC

Aquitaine, England's loss. England, for Ezra Pound. Donald Davie. CP-DaviDC

Arab Shepherd Is Searching for His Goat on Mount Zion, An. Yehuda Amichai. SP-AmicY, tr. by Chana Bloch

Arab shepherd seeks a kid goat on Mount Zion, An. Arab Shepherd Seeks a Kid on Mount Zion, A. Yehuda Amichai. SP-AmicYL, tr. by Benjamin Harshav and Barbara Harshav

Arab Shepherd Seeks a Kid on Mount Zion, A. Yehuda Amichai. SP-AmicYL, tr. by Benjamin Harshav and Barbara Harshav

Arab Steed, The. Jones Very. CP-VeryJ

Arabella. Stevie Smith. CP-SmitS

Arabella Johnson. Jones Very. CP-VeryJ

Arabella Johnson and the Texas Kid. Death in Harlem. Langston Hughes. CP-HughL; CP-HughL2

Arabia. Walter De la Mare. CP-DeLaW

Arabian Ballad. Johann Wolfgang von Goethe. CP-EmerR

Arabic Poems. George Meredith. CP-MerG2

Arable acres heave. January. Donald Davie. CP-DaviDC

Arachne. James Laughlin. CP-LaugJ

Arachne. Primo Levi. CP-LeviP, tr. by Ruth Feldman

Aran. Derek Mahon. CP-MahoD

Ararat. Charles Tomlinson. SP-TomlC

Arbatus trees, with their bark like burned skin, The. Galiano Coast: Four Entrances. Margaret Atwood. SP-AtwM2

Arbitrary roll-call, An. Norfolk. Donald Davie. CP-DaviDC

Arbor vitae, whose grooved bole. Message. Denise Levertov. SP-LeveDP

Arboreal Mystery, An. Grace Paley. CP-PalGC

Arc Inside and Out, The. A. R. Ammons. CP-AmmoA

Arc of your eyebrow ended, The. Near Finistère. Eugenio Montale. CP-MontE, tr. by Jonathan Galassi

Arcades. John Milton. CP-MiltJ

Arcades Ambo. Robert Browning. CP-BroR2

Arcades of Philadelphia the Past. Wallace Stevens. CP-StevW; CP-StevWP

Arcadia. Sir Philip Sidney.

    "All what you are still one, his own to find." SP-SidnP

Apollo Great.   SP-SidnP

"*Aurora*, now thou show'st thy blushing light."   SP-SidnP

"Beauty hath force to catch the human sight."   SP-SidnP

"Come shepherd's weeds, become your master's mind."   SP-SidnP

Complaint of Love.   SP-SidnP

Corona.   SP-SidnP

Delight of Solitariness, The.   SP-SidnP

"*Dorus*, tell me, where is thy wonted motion."   SP-SidnP

Echo.   SP-SidnP

Epithalamium: "Let mother Earth"   SP-SidnP, *tr.* by Robert Hass

"Feed on my sheep; my charge, my comfort, feed."   SP-SidnP

Fortune, Nature, Love.   SP-SidnP

Get Hence Foule Griefe.   SP-SidnP

Graven Thoughts.   SP-SidnP

"Hark, plaintful ghosts! Infernal furies, hark."   SP-SidnP

"Hateful cure with hate to heal, A."   SP-SidnP

How Is My Sun.   SP-SidnP

In Vain, Mine Eyes.   SP-SidnP

"Lady, reserved by the heav'ns to do pastors' company honour."   SP-SidnP

"Leave off my sheep: it is no time to feed."   SP-SidnP

"Like diverse flowers, whose diverse beauties serve."   SP-SidnP

Lock Up, Fair Lids.   SP-SidnP

Love and Jealousy.   SP-SidnP

Love and Reason.   SP-SidnP

"Love which is imprinted in my soul, The."   SP-SidnP

Madrigal.   SP-SidnP

"*Speech of Dorus.*"   SP-SidnP

"Merchant man, whom many seas have taught, The."   SP-SidnP

"My lute, within thyself thy tunes enclose."   SP-SidnP

"My Muse what ails this ardour."   SP-SidnP

My Sheep Are Thoughts.   SP-SidnP

"My true love hath my heart [*or* hart], and I have his."   SP-SidnP

"My words, in hope to blaze my steadfast mind."   SP-SidnP

Night.   SP-SidnP

"Now thanked be the great god *Pan*."   SP-SidnP

"Now was our heav'nly vault deprived of the light."   SP-SidnP

"O stealing time, the subject of delay."   SP-SidnP

O Words Which Fall.   SP-SidnP

Old Age.   SP-SidnP

Over These Brooks.   SP-SidnP

Phoebus Farewell.   SP-SidnP

Sapphics.   SP-SidnP

Shepherd Song.   SP-SidnP

Since So Mine Eyes.   SP-SidnP

Since That Stormy Rage.   SP-SidnP

"Since wailing is a bud of causeful sorrow."   SP-SidnP

Song Contest; Lalus and Dorus.   SP-SidnP

"Sweet glove, the witness of my secret bliss."   SP-SidnP

"Thy elder care shall from thy careful face."   SP-SidnP

"Transformed in show, but more transformed in mind."   SP-SidnP

"Unto the caitiff wretch whom long affliction holdeth."   SP-SidnP

"Virtue, beauty, and speech, did strike, wound, charm."   SP-SidnP

"What length of verse can serve brave *Mopsa*'s good to show?"   SP-SidnP

What Tongue Can Her Perfections Tell?   SP-SidnP

When Two Suns Do Appear.   SP-SidnP

Why Fear to Die?   SP-SidnP

Ye Goat-herd Gods.   SP-SidnP

"Ye living powers enclosed in stately shrine."   SP-SidnP

"You goodly pines, which still with brave ascent."   SP-SidnP

Arcadia was square and fenced.   On Going Latent.   Alan Dugan.   CP-DugaA

Arcadians the earth inhabited, The.   Sir Walter Ralegh.   CP-RaleW

Arch, The.   Herman Melville.   SP-MelvH   *Fr.* Clarel: A Poem and Pilgrimage in the Holy Land.

Arch, The.   Charles Tomlinson.   CP-TomlC

Arch of roses.   Door.   Federico García Lorca.   CP-GarcF, *tr.* by Jerome Rothenberg   *Fr.* Narcissus.

Arch traversed by divine answers.   Notre Dame.   Rainer Maria Rilke.   CP-RilkFr, *tr.* by A. Poulin, Jr.

Archaeologist's spade, The.   Archaeology.   W. H. Auden.   CP-AudeW

Archaeologists went home, The.   End of the Archaeological Season in Eyn Gedi.   Yehuda Amichai.   SP-AmicYL, *tr.* by Benjamin Harshav *and* Barbara Harshav

Archaeology.   W. H. Auden.   CP-AudeW

Archaic Figure.   Amy Clampitt.   CP-ClamA

Archangel Hope / Looks to the azure cope, The.   Ralph Waldo Emerson.   CP-EmerR

Archangel's' Song, The.   Randall Jarrell.   CP-JarrR

Archbishop is away, The. The church is gray.   Gray Stones and Gray Pigeons.   Wallace Stevens.   CP-StevW; CP-StevWP

Archduchess Anne.   George Meredith.   CP-MerG1

Archeology.   Wisława Szymborska.   SP-SzymW, *tr.* by Stanisław Barańczak *and* Clare Cavanagh

Archer.   "H. D."   CP-DoolH

Archer, The.   Charles Tomlinson.   CP-TomlC

Archer is wake, The!   Peace on Earth.   William Carlos Williams.   CP-WilW1

Archers.   Federico García Lorca.   SP-GarcF   *Fr.* Poem of the Saeta.

Arches.   James Schuyler.   CP-SchuJ

Archetype Poem, The.   Allen Ginsberg.   CP-GinsA; SP-GinsA

Archibald's Example.   Edwin Arlington Robinson.   CP-RobiE

Archie and Tina.   Stevie Smith.   CP-SmitS

Archin' here and arrachin there.   Water Music.   Hugh MacDiarmid.   SP-MacDH   *Fr.* Water Music.

Archipelago.   Arthur Sze.   SP-SzeA

Archipelago.   Louise Glück.   SP GlucL

Archipelago, The.   Herman Melville.   SP-MelvH

Architectural Masks.   Thomas Hardy.   CP-HardT

Architecture.   Andrei Codrescu.   SP-CodrA

Architecture.   Wallace Stevens.   CP-StevWP

Architecture, An.   Wendell Berry.   CP-BerrW

Architecture, The.   Robert Duncan.   SP-DuncR   *Fr.* Passages.

Architecture gives more comfort than the scenes, The.   To Draw the Warmth of Flesh from Subtle Graphite.   Olga Broumas.   SP-BrouO

Architecture of the American Mind.   Miller Williams.   CP-WillM

Architecture, sleepy Mexican, The.   Village 104.   James Tate.   CP-TateJ

Archival Print, An.   William Stafford.   SP-StafW; SP-StafWW

Arctic fox of Kiska now is quelled, The.   Homage to Binsey Poplars.   Maxine W. Kumin.   SP-KumiM

Arctic Ox, The.   Marianne Craig Moore.   CP-MoorM
   (Arctic Ox (or Goat), The.)   CP-MoorM

"Arcturus" is his other name.   Emily Dickinson.   CP-DickE

Ardella.   Langston Hughes.   CP-HughL; CP-HughL1

Arden is not Eden, but Eden's rhyme.   In Arden.   Charles Tomlinson.   CP-TomlC; SP-TomlC

Ardensteil-henarub-izabeth) / this noN.   E. E. Cummings.   CP-CummE

Ardent and white horse, bright, proud Pegasus.   Pegasus.   Rainer Maria Rilke.   CP-RilkFr, *tr.* by A. Poulin, Jr.   *Fr.* Affectionate Taxes to France.

Ardent Country.   Rainer Maria Rilke.   CP-RilkFr, *tr.* by A. Poulin, Jr.

Ardent / yet chill and formal.   Gift.   "H. D."   CP-DoolH

Ardour and Memory.   Dante Gabriel Rossetti.   CW-RossD   *Fr.* House of Life, The.

Are a stage.   Moors.   Ted Hughes.   SP-HughTN

Are all these stones.   Close-up.   A. R. Ammons.   CP-AmmoA

Are all we have. So count them as they pass. They pass / too quickly.   Few Days, A.   James Schuyler.   CP-SchuJ

Are built out of the meshing of life and space.   And Others, Vaguer Presences.   John Ashbery.   SP-AshbJ

Are eyelids on eyes lying and lifting.   Britannia Rules the Waves.   Elizabeth Bishop.   CP-BishE

Are Friends Delight or Pain?   Emily Dickinson.   CP-DickE

Are generally over or around.   Pockets.   Howard Nemerov.   CP-NemeH

Are leaving, trailing their ankles like ballads.   Skaters, The.   James Laughlin.   CP-LaugJ

Are many monsters—the ashes of the members.   On the Road to Larry Robin's Bookstore.   Eleanor Wilner.   SP-WilnE

Are more beautiful than.   Girls at the Green Hotel, The.   Charles Bukowski.   SP-BukC1

Are my poems spoken in the factories and fields.   Hugh MacDiarmid.   SP-MacDH   *Fr.* Second Hymn to Lenin.

Are not holy they are just.   Holes.   James Laughlin.   CP-LaugJ

Are not the joys of morning sweeter.   William Blake.   CP-BlakW

Are planned to make things better and not worse.   Poverty Programs, The.   Howard Nemerov.   CP-NemeH

Are souls then nothing? Must at length the die.   William Wordsworth.   MW-WorW

Are such an orderly race.   French, The.   James Laughlin.   CP-LaugJ

Are the desolate, dark weeks.   These.   William Carlos Williams.   CP-WilW1

Are the living so much use.   At the Cenotaph.   Hugh MacDiarmid.   SP-MacDH

Are the salt and the sugar at work.   Pablo Neruda.   SP-NeruP   *Fr.* Question Book.

"Are there Few that be Saved?" Luke 13:23.   Jones Very.   CP-VeryJ

Are there not twelve whole hours in every day.   Day of Denial, The.   Jones Very.   CP-VeryJ

Are there only Victories.   Ossuary.   Rainer Maria Rilke.   CP-RilkFr, *tr.* by A.

Poulin, Jr.

Are there still some. New Moon. Robert Creeley. SP-CreeR

Are there two things, of all which men possess. To Asra. Samuel Taylor Coleridge. CP-ColeS

Are these mellifluous sheep. Strictly Bucolic. Charles Simic. SP-SimiC; SP-SimiCE

Are these your presences, my clan from Heaven? Prayer to All the Dead Among Mine Own People, A. Nicholas Vachel Lindsay. CP-LindV

Are they birds or butterflies? Heights, Depths, Silence, Unceasing Sound of the Surf. Denise Levertov. SP-LeveDL

Are they blind, the lords of Gaza. Angry Samson. Robert Graves. CP-GravR

Are They Not All Ministering Spirits? Christina Georgina Rossetti. CP-RosC2

Are they sweating in the armpits. Dancing under the Stars at Nice. Clarence Major. SP-MajoC

Are those poisons / from India? Apothecary. Federico García Lorca. CP-GarcF, *tr. by* Jerome Rothenberg *Fr.* Secrets.

Are walking towards me. Five Elephants. Rita Dove. SP-DoveR

Are we still travel[l]ing? Pillow, The. Charles Simic. SP-SimiC; SP-SimiCE

Are we the only ones to have received. Rainer Maria Rilke. CP-RilkFr, *tr. by* A. Poulin, Jr. *Fr.* Fragments.

Are We Through Talking, I Hope? John Ciardi. CP-CiarJ

Are Ye Not Much Better Than They? Christina Georgina Rossetti. CP-RosC2

Are you a horror to yourself? With the Sun's Fire. David Ignatow. SP-IgnaD

Are You a Snodgrass? Ogden Nash. CP-NashO

Are you alive? Pool, The. "H. D." CP-DoolH

Are you asleep M. Valdemar. Sign. Michael Palmer. SP-PalmM

Are you awake, / Comrades, this silent night? Haunting Fingers. Thomas Hardy. CP-HardT

Are You Born? / I. Muriel Rukeyser. CP-RukeM

Are You Born? / II. Muriel Rukeyser. CP-RukeM

Are You Content. William Butler Yeats. CP-YeatW

Are you demonic, Beauty, or divine. Hymn to Beauty. Charles Baudelaire. CP-BaudC, *tr. by* Walter Martin

Are you far away? Familiar, The. Walter De la Mare. CP-DeLaW

Are You groping Your way? Xenophanes, the Monist of Colophon. Thomas Hardy. CP-HardT

Are you grown up now, John, now that it's over? John and Anne. William Meredith. SP-MereW

Are you happy? It's the only. Snatch of Sliphorn Jazz. Carl Sandburg. CP-SandC

Are you in Eden again, America? Shout, The. Anne Sexton. CP-SextA

Are you jealous of the ocean's generosity. Jelaluddin Rumi. SP-Rumi, *tr. by* Coleman Barks

Are you Mr. William Stafford? William Stafford. SP-StafWW

Are you modern. What Is Modern. W. S. Merwin. SP-MerwWF

Are you not weary. Ballet. William Carlos Williams. CP-WilW1

Are You Pining? D. H. Lawrence. CP-LawrD

Are you saying that iron understands. Rust. Lucille Clifton. SP-ClifL

Are you shaken, are you stirred. Fragment: "Are you shaken, are you stirred." Robert Graves. CP-GravR

Are You the New Person Drawn toward Me? Walt Whitman. CP-WhitW

Are you what your faire lookes expresse? Thomas Campion. CP-CampT

Are you willing to be sponged out, erased, cancelled. Phoenix. D. H. Lawrence. CP-LawrD

Are you You or Me or It? Hello Up There. Marge Piercy. SP-PierM

Are your rocks shelter for ships. Shrine, The. "H. D." CP-DoolH

Area— / no test of depth. Emily Dickinson. SP-DickE

Arena dust rusted by four bulls' blood to a dull redness. Goring, The. Sylvia Plath. CP-PlatS

Arena, The. G. K. Chesterton. CP-ChesG

Arènes de Lutèce. Samuel Beckett. CP-BeckS

Aren't you our geometry. Rainer Maria Rilke. CP-RilkFr, *tr. by* A. Poulin, Jr. *Fr.* Windows, The.

Aren't you our geometry. Window, The. Rainer Maria Rilke. CP-RilkFr, *tr. by* A. Poulin, Jr. *Fr.* Orchards.

Areopagus. Louis MacNeice. CP-MacNL

Ares at last has quit the field. Under Which Lyre, a Reactionary Tract for the Times. W. H. Auden. CP-AudeW

Arethusa. Percy Bysshe Shelley. CP-ShelP

Arethusa Meadow. Jones Very. CP-VeryJ

Argentine Round. Gabriela Mistral. SP-MistG, *tr. by* Maria Giachetti [*or* Jacketti]

Argonauts, The. D. H. Lawrence. CP-LawrD

Argonauts, The. Frank O'Hara. SP-OharF

Arguing over coffee at the station. Between Trains. Robert Graves. CP-

GravR

Argument. Elizabeth Bishop. CP-BishE

Argument ("Now lookahere, gal"). Langston Hughes. CP-HughL; CP-HughL1

Argument ("White is right, / Yellow mellow"). Langston Hughes. CP-HughL; CP-HughL3

Argument. As the true method of knowledge is experiment the true faculty of knowing must be the faculty which experiences. This faculty I treat of, The. All Religions Are One. William Blake. CP-BlakW

Argument, An. Nicholas Vachel Lindsay. CP-LindV

Argument, Th'. Sir Thomas Wyatt. CP-WyatT

Argument, The. Walter De la Mare. CP-DeLaW

Argument for Suicide. William Wordsworth. CP-WorW1

Argument. Man has no notion of moral fitness but from Education, The. There Is No Natural Religion. William Blake. CP-BlakW

Argument of His Book, The. Robert Herrick. CP-HerrR

Argument: Of the Passion of Christ, An. Thomas Merton. CP-MertT

Argument to Love as a Person. Alan Dugan. CP-DugaA

Arguments. Allen Ginsberg. SP-GinsA

Argumentum e Silentio. Paul Celan. SP-CelaP, *tr. by* John Felstiner

Argus. Alexander Pope. CP-PopeA

Argus-eyed old greenhouse is all gone where once the black banana fronds were, The. Returning Home. John Logan. CP-LogaJ

Argyll Tour. Eugenio Montale. CP-MontE, *tr. by* Jonathan Galassi

Aria. Ezra Pound. CP-PoEar

Ariadne. "H. D." CP-DoolH

Ariadne. Thomas Merton. CP-MertT

Ariadne and the Minotaur. Charles Tomlinson. CP-TomlC; SP-TomlC

Ariadne at the Labyrinth. Thomas Merton. CP-MertT

Ariadne To Theseus. Christina Georgina Rossetti. CP-RosC3

Ariadne's bird / That lone. In Midsummer Quiet. Charles Simic. SP-SimiC; SP-SimiCE

Arid that country and high, anger of sun on the mountains, but. Rattlesnake Country. Robert Penn Warren. CP-WarrR

Arides. Ezra Pound. SP-PounE

Ariel. Walter De la Mare. CP-DeLaW

Ariel. Sylvia Plath. CP-PlatS

Ariel to Miranda:—Take. With a Guitar, to Jane. Percy Bysshe Shelley. CP-ShelP

Ariel was glad he had written his poems. Planet on the Table, The. Wallace Stevens. CP-StevW; CP-StevWP

Anima leaps—glides—(smiles)—floats like a bee. Debut of the Dancer, A. B., The. Charles Baudelaire. CP-BaudC, *tr. by* Walter Martin

Arion, when, through tempests cruel wracke. Sonnet 38. Edmund Spenser. CP-Spens *Fr.* Amoretti.

Arioso and the Arabs. Jorge Luis Borges. SP-BorgJ, *tr. by* Eric McHenry

Arise, arise, arise! / There is blood on the earth that denies ye bread. Ode Written October, 1819, An. Percy Bysshe Shelley. CP-ShelP

Arise, depart, for this is not your rest. Today's Burden. Christina Georgina Rossetti. CP-RosC2

Arise, divine Urania, with new strains. On the Omniscience of the Supreme Being. Christopher Smart. SP-SmarC

Arise, dusty shadow, Mars. Dream at Arles on the Night of the Mistral, A. Thomas Merton. CP-MertT

Arise, my friend, / for the roosters are crowing! Lullaby in Death for Rosalía de Castro. Federico García Lorca. CP-GarcF, *tr. by* Catherine Brown

Arise, my soul, on wings enraptured [*or* enraptur'd], rise. Thoughts on the Works of Providence. Phillis Wheatley. CP-WheaP

Arise open the doors untie the cords. Truth. Adam Zagajewski. SP-ZagaA, *tr. by* Clare Cavanagh

Arise, up, arise. Now that it is time, shake off slumbers. Elegiac Verses. John Milton. CP-MiltJ

Arisen at Last. John Greenleaf Whittier. CP-WhitJ

Aristocracy of the Sun. D. H. Lawrence. CP-LawrD

Aristocracy, The. Wendell Berry. CP-BerrW

Aristocrat, The. G. K. Chesterton. CP-ChesG

Aristocrat among patriarchs, This. Copper Beech, The. Rita Dove. SP-DoveR

Aristodemus the Messenian. Thomas Hardy. CP-HardT

Aristomenes. Lord Byron. CP-Byron

Aristophanes' Apology. Robert Browning. CP-BroR2

Aristotle. Billy Collins. SP-CollB

Aristovoulos. Constantine P. Cavafy. CP-CavaC, *tr. by* Theoharis Constantine Theoharis

Arithmetic. Carl Sandburg. CP-SandC

Arithmetic is where numbers fly like pigeons in and out of your head. Arithmetic. Carl Sandburg. CP-SandC

Arithmetic on the Frontier. Rudyard Kipling. CP-KiplR

Arizona Desert.   Charles Tomlinson.   CP-TomlC; SP-TomlC

Arizona Highway.   Charles Tomlinson.   CP-TomlC

Arizona Midnight.   Robert Penn Warren.   CP-WarrR

Arizona wind dries out my nostrils, The.   Hitchhiker, The.   Ai.   SP-Ai

Ark, The.   Robert Graves.   CP-GravR

Ark, The.   Eugenio Montale.   CP-MontE, *tr. by* Jonathan Galassi

Ark, The.   Jones Very.   CP-VeryJ

Ark: Angelus: Anvil.   Kenneth Patchen.   CP-PatcK

Arkansas Traveller.   Charles Wright.   SP-WrigC

Arkansaw's westernmost county.   Siloam.   Donald Davie.   CP-DaviDC

Arkhangel'sk.   Norman Dubie.   CP-DubiN

Arktos.   Gary Snyder.   CP-SnydG

Arm on gigantic hammer; drunk.   Blacksmith, The.   Arthur Rimbaud.   CP-RimbA, *tr. by* Martin Sorrell

Armadillo, The.   Elizabeth Bishop.   CP-BishE

Armageddon.   John Crowe Ransom.   SP-RansJ

Armageddon, Armageddon.   Paul Muldoon.   CP-MuldP

Armah: October 12, 1990.   Alice Walker.   CP-WalkA

Armazindy;—fambily name.   James Whitcomb Riley.   CP-RileJ

Arm'd year—year of the struggle.   Eighteen Sixty-One.   Walt Whitman.   CP-WhitW

Armed with / a bass-violin.   Old-Fashioned German Christmas Card, An.   William Carlos Williams.   CP-WilW2

Armed with an indiscriminate delight.   In Memory of Donald A. Stauffer.   William Meredith.   SP-MereW

Armenian funeral on Mount Zion: the coffin, An   Yehuda Amichai.   SP-AmicY, *tr. by* Chana Bloch   *Fr.* Songs of Zion the Beautiful.

Armenian Lady's Love, The.   William Wordsworth.   CP-WorW2

Armenonville.   Edna St. Vincent Millay.   CP-MillE

Armful, The.   Robert Frost.   CP-FrosR

Armies of the Plain.   George Oppen.   CP-OppGN

Armies of the Wilderness, The.   Herman Melville.   SP-MelvH

Armistice.   Howard Nemerov.   CP-NemeH

Armistice Day, 1918.   Robert Graves.   CP-GravR

Armitage of scrap-iron for the radiations of a moon.   July seventeenth nineteen sixty eight.   Adrienne Rich.   CP-RicAE   *Fr.* Ghazals: Homage to Ghalib.

Armor.   James Dickey.   CP-DickJ

Armored in oxygen.   Astronauts.   Robert Earl Hayden.   CP-HaydR

Armored salmon jewel the ice with blood, The.   Market-Place, The.   Howard Nemerov.   CP-NemeH

Armor's Undermining Modesty.   Marianne Craig Moore.   CP-MoorM

Armour Avenue was the name of this street and door signs on empty.   Real Avenue News.   Carl Sandburg.   CP-SandC

Arms and the Boy.   Wilfred Owen.   CP-OwenW

Arms and the girl I sing—O rare.   Fearful Women.   Carolyn Kizer.   CP-KizeC

Arms and the man I sing, and sing for joy.   James Vincent Cunningham.   CP-CunnJ

Arms, and the Man I sing, the first who bore.   Virgil.   CP-WorW2   *Fr.* Aeneid [*or* Eneados *or* Aeneis], The.

Arms uplifted on the podium.   1.   Thomas Kinsella.   CP-KinsT

Army Ants.   A. K. Ramanujan.   CP-RamaA

Army Corps on the March, An.   Walt Whitman.   CP-WhitW

Army Headquarters.   Rudyard Kipling.   CP-KiplR   (Old is the song that I sing.) CP-KiplR

Army marched by for days and was admired by all, The.   Decimation before Phraäta, The.   Alan Dugan.   CP-DugaA

Army of Clouds! ye wingèd Host in troops.   To the Clouds.   William Wordsworth.   CP-WorW1

Arnica, Eyebright, the.   Todtnauberg.   Paul Celan.   SP-CelaP, *tr. by* John Felstiner

Aromas inspire me as music.   Correspondence According to Baudelaire.   Constantine P. Cavafy.   CP-CavaC, *tr. by* Theoharis Constantine Theoharis

Around, above my bed, the pitch-dark fly.   Truth.   Howard Nemerov.   CP-NemeH

Around, around the sun we go.   Mother Goose's Garland.   Archibald MacLeish.   CP-MacLA

Around bend after bend.   Not of School Age.   Robert Frost.   CP-FrosR

Around from Kentucky Fried Chicken.   Insinuations.   Yusef Komunyakaa.   CP-KomuY

Around me the images of thirty years.   Municipal Gallery Revisited, The.   William Butler Yeats.   CP-YeatW

Around Pastor Bonhoeffer.   Stanley Kunitz.   CP-KunSC

Around Sebago's lonely lake.   Funeral Tree of the Sokokis.   John Greenleaf Whittier.   CP-WhitJ

Around the cold pool in the metal light.   Hotel Normandie Pool, The.   Derek Walcott.   CP-WalcD

Around the Fire.   Ted Berrigan.   SP-BerrT

Around the fireplace, pointing at the fire.   On Falling Asleep by Firelight.

William Meredith.   SP-MereW

Around the headland, at the end.   Lives of Gulls and Children, The.   Howard Nemerov.   CP-NemeH

Around the house the flakes fly faster.   Birds at Winter Nightfall.   Thomas Hardy.   CP-HardT

Around the little park.   Back to Life.   Thom Gunn.   CP-GunnT

Around the man who seeks a noble end.   Ralph Waldo Emerson.   CP-EmerR

Around the Mountain.   Robert Graves.   CP-GravR

Around the Springs of Gray my wild root weaves.   William Blake.   CP-BlakW

Around the vase of Life at your slow pace.   Vase of Life, The.   Dante Gabriel Rossetti.   CW-RossD   *Fr.* House of Life, The.

Around them boomed the rhetoric of time.   Kairos and Logos.   W. H. Auden.   CP-AudeW

Around You, Your House.   William Stafford.   SP-StafWW

Arouse—and let thy foes disperse.   Bible, *O.T.*   *See* Let God arise, let his enemies be scattered

Arouse yrself, Bigmans.   Bigmans.   Charles Olson.   CP-OlsoC

Arranged by two's as peaches are.   Nine Nectarines,   Marianne Craig Moore.   CP-MoorM

Arrangements are changed, The.   Wedding Postponed.   Carl Sandburg.   CP-SandC

Arrangements with Earth for Three Dead Friends.   James Wright.   CP-WrigJ

Arrears of Moonlight.   Robert Graves.   CP-GravR

Arrival.   Maya Angelou.   SP-AngeM

Arrival.   Josephine Jacobsen.   CP-JacoJ

Arrival.   Philip Larkin.   CP-LarkP

Arrival.   William Stafford.   SP-StafWW

Arrival.   William Carlos Williams.   CP-WilW1

Arrival, The.   Wendell Berry.   CP-BerrW

Arrival, The.   W. S. Merwin.   SP-MerwWF

Arrival, The.   Charles Tomlinson.   CP-TomlC

Arrival, The.   Jones Very.   CP-VeryJ

Arrival and Departure.   Archibald MacLeish.   CP-MacLA

Arrival at Santos.   Elizabeth Bishop.   CP-BishE

Arrival at the Waldorf.   Wallace Stevens.   CP-StevW; CP-StevWP

Arrival (North Wales, 1897), An.   Denise Levertov.   SP-LeveDL

Arrival of Rain.   Josephine Jacobsen.   CP-JacoJ

Arrival of the Bee Box, The.   Sylvia Plath.   CP-PlatS

Arrival of the Players, The.   George Crabbe.   SP-CrabG   *Fr.* Borough, The.

Arrivals, The.   Josephine Jacobsen.   CP-JacoJ

Arrivals, Departures.   Philip Larkin.   CP-LarkP

Arrive. The Ladies from the Ladies' Betterment League.   Lovers of the Poor, The.   Gwendolyn Brooks.   SP-BrooG

Arrive to arrive and to arrive here in such thick.   If a Poem Can Be Headed into Its Proper Current.   Kenneth Patchen.   CP-PatcK

Arriving in the Country Again.   James Wright.   CP-WrigJ

Arriving Uninvited.   Clarence Major.   SP-MajoC

Arrogant young flesh kneels to his calm power.   On Dürer's Etching of Pilate Washing His Hands (1512).   Helen Pinkerton.   CP-PinkH

Arrossisce la rosa: e perchè mai?   Christina Georgina Rossetti.   CP-RosC3

Arrow.   Federico García Lorca.   SP-GarcF   *Fr.* Poem of the Saeta.

Arrow in the Wall, An.   Andrey Andreievich Voznesensky.   CP-WilbR

Arrow on the Vane.   Robert Graves.   CP-GravR

Arrow Shots.   Robert Graves.   CP-GravR

Arrow, The.   William Butler Yeats.   CP-YeatW

Arrowed, the body flies in light.   Diver.   Robert Penn Warren.   CP-WarrR

Arrows enamored of his Heart.   Emily Dickinson.   CP-DickE

Arrowy gold whose winter span, The.   Spring Morning.   Marya Alexandrovna Zaturenska.   SP-ZatuM

Arroyo.   Robert Creeley.   SP-CreeR

Arroyo Hondo.   Charles Tomlinson.   CP-TomlC

Arroyo Seco.   Charles Tomlinson.   CP-TomlC

Ars Amoris.   James Vincent Cunningham.   CP-CunnJ

Ars Gratia Artis.   James Laughlin.   CP-LaugJ

Ars Longa. Which is crueller.   Peacock Room, The.   Robert Earl Hayden.   CP-HaydR

Ars Poetica.   Jorge Luis Borges.   SP-BorgJ, *tr. by* W. S. Merwin

Ars Poetica.   Donald Davie.   CP-DaviDC

Ars Poetica.   Norman Dubie.   CP-DubiN

Ars Poetica.   Archibald MacLeish.   CP-MacLA

Ars Poetica.   Howard Nemerov.   CP-NemeH

Ars Poetica.   Charles Tomlinson.   CP-TomlC

Ars Poetica.   Eleanor Wilner.   SP-WilnE

Ars Poetica.   Charles Wright.   SP-WrigC

Ars Poetica?   Czeslaw Milosz.   CP-MiloC; CP-MiloCN, *tr. by* Lillian Vallee

Ars Poetica 2.   Charles Wright.   SP-WrigCN

Ars Poetica: Or: Who Lives in the Ivory Tower?   Thomas McGrath.   SP-

McGrT

Arse Poetica. Sam Hamill. SP-HamiS

Arsenal at Springfield, The. Henry Wadsworth Longfellow. SP-LongH

Arsenio. Eugenio Montale. CP-MontE, *tr. by* Jonathan Galassi

Art. Ralph Waldo Emerson. CP-EmerR

Art. Herman Melville. SP-MelvH

Art. Allen Tate. CP-TateA

Art, An. Charles Bukowski. SP-BukC1

Art, The. William Carlos Williams. CP-WilW2

Art above Nature, to Julia. Robert Herrick. CP-HerrR

Art and Love. James Whitcomb Riley. CP-RileJ

Art and Poetry. James Whitcomb Riley. CP-RileJ

Art Center. Lorine Niedecker. CP-NiedL

Art Colours. G. K. Chesterton. CP-ChesG

Art grows from hurt, you say. And I must own. Fountain. Charles Tomlinson. SP-TomlC

Art of a Novel, The. Marilyn Hacker. SP-HackM

Art of Contraction, The. Dan Pagis. SP-PagiD, *tr. by* Stephen Mitchell

Art of Healing, The. W. H. Auden. CP-AudeW

Art of losing isn't hard to master, The. One Art. Elizabeth Bishop. CP-BishE

Art of Love, The. Kenneth Koch. SP-KochK

Art of Love, The. Ovid.
   "Now *Dædalus*, behold, by fate assign'd." CP-JohnS

Art of Poetry, The. Nicolas Boileau-Despéaux. CP-DryJ2, *tr. by* John Dryden

Art of Poetry, The. Kenneth Koch. SP-KochK

Art of Poetry, The. Charles Tomlinson. CP-TomlC

Art of the Octopus: Variations on a Found Theme, The. Denise Levertov. SP-LeveDL

Art of writing an honest prose, The. Earthquake in the West, The. Howard Nemerov. CP-NemeH

Art Photographer Puts His Model at Ease, The. Miller Williams. CP-WillM

Art quickens Nature; Care will make a face. Neglect. Robert Herrick. CP-HerrR

Art recalls the memory. This Is about Death. Allen Ginsberg. CP-GinsA

Art Song. Howard Nemerov. CP-NemeH

Art Student. Stephen Spender. CP-SpenS

Art thou a Statesman, in the van. William Wordsworth. *See* Art thou a Statist in the van

Art thou a Statist in the van. Poet's Epitaph, A. William Wordsworth. CP-WorW1

Art thou asleep? or have thy wings. Glimpse, The. Walter De la Mare. CP-DeLaW

Art thou not destin'd? then, with hast, go on. Another. Robert Herrick. CP-HerrR

Art thou pale for weariness. To the Moon. Percy Bysshe Shelley. CP-ShelP

Art thou some individual of a kind. Another ["Art thou some individual of a kind"]. *Unknown.* CP-CowpW

Art Thou That She. *Unknown.* CP-CampT
   (Art thou that shee then whome noe fayrer is?) CP-CampT

Art thou the bird whom Man loves best. Redbreast Chasing the Butterfly, The. William Wordsworth. CP-WorW1

Art thou the thing I wanted? Emily Dickinson. CP-DickE

Art thou too fall'n? ere anger could subside. Samuel Johnson. CP-JohnS

Art thou wise, four things resign. Hafiz. CP-EmerR *Fr.* Odes.

Art to me's hear stellary. Artemisia. Louis Zukofsky. CP-ZukLS

Artaud. Raymond Carver. CP-CarvR

Arte of English Poesie, The. Sir Walter Ralegh. CP-RaleW

Artegal and Elidure. William Wordsworth. CP-WorW2

Artemis. Olga Broumas. SP-BrouO

Artemis, more passionate. After the Anthology. Kenneth Rexroth. CP-RexrK

Artemis Prologizes. Robert Browning. CP-BroR1

(Artemis speaks.). Orion Dead. "H. D." CP-DoolH

Artemisia. Alexander Pope. CP-PopeA

Artemisia. Louis Zukofsky. CP-ZukLS

Artemus of Michigan, The. James Whitcomb Riley. CP-RileJ

Arterial. Rudyard Kipling. CP-KiplR *Fr.* Muse among the Motors, The.

Arteries, red lane on lane, The. Bridges. Charles Tomlinson. CP-TomlC

Artes bred neat *An.* Another. *Unknown.* CP-BradA

Artful Pose. Maya Angelou. SP-AngeM

Arthritically bent, in black, spindle-legged. Old Women. Czeslaw Milosz. CP-MiloC; CP-MiloCN, *tr. by* Robert Hass

Arthur. Ogden Nash. CP-NashO

Arthur Allen, when he lived. Bolyai, the Geometer. Donald Davie. CP-DaviDC

Arthur Mitchell. Marianne Craig Moore. CP-MoorM

Arthur Peyton. Muriel Rukeyser. CP-RukeM

Arthur's friend's. Kyoto. Robert Creeley. SP-CreeR

Arthur's Party. Carolyn Kizer. CP-KizeC

Articulacy. Hints from the Koran. Donald Davie. CP-DaviDC

Articulation. Rae Armantrout. SP-ArmaA

Articulation & Class. Yusef Komunyakaa. CP-KomuY

Artifact. Muriel Rukeyser. CP-RukeM

Artifex in Extremis. Donald Davie. CP-DaviDC

Artificer. Czeslaw Milosz. CP-MiloC; CP-MiloCN, *tr. by* Robert Hass

Artificial Flowers. Constantine P. Cavafy. CP-CavaC, *tr. by* Theoharis Constantine Theoharis

Artificial Intelligence. Adrienne Rich. CP-RicAE; SP-RicA2

Artificial Populations. Wallace Stevens. CP-StevWP

Artillery [*or* Artillerie]. George Herbert. CP-HerbG

Artilleryman's Vision, The. Walt Whitman. CP-WhitW

Artist. Charles Bukowski. SP-BukC1

Artist. George Oppen. CP-OppGN

Artist, An. Seamus Heaney. SP-HeanSO *Fr.* Sweeney Redivivus.

Artist, An. Robinson Jeffers. CP-JefR1

Artist, The. Aleksandr Aleksandrovich Blok. SP-BlokA, *tr. by* Peter France *and* Jon Stallworthy

Artist, The. G. K. Chesterton. CP-ChesG

Artist, The. Kenneth Koch. SP-KochK

Artist, The. Stanley Kunitz. CP-KunSC

Artist, The. William Carlos Williams. CP-WilW2

Artist, Come Home. William Stafford. SP-StafWW

Artist comes next, The. Poem about Storytelling, A. Grace Paley. CP-PalGC

Artist of the Beautiful, An. John Greenleaf Whittier. CP-WhitJ

Artist sometimes sees, The. Blowpipe Game, The. James Laughlin. CP-LaugJ

Artist to Intellectual (Poet to Explainer). Denise Levertov. SP-LeveDL

Artist we now put on view, The. On a Portrait of Honoré Daumier. Charles Baudelaire. CP-BaudC, *tr. by* Walter Martin

Artists. Charles Bukowski. SP-BukC1

Artists and writers. Soul, The. Charles Olson. CP-OlsoC

Artist's Decalogue, The. Gabriela Mistral. SP-MistG, *tr. by* Maria Giachetti [*or* Jacketti]

Artists' Letters. Thomas Kinsella. CP-KinsT

Artist's Model. Robert Lowell. SP-LoweR

Artists wrestled here! Emily Dickinson. CP-DickE

Arts Council Meets in Eureka, The. Gary Snyder. CP-SnydG

Artsybashev is a Russian. Foreign. William Carlos Williams. CP-WilW1

Arunagiri, rich and spoiled, spent. Fear No Fall. A. K. Ramanujan. CP-RamaA

Arundel Tomb, An. Philip Larkin. CP-LarkP

A's. The ("A's"). Robert Creeley. SP-CreeR

As a bad orator, badly o'er-book-skilled. Fernando Pessoa. SP-PessF *Fr.* 35 Sonnets.

As a boy he was brought to Sulla's villa, The Tombs. Marcus Cato 95–42 B.C. Robert Lowell. SP-LoweR

As a child, certain skies sharpened the way I saw. War. Arthur Rimbaud. CP-RimbA, *tr. by* Martin Sorrell

As a child holds a pet. Port Bou. Stephen Spender. CP-SpenS

As a child I climbed the roof. Roofs. Philip Levine. SP-LeviP

As a child I feared the mirror might reveal. Mirror, The. Jorge Luis Borges. SP-BorgJ, *tr. by* Hoyt Rogers

As a child, they could not keep me from wells. Personal Helicon. Seamus Heaney. SP-HeanSO

As a dare-gale skylark scanted in a dull cage. Caged Skylark, The. Gerard Manley Hopkins. CP-HopkG

As a drenched, drowned bee. Baby Asleep after Pain, A. D. H. Lawrence. CP-LawrD

As a fragile and lovely flower unfolds its gleaming. Hymn 3. Marc Antony Flaminius. CP-PoEar, *tr. by* Ezra Pound

As a funny monk one is never sure where. History of the Growth of Heaven, The ("As a funny monk one is never sure where"). Andrei Codrescu. SP-CodrA

As a gigantic harp in Vermont. Play, The. Richard Eberhart. CP-EberR

As a girl no one gallantly attends. Fear of Man, The. Robert Frost. CP-FrosR

As a guest who may not stay. In Memory. John Greenleaf Whittier. CP-WhitJ

As a harvester, at dusk. Autumn. James Whitcomb Riley. CP-RileJ

As a horn of the high moon veers in clear skies over Main Street. Idyll: "As a horn of the high moon veers in clear skies over Main Street." Giorgio Bassani. CP-DaviDC, *tr. by* Donald Davie

As a horse of shell, the water's. Shapes. Kenneth Patchen. CP-PatcK

As a King, ...Unto the King. Christina Georgina Rossetti. CP-RosC2

As a Less than Robber. Robert Graves. CP-GravR

As a matter of fact, we are better than we know. Combative Spirit, The. D. H. Lawrence. CP-LawrD

As a pillar of gnats, moving up and down. Equivalence of Gnats and Mice. Richard Eberhart. CP-EberR

As a plant becomes pot-bound. Ego-Bound. D. H. Lawrence. CP-LawrD

As a poet I'm interested in religious ideas. Credo. Hugh MacDiarmid. SP-MacDH

As a queen sits down, knowing that a chair will be there. Walking to Sleep. Richard Wilbur. CP-WilbR

As a quiet little seedling. Seedling, The. Paul Laurence Dunbar. CP-DunbP

As a Real House. Michael Palmer. SP-PalmM

As a rosebud might, in dreams. Babe Herrick. James Whitcomb Riley. CP-RileJ

As a scurrying snow-flake. Casse-Noisette. Robert Graves. CP-GravR

As a short subject before the main feature. Experiment. Wisława Szymborska. SP-SzymW, tr. by Stanislaw Barańczak and Clare Cavanagh

As a sloop with a sweep of immaculate wing on her delicate spine. Buick. Karl Shapiro. SP-ShapK

As a thorn-brush or oaken bough. On Paddy's Character of "The Intelligencer." Unknown, sometimes at. to Thomas Sheridan. CP-SherT

As a thorn-bush, or oaken bough. On Paddy's Character of "The Intelligencer." Jonathan Swift. CP-SwifJ

As a War in Years of Peace. Philip Larkin. CP-LarkP

As a World Would Have It. Edwin Arlington Robinson. CP-RobiE

As Adam did in Paradise. Kenoza Lake. John Greenleaf Whittier. CP-WhitJ

As Adam Early in the Morning. Walt Whitman. CP-WhitW

As Adam lay a-dreaming beneath the Apple Tree. Four Angels, The. Rudyard Kipling. CP-KiplR

As against now the Gloucester. April Today Main Street. Charles Olson. SP-OlsoC Fr. Maximus Poems, The.

As All Must End. Robert Graves. CP-GravR

As American towns and cities I wander through. Maybe You Can't Take It with You, but Look What Happens When You Leave It Behind. Ogden Nash. CP-NashO

As an American traveler I have. Internal Migration: On Being on Tour. Alan Dugan. CP-DugaA

As an archaeologist unearths a mask with opercular teeth. Streamers. Arthur Sze. SP-SzeA

As an individual penance when my nothing speaks. "Space Is Not Merely a Background for Events, But Possesses an Autonomous Structure." —A. Einstein. Alan Dugan. CP-DugaA

As an intruder I trudged with careful innocence. Old Mansion. John Crowe Ransom. SP-RansJ

As an old traveler, I am indebted to paper-bound thrillers. Calling Spring VII-MMMC. Ogden Nash. CP-NashO

As Ann came in one summer's day. Sleeper, The. Walter De la Mare. CP-DeLaW

'As anybody seen Bill 'Awkins? Bill 'Awkins. Rudyard Kipling. CP-KiplR

As any(men's hells having wrestled with). E. E. Cummings. CP-CummE

As, at a railway junction, men. Sic Itur. Arthur Hugh Clough. SP-ClouA

As at a Theatre. Wallace Stevens. CP-StevWP

As at Funerals. Yehuda Amichai. SP-AmicYL, tr. by Benjamin Harshav and Barbara Harshav

As at the beginning of birth. Poem: "As at the beginning of birth." Yehuda Amichai. SP-AmicYL, tr. by Benjamin Harshav and Barbara Harshav

As at the bottom of a seething well. Song, A: "As at the bottom of a seething well." Richard Wilbur. CP-WilbR

As at Thy Portals Also Death. Walt Whitman. CP-WhitW

As Bad as a Mile. Philip Larkin. CP-LarkP

As balmly as the breath of her you love. Dante Gabriel Rossetti. CW-RossD

As beautiful as the hands. For Miriam. Kenneth Patchen. CP-PatcK

As Befits a Man. Langston Hughes. CP-HughL; CP-HughL3

As bronze may be much beautified. Fragment: "As bronze may be much beautified." Wilfred Owen. CP-OwenW

As by subtracting, my lady, one creates. Michelangelo Buonarroti. CP-Miche, tr. by John Frederick Nims

As by the dead we love to sit. Emily Dickinson. CP-DickE

As by the fix'd decrees of Heaven. Pignus Amoris. Lord Byron. CP-Byron

As by the quickening breath of Spring. Hymn: "As by the quickening breath of Spring." Jones Very. CP-VeryJ

As by the stream[e]s of Babylon [or Babilon]. Thomas Campion. CP-CampT

As by Water. W. S. Merwin. SP-MerwW

As cauld a wind as ever blew. Lines Written in the Kirk of Lamington. Robert Burns. CP-BurnR

As Celia rested in the shade. Pastoral[1] Dialogue, A. Thomas Carew. CP-CareT

As, certainly, it is not you who sway. Round & a Canon, A. Charles Olson. CP-OlsoC

As Children bid the Guest "Good Night." Emily Dickinson. CP-DickE

As clever Tom Clinch, while the rabble was bawling. Clever Tom Clinch Going to Be Hanged. Jonathan Swift. CP-SwifJ

As Cold Water to a Thirsty Soul, So Is Good News from a Far Country. Christina Georgina Rossetti. CP-RosC2

As Consequent, Etc. Walt Whitman. CP-WhitW

As cool as the pale wet leaves. Alba. Ezra Pound. SP-PounE

As Crazy As I Ever Was. Charles Bukowski. SP-BukC1

As Created. James Whitcomb Riley. CP-RileJ

As day was born, as night was dying. Impression: Fog Off the Coast of Dorset. Edna St. Vincent Millay. CP-MillE

As dear as freedom to the patriot breast. On the Return of Col Laurens from His Confinement in the Tower of London. Annis Boudinot Stockton. CP-StocA

As Devonshire letters, earlier in the year. To Oxford. Gerard Manley Hopkins. CP-HopkG

As down the burn they took their way. Down the Burn Davie. Robert Burns. CP-BurnR

As down the stage again. Dead Tenor, The. Walt Whitman. CP-WhitW

As dying, and behold we live! Christina Georgina Rossetti. CP-RosC2

As eager homebound traveller to the goal. After This the Judgement. Christina Georgina Rossetti. CP-RosC1

As Eichmann Said, My Brother Said. A. K. Ramanujan. CP-RamaA

As Eichmann said, the trains. As Eichmann Said, My Brother Said. A. K. Ramanujan. CP-RamaA

As Eumaeus, the swineherd, got up to attent to. Trivial Details. Yannis Ritsos. SP-RitsY, tr. by Kimon Friar

As evening shaped I found me on a moor. Meeting with Despair, A. Thomas Hardy. CP-HardT

As Expected. Thom Gunn. CP-GunnT

As fades the delicate flower of Southern skies. Arabella Johnson. Jones Very. CP-VeryJ

As far as I can see, this autumn haze. Cocoon, The. Robert Frost. CP-FrosR

As Far as It Goes, and Back. Eleanor Wilner. SP-WilnE

As far as most of what you call people, my darling, are. Suburban Homecoming. John Ciardi. CP-CiarJ

As far as statues go, so far there's not. From Trollope's Journal. Elizabeth Bishop. CP-BishE

As far from pity, as complaint. Emily Dickinson. CP-DickE

As father Adam first was fool'd. Epitaph on a Henpecked Country Squire. Robert Burns. CP-BurnR

As flames that consume the mountains, as winds that coerce the sea. Love Is Strong as Death. Christina Georgina Rossetti. CP-RosC2

As Flowers Are. Stanley Kunitz. CP-KunSC

As flowers have wars that the philosophic eye. As Flowers Are. Stanley Kunitz. CP-KunSC

As fond mother, when the day is o'er. Nature. Henry Wadsworth Longfellow. SP-LongH

As for him who. Fragment: "As for him who." William Carlos Williams. CP-WilW2

As for himself, with draggled gown. William Percival. CP-SherT Fr. Description in Answer to The Journal, A.

As for me I am a child of the god of the mountains. This Poem Is for Bear. Gary Snyder. CP-SnydG Fr. Myths and Texts.

As for me, I distrust the commonplace. Vertigo. Adrienne Rich. CP-RicAE

As for Me, I'm a Patriot. D. H. Lawrence. CP-LawrD

As for my life, I've led it. Placid Man's Epitaph, A. Thomas Hardy. CP-HardT

As for Poets. Gary Snyder. CP-SnydG

As for the liar, fear him less. Sincerity. Thomas Merton. CP-MertT

As for the World. Yehuda Amichai. SP-AmicY, tr. by Stephen Mitchell

As for the World. Yehuda Amichai. SP-AmicYL, tr. by Benjamin Harshav and Barbara Harshav

As fragile as a shell. Orphan at the Door, An. Nuala Ni Dhomhnaill. CP-MahoD, tr. by Derek Mahon

As freedom is a breakfastfood. E. E. Cummings. CP-CummE; SP-CummE

As from a freckling on. Continental Drift. Amy Clampitt. CP-ClamA

As from afar, / through ringlet of woods. Circle. Robert Creeley. CP-CreeR

As from an ancestral oak. Similes for Two Political Characters of 1819. Percy Bysshe Shelley. CP-ShelP

As from the Darkening Gloom a Silver Dove. John Keats. CP-KeatJ

As from the earth the light Balloon. Emily Dickinson. CP-DickE

As from the fall of candlelight. George Meredith. CP-MerG2

As from Thou shalt not seethe a kid in his mother's milk. Instead of a Love Poem. Yehuda Amichai. SP-AmicYL, tr. by Benjamin Harshav and Barbara Harshav

As Frost is best conceived. Emily Dickinson. CP-DickE

As froth on the face of the deep, / As foam on the crest of the sea. Christina Georgina Rossetti. CP-RosC2

As Frothing Wounds of Roses. Kenneth Patchen. CP-PatcK

As gay for you to take your father's ax. To a Young Wretch. Robert Frost. CP-FrosR

As Gilly flowers do but stay. Upon a Lady That Dyed in Child-Bed, and Left a Daughter behind Her. Robert Herrick. CP-HerrR

As God is my witness where is the difference between. Carmen 97. Catullus. CP-ZukLS *Fr.* Carmina.

As gods sometimes descend from heav'n and deign. Of the Lady Who Could Not Sleep in a Stormy Night. Alexander Pope. CP-PopeA

As golden yellow as possible. Homage to Hart Crane. Philip Whalen. SP-WhalP

As grains of sand, as stars, as drops of dew. All Saints. Christina Georgina Rossetti. CP-RosC2

As gray as that slumped. Fall Day, A. Charles Simic. SP-SimiC; SP-SimiCE

As growth of form or momentary glance. Transfigured Life. Dante Gabriel Rossetti. CW-RossD *Fr.* House of Life, The.

As happiness takes off the tie it borrowed from me. "Unfinished," The. Frank O'Hara. SP-OharF

As He Is. W. H. Auden. CP-AudeW

As he knelt by the grave of his mother and father. Milkweed and Monarch. Paul Muldoon. CP-MuldP

As he moves the mine-detector. Hunting Civil War Relics at Nimblewill Creek. James Dickey. CP-DickJ

As he passed his father's room, he glanced in a the door. Five O'Clock in the Morning. Raymond Carver. CP-CarvR

As he passes the open door. Empty Room, The. James Laughlin. CP-LaugJ

As he prowled the rim of his clearing. Hermit, The. Seamus Heaney. SP-HeanSO *Fr.* Sweeney Redivivus.

As he said vanity, so vain say I. Vanity of All Worldly Things, The. Anne Bradstreet. CP-BradA

As he stood near the plane, they heard him say. Muriel Rukeyser. CP-RukeM

As he that loves oft looks on the dear form. On the 'Vita Nuova' of Dante. Dante Gabriel Rossetti. CW-RossD

As he that sees a dark and shady grove. Holy Baptism (1). George Herbert. CP-HerbG

As he waited in front of the new invention. Opening to Satan, An. Dan Pagis. SP-PagiD, *tr. by* Stephen Mitchell

As he was standing below the altars. Ezra Pound. *See* Hudor / HUDOR et Pax

As he was walking alone in the deserted street. Nocturne. Yannis Ritsos. SP-RitsY, *tr. by* Kimon Friar

As he writes, without looking at the sea. Afternoon, An. Raymond Carver. CP-CarvR

As Hermes once took to his feathers light. On a Dream. John Keats. CP-KeatJ

As honest Jacob on a night. Patriarch, The. Robert Burns. CP-BurnR

As humans we have needs. Han-shan. CP-ColdM, *tr. by* Red Pine

As I am a Rhymer. On My Joyful Departure from the City of Cologne. Samuel Taylor Coleridge. CP-ColeS

As I approach the state of pure euphoria. Euphoria. Lawrence Ferlinghetti. SP-FerlL

As I cam down by Annan side. Trogger, The. Robert Burns. CP-BurnR

As I cam down by yon castle wa'. Song: "As I cam down by yon castle wa'." Robert Burns. CP-BurnR

As I cam in by our gate-end. Bonnie Peg. Robert Burns. CP-BurnR

As I Cam[e] O'er [the] Cairney Mount. Robert Burns. CP-BurnR

As I came out of the New York Public Library. Nuns in the Wind. Muriel Rukeyser. CP-RukeM

As I came over Windy Gap. Running to Paradise. William Butler Yeats. CP-YeatW

As I came to the edge of the woods. Come In. Robert Frost. CP-FrosR

As I cross my kitchen floor the thought of Death returns. May Days 1988. Allen Ginsberg. SP-GinsA

As I drive to the junction of lane and highway. At Castle Boterel. Thomas Hardy. CP-HardT

As I Ebb'd with the Ocean of Life. Walt Whitman. CP-WhitW

As I enter the theatre the play is going on. Ritual One. David Ignatow. SP-IgnaD

As I explained the rules. On Gaining a Soul. Alan Dugan. CP-DugaA

As I gird on for fighting. A. E. Housman. CP-HousA

As I go prowling through room. Inside the Storm. Boris Leonidovich Pasternak. SP-WeisT, *tr. by* Theodore Weiss

As I Grew Older. Langston Hughes. CP-HughL; CP-HughL1

As I Grew Up Again. Audre Lorde. SP-LordA

As I grow older, I must admit with terror. Lost Tune, The. Robert Lowell. SP-LoweR

As I grow older I perceive. Poet as Fisherman. Lawrence Ferlinghetti. SP-FerlL

As I had seen it practiced in that land. Preparation for the Highest Being.

Kenneth Patchen. CP-PatcK

As I have known them passionate and fine. Lost Follower, The. Robert Frost. CP-FrosR

As I have often told. Hugh MacDiarmid. SP-MacDH *Fr.* Snares of Varuna, The.

As I lay asleep in Italy. Mask [*or* Masque] of Anarchy, The. Percy Bysshe Shelley. CP-ShelP

As I lay awake at night-time. Revisitation, The. Thomas Hardy. CP-HardT

As I Lay Dying. Charles Bukowski. SP-BukC2

As I lay sleeping in the park. Philosophers, The. Thomas Merton. CP-MertT

As I Lay with My Head in Your Lap Camerado. Walt Whitman. CP-WhitW

As I leaned to retrieve. Savage Beast, The. William Carlos Williams. CP-WilW2

As I left my door. James Russell Lowell. Ralph Waldo Emerson. CP-EmerR

As I left the Halls at Lumley, rose the vision of a comely. As the Bell Clinks. Rudyard Kipling. CP-KiplR

As I lie here in the sun. Jonah. Randall Jarrell. CP-JarrR

As I lift the glass to drink. George Oppen. CP-OppGN

As I listened from a beach-chair in the shade. Their Lonely Betters. W. H. Auden. CP-AudeW

As I mused by the hearthside. Comfort. Walter De la Mare. CP-DeLaW

As I my little flock on Ister Bank. Shepherd Song. Sir Philip Sidney. SP-SidnP *Fr.* Arcadia.

As I one evening [*or* ev'ning] sat before my cell. Artillery [*or* Artillerie]. George Herbert. CP-HerbG

As I paint the street. Lorine Niedecker. CP-NiedL

As I pass through my incarnations in every age and race. Gods of the Copybook Headings, The. Rudyard Kipling. CP-KiplR

As I passed thru Moscow's grass lots I heard. Two Dreams. Allen Ginsberg. CP-GinsA

As I pause at the side of the bath. Grief. D. H. Lawrence. CP-LawrD

As I Ponder'd [*or* Pondered] in Silence. Walt Whitman. CP-WhitW

As I reach to close each book. Against the Evidence. David Ignatow. SP-IgnaD

As I remember it, the harbor. Belvedere. George Oppen. CP-OppGN

As I ride, as I ride. Through the Metidja to Abd-el-Kadr. Robert Browning. CP-BroR1

As I roved out impatiently. In the Ringwood. Thomas Kinsella. CP-KinsT

As I roved out this morning at daybreak. Wire. Paul Muldoon. CP-MuldP

As I said before one Saturday night. Jan, the Son of Thomas. Carl Sandburg. CP-SandC

As I sat down by Saddle Stream. Return from Town, The. Edna St. Vincent Millay. CP-MillE

As I sat smoking, alone, yesterday. Backward Look, A. James Whitcomb Riley. CP-RileJ

As I saw. George Oppen. CP-OppGN

As I sd to my / friend, because I am. I Know a Man. Robert Creeley. CP-CreeR

As I shook the dust. Lorine Niedecker. CP-NiedL

As I Sit in the Silence. James Whitcomb Riley. CP-RileJ

As I sit in twilight late alone by the flickering oak-flame. Twilight Song, A. Walt Whitman. CP-WhitW

As I sit looking out of a window of the building. Instruction Manual, The. John Ashbery. SP-AshbJ

As I sit with others at a great feast, suddenly while the music is playing. Thought. Walt Whitman. CP-WhitW

As I Sit Writing Here. Walt Whitman. CP-WhitW

As I stand here I feel myself growing older and impatient. Imaginary Splendors. Philip Whalen. SP-WhalP

As I stare at the smoothly worn portrait of. For the Egyptian Coin Today, Arden, Thank You. Raymond Carver. CP-CarvR

As I started home after dark. Winter Night Poem for Mary. Wendell Berry. CP-BerrW

As I Step over a Puddle at the End of Winter, I Think of an Ancient Chinese Governor. James Wright. CP-WrigJ

As I stood by yon roofless tower. Song: "As I stood by yon roofless tower." Robert Burns. CP-BurnR

As I stood in my room tonight, drinking a solitary toast. Tennessee Williams. CP-WillT

As I stroll the city, oft I. Character, Panegyric, and Description of the Legion Club, A. Jonathan Swift. CP-SwifJ

As I talk to these children hovering on the verge. Fledglings. William Meredith. SP-MereW

As I turn'd into the market-place. George Meredith. CP-MerG2

As I view the leaf, my theme is not the shades of meaning. My Own House. David Ignatow. SP-IgnaD

As I walk slowly along. Orphic Soul, The. Kenneth Rexroth. CP-RexrK

As I Walk These Broad Majestic Days. Walt Whitman. CP-WhitW

As I walk'd thinking through a little grove. On a Wet Day. Franco Sacchetti.

CW-RossD, *tr. by* Dante Gabriel Rossetti

As I walked at dawn in the forest. In May. Adam Zagajewski. SP-ZagaA, *tr. by* Renata Gorczynski

As I walked in the woods. Ralph Waldo Emerson. CP-EmerR

As I walked out in meadows green. Vacant Day, The. Walter De la Mare. CP-DeLaW

As I Walked Out One Evening. W. H. Auden. CP-AudeW

As I walked out that sultry night. Full Moon. Robert Graves. CP-GravR

As I wandered in the forest. Wild Flower's Song, The. William Blake. CP-BlakW

As I wandered on the beach. Great Blue Heron, The. Carolyn Kizer. CP-KizeC

As I was a wand'ring ae midsummer e'enin. Robert Burns. CP-BurnR

As I was going down that defiled staircase. On the Stairs. Constantine P. Cavafy. CP-CavaC, *tr. by* Theoharis Constantine Theoharis

As I was going whistling down the hill of Hell. Cook in Hell, A. Andrei Codrescu. SP-CodrA

As I was reading the book of nature. Book of Nature, The. Richard Eberhart. CP-EberR

As I was riding through New England. Ides of March, The. Richard Eberhart. CP-EberR

As I was spittin' into the Ditch aboard o' the *Crocodile*, Soldier an' Sailor Too. Rudyard Kipling. CP-KiplR

As I was walking. Kore. Robert Creeley. CP-CreeR

As I was walking home just now, from seeing. Departure from Hydra, The. Kenneth Koch. SP-KochK

As I was walking in the fading light. First Canto. Jaroslav Seifert. SP-SeifJ *Fr.* Robed in Light.

As I was walking through this parking. Strange Moment, A. Charles Bukowski. SP-BukC3

As I was walking up the street. O Mally's Meek, Mally's Sweet. Robert Burns. CP-BurnR

As I was wandering down the street. Any Millenniums Today, Lady? Ogden Nash. CP-NashO

As I Watch'd the Ploughman Ploughing. Walt Whitman. CP-WhitW

As I went down our street. Two-Fold. D. H. Lawrence. CP-LawrD

As I went down the hill along the wall. Meeting and Passing. Robert Frost. CP-FrosR

As I went down the road to the water, the river to the sea. Asylum Song. Muriel Rukeyser. CP-RukeM

As I went down to Rotten Lake I remembered. First Elegy. Rotten Lake. Muriel Rukeyser. CP-RukeM

As I went in and out I heard pieces. Charles Olson. CP-OlsoC

As I went out a Crow. Last Word of a Bluebird, The. Robert Frost. CP-FrosR

As I Went Out Ae May Morning. Robert Burns. CP-BurnR

As I went over fossil hill. Journey, The. Kathleen Jessie Raine. SP-RainK

As I went through the marshes. Doe at Evening, A. D. H. Lawrence. CP-LawrD

As I went up by Ovillers. Ballad of the Three Spectres. Ivor Gurney. SP-GurnI

As I went walking up and down to take the evening air. Macdougal Street. Edna St. Vincent Millay. CP-MillE

As I Would Wish You Birds. John Ciardi. CP-CiarJ

As if a cast of grain leapt back to the hand. Event, An. Richard Wilbur. CP-WilbR

As if a nail whose wide head. Of Hours. George Oppen. CP-OppGN

As If a Phantom Caress'd Me. Walt Whitman. CP-WhitW

As if a tresspasser. King of the Ditchbacks, The. Seamus Heaney. SP-HeanSO

As if an army rose out of one grave. Late Fall, Late Light. Wyatt Prunty. SP-PrunW

As if as / if a mys. E. E. Cummings. CP-CummE

As if Hallam Movius had placed a grid over it, and plumb-. Charles Olson. CP-OlsoC

As if he had been poured. Grauballe Man, The. Seamus Heaney. SP-HeanSO

As if I asked a common Alms. Emily Dickinson. CP-DickE

As if I had know you for years drink to me only if. All Over Again. Louis MacNeice. CP-MacNL

As if I were composed of dust and air. Master and Mistress. Stanley Kunitz. CP-KunSC

As if I were given a reversed telescope instead of eyes, the world moves away. Poetic State, A. Czeslaw Milosz. CP-MiloC; CP-MiloCN, *tr. by* Robert Hass

As if in a presence of an intelligence. Cold, The. Charles Simic. SP-SimiC; SP-SimiCE

As If It Happened. Tess Gallagher. SP-GallT

As if it were a scene made-up by the mind. Often I Am Permitted to Return to a Meadow. Robert Duncan. SP-DuncR

As if it were / forever that they move, that we. Merritt Parkway. Denise Levertov. SP-LeveDS

As if it were some noble thing. Mother in Wartime. Langston Hughes. CP-HughL; CP-HughL3

As if just beyond Helsinki. Thoughts on the Run 1. Hans Magnus Enzensberger. SP-EnzeH, *tr. by* Rita Dove *and* Fred Viebahn

As if planted there by giant golfers in the skies. Mt. Gabriel. Derek Mahon. CP-MahoD

As if some little Arctic flower. Emily Dickinson. CP-DickE

As if that hand. Puñal. Denise Levertov. SP-LeveDP

As if the Sea should part. Emily Dickinson. CP-DickE

As if the storme meant him. Mark 4; Why Are Yee Afraid, O Yee of Little Faith? Bible, *N.T.* CP-CrasR *Fr.* St. Mark.

As if this light boat had no keel. Sun Boat. May Sarton. SP-SartM

As if to take in ocean. Cannibals. Donald Davie. CP-DaviDC

As if we chewed dry twigs and salt grasses. Robert Lowell. SP-LoweR *Fr.* Mexico.

As if we were two. By Whose Hand. Olga Broumas. SP-BrouO

As If You Had Never Been. Richard Eberhart. CP-EberR

As imperceptibly as grief. Emily Dickinson. CP-DickE

As in a dream, strange epitaphs I see. On Stone. Ambrose Bierce. SP-BierA

As in a film by Godard: alone. Desperate Vitality, A. Pier Paolo Pasolini. SP-PasoP, *tr. by* Norman MacAfee *and* Luciano Martinengo

As in a parable the truant father. Pealing, The. Olga Broumas. SP-BrouO

As in a shoestore. False Interpretation. Yehuda Amichai. SP-AmicYL, *tr. by* Benjamin Harshav *and* Barbara Harshav

As in a silent night a lonely swain. Prologue to a Play Performed at Mr. Sheridan's School Spoke by One of His Scholars, A. Thomas Sheridan. CP-SherT

As in a Swoon. Walt Whitman. CP-WhitW

As in Gaugin's *The Loss of Virginity*. Title, The. William Carlos Williams. CP-WilW2

As in her ancient mistress' lap. Familiarity Dangerous. Vincent Bourne. CP-CowpW

As in Music / A Reprise / Across Time. James Laughlin. CP-LaugJ

As in our clothes, so likewise he who lookes. Lines Have Their Linings, and Bookes Their Buckram. Robert Herrick. CP-HerrR

As in some car chase on Sunday-night TV. Miami. John Updike. CP-UpdiJ

As in some dim baronial hall restrained. Behind the Arras. Paul Laurence Dunbar. CP-DunbP

As in the amusement park they have these streams of water. Small Birds, to Agree with the Leaves, Come in the Fall. Charles Olson. CP-OlsoC

As in the green sky. Kenneth Patchen. CP-PatcK

As In Their Time. Louis MacNeice. CP-MacNL

As is the sand upon the ocean's shore. One generation passeth away, and another generation cometh: but the earth abideth for ever. Ecclesiastes 1:4. Jones Very. CP-VeryJ

As is the sea marvelous. E. E. Cummings. CP-CummE

As is your name, so is your comely face. To the Handsome Mistresse Grace Potter. Robert Herrick. CP-HerrR

As Is / you're bearing. Written in My Dream by W. C. Williams. Allen Ginsberg. SP-GinsA

As Islam's Prophet, when his last day drew. Requital. John Greenleaf Whittier. CP-WhitJ

As it fell upon a day. Gerard Manley Hopkins. CP-HopkG

As It Happens. Denise Levertov. SP-LeveDP

As it is / in my country. We Have a Map of the World. Alice Walker. CP-WalkA

As it is, plenty. His Excellency. W. H. Auden. CP-AudeW

As It Should Be. Derek Mahon. CP-MahoD

As It Was. Yehuda Amichai. SP-AmicYL, *tr. by* Benjamin Harshav *and* Barbara Harshav

As it was with Christ, so it is with Malcolm. Abduction of Saints, The. Alice Walker. CP-WalkA

As It Was Written. Anne Sexton. CP-SextA

As it's give' me to perceive. On Any Ordenary Man in a High State of Laughture and Delight. James Whitcomb Riley. CP-RileJ

As I've carried in my heart this many a year. Michelangelo Buonarroti. CP-Miche, *tr. by* John Frederick Nims

As Joe Gould says in. E. E. Cummings. CP-CummE

As John to Patmos. Derek Walcott. CP-WalcD

As Jove will not attend on less. Epistle upon an Epistle, An. Jonathan Swift. CP-SwifJ

As Julia once a-slumbering lay. Captived Bee; or, The Little Filcher, The. Robert Herrick. CP-HerrR

As Kafka has told us, / sin always comes openly. Peccatology. Charles Wright. SP-WrigCN

As kingdoms after civil broil. Love's Parable. Robert Penn Warren. CP-

WarrR

As Kingfishers Catch Fire. Gerard Manley Hopkins. CP-HopkG

As kingfishers catch fire, dragonflies dráw flåme. As Kingfishers Catch Fire. Gerard Manley Hopkins. CP-HopkG

As late by a sodger I chanced to pass. I'll Mak You Be Fain to Follow Me. Robert Burns. CP-BurnR

As late I journey'd o'er the extensive plain. Life. Samuel Taylor Coleridge. CP-ColeS

As late I lay in slumber's shadowy vale. Burke. Samuel Taylor Coleridge. MW-ColeS *Fr.* Effusions.

As late I rambled in the happy fields. To a Friend Who Sent Me Some Roses. John Keats. CP-KeatJ

As late in wreaths gay flowers I bound. Ode in the Manner of Anacreon, An. Samuel Taylor Coleridge. CP-ColeS

As late on Skiddaw's mount I lay supine. Stanger Minstrel, A. Samuel Taylor Coleridge. CP-ColeS

As lately I a Garland bound. Upon Cupid. Robert Herrick. CP-HerrR

As lately o'er the Historick page I por'd. Thoughts on the Pythagorian System. Annis Boudinot Stockton. CP-StocA

As learn'd *Eliza*, sister of the Muse. To Eliza Plucking Laurel in Mr Pope's Gardens. Samuel Johnson. CP-JohnS

As leaves are to the tree wheron they grow. At Bologna, in Remembrance of the Late Insurrections, 1837, Continued: "As leaves are to the tree wheron they grow." William Wordsworth. CP-WorW2

As leaves fall from the trees, the body falls from the soul. Indian Summer 2. Charles Wright. SP-WrigCN

As "legal representative." Circular, A. Thomas Hardy. CP-HardT

As lemmings run into the sea. Running into Things. Miller Williams. CP-WillM

As life eternal is the sight of God. Petrarch. CP-Petra, *tr.* by J. G. Nichols

As lightning strikes the Golden Gate. Alcatraz. Peter Blue Cloud. SP-BlueP

As lone I sat one summer's day. Love Despoiled. Paul Laurence Dunbar. CP-DunbP

As Long Ago As Far Away. May Swenson. SP-SwenM

As long as Fame's imperious music rings. Three Quatrains. Edwin Arlington Robinson. CP-RobiE

As long as I stay in the village. Han-shan. CP-ColdM, *tr.* by Red Pine

As long as it took fasten it back to a place where after all he. Patriarchal Poetry. Gertrude Stein. CP-SteiG

As long as the day lasts, it will not last. Classical Tragedy. Sam Hamill. SP-HamiS

As long as they trample the sad smiles of guitars. Long Naked Walk of the Dead, The. C. K. Williams. CP-WillC

As long as we are lost. Empty Mirror. Kenneth Rexroth. CP-RexrK

As long as we look forward, all seems free. Western Approaches, The. Howard Nemerov. CP-NemeH

As long as we move at a dancing gait, my love. Yellow Bicycle. Czeslaw Milosz. CP-MiloC; CP-MiloCN, *tr.* by Robert Hass

As long as we stayed in closed rooms. Moment Between Masks. Rainer Maria Rilke. CP-RilkFr, *tr.* by A. Poulin, Jr.

As long as we're bound by the Six Extremes. Han-shan. CP-ColdM, *tr.* by Red Pine

As Long as You Can. Constantine P. Cavafy. CP-CavaC, *tr.* by Theoharis Constantine Theoharis

"As love of native land," the old man said. His Love of Home. James Whitcomb Riley. CP-RileJ

As love / that is. Bird's Companion, The. William Carlos Williams. CP-WilW1

As Lovers Do. Hugh MacDiarmid. SP-MacDH

As loving Hind that (Hartless) wants her Deer. Another. Anne Bradstreet. CP-BradA

As Mailie, an' her lambs thegither. Death and Dying Words of Poor Mailie, the Author's Only Pet Yowe, an Unco Mournfu' Tale, The. Robert Burns. CP-BurnR

"As many as I love,"—Ah Lord, Who lovest all. Whitsun Eve. Christina Georgiana Rossetti. CP-RosC2

As many flowers as can be blossom in the summer. Elegy of the Flowers. Constantine P. Cavafy. CP-CavaC, *tr.* by Theoharis Constantine Theoharis

As many Lawes and Lawyers do expresse. Prognostick, A. Robert Herrick. CP-HerrR

As Many Questions As Answers. Laura Riding Jackson. CP-RidiL

As massive and dispensable as sculpture. Sonnet: "As massive and dispensable as sculpture." Donald Davie. CP-DaviDC

As mastiff dogs in modern phrase are. Description of a Salamander, The. Jonathan Swift. CP-SwifJ

As men, for fear the stars should sleep and nod. Divinity. George Herbert. CP-HerbG

As men have loved their lovers in times past. Edna St. Vincent Millay. CP-MillE

As mercenary canting quacks. Blunder of All Blunders, on the Wonder of All

Wonders, The. *Unknown, sometimes at. to* Thomas Sheridan. CP-SherT

As Modrian knew. Summer Storm. Charles Wright. SP-WrigCN

As much as in a hundred years, she's dead. Dante Gabriel Rossetti. CW-RossD

As My Blood Was Drawn. Robert Earl Hayden. CP-HaydR

As my father died of cancer of the asshole. For Euthanasia and Pain-Killing Drugs. Alan Dugan. CP-DugaA

As my father, the late star, once told me. Portrait of the Queen in Tears. Louise Glück. SP-GlucL

As my first blow against it, I would not stay. Mad Farmer in the City, The. Wendell Berry. CP-BerrW

As my head in darkness dents pillow, the last. Tires on Wet Asphalt at Night. Robert Penn Warren. CP-WarrR

As my little Pot doth boyle. To God, His Gift. Robert Herrick. CP-HerrR

As my skin wrinkles in warning like. Thermometer. Charles Bukowski. SP-BukC2

As My Uncle Ust to Say. James Whitcomb Riley. CP-RileJ

As newer comers crowd the fore. Superseded, The. Thomas Hardy. CP-HardT

As Now It Would Be Snow. Robert Creeley. CP-CreeR

As o'er his furrowed fields which lie. Seed-Time and Harvest. John Greenleaf Whittier. CP-WhitJ

As o'er the cold sepulchral stone. Lines Written in an Album, at Malta. Lord Byron. CP-Byron

As oft as Night's is banish'd by the Morne. Dangers Wait on Kings. Robert Herrick. CP-HerrR

As often as a martyr dies. Rosa Sanguinea, The. Henry David Thoreau. CP-ThorH

As often as he let himself be seen. Rat, The. Edwin Arlington Robinson. CP-RobiE

As often as I murmur here. Poet and the Caged Turtledove, The. William Wordsworth. CP-WorW2

As often as we thought of her. Neighbors. Edwin Arlington Robinson. CP-RobiE

As often in a bun. George Meredith. CP-MerG2

As oftentimes the too resplendent sun. Silentium Amoris. Oscar Wilde. CP-WildO

As old as Woe. Emily Dickinson. CP-DickE

As on a day Sabina fell asleepe. Thomas Campion. CP-CampT

As on a hill-top rude, when closing day. John Milton. *See* As on a rugged mountain at the darkening of evening

As on a rugged mountain at the darkening of evening. Sonnet 3: "As on a rugged mountain at the darkening of evening." John Milton. CP-CowpW; CP-MiltJ

As on a window late I cast mine eye. Love-Joy. George Herbert. CP-HerbG

As on each journey there is. On Each Journey. W. S. Merwin. SP-MerwW

As once in heaven Dante looked back down. Backward Look, The. Howard Nemerov. CP-NemeH

As one by one withdraw the lofty actors. Death of General Grant. Walt Whitman. CP-WhitW

As one by the side of a pool. Shallow Pool, The. Tennessee Williams. CP-WillT

As One does Sickness over. Emily Dickinson. CP-DickE

As one in sorrow looks upon. Old Year and the New, The. James Whitcomb Riley. CP-RileJ

As one of our brightest young intellectuals said to me. What Matters. D. H. Lawrence. CP-LawrD

As one of the secretaries of the moon. Word with José Rodríguez-Feo, A. Wallace Stevens. CP-StevW; CP-StevWP

As One Put Drunk into the Packet-Boat. John Ashbery. SP-AshbJ

As one put drunk into the packet-boat. Tom May's Death. Andrew Marvell. CP-MarvA

As one red rose in a garden where all other roses are. As the Apple Tree among the Trees of the Wood. Christina Georgina Rossetti. CP-RosC2

As one speaks to stone, as / you. Radix, Matrix. Paul Celan. SP-CelaP, *tr.* by John Felstiner

As one that strives, being sick, and sick to death. To Celia, upon Love's Ubiquity. Thomas Carew. CP-CareT

As one that would draw thru the node of things. Plotinus. Ezra Pound. CP-PoEar

As one who, groping in a narrow stair. Staircase of Notre Dame, Paris, The. Dante Gabriel Rossetti. CW-RossD

As one who(having written). E. E. Cummings. CP-CummE

As one who looks from rocky dales. Theory. G. K. Chesterton. CP-ChesG

As one who 'midst a choir alone doth sing. Poet, The. Jones Very. CP-VeryJ

As one who poring on a Grecian urn. Camma. Oscar Wilde. CP-WildO

As one who shoots an arrow overhead. Arthur Hugh Clough. SP-ClouA

As one who, standing safe upon the land. Daily News, The. Jones Very. CP-VeryJ

As orange dusk-light falls on an old idea. Sunset S.S. Azemour. Allen Ginsberg. CP-GinsA

As our boat ran that dead gut, the slime. Filippo Argenti. Dante Alighieri. CP-CiarJ *Fr.* Divina Commedia.

As Our Bodies Rise, Our Names Turn into Light. Charles Wright. SP-WrigCN

As our mother the Frigate, bepainted and fine. Cruisers. Rudyard Kipling. CP-KiplR

As our planet swings and sways. Speech: For Antidraft Rally, D.C., March 22, 1980, A. Denise Levertov. SP-LeveDL

As Parmigianino did it, the right hand. Self-Portrait in a Convex Mirror. John Ashbery. SP-AshbJ

As people who appear in dreams. Museum. A. K. Ramanujan. CP-RamaA

As pilots pay attention to the air. Morning: I Know Perfectly How in a Minute You Will Stretch and Smile. John Ciardi. CP-CiarJ

As Pippa Lilted. William Stafford. SP-StafWW

As plan for Noon and plan for Night. Emily Dickinson. CP-DickE

As power and wit will me assist. Sir Thomas Wyatt. CP-WyatT

As praiseworthy / The power of breathing. Lorine Niedecker. CP-NiedL

As Puritans they prominently wax. Certain People, A. George Meredith. CP-MerG1

As rivers seek the sea. Confluents. Christina Georgina Rossetti. CP-RosC1

As Rochefoucauld his maxims drew. Verses on the Death of Dr. Swift, D.S.P.D. Jonathan Swift. CP-SwifJ

As round and soft as women. Museums in Chapultepec, The. Jay Wright. SP-WrigJ

As salt, keep your savour. In the Hills South of Capernaum, Port. Charles Olson. CP-OlsoC

As sharp as in my childhood, still. Edna St. Vincent Millay. CP-MillE

As she goes about the homestead. Land-Worker. D. H. Lawrence. CP-LawrD *Fr.* Bits.

As she laughed I was aware of becoming involved in her laughter. Hysteria. T. S. Eliot. CP-ElioT

As she rides to the station. Traveler, The. Randall Jarrell. CP-JarrR

As she walked she would look back. Melpomene in Manhattan. David Ignatow. SP-IgnaD

As She Was Thus Alone in the Clear Moonlight. Kenneth Patchen. CP-PatcK

As ships, becalmed at eve, that lay. Qua Cursum Ventus. Arthur Hugh Clough. SP-ClouA

As shows [*or* shews] the air[e], when with a rainbow graced. Upon Julia's Ribband. Robert Herrick. CP-HerrR

As sickly Plants betray a niggard Earth. Alliance of Education and Government, The. Thomas Gray. CP-GrayT

As silent as a mirror is believed. Legend. Hart Crane. CP-CranH

As Sir Saltonstall ran over. Buffalo Ode. Charles Olson. CP-OlsoC

As Sleigh Bells seem in summer. Emily Dickinson. CP-DickE

As snow lies on the hill love's blackness lies. Charles Olson. CP-OlsoC; SP-OlsoC

As Soft and as Pink as a Nursery. Eleanor Wilner. SP-WilnE

As solid-seeming as antiquity. Marriage in the 'Sixties, A. Adrienne Rich. CP-RicAE; SP-RicA1; SP-RicA2

As some bland soul, to whom a debtor says. Her Confession. Thomas Hardy. CP-HardT

As some fond virgin, whom her mother's care. Epistle to Miss [*or* Miss Teresa] Blount, on Her Leaving the Town after the Coronation. Alexander Pope. CP-PopeA

As some pale-lidded ghost that calls. I Wait. Ezra Pound. CP-PoEar

As some rapt gazer on the lowly earth. Love's Humility. Paul Laurence Dunbar. CP-DunbP

As some raw youth in country bred. To Dr. Delany, on the Libels Writ against Him. Jonathan Swift. CP-SwifJ

As some true chief of men, bowed down with stress. Sun's Shame, The ("As some true chief of men, bowed down with stress"). Dante Gabriel Rossetti. CW-RossD *Fr.* House of Life, The.

As some vast tropic Tree, itself a Wood. Tree of Mystery, The. Samuel Taylor Coleridge. CP-ColeS

As someone speaking of his mother. Rainer Maria Rilke. CP-RilkFr, *tr. by* A. Poulin, Jr. *Fr.* Valaisian Quatrains, The.

As soon as I had finished my *Last Supper*. Last Supper. Venetian, Sixteenth Century. Hans Magnus Enzensberger. SP-EnzeH

As soon as / I speak, I. Pattern, The. Robert Creeley. CP-CreeR

As soon as the blackthorn comes in flower. Order of Saying, The. Charles Tomlinson. CP-TomlC

As soon as the full moon rises, I'm going to Santiago, Cuba. Blacks Dancing to Cuban Rhythms. Federico García Lorca. CP-GarcF, *tr. by* Greg Simon *and* Steven F. White

As soon as the idea of the Flood had subsided. After the Flood. Arthur Rimbaud. CP-RimbA, *tr. by* Martin Sorrell

As soon as the old man knew he was actually dying, even before anyone else would admit it. When. C. K. Williams. SP-WillC

As spring begins the river rises. March 22, 1968. Wendell Berry. CP-BerrW

As spring flowers are promised by. Quiet Talk with Oneself, A. Charles Simic. SP-SimiC; SP-SimiCE

As spring the winter doth succeed. Anne Bradstreet. CP-BradA

As subtle as tomorrow. Emily Dickinson. CP-DickE

As sultry as the cruising hum. Muted Music. Robert Penn Warren. CP-WarrR

As Summer into Autumn slips. Emily Dickinson. CP-DickE

As Sun-beames pierce the glasse, and streaming in. Another. Robert Herrick. CP-HerrR

As sunbeams stream through liberal space. Woodnotes II ("As sunbeams stream through liberal space"). Ralph Waldo Emerson. CP-EmerR

As surely as I hold your hand in mine. Brown Boy to Brown Girl. Countee Cullen. CP-CullC

As sweet as the look of a lover. Geotheos. Ambrose Bierce. SP-BierA

As swift and dying as the forms of flame. À Constance, This Day. Charles Olson. CP-OlsoC

As swift the changing seasons come and go. Kingdom of Heaven: In Its Growth and Coming a Mystery, The. Jones Very. CP-VeryJ

As swimmers dare. Avowal, The. Denise Levertov. SP-LeveDS

As Tam the chapman on a day. Tam the Chapman. Robert Burns. CP-BurnR

As tangible a form in History. Benjamin Harrison. James Whitcomb Riley. CP-RileJ

As that named Fred. E. E. Cummings. CP-CummE

As the Apple Tree among the Trees of the Wood. Christina Georgina Rossetti. CP-RosC2

As the Asian War Begins. Robert Bly. SP-BlyR

As the Bell Clinks. Rudyard Kipling. CP-KiplR

As the builders / Planned, the city trees. Sunnyside Child. George Oppen. CP-OppGN

As the cat. Poem: "As the cat." William Carlos Williams. CP-WilW1

As the child knows not if his mother's face. From Dawn to Noon. Dante Gabriel Rossetti. CW-RossD *Fr.* House of Life, The.

As the cold aspect of a sunless way. Captivity.—Mary Queen of Scots. William Wordsworth. CP-WorW2

As the corn becomes higher. Cricket Match. Carl Sandburg. CP-SandC

As the dawn was breaking the Sambhur belled—. Hunting-Song of the Seeonee Pack. Rudyard Kipling. CP-KiplR *Fr.* Jungle Book, The.

As the Dead Prey upon Us. Charles Olson. CP-OlsoC; SP-OlsoC

As the dove which found no rest / For the sole of her foot, flew back. Christina Georgina Rossetti. CP-RosC2

As the Doves to Their Windows. Christina Georgina Rossetti. CP-RosC2

As the drop feeds its fated flower. Ralph Waldo Emerson. CP-EmerR

As the eye fails through age or disease. Robinson Jeffers. CP-JefR3

As the eye lifts, the field. Three Sonnets. William Carlos Williams. CP-WilW2

As the fireman said. Riding the Elevator into the Sky. Anne Sexton. CP-SextA; SP SextA

As the fishermen pulled up the giant manta ray. Touristic Note from the Gulf. Alan Dugan. CP-DugaA

As the fresh wine the poet pours. Ode to Apollo. William Wordsworth. CP-WorW1

As the garbage truck is backing up, one of the garbagemen is absorbed watching a pretty girl pass. Men. C. K. Williams. SP-WillC

As the gods began one world, and man another. Snakecharmer. Sylvia Plath. CP-PlatS

As the Greek's Signal Flame. Walt Whitman. CP-WhitW

As the hedges, clipt and even. Offering. William Carlos Williams. CP-WilW1

As the hostess said. Verbal Generation, The. John Ciardi. CP-CiarJ

As the Ignorant Savage will sell his own Wife. On the Great Encouragement Given By English Nobility & Gentry to Correggio Rubens Rembrandt Reynolds Gainsborough Catalani Ducrowe & Dilbury Doodle. William Blake. CP-BlakW

As the immense dew of Florida. Nomad Exquisite. Wallace Stevens. CP-StevW; CP-StevWP

As the last light. Whip-Poor-Will. Donald Hall. CP-HallD

As the Liberty Lads o'er the Sea. Lord Byron. CP-Byron

As the little white hearse went glimmering by. Little White Hearse, The. James Whitcomb Riley. CP-RileJ

As the lone, frighted user of a night-road. Fernando Pessoa. SP-PessF *Fr.* 35 Sonnets.

As the mailman walked up the hill. Pace is the Essence. Charles Bukowski. SP-BukC3

As the mind burns. For G.B.S., Old. William Carlos Williams. CP-WilW2

As the moon sidles up. He and She. William Butler Yeats. CP-YeatW

As the Ocean Changes Colour. Aleksandr Aleksandrovich Blok. SP-BlokA, *tr. by* Peter France *and* Jon Stallworthy

As the perpetual laughter about the grounds. Satyr Formalist. A. R. Ammons.

CP-AmmoA

As the plump squirrel scampers. Today I Was So Happy, So I Made this Poem. James Wright. CP-WrigJ

As the rain falls. Rain. William Carlos Williams. CP-WilW1

As the shadow closed on the face once my father's. Son. W. S. Merwin. SP-MerwWF

As the sheriff remarked: I had no business being there. On a Highway East of Selma, Alabama. Gregory Orr. SP-OrrG

As the shield goddess, Mycenae. Charles Olson. CP-OlsoC

As the shy Hind, the soft-eyed gentle Brute. Timorous Hind, The. Samuel Taylor Coleridge. CP-ColeS

As the silly shepherds. Commonplace, A. Theodore Weiss. SP-WeisT

As the snow falls I brush it away. Snowfall, A. Richard Eberhart. CP-EberR

As the Sparks Fly Upwards. Christina Georgina Rossetti. CP-RosC2

As the stars hide in the light before daybreak. Avoiding News by the River. W. S. Merwin. SP-MerwW

As the Starved Maelstrom lap the Navies. Emily Dickinson. CP-DickE

As the sun comes in the window. Monads. Kenneth Rexroth. CP-RexrK

As the sun comes up on the suffering world. Nandin's Tail. Eleanor Wilner. SP-WilnE

As the sunrise to the night. Fragment: To Italy. Percy Bysshe Shelley. CP-ShelP

As the sweet sweat of roses in a still. Comparison, The. John Donne. MW-DonnJ *Fr.* Elegies.

As the Time Draws Nigh. Walt Whitman. CP-WhitW

As the Tree Falleth. G. K. Chesterton. CP-ChesG

As the voice of many waters all saints sing as one. Before the Throne, and Before the Lamb. Christina Georgina Rossetti. CP-RosC2

As the wind breaks in from the sea again. Counsel. Charles Bukowski. SP-BukC2

As the wise men of old brought gifts. Gift, The. William Carlos Williams. CP-WilW2

As the years passed by, he began to speak bitterly; (how strange, he who had been so dedicated, or rather so submissive); not of course. Toward What? Yannis Ritsos. SP-RitsY, *tr. by* Kimon Friar

As there are such things as the liar's. Lapse of Memory, A. A. K. Ramanujan. CP-RamaA

As They Draw to a Close. Ivor Gurney. SP-GurnI

As They Draw to a Close. Walt Whitman. CP-WhitW

As they grew older. "King and Queen." Donald Hall. CP-HallD

As they lunch together at / the Boule d'Or they are. At the Boule d'Or. James Laughlin. CP-LaugJ

As they who, tossing midst the storm at night. Lost Statesman, The. John Greenleaf Whittier. CP-WhitJ

As they who watch by sick-beds find relief. Amy Wentworth. John Greenleaf Whittier. CP-WhitJ

As this comes in. Lute in the Attic, The. Kenneth Patchen. CP-PatcK

As tho' again—yea, even once again. Rhodes Memorial, Table Mountain. Rudyard Kipling. CP-KiplR

As Thomas was cudgelled [*or* cudgell'd *or* cudgel'd] one day by his wife. Three Epigrams. Jonathan Swift. CP-SwifJ

As those who are not athletic at breakfast day by day. Nature Morte. Louis MacNeice. CP-MacNL

As thou deserv'st, be proud; then gladly let. Pride Allowable in Poets. Robert Herrick. CP-HerrR

As thou wert loth to see, before thy feet. Sonnet: To a newly enriched Man; reminding him of the Wants of the Poor. Guido Cavalcanti. CW-RossD, *tr. by* Dante Gabriel Rossetti

As though a gipsy maiden with dim look. Dead Leaves. James Whitcomb Riley. CP-RileJ

As though an aged person were to wear. Elegy for the Monastery Barn. Thomas Merton. CP-MertT

As though explaining the idea of dancing. Explanation of America, An. Robert Pinsky. CP-PinsR

As though her lips. To Dorothy Maynor. Langston Hughes. CP-HughL; CP-HughL2

As Though I Was Waiting for That. W. S. Merwin. SP-MerwW

As though I'm fooled. That lacy body managed to forget. Nurse's Song. Louise Glück. SP-GlucL

As though it were the very soul of rational human intercourse which had been violated. Easter. C. K. Williams. SP-WillC

As though the mercury's under its tongue, it won't. Galatea Encore. Joseph Brodsky. CP-BrodJ

As though the skin had been stripped and pulled back onto the skull like a stocking and soldered. Scar. C. K. Williams. SP-WillC

As though there could be more than one center. Shaving without a mirror. W. S. Merwin. SP-MerwWF

As though there were no flowing. Charles Olson. CP-OlsoC

As Through the Wild Green Hills of Wyre. A. E. Housman. CP-HousA

As through the wild green hills of Wyre. As Through the Wild Green Hills of Wyre. A. E. Housman. CP-HousA

As Thucydides said. Theory, A. Thomas McGrath. SP-McGrT

As Thy Days, So Shall Thy Strength Be. Christina Georgina Rossetti. CP-RosC2

As thy friend's face, with shadow of soul o'erspread. Life the Beloved. Dante Gabriel Rossetti. CW-RossD *Fr.* House of Life, The.

As Thyself! D. H. Lawrence. CP-LawrD

As Time is not as long as Art. Bad Luck. Charles Baudelaire. CP-BaudC, *tr. by* Walter Martin

As time will turn our bodies straight. Religion Is That I Love You. Kenneth Patchen. CP-PatcK

As to a Frontispiece. Laura Riding Jackson. CP-RidiL

As to Himself at last eternity changes him. Tomb of Edgar Poe, The. Stéphane Mallarmé. CP-MallS, *tr. by* Henry Weinfield

As to How Much. Louis Zukofsky. CP-ZukLS

As to some lovely temple, tenantless. Edna St. Vincent Millay. CP-MillE

As to the fruitful tree, which, in the Spring. Tree of Liberty, The. Jones Very. CP-VeryJ

As Toilsome I Wander'd Virginia's Woods. Walt Whitman. CP-WhitW

As tomorrow as soon as it is day. Thy Gleeman Who Flattered Thee. Charles Olson. CP-OlsoC

As true as I was born into. Halfway. Maxine W. Kumin. SP-KumiM

As 'Twere To-night. Thomas Hardy. CP-HardT

As two whose love, first foolish, widening scope. Known in Vain. Dante Gabriel Rossetti. CW-RossD *Fr.* House of Life, The.

As usual i did not find him in cafes,the more dissolute atmosphere. E. E. Cummings. CP-CummE

As usual, I was desperate. Coming Home. Tess Gallagher. SP-GallT

As usual, legend got it all. Nestor's Bathtub. Rita Dove. SP-DoveR

As vain to raise a voice as a sigh. On Going Unnoticed. Robert Frost. CP-FrosR

As Venetian glass. Rainer Maria Rilke. CP-RilkFr, *tr. by* A. Poulin, Jr. *Fr.* Orchards.

As violets so be I recluse and sweet, / Cheerful as daisies unaccounted rare. Who Hath Despised the Day of Small Things? Christina Georgina Rossetti. CP-RosC2

As virtuous men pass[e] mildly away. Valediction, A: Forbidding Mourning. John Donne. CP-DonnJ; MW-DonnJ

As void as clouds that house and harbour none. Richard. Gerard Manley Hopkins. CP-HopkG

As wand'ring late o'er hill and dale. Prospect, The. By a Lady in Princeton. Annis Boudinot Stockton. CP-StocA

As watchers couched beneath a Bantine oak. Last Ode, The. Rudyard Kipling. CP-KiplR *Fr.* Debits and Credits.

As Watchers hang upon the East. Emily Dickinson. CP-DickE

As we are so wonderfully done with each other. Kenneth Patchen. CP-PatcK

As we came through the gate to look at the few new lambs. Ravens. Ted Hughes. SP-HughTN

As we drove down the ramp from the boat. Dover: Believing in Kings. James Dickey. CP-DickJ

As we hightailed it across the meadows. Journey to Cracow, A. Paul Muldoon. CP-MuldP

As we kissed good-bye. Eighteen Days without You. Anne Sexton. CP-SextA

As We Know. John Ashbery. SP-AshbJ

As we left the garden-party. Leaving. Richard Wilbur. CP-WilbR

As we lie down to sleep the world turns half away. Sleeping Standing Up. Elizabeth Bishop. CP-BishE

As / we lie side by side. E. E. Cummings. CP-CummE

As we live, we are transmitters of life. We Are Transmitters. D. H. Lawrence. CP-LawrD

As we pass Houses musing slow. Emily Dickinson. CP-DickE

As We Read Burns. James Whitcomb Riley. CP-RileJ

As We Sit. Robert Creeley. CP-CreeR

As we take nature, without permission. Emily Dickinson. SP-DickE

As we tour the field in the pause. Takeoff on Armageddon —For Ronald Reagan. Alan Dugan. CP-DugaA

As we wandered through the hill of graves. On Castle Hill. Marge Piercy. SP-PierM

As wearied pilgrims, once possessed. His Own Epitaph. Robert Herrick. CP-HerrR

As Weary Pilgrim, Now at Rest. Anne Bradstreet. CP-BradA

As Well As Any Other. Laura Riding Jackson. CP-RidiL

As well as any other, Erato. As Well As Any Other. Laura Riding Jackson. CP-RidiL

As We're Told. Rae Armantrout. SP-ArmaA

As, when a beauteous nymph decays. Stella's Birthday, 1725. Jonathan Swift. CP-SwifJ

As when a lofty pile is raised. To Stella, Who Collected and Transcribed His Poems. Jonathan Swift. CP-SwifJ

As when a ruined face. Grudging Respect. Donald Davie. CP-DaviDC

As when a tree's cut down the secret root. Prologue to *The Tempest* [or *The Enchanted Island*]. John Dryden. SP-DrydJ

As when desire, long darkling, dawns, and first. Bridal Birth. Dante Gabriel Rossetti. CW-RossD *Fr.* House of Life, The.

As when of old, some sorceress threw. Simile, A. Jonathan Swift. CP-SwifJ

As when relentless Jack the Ripper. Rose in Ice. Robert Stock. SP-StocR

As when rooting in a bin. Dick, a Maggot. Jonathan Swift. CP-SwifJ

As when someone. Position without a Magnitude. Charles Simic. SP-SimiC; SP-SimiCE

As when that Hero, who in each Campaign. Prologue to a Play for Mr. Dennis's Benefit, in 1733, when He Was Old, Blind, and in Great Distress, a Little before His Death, A. Alexander Pope. CP-PopeA

As when the deluge first began to fall. Ode to the Athenian Society. Jonathan Swift. CP-SwifJ

As when the gannet goes deep down. To H. M. Howard Nemerov. CP-NemeH

As when the last of the paid joys of love. After the French Liberation of Italy. Dante Gabriel Rossetti. CW-RossD

As When the Mystic. Robert Graves. CP-GravR

As when the new or full moon urges. Moon and the Waves, The. Samuel Taylor Coleridge. CP-ColeS

As, when the squire and tinker, Wood. Prometheus. Jonathan Swift. CP-SwifJ

As when two men have loved a woman well. Lost on Both Sides. Dante Gabriel Rossetti. CW-RossD *Fr.* House of Life, The.

As when, upon the smooth pacific deep. William Wordsworth. CP-WorW1

As white's the blossom on the rise. Love-sick Lass, The. Hugh MacDiarmid. SP-MacDH

As willing lid o'er weary eye. Emily Dickinson. CP-DickE

As winds thru a round smooth knot-hole. Ballad of Wine Skins. Ezra Pound. CP-PoEar

As wishing all about us sweet. On St. Winefred. Gerard Manley Hopkins. CP-HopkG

As with the dapper terns, or that sole cloud. Trolling for Blues. Richard Wilbur. CP-WilbR

As, working in hard stone to make the face. Michelangelo Buonarroti. CP-Miche, *tr. by* John Frederick Nims

As would any sound make. Canzone: "As would any sound make." Robert Creeley. CP-CreeR

As Wulfstan said on another occasion. Speech for the Repeal of the McCarran Act. Richard Wilbur. CP-WilbR

As ye go through these palm-trees. Song of the Virgin Mother, A. Félix Lope de Vega Carpio. CP-PoEar, *tr. by* Ezra Pound

As ye sow, so shall ye reap. Jones Very. CP-VeryJ

As years unwind now reels unwind. Casablanca. Maxine W. Kumin. SP-KumiM

As yet a stranger to the gentle fires. John Milton. *See* Not yet did I know your laws, enticing Amathusia

As yet my cheeks were not dry with flowing tears. On the Death of the Bishop of Ely. John Milton. CP-CowpW; CP-MiltJ

As yoked to her by absence as by prescence. Marilyn Hacker. SP-HackM *Fr.* Taking Notice.

As you all know, tonight is the night of the full. 12 O'Clock News. Elizabeth Bishop. CP-BishE

As you bend to touch. Sunstruck Foxglove. Ted Hughes. SP-HughTN

As You Both Shall Live. Miller Williams. CP-WillM

As You Came from the Holy Land. John Ashbery. SP-AshbJ

As You Came from the Holy Land [of Walsingham]. *Unknown, sometimes at. to* Sir Walter Ralegh. CP-RaleW

As you came with me in silence. Changes. Seamus Heaney. SP-HeanSO

As You Come. Robert Creeley. CP-CreeR

As you described your mastectomy in calm detail. American Beauty, An. Carolyn Kizer. CP-KizeC

As you grow older, it gets colder. View to the North. May Swenson. SP-SwenM

As you know mind. LZ's. Lorine Niedecker. CP-NiedL

As you lay in sleep. Cartography. Louise Bogan. CP-BogaL

As You Leave the Room. Wallace Stevens. CP-StevWP

As You Like It. Theodore Weiss. SP-WeisT

As you plaited the harvest bow. Harvest Bow, The. Seamus Heaney. SP-HeanSO

As you read, a white bear leisurely. To the Reader. Denise Levertov. SP-LeveDP

As you said, Sujata, it was not. What Was Left Over. Eleanor Wilner. SP-WilnE

As you see the large. Jack-Knife. Charles Bukowski. SP-BukC3

As you set out toward Ithaca. Ithaca. Constantine P. Cavafy. CP-CavaC, *tr. by* Theoharis Constantine Theoharis

As you sip your brand of scotch. Bosnia Tune. Joseph Brodsky. CP-BrodJ

As you would know, having lived in trouble here at my side. Plate of Steaming Fish, A. Kenneth Patchen. CP-PatcK

As you'll have heard, I'm no beginner. Tyanan Sculptor. Constantine P. Cavafy. CP-CavaC, *tr. by* Theoharis Constantine Theoharis

As yung Awrora with cristall haile. Ballat of the Abbot of Tungland, A. William Dunbar. CP-DunbW

As Zeus sent Hermes / to draw Agenor's cattle. Chronicles. Charles Olson. SP-OlsoC *Fr.* Maximus Poems, The.

Asa Gray wrote Increase Lapham. Lorine Niedecker. CP-NiedL

Ascending over Ohio. Lawrence Ferlinghetti. SP-FerlL

Ascension. Samuel Beckett. CP-BeckS

Ascension Day. Christina Georgina Rossetti. CP-RosC2

Ascension Day, 1964. W. H. Auden. CP-AudeW

Ascension Eve. Christina Georgina Rossetti. CP-RosC2

Ascension has. Emily Dickinson. SP-DickE

Ascent. W. S. Merwin. SP-MerwW

Ascent. Yannis Ritsos. *SP-RitsY, tr. by* Kimon Friar

Ascent to the Sierras. Robinson Jeffers. CP-JefR1

Asclepiades the Miser was horrified. Miser and the Mouse, The. Lucilius. SP-SmarC

Ash. W. S. Merwin. SP-MerwW

Ash-aureole behind. Paul Celan. SP-CelaP, *tr. by* John Felstiner

Ash Manor. James Tate. SP-TateJ

Ash tree / sacred to her who sails in. In the Time of the Blossoms. W. S. Merwin. SP-MerwW

Ash Wednesday. Thomas Merton. CP-MertT

Ash Wednesday. Christina Georgina Rossetti. CP-RosC2

Ash Wednesday. Christina Georgina Rossetti. CP-RosC3

Ash Wednesday [*or* Ash-Wednesday]. T. S. Eliot. CP-ElioT

Ash woods, willow, close to shore. Lorine Niedecker. CP-NiedL

Ashboughs. Gerard Manley Hopkins. CP-HopkG

Ashen skin with Titian hair. To a Red-headed Beggar. Charles Baudelaire. CP-BaudC, *tr. by* Walter Martin

Ashes. Charles Bukowski. SP-BukC1

Ashes. Philip Levine. SP-LeviP

Ashes, The. Carolyn Kizer. CP-KizeC

Ashes Ashes All Fall Down. Robert Stock. SP-StocR

Ashes Ashes We All Fall Down. C. K. Williams. CP-WillC

Ashes denote that Fire was. Emily Dickinson. SP-DickE

Ashes of Gramsci, The. Pier Paolo Pasolini. SP-PasoP, *tr. by* Norman MacAfee *and* Luciano Martinengo

Ashes of Life. Edna St. Vincent Millay. CP-MillE

Ashes of paper, ashes of a world. Annunciation, The. Thomas Merton. CP-MertT

Ashes of Soldiers. Walt Whitman. CP-WhitW

Ashes of Soldiers: Epigraph. Walt Whitman. CP-WhitW

Ashes on a Saturday Afternoon. Frank O'Hara. SP-OharF

Ashes to ashes, dust to dust. Mortality. Paul Laurence Dunbar. CP-DunbP

Ashes to ashes, spirit to the sky. Michelangelo Buonarroti. CP-Miche, *tr. by* John Frederick Nims

Ashkelon. Yehuda Amichai. SP-AmicYL, *tr. by* Benjamin Harshav *and* Barbara Harshav

Ashtray. Louis Zukofsky. CP-ZukLS

Ashtray, The. Raymond Carver. CP-CarvR

Ashurbanipal. Or the stern-view. For Cy Twombly Faced with His First Chicago & N.Y. Shows. Charles Olson. CP-OlsoC

Ashurnatsirpal III. Carl Sandburg. CP-SandC

Asia. Raymond Carver. CP-CarvR

Asian Peace Offers Rejected without Publication. Robert Bly. SP-BlyR

Asians Dying, The. W. S. Merwin. SP-MerwW

Aside. Federico García Lorca. CP-GarcF, *tr. by* Jerome Rothenberg *Fr.* Water Jets.

Aside to Husbands. Ogden Nash. CP-NashO

Asides on the Oboe. Wallace Stevens. CP-StevW

Ask at the door for the man whose name I gave you. Counsel. Tennessee Williams. CP-WillT

Ask Daddy, He Won't Know. Ogden Nash. CP-NashO

Ask Him. Raymond Carver. CP-CarvR

Ask, is Love divine. George Meredith. CP-MerG1

Ask me. On Memory. A. K. Ramanujan. CP-RamaA

Ask Me. William Stafford. SP-StafW; SP-StafWW

Ask me no more. Ode: "Ask me no more." Olga Broumas. SP-BrouO

Ask me no more, for fear I should reply. A. E. Housman. CP-HousA

Ask me to tell how it feels. Memory. Lucille Clifton. SP-ClifL

Ask not the cause why sullen Spring.   Song to a Fair Young Lady, Going Out of the Town in the Spring.   John Dryden.   SP-DrydJ

Ask not treasures from his store.   Ralph Waldo Emerson.   CP-EmerR

Ask not why hearts turn magazines of passions.   Funeral Elegy Upon that Pattern and Patron of Virtue, A.   John Norton.   CP-BradA

Ask of all-healing, all consoling thought.   Nicolas-Sébastien Roch Chamfort.   CP-BeckS

Ask of the philosopher why he philosophizes.   Role of the Idea in Poetry, The.   Wallace Stevens.   CP-StevWP

Ask the dead and they'll tell you: Come.   Shmuel HaNagid.   SP-HaNaS, *tr. by* Peter Cole

Ask the Roses.   Philip Levine.   SP-LeviP

Ask what is human life—the sage replies.   Hope.   William Cowper.   CP-CowpW

Ask why God made the GEM so small.   On Being Asked Why God Had Made Miss D——— So Little and Mrs A——— So Big.   Robert Burns.   CP-BurnR

Ask Your Mama.   Langston Hughes.   CP-HughL; CP-HughL3

Aske me what hunger is, and Ile reply.   Hunger.   Robert Herrick.   CP-HerrR

Aske me, why I do not sing.   On Himselfe.   Robert Herrick.   CP-HerrR

Ask[e] me why I send you here.   Primrose, The.   Robert Herrick.   CP-HerrR

Asked by a reporter out of questions.   On Passion as a Literary Tradition.   John Ciardi.   CP-CiarJ

Askest, 'How long thou shalt stay.'   Visit, The.   Ralph Waldo Emerson.   CP-EmerR

Asks anyone—"Where's a tag for steps?"   Epps.   Robert Browning.   CP-BroR2

Asleap / sleap / am welcome drifting.   Bride's Day.   Susan Howe.   SP-HoweS

Asleep.   Wilfred Owen.   CP-OwenW

Asleep and Awake.   Muriel Rukeyser.   CP-RukeM

Asleep in space, he labored death on time.   Adam Lay Ibounden.   Robert Stock.   SP-StocR

Asleep in the Valley.   Paul Verlaine.   CP-RimbA, *tr. by* Martin Sorrell

Asleep on the raft and forced far out to sea.   Raft, The.   Robert Graves.   CP-GravR

Asleep on your wings, Victory.   Victory Asleep.   Rainer Maria Rilke.   CP-RilkFr, *tr. by* A. Poulin, Jr.

Asleep or waking is it? for her neck.   Laus Veneris.   Algernon Charles Swinburne.   SP-SwinA

Asmodaean feat be mine, The.   Ralph Waldo Emerson.   CP-EmerR

Asmodai.   Geoffrey Hill.   CP-HillG

(Asmodeus.) CP-HillG

Asmodeus.   Geoffrey Hill.   *See* Asmodai

Asmodeus.   James Laughlin.   CP-LaugJ

Asmodeus was a singer in Naxos. He was a virtuous man.   Asmodeus.   James Laughlin.   CP-LaugJ

Asp, The.   Ogden Nash.   CP-NashO

Asparagus is back in all its glory.   Food Notes.   John Ciardi.   CP-CiarJ

Aspasia, yet pursue the sacred Theme.   Samuel Johnson.   CP-JohnS   *Fr.* Irene.

Aspect of the Air, An.   John Ciardi.   CP-CiarJ

Aspecta Medusa.   Dante Gabriel Rossetti.   CW-RossD

Aspen and the Stream, The.   Richard Wilbur.   CP-WilbR

Aspen Leaf in Windless World.   Robert Penn Warren.   CP-WarrR

Aspen tree, your leaves glance white into the dark.   Paul Celan.   SP-CelaP, *tr. by* John Felstiner

Aspen twig, The.   North to Taos.   Arthur Sze.   SP-SzeA

Aspens.   Raymond Carver.   CP-CarvR

Asphodel, An.   Allen Ginsberg.   CP-GinsA

Asphodel, That Greeny Flower.   William Carlos Williams.   CP-WilW2

Paterson, Book 5: The River of Heaven.   CP-WilW2

Asphodels.   Hans Magnus Enzensberger.   SP-EnzeH, *tr. by* Rita Dove *and* Fred Viebahn

Aspiration.   Langston Hughes.   CP-HughL; CP-HughL2

Aspirations of the Soul after God.   Jeanne Marie Bouvier de la Motte- Guyon.   CP-CowpW

Asra.   Paul Muldoon.   CP-MuldP

Ass, The.   D. H. Lawrence.   CP-LawrD

Ass, The.   Stevie Smith.   CP-SmitS

Ass But No Class.   Charles Bukowski.   SP-BukC3

Ass of Balaam, The.   George Meredith.   CP-MerG2

Assabet, The.   Henry David Thoreau.   CP-ThorH

Assassin.   Charles Tomlinson.   CP-TomlC; SP-TomlC

Assassin, An.   James Whitcomb Riley.   CP-RileJ

Assassin, The.   Richard Eberhart.   CP-EberR

Assassin, The.   James Whitcomb Riley.   CP-RileJ

Assassin, The.   Anne Sexton.   CP-SextA

Assassination Raga.   Lawrence Ferlinghetti.   SP-FerlL

Assateague.   John Logan.   CP-LogaJ

Assault.   Edna St. Vincent Millay.   CP-MillE

Ass[e], The.   Robert Herrick.   CP-HerrR

Assembled in their awful chamber.   Judges of the Secret Court, The.   James Laughlin.   CP-LaugJ

Assembly.   W. S. Merwin.   SP-MerwWF

Assembly of the Achaians.   Homer.   CP-MerG2   *Fr.* Iliad, The.

Assent to Wildflowers, An.   William Meredith.   SP-MereW

Assessment, The.   John Logan.   CP-LogaJ

Assidue ridet Lycius Clytha ut sua dormit.   In eosdem.   Thomas Campion.   CP-CampT

Assignation, The.   Walter De la Mare.   CP-DeLaW

Assignation, The.   James Wright.   CP-WrigJ

Assigned a week's good bunt, run, throw.   Baseball Team of Unknown Navy Pilots, Pacific Theater, 1944, A.   Wyatt Prunty.   SP-PrunW

Assignment.   Hayden Carruth.   CP-CarHS

Assis sur la terrasse Café Saint-Séverin.   L'Occupation Obsédée.   Lawrence Ferlinghetti.   SP-FerlL

Assisi.   Paul Celan.   SP-CelaP, *tr. by* John Felstiner

Assisi Fragments, The.   Geoffrey Hill.   CP-HillG

Assist Me, My Muse, Whilst I Labor to Limn Him.   *Unknown, sometimes at. to* Thomas Sheridan.   CP-SherT

Assist with mournful strains, assist, my Muse.   Elegy on the Deplorable Death of Mr. Thomas Sheridan, Author of *Alexander's Overthrow, or, The Downfall of Babylon*, Who Departed This Mortal Life on Thursday the 8th of March, 1721/22, An.   *Unknown.*   CP-SherT

Assistance.   Yannis Ritsos.   SP-RitsY, *tr. by* Kimon Friar

Assistants Come to Judgment In Groups.   Shmuel HaNagid.   SP-HaNaS, *tr. by* Peter Cole

Associate Professor Delivers an Exhortation to His Failing Students, The.   Miller Williams.   CP-WillM

Associate Professor (Mad Scientist) to (His Love) His Student in Physics 100 Lab.   Miller Williams.   CP-WillM

Assorted Chocolates.   Ogden Nash.   CP-NashO

Ass's hoof alone can hold, An.   On Burning a Dull Poem.   Jonathan Swift.   CP-SwifJ

Ass's Song, The.   Christopher Logue.   SP-LoguC

Assume, in a bird's eye, the world as a dainty bulge.   Two Poems, with Birds.   Mona Van Duyn.   SP-VanDM

Assuming Control.   William Stafford.   SP-StafWW

Assuming, in some dreamscape, some.   Styles.   John Ciardi.   CP-CiarJ

Assuming the Burden.   D. H. Lawrence.   CP-LawrD

Assuming the Soul Is a Bitch.   Charles Olson.   CP-OlsoC

Assurance.   Robert Frost.   CP-FrosR

Assurance.   George Herbert.   CP-HerbG

Assurance.   William Stafford.   SP-StafWW

Assurances.   Walt Whitman.   CP-WhitW

Assure us you side with order: throw.   Hymn 5: "Assure us you side with order: throw."   A. R. Ammons.   CP-AmmoA

Assured by many.   Walter Scott.   James Schuyler.   CP-SchuJ

Assured of death, of its timing, though, not so.   Michelangelo Buonarroti.   CP-Miche, *tr. by* John Frederick Nims

Assured of worthiness we do not dread.   Internal Harmony.   George Meredith.   CP-MerG1

Assuredly a lively scene.   Arthur Hugh Clough.   SP-ClouA   *Fr.* Dipsychus [and the Spirit].

Assyrian came down like the wolf on the fold, The.   Destruction of Sennacherib, The.   Lord Byron.   CP-Byron

Astarte Syriaca.   Dante Gabriel Rossetti.   CW-RossD

Aster.   Louis Zukofsky.   CP-ZukLS

Aster, a farewell-summer flower, stays long in the last fall weeks, An.   Carl Sandburg.   CP-SandC   *Fr.* People, Yes, The.

Asterisk / Says look below, as a star, The.   Games One.   Richard Wilbur.   CP-WilbR

Asters burn with the dim glow, The.   Postcards.   Adam Zagajewski.   SP-ZagaA, *tr. by* Clare Cavanagh

Astigmatic Naturalist, The.   Ogden Nash.   CP-NashO

Astonished Heart, The.   Lawrence Ferlinghetti.   SP-FerlL

Astonished Heaven looked on when man was made.   Her Seed; It Shall Bruise Thy Head.   Christina Georgina Rossetti.   CP-RosC2

Astonished stood Lucrece and Nara.   Lucrece and Nara.   Laura Riding Jackson.   CP-RidiL

Astounding subjects are the only ones, The.   Emily Dickinson.   SP-DickE

Astræa.   Ralph Waldo Emerson.   CP-EmerR

Astræa.   John Greenleaf Whittier.   CP-WhitJ

Astræa at the Capitol.   John Greenleaf Whittier.   CP-WhitJ

Astray over earth.   George Oppen.   CP-OppGN

Astride the boney jointed ridge.   Still Life.   William Carlos Williams.   CP-WilW2

Astrolabes and lexicons. Ballad: "Astrolabes and lexicons." George Oppen. CP-OppGN

Astrologer, The. Sir Thomas More. CP-CunnJ, *tr.* by James Vincent Cunningham

Astrologer's Song, An. Rudyard Kipling. CP-KiplR

Astrological Conundrums. Ted Hughes. SP-HughTN

Astrometaphysical. Robert Frost. CP-FrosR

Astronauts. Robert Earl Hayden. CP-HaydR

Astronomer. A. K. Ramanujan. CP-RamaA

Astronomer with patient, searching gaze, The. Slowness of Belief in a Spiritual World, The. Jones Very. CP-VeryJ

Astronomical Changes. D. H. Lawrence. CP-LawrD

Astronomy. A. E. Housman. CP-HousA

Astrophel. Edmund Spenser. CP-Spens

Epitaph upon the Right Honourable Sir Phillip Sidney, Knight: Lord Governor of Flushing, An. CP-Spens

Astrophil and Stella. Sir Philip Sidney. SP-SidnP

Astymelusa. Alcman. CP-GravR

Asylum, The. Hayden Carruth. CP-CarHL

Asylum Song. Muriel Rukeyser. CP-RukeM

Asylum under my tread all this day. Samuel Beckett. CP-BeckS *Fr.* Echo's Bones.

Asymmetrical face. Half of it. Bisection. Dan Pagis. SP-PagiD, *tr.* by Stephen Mitchell

Asymptotes. Charles Olson. CP-OlsoC

At a Bach Concert. Adrienne Rich. CP-RicAE; SP-RicA2

At a bend in the rocks there hung. Ritual for Eating the World. A. R. Ammons. CP-AmmoA

At a bend in the stream by willows. March Song. A. R. Ammons. CP-AmmoA

At a Bridal. Thomas Hardy. CP-HardT

At a bygone Western country fair. At a Country Fair. Thomas Hardy. CP-HardT

At a Calvary near the Ancre. Wilfred Owen. CP-OwenW

At a Certain Age. Czeslaw Milosz. CP-MiloCN, *tr.* by Robert Hass

At a certain distance I follow behind you, ashamed to come closer. Distance. Czeslaw Milosz. CP-MiloC; CP-MiloCN, *tr.* by Robert Hass

At a Country Fair. Thomas Hardy. CP-HardT

At a Country Funeral. Wendell Berry. CP-BerrW

At a Country Hotel. Howard Nemerov. CP-NemeH

At a crustal. Possibility Along a Line of Difference. A. R. Ammons. CP-AmmoA

At a Deathbed in the Year Two Thousand. Adrienne Rich. CP-RicAE

At a Fashionable Dinner. Thomas Hardy. CP-HardT

At a garden-party in Hillsborough, County Down. Bechbretha. Paul Muldoon. CP-MuldP

At a Glance. Charles Tomlinson. CP-TomlC

At a Hasty Wedding. Thomas Hardy. CP-HardT

At a House in Hampstead. Thomas Hardy. CP-HardT

At a Lecture. Joseph Brodsky. CP-BrodJ

At a literary gathering in Santa Monica. Union of Women. Carolyn Kizer. CP-KizeC

At a lonely cross where bye-roads met. Man Who Forgot, The. Thomas Hardy. CP-HardT

At a Loose End. D. H. Lawrence. CP-LawrD

(Dissolute.) CP-LawrD

At a Loss. Heather McHugh. SP-McHuH

At a Lunar Eclipse. Thomas Hardy. CP-HardT

At a March against the Vietnam War. Robert Bly. SP-BlyR

At a moment when all the discordant voices of modern society attempt to exorcize the vertigo of man. Letter to Pablo Antonio Cuadra Concerning Giants, A. Thomas Merton. CP-MertT

At a mountain inn, high above the bulky green of chestnuts. At Noon. Czeslaw Milosz. CP-MiloC; CP-MiloCN, *tr.* by Robert Hass

At a "National Encampment." Ambrose Bierce. SP-BierA

At a Parting. Countee Cullen. CP-CullC

At a Party. Louise Bogan. CP-BogaL

At a party I spy a handsome psychiatrist. Afternoon Happiness. Carolyn Kizer. CP-KizeC

At a Pause in a Country Dance. Thomas Hardy. CP-HardT

At a Private Showing in 1982. Maxine W. Kumin. SP-KumiM

At a Rehearsal of One of J.M.B.'s Plays. Thomas Hardy. CP-HardT

At a Rest Stop in Ohio. Amy Clampitt. CP-ClamA

At a Seaside Town in 1869. Thomas Hardy. CP-HardT

At a Solemn Music[k]. John Milton. CP-MiltJ

At a table in the corner two people. Revenants, The. James Laughlin. CP-LaugJ

At a Vacation Exercise [in the Col[l]e[d]ge [, Part Latin, Part English]]. John Milton. CP-MiltJ

At a Welsh Waterfall. Gerard Manley Hopkins. CP-HopkG

At a Window. Carl Sandburg. CP-SandC

At Algeciras—a Meditation upon Death. William Butler Yeats. CP-YeatW

At an Abandoned Shrine of Saint Mary Aegyptian. Robert Stock. SP-StocR

At an autumn evening bonfire. First Sonata for Karlen Paula. Carl Sandburg. CP-SandC

At an Inn. Thomas Hardy. CP-HardT

At an Intersection. Thom Gunn. CP-GunnT

At another year / I would not boggle. Birthday on the Beach. Ogden Nash. CP-NashO

At Antwerp, there is a low wall. Carillon, The. Dante Gabriel Rossetti. CW-RossD

At Apollinaire's Grave. Allen Ginsberg. CP-GinsA

At Applethwaite, near Keswick. William Wordsworth. CP-WorW1

At Auden's Grave. Karl Shapiro. SP-ShapK

At Aunty's House. James Whitcomb Riley. CP-RileJ

At Baia. "H. D." CP-DoolH

At Bald Rock with Old John. Peter Blue Cloud. SP-BlueP

At Banagher. Seamus Heaney. SP-HeanSO

At Barstow. Charles Tomlinson. CP-TomlC

At Bay. James Whitcomb Riley. CP-RileJ

At Benares. James Laughlin. CP-LaugJ

At Best, Poets. Robert Graves. CP-GravR

At Bethlehem, that city blest. Christmas Carol, A. G. K. Chesterton. CP-ChesG

At Beverly Farms, a portly, uncomfortable boulder. Terminal Days at Beverly Farms. Robert Lowell. SP-LoweR

At Billy Miller's Circus-Show. Billy Miller's Circus-Show. James Whitcomb Riley. CP-RileJ

At Blackwater Pond. Mary Oliver. SP-OlivM

At blond dawn. Jean Sans Terre Circles the Earth Seven Times. Iwan Goll. CP-WilW2

At Bologna, in Remembrance of the Late Insurrections, 1837. William Wordsworth. CP-WorW2

At Bologna, in Remembrance of the Late Insurrections, 1837, Continued: "As leaves are to the tree wheron they grow." William Wordsworth. CP-WorW2

At Bologna, in Remembrance of the Late Insurrections, 1837, Continued: "Hard task! exclaim the undisciplined, to lean." William Wordsworth. CP-WorW2

At break of dawn. Aubade: "At break of dawn." W. H. Auden. CP-AudeW *Fr.* Three Posthumous Poems.

At break of dawn the shape of life. Shuttle, The. Tennessee Williams. CP-WillT

At breakfast mother sipped her buttermilk. Magic Curtain, The. Stanley Kunitz. CP-KunSC

At Broad Ripple. James Whitcomb Riley. CP-RileJ

At Brownhill Inn. Robert Burns. CP-BurnR

At Brownhill we always get dainty good cheer. At Brownhill Inn. Robert Burns. CP-BurnR

At busy hearts in vain love's arrows fly. Ovid. CP-JohnS *Fr.* Remediae Amoris.

At Candle-Lightin' Time. Paul Laurence Dunbar. CP-DunbP

At Carol Willink's Exhibition. Joseph Brodsky. CP-BrodJ, *tr.* by Jamey Gambrell

At Casterbridge Fair. Thomas Hardy. CP-HardT

At Castle Boterel. Thomas Hardy. CP-HardT

At Cedros, thudding the dead sand. Tarpon. Derek Walcott. CP-WalcD

At certain hours when barely a breeze has blown. Remembrance of Belgian Friends. Stéphane Mallarmé. CP-MallS, *tr.* by Henry Weinfield

At Charlesgate. William Corbett. SP-CorbW

At Cheshire Cheese. Paul Laurence Dunbar. CP-DunbP

At Chinese Checkers. John Berryman. CP-BerrJ

At cliff-foot where great ledges thrust, the cave. Speleology. Robert Penn Warren. CP-WarrR

At Cocktails. John Ciardi. CP-CiarJ

At court I met it, in clothes brave enough. On Something, that Walk[e]s Somewhere. Ben Jonson. CP-JonsB; SP-JonsB

At Cove at our camp in the open canyon. At Cove on the Crooked River. William Stafford. SP-StafWW

At Cove on the Crooked River. William Stafford. SP-StafWW

At Croton. "H. D." CP-DoolH

At Crown Hill. James Whitcomb Riley. CP-RileJ

At Darien Bridge. James Dickey. CP-DickJ

At dark three o'clock. Shrivers, The. Josephine Jacobsen. CP-JacoJ

At Darragh's I. James Schuyler. CP-SchuJ

At David's Grave. Denise Levertov. SP-LeveDS

At Dawn. Czeslaw Milosz. CP-MiloC; CP-MiloCN, *tr. by* Robert Hass

At Dawn. Charles Tomlinson. CP-TomlC

At Dawn. William Carlos Williams. CP-WilW1

At dawn a certain rich man. Servant Who Loved His Prayers, The. Jelaluddin Rumi. SP-Rumi, *tr. by* Coleman Barks

At dawn a knot of sea-lions lies off the shore. Animals. Robinson Jeffers. CP-JefR3

At dawn every day a nereid comes up out of the sea. Nereid, The. James Laughlin. CP-LaugJ

At dawn, from the bedroom window: the elm tree's. Indian Summer. Gregory Orr. SP-OrrG

At Dawn in 1098. A. R. Ammons. CP-AmmoA

At dawn of morn, ere on the brake. Enchanted Goblet, The. Sir Walter Scott. SP-ScotW *Fr.* Bridal of Trierman, The.

At dawn, the crisp goodbye of friends; at night. Long Summer. Robert Lowell. SP-LoweR

At dawn the dove croons. California Spring. Charles Wright. SP-WrigC

At dawn today the spider's web was cold. End of Summer School, The. Howard Nemerov. CP-NemeH

At dawn you curl up in the top branches. Life, A. Gregory Orr. SP-OrrG

At Day-Close in November. Thomas Hardy. CP-HardT

At Daybreak. Adam Zagajewski. SP-ZagaA, *tr. by* Renata Gorczynski, Benjamin Ivry *and* C. K. Williams

At daybreak / Little one. School for Dark Thoughts. Charles Simic. SP-SimiC; SP-SimiCE

At daybreak thought. Daybreak Thought for Maria, A. Tennessee Williams. CP-WillT

At Delft. Charles Tomlinson. CP-TomlC

At Delphi. Donald Hall. CP-HallD

At Delphi. May Sarton. SP-SartM

At Delphi I prayed. Prayer, The. Denise Levertov. SP-LeveDP; SP-LeveDS

At Draw-Gloves we'l play. Draw Gloves. Robert Herrick. CP-HerrR

At Drumcliffe Churchyard, County Sligo. John Logan. CP-LogaJ

At Dublin's high feast sat Primate and Dean. Aye and No. Jonathan Swift. CP-SwifJ

At Dunbar, Castle or Arcade. Double Feature. Robert Earl Hayden. CP-HaydR

At Dusk. James Whitcomb Riley. CP-RileJ

At dusk / I went out walking. Woodcutter. Federico García Lorca. CP-GarcF, *tr. by* Jerome Rothenberg *Fr.* Secrets.

At dusk / just when. E. E. Cummings. CP-CummE

At dusk you appear, a school-girl still. Boris Leonidovich Pasternak. SP-WeisT, *tr. by* Theodore Weiss *Fr.* Illness.

At early dawn, or rather when the air. Gordale. William Wordsworth. CP-WorW2

At Ease. Walter De la Mare. CP-DeLaW

At East Lulworth the dead were friendly and pitiful, I saw them peek. Ghosts in England. Robinson Jeffers. CP-JefR2

At Easterly. Amy Clampitt. CP-ClamA

At eighteen, you stood for this faded photograph. Oval Portrait: Jessie Wilkie, The. Kathleen Jessie Raine. SP-RainK

At Eleusis. "H. D." CP-DoolH

At Eleusis. James Laughlin. CP-LaugJ

At Eleusis. Algernon Charles Swinburne. SP-SwinA

At evening, sitting on this terrace. Bat. D. H. Lawrence. CP-LawrD

At evening, something behind me. Mountain, The. Elizabeth Bishop. CP-BishE

At Eventide. John Greenleaf Whittier. CP-WhitJ

At every step, I find I must look back. Petrarch. CP-Petra, *tr. by* J. G. Nichols

At fifty I approach myself. In a Dream 2. David Ignatow. SP-IgnaD

At First. Alice Walker. CP-WalkA

At First, at Last. May Swenson. SP-SwenM

At First Flower of the Easy Day. John Ciardi. CP-CiarJ

At first he thinks the entire meadow in its abundance belongs to him. Art of Contraction, The. Dan Pagis. SP-PagiD, *tr. by* Stephen Mitchell

At first I laughed—for it was quite. My First Spectacles. James Whitcomb Riley. CP-RileJ

At first I thought a pest. Armor's Undermining Modesty. Marianne Craig Moore. CP-MoorM

At first I thought there was a superfine. Fleming Helphenstine. Edwin Arlington Robinson. CP-RobiE

At first I was given centuries. Margaret Atwood. SP-AtwM1

At first, Insult follows Injury like a choo-choo train. Marriage of Insult to Injury, The. Andrei Codrescu. SP-CodrA

At first it came easily, with the knowledge of the shadow line. Punishing the Myth. John Ashbery. SP-AshbJ

At first it seemed rather tight. Daft Little Shoe Clerk Decided It Would Be Fun to Go Up and See What Things Are Like above the Sky, The. Kenneth Patchen. CP-PatcK

At first it was as though you had passed. Many Wagons Ago. John Ashbery. SP-AshbJ

At first, it was only a trickle. Dixit Insipiens. Carolyn Kizer. CP-KizeC

At first it was only an imperceptible quivering of the skin. Divorce, The. Hans Magnus Enzensberger. SP-EnzeH, *tr. by* Michael Hamburger

At first light in the shadow, over the roach. Shaft, The. John Ciardi. CP-CiarJ

At first light, when. Eugenio Montale. CP-MontE, *tr. by* Jonathan Galassi

At first, not breathed on. Her Room. Kathleen Jessie Raine. SP-RainK

At first only cherries and the comic flight. Farewell for Zbigniew Herbert. Adam Zagajewski. SP-ZagaA, *tr. by* Clare Cavanagh

At First Sight. Robert Graves. CP-GravR

At first the dips are shallow. At First, at Last. May Swenson. SP-SwenM

At first, the euphemistic "blk." Blked. John Updike. CP-UpdiJ

At first the fences are racing under. Horses and men. Take-off over Kansas. John Ciardi. CP-CiarJ

At first, the mind feels bruised. Art of Poetry, The. Charles Tomlinson. CP-TomlC

At first, the mobiles were for multitudes. Auto. Heather McHugh. SP-McHuH

At first there was nothing. Then a closed space. Endymion. Thomas Kinsella. CP-KinsT

At first when you went away. Return, The. Louise Glück. SP-GlucL

At five in the afternoon. Lament for Ignacio Sánchez Mejías. Federico García Lorca. SP-GarcF, *tr. by* J. L. Gili *and* Stephen Spender

At five in the afternoon. Lament for Ignacio Sánchez Mejías. Federico García Lorca. CP-GarcF, *tr. by* Galway Kinnell

At five in the morning there were grey voices. Death of an Old Lady. Louis MacNeice. CP-MacNL

At five precisely in the afternoon. Crossing. Archibald MacLeish. CP-MacLA

At focus in the national. Monument and the Shrine, The. John Logan. CP-LogaJ

At Fort Worden: Calling Names. William Stafford. SP-StafWW

At Forty. A. K. Ramanujan. CP-RamaA

At forty, home from traveled intention. Firsts. John Ciardi. CP-CiarJ

At 42, Simon Rodilla, tile-setter. Nel Mezzo del Cammin di Nostra Vita. Robert Duncan. SP-DuncR

At four in the morning he wakes. More a Man Has the More a Man Wants, The. Paul Muldoon. CP-MuldP

At four o'clock. Roosters. Elizabeth Bishop. CP-BishE

At four o'clock I went by. David Ignatow. SP-IgnaD

At four this day of June I rise. Four in the Morning. Thomas Hardy. CP-HardT

At fourteen, parked / by the depot. Material. Donald Hall. CP-HallD

At fourteen you crawl through a hole. Gerry's Jazz. Yusef Komunyakaa. CP-KomuY

At Fourth and Main in Liberal, Kansas, 1932. William Stafford. SP-StafWW

At Furness Abbey. William Wordsworth. CP-WorW2

At Galway Races. William Butler Yeats. CP-YeatW

At Galway's, such / is the presence of the snows. Continuo. Hayden Carruth. CP-CarHS

At gauzy dusk, thin haze like cigarette smoke. Hospital Window. Allen Ginsberg. CP-GinsA

At ghost hour. Needle. Charles Simic. SP-SimiCE

At God's word David's kinsmen cast. Abishag. Louise Glück. SP-GlucL

At Grandmother's Wake. Kenneth Patchen. CP-PatcK

At Grass. Philip Larkin. CP-LarkP

At Half past Three, a single Bird. Emily Dickinson. CP-DickE

At Hay, or near it, 1944. Herefordshire. Donald Davie. CP-DaviDC

At her step the water-hen. Dante Gabriel Rossetti. CW-RossD

At Hertford House. Adrienne Rich. CP-RicAE

At hest, hendecasyllabics, what is this. Catullus. *See* From the quarters of the compass

At high tide / the sea—they say. Chorus of Troizenian Women. Euripides. CP-DoolH *Fr.* Hippolytus.

At his desk, lonely, Richard, his tie loose. String Puppets. Thomas Kinsella. CP-KinsT

At His Execution. Rudyard Kipling. CP-KiplR

At his incipient sun. First Love. Stanley Kunitz. CP-KunSC

At his request, after death, his brain was removed. Walt Whitman's Brain Dropped on Laboratory Floor. Thomas Lux. SP-LuxT

At His Wintry Tent. James Whitcomb Riley. CP-RileJ

At Holwell Farm. Charles Tomlinson. CP-TomlC; SP-TomlC

At Home. Andrei Codrescu. SP-CodrA

At Home. Christina Georgina Rossetti. CP-RosC1

At home, in my flannel gown, like a bear to its floe. 90 North. Randall Jarrell. CP-JarrR

At home / in the countryside. Pagan. Alice Walker. CP-WalkA

At home with my infirmities I fare. Hawkshead and Dachau in a Christmas Glass. Donald Davie. CP-DaviDC

At intermission I find her backstage. Cellist, The. Galway Kinnell. SP-KinnGN

At intersections / molecular desiring machines. Traffic. Andrei Codrescu. SP-CodrA

At Ithaca. "H. D." CP-DoolH

At its margin / the river's double willow. Ode to Arnold Schoenberg. Charles Tomlinson. CP-TomlC; SP-TomlC

At just 5 a / m i hear eng. E. E. Cummings. CP-CummE

At Kenneth Burke's Place. William Carlos Williams. CP-WilW2

At Knaresborough. Donald Davie. CP-DaviDC

At Lake Desolation. Kenneth Rexroth. CP-RexrK

At Lascaux. William Stafford. SP-StafWW

At Last. D. H. Lawrence. CP-LawrD

At Last. James Whitcomb Riley. CP-RileJ

At Last. Christina Georgina Rossetti. CP-RosC2

At Last. John Greenleaf Whittier. CP-WhitJ

At last a juggler is led out under the stars. Initiate, The. W. S. Merwin. SP-MerwW

At last, at even, to my hearth I hark. Sorrow. Charles Guérin. CP-ChesG, *tr. by* G. K. Chesterton

At last, dear friend, your letter has reached me. Elegy 1: To Charles Diodati. John Milton. CP-CowpW; CP-MiltJ

At last I entered a long dark gallery. Fragment: "At last I entered a long dark gallery." Thomas Hardy. CP-HardT

At last I hear the voice well known. Voice from the World, A. Gerard Manley Hopkins. CP-HopkG

At last I put off love. He Abjures Love. Thomas Hardy. CP-HardT

At last I realize my true position: hovering face down above the world. Self-Portrait Sad, 22:ix:58. Philip Whalen. SP-WhalP

At last! In sight of home again. Song of the Soldiers' Wives and Sweethearts. Thomas Hardy. CP-HardT

At last, someone had heard tell of Larry Durrell. Armageddon, Armageddon. Paul Muldoon. CP-MuldP

At last the poet spoke. Ralph Waldo Emerson. CP-EmerR

At last, to be identified! Resurgam. Emily Dickinson. CP DickE

At last we could keep quiet, each on his own. To Come of Age. Robert Graves. CP-GravR

At last when he had to go back. Wide Place in the Road. Miller Williams. CP-WillM

At last withdraw your cruelty. Sir Thomas Wyatt. CP-WyatT

At last you are tired of being single. Poem Read at Joan Mitchell's. Frank O'Hara. SP-OharF

At last you yielded up the album, which. Lines on a Young Lady's Photograph Album. Philip Larkin. CP-LarkP

At Least. Raymond Carver. CP-CarvR

At least at night, a streetlight. So Long. William Stafford. SP-StafW; SP-StafWW

At least let it be. Rainer Maria Rilke. CP-RilkFr, *tr. by* A. Poulin, Jr. *Fr.* Fragments.

At Least Let Me Explain. Thomas Lux. SP-LuxT

At least let me now beguile myself with false hopes. September 1903. Constantine P. Cavafy. CP-CavaC, *tr. by* Theoharis Constantine Theoharis

At least, my dear. Edna St. Vincent Millay. CP-MillE

At least, my dear. At least, my dear. Edna St. Vincent Millay. CP-MillE

At least—to pray—is left—is left. Emily Dickinson. CP-DickE

At least we cannot live to see it all; no comfort. World Will Little Note, The. Kenneth Patchen. CP-PatcK

At Least with Good Whiskey. John Ciardi. CP-CiarJ

At least you've come, sharing. From A to Z. Theodore Weiss. SP-WeisT

At leisure is the Soul. Emily Dickinson. CP-DickE

At length must *Suffolk*'s beauties shine in vain. To Lady Firebrace. Samuel Johnson. CP-JohnS

At length, my friend, the far-sent letters come. John Milton. *See* At last, dear friend, your letter has reached me

At length, my soul! thy fruitless hopes give o'er. Stanzas: "At length, my soul! thy fruitless hopes give o'er." François de Malherbe. CP-PopeA

At length revolving fates th' expected year. Ode, An: "At length revolving fates th' expected year." Francis Williams. CP-WheaP

At length their long kiss severed, with sweet smart. Nuptial Sleep. Dante Gabriel Rossetti. CW-RossD *Fr.* House of Life, The.

At length to hospital. Hospital Visits. Philip Larkin. CP-LarkP

At Liberty School. William Stafford. SP-StafWW

At Lindos. May Sarton. SP-SartM

At Loafing-Holt. Paul Laurence Dunbar. CP-DunbP

At low cost woodlands con. Lily-of-the-Valley. Louis Zukofsky. CP-ZukLS

At low tide like this how sheer the water is. Bight, The. Elizabeth Bishop. CP-BishE

At low tide, midnight, with a flashlight. Standing on an Alder Bridge over a Creek. Arthur Sze. SP-SzeA

At Lulworth Cove a Century Back. Thomas Hardy. CP-HardT

At Madame Manicure's. James Whitcomb Riley. CP-RileJ

At Madame Tussaud's in Victorian Years. Thomas Hardy. CP-HardT

At Maganosc / in the stone bedroom. William Dickey. SP-DickW *Fr.* In The Dreaming.

At Majority. Adrienne Rich. CP-RicAE

At Market Hill, as well appears. On Cutting Down the Old Thorn at Market Hill. Jonathan Swift. CP-SwifJ

At Martha's Deli. Paul Muldoon. CP-MuldP

At Mass. Nicholas Vachel Lindsay. CP-LindV

At Master McGrath's Grave. Paul Muldoon. CP-MuldP

At Mayfair Lodgings. Thomas Hardy. CP-HardT

At Melville's Tomb. Hart Crane. CP-CranH

At mid-morning her wheel-chair seems to rock. Angel of the Maze, The. James Dickey. CP-DickJ

At midday he rose on schedule from the flood. Proteus. Stanley Kunitz. CP-KunSC

At midday the birds doze. Hermit Picks Berries, The. Maxine W. Kumin. SP-KumiM

At Middle-Field Gate in February. Thomas Hardy. CP-HardT

At Midnight. D. H. Lawrence. CP-LawrD

At Midnight. Adam Zagajewski. SP-ZagaA, *tr. by* Renata Gorczynski, Benjamin Ivry *and* C. K. Williams

At midnight, after hours of love, I ate. Charles Olson. CP-OlsoC

At midnight by the stream I roved. Lewti. Samuel Taylor Coleridge. CP-ColeS

At midnight, in the month of June. Sleeper, The. Edgar Allan Poe. CP-PoeEd

At midnight, in the room where he lay dead. His Heart. Thomas Hardy. CP-HardT

At midnight / it began to rain. Arrival of Rain. Josephine Jacobsen. CP-JacoJ

At midnight on the next balcony. Lawrence Ferlinghetti. SP-FerlL *Fr.* Canti Romani.

At midnight tears. Solitary Observation Brought Back from a Sojourn in Hell. Louise Bogan. CP-BogaL

At midnight the teacher lectures on his throne. Reflections at Lake Louise. Allen Ginsberg. CP-GinsA

At midnight the world is a mediate / perspective. Two Ways of Looking in a Mirror. Robert Creeley. CP-CreeR

At midnight's hour I raised my head. Henry David Thoreau. CP-ThorH

At Midocean. Robert Bly. SP-BlyR

At Midsummer. Norman Dubie. CP-DubiN

At midsummer before dawn an orange light returns to the mountains. How We Are Spared. W. S. Merwin. SP-MerwW

At Moonrise and Onwards. Thomas Hardy. CP-HardT

At mo[o]st mischief. Sir Thomas Wyatt. CP-WyatT

At morn, at noon, at eve, and middle night. Poet, The. John Keats. CP-KeatJ

At morn—at noon—at twilight dim. Hymn: "At morn—at noon—at twilight dim." Edgar Allan Poe. CP-PoeEd

At morn I plucked a rose and gave it Thee. Rose Plant in Jericho, A. Christina Georgina Rossetti. CP-RosC1

At morn I prayed, "I fain would see." Trinitas. John Greenleaf Whittier. CP-WhitJ

At morn we placed on his funeral bier. By Callimachus. Callimachus. CP-CowpW, *tr. by* William Cowper

At morning we all look out. Hedge Life. James Dickey. CP-DickJ

At Muker, Upper Swaledale. Amy Clampitt. CP-ClamA

At Muzot. May Sarton. SP-SartM

At my age my father. Gathering, The. Wendell Berry. CP-BerrW

At my Command yon' Iron Gates unfold. Samuel Johnson. CP-JohnS *Fr.* Irene.

At My Father's Grave. Hugh MacDiarmid. SP-MacDH

At my feet the stream flows backwards. October. Gregory Orr. SP-OrrG

At my homely Country-seat. Larr's Portion, and the Poets Part. Robert Herrick. CP-HerrR

At my window / the rain raves, raves about dying. Wang Wei. Arthur Sze. SP-SzeA

At Nausicä's House. Yannis Ritsos. SP-RitsY, *tr. by* Kimon Friar

At Night. G. K. Chesterton. CP-ChesG

At Night. Paul Laurence Dunbar. CP-DunbP

At Night. Richard Eberhart. CP-EberR

At Night. Josephine Jacobsen. CP-JacoJ

At Night. William Carlos Williams. CP-WilW1

At night, alone, the animals came and shone. Animals, The. Josephine

Jacobsen. CP-JacoJ

At night Amanda's eyes. Eyes. Maxine W. Kumin. SP-KumiM

At night, as in a tomb, a pyramid. Yehuda Amichai. SP-AmicYL *Fr.* Here We Loved.

At night, back upstairs. Rainer Maria Rilke. CP-RilkFr, *tr. by* A. Poulin, Jr. *Fr.* Fragments.

At night, by the fire. Domination of Black. Wallace Stevens. CP-StevW; CP-StevWP

At night Chinamen jump. Poem: "At night Chinamen jump." Frank O'Hara. SP-OharF

At night I suddenly waken. Fernando Pessoa. SP-PessF *Fr.* Keeper of Sheep, The.

At night it was easy for me with my little candle. Keeping a Journal. William Stafford. SP-StafWW

At night, passing the open door. Fontenelle. Howard Nemerov. CP-NemeH

At night the day is constantly woken up. Work. Andrei Codrescu. SP-CodrA

At night the drawn blinds. Jockeys at Hialeah, The. Tennessee Williams. CP-WillT

At night the factories. Varick Street. Elizabeth Bishop. CP-BishE

At night—the light turned off, the filament. Burning Trash. John Updike. CP-UpdiJ

At night the monks sang softly. Shell. Adam Zagajewski. SP-ZagaA, *tr. by* Clare Cavanagh

At Night the Salmon Move. Raymond Carver. CP-CarvR

At night, toward dawn, all the lights of the shore have died. Hooded Night. Robinson Jeffers. CP-JefR2

At night we sailed past shadowed. That's Sicily. Adam Zagajewski. SP-ZagaA, *tr. by* Clare Cavanagh

At night, when I can't sleep. Career for a Child of Five. Kenneth Patchen. CP-PatcK

At nightfall, as the sea darkens. Ghost Crabs. Ted Hughes. SP-HughTN

At nine in the morning there passed a church. Faintheart in a Railway Train. Thomas Hardy. CP-HardT

At nine years a sickly boy lay down. Records. Allen Tate. CP-TateA

At Ninety in the Shade. James Whitcomb Riley. CP-RileJ

At ninety-seven my uncle found God heavy. Alec. John Ciardi. CP-CiarJ

At Noey's house—when they arrived with him. James Whitcomb Riley. CP-RileJ *Fr.* Child-World, A.

At Noon. Raymond Carver. CP-CarvR

At Noon. Czeslaw Milosz. CP-MiloC; CP-MiloCN, *tr. by* Robert Hass

At Noon—and Midnight. James Whitcomb Riley. CP-RileJ

At noon comes the lift—sunlight. William Stafford. SP-StafWW

At noon in the desert a panting lizard. At the Bomb Testing Site. William Stafford. SP-StafW; SP-StafWW

At noon in this blue cove of the Atlantic. Remembering Greece. Amy Clampitt. CP-ClamA

At noon sneaky. Cold Lunch. William Corbett. SP-CorbW

At noon, still wearing their white. Friday Lunchbreak. Gregory Orr. SP-OrrG

At noon the man was buggered and mugged downtown. God Victimized. Robert Stock. SP-StocR

At noon the sky goes off like a gun. Tropics. Thomas Merton. CP-MertT

At noon they spread their lunch on cool vineleaves. Remorse. Yannis Ritsos. SP-RitsY, *tr. by* Kimon Friar

At noon we have rain, which washes away the snow. Downstream. Raymond Carver. CP-CarvR

At noon you go back to the dust. Scarabs. Dan Pagis. SP-PagiD, *tr. by* Stephen Mitchell

At noontime under the very tall pines. In Tobey Woods. Hayden Carruth. CP-CarHS

At North Farm. John Ashbery. SP-AshbJ

At O'Hare. John Ciardi. CP-CiarJ

At once, from hence, my lines and I depart. To Mr T. W. ("At once, from hence, my lines and I depart"). John Donne. CP-DonnJ; MW-DonnJ

At once whatever happened starts receding. Whatever Happened? Philip Larkin. CP-LarkP

At one moment a few old leaves come in. Midnight in Early Spring. W. S. Merwin. SP-MerwW

At one of his readings a long time ago. Jaroslav Seifert. SP-SeifJ, *tr. by* Ewald Osers

At one of those bars where they weigh you at the door. Glass Darkly, A. Miller Williams. CP-WillM

At one the wind rose. Night-Music. Philip Larkin. CP-LarkP

At one they hurry in to eat. Waitress. Thom Gunn. CP-GunnT

At Our House. James Laughlin. CP-LaugJ

At Our House. William Stafford. SP-StafW; SP-StafWW

At peace here—I feel you about me. To the Outer World. William Carlos Williams. CP-WilW1

At Père Lachaise. Mona Van Duyn. SP-VanDM

At pet stores in Detroit, you can buy. Poem With One Fact. Donald Hall. CP-HallD

At Pleasure Bay. Robert Pinsky. CP-PinsR

At Plymouth in the friendly crowd. Ralph Waldo Emerson. CP-EmerR

At Pointe de Rompe Talon. Clarence Major. SP-MajoC

At Port Royal. John Greenleaf Whittier. CP-WhitJ

At Post and Paire, or Slam, Tom Tuck would play. Upon Tuck. Robert Herrick. CP-HerrR

At present I am a blank, and I admit it. Blank. D. H. Lawrence. CP-LawrD

At Rexroth's Grave. Sam Hamill. SP-HamiS

At Right Angles. Yehuda Amichai.

   "All my words and deeds were lost between the writing and the reading." SP-AmicYL

   "At the end of green spring, God begins." SP-AmicYL

   "Death was round and open as two halfs of an orange in sight." SP-AmicYL

   "Dust covers all the things mentioned above." SP-AmicYL

   "Electrical strings are taut over all. The world is my oud." SP-AmicYL

   "Frogs of expectation leaped out of me and came back, The." SP-AmicYL

   "Great speakers hold their microphone to their mouths." SP-AmicYL

   "I don't know what is good or bad for me hereabout." SP-AmicYL

   "I live now inside an abandoned love, like a guest." SP-AmicYL

   "I must think many stones till I have my true home." SP-AmicYL

   "I once fled, I don't recall from what God, for what wish." SP-AmicYL

   "In his prayer sands, my father saw traces of angels in heaven's gates." SP-AmicYL

   "In the end, we too will be winds from beyond the rim." SP-AmicYL

   "Most wandering thing is a heart that stopped wandering, The." SP-AmicYL

   "Now I know where they live, like the night owls." SP-AmicYL

   "Now it's autumn. All glasses broken at weddings, didn't bounce." SP-AmicYL

   "Now my love explains me as the commentators in their prime." SP-AmicYL

   "On the cover of an ancient box, a parting man and woman are drawn." SP-AmicYL

   "Once I knew answers. "Sit down!" said God. And didn't blink." SP-AmicYL

   "Sign of Gemini, star of luck, Capricorn, my star again." SP-AmicYL

   "Slowly, with the blossoms of understanding, I begin to grope." SP-AmicYL

   "Spring came. Different and quiet, anonymous blood in a spree." SP-AmicYL

   "Streets have names, pains have names, ships have names on their prow." SP-AmicYL

   "Two hopes away from the battlefield, I had a vision of peace." SP-AmicYL

   "Young soldier lies in spring, cut off from his name, A." SP-AmicYL

At Roslin Inn. Robert Burns. CP-BurnR

At Runnymede, at Runnymede. Reeds of Runnymede, The. Rudyard Kipling. CP-KiplR

At Rushy-Pond. Thomas Hardy. CP-HardT

At St. Marks Bookshop I buy. Insufficient Blue. Yusef Komunyakaa. CP-KomuY

At Saint Mary's Church. Charles Tomlinson. CP-TomlC

At Samoa, hardly unpacked, I commenced planting. Fanny. Carolyn Kizer. CP-KizeC *Fr.* Pro Femina.

At San Miguel de los Baños. Attempt to Discover Life. Wallace Stevens. CP-StevW; CP-StevWP

At Sant' Antimo. Charles Tomlinson. CP-TomlC; SP-TomlC

At School. Stevie Smith. SP-SmitS

At School-Close. John Greenleaf Whittier. CP-WhitJ

At school I always walk with Elwyn. At School. Stevie Smith. CP-SmitS

At school I loved one picture's heavy greenness. Fosterling. Seamus Heaney. SP-HeanSO

At school, I was a / squad-leader. I'd gotten enough votes. It meant. Each in a Place Apart. James McMichael. SP-McMiJ

At Sea. James Whitcomb Riley. CP-RileJ

At Sea ("Day follows day, and week succeeds to week"). Jones Very. CP-VeryJ

At Sea ("Frail woman there and childhood's tender years"). Jones Very. CP-VeryJ

At sea in the dome of St. Paul's. Homage to Wren. Louis MacNeice. CP-MacNL

At Sea, September 1833. Ralph Waldo Emerson. CP-EmerR

At secret daybreak they had met. Martins: September. Walter De la Mare. CP-DeLaW

At seventeen I'm told to write a paper. Fin-de-Siècle Blues. Carolyn Kizer. CP-KizeC

At seventeen I've come to read a poem. Twelve O'Clock. Carolyn Kizer. CP-KizeC

At seventeen women were strange & forbidden phenomenons. For Irving. Robert Creeley. CP-CreeR

At Shag's Heath. Thomas Hardy. CP-HardT

At sight of sparkling Bowls or beauteous Dames. Verses in Baretti's Commonplace Book. Samuel Johnson. CP-JohnS

At six A.M. the log cabins. Moose in the Morning, Northern Maine. Mona Van Duyn. SP-VanDM

At six / I lived in a graveyard full of dolls. Those Times. Anne Sexton. CP-SextA

At six in the morning you scratched at my porthole. Rhapsody on Irish Themes, A. Randall Jarrell. CP-JarrR

At six o'clock we were waiting for coffee. Miracle for Breakfast, A. Elizabeth Bishop. CP-BishE

At six, when April chills our hands and feet. Elektra on Third Avenue. Marilyn Hacker. SP-HackM

At sixteen I came West, riding. Living Pearl, A. Kenneth Rexroth. CP-RexrK

At 66 just learning how to take care of my body. Autumn Leaves. Allen Ginsberg. SP-GinsA

At Songfall. Federico García Lorca. CP-GarcF, tr. by Jerome Rothenberg Fr. Moments of Song.

At sound as of rushing wind, and sight as of fire. Whitsun Day. Christina Georgina Rossetti. CP-RosC2

At Sportsmen's Park, near Yakima, I crammed a hook. Kitchen, The. Raymond Carver. CP-CarvR

At start of spring I open a trench. Purification, A. Wendell Berry. CP-BerrW

At Stoke. Charles Tomlinson. CP-TomlC; SP-TomlC

At Stool-ball, Lucia, let us play. Stool-Ball. Robert Herrick. CP-HerrR

At such a time, in such a spot. Emily Jane Brontë. CP-BronE

At sun up I am up. Angel Butcher. Philip Levine. SP-LeviP

At sunrise on a pin. Radiometer. James Merrill. SP-MerrJ

At sunset I went down the western slope. Han-shan. CP-ColdM, tr. by Red Pine

At sunset my foot outreached the mounting Pacific's. Swimming in the Pacific. Robert Penn Warren. CP-WarrR

At sunset, only to his true love. Bird of Paradise. Robert Graves. CP-GravR

At Sunset Time. Paul Laurence Dunbar. CP-DunbP

At sunset, when the paralyzed street gives up. Allenby Road. Joseph Brodsky. CP-BrodJ

At ten A.M. the young housewife. Young Housewife, The. William Carlos Williams. CP-WilW1

At 10 o'clock Haydon. I'm With You. Charles Olson. CP-OlsoC

At ten one morning. Suicide. Federico García Lorca. SP-GarcF, tr. by Edwin Honig

At tennis, a missed shot meant he had MS. Seasons. Wyatt Prunty. SP-PrunW

At that time, two friends stood. Landfall among Friends. Donald Davie. CP DaviDC

At that very instant. Nostalgia for the Present. Jorge Luis Borges. SP-BorgJ, tr. by Alan S. Trueblood

At The Abbey Theatre. William Butler Yeats. CP-YeatW

At the aged. Thirteen Preludes for Pioneer Square. John Logan. CP-LoganJ

At the Airport. Howard Nemerov. CP-NemeH

At the airport, ready to leave on my little trip. Fear of Flying, The. Mona Van Duyn. SP-VanDM

At the alder-darkened brink. Hamlen Brook. Richard Wilbur. CP-WilbR

At the Anonymous Tomb of Herrera y Reissig in the Cemetery of Montevideo. Federico García Lorca. CP-GarcF, tr. by Christopher Maurer

At the antipodes of poetry, dark winter. Discovery of Thought, A. Wallace Stevens. CP-StevWP

At the Aquatic Sports. Thomas Hardy. CP-HardT

At the Autumn Equinox. Charles Tomlinson. SP-TomlC

At the back fence calling, / Mrs. Jones! Peace Conference in an American Town. Langston Hughes. CP-HughL; CP-HughL2

At the back of the houses there is the wood. House in the Wood, The. Randall Jarrell. CP-JarrR

At the Back of the North Wind. Thom Gunn. CP-GunnT

At the bad time, nothing betrays outwardly the harsh findings. December Blues. Robert Pinsky. CP-PinsR

At the Ball Game. William Carlos Williams. CP-WilW1

At the Bank in Spain. D. H. Lawrence. CP-LawrD

At the banquet tables of time. Tankards, The. Paul Celan. SP-CelaP, tr. by John Felstiner

At the Bar. William Carlos Williams. CP-WilW1

At the bar called. Chicago Scene. John Logan. CP-LoganJ

At the Barriers. Thom Gunn. CP-GunnT

At the Battery. Grace Paley. CP-PalGC

At the Beach. Yehuda Amichai. SP-AmicY, tr. by Chana Bloch

At the Beach. James Schuyler. CP-SchuJ

At the Bird Market. Raymond Carver. CP-CarvR

At the Birth of an Age. Robinson Jeffers. CP-JefR2

At the Bomb Testing Site. William Stafford. SP-StafW; SP-StafWW

At the bottom of the Arctic sea, they say. Ted Hughes. SP-HughTN

At the Boule d'Or. James Laughlin. CP-LaugJ

"At the boundary of the mighty world" H. (T) 620 foll. Charles Olson. SP-OlsoC Fr. Maximus Poems, The.

At the Brink of the Winter. William Carlos Williams. CP-WilW2

At the Café de la Terrasse. Morlaix: Into the Future with Neil Young. Lawrence Ferlinghetti. SP-FerlL

At the Café Parnasse. Donald Davie. CP-DaviDC

At the Cannon's Mouth. Herman Melville. SP-MelvH

At The Canoe Club. Richard Eberhart. CP-EberR

At the Cearne. D. H. Lawrence. CP-LawrD

At the Cenotaph. Hugh MacDiarmid. SP-MacDH

At the center of acres of snow-whiteness. Mountain Plateau. Robert Penn Warren. CP-WarrR

At the Centre. Thom Gunn. CP-GunnT

At the Chairman's Housewarming. William Stafford. SP-StafWW

At the Children's Hospital in Little Rock. Miller Williams. CP-WillM

At the Chiming of Light upon Sleep. Philip Larkin. CP-LarkP

At the Christening of an Infant the Mind of the Young Preacher Wanders Again. Miller Williams. CP-WillM

At the City Dump in Nantucket. Joseph Brodsky. CP-BrodJ

At the clear core, morning. Bead, The. Charles Tomlinson. CP-TomlC

At the Close. George Meredith. CP-MerG1

At the close of a winter day. Rhyme of the Three Captains, The. Rudyard Kipling. CP-KiplR

At the coming up of Phoebus the all-luminous charioteer. Phaéthôn. George Meredith. CP-MerG1

At the Confluence of the Colorado and the Little Colorado. William Meredith. SP-MereW

At the Core. Marge Piercy. SP-PierM

At the corner / of Forty-second and Broadway. This Street Never Sleeps. Carl Sandburg. CP-SandC

At the corner of Wood Street, when daylight appears. Reverie of Poor Susan, The. William Wordsworth. CP-WorW1

At the Cradle of Genius. Donald Davie. CP-DaviDC

At the creation of the Earth. Birth of Pleasure, The. Percy Bysshe Shelley. CP-ShelP

At the Crossroads. Thomas Kinsella. CP-KinsT

At the daydream hour my eyes were gazing / at the white page. White Page, The. "Rubén Dario." SP-DariR, tr. by Alberto Acereda and Will Derusha

At the Death of a Mongolian Peasant. Norman Dubie. CP-DubiN

At the Dinner-Table. Thomas Hardy. CP-HardT

At the dinner table, before the baked eggplant. Boast, The. Rita Dove. SP-DoveR

At the door hangs a heavy curtain. Commander's Footsteps, The. Aleksandr Aleksandrovich Blok. SP-BlokA, tr. by Peter France and Jon Stallworthy

At the door, some never; some let it be. Balance, The. Denise Levertov. SP-LeveDL

At the earliest ending of winter. Not Ideas about the Thing but the Thing Itself. Wallace Stevens. CP-StevW; CP-StevWP

At the edge. Outdoor Concert, The. Thom Gunn. CP-GunnT

At the Edge. Charles Tomlinson. CP-TomlC

At the edge of conversations. Insistence of Things, The. Charles Tomlinson. CP-TomlC

At the edge of the city the pickerel. Wreckage, The. Donald Hall. CP-HallD

At the edge of the lake, in yellow light. Sketch. Rainer Maria Rilke. CP-RilkFr, tr. by A. Poulin, Jr.

At the edge of the mariner's. Primer for the Nuclear Age. Rita Dove. SP-DoveR

At the eleventh hour he came. Vineyard, The. Rudyard Kipling. CP-KiplR Fr. Debits and Credits.

At the end a / "The Prisoner of Zenda." Prisoner of Zenda, The. Richard Wilbur. CP-WilbR

At the end, he listened only to. Late Stravinsky Listening to Late Beethoven. Stephen Spender. CP-SpenS

At the end of an unending war. Urlicht. Charles Tomlinson. CP-TomlC

At the end of green spring, God begins. Yehuda Amichai. SP-AmicYL Fr. At Right Angles.

At the end of October. Snake, The. Wendell Berry. CP-BerrW

At the end of our Ruegen holiday, that night. Sign Faehre nach Wilm, The. Stephen Spender. SP-SpenS

At the end of summer they burn the house we live in. Thieves, Seasons. Andrei Codrescu. SP-CodrA

At the end of Tarriers' Lane, which was the street. Wm. Brazier. Robert Graves. CP-GravR

At the End of the Passage. Rudyard Kipling. Fr. Life's Handicap.

At the end of the path. Grave. Rainer Maria Rilke. CP-RilkFr, tr. by A. Poulin, Jr. Fr. Affectionate Taxes to France.

At the End of the Rainbow. John Updike. CP-UpdiJ

At the end of the row. Objection to Being Stepped On, The. Robert Frost. CP-FrosR

At the end of the street stands. Still Life. Andrei Codrescu. SP-CodrA

At the End of the War. Richard Eberhart. CP-EberR

At the end of the war I arose. Driver, The. James Dickey. CP-DickJ

At the end of this sentence, rain will begin. Map of the New World. Derek Walcott. CP-WalcD

At the Entering of the New Year. Thomas Hardy. CP-HardT

At the Entrance to the Café. Constantine P. Cavafy. CP-CavaC, tr. by Theoharis Constantine Theoharis

At the Entrance to the Other World. Kenneth Patchen. CP-PatcK

At the equinox when the earth was veiled in a late rain, wreathed with wet poppies, waiting spring. Continent's End. Robinson Jeffers. CP-JefR1

At the Executed Murderer's Grave. James Wright. CP-WrigJ

At the Fair. William Stafford. SP-StafWW

At the Fall of an Age. Robinson Jeffers. CP-JefR2

At the Far End of a Long Wharf. Thomas Lux. SP-LuxT

At the far end of a trip north. Nooksack Valley. Gary Snyder. CP-SnydG

At the Faucet of June. William Carlos Williams. CP-WilW1

At the [or de] feet o' Jesus. Feet o' Jesus. Langston Hughes. CP-HughL; CP-HughL1

At the ferocious phenomenon of 5 o'clock i find myself gently decompos. E. E. Cummings. CP-CummE

At the Fillmore. Philip Levine. SP-LeviP

At the first ball his wicket fell, and sins. George Meredith. CP-MerG2

At the first chink of sunrise. Center. Billy Collins. SP-CollB

At the first strokes of the fiddle bow. Wheel, The. Wendell Berry. CP-BerrW

At the Fishhouses. Elizabeth Bishop. CP-BishE

At the foot of your dry well. Reunion. W. S. Merwin. SP-MerwW

At the Front. D. H. Lawrence. CP-LawrD

At the Funeral. George Meredith. CP-MerG2

At the Gare Bruxelles-Midi. Lawrence Ferlinghetti. SP-FerlL

At the Gate. Robert Graves. CP-GravR

At the gate, I sit in a row of blue seats. Passengers. Billy Collins. SP-CollB

At the Gates of Aerea. René Char. CP-MertT

At the Gates of Tombs. Carl Sandburg. CP-SandC

At the gay at the apple at the white sun. Winter at the Inn. Kenneth Patchen. CP-PatcK

At the German Writers Conference in Munich. Rita Dove. SP-DoveR

At the golden gate of song. Inspiration. Paul Laurence Dunbar. CP-DunbP

At the Grand Véfours in the Palais Royal. Waiters' Ballet, The. James Laughlin. CP-LaugJ

At the Grave of Burns (1803, Seven Years After His Death). William Wordsworth. CP-WorW1

At the Grave of Henry James. W. H. Auden. CP-AudeW

At the Grave of My Brother. William Stafford. SP-StafWW

At the Grave of My Brother: Bomber Pilot. William Stafford. SP-StafWW

At the Green Inn, Five P.M. Arthur Rimbaud. CP-RimbA, tr. by Martin Sorrell

At the half-way house the pony died. Half Way. Carl Sandburg. CP-SandC

At the Harbor's Edge. Yannis Ritsos. SP-RitsY, tr. by Kimon Friar and Kostas Myrsiades

At the harpsichord I see him cool-fingered, fleet. Background with Harpsichord. Marya Alexandrovna Zaturenska. SP-ZatuM

At the head of this street a gasping organ is waving moth-eaten. E. E. Cummings. CP-CummE

At the Head Table. Thomas Kinsella. CP-KinsT

At the Heart o' Me. Ezra Pound. CP-PoEar

At the height of love. Mistrust of the Beloved. William Carlos Williams. CP-WilW2

At the Helmet and Sword. Joseph Brodsky. CP-BrodJ

At the Hill Fort. Charles Tomlinson. CP-TomlC

At the hole where he went in. Rudyard Kipling. CP-KiplR Fr. Jungle Book, The.

At the Home for Unwed Mothers. James Dickey. CP-DickJ

At the hospital where I had the echocardiagram. Sonnet: "At the hospital where I had the echocardiagram." Hayden Carruth. CP-CarHS Fr. Sonnets.

At the hour when the first symptoms of mental viduity makes themselves felt. Scene. Paul Éluard. CP-BeckS

At the hour when to-day's effort changes. Cycle of Industry, The. Laura Riding Jackson. CP-RidiL

At the Indian Killer's Grave. Robert Lowell. SP-LoweR

At the Inn. John Ashbery. SP-AshbJ

At the Isle of Wight. 1793. William Wordsworth. CP-WorW1

At the Jewish New Year. Adrienne Rich. CP-RicAE; SP-RicA2

At the Justice Department November 15, 1969. Denise Levertov. SP-LeveDS Fr. Staying Alive.

At the Klamath Berry Festival. William Stafford. SP-StafWW

At the last moment you decided. Thrifty Lover, The. Marge Piercy. SP-PierM

At the last rock of the last ledge of the last climb. Leaf with Berry. Josephine Jacobsen. CP-JacoJ

At the last, tenderly. Last Invocation, The. Walt Whitman. CP-WhitW

At the last turn in the path. Saying Farewell at the Monastery After Hearing the Old Master Lecture on "Return to the Source" Gary Snyder. CP-SnydG

At the Lincoln Memorial. Archibald MacLeish. CP-MacLA

At "The Literary." James Whitcomb Riley. CP-RileJ

At the long meadow's end, where the road runs. Pond, The. Howard Nemerov. CP-NemeH

At the Maritime Museum. Yehuda Amichai. SP-AmicY, tr. by Chana Bloch

At the "Mermaid." Robert Browning. CP-BroR2

At the midnight in the silence of the sleep-time. Epilogue: "At the midnight in the silence of the sleep-time." Robert Browning. CP-BroR2

At the Mill. Thomas Hardy. CP-HardT

At the monastery of Latroun, waiting for the wine. Yehuda Amichai. SP-AmicY, tr. by Chana Bloch

At the Natural History Museum. William Meredith. SP-MereW

At the near approach of a star . . . huge tides. Robinson Jeffers. CP-JefR3

At the next vacancy for God, if I am elected. In Place of a Curse. John Ciardi. CP-CiarJ

At the noisy heart of the café. Old Man, An. Constantine P. Cavafy. CP-CavaC, tr. by Theoharis Constantine Theoharis

At the Old Place. William Stafford. SP-StafWW

At the open door of the room I stand and look at the night. Restlessness. D. H. Lawrence. CP-LawrD

At the oracle. Strait, The. A. R. Ammons. CP-AmmoA

At the outset, hysteria. Cholera. Rita Dove. SP-DoveR

At the Party. W. H. Auden. CP-AudeW

At the penultimate move, their saga nearly sung. Chess. Louis MacNeice. CP-MacNL

At the Piano. Thomas Hardy. CP-HardT

At the picnic, a fisherman. Sunday School Picnic: What Endures. Gregory Orr. SP-OrrG

At the Playground. William Stafford. SP-StafWW

At the Poem Society a black-haired man stands up to say. Fresh Air. Kenneth Koch. SP-KochK

At the Poorhouse. Federico García Lorca. CP-GarcF, tr. by Jerome Rothenberg Fr. Night (Suite for Piano and Poet's Voice).

At the Prado. William Meredith. SP-MereW

At the present rate it must come to pass. Something for Hope. Robert Frost. CP-FrosR

At the Queen's Park Hotel, with its white, high-ceilinged rooms. Derek Walcott. CP-WalcD Fr. Midsummer.

At the quick of winter. Winterpig. Denise Levertov. SP-LeveDL

At the Railway Station, Upway. Thomas Hardy. CP-HardT

At the rim of sunset waters. Being Forever. Peter Blue Cloud. SP-BlueP

At the rise of the moon. Moon Appears, The. Federico García Lorca. CP-GarcF, tr. by Alan S. Trueblood Fr. Moon Songs.

At the round / crossway. Six Capriccios. Federico García Lorca. CP-GarcF, tr. by Cola Franzen

At the Royal Academy. Thomas Hardy. CP-HardT

At the Same Time. W. S. Merwin. SP-MerwW

At the Screen Door. Yusef Komunyakaa. CP-KomuY

At the sea at the beach in the dark there was somebody. On a Night You Don't Sleep. Charles Bukowski. SP-BukC2

At the Seashore. Yehuda Amichai. SP-AmicY, tr. by Chana Bloch

At the Seashore. Yehuda Amichai. SP-AmicYL, tr. by Benjamin Harshav and Barbara Harshav

At the shiver of morning, a little before the false dawn. Honeymoon Time at an Inn. Thomas Hardy. CP-HardT

At the shower's head, high over the porcelain moonscape. Adultery At Forty. Donald Hall. CP-HallD

At the side of the road that is being paved. Beginning of Autumn in the Hills of Ephraim. Yehuda Amichai. SP-AmicY, tr. by Chana Bloch

At the sign "Fred Muffin's Antiques" they turned off the road into a. On the Towpath. John Ashbery. SP-AshbJ

At the Slackening of the Tide. James Wright. CP-WrigJ

At the small end of an illness. World Contracted to a Recognizable Image, The. William Carlos Williams. CP-WilW2

At the start, something must be arbitrarily excluded. As We're Told. Rae Armantrout. SP-ArmaA

At the stoplight waiting for the light. Two Scavengers in a Truck, Two Beautiful People in a Mercedes. Lawrence Ferlinghetti. SP-FerlL

At the street corner, hunched up. Market at Turk. Thom Gunn. CP-GunnT

At the Sun-Rise in 1848. Dante Gabriel Rossetti. CW-RossD

At the Synod in St Patrick's. Donald Davie. CP-DaviDC

At the table we say. Michael Palmer. SP-PalmM

At the tangled heart of a wood I fell asleep. Home-Coming, The. Robert Graves. CP-GravR

At the Tavern. Paul Laurence Dunbar. CP-DunbP

At the Theater. Constantine P. Cavafy. CP-CavaC, tr. by Theoharis Constantine Theoharis

At the time of nougats, the peer yellow. Forces, the Will & the Weather. Wallace Stevens. CP-StevW; CP-StevWP

At the Time of Peony Blossoming. Robert Bly. SP-BlyR

At the time when the tulip-tree, even then rare, bloomed. Old Love. Robert Penn Warren. CP-WarrR

At the Tomb of the Czech Kings. Jaroslav Seifert. SP-SeifJ, tr. by Ewald Osers

At the top of a low hill. Hampstead; the Horse Chestnut Trees. Thom Gunn. CP-GunnT

At the top of the hill you were Muriel. My Mother in Three Acts. Jane Cooper. CP-CoopJ

At the top of the world I want to go for a drive. With the Caribou. Maxine W. Kumin. SP-KumiM

At the Tourist Centre in Boston. Margaret Atwood. SP-AtwM1

At the Trade Center. Charles Tomlinson. CP-TomlC

At the Un-National Monument along the Canadian Border. William Stafford. SP-StafW; SP-StafWW

At the University of New Orleans. Yehuda Amichai. SP-AmicYL, tr. by Benjamin Harshav and Barbara Harshav

At the Versailles. In Lisbon. Charles Tomlinson. SP-TomlC Fr. Portugeuse Pieces.

At the Wailing Wall in Jerusalem. Countee Cullen. CP-CullC

At the War Office, London. Thomas Hardy. CP-HardT

At the washboard shudder. Driving Jazz. William Corbett. SP-CorbW

At the water's edge of a deserted beach. Forever. David Ignatow. SP-IgnaD

At the Wedding March. Gerard Manley Hopkins. CP-HopkG

At the Well. Robert Graves. CP-GravR

At the Wellhead. Seamus Heaney. SP-HeanSO

At the Western Ocean's Edge. Thomas Kinsella. CP-KinsT

At the wheel of the Chevrolet on the road to Sintra. Fernando Pessoa. SP-PessF, tr. by Susan M. Brown and Edwin Honig

At the Wicket-Gate. Thomas Hardy. CP-HardT

At the Window. D. H. Lawrence. CP-LawrD

At the window frame concealing. Saint. Stéphane Mallarmé. CP-MallS, tr. by Henry Weinfield

At the Word "Farewell." Thomas Hardy. CP-HardT

At the world's turning, at the hour of darkness. Luna and Leopardi. Marya Alexandrovna Zaturenska. SP-ZatuM

At the worst place in the hills above the city. Birthday Dream, The. James Dickey. CP-DickJ

At the Zoo in Spain. Clarence Major. SP-MajoC

At Thirty-One, When Some Are Rich. Philip Larkin. CP-LarkP

At Thirty-Three. Hans Magnus Enzensberger. SP-EnzeH, tr. by Hans Magnus Enzensberger and Michael Hamburger

At thirty, when the faiths give out. On When McCarthy Was a Wolf among a Nation of Queer-Queers. Alan Dugan. CP-DugaA

At This Moment. David Ignatow. SP-IgnaD

At this party heads have no noses, teeth close. HINDOO, THE: He Reads His GITA and Is Calm at All Events. A. K. Ramanujan. CP-RamaA

At This Point on the Page. William Stafford. SP-StafWW

At this wharf there are no grand landings to speak of. Winter Ship, A. Sylvia Plath. CP-PlatS

At th'Ivory Tribunall of your hand. [With Some Poems Sent to a Gentlewoman. I]. Richard Crashaw. CP-CrasR

At Thomas Hardy's Birthplace, 1953. James Wright. CP-WrigJ

At 3 A.M., if the schedule held. Whistle of the 3 A.M. Robert Penn Warren. CP-WarrR

At Three Every Thursday Afternoon. Miller Williams. CP-WillM

At three in the afternoon on a clear day. Newspaper Picture of Spectators at a Hotel Fire, A. Miller Williams. CP-WillM

At three o'clock their fingers gripped. The sun shot. Autopsy, The. Josephine Jacobsen. CP-JacoJ

At three-score winters' end I died. Another ["At three-score winters' end I died"]. Unknown. CP-CowpW

At 3:30 a.m. in the morning. 3:30 A.M. Conversation. Charles Bukowski. SP-BukC2

At times I project ahead. Michelangelo Buonarroti. CP-Miche, tr. by John Frederick Nims

At times I sit in the dunes. Van Gogh. Lorine Niedecker. CP-NiedL

At times in the day. Flight, The. W. S. Merwin. SP-MerwWF

At times our Britain cannot rest. To the Marquis of Dufferin and Ava. Alfred Tennyson. CP-TennA

At time's tail end, my great-grandchildren's great. Caveman Is Not about to Talk, The. Dan Pagis. SP-PagiD, tr. by Stephen Mitchell

At times, the wobbly top father gave me. Wobbly Top, A. A. K. Ramanujan. CP-RamaA

At times when under cover I 've said. Instructor, The. Rudyard Kipling. CP-KiplR

At Tower Peak. Gary Snyder. CP-SnydG

At Trotsky's House. Charles Tomlinson. CP-TomlC

At Truro. May Swenson. SP-SwenM

At tu quisquis eris, miseri qui cruda poetæ. Verses on the Death of His Mother. Samuel Johnson. CP-JohnS

At twelve, the disintegration of afternoon. What We See Is What We Think. Wallace Stevens. CP-StevW; CP-StevWP

At 28 I was still faithless. 28. Philip Levine. SP-LeviP

At twenty-five a man is on his way. Point of Age, A. John Berryman. CP-BerrJ

At twenty, stooping round about. With Age Wisdom. Archibald MacLeish. CP-MacLA

At twilight I went into the street. Descending Figure. Louise Glück. SP-GlucL

At two a.m. a thing, jumping out of a manhole. News Report. David Ignatow. SP-IgnaD

At two after noon for our Psyche inquire. On Psyche. Jonathan Swift. CP-SwifJ

At two o'clock in the morning, if you open your window and listen. Dawn Wind, The. Rudyard Kipling. CP-KiplR

At two, the barnyard settled. Pamela. Rita Dove. SP-DoveR

At two thousand feet the sea wrinkles like an old man's hand. Encounter. Thomas McGrath. SP-McGrT

At Ur / the lady Shub-ad's small. Enemy of the Herds, the Lion, The. Josephine Jacobsen. CP-JacoJ

At Utter Loaf. James Whitcomb Riley. CP-RileJ

At Varennes also Glioucester men had their stay. Varennes. Ivor Gurney. SP-GurnI

At various times, I have asked myself what reasons. Poem Written in a Copy of Beowulf. Jorge Luis Borges. SP-BorgJ, tr. by Alastair Reid

At Verona. Oscar Wilde. CP-WildO

At Viscount Nelson's lavish funeral. 1805. Robert Graves. CP-GravR

At Waking. Thomas Hardy. CP-HardT

At Washington. John Greenleaf Whittier. CP-WhitJ

At Wells: Polyphony. Charles Tomlinson. CP-TomlC

At Westminster, hid from the light of day. Coronation, The. Thomas Hardy. CP-HardT

At Whigham's Inn, Sanquar. Robert Burns. CP-BurnR

At White River Roadhouse in the Yukon. Gary Snyder. CP-SnydG

At whom is the rice grinning. Pablo Neruda. SP-NeruP Fr. Question Book.

At Woodlawn I heard the dead cry. Lost Son, The. Theodore Roethke. CP-RoetT

At Woodward's Gardens. Robert Frost. CP-FrosR

At Wynard's Gap. Thomas Hardy. CP-HardT

At Yale. Czeslaw Milosz. CP-MiloCN, tr. by Robert Hass

At Yorktown. Charles Olson. CP-OlsoC; SP-OlsoC

At Your Old House. William Dickey. SP-DickW

  "Do they remember me?" SP-DickW

  "Fretful and sick, you ask." SP-DickW

  "Fretful and sick, you long." SP-DickW

  "Nevertheless, sleep / And as your eyes close." SP-DickW

  "No, the night has gone." SP-DickW

  "Yes, they remember you." SP-DickW

At Zero. A. K. Ramanujan. CP-RamaA

Atalanta. Charles Olson. CP-OlsoC

Atalanta in Calydon. Algernon Charles Swinburne.

  Before the Beginning of Years. SP-SwinA

  Not as with Sundering of the Earth. SP-SwinA

  O That I Now. SP-SwinA

  We Have Seen Thee, O Love. SP-SwinA

  When the Hounds of Spring. SP-SwinA

  Who Hath Given Man Speech? SP-SwinA

Atavism. William Stafford. SP-StafWW

Atelier Cézanne. Clarence Major. SP-MajoC

Atget's Gardens. Eleanor Wilner. SP-WilnE

Athanasia. Oscar Wilde. CP-WildO

Atheism. Phillis Wheatley. CP-WheaP

Atheist, Laodicean or. Widowers. Donald Davie. CP-DaviDC

Athelstan King / Lord among Earls. Battle of Brunanburh. *Unknown*. CP-TennA, *tr. by* Alfred Tennyson

Athena. Amy Clampitt. CP-ClamA

Athena in the Front Lines. Marge Piercy. SP-PierM

Athena's Vote. Constantine P. Cavafy. CP-CavaC, *tr. by* Theoharis Constantine Theoharis

Athenian Death. Robert Penn Warren. CP-WarrR

Athenians mark the moss-grown gate, The. Garden of Metrodorus, The. Herman Melville. SP-MelvH

Atherton's Gambit. Edwin Arlington Robinson. CP-RobiE

Atkins. George Meredith. CP-MerG2

Atlantic, The. Charles Tomlinson. CP-TomlC; SP-TomlC

Atlantic City Convention, The. William Carlos Williams. CP-WilW1

Atlantic City 1939. Maxine W. Kumin. SP-KumiM

Atlantic City Waiter. Countee Cullen. CP-CullC

Atlantic is a stormy moat; and the Mediterranean, The. Eye, The. Robinson Jeffers. CP-JefR3

Atlantic Tunnel, The. Louis MacNeice. CP-MacNL

Atlantides, The. Henry David Thoreau. CP-ThorH

Atlantis. W. H. Auden. CP-AudeW

Atlantis. Wisława Szymborska. SP-SzymWM, *tr. by* Joanna Trzeciak

Atlas. George Meredith. CP-MerG2

Atlas. Jonathan Swift. CP-SwifJ

Atlas and the Fatman. Thomas Merton. CP-MertT

Atlas, How Have You Been? Carl Sandburg. CP-SandC

Atlas Immobilized. Amy Clampitt. CP-ClamA

Atlas of the Difficult World, An. Adrienne Rich. SP-RicA1

Atman, The. James Laughlin. CP-LaugJ

Atman of Sleep, The. James Laughlin. CP-LaugJ

Atmosphere. Robert Frost. CP-FrosR

Atmospheric acquaintance, The. Emily Dickinson. SP-DickE

Atom bellies like a cauliflower, The. After the Bomb Tests. Jane Cooper. CP-CoopJ

Atom displaces all atoms beside, The. Ralph Waldo Emerson. CP-EmerR

Atom from atom yawns as far. Ralph Waldo Emerson. CP-EmerR

Atop deathless narcissus. White Satyr. Federico García Lorca. CP-GarcF, *tr. by* Jerome Rothenberg *Fr.* In the Garden of the Lunar Grapefruits.

Atop each stem. End of May. Mona Van Duyn. SP-VanDM

Atop that vast dune. Dune. Federico García Lorca. CP-GarcF, *tr. by* Jerome Rothenberg *Fr.* In the Garden of the Lunar Grapefruits.

Atop the down pasture. Enniscorthy Suite. Charles Olson. CP-OlsoC

Atque in Perpetuum A.W. Louis Zukofsky. CP-ZukLS

Attack, The. D. H. Lawrence. CP-LawrD

Attack of the Squash People. Marge Piercy. SP-PierM

Attar of Roses. Donald Davie. CP-DaviDC

Attempt at the Manner of Waller, An. William Cowper. CP-CowpW

Attempt the end, and never stand to doubt. Seek[e] and Find[e]. Robert Herrick. CP-HerrR

Attempt to Discover Life. Wallace Stevens. CP-StevW; CP-StevWP

Attempt to Spell, Incantate and Annoy. Andrei Codrescu. SP-CodrA

Attempted Departure. James Dickey. CP-DickJ

Attempted Rescue, The. Alan Dugan. CP-DugaA

Attend my lays, ye ever honour'd nine. Hymn to the Morning, An. Phillis Wheatley. CP-WheaP

Attend to the music divine. Bible, *O.T.* *See* Behold, bless ye the Lord, all ye servants of the Lord

Attention. A. R. Ammons. CP-AmmoA

Attention. Rae Armantrout. SP-ArmaA

Attention. Adrienne Rich. CP-RicAE; SP-RicA2

Attention Makes Infinity. Richard Wilbur. CP-WilbR

Attentive eyes, fantastic heed. Poet, A. Thomas Hardy. CP-HardT

Attentiveness. Alice Walker. CP-WalkA

Attic, The. Raymond Carver. CP-CarvR

Attic, The. Derek Mahon. CP-MahoD

Attic maid! with honey fed. To the Swallow. Euenus. CP-CowpW, *tr. by* William Cowper

Attic Which Is Desire, The. William Carlos Williams. CP-WilW1

Attila. D. H. Lawrence. CP-LawrD

Attila. Kenneth Patchen. CP-PatcK

Attila, Hitler. Robert Lowell. SP-LoweR

Attitude. Olga Broumas. SP-BrouO

Attitudes. Richard Eberhart. CP-EberR

Attractive mansion on the avenue of Sardanapalus, An. Residence, The. Joseph Brodsky. CP-BrodJ

Atwater Kent. William Stafford. SP-StafWW

Atypical Affair, An. Allen Ginsberg. CP-GinsA

Atys. A. E. Housman. CP-HousA

Au Bout du Temps. Andrei Codrescu. SP-CodrA

Au Clair de la Lune. Hugh MacDiarmid. SP-MacDH

Au voleur, au voleur, au voleur!—. George Meredith. CP-MerG2

Aubade: "At break of dawn." W. H. Auden. CP-AudeW *Fr.* Three Posthumous Poems.

Aubade: "Beckoned anew to a World." W. H. Auden. CP-AudeW

Aubade: "Cool and beautiful as the blossom of the wild carrot." Edna St. Vincent Millay. CP-MillE

Aubade: "Having bitten on life like a sharp apple." Louis MacNeice. CP-MacNL

Aubade: "I wish for you that when you wake." Donald Davie. CP-DaviDC

Aubade: "I work all day, and get half-drunk at night." Philip Larkin. CP-LarkP

Aubade: "My dove, my doe." Stevie Smith. CP-SmitS

Aubade: "She wakes having flown." Olga Broumas. SP-BrouO

Aubade: "Today above the gull's call." Louise Glück. SP-GlucL

Aubade: Bermuda. Thomas Merton. CP-MertT

Aubade for Hope. Robert Penn Warren. CP-WarrR

Aubade for Infants. Louis MacNeice. CP-MacNL

Aubade—Harlem. Thomas Merton. CP-MertT

Aubade: Lake Erie. Thomas Merton. CP-MertT

Aubade—the Annunciation. Thomas Merton. CP-MertT

Aubade—the City. Thomas Merton. CP-MertT

Aube of the West Dawn. Venetian June. Ezra Pound. CP-PoEar

Aube Provençale. Marilyn Hacker. SP-HackM

Auburn. Carl Sandburg. CP-SandC

Auburn autumn leaves, will you come back? Auburn. Carl Sandburg. CP-SandC

Auction, The. Theodore Roethke. CP-RoetT

Auctioneer. Carl Sandburg. CP-SandC

Auctioneer of Parting, The. Emily Dickinson. CP-DickE

Audabe of the Singer and Saboteur, Marie Triste. Norman Dubie. CP-DubiN

Audacity of Bliss, said Jacob to the Angel. Emily Dickinson. SP-DickE

Audacity of the Lower Gods. Yusef Komunyakaa. CP-KomuY

Auden at Milwaukee. Stephen Spender. CP-SpenS

Auden's Funeral. Stephen Spender. CP-SpenS

Audible and the Inaudible, The. Yannis Ritsos. SP-RitsY, *tr. by* Kimon Friar

Audible smile of the leaves. Fernando Pessoa. SP-PessF, *tr. by* Susan M. Brown *and* Edwin Honig

Audible trout. Girls on the Bridge. Derek Mahon. CP-MahoD

Audience entire seemed pleased—indeed, The. Limitations of Genius. James Whitcomb Riley. CP-RileJ *Fr.* Child-World, A.

Audit at Key West. John Ciardi. CP-CiarJ

Audley Court. Alfred Tennyson. CP-TennA

Audubon. Lorine Niedecker. CP-NiedL

Audubon: A Vision. Robert Penn Warren. CP-WarrR

Auf wiedersehen! We part a little while. T.A.M. E. E. Cummings. CP-CummE

Aufilena—*bonnie, simple,* laud and they're amicable. Catullus. *See* Men always praise an honest whore, keen

Aufilena, virile content him weave her her solo. Catullus. *See* In constancy content with one man, there

Augean stables were so full of horseshit, The. Marxist Analysis of the Fifth Labor of Hercules. Alan Dugan. CP-DugaA

Augsburg Adoration, The. Randall Jarrell. CP-JarrR

Auguries of Innocence. William Blake. CP-BlakW

Augurs that watched archaic birds. Poland. G. K. Chesterton. CP-ChesG

August. John Clare. SP-ClarJ *Fr.* Shepherd's [*or* Shepheards] Calendar, The.

August. Hayden Carruth. CP-CarHS

August. Lucille Clifton. SP-ClifL

August. William Corbett. SP-CorbW

August. Primo Levi. CP-LeviP, *tr. by* Ruth Feldman

August. Louis MacNeice. CP-MacNL

August. Mary Oliver. SP-OlivM

August. Dorothy Parker. CP-ParkD

August. A. K. Ramanujan. CP-RamaA

August. Adrienne Rich. SP-RicA2

August. James Whitcomb Riley. CP-RileJ

August. Algernon Charles Swinburne. SP-SwinA

August and laurelled have been content to speak for an age, and the ages that follow. Soliloquy. Robinson Jeffers. CP-JefR1

August Darks, The. Amy Clampitt. CP-ClamA

August 8th. Anne Sexton. CP-SextA

8/8/68: i. Adrienne Rich. CP-RicAE *Fr.* Ghazals: Homage to Ghalib.

8/8/68: ii. Adrienne Rich. CP-RicAE *Fr.* Ghazals: Homage to Ghalib.

August Evening Outside of Nashville, An. Miller Williams. CP-WillM

August. / Facing the sunset. Federico García Lorca. CP-GarcF, *tr. by* Alan S.

Trueblood   *Fr.* Theories.

August First.   Hayden Carruth.   CP-CarHS

August first: it was a year ago.   For K.J., Leaving and Coming Back.   Marilyn Hacker.   SP-HackM

August First, 1974.   James Schuyler.   CP-SchuJ

8/1/68.   Adrienne Rich.   CP-RicAE   *Fr.* Ghazals: Homage to Ghalib.

August 14, 1961.   Hayden Carruth.   CP-CarHS

August fourth nineteen sixty eight.   Adrienne Rich.   CP-RicAE   *Fr.* Ghazals: Homage to Ghalib.

August, goldenrod blowing. We walk.   Maple Syrup.   Donald Hall.   CP-HallD

August Hail.   James Vincent Cunningham.   CP-CunnJ

August. Hear / the cicadas.   Speaking for Them.   Hayden Carruth.   CP-CarHS

August Holidays.   D. H. Lawrence.   CP-LawrD

August Midnight, An.   Thomas Hardy.   CP-HardT

August. Montana. The black notebook open again.   Landscape as Metaphor, Landscape as Fate and a Happy Life.   Charles Wright.   SP-WrigCN

August Moon.   Robert Penn Warren.   CP-WarrR

August Night.   James Schuyler.   CP-SchuJ

August Night, An.   Seamus Heaney.   SP-HeanSO

August, 1945.   Howard Nemerov.   CP-NemeH

August 1968.   W. H. Auden.   CP-AudeW

August, 1968.   Donald Davie.   CP-DaviDC

August 19th.   Langston Hughes.   CP-HughL; CP-HughL1

August on Sourdough, a Visit from Dick Brewer.   Gary Snyder.   CP-SnydG

August Rain.   Robert Bly.   SP-BlyR

August Rain.   Joseph Brodsky.   CP-BrodJ

August Revival: Crosby Junction.   Robert Penn Warren.   CP-WarrR

August 17th.   Anne Sexton.   CP-SextA

August, tasting of ripe grapes and afternoon sleep.   Sonnet: "August, tasting of ripe grapes and afternoon sleep."   James Schuyler.   CP-SchuJ

August, 'twas the twenty-fifth.   Bars Fight [August 28, 1746].   Lucy Terry.   CP-WheaP

August Voice, An.   Elizabeth Barrett Browning.   CP-BroEB

August was hot.   August.   A. K. Ramanujan.   CP-RamaA

August wind is shambling down the street, The.   First Debate between the Body and Soul.   T. S. Eliot.   SP-ElioT

Augustus still survives in Maro's strain.   Epigram on Colley Cibber.   Samuel Johnson.   CP-JohnS

Auld chuckie Reekie's sair distrest.   To William Creech.   Robert Burns.   CP-BurnR

Auld com'rade dear and brither sinner.   Letter to J———s T———t, Gl—nc——r.   Robert Burns.   CP-BurnR

Auld Farmer's New-Year-Morning Salutation to His Auld Mare, Maggie, on Giving Her the Accustomed Ripp of Corn to Hansel in the New-Year, The.   Robert Burns.   CP-BurnR

Auld Lang Syne.   Robert Burns.   CP-BurnR

Auld Man's Mare's Dead, The.   Robert Burns.   CP-BurnR

Auld Man's Winter Thought, The.   Robert Burns.   CP-BurnR

AULD NIBOR I'm three times, doubly, o'er your debtor.   Second Epistle to Davie.   Robert Burns.   CP-BurnR

Auld Rob Morris.   Robert Burns.   CP-BurnR

Auld wumman cam' in, a mere rickle o' banes, in a faded black dress, An.   Old Wife in High Spirits.   Hugh MacDiarmid.   SP-MacDH

Aulder than mammoth or than mastodon.   Gairmscoile.   Hugh MacDiarmid.   SP-MacDH

Aunt Edna.   James Tate.   SP-TateJ

Aunt Edna of the hills.   Aunt Edna.   James Tate.   SP-TateJ

Aunt Elsie hears / Singing in the night.   Aunt Elsie's Night Music.   Mary Oliver.   SP-OlivM

Aunt Elsie's Night Music.   Mary Oliver.   SP-OlivM

Aunt has developed carpel tunnel syndrome, An.   Kaiseki.   Arthur Sze.   SP-SzeA

Aunt Helen.   T. S. Eliot.   CP-ElioT

Aunt Imogen.   Edwin Arlington Robinson.   CP-RobiE

Aunt Jemima of the Ocean Waves.   Robert Earl Hayden.   CP-HaydR

Aunt Jennifer's Tigers.   Adrienne Rich.   CP-RicAE; SP-RicA1; SP-RicA2

Aunt Leaf.   Mary Oliver.   SP-OlivM

Aunt Lettuce, I want to peek under your skirt.   Charles Simic.   SP-SimiCE

Aunt Mabel.   William Stafford.   SP-StafW; SP-StafWW

Aunt Mary died of eating twelve red peppers.   John Ciardi.   CP-CiarJ

Aunt, my down-to-earth father's sibling, went to stay, An.   Relative and an Absolute, A.   Mona Van Duyn.   SP-VanDM

Aunt Rose—now—might I see you.   To Aunt Rose.   Allen Ginsberg.   CP-GinsA; SP-GinsA

Aunt Sue has a head full of stories.   Aunt Sue's Stories.   Langston Hughes.   CP-HughL; CP-HughL1

Aunt Sue's Stories.   Langston Hughes.   CP-HughL; CP-HughL1

Aura dolcissima, ma donde siete?   Christina Georgina Rossetti.   CP-RosC3

Aurelius Battaglia, the greatest loudmouth in the world.   In Memoriam: Aurelius Battaglia, and against His Tragic Sense of Life.   Alan Dugan.   CP-DugaA

Aurelius, father, assure that the o numb.   Catullus.   *See* Impresario of neediness

Aureng-Zebe.   John Dryden.   SP-DrydJ

Aurora.   Emily Dickinson.   CP-DickE

Aurora and Tithonus.   Euripides.   CP-BroEB   *Fr.* Trojan Women, The.

Aurora Borealis.   Rita Dove.   SP-DoveR

Aurora Est Musis Amica.   Samuel Johnson.   CP-JohnS

Aurora is the effort.   Emily Dickinson.   CP-DickE

Aurora Leigh.   Elizabeth Barrett Browning.   CP-BroEB

Aurora, now thou show'st thy blushing light.   Sir Philip Sidney.   SP-SidnP   *Fr.* Arcadia.

Aurora ushers in the glor'ous day.   Ode for Christmas Day, An.   Annis Boudinot Stockton.   CP-StocA

Auroras of Autumn, The.   Wallace Stevens.   CP-StevW; CP-StevWP

Aus Einem April.   Frank O'Hara.   SP-OharF

Aus Einer Kindheit.   Kenneth Koch.   SP-KochK

Ausonius, Epistle 7.   Kenneth Rexroth.   CP-RexrK

Auspex.   Robert Frost.   CP-FrosR

Auspice of Jewels.   Laura Riding Jackson.   CP-RidiL

Auspicious Reverence! Hush all meaner song.   Destiny of Nations, The.   Samuel Taylor Coleridge.   CP-ColeS

Austere Poem.   Richard Eberhart.   CP-EberR

Austere space. Measured words. No hint of color.   Corridor.   Yannis Ritsos.   SP-RitsY, *tr. by* N. C. Germanacos

Austerities.   Charles Simic.   SP-SimiC; SP-SimiCE

Austin! accept a grateful verse from me!   To Dr. Austin.   William Cowper.   CP-CowpW

Austin is a Poet, Austin writes a psalm.   Emily Dickinson.   SP-DickE

Austin you write all.   Prologue and Questions for St. Augustine On His Sixteenth Centenary.   John Logan.   CP-LogaJ

Authentic! Shadows of it, The.   Matins.   Denise Levertov.   SP-LeveDP

Author ad Librum.   Ben Jonson.   CP-JonsB; SP-JonsB

Author Apologizes to a Lady, for His Being a Little Man, The.   Christopher Smart.   SP-SmarC

Author of Her Misfortune, The.   Raymond Carver.   CP-CarvR

Author of light, revive my dying spright.   Thomas Campion.   CP-CampT

Author of the Jesus Papers Speaks, The.   Anne Sexton.   CP-SextA; SP-SextA

Author to Her Book, The.   Anne Bradstreet.   CP-BradA

Author to the Reader, The.   Randall Jarrell.   CP-JarrR

Author upon Himself, The.   Jonathan Swift.   CP-SwifJ

Authority of Krajova, The.   Kenneth Patchen.   CP-PatcK

Authors and actors and artists and such.   Bohemia.   Dorothy Parker.   CP-ParkD

Authors are judg'd by strange capricious Rules.   Prologue to the *Three Hours after Marriage.*   Alexander Pope.   CP-PopeA

Author's Earnest Cry and Prayer, to the Right Honorable and Honorable, the Scotch Representatives in the House of Commons, The.   Robert Burns.   CP-BurnR

Author's Manner of Living, The.   Jonathan Swift.   CP-SwifJ

Authors Motto, The.   Richard Crashaw.   CP-CrasR

Author's Prologue.   Dylan Thomas.   CP-ThomD

Authors' Residences.   John Updike.   CP-UpdiJ

Author's Voyage down the Rhine (Thirty Years Ago).   William Wordsworth.   CP-WorW2

Authours Epitaph, Made by Himself, The.   Sir Walter Ralegh.   CP-RaleW

Auto.   Heather McHugh.   SP-McHuH

Auto-Da-Fé.   D. H. Lawrence.   CP-LawrD

Auto-da-fé.   Robert Penn Warren.   CP-WarrR

Auto Mobile.   A. R. Ammons.   CP-AmmoA

Auto Poesy: On the Lam from Bloomington.   Allen Ginsberg.   CP-GinsA

Auto Wreck.   Karl Shapiro.   SP-ShapK

Autobiographia Illiteraria.   Theodore Weiss.   SP-WeisT

Autobiographia Literaria.   Frank O'Hara.   SP-OharF

Autobiographical.   Thomas Lux.   SP-LuxT

Autobiographical Libation to Erato Muse of Lyric Poetry.   Alan Dugan.   CP-DugaA

Autobiographical Note.   Kenneth Patchen.   CP-PatcK

Autobiographies.   Derek Mahon.   CP-MahoD

Autobiography.   Lawrence Ferlinghetti.   SP-FerlL

Autobiography.   Thom Gunn.   CP-GunnT

Autobiography.   Primo Levi.   CP-LeviP, *tr. by* Ruth Feldman

Autobiography.   Archibald MacLeish.   CP-MacLA

Autobiography.   Louis MacNeice.   CP-MacNL

Autobiography.   Dan Pagis.   SP-PagiD, *tr. by* Stephen Mitchell

Autobiography. Dorothy Parker. CP-ParkD

Autobiography. Jaroslav Seifert. SP-SeifJ, *tr.* by Ewald Osers

Autobiography at an Air-Station. Philip Larkin. CP-LarkP

Autobiography in the Year 1952. Yehuda Amichai. SP-AmicYL, *tr.* by Benjamin Harshav *and* Barbara Harshav

Autobiography, 1952. Yehuda Amichai. SP-AmicY, *tr.* by Stephen Mitchell

Autobiography of a Comedian. John Ciardi. CP-CiarJ

Autobiography of the Present. Laura Riding Jackson. CP-RidiL

Autograph, An. John Greenleaf Whittier. CP-WhitJ

Autographic. James Whitcomb Riley. CP-RileJ

Autolycus. Louis MacNeice. CP-MacNL

Automaton, The. Randall Jarrell. CP-JarrR

Automobile Accident. Lorine Niedecker. CP-NiedL

Autonomy these days—surprise!—is moving up. New Life, A. Amy Clampitt. CP-ClamA

Autopsy. Miller Williams. CP-WillM

Autopsy Room, The. Raymond Carver. CP-CarvR

Autopsy, The. Josephine Jacobsen. CP-JacoJ

Autopsychography. Fernando Pessoa. SP-PessF, *tr.* by Susan M. Brown *and* Edwin Honig

Autotomy. Wisława Szymborska. SP-SzymW, *tr.* by Stanisław Barańczak *and* Clare Cavanagh

Autumn. Guillaume Apollinaire. SP-MereW, *tr.* by William Meredith

Autumn. Raymond Carver. CP-CarvR

Autumn. G. K. Chesterton. CP-ChesG

Autumn. James Vincent Cunningham. CP-CunnJ

Autumn. James Dickey. CP-DickJ

Autumn. Ivor Gurney. SP-GurnI

Autumn. Philip Larkin. CP-LarkP

Autumn. Archibald MacLeish. CP-MacLA

Autumn. Walter De la Mare. CP-DeLaW

Autumn. Raissa Maritain. CP-MertT

Autumn. Edna St. Vincent Millay. CP-MillE

Autumn. Czeslaw Milosz. CP-MiloCN, *tr.* by Robert Hass

Autumn. Lorine Niedecker. CP-NiedL

Autumn. Grace Paley. CP-PalGC

Autumn. James Whitcomb Riley. CP-RileJ

Autumn. Christina Georgina Rossetti. CP-RosC1

Autumn. Christina Georgina Rossetti. CP-RosC3

Autumn. Stevie Smith. *See* He Told His Life Story to Mrs. Courtly

Autumn. Wallace Stevens. CP-StevWP

Autumn. James Tate. SP-TateJ

Autumn. Charles Tomlinson. CP-TomlC

Autumn. William Carlos Williams. CP-WilW1

Autumn. Adam Zagajewski. SP-ZagaA, *tr.* by Renata Gorczynski, Benjamin Ivry *and* C. K. Williams

Autumn 2. David Ignatow. SP-IgnaD

Autumn: A Dirge. Percy Bysshe Shelley. CP-ShelP

Autumn. A haze is gold. Gossamers, The. Charles Tomlinson. CP-TomlC

Autumn again, you wouldn't know in the city. Allen Ginsberg. SP-GinsA *Fr.* Autumn Gold: New England Fall.

Autumn Air. Charles Simic. SP-SimiCE

Autumn Air. Charles Simic. SP-SimiC

Autumn at Baiae: For Cavafy. Alan Dugan. CP-DugaA

Autumn at Taos. D. H. Lawrence. CP-LawrD

Autumn Begins in Martins Ferry, Ohio. James Wright. CP-WrigJ

Autumn blows a withered hand on. Pastoral: "Autumn blows a withered hand on." Andrei Codrescu. SP-CodrA

Autumn Burning, An. Wendell Berry. CP-BerrW

Autumn Chant. Edna St. Vincent Millay. CP-MillE

Autumn Chapter in a Novel. Thom Gunn. CP-GunnT

Autumn Crocuses. Guillaume Apollinaire. SP-MereW, *tr.* by William Meredith

Autumn Day. Aleksandr Aleksandrovich Blok. SP-BlokA, *tr.* by Peter France *and* Jon Stallworthy

Autumn Day. Rainer Maria Rilke. CP-SpenS

(Lord, it is time. The summer was so great.) CP-SpenS

Autumn Daybreak. Edna St. Vincent Millay. CP-MillE

Autumn Days. Jones Very. CP-VeryJ

Autumn, dear to walkers with your streaks and carpets. Autumn. Ivor Gurney. SP-GurnI

Autumn departs; but still his mantle's fold. Autumn on Tweedside. Sir Walter Scott. SP-ScotW *Fr.* Lord of the Isles, The.

Autumn Drought. Helen Pinkerton. CP-PinkH

Autumn Equinox. Adrienne Rich. CP-RicAE

Autumn Even-Song. George Meredith. CP-MerG1

Autumn Evening. Robinson Jeffers. CP-JefR1

Autumn Evening. W. S. Merwin. SP-MerwWF

Autumn evening in the modest square, An. Joseph Brodsky. CP-BrodJ, *tr.* by George L. Kline

Autumn feels slowed down, The. Paula Becker to Clara Westhoff. Adrienne Rich. SP-RicA2

Autumn Fire. Rainer Maria Rilke. CP-RilkFr, *tr.* by A. Poulin, Jr.

Autumn Floods. Chuang Tzu. CP-MertT

Autumn Flowers. Jones Very. CP-VeryJ

Autumn Flowers, The. Jones Very. CP-VeryJ

Autumn Freedom. Aleksandr Aleksandrovich Blok. SP-BlokA, *tr.* by Peter France *and* Jon Stallworthy

"Autumn again, you wouldn't know in the city." SP-GinsA

Autumn Gold: New England Fall. Allen Ginsberg. CP-GinsA

Autumn Hammer. Rainer Maria Rilke. CP-RilkFr, *tr.* by A. Poulin, Jr.

Autumn Has Caught Us in Our Summer Wear. Philip Larkin. CP-LarkP

Autumn has emptied heaven of its birds. Autumn Song. Thomas McGrath. SP-McGrT

Autumn has returned and we return. Past and Future Turn About. Kenneth Rexroth. CP-RexrK

Autumn Idleness. Dante Gabriel Rossetti. CW-RossD *Fr.* House of Life, The.

Autumn Imagined. Donald Davie. CP-DaviDC

Autumn in King's Hintock Park. Thomas Hardy. CP-HardT

Autumn in Norenskaia. Joseph Brodsky. CP-BrodJ, *tr.* by Daniel Weissbort

Autumn in your hemisphere whoops cranes and owls. Polonaise: A Variation. Joseph Brodsky. CP-BrodJ

Autumn is always too early. Autumn. Adam Zagajewski. SP-ZagaA, *tr.* by Renata Gorczynski, Benjamin Ivry *and* C. K. Williams

Autumn is among us. Emily Dickinson. SP-DickE

Autumn is here, and on the vineyard terrace. Relay Tower, The. Jaroslav Seifert. SP-SeifJ, *tr.* by Ewald Osers

Autumn Is Near and Memory of My Parents. Yehuda Amichai. SP-AmicYL, *tr.* by Benjamin Harshav *and* Barbara Harshav

Autumn is Near and the Memory of My Parents. Yehuda Amichai. SP-AmicY, *tr.* by Chana Bloch

Autumn is near. The last fruit ripens. Autumn Is Near and Memory of My Parents. Yehuda Amichai. SP-AmicYL, *tr.* by Benjamin Harshav *and* Barbara Harshav

Autumn is over the long leaves that love us. Falling of the Leaves, The. William Butler Yeats. CP-YeatW

Autumn is:that between there and here. E. E. Cummings. CP-CummE

Autumn Is the Crows' Time. Kenneth Patchen. CP-PatcK

Autumn Journal. Louis MacNeice. CP-MacNL

"To-day was a beautiful day, the sky was a brilliant." CP-MacNL

Autumn Lament. Stéphane Mallarmé. CP-MallS, *tr.* by Henry Weinfield

Autumn Leaf, The. Jones Very. CP-VeryJ

Autumn Leaves. Allen Ginsberg. SP-GinsA

Autumn Leaves. James Schuyler. CP-SchuJ

Autumn Leaves. Jones Very. CP-VeryJ

Autumn leaves blow from my hand. Ezra Pound. *See* Man's paradise is his good nature, A

Autumn leaves, The. Poème d'Automne. Langston Hughes. CP-HughL; CP-HughL1

Autumn Morning. Peter Blue Cloud. SP-BlueP

Autumn morning / These are the ghosts of tears. Mississippi River. Kenneth Rexroth. CP-RexrK

Autumn Movement. Carl Sandburg. CP-SandC

Autumn nibbles its leaf [right] from my hand: we are [*or* we're] friends. Corona. Paul Celan. SP-CelaP, *tr.* by John Felstiner

Autumn Night. Lorine Niedecker. CP-NiedL

Autumn 1980. Marilyn Hacker. SP-HackM

Autumn Note. Langston Hughes. CP-HughL; CP-HughL1

Autumn Notes. Ted Hughes. SP-HughTN

Autumn on Tweedside. Sir Walter Scott. SP-ScotW *Fr.* Lord of the Isles, The.

Autumn—overlooked my Knitting. Emily Dickinson. CP-DickE

Autumn Piece. Charles Tomlinson. CP-TomlC; SP-TomlC

Autumn Poem, The. "Rubén Dario." SP-DariR, *tr.* by Alberto Acereda *and* Will Derusha

Autumn Quarries. Eugenio Montale. CP-MontE, *tr.* by Jonathan Galassi

Autumn Rain. D. H. Lawrence. CP-LawrD

Autumn Rain in Tel Aviv. Yehuda Amichai. SP-AmicY, *tr.* by Chana Bloch

Autumn Rain-Scene, An. Thomas Hardy. CP-HardT

Autumn Refrain. Wallace Stevens. CP-StevW; CP-StevWP

Autumn rooms of green and bronze, The. Michaelmas. Ivor Gurney. SP-GurnI

Autumn seems ending: there is lassitude. October. Charles Tomlinson. CP-TomlC

Autumn Sequel. Louis MacNeice. CP-MacNL

Autumn Sequence. Adrienne Rich. CP-RicAE

Autumn sherbert. Columbus Square Journal. William Corbett. SP-CorbW

Autumn Song. A. R. Ammons. CP-AmmoA

Autumn Song. Federico García Lorca. CP-GarcF, tr. by Catherine Brown

Autumn Song. Thomas McGrath. SP-McGrT

Autumn Song. Dante Gabriel Rossetti. CW-RossD

Autumn Sonnet. Charles Baudelaire. CP-BaudC, tr. by Walter Martin

Autumn Sonnets, The. May Sarton.
  "If I could let you go as trees let go." SP-SartM

Autumn strewn with broken, chestnut-coloured branches, An. Hunters. Yannis Ritsos. SP-RitsY, tr. by John Stathatos

Autumn Sunshine. D. H. Lawrence. CP-LawrD

Autumn surrounds the valley, iniquity. Wanderings of the Tribe, The. Alí Chumacero. CP-WilW2

Autumn, that name of creeper falling and tea-time loving. Old Thought. Ivor Gurney. SP-GurnI

Autumn this soon! But why hanker after an eternal sun. Farewell. Arthur Rimbaud. CP-RimbA, tr. by Martin Sorrell

Autumn Thought. Langston Hughes. CP-HughL

Autumn Thoughts. John Greenleaf Whittier. CP-WhitJ

Autumn-time has come, The. My Triumph. John Greenleaf Whittier. CP-WhitJ

Autumn torture. The old signs. Antinoüs: The Diaries. Adrienne Rich. CP-RicAE; SP-RicA1; SP-RicA2

Autumn Twilight Piece. Robert Penn Warren. CP-WarrR

Autumn Valentine. Dorothy Parker. CP-ParkD

Autumn Verses. "Rubén Dario." SP-DariR, tr. by Alberto Acereda and Will Derusha

Autumn Violets. Christina Georgina Rossetti. CP-RosC1

Autumnal. Richard Eberhart. CP-EberR

Autumnal. Louise Glück. SP-GlucL

Autumnal. Denise Levertov. SP-LeveDL

Autumnal. Howard Nemerov. CP-NemeH

Autumnal. James Wright. CP-WrigJ

Autumnal breaks the flame upon the sun-set herds. Occidit. Ezra Pound. CP-PoEar

Autumnal Equinox on Mediterranean Beach. Robert Penn Warren. CP-WarrR

Autumnal Extravaganza, An. James Whitcomb Riley. CP-RileJ

Autumnal gales had wreaked their will, The. On the Esplanade. Walter De la Mare. CP-DeLaW

Autumnal Tonic, An. James Whitcomb Riley. CP-RileJ

Autumnal[l], The. John Donne. MW-DonnJ Fr. Elegies.

Autumn's Sidereal, November's a Ball and Chain. Charles Wright. SP-WrigCN

Autumnus. Ezra Pound. CP-PoEar

Aux Belles de Londres. Ezra Pound. CP-PoEar

Aux Imagistes. William Carlos Williams. CP-WilW1

Aux taureaux Dieu cornes donne. Peter Parasol. Wallace Stevens. CP-StevWP

Available Now: Archaic Torsos of Both Sexes. Gregory Orr. SP-OrrG

Avalanche. William Dickey. SP-DickW

Avalanche, The. James Laughlin. CP-LaugJ

Avarice. George Herbert. CP-HerbG

Avarice and Ambition Only Were the First Builders of Towns and Founders of Empire. Kenneth Patchen. CP-PatcK

Avarice, the noose that lets oil, oh my dear oh. Invincibility. Frank O'Hara. SP-OharF

Avarus et Plutus. John Gay. CP-CowpW

Avaunt all specious pliancy of mind. William Wordsworth. CP-WorW1

Avaunt this economic rage! To the Utilitarians. William Wordsworth. CP-WorW2

[—] avaunt! with tenfold pleasure. Vale of Esthwaite, The. William Wordsworth. CP-WorW1

Ave. Dante Gabriel Rossetti. CW-RossD

Ave Atque Vale. James Laughlin. CP-LaugJ

Ave Atque Vale. Tennessee Williams. CP-WillT

Ave Caesar. Robinson Jeffers. CP-JefR2

Ave Imperatrix. Oscar Wilde. CP-WildO

Ave Imperatrix! Rudyard Kipling. CP-KiplR

Ave Maria. G. K. Chesterton. CP-ChesG

Ave Maria. Frank O'Hara. SP-OharF

Ave Maria Gratia Plena. Oscar Wilde. CP-WildO

'Ave you 'eard o' the Widow at Windsor. Widow at Windsor, The. Rudyard Kipling. CP-KiplR

Avec Ardeur. Marianne Craig Moore. CP-MoorM

Avec Merci, Mother. Maya Angelou. SP-AngeM

Aveluy and New Year's Eve, and the time as tender. New Year's Eve. Ivor Gurney. SP-GurnI

Avenue. Federico García Lorca. CP-GarcF, tr. by Jerome Rothenberg Fr. In the Garden of the Lunar Grapefruits.

Avenue. Robert Pinsky. CP-PinsR

Avenue, The. Paul Muldoon. CP-MuldP

Avenue A. Frank O'Hara. SP-OharF

Avenue Bearing the Initial of Christ into the New World, The. Galway Kinnell. SP-KinnGN

Avenue of Poplars, The. William Carlos Williams. CP-WilW1

Avenue rises toward a city of white marble, The. Sleeping. Donald Hall. CP-HallD

Average Egyptian Faces Death, The. John Updike. CP-UpdiJ

Avert, High Wisdom, never vainly wooed. On the Danger of War. George Meredith. CP-MerG1

Avid for that dew. Our Tears. Rainer Maria Rilke. CP-RilkFr, tr. by A. Poulin, Jr.

Avigliana. Primo Levi. CP-LeviP, tr. by Ruth Feldman and Brian Swann

Avising the bright beams of these fair eyes. Sir Thomas Wyatt. CP-WyatT

Avocado. John Logan. CP-LogaJ

Avoid, you strollers in the dark street. Against Illuminations. Archibald MacLeish. CP-MacLA

Avoiding News by the River. W. S. Merwin. SP-MerwW

Avon—a precious, an immortal name! Avon, The. William Wordsworth. CP-WorW2

Avon, The. William Wordsworth. CP-WorW2

Avondale. Stevie Smith. CP-SmitS

Avondall. Stevie Smith. CP-SmitS

Avon's Harvest. Edwin Arlington Robinson. CP-RobiE

Avowal, The. Denise Levertov. SP-LeveDS

Avowal, The. Richard Wilbur. CP-WilbR

Aw, Dylan, have you left us? Have you gone? Hayden Carruth. CP-CarHS Fr. Bloomingdale Papers, The.

Aw, piss, and sing, be. Po-sy, a Po-sy, A. Charles Olson. CP-OlsoC

Aw right then. Chillens, I know you. How To. Hayden Carruth. CP-CarHS

Awa Whigs Awa. Robert Burns. CP-BurnR

Awa wi' your witchcraft o' beauty's alarms. Hey for a Lass wi' a Tocher. Robert Burns. CP-BurnR

Await. James Schuyler. CP-SchuJ

Awaiting the / light to speak. Shore, The. George Oppen. CP-OppGN

Awaiting the Swimmer. James Dickey. CP-DickJ

Awake! Walter De la Mare. CP-DeLaW

Awake, Aeolian lyre, awake. Progress of Poesy, The. Thomas Gray. CP-GrayT

Awake, Aeolian lyre, awake. Progress of Poesy, The. Thomas Gray. CP-GrayT

Awake all night with loving. Fired. Langston Hughes. CP-HughL; CP-HughL2

Awake alone in the house. Sleepless. Stephen Spender. CP-SpenS

Awake at Night. Wendell Berry. CP-BerrW

Awake! awake! how loud the stormy morning. Song by Julius Angora. Emily Jane Brontë. CP-BronE

Awake, awake, my little Boy! Land of Dreams, The. William Blake. CP-BlakW

Awake, Awake! [Thou Heavy Sprite]. Thomas Campion. CP-CampT

Awake, great Sir, the Sun shines here [or heer]. On New-Year's Day 1640, to the King. Sir John Suckling. CP-SuckJ

Awake, he loved their voices. Longfellow's Love for the Children. James Whitcomb Riley. CP-RileJ

Awake! I'm off to cities far away. Chimes Play "Life's a Bumper!"The. Thomas Hardy. CP-HardT

Awake or sleeping (for I know not which). Old-World Thicket, An. Christina Georgina Rossetti. CP-RosC2

Awake sad heart, whom sorrow ever drowns. Dawning, The. George Herbert. CP-HerbG

Awake, thou spring of speaking grace, mute rest becomes not thee. Thomas Campion. CP-CampT

Awake, Thou That Sleepest. Christina Georgina Rossetti. CP-RosC2

Awake to the cold light. March. Hart Crane. CP-CranH

Awake ye dead! the summons has gone forth. Christmas. Jones Very. CP-VeryJ

Awake ye muses nine, sing me a strain divine. Valentine, A. Emily Dickinson. CP-DickE

Awakened. Czeslaw Milosz. CP-MiloCN, tr. by Robert Hass

Awakened this morning by a voice from my childhood. Son. Raymond Carver. CP-CarvR

Awakening. Robert Bly. SP-BlyR

Awakening, The. Robert Creeley. CP-CreeR

Awakening, The. Paul Laurence Dunbar. CP-DunbP

Awakening, The. Robert Graves. CP-GravR

Awakening, The. Ivor Gurney. SP-GurnI

Awakening, The. Charles Tomlinson. CP-TomlC

Awakening, The. Alice Walker. CP-WalkA

Awakes for me and leaps from shroud. Night-Walk, The. George Meredith. CP-MerG1

Awaking. Stephen Spender. CP-SpenS

Awaking in New York. Maya Angelou. SP-AngeM

Awaking morning laughs from heaven. Emily Jane Brontë. CP-BronE

Aware. D. H. Lawrence. CP-LawrD

Aware to the dry throat of the wide hell in the world. King David Dances. John Berryman. CP-BerrJ

Away. John Berryman. CP-BerrJ

Away. Raymond Carver. CP-CarvR

Away. Robert Creeley. CP-CreeR

Away. Walter De la Mare. CP-DeLaW

Away! Robert Frost. CP-FrosR

Away. James Whitcomb Riley. CP-RileJ

Away above a harborful. Lawrence Ferlinghetti. SP-FerlL

Away, and leave me, thou thing most abhorred. To My Muse. Ben Jonson. CP-JonsB; SP-JonsB

Away! away! away! away! Henry David Thoreau. CP-ThorH

Away, away, it is the air. William Wordsworth. CP-WorW1

Away, away, resign me now. Emily Jane Brontë. CP-BronE

Away, Away, Ye Notes of Woe! Lord Byron. CP-Byron

Away, away, your flattering arts. Written in "Letters to an Italian Nun and an English Gentleman: by J.J. Rousseau: Founded on Facts." Lord Byron. CP-Byron

Away by the lands of the Japanee. Rhyme of the Three Sealers, The. Rudyard Kipling. CP-KiplR

Away despair; my gracious Lord doth hear[e]. Bag, The. George Herbert. CP-HerbG

Away down deep and away up high. At the Playground. William Stafford. SP-StafWW

Away down there, yeah. At Bald Rock with Old John. Peter Blue Cloud. SP-BlueP

Away from Home are some and I. Emily Dickinson. CP-DickE

Away from It All. Ogden Nash. CP-NashO

Away from playground games and fights. Kite, The. Wyatt Prunty. SP-PrunW

Away from the park and zoo. Fanny Howe. SP-HoweF *Fr.* Robeson Street.

Away from the shore, the roads dwindle and lose themselves. Midsummer in the Blueberry Barrens. Amy Clampitt. CP-ClamA

Away from Water. Olga Broumas. SP-BrouO

Away goes Sussex William with his pack. William Cowper. CP-CowpW

Away, haunt not thou me. Arthur Hugh Clough. SP-ClouA

Away he goes, the hour's delightful hero. She and the Muse. Denise Levertov. SP-LeveDL; SP-LeveDS

Away, Melancholy. Stevie Smith. CP-SmitS

Away! the moor is dark beneath the moon. Stanzas—April, 1814. Percy Bysshe Shelley. CP-ShelP

Away thou fondling motley humourist. Satire 1 [A London Street]. John Donne. MW-DonnJ *Fr.* Satires.

Away, through bramble, bush, and trees. Love of the Woods. Johann N. Vogl. CP-MerG2

Away with silks, away with lawn. Clothes Do But Cheat and Cozen [or Cousen] Us. Robert Herrick. CP-HerrR

Away with your fictions of flimsy romance. First Kiss of Love, The. Lord Byron. CP-Byron

Away, ye gay landscapes, ye gardens of roses! Lachin y Gair. Lord Byron. CP-Byron

Awe so quiet, An. That Passeth All Understanding. Denise Levertov. SP-LeveDS

Awed I behold once more. Ralph Waldo Emerson. CP-EmerR

Awesome in beauty, spinning. Hurricane Andrew. Peter Blue Cloud. SP-BlueP

Awf'lest boy in this-here town. Elmer Brown. James Whitcomb Riley. CP-RileJ

Awful darkness of the town, The. E. E. Cummings. CP-CummE

Awful rushes at times. Flesh. Robert Creeley. CP-CreeR

Awful shadow of some unseen Power, The. Hymn to Intellectual Beauty. Percy Bysshe Shelley. CP-ShelP

Awful Tempest mashed the air, An. Emily Dickinson. CP-DickE

Awkward as the homely are. Emily Dickinson. SP-DickE

Awkward Comparison, An. Jelaluddin Rumi. SP-Rumi, *tr.* by Coleman Barks

Awkward Silence. James Tate. SP-TateJ

Awkwardness, the grace. Siena. Charles Olson. CP-OlsoC

Awoke. James Schuyler. CP-SchuJ

Ax. Charles Simic. SP-SimiC; SP-SimiCE

Ax God:Sea Pursuit, The. James Dickey. CP-DickJ

Axe angles / from my neighbor's ashcan, An. Junk. Richard Wilbur. CP-WilbR

Axe falls on the wood in thuds, "God, God," The. Voices. G. K. Chesterton. CP-ChesG

Axe Handles. Gary Snyder. CP-SnydG

Axe-Helve, The. Robert Frost. CP-FrosR

Axed at the. Solitary's Solace in the Natural Sciences. Heather McHugh. SP-McHuH

Axes / After whose stroke the wood rings. Words. Sylvia Plath. CP-PlatS

Axes has been ringin' in de woods de blessid day, De. Back-Log Song, A. Paul Laurence Dunbar. CP-DunbP

Axiom. Margaret Atwood. SP-AtwM1

Axiom. Joseph Brodsky. CP-BrodJ, *tr.* by Jonathan Aaron

Axis, The. Arthur Sze. SP-SzeA

Axolotl. Arthur Sze. SP-SzeA

"Ay, but, Ferishtah,"—a disciple smirked. Plot-Culture. Robert Browning. CP-BroR2

Ay, his mother was a mad one. Sad Boy, The. Laura Riding Jackson. CP-RidiL

Ay, lay him 'neath the Simla pine. Possibilities. Rudyard Kipling. CP-KiplR

Ay, man is manly. Here you see. On the Photograph of Corps Commander. Herman Melville. SP-MelvH

Ay me, alas! the beautiful bright hair. Canzone: His Lament for Selvaggia. Cino da Pistoia. CW-RossD, *tr.* by Dante Gabriel Rossetti

Ay, this same midnight, by this chair of mine. With Bernard de Mandeville. Robert Browning. CP-BroR2

Ay, thou varlet! Laugh away! Laughter Holding Both His Sides. James Whitcomb Riley. CP-RileJ

Ay, Trochu, in Paris which Prussians environ. Mettle and Metal. Robert Browning. CP-BroR2

Ay Waukin O. Robert Burns. *See* Simmer's a Pleasant Time

Ayaz and the King's Pearl. Jelaluddin Rumi. SP-Rumi, *tr.* by Coleman Barks

Aye. Seamus Heaney. SP-HeanSO *Fr.* Loaning, The.

Aye and No. Jonathan Swift. CP-SwifJ

Aye and No: A Fable. Jonathan Swift. CP-SwifJ

Aye, beloved, as thou sayest, 'tis not fear nor failing will. Algernon Sydney. G. K. Chesterton. CP-ChesG

Aye, but she? Ode to Silence. Edna St. Vincent Millay. CP-MillE

Aye! I am a poet and upon my tomb. And Thus in Nineveh. Ezra Pound. CP-PoEar

Aye, lay him in his grave, the old dead year! King is Dead, The. Paul Laurence Dunbar. CP-DunbP

Aye me, an eunuch keeps my mistress chaste. Elegy 2.3: "Aye me, an eunuch keeps my mistress chaste." Ovid. CP-MarlC *Fr.* Elegies.

Aye me, that love should natures workes accuse! Thomas Campion *and* Philip Rosseter. CP-CampT

Aye sure. Letter from Ian. Lorine Niedecker. SP-NiedL

Aye, there it is! It wakes to-night. Aye there it is! It wakes tonight. Emily Jane Brontë. CP-BronE

Aye there it is! It wakes tonight. Emily Jane Brontë. CP-BronE

Aye, well I know 'tis ghastly to descend that valley. On the Same Picture. Walt Whitman. CP-WhitW

Aye, workman, make me a dream. Stephen Crane. CP-CranS

Aye you're a man that! ye old mesmerizer. Mesmerism. Ezra Pound. CP-PoEar

Ayee! Ai! This is heavy earth on our shoulders. Burying Ground by the Ties. Archibald MacLeish. CP-MacLA

Ayers Rock / Uluru Song. Allen Ginsberg. CP-GinsA; SP-GinsA

Ayres that Were Sung and Played, at *Brougham Castle* in *Westmerland*, in the Kings Entertainment, The. Thomas Campion. CP-CampT

Azalea. Louis Zukofsky. CP-ZukLS

Azalea Swamp. Jones Very. CP-VeryJ

Azazel. Robert Stock. SP-StocR

Azikiwe in Jail. Langston Hughes. CP-HughL; CP-HughL3

Aziola, The. Percy Bysshe Shelley. CP-ShelP

Azores. John Updike. CP-UpdiJ

Azrael's Count. Rudyard Kipling. CP-KiplR

Aztec. Carl Sandburg. CP-SandC

Aztec Mask. Carl Sandburg. CP-SandC

Aztec sacrifice, / beside the head of Pope, An. Le Musée Imaginaire. Charles Tomlinson. CP-TomlC

Aztec sandstone waterholes known by Moapa've. Las Vegas: Verses Improvised for El Dorado H.S. Newspaper. Allen Ginsberg. CP-GinsA

Aztecs, conquering, brough Huitzilopochtli, The. Tepoztlán. Amy Clampitt. CP-ClamA

Azure, The. Stéphane Mallarmé. CP-MallS, *tr. by* Henry Weinfield

Azure striation swirls beyond the stones. Marilyn Hacker. SP-HackM *Fr.* La Fontaine de Vaucluse.

Azure yielder, The. Naked. Alvaro Figueredo. CP-WilW2

B

B———. Robert Creeley. CP-CreeR

B.B. Robert Creeley. SP-CreeR

B.C. William Stafford. SP-StafWW

B / eLl / s? / bE. E. E. Cummings. CP-CummE

B / et / wee / n no / w dis. E. E. Cummings. CP-CummE

B is for BOMBERS, our national pride. John Ciardi. CP-CiarJ

B.W.I. John Updike. CP-UpdiJ

Babbling Child, A. Jelaluddin Rumi. SP-Rumi, *tr. by* Coleman Barks

Babe Herrick. James Whitcomb Riley. CP-RileJ

Babe is at peace within the womb, The. Fragment: Life Rounded with Sleep. Percy Bysshe Shelley. CP-ShelP

Babe, The. Charles Olson. CP-OlsoC

Babe Unborn, The. G. K. Chesterton. CP-ChesG

Babe was laid in the Manger, The. Nativity, A. Rudyard Kipling. CP-KiplR

Babel. Louis MacNeice. CP-MacNL

Babel Aboard the Hellas International Express. Amy Clampitt. CP-ClamA

Babes, when I too was young and always right. Good Grocer, The (An Apology) G. K. Chesterton. CP-ChesG

Baboon and the State, The. John Ciardi. CP-CiarJ

Baby. Langston Hughes. CP-HughL; CP-HughL1

Baby Asleep after Pain, A. D. H. Lawrence. CP-LawrD

Baby cry— / Oh fie! Christina Georgina Rossetti. CP-RosC2

Baby Face. Carl Sandburg. CP-SandC

Baby got here once who before, A. Rampage, The. C. K. Williams. CP-WillC; SP-WillC

Baby, how come you can't see me. Ultimatum. Langston Hughes. CP-HughL; CP-HughL3

Baby, I don't want. C. K. Williams. CP-WillC

Baby, if you love me. Down and Out. Langston Hughes. CP-HughL

Baby is a harmless thing / And wins our hearts with one accord, A. Christmas Day. Christina Georgina Rossetti. CP-RosC2

Baby isn't cute, The. In fact he's. Size of Spokane, The. Heather McHugh. SP-McHuH

Baby lies so fast asleep. Christina Georgina Rossetti. CP-RosC2

Baby looked toward me, The. Katharine Anne. Lorine Niedecker. CP-NiedL

Baby moon, a canoe, a silver papoose canoe sails and sails in the, The. Early Moon. Carl Sandburg. CP-SandC

Baby-Movements. D. H. Lawrence. CP-LawrD

Baby, my only husband turned away. Message of Thelma Sayles, The. Lucille Clifton. SP-ClifL

Baby picked from an ash barrel by the night police, The. Chicago Boy Baby. Carl Sandburg. CP-SandC

Baby Picture. Anne Sexton. CP-SextA

Baby Pictures of Famous Dictators. Charles Simic. SP-SimiC; SP-SimiCE

Baby Running Barefoot. D. H. Lawrence. CP-LawrD

(When the bare feet of the baby beat across the grass.) CP-LawrD

Baby-sized but skinny bronze statuette in a bronze Grecian robe, The. Autobiographical Libation to Erato Muse of Lyric Poetry. Alan Dugan. CP-DugaA

Baby Song. Thom Gunn. CP-GunnT *Fr.* Three Songs.

Baby Song of the Four Winds. Carl Sandburg. CP-SandC

Baby Songs Ten Months Old. D. H. Lawrence. CP-LawrD

Baby stood to understand, The. Five Threes (Fast Bike). Heather McHugh. SP-McHuH

Baby Toes. Carl Sandburg. CP-SandC

Baby Tortoise. D. H. Lawrence. CP-LawrD

Baby Vamps. Carl Sandburg. CP-SandC

Baby vamps, is it harder work than it used to be? Baby Vamps. Carl Sandburg. CP-SandC

Baby Villon. Philip Levine. SP-LeviP

Baby / was made in a cell, The. Nursery, The. Fanny Howe. SP-HoweF

Baby was wakened from her afternoon nap today by a fierce wind blowing up and rain, The. Muse, A. Carolyn Kizer. CP-KizeC

Baby watched a ford, whereto, A. Wagtail and Baby. Thomas Hardy. CP-HardT

Babyhood. James Whitcomb Riley. CP-RileJ

Babylon, Babylon, Babylon the Great. Nicholas Vachel Lindsay. CP-LindV

Babylon slim / -ness of / evenslicing. E. E. Cummings. CP-CummE

Babylon the Great. Christina Georgina Rossetti. CP-RosC2

Baby's cradle with no baby in it, A. Christina Georgina Rossetti. CP-RosC2

Baby's Dying. James Whitcomb Riley. CP-RileJ

Baby's flight will embellish History. Emily Dickinson. SP-DickE

Babysitters, The. Sylvia Plath. CP-PlatS

Bacardi Spreads the Eagle's Wing. Hart Crane. CP-CranH

Baccalaureate. Archibald MacLeish. CP-MacLA

Baccalaureate Hymn. Edna St. Vincent Millay. CP-MillE

Bacchae. Euripides.
Choros Translations. CP-DoolH

Bacchanalian Verse, A. Robert Herrick. CP-HerrR

Bacchic. Constantine P. Cavafy. CP-CavaC, *tr. by* Theoharis Constantine Theoharis

Bacchus. Federico García Lorca. CP-GarcF, *tr. by* Alan S. Trueblood *Fr.* Three Portraits with Shading.

Bacchus. Ralph Waldo Emerson. CP-EmerR

Bacchus and Ariadne. Hesiod. CP-BroEB *Fr.* Theogony.

Bacchus and Ariadne; 2nd Debate between the Body and Soul. T. S. Eliot. SP-ElioT

Bacchus, let me drink no more. Hymn[e] to Bacchus, A. Robert Herrick. CP-HerrR

Bach and the Sentry. Ivor Gurney. SP-GurnI

Bach Concerto, A. Jaroslav Seifert. SP-SeifJ, *tr. by* Ewald Osers

Bachanalian Verse, A. Robert Herrick. CP-HerrR

Bachelor 'e fights for one, The. Married Man, The. Rudyard Kipling. CP-KiplR

Bachelour I will, A. No Spouse but a Sister. Robert Herrick. CP-HerrR

Back. John Berryman. CP-BerrJ

Back. John Ciardi. CP-CiarJ

Back. James Schuyler. CP-SchuJ

Back, The. Karl Shapiro. SP-ShapK

Back and forth across. You ("Back and forth across"). Robert Creeley. CP-CreeR

Back and forth, back and forth. Fall 1961. Robert Lowell. SP-LoweR

Back and forth cawings between black. Crow. Peter Blue Cloud. SP-BlueP

Back at the hotel, watching her loosen, then comb out. Thermopylae. Raymond Carver. CP-CarvR

Back at the west window, Basin Creek. Returned to the Yaak Cabin, I Overhear an Old Greek Song. Charles Wright. SP-WrigCN

Back Bay. John Updike. CP-UpdiJ

Back Country. A. R. Ammons. CP-AmmoA

Back door opened, The. Reconstructing a Crime. Yusef Komunyakaa. CP-KomuY

Back from a Two-Years' Sentence. James Whitcomb Riley. CP-RileJ

Back from the cordial Grave I drag thee. Emily Dickinson. CP-DickE

Back from Town. James Whitcomb Riley. CP-RileJ

Back from Vacation. John Updike. CP-UpdiJ

Back here, old snow like lace cakes. After Reading Wang Wei, I Go Outside to the Full Moon. Charles Wright. SP-WrigCN

Back Home. William Stafford. SP-StafWW

Back Home in Pompeii. John Ciardi. CP-CiarJ

Back in a corner, alone in the clatter and babble. Old Man, An. Robert Pinsky. CP-PinsR

Back in '15, when life was harsh. Field-Postcard, The. Robert Graves. CP-GravR

Back in my youth how often did I long. Lines for the Painter Ota Janeček. Jaroslav Seifert. SP-SeifJ, *tr. by* Ewald Osers

Back in the thirties, in the midst of the Great Depression. Old Darned Man, The. Stanley Kunitz. CP-KunSC

Back in the World. Ai. SP-Ai

Back Lane, The. Thomas Kinsella. CP-KinsT

Back-Log Song, A. Paul Laurence Dunbar. CP-DunbP

Back-looking memory / And prophet hope both sprang from out. Memory and Hope. Elizabeth Barrett Browning. CP-BroEB

Back of Affluence. Donald Davie. CP-DaviDC

Back of her neck, The. She. James McMichael. SP-McMiJ

Back of my back, they talk of me. Whistling Girl, The. Dorothy Parker. CP-ParkD

Back of the dam, under. Town of Hill, The. Donald Hall. CP-HallD

Back of the door the child is playing that. Resolution. W. S. Merwin. SP-MerwW

Back of the World. Federico García Lorca.
Crazy Boy, The. CP-GarcF, *tr. by* Alan S. Trueblood
Disquiet and Night. CP-GarcF, *tr. by* Alan S. Trueblood
Leave-taking. CP-GarcF, *tr. by* Alan S. Trueblood
Marriage Vow. CP-GarcF, *tr. by* Alan S. Trueblood
Scene. CP-GarcF, *tr. by* Alan S. Trueblood
Suicide. CP-GarcF, *tr. by* Alan S. Trueblood
Voiceless Child, The. CP-GarcF, *tr. by* Alan S. Trueblood

'Back on Times Square, Dreaming of Times Square.' Allen Ginsberg. CP-GinsA

Back out of all this now too much for us. Directive. Robert Frost. CP-FrosR

Back, the yoke, the yardage, The. Lapped seams. Shirt. Robert Pinsky. CP-PinsR

Back Then. Yusef Komunyakaa. CP-KomuY

Back then, before we came. On Freedom's Ground. Richard Wilbur. CP-WilbR

Back then, when they still had gallows. Rogues' and Gonifs' Ditty, A. Paul Celan. SP-CelaP, *tr.* by John Felstiner

Back through clouds. Train Tune. Louise Bogan. CP-BogaL

Back through East Flatbush, a raw grave. Burial in Cypress Hills. Amy Clampitt. CP-ClamA

Back through the Looking Glass to This Side. John Ciardi. CP-CiarJ

Back to Carrick, the castle as plumb assured. Carrick Revisited. Louis MacNeice. CP-MacNL

Back to Life. Thom Gunn. CP-GunnT

Back to my native place. Welcome Home. Thomas Hardy. CP-HardT

Back to the Army Again. Rudyard Kipling. CP-KiplR

Back to the breast of thy mother. Alexander Crummel—Dead. Paul Laurence Dunbar. CP-DunbP

Back to the figure. Robert Duncan. SP-DuncR *Fr.* Structure of Rime, The.

Back to the great music, Scottish Gaels. Too long. Hugh MacDiarmid. SP-MacDH *Fr.* Good-bye Twilight.

Back to the Mother Breast. Laura Riding Jackson. CP-RidiL

Back Tooth. Muriel Rukeyser. CP-RukeM

Back when it took all day to come up. Hearing. W. S. Merwin. SP-MerwWF

Back wings, The. Between Walls. William Carlos Williams. CP-WilW1

Back within the valley. Home Again. Wallace Stevens. CP-StevWP

Back within the valley. Home Again. Wallace Stevens. CP-StevWP

Back Yard. Carl Sandburg. CP-SandC

Back Yard Boogie Woogie. Charles Wright. SP-WrigCN

Back yard, dry flower half-border, unpeopled landscape. Disjecta Membra. Charles Wright. SP-WrigCN

Backcountry Blues. Kenneth Patchen. CP-PatcK

Backdrop Addresses Cowboy. Margaret Atwood. SP-AtwM1

Backdrop With Lovers, 1931. Tess Gallagher. SP-GallT

Backgammon. Olga Broumas. SP-BrouO

Background and the Figure, The. Thomas Hardy. CP-HardT

Background with Harpsichord. Marya Alexandrovna Zaturenska. SP-ZatuM

Background with Revolutionaries. Archibald MacLeish. CP-MacLA

Backhoe braces itself against itself, The. Two Loves. Heather McHugh. SP-McHuH

Backlash Blues, The. Langston Hughes. CP-HughL; CP-HughL3

Backs twist with the kiss, The. "Kiss, The" Donald Hall. CP-HallD

Backside of the Academy, The. Muriel Rukeyser. CP-RukeM

Backtrack of sea, the baywater goes; flats. Conjuration. Richard Wilbur. CP-WilbR

Backward among the dusky years. Compassion. Thomas Hardy. CP-HardT

Backward Dancer. Peter Blue Cloud. SP-BlueP

Backward Glance, A. Charles Tomlinson. SP-TomlC

Backward Look, A. James Whitcomb Riley. CP-RileJ

Backward Look, The. Seamus Heaney. SP-HeanSO

Backward Look, The. Howard Nemerov. CP-NemeH

Backward Spring, A. Thomas Hardy. CP-HardT

Backwards. Robert Creeley. CP-CreeR

Backwater of air, The. Variation ("Backwater of air, The"). Federico García Lorca. CP-GarcF, *tr.* by Jerome Rothenberg *Fr.* Backwaters.

Backwaters. Federico García Lorca.

  "Cypress. / (Stagnant water)." CP-GarcF, *tr.* by Jerome Rothenberg

  Half Moon. CP-GarcF, *tr.* by Jerome Rothenberg

  Little Backwater. CP-GarcF, *tr.* by Jerome Rothenberg

  Song: "Night here already." CP-GarcF, *tr.* by Jerome Rothenberg

  Variation ("Backwater of air, The"). CP-GarcF, *tr.* by Jerome Rothenberg

Backyard in California, A. Hayden Carruth. CP-CarHS

Backyard Swingset. Thomas Lux. SP-LuxT

Bacterial War, The. Howard Nemerov. CP-NemeH

Bad Action. Charles Bukowski. SP-BukC3

Bad among the Good are here mixt ever, The. Good, and Bad. Robert Herrick. CP-HerrR

Bad are all surfeits: but Physicitians call. Surfeits. Robert Herrick. CP-HerrR

Bad are the times. *Sil.* And wors then they are we. Pastorall Sung to the King: Montano, Silvio, and Mirtillo, Shepards, A. Robert Herrick. CP-HerrR

Bad Beginning, A. D. H. Lawrence. CP-LawrD

Bad Blood. Arthur Rimbaud. CP-RimbA, *tr.* by Martin Sorrell

Bad day in Bellini country, Venetian dog high-stepper. Venetian Dog. Charles Wright. SP-WrigCN

Bad Dream. Louis MacNeice. CP-MacNL

Bad Dream, A. Kathleen Jessie Raine. SP-RainK

Bad Dreams I. Robert Browning. CP-BroR2

Bad Dreams II. Robert Browning. CP-BroR2

Bad Dreams III. Robert Browning. CP-BroR2

Bad Dreams IV. Robert Browning. CP-BroR2

Bad Example, The. Thomas Hardy. CP-HardT

Bad Heart. Federico García Lorca. CP-GarcF, *tr.* by Christopher Maurer

Bad Island, The—Easter. Robert Frost. CP-FrosR

Bad Luck. Charles Baudelaire. CP-BaudC, *tr.* by Walter Martin

Bad Luck Card. Langston Hughes. CP-HughL; CP-HughL1

Bad Man. Langston Hughes. CP-HughL; CP-HughL1

Bad May Be Better. Robert Herrick. CP-HerrR

Bad Memory Makes You a Metaphysician, a Good One Makes You a Saint, A. Charles Wright. SP-WrigCN

Bad Monk, The. Charles Baudelaire. CP-BaudC, *tr.* by Walter Martin

Bad Morning. Langston Hughes. CP-HughL; CP-HughL2

Bad Mouth. Margaret Atwood. SP-AtwM2

Bad Mouth. C. K. Williams. CP-WillC

Bad Music, The. Randall Jarrell. CP-JarrR

Bad Night, A. W. H. Auden. CP-AudeW

Bad Night on Third Avenue, A. James Laughlin. CP-LaugJ

Bad Old Days, The. Kenneth Rexroth. CP-RexrK

Bad Princes Pill Their People. Robert Herrick. CP-HerrR

Bad Season Makes the Poet Sad, The. Robert Herrick. CP-HerrR

Bad-tempered bullying bunch, the horned crows. Dehorning. Ted Hughes. SP-HughTN

Bad Thing came in the night, and, this time, ate away part of my. Story of an Olson, and Bad Thing, The. Charles Olson. CP-OlsoC

Bad times: / The cars pass. George Oppen. CP-OppGN

Bad Wages for Good Service. Robert Herrick. CP-HerrR

Badger. John Clare. SP-ClarJ

Badgers, The. Seamus Heaney. SP-HeanSO

Badlands, The. Lorine Niedecker. CP-NiedL

Baffled / by the choreography of the season. Autumn Piece. Charles Tomlinson. CP-TomlC; SP-TomlC

Baffled for just a day or two. Emily Dickinson. CP-DickE

Baffled for just a day or two. Baffled for just a day or two. Emily Dickinson. CP-DickE

Bag, The. George Herbert. CP-HerbG

Bag of the Bee, The. Robert Herrick. CP-HerrR

Bag of tricks—is it?, A. Honey and Salt. Carl Sandburg. CP-SandC

Bag-Snatching in Dublin. Stevie Smith. CP-SmitS

Bagatelles the Madrigals, The. Wallace Stevens. CP-StevW; CP-StevWP

Bagatto. Charles Olson. CP-OlsoC

Bagel, The. David Ignatow. SP-IgnaD

Baggage King, The. James Dickey. CP-DickJ

Baggot Street Deserta. Thomas Kinsella. SP-KinsT

Bagni di Lucca. Eugenio Montale. CP-MontE, *tr.* by Jonathan Galassi

Bagous, whose care doth thy mistress bridle. Elegy 2.2: "Bagous, whose care doth thy mistress bridle." Ovid. CP-MarlC *Fr.* Elegies.

Bagpipe Music. Hugh MacDiarmid. SP-MacDH

Bagpipe Music. Louis MacNeice. CP-MacNL

Bags of Meat. Thomas Hardy. CP-HardT

Bah! I have sung women in three cities. Cino. Ezra Pound. CP-PoEar; SP-PounE

Bahamas. Archibald MacLeish. CP-MacLA

Bahamas. George Oppen. CP-OppGN

Bahá'u'lláh in the Garden of Ridwan. Robert Earl Hayden. CP-HaydR

Bahia, Brazil. Raymond Carver. CP-CarvR

Baile and Aillinn. William Butler Yeats. CP-YeatW

Bailing Out—A Poem for the 1970s. Eleanor Wilner. SP-WilnE

Bailing the Boat. Mary Oliver. SP-OlivM

Bairns gat out wi' an unco shout, The. Deuks Dang o'er My Daddie, The. Robert Burns. CP-BurnR

Bait[e], The. John Donne. CP-DonnJ; CP-MarlC; MW-DonnJ

Baited / bear / on / the ashtray, The. Ashtray. Louis Zukofsky. CP-ZukLS

Baja Beatitudes. Lawrence Ferlinghetti. SP-FerlL

Baja Revisited. Lawrence Ferlinghetti. SP-FerlL

Baker, The. Raymond Carver. CP-CarvR

Baker's Island Light, The. Jones Very. CP-VeryJ

Bakery. Adam Zagajewski. SP-ZagaA, *tr.* by Clare Cavanagh

Balade of Bon Conseill. Geoffrey Chaucer. CP-ChauG (Truth.) CP-ChauG

Balade of Complaint, A. Geoffrey Chaucer. CP-ChauG

Balance. Federico García Lorca. CP-GarcF, *tr.* by Alan S. Trueblood *Fr.* Theories.

Balance, The. Denise Levertov. SP-LeveDL

Balance and Beauty. Clarence Major. SP-MajoC

Balance checkbook. / Rid lawn of onion grass. Things to Do. James Schuyler. CP-SchuJ

Balance is preserved by the snails climbing the, The. One for the Shoeshine

Man. Charles Bukowski. SP-BukC1

Balance of Europe, The. Alexander Pope. CP-PopeA

Balance Wheel, The. Anne Sexton. SP-SextA

Balancing Acts. Donald Davie. CP-DaviDC

Balancing spaces are not disturbed, The. Known Soldier, The. Kenneth Patchen. CP-PatcK

Balaustion's Adventure. Robert Browning. CP-BroR1

Balconies shut, The. Sunset at the Fair. Federico García Lorca. CP-GarcF, *tr. by* Jerome Rothenberg *Fr.* Fairs.

Balcony. Federico García Lorca. SP-GarcF *Fr.* Poem of the Saeta.

Balcony, The. Charles Baudelaire. CP-BaudC, *tr. by* Walter Martin

Balcony, The. Eugenio Montale. CP-MontE, *tr. by* Jonathan Galassi

Bald heads forgetful of their sins. Scholars, The. William Butler Yeats. CP-YeatW

Bald man in plaid playing the harpsichord, The. San Jose Symphony Reception. Lawrence Ferlinghetti. SP-FerlL

Bale-Fire, The. Sir Walter Scott. SP-ScotW *Fr.* Lay of the Last Minstrel, The.

Baler, The. Hayden Carruth. CP-CarHS

Balieff's actors from The Bat. When Fresh, It Was Sweet. William Carlos Williams. CP-WilW1

Ball, A. Czeslaw Milosz. CP-MiloCN, *tr. by* Robert Hass

Ball, The. Rainer Maria Rilke. CP-RilkFr, *tr. by* A. Poulin, Jr.

Ball Game. Richard Eberhart. CP-EberR

Ball Game, The. Robert Creeley. CP-CreeR

Ball of ropey dough, A. It's Hard to Think the Brain. Miller Williams. CP-WillM

Ball Poem, The. John Berryman. CP-BerrJ

Ball whizzed by,—It grazed his Ear, The. Epigram on an Event in Col. Evans's Redoubted Performances in Spain. William Wordsworth. CP-WorW2

Ball will bounce, but less and less. It's not, A. Juggler. Richard Wilbur. CP-WilbR

Ballad: "Astrolabes and lexicons." George Oppen. CP-OppGN

Ballad: "He passed by with another woman." Gabriela Mistral. SP-MistG, *tr. by* Maria Giachetti [*or* Jacketti]

Ballad: "I know my love is true." Paul Laurence Dunbar. CP-DunbP

Ballad: "I put my hat upon my head." Samuel Johnson. CP-JohnS (Parodies of Bishop Percy's *Hermit of Warkworth*.) CP-JohnS

Ballad: "I therefore pray thee, Renny dear." Samuel Johnson. CP-JohnS (Parodies of Bishop Percy's *Hermit of Warkworth*.) CP-JohnS

Ballad: "Of all the twice ten thousand bards." Lord Byron. CP-Byron

Ballad: "Soft white lamb in the daisy meadow." Christina Georgina Rossetti. CP-RosC3

Ballad: "Summer morning is risen." John Clare. SP-ClarJ *Fr.* Child Harold.

Ballad: "Tender infant, meek and mild, The." Samuel Johnson. CP-JohnS (Parodies of Bishop Percy's *Hermit of Warkworth*.) CP-JohnS

Ballad: "Though it may seem rude." Ben Jonson. CP-JonsB *Fr.* Masque of Augurs, The.

Ballad: "To a man and his wife." William Carlos Williams. CP-WilW2

Ballad: "What's that approaching like dusk like poverty." Charles Simic. SP-SimiC; SP-SimiCE

Ballad, A: "And will you leave me thus alone." William Wordsworth. CP-WorW1

Ballad, A: "Crowd about me, little children." James Whitcomb Riley. CP-RileJ

Ballad, A: "There was a lass and she was fair." Robert Burns. CP-BurnR

Ballad, A: "We have a song for the death in her body." Robert Creeley. CP-CreeR

Ballad, A: "While Prose-work and rhymes." Robert Burns. CP-BurnR

Ballad: Between the Boxcars [1923]. Robert Penn Warren. CP-WarrR

Ballad for Americans. Charles Olson. CP-OlsoC

Ballad for Gloom. Ezra Pound. CP-PoEar

Ballad from April, A. James Whitcomb Riley. CP-RileJ

Ballad from Childhood. Audre Lorde. SP-LordA

Ballad in Honor of the Muses of Flesh and Blood. "Rubén Dario." SP-DariR, *tr. by* Alberto Acereda *and* Will Derusha

Ballad in the Streets of Buenos Aires. Yehuda Amichai. SP-AmicYL, *tr. by* Benjamin Harshav *and* Barbara Harshav

Ballad of a Little Delta Town. Miller Williams. CP-WillM

Ballad of a Wilful Woman. D. H. Lawrence. CP-LawrD

Ballad of Abbreviations, A. G. K. Chesterton. CP-ChesG

Ballad of an Intellectual. E. E. Cummings. CP-CummE

Ballad of Another Ophelia. D. H. Lawrence. CP-LawrD

Ballad of Ballymote, The. Tess Gallagher. SP-GallT

Ballad of Basil, The. Lorine Niedecker. CP-NiedL

Ballad of Billie Potts, The. Robert Penn Warren. CP-WarrR

Ballad of Black Pain. Federico García Lorca. CP-GarcF, *tr. by* Christopher Maurer

Ballad of Blossom, The. Mona Van Duyn. SP-VanDM

Ballad of Boding, A. Christina Georgina Rossetti. CP-RosC2

Ballad of Boh Da Thone, The. Rudyard Kipling. CP-KiplR (This is the ballad of Boh Da Thone.) CP-KiplR

Ballad of Booker T. Langston Hughes. CP-HughL; CP-HughL3

Ballad of Burdens, A. Algernon Charles Swinburne. SP-SwinA

Ballad of Chaldon Down, The. Edna St. Vincent Millay. CP-MillE

Ballad of Christmas, A. Walter De la Mare. CP-DeLaW

Ballad[e] of Dead Ladies, The. François Villon. CW-RossD, *tr. by* Dante Gabriel Rossetti

Ballad of Death, A. Algernon Charles Swinburne. SP-SwinA

Ballad of East and West, The. Rudyard Kipling. CP-KiplR

Ballad of Fair Ladies in Revolt, A. George Meredith. CP-MerG1

Ballad of Faith. William Carlos Williams. CP-WilW2

Ballad of Father Gilligan, The. William Butler Yeats. CP-YeatW

Ballad of Father O'Hart, The. William Butler Yeats. CP-YeatW

Ballad of Fisher's Boardinghouse, The. Rudyard Kipling. CP-KiplR (That night, when through the mooring-chains.) CP-KiplR

Ballad of Gin Mary. Langston Hughes. CP-HughL; CP-HughL1

Ballad of God-Makers, The. G. K. Chesterton. CP-ChesG

Ballad of Harry Moore. Langston Hughes. CP-HughL; CP-HughL3

Ballad of Henry, Bridegroom. Josephine Jacobsen. CP-JacoJ

Ballad of Johnny, The. May Sarton. SP-SartM

Ballad of King Arthur, The. G. K. Chesterton. CP-ChesG

Ballad of Ladies Lost and Found. Marilyn Hacker. SP-HackM

Ballad of Levallois. Czeslaw Milosz. CP-MiloC; CP-MiloCN, *tr. by* Robert Hass

Ballad of Life, A. Algernon Charles Swinburne. SP-SwinA

Ballad of Little Sallie. Langston Hughes. CP-HughL; CP-HughL1

Ballad of Love. E. E. Cummings. CP-CummE

Ballad of Love's Skeleton, The. Thomas Hardy. CP-HardT

Ballad of Margie Polite, The. Langston Hughes. CP-HughL; CP-HughL2

Ballad of Mary's Son. Langston Hughes. CP-HughL; CP-HughL3

Ballad of Minepit Shaw, The. Rudyard Kipling. CP-KiplR

Ballad of Mister Dutcher and the Last Lynching in Gupton. Robert Penn Warren. CP-WarrR

Ballad of Moll Magee, The. William Butler Yeats. CP-YeatW

Ballad of Nat Turner, The. Robert Earl Hayden. CP-HaydR

Ballad of Negro History, A. Langston Hughes. CP-HughL; CP-HughL3

Ballad of One Doomed to Die. Federico García Lorca. SP-GarcF, *tr. by* Langston Hughes

Ballad of Orange and Grape. Muriel Rukeyser. CP-RukeM

Ballad of Our Lady of the Boat. Federico García Lorca. CP-GarcF, *tr. by* Catherine Brown

Ballad of Ozie Powell. Langston Hughes. CP-HughL; CP-HughL1

Ballad of Past Meridian, A. George Meredith. CP-MerG1

Ballad of Reading Gaol, The. Oscar Wilde. CP-WildO

Ballad of Remembrance, A. Robert Earl Hayden. CP-HaydR

Ballad of Roosevelt. Langston Hughes. CP-HughL; CP-HughL1

Ballad of Rudolph Reed, The. Gwendolyn Brooks. SP-BrooG

Ballad of Sam Solomon. Langston Hughes. CP-HughL; CP-HughL2

Ballad of Smiles and Tears, The. Lee O. Harris. CP-RileJ

Ballad of Sue Ellen Westerfield, The. Robert Earl Hayden. CP-HaydR

Ballad of the Battle of Gibeon, The. G. K. Chesterton. CP-ChesG

Ballad of the Black Sheep. Langston Hughes. CP-HughL; CP-HughL3

Ballad of the "Bolivar," The. Rudyard Kipling. CP-KiplR

Ballad of the Brown Girl. Alice Walker. CP-WalkA

Ballad of the Brown Girl, The. Countee Cullen. CP-CullC

Ballad of the Cars, The. Rudyard Kipling. CP-KiplR *Fr.* Muse among the Motors, The.

Ballad of the Clairvoyant Widow. Theodore Roethke. CP-RoetT

Ballad of the *Clampherdown*, The. Rudyard Kipling. CP-KiplR

Ballad of the Corn-Cob and the Lie, The. Archibald MacLeish. CP-MacLA

Ballad of the Dark Ladié, The. Samuel Taylor Coleridge. CP-ColeS

Ballad of the Despairing Husband. Robert Creeley. CP-CreeR

Ballad of the Enamord Image, The. Robert Duncan. SP-DuncR

Ballad of the Fool. Langston Hughes. CP-HughL; CP-HughL3

Ballad of the Fortune Teller. Langston Hughes. CP-HughL; CP-HughL2

Ballad of the Four Saints. Josephine Jacobsen. CP-JacoJ

Ballad of the Foxhunter, The. William Butler Yeats. CP-YeatW

Ballad of the Girl Whose Name Is Mud. Langston Hughes. CP-HughL; CP-HughL2

Ballad of the Goodly Fere. Ezra Pound. CP-PoEar; SP-PounE

Ballad of the Gypsy. Langston Hughes. CP-HughL; CP-HughL2

Ballad of the Harp-Weaver, The. Edna St. Vincent Millay. CP-MillE

Ballad of the Icondic. John Ciardi. CP-CiarJ

Ballad of the Killer Boy. Langston Hughes. CP-HughL; CP-HughL2

Ballad of the King's Jest, The. Rudyard Kipling. CP-KiplR

Ballad of the King's Mercy, The. Rudyard Kipling. CP-KiplR

Ballad of the Lady Eglantine, The. George Meredith. CP-MerG2

Ballad of the Landlord. Langston Hughes. CP-HughL; CP-HughL2; CP-HughL3

Ballad of the Little Square. Federico García Lorca. SP-GarcF, tr. by J. L. Gili and Stephen Spender

Ballad of the Lonely Masturbator, The. Anne Sexton. CP-SextA; SP-SextA

Ballad of the Long-legged Bait. Dylan Thomas. CP-ThomD

Ballad of the Man Who's Gone. Langston Hughes. CP-HughL; CP-HughL2

Ballad of the Marked Man. Federico García Lorca. CP-GarcF, tr. by Will Kirkland

Ballad of the Miser. Langston Hughes. CP-HughL; CP-HughL1

Ballad of the Moon Moon. Federico García Lorca. CP-GarcF, tr. by Christopher Maurer

Ballad of the Pawnbroker. Langston Hughes. CP-HughL; CP-HughL2

Ballad of the Red Earl, The. Rudyard Kipling. CP-KiplR

Ballad of the Scholar's Lament. E. E. Cummings. CP-CummE

Ballad of the Seven Songs. Langston Hughes. CP-HughL; CP-HughL2

Ballad of the Sinner. Langston Hughes. CP-HughL; CP-HughL2

Ballad of the Sixties. May Sarton. SP-SartM

Ballad of the Skeletons, The. Allen Ginsberg. SP-GinsA

Ballad of the Spanish Civil Guard. Federico García Lorca. SP-GarcF, tr. by A. L. Lloyd

Ballad of the Spanish Civil Guard. Federico García Lorca. CP-GarcF, tr. by Will Kirkland

Ballad of the Sun's Hunting. Ezra Pound. CP-PoEar

Ballad of the Three Rivers. Federico García Lorca. CP-GarcF, tr. by Robert Nasatir

Ballad of the Three Spectres. Ivor Gurney. SP-GurnI

Ballad of the Two Thieves. Langston Hughes. CP-HughL; CP-HughL3

Ballad of the Typist. Andrei Codrescu. SP-CodrA

Ballad of the Washed Hair. Yehuda Amichai. SP-AmicY, tr. by Stephen Mitchell

Ballad of the Water of the Sea. Federico García Lorca. SP-GarcF, tr. by Lloyd Mallan

Ballad of the Wheel, The. Charles Simic. SP-SimiC; SP-SimiCE

Ballad of Walter White. Langston Hughes. CP-HughL; CP-HughL3

Ballad of Will, The. Sir Thomas Wyatt. CP-WyatT

Ballad of Wine Skins. Ezra Pound. CP-PoEar

Ballad of Your Puzzlement. Robert Penn Warren. CP-WarrR

Ballad on the Game of Traffic, A. Jonathan Swift. CP-SwifJ

Ballad Rosalind. Ezra Pound. CP-PoEar

Ballad Theme, A. Muriel Rukeyser. CP-RukeM

Ballad to the Tune of the Cutpurse [or "The Cut-Purse"], A. Jonathan Swift. CP-SwifJ

Ballad Written in a Hospital. Eugenio Montale. CP-MontE, tr. by Jonathan Galassi

Ballade: "By Mystic's banks I held my dream." Paul Laurence Dunbar. CP-DunbP

Ballade: "Does something lie who'd rather stand." E. E. Cummings. CP-CummE

Ballade: "White night roared with a huge north-wind, The." E. E. Cummings. CP-CummE

Ballade at Thirty-Five. Dorothy Parker. CP-ParkD

Ballade by the Fire. Edwin Arlington Robinson. CP-RobiE

Ballade de Marguerite. Unknown. CP-WildO, tr. by Oscar Wilde

Ballade for the Duke of Orléans. Richard Wilbur. CP-WilbR

Ballade in Old French. François Villon. CP-WilbR

Ballade of a Complete Flop. Dorothy Parker. CP-ParkD

Ballade of a Great Weariness. Dorothy Parker. CP-ParkD

Ballade of a Not Insupportable Loss. Dorothy Parker. CP-ParkD

Ballade of a Talked-off Ear. Dorothy Parker. CP-ParkD

Ballade of Black Caracols. Federico García Lorca. CP-GarcF, tr. by Jerome Rothenberg Fr. Caracols / Snails.

Ballade of Broken Flutes. Edwin Arlington Robinson. CP-RobiE

Ballade of Burial, A. Rudyard Kipling. CP-KiplR

Ballade of Forgiveness. François Villon. CP-WilbR

Ballade of Jakko Hill, A. Rudyard Kipling. CP-KiplR

Ballade of Poisons. Allen Ginsberg. CP-GinsA

Ballade of Sayings. W. S. Merwin. SP-MerwW

Ballade of Soul. E. E. Cummings. CP-CummE

Ballade of the Coming Rain, The. James Whitcomb Riley. CP-RileJ

Ballade of the Ladies of Time Past. François Villon. CP-WilbR, tr. by Richard Wilbur

Ballade of the Pink Parasol. Wallace Stevens. CP-StevWP

Ballade of Understandable Ambitions. Dorothy Parker. CP-ParkD

Ballade of Unfortunate Mammals. Dorothy Parker. CP-ParkD

Ballade of White Caracols. Federico García Lorca. CP-GarcF, tr. by Jerome Rothenberg Fr. Caracols / Snails.

Ballade pour la grosse Lulu. T. S. Eliot. SP-ElioT

Ballade to be Read in the Medici Gardens. Robert Stock. SP-StocR

Ballade to End With, A. François Villon. CP-WilbR, tr. by Richard Wilbur

Ballad[e] [upon a Wedding], A. Sir John Suckling. CP-SuckJ

Ballads of Lenin. Langston Hughes. CP-HughL; CP-HughL1

Ballat [or Ballad] of Our Lady, [Ane]. William Dunbar. CP-DunbW

Ballat of the Abbot of Tungland, A. William Dunbar. CP-DunbW

Ballat of the Passioun, Ane. William Dunbar. CP-DunbW

Ballata: Concerning a Shepherd-maid. Guido Cavalcanti. CW-RossD, tr. by Dante Gabriel Rossetti

Ballata: He perceives that his highest Love is gone from him. Guido Cavalcanti. CW-RossD, tr. by Dante Gabriel Rossetti

Ballata: He reveals, in a Dialogue, his increasing Love for Mandetta. Guido Cavalcanti. CW-RossD, tr. by Dante Gabriel Rossetti

Ballata: He will gaze upon Beatrice. Dante Alighieri. CW-RossD, tr. by Dante Gabriel Rossetti

Ballata: In Exile at Sarzana. Guido Cavalcanti. CW-RossD, tr. by Dante Gabriel Rossetti

Ballata: Of a continual Death in Love. Guido Cavalcanti. CW-RossD, tr. by Dante Gabriel Rossetti

Ballata: Of his Lady among other Ladies. Guido Cavalcanti. CW-RossD, tr. by Dante Gabriel Rossetti

Ballata: Of True and False Singing. Unknown. CW-RossD, tr. by Dante Gabriel Rossetti

Ballata, Fragment. Ezra Pound. CP-PoEar

Ballatetta. Ezra Pound. CP-PoEar

Balled in the Streets of Buenos Aires. Yehuda Amichai. SP-AmicY, tr. by Chana Bloch

Ballet. William Carlos Williams. CP-WilW1

Ballet, The. Thomas Hardy. CP-HardT

Ballet, The. William Meredith. SP-MereW

Balloon Faces. Carl Sandburg. CP-SandC

Balloon of the Mind, The. William Butler Yeats. CP-YeatW

Balloons. Sylvia Plath. CP-PlatS

Balloons hang on wires in the Marigold Gardens, The. Balloon Faces. Carl Sandburg. CP-SandC

Ballroom Dark. Clarence Major. SP-MajoC

Ball's Bluff. Herman Melville. SP-MelvH

Bally Power Play. Thom Gunn. CP-GunnT

Ballydavid Pier. Thomas Kinsella. CP-KinsT

Ballyspellin. Thomas Sheridan. CP-SherT

Balm in Gilead. Christina Georgina Rossetti. CP-RosC2

Balms. Amy Clampitt. CP-ClamA

Balsa Wood. Raymond Carver. CP-CarvR

Baltasar Gracián. Jorge Luis Borges. SP-BorgJ, tr. by Alastair Reid

Baltic Fog Notes. Carl Sandburg. CP-SandC

Baltic Sea froze in 1307, The. Birds flew north. Annual of the Dark Physics, An. Norman Dubie. CP-DubiN

Baltimore bones groan maliciously under sidewalk. Haunting Poe's Baltimore. Allen Ginsberg. CP-GinsA

Balto; The Lead Dog of the Team that Brough Antitoxin to Nome. Dorothy Parker. CP-ParkD

Balustrade along my balcony, The. Beaded Balustrade. James Schuyler. CP-SchuJ

Balzac. Raymond Carver. CP-CarvR

Bamberg. Randall Jarrell. CP-JarrR

Bambini picking daisies in the new spring grass. Daisies of Florence. Kathleen Jessie Raine. SP-RainK

Ban, The. James Whitcomb Riley. CP-RileJ

Banal machines are exposing themselves, The. Ashes on a Saturday Afternoon. Frank O'Hara. SP-OharF

Banal Sojourn. Wallace Stevens. CP-StevW; CP-StevWP

Banana-stuffed, the ape behind the brain. After Sunday Dinner We Uncles Snooze. John Ciardi. CP-CiarJ

Bancroft, the message-bearing wire. Suggestion for a Telegraphic Birthday Greeting. Robert Browning. CP-BroR2

Band Concert. Carl Sandburg. CP-SandC

Band concert public square Nebraska city. Flowing and circling dresses. Band Concert. Carl Sandburg. CP-SandC

Band played Idomeneo, The. Charles Dodgson's Song. Randall Jarrell. CP-JarrR

Bandaged Shoulder, The. Constantine P. Cavafy. CP-CavaC, tr. by Theoharis Constantine Theoharis

Bandit to prince was his advance one night. Right Possessor, The. Thom Gunn. CP-GunnT

Bandol (Var). Stevie Smith. CP-SmitS

Bands of black men seem to be drifting in the air. Sick Man, The. Wallace Stevens. CP-StevWP

Bandusian Spring from glass more brightly clear. Ode 3.13: Translation of Horace's Ode 3.13. Horace. CP-WorW1 Fr. Odes.

Bang. Paul Muldoon. CP-MuldP

Bang—a burning, A. Ted Hughes. SP-HughTN

Bang dang ang S. Philip Martyr Angelus 6 P.M. or, Early Autumn in Upper Noe Valley. Philip Whalen. SP-WhalP

Banging around in a cigarette she isn't "in love." Ted Berrigan. SP-BerrT *Fr.* Sonnets, The.

Bangkok Gang, The. Maxine W. Kumin. SP-KumiM

Bangla Desh: 1. Faiz Ahmad Faiz. CP-KizeC, *tr. by* Carolyn Kizer

Bangla Desh: 2. Faiz Ahmad Faiz. CP-KizeC, *tr. by* Carolyn Kizer

Bangla Desh: 3. Faiz Ahmad Faiz. CP-KizeC, *tr. by* Carolyn Kizer

Bangle (Slight Return), The. Paul Muldoon. CP-MuldP

Bangle, The. Paul Muldoon. CP-MuldP

Bangs, The. Eugenio Montale. CP-MontE, *tr. by* Jonathan Galassi

Bangs in street. July: Fargo Street. Robert Creeley. SP-CreeR

Bangs that hide your childlike forehead, The. Bangs, The. Eugenio Montale. CP-MontE, *tr. by* Jonathan Galassi

Banish Air from Air. Emily Dickinson. CP-DickE

Banished from Massachusetts. John Greenleaf Whittier. CP-WhitJ

Banished Gods, The. Derek Mahon. CP-MahoD

Banishment. Tu Fu. CP-KizeC, *tr. by* Carolyn Kizer

Banishment in Winter. W. S. Merwin. SP-MerwW

Banjo Boomer. Wallace Stevens. CP-StevWP

Banjo done commence de shune. De Virginia Reel, A. Paul Laurence Dunbar. CP-DunbP

Banjo Song, A. Paul Laurence Dunbar. CP-DunbP

Bank Account. Robert Graves. CP-GravR

Bank feels no lameness of his knotty gout. On Bank the Usurer. Ben Jonson. CP-JonsB; SP-JonsB

Bank Fraud, A. Rudyard Kipling. *Fr.* Plain Tales from the Hills.

Bank is a matter of columns, The. Woman in Front of a Bank, A. William Carlos Williams. CP-WilW2

Bank of the Future, The. Constantine P. Cavafy. CP-CavaC, *tr. by* Theoharis Constantine Theoharis

Bank swallows veer and dip, The. Siskins, The. Theodore Roethke. CP-RoetT

Bank Thrown Down, The. Jonathan Swift. CP-SwifJ

Banked oars fell an hundred strong, The. Rowers, The. Rudyard Kipling. CP-KiplR

Banked winter cloud. Kathleen Jessie Raine. SP-RainK

Bankers Are Just Like Anybody Else, Except Richer. Ogden Nash. CP-NashO

Banking. A. R. Ammons. CP-AmmoA

Banking Potatoes. Yusef Komunyakaa. CP-KomuY

Banking to land, as readily as birds. Landing, The. Charles Tomlinson. CP-TomlC

Bankruptcy. Raymond Carver. CP-CarvR

Banks. Max Jacob. CP-BishF

Banks o' Doon, The ("Ye banks and braes o' bonie [*or* bonnie] Doon"). Robert Burns. CP-BurnR

Banks o' Doon, The ("Ye flowery banks o' bon[n]ie Doon"). Robert Burns. CP-BurnR

Banks of a Stream Where Creatures Bathe. James Merrill. SP-MerrJ

Banks of Cree. Robert Burns. CP-BurnR

Banks of Nith, The. Robert Burns. CP-BurnR

Banks of the Devon, The. Robert Burns. CP-BurnR

Bann Clay. Seamus Heaney. SP-HeanSO

Banneker. Rita Dove. SP-DoveR

Banner. Olga Broumas. SP-BrouO

Banner Bearer, The. William Carlos Williams. CP-WilW2

Banners, The. Robert Duncan. SP-DuncR

Bannocks o' Bear-Meal. Robert Burns. CP-BurnR

Banqauet, The. Dante Alighieri. CP-NemeH, *tr. by* Howard Nemerov *Fr.* Convito.

Banquet, The. George Herbert. CP-HerbG

Banquet, The. W. S. Merwin. SP-MerwWF

Banquet, The. Ogden Nash. CP-NashO

Banquet, The. Robert Stock. SP-StocR

Banquet Night. Rudyard Kipling. CP-KiplR *Fr.* Debits and Credits.

Banquo. Walter De la Mare. CP-DeLaW

Bantams in Pine-Woods. Wallace Stevens. CP-StevW; CP-StevWP

Banyan Tree, Old Year's Night, The. Derek Walcott. CP-WalcD

Baptism. Alice Walker. CP-WalkA

Baptism in the Lead Avenue Ditch. Jay Wright. SP-WrigJ

Baptismal. Norman Dubie. SP-DubiN

Baptisme. Robert Herrick. CP-HerrR

Bar. Langston Hughes. CP-HughL; CP-HughL3

Bar and Grill. Heather McHugh. SP-McHuH

Bar Giamaica, 1959-60. Charles Wright. SP-WrigC

Bar-Room Matins. Louis MacNeice. CP-MacNL

Bar-Room TV. Ted Hughes. *Fr.* Boom.

Bar Time. Billy Collins. SP-CollB

Barbara. G. K. Chesterton. CP-ChesG

Barbara Frietchie. John Greenleaf Whittier. CP-WhitJ

Barbarians. Adam Zagajewski. SP-ZagaA, *tr. by* Clare Cavanagh

Barbaric. Arthur Rimbaud. CP-RimbA, *tr. by* Martin Sorrell

Barbarity. A. George Oppen. CP-OppGN

Barbed seeds in double ranks. Sours of the Hills. Gary Snyder. CP-SnydG

Barbed wire, the plaster, the fallen windows, The. Compromises. Yannis Ritsos. SP-RitsY, *tr. by* N. C. Germanacos

Barber, A. Sir John Suckling. CP-SuckJ

Barber, barber, come and get me. I'll Get One Tomorrow. Ogden Nash. CP-NashO

Barber nurse has shaved off sensitive hair, The. On Going up to Surgery in the Morning and in Favor of Pain-Killing Drugs. Alan Dugan. CP-DugaA

Barberry Bush, The. Jones Very. CP-VeryJ

Barberry-Pickers, The. Jones Very. CP-VeryJ

Barberry-Tree, The. Samuel Taylor Coleridge. CP-ColeS; CP-WorW1

Barberry's red with ripened fruit, The. Barberry-Pickers, The. Jones Very. CP-VeryJ

Barbey tells, in verses worthy of his prose. Concerning the Cid. "Rubén Dario." SP-DariR, *tr. by* Alberto Acereda *and* Will Derusha

Barbie Doll. Marge Piercy. SP-PierM

Barcelona: February 13, 1977. Robert Creeley. SP-CreeR

Barclay of Ury. John Greenleaf Whittier. CP-WhitJ

Bard, The [A Pindaric Ode]. Thomas Gray. CP-GrayT

Bard, grown desirous of saving his pelf, A. Verses Written on One of the Windows at Delville. *Unknown, sometimes at. to* Thomas Sheridan. CP-SherT

Bard, if e'er he feel at all, The. To Mrs. King. William Cowper. CP-CowpW

Bard & mystic held me for their own, The. Rex. Ralph Waldo Emerson. CP-EmerR

Bard of the Fleece, whose skilful genius made. To the Poet, John Dyer. William Wordsworth. CP-WorW1

Bard or dunce is blest, but hard. Ralph Waldo Emerson. CP-EmerR

Bard—whose soul is meek as dawning day, The. Occasioned by the Battle of Waterloo February, 1816. William Wordsworth. CP-WorW2

Bards, The. Robert Graves. CP-GravR

Bard's Epitaph, A. Robert Burns. CP-BurnR

Bards falter in shame, their running verse, The. Bards, The. Robert Graves. CP-GravR

Bards of passion and of mirth. Ode: "Bards of passion and of mirth." John Keats. CP-KeatJ

Bards of the island city!—where of old. To a Poetical Trio in the City of Gotham. John Greenleaf Whittier. CP-WhitJ

Bards wha hae for Hellas bled—. Louis MacNeice. CP-MacNL *Fr.* Cock o' the North.

Bare Almond-Trees. D. H. Lawrence. CP-LawrD

Bare cherry tree, The. Bare Tree, The. William Carlos Williams. CP-WilW2

Bare Fig-trees. D. H. Lawrence. CP-LawrD

Bare flags. Pump water. Winter-evening cold. Scrabble. Seamus Heaney. SP-HeanSO *Fr.* Glanmore Revisited.

Bare-handed, I hand the combs. Stings. Sylvia Plath. CP-PlatS

Bare Line of the Hill, The. Ivor Gurney. SP-GurnI

Bare skin is my wrinkled sack. Shrouded Stranger, The. Allen Ginsberg. CP-GinsA; SP-GinsA

Bare Tree, The. William Carlos Williams. CP-WilW2

Bare trees / Smoky lavender twigs. Leaving L'Atelier—Aix-en-Provence. Kenneth Rexroth. CP-RexrK

Bare white marble room. Tunisian Nostalgia. Lawrence Ferlinghetti. SP-FerlL

Bare woods, you made a tight circle. December Trees. Charles Simic. SP-SimiCE

Barefoot. Anne Sexton. CP-SextA

Barefoot. Big feet. Yannis Ritsos. SP-RitsY *Fr.* First Series.

Barefoot Blues. Langston Hughes. CP-HughL; CP-HughL2

Barefoot Boy, The. John Greenleaf Whittier. CP-WhitJ

Barefoot boy! I mark him at his play, A. James Whitcomb Riley. CP-RileJ

Barefoot for a Scorpion. Alan Dugan. CP-DugaA

Barefoot Homiletics, after Wittgenstein and Boswell. Alan Dugan. CP-DugaA

Barefoot, in burgundy shorts and a salmon-pink. Paunch. Paul Muldoon. CP-MuldP

Barefoot in purple pants. Living with a Wife. John Updike. CP-UpdiJ

Barefoot, in unaccustomed clouts or skirts of raw muslin. New Saddhus, The. Robert Pinsky. CP-PinsR

Barefooted boys scud up the street. Sudden Shower, A. James Whitcomb Riley. CP-RileJ

Bareheaded / The hair blond in tight curls. Swaggering Gait, The. William Carlos Williams. CP-WilW2

Barely and *widely*. Louis Zukofsky. CP-ZukLS

Barely anything to say, everything said. Michael Palmer. SP-PalmM

Barely tolerated, living on the margin. Soonest Mended. John Ashbery. SP-AshbJ

Bark of a fox rings, sonorous and long, The. Winter Night in Woodland. Thomas Hardy. CP-HardT

Bark smells like pineapple: Jeffries. Foxtail Pine. Gary Snyder. CP-SnydG

Barking sound the shepherd hears, A. Fidelity. William Wordsworth. CP-WorW1

Barley-Break , A. Sir John Suckling. CP-SuckJ

Barley-Break; or, Last in Hell. Robert Herrick. CP-HerrR

Barley or rye / blue and white green. Charles Olson. CP-OlsoC

Barlow. Stevie Smith. CP-SmitS

Barmaids Are Diviner Than Mermaids. Ogden Nash. CP-NashO

Barmecide Feast. John Ciardi. CP-CiarJ

Barn, The. Seamus Heaney. SP-HeanSO

Barn, The. Stephen Spender. CP-SpenS

Barn Fire. Thomas Lux. SP-LuxT

Barnfloor and Winepress. Gerard Manley Hopkins. CP-HopkG

Barnsley and District. Donald Davie. CP-DaviDC

Barnsley, 1966. Donald Davie. CP-DaviDC

Barometer of my moods today, mayfly. Mayfly. Louis MacNeice. CP-MacNL

Barometer, The. Charles Tomlinson. CP-TomlC

Baron Baedeker Blew His Nose and, Sighing, Departed, The. Howard Nemerov. CP-NemeH

Baroque Comment. Louise Bogan. CP-BogaL

Baroque convent, The. Near Vienna. Eugenio Montale. CP-MontE, tr. by Jonathan Galassi

Baroque Gravure, A. Thomas Merton. CP-MertT

Baroque Image. May Sarton. SP-SartM

Baroque night advances in its clouds, A. Second Elegy. Age of Magicians. Muriel Rukeyser. CP-RukeM

Baroque sewing machine of Georg Friedrich, The. Sunday Music. Amy Clampitt. CP-ClamA

Baroque Sunburst, A. Amy Clampitt. CP-ClamA

Baroque Wall-Fountain in the Villa Sciarra, A. Richard Wilbur. CP-WilbR

Barque Aurelia of Boston, The. Jones Very. CP-VeryJ

Barque Nornen. Charles Tomlinson. CP-TomlC

Barque of phosphor. Fabliau of Florida. Wallace Stevens. CP-StevW; CP-StevWP

Barracks Apt. 14. Theodore Weiss. SP-WeisT

Barrage of Firework Poems on the Occasion of the Poet's Birthday. Federico García Lorca.

    Capriccio ("Zip! . . . / Did you just close"). CP-GarcF, tr. by Jerome Rothenberg

    Catherine Wheel. CP-GarcF, tr. by Jerome Rothenberg

    Chinese Garden. CP-GarcF, tr. by Jerome Rothenberg

    First Launching. CP-GarcF, tr. by Jerome Rothenberg

    Game of Moons, A. CP-GarcF, tr. by Jerome Rothenberg

    Rockets. CP-GarcF, tr. by Jerome Rothenberg

    Ruby Disc, The. CP-GarcF, tr. by Jerome Rothenberg

    Sunflower. CP-GarcF, tr. by Jerome Rothenberg

Bar[re] close as you can, and bolt fast too your door[e]. No Lock against Lechery. Robert Herrick. CP-HerrR

Barrel-organ / assails the suburb, A. At Trotsky's House. Charles Tomlinson. CP-TomlC

Barren. Audre Lorde. SP-LordA

Barren Leaves. Thom Gunn. CP-GunnT

Barren Spring. Dante Gabriel Rossetti. CW-RossD Fr. House of Life, The.

Barren Woman. Sylvia Plath. CP-PlatS

Barrier Snow. Robert Stock. SP-StocR

Barrier, The. Paul Laurence Dunbar. CP-DunbP

Bars. Carl Sandburg. CP-SandC

Bars are thick with drops that show, The. At Middle-Field Gate in February. Thomas Hardy. CP-HardT

Bars Fight [August 28, 1746]. Lucy Terry. CP-WheaP

Barthélémon at Vauxhall. Thomas Hardy. CP-HardT

Bartholdi Statue, The. John Greenleaf Whittier. CP-WhitJ

Bartholomew Fair. Ben Jonson.

    "My masters and friends, and good people draw near." CP-JonsB

Baruch Spinoza. Jorge Luis Borges. SP-BorgJ, tr. by Willis Barnstone

Bas Ben Adhem, A. Ogden Nash. CP-NashO

Bas-Relief. Carl Sandburg. CP-SandC

Base of All Metaphysics, The. Walt Whitman. CP-WhitW

Baseball. Wyatt Prunty. SP-PrunW

Baseball and Writing. Marianne Craig Moore. CP-MoorM

Baseball Canto. Lawrence Ferlinghetti. SP-FerlL

Baseball players know the meaning of sacrifice. Note to God Concerning a Point from an Earlier Communication, A. Miller Williams. CP-WillM

Baseball Players, The. Donald Hall. CP-HallD

Baseball Team of Unknown Navy Pilots, Pacific Theater, 1944, A. Wyatt Prunty. SP-PrunW

Bashful Arides, The. Arides. Ezra Pound. SP-PounE

Bashfulness. Robert Herrick. CP-HerrR

Bashing the Babies. John Ciardi. CP-CiarJ

Bashō. Lorine Niedecker. CP-NiedL

Bashō, coming. Snow Party, The. Derek Mahon. CP-MahoD

Basic Dialogue. Charles Wright. SP-WrigCN

Basic hatred / sometimes has a flower. Love Poem, A: "Basic hatred / sometimes has a flower." William Carlos Williams. CP-WilW2

Basic metaphor is good: blend dead, The. Garden, The. Thomas Lux. SP-LuxT

Basic Syllogism. Robert Penn Warren. CP-WarrR

Basics. James Dickey. CP-DickJ

Basil 1977-1993. William Corbett. SP-CorbW

Basilica. Ambrose Bierce. SP-BierA

Basil's turd steams. Misremembered Edwin Denby Line. William Corbett. SP-CorbW

Basket. Carl Sandburg. CP-SandC

Basket broad of woven white rods, A. Gerard Manley Hopkins. CP-HopkG

Basket of Fresh Bread, A. Jelaluddin Rumi. SP-Rumi, tr. by Coleman Barks

Baskets. Louise Glück. SP-GlucL

Basta! D. H. Lawrence. CP-LawrD

Basta una notte a maturare il fungo. Christina Georgina Rossetti. CP-RosC3

Bastard Peace, A. William Carlos Williams. CP-WilW1

Bastards. Robert Herrick. CP-HerrR

Bat. Federico García Lorca. CP-GarcF, tr. by Jerome Rothenberg Fr. Shadow.

Bat. D. H. Lawrence. CP-LawrD

Bat. Anne Sexton. CP-SextA

Bat, The. Emily Dickinson. CP-DickE

Bat, The. Ogden Nash. CP-NashO

Bat, The. James Whitcomb Riley. CP-RileJ

Bat, The. Theodore Roethke. CP-RoetT

Bat Cave. Eleanor Wilner. SP-WilnE

Bat, / elixir of shadows. Bat. Federico García Lorca. CP-GarcF, tr. by Jerome Rothenberg Fr. Shadow.

Bat is born, A. Bats. Randall Jarrell. CP-JarrR

Bat is dun with wrinkled Wings, The. Bat, The. Emily Dickinson. CP-DickE

Bat on the Road, A. Seamus Heaney. SP-HeanSO

Bath. Carl Sandburg. CP-SandC

Bath, The. Gary Snyder. CP-SnydG

Bath after Sailing. John Updike. CP-UpdiJ

Bathed in War's Perfume. Walt Whitman. CP-WhitW

Bathers, The. Hart Crane. CP-CranH

Bathing Resort. D. H. Lawrence. CP-LawrD

Bathroom tiles are very pink and new, The. 1976. Marilyn Hacker. SP-HackM

Bathtub Thoughts. W. H. Auden. CP-AudeW

Bats. Randall Jarrell. CP-JarrR

Bats at play taunt us with "guess how many" Above the Edge of Doom. Robert Graves. CP-GravR

Batsto. A. R. Ammons. CP-AmmoA

Batt he gets children, not for love to reare 'em. Upon Batt. Robert Herrick. CP-HerrR

Battalion Is Now On Rest, The. Ivor Gurney. SP-GurnI

Batter'd, wrecked old man, A. Prayer of Columbus. Walt Whitman. CP-WhitW

Battered Wife, The. Donald Davie. CP-DaviDC

Battle. G. K. Chesterton. CP-ChesG

Battle. Robinson Jeffers. See May-June, 1940

Battle, The ("Not far advanc'd was morning day"). Sir Walter Scott. SP-ScotW Fr. Marmion.

Battle Autumn of 1862, The. John Greenleaf Whittier. CP-WhitJ

Battle Continues, The. Hugh MacDiarmid.

    Major Road Ahead. SP-MacDH

    "One loves the temporal, some unique manifestation." SP-MacDH

Battle Dawn. Ezra Pound. CP-PoEar

Battle ended the moment you got there, The. Sheridan. W. S. Merwin. SP-MerwWF

Battle fought between the Soul, The. Emily Dickinson. CP-DickE

Battle Ground. Langston Hughes. CP-HughL; CP-HughL3

Battle had passed from the height, The. Emily Jane Brontë. CP-BronE

Battle is within, the. Hymn: The Good Fight. Jones Very. CP-VeryJ

Battle of Brunanburh. Unknown. CP-TennA, tr. by Alfred Tennyson

Battle of Life. D. H. Lawrence. CP-LawrD

Battle of Magnesia, The. Constantine P. Cavafy. CP-CavaC, tr. by Theoharis Constantine Theoharis

Battle of Murfreesboro. Allen Tate. CP-TateA

Battle of Sherra-Moor, The. Robert Burns. CP-BurnR

Battle of Stone River, Tennessee. Herman Melville. SP-MelvH

Battle of Unameit, The. Kenneth Patchen. CP-PatcK

Battle rent a cobweb diamond-strung, The. Range-finding. Robert Frost. CP-FrosR

Battle-Scene. Sylvia Plath. CP-PlatS

Battle Scene. Robert Stock. SP-StocR

Battlefield, A. Donald Davie. CP-DaviDC

Battleground. Robert Stock. SP-StocR

Battles whose names I do not know. Looking. Muriel Rukeyser. CP-RukeM

Battleship Newsreel. Allen Ginsberg. CP-GinsA

Battlewagon. William Meredith. SP-MereW

Batxóca. Robert Graves. CP-GravR

Baucis and Philemon. Jonathan Swift. CP-SwifJ
   (Story of Baucis & Philemon, The.) CP-SwifJ

Baudelaire knew what it was like. Lucretius, 3, 1053–1076. Kenneth Rexroth. CP-RexrK

Bavarian Gentian, The. James Laughlin. CP-LaugJ

Bavarian Gentians. D. H. Lawrence. CP-LawrD

Bawdry Embraced. Ted Hughes.
   Song: "From what dog's dish or crocodile's rotten." SP-HughTN

Bawdy Can Be Sane. D. H. Lawrence. CP-LawrD
   (What's Sane and What Isn't.) CP-LawrD

Bay Bank. A. R. Ammons. CP-AmmoA

Bay Combe. G. K. Chesterton. CP-ChesG

Bay horse is fitted with a white jade saddle, The. March, The. Li Po. CP-WilW2

Bay is frozen up, The. Historical Process. Hans Magnus Enzensberger. SP-EnzeH, tr. by Michael Hamburger

Bay is not blue but sombre yellow, The. Self-Criticism in February. Robinson Jeffers. CP-JefR2

Bay of Seven Islands, The. John Greenleaf Whittier. CP-WhitJ

Bay today breaks, The. Today. James Schuyler. CP-SchuJ

Bay Trees Were About to Bloom, The. Philip Whalen. SP-WhalP

Bayard Taylor. John Greenleaf Whittier. CP-WhitJ

Bayberry. Louis Zukofsky. CP-ZukLS

Bayonet. Anne Sexton. CP-SextA

Bayonet Charge. Ted Hughes. SP-HughTN

Bayonne Entering NYC. Allen Ginsberg. CP-GinsA

Bayonne Turnpike to Tuscarora. Allen Ginsberg. CP-GinsA

Bayou Afternoon. Amy Clampitt. CP-ClamA

Be a Demon! D. H. Lawrence. CP-LawrD

Be advised by me, darling. Advice from a Mother. Robert Graves. CP-GravR

"Be alive," they say, when I. On Rape Unattempted. Alan Dugan. CP-DugaA

Be–all. Gregory Orr. SP-OrrG

Be Angry at the Sun. Robinson Jeffers. CP-JefR3

Be angry now no more! Walter De la Mare. CP-DeLaW

Be angry yourself, as well you may. No Letter. Robert Graves. CP-GravR

Be as careful, as rational. Stone. Robert Creeley. SP-CreeR

Be assured, the Dragon is not dead. Vanity. Robert Graves. CP-GravR

Be awake mornings. See light spread across the lawn. Crystal. Ted Berrigan. SP-BerrT

Be bold my Booke, nor be abasht, or feare. To His Booke. Robert Herrick. CP-HerrR

Be-Bop Boys. Langston Hughes. CP-HughL; CP-HughL3

Be calm? And was I frantic? Clinging Vine, The. Edwin Arlington Robinson. CP-RobiE

Be calm, collected, easy. Unknown War, The. Carl Sandburg. CP-SandC

Be careful not to cross the gander. Gander, The. Ogden Nash. CP-NashO

Be careful of words. Words. Anne Sexton. CP-SextA

Be careful! Slow and careful, for you now approach. Inevitable Frontier. Robert Penn Warren. CP-WarrR

Be careful, then, and be gentle about death. All Soul's Day. D. H. Lawrence. CP-LawrD

Be careful what you say to us now. Lines to a Poet. Josephine Jacobsen. CP-JacoJ

Be composed—be at ease with me—I am Walt Whitman, liberal and lusty as Nature. To a Common Prostitute. Walt Whitman. CP-WhitW

Be diuers wyis and operatiounes. William Dunbar. CP-DunbW

Be earnest, Earth,—and kind. To Earth. Hart Crane. CP-CranH

Be faithful unto death. Christ proffers thee. That No Man Take Thy Crown. Christina Georgina Rossetti. CP-RosC2

Be fixed, you rapid orbs, that bear. Fourth Song, The. Thomas Carew. CP-CareT Fr. Carew's Masque.

Be flip with us if you want to, spring wind. Spring Wind. Carl Sandburg. CP-SandC

Be gay now. Spring Carries Surprises. Carl Sandburg. CP-SandC

Be gentle, O hands of a child. Dreams. Walter De la Mare. CP-DeLaW

Be gentle with it—Coax it. Emily Dickinson. SP-DickE

Be Glad, She Said. Shmuel HaNagid. SP-HaNaS, tr. by Peter Cole

Be gone ye blockheads, *Heraclitus* cries. Diogenes Laertius. CP-JohnS

Be-gorrie, al wor sorry. Larry Noolan's New Year. James Whitcomb Riley. CP-RileJ

Be grave, woman for love. Laura Riding Jackson. CP-RidiL

Be happy if the wind inside the orchard. On the Threshhold. Eugenio Montale. CP-MontE, tr. by Jonathan Galassi

Be happy you two. Marriage Song for Florence and Harry, A. Louis Zukofsky. CP-ZukLS

Be in me as the eternal moods. Δωρια. Ezra Pound. CP-PoEar; SP-PounE

Be it life, be it death, there is nearing the dawn of a glorious day. Requiescat. James Whitcomb Riley. CP-RileJ

Be it, Sennuccio, clearly understood. Petrarch. CP-Petra, tr. by J. G. Nichols

Be It So. D. H. Lawrence. CP-LawrD

Be it the summer-noon: a sandy space. Sea: A Summer and Winter View, The. George Crabbe. SP-CrabG Fr. Borough, The.

Be kind to your self, it is only one. Who Be Kind To. Allen Ginsberg. CP-GinsA; SP-GinsA

Be land ready. Be Ready. Carl Sandburg. CP-SandC

Be Like Me. David Ignatow. SP-IgnaD

Be literal a moment. Recollect. Seamus Heaney. SP-HeanSO Fr. Squarings.

Be loose. Be easy. Be ready. Forgotten Wars. Carl Sandburg. CP-SandC

De me a Pharaoh. For Us, Who Dare Not Dare. Maya Angelou. SP-AngeM

Be Melting Snow. Jelaluddin Rumi. SP-Rumi, tr. by Coleman Barks

Be mending still your nets, and cast not in. To the Fishermen. Jones Very. CP-VeryJ

Be mery, man, and tak nocht fer in mynd. William Dunbar. CP-DunbW

Be Mine the Doom. Emily Dickinson. CP-DickE

Be music, night, / That her sleep may go. Kenneth Patchen. CP-PatcK

Be My Defender. Thomas Merton. CP-MertT

Be natural, / wise / as you can be. Name, The. Robert Creeley. CP-CreeR

Be Nobody's Darling. Alice Walker. CP-WalkA

Be not deceived by the slow swell and lull of sea lolling. Sea Hates the Land, The. Robert Penn Warren. CP-WarrR

Be not dismaid[e], though crosses cast thee down[e]. Comforts in Crosses. Robert Herrick. CP-HerrR

Be Not Many Teachers. Jones Very. CP-VeryJ

Be not obedient of the excellent, do not prize the silly with an exceptionally pushy person or orphan. Day and Night in 1952. Frank O'Hara. SP-OharF

Be not proud, but now incline. Changes to Corinna, The. Robert Herrick. CP-HerrR

Be not thou silent now at length. Bible, O.T. See Keep not thou silence, O God

Be not too hard for life is short. September Song. Christopher Logue. SP-LoguC

Be not too wildly amorous of the far. Imagination's Pride, The. Walter De la Mare. CP-DeLaW

Be nought dismayd that her unmoved mind. Sonnet 6. Edmund Spenser. CP-Spens Fr. Amoretti.

Be of Good Cheer. Robert Creeley. SP-CreeR

Be of good cheer, brave spirit; steadfastly. Ralph Waldo Emerson. CP-EmerR

Be of Good Courage. Jones Very. CP-VeryJ

Be of love(a little). E. E. Cummings. CP-CummE

Be Off! Stevie Smith. CP-SmitS

Be Our Fortunes as They May. James Whitcomb Riley. CP-RileJ

Be patient, solemn nose. Precious Five. W. H. Auden. CP-AudeW

Be pleased, O Lord, to take a people's thanks. Matter for Gratitude. Ambrose Bierce. SP-BierA

Be proud[,] as Spaniards! [and] Leap for Pride[,] ye Fleas[!]. On Donne's First Poem. Samuel Taylor Coleridge. CP-ColeS

Be proud New-York of your prize domes. & Forty-Second Street. Archibald MacLeish. CP-MacLA

Be proud you people of these graves. City of Monuments. Muriel Rukeyser. CP-RukeM

Be, rather than be called, a child of God. On an Infant Which Died before Baptism. Samuel Taylor Coleridge. CP-ColeS

Be Ready. Carl Sandburg. CP-SandC

Be sad, be cool, be kind. Long Shadow of Lincoln: A Litany, The. Carl Sandburg. CP-SandC

Be safe, nor fear thyself so good a fame. To One that Desired Me Not to Name Him. Ben Jonson. CP-JonsB; SP-JonsB

Be showtime again. Somebody will paint beautiful faces all over. Soon It Will. Kenneth Patchen. CP-PatcK

Be Silence from your dismal cave abroad. Ode to Silence. Richard Eberhart. CP-EberR

Be slowly lifted up, thou long black arm. Sonnet: "Be slowly lifted up, thou long black arm." Wilfred Owen. CP-OwenW

Be somber with those in smoke garments. If So Hap May Be. Carl Sandburg. CP-SandC

Be Still! D. H. Lawrence. CP-LawrD

Be still as before oh pool. Old Music for Quiet Hearts. Carl Sandburg. CP-SandC

Be still, heart, cease those measured strokes. Foolish Heart, The. Countee Cullen. CP-CullC

Be still / Listen to the stones of the wall. In Silence. Thomas Merton. CP-MertT

Be still—listen to the wind! Mistral Over the Graves. Archibald MacLeish. CP-MacLA

Be still, my soul, be still; the arms you bear are brittle. A. E. Housman. CP-HousA

Be Still, Thou Busy Foolish Thing. Thomas Sheridan. CP-SherT

Be stirring, girls! we ought to have a run. On a Fine Day. Franco Sacchetti. CW-RossD, *tr. by* Dante Gabriel Rossetti

Be sure my coming was a sharp offense. Edna St. Vincent Millay. CP-MillE

Be sure, my eyes, you know. Michelangelo Buonarroti. CP-Miche, *tr. by* John Frederick Nims

Be that as it may, I'm wakened by the moans. Oscar. Paul Muldoon. CP-MuldP

Be the mistress[e] of my choice. What Kind of Mistress[e] He Would Have. Robert Herrick. CP-HerrR

Be this thing written, e'er I write. Battle. G. K. Chesterton. CP-ChesG

Be those few hours, which I have yet to spend. His Meditation upon Death. Robert Herrick. CP-HerrR

Be thou then my beauty named. Thomas Campion. CP-CampT

Be unto love as rain is unto colour^eate. E. E. Cummings. CP-CummE

Be up betimes there is no need of rest. Redeeming the Time. Jones Very. CP-VeryJ

Be warned of steps retrieved in pain. Mentor and Pupils. George Meredith. CP-MerG2

Be well assured that on our side. Song in Storm, A. Rudyard Kipling. CP-KiplR

Be who you are and will be. For Each of You. Audre Lorde. SP-LordA

Be Wise, and Fly Not. Thomas Campion. CP-CampT
    (Your faire lookes urge my desire.) CP-CampT

Be wise: / Give me to the world. Love-Song to Eunoë. Ezra Pound. CP-PoEar

Be ye an luvar, think ye nocht ye suld. William Dunbar. CP-DunbW

Be ye not many teachers; for we all. Be Not Many Teachers. Jones Very. CP-VeryJ

Be you still, be you still, trembling heart. To His Heart, Bidding It Have No Fear. William Butler Yeats. CP-YeatW

Beach. Robert Creeley. SP-CreeR

Beach, The. Robert Graves. CP-GravR

Beach, The. Robinson Jeffers. CP-JefR1

Beach Glass. Amy Clampitt. CP-ClamA

Beach Head, The. Thom Gunn. CP-GunnT

Beach Pea, The. Amy Clampitt. CP-ClamA

Beach Trip. Charles Bukowski. SP-BukC1

Beach was crowded, The. Sea Corpse, The. Anne Sexton. CP-SextA

Beaches; it is true: they go on oń. Circuit. James Dickey. CP-DickJ

Beachhead. Derek Walcott. CP-WalcD

Beacon, The. James Vincent Cunningham. CP-CunnJ

Beacon, The. Robert Stock. SP-StocR

Beacon, The. Richard Wilbur. CP-WilbR

Bead. Philip Whalen. SP-WhalP

Bead, The. Charles Tomlinson. CP-TomlC

Beaded Balustrade. James Schuyler. CP-SchuJ

Beads around / my neck / Mt. Kenya away. African Images, Glimpses from a Tiger's Back. Alice Walker. CP-WalkA

Beak of dawn's rooster pecked, The. At the Old Place. William Stafford. SP-StafWW

Beaks of Eagles, The. Robinson Jeffers. CP-JefR2

Beale Street. Langston Hughes. CP-HughL; CP-HughL2

Beale Street Love. Langston Hughes. CP-HughL; CP-HughL1

Beams of April, ere it goes, The. Silk Worm, The. Vincent Bourne. CP-CowpW

Beams of noon, like burning lances, through the tree-tops flash and glisten. Slaves of Martinique, The. John Greenleaf Whittier. CP-WhitJ

Bean Eaters, The. Gwendolyn Brooks. SP-BrooG

Bean-Feast, The. Robert Browning. CP-BroR2

Bean Field, The. John Clare. SP-ClarJ

Bean Spasms. Ted Berrigan. SP-BerrT

Bean-Stalk, The. Edna St. Vincent Millay. CP-MillE

Bean-Stripe: also, Apple-Eating, A. Robert Browning. CP-BroR2

Beanfield full in blossom smells as sweet, A. Bean Field, The. John Clare. SP-ClarJ

Beans. Maxine W. Kumin. SP-KumiM

Beanstalk Country, The. Tennessee Williams. CP-WillT

Bear, The. Robert Frost. CP-FrosR

Bear, The. Ted Hughes. SP-HughTN

Bear, The. Galway Kinnell. SP-KinnGN

Bear: A Totem Dance As Seen by Raven. Peter Blue Cloud. SP-BlueP

Bear and the Garden-Lover, The. Marianne Craig Moore. CP-MoorM *Fr.* Fables of La Fontaine.

Bear Family, A. James Whitcomb Riley. CP-RileJ

Bear Hamlet, like a soldier, to the stage. Orphic Scenario. Howard Nemerov. CP-NemeH

Bear him, comrades, to his grave. Burial of Barber. John Greenleaf Whittier. CP-WhitJ

Bear Hunt, The. Abraham Lincoln. CP-LincA

Bear in English. Heather McHugh. SP-McHuH

Bear in mind / That death is a drum. Drum. Langston Hughes. CP-HughL; CP-HughL1

Bear me to Dictaeus. Acon. "H. D." CP-DoolH

Bear mother / gives suck to the stars. Ursa Major ("Bear mother / gives suck to the stars"). Federico García Lorca. CP-GarcF, *tr. by* Jerome Rothenberg *Fr.* Night (Suite for Piano and Poet's Voice).

Bear my first thought, as waking, I hear. Night Walking. Robert Penn Warren. CP-WarrR

Bear puts both arms around the tree above her, The. Bear, The. Robert Frost. CP-FrosR

Bear sleeps in a cellarhole; pine needles, A. New Hampshire. Donald Hall. CP-HallD

Bear Story, The. James Whitcomb Riley. CP-RileJ *Fr.* Child-World, A.

Bear under the snow, A. March. James Wright. CP-WrigJ

Bear who eats with a silver spoon, A. Animal Acts. Charles Simic. SP-SimiC; SP-SimiCE

Bear with fur that appeared to have been licked backward, A. Bear and the Garden-Lover, The. Marianne Craig Moore. CP-MoorM *Fr.* Fables of La Fontaine.

Bear with us, O Great Captain, if our pride. Home-Voyage, The. James Whitcomb Riley. CP-RileJ

Bear witness, Erin! when thine injured isle. To Ireland. Percy Bysshe Shelley. CP-ShelP

Bearded goldfish move about the bowl, The. Goldfish. Howard Nemerov. CP-NemeH

Bearded Iris. Louis Zukofsky. CP-ZukLS

Bearded Oaks. Robert Penn Warren. CP-WarrR

Bearded Woman, by Ribera, The. Paul Muldoon. CP-MuldP

Beards of the grain, gray-green: the lances. Girl Dreams That She Is Giselle, The. Randall Jarrell. CP-JarrR

Beards of water. Foutains of Aix. May Swenson. SP-SwenM

Bearer, The. Hayden Carruth. CP-CarHS

Bearer of Evil Tidings, The. Robert Frost. CP-FrosR

Bearer of Freedom's holy light. Democracy. John Greenleaf Whittier. CP-WhitJ

Bearing and giving are different, it appears. Witness. Donald Davie. CP-DaviDC

Bearing leaves again. Leaf, A. David Ignatow. SP-IgnaD

Bearing Mercy. A. R. Ammons. CP-AmmoA

Bears. Adrienne Rich. CP-RicAE; SP-RicA2

Bears and Waterfalls. May Sarton. SP-SartM

Bears are kept by hundreds within fences, are fed cracked, The. Elizabeth's War with the Christmas Bear. Norman Dubie. CP-DubiN

Bears are stomping in perfect time. Circus Animals. Wisława Szymborska. SP-SzymWM, *tr. by* Joanna Trzeciak

Bears at Raspberry Time. Hayden Carruth. CP-CarHS

Bears gash the forest trees. To Be Called a Bear. Robert Graves. CP-GravR

Beast. May Swenson. SP-SwenM

Beast. Alice Walker. CP-WalkA

Beast, The. Charles Bukowski. SP-BukC2

Beast, The. Theodore Roethke. CP-RoetT

Beast, The. Mourning cloth. Sewing Machine. Charles Simic. SP-SimiCE

Beast and bird must bow aside. Epilogue for a Masque of Purcell. Adrienne Rich. CP-RicAE

Beast & Burden, The: Seven Improvisations. Yusef Komunyakaa. CP-KomuY

Beast in View. Muriel Rukeyser. SP-RukeM

Beast stands at my eye, A. Naked Land, The. Kenneth Patchen. CP-PatcK

Beasts. Richard Wilbur. CP-WilbR

Beasts Are Very Wise, The. Rudyard Kipling. CP-KiplR

Beasts' Confession to the Priest, The. Jonathan Swift. CP-SwifJ

Beasts in the schoolroom, whose transparent faces, The. Blues for Warren. Thomas McGrath. SP-McGrT

Beasts in their major freedom. Beasts. Richard Wilbur. CP-WilbR

Beasts of each kind their fellows spare. Juvenal. CP-JohnS *Fr.* Satires.

Beasts of the field, fowls likewise of the air. Ark, The. Robert Graves. CP-GravR

Beat at the bars. Bars. Carl Sandburg. CP-SandC

Beat! Beat! Drums! Walt Whitman. CP-WhitW

Beat hell out of it. Episode 17. William Carlos Williams. CP-WilW1 *Fr.* Paterson.

Beat off in our last fight were we? Rudyard Kipling. CP-KiplR *Fr.* Naulahka,

The.

Beat, Old Heart. Carl Sandburg. CP-SandC

Beat, old heart, these are the old bars. Beat, Old Heart. Carl Sandburg. CP-SandC

Beat out continuance in the choking veins. Blood is Justified, The. Muriel Rukeyser. CP-RukeM

Beat the drums of tragedy for me. Fantasy in Purple. Langston Hughes. CP-HughL; CP-HughL1

Beat-up datsun idling in the road. Kisiabaton. Gary Snyder. CP-SnydG

Beaten Path, A. G. K. Chesterton. CP-ChesG

Beatific Vision, The. G. K. Chesterton. CP-ChesG

Beating asphalt into highway potholes. Spring, The. Gary Snyder. CP-SnydG

Beating wind with a stick. Chair Gallows. Yusef Komunyakaa. CP-KomuY

Beatrice and Dante. Robert Graves. CP-GravR

Beatrice Signorini. Robert Browning. CP-BroR2; SP-BroR

Beau of the Dead. Donald Hall. CP-HallD

Beaumont! it was thy wish that I should rear. At Applethwaite, near Keswick. William Wordsworth. CP-WorW1

Beaumont to Detroit: 1943. Langston Hughes. CP-HughL; CP-HughL2

Beau's Reply. William Cowper. CP-CowpW

Beau's Reply to the Five Ladies' Answer, The. Jonathan Swift. CP-SwifJ

Beauteous rose-bud, young and gay. To Miss C**********, a Very Young Lady. Robert Burns. CP-BurnR

Beauti-ful. Charles Bukowski. SP-BukC3

Beautician, The. Thom Gunn. CP-GunnT

Beautie Without Love Deformitie. Thomas Campion. CP-CampT

Beautie's no other but a lovely Grace. Beauty. Robert Herrick. CP-HerrR

Beautiful Aeroplane, The. Charles Tomlinson. CP-TomlC

Beautiful and happy girl, A. Memories. John Greenleaf Whittier. CP-WhitJ

Beautiful and spacious green, A. Lucinda and Aminta, a Pastoral, on the Capture of Lord Cornwallis and the British Army, by General Washington. Annis Boudinot Stockton. CP-StocA

Beautiful Are the Families of Jerusalem. Yehuda Amichai. SP-AmicYL, tr. by Benjamin Harshav and Barbara Harshav

Beautiful as on a jug a painted flower. Song of the Native Land. Jaroslav Seifert. SP-SeifJ, tr. by Ewald Osers

Beautiful as the flying legend of some leopard. Judith of Bethulia. John Crowe Ransom. SP-RansJ

Beautiful as the sea. George Oppen. CP-OppGN

Beautiful Banners, The. Pier Paolo Pasolini. SP-PasoP, tr. by Norman MacAfee and Luciano Martinengo

Beautiful, bodiced, the. New Poem. John Logan. CP-LogaJ

Beautiful bodies of the dead who did not age. Desires. Constantine P. Cavafy. CP-CavaC, tr. by Theoharis Constantine Theoharis

Beautiful, bold, shaking the gold glint of sun-foil. Fatal Interview: Penthesilea and Achilles. Robert Penn Warren. CP-WarrR

Beautiful Bowel Movement, The. John Updike. CP-UpdiJ

Beautiful butterfly near, A. Rainer Maria Rilke. CP-RilkFr, tr. by A. Poulin, Jr. Fr. Valaisian Quatrains, The.

Beautiful Captive, The. Robinson Jeffers. CP-JefR3

Beautiful cashier's white face has risen once more, The. Before a Cashier's Window in a Department Store. James Wright. CP-WrigJ

Beautiful Changes, The. Richard Wilbur. CP-WilbR

Beautiful City, The. James Whitcomb Riley. CP-RileJ

Beautiful City! Forever, The. Beautiful City, The. James Whitcomb Riley. CP-RileJ

Beautiful Dove, come back to us in April. Song: "Beautiful Dove, come back to us in April." Edna St. Vincent Millay. CP-MillE

Beautiful Evelyn Hope is dead! Evelyn Hope. Robert Browning. CP-BroR1

Beautiful excess of Jesus on the waters, The. To Swim, to Believe. Maxine W. Kumin. SP-KumiM

Beautiful for Situation. Christina Georgina Rossetti. CP-RosC2

Beautiful Funerals. James Schuyler. CP-SchuJ

Beautiful girl. Lorine Niedecker. CP-NiedL

Beautiful, infinite memories. Nils Lykke. Ezra Pound. CP-PoEar

Beautiful / is the / unmea. E. E. Cummings. CP-CummE

Beautiful Lady Lu, The. Han-shan. CP-ColdM, tr. by Red Pine

Beautiful Lady where Love shows himself, The. Guido Cavalcanti. CP-CavaG, tr. by Marc Cirigliano

Beautiful Lawn Sprinkler, The. Howard Nemerov. CP-NemeH

Beautiful little children. Kyoto Born in Spring Song. Gary Snyder. CP-SnydG

Beautiful Lofty Things. William Butler Yeats. CP-YeatW

Beautiful melon, how can you be so cool. Melon. Rainer Maria Rilke. CP-RilkFr

Beautiful Mistress, A. Thomas Carew. CP-CareT

(Song: Beautiful Mistress, A.) CP-CareT

Beautiful Morning. James Laughlin. CP-LaugJ

Beautiful, my afternoon was very. Great Feast at the Home of Sosibios, A. Constantine P. Cavafy. CP-CavaC, tr. by Theoharis Constantine Theoharis

Beautiful, my delight. To Be Sung on the Water. Louise Bogan. CP-BogaL

Beautiful New / York sky harder. Blue. James Schuyler. CP-SchuJ

Beautiful Old Age. D. H. Lawrence. CP-LawrD

Beautiful One, The. James Laughlin. CP-LaugJ

Beautiful Parsi woman in your pale silk veil. Parsi Woman, The. Edna St. Vincent Millay. CP-MillE

Beautiful reed of a child, A. St. Gabriel. Federico García Lorca. CP-GarcF, tr. by Will Kirkland

Beautiful sex whose lips I know. Amberose Triste. Olga Broumas. SP-BrouO

Beautiful suicide victoriously fled, The. Stéphane Mallarmé. CP-MallS, tr. by Henry Weinfield

Beautiful swimmer the extremely shy, The. Opium for Britt Wilkie. Andrei Codrescu. SP-CodrA

Beautiful, tender, wasting away for sorrow. Luscious and Sorrowful. Christina Georgina Rossetti. CP-RosC2

Beautiful, the fair, the elegant, The. Beauty. Wilfred Owen. CP-OwenW

Beautiful the hanging cliff and the wind-thrown cedars, but they have no. On an Anthology of Chinese Poems. Robinson Jeffers. CP-JefR3

Beautiful the intricacy of body! Auto-da-fé. Robert Penn Warren. CP-WarrR

Beautiful Times. Czeslaw Milosz. Fr. Treatise on Poetry, A.

Beautiful Toilet, The. Ezra Pound. SP-PounE

Beautiful, tragical faces. Piccadilly. Ezra Pound. CP-PoEar

Beautiful woman (nor does she know it) who has already reached forty. Invisible Glory. Yannis Ritsos. SP-RitsY, tr. by Kimon Friar

Beautiful Women. Walt Whitman. CP-WhitW

Beautiful years when she was by me and we visited. Morro Bay. Robinson Jeffers. CP-JefR3

Beautiful You Are. Kenneth Patchen. CP-PatcK

Beautiful Young Girl Walking Past the Graveyard—, The. Charles Bukowski. SP-BukC1

Beautiful Young Nymph Going to Bed, A. Jonathan Swift. CP-SwifJ

Beautifully Janet slept. Janet Waking. John Crowe Ransom. SP-RansJ

Beauty. Charles Baudelaire. CP-BaudC, tr. by Walter Martin

Beauty. Ralph Waldo Emerson. CP-EmerR

Beauty. Robert Herrick. CP-HerrR

Beauty. Langston Hughes. CP-HughL; CP-HughL1

Beauty. Wilfred Owen. CP-OwenW

Beauty. Yannis Ritsos. SP-RitsY, tr. by Minas Savvas

Beauty. Jones Very. CP-VeryJ

Beauty, The. Thomas Hardy. CP-HardT

Beauty and Beauty's son and rosemary. Rosemary. Marianne Craig Moore. CP-MoorM

Beauty and Moonlight. William Wordsworth. CP-WorW1

Beauty and the Beast. Olga Broumas. SP-BrouO

Beauty and the Beast. Rita Dove. SP-DoveR

Beauty and the Beast. Eleanor Wilner. SP-WilnE

Beauty and the Bird. Dante Gabriel Rossetti. CW-RossD

Beauty and youth, with manners sweet, and friends. On the Grave. Herman Melville. SP-MelvH

Beauty be not caused—It Is. Emily Dickinson. CP-DickE

Beauty crowds me till I die. Emily Dickinson. CP-DickE

Beauty hath force to catch the human sight. Sir Philip Sidney. SP-SidnP Fr. Arcadia.

Beauty I Would Suffer For. Marge Piercy. SP-PierM

Beauty in Trouble. Robert Graves. CP-GravR

Beauty in woman; the high will's decree. Sonnet: He compares all Things with his Lady, and finds them wanting. Guido Cavalcanti. CW-RossD, tr. by Dante Gabriel Rossetti

Beauty is a shell. Song: "Beauty is a shell." William Carlos Williams. CP-WilW2

Beauty Is But a Painted Hell. Thomas Campion. CP-CampT

Beauty is in what shocks me least, The. Snail Sail. Andrei Codrescu. SP-CodrA

Beauty Is Not Bound. Thomas Campion. CP-CampT

Beauty is often timidity. Emily Dickinson. SP-DickE

Beauty is sometimes personified. On Beauty. Kenneth Koch. SP-KochK

Beauty is that Medusa's head. Archibald MacLeish. CP-MacLA Fr. Happy Marriage, The.

Beauty / is to lay hold of Love. Charles Olson. CP-OlsoC

Beauty Is Vain. Christina Georgina Rossetti. CP-RosC1

Beauty, I've seen you. Poetics. Yusef Komunyakaa. CP-KomuY

Beauty like hers is genius. Not the call. Genius in Beauty. Dante Gabriel Rossetti. CW-RossD Fr. House of Life, The.

Beauty, no other thing is, than a beam[e]. Definition of Beauty, The. Robert Herrick. CP-HerrR

Beauty of a maiden is coveted by the world, The. Ce-Lia The Immortal Beauty. William Carlos Williams. CP-WilW2

Beauty of her hair bewilders me, The. Her Hair. James Whitcomb Riley. CP-RileJ

Beauty of manhole covers—what of that? The. Manhole Covers. Karl Shapiro. SP-ShapK

Beauty of the earth is a resilient wonderful thing, The. Metamorphosis. Robinson Jeffers. CP-JefR3

Beauty of the Head, The. May Swenson. SP-SwenM

Beauty of the Ship, The. Walt Whitman. CP-WhitW

Beauty of Things, The. Robinson Jeffers. CP-JefR3

Beauty of women and wise hearts. Guido Cavalcanti. CP-CavaG, *tr. by* Marc Cirigliano

Beauty Rohtraut. Eduard Friedrich Mörike. CP-MerG1, *tr. by* George Meredith

Beauty, Since You So Much Desire. Thomas Campion. CP-CampT

Beauty (they called her) wasn't a maid. In Memoriam. Ambrose Bierce. SP-BierA

Beauty's Pageant. Dante Gabriel Rossetti. CW-RossD *Fr.* House of Life, The.

Beauty's Soliloquy during Her Honeymoon, A. Thomas Hardy. CP-HardT

Beaver. Paul Muldoon. CP-MuldP

Beaver cut his timber, The. Cobbler Keezar's Vision. John Greenleaf Whittier. CP-WhitJ

Becalmed. James Whitcomb Riley. CP-RileJ

Because. James Whitcomb Riley. CP-RileJ

Because a Lady chose to say. Arthur Hugh Clough. SP-ClouA

Because a woman. All You Can Do. Charles Olson. CP-OlsoC

Because age steals away. Michelangelo Buonarroti. CP-Miche, *tr. by* John Frederick Nims

Because / an obstreperous grin minutely floats. E. E. Cummings. CP-CummE

Because Flat-foot is the favourite of the white leghorn cock, and. Flat-Foot's Song. D. H. Lawrence. CP-LawrD

Because Great Pan is dead, Astraea gone. From the Desk of the Laureate: For Immediate Release. Howard Nemerov. CP-NemeH

Because he could not face. Founder, The. George Oppen. CP-OppGN

Because He First Loved Us. Christina Georgina Rossetti. CP-RosC2

Because he had spoken harshly to his mother. Revelation. Robert Penn Warren. CP-WarrR

Because he has been hungry for days. Three Wishes, The. Billy Collins. SP-CollB

Because he has bright white teeth, Eg- / natius whips out a. Carmen 39. Catullus. CP-ZukLS *Fr.* Carmina.

Because He loves Her. Emily Dickinson. CP-DickE

Because he puts the compromising chart. Zola. Edwin Arlington Robinson. CP-RobiE

Because he was a butcher and thereby. Reuben Bright. Edwin Arlington Robinson. CP-RobiE

Because her eyes were far too deep. Dream. James Whitcomb Riley. CP-RileJ

Because I am by nature blind. Riddle, A: "Because I am by nature blind." Thomas Sheridan. CP-SherT

Because I am drunk, this Independence Night. Fourth of July, The. Howard Nemerov. CP-NemeH

Because I am lucky, I'm a glutton. Few Licks, A. Heather McHugh. SP-McHuH

"Because I am mad about women." Wild Old Wicked Man, The. William Butler Yeats. CP-YeatW

Because I am the bullet. What the White Had to Say. Charles Simic. SP-SimiC

Because I chose to hear a special thunder in my head. Originators, The. Thomas Merton. CP-MertT

Because I expect never to return. Guido Cavalcanti. CP-CavaG, *tr. by* Marc Cirigliano

Because I feel that, in the Heavens above. To My Mother. Edgar Allan Poe. CP-PoeEd

Because I find not whom to speak withal. Sonnet: Written in Exile. Dante Alighieri. CW-RossD, *tr. by* Dante Gabriel Rossetti

Because I had loved so deeply. Compensation. Paul Laurence Dunbar. CP-DunbP

Because I have called to you. Calls. Carl Sandburg. CP-SandC

Because I have thee still kept from lies and blame. Sir Thomas Wyatt. CP-WyatT

Because I lay my. Why Is God Love, Jack? Allen Ginsberg. CP-GinsA

Because I liked you better. A. E. Housman. CP-HousA

Because I liked you better. Because I liked you better. A. E. Housman. CP-HousA

Because I love / The sun pours out its rays of living gold. Amo Ergo Sum. Kathleen Jessie Raine. SP-RainK

Because i love you)last night. E. E. Cummings. CP-CummE

Because I Sit Here So. Laura Riding Jackson. CP-RidiL

Because I sought it far from men. Rudyard Kipling. CP-KiplR *Fr.* Naulahka, The.

Because I think not ever to return. Ballata: In Exile at Sarzana. Guido Cavalcanti. CW-RossD, *tr. by* Dante Gabriel Rossetti

Because I was content with these poor fields. Musketaquid. Ralph Waldo Emerson. CP-EmerR

Because I was hungrier than sleepy. Doctor Will Be Back Too Late, The. Robert Stock. SP-StocR

Because I was whipped as a child. Eye of Heart. Olga Broumas. SP-BrouO

Because I'm nothing you can name. What the White Had to Say. Charles Simic. SP-SimiCE

Because I'm writing about the snow not the sentence. Fifth Prose. Michael Palmer. SP-PalmM

Because in the heart / of darkness I could not see. Hayden Carruth. CP-CarHS *Fr.* Clay Hill Anthology, The.

Because in Vietnam the vision of a Burning Babe. Advent 1966. Denise Levertov. SP-LeveDS

Because it is a gray day but not snowy, because traffic grinds by outside. Long, Disconsolate Lines. Jane Cooper. CP-CoopJ

Because it was a holiday, they bought a herring at the tavern. Songs in the Distance. Raymond Carver. CP-CarvR

Because it was good, we were afraid. Our Cave. William Stafford. SP-StafWW

Because it's / Spring / thingS. E. E. Cummings. CP-CummE

Because Jack was small the world had to be large. Annals of Jack. Wyatt Prunty. SP-PrunW

Because man is not virtuous in himself. Tribute. Countee Cullen. CP-CullC

Because mine eyes can never have their fill. Ballata: He will gaze upon Beatrice. Dante Alighieri. CW-RossD, *tr. by* Dante Gabriel Rossetti

Because my Brook is fluent. Emily Dickinson. CP-DickE

Because my head hasn't grown. Last Word is the Captain, The. Yehuda Amichai. SP-AmicY, *tr. by* Chana Bloch

Because my love is quick to come and go. Portrait, A. Dorothy Parker. CP-ParkD

Because my mouth. Minstrel Man. Langston Hughes. CP-HughL; CP-HughL1

Because my will is simple as a window. Blessed Virgin Mary Compared to a Window, The. Thomas Merton. CP-MertT

Because of a coolness in the air. Day, The. James Schuyler. CP-SchuJ

Because of Clothes. Laura Riding Jackson. CP-RidiL

Because of her pensive heart. Woman at Her Mirror. Rainer Maria Rilke. CP-RilkFr, *tr. by* A. Poulin, Jr.

Because of hesitations. Poem of Spring. Yehuda Amichai. SP-AmicYL, *tr. by* Benjamin Harshav *and* Barbara Harshav

Because of love and because of making love. My Son. Yehuda Amichai. SP-AmicYL, *tr. by* Benjamin Harshav *and* Barbara Harshav

Because of love's infallibility. Crab-Tree, The. Robert Graves. CP-GravR

Because of me, because of you. Randall Jarrell. CP-JarrR

Because of the change of key midway in "Come Back to Sorrento." Song of Reasons. Robert Pinsky. CP-PinsR

Because of the Influence of Spring. "Rubén Dario." SP-DariR, *tr. by* Alberto Acereda *and* Will Derusha

Because of the silent snow, we are all hushed. Winter-Lull. D. H. Lawrence. CP-LawrD

Because of the stink of the dungeons: 1344. Ezra Pound. *See* Book of the council major

Because of the unaccountable spirit of the troops. On the Civil War on the East Coast of the United States of North America 1860–64. Alan Dugan. CP-DugaA

Because of the will of the night, I left the land. Yehuda Amichai. SP-AmicY, *tr. by* Chana Bloch *Fr.* Songs of Zion the Beautiful.

Because one loves you, Helen Grey. Helen Grey. Christina Georgina Rossetti. CP-RosC3

Because one's husband is different from one's self. Causes. Mona Van Duyn. SP-VanDM

Because our life is short. Petrarch. CP-Petra, *tr. by* J. G. Nichols

Because our talk was of the cloud-control. Secret Parting. Dante Gabriel Rossetti. CW-RossD *Fr.* House of Life, The.

Because our young were drab. Think Tank. James Merrill. SP-MerrJ

Because poor PUER's both unsure and vain. Gemini. Richard Wilbur. CP-WilbR

Because she bore upon her face Love's banner. Petrarch. CP-Petra, *tr. by* J. G. Nichols

Because, straying through the wine-gardens with the grace and. Often Was It. Kenneth Patchen. CP-PatcK

Because that I am weak, my love, and ill. One Morning. Ambrose Bierce. SP-BierA

Because that stealing immortalitie. Sir Walter Ralegh. CP-RaleW

Because that you are going. Emily Dickinson. CP-DickE

Because the Bee may blameless hum. Emily Dickinson. CP-DickE

Because the gradual growth of things we see. Evolution. Jones Very. CP-VeryJ

Because the moment. Further Reasons Why Poets Do Not Tell the Truth. Hans Magnus Enzensberger. SP-EnzeH

Because the Pleasure-Bird Whistles. Dylan Thomas. CP-ThomD

Because the road to mercy is shut off. Petrarch. CP-Petra, *tr. by* J. G. Nichols

Because the snow is deep. Fox, The. Kenneth Patchen. CP-PatcK

Because the sterile arms no longer beat. Soul's Haven. Marya Alexandrovna Zaturenska. SP-ZatuM

Because the velvet image. To Hedli. Louis MacNeice. CP-MacNL

Because the wind has changed, because I guess. Clearing the Title. James Merrill. SP-MerrJ

Because there are some things. Importance of Silence, The. James Laughlin. CP-LaugJ

Because there is safety in derision. Apparitions, The. William Butler Yeats. CP-YeatW

Because there was a man somewhere in a candystripe silk shirt. Homage to the Empress of the Blues. Robert Earl Hayden. CP-HaydR

Because there was no other place. Flee on Your Donkey. Anne Sexton. CP-SextA; SP-SextA

Because there's half of me which, heaven-born. Michelangelo Buonarroti. CP-Miche, tr. by John Frederick Nims

Because there's never a time I'm not enchanted. Michelangelo Buonarroti. CP-Miche, tr. by John Frederick Nims

Because they are not. Deceptrices, The. William Carlos Williams. CP-WilW2

Because they could not give it too much ground. In a Bird Sanctuary. Richard Wilbur. CP-WilbR

Because they were prisoners. Pilots, The. Denise Levertov. SP-LeveDL

Because this world is on the wing and what cometh no man can know. Magic Psalm. Allen Ginsberg. CP-GinsA; SP-GinsA

Because Thy Love hath sought me, / All mine is Thine and Thine is mine. Christina Georgina Rossetti. CP-RosC2

Because 'twas Riches I could own. Emily Dickinson. CP-DickE

Because we couldn't sleep we went on. Morning, A. Margaret Atwood. SP-AtwM1

Because we have no type of earth for everyone. All the Day. Kenneth Patchen. CP-PatcK

Because we lived our several lives. House, The. Mary Oliver. SP-OlivM

Because we love bare hills and stunted trees. Hound Voice. William Butler Yeats. CP-YeatW

Because we met at dusk. To an Old Poet in Peru. Allen Ginsberg. CP-GinsA

Because What I Want Most Is Permanence. May Sarton. SP-SartM

Because women are expected to keep silent about. On Stripping Bark from Myself. Alice Walker. CP-WalkA

Because words have no effect upon the wind. To Stay Alive. David Ignatow. SP-IgnaD

Because you are. Against Silence. Marilyn Hacker. SP-HackM

Because you are a doormat I love you. Anti-Love Poem, An. James Laughlin. CP-LaugJ

Because you are simple people, kindly and romantic. Fourth Act. Robinson Jeffers. CP-JefR3

Because you are to me a song. Passing Love. Langston Hughes. CP-HughL; CP-HughL1

Because you found the trouble-shard. Paul Celan. SP-CelaP, tr. by John Felstiner

Because / you go away i give roses who. E. E. Cummings. CP-CummE

Because you have found me in the pitch-dark night. Ribh at the Tomb of Baile and Aillinn. William Butler Yeats. CP-YeatW

Because you have gone your individual gait. Homage to Wilfrid Scawen Blunt. Ezra Pound. CP-PoEar

Because you love me I have much achieved. Encouraged. Paul Laurence Dunbar. CP-DunbP

Because you never yet have loved me, dear. Touching "Never." Christina Georgina Rossetti. CP-RosC2

Because you take life in your stride(instead. E. E. Cummings. CP-CummE

Because you were foolish enough to love one place. Adult Grief. Louise Glück. SP-GlucL

Because you'll find how hard it can be. For a Girl I Know about to Be a Woman. Miller Williams. CP-WillM

Because you're only dead. Night. Adam Zagajewski. SP-ZagaA, tr. by Renata Gorczynski, Benjamin Ivry and C. K. Williams

Bechbretha. Paul Muldoon. CP-MuldP

Beckon to me to come. Lover to Mistress. Thomas Hardy. CP-HardT

Beckoned anew to a World. Aubade: "Beckoned anew to a World." W. H. Auden. CP-AudeW

Becoming Somebody Else. C. K. Williams. CP-WillC

Becoming Stronger. Constantine P. Cavafy. CP-CavaC, tr. by Theoharis Constantine Theoharis

Bec's Birthday. Jonathan Swift. CP-SwifJ

Bed, The. Robert Creeley. CP-CreeR

Bed, The. Thom Gunn. CP-GunnT

Bed, The. Archibald MacLeish. CP-MacLA

Bed, The. James Whitcomb Riley. CP-RileJ

Bed by the Window, The. Robinson Jeffers. CP-JefR2

Bed, glasses off, and all's. Myopia: a Night. Robert Lowell. SP-LoweR

Bed in the Sky, The. Gary Snyder. CP-SnydG

Bed is not very big, The. E. E. Cummings. CP-CummE

Bed-Man, or Grave-Maker, The. Robert Herrick. CP-HerrR

Bed of Forget-Me-Nots, A. Christina Georgina Rossetti. CP-RosC3

Bed of Old John Zeller, The. Wallace Stevens. CP-StevW; CP-StevWP

Bed the inter- / loping grass. In the Round. James Schuyler. CP-SchuJ

Beddoesque. Ezra Pound. CP-PoEar

Bedfordshire. Donald Davie. CP-DaviDC

Bedlam Revisited. John Ciardi. CP-CiarJ

Bedouin. James Whitcomb Riley. CP-RileJ

Bedouin Goes North, A. Yehuda Amichai. SP-AmicYL, tr. by Benjamin Harshav and Barbara Harshav

Bedouin in Love. Yehuda Amichai. SP-AmicYL, tr. by Benjamin Harshav and Barbara Harshav

Bedpans. Charles Bukowski. SP-BukC1

Bedridden Peasant, The. Thomas Hardy. CP-HardT

Beds of Grainne and Diarmuid, The. Robert Graves. CP-GravR

Beds, Toilets, You and Me—. Charles Bukowski. SP-BukC1

Bedside. Margaret Atwood. SP-AtwM2

Bedside Rune, A. Jane Cooper. CP-CoopJ

Bedtime. Denise Levertov. SP-LeveDP; SP-LeveDS

Bedtime Anecdote. Ted Hughes. SP-HughTN

Bedtime Stories. Mona Van Duyn. SP-VanDM

Bedtime Story. Charles Simic. SP-SimiC; SP-SimiCE

Bedtime's come fu' little boys. Lullaby: "Bedtime's come fu' little boys." Paul Laurence Dunbar. CP-DunbP

Bee, The. Charles Bukowski. SP-BukC1

Bee, The. James Dickey. CP-DickJ

Bee, The. Emily Dickinson. CP-DickE

Bee allur'd by the perfume, A. Bee and the Pine-Apple, The. William Cowper. CP-CowpW

Bee and the Pine-Apple, The. William Cowper. CP-CowpW

Bee-Bag, The. James Whitcomb Riley. CP-RileJ

Bee-Boy's Song, The. Rudyard Kipling. CP-KiplR Fr. Puck of Pook's Hill.

Bee! / drowning in, A. Grace Paley. CP-PalGC

Bee-eating bird. Disquiet and Night. Federico García Lorca. CP-GarcF, tr. by Alan S. Trueblood Fr. Back of the World.

Bee his burnished Carriage, A. Emily Dickinson. CP-DickE

Bee hit sip some honey f'om de matermony vine, De. Song: "Bee hit sip some honey f'om de matermony vine, De." Paul Laurence Dunbar. CP-DunbP

Bee Hive, The. Jones Very. CP-VeryJ

Bee! I'm expecting you! Letter to Bee. Emily Dickinson. CP-DickE

Bee is not afraid of me, The. Emily Dickinson. CP-DickE

Bee Meeting, The. Sylvia Plath. CP-PlatS

Bee rolls in the yellow rose, A. Couple, A. May Swenson. SP-SwenM

Bee Song. Carl Sandburg. CP-SandC

Bee that was searching for sweets one day, A. Two Songs. Paul Laurence Dunbar. CP-DunbP

Beech. Robert Frost. CP-FrosR

Beech, The. Charles Tomlinson. CP-TomlC

Beech, The. Charles Tomlinson. CP-TomlC

Beech leaves which might have clung. March. Richard Wilbur. CP-WilbR

Beef. Grace Paley. CP-PalGC

Beehive. Federico García Lorca. CP-GarcF, tr. by Jerome Rothenberg Fr. Water Suite.

Beekeeper Speaks., The. Howard Nemerov. CP-NemeH

Beekeeper's Daughter, The. Sylvia Plath. CP-PlatS

Been workin' on de levee. Mississippi Levee. Langston Hughes. CP-HughL; CP-HughL2

Beeny Cliff. Thomas Hardy. CP-HardT

Beeny did not quiver. Death-Day Recalled, A. Thomas Hardy. CP-HardT

Beer. Charles Bukowski. SP-BukC1

Beerbohm and Belloc. G. K. Chesterton. CP-ChesG

Bees. Emily Dickinson. CP-DickE

Bees, The. Audre Lorde. SP-LordA

Bees and a honeycomb in the dried head of a horse in a pasture corner—. In Tall Grass. Carl Sandburg. CP-SandC

Bees and lilies there were. Bring the Day! Theodore Roethke. CP-RoetT

Bees and Morning Glories. John Ciardi. CP-CiarJ

Bees and the Flies, The. Rudyard Kipling. CP-KiplR

Bees are Black, with Gilt Surcingles—. Bees. Emily Dickinson. CP-DickE

Bees are building stairways toward heaven. Nihil Obstat. Sam Hamill. SP-HamiS

Bees are eating the candy, The. Indian Market in Mexico, An. Randall Jarrell. CP-JarrR

Bees aren't humble, they don't notably bumble. Beekeeper Speaks., The. Howard Nemerov. CP-NemeH

Bees at the six-pointed junkweed blooms. Journal of Three Questions, A. Charles Wright. SP-WrigC

Bees! Bees! Hark to your bees! Bee-Boy's Song, The. Rudyard Kipling. CP-KiplR Fr. Puck of Pook's Hill.

Bees build in the crevices, The. Stare's Nest by My Window, The. William Butler Yeats. CP-YeatW *Fr.* Meditations in Time of Civil War.

Bee's 5th. Charles Bukowski. SP-BukC1

Bee's fixed hexagon, The. Come, Sleep. Louise Bogan. CP-BogaL

Bees forage where the blue ajuga's grown. Nature Morte. Howard Nemerov. CP-NemeH

Bees haven't buzzed away, nor has a horseman galloped, The. Porta San Pancrazio. Joseph Brodsky. CP-BrodJ

Bees in the late summer sun. Bee Song. Carl Sandburg. CP-SandC

Bees love grass, The. Thomas Merton. CP-MertT

Bees move between the rosemary and the rose. Alto Minho. Charles Tomlinson. SP-TomlC *Fr.* Portugeuse Pieces.

Bees stopped on the rock. A. R. Ammons. CP-AmmoA

Bees turn in a fire. Drought. A. R. Ammons. CP-AmmoA

Bees work, the. Black Workers. Langston Hughes. CP-HughL; CP-HughL1

Beethoven. Robert Lowell. SP-LoweR

Beethoven Attends the C Minor Seminar. Charles Tomlinson. CP-TomlC

Beethoven during breakfast? The human soul. C Minor. Richard Wilbur. CP-WilbR

Beethoven, Opus 111. Amy Clampitt. CP-ClamA

Beethoven Triumphant. John Berryman. CP-BerrJ

Beethoven's Death Mask. Stephen Spender. CP-SpenS

Beetle lying on his back, A. Old Revolution. Hans Magnus Enzensberger. SP-EnzeH

Beetle soars, the beetle spins, The. George Meredith. CP-MerG2

Befits me praise thine empery, Lady of Valour. Echoes. Ezra Pound. CP-PoEar

Before. Robert Browning. CP-BroR1

Before. Miller Williams. CP-WillM

Before a Cashier's Window in a Department Store. James Wright. CP-WrigJ

Before a Midnight Breaks in Storm. Rudyard Kipling. CP-KiplR

Before a sculpted stone portal. Portal, A. Czeslaw Milosz. CP-MiloC; CP-MiloCN, *tr. by* Robert Hass

Before a Statue of Cromwell. G. K. Chesterton. CP-ChesG

Before a world of tremulous green baize. Motley. George Meredith. CP-MerG2

Before and after Summer. Thomas Hardy. CP-HardT

Before and after the eye, grasses go over the long fields. Purgation. James Dickey. CP-DickJ

Before Antiochus Epiphanis. Constantine P. Cavafy. CP-CavaC, *tr. by* Theoharis Constantine Theoharis

Before Completion. Arthur Sze. SP-SzeA

Before Danger. Muriel Rukeyser. CP-RukeM

Before Dark. Wendell Berry. CP-BerrW

Before Dawn. Walter De la Mare. CP-DeLaW

Before dawn. Before we knew women. Poetics of Paperwood. Yusef Komunyakaa. CP-KomuY

Before dawn the coyotes. Manzanita. Gary Snyder. CP-SnydG

Before God died, shot while running away. Knobs and Levers. Robert Graves. CP-GravR

Before going to bed, he placed his watch under his pillow. Wonder. Yannis Ritsos. SP-RitsY, *tr. by* Minas Savvas

Before He comes we weigh the Time! Emily Dickinson. CP-DickE

Before he went to live with owls and bats. Nebuchadnezzar's Dream. John Keats. CP-KeatJ

Before I am completely shriven. Single Vision. Stanley Kunitz. CP-KunSC

Before I began life this time. Last Poem. Ted Berrigan. SP-BerrT

Before I die. Four. Robert Creeley. CP-CreeR

Before I Die. James Laughlin. CP-LaugJ

Before I got my eye put out. Emily Dickinson. CP-DickE

Before I Knocked. Dylan Thomas. CP-ThomD

Before I see another day. Complaint of a Forsaken Indian Woman, The. William Wordsworth. CP-WorW1

Before I sigh my last gasp, let me breathe. Will, The. John Donne. CP-DonnJ; MW-DonnJ

Before I was a monk I had a cat. Howdy. Andrei Codrescu. SP-CodrA

Before It Burned over: A Sioux Grass Chant. William Stafford. SP-StafWW

Before it came inside. What's That. Anne Sexton. CP-SextA; SP-SextA

Before Knowledge. Thomas Hardy. CP-HardT

Before Life and After. Thomas Hardy. CP-HardT

Before life was there a world? Vocatus atque Non Vocatus. William Stafford. SP-StafWW

Before Majesty. Czeslaw Milosz. CP-MiloC; CP-MiloCN, *tr. by* Robert Hass

Before man came to blow it right. Aim Was Song, The. Robert Frost. CP-FrosR

Before Mans fall, the Rose was born. Rose, The. Robert Herrick. CP-HerrR

Before March. Archibald MacLeish. CP-MacLA

Before Marching and After. Thomas Hardy. CP-HardT

Before Mary Magdalen, albescent in the dusk. Skull, A. Czeslaw Milosz. CP-MiloC; CP-MiloCN, *tr. by* Robert Hass

Before me a far-off time arises. Some Future Moon. Boris Leonidovich

Pasternak. CP-DaviDC, *tr. by* Donald Davie

Before me, Krakow in a gray valley. View of Krakow, A. Adam Zagajewski. SP-ZagaA, *tr. by* Clare Cavanagh

Before midsummer density. Lindenbloom. Amy Clampitt. CP-ClamA

Before morning you shall be here. Alba. Samuel Beckett. CP-BeckS

Before my closing eyes, dear Cynthia, stand. Tibullus. CP-JohnS, *tr. by* Samuel Johnson *Fr.* Elegies.

Before my drift-wood fire I sit. Burning Drift-Wood. John Greenleaf Whittier. CP-WhitJ

Before My Friend Arrived. Thomas Hardy. CP-HardT

Before my Spring I garnered Autumn's gain. Rudyard Kipling. CP-KiplR *Fr.* Life's Handicap.

Before our human dream (or terror) wove. Sea, The. Jorge Luis Borges. SP-BorgJ, *tr. by* John Updike

Before Our Lady's on Des Peres Boulevard. One Moment in Eternity. Howard Nemerov. CP-NemeH

Before our lives divide for ever. Triumph of Time, The. Algernon Charles Swinburne. SP-SwinA

Before Parting. Algernon Charles Swinburne. SP-SwinA

Before Plato told the great lie of ideals. For the Heroes Are Dipped in Scarlet. D. H. Lawrence. CP-LawrD

Before she has her floor swept. Portrait by a Neighbour. Edna St. Vincent Millay. CP-MillE

Before Sleep. Thomas Kinsella. CP-KinsT

Before sleep comes I put down. Welcome, The. James Laughlin. CP-LaugJ

Before Sunrise, ere Colour sprang. Fall'n Is Lucifer. George Meredith. CP-MerG2

Before supper we had seen three grazing deer. President's Speech, The. Hayden Carruth. CP-CarHS

Before That. W. S. Merwin. SP-MerwW

Before that thundercloud breaks from its hawsers. Derek Walcott. CP-WalcD *Fr.* Midsummer.

Before the adamantine gate, I clear my throat. Damnation, The. Carolyn Kizer. CP-KizeC

Before the Beginning. Christina Georgina Rossetti. CP-RosC2

Before the beginning of lords and kings. Liberal Party, The. G. K. Chesterton. CP-ChesG

Before the Beginning of Years. Algernon Charles Swinburne. SP-SwinA *Fr.* Atalanta in Calydon.

Before the beginning Thou hast foreknown the end. Before the Beginning. Christina Georgina Rossetti. CP-RosC2

Before the Big Storm. William Stafford. SP-StafWW

Before the Birth of One of Her Children. Anne Bradstreet. CP-BradA

Before the braces give, the cripple eased to earth. This Early Day. Kenneth Patchen. CP-PatcK

Before the Carnival. Thom Gunn. CP-GunnT

Before the cliffs I sat alone. Han-shan. CP-ColdM, *tr. by* Red Pine

Before the cock in the barnyard spoke. Hangman's Oak. Edna St. Vincent Millay. CP-MillE

Before the Concert. Charles Tomlinson. SP-TomlC

Before the Dance. Charles Tomlinson. CP-TomlC

Before the dark-brow'd sons of Spain. Inca's Daughter, The. Walt Whitman. CP-WhitW

Before the early flowers have faded quite. Columbines and Anemones. Jones Very. CP-VeryJ

Before the Elegy. Olga Broumas. SP-BrouO

Before the first visitor comes the spring. Chinese Restaurant in Portrush, The. Derek Mahon. CP-MahoD

Before the fragile gradual throne of night. E. E. Cummings. CP-CummE

Before the gate has been closed. Yehuda Amichai. SP-AmicY, *tr. by* Stephen Mitchell

Before the god Ea fashioned humankind, the earth. Chaldaic Image. Constantine P. Cavafy. CP-CavaC, *tr. by* Theoharis Constantine Theoharis

Before the grass grew over me. E. C. B. G. K. Chesterton. CP-ChesG

Before the grass is out the people are out. Paterson. William Carlos Williams. CP-WilW1

Before the House. Constantine P. Cavafy. CP-CavaC, *tr. by* Theoharis Constantine Theoharis

Before the ice is in the pools. Emily Dickinson. CP-DickE

Before the inevitable act. New Objectives, New Cadres. Kenneth Rexroth. CP-RexrK

Before the Judgment. Robert Duncan. SP-DuncR *Fr.* Passages.

Before the Night. Theodore Weiss. SP-WeisT

Before the Paling of the Stars. Christina Georgina Rossetti. CP-RosC3

Before the Press scarce one co'd see. To His Book. Robert Herrick. CP-HerrR

Before the Roman came to Rye or out to Severn strode. Rolling English Road, The. G. K. Chesterton. CP-ChesG

Before the six[t]h day of the next new year. On the Card[e]s, and Dice. Sir Walter Ralegh. CP-RaleW

Before the starry threshold of *Jove[']s* court. Comus; a Masque Presented at Ludlow Castle. John Milton. CP-MiltJ

Before the Statue of Endymion. Constantine P. Cavafy. CP-CavaC, *tr. by* Theoharis Constantine Theoharis

Before the Throne, and Before the Lamb. Christina Georgina Rossetti. CP-RosC2

Before the War. Marilyn Hacker. SP-HackM

Before the Wholesale Produce Market. Roast[ing] Potatoes. Denise Levertov. SP-LeveDS

Before the World Was Made. William Butler Yeats. CP-YeatW

Before their journeys men have dreams. Returning to Europe. Howard Nemerov. CP-NemeH

Before there was a body. Deluge, The. W. S. Merwin. SP-MerwWF

Before there was in Egypt any sound. Monadnock through the Trees. Edwin Arlington Robinson. CP-RobiE

Before This. C. K. Williams. CP-WillC

Before this longing. Her Longing. Theodore Roethke. CP-RoetT

Before this loved one. This Loved One. W. H. Auden. CP-AudeW

Before, though, Paris was wonderful. Wanderers. Years of the Dog. Archibald MacLeish. CP-MacLA

Before Time Could Change Them. Constantine P. Cavafy. CP-CavaC, *tr. by* Theoharis Constantine Theoharis

Before time had a name, when win. Young. William Stafford. SP-StafWW

Before us is the iron coin. Now let us ask. Iron Coin, The. Jorge Luis Borges. SP-BorgJ, *tr. by* Eric McHenry

Before we could call / America home. Child's Japan, A. May Sarton. SP-SartM

Before we part to alien thoughts and aims. Lines: "Before we part to alien thoughts and aims." Thomas Hardy. CP-HardT

Before word of his painting got around. Before. Miller Williams. CP-WillM

Before you can count ten. Rainer Maria Rilke. CP-RilkFr, *tr. by* A. Poulin, Jr. *Fr.* Valaisian Quatrains, The.

Before you can see the trees, you have to learn. Learning the Trees. Howard Nemerov. CP-NemeH

Before, you curled inward. Screaming Out Loud. Gregory Orr. SP-OrrG

Before you, I was living on an island. Celebration for June 24. Thomas McGrath. SP-McGrT

Before you leave her, the woman who though you lavish. Advice to a God. Mona Van Duyn. SP-VanDM

Before you thought of Spring. Emily Dickinson. CP-DickE

Before you were, America! From Chebar. Ezra Pound. CP-PoEar

Beg Song. Yusef Komunyakaa. SP-KomuY

Began under the groan of the oldest forest. Smile, The. Ted Hughes. SP-HughTN

Beggar at the Door for Fame, The. Emily Dickinson. CP-DickE

Beggar Boy. Langston Hughes. CP-HughL; CP-HughL1

Beggar Lad—dies early, The. Emily Dickinson. CP-DickE

Beggar Maid and King Cophetua, The. Robert Graves. CP-GravR

Beggar Speaks, The. Nicholas Vachel Lindsay. CP-LindV

Beggar to Beggar Cried. William Butler Yeats. CP-YeatW

Beggar to Mab, the Fairy [*or* Fairie] Queen, The. Robert Herrick. CP-HerrR

Beggars. Robert Herrick. CP-HerrR

Beggars. William Wordsworth. CP-WorW1

Beggars, The. Sylvia Plath. CP-PlatS

Beggars and Kings. W. S. Merwin. SP-MerwW

Beggar's Soliloquy, The. George Meredith. CP-MerG1

Beggar's Song. Gregory Orr. SP-OrrG

Beggar's Valentine, The. Nicholas Vachel Lindsay. CP-LindV

Begger, The. Robert Herrick. CP-HerrR

Begin a song. Lion upon the Floor, A. Charles Olson. CP-OlsoC

Begin by dipping your brush into clear light. Midsummer Mobile. Sylvia Plath. CP-PlatS

Begin. Carnation underfoot, tea splashing stars. Komboloi. James Merrill. SP-MerrJ

Begin nude, looking for the socks. Heels. Raymond Carver. CP-CarvR

Begin the story with a man; curtail. John And I. Laura Riding Jackson. CP-RidiL

Begin to charm, and as thou strok'st mine ears. To Music. Robert Herrick. CP-HerrR

Begin with a kiss[e]. Up Tail[e]s All. Robert Herrick. CP-HerrR

Begin with a pool. The deepening. Existing Pool, The. Hayden Carruth. CP-CarHS

Begin with the pain. Grief. Lucille Clifton. SP-ClifL

Begin[ne] with Jove; then is the work[e] half[e] done. Evensong. Robert Herrick. CP-HerrR

Beginner, The. Rudyard Kipling. CP-KiplR *Fr.* Muse among the Motors, The.

Beginners. Denise Levertov. SP-LeveDL; SP-LeveDS

Beginners. Walt Whitman. CP-WhitW

Beginner's Guide. Howard Nemerov. CP-NemeH

Beginner's Guide to the Ocean, A. Ogden Nash. CP-NashO

Beginning. W. S. Merwin. SP-MerwW

Beginning. Gregory Orr. SP-OrrG

Beginning. James Wright. CP-WrigJ

Beginning, A. Charles Bukowski. SP-BukC3

Beginning, The. Dan Pagis. SP-PagiD

Beginning, The. Wallace Stevens. CP-StevW; CP-StevWP

Beginning Again. Jay Wright. SP-WrigJ

Beginning and the End, The. Jones Very. CP-VeryJ

Beginning at five o'clock, just before dawn rises. My Friend Felix. Donald Hall. CP-HallD

Beginning, Difficult. Robert Herrick. CP-HerrR

Beginning My Studies. Walt Whitman. CP-WhitW

Beginning of a Long Poem of These States. Allen Ginsberg. CP-GinsA

Beginning of a Poem of These States. Allen Ginsberg. CP-GinsA

Beginning of April, The. C. K. Williams. CP-WillC; SP-WillC

Beginning of Autumn in the Hills of Ephraim. Yehuda Amichai. SP-AmicY, *tr. by* Chana Bloch

Beginning of Heliodorus, The. Heliodorus. CP-CrasR

Beginning of the Armadilloes, The. Rudyard Kipling. *Fr.* Just-So Stories.

Beginning of the End, The. Gerard Manley Hopkins. CP-HopkG

Beginning of the First Book, The [Address to Venus]. Lucretius. CP-DryJ2 *Fr.* De Rerum Natura (On the Nature of Things).

Beginning of the Plains. W. S. Merwin. SP-MerwW

Beginning of the Second Book, The. Lucretius. CP-DryJ2 *Fr.* De Rerum Natura (On the Nature of Things).

Beginning of Writing, The. Robert Duncan. SP-DuncR

Beginning—or, The. Della Primavera Transportata al Morale. William Carlos Williams. CP-WilW1

Beginning: piglet among piglets, The. Her Destiny. Denise Levertov. SP-LeveDL

Beginning to dangle beneath. In the Marble Quarry. James Dickey. CP-DickJ

Beginning to fear his own unworthiness. Soldier of Urbina, A. Jorge Luis Borges. SP-BorgJ, *tr. by* Alastair Reid

Beginning to know / how the die. Tomb of Stéphane Mallarmé, The. Charles Simic. SP-SimiC; SP-SimiCE

Beginning to Say No. Tess Gallagher. SP-GallT

Beginning to Squall. May Swenson. SP-SwenM

Beginnings. Robert Earl Hayden. CP-HaydR

Beginnings. Raymond Carver. CP-CarvR

Beginnings and Endings. Robert Herrick. CP-HerrR

Beginnings, The. Rudyard Kipling. CP-KiplR

Begins with the *ooo ooo* of a mourning dove. Holy Thursday. Charles Wright. SP-WrigC

Begirt with bombs that fall and flames that rise. After Portsmouth. Ambrose Bierce. SP-BierA

Begone, thou fond presumptuous Elf, Waterfall and the Eglantine, The. William Wordsworth. CP-WorW1; MW-WorW

Begone you slaves, you idle vermin go. On Mr Dryden's *Religio Laici*. Wentworth Dillon, 4th Earl of Roscommon. CP-DryJ2

Begot like other children, he. T the Great. W. H. Auden. CP-AudeW

Begotten of the Spleen. Charles Simic. SP-SimiC; SP-SimiCE

Beguiled into forgetfulness of care. Lines Suggested By a Portrait from the Pencil of F. Stone. William Wordsworth. CP-WorW2

Behavior. Howard Nemerov. CP-NemeH

Behaviour. D. H. Lawrence. CP-LawrD

Beheaded in the middle of the. 12:18 A.M. Charles Bukowski. SP-BukC1

Beheading. Wisława Szymborska. SP-SzymW, *tr. by* Stanisław Barańczak *and* Clare Cavanagh

Behind. G. K. Chesterton. CP-ChesG

Behind each mirror. Capriccio ("Behind each mirror"). Federico García Lorca. CP-GarcF, *tr. by* Jerome Rothenberg *Fr.* Mirror Suite.

Behind glass in Mexico / this clay doll draws. Five Poems for Dolls. Margaret Atwood. SP-AtwM2

Behind him the hotdogs split and drizzled. Suicide off Egg Rock. Sylvia Plath. CP-PlatS

Behind his back, the first wave passes over. Agent, The. Richard Wilbur. CP-WilbR

Behind His Eyes. David Ignatow. SP-IgnaD

Behind King's Chapel what the earth has kept. At the Indian Killer's Grave. Robert Lowell. SP-LoweR

Behind Me—dips Eternity. Emily Dickinson. CP-DickE

Behind me my children vanish, left asleep. Traveller. Thomas Kinsella. CP-KinsT

Behind New York there's a face. For the Chinese New Year and for Bill Berkson. Frank O'Hara. SP-OharF

Behind shut doors, in shadowy quarantine. First Time, The. Karl Shapiro. SP-ShapK

Behind Stowe. Elizabeth Bishop. CP-BishE

Behind that white brow. To a Dead Journalist. William Carlos Williams. CP-WilW1

Behind the altar in the chapel. Holy Ghost. Rainer Maria Rilke. CP-RilkFr, *tr. by* A. Poulin, Jr.

Behind the ancient wall. Indiscriminately. Yannis Ritsos. SP-RitsY, *tr. by* N. C. Germanacos

Behind the Arras. Paul Laurence Dunbar. CP-DunbP

Behind the barn the lady from the city. Admiral Fan, The. C. K. Williams. CP-WillC

Behind the church in the Isleta Pueblo, there is a courtyard. Ants. Robert Bly. SP-BlyR

Behind the dirty table where Kristofferson is having. Juggler at *Heaven's Gate*, The. Raymond Carver. CP-CarvR

Behind the Door. Philip Whalen. CP-WhalP

Behind the grid, the radiant. Death of a Painter. Donald Davie. CP-DaviDC

Behind the hills, from the city of an Etruscan gateway. Metals. Donald Davie. CP-DaviDC

Behind the house the upland falls. After the Pleasure Party. Herman Melville. SP-MelvH

Behind the Knight. Stevie Smith. CP-SmitS

Behind the lids of sleep. Kathleen Jessie Raine. SP-RainK

Behind the Line. Ivor Gurney. SP-GurnI

Behind the line there mending reserve posts, looking. Riez Bailleul ("Behind the line there mending reserve posts, looking"). Ivor Gurney. SP-GurnI

Behind the Mirror. Thom Gunn. CP-GunnT

Behind the North Wind. Donald Davie. CP-DaviDC

Behind the radio's altarlight. Compline. Philip Larkin. CP-LarkP

Behind the rigid panes. Street of the Mutes, The. Federico García Lorca. SP-GarcF, *tr. by* W. S. Merwin

Behind the Tree the hands. Blake's Baptismal Font. Denise Levertov. SP-LeveDL

Behind the unmoving glass doors. Street of the Mute, The. Federico García Lorca. CP-GarcF, *tr. by* Alan S. Trueblood *Fr.* Games.

Behind the wall of St. John's in the city. Garden at St. John's, The. May Swenson. SP-SwenM

Behind things. Sit Down. Robert Creeley. SP-CreeR

Behind us at our evening meal. Common Question, The. John Greenleaf Whittier. CP-WhitJ

Behind What Little Mirror. May Sarton. SP-SartM

Behind what they said, he always thought that they. Books, The. Wyatt Prunty. SP-PrunW

Behind yon hills where Lugar flows. Song: "Behind yon hills where Lugar flows." Robert Burns. CP-BurnR

Behine de hen-house, on my knees. Short'nin' Bread Song—Pieced Out, A. James Whitcomb Riley. CP-RileJ

Behold—a mere like a madonna's head. Water-Lilies. E. E. Cummings. CP-CummE

Behold! a proof of Irish sense! Jonathan Swift. CP-SwifJ

Behold a Shaking. Christina Georgina Rossetti. CP-RosC2

Behold an emblem of our human mind. On the Banks of a Rocky Stream. William Wordsworth. CP-WorW2

Behold around us pomp and pride. End of All, The. Walt Whitman. CP-WhitW

Behold best-selling Mr. Furneval. Lecturer in Bookstore. Ogden Nash. CP-NashO

Behold, bless ye the Lord, all ye servants of the Lord. Psalm 134: "Behold, bless ye the Lord, all ye servants of the Lord." Bible, *O.T.* SP-SmarC *Fr.* Psalms.

Behold Fiammetta, shown in Vision here. Fiammetta. Dante Gabriel Rossetti. CW-RossD

Behold, Friends, once more the Revolution has performed its famous. Note on the Late Elections, A. Thomas McGrath. SP-McGrT

Behold, from the land of the farther suns. Stephen Crane. CP-CranS

Behold He Is at Hand That Doth Betray Me. Jones Very. CP-VeryJ

Behold her, single in the field. Solitary Reaper, The. William Wordsworth. CP-WorW1; MW-WorW

Behold, I have taken at thy hands immortal wine. S.F.D. E. E. Cummings. CP-CummE

Behold, I Make All Things New. Jones Very. CP-VeryJ

Behold I make partition. Pilgrims, The. Ralph Waldo Emerson. CP-EmerR

Behold, I stand at the door and knock. Christina Georgina Rossetti. CP-RosC3

Behold in heaven a floating dazzling cloud. Thou Knewest . . . Thou Oughtest Therefore. Christina Georgina Rossetti. CP-RosC2

Behold, It Was Very Good. Christina Georgina Rossetti. CP-RosC2

Behold, love, thy power how she despiseth! Sir Thomas Wyatt. CP-WyatT

Behold my fair, where-e'er we rove. Winter's Walk, The. Samuel Johnson. CP-JohnS

Behold, my Love, how green the groves. Scotish Song. Robert Burns. CP-BurnR

Behold, O Christian! to the life displayed. On the Bunyan Tableau. Jones Very. CP-VeryJ

Behold, one faith endureth still. God's Mercy. James Whitcomb Riley. CP-RileJ

Behold, One of Several Little Christs. Kenneth Patchen. CP-PatcK

Behold that great Plotinus swim. Delphic Oracle upon Plotinus, The. William Butler Yeats. CP-YeatW

Behold the blessings of a lucky lot! Elegy: "Behold the blessings of a lucky lot!" Lord Byron. CP-Byron

Behold, the Bridegroom cometh: go ye out. Advent Sunday. Christina Georgina Rossetti. CP-RosC2

Behold the duck. / It does not cluck. Duck, The. Ogden Nash. CP-NashO

Behold the genial boy who promised much. Two Views of a Philosopher. Howard Nemerov. CP-NemeH

Behold the glow of the moon. Shih-te. CP-ColdM, *tr. by* Red Pine

Behold, the Gods are with her, and are known. George Meredith. CP-MerG1 *Fr.* France.

Behold, the grave of a wicked man. Stephen Crane. CP-CranS

Behold the hippopotamus! Hippopotamus, The. Ogden Nash. CP-NashO

Behold the hour, the boat arrive. Song: "Behold the hour, the boat arrive." Robert Burns. CP-BurnR

Behold the Lamb. Paul Muldoon. CP-MuldP

Behold the Man! Christina Georgina Rossetti. CP-RosC2

Behold the woes of matrimonial life. Wife of Bath, The. Geoffrey Chaucer. CP-PopeA *Fr.* Canterbury Tales, The.

Behold the Woman. Thomas McGrath. SP-McGrT

Behold these flowers. Henry David Thoreau. CP-ThorH

Behold this beggar, traitor, thief. And You, Too, Brutus. Robert Stock. SP-StocR

Behold this little Bane. Emily Dickinson. CP-DickE

Behold This Swarthy Face. Walt Whitman. CP-WhitW

Behold those monarch oaks that rise. Copy of Verses upon Two Celebrated Modern Poets, A. Jonathan Swift. CP-SwifJ

Behold, within the leafy shade. Sparrow's Nest, The. William Wordsworth. CP-WorW1

Behold yon mountain's hoary height. Ode 1.9: To Thaliarchus. Horace. CP-DryJ2 *Fr.* Odes.

Behold your Cross, Christians! Cross, The. D. H. Lawrence. CP-LawrD

Beholders, The. James Dickey. CP-DickJ

Beholding element, in whose pure eye. Aspen and the Stream, The. Richard Wilbur. CP-WilbR

Beholding youth and hope in mockery caught. Sun's Shame, The ("Beholding youth and hope in mockery caught"). Dante Gabriel Rossetti. CW-RossD *Fr.* House of Life, The.

Beholds the moon. Bashō. Lorine Niedecker. CP-NiedL

Bei Hennef. D. H. Lawrence. CP-LawrD

Bei Wannsee. Kenneth Rexroth. CP-RexrK

Beige sailors with large noses. Seashore through Dark Glasses (Atlantic City). Langston Hughes. CP-HughL; CP-HughL2

Bein' Back Home. Paul Laurence Dunbar. CP-DunbP

Beinecke Library. Czeslaw Milosz. CP-MiloCN, *tr. by* Robert Hass

Being, The. James Dickey. CP-DickJ

Being a father / Is quite a bother. Soliloquy in Circles. Ogden Nash. CP-NashO

Being a modest man, you wanted. For My Father. Philip Whalen. SP-WhalP

Being Alive. D. H. Lawrence. CP-LawrD

Being Alone. C. K. Williams. CP-WillC; SP-WillC

Being Altogether Literal, & Specific, and Seeking at the Same Time to be Successfully Explicit. Charles Olson. CP-OlsoC

Being an American. William Stafford. SP-StafWW

Being and Becoming. Clarence Major. SP-MajoC

Being Angry with God. Donald Davie. CP-DaviDC

Being as I Was, How Could I Help. Eleanor Wilner. SP-WilnE

Being as none is, I do complain. Sir Thomas Wyatt. CP-WyatT

Being Asked To Define Bourgeois Individuality. William Dickey. SP-DickW

Being Beauteous. Arthur Rimbaud. CP-RimbA, *tr. by* Martin Sorrell

Being Born. Thom Gunn. CP-GunnT

Being Called. John Ciardi. CP-CiarJ

Being Christlike. Ted Hughes. SP-HughTN

Being Country Bred. Mary Oliver. SP-OlivM

Being driven after the hearse thru suburbs. H.T. Louis Zukofsky. CP-ZukLS

Being expert on the zither. Ice-Blue Wind, The. Tennessee Williams. CP-WillT

Being Forever. Peter Blue Cloud. SP-BlueP

Being Here. Miller Williams. CP-WillM

Being his mother,—when he goes away. James Whitcomb Riley. CP-RileJ

Being his resting place. Dog Sleeping on My Feet, A. James Dickey. CP-DickJ

Being in this stage. Wide Awake, Full of Love. William Carlos Williams. CP-WilW2

Being in thought of love, I chanced to see. Ballata: He reveals, in a Dialogue, his increasing Love for Mandetta. Guido Cavalcanti. CW-RossD, *tr. by* Dante Gabriel Rossetti

Being kissed on the back. Knee Song. Anne Sexton. CP-SextA

Being my selfe captyved here in care. Sonnet 73. Edmund Spenser. CP-Spens *Fr.* Amoretti.

Being no longer human why should I. Paracelsus in Excelsis. Ezra Pound. CP-PoEar

Being now three or four years more than sixty. World's Wonders, The. Robinson Jeffers. CP-JefR3

Being of Three Minds. Howard Nemerov. CP-NemeH

Being Old. Langston Hughes. CP-HughL; CP-HughL1

Being old and gray, I can now remember my school days in Switzerland. I. After Lake Leman. Robinson Jeffers. CP-JefR3

Being Once Blind, His Request to Biancha. Robert Herrick. CP-HerrR

Being out of heart with government. Appointment, An. William Butler Yeats. CP-YeatW

Being serious is a / perversion of natural form. Serious Morning, A. Andrei Codrescu. SP-CodrA

Being set on the idea. Atlantis. W. H. Auden. CP AudeW

Being so hideous that the air weeps blood. Kenneth Patchen. CP-PatcK

Being so young he feels the weight of history. Conscript, The. Louis MacNeice. CP-MacNL

Being Southern. Jane Cooper. CP-CoopJ

Being the Dedication of a Morning. Nicholas Vachel Lindsay. CP-LindV

Being to timelessness as it's to time. E. E. Cummings. CP CummE

Being together is knowing. Bridging. Marge Piercy. SP PierM

Being / twelve / who hast merely. E. E. Cummings. CP-CummE

Being walkers with the dawn and morning. Walkers with the Dawn. Langston Hughes. CP-HughL; CP-HughL1

Being, whose flesh dissolves. To the Unseeable Animal. Wendell Berry. CP-BerrW

Being without quality. Vox Humana. Thom Gunn. CP-GunnT

Being Young and Green. Edna St. Vincent Millay. CP-MillE

Being(just a little). E. E. Cummings. CP-CummE

Beit Guvrin. Yehuda Amichai. SP-AmicYL, tr. by Benjamin Harshav and Barbara Harshav

Beizades to His Beloved. Constantine P. Cavafy. CP-CavaC, tr. by Theoharis Constantine Theoharis

Belated Birthday Poem, A. James Schuyler. CP-SchuJ

Belated Palinode for Dylan Thomas. Lawrence Ferlinghetti. SP-FerlL

Belated wanderer of the ways of spring. To a Violet Found on All Saints' Day. Paul Laurence Dunbar. CP-DunbP

Belfast. Louis MacNeice. CP-MacNL

Belfast on a Sunday Afternoon. Donald Davie. CP-DaviDC

Belfast Tune. Joseph Brodsky. CP-BrodJ

Belfry. Yannis Ritsos. SP-RitsY, tr. by Kimon Friar and Kostas Myrsiades

Belgium. E. E. Cummings. CP-CummE

Belief. A. R. Ammons. CP-AmmoA

Belief. D. H. Lawrence. CP-LawrD

Belief. Philip Levine. SP-LeviP

Belief in God is an inclination to listen. No Hearing. Robert Lowell. SP-LoweR

Believe, if ever the bridges of this town. Edna St. Vincent Millay. CP-MillE

Believe It. John Logan. CP-LogaJ

Believe it or not, as you choose. Catharina, the Second Part. William Cowper. CP-CowpW

Believe me, I have studied men. George Meredith. CP-MerG2

Believe me, knot of gristle, I bleed like a tree. Give Way, Ye Gates. Theodore Roethke. CP-RoetT

Believe me, Lucy Larcom, it gives me real sorrow. Letter to Lucy Larcom. John Greenleaf Whittier. CP-WhitJ

Believe me, sir, I'd like to spend whole days. Martial. CP-CunnJ, tr. by James Vincent Cunningham

Believe me, the marathon is nothing. Decathlon Man. Primo Levi. CP-LeviP, tr. by Ruth Feldman

Believe the automatic righteousness. Against the War in Vietnam. Wendell Berry. CP-BerrW

Believer. William Stafford. SP-StafWW

Believer, The. James Laughlin. CP-LaugJ

Believe't, young man, I can as eas'ly tell. Upon Two Sisters. Sir John Suckling. CP-SuckJ

Believing. Miller Williams. CP-WillM

Believing in Iron. Yusef Komunyakaa. CP-KomuY

Believing in Symbols. Miller Williams. CP-WillM

Believing in Those Inexorable Laws. Muriel Rukeyser. CP-RukeM

Believing that we are to have no Face. Emily Dickinson. SP-DickE

Belinda lived in a little white house. Tale of Custard the Dragon, The. Ogden Nash. CP-NashO

Belinda's Petition. Rita Dove. SP-DoveR

Bell, The. G. K. Chesterton. CP-ChesG

Bell Buoy, The. Rudyard Kipling. CP-KiplR

Bell dipthonging in an atmosphere, A. Dubious Night, A. Richard Wilbur. CP-WilbR

Bell doth toll, The. Knell, The. George Herbert. CP-HerbG

Bell Jar, The. Hans Magnus Enzensberger. SP-EnzeH, tr. by Michael Hamburger

Bell-looking-glass upright leaf-shells ring the. Venus's Looking-glass. Louis Zukofsky. CP-ZukLS

Bell-Man, The. Robert Herrick. CP-HerrR

Bell-man of night, if I about shall go. Cock-Crow. Robert Herrick. CP-HerrR

Bell of Haddington Road rang, The. Thomas Kinsella. CP-KinsT

Bell-Ringer, The. Stéphane Mallarmé. CP-MallS, tr. by Henry Weinfield

Bell-Ringer, The. Pablo Neruda. SP-NeruP

Bell-rope that gathers God at dawn, The. Broken Tower, The. Hart Crane. CP-CranH

Bell Speech. Richard Wilbur. CP-WilbR

Bell struck one, and shook the silent tower, The. Fair Elenor. William Blake. CP-BlakW

Bell Tower of Authenay, The. Pablo Neruda. SP-NeruP

Bell went heavy to-day, The. Premonitions. Thomas Hardy. CP-HardT

Bella. Rainer Maria Rilke. CP-RilkFr, tr. by A. Poulin, Jr.

Bella & Rosa. Donald Davie. CP-DaviDC

Bella Donna Iu. Li Yü. CP-WilW2

Belle Isle, 1949. Philip Levine. SP-LeviP

Bellerophon. George Meredith. CP-MerG1

Bellerophon and the Portable Universe. Robert Stock. SP-StocR

Bellevue Exchange. Norman Dubie. CP-DubiN

Belligerence. Andrei Codrescu. SP-CodrA

Bellis perennis daisy of history. Daisy. Louis Zukofsky. CP-ZukLS

Bellisle! that is a fabling name, but we. Gerard Manley Hopkins. CP-HopkG

Bellman, The. Robert Herrick. CP-HerrR

Bellocose. G. K. Chesterton. CP-ChesG

Bells. D. H. Lawrence. CP-LawrD

Bells, The. Walter De la Mare. CP-DeLaW

Bells, The. Edgar Allan Poe. CP-PoeEd

Bells, The. Anne Sexton. CP-SextA

Bells, The. Adam Zagajewski. SP-ZagaA, tr. by Renata Gorczynski, Benjamin Ivry and C. K. Williams

Bells and Queen Victoria, The. Rudyard Kipling. CP-KiplR

Bells for John Whiteside's Daughter. John Crowe Ransom. SP-RansJ

Bells have quit their clanging, The; here beneath. New Year Morning. Adrienne Rich. CP-RicAE

Bells in the Endtime of Gyurmey Tsultrim. Norman Dubie. CP-DubiN

Bells in tower at evening toll. A. E. Housman. CP-HousA

Bells Jangled. James Whitcomb Riley. CP-RileJ

Bells of a Chinese Temple, The. Richard Eberhart. CP-EberR

Bells that lift their yawning throats, The. New Year's Plaint, A. James Whitcomb Riley. CP-RileJ

Bells, the cannons, the houses black with crepe, The. Abduction, The. Rita Dove. SP-DoveR

Bells Toll Kindly, The. Langston Hughes. CP-HughL; CP-HughL3

Belltower's Song. Rainer Maria Rilke. CP-RilkFr, tr. by A. Poulin, Jr. Fr. Valaisian Quatrains, The.

Belly Locks Shnooks Oakie. Louis Zukofsky. CP-ZukLS

Belly's full. Sick. Robert Creeley. CP-CreeR

Beloved. D. H. Lawrence. See Bits

Beloved, Thomas Kinsella. CP-KinsT

Beloved! amid the earnest woes. To F——. Edgar Allan Poe. CP-PoeEd

Beloved Brethren, / we have before us an example of incorrect proportions. Dinosaur Skeleton. Wisława Szymborska. SP-SzymW, tr. by Stanislaw Barańczak and Clare Cavanagh

Beloved friend, who living many years. Hugh Stuart Boyd [His Death, 1848]. Elizabeth Barrett Browning. CP-BroEB

Beloved, gaze in thine own heart. Two Trees, The. William Butler Yeats. CP-YeatW

Beloved, / In what other lives or lands. Refusal. Maya Angelou. SP-AngeM

"Beloved, let us love one another," says St. John. Christina Georgina Rossetti. CP-RosC2

Beloved, may your sleep be sound. Lullaby: "Beloved, may your sleep be sound." William Butler Yeats. CP-YeatW

Beloved Sleeps on the Poet's Breast, The. Federico García Lorca. CP-GarcF, tr. by Angela Jaffray

Beloved student, what makes you think I can still teach. Assessment, The. John Logan. CP-LogaJ

"Beloved Vale!" I said, "when I shall con" William Wordsworth. CP-WorW1; MW-WorW

Beloved, yeild thy time to God, for He / Will make eternity thy recompense. Christina Georgina Rossetti. CP-RosC2

Beloved you are. For Viola: De Gustibus. William Carlos Williams. CP-WilW1

Below. Federico García Lorca. CP-GarcF, tr. by Jerome Rothenberg Fr. Night (Suite for Piano and Poet's Voice).

Below. Wendell Berry. CP-BerrW

Below a Painting. Paul Celan. SP-CelaP, tr. by John Felstiner

Below, cool grasses: over us. One Afternoon. James Whitcomb Riley. CP-RileJ

Below me, a pool gathers. To the August Fallen. James Wright. CP-WrigJ

Below me treetops and a crow. Cliff, The. Gregory Orr. SP-OrrG

Below the ridge a raven flew. Love in Barrenness. Robert Graves. CP-GravR

Below, the river scrambled like a goat. God's Little Mountain. Geoffrey Hill. CP-HillG

Below the Stairs. James Schuyler. CP-SchuJ

Below the ten thousand billionth of a centimeter. First Day, The. Howard Nemerov. CP-NemeH

Below the thunders of the upper deep. Kraken, The. Alfred Tennyson. CP-TennA

Below the wall in the lake-garden. Meben. Kenneth Patchen. CP-PatcK

Below thir stanes lie Jamie's banes. On a Noisy Polemic. Robert Burns. CP-BurnR

Below Tintern. Charles Tomlinson. CP-TomlC

Below us all day, a mile away, in a flashing. Skelpick. Donald Davie. CP-DaviDC

Below what we think we are. Underneath. D. H. Lawrence. CP-LawrD

Belsen, Day of Liberation. Robert Earl Hayden. CP-HaydR

Belshazzar! from the banquet turn. To Belshazzar. Lord Byron. CP-Byron

Belshazzar had a Letter. Emily Dickinson. CP-DickE

Belts. Rudyard Kipling. CP-KiplR

Belvedere. George Oppen. CP-OppGN

Belvoir thy coat was not more golden than thy heart. Death of the Dog Belvoir. Stevie Smith. CP-SmitS

Ben Jonson Entertains a Man from Stratford. Edwin Arlington Robinson. CP-RobiE

Ben Jonson said he was? O I could still. No Better Than a "Withered Daffodil" Marianne Craig Moore. CP-MoorM

Ben Jonson's Grace before King James. Ben Jonson. CP-JonsB

Ben Karshook's Wisdom. Robert Browning. CP-BroR2

Ben Trovato. Edwin Arlington Robinson. CP-RobiE

Benares. Jorge Luis Borges. SP-BorgJ, tr. by Charles Tomlinson

Benath yon eastern ridge, the craggy bound. For a Seat in the Groves of Coleorton. William Wordsworth. CP-WorW1

Bench of Boors, The. Herman Melville. SP-MelvH

Bend low again, night of summer stars. Summer Stars. Carl Sandburg. CP-SandC

Bend your back to it, sir: for it will snow all night. Old Man Shoveling Snow. Thomas Lux. SP-LuxT

Bend your head outside the window. Instructions for Her Voyage. Yehuda Amichai. SP-AmicYL, tr. by Benjamin Harshav and Barbara Harshav

Bended to fops who bent to him. Ralph Waldo Emerson. CP-EmerR

Bending over her bed, I saw the smile. Neverland. Galway Kinnell. SP-KinnGN

Bending staff I would not break, A. Questions of Life. John Greenleaf Whittier. CP-WhitJ

Bending the Bow. Robert Duncan. SP-DuncR

Bendix. John Updike. CP-UpdiJ

Beneath a knap where flown. Ditty: "Beneath a knap where flown." Thomas Hardy. CP-HardT

Beneath a motionless yew. Walter De la Mare. CP-DeLaW

Beneath a sky swept free of clouds. Death of Lovers, The. Charles Baudelaire. CP-BaudC, tr. by Walter Martin

Beneath Blessington's eyes. Impromptu. Lord Byron. CP-Byron

Beneath heaven's vault. Earth Your Dancing Place. May Swenson. SP-SwenM

Beneath high cliffs I live alone. Han-shan. CP-ColdM, tr. by Red Pine

Beneath My Hand and Eye the Distant Hills, Your Body. Gary Snyder. CP-SnydG

Beneath my window twilight made. Reminded. Ambrose Bierce. SP-BierA

Beneath the Apple Branches Bent Dumbly. Thomas Lux. SP-LuxT

Beneath the blaze of a tropical sun the mountain peaks are the Thrones of Frost. Blossoming of the Solitary Date-Tree, The. Samuel Taylor Coleridge. CP-ColeS

Beneath the carving drag the wood. Oaxaca. Audre Lorde. SP-LordA

Beneath the concave of an April sky. Vernal Ode. William Wordsworth. CP-WorW2; MW-WorW

Beneath the deep verandah's shade. Moon of Other Days, The. Rudyard Kipling. CP-KiplR

Beneath the hedge, or near the stream. Glow-worm, The. Vincent Bourne. CP-CowpW

Beneath the low-hung night cloud. Three Bells, The. John Greenleaf Whittier. CP-WhitJ

Beneath the moon-dark rosebay. Nu. Federico García Lorca. CP-GarcF, tr. by Alan S. Trueblood Fr. Eros with a Cane.

Beneath the moonlight and the snow. My Birthday. John Greenleaf Whittier. CP-WhitJ

Beneath the Moses of the incense. Spinster at Mass, The. Federico García Lorca. SP-GarcF, tr. by Edwin Honig

Beneath the ocean's ever-tossing breast. Triumphs of Science, and of Faith, The.

Jones Very. CP-VeryJ

Beneath the tree where M., the Frenchmen's pet. Mexican Divertimento. Joseph Brodsky. CP-BrodJ, tr. by Alan Myers

Beneath the vans of doom did men pass in. Forest History. George Meredith. CP-MerG1

Beneath the white thorn lovely May. William Blake. CP-BlakW

Beneath the wild thorn stretched upon the ground. Lost Sheep, The. Jones Very. CP-VeryJ

Beneath their flames, cities of candelabra. Chestnut Avenue: at Alton House, The. Charles Tomlinson. CP-TomlC

Beneath these fruit-tree boughs that shed. Green Linnet, The. William Wordsworth. CP-WorW1

Beneath this slab. Lather as You Go. Ogden Nash. CP-NashO

Beneath this stone does William Hazlitt lie. W. H. Eheu! Samuel Taylor Coleridge. CP-ColeS

Beneath this thorn when I was young. Three Graves, The. William Wordsworth. CP-ColeS; CP-WorW1

Beneath thy skies, November! Song, A: "Beneath thy skies, November!" John Greenleaf Whittier. CP-WhitJ

Beneath yon birch with silver bark. Ballad of the Dark Ladié, The. Samuel Taylor Coleridge. CP-ColeS

Benedicite. John Greenleaf Whittier. CP-WhitJ

Benedicta. Paul Celan. SP-CelaP, tr. by John Felstiner

Benedictine Echard, The. Vision of Echard, The. John Greenleaf Whittier. CP-WhitJ

Benediction. Charles Baudelaire. CP-BaudC, tr. by Walter Martin

Benediction. Stanley Kunitz. CP-KunSC

Benediction, A. G. K. Chesterton. CP-ChesG

(When wind and rain were like a cloak a-blow.) CP-ChesG

Benedictory. Laura Riding Jackson. CP-RidiL

Benedictus. Donald Davie. CP-DaviDC

Benefits of an Education, The. John Ciardi. CP-CiarJ

Benevolence. John Greenleaf Whittier. CP-WhitJ

Benevolent blue air. Grappling in the Central Blue. Maxine W. Kumin. SP-KumiM

Benfactors, The. Rudyard Kipling. CP-KiplR

Bengal tigress, The. In Summer. "Rubén Dario." SP-DariR, tr. by Alberto Acereda and Will Derusha

Beni Hasan. Louis MacNeice. CP-MacNL

Benison given. Unused, A. Singer Will Not Sing, The. Maya Angelou. SP-AngeM

Benjamin Banneker Helps to Build a City. Jay Wright. SP-WrigJ

Benjamin Banneker Sends His Almanac to Thomas Jefferson. Jay Wright. SP-WrigJ

Benjamin Harrison. James Whitcomb Riley. CP-RileJ

Bennelong's Blues. Yusef Komunyakaa. CP-KomuY

Benny, the albino marmoset. At Cocktails. John Ciardi. CP-CiarJ

Ben's Last Fight. Thomas Merton. CP-MertT

Bent, The. Donald Davie. CP-DaviDC

Bent and twisted by many seasons. Dedication of a Roundhouse. Peter Blue Cloud. SP-BlueP

Bent double, like old beggars under sacks. Dulce et Decorum Est. Wilfred Owen. CP-OwenW

Bent over the railing. Strange Attractor. Hans Magnus Enzensberger. SP-EnzeH

Bent over the railing in the back woodlot. So Near—And Yet. Kenneth Patchen. CP-PatcK

Bent under burdens which sometimes. Refugees. Adam Zagajewski. SP-ZagaA, tr. by Clare Cavanagh

Beowulf. Richard Wilbur. CP-WilbR

Beowulf may have killed Grendel and. Beast, The. Charles Bukowski. SP-BukC2

Beppo. Jorge Luis Borges. SP-BorgJ, tr. by Alan S. Trueblood

Beppo; a Venetian Story. Lord Byron. CP-Byron

Berceuse. Amy Clampitt. CP-ClamA

Berceuse for a Sleeping Mirror. Federico García Lorca. CP-GarcF, tr. by Jerome Rothenberg Fr. Mirror Suite.

Berceuse, mediphala. Synamism. Lorine Niedecker. CP-NiedL

Berceuse: to end the sorrow of mortals. Thomas Merton. CP-MertT

Berck-Plage. Sylvia Plath. CP-PlatS

Bereaved. James Whitcomb Riley. CP-RileJ

Bereaved of all, I went abroad. Emily Dickinson. CP-DickE

Bereaved Swan, The. Stevie Smith. CP-SmitS

Bereavement. Elizabeth Barrett Browning. CP-BroEB

Bereavement. D. H. Lawrence. CP-LawrD

Bereavement. Stevie Smith. CP-SmitS

Bereavement in their death to feel. Emily Dickinson. CP-DickE

Bereft. Robert Frost. CP-FrosR

Bereft. Thomas Hardy. CP-HardT

Bereft, She Thinks She Dreams. Thomas Hardy. CP-HardT

Berenice. James Laughlin. CP-LaugJ

Berg, The. Herman Melville. SP-MelvH

Berkeley did not forsee such misty weather. Chronic Condition, A. Richard Wilbur. CP-WilbR

Berket and the Stars. William Carlos Williams. CP-WilW1

Berkshire. Donald Davie. CP-DaviDC

Berlin: First Night & Early Morning. Robert Creeley. CP-CreeR

Berlin in Ruins. Thom Gunn. CP-GunnT

Berlin Wall Tune, The. Joseph Brodsky. CP-BrodJ, *tr. by* Joseph Brodsky

Bermuda. Jane Cooper. CP-CoopJ

Bermudas. Andrew Marvell. CP-MarvA

Bernardston. Clarence Major. SP-MajoC

Bernice said she wanted. Ballad of the Killer Boy. Langston Hughes. CP-HughL; CP-HughL2

Berries of Straw. Summer's Bounty. May Swenson. SP-SwenM

Berry Feast, A. Gary Snyder. CP-SnydG

Berry Territory. Gary Snyder. CP-SnydG

Berrying. Ralph Waldo Emerson. CP-EmerR

Berryman. Donald Davie. CP-DaviDC

Berryman. W. S. Merwin. SP-MerwWF

Bert is beguiling with his mother. Martial. CP-CunnJ, *tr. by* James Vincent Cunningham

Bertha in the Lane. Elizabeth Barrett Browning. CP-BroEB

Berthe Soucaret. Jaroslav Seifert. SP-SeifJ, *tr. by* Ewald Osers

Berthe's Eyes. Charles Baudelaire. CP-BaudC, *tr. by* Walter Martin

Bertie Goes Hunting. Amy Clampitt. CP-ClamA

Beside a running brook my lady stands. Lorenzo de' Medici. SP-ZatuM, *tr. by* Marya Alexandrovna Zaturenska

Beside a stricken field I stood. Watchers, The. John Greenleaf Whittier. CP-WhitJ

Beside an Open Grave the Mind of the Young Preacher Comes Almost to Terms. Miller Williams. CP-WillM

Beside her in the dark the chime. Archibald MacLeish. CP-MacLA *Fr.* Happy Marriage, The.

Beside her, she a limpid brook, I took. Day Song. Charles Olson. CP-OlsoC

Beside Her to Lie. Robert Creeley. SP-CreeR

Beside herself (and me, too, so help me), & she. Day Song, the Day After. Charles Olson. CP-OlsoC

Beside his father's deathbed, lost in thought. Out of the Blue. Charles Baudelaire. CP-BaudC, *tr. by* Walter Martin

Beside me,—in the car,—she sat. Natura Naturans. Arthur Hugh Clough. SP-ClouA

Beside me in this garden. Korean Mums. James Schuyler. CP-SchuJ

Beside me on the plane. Journey, The. Gregory Orr. SP-OrrG

Beside me she sat, hand hooked and hovering. Egyptian Passage, An. Theodore Weiss. SP-WeisT

Beside my cradle stood a bookcase where. Voice, The. Charles Baudelaire. CP-BaudC, *tr. by* Walter Martin

Beside our way the streams are dried. To Booker T. Washington. Paul Laurence Dunbar. CP-DunbP

Beside that milestone where the level sun. Response. John Greenleaf Whittier. CP-WhitJ

Beside the bridge's photogen- / ic lapse into air you'll. Letter from Provence. Louise Glück. SP-GlucL

Beside the Brokenstraw or Licking Creek. John Chapman. Richard Wilbur. CP-WilbR

Beside the confines of the Ægean main. Fragment from the "Monk of Athos." Lord Byron. CP-Byron

Beside the crater and the tattered palm. Dead in Melanesia, The. Randall Jarrell. CP-JarrR

Beside the door / She stood whom I had known before. Friend Revisited, A. Donald Hall. CP-HallD

Beside the fall, the moonlight spills. Death of Elizabeth Grieve, The. Charles Tomlinson. CP-TomlC

Beside the grave, a bottle in his hand. Jonathan in Mourning. Miller Williams. CP-WillM

Beside the jug of wine. Hour of Song. Yannis Ritsos. SP-RitsY, *tr. by* Kimon Friar

Beside the lumber. After Five Years. Theodore Weiss. SP-WeisT

Beside the Mare Crisium, that sea. Explorers, The. Adrienne Rich. CP-RicAE

Beside the Mead of Memories. Dead Quire, The. Thomas Hardy. CP-HardT

Beside the river Volga near the village of Anskijovka. Dun Cow and the Hag, The. Norman Dubie. CP-DubiN

Beside the sultry stream he curbs amain his smoking mare. Iconia. George Meredith. CP-MerG2

Beside this door a January tree. Purely Local. Adrienne Rich. CP-RicAE

Beside this lake / where there are no other people. Younger Sister, Going Swimming. Margaret Atwood. SP-AtwM1

Beside you, prone. Prelude to a Parting. Maya Angelou. SP-AngeM

Besides the autumn poets sing. Emily Dickinson. CP-DickE

Besides this May. Emily Dickinson. CP-DickE

Besides us two, i'th'Temple here's not one. To Julia in the Temple. Robert Herrick. CP-HerrR

Bespoke for weeks, he turned up some morning. Thatcher. Seamus Heaney. SP-HeanSO

Bess. William Stafford. SP-StafWW

Bess[y] and Her Spinning-Wheel. Robert Burns. CP-BurnR

Best. Gregory Orr. SP-OrrG

Best and brightest, come away. To Jane: The Invitation. Percy Bysshe Shelley. CP-ShelP

Best authorities are vague, The. What Is a Buslus? G. K. Chesterton. CP-ChesG

Best Beast of the Fat-Stock Show at Earls Court, The. Stevie Smith. CP-SmitS

Best Beast of the Show, The. Best Beast of the Fat-Stock Show at Earls Court, The. Stevie Smith. CP-SmitS

Best Cigarette, The. Billy Collins. SP-CollB

Best Defense Is Offensive, The. Marge Piercy. SP-PierM

Best dream I ever. Nice Try. Charles Bukowski. SP-BukC3

Best Gains—must have the Losses' Test. Emily Dickinson. CP-DickE

Best ideal is the true, The. Summa. Gerard Manley Hopkins. CP-HopkG

Best Is Good Enough, The. James Whitcomb Riley. CP-RileJ

Best is, in war or faction or ordinary vindictive life, not to take sides. Time of Disturbance. Robinson Jeffers. CP-JefR3

Best of All. James Whitcomb Riley. CP-RileJ

Best of all, / his wide, loving the old man for the memories. Theodore Weiss. SP-WeisT *Fr.* Storeroom, The.

Best of life is presence of a muse, The. Ralph Waldo Emerson. CP-EmerR

Best of School, The. D. H. Lawrence. CP-LawrD

Best of ways. That there be a law the Earth gives and the Mountain. Robert Duncan. SP-DuncR *Fr.* Structure of Rime, The.

Best She Could, The. Thomas Hardy. CP-HardT

Best Side of Me, The. Andrei Codrescu. SP-CodrA

Best Society. Philip Larkin. CP-LarkP

Best sprig of the clan. Carmen 24. Catullus. CP-ZukLS *Fr.* Carmina.

Best thing in the world but I better be quick about it, The. Biotherm [for Bill Berkson]. Frank O'Hara. SP-OharF

Best Thing in the World, The. Elizabeth Barrett Browning. CP-BroEB

Best Things dwell out of Sight. Emily Dickinson. CP-DickE

Best Time of the Day, The. Raymond Carver. CP-CarvR

Best Times. Thomas Hardy. CP-HardT

Best Times, The. James Whitcomb Riley. CP-RileJ

Best to Be Merry. Robert Herrick. CP-HerrR

Best way in (not that I've checked the map), The. Worcestershire. Donald Davie. CP-DaviDC

Best Way to Get Famous Is to Run Away, The. Charles Bukowski. SP-BukC2

Best way to wreck something is to take it seriously, The. Homage to William Seward Burroughs. Philip Whalen. SP-WhalP

Best, who could, went back—because they nursed, The. Depravity: Two Sermons. Donald Davie. CP-DaviDC

Best Witchcraft is Geometry. Emily Dickinson. CP-DickE

Bestiaries Are Out. W. H. Auden. CP-AudeW

Bestiary. Dan Pagis. SP-PagiD, *tr. by* Stephen Mitchell

Bestiary, A. Kenneth Rexroth. CP-RexrK

Bestiary for the Fingers of My Right Hand. Charles Simic. SP-SimiC; SP-SimiCE

Bethesda: A Sequel. Arthur Hugh Clough. SP-ClouA

Bethink, poor heart, what bitter kind of jest. Epitaph: "Bethink, poor heart, what bitter kind of jest." Hafiz. CP-EmerR

Betrayal. Raymond Carver. CP-CarvR

Betrayal. Walter De la Mare. CP-DeLaW

Betrayal. Sir Thomas Wyatt. CP-WyatT

Betrayal, The. Thomas Merton. CP-MertT

Betrayed by his five mechanic agents, falling. Little Odyssey of Jason Quint, of Science, Doctor, The. Thomas McGrath. SP-McGrT

Betrothal, The. Edna St. Vincent Millay. CP-MillE

Betrothal / the Bride's Lament. Olga Broumas. SP-BrouO

Betrothed. Louise Bogan. CP-BogaL

Betrothed, The. Rudyard Kipling. CP-KiplR

Betrothed to Righteousness might be. Emily Dickinson. CP-DickE

Better. Langston Hughes. CP-HughL; CP-HughL1

Better born than married, misled. Grandmother, The. Wendell Berry. CP-BerrW

Better, / despite the worms talking to. Suicide Note. Anne Sexton. CP-SextA

Better disguised than the leaf-insect. Lake, The. Ted Hughes. SP-HughTN

Better in the quiet night. Better. Langston Hughes. CP-HughL; CP-HughL1

Better is an handful with quietness. Thomas Kinsella. CP-KinsT

Better on your arse than on your feet. Nicolas-Sébastien Roch Chamfort. CP-

BeckS

Better or Worse. Heather McHugh. SP-McHuH

Better Resurrection, A. Christina Georgina Rossetti. CP-RosC1

Better So. Christina Georgina Rossetti. CP-RosC3

Better Than Counting Sheep. Robert Penn Warren. CP-WarrR

Better than flowers. William Carlos Williams. CP-WilW1 *Fr.* Paterson.

Better—than Music! For I—who heard it. Emily Dickinson. CP-DickE

Better than this she / said as we were making. I Like You. James Laughlin. CP-LaugJ

Better that every fiber crack. Monologue at 3 A.M. Sylvia Plath. CP-PlatS

Better the wind, the sea, the salt. Look-out, The. "H. D." CP-DoolH

Better this way. Yannis Ritsos. SP-RitsY *Fr.* Paper Poems 1.

Better to be the rock above the river. La Crosse at Ninety Miles an Hour. Richard Eberhart. CP-EberR

Better wait. Henry David Thoreau. CP-ThorH

Better we all were in our graves. On a Printer's Being Sent to Newgate. Jonathan Swift. CP-SwifJ

Bettine, friend of Goethe. To Bettine. Elizabeth Barrett Browning. CP-BroEB

Betuix [*or* Betwix] twell houris and ellevin [*or* eleven]. Amendis [*or* Amends] to the Telyouris [*or* Tailors] and Sowtaris [*or* Soutaris *or* Soutars *or* Shoemakers]. William Dunbar. CP-DunbW

Between. Yehuda Amichai. SP-AmicY, *tr.* by Chana Bloch

Between. John Ciardi. CP-CiarJ

Between a meadow and a cloud that sped. G. K. Chesterton. *See* In scudding cloud on high steep meadows shed

Between a smoking fire and a tolling bell. Half Truth from Cape Town. Louis MacNeice. CP-MacNL

Between Adventure. W. H. Auden. CP-AudeW

Between air and the water, glows Puente Curvo. To Puente Curvo on the Maldonado Spit in Uruguay. Pablo Neruda. SP-NeruP

Between Angels & Monsters. Yusef Komunyakaa. CP-KomuY

Between attention and attention. Easy Knowledge. W. H. Auden. CP-AudeW

Between Days. Yusef Komunyakaa. CP-KomuY

Between death and the celebration of death. On Reading "The Love and Death of Cornet Christopher Rilke." Howard Nemerov. CP-NemeH

Between / end and beginning. We sit balanced. Peter Blue Cloud. SP-BlueP

Between extremities. Vacillation. William Butler Yeats. CP-YeatW

Between five and fifty. Praise. Jane Cooper. CP-CoopJ

Between five and seven this evening. Spell. Raymond Carver. CP-CarvR

Between green / mountains. E. E. Cummings. CP-CummE

Between her breasts is my home, between her breasts. Song of a Man Who Is Loved. D. H. Lawrence. CP-LawrD

Between Holmscote and Hurstcote. Down Stream. Dante Gabriel Rossetti. CW-RossD

Between identity and difference. Being of Three Minds. Howard Nemerov. CP-NemeH

Between March and April when barrows of daffodils butter the pavement. Street Scene. Louis MacNeice. CP-MacNL

Between Me and the Rock. Stanley Kunitz. CP-KunSC

Between me and the sunset, like a dome. Man against the Sky, The. Edwin Arlington Robinson. CP-RobiE

Between Mobile and Galveston. Annie. Guillaume Apollinaire. SP-MereW, *tr.* by William Meredith

Between Moon and Moon. Robert Graves. CP-GravR

Between My Country—and the Others. Emily Dickinson. CP-DickE

Between my finger and my thumb. Digging. Seamus Heaney. SP-HeanSO

Between my husband & my people, Samson. Dalila. George Meredith. CP-MerG2

Between my right big toe, sir, and my bent. Dogmatism. John Ciardi. CP-CiarJ

Between Nose and Eyes a strange contest arose. Report of an Adjudged Case. William Cowper. CP-CowpW

Between nose-red gross. E. E. Cummings. CP-CummE

Between official letters, I doodle the wet. To a Friend Far Away. A. K. Ramanujan. CP-RamaA

Between painting a roof yesterday and the hay. Independence Day. Wendell Berry. CP-BerrW

Between plunging valleys, on a bareback of hill. Football at Slack. Ted Hughes. SP-HughTN

Between pond and sheepbarn, by maples and watery birches. Sister on the Tracks, A. Donald Hall. CP-HallD

Between Session & Session. Jane Austen. CP-AustJ

Between sets. William Corbett. SP-CorbW

Between Shade and Sun. David Ignatow. SP-IgnaD

Between / slats of the garden. During Rain. Charles Tomlinson. CP-TomlC; SP-TomlC

Between Takes. Paul Muldoon. CP-MuldP

Between the Acts. Stanley Kunitz. CP-KunSC

Between the boughs the stars showed numberless. Ivor Gurney. SP-GurnI

Between the bream with cumin and the beef with marrow. Bangle, The. Paul Muldoon. CP-MuldP

Between the breasts / of bestial. E. E. Cummings. CP-CummE

Between the brown hands of a server-lad. Maundy Thursday. Wilfred Owen. CP-OwenW

"Between the Clock and the Bed." Donald Hall. CP-HallD

Between the computer, a pencil, and a typewriter. Self-Portrait. Adam Zagajewski. SP-ZagaA, *tr.* by Clare Cavanagh

Between the dark and the daylight. Children's Hour, The. Henry Wadsworth Longfellow. SP-LongH

Between the event and the word, golden. Composition in Gold and Red-Gold. Robert Penn Warren. CP-WarrR

Between the fear. Age of Terror. Denise Levertov. SP-LeveDL

Between the folding sea-downs. Re-Enactment, The. Thomas Hardy. CP-HardT

Between the form of Life and Life. Emily Dickinson. CP-DickE

Between the fountain and the rill. Alternation. George Meredith. CP-MerG1

Between the freeway / and the gray conning towers. Walk with Tom Jefferson, A. Philip Levine. SP-LeviP

Between the Gates. John Greenleaf Whittier. CP-WhitJ

Between the hands, between the brows. Love-Lily. Dante Gabriel Rossetti. CW-RossD

Between the illuminations of great mornings. Seeming, The. Muriel Rukeyser. CP-RukeM

Between / the image of it. Face and Image. Charles Tomlinson. CP-TomlC

Between the little clouds of heaven. Pastoral: "Between the little clouds of heaven." Langston Hughes. CP-HughL; CP-HughL3

Between the living world. Cold Pane, The. Wendell Berry. CP-BerrW

Between the long wars. Peace Between Wars. Carl Sandburg. CP-SandC

Between the masques of mist and green. Rainer Maria Rilke. CP-RilkFr, *tr.* by A. Poulin, Jr. *Fr.* Orchards.

Between the perfect marriage day. Creation Day. G. K. Chesterton. CP-ChesG

Between the Porch and the Altar. Robert Lowell. SP-LoweR

Between the red-top and the rye. Hawkweed, The. Edna St. Vincent Millay. CP-MillE

Between the river and the sea. Purgatory Blind. Charles Olson. CP-OlsoC

Between the traveller and the setting sun. Henry David Thoreau. CP-ThorH

Between the walls, the brim. Terce. James McMichael. SP-McMiJ

Between the waving tufts of jungle-grass. Rudyard Kipling. CP-KiplR

Between the Window and the Screen. Howard Nemerov. CP-NemeH

Between Trains. Robert Graves. CP-GravR

Between 2 and 5 p.m. and day and any time on Sunday and. Eating My Senior Citizen's Dinner at the Sizzler. Charles Bukowski. SP-BukC3

Between two burrs on the map. Serious Step Taken Lightly, A. Robert Frost. CP-FrosR

Between Two Hills. Carl Sandburg. CP-SandC

Between Two Prisoners. James Dickey. CP-DickJ

Between two rivers. Island ("Between two rivers"). Langston Hughes. CP-HughL; CP-HughL3 *Fr.* Lenox Avenue Mural.

Between Two Seas. Olga Broumas. SP-BrouO

Between two sister moorland rills. Danish Boy; A Fragment, The. William Wordsworth. CP-WorW1

Between us, always, loved one. Troubled Water. Langston Hughes. CP-HughL; CP-HughL3

Between Us Now. Thomas Hardy. CP-HardT

Between us on our wide bed we cuddle an incubus. Marilyn Hacker. SP-HackM *Fr.* Navigators, The.

Between Walls. William Carlos Williams. CP-WilW1

Between water & sky. Palm Tree. Federico García Lorca. CP-GarcF, *tr.* by Jerome Rothenberg *Fr.* Palm Tree, The.

Between Worlds. Carl Sandburg. CP-SandC

Between You and Me. Sam Hamill. SP-HamiS

Beucolick, or Discourse of Neatherds, A. Robert Herrick. CP-HerrR

Beverly / who wished his mother wanting a girl again. On the Death of a Middle-Aged Man. Miller Williams. CP-WillM

Bewail my chance: the sad book is returned. Elegy 1.12: "Bewail my chance: the sad book is returned." Ovid. CP-MarlC *Fr.* Elegies.

Bewail not much, my parents! me, the prey. On an Infant. Lucianus. CP-CowpW

Beware! Walter De la Mare. CP-DeLaW

Beware beware beware / because because because. E. E. Cummings. CP-CummE

Beware!—breathes the faint evening wind? Shadow. Walter De la Mare. CP-DeLaW

Beware, Madam! Robert Graves. CP-GravR

Beware, madam, of the witty devil. Beware, Madam! Robert Graves. CP-GravR

Beware, my friend! of crystal brook. On an Ugly Fellow. *Unknown.* CP-CowpW

Beware o' Bonie Ann. Robert Burns. CP-BurnR

Beware, O My Dear Young Men. D. H. Lawrence. CP-LawrD

Beware of building! I intended. Epigrams on His Garden Shed. William Cowper.

CP-CowpW

Beware the ball-point lens. New Year Wishes for the English. Donald Davie. CP-DaviDC

Beware the giddy spell, ground fallen away. East Wind, An. Robert Graves. CP-GravR

Beware! The Israelite of old, who tore. Warning, The. Henry Wadsworth Longfellow. SP-LongH

Beware the Man. Stevie Smith. CP-SmitS

Beware the man who's crossed in love. Rudyard Kipling. CP-KiplR *Fr.* Naulahka, The.

Beware the Unhappy Dead! D. H. Lawrence. CP-LawrD

Beware writing of freedom: the idea is political. Many Handles. Carl Sandburg. CP-SandC

Bewcastle now must keep the Hold. Defenceless Border, The. Sir Walter Scott. SP-ScotW *Fr.* Bridal of Trierman, The.

Bewick Finzer. Edwin Arlington Robinson. CP-RobiE

Bewildered with the broken tongue. Words in Time. Archibald MacLeish. CP-MacLA

Bewildering Emotions. James Whitcomb Riley. CP-RileJ *Fr.* Child-World, A.

Beyond. Robert Creeley. SP-CreeR

Beyond. Laura Riding Jackson. CP-RidiL

Beyond. C. K. Williams. CP-WillC

Beyond a twilight of limes and willows. Evening Thrush. Ted Hughes. SP-HughTN

Beyond all this, the wish to be alone. Wants. Philip Larkin. CP-LarkP

Beyond God. Fernando Pessoa. SP-PessF, *tr.* by Susan M. Brown *and* Edwin Honig

Beyond Howth Head. Derek Mahon. CP-MahoD

Beyond impasse. Clarence Major. SP-MajoC

Beyond King Ptolemy's dream. Out There There Be Dragons. Yusef Komunyakaa. CP-KomuY

Beyond Magdalen and by the Bridge, on a place called there the Plain. Cheery Beggar. Gerard Manley Hopkins. CP-HopkG

Beyond Nagel's Funeral Parlor. Elizabethans Called It Dying, The. James Schuyler. CP-SchuJ

Beyond Reason. Stanley Kunitz. CP-KunSC

Beyond Seattle. Thomas McGrath. SP-McGrT

Beyond surprise, my ribs start up from the ground. Defeated, The. W. S. Merwin. SP-MerwW

Beyond th' old Pillars many have travelled. Sir John Wingfield. John Donne. CP-DonnJ; MW-DonnJ

Beyond that stand of firs. Late Answer, A. Philip Levine. SP-LeviP

Beyond the Alps. Robert Lowell. SP-LoweR

Beyond the bright cartoons. Far Out. Philip Larkin. CP-LarkP

Beyond the brittle towns asleep. E. E. Cummings. CP-CummE

Beyond the cornfields and the wood. Parted. Paul Laurence Dunbar. CP-DunbP

Beyond the Dark Cedars. Kenneth Patchen. CP-PatcK

Beyond the eye, grasses go over the long fields. Purgation. James Dickey. CP-DickJ

Beyond the great valley an odd instinctive rising. Ascent to the Sierras. Robinson Jeffers. CP-JefR1

Beyond the haze of alcohol and syntax and. Cocktail Party. Robert Penn Warren. CP-WarrR

Beyond the hour we counted rain that fell. Old Countryside. Louise Bogan. CP-BogaL

Beyond the Hudson's. Undertaking in New Jersey, The. George Oppen. CP-OppGN

Beyond the last flamed escarpment of mountain cloud. Eagle Descending. Robert Penn Warren. CP-WarrR

Beyond the last house, where mine was. American Portrait: Old Style. Robert Penn Warren. CP-WarrR

Beyond the Last Lamp. Thomas Hardy. CP-HardT

Beyond the meadow still where sweeps. George Meredith. CP-MerG2

Beyond the Moon. Nicholas Vachel Lindsay. CP-LindV

Beyond the moor and mountain crest. West, The. A. E. Housman. CP-HousA

Beyond the narrows of the Inner Hebrides. Now Returned Home. Robinson Jeffers. CP-JefR2

Beyond the Pale. Rudyard Kipling. *Fr.* Plain Tales from the Hills.

Beyond the path of the outmost sun through utter darkness hurled. Dedication from "Barrack-Room Ballads." Rudyard Kipling. CP-KiplR

Beyond the Pleasure Principle. Howard Nemerov. CP-NemeH

Beyond the purple, hazy trees. Used-to-Be, The. James Whitcomb Riley. CP-RileJ

Beyond the Red River. Thomas McGrath. SP-McGrT

Beyond the river, they believe. Indians' Belief in a Future State, The. Jones Very. CP-VeryJ

Beyond the Rockies. D. H. Lawrence. CP-LawrD

Beyond the sea, in a green land. How One Chose. Christina Georgina Rossetti. CP-RosC3

Beyond the Second Landing. Eleanor Wilner. SP-WilnE

Beyond the Sierras, and sage-brush Nevada ranges. Red Mountain. Robinson Jeffers. CP-JefR2

Beyond the Snow Belt. Mary Oliver. SP-OlivM

Beyond the stolid iron pond. E. E. Cummings. CP-CummE

Beyond the symbol's exactions, we transform. Poet's Bestiary. Robert Stock. SP-StocR

Beyond the trees like iron trees. Old Gentleman in the Park, The. G. K. Chesterton. CP-ChesG

Beyond the Years. Paul Laurence Dunbar. CP-DunbP

Beyond them, hill and field. Wyeth's Mild Cans. Richard Wilbur. CP-WilbR

Beyond this bitter shore there is no going. Three Poems. Robert Penn Warren. CP-WarrR

Beyond this final house. Boone. Wendell Berry CP-BerrW

Beyond this road the blackness bends. Sanine to Leda. Robert Creeley. CP-CreeR

Beyond truth, / tenacity: of those. Margaret Atwood. SP-AtwM1

Beyond What. Lorine Niedecker. CP-NiedL

Beyond What. Alice Walker. CP-WalkA

Beyond Words. Robert Frost. CP-FrosR

Beyond You. W. S. Merwin. SP-MerwW

Bheinn Naomh. Kathleen Jessie Raine. SP-RainK

Bi-Focal. William Stafford. SP-StafW; SP-StafWW

Bi-lingual. Andrei Codrescu. SP-CodrA

Bianca Among the Nightingales. Elizabeth Barrett Browning. CP-BroEB

Biancha, Let / Me pay the debt. Kissing Usurie. Robert Herrick. CP-HerrR

Biased Man, The. Yannis Ritsos. SP-RitsY, *tr.* by N. C. Germanacos

Bibber besotted, with scowl of a cur, having heart of a deer, thou! Homer. CP-MerG1 *Fr.* Iliad, The.

Bibbles. D. H. Lawrence. CP-LawrD

Bibe a Ponte all'Asse. Eugenio Montale. CP-MontE, *tr.* by Jonathan Galassi

Bibe, easy host, your brown-haired little Queen of Sheba. Bibe a Ponte all'Asse. Eugenio Montale. CP-MontE, *tr.* by Jonathan Galassi

Bible, The. Jones Very. CP-VeryJ

Bible and the other books, The. Readers, The. Laura Riding Jackson. CP-RidiL

Bible Belt. Langston Hughes. CP-HughL; CP-HughL3

Bible Does Not Sanction Polygamy, The. Jones Very. CP-VeryJ

Bible is an antique Volume, The. Emily Dickinson. CP-DickE

Bible Lady, The. James Laughlin. CP-LaugJ

Biblical Meditations. Yehuda Amichai. SP-AmicYL, *tr.* by Benjamin Harshav *and* Barbara Harshav

Biblical Tree, The. George Oppen. CP-OppGN

Bibliographers, The. Geoffrey Hill. CP-HillG

Bibulous eagle behind me at the ball game, The. One to Nothing. Carolyn Kizer. CP-KizeC

Bice laughs, when no man speaks; and doth protest. Upon Bice. Robert Herrick. CP-HerrR

Bicentennial. John Ciardi. CP-CiarJ

Bicentennial. Robert Penn Warren. CP-WarrR

Bicoastal Journal. Charles Wright. SP-WrigC

Bicycle Chain. A. John Updike. CP-UpdiJ

Bicycles and the Apex, The. George Oppen. CP-OppGN

Bid a strong ghost stand at the head. Prayer for My Son, A. William Butler Yeats. CP-YeatW

Bid adieu, my sad heart, bid adieu to thy peace. William Cowper. CP-CowpW

Bid all profane away. Ben Jonson. CP-JonsB *Fr.* Masque of Hymen.

Bid me to live, and I will live. To Anthea, Who May Command Him Anything. Robert Herrick. CP-HerrR

Bid toad sits in my writing room, The. March 7th. Anne Sexton. CP-SextA

Bidden Guest, The. Geoffrey Hill. CP-HillG

Bideford! Nothing will do. Fare Thee Well. Donald Davie. CP-DaviDC

Bifurcation. Robert Browning. CP-BroR2

Big anchor stuck in the yard, A. It will wait for eternity. Museum at Akhziv. Yehuda Amichai. SP-AmicYL, *tr.* by Benjamin Harshav *and* Barbara Harshav

Big-assed, A. American Love. Robert Creeley. SP-CreeR

Big Bang. William Stafford. SP-StafWW

Big Bastard with a Sword. Charles Bukowski. SP-BukC2

Big Beat. Allen Ginsberg. CP-GinsA

Big Billie Potts was big and stout. Ballad of Billie Potts, The. Robert Penn Warren. CP-WarrR

Big black beard. Guru. Charles Bukowski. SP-BukC1

Big Boots of Pain, The. Anne Sexton. CP-SextA

Big Boy came / Carrying a mermaid. Catch. Langston Hughes. CP-HughL; CP-HughL2

Big bud of moon hangs out of the twilight, A. Liaison. D. H. Lawrence. CP-LawrD

Big Buddy, Big Buddy. Langston Hughes. CP-HughL; CP-HughL2

Big Daddy Lipscomb, who used to help them up. Say Good-bye to Big Daddy. Randall Jarrell. CP-JarrR

Big enough for the two of us. Overcoat, The. Charles Simic. SP-SimiCE

Big family, The. Mutchmore and Not-So. Stevie Smith. CP-SmitS

Big Fat Fly, A. Charles Olson. CP-OlsoC

Big Foot. Paul Muldoon. CP-MuldP

Big guns again. / No speakee well. Imperator Victus. Hart Crane. CP-CranH

Big Harpe, Little Harpe. Theory of Evil. Robert Earl Hayden. CP-HaydR

Big Heart, The. Anne Sexton. CP-SextA

Big-hipped nature burst forth the head of god. May Swenson. SP-SwenM

Big House, The. Paul Muldoon. CP-MuldP

Big House, The. William Stafford. SP-StafWW

Big Ideas among Earthlings. Heather McHugh. SP-McHuH

Big John of Echo Park. Charles Bukowski. SP-BukC3

Big lad with too much face, The. Lunch Wagon on Highway 57. Kenneth Patchen. CP-PatcK

Big Liz. Paul Muldoon. CP-MuldP

Big Max. Charles Bukowski. SP-BukC1

Big mercy and little mercy big mercy. Cracks. C. K. Williams. CP-WillC

Big missal splayed, The. In Illo Tempore. Seamus Heaney. SP-HeanSO *Fr.* Sweeney Redivivus.

Big mountains sit still in the afternoon light, The. Sinners. D. H. Lawrence. CP-LawrD

Big part of this page (a big part of my head), A. Homage to St. Patrick, García Lorca, & the Itinerant Grocer. Philip Whalen. SP-WhalP

Big People, The. César Vallejo. CP-WrigJ

Big Picture, The. Thomas Lux. SP-LuxT

Big Rock. Richard Eberhart. CP-EberR

Big sloppy wounded dog. Winter. Charles Bukowski. SP-BukC1

Big star, and that other, The. Leaflets. Adrienne Rich. CP-RicAE; SP-RicA2

Big Steamers. Rudyard Kipling. CP-KiplR

Big stones of the cistern behind the barn, The. Twilights. James Wright. CP-WrigJ

Big Sur. Langston Hughes. CP-HughL; CP-HughL2

Big Sur: Partington Cove. John Logan. CP-LogaJ

Big Tent Under the Roof, The. Ogden Nash. CP-NashO

Big-Timer, The. Langston Hughes. CP-HughL; CP-HughL1

Big top billowing, The. Family Act, The. Wyatt Prunty. SP-PrunW

Big voices in the womanless kitchen. Aye. Seamus Heaney. SP-HeanSO *Fr.* Loaning, The.

Big Wind. Theodore Roethke. CP-RoetT

Big, wise / man. The happy. Indians. Robert Creeley. CP-CreeR

Big young bareheaded woman, A. Proletarian Portrait. William Carlos Williams. CP-WilW1

Bigger the box the more it holds, The. Boxes and Bags. Carl Sandburg. CP-SandC

Bight, The. Elizabeth Bishop. CP-BishE

Bigmans. Charles Olson. CP-OlsoC

Bigmans II. Charles Olson. CP-OlsoC

Bigness of cannon, The. E. E. Cummings. CP-CummE

Bigotry's Victim. Percy Bysshe Shelley. CP-ShelP

Bigwigs wrote from Boston: Thure. Thure Kumlien. Lorine Niedecker. CP-NiedL

Bilbea. Carl Sandburg. CP-SandC

Bilbea, I was in Babylon on Saturday night. Bilbea. Carl Sandburg. CP-SandC

Bill 'Awkins. Rudyard Kipling. CP-KiplR

Bill before his death. George Oppen. CP-OppGN

Bill Burroughs in Tangiers slowly transfiguring into sanctity season after. Fragment: The Names II. Allen Ginsberg. CP-GinsA

Bill of Fare. Hans Magnus Enzensberger. SP-EnzeH, *tr.* by Michael Hamburger

Bill on the way you saw. So Much Depends. James Laughlin. CP-LaugJ

Bill, The. Muriel Rukeyser. CP-RukeM

Billboards and Galleons. Nicholas Vachel Lindsay. CP-LindV

Billboards and the street car signs told the people, The. Bitter Summer Thoughts—No. XXII. Carl Sandburg. CP-SandC

Billet. Ivor Gurney. SP-GurnI

Billet to the Company of Players. Jonathan Swift. CP-SwifJ

Billfold. Robert Creeley. CP-CreeR

Billie Holiday. Hayden Carruth. CP-CarHS

Billings and Cooings from "The Berkeley Barb." Mona Van Duyn. SP-VanDM

Billion Freedoms, The. Kenneth Patchen. CP-PatcK

Billows on the beach are leaping around it, The. To William Shelley. Percy Bysshe Shelley. CP-ShelP

Bill's. Clarence Major. SP-MajoC

Billy and His Drum. James Whitcomb Riley. CP-RileJ

Billy Budd, Foretopman. Herman Melville.

  Billy in the Darbies. SP-MelvH

Billy Could Ride. James Whitcomb Riley. CP-RileJ

Billy Goodin'. James Whitcomb Riley. CP-RileJ

Billy in the Darbies. Herman Melville. SP-MelvH *Fr.* Billy Budd, Foretopman.

Billy Miller's Circus-Show. James Whitcomb Riley. CP-RileJ

Billy's Alphabetical Animal Show. James Whitcomb Riley. CP-RileJ

Bin a-Fishin'. James Whitcomb Riley. CP-RileJ

Binah. Kathleen Jessie Raine. SP-RainK

Bind fast my hands, they have deservéd chains. Elegy 1.7: "Bind fast my hands, they have deservéd chains." Ovid. CP-MarlC *Fr.* Elegies.

Bind me but to thee with thine haire. Bondman, The. Robert Herrick. CP-HerrR

Bind me—I still can sing. Emily Dickinson. CP-DickE

Bind up thy tresses, thou beautiful one. Stanzas: "Bind up thy tresses, thou beautiful one." John Greenleaf Whittier. CP-WhitJ

Binding the Dragon. May Sarton. SP-SartM

Bindweed. John Updike. CP-UpdiJ

Bindweed, The. Walter De la Mare. CP-DeLaW

Binnacle, The. Ambrose Bierce. SP-BierA

Binnacle, The. Charles Olson. CP-OlsoC

Binocular owl, The. Woods at Night, The. May Swenson. SP-SwenM

Binsey Poplars (Felled 1879). Gerard Manley Hopkins. CP-HopkG

Biographical Notes. Andrei Codrescu. SP-CodrA

Biographies. Dorothy Parker. CP-ParkD

Biography. John Ciardi. CP-CiarJ

Biography. Carl Sandburg. CP-SandC

Biography. William Stafford. SP-StafWW

Biography, The. Thomas Merton. CP-MertT

Biography first convinces us. Emily Dickinson. SP-DickE

Biography of a Myth, The. Laura Riding Jackson. CP-RidiL

Biography of an Artist. Czeslaw Milosz. CP-MiloCN, *tr.* by Robert Hass

Biography of Southern Rain. Kenneth Patchen. CP-PatcK

Biography of the Author: A Cento, A. Charles Tomlinson. CP-TomlC

Biography, sirs, should begin—with the breath of a man, A. Biography. Carl Sandburg. CP-SandC

Biological Reflection. Ogden Nash. CP-NashO

Biotherm [for Bill Berkson]. Frank O'Hara. SP-OharF

Birch begins to crack its outer sheath, The. Young Birch, A. Robert Frost. CP-FrosR

Birchbrook Mill. John Greenleaf Whittier. CP-WhitJ

Birches. Robert Frost. CP-FrosR

Birches are mad with green points, The. Portrait of the Author. William Carlos Williams. CP-WilW1

Birches stand in their beggar's row, The. February: The Boy Breughel. Norman Dubie. CP-DubiN

Birchington Churchyard. Christina Georgina Rossetti. CP-RosC2

Bird. Pablo Neruda. SP-NeruP

Bird. William Carlos Williams. CP-WilW2

Bird, A. Fountain Piece. May Swenson. SP-SwenM

Bird, The. Robert Creeley. CP-CreeR

Bird, The. David Ignatow. SP-IgnaD

Bird, The. Charles Simic. SP-SimiC; SP-SimiCE

Bird and the Muse. Marya Alexandrovna Zaturenska. SP-ZatuM

Bird, bird don't edge me in. Reply, The. Theodore Roethke. CP-RoetT

Bird-bones is on the roof. Seventy-eight. Sketching a Thatcher. Ted Hughes. SP-HughTN

Bird book says, common, conspicuous, The. Patch Work. Thom Gunn. CP-GunnT

Bird calls me, A. Bird, The. Charles Simic. SP-SimiC; SP-SimiCE

Bird calls rise / and drop. Theories. Rae Armantrout. SP-ArmaA

Bird came down the Walk, A. Emily Dickinson. CP-DickE

Bird-Catcher's Boy, The. Thomas Hardy. CP-HardT

Bird delegation came to Solomon complaining, A. Jelaluddin Rumi. SP-Rumi, *tr.* by Coleman Barks

Bird delicious to the taste, A. Rebus, by *I. B.*, A. James Bowdoin. CP-WheaP

Bird did prance—the Bee did play, The. Emily Dickinson. CP-DickE

Bird-dream and peeling wallpaper. Night They Took Whitey, The. Charles Bukowski. SP-BukC2

Bird feeder's. March. Lorine Niedecker. CP-NiedL

Bird fills up the, A. Center. A. R. Ammons. CP-AmmoA

Bird flew out at the break of day, A. Ballad of God-Makers, The. G. K. Chesterton. CP-ChesG

Bird flew out of a cloud, A. Woman and Emblems. Muriel Rukeyser. CP-RukeM

Bird / flies / out the / window. She / flies, The. 3 in 1. Robert Creeley. CP-CreeR

Bird Footprint. Carl Sandburg. CP-SandC

Bird Frau, The. Rita Dove. SP-DoveR

Bird half wakened in the lunar moon, A. On a Bird Singing in its Sleep. Robert Frost. CP-FrosR

Bird her punctual music brings, The. Emily Dickinson. CP-DickE

Bird in Orbit. Langston Hughes. CP-HughL; CP-HughL3

Bird in the Laurel's Song, The. Eleanor Wilner. SP-WilnE

Bird in Whatever Name, The. John Ciardi. CP-CiarJ

Bird inside a Box a box will, A. William Stafford. SP-StafWW

Bird kept saying that birds had once been men, The. On an Old Horn. Wallace Stevens. CP-StevW; CP-StevWP

Bird Killer, The. Wendell Berry. CP-BerrW

Bird-Language. W. H. Auden. CP-AudeW

Bird must sing to earn the Crumb, The. Emily Dickinson. CP-DickE

Bird of ash has appeared at windows, The. Recognition. W. S. Merwin. SP-MerwW

Bird of Endless Time, The. James Laughlin. CP-LaugJ

Bird of Night, The. Randall Jarrell. CP-JarrR

Bird of Paradise. Robert Graves. CP-GravR

Bird of the spray, the tree of bones. Loss. Randall Jarrell. CP-JarrR

Bird or Beast? Christina Georgina Rossetti. CP-RosC1

Bird / perched on a swordlike branch throws me the key, A. Discovery of Prayer, The. Andrei Codrescu. SP-CodrA

Bird-Queen, The. Kenneth Patchen. CP-PatcK

Bird Raptures. Christina Georgina Rossetti. CP-RosC1

Bird Sanctuary. Derek Mahon. CP-MahoD

Bird sat on a red handle, The. Understandings in Blue. Carl Sandburg. CP-SandC

Bird-Scene at a Rural Dwelling, A. Thomas Hardy. CP-HardT

Bird sighs for the air. Lover's Song, The. William Butler Yeats. CP-YeatW

Bird singing. Lorine Niedecker. CP-NiedL

Bird sings the selfsame song, A. Selfsame Song, The. Thomas Hardy. CP-HardT

Bird Song. William Carlos Williams. CP-WilW2

Bird Song, A. Christina Georgina Rossetti. CP-RosC1

Bird song is flute song and a glory. Thrush Song at Dawn. Richard Eberhart. CP-EberR

Bird-soul was ashamed, The. From "Bird Conversations" Farid-uddin Attar. CP-EmerR

Bird Talk. Carl Sandburg. CP-SandC

Bird that cries like a baby, The. Louis Zukofsky. CP-ZukLS

Bird that feeds from off my palm, The. Ornithology for Beginners. Dorothy Parker. CP-ParkD

Bird that has no nest, The. Fox and the Bird, The. Jones Very. CP-VeryJ

Bird that I don't know, A. Country Life, A. Randall Jarrell. CP-JarrR

Bird that sings to itself, The. Whistle or Hoot. David Ignatow. SP-IgnaD

Bird, that's fetch't from Phasis floud, The. Out of Petronius. Petronius Arbiter. CP-CrasR, tr. by Richard Crashaw

Bird, the Bird, the Bird, The. Robert Creeley. CP-CreeR

Bird was flying toward me, The. Bird, The. David Ignatow. SP-IgnaD

Bird was gone the ghastly trees, The. Ralph Waldo Emerson. CP-EmerR

Bird watchers top my honors list. Up from the Egg; the Confessions of a Nuthatch Avoider. Ogden Nash. CP-NashO

Bird Watching. John Ciardi. CP-CiarJ

Bird, who for his other sins, A. Character, A. Samuel Taylor Coleridge. CP-ColeS; MW-ColeS

Bird who watches me, The. Peaceful Kingdom. Charles Simic. SP-SimiC; SP-SimiCE

Bird-Window-Flying. Tess Gallagher. SP-GallT

Bird winging through space, A. Premonitions. David Ignatow. SP-IgnaD

Bird with a name it does not itself, A. Bird in Whatever Name, The. John Ciardi. CP-CiarJ

Bird with outstretched. Bird. William Carlos Williams. CP-WilW2

Bird with the Coppery, Keen Claws, The. Wallace Stevens. CP-StevW; CP-StevWP

Bird with the Dark Plumes, The. Robinson Jeffers. CP-JefR1

Bird-witted. Marianne Craig Moore. CP-MoorM

Bird would be a soundless thing, The. Emily Dickinson. SP-DickE

Birdbrain! Allen Ginsberg. CP-GinsA; SP-GinsA

Birdbrain runs the World! Birdbrain! Allen Ginsberg. CP-GinsA; SP-GinsA

Birdcage Walk. D. H. Lawrence. CP-LawrD

Birdcage Walk. Thomas Merton. CP-MertT

Birdham. Amy Clampitt. CP-ClamA

Birdie. W. S. Merwin. SP-MerwWF

Birdies, Don't Make Me Laugh. Ogden Nash. CP-NashO

Birdless, the bush yet shakes. Encounter. Charles Tomlinson. CP-TomlC

Birdlife. Derek Mahon. CP-MahoD

Birds. Robinson Jeffers. CP-JefR1

Birds. Clarence Major. SP-MajoC

Birds. James Schuyler. CP-SchuJ

Birds, The. William Blake. CP-BlakW

Birds, The. Robert Creeley. CP-CreeR

Birds, The. Josephine Jacobsen. CP-JacoJ

Birds, The. Ogden Nash. CP-NashO

Birds, The. Jones Very. CP-VeryJ

Birds, The. William Carlos Williams. CP-WilW1

Birds about the house pretend to be, The. Return of the Evening Grosbeaks, The. Adrienne Rich. CP-RicAE

Birds acquaint themselves with leaves. Reveille. Joseph Brodsky. CP-BrodJ

Birds afloat in air's current. In Whom We Live and Move and Have Our Being. Denise Levertov. SP-LeveDS

Birds against the April wind, The. What the Birds Said. John Greenleaf Whittier. CP-WhitJ

Birds and Fishes. Robinson Jeffers. CP-JefR3

Birds and Flowers. William Carlos Williams. CP-WilW1

Birds and periodic blood. 5:30 A.M. Adrienne Rich. CP-RicAE; SP-RicA1; SP-RicA2

Birds are flowers flying. Mirrorment. A. R. Ammons. CP-AmmoA

Birds are on fire, The. Singing Is Fire. Charles Bukowski. SP-BukC2

Birds are singing still their songs, The. Birds, The. Jones Very. CP-VeryJ

Birds—are they worth remembering?, The. Wingtip. Carl Sandburg. CP-SandC

Birds are very bold this Morning, The. Emily Dickinson. SP-DickE

Birds at Winter Nightfall. Thomas Hardy. CP-HardT

Birds begin as an isolated shower, The. Elizabeth. Paul Muldoon. CP-MuldP

Birds begun at Four o'clock, The. Emily Dickinson. CP-DickE

Birds build but not I build, no, but wipe, Time's wife. Caring for Surfaces. Mona Van Duyn. SP-VanDM

Bird's Companion, The. William Carlos Williams. CP-WilW1

Birds don't fly through my skylight nowadays. 1972. Joseph Brodsky. CP-BrodJ, tr. by Alan Myers

Birds don't just say it just once. If they like it. New Every Day. William Stafford. SP-StafWW

Birds everywhere are talking, The. For George (II). Grace Paley. CP-PalGC

Bird's-Eye View, A. Christina Georgina Rossetti. CP-RosC1

Bird's-Eye View of the Tool and Die Co. John Ashbery. SP-AshbJ

Birds' feet and baby feet. Writing on Sand. Charles Tomlinson. CP-TomlC; SP-TomlC

Birds flying high above the retreating army! Variation in V. Joseph Brodsky. CP-BrodJ

Birds from Parnassus, / swift. Euripides. CP-DoolH Fr. Ion.

Birds have a finer body and tinier brain—. Das ewig Weibliche. Robert Lowell. SP-LoweR

Birds have flown away from the mountains, The. Chung Yuan Liu. CP-WilW2

Birds have flown their summer skies to the south, The. Beyond the Red River. Thomas McGrath. SP-McGrT

Birds(/ here,inven / ting air). E. E. Cummings. CP-CummE

Birds in a whirl, drift to the rooftops, This Poem Is for Birds. Gary Snyder. CP-SnydG Fr. Myths and Texts.

Birds in Snow. "H. D." CP-DoolH

Birds in the gardens of Avignon, The. Voyage en Provence. Archibald MacLeish. CP-MacLA

Birds jab at / the evening. 6:00 p.m. Federico García Lorca. CP-GarcF, tr. by Jerome Rothenberg Fr. Summer Hours.

Birds, like Thoughts. John Ciardi. CP-CiarJ

Birds' mating-fight. Lorine Niedecker. CP-NiedL

Birds meet above the new Moon. E. E. Cummings. CP-CummE

Birds of Killingworth, The (The Poet's Tale). Henry Wadsworth Longfellow. SP-LongH Fr. Tales of a Wayside Inn.

Birds of Passage, The. Jones Very. CP-VeryJ

"Birds of Prey" March. Rudyard Kipling. CP-KiplR

Birds of the islands: in your gathering. "Rubén Dario." SP-DariR, tr. by Alberto Acereda and Will Derusha

Birds of Vietnam, The. Hayden Carruth. CP-CarHS

Birds on a Powerline. Yusef Komunyakaa. CP-KomuY

Birds on the Morning of Going, The. W. S. Merwin. SP-MerwW

Birds put off their ev'ry hue, The. On Mrs. Montagu's Feather-Hangings. William Cowper. CP-CowpW

Birds reported from the South, The. Emily Dickinson. CP-DickE

Birds return without a rhyme or reason, The. Yehuda Amichai. SP-AmicYL Fr. Here We Loved.

Birds Returning. Wisława Szymborska. SP-SzymWM, tr. by Joanna Trzeciak

Birds, singing and lamenting once again. Petrarch. CP-Petra, tr. by J. G. Nichols

Birds' Voices in the Tree Tops. Jaroslav Seifert. SP-SeifJ, tr. by Ewald Osers

Birds whistled, all. Amorous Debate, An. Thom Gunn. CP-GunnT

Birdsnest built on the palm of the high, A. Lightness. Richard Wilbur. CP-WilbR

Birdsong, The. William Carlos Williams. CP-WilW2

Birdsong brings relief. Jelaluddin Rumi. SP-Rumi, tr. by Coleman Barks

Birdsong diminishes. History of Solitude, A. Adam Zagajewski. SP-ZagaA, tr. by Renata Gorczynski, Benjamin Ivry and C. K. Williams

Birdsong from Inside the Egg. Jelaluddin Rumi. SP-Rumi, tr. by Coleman Barks

Birdsong. May. Tuscany. A house. Sunset. Bronze. James Merrill. SP-MerrJ

Birdsong of the Lesser Poet. Josephine Jacobsen. CP-JacoJ

Birdwings. Jelaluddin Rumi. SP-Rumi, *tr. by* Coleman Barks

Birks of Aberfeldy, The [Composed on the Spot]. Robert Burns. CP-BurnR (Now simmer blinks on flowery braes.) CP-BurnR

Birmingham. Louis MacNeice. CP-MacNL

Birmingham Sunday. Langston Hughes. CP-HughL; CP-HughL3

Birth. Langston Hughes. CP-HughL; CP-HughL2

Birth. Czeslaw Milosz. CP-MiloC; CP-MiloCN, *tr. by* Peter Dale Scott

Birth, A. James Dickey. CP-DickJ

Birth, A. Muriel Rukeyser. CP-RukeM

Birth, The. Paul Muldoon. CP-MuldP

Birth, The. William Carlos Williams. CP-WilW2

Birth and Death. Richard Eberhart. CP-EberR

Birth and Death. Robinson Jeffers. CP-JefR3

Birth and death are decreed. Han-shan. CP-ColdM, *tr. by* Red Pine

Birth-Bond, The. Dante Gabriel Rossetti. CW-RossD *Fr.* House of Life, The.

Birth Comes to the Archbishop. Ogden Nash. CP-NashO

Birth Day Ode, A. Annis Boudinot Stockton. CP-StocA

Birth-Day Ode. December 31st 1787, A. Robert Burns. CP-BurnR

Birth-day of the Soul how sweet its dawn! Birth-Day of the Soul, The. Jones Very. CP-VeryJ

Birth-Day of the Soul, The. Jones Very. CP-VeryJ

Birth-Dues. Robinson Jeffers. CP-JefR1

Birth I gave you in a desert. Lullaby: "Birth I gave you in a desert." Joseph Brodsky. CP-BrodJ

Birth is the starting point of passion. Fog Numbers. Carl Sandburg. CP-SandC

Birth (Near Port William), The. Wendell Berry. CP-BerrW

Birth Night. D. H. Lawrence. CP-LawrD

Birth of a Goddess. Robert Graves. CP-GravR

Birth of Angels. Robert Graves. CP-GravR

Birth of Christ, The. Federico García Lorca. CP-GarcF, *tr. by* Greg Simon *and* Steven F. White

Birth of color / out of night and the ground. April Woods: Morning. Wendell Berry. CP-BerrW

Birth of Language, The. Lucille Clifton. SP-ClifL

Birth of Love. Robert Penn Warren. CP-WarrR

Birth of Love, The. William Wordsworth. CP-WorW1

Birth of Pleasure, The. Percy Bysshe Shelley. CP-ShelP

Birth of Rainbow. Ted Hughes. SP-HughTN

Birth of Seventh Avenue, The. His Hands Have Five Knives Each. Alan Dugan. CP-DugaA

Birth of the Spirit, The. Richard Eberhart. CP-EberR

Birth of the Sun, The. Pablo Antonio Cuadra. CP-MertT, *tr. by* Thomas Merton

Birth of Venus, The. Hayden Carruth. CP-CarHS

Birth of Venus, The. Randall Jarrell. CP-JarrR

Birth of Venus, The. Muriel Rukeyser. CP-RukeM

Birth of Venus, The. William Carlos Williams. CP-WilW2

Birthday. Yehuda Amichai. SP-AmicYL, *tr. by* Benjamin Harshav *and* Barbara Harshav

Birthday. John Ciardi. CP-CiarJ

Birthday. David Ignatow. SP-IgnaD

Birthday. Robinson Jeffers. CP-JefR3

Birthday. D. H. Lawrence. CP-LawrD

Birthday. May Swenson. SP-SwenM

Birthday. Wisława Szymborska. SP-SzymW, *tr. by* Stanislaw Barańczak *and* Clare Cavanagh

Birthday, A. Robert Creeley. CP-CreeR

Birthday, A. W. S. Merwin. SP-MerwWF

Birthday, A. Christina Georgina Rossetti. CP-RosC1

Birthday, The. Jay Wright. SP-WrigJ

Birthday (Autobiography). Robinson Jeffers. CP-JefR3

Birthday Book, A. Gertrude Stein. CP-SteiG

Birthday Card for a Psychiatrist. Mona Van Duyn. SP-VanDM

Birthday Dream, The. James Dickey. CP-DickJ

Birthday Exercise, A. William Meredith. SP-MereW

Birthday Memorial to Seventh Street, A. Audre Lorde. SP-LordA

Birthday 1999. Lucille Clifton. SP-ClifL

Birthday of but a single pang. Emily Dickinson. CP-DickE

Birthday on the Acropolis. May Sarton. SP-SartM

Birthday on the Beach. Ogden Nash. CP-NashO

Birthday Party, The. Josephine Jacobsen. CP-JacoJ

Birthday Poem. Thom Gunn. CP-GunnT

Birthday Poem. Maxine W. Kumin. SP-KumiM

Birthday Poem. Philip Whalen. SP-WhalP

Birthday Poem for a Childless Man. Carolyn Kizer. CP-KizeC

Birthday Poem on the Anniversary of the Birth of the Rev. Dr. Swift, D. S. P. D.

Nov. 30, 1737, A. Thomas Sheridan. CP-SherT

Birthday Present, A. Sylvia Plath. CP-PlatS

Birthday Song. Yusef Komunyakaa. CP-KomuY

Birthday Wreath, The. John Greenleaf Whittier. CP-WhitJ

Birthdays. A. K. Ramanujan. CP-RamaA

Birthdays come and go. Birthdays. A. K. Ramanujan. CP-RamaA

Birthmark: The Pretext. Rae Armantrout. SP-ArmaA

Birthnight: To F, The. Walter De la Mare. CP-DeLaW

Birthplace, The. Robert Frost. CP-FrosR

Birthplace, The. Seamus Heaney. SP-HeanSO

Birthplace: New Rochelle. George Oppen. CP-OppGN

Birthplace of Mr. William Shakespeare author, The. Verses for a Centennial. Archibald MacLeish. CP-MacLA

Birthright. Louis MacNeice. CP-MacNL

Birthright, The. Rudyard Kipling. CP-KiplR *Fr.* Debits and Credits.

Birthright Church, The. Jones Very. CP-VeryJ

Birthright church; where shall we find its door, The. Birthright Church, The. Jones Very. CP-VeryJ

Birth's Obituary. Charles Olson. CP-OlsoC

Bisara of Pooree, The. Rudyard Kipling. *Fr.* Plain Tales from the Hills.

Bisection. Dan Pagis. SP-PagiD, *tr. by* Stephen Mitchell

Bishop, The. Paul Muldoon. CP-MuldP

Bishop Blougram's Apology. Robert Browning. CP-BroR1

Bishop Orders His Tomb at Saint Praxed's Church, The. Robert Browning. CP-BroR1; SP-BroR

Bishop Tutu's Visit to the White House: 1984. C. K. Williams. SP-WillC

Bishops of the Church of England, The. Stevie Smith. CP-SmitS

Bismillah. Jelaluddin Rumi. SP-Rumi, *tr. by* Coleman Barks

Bison Crossing Near Mt. Rushmore. May Swenson. SP-SwenM

Bison, or tiger, or whatever beast, The. In the Crevice of Time. Josephine Jacobsen. CP-JacoJ

Bit an apple on its red. Green Red Brown and White. May Swenson. SP-SwenM

Bit Different, A. James Laughlin. CP-LaugJ

Bit of talcum, A. Reflection on Babies. Ogden Nash. CP-NashO

Bit of yarrow and then of rue, A. Bouquet in Dog Time. Hayden Carruth. CP-CarHS

Bitch. Carolyn Kizer. CP-KizeC

Bitch that was full pregnant grown, A. Fable of the Bitches, The. Jonathan Swift. CP-SwifJ

Bitcheries of Madison Avenue, The. Hayden Carruth. CP-CarHS *Fr.* Bloomingdale Papers, The.

Bites and Kisses. Robert Graves. CP-GravR

Biting of Beggars. Robert Herrick. CP-HerrR

Bits. D. H. Lawrence. CP-LawrD

   Land-Worker. CP-LawrD

   (Beloved.) CP-LawrD

Bits and Pieces. Donald Davie. CP-DaviDC

Bits of Reminiscence. "Shu Ting." CP-KizeC, *tr. by* Carolyn Kizer *and* Y. H. Zhao

Bitten and burned into mirrors of thin gold. Weathercocks, The. Charles Tomlinson. CP-TomlC; SP-TomlC

Bitter blue fingers. Firing, The. Gary Snyder. CP-SnydG

Bitter Brew. Langston Hughes. CP-HughL; CP-HughL3

Bitter cold winter night, A. Who Will Take Over the Universe? Allen Ginsberg. CP-GinsA

Bitter for Sweet. Christina Georgina Rossetti. CP-RosC1

Bitter Knowledge. Yannis Ritsos. SP-RitsY, *tr. by* Kostas Myrsiades

Bitter Life, A. John Updike. CP-UpdiJ

Bitter Pleasure. Rainer Maria Rilke. CP-RilkFr, *tr. by* A. Poulin, Jr.

Bitter Reflection, A. Samuel Taylor Coleridge. CP-ColeS

Bitter River, The. Langston Hughes. CP-HughL; CP-HughL2

Bitter Strawberries. Sylvia Plath. CP-PlatS

Bitter Summer Thoughts. Carl Sandburg. CP-SandC

Bitter Summer Thoughts—No. 3. Carl Sandburg. CP-SandC

Bitter Summer Thoughts—No. XXII. Carl Sandburg. CP-SandC

Bitter-Sweet. George Herbert. CP-HerbG

Bitter-Sweet Rocks. Jones Very. CP-VeryJ

Bitter upon conviction. Interstitial Office. John Berryman. CP-BerrJ

Bitter veins reject the dream, dismiss the fire, The. Farewell to the Bluewoman. Kenneth Patchen. CP-PatcK

Bitter Waters. Walter De la Mare. CP-DeLaW

Bitter winter / Rain. Winter After, The. Charles Olson. CP-OlsoC

Bitter World of Spring, The. William Carlos Williams. CP-WilW2

Bitter year it was. What woman ever, A. Wreath, The. Robert Graves. CP-GravR

Bitterly, England, must thou grieve. How Sleep the Brave. Walter De la Mare. CP-DeLaW

Bitterly have I been contested for. Helen's Faces. Laura Riding Jackson. CP-

RidiL

Bitterness. Olga Broumas. SP-BrouO

Bitterness, A. Mary Oliver. SP-OlivM

Bitterness of Children, The. Thomas Lux. SP-LuxT

Bitterness of death is on me now, The. Cup, The. Jones Very. CP-VeryJ

Bivouac on a Mountain Side. Walt Whitman. CP-WhitW

Bix to Buxtehude to Boulez. Victor Dog, The. James Merrill. SP-MerrJ

Bixby Canyon. Allen Ginsberg. CP-GinsA

Bixby Canyon Ocean Path Word Breeze. Allen Ginsberg. CP-GinsA

Bixby's Landing. Robinson Jeffers. CP-JefR1

Bizarre. Allen Tate. CP-TateA

!blac / k / agains / t. E. E. Cummings. CP-CummE

Black. Robert Graves. CP-GravR

Black against the snow and fog. Wide-eyed. Arthur Rimbaud. CP RimbA, *tr. by* Martin Sorrell

Black are the horses. Ballad of the Spanish Civil Guard. Federico García Lorca. SP-GarcF, *tr. by* A. L. Lloyd

Black are the horses. Ballad of the Spanish Civil Guard. Federico García Lorca. CP-GarcF, *tr. by* Will Kirkland

Black Art, The. Anne Sexton. CP-SextA; SP-SextA

Black / As the gentle night. Me and My Song. Langston Hughes. CP-HughL ; CP-HughL2

Black at that depth. Pacific Lament. Charles Olson. CP OlsoC

Black bear does a strange and shuffling dance, The. Bear: A Totem Dance As Seen by Raven. Peter Blue Cloud. SP-BlueP

Black bear, pacing the shore, lollops over. Beauty of the Head, The. May Swenson. SP-SwenM

Black Beast, The. Ted Hughes. SP-HughTN

Black Berry—wears a Thorn in his side, The. Emily Dickinson. CP-DickE

Black Bile ("No writing-desk crammed full of music, twine"). Charles Baudelaire. CP-BaudC, *tr. by* Walter Martin

Black Bile ("Pluvius, venting spleen on all enclaves"). Charles Baudelaire. CP-BaudC, *tr. by* Walter Martin

Black Bile ("When heavy, threatening skies weigh like a lid"). Charles Baudelaire. CP-BaudC, *tr. by* Walter Martin

Black Bile ("Worthless and wealthy, decrepit and young"). Charles Baudelaire. CP-BaudC, *tr. by* Walter Martin

Black biplane crashes through [*or* into] the window, A [*or* The]. Love Poem: "Black biplane crashes through [*or* into] the window, A [*or* The]." Gregory Orr. SP-OrrG

Black Birch in Winter, A. Richard Wilbur. CP-WilbR

Black bird scudding. Bobolink, The. Edna St. Vincent Millay. CP-MillE

Black, black island. 7 May 1950. Yannis Ritsos. SP-RitsY *Fr.* Exile's Journals 3.

Black Boat, The. Yannis Ritsos. SP-RitsY, *tr. by* Kostas Myrsiades

Black Book, The. John Berryman.

"Grandfather, sleepless in a room upstairs." CP-BerrJ

"Lover & child, a little sing." CP-BerrJ

"*Luftmenschen* dream, the men who live on air." CP-BerrJ

Black Brightness. Charles Baudelaire. CP-BaudC, *tr. by* Walter Martin *Fr.* Phantom, A.

Black Brook is brown. It travels. Charles Tomlinson. CP-TomlC; SP-TomlC

Black bull bellowed before the sea, The. Bull of Bendylaw, The. Sylvia Plath. CP-PlatS

Black Buttercups. Amy Clampitt. CP-ClamA

Black carved desk, the two silver candlesticks, The. Poet's Space, The. Yannis Ritsos. SP-RitsY, *tr. by* Kimon Friar

Black Cat. Paul Muldoon. CP-MuldP

Black chest hairs, soft sudden mass. Lines Muttered in Sleep. Rita Dove. SP-DoveR

Black Christ, The. Countee Cullen. CP-CullC

Black clippers, tarred with whales' blood, fold their sails. Old New England. Derek Walcott. CP-WalcD

Black clouds swell up around the setting sun, The. Double Sphere, Cloven Sphere. Norman Dubie. CP-DubiN

Black Clown, The. Langston Hughes. CP-HughL; CP-HughL1

Black Coat. Ted Hughes. SP-HughTN

Black Cottage, The. Robert Frost. CP-FrosR

Black Dancers. Langston Hughes. CP-HughL; CP-HughL1

Black Day, The. Archibald MacLeish. CP-MacLA

Black Days. Charles Simic. SP-SimiCE

Black Dragon Pearl in his left hand, The. Shih-te. CP-ColdM, *tr. by* Red Pine

Black drinks the sun and draws all colours to it. Black. Robert Graves. CP-GravR

Black eyed susan. Wildflower, The. William Carlos Williams. CP-WilW1

Black Faced Sheep, The. Donald Hall. CP-HallD

Black figure dances in a black field, A. Silver Plough-Boy, The. Wallace Stevens. CP-StevWP

Black Flakes. Paul Celan. SP-CelaP, *tr. by* John Felstiner

Black flies kept nagging in the heat, The. Tao and Unfitness at Inistiogue on the River Nore. Thomas Kinsella. CP-KinsT

Black Gal. Langston Hughes. CP-HughL; CP-HughL1

Black girl going, A. Generation II. Audre Lorde. SP-LordA

Black Goddess, The. Robert Graves. CP-GravR

Black hair you'd say she had, or rather. Edna St. Vincent Millay. CP-MillE

Black hands shucked. Gristmill. Yusef Komunyakaa. CP-KomuY

Black Hawk held: In reason. Lorine Niedecker. CP-NiedL

Black Hen, The. A. K. Ramanujan. CP-RamaA

Black Holes, Black Stockings. Olga Broumas.

"Cry comes out and is the changing exterior, particles without, A." SP-BrouO

"Gods are never the same but remain the same body, The." SP-BrouO

"Hundreds of leaves inside our dreams also quiver, The." SP-BrouO

"If we were as ferries and lived only a summer, how lovely to sleep without contact." SP-BrouO

"Like the flesh of Venus is mud, every day is a good amount of time." SP-BrouO

"Remember how close we sat in Sifnos having dinner by the water!" SP-BrouO

"They drove to the far side of the island." SP-BrouO

Black Horizons. Carl Sandburg. CP-SandC

Black horizons, come up. Black Horizons. Carl Sandburg. CP-SandC

Black Hoyden. Donald Davie. CP-DaviDC

Black Humor. Archibald MacLeish. CP-MacLA

Black in blazonry means. Buffalo, The. Marianne Craig Moore. CP-MoorM

Black Jackets. Thom Gunn. CP-GunnT

Black Java Pepper. Arthur Sze. SP-SzeA

Black Jewel, The. W. S. Merwin. SP-MerwWF

Black lady, / two eyes. KE 6-8018. Anne Sexton. CP-SextA

Black lake, black boat, two black, cut-paper people. Crossing the Water. Sylvia Plath. CP-PlatS

Black Lightning. Arthur Sze. SP-SzeA

Black / like memory's wound. Paul Celan. SP-CelaP, *tr. by* John Felstiner

Black, long-tailed, The. Yellow Season, The. William Carlos Williams. CP-WilW2

Black Magdalens. Countee Cullen. CP-CullC

Black Magicians / Come home: the pink meat image. Change, The: *Kyoto-Tokyo Express.* Allen Ginsberg. CP GinsA; SP-GinsA

Black Mail. Alice Walker. CP-WalkA

Black Majesty. Countee Cullen. CP-CullC

Black man, bright nouveautés leave one, at best, pseudonymous. Nudity in the Colonies. Wallace Stevens. CP-StevW; CP-StevWP

Black man is hugging me around the throat from behind, A. Father and Son. David Ignatow. SP-IgnaD

Black Man Speaks, The. Langston Hughes. CP-HughL; CP-HughL2

Black-maned roan and coral whip, A. Han-shan. CP-ColdM, *tr. by* Red Pine

Black marble mantelpiece, The. Evening. James Schuyler. CP-SchuJ

Black March. Stevie Smith. CP-SmitS

Black Maria. Langston Hughes. CP-HughL; CP-HughL2

Black Marsh Eclogue. Sam Hamill. SP-HamiS

Black Mesa, The. James Merrill. SP-MerrJ

Black milk of daybreak we drink it at evening. Deathfugue. Paul Celan. SP-CelaP, *tr. by* John Felstiner

Black Money. Tess Gallagher. SP-GallT

Black mood, away! Winter Carol. May Sarton. SP-SartM

Black Mother Woman. Audre Lorde. SP-LordA

Black Mt. College Has a Few Words for a Visitor. Charles Olson. CP-OlsoC

Black November Turkey, A. Richard Wilbur. CP-WilbR

Black Nude. Charles Tomlinson. CP-TomlC

Black Ode. Maya Angelou. SP-AngeM

Black of grackles glints purple as, wheeling in sun-glare. Grackles, Goodbye. Robert Penn Warren. CP-WarrR

Black of my hair has gone white, The. Shmuel HaNagid. SP-HaNaS, *tr. by* Peter Cole

Black on flat water past the jonquil lawns. Black Swan, The. James Merrill. SP-MerrJ

Black Panther. Langston Hughes. CP-HughL; CP-HughL3

Black Panther and the Little Boy, The. Kenneth Patchen. CP-PatcK

Black Pierrot, A. Langston Hughes. CP-HughL; CP-HughL1

Black Pine Tree in an Orange Light. Sylvia Plath. CP-PlatS

Black Plateau, The. W. S. Merwin. SP-MerwW

Black Prince, The. Alice Walker. CP-WalkA

Black queen on the red king. Solitaire. John Updike. CP-UpdiJ

Black rain in a stubbled field. Homage to Trakl. Sam Hamill. SP-HamiS

Black relatives / you are always. Some Things I Like about My Triple Bloods. Alice Walker. CP-WalkA

Black Richard. George Meredith. CP-MerG2

Black riders came from the sea. Stephen Crane. CP-CranS

Black Road Over Which Green Trees Grow. Thomas Lux. SP-LuxT

Black rock raging that the wind has rolled, The. Tomb. Stéphane Mallarmé. CP-MallS, *tr. by* Henry Weinfield

Black Rook in Rainy Weather. Sylvia Plath. CP-PlatS

Black Samson of Brandywine. Paul Laurence Dunbar. CP-DunbP

Black Seed. Langston Hughes. CP-HughL; CP-HughL1

Black sergeant first class, The. To Have Danced with Death. Yusef Komunyakaa. CP-KomuY

Black Silk. Tess Gallagher. SP-GallT

Black smoke of sound. Air Raid: Barcelona. Langston Hughes. CP-HughL; CP-HughL1

Black Snake, The. Mary Oliver. SP-OlivM

Black snow, the winter's excrement. March Morning. John Ciardi. CP-CiarJ

Black stallion and a white mare, A. In the Rich Farmer's Field. John Ciardi. CP-CiarJ

Black Stars, The. Primo Levi. CP-LeviP, *tr. by* Ruth Feldman *and* Brian Swann

Black Stone on Top of a White Stone. César Vallejo. CP-MertT

Black String of Days. Yusef Komunyakaa. CP-KomuY

Black summer, black Vermont. Who sees. Mountain, The. Hayden Carruth. CP-CarHS

Black Swan, The. Randall Jarrell. CP-JarrR

Black Swan, The. James Merrill. SP-MerrJ

Black Tambourine. Hart Crane. CP-CranH

Black teeth / Seek the pale ropes which bind life. Lives of the Swan. Kenneth Patchen. CP-PatcK

Black thatch, black root. Falling Asleep. Robert Pinsky. CP-PinsR

Black the coniferous darkness. Passers-By on Snowy Night. Robert Penn Warren. CP-WarrR

Black Tower, The. William Butler Yeats. CP-YeatW

Black Train, The. Thomas McGrath. SP-McGrT

Black Trout, The. Eugenio Montale. CP-MontE, *tr. by* Jonathan Galassi

Black village of gravestones. Heptonstall. Ted Hughes. SP-HughTN

Black Virgin, The. G. K. Chesterton. CP-ChesG

Black Walnut Tree, The. Mary Oliver. SP-OlivM

Black was the without eye. Two Legends. Ted Hughes. SP-HughTN *Fr.* Crow.

Black Water. Wyatt Prunty. SP-PrunW

Black waters' / November / clouds. Hill. Louis Zukofsky. CP-ZukLS

Black wattles along the edge of the clearing. Keokea. Arthur Sze. SP-SzeA

Black Winds, The. William Carlos Williams. CP-WilW1

Black-winged gull, The. Song: "Black-winged gull, The." William Carlos Williams. CP-WilW1

Black Workers. Langston Hughes. CP-HughL; CP-HughL1

Black Zodiac. Charles Wright. SP-WrigCN

Blackberries. Yusef Komunyakaa. CP-KomuY

Blackberry Eating. Galway Kinnell. SP-KinnGN

Blackberry-Picking. Seamus Heaney. SP-HeanSO

Blackberry, white, The. Sobieski's Shield. Geoffrey Hill. CP-HillG

Blackberry Winter. John Crowe Ransom. SP-RansJ

Blackberrying. Sylvia Plath. CP-PlatS

Blackbird. Adam Zagajewski. SP-ZagaA, *tr. by* Clare Cavanagh

Blackbird, The. Derek Mahon. CP-MahoD

Blackbird in a wicker cage, A. Two Blackbirds, The. George Meredith. CP-MerG1

Blackbird of Derrycairn. Two from Ireland. Donald Davie. CP-DaviDC

Blackbird sat on the TV antenna, A. Blackbird. Adam Zagajewski. SP-ZagaA, *tr. by* Clare Cavanagh

Blackbird takes out, The. Script. A. R. Ammons. CP-AmmoA

Blackbirds Are Rough Today, The. Charles Bukowski. SP-BukC2

Blackbirds are scribbling in the winter heat of the trees. Amulet, The. Norman Dubie. CP-DubiN

Blackbird's song the blackbird's song, The. Ralph Waldo Emerson. CP-EmerR

Blackbirds whistle over the young. American Century, The. Kenneth Rexroth. CP-RexrK

Blackcurrant River. Arthur Rimbaud. CP-RimbA, *tr. by* Martin Sorrell

Blacked-out on a wagon, part of my life cut out forever. 7/16/68: i. Adrienne Rich. CP-RicAE *Fr.* Ghazals: Homage to Ghalib.

Blackened river ran through the park, The. Adam Zagajewski. SP-ZagaA, *tr. by* Renata Gorczynski, Benjamin Ivry *and* C. K. Williams

Blackening Sky. Robert Graves. CP-GravR

Blacker and whiter than the pages of his ledger. Hymn to Commerce. Thomas Merton. CP-MertT

Blackie, The Electric Rembrandt. Thom Gunn. CP-GunnT

Blacklisted. Carl Sandburg. CP-SandC

Blackness / Was a building blocking the [*or* my birth] moon. Mount Zion. Ted Hughes. SP-HughTN

Blacks Dancing to Cuban Rhythms. Federico García Lorca. CP-GarcF, *tr. by* Greg Simon *and* Steven F. White

Blacksmith, The. Arthur Rimbaud. CP-RimbA, *tr. by* Martin Sorrell

Blacksmith Shop. Czeslaw Milosz. CP-MiloCN, *tr. by* Robert Hass

Blacksmith's Serenade, The. Nicholas Vachel Lindsay. CP-LindV

Blackstone is gone. Law. Charles Olson. CP-OlsoC

Blackstudies. Audre Lorde. SP-LordA

Blade, The. Charles Tomlinson. SP-TomlC

Blade in the Northside, A. Jorge Luis Borges. SP-BorgJ, *tr. by* Eric McHenry

Blades. C. K. Williams. SP-WillC; SP-WillC

Blades sway. They ride, The. Reeds. Charles Tomlinson. CP-TomlC

Blaise Pascal Lip-syncs the Void. Charles Wright. SP-WrigCN

Blakes apology for His Catalogue. William Blake. CP-BlakW

(Who cries all art is a fraud & Genius a trick.) CP-BlakW

Blake's Baptismal Font. Denise Levertov. SP-LeveDL

Blame. Robert Herrick. CP-HerrR

Blame. C. K. Williams. SP-WillC

Blame me not that I refuse. George Meredith. CP-MerG2

Blame me not thou hoarse preacher. Hafiz. CP-EmerR *Fr.* Odes.

Blame Not My Cheekes. Thomas Campion. CP-CampT

Blame Not My Lute. Sir Thomas Wyatt. CP-WyatT

Blame not my lute, for he must sound [*or* sssnd *or* Sownde]. Blame Not My Lute. Sir Thomas Wyatt. CP-WyatT

Blame the Reward of Princes. Robert Herrick. CP-HerrR

Blame the Thought, Cling to the Bummer. Allen Ginsberg. CP-GinsA

Blameless as daylight I stood looking. Eye-Mote, The. Sylvia Plath. CP-PlatS

Blanch swears her Husband's lovely; when a scald. Upon Blanch. Robert Herrick. CP-HerrR

Blanche McCarthy. Wallace Stevens. CP-StevWP

Blanched her face when. Terror. James Laughlin. CP-LaugJ

Blanched tree livid behind, The. Iowa. Donald Davie. CP-DaviDC

Bland as the morning breath of June. Dream of Summer, A. John Greenleaf Whittier. CP-WhitJ

Blandly mother. Wild Orphan. Allen Ginsberg. CP-GinsA

Blandula, Tenulla [*or* Tenella], Vagula. Ezra Pound. CP-PoEar; SP-PounE

Blank. D. H. Lawrence. CP-LawrD

Blank, A. Thom Gunn. CP-GunnT

Blank Joy. Rainer Maria Rilke. CP-RilkFr, *tr. by* A. Poulin, Jr.

Blank Misgivings of a Creature Moving About in Worlds Not Realized. Arthur Hugh Clough. SP-ClouA

Blank of the wall is over against you; which, The. "St.-John Perse." CP-DaviDC, *tr. by* Donald Davie

Blank Sheet, The. Hans Magnus Enzensberger. SP-EnzeH, *tr. by* Michael Hamburger

Blank verse, as good as Marlowe's mighty line. Filling in the Blanks. Eleanor Wilner. SP-WilnE

Blanket Charge. Robert Graves. CP-GravR

Blasphemies, The. Louis MacNeice. CP-MacNL

Blasphemy. Yusef Komunyakaa. CP-KomuY

Blast from Freedom's Northern hills, upon its Southern way, The. Massachusetts to Virginia. John Greenleaf Whittier. CP-WhitJ

Blast of harsh. For John Duff. Robert Creeley. SP-CreeR

Blast skims, The. Elegy for a Jet Pilot. A. R. Ammons. CP-AmmoA

Blast the old days. Valse Triste et Sentimentale. Hans Magnus Enzensberger. SP-EnzeH

Blasted with sighs, and surrounded with tears. Twickenham [*or* Twicknam] Garden. John Donne. CP-DonnJ; MW-DonnJ

Blasting from Heaven. Philip Levine. SP-LeviP

Blasts rip Newspaper Gray [*or* grey] Mannahatta's mid day Air Spires. Friday the Thirteenth. Allen Ginsberg. CP-GinsA

Blaubeuren. Charles Tomlinson. SP-TomlC

Blazed. Ezra Pound. CP-PoEar

Blazes of color intermingled. Swinburne: A Critique. Ezra Pound. CP-PoEar

Blazing in Gold and quenching in Purple. Emily Dickinson. CP-DickE

Blazing knot which twenty-one whole years, The. Petrarch. CP-Petra, *tr. by* J. G. Nichols

Blazing shark, The. 99 to One. Charles Bukowski. SP-BukC1

Bleak January! Cold as fate. Hoosier Calendar, A. James Whitcomb Riley. CP-RileJ

Bleakness, Farewell. Philip Whalen. SP-WhalP

Bleecker Street, Summer. Derek Walcott. CP-WalcD

Bleeding. May Swenson. SP-SwenM

Bleeding Gums. James Schuyler. CP-SchuJ

Bleeding Hand: or, The Sprig of Eglantine Given to a Maid, The. Robert Herrick. CP-HerrR

Bleeding hearts in the garden, The. Me. Kenneth Rexroth. CP-RexrK

Bleeding of the mountains. Martin Luther King, Malcolm X. Muriel Rukeyser. CP-RukeM

Blemish. Paul Muldoon. CP-MuldP

Bless God, he went as soldiers. Emily Dickinson. CP-DickE

Bless J-s-s Ch———, O Cardoness. [On] Maxwell of Cardoness. Robert Burns. CP-BurnR

Bless love and hope. Full many a withered year. Love and Hope. Dante Gabriel Rossetti. CW-RossD *Fr.* House of Life, The.

Bless / something small. Prayer, A. Robert Creeley. CP-CreeR

Bless Thee, O Lord, for the living arc of the sky over me this morning. Glass House Canticle. Carl Sandburg. CP-SandC

Bless You, Mr President. James Laughlin. CP-LaugJ

Blessed, The. William Butler Yeats. CP-YeatW

Blessèd Accident. Robert Penn Warren. CP-WarrR

Blessed Are the Angels in Heaven. Richard Eberhart. CP-EberR

Blessed Are the Peacemakers. G. K. Chesterton. CP-ChesG

"Blessed are they that mourn: for they shall be comforted." Math. 5:4. Jones Very. CP-VeryJ

Blessed are they that mourn my life is theirs. Blessed Are They That Mourn. Jones Very. CP-VeryJ

Blessed are those who have not seen. In Stratis Viarum III. Arthur Hugh Clough. SP-ClouA

Blessed be the dancers! The dancers. Praise for All Dancers. Robert Bly. SP-BlyR

Blessèd be the English and all their ways and works. Jobson's Amen. Rudyard Kipling. CP-KiplR

Blessed Be the Muses. Allen Ginsberg. CP-GinsA

Blessed be the Paps which Thou hast Sucked. Bible, *N.T. Fr.* St. Luke.

Blessed be this place. Blood and the Moon. William Butler Yeats. CP-YeatW

Blessed damozel leaned out, The. Dante Gabriel Rossetti. CW-RossD

Blessed Dear & heart's Delight. 1878. Christina Georgina Rossetti. CP-RosC3

Blessed Event. W. H. Auden. CP-AudeW

Blessed is he whose transgression is forgiven, whose sin is covered. Psalm 32: "Blessed is he whose transgression is forgiven, whose sin is covered." Bible, *O.T.* CP-WyatT *Fr.* Psalms.

Blessed Is the Man. Marianne Craig Moore. CP-MoorM

Blessed is the man that walketh not in the counsel of the ungodly [*or* wicked]. Psalm 1: "Blessed is the man that walketh not in the counsel of the ungodly [*or* wicked]." Bible, *O.T.* CP-MiltJ *Fr.* Psalms.

Blessed land of Judæa! thrice hallowed of song. Palestine. John Greenleaf Whittier. CP-WhitJ

Blessed lot hath he, who having passed, A. To the Rev. George Coleridge. Samuel Taylor Coleridge. CP-ColeS; MW-ColeS

Blessed moon / noon. Full Moon. William Carlos Williams. CP-WilW1

Blessed [*or* Blesst] are your north parts, for all this long time. To Mr I. L ("Blessed [*or* Blesst] are your north parts, for all this long time"). John Donne. CP-DonnJ; MW-DonnJ

Blessed Sun. Robert Graves. CP-GravR

Blessèd Virgin Compared to the Air We Breathe, The. Gerard Manley Hopkins. CP-HopkG

Blessed Virgin Mary Compared to a Window, The. Thomas Merton. CP-MertT

Blessèd was our first age and morning-time. Consolations of Memory, The. Rudyard Kipling. CP-KiplR *Fr.* Muse among the Motors, The.

Blessèd water, blessèd man . . . . Robert Creeley. CP-CreeR

Blessed were they, who in the early time. Faith of the First Christians, The. Jones Very. CP-VeryJ

Blessed with a joy that only she. Gift of God, The. Edwin Arlington Robinson. CP-RobiE

Blessing. David Ignatow. SP-IgnaD

Blessing. Eleanor Wilner. SP-WilnE

Blessing, A. James Wright. CP-WrigJ

Blessing, A ("I live in an age of varied powers and knowledge"). G. K. Chesterton. CP-ChesG

Blessing, A ("Sunlight in a child's hair"). G. K. Chesterton. CP-ChesG

Blessing, The. Carolyn Kizer. CP-KizeC

Blessing, The. W. S. Merwin. SP-MerwW

Blessing, The. John Updike. CP-UpdiJ

Blessing in Disguise, A. John Ashbery. SP-AshbJ

Blessing in this conscious fruit, the hurt, The. Beyond Reason. Stanley Kunitz. CP-KunSC

Blessing Myself. David Ignatow. SP-IgnaD

Blessing of Rain, The. Jones Very. CP-VeryJ

Blessing the Animals. Yusef Komunyakaa. CP-KomuY

Blessing the Boats. Lucille Clifton. SP-ClifL

Blessings in abundance come. Good-Night, or Blessing, The. Robert Herrick. CP-HerrR

Blessings on thee, little man. Barefoot Boy, The. John Greenleaf Whittier. CP-WhitJ

Blessings there are of cradle and of clan. Alone. G. K. Chesterton. CP-ChesG

Blest as th'immortal Gods is he. Translation of Horace "Epode the 2d" ("Beatus Ille"). Horace. CP-JohnS *Fr.* Epodes.

Blest be McMurdo to his latest day! On John McMurdo. Robert Burns. CP-BurnR

Blest be the God of love. Evensong [*or* Even-Song]. George Herbert. CP-HerbG

Blest be thy name, who didst restore. Upon My Daughter Hannah Wiggin her Recovery from a Dangerous Fever. Anne Bradstreet. CP-BradA

Blest is the man who hath not walk'd astray. Bible, *O.T. See* Blessed is the man that walketh not in the counsel of the ungodly [*or* wicked]

Blest is the sword that leaps from sheath. George Meredith. CP-MerG2

Blest is this Isle—our native Land. To the Lady Fleming on Seeing the Foundation Preparing for the Erection of Rydal Chapel, Westmoreland. William Wordsworth. CP-WorW2

Blest Order, which in power dost so excel[l]. Priesthood, The. George Herbert. CP-HerbG

Blest pair of *Sirens*, pledges of Heav'ns [*or* Heaven's] joy. At a Solemn Music[k]. John Milton. CP-MiltJ

Blest soul, so often coming back to me. Petrarch. CP-Petra, *tr.* by J. G. Nichols

Blest Statesman He, Whose Mind's Unselfish Will. William Wordsworth. CP-WorW2

Blest was my reign, retiring Cynthia cry'd. Ovid. CP-JohnS *Fr.* Amores.

Blest! who far from all mankind. Repose in God. Jeanne Marie Bouvier de la Motte- Guyon. CP-CowpW

Blewits. Paul Muldoon. CP-MuldP

Blight. Ralph Waldo Emerson. CP-EmerR

Blight, Edna St. Vincent Millay. CP-MillE

Blight was on the oaks, A. Fanny Howe. SP-HoweF *Fr.* Robeson Street.

Blind. Langston Hughes. CP-HughL; CP-HughL2

Blind. James Whitcomb Riley. CP-RileJ

Blind, The. Charles Baudelaire. CP-BaudC, *tr.* by Walter Martin

Blind are their own brothers; we, The. Like Owls. Robert Graves. CP-GravR

Blind Arrow, A. Robert Graves. CP-GravR

Blind Boy, The. Walter De la Mare. CP-DeLaW

Blind form birth, they do not know, The. Some Lines Finished Just before Dawn at the Bedside of a Dying Student It Has Snowed All Night. Miller Williams. CP-WillM

Blind from my birth, / Where flowers are springing. Christina Georgina Rossetti. CP-RosC2

Blind Girl. Jane Cooper. CP-CoopJ

Blind Girl, The. James Whitcomb Riley. CP-RileJ

Blind girl / stares at me, A. Black Lightning. Arthur Sze. SP-SzeA

Blind girl step over the red staves, A. Fifteenth-Century Zen Master, A. Norman Dubie. CP-DubiN

Blind Highland Boy, The; A Tale Told by the Fire-side, After Returning to the Vale of Grasmere. William Wordsworth. CP-WorW1

Blind Horses. Robinson Jeffers. CP-JefR2

Blind, light- / bearded display panel. Frankfurt, September. Paul Celan. SP-CelaP, *tr.* by John Felstiner

Blind Maidens of Our Homelessness, The. Kenneth Patchen. CP-PatcK

Blind Man, A. Jorge Luis Borges. SP-BorgJ, *tr.* by Alastair Reid

Blind man, A. I can stare at him. Solitude, A. Denise Levertov. SP-LeveDP

Blind Man, The. Jorge Luis Borges. SP-BorgJ, *tr.* by Alastair Reid

Blind man living in a hollow house, A. Saturday, A. Jorge Luis Borges. SP-BorgJ, *tr.* by Eric McHenry

Blind man to the maiden said, The. Robert Browning. CP-BroR2

Blind-Man's Buff. William Blake. CP-BlakW

Blind Man's Song, The. Randall Jarrell. CP-JarrR

Blind Panorama of New York. Federico García Lorca. CP-GarcF, *tr.* by Greg Simon *and* Steven F. White

Blind Sheep, The. Randall Jarrell. CP-JarrR

Blind Spots. A. K. Ramanujan. CP-RamaA

Blind wind beats the bushes down and wild. Falling Through the Leaves. Thomas Lux. SP-LuxT

Blind with love, my daughter. Pain for a Daughter. Anne Sexton. CP-SextA; SP-SextA

Blind'd be the last of men. Kenneth Patchen. CP-PatcK

Blinded Bird, The. Thomas Hardy. CP-HardT

Blindest buzzard that I know, The. Sketch, A. Christina Georgina Rossetti. CP-RosC3

Blindman by the name of La Fontaine, A. Haec Fabula Docet. Robert Frost. CP-FrosR

Blinds are drawn because of the sun, The. Best of School, The. D. H. Lawrence. CP-LawrD

Blinds me / like the light of that surf. Your Letter. Adrienne Rich. CP-RicAE

Blinking in the light. Contraries. A. K. Ramanujan. CP-RamaA

Blisful lyf, a paisible and a swete, A. Former Age, The. Geoffrey Chaucer. CP-ChauG

Bliss is the plaything of the child. Emily Dickinson. CP-DickE

Bliss it is at break of day. Sunrise. Walter De la Mare. CP-DeLaW

Bliss of the cork abandoned to the current. Boats on the Marne. Eugenio Montale. CP-MontE, *tr.* by Jonathan Galassi

Blisse (last night drunk) did kisse his mothers knee. Upon Blisse. Robert Herrick. CP-HerrR

Blissful spirit, thanks to whom new passion. Michelangelo Buonarroti. CP-Miche, *tr. by* John Frederick Nims

Blissom. Paul Muldoon. CP-MuldP

Blithe spirit, haven't you ever been hurt. Reversibility. Charles Baudelaire. CP-BaudC, *tr. by* Walter Martin

Blithewood. Theodore Weiss. SP-WeisT

Blizzard. James Schuyler. CP-SchuJ

Blizzard. William Carlos Williams. CP-WilW1

Blizzard Notes. Carl Sandburg. CP-SandC

Blizzard sang, The. Caught by the Blizzard. Aleksandr Aleksandrovich Blok. SP-BlokA, *tr. by* Peter France *and* Jon Stallworthy

Blizzard sun upturn tulips chances. Tulip. Louis Zukofsky. CP-ZukLS

Blizzards have brought down the beech tree. Beech, The. Charles Tomlinson. CP-TomlC

Blizzards of paper. Unlearning to Not Speak. Marge Piercy. SP-PierM

Blked. John Updike. CP-UpdiJ

Block. Hayden Carruth. CP-CarHS

Blockade. Olga Broumas. SP-BrouO

Blocked-out Tree, The. Quilt-Pattern, A. Randall Jarrell. CP-JarrR

Blocked Road, The. Jelaluddin Rumi. SP-Rumi, *tr. by* Coleman Barks

Blocking the sidewalk so. Gossips, The. William Carlos Williams. CP-WilW2

Blocks. Frank O'Hara. SP-OharF

Blocks of cursive etched in softened paper, interspersed with real poems he's pasted in. Reading C. K. Williams's "The Critic." William Corbett. SP-CorbW

Blond cowl terse as a blunt threat to injure, The. Love among the Manichees. William Dickey. SP-DickW

Blond Mediterraneans, The. Tennessee Williams. CP-WillT

Blond, wholesome, serene. Photograph, Maryland Agricultural College Livestock Show, 1924. Maxine W. Kumin. SP-KumiM

Blood. Raymond Carver. CP-CarvR

Blood. James Dickey. CP-DickJ

Blood. David Ignatow. SP-IgnaD

Blood. Wyatt Prunty. SP-PrunW

Blood. Yannis Ritsos. SP-RitsY, *tr. by* Christian McEwen *and* Nikos Tsingos

Blood and Sand. Kenneth Rexroth. CP-RexrK

Blood and the Moon. William Butler Yeats. CP-YeatW

Blood began to waste into the clods, The. Book of the Dead, The. Thom Gunn. CP-GunnT

Blood blister over my thumb-moon. Fox Blood. James Dickey. CP-DickJ

Blood Flows Back, The. Stevie Smith. CP-SmitS

Blood flows in me, but what does it have to do. Living by the Red River. James Wright. CP-WrigJ

Blood from the Stone. George Oppen. CP-OppGN

Blood goes through your neck veins with a noise they call singing, The. Machine. Gun. Nest. Margaret Atwood. SP-AtwM2

Blood-Guilt, The. Robinson Jeffers. CP-JefR3

Blood has been harder to dam back than water. Flood, The. Robert Frost. CP-FrosR

Blood I foresaw. I had put by. Assassin. Charles Tomlinson. CP-TomlC; SP-TomlC

Blood in the Water. Ai. SP-Ai

Blood in your arteries is contaminated with sugar, The. Silk Road, The. Arthur Sze. SP-SzeA

Blood is blood and bone is bone. Mummy. Carl Sandburg. CP-SandC

Blood Is Justified, The. Muriel Rukeyser. CP-RukeM

Blood is more showy (gaudy) than the Breath, The. Emily Dickinson. SP-DickE

Blood-Money. Walt Whitman. CP-WhitW

Blood of the Sun. Kenneth Patchen. CP-PatcK

Blood on his torn glossy pants. Wounded Bullfighter, The. Clarence Major. SP-MajoC

Blood / Or a flag. Hero—International Brigade. Langston Hughes. CP-HughL; CP-HughL3

Blood-red turtledoves, The. From the Train. Eugenio Montale. CP-MontE, *tr. by* Jonathan Galassi

Blood-Sister. Adrienne Rich. SP-RicA2

Blood that stands the member erect, The. Yehuda Amichai. SP-AmicYL *Fr. Poems of the Land of Zion and Jerusalem.*

Blood we give the dead to drink, The. Didactic Poem. Denise Levertov. SP-LeveDP

Bloodbirth. Audre Lorde. SP-LordA

Bloodhounds look like sad old judges, The. Nice Day for a Lynching. Kenneth Patchen. CP-PatcK

Bloodless blue sky, A. 9:00 p.m. Federico García Lorca. CP-GarcF, *tr. by* Jerome Rothenberg *Fr.* Summer Hours.

Bloodletting. Yannis Ritsos. SP-RitsY, *tr. by* Kimon Friar *and* Kostas Myrsiades

Bloodroot. Jane Cooper. CP-CoopJ

Bloody and a sudden end, A. John Kinsella's Lament for Mrs. Mary Moore. William Butler Yeats. CP-YeatW

Bloody / egg yolk. A burnt hole, A. Out of the Sea, Early. May Swenson. SP-SwenM

Bloody Mary's venomous flames can curl. Martyrdom of Bishop Farrar, The. Ted Hughes. SP-HughTN

Bloody Sire, The. Robinson Jeffers. CP-JefR3

Bloom—is Result—to meet a Flower. Emily Dickinson. CP-DickE

Bloom upon the Mountain—stated. Emily Dickinson. CP-DickE

Blooming belladonna smile, A. Pool. Eugenio Montale. CP-MontE, *tr. by* Jonathan Galassi

Bloomingdale Papers, The. Hayden Carruth.

    "Aw, Dylan, have you left us? Have you gone?" CP-CarHS

    "Bitcheries of Madison Avenue, The." CP-CarHS

    "December now. Winter deepens and darkens. Stars." CP-CarHS

    "Diagnosis is / Anxiety psychoneurosis, The." CP-CarHS

    "Expectantly and fearfully I sing." CP-CarHS

    "For thon demgeorne dreorigne oft." CP-CarHS

    Hall Five. CP-CarHS

    "I know there is a country where we go." CP-CarHS

    "In deep winter the sea roams." CP-CarHS

    "In the hot high summer I came." CP-CarHS

    "Once on a night in spring." CP-CarHS

    "Rule of the majority is / strictly enforced in all matters, The." CP-CarHS

    "This all begins on a November day." CP-CarHS

    "'Tis a fine deceit." CP-CarHS

    "To dig at Luxor, to peer." CP-CarHS

Blooms of May. James Whitcomb Riley. CP-RileJ

Blossom. Mary Oliver. SP-OlivM

Blossom and greenness, making all. Birthday Wreath, The. John Greenleaf Whittier. CP-WhitJ

Blossom perhaps is an introduction, A. Emily Dickinson. SP-DickE

Blossom Themes. Carl Sandburg. CP-SandC

Blossom[e], The. John Donne. CP-DonnJ; MW-DonnJ

Blossoming are people / nimbler than Really. E. E. Cummings. CP-CummE

Blossoming Oakwood. James Schuyler. CP-SchuJ

Blossoming of the Solitary Date-Tree, The. Samuel Taylor Coleridge. CP-ColeS

Blossoms crimson, white, or blue. Blossoms on the Trees, The. James Whitcomb Riley. CP-RileJ

Blossoms crowd the branches: too beautiful to endure. Spring-Gazing Songs. Hsüeh T'ao. CP-KizeC, *tr. by* Carolyn Kizer

Blossoms of babies. Handfuls. Carl Sandburg. CP-SandC

Blossoms on the tree, The. Delay in Friendship. Henry David Thoreau. CP-ThorH

Blossoms on the Trees, The. James Whitcomb Riley. CP-RileJ

Blossoms will run away. Emily Dickinson. CP-DickE

Blotch of pallor stirs beneath the high, A. In the Dark. D. H. Lawrence. CP-LawrD

Bloud of Abel was a thing, The. Another. Robert Herrick. CP-HerrR

Blow, The. Thomas Hardy. CP-HardT

Blow is Creation, / & the Twist the Nasturtium, The. Charles Olson. SP-OlsoC *Fr. Maximus Poems, The.*

Blow out the candles of your cake. For K. R. on Her Sixtieth Birthday. Richard Wilbur. CP-WilbR

Blow, West Wind. Robert Penn Warren. CP-WarrR

Blow your cold trumpets too, Memory. From a Winter Journal. Marya Alexandrovna Zaturenska. SP-ZatuM

Blowgun and Rattlesnake. James Dickey. CP-DickJ

Blowing Eggs. Paul Muldoon. CP-MuldP

Blown of the winds whose goal is "No-man-knows." That Pass between the False Dawn and the True. Ezra Pound. CP-PoEar

Blowpipe Game, The. James Laughlin. CP-LaugJ

Blude-red rose at Yule may blaw, The. To Daunton Me. Robert Burns. CP-BurnR

Bludius et Corona [Blood and the Crown]. Andrew Marvell. CP-MarvA

Blue. Robert Creeley. CP-CreeR

Blue. Paul Laurence Dunbar. CP-DunbP

Blue. David Ignatow. SP-IgnaD

Blue. James Schuyler. CP-SchuJ

Blue. May Swenson. SP-SwenM

Blue Anchor, The. Jane Cooper. CP-CoopJ

Blue and dark. Glory of Darkness. D. H. Lawrence. CP-LawrD

Blue and white. Poems at the Porthole. Lorine Niedecker. CP-NiedL

Blue and white came out. Lake Michigan Morning. Carl Sandburg. CP-SandC

Blue anemone with a dark core, The. Mediterranean in January. D. H. Lawrence. CP-LawrD

Blue Angel, The. Allen Ginsberg. CP-GinsA

Blue Bayou. Langston Hughes. CP-HughL; CP-HughL2

Blue bell is the sweetest flower, The. Emily Jane Brontë. CP-BronE

Blue-bell springs upon the ledge, A. Spring Song. Paul Laurence Dunbar. CP-DunbP

Blue-black mountains are etched, The. Chance, The. Arthur Sze. SP-SzeA

Blue, blue is the grass about the river. Beautiful Toilet, The. Ezra Pound. SP-PounE

Blue booby lives, The. Blue Booby, The. James Tate. SP-TateJ

Blue Booby, The. James Tate. SP-TateJ

Blue Bottle, The. May Swenson. SP-SwenM

Blue Bug. Marianne Craig Moore. CP-MoorM

Blue Buildings in the Summer Air, The. Wallace Stevens. CP-StevW; CP-StevWP

Blue, but you are Rose, too. Blue. May Swenson. SP-SwenM

Blue butterflies' eyed wings. Kathleen Jessie Raine. SP-RainK

Blue-Butterfly Day. Robert Frost. CP-FrosR

Blue chair. Atelier Cézanne. Clarence Major. SP-MajoC

Blue chairs hang empty. In the Red Mountains. W. S. Merwin. SP-MerwWF

Blue Cheese and Chili Peppers. Charles Bukowski. SP-BukC1

Blue convolvulus, The. Morning Song. Wallace Stevens. CP-StevWP

Blue crabs come to the brown pond's edge, The. Crab Crack. John Updike. CP-UpdiJ

Blue devils' / Bluest. Thus. Charles Simic. SP-SimiC; SP-SimiCE

Blue Dwarfs. Margaret Atwood. SP-AtwM2

Blue Eye, The. James Merrill. SP-MerrJ

Blue-Eyed Exterminator, The. Josephine Jacobsen. CP-JacoJ

Blue-eyed grass is opening now, The. Songs for Marie's Lutebook. Kenneth Rexroth. CP-RexrK

Blue-Eyed Lassie, The. Robert Burns. CP-BurnR

Blue-eyed phantom far before, A. Fata Morgana. Christina Georgina Rossetti. CP-RosC1

Blue Eyes. Constantine P. Cavafy. CP-CavaC, *tr. by* Theoharis Constantine Theoharis

Blue-Flag in the Bog, The. Edna St. Vincent Millay. CP-MillE

Blue flax blossoming near the greenhouse. Apache Plume. Arthur Sze. SP-SzeA

Blue Flower, The. James Laughlin. CP-LaugJ

Blue Flower, The. Muriel Rukeyser. CP-RukeM

Blue Flower, The. Marya Alexandrovna Zaturenska. SP-ZatuM

Blue-Fly, The. Robert Graves. CP-GravR

Blue Footprints, The. James Laughlin. CP-LaugJ

Blue from Heaven, The. Stevie Smith. CP-SmitS

Blue garb fluttering gustily. Madge. G. K. Chesterton. CP-ChesG

Blue Ghazals, The. Adrienne Rich. CP-RicAE; SP-RicA2

Blue Girls. John Crowe Ransom. SP-RansJ

Blue go up & blue go down. American Lights, Seen from Off Abroad. John Berryman. CP-BerrJ

Blue-grained line circles a fragment of the mind, A. For L.G.: Unseen for Twenty Years. Adrienne Rich. SP-RicA2

Blue-grey, and white, and white-of-rose. Nel Biancheggiar. Ezra Pound. CP-PoEar

Blue Grotto, The. James Merrill. SP-MerrJ

Blue Hog, A. Norman Dubie. CP-DubiN

Blue house at Mills Cross, The. Radio Sky. Norman Dubie. CP-DubiN

Blue in the green trees, what are they climbing? Boys in the Branches. Muriel Rukeyser. CP-RukeM

Blue in the west the mountain stands. Vickery's Mountain. Edwin Arlington Robinson. CP-RobiE

Blue Is the Sky. George Meredith. CP-MerG2

Blue Island Intersection. Carl Sandburg. CP-SandC

Blue Jay, The. D. H. Lawrence. CP-LawrD

Blue jay scuffling in the bushes follows, The. On the Move. Thom Gunn. CP-GunnT

Blue July, bright July. July. George Meredith. CP-MerG1

Blue landing lights make. Our Ground Time Here Will Be Brief. Maxine W. Kumin. SP-KumiM

Blue Light Lounge Sutra for the Performance Poets at Harold Park Hotel. Yusef Komunyakaa. CP-KomuY

Blue light, morning. This Decoration. Hayden Carruth. CP-CarHS

Blue-lights sent up by ship forlorn. Arch, The. Herman Melville. SP-MelvH *Fr.* Clarel: A Poem and Pilgrimage in the Holy Land.

Blue Maroons. Carl Sandburg. CP-SandC

Blue Moles. Sylvia Plath. CP-PlatS

Blue Monday. Langston Hughes. CP-HughL; CP-HughL3

"Blue-Monday" at the Shoe Shop. James Whitcomb Riley. CP-RileJ

Blue Monody. Sam Hamill. SP-HamiS

Blue mountains to the north of the walls. Taking Leave of a Friend. Li Po. SP-PounE, *tr. by* Ezra Pound

Blue Movie. John Ciardi. CP-CiarJ

Blue of morning glory climbs fences and houses, The. Morning Glory Blue. Carl Sandburg. CP-SandC

Blue passionflower! Inquiry. Federico García Lorca. CP-GarcF, *tr. by* Catherine Brown

Blue pencil of the wave, The. Social. Charles Bukowski. SP-BukC1

Blue plums in the pewter bowl. Waking, The. Arthur Sze. SP-SzeA

Blue preacher / flew toward the swamp, A. Some Herons. Mary Oliver. SP-OlivM

Blue Rabbit. Robert Creeley. SP-CreeR

Blue Ribbon at Amesbury, A. Robert Frost. CP-FrosR

Blue Rider rode over The Bridge into the Bauhaus, The. Expressionist History of German Expressionism. Lawrence Ferlinghetti. SP-FerlL

Blue Ridge. Carl Sandburg. CP-SandC

Blue Rim of Memory, The. Denise Levertov. SP-LeveDL

Blue River. Federico García Lorca.
   "Blue river. / An ivory boat." CP-GarcF, *tr. by* Jerome Rothenberg
   Dreams. CP-GarcF, *tr. by* Jerome Rothenberg
   Lonesome Blues. CP-GarcF, *tr. by* Jerome Rothenberg

Blue river. / An ivory boat. Federico García Lorca. CP-GarcF, *tr. by* Jerome Rothenberg *Fr.* Blue River.

Blue river, icy sunk. Fanny Howe. SP-HoweF *Fr.* Lines Out to Silence.

Blue Roses. Rudyard Kipling. CP-KiplR *Fr.* Light That Failed, The.

Blue shot dawn, A. Themes in Contrast. Carl Sandburg. CP-SandC

Blue Skies Motel. Robert Creeley. SP-CreeR

Blue Sky, The. Gary Snyder. CP-SnydG

Blue sky. / Yellow field. Landscape Minus Song. Federico García Lorca. CP-GarcF, *tr. by* Jerome Rothenberg *Fr.* Moments of Song.

Blue Sonata. John Ashbery. SP-AshbJ

Blue Spill. James Tate. SP-TateJ

Blue Spruce. Muriel Rukeyser. CP-RukeM

Blue Starfish. Reef Mantra. Allen Ginsberg. SP-GinsA

Blue stone seems a, A. On the Gift of a Sapphire to My Wife Ann. James Laughlin. CP-LaugJ

Blue Stones, The. Raymond Carver. CP-CarvR

Blue Streak. Heather McHugh. SP-McHuH

Blue Suburban. Howard Nemerov. CP-NemeH

Blue Suede Shoes. Ai. SP-Ai

Blue sun in his red cockade, The. News and the Weather, The. Wallace Stevens. CP-StevW; CP-StevWP

Blue Sunday. Kenneth Rexroth. CP-RexrK

Blue Swallows, The. Howard Nemerov. CP-NemeH

Blue Teal's Mother. James Wright. CP-WrigJ

Blue the triangular why. E. E. Cummings. CP-CummE

Blue! 'Tis the Life of Heaven, the Domain. John Keats. CP-KeatJ

Blue Tonality. Yusef Komunyakaa. CP-KomuY

Blue took you, a wing of ash, The. At Dawn. Charles Tomlinson. CP-TomlC

Blue towel, A. James Schuyler. CP-SchuJ

Blue under sky and green under trees. Seasons in a Landscape of Woman, The. Robert Stock. SP-StocR

Blue, unstirrable, dreaming. Change, The. James Dickey. CP-DickJ

Blue water, and behind. After-Glow. E. E. Cummings. CP-CummE

Blue wave's slumber and the rocky brow, The. Olive Grove. James Merrill. SP-MerrJ

Blue windows, blue rooftops. On Rachmaninoff's Birthday. Frank O'Hara. SP-OharF

Blue Wing, The. Donald Hall. CP-HallD

Blue woman with sticking out breasts hanging, A. E. E. Cummings. CP-CummE

Bluebeard. Edna St. Vincent Millay. CP-MillE

Bluebeard. Sylvia Plath. CP-PlatS

Bluebeard. Let the gentle wife prepare. Ralph Waldo Emerson. CP-EmerR

Bluebells. Louis MacNeice. CP-MacNL

Bluebells come crowding a fellside. Metamorphosis, The. Charles Tomlinson. CP-TomlC; SP-TomlC

Blueberries. Robert Frost. CP-FrosR

Blueberry Blossoms, The. Jones Very. CP-VeryJ

Blueberrying in August. Amy Clampitt. CP-ClamA

Bluebird Houses. James Tate. SP-TateJ

Bluebird, What Do You Feed On? Carl Sandburg. CP-SandC

Bluebirds, The. Henry David Thoreau. CP-ThorH

Blueflags. William Carlos Williams. CP-WilW1

Blueness. D. H. Lawrence. CP-LawrD

Blues. Joseph Brodsky. CP-BrodJ

Blues. Robert Creeley. SP-CreeR

Blues. Kenneth Rexroth. CP-RexrK

Blues. Derek Walcott. CP-WalcD

Blues, The. Lord Byron. CP-Byron

Blues, The. Billy Collins. SP-CollB

Blues, The. Langston Hughes. CP-HughL

Blues at Dawn. Langston Hughes. CP-HughL; CP-HughL3

Blues Chant Hoodoo Rival. Yusef Komunyakaa. CP-KomuY

Blues Fantasy. Langston Hughes. CP-HughL; CP-HughL1

Blues for Casanova. Andrei Codrescu. SP-CodrA

Blues / for J.C. Olga Broumas. SP-BrouO

Blues for Jimmy. Thomas McGrath. SP-McGrT

Blues for the Old Revolutionary Woman. Thomas McGrath. SP-McGrT

Blues for Warren. Thomas McGrath. SP-McGrT

Blues in Stereo. Langston Hughes. CP-HughL; CP-HughL3

Blues is like a hardon comes right in your mouth. Hardon Blues. Allen Ginsberg. SP-GinsA

Blues may be the life you've led, The. Good Woman Feeling Bad, A. Maya Angelou. SP-AngeM

Blue's my older brother's color. Mine is brown, you see. Poem for My Brother. John Logan. CP-LogaJ

Blues on a Box. Langston Hughes. CP-HughL; CP-HughL2

Bluet. The. James Schuyler. CP-SchuJ

Bluet is a small flower, creamy-throated, that grows in patches, The. Footnote. James Schuyler. CP-SchuJ

Bluewhite birdlight. Monday Beach, Cold Day. Charles Bukowski. SP-BukC2

Bluish roofs and whitened doorways. Damned Cherub. Arthur Rimbaud. CP-RimbA, *tr.* by Martin Sorrell

Blunder is an estimate, The. Emily Dickinson. CP-DickE

Blunder of All Blunders, on the Wonder of All Wonders, The. *Unknown, sometimes at. to* Thomas Sheridan. CP-SherT

Blush as of roses, A. Le Marais du Cygne. John Greenleaf Whittier. CP-WhitJ

Blush as you stroke the curves—. Food of the Dead. Robert Graves. CP-GravR

Blush, folly, blush: here's none that fears. Ben Jonson. CP-JonsB *Fr.* Poetaster, The.

Blustering god, / Stamping across the sky. Stephen Crane. CP-CranS

Blyth Aberdeane, thow beriall of all tounis. To Aberdein. William Dunbar. CP-DunbW

Blythe, blythe and merry was she. Blythe Was She. Robert Burns. CP-BurnR

Blythe hae I been on yon hill. Song: "Blythe hae I been on yon hill." Robert Burns. CP-BurnR

Blythe Was She. Robert Burns. CP-BurnR

(Song.—Composed at Auchtertyre on Miss Euphemia Murray of Lentrose.) CP-BurnR

Bo, may you someday. Of Brook and Stone. Hayden Carruth. CP-CarHS

Bo was three when we slugged through Arizona, The. Sonnet: "Bo was three when we slugged through Arizona, The." Hayden Carruth. CP-CarHS *Fr.* Sonnets.

Boadicea: An Ode. William Cowper. CP-CowpW

Boanerges Blitzen, servant of the Queen. Man Who Could Write, The. Rudyard Kipling. CP-KiplR

Boarding House. Langston Hughes. CP-HughL; CP-HughL2

Boardwalks are empty, the cafés closed, The. Elegy of Last Resort. Howard Nemerov. CP-NemeH

Boast. Alan Dugan. CP-DugaA

Boast, The. Rita Dove. SP-DoveR

Boast not, my native spot, thy sons were first. Salem ("Boast not, my native spot, thy sons were first"). Jones Very. CP-VeryJ

Boast of Quietness. Jorge Luis Borges. SP-BorgJ, *tr.* by Stephen Kessler

Boat, A. Margaret Atwood. SP-AtwM2

Boat, The. Anne Sexton. SP-SextA *Fr.* Death of the Fathers, The.

Boat, The. Charles Olson. CP-OlsoC

Boat, The. Stevie Smith. CP-SmitS

Boat amid the ripples, drifting, rocking, A. Pastime. Christina Georgina Rossetti. CP-RosC2

Boat in the Forest, A. Thomas Lux. SP-LuxT

Boat is always going by, set afloat, The. Poem of Exile, A. Eleanor Wilner. SP-WilnE

Boat moves slowly through the fens, The. Slow Boat Ride. Richard Eberhart. CP-EberR

Boat on the Serchio, The. Percy Bysshe Shelley. CP-ShelP

Boat People. Yusef Komunyakaa. CP-KomuY

Boat Ride. Tess Gallagher. SP-GallT

Boat Song. Sir Walter Scott. *See* Lady of the Lake, The

Boat that did not rock or wobble once, A. Seamus Heaney. SP-HeanSO *Fr.* Squarings.

Boat that sails upon the sea, A. Way of the World, The. Christina Georgina Rossetti. CP-RosC3

Boat that took my love away, The. Boat, The. Stevie Smith. CP-SmitS

Boating party, The. Magic Morning. Stevie Smith. CP-SmitS

Boatman rowed into, The. Blue Grotto, The. James Merrill. SP-MerrJ

Boatmen of Santorin, The. Archibald MacLeish. CP-MacLA

Boatmen on the bay of Santorin, The. Boatmen of Santorin, The. Archibald MacLeish. CP-MacLA

Boats in a Fog. Robinson Jeffers. CP-JefR1

Boats' lights in the dawn going so swiftly the, The. Charles Olson. SP-OlsoC *Fr.* Maximus Poems, The.

Boats of Newhaven and Folkestone and Dover. French Wars, The. Rudyard Kipling. CP-KiplR

Boats on the Marne. Eugenio Montale. CP-MontE, *tr.* by Jonathan Galassi

Boats sail on the rivers, / And ships sail on the seas. Rainbow, The. Christina Georgina Rossetti. CP-RosC2

Boat's tarred and shellacked to a water-repellant finish, The. Reed Boat, A. Yusef Komunyakaa. CP-KomuY

Bob. C. K. Williams. CP-WillC; SP-WillC

Bob and I / in different rooms. Quarrel ("Bob and I / in different rooms"). Grace Paley. CP-PalGC

Bob Hope's on stage, but we want the Gold Diggers. Communiqué. Yusef Komunyakaa. CP-KomuY

Bob o' Dumblane, The. Robert Burns. CP-BurnR

Bob Visits Friends. Grace Paley. CP-PalGC

Bob-White is whirring, The. Nature's Thanksgiving. Tennessee Williams. CP-WillT

Bobber. Raymond Carver. CP-CarvR

Bobbie ("Every one"). Robert Creeley. CP-CreeR

Bobbie ("Her voice"). Robert Creeley. SP-CreeR

Bobby Delano. Robert Lowell. SP-LoweR

Bobò is dead, but don't take off your hat. Funeral of Bobò, The. Joseph Brodsky. CP-BrodJ, *tr.* by Richard Wilbur

Bobolink, The. Edna St. Vincent Millay. CP-MillE

Bobolink! / Bobolink! / Spink! Max Schling, Max Schling, Lend Me Your Green Thumb. Ogden Nash. CP-NashO

Bobolink is gone, The. Emily Dickinson. CP-DickE

Bobo's Metamorphosis. Czeslaw Milosz. CP-MiloC; CP-MiloCN, *tr.* by Richard Lourie

Bobs. Rudyard Kipling. CP-KiplR

Boccaccio: The Plague Years. Rita Dove. SP-DoveR

Bodies, sunburned, youthful—redblack earth. Yannis Ritsos. SP-RitsY, *tr.* by Athan Anagnostopoulos

Bodies / that covered the bones, The. Alyscamps at Arles, The. May Swenson. SP-SwenM

Bodiless God. D. H. Lawrence. CP-LawrD

Bodo. Thomas Lux. SP-LuxT

Body. Olga Broumas. SP-BrouO

Body. Boris Christov. CP-PinsR, *tr.* by Robert Pinsky

Body. Czeslaw Milosz. CP-MiloCN, *tr.* by Robert Hass

Body, The. Robert Herrick. CP-HerrR

Body, The. Gabriela Mistral. SP-MistG, *tr.* by Maria Giachetti [*or* Jacketti]

Body, The. C. K. Williams. SP-WillC

Body and Soul. "Anvari." CP-EmerR

Body and Soul. Olga Broumas. SP-BrouO

Body and Soul. "H. D." CP-DoolH

Body and Soul. Charles Simic. SP-SimiCE

Body and Soul: A Meditation. Maxine W. Kumin. SP-KumiM

Body Beside the Ties, The. Kenneth Patchen. CP-PatcK

Body, blind with sleep, A. Statue. Gerrit Achterberg. CP-RicAE

Body Blues. Andrei Codrescu. SP-CodrA

Body burned away the parting cloth, The. Lady, Anemone. Tennessee Williams. CP-WillT

Body cannot lie, but its betrayals, The. Handclap. Muriel Rukeyser. CP-RukeM

Body dies / little by little, The. Deaths of the Other Children, The. Margaret Atwood. SP-AtwM1

Body / Eternal Shadow of the finite Soul, The. Body Imaging Soul. Samuel Taylor Coleridge. CP-ColeS

Body grows without, The. Emily Dickinson. CP-DickE

Body Imaging Soul. Samuel Taylor Coleridge. CP-ColeS

Body Intelligence. Jelaluddin Rumi. SP-Rumi, *tr.* by Coleman Barks

Body is like a November birch facing the full moon, The. Solitude Late at Night in the Woods. Robert Bly. SP-BlyR

Body is seduced by damages, A. Tendencies. Heather McHugh. SP-McHuH

Body is the body of the Buddha, The. Ten Thousand Sutras. Sam Hamill. SP-HamiS

Body Is the Cause of Love, The. Yehuda Amichai. SP-AmicY, *tr.* by Chana Bloch

Body is the Soul's [*or* Soules] poor[e] house, or home, The. Body, The. Robert Herrick. CP-HerrR

Body keeps talking under the mind. Touching Down. A. R. Ammons. CP-AmmoA

Body Language. Charles Wright. SP-WrigCN

Body my house. Question. May Swenson. SP-SwenM

Body of God, The. D. H. Lawrence. CP-LawrD

Body of itself is clean, but the caged mind, The. Obscenity. D. H. Lawrence. CP-LawrD

Body of Jesus taken down from the cross. Loin Cloth. Carl Sandburg. CP-SandC

Body of Summer, The. Sam Hamill. SP-HamiS

Body of the youthful bronze girl, her eyes fearful, The. Spirit of the Dead Watching: after Gaugin. John Logan. CP-LogaJ

Body Politic. A. R. Ammons. CP-AmmoA

Body Politic, The. Donald Hall. CP-HallD

Body, remember not only how much you were loved. Remember, Body. Constantine P. Cavafy. CP-CavaC, tr. by Theoharis Constantine Theoharis

Body sick, the cause we seek to find, The. Cause, The. Jones Very. CP-VeryJ

Body / thin as a matchstick. Yannis Ritsos. SP-RitsY Fr. Paper Poems 2.

Body would think, A. Largesse. Paul Muldoon. CP-MuldP

Bodybuilders' Contest. Wisława Szymborska. SP-SzymW, tr. by Stanislaw Barańczak and Clare Cavanagh

Body's Beauty. Dante Gabriel Rossetti. CW-RossD Fr. House of Life, The.

Body's salt, the soule is; which when gon, The. Soul Is the Salt, The. Robert Herrick. CP-HerrR

Boeotian. Robert Frost. CP-FrosR

Boer War Bread Strike. James Schuyler. CP-SchuJ

'Boes. Carl Sandburg. CP-SandC

Bog-Face. Stevie Smith. CP-SmitS

Bog Oak. Seamus Heaney. SP-HeanSO

Bog Queen. Seamus Heaney. SP-HeanSO

Bogland. Seamus Heaney. SP-HeanSO

Boh Da Thone was a warrior bold. Ballad of Boh Da Thone, The. Rudyard Kipling. CP-KiplR

Bohemia. Dorothy Parker. CP-ParkD

Bohemian, The. Paul Laurence Dunbar. CP-DunbP

Bohemian Hymn, The. Ralph Waldo Emerson. CP-EmerR

Bohemians; A Hate Song. Dorothy Parker. CP-ParkD

Bohemians, The. Ivor Gurney. SP-GurnI

Boil. John Updike. CP-UpdiJ

Boiling Water, The. Kenneth Koch. SP-KochK

Bois seul. Samuel Beckett. CP-BeckS

Bokardo. Edwin Arlington Robinson. CP-RobiE

Bold be the critic, zealous to his trust. Epistle 2.2: "Bold be the critic, zealous to his trust." Horace. CP-JohnS Fr. Epistles.

Bold encroachers on the deep, The. Run upon the Bankers, The. Jonathan Swift. CP-SwifJ

Bold Horatius. Wilfred Owen. CP-OwenW

Bold in their cause they stood before the Czar. Mission of the Friends to the Emperor Nicholas, The. Jones Very. CP-VeryJ

Boldest thing I ever did was to save a savior, The. Oration, The. Carolyn Kizer. CP-KizeC

Boldness[e] in Love. Thomas Carew. CP-CareT

Bolero, silk-tassled, the fuchsia, The. For Kazuko. Rita Dove. SP-DoveR

"Bolinas and Me." Robert Creeley. CP-CreeR

Bolivar. John Greenleaf Whittier. CP-WhitJ

Bolsheviks. Aba Shtoltsenberg. CP-KunSC, tr. by Stanley Kunitz

Bolshevist lady is no less refined, The. True Sensibility. G. K. Chesterton. CP-ChesG

Bolt and bar the shutter. Mad as the Mist and Snow. William Butler Yeats. CP-YeatW

Bolt from the Blue. Gregory Orr. SP-OrrG

Bolt-hole of brigandage, old keep. Old Roscoff. Tristan Corbière. CP-MahoD, tr. by Derek Mahon

Bolt / In the frame. George Oppen. CP-OppGN

Bolyai, the Geometer. Donald Davie. CP-DaviDC

Bomb in the bar will explode at thirteen twenty, The. Terrorist, He's Watching, The. Wisława Szymborska. SP-SzymW, tr. by Stanislaw Barańczak and Clare Cavanagh

Bomb photographed me on the shore, A. Ground Zero [December 1982]. William Stafford. SP-StafWW

Bomb Test. Gary Snyder. CP-SnydG

Bomb (II). Pablo Neruda. SP-NeruP

Bombarded City, The. Thomas Merton. CP-MertT

Bombardment. D. H. Lawrence. CP-LawrD

Bombers spread out, temperature steady, The. War and Silence. Robert Bly. SP-BlyR

Bombing of the Town of Kralupy, The. Jaroslav Seifert. SP-SeifJ, tr. by Ewald Osers

Bombings. Lorine Niedecker. CP-NiedL

Bombings in Dixie. Langston Hughes. CP-HughL; CP-HughL3

Bon bon il est un pays. Samuel Beckett. CP-BeckS

"Bon soir, monsieur," they called to me. Street Called Crooked, The. Countee Cullen. CP-CullC

Bon Voyage. Edwin Arlington Robinson. CP-RobiE

Bonapartisme. Kenneth Rexroth. CP-RexrK

Bond and Free. Robert Frost. CP-FrosR

Bondman, The. Robert Herrick. CP-HerrR

Bonds for All. Langston Hughes. CP-HughL; CP-HughL3

Bonds: In Memoriam. Langston Hughes. CP-HughL; CP-HughL3

Bone. Thom Gunn. CP-GunnT

Bone. Charles Tomlinson. CP-TomlC

Bone Dreams. Seamus Heaney. SP-HeanSO

Bone-Flower Elegy. Robert Earl Hayden. CP-HaydR

Bone-idle, I lie listening to the rain. Dejection [Ode]. Derek Mahon. CP-MahoD

Bone Poem. Mary Oliver. SP-OlivM

Bone that has no Marrow, The. Emily Dickinson. CP-DickE

Bone-thin gent. Dance Floor. Clarence Major. SP-MajoC

Bone to his bone, grain to his grain of dust. To Every Seed His Own Body. Christina Georgina Rossetti. CP-RosC2

Bones. Ted Hughes. SP-HughTN

Bones. Carl Sandburg. CP-SandC

Bones a-gittin' achy. Chrismus Is A-Comin'. Paul Laurence Dunbar. CP-DunbP

Bones is a crazy pony. Bones. Ted Hughes. SP-HughTN

Bones of Coleridge, The. Richard Eberhart. CP-EberR

Bones of saints are praised above their flesh, The. Reliquary. Adrienne Rich. CP-RicAE

Bones of the dead are tender ice, The. Gabriela Mistral. SP-MistG, tr. by Maria Giachetti [or Jacketti]

Bones of today I am going to leave you. For Saying That It Won't Matter. W. S. Merwin. SP-MerwW

Bonfire. Tess Gallagher. SP-GallT

Bonfire, The. Robert Frost. CP-FrosR

Bonfire at Midnight. Jelaluddin Rumi. SP-Rumi, tr. by Coleman Barks

Bonfire gives the evening land, The. In Another Manner. Federico García Lorca. CP-GarcF, tr. by Alan S. Trueblood Fr. Songs to End With.

Bonfire places on the field of afternoon, The. In Another Mode. Federico García Lorca. SP-GarcF, tr. by Lysander Kemp

Bonfires, The. W. H. Auden. CP-AudeW

Bonfires, The. Rudyard Kipling. CP-KiplR

Bonhoeffer in his skylit cell. Christmas Trees. Geoffrey Hill. CP-HillG

Bonie Bell. Robert Burns. CP-BurnR

Bonie Dundee. Robert Burns. CP-BurnR

Bonie Lad That's Far Awa, The. Robert Burns. CP-BurnR

Bonie Laddie, Highland Laddie. Robert Burns. CP-BurnR

Bonie Lass Made the Bed to Me, The. Robert Burns. See Lass That Made the Bed for Me, The

Bonie Mary. Robert Burns. CP-BurnR

Bonnard's Nudes. Raymond Carver. CP-CarvR

Bonnie Broukit Bairn, The. Hugh MacDiarmid. SP-MacDH

Bonnie lassie, will ye go, will ye go, will ye go. Birks of Aberfeldy, The [Composed on the Spot]. Robert Burns. CP-BurnR

Bonnie Lesley. Robert Burns. CP-BurnR

Bonnie [or Bonny] Wee Thing, The. Robert Burns. CP-BurnR (Wishfully I look and languish.) CP-BurnR

Bonnie Peg. Robert Burns. CP-BurnR

Bonniest lad that e'er I saw, The. Highland Laddie. Robert Burns. CP-BurnR

Bonny and stout and brown, without a hat. Merry Maid. John Clare. SP-ClarJ

Bononian, sis Rufa, Rufus' lum fell at. Catullus. See Menenius' wife, / a red-headed cat from Bologna

Bonpland. Lorine Niedecker. CP-NiedL

Bonsai. Billy Collins. SP-CollB

Bonsai tree / in the attractive pot, The. Work of Artifice, A. Marge Piercy. SP-PierM

Boo hoo hoo and boo ha ha. Sarrasin's Wealth Song. Andrei Codrescu. SP-CodrA

Boobus Hierophante. Philip Whalen. SP-WhalP

Boobyhatch's bars, the guards, the nurses, the. Ontological Episode of the Asylum. Hayden Carruth. CP-CarHS

Boogah Man, The. Paul Laurence Dunbar. CP-DunbP

Boogie: 1 a.m. Langston Hughes. CP-HughL; CP-HughL3

Book. The. Rae Armantrout. SP-ArmaA

Book, The. Adrienne Rich. CP-RicAE; SP-RicA2

Book, The. John Greenleaf Whittier. CP-WhitJ

Book, The. Miller Williams. CP-WillM

Book came forth of late, called PETER BELL, A. On the Detraction Which Followed the Publication of a Certain Poem. William Wordsworth. CP-WorW2

Book goes fluttering crazily through the space of my room toward the wall like a bird, The. My Book, My Book. C. K. Williams. SP-WillC

Book in the Ruins, A. Czeslaw Milosz. CP-MiloC; CP-MiloCN, tr. by Renata

Gorczynski *and* Robert Hass

Book in which these figures grin, The. Inscription for Rhoda Bastable. G. K. Chesterton. CP-ChesG

Book is only the Heart's Portrait, A. Emily Dickinson. SP-DickE

Book of, A. Michael Palmer. SP-PalmM

Book of Ahania, The. William Blake. CP-BlakW

Book of Ancestors. Margaret Atwood. SP-AtwM1

Book of Annandale, The. Edwin Arlington Robinson. CP-RobiE

Book of Ephraim, The. James Merrill.
  Lost in Translation. SP-MerrJ

"Book of Gems," The. Henry David Thoreau. CP-ThorH

Book of Job and a Draft of a Poem to Praise the Paths of the Living, The. George Oppen. CP-OppGN

Book of Joyous Children, The. James Whitcomb Riley. CP-RileJ

Book of Kells, The. Howard Nemerov. CP-NemeH

Book of Lies, The. James Tate. SP-TateJ

Book of Life, The. Jones Very. CP-VeryJ

Book of Los, The. William Blake. CP-BlakW

Book of Nature, The. Richard Eberhart. CP-EberR

Book of nothing gives, A. Book of, A. Michael Palmer. SP-PalmM

Book of Resemblances, A. Robert Duncan. SP-DuncR

Book of the council major. Canto 25: "Book of the council major." Ezra Pound. SP-PounE *Fr.* Cantos.

Book of the Dead, The. Thom Gunn. CP-GunnT

Book of the Dead, The. Muriel Rukeyser. CP-RukeM

Book of the Duchesse, The. Geoffrey Chaucer. CP-ChauG

Book of the Yellow Castle. Michael Palmer. SP-PalmM

Book of Thel, The. William Blake. CP-BlakW

Book of Urizen [*or* First Book of Urizen], The. William Blake. CP-BlakW

Book of verses underneath the bough, A. New Omar, The. G. K. Chesterton. CP-ChesG

Book of Wild Pictures, A. G. K. Chesterton. CP-ChesG

Book opens, A. People come out, bend. *Magic Mountain, The.* William Stafford. SP-StafWW

Book thou givest, dear as such, The. Little Friend, The. Elizabeth Barrett Browning. CP-BroEB

Book was writ[t] of late called [*or* call'd] *Tetrachordon*, A. On the Detraction Which Followed upon My Writing Certain Treatises. John Milton. CP-MiltJ

Book-Worms, The. Robert Burns. CP-BurnR

Booker T. / Was a practical man. Ballad of Booker T. Langston Hughes. CP-HughL; CP-HughL3

Booker T. Washington. Paul Laurence Dunbar. CP-DunbP

Booker Washington Trilogy, The. Nicholas Vachel Lindsay. CP-LindV

Bookplate. James Vincent Cunningham. CP-CunnJ

Books. William Wordsworth. *Fr.* Prelude, The; Growth of a Poet's Mind [1850 vers.].

Books. Andrei Codrescu. SP-CodrA

Books. Billy Collins. SP-CollB

Books, The. Wyatt Prunty. SP-PrunW

Books; A Hymn of Hate. Dorothy Parker. CP-ParkD

Books, do not look at me. Sand in the Air. Louis MacNeice. CP-MacNL

Books in the Running Brooks. Christina Georgina Rossetti. CP-RosC3

Books litter the bed, / leaves the lawn. It. October. James Schuyler. CP-SchuJ

Books Men Die For. Carl Sandburg. CP-SandC

Boom. Ted Hughes.
  Bar-Room TV.
    (Public Bar TV.) SP-HughTN
  Kafka. SP-HughTN
  Tutorial. SP-HughTN

Boom! Howard Nemerov. CP-NemeH

Boom Town. William Stafford. SP-StafWW

Boomerang, on breath paths, A. Paul Celan. SP-CelaP, *tr.* by John Felstiner

Boon. Paul Muldoon. CP-MuldP

Boone. Wendell Berry. CP-BerrW

Boop-Boop-Adieup, Little Group! Ogden Nash. CP-NashO

Boor of night in middle earth cries out, A. Infernale. Wallace Stevens. CP-StevWP

Bootblack, The. Charles Tomlinson. CP-TomlC

Booth led boldly with his big bass drum. General William Booth Enters into Heaven. Nicholas Vachel Lindsay. CP-LindV

Bootlaces. G. K. Chesterton. CP-ChesG

Boots. Rudyard Kipling. CP-KiplR

Bop Lyrics. Allen Ginsberg. CP-GinsA

Border. Federico García Lorca. CP-GarcF, *tr.* by Jerome Rothenberg

Border Ballad, A. Paul Laurence Dunbar. CP-DunbP

Border halt, an hour out of Saloniki. Babel Aboard the Hellas International Express. Amy Clampitt. CP-ClamA

Border Line. Langston Hughes. CP-HughL; CP-HughL2

Borderers, The. A Tragedy. William Wordsworth. CP-WorW1

Borderland—that's where, if one knew how, The. Life of Art, The. Denise Levertov. SP-LeveDS

Bored to Choresis. Allen Tate. CP-TateA

Boredom and terror, and the older. Vase, The. Gregory Orr. SP-OrrG

Boredom, Ennui, Depression. D. H. Lawrence. CP-LawrD

Boredom of paying a call, The. Seller of Garlic and Onions, The. Stéphane Mallarmé. CP-MallS, *tr.* by Henry Weinfield

Boreman takes tole, cheats, flatters, lyes, yet Boreman. Upon Boreman. Epig. Robert Herrick. CP-HerrR

Bores; A Hymn of Hate. Dorothy Parker. CP-ParkD

Borges, The. Jorge Luis Borges. SP-BorgJ, *tr.* by Alastair Reid

Borges and I. Jorge Luis Borges. SP-BorgJ, *tr.* by Ken Krabbenhoft

Borinken Blues. Yusef Komunyakaa. CP-KomuY

Born. Wisława Szymborska. SP-SzymW, *tr.* by Stanislaw Barańczak *and* Clare Cavanagh

Born a million years ago you stay here a million years . . . watching the. Blue Ridge. Carl Sandburg. CP-SandC

Born and bred / in Wellington. Night ("Born and bred / in Wellington"). Robert Creeley. SP-CreeR

Born at 'The Bell' in Gloucester. Homage to George Whitefield. Donald Davie. CP-DaviDC

Born at the bottom of the heap. And as he grew upwards. Sacrifice. Ted Hughes. SP-HughTN

Born, died. Now bedded by the churchyard wall. Michelangelo Buonarroti. CP-Miche, *tr.* by John Frederick Nims

Born flipper-first into an icy wind. Seal. Heather McHugh. SP-McHuH

Born from ignoble stock on a day of dearth. Lack. Robert Graves. CP-GravR

Born green we were. Firesong. Sylvia Plath. CP-PlatS

Born I was to be old. Anacreontic. Robert Herrick. CP-HerrR

Born in a sour waste lot. Nasturtium. Thom Gunn. CP-GunnT

Born in December. Muriel Rukeyser. CP-RukeM

Born in the garret, in the kitchen bred. Sketch from Private Life, A. Lord Byron. CP-Byron

Born in this world. Gospel Noble Truths. Allen Ginsberg. CP-GinsA; SP-GinsA

Born like a dwarf. Speaking Bitterness. Anne Sexton. CP-SextA

Born of the buzzing hives. Wax Candle, The. Jaroslav Seifert. SP-SeifJ, *tr.* by Ewald Osers

Born of the sorrowful of heart. For Paul Laurence Dunbar. Countee Cullen. CP-CullC *Fr.* Four Epitaphs.

Born Pretty in a Poor Country. Yusef Komunyakaa. CP-KomuY

Born proud and fitful, hot and cold. Athenian Death. Robert Penn Warren. CP-WarrR

Born salesman, A. And One for My Dame. Anne Sexton. CP-SextA; SP-SextA

Born thirty years ago. Han-shan. CP-ColdM, *tr.* by Red Pine

Born Yesterday. Philip Larkin. CP-LarkP

Borne down by bitter misfortune. Carmen 68. Catullus. CP-ZukLS *Fr.* Carmina.

Borne down by the inability to lift the heaviness. Charles Olson. CP-OlsoC

Born[e] I was to meet with age. On Himself[e]. Robert Herrick. CP-HerrR

Borough, The. George Crabbe.
  Alms-House and Trustees, The. SP-CrabG
  Arrival of the Players, The. SP-CrabG
  Condemned Felon, The. SP-CrabG
  Election, The. SP-CrabG
  Poor and Their Dwellings, The. SP-CrabG
  Sea: A Summer and Winter View, The. SP-CrabG
  Vicar, The. SP-CrabG

Borrow the beloved's eyes. Checkmate. Jelaluddin Rumi. SP-Rumi, *tr.* by Coleman Barks

Borrow Urania's subtile wings. Ralph Waldo Emerson. CP-EmerR

Borrowed Ones, The. Tess Gallagher. SP-GallT

Borrowed wings on his ankles. Perseus. Louis MacNeice. CP-MacNL

Bosnia. A. K. Ramanujan. CP-RamaA

Bosnia Tune. Joseph Brodsky. CP-BrodJ

Boss came around at Christmas, The. Little Song about Charity, A. Thomas McGrath. SP-McGrT

Boss, the crane operator, one of the workers, a friend of somebody in the junkyard, The. Fire. C. K. Williams. SP-WillC

Boston. Ralph Waldo Emerson. CP-EmerR

Boston. Edwin Arlington Robinson. CP-RobiE

Boston Ballad [1854], A. Walt Whitman. CP-WhitW

Boston cleaves to the river. Crossing the Footbridge over Storrow Drive. William Corbett. SP-CorbW

Boston College team has gold helmets, under which the, The. Hockey Poem, The. Robert Bly. SP-BlyR

Boston Common. John Berryman. CP-BerrJ

Boston Evening Transcript, The. T. S. Eliot. CP-ElioT

Boston has a festival. In the Public Garden. Marianne Craig Moore. CP-MoorM

Boston Hymn. Ralph Waldo Emerson. CP-EmerR

Boston's used bookshops, anachronisms from London. Napoleon. Robert Lowell. CP-LoweR

Bosworth Field. Robert Lowell. SP-LoweR

Botanical Nomenclature. Amy Clampitt. CP-ClamA

Botanist on Alp (No. 1). Wallace Stevens. CP-StevW; CP-StevWP

Botanist on Alp (No. 2). Wallace Stevens. CP-StevW; CP-StevWP

Botched job, / the blindfold slipped, he sees, A. Newsreel: Man and Firing Squad. Margaret Atwood. SP-AtwM1

Both doors of the world. Epitaph for François. Paul Celan. SP-CelaP, *tr. by* John Felstiner

Both eaching come ghostlike. E. E. Cummings. CP-CummE

Both Erato the Muse of Lyric Poetry and Mime. Mock Translation from the Greek. Alan Dugan. CP-DugaA

Both of them were walking toward. Death Walkers, The. James Laughlin. CP-LaugJ

Both robbed of air, we both lie in one ground. Hero and Leander. John Donne. CP-DonnJ; MW-DonnJ

Both Sides of the Medal. D. H. Lawrence. CP-LawrD

Both, the company of men. Company of Men, The. Charles Olson. CP-OlsoC

Both Together and Each Apart. Yehuda Amichai. SP-AmicYL, *tr. by* Benjamin Harshav *and* Barbara Harshav

Both were jailbirds; no speechmakers at all. Jack London and O. Henry. Carl Sandburg. CP-SandC

Both you two have. To the Yew and Cypress to Grace His Funeral. Robert Herrick. CP-HerrR

Bother, The. Rudyard Kipling. CP-KiplR *Fr.* Muse among the Motors, The.

Bothering Me at Last. David Ignatow. SP-IgnaD

Bothwell Castle. William Wordsworth. CP-WorW2

Botticellian Trees, The. William Carlos Williams. CP-WilW1

Bottle, The. Walter De la Mare. CP-DeLaW

Bottle Is Drunk Out by One, The. Philip Larkin. CP-LarkP

Bottle of Aspirins, The. Stevie Smith. CP-SmitS

Bottled up for days, mostly. Charles Olson. SP-OlsoC *Fr.* Maximus Poems, The.

Bottleneck. Louis MacNeice. CP-MacNL

Bottles and bottles and bottles. Stephen Crane. CP-CranS

Bottom. Arthur Rimbaud. CP-RimbA, *tr. by* Martin Sorrell

Bottom of the air is disturbed as with an undertow, The. She, Thus. Charles Olson. CP-OlsoC

Bottom of the sea has come, The. Song: "Bottom of the sea has come, The." Thomas Merton. CP-MertT

Bottom of the second. Joe Brainard. William Corbett. SP-CorbW

Bottom of the universe and, The. Crawl. C. K. Williams. CP-WillC

Bottoms *milfoil yarrow* holm seas. Yarrow. Louis Zukofsky. CP-ZukLS

Bougainville. Donald Davie. CP-DaviDC

Bougainvillea purples burn Space Between Two Blades of Grass Meets an Intractable Ego, The. Robert Stock. SP-StocR

Bough which long has borne the winter's blast, The. Spring in the Soul. Jones Very. CP-VeryJ

Boughs being pruned, birds preenèd, show more fair. Gerard Manley Hopkins. CP-HopkG

Boughs, the boughs are bare enough, The. Winter with the Gulf Stream. Gerard Manley Hopkins. CP-HopkG

Bounce to Fop. Alexander Pope. CP-SwifJ

Bound—a trouble. Emily Dickinson. CP-DickE

Bound (almost) now of my book I see, The. On His Booke. Robert Herrick. CP-HerrR

Bound and bordered in leaf-green. Book of Joyous Children, The. James Whitcomb Riley. CP-RileJ

Bound and free. Eudaimon. Kathleen Jessie Raine. SP-RainK

Bound No'th Blues. Langston Hughes. CP-HughL; CP-HughL1

Bound to the earth. At the Zoo in Spain. Clarence Major. SP-MajoC

Bound with baling wire to the tubular jerry-built bumper of a beat-up old dump truck. Souls. C. K. Williams. SP-WillC

Boundary. Adrienne Rich. CP-RicAE

Boundary Commission, The. Paul Muldoon. CP-MuldP

Boundary Stone, The. D. H. Lawrence. CP-LawrD

Boundless Moment, A. Robert Frost. CP-FrosR

Bounty-threat of snow, The. Apple Slump. Paul Muldoon. CP-MuldP

Bouquet. Langston Hughes. CP-HughL; CP-HughL3

Bouquet, The. Wallace Stevens. CP-StevW; CP-StevWP

Bouquet in Dog Time. Hayden Carruth. CP-CarHS

Bouquet of Belle Scavoir. Wallace Stevens. CP-StevW; CP-StevWP

Bouquet of HUGE. Haiku for Mike. Philip Whalen. SP-WhalP

Bouquet of Roses in Sunlight. Wallace Stevens. CP-StevW; CP-StevWP

Bouquet of Ten Roses, A. Robert Bly. SP-BlyR

Bouquets. Constantine P. Cavafy. CP-CavaC, *tr. by* Theoharis Constantine Theoharis

Bourgeois and Bolshevist. D. H. Lawrence. CP-LawrD

Bourgeois and the bolshevist are both quite blind, The. Half-Blind, The. D. H. Lawrence. CP-LawrD

Bourgeois asserts the he owns his property by divine right, The. Property and No-Property. D. H. Lawrence. CP-LawrD

Bourgeois cowardice produces bolshevist impudence. Cowardice and Impudence. D. H. Lawrence. CP-LawrD

Bourgeois produces the bolshevist, inevitably, The. Bourgeois and Bolshevist. D. H. Lawrence. CP-LawrD

Bourn. A. R. Ammons. CP-AmmoA

Bourne, The. Christina Georgina Rossetti. CP-RosC1

Bouts-Rimeés (Written at Chawton Cottage, 1820). George Knight. CP-AustJ

Bow bent remembers home long, The. Recoil. William Stafford. SP-StafWW

Bow both your heads at once, and hearts. Ben Jonson. CP-JonsB *Fr.* Irish Masque, The.

Bow down thine ear, O Lord, hear me. Psalm 86: "Bow down thine ear, O Lord, hear me." Bible, *O.T.* CP-MiltJ *Fr.* Psalms.

Bow of black moons, A. Moonbow. Federico García Lorca. CP-GarcF, *tr. by* Jerome Rothenberg *Fr.* In the Garden of the Lunar Grapefruits.

Bow to me, bow to me. Dance of Death, The. Robert Browning. CP-BroR2

Bowed, midst a universial grief that makes. Tribute of His Home, The. James Whitcomb Riley. CP-RileJ

Bower, The. Richard Eberhart. CP-EberR

Bower-Bird. Robert Graves. CP-GravR

Bower-bird improvised a cool retreat, The. Bower-Bird. Robert Graves. CP-GravR

Bowers whereat, in dreams, I see, The. To ———: "Bowers whereat, in dreams, I see, The." Edgar Allan Poe. CP-PoeEd

Bowing he asks her the favor. Dancers. Donald Hall. CP-HallD

Bowing the Head. Donald Davie. CP-DaviDC

Bowl. Wallace Stevens. CP-StevWP

Bowl, A. Jelaluddin Rumi. SP-Rumi, *tr. by* Coleman Barks

Bowl-hollow of sandstone, beech-bounded, beech-shrouded. No Bird Does Call. Robert Penn Warren. CP-WarrR

Bowl made from a tobacco-yellow skull, The. Bells in the Endtime of Gyurmey Tsultrim. Norman Dubie. SP-DubiN

Bowl of Blood, The. Robinson Jeffers. CP-JefR3

Bowl of Progresso Minestrone. William Corbett. SP-CorbW

Bowles and Campbell. Lord Byron. CP-Byron

Bowls. D. H. Lawrence. CP-LawrD

Bowls. Marianne Craig Moore. CP-MoorM

Bows glided down, and the coast, The. Ballad of the Long-legged Bait. Dylan Thomas. CP-ThomD

Box. Robert Creeley. SP-CreeR

Box, The. Yehuda Amichai. SP-AmicY, *tr. by* Chana Bloch

Box, The. Robert Creeley. CP-CreeR

Box, The. James Laughlin. CP-LaugJ

Box cars run by a mile long. Work Gangs. Carl Sandburg. CP-SandC

Box Comes Home, A. John Ciardi. CP-CiarJ

Box of Leaves, A. Wyatt Prunty. SP-PrunW

Box of teak, a box of sandalwood, A. Plymouth. Philip Larkin. CP-LarkP

Boxers Hit Harder When Women Are Around. Kenneth Patchen. CP-PatcK

Boxes and Bags. Carl Sandburg. CP-SandC

Boxing Day. Yusef Komunyakaa. CP-KomuY

Boy. John Ciardi. CP-CiarJ

Boy, A. John Ashbery. SP-AshbJ

Boy, A. Czeslaw Milosz. CP-MiloC; CP-MiloCN, *tr. by* Robert Hass

Boy, The. Robert Creeley. CP-CreeR

Boy accepted them, The. Daedalus: The Dirge. George Oppen. CP-OppGN

Boy Alexander understands his father to be a famous lawyer, The. Boy and Father. Carl Sandburg. CP-SandC

Boy and Education. Alan Dugan. CP-DugaA

Boy and Father. Carl Sandburg. CP-SandC

Boy and the Angel, The. Robert Browning. CP-BroR1

Boy and the Bush, The. Theodore Roethke. CP-RoetT

Boy and the Man, The. E. E. Cummings. CP-CummE

Boy at the Window. Richard Wilbur. CP-WilbR

Boy bring the bowl full of wine. Hafiz. CP-EmerR *Fr.* Odes.

Boy came up the street and there was a girl, A. For Instance. John Ciardi. CP-CiarJ

Boy, Cat, Canary. Stephen Spender. CP-SpenS

Boy, don't come around here telling me you. Talking to My Mailbox. Charles Bukowski. SP-BukC3

Boy Eros mistakes me, The. Da mi basia mille. James Laughlin. CP-LaugJ

Boy-Friend, The. James Whitcomb Riley. CP-RileJ

Boy heart of Johnny Jones—aching today? Buffalo Bill. Carl Sandburg. CP-SandC

Boy His Mother, The. Grace Paley. CP-PalGC

Boy! I detest all Persian fopperies. Horace. *See* Boy, I hate their empty shows

Boy, I hate their empty shows. Ode 1.38: Simplicity. Horace. CP-CowpW; CP-HopkG *Fr.* Odes.

Boy, I played agile and difficult games, A. Nightmare Song. Robert Stock. SP-StocR

Boy in the red coat packing snow, The. On Reading Camus In Early March. John Logan. CP-LogaJ

Boy in the Roman Zoo. Archibald MacLeish. CP-MacLA

Boy is as old as the stars, A. To My God in His Sickness. Philip Levine. SP-LeviP

Boy Johnny. Christina Georgina Rossetti. CP-RosC2

Boy lives on our Farm, he's not, The. James Whitcomb Riley. CP-RileJ

Boy-Man. Karl Shapiro. SP-ShapK

Boy or Girl. John Ciardi. CP-CiarJ

Boy Patriot, The. James Whitcomb Riley. CP-RileJ

Boy, presuming on his intellect, A. At Woodward's Gardens. Robert Frost. CP-FrosR

Boy Scouts' Patrol Song, A. Rudyard Kipling. CP-KiplR

Boy severs his fingers, A. Piecemeal. Rae Armantrout. SP-ArmaA

Boy sits in the classroom, The. Learning Experience. Marge Piercy. SP-PierM

Boy steadies the air rifle on his arm, The. Peter's Diary in Goodentown. Kenneth Patchen. CP-PatcK

Boy tossed the news, The. Lorine Niedecker. CP-NiedL

Boy turned to a newt!, A. Fountain of Arethusa, The. Donald Davie. CP-DaviDC

Boy Wandering in Simms' Valley. Robert Penn Warren. CP-WarrR

Boy watched the sun, The. Driving Home after a Funeral. Gregory Orr. SP-OrrG

Boy Wearing a Dead Man's Clothes. Yusef Komunyakaa. CP-KomuY

Boy who had Gumption and Push, A. Boy and the Bush, The. Theodore Roethke. CP-RoetT

Boy with Book of Knowledge. Howard Nemerov. CP-NemeH

Boy with His Hair Cut Short. Muriel Rukeyser. CP-RukeM

Boy with honor in your heart. To a Young American the Day after the Fall of Barcelona. John Ciardi. CP-CiarJ

Boy / with the / finger in, The. Hero. Robert Creeley. CP-CreeR

Boy! / You'll fall into the river! Narcissus. Federico García Lorca. CP-GarcF, *tr.* by Alan S. Trueblood *Fr.* Three Portraits with Shading.

Boyg, Peer Gynt, the One Only One, The. Randall Jarrell. CP-JarrR

Boyhood in Tobacco Country. Robert Penn Warren. CP-WarrR

Boyhood Misremembered. Donald Davie. CP-DaviDC

Boyne at Navan swam in light, The. Evening on the Boyne. Donald Davie. CP-DaviDC

Boys, The. James Whitcomb Riley. CP-RileJ

Boys and girls, / Come out to play. Passionate Pagan and the Dispassionate Public, The. Ogden Nash. CP-NashO

Boys and Girls, Lenny Bruce, or Back from the Dead. Ai. SP-Ai

Boys and grown-up men. Han-shan. CP-ColdM, *tr.* by Red Pine

Boy's Candidate, The. James Whitcomb Riley. CP-RileJ

Boys come, each year more gallant, playing chicken, The. 1930's. Robert Lowell. SP-LoweR

Boy's Death, The. Ludwig Uhland. CP-MerG2

Boys dream of native girls who bring breadfruit. Breadfruit. Philip Larkin. CP-LarkP

Boy's Dream, The. Thomas Hardy. CP-HardT

Boy's Dream, The: A Ballad. Jones Very. CP-VeryJ

Boys i mean are not refined, The. E. E. Cummings. CP-CummE

Boys in Dresses. Yusef Komunyakaa. CP-KomuY

Boys in sporadic but tenacious droves. Horse Chestnut Tree, The. Richard Eberhart. CP-EberR

Boys in the Branches. Muriel Rukeyser. CP-RukeM

Boy's Mother, A. James Whitcomb Riley. CP-RileJ

Boys of the air, The. Sky. Federico García Lorca. CP-GarcF, *tr.* by Jerome Rothenberg *Fr.* In the Garden of the Lunar Grapefruits.

Boys of the Old Glee Club, The. James Whitcomb Riley. CP-RileJ

Boys of These Men Full Speed. Muriel Rukeyser. CP-RukeM

Boy's Room. George Oppen. CP-OppGN

Boys Summer Song, A. Paul Laurence Dunbar. CP-DunbP

Boys Then and Now. Thomas Hardy. CP-HardT

Boys with snares, The. Flux. Eugenio Montale. CP-MontE, *tr.* by Jonathan Galassi

Br-r-r-am-m-m, rackety-am-m, OM, *Am.* What the Motorcycle Said. Mona Van Duyn. SP-VanDM

Bracci born, A. From birth, born wailing, I'd. Michelangelo Buonarroti. CP-Miche, *tr.* by John Frederick Nims

Bracci, I, A. Alive because I'm dead. Michelangelo Buonarroti. CP-Miche, *tr.* by John Frederick Nims

Bracci once, A. The soul in me withdrew. Michelangelo Buonarroti. CP-Miche,

tr. by John Frederick Nims

Braccio lies here. No less a tomb could show. Michelangelo Buonarroti. CP-Miche, *tr.* by John Frederick Nims

Braccio retrieves from earth the mortal scrim. Michelangelo Buonarroti. CP-Miche, *tr.* by John Frederick Nims

Bracelet, A. Robert Graves. CP-GravR

Bracelet, The. John Donne. MW-DonnJ *Fr.* Elegies.

Bracelet invisible, A. Bracelet, A. Robert Graves. CP-GravR

Bracelet of Pearle: To Silvia, The. Robert Herrick. CP-HerrR

Bracelet to Julia, The. Robert Herrick. CP-HerrR

Bracken by the tracks. Fanny Howe. SP-HoweF *Fr.* O'Clock.

Bracken Hills in Autumn. Hugh MacDiarmid. SP-MacDH

Brackish reach of shoal off Madaket—, A. Quaker Graveyard in Nantucket, The. Robert Lowell. SP-LoweR

Braes o' Ballochmyle, The. Robert Burns. CP-BurnR

Braggart. John Clare. SP-ClarJ

Braggart. Dorothy Parker. CP-ParkD

Braggart, The. Rudyard Kipling. CP-KiplR *Fr.* Muse among the Motors, The.

Brahma. Ralph Waldo Emerson. CP-EmerR

Braiding, The. Denise Levertov. SP-LeveDS

Brain. Dan Pagis. SP-PagiD, *tr.* by Stephen Mitchell

Brain / All / Nuclei. George Oppen. CP-OppGN

Brain constructs its systems to enclose, The. Organic Bloom. Stanley Kunitz. CP-KunSC

Brain itself in its skull, The. Harsh Climate. Charles Simic. SP-SimiC; SP-SimiCE

Brain of Shelley cooks, The. Byron at Shelley's Burning. John Logan. CP-LogaJ

Brain on its descent, The. Leeway. Hans Magnus Enzensberger. SP-EnzeH, *tr.* by Michael Hamburger

Brain to the Heart, The. Yusef Komunyakaa. CP-KomuY

Brain, within its Groove, The. Emily Dickinson. CP-DickE

Brain's Dissection, The. Tennessee Williams. CP-WillT

Brainstorm. Howard Nemerov. CP-NemeH

Brainwashing. Carl Sandburg. CP-SandC

Bramble gray of stalk. Federico García Lorca. CP-GarcF, *tr.* by Alan S. Trueblood *Fr.* Andalusian Songs.

Bran. Paul Muldoon. CP-MuldP

Branch, The. Jones Very. CP-VeryJ

Branch on bird / Singing and losing leaves. Autumn. Raissa Maritain. CP-MertT

Branches. Carl Sandburg. CP-SandC

Branches bend to the river. River Between the Train and the Highway, The. Thomas Lux. SP-LuxT

Branches broken. Storm. A. R. Ammons. CP-AmmoA

Branches of Water or Desire, The. Alan Dugan. CP-DugaA

Branching head of, The. Lily, The. William Carlos Williams. CP-WilW1

Brancusi. Carl Sandburg. CP-SandC

Brancusi is a galoot; he saves tickets to take him nowhere; a galoot with. Brancusi. Carl Sandburg. CP-SandC

Brand New Clothes. Langston Hughes. CP-HughL

Brand-new heaven over outlandish earth, A. Robinsonade. Joseph Brodsky. CP-BrodJ, *tr.* by Jonathan Aaron

Branded Hand, The. John Greenleaf Whittier. CP-WhitJ

Brandons Both. Christina Georgina Rossetti. CP-RosC2

Brandy Glass, The. Louis MacNeice. CP-MacNL

Branksome Hall. Sir Walter Scott. SP-ScotW *Fr.* Lay of the Last Minstrel, The.

Brantôme. Donald Davie. CP-DaviDC

Brasen tower [*or* Tower] with doors [*or* dores] close barred [*or* bar'd], The. Horace. CP-RaleW *Fr.* Odes.

Brasilia. Sylvia Plath. CP-PlatS

Brass-green bird with grass, A. Smooth Gnarled Crape Myrtle. Marianne Craig Moore. CP-MoorM

Brass Keys. Carl Sandburg. CP-SandC

Brass medallion profile of your face I keep always, The. Medallion. Carl Sandburg. CP-SandC

Brass or bronze cup, stroked at the rim, The. Magic. Denise Levertov. SP-LeveDL

Brass Ring, The. Raymond Carver. CP-CarvR

Brass Spittoons. Langston Hughes. CP-HughL; CP-HughL1

Brass telescopes with Halley on. Retirement Catalogue, A. Wyatt Prunty. SP-PrunW

Brassiere Factory, The. Kenneth Koch. SP-KochK

Brave, brave were the soldiers (high named to-day) who lived through the fight. Bravest Soldiers, The. Walt Whitman. CP-WhitW

Brave Bull. Charles Bukowski. SP-BukC2

Brave Champions! Go On with the Farce. Lord Byron. CP-Byron

Brave Child, The. Gregory Orr. SP-OrrG

Brave Empedocles defying fools, The. Ralph Waldo Emerson. CP-EmerR

Brave infant of Saguntum, clear[e]. To the Immortal[l] Memory [or Memorie] and Friendship of That Noble Pair[e], Sir Lucius Cary and Sir H. [or Henry] Morison. Ben Jonson. CP-JonsB; SP-JonsB

Brave is the sight when a champion tall. Sonnet to J.M. George Meredith. CP-MerG2

Brave Man, The. Wallace Stevens. CP-StevW; CP-StevWP

Brave New World. Archibald MacLeish. CP-MacLA

Brave Refrain, A. James Whitcomb Riley. CP-RileJ

Brave rose, (alas!) where art thou? in the chair. Church-Rents and Schisms. George Herbert. CP-HerbG

Brave Schill! by death delivered, take thy flight. William Wordsworth. CP-WorW1

Brave you were who fought and died acclaimed. Those Who Fought for the Achaian Alliance. Constantine P. Cavafy. CP-CavaC, tr. by Theoharis Constantine Theoharis

Brave youth, to whom Fate in one hour. For a Picture Where a Queen Laments over the Tomb of a Slain Knight. Thomas Carew. CP-CareT

Bravely deckt, come forth, bright day. Thomas Campion. CP-CampT

Bravely from Fairyland he rode, on furlough. Broken Girth, The. Robert Graves. CP-GravR

Bravest Soldiers, The. Walt Whitman. CP-WhitW

Bravo. Charles Bukowski. SP-BukC3

Bravo, Paris Exposition! Walt Whitman. CP-WhitW

Braw, braw lads on Yarrow bracs. Galla Water. Robert Burns. CP-BurnR

Brawling of a sparrow in the caves, The. Sorrow of Love, The. William Butler Yeats. CP-YeatW

Braziers, It Seems, Are Preparing to Pass, The. Lord Byron. CP-Byron

Brazil. Paul Muldoon. CP-MuldP

Brazil. John Updike. CP-UpdiJ

Brazil, January 1, 1502. Elizabeth Bishop. CP-BishE

Brazilian butterflies, static and perfect as. Butterfly Piece. Robert Earl Hayden. CP-HaydR

Brazilian Tragedy. Manuel Bandeira. CP-BishE

Bread. James Dickey. CP-DickJ

Bread. W. S. Merwin. SP-MerwW

Bread. Gabriela Mistral. SP-MistG, tr. by Maria Giachetti [or Jacketti]

Bread. C. K. Williams. CP-WillC; SP-WillC

Bread and Butter. W. S. Merwin. SP-MerwW

Bread and Butter Letter, A. Kenneth Rexroth. CP-RexrK

'Bread and cheese' grow wild in the green time. Hedges. Ivor Gurney. SP-GurnI

Bread and Milk for Breakfast. Christina Georgina Rossetti. CP-RosC2

Bread at Midnight. W. S. Merwin. SP-MerwW

Bread from Heaven, The. Jones Very. CP-VeryJ

Bread Itself, The. David Ignatow. SP-IgnaD

Bread of this World; Praises III, The. Thomas McGrath. SP-McGrT

Bread thou eatest thou canst never know, The. Glutton, The. Jones Very. CP-VeryJ

Bread upon the Waters. D. H. Lawrence. CP-LawrD

Breaded Fish. A. K. Ramanujan. CP-RamaA

Breadfruit. Philip Larkin. CP-LarkP

Breadmaking. Jelaluddin Rumi. SP-Rumi, tr. by Coleman Barks

Break, The. Adrienne Rich. CP-RicAE

Break, The. Anne Sexton. CP-SextA

Break Away, The. Anne Sexton. CP-SextA

Break, Break, Break. Alfred Tennyson. CP-TennA

Break down / "innocence." Thinking of Yeats. Robert Creeley. SP-CreeR

Break, Fant'sy, from thy cave of cloud. Ben Jonson. CP-JonsB Fr. Vision of Delight, The.

Break forth in joy my soul the sea retires. Day, The. Jones Very. CP-VeryJ

Break forth in joy my soul the waves retire. Hope. Jones Very. CP-VeryJ

Break from the Bush, A. Yusef Komunyakaa. CP-KomuY

Break heart, peace. Early Reading. Robert Creeley. SP-CreeR

Break in the clouds, A. The. A blue. Simple. Raymond Carver. CP-CarvR

Break me my bounds, and let me fly. Career, A. Paul Laurence Dunbar. CP-DunbP

Break me no bread however white it be. Hunger. Countee Cullen. CP-CullC

Break not the slumbers of the bride. Hymeneal Song, on the Nuptials of the Lady Ann Wentworth and the Lord Lovelace, An. Thomas Carew. CP-CareT

Break of Day. Jorge Luis Borges. SP-BorgJ, tr. by Stephen Kessler

Break of Morning. Walter De la Mare. CP-DeLaW

Break off Delay, since we but read of one. Delay. Robert Herrick. CP-HerrR

Break off / fallen Catullus. Carmen 8. Catullus. CP-CampT; CP-ZukLS Fr. Carmina.

Break the box and shed the nard. Easter. Gerard Manley Hopkins. CP-HopkG

Breake now my heart and dye! Oh no, she may relent. Thomas Campion. CP-CampT

Break[e] of Day. John Donne. CP-DonnJ; MW-DonnJ

Breaker humps its green glass, The. Tern. Ted Hughes. SP-HughTN

Breakers at high tide shoot. World. A. R. Ammons. CP-AmmoA

Breakfast. William Carlos Williams. CP-WilW1

Breakfast Elegy. Andrei Codrescu. SP-CodrA

Breakfast in a Bowling Alley in Utica, New York. Adrienne Rich. CP-RicAE

Breakfast is an institution that I don't know who commenced it. Eight O'Clock Peril, The. Ogden Nash. CP-NashO

Breakfast is drunk down . . . Damp earth. Our Daily Bread. César Vallejo. CP-WrigJ, tr. by James Wright

Breakfast peremptorily closes. Breakfast Table. Robert Graves. CP-GravR

Breakfast Table. Robert Graves. CP-GravR

Breakfasting alone in Karachi, Delhi, Calcutta. Solitary Travel. Louis MacNeice. CP-MacNL

Breaking. Wendell Berry. CP-BerrW

Breaking and entering: from early on. Lustral Sonnet. Seamus Heaney. SP-HeanSO Fr. Glanmore Revisited.

Breaking Camp. Yusef Komunyakaa. CP-KomuY

Breaking Camp. Marge Piercy. SP-PierM

Breaking Child, The. Wyatt Prunty. SP-PrunW

Breaking every law except the one. Our City Is Guarded by Automatic Rockets. William Stafford. SP-StafWW

Breaking Ground. Thom Gunn. CP-GunnT

Breaking of Rainbows, The. Howard Nemerov. CP-NemeH

Breaking Open. Muriel Rukeyser. CP-RukeM

Breaking the Charm. Paul Laurence Dunbar. CP-DunbP

Breaking the Code. Robert Penn Warren. CP-WarrR

Breaking the nets of the world, in glimpses going. Muriel Rukeyser. CP-RukeM

Breaking Up Is Hard to Do. Robert Creeley. SP-CreeR

Breaking Webs. Louis MacNeice. CP-MacNL

Breakout. Charles Bukowski. SP-BukC2

Breaks. A. R. Ammons. CP-AmmoA

Breaks from the blue-black. Turtle, The. Mary Oliver. SP-OlivM

Breaks in splendor on / the window glass of. Morning, The. James Schuyler. CP-SchuJ

Breaks up in obelisks on the river. Ice. Ai. SP-Ai

Breakup, The. Boris Leonidovich Pasternak. SP-WeisT, tr. by Theodore Weiss

Breast, The. Anne Sexton. CP-SextA; SP-SextA

Breast she offered was full, The. Mythologies 1. A. K. Ramanujan. CP-RamaA

Breast under breast when you shall lie. Ghosts. Countee Cullen. CP CullC

Breasted, beginning his lectures. Our Home Is in the Rocks. Kenneth Rexroth. CP-RexrK

Breasts. Tess Gallagher. SP-GallT

Breasts. Yusef Komunyakaa. CP-KomuY

Breasts. Rainer Maria Rilke. CP-RilkFr, tr by A. Poulin, Jr.

Breasts. Charles Simic. SP-SimiC; SP-SimiCE

Breath. James Dickey. CP-DickJ

Breath. Philip Levine. SP-LeviP

Breath. Heather McHugh. SP-McHuH

Breath clamber-short, face sun-peeled, stones. Red-Tail Hawk and Pyre of Youth. Robert Penn Warren. CP-WarrR

Breath of a Rose. Langston Hughes. CP-HughL; CP-HughL2

Breath of Air, A. James Wright. CP-WrigJ

Breath of Life, The. D. H. Lawrence. CP-LawrD

Breath of Morning—breath of May. Morning. James Whitcomb Riley. CP-RileJ

Breath of Nature, The. Chuang Tzu. CP-MertT, tr. by Thomas Merton

Breath of Night, The. Randall Jarrell. CP-JarrR

Breath of the Briar. George Meredith. CP-MerG1

Breath of the mountains, fresh born in the regions majestic, A. Poetry of Wordsworth, The. George Meredith. CP-MerG1

Breath of What's-Out-There sags, The. Night Journal II. Charles Wright. SP-WrigC

Breath, the fragrance, and the cooling shade, The. Petrarch. CP-Petra, tr. by J. G. Nichols

Breath within us is the wind without, The. Equations of a Villanelle. Howard Nemerov. CP-NemeH

Breathe deep of the / freshly gray morning air, mild. Three Meditations. Denise Levertov. SP-LeveDP; SP-LeveDS

Breathe in experience, breathe out poetry—. Poem Out of Childhood. Muriel Rukeyser. CP-RukeM

Breathe, Julia, breathe, and Ile protest. On Julia's Breath. Robert Herrick. CP-HerrR

Breathe not, hid Heart: cease silently. To an Unborn Pauper Child. Thomas Hardy. CP-HardT

Breathe on the living. Kenneth Patchen. CP-PatcK

Breathe with me this fear. E. E. Cummings. CP-CummE

Breathed the fog from the valley. What I Did on a Rainy Day. May Swenson. SP-SwenM

Breathes there a bard who isn't moved. On Being Chosen Poet of Vermont.

Robert Frost. CP-FrosR

Breathes there the [*or* a] Man with soul so dead. Sir Walter Scott. SP-ScotW *Fr.* Lay of the Last Minstrel, The.

Breathing. James Tate. SP-TateJ

Breathing, The. Denise Levertov. SP-LeveDP

Breathing Landscape. Muriel Rukeyser. CP-RukeM

Breathless, The. Richard Eberhart. CP-EberR

Bred wild leopards—among the pale depth fungus. Canal's Drowning Black, The. Ted Hughes. SP-HughTN

Bredon Hill. A. E. Housman. CP-HousA

Breeze at dawn has secrets to tell you, The. Jelaluddin Rumi. SP-Rumi, *tr. by* Coleman Barks

Breeze blowing those blond locks and curling them. Petrarch. CP-Petra, *tr. by* J. G. Nichols

Breeze came to the aid of that wilted day, A. Other Cindy, The. John Ashbery. SP-AshbJ

Breeze discovered my open book, A. Cloud Shadow, A. Robert Frost. CP-FrosR

Breeze is blowin' 'cross de bay, De. Parted. Paul Laurence Dunbar. CP-DunbP

Breeze keeps fleshing the flag, A. Embassy. Charles Tomlinson. CP-TomlC

Breeze of the night in gentler sighs. Song: "Breeze of the night in gentler sighs." Lord Byron. CP-Byron

Breezes blowin' middlin' brisk. Speakin' o' Christmas. Paul Laurence Dunbar. CP-DunbP

Breeze's Invitation, The. Henry David Thoreau. CP-ThorH

Brekekekex? / The frogs of upstate speak. Poolville, N.Y. Charles Tomlinson. CP-TomlC

Brennende Liebe. Louise Glück. SP-GlucL

Brennoralt. Sir John Suckling. CP-SuckJ

Bresson's Movies. Robert Creeley. SP-CreeR

Brethren, The. Jones Very. CP-VeryJ

Brethren, how shall it fare with me. Question, The. Rudyard Kipling. CP-KiplR

Breton Walks. Derek Mahon.

Breughel. Stevie Smith. CP-SmitS

Breughel's Winter. Walter De la Mare. CP-DeLaW

Brewing of Soma, The. John Greenleaf Whittier. CP-WhitJ

Briar Rose (Sleeping Beauty). Anne Sexton. CP-SextA; SP-SextA

Bribes and Gifts Get All. Robert Herrick. CP-HerrR

Bric-à-Brac. Dorothy Parker. CP-ParkD

Brickenden, Hertfordshire. Stevie Smith. CP-SmitS

Bricklayer Love. Carl Sandburg. CP-SandC

Bricklayer's Lunch Hour, The. Allen Ginsberg. CP-GinsA; SP-GinsA

Bricks, The. Kenneth Koch. SP-KochK

Bricks and Sleep. Clarence Major. SP-MajoC

Bricks are stuck in earth. Fanny Howe. SP-HoweF *Fr.* Sea-Garden, The.

Bricks in a wall, The. Bricks, The. Kenneth Koch. SP-KochK

Bricks of the wall. Garden Wall, The. Denise Levertov. SP-LeveDP

Bridal Ballad. Edgar Allan Poe. CP-PoeEd

Bridal Birth. Dante Gabriel Rossetti. CW-RossD *Fr.* House of Life, The.

Bridal Measure, A. Paul Laurence Dunbar. CP-DunbP

Bridal of Pennacook, The. John Greenleaf Whittier. CP-WhitJ

Bridal of Trierman, The. Sir Walter Scott.

   Defenceless Border, The. SP-ScotW

   Enchanted Goblet, The. SP-ScotW

   Magic Castle, The. SP-ScotW

Bridal Photo, 1906. John Ciardi. CP-CiarJ

Bridal Piece. Louise Glück. SP-GlucL

Bridal Song, A: "Golden gates of Sleep unbar, The." Percy Bysshe Shelley. CP-ShelP

Bridal veils of the olive trees, you said, The. Valestrieri. Charles Tomlinson. SP-TomlC

Bridal Wish Adressed to Mr S. Stockton and His Lady the Morning after Their Maraige, The. Annis Boudinot Stockton. CP-StocA

Bride. Olga Broumas. SP-BrouO

Bride, A. James Whitcomb Riley. CP-RileJ

Bride, The. Ambrose Bierce. SP-BierA

Bride, The. D. H. Lawrence. CP-LawrD

Bride, The. Denise Levertov. SP-LeveDL

Bride, The. Charles Olson. CP-OlsoC

Bride, The. Jones Very. CP-VeryJ

Bride and Groom Lie Hidden for Three Days. Ted Hughes. SP-HughTN

Bride-Cake, The. Robert Herrick. CP-HerrR

Bride disappears, The. After twenty minutes of searching. Impossible Marriage, The. Donald Hall. CP-HallD

Bride in the 30's, A. W. H. Auden. CP-AudeW

Bride leaves her father's house, The. Bride, The. Charles Olson. CP-OlsoC

Bride loved old words, and found her pleasure marred. James Vincent Cunningham. CP-CunnJ *Fr.* Five Epigrams.

Bride-Night Fire, The. Thomas Hardy. CP-HardT

Bride of Abydos, The. Lord Byron. CP-Byron

Bride of Reason, The. Donald Davie. CP-DaviDC

Bride Song. Christina Georgina Rossetti. CP-RosC2

Bride Song, A. Christina Georgina Rossetti. CP-RosC1

Bride without a dowry, with a deep navel, A. Yehuda Amichai. SP-AmicY, *tr. by* Chana Bloch

Bridegroom Liu is eighty-two. Han-shan. CP-ColdM, *tr. by* Red Pine

Bride's Day. Susan Howe. SP-HoweS

Bride's Prelude, The. Dante Gabriel Rossetti. CW-RossD

Bride's Song, The. John Logan. CP-LogaJ *Fr.* Epilogue, Songs of the Spouses, Complaint of Love.

Bridge. A. R. Ammons. CP-AmmoA

Bridge, A. Primo Levi. CP-LeviP, *tr. by* Ruth Feldman

Bridge, The. Hart Crane. CP-CranH

Bridge, The. Walter De la Mare. CP-DeLaW

Bridge, The. Gregory Orr. SP-OrrG

Bridge, The; An Uncalled-for Apology. Yannis Ritsos. SP-RitsY, *tr. by* George Giannaris

Bridge Begins in the Trees, A. William Stafford. SP-StafWW

Bridge Fiend, The. Dorothy Parker. CP-ParkD

Bridge for the Living. Philip Larkin. CP-LarkP

Bridge-Guard in the Karroo. Rudyard Kipling. CP-KiplR

Bridge of Change, The. John Logan. CP-LogaJ

Bridge of Estador, The. Hart Crane. CP-CranH

Bridge of Lodi, The. Thomas Hardy. CP-HardT

Bridge of Time, The. Jones Very. CP-VeryJ

Bridge Passage: Variations on Two Scales. Eleanor Wilner. SP-WilnE

Bridge says: Come across, try me; see how good I am, The. Potomac Town in February. Carl Sandburg. CP-SandC

Bridge Through My Window. Audre Lorde. SP-LordA

Bridged and forgot, the river. River Bridged and Forgot, The. Wendell Berry. CP-BerrW

Bridegroom's Song, The. John Logan. CP-LogaJ *Fr.* Epilogue, Songs of the Spouses, Complaint of Love.

Bridgehead Photograph. Dan Pagis. SP-PagiD, *tr. by* Stephen Mitchell

Bridgeport Station. William Corbett. SP-CorbW

Bridges. Grace Paley. CP-PalGC

Bridges. Charles Tomlinson. CP-TomlC

Bridges, The. W. S. Merwin. SP-MerwW

Bridges, The. Arthur Rimbaud. CP-RimbA, *tr. by* Martin Sorrell

Bridges with empty niches waiting for rural madonnas. 3/6/81, Amtrack. Andrei Codrescu. SP-CodrA

Bridging. Marge Piercy. SP-PierM

Brief Cases. David Ignatow. SP-IgnaD

Brief Encounter. Langston Hughes. CP-HughL; CP-HughL2

Brief Guide to New York, A. Ogden Nash. CP-NashO

Brief Guide to Rhyming, or, How Be the Little Busy Doth?, A. Ogden Nash. CP-NashO

Brief harp of the larches. To Friend-Tree of Counted Days. René Char. CP-WilW2

Brief History (June–December 1994). Peter Blue Cloud. SP-BlueP

Brief Innocence. Maya Angelou. SP-AngeM

Brief is the day, and soon the hastening sun. Winter Night, The. Jones Very. CP-VeryJ

Brief Journey West, The. Howard Nemerov. CP-NemeH

Brief Lief. William Carlos Williams. CP-WilW2

Brief Lives. Donald Hall. CP-HallD

Brief Madrigal. Federico García Lorca. CP-GarcF, *tr. by* Alan S. Trueblood *Fr.* Love.

Brief Message. Allen Tate. CP-TateA

Brief (Remembered) *Histoire* of Rejection, A. Andrei Codrescu. SP-CodrA

Brief Reunion. Robert Graves. CP-GravR

Brief Visit to Venice. Clarence Major. SP-MajoC

Briefcase, The. W. S. Merwin. SP-MerwWF

Briefcase, The. Paul Muldoon. CP-MuldP

Briefly they are amazed. The marigold-fields. Terribilis Est Locus Iste; *Gaugin and the Pont-Aven School.* Geoffrey Hill. CP-HillG

Bright Babe! whose awfull beautyes [*or* beauties] make. In the Glorious Epiphanie of Our Lord God. Richard Crashaw. CP-CrasR

Bright baffling Soul, least capturable of themes. To Shakespeare. Thomas Hardy. CP-HardT

Bright ball of flame that through the gloom of even. Sonnet: To a Balloon Laden with Knowledge. Percy Bysshe Shelley. CP-ShelP

Bright Be the Place of Thy Soul! Lord Byron. CP-Byron

Bright Bindings. Countee Cullen. CP-CullC

BrIght / bRight s??? big / (soft). E. E. Cummings. CP-CummE

Bright clasp of her whole hand around my finger. To My Daughter. Stephen Spender. CP-SpenS

Bright cloud, / Bringer of rain to far fields. Kathleen Jessie Raine. SP-RainK

Bright clouds of reverence, sufferably bright. Veil of Light, The. Samuel Taylor Coleridge. CP-ColeS

Bright Conversation with Saint-Ex. Carl Sandburg. CP-SandC

Bright cool rose leaning. Rainer Maria Rilke. CP-RilkFr, *tr. by* A. Poulin, Jr. *Fr.* Roses, The.

Bright drop quivering on a thorn, The. Penshurst Place. Derek Mahon. CP-MahoD

Bright flower bloomed in the old fear, A. Somber Spring. Yehuda Amichai. SP-AmicYL, *tr. by* Benjamin Harshav *and* Barbara Harshav

Bright Flower! whose home is everywhere. To the Daisy ("Bright Flower! whose home is everywhere"). William Wordsworth. CP-WorW1; MW-WorW

Bright flowers! November's frosts and cold have spared. Thanksgiving Flowers. Jones Very. CP-VeryJ

Bright Goddesse, whether Jove thy father be. Out of Euphormio. Richard Crashaw. CP-CrasR

Bright image of my early years! Painted Columbine, The. Jones Very. CP-VeryJ

Bright in our minds, but in the dark earth stranded. Michelangelo Buonarroti. CP-Miche, *tr. by* John Frederick Nims

Bright is the morn, and hushed is every sound. Sabbath, The ("Bright is the morn, and hushed is every sound"). Jones Very. CP-VeryJ

Bright, jolly sunshine and clear blue skies. Signs of Spring. Langston Hughes. CP-HughL

Bright Life. Walter De la Mare. CP-DeLaW

Bright Martial Maid, Queen of the frozen zone. In Eandem Reginae Sueciae Transmissam [To Christina, Queen of Sweden]. Andrew Marvell. CP-MarvA

Bright mirror I braved: the devil in it, The. Cleopatra to the Asp. Ted Hughes. SP-HughTN

Bright mornings. Minuet, The. Raymond Carver. CP-CarvR

Bright petals of evening. Rosa Mundi. Kenneth Rexroth. CP-RexrK

Bright Sirius! that when Orion pales. Star Sirius, The. George Meredith. CP-MerG1

Bright sleep bathing breathing walking. Incantation. May Swenson. SP-SwenM

Bright soul, of whom if any country known. To the Lady Elizabeth Queen of Bohemia. George Herbert. CP-HerbG

Bright spark, shot from a brighter place. Star[re], The. George Herbert. CP-HerbG

Bright splendid head of. Comet Watch on Indian Key—Night of April 10, 1986. May Swenson. SP-SwenM

Bright Star. John Keats. CP-KeatJ

Bright starre of Majesty, oh shedd on mee. Upon the birth of the Princesse Elizabeth. Richard Crashaw. CP-CrasR

Bright Stella, form'd for universal Reign. To Miss Hickman Playing on the Spinet. Samuel Johnson. CP-JohnS

Bright / stones ride through the air, bright, The. Paul Celan. SP-CelaP, *tr. by* John Felstiner

Bright-throned, undying Aphrodite. Sappho. CP-CunnJ, *tr. by* James Vincent Cunningham

Bright Tulips, we do know. To a Bed of Tulips. Robert Herrick. CP-HerrR

Bright vocabularies are transient as rainbows. Precious Moments. Carl Sandburg. CP-SandC

Bright wanderer, fair coquette of Heaven. Fragment: To the Moon. Percy Bysshe Shelley. CP-ShelP

Brighter and clearer to me than mere daylight. Night and Day. Ludovico Ariosto. CP-MahoD, *tr. by* Derek Mahon

Brighter than crisp new money. Jonestown: More eyes for *Jadwiga's Dream.* Yusef Komunyakaa. CP-KomuY

Brightest and best are the sons of morning. Tableau de l'Inconstance des Mauvais Anges. Stevie Smith. CP-SmitS

Brightest Star's the *modestest,* The. Motto, A. James Whitcomb Riley. CP-RileJ

Brightness as a Poignant Light. David Ignatow. SP-IgnaD

Brightness is a curse upon the day. Eye of God, the Soul's First Vision, The. Jay Wright. SP-WrigJ

Brightness round the rising sun, The. Spheres, The. Jones Very. CP-VeryJ

Brighton Beach. Derek Mahon. CP-MahoD

Brigs of Ayr, a Poem. Inscribed to J. B*********, Esq; Ayr, The. Robert Burns. CP-BurnR

Brilliance. The. William Carlos Williams. CP-WilW2

Brilliance takes up residence in flaws, A. In Praise of Pain. Heather McHugh. SP-McHuH

Brilliant beard of ice, A. Icicles. Robert Pinsky. CP-PinsR

Brilliant network-lights tentacle dim suburbs. Rising Over Night-Blackened Detroit Streets. Allen Ginsberg. CP-GinsA

Brilliant Sad Sun. William Carlos Williams. CP-WilW1

Brilliant Silence. Charles Tomlinson. CP-TomlC

Brilliant, the full-bodied, the real of the world in their powers, The. Muriel Rukeyser. CP-RukeM

Brilliant, this day—a young virtuoso of a day. Celebration. Denise Levertov. SP-LeveDS

Brim. Carl Sandburg. CP-SandC

Brim Beauvais. Gertrude Stein. CP-SteiG

Brim's hammer hit a wheelbarrow; a silver of iron sent itself through the. Brim. Carl Sandburg. CP-SandC

Brimscombe. Ivor Gurney. SP-GurnI

Bring back the day the reins hung slack and free. Michelangelo Buonarroti. CP-Miche, *tr. by* John Frederick Nims

Bring bring / straight things. Horse on Fire. Charles Bukowski. SP-BukC2

Bring Down the Beams. Charles Bukowski. SP-BukC2

Bring forth, bring forth your silver! it shall be. First Shall Be Last, The. Jones Very. CP-VeryJ

Bring forth your gold and silver! They shall be. Ye have hoarded up treasure in the last days.—James 5:3. Jones Very. CP-VeryJ

Bring in the steaming bowl, my lads. Wassail for the New Year, A. George Meredith. CP-MerG2

Bring, in this timeless grave to throw. A. E. Housman. CP-HousA

Bring It Up from the Dark. Robert Duncan. SP-DuncR

Bring me all of your dreams. Dream Keeper, The. Langston Hughes. CP-HughL; CP-HughL1

Bring me my rose-buds, drawer, come. Frolic[k], A. Robert Herrick. CP-HerrR

Bring me now the bright flower. Nightsong. Carl Sandburg. CP-SandC

"Bring me soft song," said Aladdin. Aladdin and the Jinn. Nicholas Vachel Lindsay. CP-LindV

Bring me the livery of no other man. Bohemian, The. Paul Laurence Dunbar. CP-DunbP

Bring me the sunflower, let me plant it. Eugenio Montale. CP-MontE, *tr. by* Jonathan Galassi

Bring me the sunset in a cup. Emily Dickinson. CP-DickE

Bring me this day some poet of the past. To T. H. The Amphora. Ezra Pound. CP-PoEar

Bring me to see, Lord, bring me yet to see. General Assembly and Church of the Firstborn, The. Christina Georgina Rossetti. CP-RosC2

Bring me to the blasted oak. Crazy Jane and the Bishop. William Butler Yeats. CP-YeatW

Bring me wine, but wine which never grew. Bacchus. Ralph Waldo Emerson. CP-EmerR

Bring not bright candles, for his eyes. Reverie. Walter De la Mare. CP-DeLaW

Bring now ye Muses from th' Aonian grove. On Hearing of the News of the Capture of Lord Cornwallis and the British Army, by Gen. Washington. Annis Boudinot Stockton. CP-StocA

Bring on a pail of smoke. Impasse. Carl Sandburg. CP-SandC

"Bring out your dead!" The midnight street. Female Martyr, The. John Greenleaf Whittier. CP-WhitJ

Bring the Day! Theodore Roethke. CP-RoetT

Bring the holy crust of Bread. Charmes. Robert Herrick. CP-HerrR

Bring the North. William Stafford. SP-StafWW

Bring up from the dark water. Bring It up from the Dark. Robert Duncan. SP-DuncR

Bring wine release me. Hafiz. CP-EmerR *Fr.* Odes.

Bringers. Carl Sandburg. CP-SandC

Bringing. Muriel Rukeyser. CP-RukeM

Bringing a Turtle Home. Robert Lowell. SP-LoweR

Bringing Back the Trumpeter Swan. Maxine W. Kumin. SP-KumiM

Bringing in New Couples. Ted Hughes. SP-HughTN

Bringing It Home. C. K. Williams. CP-WillC

Bringing our love to the zoo to see what species. Marriage, with Beasts. Mona Van Duyn. SP-VanDM

Bringing their frozen swords, their salt-bleached eyes, their salt-bleached hair. Warriors of the North, The. Ted Hughes. SP-HughTN

Bringing to Light. Thom Gunn. CP-GunnT

Bringing you back here—. Robert Creeley. CP-CreeR

Brise Marine. Joseph Brodsky. CP-BrodJ

Brise Marine. Derek Walcott. CP-WalcD

Brisk methinks I am, and fine. Anacreontic[k] Verse. Robert Herrick. CP-HerrR

Britain. George Meredith. CP-MerG2

Britannia Rules the Waves. Elizabeth Bishop. CP-BishE

British Church, The. George Herbert. CP-HerbG

British Museum Reading Room, The. Louis MacNeice. CP-MacNL

British puss demurely mews, The. Philological. John Updike. CP-UpdiJ

British-Roman Song, A. Rudyard Kipling. CP-KiplR *Fr.* Puck of Pook's Hill.

British said to Azikiwe, The. Azikiwe in Jail. Langston Hughes. CP-HughL; CP-HughL3

British Sincerity. D. H. Lawrence. CP-LawrD

British Song, A. Stevie Smith. CP-SmitS

British Stripling's War-Song, The. Samuel Taylor Coleridge. CP-ColeS

British Workman and the Government, The. D. H. Lawrence. CP-LawrD

Britons! when last ye met, with distant streak. Verses Addressed to J. Horne Tooke and the Company Who Met on 28 June 1796 to Celebrate His Poll at the Westminster Election. Samuel Taylor Coleridge. CP-ColeS

Brittaine, the mighty Oceans lovely Bride. Upon the Duke of *Yorke* his Birth a Panegyricke. Richard Crashaw. CP-CrasR

Brittannia's Baby. D. H. Lawrence. CP-LawrD

Brittle streets, with midnight walking flung, The. Sonnet on a Still Night. J. V. Cunningham. CP-CunnJ

Broached year, The. Paul Celan. SP-CelaP, *tr.* by John Felstiner

'Broad acres, sir.' You hear them in my talk. At Knaresborough. Donald Davie. CP-DaviDC

Broad-backed hippopotamus, The. Hippopotamus, The. T. S. Eliot. CP-ElioT

Broad bald moon edged up where the sea was wide, The. On the Esplanade. Thomas Hardy. CP-HardT

Broad field darkens, but, still moving round, The. Central Park. Howard Nemerov. CP-NemeH

Broad-leaved Arrow-head, The. Lorine Niedecker. CP-NiedL

Broad Minded Bishop Rebukes the Verminous St. Francis, A. G. K. Chesterton. CP-ChesG

Broad sun-stoned beaches. Midsummer, Tobago. Derek Walcott. CP-WalcD

Broadcast. Philip Larkin. CP-LarkP

Broadcast on Ethiopia. Langston Hughes. CP-HughL; CP-HughL1

Broadcast to the West Indies. Langston Hughes. CP-HughL; CP-HughL2

Broadcasting to the G.B.P. D. H. Lawrence. CP-LawrD

Broadstone, The. Robinson Jeffers. SP-JefR2

Broadway. Carl Sandburg. CP-SandC

Broadway. Walt Whitman. CP-WhitW

Broadway Pageant, A. Walt Whitman. CP-WhitW

Broagh. Seamus Heaney. SP-HeanSO

Brocado's and damasks, and tabbies, and gauzes. Excellent New Song on a Seditious Pamphlet, An. Jonathan Swift. CP-SwifJ

Brock. Paul Muldoon. CP-MuldP

Broke. Langston Hughes. CP-HughL; CP-HughL1

Broke to every known mischance, lifted over all. France. Rudyard Kipling. CP-KiplR

Broken ALTAR, Lord, thy servant rear[e]s, A. Altar, The. George Herbert. CP-HerbG

Broken Appointment, A. Thomas Hardy. CP-HardT

Broken arm of the black oak, The. Oak Arms. Carl Sandburg. CP-SandC

Broken Back Blues. Robert Creeley. CP-CreeR

Broken Balance, The. Robinson Jeffers. CP-JefR1

Broken blood, the hunting flame, The. Machine-Gun, The. Randall Jarrell. CP-JarrR

Broken Bone Blues. Allen Ginsberg. SP-GinsA

Broken Bone Bone Bone. Broken Bone Blues. Allen Ginsberg. SP-GinsA

Broken Bowl, The. James Merrill. SP-MerrJ

Broken Bowl, The. Jones Very. CP-VeryJ

Broken Christall, The. Robert Herrick. CP-HerrR

Broken Compact. Robert Graves. CP-GravR

Broken Dark, The. Robert Earl Hayden. CP-HaydR

Broken Dreams. William Butler Yeats. CP-YeatW

Broken Drought, The. Robert Frost. CP-FrosR

Broken English. Charles Wright. SP-WrigCN

Broken-Face Gargoyles. Carl Sandburg. CP-SandC

Broken Friendship, The. Stevie Smith. CP-SmitS

Broken Girth, The. Robert Graves. CP-GravR

Broken glass on the stairs, The. Jewels of Indoor Glass. Alan Dugan. CP-DugaA

Broken Ground, The. Wendell Berry. CP-BerrW

Broken Heart, The. John Donne. CP-DonnJ; MW-DonnJ

Broken Heart, The. Stevie Smith. CP-SmitS

Broken heart, you / timeless wonder. Echo ("Broken heart, you / timeless wonder"). Robert Creeley. CP-CreeR

Broken Hearted Soprano. Carl Sandburg. CP-SandC

Broken Home, The. James Merrill. SP-MerrJ

Broken in pieces all asunder. Affliction (4). George Herbert. CP-HerbG

Broken-Link Handicap, The. Rudyard Kipling. *Fr.* Plain Tales from the Hills.

Broken Men, The. Rudyard Kipling. CP-KiplR

Broken moon on the cold water, A. Your Birthday in the California Mountains. Kenneth Rexroth. CP-RexrK

Broken Music. Dante Gabriel Rossetti. CW-RossD *Fr.* House of Life, The.

Broken near the sea. Poems of Akhziv. Yehuda Amichai. SP-AmicYL, *tr.* by Benjamin Harshav *and* Barbara Harshav

Broken Neck. Robert Graves. CP-GravR

Broken oarshaft was stuck in the hill, The. Danse Macabre. Norman Dubie. CP-DubiN

Broken part heals even stronger than the rest, The. Consolations. William Stafford. SP-StafW; SP-StafWW

Broken Pen, The. Richard Eberhart. CP-EberR

Broken pillar of the wing jags from the clotted shoulder, The. Hurt Hawks. Robinson Jeffers. CP-JefR1

Broken Promise. Archibald MacLeish. CP-MacLA

Broken Sandal. Denise Levertov. SP-LeveDS

Broken Sky. Carl Sandburg. CP-SandC

Broken snow should leave the traces, The. Snow, The. Robert Creeley. CP-CreeR

Broken Sonnet. Carl Sandburg. CP-SandC

Broken Tabernacles. Carl Sandburg. CP-SandC

Broken Tower, The. Hart Crane. CP-CranH

Broken Wing Theory. Richard Eberhart. CP-EberR

Bronchitis on the 14th Floor. Marge Piercy. SP-PierM

Broncho That Would Not Be Broken, The. Nicholas Vachel Lindsay. CP-LindV

Bronkhorst Divorce Case, The. Rudyard Kipling. *Fr.* Plain Tales from the Hills.

Bronx Zoo. George Oppen. CP-OppGN

Bronze. James Merrill. SP-MerrJ

Bronze clock brought, The. Four Small Elegies. Margaret Atwood. SP-AtwM2

Bronze David of Donatello, The. Randall Jarrell. CP-JarrR

Bronze entrance doors alive with angels' wings. Moralities. Thomas Kinsella. CP-KinsT

Bronze General Grant riding a bronze horse in Lincoln Park, The. Bronzes. Carl Sandburg. CP-SandC

Bronze Head, A. William Butler Yeats. CP-YeatW

Bronze soldier hitches a bronze cape, The. In Memoriam Francis Ledwidge. Seamus Heaney. SP-HeanSO

Bronze Sounding, The. Ivor Gurney. SP-GurnI

Bronzes. Carl Sandburg. CP-SandC

Bronzeville Man with a Belt in the Back. Gwendolyn Brooks. SP-BrooG

Bronzeville Mother Loiters in Mississippi, A. Meanwhile, a Mississippi Mother Burns Bacon. Gwendolyn Brooks. SP-BrooG

Bronzeville Woman in a Red Hat. Gwendolyn Brooks. SP-BrooG

Brooch of Lorn, The. Sir Walter Scott. SP-ScotW *Fr.* Lord of the Isles, The.

Brood mares on the block at Tipton Pavilion, The. Selling of the Slaves, The. Maxine W. Kumin. SP-KumiM

Brooder, brooder, deep beneath its walls. Dove in Spring, The. Wallace Stevens. CP-StevWP

Brooding and seated at the summit. Why Some Look up to Planets and Heroes. Thomas Merton. CP-MertT

Brooding Grief. D. H. Lawrence. CP-LawrD

Brooding Likeness. Louise Glück. SP-GlucL

Brook and road. Simplon Pass, The. William Wordsworth. CP-WorW1

Brook beneath the water mill, The. Mark Van Doren and the Brook. Archibald MacLeish. CP-MacLA

Brook glancing under green leaves, self-delighting, exulting, A. Poetry of Coleridge, The. George Meredith. CP-MerG1

Brook in the City, A. Robert Frost. CP-FrosR

Brook sings on the selfsame strain, The. Old Age. Ralph Waldo Emerson. CP-EmerR

Brook-Song, The. James Whitcomb Riley. CP-RileJ

Brook, that hast been my solace days and weeks. William Wordsworth. MW-WorW

Brook! whose society the Poet seeks. William Wordsworth. CP-WorW1

Brooke whose streame so great, so good. Epitaph. Upon Doctor Brooke, An. Richard Crashaw. CP-CrasR

Brookland Road. Rudyard Kipling. CP-KiplR

Brooklyn College Brain. Allen Ginsberg. CP-GinsA

Brooklyn Museum of Art, The. Billy Collins. SP-CollB

Brooks & Other Notions. A. R. Ammons. CP-AmmoA

Brooks are bristling in the field, The. Poesie Abrutie. Wallace Stevens. CP-StevW; CP-StevWP

Brooks Atkinson. Archibald MacLeish. CP-MacLA

Broom, The. Arthur Rimbaud. CP-RimbA, *tr.* by Martin Sorrell

Broom Besoms ["I maun hae a wife, whatsoe'er she be"]. Robert Burns. CP-BurnR

Broom Besoms ["Young and souple was I, when I lap the dyke"]. Robert Burns. CP-BurnR

Broom trees twirped by our rosewood bungalow, The. Harriet's Dream. Robert Lowell. SP-LoweR

Brooms. Charles Simic. SP-SimiC; SP-SimiCE

Broomstead a lameness got by cold and Beere. Upon One-Ey'd Broomsted. Robert Herrick. CP-HerrR

Brose and Butter. Robert Burns. CP-BurnR

Brother. Robert Graves. CP-GravR

Brother, The. Thomas Hardy. CP-HardT

Brother and Sister. D. H. Lawrence. CP-LawrD

(To Lettice, My Sister.) CP-LawrD

Brother and Sister. Walter De la Mare. CP-DeLaW

Brother Bruin. Christina Georgina Rossetti. CP-RosC2

Brother Bulleys, let us sing. Bullfinches, The. Thomas Hardy. CP-HardT

Brother Fire. Louis MacNeice. CP-MacNL

Brother, I am fire. Kin. Carl Sandburg. CP-SandC

Brother, I Am Here. "Shu Ting." CP-KizeC, *tr. by* Carolyn Kizer *and* Y. H. Zhao

Brother, my brother, whither do you pass? To a Face in the Crowd. Robert Penn Warren. CP-WarrR

Brother, no decrepitude. Ralph Waldo Emerson. CP-EmerR

Brother of Ingots—Ah Peru. Emily Dickinson. CP-DickE

Brother of Mercy, The. John Greenleaf Whittier. CP-WhitJ

Brother of Ophir. Emily Dickinson. CP-DickE

Brother of the Unknown Ancient Man. James Tate. SP-TateJ

Brother Paul! look! Suzanne. William Carlos Williams. CP-WilW2

Brother Peter Considers Mulroy Drunk under the Rosebush. Josephine Jacobsen. CP-JacoJ

Brother, that breathe the August air. If Still Your Orchards Bear. Edna St Vincent Millay. CP-MillE

Brother where dost thou dwell? Henry David Thoreau. CP-ThorH

Brotherhood. George Meredith. CP-MerG2

Brotherhood in Pain. Robert Penn Warren. CP-WarrR

Brotherhood is not by the blood certainly, The. Speech to Those Who Say Comrade. Archibald MacLeish. CP-MacLA

Brotherhood of Men. Richard Eberhart. CP-EberR

Brotherly Love. Langston Hughes. CP-HughL; CP-HughL3

Brothers. Gerard Manley Hopkins. CP-HopkG

Brothers. Langston Hughes. CP-HughL; CP-HughL2; CP-HughL3

Brothers. Thomas Kinsella. CP-KinsT

Brothers. Dan Pagis. SP-PagiD, *tr. by* Stephen Mitchell

Brothers, The. William Wordsworth. CP-WorW1; MW-WorW

Brothers and sisters, Celestine. Ballade of Forgiveness. François Villon. CP-WilbR

Brothers! between you and me. To the Republicans of North America. Percy Bysshe Shelley. CP-ShelP

Brothers in the Craft. Thomas Kinsella. CP-KinsT

Brothers share five districts. Han-shan. CP-ColdM, *tr. by* Red Pine

Brothers spoke of Ghosts,—a favourite theme, The. Lady Barbara; or, The Ghost. George Crabbe. SP-CrabG *Fr.* Tales of the Hall.

"Brothers," St. Francis called the Brutes. Poor Relations. G. K. Chesterton. CP-ChesG

Brothers, stones on this moraine of time. Toward Rationality. Robert Penn Warren. CP WarrR

Brothers, the curving grasses and their daughters. Trappist Cemetery—Gethsemani, The. Thomas Merton. CP-MertT

Brothers, / this big woman. Song at Midnight. Lucille Clifton. SP-ClifL

Brothers: Two Saltimbanques, The. John Logan. CP-LogaJ

Brought from Beyond. Amy Clampitt. CP-ClamA

Brought low in Kyoto. How to Survive Nuclear War. Maxine W. Kumin. SP-KumiM

Brought the enemy down. Lorine Niedecker. CP-NiedL

Brow burning, in cool gloom, as sundown shears. Michelangelo Buonarroti. CP-Miche, *tr. by* John Frederick Nims

Brow is that of Deity, The. Emily Dickinson. SP-DickE

Brown and furry / Caterpillar in a hurry. Caterpillar, The. Christina Georgina Rossetti. CP-RosC2

Brown and silver, the tufted. For Floss. Denise Levertov. SP-LeveDP

Brown Bess. Rudyard Kipling. CP-KiplR

Brown Boy to Brown Girl. Countee Cullen. CP-CullC

Brown bread Tom Pennie eates, and must of right. Upon Pennie. Robert Herrick. CP-HerrR

Brown, brittle, wait-a-bit weeds. Indian Cave Jerry Ramsey Found, The. William Stafford. SP-StafWW

Brown Christ. Arrow. Federico García Lorca. SP-GarcF *Fr.* Poem of the Saeta.

Brown dominates this bar. Décor. John Updike. CP-UpdiJ

Brown Dwarf of Rügen, The. John Greenleaf Whittier. CP-WhitJ

Brown enormous odor he lived by, The. Prodigal, The. Elizabeth Bishop. CP-BishE

Brown eyes, family faces, maculate giraffes. Fire. A. K. Ramanujan. CP-RamaA

Brown gas-fog, white. At the Justice Department November 15, 1969. Denise Levertov. SP-LeveDS *Fr.* Staying Alive.

Brown Girl Dead, A. Countee Cullen. CP-CullC

Brown Gold. Carl Sandburg. CP-SandC

Brown lived at such a lofty farm. Brown's Descent; or, The Willy-Nilly. Robert Frost. CP-FrosR

Brown Menace or Poem to the Survival of Roaches, The. Audre Lorde. SP-LordA

Brown muskrat, noiseless, The. Lorine Niedecker. CP-NiedL

Brown of Ossawatomie. John Greenleaf Whittier. CP-WhitJ

Brown old man with a green thumb, A. He Was. Richard Wilbur. CP-WilbR

Brown Penny. William Butler Yeats. CP-YeatW

Brown piano in diamond, A. Portland Coliseum. Allen Ginsberg. CP-GinsA

Brown stonepeaks—rockstumps. Sonora Desert-Edge. Allen Ginsberg. CP-GinsA

Brownie, The. William Wordsworth. CP-WorW2

Brownie, Brownie, let down your milk. Christina Georgina Rossetti. CP-RosC2

Brownie sits in the Scotchman's room, The. Demon of the Study, The. John Greenleaf Whittier. CP-WhitJ

Brownie's Cell, The. William Wordsworth. CP-WorW2

Browning Resolves to Be a Poet. Jorge Luis Borges. SP-BorgJ, *tr. by* Alastair Reid

Brown's Descent; or, The Willy-Nilly. Robert Frost. CP-FrosR

Browns, the olives, and the yellows died, The. Winter Song. Wilfred Owen. CP-OwenW

Browsing among the zero hours. Saint John of the Cross in Prison. James Tate. SP-TateJ

Bruce & Linley's House. Robert Creeley. SP-CreeR

Brudder Sims. James Whitcomb Riley. CP-RileJ

Brueghel. Arthur Sze. SP-SzeA

Brueghel: The Triumph of Time. Howard Nemerov. CP-NemeH

Brueghel's Two Monkeys. Wisława Szymborska. SP-SzymW, *tr. by* Stanislaw Barańczak *and* Clare Cavanagh

Brugès ("Brugès I saw attired with golden light"). William Wordsworth. MW-WorW *Fr.* Memorials of a Tour of the Continent; 1820.

Brugès I saw attired with golden light. Brugès ("Brugès I saw attired with golden light"). William Wordsworth. MW-WorW *Fr.* Memorials of a Tour of the Continent; 1820.

Brugès ("Spirit of Antiquity—enshrined, The"). William Wordsworth. MW-WorW *Fr.* Memorials of a Tour of the Continent; 1820.

Bruised Reed Shall He Not Break, A. Christina Georgina Rossetti. CP-RosC1

Brunhilde, with the young Norn soul. With a Rose, to Brunhilde. Nicholas Vachel Lindsay. CP-LindV

Brush Fire. James Wright. CP-WrigJ

Brush of a raven's, not an eagle's wing! Thyestes. Donald Davie. CP-DaviDC

Brushfires all around. Cycle of Dust. James Tate. SP-TateJ

Brushing back the curls from your famous brow. Copulating Gods, The. Carolyn Kizer. CP-KizeC

Brushy and hairy, The. October Textures. May Swenson. SP-SwenM

Brussels in Winter. W. H. Auden. CP-AudeW

Brutalization under the Heart of Peace. Alan Dugan. CP-DugaA

Brutally sheared-off cliff, A. Wiltshire. Donald Davie. CP-DaviDC

Bryan, Bryan, Bryan, Bryan. Nicholas Vachel Lindsay. CP-LindV

Bryant. James Whitcomb Riley. CP-RileJ

Bryant on His Birthday. John Greenleaf Whittier. CP-WhitJ

Bub Says. James Whitcomb Riley. CP-RileJ

Bubble; a Song, The. Robert Herrick. CP-HerrR

Bubble Bed, The. James Laughlin. CP-LaugJ

Bubble breaking, The. Shot. Robert Creeley. CP-CreeR

Bubble of Air. Muriel Rukeyser. CP-RukeM

Bubbles. Carl Sandburg. CP-SandC

Bubbling brook doth leap when I come by, The. Nature ("Bubbling brook doth leap when I come by, The"). Jones Very. CP-VeryJ

Bubbs Creek Haircut. Gary Snyder. CP-SnydG

Buck in the Snow, The. Edna St. Vincent Millay. CP-MillE

Buck Moon—From the Field Guide to Insects. Mary Oliver. SP-OlivM

Buckdancer's Choice. James Dickey. CP-DickJ

Buckinghamshire. Donald Davie. CP-DaviDC

Buckles glitter, billies lean, The. American Twilights, 1957. James Wright. CP-WrigJ

Buckwheat. Carl Sandburg. CP-SandC

Bucolick betwixt Two: Lacon and Thyrsis, A. Robert Herrick. CP-HerrR

Bucolics. W. H. Auden. CP-AudeW

Bucolics. Sylvia Plath. CP-PlatS

Bud, The. Saint Francis and the Sow. Galway Kinnell. SP-KinnGN

Bud, come here to your uncle a spell. Home-Made Fairy Tale, A. James Whitcomb Riley. CP-RileJ

Bud will soon become a flower, The. As ye sow, so shall ye reap. Jones Very. CP-VeryJ

Budapest. Billy Collins. SP-CollB

Buddha. Herman Melville. SP-MelvH

Buddha at Kamakura. Rudyard Kipling. CP-KiplR

Buddha died and. Land O'Lakes, Wisc. Allen Ginsberg. CP-GinsA

Buddha forsook the joys of rank, The. Shih-te. CP-ColdM, *tr. by* Red Pine

Buddha in the Woodpile, A. Lawrence Ferlinghetti. SP-FerlL

Buddhas and engines serve us undersea. Mermen, The. Hart Crane. CP-CranH

Buddhas care for mortal beings. Shih-te. CP-ColdM, *tr. by* Red Pine

Buddha's Last Instruction, The. Mary Oliver. SP-OlivM

Buddhas leave behind sutras. Shih-te. CP-ColdM, *tr. by* Red Pine

Buddhist monk hears all past, The. If You Talk the Talk, You Better Walk the Walk. Charles Wright. SP-WrigCN

Buddhist monks don't keep their precepts. Han-shan. CP-ColdM, *tr. by* Red Pine

Buddhist Painter Prepares to Paint, The. Hayden Carruth. CP-CarHS

Buddhists speak of an Unenlightened, The. Unenlightened Face, The. James Laughlin. CP-LaugJ

Buddy. Langston Hughes. CP-HughL; CP-HughL3

Budgerigar is baby blue, The. Budgie. Louis MacNeice. CP-MacNL

Budgie. Louis MacNeice. CP-MacNL

Budging the sluggard ripples of the Somme. Hospital Barge at Cérisy. Wilfred Owen. CP-OwenW

Budmouth Dears. Thomas Hardy. CP-HardT *Fr.* Dynasts, The.

Buds and Babies. Christina Georgina Rossetti. CP-RosC2

Bud's Fairy Tale. James Whitcomb Riley. CP-RileJ *Fr.* Child-World, A.

Bud(spiggy nuvduh fienus). E. E. Cummings. CP-CummE

Buenas noches. New York Lullaby. Joseph Brodsky. CP-BrodJ *Fr.* Shorts.

Buenos Aires. Robert Lowell. SP-LoweR

Buenos Aires has a bagpipe. Song of the Shop Boy. Federico García Lorca. CP-GarcF, *tr. by* Catherine Brown

Buenos Días. Olga Broumas. SP-BrouO

Buffalo. Eugenio Montale. CP-MontE, *tr. by* Jonathan Galassi

Buffalo, The. Marianne Craig Moore. CP-MoorM

Buffalo Bill. Charles Bukowski. SP-BukC2

Buffalo Bill. Carl Sandburg. CP-SandC

Buffalo Bill's. Portrait. E. E. Cummings. CP-CummE; SP-CummE

Buffalo, buffalo, buffalo, buffalo. Death Chant. Peter Blue Cloud. SP-BlueP

Buffalo Clouds over the Maestro Hoon. Norman Dubie. CP-DubiN

Buffalo Coat, The. Thomas McGrath. SP-McGrT

Buffalo Days / I was asleep when you waked up the buffalo. Collected Poems. Kenneth Koch. SP-KochK

Buffalo / 12.7.41 / (Late afternoon light). Pearl Harbor. Susan Howe. SP-HoweS

Buffalo Dusk. Carl Sandburg. CP-SandC

Buffalo Evening. Robert Creeley. SP-CreeR

Buffalo in Compound: Alberta. Margaret Atwood. SP-AtwM1

Buffalo Ode. Charles Olson. CP-OlsoC

Buffaloes are gone, The. Buffalo Dusk. Carl Sandburg. CP-SandC

Buffet gray marble with a deadness. Home on Rue du Bourg-Tibourg. Clarence Major. SP-MajoC

Bug, flower, bird on slipware fired and fluted. Syrinx. James Merrill. SP-MerrJ

Bug Sleep. James Tate. SP-TateJ

Bug Spots. Carl Sandburg. CP-SandC

Buggins is Drunk[e] all night, all day he sleepes. Upon Buggins. Robert Herrick. CP-HerrR

Bugler boy from barrack (it is over the hill), A. Bugler's First Communion, The. Gerard Manley Hopkins. CP-HopkG

Bugler named Dougal MacDougal, A. Edouard. Ogden Nash. CP-NashO

Bugler's First Communion, The. Gerard Manley Hopkins. CP-HopkG

Bugles Sang. Wilfred Owen. CP-OwenW

Bugs. Ogden Nash. CP-NashO

Bugs' sleep is full of lead, The. Bug Sleep. James Tate. SP-TateJ

Bui Doi, Dust of Life. Yusef Komunyakaa. CP-KomuY

Buick. Karl Shapiro. SP-ShapK

Build at Kallundborg by the sea. Kallundborg Church. John Greenleaf Whittier. CP-WhitJ

Build Soil. Robert Frost. CP-FrosR

Build up the walls about me; close each door. Sonnet: "Build up the walls about me; close each door." Wallace Stevens. CP-StevWP

Builder eternally of things. Aeterne Rerum Conditor. Saint Ambrose. CP-CunnJ, *tr. by* James Vincent Cunningham

Builder, in building the little house. Kitchen Chimney, The. Robert Frost. CP-FrosR

Builder left one narrow rent, The. Samuel Taylor Coleridge. *See* Two wedded Hearts, if e'er were such

Builder of heaven, The. Hafiz. CP-EmerR *Fr.* Odes.

Builder of Houses, The. Jane Cooper. CP-CoopJ

Builders. Constantine P. Cavafy. CP-CavaC, *tr. by* Theoharis Constantine Theoharis

Builders. Yannis Ritsos. SP-RitsY, *tr. by* Kimon Friar

Builders, The. Gregory Orr. SP-OrrG

Builders, The. Kenneth Patchen. CP-PatcK

Builders, The. Jones Very. CP-VeryJ

Builders still reject my corner stone, The. Corner Stone, The. Jones Very. CP-VeryJ

Building. Gary Snyder. CP-SnydG

Building, A. Theodore Weiss. SP-WeisT

Building, The. Philip Larkin. CP-LarkP

Building 520 at Bellevue is a temple. Building 520, Bellevue. James Laughlin. CP-LaugJ

Building 520, Bellevue. James Laughlin. CP-LaugJ

Building of the Skyscraper, The. George Oppen. CP-OppGN

Building sky-high pavilions is useless. Han-shan. CP-ColdM, *tr. by* Red Pine

Buildings. Robert Creeley. SP-CreeR

Buildings. James Schuyler. CP-SchuJ

Buildings embankment parkway grass and river. Buildings. James Schuyler. CP-SchuJ

Buildings in Harlem are brick and stone, The. Heart of Harlem, The. Langston Hughes. CP-HughL; CP-HughL2

Buildings to the horizon, an accretion. São Paulo. John Updike. CP-UpdiJ

Built long ago, old / sills rotting in mud. My Hut. Hayden Carruth. CP-CarHS

Bulbs are in the sod, The. Emily Dickinson. SP-DickE

Bulbs burn phosphorescent, white, The. Ted Berrigan. SP-BerrT *Fr.* Sonnets, The.

Bulk of it / In air, The. Chartres. George Oppen. CP-OppGN

Bulks where the barley blew, time out of mind. Long Home, The. John Berryman. CP-BerrJ

Bull, The. William Carlos Williams. CP-WilW1

Bull Moses, The. Ted Hughes. SP-HughTN

Bull of Bendylaw, The. Sylvia Plath. CP-PlatS

Bull returns from his day of work in the ring, The. Yehuda Amichai. SP-AmicY, *tr. by* Stephen Mitchell

Bull, the Fleece are crammed [*or* cramm'd], and not a room, The. Audley Court. Alfred Tennyson. CP-TennA

Bulldoze all memories and sanctuaries: our birthright. New Jerusalem. Louis MacNeice. CP-MacNL

Bulldozers come, they rip, The. Development, The. Marge Piercy. SP-PierM *Fr.* Sand Roads.

Bulletin from the Stadium, A. Thom Gunn. CP-GunnT

Bulletin Has Just Come In, A. Ogden Nash. CP-NashO

Bullet's velocity in low temperatures, A. Lines on the Winter Campaign, 1980. Joseph Brodsky. CP-BrodJ, *tr. by* Alan Myers

Bullets whine on that last afternoon. Conjectural Poem. Jorge Luis Borges. SP-BorgJ, *tr. by* Alastair Reid

Bullfinches, The. Thomas Hardy. CP-HardT

Bullock / slowly, The. Prelude: "Bullock / slowly, The." Federico García Lorca. CP-GarcF, *tr. by* Jerome Rothenberg *Fr.* Night (Suite for Piano and Poet's Voice).

Bulls. A. K. Ramanujan. CP-RamaA

Bulls and bulldozers. Bulls. A. K. Ramanujan. CP-RamaA

Bulwark. Langston Hughes. CP-HughL; CP-HughL1

Bumble Bee—the Bumble Bee, The. George Meredith. CP-MerG2

Bumblebee, The. James Whitcomb Riley. CP-RileJ

Bumblebee / is less than a stack of, The. Poem for Liz. Charles Bukowski. SP-BukC2

Bump d'Bump. Maya Angelou. SP-AngeM

Bumping against rock in the dark. Metamorphosis, The. David Ignatow. SP-IgnaD

Bumpity Road to Mutual Devotion, The. Marge Piercy. SP-PierM

Bums, on Waking. James Dickey. CP-DickJ

Buna. Primo Levi. CP-LeviP, *tr. by* Ruth Feldman *and* Brian Swann

Bunch of Flowers, The. Jones Very. CP-VeryJ

Bunch of Grapes, The. George Herbert. CP-HerbG

Buncha hardboil guys frum duh A.C. fulla. E. E. Cummings. CP-CummE

Bundle of Myrrh Is My Well-Beloved unto Me, A. Christina Georgina Rossetti. CP-RosC2

Bundle of twigs, A. From an Artist's House. Carolyn Kizer. CP-KizeC

Bundles. Carl Sandburg. CP-SandC

Bungalows, The. John Ashbery. SP-AshbJ

Bungie do's fast; looks pale; puts Sack-cloth on. Upon Bungie. Robert Herrick. CP-HerrR

Bunk Johnson Blowing. Muriel Rukeyser. CP-RukeM

Bunyan, of course. But Potton it was, or Sandy. Bedfordshire. Donald Davie. CP-DaviDC

Buona Notte. Percy Bysshe Shelley. CP-ShelP

Buoy like a man in a red sou'wester, A. Beginning to Squall. May Swenson. SP-SwenM

Buoyancy. Jelaluddin Rumi. SP-Rumi, *tr. by* Coleman Barks

Buoys begin clanging like churches. River That Is East, The. Galway Kinnell. SP-KinnGN

Bura and Helice on Achaian ground. Ovid. CP-RaleW *Fr.* Metamorphoses.

Burbank crossed a little bridge. Burbank with a Baedeker: Bleistein with a Cigar. T. S. Eliot. CP-ElioT; SP-ElioT

Burbank with a Baedeker: Bleistein with a Cigar. T. S. Eliot. CP-ElioT; SP-ElioT

Burden. Richard Eberhart. CP-EberR

Burden. Langston Hughes. CP-HughL; CP-HughL2

Burden, The. Rudyard Kipling. CP-KiplR *Fr.* Debits and Credits.

Burden of fair women. Vain delight, The. Ballad of Burdens, A. Algernon Charles Swinburne. SP-SwinA

Burden of Itys, The. Oscar Wilde. CP-WildO

Burden of Nineveh, The. Dante Gabriel Rossetti. CW-RossD

Burden of Strength, The. George Meredith. CP-MerG1

Burdened heart that bleeds and bears, A. When I Was in Trouble I Called upon the Lord. Christina Georgina Rossetti. CP-RosC2

Burdened with precious memories of the past. Old Organ of the East Society Salem, The. Jones Very. CP-VeryJ

Burdened with years and crapulous with sin. Michelangelo Buonarroti. CP-Miche, tr. by John Frederick Nims

Burdens of the world, The. Correction. A. R. Ammons. CP-AmmoA

Burdock—clawed my Gown, A. Emily Dickinson. CP-DickE

Bureaucrats: Diggers. Thomas Merton. CP-MertT

Burghers, The. Thomas Hardy. CP-HardT

Burghers of Petty Death. Wallace Stevens. CP-StevW; CP-StevWP

Burglar of Babylon, The. Elizabeth Bishop. CP-BishE

Burgundy's grasslands scale the hills. Adam Zagajewski. SP-ZagaA, tr. by Renata Gorczynski, Benjamin Ivry and C. K. Williams

Burial. Edna St. Vincent Millay. CP-MillE

Burial. May Sarton. SP-SartM

Burial. Alice Walker. CP-WalkA

Burial, A. Charles Baudelaire. CP-BaudC, tr. by Walter Martin

Burial, The. Rudyard Kipling. CP-KiplR

Burial, The. Archibald MacLeish. CP-MacLA

Burial Anthem. Christina Georgina Rossetti. CP-RosC3

Burial Ground. Charles Olson. CP-OlsoC

Burial in Cypress Hills. Amy Clampitt. CP-ClamA

Burial of Barber. John Greenleaf Whittier. CP-WhitJ

Buriall. Robert Herrick. CP-HerrR

Buried. Christina Georgina Rossetti. CP-RosC3

Buried among white rooms. Ape Experiment Room. Philip Larkin. CP-LarkP

Buried at Springs. James Schuyler. CP-SchuJ

Buried City, The. G. K. Chesterton. CP-ChesG

Buried Lake, The. Allen Tate. CP-TateA

Buried Life, The. Matthew Arnold. SP-ArnoM

Buried Light. Yusef Komunyakaa. CP-KomuY

Buried Talents, The. Robert Stock. SP-StocR

Buried temple empties through its bowels, The. Tomb of Charles Baudelaire, The. Stéphane Mallarmé. CP-MallS, tr. by Henry Weinfield

Burke. Samuel Taylor Coleridge. MW-ColeS Fr. Effusions.

Burlesque. Muriel Rukeyser. CP-RukeM

Burlesque for Palgrave on the Pronunciation of "Metamorphosis." Robert Browning. CP-BroR2

Burlesque Translation of Lines from Lope de Vega's Arcadia. Samuel Johnson. See Turnip Vendor, The

Burly, dozing, humble-bee. Humble-Bee, The. Ralph Waldo Emerson. CP-EmerR

Burly driver at my side, The. Hill-Top, The. John Greenleaf Whittier. CP-WhitJ

Burly Fading One, The. Robert Earl Hayden. CP-HaydR

Burly, provincial France. Brantôme. Donald Davie. CP-DaviDC

Burma. Paul Muldoon. CP-MuldP

Burn, The. Galway Kinnell. SP-KinnGN

Burn your literary verses. Ralph Waldo Emerson. CP-EmerR

Burne, or drowne me, choose ye whether. Song: "Burne, or drowne me, choose ye whether." Robert Herrick. CP-HerrR

Burned Child, The. Dorothy Parker. CP-ParkD

Burning. Gary Snyder. Fr. Myths and Texts.

Burning a Book. William Stafford. SP-StafWW

Burning Book [or the Contented Metaphysician], The. Edwin Arlington Robinson. CP-RobiE

Burning / burning / burning / there was finally something. Crow's Last Stand. Ted Hughes. SP-HughTN

Burning Bush. Muriel Rukeyser. CP-RukeM

Burning Child, The. Amy Clampitt. CP-ClamA

Burning Dawn. Hayden Carruth. CP-CarHS

Burning Drift-Wood. John Greenleaf Whittier. CP-WhitJ

Burning fire shakes in the night, The. Invocation: "Burning fire shakes in the night, The." Walter De la Mare. CP-DeLaW

Burning, he walks in the stream of flickering letters, clarinets. Artificer. Czeslaw Milosz. CP-MiloC; CP-MiloCN, tr. by Robert Hass

Burning Island. Gary Snyder. CP-SnydG

Burning Mystery of Anna in 1951, The. Kenneth Koch. SP-KochK

Burning of Paper instead of Children, The. Adrienne Rich. SP-RicA1; SP-RicA2

Burning Oneself In. Adrienne Rich. SP-RicA2

Burning Oneself Out. Adrienne Rich. SP-RicA2

Burning the Christmas Greens. William Carlos Williams. CP-WilW2

Burning the Holly. Thomas Hardy. CP-HardT

Burning the Leaves. Howard Nemerov. CP-NemeH

Burning the Letters. Randall Jarrell. CP-JarrR

Burning the Letters. Sylvia Plath. CP-PlatS

Burning the Small Dead. Gary Snyder. CP-SnydG

Burning Trash. John Updike. CP-UpdiJ

Burning with heat and cold. For the Seasons. Marya Alexandrovna Zaturenska. SP-ZatuM

Burnished, burned-out, still burning as the year. Public Garden, The. Robert Lowell. SP-LoweR

Burnished-head / By burnished-head. Euripides. CP-DoolH Fr. Iphigenia [or Iphigeneia] in Aulis.

Burnishing, Oakland. Muriel Rukeyser. CP-RukeM

Burns. John Greenleaf Whittier. CP-WhitJ

Burns Grace at Kirkudbright. Robert Burns. See Grace at Kirkudbright

Burns sang of bonny Lesley. To Lesley. James Whitcomb Riley. CP-RileJ

Burnt Bridge, The. Louis MacNeice. CP-MacNL

Burnt Child, The. W. S. Merwin. SP-MerwWF

Burnt Dancer, The. T. S. Eliot. SP-ElioT

Burnt Kabob. Jelaluddin Rumi. SP-Rumi, tr. by Coleman Barks

Burnt-out Spa, The. Sylvia Plath. CP-PlatS

Burnt Ship, A. John Donne. CP-DonnJ; MW-DonnJ

Burr is a smell-feast, and a man alone. Upon Burr. Robert Herrick. CP-HerrR

Burr Oaks. Richard Eberhart. CP-EberR

Burra-Boo—Shirra Sha! Song of the New Zealander among the Ruins of Old London. George Meredith. CP-MerG2

Burros, taken to Death Valley by prospectors. Stopping to Look at a Crèche in a Jewelry Store Window. Miller Williams. CP-WillM

Burrowing deep into earth until the grave is complete. Wolf. Peter Blue Cloud. SP-BlueP

Bursting Rapture. Robert Frost. CP-FrosR

Bursts from a rending East in flaws. Hard Weather. George Meredith. CP-MerG1

Bury Hope out of sight, / No book for it and no bell. Christina Georgina Rossetti. CP-RosC2

Bury me on a Sunday. Farmer Dunman's Funeral. Thomas Hardy. CP-HardT

Bury the Great Duke. Ode on the Death of the Duke of Wellington. Alfred Tennyson. CP-TennA

Bury this old Illinois farmer with respect. Illinois Farmer. Carl Sandburg. CP-SandC

Bury thy dead, dear friend. Ye Have Forgotten the Exhortation. Christina Georgina Rossetti. CP-RosC3

Bury thy sorrows, and they shall rise. Sorrows and Joys. George Meredith. CP-MerG1

Burying Blues for Janis. Marge Piercy. SP-PierM

Burying Ground by the Ties. Archibald MacLeish. CP-MacLA

Bus. Denise Levertov. SP-LeveDL

Bus along St Clair: December, A. Margaret Atwood. SP-AtwM1

Bus Ride Ballad Road to Suva. Allen Ginsberg. SP-GinsA

Bus Song. William Corbett. SP-CorbW

Bus Stopped in Fields of Misdemeanor, The. Norman Dubie. CP-DubiN

Bus to Alliston, Ontario, The. Margaret Atwood. SP-AtwM2

Busbound out of New York. Accumulation. John Updike. CP-UpdiJ

Busch and Tommy. James Whitcomb Riley. CP-RileJ

Busdriver of the Mission bus at 1 A.M. is a statistician of chance, The. Secret Training. Andrei Codrescu. SP-CodrA

Buses Headed for Scranton, The. Ogden Nash. CP-NashO

Bush. Josephine Jacobsen. CP-JacoJ

Bush which bears most briars, and bitter fruit. Barberry Bush, The. Jones Very. CP-VeryJ

Busied with private dreams, earthen, unspoken. On Correggio's Leda. James Vincent Cunningham. CP-CunnJ

Business. George Herbert. CP-HerbG

Business. David Ignatow. CP-IgnaD

Business, The. Robert Creeley. CP-CreeR

Business, The. Charles Olson. CP-OlsoC

Business Acquaintances. John Updike. CP-UpdiJ

Business enough indeed. Emily Dickinson. SP-DickE

1. Business Jacob, the Angel Wrestler. Alan Dugan. CP-DugaA

Business man the acquirer vast, The. My Legacy. Walt Whitman. CP-WhitW

Business man, the acquirer vast, The. Souvenirs of Democracy. Walt Whitman. CP-WhitW

Business Personals. John Ashbery. SP-AshbJ

Busride along waterfront down Yessler under street bridge to the old red wobbly hall. Afternoon Seattle. Allen Ginsberg. CP-GinsA

Bust of Janus Speaks, A. Jorge Luis Borges. SP-BorgJ, tr. by Alan S. Trueblood

Bust of Tiberius, The. Joseph Brodsky. CP-BrodJ, tr. by Alan Myers

Busted and booked, and all. Confessionist. Heather McHugh. SP-McHuH

Bustle in a House, The. Emily Dickinson. CP-DickE

Busy Day. James Laughlin. CP-LaugJ

Busy day has hurried by, The. Written on Returning to the P. of I. on the 10th of January, 1827. Emily Jane Brontë. CP-BronE

Busy inquiring heart, what wouldst thou know? Discharge, The. George Herbert. CP-HerbG

Busy missing you. Emily Dickinson. SP-DickE

Busy old fool, unruly sun. Sun Rising, The. John Donne. CP-DonnJ; MW-DonnJ

Busy, with an idea for a code, I write. Obsessive Combination of Ontological Inscape, Trickery and Love, An. Anne Sexton. SP-SextA

But. Robert Creeley. CP-CreeR

But a chappie needs diverting. Chappie, A. Paul Laurence Dunbar. CP-DunbP

But ah for pittie that I have thus long. Book 4, Canto 11. Edmund Spenser. CP-Spens Fr. Faerie Queene, The.

But also dying / (as well as). E. E. Cummings. CP-CummE

But as this fugitive sunlight. Ralph Waldo Emerson. CP-EmerR

But being not amazing:without love. E. E. Cummings. CP-CummE

But borne, and like a short Delight. Upon a Child. An Epitaph. Robert Herrick. CP-HerrR

But cause thou hear'st the mighty king of Spain. To Inigo, Marquess Would Be, a Corollary. Ben Jonson. CP-JonsB

But did not Adam, Eve's appointed playmate. History of the Fall. Robert Graves. CP-GravR

But do not let us quarrel any more. Andrea del Sarto. Robert Browning. CP-BroR1; SP-BroR

But does she not at times. Theodore Weiss. SP-WeisT Fr. Storeroom, The.

But don't you know it, my dear. Looking at a Picture on an Anniversary. Thomas Hardy. CP-HardT

But evil is a third thing. Doors. D. H. Lawrence. CP-LawrD

But few they were who came to see. American Aloe on Exhibition, The. Herman Melville. SP-MelvH

But first / there is this vast dinner composed. Dream (2). Andrei Codrescu. SP-CodrA

But for a brief / Moment, a poised minute. Grasshopper, A. Richard Wilbur. CP-WilbR

But for the Grace of God. Edwin Arlington Robinson. CP-RobiE

But for whom do I look? Search, The. John Logan. CP-LogaJ

But Fortune governed all their works[,] till when. Aeschylus. CP-RaleW Fr. Prometheus Bound.

But give them me, the mouth, the eyes, the brow! Eurydice to Orpheus. Robert Browning. CP-BroR1

But God will keep his promise yet. Ralph Waldo Emerson. CP-EmerR

But granted that it's nothing paradoxically enough beyond mere personal. E. E. Cummings. CP-CummE

But hark! the Curfew tolls! and lo! the night. Winter's Evening, A. William Wordsworth. CP-WorW1

"But / he" i / staring / into winter twi. E. E. Cummings. CP-CummE

But help arrives! The welcome fleet appears! Winthrop's Fleet. Jones Very. CP-VeryJ

But here no cannon thunders to the gale. Conclusion: "But here no cannon thunders to the gale." William Wordsworth. CP-WorW2 Fr. River Duddon [A Series of Sonnets], The.

But Here's an Object. Abraham Lincoln. CP-LincA

But here's an object more of dread. But Here's an Object. Abraham Lincoln. CP-LincA

But I Am Growing Old and Indolent. Robinson Jeffers. CP-JefR3

But I Say unto You: Love One Another. D. H. Lawrence. CP-LawrD

But I, too, want to be a poet. Fanny Howe. SP-HoweF Fr. Poem from a Single Pallet.

But I wish you would not hang your head. Lines for a Young Man Who Talked. John Logan. CP-LogaJ

But I would rather be horizontal. I Am Vertical. Sylvia Plath. CP-PlatS

But if a living dance upon dead minds. E. E. Cummings. CP-CummE; SP-CummE

But if I look the ice is gone from the lake. Spring of the Thief. John Logan. CP-LogaJ

But if i should say. E. E. Cummings. CP-CummE

But if / never happened. Fanny Howe. SP-HoweF Fr. Lines Out to Silence.

But if that Cerberus, my mind, should be. Utter Rim, The. Robert Graves. CP-GravR

But if thou do thy best. Ralph Waldo Emerson. CP-EmerR

But in the end one tires of the high-flown. About the Phoenix. James Merrill. SP-MerrJ

But in these years, what is free, what is strong? Muriel Rukeyser. CP-RukeM

But Islands of the Blessed, bless you, son. Answer, An. Robert Frost. CP-FrosR

But isn't talking. Hill Has Something to Say, The. Rita Dove. SP-DoveR

But It Is Purer to Die. Rainer Maria Rilke. CP-RilkFr, tr. by A. Poulin, Jr.

But, it's because the liquor of summer nights. Here Everything Is Still Floating. John Ashbery. SP-AshbJ

But it's falling already. Apple Tree in May. May Sarton. SP-SartM

But Kujany is less than a mile from Szetejnie, and there, barefoot, I used to run. I Do Not Understand. Czeslaw Milosz. CP-MiloCN, tr. by Robert Hass

But lately seen in gladsome green. Auld Man's Winter Thought, The. Robert Burns. CP-BurnR

But like love. Early Morning. Federico García Lorca. SP-GarcF Fr. Poem of the Saeta.

But little Carmine hath her face. Emily Dickinson. CP-DickE

But maybe it's just. Holy Saturday in Paris. Adam Zagajewski. SP-ZagaA, tr. by Clare Cavanagh

But Men loved Darkness[e] Rather Than [or Then] Light. Richard Crashaw. CP-CrasR

But mr can you maybe listen there's. E. E. Cummings. CP-CummE

But Murderous. Stevie Smith. CP-SmitS

But nakedness, woolen massa, concerns an innermost atom. Nudity at the Capital. Wallace Stevens. CP-StevW; CP-StevWP

But Nature whistled with all her winds. Ralph Waldo Emerson. CP-EmerR

But never yet the man was found. Ralph Waldo Emerson. CP-EmerR

But no screen would show. Travelogue. George Oppen. CP-OppGN

But not for a king's daughter? Here where Sir Patrick Spens. North Sea, The. Louis MacNeice. CP-MacNL

But Not Forgotten. Dorothy Parker. CP-ParkD

But not on a shell, she starts. Paltry Nude Starts on a Spring Voyage, The. Wallace Stevens. CP-StevW; CP-StevWP

But not with joy. Floating. James Laughlin. CP-LaugJ

But—now her pleasant gentle modest mien. Petrarch. CP-Petra, tr. by J. G. Nichols

But now "no war nor battle's sound." Henry David Thoreau. CP-ThorH

But Now They Have Seen, and Hated. Richard Crashaw. CP-CrasR

But O to see his solar eyes. Ralph Waldo Emerson. CP-EmerR

But observe;although / once is never the beginning of. E. E. Cummings. CP-CummE

But of course the poem is not an assertion. Do you see? When I wrote. Impossible Indispensability of the Ars Poetica, The. Hayden Carruth. CP-CarHS

But of Life? Kenneth Patchen. CP-PatcK

But often now the youthful eye cuts down its. God Works in a Mysterious Way. Gwendolyn Brooks. SP-BrooG

But once I dared to lift my eyes. To ———: "But once I dared to lift my eyes." Lord Byron. CP-Byron

But one stood up and said: I love. Votaries of Both Sexes Cry First to Venus. Stevie Smith. CP-SmitS

But Only Mine. James Wright. CP-WrigJ

But our escape: to what god did we owe it. Pandora. Robert Graves. CP-GravR

But outer Space. Robert Frost. CP-FrosR

But see what living glory floods the west. George Meredith. CP-MerG2

But shairly, shairly, there maun be. Hugh MacDiarmid. SP-MacDH Fr. Esplumeoir.

But she was both,—she was both loved and love. Archibald MacLeish. CP-MacLA Fr. Happy Marriage, The.

But should I not pity that poor devil. Man of Evil. Robert Graves. CP-GravR

But sithens you it assay to kill. Sir Thomas Wyatt. CP-WyatT

But so to be the denizen stingaree. Euclid Avenue. Hart Crane. CP-CranH

But sovran Jove's rapacious Bird, the regal. Pyche and the Eagle. Elizabeth Barrett Browning. CP-BroEB

But, still preserved by pious care behold. Worship ("But, still preserved by pious care behold"). Jones Very. CP-VeryJ

But still, still . . . / In stillness mystery calls. Sonnet: "But still, still . . . / In stillness mystery calls." Hayden Carruth. CP-CarHS Fr. Sonnets.

But suppose / you could, like a painter, nail down. Theodore Weiss. SP-WeisT Fr. Polish Question, The.

But tell me, child, your choice; what shall I buy You? Handsome Heart, The. Gerard Manley Hopkins. CP-HopkG

But tell me, child, your choice, your fancy; what to buy. Gerard Manley Hopkins. See But tell me, child, your choice; what shall I buy You?

But that from slow dissolving pomps of dawn. Darkness. Arthur Hugh Clough. SP-ClouA

But that Thou art my wisdom, Lord. Submission. George Herbert. CP-HerbG

But that was nothing to what things came out. Welsh Incident. Robert Graves. CP-GravR

But the hearts that once adored me. Emily Jane Brontë. CP-BronE

But the Images of His Former Dreams Still Haunted Him. Kenneth Patchen. CP-PatcK

But the little more: the little more. Little More, The. James Dickey. CP-DickJ

But the majestic river floated on. Matthew Arnold. SP-ArnoM Fr. Sohrab and Rustum.

But the other / day i am passing a certain. E. E. Cummings. CP-CummE

But there, just outside. Theodore Weiss. SP-WeisT Fr. Storeroom, The.

But they are accurate. That is a target. Game of Darts at the Chesterfield Arms,

A. Muriel Rukeyser. CP-RukeM

But this is our desire, and of its worth. Gyroscope, The. Muriel Rukeyser. CP-RukeM

But Thy Commandment Is Exceeding Broad. Christina Georgina Rossetti. CP-RosC2

But to advise thee, Ben, in this strict age. On the Magnetic Lady. Ben Jonson. CP-JonsB

But to reach the archimedean point. Mysticism Has Not the Patience To Wait for God's Revelation. Richard Eberhart. CP-EberR

But turning a corner ,i. E. E. Cummings. CP-CummE

But under the carpeting, / past the pavement's end, and. Oliverio Girondo. Pablo Neruda. SP-NeruP

But we cannot go back to Charles V. Charles Vby Titian. Robert Lowell. SP-LoweR

But we must build our walls, for what we are. Ultimatum. Philip Larkin. CP-LarkP

But we've the may / (for you are in love). Song: "But we've the may / (for you are in love)." E. E. Cummings. CP-CummE

But what avail inadequate words to reach. Utterance. John Greenleaf Whittier. CP-WhitJ

But what indeed is ask'd of me? Gerard Manley Hopkins. CP-HopkG

But what is love? Tell me, dear heart, I beg you. What is Love? Robert Graves. CP-GravR

But what woke just now at fifty-two years in narrow. Waking Up. Robert Pinsky. CP-PinsR

But what would interest you about the brook. Country Club, The. Paul Muldoon. CP-MuldP

But when he found himself in darkness. Julian at the Mysteries. Constantine P. Cavafy. CP-CavaC, *tr. by* Theoharis Constantine Theoharis

But when he heard the women crying. End of Antony, The. Constantine P. Cavafy. CP-CavaC, *tr. by* Theoharis Constantine Theoharis

But when we started singing. Singing. Primo Levi. CP-LeviP, *tr. by* Ruth Feldman *and* Brian Swann

But who died here. It's Not Who Lived Here. Charles Bukowski. SP-BukC2

But who does us? Local Matter, A. Theodore Weiss. SP-WeisT

But whose house or head. Who. Laura Riding Jackson. CP-RidiL

But why do I feel so strangely about you? Sphinx. D. H. Lawrence. CP-LawrD

"But why do you go?" said the lady, while both sat[e] under the yew. Lord Walter's Wife. Elizabeth Barrett Browning. CP-BroEB

"but why should" / the / greatest. E. E. Cummings. CP-CummE

But why so solemn when the bell tolled? Tolling Bell. Robert Graves. CP-GravR

But will you do all these things? To a City Sending Him Advertisements. Ezra Pound. CP-PoEar

But ye shall destroy their altars. Gary Snyder. *See* Ancient forests of China logged, The

But yesterday I looked away. Song of Yesterday, The. James Whitcomb Riley. CP-RileJ

But yesterday! . . . O blooms of May. Blooms of May. James Whitcomb Riley. CP-RileJ

But You. Robert Creeley. CP-CreeR

But, you see, said the handsome young man with the chamois gloves. Natural Complexion. D. H. Lawrence. CP-LawrD

But you, Thomas Jefferson. Brave New World. Archibald MacLeish. CP-MacLA

But you were wrong that desolate dusk. For Thomas Hardy. Jane Cooper. CP-CoopJ

Butcher, The! Borges, What a Shock! Alan Dugan. CP-DugaA

Butcher in China, The. Butcher's Tao. A. K. Ramanujan. CP-RamaA

Butcher knife was there, The. Clash. William Stafford. SP-StafW; SP-StafWW

Butcher Shop. Charles Simic. SP-SimiC; SP-SimiCE

Butchers and Tombs. Ivor Gurney. SP-GurnI

Butcher's Dozen. Thomas Kinsella. CP-KinsT

Butcher's Tao. A. K. Ramanujan. CP-RamaA

Butler, fetch the ruby wine. From the Persian of Hafiz. Hafiz. CP-EmerR

Butt of Winter, The. Marge Piercy. SP-PierM

Butter-and-Eggs. Louis Zukofsky. CP-ZukLS

Butter Colors. Carl Sandburg. CP-SandC

Butterandeggs. William Carlos Williams. CP-WilW1

Buttercup is like a golden cup, The. Golden Glories. Christina Georgina Rossetti. CP-RosC2

Buttercups about the rocks and the sky. Pass, The. John Logan. CP-LogaJ

Buttercups that brushed my knee, The. In the Meadow. Dorothy Parker. CP-ParkD

Buttered Greens. James Schuyler. CP-SextA

Butterflies. Rudyard Kipling. CP-KiplR

Butterflies, The. Charles Tomlinson. SP-TomlC

Butterflies are white and blue. Mariposa. Edna St. Vincent Millay. CP-MillE

Butterflies, over the map of Mexico. Mexico is a Foreign Country: Five Studies in Naturalism. Robert Penn Warren. CP-WarrR

Butterfly. D. H. Lawrence. CP-LawrD

Butterfly. Nicanor Parra. CP-MertT

Butterfly. Rainer Maria Rilke. CP-RilkFr, *tr. by* A. Poulin, Jr.

Butterfly, The. Joseph Brodsky. CP-BrodJ, *tr. by* George L. Kline

Butterfly, a cabbage-white, The. Flying Crooked. Robert Graves. CP-GravR

Butterfly Effect, The. Billy Collins. SP-CollB

Butterfly in honored Dust, The. Emily Dickinson. CP-DickE

Butterfly obtains, The. Emily Dickinson. CP-DickE

Butterfly / or falling leaf. Dancer, The. Philip Larkin. CP-LarkP

Butterfly Piece. Robert Earl Hayden. CP-HaydR

Butterfly that Stamped, The. Rudyard Kipling. CP-KiplR *Fr.* Just-So Stories.

Butterfly that, The. Butterflyweed. A. R. Ammons. CP-AmmoA

Butterfly the ancient Grecians made, The. Psyche. Samuel Taylor Coleridge. CP-ColeS

Butterfly, the wind blows sea-ward, strong beyond the garden wall! Butterfly. D. H. Lawrence. CP-LawrD

Butterfly-toed Shoes. Yusef Komunyakaa. CP-KomuY

Butterfly upon the Sky, The. Emily Dickinson. CP-DickE

Butterfly's Assumption Gown, The. Emily Dickinson. CP-DickE

Butterfly's Numidian Gown, The. Emily Dickinson. CP-DickE

Butterflyweed. A. R. Ammons. CP-AmmoA

Buttons. Carl Sandburg. CP-SandC

Buttresses of morning lift the sun, The. George Washington Brige. John Ciardi. CP-CiarJ

Buy a Bond for Grandma. Bonds for All. Langston Hughes. CP-HughL; CP-HughL3

Buy Braw Troggin. An Excellent New Song. Robert Burns. CP-BurnR *Fr.* Heron Ballads, 1795, The.

Buy, buy, buy, / Is the Peace-markt cry. Song: "Buy, buy, buy, / Is the Peace-markt cry." George Meredith. CP-MerG2

Buy me an ounce and i'll sell you a pound. E. E. Cummings. CP-CummE

Buy meat with blood still dripping. Han-shan. CP-ColdM, *tr. by* Red Pine

Buy my English posies! Flowers, The. Rudyard Kipling. CP-KiplR

Buyers and Sellers. Carl Sandburg. CP-SandC

Buying and Selling. Philip Levine. SP-LeviP

Buying and Selling. Miller Williams. CP-WillM

Buying the Whore. Anne Sexton. CP-SextA

Buzz. David Ignatow. SP-IgnaD

Buzz [*or* buz], quoth the blue fly [*or* flie]. Catch, A. Ben Jonson. CP-JonsB *Fr.* Oberon, the Fairy Prince.

Buzz-saw snarled and rattled in the yard, The. "Out, Out—." Robert Frost. CP-FrosR

Buzzard never says it is to blame, The. In Praise of Feeling Bad about Yourself. Wisława Szymborska. SP-SzymW, *tr. by* Stanisław Barańczak *and* Clare Cavanagh

Buzzards bring out their young one. High Summer. Charles Tomlinson. CP-TomlC

Buzzards over Pondy Woods, The. Pondy Woods. Robert Penn Warren. CP-WarrR

Buzzard's two-note cry falls plaintively, The. Translating the Birds. Charles Tomlinson. CP-TomlC

Bweteen Hyssop and Axe. Robert Graves. CP-GravR

By a Blest Husband Guided, Mary Came. William Wordsworth. CP-WorW2

By a bottle of fatigued blue flowers. Fanny Howe. SP-HoweF *Fr.* Vineyard, The.

By a departing light. Emily Dickinson. CP-DickE

By a face of fiery cold, I'm set aflame. Michelangelo Buonarroti. CP-Miche, *tr. by* John Frederick Nims

By a flower—By a letter. Emily Dickinson. CP-DickE

By a Lady in America to Her Husband in England. Annis Boudinot Stockton. CP-StocA

By a Lake in Minnesota. James Wright. CP-WrigJ

By a mad miracle I go intact. Street Song. Sylvia Plath. CP-PlatS

By a peninsula the wanderer sat and sketched. Emblems of Conduct. Hart Crane. CP-CranH

By a Reactionary. G. K. Chesterton. CP-ChesG

By a River in the Osage Country. William Stafford. SP-StafW; SP-StafWW

By a route obscure and lonely. Dream-Land [*or* Dreamland]. Edgar Allan Poe. CP-PoeEd

By a Stream. Czeslaw Milosz. CP-MiloCN, *tr. by* Tony Milosz

By a wall the stranger now calls his. Kiss, A. Thomas Hardy. CP-HardT

By *Abracadabra* we signify. Abracadabra. Ambrose Bierce. SP-BierA

By after long appearance. All The Time. Laura Riding Jackson. CP-RidiL

By all means sing of love, but if you do. Truest Poetry Is the Most Feigning, The [*or*, Ars Poetica for Hard Times]. W. H. Auden. CP-AudeW

By Allan-side I chanc'd to rove. Allan Water. Robert Burns. CP-BurnR

By an immense Black Man in the circular meadows of heaven. Stones Are Thrown. Tennessee Williams. CP-WillT

By an old red-pate, murdering hag pursued. Author upon Himself, The. Jonathan Swift. CP-SwifJ

By an Open Window. Constantine P. Cavafy. CP-CavaC, *tr. by* Theoharis Constantine Theoharis

By and large the monks I meet. Shih-te. CP-ColdM, *tr. by* Red Pine

By and large there is no blood. Homewreck. Karl Shapiro. SP-ShapK

By Any Other Name. James Whitcomb Riley. CP-RileJ

By art, by music, overthrilled. Ralph Waldo Emerson. CP-EmerR

By Art's bold privilege Warrior and War-horse stand. On a Portrait of the Duke of Wellington upon the Field of Waterloo, by Haydon. William Wordsworth. CP-WorW2

By banana plants, on a deck chair, by the pool. Translating Anna Swir on an Island of the Caribbean. Czeslaw Milosz. CP-MiloCN, *tr. by* Robert Hass

By Blue Ontario's Shore. Walt Whitman. CP-WhitW

By bolstered words I am borne in hand. Sir Thomas Wyatt. CP-WyatT

By breath of beds of roses drawn. Hafiz. CP-EmerR *Fr.* Odes.

By Broad Potomac's Shore. Walt Whitman. CP-WhitW

By Callimachus. Callimachus. CP-CowpW, *tr. by* William Cowper

By Candlelight. Sylvia Plath. CP-PlatS

By chance my fingers, resting on my face. Anatomy. Walter De la Mare. CP-DeLaW

By chapel bare, with walls sea-beat. Haglets, The. Herman Melville. SP-MelvH

By children's birth, and death, I am become. Niobe. John Donne. CP-DonnJ; MW-DonnJ

By Chivalries as tiny. Emily Dickinson. CP-DickE

By constantly tormenting them. Poor, The. William Carlos Williams. CP-WilW1

By Crude Rotation. Laura Riding Jackson. CP-RidiL

By Cure of—Sulfa. Charles Olson. CP-OlsoC

By dark severance the apparition head. Painted Head. John Crowe Ransom. SP-RansJ

By dawn the little owls. September. W. S. Merwin. SP-MerwW

By Day, a Lifted Study-Storehouse. Philip Larkin. CP-LarkP

By Day and by Night. W. S. Merwin. SP-MerwW

By day and night dream about happy death. Give Your Wish Light. Robinson Jeffers. CP-JefR2

By day she woo[e]s me, soft, exceeding fair. World, The. Christina Georgina Rossetti. CP-RosC1

By day the bat is cousin to the mouse. Bat, The. Theodore Roethke. CP-RoetT

By day the skyscraper looms in the smoke and sun and has a soul. Skyscraper. Carl Sandburg. CP-SandC

By day . . . tireless smokestacks . . . hungry smoky shanties hanging to. Five Towns on the B. and O. Carl Sandburg. CP-SandC

By day we pace the many decks. Estuary, The. W. S. Merwin. SP-MerwWF

By death's favor. Epitaph on an Engraver. Henry David Thoreau. CP-ThorH

By deeds not words we prove our inmost mind. Freedom and Union. Jones Very. CP-VeryJ

By Disposition of Angels. Marianne Craig Moore. CP-MoorM

By dream I saw, one of the three. Dreame, The. Robert Herrick. CP-HerrR

By duty bound, and not by custom led. To the Memory of My Dear and Ever Honored Father Thomas Dudley Esq. Who Deceased July 31, 1653, and of His Age 77. Anne Bradstreet. CP-BradA

By fate, not option, frugal Nature gave. Xenophanes. Ralph Waldo Emerson. CP-EmerR

By fire and cloud, across the desert sand. New Exodus, The. John Greenleaf Whittier. CP-WhitJ

By five o' clock—still bright in spring—I'd catch. Deep—Deeper Down. Robert Penn Warren. CP-WarrR

By following many a color-coded corridor. Aerie. John Updike. CP-UpdiJ

By footworn boards, by steps. On Quitting a Little College. William Stafford. SP-StafWW

By Frazier Creek Falls. Gary Snyder. CP-SnydG

By gifts the Macedon clave Gates a-sunder. Ode 3.16: "By gifts the Macedon clave Gates a-sunder." Horace. CP-RaleW *Fr.* Odes.

By God, I don't know what to. Prayer in Bad Weather. Charles Bukowski. SP-BukC1

By god i want above fourteenth. E. E. Cummings. CP-CummE

By-gone age appears again, A. Military surprises and the capture of capitals, are the events of a by-gone age. D'Israeli. Jones Very. CP-VeryJ

By goodness and by evil so surrounded, how can the heart. Edna St. Vincent Millay. CP-MillE

By Henstridge Cross at the Year's End. Thomas Hardy. CP-HardT

By her white bed I muse a little space. James Whitcomb Riley. CP-RileJ

By Heraclides. *Unknown.* CP-CowpW, *tr. by* William Cowper

By holding one's head stock-still and measuring. Thin Air. John Updike. CP-UpdiJ

By holy zeal inspired, and led by fame. Verses Occasioned by the Sudden Drying Up of St. Patrick's Well near Trinity College, Dublin. Jonathan Swift. CP-SwifJ

By homely gift and hindered Words. Emily Dickinson. CP-DickE

By houres we all live here, in Heaven is known. No Time in Eternity. Robert Herrick. CP-HerrR

By June or July the river flows lazily. Cottonwood. William Stafford. SP-StafWW

By June our brook's run out of song and speed. Hyla Brook. Robert Frost. CP-FrosR

By kinds I keep my kinds in check. Ralph Waldo Emerson. CP-EmerR

By Lamplight. Stanley Kunitz. CP-KunSC

By landscape reminded once of his mother's figure. Adolescence. W. H. Auden. CP-AudeW

By law of rod and cone, the closer. Numberless. Heather McHugh. SP-McHuH

By light more brilliant of a star more bright. Michelangelo Buonarroti. CP-Miche, *tr. by* John Frederick Nims

By lines fainter gray than the faintest geometry. First Dawn Light. Robert Penn Warren. CP-WarrR

By little accurate saints thickly which tread. E. E. Cummings. CP-CummE

By long observation I have understood. Wood, an Insect. Jonathan Swift. CP-SwifJ

By Love, and by Beauty. My Eppie. Robert Burns. CP-BurnR

By means of metaphor. Koan for Two Minutes of Intensive Meditation. Robert Stock. SP-StocR

By merit of grace, the cross, and all we've suffered. Michelangelo Buonarroti. CP-Miche, *tr. by* John Frederick Nims

By mistake, one day, i unplugged grammar, the refrigerator of language. Grammar. Andrei Codrescu. SP-CodrA

By mistake the evening. Landscape ("By mistake the evening"). Federico García Lorca. CP-GarcF, *tr. by* Alan S. Trueblood *Fr.* Songs for Children.

By Morning. May Swenson.

By Morning Twilight. George Meredith. CP-MerG1

By Moschus. Moschus. CP-CowpW, *tr. by* William Cowper

By Moscow Self-Devoted to a Blaze. William Wordsworth. CP-WorW2

By Mrs. Hopley. Gerard Manley Hopkins. CP-HopkG

By mutual fear. Singing Prayer, A. Christopher Logue. SP-LoguC

By my 1st you may travel with safety & speed. Charade: "By my 1st you may travel with safety & speed." Francis William Austen. CP-AustJ

By my Window have I for Scenery. Emily Dickinson. CP-DickE

By Mystic's banks I held my dream. Ballade: "By Mystic's banks I held my dream." Paul Laurence Dunbar. CP-DunbP

By night a laddered diagram. Cooling Tower, The. Amy Clampitt. CP-ClamA

By night they haunted a thicket of April mist. Spectral Lovers. John Crowe Ransom. SP-RansJ

By night, when others soundly slept. Occasional Meditations: "By night, when others soundly slept." Anne Bradstreet. CP-BradA

By Nilus Once I Knew. Hart Crane. CP-CranH

By No Means Native. Adrienne Rich. CP-RicAE

By none but me can the tale be told. White Ship, The. Dante Gabriel Rossetti. CW-RossD

By now it had gone down, the sickle moon. Saxon (A.D. 449), A. Jorge Luis Borges. SP-BorgJ, *tr. by* Alastair Reid

By now there is no way I could break loose. Petrarch. CP-Petra, *tr. by* J. G. Nichols

By now you have envisaged. Middle of the Summer, The. W. S. Merwin. SP-MerwWF

By now you will have met. Voice. W. S. Merwin. SP-MerwW

By order of hunger the starving stood in line. Song Contest. Geoffrey Hill. CP-HillG

By Oughtertyre grows the aik. Robert Burns. *See* Blythe, blythe and merry was she

By our first strange and fatal[l] interview. On His Mistress [*or* Mistris]. John Donne. MW-DonnJ *Fr.* Elegies.

By Palladas. Palladas. CP-CowpW

By Philemon. Philemon. CP-CowpW

By playful smiles, (alas! too oft). Epitaph in the Chapel Yard of Langdale, Westmoreland. William Wordsworth. CP-WorW2

By Proxy. Yusef Komunyakaa. CP-KomuY

By reason of someone's death. Deathwatch on the Southside. Jorge Luis Borges. SP-BorgJ, *tr. by* Robert Fitzgerald

By Rome's dim relics there walks a man. Roman Gravemounds, The. Thomas Hardy. CP-HardT

By Rugged Ways. Paul Laurence Dunbar. CP-DunbP

By saplings I jerked and swung. Convergences. Robert Penn Warren. CP-WarrR

By Saturday I said you would be better on Sunday. Operation, The. Robert Creeley. CP-CreeR

By September 3rd I had made my bundle. Victory. James Dickey. CP-DickJ

By service clomb I heaven. Lucifer Caditurus. Ezra Pound. CP-PoEar

By sheer dint of prayer he makes himself an archangel. Rainer Maria Rilke. CP-RilkFr, *tr. by* A. Poulin, Jr. *Fr.* Fragments.

By shores and woods and steeples. A. E. Housman. CP-HousA

By sloth on sorrow fathered. Lollocks. Robert Graves. CP-GravR

By snails, by leaps of frog, I came here, spirit. Unfold! Unfold! Theodore Roethke. CP-RoetT

By so much, vertue is the lesse. Vertue Best United. Robert Herrick. CP-HerrR

By starlight hush of wind the owl's shadow voice. Camp. Peter Blue Cloud. SP-BlueP

By such and such an offering. Emily Dickinson. CP-DickE

By ten we know the day is out of order. Heatwave. John Ciardi. CP-CiarJ

By the Arno. Oscar Wilde. CP-WildO

By the Babe Unborn. G. K. Chesterton. CP-ChesG

By the Barrows. Thomas Hardy. CP-HardT

By the Bivouac's Fitful Flame. Walt Whitman. CP-WhitW

By the brilliant ramp. 3 A.M. John Updike. CP-UpdiJ

By the bushful I have know camellias. Camellia, The. Robert Stock. SP-StocR

By the city dead-house by the gate. City Dead-House, The. Walt Whitman. CP-WhitW

By the Cloud Path. W. S. Merwin. SP-MerwW

By the cold shore we came on. Lament for Misenus. John Logan. CP-LogaJ

By the descending mountain track, soundless. Uncertain Season in High Country. Robert Penn Warren. CP-WarrR

By the Deschutes Shore. William Stafford. SP-StafWW

By the dry road the fathers cough and spit. Brief Journey West, The. Howard Nemerov. CP-NemeH

By the Earth's Corpse. Thomas Hardy. CP-HardT

By the East River and the Bronx. Ode to Walt Whitman. Federico García Lorca. CP-GarcF, tr. by Greg Simon and Steven F. White

By the eleven. I Mean, No. Charles Olson. CP-OlsoC

By the Exeter River. Donald Hall. CP-HallD

By the fire light. Pilgrim Dreaming, A. Denise Levertov. SP-LeveDL

By the Fire-Side. Robert Browning. CP-BroR1

By the first of August. I Remember. Anne Sexton. CP-SextA; SP-SextA

By the fourth (or is it the fifth?). Poisoned in Nassau. John Updike. CP-UpdiJ

By the gas-fire, kneeling. Olga Poems. Denise Levertov. SP-LeveDP; SP-LeveDS

By the gate with star and moon. Medallion. Sylvia Plath. CP-PlatS

By the great river Deschutes. Wild Life Cameo, Early Morn. Lawrence Ferlinghetti. SP-FerlL

By the highway the stream downslope. Runoff. A. R. Ammons. CP-AmmoA

By the Hoof of the Wild Goat. Rudyard Kipling. CP-KiplR Fr. Plain Tales from the Hills.

By the Isar, in the twilight. River Roses. D. H. Lawrence. CP-LawrD

By the just vengeance of incensed skies. Judas. Jonathan Swift. CP-SwifJ

By the lake at Armenonville in the Bois de Boulogne. Armenonville. Edna St. Vincent Millay. CP-MillE

By the Laws of the Family Circle 'tis written in letters of brass. Public Waste. Rudyard Kipling. CP-KiplR

By the Mango Trees. W. S. Merwin. SP-MerwWF

By the mossy brink. On a Fête at Carlton House: Fragment. Percy Bysshe Shelley. CP-ShelP

By the name of Ceran. Michael Palmer. SP-PalmM

By the next kindling of the day. To Julia, in Her Dawn, or Day-breake. Robert Herrick. CP-HerrR

By the North Gate, the wind blows full of sand. Lament of the Frontier Guard. Li Po. SP-PounE, tr. by Ezra Pound

By the Numbers. James Laughlin. CP-LaugJ

By the ocean / dawn is. Concentrations. A. R. Ammons. CP-AmmoA

By the old Bath Road Pagoda. Hymn of the I.D.K., The. G. K. Chesterton. CP-ChesG

By the old Moulmein Pagoda, lookin' lazy at [or eastward to] the sea. Mandalay. Rudyard Kipling. CP-KiplR

By the Passeyr. George Meredith. CP-MerG2

By the pool that I see in my dreams, dear love. Pool, The. Paul Laurence Dunbar. CP-DunbP

By the river. Embankment at Night, before the War: Charity. D. H. Lawrence. CP-LawrD

By the River Eden. Kathleen Jessie Raine. SP-RainK

By the rivers of Babylon, there we sat down, yea, we wept, when [or then] we remembered Zion. Psalm 137: "By the rivers of Babylon, there we sat down, yea, we wept, when [or then] we remembered Zion." Bible, O.T. CP-CowpW; CP-CrasR; SP-SmarC Fr. Psalms.

By the Rivers of Babylon We Sat Down and Wept. Lord Byron. CP-Byron

By the Riverside. Carolyn Kizer. CP-KizeC

By the road to church, Shaker Village. Religious Articles. Donald Hall. CP-HallD

By the road to the contagious hospital. Spring and All. William Carlos Williams. CP-WilW1

By the Road to Upper Midhope. Donald Davie. CP-DaviDC

By the roots of my hair some god got hold of me. Hanging Man, The. Sylvia Plath. CP-PlatS

By the Rosanna. George Meredith. CP-MerG1

By the rude bridge that arched the flood. Concord Hymn. Ralph Waldo Emerson. CP-EmerR

By the rules you stop in that pose. Living Statues. William Stafford. SP-StafWW

By the Runic Stone. Thomas Hardy. CP-HardT

By the Sea. G. K. Chesterton. CP-ChesG

By the Sea. Emily Dickinson. CP-DickE

By the Sea. Christina Georgina Rossetti. CP-RosC1

By the sea loch the island cattle. Thrush in the Gaelic Islands, The. Archibald MacLeish. CP-MacLA

By the Sea-Side. William Wordsworth. CP-WorW2

By the secret that holds the forest up. Reporting Back. William Stafford. SP-StafWW

By the Side of Rydal Mere. William Wordsworth. CP-WorW2

By the Spring at Sunset. Nicholas Vachel Lindsay. CP-LindV

By the Stream. Paul Laurence Dunbar. CP-DunbP

By the Stream. Richard Eberhart. CP-EberR

By the stream, where the ground is soft. Ex Libris. Eleanor Wilner. SP-WilnE

By the time I came around to feeling pain. Circulation. Raymond Carver. CP-CarvR

By the time I get myself out of bed, my wife has left. Tuesday, June 4, 1991. Billy Collins. SP-CollB

By the time you read this. Letter. W. S. Merwin. SP-MerwW

By the time you swear you're his. Unfortunate Coincidence. Dorothy Parker. CP-ParkD

By the unacknowledged tie. Ralph Waldo Emerson. CP-EmerR

By the water-clock it's past dawn as the day watch sounds. Adviser to the Court. Tu Fu. CP-KizeC, tr. by Carolyn Kizer

By the Waters of Babylon. Christina Georgina Rossetti. CP-RosC3

By the Waters of Babylon. B.C. 570. Christina Georgina Rossetti. CP-RosC1

By the waters of Boston we sat down and wept. Ad Amicos. G. K. Chesterton. CP-ChesG

By the weak'st means things mighty are o'rethrown. Meane Things Overcome Mighty. Robert Herrick. CP-HerrR

By the weir it says: DANGER. Girls, The. Christopher Logue. SP-LoguC

By the well, where the bullocks go. What the People Said. Rudyard Kipling. CP-KiplR

By their floating mill. Stray Pleasures. William Wordsworth. CP-WorW1; MW-WorW

By Their Works. John Greenleaf Whittier. CP-WhitJ

By then I knew my flourishing green age. Petrarch. CP-Petra, tr. by J. G. Nichols

By then the poetry is written. Not What Was. Langston Hughes. CP-HughL; CP-HughL3

By these windows we perch, tourists. Charm Against the Toothache, A. Theodore Weiss. SP-WeisT

By thine own tears thy song must tears beget. Song-Throe, The. Dante Gabriel Rossetti. CW-RossD Fr. House of Life, The.

By this exchange of eyes, this encirclement. Everywhere Is Here. Robert Graves. CP-GravR

By this eye, north of its frowning. Theodore Weiss. SP-WeisT Fr. Polish Question, The.

By those bright eyes, at whose immortal fires. Elegy, An: "By those bright eyes, at whose immortal fires." Ben Jonson. CP-JonsB

By those soft Tods of wool[l]. Conjuration, to Electra, A. Robert Herrick. CP-HerrR

By 3 P.M. the pat of snow-pads had begun. Minnesota Recollection. Robert Penn Warren. CP-WarrR

By Threes, By Fours. Paul Celan. SP-CelaP, tr. by John Felstiner

By Thy long-drawn anguish to atone. Tuesday in Holy Week. Christina Georgina Rossetti. CP-RosC2

By Time, and Counsell, doe the best we can. Event of Things Not in Our Power. Robert Herrick. CP-HerrR

By twos the dead are swimming. Paul Celan. SP-CelaP, tr. by John Felstiner

By Use Comes Easinesse. Robert Herrick. CP-HerrR

By vain affections unenthralled. Cenotaph. William Wordsworth. CP-WorW2

By way of a leak. Times Square Water Music. Amy Clampitt. CP-ClamA

By way of Fishguard, all the lying devils. Single Fare. Richard Graves. CP-GravR

By Way of Remembrance. Christina Georgina Rossetti. CP-RosC3

By what right, then, do royal rulers rule? Right. Ambrose Bierce. SP-BierA

By what sends. Children's Rhymes ("By what sends"). Langston Hughes. CP-HughL3

By what serene malevolence of names. Theophilus. Edwin Arlington Robinson. CP-RobiE

By what word's power, the key of paths untrod. Heart's Hope. Dante Gabriel Rossetti. CW-RossD Fr. House of Life, The.

By Whose Hand. Olga Broumas. SP-BrouO

By Word of Mouth. Rudyard Kipling. Fr. Plain Tales from the Hills.

By yon castle wa' at the close of the day. There'll Never Be Peace Till Jamie Comes Hame. Robert Burns. CP-BurnR

By your knees they rightly clasp you. Woman of Greece. Robert Graves. CP-GravR

Bye Baby Bother. Stevie Smith. CP-SmitS

Bye-Child. Seamus Heaney. SP-HeanSO

Bye! / I'm going to a place so thoroughly remote. Radical Departure, A. James Tate. SP-TateJ

Bygone Occasion, A. Thomas Hardy. CP-HardT

Bypassing Rue Descartes. Czeslaw Milosz. CP-MiloC; CP-MiloCN, *tr. by* Renata Gorczynski, Renata Gorczynski *and* Robert Hass

Byrnies, The. Thom Gunn. CP-GunnT

Byron and Shelley and Keats. Pig's-Eye View of Literature, A. Dorothy Parker. CP-ParkD

Byron at Shelley's Burning. John Logan. CP-LogaJ

Byron, how sweetly sad thy melody! To Lord Byron. John Keats. CP-KeatJ

Byways and bygone. Traveler, The. Maya Angelou. SP-AngeM

Byzantine Gentleman, in Exile, Composing Verses, A. Constantine P. Cavafy. CP-CavaC, *tr. by* Theoharis Constantine Theoharis

Byzantine Mosaic, A. Wisława Szymborska. SP-SzymW, *tr. by* Stanislaw Barańczak *and* Clare Cavanagh

Byzantium. Charles Tomlinson. CP-TomlC

Byzantium. William Butler Yeats. CP-YeatW

C

C B M. George Meredith. CP-MerG2

C. G. Jung's 'First Years.' Thomas Kinsella. CP-KinsT

'c-hommodating he'd bait, seeking *accomodating* willed. Catullus. *See* '*Ha*dvantageous' breathes Arrius heavily

C is for CAMEL, a very right beast. John Ciardi. CP-CiarJ

C Minor. Richard Wilbur. CP-WilbR

C33. Hart Crane. CP-CranH

Ca' the Ewes [*or* Yowes] [to the Knowes]. Robert Burns. CP-BurnR

Ca' the Yowes [to the Knowes]. Robert Burns. CP-BurnR

Cabala. May Swenson. SP-SwenM

Cabaret. Langston Hughes. CP-HughL; CP-HughL1

Cabaret, cabaret! Minnie Sings Her Blues. Langston Hughes. CP-HughL; CP-HughL1

Cabaret Girl Dies on Welfare Island. Langston Hughes. CP-HughL; CP-HughL2

Cabbage and Carrot. Joseph Brodsky. CP-BrodJ

Cabbage catch the moon. Nocturn Cabbage. Carl Sandburg. CP-SandC

Cabbage Gardens. Susan Howe. SP-HoweSE

Cabbage-Roses. D. H. Lawrence. CP-LawrD

Cabbies dozed under St. Mary's Tower. Czeslaw Milosz. CP-MiloC, *tr. by* Robert Hass *Fr.* Treatise on Poetry, A.

Cabby said: "Hey, what do you think that does," The. Tanck's Song About the Transportation Business. Hayden Carruth. CP-CarHS *Fr.* Songs About What Comes Down: The Complete Works of Mr. Septic Tank.

Cabdriver's Smile, The. Denise Levertov. SP-LeveDL

Cabin door flew open, The. Lorine Niedecker. CP-NiedL

Cabin in the Clearing, A. Robert Frost. CP-FrosR

Cabin in the Rockies. Allen Ginsberg. CP-GinsA

Cabin Tale, A. Paul Laurence Dunbar. CP-DunbP

Cabin was cozy and hollyhocks grew, The. Tennessee Williams. CP-WillT

Cabinet of Seeds Displayed, A. Howard Nemerov. CP-NemeH

Cable Hymn, The. John Greenleaf Whittier. CP-WhitJ

Cables To Rage Or I've Been Talking On This Street Corner. Audre Lorde. SP-LordA

Cables to the Ace. Thomas Merton. CP-MertT

Caboose Thoughts. Carl Sandburg. CP-SandC

"Cabron," rings in his ears as he walks down. Six Persimmons. Arthur Sze. SP-SzeA

Cacti. Tennessee Williams. CP-WillT

Cadenus and Vanessa. Jonathan Swift. CP-SwifJ

Cadenza. Ted Hughes. SP-HughTN

Cadenza. Carl Sandburg. CP-SandC

Cadenza, A. Amy Clampitt. CP-ClamA

Cadenza on Garnette. John Berryman. CP-BerrJ

Cadillacs and Poetry. Raymond Carver. CP-CarvR

Cadmus. Jones Very. CP-VeryJ

Cadwaller-Smiths, The. Pride Goeth Before a Raise or Ah, There, Mrs. Cadwallader-Smith. Ogden Nash. CP-NashO

Caedmon. Denise Levertov. SP-LeveDS

Caedmon too I was lucky to have known. Whitby-sur-Moyola. Seamus Heaney. SP-HeanSO

Caelius Aufilenus' mate, Quintius Aufilena's *am*. Catullus. *See* Undone or done up with love

Caelius, Lesbia new star, Lesbia a light. Catullus. *See* Lesbia, our Lesbia, the same old Lesbia

Caesar. W. S. Merwin. SP-MerwW

Caesar Augustus, as matter of course. Ambassador From India. Robert Stock. SP-StocR

Caesar Knifed Again, or, Culture Biz Gets Hep, Boffs Profs. Ogden Nash. CP-NashO

Caesar Mamurraque! / A peerless pair of brazen buggers. Carmen 57. Catullus. CP-ZukLS *Fr.* Carmina.

Caesar, when that the traitor of Egypt. Sir Thomas Wyatt. CP-WyatT

Caesarea. Czeslaw Milosz. CP-MiloC; CP-MiloCN, *tr. by* Lillian Vallee

Caesars' Rage. Arthur Rimbaud. CP-RimbA, *tr. by* Martin Sorrell

Café in Warsaw. Allen Ginsberg. CP-GinsA

Café Notre Dame. Lawrence Ferlinghetti. SP-FerlL

Café: 3 a.m. Langston Hughes. CP-HughL; CP-HughL3

Café Trieste: San Francisco. Joseph Brodsky. CP-BrodJ

Cafeteria in Boston. Thom Gunn. CP-GunnT

Caffè Dante in New York—1. Yehuda Amichai. SP-AmicYL, *tr. by* Benjamin Harshav *and* Barbara Harshav

Caffè Dante in New York—2. Yehuda Amichai. SP-AmicYL, *tr. by* Benjamin Harshav *and* Barbara Harshav

Caffè Dante in New York—3. Yehuda Amichai. SP-AmicYL, *tr. by* Benjamin Harshav *and* Barbara Harshav

Caffè Greco. Czeslaw Milosz. CP-MiloC; CP-MiloCN, *tr. by* Robert Hass

Cage, The. Richard Eberhart. CP-EberR

Cage, The. Walter De la Mare. CP-DeLaW

Cage, The. Walter De la Mare. CP-DeLaW

Cage, The. Gregory Orr. SP-OrrG

Cage Walker, The. Yusef Komunyakaa. CP-KomuY

Cage wires white like ribs. Caged Owl, The. Gregory Orr. SP-OrrG

Caged Bird. Maya Angelou. SP-AngeM

Caged Bird, The. May Sarton. SP-SartM

Caged Goldfinch, The. Thomas Hardy. CP-HardT

Caged Owl, The. Gregory Orr. SP-OrrG

Caged Skylark, The. Gerard Manley Hopkins. CP-HopkG

Caged Thrush Freed and Home Again, The. Thomas Hardy. CP-HardT

Cageing of Ares, The. George Meredith. CP-MerG1

Cages do not suit the Swiss. Emily Dickinson. SP-DickE

Cage's quartet no. 1—really it's a. Listen. Hayden Carruth. CP-CarHS

Cahokia. Carl Sandburg. CP-SandC

Cahoots. Carl Sandburg. CP-SandC

Cain. Howard Nemerov. CP-NemeH

Cain: A Mystery. Lord Byron. CP-Byron

Cain and Abel. Rudyard Kipling. CP-KiplR

Caïque all white, and behind it red boats, The. Probabilities. Yannis Ritsos. SP-RitsY, *tr. by* Athan Anagnostopoulos

Cairn, The. Edna St. Vincent Millay. CP-MillE

Calais, August, 1802. William Wordsworth. CP-WorW1; MW-WorW

Calais, August 15, 1802. William Wordsworth. CP-WorW1; MW-WorW

Calcium days, days when we feed our bones! Desire for Spring. Kenneth Koch. SP-KochK

Calculated Behavior. Yannis Ritsos. SP-RitsY, *tr. by* Minas Savvas

Calculations set to one side, the inevitable descent from the sky. Youth. Arthur Rimbaud. CP-RimbA, *tr. by* Martin Sorrell

Calder, A. Karl Shapiro. SP-ShapK

Calder's Hands. John Updike. CP-UpdiJ

Caledonia. Robert Burns. CP-BurnR

Caledonian Antisyzygy, The. Hugh MacDiarmid. SP-MacDH

Calef in Boston. John Greenleaf Whittier. CP-WhitJ

Calendar. John Updike. CP-UpdiJ

Calendar. Robert Penn Warren. CP-WarrR

Calendar-Watchers, or, What's So Wonderful about Being a Patriarch, The. Ogden Nash. CP-NashO

Calentures. Robert Stock. SP-StocR

Cales and Guiana. John Donne. CP-DonnJ; MW-DonnJ

Calf, The. Robert Burns. CP-BurnR

Calf, The. Thomas Hardy. CP-HardT

Calf, The. Ogden Nash. CP-NashO

Caliban Remembers. Theodore Weiss. SP-WeisT

Caliban upon Setebos; or, Natural Theology in the Island. Robert Browning. CP-BroR1; SP-BroR

Calidore. A Fragment. John Keats. CP-KeatJ

Calidus Juventa? Allen Tate. CP-TateA

California. George Oppen. CP-OppGN

California Dreaming. Charles Wright. SP-WrigC

California Is Odious but Indispensable. Philip Whalen. SP-WhalP

California Petrarchan. Karl Shapiro. SP-ShapK

California Poppy. Gabriela Mistral. SP-MistG, *tr. by* Maria Giachetti [*or* Jacketti]

California Prodigal. Maya Angelou. SP-AngeM

California rolls into. Delia Rexroth ("California rolls into"). Kenneth Rexroth.

CP-RexrK

California song, A. Song of the Redwood-Tree. Walt Whitman. CP-WhitW

California Spring. Charles Wright. SP-WrigC

Californian Summer Pictures. Ambrose Bierce. SP-BierA

Caligari. Carl Sandburg. CP-SandC

Caligula in Blue. Wyatt Prunty. SP-PrunW

Caligula's Dream. John Updike. CP-UpdiJ

Call, A. Seamus Heaney. SP-HeanSO

Call, The. George Herbert. CP-HerbG

Call, The. George Meredith. CP-MerG2

Call, The ("Come thou and labor with me I will give"). Jones Very. CP-VeryJ

Call, The ("Why art thou not awake my son?"). Jones Very. CP-VeryJ

Call, The. C. K. Williams. SP-WillC

Call a ruined shoe, the sandal. Last Poem, Snow Tree. Norman Dubie. CP-DubiN

Call down a blessing. Song: Olive Tree. Robert Graves. CP-GravR

Call down the hawk from the air. Hawk, The. William Butler Yeats. CP-YeatW

Call evil all that debases the human spirit. God. Miller Williams. CP-WillM

Call exalted green leap spider. Spider or Ribbon Plant. Louis Zukofsky. CP-ZukLS

Call friends over when you have wine. Han-shan. CP-ColdM, tr. by Red Pine

Call from, a pull in some direction (EXCELSIOR!) echoes. A. Daydream, The. Philip Whalen. SP-WhalP

Call him deluded, say that he. Homage to Paul Robeson. Robert Earl Hayden CP-HaydR

Call him not heretic whose works attest. By Their Works. John Greenleaf Whittier. CP-WhitJ

Call himself unbegun, for the sea made him; assemblages of. Ryder. Muriel Rukeyser. CP-RukeM

Call into Death. D. H. Lawrence. CP-LawrD

Call It a Day. John Ciardi. CP-CiarJ

Call It a Good Marriage. Robert Graves. CP-GravR

Call it iron discipline. But for months. NyQuil. Raymond Carver. CP-CarvR

Call it love. It's the Way You Play the Game. Charles Bukowski. SP-BukC1

Call it the first distinction. Ab Urbe Condita. Michael Palmer. SP-PalmM

Call Letters: Mrs. V.B. Maya Angelou. SP-AngeM

Call me no more. His Lachrimae or Mirth, Turn'd to Mourning. Robert Herrick. CP-HerrR

Call me to you / at siesta. Carmen 32. Catullus. CP-ZukLS Fr. Carmina.

Call me / your deepest urge. Brown Menace or Poem to the Survival of Roaches, The. Audre Lorde. SP-LordA

Call not the royal Swede unfortunate. William Wordsworth. CP-WorW1

Call of Ethiopia. Langston Hughes. CP-HughL; CP-HughL1

Call of the Christian, The. John Greenleaf Whittier. CP-WhitJ

Call of the Wild, The. Gary Snyder. CP-SnydG

Call off your eyes from care. Young Man's Exhortation, A. Thomas Hardy. CP-HardT

Call that the Public Voice which is their Error. William Blake. CP-BlakW

Call the Next Witness. Carl Sandburg. CP-SandC

Call the roller of big cigars. Emperor of Ice-Cream, The. Wallace Stevens. CP-StevW; CP-StevWP

Call to Creation. Langston Hughes. CP-HughL; CP-HughL1

Call to National Service, A. Thomas Hardy. CP-HardT

Call us back, call us with your sliding silver. Spring Cries. Carl Sandburg. CP-SandC

Callacanthus / out again (the golden fury seen), The. For a Man Gone to Stuttgart Who Left an Automobile Behind Him. Charles Olson. CP-OlsoC

Called Back. Emily Dickinson. CP-DickE

Called Back. Charles Wright. SP-WrigC

Called death, is darkness. Sans Name. Charles Olson. CP-OlsoC

Called death the sudden subway and now he has. Tennesee. James Laughlin. CP-LaugJ

Called dog men. Royals. James Schuyler. CP-SchuJ

Called Niobe high more callous. Lilies. Louis Zukofsky. CP-ZukLS

Called out on Christmas Eve for a working-party. Devil on Ice. Donald Davie. CP-DaviDC

Called Poem of the End. Michael Palmer. SP-PalmM

Called to Be Saints. Christina Georgina Rossetti. CP-RosC2

Callers, The. Marilyn Hacker. SP-HackM

Calligraphy unrestrained. Han-shan. CP-ColdM, tr. by Red Pine

Calling, A. Maxine W. Kumin. SP-KumiM

Calling, The. Jane Cooper. CP-CoopJ

Calling, The. Jones Very. CP-VeryJ

Calling all butterflies of every race. From a Milkweed Pod. Robert Frost. CP-FrosR

Calling, and Correcting. Robert Herrick. CP-HerrR

Calling and the melody all night long, The. Chapultepec Park / I. Muriel

Rukeyser. CP-RukeM

Calling Collect. Josephine Jacobsen. CP-JacoJ

Calling of Names, The. Maya Angelou. SP-AngeM

Calling Spring VII-MMMC. Ogden Nash. CP-NashO

Calling to mind[e], mine eie long went about [or my eyes went long about]. Excuse, The. Sir Walter Ralegh. CP-RaleW

Calling to Order. Czeslaw Milosz. CP-MiloC; CP-MiloCN, tr. by Lillian Vallee

Calling under the Breath, The. W. S. Merwin. SP-MerwW

Calliope. "H. D." CP-DoolH

Callisto, Ganymede, Europa, Io. Moons of Jupiter, The. John Updike. CP-UpdiJ

Calls. Carl Sandburg. CP-SandC

Calls, The. Wilfred Owen. CP-OwenW

Calls on the Heart. Elizabeth Barrett Browning. CP-BroEB

Calm. Yannis Ritsos. SP-RitsY, tr. by Athan Anagnostopoulos

Calm, The. Tess Gallagher. SP-GallT

Calm[e], The. John Donne. CP-DonnJ; MW-DonnJ

Calm and Full the Ocean. Robinson Jeffers. CP-JefR3

Calm, / Cool face of the river, The. Suicide's Note. Langston Hughes. CP-HughL; CP-HughL1

Calm Day at Drake's Bay. Robert Bly. SP-BlyR

Calm in April, A. W. S. Merwin. SP-MerwW

Calm is all nature as a resting wheel. Written in Very Early Youth. William Wordsworth. CP-WorW1

Calm is the Fragrant air, and loth to lose. William Wordsworth. CP WorW2; MW-WorW

Calm is the season, cold and clear the air. Snowstorm in January. Marya Alexandrovna Zaturenska. SP-ZatuM

Calm o'er the hills the evening star. Jupiter as the Evening Star. Jones Very. CP-VeryJ

Calm of animals for whom anxiety, The. Rainer Maria Rilke. CP-RilkFr, tr. by A. Poulin, Jr.

Calm on his charger black and tall. Richard Lionheart. George Meredith. CP-MerG2

Calm on the breast of Loch Maree. Well of Loch Maree, The. John Greenleaf Whittier. CP-WhitJ

Calm was Half-Moon Bay; we lay at anchor there. Dream of Saba. Edna St. Vincent Millay. CP-MillE

Calm was the evening, as if asleep. Spark, The. Walter De la Mare. CP-DeLaW

Calm[e] was the day, and through the trembling air [or ayre]. Prothalamion. Edmund Spenser. CP-Spens

Calming Thought of All, The. Walt Whitman. CP-WhitW

Calmly the night came down. Earthquake, The. John Greenleaf Whittier. CP-WhitJ

Calvary. Edwin Arlington Robinson. CP-RobiE

Calvary, The. G. K. Chesterton. CP-ChesG

Calverly's. Edwin Arlington Robinson. CP-RobiE

Calvert! it must not be unheard by them. To the Memory of Raisley Calvert. William Wordsworth. CP-WorW1; MW-WorW

Calves harshly parted from their mamas. Ted Hughes. SP-HughTN

Calybes plough not their barren soile, The. Sir Walter Ralegh. CP-RaleW

Calypso. Olga Broumas. SP-BrouO

Calypso. "H. D." CP-DoolH

Calypsos. William Carlos Williams. CP-WilW2

Calypso's Island. Archibald MacLeish. CP-MacLA

Calypso's Island. Thomas Merton. CP-MertT

Camargue. Kenneth Rexroth. CP-RexrK

Cambodia. James Fenton. SP-FentJ

Cambrick! with grateful blessings would I pay. To Miss Bigg. Jane Austen. CP-AustJ

Cambridge. Jorge Luis Borges. SP-BorgJ, tr. by Hoyt Rogers

Cambridge, an outdoor library stack of bricks. Vale. John Ciardi. CP-CiarJ

Cambridge ladies who live in furnished souls, The. E. E. Cummings. CP-CummE; SP-CummE

Cambridge ladies who live in furnished souls, The. Cambridge ladies who live in furnished souls, The. E. E. Cummings. CP-CummE; SP-CummE

Cambridge Revery. John Logan. CP-LogaJ

Cambridgeshire. Donald Davie. CP-DaviDC

Camden, 1892. Jorge Luis Borges. SP-BorgJ, tr. by Alastair Reid

Camden, most reverend head, to whom I owe. To William Camden. Ben Jonson. CP-JonsB; SP-JonsB

Came in my full youth to the midnight cave. Ajanta. Muriel Rukeyser. CP-RukeM

Came she not from the pages of Malory, from the Morte Darthur? Inviolable Maiden, The. James Laughlin. CP-LaugJ

Came south, tripped up by constricting manzanita. Dance, The. Robert Stock. SP-StocR

Came such a long way. Postcards from Rotterdam. Carolyn Kizer. CP-KizeC

Came suddenly & without warning. Cold, The. James Laughlin. CP-LaugJ

Came to lakes; came to dead water. Field of Light, A. Theodore Roethke. CP-RoetT

Camel, The. Ogden Nash. CP-NashO

Camel-Driver, A. Robert Browning. CP-BroR2

Camel in the Snow. Theodore Weiss. SP-WeisT

Camellia, The. Robert Stock. SP-StocR

Camellia Sabina. Marianne Craig Moore. CP-MoorM

Camel's hump is an ugly lump, The. Hump, The. Rudyard Kipling. CP-KiplR *Fr. Just-So Stories.*

Camelus Saltat. George Meredith. CP-MerG1

Camelus Saltat: Continued. George Meredith. CP-MerG1

Cameo, The. Edna St. Vincent Millay. CP-MillE

Camera. John Updike. CP-UpdiJ

Camera at the crossing sees the city. Gauley Bridge. Muriel Rukeyser. CP-RukeM

Camera Obscura. Hans Magnus Enzensberger. SP-EnzeH, *tr. by* Michael Hamburger

Camilla, good humoured, & merry, & small. On the Marriage of Miss Camilla Wallop & the Revd. [Henry] Wake. Jane Austen. CP-AustJ

Camma. Oscar Wilde. CP-WildO

Camoëns. Herman Melville. SP-MelvH

Camoëns, he the accomplished and the good. Torquato Tasso. CP-WorW1

Camomile sweetens the cliff-top grass. Response to Hopkins. Charles Tomlinson. SP-TomlC

Camouflage. Amy Clampitt. CP-ClamA

Camouflaging the Chimera. Yusef Komunyakaa. CP-KomuY

Camoufleur. May Swenson. SP-SwenM

Camp. Peter Blue Cloud. SP-BlueP

Camp in the Prussian Forest, A. Randall Jarrell. CP-JarrR

Camp-stool for chair once more and packing case for table. Work-Room. Robert Graves. CP-GravR

Campaign. Muriel Rukeyser. CP-RukeM

Campanula. Kathleen Jessie Raine. SP-RainK

Campbells Are Comin, The. Robert Burns. CP-BurnR

Camperdown Elm, The. Marianne Craig Moore. CP-MoorM

Camphene Lamp, The. Jones Very. CP-VeryJ

Camping in Madera Canyon. May Swenson. SP-SwenM

Campions. D. H. Lawrence. CP-LawrD

Campo dei Fiori. Czeslaw Milosz. CP-MiloC; CP-MiloCN, *tr. by* David Brooks *and* Louis Iribarne

Camps hold [*or* held] their distance—[of] brown chestnuts and grey smoke, The. Derek Walcott. CP-WalcD *Fr. Midsummer.*

Camps of Green. Walt Whitman. CP-WhitW

Camptown. John Ciardi. CP-CiarJ

Camus in Ulster. Derek Mahon. CP-MahoD

Can a bell ring in the heart. When Death Came April Twelve 1945. Carl Sandburg. CP-SandC

Can a mote of sunlight defeat its purpose. Louis Zukofsky. CP-ZukLS

Can another love be born. Hilda's Morning and Evening Dose of Rhyme. George Meredith. CP-MerG2

Can anything avail / Beldame, for my hid grief? Husband's View, The. Thomas Hardy. CP-HardT

Can bare fact make the cloth of a shining poem? Waiting for the Chariot. Carl Sandburg. CP-SandC

Can beauty that did prompt me first to write. Elegy, An: "Can beauty that did prompt me first to write." Ben Jonson. CP-JonsB

Can Death Be Sleep, When Life Is But a Dream. John Keats. CP-KeatJ

Can feel it in the pushing. Robert Creeley. CP-CreeR

Can flame beget white steel. She Contrasts with Herself Hippolyta. "H. D." CP-DoolH

Can historical materialism, which is only a historical method. To My Friend the Late Beatrice Hastings. Hugh MacDiarmid. SP-MacDH

Can I Catch Up with the Future? James Laughlin. CP-LaugJ

Can I cease to care. Song—(On Chloris Being Ill). Robert Burns. CP-BurnR

Can I easily say, / I know you of course now. Sisters. Adrienne Rich. CP-RicAE; SP-RicA2

Can I forget. Tennessee Williams. CP-WillT

Can I Get You a Glass of Water? or, Please Close the Glottis after You. Ogden Nash. CP-NashO

Can I know it?—Nay.— / Shall I know it?—Yea. Christina Georgina Rossetti. CP-RosC2

Can I not come to Thee, my God, for these. To His Ever-Loving God. Robert Herrick. CP-HerrR

Can I not sin, but thou wilt be. To His Conscience. Robert Herrick. CP-HerrR

Can it be. Living Alone with Jesus. Maxine W. Kumin. SP-KumiM

Can It Be? Stevie Smith. CP-SmitS

Can it be again. Lyric: "Can it be again." Tennessee Williams. CP-WillT

Can it be so? It must be so. Her Haunting-Ground. Thomas Hardy. CP-HardT

Can it be that She might forgive my continually ruined ambitions. Anguish. Arthur Rimbaud. CP-RimbA, *tr. by* Martin Sorrell

Can knowledge be conveyed that isn't felt? Lorine Niedecker. CP-NiedL

Can Language Be Taught with the Fingertips? James Laughlin. CP-LaugJ

Can Life be a blessing. John Dryden. SP-DrydJ *Fr. Troilus and Cressida.*

Can man rejoice who lives in hourly fear? Let Patience Have Her Perfect Work. Christina Georgina Rossetti. CP-RosC2

Can peach renew lost blossom, / Or violet lost perfume. Go In Peace. Christina Georgina Rossetti. CP-RosC2

Can progress pause? We know from this prediction. Logic of Progress, The. G. K. Chesterton. CP-ChesG

Can ratt-rime and ragments o' quenry. Drunk Man Looks at the Thistle, A. Hugh MacDiarmid. SP-MacDH

Can rules or tutors educate. Culture. Ralph Waldo Emerson. CP-EmerR

Can she induce a dream? Pupa. Clarence Major. SP-MajoC

Can such light offer. Rainer Maria Rilke. CP-RilkFr, *tr. by* A. Poulin, Jr. *Fr. Orchards.*

Can the Harp Shoot Through Its Propellers? Kenneth Patchen. CP-PatcK

Can the misfortune of a dog owned by vegetarians. Comrade Past & Mister Present. Andrei Codrescu. SP-CodrA

Can There Be a Female Bodhissatva? James Laughlin. CP-LaugJ

Can there be anything more mean. On Sir Joshua Reynolds. William Blake. CP-BlakW

Can this finding your presence dear. Wishing More Dear. Laura Riding Jackson. CP-RidiL

Can truth lose charm. Regret of War Ways. Laura Riding Jackson. CP-RidiL

Can we believe—by an effort. Cities. "H. D." CP-DoolH

Can we not force from wid[d]owed poetry. Elegy upon the Death of the Dean of [St.] Paul's, Dr. John Donne, An. Thomas Carew. CP-CareT

Can white birds sing? An ornithologist. No White Birds Sings. John Ciardi. CP-CiarJ

Can Ye Labor Lea. Robert Burns. CP-BurnR

Can you, after dark, bcome a darkie? After Dark. D. H. Lawrence. CP-LawrD

Can you find another market like this? Seed Market, The. Jelaluddin Rumi. SP-Rumi, *tr. by* Coleman Barks

Can You Leave Me Thus, My Katy. Robert Burns. CP-BurnR

(Canst thou leave me thus, my Katy.) CP-BurnR

Can you match with me. Jonathan Swift. CP-SwifJ

Can you still love, having once shared love's secret. Unposted Letter. Robert Graves. CP-GravR

Can you still stand out on that balcony. Pastoral. Sam Hamill. SP-HamiS

Cana. Thomas Merton. CP-MertT

Canaan. Geoffrey Hill. CP-HillG

Canada. Billy Collins. SP-CollB

Canada. Robert Creeley. CP-CreeR

Canadian Pacific. Derek Mahon. CP-MahoD

Canadians. Ivor Gurney. SP-GurnI

Canadians and Pottawatomies. Carl Sandburg. CP-SandC

Canal. Muriel Rukeyser. CP-RukeM

Canal. Charles Tomlinson. CP-TomlC; SP-TomlC

Canal Gardens. Jaroslav Seifert. SP-SeifJ, *tr. by* Ewald Osers

Canal, this one, The. Clarence Major. SP-MajoC

Canal's Drowning Black, The. Ted Hughes. SP-HughTN

Canapés, my Fabullus, at home any. Catullus. *See* I shall expect / you in to dine

Canaries in the morning, orchestras. Academic Discourse at Havana. Wallace Stevens. CP-StevW; CP-StevWP

Canary, The. Ogden Nash. CP-NashO

Canary at the Farm, A. James Whitcomb Riley. CP-RileJ

Canary Bird, The. Jones Very.

Cancel, Catullus, the expectancies of friendship. Carmen 72. Catullus. CP-ZukLS *Fr. Carmina.*

Cancelled Passage. Percy Bysshe Shelley. CP-ShelP

Cancelled Stanza. Percy Bysshe Shelley. CP-ShelP

Cancer Cells, The. Richard Eberhart. CP-EberR

Cancer Match, The. James Dickey. CP-DickJ

Cancion: "When I am the sky." Denise Levertov. SP-LeveDL

Candid Friend who strikes because he loves, The. George Meredith. CP-MerG2

Candied. Eleanor Wilner. SP-WilnE

Candle, A. Sir John Suckling. CP-SuckJ

Candle a Saint, The. Wallace Stevens. CP-StevW; CP-StevWP

Candle Hat. Billy Collins. SP-CollB

Candle Indoors, The. Gerard Manley Hopkins. CP-HopkG

Candle is made to become entirely flame, A. Just-Finishing Candle, A. Jelaluddin Rumi. SP-Rumi, *tr. by* Coleman Barks

Candle, lamp. Night. Federico García Lorca. SP-GarcF *Fr. Poem of the Saeta.*

Candle, Lamp & Firefly. Tess Gallagher. SP-GallT

Candle light blue banners incense. Land O'Lakes, Wisconsin: Vajrayana Seminary. Allen Ginsberg. CP-GinsA

Candleberry bayberry spice resinwax green. Bayberry. Louis Zukofsky. CP-ZukLS

Candlemas Dialogue, A. Christina Georgina Rossetti. CP-RosC2

Candlemas Procession, The. Thomas Merton. CP-MertT

Candles. Louis MacNeice. CP-MacNL

Candles. Constantine P. Cavafy. CP-CavaC, tr. by Theoharis Constantine Theoharis

Candles. Sylvia Plath. CP-PlatS

Candles and / Here Comes a glass box. E. E. Cummings. CP-CummE

Candles gutter in her quiet room. Obsequies for a Poetess. James Vincent Cunningham. CP-CunnJ

Candles in Babylon. Denise Levertov. SP-LeveDL; SP-LeveDS

Candles, ribbons and a cross. Twenty-Two Tremblings of the Postulant. Jay Wright. SP-WrigJ

Candor—my tepid friend. Emily Dickinson. CP-DickE

Candor of Julias Teeth, The. Robert Herrick. CP-HerrR

Candour compels me, Becher! to commend. Answer to Some Elegant Verses. Lord Byron CP-Byron

Candy / Is dandy. Reflections on Ice-breaking. Ogden Nash. CP-NashO

Candy Wrapper and Toy. Federico García Lorca. CP-GarcF, tr. by Christopher Maurer

Canebrake sends its little shoots, The. Eugenio Montale. CP-MontE, tr. by Jonathan Galassi

Canis Major. Robert Frost. CP-FrosR

Canna's Basalt Crags. Kathleen Jessie Raine. SP-RainK

Cannas shiny as slag. Flower Dump. Theodore Roethke. CP-RoetT

Cannibal Bratuscha. Muriel Rukeyser. CP-RukeM

Cannibals. Donald Davie. CP-DaviDC

Cannon his name. Napoléon. George Meredith. CP-MerG1

Cannoneer is dead, The. On Seeing an Old Civil War Painting with My Love. Charles Bukowski. SP-BukC2

Cannon's brazen lips are cold, The. To Pius IX. John Greenleaf Whittier. CP-WhitJ

Cannot Sweeten. Christina Georgina Rossetti. CP RosC3

Cannot want not to. War & Peace. Robert Creeley. SP-CreeR

Canonization, The. John Donne. CP-DonnJ; MW-DonnJ

Canossa. Howard Nemerov. CP-NemeH

Canst be idle? canst thou play? Business. George Herbert. CP-HerbG

Canst thou leave me thus, my Katy. Robert Burns. See Is this thy plighted, fond regard

Can't Be Borne. D. H. Lawrence. CP-LawrD

Can't cut it (night). February Air. Ted Berrigan. SP-BerrT

Cant first attacked as such, 1596, Count Fransesco Cenci (source:). Being Altogether Literal, & Specific, and Seeking at the Same Time to be Successfully Explicit. Charles Olson. CP-OlsoC

Can't get that tune. Ancient Tree, An. Denise Levertov. SP-LeveDL

Can't get the girl. If a Poet. James Laughlin. CP-LaugJ

Can't live / mindless. Time ("Can't live / mindless"). Robert Creeley. SP-CreeR

Can't myself / let off this. Echo Of. Robert Creeley. CP-CreeR

Can't seem to wake you, kid, guess it. Body Beside the Ties, The. Kenneth Patchen. CP-PatcK

Can't you think death lives. Pablo Neruda. SP-NeruP Fr. Question Book.

Cantab, The. Vincent Bourne. CP-CowpW

Cantabat Veneres meras Catullus. De Catullo et Martiale. Thomas Campion. CP-CampT

Cantaloupe, The. Ogden Nash. CP-NashO

Cantata, A. Jonathan Swift. CP-SwifJ

Cantata, from Metastasio. William Wordsworth. CP-WorW1

Canterbury Tales, The. Geoffrey Chaucer. CP-ChauG

   January and May, or the Merchant's Tale. CP-PopeA

   Manciple's Tale—A Modernization, The. CP-WorW1

   Prioress' Tale—A Modernization, The. CP-WorW1

   Wife of Bath, The. CP-PopeA

Canthara. William Carlos Williams. CP-WilW1

Canti Romani. Lawrence Ferlinghetti.

   "Along the Appian Way / children are playing." SP-FerlL

   "At midnight on the next balcony." SP-FerlL

Canticle. Wendell Berry. CP-BerrW

Canticle, A. Herman Melville. SP-MelvH

Canticle for Good Friday. Geoffrey Hill. CP-HillG

Canticle for the Blessed Virgin. Thomas Merton. CP-MertT

Canticle of Jack Kerouac, The. Lawrence Ferlinghetti. SP-FerlL

Canticle to Apollo, A. Robert Herrick. CP-HerrR

Cantilena Politica-Jocunda Facta Post Principis Discessum In Hispaniam. Sir John Suckling. CP-SuckJ

Canto Amor. John Berryman. CP-BerrJ

Canto One Hundred and One. Charles Olson. CP-OlsoC

Canto Primo. Thomas Campion. See Hark, All You Ladies [That Do Sleep]

Canto Quinto. Thomas Campion. See Content

Canto Secundo. Thomas Campion. See What Fair[e] Pomp[e]

Canto Tertio. Thomas Campion. See Kisses

Canto the Tenth. Lord Byron. CP-Byron Fr. Don Juan.

Cantor's Theorem: In an Infinite Class the Whole Is No Greater Than Some of Its Parts. James Vincent Cunningham. CP-CunnJ

Cantos. Ezra Pound. CP-PoCan

   Canto 1: "And then went down to the ship." SP-PounE

   Canto 2: "Hang it all, Robert Browning." SP-PounE

   Canto 3: "I sat on the Dogana's steps." SP-PounE

   Canto 4: "Palace in smoky light." SP-PounE

   Canto 9: "One year floods rose." SP-PounE

   Canto 13: "Kung walked / by the dynastic temple." SP-PounE

   Canto 14: "Io venni luogo d'ogni luce muto." SP-PounE

     ("Slough of unamiable liars, The.") SP-PounE

   Canto 17: "So that the vines burst from my fingers." SP-PounE

   Canto 20: "Sound slender, quasi tinnula." SP-PounE

     ("And from the floating bodies, the incense.") SP-PounE

   Canto 25: "Book of the council major." SP-PounE

     ("Because of the stink of the dungeons: 1344.") SP-PounE

   Canto 30: "Compleynt, compleynt I hearde upon a day." SP-PounE

   Canto 36: "Lady asks me, A / I speak in season." SP-PounE

   Canto 38: "An' that year Metevsky went over to America del Sud." SP-PounE

   Canto 45: "With Usura." SP-PounE

   Canto 47: "Who even dead, yet hath his mind entire!." SP-PounE

   Canto 49: "For the seven lakes, and by no man these verses." SP-PounE

   Canto 51: "Shines / in the mind of heaven God [or heaven God]." SP-PounE

   Canto 53: "Yeou taught men to break branches." SP-PounE

   Canto 62: "Acquit of evil intention." SP-PounE

   Canto 74: "Enormous tragedy of the dream in the peasant's bent shoulders, The." SP-PounE

   Canto 76: "And the sun high over horizon hidden in cloud bank." SP-PounE

     ("L'ara sul rostro / 20 years of the dream.") SP-PounE

   Canto 79: "Moon, cloud, tower, a patch of the battistero all of a whiteness." SP-PounE

     ("Moon has a swollen cheek, The.") SP-PounE

   Canto 80: "Ain' committed no federal crime." SP-PounE

     ("Nancy where art thou?") SP-PounE

   Canto 81: "Zeus lies in Ceres' bosom." SP-PounE

   Canto 83: "Hudor / HUDOR et Pax." SP-PounE

     ("As he was standing below the altars.") SP-PounE

   Canto 91: "Ab lo dolchor qu'al cor mi vai." SP-PounE

   Canto 93: "Man's paradise is his good nature, A." SP-PounE

     ("Autumn leaves blow from my hand.") SP-PounE

   Canto 111, Notes for: "I, one thing, as relation to one thing." CP-PoCan

     (Notes for Canto 111.) CP-PoCan

   Canto 112, From: "Owl, and wagtail / and huo-hu, the fire-fox." CP-PoCan

     (From 112.) CP-PoCan

   From Canto 115: "Scientists are in terror, The." CP-PoCan

Cantos, The. Robert Creeley. CP-CreeR

Canvas. Adam Zagajewski. SP-ZagaA, tr. by Renata Gorczynski, Benjamin Ivry and C. K. Williams

Canvass. Lorine Niedecker. CP-NiedL

Canvassing for the Election. D. H. Lawrence. CP-LawrD

Canyon Wren, The. Gary Snyder. CP-SnydG

Canzon: "Heart mine, art mine, whose embraces." Ezra Pound. CP-PoEar

Canzon: The Spear. Ezra Pound. CP-PoEar

Canzon: The Vision. Ezra Pound. CP-PoEar

Canzon: The Yearly Slain. Ezra Pound. CP-PoEar

Canzone: "As would any sound make." Robert Creeley. CP-CreeR

Canzone: "Consider the three functions of the tongue." Marilyn Hacker. SP-HackM

Canzone: "Scoffing, amorous maidens and young men." John Milton. CP-CowpW; CP-MiltJ

   (They mock my toil—the nymphs and am'rous swains.) CP-CowpW

Canzone: "When shall we learn, what should be clear as day." W. H. Auden. CP-AudeW

Canzone: A Dispute with Death. Guido Cavalcanti. CW-RossD, tr. by Dante Gabriel Rossetti

Canzone: A Song against Poverty. Guido Cavalcanti. CW-RossD, tr. by Dante Gabriel Rossetti

Canzone: A Song of Fortune. Guido Cavalcanti. CW-RossD, tr. by Dante Gabriel Rossetti

Canzone: He beseeches Death for the Life of Beatrice. Dante Alighieri. CW-RossD, tr. by Dante Gabriel Rossetti

Canzone: He laments the Presumption and Incontinence of his Youth. Guido

Cavalcanti. CW-RossD, *tr. by* Dante Gabriel Rossetti

Canzone: His Lament for Selvaggia. Cino da Pistoia. CW-RossD, *tr. by* Dante Gabriel Rossetti

Canzone: His Portrait of his Lady, Angiola of Verona. Fazio degli Uberti. CW-RossD, *tr. by* Dante Gabriel Rossetti

Canzone: Of Angels. Ezra Pound. CP-PoEar

Canzone: Of his Dead Lady. Giacomino Pugliesi. CW-RossD, *tr. by* Dante Gabriel Rossetti

Canzone: Of Incense. Ezra Pound. CP-PoEar

Canzone: Of the Gentle Heart. Guido Guinicelli. CW-RossD, *tr. by* Dante Gabriel Rossetti

Canzone: On the Death of Beatrice Portinari. Cino da Pistoia. CW-RossD, *tr. by* Dante Gabriel Rossetti

Canzonet. Oscar Wilde. CP-WildO

Cap and Bells; or, The Jealousies, The. John Keats. CP-KeatJ

Cap and Bells, The. William Butler Yeats. CP-YeatW

Cap D'Antibes. Edna St. Vincent Millay. CP-MillE

Cap of Lead across the sky, A. Emily Dickinson. CP-DickE

Capacity. John Updike. CP-UpdiJ

Cape Breton. Elizabeth Bishop. CP-BishE

Cape Elizabeth: A Photograph. John Logan. CP-LogaJ

Capercaillie, The. Eugenio Montale. CP-MontE, *tr. by* Jonathan Galassi

Capercaillies. Paul Muldoon. CP-MuldP

Capilupus Sends Greeting to Grotus. Ezra Pound. CP-PoEar

Capital, The. W. H. Auden. CP-AudeW

Capital, The. Adrienne Rich. CP-RicAE

Capital letters prompting every line. Poem: A Reminder. Robert Graves. CP-GravR

Capitalist, The. George Meredith. CP-MerG2

Capitalist was I, A. Capitalist, The. George Meredith. CP-MerG2

Capitalett. Poem: A Reminder. Robert Graves. CP-GravR

Capitals. Howard Nemerov. CP-NemeH

Capitals in bloom with Corinthian acanthus. Rainer Maria Rilke. CP-RilkFr, *tr. by* A. Poulin, Jr. *Fr.* Fragments.

Capitán profundo, capitán geloso. Revolutionists Stop for Orangeade, The. Wallace Stevens. CP-StevW; CP-StevWP

Capitol Air. Allen Ginsberg. CP-GinsA; SP-GinsA

Capo che chinasi, / Occhi che chiudonsi. Christina Georgina Rossetti. CP-RosC3

Cappadocia. Joseph Brodsky. CP-BrodJ, *tr. by* Paul Graves

Cappadocian Song. Hayden Carruth. CP-CarHS

Capper Kaplinski at the North Side Cue Club. Hayden Carruth. CP-CarHS

Capri. Czeslaw Milosz. CP-MiloCN, *tr. by* Robert Hass

Capriccio ("Behind each mirror"). Federico García Lorca. CP-GarcF, *tr. by* Jerome Rothenberg *Fr.* Mirror Suite.

Capriccio ("In the net of moon"). Federico García Lorca. CP-GarcF, *tr. by* Jerome Rothenberg *Fr.* Sublunar Cantos.

Capriccio ("Zip! . . . / Did you just close"). Federico García Lorca. CP-GarcF, *tr. by* Jerome Rothenberg *Fr.* Barrage of Firework Poems on the Occasion of the Poet's Birthday.

Capriccios. Federico García Lorca.
  Pirouette. CP-GarcF, *tr. by* Jerome Rothenberg
  Sun. CP-GarcF, *tr. by* Jerome Rothenberg
  "Tree / The *tee* gives you leaves." CP-GarcF, *tr. by* Jerome Rothenberg

Caprice, a Fragment. Annis Boudinot Stockton. CP-StocA

Capricious fortune ever joys. Seneca. CP-JohnS *Fr.* Hercules Furens.

Capricorn (of sizable thirst). Year Is a Great Circle or the Year Is a Great Mistake, The. Charles Olson. CP-OlsoC

Capt. Samuel Cook. Jones Very. CP-VeryJ

Captain Ahab's desire was the White Whale. Why the Postman Has to Ring Twice, or, Yellow Envelope, Where Have You Gone? Ogden Nash. CP-NashO

Captain Bada. Frank O'Hara. SP-OharF

Captain Carpenter. John Crowe Ransom. SP-RansJ

Captain Craig. Edwin Arlington Robinson. CP-RobiE

Captain Diable's Receptionist. Yusef Komunyakaa. CP-KomuY

Captain Holm. May Swenson. SP-SwenM

Captain in Time of Peace. Thom Gunn. CP-GunnT

Captain John Smith. Ogden Nash. CP-NashO

Captain Nicholas Strong. John Ciardi. CP-CiarJ

Captain or Colonel, or Knight in Arms. When the Assault Was Intended to the City. John Milton. CP-MiltJ

Captain Sword and Dr Gunn. Fairy-Tale. G. K. Chesterton. CP-ChesG

Captain's Lady, The. Robert Burns. CP-BurnR

Captain's Song. John Berryman. CP-BerrJ

Captain's Well, The. John Greenleaf Whittier. CP-WhitJ

Caption for a Photograph of Four Organized Criminals. François Villon. SP-LoguC, *tr. by* Christopher Logue

Captive, The. Rudyard Kipling. CP-KiplR

Captive, The. Walter De la Mare. CP-DeLaW

Captive, The. Walter De la Mare. CP-DeLaW

Captive. Federico García Lorca. CP-GarcF, *tr. by* Christopher Maurer

Captive flourished like, The. Portrait. Alan Dugan. CP-DugaA

Captive mahogany of a private Roman, The. Roman Elegies. Joseph Brodsky. CP-BrodJ, *tr. by* Joseph Brodsky

Captive on a foreign shore. Cassandra. George Meredith. CP-MerG1

Captived Bee, The. Little Filcher, The. Robert Herrick. CP-HerrR

Captives—a Psalm, The. Thomas Merton. CP-MertT

Captivity.—Mary Queen of Scots. William Wordsworth. CP-WorW2

Captivity of the Fly. Archibald MacLeish. CP-MacLA

Capture. Ai. SP-Ai

Capture, The. Paul Laurence Dunbar. CP-DunbP

Capuchin—long acquaintance with the dead, A. Catacomb. Charles Tomlinson. SP-TomlC

Caput Mortuum. Edwin Arlington Robinson. CP-RobiE

Car, The. Raymond Carver. CP-CarvR

Car Crash. Allen Ginsberg. CP-GinsA

Car is heavy with children, The. Road Back, The. Anne Sexton. CP-SextA

Car / moving / the hill / down, The. Robert Creeley. CP-CreeR

Car turned over three times, The. For Mike and Jeannie: Resisters Fifteen Years Later. Grace Paley. CP-PalGC

Car wheels roar over freeway concrete. Guru Om. Allen Ginsberg. CP-GinsA

Car with a cracked windshield, The. Car, The. Raymond Carver. CP-CarvR

Caracol, now / hold still. Federico García Lorca. CP-GarcF, *tr. by* Jerome Rothenberg *Fr.* Caracols / Snails.

Caracols / Snails. Federico García Lorca.
  Ballade of Black Caracols. CP-GarcF, *tr. by* Jerome Rothenberg
  Ballade of White Caracols. CP-GarcF, *tr. by* Jerome Rothenberg
  "Caracol, now / hold still." CP-GarcF, *tr. by* Jerome Rothenberg
  Spiral. CP-GarcF, *tr. by* Jerome Rothenberg

Caradoc. Thomas Gray. CP-GrayT

Caravan. John Berryman. CP-BerrJ

Caravan of Silence. Richard Eberhart. CP-EberR

Caraway Seed, The. Ogden Nash. CP-NashO

Carbon of everything that ever went on meets the manuscript of the future, The. 5 Ways of Saying the Same Thing. Andrei Codrescu. SP-CodrA

Card, A. William Cowper. CP-CowpW

Card-Dealer, The. Dante Gabriel Rossetti. CW-RossD

Card-house over the fault, The. Rising Sun, The. Randall Jarrell. CP-JarrR

Card in pew pocket. Way, The. Rae Armantrout. SP-ArmaA

Card-Players, The. Philip Larkin. CP-LarkP

Card table in the library stands ready, A. Lost in Translation. James Merrill. SP-MerrJ *Fr.* Book of Ephraim, The.

Cardiac Autoscope, The. James Laughlin. CP-LaugJ

Cardin o't, The. Robert Burns. CP-BurnR

Cardinal, A. James Schuyler. CP-SchuJ

Cardinal and the Dog, The. Robert Browning. CP-BroR2

Cardinal Bembo's Epitaph on Raphael. Thomas Hardy. CP-HardT

Cardinal Newman. Christina Georgina Rossetti. CP-RosC3

Cardplayers. Yannis Ritsos. SP-RitsY, *tr. by* Kostas Myrsiades

Cards that brighten the New Year, The. For the Visitors' Book. Kathleen Jessie Raine. SP-RainK

Cardtable is black, the cards are played face down, The. Draw. Robert Lowell. SP-LoweR

Care a Good Keeper. Robert Herrick. CP-HerrR

Care and Feeding of a Poet, The. James Laughlin. CP-LaugJ

Care and Generosity. Christopher Smart. SP-SmarC

Care, carefully chosen, even. Thoughts of a Retired Diamond Cutter. Eleanor Wilner. SP-WilnE

Care flieth, / Hope and fear together. Christina Georgina Rossetti. CP-RosC3

Care in Calling. Laura Riding Jackson. CP-RidiL

Care keepes the Conquest; 'tis no lesse renown[e]. Care a Good Keeper. Robert Herrick. CP-HerrR

Career, A. Paul Laurence Dunbar. CP-DunbP

Career for a Child of Five. Kenneth Patchen. CP-PatcK

Career in vestige management, A. Manufacturing. Rae Armantrout. SP-ArmaA

Career of flowers differs from ours, The. Emily Dickinson. SP-DickE

Career was feminine, resourcesful, clever. James Vincent Cunningham. CP-CunnJ

Carefree Corpse, The. Charles Baudelaire. CP-BaudC, *tr. by* Walter Martin

Careful examination of the past. Summer Evening at the Window with Psalms. Yehuda Amichai. SP-AmicYL, *tr. by* Benjamin Harshav *and* Barbara Harshav

Careful observers may foretell the hour. Description of a City Shower, A. Jonathan Swift. CP-SwifJ

Careful text-books measure, The. Hymn of Breaking Strain. Rudyard Kipling.

CP-KiplR

Careful, they said: don't slip. Danger, The. Pablo Neruda. SP-NeruP

Carefully, sending leaves always toward the sun. Living on the Plains ("Carefully, sending leaves always toward the sun"). William Stafford. SP-StafWW

Carefully / the leaves of autumn. Late October. Maya Angelou. SP-AngeM

Careless and still. Rabbit Hunter, The. Robert Frost. CP-FrosR

Careless Love. Stanley Kunitz. CP-KunSC

Careless Lover, The. Sir John Suckling. CP-SuckJ

Careless Night. Robert Lowell. SP-LoweR

Carelessly all fixed up a can of beer. Friendship Greetings. Philip Whalen. SP-WhalP

Cares o' love are sweeter far, The. Robert Burns. CP-BurnR

Carew's Masque. Thomas Carew. CP-CareT

    Coelum Britannicum. CP-CareT

    First Song, The. CP-CareT

    Fourth Song, The. CP-CareT

    Second Song, The. CP-CareT

    Third Song, The. CP-CareT

Caria and Philistia considered. Cry Faugh! Robert Graves. CP-GravR

Caribbean Sea. Gabriela Mistral. SP-MistG, tr. by Maria Giachetti [or Jacketti]

Caribbean Sunset. Langston Hughes. CP-HughL; CP-HughL1

Caribou. Robert Penn Warren. CP-WarrR

Caribou, The. Ogden Nash. CP-NashO

Caricature, The. Thomas Hardy. CP-HardT

Caridad para los pobrecitos. Los Pobrecitos. Charles Tomlinson. CP-TomlC

Carillon, The. Dante Gabriel Rossetti. CW-RossD

Caring: A Dream. Maxine W. Kumin. SP-KumiM

Caring for Surfaces. Mona Van Duyn. SP-VanDM

Caritas. Olga Broumas. SP-BrouO

Carkanet, The. Robert Herrick. CP-HerrR

Carl an the King Come. Robert Burns. CP-BurnR

Carla bought an old horse. Carla Is a Horse Lover. Alan Dugan. CP-DugaA

Carla Is a Horse Lover. Alan Dugan. CP-DugaA

Carlos, keep calm, love. Don't Kill Yourself. Carlos Drummond de Andrade. CP-BishE, tr. by Elizabeth Bishop

Carlos Trujillo / killed this mountain wolf. Anecdote. Charles Tomlinson. CP-TomlC

Carlos, your art is embryos. For a Mexican Painter. Muriel Rukeyser. CP-RukeM

Carlotta's Confession. Donald Hall. CP-HallD

Carlovingian Dreams. Carl Sandburg. CP-SandC

Carly Simon / on the juke. Mike. James Schuyler. CP-SchuJ

Carmel. Robinson Jeffers. CP-JefR3

Carmel Point. Robinson Jeffers. CP-JefR3

Carmel: Point Lobos. John Logan. CP-LogaJ

Carmel Valley. Allen Ginsberg. CP-GinsA

Carmen 1–116. Catullus. CP-ZukLS Fr. Carmina.

Carmen Circulare. Rudyard Kipling. CP-KiplR Fr. Muse among the Motors, The.

Carmen de Boheme. Hart Crane. CP-CranH

Carmen Saeculare. Charles Hubert Sisson. SP-SmarC, tr. by Christopher Smart (Secular Ode, The.) SP-SmarC

Carmencita loves Patrick. Little Song ("Carmencita loves Patrick"). Langston Hughes. CP-HughL

Carmina. Catullus. CP-Catul

    Carmen 1. CP-ZukLS

      ("Whom do I give my neat little volume.") CP-ZukLS

    Carmen 2. CP-ZukLS

      ("Sparrow, my girl's pleasure, delight of my girl.") CP-ZukLS

    Carmen 3. CP-ZukLS

      (Death of a Starling, The.) CP-WorW1

      ("Lament, o graces of Venus, and Cupids.") CP-ZukLS

      ("Pity mourns in plaintive tone.") CP-WorW1

      (Translation from Catullus.) CP-Byron

      ("Ye Cupids, droop each little head.") CP-Byron

    Carmen 4. CP-ZukLS

      ("Facile as can be the boat you see, my guests, says.") CP-ZukLS

    Carmen 5. CP-CampT; CP-ZukLS

      (Lesbia.) CP-WorW1

      ("May we live, my Lesbia, love while we may.") CP-ZukLS

      ("My Lesbia let us love and live.") CP-WorW1

      ("My sweetest Lesbia, let us live and love.") CP-CampT, tr. by Thomas Campion

      (My Sweetest Lesbia [Let Us Live and Love].) CP-CampT, tr. by Thomas Campion

      Sun May Set, The. CP-RaleW, tr. by Sir Walter Alexander Raleigh

    Carmen 6. CP-ZukLS

      ("Flavius—that delicate lass—to Catullus.") CP-ZukLS

    Carmen 7. CP-ZukLS

      ("Queries, you ask how many times must I kiss.") CP-ZukLS

    Carmen 8. CP-CampT; CP-ZukLS

      ("Harden now thy tyred hart, with more than flinty rage.") CP-CampT, tr. by Thomas Campion

      ("Miss her, Catullus? don't be so inept to rail.") CP-ZukLS

    Carmen 9. CP-ZukLS

      ("Veranius of all my beloved friends.") CP-ZukLS

    Carmen 10. CP-ZukLS

      ("Varus old crony had me visit his love.") CP-ZukLS

    Carmen 11. CP-ZukLS

      ("Furius, Aurelius: comities—Catullus.") CP-ZukLS

    Carmen 12. CP-ZukLS

      ("Marrucinus Asinius, that sinister.") CP-ZukLS

    Carmen 13. CP-ZukLS

      ("Canapés, my Fabullus, at home any.") CP-ZukLS

    Carmen 14. CP-ZukLS

      ("Not that I look to my eyes more than your love.") CP-ZukLS

    Carmen 15. CP-ZukLS

      ("Commend to you my cares for the love I love.") CP-ZukLS

    Carmen 16. CP-ZukLS

      ("Piping, beaus, I'll go whoosh and I'll rumble you.") CP-ZukLS

    Carmen 17. CP-ZukLS

      ("O Colonia, whose wishes build a long bridge to dance on.") CP-ZukLS

    Carmen 21. CP-ZukLS

      ("Aurelius, father, assure that the o numb.") CP-ZukLS

    Carmen 22. CP-ZukLS

      ("Suffenus is, stay Varus,—whom you've proven—is the.") CP-ZukLS

    Carmen 23. CP-ZukLS

      ("Furius, with no key to service, no key.") CP-ZukLS

    Carmen 24. CP-ZukLS

      ("O quick floss silk of the Juventii, form.") CP-ZukLS

    Carmen 25. CP-ZukLS

      ("Conniving Thallus, mulley, you, cony cully, cop below.") CP-ZukLS

    Carmen 26. CP-ZukLS

      ("Furius, "Little Villa" has no nod for Auster.") CP-ZukLS

    Carmen 27. CP-ZukLS

      ("Minister wet to lee, pour the Falernian.") CP-ZukLS

    Carmen 28. CP-ZukLS

      ("Piso's own comates, his, corps an inane as.") CP-ZukLS

    Carmen 29. CP-ZukLS

      ("Whose hoax to put up with, outstare, protest patience.") CP-ZukLS

    Carmen 30. CP-ZukLS

      ("Alfenus, remember kind intimacies? false? They elated us.") CP-ZukLS

    Carmen 31.

      (Catullus: XXXI.) CP-HardT

      (Dear Little Sirmio.) CP-SmitS

    Carmen 32. CP-ZukLS

      ("I'm a bow, my dual kiss, Ipsithilla.") CP-ZukLS

    Carmen 33. CP-ZukLS

      ("Offer 'em up to me—bullneck crook of the baths.") CP-ZukLS

    Carmen 34. CP-ZukLS

      ("Diana, sum us in faith a.") CP-ZukLS

    Carmen 35. CP-ZukLS

      ("Poet I'm too near your and my sod daily.") CP-ZukLS

    Carmen 36. CP-ZukLS

      ("Annals of Volusius, cock at his offal.") CP-ZukLS

    Carmen 37. CP-ZukLS

      ("Salt hacks, tavern boys, what skews, can't you burn alleys.") CP-ZukLS

    Carmen 38. CP-ZukLS

      ("My last—Cornificius—your Catullus'.") CP-ZukLS

    Carmen 39. CP-ZukLS

      ("Egnatius, candid as his horse-bit white dentures.") CP-ZukLS

    Carmen 40. CP-ZukLS

      ("What demented malice, my silly Ravidus.") CP-ZukLS

    Carmen 41. CP-ZukLS

      ("Ameana pulling, a foot touted high.") CP-ZukLS

    Carmen 42. CP-ZukLS

      ("At hest, hendecasyllabics, what is this.") CP-ZukLS

    Carmen 43. CP-ZukLS

      ("Salvé, next, minimal, poor little nosey.") CP-ZukLS

    Carmen 44. CP-ZukLS

      ("O farm, dear nest, or say Sabine, ah say Tibur's.") CP-ZukLS

    Carmen 45. CP-ZukLS

      ("Acme, Septimius, sighs so amorous.") CP-ZukLS

(Septimius and Acme.) CP-WorW1

("Septimius thus his love addressed.") CP-WorW1

Carmen 46. CP-ZukLS

("Warm gale, a dose of spring—revert to the pores.") CP-ZukLS

Carmen 47. CP-ZukLS

("Porky and Socration, two-eye sins as try.") CP-ZukLS

Carmen 48. CP-Byron; CP-ZukLS

("Mellowed *those*, I call *those* eyes, Juventius.") CP-ZukLS

("Oh! might I kiss those eyes of fire.") CP-Byron

Carmen 49. CP-ZukLS

(Disertissime Romuli Nepotum.) SP-SmarC

("Master of eloquence and Rome's potent line.") CP-ZukLS

("O Thou, of British Orators the chief.") SP-SmarC

Carmen 50. CP-ZukLS

("Yesterday, Licinius, what a day it was.") CP-ZukLS

Carmen 51. CP-ZukLS

("Equal to Jove that youth must be.") CP-Byron

("He'll hie me, par *is* he? the God divide her.") CP-ZukLS

(Translation from Catullus.) CP-Byron

Carmen 52. CP-ZukLS

("Quick death, Catullus! what more horrors may hurry!") CP-ZukLS

Carmen 53. CP-ZukLS

("Risible nice go when from mud a crony.") CP-ZukLS

Carmen 54. CP-ZukLS

("Otho's scooped nut its pusillanimity.") CP-ZukLS

Carmen 55. CP-ZukLS

("Rum asks—see, fortune won't molest you.") CP-ZukLS

Carmen 56. CP-ZukLS

("O ram ridicule home, Cato, the jokes some.") CP-ZukLS

Carmen 57. CP-ZukLS

("Pull! crew" 's convenient to reprobate kin hides.") CP-ZukLS

Carmen 58. CP-ZukLS

("Caelius, Lesbia new star, Lesbia a light.") CP-ZukLS

Carmen 59. CP-ZukLS

("Bononian, sis Rufa, Rufus' lum fell at.") CP-ZukLS

Carmen 60. CP-ZukLS

("None but a lioness moaned this, Libya's mountains.") CP-ZukLS

Carmen 61. CP-ZukLS

("Who lives o on Helicon hill.") CP-ZukLS

Carmen 62. CP-ZukLS

("Vesper out there, you vain knees can sure get up: Vesper, Olympus.") CP-ZukLS

Carmen 63. CP-ZukLS

("Spurred altering wake toss Attis his craft racing till marled in the.") CP-ZukLS

Carmen 64. CP-ZukLS

("Pelion could one time prong its top worthy keel in pines.") CP-ZukLS

Carmen 65. CP-ZukLS

("Yet see (may as I do) a confect of my cure—a dolor.") CP-ZukLS

Carmen 66. CP-ZukLS

("Human all key mog knee this pecks it loom in a moon the.") CP-ZukLS

Carmen 67. CP-ZukLS

("O dear cool you couldn't be virile—you couldn't a parent he.") CP-ZukLS

Carmen 68. CP-ZukLS

("Cold how mean, fortune consuming you oppresses your care, your.") CP-ZukLS

Carmen 69. CP-ZukLS

("No lift odd mere horror, harrowed (why boy?) that no woman will.") CP-ZukLS

Carmen 70. CP-ZukLS

("Newly say dickered my love air my own would marry me all.") CP-ZukLS

Carmen 71. CP-ZukLS

("Securer a bo? no sacred armpits lair hops as that he-goat's.") CP-ZukLS

Carmen 72. CP-ZukLS

("Decay bars one time, 'solely to know, see Catullus'") CP-ZukLS

Carmen 72. CP-ZukLS

("Day, see no day—choke, qualm, quick qualm—benevolence, merit are.") CP-ZukLS

Carmen 74. CP-ZukLS

("Gellius how he'd rare at pot true uncle objurgate soul array.") CP-ZukLS

Carmen 75. CP-ZukLS

("How cast down is the mind that took to my Lesbia, culprit.") CP-ZukLS

Carmen 76. CP-ZukLS

("Seek or record then the benefactor—pree or voluptuous.") CP-ZukLS

Carmen 77. CP-ZukLS

("Rufey my how frustrate unquickened and craved the tie I'm equal.") CP-ZukLS

Carmen 78. CP-ZukLS

("Gallus ha' but brothers: bro one's lady slip's make so young she's.") CP-ZukLS

Carmen 79. CP-ZukLS

("Lesbius has pooled her: kidney? whom Lesbia my—lit.") CP-ZukLS

Carmen 80. CP-ZukLS

("Quiddity, Gelli, quarry, rosy as these too lips belie.") CP-ZukLS

Carmen 81. CP-ZukLS

("Not many enchant you (put to it) popular is he, Juventi.") CP-ZukLS

Carmen 82. CP-ZukLS

("Quinti, see if't be wish of cool eyes day bear your Catullus.") CP-ZukLS

Carmen 83. CP-ZukLS

("Lesbia (my price scent t'her hero) mauls and deplores me, '*dig it*'.") CP-ZukLS

Carmen 84. CP-ZukLS

("'*C-hommodating* he'd bait, seeking *accomodating* willed.") CP-ZukLS

Carmen 85. CP-ZukLS

("O th'hate I move love. Quarry it fact I am, for that's so re queries.") CP-ZukLS

Carmen 86. CP-ZukLS

("Quintia's *foremost* to multitudes; my eye can deed her *long, e—*.") CP-ZukLS

Carmen 87. CP-ZukLS

("No love by test, my love, 'll air then, time, say the care of all my time.") CP-ZukLS

Carmen 88. CP-ZukLS

("Quid, fact it is Gelli? quick'ning mother, at (queer) sis, all three.") CP-ZukLS

Carmen 89. CP-ZukLS

("Gellius is thin why yes: kiddin'? quite a bonny mater.") CP-ZukLS

Carmen 90. CP-ZukLS

("Now seed their Magus (of Gelli's mother wrestling confounded.") CP-ZukLS

Carmen 91. CP-ZukLS

("No idea, Gelli, spurred me to mirror you faithful.") CP-ZukLS

Carmen 92. CP-ZukLS

(Lesbia.) CP-SwifJ

("Lesbia forever on me rails.") CP-SwifJ, *tr. by* Jonathan Swift

("Lesbia may dicker simper maul or nag talk at whom, come.") CP-ZukLS

Carmen 93. CP-ZukLS

("Nil, not my aim to study you, Caesar, to be—well, a placater.") CP-ZukLS

Carmen 94. CP-ZukLS

("Meantool amuck with her. Muck with her mean tool ah? Geared I.") CP-ZukLS

Carmen 95. CP-ZukLS

("*Zmyrna*, my own Cinna, nine harvests passed making his hymn.") CP-ZukLS

Carmen 96. CP-ZukLS

("See quick calm moot as gratifying the tombed—sepulchres.") CP-ZukLS

Carmen 97. CP-ZukLS

("No it would not mean a damn (quick whim referred to pure.") CP-ZukLS

Carmen 98. CP-ZukLS

("In the, same in (when qualm?) thick wee poetry, putrid Victi.") CP-ZukLS

Carmen 99. CP-ZukLS

("Surreptitious you at bay doom loot is, my little Juventi.") CP-ZukLS

Carmen 100. CP-ZukLS

("Caelius Aufilenus' mate, Quintius Aufilena's *am*.") CP-ZukLS

Carmen 101. CP-ZukLS

(Adaption of a Theme from Catullus.) CP-TateA

("Mulled hosts their countries yet mulled there by a core of wake tossed.") CP-ZukLS

("Past towns, states, deserts, hills, and rivers borne.") CP-TateA

Carmen 102. CP-ZukLS

("Secret I take it a commitment hushed to feed amic—.") CP-ZukLS

Carmen 103. CP-ZukLS

("*Out*—so this means you render them, ten sestertia, Silo.") CP-ZukLS

Carmen 104. CP-ZukLS

("Credit me poor to say of my life *maledictory weed die*.") CP-ZukLS

Carmen 105. CP-ZukLS

("Meantool reconnoiters Pipléa scanning Their mountain.") CP-ZukLS

Carmen 106. CP-ZukLS

("Cute boy arm in elbow prize con man, kid, what do we see.") CP-ZukLS

Carmen 107. CP-ZukLS

("See could we quit coveting hope taunting where hope hid and.") CP-ZukLS

Carmen 108. CP-ZukLS

("See, Comini, popular arbitrer turned on uncanny senescence.") CP-ZukLS

Carmen 109. CP-ZukLS

("You could then, my heart, wit, eye, mean in proposing love our aim.") CP-ZukLS

Carmen 110. CP-ZukLS

("Aufilena—*bonnie, simple,* laud and they're amicable.") CP-ZukLS

Carmen 111. CP-ZukLS

("Aufilena, virile content him weave her her solo.") CP-ZukLS

Carmen 112. CP-ZukLS

("Mool 'tis homos,' Naso 'n' queer take 'im mool 'tis ho most *he.*") CP-ZukLS

Carmen 113. CP-ZukLS

("Consul (ere) Pompei O preened a duo, Cinna, so lay bound.") CP-ZukLS

Carmen 114. CP-ZukLS

("Firmum is all too known fails so Meantool a Dives.") CP-ZukLS

Carmen 115. CP-ZukLS

("Meantool inhabits in style three times ten hewed acres, forty.") CP-ZukLS

Carmen 116. CP-ZukLS

("Sigh paid to be studious when I moved went on to (queer) once.") CP-ZukLS

Carmina Gemina. James Laughlin. CP-LaugJ

Carmine defunctum, Breto, caute inducis Amorem. In Bretonem. Thomas Campion. CP-CampT

Carnal Knowledge. Thom Gunn. CP-GunnT

Carnal Word. Yannis Ritsos. SP-RitsY, *tr.* by Kimon Friar

Carnality, the organic ruffles of / opening pink and white and red. Carnations. Hayden Carruth. CP-CarHS

Carnations. Hayden Carruth. CP-CarHS

Carnations. Theodore Roethke. CP-RoetT

Carnegie Hall: Rescued. Marianne Craig Moore. CP-MoorM

Carnegie Hall, the great musicbox. Violin Debut. Lorine Niedecker. CP-NiedL

Carnegie Library, Juvenile Division, The. Randall Jarrell. CP-JarrR

Carnet de Voyage. Wallace Stevens. CP-StevWP

Carney Elegy. Josephine Jacobsen. CP-JacoJ

Carnival, The. Robert Creeley. CP-CreeR

Carnival, and the odd light. Flashes from you. Michael Palmer. SP-PalmM

Carob's mare's-nest that stands stark, The. Another Moon Effect. Eugenio Montale. CP-MontE, *tr.* by Jonathan Galassi

Carol: "Flocks feed by darkness with a noise of whispers." Thomas Merton. CP-MertT

Carol: "Now is the world withdrawn all." Howard Nemerov. CP-NemeH

Carol: "To end all carols, darling." Louis MacNeice. CP-MacNL

Carol, A: "Our Lord Who did the Ox command." Rudyard Kipling. CP-KiplR

Carol, A: "When Jesus got my broken back for Christmas, Juniors." Thomas Merton. CP-MertT

Carol, A. Donald Hall. CP-HallD

Carol Closing Sixty-Nine. Walt Whitman. CP-WhitW

Carol for Children, A. Ogden Nash. CP-NashO

Carol of Jack Frost, A. George Meredith. CP-MerG2

Carol of Patience. Robert Graves. CP-GravR

Carol of the Brown King. Langston Hughes. CP-HughL; CP-HughL3

Carol said, "I looked at all my cells today." Soufflé. Philip Whalen. SP-WhalP

Carole, si quid habes longo quod tempore coctum. Ad Carolum Fitz Geofridum. Thomas Campion. CP-CampT

Carolina Cabin. Langston Hughes. CP-HughL; CP-HughL2

Carols nature, counsel men. Three Singers to Young Blood, The. George Meredith. CP-MerG1

Carp are secrets, The. Lifting Illegal Nets by Flashlight. James Wright. CP-WrigJ

Carpe Diem. Robert Frost. CP-FrosR

Carpel / filament the brilliant. Poem about the Garden, A. George Oppen. CP-OppGN

Carpenter, The. G. K. Chesterton. CP-ChesG

Carpentered hen, The. Wooden Darning Egg, A. John Updike. CP-UpdiJ

Carpenter's Boat. George Oppen. CP-OppGN

Carpenter's made a hole, The. Hole in the Floor, A. Richard Wilbur. CP-WilbR

Carpenter's Son, The. A. E. Housman. CP-HousA

Carpet Not Bought, A. James Merrill. SP-MerrJ

Carrara, Looking Seaward. Lawrence Ferlinghetti. SP-FerlL

Carrara Revisited. Charles Tomlinson. SP-TomlC

Carriage from Sweden, A. Marianne Craig Moore. CP-MoorM

Carrick Revisited. Louis MacNeice. CP-MacNL

Carrickfergus. Louis MacNeice. CP-MacNL

Carried lonely up the aisle. Funeral. Langston Hughes. CP-HughL; CP-HughL2

Carried me to de court. Ballad of Gin Mary. Langston Hughes. CP-HughL; CP-HughL1

Carried this morning in the dodge and swoop. Cougar Meat. Tess Gallagher. SP-GallT

Carrier. William Meredith. SP-MereW

Carrier, The. Thomas Hardy. CP-HardT

Carrier Letter. Hart Crane. CP-CranH

(Exile.) CP-CranH

Carrion. Charles Baudelaire. CP-BaudC, *tr.* by Walter Martin

Carrion, A. Charles Baudelaire. CP-TateA, *tr.* by Allen Tate

Carrion Comfort. Gerard Manley Hopkins. CP-HopkG

Carrion Crow, The. Archibald MacLeish. CP-MacLA

Carrots grow happily into the earth. I'm in Great Trouble. Yehuda Amichai. SP-AmicYL, *tr.* by Benjamin Harshav *and* Barbara Harshav

Carry me back to Ole Virginny. First Families Move Over! Ogden Nash. CP-NashO

Carrying a bunch of marigolds. Negro Woman, A. William Carlos Williams. CP-WilW2

Carrying Food Home in Winter. Margaret Atwood. SP-AtwM1

Carrying the guidebook you marked. At the Prado. William Meredith. SP-MereW

Carrying their deckhands' bicycles. Tugs of Hull, The. George Oppen. CP-OppGN

Carrying water to the Youth in Honor of Sappho Jane Harrison & Miss Duncan if She Had. Charles Olson. CP-OlsoC

Carrying you, a little model carefully dressed. Ceremony, A: Doing the Needful. William Stafford. SP-StafWW

Cars collide and erupt luggage and babies. In Laughter. Ted Hughes. SP-HughTN

Cars in Caracas, The. John Updike. CP-UpdiJ

Cars slide minute down asphalt lanes in front of. Thoughts on a Breath. Allen Ginsberg. CP-GinsA

Carscape. Charles Tomlinson. CP-TomlC

Cart, The. W. S. Merwin. SP-MerwWF

Cartagena. Gary Snyder. CP-SnydG

Carteret was welcomed to the shore. Epigram on Wood's Brass Money, An. Jonathan Swift. CP-SwifJ

Carter's trophy, A. Bog Oak. Seamus Heaney. SP-HeanSO

Cartographer of meadows does not rose, The. John Ciardi. CP-CiarJ

Cartographer's Wedding, The. Sam Hamill. SP-HamiS

Cartographies of Silence. Adrienne Rich. SP-RicA2

Cartography. Louise Bogan. CP-BogaL

Cartoon. Carl Sandburg. CP-SandC

Carts of the wee blind lass, The. Kenneth Patchen. CP-PatcK

Carts plod toward the valley, The. Toward the Valley. Primo Levi. CP-LeviP, *tr.* by Ruth Feldman

Caruso: a voice. Sleeping with Women. Kenneth Koch. SP-KochK

Carved living wood face, A. Mask. Philip Whalen. SP-WhalP

Carved, Matthew, with a master's skill. William Wordsworth. MW-WorW

Carver, having loved too long in vain, A. Carver. To His Mistress, The. Thomas Carew. CP-CareT

Carver. To His Mistress, The. Thomas Carew. CP-CareT

Carving on the jamb of an embrasure, A. Priory of St Saviour, Glendalough, The. Donald Davie. CP-DaviDC

Carving the Turkey. John Ciardi. CP-CiarJ

Caryophyllaceae / like a scroungy, The. Spring Coming. A. R. Ammons. CP-AmmoA

Casa Guidi Windows. Elizabeth Barrett Browning. CP-BroEB

Casabianca. Elizabeth Bishop. CP-BishE

Casablanca. Maxine W. Kumin. SP-KumiM

Casarola. Charles Tomlinson. CP-TomlC; SP-TomlC

Cascades and Fountains. Marya Alexandrovna Zaturenska. SP-ZatuM

Cascadilla Falls. A. R. Ammons. CP-AmmoA

Cascando. Samuel Beckett. CP-BeckS

Case for Jefferson, A. Robert Frost. CP-FrosR

Case History. A. K. Ramanujan. CP-RamaA

Case in P'int, A. James Whitcomb Riley. CP-RileJ

Case is a Lawyer, that near pleads alone. Upon Case. Robert Herrick. CP-HerrR

Case of the Crushed Petunias, The: A Lyrical Fantasy. Tennessee Williams. "How grimly do petunias look." CP-WillT

Case of The, The. Mona Van Duyn. SP-VanDM

Caserta Garden. Richard Wilbur. CP-WilbR

Casida of the Boy Wounded by the Water. Federico García Lorca. SP-GarcF, *tr.* by Edwin Honig

Casida of the Branches. Federico García Lorca. SP-GarcF, *tr.* by J. L. Gili *and* Stephen Spender

Casida of the Dark Doves. Federico García Lorca. SP-GarcF, *tr.* by W. S. Merwin

Casida of the Golden Girl. Federico García Lorca. SP-GarcF, *tr. by* W. S. Merwin

Casida of the Lament. Federico García Lorca. SP-GarcF, *tr. by* J. L. Gili *and* Stephen Spender

Casida of the Reclining Woman. Federico García Lorca. SP-GarcF, *tr. by* W. S. Merwin

Casino. W. H. Auden. CP-AudeW

Casino Pierre. Andrei Codrescu. SP-CodrA

Cask of Hate, The. Charles Baudelaire. CP-BaudC, *tr. by* Walter Martin

Casket of Pandora, The. Marya Alexandrovna Zaturenska. SP-ZatuM

Cass and Me. Paul Muldoon. CP-MuldP

"Cassander! *O* Cassander!"—her mother's voice seems cle'r. James Whitcomb Riley. CP-RileJ

Cassandra. Louise Bogan. CP-BogaL

Cassandra. "H. D." CP-DoolH

Cassandra. Robinson Jeffers. CP-JefR3

Cassandra. George Meredith. CP-MerG1

Cassandra. Edwin Arlington Robinson. CP-RobiE

Cassandra. Dante Gabriel Rossetti. CW-RossD

Cassandra Drops into Verse. Dorothy Parker. CP-ParkD

Cassandra Southwick. John Greenleaf Whittier. CP-WhitJ

Casse-Noisette. Robert Graves. CP-GravR

Cassinus and Peter. Jonathan Swift. CP-SwifJ

Cast a bronze of my head and legs and put them on the king's street. Savoir Faire. Carl Sandburg. CP-SandC

Cast down but not destroyed, chastened not slain. Christina Georgina Rossetti. CP-RosC2

Cast her in outer darkness old. To Frances. G. K. Chesterton. CP-ChesG

Cast Off, The. Marge Piercy. SP-PierM

Cast out among your impatient. Youngest Son, The. Theodore Weiss. SP-WeisT

Cast your bread for it's good to give. Shmuel HaNagid. SP-HaNaS, *tr. by* Peter Cole

Castara Victrix. Gerard Manley Hopkins. CP-HopkG

Castaway, The. William Cowper. CP-CowpW

Castaway, The. Derek Walcott. CP-WalcD

Castaways, The. Marya Alexandrovna Zaturenska. SP-ZatuM

Caste Wife Speaks to the Enigmatic Parabolas, The. Norman Dubie. CP-DubiN

Casterbridge Captains, The. Thomas Hardy. CP-HardT

Casting. Andrei Codrescu. SP-CodrA

Casting. Howard Nemerov. CP-NemeH

Casting the times with their stong signes. Sospetto d'Herode. Giovanni Giambattista. CP-CrasR *Fr.* Strage degli innocenti, La.

Castle. Adam Zagajewski. SP-ZagaA, *tr. by* Clare Cavanagh

Castle, The. Robert Graves. CP-GravR

Castle, The. Stevie Smith. CP-SmitS

Castle, The. Charles Tomlinson. CP-TomlC

Castle-Builder's World, A. Christina Georgina Rossetti. CP-RosC2

Castle Gordon—*Intended to Be Sung to Morag.* Robert Burns. CP-BurnR

Castle has gone into the cliff, The. Near Ceibwr. Charles Tomlinson. CP-TomlC

Castle on the rock briny from surf, The. From the Chronicles of the Town of Pornic. Czeslaw Milosz. CP-MiloC; CP-MiloCN, *tr. by* Lillian Vallee

Castle Wood. Emily Jane Brontë. CP-BronE

Castles and Distances. Richard Wilbur. CP-WilbR

Casual. Langston Hughes. CP-HughL; CP-HughL3

Casual Acquaintance, The. Thomas Hardy. CP-HardT

Casual, sudsy. Laundromat. Lorine Niedecker. CP-NiedL

Casualties. Robert Herrick. CP-HerrR

Casualty. Seamus Heaney. SP-HeanSO

Casualty. Langston Hughes. CP-HughL; CP-HughL3

Casualty, The. Ted Hughes. SP-HughTN

Casualty, The. Louis MacNeice. CP-MacNL

Cat. Charles Baudelaire. CP-BaudC, *tr. by* Walter Martin

Cat. Emily Dickinson. CP-DickE

Cat. Rainer Maria Rilke. CP-RilkFr, *tr. by* A. Poulin, Jr.

Cat, The. Charles Baudelaire. CP-CullC

Cat, The. Constantine P. Cavafy. CP-CavaC, *tr. by* Theoharis Constantine Theoharis

Cat, The. Lawrence Ferlinghetti. SP-FerlL

Cat, The. Galway Kinnell. SP-KinnGN

Cat and Mouse. Ted Hughes. SP-HughTN

Cat and the Meat, The. Jelaluddin Rumi. SP-Rumi, *tr. by* Coleman Barks

Cat and the Moon, The. William Butler Yeats. CP-YeatW

Cat and the Saxophone (2 a.m.), The. Langston Hughes. CP-HughL; CP-HughL1

Cat and the Wind, The. Thom Gunn. CP-GunnT

Cat as Cat, The. Denise Levertov. SP-LeveDP; SP-LeveDS

Cat Asks Mouse Out. Stevie Smith. CP-SmitS

Cat bird singing / makes music like sounds coming. Air: "Cat Bird Singing"

Robert Creeley. CP-CreeR

Cat gave birth to an adder, The. The dog died. Domestic Sonnet. John Ciardi. CP-CiarJ

Cat Ghosts. W. S. Merwin. SP-MerwW

Cat-Goddesses. Robert Graves. CP-GravR

Cat in an Empty Apartment. Wisława Szymborska. SP-SzymW, *tr. by* Stanislaw Barańczak *and* Clare Cavanagh

Cat in an Empty Apartment. Wisława Szymborska. SP-SzymWM, *tr. by* Joanna Trzeciak

Cat in distress, A. Verses on a Cat. Percy Bysshe Shelley. CP-ShelP

Cat in the wood cried farewell cried farewell, The. Cat in the Wood, The. Archibald MacLeish. CP-MacLA

Cat in the Wood, The. Archibald MacLeish. CP-MacLA

Cat is killed, The. Hole Filler. Heather McHugh. SP-McHuH

Cat / licks its paw and, The. Cat, The. Lawrence Ferlinghetti. SP-FerlL

Cat like he creeps along where ways are dim. Assassin, An. James Whitcomb Riley. CP-RileJ

Cat meanders through my brain, A. Cat. Charles Baudelaire. CP-BaudC, *tr. by* Walter Martin

Cat Naps Are Too Good for Cats. Ogden Nash. CP-NashO

Cat on its hind legs, The. Another Cat Poem: A Cat Is Not a Dancer but a Hunter. Alan Dugan. CP-DugaA

Cat on my bosom, The. Cat as Cat, The. Denise Levertov. SP-LeveDP; SP-LeveDS

Cat provokes antipathy in common men, The. Cat, The. Constantine P. Cavafy. CP-CavaC, *tr. by* Theoharis Constantine Theoharis

Cat sits on the pavement by the house, A. Lonely Man, The. Randall Jarrell. CP-JarrR

Cat stirs in the material world, A. From the Japanese. Louise Glück. SP-GlucL

Cat That Walked by Himself, The. Rudyard Kipling. *Fr.* Just-So Stories.

Cat took fright, The. Annunciation. Charles Tomlinson. SP-TomlC

Cat was observing the Rule of Silence, The. Human Touch Misunderstood, A. Andrei Codrescu. SP-CodrA

Cat went here and there, The. Cat and the Moon, The. William Butler Yeats. CP-YeatW

Cat! who hast passed [*or* pass'd] thy grand climacteric. To a Cat. John Keats. CP-KeatJ

Cat, you tumble down the street. Fernando Pessoa. SP-PessF, *tr. by* Susan M. Brown *and* Edwin Honig

Catacomb. Charles Tomlinson. SP-TomlC

Catalogues of seeds flood him. Next Summer. Josephine Jacobsen. CP-JacoJ

Catalonian Woman. Gabriela Mistral. SP-MistG, *tr. by* Maria Giachetti [*or* Jacketti]

Catalpa, The. John Ciardi. CP-CiarJ

Catalpa's white week is ending there, The. Catalpa, The. John Ciardi. CP-CiarJ

Catalyst. A. R. Ammons. CP-AmmoA

Catarina to Camoens. Elizabeth Barrett Browning. CP-BroEB

Catastrophic Birth. William Carlos Williams. CP-WilW2

Catbird cadenzas from the bushes. Alongside. Denise Levertov. SP-LeveDL

Catbird in redbud this morning. May Swenson. SP-SwenM

Catch. Langston Hughes. CP-HughL; CP-HughL2

Catch, A. Ben Jonson. CP-JonsB *Fr.* Oberon, the Fairy Prince.

Catch, The. Raymond Carver. CP-CarvR

Catch, The. Stanley Kunitz. CP-KunSC

Catch, The. Richard Wilbur. CP-WilbR

Catch a moth in the Amazon; pin it under glass. Every Where and Every When. Arthur Sze. SP-SzeA

Catch and let go, leaves take sunlight. Cro-Magnon. William Stafford. SP-StafWW

Catch of Shy Fish, A. Gwendolyn Brooks. SP-BrooG

Catch the old one first. Man and Boy. Seamus Heaney. SP-HeanSO

Catch with Reuben. Miller Williams. CP-WillM

Catching Ballet of the Wedding Clothes, The. Thomas Hardy. CP-HardT

Catching Cold. Robert Creeley. CP-CreeR

Catching yourself, hands lathery. In the Round. Theodore Weiss. SP-WeisT

Catchment. Maxine W. Kumin. SP-KumiM

Catechism, A. William Stafford. SP-StafW; SP-StafWW

Catechism, The. Walter De la Mare. CP-DeLaW

Caterpillar. Emily Dickinson. CP-DickE

Caterpillar. Emily Dickinson. CP-DickE

Caterpillar, A. Robert Bly. SP-BlyR

Caterpillar, The. Christina Georgina Rossetti. CP-RosC2

Caterpillar, The. Miller Williams. CP-WillM

Catfish River Lullaby. Kenneth Patchen. CP-PatcK

Catharina. William Cowper. CP-CowpW

Catharina, the Second Part. William Cowper. CP-CowpW

Catharsis builds across the dreadful air. Oedipus Tyrannus. John Ciardi. CP-CiarJ

Cathedral. John Ciardi. CP-CiarJ

Cathedral Bells, The. Karl Shapiro. SP-ShapK

Cathedral evening, tinkle of candles. Beautiful You Are. Kenneth Patchen. CP-PatcK

Cathedral Façade at Midnight, A. Thomas Hardy. CP-HardT

Cathedral of my enchantments, autumn wind, I grew old giving thanks. Autumn. Czeslaw Milosz. CP-MiloCN, *tr.* by Robert Hass

Cathedral, The. Robert Stock. SP-StocR

Cathedrals are not built along the sea. Wallace Stevens. CP-StevWP

Catherine of Alexandria. Rita Dove. SP-DoveR

Catherine of Siena. Rita Dove. SP-DoveR

Catherine Wheel. Federico García Lorca. CP-GarcF, *tr.* by Jerome Rothenberg *Fr.* Barrage of Firework Poems on the Occasion of the Poet's Birthday.

Catholic Bells, The. William Carlos Williams. CP-WilW1

Catpig, The. Denise Levertov. SP-LeveDL

Catprints, dogprints, marks. Roominghouse, Winter. Margaret Atwood. SP-AtwM1

Catrine woods were yellow seen, The. Braes o' Ballochmyle, The. Robert Burns. CP-BurnR

Cats. Charles Baudelaire. CP-BaudC, *tr.* by Walter Martin

Cats. Charles Baudelaire. CP-CullC

Cats and a Cock. Muriel Rukeyser. CP-RukeM

Cats are full of death. Christopher Logue. SP-LoguC

Cats, as a rule, don't take to travel. Spruce Has No Taproot, The. Amy Clampitt. CP-ClamA

Cat's asleep; I whisper *kitten*, The. Happy Cat, The. Randall Jarrell. CP-JarrR

Cats Like Angels. Marge Piercy. SP-PierM

Cats' Month, The. William Carlos Williams. CP-WilW1

Cats of Greece, The. Marge Piercy. SP-PierM

Cats walk the floor at midnight; that enemy of fog. Retroduction to American History. Allen Tate. CP-TateA

Cattail fluff / blows in. Porous. William Carlos Williams. CP-WilW1

Cattivo Tempo. W. H. Auden. CP-AudeW

Cattle are crowding the salt-lick. In December. Charles Tomlinson. CP-TomlC

Cattle crowding round this beverage clear, The. Nun's Well, Brigham. William Wordsworth. CP-WorW2

Cattle in the slaughter-pens, laboratory dogs. King of Beasts, The. Robinson Jeffers. CP-JefR3

Catullian Hendecasyllables. Samuel Taylor Coleridge. CP-ColeS

Catullus viii. Louis Zukofsky. CP-ZukLS

Catullus is my master and I mix. Technical Notes. James Laughlin. CP-LaugJ

Catullus on Friendship. Donald Davie. CP-DaviDC

Catullus: XXXI. Catullus. *See* Carmina

Caucasus: A Romance, The. Raymond Carver. CP-CarvR

Caught by the Blizzard. Aleksandr Aleksandrovich Blok. SP-BlokA, *tr.* by Peter France *and* Jon Stallworthy

Caught by the lure of marriage. Name. Robert Graves. CP-GravR

Caught in a Net. Nicholas Vachel Lindsay. CP-LindV

Caught in the centre of a soundless field. Myxomatosis. Philip Larkin. CP-LarkP

Caught in the homeland-trap of a Chosen People. National Thoughts. Yehuda Amichai. SP-AmicYL, *tr.* by Benjamin Harshav *and* Barbara Harshav

Caught off first, he leaped to run to second, but. Ball Game. Richard Eberhart. CP-EberR

Caught on the move—no knowing·what year it was. Sed de Correr. Amy Clampitt. CP-ClamA

Caught Susanner whistlin'; well. Breaking the Charm. Paul Laurence Dunbar. CP-DunbP

Caught—the bubble. Sonnet: "Caught—the bubble." Elizabeth Bishop. CP-BishE

Caught upon a thousand thorns, I sing. 1934. Richard Eberhart. CP-EberR

Caul Gate, Farewell, that hath me bound. Michtam. Louis Zukofsky. CP-ZukLS

Cauld blaws the wind frae east to west. Up in the Morning Early. Robert Burns. CP-BurnR

Cauld Frosty Morning. Robert Burns. CP-BurnR

Cauld Is the E'enin Blast. Robert Burns. CP-BurnR

Cauliflower-eared Spartan. Reading and Talking. Louis Zukofsky. CP-ZukLS

Cauliflowers. Paul Muldoon. CP-MuldP

Cause, The. Jones Very. CP-VeryJ

Cause, the Cause, The. Charles Olson. CP-OlsoC

'Cause Herbert Graham's a' only child. Spoiled Child, The. James Whitcomb Riley. CP-RileJ

Cause Won, The. Vincent Bourne. CP-CowpW

Cause you don't love me. Bad Luck Card. Langston Hughes. CP-HughL; CP-HughL1

Causerie. Allen Tate. CP-TateA

Causes. Mona Van Duyn. SP-VanDM

Causes, The. Jorge Luis Borges. SP-BorgJ, *tr.* by Willis Barnstone

Causes are in Time; only their issue, The. Allegory of the Wolf Boy, The. Thom Gunn. CP-GunnT

Caution. Raymond Carver. CP-CarvR

Caution. Miller Williams. CP-WillM

Caution, A. Robert Herrick. CP-HerrR

Caution in Councell. Robert Herrick. CP-HerrR

Caution to Everybody, A. Ogden Nash. CP-NashO

Cautionary, The. C. K. Williams. SP-WillC

Cautionless flagon threw the heart unphrased, A. Desecration of the Gravestone of Rose P. Robert Pinsky. CP-PinsR

Cautiously the wind explores. Federico García Lorca. CP-GarcF, *tr.* by Christopher Maurer

Cavalier Tunes. Robert Browning. CP-BroR1

Cavalli marittimi / Urtansi in guerra. Christina Georgina Rossetti. CP-RosC3

Cavalry Crossing a Ford. Walt Whitman. CP-WhitW

Cavatina of broken parlando utterances, A. *Firenze*, a Lifetime Later. Lawrence Ferlinghetti. SP-FerlL

Cave, The. Wisława Szymborska. SP-SzymWM, *tr.* by Joanna Trzeciak

Cave, The. C. K. Williams. CP-WillC; SP-WillC

Cave Canem. Edna St. Vincent Millay. CP-MillE

Cave downstairs, The. Above the Cave. Denise Levertov. SP-LeveDP

Cave looked much like any other, The. Bat Cave. Eleanor Wilner. SP-WilnE

Cave Painting. Hayden Carruth. CP-CarHS

Cave Painting. William Stafford. SP-StafWW

Cave / wall the cave lion's, The. On All Sides. Charles Olson. CP-OlsoC

Caveman Is Not about to Talk, The. Dan Pagis. SP-PagiD, *tr.* by Stephen Mitchell

Cavern, The. Charles Tomlinson. CP-TomlC; SP-TomlC

Caverns of the Grave Ive seen, The. William Blake. CP-BlakW

Caw Caw, Caw Caw Caw. Fauve. Arthur Sze. SP-SzeA

Caw Caw Caw / on a far shingle long ago. Sea and Ourselves at Cape Ann, The. Lawrence Ferlinghetti. SP-FerlL

Cawdor. Robinson Jeffers. CP-JefR1

Ce bruit da la mer. Denise Levertov. SP-LeveDP

Ce-Lia The Immortal Beauty. William Carlos Williams. CP-WilW2

Ce n'est pas pour qu'on se dégoute. Petit Epître. T. S. Eliot. SP-ElioT

Ce qu'a de pis. Samuel Beckett. SP-BeckS

Ce qu'ont les yeux. Samuel Beckett. CP-BeckS

Cease lovely warbler cease thy fond complaint. On Hearing the Cooing of a Dove, a Song. Annis Boudinot Stockton. CP-StocA

Cease, thou afflicted soul, to mourn. Lover, in the Disguise of an Amazon, Is Dearly Beloved of His Mistress, A. Thomas Carew. CP-CareT

Cease, ye prudes, your envious railing. Written under the Picture of the Celebrated Miss Burns. Robert Burns. CP-BurnR

Cebu. Robert Creeley. SP-CreeR

Cecchino here has laid his body low. Michelangelo Buonarroti. CP-Miche, *tr.* by John Frederick Nims

Ceci est digne de gens sans dieu. Stevie Smith. CP-SmitS

Ceci n'est pas une Pipe. Charles Tomlinson. CP-TomlC

Cedar fires burn in my heart. Arthur Sze. SP-SzeA

Cedars and the westward sun. Curse, The. John Berryman. CP-BerrJ

Ceiling, The. Theodore Roethke. CP-RoetT

Celebrants came chanting "God is dead!", The. Death of God, The. Howard Nemerov. CP-NemeH

Celebrating Giacometti. René Char. CP-MertT

Celebration. Denise Levertov. SP-LeveDS

Celebration. Thomas McGrath. SP-McGrT

Celebration. Helen Pinkerton. CP-PinkH

Celebration, A. William Carlos Williams. CP-WilW1

Celebration, The. James Dickey. CP-DickJ

Celebration for George Sarton, A. May Sarton. SP-SartM

Celebration for June 24. Thomas McGrath. SP-McGrT

Celebration in the Plaza, The. Adrienne Rich. CP-RicAE

Celebration of Charis in Ten Lyric[k] Pieces [*or* Peeces], A. Ben Jonson. CP-JonsB; SP-JonsB

Celebration of Failure. Laura Riding Jackson. CP-RidiL

Celery. Ogden Nash. CP-NashO

Celery. John Updike. CP-UpdiJ

Celestial. A. R. Ammons. CP-AmmoA

Celestial choir! enthroned [*or* enthron'd] in realms of light. To His Excellency General Washington. Phillis Wheatley. CP-WheaP

Celestial Circus, The. Nicholas Vachel Lindsay. CP-LindV

Celestial Desolations. Gregory Orr. SP-OrrG

Celestial Evening, October 1967. Charles Olson. SP-OlsoC *Fr.* Maximus Poems, The.

Celestial Globe. Howard Nemerov. CP-NemeH

Celestial muse! for sweetness fam'd inspire. To a Gentleman of the Navy. Phillis Wheatley. CP-WheaP

Celestial muse! sublimest of the nine. Answer, The [By the Gentleman of the Navy]. *Unknown.* CP-WheaP

Celestial pow'rs! that piety regard. Samuel Johnson. CP-JohnS

Celestials at the Board of Projects burst into laughter. Creating the World. Czeslaw Milosz. CP-MiloCN, *tr.* by Robert Hass

Celia Bleeding, to the Surgeon. Thomas Carew. CP-CareT

Celia Singing. Thomas Carew. CP-CareT

Celia's Birthday Poem. Louis Zukofsky. CP-ZukLS

Celibate white cat surveys himself, The. Beppo. Jorge Luis Borges. SP-BorgJ, *tr.* by Alan S. Trueblood

Cell, The. Louise Glück. SP-GlucL

Cell by cell the baby made herself, the cells. Sara in Her Father's Arms. George Oppen. CP-OppGN

Cellar Stairs. Thomas Lux. SP-LuxT

Celle Qui Fût Héaulmiette. Wallace Stevens. CP-StevW; CP-StevWP

Celles. Marilyn Hacker. SP-HackM

Cellist, The. Galway Kinnell. SP-KinnGN

Cello. Adam Zagajewski. SP-ZagaA, *tr.* by Clare Cavanagh

Cellophane. C. K. Williams. CP-WillC

Cells. Rudyard Kipling. CP-KiplR

Celluloid boats scoot across the lake because (I think) someone, The. Journal Entry (April 1969, Villa Serbelloni). William Meredith. SP-MereW

Celluloid of a photograph holds them well, The. Six Young Men. Ted Hughes. SP-HughTN

Celt in all his variants from Builth to Ballyhoo, The. Puzzler, The. Rudyard Kipling. CP-KiplR

Celtic Fringe, The. Stevie Smith. CP-SmitS

Celtic genius—Cornwall, Scotland, Ireland, Wales—, The. Hugh MacDiarmid. SP-MacDH *Fr.* Cornish Heroic Song for Valda Trevlyn.

Celtic spearman forcing the cromlech-builder's brown daughter, A. Second-Best. Robinson Jeffers. CP-JefR2

Celts, The. Stevie Smith. CP-SmitS

Cemetary. Rainer Maria Rilke. CP-RilkFr, *tr.* by A. Poulin, Jr.

Cemetary Angels. Galway Kinnell. SP-KinnGN

Cemetary in Flaach. Rainer Maria Rilke. CP-RilkFr, *tr.* by A. Poulin, Jr.

Cemetary in Ragaz. Rainer Maria Rilke. CP-RilkFr, *tr.* by A. Poulin, Jr.

Cemetery, A. Emily Dickinson. CP-DickE

Cemetery at Academy, California, The. Philip Levine. SP-LeviP

Cemetery in Pernambuco: Our Lady of Light. João Cabral de Melo Neto. CP-CoopJ, *tr.* by Jane Cooper

Cemetery of Childhood. Joaquim Cardozo. CP-BishE

Cemetery of Harmony Grove, The. Jones Very. CP-VeryJ

Cemetery suburb was, The. Kind of Poor. Heather McHugh. SP-McHuH

Cemetery where the college, The. What It Really Means. Alan Dugan. CP-DugaA

Cenci, The. Percy Bysshe Shelley. CP-ShelP

Cenciaja. Robert Browning. CP-BroR2

Cenotaph. Yusef Komunyakaa. CP-KomuY

Cenotaph. William Wordsworth. CP-WorW2

Cenotaph, The. James Schuyler. CP-SchuJ

Cenotaph for Two Butterflies. Robert Stock. SP-StocR

Censer-Moon, The. Nicholas Vachel Lindsay. CP-LindV

Censers are swinging / Over the town. Soul of the City Receives the Gift of the Holy Spirit, The. Nicholas Vachel Lindsay. CP-LindV

Censors. D. H. Lawrence. CP-LawrD

Censorship. John Ciardi. CP-CiarJ

Censure not sharply then, but me advise. Epistle to a Friend, An ("Censure not sharply then, but me advise"). Ben Jonson. CP-JonsB

Census man, The. Madam and the Census Man. Langston Hughes. CP-HughL; CP-HughL2

Census-Taker, The. Robert Frost. CP-FrosR

Centaur, The. May Swenson. SP-SwenM

Centaur has good reason, The. Rainer Maria Rilke. CP-RilkFr, *tr.* by A. Poulin, Jr. *Fr.* Orchards.

Centaur Song. "H. D." CP-DoolH

Centaurs, The. Rudyard Kipling. CP-KiplR *Fr.* Debits and Credits.

Centaurs, The. Paul Muldoon. CP-MuldP

Centaurs 1. Joseph Brodsky. CP-BrodJ

Centaurs 2. Joseph Brodsky. CP-BrodJ

Centaurs 3. Joseph Brodsky. CP-BrodJ

Centaurs 4. Joseph Brodsky. CP-BrodJ

Centenarian, The. William Carlos Williams. CP-WilW1

Centenarian's Story, The. Walt Whitman. CP-WhitW

Centenary forest, A. City. Federico García Lorca. CP-GarcF, *tr.* by Jerome Rothenberg *Fr.* Palimpsests.

Centenary Note: Inscribed to Little Crow, Leader of the Sioux Rebellion in Minnesota, 1862, A. James Wright. CP-WrigJ

Centenary of Garibaldi, The. George Meredith. CP-MerG2

Centennial Bell that will not ring. Conversation in a Belfry. Archibald MacLeish. CP-MacLA

Centennial For Whitman. Richard Eberhart. CP-EberR

Centennial Hymn. John Greenleaf Whittier. CP-WhitJ

Center. A. R. Ammons. CP-AmmoA

Center. Billy Collins. SP-CollB

Center, The. Yannis Ritsos. SP-RitsY, *tr.* by Kimon Friar

Center is known weak sighted, and he sells. Upon Center a Spectacle-Maker with a Flat Nose. Robert Herrick. CP-HerrR

Center of the Fire, The. Jelaluddin Rumi. SP-Rumi, *tr.* by Coleman Barks

Center Piece. Andrei Codrescu. SP-CodrA

Centipede. Rita Dove. SP-DoveR

Centipede, The. Ogden Nash. CP-NashO

Cento Made By Wordsworth, A. William Wordsworth. CP-WorW2

Central Park. Robert Lowell. SP-LoweR

Central Park. Howard Nemerov. CP-NemeH

Central Park, Twilight. Dan Pagis. SP-PagiD, *tr.* by Stephen Mitchell

Central stone is small, small, The. Gifts Accompaniment, A. Alan Dugan. CP-DugaA

"Centre of Earth!" a Chinaman he said. Chinaman, The. Christina Georgina Rossetti. CP-RosC3

Centre of equal daughters, equal sons. America. Walt Whitman. CP-WhitW

Centre that he sought was a state of mind, The. Artificial Populations. Wallace Stevens. CP-StevWP

Centre: the Emperor, apotheosis. Arthur Rimbaud. CP-RimbA, *tr.* by Martin Sorrell

Centurion of the Thirtieth, A. Rudyard Kipling. *Fr.* Puck of Pook's Hill.

Century Dying, A. Pablo Neruda. SP-NeruP

Century Piece for Poor Heine, A. John Logan. CP-LogaJ

Century-plant has flowered, its golden blossom, The. Flowering Aloe, The. Robert Graves. CP-GravR

Century will soon be over, but sooner it will be me, The. Fin de Siècle. Joseph Brodsky. CP-BrodJ

Century's Decline, The. Wisława Szymborska. SP-SzymW, *tr.* by Stanisław Barańczak *and* Clare Cavanagh

Cerebral Emotions. D. H. Lawrence. CP-LawrD

Ceremonial. Richard Eberhart. CP-EberR

Ceremonial rose in the lapel, A. Bridal Photo, 1906. John Ciardi. CP-CiarJ

Ceremonies for Candlemasse Day, The. Robert Herrick. CP-HerrR

Ceremonies for Candlemas[se] Eve. Robert Herrick. CP-HerrR

Ceremonies for Christmas[se]. Robert Herrick. CP-HerrR

Ceremony. William Stafford. SP-StafW; SP-StafWW

Ceremony. Richard Wilbur. CP-WilbR

Ceremony, A: Doing the Needful. William Stafford. SP-StafWW

Ceremony after a Fire Raid. Dylan Thomas. CP-ThomD

Ceremony and Vision. John Berryman. CP-BerrJ

Ceremony By the Sea, A. Richard Eberhart. CP-EberR

Ceremony for Any Beginning. Robert Pinsky. CP-PinsR

Ceremony for Edward Dahlberg. Thomas Merton. CP-MertT

Ceremony upon Candlemas Eve. Robert Herrick. CP-HerrR

Cernis ut eoi descendat gemmula roris. Ros. Andrew Marvell. CP-MarvA

Certain branches cut. October. Denise Levertov. SP-LeveDP

Certain Days. Grace Paley.

Certain Democrat, A. A. K. Ramanujan. CP-RamaA

Certain faces seem to be ours. November Talks. Michael Palmer. SP-PalmM

Certain Lady, A. Dorothy Parker. CP-ParkD

Certain man had a jealous wife, A. Two Ways of Running. Jelaluddin Rumi. SP-Rumi, *tr.* by Coleman Barks

Certain Maxims of Hafiz. Rudyard Kipling. CP-KiplR

Certain Mercies. Robert Graves. CP-GravR

Certain Music, A. Muriel Rukeyser. CP-RukeM

Certain neighbour lying sick to death, A. Family, The. Robert Browning. CP-BroR2

Certain of death, though not yet of the hour. Michelangelo Buonarroti. CP-MahoD, *tr.* by Derek Mahon

Certain Paralipomena to an Unbegun Epic. Robert Stock. SP-StocR

Certain People, A. George Meredith. CP-MerG1

Certain people would not clean their buttons. Bohemians, The. Ivor Gurney. SP-GurnI

Certain person came to the Friend's door, A. Two Friends. Jelaluddin Rumi. SP-Rumi, *tr.* by Coleman Barks

Certain Phenomena of Sound. Wallace Stevens. CP-StevW; CP-StevWP

Certain poems enclose. Lucky. Gregory Orr. SP-OrrG

Certain poet in outlandish clothes, A. Old Age of Queen Maeve, The. William Butler Yeats. CP-YeatW

Certain presuppositions are altered. Upland. A. R. Ammons. CP-AmmoA

Certain Pretexts. Robert Stock. SP-StocR

Certain saurian species, notably the skink, are capable of shedding their tails in self-defense when threatened. Three Small Parables for My Poet Friends. Stanley Kunitz. CP-KunSC

Certain Sharpness in the Morning Air, A. Mary Oliver. SP-OlivM

Certain Slant of Sunlight, A. Ted Berrigan. SP-BerrT

Certain student in the city of Paris, A. Lecture, A. Czeslaw Milosz. CP-MiloCN, *tr. by* Robert Hass

Certain things here are quietly American. Midsummer. Derek Walcott. CP-WalcD *Fr.* Midsummer.

Certain traveler, who believed in nothing, A. Traveler. Adam Zagajewski. SP-ZagaA, *tr. by* Clare Cavanagh

Certain Village, A. Theodore Weiss. SP-WeisT

Certain waters are as blue as metal. On the Anniversary of My Baptism. Thomas Merton. CP-MertT

Certain young man was asking around, A. Sheikh Who Played with Children, The. Jelaluddin Rumi. SP-Rumi, *tr. by* Coleman Barks

Certain youthful lady in Thoulouse, A. Sonnet: Of the Eyes of a certain Mandetta, of Thoulouse, which resemble those of his Lady Joan, of Florence. Guido Cavalcanti. CW-RossD, *tr. by* Dante Gabriel Rossetti

Certainly, Lean-shanks, you have forced the pace. Mens Sana in Corpore Sano. Donald Davie. CP-DaviDC

Certainly sought: one quiet time. Dogs, The. Charles Bukowski. SP-BukC2

Certainly we have much in common. For Jan Lebenstein. Czeslaw Milosz. CP-MiloC; CP-MiloCN, *tr. by* Robert Hass

Certainty Before Lunch. John Berryman. CP-BerrJ

Certainty of wings: a child's bold heart, The. Wings in the Pedlar's Pack. Denise Levertov. SP-LeveDS

César Franck walks between rows of radishes & scallions. California Is Odious but Indispensable. Philip Whalen. SP-WhalP

Cessible / Inack. Park in the Public's or in the Public, Parks. Kenneth Rexroth. CP-RexrK

'Cession's stahted on de gospel way, De. Spiritual, A. Paul Laurence Dunbar. CP-DunbP

C'est un grand Monsieur Pussy-Cat. Monsieur Pussy-Cat, Blackmailer. Stevie Smith. CP-SmitS

Ceux Qui Luttent. Stevie Smith. CP-SmitS

Cézanne. John Ciardi. CP-CiarJ

Cézanne. William Carlos Williams. CP-WilW2

Cézanne at Aix. Charles Tomlinson. CP-TomlC; SP-TomlC

Cézanne's Ports. Allen Ginsberg. CP-GinsA

Chaconne for Unaccompanied Violin. Charles Tomlinson. CP-TomlC

Chacun à Son Berlitz. Ogden Nash. CP-NashO

Chaeronean Plutarch, to thy deathless praise. Epigram on Plutarch, An. Agathias. CP-DryJ2, *tr by* John Dryden

Chafed ocean, a chadored moon. Walk on the Water. Olga Broumas. SP-BrouO

Chaff, The. W. S. Merwin. SP-MerwW

Chagall. Raissa Maritain. CP-MertT

Chagall's sweet lovers mounting into blue. Lovers Are like Children. Adrienne Rich. CP-RicAE

Chain, The. Maxine W. Kumin. SP-KumiM

Chain I Gave, The. Lord Byron. CP-Byron

Chain is on the door, The. One Hundred and Ninety-Nine Pounds of Clay Leaning Forward. Charles Bukowski. SP-BukC2

Chain of memory is resurrection I am a vain man, The. Charles Olson. CP-OlsoC; SP-OlsoC

Chain Saw at Dawn in Vermont in Time of Drouth. Robert Penn Warren. CP-WarrR

Chair, The. Theodore Roethke. CP-RoetT

Chair Gallows. Yusef Komunyakaa. CP-KomuY

Chair grows from the floor, A. Night Sky, The. Michael Palmer. SP-PalmM

Chair squeaks in a high wind, The. Nostalgias. Derek Mahon. CP-MahoD

Chair was placed, A. Seeing Jupiter. May Swenson. SP-SwenM

Chairley Burke's in Town. James Whitcomb Riley. CP-RileJ

Chairs. Charles Simic. SP-SimiCE

Chaldaic Image. Constantine P. Cavafy. CP-CavaC, *tr. by* Theoharis Constantine Theoharis

Chalices hammered into sword and helmet! Michelangelo Buonarroti. CP-Miche, *tr. by* John Frederick Nims

Chalk-white, light dazzled on the stone. Twice Lovely. Walter De la Mare. CP-DeLaW

Chalkley Hall. John Greenleaf Whittier. CP-WhitJ

Chalky swallow shit. Poem: "Chalky swallow shit." William Corbett. SP-CorbW

Challenge: A Court Ballad, The. Alexander Pope. CP-PopeA

Challenge is always to find the ultimate, The. South End. James Tate. SP-TateJ

Challenge to Poets, A. Tennessee Williams. CP-WillT

Challenged once more to reunite. Song: Twinned Heart. Robert Graves. CP-GravR

Challenger, The. Mona Van Duyn. SP-VanDM

Chambermaid's First Song, The. William Butler Yeats. CP-YeatW

Chambermaid's Second Song, The. William Butler Yeats. CP-YeatW

Chambers of my heart are many, dear, The. George Meredith. CP-MerG2

Chameleon who wistfully, The. Wanderer, The. Denise Levertov. SP-LeveDS

Chameleons feed on light and air. Exhortation, An. Percy Bysshe Shelley. CP-ShelP

Chamfort. Carl Sandburg. CP-SandC

Champagne. Rita Dove. SP-DoveR

Champion of those who groan beneath. To William Lloyd Garrison. John Greenleaf Whittier. CP-WhitJ

Chance. Ai. SP-Ai

Chance. "H. D." CP-DoolH

Chance. Charles Tomlinson. SP-TomlC

Chance, The. Robert Creeley. CP-CreeR

Chance, The. Arthur Sze. SP-SzeA

Chance and chance and thereby starlit. Animula. George Oppen. CP-OppGN

Chance is the remotest, The. Some Science Fiction. Robert Frost. CP-FrosR

Chance Meeting. "H. D." CP-DoolH

Chance of a few morning sprinkles, A. October 5, 1981. James Schuyler. CP-SchuJ

Chancellor once was a tree full of fruit, The. On Thurlow. William Cowper. CP-CowpW

Chances, The. Wilfred Owen. CP-OwenW

Chances are we will sink quietly back. Clay out of Silence. C. K. Williams. CP-WillC; SP-WillC

Chances of rhyme are like the chances of meeting, The. Charles Tomlinson. CP-TomlC; SP-TomlC

Chances "R." Allen Ginsberg. CP-GinsA

Chance's / zodiac. Fan. Federico García Lorca. CP-GarcF, *tr. by* Jerome Rothenberg *Fr.* Wheels of Fortune.

Chandelier. Constantine P. Cavafy. CP-CavaC, *tr. by* Theoharis Constantine Theoharis

Chang Yuen is on the threshold of a remarkable career. Very Early Morning Exercise, A. Kenneth Rexroth. CP-RexrK

Change. John Donne. MW-DonnJ *Fr.* Elegies.

Change. Robert Creeley. CP-CreeR

Change. Robert Graves. CP-GravR

Change. Langston Hughes. CP-HughL; CP-HughL1

Change. Stanley Kunitz. CP-KunSC

Change. D. H. Lawrence. CP-LawrD

Change. Jones Very. CP-VeryJ

Change, The. James Dickey. CP-DickJ

Change, The. Paul Laurence Dunbar. CP-DunbP

Change, The. Ivor Gurney. SP-GurnI

Change, The. Thomas Hardy. CP-HardT

Change, The. Denise Levertov. SP-LeveDS

Change, The: *Kyoto-Tokyo Express*. Allen Ginsberg. CP-GinsA; SP-GinsA

Change and chancefulness in my flowering youthtime. Temporary the All, The. Thomas Hardy. CP-HardT

Change Common to All. Robert Herrick. CP-HerrR

Change Gives Content. Robert Herrick. CP-HerrR

Change Has Come, The. Paul Laurence Dunbar. CP-DunbP

Change Here for Wichita Falls, or, Has Anybody Seen My Wanderlust? Ogden Nash. CP-NashO

Change in Recurrence. George Meredith. CP-MerG1

Change in the Seasons. Jones Very. CP-VeryJ

Change Me, Some God, Into That Breathing Rose! William Wordsworth. CP-WorW2 *Fr.* River Duddon [A Series of Sonnets], The.

Change of Air, A. W. H. Auden. CP-AudeW

Change of Government. D. H. Lawrence. CP-LawrD

Change of Habit, A. Charles Bukowski. SP-BukC1

Change of Life. D. H. Lawrence. CP-LawrD

Change of Season. Audre Lorde. SP-LordA

Change of self in wide address of self, The. Growth. Laura Riding Jackson. CP-RidiL

Change of World, A. Adrienne Rich. CP-RicAE

Change the glacier's loneliness and the ice melts. Late Romantic. A. R. Ammons. CP-AmmoA

Change Upon Change. Elizabeth Barrett Browning. CP-BroEB

Changed by this last enchantment of our kind. Men of My Century Loved Mozart. Archibald MacLeish. CP-MacLA

Changed Woman, The. Louise Bogan. CP-BogaL

Changelessness / is Nature's change. Emily Dickinson. SP-DickE

Changeling. Tennessee Williams. CP-WillT

Changeling, The. Thomas McGrath. SP-McGrT

Changeling, The. Theodore Roethke. CP-RoetT

Changeling, The. John Greenleaf Whittier. CP-WhitJ

Changelings, The. Rudyard Kipling. CP-KiplR *Fr.* Debits and Credits.

Changes. Maya Angelou. SP-AngeM

Changes. Seamus Heaney. SP-HeanSO

Changes, The. Robert Creeley. CP-CreeR

Changes, The. Robert Pinsky. CP-PinsR

Changes; or, Reveries at a Window Overlooking a Country Road, with Two Women Talking Blues in the Kitchen. Yusef Komunyakaa. CP-KomuY

Changes, Mistakes, Loves. Yehuda Amichai. SP-AmicYL, tr. by Benjamin Harshav and Barbara Harshav.

Changes to Corinna, The. Robert Herrick. CP-HerrR

Changing Chimes. Christina Georgina Rossetti. CP-RosC2

Changing Diapers. Gary Snyder. CP-SnydG

Changing guests, each in a different mood, The. Inclusiveness. Dante Gabriel Rossetti. CW-RossD Fr. House of Life, The.

Changing Light Winds. Carl Sandburg. CP-SandC

Changing skyline, A. Sequence, A. Denise Levertov. SP-LeveDP

Changing the Children. Maxine W. Kumin. SP-KumiM

Changing the Imperatives. Eleanor Wilner. SP-WilnE

Changing Time. Paul Laurence Dunbar. CP-DunbP

Channel Crossing. Sylvia Plath. CP-PlatS

Channel Firing. Thomas Hardy. CP-HardT

Channel 13. James Merrill. SP-MerrJ

Channing. John Greenleaf Whittier. CP-WhitJ

Chanson. Robert Creeley. CP-CreeR

Chanson. Oscar Wilde. CP-WildO

Chanson. William Carlos Williams. CP-WilW2

Chanson d'Outre Tombe. Philip Whalen. SP-WhalP

Chanson un Peu Naïve. Louise Bogan. CP-BogaL

Chant for Dark Hours. Dorothy Parker. CP-ParkD

Chant for May Day. Langston Hughes. CP-HughL; CP-HughL1

Chant for Tom Mooney. Langston Hughes. CP-HughL; CP-HughL1

Chant me a rhyme of Christmas. Song for Christmas, A. James Whitcomb Riley. CP-RileJ

Chant of the Cross-bearing Child, The. James Whitcomb Riley. CP-RileJ

Chant of the Frontiersman. Wang Ch'ang-ling. CP-WilW2

Chant-Pagan. Rudyard Kipling. CP-KiplR

Chant: Sunset, Somerville, Late Fall '75. Denise Levertov. SP-LeveDL

Chant to Be Used in Processions around a Site with Furnaces. Thomas Merton. CP-MertT

Chant we the story now. Eden in Winter. Nicholas Vachel Lindsay. CP-LindV

Chant you loud of punishments. Stephen Crane. CP-CranS

Chanterelles, The. Josephine Jacobsen. CP-JacoJ

Chantey. Dorothy Parker. CP-ParkD

Chanting at the Crystal Sea. Susan Howe. SP-HoweSE

Chanting the Square Deific. Walt Whitman. CP-WhitW

Chaos in Motion and Not in Motion. Wallace Stevens. CP-StevW

Chaos Staggered Up the Hill. A. R. Ammons. CP-AmmoA

Chaos was happy. Han-shan. CP-ColdM, tr. by Red Pine

Chaparral. Federico García Lorca. CP-GarcF, tr. by Jerome Rothenberg Fr. In the Forest of Clocks.

Chapel, A. James Schuyler. CP-SchuJ

Chapel has fallen into ruins, A. Chemin de Fer. Norman Dubie. CP-DubiN

Chapel of the Hermits, The. John Greenleaf Whittier. CP-WhitJ

Chapel-Organist, The. Thomas Hardy. CP-HardT

Chapel's cowbell, The. Crusoe's Island. Derek Walcott. CP-WalcD

Chaplet for Judith Landry, A. Marilyn Hacker. SP-HackM

Chaplet of Sage, A. Jaroslav Seifert. CP-SeifJ, tr. by Ewald Osers

Chaplinesque. Hart Crane. CP-CranH

Chapman. Muriel Rukeyser. CP-RukeM

Chappie, A. Paul Laurence Dunbar. CP-DunbP

Chapter Six. William Blake. Fr. Island in the Moon, An.

Chapultepec Castle. Jay Wright. SP-WrigJ

Chapultepec Park / I. Muriel Rukeyser. CP-RukeM

Chapultepec Park / II. Muriel Rukeyser. CP-RukeM

Chaque jour envie. Samuel Beckett. CP-BeckS

Character. Ralph Waldo Emerson. CP-EmerR

Character, A. Samuel Taylor Coleridge. CP-ColeS; MW-ColeS

Character, A. Alfred Tennyson. CP-TennA

Character, A. William Wordsworth. CP-WorW1; MW-WorW

Character, indistinct, entered, A. Songs of the Psyche. Thomas Kinsella. CP-KinsT

Character of Charles Brown. John Keats. See Portrait, A

Character of Holland, The. Andrew Marvell. CP-MarvA

Character of Love Seen as a Search for the Lost, The. Kenneth Patchen. CP-PatcK

Character of Marlborough, A. Alexander Pope. CP-PopeA Fr. Essay on Man, An.

Character of Sir Robert Walpole, The. Jonathan Swift. CP-SwifJ

Character of the Happy Warrior. William Wordsworth. CP-WorW1

Character of Wallenstein, The. Samuel Taylor Coleridge. CP-ColeS Fr. Death of Wallenstein, The.

Character, Panegyric, and Description of the Legion Club, A. Jonathan Swift. CP-SwifJ

Characteristic, nevertheless strange. Strayed Message, The. Robert Graves. CP-GravR

Characteristic of the mind, The. Mind and Nature. Richard Eberhart. CP-EberR

Characteristically. Robert Creeley. CP-CreeR

Characteristics of a Child Three Years Old. William Wordsworth. CP-WorW1; MW-WorW

Characters are sounds made by various sizes and kinds of engines, The. Rehearsal. Rae Armantrout. SP-ArmaA

Charade. Christina Georgina Rossetti. CP-RosC3

Charade: "By my 1st you may travel with safety & speed." Francis William Austen. CP-AustJ

Charade: "I with a Housemaid once was curst." Henry Thomas Austen. CP-AustJ

Charade: "In my first that he may not be tardy & late." James Austen. CP-AustJ

Charade: "My first displays the wealth and pomp of kings." Jane Austen. CP-AustJ Fr. Emma.

Charade: "Without me divided, fair ladies I ween." Charles John Austen. CP-AustJ

Charade on Dr Thomas Barnard. Samuel Johnson. CP-JohnS

Charades. Christina Georgina Rossetti. CP-RosC3

Charades. William Stafford. SP-StafWW

Charades: "Should you chance to suffer thirst." Cassandra Elizabeth Austen. CP-AustJ

Charge, The. Jones Very. CP-VeryJ

Charge of the Light Brigade, The. Alfred Tennyson. CP-TennA

Chariot. Stanley Kunitz. CP-KunSC

Chariot, The. Philip Whalen. SP-WhalP

Chariot so strict chariot. Day. Allen Tate. CP-TateA

Charioteer. "H. D." CP-DoolH

Charioteer 1970. Yannis Ritsos. SP-RitsY, tr. by N. C. Germanacos

Charioteer of Delphi, The. James Merrill. SP-MerrJ

Charisma. Ai. SP-Ai

Charisma. Lewis Hyde. SP-BrouO, tr. by Olga Broumas

C[h]aritas Nimia; or, The Dear[e] Bargain. Richard Crashaw. CP-CrasR

Charity. William Cowper. CP-CowpW

Charity. Paul Laurence Dunbar. CP-DunbP

Charity. Christina Georgina Rossetti. CP-RosC3

Charity. Jones Very. CP-VeryJ

Charity in Thought. Samuel Taylor Coleridge. CP-ColeS

Charity Never Faileth. Christina Georgina Rossetti. CP-RosC2

Charity Overcoming Envy. Marianne Craig Moore. CP-MoorM

Charity, thou art a lie. Stephen Crane. CP-CranS

Charivari. Margaret Atwood. SP-AtwM1

Charles—and I say it wond'ring—thou must know. To Charles Diodati. John Milton. CP-CowpW, tr. by William Cowper

Charles Carville's Eyes. Edwin Arlington Robinson. CP-RobiE

Charles Cavendish to His Posterity. Ben Jonson. CP-JonsB

Charles comes out among his people, looks. Morning of 1649, A. Jorge Luis Borges. SP-BorgJ, tr. by Alastair Reid

Charles Dodgson's Song. Randall Jarrell. CP-JarrR

Charles H. Philips. James Whitcomb Riley. CP-RileJ

Charles Ives, I have heard. Ives. Richard Eberhart. CP-EberR

Charles Main, of Main & Winchester, attend. Word to the Unwise, A. Ambrose Bierce. SP-BierA

Charles! my slow heart was only sad, when first. Sonnet to a Friend Who Asked How I Felt When the Nurse First Presented My Infant to Me. Samuel Taylor Coleridge. CP-ColeS

Charles on Fire. James Merrill. SP-MerrJ

Charles on the Trevisan, night bridge. Self-Portrait. Charles Wright. SP-WrigC

Charles Simic. Charles Simic. SP-SimiC; SP-SimiCE

Charles V by Titian. Robert Lowell. SP-LoweR

Charles the First. Percy Bysshe Shelley. CP-ShelP

Charleston. John Updike. CP-UpdiJ

Charleston in the Eighteen-Sixties. Adrienne Rich. CP-RicAE; SP-RicA2

Charleston Plantations. May Sarton. SP-SartM

Charlie. Thomas Kinsella. CP-KinsT

Charlie bends to feed the stove. Storm Mountain Face. Peter Blue Cloud. SP-BlueP

Charlie He's My Darling. Robert Burns. CP-BurnR

Charlie Parker running a towline. Somebody'll Hav' to Shoot Ya Down. Norman Dubie. CP-DubiN

Charlock per Winkle. Louis Zukofsky. CP-ZukLS

Charlotte Corday. Charles Tomlinson. CP-TomlC; SP-TomlC

Charlotte, "the angel of / assassination," is unrelaxed. "Marat's Death." Donald Hall. CP-HallD

Charm, A. Robert Herrick. CP-HerrR

(Another.) CP-HerrR

Charm, A. Rudyard Kipling. CP-KiplR

Charm, The. Robert Creeley. CP-CreeR

Charm, The. Rita Dove. SP-DoveR

Charm Against the Toothache, A. Theodore Weiss. SP-WeisT

Charm for Cantinflas, A. Muriel Rukeyser. CP-RukeM

Charm for Sound Sleeping, A. Robert Graves. CP-GravR

Charm invests a face, A. Emily Dickinson. CP-DickE

Charm me asleep, and melt me so. To Music, to Becalm His Fever. Robert Herrick. CP-HerrR

Charm with your stainlessness these winter nights. Advent. Thomas Merton. CP-MertT

Charm[e]. Ben Jonson. CP-JonsB *Fr.* Masque of Queens, The.

Charme, or an Allay for Love, A. Robert Herrick. CP-HerrR

Charmed. Yusef Komunyakaa. CP-KomuY

Charmes. Robert Herrick. CP-HerrR

Charmes. Robert Herrick. CP-HerrR

Charmides. Oscar Wilde. CP-WildO

Charming lady, she whose beautiful name honors. Sonnet 2: "Charming lady, she whose beautiful name honors." John Milton. CP-CowpW; CP-MiltJ

Charming pallor clothing her sweet smile, The. Petrarch. CP-Petra, *tr. by* J. G. Nichols

Charming, the movement of girls about a May-pole in May. Men Working. Edna St. Vincent Millay. CP-MillE

Charms. James Whitcomb Riley. CP-RileJ

Charms and Knots. George Herbert. CP-HerbG

Charms, that call down the moon from out her sphere. To Music, to Becalm a Sweet-sick Youth. Robert Herrick. CP-HerrR

Charnel Ground, The. Allen Ginsberg. SP-GinsA

Charolais, the new cow-calf, A. From Strength to Strength. Paul Muldoon. CP-MuldP

Charon. Louis MacNeice. CP-MacNL

Charon. Christina Georgina Rossetti. CP-RosC3

Charon and Phylomel, a Dialogue Sung. Robert Herrick. CP-HerrR

Charon, indeed, your dreaded oar. Sappho Crosses the Dark River into Hades. Edna St. Vincent Millay. CP-MillE

Charon, O Charon, draw thy Boat to th'shore. New Charon, The. Robert Herrick. CP-HerrR

Charon! O gentle Charon! let me wooe thee. Charon and Phylomel, a Dialogue Sung. Robert Herrick. CP-HerrR

Charon! receive a family on board. On Niobe. *Unknown.* CP-CowpW, *tr. by* William Cowper

Charon's Cosmology. Charles Simic. SP-SimiC; SP-SimiCE

(With only his dim lantern.) SP-SimiC

Charroll Presented to Dr. Williams Bp. of Lincolne as a Newyears Guift, A. Robert Herrick. CP-HerrR

Charterhouse, The. "Rubén Dario." SP-DariR, *tr. by* Alberto Acereda

Chartist's Complaint, The. Ralph Waldo Emerson. CP-EmerR

Chartres. Archibald MacLeish. CP-MacLA

Chartres. George Oppen. CP-OppGN

Chartres Annunciation, The. Kathleen Jessie Raine. SP-RainK

Chartres Windows. Rudyard Kipling. CP-KiplR

Chas sing does(who). E. E. Cummings. CP-CummE

Chase, The. Sir Walter Scott. *Fr.* Lady of the Lake, The.

Chase, The. James Vincent Cunningham. CP-CunnJ

Chase, The. Paul Laurence Dunbar. CP-DunbP

Chase, The. W. S. Merwin. SP-MerwW

Chase in Spring, The. Hayden Carruth. CP-CarHS

Chasers. Carl Sandburg. CP-SandC

Chasing the Bird. Robert Creeley. CP-CreeR

Chasm. A. R. Ammons. CP-AmmoA

Chaste and kind . . . 'a pattern.' Master & Man. Donald Davie. CP-DaviDC

Chaste Stranger, The. James Tate. SP-TateJ

Chastely to write these eclogues I need to lie. Yellow Book, The. Derek Mahon. CP-MahoD

Chastity. D. H. Lawrence. CP-LawrD

Château de Muzot. Charles Tomlinson. CP-TomlC

Chateau Hardware, The. John Ashbery. SP-AshbJ

Château Jackson. Louis MacNeice. CP-MacNL

Chateaubriand on the Niagara Frontier, 1791. Gregory Orr. SP-OrrG

Chatham was my depot. Kent. Donald Davie. CP-DaviDC

Chatsworth! thy stately mansion, and the pride. 1830. William Wordsworth. CP-WorW2

Chatter of a death-demon from a tree-top, The. Stephen Crane. CP-CranS

Chatter of birds two by two raises a night song joining a litany of running water. Prairie Waters by Night. Carl Sandburg. CP-SandC

Chattering finch and water-fly. Skeleton, The. G. K. Chesterton. CP-ChesG

"Chattering, gum snapping audience," A. Miss Moore at Assembly. John Updike. CP-UpdiJ

Chaucer. E. E. Cummings. CP-CummE

Chaucer. Ted Hughes. SP-HughTN

Chaucer, Langland, Douglas, Dunbar, with all your. Ode to the Medieval Poets. W. H. Auden. CP-AudeW

Chaucer's Wordes unto Adam, his Owne Scriveyn. Geoffrey Chaucer. CP-ChauG

Che. Derek Walcott. CP-WalcD

Che Di Lor Suona Su Nella Tua Vita. Louis Zukofsky. CP-ZukLS

Che Farò Senza Euridice. Randall Jarrell. CP-JarrR

Che Fece . . . Il Gran Rifiuto. Constantine P. Cavafy. CP-CavaC, *tr. by* Theoharis Constantine Theoharis

Cheap Blue. Carl Sandburg. CP-SandC

Cheap little rhymes. Sliver. Langston Hughes. CP-HughL; CP-HughL3

Cheap Rent. Carl Sandburg. CP-SandC

Cheap Thrill. Robert Creeley. SP-CreeR

Chearful sage, when solemn dictates fail. Horace, *See* This was the summit of my views

Cheat of Cupid; or, The Ungentle Guest, The. Robert Herrick. CP-HerrR

Cheating Mirror, The. Federico García Lorca. CP-GarcF, *tr. by* Alan S. Trueblood *Fr.* Songs to End With.

Check. Thomas Kinsella. CP-KinsT

Check out the humpback, Manny. Guido Cavalcanti. CP-CavaG, *tr. by* Marc Cirigliano

Checkmate. Jelaluddin Rumi. SP-Rumi, *tr. by* Coleman Barks

Cheer, The. William Meredith. SP-MereW

Cheerful soldiers, with new stores supplied, The. John Dryden. SP-DrydJ *Fr.* Annus Mirabilis.

Cheerful youth joined Coleridge on his walk, A. Keats at Highgate. Thom Gunn. CP-GunnT

Cheerfulness in lordly. Sing unto the Lord a New Song. Donald Davie. CP-DaviDC

Cheerfulness Taught by Reason. Elizabeth Barrett Browning. CP-BroEB

Cheerfulnesse in Charitie; or, The Sweet Sacrifice. Robert Herrick. CP-HerrR

Cheers. Raymond Carver. CP-CarvR

Cheery Beggar. Gerard Manley Hopkins. CP-HopkG

Chee$e. Thomas Merton. CP-MertT

Cheesecake. Paul Muldoon. CP-MuldP

Chekhov on Sakhalin. Seamus Heaney. SP-HeanSO

Chekhov on the West Heath. Denise Levertov. SP-LeveDL; SP-LeveDS

Chelsea Naval Hospital. John Ciardi. CP-CiarJ

Chemical conviction, The. Emily Dickinson. CP-DickE

Chemicals ripen the citrus. In California. Donald Davie. CP-DaviDC

Chemin de Fer. Elizabeth Bishop. CP-BishE

Chemin de Fer. Norman Dubie. CP-DubiN

Chemist creates, The. Tradition. Lorine Niedecker. CP-NiedL

Chemist of love, The. Hafiz. CP-EmerR *Fr.* Odes.

Chenille. James Dickey. CP-DickJ

Cheops, to sail eternity. Ship in the Tomb. Archibald MacLeish. CP-MacLA

Chérie / the very,picturesque,last Day. E. E. Cummings. CP-CummE

Cherish. Raymond Carver. CP-CarvR

Cherish the Ladies. Paul Muldoon. CP-MuldP

Cherish you then the hope I shall forget. Edna St. Vincent Millay. CP-MillE

Cherishing that is speechless, The. Emily Dickinson. SP-DickE

Chernobyl. A Disaster. Donald Davie. CP-DaviDC

Cherrie-Ripe. Robert Herrick. CP-HerrR

Cherrie-Ripe, Ripe, Ripe, I cry. Cherrie-Ripe. Robert Herrick. CP-HerrR

Cherries. Robert Browning. CP-BroR2

Cherries. Pablo Neruda. SP-NeruP

Cherry Birds, The. Jones Very. CP-VeryJ

Cherry Blossoms at Evening. William Carlos Williams. CP-WilW2

Cherry-colored picture hat, A. Hats. James Schuyler. CP-SchuJ

Cherry-Pit. Robert Herrick. CP-HerrR

Cherry red chrome dazzle, A. Craft. John Ciardi. CP-CiarJ

Cherry-red her mouth was. Eleanor. Christina Georgina Rossetti. CP-RosC3

Cherry Ripe. Donald Davie. CP-DaviDC

Cherry Robbers. D. H. Lawrence. CP-LawrD

Cherry Tree, The. Thom Gunn. CP-GunnT

Cherry Tree, The. Howard Nemerov. CP-NemeH

Cherry Trees, The. Walter De la Mare. CP-DeLaW

Cherry White. Dorothy Parker. CP-ParkD

Cherrylog Road. James Dickey. CP-DickJ

Cherub, The. Ogden Nash. CP-NashO

Cheshire. Donald Davie. CP-DaviDC

Chess. Jorge Luis Borges. SP-BorgJ, *tr.* by Alastair Reid

Chess. Primo Levi. CP-LeviP, *tr.* by Ruth Feldman

Chess. Louis MacNeice. CP-MacNL

Chess 2. Primo Levi. CP-LeviP, *tr.* by Ruth Feldman

Chess under Trees. A. K. Ramanujan. CP-RamaA

Chestnut Avenue: at Alton House, The. Charles Tomlinson. CP-TomlC

Chestnut casts his flambeaux, and the flowers, The. A. E. Housman. CP-HousA

Chestnut flowers are falling. Blue Sunday. Kenneth Rexroth. CP-RexrK

Chestnut splits its padded cell, The. Autumn Notes. Ted Hughes. SP-HughTN

Cheval-Glass, The. Thomas Hardy. CP-HardT

Cheval-glass is empty, The. Montage. Charles Tomlinson. CP-TomlC

Cheveril [*or* Cheverel] cries out, my verses libels are. On Cheveril [*or* Cheverel]. Ben Jonson. CP-JonsB; SP-JonsB

Cheville. Hugh MacDiarmid. SP-MacDH

Chewing [of] the Cud, The. Robert Herrick. CP-HerrR

Chez Jane. Frank O'Hara. SP-OharF

Chi Hsing Tzu was a trainer of fighting cocks. Fighting Cock, The. Chuang Tzu. CP-MertT

Chiami il mio core / Crudele, altero. Amore E Dovere. Christina Georgina Rossetti. CP-RosC3

Chiami il mio core / Crudele, altero. Tirsi, A. Christina Georgina Rossetti. CP-RosC3

Chiaroscuro. Wallace Stevens. CP-StevWP

Chic Freedom's Reflection. Alice Walker. CP-WalkA

Chicadee, The. Henry David Thoreau. CP-ThorH

Chicago. Charles Bukowski. SP-BukC1

Chicago. Robert Creeley. CP-CreeR

Chicago. Langston Hughes. CP-HughL; CP-HughL3

Chicago. John Greenleaf Whittier. CP-WhitJ

Chicago Airport / O'Hare, The. Illegal Aliens. Grace Paley. CP-PalGC

Chicago Blues. Langston Hughes. CP-HughL; CP-HughL3

Chicago Boy Baby. Carl Sandburg. CP-SandC

Chicago Cabaret. Kenneth Rexroth. CP-RexrK

Chicago *Defender* Sends a Man to Little Rock, The. Gwendolyn Brooks. SP-BrooG

Chicago English Afternoon. Ted Berrigan. SP-BerrT

Chicago is a town. Chicago Blues. Langston Hughes. CP-HughL; CP-HughL3

Chicago Morning. Ted Berrigan. SP-BerrT

Chicago Poet. Carl Sandburg. CP-SandC

Chicago Scene. John Logan. CP-LogaJ

Chicago to Salt Lake by Air. Allen Ginsberg. CP-GinsA

Chicago Train, The. Louise Glück. SP-GlucL

Chicago Zen. A. K. Ramanujan. CP-RamaA

Chicago's avenues, as white as Poland. Derek Walcott. CP-WalcD *Fr.* Midsummer.

Chichester. Amy Clampitt. CP-ClamA

Chickamauga. Charles Wright. SP-WrigCN

Chicken. How shall I tell you what it is. Presentation of Two Birds to My Son, A. James Wright. CP-WrigJ

Chicken-Licken. Maya Angelou. SP-AngeM

Chicken Without a Head, The. Charles Simic. SP-SimiC; SP-SimiCE

Chickens in San Francisco. William Dickey. SP-DickW

Chickpea leaps almost over the rim of the pot, A. Chickpea to Cook. Jelaluddin Rumi. SP-Rumi, *tr.* by Coleman Barks

Chickpea to Cook. Jelaluddin Rumi. SP-Rumi, *tr.* by Coleman Barks

Chicks. Carl Sandburg. CP-SandC

Chicks in the egg picks at the shell, cracks open one oval world, and, The. Chicks. Carl Sandburg. CP-SandC

Chicory. Hayden Carruth. CP-CarHS

Chicory. Louis Zukofsky. CP-ZukLS

Chicory and Daisies. William Carlos Williams. CP-WilW1

Chicory Flower / on Campus. Lorine Niedecker. SP-NiedL

Chiddingly, pronounced. Sussex. Donald Davie. CP-DaviDC

Chide not; let me breathe a little. Death's Chill Between. Christina Georgina Rossetti. CP-RosC3

Chief is silent, The. Urn with a Political Profile. Pablo Antonio Cuadra. CP-MertT

Chief Joseph of the Nez Perce. Robert Penn Warren. CP-WarrR

Chief Mystery, The. D. H. Lawrence. CP-LawrD

Chief of organic numbers! On Seeing a Lock of Milton's Hair. John Keats. CP-KeatJ

Chief of the civil administration, The. Pilate. Donald Davie. CP-DaviDC

Chief Standing Water. Charles Tomlinson. CP-TomlC

Chiefest among Ten Thousand, The. Christina Georgina Rossetti. CP-RosC2

Chiefest among Ten Thousand, The. Christina Georgina Rossetti. *See* I Will Lift Up Mine Eyes unto the Hills

Chiefly I prize this loss of patience, deep. Among Ourselves and with All Nations. Kenneth Patchen. CP-PatcK

Chieftain Iffucan of Azcan in caftan. Bantams in Pine-Woods. Wallace Stevens. CP-StevW; CP-StevWP

Chiesa E Signore. Christina Georgina Rossetti. CP-RosC3

Child. Sylvia Plath. CP-PlatS

Child. Carl Sandburg. CP-SandC

Child, The. Raymond Carver. CP-CarvR

Child, The. G. K. Chesterton. CP-ChesG

Child, The. Richard Eberhart. CP-EberR

Child, The. Donald Hall. CP-HallD

Child, The. Randall Jarrell. CP-JarrR

Child, The. James Laughlin. CP-LaugJ

Child, The. W. S. Merwin. SP-MerwW

Child, The. Rainer Maria Rilke. CP-RilkFr, *tr.* by A. Poulin, Jr.

Child (a boy) bouncing, A. To. William Carlos Williams. CP-WilW1

Child among his powers gathering, The. Another Day (Child among his powers). Muriel Rukeyser. CP-RukeM

Child and Mother. Muriel Rukeyser. CP-RukeM

Child and the Sage, The. Thomas Hardy. CP-HardT

Child and Vegetables. William Carlos Williams. CP-WilW1

Child Asleep, A. Elizabeth Barrett Browning. CP-BroEB

Child Asleep, A. Walter De la Mare. CP-DeLaW

Child Asleep in Its Own Life, A. Wallace Stevens. CP-StevWP

Child at One or Two, The. Shmuel HaNagid. SP-HaNaS, *tr.* by Peter Cole

Child at the Mirror, The. Rainer Maria Rilke. CP-RilkFr, *tr.* by A. Poulin, Jr.

Child at the window sill waits for his mother's, The. Rainer Maria Rilke. CP-RilkFr, *tr.* by A. Poulin, Jr.

Child Bearers, The. Anne Sexton. CP-SextA

Child Beater. Ai. SP-Ai

Child begins to walk, The. Poem for the Sandman. James Tate. SP-TateJ

Child beheld the o'er arching heaven, A. Child's Dream of Reaching the Horizon, The. Jones Very. CP-VeryJ

Child comes sometimes with his mother's needle, The. Voyage of the Needle, The. James Dickey. CP-DickJ

Child crying in the night, A. Terms, The. Charles Simic. SP-SimiC; SP-SimiCE

Child Dead in Old Seas. Maya Angelou. SP-AngeM

Child disturbs our view, The. Tow-head bent, she. Three Valentines to the Wide World. Mona Van Duyn. SP-VanDM

Child draws the outline of a body, A. Portrait. Louise Glück. SP-GlucL

Child dreaming along a crowded street, The. Sweet-Shop Round The Corner, The. Robert Graves. CP-GravR

Child Face. Carl Sandburg. CP-SandC

Child goes seeking his voice, The. Voiceless Child, The. Federico García Lorca. CP-GarcF, *tr.* by Alan S. Trueblood *Fr.* Back of the World.

Child Harold. John Clare.

    Ballad: "Summer morning is risen." SP-ClarJ

    Song: "Dying gales of sweet even." SP-ClarJ

    Song: "Say What Is Love—To Live In Vain." SP-ClarJ

Child in Red. Rainer Maria Rilke. CP-RilkFr, *tr.* by A. Poulin, Jr.

Child in the Crystal. Marya Alexandrovna Zaturenska. SP-ZatuM

Child in the Great Wood. Muriel Rukeyser. CP-RukeM

Child in the Sabbath peace, there, A. Sunday, A. Walter De la Mare. CP-DeLaW

Child in the womb. How to Sleep. Philip Larkin. CP-LarkP

Child / Is bathing in the mud, The. Three Generations. K'o Chia Tsang. CP-WilW2

Child is born, they cry, a child, A. Christmas. Stevie Smith. CP-SmitS

Child Is Father to the Man, But with More Authority, The. Ogden Nash. CP-NashO

Child is sleeping in His golden house, The. Song for the Blessed Sacrament. Thomas Merton. CP-MertT

Child is something else again, A. Wakes up. Yehuda Amichai. SP-AmicY, *tr.* by Chana Bloch

Child like mustard seed, The. War-Baby. D. H. Lawrence. CP-LawrD

Child looked through the lattice old, The. Sunset and Dawn. G. K. Chesterton. CP-ChesG

Child looking at ruins grows younger, A. Love for October, The. W. S. Merwin. SP-MerwWF

Child Margaret. Carl Sandburg. CP-SandC

Child Margaret begins to write numbers on a Saturday morning, the, The. Child Margaret. Carl Sandburg. CP-SandC

Child Moon. Carl Sandburg. CP-SandC

Child, no-one to stare, I'd run full tilt to a tree, A. Metamorphic Journal. Denise Levertov. SP-LeveDL

Child of a line accurst / And old as Troy. Bon Voyage. Edwin Arlington Robinson. CP-RobiE

Child of Europe. Czeslaw Milosz. CP-MiloC; CP-MiloCN, *tr.* by Jan Darowski

Child of God Longing To See Him Beloved, A. Jeanne Marie Bouvier de la

Motte Guyon. CP-CowpW, *tr. by* William Cowper

Child of loud-throated War! the mountain Stream. Address to Kilchurn Castle, upon Loch Awe. William Wordsworth. CP-WorW1

Child of Mary Queen of Scots, The. James I. Rudyard Kipling. CP-KiplR

Child of my parents! Sister of my soul! Prelude, The; Growth of a Poet's Mind [1805 vers.]. William Wordsworth. CP-WorW3; MW-WorW

Child of St. Catherine—none shall groan. To a Catherine Wheel. G. K. Chesterton. CP-ChesG

Child of the Aztec gods. Dusty Doors. Carl Sandburg. CP-SandC

Child of the Moon. Pablo Neruda. SP-NeruP

Child of the Romans. Carl Sandburg. CP-SandC

Child of the root, among your apples and forests. Muriel Rukeyser. CP-RukeM

Child of the sunlight in the tower room. Hero with Girl and Gorgon. Howard Nemerov. CP-NemeH

Child on Top of a Greenhouse. Theodore Roethke. CP-RoetT

Child played being a gravedigger, A. Game, The. Charles Simic. SP-SimiC; SP-SimiCE

Child Poems. "H. D." CP-DoolH

Child Psychology. C. K. Williams. SP-WillC

Child riding the stormy mane of noon, A. Are You Born? / II. Muriel Rukeyser. CP-RukeM

Child runs in to play, A. Invaders, The. Marya Alexandrovna Zaturenska. SP-ZatuM

Child said:"Pretty bird, The" Three Moments. Christina Georgina Rossetti. CP-RosC3

Child saw the bombers skate like stones across the fields, The. Come to the Stone. Randall Jarrell. CP-JarrR

Child signed the steamed pane, The. Variation on Themes by Roethke and Eliot. Alan Dugan. CP-DugaA

Child sits in a sunny place, A. Ancient of Days, The. G. K. Chesterton. CP-ChesG

Child-Songs. John Greenleaf Whittier. CP-WhitJ

Child Stealer. Yusef Komunyakaa. CP-KomuY

Child, the current of your breath is six days long. Unknown Girl in the Maternity Ward. Anne Sexton. CP-SextA; SP-SextA

Child, the poems, the child, the poems, the journeys, The. Gift. Muriel Rukeyser. CP-RukeM

Child, the temptation please resist. If Fun Is Fun, Isn't That Enough? Ogden Nash. CP-NashO

Child wakes in the morning to enter a country, The. Muriel Rukeyser. CP-RukeM

Child, were I king, I'd yield my royal rule. From Victor Hugo. Thomas Hardy. CP-HardT

Child, what can those old men bring you? Let Them Ask Your Pardon. Carl Sandburg. CP-SandC

Child who doesn't have a teacher, A. Han-shan. CP-ColdM, *tr. by* Red Pine

Child who picked up bullets, Pubescent Lad, The. Arthur Rimbaud. CP-RimbA, *tr. by* Martin Sorrell

Child with a chip of mirror in his eye. Snow Queen, The. Adrienne Rich. CP-RicAE; SP-RicA2

Child with Veteran. Robert Graves. CP-GravR

Child-World, A. James Whitcomb Riley. CP-RileJ

    "At Noey's house—when they arrived with him." CP-RileJ

    Bear Story, The. CP-RileJ

    Bewildering Emotions. CP-RileJ

    Bud's Fairy Tale. CP-RileJ

    Child-World, The. CP-RileJ

    Cousin Rufus' Story. CP-RileJ

    Delicious Interruption, A. CP-RileJ

    Evening Company, The. CP-RileJ

    Floretty's Musical Contribution. CP-RileJ

    Heat-Lightning. CP-RileJ

    Hired Man and Floretty, The. CP-RileJ

    Limitations of Genius. CP-RileJ

    Little Jack Janitor. CP-RileJ

    Loehrs and the Hammonds, The. CP-RileJ

    Maymie's Story of Red Riding-Hood. CP-RileJ

    Mr. Hammond's Parable. CP-RileJ

    Noey's Night-Piece. CP-RileJ

    Old Home-Folks, The. CP-RileJ

    Pathos of Applause, The. CP-RileJ

    Proem: "Child-World—long and long since lost to view, The." CP-RileJ

    Prospective Visit, A. CP-RileJ

    St. Lirriper. CP-RileJ

    Told by "The Noted Traveler." CP-RileJ

    Uncle Mart's Poem. CP-RileJ

Child-World, The. James Whitcomb Riley. CP-RileJ *Fr.* Child-World, A.

Child-World—long and long since lost to view, The. Proem: "Child-World—

long and long since lost to view, The." James Whitcomb Riley. CP-RileJ *Fr.* Child-World, A.

Child-World, yet a wondrous world no less, A. Child-World, The. James Whitcomb Riley. CP-RileJ *Fr.* Child-World, A.

Childe Harold to the Round Tower Came. William Carlos Williams. CP-WilW2

Childe Harold's Pilgrimage. Lord Byron. CP-Byron

Childe Horvald to the Dark Tower Came. John Ciardi. CP-CiarJ

Childe Roland to the Dark Tower Came. Robert Browning. CP-BroR1; SP-BroR

Childe Rolandine. Stevie Smith. CP-SmitS

Childhood. Randall Jarrell. CP-JarrR

Childhood. Kathleen Jessie Raine. SP-RainK

Childhood. Rainer Maria Rilke. CP-NemeH

Childhood. Arthur Rimbaud. CP-RimbA, *tr. by* Martin Sorrell

Childhood among the Ferns. Thomas Hardy. CP-HardT

Childhood and Death. Federico García Lorca. CP-GarcF, *tr. by* Greg Simon *and* Steven F. White

Childhood dotted with bodies. Origin of the Marble Forest. Gregory Orr. SP-OrrG

Childhood Friends. Jelaluddin Rumi. SP-Rumi, *tr. by* Coleman Barks

Childhood in Jacksonville, Florida. Jane Cooper. CP-CoopJ

Childhood Is the Kingdom Where Nobody Dies. Edna St. Vincent Millay. CP-MillE

Childhood Memory. Kathleen Jessie Raine. SP-RainK

Childhood of Parmenides, The. Charles Simic. SP-SimiC; SP-SimiCE

Childhood of the Hero. Kenneth Patchen. CP-PatcK

Childhood's Body. Charles Wright. SP-WrigC

Childhood's End. Denise Levertov. SP-LeveDS

Childhood's Songs. Jones Very. CP-VeryJ

Childish. Robert Creeley. SP-CreeR

Childish Prank, A. Ted Hughes. SP-HughTN

Childish Recollections. Lord Byron. CP-Byron

Childless Father, The. William Wordsworth. CP-WorW1; MW-WorW

Childless Woman. Sylvia Plath. CP-PlatS

Childlessness. James Merrill. SP-MerrJ

    (Weather of this winter night, my dream-wife, The.) SP-MerrJ

Children. Ted Hughes. SP-HughTN

Children. Carolyn Kizer. CP-KizeC

Children, The. Robert Creeley. SP-CreeR

Children, The. Rudyard Kipling. CP-KiplR

Children, The. Anne Sexton. CP-SextA

Children, The. Jones Very. CP-VeryJ

Children, The. William Carlos Williams. CP-WilW2

Children and Sir Nameless, The. Thomas Hardy. CP-HardT

Children are all crying in their pens, The. Children, The. Anne Sexton. CP-SextA

Children are dumb to say how hot the day is. Cool Web, The. Robert Graves. CP-GravR

Children are healthy, The. Note to Grandparents. Grace Paley. CP-PalGC

Children are off somewhere, The. Lights I Have Seen Before. Philip Levine. SP-LeviP

Children are planting their shoots. Poem for Arbor Day. Yehuda Amichai. SP-AmicY, *tr. by* Stephen Mitchell

Children aren't happy with nothing to ignore. Parent, The. Ogden Nash. CP-NashO

Children begin at green dawn nimbly to build. Altars in the Street, The. Denise Levertov. SP-LeveDP

Children, come to my knee. News. Randall Jarrell. CP-JarrR

Children do not always mean. Christmas Carols. Margaret Atwood. SP-AtwM2

Children go forward with their little satchels, The. School Children, The. Louise Glück. SP-GlucL

Children have colds and snore, The. Aix-en-Provence. Kenneth Rexroth. CP-RexrK

Children hung around, The. On a Party. Alan Dugan. CP-DugaA

Children, I come back today. Negro Mother, The. Langston Hughes. CP-HughL; CP-HughL1

Children, I crave your kind forbearance. Child's Guide to Parents, A. Ogden Nash. CP-NashO

Children I implore you. Han-shan. CP-ColdM, *tr. by* Red Pine

Children, if you dare to think. Warning to Children. Robert Graves. CP-GravR

Children in Exile. James Fenton. SP-FentJ

Children in the street play hard, The. Warning: Children at Play. Howard Nemerov. CP-NemeH

Children nurs'd woods tilled rock. Yaupon. Louis Zukofsky. CP-ZukLS

Children of Darkness. Robert Graves. CP-GravR

Children of Darkness. Richard Wilbur. CP-WilbR

Children of mine, not mine but lent. Godchildren. William Meredith. SP-MereW

Children of my happier prime. Immolated. Herman Melville. SP-MelvH

Children of Our Age. Wisława Szymborska. SP-SzymW, *tr. by* Stanislaw Barańczak *and* Clare Cavanagh

Children of Our Era. Wisława Szymborska. SP-SzymWM, *tr. by* Joanna Trzeciak

Children of Stare, The. Walter De la Mare. CP-DeLaW

Children of the Childless, The. James Whitcomb Riley. CP-RileJ

Children of the Childless!—Yours—and mine, The. Children of the Childless, The. James Whitcomb Riley. CP-RileJ

Children of the Cross, The. Stevie Smith. CP-SmitS

Children of the early / Countryside. Penobscot. George Oppen. CP-OppGN

Children of the future Age. Little Girl Lost, A. William Blake. CP-BlakW *Fr.* Songs of Experience.

Children of the Triple World. Han-shan. CP-ColdM, *tr. by* Red Pine

Children on the lawn / joined hand to hand, The. Circle Game, The. Margaret Atwood. SP-AtwM1

Children picking up our bones. Postcard from the Volcano, A. Wallace Stevens. CP-StevW; CP-StevWP

Children play at the Luxembourg fountain, The. Bridge of Change, The. John Logan. CP-LogaJ

Children play on into. Hide and Seek. Thom Gunn. CP-GunnT

Children play under, The. Ballade of White Caracols. Federico García Lorca. CP-GarcF, *tr. by* Jerome Rothenberg *Fr.* Caracols / Snails.

Children remembering sadness grieve, they grieve. Facing Sentencing. Muriel Rukeyser. CP-RukeM

Children, seated, The. Ballade of Black Caracols. Federico García Lorca. CP-GarcF, *tr. by* Jerome Rothenberg *Fr.* Caracols / Snails.

Children Selecting Books in a Library. Randall Jarrell. CP-JarrR

Children sing, The. Ballad of the Little Square. Federico García Lorca. SP-GarcF, *tr. by* J. L. Gili *and* Stephen Spender

Children Singing in School. D. H. Lawrence. CP-LawrD

Children stood watch by the crematorium, The. Yellow Newspaper and a Wooden Leg. James Tate. SP-TateJ

Children—take 'em as they run. Raggedy Man on Children, The. James Whitcomb Riley. CP-RileJ

Children, the Sandbar, That Summer. Muriel Rukeyser. CP-RukeM

Children the time of angry fathers. Round and a Hope for Smithgirls, A. Thomas Merton. CP-MertT

Children walking with their grandmothers. Nature of This City, The. Grace Paley. CP-PalGC

Children we have not borne. To My Daughter the Junkie on a Train. Audre Lorde. SP-LordA

Children who explored the brook and found, The. To Walter de la Mare. T. S. Eliot. CP-ElioT

Children who paddle where the ocean bed shelves steeply. Advice to Young Children. Stevie Smith. CP-SmitS

Children's Crusade, The. Philip Levine. SP-LeviP

Children's eyes were like lakes of the sea, The. Triumph of Education, The. Howard Nemerov. CP-NemeH

Children's Game, A. Jelaluddin Rumi. SP-Rumi, *tr. by* Coleman Barks

Children's Games. Louis MacNeice. CP-MacNL

Children's Games. Miller Williams. CP-WillM

Children's Hour, The. Henry Wadsworth Longfellow. SP-LongH

Children's Orchard, The. Muriel Rukeyser. CP-RukeM

Children's Party. Ogden Nash. CP-NashO

Children's Procession. Yehuda Amichai. SP-AmicY, *tr. by* Stephen Mitchell

Children's Rhymes ("By what sends"). Langston Hughes. CP-HughL3

Children's Rhymes ("When I was a chile we used to play"). Langston Hughes. CP-HughL; CP-HughL3

Children's Song, The. Rudyard Kipling. *See* Puck of Pook's Hill

Children's Ward, The. Jane Cooper. CP-CoopJ

Child's Amaze, A. Walt Whitman. CP-WhitW

Child's Answer, The. Jones Very. CP-VeryJ

Child's Chistmas in Georgia, A. Wyatt Prunty. SP-PrunW

Child's Christmas Carol. James Whitcomb Riley. CP-RileJ

Child's Dream of Reaching the Horizon, The. Jones Very. CP-VeryJ

Child's Evening Prayer, A. Samuel Taylor Coleridge. CP-ColeS

Child's faith is new, The. Emily Dickinson. CP-DickE

Child's Garden, A. Rudyard Kipling. CP-KiplR *Fr.* Muse among the Motors, The.

Child's Garden, A. Donald Hall. CP-HallD

Child's Grave at Florence, A. Elizabeth Barrett Browning. CP-BroEB

Child's Guide to Parents, A. Ogden Nash. CP-NashO

Child's Home—Long Ago, A. James Whitcomb Riley. CP-RileJ

Child's Japan, A. May Sarton. SP-SartM

Child's Park Stones. Sylvia Plath. CP-PlatS

Child's Play. Yusef Komunyakaa. CP-KomuY

Child's Prayer, A. George Meredith. CP-MerG2

Child's Song. Robert Lowell. SP-LoweR

Child's song sounds behind the mud walls, A. Air. Alfonso Cortes. CP-MertT

Child's Talk in April. Christina Georgina Rossetti. CP-RosC1

Child's Thought of God, A. Elizabeth Barrett Browning. CP-BroEB

Child's wonder, the. Child Moon. Carl Sandburg. CP-SandC

Chile, these steps is hard to climb. Dime. Langston Hughes. CP-HughL; CP-HughL3

Chilean Earth. Gabriela Mistral. SP-MistG, *tr. by* Maria Giachetti [*or* Jacketti]

Chill, A. Christina Georgina Rossetti. CP-RosC1

Chill, The. Denise Levertov. SP-LeveDL

Chill and mirk is the nightly blast. Stanzas: "Chill and mirk is the nightly blast." Lord Byron. CP-Byron

Chill blank world. Yet over the utmost sea, A. Christina Georgina Rossetti. CP-RosC2

Chill to the marrow. Sparrow. Thom Gunn. CP-GunnT *Fr.* Three Songs.

Chill wind sweeps the high places, A. Blackstudies. Audre Lorde. SP-LordA

Chillianwallah. George Meredith. CP-MerG2

Chillicothe. Carl Sandburg. CP-SandC

Chilly,murky night, A. E. E. Cummings. CP-CummE

Chilly Night, A. Christina Georgina Rossetti. CP-RosC3

Chilly Peace infests the Grass, A. Emily Dickinson. CP-DickE

Chil's Song. Rudyard Kipling. CP-KiplR *Fr.* Second Jungle Book, The.

Chimaera. D. H. Lawrence. CP-LawrD

Chimaeras, The. W. H. Auden. CP-AudeW

Chime of the bells, and the church clock striking eight, The. Little Town at Evening, The. D. H. Lawrence. CP-LawrD

Chimeras of Saint Helena, The. James Laughlin. CP-LaugJ

Chimes. Dante Gabriel Rossetti. CW-RossD

Chimes, The. Thomas Hardy. CP-HardT

Chimes called midnight, just at interlune, The. Aquae Sulis. Thomas Hardy. CP-HardT

Chimes for Yahya. James Merrill. SP-MerrJ

Chimes Play "Life's a Bumper!", The. Thomas Hardy. CP-HardT

Chiming seas may clang; and Tubal Cain, The. To the Cricket. James Whitcomb Riley. CP-RileJ

Chimney, breathing a little smoke, A. February. James Schuyler. CP-SchuJ

Chimney Sweep. Lorine Niedecker. CP-NiedL

Chimney Sweeper, The. William Blake. CP-BlakW *Fr.* Songs of Experience.

China Bronchitis. Allen Ginsberg. SP-GinsA *Fr.* Reading Bai Juyi.

China-going P. & O.'s. Rudyard Kipling. CP-KiplR *Fr.* Just-So Stories.

China Journal. Charles Wright. SP-WrigC

China Mail. Charles Wright. SP-WrigCN

China moon in the northeast, egg-like, 9:10 p.m. St. Augustine and the Arctic Bear. Charles Wright. SP-WrigCN

Chinaman, The. Christina Georgina Rossetti. CP-RosC3

Chinaman said don't take the hardware, The. Hello, Willie Shoemaker. Charles Bukowski. SP-BukC2

Chinese Art and Greek Art. Jelaluddin Rumi. SP-Rumi, *tr. by* Coleman Barks

Chinese Banyan, The. William Meredith. SP-MereW

Chinese England. Christopher Logue. SP-LoguC

Chinese Garden. Federico García Lorca. CP-GarcF, *tr. by* Jerome Rothenberg *Fr.* Barrage of Firework Poems on the Occasion of the Poet's Birthday.

Chinese History of Colden Water. Ted Hughes. SP-HughTN

Chinese Journal. Charles Wright. SP-WrigC

Chinese, Koreans, The. If You're Going to Have One. Robert Creeley. SP-CreeR

Chinese Nightingale. Ted Berrigan. SP-BerrT

Chinese Nightingale. William Carlos Williams. CP-WilW1

Chinese Nightingale, The. Nicholas Vachel Lindsay. CP-LindV

Chinese Poem. Adam Zagajewski. SP-ZagaA, *tr. by* Clare Cavanagh

Chinese Restaurant in Portrush, The. Derek Mahon. CP-MahoD

Chinese Tomb Guardians. Robert Bly. SP-BlyR

Chinese Toy, A. William Carlos Williams. CP-WilW1

Chinese windchimes, The. Wind in the Sunporch, The. Josephine Jacobsen. CP-JacoJ

Chink, The. Robert Graves. CP-GravR

Chinook. Paul Muldoon. CP-MuldP

Chipmunk, The. Ogden Nash. CP-NashO

Chipmunk chewing the Chippendale. Exit, Pursued by a Bear. Ogden Nash. CP-NashO

Chipmunk's Day, The. Randall Jarrell. CP-JarrR

Chippy. Langston Hughes. CP-HughL; CP-HughL2

Chirotherium tracks occur. Fact ("Chirotherium tracks occur"). Kenneth Rexroth. CP-RexrK

Chivalry. Aleksandr Aleksandrovich Blok. SP-BlokA, *tr. by* Peter France *and* Jon Stallworthy

Chivalry. George Meredith. CP-MerG2

Chivalry, honour, exploits, fame. Chivalry. Aleksandr Aleksandrovich Blok. SP-BlokA, *tr. by* Peter France *and* Jon Stallworthy

Chladni strewed on glass the sand. Ralph Waldo Emerson. CP-EmerR

Chloe. Robert Burns. CP-BurnR
  (Song, Altered from an Old English One.) CP-BurnR
Chloe or her modern sister, Lil. Laura Riding Jackson. CP-RidiL
Chloe's hair, no doubt, was brighter. Renunciation. Dorothy Parker. CP-ParkD
Chloë's Poem. John Updike. CP-UpdiJ
Chloride of Lime and Charcoal. Louis Zukofsky. CP-ZukLS
Chloridia. Ben Jonson.
  "Come forth, come forth, the gentle Spring." CP-JonsB
Chocorua to Its Neighbor. Wallace Stevens. CP-StevW; CP-StevWP
Choice. A. R. Ammons. CP-AmmoA
Choice. James Vincent Cunningham. CP-CunnJ
Choice. Emily Dickinson. CP-DickE
Choice. D. H. Lawrence. CP-LawrD
Choice. Yannis Ritsos. SP-RitsY, tr. by Kimon Friar
Choice, A. Paul Laurence Dunbar. CP-DunbP
Choice, The. Rudyard Kipling. CP-KiplR
Choice, The. Dorothy Parker. CP-ParkD
Choice, The. Ezra Pound. CP-PoEar
Choice, The. William Butler Yeats. CP-YeatW
Choice, The ("Eat thou and drink; to-morrow thou shalt die"). Dante Gabriel Rossetti. CW-RossD Fr. House of Life, The.
Choice, The ("Think thou and act; to-morrow thou shalt die"). Dante Gabriel Rossetti. CW-RossD Fr. House of Life, The.
Choice, The ("Watch thou and fear; to-morrow thou shalt die"). Dante Gabriel Rossetti. CW-RossD Fr. House of Life, The.
Choice of Evils. D. H. Lawrence. CP-LawrD
Choice of you shuts up that peacock-fan. To My Wife. Philip Larkin. CP-LarkP
Choice proposed: ascends, the nervy conductor, The. Trophies. Muriel Rukeyser. CP-RukeM
Choices. Carl Sandburg. CP-SandC
Choir, The. Olga Broumas. SP-BrouO
Choir of bright beauties in spring did appear, A. Lady's Song, The. John Dryden. SP-DrydJ
Choir Singing, The. Grace Paley. CP-PalGC
Choirmaster's Burial, The. Thomas Hardy. CP-HardT
Choke cherry blossoms on the Back. On the Shore. Charles Olson. CP-OlsoC
Chokecherries. Peter Blue Cloud. SP-BlueP
Chokecherry. Louis Zukofsky. CP-ZukLS
Cholera. Rita Dove. SP-DoveR
Cholera Camp. Rudyard Kipling. CP-KiplR
Chommoda. Ezra Pound. CP-PoEar
Choose. Carl Sandburg. CP-SandC
Choose Flowers that have no Fang, Dear. Emily Dickinson. SP-DickE
Choose for the Best. Robert Herrick. CP-HerrR
Choose me your Valentine. To His Mistress[e]. Robert Herrick. CP-HerrR
Choose one set of tracks and track a hare. Seamus Heaney. SP-HeanSO Fr. Squarings.
Choose Something like a Star. Robert Frost. CP-FrosR
  (Take Something Like a Star.) CP-FrosR
Choose your own difference between surgery. Differences. John Ciardi. CP-CiarJ
Choosers, The. Stevie Smith. CP-SmitS
Choosing a Dog. William Stafford. SP-StafWW
Chop-Cherry. Robert Herrick. CP-HerrR
Chopin Bukowski. Charles Bukowski. SP-BukC1
Choral Song: "Soft sleep, thou stranger to all pain." Sophocles. CP-SherT Fr. Philoctetes.
Choral: The Pink Church. William Carlos Williams. CP-WilW2
Chorale, The. Christopher Logue. SP-LoguC Fr. Lily-White Boys, The.
Chorale for Autumn. Marya Alexandrovna Zaturenska. SP-ZatuM
Chorale for the Seasons. Marya Alexandrovna Zaturenska. SP-ZatuM
Chord. Langston Hughes. CP-HughL; CP-HughL3
Chords. Carl Sandburg. CP-SandC
Choros Sequence. "H. D." CP-DoolH
Choros Translations. Euripides. CP-DoolH Fr. Bacchae.
Chorus: "I heard of those eternal pains." Sophocles. CP-SherT Fr. Philoctetes.
Chorus: "What man is he that yearneth." Sophocles. SP-HousA Fr. Oedipus at Colonus.
Chorus for a Play. G. K. Chesterton. CP-ChesG
Chorus for One Voice. Charles Simic. SP-SimiC; SP-SimiCE
Chorus from Antigone, A. Sophocles. SP-LoguC Fr. Antigone.
Chorus of Old Men in "Ægeus," The. Edwin Arlington Robinson. CP-RobiE
Chorus of the Pities. Thomas Hardy. CP-HardT Fr. Dynasts, The.
Chorus of the weeds, unnameably, The. Weeds as Partial Survivors. Alan Dugan. CP-DugaA
Chorus of the Women of Chalkis. Euripides. CP-DoolH Fr. Iphigenia [or Iphigeneia] in Aulis.
Chorus of Troizenian Women. Euripides. CP-DoolH Fr. Hippolytus.

Chorus sing of escape, The. Euripides. CP-DoolH Fr. Hippolytus.
Chorus? / Words and silence, standing face to face. Responsory, A. Thomas Merton. CP-MertT
Choruses from "The Rock." T. S. Eliot. CP-ElioT
Chosen. G. K. Chesterton. CP-ChesG
Chosen. William Butler Yeats. CP-YeatW
Chosen, The. Thomas Hardy. CP-HardT
Chosen, The. Josephine Jacobsen. CP-JacoJ
Chosun. James Fenton. SP-FentJ
Chris-Cross; On Confusing Messrs. Morley and Robin. Dorothy Parker. CP-ParkD
Chrismus Is A-Comin'. Paul Laurence Dunbar. CP-DunbP
Chrismus on the Plantation. Paul Laurence Dunbar. CP-DunbP
Christ. Robert Herrick. CP-HerrR
Christ, The. James Whitcomb Riley. CP-RileJ
Christ, The. Jones Very. CP-VeryJ
Christ, / a mirror. Symbol. Federico García Lorca. CP-GarcF, tr. by Jerome Rothenberg Fr. Mirror Suite.
Christ Abiding Forever. Jones Very. CP-VeryJ
Christ bids the dumbe tongue speake, it speakes; the sound. Mark 7; The Dumbe Healed, and the People Enjoyned Silence. Bible, N.T. CP-CrasR Fr. St. Mark.
Christ broods over our heads. In a Greek Orthodox Church near Daphne. Raymond Carver. CP-CarvR
Christ but they're few. E. E. Cummings. CP-CummE
Christ but this earth goes over to the squall of time! Sunset Piece, The. Archibald MacLeish. CP-MacLA
Christ! Christ! Christ! that the world. Kenneth Patchen. CP-PatcK
Christ Church Meadows, [Oxford]. Donald Hall. CP-HallD
Christ crucified at daybreak. Palm Sunday. Adam Zagajewski. SP-ZagaA, tr. by Renata Gorczynski
Christ died for God and me. Conviction (i). Stevie Smith. CP-SmitS
Christ, dost thou live indeed? or are thy bones. Sonnet on the Massacre of the Christians in Bulgaria. Oscar Wilde. CP-WildO
Christ God who savest man, save most. Count Gismond. Robert Browning. CP-BroR1
Christ harrowed Hell in pity for all damned souls. Descent into Hell. Robert Graves. CP-GravR
Christ, He requires still, wheresoere He comes. Christs Part. Robert Herrick. CP-HerrR
Christ, I have read, did to His chaplains say. Salutation. Robert Herrick. CP-HerrR
Christ in Alabama. Langston Hughes. CP-HughL; CP-HughL3
Christ is a nigger, / Beaten and black. Christ in Alabama. Langston Hughes. CP-HughL; CP-HughL3
Christ is risen the preachers say, The. Easter Sunday. G. K. Chesterton. CP-ChesG
Christ is the population of the world. Jelaluddin Rumi. SP-Rumi, tr. by Coleman Barks
Christ is walking in your blood today. Villanelle: "Christ is walking in your blood today." Richard Eberhart. CP-EberR
Christ never did so great a work, but there. Christs Action. Robert Herrick. CP-HerrR
Christ on the cross; his feet touch the earth. Jorge Luis Borges. SP-BorgJ, tr. by Alexander Coleman
Christ passed before my shop, and as I spat. Ahasuerus. Howard Nemerov. CP-NemeH
Christ sprang from David Shepherd, and even so. Seed of David, The. Dante Gabriel Rossetti. CW-RossD
Christ that as the maggot. Vision and Prayer. Miller Williams. CP-WillM
Christ the dew in the clod. Johnny Appleseed's Hymn to the Sun. Nicholas Vachel Lindsay. CP-LindV
Christ the Judge, supposedly. On the Highest Column. Eugenio Montale. CP-MontE, tr. by Jonathan Galassi
Christ took our Nature on Him, not that He. Christs Incarnation. Robert Herrick. CP-HerrR
Christ used to be like you and me. Child's Christmas Carol. James Whitcomb Riley. CP-RileJ
Christ was not sad, i'th garden, for His own. Christs Sadnesse. Robert Herrick. CP-HerrR
Christ when he dy'd. Christs Victory. Richard Crashaw. CP-CrasR
Christ, when He hung the dreadfull Crosse upon. Christs Words on the Crosse, My God, My God. Robert Herrick. CP-HerrR
Christabel. Samuel Taylor Coleridge. CP-ColeS; MW-ColeS
Christall Violl Cupid brought, A. Upon Love. Robert Herrick. CP-HerrR
Christening, A. Donald Davie. CP-DaviDC
Christening, The. Thomas Hardy. CP-HardT
Christian. Ambrose Bierce. SP-BierA
Christian and Jew. A Dialogue. Christina Georgina Rossetti. CP-RosC1

Christian coin, The. Threnody: "Christian coin, The." William Carlos Williams. CP-WilW2

Christian Commonwealth, A. Jones Very. CP-VeryJ

Christian Country, A. Langston Hughes. CP-HughL; CP-HughL1

Christian Forbearance. William Blake. *See* Songs of Experience

Christian! going, gone!, A. Christian Slave, The. John Greenleaf Whittier. CP-WhitJ

Christian Hero, A. Donald Davie. CP-DaviDC

Christian Influence. Jones Very. CP-VeryJ

Christian Militant. Robert Herrick. CP-HerrR

Christian Slave, The. John Greenleaf Whittier. CP-WhitJ

Christian Social Union here, The. Christian Social Union, Nottingham, The. G. K. Chesterton. CP-ChesG

Christian Social Union, Nottingham, The. G. K. Chesterton. CP-ChesG

Christian Tourists, The. John Greenleaf Whittier. CP-WhitJ

Christina. Thomas Merton. CP-MertT

Christina, maiden of heroic mien! To Christina. John Milton. CP-CowpW

Christina (seven) skipped a stone. Homage to Christina Rossetti. John Logan. CP-LogaJ

Christine. James Whitcomb Riley. CP-RileJ

Christine's Song. James Whitcomb Riley. CP-RileJ

Christmas. Paul Laurence Dunbar. CP-DunbP

Christmas. George Herbert. CP-HerbG

Christmas. Laura Riding Jackson. CP-RidiL

Christmas. Robert Lowell. SP-LoweR

Christmas. Charles Olson. CP-OlsoC

Christmas. Fernando Pessoa. SP-PessF, *tr. by* Susan M. Brown *and* Edwin Honig

Christmas. A. K. Ramanujan. CP-RamaA

Christmas. Stevie Smith. CP-SmitS

Christmas. Jones Very. CP-VeryJ

Christmas Afterthought. James Whitcomb Riley. CP-RileJ

Christmas Alone in Key West. John Ciardi. CP-CiarJ

Christmas along the Wires. James Whitcomb Riley. CP-RileJ

Christmas as to People. Thomas Merton. CP-MertT

Christmas Canticle. Edna St. Vincent Millay. CP-MillE

Christmas Card, A. Thomas Merton. CP-MertT

Christmas Card, After the Assassinations, A. Mona Van Duyn. SP-VanDM

Christmas Carmen, A. John Greenleaf Whittier. CP-WhitJ

Christmas Carol: "Ring out, ye bells!" Paul Laurence Dunbar. CP-DunbP

Christmas Carol, A. G. K. Chesterton. CP-ChesG

Christmas Carol, A. Algernon Charles Swinburne. *See* Christmas Carol, A: "Three damsels in the queen's chamber"

Christmas Carol, A: "God rest you merry gentlemen." G. K. Chesterton. CP-ChesG

Christmas Carol, A: "In the bleak mid-winter." Christina Georgina Rossetti. CP-RosC1

Christmas Carol, A: "Shepherds went their hasty way, The." Samuel Taylor Coleridge. CP-ColeS

Christmas Carol, A: "Stores wore Christmas perfectly, The." John Ciardi. CP-CiarJ

Christmas Carol, A: "Thank God, thank God, we do believe." Christina Georgina Rossetti. CP-RosC3

Christmas Carol, A: "Three damsels in the queen's chamber." Algernon Charles Swinburne. SP-SwinA

  (Christmas Carol, A.) SP-SwinA

Christmas Carol, for My Godchildren, A. Christina Georgina Rossetti.

Christmas Caroll Sung to the King in the Presence at White-Hall, A. Robert Herrick. CP-HerrR

Christmas Carols. Christina Georgina Rossetti. CP-RosC2

Christmas Carols. Margaret Atwood. SP-AtwM2

Christmas Crown, A. Marilyn Hacker. SP-HackM

Christmas Day. Christina Georgina Rossetti. CP-RosC2

Christmas East of the Blue Ridge. Charles Wright. SP-WrigCN

Christmas-Eve. Robert Browning. CP-BroR1

Christmas Eve. A. R. Ammons. CP-AmmoA

Christmas Eve. John Ciardi. CP-CiarJ

Christmas Eve. Christina Georgina Rossetti. CP-RosC2

Christmas Eve. Muriel Rukeyser. CP-RukeM

Christmas Eve. Anne Sexton. CP-SextA

Christmas Eve, Alone. Charles Bukowski. SP-BukC1

Christmas Eve, and twelve of the clock. Oxen, The. Thomas Hardy. CP-HardT

Christmas Eve in Whitneyville, 1955. Donald Hall. CP-HallD

Christmas Eve: Nearing Midnight in New York. Langston Hughes. CP-HughL; CP-HughL3

Christmas Eve Service at Midnight at St. Michael's. Robert Bly. SP-BlyR

Christmas Eve, unseasonably cold. Leda Hidden. Kenneth Rexroth. CP-RexrK

Christmas Folksong, A. Paul Laurence Dunbar. CP-DunbP

Christmas Ghost-Story, A. Thomas Hardy. CP-HardT

Christmas Gifts. Elizabeth Barrett Browning. CP-BroEB

Christmas Glee, A. James Whitcomb Riley. CP-RileJ

Christmas Greeting. James Whitcomb Riley. CP-RileJ

Christmas Greeting, A. Walt Whitman. CP-WhitW

Christmas Greeting, A. James Wright. CP-WrigJ

Christmas hath a darkness. Christmas Eve. Christina Georgina Rossetti. CP-RosC2

Christmas His Masque. Ben Jonson.

  "Hum drum, sauce for a cony." CP-JonsB

  "Nor do you think that their legs is all." CP-JonsB

Christmas Hymn, A. Richard Wilbur. CP-WilbR

Christmas in India. Rudyard Kipling. CP-KiplR

Christmas in New York. Andrei Codrescu. SP-CodrA

Christmas in the Elgin Room. Thomas Hardy. CP-HardT

Christmas in the gleaming. Poems for Camillo Sbarbaro. Eugenio Montale. CP-MontE, *tr. by* Jonathan Galassi

Christmas in the Heart. Paul Laurence Dunbar. CP-DunbP

Christmas is as Christmas does. Christmas as to People. Thomas Merton. CP-MertT

Christmas Letter to a Psychiatrist. May Sarton. SP-SartM

Christmas Long Ago, The. James Whitcomb Riley. CP-RileJ

Christmas: May 10, 1970. Robert Creeley. CP-CreeR

Christmas Memory, A. James Whitcomb Riley. CP-RileJ

Christmas Morning. Howard Nemerov. CP-NemeH

Christmas 1950. William Carlos Williams. CP-WilW2

Christmas 1944. "H. D." CP-DoolH

Christmas, 1937. Laura Riding Jackson. CP-RidiL

Christmas: 1924. Thomas Hardy. CP-HardT

Christmas, 1921. Dorothy Parker. CP-ParkD

Christmas Note for Geraldine Udell, A. Kenneth Rexroth. CP-RexrK

Christmas of 1888, The. John Greenleaf Whittier. CP-WhitJ

Christmas on the Hudson. Federico García Lorca. CP-GarcF, *tr. by* Greg Simon *and* Steven F. White

Christmas Poem, A. Miller Williams. CP-WillM

Christmas Rhyme, A. G. K. Chesterton. CP-ChesG

Christmas Robin, The. Robert Graves. CP-GravR

Christmas Roses, The. Randall Jarrell. CP-JarrR

Christmas Season. James Whitcomb Riley. CP-RileJ

Christmas Shopping. Louis MacNeice. CP-MacNL

Christmas Star, The. Gabriela Mistral. SP-MistG, *tr. by* Maria Giachetti [*or* Jacketti]

Christmas Story, The. Langston Hughes. CP-HughL; CP-HughL3

Christmas Syllabics for a Wife. Donald Davie. CP-DaviDC

Christmas-Time Jingle, A. James Whitcomb Riley. CP-RileJ

Christmas Tree. Richard Eberhart. CP-EberR

Christmas Tree. Robert Lowell. SP-LoweR

Christmas Trees. Robert Frost. CP-FrosR

Christmas Trees. Geoffrey Hill. CP-HillG

Christmas trees are almost all sold, The. Christmas Eve: Nearing Midnight in New York. Langston Hughes. CP-HughL; CP-HughL3

Christmas Week, 1948. Donald Davie. CP-DaviDC

Christmasse-Eve, Another Ceremonie. Robert Herrick. CP-HerrR

Christmastide. Thomas Hardy. CP-HardT

Christmastide. Christina Georgina Rossetti. CP-RosC2

Christofo Colombo was a hungry man. Mysterious Biography. Carl Sandburg. CP-SandC

Christoper Robin. Czeslaw Milosz. CP-MiloCN, *tr. by* Robert Hass

Christopher Columbus. Thomas Merton. CP-MertT

Christopher Morley goes hippotty, hoppetty. Chris-Cross; On Confusing Messrs. Morley and Robin. Dorothy Parker. CP-ParkD

Christophori Columbi Tumulus. Hippolytus Capilupus. CP-PoEar, *tr. by* Ezra Pound

Christo's. Paul Muldoon. CP-MuldP

Christs Action. Robert Herrick. CP-HerrR

Christs Birth. Robert Herrick. CP-HerrR

Christ's Capture in the Garden: A Paraphrase. Jones Very. CP-VeryJ

Christ's Compassion. Jones Very. CP-VeryJ

Christ's Final Victory. Jones Very. CP-VeryJ

Christ's first portrait was a donkey's head. Words. Robert Lowell. SP-LoweR

Christ's Heart was wrung for me, if mine is sore. Surely He Hath Borne Our Griefs. Christina Georgina Rossetti. CP-RosC2

Christs Incarnation. Robert Herrick. CP-HerrR

Christs Part. Robert Herrick. CP-HerrR

Christs Sadnesse. Robert Herrick. CP-HerrR

Christs Suffering. Robert Herrick. CP-HerrR

Christs Twofold Coming. Robert Herrick. CP-HerrR

Christs Victory. Richard Crashaw. CP-CrasR

Christs Words on the Crosse, My God, My God. Robert Herrick. CP-HerrR

Christus Natus Est. Countee Cullen. CP-CullC

Christus of Guadalajara, The. Tennessee Williams. CP-WillT

Chromium-Plated Hat. Inlaid with Scenes from Siegfried, A. Howard Nemerov. CP-NemeH

Chromo. Carl Sandburg. CP-SandC

Chronic Condition, A. Richard Wilbur. CP-WilbR

"Chronic Kicker," The. Paul Laurence Dunbar. CP-DunbP

Chronicler is breathing, his heart is beating, The. Far Away. Czeslaw Milosz. CP-MiloCN, tr. by Robert Hass

Chronicles. Charles Olson. SP-OlsoC Fr. Maximus Poems, The.

Chronos, Chronos, mend thy pace. Secular Masque, The. John Dryden. SP-DrydJ

Chruchyard Song of Patient Hope, A. Christina Georgina Rossetti. CP-RosC2

Chrysalides. Thomas Kinsella. CP-KinsT

Chrysalis. Laura Riding Jackson. CP-RidiL

Chrysalis. Eugenio Montale. CP-MontE, tr. by Jonathan Galassi

Chrysanthemum. Louis Zukofsky. CP-ZukLS

Chrysanthemum, The. William Carlos Williams. CP-WilW2

Chrysanthemum and nightshade. Talking to IIis Reflection in a Shallow Pond. Ai. SP-Ai

Chrysanthemums become a cult because. Donald Davie. CP-DaviDC

Chrysanthemums last too long for these ravenous ladies. Starved Lovers. Archibald MacLeish. CP-MacLA

Chuang Tzu and Hui Tzu. Joy of Fishes, The. Chuang Tzu. CP-MertT

Chuang-tzu said for his funeral. Han-shan. CP-ColdM, tr. by Red Pine

Chuang Tzu with his bamboo pole. Turtle, The. Chuang Tzu. CP-MertT

Chuff, lately rich in name, in chattels, goods. On Chuff, Banks the Usurer's Kinsman. Ben Jonson. CP-JonsB

Ch'ui the draftsman / Could draw more perfect circles freehand. When the Shoe Fits. Chuang Tzu. CP-MertT

Chums, The. Theodore Roethke. CP-RoetT

Church, The. D. H. Lawrence. CP-LawrD

Church, The. W. S. Merwin. SP-MerwW

Church, The. Jones Very. CP-VeryJ

Church and State. William Butler Yeats. CP-YeatW

Church and the Wedding, The. Thomas Hardy. CP-HardT

Church bells toll a melancholy round, The. Written in Disgust of Vulgar Superstition. John Keats. CP-KeatJ

Church-Builder, The. Thomas Hardy. CP-HardT

Church flings forth a battled shade, The. Church-Builder, The. Thomas Hardy. CP-HardT

Church-Floor[e], The. George Herbert. CP-HerbG

Church Going. Philip Larkin. CP-LarkP

Church I hate, and have good reason, The. Verses on the Upright Judge. Jonathan Swift. CP-SwifJ

Church in the forest, The. Ash. W. S. Merwin. SP-MerwW

Church Interior. George Oppen. CP-OppGN

Church is a business, and the rich, The. After Lorca. Robert Creeley. CP-CreeR

Church is an iceberg, The. Winter Night. Charles Simic. SP-SimiC; SP-SimiCE

Church-Lock and Key. George Herbert. CP-HerbG

Church Militant. Donald Davie. CP-DaviDC

Church Militant, The. George Herbert. CP-HerbG

Church Monuments. George Herbert. CP-HerbG

Church-Music[k]. George Herbert. CP-HerbG

Church of Ireland. Donald Davie. CP-DaviDC

Church of Vico-Morcote [or Vice-Morcate], The. View by Color Photography on a Commercial Calendar. William Carlos Williams. CP-WilW2

Church Porch 1, The. Dante Gabriel Rossetti. CW-RossD

Church Porch 2, The. Dante Gabriel Rossetti. CW-RossD

Church-Porch, The. George Herbert. CP-HerbG

Church-Rents and Schisms. George Herbert. CP-HerbG

Church Romance, A. Thomas Hardy. CP-HardT

Churches of France, more welcoming than its inns and its poems, The. Adam Zagajewski. SP-ZagaA, tr. by Clare Cavanagh

Churchill's Death. Lorine Niedecker. CP-NiedL

Churchill's Funeral. Geoffrey Hill. CP-HillG

Churchill's Grave. Lord Byron. CP-Byron

Church's compass, if you please, The. Binnacle, The. Ambrose Bierce. SP-BierA

Churchyard Wall, The. Charles Tomlinson. CP-TomlC; SP-TomlC

Churning Day. Seamus Heaney. SP-HeanSO

Ci-gît l Foetus(unborn to not die). E. E. Cummings. CP-CummE

Ciano's. Robert Creeley. SP-CreeR

Cicada. Charles Wright. SP-WrigCN

Cicada Blue. Charles Wright. SP-WrigCN

Cicada fill up the bamboo thickets. Rainbow Body. Gary Snyder. CP-SnydG

Cicada! / Oh happy cicada! Federico García Lorca. CP-GarcF, tr. by Catherine Brown

Cicadas. Richard Wilbur. CP-WilbR

Cicadas are singing in the mulberry forest, The. Chant of the Frontiersman. Wang Ch'ang-ling. CP-WilW2

Cicero, the Sacrificial Killing. Robert Lowell. SP-LoweR

Cider. Paul Muldoon. CP-MuldP

Cider 5¢ A Glass. Donald Hall. CP-HallD

Cigarette smoke hanging on. Tomorrow. Raymond Carver. CP-CarvR

Cigarettes and Whiskey and Wild, Wild Women. Anne Sexton. CP-SextA

Cigarettes in my mouth. End of an Ethnic Dream, The. Jay Wright. SP-WrigJ

Cigarettes wetted with beer from. Coupons. Charles Bukowski. SP-BukC1

Cincinnatus in Utah. James Laughlin. CP-LaugJ

Cinder Hill. Tennessee Williams. CP-WillT

Cinderella. Olga Broumas. SP BrouO

Cinderella. Randall Jarrell. CP-JarrR

Cinderella. Sylvia Plath. CP-PlatS

Cinderella. Anne Sexton. CP-SextA

Cinderella at Big Sur. Yusef Komunyakaa. CP-KomuY

Cinderella's Story. Mona Van Duyn. SP-VanDM

Cindy, I've used my writing all my life. Sonnet: "Cindy, I've used my writing all my life." Hayden Carruth. CP CarHS Fr. Sonnets.

Cindy, the secret's out. Yes, you're addict-. Sonnet: "Cindy, the secret's out. Yes, you're addict-" Hayden Carruth. CP-CarHS Fr. Sonnets

Cinema is cruel, the. Image of Leda, An. Frank O'Hara. SP-OharF

Cinema of a Man. Archibald MacLeish. CP-MacLA

Cinna, give me the man, when all is done. Martial. CP-SherT, tr. by Thomas Sheridan

Cinnabar Hills rise up to the clouds, The. Han-shan. CP-ColdM, tr. by Red Pine

Cinnamon and rayon. Graduation. Langston Hughes. CP-HughL; CP-HughL2

Cino. Ezra Pound. CP-PoEar; SP-PounE

Cinos. Charles Olson. CP-OlsoC

Cinque Terre. Kenneth Rexroth. CP-RexrK

Cinquefoil. Louis Zukofsky. CP-ZukLS

Circe. W. H. Auden. CP-AudeW

Circe. Olga Broumas. SP-BrouO

Circe. "H. D." CP-DoolH

Circe. Louis MacNeice. CP-MacNL

Circe. Robert Stock. SP-StocR

Circe / Mud Poems. Margaret Atwood. SP-AtwM1

Circle. Robert Creeley. CP-CreeR

Circle, The. Robert Creeley. CP-CreeR

Circle, The. Fernando Pessoa. SP-PessF

Circle, a Square, a Triangle and a Ripple of Water, A. Jane Cooper. CP-CoopJ

Circle Game, The. Margaret Atwood. SP-AtwM1

Circle is broken, one seat is forsaken, The. Lament, A: "Circle is broken, one seat is forsaken, The." John Greenleaf Whittier. CP-WhitJ

Circle Jerk. Andrei Codrescu. SP-CodrA

Circle of Breath. William Stafford. SP-StafWW

Circle of Doors. Carl Sandburg. CP-SandC

Circle of her arms could be, The. Glaphira 3. Donald Davie. CP-DaviDC

Circle of saints, all, A. Weeper in Jalisco. Charles Tomlinson. CP-TomlC

Circle the mountain gently. For a Child. Peter Blue Cloud. SP-BlueP

Circles. A. R. Ammons. CP-AmmoA

Circles. Robert Creeley. SP-CreeR

Circles. Ralph Waldo Emerson. CP-EmerR

(Motto to "Circles.") CP-EmerR

Circles. Langston Hughes. CP-HughL; CP-HughL2

Circles spin round, The. Circles. Langston Hughes. CP-HughL; CP-HughL2

Circling the Sun, at a respectful distance. Problems Of Gender. Robert Graves. CP-GravR

Circuit. James Dickey. CP-DickJ

Circular, A. Thomas Hardy. CP-HardT

Circular moon saw-wheels through the oak-grove. 1930's. Robert Lowell. SP-LoweR

Circulation. Raymond Carver. CP-CarvR

Circulations of the Song. Robert Duncan. SP-DuncR

Circumambulating Arunachala. Gary Snyder. CP-SnydG

Circumference thou Bride of Awe. Emily Dickinson. CP-DickE

Circumstance. Unknown. CP-ShelP

Circumstance, The. Hart Crane. CP-CranH

Circumstances Alter Cases. Paul Laurence Dunbar. CP-DunbP

Circus. Louis MacNeice. CP-MacNL

Circus. Heather McHugh. SP-McHuH

Circus. Adam Zagajewski. SP-ZagaA, tr. by Clare Cavanagh

Circus, The. Kenneth Koch. SP-KochK

Circus Animals. Wisława Szymborska. SP-SzymWM, *tr.* by Joanna Trzeciak

Circus Animals' Desertion, The. William Butler Yeats. CP-YeatW

Circus-Day Parade, The. James Whitcomb Riley. CP-RileJ

Circus in Three Rings. Sylvia Plath. CP-PlatS

Circus Parade, The. James Whitcomb Riley. CP-RileJ

Circus-Rider to Ringmaster. Thomas Hardy. CP-HardT

Circus Ring. Robert Graves. CP-GravR

Circus Ringmaster's Apology to God, The. Norman Dubie. CP-DubiN

Circus!—The Circus!—The throb of the drums, The. Circus Parade, The. James Whitcomb Riley. CP-RileJ

Cirque d'Hiver. Elizabeth Bishop. CP-BishE

Cisma de Inglaterra. Pedro Calderón de la Barca. "Hast thou not seen, officious with delight." CP-ShelP

Cistercians might crack their sides. Hernani. George Meredith. CP-MerG1

Citation for Horace Gregory. Muriel Rukeyser. CP-RukeM

Cities. "H. D." CP-DoolH

Cities ("Official acropolis surpasses the most colossal conceptions of modern barbarity, The"). Arthur Rimbaud. CP-RimbA, *tr.* by Martin Sorrell

Cities ("These are cities! This is a people for whom these dream Alleghenies and these Lebanons have risen into being!"). Arthur Rimbaud. CP-RimbA, *tr.* by Martin Sorrell

Cities and Thrones and Powers. Rudyard Kipling. CP-KiplR *Fr.* Puck of Pook's Hill.

Cities are full of pride, The. To the City of Bombay. Rudyard Kipling. CP-KiplR

Cities arise . . . . Underground, The. Thomas McGrath. SP-McGrT

Cities of the Plain, The. Mona Van Duyn. SP-VanDM

Cities of the Plain, The. John Greenleaf Whittier. CP-WhitJ

Citizen. Robert Creeley. CP-CreeR

Citizen Dreaming, The. Thomas McGrath. SP-McGrT

Citizen, enemy, mama's boy, sucker, utter. Letter to an Archaeologist. Joseph Brodsky. CP-BrodJ

City. Gerrit Achterberg. CP-RicAE

City. Federico García Lorca. CP-GarcF, *tr.* by Jerome Rothenberg *Fr.* Palimpsests.

City. Langston Hughes. CP-HughL

City. W. S. Merwin. SP-MerwWF

City. Arthur Rimbaud. CP-RimbA, *tr.* by Martin Sorrell

City, The. Constantine P. Cavafy. CP-CavaC, *tr.* by Theoharis Constantine Theoharis

City, The. Robert Creeley. CP-CreeR

City, The. Czeslaw Milosz. CP-MiloC; CP-MiloCN, *tr.* by Robert Hass

City, The. Ogden Nash. CP-NashO

City, The. Jones Very. CP-VeryJ

City, a mountain, a river, A. Dr. Williams' Garden. Wyatt Prunty. SP-PrunW

City after Noon, The. Thomas Merton. CP-MertT

City, City! Randall Jarrell. CP-JarrR

City comes to a standstill, The. It Comes to a Standstill. Adam Zagajewski. SP-ZagaA

City Dark, The. Robert Pinsky. CP-PinsR

City Dead-House, The. Walt Whitman. CP-WhitW

City dense with covered passageways, narrow, A. For My Eighty-eighth Birthday. Czeslaw Milosz. CP-MiloCN, *tr.* by Robert Hass

City Dog goes to the drinking trough, The. Wild Dog, The. Stevie Smith. CP-SmitS

City Elegies. Robert Pinsky. CP-PinsR

City exulted, all in flowers, The. City, The. Czeslaw Milosz. CP-MiloC; CP-MiloCN, *tr.* by Robert Hass

City Flats, Coal yards and brown rivers. Wings Lifted over the Black Pit. Allen Ginsberg. CP-GinsA

City Garden in April, A. May Swenson. SP-SwenM

City had withdrawn into itself, The. Christmas Trees. Robert Frost. CP-FrosR

City has tits in rows, The. Grotesque. William Carlos Williams. CP-WilW1

City in the Sea, The. Edgar Allan Poe. CP-PoeEd

City is empty, like a dangerous area, The. Untitled Poem: "City is empty, like a dangerous area, The." Alan Dugan. CP-DugaA

City is quiet at dusk, The. City Where I Want to Live, The. Adam Zagajewski. SP-ZagaA, *tr.* by Clare Cavanagh

City lies grey and sopping like a dead rat, The. Butt of Winter, The. Marge Piercy. SP-PierM

City-Life. D. H. Lawrence. CP-LawrD

City lifts toward heaven from the continent of sleep, The. Dawn Song. Thomas McGrath. SP-McGrT

City Limits, The. A. R. Ammons. CP-AmmoA

City man got dust on his shoes and carried, The. Holcomb, Kansas. William Stafford. SP-StafWW

City Midnight Junk Strains. Allen Ginsberg. CP-GinsA; SP-GinsA

City Mouse and the Garden Mouse, The. Christina Georgina Rossetti. CP-RosC2

City mouse lives in a house, The. City Mouse and the Garden Mouse, The.

Christina Georgina Rossetti. CP-RosC2

City Number. Carl Sandburg. CP-SandC

City of Brass, The. Rudyard Kipling. CP-KiplR

City of factory owners, boxers, millionaires, The. Sinful City. Jaroslav Seifert. SP-SeifJ, *tr.* by Ewald Osers

City of God, The. Jones Very. CP-VeryJ

City of Keansburg, The. George Oppen. CP-OppGN

City of Monuments. Muriel Rukeyser. CP-RukeM

City of My Youth. Czeslaw Milosz. CP-MiloCN, *tr.* by Robert Hass

City of Orgies. Walt Whitman. CP-WhitW

City of Salt, The. Gregory Orr. SP-OrrG

City of Ships. Walt Whitman. CP-WhitW

City of Sleep, The. Rudyard Kipling. CP-KiplR

City of the corporations, A. Language of New York, A. George Oppen. CP-OppGN

City of the heart, The. Chapultepec Park / II. Muriel Rukeyser. CP-RukeM

City of the Moon, The. Kenneth Rexroth. CP-RexrK

City of the Olesha Fruit, The. Norman Dubie. CP-DubiN

City Planners, The. Margaret Atwood. SP-AtwM1

City plum is not a plum, A. Christina Georgina Rossetti. CP-RosC2

City Psalm. Denise Levertov. SP-LeveDP

City squats on my back, The. Route Six. Stanley Kunitz. CP-KunSC

City Talk. Lorine Niedecker. CP-NiedL

City That Will Not Repent, The. Nicholas Vachel Lindsay. CP-LindV

City Trees. Edna St. Vincent Millay. CP-MillE

City Unknown. Adam Zagajewski. SP-ZagaA, *tr.* by Renata Gorczynski

City we shared without knowing. Poem about Oxford. Philip Larkin. CP-LarkP

City Where I Want to Live, The. Adam Zagajewski. SP-ZagaA, *tr.* by Clare Cavanagh

City where I was born was destroyed by cannons, The. Yehuda Amichai. SP-AmicYL *Fr.* Poems of the Land of Zion and Jerusalem.

City where I was born was destroyed by gunfire, The. Yehuda Amichai. SP-AmicY, *tr.* by Chana Bloch *Fr.* Songs of Zion the Beautiful.

City without a Name. Czeslaw Milosz. CP-MiloC; CP-MiloCN, *tr.* by Renata Gorczynski, Robert Hass *and* Robert Pinsky

City without Walls. W. H. Auden. CP-AudeW

City's Death by Fire, A. Derek Walcott. CP-WalcD

City's Spring, The. Thomas Merton. CP-MertT

Civics. A. R. Ammons. CP-AmmoA

Civil Song. Pier Paolo Pasolini. SP-PasoP, *tr.* by Norman MacAfee *and* Luciano Martinengo

Civil War [Bellum Civile] *or* Pharsalia. Lucan. "Amid the storms of war, with curious eyes." CP-JohnS

Coracle, The. CP-RaleW

In the French Translation of Lucan by Monsieur De Brebeuf Are These Verses: Lib 3. CP-MarvA

"Just and fit actions, Ptolemy (he saith)." CP-JonsB, *tr.* by Ben Jonson

"No faith of partnership dominion owns." CP-JohnS

"None dares with impious steel the grove to rend." CP-JohnS

"O wastfull Riot, never well content." CP-RaleW

"Phoenicians first (if Fame may credit have)." CP-RaleW

"Wars worse than civil on Thessalian plains." CP-MarlC

"Why? thou great ruler of Olympus, why." CP-SherT

Civil War, The. Charles Olson. CP-OlsoC

Civil War, The. Anne Sexton. CP-SextA

Civil war photo. George Oppen. CP-OppGN

Civil world will much forgive, The. Ralph Waldo Emerson. CP-EmerR

Civilian for a pause of hours. Goodmorning with Light. John Ciardi. CP-CiarJ

Civilisation is hooped together, brought. Meru. William Butler Yeats. CP-YeatW

Civilities of Lamplight. Charles Tomlinson. CP-TomlC; SP-TomlC

Civility of nature overthrown, the. Autumn. Charles Tomlinson. CP-TomlC

Civilization—spurns—the Leopard! Emily Dickinson. CP-DickE

Civilizations are set up and knocked down. At the Gates of Tombs. Carl Sandburg. CP-SandC

Civilized, crying how to be human again: this will tell you how. Sign-Post. Robinson Jeffers. CP-JefR2

Clack, clack, clack, went the mill-wheel as I came. Second Visit, The. Thomas Hardy. CP-HardT

Clad All in Brown. Jonathan Swift. CP-SwifJ

Claim, The. Elizabeth Barrett Browning. CP-BroEB

Claims. Louis Zukofsky. CP-ZukLS

Claims of the sea, of the tide, move out, The. Nocturn 4: "Claims of the sea, of the tide, move out, The." Carl Sandburg. CP-SandC

Claire O'Reilly used her granny's stick. Two Stick Drawings. Seamus Heaney. SP-HeanSO

Clairvaux. Thomas Merton. CP-MertT

Clairvaux Prison. Thomas Merton. CP-MertT

Clam Diggers and Diggers of Sea Worms, The. Richard Eberhart. CP-EberR

Clam Man. Mary Oliver. SP-OlivM

Clambering up the Cold Mountain path. Han-shan. CP-SnydG

Clamminess hangs all over like a clout, A. Suspense. Thomas Hardy. CP-HardT

Clamor of gulls / outside the French windows, A. Triste Corbiére. Lawrence Ferlinghetti. SP-FerlL

Clamorous evenings, when the swing. Low Tide. Eugenio Montale. CP-MontE, *tr. by* Jonathan Galassi

Clan, The. John Updike. CP-UpdiJ

Clan of imps—morose and ugly things, A. Paper Palace, The. E. E. Cummings. CP-CummE

Clang clang / The air, having been killed. Portico ("Clang clang / The air, having been killed"). Federico García Lorca. CP GarcF, *tr. by* Jerome Rothenberg *Fr.* In the Garden of the Lunar Grapefruits.

Clapper hovers, but why run so hard?, The. Surviving Love. John Berryman. CP-BerrJ

Clapping blackness of the wings of pointed cormorants, the great indolent planes, The. Cycle, The. Robinson Jeffers. CP-JefR1

Clara, there's a hole. Street Cool Clara. Yusef Komunyakaa. CP-KomuY

Clara walked in the garden with the children. Memories of the Ancient World. Carlos Drummond de Andrade. CP-MertT

Clarabelle has golden hair. Song: "Clarabelle has golden hair." Dorothy Parker. CP-ParkD

Clarance Mangan. Thomas Kinsella. CP-KinsT

Clare was the friend of Francis. To Clare Nicholl. G. K. Chesterton. CP-ChesG

Clarel: A Poem and Pilgrimage in the Holy Land. Herman Melville.
  Arch, The. SP-MelvH
  Empty Stirrups. SP-MelvH
  Epilogue: "If Luther's day expand to Darwin's year." SP-MelvH
  Inscription, The: "While yet Rolfe's foot in stirrup stood." SP-MelvH
  Mortmain Reappears. SP-MelvH
  Of Wickedness the Word. SP-MelvH
  Prelusive. SP-MelvH
  Sketch, A. SP-MelvH
  Ungar and Rolfe. SP-MelvH
  Via Crucis. SP-MelvH
  Vine and Clarel. SP-MelvH

Clarence, my boy-friend, hale and strong! Boy-Friend, The. James Whitcomb Riley. CP-RileJ

Clarinda. Robert Burns. CP-BurnR

Clarinda, mistress of my soul. Clarinda. Robert Burns. CP-BurnR

Clarissa draws her scissors from their case. Another Picture of Dun. Thomas Sheridan. CP-SherT

Claritas. Denise Levertov. SP-LeveDP; SP-LeveDS

Clarity. A. R. Ammons. CP-AmmoA

(Clarity! clarity!) a semblance of motion, omniscience. Ted Berrigan. SP-BerrT *Fr.* Sonnets, The.

Clark Street Bridge. Carl Sandburg. CP-SandC

Clarkson! it was an obstinate hill to climb. To Thomas Clarkson, on the Final Passing of the Bill for the Abolition of the Slave Trade. March, 1807. William Wordsworth. CP-WorW1

Clash. William Stafford. SP-StafW; SP-StafWW

Clash in Arms of the Achaians and Trojans. Homer. CP-MerG1, *tr. by* George Meredith *Fr.* Iliad, The.

Clash of arms, which shook the Persian state, The. Abdolonymus—The Sidonian. Jones Very. CP-VeryJ

Clasped Skeleton, The. Thomas Hardy. CP-HardT

Clasping her magic. After the ball. James Merrill. SP-MerrJ

Clasping of Hands. George Herbert. CP-HerbG

Class. Jane Cooper. CP-CoopJ

Class. Charles Tomlinson. CP-TomlC

Class, The. Josephine Jacobsen. CP-JacoJ

Class-children are singing in school. Children Singing in School. D. H. Lawrence. CP-LawrD

Class of 1934. Kenneth Patchen. CP-PatcK

Class Will Come to Order, The. Stanley Kunitz. CP-KunSC

Classes. D. H. Lawrence. CP-LawrD

Classic. A. R. Ammons. CP-AmmoA

Classic, The. Wisława Szymborska. SP-SzymW, *tr. by* Stanisław Barańczak *and* Clare Cavanagh

Classic Ballroom Dances. Charles Simic. SP-SimiC; SP-SimiCE

Classic Picture. William Carlos Williams. CP-WilW2

Classic Scene. William Carlos Williams. CP-WilW1

Classical ballet, let's say, is beauty's keep, The. Joseph Brodsky. CP-BrodJ, *tr. by* Alan Myers

Classical Optical. John Updike. CP-UpdiJ

Classical Proportions of the Heart. Eleanor Wilner. SP-WilnE

Classical Tragedy. Sam Hamill. SP-HamiS

Classicality Applied to Tea-Dealing: A Fancy Inspired by Westbourne Grove. Robert Browning. CP-BroR2

Classmate, The. Adrienne Rich. CP-RicAE

Clatter of hooves on cobblestone, The. Treblinka Lights. Sam Hamill. SP-HamiS

Claude Matthews. James Whitcomb Riley. CP-RileJ

Claudia is a multitude of Jews. Two Poets in Mexico. Yehuda Amichai. SP-AmicYL, *tr. by* Benjamin Harshav *and* Barbara Harshav

Claus von Stauffenberg. Thom Gunn. CP-GunnT

Clavering. Edwin Arlington Robinson. CP-RobiE

Clavichord. Walter De la Mare. CP-DeLaW

Clavichord, The. May Sarton. SP-SartM

Claw at his eyes, O carrion crow. Carrion Crow, The. Archibald MacLeish. CP-MacLA

Clay. Ivor Gurney. SP-GurnI

Clay, The. Jones Very. CP-VeryJ

Clay Bison in a Cave. Clarence Major. SP-MajoC

Clay Hill Anthology, The. Hayden Carruth.
  "Again on dark looms." CP-CarHS
  "Against the wall he / gropes like ivy, you pray, I." CP-CarHS
  "All my life that's been / the watchword: Resist! Resist!" CP-CarHS
  "Always this special / secret feeling, the failure." CP-CarHS
  "Am I wrong? The roads." CP-CarHS
  "Because in the heart / of darkness I could not see." CP-CarHS
  "Coarse leaf, alder leaf." CP-CarHS
  "Dawn. Hoar on the grass." CP-CarHS
  "Ducks, waking at sea." CP-CarHS
  "Ecstasy is the / disaster of pleasure": this." CP-CarHS
  "Electroshock. Bang—" CP-CarHS
  "Emptiness—you know." CP-CarHS
  "Excellence requires / leaf-rakers to sweep one spot." CP-CarHS
  "Fathers die, but sons." CP-CarHS
  "For your love given." CP-CarHS
  "Forward! You must. Keep." CP-CarHS
  "Hard journey—yes, A." CP-CarHS
  "Have you ever seen." CP-CarHS
  "He: Life is an old / casino in the park. I." CP-CarHS
  "Hey, Basho, you there!" CP-CarHS
  "I live where Frost lived." CP-CarHS
  "Ideas hit life like / planks hitting water. Some skim." CP-CarHS
  "Imagine bird bones." CP-CarHS
  "Last year of youth, The." CP-CarHS
  "Let my snow-tracks lead." CP-CarHS
  "Look, a cypress tree." CP-CarHS
  "Mansion burned. Maids, The." CP-CarHS
  "Niobe, your tears." CP-CarHS
  "No, I was wrecked here." CP-CarHS
  "October. Twilight / flutters like cloth of silver." CP-CarHS
  "Of course make love not." CP-CarHS
  "One ant turns backward." CP-CarHS
  "Out of the garden." CP-CarHS
  "Over and over." CP-CarHS
  "Parting up/down from / one on the shore, two egrets—." CP-CarHS
  "Reversions, always." CP-CarHS
  "Sanskrit root word, The." CP-CarHS
  "Shadow sprang out, The." CP-CarHS
  "She lay like a book." CP-CarHS
  "Shirt, britches, paper." CP-CarHS
  "Sigh, you seven seas." CP-CarHS
  "Steeple bush, hardhack." CP-CarHS
  "There! Whitman's skull—." CP-CarHS
  "Therefore to us, time's / final lesson: be content." CP-CarHS
  "They gave me in trust." CP-CarHS
  "Today my poems seem / only the spells I muttered." CP-CarHS
  "Trees, the naked trees." CP-CarHS
  "True, I happen. So." CP-CarHS
  "Tsar, who knew you? Who." CP-CarHS
  "Well, beat on, beat on." CP-CarHS
  "Why speak of the use / of poetry? Poetry." CP-CarHS
  "Wise child is born, The." CP-CarHS
  "Women like new brooms." CP-CarHS
  "You—Spanish-speaking." CP-CarHS

Clay our mothers feed us with is taken, The. Clay. Ivor Gurney. SP-GurnI

Clay out of Silence. C. K. Williams. CP-WillC; SP-WillC

Clay somnambule returned / after many years away. Paris Transformations. Lawrence Ferlinghetti. SP-FerlL

Clay-tan, eyeless. Clay Bison in a Cave. Clarence Major. SP-MajoC

Clay tone your purple arrives. Grassflower. Louis Zukofsky. CP-ZukLS

Cle— / 1600 men to a stone. Please mention. Egypt. Kenneth Patchen. CP-PatcK

Clean Conscience Never Relaxes, A. Ogden Nash. CP-NashO

Clean Curtains. Carl Sandburg. CP-SandC

Clean Hands. Carl Sandburg. CP-SandC

Clean Old Man. Charles Bukowski. SP-BukC1

Clean Platter, The. Ogden Nash. CP-NashO

Clean the spittoons, boy. Brass Spittoons. Langston Hughes. CP-HughL; CP-HughL1

Clean used ones, of course. Also a dresser scarf, woven with a pattern. "Used Handkerchiefs 5¢." James Schuyler. CP-SchuJ

Cleaned all surfaces. Lorine Niedecker. CP-NiedL

Clear and Colder. Robert Frost. CP-FrosR

Clear blue temple I'm taken in. Flower Parry. Olga Broumas. SP-BrouO

Clear bright morning, with its scented air, The. Fair Morning, The. Jones Very. CP-VeryJ

Clear Day and No Memories, A. Wallace Stevens. CP-StevWP

Clear Days, The. Wendell Berry. CP-BerrW

Clear Eyes. Walter De la Mare. CP-DeLaW

Clear fountain. / Clear sky. Front Page. Federico García Lorca. CP-GarcF, tr. by Jerome Rothenberg Fr. Palimpsests.

Clear, fresh, and pleasant water. Petrarch. CP-Petra, tr. by J. G. Nichols

Clear green stars / Rise and set: / Peaceful dragon. Submerged Dragon. Thomas Merton. CP-MertT

Clear is my love but shadowed. Madrigale: "Clear is my love but shadowed." Ezra Pound. CP-PoEar

Clear knowledge having come. Logic. Robert Graves. CP-GravR

Clear lamps and dim stars. London. Ivor Gurney. SP-GurnI

Clear Midnight, A. Walt Whitman. CP-WhitW

Clear moments are so short. Moment. Adam Zagajewski. SP-ZagaA, tr. by Renata Gorczynski

Clear night after four days' rain. Sky Diving. Charles Wright. SP-WrigCN

Clear [or Cleere] are her eyes. Upon Her Eyes. Robert Herrick. CP-HerrR

Clear running stream. Running Water Music II. Gary Snyder. CP-SnydG

Clear Skies, The. W. S. Merwin. SP-MerwW

Clear smoke, / a fire in the far off. Fire. Robert Creeley. CP-CreeR

Clear the music, clear the message, the mind clear. Placation of Reality. Richard Eberhart. CP-EberR

Clear Vision, The. John Greenleaf Whittier. CP-WhitJ

Clear water in a brilliant bowl. Poems of Our Climate, The. Wallace Stevens. CP-StevW; CP-StevWP

Clear water; salty as childhood tears. Memory. Arthur Rimbaud. CP-RimbA, tr. by Martin Sorrell

Clear weather of juniper, The. Sloe Gin. Seamus Heaney. SP-HeanSO

Clearances. Seamus Heaney. SP-HeanSO

Cleared. Rudyard Kipling. CP-KiplR

Clearing. A. R. Ammons. CP-AmmoA

Clearing. Tess Gallagher. SP-GallT

Clearing, The. Wendell Berry. CP-BerrW

Clearing, The. Thomas Kinsella. CP-KinsT

Clearing her forehead, A. Brisk wilderness. Sketch for a Landscape. May Swenson. SP-SwenM

Clearing the Dark Symbiosis. A. R. Ammons. CP-AmmoA

Clearing the Title. James Merrill. SP-MerrJ

Clearlit the seeds / I swam unto. Paul Celan. SP-CelaP, tr. by John Felstiner

Clearly my ruined garden as it stood. Edna St. Vincent Millay. CP-MillE

Clearness. Richard Wilbur. CP-WilbR

Cleavage. A. R. Ammons. CP-AmmoA

Clefs. Carl Sandburg. CP-SandC

Clemency. Robert Herrick. CP-HerrR

Clemency in Kings. Robert Herrick. CP-HerrR

Clementene. Jane Cooper. CP-CoopJ

Cleon. Robert Browning. CP-BroR1; SP-BroR

Cleon the poet (from the sprinkled isles). Cleon. Robert Browning. CP-BroR1; SP-BroR

Cleopatra. Anna Andreyevna Akhmatova. CP-KunSC, tr. by Max Hayward and Stanley Kunitz

Cleopatra. George Meredith. CP-MerG2

Cleopatra built / like a smooth arrow or. E. E. Cummings. CP-CummE

Cleopatra to the Asp. Ted Hughes. SP-HughTN

Cleopompus and Heliodemus, whose philosophy. "Rubén Dario." SP-DariR, tr. by Alberto Acereda and Will Derusha

Clepsydra. John Ashbery. SP-AshbJ

Clergyman's Second Tale, The. Arthur Hugh Clough. SP-ClouA Fr. Mari Magno.

Cleric, The. Seamus Heaney. SP-HeanSO Fr. Sweeney Redivivus.

Clerical Oppressors. John Greenleaf Whittier. CP-WhitJ

Clerihew for Alan Gaylord, A. Richard Eberhart. CP-EberR

Clerk Bukashkin is our neighbor, The. Antiworlds. Andrey Andreievich Voznesensky. CP-WilbR

Clerk half skips away in his jaunty-officious hurry, The. Writing. Rae Armantrout. SP-ArmaA

Clerks, The. Edwin Arlington Robinson. CP-RobiE

Clerks and the Bells, The. Rudyard Kipling. CP-KiplR

Cleveland, Oh? Kenneth Patchen. CP-PatcK

Cleveland, the Flats. Allen Ginsberg. CP-GinsA

Clever, defensive, seasoned animals. Winter Day in Ohio, A. James Wright. CP-WrigJ

Clever little Willie wee, / Bright eyed, blue eyed little fellow. Christina Georgina Rossetti. CP-RosC2

Clever Tom Clinch Going to Be Hanged. Jonathan Swift. CP-SwifJ

Click here / to express your view. Words. Rae Armantrout. SP-ArmaA

Clicking in rock pasturage. Idyll of Ascension. Alan Dugan. CP-DugaA

Cliff, The. Gregory Orr. SP-OrrG

Cliff and Wave. Robert Graves. CP-GravR

Cliff Dwelling. A. Robert Frost. CP-FrosR

Cliff Edge, The. Robert Graves. CP-GravR

Cliff Klingenhagen. Edwin Arlington Robinson. CP-RobiE

Cliff Temple, The. "H. D." CP-DoolH

Cliffs. Henry David Thoreau. CP-ThorH

Cliffs come sheering down into woodland here. Casarola. Charles Tomlinson. CP-TomlC; SP-TomlC

Climate and Lyre. Radovan Pavlovski. CP-KizeC, tr. by Carolyn Kizer

Climate of Thought, The. Robert Graves. CP-GravR

Climate of War, The. Kenneth Patchen. CP-PatcK

Climatic Sorcery. James Whitcomb Riley. CP-RileJ

Climb at court for me that will. Seneca. CP-MarvA, tr. by Andrew Marvell Fr. Thyestes.

Climb Down, O Lordly Mind. D. H. Lawrence. CP-LawrD

Climb / into a jar. Pithos. Rita Dove. SP-DoveR

Climb / through my hair, climb in. Rapunzel. Olga Broumas. SP-BrouO

Climbed from the road and found. Latitude, Longitude. George Oppen. CP-OppGN

Climbing a path which leads back never more. O. W. Holmes on His Eightieth Birthday. John Greenleaf Whittier. CP-WhitJ

Climbing alone all day long. Incarnation. Kenneth Rexroth. CP-RexrK

Climbing along the River. William Stafford. SP-StafWW

Climbing Down. D. H. Lawrence. CP-LawrD

Climbing Milestone Mountain, August 22, 1937. Kenneth Rexroth. CP-RexrK

Climbing northward. Herds. The. W. S. Merwin. SP-MerwW

Climbing the heights of Berkeley. City That Will Not Repent, The. Nicholas Vachel Lindsay. CP-LindV

Climbing the Hill within the Deafening Wind. Philip Larkin. CP-LarkP

Climbing the stairway gray with urban midnight. Effort at Speech. William Meredith. SP-MereW

Climbing through the January snow, into the Lobo canyon. Mountain Lion. D. H. Lawrence. CP-LawrD

Climbing to Colonnata past ravines. Above Carrara. Charles Tomlinson. CP-TomlC; SP-TomlC

Climbing to reach the costly Hearts. Emily Dickinson. CP-DickE

Climbing Up. D. H. Lawrence. CP-LawrD

Clinging Vine, The. Edwin Arlington Robinson. CP-RobiE

Clings to the shadows, a wan silhouette. Frost. Charles Tomlinson. CP-TomlC

Clinton South of Polk. Carl Sandburg. CP-SandC

Clip cuticle; drink orange juice. Epigrams & Imitations. Philip Whalen. SP-WhalP

Clive. Robert Browning. CP-BroR2; SP-BroR

Cloak, A. Denise Levertov. SP-LeveDS

Cloak, The. Robert Graves. CP-GravR

Cloak, the Boat, and the Shoes, The. William Butler Yeats. CP-YeatW

Cloakroom pegs are empty now, The. School in August, The. Philip Larkin. CP-LarkP

Cloathes, Are Conspirators. Robert Herrick. CP-HerrR

Cloaths for Continuance. Robert Herrick. CP-HerrR

Clochard. Wisława Szymborska. SP-SzymW, tr. by Stanislaw Barańczak and Clare Cavanagh

Clock. Robert Creeley. SP-CreeR

Clock, The. Charles Baudelaire. CP-BaudC, tr. by Walter Martin

Clock, The. Thom Gunn. CP-GunnT

Clock, The. Josephine Jacobsen. CP-JacoJ

Clock, The. Jones Very. CP-VeryJ

Clock Echo. Federico García Lorca. CP-GarcF, tr. by Jerome Rothenberg Fr. In the Forest of Clocks.

Clock in the Mirror, The. John Ciardi. CP-CiarJ

Clock in the Square, A. Adrienne Rich. CP-RicAE

Clock in the Tower of the Church, The. Randall Jarrell. CP-JarrR

Clock is getting ready to strike forever o'clock, A. Forever O'Clock. Robert Penn Warren. CP-WarrR

Clock of my days winds down, The. Alligator Bride, The. Donald Hall. CP-HallD

Clock of the Years, The. Thomas Hardy. CP-HardT

Clock of the Years, The. William Carlos Williams. CP-WilW2

Clock on the parlor wall, stout as a mariner's clock, The. Day I Was Older, The. Donald Hall. CP-HallD

Clock stopped, A. Emily Dickinson. CP-DickE

Clock strikes one one one, The. News of the Assassin. W. S. Merwin. SP-MerwW

Clock strikes one that just struck two, The. Emily Dickinson. CP-DickE

Clock-Winder, The. Thomas Hardy. CP-HardT

Clock With No Hands, A. Howard Nemerov. CP-NemeH

Clocks. Carl Sandburg. CP-SandC

Clocks are wrong, watches. After the Blackout (1965). Jane Cooper. CP-CoopJ

Clocks begin, civicly simultaneous, The. At Delft. Charles Tomlinson. CP-TomlC

Clocks belled twelve. Main Street showed otherwise. Owl. Sylvia Plath. CP-PlatS

Clocks cannot tell our time of day. W. H. Auden. CP-AudeW

Clocks cry: stillness is a lie, my dear. To Eva Descending the Stair. Sylvia Plath. CP-PlatS

Clocks lose their tongues. At Zero. A. K. Ramanujan. CP-RamaA

Clocks of time divide us, The. Song: The Clocks of Time. Robert Graves. CP-GravR

Clock's untiring fingers wind the wool of darkness, The. Cradle Song: "Clock's untiring fingers wind the wool of darkness, The." Louis MacNeice. CP-MacNL

Clod and the Pebble, The. William Blake. CP-BlakW Fr. Songs of Experience.

Cloister gardens, secluded, and poppies: a drowsy noon. Siege. Dan Pagis. SP-PagiD, tr. by Stephen Mitchell

Cloistered. Sam Hamill. SP-HamiS

Cloistered. Seamus Heaney. SP-HeanSO

Cloistered as the snail and conch. Lady in the Single, The. Louise Glück. SP-GlucL

Cloisters, The. Jorge Luis Borges. SP-BorgJ, tr. by W. S. Merwin

Clonfeacle. Paul Muldoon. CP-MuldP

Clora come view my Soul, and tell. Gallery, The. Andrew Marvell. CP-MarvA

Clorinda and Damon. Andrew Marvell. CP-MarvA

Close as I ever came to seeing things. Seeing Things. Howard Nemerov. CP-NemeH

Close bound in a familiar bed. Prometheus. Robert Graves. CP-GravR

Close by the threshold of a door nail'd fast. Colubriad, The. William Cowper. CP-CowpW

Close Echo hears the woodman's axe. Woodman and Echo. George Meredith. CP-MerG1

Close, eyes, and soul, come home! Lent. Thomas Merton. CP-MertT

Close keep your lips, if that you meane. To Women, to Hide Their Teeth, if They Be Rotten or Rusty. Robert Herrick. CP-HerrR

Close-mouthed lexicon of facts, A. Hard Facts. Robert Stock. SP-StocR

Close-mouthed you sat five thousand years and never let out a whisper. Sphinx, A. Carl Sandburg. CP-SandC

Close of Summer, The. Adam Zagajewski. SP-ZagaA, tr. by Renata Gorczynski, Benjamin Ivry and C. K. Williams

Close the book and dim the light. His Vigil. James Whitcomb Riley. CP-RileJ

Close the book, and leave the tale. James Whitcomb Riley. CP-RileJ

Close the shutters. Let the ceiling fly. La Foce. Archibald MacLeish. CP-MacLA

Close to each other, the coffeehouse, the drug strore, the candy shop. Reverential Comparison. Yannis Ritsos. SP-RitsY, tr. by Kimon Friar

Close to Me. Gabriela Mistral. SP-MistG, tr. by Maria Giachetti [or Jacketti]

Close to the best known Author, Umbra sits. Umbra. Alexander Pope. CP-PopeA

Close to the gates a spacious garden lies. Gardens of Alcinous, The. Homer. CP-PopeA, tr. by Alexander Pope Fr. Odyssey.

Close-up. A. R. Ammons. CP-AmmoA

Close Up. Fanny Howe. SP-HoweF

Close up the casement, draw the blind. Shut Out That Moon. Thomas Hardy. CP-HardT

Close your eyes, my love, let me make you blind! These Clever Women. D. H. Lawrence. CP-LawrD

Closed car—closed in glass. George Oppen. CP-OppGN

Closed coaches were coming. Saint Raphael (Córdoba). Federico García Lorca. SP-GarcF, tr. by Rolfe Humphries

Closed coaches were coming. St. Raphael. Federico García Lorca. CP-GarcF, tr. by Will Kirkland

Closed for Good. Robert Frost. CP-FrosR

Closed Gentian Distances. James Schuyler. CP-SchuJ

Closed House. Charles Simic. SP-SimiCE

Closed in a final rain. Distinctions at Dusk. James Vincent Cunningham. CP-CunnJ

Closed like confessionals, they thread. Ambulances. Philip Larkin. CP-LarkP

Closed now his shining eyes, that dazzled so. Michelangelo Buonarroti. CP-Miche, tr. by John Frederick Nims

Closed up like a mouth after a cry. After Rilke. Heather McHugh. SP-McHuH

Closed World, The. Denise Levertov. SP-LeveDP; SP-LeveDS

Closeness of life to death. First Rain on a Burned Car. Yehuda Amichai. SP-AmicY, tr. by Chana Bloch

Closer that I come to that last day, The. Petrarch. CP-Petra, tr. by J. G. Nichols

Closest at lampfall. Lampfall. Derek Walcott. CP-WalcD

Closing Album, The. Louis MacNeice. CP-MacNL

Closing Ceremonies for the Bicentennial. Eleanor Wilner. SP-WilnE

Closing the book, I find I have left my head. Afternoon in the Stacks, An. William Stafford. SP-StafWW

Closing the heavy volume of Montaigne. Emerson. Jorge Luis Borges. SP-BorgJ, tr. by Alastair Reid

Closing the House. Miller Williams. CP-WillM

Closing the Jaffa Port. Yehuda Amichai. SP-AmicYL, tr. by Benjamin Harshav and Barbara Harshav

Closing Time. Langston Hughes. CP-HughL; CP-HughL1

Closing Time at the Second Avenue Deli. Alan Dugan. CP-DugaA

Cloth of the Tempest, The. Kenneth Patchen. CP-PatcK

Clothed upon with house from heaven. Hymn: The Spiritual Body. Jones Very. CP-VeryJ

Clothed with the wind, light in the light. Lady on a Balcony, A. Randall Jarrell. CP-JarrR

Clother of the lily, Feeder of the sparrow. They Toil Not, Neither Do They Spin. Christina Georgina Rossetti. CP-RosC2

Clothes. Hans Magnus Enzensberger. SP-EnzeH

Clothes. Anne Sexton. CP-SextA; SP-SextA

Clothes. Wisława Szymborska. SP-SzymW, tr. by Stanislaw Barańczak and Clare Cavanagh

Clothes and the inscrutable small jack are white, The. Lawn Bowlers, The. Josephine Jacobsen. CP-JacoJ

Clothes Do But Cheat and Cozen [or Cousen] Us. Robert Herrick. CP-HerrR

Clothes Maketh the Man. Theodore Weiss. SP-WeisT

Clothesline post is set, The. Lorine Niedecker. CP-NiedL

Clothing of green, deep crimson, black, or purple. Petrarch. CP-Petra, tr. by J. G. Nichols

Clotted cream and heather, Bronte way to heavenshire. Fanny Howe. SP-HoweF Fr. O'Clock.

Cloud. Kathleen Jessie Raine. SP-RainK

Cloud, The. Ivor Gurney. SP-GurnI

Cloud, The. Robert Herrick. CP-HerrR

Cloud, The. Raissa Maritain. CP-MertT

Cloud, The. Percy Bysshe Shelley. CP-ShelP

Cloud and Flame. John Berryman. CP-BerrJ

Cloud and Wind. Dante Gabriel Rossetti. CW-RossD Fr. House of Life, The.

Cloud Chamber, The. Arthur Sze. SP-SzeA

Cloud Change. Charles Tomlinson. CP-TomlC

Cloud—cloud—cloud— hurls. It. Gary Snyder. CP-SnydG

Cloud Confines, The. Dante Gabriel Rossetti. CW-RossD

Cloud creates the face of a man who, happening to look up, A. David Ignatow. SP-IgnaD

Cloud fell down from the heavens, A. Starry Night, A. Paul Laurence Dunbar. CP-DunbP

Cloud formation looks, The. From 20,000 Feet. Heather McHugh. SP-McHuH

Cloud in the morning. Fate. W. S. Merwin. SP-MerwWF

Cloud in the sky, A. Cloud, The. Raissa Maritain. CP-MertT

Cloud is free only, The. Law That Marries All Things, The. Wendell Berry. CP-BerrW

Cloud, like that the old-time Hebrew saw, A. Storm on Lake Asquam. John Greenleaf Whittier. CP-WhitJ

Cloud looked in at the window, The. Changing Time. Paul Laurence Dunbar. CP-DunbP

Cloud-maidens that float on for ever [or forever]. Aristophanes. CP-WildO Fr. Clouds, The.

Cloud-Mobile, The. May Swenson. SP-SwenM

Cloud moved close, A. The bulk of the wind shifted. Visitant, The. Theodore Roethke. CP-RoetT

Cloud of dusk gathers in the room, The. Three Voices. Adam Zagajewski. SP-ZagaA, tr. by Renata Gorczynski

Cloud Poems. Denise Levertov. SP-LeveDL

Cloud-puffball, torn tufts, tossed pillows flaunt forth, then chevy on an air-. That

Nature Is a Heraclitean Fire and of the Comfort of the Resurrection. Gerard Manley Hopkins. CP-HopkG

Cloud Seeding. Howard Nemerov. CP-NemeH

Cloud Shadow, A. Robert Frost. CP-FrosR

Cloud Shadows. John Updike. CP-UpdiJ

Cloud that shifts. Shade. Rainer Maria Rilke. CP-RilkFr, *tr.* by A. Poulin, Jr.

Cloud upon cloud / Clouds after rain. Ralph Waldo Emerson. CP-EmerR

Cloud upon cloud / The world is seeming. Ralph Waldo Emerson. CP-EmerR

Cloud was on the mind of men, and wailing went the weather, A. To Edmund Clerihew Bentley. G. K. Chesterton. CP-ChesG

Cloud withdrew from the Sky, A. Emily Dickinson. CP-DickE

Cloudberry Summer. Amy Clampitt. CP-ClamA

Cloudburst and steady downpour now. Gifts of Rain. Seamus Heaney. SP-HeanSO

Clouded Morning, The ("Morning comes, and thickening clouds prevail, The"). Jones Very. CP-VeryJ

Clouded Morning, The ("Morning comes; and thickening fogs prevail, The"). Jones Very. CP-VeryJ

Clouded with snow / The cold winds blow. Winter. Walter De la Mare. CP-DeLaW

Cloudless night like this, A. Walk After Dark, A. W. H. Auden. CP-AudeW

Clouds ("High in the air these placid mountains or"). Jorge Luis Borges. SP-BorgJ, *tr.* by Willis Barnstone

Clouds ("There cannot be a single thing which is"). Jorge Luis Borges. SP-BorgJ, *tr.* by Willis Barnstone

Clouds. Joseph Brodsky. CP-BrodJ

Clouds. Robert Herrick. CP-HerrR

Clouds. Denise Levertov. SP-LeveDP

Clouds. Philip Levine. SP-LeviP

Clouds. Rainer Maria Rilke. CP-RilkFr, *tr.* by A. Poulin, Jr.

Clouds. Wisława Szymborska. SP-SzymWM, *tr.* by Joanna Trzeciak

Clouds. Charles Tomlinson. CP-TomlC

Clouds, The. Aristophanes.
  "Cloud-maidens that float on for ever [*or* forever]." CP-WildO

Clouds, The. Charles Olson. CP-OlsoC

Clouds, The. William Carlos Williams. CP-WilW2

Cloud's a clue. O cloud!, The. Solving the Riddle. Charles Simic. SP-SimiC

Clouds above, as white as wool. In Swimming-Time. James Whitcomb Riley. CP-RileJ

Clouds across the azure sky, The. Song of the Early Spring. Jones Very. CP-VeryJ

Clouds, Airs, Carried me Away. Muriel Rukeyser. CP-RukeM

Clouds and the stars didn't wage this war, The. For the Record. Adrienne Rich. SP-RicA2

Clouds are electric in this university, The. 7/12/68. Adrienne Rich. CP-RicAE *Fr.* Ghazals: Homage to Ghalib.

Clouds are pushing in grey reluctance slowly northward to you, The. Letter from Town: On a Grey Morning in March. D. H. Lawrence. CP-LawrD

Clouds are withdrawn, The. Sunrise. George Meredith. CP-MerG1

Clouds as I see them, rising, The. Clouds. Denise Levertov. SP-LeveDP

Clouds before the sun when the sun rose, The. Meditation. John Berryman. CP-BerrJ

Clouds came from the south, the Nile. Akhziv. Yehuda Amichai. SP-AmicYL, *tr.* by Benjamin Harshav *and* Barbara Harshav

Clouds clamber, turgid, the mountain, peakward. Sunset. Robert Penn Warren. CP-WarrR

Clouds do not always viel the skies. Ode 2.9: Translation of Horace: *Odes* 2.9. Horace. CP-JohnS *Fr.* Odes.

Clouds dripped poisonous dew to spite, The. Poisoned Day. Robert Graves. CP-GravR

Clouds fly fast across the moon, The. Marian: "Clouds fly fast across the moon, The." George Meredith. CP-MerG2

Clouds glow like coals just fresh from fire, a flare. Unextinguished, The. Theodore Roethke. CP-RoetT

Clouds hang loosely over this mountain range. Rest, The. Raymond Carver. CP-CarvR

Clouds have deepened o'er the night, The. Light of Love, The. James Whitcomb Riley. CP-RileJ

Clouds, lingering yet, extend in solid bars. Composed by the Side of Grasmere Lake. William Wordsworth. CP-WorW1

Clouds of Evening. Robinson Jeffers. CP-JefR1

Clouds of Magellan (Aphorisms of Mr. Canon Aspirin), The. Norman Dubie. CP-DubiN

Clouds on the mountains. Who is to blame? What is to blame? Silent, tired. Unaccomplished. Yannis Ritsos. SP-RitsY, *tr.* by Kimon Friar

Clouds' silent shadows passing across the Sun above Teton's mountaintop. What's Dead? Allen Ginsberg. CP-GinsA

Clouds spout upon her. Rain on a Grave. Thomas Hardy. CP-HardT

Clouds that touch us out of clear skies, The. Clear Skies, The. W. S. Merwin. SP-MerwW

Clouds, the source of rain, one stormy night, The. Lost in Heaven. Robert Frost. CP-FrosR

Clouds their Backs together laid, The. Emily Dickinson. CP-DickE

Clouds weave a shawl, The. Garment. Langston Hughes. CP-HughL

Clouds, which rise with thunder, slake, The. All's Well. John Greenleaf Whittier. CP-WhitJ

Clouds within the Milky Way, The. Skyey Developments. John Updike. CP-UpdiJ

Cloudy luminous rose-mallow sundown, suffusing the whole. Chant: Sunset, Somerville, Late Fall '75. Denise Levertov. SP-LeveDL

Cloudy sky, The. Song of November and April. Federico García Lorca. CP-GarcF, *tr.* by Alan S. Trueblood *Fr.* Songs to End With.

Clover. Herman Melville. SP-MelvH

Clover. Tennessee Williams. CP-WillT

Clover. Louis Zukofsky. CP-ZukLS

Clover, The. James Whitcomb Riley. CP-RileJ

Clover blossom's a province, A. Mechanics. A. R. Ammons. CP-AmmoA

Clover Patch. Gabriela Mistral. SP-MistG, *tr.* by Maria Giachetti [*or* Jacketti]

Clover's simple Flame, The. Emily Dickinson. CP-DickE

Clown, The. John Clare. SP-ClarJ

Clown, The. Donald Hall. CP-HallD

Clown Chastised, The. Stéphane Mallarmé. CP-MallS, *tr.* by Henry Weinfield

Clown kite, my, A. Up. A. R. Ammons. CP-AmmoA

Clownlike, happiest on your hands. You're. Sylvia Plath. CP-PlatS

Clowns are demolishing the circus, The. The elephants have run off to India. MCMXCV. Joseph Brodsky. CP-BrodJ

Clown's smirk in the skull of a baboon, A. E. E. Cummings. CP-CummE; SP-CummE

Club Car, The. Ogden Nash. CP-NashO

Club-footed woman was mangled by the train, The. Not Both. William Meredith. SP-MereW

Club 26. Lorine Niedecker. CP-NiedL

Clues. Muriel Rukeyser. CP-RukeM

Clumped murmuring above a sump of loam. Woodlot, The. Amy Clampitt. CP-ClamA

Clumsily, with a thick needle, with thick thread. Fundamentals, The. Yannis Ritsos. SP-RitsY, *tr.* by N. C. Germanacos

Clumsy at first, fitting together. Kentucky River Junction. Wendell Berry. CP-BerrW

Clumsy futility, drown yourself. Calypso. "H. D." CP-DoolH

Clunton and Clunbury. A. E. Housman. CP-HousA

Cluster of faith and frost, the mistletoe. Metropolitan Christmas, A. Eugenio Montale. CP-MontE, *tr.* by Jonathan Galassi

Cluster of rocks far from the trade routes, A. St Paul's Rocks: 16 February 1832. Thomas Kinsella. CP-KinsT

Clustered / berries at dusk. Context. Rae Armantrout. SP-ArmaA

Clusters which invite the morning sun. Chokecherries. Peter Blue Cloud. SP-BlueP

Clutching at trees and clawing rocks. For an Indian Screen. Langston Hughes. CP-HughL; CP-HughL1

Clutter of Silence: Invention for Two Voices. Miller Williams. CP-WillM

Clutter-up People. Alice Walker. CP-WalkA

Clydesider. D. H. Lawrence. CP-LawrD

C'mon Jack. Allen Ginsberg. CP-GinsA

C'mon Pigs of Western Civilization Eat More Grease. Allen Ginsberg. SP-GinsA

C'mon said the pilot and. Small Plane in Kansas. Thom Gunn. CP-GunnT

Coach. Wyatt Prunty. SP-PrunW

Coagula. Paul Celan. SP-CelaP, *tr.* by John Felstiner

Coal. Audre Lorde. SP-LordA
  (I is the total black.) SP-LordA

Coal Fire, The. Donald Hall. CP-HallD

Coal fire burned in a basket grate, A. Coal Fire, The. Donald Hall. CP-HallD

Coal Fire in Winter, A. Thomas McGrath. SP-McGrT

Coal mine is a hollow tree, A. Portrait in the Form of an Extended Conceit. Alan Dugan. CP-DugaA

Coals work in a stove like. Live. Heather McHugh. SP-McHuH

Coarse leaf, alder leaf. Hayden Carruth. CP-CarHS *Fr.* Clay Hill Anthology, The.

Coast hills at Sovranes Creek, The. Place for No Story, The. Robinson Jeffers. CP-JefR2

Coast Hillside. Helen Pinkerton. CP-PinkH

Coast-Nightmare, A. Christina Georgina Rossetti. CP-RosC3

Coast of Maine. Richard Eberhart. CP-EberR

Coast-Road, The. Robinson Jeffers. CP-JefR2

Coast-road was being straightened and repaired again, The. Thurso's Landing. Robinson Jeffers. CP-JefR2

Coastal Strip. George Oppen. CP-OppGN

Coasters, The. Jones Very. CP-VeryJ

Coastwise Lights, The. Rudyard Kipling. CP-KiplR

Coat, A. William Butler Yeats. CP-YeatW

Coat of Arms. Alan Dugan. CP-DugaA

Coats, The. Tess Gallagher. SP-GallT

Cob clouts his shooes, and as the story tells. Upon Cob. Robert Herrick. CP-HerrR

Cob, thou nor soldier, thief, nor fencer art. To Pertinax Cob. Ben Jonson. CP-JonsB; SP-JonsB

Cobble thrown a hundred years ago, A. Clearances. Seamus Heaney. SP-HeanSO

Cobbler Keezar's Vision. John Greenleaf Whittier. CP-WhitJ

Coblers Catch, The. Robert Herrick. CP-HerrR

Cobra, The. Ogden Nash. CP-NashO

Cobweb, The. Raymond Carver. CP-CarvR

Cobwebs. Christina Georgina Rossetti. CP-RosC3

Cochiti. Charles Tomlinson. CP-TomlC

Cock-a-Doo. Stevie Smith. CP-SmitS

Cock-a-doodle-doo the brass-lined rooster goes [or says]. Dog. John Crowe Ransom. SP RansJ

Cock and cunt. Hymn to the Word. Charles Olson. CP-OlsoC

Cock and the Hen, The. Stevie Smith. CP-SmitS

Cock calls his Wife his Hen: when Cock goes too't. Upon Cock. Robert Herrick. CP-HerrR

Cock-Crow. Robert Herrick. CP-HerrR

Cock-crowing. Henry David Thoreau. CP-ThorH

Cock-Crows. Ted Hughes. SP-HughTN

Cock crows / But no queen rises, The. Depression before Spring. Wallace Stevens. CP-StevW; CP-StevWP

Cock-Fighters Garland. William Cowper. CP-CowpW

Cock in Pullet's Feathers. Robert Graves. CP-GravR

Cock is crowing, The. Written in March [While Resting on the Bridge at the Foot of Brother's Water]. William Wordsworth. CP-WorW1; MW-WorW

Cock o' the North. Louis MacNeice. CP-MacNL

"Bards wha hae for Hellas bled—." CP-MacNL

Cock of the North, The. Cock and the Hen, The. Stevie Smith. CP-SmitS

Cock on the weather vane, The. Weathercock on the Cathedral of Quito, The. Jorge Carrera Andrade. CP-MertT

Cock up Your Beaver. Robert Burns. CP-BurnR

Cock was working very hard, A. Fables: "Cock was working very hard, A." Mrs. Austen. CP-AustJ

Cocker. English. Fifteen years old. Tumor. Old Dog Dead. Robert Penn Warren. CP-WarrR

Cockfighter's Daughter, The. Ai. SP-Ai

Cockle. Louis Zukofsky. CP-ZukLS

Cockleburs came on the burdocks, The. Suburban Sicilian Sketches. Carl Sandburg. CP-SandC

Cocklorel would needs have the devil his guest. Dinner for the Devil. Ben Jonson. CP-JonsB Fr. Gypsies Metamorphosed, The.

Cockroach. Charles Bukowski. SP-BukC1

Cockroach. Anne Sexton. CP-SextA

Cockroach. Charles Simic. SP-SimiCE

Cockroach crouched, The. Cockroach. Charles Bukowski. SP-BukC1

Cocks crow / Dogs bark / This all men know. Tao. Chuang Tzu. CP-MertT

Cocktail Party. Robert Penn Warren. CP-WarrR

Cocoa-nut naught. On the High Price of Fish. William Cowper. CP-CowpW

Cocoa Tree. Jorge Carrera Andrade. CP-MertT

Coconut Palms, The. Gabriela Mistral. SP-MistG, tr. by Maria Giachetti [or Jacketti]

Cocoon, The. Robert Frost. CP-FrosR

Cocoon above! Cocoon below! Emily Dickinson. CP-DickE

Cod Head, The. William Carlos Williams. CP-WilW1

Cod Summer. Marge Piercy. SP-PierM

Coda: "Love is not worth so much." James Tate. SP-TateJ

Coda: "Maybe we knew each other better." Louis MacNeice. CP-MacNL

Coda: "Nine are the enabling elements." Thomas Kinsella. CP-KinsT

Coda: "O My songs." Ezra Pound. SP-PounE

Coda: "There's little in taking or giving." Dorothy Parker. CP-ParkD

Coda, Overture. Eleanor Wilner. SP-WilnE

Coda: Song. Ted Berrigan. SP-BerrT

Code, The. Robert Frost. CP-FrosR

Code, The. John Updike. CP-UpdiJ

Code Book Lost. Robert Penn Warren. CP-WarrR

Code of Morals, A. Rudyard Kipling. CP-KiplR

(Lest you should think this story true.) CP-KiplR

Codicil. Kenneth Rexroth. CP-RexrK

Codicil. Derek Walcott. CP-WalcD

Coelum Britannicum. Thomas Carew. CP-CareT Fr. Carew's Masque.

Coeur Simple. Stevie Smith. CP-SmitS

Coffee. James Vincent Cunningham. CP-CunnJ

Coffee Cup, The. Donald Hall. CP-HallD

Coffee with the Meal. Ogden Nash. CP-NashO

Coffeepot percolates, The. Waiting for a Tree through a Window. Yusef Komunyakaa. CP-KomuY

Coffin—is a small Domain, A. Emily Dickinson. CP-DickE

Coffin sealer is fanatical, The. For Thom Gunn. Andrei Codrescu. SP-CodrA

Cogimur; invitis (Clarissime) parce quaerelis. Illustrissimo, Potentissimoque Principi, Frederico Quinto, Rheni Comiti Palatino, Duci Bavariae, &c. Thomas Campion. CP-CampT

Cogis ut inspidus sapiat, damnose Cupido. Ad Amorem. Thomas Campion. CP-CampT

Coheires. Robert Herrick. CP-HerrR

Cohere Britannia. Andrei Codrescu. SP-CodrA

Coil of space the cones of light, The. Ralph Waldo Emerson. CP-EmerR

Coiled in the azimuth, Vipère. Mix the Ingredients. Hayden Carruth. CP-CarHS

Coiled into myself, I was not a seashell for your voice. Seashell. Dan Pagis. SP-PagiD, tr. by Stephen Mitchell

Coin, A. Carl Sandburg. CP-SandC

Coin, The. Ivor Gurney. SP-GurnI

Coin, The. W. S. Merwin. SP-MerwWF

Coin the daydawn into lines. Ralph Waldo Emerson. CP-EmerR

Coincidentally. Yannis Ritsos. SP-RitsY, tr. by John Stathatos

Coiner, The. Rudyard Kipling. CP-KiplR

Coins. Yannis Ritsos. SP-RitsY Fr. Monovasia.

Coins. Constantine P. Cavafy. CP-CavaC, tr. by Theoharis Constantine Theoharis

Coins with Indian inscriptions. Coins. Constantine P. Cavafy. CP-CavaC, tr. by Theoharis Constantine Theoharis

Coitus. Ezra Pound. SP-PounE

Cold. Pablo Neruda. SP-NeruP

Cold. Wyatt Prunty. SP-PrunW

Cold, The. Wendell Berry. CP-BerrW

Cold, The. James Laughlin. CP-LaugJ

Cold, The. Robert Pinsky. CP-PinsR

Cold, The. Charles Simic. SP-SimiC; SP-SimiCE

Cold and final, the imagination. Two Lovers and a Beachcomber by the Real Sea. Sylvia Plath. CP-PlatS

Cold and stormy the night I sailed from Montevideo. To a Coin. Jorge Luis Borges. SP-BorgJ, tr. by Alastair Reid

Cold and violent winds of March, The. O Lyric March. Marya Alexandrovna Zaturenska. SP-ZatuM

Cold as no love, and wild with all negation. Quand on n'a pas ce que l'on aime, il faut aimer ce que l'on a—. Stevie Smith. CP-SmitS

Cold as No Plea. Death Sentence, The. Stevie Smith. CP-SmitS

Cold August. Time of Tree Cutting. W. S. Merwin. SP-MerwWF

Cold before dawn. Earth Sky Sea Trees Birds House Beasts Flowers. Kenneth Rexroth. CP-RexrK

Cold before the Moonrise, The. W. S. Merwin. SP-MerwW

Cold Blood. D. H. Lawrence. CP-LawrD

Cold blood or warm, crawling or fluttering. Pet Shop. Louis MacNeice. CP-MacNL

Cold Blue Tinge. Charles Simic. SP-SimiC; SP-SimiCE

Cold came. It has photographed the scene, The. In the Balance. Charles Tomlinson. CP-TomlC

Cold, clear, and blue, the morning heaven. Morning Star, The. Emily Jane Brontë. CP-BronE

Cold Cliff's remoteness is what I like. Han-shan. CP-ColdM, tr. by Red Pine

Cold, cold, cold. Cortege. Tennessee Williams. CP-WillT

Cold cold cold of a special night. Rock-Study with Wanderer. John Berryman. CP-BerrJ

Cold / cold / on the bold. Other Than. Charles Olson. CP-OlsoC

Cold cold thy lips my gentle boy. Jones Very. CP-VeryJ

Cold Colloquy. Robert Penn Warren. CP-WarrR

Cold Comfort. Hans Magnus Enzensberger. SP-EnzeH

Cold coming we had of it, A. Journey of the Magi. T. S. Eliot. CP-ElioT

Cold dawn Harrow-On-The-Hill. Death of Southwell, The. John Logan. CP-LogaJ

Cold / December nights I'd go. Touched. Olga Broumas. SP-BrouO

Cold Divinities, The. James Wright. CP-WrigJ

Cold earth slept below, The. Lines: "Cold earth slept below, The." Percy Bysshe Shelley. CP-ShelP

Cold-eyed, in Naples Once. Lincoln Relics, The. Stanley Kunitz. CP-KunSC

Cold felt cold until our blood, The. Phantasia for Elvira Shatayev. Adrienne Rich. SP-RicA1; SP-RicA2

Cold Fire, A. Sam Hamill. SP-HamiS

Cold fountain / before which Christ's. Fountain. Federico García Lorca. CP-

GarcF, *tr. by* Jerome Rothenberg *Fr.* Secrets.

Cold Front, A. William Carlos Williams. CP-WilW2

Cold hand among the clouds, A. Fourth of October, 1963, The. Philip Whalen. SP-WhalP

Cold Heaven, The. William Butler Yeats. CP-YeatW

Cold holds everything in abeyance, The. Commas in Wintertime. Richard Eberhart. CP-EberR

Cold how mean, fortune consuming you oppresses your care, your. Catullus. *See* Borne down by bitter misfortune

Cold in cathedral the old women pray. Old Country, The. Howard Nemerov. CP-NemeH

Cold in the earth—and the deep snow piled above thee! Remembrance. Emily Jane Brontë. CP-BronE

Cold Iron. Rudyard Kipling. CP-KiplR

Cold / like Grandfather's icehouse. God's Backside. Anne Sexton. CP-SextA

Cold Lunch. William Corbett. SP-CorbW

Cold moon hangs to the sky by its horn, The. Night of the Dance, The. Thomas Hardy. CP-HardT

Cold moons withdraw, refusing to come to terms. Metamorphoses of the Moon. Sylvia Plath. CP-PlatS

Cold Morning Sky. Marya Alexandrovna Zaturenska. SP-ZatuM

Cold Mountain has so many wonders. Han-shan. CP-ColdM, *tr. by* Red Pine

Cold Mountain is a cold mountain. Shih-te. CP-ColdM, *tr. by* Red Pine

Cold Mountain is a house. Han-shan. CP-SnydG, *tr. by* Gary Snyder

Cold Mountain is a leakproof cliff. Han-shan. CP-ColdM, *tr. by* Red Pine

Cold Mountain is nothing but clouds. Han-shan. CP-ColdM, *tr. by* Red Pine

Cold Mountain is so cold. Han-shan. CP-ColdM, *tr. by* Red Pine

Cold Mountain owns a house. Han-shan. CP-ColdM, *tr. by* Red Pine

Cold Mountain Road is strange, The. Han-shan. CP-ColdM, *tr. by* Red Pine

Cold Mountain speaks these words. Han-shan. CP-ColdM, *tr. by* Red Pine

Cold Mountain's remoteness. Han-shan. CP-ColdM, *tr. by* Red Pine

Cold Night, The. William Carlos Williams. CP-WilW1

Cold night, the sidewalk we walk on icy, A. Christmas Eve Service at Midnight at St. Michael's. Robert Bly. SP-BlyR

Cold nights on the farm, a sock-shod. On the Disadvantages of Central Heating. Amy Clampitt. CP-ClamA

Cold nights outside the taverns in Wyoming. Accountability. William Stafford. SP-StafWW

Cold on my narrow cot I lie. To a Jilted Lover. Sylvia Plath. CP-PlatS

Cold Pane, The. Wendell Berry. CP-BerrW

Cold Pastoral. Allen Tate. CP-TateA

Cold Plums. Charles Bukowski. SP-BukC1

Cold rain falls through empty nests, a cold rain, A. Old Night and Sleep. Norman Dubie. CP-DubiN

Cold remote islands, The. Night. Louise Bogan. CP-BogaL

Cold rises around / our house, the wind, The. Midwinter, Presolstice. Margaret Atwood. SP-AtwM1

Cold rosy dawn in New York City. American Express. Ted Berrigan. SP-BerrT

Cold, sharp and very lean, the wind. Incense. Peter Blue Cloud. SP-BlueP

Cold slope is standing in darkness, The. December Night. W. S. Merwin. SP-MerwW

Cold, slow, silent, but returning, after so many hours. Prayer at Morning, A. Randall Jarrell. CP-JarrR

Cold snare taps on the skylight, / ice like a new conk on the trees. Freezing Rain. Charles Wright. SP-WrigCN

Cold so keen, A. Nightgown. James Merrill. SP-MerrJ

Cold Spring, A. Elizabeth Bishop. CP-BishE

Cold Spring, The. Denise Levertov. SP-LeveDS

Cold spring, The. Hippocrene. Amy Clampitt. CP-ClamA

Cold Spring Harbor. Derek Walcott. CP-WalcD

Cold Spring in Essex. Donald Davie. CP-DaviDC

Cold Spring in North Salem, The. Jones Very. CP-VeryJ

Cold spring morning sees, A. Operation, The. Charles Tomlinson. SP-TomlC

Cold stars / over our highways. North. Federico García Lorca. CP-GarcF, *tr. by* Jerome Rothenberg *Fr.* Cross.

Cold stone, none knows but you, my gaol forever. Michelangelo Buonarroti. CP-Miche, *tr. by* John Frederick Nims

Cold Sunbeams. Nicholas Vachel Lindsay. CP-LindV

Cold the day and cold the drifted snow. Months: A Pageant, The. Christina Georgina Rossetti. CP-RosC2

Cold, the day you leave. Thelonious Sphere Monk. William Corbett. SP-CorbW

Cold tremor, A. Landscape Seen with the Nose. Federico García Lorca. CP-GarcF, *tr. by* Jerome Rothenberg *Fr.* Suite.

Cold Water. Donald Hall. CP-HallD

Cold whip-adder unespied, The. Gerard Manley Hopkins. CP-HopkG

Cold wife lay with her husband after his death, The. Widow, The. Wallace Stevens. CP-StevWP

Cold wind freezes me inside, A. Smallest Blessing, The. James Laughlin. CP-LaugJ

Cold wind of autumn, blowing loud. Autumn Daybreak. Edna St. Vincent Millay. CP-MillE

Cold wind stirs the blackthorn, A. Endure Hardness. Christina Georgina Rossetti. CP-RosC2

Colder the Air, The. Elizabeth Bishop. CP-BishE

Coldest, wettest spring within living memory, The. In Umbria: A Snapshot. Amy Clampitt. CP-ClamA

Coldly, bleakly, drearily. Emily Jane Brontë. CP-BronE

Coldness in Love. D. H. Lawrence. CP-LawrD

Coleorton. Amy Clampitt. CP-ClamA

Coleridge. Robert Lowell. SP-LoweR

Coleridge and Richard II. Robert Lowell. SP-LoweR

Coleridge Crossing the Plain of Jars [1833]. Norman Dubie. CP-DubiN

Coleridge received the Person from Porlock. Thoughts about the Person from Porlock. Stevie Smith. CP-SmitS

Coleridge stands, he flamed for the one friend . . . . Coleridge. Robert Lowell. SP-LoweR

Coleridge wasn't flatter-blinded by. Coleridge and Richard II. Robert Lowell. SP-LoweR

Cole's Island. Charles Olson. SP-OlsoC *Fr.* Maximus Poems, The.

Coleus. Louis Zukofsky. CP-ZukLS

Coleus *foliage plant* coleus bloom. Coleus. Louis Zukofsky. CP-ZukLS

Colin Clouts Come Home Againe. Edmund Spenser. CP-Spens

Coliseum, The. Edgar Allan Poe. CP-PoeEd

Collapse of a civil privacy of manner. Replying to Reviewers. Donald Davie. CP-DaviDC

Collar, The. George Herbert. CP-HerbG

Collarbone. William Corbett. SP-CorbW

Collarbone [*or* Collar-Bone] of a Hare, The. William Butler Yeats. CP-YeatW

Collected from childhood's high October. Box of Leaves, A. Wyatt Prunty. SP-PrunW

Collected Poems. Kenneth Koch. SP-KochK

Collected Poems of, The. Charles Olson. CP-OlsoC

Collectivist State, The. Sociological Triolets. G. K. Chesterton. CP-ChesG

Collector Cleans His Picture, The. Thomas Hardy. CP-HardT

College Boys; A Hymn of Hate. Dorothy Parker. CP-ParkD

College Colonel, The. Herman Melville. CP-MelvH

College Formal: Renaissance Casino. Langston Hughes. CP-HughL; CP-HughL3

Collier's Wife, The. D. H. Lawrence. CP-LawrD

Collision with the earth has finally come. Ted Hughes. SP-HughTN

Colloque Sentimental. Frank O'Hara. SP-OharF

Colloquy. Josephine Jacobsen. CP-JacoJ

Colloquy for the States. Archibald MacLeish. CP-MacLA

Colloquy in Black Rock. Robert Lowell. SP-LoweR

Colloquy of the Centaurs. "Rubén Dario." SP-DariR, *tr. by* Alberto Acereda *and* Will Derusha

Colloquy with a Polish Aunt. Wallace Stevens. CP-StevW; CP-StevWP

Cologna Veneta - / where the good folk. Carmen 17. Catullus. CP-ZukLS *Fr.* Carmina.

Cologne. Samuel Taylor Coleridge. CP-ColeS

Cologne, at the Station. Paul Celan. SP-CelaP, *tr. by* John Felstiner

Colonel Martin. William Butler Yeats. CP-YeatW

Colonel went out sailing, The. Colonel Martin. William Butler Yeats. CP-YeatW

Colonel's Soliloquy, The. Thomas Hardy. CP-HardT

Colonist's 'they' that needs no antecedent, The. Monmouthshire. Donald Davie. CP-DaviDC

Colonnades of Nature's temple live, The. Universal Analogies. Charles Baudelaire. CP-BaudC, *tr. by* Walter Martin

Colonus' Praise. Sophocles. CP-YeatW *Fr.* Oedipus at Colonus.

Colony of the Sun, The. Kenneth Patchen. CP-PatcK

Colophon. Robert Graves. CP-GravR

Colophon. Adrienne Rich. CP-RicAE

Color. Langston Hughes. CP-HughL; CP-HughL3
  (I would wear it.) CP-HughL2

Color-bearers facing death, The. Rebel Color-Bearers at Shiloh. Herman Melville. CP-MelvH

Color, Caste, Denomination. Emily Dickinson. CP-DickE

Color floods to the spot, dull purple. Contusion. Sylvia Plath. CP-PlatS

Color is image. Charles Olson. CP-OlsoC

Color of a House, The. Tennessee Williams. CP-WillT

Color of lemon, mango, peach. Southern Sunrise. Sylvia Plath. CP-PlatS

Color of the Grave is Green, The. Emily Dickinson. CP-DickE

Color of the sac and stinger of the scorpion, The. Barefoot for a Scorpion. Alan Dugan. CP-DugaA

Color of Time, The. C. K. Williams. CP-WillC

Color, taste, and smell, smaragdus, sugar, and musk. Abu Nadhar 'Abdu'l 'Aziz.

CP-EmerR

Colorado. Mona Van Duyn. SP-VanDM

Coloratura. Wisława Szymborska. SP-SzymW, *tr. by* Stanislaw Barańczak *and* Clare Cavanagh

Colored Band, The. Paul Laurence Dunbar. CP-DunbP

Colored Blues Singer. Countee Cullen. CP-CullC

Colored Soldier, The. Langston Hughes. CP-HughL; CP-HughL1

Colored Soldiers, The. Paul Laurence Dunbar. CP-DunbP

Colors. Federico García Lorca. CP-GarcF, *tr. by* Jerome Rothenberg *Fr. Sublunar* Cantos.

Colors. Robert Creeley. CP-CreeR

Colors. Countee Cullen. CP-CullC

Colors. Wallace Stevens. CP-StevWP

Colors of stars. Colors. Robert Creeley. CP-CreeR

Colors take bodies. Another Spring Uncovered. May Swenson. SP-SwenM

Colossal leagues of powers. Daisy, The. G. K. Chesterton. CP-ChesG

Colossians 3:3. George Herbert. *See* Our Life Is Hid with Christ in God

Colossus in Quicksand, The. John Ciardi. CP-CiarJ

Colossus, The. Sylvia Plath. CP-PlatS

Colour, The. Thomas Hardy. CP-HardT

Colour fulfills where Music has no power. Chartres Windows. Rudyard Kipling. CP-KiplR

Colour Machine, The. Thom Gunn. CP-GunnT

Colours drain, shapes blur, resisting. Kiss at Bayreuth, The. Thom Gunn. CP-GunnT

Colours of Night, The. Robert Graves. CP-GravR

Colours of October. Transition. Lorine Niedecker. CP-NiedL

Colubriad, The. William Cowper. CP-CowpW

Columbia. Langston Hughes. CP-HughL; CP-HughL1

Columbian Ode. Paul Laurence Dunbar. CP-DunbP

Columbian's Song, The. Walt Whitman. CP-WhitW

Columbine, The. Jones Very. CP-VeryJ

Columbines. Kathleen Jessie Raine. SP-RainK

Columbines and Anemones. Jones Very. CP-VeryJ

Columbo and Bolo Verses. T. S. Eliot. SP-ElioT

Columbo he lived over in Spain. Columbo and Bolo Verses. T. S. Eliot. SP-ElioT

Columbus. Thomas McGrath. SP-McGrT

Columbus. Ogden Nash. CP-NashO

Columbus may have worked the wind. America Is Hard to See. Robert Frost. CP-FrosR

Columbus Square Journal. William Corbett. SP-CorbW

Columbus, wearing a night-gown made from a treasure map. Columbus. Thomas McGrath. SP-McGrT

Column and the Laurel-tree are broken, The. Petrarch. CP-Petra, *tr. by* J. G. Nichols

Column of glory, strong stay and support. Petrarch. CP-Petra, *tr. by* J. G. Nichols

Column of your book titles, The. Rival Poet, The. Billy Collins. SP-CollB

Columns. Rudyard Kipling. CP-KiplR

Columns and Caryatids. Carolyn Kizer. CP-KizeC

Columns glow faintly white, The. These Unreturning Destinies. Kenneth Patchen. CP-PatcK

Columns of grandsons, stiff at attention. On the Death of Zhukov. Joseph Brodsky. CP-BrodJ, *tr. by* George L. Kline

Columns of the Parthenon, The. Donald Hall. CP-HallD

Comanches tell how the buffalo. Paso por Aquí. William Stafford. SP-StafWW

Comb, The. Hans Magnus Enzensberger. SP-EnzeH, *tr. by* Michael Hamburger

Combat. C. K. Williams. CP-WillC; SP-WillC

Combat Cultural. Marianne Craig Moore. CP-MoorM

Combat Pay for Jody. Yusef Komunyakaa. CP-KomuY

Combative Spirit, The. D. H. Lawrence. CP-LawrD

Come. Dan Pagis. SP-PagiD, *tr. by* Stephen Mitchell

Come. Stevie Smith. CP-SmitS

Come! David Ignatow. SP-IgnaD

Come a little further—why be afraid. E. E. Cummings. CP-CummE

"Come aboard" the old man used to say. Rosy, It Was. Charles Olson. CP-OlsoC

Come admire this hour turning silver. Rainer Maria Rilke. CP-RilkFr, *tr. by* A. Poulin, Jr. *Fr.* Fragments.

Come again next winter. Yehuda Amichai. SP-AmicYL *Fr.* Poems on the Shore of Caesarea.

Come again to the place. After the Visit. Thomas Hardy. CP-HardT

Come All Ye Brave Boys. Allen Ginsberg. CP-GinsA

Come all ye weary. I will give you rest. Come Unto Me. Jones Very. CP-VeryJ

Come all you Jewish boy friends / that live here in New York. NY Youth Call Annunciation. Allen Ginsberg. SP-GinsA

Come all you young men that proudly display. Come All Ye Brave Boys. Allen Ginsberg. CP-GinsA

Come along, everybody, see the pretty baby. After the Christening. Ogden Nash. CP-NashO

Come along in then, little girl! From a Very Little Sphinx. Edna St. Vincent Millay. CP-MillE

Come, And Be My Baby. Maya Angelou. SP-AngeM

Come, and enter Heaven, O soul! Soul's Invitation, The. Jones Very. CP-VeryJ

Come and Kiss Me Sweet and Twenty. Paul Laurence Dunbar. CP-DunbP

Come and let us live my Deare. Out of Catullus. Ausonius. CP-CrasR

Come and let's in solemn wise. Sacrifice, by Way of Discourse betwixt Himselfe and Julia, The. Robert Herrick. CP-HerrR

Come Anthea, know thou this. To Anthea. Robert Herrick. CP-HerrR

Come Anthea let us two. Wake, The. Robert Herrick. CP-HerrR

Come Arabella, fetch the cake. Party, The. Ogden Nash. CP-NashO

Come as my doctor. Invitation to Bristol. Robert Graves. CP-GravR

Come away, arm'd with loves delights. Thomas Campion. CP-CampT

Come away! come away! there's a frost along the marshes. Wilderness, The. Edwin Arlington Robinson. CP-RobiE

Come away, / Make no delay. Doomsday. George Herbert. CP-HerbG

Come away to dreamin' town. Dreamin' Town. Paul Laurence Dunbar. CP-DunbP

Come Back. W. S. Merwin. SP-MerwW

Come back and you will find me just the same. Randall Jarrell, Office Hours 10-11. Randall Jarrell. CP-JarrR

Come Back Christmas: Blues Stanza. Allen Ginsberg. SP-GinsA

Come back Mother, come back from. Eternity, An. William Carlos Williams. CP-WilW2

Come back when fog drifts out over the city. He Was Alone (As in Reality) Upon His Humble Bed. Kenneth Patchen. CP-PatcK

Come, be content, since out it must. To Charles Ford, Esq. on His Birthday. Jonathan Swift. CP-SwifJ

Come, be happy!—sit near me. Invocation to Misery. Percy Bysshe Shelley. CP-ShelP

Come blessed sleep, most full, most perfect, come. There Remaineth Therefore a Rest for the People of God. Christina Georgina Rossetti. CP-RosC3

Come blithefull Neatherds, let us lay. Beucolick, or Discourse of Neatherds, A. Robert Herrick. CP-HerrR

Come, blunt your spear with us. Huntress. "H. D." CP-DoolH

Come boat me o'er, come row me o'er. O'er the Water to Charlie. Robert Burns. CP-BurnR

Come, brave soldjers, come, and see. In Cicatrices Domini Jesu. Richard Crashaw. CP-CrasR

Come, Break with Time. Louise Bogan. CP-BogaL

Come, bring thy gift. If blessings were as slow. Offering, An. George Herbert. CP-HerbG

Come, bring with a noise. Ceremonies for Christmas[se]. Robert Herrick. CP-HerrR

Come bring your sampler, and with Art. Wounded Heart, The. Robert Herrick. CP-HerrR

Come, bumpers high, express your joy. You're Welcome, Willie Stewart. Robert Burns. CP-BurnR

Come, Capsicum, cast off thy membranous pods. Sensualist, The. John Updike. CP-UpdiJ

Come, Celia, fix thine eyes on mine. To a Lady, Not Yet Enjoyed by Her Husband. Thomas Carew. CP-CareT

Come, chearfull day, part of my life, to mee. Thomas Campion. *See* Come, Cheerful Day!

Come cheer up, my lads, 'tis to glory we steer! Christina Georgina Rossetti. CP-RosC3

Come, Cheerful Day! Thomas Campion. CP-CampT

(Come, chearfull day, part of my life, to mee.) CP-CampT

Come, child, while rambling through the nation. Club Car, The. Ogden Nash. CP-NashO

Come children, gather round my knee. Good Riddance, but Now What? Ogden Nash. CP-NashO

Come close to me, dear friends; still closer; thus! Paracelsus. Robert Browning. CP-BroR1

Come closer, hat in the dust. Wars, The. Pablo Neruda. SP-NeruP

Come closer yet, my honeysuckle, my sweetheart Jinny. Land of Whipperginny, The. Robert Graves. CP-GravR

Come, come away / Or let me go. Upon a Delaying Lady. Robert Herrick. CP-HerrR

Come, come, thou bleak December Wind. Death Wish, A. Samuel Taylor Coleridge. CP-ColeS

Come crown my brows with leaves of myrtle. Tortoise, The. Ogden Nash. CP-NashO

Come, cruel tigress, bask and purr. Lethe. Charles Baudelaire. CP-BaudC, *tr. by* Walter Martin

Come, cuckoo, come; / Come again, swift swallow. Summer. Christina Georgina Rossetti. CP-RosC3

Come Dance in Baronies. René Char. CP-MertT

Come, dear children, let us away. Forsaken Merman, The. Matthew Arnold. SP-ArnoM

Come, Death (1). Stevie Smith. CP-SmitS

Come, Death (2). Stevie Smith. CP-SmitS

Come death, come bands, nor do you shrink, my eares. Acts 21; I Am Ready Not Onely To Be Bound but To Dye. Richard Crashaw. CP-CrasR

Come, Death, I'd have a word with thee. Motley. Walter De la Mare. CP-DeLaW

Come, Doctor, we must fly someotherwhere. William Dickey. SP-DickW *Fr.* Part Song, With Concert of Recorders.

Come, *Dorus*, come, let the songs thy sorrows signify. Song Contest: Lalus and Dorus. Sir Philip Sidney. SP-SidnP *Fr.* Arcadia.

Come down, and dance ye in the toyle. Song to the Maskers, A. Robert Herrick. CP-HerrR

Come down Canyon Creek trail on a summer afternoon. How to Regain Your Soul. William Stafford. SP-StafW

Come down, O Christ, and help me! reach thy hand. E Tenebris. Oscar Wilde. CP-WildO

Come, drink a stirrup cup with me. Stirrup Cup, The. Paul Laurence Dunbar. CP-DunbP

Come, drunks and drug-takers; come, perverts unnerved! Several Voices Out of a Cloud. Louise Bogan. CP-BogaL

Come, eat the bread of idleness. Beggar Speaks, The. Nicholas Vachel Lindsay. CP-LindV

Come, *Espilus*, come now declare thy skill. Sir Philip Sidney. SP-SidnP *Fr.* Lady of May, The.

Come, essay a sprightly measure. Bridal Measure, A. Paul Laurence Dunbar. CP-DunbP

Come, fair muse of Grub Street, the dialogue write. Dialogue between Captain Tom and Sir Henry Dutton Colt, A. Jonathan Swift. CP-SwifJ

Come, follow me by the smell. Onyons. Jonathan Swift. CP-SwifJ *Fr.* Verses Made for the Women Who Cry Apples, etc.

Come, follow me into the realms of music. Here is the gate. Hugh MacDiarmid. SP-MacDH *Fr.* Plaited Like the Generations of Men.

Come Forth. James Wright. CP-WrigJ

Come forth, come forth my people from the place. Flight, The. Jones Very. CP-VeryJ

Come forth, come forth, the gentle Spring. Ben Jonson. CP-JonsB *Fr.* Chloridia.

Come, freighted heart, within this port. Lovemusic. Carolyn Kizer. CP-KizeC

Come friend / I have an old story to tell you. Wallflower. Anne Sexton. CP-SextA

Come, frog, reveal yourself. Agnostic Speaks to Her Horse's Hoof, The. Maxine W. Kumin. SP-KumiM

Come from his gal's. E. E. Cummings. CP-CummE

Come Gather Round Me Parnellites. William Butler Yeats. CP-YeatW

Come,gaze with me upon this dome. E. E. Cummings. CP-CummE

Come, gentle Air! th' Æolian shepherd said. On a Fan of the Author's Design, in Which Was Painted the Story of CEPHALUS and PROCRIS, with the Motto, AURA VENI. Alexander Pope. CP-PopeA

Come, gentle sleep, death's image though thou art. Thomas, the Younger Warton. CP-WorW1

Come guard this night the Christmas-Pie. Christmasse-Eve, Another Ceremonie. Robert Herrick. CP-HerrR

Come heavenly Muse a suppliant asks thine aid. Lines on the Death of Miss M. B. Farnham. Ralph Waldo Emerson. CP-EmerR

Come heavenly Muse my voice inspire. No. 13 Hymn Written in Concord Sept. 1814. Ralph Waldo Emerson. CP-EmerR

Come here, I want to show you something. Sightseeing. Rita Dove. SP-DoveR

Come hither all sweet maidens soberly. On a Leander Gem which Miss Reynolds, My Kind Friend, Gave Me. John Keats. CP-KeatJ

Come hither, child—who gifted thee. Emily Jane Brontë. CP-BronE

Come hither, Fisher Unwin. Lines to Waterloo Station. G. K. Chesterton. CP-ChesG

Come hither, gently rowing. Water Ballad. Samuel Taylor Coleridge. CP-ColeS

Come hither my boy tell me what thou seest here. Lacedemonian Instruction. William Blake. CP-BlakW

Come hither my sparrows. Fairy, The. William Blake. CP-BlakW

Come hither, my sweet Rosalind. Rosalind and Helen; A Modern Eclogue. Percy Bysshe Shelley. CP-ShelP

Come, holy Silence, come. Silence. D. H. Lawrence. CP-LawrD

Come, Holy Spirit. Veni Creator. Czeslaw Milosz. CP-MiloC; CP-MiloCN, *tr. by* Robert Pinsky

Come Home, Come Home! Arthur Hugh Clough. SP-ClouA

Come home, come home! and where an home hath he. Come Home, Come Home! Arthur Hugh Clough. SP-ClouA

Come home, victorious wounded!—let the dead. For You O Democracy. Edna St. Vincent Millay. CP-MillE

Come, I will make the continent indissoluble. For You O Democracy. Walt Whitman. CP-WhitW

Come In. Robert Frost. CP-FrosR

Come In. Lorine Niedecker. CP-NiedL

Come in a week. Return of Returns. D. H. Lawrence. CP-LawrD

Come in, dear guests, we've got a treat for you. Out Is Out. Ogden Nash. CP-NashO

Come in Go Out. May Swenson. SP-SwenM

Come into Animal Presence. Denise Levertov. SP-LeveDP; SP-LeveDS

Come into My Parlour. Paul Muldoon. CP-MuldP

Come, Kings, and listen to my song. Gwin, King of Norway. William Blake. CP-BlakW

Come knock your heads against this stone. Epitaph, An: "Come knock your heads against this stone." William Blake. CP-BlakW

Come lady, bring that pot. Tinker Jack and the Tidy Wives. Sylvia Plath. CP-PlatS

Come laughing when the wind. Folly of Clowns. Kenneth Patchen. CP-PatcK

Come leave the loathèd stage. Ode to Himself[e]. Ben Jonson. CP-JonsB

Come, leave this loathed Country-life, and then. Upon Himself. Robert Herrick. CP-HerrR

Come, let me sing into your ear. Those Dancing Days Are Gone. William Butler Yeats. CP-YeatW

Come, let us blow up the whole business. Come! David Ignatow. SP-IgnaD

Come, let us break our leafy caskets here. On the Celebration of the Birth of the Dauphin of France. Annis Boudinot Stockton. CP-StocA

Come, let us build a temple to oblivion. Tabernacle. D. H. Lawrence. CP-LawrD

Come, let us here enjoy the shade. Song, A: "Come, let us here enjoy the shade." Ben Jonson. CP-JonsB

Come, let us pity those who are better off than we are. Garret, The. Ezra Pound. SP-PounE

Come, let us plant our love as farmers plant. Love Tree, The. Countee Cullen. CP-CullC

Come let us play with our own toys. Xenia ("Come let us play with our own toys"). Ezra Pound. CP-PoEar

Come, / Let us roam the night together. Harlem Night Song. Langston Hughes. CP-HughL; CP-HughL1

Come Let Us Sound With Melodie. Thomas Campion. CP-CampT

Come let us strew roses. Hafiz. CP-EmerR *Fr.* Odes.

Come, let us tell the weeds in ditches. Last Hill in a Vista. Louise Bogan. CP-BogaL

Come let's roam the breezy pastures. Breeze's Invitation, The. Henry David Thoreau. CP-ThorH

Come, let's to Culliford Hill and Wood. Ballad of Love's Skeleton, The. Thomas Hardy. CP-HardT

Come lie with me and be my love. Lawrence Ferlinghetti. SP-FerlL

Come listen, good people, while a story I do tell. Ezra House. James Whitcomb Riley. CP-RileJ

Come Little Birds. Robinson Jeffers. CP-JefR3

Come, little infant, love me now. Young Love. Andrew Marvell. CP-MarvA

Come, live in Now and occupy it well. Non Cogunt Astra. Robert Graves. CP-GravR

Come live with me and be my dear. Another of the Same Nature, Made Since. *Unknown.* CP-MarlC, *tr. by* Christopher Marlowe

Come live with me and be my love. Further Proposal, A. Allen Ginsberg. CP-GinsA

Come live with me and be my love. War Resisters' Song. Thomas McGrath. SP-McGrT

Come live with me[e] and be my Love. Passionate Shepherd To His Love, The. Christopher Marlowe. CP-MarlC

Come live with me[e], and be[e] my love. Bait[e], The. John Donne. CP-DonnJ; CP-MarlC; MW-DonnJ

Come look they said. In San Salvador (I). Grace Paley. CP-PalGC

Come Lord, my head doth burn, my heart is sick. Home. George Herbert. CP-HerbG

Come, Madam, come, all rest my powers defy [or defie]. To His Mistress Going to Bed. John Donne. MW-DonnJ *Fr.* Elegies.

Come meek ey'd resignation child of peace. Resignation, an Elegiac Ode, February the 28th, 1788. Annis Boudinot Stockton. CP-StocA

Come, megrims, mollygrubs and collywobbles! So Penseroso. Ogden Nash. CP-NashO

Come, merry May, on this first day. May Song. George Meredith. CP-MerG2

Come moo, dear moo, let's you and me. Due Respect. John Updike. CP-UpdiJ

Come Morning. John Ciardi. CP-CiarJ

Come my Alexis with thy mother share. To Richard John Stockton Esqr, Inclosing the Preceding Elegy [Feb. 28, 1787]. Annis Boudinot Stockton. CP-StocA

Come my Amanda, leave thy downy bed. Lavinia and Amanda, a Pastoral. Annis Boudinot Stockton. CP-StocA

Come, my beloved. From the Garden. Anne Sexton. CP-SextA

Come my Celia, let us prove. Song. To Celia ("Come my Celia, let us prove"). Ben Jonson. CP-JonsB; SP-JonsB, *tr. by* Ben Jonson *Fr.* Volpone.

Come, my little one, closer up against me. Wedlock. D. H. Lawrence. CP-LawrD

Come my servant, follow me. Dialogue Entitled the Kind Master and Dutiful Servant, A. Jupiter Hammon. CP-WheaP

Come, my songs, let us speak of perfection. Salvationists. Ezra Pound. SP-PounE

Come my tan-faced children. Pioneers! O Pioneers! Walt Whitman. CP-WhitW

Come, my Way, my Truth, my Life. Call, The. George Herbert. CP-HerbG

Come, noble nymphs, and do not hide. Ben Jonson. CP-JonsB *Fr.* Neptune's Triumph.

Come not with kisses. Leda. D. H. Lawrence. CP-LawrD

Come Not; Yet Come! Thomas Hardy. CP-HardT

Come nothing to my comparable soul. E. E. Cummings. CP-CummE

Come now, all you who are singers. Song of Spain. Langston Hughes. CP-HughL; CP-HughL1

"Come now," I said, "put off these webs of death." Bright Life. Walter De la Mare. CP-DeLaW

Come, O come, my life's delight. My Life's Delight. Thomas Campion. CP-CampT

Come, O King of the Lacedaimonians. Constantine P. Cavafy. CP-CavaC, *tr. by* Theoharis Constantine Theoharis

Come, O my love, and lay you down. Sharp in My Heart. Kenneth Rexroth. CP-RexrK

Come October, if I close my eyes. House Fly, The. James Merrill. SP-MerrJ

Come On! William Carlos Williams. CP-WilW2

Come On, Come Back. Stevie Smith. CP-SmitS

Come on, come on! And where you go. Ben Jonson. CP-JonsB *Fr.* Pleasure Reconciled to Virtue.

Come On In, the Senility Is Fine. Ogden Nash. CP-NashO

Come on, stretch out on my warm heart. Cat. Charles Baudelaire. CP-BaudC, *tr. by* Walter Martin

Come on walkin' wid me, Lucy. Spring Wooing, A. Paul Laurence Dunbar. CP-DunbP

Come, or the stellar tide will slip away. Needle, The. Ezra Pound. CP-PoEar

Come out my lads, make haste, come out and play. Prologue Spoken before a Greek Play, at the Reverend Dr. Sheridan's School, at the Breaking-Up of His Scholars for Christmas, 1728. Thomas Sheridan. CP-SherT

Come out of the dark earth. Invocation: "Come out of the dark earth." May Sarton. SP-SartM

Come out of your astrology, the order. Come. Dan Pagis. SP-PagiD, *tr. by* Stephen Mitchell

Come pass the cup, Debaters all. J.D.C.: Chaunt of the Junior Debating Club. G. K. Chesterton. CP-ChesG

Come, peace of mind, delightful guest! Ode to Peace. William Cowper. CP-CowpW

Come pity [or pitie] us, all ye, who see. Widow's Tears [or Widdowes Teares]: or, Dirge of Dorcas, The. Robert Herrick. CP-HerrR

Come play with me. To a Squirrel at Kyle-Na-No. William Butler Yeats. CP-YeatW

Come pleasant thoughts; sweet thoughts, at will. Arthur Hugh Clough. SP-ClouA

Come, ponder well, for 'tis no jest. Yearly Distress, The. William Cowper. CP-CowpW

Come praise Colonus' horses and come praise. Colonus' Praise. Sophocles. CP-YeatW *Fr.* Oedipus at Colonus.

Come Prima. A. R. Ammons. CP-AmmoA

Come rain down words as does. God of Details, The. Boris Leonidovich Pasternak. CP-DaviDC, *tr. by* Donald Davie

Come rede me, dame, come tell me, dame. Nine Inch Will Please a Lady. Robert Burns. CP-BurnR

Come, Robin, come, and sing to me. Invitation to the Robin. Jones Very. CP-VeryJ

Come round me, little childer. Ballad of Moll Magee, The. William Butler Yeats. CP-YeatW

Come, said my soul. Walt Whitman. CP-WhitW

Come said the Muse. Song of the Universal. Walt Whitman. CP-WhitW

Come, said the world, thy youth is not all play. Wallace Stevens. CP-StevWP

Come, selfsame and ageless Night. Fernando Pessoa. SP-PessF *Fr.* Ode.

Come shepherd's weeds, become your master's mind. Sir Philip Sidney. SP-SidnP *Fr.* Arcadia.

Come show thy Durham Breast. Emily Dickinson. CP-DickE

Come, sing a hale Heigh-ho. Christmas Long Ago, The. James Whitcomb Riley. CP-RileJ

Come sing the name that brings all hearts. Fireside. George Meredith. CP-MerG2

Come singing in your chains. Faith Healer. Yusef Komunyakaa. CP-KomuY

Come sit beneath the tariff walls. Economist's Song, The. Stanley Kunitz. CP-KunSC

Come sit by my side, while this picture I draw. Portrait from the Life, A.

Jonathan Swift. CP-SherT; CP-SwifJ

Come sit we by the fires side. Coblers Catch, The. Robert Herrick. CP-HerrR

Come sit we under yonder Tree. To the Maids to Walke Abroad. Robert Herrick. CP-HerrR

Come, skilfull Lupo, now, and take. To the Painter, To Draw Him a Picture. Robert Herrick. CP-HerrR

Come, Sleep. Louise Bogan. CP-BogaL

Come slowly—Eden! Emily Dickinson. CP-DickE

Come small creatures of low estate, friskily moving. To the Field Mice. Richard Eberhart. CP-EberR

Come something come blood sunlight come and they break. Eye-Beaters, The. James Dickey. CP-DickJ

Come, sons of summer, by whose toil[e]. Hock-Cart, or Harvest Home, The. Robert Herrick. CP-HerrR

Come, spread foam rubber on the floor. I Can't Have a Martini, Dear, but You Take One, or, Are You Going to Sit THere Guzzling All Night? Ogden Nash. CP-NashO

Come Spring, Come Sorrow. D. H. Lawrence. CP-LawrD

Come suddenly, O Lord, or slowly come. Take ye heed, watch and pray: for ye know not when the time is. Mark 13:33. Jones Very. CP-VeryJ

Come, surly fellow, come: a song! Haunted House, The. Robert Graves. CP-GravR

Come swish around my pretty punk. Drunken Man's Praise of Sobriety, A. William Butler Yeats. CP-YeatW

Come!—the palace of heaven rests on aëry pillars. Hafiz. CP-EmerR *Fr.* Odes.

Come, the wind may never again. D.G.C. to J.A. Emily Jane Brontë. CP-BronE

Come then in robe of darkest blue. To Melpomene. William Wordsworth. CP-WorW1

Come Then to Prayers. Philip Larkin. CP-LarkP

Come, then, with showers; I love thy cloudy face. April. Walter De la Mare. CP-DeLaW

Come thou and labor with me I will give. Call, The ("Come thou and labor with me I will give"). Jones Very. CP-VeryJ

Come, thou awakener of the spirit's ocean. Fragment: Zephyrus the Awakener. Percy Bysshe Shelley. CP-ShelP

"Come," thou dost say to Angels. Advent. Christina Georgina Rossetti. CP-RosC3

Come thou not neere those men, who are like Bread. To His Booke. Robert Herrick. CP-HerrR

Come, thou, who art the wine and wit. His Winding-Sheet. Robert Herrick. CP-HerrR

Come, tinkers, among droves of acorn trees. Fanny Howe. SP-HoweF *Fr.* Introduction to the World.

Come to me darling little Ben. Farewell Rehearsed. Allen Tate. CP-TateA

Come to me God; but do not come. To God. Robert Herrick. CP-HerrR

Come to me in any shape! Song: "Come to me in any shape!" George Meredith. CP-MerG1

Come to me in the silence of the night. Echo. Christina Georgina Rossetti. CP-RosC1

Come to me only with playthings now. Murmurings in a Field Hospital. Carl Sandburg. CP-SandC

Come to Rio, oh come to Rio. Rio Samba. Joseph Brodsky. CP-BrodJ

Come to Sunny Prestatyn. Sunny Prestatyn. Philip Larkin. CP-LarkP

Come to the Edge. Christopher Logue. SP-LoguC

Come to the luminous beaches—he murmured to himself. Small Invitation, A. Yannis Ritsos. SP-RitsY, *tr. by* Kimon Friar

Come to the orchard in Spring. Jelaluddin Rumi. SP-Rumi, *tr. by* Coleman Barks

Come to the pane, draw the curtain apart. My Little March Girl. Paul Laurence Dunbar. CP-DunbP

Come to the Stone. Randall Jarrell. CP-JarrR

Come Unto Me. Christina Georgina Rossetti. CP-RosC3

Come Unto Me. Jones Very. CP-VeryJ

Come up and see the court of the patron. Shmuel HaNagid. SP-HaNaS, *tr. by* Peter Cole

Come Up from the Fields Father. Walt Whitman. CP-WhitW

Come up from the fields father, here's a letter from our Pete. Come Up from the Fields Father. Walt Whitman. CP-WhitW

'Come up now into / the world' no need to light. To the Poets: To Make Much of Life. George Oppen. CP-OppGN

Come up, thou red thing. Southern Night. D. H. Lawrence. CP-LawrD

Come virgin Tapers of pure waxe. Epithalamium: "Come virgin Tapers of pure waxe." Richard Crashaw. CP-CrasR

Come, walk with me. Emily Jane Brontë. CP-BronE

Come, wander forth with me! the orange flowers. Serenade. Christina Georgina Rossetti. CP-RosC3

Come (we say) Clemenceau. Dead to Clemenceau: November 1929, The. Robinson Jeffers. CP-JefR2

Come we shepheards whose blest Sight. In the Holy Nativity of Our Lord God. Richard Crashaw. CP-CrasR

Come, wed me, Lady Singleton. Lady "Rogue" Singleton. Stevie Smith. CP-SmitS

Come wee Shepheards who have seene. Hymne of the Nativity, Sung by the Shepheards, A. Richard Crashaw. CP-CrasR

Come were the times of Ceres' sacrifice. Elegy 3.9: "Come were the times of Ceres' sacrifice." Ovid. CP-MarlC *Fr.* Elegies.

Come, when no graver cares employ. To the Rev. F. D. Maurice. Alfred Tennyson. CP-TennA

Come when the nights are bright with stars. Invitation to Love. Paul Laurence Dunbar. CP-DunbP

Come where the grieving rivers of the night. Song: "Come where the grieving rivers of the night." Thomas Merton. CP-MertT

Come with me / into the field of sunflowers. Sunflowers, The. Mary Oliver. SP-OlivM

Come with our voices, let us war. Musical Strife, The; in a Pastoral Dialogue. Ben Jonson. CP-JonsB; SP-JonsB

Come with rain, O loud Southwester! To the Thawing Wind. Robert Frost. CP-FrosR

Come with the cannon-wheel. Hatton's "God of War." George Meredith. CP-MerG2

Come with the Spring-time, forth fair maid, and be. Meddow Verse; or, Aniversary to Mistris Bridget Lowman, The. Robert Herrick. CP-HerrR

Come with us and play! From "The Birth of Venus," Song. William Carlos Williams. CP-WilW1

Come, words, away from mouths. Laura Riding Jackson. CP-RidiL

Come ye hither all, whose taste. Invitation, The. George Herbert. CP-HerbG

Come ye that are disturbed, this steady voice. William Wordsworth. CP-WorW1

Come ye—who, if (which Heaven avert!) the Land. Lines on the Expected Invasion 1803. William Wordsworth. CP-WorW1

Come you, cartoonists. Halsted Street Car. Carl Sandburg. CP-SandC

Come, you pretty false-eyed wanton [*or* false-ey'd wanton]. Thomas Campion. CP-CampT

Come(all your mischief- / hatchers hatch). E. E. Cummings. CP-CummE

Comedian as the Letter C, The. Wallace Stevens. CP-StevW; CP-StevWP

Comedian stands on a corner,the sky is, The. E. E. Cummings. CP-CummE

Comedy. Charles Tomlinson. CP-TomlC

Comedy Card for a Serious Case. Thomas Merton. CP-MertT

Comedy like That, A. Gertrude Stein. CP-SteiG

Comedy of Thirst. Arthur Rimbaud. CP-RimbA, *tr.* by Martin Sorrell

Comely Acts well; and when he speaks his part. Upon Comely a Good Speaker but an Ill Singer. Robert Herrick. CP-HerrR

Comely and capable one of our race. On the Portrait of a Woman About to Be Hanged. Thomas Hardy. CP-HardT

Comes home dull with coal-dust deliberately. Her Husband. Ted Hughes. SP-HughTN

Comes, if he comes at all, among sumach. Big Foot. Paul Muldoon. CP-MuldP

Comes the time when it's later. Wicker Basket, A. Robert Creeley. CP-CreeR

Comes to mind as another small upheaval. Frog, The. Paul Muldoon. CP-MuldP

Comes Winter, the Sea Hunting. Norman Dubie. CP-DubiN

Comet. Federico García Lorca. CP-GarcF, *tr.* by Jerome Rothenberg *Fr.* Night (Suite for Piano and Poet's Voice).

Comet, The. Michael Palmer. SP-PalmM

Comet, The. Jones Very. CP-VeryJ

Comet at Yell'ham, The. Thomas Hardy. CP-HardT

Comet of Prophecy, The. Nicholas Vachel Lindsay. CP-LindV

Comet Watch on Indian Key—Night of April 10, 1986. May Swenson. SP-SwenM

Comets and Princes. Samuel Johnson. CP-JohnS
  (Translation of a Distich on the Duke of Modena.) CP-JohnS

Comets you say shoot from nothing? Kepler. Lorine Niedecker. CP-NiedL *Fr.* Element Mother, The.

Comfort. Elizabeth Barrett Browning. CP-BroEB

Comfort. Robert Creeley. CP-CreeR

Comfort. Walter De la Mare. CP-DeLaW

Comfort. Jones Very. CP-VeryJ

Comfort. William Carlos Williams. CP-WilW2

Comfort at hand! Pluck up thy heart. Sir Thomas Wyatt. CP-WyatT ·

Comfort for Communists. G. K. Chesterton. CP-ChesG

Comfort In Calamity. Robert Herrick. CP-HerrR

Comfort me from wherever you are. Rainer Maria Rilke. CP-RilkFr, *tr.* by A. Poulin, Jr.

Comfort thyself, my wo[e]ful heart. Sir Thomas Wyatt. CP-WyatT

Comfort to a Lady Upon the Death of Her Husband. Robert Herrick. CP-HerrR

Comfort to a Youth That Had Lost His Love. Robert Herrick. CP-HerrR

Comfort with a purring cat. Ralph Waldo Emerson. CP-EmerR

Comfortable craggy slope, The. Going. Richard Eberhart. CP-EberR

Comforter, The. Donald Davie. CP-DaviDC

Comforter and the Betrayer, The. Tennessee Williams. CP-WillT

Comforters, The. Rudyard Kipling. CP-KiplR

Comforters, The. George Oppen. CP-OppGN

Comforting Reflection, A. G. K. Chesterton. CP-ChesG *Fr.* Thought and Reflections.

Comforts in Contentions. Robert Herrick. CP-HerrR

Comforts in Crosses. Robert Herrick. CP-HerrR

Comic Books vs. History. Margaret Atwood. SP-AtwM1

Coming. Philip Larkin. CP-LarkP

Coming. Heather McHugh. SP-McHuH

Coming, The. Josephine Jacobsen. CP-JacoJ

Coming, The. Jones Very. CP-VeryJ

Coming about / When the squall knocked her. Squall. George Oppen. CP-OppGN

Coming around the corner of the dark trail . . . what was wrong with the. Inquisitors, The. Robinson Jeffers. CP-JefR3

Coming at Last to Night's Most Thankful Springs. Philip Larkin. CP-LarkP

Coming Awake. D. H. Lawrence. CP-LawrD

Coming Back. Pablo Neruda. SP-NeruP

Coming Back in the Spring. W. S. Merwin. SP-MerwWF

Coming back over the col between. Strength through Joy. Kenneth Rexroth. CP-RexrK

Coming Back to America. James Dickey. CP-DickJ

Coming by evening through the wintry city. At a Bach Concert. Adrienne Rich. CP-RicAE; SP-RicA2

Coming by noon to all the branches. What Troubles I Have Seen in Birdlegged Spring. Thomas Merton. CP-MertT

Coming, clean from the Maryland-end. Told by "The Noted Traveler." James Whitcomb Riley. CP-RileJ *Fr.* Child-World, A.

Coming Down Cleveland Avenue. James Tate. SP-TateJ

Coming down / out of the freezing sky. White Owl Flies Into and Out of the Field. Mary Oliver. SP-OlivM

Coming down the hill into this town. Address to the Senior Class. William Stafford. SP-StafWW

Coming down the mountain in the twilight. Where the Hayfields Were. Archibald MacLeish. CP-MacLA

Coming down the village lane. Sacks, The. James Laughlin. CP-LaugJ

Coming Down through Somerset. Ted Hughes. SP-HughTN

Coming Down to the Desert at Lordsburg, N.M. Hayden Carruth. CP-CarHS

Coming Fall, The. Denise Levertov. SP-LeveDP

Coming from the deli / a block away today I. This Dark Apartment. James Schuyler. CP-SchuJ

Coming here, we were like that mountain whose base. Seanchas. Paul Muldoon. CP-MuldP

Coming Home. Robert Creeley. SP-CreeR

Coming Home. Tess Gallagher. SP-GallT

Coming Home, *Detroit,* 1968. Philip Levine. SP-LeviP

Coming home, I find you still in bed. Abortion. Ai. SP-Ai

Coming home on a summer night. Small Moon. Howard Nemerov. CP-NemeH

Coming home with the last load I ride standing. Emergency Haying. Hayden Carruth. CP-CarHS

Coming late, as always. Poem, The: "Coming late, as always." W. S. Merwin. SP-MerwW

Coming of Age. John Logan. CP-LogaJ

Coming of Fox, The. Lucille Clifton. SP-ClifL

Coming of Good Luck, The. Robert Herrick. CP-HerrR

Coming of May, The. E. E. Cummings. CP-CummE

Coming of Quetzalcoatl, The. D. H. Lawrence. CP-LawrD

Coming of Spring, The. James Laughlin. CP-LaugJ

Coming of the Cold, The. Theodore Roethke. CP-RoetT

Coming of the End, The. Thomas Hardy. CP-HardT

Coming of War, The; Actaeon. Ezra Pound. SP-PounE

Coming of Wisdom with Time, The. William Butler Yeats. CP-YeatW

Coming Out. Miller Williams. CP-WillM

Coming out of Sleep. Lorine Niedecker. CP-NiedL

Coming out of the earth and going. Two Possibilities. A. R. Ammons. CP-AmmoA

Coming Storm, The. Herman Melville. SP-MelvH

Comin[g] thro' [*or* through] the Rye. Robert Burns. CP-BurnR

Coming To. A. R. Ammons. CP-AmmoA

Coming to a pinywoods. Interval. A. R. Ammons. CP-AmmoA

Coming to a rockwall. Terminus. A. R. Ammons. CP-AmmoA

Coming to Christ. Robert Herrick. CP-HerrR

Coming to cottonwoods, an. Prospecting. A. R. Ammons. CP-AmmoA

Coming to Sumer and the tamarisks on the river. A. R. Ammons. CP-AmmoA

Coming up England by a different line. I Remember, I Remember. Philip Larkin. CP-LarkP

Coming Up Oxford Street: Evening. Thomas Hardy. CP-HardT

Coming up to the mountaintop. Mountaintop. Federico García Lorca. CP-GarcF, *tr. by* Jerome Rothenberg *Fr.* Shadow.

Comings on of Faith, The. Faith and Light. Jones Very. CP-VeryJ

Command the Roofe great Genius, and from thence. To the Genius of His House. Robert Herrick. CP-HerrR

Commandant, Black Chen, has walked, The. On the Chinese Abduction of Tibet's Child Panchen Lama. Norman Dubie. CP-DubiN

Commander Lowell. Robert Lowell. SP-LoweR

Commander's Footsteps, The. Aleksandr Aleksandrovich Blok. SP-BlokA, *tr. by* Peter France *and* Jon Stallworthy

Commandments. D. H. Lawrence. CP-LawrD

Commas in Wintertime. Richard Eberhart. CP-EberR

Commemoration. Wisława Szymborska. SP-SzymWM, *tr. by* Joanna Trzeciak

Commemorative of a Naval Victory. Herman Melville. SP-MelvH

Commencement, Pingree School. John Updike. CP-UpdiJ

Commend to you my cares for the love I love. Catullus. *See My love & I* are yours to command

Commendatory Sonnets. Edmund Spenser. CP-Spens

Commendatory Verses to Edmund Spenser's Fairy Queen. Sir Walter Ralegh. Another of the Same. CP-RaleW

    Vision upon This Concei[p]t of the Faerie [*or* Faery] Queen[e], A. CP-RaleW

Commendo tibi, Nashe, Puritanum. Ad Nashum. Thomas Campion. CP-CampT

Comment. Langston Hughes. CP-HughL; CP-HughL2

Comment. Dorothy Parker. CP-ParkD

Comment against Lamp Post. Langston Hughes. CP-HughL3

2. Comment on "Business Jacob, the Angel Wrestler." Alan Dugan. CP-DugaA

Comment on Curb. Langston Hughes. CP-HughL; CP-HughL3 *Fr.* Lenox Avenue Mural.

2. Comment on 1. Alan Dugan. CP-DugaA

Comment on Stoop. Langston Hughes. CP-HughL3

Comment on the Relevance of Modern Science to the Everyday Lives of the Larger Animals, A. Eleanor Wilner. SP-WilnE

Comment on War. Langston Hughes. CP-HughL; CP-HughL1

Commerce. Raymond Carver. CP-CarvR

Commerce Has Markets. Shmuel HaNagid. SP-HaNaS, *tr. by* Peter Cole

Commercial Candour. G. K. Chesterton. CP-ChesG

Commercial Leech Farming Today. Thomas Lux. SP-LuxT

Commercial Variations. Frank O'Hara. SP-OharF

Commingling sky, A. Freely Espousing. James Schuyler. CP-SchuJ

Comminuit brum a rainy day / when he can't play outside. Saxo Cere. James Laughlin. CP-LaugJ

Commitment, A. Richard Eberhart. CP-EberR

Committee, The—now a permanent body. Dream. Marianne Craig Moore. CP-MoorM

Committee's fat, The. Un-American Investigators. Langston Hughes. CP-HughL; CP-HughL3

Committing crimes behind closed doors. Shih-te. CP-ColdM, *tr. by* Red Pine

Commodore Barry. Donald Davie. CP-DaviDC

Common Cold, The. Ogden Nash. CP-NashO

Common enough mistake, A. Entrance to the Underworld, The. Gregory Orr. SP-OrrG

Common Grave, The. James Dickey. CP-DickJ

Common Ground, A. Denise Levertov. SP-LeveDP; SP-LeveDS

Common Holly bears a berry. Golden Holly. Christina Georgina Rossetti. CP-RosC3

Common Life, The. Wallace Stevens. CP-StevW; CP-StevWP

Common Miracles. Yannis Ritsos. SP-RitsY, *tr. by* Kimon Friar *and* Kostas Myrsiades

Common Place. Charles Olson. CP-OlsoC

Common Question, The. John Greenleaf Whittier. CP-WhitJ

Common Saw, A. Howard Nemerov. CP-NemeH

Common School, The. Jones Very. CP-VeryJ

Common Things. Paul Laurence Dunbar. CP-DunbP

Common Wisdom, The. Howard Nemerov. CP-NemeH

Commonplace, A. Theodore Weiss. SP-WeisT

Commonplace Day, A. Thomas Hardy. CP-HardT

Commonplace miracle. Miracle Fair. Wisława Szymborska. SP-SzymWM, *tr. by* Joanna Trzeciak

Commonplace miracle, The. Miracle Fair. Wisława Szymborska. SP-SzymW, *tr. by* Stanisław Barańczak *and* Clare Cavanagh

Commonplace, The. Walt Whitman. CP-WhitW

Communication. A. R. Ammons. CP-AmmoA

Communication I. Maya Angelou. SP-AngeM

Communication II. Maya Angelou. SP-AngeM

Communications of Meaning. Wallace Stevens. CP-StevWP

Communion. Charles Bukowski. SP-BukC1

Communion. Paul Laurence Dunbar. CP-DunbP

Communion. Langston Hughes. CP-HughL; CP-HughL2

Communion 1. David Ignatow. SP-IgnaD

Communion 2. David Ignatow. SP-IgnaD

Communion, The. Thomas Merton. CP-MertT

Communion, The. Jones Very. CP-VeryJ

Communiqué. Langston Hughes. CP-HughL; CP-HughL3

Communiqué. Yusef Komunyakaa. CP-KomuY

Communist. John Berryman. CP-BerrJ

Community. John Donne. CP-DonnJ; MW-DonnJ

Community. Marge Piercy. SP-PierM

Community of the Spirit, A. Jelaluddin Rumi. SP-Rumi, *tr. by* Coleman Barks

Commuted Sentence, The. Stevie Smith. CP-SmitS

Commuter train speeds through detachments, The. Close of Summer, The. Adam Zagajewski. SP-ZagaA, *tr. by* Renata Gorczynski, Benjamin Ivry *and* C. K. Williams

Commuter's Entry in a Connecticut Diary. Robert Penn Warren. CP-WarrR

Comp. Religion. John Updike. CP-UpdiJ

Compact. Robert Graves. CP-GravR

Compact, The: at Volterra. Charles Tomlinson. CP-TomlC; SP-TomlC

Companion, The. Marilyn Hacker. SP-HackM

Companion, The. Edwin Arlington Robinson. CP-RobiE

Companion in Rome, whom Rome makes as old as Rome. Derek Walcott. CP-WalcD *Fr.* Midsummer.

Companion—North-East Dug-Out. Ivor Gurney. SP-GurnI

Companion to the Foregoing [Love Lies Bleeding]. William Wordsworth. CP-WorW2

Companionable Ills, The. Sylvia Plath. CP-PlatS

Companionless / Without trace you are. Wind. Kathleen Jessie Raine. SP-RainK

Companions. Archibald MacLeish. CP-MacLA

Companions, The. Wendell Berry. CP-BerrW

Companions, The. Ivor Gurney. SP-GurnI

Companions, The. Howard Nemerov. CP-NemeH

Companions, all day long we've stood. Emily Jane Brontë. CP-BronE

Companion's Progress, A. Paul Laurence Dunbar. CP-DunbP

Company. Raymond Carver. CP-CarvR

Company. Rita Dove. SP-DoveR

Company. Stevie Smith. CP-SmitS

Company Manners. James Whitcomb Riley. CP-RileJ

Company of Men, The. Charles Olson. CP-OlsoC

Comparative Iconography. Hayden Carruth. CP-CarHS

Compari. D. H. Lawrence. CP-LawrD

Comparison. Paul Laurence Dunbar. CP-DunbP

Comparison, A. William Cowper. CP-CowpW

Comparison, The. John Donne. MW-DonnJ *Fr.* Elegies.

Comparison, The. Thomas Carew. CP-CareT

Comparison of Love to a Streame Falling from the Alpes. Sir Thomas Wyatt. CP-WyatT

Comparisons. G. K. Chesterton. CP-ChesG

Comparisons. Christina Georgina Rossetti. CP-RosC2

Compass. Jorge Luis Borges. SP-BorgJ, *tr. by* Alastair Reid

Compass. Jorge Luis Borges. CP-WilbR, *tr. by* Richard Wilbur

Compassion. Thomas Hardy. CP-HardT

Compassion. Jones Very. CP-VeryJ

Compassion. Miller Williams. CP-WillM

Compassion in the world again is bred. Ralphius. John Donne. CP-DonnJ; MW-DonnJ

Compelled by calamity's magnet. Aftermath. Sylvia Plath. CP-PlatS

Compendium. Rita Dove. SP-DoveR

Compensation. Paul Laurence Dunbar. CP-DunbP

Compensation. Ralph Waldo Emerson. CP-EmerR

Compensations. Ivor Gurney. SP-GurnI

Compensations. A. K. Ramanujan. CP-RamaA

Competitions of the sky, The. Emily Dickinson. CP-DickE

Complacencies of the peignoir, and late. Sunday Morning. Wallace Stevens. CP-StevW; CP-StevWP

Complacency! My Father! Emily Dickinson. SP-DickE

Complacency of this student, late, The. Monday Morning. Billy Collins. SP-CollB

Complaining. George Herbert. CP-HerbG

Complaining, alas, without redress. Sir Thomas Wyatt. CP-WyatT

Complaint. Richard Wilbur. CP-WilbR

Complaint. William Carlos Williams. CP-WilW1

Complaint. James Wright. CP-WrigJ

Complaint, A. Gerard Manley Hopkins. CP-HopkG

Complaint, A. William Wordsworth. CP-WorW1; MW-WorW

Complaint, The. John Logan. CP-LogaJ *Fr.* Epilogue, Songs of the Spouses, Complaint of Love.

Complaint, The. Jones Very. CP-VeryJ

Complaint and Reply. Robert Graves. CP-GravR

Complaint of a Forsaken Indian Woman, The. William Wordsworth. CP-WorW1

Complaint of Annelida to False Arcite, The. Geoffrey Chaucer. CP-BroEB

Complaint of Chaucer to His Empty Purse, The. Geoffrey Chaucer. CP-ChauG (Complaint of Chaucer to His Purse, The.) CP-ChauG

Complaint of Chaucer to His Purse, The. Geoffrey Chaucer. *See* Complaint of Chaucer to His Empty Purse, The

Complaint of Love. Sir Philip Sidney. SP-SidnP *Fr.* Arcadia.

Complaint of Mars, The. Geoffrey Chaucer. CP-ChauG

Complaint of the Fair Armoress [*or* Armouress], The. François Villon. SP-SwinA, *tr. by* Algernon Charles Swinburne

Complaint of the Skeleton to Time. Allen Ginsberg. CP-GinsA

Complaint of Venus, The. Geoffrey Chaucer. CP-ChauG

Complaint on the Miseries of Life, A. James Thomson. CP-ThomD

Complaint to Four Angels. Ogden Nash. CP-NashO

Complaint: To the Muse. Philip Whalen. SP-WhalP

Complaint unto His Lady, A. Geoffrey Chaucer. CP-ChauG

Complaint unto Pity, The. Geoffrey Chaucer. CP-ChauG

Complane I wald, wist I quhome till. William Dunbar. CP-DunbW

Complaynt d'Amours. Geoffrey Chaucer. CP-ChauG

Complaynt of Schir David Lindesay, The. Sir David Lyndsay. SP-LyndD

Complement, The. Thomas Carew. CP-CareT

Complete Destruction. William Carlos Williams. CP-WilW1

Completely New Set of Objects, A. Wallace Stevens. CP-StevW; CP-StevWP

Completely protected on all sides. Observer, The. Adrienne Rich. CP-RicAE; SP-RicA2

Complex, The. David Ignatow. SP-IgnaD

Complex Autumnal. Carolyn Kizer. CP-KizeC

Complexity o'erwhelms the gist. Even. A. R. Ammons. CP-AmmoA

Complexity, The. William Carlos Williams. CP-WilW2

Compleyne ne koude, ne might myn herte never. Balade of Complaint, A. Geoffrey Chaucer. CP-ChauG

Compleynt Blossoms April to July. Charles Olson. CP-OlsoC

Compleynt, compleynt I hearde upon a day. Canto 30: "Compleynt, compleynt I hearde upon a day." Ezra Pound. SP-PounE *Fr.* Cantos.

Compliance. Ambrose Bierce. SP-BierA

Compliment to the Ladies, A. William Blake. CP-BlakW (Imitation of Pope A Compliment to the Ladies.) CP-BlakW

Complimentary Pieces to Milton. *Various authors.* CP-CowpW

Compliments of a Friend. Ogden Nash. CP-NashO

Compline. John Berryman. CP-BerrJ

Compline. Richard Crashaw. CP-CrasR

Compline. Philip Larkin. CP-LarkP

Compline. James McMichael. SP-McMiJ

Compos'd in a Dancing Room, December 69. Annis Boudinot Stockton. CP-StocA

Composed after a Journey across the Hambleton [*or* Hamilton] Hills, Yorkshire. William Wordsworth. CP-WorW1 (Ere we had reached the wished-for place, night fell.) MW-WorW

Composed after Reading a Newspaper of the Day. William Wordsworth. CP-WorW2

Composed among the Ruins of a Castle in North Wales. William Wordsworth. CP-WorW2; MW-WorW

Composed as I am, like others. Elements of Composition. A. K. Ramanujan. CP-RamaA

Composed at Cora Linn in Sight of Wallace's Tower. William Wordsworth. CP-WorW2

Composed at Neidpath Castle, the Property of Lord Queensberry,1803. William Wordsworth. CP-WorW1 (Sonnet Composed at—Castle.) CP-WorW1

Composed at the Same Time and on the Same Occasion. William Wordsworth. *See* Sonnet: Composed While the Author Was Engaged in Writing a Tract Occasioned by the Convention of Cintra

Composed by the Sea-Shore. William Wordsworth. CP-WorW2

Composed by the Sea-Side, near Calais, August, 1802. William Wordsworth. CP-WorW1; MW-WorW

Composed by the Side of Grasmere Lake. William Wordsworth. CP-WorW1

Composed During a Storm. William Wordsworth. CP-WorW2

Composed in One of the Valleys of Westmoreland, on Easter Sunday. William Wordsworth. CP-WorW2

Composed in Roslin Chapel, During a Storm. William Wordsworth. CP-WorW2

Composed in the Glen of Loch Etive. William Wordsworth. CP-WorW2

Composed in the Valley near Dover, on the Day of Landing. William Wordsworth. CP-WorW1 (Dear fellow Traveller! here we are once more.) MW-WorW

Composed near Calais, on the Road Leading to Ardres, August 7, 1802. William Wordsworth. CP-WorW1

Composed of horny, jagged *black Tropical* Beetles. John Updike. CP-UpdiJ

Composed of priests and laymen, a procession. *Grand Procession* of Priests and Laymen. Constantine P. Cavafy. CP-CavaC, *tr. by* Theoharis Constantine Theoharis

Composed on a May Morning. William Wordsworth. CP-WorW2

Composed on the Banks of a Rocky Stream. William Wordsworth. CP-WorW2

Composed on the Eve of the Marriage of a Friend in the Vale of Grasmere, 1812. William Wordsworth. CP-WorW1

Composed / solely of carbon and soot-roses. Night-Train, The. Charles Tomlinson. CP-TomlC

Composed upon an Evening of Extraordinary Splendour and Beauty. William Wordsworth. CP-WorW2; MW-WorW

Composed upon Westminster Bridge, September 3, 1802. William Wordsworth. CP-WorW1; MW-WorW

Composed When a Probability Existed of Our Being Obliged to Quit Rydal Mount as a Residence. William Wordsworth. CP-WorW2

Composed While the Author Was Engaged in Writing a Tract, Occasioned by the Convention of Cintra. William Wordsworth. CP-WorW1

Composer, The. W. H. Auden. CP-AudeW

Composer's Winter Dream, The. Norman Dubie. CP-DubiN

Composing. A. R. Ammons. CP-AmmoA

Composition. May Sarton. SP-SartM

Composition. Charles Tomlinson. CP-TomlC

Composition. Philip Whalen. SP-WhalP

Composition. William Carlos Williams. CP-WilW1

Composition / Beginning to write. Continuing finally to write. Writing finally to continue beginning, A. Beginning of Writing, The. Robert Duncan. SP-DuncR

Composition in Gold and Red-Gold. Robert Penn Warren. CP-WarrR

Composition in Grey and Pink. Charles Wright. SP-WrigC

Compound bass roar, A. Song of the Night. Thomas Kinsella. CP-KinsT

Compra? Compra?—the street cry. Teotihuacán. Charles Tomlinson. CP-TomlC

Comprehension of good and evil is given in the running of the blood. One More Day. Czeslaw Milosz. CP-MiloC; CP-MiloCN, *tr. by* Robert Hass

Compromises. Yannis Ritsos. SP-RitsY, *tr. by* N. C. Germanacos

Compulsive Obligatory Paranoia Flashes. Philip Whalen. SP-WhalP

Compulsory Chapel. Alice Walker. CP-WalkA

Compunction at presumption. Woe unto Thee! Donald Davie. CP-DaviDC

Computation, The. John Donne. CP-DonnJ; MW-DonnJ

Comrade. Paul Laurence Dunbar. CP-DunbP

Comrade Lenin of Russia. Ballads of Lenin. Langston Hughes. CP-HughL; CP-HughL1

Comrade locust sings / With a splinter in his throat. Radicals. Jorge Carrera Andrade. CP-MertT

Comrade of the snow & wind. Ralph Waldo Emerson. CP-EmerR

Comrade or the book is good, The. Ralph Waldo Emerson. CP-EmerR

Comrade Past & Mister Present. Andrei Codrescu. SP-CodrA

Comraderie. Ezra Pound. CP-PoEar

Comrades, leave me here a little, while as yet 'tis early morn. Locksley Hall. Alfred Tennyson. CP-TennA

Comus; a Masque Presented at Ludlow Castle. John Milton. CP-MiltJ (Mask, A.) CP-MiltJ

Con Brio. William Carlos Williams. CP-WilW1

Con the dead page as 'twere live love: press on! Her Reproach. Thomas Hardy. CP-HardT

Conan. Thomas Gray. CP-GrayT

Concealment, The: Ishi, the Last Wild Indian. William Stafford. SP-StafW; SP-StafWW

Concei[p]t begotten by the eyes. Poesie to Prove Affection is Not Love, A. Sir Walter Ralegh. CP-RaleW

Conceit. D. H. Lawrence. CP-LawrD

Conceit, A. Maya Angelou. SP-AngeM

Conceive a man,should he have anything. E. E. Cummings. CP-CummE; SP-CummE

Concentrate on the top of the mast, father. Fanny Howe. SP-HoweF *Fr.* Introduction to the World.

Concentrations. A. R. Ammons. CP-AmmoA

Concepción. Gabriela Mistral. SP-MistG, *tr. by* Maria Giachetti [*or* Jacketti]

Concept is interesting, The: to see, as though reflected. Wet Casements. John Ashbery. SP-AshbJ

Concept Self-Conceived, A. Robert Frost. CP-FrosR

Conception. Galway Kinnell. SP-KinnGN

Conception. Hugh MacDiarmid. SP-MacDH

Concerned, against our wish, with a sick world. Fetter, The. Robert Graves. CP-GravR

Concerned as I am with the West Highlands and Hebrides. Why. Hugh MacDiarmid. SP-MacDH

Concerning a Jackass. Charles Baudelaire. CP-BaudC, *tr. by* Walter Martin

RaleW

Conjectural Poem. Jorge Luis Borges. SP-BorgJ, *tr. by* Alastair Reid

Conjecture. Thomas Hardy. CP-HardT

Conjecturing a Climate. Emily Dickinson. CP-DickE

Conjugation of the Paramecium, The. Muriel Rukeyser. CP-RukeM

Conjugations of the verb "to be." Firesticks. Stanley Kunitz. CP-KunSC

Conjunction. Robert Graves. CP-GravR

Conjunction "Or," The. Yannis Ritsos. SP-RitsY, *tr. by* Kimon Friar

Conjunctions. William Butler Yeats. CP-YeatW

Conjuration. Richard Wilbur. CP-WilbR

Conjuration, to Electra, A. Robert Herrick. CP-HerrR

Conjuring in Heaven. Ted Hughes. SP-HughTN

Conjuring Roethke. James Tate. SP-TateJ

Connais-tu peut-être la chanson ancienne "C'était un étranger." Petit Poème en Prose. Frank O'Hara. SP-OharF

Connect! Connect! cries my disconnecting. A. K. Ramanujan. CP-RamaA

Connection, The. Charles Olson. CP-OlsoC

Connections. Stephen Dobyns. SP-DoveR

Connections. William Stafford. SP-StafWW

Connections: Vermont Vietnam (I). Grace Paley. CP-PalGC

Connections: Vermont Vietnam (II). Grace Paley. CP-PalGC

Conniving Thallus, mulley, you, cony cully, cop below. Catullus. *See* From Thallus the pederast

Connoisseur of Chaos. Wallace Stevens. CP-StevW; CP-StevWP

Connotation of infinity, A. E. E. Cummings. CP-CummE

Connubial. Heather McHugh. SP-McHuH

Connubii Flores, or the Well-Wishes at Weddings. Robert Herrick. CP-HerrR

Conquer we shall, but we must first contend. End, The. Robert Herrick. CP-HerrR

Conqueror. Charles Olson. CP-OlsoC

Conqueror, The. James Whitcomb Riley. CP-RileJ

Conqueror, The. Yannis Ritsos. SP-RitsY, *tr. by* Kimon Friar

Conqueror Worm, The. Edgar Allan Poe. CP-PoeEd

Conquerors, The. Paul Laurence Dunbar. CP-DunbP

Conquest. William Carlos Williams. CP-WilW1

Conquest, The. Lord Byron. CP-Byron

Conquest by Flight. Thomas Carew. CP-CareT

Conquest of Finland, The. John Greenleaf Whittier. CP-WhitJ

Conquest of Granada, The. John Dryden.

    Epilogue to the Second Part of *The Conquest of Granada.* SP-DrydJ

    Song: "Wherever I am, and whatever I do." SP-DrydJ

Conquistador. Archibald MacLeish. CP-MacLA

Conquistador! Live dangerously, my Byron. To Thom Gunn in Los Altos, California. Donald Davie. CP-DaviDC

Conscience. George Herbert. CP-HerbG

Conscience. D. H. Lawrence. CP-LawrD

Conscience. C. K. Williams. SP-WillC

Conscience and Remorse. Paul Laurence Dunbar. CP-DunbP

Conscience is instinct bred in the house. Henry David Thoreau. CP-ThorH

Conscientious Objection. Sam Hamill. SP-HamiS

Conscientious Objector. Edna St. Vincent Millay. CP-MillE

Conscientious Objector, The. Karl Shapiro. SP-ShapK

Conscientiously bringing my mind to bear on this problem. Carmen 116. Catullus. CP-ZukLS *Fr.* Carmina.

Conscious. Wilfred Owen. CP-OwenW

Conscious am I in my Chamber. Emily Dickinson. CP-DickE

Consciousness. Robinson Jeffers. CP-JefR1

Consciousness. Czeslaw Milosz. CP-MiloC; CP-MiloCN, *tr. by* Robert Hass

Consciousness enclosed in itself every separate birch. Consciousness. Czeslaw Milosz. CP-MiloC; CP-MiloCN, *tr. by* Robert Hass

Consciousness / in itself. Who Shall Doubt. George Oppen. CP-OppGN

Consciousness is the only home. Emily Dickinson. SP-DickE

Conscript. Philip Larkin. CP-LarkP

Conscript, The. Louis MacNeice. CP-MacNL

Conscript, The. Stephen Spender. CP-SpenS

Consecrating Mother, The. Anne Sexton. CP-SextA; SP-SextA

Consent, The. Howard Nemerov. CP-NemeH

Consequences. Rudyard Kipling. *Fr.* Plain Tales from the Hills.

Consequences. William Meredith. SP-MereW

Conservative heart, outdone by all unpheaval. Variations on Variety. Josephine Jacobsen. CP-JacoJ

Conservatory Student Struggles with Higher Instrumentation. Langston Hughes. CP-HughL; CP-HughL2

Conserved in dews. Its Time. James McMichael. SP-McMiJ

Conserving the Magnitude of Uselessness. A. R. Ammons. CP-AmmoA

Consider. W. H. Auden. CP-AudeW

Consider. Lorine Niedecker. CP-NiedL

Consider. Christina Georgina Rossetti. CP-RosC1

Consider a fact: an olive. How the Elephant Got His Hump. Miller Williams. CP-WillM

Consider / a girl who keeps slipping off. Briar Rose (Sleeping Beauty). Anne Sexton. CP-SextA; SP-SextA

Consider a lady gone reckless in love. Verse Reporting Late Arrival at a Conclusion. Dorothy Parker. CP-ParkD

Consider at the outset. Lorine Niedecker. CP-NiedL

Consider big-city. Medicine for Tight Spots. A. R. Ammons. CP-AmmoA

Consider greatness. Great Men. Robinson Jeffers. CP-JefR3

Consider Icarus, pasting those sticky wings on. To a Friend Whose Work Has Come to Triumph. Anne Sexton. CP-SextA; SP-SextA

Consider me, / A colored boy. Langston Hughes. CP-HughL; CP-HughL3

Consider now, stranger, how the new land lies. New Land. Mona Van Duyn. SP-VanDM

Consider now that Troy has burned. Second-Best Bed, The. Howard Nemerov. CP-NemeH

Consider O / woman this / my body. E. E. Cummings. CP-CummE

Consider sorrowes, how they are aright. Griefe. Robert Herrick. CP-HerrR

Consider the auk. Caution to Everybody, A. Ogden Nash. CP-NashO

Consider the banker. / He was once a financial anchor. Anybody for Money? or, Just Bring Your Own Basket. Ogden Nash. CP-NashO

Consider the breaking of waves on a shore. The measure. Measure of Poetry, The. Howard Nemerov. CP-NemeH

Consider the case of Mr. Suggs. Strange Case of the Entomologist's Heart, The. Ogden Nash. CP-NashO

Consider the difference. Emptiness. Jelaluddin Rumi. SP-Rumi, *tr. by* Coleman Barks

Consider the Lapel, Sir. Ogden Nash. CP-NashO

Consider the Lilies of the Field. Christina Georgina Rossetti. CP-RosC1

Consider the Lilies of the Field. Christina Georgina Rossetti. CP-RosC2

Consider the man without a watch. I Had No Idea It Was So Late. Ogden Nash. CP-NashO

Consider the mysterious salt. In Time Like Air. May Sarton. SP-SartM

Consider the sea's listless chime. Sea-Limits, The. Dante Gabriel Rossetti. CW-RossD

Consider the three functions of the tongue. Canzone: "Consider the three functions of the tongue." Marilyn Hacker. SP-HackM

Consider this and in our time. Consider. W. H. Auden. CP-AudeW

Considerable Speck, A. Robert Frost. CP-FrosR

Considered by the logical brief clock. Strange Calendar. Stanley Kunitz. CP-KunSC

Considering the Snail. Thom Gunn. CP-GunnT

Consignee. A. R. Ammons. CP-AmmoA

Consistencies rise. Saliences. A. R. Ammons. CP-AmmoA

Consistency. Hans Magnus Enzensberger. SP-EnzeH, *tr. by* Michael Hamburger

Consistency is terrific. Killer, A. Charles Bukowski. SP-BukC1

Consolatio Nova. James Vincent Cunningham. CP-CunnJ

Consolation. Elizabeth Barrett Browning. CP-BroEB

Consolation. Billy Collins. SP-CollB

Consolation. David Ignatow. SP-IgnaD

Consolation. William Butler Yeats. CP-YeatW

Consolation of Philosophy, The ("De Consolacione Philosophie"). Boethius. CP-ChauG

    Book III. Metre 6. CP-JohnS

    "Give me, O Father! to thy throne access." CP-JohnS

    "Happy he whose eyes have view'd." CP-JohnS

    "Man who pants for ample Sway, The." CP-JohnS

    "O thou, whose all-creating hands sustain." CP-PopeA

    "O thou whose pow'r o'er moving worlds presides." CP-JohnS

    "Prudent Hind intent on Gain, The." CP-JohnS

    "Though countless as the Grains of Sand." CP-JohnS

    "Through Gripus Grounds let rich Pactolus roll." CP-JohnS

    "Truth in platonic ornaments bedeck'd." CP-JohnS

    "Unless the soul, to vice a thrall." CP-JohnS

    "Vainly the Tyrian Purple bright." CP-JohnS

    "Wouldst thou to some stedfast Seat." CP-JohnS

Consolation Sonata. Carl Sandburg. CP-SandC

Consolations. William Stafford. SP-StafW; SP-StafWW

Consolations for Double Bass. Charles Tomlinson. CP-TomlC

Consolations of Memory, The. Rudyard Kipling. CP-KiplR *Fr.* Muse among the Motors, The.

Consolations of Philosophy. Derek Mahon. CP-MahoD

Consolidation / of voices in the street, A. Square, The. Charles Tomlinson. CP-TomlC

Consorting with Angels. Anne Sexton. CP-SextA; SP-SextA

Consortium of Stones. Robert Graves. CP-GravR

Conspiracy, The. Robert Creeley. CP-CreeR

Conspiracy, The. Charles Tomlinson. CP-TomlC

Conspiracy, The. Jones Very. CP-VeryJ

Conspiracy of Two against the World. Alan Dugan. CP-DugaA

Conspirators. Raymond Carver. CP-CarvR

Constancy. Joseph Brodsky. CP-BrodJ

Constancy. George Herbert. CP-HerbG

Constancy is an evolution of one's living quarters into. Constancy. Joseph Brodsky. CP-BrodJ

Constancy to an Ideal Object. Samuel Taylor Coleridge. CP-ColeS; MW-ColeS

Constant. Louis MacNeice. CP-MacNL

Constant, The. A. R. Ammons. CP-AmmoA

Constant Bridegrooms, The. Kenneth Patchen. CP-PatcK

Constant Conversation. Jelaluddin Rumi. SP-Rumi, tr. by Coleman Barks

Constant cry against an old order, The. Polo Ponies Practicing. Wallace Stevens. CP-StevWP

Constant Defender. James Tate. SP-TateJ

Constant the waterman. Late Anniversary, A. Donald Davie. CP-DaviDC

Constant X, The. Fanny Howe. SP-HoweF Fr. In the Spirit There Are No Accidents.

Constantine the Great. Nathaniel Lee.

Epilogue: "Our hero's happy in the play's conclusion." CP-DryJ2

Constantly near you, I never in my entire. Horse Show, The. William Carlos Williams. CP-WilW2

Constantly Risking Absurdity. Lawrence Ferlinghetti. SP-FerlL

Constantly risking absurdity. Constantly Risking Absurdity. Lawrence Ferlinghetti. SP-FerlL

Consternation in household! Untitled Poem: "Consternation in household!" Alan Dugan. CP-DugaA

Constitution Day. Charles Tomlinson. CP-TomlC

Constricted by my tortured thought. Prayer before Study. Theodore Roethke. CP-RoetT

Construction. William Carlos Williams. CP-WilW2

Constructive. Heather McHugh. SP-McHuH

Consul (ere) Pompei O preened a duo, Cinna, so lay bound. Catullus. See In The Year of Pompey's First Consulate, Cinna

Consult ere thou begin'st, that done, go on. Consultation. Robert Herrick. CP-HerrR

Consultation. Robert Herrick. CP-HerrR

Consulting I Ching Smoking Pot Listening to the Fugs Sing Blake. Allen Ginsberg. CP-GinsA

Consulting summer's clock. Emily Dickinson. CP-DickE

Consulting the Oracle. Denise Levertov. SP-LeveDL

Consumed. James Tate. SP-TateJ

Consumed. Eaten away. And love across the street. Arthur Peyton. Muriel Rukeyser. CP-RukeM

Consumer, The. Marge Piercy. SP-PierM

Consummation is the hurry of fools. Emily Dickinson. SP-DickE

Consumptive, The. Langston Hughes. CP-HughL; CP-HughL1

Cont) / in / this / crazily. E. E. Cummings. CP-CummE

Contact, A. Louis MacNeice. CP-MacNL

Contact, The. Raymond Carver. CP-CarvR

Contagion. James Tate. SP-TateJ

Contained in this short Life. Emily Dickinson. CP-DickE

Contemplate, when the sun declines. Sunset and Sunrise. William Cowper. CP-CowpW

Contemplation. Federico García Lorca. CP-GarcF, tr. by Jerome Rothenberg Fr. Seaside Prints.

Contemplation, The. Olga Broumas. SP-BrouO

Contemplation of the Sword. Robinson Jeffers. CP-JefR2

Contemplation would make a good life, keep it strict, only. Cruel Falcon, The. Robinson Jeffers. CP-JefR2

Contemplations. Anne Bradstreet. CP-BradA

Contemporania. Ezra Pound.

Tenzone. SP-PounE

Contemporania. William Carlos Williams. CP-WilW1

Contemporary, A. W. S. Merwin. SP-MerwWF

Contemporary Announcement. Maya Angelou. SP-AngeM

Contemporary Portrait. Archibald MacLeish. CP-MacLA

Contempt and pangs and haunting fears— / Too late for hope, too late for ease. Exceeding Bitter Cry, An. Christina Georgina Rossetti. CP-RosC2

Contemptuous of his home beyond. Frog's Fate, A. Christina Georgina Rossetti. CP-RosC3

Contend in a sea which the land partly encloses. Yachts, The. William Carlos Williams. CP-WilW1

Contender, The. Ted Hughes. SP-HughTN

Content. Thomas Campion. CP-CampT

(Canto Quinto.) CP-CampT

Content. Paul Laurence Dunbar. CP-DunbP

Content. George Herbert. CP-HerbG

Content. David Ignatow. SP-IgnaD

Content in you. New Legends. Robert Graves. CP-GravR

Content, Not Cates. Robert Herrick. CP-HerrR

Content thee, greedy heart. Size, The. George Herbert. CP-HerbG

Content to come, content to go, / Content to wrestle or to race. Do This, and He Doeth It. Christina Georgina Rossetti. CP-RosC2

Contented Peasant, The. George Crabbe. SP-CrabG Fr. Parish Register, The.

Contented wi' Little. Robert Burns. CP-BurnR

(Song.) CP-BurnR

Contention. Robert Herrick. CP-HerrR

Contentment. Ambrose Bierce. SP-BierA

Contentment is seen at the tip, The. I am so. Old Cities. Andrei Codrescu. SP-CodrA

Contest, The. "H. D." CP-DoolH

Contest of Bards. Allen Ginsberg. CP-GinsA

"Youth the color of the hills laughed delighted at his Vanity, The." SP-GinsA

Context. Rae Armantrout. SP-ArmaA

Continent. Denise Levertov. SP-LeveDl

Continental Drift. Amy Clampitt. CP-ClamA

Continent's a tamed ox, with all its mountains, The. July Fourth by the Ocean. Robinson Jeffers. CP-JefR1

Continent's End. Robinson Jeffers. CP-JefR1

Contingency. A. R. Ammons. CP-AmmoA

Continous fabric (nerve movie?) exactly as wide as these lines, A. Preface, The: "Continous fabric (nerve movie?) exactly as wide as these lines, A." Philip Whalen. SP-WhalP

Continual Conversation with a Silent Man. Wallace Stevens. CP-StevW; CP-StevWP

Continual Ministry of Thy Anger, The. Kenneth Patchen. CP-PatcK

Continuation of a Long Poem of These States. Allen Ginsberg. CP-GinsA

Continuation of R. Garnett's Nix. Gerard Manley Hopkins. CP-HopkG

Continuation of the Landscape. Kenneth Patchen. CP-PatcK

Continuing forward with a trembling. Robert Creeley. CP-CreeR

Continuing to Live. Philip Larkin. CP-LarkP

Continuities. Walt Whitman. CP-WhitW

Continuo. Hayden Carruth. CP-CarHS

Continuo, The. Olga Broumas. SP-BrouO

Continuo, The. W. S. Merwin. SP-MerwW

Continuous Is Broken, and Resumes, The. Eleanor Wilner. SP-WilnE

Continuum. Denise Levertov. SP-LeveDL

Continuum. Adrienne Rich. CP-RicAE

Continuum: a Love Poem. Maxine W. Kumin. SP-KumiM

Contours and the shine, The. Sea-Trout and Butterfish. William Carlos Williams. CP-WilW1

Contra Mortem. Hayden Carruth. CP-CarHL

Contradictions. Rudyard Kipling. CP-KiplR Fr. Muse among the Motors, The.

Contradictions. Yannis Ritsos. SP-RitsY, tr. by Gwendolyn MacEwen and Nikos Tsingos

Contradictions: Tracking Poems. Adrienne Rich.

"Dear Adrienne, / I feel signified by pain." SP-RicA1

"Dear Adrienne: / I'm calling you up tonight." SP-RicA1

"My mouth hovers across your breasts." SP-RicA1

"Problem, unstated until now, is how, The." SP-RicA1

"This high summer we love will put its light." SP-RicA1

"You: air-driven reft from the tuber-bitten soil." SP-RicA1

"You who think I find words for everything." SP-RicA1

Contrapuntalist, A/ composer of chorales. Melchior Vulpius. Marianne Craig Moore. CP-MoorM

Contraries. A. K. Ramanujan. CP-RamaA

Contrariness of the Mad Farmer, The. Wendell Berry. CP-BerrW

Contrary Theses (I). Wallace Stevens. CP-StevW; CP-StevWP

Contrary Theses (II). Wallace Stevens. CP-StevW; CP-StevWP

Contrary to / tales you told us. Anti-Father. Rita Dove. SP-DoveR

Contrary to the views. Good Author, The. Carolyn Kizer. CP-KizeC

Contrast. Robinson Jeffers. CP-JefR1

Contrast, A. W. H. Auden. CP-AudeW

Contrast; the Parrot and the Wren, The. William Wordsworth. CP-WorW2

Contretemps, The. Thomas Hardy. CP-HardT

Contrite Heart, The. William Cowper. See Olney Hymns

Control Burn. Gary Snyder. CP-SnydG

Control of the passes was, he saw, the key. Secret Agent, The. W. H. Auden. CP-AudeW

Controversy. Ambrose Bierce. SP-BierA

Controversy, The. William Carlos Williams. CP-WilW2

Contusion. Sylvia Plath. CP-PlatS

Conundrum of the Workshops, The. Rudyard Kipling. CP-KiplR

Conundrums. D. H. Lawrence. CP-LawrD

Convalescence. James Vincent Cunningham. CP-CunnJ

Convalescent. Dorothy Parker. CP-ParkD

Convent. Langston Hughes. CP-HughL; CP-HughL2

Convent Threshold, The. Christina Georgina Rossetti. CP-RosC1

Conventional Ballad. William Carlos Williams. CP-WilW2

Conventionalist, The. Stevie Smith. CP-SmitS

Conventions of Despair. A. K. Ramanujan. CP-RamaA

Convergence. A. R. Ammons. CP-AmmoA

Convergence of the Many. René Char. CP-MertT

Convergence of the Twain, The. Thomas Hardy. CP-HardT

Convergences. Robert Penn Warren. CP-WarrR

Conversation. Ai. SP-Ai

Conversation. Charles Baudelaire. CP-BaudC, tr. by Walter Martin

Conversation. John Berryman. CP-BerrJ

Conversation. William Cowper. CP-CowpW

Conversation. Louis MacNeice. CP-MacNL

Conversation. Dan Pagis. SP-PagiD, tr. by Stephen Mitchell

Conversation. John Updike. CP-UpdiJ

Conversation, A. Margaret Atwood. SP-AtwM2

Conversation, A. Robert Bly. SP-BlyR

Conversation, The. Thom Gunn. CP-GunnT

Conversation among the Ruins. Sylvia Plath. CP-PlatS

Conversation at Dawn, A. Thomas Hardy. CP-HardT

Conversation begins / with a lie. And each, A. Cartographies of Silence. Adrienne Rich. SP-RicA2

Conversation by the Body's Light. Jane Cooper. CP-CoopJ

Conversation Galante. T. S. Eliot. CP-ElioT; SP-ElioT (Short Romance.) SP-ElioT

Conversation Galante. Charles Olson. CP-OlsoC

Conversation in a Belfry. Archibald MacLeish. CP-MacLA

Conversation in a Cheap Room. Charles Bukowski. SP-BukC2

Conversation in Moscow. Denise Levertov. SP-LeveDL

Conversation of Old Men, The. Thom Gunn. CP-GunnT

Conversation of Prayer, The. Dylan Thomas. CP-ThomD

Conversation on Morality, Eternity and Copulation, A. Charles Bukowski. SP-BukC2

Conversation with a Dirty-Minded Little Girl. Alan Dugan. CP-DugaA

Conversation with a Fireman from Brooklyn. Tess Gallagher. SP-GallT

Conversation with a Holy Woman Not Seen for Many Years. Robert Bly. SP-BlyR

Conversation with a Japanese Student. Eleanor Wilner. SP-WilnE

Conversation with a Rock. Wisława Szymborska. SP-SzymWM, tr. by Joanna Trzeciak

Conversation with a Stone. Wisława Szymborska. SP-SzymW, tr. by Stanislaw Barańczak and Clare Cavanagh

Conversation with Jeanne. Czeslaw Milosz. CP-MiloCN Fr. Two Poems.

Conversation with Leonardo, A. John Ciardi. CP-CiarJ

Conversation with my friend is particularly. E. E. Cummings. CP-CummE

Conversation with the Devil, A. Randall Jarrell. CP-JarrR

Conversation with Three Women of New England. Wallace Stevens. CP-StevWP

Conversations. Thomas Merton. CP-MertT

Conversations are simple: about food, The. Under the Window: Ouro Prêto. Elizabeth Bishop. CP-BishE

Conversations in Crisis. Audre Lorde. SP-LordA

Conversations of the French, The. Virgin Mule. Andrei Codrescu. SP-CodrA

Converse airwaves. Fanny Howe. SP-HoweF Fr. O'Clock.

Conversing with Paradise. Howard Nemerov. CP-NemeH

Conversion of Aurelian McGoggin, The. Rudyard Kipling. Fr. Plain Tales from the Hills.

Conversion of Brother Lawrence. Denise Levertov. SP-LeveDS

Conversion of St. Paul. Christina Georgina Rossetti. CP-RosC2

Convict, The. William Wordsworth. CP-WorW1

Conviction (i). Stevie Smith. CP-SmitS

Conviction (ii). Stevie Smith. CP-SmitS

Conviction (iii). Stevie Smith. CP-SmitS

Conviction (iv). Stevie Smith. CP-SmitS

Convictions, beliefs, opinions. After. Czeslaw Milosz. CP-MiloCN, tr. by Robert Hass

Convictions (Curtain Raiser). T. S. Eliot. SP-ElioT

Convinced of decrepitude. Recoleta Cemetary. Jorge Luis Borges. SP-BorgJ, tr. by Stephen Kessler

Convito. Dante Alighieri.
  Banqauet, The. CP-NemeH, tr. by Howard Nemerov

Convivio. William Carlos Williams. CP-WilW2

Convoy. Louis MacNeice. CP-MacNL

Convulsions came; and, where the field. Apparition, The—A Retrospect. Herman Melville. SP-MelvH

Conway Burying Ground. Archibald MacLeish. CP-MacLA

Coo-saw kin-ens sees seas season. Dogwood. Louis Zukofsky. CP-ZukLS

Cook County. Archibald MacLeish. CP-MacLA

Cook in Hell, A. Andrei Codrescu. SP-CodrA

Cook left his pots, The. 7 December 1948. Yannis Ritsos. SP-RitsY Fr. Exile's Journals 2.

Cook named McMurray, A. Second Limick. Ogden Nash. CP-NashO

Cooking. Sam Hamill. SP-HamiS

Cooking Egg, A. T. S. Eliot. CP-ElioT; SP-ElioT

Cool and beautiful as the blossom of the wild carrot. Aubade: "Cool and beautiful as the blossom of the wild carrot." Edna St. Vincent Millay. CP-MillE

Cool and Plain. Stevie Smith. CP-SmitS

Cool around the Fire, The. Gary Snyder. CP-SnydG

Cool as a Cucumber. Stevie Smith. CP-SmitS

Cool black night thru the redwoods. First Party at Ken Kesey's with Hell's Angels. Allen Ginsberg. CP-GinsA; SP-GinsA

Cool is the wind, for the summer is waning. To the Road. Paul Laurence Dunbar. CP-DunbP

Cool northern waters. Engine Room, S.S. Sappa Creek, The. Gary Snyder. CP-SnydG

Cool of an oak's unchequered shade, The. Last Hours. D. H. Lawrence. CP-LawrD

Cool small evening shrunk to a dog bark and the clank of a bucket, A. Full Moon and Little Frieda. Ted Hughes. SP-HughTN

Cool summer nights. Best Time of the Day, The. Raymond Carver. CP-CarvR

Cool Tombs. Carl Sandburg. CP-SandC

Cool Web, The. Robert Graves. CP-GravR

Cool with the touch of autumn, waters break. Lament for My Brother on a Hayrake. James Wright. CP-WrigJ

Cool you proceed at speed. George Meredith. CP-MerG2

Cool your heels on the rail of an observation car. Still Life. Carl Sandburg. CP-SandC

Coole Park and Ballylee, 1931. William Butler Yeats. CP-YeatW

Coole Park, 1929. William Butler Yeats. CP-YeatW

Coolea: 6 October 1971. Thomas Kinsella. CP-KinsT Fr. Selected Life, A.

Cooled Heels Lament against Frivolity, the Mask of Despair. Alan Dugan. CP-DugaA

Cooling Board, The. Yusef Komunyakaa. CP-KomuY

Cooling Tower, The. Amy Clampitt. CP-ClamA

Coolness, like the evening tide. Brother, I Am Here. "Shu Ting." CP-KizeC, tr. by Carolyn Kizer and Y. H. Zhao

Coomb-Firtrees say that Life is a moan. Yell'ham-Wood's Story. Thomas Hardy. CP-HardT

"Coon-Dog Wess"—he allus went. James Whitcomb Riley. CP-RileJ

Coon Showman. Clarence Major. SP-MajoC

Coon Song. A. R. Ammons. CP-AmmoA

Coon, why did you come to this dance. Raccoon. Anne Sexton. CP-SextA

Coopered at Fish Creek. Lorine Niedecker. CP-NiedL

Cootchie. Elizabeth Bishop. CP-BishE

Cootchie, Miss Lula's servant, lies in marl. Cootchie. Elizabeth Bishop. CP-BishE

Cop-Shooting: On a Newspaper Photograph. Alan Dugan. CP-DugaA

Copacetic Mingus. Yusef Komunyakaa. CP-KomuY

Coping. Miller Williams. CP-WillM

Copper Beech, The. Rita Dove. SP-DoveR

Copper Vat, A. A. K. Ramanujan. CP-RamaA

Coppice, The. Ivor Gurney. SP-GurnI

Cops and Robbers. Donald Hall. CP-HallD

Cops Call Him Charlie, The. Yusef Komunyakaa. CP-KomuY

Cops want me to come down and identify, The. She Came Out of the Bathroom With Her Flaming Red Hair and Said—. Charles Bukowski. SP-BukC1

Copulating Gods, The. Carolyn Kizer. CP-KizeC

Copy of a Copy of Verses from Thomas Sheridan, Clerk, to George Nim-Dan-Dean, Esq., A. Thomas Sheridan. CP-SherT

Copy of the first edition of the Edda Islandorum, by Snorri, printed in Denmark. Talismans. Jorge Luis Borges. SP-BorgJ, tr. by Alastair Reid

Copy of Verses upon Two Celebrated Modern Poets, A. Jonathan Swift. CP-SwifJ

Copying Architecture in an Old Minster. Thomas Hardy. CP-HardT

Coq au Vin. John Ciardi. CP-CiarJ

Coquette, and After, The. Thomas Hardy. CP-HardT

Coquette Conquered, A. Paul Laurence Dunbar. CP-DunbP

Cor Cordium. Countee Cullen. CP-CullC

Cor cordium is written there. Cor Cordium. Countee Cullen. CP-CullC

Cor Mio. Christina Georgina Rossetti. CP-RosC3

Cor mio, cor mio / Più non ti veggo, ma mi rammento. Christina Georgina Rossetti. CP-RosC3

Cora. Langston Hughes. CP-HughL; CP-HughL1

Coracle, The. Lucan. CP-RaleW *Fr.* Civil War [Bellum Civile] *or* Pharsalia.

Coral. Derek Walcott. CP-WalcD

Coral and clear emerald. Spirit of air, The. Walter De la Mare. CP-DeLaW

Coral worm beneath the sea, The. Ralph Waldo Emerson. CP-EmerR

Cordelia. James Laughlin. CP-LaugJ

Cordial lyre of glowing silver. Sonnet in Homage to Manuel de Falla Offering Him Some Flowers. Federico García Lorca. CP-GarcF, *tr. by* Christopher Maurer

Córdoba. / Distant and lonely. Rider's Song. Federico García Lorca. CP-GarcF, *tr. by* Alan S. Trueblood *Fr.* Andalusian Songs.

Córdoba. / Far away and alone. Rider's Song. Federico García Lorca. SP-GarcF, *tr. by* J. L. Gili *and* Stephen Spender

Corduroy Road. Rita Dove. SP-DoveR

Core of conversations we never had, A. Sister, Morning Is a Time for Miracles. Audre Lorde. SP-LordA

Core of masculinity does not derive [from being male], The. Jelaluddin Rumi. SP-Rumi, *tr. by* Coleman Barks

Core of the strong hill: not understood, The. Natural Resources. Adrienne Rich. SP-RicA2

Corinna. Jonathan Swift. CP-SwifJ

Corinna foots it in bare feet. Young Matrons Dancing. John Updike. CP-UpdiJ

Corinna, pride of Drury Lane. Beautiful Young Nymph Going to Bed, A. Jonathan Swift. CP-SwifJ

Corinna's Going a-Maying. Robert Herrick. CP-HerrR

Corinth, Argos, Sparta, Athens, Sicyon, and how many other smaller city-states. After the Breakdown of the Treaty between the Lacedaemonians and the Athenians. Yannis Ritsos. SP-RitsY, *tr. by* Kimon Friar *and* Karelisa Hartigan

Coriolan. T. S. Eliot. CP-EliotT

Cormorant, A. Ted Hughes. SP-HughTN

Cormorant in Its Element, The. Amy Clampitt. CP-ClamA

Cormorant still screams, The. Late. Louise Bogan. CP-BogaL

Corn and Beans. Carl Sandburg. CP-SandC

Corn Close. Robert Creeley. SP-CreeR

Corn has turned from grey to red, The. Rome Unvisited. Oscar Wilde. CP-WildO

Corn Hut Talk. Carl Sandburg. CP-SandC

Corn is coming along, The. Cain. Howard Nemerov. CP-NemeH

Corn Prattlings. Carl Sandburg. CP-SandC

Corn-Song, A. Paul Laurence Dunbar. CP-DunbP

Corn-Stalk Fiddle, THe. Paul Laurence Dunbar. CP-DunbP

Corn wave swarming with ravens. Below a Painting. Paul Celan. SP-CelaP, *tr. by* John Felstiner

Cornelian, The. Lord Byron. CP-Byron

Corner, The. Donald Hall. CP-HallD

Corner Meeting. Langston Hughes. CP-HughL; CP-HughL3

Corner of a great rain, The. Contemporania. William Carlos Williams. CP-WilW1

Corner of the Eye, The. Robert Penn Warren. CP-WarrR

Corner Seat. Louis MacNeice. CP-MacNL

Corner Stone, The. Walter De la Mare. CP-DeLaW

Corner Stone, The. Jones Very. CP-VeryJ

Corners of Night. Yusef Komunyakaa. CP-KomuY

Corners / Of South Parkway. Jitney. Langston Hughes. CP-HughL; CP-HughL2

Cornet Cornelius Rilke. Stephen Spender. CP-SpenS

Cornfield, The. Muriel Rukeyser. CP-RukeM

Cornfield Ridge and Stream. Carl Sandburg. CP-SandC

Cornfields, The. Nicholas Vachel Lindsay. CP-LindV

Cornflowers. James Schuyler. CP-SchuJ

Cornish Heroic Song for Valda Trevlyn. Hugh MacDiarmid.
     "Celtic genius—Cornwall, Scotland, Ireland, Wales—, The." SP-MacDH
     "His attitude towards woman is the basic point." SP-MacDH
     "I sing of Cornwall." SP-MacDH

Cornkind. Frank O'Hara. SP-OharF

Cornpicker Poem. Robert Bly. SP-BlyR

Corns, heartburn, sinus headaches, such minor ailments. Change of Air, A. W. H. Auden. CP-AudeW

Cornstarch, The. Food for Thought; or, Death Is Physical. Clarence Major. SP-MajoC

Cornucopia. Rainer Maria Rilke. CP-RilkFr, *tr. by* A. Poulin, Jr. *Fr.* Orchards.

Cornucopia. Carl Sandburg. CP-SandC

Cornucopia, The. Arthur Sze. SP-SzeA

Cornwall, the unreality. Donald Davie. CP-DaviDC

Corona. Sir Philip Sidney. SP-SidnP *Fr.* Arcadia.

Corona. Paul Celan. SP-CelaP, *tr. by* John Felstiner

Corona. Tess Gallagher. SP-GallT

Corona, The. Arthur Sze. SP-SzeA

Coronach. Sir Walter Scott. SP-ScotW *Fr.* Lady of the Lake, The.

Coronal, A. William Carlos Williams. CP-WilW1

Coronation, The. Thomas Hardy. CP-HardT

Coronation Murder, The. Robert Graves. CP-GravR

Coroner said a white picket fence, The. Open Happens in the Midst of Beings, The. Norman Dubie. CP-DubiN

Coroner's merry little children, The. Hic Jacet. William Carlos Williams. CP-WilW1

Coronet, The. Andrew Marvell. CP-MarvA

Coronet of Moonlight. Robert Graves. CP-GravR

Corot. D. H. Lawrence. CP-LawrD
     (Music of music is stillness, you birds, The.) CP-LawrD

Corporal, The. Thom Gunn. CP-GunnT

Corporate Entity. Archibald MacLeish. CP-MacLA

Corpse has walked across my shadow, A. Into the Known. Tess Gallagher. SP-GallT

Corpse my mother made, The. Addio. John Ciardi. CP-CiarJ

Corpse-Plant, The. Adrienne Rich. CP-RicAE; SP-RicA2

Corpses are cold in the tomb. Lines Written During the Castlereagh Administration. Percy Bysshe Shelley. CP-ShelP

Corpses below wooden crosses. At night. Yannis Ritsos. SP-RitsY *Fr.* Third Series.

Corpulent man is my bachelor chum, A. My Bachelor Chum. James Whitcomb Riley. CP-RileJ

Corpus Christi. John Ciardi. CP-CiarJ

Corpuscle, skin. Towards Simplicity. A. K. Ramanujan. CP-RamaA

Correct death is written in, The. Assassin, The. Anne Sexton. CP-SextA

Correction. A. R. Ammons. CP-AmmoA

Correction. Robert Herrick. CP-HerrR

Correction: *Eve* Delved and *Adam* Span. Ogden Nash. CP-NashO

Correspondence According to Baudelaire. Constantine P. Cavafy. CP-CavaC, *tr. by* Theoharis Constantine Theoharis

Correspondence between Mr. Harrison in Newcastle and Mr. Sholto Peach Harrison in Hull. Stevie Smith. CP-SmitS

Correspondence in After Years. D. H. Lawrence. CP-LawrD

Correspondences. Charles Baudelaire. CP-TateA, *tr. by* Allen Tate

Correspondences. Eugenio Montale. CP-MontE, *tr. by* Jonathan Galassi

Correspondences. Muriel Rukeyser. CP-RukeM

Corrib. An Emblem. Donald Davie. CP-DaviDC

Corridor. Federico García Lorca. CP-GarcF, *tr. by* Jerome Rothenberg *Fr.* Palimpsests.

Corridor. Yannis Ritsos. SP-RitsY, *tr. by* N. C. Germanacos

Corridor, The. Thom Gunn. CP-GunnT

Corridor, The. Edwin Arlington Robinson. CP-RobiE

Corrigan knew that loneliness is the one human passion. Birds, The. Josephine Jacobsen. CP-JacoJ

Corrigenda. Yusef Komunyakaa. CP-KomuY

Corrugated roof, The. Everybody Lying on Their Stomachs, Head toward the Candle, Reading, Sleeping, Drawing. Gary Snyder. CP-SnydG

Corrupt Tree, The. Jones Very. CP-VeryJ

Corruptible if all things are. Tricked by Eternity the Heart. Archibald MacLeish. CP-MacLA

Corruption reaps the young; you dread. Feud. Theodore Roethke. CP-RoetT

Corruptions of war and peace, the public and wholesale crimes that, The. Skunks. Robinson Jeffers. CP-JefR3

Corsair, The. Lord Byron. CP-Byron

Corsons Inlet. A. R. Ammons. CP-AmmoA

Cortège. Edwin Arlington Robinson. CP-RobiE

Cortege. Tennessee Williams. CP-WillT

Cortège for Rosenbloom. Wallace Stevens. CP-StevW; CP-StevWP

Corydon's Lament and Resolution. Christina Georgina Rossetti. CP-RosC3

Cosmic Comics. Howard Nemerov. CP-NemeH

Cosmic Factories, The. G. K. Chesterton. CP-ChesG

Cosmic Gall. John Updike. CP-UpdiJ

Cosmologist says, The. Americans, The. Charles Olson. CP-OlsoC

Cosmopolitan Greetings. Allen Ginsberg. SP-GinsA

Cosmopolites without a plea. Emily Dickinson. CP-DickE

Costa Rican Pastoral. Robert Stock. SP-StocR

Costa San Giorgio. Eugenio Montale. CP-MontE, *tr. by* Jonathan Galassi

Cosway Frazer & Baldwin of Egypts Lake. William Blake. CP-BlakW

Cot, The. Seamus Heaney. SP-HeanSO *Fr.* Glanmore Revisited.

Cot of an old lady. At Grandmother's Wake. Kenneth Patchen. CP-PatcK

Cotswold Ways. Ivor Gurney. SP-GurnI

Cottage, The. Jones Very. CP-VeryJ

Cottage Street, 1953. Richard Wilbur. CP-WilbR

Cottager and His Landlord, The. John Milton. *See* Fable of the Peasant and the Overlord, The

Cottager to Her Infant, (By My Sister), The. Dorothy Wordsworth. CP-WorW1

Cotter's Saturday Night [nscribed to Robert Aiken [*or* R. A****], Esq.], The. Robert Burns. CP-BurnR

Cotton Club, The. Clarence Major. SP-MajoC

Cotton Mather died when I was a boy. The books. Blue Buildings in the Summer Air, The. Wallace Stevens. CP-StevW; CP-StevWP

Cotton rows crisscross the world. Memory, The. Maya Angelou. SP-AngeM

Cottonmouth Country. Louise Glück. SP-GlucL

Cottonwood. William Stafford. SP-StafWW

Cottum perfidiae haud satis pudenter. Ad Ge. Chapmannum. Thomas Campion. CP-CampT

Cougar. A. R. Ammons. CP-AmmoA

Cougar, The. Raymond Carver. CP-CarvR

Cougar Meat. Tess Gallagher. SP-GallT

Coughing in the Morning. Autumn Gold: New England Fall. Allen Ginsberg. CP-GinsA

Could a more dreadful vision ever be? Petrarch. CP-Petra, *tr. by* J. G. Nichols

Could all we little folks that wait. Panegyric on the Reverend Dean Swift, A. Jonathan Swift. CP-SwifJ

Could be Hastings Street. Langston Hughes. CP-HughL; CP-HughL2

Could Have. Wisława Szymborska. SP-SzymW, *tr. by* Stanisław Barańczak *and* Clare Cavanagh

Could have made Priscilla share. Llewellyn and the Tree. Edwin Arlington Robinson. CP-RobiE

Could he possess an idea? Difficulty of Ideas, The. Richard Eberhart. CP-EberR

Could Homer come himself, distressed and poor. Epigram on the Refusal of the University of Oxford to Subscribe to His Translation of Homer. William Cowper. CP-CowpW

Could Hope inspect her Basis. Emily Dickinson. CP-DickE

Could I be sure that I shall see the day. Sonnet: "Could I be sure that I shall see the day." Allen Tate. CP-TateA

Could I but live again. Pisgah-Sights. II. Robert Browning. CP-BroR2

Could I but pour out into powerful rhyme. Petrarch. CP-Petra, *tr. by* J. G. Nichols

Could I but ride indefinite. Emily Dickinson. CP-DickE

Could I but take revenge upon that one. Petrarch. CP-Petra, *tr. by* J. G. Nichols

Could I but Will. Thomas Hardy. CP-HardT

Could—I do more—for Thee. Emily Dickinson. CP-DickE

Could I envy Maria I certainly shou'd. To Miss Mary Stockton, an Epistle upon Some Gentleman Refusing to Admit Ladies of Their Circle into the Parlour till Supper Where They Met for Conversation and Business Once a Week. Annis Boudinot Stockton. CP-StocA

Could I, from heav'n inspir'd, as sure presage. On a Similar Occasion for the Year 1788. William Cowper. CP-CowpW

Could I, heart-broken, reach his place of birth. On Correggio. Robert Browning. CP-BroR2

Could I pour out the nectar the gods only can. Traveling Man, The. James Whitcomb Riley. CP-RileJ

Could I remount the river of my years. Fragment, A: "Could I remount the river of my years." Lord Byron. CP-Byron

Could I say what I think, could I express. Sonnet: "Could I say what I think, could I express." Fernando Pessoa. SP-PessF

Could I the priest's consent have gained. William Wordsworth. CP-WorW1; MW-WorW

Could I—then—shut the door. Emily Dickinson. CP-DickE

Could I visit the Beds. Emily Dickinson. SP-DickE

Could it be that I am the one. Shard of History, A. James Laughlin. CP-LaugJ

Could Juno's self more sovereign presence wear. Venus Victrix. Dante Gabriel Rossetti. CW-RossD *Fr.* House of Life, The.

Could Kings Right a People Gone Bad. Shmuel HaNagid. SP-HaNaS, *tr. by* Peter Cole

Could live—did live. Emily Dickinson. CP-DickE

Could Love for ever. Stanzas: "Could Love for ever." Lord Byron. CP-Byron

Could man be drunk for ever. A. E. Housman. CP-HousA

Could mortal lip divine. Emily Dickinson. CP-DickE

Could my heart more tongues imploy. Thomas Campion. CP-CampT

Could my poore hart whole worlds of toungs employ. Thomas Campion. CP-CampT

Could not once blinding me, cruel[l], suffice? Samson to His Delilah. Richard Crashaw. CP-CrasR

Could one choose a more absurd route? Dark Band. Primo Levi. CP-LeviP, *tr. by* Ruth Feldman

Could She See the Whole Real World with Her Ghost Breast Eyes Shut under a Blouse Lid? Gary Snyder. CP-SnydG

Could some descending escalator. Snark Was a Boojum Was a Prawn, The. Ogden Nash. CP-NashO

Could that sweet Darkness where they dwell. Emily Dickinson. CP-DickE

"Could that"i marveled"be / you?" E. E. Cummings. CP-CummE

Could time turn on its scholars? House of Prayer, The. Shmuel HaNagid. SP-HaNaS, *tr. by* Peter Cole

Could walk on water backwards. Provincetown. Robert Creeley. SP-CreeR

Could we know how kin we are. George Meredith. CP-MerG2

Could we like youth consume the stolen night? Horologikos. Hayden Carruth. CP-CarHS

Could write of fucking—. Robert Creeley. CP-CreeR

Could ye be very blest in hearkening. Vanities. Elizabeth Barrett Browning. CP-BroEB

Could You Be Right. Lorine Niedecker. CP-NiedL

Could you not drink her gaze like wine? Card-Dealer, The. Dante Gabriel Rossetti. CW-RossD

Could you tell me how to grow. Emily Dickinson. SP-DickE

Couldn't guess it. Ambition. Robert Creeley. SP-CreeR

Council, The. W. H. Auden. CP-AudeW

Councils. Marge Piercy. SP-PierM

Counsel. Charles Bukowski. SP-BukC2

Counsel. Tennessee Williams. CP-WillT

Counsel, A. Christina Georgina Rossetti. CP-RosC3

Counsell. Robert Herrick. CP-HerrR

Counselor, The. Dorothy Parker. CP-ParkD

Counsels. Czeslaw Milosz. CP-MiloC; CP-MiloCN

Count Flanders / Was eaten up with pride. Après la Politique, la Haine des Bourbons. Stevie Smith. CP-SmitS

Count Gismond. Robert Browning. CP-BroR1

Count it anyway he wants. Variation on Guilt. Rita Dove. SP-DoveR

Count not that far that can be had. Emily Dickinson. CP-DickE

Count the number of times boards crack. Insomnia. Wyatt Prunty. SP-PrunW

Count them unclean, these tears that turn no mill. Edna St. Vincent Millay. CP-MillE

Count them. / You are able to count them. They. In the Full Severity of Mercy. Yehuda Amichai. SP-AmicY, *tr. by* Stephen Mitchell

Count them. / You may count them. They. With All the Rigor of Pity. Yehuda Amichai. SP-AmicYL, *tr. by* Benjamin Harshav *and* Barbara Harshav

Count these reminiscences like money. Carlovingian Dreams. Carl Sandburg. CP-SandC

Count up the almonds. Paul Celan. SP-CelaP, *tr. by* John Felstiner

Countenance, A. Thomas Hardy. CP-HardT

Countenance is grave but graced by candor, The. On the Southworth and Hawes Daguerreotype of Massachusetts Supreme Court Chief Justice Lemuel Shaw (1851). Helen Pinkerton. CP-PinkH

Counter. Rae Armantrout. SP-ArmaA

Counter, The. William Carlos Williams. CP-WilW2

Counter and Clubb were men in trade, whose pains. Wager, The. George Crabbe. SP-CrabG *Fr.* Tales.

Counter Mood. Countee Cullen. CP-CullC

Counterblast on Penny Trumpet. Christina Georgina Rossetti. CP-RosC3

Counterfeit—a Plated Person, A. Emily Dickinson. CP-DickE

Counterfeit Eden. Tropical Greenhouse. Dan Pagis. SP-PagiD, *tr. by* Stephen Mitchell

Countering. A. R. Ammons. CP-AmmoA

Counterpoint, A. Robert Creeley. CP-CreeR

Countess, The. John Greenleaf Whittier. CP-WhitJ

Countess Cathleen in Paradise, The. William Butler Yeats. CP-YeatW

Countess' Pillar. William Wordsworth. CP-WorW2

Counting. Philip Larkin. CP-LarkP

Counting. Carl Sandburg. CP-SandC

Counting Houses, The. W. S. Merwin. SP-MerwWF

Counting on Flowers. John Ciardi. CP-CiarJ

Counting-out Rhyme. Edna St. Vincent Millay. CP-MillE

Counting-Out Song, A. Rudyard Kipling. CP-KiplR *Fr.* Land and Sea Tales.

Counting Small-Boned Bodies. Robert Bly. SP-BlyR

Counting the Beats. Robert Graves. CP-GravR

Countless gold of a merry heart, The. Riches. William Blake. CP-BlakW

Countless these crosses and these ruinous stones. Taciturn, The. Walter De la Mare. CP-DeLaW

Countries. Federico García Lorca.

    Snows. CP-GarcF, *tr. by* Jerome Rothenberg

    Worlds. CP-GarcF, *tr. by* Jerome Rothenberg

Countries we depart will manage without us, The. Goodbye, Göteborg. John Updike. CP-UpdiJ

Country. Langston Hughes. CP-HughL

Country & Western II. Marilyn Hacker. SP-HackM

Country Bath. Josephine Jacobsen. CP-JacoJ

Country beneath / the earth has a green sun, The. Procedures for Underground. Margaret Atwood. SP-AtwM1

Country Club, The. Paul Muldoon. CP-MuldP

Country Drive-In. Josephine Jacobsen. CP-JacoJ

Country Editor, The. James Whitcomb Riley. CP-RileJ

Country Excursion. Kenneth Patchen. CP-PatcK

Country is a funny place, The. Nine Miles to the Railroad. Ogden Nash. CP-NashO

Country is so populous that polygamists and serial, The. Postcard, A. Joseph Brodsky. CP-BrodJ

Country Lassie. Robert Burns. CP-BurnR

Country Life, A. Randall Jarrell. CP-JarrR

Country Life: To His Brother, M. Tho: Herrick. Robert Herrick. CP-HerrR

Country Life, to the Honored Mr. Endymion Porter[, Groome of the Bed-Chamber to His Maj.], The. Robert Herrick. CP-HerrR

Country Lover. Maya Angelou. SP-AngeM

Country Mansion, A. Robert Graves. CP-GravR

Country Matters. Raymond Carver. CP-CarvR

Country Midwife, The: A Day. Ai. SP-Ai

Country of a Thousand Years of Peace, The. James Merrill. SP-MerrJ

Country of hunchbacks!—where the strong, straight spine. Sonnet to Gath. Edna St. Vincent Millay. CP-MillE

Country of Marriage, The. Wendell Berry. CP-BerrW

Country Pathway, A. James Whitcomb Riley. CP-RileJ

Country singing while working. Rainer Maria Rilke. CP-RilkFr, tr. by A. Poulin, Jr. Fr. Valaisian Quatrains, The.

Country Squire and the Mandrake, The. Christopher Smart. SP-SmarC

Country Stars. William Meredith. SP-MereW

Country surrounds the city, The. Revolution in the Revolution in the Revolution. Gary Snyder. CP-SnydG

Country Walk, A. Thomas Kinsella. CP-KinsT

Country Was, The. Randall Jarrell. CP-JarrR

Country Wedding, The. Thomas Hardy. CP-HardT

Country Week-End. Louis MacNeice. CP-MacNL

Country Western. Robert Creeley. SP-CreeR

Country & Western. Marilyn Hacker. SP-HackM

Country Woman. Yannis Ritsos. SP-RitsY, tr. by Kimon Friar

Country Words. Wallace Stevens. CP-StevW; CP-StevWP

Countryman, The. Wallace Stevens. CP-StevW; CP-StevWP

Country's economics sick, A. Lorine Niedecker. CP-NiedL

'Country's love- / liness,' it said, The. Hyphens. Charles Tomlinson. CP-TomlC

Countryside. Charles Bukowski. SP-BukC2

County Durham. Donald Davie. CP-DaviDC

Couper o' Cuddy cam here awa, The. We'll Hide the Couper behint the Door. Robert Burns. CP-BurnR

Couple, A. Carl Sandburg. CP-SandC

Couple, A. May Swenson. SP-SwenM

Couple, The. Maya Angelou. SP-AngeM

Couple, The. Robert Lowell. SP-LoweR

Couple, The. Tennessee Williams. CP-WillT

Couple in the Next Room, The. John Ashbery. SP-AshbJ

Couple of Trees, A. William Meredith. SP-MereW

Couple of women is one too many, A. Fool, The. Stevie Smith. CP-SmitS

Couple Overhead, The. William Meredith. SP-MereW

Couples. Carl Sandburg. CP-SandC

Couples on the boat to the Isola di Giglio. Light, The. Lawrence Ferlinghetti. SP-FerlL

Couples sought (enclose photographs please). Billings and Cooings from "The Berkeley Barb." Mona Van Duyn. SP-VanDM

Couplet. Donald Hall. CP-HallD

  (Old Timer's Day.) CP-HallD

Couplet. Charles Tomlinson. CP-TomlC

Couplet about Birds. Thomas Gray. See Fragment: "There pipes the woodlark, and the song[-]thrush there"

Couplet for Furnivall on Two Publishers. Robert Browning. CP-BroR2

Coupling. David Ignatow. SP-IgnaD

Couplings buckled, cracked, collapsed. Wreck of the Circus Train, The. Hayden Carruth. CP-CarHS

Coupons. Charles Bukowski. SP-BukC1

Courage. D. H. Lawrence. CP-LawrD

Courage. Walter De la Mare. CP-DeLaW

Courage. Anne Sexton. CP-SextA

Courage, a Tale. Thom Gunn. CP-GunnT

Courage Cool'd. Robert Herrick. CP-HerrR

"Courage!" he said, and pointed toward the land. Lotus-Eaters, The. Alfred Tennyson. CP-TennA

"Courage!" I say. Thus exhorting myself. Self-Exhortation on Military Themes. Alan Dugan. CP-DugaA

Courage, my chieftain, and strike the blow. Field-Marshal Radetzky. Franz Grillparzer. CP-MerG2

Courage my Soul, now learn to wield. Dialogue between the Resolved Soul and Created Pleasure, A. Andrew Marvell. CP-MarvA

Courage of Shutting-Up, The. Sylvia Plath. CP-PlatS

Courage of the shut mouth, in spite of artillery!, The. Courage of Shutting-Up, The. Sylvia Plath. CP-PlatS

Courage or Ignorance. Yannis Ritsos. SP-RitsY, tr. by Thanasis Maskaleris

Courage that my mother had, The. Edna St. Vincent Millay. CP-MillE

Courage to Be New, The. Robert Frost. CP-FrosR

Courage yet, my brother or my sister! To a Foil'd European Revolutionaire. Walt Whitman. CP-WhitW

Courage: your tongue has left. Stutterer. Alan Dugan. CP-DugaA

Courageous fool—the peril's strength unknown. Two Types. Ambrose Bierce. SP-BierA

Courbet might have painted this. Composition. Charles Tomlinson. CP-TomlC

Couriers, The. Sylvia Plath. CP-PlatS

Course. Muriel Rukeyser. CP-RukeM

Course in Creative Writing, A. William Stafford. SP-StafWW

Course of a day is never steady, The. And a Day. Laura Riding Jackson. CP-RidiL

Course of a Life, The. Yehuda Amichai. SP-AmicY, tr. by Chana Bloch

Course of a Particular, The. Wallace Stevens. CP-StevWP

Court is far away, The. Emily Dickinson. CP-DickE

Court Lady, A. Elizabeth Barrett Browning. CP-BroEB

Court of First Appeal. Kenneth Patchen. CP-PatcK

Court of Love, A. Robert Graves. CP-GravR

Court Revolt, The. Thom Gunn. CP-GunnT

Courteous handsome young man, A. Han-shan.

Courteously self-assured, although alone. Charlotte Corday. Charles Tomlinson. CP-TomlC; SP-TomlC

Courtesies of Authorship, The. Laura Riding Jackson. CP-RidiL

Courtesies of good-morning and good-evening. On Dwelling. Robert Graves. CP-GravR

Courtesies of the Interregnum. Thom Gunn. CP-GunnT

Courtesy Call. John Updike. CP-UpdiJ

Courtier's Life, The. Sir Thomas Wyatt. CP-WyatT

Courting of Dinah Shadd, The. Rudyard Kipling. Fr. Life's Handicap.

Courting Song: Attack! Attack! Attack! Alan Dugan. CP-DugaA

Courtling, I rather thou shouldst utterly. To Censorious Courtling. Ben Jonson. CP-JonsB; SP-JonsB

Courtship. Rita Dove. SP-DoveR

Courtship, The. James Dickey. CP-DickJ

Courtship, Diligence. Rita Dove. SP-DoveR

Courtship of Miles Standish, The. Henry Wadsworth Longfellow. SP-LongH

Courtyard Thaw, A. Richard Wilbur. CP-WilbR

Courtyards in Delft. Derek Mahon. CP-MahoD

Cousin, The. Stevie Smith. CP-SmitS

Cousin Euphemia Knows Best, or, Physician, Heal Somebody Else. Ogden Nash. CP-NashO

Cousin Florence. Richard Eberhart. CP-EberR

Cousin Kate. Christina Georgina Rossetti. CP-RosC1

Cousin Nancy. T. S. Eliot. CP-ElioT

Cousin Rufus' Story. James Whitcomb Riley. CP-RileJ Fr. Child-World, A.

Cousins, Brothers, Sisters. Wyatt Prunty. SP-PrunW

Cove, The. Amy Clampitt. CP-ClamA

Covenant. Tennessee Williams. CP-WillT

Covenant. Adam Zagajewski. SP-ZagaA, tr. by Renata Gorczynski, Benjamin Ivry and C. K. Williams

Covenant, The. Rudyard Kipling. CP-KiplR

Covenant, The. C. K. Williams. SP-WillC

Covenanters, The. Hugh MacDiarmid. SP-MacDH

Cover Her Face. Thomas Kinsella. CP-KinsT

Cover him over with daisies white. Death of the First Born, The. Paul Laurence Dunbar. CP-DunbP

Cover Me Over. Richard Eberhart. CP-EberR

Cover me over. Bringers. Carl Sandburg. CP-SandC

Cover up / Oh, quickly cover up. Mask, The. Laura Riding Jackson. CP-RidiL

Covered Bridge. Robert Penn Warren. CP-WarrR

Covered in quicklime in his native soil. Salute to the Madrid Barricades. Jaroslav Seifert. SP-SeifJ, tr. by Ewald Osers

Covered the flowered linen. Home, and I've. Marilyn Hacker. SP-HackM

Covered with yellow leaves. Memory Gardens. Allen Ginsberg. CP-GinsA; SP-GinsA

Covers. Rae Armantrout. SP-ArmaA

Covetous Still Captives, The. Robert Herrick. CP-HerrR

Covined Bird, The. Wyatt Prunty. SP-PrunW

Cow. Federico García Lorca. CP-GarcF, tr. by Greg Simon and Steven F. White

Cow, The. John Ciardi. CP-CiarJ

Cow, The. W. S. Merwin. SP-MerwWF

Cow, The. Ogden Nash. CP-NashO

Cow, The. Theodore Roethke. CP-RoetT

Cow in Apple Time, The. Robert Frost. CP-FrosR

Cow so massive, so hilly, it was a massacre!, A. Slaughtering the Cow. Robert Stock. SP-StocR

Cow wandering in the bare field, The. Randall Jarrell. CP-JarrR

Cowan Bridge; At the Site of 'Lowood School' Geoffrey Hill. CP-HillG

Coward, The. Stephen Spender. CP-SpenS

Coward ever sings no song, The. Henry David Thoreau. CP-ThorH

Coward thought has struck me: "See poor soul," A. Vincenzo Monti. SP-ZatuM, *tr. by* Marya Alexandrovna Zaturenska

Cowardice and Impudence. D. H. Lawrence. CP-LawrD

Cowards. D. H. Lawrence. CP-LawrD

Cowards fear to die, but Courage stout. On the Snuff of a Candle. Sir Walter Ralegh. CP-RaleW

Cowdung-colored mud, The. Five Poems from Mexico. Denise Levertov. SP-LeveDP

Cowhorn-crowned, shockheaded, cornshuck-bearded. Knight, Death, and the Devil, The. Randall Jarrell. CP-JarrR

Cowper had sinn'd with some excuse. On a Mistake in His Translation of Homer. William Cowper. CP-CowpW

Cowper, whose silver voice, task'd sometimes hard. Sonnet to Henry Cowper. William Cowper. CP-CowpW

Cowper's Grave. Elizabeth Barrett Browning. CP-BroEB

Cowper's 'Yardley Oak': A Continuation. Donald Davie. CP-DaviDC

Cows. Paul Muldoon. CP-MuldP

Cows, a Vision. Tess Gallagher. SP-GallT

Cows at Night, The. Hayden Carruth. CP-CarHS

Cows bring in the last light, The. Black Plateau, The. W. S. Merwin. SP-MerwW

Cows go around saying Moo. Word on Wind, A. Ogden Nash. CP-NashO

Cows in Art Class. Charles Bukowski. SP-BukC2

Cows Waiting at the Pasture Gate, The. Jones Very. CP-VeryJ

Cowshed Blues, The. Hayden Carruth. CP-CarHS

Coyote. William Stafford. SP-StafWW

Coyote Creek. Norman Dubie. CP-DubiN

Coyote eats chunks of the moon, A. I Can't Get Started. Ai. SP-Ai

Coyote in the Zoo, The. William Stafford. SP-StafWW

Coyote's Song. William Dickey. SP-DickW

Crab Crack. John Updike. CP-UpdiJ

Crab faces gownes with sundry Furres; 'tis known. Upon Crab. Robert Herrick. CP-HerrR

Crab Orchard Sanctuary, Late October. Thomas Kinsella. CP-KinsT

Crab That Played with the Sea, The. Rudyard Kipling. *Fr.* Just-So Stories.

Crab-Tree, The. Robert Graves. CP-GravR

Crabapple Blossoms. Carl Sandburg. CP-SandC

Crabapples. Carl Sandburg. CP-SandC

Crabbing. Lucille Clifton. SP-ClifL

Crabs. Marge Piercy. SP-PierM

Crack. Yusef Komunyakaa. CP-KomuY

Crack, The. Denise Levertov. SP-LeveDP

Crack in the stone, the black filament, The. Compact, The: at Volterra. Charles Tomlinson. CP-TomlC; SP-TomlC

Cracked Bell, The. Charles Baudelaire. CP-BaudC, *tr. by* Walter Martin

Cracked walk in the garden, A. Flesh and Blood. Adrienne Rich. CP-RicAE

Cracking the Safe. Chuang Tzu. CP-MertT

Cracks. C. K. Williams. CP-WillC

Cradle Song: "Clock's untiring fingers wind the wool of darkness, The." Louis MacNeice. CP-MacNL

   (Cradle Song for Miriam.) CP-MacNL

Cradle Song: "Sleep, my darling, sleep." Louis MacNeice. CP-MacNL

   (Cradle Song for Eleanor.) CP-MacNL

Cradle Song, A: "Angels are stooping, The." William Butler Yeats. CP-YeatW

Cradle Song, A: "Sleep, sleep, beauty bright." William Blake. CP-BlakW

   (Sleep Sleep; in thy sleep.) CP-BlakW

Cradle Song for Eleanor. Louis MacNeice. *See* Cradle Song: "Sleep, my darling, sleep"

Cradle Song for Mercedes, in Death. Federico García Lorca. CP-GarcF, *tr. by* Christopher Maurer

Cradle Song for Miriam. Louis MacNeice. *See* Cradle Song: "Clock's untiring fingers wind the wool of darkness, The"

Cradock Newton: From an Epitaph. Charles Tomlinson. CP-TomlC

Craft. John Ciardi. CP-CiarJ

Craftsman. Czeslaw Milosz. CP-MiloCN, *tr. by* Robert Hass

Craftsman, The. Rudyard Kipling. CP-KiplR

Craftsman, The. Yannis Ritsos. SP-RitsY, *tr. by* Kimon Friar

Craftsman of Winebowls. Constantine P. Cavafy. CP-CavaC, *tr. by* Theoharis Constantine Theoharis

Craftsman, prepare your instruments. Craftsman. Czeslaw Milosz. CP-MiloCN, *tr. by* Robert Hass

Craftsman pulled a reed from the reedbed, A. Jelaluddin Rumi. SP-Rumi, *tr. by* Coleman Barks

Craftsmanship and Emptiness. Jelaluddin Rumi. SP-Rumi, *tr. by* Coleman Barks

Crafty boy that had full oft assay'd, The. Song: "Crafty boy that had full oft assay'd, The." Sir John Suckling. CP-SuckJ

Craigdarroch, fam'd for speaking art. Sketch for an Elegy. Robert Burns. CP-BurnR

Craigieburn-Wood—A Song. Robert Burns. CP-BurnR

Craigvara House. Derek Mahon. CP-MahoD

Cramped in that funnelled hole, they watched the dawn. Fragment: "Cramped in that funnelled hole, they watched the dawn." Wilfred Owen. CP-OwenW

Cranach's Lot and His Daughter. Paintings in the Museums of Munich and Vienna. James Laughlin. CP-LaugJ

Crane, The. Robert Graves. CP-GravR

Crane, The. Charles Tomlinson. CP-TomlC; SP-TomlC

Crane lounes loudly in his need, The. Crane, The. Robert Graves. CP-GravR

Cranefly in September, A. Ted Hughes. SP-HughTN

Cranes along the scaffolding are gorged, The. Man. Randall Jarrell. CP-JarrR

Cranes lifting up out of the marshland. Cranes, The. Raymond Carver. CP-CarvR

Cranes, The. Raymond Carver. CP-CarvR

Crankadox leaned o'er the edge of the moon, The. Craqueodoom. James Whitcomb Riley. CP-RileJ

Cranston Near the City Line. Ted Berrigan. SP-BerrT

Crap Game. Langston Hughes. CP-HughL; CP-HughL1

Crapshooters. Carl Sandburg. CP-SandC

Craqueodoom. James Whitcomb Riley. CP-RileJ

Crash. Allen Ginsberg. CP-GinsA

Crash. Gary Snyder. CP-SnydG

Crash on crash of the sea. Sea Heroes. "H. D." CP-DoolH

Crash / Take Valium Sleep. Things To Do in Providence. Ted Berrigan. SP-BerrT

Crashed through the woods that lumbering Coach. The dust. Last Coachload, The. Walter De la Mare. CP-DeLaW

Crassis invideo tenuis nimis ipse, videtur. Ad Lucium. Thomas Campion. CP-CampT

Crate of Sterling Loving Cups, A. John Ciardi. CP-CiarJ

Craters. James Dickey. CP-DickJ

Craved, having so long gone. Seconds. Louise Glück. SP-GlucL

Craving. Denise Levertov. SP-LeveDL

Craving for Spring. D. H. Lawrence. CP-LawrD

Craw cracks in sirrop; and do's stinking say. Upon Craw. Robert Herrick. CP-HerrR

Crawl. C. K. Williams. CP-WillC

Crawling down headfirst into the hole. Tunnels. Yusef Komunyakaa. CP-KomuY

Crayon House. Muriel Rukeyser. CP-RukeM

Crazed. Walter De la Mare. CP-DeLaW

Crazed Girl, A. William Butler Yeats. CP-YeatW

Crazed Moon, The. William Butler Yeats. CP-YeatW

Crazed through much child-bearing. Crazed Moon, The. William Butler Yeats. CP-YeatW

Crazy Boy, The. Federico García Lorca. CP-GarcF, *tr. by* Alan S. Trueblood *Fr.* Back of the World.

Crazy Carlson cleared this meadow alone. Crazy Carlson's Meadow. Robert Bly. SP-BlyR

Crazy Carlson's Meadow. Robert Bly. SP-BlyR

Crazy, girls, crazy. Don is gone. Epitaph: "Crazy, girls, crazy. Don is gone." Howard Nemerov. CP-NemeH

Crazy Horse Monument. Peter Blue Cloud. SP-BlueP

Crazy Jane and Jack the Journeyman. William Butler Yeats. CP-YeatW

Crazy Jane and the Bishop. William Butler Yeats. CP-YeatW

Crazy Jane Grown Old Looks at the Dancers. William Butler Yeats. CP-YeatW

Crazy Jane on God. William Butler Yeats. CP-YeatW

Crazy Jane on the Day of Judgment. William Butler Yeats. CP-YeatW

Crazy Jane Reproved. William Butler Yeats. CP-YeatW

Crazy Jane Talks with the Bishop. William Butler Yeats. CP-YeatW

Crazy jay blue) / demon laughshriek. E. E. Cummings. CP-CummE

Crazy kid-face. B———. Robert Creeley. CP-CreeR

Crazy Spiritual, A. Allen Ginsberg. CP-GinsA; SP-GinsA

Crazy Weather. John Ashbery. SP-AshbJ

Crazy Woman, The. Gwendolyn Brooks. SP-BrooG

Creak, little wood thing, creak. Little Old Table, The. Thomas Hardy. CP-HardT

Creamcheese babies square and downy as bolsters. Peaceable Kingdom, The. Marge Piercy. SP-PierM

Creams. C. K. Williams. CP-WillC

Created by the poet to sing my song. Reaper, The. Robert Duncan. SP-DuncR

Created purely from glass the saint stands. In Piam Memoriam. Geoffrey Hill. CP-HillG

Creating the World. Czeslaw Milosz. CP-MiloCN, *tr. by* Robert Hass

Creation. Ambrose Bierce. SP-BierA

Creation. Kenneth Patchen. CP-PatcK

Creation, The. Rae Armantrout. SP-ArmaA

Creation, The. Mona Van Duyn. SP-VanDM

Creation, The. Jones Very. CP-VeryJ

Creation According to Ovid. Robert Pinsky. CP-PinsR

Creation and the Prophet. George Meredith. CP-MerG2

Creation basks in this man's fire. Alchemist of Sorrows, The. Charles Baudelaire. CP-BaudC, *tr. by* Walter Martin

Creation Day. G. K. Chesterton. CP-ChesG

Creation Myth. Wendell Berry. CP-BerrW

Creation Myth on a Moebius Band. Howard Nemerov. CP-NemeH

Creation of Anguish. Howard Nemerov. CP-NemeH

Creation of the World, The. Adam Zagajewski. SP-ZagaA, *tr. by* Renata Gorczynski, Benjamin Ivry *and* C. K. Williams

Creation quaked voices. Crow Tyrannosaurus. Ted Hughes. SP-HughTN

Creation was the end that preceded means. Fanny Howe. SP-HoweF *Fr. Q.*

Creations of Sound, The. Wallace Stevens. CP-StevW; CP-StevWP

Creator. Archibald MacLeish. CP-MacLA

Creator of night and of birth, The. Special Starlight. Carl Sandburg. CP-SandC

Creator, The. G. K. Chesterton. CP-ChesG
     (Utmost sign of the inmost, The) CP-ChesG

Creature David, The. Donald Davie. CP-DaviDC

Creature Has a Purpose, The. Thomas Lux. SP-LuxT

"Creature," I said to the blue jay nesting. Socializing with a Creature. John Ciardi. CP-CiarJ

Creature of God, thy coat. Hymn to the Seal. Stevie Smith. SP-SmitS

Creature was limber once, The. It came to grief. Heartmoss, The. Robert Pinsky. CP-PinsR

Creatures. Maxine W. Kumin. SP-KumiM

Creatures of Prometheus, The. James Laughlin. CP-LaugJ

Credences of Summer. Wallace Stevens. CP-StevW; CP-StevWP

Credibility. John Ciardi. CP-CiarJ

Credit me poor to say of my life *maledictory weed die.* Catullus. *See* Do you really believe I could blacken my life

Credit of the Conquerer, The. Robert Herrick. CP-HerrR

Creditor, The. Louis MacNeice. CP-MacNL

Credo. Alan Dugan. CP-DugaA

Credo. Robinson Jeffers. CP-JefR1

Credo. Hugh MacDiarmid. SP-MacDH

Credo. Edwin Arlington Robinson. CP-RobiE

Credo ("I asked the doctor who had pronounced me dead"). John Ciardi. CP-CiarJ

Credo in Intellectum Videntem. Allen Tate. CP-TateA

Credo ("Today / Dr. William Carlos Williams"). John Ciardi. CP-CiarJ

Credo ut intelligam. Little Dog Laughs, The. James Laughlin. CP-LaugJ

Creed. George Meredith. CP-MerG2

Creeks. Mary Oliver. SP-OlivM

Creep up, moon, on the south sky. Moon Path. Carl Sandburg. CP-SandC

Creeps and Crawls. Ogden Nash. CP-NashO

Cremation. Robinson Jeffers. CP-JefR3

Creon's Mouse. Donald Davie. CP-DaviDC

Crepe de Chine. Tennessee Williams. CP-WillT

Crêpes Flambeau. Tess Gallagher. SP-GallT

Crépuscule Provençale. Marilyn Hacker. SP-HackM

Crescent Moon Like a Canoe. Marge Piercy. SP-PierM

Crescent-Moon, the Star of Love, The. William Wordsworth. CP-WorW2

Crescenzago. Primo Levi. CP-LeviP, *tr. by* Ruth Feldman *and* Brian Swann

Crescenzio, the Pope's Legate at the High Council, Trent. Cardinal and the Dog, The. Robert Browning. CP-BroR2

Cretan Woman, The. Robinson Jeffers. CP-JefR3

Cretians ever lyars were, they care not what they say, The. Sir Walter Ralegh. CP-RaleW

Crevice. A. R. Ammons. CP-AmmoA

Crewcut et Ux. have raised their long-haired pup. History of Hair from World War II to the Present. Howard Nemerov. CP-NemeH

Cri / C / k / et / in. E. E. Cummings. CP-CummE

Crib stock fothered, horses suppered up, The. Winter Evening. John Clare. SP-ClarJ

Cribs loaded with roughage huddle together. From a Bus Window in Central Ohio, Just before a Thunder Shower. James Wright. CP-WrigJ

Cricket, The. Vincent Bourne. CP-CowpW

Cricket in the telephone is still, The. Certain Phenomena of Sound. Wallace Stevens. CP-StevW; CP-StevWP

Cricket Match. Carl Sandburg. CP-SandC

Cricket-song. Lorine Niedecker. CP-NiedL

Crickets call through the long, long night, The. Johnny Appleseed's Wife from the Palace of Eve. Nicholas Vachel Lindsay. CP-LindV

Crickets cranking shifting gears. Heartland Music. Clarence Major. SP-MajoC

Crickets on a Strike. Nicholas Vachel Lindsay. CP-LindV

Crickets sang, The. Emily Dickinson. CP-DickE

Cried Innocence, "Mother, my thumbs, my thumbs!" Tortured, The. May Sarton. SP-SartM

Cried Out with Tears. Christina Georgina Rossetti. CP-RosC2

Cried the Fox. Tennessee Williams. CP-WillT

Cried when she could not. Berenice. James Laughlin. CP-LaugJ

Cries From Chiapas. Muriel Rukeyser. CP-RukeM

Cries / of the eagle / dancers at Cochiti, The. Cochiti. Charles Tomlinson. CP-TomlC

Crime. Robert Penn Warren. CP-WarrR

Crime. C. K. Williams. SP-WillC

Crime, The. C. K. Williams. SP-WillC

Crime of 1903, The. Ambrose Bierce. SP-BierA

Crimes of Bernard, The. Alan Dugan. CP-DugaA

Criminal possession of a controlled substance. News Bulletin. Allen Ginsberg. CP-GinsA

Crimson. Carl Sandburg. CP-SandC

Crimson as the rubies, crimson as the roses, / Crimson as the sinking sun. Let Them Rejoice in Their Beds. Christina Georgina Rossetti. CP-RosC2

Crimson blossom charms the bee, The. To Miss Isabella Macleod. Robert Burns. CP-BurnR

Crimson Changes People. Carl Sandburg. CP-SandC

Crimson curtains round my mother's bed. Christina Georgina Rossetti. CP-RosC2

Crimson Cyclamen, The. William Carlos Williams. CP-WilW1

Crimson is the slow smolder of the cigar end I hold. Crimson. Carl Sandburg. CP-SandC

Crimson Rambler. Carl Sandburg. CP-SandC

Crinkled paper makes a brilliant sound, A. Extracts from Addresses to the Academy of Fine Ideas. Wallace Stevens. CP-StevW; CP-StevWP

Cripple. Carl Sandburg. CP-SandC

Cripple aches in his lost limb, The. Spring Cleaning. Louis MacNeice. CP-MacNL

Cripple every step Drudges & labours, The. William Blake. CP-BlakW

Cripple in the Subway, The. Louise Glück. SP-GlucL

Cripple in the wheelchair, The. Busy Day. James Laughlin. CP-LaugJ

Crippled angel bent in a scythe of grief, A. A. R. Ammons. CP-AmmoA

Cripples and Other Stories. Anne Sexton. CP-SextA; SP-ScxtA

Crippling, The. Marge Piercy. SP-PierM

Crisis. John Berryman. CP-BerrJ

Crisis, The. Kenneth Rexroth. CP-RexrK

Crisis, The. Robert Creeley. CP-CreeR

Crisis, The. Paul Laurence Dunbar. CP-DunbP

Crisis, The. George Meredith. CP-MerG2

Crisis, The. Jones Very. CP-VeryJ

Crisis, The. John Greenleaf Whittier. CP-WhitJ

Crisis is a Hair. Emily Dickinson. CP-DickE

Crisis is sweet and yet the Heart. Emily Dickinson. CP-DickE

Crisis they call it?—when. Universe is One Place. William Stafford. SP-StafWW

Crisp, curling invitation, A. Meditation of Leaves, A. Peter Blue Cloud. SP-BlueP

Crispus Attucks. Robert Earl Hayden. CP-HaydR

Crispus Attucks. Jay Wright. SP-WrigJ

Criss Cross Apple Sauce. Thomas Lux. SP-LuxT

Crisscross. Carl Sandburg. CP-SandC

Cristina. Robert Browning. CP-BroR1

Cristina and Monaldeschi. Robert Browning. CP-BroR2

Critic. Howard Nemerov. CP-NemeH

Critic, The. Frank O'Hara. SP-OharF

Critic, The. C. K. Williams. SP-WillC

Critic With His Pained Eye, The. Richard Eberhart. CP-EberR

Critical Minute, The. Michael Tracey.
     "O Thou! What e'er may thy attention draw." CP-SherT

Criticism of Bergson and Darwin. Alan Dugan. CP-DugaA

Critics and Connoisseurs. Marianne Craig Moore. CP-MoorM

Critics on the Lawn. Archibald MacLeish. CP-MacLA

Critics, right honourable Bard, decree. Two Epigrams on Byron's *Cain*. William Wordsworth. CP-WorW2

Critique, The. Shmuel HaNagid. SP-HaNaS, *tr. by* Peter Cole

Critters' Dance, De. Paul Laurence Dunbar. CP-DunbP

Cro-Magnon. William Stafford. SP-StafWW

Cro-Magnons. Lawrence Ferlinghetti. SP-FerlL

Croak, croak, croak. Bird's-Eye View, A. Christina Georgina Rossetti. CP-RosC1

Croce e Delizia al Cor. Tess Gallagher. SP-GallT

Crocodile. John Crowe Ransom. *See* Amphibious Crocodile

Crocodile at the Ancient Tombs. Howard Nemerov. CP-NemeH

Crocus. Louis Zukofsky. CP-ZukLS

Crocus, The. Jones Very. CP-VeryJ

Crocus armies from the dead, The. Veni Coronaberis. Geoffrey Hill. CP-HillG

Crocus Night. James Schuyler. CP-SchuJ

Crocus, spotted from a. Paul Celan. SP-CelaP, *tr.* by John Felstiner

Crocuses and snowdrops wither. Seasons. Christina Georgina Rossetti. CP-RosC3

Crocuses are springing. Somewhat Delayed Spring Song. Dorothy Parker. CP-ParkD

Croesus in Autumn. Robert Penn Warren. CP-WarrR

Croft. Stevie Smith. CP-SmitS

Cr[omek] loves artists as he loves his Meat. William Blake. CP-BlakW

Cromek Speaks. William Blake. CP-BlakW

Cromlech, The. Louis MacNeice. CP-MacNL

Cromwell, our chief [*or* cheif] of men, who through a cloud. To the Lord General Cromwell. John Milton. CP-MiltJ

Cronkhite Beach. Charles Tomlinson. CP-TomlC

Crooked, black tree. Trees. William Carlos Williams. CP-WilW1

Crooked you are, but that dislikes not me. Upon a Crooked Maid. Robert Herrick. CP-HerrR

Croon. Langston Hughes. CP-HughL; CP-HughL3

Crooner, The. G. K. Chesterton. CP-ChesG

Crops fall apart. Breaking Camp. Yusef Komunyakaa. CP-KomuY

Cross. Federico García Lorca.

  East. CP-GarcF, *tr.* by Jerome Rothenberg

  North. CP-GarcF, *tr.* by Jerome Rothenberg

  South. CP-GarcF, *tr.* by Jerome Rothenberg

  West. CP-GarcF, *tr.* by Jerome Rothenberg

Cross. Langston Hughes. CP-HughL; CP-HughL1

Cross, The. John Donne. CP-DonnJ; MW-DonnJ

Cross, The. D. H. Lawrence. CP-LawrD

Cross, The. Allen Tate. CP-TateA

Cross, The. Robert Penn Warren. CP-WarrR

Cross, The. John Greenleaf Whittier. CP-WhitJ

Cross begot me on the stone, The. Ah, Will the Saviour . . . ? Stevie Smith. CP-SmitS

Cross-country, out of sea fog. Message, The. Denise Levertov. SP-LeveDP

Cross-Currents. Thomas Hardy. CP-HardT

Cross-fade of grief to nothingness. Unoccupied Zone, The. Louis Aragon. CP-MacNL

Cross-hatching technique which allowed our ancestors to exchange, The. Whatever It Is, Wherever You Are. John Ashbery. SP-AshbJ

Cross-Legged, the Spider and the Web. Charles Olson. CP-OlsoC; SP-OlsoC

Cross My Heart and Hope to Die, It Was the Very Same Song Exactly. Hayden Carruth. CP-CarHS

Cross not, cross not, merry men of France. To the Merry Men of France. George Meredith. CP-MerG2

Cross of boy with man within is an, The. On a Prize Crucifix by a Student Sculptor. John Logan. CP-LoganJ

Cross of Snow, The. Henry Wadsworth Longfellow. SP-LongH

Cross staggered him. At the cliff-top, The. Canticle for Good Friday. Geoffrey Hill. CP-HillG

Cross, the Cross, The. Tortoise-Shell. D. H. Lawrence. CP-LawrD

Cross the hands over the breaest here—so. Anna Imroth. Carl Sandburg. CP-SandC

Cross, The ("I must go on, till in my tearful line"). Jones Very. CP-VeryJ

Cross, The ("Raised on high, above the city"). Jones Very. CP-VeryJ

Cross-tree, The. Robert Herrick. CP-HerrR

Crossbow wanted a child. Children's Crusade, The. Philip Levine. SP-LeviP

Cross[e], the. George Herbert. CP-HerbG

Crosse and Pile. Robert Herrick. CP-HerrR

Crossed Apple, The. Louise Bogan. CP-BogaL

Crossed Hands. Andrei Codrescu. SP-CodrA

Crossed Numbers. Carl Sandburg. CP-SandC

Crossed-over dreams, or infertile. He, Who, in His Abandnoned Infancy, Spoke of Jesus, Caesar, Those Who Beg, and Hell. Charles Olson. CP-OlsoC

Crossed shadow of the kestrel seems unknown, The. Summer. Eugenio Montale. CP-MontE, *tr.* by Jonathan Galassi

Crosses. Robert Herrick. CP-HerrR

Crosses. Robert Herrick. CP-HerrR

Crosses on the convent roofs, The. Botanist on Alp (No. 2). Wallace Stevens. CP-StevW; CP-StevWP

Crossing. Rae Armantrout. SP-ArmaA

Crossing. Langston Hughes. CP-HughL; CP-HughL2

Crossing. Archibald MacLeish. CP-MacLA

Crossing, The. Howard Nemerov. CP-NemeH

Crossing, The. May Swenson. SP-SwenM

Crossing alone the nighted ferry. Crossing Alone the Nighted Ferry. A. E. Housman. CP-HousA

Crossing at rush hour the Walt Whitman Bridge. Modern Poet, A. Howard Nemerov. CP-NemeH

Crossing Borders. William Corbett. SP-CorbW

Crossing Brooklyn Ferry. Walt Whitman. CP-WhitW

Crossing Brooklyn Ferry. Charles Tomlinson. CP-TomlC

Crossing from a chore as the day. Long Shadow. John Updike. CP-UpdiJ

Crossing Nation. Allen Ginsberg. CP-GinsA

Crossing on Staten Island Ferry. Kenneth Patchen. CP-PatcK

Crossing Our Campground. William Stafford. SP-StafWW

Crossing Over. William Meredith. SP-MereW

Crossing Place. W. S. Merwin. SP-MerwWF

Crossing the Atlantic. Anne Sexton. CP-SextA

Crossing the Bar. Alfred Tennyson. CP-TennA

Crossing the Border. Ogden Nash. CP-NashO

Crossing the Footbridge over Storrow Drive. William Corbett. SP-CorbW

Crossing the Line. Paul Muldoon. CP-MuldP

Crossing the Ohio When Poppies Bloom in Ashtabula. Carl Sandburg. CP-SandC

Crossing the Paces. Carl Sandburg. CP-SandC

Crossing the Pedregal. Helen Pinkerton. CP-PinkH

Crossing the Public Garden. William Corbett. SP-CorbW

Crossing the sound I summoned you in thought. Kathleen Jessie Raine. SP-RainK

Crossing the street. Broken Home, The. James Merrill. SP-MerrJ

Crossing the Swamp. Mary Oliver. SP-OlivM

Crossing the Water. Sylvia Plath. CP-PlatS

Crossings. Seamus Heaney. SP-HeanSO *Fr.* Squarings.

Crosspurposes. Denise Levertov. SP-LeveDL

Crossroad. Federico García Lorca. CP-GarcF, *tr.* by Catherine Brown

Crossroads, dusty, virgin, A. Singing, The. Robert Stock. SP-StocR

Crossroads of the World Etc., The. W. S. Merwin. SP-MerwW

Crosswords. Wyatt Prunty. SP-PrunW

Crouched at the corner of the street. Deformed. James Whitcomb Riley. CP-RileJ

Crouched beneath a snowbound sky. Grey Ones, The. Louis MacNeice. CP-MacNL

Crouched down by a roadside windbreak. Listening to the Mourners. James Wright. CP-WrigJ

Crouched on wet shingle at the cove. Judges, The. Robert Graves. CP-GravR

Crouched under my desk, at a bad clap. Out in It. Maxine W. Kumin. SP-KumiM

Crow. Ted Hughes.

  Dawn's Rose. SP-HughTN

  Littleblood. SP-HughTN

  That Moment. SP-HughTN

  Two Legends. SP-HughTN

Crow. Peter Blue Cloud. SP-BlueP

Crow. Charles Tomlinson. CP-TomlC

Crow, The. Robert Creeley. CP-CreeR

Crow and the Birds. Ted Hughes. SP-HughTN

Crow Blacker than Ever. Ted Hughes. SP-HughTN

Crow flew into the tree outside my window, A. My Crow. Raymond Carver. CP-CarvR

Crow Goes, Too. Langston Hughes. CP-HughL; CP-HughL3

Crow Hill. Ted Hughes. SP-HughTN

Crow in the cage in the dining-room, The. Crow, The. Robert Creeley. CP-CreeR

Crow on the Beach. Ted Hughes. SP-HughTN

Crow Spring. Denise Levertov. SP-LeveDS

Crow Tyrannosaurus. Ted Hughes. SP-HughTN

Crow Wakes. Ted Hughes. SP-HughTN

Crowd about me, little children. Ballad, A: "Crowd about me, little children." James Whitcomb Riley. CP-RileJ

Crowd and Company, The. Robert Herrick. CP-HerrR

Crowd at the ball game, The. At the Ball Game. William Carlos Williams. CP-WilW1

Crowd at the ballpark sing, the cantor sings, The. Uncreation, The. Robert Pinsky. CP-PinsR

Crowd moves forward on the midway, back, The. World's Fair. John Berryman. CP-BerrJ

Crowd of the Greek force, The. Euripides. CP-DoolH *Fr.* Iphigenia [*or* Iphigeneia] in Aulis.

Crowd the horizons, poised, wings. Poets. Ted Hughes. SP-HughTN

Crowded. Philip Whalen. SP-WhalP

Crowded Countries of the Bomb, The. George Oppen. CP-OppGN

Crowded Net, The. Kenneth Patchen. CP-PatcK

Crowded steps, a sea of white faces. Sacrifice. Thomas Kinsella. CP-KinsT

Crowdieknowe. Hugh MacDiarmid. SP-MacDH

Crowding. David Ignatow. SP-IgnaD

Crowding everywhere. New People, The. George Oppen. CP-OppGN

Crowding this beach. Stone Speech. Charles Tomlinson. CP-TomlC; SP-TomlC

Crowds, streetcars stopped—is it a demonstration? Human Fly, A. Czeslaw Milosz. CP-MiloCN, *tr. by* Robert Hass

Crowing Hen Blues. Langston Hughes. CP-HughL; CP-HughL2

Crown, a crown for Love's bright head, A. Ben Jonson. CP-JonsB *Fr.* Love Freed from Ignorance and Folly.

Crown of Bays, The. Stevie Smith. CP-SmitS

Crown of Gold, The. Stevie Smith. CP-SmitS

Crown of Love, The. George Meredith. CP-MerG1

Crown of Windflowers, A. Christina Georgina Rossetti. CP-RosC2

Crown of Woman, The. G. K. Chesterton. CP-ChesG

Crowned and Buried. Elizabeth Barrett Browning. CP-BroEB

Crowned and Wedded. Elizabeth Barrett Browning. CP-BroEB

Crowned king, A. William Blake. CP-BlakW *Fr.* Island in the Moon, An.

Crowned out, / spit out into night. Paul Celan. CP-CelaP, *tr. by* John Felstiner

Crowning a bluff where gleams the lake below. Pontoosuce. Herman Melville. SP-MelvH

Crowning hour when bodies vie with souls, The. Ralph Waldo Emerson. CP-EmerR

Crowns and Garlands. Langston Hughes. CP-HughL; CP-HughL3

Crows. Mary Oliver. SP-OlivM

Crows. Marge Piercy. SP-PierM

Crows. Arthur Rimbaud. CP-RimbA, *tr. by* Martin Sorrell

Crows. Charles Simic. SP-SimiC; SP-SimiCE

Crows, The. Louise Bogan. CP-BogaL

Crows, The. Wyatt Prunty. SP-PrunW

Crow's Account of the Battle. Ted Hughes. SP-HughTN

Crows are flying above the foyer of summer, The. Novel, The. Wallace Stevens. CP-StevW; CP-StevWP

Crows are tossing themselves, The. Crow Spring. Denise Levertov. SP-LeveDS

Crow's Battle Fury. Ted Hughes. SP-HughTN

Crow's Elephant Totem Song. Ted Hughes. SP-HughTN

Crow's Fall. Ted Hughes. SP-HughTN

Crow's First Lesson. Ted Hughes. SP-HughTN

Crow's Flight. Peter Blue Cloud. SP-BlueP

Crow's Last Stand. Ted Hughes. SP-HughTN

Crow's Mark. Hayden Carruth. CP-CarHS

Crows of Boston and New York, The. Thomas Lux. SP-LuxT

Crows on the North Slope. W. S. Merwin. SP-MerwW

Crows scoured the wet evening clean. Entrance. Thomas Kinsella. CP-KinsT

Crows see me. / They stretch their glossy necks, The. Entering the Kingdom. Mary Oliver. SP-OlivM

Crow's Song 2, The. Primo Levi. CP-LeviP, *tr. by* Ruth Feldman *and* Brian Swann

Crow's Song, The. Primo Levi. CP-LeviP, *tr. by* Ruth Feldman *and* Brian Swann

Crow's Vanity. Ted Hughes. SP-HughTN

Crucible. Carl Sandburg. CP-SandC

Crucibles of Love. Robert Graves. CP-GravR

Crucified, The. G. K. Chesterton. CP-ChesG

Crucifix in the Filing Cabinet, The. Karl Shapiro. SP-ShapK

Crucifixion. Hayden Carruth. CP-CarHS

Crucifixion. Federico García Lorca. CP-GarcF, *tr. by* Greg Simon *and* Steven F. White

Crucifixion, The. John Greenleaf Whittier. CP-WhitJ

Crucifixion in the Desert. James Laughlin. CP-LaugJ

Crude Foyer. Wallace Stevens. CP-StevW; CP-StevWP

Crude Lament. William Carlos Williams. CP-WilW1

Crudely continues what has been begun. Captain in Time of Peace. Thom Gunn. CP-GunnT

Cruel. Adam Zagajewski. SP-ZagaA, *tr. by* Renata Gorczynski, Benjamin Ivry *and* C. K. Williams

Cruel Cerinthus! does the fell disease. Imitation of Tibullus. Lord Byron. CP-Byron

Cruel Falcon, The. Robinson Jeffers. CP-JefR2

Cruel Mistress, A. Thomas Carew. CP-CareT

Cruel of heart, lay down my song. To Those Without Pity. Edna St. Vincent Millay. CP-MillE

Cruel Song. Rainer Maria Rilke. CP-RilkFr, *tr. by* A. Poulin, Jr.

Cruel the star (if stars are powerful). Petrarch. CP-Petra, *tr. by* J. G. Nichols

Cruelkind Swans, The. Kenneth Patchen. CP-PatcK

Cruell Maid, The. Robert Herrick. CP-HerrR

Cruelly,love / walk the autumn long. E. E. Cummings. CP-CummE

Cruelties. Robert Herrick. CP-HerrR

Cruelties of the Sportive Power. Kenneth Patchen. CP-PatcK

Cruelty. Ai. SP-Ai

Cruelty. Robert Herrick. CP-HerrR

Cruelty Base in Commanders. Robert Herrick. CP-HerrR

Cruelty is rarely conscious. Photograph of the Unmade Bed, The. Adrienne Rich. CP-RicAE; SP-RicA2

Cruise, The. Muriel Rukeyser. CP-RukeM

Cruisers. Rudyard Kipling. CP-KiplR

Cruising these residential Sunday / streets in dry August sunlight. City Planners, The. Margaret Atwood. SP-AtwM1

Crumb, a Crumb, and a Little Seed, A. Paul Laurence Dunbar. CP-DunbP

Crumb or maybe a peanut dropped in the suburb, A. Dead Pigeon on South Street. John Ciardi. CP-CiarJ

Crumbling elms and evergreens, The. Emily Dickinson. SP-DickE

Crumbling is not an instant's Act. Emily Dickinson. CP-DickE

Crumbs or the Loaf. Robinson Jeffers. CP-JefR2

Crunch, The. Charles Bukowski. SP-BukC1

Crusade. Robert Penn Warren. CP-WarrR

Crusader Returns from Captivity, The. G. K. Chesterton. CP-ChesG

Crusoe. Thomas Merton. CP-MertT

Crusoe in England. Elizabeth Bishop. CP-BishE

Crusoe's Island. Derek Walcott. CP-WalcD

Crusoe's Journal. Derek Walcott. CP-WalcD

Crust of bread and a corner to sleep in, A. Life. Paul Laurence Dunbar. CP-DunbP

Crustaceous / wedge / of sweaty kitchens. Agonized Spires, The. William Carlos Williams. CP-WilW1

Crutches. Robert Herrick. CP-HerrR

Cry, The. W. S. Merwin. SP-MerwW

Cry comes out and is the changing exterior, particles without, A. Olga Broumas. SP-BrouO *Fr.* Black Holes, Black Stockings.

Cry Faugh! Robert Graves. CP-GravR

Cry for me, ladies, your servant. Guillaume de Machault (1300-1377) Ballade: Plourès, dames. Louis Zukofsky. CP-ZukLS

Cry from the green-grained sticks of the fire, A. Surview [*or* Surview: Cogitavi Vias Meas]. Thomas Hardy. CP-HardT

Cry Going Out over Pastures, The. Robert Bly. SP-BlyR

Cry I bring down from the hills, The. You and I Are Disappearing. Yusef Komunyakaa. CP-KomuY

Cry "Murder" in the market-place, and each. Rudyard Kipling. CP-KiplR *Fr.* Plain Tales from the Hills.

Cry of a Lost Soul, The. John Greenleaf Whittier. CP-WhitJ

Cry of the Children, The. Elizabeth Barrett Browning. CP-BroEB

Cry of the Eyes, The. Ezra Pound. CP-PoEar

Cry of the Homeless. Thomas Hardy. CP-HardT

Cry of the Human, The. Elizabeth Barrett Browning. CP-BroEB

Cry of the Masses. D. H. Lawrence. CP-LawrD

Cry of the Spectres, The. Jaroslav Seifert. SP-SeifJ, *tr. by* Ewald Osers

Cry Out in Your Weakness. Jelaluddin Rumi. SP-Rumi, *tr. by* Coleman Barks

Cry pain, & the dogs of yrself devour. Charles Olson. CP-OlsoC

Cry to Rome. Federico García Lorca. CP-GarcF, *tr. by* Greg Simon *and* Steven F. White

Crying from exile, I. Elegy: "Crying from exile, I." Marilyn Hacker. SP-HackM

Crying, my little one, footsore and weary? Christina Georgina Rossetti. CP-RosC2

Cryopexy. Charles Wright. SP-WrigC

Crystal. Ted Berrigan. SP-BerrT

Crystal. Paul Celan. SP-CelaP, *tr. by* John Felstiner

Crystal, The. G. K. Chesterton. CP-ChesG

Crystal, The. Robert Graves. CP-GravR

Crystal Cabinet, The. William Blake. CP-BlakW

Crystal Cage, The. Stanley Kunitz. CP-KunSC

Crystal Gazer. Sylvia Plath. CP-PlatS

Crystal Lithium, The. James Schuyler. CP-SchuJ

Crystal Maze, A. William Carlos Williams. CP-WilW1

Crystal of reason, The. Countering. A. R. Ammons. CP-AmmoA

Crystal Palace Market. James Laughlin. CP-LaugJ

Crystals like Blood. Hugh MacDiarmid. SP-MacDH

Cuba. Paul Muldoon. CP-MuldP

Cuba, 1962. Ai. SP-Ai

Cuban Doctor, The. Wallace Stevens. CP-StevW; CP-StevWP

Cubes. Langston Hughes. CP-HughL; CP-HughL1

Cubism. Yusef Komunyakaa. CP-KomuY

Cuccurucù! Cuccurucù! / All'alba il gallo canta. Christina Georgina Rossetti. CP-RosC3

Cuchulain. William Carlos Williams. CP-WilW2

Cuchulain Comforted. William Butler Yeats. CP-YeatW

Cuchulain's Fight with the Sea. William Butler Yeats. *See* Death of Cuchulain, The

Cuckoo. Louis MacNeice. CP-MacNL

Cuckoo. Rainer Maria Rilke. CP-RilkFr, *tr. by* A. Poulin, Jr.

Cuckoo, The. Gerard Manley Hopkins. CP-HopkG
(Repeat That, Repeat.) CP-HopkG

Cuckoo, The. Ogden Nash. CP-NashO

Cuckoo across the poppies. Cuckoo. Louis MacNeice. CP-MacNL

Cuckoo and the coo-dove's ceaseless calling, The. Sigh No More. D. H. Lawrence. CP-LawrD

Cuckoo and the Nightingale, The. William Wordsworth. CP-WorW1

Cuckoo-Clock, The. William Wordsworth. CP-WorW2

Cuckoo Corn. Paul Muldoon. CP-MuldP

Cúckoo-Cuckoo-Cuckóo. Federico García Lorca.
"Cuckoo divides the night, The." CP-GarcF, *tr. by* Jerome Rothenberg
Cuckoo's First Nocturne. CP-GarcF, *tr. by* Jerome Rothenberg
Cuckoo's Second Nocturne. CP-GarcF, *tr. by* Jerome Rothenberg
Last Nocturne. CP-GarcF, *tr. by* Jerome Rothenberg
Old Cuckoo's Song, The. CP-GarcF, *tr. by* Jerome Rothenberg

Cuckoo divides the night, The. Federico García Lorca. CP-GarcF, *tr. by* Jerome Rothenberg *Fr.* Cúckoo-Cuckoo-Cuckóo.

Cuckoo in the singing nest betrays, A. Elders and Betters. Donald Davie. CP-DaviDC

Cuckoo King, The. Howard Nemerov. CP-NemeH

Cuckoo Myth. W. S. Merwin. SP-MerwW

Cuckoo says Yes, The. Cuckoo's Second Nocturne. Federico García Lorca. CP-GarcF, *tr. by* Jerome Rothenberg *Fr.* Cúckoo-Cuckoo-Cuckóo.

Cuckoo Song. "H. D." CP-DoolH

Cuckoo Song. Rudyard Kipling. CP-KiplR

Cuckoo-throb, the heartbeat of the Spring, The. Ardour and Memory. Dante Gabriel Rossetti. CW-RossD *Fr.* House of Life, The.

Cuckoo's First Nocturne. Federico García Lorca. CP-GarcF, *tr. by* Jerome Rothenberg *Fr.* Cúckoo-Cuckoo-Cuckóo.

Cuckoo's Second Nocturne. Federico García Lorca. CP-GarcF, *tr. by* Jerome Rothenberg *Fr.* Cúckoo-Cuckoo-Cuckóo.

Cucumbers are thirsty, their big leaves turn away from, The. Glimpse of the Waterer. Robert Bly. SP-BlyR

Cud's a locus in time, a staying change, moving, A. Hibernaculum. A. R. Ammons. CP-AmmoA

Cuffe comes to Church much; but he keeps his bed. Upon Cuffe. Epig. Robert Herrick. CP-HerrR

Cuirassiers of the Frontier, The. Robert Graves. CP-GravR

Cuisine Bourgeoise. Wallace Stevens. CP-StevW; CP-StevWP

Cujus pulchritudinem / Sol et luna mirantur. St. Agnes: A Responsory. Thomas Merton. CP-MertT

Cul de Sac. Josephine Jacobsen. CP-JacoJ

Cul-de-Sac. Allen Tate. CP-TateA

Culled from the brambled ceiling of my wide. Marilyn Hacker. SP-HackM *Fr.* Separations.

Culprit, The. A. E. Housman. CP-HousA

Cultivation of Christmas Trees, The. T. S. Eliot. CP-ElioT

Cultural Evolution. Carolyn Kizer. CP-KizeC

Cultural Exchange ("IN THE / IN THE QUARTER / IN THE QUARTER OF THE NEGROES"). Langston Hughes. CP-HughL; CP-HughL3

Cultural Exchange ("In the Quarter of the Negroes / Where the doors are doors of paper"). Langston Hughes. CP-HughL3

Cultural Note. James Laughlin. CP-LaugJ

Cultural Triumph, A. George Oppen. CP-OppGN

Culture. Ralph Waldo Emerson. CP-EmerR

Culture and Anarchy. Adrienne Rich. SP-RicA2

Culture / Of the draft-pool, an oblique poetry. Modern Incident, A. George Oppen. CP-OppGN

Cum caput Hesperiis attollit Phœbus ab undis. Aurora Est Musis Amica. Samuel Johnson. CP-JohnS

Cum tibi vilescat doctus lepidusque Catullus. In Cambrum. Thomas Campion. CP-CampT

Cum tot sustineat reges et tanta, neque ulla. On Loyalty. William Cowper. CP-CowpW

Cumaean Sibyl, charming Ogress. Our Doom to Bloom. Robert Frost. CP-FrosR

Cumberland. Donald Davie. CP-DaviDC

Cumhal called out, bending his head. Blessed, The. William Butler Yeats. CP-YeatW

Cummings. Archibald MacLeish. CP-MacLA

Cumulatives. Carl Sandburg. CP-SandC

Cumuli. May Swenson. SP-SwenM

Cunctation in Correction. Robert Herrick. CP-HerrR

Cunning. Arthur Rimbaud. CP-RimbA, *tr. by* Martin Sorrell

Cunning sures & the Aim at yours, The. William Blake. CP-BlakW

Cunts. John Updike. CP-UpdiJ

Cuored o' Skeerin. James Whitcomb Riley. CP-RileJ

Cup, The. Jones Very. CP-VeryJ

Cup for hope! she said, A. Three Seasons. Christina Georgina Rossetti. CP-RosC1

Cup, ignorant and cruel. To Wine. Louise Bogan. CP-BogaL

Cup of life is not so shallow, The. Ralph Waldo Emerson. CP-EmerR

Cup of Tea, A. James Whitcomb Riley. CP-RileJ

Cup with a Jaguar for the Drinking of Health. Pablo Antonio Cuadra. CP-MertT

Cupid & Skull. Charles Baudelaire. CP-BaudC, *tr. by* Walter Martin

Cupid and Venus. Mark Alexander Boyd. CP-KizeC, *tr. by* Carolyn Kizer

Cupid as he lay among. Wounded Cupid, The. Robert Herrick. CP-HerrR

Cupido. Ralph Waldo Emerson. CP-EmerR

Cupid's Arrows. Rudyard Kipling. *Fr.* Plain Tales from the Hills.

Cupola, The. Louise Bogan. CP-BogaL

Cups. D. H. Lawrence. CP-LawrD

Cups of Coffee. Carl Sandburg. CP-SandC

Cur foretells the knell of parting day, The. Elegy: "Cur foretells the knell of parting day, The." Ambrose Bierce. SP-BierA *Fr.* Devil's Dictionary, The.

Cur Me Bespateras, Blaterans Furiosè Poeta. Thomas Sheridan. CP-SherT, *tr. by* Robert Hogan

Curate and churchwarden, The. Tom Raban. William Cowper. CP-CowpW

Curate's Kindness, The. Thomas Hardy. CP-HardT

Curator, The. Miller Williams. CP-WillM

Curb Science? Robinson Jeffers. CP-JefR3

Cure, The. Robert Graves. CP-GravR

Curé, The. Rudyard Kipling. CP-KiplR

Cure, The. Theodore Weiss. SP-WeisT

Cure, The. William Carlos Williams. CP-WilW2

Curé and pastor, dead at the one time. Jesuits in North America, The. Donald Davie. CP-DaviDC

Cure at Porlock, A. Amy Clampitt. CP-ClamA

Cure for Warts, The. Paul Muldoon. CP-MuldP

Cure of Ignorance. Laura Riding Jackson. CP-RidiL

Cure of Souls, A. Denise Levertov. SP-LeveDP

Curfew. Paul Éluard. CP-WilW2

Curfew, A. Amy Clampitt. CP-ClamA

Curfew tolls the knell of parting day, The. Elegy Written in a Country Churchyard. Thomas Gray. CP-GrayT

Curiosity. Paul Laurence Dunbar. CP-DunbP

Curious. Langston Hughes. CP-HughL; CP-HughL2

Curious Cloud surprised the Sky, A. Emily Dickinson. CP-DickE

Curious Ghost, A. Derek Mahon.

Curious heart plays with its fears:, The. Shot, The. Robert Graves. CP-GravR

Curious Man's Dream, A. Charles Baudelaire. CP-BaudC, *tr. by* Walter Martin

Curious reticence afflicts my generation, faced with the holocaust, A. Event Itself, The. Hayden Carruth. CP-CarHS

Curious Romance, A. James Laughlin. CP-LaugJ

Curious to learn / how many kiss- / es of your lips. Carmen 7. Catullus. CP-ZukLS *Fr.* Carmina.

Curious to see oneself irresistibly alive in the middle of death. Prologo. Thomas Merton. CP-MertT

Curious upward stumbling motion, The. Thoughts to a Concerto of Telemann. Lawrence Ferlinghetti. SP-FerlL

Curiously enough. actual revolutions are made by robots. Revolutions as Such! D. H. Lawrence. CP-LawrD

Curl Up and Diet. Ogden Nash. CP-NashO

Curled, too much curled, he was sleeping. Fathers and Sons. James Dickey. CP-DickJ

Curlews [Lift]. Ted Hughes. SP-HughTN

Curlicue Ego bends its own way, The. Figure Drawn in Wire, The. John Ciardi. CP-CiarJ

Curly Blue Buppo, The. Kenneth Patchen. CP-PatcK

Curly Locks! Curly Locks! wilt thou be mine? James Whitcomb Riley. CP-RileJ

Curly mousetail, mousetail, curly. By Threes, By Fours. Paul Celan. SP-CelaP, *tr. by* John Felstiner

Currants on a bush, / And figs upon a stem. Christina Georgina Rossetti. CP-RosC2

Current, The. Wendell Berry. CP-BerrW

Current, The. Raymond Carver. CP-CarvR

Current, The. James Merrill. SP-MerrJ

Current, The. W. S. Merwin. SP-MerwW

Currente Calamo. Arthur Hugh Clough. SP-ClouA *Fr. Mari Magno.*

Currents figure. Brooks & Other Notions. A. R. Ammons. CP-AmmoA

Curricle and hansom, The. Great Garret, or 100 Wheels, The. James McMichael. SP-McMiJ

Curriculum Vitae. Robert Stock. SP-StocR

Curs'd be the man, the poorest wretch in life. Henpeck'd Husband, The. Robert Burns. CP-BurnR

Curse. Robert Creeley. CP-CreeR

Curse, A. W. H. Auden. CP-AudeW

Curse, A. Shmuel HaNagid. SP-HaNaS, *tr. by* Peter Cole

Curse. A Song, The. Robert Herrick. CP-HerrR

Curse, The. John Berryman. CP-BerrJ

Curse, The. John Donne. CP-DonnJ; MW-DonnJ

Curse, The. Edna St. Vincent Millay. CP-MillE

Curse against Elegies, A. Anne Sexton. CP-SextA

Curse for Kings, A. Nicholas Vachel Lindsay. CP-LindV

Curse in Free Verse, A. G. K. Chesterton. CP-ChesG

Curse not the mice, no grist of thine they eat. Upon Ralph. Robert Herrick. CP-HerrR

Curse of a Rich Polish Peasant on His Sister Who Ran Away with a Wild Man. Carl Sandburg. CP-SandC

Curse of Cromwell, The. William Butler Yeats. CP-YeatW

Curse of Minerva, The. Lord Byron. CP-Byron

Curse of the Charter-Breakers, The. John Greenleaf Whittier. CP-WhitJ

Curse of the Earth Magician on a Metal Land. Marge Piercy. SP-PierM

Curse of the Wandering Foot, The. James Whitcomb Riley. CP-RileJ

Curse on ungrateful man, that can be pleas'd. On Fergusson. Robert Burns. CP-BurnR

Curse thee, Life, I will live with thee no more! Suicide, The. Edna St. Vincent Millay. CP-MillE

Curse upon each king who leads his state, A. Curse for Kings, A. Nicholas Vachel Lindsay. CP-LindV

Cursed Child. Rainer Maria Rilke. CP-RilkFr, *tr. by* A. Poulin, Jr.

Cursing rogue with a merry face, A. Hour before Dawn, The. William Butler Yeats. CP-YeatW

Cursing this mistral. Crépuscule Provençale. Marilyn Hacker. SP-HackM

Cursive crawl, the squared-off characters, The. Writing. Howard Nemerov. CP-NemeH

Curtain. Paul Laurence Dunbar. CP-DunbP

Curtain Call. Charles Tomlinson. CP-TomlC

Curtains! Donald Davie. CP-DaviDC

Curtains belly in the waking room, The. Landfall. Alan Dugan. CP-DugaA

Curtains forcing their will. Awaking in New York. Maya Angelou. SP-AngeM

Curtains in the House of the Metaphysician, The. Wallace Stevens. CP-StevW; CP-StevWP

Curtains Now Are Drawn, The. Thomas Hardy. CP-HardT

Curtains part) / the peacockappareled. E. E. Cummings. CP-CummE

Curtains were half drawn, the floor was swept, The. After Death. Christina Georgina Rossetti. CP-RosC1

Curtis and I sit drinking auburn sherry. Five O'Clock, Beacon Hill. Adrienne Rich. CP-RicAE

Curtis, you've been American too long. Letter to Curtis Bradford, A. Donald Davie. CP-DaviDC

Curtly the sky. Scornful Reprieve. Denise Levertov. SP-LeveDL

Curvd lines toe-drawn, round cornerd squares, The. Hop, Skip, and Jump. Gary Snyder. CP-SnydG

Curve. Federico García Lorca. CP-GarcF, *tr. by* Jerome Rothenberg *Fr. Water Suite.*

Curve. Heather McHugh. SP-McHuH

Curve of lamps that climbs into the dark, The. Question, The. Charles Tomlinson. CP-TomlC

Curve of the earth in emerald water. Rattlesnake Glyph. Arthur Sze. SP-SzeA

Curve of the two steel spring-up prongs on. Wild Edge, The. Gary Snyder. CP-SnydG

Cushing. Robert Stock. SP-StocR

Custard, The. Robert Herrick. CP-HerrR

Custodian. Maxine W. Kumin. SP-KumiM

Customs Collector's Report, The. Stanley Kunitz. CP-KunSC

Customs Men, The. Arthur Rimbaud. CP-RimbA, *tr. by* Martin Sorrell

Cut. Sylvia Plath. CP-PlatS

Cut a cane that once. In the Bulrush. Rita Dove. SP-DoveR

"Cut." / An actress feigning death for one hundred seconds gasps. Great Square Has No Corners, A. Arthur Sze. SP-SzeA

Cut down by the sky. After a Walk. Federico García Lorca. CP-GarcF, *tr. by* Greg Simon *and* Steven F. White

Cut Flower, A. Karl Shapiro. SP-ShapK

Cut from the green hedge a forked hazel stick. Diviner, The. Seamus Heaney. SP-HeanSO

Cut Grass. Philip Larkin. CP-LarkP

Cut if you will, with Sleep's dull knife. Midnight Oil. Edna St. Vincent Millay. CP-MillE

Cut into by doors. Venice. Charles Tomlinson. CP-TomlC; SP-TomlC

Cut rhododendron branches, The. Argument to Love as a Person. Alan Dugan. CP-DugaA

Cut the bank for the fill. Defective Record, The. William Carlos Williams. CP-WilW1

Cut the Grass. A. R. Ammons. CP-AmmoA

Cut the lemon and let two drops fall into the glass. Naked Face. Yannis Ritsos. SP-RitsY, *tr. by* Kimon Friar *and* Kostas Myrsiades

Cute boy arm in elbow prize con man, kid, what do we see. Catullus. *See* When an auctioneer's seen with a good-looking boy

Cutlery. Raymond Carver. CP-CarvR

Cutting across a vacant lot. House in the Vacant Lot, The. Miller Williams CP-WillM

Cutting off the. Lion::Mouse. A. R. Ammons. CP-AmmoA

Cutting the stems from a quart. Memory 1. Raymond Carver. CP-CarvR

Cutting up an Ox. Chuang Tzu. CP-MertT, *tr. by* Thomas Merton

Cuttings. Theodore Roethke. CP-RoetT

Cuttings. Theodore Roethke. CP-RoetT

Cwa een like milk-wort and bog-cotton hair! Milk-Wort and Bog Cotton Hugh MacDiarmid. SP-MacDH

Cy Est Pourtraicte, Madame Ste Ursule, et Les Unze Mille Vierges. Wallace Stevens. CP-StevW; CP-StevWP

Cybernetics. Howard Nemerov. CP-NemeH

Cycle. Geoffrey Hill. CP-HillG

Cycle. Robert Penn Warren. CP-WarrR

Cycle, The. Robinson Jeffers. CP-JefR1

Cycle, The. Dan Pagis. SP-PagiD, *tr. by* Stephen Mitchell

Cycle, The. Theodore Roethke. CP-RoetT

Cycle for Mother Cabrini, A. John Logan. CP-LogaJ

Cycle of Dust. James Tate. SP-TateJ

Cycle of Industry, The. Laura Riding Jackson. CP-RidiL

Cycles of Strangeness. Laura Riding Jackson. CP-RidiL

Cyclical Night, The. Jorge Luis Borges. SP-BorgJ, *tr. by* Alastair Reid

Cyclist, The. Louis MacNeice. CP-MacNL

Cyclist, The. Marge Piercy. SP-PierM

Cyclone, The. James Whitcomb Riley. CP-RileJ

Cyclops. Margaret Atwood. SP-AtwM1

Cyclops, The. Euripides. CP-ShelP, *tr. by* Percy Bysshe Shelley

Cyclops, The. Theocritus. CP-BroEB *Fr.* Idylls.

Cydonian Spring with her attendant train. Spring, The. Ezra Pound. SP-PounE

Cygnets dark; their black feet. Menagerie at Versailles in 1775, The. John Updike. CP-UpdiJ

Cynic perforce from studying mankind. Ambrose Bierce. SP-BierA

Cynic's Epitaph. Thomas Hardy. CP-HardT

Cynthia in California. James Laughlin. CP-LaugJ

Cynthia Matz, with my finger in your cunt. Each Day. David Ignatow. SP-IgnaD

Cynthia's Revels. Ben Jonson.

   Echo's [*or* Eccho's] Song. CP-JonsB; SP-JonsB

   Glove, The. CP-JonsB

   Hymn[e] to Cynthia. CP-JonsB; SP-JonsB

   "O, that joy so soon should waste!" CP-JonsB

Cynthius pluck ye by the eare. Disswasions from Idlenesse. Robert Herrick. CP-HerrR

Cypassis, that a thousand ways trim'st hair. Elegy 2.8: "Cypassis, that a thousand ways trim'st hair." Ovid. CP-MarlC, *tr. by* Christopher Marlowe *Fr.* Elegies.

Cypress Avenue, The. Donald Davie. CP-DaviDC

Cypress. / (Stagnant water). Federico García Lorca. CP-GarcF, *tr. by* Jerome Rothenberg *Fr.* Backwaters.

Cypress stood up like a church, The. Bianca Among the Nightingales. Elizabeth Barrett Browning. CP-BroEB

Cypress-Tree of Ceylon, The. John Greenleaf Whittier. CP-WhitJ

Cypresses. D. H. Lawrence. CP-LawrD

Cyrano. G. K. Chesterton. CP-ChesG

Cyrano, allez aux chiens. Cyrano. G. K. Chesterton. CP-ChesG

Cyriack, this three years['] day these eyes, though clear. To Mr. Cyriack Skinner upon His Blindness. John Milton. CP-MiltJ

Cyril Connolly. Stephen Spender. CP-SpenS

Cythera's pearls were dim. Psyche. "H. D." CP-DoolH

Cywydd. Gerard Manley Hopkins. CP-HopkG

Czar Alexander the Second. Dante Gabriel Rossetti. CW-RossD

Czar's Last Christmas Letter, The: A Barn in the Urals. Norman Dubie. CP-DubiN

Czech Refugee in London, A. Yehuda Amichai. SP-AmicYL, *tr.* by Benjamin Harshav *and* Barbara Harshav

Czecho-Slovakia. Edna St. Vincent Millay. CP-MillE

Czechoslovakia lynched on a swastika cross! Song for Ourselves. Langston Hughes. CP-HughL; CP-HughL1

D

D.G.C. to J.A. Emily Jane Brontë. CP-BronE

D-re-A-mi-N-gl-Y / leaves / (sEe). E. E. Cummings. CP-CummE

Da Boyg. Charles Olson. CP-OlsoC

Da Capo. Charles Tomlinson. CP-TomlC

Da. Da. Da da. So There. Robert Creeley. SP-CreeR

Da mi basia mille. James Laughlin. CP-LaugJ

Da Tagte Es. Samuel Beckett. CP-BeckS

Da Vinci, Raphael, Michelangelo—they committed. Vatican Museum. Yannis Ritsos. SP-RitsY, *tr.* by Kostas Myrsiades

D'abord / à plat sur du dur. Samuel Beckett. CP-BeckS

Dactyls. Olga Broumas. SP-BrouO

Dad was saying they've duplicated us. Visitation. Yusef Komunyakaa. CP-KomuY

Daddy. Sylvia Plath. CP-PlatS

Daddy-Do-Nothing. D. H. Lawrence. CP-LawrD

Daddy, / don't let your dog. Warning ("Daddy, / don't let your dog"). Langston Hughes. CP-HughL

Daddy-o / Buddy-o. Migrant. Langston Hughes. CP-HughL; CP-HughL2

"Daddy" Warbucks. Anne Sexton. CP-SextA

Daddy would drop purple-veined vines. Banking Potatoes. Yusef Komunyakaa. CP-KomuY

Daedalus in Sicily. Joseph Brodsky. CP-BrodJ

Daedalus: The Dirge. George Oppen. CP-OppGN

Daemon initiate, spirit. Euripides. CP-DoolH *Fr.* Hippolytus.

Daemon of the World, The; A Fragment. Percy Bysshe Shelley. CP-ShelP

Daemon, The. Louise Bogan. CP-BogaL

Daemons. John Ciardi. CP-CiarJ

Daffodil from Emily's lot, A. Daffodildo. May Swenson. SP-SwenM

Daffodil Poem. Gregory Orr. SP-OrrG

Daffodildo. May Swenson. SP-SwenM

Daffodils, The. Rae Armantrout. SP-ArmaA

Daffy Duck in Hollywood. John Ashbery. SP-AshbJ

Daft Little Shoe Clerk Decided It Would Be Fun to Go Up and See What Things Are Like above the Sky, The. Kenneth Patchen. CP-PatcK

Dagger lies in a drawer, A. Dagger, The. Jorge Luis Borges. SP-BorgJ, *tr.* by Alastair Reid

Dagger, The. Jorge Luis Borges. SP-BorgJ, *tr.* by Alastair Reid

Dago shovelman sits by the railroad track, The. Child of the Romans. Carl Sandburg. CP-SandC

Daguerreotype Taken in Old Age. Margaret Atwood. SP-AtwM1

Dagwood and Blondie. Charles Bukowski. SP-BukC3

Dahlia. Louis Zukofsky. CP-ZukLS

Dahlia Gardens, The. Amy Clampitt. CP-ClamA

Dah's Brudder Sims! Dast slam yo' Bible shet. Brudder Sims. James Whitcomb Riley. CP-RileJ

Daie, a night, an houre of sweete content, A. Thomas Campion. *See* Day, a night, an hour of sweet content, A

Daih's a moughty soothin' feelin'. 'Long To'ds Night. Paul Laurence Dunbar. CP-DunbP

Daily, and therefore calmly, one reads. One Reads. A. K. Ramanujan. CP-RamaA

Daily concerns are endless. Han-shan. CP-ColdM, *tr.* by Red Pine

Daily dawns another day. Inscription for the Ceiling of a Bedroom. Dorothy Parker. CP-ParkD

Daily Globe, The. Howard Nemerov. CP-NemeH

Daily I listen to wonder and woe. Ballade of a Talked-off Ear. Dorothy Parker. CP-ParkD

Daily Life of the Worker Bee, The. Marge Piercy. SP-PierM

Daily News, The. Jones Very. CP-VeryJ

Daily—Old Tale. Ivor Gurney. SP-GurnI

Daily, out of that unfamiliar. Horned Rampion, The. Amy Clampitt. CP-ClamA

Daily the cortege of crumpled. Salvage. Amy Clampitt. CP-ClamA

Daily, the kindergarteners. Better or Worse. Heather McHugh. SP-McHuH

Daily the / sledgehammers and the. Sad-Eyed Mules of Men. Charles Bukowski. SP-BukC2

Daily the wind-flowers age, and so do I. Weaving Love-Knots. Hsüeh T'ao. CP-KizeC, *tr.* by Carolyn Kizer

Daily Things We Do, The. Philip Larkin. CP-LarkP

Daily way for looking is inside, The. Window Washer, The. Wyatt Prunty. SP-PrunW

Daimon or angel, in her wrath. On Emily Dickinson. Helen Pinkerton. CP-PinkH

Daintiest of Manicures! At Madame Manicure's. James Whitcomb Riley. CP-RileJ

Dainty Baby Austin! King of Oo-Rinktum-Jing, The. James Whitcomb Riley. CP-RileJ

Dainty Davie. Robert Burns. CP-BurnR

Daisies, The. Charles Tomlinson. CP-TomlC

Daisies are broken. Love Song: "Daisies are broken." William Carlos Williams. CP-WilW1

Daisies of Florence. Kathleen Jessie Raine. SP-RainK

Daisy. William Carlos Williams. CP-WilW1

Daisy. Louis Zukofsky. CP-ZukLS

Daisy, The. G. K. Chesterton. CP-ChesG

Daisy, The. Walter De la Mare. CP-DeLaW

Daisy, The. Alfred Tennyson. CP-TennA

Daisy, The. Marya Alexandrovna Zaturenska. SP-ZatuM

Daisy and dandelion, speedwell, daffodil. Demi-Exile. Howth. Donald Davie. CP-DaviDC

Daisy follows soft the Sun, The. Emily Dickinson. CP-DickE

Daisy now is out upon the green, The. Song: "Daisy now is out upon the green, The." George Meredith. CP-MerG1

Daisy-Song. G. K. Chesterton. CP-ChesG

Dakar Doldrums. Allen Ginsberg. CP-GinsA

Da'kest hour, dey allus say, De. Joggin' Erlong. Paul Laurence Dunbar. CP-DunbP

Dakota, The. Amy Clampitt. CP-ClamA

Dalhousie Farm. William Meredith. SP-MereW

Dalila. George Meredith. CP-MerG2

Dallas–Fort Worth: Redbud and Mistletoe. Amy Clampitt. CP-ClamA

Dalliance of the Eagles, The. Walt Whitman. CP-WhitW

Dalqak's Message. Jelaluddin Rumi. SP-Rumi, *tr.* by Coleman Barks

Dam, The. Muriel Rukeyser. CP-RukeM

Dam Neck, Virginia. Richard Eberhart. CP-EberR

Damaetas. Lord Byron. CP-Byron

Damask. Wallace Stevens. CP-StevWP

Dame Kind. W. H. Auden. CP-AudeW

Dame of Athelhall, The. Thomas Hardy. CP-HardT

Dames du Temps Jadis. Robert Lowell. SP-LoweR

Damn Her. John Ciardi. CP-CiarJ

Damn it all! all this our South stinks peace. Sestina: Altaforte. Ezra Pound. CP-PoEar; SP-PounE

Damn near where'er you look, a writer's ghost. Literary Dublin. John Updike. CP-UpdiJ

Damn that celibate farm, that cracker-box house. Censorship. John Ciardi. CP-CiarJ

Damn the snow. Elegy for Thelonious. Yusef Komunyakaa. CP-KomuY

Damn You, Jim D., You Woke Me Up. John Berryman. CP-BerrJ

"Damn!" you would say if I were to write the best. Casualty, The. Louis MacNeice. CP-MacNL

Damnation, The. Carolyn Kizer. CP-KizeC

Damnation of Doves, A. John Ciardi. CP-CiarJ

Damned. John Berryman. CP-BerrJ

Damned Cherub. Arthur Rimbaud. CP-RimbA, *tr.* by Martin Sorrell

Damned. Lost & *damned*. And I find I'm pregnant. Damned. John Berryman. CP-BerrJ

Damned ugly things. Tanck's Song About Brains. Hayden Carruth. CP-CarHS *Fr.* Songs About What Comes Down: The Complete Works of Mr. Septic Tanck.

Damned Women ("Half-hidden in the dying light's caress"). Charles Baudelaire. CP-BaudC, *tr.* by Walter Martin

Damned Women ("Like ruminating cattle on the sand"). Charles Baudelaire. CP-BaudC, *tr.* by Walter Martin

Damon, come drive thy flocks this way. Clorinda and Damon. Andrew Marvell. CP-MarvA

Damon & Pythias. Robert Creeley. CP-CreeR

Damon the artisan in all the Peloponnese. Procession of Dionysus. Constantine P. Cavafy. CP-CavaC, *tr.* by Theoharis Constantine Theoharis

Damon the Mower. Andrew Marvell. CP-MarvA

Damon's Epitaph. John Milton. CP-MiltJ

(On the Death of Damon.) CP-CowpW

Damp[e], The. John Donne. CP-DonnJ; MW-DonnJ

Dam's broke. Morning ("Dam's broke"). Robert Creeley. SP-CreeR

Damson. Seamus Heaney. SP-HeanSO

Dan. Carl Sandburg. CP-SandC

Dan Jackson's Reply. Jonathan Swift. CP-SwifJ

Dan O'Sullivan: It's your. James Whitcomb Riley. CP-RileJ

Dan Paine. James Whitcomb Riley. CP-RileJ

Dan Wallingford, my jo Dan! To the Boy with a Country. James Whitcomb Riley. CP-RileJ

Danaan children laugh, in cradles of wrought gold, The. Unappeasable Host, The. William Butler Yeats. CP-YeatW

Dance, A. Wendell Berry. CP-BerrW

Dance, The. Thomas Campion. CP-CampT *Fr.* Ayres that Were Sung and Played, at *Brougham Castle* in *Westmerland*, in the Kings Entertainment, The.

Dance, The. Wendell Berry. CP-BerrW

Dance, The. Elizabeth Barrett Browning. CP-BroEB

Dance, The. Paul Laurence Dunbar. CP-DunbP

Dance, The. Thomas Kinsella. CP-KinsT

Dance, The. Philip Larkin. CP-LarkP

Dance, The. Robert Stock. SP-StocR

Dance, The. William Carlos Williams. CP-WilW2

Dance, The. William Carlos Williams. CP-WilW2

Dance a little. All the Way. Robert Creeley. SP-CreeR

Dance at the Phoenix, The. Thomas Hardy. CP-HardT

Dance begins. to end about a form, The. Desert Music, The. William Carlos Williams. CP-WilW2

Dance begins with the sun descending, The. Marrakech. Richard Eberhart. CP-EberR

Dance Called David, The. Theodore Weiss. SP-WeisT

Dance Figure. Ezra Pound. SP-PounE

Dance Floor. Clarence Major. SP-MajoC

"Dance for a year and a day!" he cried. Priest's Curse on Dancing, The. Howard Nemerov. CP-NemeH

Dance in Jinotega, The. Grace Paley. CP-PalGC

Dance / is not yet / and when it will begin, The. Before the Dance. Charles Tomlinson. CP-TomlC

Dance like a jackrabbit. Inside Chance, The. Marge Piercy. SP-PierM

Dance of Death. Federico García Lorca. CP-GarcF, *tr. by* Greg Simon *and* Steven F. White

Dance of Death, The. Robert Browning. CP-BroR2

Dance of the Girls' Chemises. Jaroslav Seifert. SP-SeifJ, *tr. by* Ewald Osers

Dance, of the Grizzly Bear, The. Charles Olson. CP-OlsoC

Dance of the Macabre Mice. Wallace Stevens. SP-StevW; CP-StevWP

Dance of the Moon in Santiago. Federico García Lorca. SP-GarcF, *tr. by* Norman Thomas Di Giovanni

Dance of the Moon in Santiago. Federico García Lorca. CP-GarcF, *tr. by* Catherine Brown

Dance of the Skin, The. James Laughlin. CP-LaugJ

Dance of Words. Robert Graves. CP-GravR

Dance on, dance on, we see, we see. Arthur Hugh Clough. SP-ClouA

Dance on the Staircase, The. Rainer Maria Rilke. CP-RilkFr, *tr. by* A. Poulin, Jr.

Dance the Orange. Robert Earl Hayden. CP-HaydR

Dance there upon the shore. To a Child Dancing in the Wind. William Butler Yeats. CP-YeatW

Dance Unmacabre. Ogden Nash. CP-NashO

Dance, when you're broken open. Jelaluddin Rumi. SP-Rumi, *tr. by* Coleman Barks

Dance, yellows and whites and reds. Spring Song. Robert Browning. SP-BroR

Dancer. Langston Hughes. CP-HughL; CP-HughL3

Dancer. Carl Sandburg. CP-SandC

Dancer, The. "H. D." CP-DoolH

Dancer, The. Philip Larkin. CP-LarkP

Dancer at Cruachan and Cro-Patrick, The. William Butler Yeats. CP-YeatW

Dancers. Donald Hall. CP-HallD

Dancers. Langston Hughes. CP-HughL; CP-HughL2

Dancers at the Moy. Paul Muldoon. CP-MuldP

Dancers danced in a quiet meadow, The. Ivor Gurney. SP-GurnI

Dancers Exercising. Amy Clampitt. CP-ClamA

Dancers in a Hospital. A. K. Ramanujan. CP-RamaA

Dancer's Reply, The. Howard Nemerov. CP-NemeH

Dancers strapped to canoes is. Sea Sickness. Andrei Codrescu. SP-CodrA

Dances beautifully. Night. Adam Zagajewski. SP-ZagaA, *tr. by* Clare Cavanagh

Dances of Death. Aleksandr Aleksandrovich Blok. Scene, The. CP-KunSC

Dances of Death. Aleksandr Aleksandrovich Blok. SP-BlokA, *tr. by* Peter France *and* Jon Stallworthy

Dancin' the funky chicken. Ain't That Bad. Maya Angelou. SP-AngeM

Dancing. Robert Creeley. CP-CreeR

Dancing Bear grotesque and funny, A. Brother Bruin. Christina Georgina Rossetti. CP-RosC2

Dancing Death. Charles Baudelaire. CP-BaudC, *tr. by* Walter Martin

Dancing Flame. Robert Graves. CP-GravR

Dancing for a Prize. Nicholas Vachel Lindsay. CP-LindV

Dancing girls here . . . after a long night of it . . . , The. Branches. Carl Sandburg. CP-SandC

Dancing lamely on a laquered plain. Tillaquils, The. Laura Riding Jackson. CP-RidiL

Dancing Measures. Donald Davie. CP-DaviDC

Dancing on the hill-tops, / Singing in the valleys. Christina Georgina Rossetti. CP-RosC2

Dancing Serpent, The. Charles Baudelaire. CP-BaudC, *tr. by* Walter Martin

Dancing toward Bethlehem. Billy Collins. SP-CollB

Dancing under the Stars at Nice. Clarence Major. SP-MajoC

Dandelion. Louis Zukofsky. CP-ZukLS

Dandelion cavalry, light little saviors. On a Church Lawn. William Stafford. SP-StafWW

Dandelion, The. Nicholas Vachel Lindsay. CP-LindV

Dandelions. Howard Nemerov. CP-NemeH

Dandelion's pallid tube, The. Emily Dickinson. CP DickE

Dane-Geld. Rudyard Kipling. CP-KiplR

Danger, The. Pablo Neruda. SP-NeruP

Danger, danger of dying. Winter Landscapes. Donald Davie. CP-DaviDC

Danger in the Air, The. Archibald MacLeish. CP-MacLA

Danger is not at first. Emily Dickinson. SP-DickE

Danger not an inch outside, The. Assurance. Robert Frost. CP-FrosR

Danger of Loss, The. Robert Bly. SP-BlyR

Danger of Writing Defiant Verse, The. Dorothy Parker. CP-ParkD

Danger Outstripped. Yannis Ritsos. SP-RitsY, *tr. by* Kimon Friar

Danger / Road under Repair. James Laughlin. CP-LaugJ

Danger stalks on such nights, the moon is dangerous. Lunar Tides, The. Marya Alexandrovna Zaturenska. SP-ZatuM

Dangerous / Are the western waters now. To Captain Mulzac. Langston Hughes. CP-HughL; CP-HughL2

Dangerous country. Full of suspect objects. Yehuda Amichai. SP-AmicYL, *tr. by* Benjamin Harshav *and* Barbara Harshav

Dangerous Games. Carolyn Kizer. CP-KizeC

Dangerous gift & grace is mine, A. Ralph Waldo Emerson. CP-EmerR

Dangerous Gift, The. Robert Graves. CP-GravR

Dangerous Little Boy Fairies, The. Nicholas Vachel Lindsay. CP-LindV

Dangerous Painters, The. Tennessee Williams. CP-WillT

Dangerous Remarks. Constantine P. Cavafy. CP-CavaC, *tr. by* Theoharis Constantine Theoharis

Dangerous Year, The. John Berryman. CP-BerrJ

Dangers. Yannis Ritsos. SP-RitsY, *tr. by* Andonis Decavalles

Dangers Wait on Kings. Robert Herrick. CP-HerrR

Daniel. Nicholas Vachel Lindsay. CP-LindV

Daniel Boone, the father of Kentucky. Poem: "Daniel Boone, the father of Kentucky." William Carlos Williams. CP-WilW1

Daniel Neall. John Greenleaf Whittier. CP-WhitJ

Daniel Wheeler. John Greenleaf Whittier. CP-WhitJ

Danish Boy; A Fragment, The. William Wordsworth. CP-WorW1

Danish Conqueror, on his royal chair, The. Fact, and an Imagination or, Canute and Alfred, on the Sea-Shore, A. William Wordsworth. CP-WorW2

Danish native, The. Smiling Dane, A. William Carlos Williams. CP-WilW2

Danny dead of heart attack. Landed Fish. Marge Piercy. SP-PierM

Danny Deever. Rudyard Kipling. CP-KiplR

Dans le Restaurant. T. S. Eliot. CP-ElioT; SP-ElioT

Dans un Seul Lit. Robert Graves. CP-GravR

Danse Africaine. Langston Hughes. CP-HughL; CP-HughL1

Danse Macabre. W. H. Auden. CP-AudeW

Danse Macabre. Norman Dubie. CP-DubiN

Danse Macabre. Sylvia Plath. CP-PlatS

Danse Russe. William Carlos Williams. CP-WilW1

Dante. Anna Andreyevna Akhmatova. CP-KunSC, *tr. by* Max Hayward *and* Stanley Kunitz

Dante. Czeslaw Milosz. CP-MiloCN, *tr. by* Robert Hass

Dante, a sigh that rose from the heart's core. Sonnet: He reports, in a feigned Vision, the successful Issue of Lapo Gianni's Love. Guido Cavalcanti. CW-RossD, *tr. by* Dante Gabriel Rossetti

Dante, a sighing messenger of the heart. Guido Cavalcanti. CP-CavaG, *tr. by* Marc Cirigliano

Dante and I are come to learn of thee. To Guido Cavalcanti. Ezra Pound. CP-PoEar

Dante at Verona. Dante Gabriel Rossetti. CW-RossD

Dante Études. Robert Duncan.
  Everything Speaks to Me. SP-DuncR
  Household, The. SP-DuncR

Dante himself endured. Her Wrath. Theodore Roethke. CP-RoetT

Dante, since I from my own native place. Sonnet: He answers Dante, confessing his unsteadfast Heart. Cino da Pistoia. CW-RossD, *tr. by* Dante Gabriel Rossetti

Dante 3. Buonconte. Robert Lowell. SP-LoweR

Dante, whenever this thing happeneth. Sonnet: He conceives of some Compensation in Death. Cino da Pistoia. CW-RossD, *tr. by* Dante Gabriel Rossetti

Dante's Tomb. John Berryman. CP-BerrJ

Dante's Vita Nuova. Dante Alighieri. CP-EmerR, *tr. by* Ralph Waldo Emerson

Dantis Tenebræ (In Memory of my Father). Dante Gabriel Rossetti. CW-RossD

Danton. G. K. Chesterton. CP-ChesG

Daphnaïda. Edmund Spenser. CP-Spens

Daphne. Gerard Manley Hopkins. CP-HopkG

Daphne. George Meredith. CP-MerG1

Daphne. Edna St. Vincent Millay. CP-MillE

Daphne. Jonathan Swift. CP-SwifJ

Daphne. Marya Alexandrovna Zaturenska. SP-ZatuM

Daphne (age 2) can't say. My Granddaughter. James Laughlin. CP-LaugJ

Daphne knows, with equal ease. Daphne. Jonathan Swift. CP-SwifJ

Daphnis and Chloe. Andrew Marvell. CP-MarvA

Daphnis must from Chloe part. Daphnis and Chloe. Andrew Marvell. CP-MarvA

Dappled bird, A. Grace. Gabriela Mistral. SP-MistG, *tr. by* Maria Giachetti [*or* Jacketti]

Dappled die-away, The. Morning, Midday, and Evening Sacrifice. Gerard Manley Hopkins. CP-HopkG

Dare. Langston Hughes. CP-HughL; CP-HughL2

Dare you dispute / You saucy brute. Answer to the Ballyspellin Ballad, An. Jonathan Swift. CP-SwifJ

Dare you see a Soul *at the White Heat?* Emily Dickinson. CP-DickE

Dared and done: at last I stand upon the summit, Dear and True! La Saisiaz. Robert Browning. CP-BroR2

Dareios. Constantine P. Cavafy. CP-CavaC, *tr. by* Theoharis Constantine Theoharis

Dares the lama, most fleet of the sons of the wind. Bigotry's Victim. Percy Bysshe Shelley. CP-ShelP

Darest Thou Now O Soul. Walt Whitman. CP-WhitW

Darien. Robert Graves. CP-GravR

Darius the Mede was a king and a wonder. Daniel. Nicholas Vachel Lindsay. CP-LindV

Darjeeling. Thomas Merton. CP-MertT

Dark accurate plunger down the successive knell. Subway, The. Allen Tate. CP-TateA

Dark Age Glosses. Louis MacNeice. CP-MacNL

Dark ages, calm and merry. North Sea, in a Snowstorm, The. Donald Davie. CP-DaviDC

Dark ancestral fields. Northern Heather. Robinson Jeffers. CP-JefR2

Dark and deafening skies are bowed, The. Rain, The. G. K. Chesterton. CP-ChesG

Dark and intent, you sit. Confidence. William Dickey. SP-DickW

Dark and more dark the shades of evening fell. Composed after a Journey across the Hambleton [*or* Hamilton] Hills, Yorkshire. William Wordsworth. CP-WorW1

Dark and the Fair, The. Stanley Kunitz. CP-KunSC

Dark archers / approaching Seville. Poem of the *Saeta.* Federico García Lorca. CP-GarcF, *tr. by* Cola Franzen *and* Robert Nasatir

Dark archers, The. Archers, The. Federico García Lorca. SP-GarcF *Fr.* Poem of the Saeta.

Dark Arm, Hanging over the Edge of Infinity. Tennessee Williams. CP-WillT

Dark as a gypsy, berry. Old Meg. Thom Gunn. CP-GunnT

Dark August. Derek Walcott. CP-WalcD

Dark Band. Primo Levi. CP-LeviP, *tr. by* Ruth Feldman

Dark blood of night-time, The. Nocturne: "Dark blood of night-time, The." Louis MacNeice. CP-MacNL

Dark blue wind of early autumn, The. Sleep Impression. Carl Sandburg. CP-SandC

Dark blush of anger, The. Three Talks on Civilization. Czeslaw Milosz. CP-MiloC; CP-MiloCN, *tr. by* Jan Darowski

Dark brown pinstripe, the trousers. Suit, The. Philip Levine. SP-LeviP

Dark-Buffalo, are you out on the plains. Old Friends. Peter Blue Cloud. SP-BlueP

Dark building, A. Crossed boards, nailed up, create. Book in the Ruins, A. Czeslaw Milosz. CP-MiloC; CP-MiloCN, *tr. by* Renata Gorczynski *and* Robert Hass

Dark came first and settled in. Hundred Nights, A. Maxine W. Kumin. SP-KumiM

Dark Château, The. Walter De la Mare. CP-DeLaW

Dark child in my arms, eyes. To a Child in Calcutta. Galway Kinnell. SP-KinnGN

Dark children of the mere and marsh. Rudyard Kipling. CP-KiplR

Dark Comes On In Blocks, In Cubes, The. Thomas Lux. SP-LuxT

Dark curtain of rain sweeps slowly over the sunlit mountain, A. Summer Rain in Mountains. Robert Penn Warren. CP-WarrR

Dark damp night and a sudden hatch, A. Moths, The. James Laughlin. CP-LaugJ

Dark. Dark. And dark winds. End of the Road from Nantucket, The. Sam Hamill. SP-HamiS

Dark Day, A. Dante Gabriel Rossetti. CW-RossD *Fr.* House of Life, The.

Dark day / hard, swarming. Flashes. James Schuyler. CP-SchuJ

Dark Day, The. Jones Very. CP-VeryJ
 (Spiritual Darkness.) CP-VeryJ

Dark Day, The. William Carlos Williams. CP-WilW1

Dark / days are past. Mysteries, The. "H. D." CP-DoolH

Dark, deeply. A red. Inside the River. James Dickey. CP-DickJ

Dark Diana of the groves, The. White Witch, The. G. K. Chesterton. CP-ChesG

Dark eleventh hour, The. Ulster. Rudyard Kipling. CP-KiplR

Dark Encounter, The. Thomas Merton. CP-MertT

Dark-Eyed Gentleman, The. Thomas Hardy. CP-HardT

Dark eyed, / O woman of my dreams. Dance Figure. Ezra Pound. SP-PounE

Dark Flower of Cheshire garden. Ralph Waldo Emerson. CP-EmerR

Dark fossil flower! I see thy leaves unrolled. Fossil Flower, The. Jones Very. CP-VeryJ

Dark frost was in the air without. Winter Dusk. Walter De la Mare. CP-DeLaW

Dark geese treading blowing Dakota snows, The. Snow Geese. Robert Bly. SP-BlyR

Dark Girl's Rhyme, The. Dorothy Parker. CP-ParkD

Dark Glass, The. Dante Gabriel Rossetti. CW-RossD *Fr.* House of Life, The.

Dark God, the Light God, The. Adam Zagajewski. SP-ZagaA, *tr. by* Renata Gorczynski

Dark-green upon distant heights. Prologue at Sixty. W. H. Auden. CP-AudeW

Dark hair of summer, The. Beech leaves as tense. Vacation. Adam Zagajewski. SP-ZagaA, *tr. by* Renata Gorczynski, Benjamin Ivry *and* C. K. Williams

Dark Hills, The. Edwin Arlington Robinson. CP-RobiE

Dark House, The. Edwin Arlington Robinson. CP-RobiE

Dark illumination of a storm, The. English Accounts. William Meredith. SP-MereW

Dark in the cubicle boxed from snow-darkness of night. History during Nocturnal Snowfall. Robert Penn Warren. CP-WarrR

Dark is dividing, the sun is coming past the wall, The. Dawn Verse, The. D. H. Lawrence. CP-LawrD

Dark is the night. Vigil. Walter De la Mare. CP-DeLaW

Dark Lady, when you lie in your dark tomb. Posthumous Remorse. Charles Baudelaire. CP-BaudC, *tr. by* Walter Martin

Dark lean face, a narrow, slanting eye, A. Iago. Walter De la Mare. CP-DeLaW

Dark mind dark soul dark age. History of the World: a TV Docu-Drama. Lawrence Ferlinghetti. SP-FerlL

Dark Morning, The. Thomas Merton. CP-MertT

Dark Mutinous Shannon Waves, The. James Laughlin. CP-LaugJ

Dark Night, A. Gregory Orr. SP-OrrG

Dark of the moon, bear's tail through triage of winter trees. Step-Children of Paradise. Charles Wright. SP-WrigCN

Dark on the ridge of the cold salt wave. George Meredith. CP-MerG2

Dark One in lightning, The. Dark God, the Light God, The. Adam Zagajewski. SP-ZagaA, *tr. by* Renata Gorczynski

Dark Ones. James Dickey. CP-DickJ

Dark-out Lucifer detesting this, The. Gerard Manley Hopkins. CP-HopkG

Dark plume fetch me from yon blasted yew, A. Return. William Wordsworth. CP-WorW2 *Fr.* River Duddon [A Series of Sonnets], The.

Dark Portrait, A. Lawrence Ferlinghetti. SP-FerlL

Dark rain at. Sun. W. S. Merwin. SP-MerwWF

Dark, rainsoaked. Romance. Denise Levertov. SP-LeveDL

Dark rainy night, A. Yannis Ritsos. SP-RitsY *Fr.* First Series.

Dark road home. Peace. Lorine Niedecker. CP-NiedL

Dark rose grew in the desert, A. Saint Anthony and the Rose of Life. Stevie Smith. CP-SmitS

Dark Satanic Mills. D. H. Lawrence. CP-LawrD

Dark Shades. Charles Bukowski. SP-BukC1

Dark Song. A. R. Ammons. CP-AmmoA

Dark stone statue of Goya, The. Goya & the Sleep of Reason. Lawrence Ferlinghetti. SP-FerlL

Dark Summer. Louise Bogan. CP-BogaL

Dark swallows will doubtless come back killing. Will Not Come Back. Robert Lowell. SP-LoweR

Dark, tempestuous night; the stars shut in, A. At Last. James Whitcomb Riley. CP-RileJ

Dark the halls, and cold the feast. New Wife and the Old, The. John Greenleaf Whittier. CP-WhitJ

Dark the sea was: but I saw him. Fish, The. G. K. Chesterton. CP-ChesG

Dark theme keeps me here, A. In Evening Air. Theodore Roethke. CP-RoetT

Dark, thick branch in the last light is like, A. Hour, The. Norman Dubie. CP-DubiN

Dark things of the wood, The. Family, The. Mary Oliver. SP-OlivM

Dark through the clouds, they are silver-lined. Far-Sighted Muse, The. Dorothy Parker. CP-ParkD

Dark to my mind. Tremor. Federico García Lorca. CP-GarcF, tr. by Jerome Rothenberg Fr. Water Suite.

Dark Tower, The. Alan Dugan. CP-DugaA

Dark Tree, The. Ivor Gurney. SP-GurnI

Dark, underground, is furnished with the bone. Sonnet: "Dark, underground, is furnished with the bone." Louise Bogan. CP-BogaL

Dark was that day when Diesel. Curse, A. W. H. Auden. CP-AudeW

Dark was the day for Childe Rolandine the artist. Childe Rolandine. Stevie Smith. CP-SmitS

Dark was thick, The. A boy he seemed at that time. Seven Times, The. Thomas Hardy. CP-HardT

Dark water, underground. Cycle, The. Theodore Roethke. CP-RoetT

Dark waterfalls. Black fleece. Cascading curls. Her Hair. Charles Baudelaire. CP-BaudC, tr. by Walter Martin

Dark waters churn amongst us. C. G. Jung's 'First Years'. Thomas Kinsella. CP-KinsT

Dark will come, I said, The. Moonset. Hayden Carruth. CP-CarHS

Dark with power. Wendell Berry. CP-BerrW

Dark woman, head bent, listening for something, A. Atlas of the Difficult World, An. Adrienne Rich. SP-RicA1

Dark Wood, Dark Water. Sylvia Plath. CP-PlatS

Dark woods, I give myself entirely over. December Trees. Charles Simic. SP-SimiC

Dark Year, The. Marya Alexandrovna Zaturenska. SP-ZatuM

Dark Years, The. W. H. Auden. CP-AudeW

Dark Youth of the U.S.A. Langston Hughes. CP-HughL; CP-HughL1

Darkened by time, the masters, like our memories, mix. Black Zodiac. Charles Wright. SP-WrigCN

Darkening the edges of the land. Suggestions for the Improvement of a Sunset. Charles Tomlinson. CP-TomlC

Darker than night; and, oh, much darker, she. Shade, The. Walter De la Mare. CP-DeLaW

Darkest hour that falls upon the earth, The. Hour Before the Dawn, The. Jones Very. CP-VeryJ

Darklight. Adrienne Rich.
"When heat leaves the walls at last." SP-RicA1

Darkling Thrush, The. Thomas Hardy. CP-HardT

Darkly against the winter's white. Fall Song. Howard Nemerov. CP-NemeH

Darkness. Lord Byron. CP-Byron

Darkness. Paul Celan. SP-CelaP, tr. by John Felstiner

Darkness. Arthur Hugh Clough. SP-ClouA

Darkness and light are both alike to Thee. Christina Georgina Rossetti. CP-RosC2

Darkness and light define here one another. On Caravaggio's Conversion of St. Paul (1600) in Santa Maria del Popolo, Rome. Helen Pinkerton. CP-PinkH

Darkness—and white. Twelve, The. Aleksandr Aleksandrovich Blok. SP-BlokA, tr. by Peter France and Jon Stallworthy

Darkness / as black as your eyelid. Fury of Sunrises, The. Anne Sexton. SP-SextA Fr. Furies, The.

Darkness comes out of the earth. Twilight. D. H. Lawrence. CP-LawrD

Darkness falls like a wet sponge. Picture of Little J. A. in a Prospect of Flowers, The. John Ashbery. SP-AshbJ

Darkness gathering in the branches. Grandmother in Heaven. Philip Levine. SP-LeviP

Darkness, giving us dream's black unity. Seventh Elegy. Dream-Singing Elegy. Muriel Rukeyser. CP-RukeM

Darkness had fallen. I opened the door. Unforeseen. Walter De la Mare. CP-DeLaW

Darkness Has Cheating Swiftness. Ivor Gurney. SP-GurnI

Darkness has cheating swiftness. Darkness Has Cheating Swiftness. Ivor Gurney. SP-GurnI

Darkness lifts, imagine, in your lifetime, The. Undertaking, The. Louise Glück. SP-GlucL

Darkness like the middle of the night, A. Dark Day, The. Jones Very. CP-VeryJ

Darkness Music. Muriel Rukeyser. CP-RukeM

Darkness of the year begins, The. Political Song for the Year's End. Thomas McGrath. SP-McGrT

Darkness steals the forms of all the queens, The. Firelight and Nightfall. D. H. Lawrence. CP-LawrD

Darkness waits apart from any occasion for it. Interlunar. Margaret Atwood. SP-AtwM2

Darkness was bad as weariness, till Grimes said. Puncture. John Crowe Ransom. SP-RansJ

Darkness was overtraced on every face. Emily Jane Brontë. CP-BronE

Darlene's Hospital. John Ashbery. SP-AshbJ

Darling. John Ciardi. CP-CiarJ

Darling!because my blood can sing. E. E. Cummings. CP-CummE; SP-CummE

Darling Daughter of Babylon. Nicholas Vachel Lindsay. CP-LindV

Darling Daughters. Stevie Smith. CP-SmitS

Darling, I had my hand on your khaki. All the Leaves Were Green. Jane Cooper. CP-CoopJ

Darling, I understand. Syzygy. Yusef Komunyakaa. CP-KomuY

Darling, if ever on some night of fever. First Love. Robert Graves. CP-GravR

Darling little baby child. Sad Mother, The. Stevie Smith. CP-SmitS

Darling little Cousin, / With your thoughtful look. To Lalla, Reading My Verses Topsy-Turvy. Christina Georgina Rossetti. CP-RosC3

Darling, my darling, my heart is on the wing. Morning Song of Love. Paul Laurence Dunbar. CP-DunbP

Darling of Milton—when that marble man. To Eve, Man's Dream of Wifehood as Described by Milton. Nicholas Vachel Lindsay. CP-LindV

Darling of our hearts, drowning. Elegy for Margaret. Stephen Spender. CP SpenS

Darling, the plates have been cleared away. Beauty and the Beast. Rita Dove. SP-DoveR

Darling, what is that? Drop of a Hat, The. Ogden Nash. CP-NashO

Darling, you think it's love, it's just a midnight journey. Seaward. Joseph Brodsky. CP-BrodJ

Darlings. Charles Bukowski. SP-BukC3

Dar'st thou amid the varied multitude Solitary, The. Percy Bysshe Shelley. CP-ShelP

Dart, The. Thomas Carew CP CareT

Darting fear, a pomp, a tear, A. Emily Dickinson. CP-DickE

Daruma. Louis Zukofsky. CP-ZukLS

Daruma / found object / that is art. Daruma. Louis Zukofsky. CP-ZukLS

Darwin. Lorine Niedecker. CP-NiedL

Darwinians at Play. G. K. Chesterton. CP-ChesG

Darwin's Dream. Clarence Major. SP-MajoC

Darzee's Chaunt. Rudyard Kipling. CP-KiplR Fr. Jungle Book, The.

Das Babenzorn. Ezra Pound. CP-PoEar

Das ewig Weibliche. Robert Lowell. SP-LoweR

Das Kleine Weinjahr. Rainer Maria Rilke. CP-RilkFr, tr. by A. Poulin, Jr.

Das Krist Kindel. James Whitcomb Riley. CP-RileJ

Dashing in glass we race. Eccentric Motion. Muriel Rukeyser. CP-RukeM

Dat Ol' Mare o' Mine. Paul Laurence Dunbar. CP-DunbP

Data in the glass beaker: a dozen scorpions, The. In the Laboratory. Dan Pagis. SP-PagiD, tr. by Stephen Mitchell

Date of my birth is probably 903 B.C.—but also quite probably, The. Items of Identification. Yannis Ritsos. SP-RitsY Fr. Monovasia.

Dateline Saigon: Marines wait in the rain. First of June Again, The. Carolyn Kizer. CP-KizeC

Dates. Gertrude Stein. CP-SteiG

Dates: Penkhull New Road. Charles Tomlinson. CP-TomlC

Dative Haruspices. Kenneth Rexroth. CP-RexrK

Daughter. James Dickey. CP-DickJ

Daughter. Robert Pinsky. CP-PinsR

Daughter. John Updike. CP-UpdiJ

Daughter (1), A. Denise Levertov. SP-LeveDL

Daughter (2), A. Denise Levertov. SP-LeveDL

Daughter is mad, and so, The. Anne. Mary Oliver. SP-OlivM

Daughter-my-mother. Blessing, The. Carolyn Kizer. CP-KizeC

Daughter of Chaos' doting years. Ode to the Departed Regency-Bill—1789. Robert Burns. CP-BurnR

Daughter of Eve, A. Christina Georgina Rossetti. CP-RosC1

Daughter of Heaven and Earth, coy Spring. May-Day. Ralph Waldo Emerson. CP-EmerR

Daughter of Jove, relentless Power. Hymn to Adversity. Thomas Gray. CP-GrayT

Daughter of music. Song for the Year's End, A. Louis Zukofsky. CP-ZukLS

Daughter Returns, A. Thomas Hardy. CP-HardT

"Daughter, thou art come to die." Very Old Song, A. "William Laird." CP-HerrR

Daughter to Archeologist. Josephine Jacobsen. CP-JacoJ

Daughter to that good Earl[e], once President. To the Lady Margaret Ley. John Milton. CP-MiltJ

Daughters of Pandarus, The. Homer. CP-BroEB Fr. Odyssey.

Daughters of the horseleech crying "Give! Give!", The. Stanley Kunitz. CP-KunSC

Daughters of the subtle flood. Ben Jonson. CP-JonsB Fr. Masque of Blackness, The.

Daughters of Time, the hypocritic Days. Days. Ralph Waldo Emerson. CP-EmerR

Davao Insular Hotel. Robert Creeley. SP-CreeR

Dave Field. James Whitcomb Riley. CP-RileJ

David Dancing. Donald Davie. CP-DaviDC

David Walker (1785–1830). Rita Dove. SP-DoveR

David's Lamentation for Saul and Jonathan. Anne Bradstreet. CP-BradA

David's Night in Veliès. James Merrill. SP-MerrJ

Dawdling into glory; / or with hammer-strokes. Antitheses. John Berryman. CP-BerrJ

Dawlish Fair. John Keats. CP-KeatJ
(Over the Hill and Over the Dale.) CP-KeatJ

Dawn. Gerard Manley Hopkins. CP-HopkG

Dawn. Peter Blue Cloud. SP-BlueP

Dawn. Paul Laurence Dunbar. CP-DunbP

Dawn. Robinson Jeffers. CP-JefR3

Dawn. Philip Larkin. CP-LarkP

Dawn. Federico García Lorca. CP-GarcF, tr. by Greg Simon and Steven F. White

Dawn. Walter De la Mare. CP-DeLaW

Dawn. Edna St. Vincent Millay. CP-MillE

Dawn. Gabriela Mistral. SP-MistG, tr. by Maria Giachetti [or Jacketti] and Maria Jacketti

Dawn. Robert Penn Warren. CP-WarrR

Dawn. William Carlos Williams. CP-WilW1

Dawn. C. K. Williams. SP-WillC

Dawn. First light tearing. Clouds. Philip Levine. SP-LeviP

Dawn. Hoar on the grass. Hayden Carruth. CP-CarHS Fr. Clay Hill Anthology, The.

Dawn. The river thins. Strangers. Ted Hughes. SP-HughTN

Dawn, The. Federico García Lorca. SP-GarcF, tr. by J. L. Gili and Stephen Spender

Dawn, The. William Butler Yeats. CP-YeatW

Dawn—a smouldering fume of dry frost. Earth-Numb. Ted Hughes. SP-HughTN

Dawn after the Dance, The. Thomas Hardy. CP-HardT

Dawn alps, The. Perspectives. Denise Levertov. SP-LeveDP

Dawn an unsympathetic yellow. Electrical Storm. Elizabeth Bishop. CP-BishE

Dawn and a Woman. John Logan. CP-LogaJ

Dawn and Dew my Bearers be. Emily Dickinson. SP-DickE

Dawn and, distant, the steel-snarl and lyric. Chain Saw at Dawn in Vermont in Time of Drouth. Robert Penn Warren. CP-WarrR

Dawn: and foot on the cold stair treading or. Aubade for Hope. Robert Penn Warren. CP-WarrR

Dawn / and now.begins / feeling. E. E. Cummings. CP-CummE

Dawn and Sunrise. Sir Walter Scott. SP-ScotW Fr. Rokeby.

Dawn; and the jew's-harp's sawing seesaw song. Pilots, Man Your Planes. Randall Jarrell. CP-JarrR

Dawn, and the scent of clover rises from low meadows. Anton Bruckner. Adam Zagajewski. SP-ZagaA, tr. by Renata Gorczynski, Benjamin Ivry and C. K. Williams

Dawn at Saint Patrick's. Derek Mahon. CP-MahoD

Dawn Bombardment. Robert Graves. CP-GravR

Dawn brings lovely playthings to the mind. Lovely Playthings. Ivor Gurney. SP-GurnI

Dawn brings us the smell. Second Anniversary ("Dawn brings us the smell"). Federico García Lorca. CP-GarcF, tr. by Christopher Maurer

Dawn came at six today. To the Man in the Yellow Terry. Alice Walker. CP-WalkA

Dawn Chorus, The. Derek Mahon. CP-MahoD

Dawn in New York has / four columns of mire. Dawn. Federico García Lorca. CP-GarcF, tr. by Greg Simon and Steven F. White

Dawn in Threshing Time. Robert Bly. SP-BlyR

Dawn is no longer in the house of the Fish. Astronomical Changes. D. H. Lawrence. CP-LawrD

Dawn, noon and dewfall! Bluebird and robin. James Whitcomb Riley. CP-RileJ

Dawn of the day was dreary, The. Rainy Morning, The. James Whitcomb Riley. CP-RileJ

Dawn of the Space Age. John Ciardi. CP-CiarJ

Dawn off the Foreland—the young flood making. Mine Sweepers. Rudyard Kipling. CP-KiplR

Dawn offers / innocence to a half-mad city. Brief Innocence. Maya Angelou. SP-AngeM

Dawn on the Night-Journey. Dante Gabriel Rossetti. CW-RossD

Dawn Song. Thomas McGrath. SP-McGrT

Dawn Song, A. Ezra Pound. CP-PoEar

Dawn that cares for nobody. February. W. S. Merwin. SP-MerwW

Dawn this morning burned all red. Yankee Doodle. Nicholas Vachel Lindsay. CP-LindV

Dawn Verse, The. D. H. Lawrence. CP-LawrD

Dawn Walk and Prayer. Thomas Lux. SP-LuxT

Dawn was a dawn of splendor, The. Windy Day, A. James Whitcomb Riley. CP-RileJ

Dawn was apple-green, The. Green. D. H. Lawrence. CP-LawrD

Dawn Wind, The. Rudyard Kipling. CP-KiplR

Dawnbreaker. Robert Earl Hayden. CP-HaydR

Dawning, The. George Herbert. CP-HerbG

Dawnlight freezes against the east-wire. I Had Hope When Violence Was Ceas't. Geoffrey Hill. CP-HillG

Dawns. Czeslaw Milosz. CP-MiloC; CP-MiloCN, tr. by Robert Hass

Dawn's orb orange-raw shining over Palisades. We Rise on Sun Beams and Fall in the Night. Allen Ginsberg. CP-GinsA

Dawn's Rose. Ted Hughes. SP-HughTN Fr. Crow.

Dawnward I wake. In darkness wait. Dawn. Robert Penn Warren. CP-WarrR

Day. A. R. Ammons. CP-AmmoA

Day. William Blake. CP-BlakW

Day. Paul Laurence Dunbar. CP-DunbP

Day. Langston Hughes. CP-HughL; CP-HughL1

Day. Allen Tate. CP-TateA

Day. Jones Very. CP-VeryJ

Day, A. John Greenleaf Whittier. CP-WhitJ

Day! A, Help! Help! Another Day! Emily Dickinson. CP-DickE

Day, The. W. S. Merwin. SP-MerwW

Day, The. James Schuyler. CP-SchuJ

Day, The. James Schuyler. CP-SchuJ

Day, The. Jones Very. CP-VeryJ

Day, a night, an hour of sweet content, A. Content. Thomas Campion. CP-CampT

Day after day, day after still day. Summer's Elegy. Howard Nemerov. CP-NemeH

Day after day I work. For this I've come. Recoveries. Theodore Weiss. SP-WeisT

Day after day in a high room between. Winter Words. Philip Levine. SP-LeviP

Day after day up there beating my wings. Lit Instructor. William Stafford. SP-StafWW

Day after somber day. Plaint. Theodore Roethke. CP-RoetT

Day after the first rain, The. Ecology. A. K. Ramanujan. CP-RamaA

Day and Night. Eugenio Montale. CP-MontE, tr. by Jonathan Galassi

Day and night are never weary. Greek Epigram. Ezra Pound. CP-PoEar

Day and night as a child. Fishing. W. S. Merwin. SP-MerwWF

Day and Night in 1952. Frank O'Hara. SP-OharF

Day and night the Accuser makes no pause. Christina Georgina Rossetti. CP-RosC2

Day and the Night speak, and what they say is, The. Michelangelo Buonarroti. CP-Miche, tr. by John Frederick Nims

Day arrives of the autumn fair, The. Sheep Fair, A. Thomas Hardy. CP-HardT

Day astonishes and the night fills me with fear, The. Wolf, A. Paul Éluard. CP-WilW2

Day-Bed, The. Richard Eberhart. CP-EberR

Day before divorce, I take my children, The. My Children at the Dump. John Updike. CP-UpdiJ

Day before he died, a burnet moth, The. In Memory of Boris Pasternak. Denise Levertov. SP-LeveDP

Day before I died, The. Tragic Detail. William Carlos Williams. CP-WilW2

Day Begins. Denise Levertov. SP-LeveDP

Day begins—it comes—the appointed day!, The. Coming, The. Jones Very. CP-VeryJ

Day begins to dawn, O blessed word!, The. Day Begins to Dawn, The. Jones Very. CP-VeryJ

Day Begins to Dawn, The. Jones Very. CP-VeryJ

Day being humid and my head, The. Ovid in Love. Ovid. CP-MahoD Fr. Amores.

Day brings what is going to be. Trees. Letting You Go. William Stafford. SP-StafWW

Day by day for her darlings to her much she added more. Nature. Ralph Waldo Emerson. CP-EmerR

Day by day he disarmed himself. First he stripped off his clothing. Process. Yannis Ritsos. SP-RitsY, tr. by Kimon Friar

Day by day, such rewards. Prolific Spell, The. Donald Davie. CP-DaviDC

Day by day the acacia tree. Acacia Tree. Kathleen Jessie Raine. SP-RainK

Day by day your estimation clocks up. Administration. Philip Larkin. CP-LarkP

Day Calling Us to a New Life, The. Jones Very. CP-VeryJ

Day came slow—till Five o'clock, The. Emily Dickinson. CP-DickE

Day Can Become a Zen Garden of Raked Sand, The. Arthur Sze. SP-SzeA

Day comes and goes, The. Robert Creeley. CP-CreeR

Day creeps down. The moon is creeping up. Man on the Dump, The. Wallace Stevens. CP-StevW; CP-StevWP

Day dawns again, with wondering gaze they see. Petrels, The. Jones Very. CP-VeryJ

Day dawns with scent of must and rain, The. Mirror in February. Thomas Kinsella. CP-KinsT

Day / / diminutive / Night is the Mother, is the / Fixer of Change. Littleton, N.H.

Robert Creeley. CP-CreeR

Day Dr. Knox Did It, The. Robert Penn Warren. CP-WarrR

Day Dream, A. Emily Jane Brontë. CP-BronE

Day-Dream, A. Samuel Taylor Coleridge. CP-ColeS

Day-Dream, The. Samuel Taylor Coleridge. CP-ColeS

Day-Dream, The. Dante Gabriel Rossetti. CW-RossD

Day-Dreams. Dorothy Parker. CP-ParkD

Day / drunk with the nectar of, A. Wonder. Maya Angelou. SP-AngeM

Day! / Faster and more fast. Pippa Passes. Robert Browning. CP-BroR1

Day follows day, and week succeeds to week. At Sea ("Day follows day, and week succeeds to week"). Jones Very. CP-VeryJ

Day for Anne Frank, A. C. K. Williams. CP-WillC; SP-WillC

Day goes on, but we are left behind, The. Day Calling Us to a New Life, The. Jones Very. CP-VeryJ

Day grew small, surrounded tight, The. Emily Dickinson. CP-DickE

Day hanging by its feet with a hole, The. Invocation: "Day hanging by its feet with a hole, The." W. S. Merwin. SP-MerwW

Day hangs heavy, The. Greyday. Maya Angelou. SP-AngeM

Day has found next door another, The. Nones. James McMichael. SP-McMiJ

Day has gone, the summer day, The. Song: The Summer Day. Jones Very. CP-VeryJ

Day! hast thou two faces. Chartist's Complaint, The. Ralph Waldo Emerson. CP-EmerR

Day He Died, The. Ted Hughes. SP-HughTN

Day hot in the terror of her head. Dusk. Allen Tate. CP-TateA

Day I Kicked Away a Bankroll, The. Charles Bukowski. SP-BukC2

Day I lament that none can hymn thy praise. Day. Jones Very. CP-VeryJ

Day I Was Older, The. Donald Hall. CP-HallD

Day in, day out, from childhood long ago. Michelangelo Buonarroti. CP-Miche, tr. by John Frederick Nims

Day in Late October, A. Mona Van Duyn. SP-VanDM

Day in the Death, A. Miller Williams. CP-WillM

Day in the Sun, A. John Logan. CP-LogaJ

Day is a Poem, The. Robinson Jeffers. CP-JefR3

Day Is At Hand, The. Christina Georgina Rossetti. CP-RosC2

Day is awake. The bark calls to the rain still in the cloud, The. July Morning. Robert Bly. SP-BlyR

Day is closing dark and cold, The. Legend of St. Mark, The. John Greenleaf Whittier. CP-WhitJ

Day is colorless like Swiss characters in a novel, The. For Guillaume Apollinaire. William Meredith. SP-MereW

Day is dark and the night, The. Cloud Confines, The. Dante Gabriel Rossetti. CW-RossD

Day is dawning, I can tell. Like a Fantasia. Eugenio Montale. CP-MontE, tr. by Jonathan Galassi

Day is done, and the darkness, The. Day Is Done, The. Henry Wadsworth Longfellow. SP-LongH

Day Is Done, The. Henry Wadsworth Longfellow. SP-LongH

Day is done, the winter sun, The. Castle Wood. Emily Jane Brontë. CP-BronE

Day is drawing to its fall, A. First Sight of Her and After. Thomas Hardy. CP-HardT

Day is ending, the night descending, The. Old Song. D. H. Lawrence. CP-LawrD

Day is full of people, Sun, The. Noon's World. Alan Dugan. CP-DugaA

Day is going, now 'tis noon. George Meredith. CP-MerG2

Day Is Gone and All Its Sweets Are Gone, The. John Keats. CP-KeatJ

Day is gone, the night is come, The. Child's Prayer, A. George Meredith. CP-MerG2

Day is gray / as stone: the stones, The. Day, The. James Schuyler. CP-SchuJ

Day is great and strong, The. World without Peculiarity. Wallace Stevens. CP-StevW; CP-StevWP

Day Is Laid By, A. May Swenson. SP-SwenM

Day is spent, and hath his will on me, The. Evensong. George Herbert. CP-HerbG

Day is the children's friend. Prejudice against the Past, The. Wallace Stevens. CP-StevW; CP-StevWP

Day is turning ghost, The. Commonplace Day, A. Thomas Hardy. CP-HardT

Day is uncertain, night is ephemeral. Rainer Maria Rilke. CP-RilkFr, tr. by A. Poulin, Jr. Fr. Fragments.

Day Lady Died, The. Frank O'Hara. SP-OharF

Day Like Rousseau's Dream, A. May Swenson. SP-SwenM

Day lilies, yellow daisies, Queen Anne's lace. A barrel, a box of. Another Day (Day Lilies, Yellow Daisies). Muriel Rukeyser. CP-RukeM

Day Lily, The. Jones Very. CP-VeryJ

Day Marked with a Small White Stone, A. Charles Simic. SP-SimiC; SP-SimiCE

Day? Memorial, The. Grape Sherbet. Rita Dove. SP-DoveR

Day Millicent Found the World, The. William Stafford. SP-StafWW

Day moon, a half ball of snow vaulting, The. Day Moon, The. May Swenson.

SP-SwenM

Day Moon, The. May Swenson. SP-SwenM

Day not for Gain, The. Jones Very. CP-VeryJ

Day of Battle, The. A. E. Housman. CP-HousA

Day of Denial, The. Jones Very. CP-VeryJ

Day of distress and anguish, A. Shmuel HaNagid. SP-HaNaS, tr. by Peter Cole

Day of Foreboding. Stanley Kunitz. CP-KunSC

Day of Freedom is each dawning day, A. Every Day a Day of Freedom. Jones Very. CP-VeryJ

Day of Generation. Czeslaw Milosz. CP-MiloC; CP-MiloCN

Day of gusts and puddles, the vivid, A. Manhattan. Amy Clampitt. CP-ClamA

Day of harsh south wind built up the black clouds. House to the West, A. W. S. Merwin. SP-MerwWF

Day of Judgement, The. Jonathan Swift. CP-SwifJ

(On the Day of Judgement.) CP-SwifJ

Day of life and death offers its flowers, The. All Souls. Muriel Rukeyser. CP-RukeM

Day of Love, A. Dante Gabriel Rossetti. CW-RossD Fr. House of Life, The.

Day of mist: day of tarnish. Resolve. Sylvia Plath. CP-PlatS

Day of Rabblement. Kenneth Patchen. CP-PatcK

Day of Renewal. Louis MacNeice. CP-MacNL

Day of Returning. Louis MacNeice. CP-MacNL

Day of Satan's painful duty! Dies Iræ (The Day of Wrath). Unknown. SP-BierA, tr. by Ambrose Bierce

Day of stone, words of stone, A. 24 November 1948. Yannis Ritsos. SP-RitsY Fr. Exile's Journals 2.

Day of the cloud in fleets! O day. South-Wester, The. George Meredith. CP-MerG1

Day of the Daughter of Hades, The. George Meredith. CP-MerG1

Day of the strong rap, The. Guy I Know on 47th and Cottage, A. Clarence Major. SP-MajoC

Day of torpor in the sullen heat, A. August. James Whitcomb Riley. CP-RileJ

Day of wild beauty, A. First of September. William Corbett. SP-CorbW

Day on the Big Branch, A. Howard Nemerov. CP-NemeH

Day on the boulevards chosen out of ten years of, A. Berket and the Stars. William Carlos Williams. CP-WilW1

Day Poems. Federico García Lorca. CP-GarcF, tr. by Jerome Rothenberg

Day red like the cardinal, The. Said Adam. Charles Olson. CP-OlsoC

Day returns again, my natal day, The. To the Memory of Mrs. Lefroy. Jane Austen. CP-AustJ

Day returns, my bosom burns, The. Seventh of November, The. Robert Burns. CP-BurnR

Day, see no day—choke, qualm, quick qualm—benevolence, merit are. Catullus. See Cancel, Catullus, the expectancies of friendship

Day set on Norham's castled steep. Norham Castle. Sir Walter Scott. SP-ScotW Fr. Marmion.

Day she goes, The. Emily Dickinson. CP-DickE

Day she visited the dissecting room, The. Two Views of a Cadaver Room. Sylvia Plath. CP-PlatS

Day shines down in waves, The. Shades. Heather McHugh. SP-McHuH

Day shone brand new, in contrast to your disbelief, The. Revival. Yannis Ritsos. SP-RitsY, tr. by Kimon Friar

Day so happy, A. Gift. Czeslaw Milosz. CP-CarvR; CP-MiloC; CP-MiloCN

Day so lovely it could be Eden, A. Fall. Gregory Orr. SP-OrrG

Day Song. Charles Olson. CP-OlsoC

Day Song, the Day After. Charles Olson. CP-OlsoC

Day that hath no tinge of night. As Thy Days, So Shall Thy Strength Be. Christina Georgina Rossetti. CP-RosC2

Day that I was christened, The. Godmother. Dorothy Parker. CP-ParkD

Day that I was crowned, The. Emily Dickinson. CP-DickE

Day that is the night of days, The. England before the Storm. George Meredith. CP-MerG1

Day that passes. Que J'ay Dit Devant. Louis Zukofsky. CP-ZukLS

Day, the day, 'tis changed to darkest night!, The. Then shall all the tribes of the earth mourn. Jones Very. CP-VeryJ

Day the Epileptic Spoke, The. Charles Bukowski. SP-BukC3

Day They Eulogized Mahalia, The. Audre Lorde. SP-LordA

Day Trip to Donegal. Derek Mahon. SP-MahoD

Day turning to night. Eternal City. Hayden Carruth. CP-CarHS

Day turns holy as though a god moved through it, The. Separate Poem, A. Tennessee Williams. CP-WillT

Day undressed—Herself, The. Emily Dickinson. CP-DickE

Day Unto Day Uttereth Speech. Jones Very. CP-VeryJ

Day was gathered on waking, The. Robert Creeley. CP-CreeR

Day was here when it was his to know, The. New Tenants, The. Edwin Arlington Robinson. CP-RobiE

Day was mild, the light was generous, The. Mysticism for Beginners. Adam Zagajewski. SP-ZagaA, tr. by Clare Cavanagh

Day we went to visit the house of the poet, The. Things. Miller Williams. CP-WillM

Day Went Dark, The. A. K. Ramanujan. CP-RamaA

Day, what a hard time I have. Song of Departing Day. Federico García Lorca. CP-GarcF, *tr. by* Alan S. Trueblood *Fr.* Songs to End With.

Day when the under-cover writings, The. And Who Do You Think "They" Are? William Carlos Williams. CP-WilW2

Day which never could be yesterday, A. Impossible Day, The. Robert Graves. CP-GravR

Day with well-known duties now is o'er, The. Influence of the Night on Faith and Imagination, The. Jones Very. CP-VeryJ

Day Without Night. Louise Glück. SP-GlucL

Day works on, The. Mexican Valley. James Dickey. CP-DickJ

Day you came, The. Breasts. Tess Gallagher. SP-GallT

Day you died I went into the dirt, The. Electra on Azalea Path. Sylvia Plath. CP-PlatS

Daybreak. James Dickey. CP-DickJ

Daybreak. Galway Kinnell. SP-KinnGN

Daybreak. W. S. Merwin. SP-MerwW

Daybreak. Carl Sandburg. CP-SandC

Daybreak. William Carlos Williams. CP-WilW1

Daybreak comes first. Daybreak. Carl Sandburg. CP-SandC

Daybreak in Alabama. Langston Hughes. CP-HughL; CP-HughL2; CP-HughL3 (When I get to be a colored composer.) CP-HughL2

Daybreak / in the orange grove. Sevillian Ditty. Federico García Lorca. CP-GarcF, *tr. by* Alan S. Trueblood *Fr.* Songs for Children.

Daybreak Thought for Maria, A. Tennessee Williams. CP-WillT

Daydream, The. Philip Whalen. SP-WhalP

Daydream the old Indian medicine man. Ghost Chant, et alii. Yusef Komunyakaa. SP-KomuY

Daydreaming child on the tenement roof. Future in Miniature. Marya Alexandrovna Zaturenska. SP-ZatuM

Daydreams of a River. Federico García Lorca. CP-GarcF, *tr. by* Jerome Rothenberg

Daylight. James Schuyler. CP-SchuJ

Daylight clears after rain to show cool mornings. Walking into Autumn. W. S. Merwin. SP-MerwWF

Daylight, full of small dancing particles. Jelaluddin Rumi. SP-Rumi, *tr. by* Coleman Barks

Daylight leaks in, and sluggishly I surface. Waking Up. Jorge Luis Borges. SP-BorgJ, *tr. by* Alastair Reid

Daylight Savings. Dorothy Parker. CP-ParkD

Daylong this tomcat lies stretched flat. Esther's Tomcat. Ted Hughes. SP-HughTN

Dayly when I do seeke and sew for peace. Sonnet 11. Edmund Spenser. CP-Spens *Fr.* Amoretti.

Days. John Ciardi. CP-CiarJ

Days. Billy Collins. SP-CollB

Days. Ralph Waldo Emerson. CP-EmerR

Days. Philip Larkin. CP-LarkP

Days, The. Donald Hall. CP-HallD

Days and Days. Robert Creeley. CP-CreeR

Days and Nights. Kenneth Koch. SP-KochK

Days are bright. Seesaw. Thom Gunn. CP-GunnT

Days are clear, / Day after day, The. Christina Georgina Rossetti. CP-RosC2

Days are cold. Cottager to Her Infant, (By My Sister), The. Dorothy Wordsworth. CP-WorW1

Days are incestuous, each with its yesterday, The. Sundays, They Sleep Late. Muriel Rukeyser. CP-RukeM

Days are over, I leave after breakfast, The. Purgatory. John Berryman. CP-BerrJ

Days are so vivid, so bright, The. Little Waltz. Adam Zagajewski. SP-ZagaA, *tr. by* Clare Cavanagh

Days bury days, then weeks, month, years. Inscribed on a Prayer Wheel and Spun. William Stafford. SP-StafWW

Days come and go without haste, without surprises. Stones. Yannis Ritsos. SP-RitsY, *tr. by* Kimon Friar

Day's crest / first appearing. Fifth Page. Federico García Lorca. CP-GarcF, *tr. by* Jerome Rothenberg *Fr.* White Album.

Days draw in, The. Calendar. Robert Penn Warren. CP-WarrR

Days git wa'm an' wa'mah. Wadin' in de Crick. Paul Laurence Dunbar. CP-DunbP

Days Gone By, The. James Whitcomb Riley. CP-RileJ

Days grow and the stars cross over, The. Darkness Music. Muriel Rukeyser. CP-RukeM

Days in the train, a. Robert Creeley. CP-CreeR

Day's Journey, A. John Greenleaf Whittier. CP-WhitJ

Days later—neither having. Robert Creeley. CP-CreeR

Days of Argument and Blossom. Olga Broumas. SP-BrouO

Days of 1896. Constantine P. Cavafy. CP-CavaC, *tr. by* Theoharis Constantine Theoharis

Days of eyes of eyes. Prayer with Martial Stance. Olga Broumas. SP-BrouO

Days of 1986. Carolyn Kizer. CP-KizeC

Days of 1959. Marilyn Hacker. SP-HackM

Days of 1944: Three Friends. Marilyn Hacker. SP-HackM

Days of 1941 and '44. James Merrill. SP-MerrJ

Days of 1908. Constantine P. Cavafy. CP-CavaC, *tr. by* Theoharis Constantine Theoharis

Days of 1909, '10 and '11. Constantine P. Cavafy. CP-CavaC, *tr. by* Theoharis Constantine Theoharis

Days of 1901. Constantine P. Cavafy. CP-CavaC, *tr. by* Theoharis Constantine Theoharis

Days of 1903. Constantine P. Cavafy. CP-CavaC, *tr. by* Theoharis Constantine Theoharis

Days of 1971. James Merrill. SP-MerrJ

Days of 1964. James Merrill. SP-MerrJ

Days of 1935. James Merrill. SP-MerrJ

Days of the dead men, Danny. Drumnotes. Carl Sandburg. CP-SandC

Days of Vanity. Christina Georgina Rossetti. CP-RosC1

Days of Yore, The. Stevie Smith. CP-SmitS

Days pass over me, The. Ralph Waldo Emerson. CP-EmerR

Days pass when I forget the mystery. Primary Wonder. Denise Levertov. SP-LeveDS

Day's Ration, The. Ralph Waldo Emerson. CP-EmerR

Day's sharp strife is ended now, The. After Election. John Greenleaf Whittier. CP-WhitJ

Days shorten, the south blows wide for showers now, The. Salmon Fishing. Robinson Jeffers. CP-JefR1

Days: Spring, The. Adrienne Rich. CP-RicAE

Days that cannot bring you near. Argument. Elizabeth Bishop. CP-BishE

Days that we can spare, The. Emily Dickinson. CP-DickE

Days to come are a watershed, The. We Hesitate. John Ashbery. SP-AshbJ

Days to Recollect. Thomas Hardy. CP-HardT

Days undefiled by luxury or sloth. To the Pennsylvanians. William Wordsworth. CP-WorW2

Days, when the ball of our vision. Youth in Memory. George Meredith. CP-MerG1

Days will rally, wreathing, The. Braggart. Dorothy Parker. CP-ParkD

Dayseye hugging the earth, The. Daisy. William Carlos Williams. CP-WilW1

Daystar. Rita Dove. SP-DoveR

Daytime / wonder at / the quieter possibilities. Plan, The. Robert Creeley. CP-CreeR

Dazzle of Darkness. Robert Graves. CP-GravR

Dazzle on the sea, my darling, The. Leaving Barra. Louis MacNeice. CP-MacNL

Dazzled. Arthur Sze. SP-SzeA

Dazzled blood, The. Faustust Triumphant. Thom Gunn. CP-GunnT

Dazzling Burden, The. Kenneth Patchen. CP-PatcK

D-Day 1989. William Corbett. SP-CorbW

De Anima. Howard Nemerov. CP-NemeH

De Arte Poetica. Robert Graves. CP-GravR

De Catullo et Martiale. Thomas Campion. CP-CampT

De Contemptu Mundi. James Laughlin. CP-LaugJ

De-daddle-dy! Figurette. Langston Hughes. CP-HughL3

DE— / DELIGHT— / DELIGHTED! INTRODUCE ME TO EARTHA. Bird in Orbit. Langston Hughes. CP-HughL; CP-HughL3

De-dop! Figurine. Langston Hughes. CP-HughL3

De Epigrammate. Thomas Campion. CP-CampT

De Fera Dormita. Kenneth Rexroth. CP-RexrK

De Fran. Draco. Thomas Campion. CP-CampT

De Gustibus. Robert Browning. CP-BroR1

De horologio portabili. Thomas Campion. CP-CampT

De Jure Belli ac Pacis. Geoffrey Hill. CP-HillG

De là où nous sommes assis plus haut que les gradins. Arènes de Lutèce. Samuel Beckett. CP-BeckS

De lady I work for. Present. Langston Hughes. CP-HughL; CP-HughL2

De Los Cantares. Charles Olson. CP-OlsoC

De minimus curat non Lex, utcumque poetica. De Arte Poetica. Robert Graves. CP-GravR

De Natura Rerum. Andrei Codrescu. SP-CodrA

De obitu Phil. Sydnaei equitis aurati generosissimi. Thomas Campion. CP-CampT

De penetratione aperturae vulvularis. Ravings of the Depraved Monk Benno of St. Gall Who Went Mad from Carnal Longing in His Cell and Forgot How to Write Good Latin. James Laughlin. CP-LaugJ

De pied ferme. Samuel Beckett. CP-BeckS

De Profundis. Elizabeth Barrett Browning. CP-BroEB

De Profundis. Dorothy Parker. CP-ParkD

De Profundis. Christina Georgina Rossetti. CP-RosC2

De Profundis. Georg Trakl. CP-WrigJ, tr. by James Wright

De Quincey in Later Life. Derek Mahon. CP-MahoD

De railroad bridge's. Homesick Blues. Langston Hughes. CP-HughL; CP-HughL1

De Regis reditu e Scotia. Thomas Campion. CP-CampT

De Rerum Natura (On the Nature of Things). Lucretius.
    Against the Fear of Death. CP-DryJ2, tr. by John Dryden
    "All men of mirth and sense admire and love." CP-SherT
    Beginning of the First Book, The [Address to Venus]. CP-DryJ2
    Beginning of the Second Book, The. CP-DryJ2
    Concerning the Nature of Love. CP-DryJ2
    "If all this world had no original[l]." CP-RaleW
    "Principle of all things; entrails made, The." CP-EmerR
    "Thus like a sailor [or Sayler] by the tempest hurled [or hurl'd]." CP-DryJ2

De Rerum Virtute. Robinson Jeffers. CP-JefR3

De Sade's rent walls let in, Lacoste. Charles Tomlinson. CP-TomlC

De Secretis Mulierum. Paul Muldoon. CP-MuldP

De shepherd shrieves in Egyptian light. Pocomania. Derek Walcott. CP-WalcD

De Síntoma Profundo. Yusef Komunyakaa. CP-KomuY

De Sole. Charles Tomlinson. CP-TomlC

De Votre Bonheur Il ne Reste Que Vos Photos. Archibald MacLeish. CP-MacLA

Dea ex Machina. John Updike. CP-UpdiJ

Deacon Jones' Grievance. Paul Laurence Dunbar. CP-DunbP

Deacon thought. "I know them," he began, The. Ben Trovato. Edwin Arlington Robinson. CP-RoblE

Dead. Paul Laurence Dunbar. CP-DunbP

Dead, The. Yannis Ritsos. SP-RitsY Fr. Monovasia.

Dead, The. Billy Collins. SP-CollB

Dead, The. Randall Jarrell. CP-JarrR

Dead, The. Denise Levertov. SP-LeveDS

Dead, The. Eugenio Montale. CP-MontE, tr. by Jonathan Galassi

Dead, The. Sylvia Plath. CP-PlatS

Dead, The. Kathleen Jessie Raine. SP-RainK

Dead, The. Rainer Maria Rilke. CP-RilkFr, tr. by A. Poulin, Jr.

Dead, The. Jones Very. CP-VeryJ

Dead and the Living One, The. Thomas Hardy. CP-HardT

Dead! / And the Muses cried with a stormy cry. Dead Prophet, The. Alfred Tennyson. CP-TennA

Dead are always looking down on us, they say, The. Dead, The. Billy Collins. SP-CollB

Dead are hovering on the air, The. Nexus. Richard Eberhart. CP-EberR

Dead are on their journey, the way is dark, The. Song of the Dead. D. H. Lawrence. CP-LawrD

Dead / are the departed therefrom. Whose, The. Human Communion. Traces, The. Robert Duncan. SP-DuncR

Dead at Daybreak. Federico García Lorca. CP-GarcF, tr. by Alan S. Trueblood Fr. Moon Songs.

Dead at Quang Tri, The. Yusef Komunyakaa. CP-KomuY

Dead Baby, The. William Carlos Williams. CP-WilW1

Dead Bastard, The. Thomas Hardy. CP-HardT

Dead-Beat, The. Wilfred Owen. CP-OwenW

Dead beetle lies on a dirt road, A. Seen from Above. Wisława Szymborska. SP-SzymWM, tr. by Joanna Trzeciak

Dead beetle lies on the path through the field, A. Seen from Above. Wisława Szymborska. SP-SzymW, tr. by Stanisław Barańczak and Clare Cavanagh

Dead before Death. Christina Georgina Rossetti. CP-RosC1

Dead birds fell, but no one had seen them fly, The. Some Dreams They Forgot. Elizabeth Bishop. CP-BishE

Dead books exposed like mummies' tombs. Posthumous Work. Charles Baudelaire. CP-BaudC, tr. by Walter Martin

Dead Boy. John Crowe Ransom. SP-RansJ

Dead boy living among men as a man, A. Head, A. James Schuyler. CP-SchuJ

Dead boy, the. Precedence. Rae Armantrout. SP-ArmaA

Dead Bride, The. Christina Georgina Rossetti. CP-RosC3

Dead brood over Europe, the cloud and vision descends over chearful France, The. French Revolution, The. William Blake. CP-BlakW

Dead by the Side of the Road, The. Gary Snyder. CP-SnydG

Dead child lay in the shroud, The. Gift of the Sea, The. Rudyard Kipling. CP-KiplR

Dead City, The. Christina Georgina Rossetti. CP-RosC3

Dead city waited, The. Quarry, Pigeon Cove. Maxine W. Kumin. SP-KumiM

Dead Color. Charles Wright. SP-WrigC

Dead! Dead! Dead! Dead in Sight of Fame. James Whitcomb Riley. CP-RileJ

Dead, dead, dead, dead. Winter. Adrienne Rich. CP-RicAE

Dead do not need, The. Everything. Charles Bukowski. SP-BukC2

Dead Dog. Pablo Neruda. SP-NeruP

Dead Elm, The. Jones Very. CP-VeryJ

Dead Emperor, The. Walt Whitman. CP-WhitW

Dead-ends at 19th one / block over from Dolores. Blossoming Oakwood. James Schuyler. CP-SchuJ

Dead every enormous piece. E. E. Cummings. CP-CummE

Dead falls the Cause, if once the Hand be mute. Bribes and Gifts Get All. Robert Herrick. CP-HerrR

Dead Feast of the Kol-Folk, The. John Greenleaf Whittier. CP-WhitJ

Dead from Love. Federico García Lorca. CP-GarcF, tr. by Will Kirkland

Dead grasshoppers' / bone-white. Desert Autumn. Charles Tomlinson. CP-TomlC

Dead Hand. Robert Graves. CP-GravR

Dead Hand. W. S. Merwin. SP-MerwW

Dead have been awaken'd—shall I sleep?, The. Journal in Cephalonia. Lord Byron. CP-Byron

Dead Heart, The. Anne Sexton. CP-SextA

Dead Hero, The. G. K. Chesterton. CP-ChesG

Dead Hive, The. W. S. Merwin. SP-MerwW

Dead Hope. Christina Georgina Rossetti. CP-RosC1

Dead Horse in Field. Robert Penn Warren. CP-WarrR

Dead in Melanesia, The. Randall Jarrell. CP-JarrR

Dead in Sight of Fame. James Whitcomb Riley. CP-RileJ

Dead in the cold, a song-singing thrush. Last Rites. Christina Georgina Rossetti. CP-RosC2

Dead in the year—. Robert Creeley. CP-CreeR

Dead in their dressing rooms, The. Curtain Call. Charles Tomlinson. CP-TomlC

Dead in There. Langston Hughes. CP-HughL; CP-HughL3

Dead in via, The. La Préface. Charles Olson. CP-OlsoC

Dead inhabit such a crowded city, The. Problem. Tennessee Williams. CP-WillT

Dead Joke and the Funny Man, The. James Whitcomb Riley. CP-RileJ

Dead King, The [Edward VII; 1910]. Rudyard Kipling. CP-KiplR

Dead Leaves. James Whitcomb Riley. CP-RileJ

Dead leaves nest in the crown and the word. Poem to the Mother. Gregory Orr. SP-OrrG

Dead Letter. Sam Hamill. SP-HamiS

Dead Liebknecht, The. Hugh MacDiarmid. SP-MacDH

Dead Lover, The. James Whitcomb Riley. CP-RileJ

Dead maiden, The. Venus ("Dead maiden, The"). Federico García Lorca. CP-GarcF, tr. by Alan S. Trueblood Fr. Three Portraits with Shading.

Dead Man, The. Paul Celan. SP-CelaP, tr. by John Felstiner

Dead Man Walking, The. Thomas Hardy. CP-HardT

Dead Man's Room, The. John Logan. CP-LogaJ

Dead men are wisest, for they know. Wise, The. Countee Cullen. CP-CullC

Dead Men's Child, The. Robinson Jeffers. CP-JefR1

Dead mosquito, flattened against a door, A. 7/26/68: II. Adrienne Rich. CP-RicAE Fr. Ghazals: Homage to Ghalib.

Dead, my lords and gentlemen! James Whitcomb Riley. CP-RileJ

Dead! my wayward boy—my own. His Mother. James Whitcomb Riley. CP-RileJ

Dead nailed to the walls, next to the advertisements, The. Dangers. Yannis Ritsos. SP-RitsY, tr. by Andonis Decavalles

Dead Now. Charles Bukowski. SP-BukC1

Dead of Lidice, The. Jaroslav Seifert. SP-SeifJ, tr. by Ewald Osers

Dead of night's auto-da-fé, The. Examination of Conscience, The. Charles Baudelaire. CP-BaudC, tr. by Walter Martin

Dead of '92 and '93, The. Arthur Rimbaud. CP-RimbA, tr. by Martin Sorrell

Dead of Winter. William Corbett. SP-CorbW

Dead on one side. Walking the Fire Line. James Dickey. CP-DickJ

Dead! One of them shot by the sea in the east. Mother and Poet. Elizabeth Barrett Browning. CP-BroEB

Dead Pan, The. Elizabeth Barrett Browning. CP-BroEB

Dead People. D. H. Lawrence. CP-LawrD

Dead Petra in her hill-tomb sleeps. "Rock" in El Ghor, The. John Greenleaf Whittier. CP-WhitJ

Dead Pigeon on South Street. John Ciardi. CP-CiarJ

Dead poets stalk the air. Rainy Night at the Writers' Colony. Josephine Jacobsen. CP-JacoJ

Dead Priestess Speaks, A. "H. D." CP-DoolH

Dead Prophet, The. Alfred Tennyson. CP-TennA

Dead Quire, The. Thomas Hardy. CP-HardT

Dead River. Howard Nemerov. CP-NemeH

Dead Rose, A. Elizabeth Barrett Browning. CP-BroEB

Dead Seal [near McClure's Beach], The. Robert Bly. SP-BlyR

Dead Season. Michael Palmer. SP-PalmM

Dead Selves. James Whitcomb Riley. CP-RileJ

Dead Shall Be Raised Incorruptible, The. Galway Kinnell. SP-KinnGN

Dead shalt thou lie; and nought. Sapphic Fragment. Sappho. CP-HardT, *tr. by* Thomas Hardy

Dead, she became space-earth. Ted Hughes. SP-HughTN *Fr.* Seven Dungeon Songs.

Dead / she now lay deaf to death. Lorine Niedecker. CP-NiedL

Dead Ship of Harpswell, The. John Greenleaf Whittier. CP-WhitJ

Dead Skunk. Richard Eberhart. CP-EberR

Dead Soldiers. James Fenton. SP-FentJ

Dead soldiers rise and walk into the trees, The. Reader of the Sentences, The. Norman Dubie. CP-DubiN

Dead Sparrow. Adam Zagajewski. SP-ZagaA, *tr. by* Clare Cavanagh

Dead Still. Andrey Andreievich Voznesensky. CP-WilbR, *tr. by* Richard Wilbur

Dead Tenor, The. Walt Whitman. CP-WhitW

Dead! the dead! they throw their grave clothes by, The. Resurrection, The. Jones Very. CP-VeryJ

Dead! Thirteen a month ago! Little Mattie. Elizabeth Barrett Browning. CP-BroEB

Dead? this peerless man of men. John Boyle O'Reilly. James Whitcomb Riley. CP-RileJ

Dead to Clemenceau: November 1929, The. Robinson Jeffers. CP-JefR2

Dead truck sits in the shimmering wheat, The. La Pampa. Norman Dubie. CP-DubiN

Dead Village, The. Edwin Arlington Robinson. CP-RobiE

Dead "Wessex" the Dog to the Household. Thomas Hardy. CP-HardT

Dead Wife, The. James Whitcomb Riley. CP-RileJ

Dead Wingman, The. Randall Jarrell. CP-JarrR

Dead woman lay in her first night's grave, The. Dead and the Living One, The. Thomas Hardy. CP-HardT

Deader they die here, or at least. Fall Comes in Back-Country Vermont. Robert Penn Warren. CP-WarrR

Deadhouse at the Workhouse, The. Thomas Lux. SP-LuxT

Deadlines. James Tate. SP-TateJ

Deadly Victorians, The. D. H. Lawrence. CP-LawrD

Deadly Victory. Yannis Ritsos. SP-RitsY, *tr. by* Minas Savvas

Deadsong for a Neighbor Child Who Ran Away to the Woods. Miller Williams. CP-WillM

Deaf and Dumb. Robert Browning. CP-BroR1

Deaf children were monkey-nimble, fish-tremulous and sudden, The. Deaf School. Ted Hughes. SP-HughTN

Deaf, giddy, odious to my friends. On His Own Deafness. Jonathan Swift. CP-SwifJ

Deaf Girl Playing. James Tate. SP-TateJ

Deaf-mute was waving his hands—he didn't hide his fear, The. At the Harbor's Edge. Yannis Ritsos. SP-RitsY, *tr. by* Kimon Friar *and* Kostas Myrsiades

Deaf-Mutes at the Ballgame. Josephine Jacobsen. CP-JacoJ

Deaf School. Ted Hughes. SP-HughTN

Deal not with me God as I have dealt with Man. Death-Bed of a Financier. Stevie Smith. CP-SmitS

Deal table where he wrote, so small and plain, The. Birthplace, The. Seamus Heaney. SP-HeanSO

Dean, adult education may seem silly. Lucretius versus the Lake Poets. Robert Frost. CP-FrosR

Dean and the Duke, The. Jonathan Swift. CP-SwifJ

Dean-Bourn, farewell; I never look to see. To Dean-bourn, a Rude River in Devon, by Which Sometimes He Lived. Robert Herrick. CP-HerrR

Dean must die?—Our idiots to maintain!, The. On the Revd. Dr. Swift, D. S. P. D. Leaving His Fortune to Build an Hospital for Idiots and Lunatics. *Unknown, sometimes at. to* Thomas Sheridan. CP-SherT

Dean of Faculty—a New Ballad, The. Robert Burns. CP-BurnR

Dean of St. Patrick's to Thomas Sheridan, The. Jonathan Swift. CP-SwifJ

Dean Smedley Gone to Seek His Fortune. Jonathan Swift. CP-SherT; CP-SwifJ

Dean Swift's Answer to the Reverend Dr. Sheridan. Jonathan Swift. CP-SwifJ

Dean to Himself on St. Cecilia's Day, The. Jonathan Swift. CP-SwifJ

Dean to Thomas Sheridan, The. Jonathan Swift. CP-SwifJ

Dean would visit Market Hill, The. Lady Acheson Weary of the Dean. Jonathan Swift. CP-SwifJ

Dean's Answer to "Upon Stealing a Crown," The. Jonathan Swift. CP-SwifJ

Dean's Reasons for Not Building at Drapier's Hill, The. Jonathan Swift. CP-SwifJ

Dear. Robert Creeley. SP-CreeR

Dear, The. Thomas Hardy. CP-HardT

Dear Adrienne, / I feel signified by pain. Adrienne Rich. SP-RicA1 *Fr.* Contradictions: Tracking Poems.

Dear Adrienne: / I'm calling you up tonight. Adrienne Rich. SP-RicA1 *Fr.* Contradictions: Tracking Poems.

Dear, all benevolence of fingering lips. In Sickness and in Health. W. H. Auden. CP-AudeW

Dear and great Angel, wouldst thou only leave. Guardian-Angel, The. Robert Browning. CP-BroR1

Dear Angels and dear disembodied Saints. Christina Georgina Rossetti. CP-RosC2

Dear Anna—between friend and friend. Epistle to Lady Austen. William Cowper. CP-CowpW

Dear architect of fine *Chateaux en l'air.* To William Hayley, Esq.: In Reply to His Solicitation to Write with Him in a Literary Work. William Cowper. CP-CowpW

Dear are the pleasant memories. Ralph Waldo Emerson. CP-EmerR

Dear arrears of tenderness. Emily Dickinson. SP-DickE

Dear beast, luxurious of pelt. Bertie Goes Hunting. Amy Clampitt. CP-ClamA

Dear Becher, you tell me to mix with mankind. Lines: "Dear Becher, you tell me to mix with mankind." Lord Byron. CP-Byron

Dear boy, you will not hear me speak. Pangloss's Song: A Comic-Opera Lyric. Richard Wilbur. CP-WilbR

Dear Brother at home. Letter from Spain. Langston Hughes. CP-HughL; CP-HughL1

Dear brother, would you know the life. Ralph Waldo Emerson. CP-EmerR

Dear Carolyn: / I'm attempting to put together a Study Club paper on the subject of your father Ben. My Good Father. Carolyn Kizer. CP-KizeC

Dear CHARLES, My Muse, Asleep or Dead. Philip Larkin. CP-LarkP

Dear Charles! whilst yet thou wert a babe, I ween. To a Friend [Charles Lamb] Who Had Declared His Intention of Writing No More Poetry. Samuel Taylor Coleridge. CP-ColeS

Dear Child of God. Stevie Smith. CP-SmitS

Dear Child of Nature, let them rail! To a Young Lady Who Had Been Reproached for Taking Long Walks in the Country. William Wordsworth. CP-WorW1

DEAR CHRIS / It is 3:17 a.m. in New York city, yes, it is. Sonnet LXXVII: "DEAR CHRIS / It is 3:17 a.m. in New York city, yes, it is." Ted Berrigan. SP-BerrT *Fr.* Sonnets, The.

Dear Col'nel, COBHAM's and your country's Friend! Second Epistle of the Second Book of Horace Imitated, The. Alexander Pope. CP-PopeA

Dear Cousin Nancy: / You probably never heard of me or Cousin Beauregard. Ms. Found under a Serviette in a Lovely Home. Ogden Nash. CP-NashO

Dear Craoibhin Aoibhin, look into our case. At The Abbey Theatre. William Butler Yeats. CP-YeatW

Dear critic, who my lightness so deplores. To a Captious Critic. Paul Laurence Dunbar. CP-DunbP

Dear, damn'd, distracting Town, farewell! Farewell to London in the Year 1715, A. Alexander Pope. CP-PopeA

Dear Dan, it does amaze me quite. Sheridan to Dan Jackson. Thomas Sheridan. CP-SherT

Dear dead Victoria. Victoria. Dorothy Parker. CP-ParkD

Dear Dean, if e'er again you write. Letter from Dean Swift to Dean Smedley, A. Jonathan Swift. CP-SwifJ

Dear Dean, I'm in a sad condition. To the Dean of St. Patrick's ("Dear Dean, I'm in a sad condition"). Thomas Sheridan. CP-SherT

Dear Dean, since in cruxes and puns you and I deal. To Dean Swift. Thomas Sheridan. CP-SherT

Dear Dean, since you in sleepy wise. Upon Stealing a Crown when the Dean Was Asleep. Thomas Sheridan. CP-SherT

Dear Death: / I got your message. Official Notice. Langston Hughes. CP-HughL; CP-HughL3

Dear Dick, prithee tell by what passion you move? On the Archbishop of Cashel and Bettesworth. Jonathan Swift. CP-SwifJ

Dear Doctor—Being you're so kind. Invitation, The. Thomas Sheridan. CP-SherT

Dear Doctor, I Have Read Your Play. Lord Byron. CP-Byron

Dear Dorothy. Robert Creeley. CP-CreeR

Dear Dorothy, forgive me now. Happy Xmas, A. G. K. Chesterton. CP-ChesG

Dear Eavan, / Just yesterday afternoon. Late August Letter. Marilyn Hacker. SP-HackM

Dear Editors. Andrei Codrescu. SP-CodrA

Dear Elizabeth. May Swenson. SP-SwenM

Dear Ellen, many a golden year. Ralph Waldo Emerson. CP-EmerR

Dear Father: / You were a doctor. Perhaps your avocation. Daughter to Archeologist. Josephine Jacobsen. CP-JacoJ

Dear Fellow Americans. Will V-Day Be Me-Day Too? Langston Hughes. CP-HughL; CP-HughL2

Dear fellow-artist, why so free. To a Young Beauty. William Butler Yeats. CP-YeatW

Dear fellow Traveller! here we are once more. William Wordsworth. *See* Here, on our native soil, we breathe once more

Dear Female Heart. Stevie Smith. CP-SmitS

Dear Folks at home. Postcard from Spain. Langston Hughes. CP-HughL; CP-HughL1

Dear Fox. Lucille Clifton. SP-ClifL

Dear Friend. Charles Bukowski. SP-BukC2

Dear Friend. When You Asked for It. Kenneth Rexroth. CP-RexrK

Dear friend, a letter not yet written. Letter to Any Friend, A. Laura Riding

Jackson. CP-RidiL

Dear friend, can you walk. Emily Dickinson. SP-DickE

Dear friend: If the poem. Otherwise. Lorine Niedecker. CP-NiedL

Dear Friends. Edwin Arlington Robinson. CP-RobiE

Dear Friends and Gentle Hearts. Countee Cullen. CP-CullC

Dear friends, and here I say friends. To my Friends. Primo Levi. CP-LeviP, *tr. by* Ruth Feldman

Dear friends, stay! / Lamplit wafts of wit keep sorrow. Queen Caroline to Her Guests. Thomas Hardy. CP-HardT

Dear friends, who read the world aright. Wordsworth. John Greenleaf Whittier. CP-WhitJ

Dear George, behold the portentous day. Advice outside a Church. Ogden Nash. CP-NashO

Dear grandpapa, / To be obedient. Lines to My Grandfather. Christina Georgina Rossetti. CP-RosC3

Dear, had the world in its caprice. Respectability. Robert Browning. CP-BroR1

Dear Hands. James Whitcomb Riley. CP-RileJ

Dear heart, good-night! Premonition. Paul Laurence Dunbar. CP-DunbP

Dear Heart I think the young impassioned priest. Quia Multum Amavi. Oscar Wilde. CP-WildO

Dear Heaven! for this sweet pledge of life. George Meredith. CP-MerG2

Dear, heavn-designing [*or* heavn-designed] soul! To a Young Gentle-Woman, Councel Concerning Her Choice. Richard Crashaw. CP-CrasR

Dear Herries, let's hope, by impounding your Pope. Dogma Triumphant, The. Robert Browning. CP-BroR2

Dear home, thou scene of earliest hopes and joys. Fragment: Home. Percy Bysshe Shelley. CP-ShelP

Dear Hosmer; or still dearer Hatty. Round Robin, A. Robert Browning. CP-BroR2

Dear, I must be gone. Parting. William Butler Yeats. CP-YeatW

Dear, I ventured out of the house late this evening, merely. Brise Marine. Joseph Brodsky. CP-BrodJ

Dear, if I never saw your face again. To Nanine. Ambrose Bierce. SP-BierA

Dear If I with Guile. Thomas Campion. CP-CampT

Dear———, I'll gie ye some advice. To an Artist. Robert Burns. CP-BurnR

Dear individual soul, this is the Styx. On the Banks of the Styx. Wisława Szymborska. SP-SzymW, *tr. by* Stanislaw Barańczak *and* Clare Cavanagh

Dear Joe. William Corbett. SP-CorbW

Dear Joe. James Schuyler. CP-SchuJ

Dear Jonno / there are pigeons who nest. Trip on the Staten Island Ferry, A. Audre Lorde. SP-LordA

Dear Jool, I Miss You in Saint-Saturnin. Marilyn Hacker. SP-HackM

Dear Joseph—five and twenty years ago. Epistle to Hill. William Cowper. CP-CowpW

Dear Judas. Robinson Jeffers. CP-JefR2

Dear Judith: In sincerest gratitude. Chaplet for Judith Landry, A. Marilyn Hacker. SP-HackM

Dear Karl. Stevie Smith. CP-SmitS

Dear Kelly, when I was a kid. To Kelly Miller, Jr. Paul Laurence Dunbar. CP-DunbP

Dear Kenward. Stone Knife, A. James Schuyler. CP-SchuJ

Dear language, English, whose. Strathnaver. Donald Davie. CP-DaviDC

Dear Lexicon, I died in you. Michael Palmer. SP-PalmM

Dear little Bog-Face. Bog-Face. Stevie Smith. SP-SmitS

Dear Little Sirmio. Catullus. *See* Carmina

Dear Lizbie Browne. To Lizbie Browne. Thomas Hardy. CP-HardT

Dear Long, in this sequestr'd scene. To Edward Noel Long, Esq. Lord Byron. CP-Byron

Dear Lord! kind Lord! Prayer Perfect, The. James Whitcomb Riley. CP-RileJ

Dear Lord, let me recount to Thee. It Is Finished. Christina Georgina Rossetti. CP-RosC2

Dear Lord, observe this bended knee. Prayer at the End of a Rope. Ogden Nash. CP-NashO

Dear Lord, to Thee my knee is bent. Kneeling with Herrick. James Whitcomb Riley. CP-RileJ

Dear love, since the impossible proves. Impossible, The. Robert Graves. CP-GravR

"Dear love, why should you weep" Lost World, A. Robert Graves. CP-GravR

Dear Lovely Death. Langston Hughes. CP-HughL; CP-HughL1

Dear M. Michael Palmer. SP-PalmM

Dear M ("Look this figure half-hidden is not a book"). Michael Palmer. SP-PalmM

Dear M ("Sky today yes and no, The. I am writing a play about a man with a pebble"). Michael Palmer. SP-PalmM

Dear Mama, / Time I pay rent and get my food. Letter ("Dear Mama, / Time I pay rent and get my food"). Langston Hughes. CP-HughL; CP-HughL3 *Fr.* Lenox Avenue Mural.

Dear March, Come in. Emily Dickinson. CP-DickE

Dear Margie, hello. It is 5:15 a.m. Ted Berrigan. SP-BerrT *Fr.* Sonnets, The.

Dear Masoch doodling with his contracts. Andrei Codrescu. SP-CodrA

Dear Max. I call you that because. Postscript. Eleanor Wilner. SP-WilnE

Dear mermaids, it was bound to happen. Thomas Mann. Wisława Szymborska. SP-SzymW, *tr. by* Stanislaw Barańczak *and* Clare Cavanagh

Dear mermaids, this is how it had to be. Thomas Mann. Wisława Szymborska. SP-SzymWM, *tr. by* Joanna Trzeciak

Dear Miss Dix, I am a young lady of Scandinavian origin, and I. Strange Case of the Lovelorn Letter Writer, The. Ogden Nash. CP-NashO

Dear Miss Dix, I am a young man of half-past thirty-seven. Two and One Are a Problem. Ogden Nash. CP-NashO

Dear Miss Lucy: I been t'inkin' dat I'd write you long fo' dis. Letter, A. Paul Laurence Dunbar. CP-DunbP

Dear Miss Unger. To Miss Unger. Robert Browning. CP-BroR2

Dear Mr. Bowles found out too late. Emily Dickinson. SP-DickE

Dear Mr. President. Langston Hughes. CP-HughL; CP-HughL2

Dear Mr President. Philip Whalen. SP-WhalP

Dear Mr. Worldly Wiseman. Robert Stock. SP-StocR

Dear Mona, Mary and all. Lorine Niedecker. CP-NiedL

Dear Mother, dear Mother, the Church is cold. Little Vagabond, The. William Blake. CP-BlakW *Fr.* Songs of Experience.

Dear Mother Goose! most motherly and dear. Mother Goose. James Whitcomb Riley. CP-RileJ

Dear Mother, in a dream. Escape, The. Gabriela Mistral. SP-MistG, *tr. by* Maria Giachetti [*or* Jacketti]

Dear Muse. Stevie Smith. CP-SmitS

Dear my friend and fellow-student, I would lean my spirit o'er you! Lady Geraldine's Courtship. Elizabeth Barrett Browning. CP-BroEB

Dear, my friend & honour'd madam! of hard facts I'm not a hoarder. George Meredith. CP-MerG2

Dear native brook! wild streamlet of the West! Sonnet to the River Otter. Samuel Taylor Coleridge. CP-ColeS; MW-ColeS

Dear native brooks, your ways I have pursued. William Wordsworth. MW-WorW

Dear native regions, I foretell. Extract from the Conclusion of a Poem, Composed in Anticipation of Leaving School. William Wordsworth. CP-WorW1

Dear nut / Uncrackable by nuance or debate. To My Greek. James Merrill. SP-MerrJ

Dear object of defeated care! Lines Written beneath a Picture. Lord Byron. CP-Byron

Dear Obour / Our crossing was without. Letter from Phillis Wheatley, A. Robert Earl Hayden. CP-HaydR

Dear old friend of us all in need. To the Quiet Observer. James Whitcomb Riley. CP-RileJ

Dear old woman in the lane, The. Christina Georgina Rossetti. CP-RosC2

Dear ones in the house of the dead. Kathleen Jessie Raine. SP-RainK

Dear ones, in those days it was otherwise. Woman Who Raised Goats, The. Tess Gallagher. SP-GallT

Dear Pa and Ma. Charles Bukowski. SP-BukC3

Dear Paul: / the sheets of your father's book of poetry. Lorine Niedecker. CP-NiedL

Dear Peter, Dear Peter. To Peter Stuart. Robert Burns. CP-BurnR

Dear Philip: "Thank God for boozy godfathers" Epistle to a Godson. W. H. Auden. CP-AudeW

Dear Poetry Editor. Death Threat Note. Yusef Komunyakaa. CP-KomuY

Dear possible, and if you drown. Laura Riding Jackson. CP-RidiL

Dear President whose art sublime. To Sir Joshua Reynolds. William Cowper. CP-CowpW

Dear pursuing presence. Hindu to His Body, A. A. K. Ramanujan. CP-RamaA

Dear queen and mother—what do the archers now! Niobe. Kenneth Patchen. CP-PatcK

Dear Ralph, to your Great Stone Face. Emerson's Concord. Richard Eberhart. CP-EberR

Dear Reader. James Tate. SP-TateJ

Dear Reliques! from a pit of vilest mould. Feelings of a French Royalist, on the Disinterment of the Remains of the Duke D'Enghien. William Wordsworth. CP-WorW2

Dear Reliques of a dislodg'd Soul, whose lack. Death's Lecture. Richard Crashaw. CP-CrasR

Dear Reynolds! as last night I lay in bed. To J. H. Reynolds, Esq. John Keats. CP-KeatJ

Dear Robert, Thank you for trying to rig. Ice-Storm, The. Robert Pinsky. CP-PinsR

Dear Ron: hello. Your name is now a household name. Ted Berrigan. SP-BerrT *Fr.* Sonnets, The.

Dear Ron: Keats was a baiter of bears etc. Ted Berrigan. SP-BerrT *Fr.* Sonnets, The.

Dear San: Everybody doesn't write poetry. Feeling and Form. Marilyn Hacker. SP-HackM

Dear savages, though I've never mastered your tongue, free of pronouns and gerunds. Infinitive. Joseph Brodsky. CP-BrodJ

"Dear! Shall I see thy face," she said. Dame of Athelhall, The. Thomas Hardy. CP-HardT

Dear Sheridan, a loving pair. George Nim-Dan-Dean, Esq. to Mr. Sheridan. Jonathan Swift. CP-SwifJ

Dear Sherry, I'm sorry for your bloodshedded sore eye. To Thomas Sheridan. Patrick Delany. CP-SherT

Dear Silent Ghost. Tennessee Williams. CP-WillT

Dear, simple girl, those flattering airs. Answer to the Foregoing, Addressed to Miss————. Lord Byron. CP-Byron

Dear Sir, at ony time or tide. Reply to Robert Riddell. Robert Burns. CP-BurnR

Dear, Sir, I trust you will pardon this intrusion of an Old Subscriber. Letter to Ogden Nash. Dorothy Parker. CP-ParkD

Dear Sir: / In Washington we are breathing very sincerely. New Letters from Thomas Jefferson. William Stafford. SP-StafWW

Dear Sir, of late delighted with the sight. To Her Most Honored Father Thomas Dudley, Esquire, These Humbly Presented. Anne Bradstreet. CP-BradA

Dear Sir, / our Lucky humbly begs. To Alexander Findlater. Robert Burns. CP-BurnR

Dear Sir, since you in humble wise. To the Dean of St. Patrick's ("Dear Sir, since you in humble wise"). Thomas Sheridan. CP-SherT

Dear Sir, We beseech & intreat & request. Humble Petition of Rd Buller & W. Goodenough, The. Mrs. Austen. CP-AustJ

Dear Sir: We haven't met but my father knew you. John Ciardi. CP-CiarJ

Dear Sister! while the wise and sage. To My Sister. John Greenleaf Whittier. CP-WhitJ

Dear Smed, I read thy brilliant lines. His Grace's Answer to Jonathan. Jonathan Swift. CP-SwifJ

Dear Smith [or S****], the sleest, paukie thief. To James Smith. Robert Burns. CP-BurnR

Dear, think not that they will forget you. Her Temple. Thomas Hardy. CP-HardT

Dear tho' unseen! tho' I have left behind. To Mary Pridham. Samuel Taylor Coleridge. CP-ColeS

Dear Tim, no more such angry speeches. Jonathan Swift. CP-SherT Fr. Tim and the Fables.

Dear to each Muse, and to thy Country dear. To the Honourable Col. Peter Schuyler. Annis Boudinot Stockton. CP-StocA

Dear Tom, I'm surprised that your verse did not jingle. To Thomas Sheridan. Jonathan Swift. CP-SherT, tr. by Robert Hogan

Dear Tom, I'm surprised that your verse did not jingle. To Thomas Sheridan. Jonathan Swift. CP-SherT; CP-SwifJ

Dear Tom, Nor turkey fat, nor goose from country-hut. Letter to Tom Punsibi, Occasioned by Reading His Excellent Farce, Called Alexander's Overthrow, or, The Downfall of Babylon, A. Unknown. CP-SherT

Dear Tom, this verse, which however the beginning may appear. George Nim-Dan-Dean's Invitation to Mr. Thomas Sheridan. Jonathan Swift. CP-SwifJ

Dear Tom, / When my next volume (granted: slender). Riposte. Marilyn Hacker. SP-HackM

Dear Tomasito. In Dream Time. Thomas McGrath. SP-McGrT

Dear Toni Instead of a Letter of Congratulation. Audre Lorde. SP-LordA

Dear Voyager: / This is to thank you for. Open Letter to Voyager II, An. John Updike. CP-UpdiJ

Dear welcomer, I think you must agree. Invitation, An. Thom Gunn. CP-GunnT

Dear Whizz, I remember you at St. Mark's in '39. To Auden on His Fiftieth. Richard Eberhart. CP-EberR

Dear Whoever-You-Are-That-You-Are. Letter from the Pygmies, A. Theodore Weiss. SP-WeisT

Dear wolfgang: / the asshole of the devil. Telegram. Andrei Codrescu. SP-CodrA

Dear woman, you never let me forget. Love Poem for a Wife and Her Trees. A. K. Ramanujan. CP-RamaA

Dear X, you wouldn't believe how curious. To a Dead Flame. John Updike. CP-UpdiJ

Dear[e] friend, sit down: the tale is long and sad. Love Unknown. George Herbert. CP-HerbG

Deare, if I with guile would guild a true intent. Dear If I with Guile. Thomas Campion. CP-CampT

Dear[e] love, for nothing less[e] than thee. Dream[e], The. John Donne. CP-DonnJ; MW-DonnJ

Deare Perenna, prethee come. To Perenna, A Mistresse. Robert Herrick. CP-HerrR

Dear[e], though to part it be a hell. To Dianeme. Robert Herrick. CP-HerrR

Dearest, best and brightest. Pine Forest of the Cascine Near Pisa, The. Percy Bysshe Shelley. CP-ShelP

Dearest Dimpling, we believe. George Meredith. CP-MerG2

Dearest Evelyn, I often think of you. Jungle Husband, The. Stevie Smith. CP-SmitS

Dearest Foxxy, / I am in a crate. Love Letter Written in a Burning Building. Anne Sexton. CP-SextA

Dearest, I never knew such loving. There. Sonnet: "Dearest, I never knew such

loving. There." Hayden Carruth. CP-CarHS Fr. Sonnets.

Dearest, it was a night. Birthnight: To F, The. Walter De la Mare. CP-DeLaW

Dearest love: The roses are in bloom again. Brennende Liebe. Louise Glück. SP-GlucL

Dearest of thousands, now the time drawes neere. His Charge to Julia at His Death. Robert Herrick. CP-HerrR

Dearest one, daughter! at glance of your brow-shaded eye. Glance, The. Walter De la Mare. CP-DeLaW

Dearest one, when I am dead. Prayer for a Prayer. Dorothy Parker. CP-ParkD

Dearest Reader. Michael Palmer. SP-PalmM

Dearest, thy tresses are not threads of gold. Comparison, The. Thomas Carew. CP-CareT

Dearest was the one to whom it fell, The. Hilda. John Crowe Ransom. SP-RansJ

Dearest, whatever others see. Frances ("Dearest, whatever others see"). G. K. Chesterton. CP-ChesG

Dearest, where thy shadow falls. Hafiz. CP-EmerR

Dearly-beloved Mr Squire. Mr Squire. D. H. Lawrence. CP-LawrD

Dearth. James Whitcomb Riley. CP-RileJ

Death. Thomas Kinsella. CP-KinsT

Death. Emily Jane Brontë. CP-BronE

Death. Robert Creeley. SP-CreeR

Death. Paul Laurence Dunbar. CP-DunbP

Death. George Herbert. CP-HerbG

Death. Randall Jarrell. CP-JarrR

Death. D. H. Lawrence. CP-LawrD

Death. Federico García Lorca. CP-GarcF, tr. by Greg Simon and Steven F. White

Death. Thomas Merton. CP-MertT

Death. James Whitcomb Riley. CP-RileJ

Death. Christina Georgina Rossetti. CP-RosC3

Death. Percy Bysshe Shelley. CP-ShelP

Death. Percy Bysshe Shelley. CP-ShelP

Death. Jones Very. CP-VeryJ

Death. William Carlos Williams. CP-WilW1

Death. William Carlos Williams. CP-WilW2

Death. William Butler Yeats. CP-YeatW

Death also is trying to be life. Life Is Trying to Be Life. Ted Hughes. SP-HughTN

Death and Burial of McDonald Clarke, a Parody, The. Walt Whitman. CP-WhitW

Death and Co. Sylvia Plath. CP-PlatS

Death and Daphne. Jonathan Swift. CP-SwifJ

Death and Doctor Hornbook [A True Story]. Robert Burns. CP-BurnR

Death and Dying Words of Poor Mailie, the Author's Only Pet Yowe, an Unco Mournfu' Tale, The. Robert Burns. CP-BurnR

Death and Life of a Severino, The. João Cabral de Melo Neto.

"All the heaven and earth." CP-BishE

"My name is Severino." CP-BishE

"Whom are you carrying." CP-BishE

Death and the Bridge. Robert Lowell. SP-LoweR

Death and the Good Citizen. A. K. Ramanujan. CP-RamaA

Death and the Lovers. May Sarton. SP-SartM

Death and the Maiden. Howard Nemerov. CP-NemeH

Death and the Professor. Thomas Kinsella. CP-KinsT

Death and the Turtle. Josephine Jacobsen. CP-JacoJ

Death, are you well? I trust you have no cough. Guest, A. Ambrose Bierce. SP-BierA

Death as Death. Laura Riding Jackson. CP-RidiL

Death Baby, The. Anne Sexton. CP-SextA; SP-SextA

Death Ballad. John Berryman. CP-BerrJ

Death Bed. Thomas Kinsella. CP-KinsT

Death-Bed, A. Rudyard Kipling. CP-KiplR

Death-Bed of a Financier. Stevie Smith. CP-SmitS

Death Bereaves Our Common Mother Nature Grieves for My Dead Brother. Stevie Smith. CP-SmitS

Death blow is a Life blow to Some, A. Emily Dickinson. CP-DickE

Death By Aesthetics. Mona Van Duyn. SP-VanDM

Death by Drums. Robert Graves. CP-GravR

Death by Radio. William Carlos Williams. CP-WilW2

Death Came to Me. Stevie Smith. CP-SmitS

Death can have no alternative but Love. Song: Cherries or Lilies. Robert Graves. CP-GravR

Death cannot come too soon. Henry David Thoreau. CP-ThorH

Death cannot plunder half so fast. Emily Dickinson. SP-DickE

Death Chant. Peter Blue Cloud. SP-BlueP

Death Chant. Langston Hughes. See Stony Lonesome

Death comes once, let it be easy. Finish. Carl Sandburg. CP-SandC

Death covers me with fine dust. Books. Andrei Codrescu. SP-CodrA

Death-Day Recalled, A. Thomas Hardy. CP-HardT

Death Decay and Change. Jones Very. CP-VeryJ

Death devours all lovely things. Passer Mortuus Est. Edna St. Vincent Millay. CP-MillE

Death didn't wish to lay Cecchino low. Michelangelo Buonarroti. CP-Miche, tr. by John Frederick Nims

Death don't ring no doorbells. Casual. Langston Hughes. CP-HughL; CP-HughL3

Death-Dream, The. Walter De la Mare. CP-DeLaW

Death Embrace, The. Tennessee Williams. CP-WillT

Death Ends All Woe. Robert Herrick. CP-HerrR

Death extends his hand. Death of a General. Constantine P. Cavafy. CP-CavaC, tr. by Theoharis Constantine Theoharis

Death for the Dark Stranger. Thomas McGrath. SP-McGrT

Death, from a Distance. Jorge Guillén. CP-WilbR

Death from Cancer. Robert Lowell. SP-LoweR Fr. In Memory of Arthur Winslow.

Death gallops up the bridge of red railtie girders. Death and the Bridge. Robert Lowell. SP-LoweR

Death goes far around. Emily Dickinson. SP-DickE

Death / goes in and out. Three Cities. Federico García Lorca. CP-GarcF, tr. by Cola Franzen

Death Grapple, The. Robert Graves. CP-GravR

Death, Great Smoothener. May Swenson. SP-SwenM

Death-grip of the chalky clouds lets slip, The. Landing in the Rain at La Guardia. John Updike. CP-UpdiJ

Death has no power to make that sweet face bitter. Petrarch. CP-Petra, tr. by J. G. Nichols

Death has only to touch a trifle. Emily Dickinson. SP-DickE

Death has put out the sun which dazed my eyes. Petrarch. CP-Petra, tr. by J. G. Nichols

Death himself. L M F B R. Gary Snyder. CP-SnydG

Death I recant, and say, unsaid by me. Elegy on Mistress Boulstred. John Donne. CP-DonnJ; MW-DonnJ

Death, I say, my heart is bowed. Shroud, The. Edna St. Vincent Millay. CP-MillE

Death in Africa. Langston Hughes. CP-HughL; CP-HughL2

Death in Harlem. Langston Hughes. CP-HughL; CP-HughL2

Death-in-Love. Dante Gabriel Rossetti. CW-RossD Fr. House of Life, The.

Death in Mexico. Denise Levertov. SP-LeveDL

Death in Search of a Comfortable Metaphor. A. K. Ramanujan. CP-RamaA

Death in the Desert, A. Robert Browning. CP-BroR1; SP-BroR

Death in the Desert, A. Charles Tomlinson. CP-TomlC; SP-TomlC

Death in the Mines. Richard Eberhart. CP-EberR

Death in the Rose Garden. Stevie Smith. CP-SmitS

Death in the West, A. Donald Davie. CP-DaviDC

Death in Venice. Charles Tomlinson. CP-TomlC

Death in war begins. From Man You Came and to Man You Shall Return. Yehuda Amichai. SP-AmicYL, tr. by Benjamin Harshav and Barbara Harshav

Death in Yorkville. Langston Hughes. CP-HughL; CP-HughL3

Death Invited. May Swenson. SP-SwenM

Death is a dead, at least that's what Freud said. Einstein & Freud & Jack. Howard Nemerov. CP-NemeH

Death is a Dialogue between. Emily Dickinson. CP-DickE

Death is a tower. Tower. Langston Hughes. CP-HughL; CP-HughL1

Death Is Dead. James Whitcomb Riley. CP-RileJ

Death is everywhere in it. Yet. Poetry. John Ciardi. CP-CiarJ

Death is here and death is there. Death. Percy Bysshe Shelley. CP-ShelP

Death Is High. Tennessee Williams. CP-WillT

Death is like the insect. Emily Dickinson. CP-DickE

Death is more than. One X. E. E. Cummings. CP-CummE

Death is no escape, ah no! only a doorway to the inevitable. Death. D. H. Lawrence. CP-LawrD

Death is perhaps an intimate friend. Emily Dickinson. SP-DickE

Death is potential to that Man. Emily Dickinson. CP-DickE

Death is serious. Small Moment. Howard Nemerov. CP-NemeH

Death is stronger than all the governments. Death Snips Proud Men. Carl Sandburg. CP-SandC

Death Is Swallowed Up in Victory. Christina Georgina Rossetti. CP-RosC3

Death is the poor man's consolation prize. Death of the Poor, The. Charles Baudelaire. CP-BaudC, tr. by Walter Martin

Death Is the Serpent. Marya Alexandrovna Zaturenska. SP-ZatuM

Death is the supple Suitor. Emily Dickinson. CP-DickE

Death is the tranquil night. From Heine. Heinrich Heine. CP-BogaL, tr. by Louise Bogan

Death is the twin of Sleep, they say. Twin of Sleep, The. Robert Graves. CP-GravR

Death, Judgment, Heaven, Hell. Kenneth Rexroth. CP-RexrK

Death King, The. Anne Sexton. CP-SextA

Death knell is ringing, The. Percy Bysshe Shelley. CP-ShelP

Death leaves Us homesick, who behind. Emily Dickinson. CP-DickE

Death makes his / obeisance. Festival, The. Robert Creeley. CP-CreeR

Death mask is prepared, The. How To. Dan Pagis. SP-PagiD, tr. by Stephen Mitchell

Death Mask of a Young Man. Robert Penn Warren. CP-WarrR

Death News. Allen Ginsberg. CP-GinsA

Death obtains the Rose. Emily Dickinson. SP-DickE

Death of a Bomber. John Ciardi. CP-CiarJ

Death of a Favorite Bird. W. S. Merwin. SP-MerwW

Death of a First-Born, A. Christina Georgina Rossetti. CP-RosC3

Death Of A.G.A., The. Emily Jane Brontë. CP-BronE

Death of a General. Constantine P. Cavafy. CP-CavaC, tr. by Theoharis Constantine Theoharis

Death of a Lawn Mower. David Ignatow. SP-IgnaD

Death of a man is like the fall of a mighty nation, The. Fall, The. Czeslaw Milosz. CP-MiloC; CP-MiloCN, tr. by Lillian Vallee

Death of a Naturalist. Seamus Heaney. SP-HeanSO

Death of a Painter. Donald Davie. CP-DaviDC

Death of a Pianist. Adam Zagajewski. SP-ZagaA, tr. by Clare Cavanagh

Death of a Public Servant, The. Carolyn Kizer. CP-KizeC

Death of a Soldier, The. Wallace Stevens. CP-StevW; CP-StevWP

Death of a Starling, The. Catullus. See Carmina

Death of a Toad, The. Richard Wilbur. CP-WilbR

Death of a Voice. Boris Leonidovich Pasternak. CP-DaviDC, tr. by Donald Davie

Death of a Young Son by Drowning. Margaret Atwood. SP-AtwM1

Death of Alexander. Robert Lowell. SP-LoweR

Death of Allegory, The. Billy Collins. SP-CollB

Death of an Actress. Louis MacNeice. CP-MacNL

Death of an Old Lady. Louis MacNeice. CP-MacNL

Death of an Old Seaman. Langston Hughes. CP-HughL; CP-HughL1

Death of an Unfamiliar Sister, The. Jay Wright. SP-WrigJ

Death of Anne Boleyn. Robert Lowell. SP-LoweR

Death of Antonito el Camborio, The. Federico García Lorca. SP-GarcF, tr. by J. L. Gili and Stephen Spender

Death of Argentine, The. Sir Walter Scott. SP-ScotW Fr. Lord of the Isles, The.

Death of Artists, The. Charles Baudelaire. CP-BaudC, tr. by Walter Martin

Death of Assia G., The. Yehuda Amichai. SP-AmicYL, tr. by Benjamin Harshav and Barbara Harshav

Death of Autumn, The. Edna St. Vincent Millay. CP-MillE

Death of Chet Baker, The. Miller Williams. CP-WillM

Death of Count Roland. Robert Lowell. SP-LoweR

Death of Cuchulain, The. William Butler Yeats. CP-YeatW (Cuchulain's Fight with the Sea.) CP-YeatW

Death of Do Dirty: A Rounder's Song. Langston Hughes. CP-HughL; CP-HughL1

Death of Elizabeth Grieve, The. Charles Tomlinson. CP-TomlC

Death of Europe, The. Charles Olson. CP-OlsoC; SP-OlsoC

Death of Fathers, The. Theodore Weiss. SP-WeisT

Death of Franco of Cologne, The: His Prophecy of Beethoven. William Carlos Williams. CP-WilW1

Death of Fred Clifton, The. Lucille Clifton. SP-ClifL

Death of General Grant. Walt Whitman. CP-WhitW

Death of God, The. Howard Nemerov. CP-NemeH

Death of Grant, The. Ambrose Bierce. SP-BierA

Death of Hoel, The. Thomas Gray. CP-GrayT

Death of Lafayette. Jones Very. CP-VeryJ

Death of Little Boys. Allen Tate. CP-TateA

Death of Little Tony Camborio, The. Federico García Lorca. CP-GarcF, tr. by Will Kirkland

Death of love comes from reiteration, The. Reiteration, The. Robert Graves. CP-GravR

Death of Lovers, The. Charles Baudelaire. CP-BaudC, tr. by Walter Martin

Death of Man, The. Jones Very. CP-VeryJ

Death of Marmion, The. Sir Walter Scott. SP-ScotW Fr. Marmion.

Death of Mr. Mounsel. Stevie Smith. CP-SmitS

Death of my poor father, The. Lorine Niedecker. CP-NiedL

Death of Myth-making, The. Sylvia Plath. CP-PlatS

Death of / one is, The. Robert Creeley. CP-CreeR

Death of Our Era, The. D. H. Lawrence. CP-LawrD

Death of Regret, The. Thomas Hardy. CP-HardT

Death of See, The. William Carlos Williams. CP-WilW1

Death of Sir Nihil, book the nth. Tywater. Richard Wilbur. CP-WilbR

Death of Southwell, The. John Logan. CP-LogaJ

Death of the Ball Turret Gunner, The. Randall Jarrell. CP-JarrR

Death of the Baron, The. D. H. Lawrence. CP-LawrD

Death of the Dog Belvoir. Stevie Smith. CP-SmitS

Death of the Emperor Tacitus, The. Constantine P. Cavafy. CP-CavaC, tr. by Theoharis Constantine Theoharis

Death of the Fathers, The. Anne Sexton. CP-SextA

  Boat, The. SP-SextA

  How We Danced. SP-SextA

  Oysters. SP-SextA

  Santa. SP-SextA

Death of the First Born, The. Paul Laurence Dunbar. CP-DunbP

Death of the Hat, The. Billy Collins. SP-CollB

Death of the Hired Man, The. Robert Frost. CP-FrosR

Death of the Horses by Fire. Tess Gallagher. SP-GallT

Death of the Infanta, The. Charles Tomlinson. CP-TomlC

Death of the Nature-Lover, The. Walt Whitman. CP-WhitW

Death of the Poor, The. Charles Baudelaire. CP-BaudC, tr. by Walter Martin

Death of the Race Car Driver, The. Norman Dubie. CP-DubiN

Death of the Sheriff, The. Robert Lowell. CP-LoweR

Death of the Small Commune, The. Marge Piercy. SP-PierM

Death, of thee do I make my moan. To Death, of His Lady. François Villon. CW-RossD, tr. by Dante Gabriel Rossetti

Death of Thelma Sayles. Lucille Clifton. SP-ClifL

Death of Venus, The. Robert Creeley. CP-CreeR

Death of Wallenstein, The. Samuel Taylor Coleridge. Character of Wallenstein, The. CP-ColeS

Death of Will, The. Charles Tomlinson. CP-TomlC

Death of Winter, The. George Meredith. CP-MerG1

Death on All Fronts. Allen Ginsberg. CP-GinsA

Death-Parting, A. Dante Gabriel Rossetti. CW-RossD

Death Piece. Theodore Roethke. CP-RoetT

Death Psalm: O Lord of Mysteries. Denise Levertov. SP-LeveDL

Death, removal of names, disappearance. Then Wherefore Death. Laura Riding Jackson. CP-RidiL

Death Room, The. Robert Graves. CP-GravR

Death Scene, A. Emily Jane Brontë. CP-BronE

  (From a D— W— in the N. C.) CP-BronE

Death Sentence, The. Stevie Smith. CP-SmitS

Death sets a Thing significant. Emily Dickinson. CP-DickE

Death shut those eyes, him too it shut below. Michelangelo Buonarroti. CP-Miche, tr. by John Frederick Nims

Death, since I find not one with whom to grieve. Canzone: He beseeches Death for the Life of Beatrice. Dante Alighieri. CW-RossD, tr. by Dante Gabriel Rossetti

Death Snips Proud Men. Carl Sandburg. CP-SandC

Death Song[, A]. Paul Laurence Dunbar. CP-DunbP

Death squats on the bottom stair. Praises for Mrs. Dodd. Robert Penn Warren. CP-WarrR

Death stretched an arm, stole fruit not ripened yet. Michelangelo Buonarroti. CP-Miche, tr. by John Frederick Nims

Death swooped suddenly on men in Flanders. Swift and Slow. Ivor Gurney. SP-GurnI

Death, that struck when I was most confiding. Death. Emily Jane Brontë. CP-BronE

Death the Barber. William Carlos Williams. CP-WilW1

Death, thou wast once an uncouth hideous thing. Death. George Herbert. CP-HerbG

Death Threat Note. Yusef Komunyakaa. CP-KomuY

Death to the first-born sons, always. Miriam's Song. Eleanor Wilner. SP-WilnE

Death to the Poor. Charles Baudelaire. CP-CullC

Death to Van Gogh's Ear! Allen Ginsberg. CP-GinsA; SP-GinsA

Death took my father. Manos Karastefanís. James Merrill. SP-MerrJ

Death Walkers, The. James Laughlin. CP-LaugJ

Death Wants More Death. Charles Bukowski. SP-BukC2

Death warrants are supposed to be. Emily Dickinson. CP-DickE

Death was round and open as two halfs of an orange in sight. Yehuda Amichai. SP-AmicYL Fr. At Right Angles.

Death-Watches. Christina Georgina Rossetti. CP-RosC2

Death went upon a solemn day. Death and Daphne. Jonathan Swift. CP-SwifJ

Death, what dost? ô hold thy Blow. Upon the Death of the Most Desired Mister Herrys. Richard Crashaw. CP-CrasR

Death, when I am ready, I. Pause en Route. Thomas Kinsella. CP-KinsT

Death! where is thy victory? To Death. Percy Bysshe Shelley. CP-ShelP

Death / White hand. Looking East at Night. W. S. Merwin. SP-MerwW

Death, why hast thou made life so hard to bear. Canzone: Of his Dead Lady. Giacomino Pugliesi. CW-RossD, tr. by Dante Gabriel Rossetti

Death Will Amuse Them. Kenneth Patchen. CP-PatcK

Death will come and it will have your eyes. Homage to Cesare Pavese. Charles Wright. SP-WrigC

Death Wish, A. Samuel Taylor Coleridge. CP-ColeS

Death-Wish, The. Louis MacNeice. CP-MacNL

Death, you have left this world, without its sun. Petrarch. CP-Petra, tr. by J. G. Nichols

Deathfear. James Laughlin. CP-LaugJ

Deathfugue. Paul Celan. SP-CelaP, tr. by John Felstiner

Death(having lost)put on his universe. E. E. Cummings. CP-CummE; SP-CummE

Deathly Child, The. Stevie Smith. CP-SmitS

Deaths. Denise Levertov. SP-LeveDP

Deaths about You when You Stir in Sleep, The. John Ciardi. CP-CiarJ

Deaths and Entrances. Dylan Thomas. CP-ThomD

Death's Chicken, Named Amelia. Alan Dugan. CP-DugaA

Death's Chill Between. Christina Georgina Rossetti. CP-RosC3

Death's Chimney. E. E. Cummings. CP-CummE

Death's Door. Thom Gunn. CP-GunnT

Death's Echo. W. H. Auden. CP-AudeW

Deaths everywhere. George Oppen. CP-OppGN

Death's head of realism, The. Fyodor. Allen Ginsberg. CP-GinsA; SP-GinsA

Death's Lecture. Richard Crashaw. CP-CrasR

Deaths of the Other Children, The. Margaret Atwood. SP-AtwM1

Deaths of the Uncles, The. Maxine W. Kumin. SP-KumiM

Death's Ostracism. Stevie Smith. CP-SmitS

Death's Songsters. Dante Gabriel Rossetti. CW-RossD Fr. House of Life, The.

Death's taxi crackles through the mist. The cheeks. To the Airport. Adrienne Rich. CP-RicAE

Death's the lover that I'd be taking. Trifler, The. Dorothy Parker. CP-ParkD

Death's Valley. Walt Whitman. CP-WhitW

Death's Waylaying not the sharpest. Emily Dickinson. CP-DickE

Deathsong for a Maiden. Kenneth Patchen. CP-PatcK

Deathwatch on the Southside. Jorge Luis Borges. SP-BorgJ, tr. by Robert Fitzgerald

Débâcle. Louis MacNeice. CP-MacNL

Debate, The. Raymond Carver. CP-CarvR

Debate, The. David Ignatow. SP-IgnaD

Debate with the Rabbi. Howard Nemerov. CP-NemeH

Debauchery and Death—compliant pair! Sisters of Mercy. Charles Baudelaire. CP-BaudC, tr. by Walter Martin

Debet multa tibi veneranda (Bacone) poesis. Ad ampliss. totius Angliae Cancellarium, Fr. Ba. Thomas Campion. CP-CampT

Debits and Credits. Rudyard Kipling.

  Alnaschar and the Oxen. CP-KiplR

  Banquet Night. CP-KiplR

  Birthright, The. CP-KiplR

  Burden, The. CP-KiplR

  Centaurs, The. CP-KiplR

  Changelings, The. CP-KiplR

  Gipsy Vans. CP-KiplR

  Jane's Marriage. CP-KiplR

  Last Ode, The. CP-KiplR

  Late Came the God. CP-KiplR

  Legend of Truth, A. CP-KiplR

  Portent, The. CP-KiplR

  Rahere. CP-KiplR

  Supports, The. CP-KiplR

  after Horace, Book 5, Ode 22. CP-KiplR

  To the Companions. CP-KiplR

  Untimely. CP-KiplR

  Vineyard, The. CP-KiplR

  We and They. CP-KiplR

Deborah as Scion. James Dickey. CP-DickJ

Debris. Walt Whitman. CP-WhitW

Debris of Life and Mind. Wallace Stevens. CP-StevW; CP-StevWP

Debt. George Oppen. CP-OppGN

Debt. Allen Tate. CP-TateA

Debt, A. W. S. Merwin. SP-MerwW

Debt, The. Paul Laurence Dunbar. CP-DunbP

Debt is paid, The. Past, The. Ralph Waldo Emerson. CP-EmerR

Debtor Sheikh, The. Jelaluddin Rumi. SP-Rumi, tr. by Coleman Barks

Debtor's Prison Road. Heather McHugh. SP-McHuH

Debts. Andrei Codrescu. SP-CodrA

Debussy. Federico García Lorca. CP-GarcF, tr. by Alan S. Trueblood Fr. Three Portraits with Shading.

Debut of the Dancer, A. B., The. Charles Baudelaire. CP-BaudC, tr. by Walter Martin

Deep Fishing. Richard Eberhart. CP-EberR

Deep-founded bathylites their heavings fault. Visitation. Robert Stock. SP-StocR

Deep-green tree, The. Chrysalis. Eugenio Montale. CP-MontE, *tr.* by Jonathan Galassi

Deep in a forest where the kestrel screamed. Dwelling-Place, The. Walter De la Mare. CP-DeLaW

Deep in a time that cannot come again. Lines & Circularities. Howard Nemerov. CP-NemeH

Deep in Alabama earth. Alabama Earth. Langston Hughes. CP-HughL; CP-HughL1

Deep in distant waters. Diver. Tennessee Williams. CP-WillT

Deep in earth's opaque mirror. Symmetries & Asymmetries. W. H. Auden. CP-AudeW

Deep in liquid indigo. Aquatic Nocturne. Sylvia Plath. CP-PlatS

Deep in my heart that aches with the repression. Unexpressed. Paul Laurence Dunbar. CP-DunbP

Deep in the back ways of my mind I see them. My Great-Grandfather's Slaves. Wendell Berry. CP-BerrW

Deep in the Century of Opposites. Muriel Rukeyser. CP-RukeM

Deep in the inner space denuded of trees. Deterioration. Yannis Ritsos. SP-RitsY, *tr.* by Kimon Friar

Deep in the man sits fast his fate. Fate. Ralph Waldo Emerson. CP-EmerR

Deep in the muck of unregarded doom. Edna St. Vincent Millay. CP-MillE

Deep in the shady sadness of a vale. Hyperion. John Keats. CP-KeatJ

Deep in the soul a strong delusion dwells. Idealism. Ralph Waldo Emerson. CP-EmerR

Deep in the still mysterious waters of the lake a world lies drowned. Abominable Lake, The. Stevie Smith. CP-SmitS

Deep in the study / of Eugenics. Phœnix, The. Ogden Nash. CP-NashO

Deep Measure. Charles Wright. SP-WrigCN

Deep Pool, the. James Laughlin. CP-LaugJ

Deep pools of shade beneath dense maples. July. John Updike. CP-UpdiJ

Deep prolonged entry with the strong pink cock. She Loves. Olga Broumas. SP-BrouO

Deep-red apples / curve down the royal trunk like a harp. Apple Tree with Cobweb Strings. Jaroslav Seifert. SP-SeifJ, *tr.* by Ewald Osers

Deep Religious Faith. William Carlos Williams. CP-WilW2

Deep-Sea Cables, The. Rudyard Kipling. CP-KiplR

Deep-sea frost, and. Lily at Noon, A. Donald Davie. CP-DaviDC

Deep-sea salmon far at sea, The. Old Man's Journey. Archibald MacLeish. CP-MacLA

Deep Sea Wandering. Carl Sandburg. CP-SandC

Deep sea was the wandering. Deep Sea Wandering. Carl Sandburg. CP-SandC

Deep South. Thomas McGrath. SP-McGrT

Deep-sworn Vow, A. William Butler Yeats. CP-YeatW

Deep, tender, firm and true, the Nation's heart. Silent Victors, The. James Whitcomb Riley. CP-RileJ

Deep were the woods and the birdsong. Interview in Midsummer. Marya Alexandrovna Zaturenska. SP-ZatuM

Deep Winter. James Schuyler. CP-SchuJ

Deep wooden note, A. Overheard. Denise Levertov. SP-LeveDP

Deep Woods. Howard Nemerov. CP-NemeH

Deeper Than a Dream. Peter Blue Cloud. SP-BlueP

Deeper Than Love. D. H. Lawrence. CP-LawrD

Deeper Than Love. D. H. Lawrence. CP-LawrD

Deeper than sleep but not so deep as death. Night Feeding. Muriel Rukeyser. CP-RukeM

Deepest Sensuality, The. D. H. Lawrence. CP-LawrD

Deepfreeze, The. Fourteen degrees. Ducks. February 29th. William Corbett. SP-CorbW

Deeply Morbid. Stevie Smith. CP-SmitS

Deer among Cattle. James Dickey. CP-DickJ

Deer and the dachshund are one, The. Loneliness in Jersey City. Wallace Stevens. CP-StevW; CP-StevWP

Deer and the Snake, The. Kenneth Patchen. CP-PatcK

Deer carcass hangs from a rafter, The. Gathering the Bones Together. Gregory Orr. SP-OrrG

Deer have stood around our house. Deer Stolen. William Stafford. SP-StafWW

Deer in the body, A. Ten Speeds. Yusef Komunyakaa. CP-KomuY

Deer is humble, lovely as God made her, The. Deer and the Snake, The. Kenneth Patchen. CP-PatcK

Deer Lay Down Their Bones, The. Robinson Jeffers. CP-JefR3

Deer live deep in the forest. Han-shan. CP-ColdM, *tr.* by Red Pine

Deer [*or* Dear] God, / If thy smart Rod. Ode, or Psalme, to God, An. Robert Herrick. CP-HerrR

Deer stand black by water, the Lion's head, The. Sleep (by Rousseau), A. John Ciardi. CP-CiarJ

Deer Stolen. William Stafford. SP-StafWW

Deer were bounding like blown leaves, The. Fire on the Hills. Robinson Jeffers. CP-JefR2

Defamed guiltiness by silence unkempt. Sir Thomas Wyatt. CP-WyatT

Defeat. Charles Bukowski. SP-BukC1

Defeat. Walter De la Mare. CP-DeLaW

Defeated. Robert Bly. SP-BlyR

Defeated, The. A. E. Housman. CP-HousA

Defeated, The. W. S. Merwin. SP-MerwW

Defective Circles. Philip Whalen. SP-WhalP

Defective Record, The. William Carlos Williams. CP-WilW1

Defective Santa Claus, A. James Whitcomb Riley. CP-RileJ

Defence for Women, A. Robert Herrick. CP-HerrR

Defenceless Border, The. Sir Walter Scott. SP-ScotW *Fr.* Bridal of Trierman, The.

Defendant. Alan Dugan. CP-DugaA

Defending the Faith. Allen Ginsberg. CP-GinsA; SP-GinsA

Defense. William Carlos Williams. CP-WilW2

Defense of the Islands. T. S. Eliot. CP-ElioT

Defensio in Extremis. John Berryman. CP-BerrJ

Deferred. Langston Hughes. CP-HughL; CP-HughL3

Defiance to Cupid. William Carlos Williams. CP-WilW2

Definite motion is accomplished. Continuation of the Landscape. Kenneth Patchen. CP-PatcK

Definition. Grace Paley. CP-PalGC

Definition in the Face of Unnamed Fury. Rita Dove. SP-DoveR

Definition of Beauty is, The. Emily Dickinson. CP-DickE

Definition of Beauty, The. Robert Herrick. CP-HerrR

Definition of love in many languages, The. Laura Riding Jackson. CP-RidiL

Definition of Love, The. Andrew Marvell. CP-MarvA

Definition of the Frontiers. Archibald MacLeish. CP-MacLA

Definitions. A. R. Ammons. CP-AmmoA

Definitions of Old Age. Archibald MacLeish. CP-MacLA

Deflowering. Lawrence Ferlinghetti. SP-FerlL

Deformed. James Whitcomb Riley. CP-RileJ

Deformed Mistress, The. Sir John Suckling. CP-SuckJ

Deformed Transformed, The. Lord Byron. CP-Byron

Defrauded I a Butterfly. Emily Dickinson. CP-DickE

Deganya. Yehuda Amichai. SP-AmicYL, *tr.* by Benjamin Harshav *and* Barbara Harshav

Degas: *The Milliner's Shop*. Adam Zagajewski. SP-ZagaA, *tr.* by Clare Cavanagh

Degenerate Douglas! O [*or* oh,] the unworthy lord! Composed at Neidpath Castle, the Property of Lord Queensberry,1803. William Wordsworth. CP-WorW1

Degrade first the Arts if you'd Mankind degrade. Advice of the Popes Who Succeeded the Age of Rafael. William Blake. CP-BlakW

Degrees of Shade. Helen Pinkerton. CP-PinkH

Dehorning. Ted Hughes. SP-HughTN

Deign, Sovereign Mistress! to accept a Lay. Lines Inscribed in a Copy of His Poems Sent to the Queen for the Royal Library at Windsor. William Wordsworth. CP-WorW2

Deil [*or* De'il] cam fiddling through the town, The. De'il's [*or* Deil's] Awa wi' th' [*or* the] Exciseman, The. Robert Burns. CP-BurnR

De'il's [*or* Deil's] Awa wi' th' [*or* the] Exciseman, The. Robert Burns. CP-BurnR

Deir Ayub, a Heap of Watermelons and the Rest of My Life. Yehuda Amichai. SP-AmicYL, *tr.* by Benjamin Harshav *and* Barbara Harshav

Deism. Phillis Wheatley. CP-WheaP

Deities and Beasts. John Updike. CP-UpdiJ

Deity, The. John Greenleaf Whittier. CP-WhitJ

Déjà, Indeed. John Updike. CP-UpdiJ

  (I sometimes fear that I shall never view.) CP-UpdiJ

Déjà Vu. Louis MacNeice. CP-MacNL

Dejection: A Footnote. Amy Clampitt. CP-ClamA

Dejection: An Ode. Samuel Taylor Coleridge. CP-ColeS; MW-ColeS

Dejection [Ode]. Derek Mahon. CP-MahoD

Déjeuner sur l'herbe. Tu Fu. CP-KizeC, *tr.* by Carolyn Kizer

DeKooning, Jack "The Dripper" Painters, The. William Corbett. SP-CorbW

Delany, most learned of men. Ad Te, Doctissime Delany. Thomas Sheridan. CP-SherT, *tr.* by Robert Hogan

Delaware Water Gap. A. R. Ammons. CP-AmmoA

Delay. Robert Herrick. CP-HerrR

Delay. Henry David Thoreau. CP-ThorH

Delay in Friendship. Henry David Thoreau. CP-ThorH

Delay responsible? Why, then, my friend. To a Censor. Ambrose Bierce. SP-BierA

Delay, well, travellers must expect. Autobiography at an Air-Station. Philip

Larkin. CP-LarkP

Delay Your Speech. Shmuel HaNagid. SP-HaNaS, *tr. by* Peter Cole

Delayed till she had ceased to know. Emily Dickinson. CP-DickE

Delaying Bride, The. Robert Herrick. CP-HerrR

Delete the Inapplicable. Hans Magnus Enzensberger. SP-EnzeH, *tr. by* Michael Hamburger

Deleted Passage. Amy Clampitt. CP-ClamA

Delft. Rita Dove. SP-DoveR

Delia. Robert Burns. CP-BurnR

Delia excuse this falling tear. Tears of Friendship, The. Elegy the 4th. Annis Boudinot Stockton. CP-StocA

Delia Rexroth ("California rolls into"). Kenneth Rexroth. CP-RexrK

Delia Rexroth ("Under your illkempt yellow roses"). Kenneth Rexroth. CP-RexrK

Delia Sequence, The. James Laughlin. CP-LaugJ

Delia, th' unkindest girl on earth. William Cowper. CP-CowpW

Deliberate motion and the blue sound. Soldier Who Lived Through the War, The. Howard Nemerov. CP-NemeH

Deliberately, long ago / the carcasses. From an Old House in America. Adrienne Rich. SP-RicA1; SP-RicA2

Deliberation. Jelaluddin Rumi. SP-Rumi, *tr. by* Coleman Barks

Delicacies, The. William Carlos Williams. CP-WilW1

Delicate Cluster. Walt Whitman. CP-WhitW

Delicate Conspiracy, A. Yusef Komunyakaa. CP-KomuY

Delicate eyes that blinked blue Rookies all ach. On Neal's Ashes. Allen Ginsberg. CP-GinsA; SP-GinsA

Delicate french girl jukebox husky lament, The. Growing Old Again. Allen Ginsberg. CP-GinsA

Delicate lepidopteran tongue, The. Hearts' and Flowers'. Archibald MacLeish. CP-MacLA

Delicate omens traced in air. Motto to "Fate" Ralph Waldo Emerson. CP-EmerR

Delicate Riders, The. James Tate. SP-TateJ

Delicate the syllables that release the repression. Gentle, The. Theodore Roethke. CP-RoetT

Delicious Interruption, A. James Whitcomb Riley. CP-RileJ *Fr.* Child-World, A.

Delicious, white, refined. Domino. James Merrill. SP-MerrJ

Delight. Robert Penn Warren. CP-WarrR

Delight—becomes pictorial. Emily Dickinson. CP-DickE

Delight dances. Robert Creeley. CP-CreeR

Delight has no Competitor. Emily Dickinson. SP-DickE

Delight in Disorder. Robert Herrick. CP-HerrR

Delight is as the flight. Emily Dickinson. CP-DickE

Delight it is in youth and May. A. E. Housman. CP-HousA

Delight of Being Alone. D. H. Lawrence. CP-LawrD

Delight of human[e] kind, and gods above. Beginning of the First Book, The [Address to Venus]. Lucretius. CP-DryJ2 *Fr.* De Rerum Natura (On the Nature of Things).

Delight of Solitariness, The. Sir Philip Sidney. SP-SidnP *Fr.* Arcadia.

Delighted with Bluepink. Kenneth Patchen. CP-PatcK

Delightful Evening. Wallace Stevens. CP-StevW; CP-StevWP

Delight's Despair at setting. Emily Dickinson. CP-DickE

Delights of our childhood is soon passed away, The. Old Man's Memory, An. James Whitcomb Riley. CP-RileJ

Delilah. Rudyard Kipling. CP-KiplR

(We have another Viceroy now,—those days are dead and done.) CP-KiplR

Delilah. Primo Levi. CP-LeviP, *tr. by* Ruth Feldman

Delilah Aberyswith was a lady—not too young. Delilah. Rudyard Kipling. CP-KiplR

Delinquent. Langston Hughes. CP-HughL; CP-HughL3

Delinquent, The. Paul Laurence Dunbar. CP-DunbP

Delinquent Travellers, The. Samuel Taylor Coleridge. CP-ColeS

Delirium. Federico García Lorca. CP-GarcF, *tr. by* Jerome Rothenberg *Fr.* Six Songs at Nightfall.

Deliverance. Robert Graves. CP-GravR

Deliverance from a Fit of Fainting. Anne Bradstreet. CP-BradA

Delivered out of raw continual pain. St. Peter and the Angel. Denise Levertov. SP-LeveDS

Delivery to the Secular Arm, The: A Scene During the Existence of the Spanish Inquisition at Antwerp, 1570. Robert Browning. CP-BroR2

Della Primavera Transportata al Morale. William Carlos Williams. CP-WilW1

Dellius, that car which, night and day. Carmen Circulare. Rudyard Kipling. CP-KiplR *Fr.* Muse among the Motors, The.

Delphi. "H. D." CP-DoolH

Delphic Oracle upon Plotinus, The. William Butler Yeats. CP-YeatW

Delphinium flings a shadow, A. Out of the Rainbow End. Carl Sandburg. CP-SandC

Delphiniums are born. Crossed Numbers. Carl Sandburg. CP-SandC

Delta. Eugenio Montale. CP-MontE, *tr. by* Jonathan Galassi

Delta. Adrienne Rich. SP-RicA1

Delta Poems. Muriel Rukeyser. CP-RukeM

Deluded mortals, whom the great. Libel on the Reverend Dr. Delany and His Excellency John, Lord Carteret. Jonathan Swift. CP-SwifJ

Deluge, The. Robert Herrick. CP-HerrR

Deluge, The. W. S. Merwin. SP-MerwWF

Deluge, The ("Though giant rains put out the sun"). G. K. Chesterton. CP-ChesG

Deluge, The ("When dark and deafening skies are bowed"). G. K. Chesterton. CP-ChesG

Delusion?—No! Robert Penn Warren. CP-WarrR

Delusion of Saints. Robinson Jeffers. CP-JefR2

Dely. Paul Laurence Dunbar. CP-DunbP

Dem good old days done past and gone. My White Bread. James Whitcomb Riley. CP-RileJ

Demand. Langston Hughes. CP-HughL; CP-HughL1

Demands of Exile. Andrei Codrescu. SP-CodrA

Demeter. Olga Broumas. SP-BrouO

Demeter. "H. D." CP-DoolH

Demeter devastated our good land. Appeasement of Demeter, The. George Meredith. CP-MerG1

Demi-Exile. Howth. Donald Davie. CP-DaviDC

Demiurge. D. H. Lawrence. CP-LawrD

Demiurge's Laugh, The. Robert Frost. CP-FrosR

Democracy. Langston Hughes. *See* Freedom ("Freedom will not come")

Democracy. D. H. Lawrence. CP-LawrD

Democracy. Arthur Rimbaud. CP-RimbA, *tr. by* Martin Sorrell

Democracy. John Greenleaf Whittier. CP-WhitJ

Democracy Is Serivce. D. H. Lawrence. CP-LawrD

Democracy will not come. Langston Hughes. *See* Freedom will not come

Democratic Order, The: Such Things in Twenty Years I Understood. Alice Walker. CP-WalkA

Democrats. Donald Davie. CP-DaviDC

Democritus laughed when he. Correspondences. Muriel Rukeyser. CP-RukeM

Demolition Report. Jaroslav Seifert. SP-SeifJ, *tr. by* Ewald Osers

Demon. Anne Sexton. CP-SextA

Demon and Beast. William Butler Yeats. CP-YeatW

Demon Justice. D. H. Lawrence. CP-LawrD

Demon Lover, The. Adrienne Rich. CP-RicAE; SP-RicA1; SP-RicA2

Demon of Analogy, The. Stéphane Mallarmé. CP-MallS, *tr. by* Henry Weinfield

Demon of the Study, The. John Greenleaf Whittier. CP-WhitJ

Demon Smoke. Tennessee Williams. CP-WillT

Demon who throughout our late estrangement, The. This Holy Month. Robert Graves. CP-GravR

Demonstration. Langston Hughes. CP-HughL; CP-HughL3

Demonstration. Kenneth Patchen. CP-PatcK

Demonstration, The. Gregory Orr. SP-OrrG

Demos. Edwin Arlington Robinson. CP-RobiE

Demure apothecary / Whose early reverend genius my young eye. S. R. Ralph Waldo Emerson. CP-EmerR

Denial, A. Elizabeth Barrett Browning. CP-BroEB

Denial—is the only fact. Emily Dickinson. CP-DickE

Denial[l]. George Herbert. CP-HerbG

Deniall in Women No Disheartning to Men. Robert Herrick. CP-HerrR

Denied night's face / have shadowless they? E. E. Cummings. CP-CummE

Denis, / Whose motionable, alert, most vaulting wit. Gerard Manley Hopkins. CP-HopkG

Denner's Old Woman. Vincent Bourne. CP-CowpW

Dennis Shand. Dante Gabriel Rossetti. CW-RossD

Dennis Was Very Sick. Yehuda Amichai. SP-AmicYL, *tr. by* Benjamin Harshav *and* Barbara Harshav

Denomination. Heather McHugh. SP-McHuH

Denouement. Sylvia Plath. CP-PlatS

Dense dark day, two sun chairs. Held Breath, A. James Schuyler. CP-SchuJ

Dense fog shuts down. Privacy. Kenneth Rexroth. CP-RexrK

Dense icon of time's passing: hyacinth. On Jan van Huysum's *Vase of Flowers* (1722) in the J. Paul Getty Museum. Helen Pinkerton. CP-PinkH

Dense, low, irregular overcast is flowing rapidly in over the city from the middle South, A. Storm, The. C. K. Williams. SP-WillC

Dense ravine, no inch, A. Portola Valley. Amy Clampitt. CP-ClamA

Denver tower blocks group'd under gray haze. Flying Elegy. Allen Ginsberg. CP-GinsA

Deny yourself all. Thoughtful Lover, The. William Carlos Williams. CP-WilW2

Departed Child! I could forget thee once. Maternal Grief. William Wordsworth. CP-WorW1

Departed, The. Donald Davie. CP-DaviDC

Departed—to the Judgment. Emily Dickinson. CP-DickE

Departing summer hath assumed. September, 1819. William Wordsworth. CP-WorW2

Departmental. Robert Frost. CP-FrosR

Departure. Louise Glück. SP-GlucL

Departure. Thomas Hardy. CP-HardT

Departure. Langston Hughes. CP-HughL; CP-HughL3

Departure. D. H. Lawrence. CP-LawrD

Departure. Edna St. Vincent Millay. CP-MillE

Departure. Sylvia Plath. CP-PlatS

Departure. Rainer Maria Rilke. CP-RilkFr, tr. by A. Poulin, Jr.

Departure. Arthur Rimbaud. CP-RimbA, tr. by Martin Sorrell

Departure. Charles Tomlinson. CP-TomlC

Departure. Robert Penn Warren. CP-WarrR

Departure, A. Rudyard Kipling. CP-KiplR Fr. Land and Sea Tales.

Departure, The. Henry David Thoreau. CP-ThorH

Departure, The. Jones Very. CP-VeryJ

Departure from Hydra, The. Kenneth Koch. SP-KochK

Departure from the Bush. Margaret Atwood. SP-AtwM1

Departure from the Vale of Grasmere. August, 1803. William Wordsworth. CP-WorW1

Departure of the Good Daemon, The. Robert Herrick. CP-HerrR

Departure of the Ships. Howard Nemerov. CP-NemeH

Departure Platforms. Thomas Kinsella. CP-KinsT

Departures 1. Yannis Ritsos. SP-RitsY, tr. by N. C. Germanacos

Departures 2. Yannis Ritsos. SP-RitsY, tr. by N. C. Germanacos

Departures 3. Yannis Ritsos. SP-RitsY, tr. by N. C. Germanacos

Departure's Girl-Friend. W. S. Merwin. SP-MerwW

Dependence . . . the male. Demeter. Olga Broumas. SP-BrouO

Dependencies, The. Howard Nemerov. CP-NemeH

Deploratioun of the Deith of Quene Magdalene, The. Sir David Lyndsay. SP-LyndD

Deposition from Love, A. Thomas Carew. CP-CareT

Deposition, The. Howard Nemerov. CP-NemeH

Depravity: Two Sermons. Donald Davie. CP-DaviDC

Depressed by a Book of Bad Poetry, I Walk toward an Unused Pasture and Invite the Insects to Join Me. James Wright. CP-WrigJ

Depression before Spring. Wallace Stevens. CP-StevW; CP-StevWP

Depression, the War, and Gypsy Rose Lee, The. Wyatt Prunty. SP-PrunW

Depression Years. Lorine Niedecker. CP-NiedL

Deprivation. Thomas McGrath. SP-McGrT

Deprived like the cougar. Cougar. A. R. Ammons. CP-AmmoA

Deprived of learning and. Catherine of Alexandria. Rita Dove. SP-DoveR

Deprived of other Banquet. Emily Dickinson. CP-DickE

Deprived though we were of your climatic privileges. Camus in Ulster. Derek Mahon. CP-MahoD

Dept. of Philosophy. Hans Magnus Enzensberger. SP-EnzeH

Depth of Field, A. Norman Dubie. CP-DubiN

Depth of Love. Robert Graves. CP-GravR

Depths, The. Ivor Gurney. SP-GurnI

Depths, The. Denise Levertov. SP-LeveDP

Der Abschied. May Sarton. SP-SartM

Derbyshire. Donald Davie. CP-DaviDC

Derbyshire Turf. Donald Davie. CP-DaviDC

Derelict, The. Rudyard Kipling. CP-KiplR

Derelict who lives on our street, The. Poem in New York. Gregory Orr. SP-OrrG

Derne. John Greenleaf Whittier. CP-WhitJ

Derry Morning. Derek Mahon. CP-MahoD

Dervish at the Door. Jelaluddin Rumi. SP-Rumi, tr. by Coleman Barks

Dervish—(though yet un-dervished, call him so). Eagle, The. Robert Browning. CP-BroR2

Dervish whined to *Said*, The. Ralph Waldo Emerson. CP-EmerR

Descartes. Jorge Luis Borges. SP-BorgJ, tr. by Alastair Reid

Descartes and the Stove. Charles Tomlinson. CP-TomlC; SP-TomlC

Descend O radiant God!—the plains are thirsting. Evening, after a Picture. Johann Christoph Friedrich von Schiller. CP-MerG2

Descend, ye Nine! descend and sing. Ode for Music on St. Cecilia's Day. Alexander Pope. CP-PopeA

Descendant of Solomon and the Queen of Sheba. Clarence Major. SP-MajoC

Descendants of the Puritans! whose fame. Conclusion: "Descendants of the Puritans! whose fame." Jones Very. CP-VeryJ

Descended of an ancient line. Ode 3.29: To Maecenas. Horace. CP-DryJ2, tr. by John Dryden Fr. Odes.

Descending Figure. Louise Glück. SP-GlucL

Descending from the sky I see Aurora. Petrarch. CP-Petra, tr. by J. G. Nichols

Descending hillsides in. Across Lamarck Col. Gary Snyder. CP-SnydG

Descending out of the grey. Elephant Trunk. Louis MacNeice. CP-MacNL

Descent. Peter Blue Cloud. SP-BlueP

Descent. Ted Hughes. SP-HughTN

Descent. Yannis Ritsos. SP-RitsY, tr. by Kostas Myrsiades

Descent. Tennessee Williams. CP-WillT

Descent. William Carlos Williams. CP-WilW2

Descent, The. William Carlos Williams. CP-WilW2

Descent beckons, The. Descent, The. William Carlos Williams. CP-WilW2

Descent from the Cross, The. Christina Georgina Rossetti. CP-RosC2

Descent Into Hades. Kathleen Jessie Raine. SP-RainK

Descent into Hell. Robert Graves. CP-GravR

Descent into the Hours of the Peregrine. Norman Dubie. CP-DubiN

Descent of Mr. Aldez, The. John Updike. CP-UpdiJ

Descent of Odin, The. Thomas Gray. CP-GrayT

Descent of Winter, The. William Carlos Williams. CP-WilW1

Deschutes River. Raymond Carver. CP-CarvR

Describe: The Rain on Dasaswamedh Ghat. Allen Ginsberg. CP-GinsA; SP-GinsA

Describes the Rolling Meadows Club but things are slipping. Gracious Living. James Laughlin. CP-LaugJ

Describing circle after circle. Kite, The. Aleksandr Aleksandrovich Blok. SP-BlokA, tr. by Peter France and Jon Stallworthy

Descripcion; of a Woman, The. Robert Herrick. CP-HerrR

Description. Charles Simic. SP-SimiC; SP-SimiCE

Description in Answer to *The Journal*, A. William Percival. "As for himself, with draggled gown." CP-SherT

Description of a City Shower, A. Jonathan Swift. CP-SwifJ

Description of a Maske: Presented in the Banqueting Roome at *Whitehall*, on Saint Stephens Night Last, at the Marriage of the Right Honourable the Earle of *Somerset*: and the Right Noble the Lady FRANCES *Howard*. Thomas Campion. CP-CampT

Description of a Religious House and Condition of Life. Richard Crashaw. CP-CrasR

Description of a Salamander, The. Jonathan Swift. CP-SwifJ

Description of an Irish Feast, The. Hugh MacGowran. CP-SwifJ, tr. by Jonathan Swift

Description of an Irish Feast, The. Jonathan Swift. CP-SwifJ

Description of Doctor Delany's Villa, A. Thomas Sheridan. CP-SherT

Description of Love, A. Sir Walter Ralegh. CP-RaleW

Description of Mother Ludwell's Cave, A. Jonathan Swift. CP-SwifJ

Description of Some Confederate Soldiers, A. Randall Jarrell. CP-JarrR

Description of the Contrarious Passions in a Lover. Petrarch. CP-WyatT, tr. by Sir Thomas Wyatt Fr. Sonnets to Laura.

Description of the Morning, A. Jonathan Swift. CP-SwifJ

Description of the sensuous, A. Question, The. Robert Creeley. CP-CreeR

Description, Speeches, and Songs, of the Lords Maske, Presented in the Banquetting-House on the Marriage Night of the High and Mightie Count Palatine, *and the Royally Descended the Ladie* ELISABETH. Thomas Campion. *See* Lords Mask[e], The

Description without Place. Wallace Stevens. CP-StevW; CP-StevWP

Descriptions of Imaginary Poetries. Robert Duncan. SP-DuncR

Descriptive Sketches Taken During a Pedestrian Tour among the Alps. William Wordsworth. CP-WorW1

Desdain. Sir John Suckling. CP-SuckJ

Desdain. Sir John Suckling. CP-SuckJ

Desdichada. Muriel Rukeyser. SP-RukeM

Desecraters, The. G. K. Chesterton. CP-ChesG

Desecration of the Gravestone of Rose P. Robert Pinsky. CP-PinsR

Desert. Langston Hughes. CP-HughL; CP-HughL2

Desert, The. Jones Very. CP-VeryJ

Desert as Garden of Paradise, The. Adrienne Rich. SP-RicA1

Desert Autumn. Charles Tomlinson. CP-TomlC

Desert Deportation of 1915, The. Norman Dubie. CP-DubiN

Desert dreamer, telepathic. Man Who Carries the Desert Around Inside Himself, The: For Wally. Yusef Komunyakaa. CP-KomuY

Desert Fringe. Robert Graves. CP-GravR

Desert moves out on half the horizon, The. Supper after the Last, The. Galway Kinnell. SP-KinnGN

Desert Music, The. William Carlos Williams. CP-WilW2

Desert of weed and water-darkened stone under my western windows, A. People and a Heron. Robinson Jeffers. CP-JefR1

Desert Parable. Eleanor Wilner. SP-WilnE

Desert Places. Robert Frost. CP-FrosR

Desert Storm. William Corbett. SP-CorbW

Desert vulture / jealousy, The. George Meredith. CP-MerG2

Desert Wasn't Loved Enough said Reich, The. Grace Paley. CP-PalGC

Deserted Garden, The. Elizabeth Barrett Browning. CP-BroEB

Deserted harbour stillness. Every stone. Seamus Heaney. SP-HeanSO Fr. Squarings.

Deserted Plantation, The. Paul Laurence Dunbar. CP-DunbP

Deserter, The. A. E. Housman. CP-HousA

Deserter, The. Stevie Smith. CP-SmitS

Deserts of Love, The. Arthur Rimbaud. CP-RimbA, *tr. by* Martin Sorrell

Design. Billy Collins. SP-CollB

Design. Robert Frost. CP-FrosR

Design for November. William Carlos Williams. CP-WilW2

Design in Living Colors. Adrienne Rich. CP-RicAE

Design of a House, The. Wendell Berry. CP-BerrW

Designed by Mikhail Kalashnikov, who, if alive. Kalashnikov. Thomas Lux. SP-LuxT

Designs. Andrei Codrescu. SP-CodrA

Desire. Samuel Taylor Coleridge. CP-ColeS

Desire. Langston Hughes. CP-HughL; CP-HughL2

Desire. D. H. Lawrence. CP-LawrD

Desire. Federico García Lorca. CP-GarcF, *tr. by* Catherine Brown

Desire / The. The. Louis Zukofsky. CP-ZukLS

Desire, alas, my master and my foe. Sir Thomas Wyatt. CP-WyatT

Desire and act were a combination known as sin. Sheffield Ghazal 5: Passing the Cemetary. Galway Kinnell. SP-KinnGN

Desire and Possession. Jonathan Swift. CP-SwifJ

Desire & the Object. Wallace Stevens. CP-StevWP

Desire, first, by a natural miracle. Snapped Thread, The. Robert Graves. CP-GravR

Desire for Oblivion. Charles Baudelaire. CP-BaudC, *tr. by* Walter Martin

Desire for Spring. Kenneth Koch. SP-KochK

Desire Goes Down into the Sea. D. H. Lawrence. CP-LawrD

Desire has failed, desire has failed. Grasshopper Is a Burden. D. H. Lawrence. CP-LawrD

Desire Is a World by Night. John Berryman. CP-BerrJ

Desire Is Dead. D. H. Lawrence. CP-LawrD

Desire no bread, forsake the guest hall of the earth. Hafiz. CP-EmerR *Fr.* Odes.

Desire of a Statue. Federico García Lorca. SP-GarcF, *tr. by* W. S. Merwin

Desire to Make Love in a Pagoda, The. Wallace Stevens. CP-StevWP

Desire to sorrow doth me constrain. Sir Thomas Wyatt. CP-WyatT

Desire to us. Desire. Langston Hughes. CP-HughL; CP-HughL2

Desire was a quotation from someone. Michael Palmer. SP-PalmM

Desire weaves its fantasy of dreams. Spring for Lovers. Langston Hughes. CP-HughL; CP-HughL1

Desired as Summer rain. George Meredith. CP-MerG2

Desires. Constantine P. Cavafy. CP-CavaC, *tr. by* Theoharis Constantine Theoharis

Desires of Men and Women. John Berryman. CP-BerrJ

Desmond, what of the blue nights. Sea in Winter, The. Derek Mahon. CP-MahoD

Desolate and lone. Lost. Carl Sandburg. CP-SandC

Desolate Field, The. William Carlos Williams. CP-WilW1

Desolate lemons, hold. Sunday Lemons. Derek Walcott. CP-WalcD

Desolate Light. Denise Levertov. SP-LeveDL

Desolation. Wendell Berry. CP-BerrW

Desolation, A. Allen Ginsberg. CP-GinsA

Desolation Dreamed Of. Edna St. Vincent Millay. CP-MillE

Despair. John Berryman. CP-BerrJ

Despair. Samuel Taylor Coleridge. CP-ColeS

Despair. Paul Laurence Dunbar. CP-DunbP

Despair. Richard Eberhart. CP-EberR

Despair. Christina Georgina Rossetti. CP-RosC3

Despair. Anne Sexton. CP-SextA

Despair, anger, grief. Black Java Pepper. Arthur Sze. SP-SzeA

Despair is big with friends I love. Consequences. William Meredith. SP-MereW

Despaire takes heart, when ther's no hope to speed. Fear[e] Gets Force. Robert Herrick. CP-HerrR

Despairing Man Draws a Serpent, The. Pablo Antonio Cuadra. CP-MertT

Despairing of Understanding We Fall Into Decadence. Miller Williams. CP-WillM

Despair's advantage is achieved. Emily Dickinson. CP-DickE

Desperate, at last I stand. At Bay. James Whitcomb Riley. CP-RileJ

Desperate Vitality, A. Pier Paolo Pasolini. SP-PasoP, *tr. by* Norman MacAfee *and* Luciano Martinengo

Desperate young man. Halfworld, The. William Carlos Williams. CP-WilW1

Desperation. Constantine P. Cavafy. CP-CavaC, *tr. by* Theoharis Constantine Theoharis

Despisals. Muriel Rukeyser. CP-RukeM

Despised and Rejected. Christina Georgina Rossetti. CP-RosC1

Despite all the gypsum. Ghazal of Marvelous Love. Federico García Lorca. CP-GarcF, *tr. by* Catherine Brown *Fr.* Ghazals.

Despite and Still. Robert Graves. CP-GravR

Despite his name, the dog's. Spot in Space and Time. Heather McHugh. SP-McHuH

Despite its being invisible, a ghost has enough mass. Black Cat. Paul Muldoon. CP-MuldP

Despite our infractions. Story, A. Rae Armantrout. SP-ArmaA

Despite that it is summer and the sun. Alf Burt, Tenant Farmer. Robert Penn Warren. CP-WarrR

Despite the lonesome look. On the London Train. John Berryman. CP-BerrJ

Despite the Plainness of the Day. David Ignatow. SP-IgnaD

Despite the sky that is still. Some Perfume. Rainer Maria Rilke. CP-RilkFr, *tr. by* A. Poulin, Jr.

Despite the times, the tedious self. Never Apologize for Poetry. Eleanor Wilner. SP-WilnE

Despite this learned cult's official. Apollo of the Physiologists. Robert Graves. CP-GravR

Despoiled and machine-honed as I am, I guess. Poem Written on the Typewriter. Robert Stock. SP-StocR

Despoiled of speech, defended poorly by birds. Dear Mr. Worldly Wiseman. Robert Stock. SP-StocR

Despondency, an Ode. Robert Burns. CP-BurnR

Desponding Father! Mark This Altered Bough. William Wordsworth. CP-WorW2

Desponding Phyllis was endued. Phyllis [or Phillis] [or Progress of Love, The]. Jonathan Swift. CP-SwifJ

Despots of Manchester, Oligarchs! George Meredith. CP-MerG2

Destination: Accomplished. Jay Wright. SP-WrigJ

Destination Zero. Sam Hamill. SP-HamiS

Destined lover, whom his stars, The. Lover's Stars, The. Gerard Manley Hopkins. CP-HopkG

Destined Pair, The. Thomas Hardy. CP-HardT

Destined to great things, he lies on his belly and confidently. Pages in an Album. Dan Pagis. SP-PagiD, *tr. by* Stephen Mitchell

Destined to war from very infancy. Gabriello Chiabrera. CP-WorW1

Destiny. D. H. Lawrence. CP-LawrD

Destiny of Nations, The. Samuel Taylor Coleridge. CP-ColeS

Destroyers. Carl Sandburg. CP-SandC

Destroyers, The. Rudyard Kipling. CP-KiplR

Destroying Angel, The. Paul Muldoon. CP-MuldP

Destroying Beauty. Charles Bukowski. SP-BukC2

Destruction of Carthage, The. Kenneth Patchen. CP-PatcK

Destruction of Grief. Muriel Rukeyser. CP-RukeM

Destruction of Public Property by Mobs, The. Jones Very. CP-VeryJ

Destruction of Sennacherib, The. Lord Byron. CP-Byron

Destruction of the Bastile. Samuel Taylor Coleridge. CP-ColeS

Desultory Days. Robert Creeley. SP-CreeR

Detached, The. Maya Angelou. SP-AngeM

Detachment, Wisdom and Compassion. Philip Whalen. SP-WhalP

Detail. William Carlos Williams. CP-WilW2

Detail. William Carlos Williams. CP-WilW2

Detail. William Carlos Williams. CP-WilW2

Detail. William Carlos Williams. CP-WilW2

Details for Paterson. William Carlos Williams. CP-WilW2

Detective Story. W. H. Auden. CP-AudeW

Detective, The. Ai. SP-Ai

Detective, The. Sylvia Plath. CP-PlatS

Detectives from the vice squad. Café: 3 a.m. Langston Hughes. CP-HughL; CP-HughL3

Deterioration. Yannis Ritsos. SP-RitsY, *tr. by* Kimon Friar

Detestable race, continue to expunge yourself, die out. Apostrophe to Man. Edna St. Vincent Millay. CP-MillE

Detraction Execrated. Sir John Suckling. CP-SuckJ

Detroit Grease Shop Poem. Philip Levine. SP-LeviP

Deuks Dang o'er My Daddie, The. Robert Burns. CP-BurnR

Deutsch ueber Freud. Randall Jarrell. CP-JarrR

Deutzia. Louis Zukofsky. CP-ZukLS

Devastating flame of that fierce plague, The. Canzone: He laments the Presumption and Incontinence of his Youth. Guido Cavalcanti. CW-RossD, *tr. by* Dante Gabriel Rossetti

Developing. / Forty-five years developing. Birthday. Yehuda Amichai. SP-AmicYL, *tr. by* Benjamin Harshav *and* Barbara Harshav

Development. Robert Browning. CP-BroR2

Development, The. Marge Piercy. SP-PierM *Fr.* Sand Roads.

Devil As Friend, The. Laura Riding Jackson. CP-RidiL

Devil believes that the Lord will come, The. Two Round Spaces on the Tombstone, The. Samuel Taylor Coleridge. CP-ColeS

Devil crept in eden wood. E. E. Cummings. CP-CummE

Devil got notice that GROSE was a-dying, The. Epigram on Capt. Francis Grose, the Celebrated Antiquary. Robert Burns. CP-BurnR

Devil, had he fidelity, The. Emily Dickinson. CP-DickE

Devil is a gentleman, and asks you down to stay, The. Aristocrat, The. G. K. Chesterton. CP-ChesG

Devil-My-Wife, The. Stevie Smith. CP-SmitS

Devil on Ice. Donald Davie. CP-DaviDC

Devil return'd to hell by two, The. Devil's Drive, The. Lord Byron. CP-Byron

Devilish and the dark, the dying and diseas'd, The. Rounded Catalogue Divine Complete, The. Walt Whitman. CP-WhitW

Devil's Advice to Story-Tellers, The. Robert Graves. CP-GravR

Devil's Dictionary, The. Ambrose Bierce.

   Egotist. SP-BierA

   Elegy: "Cur foretells the knell of parting day, The." SP-BierA

   Freedom. SP-BierA

   Orthography. SP-BierA

Devil's Drive, The. Lord Byron. CP-Byron

Devil's Thoughts, The. Samuel Taylor Coleridge. CP-ColeS

Devil's Walk, The. Percy Bysshe Shelley. CP-ShelP

Devine philosopher to thee tis given. On Reading Dr Beaties Hermit. Annis Boudinot Stockton. CP-StocA

Devising. A. R. Ammons. CP-AmmoA

Devonshire. Donald Davie. CP-DaviDC

Devonshire Road, A. Samuel Taylor Coleridge. CP-ColeS

Devoted to the compost pile. Crosswords. Wyatt Prunty. SP-PrunW

Devotee's Complaint, A. A. K. Ramanujan. CP-RamaA

Devotion. Robert Frost. CP-FrosR

Devotion. Dan Pagis. SP-PagiD, tr. by Stephen Mitchell

Devotion, A. Kenneth Patchen. CP-PatcK

Devotion, I had thought, to my vocation. From Wherever I Am. Robert Stock. SP-StocR

Devotion Makes the Deity. Robert Herrick. CP-HerrR

Devotion should always wear a fence. Emily Dickinson. SP-DickE

Devotion: That It Flow; That There Be Concentration. Tess Gallagher. SP-GallT

Devotional Incitements. William Wordsworth. CP-WorW2

Devotions. Arthur Rimbaud. CP-RimbA, tr. by Martin Sorrell

Devotions. Charles Simic. SP-SimiCE

Devotions. James Wright. CP-WrigJ

Dew. And I lay with you, you, in the trash. Paul Celan. SP-CelaP, tr. by John Felstiner

Dew in the morning, dust at noon. Barefoot Homiletics, after Wittgenstein and Boswell. Alan Dugan. CP-DugaA

Dew—is the Freshet in the Grass. Emily Dickinson. CP-DickE

Dew Sat on Julia's Hair. Robert Herrick. CP-HerrR

   (Upon Julia's Haire Fill'd with Dew.) CP-HerrR

Dew suffced itself, A. Emily Dickinson. CP-DickE

Dew, the rain and moonlight, The. Net to Snare the Moonlight, A. Nicholas Vachel Lindsay. CP-LindV

Dew was falling fast, the stars began to blink, The. Pet Lamb, The; A Pastoral. William Wordsworth. CP-WorW1

Dews drop slowly and dreams gather: unknown spears, The. Valley of the Black Pig, The. William Butler Yeats. CP-YeatW

Dexery-Tethery! down in the dike. Wrangdillion, A. James Whitcomb Riley. CP-RileJ

Dexter Gordon's tenor sax. February in Sydney. Yusef Komunyakaa. CP-KomuY

Dey been speakin' at de cou't-house. Speakin' at de Cou't-House. Paul Laurence Dunbar. CP-DunbP

Dey had a gread big pahty down to Tom's de othah night. Party, The. Paul Laurence Dunbar. CP-DunbP

Dey is snow upon de meddahs. Snowin'. Paul Laurence Dunbar. CP-DunbP

Dey is times in life when Nature. When de Co'n Pone's Hot. Paul Laurence Dunbar. CP-DunbP

Dey was oncet a awful quoil. Trouble in de Kitchen. Paul Laurence Dunbar. CP-DunbP

Dey was talkin' in de cabin, dey was talkin' in de hall. When Dey 'Listed Colored Soldiers. Paul Laurence Dunbar. CP-DunbP

Dey's a so't o' threatenin' feelin' in de blowin' of de breeze. Soliloquy of a Turkey. Paul Laurence Dunbar. CP-DunbP

Dezembrum. Wallace Stevens. CP-StevW; CP-StevWP

Dharma. Billy Collins. SP-CollB

Dharma Youth League, The. Philip Whalen. SP-WhalP

Dharmakaya. Philip Whalen. SP-WhalP

Diabetes. James Dickey. CP-DickJ

Diagnosis is / Anxiety psychoneurosis, The. Hayden Carruth. CP-CarHS Fr. Bloomingdale Papers, The.

Diagonal white city dreamed by a Frenchman. Washington. John Updike. CP-UpdiJ

Diagram. Robinson Jeffers. CP-JefR3

Diagram of Abandoned Mosque. Olga Broumas. SP-BrouO

Diagrams. Thom Gunn. CP-GunnT

Dial Tone, The. Howard Nemerov. CP-NemeH

Dialectic. Charles Tomlinson. CP-TomlC

Dialectical Songs. Howard Nemerov. CP-NemeH

Dialog betwix Experience and ane Courteour, Ane. Sir David Lyndsay.

   Epistill, The: "Thou, lytil quair, of mater miserabyll." SP-LyndD

   Exclamatioun to the Redar, Tuycheyng the Wryttyng of Vulgare and Maternall Language, Ane. SP-LyndD

   Heir endis the Prologe. And beginnis the Mater. SP-LyndD

   Prologe, The: "Musing and marvelling on the miserie." SP-LyndD

Dialogue. John Ciardi. CP-CiarJ

Dialogue. Howard Nemerov. CP-NemeH

Dialogue. Adrienne Rich. SP-RicA2

Dialogue. Carl Sandburg. CP-SandC

Dialogue. Jaroslav Seifert. SP-SeifJ, tr. by Ewald Osers

Dialogue. Charles Tomlinson. CP-TomlC

Dialogue. Marya Alexandrovna Zaturenska. SP-ZatuM

Dialogue, A. George Herbert. CP-HerbG

Dialogue, A. Alexander Pope. CP-PopeA

Dialogue, A. Percy Bysshe Shelley. CP-ShelP

Dialogue-Anthem, A. George Herbert. CP-HerbG

Dialogue between an Eminent Lawyer and Dr. Swift, Dean of St. Patrick's. Jonathan Swift. CP-SwifJ

Dialogue between Captain Tom and Sir Henry Dutton Colt, A. Jonathan Swift. CP-SwifJ

Dialogue between Death and Mrs A. Mrs. Austen. CP-AustJ

Dialogue between Father and Daughter. Robert Browning. CP-BroR2

Dialogue between Ghost and Priest. Sylvia Plath. CP-PlatS

Dialogue between Old England and New, A. Anne Bradstreet. CP-BradA

Dialogue between Soul and Body, A. Randall Jarrell. CP-JarrR

Dialogue Between The Resolved Soul and Created Pleasure, A. Andrew Marvell. CP-MarvA

Dialogue between the Soul and [the] Body, A. Andrew Marvell. CP-MarvA

Dialogue between Thyrsis and Dorinda, A. Andrew Marvell. CP-MarvA

Dialogue Betwixt Himselfe and Mistresse Eliza: Wheeler, Under the Name of Amarillis, A. Robert Herrick. CP-HerrR

Dialogue En Route. Sylvia Plath. CP-PlatS

Dialogue Entitled the Kind Master and Dutiful Servant, A. Jupiter Hammon. CP-WheaP

Dialogue in the Shade, A. John Ciardi. CP-CiarJ

Dialogue of Amargo. Federico García Lorca. CP-GarcF, tr. by Christopher Maurer

Dialogue of Self and Soul, A. William Butler Yeats. CP-YeatW

Dialogue of Watching, A. Kenneth Rexroth. CP-RexrK

Dialogue on the Headland. Robert Graves. CP-GravR

Dialogue with La Mettrie, A. John Logan. CP-LoganJ

Dialogue with Outer Space. John Ciardi. CP-CiarJ

Dialysis. Lucille Clifton. SP-ClifL

Diameter of the bomb was thirty centimeters, The. Yehuda Amichai. SP-AmicY, tr. by Chana Bloch

Diamond. Federico García Lorca. CP-GarcF, tr. by Catherine Brown

Diamond Cutters, The. Adrienne Rich. CP-RicAE; SP-RicA1; SP-RicA2

Diamond of a star, The. Diamond. Federico García Lorca. CP-GarcF, tr. by Catherine Brown

Diamond on the Hand, A. Emily Dickinson. CP-DickE

Diamond or a coal? / A diamond, if you please, A. Christina Georgina Rossetti. CP-RosC2

Diamond Persona, The. Norman Dubie. CP-DubiN

Diamond Point, The. Arthur Sze. SP-SzeA

Diamonds on Liz's Bosom, The. Alice Walker. CP-WalkA

Diamonds or broken saucepans interchangeable. Tiger. Josephine Jacobsen. CP-JacoJ

Diana did not more delight her lover. Petrarch. CP-Petra, tr. by J. G. Nichols

Diana sleeping under the flowering apple tree. Theme from Louise Labé, A. Marya Alexandrovna Zaturenska. SP-ZatuM

Diana, sum us in faith a. Catullus. See Moving in her radiant care

Diapason of fragrances. East. Federico García Lorca. CP-GarcF, tr. by Jerome Rothenberg Fr. Cross.

Diapason of moon. West. Federico García Lorca. CP-GarcF, tr. by Jerome Rothenberg Fr. Cross.

Diaries of Death. Charles Olson. CP-OlsoC

Diary Entry. John Ciardi. CP-CiarJ

Diaspora. W. H. Auden. CP-AudeW

Diatribe Against the Old Gods. Clement of Alexandria.

   Idol of Sarapis, The. CP-MertT

   Priests of the Old Gods, The. CP-MertT

   Zeus Is Dead. CP-MertT

Diatribe of the Kite, The. Norman Dubie. CP-DubiN

Dichtung und Wahrheit. W. H. Auden. CP-AudeW

Dick, a Maggot. Jonathan Swift. CP-SwifJ

Dick King. Thomas Kinsella. CP-KinsT

Dick Mid's large bluish face without eyebrows. E. E. Cummings. CP-CummE

Dick, thou'rt resolved, as I am told. First Ode of the Second Book of Horace Paraphrased and Addressed to Richard Steele, Esq, The. Jonathan Swift. CP-SwifJ

Dick's Variety. Jonathan Swift. CP-SwifJ

"Dicky the Stick"—. Robert Creeley. CP-CreeR

Dicky was hurt. Yehuda Amichai. SP-AmicYL *Fr.* Elegies on the War Dead.

Dictic. One Word as the Complete Poem. Charles Olson. CP-OlsoC

Diction. Robert Creeley. CP-CreeR

Dictum. Countee Cullen. CP-CullC

Did all the lets and bars appear. March into Virginia, The. Herman Melville. SP-MelvH

Did any bird come flying. Bird or Beast? Christina Georgina Rossetti. CP-RosC1

Did Cytherea to the skies. On a Bath. Plato. CP-CowpW

Did ever problem thus perplex. Problem, The. Jonathan Swift. CP-SwifJ

Did Fear and Danger so perplex your Mind. On Messrs Hussey and Coffin. Phillis Wheatley. CP-WheaP

Did he imagine that her letters. Her Letters. James Laughlin. CP-LaugJ

Did he who drew her in the years ago. To an Imposter of Rosalind. Thomas Hardy. CP-HardT

Did Helen steal my love from me? Gerard Manley Hopkins. CP-HopkG

Did I believe I had a clear mind? Breaking. Wendell Berry. CP-BerrW

Did I fulfill what I had to, here, on earth? One More Contradiction. Czeslaw Milosz. CP-MiloCN, *tr. by* Robert Hass

Did I? Is it? ID. Heather McHugh. SP-McHuH

Did I mistake the house or the street. Album of Dreams. Czeslaw Milosz. CP-MiloCN, *tr. by* Lawrence Davis

Did I not *once* have a pleasant childhood, heroic and fabulous. Morning. Arthur Rimbaud. CP-RimbA, *tr. by* Martin Sorrell

Did I or love, or could I others draw. To His Honoured Friend, M. John Weare, Councellour. Robert Herrick. CP-HerrR

Did I see a crucifix in your eyes. Crimson Changes People. Carl Sandburg. CP-SandC

Did I see it go by. Wish to Comply, A. Robert Frost. CP-FrosR

Did I write this. C. K. Williams. SP-WillC

Did it come from. Kušiwoqqób. Gary Snyder. CP-SnydG

Did life's penurious length. Emily Dickinson. CP-DickE

Did music help him? Indeed it helped him. Lines about Elias. Ted Hughes. SP-HughTN

Did no one else, then, see them, man. Single Witness, The. Thomas Hardy. CP-HardT

Did not my muse (what can she less?). Apology, An. William Cowper. CP-CowpW

Did not thy reason and thy sense. Attempt at the Manner of Waller, An. William Cowper. CP-CowpW

Did one look at what one saw. Hieroglyphic. Hart Crane. CP-CranH

Did Our Best Moment last. Emily Dickinson. CP-DickE

Did she in summer write it, or in spring. Words on the Window-Pane. Dante Gabriel Rossetti. CW-RossD

Did she suffer—except to leave you? Emily Dickinson. SP-DickE

Did someone say that there would be an end. All Souls. May Sarton. SP-SartM

Did ter notice that lass, sister, as stood away back. Violets for the Dead. D. H. Lawrence. CP-LawrD

Did the Harebell loose her girdle. Emily Dickinson. CP-DickE

Did the long goodbyes of dying water lilies. Rainer Maria Rilke. CP-RilkFr, *tr. by* A. Poulin, Jr. *Fr.* Fragments.

Did the people of Viet Nam. What Were They Like? Denise Levertov. SP-LeveDP

Did these night-hung houses. Suicide, The. Walter De la Mare. CP-DeLaW

Did they catch as it were in a Vision at shut of the day. Jezreel. Thomas Hardy. CP-HardT

Did they expect to find. Raw Data for an Unfinished Questionnaire. Yusef Komunyakaa. CP-KomuY

Did they send me away from my cat and my wife. Gunner. Randall Jarrell. CP-JarrR

Did This Happen to Your Mother? Did Your Sister Throw Up a Lot? Alice Walker. CP-WalkA

Did We abolish Frost. Emily Dickinson. CP-DickE

Did we count great, O soul, to penetrate the themes of mighty books. My Canary Bird. Walt Whitman. CP-WhitW

Did we disobey Him? Emily Dickinson. CP-DickE

Did we love each other, sweetest. Fantasy. Dorothy Parker. CP-ParkD

Did you ask dulcet rhymes from me? To a Certain Civilian. Walt Whitman. CP-WhitW

Did you bring the bottle, Mr. J.? And in Another Place Uses the Same Phrase. Kenneth Patchen. CP-PatcK

Did you ever go down to the river. Reverie on the Harlem River. Langston Hughes. CP-HughL; CP-HughL2

Did you ever have a grey knot topped symbolically with lightning bolts. Port of Call. Andrei Codrescu. SP-CodrA

Did you ever see someone coldcock a blind nun? Election Day, 1984. Carolyn Kizer. CP-KizeC

Did you ever stand in a Cavern's Mouth. Emily Dickinson. CP-DickE

Did you ever walk into a firehose. Demonstration. Langston Hughes. CP-HughL; CP-HughL3

Did you exist. Lake, The. W. S. Merwin. SP-MerwW

Did you hear? Old Warrior Terror, The. Alice Walker. CP-WalkA

Did you kill anyone over there? Nude Interrogation. Yusef Komunyakaa. CP-KomuY

Did you know that hair is flying around in the universe? Hair. David Ignatow. SP-IgnaD

Did you know that the earth, not like a top on its point. Not Quite Like a Top. Robert Penn Warren. CP-WarrR

Did you like the city that the water. Poet Asks His Love about the "Enchanted City" of Cuenca, The. Federico Garcia Lorca. CP-GarcF, *tr. by* Angela Jaffray

Did you like your piece of pineapple would you like a napkin. Questions to Tourists Stopped by a Pineapple Field. W. S. Merwin. SP-MerwWF

Did you notice all the water. Knokke. Robert Creeley. CP-CreeR

Did you see something within the house. She Who Saw Not. Thomas Hardy. CP-HardT

Did you stay up last night (the Magi did). Loose Mountain, A. Robert Frost. CP-FrosR

Did you think I was talking about my life? 7/14/68: i. Adrienne Rich. CP-RicAE *Fr.* Ghazals: Homage to Ghalib.

Did your father leave you glory and then die? Shmuel HaNagid. SP-HaNaS, *tr. by* Peter Cole

Didactic Laurel, loose your reasoning leaf. Maimed Man, The. Allen Tate. CP-TateA

Didactic Piece. Louise Bogan. CP-BogaL

Didactic Poem. Denise Levertov. SP-LeveDP

Dido am I, the founder first of Carthage. Sir Thomas Wyatt. CP-WyatT

Dido at wit's end of Dido, your fates dispersed. Beacon, The. Robert Stock. SP-StocR

Dido cried at the innocent fact. Speech for Aeneas. Alan Dugan. CP-DugaA

Dido's Farewell to Aeneas. Stevie Smith. CP-SmitS

Didst thou not find the place inspired [*or* inspir'd]. Upon My Lady Carlisle's Walking in Hampton Court Garden. Sir John Suckling. CP-SuckJ

Didymus. Louis MacNeice. CP-MacNL

Die Älte Frau, Die Älte Marschallin. William Dickey. SP-DickW

Die and be buried who will. Henry David Thoreau. CP-ThorH

Die, Boreas, / And drown your ruins in the gaudy sea. Canticle for the Blessed Virgin. Thomas Merton. CP-MertT

Die ere long I'm sure, I shall. After Autumne, Winter. Robert Herrick. CP-HerrR

Die, Florence, Judas, disappear. Florence. Aleksandr Aleksandrovich Blok. SP-BlokA, *tr. by* Peter France and Jon Stallworthy

Die Heimat. James Laughlin. CP-LaugJ

Die in the grain. King of the Wood / King of the Dead. Charles Olson. CP-OlsoC

Die Lorelei. Stevie Smith. CP-SmitS

Die Neuen Heiligen. John Updike. CP-UpdiJ

Die when you go a world. And Will That Magic World. James Laughlin. CP-LaugJ

Die—you can't do that to a cat. Cat in an Empty Apartment. Wisława Szymborska. SP-SzymW, *tr. by* Stanislaw Barańczak and Clare Cavanagh

Died. Elizabeth Barrett Browning. CP-BroEB

Died in a dust of lions; her Africa. My Small Aunt. Josephine Jacobsen. CP-JacoJ

Died in the meadow, there. Green Fires, The. Kenneth Patchen. CP-PatcK

Dien Bien Phu. Adrienne Rich. SP-RicA2

Dieppe. Samuel Beckett. CP-BeckS

Dieppe. Samuel Beckett. CP-BeckS

Dies Illa. D. H. Lawrence. CP-LawrD

Dies Irae. Thomas of Celano. CP-CrasR, *tr. by* Richard Crashaw

Dies Irae. D. H. Lawrence. CP-LawrD

Dies Iræ (The Day of Wrath). *Unknown.* SP-BierA, *tr. by* Ambrose Bierce

Diet. Robert Herrick. CP-HerrR

Dieu Qu'il la Fait. Charles, Duc d' Orléans. CP-PoEar, *tr. by* Ezra Pound

Difference between Despair, The. Emily Dickinson. CP-DickE

Difference between you and her, The. Song: Dew-Drop and Diamond. Robert Graves. CP-GravR

Difference Betwixt King and Subjects, The. Robert Herrick. CP-HerrR

Difference, finding the, The. Account, The. A. R. Ammons. CP-AmmoA

Difference, The. Thomas Hardy. CP-HardT

Difference, The. D. H. Lawrence. CP-LawrD

Difference, The. A. K. Ramanujan. CP-RamaA

Differences. John Ciardi. CP-CiarJ

Differences. Paul Laurence Dunbar. CP-DunbP

Differences, The. Andrei Codrescu. SP-CodrA

Differences, The. Thom Gunn. CP-GunnT

Different Holofernes says: Judith, A. Ancient Complaint, An. Dan Pagis. SP-PagiD, *tr. by* Stephen Mitchell

Different kind of thought, A. Come On! William Carlos Williams. CP-WilW2

Different Kinds of Good-by. Carl Sandburg. CP-SandC

Different Ship, A. Pablo Neruda. SP-NeruP, *tr. by* Ben Belitt

Different Stars, The. W. S. Merwin. SP-MerwW

Different Story, A. Yusef Komunyakaa. CP-KomuY

Different Things. William Stafford. SP-StafWW

Difficult achievement for true lovers, A. Starred Coverlet, The. Robert Graves. CP-GravR

Difficult Death. D. H. Lawrence. CP-LawrD

Difficult hours, difficult in our land. And this proud. Final Obol, The. Yannis Ritsos. SP-RitsY, *tr. by* Kimon Friar

"Difficult ordinary happiness," / no one nowadays believes in you. In the Woods. Adrienne Rich. CP-RicAE; SP-RicA1; SP-RicA2

Difficult part of love, The. Love. Philip Larkin. CP-LarkP

Difficult Resolution, The. Randall Jarrell. CP-JarrR

Difficulties, the impossibilities, The. Robert Lowell. SP-LoweR *Fr.* Mexico.

Difficulty. A. K. Ramanujan. CP-RamaA

Difficulty of Ideas, The. Richard Eberhart. CP-EberR

Difficulty to think at the end of day, The. Rabbit as King of the Ghosts, A. Wallace Stevens. CP-StevW; CP-StevWP

Diffidently, when asked who might I be. Powers Unconfessed. Robert Graves. CP-GravR

Diffugere Nives. A. E. Housman. CP-HousA

Diffuse the outpourings of the spiritual coward. Prognosis. Theodore Roethke. CP-RoetT

Dig and you'll find my bones. Elephant, The. Primo Levi. CP-LeviP, *tr. by* Ruth Feldman

Digby D'Avigdor. G. K. Chesterton. CP-ChesG

Digestibles of Sun. Olga Broumas. SP-BrouO

Diggers, The. W. S. Merwin. SP-MerwW

Digging. Margaret Atwood. SP-AtwM1

Digging. Donald Hall. CP-HallD

Digging. Seamus Heaney. SP-HeanSO

Digging Down to China. James Laughlin. CP-LaugJ

Digging for China. Richard Wilbur. CP-WilbR

Digging In. Marge Piercy. SP-PierM

Digging in the Garden of Age I Uncover a Live Root. May Swenson. SP-SwenM

Digging my claws in sand, I crawled ashore. Voyager. Carolyn Kizer. CP-KizeC

Digging potatoes east of Sapporo. Surrounded by Mountains. William Stafford. SP-StafWW

Digging Worms. Robert Bly. SP-BlyR

Diggon Davie, I bidde her god day. September. Edmund Spenser. CP-Spens *Fr.* Shepheardes [*or* Shepeards *or* Shepherd's] Calender, The.

Dignissimo Suo Amico Doctori Witty. Andrew Marvell. CP-MarvA

Dilapidation at erected original. THEIR / Book of Stella. Susan Howe. SP-HoweS

Dilemma. David Ignatow. SP-IgnaD

Dilemma. Dorothy Parker. CP-ParkD

Dilemma in the Delta. John Updike. CP-UpdiJ

Dilemma / my suit, continuous. Tea. Lorine Niedecker. CP-NiedL

Dilemma, The. Robert Graves. CP-GravR

Dilemmist, The. Laura Riding Jackson. CP-RidiL

Dilettante, The: A Modern Type. Paul Laurence Dunbar. CP-DunbP

Dillingham, Alaska, the Willow Tree Bar. Gary Snyder. CP-SnydG

Diluculo surgit Sapiens, et per juga nigra. Philosophus et Phasiani. John Gay. CP-CowpW

Dim as the borrowed beams of moon and stars. Religio Laici. John Dryden. CP-DryJ2; SP-DrydJ

Dim-berried is the mistletoe. Before Dawn. Walter De la Mare. CP-DeLaW

Dim dawn behind the tamarisks—the sky is saffron-yellow. Christmas in India. Rudyard Kipling. CP-KiplR

Dim deep of a yellow evening slides, The. Vision. E. E. Cummings. CP-CummE

Dim Hour! that sleep'st on pillowing clouds afar. Hour When We Shall Meet Again, The. Samuel Taylor Coleridge. CP-ColeS

Dim House, Bright Face. Tess Gallagher. SP-GallT

Dim / i / nu / tiv / e this park is e. E. E. Cummings. CP-CummE

Dim in the glimmering room. My Father's Honour. Donald Davie. CP-DaviDC

Dim vales—and shadowy floods. Fairyland [*or* Fairy-Land]. Edgar Allan Poe. CP-PoeEd

Dim-winged spirits of the night, The. What the Scarecrow Said. Nicholas Vachel Lindsay. CP-LindV

Dimaratos. Constantine P. Cavafy. CP-CavaC, *tr. by* Theoharis Constantine Theoharis

Dime. Langston Hughes. CP-HughL; CP-HughL3

Dime Found in the Snow, A. James Tate. SP-TateJ

Dimensions. Robert Creeley. CP-CreeR

Dimensions. C. K. Williams. CP-WillC; SP-WillC

Dimitrios Selefkides was displeased. Displeasure of Selefkides, The. Constantine P. Cavafy. CP-CavaC, *tr. by* Theoharis Constantine Theoharis

Dimly Outlined by a Police Artist. Charles Simic. SP-SimiC *Fr.* Rosalia.

Dimout in Harlem. Langston Hughes. CP-HughL; CP-HughL2

Dimple-cheeked and rosy-lipped. Tommy Smith. James Whitcomb Riley. CP-RileJ

Dimple in the Tomb, A. Emily Dickinson. CP-DickE

Din of work is subdued, The. Lullaby: "Din of work is subdued, The." W. H. Auden. CP-AudeW

Dinah in Heaven. Rudyard Kipling. CP-KiplR

Dinah Kneading Dough. Paul Laurence Dunbar. CP-DunbP

Dinah stan' befo' de glass. Looking-Glass, The. Paul Laurence Dunbar. CP-DunbP

Dined with Auden. He'd been at Milwaukee. Auden at Milwaukee. Stephen Spender. CP-SpenS

Diner, The. David Ignatow. SP-IgnaD

"Ding a ding," / The sweet bells sing. Christina Georgina Rossetti. CP-RosC2

Ding-dong, ding-dong, ding-dong. Dirge for a Righteous Kitten, A. Nicholas Vachel Lindsay. CP-LindV

Ding-Donging. Laura Riding Jackson. CP-RidiL

Dingley and Brent. Jonathan Swift. CP-SwifJ

Dining Out with Doug and Frank. James Schuyler. CP-SchuJ

Dining room is empty at the country inn, The. Most, The. Heather McHugh. SP-McHuH

Dinky. Theodore Roethke. CP-RoetT

Dinner at George & Katie Schneeman's. Ted Berrigan. SP-BerrT

Dinner Bell in the Woods. Wallace Stevens. CP-StevWP

Dinner for the Devil. Ben Jonson. CP-JonsB *Fr.* Gypsies Metamorphosed, The.

Dinner Guest: Me. Langston Hughes. CP-HughL; CP-HughL3

Dinner Party. Eleanor Wilner. SP-WilnE

Dinner, The. Gregory Orr. SP-OrrG

Dinner was duckling with tangerine sauce. Limits of Friendship, The. John Ciardi. CP-CiarJ

Dinosaur bones are dusted every day, The. Dinosaur Bones, The. Carl Sandburg. CP-SandC

Dinosaur Bones, The. Carl Sandburg. CP-SandC

Dinosaur died, and small, The. Naked Ape, The. John Updike. CP-UpdiJ

Dinosaur Skeleton. Wisława Szymborska. SP-SzymW, *tr. by* Stanisław Barańczak *and* Clare Cavanagh

Diodati, and I will say it to you with wonder. Sonnet 4: "Diodati, and I will say it to you with wonder." John Milton. CP-MiltJ

Diodorus Siculus tells the story of a god who had been cut into pieces and then scattered. Paradiso 31, 108. Jorge Luis Borges. SP-BorgJ, *tr. by* Ken Krabbenhoft

Dion. William Wordsworth. CP-WorW2

Dionysiaca. Nonnus.

    How Bacchus Comforts Ariadne. CP-BroEB

    How Bacchus Finds Ariadne Sleeping. CP-BroEB

Dioscuri guardyou in this passing, The. Self Prepares for an Unwilling Journey, The. William Dickey. SP-DickW

Diplomacy. Paul Laurence Dunbar. CP-DunbP

Dipper, small dust-colored bird with robin, The. Three Praises. Margaret Atwood. SP-AtwM2

Dipping spruce branches into the calm water. Halibut, The. Arthur Sze. SP-SzeA

Dipsychus [and the Spirit]. Arthur Hugh Clough.

    "Assuredly a lively scene." SP-ClouA

    There Is No God. SP-ClouA

Dire was the hate at old Harlaw. Dean of Faculty—a New Ballad, The. Robert Burns. CP-BurnR

Direadh III. Hugh MacDiarmid. SP-MacDH

Direct address to the swans: you, whose feet. You, Failed Pronoun. Eleanor Wilner. SP-WilnE

Direction. W. S. Merwin. SP-MerwWF

Directions. Billy Collins. SP-CollB

Directions for a Birthday Song. Jonathan Swift. CP-SwifJ

Directions for Finding the Bard. Dorothy Parker. CP-ParkD

Directions for Laughing. *Unknown, sometimes at. to* Thomas Sheridan. CP-SherT

Directive. Robert Frost. CP-FrosR

Directly on the right as you enter the library. Tomb of the Grammarian Lysias. Constantine P. Cavafy. CP-CavaC, *tr. by* Theoharis Constantine Theoharis

Director of Alienation. Lawrence Ferlinghetti. SP-FerlL

Dirge, A. Derek Mahon. CP-MahoD

Dirge, A. Christina Georgina Rossetti. CP-RosC3

Dirge, A: "Rough wind, that moanest loud." Percy Bysshe Shelley. CP-ShelP

Dirge, A: "Why were you born when the snow was falling?" Christina Georgina Rossetti. CP-RosC1

Dirge for a Joker. Sylvia Plath. CP-PlatS

Dirge for a Righteous Kitten, A. Nicholas Vachel Lindsay. CP-LindV

Dirge for a Soldier. Paul Laurence Dunbar. CP-DunbP

Dirge for a Town in France. Thomas Merton. CP-MertT

Dirge for the City of Miami. Thomas Merton. CP-MertT

Dirge for the Proud World. Thomas Merton. CP-MertT

Dirge for the World Joyce Died In. Thomas Merton. CP-MertT

Dirge for the Year. Percy Bysshe Shelley. CP-ShelP

Dirge for Two Veterans. Walt Whitman. CP-WhitW

Dirge: "From a friend's friend I taste friendship." Stevie Smith. CP-SmitS

Dirge: "He has hid his face, and he's gone!" George Meredith. CP-MerG2

Dirge: "I bring ye little noisy crew!" William Wordsworth. MW-WorW

Dirge in Woods. George Meredith. CP-MerG1

Dirge is wailing from the Gulf of storm-vexed Mexico, A. Bolivar. John Greenleaf Whittier. CP-WhitJ

Dirge: "Knows he who tills this lonely field." Ralph Waldo Emerson. CP-EmerR

Dirge of Dead Sisters. Rudyard Kipling. CP-KiplR

Dirge of Jephthah's Daughter, The. Robert Herrick. CP-HerrR

Dirge: "Place this bunch of mignonette." Paul Laurence Dunbar. CP-DunbP

Dirge: "Some one who hears the bugle neigh will know." Thomas Merton. CP-MertT

Dirge Sung by a Minstrel. William Wordsworth. CP-WorW1

Dirge upon the Death of the Right Valiant Lord, Bernard Stuart, A. Robert Herrick. CP-HerrR

Dirge Without Music. Edna St. Vincent Millay. CP-MillE

Dirt & Slime. James Edward Austen-Leigh. CP-AustJ

Dirt and stone, if I may know you as you know yourselves. Invocation: "Dirt and stone, if I may know you as you know yourselves." David Ignatow. SP-IgnaD

Dirt feels sweet, The. Fanny Howe. SP-HoweF Fr. O'Clock.

Dirty Christmas / which Origen. Christmas. Charles Olson. CP-OlsoC

Dirty colours of her kiss have just, The. E. E. Cummings. CP-CummE

Dirty dogs of Egypt stride down my bones, The. Dogs of Egypt, The. Charles Bukowski. SP-BukC2

Dirty money and the sleazy hearts, The. Matadors, The. Josephine Jacobsen. CP-JacoJ

Dirty picture, a photograph, possibly a tintype, from the turn of the century, even before:, A. Floor. C. K. Williams. CP-WillC; SP-WillC

Dirty river by religious explorers, The. Mystic River. John Ciardi. CP-CiarJ

Dirty socks in dirty sneakers. Sorting, Wrapping, Packing, Stuffing. James Schuyler. CP-SchuJ

Dirty Souls. Alfonso Cortes. CP-MertT

Dirty Talker: D Line, Boston, The. C. K. Williams. SP-WillC

Dirty windows in March glare. Nine Lives. William Corbett. SP-CorbW

Dirty word hops in the cage of the mind like the Pondicherry vulture, The. Dirty Word, The. Karl Shapiro. SP-ShapK

Dirty Word, The. Karl Shapiro. SP-ShapK

Dîs Aliter Visum; or, Le Byron de Nos Jours. Robert Browning. CP-BroR1; SP-BroR

Dis-easted, a grave- / tree split into. Solve. Paul Celan. SP-CelaP, tr. by John Felstiner

Dis is gospel weathah sho'. Song of Summer. Paul Laurence Dunbar. CP-DunbP

Disabled. Wilfred Owen. CP-OwenW

Disagreeable Advice. D. H. Lawrence. CP-LawrD

Disappearances in the Guarded Sector. Tess Gallagher. SP-GallT

Disappearee's Song. Heather McHugh. SP-McHuH

Disappearing Island, The. Seamus Heaney. SP-HeanSO

Disappointed. Paul Laurence Dunbar. CP-DunbP

Disappointed impoverished scholars. Han-shan. CP-ColdM, tr. by Red Pine

Disappointment, an Ode 1756 to Mr Stockton, The. Annis Boudinot Stockton. CP-StocA

Disappointment, The. Thomas Southerne.
   Prologue: "How comes it, gentlemen, that nowadays." CP-DryJ2

Disappointment, The. Robert Creeley. CP-CreeR

Disarmament. John Greenleaf Whittier. CP-WhitJ

Disarming hour! the underworld's ally. Last Light. Charles Baudelaire. CP-BaudC, tr. by Walter Martin

Disaster does not abate however much you speak of it. Love, A. Constantine P. Cavafy. CP-CavaC, tr. by Theoharis Constantine Theoharis

Disasters. George Oppen. CP-OppGN

Disasters numb within us, The. Life at War. Denise Levertov. SP-LeveDP; SP-LeveDS

Disbeliever walked the moonlit place, The. Palace of the Babies. Wallace Stevens. CP-StevW; CP-StevWP

Discard the fear and what. Couple, The. Maya Angelou. SP-AngeM

Discarded Love Poem, The. Robert Graves. CP-GravR

Discerning friend, A. Lady Asks Me, A. James Laughlin. CP-LaugJ

Discharge, The. George Herbert. CP-HerbG

Discharged Soldier, The. William Wordsworth. MW-WorW

Discharged upon the body of the world. Devonshire. Donald Davie. CP-DaviDC

Disciple, The. John Berryman. CP-BerrJ

Disciple, The. Rudyard Kipling. CP-KiplR

Disciple, The. Jones Very. CP-VeryJ

Disciple complained to Keng, A. Keng's Disciple. Chuang Tzu. CP-MertT

Discipline. George Herbert. CP-HerbG

Discipline. D. H. Lawrence. CP-LawrD

Discipline, A. Wendell Berry. CP-BerrW

Discipline of Wisdom, The. George Meredith. CP-MerG1

Disclaimer of the Person. Laura Riding Jackson. CP-RidiL

Disclosure, The. Denise Levertov. SP-LeveDP; SP-LeveDS

Discomfort marks the boundary. Natural History. Rae Armantrout. SP-ArmaA

Discontent. Elizabeth Barrett Browning. CP-BroEB

Discontent. Jones Very. CP-VeryJ

Discontent with that first draft. Where one's own. Before the Judgment. Robert Duncan. SP-DuncR Fr. Passages.

Discontented Poet: A Masque, The. Ralph Waldo Emerson. CP-EmerR

Discontents in Devon. Robert Herrick. CP-HerrR

Discord in Childhood. D. H. Lawrence. CP-LawrD

Discord Not Disadvantageous. Robert Herrick. CP-HerrR

Discouragement. Thomas Hardy. CP-HardT

Discouraging Model, A. James Whitcomb Riley. CP-RileJ

Discourse / of sun and moon. Wrestling. Thom Gunn. CP-GunnT

Discourse was deemed Man's noblest attribute. Illustrated Books and Newspapers. William Wordsworth. CP-WorW2

Discover it not so easy (oh, I do!). Going Too Far. Robert Stock. SP-StocR

Discovered. Paul Laurence Dunbar. CP-DunbP

Discoverer. A. R. Ammons. CP-AmmoA

Discovering, discovering trees light up green at night. No Hearing. Robert Lowell. SP-LoweR

Discovery. Amy Clampitt. CP-ClamA

Discovery. Edwin Arlington Robinson. CP-RobiE

Discovery. Wisława Szymborska. SP-SzymW, tr. by Stanislaw Barańczak and Clare Cavanagh

Discovery, A. Christina Georgina Rossetti. CP-RosC3

Discovery, The. Paul Laurence Dunbar. CP-DunbP

Discovery, The. Thomas Hardy. CP-HardT

Discovery, The. Jonathan Swift. CP-SwifJ

Discovery of Prayer, The. Andrei Codrescu. SP-CodrA

Discovery of the Madeiras, The. Robert Frost. CP-FrosR

Discovery of the Pacific, The. Thom Gunn. CP-GunnT

Discovery of Thought, A. Wallace Stevens. CP-StevWP

Discreet and prudent we that Discord call. Contention. Robert Herrick. CP-HerrR

Discreet householder exclaims on the grandsire, A. Old Man Playing with Children. John Crowe Ransom. SP-RansJ

Discrepancies. Charles Tomlinson. CP-TomlC

Discrete Gloss, A. Charles Olson. CP-OlsoC

Discretions of Alcibiades. Robert Pinsky. CP-PinsR

Discrimination. Kenneth Rexroth. CP-RexrK

Discriminations. Philip Whalen. SP-WhalP

Discription of a Maske, Presented before the Kinges Majestie at Whitehall, on Twelfth Night Last, in Honour of the Lord HAYES, and His Bride, Daughter and Heire to the Honourable the Lord Dnnye, their Marriage Having Been t. Thomas Campion.

Discussion, A. David Ignatow. SP-IgnaD

Disdain. Sir Thomas Wyatt. CP-WyatT

Disdain me not without desert. Sir Thomas Wyatt. CP-WyatT

Disdain not, madam, on him to look. Sir Thomas Wyatt. CP-WyatT

Disdain Returned. Thomas Carew. CP-CareT

Disease, The. Muriel Rukeyser. CP-RukeM

Disease: After-Effects, The. Muriel Rukeyser. CP-RukeM

Disease of civilization is not tools, citizen, The. Philosophical Poem. John Ciardi. CP-CiarJ

Disease that on thy body feeds. Decay. Jones Very. CP-VeryJ

Diseased or unwanted / trees, cut into pieces, thrown. Marsh, Hawk. Margaret Atwood. SP-AtwM2

Diseases, famine, enemies, in us no change have wrought. Sir Walter Ralegh. CP-RaleW

Disembarking at Quebec. Margaret Atwood. SP-AtwM1

Disenthralled, The. John Greenleaf Whittier. CP-WhitJ

Disertissime Romuli Nepotum. Catullus. *See* Carmina

Disguise, The. Walter De la Mare. CP-DeLaW

Dish of Fruit, The. William Carlos Williams. CP-WilW2

Dish of Peaches in Russia, A. Wallace Stevens. CP-StevW; CP-StevWP

Dishes are apples are guitars. Still Life II. Howard Nemerov. CP-NemeH

Dishevelled leaves creep down. Where They Lived. Thomas Hardy. CP-HardT

Dishonest Mailmen, The. Robert Creeley. CP-CreeR

Dishonoured Rock and Ruin! that, by law. Eagles. William Wordsworth. CP-WorW2

Dishwasher as Absolution. Josephine Jacobsen. CP-JacoJ

Disillusion. Langston Hughes. CP-HughL; CP-HughL1

Disillusionment of Ten O'Clock. Wallace Stevens. CP-StevW; CP-StevWP

Disindividuating Chaos. Passage, The. Richard Eberhart. CP-EberR

Disinherited. John Donne. CP-DonnJ; MW-DonnJ

Disintegration. Philip Larkin. CP-LarkP

Disjecta Membra. Charles Wright. SP-WrigCN

Dismal bell hung in the belfry, A. Fairy Bell, The. Stevie Smith. CP-SmitS

Dismal fog-hoarse siren howls at dawn, A. Calls, The. Wilfred Owen. CP-OwenW

Dismal Moment Passing. Clarence Major. SP-MajoC

Dismantled Ship, The. Walt Whitman. CP-WhitW

Dismantling the Silence. Charles Simic. SP-SimiC; SP-SimiCE

Disown. Rae Armantrout. SP-ArmaA

Displacement. Yannis Ritsos. SP-RitsY, *tr. by* Kimon Friar

Display thy breasts, my Julia. Upon Julia's Breasts. Robert Herrick. CP-HerrR

Displeas'd with my self with my bosom at war. Caprice, a Fragment. Annis Boudinot Stockton. CP-StocA

Displeased Viewer, A. Constantine P. Cavafy. CP-CavaC, *tr. by* Theoharis Constantine Theoharis

Displeasure of Selefkides, The. Constantine P. Cavafy. CP-CavaC, *tr. by* Theoharis Constantine Theoharis

Disposings of the heart in man, The. Creature David, The. Donald Davie. CP-DaviDC

Disposition, The. Charles Olson. CP-OlsoC

Dispossess me of belief. This Black Rich Country. A. R. Ammons. CP-AmmoA

Dispossessed, The. John Berryman. CP-BerrJ

Dispossessed, The. Thomas Kinsella. CP-KinsT

Dispossessed, The. Sylvia Plath. CP-PlatS

Dispossessions. Jane Cooper. CP-CoopJ

Disputants, The. William Carlos Williams. CP-WilW1

Dispute, The. Clarence Major. SP-MajoC

Disquiet and Night. Federico García Lorca. CP-GarcF, *tr. by* Alan S. Trueblood *Fr.* Back of the World.

Disquieting Muses, The. Sylvia Plath. CP-PlatS

Disquieting muses again: what are "leftovers?", The. Business Personals. John Ashbery. SP-AshbJ

Dissecto Nervae capite, haud (chirurge) cerebrum. In Nervam. Thomas Campion. CP-CampT

Dissemblers, The. Thomas Hardy. CP-HardT

Dissentient Voice, A. Donald Davie. CP-DaviDC

Dissolute. D. H. Lawrence. *See* At a Loose End

Dissolution, The. John Donne. CP-DonnJ; MW-DonnJ

Dissolver of sugar, dissolve me. Jelaluddin Rumi. SP-Rumi, *tr. by* Coleman Barks

Dissolving in the chemic vat. Change. Stanley Kunitz. CP-KunSC

Dissolving, the coals shift. Rain swaddles us. Ruin, The. Charles Tomlinson. CP-TomlC

Dissonant music of the night. Transformation, The. John Logan. CP-LogaJ

Disswasions from Idlenesse. Robert Herrick. CP-HerrR

Distance. Robert Creeley. CP-CreeR

Distance. Josephine Jacobsen. CP-JacoJ

Distance. Maxine W. Kumin. SP-KumiM

Distance. Czeslaw Milosz. CP-MiloC; CP-MiloCN, *tr. by* Robert Hass

Distance. Dorothy Parker. CP-ParkD

Distance, The. Denise Levertov. SP-LeveDL

Distance Betters Dignities. Robert Herrick. CP-HerrR

Distance Between, The: Picnic of Old Friends. Robert Penn Warren. CP-WarrR

Distance brings proportion. From here. Tao in the Yankee Stadium Bleachers. John Updike. CP-UpdiJ

Distance / Dappled with diminish'd trees. Gerard Manley Hopkins. CP-HopkG

Distance into Place, The. Wyatt Prunty. SP-PrunW

Distance is dead. At Gatwick, at Heathrow. Westward. Amy Clampitt. CP-ClamA

Distance—is not the Realm of Fox. Emily Dickinson. CP-DickE

Distance / is where we were. Words from a Totem Animal. W. S. Merwin. SP-MerwW

Distance that lies from here, The. Space Song. Alfonso Cortes. CP-MertT, *tr. by* Thomas Merton

Distance that the dead have gone, The. Emily Dickinson. CP-DickE

Distances, The. W. S. Merwin. SP-MerwW

Distances, The. Charles Olson. CP-OlsoC; SP-OlsoC

Distances They Keep, The. Howard Nemerov. CP-NemeH

Distant, The. Yannis Ritsos. SP-RitsY, *tr. by* Edmund Keeley

Distant, The. Jones Very. CP-VeryJ

Distant Fury of Battle, The. Geoffrey Hill. CP-HillG

Distant, I was with you when your father. Eugenio Montale. CP-MontE, *tr. by* Jonathan Galassi

Distant on the meridian verges. Ice Shall Cover Nineveh. Kenneth Rexroth. CP-RexrK

Distant Rainfall. Robinson Jeffers. CP-JefR2

Distant Song. Rainer Maria Rilke. CP-RilkFr, *tr. by* A. Poulin, Jr.

Distinct Motion. Yannis Ritsos. SP-RitsY, *tr. by* Kostas Myrsiades

Distinction. Paul Laurence Dunbar. CP-DunbP

Distinctions. Charles Tomlinson. CP-TomlC

Distinctions at Dusk. James Vincent Cunningham. CP-CunnJ

Distinguishing Marks. Constantine P. Cavafy. CP-CavaC, *tr. by* Theoharis Constantine Theoharis

Distraction. James Vincent Cunningham. CP-CunnJ

Distraction. Howard Nemerov. CP-NemeH

Distraction Fit, A. Philip Whalen. CP-WhalP

Distractions. William Stafford. SP-StafWW

Distractions and the Human Crowd. Stevie Smith. CP-SmitS

Distress Sale. Raymond Carver. CP-CarvR

Distressed Travellers, The. William Cowper. CP-CowpW

Distressful gift! this Book receives. William Wordsworth. CP-WorW1; MW-WorW

Distrust. Robert Herrick. CP-HerrR

Distrust. Robert Herrick. CP-HerrR

Distrustful of the Gentian. Emily Dickinson. CP-DickE

Disturb the balance, broken bird. Birdsong, The. William Carlos Williams. CP-WilW2

Disturber, The. Paul Laurence Dunbar. CP-DunbP

Disused Shed in Co. Wexford, A. Derek Mahon. CP-MahoD

Ditch, The. Gregory Orr. SP-OrrG

Ditch is dear to the Drunken man, The. Emily Dickinson. CP-DickE

Dithyramb. Czeslaw Milosz. CP-MiloC; CP-MiloCN, *tr. by* Peter Dale Scott

Ditto. Thomas Lux. SP-LuxT

Ditty: "Beneath a knap where flown." Thomas Hardy. CP-HardT

Ditty: "Moon will run all consciences to cover, The." Allen Tate. CP-TateA

Ditty of First Desire. Federico García Lorca. CP-GarcF, *tr. by* Alan S. Trueblood *Fr.* Love.

Ditty of No Tone, A. James Whitcomb Riley. CP-RileJ

Dive. Langston Hughes. CP-HughL; CP-HughL3

Dive for dreams / or a slogan may topple you. E. E. Cummings. CP-CummE

Diver. Robert Penn Warren. CP-WarrR

Diver. Tennessee Williams. CP-WillT

Diver, The. Robert Earl Hayden. CP-HaydR

Diver's Clothes Lying Empty, The. Jelaluddin Rumi. SP-Rumi, *tr. by* Coleman Barks

Divers[e] [*or* Dyvers] doth[e] use, as I have heard and kno[w]. Sir Thomas Wyatt. CP-WyatT

Diverted Tragedy, A. James Whitcomb Riley. CP-RileJ

Divertimiento. William Carlos Williams. CP-WilW1

Divestment of Beauty. Laura Riding Jackson. CP-RidiL

Divided Destinies. Rudyard Kipling. CP-KiplR

Divina Commedia. Dante Alighieri.

  Inferno: Canto 1.

    "And now, *Vexilla regis produent*." CP-PinsR

    Filippo Argenti. CP-CiarJ

    Francesca da Rimini. CW-RossD

    Francesca of Rimini. CP-Byron

    Ugolino. SP-HeanSO, *tr. by* Seamus Heaney

    Ugolino. CP-ShelP

    Underworld of Dante, The. CP-ClamA

  Purgatorio.

    La Pia. CW-RossD

    Matilda Gathering Flowers. CP-ShelP

Divination by a Daffadill [*or* Daffodil]. Robert Herrick. CP-HerrR

Divine and Human Pleading. Christina Georgina Rossetti. CP-RosC3

Divine Compassion. John Greenleaf Whittier. CP-WhitJ

Divine Disgrace. Rainer Maria Rilke. CP-RilkFr, *tr. by* A. Poulin, Jr.

Divine Falling of Leaves, A. César Vallejo. CP-WrigJ

Divine Inviters! I accept. Ralph Waldo Emerson. CP-EmerR

Divine Justice Amiable. Jeanne Marie Bouvier de la Motte- Guyon. CP-CowpW

Divine Law: A Blue Beach Sermon. Clarence Major. SP-MajoC

Divine Love, A. Thomas Carew. CP-CareT

Divine Love Endures No Rival. Jeanne Marie Bouvier de la Motte- Guyon. CP-CowpW

Divine Mistress, A. Thomas Carew. CP-CareT

Divine Psyche, sweet invisible Butterfly. "Rubén Dario." SP-DariR, tr. by Alberto Acereda and Will Derusha

Divine sea rocks its, The. Rocking. Gabriela Mistral. SP-MistG, tr. by Maria Giachetti [or Jacketti] and Maria Jacketti

Divinely Superfluous Beauty. Robinson Jeffers. CP-JefR1

Diviner, The. Seamus Heaney. SP-HeanSO

Divines, especially your old ones. Verses on a Wooden Leg. Unknown, sometimes at. to Thomas Sheridan. CP-SherT

Diving Bell, The. Tennessee Williams. CP-WillT

Diving into the Wreck. Adrienne Rich. SP-RicA1; SP-RicA2

Diving / through bedrooms. Moon, The. William Carlos Williams. CP-WilW1

Divining Water. Muriel Rukeyser. CP-RukeM

Divinities. W. S. Merwin. SP-MerwW

Divinity. George Herbert. CP-HerbG

Divinity of the sleep of cats. Rainer Maria Rilke. CP-RilkFr, tr. by A. Poulin, Jr. Fr. Fragments.

Division. Louise Bogan. CP-BogaL

Division. W. S. Merwin. SP-MerwW

Division, The. Thomas Hardy. CP-HardT

Division, mother of pain. From a Series. W. S. Merwin. SP-MerwW

Division of Parts, The. Anne Sexton. CP-SextA; SP-SextA

Divisions. Robert Creeley. CP-CreeR

Divorce. Anne Sexton. CP-SextA

Divorce. Miller Williams. CP-WillM

Divorce, The. Hans Magnus Enzensberger. SP-EnzeH, tr. by Michael Hamburger

Divorce of Lovers, A. May Sarton.
   "I shall not see the end of this unweaving." SP-SartM

Divorce, Thy Name Is Woman. Anne Sexton. CP-SextA; SP-SextA

Divorced, Husband Demolishes House. John Ciardi. CP-CiarJ

Divorcing. Denise Levertov. SP-LeveDL; SP-LeveDS

Dixie Man to Uncle Sam. Langston Hughes. CP-HughL; CP-HughL3

Dixie South Africa. Langston Hughes. CP-HughL; CP-HughL3

Dixit Insipiens. Carolyn Kizer. CP-KizeC

Do' a-stan'in' on a jar, fiah a-shinin' thoo. Howdy, Honey, Howdy! Paul Laurence Dunbar. CP-DunbP

Do all thy acts with strictest justice square. Just, The. Jones Very. CP-VeryJ

Do animals expect spring? First Woman. Josephine Jacobsen. CP-JacoJ

Do any of you old fogies remember Mrs. Hauksbee? How to Be Married without a Spouse, or, Mr. Kipling, What Have You Done with Mr. Hauksbee? Ogden Nash. CP-NashO

Do, Do, Do What You Done, Done, Done Before, Before, Before. Ogden Nash. CP-NashO

Do duty feeling nought and truth believe. Arthur Hugh Clough. SP-ClouA

Do I hear them? Yes, I hear the children singing—and what of it? London Bridge. Edwin Arlington Robinson. CP-RobiE

Do I know how I feel? Do I know what I think? T. S. Eliot. SP-ElioT

Do I know these, slack-shaped and wan. In a Former Resort after Many Years. Thomas Hardy. CP-HardT

Do I not deal with angels. For Miriam. Kenneth Patchen. CP-PatcK

Do I not know what savage blossom only under the pitting hail. What Savage Blossom. Edna St. Vincent Millay. CP-MillE

Do I regret each thing. Near Rhyme. Rae Armantrout. SP-ArmaA

Do I say no-one has loved as I love? Love: "Do I say no-one has loved as I love?" G. K. Chesterton. CP-ChesG

Do it just right, anything will grow. Now If You. Kenneth Patchen. CP-PatcK

Do me that love. Kenneth Patchen. CP-PatcK

Do Nations Ever Become Insane? Jones Very. CP-VeryJ

Do Not! Stevie Smith. CP-SmitS

Do not accept these rains that come too late. Yehuda Amichai. SP-AmicYL, tr. by Benjamin Harshav and Barbara Harshav

Do not, at this high time, desert. Quatrain: "Do not, at this high time, desert." Charles Olson. CP-OlsoC

Do not bake bread in an oven that is not made of stone. Some General Instructions. Kenneth Koch. SP-KochK

Do not be afraid / O my people. I Have Called You. Thomas Merton. CP-MertT

Do Not Be Ashamed. Wendell Berry. CP-BerrW

Do not because this day I have grown saturnine. Under Saturn. William Butler Yeats. CP-YeatW

Do not beguile my heart. Complaining. George Herbert. CP-HerbG

Do not call me Dr. Poem for an Intellectual on the Way Up to Submit to His Lady. Langston Hughes. CP-HughL; CP-HughL2

Do not call to her there. Hill, The. Charles Tomlinson. CP-TomlC

Do not deny. Incarnations. Laura Riding Jackson. CP-RidiL

Do Not Die. W. S. Merwin. SP-MerwW

Do not disdain, O straight upraised pine. Graven Thoughts. Sir Philip Sidney. SP-SidnP Fr. Arcadia.

Do Not Embrace Your Mind's New Negro Friend. William Meredith. SP-MereW

Do not enquire from the centurion nodding. Silver Age, The. Thom Gunn. CP-GunnT

Do Not Go Gentle into That Good Night. Dylan Thomas. CP-ThomD

Do not go to the Charles St. Jail. When I Was Drunk and Disorderly the Boston Policeman Told Me. Alan Dugan. CP-DugaA

Do not guard this as rich stuff without mark. Memory. Louise Bogan. CP-BogaL

Do not hold me, Siegmund. Love-Passage, A. D. H. Lawrence. CP-LawrD

Do not hold my few years / against me. So We've Come at Last to Freud. Alice Walker. CP-WalkA

Do not imagine his father lying. Voice of America. Miller Williams. CP-WillM

Do not imagine that Jack and Rose apart. Jack's Letter. John Crowe Ransom. SP-RansJ

Do not lecture me, doctor, about your science. Ekstase, Alptraum, Schlaf in einem Nest von Flammen. Hayden Carruth. CP-CarHS

Do not lie there in the darkness silent. Thunderhead. Archibald MacLeish. CP-MacLA

Do not mistake me: I was never a rival. To the Teumessian Vixen. Robert Graves. CP-GravR

Do not need wings because. Apsarases. James Laughlin. CP-LaugJ

Do not, O do not prize thy beauty at too high a rate. Unknown. See Do Not, Oh, Do Not Prize

Do Not, Oh, Do Not Prize. Unknown. CP-CampT
  (Do not, O do not prize thy beauty at too high a rate.) CP-CampT

Do not pick my rosemary. Mother Goose. Kenneth Rexroth. CP-RexrK

Do Not Pick Up the Telephone. Ted Hughes. SP-HughTN

Do not seek your mouth on my lips. Crystal. Paul Celan. SP-CelaP, tr. by John Felstiner

Do not sell me out, baby. In a Troubled Key. Langston Hughes. CP-HughL; CP-HughL2

Do Not Speak Keresan to a Mescalero Apache. Arthur Sze. SP-SzeA

Do not speak of guilt, do not speak of responsibility. Regiment of Pleasure, The. Constantine P. Cavafy. CP-CavaC, tr. by Theoharis Constantine Theoharis

Do not think I am not grateful for your small. Gratitude. Louise Glück. SP-GlucL

Do not think me gentle. Warning to My Readers, A. Wendell Berry. CP-BerrW

Do not weep, maiden, for war is kind. Stephen Crane. CP-CranS

Do not wonder when the wench declines. Carmen 69. Catullus. CP-ZukLS Fr. Carmina.

Do not work ahead. Paul Celan. SP-CelaP, tr. by John Felstiner

Do. / omful / relaxing. E. E. Cummings. CP-CummE

Do our humble things. Rainer Maria Rilke. CP-RilkFr, tr. by A. Poulin, Jr. Fr. Orchards.

Do People moulder equally. Emily Dickinson. CP-DickE

Do poets really suffer more. Words Continue Their Journey, The. Margaret Atwood. SP-AtwM2

Do Sphinxes Think? Dorothy Nash. CP-NashO

Do squamous and squiggling fish. Nocturne: "Do squamous and squiggling fish." W. H. Auden. CP-AudeW

"Do such, wait so," you said; I waited. Did you wait? Randall Jarrell. CP-JarrR

Do Take Muriel Out. Stevie Smith. CP-SmitS

Do that which you can do. Ralph Waldo Emerson. CP-EmerR

Do the Dead Know What Time It Is? Kenneth Patchen. CP-PatcK

Do the Meditation Rock. Allen Ginsberg. SP-GinsA

Do the prairie flowers, the huge autumn. Christmas Note for Geraldine Udell, A. Kenneth Rexroth. CP-RexrK

Do the wife and baby travelling to see. Sick Nought, The. Randall Jarrell. CP-JarrR

Do these leaves know as much as I? They must. For Brother Antoninus. Philip Whalen. SP-WhalP

Do these poems remember. Tu Fu in English. William Corbett. SP-CorbW

Do they block the way? Softly, Then, Softly. D. H. Lawrence. CP-LawrD

Do they remember me? William Dickey. SP-DickW Fr. At Your Old House.

Do This, and He Doeth It. Christina Georgina Rossetti. CP-RosC2

Do way, do way, ye little wily prat! Sir Thomas Wyatt. CP-WyatT

Do We Understand Each Other? Allen Ginsberg. CP-GinsA

Do what you come for, captain, with your news. To Captain Hungry. Ben Jonson. CP-JonsB; SP-JonsB

Do with me, God! as Thou didst deal with John. To God. Robert Herrick. CP-HerrR

Do ye hear the children weeping, O my brothers. Cry of the Children, The. Elizabeth Barrett Browning. CP-BroEB

Do you ask what the birds say? The sparrow, the dove. Answer to a Child's Question. Samuel Taylor Coleridge. CP-ColeS; MW-ColeS

Do you believe in a God. Ordinary God. Donald Davie. CP-DaviDC

Do you blame me that I sit hours before this picture? Nativity by Botticelli, The. G. K. Chesterton. CP-ChesG

Do you call the ideal the impossible? Permanence. G. K. Chesterton. CP-ChesG

"Do you delude yourself?" a neighbor asks. Troughs of Sea. Robert Graves. CP-GravR

Do you exist. Unknown, The. William Carlos Williams. CP-WilW2

Do you forget the shifting hole. To a Defeated Savior. James Wright. CP-WrigJ

Do you hanker for April showers. Here We Go Quietly Nuts in May. Ogden Nash. CP-NashO

Do you hear the low winds singing. For Rosaline's Album. Christina Georgina Rossetti. CP-RosC3

Do you hear yellow detonations. Pablo Neruda. SP-NeruP *Fr.* Question Book.

Do you imagine, wakeful late in bed. Partial Analysis. Marilyn Hacker. SP-HackM

Do you know Dr. Nott? New Vicar of Bray, The. Lord Byron. CP-Byron

Do you know Hitler? Does he like you? Muriel Rukeyser. CP-RukeM

Do you know how much pain is left. After That. C. K. Williams. CP-WillC

Do you know how the dream looms? how if summer misses one of us. Silver Wind. Carl Sandburg. CP-SandC

Do you know Mr. Ganderdonk, he is no Einstein, he has no. Slow Down, Mr. Ganderdonk, You're Late. Ogden Nash. CP-NashO

Do you know my friend Mr. Betts? Mr. Betts's Mind a Kingdom Is. Ogden Nash. CP-NashO

Do you know the name of the average animal? Drunken Girl. Muriel Rukeyser. CP-RukeM

Do you know what. Fancy. Robert Creeley. CP-CreeR

Do you know what I play to be, in bed at night? Muriel Rukeyser. CP-RukeM

Do you know why your soul-mirror. King and the Handmaiden and the Doctor, The. Jelaluddin Rumi. SP-Rumi, *tr. by* Coleman Barks

Do you like me? Lessons in Hunger. Anne Sexton. CP-SextA

Do you like your life? Three A.M. and Then Five. John Ciardi. CP-CiarJ

Do You Not Father Me. Dylan Thomas. CP-ThomD

Do you not hear me calling, white deer with no horns? Mongan Laments the Change That Has Come upon Him and His Beloved. William Butler Yeats. CP-YeatW

Do you not hear the Aziola cry? Aziola, The. Percy Bysshe Shelley. CP-ShelP

Do You Plan to Speak Bantu? or Abbreviation is the Thief of Sanity. Ogden Nash. CP-NashO

Do you really believe I could blacken my life. Carmen 104. Catullus. CP-ZukLS *Fr.* Carmina.

Do you recall how we sat by the smokily-burning. Memory of Cassis. Edna St. Vincent Millay. CP-MillE

Do you recall / That day in Fall. Days to Recollect. Thomas Hardy. CP-HardT

Do you recall the night we flung. Night Transfigured. Charles Tomlinson. CP-TomlC

Do You Reckon? Langston Hughes. CP-HughL; CP-HughL3

Do you recognize us? We are the ghetto sheep. Gedale's Song. Primo Levi. CP-LeviP, *tr. by* Ruth Feldman

Do you remember. Reminder. D. H. Lawrence. CP-LawrD

Do you remember by morning when the sun. Spring Song ("Do you remember by morning when the sun"). John Ciardi. CP-CiarJ

Do you remember, dear friend, the many snowstorms. Another Snowstorm. Marya Alexandrovna Zaturenska. SP-ZatuM

Do you remember how I beat on the door. Door, A ("Do you remember how I beat on the door"). W. S. Merwin. SP-MerwW

Do you remember how last year we walked. Bizarre. Allen Tate. CP-TateA

Do you remember how the rocket went on. Two Tales of Liadoff. Wallace Stevens. CP-StevW; CP-StevWP

Do you remember learning to tie your shoes? Spirit the Triumph, The. C. K. Williams. CP-WillC; SP-WillC

Do you remember me, Cass. Cass and Me. Paul Muldoon. CP-MuldP

Do you remember? (one said) and they rose from their long sleep. Voices in Air. Marya Alexandrovna Zaturenska. SP-ZatuM

Do you remember the first raw winter. Bumpity Road to Mutual Devotion, The. Marge Piercy. SP-PierM

Do you remember—the green water. Aleksandr Aleksandrovich Blok. SP-BlokA, *tr. by* Peter France *and* Jon Stallworthy

Do you remember things you've lost, the next day? Lost Things. Rainer Maria Rilke. CP-RilkFr, *tr. by* A. Poulin, Jr.

Do you remember when the fluttering dusk. E. E. Cummings. CP-CummE

Do you remember when we dreamed about the owl. Hard Part, The. C. K. Williams. CP-WillC

Do you remember, when you were first a child. Message from Home. Kathleen Jessie Raine. SP-RainK

Do you see? Musical Toys. Lorine Niedecker. CP-NiedL

Do you see that slowly walking, happy. Summer Passer-By. Rainer Maria Rilke. CP-RilkFr, *tr. by* A. Poulin, Jr. *Fr.* Orchards.

Do you see the sea, breaking itself to bits against the islands. Mana of the Sea.

D. H. Lawrence. CP-LawrD

Do you set yourself up as example? Rainer Maria Rilke. CP-RilkFr, *tr. by* A. Poulin, Jr. *Fr.* Roses, The.

Do you still remember what the house was like? House, The. Adam Zagajewski. SP-ZagaA, *tr. by* Clare Cavanagh

"Do You Think." Robert Creeley. CP-CreeR

Do you think / Death is an answer then? Interrogate the Stones. Archibald MacLeish. CP-MacLA

Do you think he likes me I have. Hope Springs. James Laughlin. CP-LaugJ

Do you think I know what I'm doing? Jelaluddin Rumi. SP-Rumi, *tr. by* Coleman Barks

Do you think it is easy to change? Change. D. H. Lawrence. CP-LawrD

Do you think of me as I think of you. L.E.L.'s Last Question. Elizabeth Barrett Browning. CP-BrowE

Do you think of me at all. Dead "Wessex" the Dog to the Household. Thomas Hardy. CP-HardT

Do you think old people should be put away. Question. Grace Paley. CP-PalGC

Do you understand the managing. Into the Shandy Westerness. Kenneth Rexroth. CP-RexrK

Do You Want Affidavits? Carl Sandburg. CP-SandC

Do you? / Yes. Dialogue with Outer Space. John Ciardi. CP-CiarJ

Dobermans run the tiny park. Neighborhood. William Corbett. SP-CorbW

Doc, I bin lookin' for you. Detail. William Carlos Williams. CP-WilW2

Doc Sifers. James Whitcomb Riley. CP-RileJ

Dockery and Son. Philip Larkin. CP-LarkP

Dockery was junior to you. Dockery and Son. Philip Larkin. CP-LarkP

Docks. Carl Sandburg. CP-SandC

Doctor———. Robert Browning. CP-BroR2

Doctor, The. James Whitcomb Riley. CP-RileJ

Doctor, The. Stevie Smith. CP-SmitS

Doctor and Dean, Pope, Parnell and Gay, The. Scriblerian Verses. Jonathan Swift. CP-SwifJ

Doctor and I have become intimate, The. Untitled Poem: "Doctor and I have become intimate, The." Alan Dugan. CP-DugaA

Doctor arrives to inject the movie star against, The. Conversation, A. Robert Bly. SP-BlyR

Doctor calls it "revenge of the nerves," The. Emily Dickinson. SP-DickE

Doctor Faustus. Geoffrey Hill. CP-HillG

Dr. Fell and Points West. Ogden Nash. CP-NashO

Doctor Fell? I Thought So. Ogden Nash. CP-NashO

Dr. Fell is at the door and my *mens sana* is about to depart from. Visit From Dr. Fell, A. Ogden Nash. CP-NashO

Doctor flicks on a light, The. Murmur, The. Arthur Sze. SP-SzeA

Doctor Frolic. Robert Pinsky. CP-PinsR

Doctor gets you when you're born, The. I Yield to My Learned Brother or Is There a Candlestick Maker in the HOuse? Ogden Nash. CP-NashO

Doctor Gliedschirm, skin specialist, surgeries 14–16 hours or by appointment. James Fenton. SP-FentJ *Fr.* German Requiem, A.

Doctor, I did not see that you were there. William Dickey. SP-DickW *Fr.* Part Song, With Concert of Recorders.

Dr. King's photograph. Report from the Skull's Diorama. Yusef Komunyakaa. CP-KomuY

Doctor Mohawk. Nicholas Vachel Lindsay. CP-LindV

Doctor of Billiards. Edwin Arlington Robinson. CP-RobiE

Doctor of Geneva stamped the sand, The. Wallace Stevens. CP-StevW; CP-StevWP

Doctor of the Heart, The. Anne Sexton. CP-SextA

Doctor punched my vein, The. Scyros. Karl Shapiro. SP-ShapK

Dr. Sigmund Freud Discovers the Sea Shell. Archibald MacLeish. CP-MacLA

Dr. Swift to Mr. Pope. Jonathan Swift. CP-SwifJ

Dr. Swift's Answer to Dr. Sheridan. Jonathan Swift. CP-SwifJ

Doctor Will Be Back Too Late, The. Robert Stock. SP-StocR

Doctors. Rudyard Kipling. CP-KiplR

Doctors. Anne Sexton. CP-SextA

Doctors, The. Muriel Rukeyser. CP-RukeM

Doctors, in the Talmud, say, The. Penitence. Robert Herrick. CP-HerrR

Doctors tell me that some people wonder who they are, they don't. You Bet Travel Is Broadening. Ogden Nash. CP-NashO

Documentation. Michael Palmer. SP-PalmM

Documenting It. Miller Williams. CP-WillM

Dodona. "H. D." CP-DoolH

Dodona: Asked of the Oracle. Amy Clampitt. CP-ClamA

Doe: A Fragment, The. George Meredith. CP-MerG1

Doe, The. Rainer Maria Rilke. CP-RilkFr, *tr. by* A. Poulin, Jr. *Fr.* Orchards.

Doe at Evening, A. D. H. Lawrence. CP-LawrD

Do[e] but consider this small dust. Hour-Glass [*or* Houre-Glasse], The. Ben Jonson. CP-JonsB; SP-JonsB

Doe I not see that fayrest ymages. Sonnet 51. Edmund Spenser. CP-Spens *Fr.*

Amoretti.

Doeg, though without knowing how or why. Nahum Tate. SP-DrydJ *Fr.* Absalom and Achitophel, Part 2.

Does a jazz-band ever sob? Cabaret. Langston Hughes. CP-HughL; CP-HughL1

Does anybody listen to advice? Three on Luck. Robert Pinsky. CP-PinsR

Does anybody mind if I don't live in a house that is quaint? No Wonder Our Fathers Died. Ogden Nash. CP-NashO

Does anything get more tangled and higgeldy-piggeldy than the days as they drop. Post-Impressionist Susurration for the First of November, 1983, A. Hayden Carruth. CP-CarHS

Does haughty Gaul invasion threat. Dumfires Volunteers, The. Robert Burns. CP-BurnR

Does he want you down there. To My Father's Violin. Thomas Hardy. CP-HardT

Does my blood need a motive. Blood. David Ignatow. SP-IgnaD

Does No Love Last? Stevie Smith. CP-SmitS

Does No One at All Ever Feel This Way in the Least? Robert Frost. CP-FrosR

Does not show his. His Shirt. Rita Dove. SP-DoveR

Does Pride at evening always fume. Stéphane Mallarmé. CP-MallS, *tr.* by Henry Weinfield

Does she dance? . . . in the first blue hours. Arthur Rimbaud. CP-RimbA, *tr.* by Martin Sorrell

Does something lie who'd rather stand. Ballade: "Does something lie who'd rather stand." E. E. Cummings. CP-CummE

Does sunset sometimes look like the sun's coming up? Jelaluddin Rumi. SP-Rumi, *tr.* by Coleman Barks

Does that lamp still burn in my Father's house. Prodigal Son, A. Christina Georgina Rossetti. CP-RosC2

Does the court pucell then so censure me. Epigram on the Court Pucell, An. Ben Jonson. CP-JonsB

Does the road wind up-hill all the way? Uphill. Christina Georgina Rossetti. CP-RosC1

Does yesterday's perfection seem not quite. E. E. Cummings. CP-CummE

Doesn't anyone see. Shih-te. CP-ColdM, *tr.* by Red Pine

Doesn't he *see* / in the tree / something of *me*? Look. Robert Creeley. CP-CreeR

Doesn't, when we touch it, that sheen of infinitesimally pebbled steel, doesn't it, perhaps. New Car. C. K. Williams. SP-WillC

Doeth Well . . . Doeth Better. Christina Georgina Rossetti. CP-RosC2

Dog. Charles Bukowski. SP-BukC1

Dog. Lawrence Ferlinghetti. SP-FerlL

Dog. John Crowe Ransom. SP-RansJ

Dog, The. Buddhadeva Bose. CP-OppGN, *tr.* by George Oppen

Dog, The. C. K. Williams. CP-WillC; SP-WillC

Dog Act, The. Yusef Komunyakaa. CP-KomuY

Dog After Love, A. Yehuda Amichai. SP-AmicY, *tr.* by Chana Bloch

Dog—An Idyllium, The. William Wordsworth. CP-WorW1

Dog and the Thief, The. Jonathan Swift. CP-SwifJ

Dog and the Water-Lily, The. William Cowper. CP-CowpW

Dog barked, The. Yannis Ritsos. SP-RitsY *Fr.* So?

Dog barked; then the woman stood in the doorway, and hearing iron strike stone down the steep road, The. Roan Stallion. Robinson Jeffers. CP-JefR1

Dog barks far out, A. Ernesto Cardenal. CP-MertT *Fr.* Gethsemani, KY.

Dog barks from a cloud, The. Adolescence. Gregory Orr. SP-OrrG

Dog Day Vespers. Charles Wright. SP-WrigC

Dog, don't look to me! Dog, The. Buddhadeva Bose. CP-OppGN, *tr.* by George Oppen

Dog go howlin' 'long de road, De. Hope. Paul Laurence Dunbar. CP-DunbP

Dog howled, A. Suburban Evening. Langston Hughes. CP-HughL; CP-HughL3

Dog in a Cornfield. James Wright. CP-WrigJ

Dog in the Doorway, The. Jelaluddin Rumi. SP-Rumi, *tr.* by Coleman Barks

Dog in the Sky, The. Robinson Jeffers. CP-JefR3

Dog lies in his kennel, The. Christina Georgina Rossetti. CP-RosC2

Dog pauses before the fire, The. Politics. Heather McHugh. SP-McHuH

Dog Poem. Philip Levine. SP-LeviP

Dog ran down the street, The. Silly Animals. Langston Hughes. CP-HughL

Dog Sleeping on My Feet, A. James Dickey. CP-DickJ

Dog snout puzzles out the look of a man, A. Baboon and the State, The. John Ciardi. CP-CiarJ

Dog surrounding howls, A. Morning, A. James Dickey. CP-DickJ

Dog that spoke, a monster born of sheep, A. Mongolian Idiot. Karl Shapiro. SP-ShapK

Dog-Tired. D. H. Lawrence. CP-LawrD

Dog-tired, suisired, will now my body down. Poet's Final Instructions, The. John Berryman. CP-BerrJ

Dog trots freely in the street, The. Dog. Lawrence Ferlinghetti. SP-FerlL

Dog Under False Pretences. William Dickey. SP-DickW

Dog Wants His Dinner, The. James Schuyler. CP-SchuJ

Dog Was Crying Tonight in Wicklow Also, A. Seamus Heaney. SP-HeanSO

Dog writes on the window with his nose, The. Early Spring. Philip Whalen. SP-WhalP

Dog Yoga. Charles Wright. SP-WrigC

Dogbrothers. Denise Levertov. SP-LeveDL

Dogdays. James Vincent Cunningham. CP-CunnJ

Dogfish. Mary Oliver. SP-OlivM

Doggerel by a Senior Citizen. W. H. Auden. CP-AudeW

Doggerel for My Seventieth Birthday, A. Charles Tomlinson. SP-TomlC

"Doggerel," he thought, "will do for churchwardens." Shakespeare's Grave. Robinson Jeffers. CP-JefR2

Doggie Bags. Robert Creeley. CP-CreeR

Dogheads. Carl Sandburg. CP-SandC

Dogma Triumphant, The. Robert Browning. CP-BroR2

Dogmatic Teachers, of the snow-white fur! Composed on the Banks of a Rocky Stream. William Wordsworth. CP-WorW2

Dogmatism. John Ciardi. CP-CiarJ

Dogs. Charles Bukowski. SP-BukC3

Dogs. W. S. Merwin. SP-MerwW

Dogs, The. Charles Bukowski. SP-BukC2

Dogs, The. Josephine Jacobsen. CP-JacoJ

Dogs and angels are not. Plate Glass Window, A. Charles Bukowski. SP-BukC1

Dogs Are Eating Your Mother, The. Ted Hughes. SP-HughTN

Dog's Best Friend Is His Illiteracy, A. Ogden Nash. CP-NashO

Dog's / body zipped, A. At the Crossroads. Thomas Kinsella. CP-KinsT

Dog's Death. John Updike. CP-UpdiJ

Dogs have nothing better, The. Three Days of Forest, a River, Free. Rita Dove. SP-DoveR

Dogs, I contend, is jes' about. Hired Man's Dog-Story, The. James Whitcomb Riley. CP-RileJ

Dogs in the Park. Louis MacNeice. CP-MacNL

Dog's laughing mouth and happy eye. High-tension on Low-pressure Non-accomplishment Blues. Philip Whalen. SP-WhalP

Dogs of Egypt, The. Charles Bukowski. SP-BukC2

Dogs of hell have claws like cats, The. How Do They Get Your Number? Charles Bukowski. SP-BukC3

Dogs of indecision, The. Clear Days, The. Wendell Berry. CP-BerrW

Dogs, Sheep, Cows, Goats. Gary Snyder. CP-SnydG

Dogs still bark, The. Cure of Ignorance. Laura Riding Jackson. CP-RidiL

Dogs' tails tick like metronomes, The. Lugubrious, Salubrious Seaside, The. Louis MacNeice. CP-MacNL

Dog's Theology, The. Yusef Komunyakaa. CP-KomuY

Dog's thigh, the absurd heaven, The. Grey August. Denise Levertov. SP-LeveDL

Dogwood. Louis Zukofsky. CP-ZukLS

Dogwood Blossoms. Peter Blue Cloud. SP-BlueP

Dogwood Comes Out Yellow, The. Charles Olson. CP-OlsoC

Dogwood flakes / what is green. Variations Done for Gerald Van De Wiele. Charles Olson. CP-OlsoC; SP-OlsoC

Dogwood Trees, The. Robert Earl Hayden. CP-HaydR

Dogwood's snow. In the Yard. May Swenson. SP-SwenM

Doing, a filthy pleasure is, and short. Petronius Arbiter. CP-JonsB; SP-JonsB, *tr.* by Ben Jonson

Doing It Differently. Marge Piercy. SP-PierM

Dole of Jarl Thorkell, The. John Greenleaf Whittier. CP-WhitJ

Dole of the King's Daughter, The. *Unknown.* CP-WildO, *tr.* by Oscar Wilde *and* Oscar Wilde

Doll, The. Gregory Orr. SP-OrrG

Doll Believers, The. Clarence Major. SP-MajoC

Doll in the doll-maker's house, A. Dolls, The. William Butler Yeats. CP-YeatW

Doll she so soone began the wanton trade. Upon Doll. Robert Herrick. CP-HerrR

Doll told me / to exist, The. Veil. Rae Armantrout. SP-ArmaA

Dollar Air. Andrei Codrescu. SP-CodrA

Dollar Dance. Andrei Codrescu. SP-CodrA

Dollmaker, The. Robert Stock. SP-StocR

Dolls. Wallace Stevens. CP-StevWP

Dolls, The. John Ciardi. CP-CiarJ

Dolls, The. Thomas Hardy. CP-HardT

Dolls, The. William Butler Yeats. CP-YeatW

Doll's "Arabian Nights," A. Nicholas Vachel Lindsay. CP-LindV

Doll's boy's asleep / under a stile. E. E. Cummings. CP-CummE

Dolls, / by the thousands. Falling Dolls, The. Anne Sexton. CP-SextA

Doll's hair concealing, A. Partial Resemblance. Denise Levertov. SP-LeveDP

Dolls in gallery along her walls. Distance into Place, The. Wyatt Prunty. SP-PrunW

Dolls Play at Hansel and Gretel, The. William Dickey. SP-DickW

Dolly. Thom Gunn. CP-GunnT

Dolly sits a-quilting by her mother, stitch by stitch. Quilting, The. Paul Laurence Dunbar. CP-DunbP

Dolor. Theodore Roethke. CP-RoetT

Dolores. James Whitcomb Riley. CP-RileJ

Dolour of Autumn. D. H. Lawrence. CP-LawrD

Dolphin. Robert Lowell. SP-LoweR

Dolphin plunge, fountain play. Invocation: "Dolphin plunge, fountain play." Louis MacNeice. CP-MacNL

Dolphin / walked upon the land a little while, The. Living on the Surface. Miller Williams. CP-WillM

Dolphy's Aviary. Yusef Komunyakaa. CP-KomuY

Dolus. Thomas Campion. CP-CampT

Dom Pedro, Emperor of far Brazil. False Prophecy, A. Ambrose Bierce. SP-BierA

Dome of Sunday, The [or A]. Karl Shapiro. SP-ShapK

Dome of the capitol looks to the Potomac river, The. Smoke Rose Gold. Carl Sandburg. CP-SandC

Dome of the Observatory, The. Jaroslav Seifert. SP-SeifJ, tr. by Ewald Osers

Domestic and Unavoidable. Lorine Niedecker. CP-NiedL

Domestic Life. Gregory Orr. SP-OrrG

Domestic of the Outer Banks. Wyatt Prunty. SP-PrunW

Domestic Sonnet. John Ciardi. CP-CiarJ

Domicilium. Thomas Hardy. CP-HardT

Dominant marble, neither will I yield! Don Juan to the Statue. Howard Nemerov. CP-NemeH

Dominant Woman. D. H. Lawrence. CP-LawrD

Domination of Black. Wallace Stevens. CP-StevW; CP-StevWP

Dominic has / a doll wired. E. E. Cummings. CP-CummE

Dominion. A. R. Ammons. CP-AmmoA

Dominion: Depression. C. K. Williams. SP-WillC

Dominion lasts until obtained. Emily Dickinson. CP-DickE

Domino. James Merrill. SP-MerrJ

Don Baty, the Draft Resister. Muriel Rukeyser. CP-RukeM

Don Carlos in a merry spite. Stella at Woodpark. Jonathan Swift. CP-SwifJ

Don John of Chesterton was riding to the wars. Forests of Lithuania, The. Donald Davie. CP-DaviDC

Don Juan. Lord Byron. CP-Byron

Don Juan. John Clare.
  "Poets are born"—and so are whores—the trade is." SP-ClarJ

Don Juan. D. H. Lawrence. CP-LawrD

Don Juan in the Underworld. Charles Baudelaire. CP-BaudC, tr. by Walter Martin

Don Juan to the Statue. Howard Nemerov. CP-NemeH

Don Ramón don't drink, don't smoke. Song to the Tune of *La Cucaracha*. D. H. Lawrence. CP-LawrD

Don Sebastian. John Dryden.
  Prologue to *Don Sebastian*. SP-DrydJ

Don Surly, to aspire the glorious name. On Don Surly. Ben Jonson. CP-JonsB; SP-JonsB

Don, the divinest women that have walked. With Daniel Bartoli. Robert Browning. CP-BroR2

Doña Catalina / had a single gold hair. Catherine Wheel. Federico García Lorca. CP-GarcF, tr. by Jerome Rothenberg Fr. Barrage of Firework Poems on the Occasion of the Poet's Birthday.

Donaghadee. Thomas Hardy. CP-HardT

Donahue's Sister. Thom Gunn. CP-GunnT

Donald. Robert Browning. CP-BroR2; SP-BroR

Done are the toils and the wearisome marches. Ode for Memorial Day. Paul Laurence Dunbar. CP-DunbP

Done, Finished with the Biggest Cock. Allen Ginsberg. CP-GinsA

Done for the Doing. John Ciardi. CP-CiarJ

Done is a battell [or battle] on the dragon blak [or black]. William Dunbar. CP-DunbW

Donegal Triptych. Louis MacNeice. CP-MacNL

Donkey, The. G. K. Chesterton. CP-ChesG

Donkey, The. Theodore Roethke. CP-RoetT

Donkey, The. Stevie Smith. CP-SmitS

Donkey's tail is very nice, A. Monotony Song, The. Theodore Roethke. CP-RoetT

Donn Piatt of Mac-o-chee. James Whitcomb Riley. CP-RileJ

Donne Ch'avete Intellètto d'Amore. John Ciardi. CP-CiarJ

Donne, the delight of Phoebus, and each Muse. To John Donne ("Donne, the delight of Phoebus, and each Muse"). Ben Jonson. CP-JonsB; SP-JonsB

Donnez à manger aux affamées. Film Star, The. Stevie Smith. CP-SmitS

Donor. Lucille Clifton. SP-ClifL

Don't. C. K. Williams. CP-WillC

Don't Allow the Lucid Moment to Dissolve. Adam Zagajewski. SP-ZagaA, tr. by Renata Gorczynski

Don't ask for the true story. True Stories. Margaret Atwood. SP-AtwM2

Don't ask us for the word to frame. Eugenio Montale. CP-MontE, tr. by Jonathan Galassi

Don't be afraid if the work is hard. Proxy. Primo Levi. CP-LeviP, tr. by Ruth Feldman

Don't Be Cross, Amanda. Ogden Nash. CP-NashO

Don't be dismayed, woman, by my fierce form. Annunciation. Primo Levi. CP-LeviP, tr. by Ruth Feldman

Don't be too long now, the next time. High Road, The. Thomas Kinsella. CP-KinsT

Don't believe yourself sterile, although, an exile from women. Upon an Eunuch: A Poet. Andrew Marvell. CP-MarvA

Don't bother me. / I've just / been born. One or Two Things. Mary Oliver. SP-OlivM

Don't care for it. Berkshire. Donald Davie. CP-DaviDC

Don't cries to please my. E. E. Cummings. CP-CummE

Don't Cry, Darling, It's Blood All Right. Ogden Nash. CP-NashO

Don't escape into the shade. Eugenio Montale. CP-MontE, tr. by Jonathan Galassi

Don't Even Tell Your Wife, Particularly. Ogden Nash. CP-NashO

Don't ever cut me from your hands. Digestibles of Sun. Olga Broumas. SP-BrouO

Don't / ever refuse / the. Easter. Robert Creeley. CP-CreeR

Don't forget, dear departing saint. One, Two, Maybe Three, Arguments against Suicide. A. K. Ramanujan. CP-RamaA

Don't get me wrong oblivion. E. E. Cummings. CP-CummE

Don't go anywhere without me. In the Arc of Your Mallet. Jelaluddin Rumi. SP-Rumi, tr. by Coleman Barks

Don't go to sleep one night. Vigil, The. Jelaluddin Rumi. SP-Rumi, tr. by Coleman Barks

Don't go / to the mountains. Then ("Don't go / to the mountains"). Robert Creeley. SP-CreeR

Don't grieve. Anything you lose comes round. Unmarked Boxes. Jelaluddin Rumi. SP-Rumi, tr. by Coleman Barks

Don't Grin, or You'll Have to Bear It. Ogden Nash. CP-NashO

Don't Grow Old. Allen Ginsberg. CP-GinsA

Don't Guess, Let Me Tell You. Ogden Nash. CP-NashO

Don't hate your parents, or your children will hire. Hard Way, The. Robert Lowell. SP-LoweR

Don't hold me back, friends, let me set out. Pliny. Primo Levi. CP-LeviP, tr. by Ruth Feldman

Don't hoot at the poor dear basilisk. Flabbergasting of the True & False Basilisk, The. Robert Stock. SP-StocR

Don't kid yourself: / something kills them all—. Kind of Lecture on a Dull Day When There Isn't Even a Fly Around to Kill, A. Charles Bukowski. SP-BukC2

Don't Kill Yourself. Carlos Drummond de Andrade. CP-BishE, tr. by Elizabeth Bishop

Don't know why I. Angola Question Mark. Langston Hughes. CP-HughL; CP-HughL3

Don't let it mean anything. Rifkin Movement. Richard Eberhart. CP-EberR

Don't Let That Horse. Lawrence Ferlinghetti. SP-FerlL

Don't let that horse. Don't Let That Horse. Lawrence Ferlinghetti. SP-FerlL

Don't let your dog curb you! Warning: Augmented. Langston Hughes. CP-HughL; CP-HughL3

Don't let your throat tighten. Jelaluddin Rumi. SP-Rumi, tr. by Coleman Barks

Don't lock me in wedlock, I want. About Marriage. Denise Levertov. SP-LeveDP; SP-LeveDS

Don't Look at Me. D. H. Lawrence. CP-LawrD

Don't look at me. Sheikh Kharraqani and His Wretched Wife. Jelaluddin Rumi. SP-Rumi, tr. by Coleman Barks

Don't look at me. Shy One, The. James Tate. SP-TateJ

Don't Look for the Silver Lining, Just Wait for It. Ogden Nash. CP-NashO

Don't Look Now. Ogden Nash. CP-NashO

Don't look now, God, we're all right. May 30th. Anne Sexton. CP-SextA

Don't mix me up with that rascal Eros. King's Bowman, The. James Laughlin. CP-LaugJ

Don't play with sharp tools, these are edge 'uns. Rhyme on Edward Burne-Jones. Robert Browning. CP-BroR2

Don't prepare for tomorrow. Turn your face to the narrow alley. Yehuda Amichai. SP-AmicYL, tr. by Benjamin Harshav *and* Barbara Harshav

Don't put up my Thread and Needle. Emily Dickinson. CP-DickE

Don't Run. Raymond Carver. CP-CarvR

Don't run anymore. Quiet. How softly it rains. After Paradise. Czeslaw Milosz. CP-MiloC; CP-MiloCN, tr. by Robert Hass

Don't run around this world. Tending Two Shops. Jelaluddin Rumi. SP-Rumi, tr. by Coleman Barks

Don't sail, Tui, where krait and coconut-crab. To Tui: Not to Hie Herself Off To Only God Knows How Dire & Pestilential A South Sea Island, But to Come With Us To Found Her Community in Brazil; Together With Some Preposterous Notes Toward an Ornithomancy of Lovingkindness. Robert

Stock. SP-StocR

Don't say, don't say there is no water. Fountain, The. Denise Levertov. SP-LeveDP

Don't say, "humbly" Graph for Action. William Carlos Williams. CP-WilW1

Don't shoot the rail! Lorine Niedecker. CP-NiedL

Don't Sign Anything. Robert Creeley. CP-CreeR

Don't sing: your tongue. Drops of Gall. Gabriela Mistral. SP-MistG, tr. by Maria Giachetti [or Jacketti]

Don't smell, said the little girl. Two Holidays. Heather McHugh. SP-McHuH

Dont smoke dont smoke dont smoke. Put Down Your Cigarette Rag (Dont Smoke). Allen Ginsberg. SP-GinsA

Don't spill the salt, for it is the landmark. Spilling the Salt. D. H. Lawrence. CP-LawrD

Don't stand out there, man, in all that howllllllll. Six Inch Chapter—in Verse, A. Charles Olson. CP-OlsoC

Don't stay poor my friend. Han-shan. CP-ColdM, tr. by Red Pine

Don't stir from that profound repose. Girandole, The. Charles Baudelaire. CP-BaudC, tr. by Walter Martin

Don't take jesters into outer space. Warning. Wisława Szymborska. SP-SzymW, tr. by Stanislaw Barańczak and Clare Cavanagh

Don't take / the steak. Doggie Bags. Robert Creeley. SP-CreeR

Don't take your love. Breaking Up Is Hard to Do. Robert Creeley. SP-CreeR

Don't take your memory with you. Ghazal of the Memory of Love. Federico García Lorca. CP-GarcF, tr. by Catherine Brown Fr. Ghazals.

Don't talk to me about trees having branches and roots. On Trees. Alan Dugan. CP-DugaA

Don't tell me property is sacred! Lorine Niedecker. CP-NiedL

Don't think / because her petal thighs. Girl in White. Marge Piercy. SP-PierM

Don't think I'm willing to pay cash. Woman Selling Aromatic Herbs, The. Stéphane Mallarmé. CP-MallS Fr. Street Songs.

Don't think I'm willing to pay cash. Woman Selling Aromatic Herbs, The. Stéphane Mallarmé. CP-MallS, tr. by Henry Weinfield

Don't think of it. Praise. Wendell Berry. CP-BerrW

Don't think these few lines which I send a reproach. To the Dean. Thomas Sheridan. CP-SherT

Don't Think You Know My Name! Thomas McGrath. SP-McGrT

Don't Touch the Girls. Charles Bukowski. SP-BukC1

Don't undress my love. Trapped. Charles Bukowski. SP-BukC1

Don't unstring the bow. All Rivers at Once. Jelaluddin Rumi. SP-Rumi, tr. by Coleman Barks

Don't Wait for Me. Andrei Codrescu. SP-CodrA

Don't Wait, Hit Me Now! Ogden Nash. CP-NashO

Don't walk barefoot in the bathroom. Note of Quits. Alan Dugan. CP-DugaA

Don't Wash Your Hair in the Streetcar, Nora Dear. Kenneth Patchen. CP-PatcK

Don't waste your time, Leuconoë, living in fear and hope. Ode 1.2: How to Live. Horace. CP-MahoD Fr. Odes.

Don't worry about rejections, pard. For Al—. Charles Bukowski. SP-BukC1

Don't worry about saving these songs! Where Everything Is Music. Jelaluddin Rumi. SP-Rumi, tr. by Coleman Barks

Don't write yourself. Paul Celan. SP-CelaP, tr. by John Felstiner

Don't you also feel danger. Pablo Neruda. SP-NeruP Fr. Question Book.

Don't you care for my love? she said bitterly. Intimates. D. H. Lawrence. CP-LawrD

Don't You Hear that Whistle Blowin'. Denise Levertov. SP-LeveDL

Don't you see? Alternatives. James Tate. SP-TateJ

Don'ts. D. H. Lawrence. CP-LawrD

Donut Dollies. Yusef Komunyakaa. CP-KomuY

Donzella Beata. Ezra Pound. CP-PoEar

Doodle-Bug's Charm, The. James Whitcomb Riley. CP-RileJ

Doodler, The. James Merrill. SP-MerrJ

Doom and She. Thomas Hardy. CP-HardT

Doom and Siesta Time. Charles Bukowski. SP-BukC1

Doom in Bloom. Laura Riding Jackson. CP-RidiL

Doom is dark and deeper than any sea-dingle. Wanderer, The. W. H. Auden. CP-AudeW

Doom is the House without the Door. Emily Dickinson. CP-DickE

Doom of Exiles. Sylvia Plath. CP-PlatS

Doom of Fruit without the Bloom, A. Emily Dickinson. SP-DickE

Doom'd as I am in solitude to waste. On the Death of Russell. William Cowper. CP-CowpW

Doomed gunman, surrounded, The. Margins of Choice. Josephine Jacobsen. CP-JacoJ

Doomed—regard the Sunrise, The. Emily Dickinson. CP-DickE

Doomes-Day. Robert Herrick. CP-HerrR

Dooms menace from tumults. Who's immune. Beethoven Triumphant. John Berryman. CP-BerrJ

Doomsday. George Herbert. CP-HerbG

Doomsday. Sylvia Plath. CP-PlatS

Doomsday Books, The. Howard Nemerov. CP-NemeH

Door. Federico García Lorca. CP-GarcF, tr. by Jerome Rothenberg Fr. Narcissus.

Door, A ("Do you remember how I beat on the door"). W. S. Merwin. SP-MerwW

Door, A ("This is a place where a door might be"). W. S. Merwin. SP-MerwW

Door, A ("What is dying all over the world"). W. S. Merwin. SP-MerwW

Door, A ("You walk on"). W. S. Merwin. SP-MerwW

Door, The. Jane Cooper. CP-CoopJ

Door, The. Robert Creeley. CP-CreeR

Door, The. Robert Creeley. CP-CreeR

Door, The. Robert Graves. CP-GravR

Door, The. Charles Tomlinson. CP-TomlC; SP-TomlC

Door-bell jangled in evening's peace, The. Owl, The. Walter De la Mare. CP-DeLaW

Door in the Dark, The. Robert Frost. CP-FrosR

Door in the Wall, The. Charles Tomlinson. SP-TomlC

Door is shut. / The red rider, The. Sense of Distance, A. Charles Tomlinson. CP-TomlC; SP-TomlC

Door just opened on a street, A. Emily Dickinson. CP-DickE

Door of Death is made of Gold, The. Dedication of the Illustrations to Blair's "Grave" William Blake. CP-BlakW

Door of the house opened by mistake, The. Yehuda Amichai. SP-AmicYL, tr. by Benjamin Harshav and Barbara Harshav

Door opens, The. Enters Éri. Two cherries, Unexpectedly Yannis Ritsos. SP RitsY, tr. by Kimon Friar

Door: / PER L'UNIVERSO / is what it says, A. Idyll. "Door: / PER L'UNIVERSO / is what it says, A." Charles Tomlinson. CP-TomlC; SP-TomlC

Door sunk in a hillside, with a bolt, A. Icehouse in Summer, The. Howard Nemerov. CP-NemeH

Door was shut. I looked between, The. Shut Out. Christina Georgina Rossetti. CP-RosC1

Doorkeepers of Zion, The. Zion. Rudyard Kipling. CP-KiplR

Doorknobs. Langston Hughes. CP-HughL; CP-HughL3

Doors. D. H. Lawrence. CP-LawrD

Doors. Carl Sandburg. CP-SandC

Doors are down before the ancient tombs, The. Pride of the Dead, The. Thomas Merton. CP-MertT

Doors, Doors, Doors. Anne Sexton. CP-SextA

Doors in the Wind and the Water. Marge Piercy. SP-PierM

Doors of the morning must open, The. Pass, Friend. Carl Sandburg. CP-SandC

Doors open in the mind. Doors in the Wind and the Water. Marge Piercy. SP-PierM

Doors open, The. In the Beach House. Anne Sexton. CP-SextA; SP-SextA

Doors take in air, exhale steam; you, however, won't, The. December in Florence. Joseph Brodsky. CP-BrodJ

Doors to the left and right. A woman appeared in the corridor. Yannis Ritsos. SP-RitsY Fr. First Series.

Doors were wide, the story saith, The. Rudyard Kipling. CP-KiplR Fr. Life's Handicap.

Doorstep, Lightning, Waif-Dreaming. James Dickey. CP-DickJ

Dope Fiend Blues. Allen Ginsberg. SP-GinsA

Doppelgaengers, The. James Laughlin. CP-LaugJ

Doppelgängers. Yusef Komunyakaa. CP-KomuY

Dora Markus. Eugenio Montale. CP-MontE, tr. by Jonathan Galassi

Dorabella's Naples Watercolor. James Schuyler. CP-SchuJ

Dora's gone to Ireland. How She Went to Ireland. Thomas Hardy. CP-HardT

Δωρια. Ezra Pound. CP-PoEar; SP-PounE

Dorinda dreams of dress abed. Jonathan Swift. CP-SwifJ

Dormi, Jesu! Mater ridet. Samuel Taylor Coleridge. See Sleep, sweet babe! my cares beguiling

Dorothy Wordsworth, dying, did not want to read. My Sisters, O My Sisters. May Sarton. SP-SartM

Dorset. Donald Davie. CP-DaviDC

Dorset, the Grace of Courts, the Muses' Pride. Epitaph on Charles Earl of Dorset. Alexander Pope. CP-PopeA

Dorset! whose early steps with mine have stray'd. To the Duke of Dorset. Lord Byron. CP-Byron

Dortmunder. Samuel Beckett. CP-BeckS

Dorus, tell me, where is thy wonted motion. Sir Philip Sidney. SP-SidnP Fr. Arcadia.

Do's Fortune rend thee? Beare with thy hard Fate. Suffer Thou that Canst not Shift. Robert Herrick. CP-HerrR

Dose of death occupied your body, A. Light of Lamps, The. Adam Zagajewski. SP-ZagaA, tr. by Renata Gorczynski, Benjamin Ivry and C. K. Williams

Dosn't thou 'ear my 'erse's legs, as they canters awaäy? Northern Farmer: New Style. Alfred Tennyson. CP-TennA

Dost ask, dear Captain, why from Syme. To Captain G———, on Being Asked

Why I Was Not to Be of the Party with Him and His Brother K-nm-re at Syme's. Robert Burns. CP-BurnR

Dost ask me, why I send thee here. Primrose, The. Robert Burns. CP-BurnR

Dost me of new crimes always guilty frame? Elegy 2.7: "Dost me of new crimes always guilty frame?" Ovid. CP-MarlC *Fr.* Elegies.

Dos't o' Blues, A. James Whitcomb Riley. CP-RileJ

Dost see how unregarded now. Sonnet: "Dost see how unregarded now." Sir John Suckling. CP-SuckJ

Dost tha hear my horse's feet, as he canters away? Lord Tennyson and Lord Melchett. D. H. Lawrence. CP-LawrD

Dost thou behold some woeful soul. George Meredith. CP-MerG2

Dost thou love me, my Belovèd? Proof and Disproof. Elizabeth Barrett Browning. CP-BroEB

Dost Thou Not Care? Christina Georgina Rossetti. CP-RosC1

Dost thou not hear me Ellen. Ralph Waldo Emerson. CP-EmerR

Dost thou not rise, indignant Shade. Extempore—on Some Commemorations of Thomson. Robert Burns. CP-BurnR

Dost thou weep, mourning mother. Mourning Mother, The. Elizabeth Barrett Browning. CP-BroEB

Dostoyevsky. Kenneth Patchen. CP-PatcK

Dot Leedle Boy. James Whitcomb Riley. CP-RileJ

Dotage. George Herbert. CP-HerbG

Doth most humbly show it. Humble Petition of Poor Ben to the Best of Monarchs, Masters, Men, King Charles, The. Ben Jonson. CP-JonsB

Dotted line my father's ashplant made, The. Strand, The. Seamus Heaney. SP-HeanSO

Dotty had / Great Big. When We Were Very Sore; Lines on Discovering that You Have Been Advertised as America's A.A. Milne. Dorothy Parker. CP-ParkD

D'où / la voix qui dit. Samuel Beckett. CP-BeckS

Double. Rae Armantrout. SP-ArmaA

Double Agent. Heather McHugh. SP-McHuH

Double Axe, The. Robinson Jeffers. CP-JefR3

Double Ballade of Newfangled Ladies, A. Robert Stock. SP-StocR

Double Bass. Robert Graves. CP-GravR

Double Condemnation. Yannis Ritsos. SP-RitsY, *tr. by* N. C. Germanacos

Double Dialogue: *Homage to Robert Frost.* Muriel Rukeyser. CP-RukeM

Double, diverse, sullen, and strange. Sir Thomas Wyatt. CP-WyatT

Double, double, root and branch. Charles Olson. CP-OlsoC

Double, double, twice the face. Bagatto. Charles Olson. CP-OlsoC

Double Feature. Robert Earl Hayden. CP-HaydR

Double Feature. Theodore Roethke. CP-RoetT

Double-Headed Snake of Newbury, The. John Greenleaf Whittier. CP-WhitJ

Double Image, The. Anne Sexton. CP-SextA; SP-SextA

Double in the mirror is confused, The. Rainer Maria Rilke. CP-RilkFr

Double Limbo. Yusef Komunyakaa. CP-KomuY

Double Monologue. Adrienne Rich. CP-RicAE

Double moon, one on the high backdrop of the west, one on the, The. River Moons. Carl Sandburg. CP-SandC

Double Ode. Muriel Rukeyser. CP-RukeM

Double Poem of Lake Eden. Federico García Lorca. CP-GarcF, *tr. by* Greg Simon *and* Steven F. White

Double Rainbow, The. Charles Tomlinson. CP-TomlC

Double Shame, The. Stephen Spender. CP-SpenS

Double Sphere, Cloven Sphere. Norman Dubie. CP-DubiN

Double Vision. Robert Lowell. SP-LoweR

Double Vision of Michael Robartes, The. William Butler Yeats. CP-YeatW

Double Voice, The. Margaret Atwood. SP-AtwM1

Doubled Mirrors. Kenneth Rexroth. CP-RexrK

Doubleness coils in Time like. Robert Penn Warren. CP-WarrR

Doubling and doubling with laborious walk. Rest and Be Thankful! William Wordsworth. CP-WorW2

Doubling the Nerve. A. R. Ammons. CP-AmmoA

Doubt. G. K. Chesterton. CP-ChesG

Doubt. Rainer Maria Rilke. CP-RilkFr, *tr. by* A. Poulin, Jr.

Doubt, a Pastoral Ballad—1762. Annis Boudinot Stockton. CP-StocA

Doubt and the passion, The. Oath, The. Robert Graves. CP-GravR

Doubt if it be Us, A. Emily Dickinson. CP-DickE

Doubt Me. Surrender. Emily Dickinson. CP-DickE

Doubt No More that Oberon. Edna St. Vincent Millay. CP-MillE

Doubt to which a wavering hope had clung, The. Composed When a Probability Existed of Our Being Obliged to Quit Rydal Mount as a Residence. William Wordsworth. CP-WorW2

Doubt you fought so long, The. Whip, The. Edwin Arlington Robinson. CP-RobiE

Doubtful Encounters. Yannis Ritsos. SP-RitsY, *tr. by* Kostas Myrsiades

Doubtless, sweet girl! the hissing lead. Lines Addressed to a Young Lady. Lord Byron. CP-Byron

Doughnut is no sculpture, A. Two for Gertrude Kasle. John Ciardi. CP-CiarJ

Douglas and Marmion. Sir Walter Scott. *See* Marmion

Douglass. Paul Laurence Dunbar. CP-DunbP

Douglas's Ride. Emily Jane Brontë. CP-BronE

Douglass was someone who. Frederick Douglass: 1817–1895. Langston Hughes. CP-HughL; CP-HughL3

Dove, A. Ted Hughes. SP-HughTN

Dove, The. Paul Laurence Dunbar. CP-DunbP

Dove, The. Langston Hughes. CP-HughL; CP-HughL3

Dove, The. Walter De la Mare. CP-DeLaW

Dove flew with an Olive Branch, A. Olive Branch, The. George Meredith. CP-MerG1

Dove in Spring, The. Wallace Stevens. CP-StevWP

Dove in the Belly, The. Wallace Stevens. CP-StevW; CP-StevWP

Dove in the Eaves, A. Jelaluddin Rumi. SP-Rumi, *tr. by* Coleman Barks

Dove-melting mountains, ridges gashed with water. No More Sea. Louis MacNeice. CP-MacNL

Dove of Dacca, The. Rudyard Kipling. CP-KiplR

Dove of liberty sat on an egg, The. American Eagle, The. D. H. Lawrence. CP-LawrD

Dove sta amore / Where lies love. Lawrence Ferlinghetti. SP-FerlL

Dove that lets the silence answer. Wood Dove at Sandy Spring, The. Archibald MacLeish. CP-MacLA

Dove-twirl in the tall grass. Chickamauga. Charles Wright. SP-WrigCN

Dove walks with sticky feet, The. Pastoral: "Dove walks with sticky feet, The." Kenneth Patchen. CP-PatcK

Dove-white gulls / on the wet lawn in Washington Square, The. I Genitori Perduti. Lawrence Ferlinghetti. SP-FerlL

Doveglion. E. E. Cummings. CP-CummE

Dover. W. H. Auden. CP-AudeW

Dover Beach. Matthew Arnold. SP-ArnoM

"Dover Beach"—a Note to That Poem. Archibald MacLeish. CP-MacLA

Dover: Believing in Kings. James Dickey. CP-DickJ

Doverrit with dreme, devysing in my slummer. William Dunbar. CP-DunbW

Doves, The. William Cowper. CP-CowpW

Doves sit on shoulder and on window sill. Yehuda Amichai. SP-AmicYL *Fr.* Here We Loved.

Doves the speckled doves, The. In Aix. Grace Paley. CP-PalGC

Dow Jones: Down. Charles Bukowski. SP-BukC2

Down. Robert Graves. CP-GravR

Down a rope of. Plunge, The. Thom Gunn. CP-GunnT

Down among strict roots and rocks. Danse Macabre. Sylvia Plath. CP-PlatS

Down among the roots. Thomas Kinsella.

Down and down into your own regard. In a World of Taking, the Mistake. Heather McHugh. SP-McHuH

Down and Out. Langston Hughes. CP-HughL

Down around the River. James Whitcomb Riley. CP-RileJ

Down at the Docks. Kenneth Koch. SP-KochK

Down & Back. John Berryman. CP-BerrJ

Down below the window, on the deck, some ragged-looking. Through the Boughs. Raymond Carver. CP-CarvR

Down between the walls of shadow. Subway. Carl Sandburg. CP-SandC

Down by La Perla. Borinken Blues. Yusef Komunyakaa. CP-KomuY

Down by the bay I. Attention. A. R. Ammons. CP-AmmoA

Down by the Nile water. Moses. Howard Nemerov. CP-NemeH

Down by the Salley Gardens. William Butler Yeats. CP-YeatW

Down by the waters of the sea. Never-To-Be. Walter De la Mare. CP-DeLaW

Down comes the winter rain. Unrealized. Thomas Hardy. CP-HardT

Down, down beneath the daisy beds. Song of the Garden-Toad, The. Nicholas Vachel Lindsay. CP-LindV

Down, down, down! Finding Your Level. D. H. Lawrence. CP-LawrD

Down, down there in the great green sea. Song of the Sea-Wealth, The. G. K. Chesterton. CP-ChesG

Down drop of the blackbird, The. Three Spring Notations on Bipeds. Carl Sandburg. CP-SandC

Down East people, not being botanists. Botanical Nomenclature. Amy Clampitt. CP-ClamA

Down from Chicago Bryan came. Muriel Rukeyser. CP-RukeM

Down From Colonnata. Charles Tomlinson. SP-TomlC

Down from the realms of light above. Amore Fuggitivo. Torquato Tasso. CP-SherT, *tr. by* Thomas Sheridan

Down gently / through the smokehole down. Descent. Peter Blue Cloud. SP-BlueP

Down Home. Robert Creeley. CP-CreeR

Down home / he sets on a stoop. Neighbor. Langston Hughes. CP-HughL; CP-HughL3

Down in a pale plain dry as chaff. As the Tree Falleth. G. K. Chesterton. CP-ChesG

Down in Ol' Dontcaradama. Kenneth Patchen. CP-PatcK

Down in the bass. Easy Boogie. Langston Hughes. CP-HughL; CP-HughL3

Down in the lobby three elderly women, bored. Lagoon. Joseph Brodsky. CP-BrodJ, *tr.* by Anthony Hecht

Down in the Lone Valley. Kenneth Patchen. CP-PatcK

Down in the night I hear them. Voices, The. James Whitcomb Riley. CP-RileJ

Down in the street there are ice-cream parlors to go to. Thank You for Not Cooperating. John Ashbery. SP-AshbJ

Down in West Texas where the [*or* de] sun. West Texas. Langston Hughes. CP-HughL; CP-HughL2

Down lay Karl Onyx for his end of time. Karl Onyx. George Meredith. CP-MerG2

Down Narrow Stairs from a Thin Eye. John Ciardi. CP-CiarJ

Down on the ancient wharf, the sand, I sit with a new-comer chatting. Twenty Years. Walt Whitman. CP-WhitW

Down on the riverbanks. Serenade: "Down on the riverbanks." Federico García Lorca. CP-GarcF, *tr.* by Alan S. Trueblood *Fr.* Eros with a Cane.

Down on the sidewalk recurrent. Children, The. Robert Creeley. SP-CreeR

Down on the tongue of black rock. Sea Cliffs at Kailua in December, The. W. S. Merwin. SP-MerwWF

Down on '33rd Street. Statement. Langston Hughes. CP-HughL; CP-HughL2

Down on Wriggle Crick. James Whitcomb Riley. CP-RileJ

Down. Shovelled. Can hear. Alternate Thoughts from Underground. Margaret Atwood. SP-AtwoM1

Down Stream. Dante Gabriel Rossetti. CW-RossD

Down stucco sidestreets. Dublinesque. Philip Larkin. CP-LarkP

Down the Burn Davie. Robert Burns. CP-BurnR

Down the church gravel where the bridal car. Wedding Morning. Thomas Kinsella. CP-KinsT

Down the close, darkening lanes they sang their way. Send-Off, The. Wilfred Owen. CP-OwenW

Down the dawn-brown. Current, The. James Merrill. SP-MerrJ

Down the façade lean statues listening. Thunder in Tuscany. Charles Tomlinson. CP-TómlC; SP-TomlC

Down the golden mountains. In the Sun. Wallace Stevens. CP-StevWP

Down the long curving walk you trudge to the street. Gerda. Carolyn Kizer. CP-KizeC

Down the long library each marble bust. St. Patrick's Day. Derek Mahon. CP-MahoD

Down the Mousehole, and What Science Missed There. Ogden Nash. CP-NashO

Down the river, on rafts you came. Rafts, The. Adrienne Rich. CP-RicAE

Down the road someone is practising scales. Sunday Morning. Louis MacNeice. CP-MacNL

Down the rock chute into the tombs of the kings they grope these battling sandalled. This Is the Life. Louis MacNeice. CP-MacNL

Down the small and crooked road. Poem: "Down the small and crooked road." Thomas McGrath. SP-McGrT

Down the stair had creaked the doctor's feet. Death Mask of a Young Man. Robert Penn Warren. CP-WarrR

Down the stairs flying, looks at the surfaces. Muriel Rukeyser. CP-RukeM

Down the stone stairs. After the Opera. D. H. Lawrence. CP-LawrD

Down the street young Harlem. Dimout in Harlem. Langston Hughes. CP-HughL; CP-HughL2

Down the track of a Philippine Island. Enclosure, The. James Dickey. CP-DickJ

Down the wet-leaves steps comes the tiger-head. Allhallows Party. Josephine Jacobsen. CP-JacoJ

Down there along the Maldonado. Blade in the Northside, A. Jorge Luis Borges. SP-BorgJ, *tr.* by Eric McHenry

Down there in those islands. Bahamas. Archibald MacLeish. CP-MacLA

Down this old well. Well, The. Adrienne Rich. CP-RicAE

Down through the generations. History of the Night. Jorge Luis Borges. SP-BorgJ, *tr.* by Charles Tomlinson

Down through the latticework of leaves. Basic Syllogism. Robert Penn Warren. CP-WarrR

Down through the rocks where the dark roots dry. Grave of Arthur, The. G. K. Chesterton. CP-ChesG

Down through the tomb's inward arch. Ikon: The Harrowing of Hell. Denise Levertov. SP-LeveDS

Down, throw down his like who eat. Cinos. Charles Olson. CP-OlsoC

Down Time's quaint stream. Emily Dickinson. CP-DickE

(Down, / to my soul. Love. Charles Olson. CP-OlsoC

Down to the Capital. James Whitcomb Riley. CP-RileJ

Down to the Dregs. César Vallejo. CP-WrigJ, *tr.* by James Wright *and* James Wright

Down to the stream to watch the jade flow. Han-shan. CP-ColdM, *tr.* by Red Pine

Down to this north end of the verandah, across the view. Flower Path, The. Arthur Sze. SP-SzeA

Down valley a smoke haze. Mid-August at Sourdough Mountain Lookout. Gary Snyder. CP-SnydG

Down Wall Street. Workers Rose on May Day or Postcript to Karl Marx, The. Audre Lorde. SP-LordA

Down, Wanton, Down! Robert Graves. CP-GravR

Down We Go. James Laughlin. CP-LaugJ

Down went the grand "Queen Mary." Sea Fight, The. Thomas Hardy. CP-HardT

Down Wessex way, when spring's a-shine. Spring Call, The. Thomas Hardy. CP-HardT

Down Where I Am. Langston Hughes. CP-HughL; CP-HughL3

Down where the dog-toothed tide. Art Song. Howard Nemerov. CP-NemeH

Down with the Rosemary and Bay[e]s. Ceremonies for Candlemas[se] Eve. Robert Herrick. CP-HerrR

Down with the rosemary, and so. Ceremony upon Candlemas Eve. Robert Herrick. CP-HerrR

Down, you mongrel, Death! Poet and His Book, The. Edna St. Vincent Millay. CP-MillE

Downhill, any gait will serve. Wild Horse Love. William Stafford. SP-StafWW

Downstairs a clock had chimed, two o'clock only. Down. Robert Graves. CP-GravR

Downstairs I laugh, I sport and jest with all. L. E. L. Christina Georgina Rossetti. CP-RosC1

Downstream. Raymond Carver. CP-CarvR

Downstream on impassive rivers suddenly. Drunken Boat. Arthur Rimbaud. CP-BeckS, *tr.* by Samuel Beckett

Downstream they have killed the river and built a dam. Fish Counter at Bonneville, The. William Stafford. SP-StafWW

Downstream ("We gave our craft to the slow-moving stream"). Thomas Kinsella. CP-KinsT

Downtown, an office tower is going up. Diagrams. Thom Gunn. CP-GunnT

Downtown Bus, The. Wyatt Prunty. SP-PrunW

Downtrodden sailor's quarter, A. The light globes sleepy. Moment. Yannis Ritsos. SP-RitsY, *tr.* by Kimon Friar

Downward. May Swenson. SP-SwenM

Downward through the evening twilight. Hiawatha's Childhood. Henry Wadsworth Longfellow. SP-LongH *Fr.* Song of Hiawatha, The.

Downwards. C. K. Williams. CP-WillC; SP-WillC

Downwind. Clarence Major. SP-MajoC

Dowser, The. Louis MacNeice. CP-MacNL

Doxology. A. R. Ammons. CP-AmmoA

Doxology. Yannis Ritsos. SP-RitsY, *tr.* by Kimon Friar

Dozen girls' chemises, A. Dance of the Girls' Chemises. Jaroslav Seifert. SP-SeifJ, *tr.* by Ewald Osers

Dozens, The. Audre Lorde. SP-LordA

Dozing on the Lawn. Archibald MacLeish. CP-MacLA

Dr. Goebbels did not go to heaven. The mundane. Dr. Goebbel's Novels. Thomas Lux. SP-LuxT

Dr. Goebbel's Novels. Thomas Lux. SP-LuxT

Dr. Williams' Garden. Wyatt Prunty. SP-PrunW

Dr. Y. / I need a thin hot wire. Letters to Dr. Y. Anne Sexton. CP-SextA

Drab Habitation of Whom? Emily Dickinson. CP-DickE

Drab look'd long at his neighbour's note. Song of Drab, The. George Meredith. CP-MerG2

Drachms and Scruples. Ivor Gurney. SP-GurnI

Draft Horse, The. Robert Frost. CP-FrosR

Draft of a Reparations Agreement. Dan Pagis. SP-PagiD, *tr.* by Stephen Mitchell

Draft of love was cool and sweet, The. Love's Draft. Paul Laurence Dunbar. CP-DunbP

Draftees. Langston Hughes. CP-HughL; CP-HughL3

Drafts. A. K. Ramanujan. CP-RamaA

Dragging his hunger through the sky. Vulture, The. Samuel Beckett. CP-BeckS *Fr.* Echo's Bones.

Dragon and the Unicorn, The. Kenneth Rexroth. CP-RexrK

Dragon-Fly, The. Charles Olson. CP-OlsoC

Dragon in the Clouds, A. Sam Hamill. SP-HamiS

Dragon of Revolutionary Love. Denise Levertov. SP-LeveDL

Dragon-Tree. Robert Penn Warren. CP-WarrR

Dragon was pulling a bear into its terrible mouth, A. Cry Out in Your Weakness. Jelaluddin Rumi. SP-Rumi, *tr.* by Coleman Barks

Dragonfly, The. Louise Bogan. CP-BogaL

Dragonfly, The. Stanley Kunitz. CP-KunSC

Dragonfly, The. W. S. Merwin. SP-MerwW

Dragonfly, The. Edna St. Vincent Millay. CP-MillE

Dragonfly, The. Howard Nemerov. CP-NemeH

Dragonfly-Mother, The. Denise Levertov. SP-LeveDL; SP-LeveDS

Dragons are not the only beasts. John Ciardi. CP-CiarJ

Dragons Are Too Seldom. Ogden Nash. CP-NashO

Dragons on the back of a circular bronze mirror, The. Redshifting Web, The. Arthur Sze. SP-SzeA

Dragon's Proteus. He must be fought, The. Binding the Dragon. May Sarton. SP-SartM

Dragoons, I tell you the white hydrangeas turn rust and go soon. Carl Sandburg. CP-SandC

Drained Cup, The. D. H. Lawrence. CP-LawrD

Drake in the Southern Sea. Ernesto Cardenal. CP-MertT

Drama. Howard Nemerov. CP-NemeH

Drama, A. D. H. Lawrence. CP-LawrD

Drama, The; A Hymn of Hate. Dorothy Parker. CP-ParkD

Drama for Winter Night (Fifth Avenue). Langston Hughes. CP-HughL; CP-HughL1

Drama of Exile, A. Elizabeth Barrett Browning. CP-BroEB

Drama's Vitallest Expression is the Common Day. Emily Dickinson. CP-DickE

Dramatic light, gold and rose. Untitled, 6 September 1969. Kenneth Rexroth. CP-RexrK

Dramatis Personae. Charles Olson. CP-OlsoC

Dramatists, The. Dorothy Parker. CP-ParkD

Drapier's Ballad, The. Thomas Sheridan. CP-SherT

Drapier's Hill. Jonathan Swift. CP-SwifJ

Draw. Robert Lowell. SP-LoweR

Draw, and Drinke. Robert Herrick. CP-HerrR

Draw as you will there are no images. In a Room with Picassos. Jane Cooper. CP-CoopJ

Draw Gloves. Robert Herrick. CP-HerrR

Draw over and dig. Roots. Gary Snyder. CP-SnydG

Drawbridge blinks red, yawns, The. The airport limo. Leaving Longboat Key. John Ciardi. CP-CiarJ

Drawing. George Oppen. CP-OppGN

Drawing Board, The. Derek Mahon. CP-MahoD

Drawing Details in an Old Church. Thomas Hardy. CP-HardT

Drawing from Life. Clarence Major. SP-MajoC

Drawing Lesson, The. James Laughlin. CP-LaugJ

Drawing Lessons. Howard Nemerov. CP-NemeH

Drawing-Room. D. H. Lawrence. CP-LawrD

Drawing the Triangle. Charles Simic. SP-SimiC; SP-SimiCE

Drawn by the annual call, we now behold. Arrival of the Players, The. George Crabbe. SP-CrabG *Fr.* Borough, The.

Drawn from deep sleep, the dark, dim waters run. Cascades and Fountains. Marya Alexandrovna Zaturenska. SP-ZatuM

Drawn to each lovely thing, my doting eyes. Michelangelo Buonarroti. CP-MicheE, *tr. by* John Frederick Nims

Drawn to Perspective. Charles Simic. SP-SimiC; SP-SimiCE

Dread Mother of Forgetfulness. Hymn to Physical Pain. Rudyard Kipling. CP-KiplR

Dread Nay. Samuel Beckett. CP-BeckS

Dread not the shackles: on with thine intent. Wit Punisht, Prospers Most. Robert Herrick. CP-HerrR

Dread of an impending umptieth. Ouzo for Robin. James Merrill. SP-MerrJ

Dread spirit in me that I ever try. Vision 1948. Allen Ginsberg. CP-GinsA

Dreadful burden of our sins we feel, The. Fragment, A: "Dreadful burden of our sins we feel, The." John Greenleaf Whittier. CP-WhitJ

Dream. Jorge Luis Borges. SP-BorgJ, *tr. by* Alastair Reid

Dream. Norman Dubie. CP-DubiN

Dream. Langston Hughes. CP-HughL; CP-HughL2

Dream. Thomas Kinsella. CP-KinsT

Dream. Federico García Lorca. CP-GarcF, *tr. by* Catherine Brown

Dream. Marianne Craig Moore. CP-MoorM

Dream. Robert E. Penn. CP-WarrR

Dream. Kathleen Jessie Raine. SP-RainK

Dream. James Whitcomb Riley. CP-RileJ

Dream. Stevie Smith. CP-SmitS

Dream. Philip Whalen. SP-WhalP

Dream 2: Brian the Still-Hunter. Margaret Atwood. SP-AtwM1

Dream 3: Night Bear Which Frightened Cattle. Margaret Atwood. SP-AtwM1

Dream (1). Andrei Codrescu. SP-CodrA

Dream (2). Andrei Codrescu. SP-CodrA

Dream, A. Robert Burns. CP-BurnR

Dream, A. John Ciardi. CP-CiarJ

Dream, A. Richard Eberhart. CP-EberR

Dream, A. Hans Magnus Enzensberger. SP-EnzeH

Dream, A. Allen Ginsberg. CP-GinsA

Dream, A. Walter De la Mare. CP-DeLaW

Dream, A. Edgar Allan Poe. CP-PoeEd

Dream, A. James Whitcomb Riley. CP-RileJ

Dream, A. Christina Georgina Rossetti. CP-RosC3

Dream, A. May Swenson. SP-SwenM

Dream, A. Wisława Szymborska. SP-SzymWM, *tr. by* Joanna Trzeciak

Dream, A. Charles Tomlinson. CP-TomlC

Dream, A / we dreamed. Perpetuum Mobile: The City. William Carlos Williams. CP-WilW1

Dream, The. John Donne. MW-DonnJ *Fr.* Elegies.

Dream, The. Wendell Berry. CP-BerrW

Dream, The. Louise Bogan. CP-BogaL

Dream, The. Jorge Luis Borges. SP-BorgJ, *tr. by* Alastair Reid

Dream, The. Lord Byron. CP-Byron

Dream, The. Robert Creeley. CP-CreeR

Dream, The. Robert Creeley. CP-CreeR

Dream, The. Richard Eberhart. CP-EberR

Dream, The. Ivor Gurney. SP-GurnI

Dream, The. Shmuel HaNagid. SP-HaNaS, *tr. by* Peter Cole

Dream, The. Robert Earl Hayden. CP-HaydR

Dream, The. Robert Herrick. CP-HerrR

Dream, The. David Ignatow. SP-IgnaD

Dream, The. Randall Jarrell. CP-JarrR

Dream, The. Edna St. Vincent Millay. CP-MillE

Dream, The. George Oppen. CP-OppGN

Dream, The. Sylvia Plath. CP-PlatS

Dream, The. Theodore Roethke. CP-RoetT

Dream, The. Christina Georgina Rossetti. CP-RosC3

Dream, The. Stephen Spender. CP-SpenS

Dream, The. Charles Tomlinson. CP-TomlC

Dream, The. C. K. Williams. SP-WillC

Dream, The. Marya Alexandrovna Zaturenska. SP-ZatuM

Dream, The: A Reflection on Morris Graves's Paintings. John Logan. CP-LogaJ

Dream after Nanook. May Swenson. SP-SwenM

Dream, after Reading Dante's Episode of Paolo and Francesca, A. John Keats. *See* On a Dream

Dream Again, The. W. S. Merwin. SP-MerwW

Dream, an Ode, 1756, The. Annis Boudinot Stockton. CP-StocA

Dream and Reality. John Updike. CP-UpdiJ

Dream Animal. Yusef Komunyakaa. CP-KomuY

Dream at Arles on the Night of the Mistral, A. Thomas Merton. CP-MertT

Dream Boogie. Langston Hughes. CP-HughL; CP-HughL3

Dream Boogie: Variation. Langston Hughes. CP-HughL; CP-HughL3

Dream Called "The House of Jews", A. Michael Palmer. SP-PalmM

Dream-Confused. D. H. Lawrence. CP-LawrD

Dream days of fond delight and hours. Madrigal, A: "Dream days of fond delight and hours." Paul Laurence Dunbar. CP-DunbP

Dream Deferred. Langston Hughes. *See* Lenox Avenue Mural

Dream Dogs. Andrei Codrescu. SP-CodrA

Dream-Drumming. Muriel Rukeyser. CP-RukeM

Dream, Dump-Heap, and Civilization. Robert Penn Warren. CP-WarrR

Dream Dust. Langston Hughes. CP-HughL; CP-HughL2; CP-HughL3

Dream (Escape from the Sculpture Museum) and Waking. James Merrill. SP-MerrJ

Dream & Excursus, Arlington Massachusetts. Philip Whalen. SP-WhalP

Dream Flood, The. James Dickey. CP-DickJ

Dream-flowers. Kathleen Jessie Raine. SP-RainK

Dream fluently, still brothers, who when young. To the Etruscan Poets. Richard Wilbur. CP-WilbR

Dream-Follower, The. Thomas Hardy. CP-HardT

Dream Forest. Donald Davie. CP-DaviDC

Dream Girl. Carl Sandburg. CP-SandC

Dream Habitués, The. Josephine Jacobsen. CP-JacoJ

Dream in a dream the heavy soul somewhere. Canto Amor. John Berryman. CP-BerrJ

Dream in an Old Language. A. K. Ramanujan. CP-RamaA

Dream in Which the Routine Quality of My Imagination Is Fully Exposed. Jane Cooper. CP-CoopJ

Dream Inscape. Denise Levertov. SP-LeveDL

Dream is a cocktail at Sloppy Joe's, The. Havana Dreams. Langston Hughes. CP-HughL; CP-HughL2

Dream is blood: I swim, The. Her Nightmare. Denise Levertov. SP-LeveDL

Dream is vague, The. Beale Street. Langston Hughes. CP-HughL; CP-HughL2

Dream Is—Which? The. Thomas Hardy. CP-HardT

Dream Journey of the Head and Heart. Richard Eberhart. CP-EberR

Dream Keeper, The. Langston Hughes. CP-HughL; CP-HughL1

Dream Land. Christina Georgina Rossetti. CP-RosC1

Dream-Land [*or* Dreamland]. Edgar Allan Poe. CP-PoeEd

Dream lies dead here, A. May you softly go. Dorothy Parker. CP-ParkD

Dream-Love. Christina Georgina Rossetti. CP-RosC1

Dream-March. James Whitcomb Riley. CP-RileJ

Dream Message. Marya Alexandrovna Zaturenska. SP-ZatuM

Dream Movement. Rainer Maria Rilke. CP-RilkFr, *tr.* by A. Poulin, Jr.

Dream not, O Soul, that easy is the task. Help. John Greenleaf Whittier. CP-WhitJ

Dream Not of Other Worlds. James Laughlin. CP-LaugJ

Dream Objects. John Updike. CP-UpdiJ

Dream of a Brother, A. Robert Bly. SP-BlyR

Dream of a Dream. Robert Penn Warren. CP-WarrR

Dream of a Large Lady. Carolyn Kizer. CP-KizeC

Dream of All the Springfield Writers, The. Nicholas Vachel Lindsay. CP-LindV

Dream of Autumn, A. James Whitcomb Riley. CP-RileJ

Dream of Burial, A. James Wright. CP-WrigJ

Dream of coffee beans rice codfish and bananas. In the Armpit of the Hill. Clarence Major. SP-MajoC

Dream of Comparison, A. Stevie Smith. CP-SmitS

Dream of Death, A. William Butler Yeats. CP-YeatW

Dream of Death, The. James Whitcomb Riley. CP-RileJ *Fr.* Adjustable Lunatic, An.

Dream of Fair Women, A. Alfred Tennyson. CP-TennA

Dream of Fifty, A. Gregory Orr. SP-OrrG

Dream of Flying Comes of Age, The. Howard Nemerov. CP-NemeH

Dream of Foxes, A. Lucille Clifton. SP-ClifL

Dream of Frances Speedwell, A. Robert Graves. CP-GravR

Dream of Freedom. Langston Hughes. CP-HughL; CP-HughL3

Dream of Games, A. Josephine Jacobsen. CP-JacoJ

Dream of Hell, A. Robert Graves. CP-GravR

Dream of Inspiration, A. James Whitcomb Riley. CP-RileJ

Dream of Jealousy, A. Seamus Heaney. SP-HeanSO

Dream of life a dream of birth, A. Wait for Me. James Tate. SP-TateJ

Dream of limestone in sea-light, A. Thinking of Inis Oírr in Cambridge, Mass. Derek Mahon. CP-MahoD

Dream of Long Ago, A. James Whitcomb Riley. CP-RileJ

Dream of Mind: The Gap, A. C. K. Williams. SP-WillC (Gap, The.) SP-WillC

Dream of mine flew over the mead, A. Dream-Follower, The. Thomas Hardy. CP-HardT

Dream of Mourning, The. Louise Glück. SP-GlucL

Dream of Nourishment, A. Stevie Smith. CP-SmitS

Dream of Now, The. William Stafford. SP-StafWW

Dream of Pedro Henríquez Ureña, The. Jorge Luis Borges. SP-BorgJ, *tr.* by Alastair Reid

Dream of Pio Nono, The. John Greenleaf Whittier. CP-WhitJ

Dream of Politics, A. George Oppen. CP-OppGN

Dream of reclusive life, a strict, essential solitude, The. Reply to Wang Wei. Charles Wright. SP-WrigCN

Dream of Retarded Children, A. Robert Bly. SP-BlyR

Dream of Roses, A. Kathleen Jessie Raine. SP-RainK

Dream of Saba. Edna St. Vincent Millay. CP-MillE

Dream of Summer, A. John Greenleaf Whittier. CP-WhitJ

Dream of the City Shopwoman. Thomas Hardy. CP-HardT

Dream of the Little Princess, The. James Whitcomb Riley. CP-RileJ

Dream of the Old Tortoise, The. Wisława Szymborska. SP-SzymWM, *tr.* by Joanna Trzeciak

Dream of the world / speaking to me. Recovering. Muriel Rukeyser. CP-RukeM

Dream of Three Sisters, A. Norman Dubie. CP-DubiN

Dream of Trees, A. Mary Oliver. SP-OlivM

Dream of Waking, The. Randall Jarrell. CP-JarrR

Dream of What Is Missing, A. Robert Bly. SP-BlyR

Dream of yesterday. Motherland. Langston Hughes. CP-HughL; CP-HughL2

Dream on, for dreams are sweet. Dreams. Paul Laurence Dunbar. CP-DunbP

Dream on the Night of First Snow, A. Robert Bly. SP-BlyR

Dream 1: the Bush Garden. Margaret Atwood. SP-AtwM1

Dream or No, A. Thomas Hardy. CP-HardT

Dream Pang, A. Robert Frost. CP-FrosR

Dream: pigeon— / rooftop, water. For Walter Chappell. Robert Creeley. CP-CreeR

Dream Play, The. Derek Mahon. CP-MahoD

Dream please / no favors. Long Bells, The. C. K. Williams. CP-WillC

Dream Poems. Philip Whalen. SP-WhalP

Dream Question, A. Thomas Hardy. CP-HardT

Dream Range, The. Thomas McGrath. SP-McGrT

Dream Recalled on Waking. Robert Graves. CP-GravR

Dream Record: June 8 1955. Allen Ginsberg. CP-GinsA; SP-GinsA

Dream-singers, / Story-tellers. Laughers. Langston Hughes. CP-HughL; CP-HughL1

Dream Song I. Paul Laurence Dunbar. CP-DunbP

Dream Song II. Paul Laurence Dunbar. CP-DunbP

Dream That Must Be Interpreted, The. Jelaluddin Rumi. SP-Rumi, *tr.* by Coleman Barks

Dream that waketh, A. Days of Vanity. Christina Georgina Rossetti. CP-RosC1

Dream tree, Polly's tree, A. Polly's Tree. Sylvia Plath. CP-PlatS

Dream Unfinished, A. James Whitcomb Riley. CP-RileJ

Dream Variation[s]. Langston Hughes. CP-HughL; CP-HughL1

Dream went on like a rake of sliced bamboo, The. Randall Jarrell 3. Robert Lowell. SP-LoweR

Dream which Pedro Henríquez Ureña dreamed close to dawn one day, The. Dream of Pedro Henríquez Ureña, The. Jorge Luis Borges. SP-BorgJ, *tr.* by Alastair Reid

Dream with Clam-Diggers. Sylvia Plath. CP-PlatS

Dream within a Dream, A. Edgar Allan Poe. CP-PoeEd

Dreambook Bestiary. Yusef Komunyakaa. CP-KomuY

Dream[e], The. John Donne. CP-DonnJ; MW-DonnJ

Dreame, The. Robert Herrick. CP-HerrR

Dream[e], The. Ben Jonson. CP-JonsB

Dreamed Grail found as if in dreams, The. On Finding the Meaning of "Radiance" Alan Dugan. CP-DugaA

Dreamed the thong of my sandal broke. Broken Sandal. Denise Levertov. SP-LeveDS

Dreamer. Langston Hughes. CP-HughL; CP-HughL1

Dreamer, The. Paul Laurence Dunbar. CP-DunbP

Dreamer, The. Walter De la Mare. CP-DeLaW

Dreamer, The. Walter De la Mare. CP-DeLaW

Dreamer, The. Robert Pinsky. CP-PinsR

Dreamer, say, will you dream for me. James Whitcomb Riley. CP-RileJ

Dreamer, the Dream, The. Maxine W. Kumin. SP-KumiM

Dreamers, The. Robert Duncan. SP-DuncR

Dreamers, The. W. S. Merwin. SP-MerwW

Dream[e]s. Robert Herrick. CP-HerrR

Dreamin' Town. Paul Laurence Dunbar. CP-DunbP

Dreaming Children. Robert Graves. CP-GravR

Dreaming Fool. Carl Sandburg. CP-SandC

Dreaming I am in Egypt trying to convince. Rain. Andrei Codrescu. SP-CodrA

Dreaming, I rush. Emblem (1). Denise Levertov. SP-LeveDL

Dreaming in Daylight. Robert Penn Warren. CP-WarrR

Dreaming in marble all the castle lay. Of Nicolette. E. E. Cummings. CP-CummE

Dreaming of Africa. Words for the Unknown Makers. Stanley Kunitz. CP-KunSC

Dreaming of grips at her heart. Rain Winds Blow Doors Open. Carl Sandburg. CP-SandC

Dreaming the Breasts. Anne Sexton. CP-SextA; SP-SextA

Dreaming Trader, The. Thomas Merton. *See* Hymn to Commerce

Dreaming, we turn the gods into such shapes. Sunflowers, Repossessed. Eleanor Wilner. SP-WilnE

Dreaming we were awake, we heard the rivers. Muriel Rukeyser. CP-RukeM

Dreams. Edgar Allan Poe. CP-PoeEd

Dreams. Federico García Lorca. CP-GarcF, *tr.* by Jerome Rothenberg *Fr.* Blue River.

Dreams ("I was supposed to wake"). Robert Creeley. SP-CreeR

Dreams ("Tunneling through the earth"). Robert Creeley. CP-CreeR

Dreams. Paul Laurence Dunbar. CP-DunbP

Dreams. Paul Laurence Dunbar. CP-DunbP

Dreams. Langston Hughes. CP-HughL; CP-HughL1

Dreams. Randall Jarrell. CP-JarrR

Dreams. Walter De la Mare. CP-DeLaW

Dreams. Walter De la Mare. CP-DeLaW

Dreams. Mary Oliver. SP-OlivM

Dreams. Kathleen Jessie Raine. SP-RainK

Dreams. James Schuyler. CP-SchuJ

Dreams About Clothes. James Merrill. SP-MerrJ

Dreams are the subtle Dower. Emily Dickinson. CP-DickE

Dreams—are well—but Waking's better. Emily Dickinson. CP-DickE

Dreams Bite. Audre Lorde. SP-LordA

Dream's blue bird, The. "Rubén Dario." SP-DariR

Dreams fled away, this country bedroom, raw. Another September. Thomas Kinsella. CP-KinsT

Dreams flickered on a white cloth. Leaving the Cinema. Wisława Szymborska. SP-SzymWM, *tr.* by Joanna Trzeciak

Dreams, graves, pools, growing. So to Speak. Carl Sandburg. CP-SandC

Dreams in Middle Age. Louis MacNeice. CP-MacNL

Dreams in the Dusk. Carl Sandburg. CP-SandC

Dream's matterless, it dips. Connubial. Heather McHugh. SP-McHuH

Dreams of a child are peace, The. Peace. Yannis Ritsos. SP-RitsY, *tr.* by Kimon Friar

Dreams of morning, The. Beautiful Banners, The. Pier Paolo Pasolini. SP-PasoP, *tr. by* Norman MacAfee *and* Luciano Martinengo

Dreams of Suicide. William Meredith. SP-MereW

Dreams of the Animals. Margaret Atwood. SP-AtwM1

Dreams of Wild Horses, The. Thomas McGrath. SP-McGrT

Dreams Old and Nascent. D. H. Lawrence. CP-LawrD

Dreams Old and Nascent: Nascent. D. H. Lawrence. CP-LawrD

Dreams Old and Nascent: Old. D. H. Lawrence. CP-LawrD

Dreamtigers. Jorge Luis Borges. SP-BorgJ, *tr. by* Alastair Reid

Dreamwood. Adrienne Rich. SP-RicA1

Dreamwork, the mnemonic flicker. Burning Child, The. Amy Clampitt. CP-ClamA

Dreamy Cars Graze on the Dewy Boulevard. James Tate. SP-TateJ

Drear and desolate shore!, A. Rock-Tomb of Bradore, The. John Greenleaf Whittier. CP-WhitJ

Dreary, heavy / accumulation. Robert Creeley. CP-CreeR

Dremand me thocht that I did heir. William Dunbar. CP-DunbW

Dreme, The. Sir David Lyndsay. SP-LyndD

Drenched, the roofs glisten in the moon's light. The women. Same Star, The. Yannis Ritsos. SP-RitsY, *tr. by* Edmund Keeley

Drenched with purple. Simaetha. "H. D." CP-DoolH

Dresden Cattle. Sam Hamill. SP-HamiS

Dress was a suspicious madder,importing the cruelty of roses, The. E. E. Cummings. CP-CummE

Dressed in sky-flower clothes. Han-shan. CP-ColdM, *tr. by* Red Pine

Dressed to Kill. Clarence Major. SP-MajoC

Dressed Up. Langston Hughes. CP-HughL; CP-HughL1

Dresser, The. Arthur Rimbaud. CP-RimbA, *tr. by* Martin Sorrell

Dribble lights a shelf, A. Aqueduct. Thom Gunn. CP-GunnT

Dried Sturgeon, The. Robert Bly. SP-BlyR

Drifting. James Dickey. CP-DickJ

Drifting, drifting, a single gull between sky and earth. Thinking About the Night Sky, I Remember a Poem by Tu Fu. Charles Wright. SP-WrigCN

Drifting night in the Georgia pines. O Daedalus, Fly Away Home. Robert Earl Hayden. CP-HaydR

Drifting Off. Seamus Heaney. SP-HeanSO *Fr.* Sweeney Redivivus.

Drifting outside in a pall of smoke. Forever. Raymond Carver. CP-CarvR

Driftwood. Richard Wilbur. CP-WilbR

Driftwood gathered here and there. To Pfrimmer. Paul Laurence Dunbar. CP-DunbP

Drill, The. Charles Bukowski. SP-BukC1

Drills chatter full of mud and compressed air. Dillingham, Alaska, the Willow Tree Bar. Gary Snyder. CP-SnydG

Drink. William Carlos Williams. CP-WilW1

Drink and dance and laugh and lie. Flaw in Paganism, The. Dorothy Parker. CP-ParkD

Drink black coffee from a thermos. Cool around the Fire, The. Gary Snyder. CP-SnydG

Drink, hear my counsel, my son, that the world fret thee not. Hafiz. CP-EmerR *Fr.* Odes.

Drink of Water, A. Seamus Heaney. SP-HeanSO

Drink, sex and jazz all sweet things, brother: far. Dance, The. Philip Larkin. CP-LarkP

Drink till the turbans are all unbound. Hafiz. CP-EmerR *Fr.* Odes.

Drink to me only with thine eyes. Song. To Celia ("Drink to me only with thine eyes"). Ben Jonson. CP-JonsB; SP-JonsB

Drink Wine, and live here blithefull, while ye may. To Youth. Robert Herrick. CP-HerrR

Drink wine, and the heaven. Hafiz. CP-EmerR *Fr.* Odes.

Drink with Something in It, A. Ogden Nash. CP-NashO

Drink ye a skoal for the gallows tree! Villonauld, A. Ballad of the Gibbet. Ezra Pound. CP-PoEar

Drinke up / Your cup. Bachanalian Verse, A. Robert Herrick. CP-HerrR

Drinker, The. Robert Lowell. SP-LoweR

Drinking 15 dollar champagne—. Price, The. Charles Bukowski. SP-BukC1

Drinking from a Helmet. James Dickey. CP-DickJ

Drinking German beer. Ah. Charles Bukowski. SP-BukC1

Drinking Song. Thomas Hardy. CP-HardT

Drinking Song, A. William Butler Yeats. CP-YeatW

Drinking the seconal dissolved in bourbon. Case of The, The. Mona Van Duyn. SP-VanDM

Drinking Together. Li Po. CP-WilW2

Drinking versus Thinking. Samuel Taylor Coleridge. CP-ColeS

Drinking While Driving. Raymond Carver. CP-CarvR

Drinking Wine. Wisława Szymborska. SP-SzymWM, *tr. by* Joanna Trzeciak

Dripped a chill virulence. Rhododendrons. Ted Hughes. SP-HughTN

Dripping / words / off. (Ryokan's scroll). Louis Zukofsky. CP-ZukLS

Drive. Charles Tomlinson. CP-TomlC

"Drive All Blames into One" Allen Ginsberg. CP-GinsA

Drive, fast kisses. Louis Zukofsky. CP-ZukLS

Drive Home, The. William Corbett. SP-CorbW

Drive Home, The. W. S. Merwin. SP-MerwWF

Drive the bolt home: There. Wolfsbean. Paul Celan. SP-CelaP, *tr. by* John Felstiner

Drive to Los Alamos, A. Thom Gunn. CP-GunnT

Driven, at midnight, to growth, the city's wistful turnings. Lover as Fox. Muriel Rukeyser. CP-RukeM

Driven by desire, I did this deed. Sir Thomas Wyatt. CP-WyatT

Driven by desire to set affection. Sir Thomas Wyatt. CP-WyatT

Driven in by Autumn's sharpening air. Redbreast, The [Suggested in a Westmoreland Cottage]. William Wordsworth. CP-WorW2

Driven out of Paradise. To the Babylonians. Howard Nemerov. CP-NemeH

Driven to my shelves for Plato, aware. Wherein the Maker's Right Hand Moralizes the Way to a Familiar but Rare Felicity, Whatwhile the Left Hand Seemingly Knoweth Not Its Brother's Ambages and So Falleth in the Way of an Undiscerning Subtraction. Robert Stock. SP-StocR

Driver, The. James Dickey. CP-DickJ

Driver Ant, The. Thomas Lux. SP-LuxT

Driver asked, The. We answered, All the way. Yehuda Amichai. SP-AmicY *Fr.* In a Right Angle: A Cycle of Quatrains.

Drives sheep through ravine. Maid, The. *Unknown*. CP-WilW2

Driveway. Muriel Rukeyser. CP-RukeM

Driving across the American Desert and Thinking of the Sahara. John Ciardi. CP-CiarJ

Driving across the huge bridge. Light on the Pewter Dish, The. Kenneth Rexroth. CP-RexrK

Driving along the coast road. Mobile Homes. Robert Creeley. CP-CreeR

Driving along the road and looking. Driving through Snow. Stephen Spender. CP-SpenS

Driving back from the market. Green Shelf, The. Donald Hall. CP-HallD

Driving Home after a Funeral. Gregory Orr. SP-OrrG

Driving Jazz. William Corbett. SP-CorbW

Driving lickety-split to make the ferry! Movement. Raymond Carver. CP-CarvR

Driving north, I catch the hillshapes, Gurney. To Ivor Gurney. Charles Tomlinson. CP-TomlC; SP-TomlC

Driving on the road to Stinson Beach. Promising Author. Carolyn Kizer. CP-KizeC

Driving once more / on Central—though what. Albuquerque. Charles Tomlinson. CP-TomlC

Driving south on U.S. 71. Muse, The. Miller Williams. CP-WillM

Driving the new road to Buck's Lake. Coming of Age. John Logan. CP-LogaJ

Driving Through. A. R. Ammons. CP-AmmoA

Driving through Minnesota during the Hanoi Bombings. Robert Bly. SP-BlyR

Driving through Snow. Stephen Spender. CP-SpenS

Driving through Tennessee. Charles Wright. SP-WrigC

Driving to desire, adread also to dare. Sir Thomas Wyatt. CP-WyatT

Driving to Passalacqua, 1960. Charles Wright. SP-WrigC

Driving toward Boston I Run across One of Robert Bly's Old Poems. Thomas McGrath. SP-McGrT

Driving toward the Lac Qui Parle River. Robert Bly. SP-BlyR

Driving up from Tees-side. County Durham. Donald Davie. CP-DaviDC

Driving with mother to the shore. Native. Olga Broumas. SP-BrouO

Drizzle. Paul Laurence Dunbar. CP-DunbP

Drizzle hangs in the air, A. Rocks Push. Yusef Komunyakaa. CP-KomuY

Drizzle off the Ocean. Andrei Codrescu. SP-CodrA

Drizzling Easter Morning, A. Thomas Hardy. CP-HardT

Dromedary, The. Primo Levi. CP-LeviP, *tr. by* Ruth Feldman

Drone and Ostinato. Charles Wright. SP-WrigCN

Drone, dove, that rounded woe again. Adagio. Wallace Stevens. CP-StevWP

Droning a drowsy syncopated tune. Weary Blues, The. Langston Hughes. CP-HughL; CP-HughL1

Droop, droop no more, or hang the head. Upon Julias Recovery. Robert Herrick. CP-HerrR

Drop after drop. Leaky Tap after a Sister's Wedding, A. A. K. Ramanujan. CP-RamaA

Drop dead, Catullus, lie right down where you are & die. Carmen 52. Catullus. CP-ZukLS *Fr.* Carmina.

Drop fell on the Apple Tree, A. Emily Dickinson. CP-DickE

Drop of a Hat, The. Ogden Nash. CP-NashO

Drop of color, A. KMnO₄ in Grandfather's Shaving Class. A. K. Ramanujan. CP-RamaA

Drop of water fell on my hand, A. Water. Wisława Szymborska. SP-SzymW, *tr. by* Stanislaw Barańczak *and* Clare Cavanagh

Drop on the window, once, twice, A. November. Archibald MacLeish. CP-MacLA

Drop, one drop, how sweetly one fair[e] drop, A. Luke 16; Dives *Asking a Drop.*

Bible, *N.T.* CP-CrasR *Fr.* St. Luke.

Drop, that wrestles in the Sea, The. Emily Dickinson. CP-DickE

Dropkick Me Jesus. James Laughlin. CP-LaugJ

Dropout. William Stafford. SP-StafWW

Dropped into the Ether Acre. Emily Dickinson. CP-DickE

Dropping Eyelids Among the Aerial Ash. A. R. Ammons. CP-AmmoA

Drops of Gall. Gabriela Mistral. SP-MistG, *tr. by* Maria Giachetti [*or* Jacketti]

Dross of verse. Rhyme!, The. I, Mencius, Pupil of the Master. Charles Olson. CP-OlsoC

Drought. A. R. Ammons. CP-AmmoA

Drought. C. K. Williams. SP-WillC

Drought continuing. Return. A. R. Ammons. CP-AmmoA

Drovers, The. John Greenleaf Whittier. CP-WhitJ

Drowned Children, The. Louise Glück. SP-GlucL

Drowned Man: Death Between Two Rivers, The. Thomas McGrath. SP-McGrT

Drowning (I). Grace Paley. CP-PalGC

Drowning (II). Grace Paley. CP-PalGC

Drowning Another Peasant Inquisition. Andrei Codrescu. SP-CodrA

Drowning, drowning, I espie. Deluge, The. Robert Herrick. CP-HerrR

Drowning is not so pitiful. Emily Dickinson. CP-DickE

Drowning with Others. James Dickey. CP-DickJ

Drowning Young Man, The. Muriel Rukeyser. CP-RukeM

Drowse Murmurs. Allen Ginsberg. CP-GinsA

Drowsing in my chair of disbelief. Visitation, The. Robert Graves. CP-GravR

Drowsing over *The Arabian Nights*. Thomas Kinsella. CP-KinsT

Drowsy. Carl Sandburg. CP-SandC

Drowsy carrier sways, The. Contradictions. Rudyard Kipling. CP-KiplR *Fr.* Muse among the Motors, The.

Drowsy Day, A. Paul Laurence Dunbar. CP-DunbP

Drug Store. Karl Shapiro. SP-ShapK

Drugged. Walter De la Mare. CP-DeLaW

Drugs Alcohol Little Sister. John Berryman. CP-BerrJ

Drugs Made Pauline Vague. Stevie Smith. CP-SmitS

Drugstore Library. William Carlos Williams. CP-WilW2

Druid Love. Robert Graves. CP-GravR

Druida. Laura Riding Jackson. CP-RidiL

Druidic Rimes. Howard Nemerov. CP-NemeH

Druids waved their golden knives, The. Song of the Oak, The. G. K. Chesterton. CP-ChesG

Drum. Federico García Lorca. CP-GarcF, *tr. by* Jerome Rothenberg *Fr.* Fairs.

Drum. Langston Hughes. CP-HughL; CP-HughL1

Drum, The. Louise Bogan. CP-BogaL

Drum, The. James Whitcomb Riley. CP-RileJ

Drum is played. / From here a rose, A. June. James Schuyler. CP-SchuJ

Drum / is the heart, The. Drum. Federico García Lorca. CP-GarcF, *tr. by* Jerome Rothenberg *Fr.* Fairs.

Drum-Majors in the Labor Day Parade, The. Wallace Stevens. CP-StevWP

Drum on your drums, batter on your banjos. Jazz Fantasia. Carl Sandburg. CP-SandC

Drum roars up, The. Drum, The. Louise Bogan. CP-BogaL

Drum upon the table you drum. For My Friend. Charles Olson. CP-OlsoC

Drum World, The. Charles Olson. CP-OlsoC

Drumlin Woodchuck, A. Robert Frost. CP-FrosR

Drummer Hodge. Thomas Hardy. CP-HardT

Drumming started in the cool of the evening, The. July. Seamus Heaney. SP-HeanSO

Drumnotes. Carl Sandburg. CP-SandC

Drums. Langston Hughes. CP-HughL; CP-HughL3

Drums gather and humble us beyond escape. Belief. A. R. Ammons. CP-AmmoA

Drums of the early evening wake. La Comparsa en Oriente. Thomas Merton. CP-MertT

Drums, The. Robert Creeley. CP-CreeR

Drumsound rises on the air. Jelaluddin Rumi. SP-Rumi, *tr. by* Coleman Barks

Drunk. D. H. Lawrence. CP-LawrD

'Drunk again! Where do you think you are?' Louis MacNeice. CP-MacNL *Fr.* Kingdom, The.

Drunk and the Sailor, The. William Carlos Williams. CP-WilW2

Drunk and writing poems. As Crazy As I Ever Was. Charles Bukowski. SP-BukC1

Drunk as drunk on turpentine. Pablo Neruda. SP-LoguC, *tr. by* Christopher Logue *Fr.* Red Bird.

Drunk at 3 a.m. at the bottom of my 2nd bottle. Here I Am. Charles Bukowski. SP-BukC3

Drunk crowd hoots the fat emcee, The. Act, The. Heather McHugh. SP-McHuH

Drunk, drunk, drunk, amid the blaze of noon. Folly on Royal Street before the Raw Face of God. Robert Penn Warren. CP-WarrR

Drunk Man Looks at the Thistle, A. Hugh MacDiarmid. SP-MacDH

Drunk on delusion greed and anger. Shih-te. CP-ColdM, *tr. by* Red Pine

Drunk ones lay down; they fell asleep immediately, The. He. Striding Over. Yannis Ritsos. SP-RitsY, *tr. by* Edmund Keeley

Drunk / Skunk. Stupidities—Second Series. Arthur Rimbaud. CP-RimbA, *tr. by* Martin Sorrell

Drunkard. Langston Hughes. CP-HughL; CP-HughL3

Drunkard, The. Louis MacNeice. CP-MacNL

Drunkard, The. William Carlos Williams. CP-WilW1

Drunkard cannot meet a Cork, A. Emily Dickinson. CP-DickE

Drunkard to His Bottle, The. John Greenleaf Whittier. CP-WhitJ

Drunkard's Funeral, The. Nicholas Vachel Lindsay. CP-LindV

Drunkards in the Street, The. Nicholas Vachel Lindsay. CP-LindV

Drunken Boat. Arthur Rimbaud. CP-RimbA, *tr. by* Martin Sorrell

Drunken Boat. Arthur Rimbaud. CP-BeckS, *tr. by* Samuel Beckett

Drunken Boat [*or* Barge], The. Arthur Rimbaud.
  "Hearing the thunder of the intransitive weirs." CP-MahoD

Drunken Charlie. Robinson Jeffers. CP-JefR3

Drunken Fiddler, The. Tennessee Williams. CP-WillT *Fr.* Night of the Iguana, The.

Drunken Fisherman, The. Robert Lowell. SP-LoweR

Drunken Girl. Muriel Rukeyser. CP-RukeM

Drunken laughter escapes. Moonshine. Yusef Komunyakaa. CP-KomuY

Drunken man, The. Night Scene. George Oppen. CP-OppGN

Drunken Man's Praise of Sobriety, A. William Butler Yeats. CP-YeatW

Drunken Memories of Anne Sexton. Alan Dugan. CP-DugaA

Drunken night in my house with a, A. Dream Record: June 8 1955. Allen Ginsberg. CP-GinsA; SP-GinsA

Drunkenness. Robert Stock. SP-StocR

Drunks. John Berryman. CP-BerrJ

Drunks fear the police. Jelaluddin Rumi. SP-Rumi, *tr. by* Coleman Barks

Drunks leaning on your arm. Later ("Drunks leaning on your arm"). Robert Creeley. SP-CreeR

Drusilla. Ogden Nash. CP-NashO

Dry August Burned. Walter De la Mare. CP-DeLaW

Dry birch logs. Near Pah-Gotzin-Kay. Thomas McGrath. SP-McGrT

Dry Cup. James Tate. SP-TateJ

Dry is the word for a life of solitude. Fanny Howe. SP-HoweF *Fr.* Lines Out to Silence.

Dry land, / quiet land. Poem of the *Soleá*. Federico García Lorca. CP-GarcF, *tr. by* Cola Franzen, Christopher Maurer *and* Robert Nasatir

Dry Loaf. Wallace Stevens. CP-StevW; CP-StevWP

Dry Ode, The. Charles Olson. CP-OlsoC

Dry Places. Thomas Merton. CP-MertT

Dry rot intruding where the wood is wet. Enemies of a House. John Updike. CP-UpdiJ

Dry Rot, The. Richard Eberhart. CP-EberR

Dry season. Block. So, rain. Though Dry, Not Dry. Donald Davie. CP-DaviDC

Dry spring, no rain for five weeks. After Reading T'ao Ch'ing, I Wander Untethered through the Short Grass. Charles Wright. SP-WrigCN

Dry Stone Mason, The. W. S. Merwin. SP-MerwW

Dry summers flaw the leaf to a rose flame. Nature Note: The California Poison Oak. Helen Pinkerton. CP-PinkH

Dry the tears for holy Eva. Eva. John Greenleaf Whittier. CP-WhitJ

Dry they call him, and dry is what he hopes. John Dryden. Hayden Carruth. CP-CarHS

Dry timber under that rich foliage. Her Vision in the Wood. William Butler Yeats. CP-YeatW

Dry Time. Heather McHugh. SP-McHuH

Dry walls, and nettles battered by the dust. Fantasia on 'Horbury'; John Bacchus Dykes, 1859. Geoffrey Hill. CP-HillG

Dry your sweet cheek, long drown'd with sorrows raine. Comfort to a Lady Upon the Death of Her Husband. Robert Herrick. CP-HerrR

Drying Their Wings. Nicholas Vachel Lindsay. CP-LindV

Dryness is upon the house, A. In Honor of David Anderson Brooks, My Father. Gwendolyn Brooks. SP-BrooG

Du Bay. Lorine Niedecker. CP-NiedL

Du rêve, de la mathématique, et de la mort. Howard Nemerov. CP-NemeH

Dubiety. Robert Browning. CP-BroR2

Dubious daylight ended, The. Two Rosalinds, The. Thomas Hardy. CP-HardT

Dubious light sad glimmers o'er the sky, The. Lover's Complaint to His Mistress, A. Samuel Taylor Coleridge. CP-ColeS

Dubious Night, A. Richard Wilbur. CP-WilbR

Dubious "Old Kriss," A. James Whitcomb Riley. CP-RileJ

Dublin Georgian. Donald Davie. CP-DaviDC

Dublin Georgian ("Thin brown orphan in his washed-out blue, A"). Donald Davie. CP-DaviDC

Dublin Suite: Homage to James Joyce. John Logan. CP-LogaJ

Dublinesque. Philip Larkin. CP-LarkP

Duc de Berry usually wore a robe, The. Marginal Employment. Amy Clampitt. CP-ClamA

Duchesse's Red Shoes, The. Norman Dubie. CP-DubiN

Duck come switchin' 'cross de lot. Capture, The. Paul Laurence Dunbar. CP-DunbP

Duck, The. Ogden Nash. CP-NashO

Ducking Stool, The. Paul Muldoon. CP-MuldP

Ducks in the pond. Picnic, The. Robert Creeley. CP-CreeR

Ducks require no ship and sail. What Ducks Require. John Crowe Ransom. SP-RansJ

Ducks, waking at sea. Hayden Carruth. CP-CarHS *Fr.* Clay Hill Anthology, The.

Dudwood. Donald Davie. CP-DaviDC

Due Respect. John Updike. CP-UpdiJ

Due to weekend conditions, and although there's. Sundays Kill More Men Than Bombs. Charles Bukowski. SP-BukC2

Duel, The. Lord Byron. CP-Byron

Duel, The. Thomas Hardy. CP-HardT

Duerden's Garage, Stinson Beach. Philip Whalen. SP-WhalP

Duet. Theodore Roethke. CP-RoetT

Duet, The. W. H. Auden. CP-AudeW

Duet, with Muffled Brake Drums. John Updike. CP-UpdiJ

Duettist to her Pianoforte, A. Thomas Hardy. CP-HardT

Duffy's Circus. Paul Muldoon. CP-MuldP

Dugan's deathward, darling: you. Cooled Heels Lament against Frivolity, the Mask of Despair. Alan Dugan. CP-DugaA

Duke Hwan and the Wheelwright. Chuang Tzu. CP-MertT

Duke insists you stay; you could do worse, The. Tuscan Brutus, The. Donald Davie. CP-DaviDC

Duke of Guise, The. Nathaniel Lee.
    Another Epilogue: "Two houses joined, two poets to a play?." CP-DryJ2
    Epilogue: "Much time and trouble this poor play has cost." CP-DryJ2
    Prologue: "Our play's a parallel: the Holy League." CP-DryJ2
    Song: "Malicorn, Malicorn, Malicorn, ho!." CP-DryJ2
    Song: "Tell me Thirsis, tell your anguish." CP-DryJ2

Dulce et Decorum Est. Wilfred Owen. CP-OwenW

Dulcy, take our gratitude. Lynn Fontanne. Dorothy Parker. CP-ParkD

Dule of a Dewsbury Matron. Donald Davie. CP-DaviDC

Dull conclave of crows'-footed faces, The. Hitch Your Wagon to a Star. Allen Tate. CP-TateA

Dull-headed, with dull fingers. To Judith, Taking Leave. Adrienne Rich. CP-RicAE; SP-RicA2

Dull knife cuts our hand, The. Deprivation. Thomas McGrath. SP-McGrT

"Dull Knife," that sound, his name, surrounded. One Man. William Stafford. SP-StafWW

Dull, sluggish, Ile! what more than Lethargy. On the Gunpowder-Treason. Richard Crashaw. CP-CrasR

Dull to myself [*or* my self] and almost dead to these. Bad Season Makes the Poet Sad, The. Robert Herrick. CP-HerrR

Dull uncertain brain, A. Ralph Waldo Emerson. CP-EmerR

Dull uniformity in fools. Dick's Variety. Jonathan Swift. CP-SwifJ

Dullness in February: Japan. Gary Snyder. CP-SnydG

Dulness[e]. George Herbert. CP-HerbG

Duly with knees that feign to quake. Rimmon. Rudyard Kipling. CP-KiplR

Dumb aura, The. Two. Yusef Komunyakaa. CP-KomuY

Dumb Friend, A. Christina Georgina Rossetti. CP-RosC3

Dumbaris Dirige to the King. William Dunbar. CP-DunbW

Dumbass clunk plane "American" Oh Max. Robert Creeley. SP-CreeR

Dumfires Volunteers, The. Robert Burns. CP-BurnR

Dumfries Epigrams. Robert Burns. CP-BurnR

Dummies. Randall Jarrell. CP-JarrR

Dump, The. Donald Hall. CP-HallD

Dumped in the dunes snatched from the witless Finns. Kellomäki. Joseph Brodsky. CP-BrodJ

Dun Cow and the Hag, The. Norman Dubie. CP-DubiN

D'un sonno profondissimo. Christina Georgina Rossetti. CP-RosC3

Dunbarton. Robert Lowell. SP-LoweR

Duncan Davison. Robert Burns. CP-BurnR

Duncan Gibb o' Focherty's. Focherty. Hugh MacDiarmid. SP-MacDH

Duncan Gray. Robert Burns. CP-BurnR

Duncan Gray ["Weary fa' you, Duncan Gray"]. Robert Burns. CP-BurnR

Dunciad, The. Alexander Pope. CP-PopeA

Dundrige his Issue hath; but is not styl'd. Upon Dundrige. Robert Herrick. CP-HerrR

Dune. Federico García Lorca. CP-GarcF, *tr. by* Jerome Rothenberg *Fr.* In the Garden of the Lunar Grapefruits.

Dunes. A. R. Ammons. CP-AmmoA

Dunes. Carl Sandburg. CP-SandC

Dungeon, The. Samuel Taylor Coleridge. CP-ColeS

Dunkirk to be Let. Jonathan Swift.
    "Old Lewis thus the terms of peace to burnish." CP-SwifJ

Dunna thee tell me it's his'n, mother. Whether or Not. D. H. Lawrence. CP-LawrD

Duns Scotus. Thomas Merton. CP-MertT

Duns Scotus's Oxford. Gerard Manley Hopkins. CP-HopkG

Dünya Güzeli. Constantine P. Cavafy. CP-CavaC, *tr. by* Theoharis Constantine Theoharis

Duplicity in Prayer. Donald Davie. CP-DaviDC

Dupont's Round Fight. Herman Melville. SP-MelvH

Dura. Charles Olson. CP-OlsoC

Dura Mater. Thomas Kinsella. CP-KinsT

Durban, Birmingham. Question and Answer. Langston Hughes. CP-HughL; CP-HughL3

Dürer, I like that horse of yours. Travel[l]ing Slaughterhouse. Charles Simic. SP-SimiC; SP-SimiCE

Dürer would have seen a reason for living. Steeple-Jack, The. Marianne Craig Moore. CP-MoorM *Fr.* Part of a Novel, Part of a Poem, Part of a Play.

Duress of pains and grievous smart. Sir Thomas Wyatt. CP-WyatT

During a Funeral Service the Mind of the Young Preacher Wanders Again. Miller Williams. CP-WillM

During a lull at dinner the vampire frankly. Narrow Escape, A. James Merrill. SP-MerrJ

During a Son's Dangerous Illness. Denise Levertov. SP-LeveDS

During a war the poets turn to war. Ordonnance. Thomas McGrath. SP-McGrT

During an Absence. Thom Gunn. CP-GunnT

During Fever. Robert Lowell. SP-LoweR

During Music. Dante Gabriel Rossetti. CW-RossD

During Rain. Charles Tomlinson. CP-TomlC; SP-TomlC

During that long time, in those places. Wedding, The. James Dickey. CP-DickJ

During the eastering of untainted morns. Gerard Manley Hopkins. CP-HopkG

During the Eichmann Trial. Denise Levertov. SP-LeveDP
    When We Look Up. SP-LeveDS

During the Hymn Before the Christmas Sermon the Mind of the Young Preacher Wanders Again. Miller Williams. CP-WillM

During the journey there come moments of waking. Muriel Rukeyser. CP-RukeM

During the twentieth century chance. Blue Streak. Heather McHugh. SP-McHuH

During Wind and Rain. Thomas Hardy. CP-HardT

Dusk. Rae Armantrout. SP-ArmaA

Dusk. Langston Hughes. CP-HughL; CP-HughL2

Dusk. Gabriela Mistral. SP-MistG, *tr. by* Maria Giachetti [*or* Jacketti]

Dusk. Stephen Spender. CP-SpenS

Dusk. Allen Tate. CP-TateA

Dusk dark / On Railroad Avenue. Railroad Avenue. Langston Hughes. CP-HughL; CP-HughL1

Dusk-haired and gold-robed o'er the golden wine. For 'The Wine of Circe' by Edward Burne Jones. Dante Gabriel Rossetti. CW-RossD

Dusk— / He's spearing from a boat. Lorine Niedecker. CP-NiedL

Dusk in Winter. W. S. Merwin. SP-MerwW

Dusk, iridescent gasoline floats on the. Going Back to the River. Marilyn Hacker. SP-HackM

Dusk of evening comes on, The. Earlier a little rain. Afterglow. Raymond Carver. CP-CarvR

Dusk of Horses, The. James Dickey. CP-DickJ

Dusk of this box wood, The. Hoof Dusk. Carl Sandburg. CP-SandC

Dusk Song—The Beetle. James Whitcomb Riley. CP-RileJ

Dust. James Dickey. CP-DickJ

Dust. Primo Levi. CP-LeviP, *tr. by* Ruth Feldman

Dust. Carl Sandburg. CP-SandC

Dust. Miller Williams. CP-WillM

Dust always blowing about the town. Peck of Gold, A. Robert Frost. CP-FrosR

Dust and a blast soon broken. Rhyme of Dust, A. G. K. Chesterton. CP-ChesG

Dust As We Are. Ted Hughes. SP-HughTN

Dust behind I strove to join, The. Emily Dickinson. CP-DickE

Dust covers all the things mentioned above. Yehuda Amichai. SP-AmicYL *Fr.* At Right Angles.

Dust flies smothering, as on clatt'ring Wheels. Perspiration: A Travelling Eclogue. Samuel Taylor Coleridge. CP-ColeS

Dust in a cloud, blinding weather. Apples and Water. Robert Graves. CP-GravR

Dust in the Eyes. Robert Frost. CP-FrosR

Dust is the only Secret. Emily Dickinson. CP-DickE

Dust like the Mosquito, The. Emily Dickinson. SP-DickE

Dust Now Is. Hart Crane. CP-CranH

Dust of Snow. Robert Frost. CP-FrosR

Dust of the feet / And dust of the wheels. Clark Street Bridge. Carl Sandburg. CP-SandC

"Dust," she said. "What is it? Where does it come from?" How Lewisburg, Pa., Escaped the Avenging Angel. Hayden Carruth. CP-CarHS

Dust thrown into eyes. In the Life of Dust. W. S. Merwin. SP-MerwW

Dust to Dust. Walter De la Mare. CP-DeLaW

Dust unto dust! and shall no more be said. Ralph Waldo Emerson. CP-EmerR

Dustbowl. Langston Hughes. CP-HughL; CP-HughL2

Dusting. Rita Dove. SP-DoveR

Dusty Doors. Carl Sandburg. CP-SandC

Dusty Miller. Robert Burns. CP-BurnR

Dutch Cleanser. John Updike. CP-UpdiJ

Dutch Courtyard, A. Richard Wilbur. CP-WilbR

Dutch Graves in Bucks County. Wallace Stevens. CP-StevW; CP-StevWP

Dutch in the Medway, The. Rudyard Kipling. CP-KiplR

Dutch Interior. May Sarton. SP-SartM

Dutch Mistress. Joseph Brodsky. CP-BrodJ

Dutch Painters. Adam Zagajewski. SP-ZagaA, tr. by Clare Cavanagh

Dutch White Iris. Louis Zukofsky. CP-ZukLS

Duties of the Wind are few, The. Emily Dickinson. CP-DickE

Dutifully I close this book. Colophon. Robert Graves. CP-GravR

Duty. Arthur Hugh Clough. SP-ClouA

Duty Surviving Self-Love. Samuel Taylor Coleridge. CP-ColeS; MW-ColeS

Duty—that's to say, complying. Duty. Arthur Hugh Clough. SP-ClouA

Duty to Tyrants. Robert Herrick. CP-HerrR

Duty Was His Lodestar. Stevie Smith. CP-SmitS

Duty was my Lobster, my Lobster was she. Duty Was His Lodestar. Stevie Smith. CP-SmitS

Dwarf, The. Wallace Stevens. CP-StevW; CP-StevWP

Dwarf in the Woods. Mona Van Duyn. SP-VanDM

Dwarfcypress silva evergreen spineranks branchlets. Lavender Cotton. Louis Zukofsky. CP-ZukLS

Dwarfs shuffle up the white steps, The. We Are Not Worthy, Lord. Kenneth Patchen. CP-PatcK

Dweller in yon dungeon dark. Ode, Sacred to the Memory of Mrs. ——— of ———. Robert Burns. CP-BurnR

Dwellers at the Hermitage. Denise Levertov. SP-LeveDL

Dwelling-Place, The. Walter De la Mare. CP-DeLaW

Dwellings of the Just, The. Jones Very. CP-VeryJ

Dwindled creeks of summer, The. Creeks. Mary Oliver. SP-OlivM

Dwindling body of ageing fish, A. Friends of the River Trent. Stevie Smith. CP-SmitS

Dwindling pole, The. Eagle. Stanley Kunitz. CP-KunSC

Dwingelo. Gerrit Achterberg. SP-RicAE

Dying. Robert Creeley. CP-CreeR

Dying. Pablo Neruda. SP-NeruP

Dying. Robert Pinsky. CP-PinsR

Dying Art, A. Derek Mahon. CP-MahoD

Dying at my music! Emily Dickinson. CP-DickE

Dying Away. William Meredith. SP-MereW

Dying Beast. Langston Hughes. CP-HughL; CP-HughL1

Dying Chauffer, The. Rudyard Kipling. CP-KiplR Fr. Muse among the Motors, The.

Dying Child, The. John Clare. SP-ClarJ

Dying Christian peaceful lay, The. Dying Words of John Foster: "I Can Pray, and That's a Glorious Thing" Jones Very. CP-VeryJ

Dying! Dying in the night! Emily Dickinson. CP-DickE

Dying Earth, The. Hugh MacDiarmid. SP-MacDH

Dying gales of sweet even. Song: "Dying gales of sweet even." John Clare. SP-ClarJ Fr. Child Harold.

Dying Goddess, The. Carolyn Kizer. CP-KizeC

Dying in a Mirthful Place. A. R. Ammons. CP-AmmoA

Dying is a wild Night. Emily Dickinson. SP-DickE

Dying is fine)but Death. E. E. Cummings. CP-CummE

Dying, Laughing. Jelaluddin Rumi. SP-Rumi, tr. by Coleman Barks

Dying Leaf, The. Jones Very. CP-VeryJ

Dying Man, The. Theodore Roethke. CP-RoetT

Dying man / Lifts his head, The. People Are So Busy; Or: That's Life! Thomas McGrath. SP-McGrT

Dying man on his pillow, The. Satire, The. Walter De la Mare. CP-DeLaW

Dying Man to His Betrothed, The. Christina Georgina Rossetti. CP-RosC3

Dying need but little, Dear, The. Emily Dickinson. CP-DickE

Dying now, or already dead. Paul Blackburn. Ted Berrigan. SP-BerrT

Dying of the day in the dying of the year, The. Return, The. Charles Olson. CP-OlsoC

Dying sun, shine warm a little longer! Lament for Pasiphaë. Robert Graves. CP-GravR

Dying Swan, The. Alfred Tennyson. CP-TennA

Dying Tiger—moaned for Drink, A. Emily Dickinson. CP-DickE

Dying! To be afraid of thee. Emily Dickinson. CP-DickE

Dying Tooth Song. Philip Whalen. SP-WhalP

Dying Veteran, The. Walt Whitman. CP-WhitW

Dying Words of John Foster: "I Can Pray, and That's a Glorious Thing" Jones Very. CP-VeryJ

Dying—you wouldn't do that to a cat. Cat in an Empty Apartment. Wisława Szymborska. SP-SzymWM, tr. by Joanna Trzeciak

Dykes, The. Rudyard Kipling. CP-KiplR

Dylan. James Laughlin. CP-LaugJ

Dylan Thomas, and Now Matthew Mead—as He Himself, "To Edward Thomas" Charles Olson. CP-OlsoC

Dymchurch Flit. Rudyard Kipling. Fr. Puck of Pook's Hill.

Dynamiter. Carl Sandburg. CP-SandC

Dynasts, The. Thomas Hardy.
  Budmouth Dears. CP-HardT
  Chorus of the Pities. CP-HardT
    Last Chorus. CP-HardT
  Epilogue: "We have now set forth, in our imperfect way." CP-HardT
  Eve of Waterloo, The. CP-HardT
  My Love's Gone a-Fighting. CP-HardT
  Night of Trafalgar, The. CP-HardT
  Prologue: "In these stern times of ours, when crimson strife." CP-HardT

Dying Seagull and the Great Whore of the World, The. Alan Dugan. CP-DugaA

Dytiscus. Hugh MacDiarmid. SP-MacDH

E

E babbo e mamma ha il nostro figliolino. Christina Georgina Rossetti. CP-RosC3

E. C. B. G. K. Chesterton. CP-ChesG

E / cco the uglies / t. E. E. Cummings. CP-CummE

E.G. to M.R. Emily Jane Brontë. CP-BronE

E-mail. Miller Williams. CP-WillM

E multis aliquos si non despexit amantes. Ad Cambricum. Thomas Campion. CP-CampT

E Nihilo Nihil. Lord Byron. CP-Byron

E Pluribus Unum. Jones Very. CP-VeryJ

E Tenebris. Oscar Wilde. CP-WildO

E.W. to A.G.A. Emily Jane Brontë. CP-BronE

'E was warned agin 'er. Sergeant's Weddin', The. Rudyard Kipling. CP-KiplR

Each act of criticism is general. Their Day. John Ashbery. SP-AshbJ

Each afternoon in Granada. Gacela of the Dead Child. Federico García Lorca. SP-GarcF, tr. by Edwin Honig

Each and All. Ralph Waldo Emerson. CP-EmerR

Each barge on the river easily tows. Quai d'Orléans. Elizabeth Bishop. CP-BishE

Each Bird Walking. Tess Gallagher. SP-GallT

Each blest drop, on each blest limb [or limme]. On the Water of Our Lord's Baptism[e]. Richard Crashaw. CP-CrasR

Each body has its art, its precious prescribed. Still Do I Keep My Look, My Identity . . . . Gwendolyn Brooks. SP-BrooG

Each care-worn face is but a book. Strangers, The. Jones Very. CP-VeryJ

Each city is a solitary reef. Flying at Night. Wyatt Prunty. SP-PrunW

Each creature holds an insular point in space. Life. Elizabeth Barrett Browning. CP-BroEB

Each dawn is clear. Gary Snyder. CP-SnydG Fr. Myths and Texts.

Each Day. David Ignatow. SP-IgnaD

Each Day a Prophecy. Jones Very. CP-VeryJ

Each day another installment of the old. Daily Globe, The. Howard Nemerov. CP-NemeH

Each day brings its toad, each night its dragon. Jerome. Randall Jarrell. CP-JarrR

Each day I come to you an infinity of times. Guido Cavalcanti. CP-CavaG, tr. by Marc Cirigliano

Each day now more precious will dawn. Paradox of Time. Robert Penn Warren. CP-WarrR

Each day / the cardinals call and call in the rain. April in Ohio. Denise Levertov. SP-LeveDL

Each day the tide withdraws; chills us; pastes. Wreaths. Geoffrey Hill. CP-HillG

Each day with so much ceremony. Anaphora. Elizabeth Bishop. CP-BishE

Each day's terror, almost. Concurrence. Denise Levertov. SP-LeveDL; SP-LeveDS

Each evening an eagle soars down from the snowy. Caucasus: A Romance, The. Raymond Carver. CP-CarvR

Each evening, the sins of the whole world collect here like a dew. There Is No Shelter. Charles Wright. SP-WrigCN

Each face in the street is a slice of bread. Bread. W. S. Merwin. SP-MerwW

Each for himself is still the rule. In the Great Metropolis. Arthur Hugh Clough. SP-ClouA

Each fresh and sweet source. Guido Cavalcanti. CP-CavaG, *tr. by* Marc Cirigliano

Each gesture / is a common one, a. Reason, A. Robert Creeley. CP-CreeR

Each hired hand places. Vigilante. Yusef Komunyakaa. CP-KomuY

Each hour until we meet is as a bird. Winged Hours. Dante Gabriel Rossetti. CW-RossD *Fr.* House of Life, The.

Each hurt swallowed. Promises. Rita Dove. SP-DoveR

Each in a Place Apart. James McMichael. SP-McMiJ

Each inly murm'ring at th'unequal meed. Epistle 2.1: "Each inly murm'ring at th'unequal meed." Horace. CP-JohnS *Fr.* Epistles.

Each Is Alone, Each Is Everything. Kenneth Patchen. CP-PatcK

Each Life Converges to some Centre. Emily Dickinson. CP-DickE

Each like a Leaf. May Swenson. SP-SwenM

Each little room. Room. Langston Hughes. CP-HughL; CP-HughL3

Each lover has a theory of his own. Alone. W. H. Auden. CP-AudeW

Each lover's longing leads him naturally. Sonnet: He interprets Dante's Dream, related in the first Sonnet of the Vita Nuova. Cino da Pistoia. CW-RossD, *tr. by* Dante Gabriel Rossetti

Each Man is in His Spectres power. William Blake. CP-BlakW

Each man me telleth I change most my device [*or* devise]. Sonnet: 'Each man me telleth.' Sir Thomas Wyatt. CP-WyatT

Each man pictures his hell or heaven different. Hells and Heavens. Carl Sandburg. CP-SandC

Each more melodious note I hear. Henry David Thoreau. CP-ThorH

Each morning my characters. Marching through a Novel. John Updike. CP-UpdiJ

Each morning when I break my buttered toast. Keeping Informed in D.C. Howard Nemerov. CP-NemeH

Each movement of the Mozart has a soloist and as each appears the conductor tunes her instrument. Junior High School Concert: Salle Rossini. C. K. Williams. SP-WillC

Each must, in vertue, strive for to excell. Vertue. Robert Herrick. CP-HerrR

Each naked branch, the yellow leaf or brown. Robe, The. Jones Very. CP-VeryJ

Each night for seven nights beyond the gulf. Oleaster, The. Robert Graves. CP-GravR

Each night, this adroit young lady. Aerialist. Sylvia Plath. CP-PlatS

Each Note. Jelaluddin Rumi. SP-Rumi, *tr. by* Coleman Barks

Each of these hours has been to you first. On the Silent Anniversary of a Reunion. W. S. Merwin. SP-MerwW

Each of these weeds is a day. Lot's Wife 1988. Lucille Clifton. SP-ClifL

Each of Us. David Ignatow. SP-IgnaD

Each of us has the time. Treviso, the Pescheria. Donald Davie. CP-DaviDC

Each of us is like you. Adonis. "H. D." CP-DoolH

Each of us waking to the window's light. Exile. Donald Hall. CP-HallD

Each one *is* a gift, no doubt. Days. Billy Collins. SP-CollB

Each One, Pull One. Alice Walker. CP-WalkA

Each one shall sit at table with his own cup and spoon. Practical Program for Monks, A. Thomas Merton. CP-MertT

Each person's own particular angel (so believe, nations). To Leonora Singing in Rome. John Milton. CP-MiltJ

Each red seed bursts. Hymn to Proserpine. Charles Olson. CP-OlsoC

Each return is a blessing. Gnostology. Sam Hamill. SP-HamiS

Each Scar I'll keep for Him. Emily Dickinson. CP-DickE

Each Second is the last. Emily Dickinson. CP-DickE

Each servant stamps the reader with a look. Sonnet: "Each servant stamps the reader with a look." John Ashbery. SP-AshbJ

Each shift you make in the sunlight somewhere. Sunlight Is Imagination. Richard Wilbur. CP-WilbR

Each small gleam was a voice. Stephen Crane. CP-CranS

Each spot where tulips prank their state. From Omar Chiam. Omar Khayyám. CP-EmerR

Each step is to and from an object. From the Observatory. David Ignatow. SP-IgnaD

Each stone its shape. David Ignatow. SP-IgnaD

Each summer sound. Henry David Thoreau. CP-ThorH

Each Summer's Swallows. John Updike. CP-UpdiJ

Each sword of the plant is burning. Labor. Heather McHugh. SP-McHuH

Each that I loved is now my enemy. Epigrams: A Journal. James Vincent Cunningham. CP-CunnJ

Each that we lose takes part of us. Emily Dickinson. CP-DickE

Each thing, / you didn't even taste it. Post Cards. Robert Creeley. CP-CreeR

Each time I call to mind the hour, the place. Petrarch. CP-Petra, *tr. by* J. G. Nichols

Each time I look up from the board to the rusty vineyards. Game of Monopoly in Chavannes. Maxine W. Kumin. SP-KumiM

Each time I order her to go. Forgiveness. Alice Walker. CP-WalkA

Each time it happened recklessly. Moon's Tear, The. Robert Graves. CP-GravR

Each time it rings. Thing, The. William Carlos Williams. CP-WilW2

Each time we meet. Family Reunion. Jay Wright. SP-WrigJ

Each traveller prays, "Let me be far from any" Journey to Iceland. W. H. Auden. CP-AudeW

Each tree stands alone in stillness. Ted Berrigan. SP-BerrT *Fr.* Sonnets, The.

Each voice which was asked. Hero, The. Robert Creeley. CP-CreeR

Each way the turn. Turn, The. Robert Creeley. CP-CreeR

Each word of love a child doth speak. Song: Words of Love to a Parent. Jones Very. CP-VeryJ

Each year at this time I shall be telling you of the Lord. May Day Sermon to the Women of Gilmer County, Georgia, by a Woman Preacher Leaving the Baptist Church. James Dickey. CP-DickJ

Each year for a short season. Folk Wisdom. Thomas Kinsella. CP-KinsT

Each year is like a snake that swallows its tail. Paradigm of Seasons. Robert Penn Warren. CP-WarrR

Each year, just as the blossoms. All or None. Randall Jarrell. CP-JarrR

Eager note on my door said "Call me", The. Poem: "Eager note on my door said 'Call me', The." Frank O'Hara. SP-OharF

Eager Youths to a Dead Girl. Allen Tate. CP-TateA

Eagerness of objects to, The. Interior (With Jane). Frank O'Hara. SP-OharF

Eagle. Stanley Kunitz. CP-KunSC

Eagle, The. Robert Browning. CP-BroR2

Eagle, The. E. E. Cummings. CP-CummE

Eagle, The. Allen Tate. CP-TateA

Eagle, The. Alfred Tennyson. CP-TennA

Eagle and hawk with their great claws and hooked heads. Robinson Jeffers. CP-JefR3

Eagle and the Dove, The. William Wordsworth. CP-WorW2

Eagle and the Tortoise, The. Samuel Taylor Coleridge. CP-ColeS

Eagle Descending. Robert Penn Warren. CP-WarrR

Eagle Exterminating Company, The. James Tate. SP-TateJ

Eagle in New Mexico. D. H. Lawrence. CP-LawrD

Eagle of Austerlitz! where were thy wings. Louis Napoleon. Oscar Wilde. CP-WildO

Eagle Rock. Alice Walker. CP-WalkA

Eagle, stooping from yon snow-blown peaks, The. Inscription: "Eagle, stooping from yon snow-blown peaks, The." John Greenleaf Whittier. CP-WhitJ

Eagle That Is Forgotten, The. Nicholas Vachel Lindsay. CP-LindV

Eagle Valor, Chicken Mind. Robinson Jeffers. CP-JefR3

Eagle! why soarest thou above that tomb? Spirit of Plato. *Unknown.* CP-ShelP

Eagles. Raymond Carver. CP-CarvR

Eagles. James Dickey. CP-DickJ

Eagles. William Wordsworth. CP-WorW2

Eagles, The. Jones Very. CP-VeryJ

Eagles and Alone. George Oppen. CP-OppGN

Eagles gather on the place of death, The. Eagles, The. Jones Very. CP-VeryJ

Eagle's Mile, The. James Dickey. CP-DickJ

Eagle's nest on the head of an old redwood on one of the, An. Beaks of Eagles, The. Robinson Jeffers. CP-JefR2

EAMD. Philip Whalen. SP-WhalP

Ear, The. Robert Creeley. CP-CreeR

Ear, The. Louis MacNeice. CP-MacNL

Ear threading, The. Stream, The. Charles Simic. SP-SimiC; SP-SimiCE

Eare-rings. Robert Herrick. CP-HerrR

Earl of Breadalbane's Ruined Mansion, and Family Burial-Place, near Killin, The. William Wordsworth. CP-WorW2

Earlier in the evening the moon. Moon, The. Robert Creeley. CP-CreeR

Earlier Lovers. Robert Graves. CP-GravR

Earlier than I could learn. Reincarnation of Captain Cook, The. Margaret Atwood. SP-AtwM1

Earliest flower of Spring, The. Crocus, The. Jones Very. CP-VeryJ

Earliest morning hot moonlight. Discriminations. Philip Whalen. SP-WhalP

Earliest morning, switching all the tracks. Love Lies Sleeping. Elizabeth Bishop. CP-BishE

Earliest sportsman in the earliest dawn, The. Worst Sinner, Jonathan Edwards' God, The. Robert Lowell. SP-LoweR

Earliest Spring. Denise Levertov. SP-LeveDL

Early after the night long revel. Hafiz. CP-EmerR *Fr.* Odes.

Early Autumn. Arthur Sze. SP-SzeA

Early Autumn in Upper Noe Valley. Philip Whalen. SP-WhalP

Early Blizzard. Thomas Merton. CP-MertT

Early blue evening. Wonder. Langston Hughes. CP-HughL; CP-HughL3

Early Companions. Jones Very. CP-VeryJ

Early Copper. Carl Sandburg. CP-SandC

Early December in Croton-on-Hudson. Louise Glück. SP-GlucL

Early, early in the morning, even before five o'clock, the. Hanging of the

Mouse, The. Elizabeth Bishop. CP-BishE

Early electric people had domesticated the wild ass, The. Electric Orchard, The. Paul Muldoon. CP-MuldP

Early Evening Quarrel. Langston Hughes. CP-HughL; CP-HughL2

Early Fix. Andrei Codrescu. SP-CodrA

Early Hours. Carl Sandburg. CP-SandC

Early Hours, The. Adam Zagajewski. SP-ZagaA, *tr. by* Clare Cavanagh

Early hours of morning; you still aren't writing, The. Early Hours, The. Adam Zagajewski. SP-ZagaA, *tr. by* Clare Cavanagh

Early in the Morning. Kenneth Patchen. CP-PatcK

Early in the morning, you lean on the wall of an old house. Yehuda Amichai. SP-AmicYL, *tr. by* Benjamin Harshav *and* Barbara Harshav

Early January. W. S. Merwin. SP-MerwW

Early Legend, The. Thomas Merton. CP-MertT

Early Losses: a Requiem. Alice Walker. CP-WalkA

Early Lynching. Carl Sandburg. CP-SandC

Early Martyr, An. William Carlos Williams. CP-WilW1

Early Mass. Thomas Merton. CP-MertT

Early May (a late spring) a field. Industrial Archaeology. James Schuyler. CP-SchuJ

Early May, after cold rain the sun baffling cold wind. Dan. Carl Sandburg. CP-SandC

Early mist. Calm in April, A. W. S. Merwin. SP-MerwW

Early Moon. Carl Sandburg. CP-SandC

Early Morning. Federico García Lorca. SP-GarcF *Fr.* Poem of the Saeta.

Early Morning. Czeslaw Milosz. CP-MiloC; CP-MiloCN, *tr. by* Robert Hass

Early Morning: Cape Cod. May Swenson. SP-SwenM

Early morning corn. Fall. Lorine Niedecker. CP-NiedL

Early Morning in Early April. A. R. Ammons. CP-AmmoA

Early Morning on the Tel Aviv-Haifa Freeway. Rita Dove. SP-DoveR

Early mornings, in the light still. Sound, The. Robert Creeley. SP-CreeR

Early November in the soul, / a hard rain, and dusky gold. North American Bear. Charles Wright. SP-WrigCN

Early On, This Decade's Light Smelled. Thomas Lux. SP-LuxT

Early one day a mountain uprose, all cased in silver. Index, a Mountain. Carolyn Kizer. CP-KizeC

Early One Summer. W. S. Merwin. SP-MerwW

Early one Sunday morning everything outside. Distress Sale. Raymond Carver. CP-CarvR

Early Pompeian. Derek Walcott. CP-WalcD

Early Queen of Light arise. Ode, An: "Early Queen of Light arise." Thomas Sheridan. CP-SherT

Early Reading. Robert Creeley. SP-CreeR

Early Saturday Afternoon, Early Evening. Charles Wright. SP-WrigCN

Early Spring. D. H. Lawrence. *See* Amour

Early Spring. Philip Whalen. SP-WhalP

Early Spring Between Madison and Bellingham. Robert Bly. SP-BlyR

Early Spring Dawn. Ivor Gurney. SP-GurnI

Early Summer Sketch. E. E. Cummings. CP-CummE

Early violets we saw together, The. Approach of Autumn. Stanley Kunitz. CP-KunSC

Early wagons left no sign, The. Trail into Kansas, The. W. S. Merwin. SP-MerwW

Early Warning. Paul Muldoon. CP-MuldP

Early Winter, Long Island. Dan Pagis. SP-PagiD, *tr. by* Stephen Mitchell

Earnest, earthless, equal, attuneable, vaulty, voluminous, stupendous. Spelt from Sibyl's Leaves. Gerard Manley Hopkins. CP-HopkG

Earnest man, in long-forgotten years, An. Story of Sir Arnulph, The. George Meredith. CP-MerG2

Earnestly I looked. Dead, The. Denise Levertov. SP-LeveDS

Earrings of Madame de, The. William Corbett. SP-CorbW

Earrings, The. Eugenio Montale. CP-MontE, *tr. by* Jonathan Galassi

Ears in the Turrets Hear. Dylan Thomas. CP-ThomD

Ears of the forest, The. What Splendid Birthdays. Kenneth Patchen. CP-PatcK

Ears stung with cold, The. Finches, The. Wendell Berry. CP-BerrW

Earth. Laura Riding Jackson. CP-RidiL

Earth. Czeslaw Milosz. CP-MiloC; CP-MiloCN, *tr. by* Robert Hass

Earth. Pablo Neruda. SP-NeruP

Earth, The. Ralph Waldo Emerson. CP-EmerR

Earth, The. Boris Leonidovich Pasternak. CP-MahoD, *tr. by* Derek Mahon

Earth, The. Anne Sexton. CP-SextA; SP-SextA

Earth, The. Henry David Thoreau. CP-ThorH

Earth, The. Jones Very. CP-VeryJ

Earth a flower. For Nothing. Gary Snyder. CP-SnydG

Earth again like a ship steams out of the dark sea over, The. Shadow of Death, The. D. H. Lawrence. CP-LawrD

Earth and a Wedded Woman. George Meredith. CP-MerG1

Earth and Creation. Peter Blue Cloud. SP-BlueP

Earth and Fire. Wendell Berry. CP-BerrW

Earth and Heaven. Christina Georgina Rossetti. CP-RosC3

Earth and heaven, so little known, The. Gerard Manley Hopkins. CP-HopkG

Earth and Her Praisers. Elizabeth Barrett Browning. CP-BroEB

Earth and Man. George Meredith. CP-MerG1

Earth and Moon. Federico García Lorca. CP-GarcF, *tr. by* Greg Simon *and* Steven F. White

Earth and water air. Martha Graham. James Laughlin. CP-LaugJ

Earth-animal tastes, The. In the Courtyard of Secret Life. Kenneth Patchen. CP-PatcK

Earth, bind us close, and time ; nor, sky, deride. Preamble. Muriel Rukeyser. CP-RukeM

Earth cannot bar flame from ascending, / Hell cannot bind light from descending. St. John, Apostle. Christina Georgina Rossetti. CP-RosC2

Earth does not understand her child. Return, The. Edna St. Vincent Millay. CP-MillE

Earth doth with the heavens sympathise!, The. Signs in the Natural World. Jones Very. CP-VeryJ

Earth Dweller. William Stafford. SP-StafW; SP-StafWW

Earth, earth! This Bright Day. A. R. Ammons. CP-AmmoA

Earth, earth, / riding your merry-go-round. As It Was Written. Anne Sexton. CP-SextA

Earth Falls Down, The. Anne Sexton. CP-SextA

Earth feels old tonight, The. Greeting. May Sarton. SP-SartM

Earth flows away from the shore where I stand. Song, The: "Earth flows away from the shore where I stand." Czeslaw Milosz. CP-MiloC; CP-MiloCN

Earth gave me body; strong through fire am I. Some Riddles from Symphosius. Richard Wilbur. CP-WilbR

Earth gave up her dead that tide, The. Rudyard Kipling. CP-KiplR *Fr.* Life's Handicap.

Earth ("Girls of the breeze, The"). Federico García Lorca. CP-GarcF, *tr. by* Jerome Rothenberg *Fr.* In the Garden of the Lunar Grapefruits.

Earth grown old, yet still so green. Advent. Christina Georgina Rossetti. CP-RosC2

Earth hard to my heels. David Ignatow. SP-IgnaD

Earth has been unkind to him, The. Toothache Man. John Updike. CP-UpdiJ

Earth has clear call of daily bells, / A chancel-vault of gloom and star. Christina Georgina Rossetti. CP-RosC2

Earth has covered Sicilian Syracuse, there asphodel grows, The. What are Cities For? Robinson Jeffers. CP-JefR2

Earth has many keys, The. Emily Dickinson. CP-DickE

Earth has not anything to show [*or* shew] more fair. Composed upon Westminster Bridge, September 3, 1802. William Wordsworth. CP-WorW1; MW-WorW

Earth has turned over; our side feels the cold. Through the Looking-Glass. W. H. Auden. CP-AudeW

Earth in beauty dressed. Her Anxiety. William Butler Yeats. CP-YeatW

Earth Is a Living Thing, The. Lucille Clifton. SP-ClifL

Earth is a prey of the hours. Impermanence. G. K. Chesterton. CP-ChesG

Earth is become the seat of a new sea. Mist. E. E. Cummings. CP-CummE

Earth is bright though the boughs of the moon like a, The. Cinema of a Man. Archibald MacLeish. CP-MacLA

Earth is for the living OR, The. Canto One Hundred and One. Charles Olson. CP-OlsoC

Earth is full of anger, The. Hymn before Action. Rudyard Kipling. CP-KiplR

Earth is God's, with all she bears, The. Bible, *O.T. See* Earth is the Lord's and the fulness thereof, The

Earth is near tonight; O slow, The. Other Side: The Green Home, The. Kenneth Patchen. CP-PatcK

Earth is old, The. Earth and Her Praisers. Elizabeth Barrett Browning. CP-BroEB

Earth is parched with heat, flowers droop and die, The. Jones Very. CP-VeryJ

"Earth is the birth of the blues," sang Yellow Bertha. Passing Through. Ai. SP-Ai

Earth is the Lord's and the fulness thereof, The. Psalm 24: "Earth is the Lord's and the fulness thereof, The." Bible, *O.T.* SP-SmarC, *tr. by* Christopher Smart *Fr.* Psalms.

Earth lay golden green, The. Going from Battle to Battle. Charles Olson. CP-OlsoC

Earth lends us flesh, heaven lends the soul, the two. Michelangelo Buonarroti. CP-Miche, *tr. by* John Frederick Nims

Earth like a tipsy. E. E. Cummings. CP-CummE

Earth locked out the light, The. Ted Hughes. SP-HughTN *Fr.* Seven Dungeon Songs.

Earth loves her young: a preference manifest. Earth's Preference. George Meredith. CP-MerG1

Earth-meaning, The. Fulfillment. Langston Hughes. CP-HughL; CP-HughL2

Earth, My Likeness. Walt Whitman. CP-WhitW

Earth, not flat, not round, your skin loose as a dog's. Once There Were Glaciers. May Swenson. SP-SwenM

Earth-Numb. Ted Hughes. SP-HughTN

Earth, ocean, air, belovèd brotherhood! Alastor; or, The Spirit of Solitude. Percy Bysshe Shelley. CP-ShelP

Earth owls in ancient burrows clumpt. Sentinels, The. Robert Duncan. SP-DuncR

Earth Psalm. Denise Levertov. SP-LeveDP

Earth rais'd up her head. Earth's Answer. William Blake. CP-BlakW *Fr.* Songs of Experience.

Earth says have a place, be what that place, The. In Response to a Question. William Stafford. SP-StafWW

Earth Shall Tremble at the Look of Him, The. Christina Georgina Rossetti. CP-RosC2

Earth Sky Sea Trees Birds House Beasts Flowers. Kenneth Rexroth. CP-RexrK

Earth Song. Langston Hughes. CP-HughL; CP-HughL2

Earth spins to my fingertips and, The. Globe in [North] Carolina, The. Derek Mahon. CP-MahoD

Earth, still heavy and warm with afternoon, The. Nocturne: "Earth, still heavy and warm with afternoon, The." Archibald MacLeish. CP-MacLA

Earth, sweet Earth, sweet landscape, with leavès throng. Ribblesdale. Gerard Manley Hopkins. CP-HopkG

Earth, the rock and the oil of the earth, the slippery frozen places of, The. Four Steichen Prints. Carl Sandburg. CP-SandC

Earth! thou mother of numberless children, the nurse and the mother. Hymn to the Earth. Samuel Taylor Coleridge. CP-ColeS

Earth to Man. Shmuel HaNagid. SP-HaNaS, *tr. by* Peter Cole

Earth Tremors Felt in Missouri. Mona Van Duyn. SP-VanDM

Earth turns. Sleeping Overnight on the Shore. May Swenson. SP-SwenM

Earth upon earth. Crisis, The. Kenneth Rexroth. CP-RexrK

Earth Walk. William Meredith. SP-MereW

Earth was green, the sky was blue, The. Green Cornfield, A. Christina Georgina Rossetti. CP-RosC1

Earth was my home, but even there I was a stranger. Flight of Apollo, The. Stanley Kunitz. CP-KunSC

Earth was not Earth before her sons appeared. Appreciation. George Meredith. CP-MerG1

Earth water stars and flesh—the seamless coat. Place of a Skull. Louis MacNeice. CP-MacNL

Earth ("We walk on / an unsilvered"). Federico García Lorca. CP-GarcF, *tr. by* Jerome Rothenberg *Fr.* Mirror Suite.

Earth will be going on a long time, The. Lute Music. Kenneth Rexroth. CP-RexrK

Earth will become a wicked stepmother, The. God Wills It. Gabriela Mistral. SP-MistG, *tr. by* Maria Giachetti [*or* Jacketti]

Earth Worm, The. Denise Levertov. SP-LeveDP

Earth would not seem homelike without. Emily Dickinson. SP-DickE

Earth Your Dancing Place. May Swenson. SP-SwenM

Earthenware Head, The. Ted Hughes. SP-HughTN

Earthfault we stand on is nobody's fault, The. Here. Andrei Codrescu. SP-CodrA

Earthling. Billy Collins. SP-CollB

Earthly doctor fiddled with his beard, The. Fables of the Moscow Subway. Howard Nemerov. CP-NemeH

Earthquake. Thomas Merton. CP-MertT

Earthquake, The. Jane Cooper. CP-CoopJ

Earthquake, The. Shmuel HaNagid. SP-HaNaS, *tr. by* Peter Cole

Earthquake, The. Paul Muldoon. CP-MuldP

Earthquake, The. James Whitcomb Riley. CP-RileJ

Earthquake, The. John Greenleaf Whittier. CP-WhitJ

Earthquake in the West, The. Howard Nemerov. CP-NemeH

Earthrise. Theodore Weiss. SP-WeisT

Earth's Answer. William Blake. CP-BlakW *Fr.* Songs of Experience.

Earth's Attraction, The. Yannis Ritsos. SP-RitsY, *tr. by* Kimon Friar *and* Kostas Myrsiades

Earth's Champion. G. K. Chesterton. CP-ChesG

Earth's Festival, The ("Let the wind be a whirl of trumpets"). G. K. Chesterton. CP-ChesG

Earth's Festival, The ("Walls and the dome of the evening, The"). G. K. Chesterton. CP-ChesG

Earth's Heart Is Growing Cold Again. Aleksandr Aleksandrovich Blok. SP-BlokA, *tr. by* Peter France *and* Jon Stallworthy

Earth's Holocaust. James Schuyler. CP-SchuJ

Earth's icy dome, the skull that wears. Hope of the Year, The. G. K. Chesterton. CP-ChesG

Earth's Immortalities. Robert Browning. CP-BroR1

Earth's Preference. George Meredith. CP-MerG1

Earth's Secret. George Meredith. CP-MerG1

Earth's Shame, The. G. K. Chesterton. CP-ChesG

Earth's Vigil, The. G. K. Chesterton. CP-ChesG

Earth's winter cometh. Invern. Ezra Pound. CP-PoEar

Earthwoman and the Waterwoman, The. Denise Levertov. SP-LeveDS

Earthwoman by her oven, The. Earthwoman and the Waterwoman, The. Denise Levertov. SP-LeveDS

Earthworks. James Tate. SP-TateJ

Earthworm. Anne Sexton. CP-SextA

Earthworm. John Updike. CP-UpdiJ

Earthy Anecdote. Wallace Stevens. CP-StevW; CP-StevWP

Earwigs. Raymond Carver. CP-CarvR

Ease. Robert Herrick. CP-HerrR

Ease is the weary merchant's pray'r. Horace. *See* When o'er the Aegean vast he sails

Easedale Tarn. Amy Clampitt. CP-ClamA

Easily, almost matter-of-factly they step. Performers, The. Robert Earl Hayden. CP-HaydR

Easily as the moon. Making It. Theodore Weiss. SP-WeisT

Easily you confound. Michelangelo Buonarroti. CP-Miche, *tr. by* John Frederick Nims

Easily you move, easily your head. Bride in the 30's, A. W. H. Auden. CP-AudeW

East. Federico García Lorca. CP-GarcF, *tr. by* Jerome Rothenberg *Fr.* Cross.

East Bronx. David Ignatow. SP-IgnaD

East Coocoo. William Carlos Williams. CP-WilW2

East-End Curate, An. Thomas Hardy. CP-HardT

East Hampton—Boston by Air. John Updike. CP-UpdiJ

East India Marine Museum, The. Jones Very. CP-VeryJ

East Mauch Chunk - Jim Thorpe. William Corbett. SP-CorbW

East of me, west of me, full summer. After Reading Tu Fu, I Go Outside to the Dwarf Orchard. Charles Wright. SP-WrigCN

East of the Blue Ridge, Our Tombs Are in the Dove's Throat. Charles Wright. SP-WrigCN

East of the Sun, West of the Moon. Eleanor Wilner. SP-WilnE

East of town, the countryside unwrinkles and smooths out. Stray Paragraphs in February, Year of the Rat. Charles Wright. SP-WrigCN

East Side West. David Ignatow. SP-IgnaD

East Sixty-seventh Street. John Ciardi. CP-CiarJ

East Wind, An. Robert Graves. CP-GravR

East wind finds the gap bringing rain, The. Return, The: An Elegy. Robert Penn Warren. CP-WarrR

East winde with Aurora hath abiding, The. Ovid. CP-RaleW *Fr.* Metamorphoses.

East Window on Elizabeth Street, An. James Schuyler. CP-SchuJ

Eastbourne. Eugenio Montale. CP-MontE, *tr. by* Jonathan Galassi

Easter. Olga Broumas. SP-BrouO

Easter. Robert Creeley. CP-CreeR

Easter. George Herbert. CP-HerbG

Easter. Gerard Manley Hopkins. CP-HopkG

Easter. Lorine Niedecker. CP-NiedL

Easter. Frank O'Hara. SP-OharF

Easter. Charles Olson. CP-OlsoC

Easter. Derek Walcott. CP-WalcD

Easter. C. K. Williams. SP-WillC

Easter again, and a small rain falls. Other Side of the River, The. Charles Wright. SP-WrigC

Easter Carol, An. Christina Georgina Rossetti. CP-RosC2

Easter Communion. Gerard Manley Hopkins. CP-HopkG

Easter-Day. Robert Browning. CP-BroR1

Easter Day. Richard Crashaw. CP-CrasR

Easter Day. Christina Georgina Rossetti. CP-RosC2

Easter Day. Oscar Wilde. CP-WildO

Easter Day II. Arthur Hugh Clough. SP-ClouA

Easter Day. Naples, 1849. Arthur Hugh Clough. SP-ClouA

Easter Eve 1945. Muriel Rukeyser. SP-RukeM

Easter Even. Christina Georgina Rossetti. CP-RosC2

Easter Even. Christina Georgina Rossetti. CP-RosC3

Easter Flower Gift, An. John Greenleaf Whittier. CP-WhitJ

Easter Greeting. Lorine Niedecker. CP-NiedL

Easter Hymn. A. E. Housman. CP-HousA

Easter in Pittsburgh. James Laughlin. CP-LaugJ

Easter Island. Paul Muldoon. CP-MuldP

Easter Monday. Christina Georgina Rossetti. CP-RosC2

Easter Morning. Amy Clampitt. CP-ClamA

Easter Morning. Christina Georgina Rossetti. CP-RosC3

Easter Morning. May Sarton. SP-SartM

Easter Morning. William Stafford. SP-StafWW

Easter Morning: Crosby Junction. Robert Penn Warren. CP-WarrR

Easter 1989. Charles Wright. SP-WrigCN

Easter 1916. William Butler Yeats. CP-YeatW

Easter, 1968. May Sarton. SP-SartM

Easter Ode, An. Paul Laurence Dunbar. CP-DunbP

Easter Returns. Louis MacNeice. CP-MacNL

Easter Season. Louise Glück. SP-GlucL

Easter: Sensations of April. T. S. Eliot. SP-ElioT

Easter stars are shining, The. Flight to the City. William Carlos Williams. CP-WilW1

Easter Sunday. G. K. Chesterton. CP-ChesG

Easter Sunday. Allen Ginsberg. CP-GinsA

Easter Tuesday. Christina Georgina Rossetti. CP-RosC2

Easter Wings. George Herbert. CP-HerbG

Eastern Ballad, An. Allen Ginsberg. CP-GinsA

East[ern] European Cooking. Charles Simic. SP-SimiC; SP-SimiCE

Eastern European Eclogues. Rita Dove. SP-DoveR

Eastern mail comes lumbering in, The. Evening Wind, The. Henry David Thoreau. CP-ThorH

Eastern Question, The. Ambrose Bierce. SP-BierA

Eastern sky at sunset taking, The. Coming Fall, The. Denise Levertov. SP-LeveDP

Eastern tip of the Empire dives into night, The. Lullaby of Cape Cod. Joseph Brodsky. CP-BrodJ, tr. by Anthony Hecht

Eastern War Time. Adrienne Rich.
 "Memory says: Want to do right? Don't count on me." SP-RicA1

Easters of childhood heaped in motley shards. Easter Returns. Louis MacNeice. CP-MacNL

Eastport. Heather McHugh. SP-McHuH

Eastport to Block Island. Adrienne Rich. CP-RicAE

Eastward from here. Blue Sky, The. Gary Snyder. CP-SnydG

Eastward the city with scarcely even a murmur. Soft City, The. Tennessee Williams. CP-WillT

Easy. Stevie Smith. CP-SmitS

Easy as cove-water rustles its pebbles and shells. Part of a Letter. Richard Wilbur. CP-WilbR

Easy Boogie. Langston Hughes. CP-HughL; CP-HughL3

Easy Decision, An. Kenneth Patchen. CP-PatcK

Easy, easy, watch that belly! News Photo. Robert Penn Warren. CP-WarrR

Easy-Goin' Feller, An. Paul Laurence Dunbar. CP-DunbP

Easy in their ugly skins. Easy. Stevie Smith. CP-SmitS

Easy Knowledge. W. H. Auden. CP-AudeW

Easy lazy length of limb, An. Portraits. Christina Georgina Rossetti. CP-RosC3

Easy Lessons in Geophagy. Kenneth Rexroth. CP-RexrK

Easy Rider. Kenneth Patchen. CP-PatcK

Easy to match what others do. Ralph Waldo Emerson. CP-EmerR

Eat. Charles Bukowski. SP-BukC2

Eat Eat more marbled Sirloin more Pork'n / gravy! C'mon Pigs of Western Civilization Eat More Grease. Allen Ginsberg. SP-GinsA

Eat, race of Abel, drink and sleep! Abel and Cain. Charles Baudelaire. CP-BaudC, tr. by Walter Martin

Eat the bit of cake in your garden. Emily Dickinson. SP-DickE

Eat the crust and drink the water, use the simple homely store. J.D.C., The. G. K. Chesterton. CP-ChesG

Eat thou and drink; to-morrow thou shalt die. Choice, The ("Eat thou and drink; to-morrow thou shalt die"). Dante Gabriel Rossetti. CW-RossD Fr. House of Life, The.

Eat Your Heart Out. Charles Bukowski. SP-BukC1

Eaten by Butterflies. Charles Bukowski. SP-BukC2

Eaten I have; and though I had good cheere. Meat without Mirth. Robert Herrick. CP-HerrR

'Eathen, The. Rudyard Kipling. CP-KiplR

Eating a sandwich. We Make Our Vows Together with All Beings. Gary Snyder. CP-SnydG

Eating, being eaten. Questions. A. K. Ramanujan. CP-RamaA

Eating cold plums in bed. Cold Plums. Charles Bukowski. SP-BukC1

Eating Fire. Margaret Atwood. SP-AtwM1

Eating My Senior Citizen's Dinner at the Sizzler. Charles Bukowski. SP-BukC3

Eating Snake. Margaret Atwood. SP-AtwM2

Eating the living germs of grasses. Song of the Taste. Gary Snyder. CP-SnydG

Eating the Pig. Donald Hall. CP-HallD

Eats meat exclusively. Can't bear. Driver Ant, The. Thomas Lux. SP-LuxT

Eats with one stomach but. Believer, The. James Laughlin. CP-LaugJ

Eavesdropper. Sylvia Plath. CP-PlatS

Ebb. Edna St. Vincent Millay. CP-MillE

Ebb slips from the rock, the sunken, The. Night. Robinson Jeffers. CP-JefR1

Eben Haëzer. Gerrit Achterberg. CP-RicAE

Ecce Homo. John Berryman. CP-BerrJ

Ecce quam leve et quam jocosum. Psalm 132: A Modern Monastic Revision.

Thomas Merton. CP-MertT

Ecce Sponsus. "H. D." CP-DoolH

Eccentric Motion. Muriel Rukeyser. CP-RukeM

Ecclesiast, The. John Ashbery. SP-AshbJ

Ecclesiastes. G. K. Chesterton. CP-ChesG

Ecclesiastes. Derek Mahon. CP-MahoD

Ecclesiastic, The. Stéphane Mallarmé. CP-MallS, tr. by Henry Weinfield

Ecclesiastical Polity. Donald Davie. CP-DaviDC

Ecclesiastical Sonnets. William Wordsworth. CP-WorW2
 Conclusion: "Why Sleeps the future, as a snake enrolled." CP-WorW2
 Mutability. MW-WorW

Ecco a letter starting "dearest we." E. E. Cummings. CP-CummE

Echetlos. Robert Browning. CP-BroR2

Echo. Sir Philip Sidney. SP-SidnP Fr. Arcadia.

Echo. Federico García Lorca. CP-GarcF, tr. by Alan S. Trueblood Fr. Love.

Echo. Audre Lorde. SP-LordA

Echo. Walter De la Mare. CP-DeLaW

Echo. Michael Palmer. SP-PalmM

Echo. Michael Palmer. SP-PalmM

Echo. Christina Georgina Rossetti. CP-RosC1

Echo ("Broken heart, you / timeless wonder"). Robert Creeley. CP-CreeR

Echo-Elf Answers, The. Thomas Hardy. CP-HardT

Echo ("Faint, persistent"). Robert Creeley. SP-CreeR

Echo for the Promise of Georg Trakl's Life. James Wright. CP-WrigJ

Echo from Willowwood, An. Christina Georgina Rossetti. CP-RosC3

Echo ("I'm almost / done, the hour"). Robert Creeley. CP-CreeR

Echo in the mirror's not potential. Signing the Poem. Robert Stock. SP-StocR

Echo Of. Robert Creeley. CP-CreeR

Echo of the Sabbath Bell, The. Henry David Thoreau.

Echo, the beating of the tide. Prophecy on Lethe. Stanley Kunitz. CP-KunSC

Echo ("Two poles, The. We didn't disagree"). Michael Palmer. SP-PalmM

Echo ("Yes but your sweetness"). Robert Creeley. CP-CreeR

Echoes. John Ciardi. CP-CiarJ

Echoes. Hart Crane. CP-CranH

Echoes. Laura Riding Jackson. CP-RidiL

Echoes. Thomas Kinsella. CP-KinsT

Echoes. Ezra Pound. CP-PoEar

Echoes ("Eight panes"). Robert Creeley. SP-CreeR

Echoes of voices stilled may linger on. Assignation, The. Walter De la Mare. CP-DeLaW

Echoes ("Step through the mirror"). Robert Creeley. SP-CreeR

Echoes ("Sudden / loss of hope, A"). Robert Creeley. CP-CreeR

Echo's Bones. Samuel Beckett.
 "Asylum under my tread all this day." CP-BeckS
 Vulture, The. CP-BeckS

Echo's [or Eccho's] Song. Ben Jonson. CP-JonsB; SP-JonsB Fr. Cynthia's Revels.

Eclipse. Ted Hughes. SP-HughTN

Eclipse, The. Robert Herrick. CP-HerrR

Eclogue 4: Winter. Joseph Brodsky. CP-BrodJ, tr. by Joseph Brodsky

Eclogue 5: Summer. Joseph Brodsky. CP-BrodJ, tr. by George L. Kline

Eclogue at Daybreak. Yusef Komunyakaa. CP-KomuY

Eclogue at Nash's Grove. James Wright. CP-WrigJ

Eclogue at Twilight. Yusef Komunyakaa. CP-KomuY

Eclogue between the Motherless. Louis MacNeice. CP-MacNL

Eclogue by a Five-Barred Gate. Louis MacNeice. CP-MacNL

Eclogue for Christmas, An. Louis MacNeice. CP-MacNL

Eclogue from Iceland. Louis MacNeice. CP-MacNL

Eclogue: "It was good getting lost." Eugenio Montale. CP-MontE, tr. by Jonathan Galassi

Eclogue: "JANE SNEED BEGAN IT: My poor John, alas." John Crowe Ransom. SP-RansJ

Eclogue: "Lying in the mint." Wallace Stevens. CP-StevWP

Eclogue: "Men talking, The." George Oppen. CP-OppGN

Eclogue of the Liberal and the Poet. Allen Tate. CP-TateA

Eclogue, or Pastorall between Endimion Porter and Lycidas Herrick, An. Robert Herrick. CP-HerrR

Eclogues. Virgil.
 Eclogue 2.
 "With me retire and leave the pomp of courts." CP-JohnS
 Eclogue 4: The Messiah. CP-DryJ2
 Eclogue 9: Lycidas and Moeris. CP-DryJ2, tr. by John Dryden
 Eclogue 10.
 "Melodious Arethusa, o'er my verse." CP-ShelP

Ecologue. Allen Ginsberg. CP-GinsA

Ecology. A. K. Ramanujan. CP-RamaA

Ecology, An. David Ignatow. SP-IgnaD

Ecology of Jerusalem. Yehuda Amichai. SP-AmicY, *tr.* by Chana Bloch

"Economic secu / rity" is a cu. E. E. Cummings. CP-CummE

Economics. G. K. Chesterton. CP-ChesG

Economics. Mona Van Duyn. SP-VanDM

Economist's Song, The. Stanley Kunitz. CP-KunSC

Economy. W. S. Merwin. SP-MerwW

Écoute-les / s'ajouter. Samuel Beckett. CP-BeckS

Ecquis Binas. Gerard Manley Hopkins. CP-HopkG

Ecstasies of Dialectic, The. Howard Nemerov. CP-NemeH

Ecstasy, The. John Donne. CP-DonnJ; MW-DonnJ

"Ecstasy is the / disaster of pleasure": this. Hayden Carruth. CP-CarHS *Fr.* Clay Hill Anthology, The.

Ecstasy of Chaos. Robert Graves. CP-GravR

Ecstasy of the Pure. Kenneth Patchen. CP-PatcK

Ecstasy to guess, The. Emily Dickinson. CP-DickE

Ecstatic bird songs pound. Dawn. William Carlos Williams. CP-WilW1

Ed. William Corbett. SP-CorbW

Ed Stiles and old Tom Birnam went up to their cattle on the bare hills. Wind-Struck Music, The. Robinson Jeffers. CP-JefR2

Edain came out of Midhir's hill, and lay. Harp of Aengus, The. William Butler Yeats. CP-YeatW

Eddi, priest of St. Wilfrid. Eddi's Service. Rudyard Kipling. CP-KiplR

Eddie and Charlie and Jack and Ted. Bonds: In Memoriam. Langston Hughes. CP-HughL; CP-HughL3

Eddi's Service. Rudyard Kipling. CP-KiplR

Eden. Donald Davie. CP-DaviDC

Eden. Charles Tomlinson. CP-TomlC; SP-TomlC

Eden. Jones Very. CP-VeryJ

Eden Bower. Dante Gabriel Rossetti. CW-RossD

Eden in Winter. Nicholas Vachel Lindsay. CP-LindV

Eden is that Old-Fashioned House. Emily Dickinson. CP-DickE

Eden is that old-fashioned house. Eden is that Old-Fashioned House. Emily Dickinson. CP-DickE

Eden land, an Eden in the west, An. On the Nebraska Bill. Jones Very. CP-VeryJ

Edgar Allan Poe Meets Sarah Hale (Author of "Mary Had a Little Lamb"). Thomas Lux. SP-LuxT

Edgar Lee Masters. Richard Eberhart. CP-EberR

Edgar Wilson Nye. James Whitcomb Riley. CP-RileJ

Edge. Sylvia Plath. CP-PlatS

Edge, The. Louise Glück. SP-GlucL

Edge, The. Yusef Komunyakaa. CP-KomuY

Edge, The ("Long over whatever edge"). Robert Creeley. SP-CreeR

Edge, The ("Place it, / make the space"). Robert Creeley. CP-CreeR

Edge of autumn touches leaves, The. Sweet Corn. Peter Blue Cloud. SP-BlueP

Edge of the cancer, The. Front Lines. Gary Snyder. CP-SnydG

Edge of the dome is slipping, The. Fanny Howe. SP-HoweF *Fr.* O'Clock.

Edge of the green wave whitely doth hiss, The. Fernando Pessoa. SP-PessF *Fr.* 35 Sonnets.

Edge of the Hurricane, The. Amy Clampitt. CP-ClamA

Edge of the ocean, The. George Oppen. CP-OppGN

Edge of the River, The. Thomas McGrath. SP-McGrT

Edge of the wind, The. James Whitcomb Riley. CP-RileJ

Edgehill Fight. Rudyard Kipling. CP-KiplR

Edges. Allen Tate. CP-TateA

Edging each other towards consummation. In the Borghese Gardens. Charles Tomlinson. SP-TomlC

Edgy, perhaps. *Not* on the point of bursting-forth. How Do You Do, Dr Berryman, Sir? John Berryman. CP-BerrJ

Edina! *Scotia's* darling seat! Address to Edinburgh. Robert Burns. CP-BurnR

Edinburgh From Blackford Hill. Sir Walter Scott. *See* Marmion

Edinburgh from the Pentland Hills. Sir Walter Scott. SP-ScotW *Fr.* Marmion.

Edison. Robinson Jeffers. CP-JefR2

Editorial Office. D. H. Lawrence. CP-LawrD

Editorially / We wonder why we. Poet Scratches His Head, The. John Logan. CP-LogaJ

Edmonton, Thy Cemetery. Stevie Smith. CP-SmitS

Edmund Husserl, modern philosopher. Name Edmund, The. Adam Zagajewski. SP-ZagaA, *tr.* by Clare Cavanagh

Edmund! thy grave with aking eye I scan. Lines on a Friend. Samuel Taylor Coleridge. CP-ColeS

Edmund's Songs. Sir Walter Scott. SP-ScotW *Fr.* Rokeby.

Edna Bay. Arthur Sze. SP-SzeA

Edouard. Ogden Nash. CP-NashO

Edouard shall we leave. W. S. Merwin. SP-MerwW

Education. G. K. Chesterton. CP-ChesG

Education. Kenneth Rexroth. CP-RexrK

Education. Jones Very. CP-VeryJ

Education a Failure. William Carlos Williams. CP-WilW2

Education, kindness. Come In. Lorine Niedecker. CP-NiedL

Education of a Novelist. Adrienne Rich. SP-RicA2

Edward and Jane a married couple were. Clergyman's Second Tale, The. Arthur Hugh Clough. SP-ClouA *Fr.* Mari Magno.

Edward Kienholz: *The State Hospital.* Paul Muldoon. CP-MuldP

Edward Lear. W. H. Auden. CP-AudeW

Edward Shore. George Crabbe. SP-CrabG *Fr.* Tales.

Edwardian pillar boxes wait for Edwardian letters; the Museum. October in Bloomsbury. Louis MacNeice. CP-MacNL

Edward's Anecdote. Donald Hall. CP-HallD

Edwards' great millstone and rock. Jonathan Edwards in Western Massachusetts. Robert Lowell. SP-LoweR

Edwin Morris. Alfred Tennyson. CP-TennA

Edwin Muir. Archibald MacLeish. CP-MacLA

Eel. Muriel Rukeyser. CP-RukeM

Eel, An. Ted Hughes. SP-HughTN

Eel, The. Eugenio Montale. CP-MontE, *tr.* by Jonathan Galassi

Eel, The. Ogden Nash. CP-NashO

Eel-Grass. Edna St. Vincent Millay. CP-MillE

Eel, siren, The. Eel, The. Eugenio Montale. CP-MontE, *tr.* by Jonathan Galassi

Eeles winds and turnes. and cheats and steales; yet Eeles. Upon Eeles. Robert Herrick. CP-HerrR

Eemis-Stane, The. Hugh MacDiarmid. SP-MacDH

E'en all Religious courses to be rich. Any Way for Wealth. Robert Herrick. CP-HerrR

E'er bribes convince you whom to choose. Elephant, The. Jonathan Swift. CP-SwifJ

Ef dey's anyt'ing dat riles me. Possum. Paul Laurence Dunbar. CP-DunbP

Ef you's only got de powah fe' to blow a little whistle. Limitations. Paul Laurence Dunbar. CP-DunbP

Effacement. Denise Levertov. SP-LeveDS

Effects of Music upon a Company of People. Ezra Pound. CP-PoEar

Effervescent Mrs. G, The. Wyatt Prunty. SP-PrunW

Effort. Jones Very. CP-VeryJ

Effort at Speech. William Meredith. SP-MereW

Effort at Speech between Two People. Muriel Rukeyser. CP-RukeM

Effort of Love, The. D. H. Lawrence. CP-LawrD

Effort to put my essence in me, The. Signature, The. Laura Riding Jackson. CP-RidiL

Efforts of Affection. Marianne Craig Moore. CP-MoorM

Effusion in the Pleasure-Ground on the Banks of the Bran, Near Dunkeld. William Wordsworth. CP-WorW2

Effusions. Samuel Taylor Coleridge. CP-ColeS

  Burke. MW-ColeS

  Eolian Harp, The. MW-ColeS

  Genevieve. MW-ColeS

  Pitt. MW-ColeS

  Priestley. CP-ColeS; MW-ColeS

  To an Infant. MW-ColeS

  To Richard Brinsley Sheridan, Esq. CP-ColeS

  To the Rev. [*or* Reverend] W. L. Bowles. MW-ColeS

Effusions of a School-Patriarch, The. Arthur Hugh Clough. SP-ClouA

Eftir geving I speik of taking. William Dunbar. CP-DunbW

Egg, The. Louise Glück. SP-GlucL

Egg, The. Sam Hamill. SP-HamiS

Egg, The. Gary Snyder. CP-SnydG

Egg a chick pokes its head out of, The. Eggs. John Ciardi. CP-CiarJ

Egg and the Machine, The. Robert Frost. CP-FrosR

Egg-Head. Ted Hughes. SP-HughTN

Egg-Shell, The. Rudyard Kipling. CP-KiplR

Eggs. John Ciardi. CP-CiarJ

Eggs. Dates and camel's milk. From Dread in the Eyes of Horses. Tess Gallagher. SP-GallT

Eggs of Pheasants wrie-nos'd Tooly sells, The. Upon Tooly. Robert Herrick. CP-HerrR

Egnatius, candid as his horse-bit white dentures. Catullus. *See* Because he has bright white teech, Eg- / natius whips out a

Ego. G. K. Chesterton. CP-ChesG

Ego. John Greenleaf Whittier. CP-WhitJ

Ego-Bound. D. H. Lawrence. CP-LawrD

Ego-Bound Women. D. H. Lawrence. CP-LawrD

Ego Confession. Allen Ginsberg. CP-GinsA; SP-GinsA

Ego Dominus Tuus. William Butler Yeats. CP-YeatW

Egocentric. Stevie Smith. CP-SmitS

Egoist. Pablo Neruda. SP-NeruP

Egoists, The. D. H. Lawrence. CP-LawrD

Egon Schiele knew that he was two people. Doppelgaengers, The. James Laughlin. CP-LaugJ

Ego's county he inheritied, The. Conscript. Philip Larkin. CP-LarkP

Egotism. A Letter to J.T. Becher. Lord Byron. CP-Byron

Egotist. Ambrose Bierce. SP-BierA *Fr.* Devil's Dictionary, The.

Egregious was the egret's error, very. Even Egrets Err. John Updike. CP-UpdiJ

Egress. Raymond Carver. CP-CarvR

Egret, The. Mary Oliver. SP-OlivM

Egrets. Mary Oliver. SP-OlivM

Egypt. "H. D." CP-DoolH

Egypt. Kenneth Patchen. CP-PatcK

Egypt That Doesn't Exist, An. Jelaluddin Rumi. SP-Rumi, *tr. by* Coleman Barks

Egypt, Tobago. Derek Walcott. CP-WalcD

Egyptian Maid; or, The Romance of the Water Lilly, The. William Wordsworth. CP-WorW2

Egyptian Passage, An. Theodore Weiss. SP-WeisT

Egyptian Pulled Glass Bottle in the Shape of a Fish, An. Marianne Craig Moore. CP-MoorM

Egyptians [*or* Aegyptians] think[e] it sin[ne] to root[e] up, or to bite. Juvenal. CP-RaleW *Fr.* Satires.

"Eh bien! Marche!," fit le Majeur Ydow. Le Majeur Ydow. Stevie Smith. CP-SmitS

Eheu! "Rubén Darío." SP-DariR, *tr. by* Alberto Acereda *and* Will Derusha

Eheu Fugaces. G. K. Chesterton. CP-ChesG

Eheu! Fugaces, or, What a Difference a Lot of Days Make. Ogden Nash. CP-NashO

Eheu! fugaces, Posthume, Posthume, Labuntur anni. Jones Very. CP-VeryJ

Eheu fugaces, Postume. Eheu Fugaces. G. K. Chesterton. CP-ChesG

Ei Men Een Mathein. Sir John Suckling. CP-SuckJ

Eider afloat in the bay. Kathleen Jessie Raine. SP-RainK

Eidolon. Robert Penn Warren. CP-WarrR

Eidolons. Walt Whitman. CP-WhitW

8 BLACK BOYS IN A SOUTHERN JAIL. Scottsboro. Langston Hughes. CP-HughL; CP-HughL1

Eight Early Poems. Kenneth Patchen. CP-PatcK

Eight hours between us, eight. England. Donald Davie. CP-DaviDC

851. Alan Dugan. CP-DugaA

Eight Months Later. Robert Lowell. SP-LoweR

Eight Observations on the Nature of Eternity. Charles Tomlinson. CP-TomlC

Eight O'Clock. A. E. Housman. CP-HousA

Eight o'clock, no later. Lamps, The. Mary Oliver. SP-OlivM

Eight O'Clock Peril, The. Ogden Nash. CP-NashO

Eight o'clock; / The postman's knock! Postman, The. Christina Georgina Rossetti. CP-RosC2

Eight of 'em hyeah all tol' an' yet. Puttin' the Baby Away. Paul Laurence Dunbar. CP-DunbP

Eight panes. Echoes ("Eight panes"). Robert Creeley. SP-CreeR

8:00 p.m. Federico García Lorca. CP-GarcF, *tr. by* Jerome Rothenberg *Fr.* Summer Hours.

Eight Poems on Portraits of the Foot. John Logan. CP-LogaJ

Eight Riddles from Symphosius. Richard Wilbur. CP-WilbR

8/12/70. James Schuyler. CP-SchuJ

Eight Years After. Donald Davie. CP-DaviDC

Eight years difference in age seems now, The. Terminal. Thom Gunn. CP-GunnT

Eight years removed from them, I sit among. Widener Library, Reading Room. John Updike. CP-UpdiJ

Eighteen Days without You. Anne Sexton. CP-SextA

    December 18th. SP-SextA

    December 11th. SP-SextA

    December 2nd. SP-SextA

Eighteen-Dollar Taxi Trip to Tizapan and Back to Chapala. Clarence Major. SP-MajoC

1880. Christina Georgina Rossetti. *See* Valentines to My Mother, 1880

1885. St. Valentine's Day. Christina Georgina Rossetti. CP-RosC3

1884. Christina Georgina Rossetti. CP-RosC3

1887. A. E. Housman. CP-HousA

1886, St. Valentine's Day. Christina Georgina Rossetti. CP-RosC3

1811. William Wordsworth. CP-WorW1

1805. Robert Graves. CP-GravR

1811. William Wordsworth. CP-WorW1

1801. William Wordsworth. CP-WorW1

1810. William Wordsworth. CP-WorW1

1810. William Wordsworth. CP-WorW1

1891. Jorge Luis Borges. SP-BorgJ, *tr. by* Alastair Reid

1892—19—. Archibald MacLeish. CP-MacLA

1892-1941. Louis Zukofsky. CP-ZukLS

1801. William Wordsworth. MW-WorW

1878. Christina Georgina Rossetti. CP-RosC3

1879. Christina Georgina Rossetti. CP-RosC3

Eighteen Sixty-One. Walt Whitman. CP-WhitW

1830. William Wordsworth. CP-WorW2

1837 War in Retrospect. Margaret Atwood. SP-AtwM1

18 West 11th Street. James Merrill. SP-MerrJ

Eighteen years I've spent in Manhattan. Blues. Joseph Brodsky. CP-BrodJ

Eighth Air Force. Randall Jarrell. CP-JarrR

Eighth Elegy. Children's Elegy. Muriel Rukeyser. CP-RukeM

Eighth Psalm. Anne Sexton. SP-SextA *Fr.* O Ye Tongues.

Eighty-eight thousand six-hundred. Buck Moon—From the Field Guide to Insects. Mary Oliver. SP-OlivM

'Eighty-Nine. Amy Clampitt. CP-ClamA

86'd. Charles Bukowski. SP-BukC2

Eileann Chanaidh. Kathleen Jessie Raine. SP-RainK

Ein Feste Burg Ist Unser Gott. John Greenleaf Whittier. CP-WhitJ

Ein Kitzbuehler Tag (1947). James Laughlin. CP-LaugJ

Ein Leben. Dan Pagis. SP-PagiD, *tr. by* Stephen Mitchell

Eine Kleine Nachtmusik. Randall Jarrell. CP-JarrR

Eine Kleine Snailmusik. May Sarton. SP-SartM

Einstein. Archibald MacLeish. CP-MacLA

Einstein & Freud & Jack. Howard Nemerov. CP-NemeH

Eisenhower's Visit to Franco, 1959. James Wright. CP-WrigJ

Either give me my hundred pounds back, Silo. Carmen 103. Catullus. CP-ZukLS *Fr.* Carmina.

Either heard or taught. Song for a Thin Sister. Audre Lorde. SP-LordA

Either in or out of. Finger, The. Robert Creeley. CP-CreeR

Either-Or. Czeslaw Milosz. CP-MiloCN, *tr. by* Robert Hass

Either she was foul, or her attire was bad. Elegy 3.6: "Either she was foul, or her attire was bad." Ovid. CP-MarlC, *tr. by* Christopher Marlowe *Fr.* Elegies.

Either they treed me, or I hid. High Jinx. Heather McHugh. SP-McHuH

Either we blow ourselves up now and die, like the old tribe of man, arguing among neutrons. Allen Ginsberg. SP-GinsA *Fr.* Television Was a Baby Crawling toward That Deathchamber.

Either we lodge diurnally here together. Elsewhere. Robert Graves. CP-GravR

Either you will / go through this door. Prospective Immigrants Please Note. Adrienne Rich. CP-RicAE; SP-RicA1; SP-RicA2

Eiusdem ad Authorem. Thomas Campion. CP-CampT

Ejected Indians haunt the lawns. West Virginia's Auburn. Donald Davie. CP-DaviDC

Ekstase, Alptraum, Schlaf in einem Nest von Flammen. Hayden Carruth. CP-CarHS

El camino de amor. James Laughlin. CP-LaugJ

El-Hajj Malik El-Shabazz. Robert Earl Hayden. CP-HaydR

El Hombre. William Carlos Williams. CP-WilW1

Elaine. Edna St. Vincent Millay. CP-MillE

Elaine, the counter-girl from the hat department. John Ciardi. CP-CiarJ

Elbows on dry books, we dreamed. Spring in the Classroom. Mary Oliver. SP-OlivM

Elder Father, though thine eyes. Holy of Holies, The. G. K. Chesterton. CP-ChesG

Elder folks shook hands at last, The. Meeting, The. John Greenleaf Whittier. CP-WhitJ

Elderly Discontented Women. D. H. Lawrence. CP-LawrD

Elderly Lady Crossing on Green. Wyatt Prunty. SP-PrunW

Elderly Leaders. Langston Hughes. CP-HughL; CP-HughL3

Elderly policemen stands beside my statue of him, An. Nausea, Coincidence. James Tate. SP-TateJ

Elderly Sex. John Updike. CP-UpdiJ

Elders and Betters. Donald Davie. CP-DaviDC

Elders at their services begin, The. James Vincent Cunningham. CP-CunnJ

Eldest-born of pow'rs divine! To Health. *Unknown.* CP-CowpW

Eldest son bestrides him, The. Undertaker's Horse, The. Rudyard Kipling. CP-KiplR

Eldorado. Edgar Allan Poe. CP-PoeEd

Eleanor. Christina Georgina Rossetti. CP-RosC3

Eleanor's Letters. Donald Hall. CP-HallD

Elecampane has no hope, but it has a connection. Elecampane, Jasmine, Vine, and Oleander. Yehuda Amichai. SP-AmicYL, *tr. by* Benjamin Harshav *and* Barbara Harshav

Elecampane, Jasmine, Vine, and Oleander. Yehuda Amichai. SP-AmicYL, *tr. by* Benjamin Harshav *and* Barbara Harshav

Elect, The. Donald Davie. CP-DaviDC

Elected Silence, sing to me. Habit of Perfection, The. Gerard Manley Hopkins. CP-HopkG

Election. Andrei Codrescu. SP-CodrA

Election: A New Song, The. Robert Burns. CP-BurnR *Fr.* Heron Ballads, 1795,

The.

Election, The. George Crabbe. SP-CrabG *Fr.* Borough, The.

Election Day. William Carlos Williams. CP-WilW2

Election Day Is a Holiday. Ogden Nash. CP-NashO

Election Day, 1984. Carolyn Kizer. CP-KizeC

Election Day, November, 1884. Walt Whitman. CP-WhitW

Election Echo, An. G. K. Chesterton. CP-ChesG

Elections to the Academy: referred from. Heroine of the Academy, A. Donald Davie. CP-DaviDC

Elective Affiniites. Josephine Jacobsen. CP-JacoJ

Electra. Sophocles.
Reverie. CP-CummE

Electra Becomes Morbid. Ogden Nash. CP-NashO

Electra on Azalea Path. Sylvia Plath. CP-PlatS

Electra-Orestes. "H. D."
"He marked the pattern of the sky." CP-DoolH
"Lovers may come and go." CP-DoolH
"Never let it be said." CP-DoolH
"No one knows, / the heart of a child." CP-DoolH
"She is dead." CP-DoolH
"To love, one must slay." CP-DoolH

Electric clock died in the night. Defective Circles. Philip Whalen. SP-WhalP

Electric Elegy. Adam Zagajewski. SP-ZagaA, *tr. by* Renata Gorczynski, Benjamin Ivry *and* C. K. Williams

Electric lines are ripped from trees. Faith. Heather McHugh. SP-McHuH

Electric Orchard, The. Paul Muldoon. CP-MuldP

Electric Sign Goes Dark, An. Carl Sandburg. CP-SandC

Electrical Storm. Elizabeth Bishop. CP-BishE

Electrical Storm. Robert Earl Hayden. CP-HaydR

Electrical strings are taut over all. The world is my oud. Yehuda Amichai. SP-AmicYL *Fr.* At Right Angles.

Electronic watch runs backwards to five A.M., The. What Are You Studying, These Days? Philip Whalen. SP-WhalP

Electroshock. Bang—. Hayden Carruth. CP-CarHS *Fr.* Clay Hill Anthology, The.

Eleemosynary. Yusef Komunyakaa. CP-KomuY

Elegant bird— / delicate claws, An. Bird. Pablo Neruda. SP-NeruP

Elegant office girl, The. Lorine Niedecker. CP-NiedL

Elegeia I (1595). Thomas Campion. CP-CampT

Elegia I (1619). Thomas Campion. CP-CampT

Elegiac Calculation. Wisława Szymborska. SP-SzymW, *tr.* Stanislaw Barańczak *and* Clare Cavanagh

Elegiac Musings in the Grounds of Coleorton Hall, the Seat of the Late Sir G.H. Beaumont, BART. William Wordsworth. CP-WorW2

Elegiac Poem, on the Death of That Celebrated Divine, and Eminent Servant of Jesus Christ, the Late Reverend, and Pious George Whitefield, An. Phillis Wheatley. *See* On the Death of the Rev. Mr. George Whitefield [1770]

Elegiac Stanzas (Addressed to Sir G.H.B. upon the Death of His Sister-in-Law). William Wordsworth. CP-WorW2

Elegiac Stanzas Composed in the Churchyard of Grasmere. William Wordsworth. CP-WorW1

Elegiac Stanzas: On a Visit to Dove Cottage. Geoffrey Hill. CP-HillG

Elegiac Stanzas on the Death of Sir Peter Parker, Bart. Lord Byron. CP-Byron

Elegiac Stanzas Suggested by a Picture of Peele Castle, in a Storm, Painted by Sir George Beaumont. William Wordsworth. CP-WorW1; MW-WorW

Elegiac Verses. John Milton. CP-MiltJ

Elegiac Verses in Memory of My Brother, John Wordsworth. William Wordsworth. CP-WorW1

Elegiack Ode on the 28th Day of February 1782, An. The Anniversary of Mr. Stockton's Death. Annis Boudinot Stockton. CP-StocA

Elegiacs. Gerard Manley Hopkins. CP-HopkG

Elegie on the Death of Doctor Porter, An. Richard Crashaw. CP-CrasR

Elegie upon the Untimely Death of Prince *Henry*, An. Thomas Campion. CP-CampT

Elegies. John Donne. CP-DonnJ
Anagram, The. MW-DonnJ
Autumnal[l], The. MW-DonnJ
Bracelet, The. MW-DonnJ
Change. MW-DonnJ
Comparison, The. MW-DonnJ
Dream, The. MW-DonnJ
His Picture. MW-DonnJ
Jealousy [*or* Jealousie]. MW-DonnJ
Love's Progress. MW-DonnJ
Love's War. MW-DonnJ
"Nature's lay idiot [*or* ideot], I taught thee to love." MW-DonnJ
"Oh, let me not serve so, as those men serve." MW-DonnJ
On His Mistress [*or* Mistris]. MW-DonnJ

Perfume, The. MW-DonnJ
Sappho to Philaenis. MW-DonnJ
To His Mistress Going to Bed. MW-DonnJ

Elegies. Ovid.
Elegy 1.1: "We which were Ovid's five books now are three." CP-MarlC
Elegy 1.2: "What makes my bed seem hard seeing it is soft?." CP-MarlC, *tr. by* Christopher Marlowe
Elegy 1.3: "I ask but right: let her that caught me late." CP-MarlC, *tr. by* Christopher Marlowe
Elegy 1.4: "Thy husband to a banquet goes with me." CP-MarlC
Elegy 1.5: "In summer's heat[e] and mid-time of the day." CP-MarlC, *tr. by* Christopher Marlowe
Elegy 1.6: "Unworthy porter, bound in chains full sore." CP-MarlC
Elegy 1.7: "Bind fast my hands, they have deservéd chains." CP-MarlC
Elegy 1.8: "There is—whoe'er will know a bawd aright." CP-MarlC
Elegy 1.9: "All lovers war, and Cupid hath his tent." CP-MarlC
Elegy 1.10: "Such as the cause was of two husbands' war." CP-MarlC
Elegy 1.11: "In skilful gathering ruffled hairs in order." CP-MarlC
Elegy 1.12: "Bewail my chance: the sad book is returnéd." CP-MarlC
Elegy 1.13: "Now o'er the sea from her old love comes she." CP-MarlC
Elegy 1.14: "'Leave colouring thy tresses', I did cry." CP-MarlC
Elegy 1.15: "Envy, why carp'st [*or* carpest] thou my time is spent so ill." CP-MarlC, *tr. by* Christopher Marlowe
Elegy 2.1: "I, Ovid, poet of my wantonness." CP-MarlC, *tr. by* Christopher Marlowe
Elegy 2.2: "Bagous, whose care doth thy mistress bridle." CP-MarlC
Elegy 2.3: "Aye me, an eunuch keeps my mistress chaste." CP-MarlC
Elegy 2.4: "I mean not to defend the scapes of any." CP-MarlC
Elegy 2.5: "No love is so dear (quivered Cupid, fly!)." CP-MarlC
Elegy 2.6: "Parrot, from east India to me sent, The." CP-MarlC
Elegy 2.7: "Dost me of new crimes always guilty frame?." CP-MarlC
Elegy 2.8: "Cypassis, that a thousand ways trim'st hair." CP-MarlC, *tr. by* Christopher Marlowe
Elegy 2.9: "O Cupid, that dost never cease my smart." CP-MarlC
Elegy 2.10: "Graecinus (well I wot) thou told'st me once." CP-MarlC, *tr. by* Christopher Marlowe
Elegy 2.11: "Lofty pine, from high Mount Pelion raught, The." CP-MarlC
Elegy 2.12: "About my temples go, triumphant bays!." CP-MarlC
Elegy 2.13: "While rashly her womb's burden she casts out." CP-MarlC
Elegy 2.14: "What helps it woman to be free from war." CP-MarlC
Elegy 2.15: "Thou ring that shalt my fair girl's finger bind." CP-MarlC
Elegy 2.16: "Sulmo, Peligny's third part, me contains." CP-MarlC
Elegy 2.17: "To serve a wench if any think it shame." CP-MarlC
Elegy 2.18: "To tragic verse while thou Achilles train't." CP-MarlC
Elegy 2.19: "Fool, if to keep thy wife thou hast no need." CP-MarlC
Elegy 2.19: "If for thyself thou wilt not watch thy whore." CP-DryJ2, *tr. by* John Dryden
Elegy 3.1: "Old wood stands uncut, of long years' space, An." CP-MarlC
Elegy 3.2: "I sit not here the noble horse to see." CP-MarlC
Elegy 3.3: "What, are there gods? herself she hath forswore." CP-MarlC
Elegy 3.4: "Rude man, 'tis vain thy damsel to commend." CP-MarlC
Elegy 3.5: "Flood with reed-grown slime banks, till I be past." CP-MarlC
Elegy 3.6: "Either she was foul, or her attire was bad." CP-MarlC, *tr. by* Christopher Marlowe
Elegy 3.7: "What man will now take liberal arts in hand." CP-MarlC
Elegy 3.8: "If Thetis and the Morn their sons did wail." CP-MarlC
Elegy 3.9: "Come were the times of Ceres' sacrifice." CP-MarlC
Elegy 3.10: "Long have I borne much, mad thy faults me make." CP-MarlC
Elegy 3.11: "What day was that which, all sad haps to bring." CP-MarlC
Elegy 3.12: "When fruit-filled Tuscia should a wife give me." CP-MarlC
Elegy 3.13: "Seeing thou art fair[e], I bar[re] not thy false playing." CP-MarlC, *tr. by* Christopher Marlowe
Elegy 3.14: "Tender Love's mother, a new poet get." CP-MarlC
Elegy 5.12: "You bid me write t'amuse the tedious hours." CP-CowpW, *tr. by* William Cowper

Elegies. Tibullus.
"Before my closing eyes, dear Cynthia, stand." CP-JohnS, *tr. by* Samuel Johnson
"How sweet in sleep to pass the careless hours." CP-JohnS, *tr. by* Samuel Johnson

Elegies for Paradise Valley. Robert Earl Hayden. CP-HaydR

Elegies for the Ocher Deer on the Walls at Lascaux. Norman Dubie. CP-DubiN

Elegies on the War Dead. Yehuda Amichai.
"Dicky was hurt." SP-AmicYL
"I found an old book on animals." SP-AmicYL
"Mister Beringer, whose son." SP-AmicYL

Elegy. Wendell Berry. CP-BerrW

Elegy 3: On the Death of the Bishop of Winchester. John Milton. CP-CowpW; CP-MiltJ
   (Silent I sat, dejected, and alone.) CP-CowpW
Elegy 4: To Thomas Young. John Milton. CP-CowpW; CP-MiltJ
   (Hence my epistle—skim the deep—fly o'er.) CP-CowpW
Elegy 6: To Charles Deodati. John Milton. CP-CowpW; CP-MiltJ
   (With no rich viands overcharg'd, I send.) CP-CowpW
Elegy 7: "Not yet did I know your laws, enticing Amathusia." John Milton. CP-CowpW; CP-MiltJ
   (As yet a stranger to the gentle fires.) CP-CowpW
Elegy: "About a year has passed. I've returned to the place of battle." Joseph Brodsky. CP-BrodJ, tr. by Joseph Brodsky
Elegy: "All day our eyes could find no resting place." Wendell Berry. CP-BerrW
Elegy: "Always, the world we invent or build." Sam Hamill. SP-HamiS
Elegy, An: "By those bright eyes, at whose immortal fires." Ben Jonson. CP-JonsB
Elegy, An: "Can beauty that did prompt me first to write." Ben Jonson. CP-JonsB
Elegy [or Elegie], An: "Let me be what I am, as Virgil cold." Ben Jonson. CP-JonsB; SP-JonsB
Elegy, An: "Since you must go, and I must bid farewell." Ben Jonson. CP-JonsB
Elegy, An: "That love's a bitter sweet, I ne'er conceive." Ben Jonson. CP-JonsB
Elegy, An: "Though beauty be the mark of praise." Ben Jonson. CP-JonsB
Elegy and Nocturne for Lora Baxter. Marya Alexandrovna Zaturenska. SP-ZatuM
Elegy Asking that It Be the Last. Norman Dubie. CP-DubiN
Elegy at Beaverhead County, Montana. Helen Pinkerton. CP-PinkH
Elegy before Death. Edna St. Vincent Millay. CP-MillE
Elegy Before the Time. William Dickey. SP-DickW
Elegy: "Behold the blessings of a lucky lot!" Lord Byron. CP-Byron
Elegy Che Guevara. Allen Ginsberg. CP-GinsA
Elegy: "Crying from exile, I." Marilyn Hacker. SP-HackM
Elegy: "Cur foretells the knell of parting day, The." Ambrose Bierce. SP-BierA
   Fr. Devil's Dictionary, The.
Elegy 5: On the Coming of Spring. John Milton. CP-CowpW; CP-MiltJ
   (Time, never wand'ring from his annual round.) CP-CowpW
Elegy for a Cave Full of Bones. John Ciardi. CP-CiarJ
Elegy for a Cricket. James Vincent Cunningham. CP-CunnJ
Elegy for a Gifted Child. Alan Dugan. CP-DugaA
Elegy for a Jet Pilot. A. R. Ammons. CP-AmmoA
Elegy for a Magician. Alan Dugan. CP-DugaA
Elegy for a Nature Poet. Howard Nemerov. CP-NemeH
Elegy for a Park. Jorge Luis Borges. SP-BorgJ, tr. by Alastair Reid
Elegy for a Puritan Conscience. Alan Dugan. CP-DugaA
Elegy for a Sweet Sharpy. John Ciardi. CP-CiarJ
Elegy for a Trappist. Thomas Merton. CP-MertT
Elegy for a Writer. Eleanor Wilner. SP-WilnE
Elegy for D.H. Lawrence, An. William Carlos Williams. CP-WilWI
Elegy for Dylan Thomas. John Logan. CP-LogaJ
Elegy for Ernest Hemingway, An. Thomas Merton. CP-MertT
Elegy for Eugenesis. Allen Tate. CP-TateA
Elegy for Five Old Ladies, An. Thomas Merton. CP-MertT
Elegy for Frank Stanford. Thomas Lux. SP-LuxT
Elegy for G. B. Shaw. John Ciardi. CP-CiarJ
Elegy for Hassan Nasir. Faiz Ahmad Faiz. CP-KizeC, tr. by Carolyn Kizer
Elegy for Henry Street. Charles Tomlinson. CP-TomlC
Elegy for Integral Domains, The. Norman Dubie. CP-DubiN
Elegy for James Thurber. Thomas Merton. CP-MertT
Elegy for Jane. Theodore Roethke. CP-RoetT
Elegy for Jog. John Ciardi. CP-CiarJ
Elegy for Margaret. Stephen Spender. CP-SpenS
Elegy for Maria Alves. Joaquim Cardozo. CP-BishE
Elegy for Minor Poets. Louis MacNeice. CP-MacNL
Elegy for Moral Self-Assurance and Country Virtue, An. John Ciardi. CP-CiarJ
Elegy for My Brother. Norman Dubie. CP-DubiN
Elegy for N. N. Czeslaw Milosz. CP-MiloC; CP-MiloCN, tr. by Larence Davis and Lawrence Davis
Elegy for Neal Cassady. Allen Ginsberg. CP-GinsA; SP-GinsA
Elegy: For Robert Lowell. Joseph Brodsky. CP-BrodJ
Elegy for Robert Winner. Thomas Lux. SP-LuxT
Elegy for Sam. John Ciardi. CP-CiarJ
Elegy for the Face at Your Elbow. John Ciardi. CP-CiarJ
Elegy for the Giant Tortoises. Margaret Atwood. SP-AtwM1
Elegy for the Living. Adam Zagajewski. SP-ZagaA, tr. by Renata Gorczynski, Benjamin Ivry and C. K. Williams
Elegy for the Monastery Barn. Thomas Merton. CP-MertT
Elegy for the Poet Morgan Blum, An. James Wright. CP-WrigJ

Elegy for the Rev. Mr. James B. Hodgson (1892–1963). John Logan. CP-LogaJ
Elegy for the Silent Voices and the Joiners of Everything. Kenneth Patchen. CP-PatcK
Elegy: "For thee I drop the tender tear." Annis Boudinot Stockton. CP-StocA
Elegy for Thelonious. Yusef Komunyakaa. CP-KomuY
Elegy for Wesley Wells. Donald Hall. CP-HallD
Elegy for Wright & Hugo. Norman Dubie. CP-DubiN
Elegy for Y. Z. Czeslaw Milosz. CP-MiloC; CP-MiloCN, tr. by Robert Hass
Elegy: For You, Father. John Ciardi. CP-CiarJ
Elegy: "Grown son's tears in a restaurant mix their salt, A." A. K. Ramanujan. CP-RamaA
Elegy: "Her face like a rain-beaten stone on the day she rolled off." Theodore Roethke. CP-RoetT
Elegy: "Here are consoling pieties." Gregory Orr. SP-OrrG
Elegy: "Hundreds of flies." Ai. SP-Ai
Elegy: "I can almost see it." Thom Gunn. CP-GunnT
Elegy: "I know but will not tell." Alan Dugan. CP-DugaA
Elegy: "I lay down in my grave." Maya Angelou. SP-AngeM
Elegy Imitated from One of Akenside's Blank-Verse Inscriptions. Samuel Taylor Coleridge. CP-ColeS
Elegy in a Country Churchyard. G. K. Chesterton. CP-ChesG
Elegy in a Firelit Room. James Wright. CP-WrigJ
Elegy in a Spider's Web. Laura Riding Jackson. CP-RidiL
Elegy in April and September. Wilfred Owen. CP-OwenW
Elegy in the Classroom. Anne Sexton. CP-SextA
Elegy in the Extreme Illness of a Friend Whose Disorder Was the Bursting of a Blood Vesel in His Breast, An. Annis Boudinot Stockton. CP-StocA
Elegy: "In the May breeze." M. Safdar Mir. CP-KizeC, tr. by Carolyn Kizer
Elegy Inscribed to Richard J Stockton Esqr [Feb. 28, 1787]. Annis Boudinot Stockton. CP-StocA
Elegy: "It is almost dawn." Sam Hamill. SP-HamiS
Elegy: "It was a gray landscape, houses small." Adam Zagajewski. SP-ZagaA, tr. by Clare Cavanagh
Elegy Just in Case. John Ciardi. CP-CiarJ
Elegy: "Like a censer filled with desire." Federico García Lorca. CP-GarcF, tr. by Catherine Brown
Elegy: "My father was born with a spade in his hand and traded it." John Ciardi. CP-CiarJ
Elegy: "No more the white refulgent streets." Allen Tate. CP-TateA
Elegy? No muse, it asks a strain, An. Proludium. Ben Jonson. CP-JonsB
Elegy: "Not only doesn't the Ohio." Gregory Orr. SP-OrrG
Elegy: "Note / as it gets darker." Charles Simic. SP-SimiC; SP-SimiCE
Elegy 3, Cavalcante. John Ciardi. CP-CiarJ
Elegy of Last Resort. Howard Nemerov. CP-NemeH
Elegy of the Flowers. Constantine P. Cavafy. CP-CavaC, tr. by Theoharis Constantine Theoharis
Elegy: "Oh destiny of Borges." Jorge Luis Borges. SP-BorgJ, tr. by Alastair Reid
Elegy on an Abandoned Village. Yehuda Amichai. SP-AmicY, tr. by Stephen Mitchell
Elegy on Captain Matthew Henderson [or Capt. M——— H———] [A Gentleman Who Held the Patent for His Honours Immediately from Almighty God!]. Robert Burns. CP-BurnR
Elegy on Dicky and Dolly, An. Jonathan Swift. CP-SwifJ
Elegy on Leaving, An. Phillis Wheatley. CP-WheaP
Elegy on Mister William Cruikshank A. M. Robert Burns. CP-BurnR
Elegy on Mistress Boulstred. John Donne. CP-DonnJ; MW-DonnJ
Elegy on Newstead Abbey. Lord Byron. CP-Byron
Elegy on Peg Nicholson. Robert Burns. CP-BurnR
Elegy on Prince Henry. John Donne. See Elegy upon the Untimely Death of the Incomparable Prince Henry
Elegy on the Death of a Young Lady, An. Annis Boudinot Stockton. CP-StocA
Elegy on the Death of Kenneth Patchen, An. Lawrence Ferlinghetti. SP-FerlL
Elegy on the Death of Miss Chandler, as if Written in Her Fathers Church Yard. Annis Boudinot Stockton. CP-StocA
Elegy on the Death of Mrs Dickinson. The Event Was Communicated at the Sea Shore. Annis Boudinot Stockton. CP-StocA
Elegy on the Death of Mrs Wilson, April the 19, 1786, An. Annis Boudinot Stockton. CP-StocA
Elegy on the Death of Robert Ruisseaux. Robert Burns. CP-BurnR
Elegy on the Deplorable Death of Mr. Thomas Sheridan, Author of Alexander's Overthrow, or, The Downfall of Babylon, Who Departed This Mortal Life on Thursday the 8th of March, 1721/22, An. Unknown. CP-SherT
Elegy on the Destruction of the Trees by the Isicles Sunday and Monday of Feb, the 17th and 18th, 1788. Annis Boudinot Stockton. CP-StocA
Elegy on the L. C. John Donne. CP-DonnJ; MW-DonnJ
Elegy on the La: Pen: Sent to My Mistress Out of France, An. Thomas Carew. CP-CareT
Elegy [or Elegie] on the Lady Jane Pawlet [or Paulet], [Marchioness of Winton],

An. Ben Jonson. CP-JonsB

Elegy on the Lady Markham. John Donne. CP-DonnJ; MW-DonnJ

Elegy on the Lost Child. Yehuda Amichai. SP-AmicYL, *tr.* by Benjamin Harshav *and* Barbara Harshav

Elegy on the Lost Child, The. Yehuda Amichai. SP-AmicY, *tr.* by Stephen Mitchell

Elegy on the Much Lamented Death of Mr. Demar, the Famous Rich Usurer [*or* Man], An. Patrick Delany. CP-SherT; CP-SwifJ

Elegy On the Supposed Death of Mr. Partridge, the Almanac Maker. Jonathan Swift. CP-SwifJ

Elegy on the Year 1788. Robert Burns. CP-BurnR

Elegy: "Our hammock swung between Americas." Derek Walcott. CP-WalcD

Elegy: "Responsible sound of the lawnmower, The." William Stafford. SP-StafWW

Elegy, Sacred to the Memory of that Great Divine, the Reverend and Learned Dr. Samuel Cooper, An. Phillis Wheatley. CP-WheaP

Elegy Sacred to the Memory of the Rev'd Samuel Cooper, D.D., An. Phillis Wheatley. CP-WheaP

Elegy: "Should every creature be as I have been." Theodore Roethke. CP-RoetT

Elegy: "Since louely sweete, much like unto a Dewe." Robert Herrick. CP-HerrR

Elegy: "Some gone like boys to school wearing their badges." John Ciardi. CP-CiarJ

Elegy: "Somebody left the world last night, I felt it." Olga Broumas. SP-BrouO

Elegy: "Sun immense and rosy, The." D. H. Lawrence. CP-LawrD

Elegy: "Sweetheart, losing your looks, go to live in a village." Joseph Brodsky. CP-BrodJ

Elegy: "This is the body of my good gray practical dead." John Ciardi. CP-CiarJ

Elegy: "Three very ancient faces stay with me." Jorge Luis Borges. SP-BorgJ, *tr.* by Alastair Reid

Elegy [*or* Elegie], An: "'Tis true, I'm broke! Vows, oaths, and all I had." Ben Jonson. CP-JonsB

Elegy to Dispel Gloom, An. Lawrence Ferlinghetti. SP-FerlL

Elegy, To Miss. Mary Moorhead, on the Death of Her Father, The Rev. Mr. John Moorhead, An. Phillis Wheatley. CP-WheaP

Elegy: To Silence. Federico García Lorca. CP-GarcF, *tr.* by Catherine Brown

Elegy to the Memory of an Unfortunate Lady. Alexander Pope. CP-PopeA

Elegy to the Pulley of Superior Oblique. Norman Dubie. CP-DubiN

Elegy to the Sioux. Norman Dubie. CP-DubiN

Elegy: "Too proud to die; broken and blind he died." Dylan Thomas. CP-ThomD

Elegy Upon that Honorable and Reknowned Knight Sir Philip Sydney, An. Anne Bradstreet. CP-BradA

Elegy upon the Death of Doctor [*or* Dr.] Donne, Dean of Paul's, An. Thomas Carew. *See* Elegy upon the Death of the Dean of [St.] Paul's, Dr. John Donne, An

Elegy upon the Death of Mistress Boulstred, An. John Donne. CP-DonnJ; MW-DonnJ

Elegy upon the Death of Mr. Stanninow Fellow of Queenes Colledge. Richard Crashaw. CP-CrasR

Elegy upon the Death of My Lord Francis Villiers, An. Andrew Marvell. CP-MarvA

Elegy upon the Death of the Dean of [St.] Paul's, Dr. John Donne, An. Thomas Carew. CP-CareT

(Elegy upon the Death of Doctor [*or* Dr.] Donne, Dean of Paul's, An.) CP-CareT

Elegy upon the Untimely Death of the Incomparable Prince Henry. John Donne. CP-DonnJ

(Elegy on Prince Henry.) MW-DonnJ

Elegy: "Whether you fished me bravely out of the Pacific." Joseph Brodsky. CP-BrodJ

Elegy: "Who would I show it to." W. S. Merwin. SP-MerwW

Elegy: "Wind won't come to draw smiles in the sand of dreams, The." Yehuda Amichai. SP-AmicY, *tr.* by Stephen Mitchell

Elegy Written in a Country Churchyard. Thomas Gray. CP-GrayT

Elegy Written in the Same Place upon the Same Occasion. William Wordsworth. CP-WorW1; MW-WorW

Elektra on Third Avenue. Marilyn Hacker. SP-HackM

Element in which they live, The. Skeleton, The. Robert Creeley. CP-CreeR

Element Mother, The. Lorine Niedecker.

Graves, The. CP-NiedL

Kepler. CP-NiedL

She's Dead.

(Mother Is Dead.) CP-NiedL

Element of air was out of hand, The. Interlude. Theodore Roethke. CP-RoetT

Element of Elegy, The. Emily Dickinson. SP-DickE

Element of mischief contributed, An. Summer Breezes. Frank O'Hara. SP-OharF

Elemental. D. H. Lawrence. CP-LawrD

Elemental. Charles Tomlinson. CP-TomlC

Elemental Trust. Robert Stock. SP-StocR

Elementals, The. Kathleen Jessie Raine. SP-RainK

Elementary Attitudes. Mona Van Duyn. SP-VanDM

Elementary Cosmogony. Charles Simic. SP-SimiC; SP-SimiCE

Elementary Scene, The. Randall Jarrell. CP-JarrR

Elementary School Classroom in a Slum, An. Stephen Spender. CP-SpenS

Elements. Robert Creeley. SP-CreeR

Elements have merged into solicitude, The. Racer's Widow, The. Louise Glück. SP-GlucL

Elements of clothes, an arm and hand the head of a cock. Charles Olson. CP-OlsoC

Elements of Composition. A. K. Ramanujan. CP-RamaA

Elements on my table. Ghost May Come, A. Allen Ginsberg. CP-GinsA

Elements respect their Maker's seal!, The. Fragment from the Wandering Jew. Percy Bysshe Shelley. CP-ShelP

Elements, The. D. H. Lawrence. CP-LawrD

Elephant. D. H. Lawrence. CP-LawrD

Elephant, The. Rudyard Kipling. CP-KiplR *Fr.* Jungle Book, The.

Elephant, The. Primo Levi. CP-LeviP, *tr.* by Ruth Feldman

Elephant, The. Jonathan Swift. CP-SwifJ

Elephant, a crusty old general, scarred, The. Bestiary. Dan Pagis. SP-PagiD, *tr.* by Stephen Mitchell

Elephant / comes past the Visitor two feet away, The. Short Views in Africa. Josephine Jacobsen. CP-JacoJ

Elephant in the Dark. Jelaluddin Rumi. SP-Rumi, *tr.* by Coleman Barks

Elephant Is Slow to Mate, The. D. H. Lawrence. CP-LawrD

Elephant made of cotton, An. Grand Palace of Versailles, The. Kenneth Patchen. CP-PatcK

Elephant, say, scraping its dry sides. West. George Oppen. CP-OppGN

Elephant, the huge old beast, The. Elephant Is Slow to Mate, The. D. H. Lawrence. CP-LawrD

Elephant Trunk. Louis MacNeice. CP-MacNL

Elephants. Marianne Craig Moore. CP-MoorM

Elephants Are Different to Different People. Carl Sandburg. CP-SandC

Elephant's Child, The. Rudyard Kipling. *Fr.* Just-So Stories.

Elephants in the Circus. D. H. Lawrence. CP-LawrD

Elephants Plodding. D. H. Lawrence. CP-LawrD

Eleusis. Eleanor Wilner. SP-WilnE

Eleutheria. Carolyn Kizer. CP-KizeC

Eleutheria. James Wright. CP-WrigJ

Elevator Boy. Langston Hughes. CP-HughL; CP-HughL1

Elevator, moving through the stories of the dream. Dream Movement. Rainer Maria Rilke. CP-RilkFr, *tr.* by A. Poulin, Jr.

Eleven. Archibald MacLeish. CP-MacLA

Eleven Addresses to the Lord. John Berryman. CP-BerrJ

11 February 1946. Primo Levi. CP-LeviP, *tr.* by Ruth Feldman *and* Brian Swann

Eleven horsemen gather at the hollow bridge. In the Pass. W. S. Merwin. SP-MerwWF

11:02 A.M. The Bird Disappeared. John Ciardi. CP-CiarJ

Eleven Occasional Poems. W. H. Auden. CP-AudeW

Eleven palm trees stand up between me. Sunbathing on a Rooftop in Berkeley. Maxine W. Kumin. SP-KumiM

Eleven rogues and he to judge a fool. Mr. High-Mind. John Updike. CP-UpdiJ

Eleven stars and clusters on a flying gun. Letter from a Rubber Raft. John Ciardi. CP-CiarJ

Eleven-thirty and hot. Cyclist, The. Marge Piercy. SP-PierM

Elevens. Marilyn Hacker. SP-HackM

11th: and Last Booke of the Ocean to Scinthia, The. Sir Walter Ralegh. CP-RaleW *Fr.* Ocean's Love to Cynthia, The.

Eleventh Avenue Racket. Carl Sandburg. CP-SandC

Eleventh Hour, The. Christina Georgina Rossetti. CP-RosC3

Eleventh of progressional, The. Lorine Niedecker. CP-NiedL

Elf-locked, elf-eyed, exquisite Barbara. Barbara. G. K. Chesterton. CP-ChesG

Elgin Marbles, The. Amy Clampitt. CP-ClamA

Elias—Variations on a Theme. Thomas Merton. CP-MertT

Elijah's Wagon knew no thill. Emily Dickinson. CP-DickE

Elise, I have your valentine with the red shoes. I have. Grandfather's Last Letter, A. Norman Dubie. CP-DubiN

Elixir. D. H. Lawrence. CP-LawrD

Elixir [*or* Elixer], The. George Herbert. CP-HerbG

Eliza, what fools are the Mussulman sect. To Eliza. Lord Byron. CP-Byron

Elizabeth. Robert Lowell. SP-LoweR

Elizabeth. Paul Muldoon. CP-MuldP

Elizabeth. James Whitcomb Riley. CP-RileJ

Elizabeth! Elizabeth! / The first May-morning whispereth. Elizabeth. James Whitcomb Riley. CP-RileJ

Elizabeth Gone. Anne Sexton. CP-SextA; SP-SextA

Elizabeth Hoar. Ralph Waldo Emerson. CP-EmerR

Elizabeth Swados. Yehuda Amichai. SP-AmicYL, *tr. by* Benjamin Harshav *and* Barbara Harshav

Elizabeth told Essex. Emily Dickinson. CP-DickE

Elizabethans Called It Dying, The. James Schuyler. CP-SchuJ

Elizabeth's War with the Christmas Bear. Norman Dubie. CP-DubiN

Elk Camp. Raymond Carver. CP-CarvR

Elk discards his antlers every spring, The. On Being Asked to Write a Poem in Memory of Anne Sexton. Maxine W. Kumin. SP-KumiM

Elk Trails. Gary Snyder. CP-SnydG

Ella Mason and Her Eleven Cats. Sylvia Plath. CP-PlatS

Ellen. George Crabbe. SP-CrabG *Fr.* Tales of the Hall.

Ellen Irwin; or, The Braes of Kirtle. William Wordsworth. CP-WorW1

Ellen Middleton. Christina Georgina Rossetti. CP-RosC3

Ellen's Song. Sir Walter Scott. SP-ScotW *Fr.* Lady of the Lake, The.

Elles viennent. Samuel Beckett. CP-BeckS

Elliott. John Greenleaf Whittier. CP-WhitJ

Elm. Sylvia Plath. CP-PlatS

Elm. John Updike. CP-UpdiJ

Elm Buds. Carl Sandburg. CP-SandC

Elm buds are out. Elm Buds. Carl Sandburg. CP-SandC

Elm Seed, The. Jones Very. CP-VeryJ

Elm tree is our highest mountain peak, The. In Praise of Prairie. Theodore Roethke. CP-RoetT

Elmer Brown. James Whitcomb Riley. CP-RileJ

Elms. Louise Glück. SP-GlucL

Elms. C. K. Williams. SP-WillC

Elms' silhouettes, The. Late January. John Updike. CP-UpdiJ

Elocution, logic, political science. Antigone Riddle, The. Derek Mahon. CP-MahoD

Eloi, Eloi, Lama Sabachthani? D. H. Lawrence. CP-LawrD

Eloisa to Abelard. Alexander Pope. CP-PopeA

Elopement, The. Thomas Hardy. CP-HardT

Elopement, The. Gerard Manley Hopkins. CP-HopkG

Else a great Prince in prison lies. Denise Levertov. SP-LeveDP

Else has blown away on the east wind, Richard went away with the wind from the west. Three Children, The. Josephine Jacobsen. CP-JacoJ

Elsewhere. Robert Graves. CP-GravR

Elsie Flimmerwon, you got a job now with a jazz outfit in vaudeville. Vaudeville Dancer. Carl Sandburg. CP-SandC

Elsie Mingus *lisps*, she does! Lisper, The. James Whitcomb Riley. CP-RileJ

Elsie's mirror only shows. Wallace Stevens. CP-StevWP

Elsinore in the Late Ancient Autumn. Norman Dubie. CP-DubiN

Elusive. Denise Levertov. SP-LeveDS

Elusive / This godfather who mostly forgets one's birthday. Godfather. Louis MacNeice. CP-MacNL

Elusive Time. James Laughlin. CP-LaugJ

Elves, The. Denise Levertov. SP-LeveDP

Elves are no smaller. Elves, The. Denise Levertov. SP-LeveDP

Elvira, by love's grace. Homage. William Carlos Williams. CP-WilW1

Elvis Presley. Thom Gunn. CP-GunnT

Ely Place. Thomas Kinsella. CP-KinsT

Elysium. D. H. Lawrence. CP-LawrD

Elysium is as far as to. Suspense. Emily Dickinson. CP-DickE

Emancipation. Paul Laurence Dunbar. CP-DunbP

Emancipation: 1865. Long View: Negro. Langston Hughes. CP-HughL; CP-HughL3

Emancipation Group, The. John Greenleaf Whittier. CP-WhitJ

Emancipation of Mr. Poplin, or, Skoal to the Skimmerless. Ogden Nash. CP-NashO

Emancipators, The. Randall Jarrell. CP-JarrR

Emanuel Swedenborg. Jorge Luis Borges. SP-BorgJ, *tr. by* Willis Barnstone

Emasculation. D. H. Lawrence. CP-LawrD

Embankment at Night, before the War: Charity. D. H. Lawrence. CP-LawrD

Embankment at Night, before the War: Outcasts. D. H. Lawrence. CP-LawrD

Embarcation. Thomas Hardy. CP-HardT

Embarking on the Study of Anglo-Saxon Grammer. Jorge Luis Borges. SP-BorgJ, *tr. by* Alastair Reid

Embarrassment of one another. Emily Dickinson. CP-DickE

Embassy. Charles Tomlinson. CP-TomlC

Embertide. Christina Georgina Rossetti. CP-RosC2

Emblem. Olga Broumas. SP-BrouO

Emblem. Richard Eberhart. CP-EberR

Emblem (1). Denise Levertov. SP-LeveDL

Emblem (2). Denise Levertov. SP-LeveDL

Emblem of blasted hope and lost desire. Sonnet: "Emblem of blasted hope and lost desire." Paul Laurence Dunbar. CP-DunbP

Emblems. Allen Tate. CP-TateA

Emblems of Conduct. Hart Crane. CP-CranH

Emblems of Exile. Thomas McGrath. SP-McGrT

Embowering rose, the acacia, and the pine, The. *see also* Written at the Request of Sir George Beaumont, BART., and in His Name, for an Urn, Placed by Him at the Termination of a Newly-Planted Avenue, in the Same Grounds *and* Inscription in a Garden of the Same. William Wordsworth. CP-WorW1

Embrace, The. Louise Glück. SP-GlucL

Embracing in the road. Hawk's Shadow. Louise Glück. SP-GlucL

Embroidered in a tapestry of green. Design in Living Colors. Adrienne Rich. CP-RicAE

Emerald is as green as grass, An. Flint. Christina Georgina Rossetti. CP-RosC2

Emergency Haying. Hayden Carruth. CP-CarHS

Emerges daintily, the skunk. Wood Weasel, The. Marianne Craig Moore. CP-MoorM

Emerging from aeons of ocean on to the shore. Vistas. Louis MacNeice. CP-MacNL

Emeritus Addresses the School, An. John Ciardi. CP-CiarJ

Emerson. Jorge Luis Borges. SP-BorgJ, *tr. by* Alastair Reid

Emerson. James Whitcomb Riley. CP-RileJ

Emerson thought the bride had one eye. New England, Springtime. Norman Dubie. CP-DubiN

Emerson's Concord. Richard Eberhart. CP-EberR

Emerson's intimacy with his "Bee" Emily Dickinson. SP-DickE

Emigrant Mother, The. William Wordsworth. CP-WorW1

Emigrant, to the Receding Shore. Donald Davie. CP-DaviDC

Emigration. Eleanor Wilner. SP-WilnE

Émigré. W. S. Merwin. SP-MerwWF

Émigrée from the Bronx, a married child. Nights of 1962: The River Merchant's Wife. Marilyn Hacker. SP-HackM

Émigrés, The. Marya Alexandrovna Zaturenska. SP-ZatuM

Emily and Kate. Cage, The. Richard Eberhart. CP-EberR

Emily Brontë. Ted Hughes. SP-HughTN

Emily Dickenson: / You gave us the bumblebee who has a soul. Letters to Dead Imagists. Carl Sandburg. CP-SandC

Emily Dickinson. Richard Eberhart. CP-EberR

Emily Hardcastle, Spinster. John Crowe Ransom. SP-RansJ

Emily, this Place, and You. William Stafford. SP-StafWW

Emily Writes Such a Good Letter. Stevie Smith. CP-SmitS

Emily, you were sick. North & South. Donald Davie. CP-DaviDC

Emily's Mom. Thomas Lux. SP-LuxT

Emissary, The. Denise Levertov. SP-LeveDL

Emlyn reads in Dickens' clothes. Clan, The. John Updike. CP-UpdiJ

Emma. Jane Austen.
  Charade: "My first displays the wealth and pomp of kings." CP-AustJ

(E)Motion. Yusef Komunyakaa. CP-KomuY

Emotion is to be found in the clouds, The. Student of Clouds. Billy Collins. SP-CollB

Emotional Friend, The. D. H. Lawrence. CP-LawrD

Emotional Lies. D. H. Lawrence. CP-LawrD

Emp Lace. Gertrude Stein. CP-SteiG

Empathy and New Year. James Schuyler. CP-SchuJ

Empedocles. George Meredith. CP-MerG1

Empedocles on Etna. Matthew Arnold. SP-ArnoM

Emperor, Emperor! Napoleon III in Italy. Elizabeth Barrett Browning. CP-BroEB

Emperor Frederick of Our Time, The. George Meredith. CP-MerG1

Emperor Haile Selassie. Langston Hughes. CP-HughL; CP-HughL3

Emperor Manuel Komninos, The. Manuel Komninos. Constantine P. Cavafy. CP-CavaC, *tr. by* Theoharis Constantine Theoharis

Emperor of Ice-Cream, The. Wallace Stevens. CP-StevW; CP-StevWP

Emperor / sleeps in a palace of porphyry, The. E. E. Cummings. CP-CummE

Emperor Tacitus is ill, The. Death of the Emperor Tacitus, The. Constantine P. Cavafy. CP-CavaC, *tr. by* Theoharis Constantine Theoharis

Emperor Wu of the Han they say. Han-shan. P'o-ch'ang. CP-ColdM, *tr. by* Red Pine

Emperors and Kings, How Oft Have Temples Rung. William Wordsworth. CP-WorW2

Emperor's Cook, The. Josephine Jacobsen. CP-JacoJ

Emperors' heads around the Sheldonian, The. Oxford, Thirty Years After. John Updike. CP-UpdiJ

Empire. Robert Penn Warren. CP-WarrR

Empire Builders. Archibald MacLeish. CP-MacLA

Empire of Coins, An. Charles Bukowski. SP-BukC2

Empire of Dreams. Charles Simic. SP-SimiC; SP-SimiCE

Empire of Persia, The. Kenneth Patchen. CP-PatcK

Empires. Robert Herrick. CP-HerrR

Empires of Kings, are now, and ever were. Empires. Robert Herrick. CP-HerrR

Empirical Scene. Alan Dugan. CP-DuganA

Emplacement. A. R. Ammons. CP-AmmoA

Employee, The. Hans Magnus Enzensberger. SP-EnzeH, *tr. by* Michael Hamburger

Employment: "He that is weary, let him sit." George Herbert. CP-HerbG (Employment (2).) CP-HerbG

Employment (1). George Herbert. CP-HerbG

Employment (2). George Herbert. *See* Employment: "He that is weary, let him sit"

Empress Marie Louise, The. Marya Alexandrovna Zaturenska. SP-ZatuM

'Empress of China'! I nor rule nor reign. Voice from Pekin, A. Ambrose Bierce. SP-BierA

Emptied.hills.listen. E. E. Cummings. CP-CummE

Emptiness. Jelaluddin Rumi. SP-Rumi, *tr. by* Coleman Barks

Emptiness—you know. Hayden Carruth. CP-CarHS *Fr.* Clay Hill Anthology, The.

Empty battlefields keep their phantoms. New Feet. Carl Sandburg. CP-SandC

Empty Boat, The. Chuang Tzu. CP-MertT

Empty Boats, The. Nicholas Vachel Lindsay. CP-LindV

Empty can on a rock, An. Summer Evening in the Jerusalem Mountains. Yehuda Amichai. SP-AmicYL, *tr. by* Benjamin Harshav *and* Barbara Harshav

Empty Drawing Room. Jorge Luis Borges. SP-BorgJ, *tr. by* W. S. Merwin

Empty faces of / and tomorrow's alternate idea. False Portrait of Hanna H. Michael Palmer. SP-PalmM

Empty Garlic, An. Jelaluddin Rumi. SP-Rumi, *tr. by* Coleman Barks

Empty glove—long withering in the grasp, An. James Whitcomb Riley. CP-RileJ

Empty House. Langston Hughes. CP-HughL; CP-HughL1

Empty House. Stephen Spender. CP-SpenS

Empty house on a horizon. Heap of Broken Images, A. Lawrence Ferlinghetti. SP-FerlL

Empty House, The. Walter De la Mare. CP-DeLaW

Empty, I echo to the least footfall. Barren Woman. Sylvia Plath. CP-PlatS

Empty Mirror. Kenneth Rexroth. CP-RexrK

Empty my Heart, of Thee. Emily Dickinson. CP-DickE

Empty Nest, An. James Whitcomb Riley. CP-RileJ

Empty Pitchforks. Thomas Lux. SP-LuxT

Empty Place, An. Robert Bly. SP-BlyR

Empty Purse: A Sermon to our Later Prodigal Son, The. George Meredith. CP-MerG1

Empty Purse, The. George Meredith. CP-MerG1

Empty Room, The. James Laughlin. CP-LaugJ

Empty soda can on a rock, An. Summer Evening in the Jerusalem Mountains. Yehuda Amichai. SP-AmicY, *tr. by* Chana Bloch

Empty Song, The. James Whitcomb Riley. CP-RileJ

Empty Stirrups. Herman Melville. SP-MelvH *Fr.* Clarel: A Poem and Pilgrimage in the Holy Land.

Empty the last drop. Plunger. Carl Sandburg. CP-SandC

Empty Threat, An. Robert Frost. CP-FrosR

Empty Vessel. Hugh MacDiarmid. SP-MacDH

Empty White Blotch on Map of Universe: A Possible View. Robert Penn Warren. CP-WarrR

Empty Woman, The. Gwendolyn Brooks. SP-BrooG

Empty Words. Arthur Sze. SP-SzeA

En Amérique, professeur; / En Angleterre, journaliste. Mélange Adultère de Tout. T. S. Eliot. CP-ElioT

En-Dor. Rudyard Kipling. CP-KiplR

En face. Samuel Beckett. CP-BeckS

En ma Provence le blé est toujours vert. Ma Provence. Kenneth Koch. SP-KochK

En Masse. D. H. Lawrence. CP-LawrD

En Passant. Andrei Codrescu. SP-CodrA

En Promenade des Anglais. Clarence Major. SP-MajoC

En Route to Southampton. James Schuyler. CP-SchuJ

Enabling love, roof of this drafty hutch. Ghosts of the House, The. William Meredith. SP-MereW

Enacting someone's notion of themselves. Aunt Jemima of the Ocean Waves. Robert Earl Hayden. CP-HaydR

Enamour'd, artless, young, on foreign ground. John Milton. *See* Young, gentle, and candid lover that I am

Enamoured by / Brevity in method. Epitaph: "Enamoured by / Brevity in method." Charles Tomlinson. CP-TomlC

Encampment at Morning, An. W. S. Merwin. SP-MerwWF

Encased in talent like a uniform. Novelist, The. W. H. Auden. CP-AudeW

Enchanted Goblet, The. Sir Walter Scott. SP-ScotW *Fr.* Bridal of Trierman, The.

Encinctured with a twine of leaves. Fruit Plucker, The. Samuel Taylor Coleridge. CP-ColeS

Encircled by her arms as by a shell. Narcissus. Rainer Maria Rilke. CP-RilkFr, *tr. by* A. Poulin, Jr.

Enclave where new mythologies. Zeus over Redeye. Robert Earl Hayden. CP-HaydR

Enclos'd My Dears the promised glass. To a Little Miss, with a Toy Lookingglass. Annis Boudinot Stockton. CP-StocA

Enclosed and hidden in a monstrous stone. Michelangelo Buonarroti. CP-Miche, *tr. by* John Frederick Nims

Enclosed in this disturbing mutual wood. Prisoners, The. Adrienne Rich. CP-RicAE; SP-RicA2

Enclosure, The. James Dickey. CP-DickJ

Encore le dernier reflux. Dieppe. Samuel Beckett. CP-BeckS

Encounter. John Ciardi. CP-CiarJ

Encounter. Langston Hughes. CP-HughL; CP-HughL3

Encounter. Thomas McGrath. SP-McGrT

Encounter. W. S. Merwin. SP-MerwW

Encounter. Czeslaw Milosz. CP-MiloC; CP-MiloCN, *tr. by* Lillian Vallee

Encounter. Eugenio Montale. CP-MontE, *tr. by* Jonathan Galassi

Encounter. Mary Oliver. SP-OlivM

Encounter. Yannis Ritsos. SP-RitsY, *tr. by* Kimon Friar

Encounter. Charles Tomlinson. CP-TomlC

Encounter, An. W. H. Auden. CP-AudeW

Encounter, An. Robert Frost. CP-FrosR

Encounter, The. Robert Graves. CP-GravR

Encounter, The. Walter De la Mare. CP-DeLaW

Encounter, The. Charles Olson. CP-OlsoC

Encounter, The. Ezra Pound. SP-PounE

Encounter at Nightfall. Kenneth Patchen. CP-PatcK

Encounter at the Casino, Aix-les-Bains. James Laughlin. CP-LaugJ

Encounter in August. Maxine W. Kumin. SP-KumiM

Encounter in the Cage Country. James Dickey. CP-DickJ

Encounter ("María del Reposo, / again I encounter"). Federico García Lorca. CP-GarcF, *tr. by* Jerome Rothenberg *Fr.* Garden in Umber; or The Garden of the Brownhaired Girls.

Encounter ("Sun flower. / River flower"). Federico García Lorca. CP-GarcF, *tr. by* Jerome Rothenberg *Fr.* In the Garden of the Lunar Grapefruits.

Encounters. Dan Pagis. SP-PagiD, *tr. by* Stephen Mitchell

Encounters. Yannis Ritsos. SP-RitsY, *tr. by* Kostas Myrsiades

Encouraged. Paul Laurence Dunbar. CP-DunbP

Encouragement. Paul Laurence Dunbar. CP-DunbP

Encouragement meant nothing. Pieces for Other Lives. W. S. Merwin. SP-MerwW

Encyclopædia, The. Nicholas Vachel Lindsay. CP-LindV

End. Federico García Lorca. CP-GarcF, *tr. by* Jerome Rothenberg *Fr.* Shadow.

End. Robert Creeley. SP-CreeR

End. Langston Hughes. CP-HughL; CP-HughL2

End, An. James Whitcomb Riley. CP-RileJ

End, An. Christina Georgina Rossetti. CP-RosC1

End, The. Charles Bukowski. SP-BukC2

End, The. Robert Creeley. CP-CreeR

End, The. Allen Ginsberg. CP-GinsA; SP-GinsA

End, The. Robert Herrick. CP-HerrR

End, The. Robert Herrick. CP-HerrR

End, The. D. H. Lawrence. CP-LawrD

End, The. Wilfred Owen. CP-OwenW

End, The. Charles Tomlinson. CP-TomlC

End and Beginning. Wisława Szymborska. CP-BrodJ, *tr. by* Joseph Brodsky

End and the Beginning, The. Wisława Szymborska. SP-SzymWM, *tr. by* Joanna Trzeciak

End and the Beginning, The. Wisława Szymborska. SP-SzymW, *tr. by* Stanislaw Barańczak *and* Clara Cavanagh, Stanislaw Baranczak *and* Clare Cavanagh

End Decreed, An. Robert Herrick. CP-HerrR

End Games. Andrei Codrescu. SP-CodrA

End has come, as come it must, The. At School-Close. John Greenleaf Whittier. CP-WhitJ

End in Spring, An. W. S. Merwin. SP-MerwW

End is a happy end only, An. Unread Pages. Laura Riding Jackson. CP-RidiL

End Is Not Yet, The. Christina Georgina Rossetti. CP-RosC2

End, Middle, Beginning. Anne Sexton. CP-SextA

End now the White-loafe, & the Pye. Upon Candlemasse Day. Robert Herrick. CP-HerrR

End of a Beautiful Era, The. Joseph Brodsky. CP-BrodJ, *tr. by* David Rigsbee

End of a Day, The. Yannis Ritsos. SP-RitsY, *tr. by* Kimon Friar

End of a Short Affair, The. Charles Bukowski. SP-BukC1

End of All, The. Walt Whitman. CP-WhitW

End of all things is at hand. We all, The. Sunday Before Advent. Christina Georgina Rossetti. CP-RosC2

End of all thou seest is near, The. World, The ("End of all thou seest is near, The"). Jones Very. CP-VeryJ

End of an Ethnic Dream, The. Jay Wright. SP-WrigJ

End of Another Home Holiday. D. H. Lawrence. CP-LawrD

End of Antony, The. Constantine P. Cavafy. CP-CavaC, *tr. by* Theoharis Constantine Theoharis

End of Camp Alamoosook. Robert Lowell. SP-LoweR

End of Childhood. Eugenio Montale. CP-MontE, *tr. by* Jonathan Galassi

End of Drought. C. K. Williams. SP-WillC

End of Elul. Yehuda Amichai. SP-AmicYL, *tr. by* Benjamin Harshav *and* Barbara Harshav

End of Fear, The. G. K. Chesterton. CP-ChesG

End of His Work, The. Robert Herrick. CP-HerrR

End of It All, The. James Laughlin. CP-LaugJ

End of March, The. Elizabeth Bishop. CP-BishE

End of May. Mona Van Duyn. SP-VanDM

End of Owls, The. Hans Magnus Enzensberger. SP-EnzeH, *tr. by* Michael Hamburger

End of page. End. Robert Creeley. SP-CreeR

End of Play. Robert Graves. CP-GravR

End of Season. Robert Penn Warren. CP-WarrR

End of Summer. Stanley Kunitz. CP-KunSC

End of Summer. W. S. Merwin. SP-MerwW

End of summer in the Judean mountains. The ground lies there. Yehuda Amichai. SP-AmicY, *tr. by* Chana Bloch

End of Summer School, The. Howard Nemerov. CP-NemeH

End of the affair is always death, The. Ballad of the Lonely Masturbator, The. Anne Sexton. CP-SextA; SP-SextA

End of the Archaeological Season in Eyn Gedi. Yehuda Amichai. SP-AmicYL, *tr. by* Benjamin Harshav *and* Barbara Harshav

End of the Boo[c]k[e]s, of the Ocean's Love to Cynthia [*or* Scinthia], and the Beginning[e] of the 12 [*or* 22] Boo[c]k, Entreating of Sorrow, The. Sir Walter Ralegh. CP-RaleW *Fr.* Ocean's Love to Cynthia, The.

End of the Chapter, The. Paul Laurence Dunbar. CP-DunbP

End of the Day, The. Charles Baudelaire. CP-BaudC, *tr. by* Walter Martin

End of the Day, The. Robert Creeley. CP-CreeR

End of the Episode, The. Thomas Hardy. CP-HardT

End of the Line, The. Thomas McGrath. SP-McGrT

End of the Line, The. James Tate. SP-TateJ

End of the Line, The. Eleanor Wilner. SP-WilnE

End of the Parade, The. William Carlos Williams. CP-WilW2

End of the Questionnaire. Dan Pagis. SP-PagiD, *tr. by* Stephen Mitchell

End of the Rainbow, The. Randall Jarrell. CP-JarrR

End of the Road from Nantucket, The. Sam Hamill. SP-HamiS

End of the Rope, The. William Carlos Williams. CP-WilW2

End of the world. End. Federico García Lorca. CP-GarcF, *tr. by* Jerome Rothenberg *Fr.* Shadow.

End of the World. Robinson Jeffers. CP-JefR3

End of the World / is the Turn-About, The. Charles Olson. CP-OlsoC

End of the World, The. Louise Glück. SP-GlucL

End of the World, The. Archibald MacLeish. CP-MacLA

End of the World, The. Thomas McGrath. SP-McGrT

End of the year fell chilly, The. New Year's Eve. A. E. Housman. CP-HousA

End of the Year 1912. Thomas Hardy. CP-HardT

End of the year wears its face in the moon against the disguises one would otherwise put upon it. New Year's. Robert Creeley. CP-CreeR

End of Time, The. Christina Georgina Rossetti. CP-RosC3

End of Winter, The. Dan Pagis. SP-PagiD, *tr. by* Stephen Mitchell

End, The Beginning, The. D. H. Lawrence. CP-LawrD

End was more of a melting, The. Death of Will, The. Charles Tomlinson. CP-TomlC

Endanger it, and the Demand. Emily Dickinson. CP-DickE

Endecott. Jones Very. CP-VeryJ

Ended Day, An. Walt Whitman. CP-WhitW

Ended, ere it begun. Emily Dickinson. CP-DickE

Endegeeste. Howard Nemerov. CP-NemeH

Ending. Alice Walker. CP-WalkA

Ending, An. Howard Nemerov. CP-NemeH

Endings. Derek Walcott. CP-WalcD

Endive. Thomas Lux. SP-LuxT

Endless. Muriel Rukeyser. CP-RukeM

Endless and flooded, An. Sunday, 4 A.M. Elizabeth Bishop. CP-BishE

Endless Anxiety. D. H. Lawrence. CP-LawrD

Endless Life. Lawrence Ferlinghetti. SP-FerlL

Endless line of splendor, An. Foreign Missions in Battle Array. Nicholas Vachel Lindsay. CP-LindV

Endless line of tubs, all in an endless row, An. Age of Reason, The. G. K. Chesterton. CP-ChesG

"Endless" meaning soul. Counter. Rae Armantrout. SP-ArmaA

Endless Mirrors, The. James Laughlin. CP-LaugJ

Endless part of disintegration, The. Wisdom of Insecurity, The. Richard Eberhart. CP-EberR

Endless Pavement. Robert Graves. CP-GravR

Endless rain is just beginning, An. Into the Ark. Wisława Szymborska. SP-SzymW, *tr. by* Stanisław Barańczak *and* Clare Cavanagh

Endless the splendid life of the world. Endless Life. Lawrence Ferlinghetti. SP-FerlL

Endlessly to no end wending. Between Me and the Rock. Stanley Kunitz. CP-KunSC

Endor. Howard Nemerov. CP-NemeH

Endorsement to the Deed of Separation, in the April of 1816. Lord Byron. CP-Byron

Endow the Living—with the Tears. Emily Dickinson. CP-DickE

Ends. Robert Frost. CP-FrosR

Ends for Which a Nation Exists, The. Jones Very. CP-VeryJ

Endure friend-parting yet, old soldier. To a Friend Parting. Robert Penn Warren. CP-WarrR

Endure Hardness. Christina Georgina Rossetti. CP-RosC2

Enduring Love. Denise Levertov. SP-LeveDS

Enduring, The. James Whitcomb Riley. CP-RileJ

Endymion. Thomas Kinsella. CP-KinsT

Endymion. Oscar Wilde. CP-WildO

Endymion: A Poetic Romance. John Keats. CP-KeatJ

Endymion, your star is steadfast now. To Endymion. Countee Cullen. CP-CullC

Enemies. The. Constantine P. Cavafy. CP-CavaC, *tr. by* Theoharis Constantine Theoharis

Enemies of a House. John Updike. CP-UpdiJ

Enemies of the Angels, The. John Berryman. CP-BerrJ

Enemy. Langston Hughes. CP-HughL; CP-HughL2

Enemy, The. Charles Baudelaire. CP-BaudC, *tr. by* Walter Martin

Enemy, The. Thomas McGrath. SP-McGrT

Enemy, The. Alice Walker. CP-WalkA

Enemy coming on roads, The. Cabbage Gardens. Susan Howe. SP-HoweSE

Enemy Number One. Carl Sandburg. CP-SandC

Enemy [*or* en'my] of life, decayer of all kind, The [*or* Th']. Sir Thomas Wyatt. CP-WyatT

Enemy of the Herds, the Lion, The. Josephine Jacobsen. CP-JacoJ

Enemy the Wind, The. Thomas Lux. SP-LuxT

Enemy's Portrait, The. Thomas Hardy. CP-HardT

Energetic and long. Days of Argument and Blossom. Olga Broumas. SP-BrouO

Energetic Women. D. H. Lawrence. CP-LawrD

Energies. Donald Davie. CP-DaviDC

Energies of this particu- / lar poet are directed about, The. Metropolitan Bard. James Laughlin. CP-LaugJ

Energy. Raymond Carver. CP-CarvR

Energy: A Villanelle. John Updike. CP-UpdiJ

Energy glows at the lips. Lorine Niedecker. CP-NiedL

Enfranchising cable, silvered by the sea. Granite and Steel. Marianne Craig Moore. CP-MoorM

Eng. Stevie Smith. CP-SmitS

Engagement. A. K. Ramanujan. CP-RamaA

Engagement, The. May Swenson. SP-SwenM

Engine, The. T. S. Eliot. SP-ElioT

Engine and transmission and the wheels, The. Great Society, Mark X, The. Howard Nemerov. CP-NemeH

Engine Drain, The. Stevie Smith. CP-SmitS

Engine hammered and hummed, The. Flat faces of American business men. Engine, The. T. S. Eliot. SP-ElioT

Engine is killing the track, the track is silver, The. Totem. Sylvia Plath. CP-PlatS

Engine Room, S.S. Sappa Creek, The. Gary Snyder. CP-SnydG

Engine screams and Murphy, isolate, The. Song: "Engine screams and Murphy, isolate, The." Thomas Kinsella. CP-KinsT

Engines. Ron Silliman. SP-ArmaA

Engines of burning took him there. Letters from Jerusalem. Amy Clampitt. CP-ClamA

England. Donald Davie. CP-DaviDC

England. Walter De la Mare. CP-DeLaW

England. Marianne Craig Moore. CP-MoorM

England before the Storm. George Meredith. CP-MerG1

England, confess your sins! toward the poor. Exultation, An. William Carlos Williams. CP-WilW2

England, for Ezra Pound. Donald Davie. CP-DaviDC

England in 1819. Percy Bysshe Shelley. CP-ShelP

(Sonnet: England in 1819.) CP-ShelP

England in 1929. D. H. Lawrence. CP-LawrD

England is a cosy little country. Open Door, The. Rudyard Kipling. CP-KiplR

England Is Our Enemy. Hugh MacDiarmid.

"It is possible that a change may come." SP-MacDH

"To distinctly English writers in England." SP-MacDH

England seems full of graves to me. Spirits Summoned West. D. H. Lawrence. CP-LawrD

England! the time is come when thou shouldst wean. Sonnet: "England! the time is come when thou shouldst wean." William Wordsworth. CP-WorW1; MW-WorW

England to Germany in 1914. Thomas Hardy. CP-HardT

England was always a country of men. England in 1929. D. H. Lawrence. CP-LawrD

England, you had better go. Voices against England in the Night. Stevie Smith. CP-SmitS

England's Answer. Rudyard Kipling. CP-KiplR

England's Difficulty. Seamus Heaney. CP-HeanSO

England's Double Knavery. Hugh MacDiarmid.

"Left-wing poetry represents a rise in the price of bread." SP-MacDH

England's lads are miniature men. Boy-Man. Karl Shapiro. SP-ShapK

England's on the anvil—hear the hammers ring. Anvil, The. Rudyard Kipling. CP-KiplR

English A. John Ciardi. CP-CiarJ

English, The. Langston Hughes. CP-HughL; CP-HughL1

English, The. Stevie Smith. CP-SmitS

English Accounts. William Meredith. SP-MereW

English Advance at Flodden, The. Sir Walter Scott. SP-ScotW *Fr.* Marmion.

English Are So Nice!, The. D. H. Lawrence. CP-LawrD

English Bards and Scotch Reviewers. Lord Byron. CP-Byron

English Cocker: Old and Blind. Robert Penn Warren. CP-WarrR

English Downs. Walter De la Mare. CP-DeLaW

English Encouragement of Art Cromeks Opinions Put Into Rhyme. William Blake. CP-BlakW

English Field in the Nuclear Age, An. Denise Levertov. SP-LeveDL

English Flag, The. Rudyard Kipling. CP-KiplR

English Garden in Austria, An. Randall Jarrell. CP-JarrR

English Graves, The. G. K. Chesterton. CP-ChesG

English heart, my commandant, An. To Colonel Charles. George Meredith. CP-MerG1

English Horn. Eugenio Montale. CP-MontE, *tr. by* Jonathan Galassi

English is a language than which none is sublimer. Brief Guide to Rhyming, or, How Be the Little Busy Doth?, A. Ogden Nash. CP-NashO

English May. Dante Gabriel Rossetti. CW-RossD

English Revenant, An. Donald Davie. CP-DaviDC

English Song. Robert Burns. CP-BurnR

English Song. Robert Burns. CP-BurnR

   (O wert thou, Love, but near me.) CP-BurnR

English Sparrows. Edna St. Vincent Millay. CP-MillE

English Sparrows. Jones Very. CP-VeryJ

English Train Compartment. John Updike. CP-UpdiJ

English Visitor, The. Stevie Smith. CP-SmitS

English Way, The. Rudyard Kipling. CP-KiplR

Englishman in Italy, The. Robert Browning. CP-BroR1

Engraved. Denise Levertov. SP-LeveDL

Engraving of expansive gold, An. Paradise. Gabriela Mistral. SP-MistG, *tr. by* Maria Giachetti [*or* Jacketti]

Engravings of the Garden. Federico García Lorca. CP-GarcF, *tr. by* Jerome Rothenberg *Fr.* In the Garden of the Lunar Grapefruits.

Enhanced in a tower, asleep, dreaming about him. Garden, The. Robert Graves. CP-GravR

Enid, An Invitation. G. K. Chesterton. CP-ChesG

Enigma. *Unknown, sometimes at. to* Thomas Sheridan. CP-SherT

Enigma, An. Edgar Allan Poe. CP-PoeEd

1. Enigma: Calm: Addressed to the Air. Alan Dugan. CP-DugaA

Enigma in the Last *Mercury* Explained, The. *Unknown, sometimes at. to* Thomas Sheridan. CP-SherT

Enigma of a Final Scene. Robert Stock. SP-StocR

Enigma, The. Richard Eberhart. CP-EberR

Enigmas, The. Jorge Luis Borges. SP-BorgJ, *tr. by* John Updike

Enjoyable clouds, and a man comes. Expanses. James Dickey. CP-DickJ

Enkindled Spring, The. D. H. Lawrence. CP-LawrD

Enlacement, The. James Laughlin. CP-LaugJ

Enlightened / a conscience rams through. For Eric. Paul Celan. SP-CelaP, *tr. by* John Felstiner

Enlightened Teacher, gladly from thy hand. To the Rev. Christopher Wordsworth, D.D., Master of Harrow School. William Wordsworth. CP-WorW2

Enniscorthy Suite. Charles Olson. CP-OlsoC

Ennui. Langston Hughes. CP-HughL; CP-HughL2

Eno aged Mother. Book of Los, The. William Blake. CP-BlakW

Enoch. Jones Very. CP-VeryJ

Enoch Arden. Alfred Tennyson. CP-TennA

Enormous and solid. Grove, The. Octavio Paz. CP-BishE, *tr. by* Elizabeth Bishop

Enormous and strong monks who from their place. Rainer Maria Rilke. CP-RilkFr, *tr. by* A. Poulin, Jr. *Fr.* Fragments.

Enormous cloud-mountains that form over Point Lobos and into the sunset. Clouds of Evening. Robinson Jeffers. CP-JefR1

Enormous Love, it's no good asking. Randall Jarrell. CP-JarrR

Enormous moon, that rise behind these hills. Edna St. Vincent Millay. CP-MillE

Enormous mortgage must be paid somehow, The. Dispossessed, The. Sylvia Plath. CP-PlatS

Enormous, the upper brain. Laurels. Eleanor Wilner. SP-WilnE

Enormous tragedy of the dream in the peasant's bent shoulders, The. Canto 74: "Enormous tragedy of the dream in the peasant's bent shoulders, The." Ezra Pound. SP-PounE *Fr.* Cantos.

Enough. One Fond Embrace. Thomas Kinsella. CP-KinsT

Enough. Robert Creeley. CP-CreeR

Enough. Laura Riding Jackson. CP-RidiL

Enough. Marianne Craig Moore. CP-MoorM

Enough. Marianne Craig Moore. CP-MoorM

Enough: and leave the rest to fame. Epitaph upon —, An. Andrew Marvell. CP-MarvA

Enough is done highminded friend go sleep. Ralph Waldo Emerson. CP-EmerR

Enough is enough. If you got. Tanck's Epilogue. Hayden Carruth. CP-CarHS *Fr.* Songs About What Comes Down: The Complete Works of Mr. Septic Tanck.

Enough is so vast a sweetness. Emily Dickinson. SP-DickE

Enough of climbing toil!—Ambition treads. Ode to Lycoris. William Wordsworth. CP-WorW2

Enough of garlands, of the Arcadian crook. Suggested at Tyndrum in a Storm. William Wordsworth. CP-WorW2

Enough of rose-bud lips, and eyes. Russian Fugitive, The. William Wordsworth. CP-WorW2

Enough of Thought, Philosopher. Philosopher, The. Emily Jane Brontë. CP-BronE

Enough seen. The vision has been met in every air. Departure. Arthur Rimbaud. CP-RimbA, *tr. by* Martin Sorrell

Enough, small Room,—though all too true. Arthur Hugh Clough. SP-ClouA

Enough! we're tired, my heart and I. My Heart and I. Elizabeth Barrett Browning. CP-BroEB

Enough Words? Jelaluddin Rumi. SP-Rumi, *tr. by* Coleman Barks

Enquiring fields, courtesies, The. Pastoral: "Enquiring fields, courtesies, The." Allen Tate. CP-TateA

Enraged by what he called. Spring, 480 BC. Raymond Carver. CP-CarvR

Enrica, 1865. Christina Georgina Rossetti. CP-RosC1

Enrich My Resignation. Hart Crane. CP-CranH

Enriching the Earth. Wendell Berry. CP-BerrW

Enrique, / Emilio. Fable and Round of the Three Friends. Federico García Lorca. SP-GarcF, *tr. by* Ben Belitt

Enrique, / Emilio, / Lorenzo. Fable of Three Friends to Be Sung in Rounds. Federico García Lorca. CP-GarcF, *tr. by* Greg Simon *and* Steven F. White

Entangled in one motion. Tuesday Night at the Savoy Ballroom. Yusef Komunyakaa. CP-KomuY

Enter a five-cornered room. Saturdays. A. K. Ramanujan. CP-RamaA

Enter April, laughingly. Spring Song. Dorothy Parker. CP-ParkD

"Enter my palace," if a prince should say. Founder of the Feast, The. Robert Browning. CP-BroR2

Enter no(silence is the blood whose flesh). E. E. Cummings. CP-CummE

Enter the chilly no-man's land of about. Ghost's Leavetaking, The. Sylvia Plath. CP-PlatS

Enter the darkest room. If I Should. Lucille Clifton. SP-ClifL

Enter the siren quiet, wave upon glittering wave. Silence and the Wayfarer. Marya Alexandrovna Zaturenska. SP-ZatuM

Enter these enchanted woods. Woods of Westermain, The. George Meredith. CP-MerG1

Enter with him. Legend. W. H. Auden. CP-AudeW

Entered in the Minutes. Louis MacNeice. CP-MacNL

Entered that brilliant intimate. Only Alice. Josephine Jacobsen. CP-JacoJ

Entering History. William Stafford. SP-StafWW

Entering Minetta's soft yellow chrome, to the acrid bathroom. Old Village before I Die, The. Allen Ginsberg. CP-GinsA

Entering my room this morning. Mask, The. Rainer Maria Rilke. CP-RilkFr, *tr. by* A. Poulin, Jr.

Entering the Kingdom. Mary Oliver. SP-OlivM

Entering the midnight. Talking Late with the Governor about the Budget. Gary Snyder. CP-SnydG

Enters give / whose lost is his found. E. E. Cummings. CP-CummE

Entertainment, or Porch-Verse, at the Marriage of Mr. Henry Northleigh [*or* Hen.

Northly] and the Most Witty Mrs. Lettice Yard, The. Robert Herrick. CP-HerrR

Enthroned in plastic, shrouded in wool, diamond crowned. To the Body. Allen Ginsberg. CP-GinsA

Enthroned upon the mighty truth. Justice. Paul Laurence Dunbar. CP-DunbP

Enthused I went to Yale, enthused. Story of My Life, The. John Updike. CP-UpdiJ

"Enthusiasm," An. Charles Olson. CP-OlsoC

Enthusiasm for Hats. Howard Nemerov. CP-NemeH

Enthusiast, The. Herman Melville. SP-MelvH

Enthusiast Is a Devotee Is a Rooter, or, Mr. Hemingway, Meet Mr. Stengel, An. Ogden Nash. CP-NashO

Entire household suffered, The. Anathema. Raymond Carver. CP-CarvR

Entire island, The. No Man Is an Island. A. K. Ramanujan. CP-RamaA

Entire soul evoked, The. Stéphane Mallarmé. CP-MallS, tr. by Henry Weinfield

Entire Surrender, The. Jeanne Marie Bouvier de la Motte- Guyon. CP-CowpW

Entirely. Louis MacNeice. CP-MacNL

Entity, The. William Carlos Williams. CP-WilW1

Entraining to Southampton in the parlor car with Jap and Vincent, I. Joe's Jacket. Frank O'Hara. SP-OharF

Entrance. Thomas Kinsella. CP-KinsT

Entrance. Kenneth Rexroth. CP-RexrK

Entrance to the Underworld, The. Gregory Orr. SP-OrrG

Entre deux belles femmes dans un seul lit. Dans un Seul Lit. Robert Graves. CP-GravR

Entre la scène et moi. La Mouche. Samuel Beckett. CP-BeckS

Entre Nous. Robert Creeley. CP-CreeR

Entretien dans un parc. T. S. Eliot. SP-ElioT

Entries for a Catalogue of Fears. A. K. Ramanujan. CP-RamaA

Entropy. Miller Williams. CP-WillM

Enueg II. Samuel Beckett. CP-BeckS

Enueg I. Samuel Beckett. CP-BeckS

Envelope, The. Maxine W. Kumin. SP-KumiM

Envelopes arrive from everywhere and they are filled with earth. Mail. Andrei Codrescu. SP-CodrA

Enviable Isles, The. Herman Melville. SP-MelvH

Envious and foul disease, could there not be. Epigram. To the Small-Pox, An. Ben Jonson. CP-JonsB

Envisage it: the Atlantic. Behind the North Wind. Donald Davie. CP-DaviDC

Envision Artemis in hunting gear. Sisina. Charles Baudelaire. CP-BaudC, tr. by Walter Martin

Envoi: "Go, little book. If anybody asks." William Meredith. SP-MereW

Envoi: "Hear me, whom I betrayed." James Vincent Cunningham. CP-CunnJ

Envoi: "Particulars they want." Robert Creeley. CP-CreeR

Envoi: "Strange judgment upon me." David Ignatow. SP-IgnaD

Envoi: "There is no now for us but always." Robert Graves. CP-GravR

Envoi: "There's a whisper down the field where the year has shot her yield." Rudyard Kipling. CP-KiplR
  (Long Trail, The.) CP-KiplR

Envoi: "Well have I loved ye, / little songs of mine." Ezra Pound. CP-PoEar

Envoy from d'Aubigné. W. S. Merwin. SP-MerwW

Envoy: "Love, all day there has been at the edge of my mind." Wendell Berry. CP-BerrW

Envoy: "So, to complete the spectrum." Theodore Weiss. SP-WeisT Fr. Polish Question, The.

Envoy to Africa. Langston Hughes. CP-HughL; CP-HughL3

Envoys from Alexandria. Constantine P. Cavafy. CP-CavaC, tr. by Theoharis Constantine Theoharis

Envy. "H. D." See Fragment 68: "I envy you your chance of death"

Envy, if thy jaundiced eye. At Whigham's Inn, Sanquar. Robert Burns. CP-BurnR

Envy of Natural Formal Liberties, An. Alan Dugan. CP-DugaA

Envy of the elegant, The. This Pair. A. K. Ramanujan. CP-RamaA

Envy the mad killer who lies in the ditch and grieves. Crime. Robert Penn Warren. CP-WarrR

Envy, why carp'st [or carpest] thou my time is spent so ill. Elegy 1.15: "Envy, why carp'st [or carpest] thou my time is spent so ill." Ovid. CP-MarlC, tr. by Christopher Marlowe Fr. Elegies.

Eolian Harp, The. Samuel Taylor Coleridge. MW-ColeS Fr. Effusions.

Eolith. A. R. Ammons. CP-AmmoA

Ep on a Good Man. Henry David Thoreau. CP-ThorH

Epeisodia. Thomas Hardy. CP-HardT

Ephemera. William Butler Yeats. CP-YeatW

Ephemeron! It's over! All. Elegy for a Gifted Child. Alan Dugan. CP-DugaA

Ephesians 4:30. Grieve not the Holy Spirit, etc. George Herbert. See Grieve Not the Holy Spirit, etc

Epi-strauss-ium. Arthur Hugh Clough. SP-ClouA

Epic. Robert Creeley. SP-CreeR

"Epic epigram," I heard you say, An. Martial. CP-CunnJ, tr. by James Vincent Cunningham

Epic Expands, The. Robert Creeley. CP-CreeR

Epic in the Heart. Constantine P. Cavafy. CP-CavaC, tr. by Theoharis Constantine Theoharis

Epic Stars, The. Robinson Jeffers. CP-JefR3

Epicoene; or, The Silent Woman. Ben Jonson.
  "Modest, and fair, for fair and good are near." CP-JonsB
  "Still to be neat, still to be dressed [or Drest]." CP-JonsB; SP-JonsB

Epicure From My Staircase, The. Adam Zagajewski. SP-ZagaA, tr. by Clare Cavanagh

Epidermal Macabre. Theodore Roethke. CP-RoetT

Epigon. Charles Olson. CP-OlsoC

Epigoni, The. W. H. Auden. CP-AudeW

Epigram Addressed to Two Clergymen Who Had Been Trying in Jest to Put Some Constructions on the Conversation That Was Not Meant, An. Annis Boudinot Stockton. CP-StocA

Epigram, An: "Friend Rundle fell with grievous bump." Jonathan Swift. CP-SwifJ

Epigram, An: "In your indignation what mercy appears." Jonathan Swift. CP-SwifJ

Epigram, An: "That you have seen the pride, beheld the sport." Ben Jonson. CP-JonsB

Epigram: "And what is love? Misunderstanding, pain." James Vincent Cunningham. CP-CunnJ

Epigram does many things require, An. Of Epigram. Thomas Sheridan. CP-SherT

Epigram from the French: "Sir, I admit your general [or gen'ral] Rule." Alexander Pope. CP-PopeA

Epigram: "Golden one is gone from the banquets, The." "H. D." CP-DoolH

Epigram: "Good Fortune, when I hailed her recently." James Vincent Cunningham. CP-CunnJ

Epigram: "Here lies my wife. Eternal peace." James Vincent Cunningham. CP-CunnJ

Epigram: "Here lies New Critic who would fox us." James Vincent Cunningham. CP-CunnJ

Epigram: "I had gone broke, and got set to come back." James Vincent Cunningham. CP-CunnJ

Epigram: "I have been insulted in St Peter's." George Oppen. CP-OppGN

Epigram in a Maid of Honour's Prayer-Book. Alexander Pope. CP-PopeA

Epigram is but a feeble thing, An. William Cowper. CP-CowpW

Epigram: "Lord Pam in the church (could [or cou'd] you think it) kneeled [or kneel'd] down." Jonathan Swift. CP-SwifJ

Epigram: "My Lord complains, that Pope, stark mad with gardens." Alexander Pope. CP-PopeA

Epigram of Homer, An. Homer. CP-CowpW

Epigram on a Painting of Golgotha. Allen Ginsberg. CP-GinsA

Epigram on an Event in Col. Evans's Redoubted Performances in Spain. William Wordsworth. CP-WorW2

Epigram on an Old Lady Who Had Some Curious Notions Respecting the Soul. Lord Byron. CP-Byron

Epigram on Capt. Francis Grose, the Celebrated Antiquary. Robert Burns. CP-BurnR

Epigram on Colley Cibber. Samuel Johnson. CP-JohnS

Epigram on Doctor Babington. Robert Burns. See Parson's Looks, The

Epigram on Fasting. Jonathan Swift. CP-SwifJ

Epigram on Plutarch, An. Agathias. CP-DryJ2, tr. by John Dryden

Epigram on Rough Roads. Robert Burns. CP-BurnR

Epigram on Said Occasion. Robert Burns. CP-BurnR

Epigram on School Days. Robert Browning. CP-BroR2

Epigram on Scolding, An. Jonathan Swift. CP-SwifJ

Epigram on Sir Edward Coke, when He Was Lord Chief Justice of England, An. Ben Jonson. CP-JonsB

Epigram on the Court Pucell, An. Ben Jonson. CP-JonsB

Epigram on the Hermitage at Richmond. Jonathan Swift. CP-SwifJ

Epigram on the Prince's Birth. 1630, An. Ben Jonson. CP-JonsB

Epigram on the Refusal of the University of Oxford to Subscribe to His Translation of Homer. William Cowper. CP-CowpW

Epigram on the Toasts of the Kit-Cat Club, Anno 1716. Alexander Pope. CP-PopeA

Epigram on William, Lord Burl[eigh], Lo[rd] High Treasurer of England, An. Ben Jonson. CP-JonsB

Epigram on Wood's Brass Money, An. Jonathan Swift. CP-SwifJ

Epigram: "Peter complains, that God has given." Alexander Pope. CP-PopeA

Epigram. To a Friend and Son. Ben Jonson. CP-JonsB

Epigram to Fidelia. Annis Boudinot Stockton. CP-StocA

Epigram. To K[ing] Charles for a[n] Hundred Pounds He Sent Me in My Sickness. 1629, An. Ben Jonson. CP-JonsB

Epigram to My Bookseller. Ben Jonson. CP-JonsB

Epigram to My Jovial Good Friend Mr Robert Dover, on His Great Instauration of His Hunting and Dancing at Cotswold, An. Ben Jonson. CP-JonsB

Epigram to My Muse, the Lady Digby, on Her Husband, Sir Kenelm Digby, An. Ben Jonson. CP-JonsB

Epigram. To our Great and Good K[ing] Charles on his Anniversary Day. 1629, An. Ben Jonson. CP-JonsB

Epigram: "To purify their wine some people bleed." William Cowper. CP-CowpW

Epigram to the Coucillor That Pleaded and Carried the Cause, An. Ben Jonson. CP-JonsB

Epigram. To the Honoured——, Countess of——, An. Ben Jonson. CP-JonsB

Epigram. To the Household. 1630, An. Ben Jonson. CP-JonsB

Epigram to the Queen, Then Lying In. 1630, An. Ben Jonson. CP-JonsB

Epigram. To the Small-Pox, An. Ben Jonson. CP-JonsB

Epigram. To Thomas Lo[rd] Ellsmere, the Last Term He Sat Chancellor, An. Ben Jonson. CP-JonsB

Epigram. To William, Earl of Newcastle, An. Ben Jonson. CP-JonsB

Epigram. To William, Earl of Newcastle, An. Ben Jonson. CP-JonsB

Epigram: "When other Ladies to the Groves go down." Alexander Pope. CP-PopeA

Epigram: "Whoe'er he be that sojourns here." Robert Burns. CP-BurnR

Epigram: "You ask me how Contempt who claims to sleep." James Vincent Cunningham. CP-CunnJ

Epigram: "You wonder why Drab sells her love for gold?" James Vincent Cunningham. CP-CunnJ

Epigramma in Duos Montes Amosclivium et Bilboreum: Farfacio [Epigram on Two Mountains, Almscliff and Bilbrough: To Fairfax]. Andrew Marvell. CP-MarvA

Epigramma Martialis. Lib. VIII. lxxvii. The Same Translated. Ben Jonson. CP-JonsB

Epigramme: "Hast ever seen a man." William Carlos Williams. CP-WilW1

Epigrams. Edmund Spenser. CP-Spens Fr. Amoretti.

Epigrams. "H. D." CP-DoolH

Epigrams. Martial.
    "Gaurus pretends to Cato's fame." CP-JohnS
    "Not him I prize who poorly gains." CP-JohnS

Epigrams. Howard Nemerov. CP-NemeH

Epigrams: A Journal. James Vincent Cunningham. CP-CunnJ

Epigrams & Imitations. Philip Whalen. SP-WhalP

Epigrams: "O ivory, delicate hands!" Ezra Pound. CP-PoEar

Epigrams Occasion'd by an Invitation to Court. Alexander Pope. CP-PopeA

Epigrams Occasioned by Cibber's Verses in Praise of Nash. Alexander Pope. CP-PopeA

Epigrams: "Oh, Castlereagh! thou art a patriot now." Lord Byron. CP-Byron

Epigrams: "Old dissembler who lived out his lie, An." James Vincent Cunningham. CP-CunnJ

Epigrams on His Garden Shed. William Cowper. CP-CowpW

Epigrams on Lord Galloway. Robert Burns. CP-BurnR
    On Lord Galloway.
    (On the Same Nobleman.) CP-BurnR
    To the Same, on the Author Being Threatened with His Resentment. CP-BurnR

Epigrams: "Phony now has good fortune and a wife." Helen Pinkerton. CP-PinkH

Epigraph. William Blake. Fr. Jerusalem.

Epigraph for a Condemned Book. Charles Baudelaire. CP-BaudC, tr. by Walter Martin

Epigraph: "Lot's wife, / married to chance." Robert Creeley. CP-CreeR

Epigraph to Call Me Ishmael. Charles Olson. CP-OlsoC

Epigraph to "The Woodlanders" Thomas Hardy. CP-HardT

Epilogue. John Logan. CP-LoganJ Fr. Epilogue, Songs of the Spouses, Complaint of Love.

Epilogue. Langston Hughes. See I, too, sing America

Epilogue: "After our Aesop's fable shown today." John Dryden. CP-DryJ2 Fr. Albion and Albanius.

Epilogue: "At the midnight in the silence of the sleep-time." Robert Browning. CP-BroR2

Epilogue Designed to Be Spoken by Alonzo, at the Acting of The Revenge by Some Schoolboys. Unknown, sometimes at. to Thomas Sheridan. CP-SherT

Epilogue for a Masque of Purcell. Adrienne Rich. CP-RicAE

Epilogue: "He died in December. He must descend." John Berryman. CP-BerrJ

Epilogue: "I bring you the spoils, my nation." Ezra Pound. CP-PoEar

Epilogue: "If Luther's day expand to Darwin's year." Herman Melville. SP-MelvH Fr. Clarel: A Poem and Pilgrimage in the Holy Land.

Epilogue: "Lily, being white not red, The." Countee Cullen. CP-CullC

Epilogue: "Much time and trouble this poor play has cost." Nathaniel Lee. CP-DryJ2 Fr. Duke of Guise, The.

Epilogue: "Now that the number of steps you were given." Jorge Luis Borges. SP-BorgJ, tr. by Stephen Kessler

Epilogue: "Oh, Love—no, Love! All the noise below, Love." Robert Browning. CP-BroR2

Epilogue: "On the first of the Feast of Feasts." Robert Browning. CP-BroR1; SP-BroR

Epilogue: "Our hero's happy in the play's conclusion." Nathaniel Lee. CP-DryJ2 Fr. Constantine the Great.

Epilogue: "Poets pour us wine, The." Robert Browning. CP-BroR2

Epilogue: "Qualm of conscience brings me back again, A." Nathaniel Lee. CP-DryJ2 Fr. Princess of Cleves, The.

Epilogue, Songs of the Spouses, Complaint of Love. John Logan. CP-LogaJ
    Bride's Song, The. CP-LogaJ
    Bridgeroom's Song, The. CP-LogaJ
    Complaint, The. CP-LogaJ
    Epilogue. CP-LogaJ
    Tale of Courtship. CP-LogaJ

Epilogue Spoken by Mrs. Boutell. John Dryden. SP-DrydJ
    (Epilogue to the University of Oxford, 1674.) SP-DrydJ

Epilogue, The: "It was a dream delivered the epilogue." Charles Tomlinson. CP-TomlC; SP-TomlC

Epilogue, The: "Now all is done, learned spectators, tell." Thomas Sheridan. CP-SherT

Epilogue, The: "Virgin poet was served up today, A." Thomas Southerne. CP-DryJ2 Fr. Loyal Brother, The.

Epilogue: "There's something in a stupid ass." Lord Byron. CP-Byron

Epilogue to a Human Drama. Stephen Spender. CP-SpenS

Epilogue to a Play for the Benefit of the Weavers in Ireland, An. Jonathan Swift. CP-SwifJ

Epilogue to Horace's Carmen Seculare. Samuel Johnson. CP-JohnS

Epilogue to Julius Caesar, The. Thomas Sheridan. CP-SherT

Epilogue to Mr. Rowe's Jane Shore. Alexander Pope. CP-PopeA

Epilogue to Mother's Day, Which Is To Be Published on Any Day But Mother's Day. Ogden Nash. CP-NashO

Epilogue to Robinson Crusoe. Dan Pagis. SP-PagiD, tr. by Stephen Mitchell

Epilogue to the Adventures While Preaching the Gospel of Beauty. Nicholas Vachel Lindsay. CP-LindV

Epilogue to The Distrest Mother, An. Samuel Johnson. CP-JohnS

Epilogue to the King and Queen. John Dryden. CP-DryJ2

Epilogue to the Opera of Dead on Arrival. Yusef Komunyakaa. CP-KomuY

Epilogue to the Satires, in Two Dialogues. Alexander Pope. CP-PopeA

Epilogue to the Second Part of The Conquest of Granada. John Dryden. SP-DrydJ Fr. Conquest of Granada, The.

Epilogue to the Sultan. James Austen. CP-AustJ

Epilogue to the University of Oxford, 1674. John Dryden. See Epilogue Spoken by Mrs. Boutell.

Epilogue to Tyrannic[k] Love. John Dryden. SP-DrydJ Fr. Tyrannic Love.

Epilogue: "Trees are tall gods, The." David Ignatow. SP-IgnaD

Epilogue: "We have now set forth, in our imperfect way." Thomas Hardy. CP-HardT Fr. Dynasts, The.

Epiphany. A. R. Ammons. CP-AmmoA

Epiphany. Christina Georgina Rossetti. CP-RosC2

Epiphanytide. Christina Georgina Rossetti. CP-RosC2

Epipsychidion. Percy Bysshe Shelley. CP-ShelP

Episcopal, that church I visited at first. To a Christian. Heather McHugh. SP-McHuH

Episode. Yannis Ritsos. SP-RitsY, tr. by Minas Savvas

Episode of Hands. Hart Crane. CP-CranH

Episode of Nisus and Euryalus, The. Lord Byron. CP-Byron

Episode of Sarpedon, The. Homer. CP-PopeA Fr. Iliad, The.

Episode 17. William Carlos Williams. CP-WilW1 Fr. Paterson.

Episodes. Walter De la Mare. CP-DeLaW

Epistemology. Richard Wilbur. CP-WilbR

Epistill, The: "Thou, lytil quair, of mater miserabyll." Sir David Lyndsay. SP-LyndD Fr. Dialog betwix Experience and ane Courteour, Ane.

Epistle 1.4: "Tibullus, whom I love and praise." Horace. SP-SmarC Fr. Epistles.

Epistle 1.6. Horace. Fr. Epistles.

Epistle 1.20: "You seem to cast, my vent'rous book." Horace. SP-SmarC Fr. Epistles.

Epistle 2.1: "Each inly murm'ring at th'unequal meed." Horace. CP-JohnS Fr. Epistles.

Epistle 2.2: "Bold be the critic, zealous to his trust." Horace. CP-JohnS Fr. Epistles.

Epistle Answering to One That Asked to Be Sealed of the Tribe of Ben, An. Ben Jonson. CP-JonsB; SP-JonsB

Epistle Containing the Strange Medical Experience of Karshish, the Arab Physician, An. Robert Browning. CP-BroR1; SP-BroR

Epistle V, to Mr. Addison. Alexander Pope. CP-PopeA

Epistle IV, to Richard Boyle, Earl of Burlington. Alexander Pope. CP-PopeA

Epistle in Behalf of Our Irish Poets to the Right Hon. Lady C——t, An. *Unknown*.
  "There's punning Tom Sh-r-d-n, Phoebus's darling." CP-SherT

Epistle: "Jesus loved the sunsets on Galilee." Carl Sandburg. CP-SandC

Epistle I, to Sir Richard Temple, Lord Cobham. Alexander Pope. CP-PopeA

Epistle III, to Allen Lord Bathurst. Alexander Pope. CP-PopeA

Epistle to a Friend. Lord Byron. CP-Byron

Epistle to a Friend. Ben Jonson. CP-JonsB

Epistle to a Friend, An ("Censure not sharply then, but me advise"). Ben Jonson. CP-JonsB

Epistle to a Friend, An ("Sir, I am thankful, first, to heaven, for you"). Ben Jonson. CP-JonsB

Epistle to a Friend, to Persuade [or Perswade] Him to the Wars [or Warres], An. Ben Jonson. CP-JonsB; SP-JonsB

Epistle to a Friend Who Urg'd to Have Some Poetry Sent Her in the Year 1759, in the Winter, An. Annis Boudinot Stockton. CP-StocA

Epistle to a Godson. W. H. Auden. CP-AudeW

Epistle to a Protestant Lady in France, An. William Cowper. CP-CowpW

Epistle to a Young Friend. Robert Burns. CP-BurnR

Epistle to Augusta. Lord Byron. CP-Byron

Epistle to Be Left in the Earth. Archibald MacLeish. CP-MacLA

Epistle to Captn Willm Logan at Park. Robert Burns. CP-BurnR

Epistle to Davie, a Brother Poet. Robert Burns. CP-BurnR

Epistle to Dr. Arbuthnot. Alexander Pope. CP-PopeA

Epistle to Dr. Nares. Christopher Smart. SP-SmarC

Epistle to Elizabeth, Countess of Rutland. Ben Jonson. CP-JonsB; SP-JonsB

Epistle. To Enrique Caracciolo Trejo. Donald Davie. CP-DaviDC

Epistle to G. East Esq. Mrs. Austen. CP-AustJ

Epistle to General Washington [May 26, 1787]. Annis Boudinot Stockton. CP-StocA

Epistle to Hill. William Cowper. CP-CowpW

Epistle to Hugh Parker. Robert Burns. CP-BurnR

Epistle to J. L*****k, an Old Scotch Bard. Robert Burns. *See* Epistle to John Lapraik

Epistle to J. R******, Enclosing Some Poems. Robert Burns. CP-BurnR

Epistle to James Craggs, Esq., Secretary of State. Alexander Pope. CP-PopeA

Epistle to John Goldie in Kilmarnock, Author of, the Gospel Recovered. Robert Burns. CP-BurnR

Epistle to John Lapraik. Robert Burns. CP-BurnR
  (Epistle to J. L*****k, an Old Scotch Bard.) CP-BurnR

Epistle to John Sherratt, Esq, An. Christopher Smart. SP-SmarC

Epistle. To Katharine, Lady Aubigny. Ben Jonson. CP-JonsB

Epistle to Lady Austen. William Cowper. CP-CowpW

Epistle to Léon-Paul Fargue. Archibald MacLeish. CP-MacLA

Epistle—To Lucius. Annis Boudinot Stockton. CP-StocA

Epistle to Master Arth[ur] Squib, An. Ben Jonson. CP-JonsB

Epistle to Master John Selden, An. Ben Jonson. CP-JonsB; SP-JonsB

Epistle to Miss Blount, with the Works of Voiture. Alexander Pope. CP-PopeA

Epistle to Miss [or Miss Teresa] Blount, on Her Leaving the Town after the Coronation. Alexander Pope. CP-PopeA

Epistle to Mr Arthur Squib. Ben Jonson. CP-JonsB

Epistle to Mr. Jervas, with Dryden's Translation of Fresnoy's *Art of Painting*. Alexander Pope. CP-PopeA

Epistle to Mr Tytler of Woodhouselee, Author of a Defence of Mary Queen of Scots. Robert Burns. CP-BurnR

Epistle. To My Lady Covell. Ben Jonson. CP-JonsB

Epistle to Prescott S. Liddell. Robert Stock. SP-StocR

Epistle to Robert Earl of Oxford and Earl Mortimer. Alexander Pope. CP-PopeA

Epistle to Robt. Graham Esq: of Fintry on the Election for the Dumfries String of Boroughs, Anno 1790. Robert Burns. CP-BurnR

Epistle to Robert Lloyd, Esq, An. William Cowper. CP-CowpW

Epistle to Simon Perchik. Robert Stock. SP-StocR

Epistle to Sir Edward Sackville, now Earl of Dorset, An. Ben Jonson. CP-JonsB

Epistle to Sir George Howland Beaumont, BART. William Wordsworth. CP-WorW1

Epistle to Spencer Holst. Robert Stock. SP-StocR

Epistle to Suzanne Joslyn Fosberg. Robert Stock. SP-StocR

Epistle [II,] to a Lady[: Of the Characters of Women]. Alexander Pope. CP-PopeA

Epistle [II,] to a Lady[: Of the Characters of Women]. Alexander Pope. CP-PopeA

Epistle upon an Epistle, An. Jonathan Swift. CP-SwifJ

Epistles. Horace.
  Epistle 1.4: "Tibullus, whom I love and praise." SP-SmarC
  Epistle 1.6.
    "If any man can better rules impart." CP-SherT

Epistle 1.20: "You seem to cast, my vent'rous book." SP-SmarC

Epistle 2.1: "Each inly murm'ring at th'unequal meed." CP-JohnS

Epistle 2.2: "Bold be the critic, zealous to his trust." CP-JohnS

Epitaph. A. E. Housman. CP-HousA

Epitaph (1): "Julio hernadez does not lie here." Andrei Codrescu. SP-CodrA

Epitaph (2): "He was a young guy with surrealist connections." Andrei Codrescu. SP-CodrA

Epitaph: "Again, traveller, you have come a long way led by that star." Thomas McGrath. SP-McGrT

Epitaph, An: "Come knock your heads against this stone." William Blake. CP-BlakW

Epitaph, An: "Here lies a most beautiful lady." Walter De la Mare. CP-DeLaW

Epitaph, An: "Here lies one, who never drew." William Cowper. CP-CowpW

Epitaph, An: "I was buried near this dyke [or Dike]." William Blake. CP-BlakW (Another [Epitaph].) CP-BlakW

Epitaph, An: "Last, Stone, a little yet." Walter De la Mare. CP-DeLaW

Epitaph, An: "My name my country—what are they to thee" Paulus Silentiarius.

Epitaph, An: "Stay, if you list, O passer by the way." A. E. Housman. CP-HousA

Epitaph, An: "What beauty would have lovely styled." Ben Jonson. CP-JonsB

Epitaph: "Bethink, poor heart, what bitter kind of jest." Hafiz. CP-EmerR

Epitaph by a Young Lady, Design'd by Herself, An. Annis Boudinot Stockton. CP-StocA

Epitaph: "Crazy, girls, crazy. Don is gone." Howard Nemerov. CP-NemeH

Epitaph: "Enamoured by / Brevity in method." Charles Tomlinson. CP-TomlC

Epitaph Ending in And, The. William Stafford. SP-StafWW

Epitaph Extempore, on a Person Nicknamed the Marquis, Who Desired Burns to Write One on Him. Robert Burns. CP-BurnR

Epitaph: "First time I died, I walked my ways, The." Dorothy Parker. CP-ParkD

Epitaph for a Bird. Federico García Lorca.
  "And its eyes as deep." CP-GarcF, *tr.* by Jerome Rothenberg
  Memento ("I have laid out the singer"). CP-GarcF, *tr.* by Jerome Rothenberg
  Thanksgiving. CP-GarcF, *tr.* by Jerome Rothenberg

Epitaph for a Careless Beauty. Marya Alexandrovna Zaturenska. SP-ZatuM

Epitaph for a Centaur. Joseph Brodsky. CP-BrodJ

Epitaph for a Darling Lady. Dorothy Parker. CP-ParkD

Epitaph for a Public Servant. Thomas Merton. CP-MertT

Epitaph for a Tyrant. Joseph Brodsky. CP-BrodJ *Fr.* Shorts.

Epitaph for Fire and Flower. Sylvia Plath. CP-PlatS

Epitaph for François. Paul Celan. SP-CelaP, *tr.* by John Felstiner

Epitaph for G. K. Chesterton. Thomas Hardy. CP-HardT

Epitaph for George Moore. Thomas Hardy. CP-HardT

Epitaph for H—— L——, Esq., of L——. Robert Burns. CP-BurnR

Epitaph for Isaac Albéniz. Federico García Lorca. CP-GarcF, *tr.* by Christopher Maurer

Epitaph for J. H. Writer in Ayr. Robert Burns. CP-BurnR

Epitaph for John McCutcheon. Archibald MacLeish. CP-MacLA

Epitaph for Joseph Blacket. Lord Byron. CP-Byron

Epitaph for Liberal Poets. Louis MacNeice. CP-MacNL

Epitaph for One Who Would Not Be Buried in Westminster Abbey. Alexander Pope. CP-PopeA

Epitaph for One Who Would Not Be Buried in Westminster Abbey. Alexander Pope. CP-PopeA

Epitaph for Someone or Other. James Vincent Cunningham. CP-CunnJ *Fr.* Five Epigrams.

Epitaph for the Race of Man. Edna St. Vincent Millay. CP-MillE
  "He heard the coughing tiger in the night." CP-MillE

Epitaph for William Nicol. Robert Burns. CP-BurnR

Epitaph: "Grieve not for happy Claudius, he is dead." Edna St. Vincent Millay. CP-MillE

Epitaph: "Heap not on this mound." Edna St. Vincent Millay. CP-MillE *Fr.* Memorial to D. C.

Epitaph: "Here lies an honest man." Henry David Thoreau. CP-ThorH

Epitaph: "Here lies our freind who having promis-ed." Jane Austen. CP-AustJ

Epitaph. Here Lies Robert Fergusson, Poet. Robert Burns. CP-BurnR

Epitaph: "Here, time concurring (and it does)." John Ciardi. CP-CiarJ

Epitaph: "I am old." Christopher Logue. SP-LoguC

Epitaph: "I never cared for Life: Life cared for me." Thomas Hardy. CP-HardT

Epitaph in Form of a Ballad, The. François Villon. SP-SwinA, *tr.* by Algernon Charles Swinburne

Epitaph in Grasmere Church. William Wordsworth. CP-WorW2

Epitaph in the Chapel Yard of Langdale, Westmoreland. William Wordsworth. CP-WorW2

Epitaph in Three Parts. Sylvia Plath. CP-PlatS

Epitaph Intended for Mr. Rowe, in Westminster Abbey. Alexander Pope. CP-PopeA

Epitaph Intended for Sir Isaac Newton, in Westminster Abbey. Alexander Pope. *See* Intended for Sir Isaac Newton

Epitaph: "Lo worms enjoy the seat of bliss." Robert Burns. CP-BurnR

Epitaph of Antiochus, King of Kommagini. Constantine P. Cavafy. CP-CavaC, *tr. by* Theoharis Constantine Theoharis

Epitaph of Sir Thomas Gravener, [Knight], An. Sir Thomas Wyatt. CP-WyatT

Epitaph: "Of the Great World he knew not much." Howard Nemerov. CP-NemeH

Epitaph: "Oh you, passing by this hill—one." Primo Levi. CP-LeviP, *tr. by* Ruth Feldman *and* Brian Swann

Epitaph: "Old willow with hollow branches, An." William Carlos Williams. CP-WilW1

Epitaph on a Child. Thomas Gray. CP-GrayT

Epitaph on a Free but Tame Redbreast. William Cowper. CP-CowpW

Epitaph on a Friend. Lord Byron. CP-Byron

Epitaph on a Hare. William Cowper. CP-CowpW

Epitaph on a Henpecked Country Squire. Robert Burns. CP-BurnR

Epitaph on a Man who Had a Scold to His Wife. Robert Herrick. CP-HerrR

Epitaph on a Pessimist. Thomas Hardy. CP-HardT

Epitaph on a Philosopher the Reports of Whose Death Have Been Grossly Minimized. Howard Nemerov. CP-NemeH

Epitaph on a Schoolmaster. Robert Burns. CP-BurnR
(On a Schoolmaster in Cleish Parish, Fifeshire.) CP-BurnR

Epitaph on a Street Dog. A. K. Ramanujan. CP-RamaA

Epitaph on a Tyrant. W. H. Auden. CP-AudeW

Epitaph on a Wag in Mauchline. Robert Burns. CP-BurnR

Epitaph on an Army of Mercenaries. A. E. Housman. CP-HousA

Epitaph on an Engraver. Henry David Thoreau. CP-ThorH

Epitaph on an Infant. Samuel Taylor Coleridge. CP-ColeS; MW-ColeS

Epitaph on an Infant. Samuel Taylor Coleridge. CP-ColeS

Epitaph on Charles Earl of Dorset. Alexander Pope. CP-PopeA

see also Epitaph on the Count of Mirandula. Alexander Pope. CP-PopeA

Epitaph on Claudy Phillips, a Musician, An. Samuel Johnson. *See* Epitaph upon the Celebrated Claudy Phillips, Musician, Who Died Very Poor, An

Epitaph on D——— C———. Robert Burns. CP-BurnR

Epitaph on Dr. Francis Atterbury, Bishop of Rochester, Who Died in Exile at Paris, 1732; a Dialogue. Alexander Pope. CP-PopeA

Epitaph on Dr. Johnson. William Cowper. CP-CowpW

Epitaph on Edmund Duke of Buckingham, Who Died in the Nineteenth Year of His Age, 1735. Alexander Pope. CP-PopeA

Epitaph on Elizabeth, L. H. Ben Jonson. CP-JonsB; SP-JonsB

Epitaph on Fop. William Cowper. CP-CowpW

Epitaph on General Henry Withers, in Westminster-Abbey, 1729. Alexander Pope. CP-PopeA

Epitaph on Henry Fielding, Esq. Christopher Smart. SP-SmarC

Epitaph, on Henry L[ord] La-ware. To the Passer-By, An. Ben Jonson. CP-JonsB

Epitaph on Himself. John Donne. CP-DonnJ; MW-DonnJ

Epitaph on Holy Willie. Robert Burns. CP-BurnR

Epitaph on James Craggs, Esq., in Westminster Abbey. Alexander Pope. CP-PopeA

Epitaph on James Grieve, Laird of Boghead. Robert Burns. CP-BurnR
(On Jas. Grieve, Laird of Boghead, Tarbolton.) CP-BurnR

Epitaph on John Adams, of Southwell. Lord Byron. CP-Byron

Epitaph on J-hn B-shby. Robert Burns. CP-BurnR

Epitaph on John Dove [Innkeeper, Mauchline]. Robert Burns. CP-BurnR

Epitaph on John Knight, Who Died Oct. 2, 1733. Alexander Pope. CP-PopeA

Epitaph on Katherine, Lady Ogle. Ben Jonson. CP-JonsB

Epitaph on Master Philip Gray, An. Ben Jonson. CP-JonsB

Epitaph on Master Vincent Corbet[t], An. Ben Jonson. CP-JonsB

Epitaph on Mr. Burton. Robert Burns. CP-BurnR

Epitaph on Mr. Chester. William Cowper. CP-CowpW

Epitaph on Mr. Elijah Fenton, at Easthamstead in Berks, 1730. Alexander Pope. CP-PopeA

Epitaph on Mrs. Corbet, Who Died of a Cancer in Her Breast. Alexander Pope. CP-PopeA

Epitaph on Mrs. Higgins. William Cowper. CP-CowpW

Epitaph on Mrs Jane Clarke. Thomas Gray. CP-GrayT

Epitaph on my Dear and Ever Honored Mother Mrs. Dorothy Dudley. Anne Bradstreet. CP-BradA

Epitaph on My Own Friend, and My Father's Friend, Wm Muir in Tarbolton Miln. Robert Burns. CP-BurnR

Epitaph on Pursy. Henry David Thoreau. CP-ThorH

Epitaph on R. Muir. Robert Burns. CP-BurnR

Epitaph on S. P. [*or* Salomon Pavy], a Child of Q[ueen] El[izabeth's] Chapel. Ben Jonson. CP-JonsB; SP-JonsB

Epitaph on Sir Godfrey Kneller, in Westminster-Abbey, 1723. Alexander Pope. CP-PopeA

Epitaph on Sir Philip Sidney. Sir Walter Ralegh. CP-RaleW
(Epitaph upon the Right Hono[u]rable Sir Philip Sidney Knight, Lord Governor of Flushing, An.) CP-RaleW

Epitaph on Sir William Trumbal. Alexander Pope. CP-PopeA

Epitaph on Sir William Williams. Thomas Gray. CP-GrayT

Epitaph on the Count of Mirandula. Alexander Pope. CP-PopeA

Epitaph on the Earl of Leicester [*or* Leceister]. Sir Walter Ralegh. CP-RaleW

Epitaph on the Earl of Salisbury. *Unknown, sometimes at. to* Sir Walter Ralegh. CP-RaleW

Epitaph on the Hon. Simon Harcourt. Alexander Pope. CP-PopeA

Epitaph on the Lady Mary Villiers. Thomas Carew. CP-CareT

Epitaph on the Lady Mary Villiers, An. Thomas Carew. CP-CareT
(Another [Epitaph on Lady Mary Villiers].) CP-CareT

Epitaph on the Lady S.: Wife of Sir W.S. Thomas Carew. CP-CareT

Epitaph on the Marchioness of Winchester, An. John Milton. CP-MiltJ

Epitaph on the Monument of the Honourable Robert Digby, and of his Sister Mary, erected by their Father the Lord Digby, in the Church of Sherborne in Dorsetshire, 1727. Alexander Pope. CP-PopeA

Epitaph on the Tomb of Sir Edward Giles and His Wife in the South Aisle of Dean Prior Church. Robert Herrick. CP-HerrR

Epitaph on the Tombstone of James Christopher Wilson. George Meredith. CP-MerG2

Ep[itaph] on the World. Henry David Thoreau. CP-ThorH

Epitaph on William Hogarth, An. Samuel Johnson. CP-JohnS

Epitaph: "She leans across a golden table." Countee Cullen. CP-CullC

Epitaph: "Six months to six years added he remained." William Wordsworth. CP-WorW1

Epitaph: "Slave yet wearing on my head a crown, A." Christina Georgina Rossetti. CP-RosC3

Epitaph: "So I may say." "H. D." CP-DoolH

Epitaph: "Stop, Christian passer-by!—Stop, child of God." Samuel Taylor Coleridge. CP-ColeS; MW-ColeS

Epitaph: "Stranger, beside the Ganges I lie, a man." Constantine P. Cavafy. CP-CavaC, *tr. by* Theoharis Constantine Theoharis

Epitaph: "There were no hidden motives to his life." David Ignatow. SP-IgnaD

Epitaph: "These are two friends whose lives were undivided." Percy Bysshe Shelley. CP-ShelP

Epitaph to a Tyrant. Joseph Brodsky. CP-BrodJ *Fr.* Shorts.

Epitaph: "Uncle Tom, / When he was alive." Langston Hughes. CP-HughL; CP-HughL3

Epitaph upon a Child, An. Robert Herrick. CP-HerrR

Epitaph upon a Sober Matron, An. Robert Herrick. CP-HerrR

Epitaph upon a Virgin, An. Robert Herrick. CP-HerrR

Epitaph upon a Young Married Couple, An. Richard Crashaw. *See* Epitaph Upon Husband and Wife Who Died and Were Buried Together, An

Epitaph upon —, An. Andrew Marvell. CP-MarvA

Epitaph. Upon Doctor Brooke, An. Richard Crashaw. CP-CrasR

Epitaph Upon Husband and Wife Who Died and Were Buried Together, An. Richard Crashaw. CP-CrasR
(Epitaph upon a Young Married Couple, An.) CP-CrasR

Epitaph upon Mr. Ashton, a Conformable Citizen, An. Richard Crashaw. CP-CrasR

Epitaph upon the Celebrated Claudy Phillips, Musician, Who Died Very Poor, An. Samuel Johnson. CP-JohnS
(Epitaph on Claudy Phillips, a Musician, An.) CP-JohnS

Epitaph upon the Right Hono[u]rable Sir Philip Sidney Knight, Lord Governor of Flushing, An. Sir Walter Ralegh. *See* Epitaph on Sir Philip Sidney

Epitaph upon the Right Honourable Sir Phillip Sidney, Knight: Lord Governor of Flushing, An. Edmund Spenser. CP-Spens *Fr.* Astrophel.

Epitaph: "Well then, poor G——— lies under ground!" Alexander Pope. CP-PopeA

Epitaph: "Within this grave lie." Langston Hughes. CP-HughL; CP-HughL1

Epitaph: "Young then, / we were bored already." Eleanor Wilner. SP-WilnE

Epitaphium. Percy Bysshe Shelley. CP-ShelP

Epitaphium Alterum. William Cowper. CP-CowpW

Epitaphium Testamentarium. Samuel Taylor Coleridge. CP-ColeS

Epitaphs for Two Players. Nicholas Vachel Lindsay. CP-LindV

Epitaphs: "Fu I loved the high cloud and the hill." Ezra Pound. SP-PounE

Epitaphs of the War [1914–1918]. Rudyard Kipling. CP-KiplR

Epithalamion at the Marriage of the Earl of Somerset. John Donne. CP-DonnJ; MW-DonnJ

Epithalamion for Tyler. James Tate. SP-TateJ

Epithalamion: "Glad time is at his point arrived." Ben Jonson. CP-JonsB *Fr.* Masque of Hymen.

Epithalamion: "Hark, hearer, hear what I do; lend a thought now, make believe." Gerard Manley Hopkins. CP-HopkG

Epithalamion Made at Lincoln's Inn [*or* Lincolnes Inne]. John Donne. CP-

DonnJ; MW-DonnJ

Epithalamion: or, a Song. Ben Jonson. CP-JonsB

Epithalamion, or Marriage Song on the Lady Elizabeth and Count Palatine Being Married on St. Valentine's Day, An. John Donne. CP-DonnJ; MW-DonnJ

Epithalamion: "Our mound of earth dug up." Olga Broumas. SP-BrouO

Epithalamion: "Pussy put her paw into the pail of paint." Ted Berrigan. SP-BerrT

Epithalamion: "Thou aged unreluctant earth who dost." E. E. Cummings. CP-CummE

Epithalamion: "Up, youths and virgins, up, and praise." Ben Jonson. CP-JonsB Fr. Haddington Masque, The.

Epithalamion: "Ye learned sisters which have oftentimes." Edmund Spenser. CP-Spens

Epithalamion: "You left me gasping on the shore." Carolyn Kizer. CP-KizeC

Epithalamium Argentum. G. K. Chesterton. CP-ChesG

Epithalamium at St. Michael's Cemetary. John Ciardi. CP-CiarJ

Epithalamium: "Come virgin Tapers of pure waxe." Richard Crashaw. CP-CrasR

Epithalamium: "He is here, Urania's son." A. E. Housman. CP-HousA

Epithalamium: "Let mother Earth" Sir Philip Sidney. SP-SidnP, tr. by Robert Hass Fr. Arcadia.

Epithalamium: "Night, with all thine eyes look down!" Percy Bysshe Shelley. CP-ShelP

Epithalamium, The: "Ye woodland choirs come consecrate the lay." Annis Boudinot Stockton. CP-StocA

Epithalamium: "There were others; their bodies." Louise Glück. SP-GlucL

Epithalamy to Sir Thomas Southwell and His Lady, An. Robert Herrick. CP-HerrR

Eplenor. Archibald MacLeish. CP-MacLA

Epoch of a streetcar drawn by horses, The. Baby Pictures of Famous Dictators. Charles Simic. SP-SimiC; SP-SimiCE

Epode 2: "How happy in his low degree." Horace. CP-DryJ2 Fr. Epodes.

Epode: "Not to know vice at all, and keep[e] true state." Ben Jonson. CP-JonsB; SP-JonsB

Epodes. Horace.
　　Epode 2: "How happy in his low degree." CP-DryJ2
　　Praises of a Country Life, The. CP-JonsB; SP-JonsB, tr. by Ben Jonson
　　Translation of Horace "Epode the 2d" ("Beatus Ille"). CP-JohnS
　　Translation of Horace: Epode xi. CP-JohnS

Epona. Paul Muldoon. CP-MuldP

Eppie McNab. Robert Burns. CP-BurnR

Epps. Robert Browning. CP-BroR2

Epstein, Spare That Yule Log! Ogden Nash. CP-NashO

Equal to Jove that youth must be. Catullus. See Godlike the man who

Equal Troth. Dante Gabriel Rossetti. CW-RossD Fr. House of Life, The.

Equalizer, An. Robert Frost. CP FrosR

Equally dismal rain and sunshine. Meanwhile. Laura Riding Jackson. CP-RidiL

Equally innocent. Song: Victims of Calumny. Robert Graves. CP-GravR

Equation for Marie, An. Kenneth Rexroth. CP-RexrK

Equations of a Villanelle. Howard Nemerov. CP-NemeH

Equestrian Sestina. Donald Davie. CP-DaviDC

Equilibrists, The. John Crowe Ransom. SP-RansJ

Equinox. Mateja Matevski.
　　"This is an hour of calm, a quiet hour." CP-KizeC, tr. by Carolyn Kizer

Equinox. A. R. Ammons. CP-AmmoA

Equinox. Audre Lorde. SP-LordA

Equipment. Paul Laurence Dunbar. CP-DunbP

Equipoise: becalmed / Trees, a dome of kindness. Evening in Connecticut. Louis MacNeice. CP-MacNL

Equity—? James Whitcomb Riley. CP-RileJ

Equivalence of Gnats and Mice. Richard Eberhart. CP-EberR

Er-Heb beyond the Hills of Ao-Safai. Sacrifice of Er-Heb, The. Rudyard Kipling. CP-KiplR

Era mea / In qua terra. Ezra Pound. CP-PoEar

Erase the lines: I pray you not to love classifications. Monument. Robinson Jeffers. CP-JefR3

Eraser. Charles Simic. SP-SimiC; SP-SimiCE

Eraser, The. James Laughlin. CP-LaugJ

Erasmus. Edwin Arlington Robinson. CP-RobiE

Erasmus Wilson. James Whitcomb Riley. CP-RileJ

Erasure. Marge Piercy. SP-PierM

Erat Hora. Ezra Pound. CP-PoEar; SP-PounE

Erato popped in. What a talent for suspicion! Apology for Not Invoking the Muse, An. John Ciardi. CP-CiarJ

Ere cherries ripe, and strawberries be gone. New Cry, The. Ben Jonson. CP-JonsB; SP-JonsB

Ere down yon blue Carpathian hills. Knight of St. John, The. John Greenleaf Whittier. CP-WhitJ

Ere elfish Night shall sift another day. Sonnet: "Ere elfish Night shall sift another day." Hart Crane. CP-CranH

Ere I goe hence and bee noe more. Mr. Hericke his Daughter's Dowrye. Robert Herrick. CP-HerrR

Ere I Went Mad. James Whitcomb Riley. CP-RileJ

Ere Mor the Peacock flutters, ere the Monkey People cry. Song of the Little Hunter, The. Rudyard Kipling. CP-KiplR Fr. Second Jungle Book, The.

Ere on my bed my limbs I lay. Pains of Sleep, The. Samuel Taylor Coleridge. CP-ColeS; MW-ColeS

Ere on my bed my limbs I lay. Child's Evening Prayer, A. Samuel Taylor Coleridge. CP-ColeS

Ere Sin could blight or Sorrow fade. Epitaph on an Infant. Samuel Taylor Coleridge. CP-ColeS; MW-ColeS

Ere Sleep Comes Down to Soothe the Weary Eyes. Paul Laurence Dunbar. CP-DunbP

Ere stopping or turning, to put forth a hande. Four Points, The. Rudyard Kipling. CP-KiplR Fr. Muse among the Motors, The.

Ere the birth of my life, if I wished it or no. Suicide's Argument, The. Samuel Taylor Coleridge. CP-ColeS

Ere the Brothers through the gateway. Horn of Egremont Castle, The. William Wordsworth. CP-WorW1

Ere the cock has crowed. Forsaken Girl, The. Eduard Friedrich Mörike. CP-JarrR, tr. by Randall Jarrell

Ere the daughter of Brunswick is cold in her grave. Irish Avatar, The. Lord Byron. CP-Byron

Ere the mother's milk had dried. Totem, The. Rudyard Kipling. CP-KiplR

Ere the steamer bore him Eastward, Sleary was engaged to marry. Post That Fitted, The. Rudyard Kipling. CP-KiplR

Ere we had reached the wished-for place, night fell. William Wordsworth. See Dark and more dark the shades of evening fell

Ere-while of Musick, and Ethereal mirth. Passion, The. John Milton. CP-MiltJ

Ere with Cold Beads of Midnight Dew. William Wordsworth. CP-WorW2

Ere yet the morn its lovely blushes spread. On the Death of the Rev. Dr. Sewell. 1769. Phillis Wheatley. CP-WheaP

E're [or E'r or E'er] yet the morning heav'd its Orient head. Phillis Wheatley. See Ere yet the morn its lovely blushes spread

Erect, meticulous within the mirror. Mirror, The. Robert Penn Warren. CP-WarrR

Erect was the old Hellenistic head. When Life Begins. Robert Penn Warren. CP-WarrR

Erecting beyond the boundaries of all government. Robert Duncan. SP-DuncR Fr. Structure of Rime, The.

Eric—we used to call him Eric. Men of Sheepshead, The. George Oppen. CP-OppGN

Erica is eight, a factory of will. Look at Me! Look at Me! William Meredith. SP-MereW

Erige Cor Tuum ad Me in Caelum. "H. D." CP-DoolH

Erinna to Sappho. James Wright. CP-WrigJ

Erinnyes. D. H. Lawrence. CP-LawrD

Erishkigal, Ishtar's fresh sister sky. Pitch Lake. Josephine Jacobsen. CP-JacoJ

Ermine, The. James Laughlin. CP-LaugJ

Eroica. Allen Ginsberg. CP-GinsA

Eros. Rainer Maria Rilke. CP-RilkFr, tr. by A. Poulin, Jr. Fr. Orchards.

Eros. Olga Broumas. SP-BrouO

Eros. Robert Creeley. CP-CreeR

Eros. "H. D." CP-DoolH

Eros. Ralph Waldo Emerson. CP-EmerR

Eros. Denise Levertov. SP-LeveDP

Eros. George Oppen. CP-OppGN

Eros. James Whitcomb Riley. CP-RileJ

Eros aei lalethros hetairos. Samuel Taylor Coleridge. CP-ColeS

Eros as Archaeologist. James Laughlin. CP-LaugJ

Eros at Temple Stream. Denise Levertov. SP-LeveDP; SP-LeveDS

Eros to Howard Nemerov. Mona Van Duyn. SP-VanDM

Eros Turannos. Edwin Arlington Robinson. CP-RobiE

Eros with a Cane. Federico García Lorca.
　　Fright in the Dining Room. CP-GarcF, tr. by Alan S. Trueblood
　　In Málaga. CP-GarcF, tr. by Alan S. Trueblood
　　Interior ("I want to be neither a poet"). CP-GarcF, tr. by Alan S. Trueblood
　　Lucía Martínez. CP-GarcF, tr. by Alan S. Trueblood
　　Nu. CP-GarcF, tr. by Alan S. Trueblood
　　Serenade: "Down on the riverbanks." CP-GarcF, tr. by Alan S. Trueblood
　　Unmarried Woman at Mass, The. CP-GarcF, tr. by Alan S. Trueblood

Erotic. D. H. Lawrence. CP-LawrD

Erotic Epigrams. John Updike. CP-UpdiJ

Erotic Philosophers, The. Carolyn Kizer. CP-KizeC Fr. Pro Femina.

Erotic sleep, after the act of love. Sweaty bedsheets. Carnal Word. Yannis Ritsos. SP-RitsY, tr. by Kimon Friar

Erotica. Robert Creeley. SP-CreeR

Err shall they not, who resolute explore. Translations from the *Medea* of Euripides. Euripides. CP-JohnS *Fr.* Medea.

Errand, The. Seamus Heaney. SP-HeanSO

Errand, The. Anne Sexton. CP-SextA

Errand Boy 1, The. David Ignatow. SP-IgnaD

Errant Mole and the Loveliest of Hawks, The. Robert Stock. SP-StocR

Errat adhuc vitreus per prata virentia rivus. In Rivum a Mola Stoana Lichfeldiæ Diffluentem. Samuel Johnson. CP-JohnS

Errata. Paul Muldoon. CP-MuldP

Errata. Charles Simic. SP-SimiC; SP-SimiCE

Error, An. Ambrose Bierce. SP-BierA

Error, The. Ted Hughes. SP-HughTN

Error, disease, snow, sudden weather. Cornfield, The. Muriel Rukeyser. CP-RukeM

Error Pursued. Helen Pinkerton. CP-PinkH

Errors. John Ashbery. SP-AshbJ

Errors of a Wise Man make your Rule, The. William Blake. CP-BlakW

Eruptive lightnings flutter to and fro. Summer Silence. E. E. Cummings. CP-CummE

Es War Einmal. Stevie Smith. CP-SmitS

Es war einmal . . . No, it's too heavy. Märchenbilder. John Ashbery. SP-AshbJ

Escalator. Adam Zagajewski. SP-ZagaA, *tr. by* Clare Cavanagh

Escape. D. H. Lawrence. CP-LawrD

Escape, The. Charles Bukowski. SP-BukC1

Escape, The. G. K. Chesterton. CP-ChesG

Escape, The. James Dickey. CP-DickJ

Escape, The. Ivor Gurney. SP-GurnI

Escape, The. James Laughlin. CP-LaugJ

Escape, The. Gabriela Mistral. SP-MistG, *tr. by* Maria Giachetti [*or* Jacketti]

Escape from the black widow spider. Escape, The. Charles Bukowski. SP-BukC1

Escape in Ice. Josephine Jacobsen. CP-JacoJ

Escape is such a thankful Word. Emily Dickinson. CP-DickE

Escape me? / Never. Life in a Love. Robert Browning. CP-BroR1

Escape to the Mountain. Christina Georgina Rossetti. CP-RosC2

Escaping backward to perceive. Emily Dickinson. CP-DickE

Escaping from allegories / in the misty east, where inherited events. Migration: C.P.R. Margaret Atwood. SP-AtwM1

Escaping through a hole I've peered in time. Taking Stock of Lot. Robert Stock. SP-StocR

Escapist—Never. Robert Frost. CP-FrosR

Escorial, The. Gerard Manley Hopkins. SP-HopkG

Eskimo Song. G. K. Chesterton. CP-ChesG

Eskimos in Manitoba. Recital. John Updike. CP-UpdiJ

Especially forlorn human specimen, An. Dimly Outlined by a Police Artist. Charles Simic. SP-SimiC *Fr.* Rosalia.

Especially the fallen tree. Snow Log. A. R. Ammons. CP-AmmoA

Especially When the October Wind. Dylan Thomas. CP-ThomD

Esplumeoir. Hugh MacDiarmid.

"But shairly, shairly, there maun be." SP-MacDH

Esprit D'Escalier. Adam Zagajewski. SP-ZagaA, *tr. by* Renata Gorczynski

Esquimos Have No Word for "War," The. Mary Oliver. SP-OlivM

Essay. Hayden Carruth. CP-CarHS

Essay on Chess. Karl Shapiro. SP-ShapK

Essay on Criticism, An. Alexander Pope. CP-PopeA

Essay on Criticism, An. Mona Van Duyn. SP-VanDM

Essay on Death. Hayden Carruth. CP-CarHS

Essay on Love. Hayden Carruth. CP-CarHS

Essay on Man, An. Alexander Pope. CP-PopeA
   Character of Marlborough, A. CP-PopeA

Essay on Marriage. Hayden Carruth. CP-CarHS

Essay on Poetics. A. R. Ammons. CP-AmmoA

Essay on Psychiatrists. Robert Pinsky. CP-PinsR

Essay on Stone. Hayden Carruth. CP-CarHS

Essay on Style. Frank O'Hara. SP-OharF

Essay on the Human Will, An. Randall Jarrell. CP-JarrR

Esse. Czeslaw Milosz. CP-MiloC; CP-MiloCN, *tr. by* Robert Pinsky

Essential Beauty. Philip Larkin. CP-LarkP

Essential oils—are wrung. Emily Dickinson. CP-DickE

Essential poem at the center [*or* centre] of things, The. Primitive like an Orb, A. Wallace Stevens. CP-StevW; CP-StevWP

Essential Resources. Adrienne Rich. SP-RicA2

Essential tears wash green. My Little Lovebirds. Arthur Rímbaud. CP-RimbA, *tr. by* Martin Sorrell

Essex. Donald Davie. CP-DaviDC

Establishment is shocked. Stir no adventure. Edna St. Vincent Millay. CP-MillE

Estais Muertos. César Vallejo. CP-MertT

Esteem. Yannis Ritsos. SP-RitsY, *tr. by* Kostas Myrsiades

Esterina, twenty's out for you. Falsetto. Eugenio Montale. CP-MontE, *tr. by* Jonathan Galassi

Esther's Tomcat. Ted Hughes. SP-HughTN

Esthetic Theories: Art as Expression. Randall Jarrell. CP-JarrR

Esthetics of Circumcision, The. Alan Dugan. CP-DugaA

Esthétique du Mal. Wallace Stevens. CP-StevW; CP-StevWP

Estimable sophist, now that you are departing from Syria. Sophist Departing from Syria. Constantine P. Cavafy. CP-CavaC, *tr. by* Theoharis Constantine Theoharis

Estivation means passing the summer in a torpid condition, which is why I love to estivate. I Always Say There's No Place Like New York in the Summer, or, That Cottage Small by a Waterfall Was Snapped Up Last February. Ogden Nash. CP-NashO

Estranged. Walter De la Mare. CP-DeLaW

Estranged from Beauty, none can be. Emily Dickinson. CP-DickE

Estranged in site. Parthenon, The. Herman Melville. SP-MelvH

Estrangement. Jane Cooper. CP-CoopJ

Estuary, The. W. S. Merwin. SP-MerwWF

Et Dona Ferentes. Rudyard Kipling. CP-KiplR

Et Faim Sallir les Loups des Boys. Ezra Pound. CP-PoEar

Et in Arcadia Ego. W. H. Auden. CP-AudeW

Et là être là encore là. Mort de A.D. Samuel Beckett. CP-BeckS

Et miser atque vorax optat sibi Nerva podagram. In Nervam. Thomas Campion. CP-CampT

Et pour Eux Seuls, les Paradis Chantent Encore. Kenneth Rexroth. CP-RexrK

Etched away by the. Paul Celan. SP-CelaP, *tr. by* John Felstiner

Eternal Child, The. Kathleen Jessie Raine. SP-RainK

Eternal City. Hayden Carruth. CP-CarHS

Eternal City, The. A. R. Ammons. CP-AmmoA

Eternal Dice, The. César Vallejo. CP-WrigJ

Eternal God, (for whom who ever [*or* whoever] dare). Upon the Translation of the Psalms by Sir Philip Sidney, and the Countess of Pembroke His Sister. John Donne. CP-DonnJ; MW-DonnJ

Eternal Goodness, The. John Greenleaf Whittier. CP-WhitJ

Eternal Heart, The. G. K. Chesterton. CP-ChesG

Eternal Life. Jones Very. CP-VeryJ

Eternal mystery of oars, The. Yehuda Amichai. SP-AmicYL, *tr. by* Benjamin Harshav *and* Barbara Harshav

Eternal Spirit of the chainless Mind! Prisoner of Chillon, The. Lord Byron. CP-Byron

Eternal Vernal, or, In All My Dreams My Fair Face Beams, The. Ogden Nash. CP-NashO

Eternal Watcher, who doth wake, The. Fayzi. CP-EmerR

Eternal Window, An. Yehuda Amichai. SP-AmicY, *tr. by* Chana Bloch

Eternal Writing, Isaac Luris maintains, The. To Manuel Mujica Lainez. Jorge Luis Borges. SP-BorgJ, *tr. by* Eric McHenry

Eternally given. Seek / The flowers of the. To Be Holy, Be Wholly Your Own. Kenneth Patchen. CP-PatcK

Eternities. G. K. Chesterton. CP-ChesG

Eternity. Constantine P. Cavafy. CP-CavaC, *tr. by* Theoharis Constantine Theoharis

Eternity. Hart Crane. CP-CranH

Eternity. Emily Dickinson. CP-DickE

Eternity. James Whitcomb Riley. CP-RileJ

Eternity. William Carlos Williams. CP-WilW2

Eternity, An. Archibald MacLeish. CP-MacLA

Eternity, An. William Carlos Williams. CP-WilW2

Eternity Blues. Hayden Carruth. CP-CarHS

Eternity is passion, girl or boy. Whence Had They Come? William Butler Yeats. CP-YeatW

Eternity may imitate. Emily Dickinson. SP-DickE

Eternity of Love Protested. Thomas Carew. CP-CareT

Eternity [*or* Eternitie]. Robert Herrick. CP-HerrR

Etesian Winds. Yannis Ritsos. SP-RitsY, *tr. by* Kimon Friar

Ethereal clouds. To the Clouds. Gabriela Mistral. SP-MistG, *tr. by* Maria Giachetti [*or* Jacketti]

Ethereal minstrel! pilgrim of the sky! To a Skylark. William Wordsworth. CP-WorW2

Etherealizing. Robert Frost. CP-FrosR

Ethics. C. K. Williams. SP-WillC

Ethiopia / Lift your night-dark face. Call of Ethiopia. Langston Hughes. CP-HughL; CP-HughL1

Ethiopia Saluting the Colors. Walt Whitman. CP-WhitW

Ethnic Jammies. Andrei Codrescu. SP-CodrA

Ethnobotany. Gary Snyder. CP-SnydG

Ethography. Yannis Ritsos. SP-RitsY, *tr. by* Kostas Myrsiades

Etienne de la Boéce. Ralph Waldo Emerson. CP-EmerR

Être là sans mâchoires sans dents. Samuel Beckett. CP-BeckS

Etruria Vale. Charles Tomlinson. CP-TomlC

Études de Plusiers Paysages de l'Âme. Hayden Carruth. CP-CarHS

Etymology. Olga Broumas. SP-BrouO

Eucharist, The. Robert Herrick. CP-HerrR

Euclia's Hymn. Ben Jonson. CP-JonsB *Fr.* Love's Triumph through Callipolis.

Euclid. Nicholas Vachel Lindsay. CP-LindV *Fr.* Poems about the Moon.

Euclid Alone Has Looked on Beauty Bare. Edna St. Vincent Millay. CP-MillE

Euclid, alone, who looked in beauty's heart. Cantor's Theorem: In an Infinite Class the Whole Is No Greater Than Some of Its Parts. James Vincent Cunningham. CP-CunnJ

Euclid Avenue. Hart Crane. CP-CranH

Euclid Avenue. Charles Simic. SP-SimiC; SP-SimiCE

Eudaimon. Kathleen Jessie Raine. SP-RainK

Eugene Field. James Whitcomb Riley. CP-RileJ

Eugenio Montale in California. Andrei Codrescu. SP-CodrA

Euglena. Miller Williams. CP-WillM

Eulalie—A Song. Edgar Allan Poe. CP-PoeEd

Eulenspiegelei. Stevie Smith. CP-SmitS

Eulogy to a Hell of a Dame—. Charles Bukowski. SP-BukC3

Eunice. Thomas Hardy. CP-HardT

Eunuch and the unicorn, The. Primrose Bed, The. Robert Graves. CP-GravR

Eunuch is a silly fat, The. Still Life I. Howard Nemerov. CP-NemeH

Eupheme. Ben Jonson. CP-JonsB

Euphoria. Lawrence Ferlinghetti. SP-FerlL

Euphrasy, Walter De la Mare. CP-DeLaW

Europa. Derek Walcott. CP-WalcD

Europa, / your red-haired. For the West. Gary Snyder. CP-SnydG

Europe. Howard Nemerov. CP-NemeH

Europe; A Prophecy. William Blake. CP-BlakW

Europe already sleeps beneath a coarse plaid of borders. Houston, 6 P.M. Adam Zagajewski. SP-ZagaA, *tr. by* Clare Cavanagh

Europe and America. David Ignatow. SP-IgnaD

Europe! Europe! Allen Ginsberg. CP-GinsA

Europe goes to sleep; in Lisbon aging. Adam Zagajewski. SP-ZagaA, *tr. by* Clare Cavanagh

Europe has run its course, and whether to fall by its own sickness or ours. Invasion. Robinson Jeffers. CP-JefR3

Europe in Winter. Adam Zagajewski. SP-ZagaA, *tr. by* Clare Cavanagh

Europe, Late. Dan Pagis. SP-PagiD, *tr. by* Stephen Mitchell

Europe 1953. For Ethel Rosenberg. Adrienne Rich. SP-RicA1; SP-RicA2

Europe, the 72d and 73d Year of These States. Walt Whitman. CP-WhitW

European Travel / (Nazi New Order). Lorine Niedecker. CP-NiedL

European Trib. boy's face photo'd eyes opened. Elegy Che Guevara. Allen Ginsberg. CP-GinsA

Europeans, The. Robert Creeley. CP-CreeR

Euryálos' improper words wrongfully enraged Odysseus. Gradations. Yannis Ritsos. SP-RitsY, *tr. by* Kimon Friar

Euryclea's Tale. Adrienne Rich. CP-RicAE

Eurydice. "H. D." CP-DoolH

Eurydice. Margaret Atwood. SP-AtwM2

Eurydice. Robert Graves. CP-GravR

Eurydice. Raissa Maritain. CP-MertT

Eurydice. John Updike. CP-UpdiJ

"Eurydice," he called. Hurriedly he descended the stairs. Descent. Yannis Ritsos. SP-RitsY, *tr. by* Kostas Myrsiades

Eurydice—it concerned thee, O Lord, The. Loss of the Eurydice, The. Gerard Manley Hopkins. CP-HopkG

Eurydice to Orpheus. Robert Browning. CP-BroR1

Euthanasia. Lord Byron. CP-Byron

Euthanasia. Allen Tate. CP-TateA

Ev erythingex Cept: / that / 's what she's. E. E. Cummings. CP-CummE

Eva. Christina Georgina Rossetti. CP-RosC3

Eva. John Greenleaf Whittier. CP-WhitJ

Evadne. "H. D." CP-DoolH

Evagene Baker. James Whitcomb Riley. CP-RileJ

Evaluation. Yannis Ritsos. SP-RitsY, *tr. by* Kimon Friar

Evaluation of an Unwritten Poem. Wisława Szymborska. SP-SzymW, *tr. by* Stanisław Barańczak *and* Clare Cavanagh

Evaluation Under a Pine Tree, Lying On Pine Needles, An. Richard Eberhart. CP-EberR

Evangelie, or, The Figure of Literary Corruption, Seeking Glory Not Truth. Stevie Smith. CP-SmitS

Evangeline, a Tale of Acadie. Henry Wadsworth Longfellow. SP-LongH

Evangelist, The. Donald Davie. CP-DaviDC

Evangelists, The. Robert Stock. SP-StocR

Evangelist's Wife, An. Edwin Arlington Robinson. CP-RobiE

Evarra and His Gods. Rudyard Kipling. CP-KiplR

Evasive souls, of whom the wise lose track. Imaginative Life, The. Geoffrey Hill. CP-HillG

Eve. Jane Cooper. CP-CoopJ

Eve. D. H. Lawrence. CP-LawrD

Eve. Howard Nemerov. CP-NemeH

Eve. Christina Georgina Rossetti. CP-RosC1

Eve. William Carlos Williams. CP-WilW1

Eve & her envy roving slammed me down. Gislebertus' Eve. John Berryman. CP-BerrJ

Eve is a twofold mystery. Poet's Vow, The. Elizabeth Barrett Browning. CP-BroEB

Eve of Battle, The. Raymond Carver. CP-CarvR

Eve of Election, The. John Greenleaf Whittier. CP-WhitJ

Eve of Rosh Hashanah. At the house that's being built, The. Yehuda Amichai. SP-AmicY, *tr. by* Chana Bloch

Eve of St Agnes, The. John Keats. CP-KeatJ

Eve of St. Agony, or the Middle Class Was Sitting on Its Fat. Kenneth Patchen. CP-PatcK

Eve of St. Mark, The. John Keats. CP-KeatJ

Eve of Waterloo, The. Thomas Hardy. CP-HardT *Fr.* Dynasts, The.

Eve roved in Paradise, I've heard. Ralph Waldo Emerson. CP-EmerR

Eve Thinking. Lucille Clifton. SP-ClifL

Evelyn G of Christminster. Thomas Hardy. CP-HardT

Evelyn Hope. Robert Browning. CP-BroR1

Even. A. R. Ammons. CP-AmmoA

Even a Dawn too numb. Homage: "Even a Dawn too numb." Stéphane Mallarmé. CP-MallS, *tr. by* Henry Weinfield

Even a pencil has fear to. E. E. Cummings. CP-CummE

Even a thing like this takes pathos. Old Warplane, An. Howard Nemerov. CP-NemeH

Even after his death he did not return. Dante. Anna Andreyevna Akhmatova. CP-KunSC, *tr. by* Max Hayward *and* Stanley Kunitz

Even after the letters, there is work. Juanita Tinsley. Muriel Rukeyser. CP-RukeM

Even as a child, of sorrow that we give. Pride of Youth. Dante Gabriel Rossetti. CW-RossD *Fr.* House of Life, The.

Even as a child that weeps. Young Girl, The. Niccolò Tommaseo. CW-RossD, *tr. by* Dante Gabriel Rossetti

Even as a child to whom sad neighbors speak. James Whitcomb Riley. CP-RileJ

Even as a dragon's eye that feels the stress. William Wordsworth. CP-WorW1

Even as children they were late sleepers. Undead, The. Richard Wilbur. CP-WilbR

Even as I dream of home again. Poem Recalled, A. Theodore Weiss. SP-WeisT

Even as I Hold You. Alice Walker. SP-WalkA

Even as I rage, I see my daughter. My Father's Voice. Gregory Orr. SP-OrrG

Even as it thrills. Valaisian Sky. Rainer Maria Rilke. CP-RilkFr, *tr. by* A. Poulin, Jr. *Fr.* Valaisian Quatrains, The.

Even as lame things thirst their perfection, so. To Mr E. G. John Donne. CP-DonnJ; MW-DonnJ

Even as the last bars clang. Solitary Confinement. Gregory Orr. SP-OrrG

Even as the moon grows queenlier in mid-space. Gracious Moonlight. Dante Gabriel Rossetti. CW-RossD *Fr.* House of Life, The.

Even as we speak, there's a smoker's cough. Cows. Paul Muldoon. CP-MuldP

Even as when you behold hot swarms of the tribes of the wild bees. Assembly of the Achaians. Homer. CP-MerG2 *Fr.* Iliad, The.

Even as you are dying, a part of the world. You Don't Know the End. William Stafford. SP-StafWW

Even as you went over, Nietzche. Giant Yea, The. Theodore Weiss. SP-WeisT

Even at night the air rang and rang. Boccaccio: The Plague Years. Rita Dove. SP-DoveR

Even at night, the objects kept vigil. Morandi. Adam Zagajewski. SP-ZagaA, *tr. by* Renata Gorczynski, Benjamin Ivry *and* C. K. Williams

Even at sea the bodies of the unborn and the dead. Changes, The. Robert Pinsky. CP-PinsR

Even before his book came out. Ars Poetica. Howard Nemerov. CP-NemeH

Even culture / ought to. Whole World, The. Charles Olson. CP-OlsoC

Even Egrets Err. John Updike. CP-UpdiJ

Even from the train the hill looked empty. Story, A. Randall Jarrell. CP-JarrR

Even here, in a forest in the foothills of a range of mountains, lucent air, the purest dawn. Insult, The. C. K. Williams. SP-WillC

Even I can't help but notice, my sweet. Throwback, The. Paul Muldoon. CP-MuldP

Even if a man has been. On Visiting a Veterans Hospital. Alan Dugan. CP-DugaA

Even if all desires things moments be. E. E. Cummings. CP-CummE

Even If I Could. C. K. Williams. CP-WillC; SP-WillC

Even if it keeps you up all night. Advice to Writers. Billy Collins. SP-CollB

Even if love convey. Louis Zukofsky. CP-ZukLS

Even if there had been a crescent moon. Two Letters. Wallace Stevens. CP-StevWP

Even if we knew the children were all asleep. Poetry: III. Adrienne Rich. SP-RicA1

Even if you are relatively young—say. Blessèd Accident. Robert Penn Warren. CP-WarrR

Even in a country you know by heart. Traveling at Home. Wendell Berry. CP-BerrW

Even in bed I pose: desire may grow. Carnal Knowledge. Thom Gunn. CP-GunnT

Even in childhood. Liadan and Curithir. Robert Graves. CP-GravR

Even in death they prosper; even in the death. Necropolis. Karl Shapiro. SP-ShapK

Even in mild Devon, that spring, the lung. Teignmouth. Amy Clampitt. CP-ClamA

Even in spring, even in first. April in November. Archibald MacLeish. CP-MacLA

Even in the cave of the night when you. Waking at 3 A.M.. William Stafford. SP-StafWW

Even In The Grave. Walter De la Mare. CP-DeLaW

Even in the middle of the night. Habits. W. S. Merwin. SP-MerwW

Even in the moment of our earliest kiss. Edna St. Vincent Millay. CP-MillE

Even in the pink crib. One-Eye, Two-Eyes, Three-Eyes. Anne Sexton. CP-SextA; SP-SextA

Even in the time when as yet. Wanderer, The: A Rococo Study. William Carlos Williams. CP-WilW1

Even iron can put forth. Almond Blossom. D. H. Lawrence. CP-LawrD

Even love must pass through loneliness. Setting Out. Wendell Berry. CP-BerrW

Even my loves are measured by the wars. Yehuda Amichai. SP-AmicYL Fr. Poems of the Land of Zion and Jerusalem.

Even my loves are measured by wars. Yehuda Amichai. SP-AmicY, tr. by Chana Bloch Fr. Songs of Zion the Beautiful.

Even now in my hands the feel of the shovel comes back. Life Work. William Stafford. SP-StafWW

Even now there are places where a thought might grow. Disused Shed in Co. Wexford, A. Derek Mahon. CP-MahoD

Even now this landscape is assembling. All Hallows. Louise Glück. SP-GlucL

Even Now You Are Leaving. Tess Gallagher. SP-GallT

Even Numbers. Carl Sandburg. CP-SandC

Even on Easter Sunday. Easter in Pittsburgh. James Laughlin. CP-LaugJ

Even on mountainsides. Saxifrage. Robert Stock. SP-StocR

Even on the quietest days the distant. Ford Manor. Derek Mahon. CP-MahoD

Even Sea, The. May Swenson. SP-SwenM

Even she too dead! all languor on her brow. Imogen. Walter De la Mare. CP-DeLaW

Even sleeping you astonish me. Russia. Aleksandr Aleksandrovich Blok. SP-BlokA, tr. by Peter France and Jon Stallworthy

Even So. Dante Gabriel Rossetti. CW-RossD

Even so—as a man at the end tries no more. Wreck of the Swan, The. Hugh MacDiarmid. SP-MacDH

Even so bewails, the poplar groves among. Virgil. CP-WorW2, tr. by William Wordsworth Fr. Georgics.

Even so distant, I can taste the grief. Deceptions. Philip Larkin. CP-LarkP

Even so for me a Vision sanctified. November, 1836. William Wordsworth. CP-WorW2; MW-WorW

Even so it was. From Flodden ridge. English Advance at Flodden, The. Sir Walter Scott. SP-ScotW Fr. Marmion.

Even so, let us bring all that feeds. Rainer Maria Rilke. CP-RilkFr, tr. by A. Poulin, Jr. Fr. Valaisian Quatrains, The.

Even such is Time, which takes in trust. Authours Epitaph, Made by Himself, The. Sir Walter Ralegh. CP-RaleW

Even sunlight dares. Prisoner. Maya Angelou. SP-AngeM

Even the barnacle has certain rights. This Octopus Exploits Women. James Fenton. SP-FentJ

Even the beauty of the rose doth cast. Shadow. Walter De la Mare. CP-DeLaW

Even the bravest that are slain. Trial by Existence, The. Robert Frost. CP-FrosR

Even the dignity of Christ. Red Branch, The. Donald Hall. CP-HallD

Even the flaws were good. At the Fair. William Stafford. SP-StafWW

Even the liveliest of us had. Another and Another and. Theodore Weiss. SP-WeisT

Even the mountaineer came back. Bell-Ringer, The. Pablo Neruda. SP-NeruP

Even the old emotions are finished. Dies Irae. D. H. Lawrence. CP-LawrD

Even the old priest, in his long black robe and silvery hair. At the Bank in Spain. D. H. Lawrence. CP-LawrD

Even the rainbow has a body. Rainbow, The. D. H. Lawrence. CP-LawrD

Even the raven belongs to the songbird family. In an Empty Room. Jaroslav Seifert. SP-SeifJ, tr. by Ewald Osers

Even the shrewd and bitter. Prologue to "Rhymes to be Traded for Bread" Nicholas Vachel Lindsay. CP-LindV

Even the sun-clouds this morning cannot manage such skirts. Poppies in October. Sylvia Plath. CP-PlatS

Even the walls are flowing, even the ceiling. Variation on Heraclitus. Louis MacNeice. CP-MacNL

Even these stones I placed crudely once. Little Fire in the Woods, The. Hayden Carruth. CP-CarHS

Even they that have no murdrous will. Sir Walter Ralegh. CP-RaleW

Even though the house is deeply silent. Insomnia. Billy Collins. SP-CollB

Even to think / of installing an air-conditioner. Song: Luxury. Hayden Carruth. CP-CarHS

Even today, in this melancholy physicality. Plan of Future Works. Pier Paolo Pasolini. SP-PasoP, tr. by Norman MacAfee and Luciano Martinengo

Even two weeks after her fall. Death in Mexico. Denise Levertov. SP-LeveDL

Even unto the End of the World. G. K. Chesterton. CP-ChesG

Even water, infused with lilies-of-the-valley. Window on Birds' Wings. Jaroslav Seifert. SP-SeifJ, tr. by Ewald Osers

Even when death has taken. For Dudley. Richard Wilbur. CP-WilbR

Even when first her face. Someone Talking to Himself. Richard Wilbur. CP-WilbR

Even when he was a child, the Emperor. Memoirs. William Meredith. SP-MereW

Even when I thought I prayed, I was talking to myself; when I. Ghazal V. Adrienne Rich. SP-RicA2 Fr. Shooting Script.

Even when the dry wells of black honey. Beyond You. W. S. Merwin. SP-MerwW

Even when you lust, ye may refrain. Answer, The. Sir Thomas Wyatt. CP-WyatT

Even wisteria, sufficiently looked at. Everywhere That Universe. John Ciardi. CP-CiarJ

Even with its own ax to grind, sometimes. Mind, Intractable Thing, The. Marianne Craig Moore. CP-MoorM

Even you, Sweet Basil: even you. Steepletop. Edna St. Vincent Millay. CP-MillE

Evenin' Air Blues. Langston Hughes. CP-HughL; CP-HughL2

Evening. Sir Walter Scott. SP-ScotW Fr. Rokeby.

Evening. Raymond Carver. CP-CarvR

Evening. G. K. Chesterton. CP-ChesG

Evening. John Clare. SP-ClarJ

Evening. John Clare. SP-ClarJ

Evening. Robert Creeley. SP-CreeR

Evening. "H. D." CP-DoolH

Evening. Emily Dickinson. CP-DickE

Evening. Paul Laurence Dunbar. CP-DunbP

Evening. Randall Jarrell. CP-JarrR

Evening. Walter De la Mare. CP-DeLaW

Evening. Walter De la Mare. CP-DeLaW

Evening. Thomas Merton. CP-MertT

Evening. W. S. Merwin. SP-MerwW

Evening. Czeslaw Milosz. CP-MiloCN, tr. by Robert Hass

Evening. James Schuyler. CP-SchuJ

Evening. Charles Simic. SP-SimiC; SP-SimiCE

Evening. Tennessee Williams. CP-WillT

Evening. James Wright. CP-WrigJ

Evening: A Studio in Rome. Miller Williams. CP-WillM

Evening, after a Picture. Johann Christoph Friedrich von Schiller. CP-MerG2

Evening as dark as an empty pocket, An. Deep in the pocket. Inevitables. Yannis Ritsos. SP-RitsY, tr. by Andonis Decavalles

Evening at the calm. Sea Storm. Richard Eberhart. CP-EberR

Evening Bird Song. Richard Eberhart. CP-EberR

Evening came, a paw, to the gray hut by the river. Fall Journey. William Stafford. SP-StafW; SP-StafWW

Evening Choir, The. Jones Very. CP-VeryJ

Evening clouds; the lighted clock in the church in the square. News Report. Yannis Ritsos. SP-RitsY, tr. by Gwendolyn MacEwen and Nikos Tsingos

Evening come apart. Delirium. Federico García Lorca. CP-GarcF, tr. by Jerome Rothenberg Fr. Six Songs at Nightfall.

Evening comes on and the hills thicken. Boat, A. Margaret Atwood. SP-AtwM2

Evening Company, the. James Whitcomb Riley. CP-RileJ Fr. Child-World, A.

Evening Ebb. Robinson Jeffers. CP-JefR2

Evening faultless interval when, An. Sanctuary. John Berryman. CP-BerrJ

Evening folds about itself the dark, The. Evening. Randall Jarrell. CP-JarrR

Evening Harmony. Charles Baudelaire. CP-BaudC, tr. by Walter Martin

Evening has brought its. Witnesses. W. S. Merwin. SP-MerwW

Evening Hawk. Robert Penn Warren. CP-WarrR

Evening Hour. Robert Penn Warren. CP-WarrR

Evening hours of the soul. Yehuda Amichai. SP-AmicYL, tr. by Benjamin Harshav and Barbara Harshav

Evening in a Sugar Orchard. Robert Frost. CP-FrosR

Evening in Burmah. John Greenleaf Whittier. CP-WhitJ

Evening in Connecticut. Louis MacNeice. CP-MacNL

Evening in Galilee, An. Thomas Hardy. CP-HardT

Evening in the Sanitarium. Louise Bogan. CP-BogaL

Evening Indoors. Louis MacNeice. CP-MacNL

Evening is her name. Evening. Tennessee Williams. CP-WillT

Evening is lying at the horizon, donating blood, The. Yehuda Amichai. SP-AmicYL, *tr. by* Benjamin Harshav *and* Barbara Harshav

Evening is, The. Three Crepuscular Poems. Federico García Lorca. CP-GarcF, *tr. by* Jerome Rothenberg

Evening ("It's now the hour / for being sincere"). Federico García Lorca. CP-GarcF, *tr. by* Jerome Rothenberg

Evening Land, The. D. H. Lawrence. CP-LawrD

Evening like Doomsday. Sunset over Villa Ortúzar. Jorge Luis Borges. SP-BorgJ, *tr. by* W. S. Merwin

Evening Love Song. Rainer Maria Rilke. CP-RilkFr, *tr. by* A. Poulin, Jr.

Evening Lull, An. Walt Whitman. CP-WhitW

Evening Music. May Sarton. SP-SartM

Evening News, The. Audre Lorde. SP-LordA

Evening Ode, An. Samuel Johnson. CP-JohnS

Evening of the Private Eye, An. John Ciardi. CP-CiarJ

Evening of the Pyramids, The. Norman Dubie. CP-DubiN

Evening of the Visitation, The. Thomas Merton. CP-MertT

Evening on Lesbos. Edna St. Vincent Millay. CP-MillE

Evening on the Boyne. Donald Davie. CP-DaviDC

Evening Out, The. Ogden Nash. CP-NashO

Evening paper under one arm. Intermittent Light, An. Wyatt Prunty. SP-PrunW

Evening Particulier. Andrei Codrescu. SP-CodrA

Evening passes fast away, The. Self-Interrogation. Emily Jane Brontë. CP-BronE

Evening Plaza, San Miguel. Muriel Rukeyser. CP-RukeM

Evening: Ponte al Mare, Pisa. Percy Bysshe Shelley. CP-ShelP

Evening Prayer. Thomas Merton. CP-MertT

Evening Prayers. Arthur Rimbaud. CP-RimbA, *tr. by* Martin Sorrell

Evening Primrose, The. Dorothy Parker. CP-ParkD

Evening Procession. Yannis Ritsos. SP-RitsY, *tr. by* N. C. Germanacos

Evening Questions. Carl Sandburg. CP-SandC

Evening ("Rainy evening in exhausted gray"). Federico García Lorca. CP-GarcF, *tr. by* Catherine Brown

Evening Sea Wind. Carl Sandburg. CP-SandC

Evening Shadows. Thomas Hardy. CP-HardT

Evening Song. Langston Hughes. CP-HughL; CP-HughL3

Evening Star. Louise Bogan. CP-BogaL

Evening Star. Edgar Allan Poe. CP-PoeEd

Evening Star (Georgia O'Keeffe). Jane Cooper. CP-CoopJ

Evening Star, The. Randall Jarrell. CP-JarrR

Evening Star unfurling like an embryo. *Evening Star* (Georgia O'Keeffe). Jane Cooper. CP-CoopJ

Evening Stroll in the Suburbs. Mona Van Duyn. SP-VanDM

Evening sulks along the shore, the reddening sun, The. Forte Dei Marmi. D. H. Lawrence. CP-LawrD

Evening Sun, The. Emily Jane Brontë. CP-BronE

Evening sun was sinking down, The. Evening Sun, The. Emily Jane Brontë. CP-BronE

Evening Sunsets Witness and Pass On, The. Carl Sandburg. CP-SandC

Evening, the edge of the city, a whole day. Late Feast. Adam Zagajewski. SP-ZagaA, *tr. by* Renata Gorczynski, Benjamin Ivry *and* C. K. Williams

Evening Thought, An. Salvation by Christ with Penetential Cries. Jupiter Hammon. CP-WheaP

Evening ("Three looming poplars"). Federico García Lorca. CP-GarcF, *tr. by* Alan S. Trueblood *Fr.* Andalusian Songs.

Evening Thrush. Ted Hughes. SP-HughTN

Evening: To Harriet. Percy Bysshe Shelley. CP-ShelP

Evening Train. Denise Levertov. SP-LeveDS

Evening twirling. Bei Wannsee. Kenneth Rexroth. CP-RexrK

Evening Walk, An. Jones Very. CP-VeryJ

Evening Walk, An; Addressed to a Young Lady. William Wordsworth. CP-WorW1; MW-WorW

Evening Walk in France. May Sarton. SP-SartM

Evening, water in a glass, The. George Oppen. CP-OppGN

Evening Waterfall. Carl Sandburg. CP-SandC

Evening When the Full Moon Rose as the Sun Set, An. Robert Bly. SP-BlyR

Evening Wind. James Schuyler. CP-SchuJ

Evening Wind, The. Henry David Thoreau. CP-ThorH

Evening with the Master, An. Charles Simic. SP-SimiCE

Evening with the Master, An. Charles Simic. SP-SimiC

Evening without Angels. Wallace Stevens. CP-StevW; CP-StevWP

Evening: Zero Weather. Thomas Merton. CP-MertT

Evenings I hear. Plague of Starlings, A. Robert Earl Hayden. CP-HaydR

Evenings in Vermont. James Schuyler. CP-SchuJ

Evening's Love, An. John Dryden.
  Song: "You charmed [*or* charm'd] me not with that fair face." SP-DrydJ

Evenings seem endless, now. Roots. Adrienne Rich. CP-RicAE; SP-RicA2

Evenings, we call quail. Survival. William Stafford. SP-StafWW

Evensong. Olga Broumas. SP-BrouO

Evensong. John Ciardi. CP-CiarJ

Evensong. Richard Crashaw. CP-CrasR

Evensong. George Herbert. CP-HerbG

Evensong. Robert Herrick. CP-HerrR

Evensong. James Whitcomb Riley. CP-RileJ

Evensong [*or* Even-Song]. George Herbert. CP-HerbG

Event. A. R. Ammons. CP-AmmoA

Event. Sylvia Plath. CP-PlatS

Event. Charles Tomlinson. CP-TomlC; SP-TomlC

Event / a reflection. Shenandoah. Charles Olson. CP-OlsoC

Event, An. Richard Wilbur. CP-WilbR

Event at Konna, The. Kenneth Patchen. CP-PatcK

Event Itself, The. Hayden Carruth. CP-CarHS

Event of Things Not in Our Power. Robert Herrick. CP-HerrR

Event, The. Rita Dove. SP-DoveR

Event was directly behind Him, The. Emily Dickinson. CP-DickE

Events in a Rustic Mirror. George Meredith. CP-MerG2

Events proceed in different localities. Tennessee Williams. CP-WillT

Events reported by the ear. Heard and Seen. W. H. Auden. CP-AudeW

Eventual Love. Laura Riding Jackson. CP-RidiL

Eventual Proteus. Margaret Atwood. SP-AtwM1

Eventually he dies. Flaubert's Early Prose. Robert Creeley. SP-CreeR

Eventually one finds / There is no environment. Place, The. Richard Eberhart. CP-EberR

Eventually we must combine nightmares. Fuck the Astronauts. James Tate. SP-TateJ

Ever a Seeker. Carl Sandburg. CP-SandC

Ever After. Tess Gallagher. SP-GallT

Ever again to breathe pure happiness. Happiness. Wilfred Owen. CP-OwenW

Ever and ever, on and on. To a Poet on His Marriage. James Whitcomb Riley. CP-RileJ

Ever as now with Love and Virtue's glow. Fragment of a Sonnet: To Harriet. Percy Bysshe Shelley. CP-ShelP

Ever before my face there went. Vain Finding. Walter De la Mare. CP-DeLaW

Ever exulting in thyself, on fire. Humanity. Walter De la Mare. CP-DeLaW

Ever honoured Mistress mine. Tyger's Letter to Caroline 1812. James Austen. CP-AustJ

Ever I view those people dumbly. Our Cousins. Dorothy Parker. CP-ParkD

Ever invoking fire from heaven, the fire. George Meredith. CP-MerG1 *Fr.* France.

Ever let the Fancy roam. Fancy. John Keats. CP-KeatJ

Ever mine [*or* myn] hap[pe] is slack and slo[w] in coming [*or* commyng]. Petrarch. CP-WyatT

Ever musing I delight to tread. Ode to Pity. Jane Austen. CP-AustJ

Ever restless, restless, craving rest. Camoëns. Herman Melville. SP-MelvH

Ever Since. Archibald MacLeish. CP-MacLA

Ever since the abandonment of courtship. Breakfast Elegy. Andrei Codrescu. SP-CodrA

Ever since the old days. Lament of a Maiden for the Warrior's Death. Pablo Antonio Cuadra. CP-MertT

Ever since the seriously ill were sent away. Taking Down, The. Wyatt Prunty. SP-PrunW

Ever since they'd left the Tennessee ridge. Event, The. Rita Dove. SP-DoveR

Ever So. James Laughlin. CP-LaugJ

Ever that Everest. Time. James Merrill. SP-MerrJ

Ever the Rock of Ages melts. Ralph Waldo Emerson. CP-EmerR

Ever the Same. Charles Baudelaire. CP-BaudC, *tr. by* Walter Martin

Ever the same, forever new! Awaking. Stephen Spender. CP-SpenS

Ever the undiscouraged, resolute, struggling soul of man. Life. Walt Whitman. CP-WhitW

Ever / to sleep. Sea ("Ever / to sleep"). Robert Creeley. SP-CreeR

Evergreen, The. Jones Very. CP-VeryJ

Everlasting Contenders, The. Kenneth Patchen. CP-PatcK

Everlasting Flowers. D. H. Lawrence. CP-LawrD

Everlasting Gospel, The. William Blake. CP-BlakW

Everlasting layers / Of ideas, images, feelings. Hugh MacDiarmid. SP-MacDH *Fr.* Plaited Like the Generations of Men.

Everlasting Monday, The. Sylvia Plath. CP-PlatS

Everlasting universe of things, The. Mont Blanc. Percy Bysshe Shelley. CP-ShelP

Komunyakaa. CP-KomuY

Everyman. Tennessee Williams. CP-WillT

Everyone. David Ignatow. SP-IgnaD

Everyone Dies in a Light Rain. Miller Williams. CP-WillM

Everyone else says otherwise. They take me. I Was Born in Lucerne. Philip Levine. SP-LeviP

Everyone else sleeping when I step. Elk Camp. Raymond Carver. CP-CarvR

Everyone had to know something, and what they said. In Memory of Robert Frost. William Meredith. SP-MereW

Everyone has eaten and fallen asleep. The house is empty. Spring Is Christ. Jelaluddin Rumi. SP-Rumi, tr. by Coleman Barks

Everyone has only one leg. Great Infirmities. Charles Simic. SP-SimiC; SP-SimiCE

Everyone here knows how it ends, in the stone. Classical Proportions of the Heart. Eleanor Wilner. SP-WilnE

Everyone in me is a bird. In Celebration of My Uterus. Anne Sexton. CP-SextA; SP-SextA

Everyone in my tribe hates. My Tribe. John Ciardi. CP-CiarJ

Everyone looked, and, passing, revealed. 3 A.M. The Girl with the Honey Colored Hair. William Carlos Williams. CP WilW2

Everyone notices they are inseparable. Sisters, The. Josephine Jacobsen. CP-JacoJ

Everyone sitting alone with a sorrow. Grief of Cafeterias, The. John Updike. CP-UpdiJ

Everyone touch everybody's lips. It's ritual, it's important. Everyone. David Ignatow. SP-IgnaD

Everyone whacks her with tiny blows. Sweet Breakdowns of Abigail, The. Yehuda Amichai. SP AmicY, tr. by Chana Bloch

Everything. Charles Bukowski. SP-BukC2

Everything. Gregory Orr. SP-OrrG

Everything ages, wears out, becomes useless—he said. What's the Use? Yannis Ritsos. SP-RitsY, tr. by N. C. Germanacos

Everything and Nothing. Jorge Luis Borges. SP-BorgJ, tr. by Ken Krabbenhoft

Everything begins at the tip-end, the dying-out. Peak. A. R. Ammons. CP-AmmoA

Everything but confessions. My own life. Prescription. Czeslaw Milosz. CP-MiloCN, tr. by Robert Hass

Everything changes; nothing does. I am back. After the Fire. James Merrill. SP-MerrJ

Everything Comes. Thomas Hardy. CP-HardT

Everything: Eloy, Arizona, 1956. Ai. SP-Ai

Everything flows. Even a solid man. Crossings. Seamus Heaney. SP-HeanSO Fr. Squarings.

Everything goes / into the stove, a kind of detox where. Household. Heather McHugh. SP-McHuH

Everything happens a little. Rainer Maria Rilke. CP-RilkFr, tr. by A. Poulin, Jr. Fr. Orchards.

Everything has its limit, including sorrow. To Urania. Joseph Brodsky. CP-BrodJ, tr. by Joseph Brodsky

Everything here has a price. In the Commercial Gardens. Howard Nemerov. CP-NemcII

Everything here is alive, / working at something. Child of the Moon. Pablo Neruda. SP-NeruP

Everything here is real and of our joy. Muriel Rukeyser. CP-RukeM

Everything here is yellow and green. It is a Spring Afternooon. Anne Sexton. CP-SextA; SP-SextA

Everything hidden you know and explain. Shmuel HaNagid. SP-HaNaS, tr. by Peter Cole

Everything I do. Pigheaded Poet. William Carlos Williams. CP-WilW2

Everything I do is against meaning. Against Meaning. Andrei Codrescu. SP-CodrA

Everything I steal, I give away. Gift of Tongues, The. Sam Hamill. SP-HamiS

Everything in Order. Thomas McGrath. SP-McGrT

Everything is blowing, his. Jittoku, Buddhist Mystic—15th Century. Jane Cooper. CP-CoopJ

Everything Is Fine Here. How Are You? Miller Williams. CP-WillM

Everything Is Going to Be All Right. Derek Mahon. CP-MahoD

Everything is regional. Long Branch, New Jersey. Robert Pinsky. CP-PinsR

Everything Is Swimming. Stevie Smith. CP-SmitS

Everything seemed already dry and burnt at. Morning Melancholy. Rainer Maria Rilke. CP-RilkFr, tr. by A. Poulin, Jr.

Everything sounds funny in a funny magazine. Paper on Humor. Andrei Codrescu. SP-CodrA

Everything Speaks to Me. Robert Duncan. SP-DuncR Fr. Dante Études.

Everything That Acts Is Actual. Denise Levertov. SP-LeveDS

Everything that happens. Angels' Surprise. Rainer Maria Rilke. CP-RilkFr, tr. by A. Poulin, Jr.

Everything that happens is the messsage. Message from Space, A. William Stafford. SP-StafWW

Everything that has beauty has a body, and is a body. Bodiless God. D. H. Lawrence. CP-LawrD

Everything that is born must die. Christina Georgina Rossetti. CP-RosC2

Everything that lives has its own proper pride. Proper Pride. D. H. Lawrence. CP-LawrD

Everything went in the car. Egg, The. Louise Glück. SP-GlucL

Everything you/I/we do in the natural course. Tragedy-Maker, The. John Ciardi. CP-CiarJ

Everything's a fan. Rays. Federico García Lorca. CP-GarcF, tr. by Jerome Rothenberg Fr. Mirror Suite.

Everything's Haggis in HOboken, or, Scots Wha Hae Hae. Ogden Nash. CP-NashO

Everything's mine but just on loan. Travel Elegy. Wisława Szymborska. SP-SzymW, tr. by Stanislaw Barańczak and Clare Cavanagh

Everywhere he went that day he walked. Where They'd Lived. Raymond Carver. CP-CarvR

Everywhere Is Here. Robert Graves. CP-GravR

Everywhere of Silver, An. Emily Dickinson. CP-DickE

Everywhere people love their children. It's True. Grace Paley. CP-PalGC

Everywhere reality offers / the old, old man. Song: The Old, Old Man. Hayden Carruth. CP-CarHS

Everywhere, snow is falling. Your bandaged foot. For a Russian Poet. Adrienne Rich. CP-RicAE; SP-RicA2

Everywhere That Universe. John Ciardi. CP-CiarJ

Everywhere / The first bird of the year. Winter Solstice. Kathleen Jessie Raine. SP-RainK

Everywhere you are coaxing the mad. Companion, The. Marilyn Hacker. SP-HackM

Eve's version. Lucille Clifton. SP-ClifL

Evicted from sleep's mute palace. Shaker, Why Don't You Sing? Maya Angelou. SP-AngeM

Evidence. Yehuda Amichai. SP-AmicY, tr. by Chana Bloch

Evidence. Yehuda Amichai. SP-AmicYL, tr. by Benjamin Harshav and Barbara Harshav

Evidence. William Stafford. SP-StafWW

Evidence? What Evidence . . . ? Kenneth Patchen. CP-PatcK

Evil. Richard Eberhart. CP-EberR

Evil. Langston Hughes. CP-HughL; CP-HughL2

Evil. Charles Olson. CP-OlsoC

Evil. Arthur Rimbaud. CP-RimbA, tr. by Martin Sorrell

Evil days have come, the poor, The. In the Evil Days. John Greenleaf Whittier. CP-WhitJ

Evil Eye, The. John Ciardi. CP-CiarJ

Evil Eye, The. Anne Sexton. CP-SextA

Evil grigri: / taste acid in the word sybaritic. Arthur Sze. SP-SzeA

Evil is any this or this. Haecceity. James Vincent Cunningham. CP-CunnJ

Evil Is Homeless. D. H. Lawrence. CP-LawrD

Evil is such a great structure you can't surround it. Laocoön. Richard Eberhart. CP-EberR

Evil Morning. Langston Hughes. CP-HughL; CP-HughL2

Evil Seekers, The. Anne Sexton. CP-SextA

Evil Woman. Langston Hughes. CP-HughL; CP-HughL1

Evil World-Soul, The. D. H. Lawrence. CP-LawrD

Evill. Robert Herrick. CP-HerrR

Evill no Nature hath; the losse of good. Evill. Robert Herrick. CP-HerrR

Ev'n one who has little travelled in. Dreams. Walter De la Mare. CP-DeLaW

Ev'n yet his voice from Hell's dread shades we hear. Virgil. CP-JohnS Fr. Aeneid [or Eneados or Aeneis], The.

Ev'ning, now, from purple wings. Evening Ode, An. Samuel Johnson. CP-JohnS

Evolution. G. K. Chesterton. CP-ChesG

Evolution. May Swenson. SP-SwenM

Evolution. Jones Very. CP-VeryJ

Evolutionist to His Lady, The. G. K. Chesterton. CP-ChesG

Ev'ry Dame affects good fame, what ere her doings be. Thomas Campion. CP-CampT

Ewigkeit. Jorge Luis Borges. CP-WilbR, tr. by Richard Wilbur

Ex-Basketball Player. John Updike. CP-UpdiJ

Ex Libris. Eleanor Wilner. SP-WilnE

Ex Vermibus. Hugh MacDiarmid. SP-MacDH

Ex Voto. Joseph Brodsky. CP-BrodJ

Exact / second, The. Sitting in a Rocking Chair, Going Blind. Yusef Komunyakaa. CP-KomuY

Exactly at one o'clock your arms broach. Tarquin. Frank O'Hara. SP-OharF

Exactly like a rain cloud. Ever After. Tess Gallagher. SP-GallT

Exaggeration. Elizabeth Barrett Browning. CP-BroEB

Examination at the Womb-Door. Ted Hughes. SP-HughTN

Examination into Life and Death, An. Kenneth Patchen. CP-PatcK

Examination of Conscience, The. Charles Baudelaire. CP-BaudC, tr. by Walter

Martin

Examination of Psyche: Thoughts of Home. Richard Eberhart. CP-EberR

Examination of the Hero in a Time of War. Wallace Stevens. CP-StevW; CP-StevWP

Examine a big stone across the creek outside the kitchen window. Hot Springs Infernal in the Human Beast. Philip Whalen. SP-WhalP

Examine Me, I Am Continuous. David Ignatow. SP-IgnaD

Example. Czeslaw Milosz. CP-MiloCN, *tr. by* Robert Hass

Examples—for Richard Bridgeman. Charles Olson. CP-OlsoC

Examples of Created Systems. William Meredith. SP-MereW

Examples, or Like Prince, Like People. Robert Herrick. CP-HerrR

Exasperated, worn, you conjure a mansion. Desires of Men and Women. John Berryman. CP-BerrJ

Exasperations of a Novelist. Howard Nemerov. CP-NemeH

Excavation for the new, The. Dedication for a Building. Alan Dugan. CP-DugaA

Excavation of Troy. Archibald MacLeish. CP-MacLA

Excavation, The. Gregory Orr. SP-OrrG

Exceeding All. James Whitcomb Riley. CP-RileJ

Exceeding Bitter Cry, An. Christina Georgina Rossetti. CP-RosC2

Exceeding brightness of this early sun, The. Sun This March, The. Wallace Stevens. CP-StevW; CP-StevWP

Excellence is sparse. Ezra Pound in Pisa. Donald Davie. CP-DaviDC

Excellence requires / leaf-rakers to sweep one spot. Hayden Carruth. CP-CarHS *Fr.* Clay Hill Anthology, The.

Excellent herbs had our fathers of old. Our Fathers of Old. Rudyard Kipling. CP-KiplR

Excellent New Ballad, An. Jonathan Swift. CP-SwifJ

Excellent New Song, An. Jonathan Swift. CP-SwifJ

Excellent New Song on a Seditious Pamphlet, An. Jonathan Swift. CP-SwifJ

Excellent New Song upon His Grace Our Good Lord Archbishop of Dublin, An. Jonathan Swift. CP-SwifJ

Excelsior. Walt Whitman. CP-WhitW

Except. Wendell Berry. CP-BerrW

Except for the dog, that she wouldn't have him put away, wouldn't let him die, I'd have liked her. Dog, The. C. K. Williams. CP-WillC; SP-WillC

Except for the little girl. Even If I Could. C. K. Williams. CP-WillC; SP-WillC

Except for the undeniable flash of envy I feel, the reflexive competitiveness, he's inconsequential. Love: Youth. C. K. Williams. SP-WillC

Except from your inner. Rainer Maria Rilke. CP-RilkFr, *tr. by* A. Poulin, Jr. *Fr.* Roses, The.

Except in idea, perfection is as wild. Design of a House, The. Wendell Berry. CP-BerrW

Except in your / honour. E. E. Cummings. CP-CummE; SP-CummE

Except, returning, by the Marlboro. Henry David Thoreau. CP-ThorH

Except that through the wet panes. Variant on a Scrap of Conversation. Charles Tomlinson. CP-TomlC

Except the Heaven had come so near. Emily Dickinson. CP-DickE

Except the Lord build the house. Psalm 127: "Except the Lord build the house." Bible, *O.T.* SP-SmarC *Fr.* Psalms.

Except the Lord Build the House. Donald Davie. CP-DaviDC

Except the occasional auxilary horse or hound. Silent Shepherds, The. Robinson Jeffers. CP-JefR3

Except the smaller size. Emily Dickinson. CP-DickE

Except to Heaven, she is nought. Emily Dickinson. CP-DickE

Except when he enters my son. String, The. James Dickey. CP-DickJ

Except where blast-furnaces and generating-stations. Forty Years On. W. H. Auden. CP-AudeW

Exceptional / even deviant / you draw your long skirts. Heroines. Adrienne Rich. SP-RicA2

Excerpt from an Argument with Enthusiasts, Concerning Inspiration. Heather McHugh. SP-McHuH

Excerpts from a Father's Wisdom. A. K. Ramanujan. CP-RamaA

Excesse. Robert Herrick. CP-HerrR

Excesses of God, The. Robinson Jeffers. CP-JefR1

Exchange of Gifts, An. May Sarton. SP-SartM

Exchange Student Awaits the Arrival of an African Princess, An. Yusef Komunyakaa. CP-KomuY

Exchange, The. Samuel Taylor Coleridge. CP-ColeS

Exchange, The. May Swenson. SP-SwenM

Exchanges. James Dickey. CP-DickJ

Exchanges and repayments. We cheated no one. Coincidentally. Yannis Ritsos. SP-RitsY, *tr. by* John Stathatos

Exchanging gentle grips, the men retire. Imaginable Conference, An. John Updike. CP-UpdiJ

Exchanging Hats. Elizabeth Bishop. CP-BishE

Excitement of being someone else about whom. Fiction ("Excitement of being someone else about whom"). Rae Armantrout. SP-ArmaA

Exclamatioun to the Redar, Tuycheyng the Wryttyng of Vulgare and Maternall

Language, Ane. Sir David Lyndsay. SP-LyndD *Fr.* Dialog betwix Experience and ane Courteour, Ane.

Exclusiveness of such things as policemen's, The. Certain Democrat, A. A. K. Ramanujan. CP-RamaA

Excrement Poem, The. Maxine W. Kumin. SP-KumiM

Excursion Into Assonance. Dorothy Parker. CP-ParkD

Excursion: Or: O Columbus!, The. Thomas McGrath. SP-McGrT

Excursion, The. William Wordsworth. CP-WorW2

Excursion Train. D. H. Lawrence. CP-LawrD
  (Honeymoon.) CP-LawrD

Excursions, Incursions. Marge Piercy. SP-PierM

Excursus of Reassurance in Begonia Time, An. Hayden Carruth. CP-CarHS

Excuse. Alice Walker. CP-WalkA

Excuse is needless when with love sincere. To S.H. William Wordsworth. CP-WorW2

Excuse Me. Miller Williams. CP-WillM

Excuse me, but are you a superior person? Canvassing for the Election. D. H. Lawrence. CP-LawrD

Excuse, my lord, the liberty I take. Letter to Lord Byron. W. H. Auden. CP-AudeW

Excuse, The. Sir Walter Ralegh. CP-RaleW

Excuse the unromantic place. Bernardston. Clarence Major. SP-MajoC

Exeat. Stevie Smith. CP-SmitS

Execration upon Vulcan, An. Ben Jonson. CP-JonsB; SP-JonsB

Execution of Maximilian, The. Arthur Sze. SP-SzeA

Executioner, The. Ted Hughes. SP-HughTN

Executions in Moscow, The. Kenneth Patchen. CP-PatcK

Executive speed is poetry! Whereas. Savannah. Donald Davie. CP-DaviDC

Executive's Death, The. Robert Bly. SP-BlyR

Exempla. James Fenton. SP-FentJ

Exeo in a spasm. Enueg I. Samuel Beckett. CP-BeckS

Exercise. W. S. Merwin. SP-MerwW

Exercise. William Carlos Williams. CP-WilW2

Exercise, An. William Carlos Williams. CP-WilW2

Exercise, The. Thom Gunn. CP-GunnT

Exercise for Professor X, An. Wallace Stevens. CP-StevWP

Exercise No. 2. William Carlos Williams. CP-WilW2

Exercises on Themes from Life. Alice Walker. CP-WalkA

Exeter Revisited. Joseph Brodsky. CP-BrodJ

Exeunt. Richard Wilbur. CP-WilbR

Exeunt Omnes. Thomas Hardy. CP-HardT

Exeunt the Viols. Rita Dove. SP-DoveR

Exhaust your mind for profit and fame. Han-shan. CP-ColdM, *tr. by* Red Pine

Exhaustion among rocks. Mirages, The. Robert Earl Hayden. CP-HaydR

Exhibits. Yannis Ritsos. SP-RitsY, *tr. by* Kostas Myrsiades

Exhilarated flowers, and lucky grasses. Petrarch. CP-Petra, *tr. by* J. G. Nichols

Exhiliration is the Breeze. Emily Dickinson. CP-DickE

Exhiliration—is within. Emily Dickinson. CP-DickE

Exhortation. Louise Bogan. CP-BogaL

Exhortation, An. Percy Bysshe Shelley. CP-ShelP

Exile. Hart Crane. *See* Carrier Letter

Exile. Louise Glück. SP-GlucL

Exile. Donald Hall. CP-HallD

Exile. Walter De la Mare. CP-DeLaW

Exile. Robert Pinsky. CP-PinsR

Exile. Derek Walcott. CP-WalcD

Exile, An. Samuel Taylor Coleridge. CP-ColeS

Exile, The. Khvaju of Kerman. CP-EmerR

Exile, The. Walter De la Mare. CP-DeLaW

Exile (1977), The. Jorge Luis Borges. SP-BorgJ, *tr. by* Alastair Reid

Exile of Music. Muriel Rukeyser. CP-RukeM

Exiled. Edna St. Vincent Millay. CP-MillE

Exiles. Constantine P. Cavafy. CP-CavaC, *tr. by* Theoharis Constantine Theoharis

Exiles. Marilyn Hacker. SP-HackM

Exiles. Arthur Rimbaud. CP-RimbA, *tr. by* Martin Sorrell

Exiles, The. W. H. Auden. CP-AudeW

Exiles, The. Stephen Spender. CP-SpenS

Exiles, The. John Greenleaf Whittier. CP-WhitJ

Exile's Departure, The. John Greenleaf Whittier. CP-WhitJ

Exile's Journals 1. Yannis Ritsos.
  17 Novemeber 1948. SP-RitsY
  6 November 1948. SP-RitsY
  12 November 1948. SP-RitsY
  21 November 1948. SP-RitsY

Exile's Journals 2. Yannis Ritsos.

1 December 1948. SP-RitsY

7 December 1948. SP-RitsY

30 January 1949. SP-RitsY

30 November 1948. SP-RitsY

24 November 1948. SP-RitsY

27 November 1948. SP-RitsY

26 January 1949. SP-RitsY

26 November 1948. SP-RitsY

23 January 1949. SP-RitsY

Exile's Journals 3. Yannis Ritsos.

19 May 1950. SP-RitsY

1 May 1950. SP-RitsY

7 May 1950. SP-RitsY

6 May 1950. SP-RitsY

30 May 1950. SP-RitsY

24 May 1950. SP-RitsY

Exile's Letter. Li Po. SP-PounE, tr. by Ezra Pound

Exiles' Line, The. Rudyard Kipling. CP-KiplR

Exile's Return, The. Elizabeth Barrett Browning. CP-BroEB

Exile's Return, The. Robert Lowell. SP-LoweR

Exiles, the proverb says, subsist on hope. Euripides. CP-JohnS Fr. Pheonician Women, The [or Phœnissae].

Existence Before Essence. Hayden Carruth. CP-CarHS

Existences. William Stafford. SP-StafWW

Existing Pool, The. Hayden Carruth. CP-CarHS

Exit. Thomas Kinsella. CP-KinsT

Exit. Edwin Arlington Robinson. CP-RobiE

Exit a kind of unkindness exit. E. E. Cummings. CP-CummE

Exit, Pursued by a Bear. Ogden Nash. CP-NashO

Exits. Langston Hughes. CP-HughL; CP-HughL2

Exmoor. Amy Clampitt. CP-ClamA

Exodus. Carolyn Kizer. CP-KizeC

Exodus. George Oppen. CP-OppGN

Exonerated. Yannis Ritsos. SP-RitsY, tr. by Kimon Friar and Kostas Myrsiades

Exorcists, The. Anne Sexton. CP-SextA

Exotic. A. R. Ammons. CP-AmmoA

Exotic Scent. Charles Baudelaire. CP-BaudC, tr. by Walter Martin

Expanded Composition, The. Clarence Major. SP-MajoC

Expanse cannot be lost. Emily Dickinson. CP-DickE

Expanses. James Dickey. CP-DickJ

Expatiation on the Combining of Weathers at Thirty-Seventh and Indiana Where the Southern More or Less Crosses the Dog, An. Hayden Carruth. CP-CarHS

Expatriates, The. Anne Sexton. CP-SextA

Expatriates of the, The. Lost Etc. Kenneth Rexroth. CP-RexrK

Expect na, Sir, in this narration. Dedication to G**** H******* Esq. A. Robert Burns. CP-BurnR

Expect not here a curious river fine. Prologue of the Author's to a Masque at Witten, A. Sir John Suckling. CP-SuckJ

Expect Nothing. Robert Graves. CP-GravR

Expect Nothing. Alice Walker. CP-WalkA

Expect nothing. Live frugally. Expect Nothing. Alice Walker. CP-WalkA

Expect the unexpected. Greeting Card. Robert Creeley. SP-CreeR

Expectant, hushed the air. Sounds heard when the earthly ear. Forest of Arden. Marya Alexandrovna Zaturenska. SP-ZatuM

Expectant Shelters, The. Kenneth Patchen. CP-PatcK

Expectant yet relaxed, he. Hotblood on Friday. Thom Gunn. CP-GunnT

Expectantly and fearfully I sing. Hayden Carruth. CP-CarHS Fr. Bloomingdale Papers, The.

Expectation. Paul Laurence Dunbar. CP-DunbP

Expectation and Experience. Thomas Hardy. CP-HardT

Expectation—is Contentment. Emily Dickinson. CP-DickE

Expecting rain, the profile of a day. Frontispiece. John Ashbery. SP-AshbJ

Expecting Silence. Donald Davie. CP-DaviDC

Expecting to see him anytime. Between Days. Yusef Komunyakaa. CP-KomuY

Expecting your arrival tomorrow, I find myself thinking I love You. Dichtung und Wahrheit. W. H. Auden. CP-AudeW

Expedient, An—Leonardo da Vinci's—and a Query. Marianne Craig Moore. CP-MoorM

Expedition. Peter Blue Cloud. SP-BlueP

Expendability. John Ciardi. CP-CiarJ

Expendable. Langston Hughes. CP-HughL; CP-HughL3

Expenses. Alan Dugan. CP-DugaA

Expenses Exhaust. Robert Herrick. CP-HerrR

Experience. Charles Bukowski. SP-BukC2

Experience. Ralph Waldo Emerson. CP-EmerR

Experience. Dorothy Parker. CP-ParkD

Experience. C. K. Williams. SP-WillC

Experience, An. Thomas Hardy. CP-HardT

Experience bows a sweet contented face. Christina Georgina Rossetti. CP-RosC2

Experience Evoked. Richard Eberhart. CP-EberR

Experience is the Angled Road. Emily Dickinson. CP-DickE

Experience is the mistress of old age. On a Line from Bodenham's "Belvedere" James Vincent Cunningham. CP-CunnJ

Experience, like a pale musician, holds. Perplexed Music. Elizabeth Barrett Browning. CP-BroEB

Experience of Blood. James Laughlin. CP-LaugJ

Experience to Let. Ogden Nash. CP-NashO

Experienced words, dense, defined. Same Meaning, The. Yannis Ritsos. SP-RitsY, tr. by N. C. Germanacos

Experiences. Yannis Ritsos. SP-RitsY, tr. by N. C. Germanacos

Experiment. Wisława Szymborska. SP-SzymW, tr. by Stanisław Barańczak and Clare Cavanagh

Experiment escorts us last. Emily Dickinson CP-DickE

Experiment That Failed, The. John Logan. CP-LogaJ

Experiment to me. Emily Dickinson. CP-DickE

Expert, The. Rudyard Kipling. CP-KiplR

Expert coachdog when other things go slack. He Is an. Kenneth Patchen. CP-PatcK

Expiration, The. John Donne. CP-DonnJ; MW-DonnJ

Explain It, Please. Langston Hughes. CP-HughL; CP-HughL3

Explain my spirit—adding word to word. Sonnet: "Explain my spirit—adding word to word." Wallace Stevens. CP-StevWP

Explaining the Big One. William Stafford. SP-StafWW

Explanation. Wallace Stevens. CP-StevW; CP-StevWP

Explanation of America, An. Robert Pinsky. CP-PinsR

Explanation of the Grasshopper, An. Nicholas Vachel Lindsay. CP-LindV

Explanation, The. Rudyard Kipling. CP-KiplR

Explanations of Love. Carl Sandburg. CP-SandC

Explodes / From one posture to the next. The basic. Squirrel's Stance, The. George Oppen. CP-OppGN

Exploit in the Bullring. "Rubén Dario." SP-DariR, tr. by Alberto Acereda and Will Derusha

Exploits of a Machine Age. Thomas Merton. CP-MertT

Explorations. Louis MacNeice. CP-MacNL

Explorer. Josephine Jacobsen. CP-JacoJ

Explorer, The. Rudyard Kipling. CP-KiplR

Explorer on Main Street, The. Richard Eberhart. CP-EberR

Explorers. Charles Simic. SP-SimiC; SP-SimiCE

Explorers, The. Margaret Atwood. SP-AtwM1

Explorers, The. Adrienne Rich. CP-RicAE

Explorers will come, The. Explorers, The. Margaret Atwood. SP-AtwM1

Explosion. Robinson Jeffers. CP-JefR3

Explosion of a bomb, The. Perhaps. Stephen Spender. CP-SpenS

Explosion, The. Philip Larkin. CP-LarkP

Exposé. John Updike. CP-UpdiJ

Exposed Nest, The. Robert Frost. CP-FrosR

Exposed to grief too long. Reprieve and Admixture. Charles Bukowski. SP-BukC2

Exposition of the Contents of a Cab. Wallace Stevens. CP-StevWP

Expostulation. William Cowper. CP-CowpW

Expostulation. John Greenleaf Whittier. CP-WhitJ

Expostulation, An. Thomas Hardy. CP-HardT

Expostulation and Reply. William Wordsworth. CP-WorW1; MW-WorW

Expostulation, The. Sir John Suckling. CP-SuckJ

Expostulation with Inigo Jones, An. Ben Jonson. CP-JonsB; SP-JonsB

Exposure. Wilfred Owen. CP-OwenW

Exposure. Dan Pagis. SP-PagiD, tr. by Stephen Mitchell

Exposure. John Updike. CP-UpdiJ

Express, The. Stephen Spender. CP-SpenS

Expression. Thom Gunn. CP-GunnT

"Expression," he says, "does not mean to say something." Places of Refuge. Yannis Ritsos. SP-RitsY, tr. by Kimon Friar

Expressionist History of German Expressionism. Lawrence Ferlinghetti. SP-FerlL

Expressions of Sea Level. A. R. Ammons. CP-AmmoA

Expulsion from Eden grows indistinct. Emily Dickinson. SP-DickE

Exquisite / Jeremiah! Willow. Federico García Lorca. CP-GarcF, tr. by Jerome Rothenberg Fr. Shadow.

Exquisite loneliness / Bound of mine own caprice. Anima Sola. Ezra Pound. CP-PoEar

Extemporal Ode in a Sleepless Night, An. By a Lady, (Mrs. S. of New-Jersey) while Attending on Her Husband in a Long and Painful Illness. Annis Boudinot Stockton. CP-StocA

Extemporaneous Effusion on Being Appointed to the Excise, An. Robert Burns. CP-BurnR

Extempore. Robert Burns. CP-BurnR

Extempore Effusion upon the Death of James Hogg. William Wordsworth. CP-WorW2; MW-WorW

Extempore Elegy, An. Samuel Johnson. CP-JohnS

Extempore Epistle to Mr. McAdam of Craigengillian, (Wrote in Nanse Tinnock's, Mauchline) in Answer to an Obliging Letter He Sent in the Commencement of My Poetic Career. Robert Burns. CP-BurnR

Extempore, in the Court of S———. Robert Burns. CP-BurnR

Extempore—On Being Shown a Beautiful County Seat Belonging to the Same [Maxwell of Cardoness]. Robert Burns. CP-BurnR

Extempore—on Some Commemorations of Thomson. Robert Burns. CP-BurnR

Extempore [on the *Loyal Natives'* Verses]. Robert Burns. CP-BurnR

Extempore Pinned to a Lady's Coach. Robert Burns. CP-BurnR
    (Pinned to Mrs R———'s Carriage.) CP-BurnR

Extempore Reply to an Invitation. Robert Burns. CP-BurnR

Extempore—To Mr. Gavin Hamilton. Robert Burns. CP-BurnR

Extempore Verses on Dining with Lord Daer. Robert Burns. CP-BurnR

Extended Family. A. K. Ramanujan. CP-RamaA

Exterminator has arrived. He has not intruded. He was summoned, The. Blue-Eyed Exterminator, The. Josephine Jacobsen. CP-JacoJ

Extinct animals are still looking for home, The. In Autumn. W. S. Merwin. SP-MerwW

Extinct Vertebrate, An. Robinson Jeffers. CP-JefR3

Extinction. Yannis Ritsos. SP-RitsY, *tr. by* Kimon Friar *and* Kostas Myrsiades

Extirpation. Raymond Carver. CP-CarvR

Extol thee—could I? Then I will. Emily Dickinson. CP-DickE

Extra-Terrestrial Function of Spokes. Robert Stock. SP-StocR

Extract from "A New England Legend" John Greenleaf Whittier. CP-WhitJ

Extract from Memoirs. Howard Nemerov. CP-NemeH

Extract from the Conclusion of a Poem, Composed in Anticipation of Leaving School. William Wordsworth. CP-WorW1

Extracts from Addresses to the Academy of Fine Ideas. Wallace Stevens. CP-StevW; CP-StevWP

Extracts from an Opera. John Keats. CP-KeatJ

Extraordinary. A house. Tall. Surrounded by air. It stands. In the middle of a blue sky. From My Dentist's Window. Czeslaw Milosz. CP-MiloCN, *tr. by* Robert Hass

Extraordinary. Our friends. Love Uncommanded. Eleanor Wilner. SP-WilnE

Extraordinary patience of things!, The. Carmel Point. Robinson Jeffers. CP-JefR3

Extraordinary References. Wallace Stevens. CP-StevW; CP-StevWP

Extravagant Love. Wyatt Prunty. SP-PrunW

Extreme delicacy of this Easter morning, The. Easter Morning. May Sarton. SP-SartM

Extremely logical circumstances are in effect. Momentary Bafflement with Return Home at Dawn. Andrei Codrescu. SP-CodrA

Extremes. James Whitcomb Riley. CP-RileJ

Extremes and Moderations. A. R. Ammons. CP-AmmoA

Extremities. Rae Armantrout. SP-ArmaA

Extremity. Richard Eberhart. CP-EberR

Exuberance: joy to the last. Open. A. R. Ammons. CP-AmmoA

Exuding someone's Scotch in a moving mist. Birdsong of the Lesser Poet. Josephine Jacobsen. CP-JacoJ

Exultate Deo. Christina Georgina Rossetti. CP-RosC2

Exultation. Yannis Ritsos. SP-RitsY, *tr. by* Andonis Decavalles

Exultation, An. William Carlos Williams. CP-WilW2

Exultation is the going. Emily Dickinson. CP-DickE

Eye, The. Robert Creeley. CP-CreeR

Eye, The. Robert Creeley. CP-CreeR

Eye, The. Robert Herrick. CP-HerrR

Eye, The. Robert Herrick. CP-HerrR

Eye, The. Robinson Jeffers. CP-JefR3

Eye, The. Skopus. May Swenson. SP-SwenM

Eye, The. Allen Tate. CP-TateA

Eye, The. Richard Wilbur. CP-WilbR

Eye Altering Alters All, The. Allen Ginsberg. CP-GinsA

Eye and Ear, The. Jones Very. CP-VeryJ

Eye and Tooth. Robert Lowell. SP-LoweR

Eye-Beaters, The. James Dickey. CP-DickJ

Eye can hardly pick them out, The. At Grass. Philip Larkin. CP-LarkP

Eye closes, The. At Night. Josephine Jacobsen. CP-JacoJ

Eye, dark, The. Tabernacle Window. Paul Celan. SP-CelaP, *tr. by* John Felstiner

Eye-dazzlers the Indians weave. Three colors. Navajo Blanket, The. Maurice Sendak. SP-SwenM

Eye / drinks the dry orange ground. Arizona Desert. Charles Tomlinson. CP-TomlC; SP-TomlC

Eye follows, the land, The. California Prodigal. Maya Angelou. SP-AngeM

Eye Hath Not Seen. Christina Georgina Rossetti. CP-RosC3

"Eye hath not seen:"—yet man hath known and weighed. That Which Hath Been Is Named Already, and It Is Known That It Is Man. Christina Georgina Rossetti. CP-RosC2

Eye I look out of, The. Eye, The. Robert Creeley. CP-CreeR

Eye Is a Dog Howling in the Distance, The. Pablo Antonio Cuadra. CP-MertT

Eye is meant to see things, An. Someone Digging in the Ground. Jelaluddin Rumi. SP-Rumi, *tr. by* Coleman Barks

Eye is trapped in a cul-de-sac, The. Love of What Is Not, The. Eleanor Wilner. SP-WilnE

Eye-Mote, The. Sylvia Plath. CP-PlatS

Eye o' the Storm. Robert Creeley. SP-CreeR

Eye of God, the Soul's First Vision, The. Jay Wright. SP-WrigJ

Eye of Heart. Olga Broumas. SP-BrouO

Eye of looking back were well, An. Ben Jonson. CP-JonsB *Fr.* Pleasure Reconciled to Virtue.

Eye on the object, eye on the congeries. Warwickshire. Donald Davie. CP-DaviDC

Eye, Open, An. Paul Celan. SP-CelaP, *tr. by* John Felstiner

Eye remembers history by the pages of the house in flames, rolls for, An. Notes for Echo Lake 11. Michael Palmer. SP-PalmM

Eye roves / back and forth, as, The. Admission. Rae Armantrout. SP-ArmaA

Eye unacquitted by whatever it holds in allegiance, The. Didactic Piece. Louise Bogan. CP-BogaL

Eye which made this saw no pallor, The. Museum Piece. Hayden Carruth. CP-CarHS

Eye Witness. Yusef Komunyakaa. CP-KomuY

Eyeball Television. Yusef Komunyakaa. CP-KomuY

Eyeglasses, The. William Carlos Williams. CP-WilW1

Eyeing the grass for mushrooms, you will find. Mushrooms. Charles Tomlinson. CP-TomlC; SP-TomlC

Eyeing the World. Wyatt Prunty. SP-PrunW

Eyelid, shadowing, doesn't interfere, The. Michelangelo Buonarroti. CP-Miche, *tr. by* John Frederick Nims

Eyelids meet. He'll catch a little nap, The. In the Smoking-Car. Richard Wilbur. CP-WilbR

Eyelids of eve fall together at last, The. Eve of Waterloo, The. Thomas Hardy. CP-HardT *Fr.* Dynasts, The.

Eyes. Federico García Lorca. CP-GarcF, *tr. by* Jerome Rothenberg *Fr.* Mirror Suite.

Eyes. Robert Creeley. SP-CreeR

Eyes. Maxine W. Kumin. SP-KumiM

Eyes. Walter De la Mare. CP-DeLaW

Eyes. James Schuyler. CP-SchuJ

Eyes: A Fragment. Percy Bysshe Shelley. CP-ShelP

Eyes, The. Robert Herrick. CP-HerrR

Eyes, The. Tennessee Williams. CP-WillT

Eyes aloft, over dangerous places. Butterflies. Rudyard Kipling. CP-KiplR

Eyes and No-Eyes. Denise Levertov. SP-LeveDL

Eyes and Tears. Andrew Marvell. CP-MarvA

Eyes are clouded where, The. Squince. Derek Mahon. CP-MahoD

Eyes are drawn to the dusty ground in fall, The. Empty Place, An. Robert Bly. SP-BlyR

Eyes are fog. Eyes, Ears, Noses, and a Thing about Touch. A. K. Ramanujan. CP-RamaA

Eyes are last to go out, The. Eyes, The. Tennessee Williams. CP-WillT

Eyes Are the Guides of Love. James Laughlin. CP-LaugJ

Eyes at the Window. James Schuyler. CP-SchuJ

Eyes at the window are Norma Shearer's, The. Eyes at the Window. James Schuyler. CP-SchuJ

Eyes before the Eares, The. Robert Herrick. CP-HerrR

Eyes, calm beside thee, (Lady couldst thou know!). Sonnet: "Eyes, calm beside thee, (Lady couldst thou know!)." Robert Browning. CP-BroR2

Eyes cannot follow. Blind Spots. A. K. Ramanujan. CP-RamaA

Eyes closed. Lines after Cummings. James Laughlin. CP-LaugJ

Eyes, Ears, Noses, and a Thing about Touch. A. K. Ramanujan. CP-RamaA

Eyes Fastened with Pins. Charles Simic. SP-SimiC; SP-SimiCE

Eyes, lakes with my simple lust to be reborn. Clown Chastised, The. Stéphane Mallarmé. CP-MallS, *tr. by* Henry Weinfield

Eyes, not bleared but blue. Safe in Shade. Robert Penn Warren. CP-WarrR

Eyes of a Blind Man. Edwin Rolfe. CP-CareT

Eyes of grey—a sodden quay. Lovers' Litany, The. Rudyard Kipling. CP-KiplR

Eyes of kindness that the dog had. Kindness. Denise Levertov. SP-LeveDL

Eyes of Night-Time. Muriel Rukeyser. CP-RukeM

Eyes of strangers, The. Strangers. Philip Larkin. CP-LarkP

Eyes of Summer. W. S. Merwin. SP-MerwW

Eyes of that gentle country girl, The. Guido Cavalcanti. CP-CavaG, *tr. by* Marc Cirigliano

Eyes of the Children at the Brink of the Sea's Grasp, The. Josephine Jacobsen. CP-JacoJ

Eyes of the children at the brink of the sea's, The. Eyes of the Children at the Brink of the Sea's Grasp, The. Josephine Jacobsen. CP-JacoJ

Eyes of the crow and the eye of the camera open, The. Memorial for the City. W. H. Auden. CP-AudeW

Eyes of the eagle are yours, eyes of the dove are yours. Being the Dedication of a Morning. Nicholas Vachel Lindsay. CP-LindV

Eyes of the Statue, The. Yannis Ritsos. SP-RitsY, *tr. by* Kimon Friar *and* Kostas Myrsiades

Eyes of this dead lady speak to me, The. Picture, The. Ezra Pound. CP-PoEar

Eyes open to a cry of pulleys, The. Love Calls Us to the Things of This World. Richard Wilbur. CP-WilbR

Eye's plain version is a thing apart, The. Ordinary Evening in New Haven, An. Wallace Stevens. CP-StevW; CP-StevWP

Eyes round between the bars. Speech-Grille. Paul Celan. SP-CelaP, *tr. by* John Felstiner

Eyes searching thru hills of gravel. Shady Creek. Peter Blue Cloud. SP-BlueP

Eyes talked in- / to blindness. Tübingen, January. Paul Celan. SP-CelaP, *tr. by* John Felstiner

Eyes / That are frozen. Grief. Langston Hughes. CP-HughL; CP-HughL2

Eyes that glass fear, though fear on furtive foot. Hare, A. Walter De la Mare. CP-DeLaW

Eyes That Last I Saw in Tears. T. S. Eliot. CP-ElioT

Eyes that would my garden see, The. My Garden. Jones Very. CP-VeryJ

Eyesight. A. R. Ammons. CP-AmmoA

Eyewitness. Yannis Ritsos. SP-RitsY, *tr. by* Kimon Friar *and* Kostas Myrsiades

Eyn Gedi Preserve. Yehuda Amichai. SP-AmicYL, *tr. by* Benjamin Harshav *and* Barbara Harshav

Ezekiel. John Greenleaf Whittier. CP-WhitJ

Ezekiel Saw the Wheel. Eugenio Montale. CP-MontE, *tr. by* Jonathan Galassi

Ezekiel's Rabbit. William Dickey. SP-DickW

Ezra Æsop, at eighty-eight. Parable for Sports Writers, Society Columnists, Bond Salesmen, and Poets or Go Get a Reputation, A. Ogden Nash. CP-NashO

Ezra House. James Whitcomb Riley. CP-RileJ

Ezra on the Strike. Ezra Pound. CP-PoEar

Ezra Pound in Pisa. Donald Davie. CP-DaviDC

Ezry. Archibald MacLeish. CP-MacLA

F

F. de Samara to A. G. A. Emily Jane Brontë. CP-BronE

F / eeble a blu / r of cr. E. E. Cummings. CP-CummE

F = ci² Keats: the intensity of object The trouble. Post Virginal, The. Charles Olson. CP-OlsoC

F is for foetus(a). E. E. Cummings. CP-CummE

F. (Missive & Walk) I. #53. Frank O'Hara. SP-OharF

F.O.M. Muriel Rukeyser. CP-RukeM

Fabergé. James Schuyler. CP-SchuJ

Fabien dei Franchi. Oscar Wilde. CP-WildO

Fable. Heather McHugh. SP-McHuH

Fable, A. Richard Wilbur. CP-WilbR

Fable, A: "Raven, while with glossy breast, A." William Cowper. CP-CowpW

Fable and Round of the Three Friends. Federico García Lorca. SP-GarcF, *tr. by* Ben Belitt

Fable for a War. Thomas Merton. CP-MertT

Fable for Slumber. Charles Olson. CP-OlsoC

Fable for When There's No Way Out. May Swenson. SP-SwenM

Fable: "In my favorite one." Charles Simic. SP-SimiCE

Fable: "Mountain and the squirrel, The." Ralph Waldo Emerson. CP-EmerR

Fable of Dryope, The. Ovid. CP-PopeA *Fr.* Metamorphoses.

Fable of Midas, The. Jonathan Swift. CP-SwifJ

Fable of Survival, A. John Ciardi. CP-CiarJ

Fable of the Bitches, The. Jonathan Swift. CP-SwifJ

Fable of the Lion and Other Beasts, A. *Unknown, sometimes at. to* Thomas Sheridan. CP-SherT

Fable of the Peasant and the Overlord, The. John Milton. CP-MiltJ (Cottager and His Landlord, The.) CP-CowpW

Fable of the Rhododendron Stealers. Sylvia Plath. CP-PlatS

Fable of the War, A. Howard Nemerov. CP-NemeH

Fable of the Widow and Her Cat, A. Jonathan Swift. CP-SwifJ

Fable of Three Friends to Be Sung in Rounds. Federico García Lorca. CP-GarcF, *tr. by* Greg Simon *and* Steven F. White

Fable: "Oh, there once was a lady, and so I've been told." Dorothy Parker. CP-ParkD

Fable: "Unicorns and cyclops." Federico García Lorca. CP-GarcF, *tr. by* Alan S. Trueblood *Fr.* Theories.

Fable: "Unicorns and cyclopses." Federico García Lorca. SP-GarcF, *tr. by* Roy Campbell

Fable: "Yes it was the prince's kiss." Muriel Rukeyser. CP-RukeM

Fables about Error. William Meredith. SP-MereW

Fables Bullfinch Forgot. Ogden Nash. CP-NashO

Fables: "Cock was working very hard, A." Mrs. Austen. CP-AustJ

Fables of La Fontaine. Marianne Craig Moore.

  Animals Sick of the Plague, The. CP-MoorM

  Bear and the Garden-Lover, The. CP-MoorM

  Fox and the Grapes, The. CP-MoorM

  Lion In Love, The. CP-MoorM

  Mouse Metamorphosed Into a Maid, The. CP-MoorM

Fables of the Moon. Richard Eberhart. CP-EberR

Fables of the Moscow Subway. Howard Nemerov. CP-NemeH

Fabliau of Florida. Wallace Stevens. CP-StevW; CP-StevWP

Fabrication of Ancestors. Alan Dugan. CP-DugaA

Fabulae. Phaedrus.

  "Let those whom folly prompts to sneer." CP-JohnS

  "Through all the town the busy triflers swarm." CP-JohnS

  "Tinsel glitter, and the specious mein, The." CP-JohnS

  "Two-fold gift in this my volume lies, A." CP-JohnS

  "Wretch that often has deceiv'd, The." CP-JohnS

Fabulists, The. Rudyard Kipling. CP-KiplR

Fabulous against ,a,fathoming jelly. E. E. Cummings. CP-CummE

Facades for Norma Cole. Michael Palmer. SP-PalmM

Face. Denise Levertov. SP-LeveDL

Face. Adrienne Rich. CP-RicAE

Face. Carl Sandburg. CP-SandC

Face, A. Robert Browning. CP-BroR1

Face, A. Marianne Craig Moore. CP-MoorM

Face, The. Randall Jarrell. CP-JarrR

Face, The. Philip Levine. SP-LeviP

Face, The. Stevie Smith. CP-SmitS

Face and Image. Charles Tomlinson. CP-TomlC

Face at the Casement, The. Thomas Hardy. CP-HardT

Face devoid of love or grace, A. Emily Dickinson. CP-DickE

Face-down; odor. Terror. Denise Levertov. SP-LeveDS

Face I carry with me—last, The. Emily Dickinson. CP-DickE

Face in evanescence lain, The. Emily Dickinson. CP-DickE

Face in stone and / Stone in face. Portrait in Stone. Charles Tomlinson. CP-TomlC

Face in the crook of her neck. Gary Snyder. CP-SnydG *Fr.* Myths and Texts.

Face in the Mirror, The. Robert Graves. CP-GravR

Face Lift. Sylvia Plath. CP-PlatS

Face like a chocolate bar. 125th Street. Langston Hughes. CP-HughL; CP-HughL3

Face narrows, The. How Does It Look? James Laughlin. CP-LaugJ

Face, Ocean. Richard Eberhart. CP-EberR

Face of (a woman). Signs and Evidence in the Orchard of Gan-Hayim. Yehuda Amichai. SP-AmicYL, *tr. by* Benjamin Harshav *and* Barbara Harshav

Face of the Dam: Vivian Jones. Muriel Rukeyser. CP-SpenS

Face of the Precipice is Black with Lovers, The. Thomas McGrath. SP-McGrT

Face of war is my face, The. War. Langston Hughes. CP-HughL; CP-HughL3

Face of you, already face of dreaming. Farewell. Yehuda Amichai. SP-AmicY, *tr. by* Stephen Mitchell

Face of youth mature; a mouth of tender, A. On a Youthful Portrait of Stevenson. James Whitcomb Riley. CP-RileJ

Face or Mask? Yannis Ritsos. SP-RitsY, *tr. by* Kostas Myrsiades

Face-Paintings of the Caduveo Indians. William Dickey. SP-DickW

Face Portrait. Andrei Codrescu. SP-CodrA

Face that should content me wonders [*or* wondrous] well, A. Sir Thomas Wyatt. CP-WyatT

Face to Face. Denise Levertov. SP-LeveDP

Face to Face. Adrienne Rich. CP-RicAE; SP-RicA1; SP-RicA2

Face to face in my chamber, my silent chamber, I saw her. Confessions. Elizabeth Barrett Browning. CP-BroEB

Face to the wall and behind him. Wall, The. Louis MacNeice. CP-MacNL

Face / was / beautiful, The. Was. Robert Creeley. CP-CreeR

Face was necessary—I found face. Ted Hughes. SP-HughTN *Fr.* Seven Dungeon Songs.

Face we choose to miss, The. Emily Dickinson. CP-DickE

Face While Shaving. Charles Bukowski. SP-BukC2

Faced to the island, Mackinnon's boat. Mackinnon's Boat. Charles Tomlinson. CP-TomlC

Faced with furnace demands during its education. Burning Bush. Muriel Rukeyser. CP-RukeM

Faces. Maya Angelou. SP-AngeM

Faces. John Ciardi. CP-CiarJ

Faces. Grace Paley. CP-PalGC

Faces. Walt Whitman. CP-WhitW

Faces and more remember. Faces. Maya Angelou. SP-AngeM

Faces greying faster than loam-crumbs on a harrow. Judge Not. Theodore Roethke. CP-RoetT

Faces of children turn like sunflowers to death, The. Innocents, The. Josephine Jacobsen. CP-JacoJ

Faces of Girls Looking at Themselves in the River. Pablo Antonio Cuadra. CP-MertT

Faces of two eternities keep looking at me. Two Neighbors. Carl Sandburg. CP-SandC

Faces Seen Once. James Dickey. CP-DickJ

Faces seen once are seen. Faces Seen Once. James Dickey. CP-DickJ

Faces there at the center, ruinous, The. Island (VIII), The. Pablo Neruda. SP-NeruP *Fr.* Separate Rose, The.

Faces with anticipated youth, The. Robert Creeley. SP-CreeR

Facile as can be the boat you see, my guests, says. Catullus. *See* My bean-pod boat you see here

Facing Africa. James Dickey. CP-DickJ

Facing into It. Eleanor Wilner. SP-WilnE

Facing It. Yusef Komunyakaa. CP-KomuY

Facing Sentencing. Muriel Rukeyser. CP-RukeM

Facing the Chair. Hugh MacDiarmid. SP-MacDH

Facing the deserted fair. Variation ("Facing the deserted fair"). Federico García Lorca. CP-GarcF, *tr. by* Jerome Rothenberg *Fr.* Fairs.

Facing the Way. Alice Walker. CP-WalkA

Facing West from California's Shores. Walt Whitman. CP-WhitW

Fact. Langston Hughes. CP-HughL; CP-HughL3

Fact, The. Robert Creeley. SP-CreeR

Fact, The. Laura Riding Jackson. CP-RidiL

Fact ("Chirotherium tracks occur"). Kenneth Rexroth. CP-RexrK

Fact ("In the encyclopedia"). Kenneth Rexroth. CP-RexrK

Fact, and an Imagination or, Canute and Alfred, on the Sea-Shore, A. William Wordsworth. CP-WorW2

Fact of a Doorframe, The. Adrienne Rich. SP-RicA1

Fact of the Act. Robert Graves. CP-GravR

Fact of the Matter, The. Hayden Carruth. CP-CarHS

Fact that Earth is Heaven, The. Emily Dickinson. CP-DickE

Faction du Muet. René Char. CP-MertT

Factions. Robert Herrick. CP-HerrR

Factories close, the harbor stinks. Dead of Winter. William Corbett. SP-CorbW

Factory Cities, The. D. H. Lawrence. CP-LawrD

Factory off Santa Fe Ave. was, The. Sparks. Charles Bukowski. SP-BukC3

Factory, The. Aleksandr Aleksandrovich Blok. SP-BlokA, *tr. by* Peter France *and* Jon Stallworthy

Factory Windows Are Always Broken. Nicholas Vachel Lindsay. CP-LindV

Facts by our side are never sudden. Emily Dickinson. CP-DickE

Facts have no eyes. One must. Observation of Facts. Charles Tomlinson. CP-TomlC

Facts & Issues, The. John Berryman. CP-BerrJ

Fade tender lily, / Fade O crimson rose. Autumn. Christina Georgina Rossetti. CP-RosC3

Faded. Randall Jarrell. CP-JarrR

Faded back last night. Talking. Robert Creeley. SP-CreeR

Faded Boy—in sallow Clothes, A. Emily Dickinson. CP-DickE

Faded Face, The. Thomas Hardy. CP-HardT

Faded man shines in a novel, A. Sadness Unhinged. Andrei Codrescu. SP-CodrA

Faded mind, / fading colors. Place ("Faded mind, / fading colors"). Robert Creeley. CP-CreeR

Faded Offering. Rainer Maria Rilke. CP-RilkFr, *tr. by* A. Poulin, Jr.

Fading of the Sun, A. Wallace Stevens. CP-StevW; CP-StevWP

Fading Rose, The. Thomas Hardy. CP-HardT

Faerie Queene, The. Edmund Spenser. CP-Spens

  Book 2. CP-Spens

  Book 2, Canto 6. CP-Spens

  Book 2, Canto 8. CP-Spens

  Book 2, Canto 12. CP-Spens

  Book 3. CP-Spens

  Book 3, Canto 9. CP-Spens

  Book 4. CP-Spens

    Book 4, Canto 1. CP-Spens

  Book 4, Canto 9. CP-Spens

  Book 4, Canto 11. CP-Spens

  Book 4, Canto 12. CP-Spens

  Book 5. CP-Spens

  Book 5, Canto 2. CP-Spens

  Book 6. CP-Spens

  Book 7. CP-Spens

Faery Beam upon You, The. Ben Jonson. CP-JonsB *Fr.* Gypsies Metamorphosed, The.

Faery Bird's Song. John Keats. *See* Fairy Song

Faery Chasm, The. William Wordsworth. CP-WorW2 *Fr.* River Duddon [A Series of Sonnets], The.

Faery Song. John Keats. CP-KeatJ

Faery Song, A. William Butler Yeats. CP-YeatW

Faeryland. Robert Pinsky. CP-PinsR

Fafnir and the Knights. Stevie Smith. CP-SmitS

Faggot, The. Jonathan Swift. CP-SwifJ

Fagots blazed, the caldron's smoke, The. Brewing of Soma, The. John Greenleaf Whittier. CP-WhitJ

Fags and their gay dogs are patrolling, The. Sunday in Boston. John Updike. CP-UpdiJ

Fahrenheit *Gesundheit*. Ogden Nash. CP-NashO

Failed Spirit, The. Stevie Smith. CP-SmitS

Failed Tribute to the Stonemason of Tor House, Robinson Jeffers. James Tate. SP-TateJ

Failing. Philip Whalen. SP-WhalP

Failing impartial measure to dispense. Plea for Authors, May, 1838, A. William Wordsworth. CP-WorW2

Failure. Dan Pagis. SP-PagiD, *tr. by* Stephen Mitchell

Failure. C. K. Williams. SP-WillC

Failure, A. D. H. Lawrence. CP-LawrD

Failure of Communication in the Animal Kingdom, A. James Laughlin. CP-LaugJ

Failure to go far enough, The. Plighted to Shame. Laura Riding Jackson. CP-RidiL

Failure, worse failure, nothing seen. World, World—. George Oppen. CP-OppGN

Failures. One after the. 35 Seconds. Charles Bukowski. SP-BukC2

Fain would I kiss my Julia's dainty leg. Her Legs. Robert Herrick. CP-HerrR

Fain Would I Wed. Thomas Campion. CP-CampT

  (Faine would I wed a faire yong man that day and night could please mee.) CP-CampT

Fain would my Muse the flow'ry Treasures sing. Garden, The. Alexander Pope. CP-PopeA

Faine would I my love disclose. Thomas Campion. CP-CampT

Faine would I wed a faire yong man that day and night could please mee. Thomas Campion. *See* Fain Would I Wed

Faint and worn and aged. Eleventh Hour, The. Christina Georgina Rossetti. CP-RosC3

Faint as leaf shadow does he fade. Tennessee Williams. CP-WillT

Faint dusky light. Country Western. Robert Creeley. SP-CreeR

Faint Music. Walter De la Mare. CP-DeLaW

Faint now the colours in the West. Tryst, The. Walter De la Mare. CP-DeLaW

Faint, persistent. Echo ("Faint, persistent"). Robert Creeley. SP-CreeR

Faint Praise. C. K. Williams. CP-WillC

Faint, sickening scent of irises, A. Scent of Irises. D. H. Lawrence. CP-LawrD

Faint sighings sounded, not of wind, amid. Image, The. Walter De la Mare. CP-DeLaW

Faint smile of distraction, moist response, A. James Vincent Cunningham. CP-CunnJ

Faint white pillars that seem to fade. Fragment: "Faint white pillars that seem to fade." Edwin Arlington Robinson. CP-RobiE

Faint with love, the Lady of the South. Fragment: The Lady of the South. Percy Bysshe Shelley. CP-ShelP

Faint, Yet Pursuing. Christina Georgina Rossetti. CP-RosC3

Faintheart in a Railway Train. Thomas Hardy. CP-HardT

Faintly the ne'er-do-well. Flute of the Lonely, The. Nicholas Vachel Lindsay. CP-LindV

Fair Amy of the terraced house. Amy's Cruelty. Elizabeth Barrett Browning. CP-BroEB

Fair and false! No dawn will greet. Song: "Fair and false! No dawn will greet." George Meredith. CP-MerG1

Fair Bedfellow, The. George Meredith. CP-MerG2

Fair, but of fairness as a vision dream'd. Fragment of Anything You Like, A. Gerard Manley Hopkins. CP-HopkG

Fair by Starlight. Federico García Lorca. CP-GarcF, *tr. by* Jerome Rothenberg *Fr.* Fairs.

Fair Caroline, I wonder what. To C.F.H. Thomas Hardy. CP-HardT

Fair Charmer, cease, nor make your voice's prize. Of a Lady Singing to Her Lute. Alexander Pope. CP-PopeA

Fair copy of my Celia's face. To T. H., a Lady Resembling My Mistress. Thomas Carew. CP-CareT

Fair Cuirass Shattered. Allen Tate. CP-TateA

Fair damask roses! that, from year to year. On the Beautiful Roses, in front of the Mansion of John Hodges, Esq. Jones Very. CP-VeryJ

Fair Division, A. Ambrose Bierce. SP-BierA

Fair Doris, break thy glass, it hath perplex'd. To A.D., Unreasonable, Distrustful of Her Own Beauty. Thomas Carew. CP-CareT

Fair Elenor. William Blake. CP-BlakW

Fair Eliza. Robert Burns. CP-BurnR

Fair Ellen Irwin, when she sate. Ellen Irwin; or, The Braes of Kirtle. William Wordsworth. CP-WorW1

Fair Empress of the Poet's soul. To Clarinda. Robert Burns. CP-BurnR

Fair fa' your honest, sonsie face. To a Haggis. Robert Burns. CP-BurnR

Fair faces crowd on Christmas night. Portrait, A ("Fair faces crowd on Christmas night"). G. K. Chesterton. CP-ChesG

Fair fall thy soft heart! Hafiz. CP-EmerR *Fr.* Odes.

Fair flower! from one who toils in distant land. On Receiving a Flower from the Rev. C. H. A. Dall, in India. Jones Very. CP-VeryJ

Fair flower! that, from the southern skies. On a Hyacinth from Georgia. Jones Very. CP-VeryJ

Fair flowers! that open to the April sun. On Some Beautiful Crocuses: In Front of the House of B. H. Silsbee, Esq. Jones Very. CP-VeryJ

Fair friend, 'tis true, your beauties move. Ben Jonson. CP-JonsB

Fair girl, fond wife, and dear. Mother Sainted, The. James Whitcomb Riley. CP-RileJ

Fair, great, and good, since seeing you, we see. To the Countess of Salisbury. John Donne. CP-DonnJ; MW-DonnJ

Fair Haven ("When little hills like lambs did skip"). Henry David Thoreau. CP-ThorH

Fair Haven ("When Winter fringes every bough"). Henry David Thoreau. CP-ThorH

Fair Head in Antrim, long dark waves of wet heather to the black lips of the height. Irish Headland, An. Robinson Jeffers. CP-JefR2

"Fair Helena." by Rackham. Ezra Pound. CP-PoEar

Fair in the Woods, The. Thom Gunn. CP-GunnT

Fair is our lot—O goodly is our heritage! Song of the English, A. Rudyard Kipling. CP-KiplR

Fair Isabel, poor simple Isabel! Isabella; or, The Pot of Basil. John Keats. CP-KeatJ

Fair isle, that from the fairest of all flowers. Sonnet to Zante. Ugo Foscolo. CP-PoeEd

Fair Jenny. Robert Burns. CP-BurnR

Fair ladies, number five. On the Five Ladies at Sot's Hole, with the Doctor at Their Head. Jonathan Swift. CP-SwifJ

Fair ladies tall lovers / riding are through the. E. E. Cummings. CP-CummE

Fair Lady! can I sing of flowers. To a Lady. William Wordsworth. CP-WorW2

Fair Lady! whose harmonious name the Rhine. John Milton. *See* Charming lady, she whose beautiful name honors

Fair maid, you need not take the hint. To a Lady. Robert Burns. CP-BurnR

Fair Margaret. Christina Georgina Rossetti. CP-RosC3

Fair Marg'ret sat in her bower. Lord Thomas and Fair Margaret. Christina Georgina Rossetti. CP-RosC3

Fair Morning, The. Jones Very. CP-VeryJ

Fair Mother Earth lay on her back last night. Ode to the Spirit of Earth in Autumn. George Meredith. CP-MerG1

Fair Nature's priestesses! to whom. To ———: "Fair Nature's priestesses! to whom." John Greenleaf Whittier. CP-WhitJ

Fair of face, full of pride. Lyke-Wake Song, A. Algernon Charles Swinburne. SP-SwinA

Fair ones! To you who hearts command. Punch's Petition to the Ladies. *Unknown, sometimes at. to* Thomas Sheridan. CP-SherT

Fair[e] pledges of a fruitful tree. To Blossoms. Robert Herrick. CP-HerrR

Fair Pomona flourish'd in his reign, The. Vertumnus and Pomona. Ovid. CP-PopeA *Fr.* Metamorphoses.

Fair Prime of Life! Were It Enough to Gild. William Wordsworth. CP-WorW2

Fair Quakeress, The. John Greenleaf Whittier. CP-WhitJ

Fair rise the Morn that gave our heroe birth. Ode on the Birth Day of the Illustrious George Washington President of the United States, An. Annis Boudinot Stockton. CP-StocA

Fair rise the morn that gave to stanhope birth. To Doctor Smith on His Birth Day March the 16th, 1790. Annis Boudinot Stockton. CP-StocA

Fair river! in thy bright, clear flow. To the River ———. Edgar Allan Poe. CP-PoeEd

Fair rocks, goodly rivers, sweet woods, when shall I see peace? Echo. Sir Philip Sidney. SP-SidnP *Fr.* Arcadia.

Fair Singer, The. Andrew Marvell. CP-MarvA

Fair sinks the summer evening now. Emily Jane Brontë. CP-BronE

Fair slim boy not made for this world's pain, A. Wasted Days. Oscar Wilde. CP-WildO

Fair soul, which wast, not only, as all souls be. Obsequies to the Lord Harrington, Brother to the Lady Lucy, Countess of Bedford. John Donne. CP-DonnJ; MW-DonnJ

Fair, square Harvard, crib of the pilgrim mind. Apologies to Harvard. John Updike. CP-UpdiJ

Fair Star of evening, Splendo[u]r of the west. Composed by the Sea-Side, near Calais, August, 1802. William Wordsworth. CP-WorW1; MW-WorW

Fair, sweet and young, receive a prize. Song: "Fair, sweet and young, receive a prize." John Dryden. SP-DrydJ

Fair the face of orient day. Delia. Robert Burns. CP-BurnR

Fair the sun riseth, / Bright as bright can be. Moonshine. Christina Georgina Rossetti. CP-RosC3

Fair waved the golden corn. In Canaan's Happy Land. Stevie Smith. CP-SmitS

Fair Weather. Dorothy Parker. CP-ParkD

Fair weather for your journey! whither away. Jack & Harry. George Meredith. CP-MerG2

Fair World Tho' a Fallen, A. Christina Georgina Rossetti. CP-RosC3

Faire after Foule. Robert Herrick. CP-HerrR

Faire and foule dayes trip Crosse and Pile; The faire. Crosse and Pile. Robert Herrick. CP-HerrR

Fair[e] daffodils [*or* daffadills], we weep to see. To Daffodils [*or* Daffadills]. Robert Herrick. CP-HerrR

Fair[e] Days; or, Dawn[e]s Deceitful[l]. Robert Herrick. CP-HerrR

Faire If You Expect Admiring. Thomas Campion. CP-CampT

Faire Shewes Deceive. Robert Herrick. CP-HerrR

Fair[e] was the dawn[e], and but e'ne now the skies. Fair[e] Days; or, Dawn[e]s Deceitful[l]. Robert Herrick. CP-HerrR

Fairer than younger beauties, more beloved. Valentines From C.G.R. Christina Georgina Rossetti. CP-RosC3

Fairer through Fading—as the Day. Emily Dickinson. CP-DickE

Fairest and foremost of the train, that wait. Charity. William Cowper. CP-CowpW

Fairest, brightest, hues of ether fade, The. William Wordsworth. CP-WorW1

Fairest day that ever yet has shone, The. Lost, The ("Fairest day that ever yet has shone, The"). Jones Very. CP-VeryJ

Fairest Home I ever knew, The. Emily Dickinson. CP-DickE

Fairest isle, all isles excelling. Song of Venus. John Dryden. SP-DrydJ *Fr.* King Arthur.

Fairest maid on Devon banks. Robert Burns. *See* Full well thou knowest I love thee dear

Fairest of the Destinies. Fragments Written for Hellas. Percy Bysshe Shelley. CP-ShelP

Fairground. W. H. Auden. CP-AudeW

Fairies. Langston Hughes. CP-HughL

Fairies, The. Robert Herrick. CP-HerrR

Fairies Break Their Dances, The. A. E. Housman. CP-HousA

Fairies break their dances, The. Fairies Break Their Dances, The. A. E. Housman. CP-HousA

Fairies' Siege, The. Rudyard Kipling. CP-KiplR *Fr.* Kim.

Fairly Sad Tale, A. Dorothy Parker. CP-ParkD

Fairs. Federico García Lorca.

    All Night Fair. CP-GarcF, *tr. by* Jerome Rothenberg

    Confusion ("Over wide awake houses"). CP-GarcF, *tr. by* Jerome Rothenberg

    Drum. CP-GarcF, *tr. by* Jerome Rothenberg

    Fair by Starlight. CP-GarcF, *tr. by* Jerome Rothenberg

    Moon at the Fair, A. CP-GarcF, *tr. by* Jerome Rothenberg

    On the Swing. CP-GarcF, *tr. by* Jerome Rothenberg

    Paper Roses. CP-GarcF, *tr. by* Jerome Rothenberg

    Poem at the Fairground. CP-GarcF, *tr. by* Jerome Rothenberg

    Scream. CP-GarcF, *tr. by* Jerome Rothenberg

    Song in Brown. CP-GarcF, *tr. by* Jerome Rothenberg

    Sunset at the Fair. CP-GarcF, *tr. by* Jerome Rothenberg

    Variation ("Facing the deserted fair"). CP-GarcF, *tr. by* Jerome Rothenberg

    Wooden Horses. CP-GarcF, *tr. by* Jerome Rothenberg

Fairy. Arthur Rimbaud. CP-RimbA, *tr. by* Martin Sorrell

Fairy, The. William Blake. CP-BlakW

Fairy Bell, The. Stevie Smith. CP-SmitS

Fairy Bridal Hymn, The. Nicholas Vachel Lindsay. CP-LindV

Fairy fixes his hair, The. Song of the Fairy. Federico García Lorca. CP-GarcF, *tr. by* Alan S. Trueblood *Fr.* Games.

Fairy from the Apple-Seed, The. Nicholas Vachel Lindsay. CP-LindV

Fairy in Winter, The. Walter De la Mare. CP-DeLaW

Fairy [*or* Faery *or* Faiery] beam[e] upon you, The. Faery Beam upon You, The. Ben Jonson. CP-JonsB *Fr.* Gypsies Metamorphosed, The.

Fairy skipd [*or* leapt] upon my knee, A. William Blake. CP-BlakW

Fairy Song. Randall Jarrell. CP-JarrR

Fairy Song. John Keats. CP-KeatJ

(Faery Bird's Song.) CP-KeatJ
Fairy Story. Donald Davie. CP-DaviDC
Fairy Story. Stevie Smith. CP-SmitS
Fairy-Tale. G. K. Chesterton. CP-ChesG
Fairy Tale, A. G. K. Chesterton. CP-ChesG
Fairy Temple; or, Oberon's Chapel, The. Robert Herrick. CP-HerrR
Fairyland [or Fairy-Land]. Edgar Allan Poe. CP-PoeEd
Faith. Thomas Kinsella. CP-KinsT
Faith. Paul Laurence Dunbar. CP-DunbP
Faith. George Herbert. CP-HerbG
Faith. Robert Herrick. CP-HerrR
Faith. Robinson Jeffers. CP-JefR3
Faith. Heather McHugh. SP-McHuH
Faith. James Whitcomb Riley. CP-RileJ
Faith ("There is no faith; the mountain stands within"). Jones Very. CP-VeryJ
Faith ("Hast thou but faith thou shalt the mountain bid"). Jones Very. CP-VeryJ
Faith and Hope are wings to Love. Christina Georgina Rossetti. CP-RosC3
Faith and Light. Jones Very. CP-VeryJ
Faith Four-square. Robert Herrick. CP-HerrR
Faith Healer. Yusef Komunyakaa. CP-KomuY
Faith Healing. Philip Larkin. CP-LarkP
Faith, Hope, and Charity. Samuel Taylor Coleridge. CP-ColeS
Faith, Hope, and Love. Of these three is Love all? 1 Corinthians 13: Commentary. James Vincent Cunningham. CP-CunnJ
Faith in the Lord how can I find? How Faith Comes. Jones Very. CP-VeryJ
Faith in the Resurrection Confirmed. Jones Very. CP-VeryJ
Faith in Time of War. Jones Very. CP-VeryJ
"Faith" is a fine invention. Emily Dickinson. CP-DickE
Faith is a thing that's four-square; let it fall. Faith Four-square. Robert Herrick. CP-HerrR
Faith is the evidence of things I've wasted. Faith Relearned. Andrei Codrescu. SP-CodrA
Faith—is the Pierless Bridge. Emily Dickinson. CP-DickE
Faith of the First Christians, The. Jones Very. CP-VeryJ
Faith of years is broken. Fair Margaret. Christina Georgina Rossetti. CP-RosC3
Faith on Trial, A. George Meredith. CP-MerG1
Faith Relearned. Andrei Codrescu. SP-CodrA
Faith Upon the Waters. Laura Riding Jackson. CP-RidiL
Faithful, The. Jane Cooper. CP-CoopJ
Faithful Friend, The. William Cowper. CP-CowpW
Faithful "I am sorry," A. Emily Dickinson. SP-DickE
Faithful Inventory of the Furniture Belonging to ——— Room in T. C. D., A. Unknown, sometimes at. to Thomas Sheridan. CP-SherT
Faithful mother tongue, / I have been serving you. My Faithful Mother Tongue. Czeslaw Milosz. CP-MiloC; CP-MiloCN, tr. by Robert Pinsky
Faithful One. Langston Hughes. CP-HughL; CP-HughL2
Faithful Swallow, The. Thomas Hardy. CP-HardT
"Faithful to the end" Amended. Emily Dickinson. CP-DickE
Faithful Wilson. Thomas Hardy. CP-HardT
Faithful youth, A. Crazy Spiritual, A. Allen Ginsberg. CP-GinsA; SP-GinsA
Faithfully tinying at twilight voice. E. E. Cummings. CP-CummE
Faithless. Walter De la Mare. CP-DeLaW
Faithless Shepherdess, The. Christina Georgina Rossetti. CP-RosC3
Faithless, we have come here. Transformation. Raymond Carver. CP-CarvR
Faithless Wife, The. Federico García Lorca. SP-GarcF, tr. by J. L. Gili and Stephen Spender
Faithlesse and fond mortality. Upon the Death of a Gentleman. Richard Crashaw. CP-CrasR
Falcon Woman, The. Robert Graves. CP-GravR
Falcons have come to the city, The. Sky Sign. Charles Bukowski. SP-BukC3
Falcons, The. W. S. Merwin. SP-MerwWF
Falernian, / old Falernian! Carmen 27. Catullus. CP-ZukLS Fr. Carmina.
Fall. Wendell Berry. CP-BerrW
Fall. Robert Creeley. CP-CreeR
Fall. Mona Van Duyn. SP-VanDM
Fall. Lorine Niedecker. CP-NiedL
Fall. Gregory Orr. SP-OrrG
Fall. Rainer Maria Rilke. CP-RilkFr, tr. by A. Poulin, Jr.
Fall. John Updike. CP-UpdiJ
Fall, The. A. R. Ammons. CP-AmmoA
Fall, The. Heather McHugh. SP-McHuH
Fall, The. Thomas Merton. CP-MertT
Fall, The. Czeslaw Milosz. CP-MiloC; CP-MiloCN, tr. by Lillian Vallee
Fall, The. A. K. Ramanujan. CP-RamaA
Fall Again, The. Howard Nemerov. CP-NemeH
Fall Comes in Back-Country Vermont. Robert Penn Warren. CP-WarrR

Fall Creek. A. R. Ammons. CP-AmmoA
Fall-Crick View of the Earthquake, A. James Whitcomb Riley. CP-RileJ
Fall Day, A. Charles Simic. SP-SimiC; SP-SimiCE
Fall has come, clear as the eyes of chickens, The. Silence. Robert Bly. SP-BlyR
Fall in Connecticut. Yehuda Amichai. SP-AmicY, tr. by Chana Bloch
Fall in Corrales. Richard Wilbur. CP-WilbR
Fall Journey. William Stafford. SP-StafW; SP-StafWW
Fall, leaves, fall; die, flowers, away; Song. Emily Jane Brontë. CP-BronE
Fall 1970. William Corbett. SP-CorbW
Fall 1961. Robert Lowell. SP-LoweR
Fall of a Wall. John Donne. CP-DonnJ; MW-DonnJ
Fall of Day, The. D. H. Lawrence. CP-LawrD
Fall of Hyperion, The; A Dream. John Keats. CP-KeatJ
Fall of Jock Gillespie, The. Rudyard Kipling. CP-KiplR
Fall of Night, The. Thomas Merton. CP-MertT
Fall of Rome, The. W. H. Auden. CP-AudeW
Fall of the Evening Star. Kenneth Patchen. CP-PatcK
Fall of the Leaf, The ("Grown tired of this rank summer's wealth"). Henry David Thoreau. CP-ThorH
Fall Out. Charles Bukowski. SP-BukC3
Fall rings in the empty leaves. Fall. Rainer Maria Rilke. CP-RilkFr, tr. by A. Poulin, Jr.
Fall '66. Thomas Merton. CP-MertT
Fall Song. Howard Nemerov. CP-NemeH
Fall stream from Heaven to bless: return as well. Inscription on a Well in Memory of the Martyrs of the War. Ralph Waldo Emerson. CP-EmerR
Fall the deep curtains. Archer. "H. D." CP-DoolH
Fall we moved to the farm, I was thirteen, The. Solitary Pond, The. John Updike. CP-UpdiJ
Fall Weekend at Milgate. Robert Lowell. SP-LoweR
Fall Wind. William Stafford. SP-StafWW
Fall with me / Through the frigid stars. Medusa. Hart Crane. CP-CranH
Fall work almost done . . . . Another Season. Thomas McGrath. SP-McGrT
Fall, yellow leaf, for thy brief work is done! Falling Leaf, The. Jones Very. CP-VeryJ
Fallen Angels, The. Anne Sexton. CP-SextA
Fallen, Fallen. Stevie Smith. CP-SmitS
Fallen from heaven, lies across. River. Ted Hughes. SP-HughTN
Fallen from the clouds, well-met. Days of 1971. James Merrill. SP-MerrJ
Fallen immortal found this valley, A. Chinese History of Colden Water. Ted Hughes. SP-HughTN
Fallen in between the tendons and bones. Hand. Robinson Jeffers. CP-JefR3
Fallen Leaves. D. H. Lawrence. CP-LawrD
Fallen Majesty. William Butler Yeats. CP-YeatW
Fallen Oak, A. Peter Blue Cloud. SP-BlueP
Fallen, so freshly fallen. Dragonfly, The. Stanley Kunitz. CP-KunSC
Fallen Tower of Siloam, The. Robert Graves. CP-GravR
Fallen volume, hidden by the others, The. Things ("Fallen volume, hidden by the others, The"). Jorge Luis Borges. SP-BorgJ, tr. by Alastair Reid
Fallen Weathervane, The. Federico García Lorca. CP-GarcF, tr. by Catherine Brown
Fallgrief's Girlfriends. Ted Hughes. SP-HughTN
Falling. Robert Creeley. CP-CreeR
Falling. James Dickey. CP-DickJ
Falling: 1. Rae Armantrout. SP-ArmaA
Falling: 2. Rae Armantrout. SP-ArmaA
Falling Asleep. Wendell Berry. CP-BerrW
Falling Asleep. Robert Bly. SP-BlyR
Falling Asleep. Robert Pinsky. CP-PinsR
Falling Asleep in America. Allen Ginsberg. CP-GinsA
Falling Dolls, The. Anne Sexton. CP-SextA
Falling-Down Song, The. Yusef Komunyakaa. CP-KomuY
Falling downhill—. Robert Creeley. CP-CreeR
Falling / from grace—. Falling. Robert Creeley. CP-CreeR
Falling, I caught the curtain. On the Other Side. Czeslaw Milosz. CP-MiloC; CP-MiloCN, tr. by Jan Darowski
Falling, / I think of a man falling. Fall, The. A. K. Ramanujan. CP-RamaA
Falling in love is never as simple. Randall Jarrell. CP-JarrR
Falling Leaf, The. Jones Very. CP-VeryJ
Falling Leaves. Kathleen Jessie Raine. SP-RainK
Falling Leaves and Early Snow. Kenneth Rexroth. CP-RexrK
Falling of Sally, The. George Meredith. CP-MerG2
Falling of the Leaves, The. William Butler Yeats. CP-YeatW
Falling out of love. Erasure. Marge Piercy. SP-PierM
Falling separate into the dark. Late at Night ("Falling separate into the dark"). William Stafford. SP-StafWW
Falling snow has made her thoughtful, The. My Mother Remembers That She

Was Beautiful. Tess Gallagher. SP-GallT

Falling star, or worse, a planet (true or bogus), A. Fifth Anniversary, The. Joseph Brodsky. CP-BrodJ

Falling Through the Ice. Wyatt Prunty. SP-PrunW

Falling Through the Leaves. Thomas Lux. SP-LuxT

Fall'n Is Lucifer. George Meredith. CP-MerG2

Fallow between the horny trees. Dog in a Cornfield. James Wright. CP-WrigJ

Fallow Deer at the Lonely House, The. Thomas Hardy. CP-HardT

Falltime. Carl Sandburg. CP-SandC

False and impenetrable. Benares. Jorge Luis Borges. SP-BorgJ, tr. by Charles Tomlinson

False and True. James Whitcomb Riley. CP-RileJ

False, cruel, disappointed, stung to th' heart. In Seditionem Horrendum. William Cowper. CP-CowpW

False Dawn. Rudyard Kipling. Fr. Plain Tales from the Hills.

False Democracy and Real. D. H. Lawrence. CP-LawrD

False Friends, The. Dorothy Parker. CP-ParkD

False glozing pleasures, casks of happiness. Dotage. George Herbert. CP-HerbG

False Gods, The. Edwin Arlington Robinson. CP-RobiE

False Interpretation. Yehuda Amichai. SP-AmicYL, tr. by Benjamin Harshav and Barbara Harshav

False Leads. Yusef Komunyakaa. CP-KomuY

False Mourning. Robert Herrick. CP-HerrR

False Portrait. Michael Palmer. SP-PalmM

False Portrait of D.B. as Niccolò Paganini. Michael Palmer. SP-PalmM

False Portrait of Hanna H. Michael Palmer. SP-PalmM

False Prophecy, A. Ambrose Bierce. SP-BierA

False Solomon's Seal. Howard Nemerov. CP-NemeH

False Step, A. Elizabeth Barrett Browning. CP-BroEB

False strawberry is. Grace Paley. CP-PalGC

False Witness. Ai. SP-Ai

False world, good night: since thou hast brought. To the World [A Farewell for a Gentlewoman, Virtuous and Noble]. Ben Jonson. CP-JonsB; SP-JonsB

False Youth: Autumn: Clothes of the Age. James Dickey. CP-DickJ

False Youth: Two Seasons. James Dickey. CP-DickJ

Falsehood of Thee could I suppose. Emily Dickinson. CP-DickE

Falsetto. Eugenio Montale. CP-MontE, tr. by Jonathan Galassi

Falstaff. Walter De la Mare. CP-DeLaW

Famam Librosque Cano. Ezra Pound. CP-PoEar

Famam, posteritas quam dedit Orpheo. To. Campiani Epigramma de Instituto Authoris. Thomas Campion. CP-CampT

Fame. Jorge Luis Borges. SP-BorgJ, tr. by Alastair Reid

Fame. Ralph Waldo Emerson. CP-EmerR

Fame. Robert Herrick. CP-HerrR

Fame. James Whitcomb Riley. CP-RileJ

Fame and honor and high degree. Ballade of Understandable Ambitions. Dorothy Parker. CP-ParkD

Fame If Not Fortune. Carl Sandburg. CP-SandC

Fame is a bee. Emily Dickinson. CP-DickE

Fame is a fickle food. Emily Dickinson. CP-DickE

Fame is the one that does not stay. Emily Dickinson. CP-DickE

Fame is the tint that Scholars leave. Emily Dickinson. CP-DickE

Fame keeps the epitaphs where they lie. Michelangelo Buonarroti. CP-Miche, tr. by John Frederick Nims

Fame, like a wayward girl, will still be coy. On Fame. John Keats. CP-KeatJ Fr. Two Sonnets on Fame.

Fame Makes Us Forward. Robert Herrick. CP-HerrR

Fame of Myself, to justify. Emily Dickinson. CP-DickE

Fame Speaks. E. E. Cummings. CP-CummE

Fame tells of groves—from England far away. June, 1820. William Wordsworth. CP-WorW2

Fame, wisdom, love, and power were mine. 'All Is Vanity, Saith the Preacher' Lord Byron. CP-Byron

"Fame!" Yes, I said it and you read it. First. Two Poets of Croisic, The. Robert Browning. CP-BroR2

Famed for contemptuous breach of sacred ties. Windsor Poetics. Lord Byron. CP-Byron

Famed for their civil and domestic quarrels. On a Royal Visit to the Vaults. Lord Byron. CP-Byron

Fame's Boys and Girls, who never die. Emily Dickinson. CP-DickE

Fame's pillar here at last we set. Pillar of Fame, The. Robert Herrick. CP-HerrR

Fame's Vanity. Walt Whitman. CP-WhitW

Familiar, The. Wendell Berry. CP-BerrW

Familiar, The. Walter De la Mare. CP-DeLaW

Familiar, The. Marya Alexandrovna Zaturenska. SP-ZatuM

Familiar Things. George Meredith. CP-MerG2

Familiarity Dangerous. Vincent Bourne. CP-CowpW

Families. Grace Paley. CP-PalGC

Families & dreams chained. New Gold Mountain. Yusef Komunyakaa. CP-KomuY

'Families', I said, conscious that I could not find. To My Daughter. Charles Tomlinson. SP-TomlC Fr. For A Granddaughter.

Familist's Hymn, The. John Greenleaf Whittier. CP-WhitJ

Family. Yehuda Amichai. SP-AmicYL, tr. by Benjamin Harshav and Barbara Harshav

Family. Olga Broumas. SP-BrouO

Family. William Corbett. SP-CorbW

Family. Grace Paley. CP-PalGC

Family, A. W. S. Merwin. SP-MerwWF

Family, A. Czeslaw Milosz. CP-MiloC; CP-MiloCN, tr. by Robert Hass

Family, The. Robert Browning. CP-BroR2

Family, The. Robert Creeley. CP-CreeR

Family, The. Donald Hall. CP-HallD

Family, The. Mary Oliver. SP-OlivM

Family, The. Kenneth Rexroth. CP-RexrK

Family Act, The. Wyatt Prunty. SP-PrunW

Family Affairs. Maya Angelou. SP-AngeM

Family Album. Wisława Szymborska. SP-SzymW, tr. by Stanislaw Barańczak and Clare Cavanagh

Family Council of the Yakovlevs, The. James Laughlin. CP-LaugJ

Family Court. Ogden Nash. CP-NashO

Family Ghosts. W. H. Auden. CP-AudeW

Family Group. Archibald MacLeish. CP-MacLA

Family had buried him, The. After the Burial. Thomas Hardy. CP-HardT

Family Of. Alice Walker. CP-WalkA

Family [or Familie], The. George Herbert. CP-HerbG

Family Portrait. Carlos Drummond de Andrade. CP-BishE

Family Portrait. Kenneth Patchen. CP-PatcK

Family Portrait for Our Daughter, A. Wyatt Prunty. SP-PrunW

Family Portrait, The. James Laughlin. CP-LaugJ

Family Portraits. Thomas Hardy. CP-HardT

Family Resemblance, A. Audre Lorde. SP-LordA

Family Reunion. Hayden Carruth. CP-CarHS

Family Reunion. Maxine W. Kumin. SP-KumiM

Family Reunion. Sylvia Plath. CP-PlatS

Family Reunion. Jay Wright. SP-WrigJ

Family Statements. Alan Dugan. CP-DugaA

Family story tells, and it was told true, The. Funnel. Anne Sexton. CP-SextA

Family Tree. Yusef Komunyakaa. CP-KomuY

Family Turn, A. William Stafford. SP-StafW; SP-StafWW

Famous engines support type B network. Thomas Merton. CP-MertT

Famous kingdom of the birds, The. Somewhere Is Such a Kingdom. John Crowe Ransom. SP-RansJ

Famous man is Robin Hood, A. Rob Roy's Grave. William Wordsworth. CP-WorW1; MW-WorW

Famous Poet. Ted Hughes. SP-HughTN

Famous Prediction of Merlin, A. Jonathan Swift. "Seven and Ten addyd to nyne." CP-SwifJ

Famous torturer takes a walk, The. Rough Outline. Charles Simic. SP-SimiC; SP-SimiCE

Famous warriors of the anticke world, The. Sonnet 69. Edmund Spenser. CP-Spens Fr. Amoretti.

Famous Writer, The. Charles Bukowski. SP-BukC3

Fan. Federico García Lorca. CP-GarcF, tr. by Jerome Rothenberg Fr. Wheels of Fortune.

Fan, A; of Madame Mallarmé. Stéphane Mallarmé. CP-MallS, tr. by Henry Weinfield

Fan, A; of Méry Laurent. Stéphane Mallarmé. CP-MallS, tr. by Henry Weinfield

Fan, The. Eugenio Montale. CP-MontE, tr. by Jonathan Galassi

Fan, The. Jaroslav Seifert. SP-SeifJ, tr. by Ewald Osers

Fan surrender'd to a meaning look, The. Restoration of a Stolen Fan, The. To —— ——. Annis Boudinot Stockton. CP-StocA

Fanatic, The. G. K. Chesterton. CP-ChesG

Fanaticism? No. Writing is exciting. Baseball and Writing. Marianne Craig Moore. CP-MoorM

Fanatics have their dreams, wherewith they weave. Fall of Hyperion, The; A Dream. John Keats. CP-KeatJ

Fancies at Navesink. Walt Whitman. CP-WhitW

Fancy. Robert Creeley. CP-CreeR

Fancy. James Vincent Cunningham. CP-CunnJ

Fancy. John Keats. CP-KeatJ

Fancy, A. Thomas Carew. CP-CareT

Fancy and Tradition. William Wordsworth. CP-WorW2

Fancy Another Day Gone. Lorine Niedecker. CP-NiedL

Fancy I had today, The. Amphibian. Robert Browning. CP-BroR2

Fancy in Nubibus. Samuel Taylor Coleridge. CP-ColeS; MW-ColeS

Fancy, who leads the pastimes of the glad. Morning Exercise, A. William Wordsworth. CP-WorW2

Fancy's Knell. A. E. Housman. CP-HousA

Fanfan returns the victor; Molly's sold. Keepsake. Eugenio Montale. CP-MontE, *tr. by* Jonathan Galassi

Fanning his amorous eagerness inside. Tartufe's Punishment. Arthur Rimbaud. CP-RimbA, *tr. by* Martin Sorrell

Fanny. Carolyn Kizer. CP-KizeC *Fr.* Pro Femina.

Fans and the beltings they roar round me, The. Song of the Lathes, The. Rudyard Kipling. CP-KiplR

Fantaisies Décoratives. Oscar Wilde. CP-WildO

Fantasia on 'Horbury'; John Bacchus Dykes, 1859. Geoffrey Hill. CP-HillG

Fantasia on "The Nut-Brown Maid." John Ashbery. "Unless this is the shelf of whatever happens?" SP-AshbJ

Fantasies / indulged, great. Robert Creeley. CP-CreeR

Fantastic Engraving, A. Charles Baudelaire. CP-BaudC, *tr. by* Walter Martin

Fantasy. James Whitcomb Riley. CP-RileJ *Fr.* Adjustable Lunatic, An.

Fantasy. Robinson Jeffers. CP-JefR3

Fantasy. Frank O'Hara. SP-OharF

Fantasy. Dorothy Parker. CP-ParkD

Fantasy, A. James Whitcomb Riley. CP-RileJ

Fantasy and Conversation. Audre Lorde. SP-LordA

Fantasy in Purple. Langston Hughes. CP-HughL; CP-HughL1

Fantasy of a Small Idea. Richard Eberhart. CP-EberR

Fantasy that came to me, A. Fantasy. James Whitcomb Riley. CP-RileJ *Fr.* Adjustable Lunatic, An.

Fantasy that came to me, A. Fantasy, A. James Whitcomb Riley. CP-RileJ

Far above the dome. It Pleases. Gary Snyder. CP-SnydG

Far are the shades of Arabia. Arabia. Walter De la Mare. CP-DeLaW

Far are those tranquil hills. Three Strangers, The. Walter De la Mare. CP-DeLaW

Far Away. Czeslaw Milosz. CP-MiloCN, *tr. by* Robert Hass

Far away in the twilight time. Double-Headed Snake of Newbury, The. John Greenleaf Whittier. CP-WhitJ

Far away is close at hand. Song of Contrariety. Robert Graves. CP-GravR

Far away is the land of rest. Lines: "Far away is the land of rest." Emily Jane Brontë. CP-BronE

Far away under us, they are mowing on the green steps. Beholders, The. James Dickey. CP-DickJ

Far back, in the most remote times with their fresh colors. Garden, The. Robert Pinsky. CP-PinsR

Far back, related on my mother's side. Old Salt Kossabone. Walt Whitman. CP-WhitW

Far back when I went zig-zagging. Orion. Adrienne Rich. CP-RicAE; SP-RicA1; SP-RicA2

Far below, plowed fields vibrated. Gregory Orr. SP-OrrG

Far court opens for us all July, The. Prothalamion. Maxine W. Kumin. SP-KumiM

Far Cry from Africa, A. Derek Walcott. CP-WalcD

Far down the purple wood. Constant Bridegrooms, The. Kenneth Patchen. CP-PatcK

"Far enough down is China," somebody said. Digging for China. Richard Wilbur. CP-WilbR

Far-Far-Away. Alfred Tennyson. CP-TennA

Far, far away is mirth withdrawn. Emily Jane Brontë. CP-BronE

Far, far away, O ye. Lines: "Far, far away, O ye." Percy Bysshe Shelley. CP-ShelP

Far far from gusty waves these children's faces. Elementary School Classroom in a Slum, An. Stephen Spender. CP-SpenS

Far far o'er city and field thou art flying. Passage Bird, The. Jones Very. CP-VeryJ

Far, far southward, the forest is white, not merely. Caribou. Robert Penn Warren. CP-WarrR

Far far the least of all, in want. Prisoners, The. Stephen Spender. CP-SpenS

Far from a you it is always early. Home Movies. Olga Broumas. SP-BrouO

Far from birds, flocks, from village girls. Tear. Arthur Rimbaud. CP-RimbA, *tr. by* Martin Sorrell

Far from here but still in sight. Ship. W. S. Merwin. SP-MerwW

Far from his close and noisome cell. Human Sacrifice, The. John Greenleaf Whittier. CP-WhitJ

Far from his early charge, at four score years. Oliver C. Felton, Esq., of Brookfield. Jones Very. CP-VeryJ

Far from home Grotus dedicated an alter to Coventina. Grotus and Coventina. Seamus Heaney. SP-HeanSO

Far from Love the Heavenly Father. Emily Dickinson. CP-DickE

Far from me. She Is. Robert Creeley. SP-CreeR

Far from my dearest Friend, 'tis mine to rove. Evening Walk, An; Addressed to a Young Lady. William Wordsworth. CP-WorW1; MW-WorW

Far from normal far from normal far from normal I am. I Am. Stevie Smith. CP-SmitS

Far from our home by Grasmere's quiet Lake. Epistle to Sir George Howland Beaumont, BART. William Wordsworth. CP-WorW1

Far from the clams and fogs and bogs. End of the Rainbow, The. Randall Jarrell. CP-JarrR

Far from the marketplace, the city's roar. Jonathan Edwards. Jorge Luis Borges. SP-BorgJ, *tr. by* Alan S. Trueblood

Far from the Player's Club but not in play. Player's Club, The. G. K. Chesterton. CP-ChesG

Far from the Rappahannock, the silent. Into the Dusk-Charged Air. John Ashbery. CP-AshbJ

Far from the sea far from the sea. Canticle of Jack Kerouac, The. Lawrence Ferlinghetti. SP-FerlL

Far from the steamy parlors of the north. Little Robber Girl Considers the Wide World, The. Marilyn Hacker. SP-HackM

Far from the world, poetic magic intoxicates him. Singer. Constantine P. Cavafy. CP-CavaC, *tr. by* Theoharis Constantine Theoharis

Far from this atmosphere that music sounds. Music. Henry David Thoreau. CP-ThorH

Far happier are the dead, methinks, than they. On Invalids. *Unknown.* CP-CowpW

Far hence amid an isle of wondrous beauty. Old Ireland. Walt Whitman. CP-WhitW

Far I hear the bugle blow. Day of Battle, The. A. E. Housman. CP-HousA

Far in a western brookland. A. E. Housman. CP-HousA

Far in the chambers of the west. Dawn and Sunrise. Sir Walter Scott. SP-ScotW *Fr.* Rokeby.

Far in the dim past, the dark house of childhood. Past and Present. G. K. Chesterton. CP-ChesG

Far in the night, and yet no rest for him! The pillow next his own. At Noon—and Midnight. James Whitcomb Riley. CP-RileJ

Far in the sunlit eastward. Creator, The. G. K. Chesterton. CP-ChesG

Far inland here Death's pinions mocked the roar. Truce. Walter De la Mare. CP-DeLaW

Far islands . . . veiled by cold rain. Beyond Seattle. Thomas McGrath. SP-McGrT

Far known to sea and shore. A. E. Housman. CP-HousA

Far Memory. Lucille Clifton. SP-ClifL

Far moon maketh lovers wise, The. Moonlight. Walter De la Mare. CP-DeLaW

Far Mosque, The. Jelaluddin Rumi. SP-Rumi, *tr. by* Coleman Barks

Far north a crossroad in mud. Junction. W. S. Merwin. SP-MerwWF

Far oer The bow. Henry David Thoreau. CP-ThorH

Far Off. Constantine P. Cavafy. CP-CavaC, *tr. by* Theoharis Constantine Theoharis

Far off, above the plain the summer dries. Second Air Force. Randall Jarrell. CP-JarrR

Far off, among the distant hills. Arethusa Meadow. Jones Very. CP-VeryJ

Far-off / at the core of space. Swan. D. H. Lawrence. CP-LawrD

Far off, from the burned fields. Ashes. Philip Levine. SP-LeviP

Far off I see, like a dim cloud, the hills. On Seeing the White Mountains from Cook's Hill, in West Peabody. Jones Very. CP-VeryJ

Far-off, most secret, and inviolate Rose. Secret Rose, The. William Butler Yeats. CP-YeatW

Far Off-Shore. Herman Melville. SP-MelvH

Far-off the lily-statues stand white-ranked in the garden at home. At the Front. D. H. Lawrence. CP-LawrD

Far off the road on the left on a slight rolling hill. John Logan. CP-LogaJ *Fr.* Monologues of the Son of Saul.

Far Out. Philip Larkin. CP-LarkP

Far Out, Far In. Theodore Weiss. SP-WeisT

Far overhead—the glass set fair. Omen, The. Walter De la Mare. CP-DeLaW

Far Point. Charles Tomlinson. SP-TomlC

Far-removed Mountain Men, The. Hayden Carruth. CP-CarHS

Far roam the death-faces. Second-Death. Laura Riding Jackson. CP-RidiL

Far Rockaway Night Till Morning. Carl Sandburg. CP-SandC

Far seen the river glides below. Ralph Waldo Emerson. CP-EmerR

Far side of your moon is black, The. Song: The Far Side of Your Moon. Robert Graves. CP-GravR

Far-Sighted Muse, The. Dorothy Parker. CP-ParkD

Far star that tickles for me my sensitive plate. Skeptic. Robert Frost. CP-FrosR

Far West. Czeslaw Milosz. CP-MiloC; CP-MiloCN, *tr. by* Robert Hass

Far West Once. Robert Penn Warren. CP-WarrR

Farallones seals clubbed, The. Visiting the Farallones. Robert Bly. SP-BlyR

Fare Thee Well. Lord Byron. CP-Byron

Fare Thee Well. Donald Davie. CP-DaviDC

Fare thee well, it was your face, and now the face of memory. Farewell: "Fare thee well, it was your face, and now the face of memory." Yehuda Amichai. SP-AmicYL, *tr. by* Benjamin Harshav *and* Barbara Harshav

Fare Well. John Berryman. CP-BerrJ

Fare Well. Walter De la Mare. CP-DeLaW

Fareweel to a' our Scotish fame. Such a Parcel of Rogues in a Nation. Robert Burns. CP-BurnR

Farewel D..r Friend! may Guid-luck hit you. To John Kennedy. Robert Burns. CP-BurnR

Farewel! ye friendly bow'rs, ye streams adieu. Elegy on Leaving, An. Phillis Wheatley. CP-WheaP

Farewell. Sir Walter Scott. *See* Lady of the Lake, The

Farewell. Yehuda Amichai. SP-AmicY, *tr. by* Stephen Mitchell

Farewell. Arthur Rimbaud. CP-RimbA, *tr. by* Martin Sorrell

Farewell. Henry David Thoreau. CP-ThorH

Farewell, A. Langston Hughes. CP-HughL; CP-HughL1

Farewell, A. Niccolò Tommaseo. CW-RossD, *tr. by* Dante Gabriel Rossetti

Farewell, A: "Farewell thou little Nook of mountain-ground." William Wordsworth. CP-WorW1; MW-WorW

Farewell, A: "Flow down, cold rivulet, to the sea." Alfred Tennyson. CP-TennA

Farewell, A: "My horse's feet beside the lake." Matthew Arnold. SP-ArnoM *Fr.* Switzerland.

Farewell, A: "What shall I say, dear friends, to whom I owe." John Greenleaf Whittier. CP-WhitJ

Farewell, The: "Farewell, old Scotia's bleak domains." Robert Burns. CP-BurnR

Farewell, The: "Sweetest Loue since wee must part." Robert Herrick. CP-HerrR

Farewell, The: "Gone, gone,—sold and gone." John Greenleaf Whittier. CP-WhitJ

Farewell, Age Ten, A. William Stafford. SP-StafWW

Farewell, all my welfare. Sir Thomas Wyatt. CP-WyatT

Farewell and adieu to you, Harwich Ladies. Rudyard Kipling. CP-KiplR

Farewell and adieu to you noble hearties. Tom Deadlight. Herman Melville. SP-MelvH

Farewell!—But not for ever, Hope replies. Translation of Epitaph to Northcot. William Cowper. CP-CowpW

Farewell, clear and profound. Image of a Friend. Marya Alexandrovna Zaturenska. SP-ZatuM

Farewell dear babe, my heart's too much content. In Memory of My Dear Grandchild Elizabeth Bradstreet Who Deceased August, 1665, Being a Year and Half Old. Anne Bradstreet. CP-BradA

Farewell dear England, and thy Church farewell! Farewell: "Farewell dear England, and thy Church farewell!" Jones Very. CP-VeryJ

Farewell dear friends. Farewell: "Farewell dear friends." Stevie Smith. CP-SmitS

Farewell, dear scenes, for ever closed to me. Lines Written upon a Window-Shutter at Weston. William Cowper. CP-CowpW

Farewell! endued with all that could engage. Lines for a Memorial of Ashley Cowper. William Cowper. CP-CowpW

Farewell fair Arminda, my joy and my grief. Song: "Farewell fair Arminda, my joy and my grief." John Dryden. SP-DrydJ

Farewell fair Saint, may not the seas and wind. On His Mistress[e] Going to Sea. Thomas Cary. CP-CareT

Farewell, false hearts! whose best affections fail. Valediction, The: "Farewell, false hearts! whose best affections fail." William Cowper. CP-CowpW

Farewell, false love, the oracle of lies. Farewell to False Love, A. Sir Walter Ralegh. CP-RaleW

Farewell: "Fare thee well, it was your face, and now the face of memory." Yehuda Amichai. SP-AmicYL, *tr. by* Benjamin Harshav *and* Barbara Harshav

Farewell: "Farewell dear England, and thy Church farewell!" Jones Very. CP-VeryJ

Farewell: "Farewell dear friends." Stevie Smith. CP-SmitS

Farewell, Farewell, *Despedida!* Jesus' Farewell. D. H. Lawrence. CP-LawrD

Farewell, farewell, my love Irene. My Love Irene. Paul Laurence Dunbar. CP-DunbP

Farewell, Foolish Objects. Charles Bukowski. SP-BukC2

Farewell for ever, well for ever fare. Murder. Stevie Smith. CP-SmitS

Farewell for Zbigniew Herbert. Adam Zagajewski. SP-ZagaA, *tr. by* Clare Cavanagh

Farewell Frost; or, Welcome the Spring. Robert Herrick. CP-HerrR

Farewell, German radio with your green eye. Electric Elegy. Adam Zagajewski. SP-ZagaA, *tr. by* Renata Gorczynski, Benjamin Ivry *and* C. K. Williams

Farewell: "I speak to you, my son." Czeslaw Milosz. CP-MiloC; CP-MiloCN, *tr. by* Renata Gorczynski *and* Robert Hass

Farewell! If Ever Fondest Prayer. Lord Byron. CP-Byron

Farewell: "If I die." Federico García Lorca. SP-GarcF, *tr. by* W. S. Merwin

Farewell Lines. William Wordsworth. CP-WorW2

Farewell, my Highland lassie! when the year returns around. O Theos Meta Sou. Arthur Hugh Clough. SP-ClouA

Farewell, old Scotia's bleak domains. Farewell, The: "Farewell, old Scotia's bleak domains." Robert Burns. CP-BurnR

Farewell parental scenes! a sad farewell! Sonnet on Quitting Christ's Hospital. Samuel Taylor Coleridge. CP-ColeS

Farewell Petition to J.C.H., Esq. Lord Byron. CP-Byron

Farewell Rehearsed. Allen Tate. CP-TateA

"Farewell, Romance!" the Cave-men said. King, The. Rudyard Kipling. CP-KiplR

Farewell,runaway snows! For the meadow is green,and the tree stands. Ode 4.7: "Farewell,runaway snows! For the meadow is green,and the tree stands." Horace. CP-CummE *Fr.* Odes.

Farewell sadness. Scarcely Disfigured. Paul Éluard. CP-BeckS

Farewell Song. Paul Laurence Dunbar. CP-DunbP

Farewell, sweet Love! yet blame you not my truth. Farewell to Love. Samuel Taylor Coleridge. CP-ColeS

Farewell Symphony, The. Randall Jarrell. CP-JarrR

Farewell, the reign of cruelty! Sir Thomas Wyatt. CP-WyatT

Farewell Thing While Breathing, A. Charles Bukowski. SP-BukC2

Farewell, thou child of my right hand and joy On My First Son[ne]. Ben Jonson. CP-JonsB; SP-JonsB

Farewell, thou fair day; thou green earth; and ye skies. Orananaoig, or, the Song of Death. Robert Burns. CP-BurnR

Farewell thou little Nook of mountain-ground. Farewell, A: "Farewell thou little Nook of mountain-ground." William Wordsworth. CP-WorW1; MW-WorW

Farewell, thou stream that winding flows. Song: "Farewell, thou stream that winding flows." Robert Burns. CP-BurnR

Farewell, thou Thing, time-past so knowne, so dear. His Farewell [*or* Fare-well] to Sack. Robert Herrick. CP-HerrR

Farewell to a name and a number. A. E. Housman. CP-HousA

Farewell To Alexandria, A. Emily Jane Brontë. CP-BronE

Farewel[l] to America, A. To Mrs. S. W. Phillis Wheatley. CP-WheaP

(To the Empire of America, beneath the Western Hemisphere. Farewell to America. To Mrs. S. W.) CP-WheaP

Farewell to Anactoria. Sappho. CP-TateA, *tr. by* Allen Tate

Farewell to Arcady. Paul Laurence Dunbar. CP-DunbP

Farewell to Bædeker. Robert Stock. SP-StocR

Farewell to barn and stack and tree. A. E. Housman. CP-HousA

Farewell to False Love, A. Sir Walter Ralegh. CP-RaleW

Farewell to Florida. Wallace Stevens. CP-StevW; CP-StevWP

Farewell to London in the Year 1715, A. Alexander Pope. CP-PopeA

Farewell to Love. Samuel Taylor Coleridge. CP-ColeS

Farewell to Love. John Donne. CP-DonnJ; MW-DonnJ

Farewell to Love. Sir John Suckling. CP-SuckJ

(Well-shadow'd landskip, fare ye well.) CP-SuckJ

Farewell to Malta. Lord Byron. CP-Byron

Farewell to Miles. John Berryman. CP-BerrJ

Farewell to the Bluewoman. Kenneth Patchen. CP-PatcK

Farewell. To the Brethren of St. James' Lodge, Tarbolton, The. Robert Burns. CP-BurnR

Farewell to the Court. Sir Walter Ralegh. CP-RaleW

Farewell to the Glen. Dante Gabriel Rossetti. CW-RossD *Fr.* House of Life, The

Farewell to the Land where the gloom of my Glory. Napoleon's Farewell. Lord Byron. CP-Byron

Farewell to the Muse. Lord Byron. CP-Byron

Farewell to the Shopping District of Antibes. John Updike. CP-UpdiJ

Farewell to Van Gogh. Charles Tomlinson. CP-TomlC; SP-TomlC

Farewell, too little and too lately known. To the Memory of Mr Oldham. John Dryden. CP-DryJ2; SP-DrydJ

Farewell ungrateful[l] traitor [*or* traytor], / Farewell my perjured swain. John Dryden. SP-DrydJ *Fr.* Spanish Friar [*or* Fryar], The.

Farewell without a Guitar. Wallace Stevens. CP-StevWP

Farewell, ye dungeons dark and strong. Macpherson's Farewell. Robert Burns. CP-BurnR

Farewell, ye lofty spires. Last Farewell, The. Edward Bliss Emerson. CP-EmerR

Farewells, whistling in the dark, waves, coughs. Eugenio Montale. CP-MontE, *tr. by* Jonathan Galassi

Fargo. John Updike. CP-UpdiJ

Faring, The. Charles Tomlinson. CP-TomlC; SP-TomlC

Farm, The. Robert Creeley. CP-CreeR

Farm, The. Donald Hall. CP-HallD

Farm, The. Archibald MacLeish. CP-MacLA

Farm afternoons, there's much too much blue air. Sonnet of Intimacy. Vinícius de Moraes. CP-BishE

Farm boy lost in the snow, A. Or, Solitude. Donald Davie. CP-DaviDC

Farm boys wild to couple. Sheep Child, The. James Dickey. CP-DickJ

Farm Child's Lullaby, The. Paul Laurence Dunbar. CP-DunbP

Farm Country. Mary Oliver. SP-OlivM

Farm Implements and Rutabagas in a Landscape. John Ashbery. SP-AshbJ

Farm on the Great Plains, The. William Stafford. SP-StafW; SP-StafWW

Farm Picture, A. Walt Whitman. CP-WhitW

Farm Walk, A. Christina Georgina Rossetti. *See* Milking-Maid, The

Farm-Woman's Winter, The. Thomas Hardy. CP-HardT

Farmer. Yannis Ritsos. SP-RitsY, *tr.* by Kimon Friar

Farmer Among the Tombs, The. Wendell Berry. CP-BerrW

Farmer and the Sea, The. Wendell Berry. CP-BerrW

Farmer drags two lashed poles through a storm, A. Tomb Pond. Norman Dubie. CP-DubiN

Farmer Dunman's Funeral. Thomas Hardy. CP-HardT

Farmer in deep thought, The. Farmer, The. William Carlos Williams. CP-WilW1

Farmer, in the pride of sea-won acres, The. Sunday in October. Richard Eberhart. CP-EberR

Farmer of the Augustan Age, A. Bees and the Flies, The. Rudyard Kipling. CP-KiplR

Farmer of Tilsbury Vale, The. William Wordsworth. CP-WorW1

Farmer sings about the Fourth Moon, A. Buried Light. Yusef Komunyakaa. CP-KomuY

Farmer, Speaking of Monuments, The. Wendell Berry. CP-BerrW

Farmer, The. William Carlos Williams. CP-WilW1

Farmer Whipple—Bachelor. James Whitcomb Riley. CP-RileJ

Farmer with acres of mulberry groves, A. Han-shan. CP-ColdM, *tr.* by Red Pine

Farmer with his milk pail, The. At Muker, Upper Swaledale. Amy Clampitt. CP-ClamA

Farmers. James Dickey. CP-DickJ

Farmers. Thomas Lux. SP-LuxT

Farmer's goose, who in the stubble, The. Progress of Poetry, The. Jonathan Swift. CP-SwifJ

Farmers in the fields, housewives behind. Casualty, The. Ted Hughes. SP-HughTN

Farmer's Wife: at Fostons Ash, The. Charles Tomlinson. CP-TomlC

Farmer's wife missed the tails entirely, The. On Word That the Old Children's Stories Have Been Brought Up to Date. Miller Williams. CP-WillM

Farmer's Wife, The. Anne Sexton. CP-SextA

Farmhouse lingers, though averse to square, The. Brook in the City, A. Robert Frost. CP-FrosR

Farmhouses north of Driggs, The. Itinerary. James McMichael. SP-McMiJ

Farms are oozing [*or* stinking] craters in, The. Crow Hill. Ted Hughes. SP-HughTN

Farms of home lie lost in even, The. A. E. Housman. CP-HousA

Farther up the gorge the sea's voice fainted and ceased. All the Little Hoof-Prints. Robinson Jeffers. CP-JefR2

Farthest am I from perfection's heights. Invictus. Dorothy Parker. CP-ParkD

Farthest Thunder that I heard, The. Emily Dickinson. CP-DickE

Fascinating chill that music leaves, The. Emily Dickinson. CP-DickE

Fascination. Andrei Codrescu. SP-CodrA

Fascination. Langston Hughes. CP-HughL; CP-HughL1

Fascination of What's Difficult, The. William Butler Yeats. CP-YeatW

Fashions are changing in the sphere. Change of World, A. Adrienne Rich. CP-RicAE

Fast. Olga Broumas. SP-BrouO

Fast. Heather McHugh. SP-McHuH

Fast, The. Gregory Orr. SP-OrrG

Fast-Anchor'd Eternal O Love! Walt Whitman. CP-WhitW

Fast as You Can Count to Ten. John Ciardi. CP-CiarJ

Fast asleep, mine own familiar friend. Better So. Christina Georgina Rossetti. CP-RosC3

Fast Bound Together. Robert Graves. CP-GravR

Fast breaks. Lay ups. With Mercury's. Slam, Dunk, & Hook. Yusef Komunyakaa. CP-KomuY

Fast Food. C. K. Williams. SP-WillC

Fast friends, the best friends to my ease. Sitting for a Self-Portrait. Robert Stock. SP-StocR

Fast from thine evil growing will within. Corrupt Tree, The. Jones Very. CP-VeryJ

Fast, or Lent, The. Robert Herrick. CP-HerrR

Fast rode the knight. Stephen Crane. CP-CranS

Fast this Life of mine was dying. Life and Love. Elizabeth Barrett Browning. CP-BroEB

Fasten black eyes on me. Spanish. Carl Sandburg. CP-SandC

Fasten your hair with a golden pin. He Gives His Beloved Certain Rhymes. William Butler Yeats. CP-YeatW

Faster, faster with no loss of ritual. Procession. Allen Tate. CP-TateA

Fastest of our machines, The. Hare in the Data Processing Centre, A. Hans Magnus Enzensberger. SP-EnzeH

Fasting. Jelaluddin Rumi. SP-Rumi, *tr.* by Coleman Barks

Fastness. Rudyard Kipling. CP-KiplR *Fr.* Muse among the Motors, The.

Fat. C. K. Williams. SP-WillC

Fat, aging, the child clinging to her hand. Randall Jarrell. CP-JarrR

Fat and bored, pedestrian. Gnostic at the Zoo, The. Wyatt Prunty. SP-PrunW

Fat be my Hinde; unlearned be my wife. His Wish. Robert Herrick. CP-HerrR

Fat black bucks in a wine-barrel room. Congo, The. Nicholas Vachel Lindsay. CP-LindV

Fat hands, no longer guided, rest their talons. Tyrant Dying. Thomas Kinsella. CP-KinsT

Fat-kneed god! Feeder of mangy leopards! You Also, Gaius Valerius Catullus. Archibald MacLeish. CP-MacLA

Fat Lady, The. Hayden Carruth. CP-CarHS

Fat lady came first, The. Landscape of a Vomiting Multitude. Federico García Lorca. CP-GarcF, *tr.* by Greg Simon *and* Steven F. White

Fat Man in the Mirror, The. Robert Lowell. SP-LoweR

Fat robin redbreast getting fatter. Academy of Sincerity. Robert Stock. SP-StocR

Fat singer in three keys. Rhythm, Charts and Changes. Jay Wright. SP-WrigJ

Fat sixty-year-old man woke me, A. "Hello" Birthday. John Ciardi. CP-CiarJ

Fat Woman, The. Walter De la Mare. CP-DeLaW

Fata Morgana. Christina Georgina Rossetti. CP-RosC1

Fatal Interview. Edna St. Vincent Millay. CP-MillE

Fatal Interview: Penthesilea and Achilles. Robert Penn Warren. CP-WarrR

Fatal Lamp! whose brilliant ray. Camphene Lamp, The. Jones Very. CP-VeryJ

Fatal Sisters, The. Thomas Gray. CP-GrayT

Fatality. D. H. Lawrence. CP-LawrD

Fate. Ralph Waldo Emerson. CP-EmerR

Fate. Ralph Waldo Emerson. CP-EmerR

Fate. Kenneth Koch. SP-KochK

Fate. W. S. Merwin. SP-MerwWF

Fate. Carl Sandburg. CP-SandC

Fate and the Younger Generation. D. H. Lawrence. CP-LawrD

Fate comes with pennies or dollars. Fate. Carl Sandburg. CP-SandC

Fate gave the word, the arrow sped. Mother's Lament for the Death of Her Son, A. Robert Burns. CP-BurnR

Fate hired me once to play a villain's part. Between the Acts. Stanley Kunitz. CP-KunSC

Fate is dead. God is in man. Truth, The. Alfonso Cortes. CP-MertT

Fate lifts us up so she can hurl. In Memoriam. John Updike. CP-UpdiJ

Fate of Actaeon, The. James Laughlin. CP-LaugJ

Fate of the Observer, The. Yannis Ritsos. SP-RitsY, *tr.* by N. C. Germanacos

Fate slew Him, but He did not drop. Emily Dickinson. CP-DickE

Fate succumbs. Marginalia. W. H. Auden. CP-AudeW

Fate summoned, in gray-bearded age, to act. Thiers. John Greenleaf Whittier. CP-WhitJ

Fateless Ones, The. Kathleen Jessie Raine. SP-RainK

Fately alone with you once more. That Other World. Robert Graves. CP-GravR

Fates, The. Wilfred Owen. CP-OwenW

Fates and the Mothers, The. Laura Riding Jackson. CP-RidiL

Fate's now grown merciful to men. Tooth-Ache Cured by a Kiss, The. Thomas Carew. CP-CareT

Father. A. R. Ammons. CP-AmmoA

Father. David Ignatow. SP-IgnaD

Father. Robert Lowell. SP-LoweR

Father. James Wright. CP-WrigJ

Father, The. Jones Very. CP-VeryJ

Father all bountiful, in mercy bear. America's Thanksgiving. James Whitcomb Riley. CP-RileJ

Father and Child. William Butler Yeats. CP-YeatW

Father and I drove to the sand-quarry across the ruined marshlands. Sand-Quarry with Moving Figures. Muriel Rukeyser. CP-RukeM

Father and master magician, divine lyre-bearer. Prayer for the Dead (To Verlaine). "Rubén Dario." SP-DariR, *tr.* by Alberto Acereda *and* Will Derusha

Father / and mother / and sister. Family, The. Robert Creeley. CP-CreeR

Father and mother sat, and the sister beside her, The. Four in a Family. Muriel Rukeyser. CP-RukeM

Father and Son. David Ignatow. SP-IgnaD

Father and Son. Stanley Kunitz. CP-KunSC, *tr.* by Jack Bevan

Father and Son. William Stafford. SP-StafWW

Father asks for the salt. Suppertime. Grace Paley. CP-PalGC

Father capers across the yard cobbles, The. Last of the 1st/5th Lancashire Fusiliers, The. Ted Hughes. SP-HughTN

Father Ch., Many Years Later. Czeslaw Milosz. CP-MiloC; CP-MiloCN, *tr.* by Robert Hass

Father Chomski, the vicar of Vaidotai parish. Father Ch., Many Years Later. Czeslaw Milosz. CP-MiloC; CP-MiloCN, *tr.* by Robert Hass

Father Christmas. For Noel. Gabriela Mistral. SP-MistG, *tr.* by Maria Giachetti [*or* Jacketti]

Father-confessor / Of the fat hen. Knife. Charles Simic. SP-SimiC; SP-SimiCE

Father, Dear Father, Go Jump in the Lake, or, You're Costlier than You Think. Ogden Nash. CP-NashO

Father dreams that he was hid in a tree, The. Muriel Rukeyser. CP-RukeM

Father, Father, I am overwhelmed. Prayer After All, A. John Berryman. CP-BerrJ

Father fell backwards off the stool. Father. David Ignatow. SP-IgnaD

Father for a Fool, A. Stevie Smith. CP-SmitS

Father Guru. Allen Ginsberg. CP-GinsA

Father Guru unforlorn. Father Guru. Allen Ginsberg. CP-GinsA

Father has given his year-old son *Le Monde* to play with in his stroller and the baby does, The. Reading: Early Sorrow. C. K. Williams. SP-WillC

Father has his arm around Tereze. Still Life. Louise Glück. SP-GlucL

Father / (he calls himself). Boat, The. Anne Sexton. SP-SextA *Fr.* Death of the Fathers, The.

Father! help them who walk in their own light. Prayer, The ("Father! help them who walk in their own light"). Jones Very. CP-VeryJ

Father, I fear your trade. Bird-Catcher's Boy, The. Thomas Hardy. CP-HardT

Father, I scarcely could believe you dead. From an Asian Tent. Thom Gunn. CP-GunnT

Father, I thank Thee that the day begins. Laborer, The. Jones Very. CP-VeryJ

Father, / I wait for you in oceans. Child Dead in Old Seas. Maya Angelou. SP-AngeM

Father! I wait thy word—the sun doth stand. Son, The. Jones Very. CP-VeryJ

Father in a Dream. Robert Lowell. SP-LoweR

Father is the Void, The. No Matter, Never Mind. Gary Snyder. CP-SnydG

Father John Burges, / Necessity urges. To Master John Burges. Ben Jonson. CP-JonsB; SP-JonsB

Father, Mother, and me. We and They. Rudyard Kipling. CP-KiplR *Fr.* Debits and Credits.

Father of all! in every [*or* ev'ry] age. Universal Prayer [Deo Opt. Max.], The. Alexander Pope. CP-PopeA

Father of heaven, and him, by whom. Litany, A. John Donne. CP-DonnJ; MW-DonnJ

Father of heaven, for all the days now lost. Petrarch. CP-Petra, *tr.* by J. G. Nichols

Father of his country stood, The. Washington. Jones Very. CP-VeryJ

Father of Light! great God of Heaven! Prayer of Nature, The. Lord Byron. CP-Byron

Father out Walking on the Lawn, A. Rita Dove. SP-DoveR

Father Reason. Jelaluddin Rumi. SP-Rumi, *tr.* by Coleman Barks

Father shall shine. The father shall stand at home. Now, The. Another Day. A Game of Toys. Paul, Telling the Game. Muriel Rukeyser. CP-RukeM

"Father!" (so The Word) He cried. Christ, The. James Whitcomb Riley. CP-RileJ

Father Son and Holy Ghost. Audre Lorde. SP-LordA

Father, the Cavalier. Donald Davie. CP-DaviDC

Father, / the Santa Claus suit. Santa. Anne Sexton. SP-SextA *Fr.* Death of the Fathers, The.

Father, the Year Has Fallen. Audre Lorde. SP-LordA

Father! there is no change to live with Thee. Change. Jones Very. CP-VeryJ

Father, this year's jinx rides us apart. All My Pretty Ones. Anne Sexton. CP-SextA; SP-SextA

Father, Thou wilt accept the pure in heart. Pure in Heart, The. Jones Very. CP-VeryJ

Father! Thy wonders do not singly stand. Spirit Land, The ("Father! Thy wonders do not singly stand"). Jones Very. CP-VeryJ

Father! Thy wonders do not singly stand. God Not Afar Off. Jones Very. CP-VeryJ

Father! to Thy suffering poor. Familist's Hymn, The. John Greenleaf Whittier. CP-WhitJ

Father, under the stone, accept your ruin. Elegy: For You, Father. John Ciardi. CP-CiarJ

Father, what are you doing. Closed House. Charles Simic. SP-SimiCE

Father, when he passed on. Obituary. A. K. Ramanujan. CP-RamaA

Father! whose hard and cruel law. Death of Grant, The. Ambrose Bierce. SP-BierA

Father William. Lee O. Harris. CP-RileJ

Father, you must have been. Offering. Thomas McGrath. SP-McGrT

Father, you seem to have been sleeping fair? Last Journey, A. Thomas Hardy. CP-HardT

Fatherhood. Donald Davie. CP-DaviDC

Fathers, The. Charles Olson. CP-OlsoC

Fathers and Sons. James Dickey. CP-DickJ

Fathers and Sons. Donald Hall. CP-HallD

Father's Bedroom. Robert Lowell. SP-LoweR

Father's dead. Friend. Robert Creeley. SP-CreeR

Fathers die, but sons. Hayden Carruth. CP-CarHS *Fr.* Clay Hill Anthology, The.

Father's letter to your father said. Anne Dick 1. 1936. Robert Lowell. SP-LoweR

Fathers never fit in poems. Non-Birthday Poem for My Father, A. Jay Wright. SP-WrigJ

Father's Song. Gregory Orr. SP-OrrG

Father's Voice. William Stafford. SP-StafW; SP-StafWW

Fatigue. D. H. Lawrence. CP-LawrD

Fatigue of Objects, The. Thomas McGrath. SP-McGrT

Fatigue, regrets. The lights. Demon Lover, The. Adrienne Rich. CP-RicAE; SP-RicA1; SP-RicA2

Fatima. Alfred Tennyson. CP-TennA

Fatted / on herbs, swollen on crabapples. Porcupine, The. Galway Kinnell. SP-KinnGN

Faucet drips all night, the plumber forgot it, The. Dragon-Tree. Robert Penn Warren. CP-WarrR

Fault of It, The. Ezra Pound. CP-PoEar

Faun. Sylvia Plath. CP-PlatS

Faun's Head. Arthur Rimbaud. CP-RimbA, *tr.* by Martin Sorrell

Fauré Ballade, The. James Schuyler. CP-SchuJ

Fauré's Second Piano Quartet. James Schuyler. CP-SchuJ

Faust. Johann Wolfgang von Goethe.
   Prologue in Heaven. CP-ShelP
   "Would you not like a broomstick? As for me." CP-ShelP

Faust. John Ashbery. SP-AshbJ

Faustina, or Rock Roses. Elizabeth Bishop. CP-BishE

Faustus and I. Anne Sexton. CP-SextA

Faustus Triumphant. Thom Gunn. CP-GunnT

Faut de Mieux. Dorothy Parker. CP-ParkD

Fauve. Arthur Sze. SP-SzeA

Favor of Alexander Valas, The. Constantine P. Cavafy. CP-CavaC, *tr.* by Theoharis Constantine Theoharis

Favorite, The. Theodore Roethke. CP-RoetT

Fawn, The. Shmuel HaNagid. SP-HaNaS, *tr.* by Peter Cole

Fawn, The. Edna St. Vincent Millay. CP-MillE

Fawn's Foster-Mother. Robinson Jeffers. CP-JefR1

Fayette beside King Lewis stood. William Blake. CP-BlakW

Fayne Would I But I Dare Not. Sir Walter Ralegh. CP-RaleW

Fayre cruell, why are ye so fierce and cruell? Sonnet 49. Edmund Spenser. CP-Spens *Fr.* Amoretti.

Fayre eyes, the myrrour of my mazed hart. Sonnet 7. Edmund Spenser. CP-Spens *Fr.* Amoretti.

Fayre Mayd, you did but cast your eyes erewhile. To a Mayd. Robert Herrick. CP-HerrR

Fea / therr / ain / :dreamin. E. E. Cummings. CP-CummE

Feacie (some say) doth wash her clothes i'th'Lie. Upon a Cheap Laundresse: Epigram. Robert Herrick. CP-HerrR

Fear. Charles Bukowski. SP BukC1

Fear. Raymond Carver. CP-CarvR

Fear. Andrei Codrescu. SP-CodrA

Fear. Hart Crane. CP-CranH

Fear. James Vincent Cunningham. CP-CunnJ

Fear. Randall Jarrell. CP-JarrR

Fear. Walter De la Mare. CP-DeLaW

Fear. W. S. Merwin. SP-MerwW

Fear. Grace Paley. CP-PalGC

Fear. A. K. Ramanujan. CP-RamaA

Fear. Charles Simic. SP-SimiC; SP-SimiCE

Fear, The. Robert Frost. CP-FrosR

Fear and Trembling. Robert Penn Warren. CP-WarrR

Fear death?—to feel the fog in my throat. Prospice. Robert Browning. CP-BroR1

Fear-Dream (1918). Czeslaw Milosz. CP-MiloC; CP-MiloCN, *tr.* by Robert Hass

Fear-dulled eyes in the pallid face, The. In Disgrace. Walter De la Mare. CP-DeLaW

Fear, Faith, and Hope have sent their hearts above. Ye Are Come unto Mount Sion. Christina Georgina Rossetti. CP-RosC2

Fear Five to the Power of Five. Shmuel HaNagid. SP-HaNaS, *tr.* by Peter Cole

Fear is a monster vast as night. Two Poems from *The Two-Character Play*. Tennessee Williams. CP-WillT

Fear is my way / of not being here although. Fear. Andrei Codrescu. SP-CodrA

Fear Is What Quickens Me. James Wright. CP-WrigJ

Fear, jealousy and murder are the same. Gamecock. James Dickey. CP-DickJ

Fear, like a living fire that only death. Avon's Harvest. Edwin Arlington Robinson. CP-RobiE

Fear—like Dying, dilates trust. Emily Dickinson. SP-DickE

Fear No Fall. A. K. Ramanujan. CP-RamaA

Fear no more, thou timid Flower! Snow-Drop, The. Samuel Taylor Coleridge. CP-ColeS

Fear Not. Gary Snyder. CP-SnydG

Fear not, dear love, that I'll reveal. Secrecy [*or* Secresie] Protested. Thomas Carew. CP-CareT

Fear not, fear not, my children. Plakkopytrixophylisperambulantiobatrix. G. K. Chesterton. CP-ChesG

Fear not: for they that are with us are more than they that are with them. 2

Kings 6:16. Jones Very. CP-VeryJ

Fear of Angels, The. May Sarton. SP-SartM

Fear of Beasts, The. William Meredith. SP-MereW

Fear of Darkness, The. Wendell Berry. CP-BerrW

Fear of death! Who'd shove, The. Michelangelo Buonarroti. CP-Miche, *tr. by* John Frederick Nims

Fear / of drowning. Imitations of Drowning. Anne Sexton. CP-SextA

Fear of falling is why the old men walk. Sonnet: "Fear of falling is why the old men walk." Hayden Carruth. CP-CarHS *Fr.* Sonnets.

Fear of Flying, The. Mona Van Duyn. SP-VanDM

Fear of God, The. Robert Frost. CP-FrosR

Fear of Love, The. Wendell Berry. CP-BerrW

Fear of Man, The. Robert Frost. CP-FrosR

Fear of poetry is the, The. Reading Time : 1 Minute 26 Seconds. Muriel Rukeyser. CP-RukeM

Fear of seeing a police car pull into the drive. Fear. Raymond Carver. CP-CarvR

Fear of Society Is the Root of All Evil. D. H. Lawrence. CP-LawrD

Fear / there is. Fear. W. S. Merwin. SP-MerwW

Fear threads its song. Beast & Burden, The: Seven Improvisations. Yusef Komunyakaa. CP-KomuY

Fear. Three bears / are not fear, mother. Bears at Raspberry Time. Hayden Carruth. CP-CarHS

Fear was always there, The. It lurked in early love. Affliction of William Cowper, The. Marya Alexandrovna Zaturenska. SP-ZatuM

Fear was on the cattle, for the gale was on the sea, The. Mulholland's Contract. Rudyard Kipling. CP-KiplR

Feare. Robert Herrick. CP-HerrR

Fear[e] Gets Force. Robert Herrick. CP-HerrR

Fearful, The. Sylvia Plath. CP-PlatS

Fearful with them gathered about my bed on that dreary autumn. Rising a Little. Kenneth Patchen. CP-PatcK

Fearful Women. Carolyn Kizer. CP-KizeC

Fearlessandbosomy / this / grand:gal. E. E. Cummings. CP-CummE

Fears and Scruples. Robert Browning. CP-BroR2

Fears in Solitude [Written in April, 1798, during the Alarm of an Invasion]. Samuel Taylor Coleridge. CP-ColeS; MW-ColeS

Feast. Edna St. Vincent Millay. CP-MillE

Feast, The. Jones Very. CP-VeryJ

Feast of Friends, A. John Logan. CP-LogaJ

Feast of the Annunciation. Christina Georgina Rossetti. CP-RosC2

Feast of the Presentation. Christina Georgina Rossetti. CP-RosC2

Feast on wine or fast on water. Song of Right and Wrong, The. G. K. Chesterton. CP-ChesG

Feast was over in Branksome tower, The. Branksome Hall. Sir Walter Scott. SP-ScotW *Fr.* Lay of the Last Minstrel, The.

Feasts. John Ciardi. CP-CiarJ

Feather from the Whippoorwill, A. Emily Dickinson. CP-DickE

Feather Lights. Carl Sandburg. CP-SandC

Feather'd battalions, squadrons on the wing. Translation of Addison's Pugmaiogeranomachia; The Battle of the Pygmies and Cranes. Samuel Johnson. CP-JohnS

Feathered Robe, The. Gary Snyder. CP-SnydG

Feathers up fast, and steeples; then in clods. Fountain, The. Donald Davie. CP-DaviDC

Featureless ghost under the wall cannot jerk out at us, The. Elegy for the Silent Voices and the Joiners of Everything. Kenneth Patchen. CP-PatcK

February. John Clare. SP-ClarJ *Fr.* Shepherd's [*or* Shepheards] Calendar, The.

February. Ted Hughes. SP-HughTN

February. Maxine W. Kumin. SP-KumiM

February. W. S. Merwin. SP-MerwW

February. Paul Muldoon. CP-MuldP

February. James Schuyler. CP-SchuJ

February. Charles Simic. SimiC; SP-SimiCE

February: A Thaw. John Clare. *See* Shepherd's [*or* Shepheards] Calendar, The

February Air. Ted Berrigan. SP-BerrT

February almost March bites the cold. Lorine Niedecker. CP-NiedL

February Awakening. John Logan. CP-LogaJ

February Beach. A. R. Ammons. CP-AmmoA

February Dawn. Ivor Gurney. SP-GurnI

February 11th. Anne Sexton. CP-SextA

February 14. William Meredith. SP-MereW

February 14. 1883. Christina Georgina Rossetti. CP-RosC3

February 4th. Anne Sexton. CP-SextA

February in Sydney. Yusef Komunyakaa. CP-KomuY

February Midnight. Josephine Jacobsen. CP-JacoJ

February of the merely real, A. Marilyn Hacker. SP-HackM *Fr.* Separations.

February 17th. Ted Hughes. SP-HughTN

February 17th. Anne Sexton. CP-SextA

February 10, One Year Too Late. Charles Olson. CP-OlsoC

February: The Boy Breughel. Norman Dubie. CP-DubiN

February 3rd. Anne Sexton. CP-SextA; SP-SextA

February 13, 1975. James Schuyler. CP-SchuJ

February Twelfth Birthday Statement. Alan Dugan. CP-DugaA

February 20th. Anne Sexton. CP-SextA

February 21st. Anne Sexton. CP-SextA; SP-SextA

February 29, 1988. William Corbett. SP-CorbW

February 29th. William Corbett. SP-CorbW

February 22. John Updike. CP-UpdiJ

February 2, 1968. Wendell Berry. CP-BerrW

Feckless Dinner-Party, The. Walter De la Mare. CP-DeLaW

Fee, faw, fum! bubble and squeak! Holy-Cross Day. Robert Browning. CP-BroR1

Fee Fi Ho Hum, No Wonder Baby Sucks Her Thumb. Ogden Nash. CP-NashO

Feeble Caligula! To say. August, 1945. Howard Nemerov. CP-NemeH

Feeble claw blanket grab disappear foot hog. Allegorical Painting: Capitalistic Society Destroyed by the Contradiction Within Itself. (Second Five-Year Plan). Philip Whalen. SP-WhalP

Feeble sistrum in the wind. Eugenio Montale. CP-MontE, *tr. by* Jonathan Galassi

Feed on my sheep; my charge, my comfort, feed. Sir Philip Sidney. SP-SidnP *Fr.* Arcadia.

Feeders, The. Donald Davie. CP-DaviDC

Feeding Time. Maxine W. Kumin. SP-KumiM

Feel for the Wrongs of Universal Ken. William Wordsworth. CP-WorW2

Feel for your bad fall how could I fail. Sympathy, A Welcome, A. John Berryman. CP-BerrJ

Feel in the Chris'mas-Air, A. James Whitcomb Riley. CP-RileJ

Feel like a Bird. May Swenson. SP-SwenM

Feel Me. May Swenson. SP-SwenM

"Feel me to do right," our father said on his deathbed. Feel Me. May Swenson. SP-SwenM

Feel of Hands, The. Thom Gunn. CP-GunnT

Feeling and Form. Marilyn Hacker. SP-HackM

Feeling chilled in that cold country. Poem: "Feeling chilled in that cold country." Kenneth Patchen. CP-PatcK

Feeling good, green light, the earthly paradise. Poet Redeemed & Dead. Donald Davie. CP-DaviDC

Feeling is believing. Sayings of the Blind. William Stafford. SP-StafWW

Feeling it with me. Walking on Water. James Dickey. CP-DickJ

Feeling the icy kick, the endless waves. Swimming Lesson, The. Mary Oliver. SP-OlivM

Feelings I don't have I don't have, The. To Women, as Far as I'm Concerned. D. H. Lawrence. CP-LawrD

Feelings of a French Royalist, on the Disinterment of the Remains of the Duke D'Enghien. William Wordsworth. CP-WorW2

Feelings of a Noble Biscayan at One of Those Funerals 1810. William Wordsworth. CP-WorW1

Feelings of a Republican on the Fall of Bonaparte. Percy Bysshe Shelley. CP-ShelP

Feelings of the Tyrolese. William Wordsworth. CP-WorW1

Feels about his new poem. I Know How Every Poet. James Laughlin. CP-LaugJ

Feet have left the wormholed flooring, The. Song to an Old Burden. Thomas Hardy. CP-HardT

Feet Nailed to the Floor. Yusef Komunyakaa. CP-KomuY

Feet o' Jesus. Langston Hughes. CP-HughL; CP-HughL1

Feet of Cheese. Love Is a Dog from Hell. Charles Bukowski. SP-BukC1

Feet of people walking home, The. Emily Dickinson. CP-DickE

Feet of the Young Men, The. Rudyard Kipling. CP-KiplR

Feet waiting in pairs ways of sitting in subways. Going. W. S. Merwin. SP-MerwWF

Felicia Hemans. Elizabeth Barrett Browning. CP-BroEB

Felicitie Knowes No Fence. Robert Herrick. CP-HerrR

Felicitous Life, A. Czeslaw Milosz. CP-MiloC; CP-MiloCN, *tr. by* Lillian Vallee

Felicity of Grief!—even Death being kind. Edna St. Vincent Millay. CP-MillE

Felicity, Quick of Flight. Robert Herrick. CP-HerrR

Felicity the healer isn't young. Doctor Frolic. Robert Pinsky. CP-PinsR

Felicity's Fourth Order. Donald Davie. CP-DaviDC

Feliksowa has gone again from our house and this time for good, I hope. Curse of a Rich Polish Peasant on His Sister Who Ran Away with a Wild Man. Carl Sandburg. CP-SandC

Felix Baran / Hugo Gerlot. Gary Snyder. CP-SnydG *Fr.* Myths and Texts.

Felix Randal. Gerard Manley Hopkins. CP-HopkG

Fellatio. John Updike. CP-UpdiJ

Felled Elm and She, The. Thomas Hardy. CP-HardT

Felled in my tracks by your tremendous horse. Lines to Mr Frost. John Berryman. CP-BerrJ

Felling a Tree. Ivor Gurney. SP-GurnI

Fellow Citizens. Carl Sandburg. CP-SandC

Fellow humans, to whom a year is a long time. In the Beginning. Primo Levi. CP-LeviP, tr. by Ruth Feldman and Brian Swann

Fellow-Men. D. H. Lawrence. CP-LawrD

Fellow no one ever looked at twice, The. Small Wonders. Charles Simic. SP-SimiCE

Fellow Passengers. Denise Levertov. SP-LeveDL

Fellow Soul, Sound Hunting to Thy Immeasurable Heart. Kenneth Patchen. CP-PatcK

Fellows, my teeth hurt. Black Days. Charles Simic. SP-SimiCE

Female. Lucille Clifton. SP-ClifL

Female Author. Sylvia Plath. CP-PlatS

Female body, its creases and declivities, The. Dodona: Asked of the Oracle. Amy Clampitt. CP-ClamA

Female Coercion. D. H. Lawrence. CP-LawrD

Female Martyr, The. John Greenleaf Whittier. CP-WhitJ

Female of the Species, The. Rudyard Kipling. CP-KiplR

Femina Contra Mundum. G. K. Chesterton. CP-ChesG

Feminine Charm. Stevie Smith. CP-SmitS

Femmes Damnees. Philip Larkin. CP-LarkP

Fence, A. Carl Sandburg. CP-SandC

Fence, A. Chestnut trees. Bindweed. God. Adam Zagajewski. SP-ZagaA, tr. by Renata Gorczynski, Benjamin Ivry and C. K. Williams

Fence Posts. Gary Snyder. CP-SnydG

Fence Wire. James Dickey. CP-DickJ

Fennel. Thom Gunn. CP-GunnT

Fennel, serpent and rush. Schematic Nocturne. Federico García Lorca. SP-GarcF, tr. by Stanley Read

Fennel, serpent, and rushes. Nocturne in Outline. Federico García Lorca. CP-GarcF, tr. by Alan S. Trueblood Fr. Theories.

Fer any boy 'at's little as me. Schoolboy's Favorite, The. James Whitcomb Riley. CP-RileJ

Fer forty year and better you have been a friend to me. To My Old Friend, William Leachman. James Whitcomb Riley. CP-RileJ

Fergus and the Druid. William Butler Yeats. CP-YeatW

Fergus Falling. Galway Kinnell. SP-KinnGN

Fern. Ted Hughes. SP-HughTN

Fern-Beds in Hampshire County. Richard Wilbur. CP-WilbR

Fern, Coal, Diamond. Arthur Sze. SP-SzeA

Fern coming up shyly, A. Velvet Rocks. Richard Eberhart. CP-EberR

Fern Hill. Dylan Thomas. CP-ThomD

Fernery, The. Hart Crane. CP-CranH

Ferns. Robert Bly. SP-BlyR

Ferocious as a Bee without a wing. Emily Dickinson. SP-DickE

Ferrini—I. Charles Olson. CP-OlsoC

Ferris Wheel, The. Wyatt Prunty. SP-PrunW

Ferry Me across the Water. Christina Georgina Rossetti. CP-RosC2

Ferry Port. W. S. Merwin. SP-MerwWF

Fertile. William Carlos Williams. CP-WilW2

Fertilest soil this side of the Tigris, The. Fargo. John Updike. CP-UpdiJ

Fessler's Bees. James Whitcomb Riley. CP-RileJ

Festina Lentè. Samuel Johnson. CP-JohnS

Festival lights go on. Fête. Donald Hall. CP-HallD

Festival of massacre: how make it vivid?, The. Bangla Desh: 1. Faiz Ahmad Faiz. CP-KizeC, tr. by Carolyn Kizer

Festival, The. Robert Creeley. CP-CreeR

Festivals have I seen that were not names. Calais, August 15, 1802. William Wordsworth. CP-WorW1; MW-WorW

Festivals of Hunger. Arthur Rimbaud. CP-RimbA, tr. by Martin Sorrell

Festivals of Patience. Arthur Rimbaud. CP-RimbA, tr. by Martin Sorrell

Festivals, The. Robert Duncan. SP-DuncR

Festung, Salzburg, The. Maxine W. Kumin. SP-KumiM

Fetch, papyrus / our soft-measured poet. Carmen 35. Catullus. CP-ZukLS Fr. Carmina.

Fetching Her. Thomas Hardy. CP-HardT

Fête. Donald Hall. CP-HallD

Fête Champetre, The. Robert Burns. CP-BurnR

Fête Galante. Arthur Rimbaud. CP-RimbA, tr. by Martin Sorrell

Fetish. Hans Magnus Enzensberger. SP-EnzeH

Fetter, The. Robert Graves. CP-GravR

Fetters of winter are shattered,shatter, The. Ode 1.4: "Fetters of winter are shattered,shatter, The." Horace. CP-CummE Fr. Odes.

F[o]etus in an acrobat's womb, A. Alien. A. K. Ramanujan. CP-RamaA

Feud. Theodore Roethke. CP-RoetT

Feud, The. Federico García Lorca. CP-GarcF, tr. by Christopher Maurer

Feuer-Nacht. Louise Bogan. CP-BogaL

Fever. Norman Dubie. CP-DubiN

Fever. Thom Gunn. CP-GunnT

Fever. Yusef Komunyakaa. CP-KomuY

Fever. John Updike. CP-UpdiJ

Fever. Hendrik de Vries. CP-RicAE

Fever. Adam Zagajewski. SP-ZagaA, tr. by Renata Gorczynski

Fever, A. John Donne. CP-DonnJ; MW-DonnJ

Fever of afternoon, The. Afternoon. Laura Riding Jackson. CP-RidiL

Fever 103°. Sylvia Plath. CP-PlatS

Fever, the clang in the beleaguered pumproom. Curfew, A. Amy Clampitt. CP-ClamA

Fevers fled with great joy to the hawsers of mooted ships, The. Jewish Cemetery. Federico García Lorca. CP-GarcF, tr. by Greg Simon and Steven F. White

Few and Simple. W. H. Auden. CP-AudeW

Few are free / All might be. Ralph Waldo Emerson. CP-EmerR

Few are my fellow men, A. Fellow-Men. D. H. Lawrence. CP-LawrD

Few Ashes for Sunday Morning, A. Marge Piercy. SP-PierM

Few Axioms for a Young Man, A. Robert Penn Warren. CP-WarrR

Few bold Patriots, Reliques of the Fight, A. Pelayo. William Wordsworth. CP-WorW1

Few brief years have passed away, A. Freed Islands, The. John Greenleaf Whittier. CP-WhitJ

Few clods of dirt, and his life will be forgotten, A. Classic, The. Wisława Szymborska. SP-SzymW, tr. by Stanisław Barańczak and Clare Cavanagh

Few come this way; not that the darkness. Edna St. Vincent Millay. CP-MillE

Few Days, A. James Schuyler. CP-SchuJ

Few Drops Known, The. Walt Whitman. CP-WhitW

Few Easter Eggs, A. Rainer Maria Rilke. CP-RilkFr, tr. by A. Poulin, Jr.

Few footsteps stray when dusk droops o'er. Tailor, The. Walter De la Mare. CP-DeLaW

Few Fortunate. Robert Herrick. CP-HerrR

Few leaves remain, A. Long Goodbye. Thomas McGrath. SP-McGrT

Few Licks, A. Heather McHugh. SP-McHuH

Few light flakes of snow, A. Kyoto: March. Gary Snyder. CP-SnydG

Few miles ago, a year, a year, A. Farewell Symphony, The. Randall Jarrell. CP-JarrR

Few minutes ago, I stepped onto the deck, A. Cobweb, The. Raymond Carver. CP-CarvR

Few nightbirds scissor dusk into silhouettes . . . distant voices harmonize silences, A. Shrines. Yusef Komunyakaa. CP-KomuY

Few nights ago I was half-watching the news on television and half-reading to my daughter, A. Last Deaths, The. C. K. Williams. CP-WillC; SP-WillC

Few of the Bird-Family, A. James Whitcomb Riley. CP-RileJ

Few of them made it to thirty. Our Ancestors' Short Lives. Wisława Szymborska. SP-SzymW, tr. by Stanisław Barańczak and Clare Cavanagh

Few sashay, a few finagle, A. I Knew I'd Sing. Heather McHugh. SP-McHuH

Few Sirens, A. Alice Walker. CP-WalkA

Few Snorts from a Wild One, A. William Stafford. SP-StafWW

Few strokes of ink and there it is, A. Reading the Japanese Poet Issa (1762–1826). Czeslaw Milosz. CP-MiloC; CP-MiloCN, tr. by Robert K. Haas

Few tasks more difficult. Photograph, A. Czeslaw Milosz. CP-MiloCN, tr. by Robert Hass

Few things are duller. When the Devil Was Sick Could He Prove It? Ogden Nash. CP-NashO

Few things are less endearing than a personal comparison. Nymph and the Shepherd, or She Went That-a-Way, The. Ogden Nash. CP-NashO

Few things are more liberating to learn. Truth and Truthfulness. Miller Williams. CP-WillM

Few things for themselves, A. O Florida, Venereal Soil. Wallace Stevens. CP-StevW; CP-StevWP

Few Words, and Some His, In Memory of Clayton Stafford, A. James Vincent Cunningham. CP-CunnJ

Few years have pass'd since thou and I. To a Youthful Friend. Lord Byron. CP-Byron

Few, yet enough. Emily Dickinson. CP-DickE

F[f]rom depth of[f] sin[n] and from a deep [or diepe] despair [or dispaire]. Psalm 130: "Out of the deep [or depths] have I called [or cried unto] thee, O Lord." Bible, O.T. Fr. Psalms.

Fiammetta. Dante Gabriel Rossetti. CW-RossD

Fiammetta Breaks Her Peace. Rita Dove. SP-DoveR

Fiascherino. Charles Tomlinson. CP-TomlC; SP-TomlC

Fiat Voluntas Tua. Oaxaca Bus, The. Charles Tomlinson. CP-TomlC; SP-TomlC

Fickle comfort steals away. Changes. Maya Angelou. SP-AngeM

Fickle crowd with fortune comes and goes, The. Juvenal. CP-JohnS Fr. Satires.

Fickle mankind! Hymn in Adversity. James Vincent Cunningham. CP-CunnJ

Fiction. Howard Nemerov. CP-NemeH

Fiction. William Stafford. SP-StafWW

Fiction and the Reading Public. Philip Larkin. CP-LarkP

Fiction ("Excitement of being someone else about whom"). Rae Armantrout. SP-ArmaA

Fiction ("When the woman's face contorted and she clutched the railing for support, we knew she would die"). Rae Armantrout. SP-ArmaA

Fiddlehead ferns down by our pond, The. Spring Song. John Updike. CP-UpdiJ

Fiddler, The. Thomas Hardy. CP-HardT

Fiddler crab fiddles, glides and dithers. Josephine Jacobsen. CP-JacoJ

Fiddler of Dooney, The. William Butler Yeats. CP-YeatW

Fidelity. D. H. Lawrence. CP-LawrD

Fidelity. William Wordsworth. CP-WorW1

Fidelity never flickers. Emily Dickinson. SP-DickE

Fie, Aphrodite, shamming you are no mother. Bad Example, The. Thomas Hardy. CP-HardT

Fie, Mr. Coleridge!—and can this be you? Reproof and Reply, The. Samuel Taylor Coleridge. CP-ColeS

Fie My Fum. Allen Ginsberg. CP-GinsA

Fie, (quoth my Lady) what a stink is here? Upon a Sowre-Breath Lady. Robert Herrick. CP-HerrR

Fie upon hearts that burn with mutual fire[!]. Against Fruition. Sir John Suckling. CP-SuckJ

Field. Olga Broumas. SP-BrouO

Field, The. Heather McHugh. SP-McHuH

Field and Forest. Randall Jarrell. CP-JarrR

Field and Wood, The. Jones Very. CP-VeryJ

Field Asters. Herman Melville. SP-MelvH

Field got no roads. Snows. Federico García Lorca. CP-GarcF, *tr. by* Jerome Rothenberg *Fr.* Countries.

Field Hospital, A. Randall Jarrell. CP-JarrR

Field Hospital, The. Paul Muldoon. CP-MuldP

Field in New England, A. Gregory Orr. SP-OrrG

Field-Marshal Radetzky. Franz Grillparzer. CP-MerG2

Field mouse flickers, The. Where. Wendell Berry. CP-BerrW

Field near Linden, Alabama. Mary Oliver. SP-OlivM

Field of blond sage, A. Albino. Yusef Komunyakaa. CP-KomuY

Field of Glory, The. Edwin Arlington Robinson. CP-RobiE

Field of Light, A. Theodore Roethke. CP-RoetT

Field / of olive trees, The. Poem of the Gypsy *Siguiriya*. Federico García Lorca. CP-GarcF, *tr. by* Cola Franzen

Field of Stubble, lying sere, A. Emily Dickinson. CP-DickE

Field of Vision. Seamus Heaney. SP-HeanSO

Field Pansy, The. Amy Clampitt. CP-ClamA

Field People. Carl Sandburg. CP-SandC

Field-Postcard, The. Robert Graves. CP-GravR

Field tipped over pleasantly and he, The. Nap. Mona Van Duyn. SP-VanDM

Field where my brother died, The. Moment, A. Gregory Orr. SP-OrrG

Field Work. Seamus Heaney. SP-HeanSO

Fields, The. Raymond Carver. CP-CarvR

Fields, The. W. S. Merwin. SP-MerwWF

Fields are black once more, The. Reading in Fall Rain. Robert Bly. SP-BlyR

Fields are white to harvest, look and see, The. When My Heart Is Vexed I Will Complain. Christina Georgina Rossetti. CP-RosC2

Fields of Earth. Kenneth Patchen. CP-PatcK

Fields of sunflowers, ripe and withering. Yehuda Amichai. SP-AmicY, *tr. by* Chana Bloch

Fields of the sky, The. Thoughts of the Time. Charles Olson. CP-OlsoC

Fields parched, the leaves, The. Words Lying Idle, The. William Carlos Williams. CP-WilW2

Fields rattle / with red birds, the. 4:30 A.M. Charles Bukowski. SP-BukC2

Fields sloping down and a trumpet. Bobo's Metamorphosis. Czeslaw Milosz. CP-MiloC; CP-MiloCN, *tr. by* Richard Lourie

Fields took on their final. Gregory Orr. SP-OrrG

Fields where we slept. Muriel Rukeyser. CP-RukeM

Fields which with covetous spirit we sold, The. Repentance; A Pastoral Ballad. William Wordsworth. CP-WorW1

Fiend slays the children of the messenger, A. Intimate Guest, The. Kenneth Patchen. CP-PatcK

Fiend, The. James Dickey. CP-DickJ

Fiend's Weather. Louise Bogan. CP-BogaL

Fierce and stupid all dogs are. Dog Poem. Philip Levine. SP-LeviP

Fierce beasts of the woods and wildernesses, The. Fragment: The Lake's Margin. Percy Bysshe Shelley. CP-ShelP

Fierce bodily control, constant routine. Two Disciplines. Robert Graves. CP-GravR

Fierce Horsemen, The. Robert Penn Warren. CP-WarrR

Fierce indignation is best understood by those. Sonnet—September 1922. Ivor Gurney. SP-GurnI

Fierce musical cries of a couple of sparrowhawks hunting on the headland, The.

Birds. Robinson Jeffers. CP-JefR1

Fierce, seraphic, savage-eyed. Living Dead, The. Charles Baudelaire. CP-BaudC, *tr. by* Walter Martin

Fierce though your love of her may be. To Myrto About Herself. Robert Graves. CP-GravR

Fierceness of Female, The. Anne Sexton. CP-SextA

Fiery Cross, The. Sir Walter Scott. SP-ScotW *Fr.* Lady of the Lake, The.

Fiery mountains answer each other, The. Liberty. Percy Bysshe Shelley. CP-ShelP

Fiesole Window. Eugenio Montale. CP-MontE, *tr. by* Jonathan Galassi

Fiesta Melons. Sylvia Plath. CP-PlatS

Fifine Answers. Ezra Pound. CP-PoEar

Fifine at the Fair. Robert Browning. CP-BroR2

Fifteen. William Stafford. SP-StafW; SP-StafWW

Fifteen. C. K. Williams. SP-WillC

Fifteen nights I have lain awake and called you. Elegy for a Cricket. James Vincent Cunningham. CP-CunnJ

Fifteen to Eighteen. Marilyn Hacker. SP-HackM

15 Years Later. William Carlos Williams. CP-WilW2

Fifteenth-Century Zen Master, A. Norman Dubie. CP-DubiN

Fifteenth Farewell. Louise Bogan. CP-BogaL

Fifteenth of May. Cherry blossom. The swifts. Swifts. Ted Hughes. SP-HughTN

Fifth Anniversary, The. Joseph Brodsky. CP-BrodJ

Fifth Dimension. Kenneth Patchen. CP-PatcK

Fifth Elegy. A Turning Wind. Muriel Rukeyser. CP-RukeM

Fifth Month, The. Gregory Orr. SP-OrrG

Fifth Ode of Horace, The. Horace. *See* Odes

Fifth Page. Federico García Lorca. CP-GarcF, *tr. by* Jerome Rothenberg *Fr.* White Album.

5th Position. Philip Whalen. SP-WhalP

Fifth Prose. Michael Palmer. SP-PalmM

Fifth spring of war is beginning, The. Songs of Adrian Zieliński. Czeslaw Milosz. CP-MiloC; CP-MiloCN, *tr. by* Renata Gorczynski *and* Robert Hass

Fifth Sunday after Easter. Thomas Kinsella. CP-KinsT

Fifty. Kenneth Rexroth. CP-RexrK

Fifty. Miller Williams. CP-WillM

50–50. Langston Hughes. CP-HughL; CP-HughL2

Fifty-Fifty. Carl Sandburg. CP-SandC

Fifty Males Sitting Together. Robert Bly. SP-BlyR

Fifty North and Forty West. Rudyard Kipling. CP-KiplR *Fr.* Just-So Stories.

Fifty-odd years ago if you. Part of What Might Have Been a Short Story, Almost Forgotten. Robert Penn Warren. CP-WarrR

56 and *tomato*. History in a Minor Key. Kenneth Patchen. CP-PatcK

56 lb. weight, The. A solid iron. Weighing In. Seamus Heaney. SP-HeanSO

56 Year Old Poem, A. Charles Bukowski. SP-BukC1

52 Oswald Street. Galway Kinnell. SP-KinnGN

Fifty years' flight! Wherein should he rejoice. Lines for the Jubilee Window. Robert Browning. CP-BroR2

Fig, The. Gabriela Mistral. SP-MistG, *tr. by* Maria Giachetti [*or* Jacketti]

Fig, The. May Sarton. SP-SartM

Fig Tree, The. W. S. Merwin. SP-MerwWF

Fig Tree, The. Jones Very. CP-VeryJ

Fig-trees, weird fig-trees. Bare Fig-trees. D. H. Lawrence. CP-LawrD

Fight. Carl Sandburg. CP-SandC

Fight, The. William Carlos Williams. CP-WilW2

Fight! O My Young Men. D. H. Lawrence. CP-LawrD

Fight on Dunnover Moor, The. Thomas Hardy. CP-HardT

Fight thou with shafts of silver, and o'[e]rcome. Money Gets the Mastery [*or* Masterie]. Robert Herrick. CP-HerrR

Fight your little fight, my boy. Don'ts. D. H. Lawrence. CP-LawrD

Fighters. René Char. CP-MertT

Fighting Cock, The. Chuang Tzu. CP-MertT

Fighting for Roses. Muriel Rukeyser. CP-RukeM

Fighting Words. Dorothy Parker. CP-ParkD

Figlia, la madre disse. Versi. Christina Georgina Rossetti. CP-RosC3

Figlio Mio. James Laughlin. CP-LaugJ

Figs. D. H. Lawrence. CP-LawrD

Figs on the fig tree in the yard are green, The. Departure. Sylvia Plath. CP-PlatS

Figueras Castle. William Carlos Williams. CP-WilW2

Figurative Description of the Procedure of Divine Love, A. Jeanne Marie Bouvier de la Motte- Guyon. CP-CowpW

Figure. Josephine Jacobsen. CP-JacoJ

Figure Drawn in Wire, The. John Ciardi. CP-CiarJ

Figure in the Doorway, The. Robert Frost. CP-FrosR

Figure in the Scene, The. Thomas Hardy. CP-HardT

Figure Motioned with Its Mangled Hand Toward the Wall Behind It, The. Kenneth Patchen. CP-PatcK

Figure of Eight. Louis MacNeice. CP-MacNL

Figure of my Lady, A. Guido Cavalcanti. CP-CavaG, *tr. by* Marc Cirigliano

Figure / of tall, The. Province, The. William Carlos Williams. CP-WilW2

Figure of Time, A. Denise Levertov. CP-LeveDP

Figure on the Far Side, The. Jane Cooper. CP-CoopJ

Figure or figures unknown. Grocery. Charles Simic. SP-SimiC; SP-SimiCE

Figured wheel rolls through shopping malls and prisons, The. Robert Pinsky. CP-PinsR

Figurehead, The. Karl Shapiro. SP-ShapK

Figures, The. Robert Creeley. CP-CreeR

Figures for an Apocalypse. Thomas Merton. CP-MertT

Figures in Popular Literature. Dorothy Parker. CP-ParkD

Figures of Speech. Thomas Sheridan. CP-SherT

Figures of the Human. David Ignatow. SP-IgnaD

Figures of Thought. Howard Nemerov. CP-NemeH

Figures on a silent screen. Woman-Enough. Tess Gallagher. SP-GallT

Figurette. Langston Hughes. CP-HughL3

Figurine. Langston Hughes. CP-HughL3

Figuring. Charles Simic. SP-SimiC; SP-SimiCE

Filament carrying morning through the waves, A. Muriel Rukeyser. CP-RukeM

Files on files of Prairie Maize. Trophies of Peace. Herman Melville. SP-MelvH

FIles, The. Rudyard Kipling. CP-KiplR

Files— / The Files— / Office Files! FIles, The. Rudyard Kipling. CP-KiplR

Filial Piety. William Wordsworth. CP-WorW2

Filina. Czeslaw Milosz. CP-MiloC; CP-MiloCN, *tr. by* Robert Hass

Filippo Argenti. Dante Alighieri. CP-CiarJ *Fr.* Divina Commedia.

Filippo Baldinucci on the Privilege of Burial. Robert Browning. CP-BroR2

Fill for Me a Brimming Bowl. John Keats. CP-KeatJ

Fill in blanks: Your name is. Final Exam: American Renaissance. William Stafford. SP-StafWW

Fill me a mighty Bowle. Bacchanalian Verse, A. Robert Herrick. CP-HerrR

Fill me my Wine in Christall; thus, and thus. How He Would Drinke His Wine. Robert Herrick. CP HerrR

Fill the air with their. Creatures of Prometheus, The. James Laughlin. CP-LaugJ

Fill the Goblet. Lord Byron. CP-Byron

Filling in the Blanks. Eleanor Wilner. SP-WilnE

Filling Night with the Name: Funeral as Local Color. Robert Penn Warren. CP-WarrR

Filling Station. Elizabeth Bishop. CP-BishE

Filling the mind. Clouds, The. William Carlos Williams. CP-WilW2

Fills up / Sun, moon, stars, he fills them up. Executioner, The. Ted Hughes. SP-HughTN

Film, The. Denise Levertov. SP-LeveDP

Film and filament, no. Dative Haruspices. Kenneth Rexroth. CP-RexrK

Film Passion. D. H. Lawrence. CP-LawrD

Film Star, The. Stevie Smith. CP-SmitS

Films. Carl Sandburg. CP-SandC

Fin de Siècle. Joseph Brodsky. CP-BrodJ

Fin-de-Siècle Blues. Carolyn Kizer. CP-KizeC

Fin di Maggio. Dante Gabriel Rossetti. CW-RossD

Fin fond du néant. Samuel Beckett. CP-BeckS

Final. Pablo Neruda. SP-NeruP, *tr. by* Ben Belitt

Final Agreement. Yannis Ritsos. SP-RitsY, *tr. by* Kimon Friar

Final Call. Langston Hughes. CP-HughL; CP-HughL3

Final Curve. Langston Hughes. CP-HughL; CP-HughL2

Final Exam: American Renaissance. William Stafford. SP-StafWW

Final Examination. Dan Pagis. SP-PagiD, *tr. by* Stephen Mitchell

Final Hour. Yannis Ritsos. SP-RitsY, *tr. by* Kimon Friar

Final Inch, The. Emily Dickinson. CP-DickE

Final Meeting. Carolyn Kizer. CP-KizeC

Final Notations. Adrienne Rich. SP-RicA1

Final Note to Clark. Lucille Clifton. SP-ClifL

Final Obol, The. Yannis Ritsos. SP-RitsY, *tr. by* Kimon Friar

Final Page. Federico García Lorca. CP-GarcF, *tr. by* Jerome Rothenberg *Fr.* White Album.

Final Report. Dan Pagis. SP-PagiD, *tr. by* Stephen Mitchell

Final Soliloquy of the Interior Paramour. Wallace Stevens. CP-StevW; CP-StevWP

Final Sonnet, A. Ted Berrigan. SP-BerrT *Fr.* Sonnets, The.

Finality broods upon the things that pass. Walk by the Charles, A. Adrienne Rich. CP-RicAE; SP-RicA2

Finally. David Ignatow. SP-IgnaD

Finally. Laura Riding Jackson. CP-RidiL

Finally. W. S. Merwin. SP-MerwW

Finally a Valentine. Louis Zukofsky. CP-ZukLS

Finally bigness turned into the sun. Finally. Laura Riding Jackson. CP-RidiL

Finally got the horse broken in. It took years. Horse. May Swenson. SP-SwenM

Finally, he decided there was too much pain. 21st Century Man. Richard Eberhart. CP-EberR

Finally I have a house. Homesick. Marge Piercy. SP-PierM

Finally, I have reduced you to a human being. Meeting. David Ignatow. SP-IgnaD

Finally, I'm sitting here at my desk because I'm afraid to venture into the street. Finally. David Ignatow. SP-IgnaD

Finally, in the last year of her age. Pastoral Nun, A. Wallace Stevens. CP-StevW; CP-StevWP

Finally in white innocence. Fantasy. Robinson Jeffers. CP-JefR3

Finally that Blue Receding Sphere. John Ciardi. CP-CiarJ

Finally / the mirror reflects. 23 January 1949. Yannis Ritsos. SP-RitsY *Fr.* Exile's Journals 2.

Finally, to forgo love is to kiss a leaf. Rescue the Dead. David Ignatow. SP-IgnaD

Finches, The. Wendell Berry. CP-BerrW

Finches at the feeder, The. Us. George Oppen. CP-OppGN

Find me diffuse, leached colorless. Look for My White Self. A. R. Ammons. CP-AmmoA

Find Meat on Bones. Dylan Thomas. CP-ThomD

Find the Favorite. James Whitcomb Riley. CP-RileJ

Find the place. Pulse, A. Rae Armantrout. SP-ArmaA

Finding a Teacher. W. S. Merwin. SP-MerwW

Finding in a friend's garden columbines. Columbines. Kathleen Jessie Raine. SP-RainK

Finding is the first Act. Emily Dickinson. CP-DickE

Finding of Love, The. Robert Graves. CP-GravR

Finding of Reasons, The. W. S. Merwin. SP-MerwW

Finding the Father. Robert Bly. SP-BlyR

Finding Your Level. D. H. Lawrence. CP-LawrD

Findings testify to a complete disregard, The. Final Report. Dan Pagis. SP-PagiD, *tr. by* Stephen Mitchell

"Fine China." Robert Creeley. CP-CreeR

Fine cloth of your love might be a fabric of Egypt, The. They Buy with an Eye to Looks. Carl Sandburg. CP-SandC

Fine clouds open their outfits. T'ang Notebook. Charles Wright. SP-WrigC

Fine delight that fathers thought; the strong, The. To R. B. Gerard Manley Hopkins. CP-HopkG

Fine drizzle blew, A. Coolea: 6 October 1971. Thomas Kinsella. CP-KinsT *Fr.* Selected Life, A.

Fine evening may I have. Courtship. Rita Dove. SP-DoveR

Fine lass or lady, they. Michelangelo Buonarroti. CP-Miche, *tr. by* John Frederick Nims

Fine living . . . à la carte?? Advertisement for the Waldorf-Astoria. Langston Hughes. CP-HughL; CP-HughL1

Fine Madam Would-Be, wherefore should you fear. To Fine Lady Would-Be. Ben Jonson. CP-JonsB; SP-JonsB

Fine old house with the Georgian Door, The. Population Explosion. Archibald MacLeish. CP-MacLA

Fine powder of the dry rot, The. Dry Rot, The. Richard Eberhart. CP-EberR

Fine presentiments controlled him. Ralph Waldo Emerson. CP-EmerR

Fine rain along mountains to the south of me. Guardians. W. S. Merwin. CP-MerwWF

Fine songs, fair songs, these golden usuries. Octave. Ezra Pound. CP-PoEar

Fine Work with Pitch and Copper. William Carlos Williams. CP-WilW1

Fine young man on horseback, A. Han-shan. CP-ColdM, *tr. by* Red Pine

Finest / lad of all is Mr, The. It Depends on Whose Science. Kenneth Patchen. CP-PatcK

Finger, The. Robert Creeley. CP-CreeR

Fingerprints. Jaroslav Seifert. SP-SeifJ, *tr. by* Ewald Osers

Fingers of the Light, The. Emily Dickinson. CP-DickE

Fingers turn the pages, The. Ever a Seeker. Carl Sandburg. CP-SandC

Fingertips just tipping you would send you. Swing, The. Seamus Heaney. SP-HeanSO

Finis. E. E. Cummings. CP-CummE

Finis. Dorothy Parker. CP-ParkD

Finis Æternitatis. Ambrose Bierce. SP-BierA

Finis, apparent on an earlier page. Leaving the Rest Unsaid. Robert Graves. CP-GravR

Finish. Carl Sandburg. CP-SandC

Finished. Ai. SP-Ai

Finished Man, A. Richard Wilbur. CP-WilbR

Finishing the Work. Jones Very. CP-VeryJ

Finishing Touch. Yannis Ritsos. SP-RitsY *Fr.* Monovasia.

Finisterre. Sylvia Plath. CP-PlatS

Finite and Infinite. Elizabeth Barrett Browning. CP-BroEB

Finite life, little sister, A. Emily Dickinson. SP-DickE

Finite—to fail, but infinite to Venture. Emily Dickinson. CP-DickE

Fins. Carl Sandburg. CP-SandC

Fintry, my stay in worldly strife. Epistle to Robt. Graham Esq: of Fintry on the Election for the Dumfries String of Boroughs, Anno 1790. Robert Burns. CP-BurnR

Fiordispina. Percy Bysshe Shelley. CP-ShelP

Fire. Robert Creeley. CP-CreeR

Fire. Robinson Jeffers. CP-JefR3

Fire. D. H. Lawrence. CP-LawrD

Fire. D. H. Lawrence. CP-LawrD

Fire. A. K. Ramanujan. CP-RamaA

Fire. C. K. Williams. SP-WillC

Fire. Adam Zagajewski. SP-ZagaA, *tr.* by Renata Gorczynski

Fire, The. Robert Duncan. SP-DuncR *Fr.* Passages.

Fire, The. Robert Creeley. CP-CreeR

Fire, The. Louise Glück. SP-GlucL

Fire advances along the log, The. Logs on the Hearth. Thomas Hardy. CP-HardT

Fire and Deluge, rival pretenders. Mist. Robert Graves. CP-GravR

Fire and Ice. Robert Frost. CP-FrosR

Fire and smoke raged within. Han-shan. CP-ColdM, *tr.* by Red Pine

Fire and wings, De Bosis, soaring above. Poem in the Form of a Letter: to Lauro de Bosis. Kenneth Patchen. CP-PatcK

Fire at Alexandria, The. Theodore Weiss. SP-WeisT

Fire at Night. James Whitcomb Riley. CP-RileJ

Fire at the Waxworks, The. Randall Jarrell. CP-JarrR

Fire back of grate. Bruce & Linley's House. Robert Creeley. SP-CreeR

Fire: because it is quick, and can destroy. If You Could Write One Great Poem, What Would You Want It to Be About? Robert Pinsky. CP-PinsR

Fire bites, the fire bites. Bites, The. Circe. Olga Broumas. SP-BrouO

Fire-Caught. Langston Hughes. CP-HughL; CP-HughL1

Fire Dreams. Carl Sandburg. CP-SandC

Fire-Eater. Ted Hughes. SP-HughTN

Fire, Famine, and Slaughter. Samuel Taylor Coleridge. CP-ColeS; MW-ColeS

Fire, Fire. Adam Zagajewski. SP-ZagaA, *tr.* by Renata Gorczynski

Fire, fire, fire, fire! Thomas Campion. CP-CampT

Fire, / Fire, Lord! Langston Hughes. CP-HughL; CP-HughL1

Fire! Fire! Ring! and ring! Fire at Night. James Whitcomb Riley. CP-RileJ

Fire flickers on the deep hearth in the dark hall. Fire. Robinson Jeffers. CP-JefR3

Fire from a fixèd star. World of the Perfect Tear, The. Thomas McGrath. SP-McGrT

Fire in a Dark Landscape. Charles Tomlinson. CP-TomlC

Fire in her ashes Ireland feels. Ireland. George Meredith. CP-MerG2

Fire in leaf and grass, The. Living. Denise Levertov. SP-LeveDP; SP-LeveDS

Fire in Luna Park. Galway Kinnell. SP-KinnGN

Fire in the Hole. Gary Snyder. CP-SnydG

Fire Is. Charles Olson. CP-OlsoC

Fire is ash, The: the early morning sun. Femmes Damnees. Philip Larkin. CP-LarkP

Fire is lit in the hearth, and flickers, The. Dinner Party. Eleanor Wilner. SP-WilnE

Fire-Logs. Carl Sandburg. CP-SandC

Fire looked real good, The. Old Tom would tell us. Peter Blue Cloud. SP-BlueP

Fire makes noises like snow on wet panes, The. Li Po. Charles Olson. CP-OlsoC

Fire of Descartes, the fire of Pascal, The. Fire, Fire. Adam Zagajewski. SP-ZagaA, *tr.* by Renata Gorczynski

Fire of Despair Has Been Our Savior, The. Robert Bly. SP-BlyR

Fire of Drift-Wood, The. Henry Wadsworth Longfellow. SP-LongH

Fire of Hell this strange condition hath, The. Hell Fire. Robert Herrick. CP-HerrR

Fire of the seed is in her pose, The. Child and Vegetables. William Carlos Williams. CP-WilW1

Fire of winter sunset. Aloof. Carl Sandburg. CP-SandC

Fire on the Hills. Robinson Jeffers. CP-JefR2

Fire Pages. Carl Sandburg. CP-SandC

Fire shimmied & reached up. Temples of Smoke. Yusef Komunyakaa. CP-KomuY

Fire Spirit. William Carlos Williams. CP-WilW1

Fire stop thief help murder save the world. E. E. Cummings. CP-CummE

Fire that must flame is with apt fuell fed. Thomas Campion. CP-CampT

Fire Thief, The. Anne Sexton. CP-SextA

Fire took the house. Black bricks. Salvaged Parts. William Stafford. SP-StafW; SP-StafWW

Fire-Truck, A. Richard Wilbur. CP-WilbR

Fire wakes with a burst in the tower of leaf. Fire Will Not Change. Josephine Jacobsen. CP-JacoJ

Fire Walker. Robert Graves. CP-GravR

Fire Will Not Change. Josephine Jacobsen. CP-JacoJ

Firebombers, The. Anne Sexton. CP-SextA

Firebombing, The. James Dickey. CP-DickJ

Fireborn Are at Home in Fire, The. Carl Sandburg. CP-SandC

Firebreathers at the Café Deux Magots, The. Miller Williams. CP-WillM

Firecrackers came from China. Bitter Summer Thoughts—No. 3. Carl Sandburg. CP-SandC

Fired. Langston Hughes. CP-HughL; CP-HughL2

Fired in sanguine clay, the model head. Lady and the Earthenware Head, The. Sylvia Plath. CP-PlatS

Fireflies. Charles Tomlinson. CP-TomlC; SP-TomlC

Fireflies, The. Jones Very. CP-VeryJ

Fireflies and the stars our only light, The. Spinning Heart, The. John Berryman. CP-BerrJ

Fireflies in the Corn. D. H. Lawrence. CP-LawrD

Fireflies in the Garden. Robert Frost. CP-FrosR

Firefly, The. James Laughlin. CP-LaugJ

Firelight. Edwin Arlington Robinson. CP-RobiE

Firelight and Nightfall. D. H. Lawrence. CP-LawrD (Grief.) CP-LawrD

Firelight in Sunlight. Howard Nemerov. *See* Marriage of Heaven and Earth, The

Firelight in sunlight, silver-pale. Marriage of Heaven and Earth, The. Howard Nemerov. CP-NemeH

Firenze, a Lifetime Later. Lawrence Ferlinghetti. SP-FerlL

Fire's Reflection. Rainer Maria Rilke. CP-RilkFr, *tr.* by A. Poulin, Jr.

Fires, The. Rudyard Kipling. CP-KiplR

Firescreen at Mount Vernon, A. William Meredith. SP-MereW

Fireside. Seamus Heaney. SP-HeanSO

Fireside. George Meredith. CP-MerG2

Fireside Reverie. George Meredith. CP-MerG2

Firesong. Sylvia Plath. CP-PlatS

Firesticks. Stanley Kunitz. CP-KunSC

Fireweed. Amy Clampitt. CP-ClamA

Fireweed. W. S. Merwin. SP-MerwWF

Fireweed now. For Albert Saijo. Philip Whalen. SP-WhalP

Firewood under the eaves. Aged Tamba Temple Plum Tree Song. Gary Snyder. CP-SnydG

Fireworks. John Updike. CP-UpdiJ

Firing, The. Kenneth Patchen. CP-PatcK

Firing, The. Gary Snyder. CP-SnydG

Firm-lipped, high-bosomed, slender Queen of Beanstalk Land. Batxóca. Robert Graves. CP-GravR

Firmament breaks up. In black eclipse, The. Word for the Hour, A. John Greenleaf Whittier. CP-WhitJ

Firmum is all too known fails so Meantool a Dives. Catullus. *See* O'Toole is generally maintained

First. Clarence Major. SP-MajoC

First, a female buffalo gnat of the genus *Simulium* bites you. River Blindness (Onchocerciasis). Thomas Lux. SP-LuxT

First, a look. "Rubén Dario." SP-DariR, *tr.* by Alberto Acereda *and* Will Derusha

First a monkey, then a man. Dawn of the Space Age. John Ciardi. CP-CiarJ

First a sea: soft sands, muds, and marls. What Happened Here Before. Gary Snyder. CP-SnydG

First a word was fuzzy, and was nothing. Words. Richard Eberhart. CP-EberR

First Advent of Love. Samuel Taylor Coleridge. CP-ColeS

First age of the world was counterpoint, The. Four Ages, The. Howard Nemerov. CP-NemeH

First and best of earthly joys. Grampa's Choice. James Whitcomb Riley. CP-RileJ

First and last time I met, The. Drunken Memories of Anne Sexton. Alan Dugan. CP-DugaA

First Anniversary. Federico García Lorca. CP-GarcF, *tr.* by Alan S. Trueblood *Fr.* Moon Songs.

First Anniversary of the Government under His Highness the Lord Protector, 1655, The. Andrew Marvell. CP-MarvA

First, April, she with mellow show[e]rs. Four Sweet Months, The. Robert Herrick. CP-HerrR

First, are you our sort of a person? Applicant, The. Sylvia Plath. CP-PlatS

First Atlantic Telegraph, The. Jones Very. CP-VeryJ

First Atlas, The. Primo Levi. CP-LeviP, *tr.* by Ruth Feldman

First Autumn, The. May Sarton. SP-SartM

1st Avenue Basics. Andrei Codrescu. SP-CodrA

First blossom was the best blossom, The. Apple Blossom. Louis MacNeice. CP-MacNL

First Bluebird, The. James Whitcomb Riley. CP-RileJ

First-Born of Egypt, The. Robert Browning. CP-BroR2

First-Born, The. George Meredith. CP-MerG2

First bridge, Constitution Station, The. At my feet. Matthew 25:30. Jorge Luis

Borges. SP-BorgJ, *tr.* by Alastair Reid

First Brother. Peter Blue Cloud. SP-BlueP

First came fine words softening our souls for magic. Earlier Lovers. Robert Graves. CP-GravR

First came the Lion-Rider, across the green fields of the morning. Kenneth Patchen. CP-PatcK

First Canto. Jaroslav Seifert. SP-SeifJ *Fr.* Robed in Light.

First Canzone of the Convito, The. Dante Alighieri. CP-ShelP, *tr.* by Percy Bysshe Shelley

First Caprice in North Cambridge. T. S. Eliot. SP-ElioT

First Carolina Said-Song. A. R. Ammons. CP-AmmoA

First chainsaw I owned was years ago, The. Regarding Chainsaws. Hayden Carruth. CP-CarHS

First Chantey, The. Rudyard Kipling. CP-KiplR

First clear faint unlocated call, The. Insomniac's Bird. Josephine Jacobsen. CP-JacoJ

First cocks begin clearing the throat of morning—, The. Valley Where I Don't Belong, A. Marge Piercy. SP-PierM

First Coffin Poem. David Ignatow. SP-IgnaD

First cold front came in, The. Winter's Onset from an Alienated Point of View. Alan Dugan. CP-DugaA

First cold front came through Indian Summer, The. Variation on "Winter's Onset from an Alienated Point of View" Alan Dugan. CP-DugaA

First comes the flight, of course. Hope gleams in steel. Guide for Survivors, Josephine Jacobsen. CP-JacoJ

First commandment of the wind. From the Inside. Paul Éluard. CP WilW2

First Communions. Arthur Rimbaud. CP-RimbA, *tr.* by Martin Sorrell

First composer, The. Memory of Spring. W. S. Merwin. SP-MerwW

First Confession, A. William Butler Yeats. CP-YeatW

First Crusades, The! Kenneth Patchen. CP-PatcK

First Dances. Frank O'Hara. SP-OharF

First Dandelion, The. Walt Whitman. CP-WhitW

First Darkness, The. W. S. Merwin. SP-MerwW

First Date. Miller Williams. CP-WillM

First Dawn Light. Robert Penn Warren. CP-WarrR

First Day, The. Howard Nemerov. CP-NemeH

First day each fall she lectured. Miss Lucy. Wyatt Prunty. SP-PrunW

First Day of the Future. Galway Kinnell. SP-KinnGN

First day sleet, the second ice, The. Sneeze, The. Wyatt Prunty. SP-PrunW

First Day that I was a Life, The. Emily Dickinson. CP-DickE

First-Day Thoughts. John Greenleaf Whittier. CP-WhitJ

First daylight on the bittersweet-hung. Meridian. Amy Clampitt. CP-ClamA

First Day's Night had come, The. Emily Dickinson. CP-DickE

First Death in Nova Scotia. Elizabeth Bishop. CP-BishE

First Debate between the Body and Soul. T. S. Eliot. SP-ElioT

First Delirium. The Foolish Virgin. The Infernal Bridegroom. Arthur Rimbaud. CP-RimbA, *tr.* by Martin Sorrell

First Desires. C. K. Williams. SP-WillC

First disappointment, The. Fanny Howe. SP-HoweF *Fr.* In the Spirit There Are No Accidents.

First drops of rain struck the sea, The. Being young, they didn't mind. Misconstructions. Yannis Ritsos. SP-RitsY, *tr.* by Kimon Friar

First drumroll—and he is a coil of air, his limbs four rubber, A. Acrobatics. Dan Pagis. SP-PagiD, *tr.* by Stephen Mitchell

First Early Mornings Together. Robert Pinsky. CP-PinsR

First Elegy. Rotten Lake. Muriel Rukeyser. CP-RukeM

First Epistle of the First Book of Horace Imitated, The. Alexander Pope. CP-PopeA

First Epistle of the Second Book of Horace Imitated, The. Alexander Pope. CP-PopeA

First Families Move Over! Ogden Nash. CP-NashO

First Fig. Edna St. Vincent Millay. CP-MillE

First Figure. Michael Palmer. SP-PalmM

First fire since the summer is lit, and is smoking into the room, The. Shortening Days at the Homestead. Thomas Hardy. CP-HardT

First fish / I ever caught, The. Fish, The. Mary Oliver. SP-OlivM

First Flight. Mona Van Duyn. SP-VanDM

First Flight, The. Seamus Heaney. SP-HeanSO *Fr.* Sweeney Redivivus.

First flower, / Fields' document, The. Palms for a Catholic Child. Kenneth Patchen. CP-PatcK

First Flowers, The. John Greenleaf Whittier. CP-WhitJ

First flowret of the year is that which shows. In the First Page of an Album by One Whose Handwriting Is Wretchedly Bad. William Wordsworth. CP-WorW2

First, for effusions due unto the dead. Upon His Sister-in-Law, Mistress Elizabeth Herrick. Robert Herrick. CP-HerrR

First, for your shape, the curious cannot shew. Another Upon Her. Robert Herrick. CP-HerrR

First forget what time it is. Exercise. W. S. Merwin. SP-MerwW

First frost, and I walk among the rose-fruit, the marble toes. Private Ground. Sylvia Plath. CP-PlatS

First frost is weeks off, but the prudent man. Discretions of Alcibiades. Robert Pinsky. CP-PinsR

First Gloss, The. Seamus Heaney. SP-HeanSO *Fr.* Sweeney Redivivus.

First Grade. William Stafford. SP-StafW; SP-StafWW

First having read the book of myths. Diving into the Wreck. Adrienne Rich. SP-RicA1; SP-RicA2

First hay is down, The. Haying. William Corbett. SP-CorbW

First he could not remember. Documenting It. Miller Williams. CP-WillM

First he gave me. Pomegranate. Louise Glück. SP-GlucL

First he must go where / Not even the birds will brave his solitude. Buddhist Painter Prepares to Paint, The. Hayden Carruth. CP-CarHS

First he said. Transitional. William Carlos Williams. CP-WilW1

First hear the story of Kaspar the rosy-cheeked. Fräulein Reads Instructive Rhymes. Maxine W. Kumin. SP-KumiM

First heaven is a flowery plain, The. Green Castle, The. Robert Graves. CP-GravR

First, her tippet made of tulle. Taking Off Emily Dickinson's Clothes. Billy Collins. SP-CollB

First horn lifts its arm over the dew-lit grass, The. House Slave, The. Rita Dove. SP-DoveR

First I locked hands with myself. What a Circus. Alan Dugan. CP DugaA

First I looked on, after a long time far from home, The. American Change. Allen Ginsberg. CP-GinsA

First I salute this soil of the blessed, river and rock! Pheidippides. Robert Browning. CP-BroR2

First I saw the surface. Surface, The. May Swenson. SP-SwenM

First, I tell you who I am. In the First Stanza. Carolyn Kizer. CP-KizeC

First I will tell you something of these two. Archibald MacLeish. CP-MacLA *Fr.* Happy Marriage, The.

First I would like to write for you a poem to be shouted in the teeth. Horse Fiddle. Carl Sandburg. SP-SandC

First Icon with Gun, The. Andrei Codrescu. SP-CodrA

First Invention on the Theme of the Adam. Robert Duncan. SP-DuncR

First is female, The. Terminal Tramps. Charles Tomlinson. CP-TomlC

First Jock he / was kilt a handsome. E. E. Cummings. CP-CummE

First, Jollies wife is lame; then next, loose-hipt. Upon Jollies Wife. Robert Herrick. CP-HerrR

First Kingdom, The. Seamus Heaney. SP-HeanSO *Fr.* Sweeney Redivivus.

First Kiss. Rita Dove. SP-DoveR

First Kiss of Love, The. Lord Byron. CP-Byron

First, last, and dearest, / My love, mine own. From Mestastasio. Christina Georgina Rossetti. CP-RosC3

First/Last Meditation. Federico García Lorca. CP GarcF, *tr.* by Jerome Rothenberg *Fr.* In the Forest of Clocks.

First Last Will & Testament. Robert Stock. SP-StocR

First Launching. Federico García Lorca. CP-GarcF, *tr.* by Jerome Rothenberg *Fr.* Barrage of Firework Poems on the Occasion of the Poet's Birthday.

First Leaf, The. Howard Nemerov. CP-NemeH

First Lesson. James Tate. SP-TateJ

First Lesson about Man. Thomas Merton. CP-MertT

First lesson: Don't. Articulacy. Hints from the Koran. Donald Davie. CP-DaviDC

First Light. Charles Baudelaire. CP-BaudC, *tr.* by Walter Martin

First Light. Peter Blue Cloud. SP-BlueP

First Light. Thomas Kinsella. CP-KinsT

First light, a dark outline. First Light. Peter Blue Cloud. SP-BlueP

First light—call it. Cloud Change. Charles Tomlinson. CP-TomlC

First light strikes / across a landmass. Drive. Charles Tomlinson. CP-TomlC

First Limick. Ogden Nash. CP-NashO

First Love. Thomas Campion. CP-CampT

First Love. Robert Graves. CP-GravR

First Love. Stanley Kunitz. CP-KunSC

First Love. Denise Levertov. SP-LeveDS

First Love. Robert Lowell. SP-LoweR

First Love. Hugh MacDiarmid. SP-MacDH

First Love. Derek Mahon. CP-MahoD

First Love Remembered. Dante Gabriel Rossetti. CW-RossD

First man who whistled, The. First, The. Wendell Berry. CP-BerrW

First March. Ivor Gurney. SP-GurnI

First Marrs or Makes, The. Robert Herrick. CP-HerrR

First, may the hand of bounty bring. Happinesse to Hospitalitie, or a Hearty Wish to Good House-Keeping. Robert Herrick. CP-HerrR

First Meeting with a Possible Mother-in-Law. Thom Gunn. CP-GunnT

First Moment of Autumn Recognized. Robert Penn Warren. CP-WarrR

First Morning. D. H. Lawrence. CP-LawrD

First morning after anyone's death, is it important, The. Thomas Hardy. Norman Dubie. CP-DubiN

First morning of mist after days of draining, unwavering heat along the shore: a *breath*, The. Dawn. C. K. Williams. SP-WillC

First morning of Three Mile Island: those first disquieting, uncertain, mystifying hours, The. Tar. C. K. Williams. CP-WillC; SP-WillC

First morning, The. Morning, The. W. S. Merwin. SP-MerwWF

First movie I ever saw was the Walt Disney Cartoon *The Three Little Pigs* , The. Lonedale Operator, The. John Ashbery. SP-AshbJ

First Mute Coming, A. Emily Dickinson. CP-DickE

First name cut on a rock, a King's, The. Uncalendared Love. Robert Graves. CP-GravR

First Neighbours. Margaret Atwood. SP-AtwM1

First News from Villafranca. Elizabeth Barrett Browning. CP-BroEB

First Night. Arthur Rimbaud. CP-RimbA, *tr. by* Martin Sorrell

First Night at Sea. John Berryman. CP-BerrJ

First night God created was too weak, The. Reunions with a Ghost. Ai. SP-Ai

First night. / Mid-winter. Rumpelstiltskin. Olga Broumas. SP-BrouO

First Night, The. James Laughlin. CP-LaugJ

First O Songs for a Prelude. Walt Whitman. CP-WhitW

First Ode of the Fourth Book of Horace Imitated, The. Alexander Pope. CP-PopeA

First Ode of the Second Book of Horace Paraphrased and Addressed to Richard Steele, Esq, The. Jonathan Swift. CP-SwifJ

First of all is God, and the same last is he, The. Sir Walter Ralegh. CP-RaleW

First of all my dreams was of, The. E. E. Cummings. CP-CummE

First of April, The. Jonathan Swift. CP-SwifJ

First, of course, you think of Robin Hood. Romance. Miller Williams. CP-WillM

First of June Again, The. Carolyn Kizer. CP-KizeC

First of May. Langston Hughes. CP-HughL; CP-HughL2

First of May, The. A. E. Housman. CP-HousA

First of May, The. Chant for May Day. Langston Hughes. CP-HughL; CP-HughL1

First of May, The. Jones Very. CP-VeryJ

First of September. William Corbett. SP-CorbW

First of several good hours, The. Imaginary Sufi Garden. Olga Broumas. SP-BrouO

First of the seals was opened; the gold of the dawn unsealed, The. Apocalypse ("First of the seals was opened; the gold of the dawn unsealed, The"). G. K. Chesterton. CP-ChesG

First of the undecoded messages read: Popeye sits in thunder, The. Farm Implements and Rutabagas in a Landscape. John Ashbery. SP-AshbJ

First off, I have to say I can't talk good. Marvin McCabe. Hayden Carruth. CP-CarHS

First offer Incense, then thy field and meads. Pray and Prosper. Robert Herrick. CP-HerrR

First on TV, A. David Ignatow. SP-IgnaD

First or Last. Thomas Hardy. CP-HardT

First Page. Federico García Lorca. CP-GarcF, *tr. by* Jerome Rothenberg *Fr.* White Album.

First Panel is occupied with Storm and Night Battle, The. Murals Not Yet Dreamed. Philip Whalen. SP-WhalP

First Party at Ken Kesey's with Hell's Angels. Allen Ginsberg. CP-GinsA; SP-GinsA

First Payment Deferred. Ogden Nash. CP-NashO

First, plain speech in the mother tongue. Treatise on Poetry, A. Czeslaw Milosz. CP-MiloCN, *tr. by* Robert Hass

First, plain speech in the mother tongue. Preface: "First, plain speech in the mother tongue." Czeslaw Milosz. CP-MiloC, *tr. by* Robert Hass *Fr.* Treatise on Poetry, A.

First Poem. Ivor Gurney. SP-GurnI

First Point of Aries, The. Howard Nemerov. CP-NemeH

First point of the shell, The. Natural Enemies of the Conch, The. Alan Dugan. CP-DugaA

First Praise. William Carlos Williams. CP-WilW1

First Prelude. Dream in Ohio: The Father. John Logan. CP-LogaJ *Fr.* Poem in Progress.

First president to be loved by his, The. E. E. Cummings. CP-CummE

First Principles. Jay Wright. SP-WrigJ

First Psalm. Anne Sexton. SP-SextA *Fr.* O Ye Tongues.

First Psalm, The. Robert Burns. CP-BurnR

First Rain. Robert Creeley. SP-CreeR

First Rain of Spring, The. Maxine W. Kumin. SP-KumiM

First Rain on a Burned Car. Yehuda Amichai. SP-AmicY, *tr. by* Chana Bloch

First Rain on a Burned Car, The. Yehuda Amichai. SP-AmicYL, *tr. by* Benjamin Harshav *and* Barbara Harshav

First rain reminds me, The. Yehuda Amichai. SP-AmicYL, *tr. by* Benjamin Harshav *and* Barbara Harshav

First Reader. Billy Collins. SP-CollB

First real grip I ever got on things, The. Wheels within Wheels. Seamus Heaney. SP-HeanSO

First retainer / he gave to her, The. Marriage, A. Robert Creeley. CP-CreeR

First robin the; / you say something. E. E. Cummings. CP-CummE

First rose a low shore pastures green to the water. Waving of a Hand, The. W. S. Merwin. SP-MerwWF

First rose on my rose-tree, The. Three Songs of Shattering. Edna St. Vincent Millay. CP-MillE

First Row, The. Robert Stock. SP-StocR

First Satire of the Second Book of Horace [Imitated], The. Alexander Pope. CP-PopeA

First, scattering rain on the Polish cities, The. 1 September 1939. John Berryman. CP-BerrJ

First Sensual Delight, The. Yannis Ritsos. SP-RitsY, *tr. by* Kimon Friar

First Series. Yannis Ritsos.
   "Barefoot. Big feet." SP-RitsY
   "Dark rainy night, A." SP-RitsY
   "Doors to the left and right. A woman appeared in the corridor." SP-RitsY
   "From a beautiful mouth." SP-RitsY
   "In the fog, lemon trees hang their lanterns." SP-RitsY
   "Kisses and poetry you endured." SP-RitsY
   "Long summer nights." SP-RitsY
   "Monday, Tuesday: thorns. Thursday: iron." SP-RitsY
   "Oranges fell to the ground, The." SP-RitsY
   "Parades, heroes, wreathes." SP-RitsY
   "Small moon, The." SP-RitsY
   "Sunday moon, A." SP-RitsY
   "You punched a hole in the paper." SP-RitsY

First Shall Be Last, The. Jones Very. CP-VeryJ

First Shaman Song. Gary Snyder. CP-SnydG *Fr.* Myths and Texts.

First she come to our house. Stepmother, The. James Whitcomb Riley. CP-RileJ

First she died then on the bus. I See My Friend Everywhere. Grace Paley. CP-PalGC

First she like a piece of ill-oiled. E. E. Cummings. CP-CummE

First: She's a listener. Learning from Barbara Deming. Grace Paley. CP-PalGC

First showing of herself was foolish, The. Biography of a Myth, The. Laura Riding Jackson. CP-RidiL

First Sight. Philip Larkin. CP-LarkP

First Sight of Her and After. Thomas Hardy. CP-HardT

First signs of the death of the boom came in the summer, The. Tampa Stomp. John Berryman. CP-BerrJ

First Six Verses of the Ninetieth Psalm, The. Robert Burns. CP-BurnR

First Snow. Sam Hamill. SP-HamiS

First Snow. Howard Nemerov. CP-NemeH

First Snow. Mary Oliver. SP-OlivM

First Snow. May Sarton. SP-SartM

First Snow in Alsace. Richard Wilbur. CP-WilbR

First Sonata for Karlen Paula. Carl Sandburg. CP-SandC

First Song. Galway Kinnell. SP-KinnGN

First Song, The. Thomas Carew. CP-CareT *Fr.* Carew's Masque.

First Song of Huitzilopochtli. D. H. Lawrence. CP-LawrD

First soothsayers of the land, the man, The. Americana. Wallace Stevens. CP-StevWP

First Spring Day, The. Christina Georgina Rossetti. CP-RosC1

First star out. 7:00 p.m. Federico García Lorca. CP-GarcF, *tr. by* Jerome Rothenberg *Fr.* Summer Hours.

First Step, The. Constantine P. Cavafy. CP-CavaC, *tr. by* Theoharis Constantine Theoharis

First, suicide notes should be. Suicide. Alice Walker. CP-AudeW

First Telegraphic Message, The. Jones Very. CP-VeryJ

First that beautiful mad exploration. Journey toward Poetry. May Sarton. SP-SartM

First, The. Wendell Berry. CP-BerrW

First the dirt road. Drive Home, The. William Corbett. SP-CorbW

First the elaborate letters, then their sounds. Learning Russian. Miller Williams. CP-WillM

First the statues left. A little later. Return. Yannis Ritsos. SP-RitsY, *tr. by* N. C. Germanacos

First—the sun coming closer, growing by the minute. Notes for a Little Play. Ted Hughes. SP-HughTN

First the teacher called the roll. By Any Other Name. James Whitcomb Riley. CP-RileJ

First the warmth, variability. Rose, The. William Carlos Williams. CP-WilW1

First then made he a big strong shield, with his cunningest craft-skill. Shield of Achilles, The. Homer. CP-MerG2 *Fr.* Iliad, The.

First there is my little grandfather, I think he is no more than four or five. How Can I Speak for Her. Jane Cooper. CP-CoopJ

First, there is the memory of the dead priest in Norway. *Sun and Moon Flowers: Paul Klee, 1879–1940.* Norman Dubie. CP-DubiN

First there is the wind but not like the familiar wind but long. Definition of the Frontiers. Archibald MacLeish. CP-MacLA

First there were the trips, the cars, then girls. Sorrows of Lester Buster, The. Wyatt Prunty. SP-PrunW

First, They Said. Alice Walker. CP-WalkA

First thing he said, The. James Laughlin. CP-LaugJ *Fr.* America I Love You.

First thing that happened, The. Cat, The. Galway Kinnell. SP-KinnGN

First thing to do in Zurich. In Switzerland. Raymond Carver. CP-CarvR

First Things. Robert Lowell. SP-LoweR

First Things. Adrienne Rich. CP-RicAE

First Things First. W. H. Auden. CP-AudeW

First, this face—history did it. Evidence. William Stafford. SP-StafWW

First three deer bounding. Three Deer One Coyote Running in the Snow. Gary Snyder. CP-SnydG

First three-quarters of its century, The. From the Bunkers. Sam Hamill. SP-HamiS

First three roses / opened up today, the outer petals, The. For Bob Dash. James Schuyler. CP-SchuJ

First time, The. In School and at the University. Federico García Lorca. CP-GarcF, *tr. by* Alan S. Trueblood *Fr.* Love.

First Time, The. Robert Creeley. CP-CreeR

First Time, The. Karl Shapiro. SP-ShapK

First Time, The. Robert Penn Warren. CP-WarrR

First time ever I saw Johnny Spain was, The. Johnny Spain's White Heifer. Hayden Carruth. CP-CarHS

First time I died, I walked my ways, The. Epitaph: "First time I died, I walked my ways, The." Dorothy Parker. CP-ParkD

First time I met him Henry Moore was sixty. Before tea, The. Notes For Nobody. Donald Hall. CP-HallD

First time I went, The. Gregory Corso's Story. Allen Ginsberg. CP-GinsA

First Time In. Ivor Gurney. SP-GurnI

First / time is / the first, The. Robert Creeley. CP-CreeR

First time out. Lives. Derek Mahon. CP-MahoD

First time that I dreamed, we were in flight, The. Lesson, The. W. H. Auden. CP-AudeW

First time that Peter denied his Lord, The. Song at Cock-Crow, A. Rudyard Kipling. CP-KiplR

First Travels of Max. John Crowe Ransom. SP-RansJ

First under up and then again down under. On Our Sympathy with the Under Dog. Robert Frost. CP-FrosR

First ventured into. Cloudberry Summer. Amy Clampitt. CP-ClamA

First waking to the gray. February. Maxine W. Kumin. SP-KumiM

First war resembles. Shmuel HaNagid. SP-HaNaS, *tr. by* Peter Cole

First Warmth. Wallace Stevens. CP-StevWP

First was like a dream thro' summer heat, The. From House to Home. Christina Georgina Rossetti. CP-RosC1

First was the world as one great cymbal made. Music's Empire. Andrew Marvell. CP-MarvA

First We knew of Him was Death, The. Emily Dickinson. CP-DickE

First when Maggie [*or* Maggy] was my care. Whistle o'er the Lave o't. Robert Burns. CP-BurnR

First white hair coils in my hand, The. Sign. Marge Piercy. SP-PierM

First windsnake twists, The. Situation. Federico García Lorca. CP-GarcF, *tr. by* Jerome Rothenberg *Fr.* In the Forest of the Lunar Grapefruits.

First Winter. Pablo Neruda. SP-NeruP

First Woman. Josephine Jacobsen. CP-JacoJ

First Work, and Then Wages. Robert Herrick. CP-HerrR

First, worms begin with a man's mind. In the Background of Silence. Yusef Komunyakaa. CP-KomuY

First year was like icing, The. More Pleasant Adventures. John Ashbery. SP-AshbJ

First you are hot. Swan Song. Dorothy Parker. CP-ParkD

First you must have. Instructions for Building Straw Huts. Yusef Komunyakaa. CP-KomuY

Firstborn. Louise Glück. SP-GlucL

Firste stok, fader of gentilesse, The. Gentilesse. Geoffrey Chaucer. CP-ChauG

Firstly Inclined to Take What It Is Told. Gwendolyn Brooks. SP-BrooG

Firsts. John Ciardi. CP-CiarJ

Fish. D. H. Lawrence. CP-LawrD

Fish. William Carlos Williams. CP-WilW1

Fish. / Bequeath fish. Dates. Gertrude Stein. CP-SteiG

Fish, The. Elizabeth Bishop. CP-BishE

Fish, The. G. K. Chesterton. CP-ChesG

Fish, The. Norman Dubie. CP-DubiN

Fish, The. Marianne Craig Moore. CP-MoorM

Fish, The. Ogden Nash. CP-NashO

Fish, The. Mary Oliver. SP-OlivM

Fish, The. William Butler Yeats. CP-YeatW

Fish are subtle. Fishermen. Of Fish and Fishermen. John Ciardi. CP-CiarJ

Fish are very good at swimming. Barmaids Are Diviner Than Mermaids. Ogden Nash. CP-NashO

Fish bones walked the waves off Hatteras. Cottonmouth Country. Louise Glück. SP-GlucL

Fish Counter at Bonneville, The. William Stafford. SP-StafWW

Fish Crier. Carl Sandburg. CP-SandC

Fish, Fish. Stevie Smith. CP-SmitS

Fish float belly-up, for real—, The. Bomb Test. Gary Snyder. CP-SnydG

Fish / fowl. Paean to Place. Lorine Niedecker. CP-NiedL

Fish has laid her succulent eggs. Vicissitudes of the Creator. Archibald MacLeish. CP-MacLA

Fish in the Stone, The. Rita Dove. SP-DoveR

Fish is speech, or see, The. Abstract #1, Yucatan. Charles Olson. CP-OlsoC

Fish is the Flower of Water, A. Charles Olson. CP-OlsoC

Fish never sleep. Mondo Angelico. Charles Wright. SP-WrigCN

Fish Peddler and Cobbler. Kenneth Rexroth. CP-RexrK

Fish-Scale Sunrise, A. Wallace Stevens. CP-StevW; CP-StevWP

Fish scales, old newspapers, unopened cans. Sources. Philip Levine. SP-LeviP

Fish-sky at morning. Mock Confessional. Lawrence Ferlinghetti. SP-FerlL

Fish Tank Room, The. Josephine Jacobsen. CP-JacoJ

Fish That Lives at the Bottom, The. David Ignatow. SP-IgnaD

Fish That Walked, The. Anne Sexton. CP-SextA

Fishbone pattern of flint arrows flattened, A. Outline of History. G. K. Chesterton. CP-ChesG

Fisher Cat, The. Richard Eberhart. CP-EberR

Fisher Child's Lullaby, The. Paul Laurence Dunbar. CP-DunbP

Fisher-Wife, A. Christina Georgina Rossetti. CP-RosC2

Fisherman, The. William Butler Yeats. CP-YeatW

Fisherman took his gear and left, The. Private Place. Yannis Ritsos. SP-RitsY, *tr. by* Kimon Friar

Fisherman's swapping a yarn for a yarn, The. Flower Boat, The. Robert Frost. CP-FrosR

Fishermen. Federico García Lorca. CP-GarcF, *tr. by* Jerome Rothenberg *Fr.* Six Songs at Nightfall.

Fishermen at Ballyshannon. Limbo. Seamus Heaney. SP-HeanSO

Fishermen on Lake Michigan, sometimes, The. Kicks. Howard Nemerov. CP-NemeH

Fishermen rowing homeward in the dusk, The. Harbour, The. Derek Walcott. CP-WalcD

Fishermen, The. John Greenleaf Whittier. CP-WhitJ

Fishermen, The. James Wright. CP-WrigJ

Fisher's Son, The. Henry David Thoreau. CP-ThorH

Fisherwoman, The. David Ignatow. SP-IgnaD

Fisherwoman, The. James Laughlin. CP-LaugJ

Fishes are born in water. Man Is Born in Tao. Chuang Tzu. CP-MertT, *tr. by* Thomas Merton

Fishes swam here through the Eocene. Quarry, The. Amy Clampitt. CP-ClamA

Fishing. Paul Laurence Dunbar. CP-DunbP

Fishing. W. S. Merwin. SP-MerwWF

Fishing for Eel Totems. Margaret Atwood. SP-AtwM1

Fishing in Lough Arrow is piss-poor, The. Schooldesk, The. Raymond Carver. CP-CarvR

Fishing on the Susquehanna in July. Billy Collins. SP-CollB

Fishing Party, The. James Whitcomb Riley. CP-RileJ

Fishing Pole of the Drowned Man, The. Raymond Carver. CP-CarvR

Fishnet. Robert Lowell. SP-LoweR

Fishvendor, The. William Meredith. SP-MereW

Fission has turned our barracks ghostly. Elemental Trust. Robert Stock. SP-StocR

Fist. Philip Levine. SP-LeviP

Fist, The. Derek Walcott. CP-WalcD

Fistulae. Ezra Pound. CP-PoEar

Fit against the Country, A. James Wright. CP-WrigJ

Fit emblem of th' immortal soul! though thou. Lines Suggested by Seeing a Butterfly Sculptured Upon a Tomb. Jones Very. CP-VeryJ

Fit for the Pleiads' azure chord. Hafiz. CP-EmerR *Fr.* Odes.

Fit of Rhyme [*or* Rime] against Rhyme [*or* Rime], A. Ben Jonson. CP-JonsB; SP-JonsB

Fitful alternations of the rain, The. Fragment: Rain. Percy Bysshe Shelley. CP-ShelP

Fitter to see Him, I may be. Emily Dickinson. CP-DickE

Fittest, The. Josephine Jacobsen. CP-JacoJ

Fitting, The. Edna St. Vincent Millay. CP-MillE

Fitting of the Mask, The. Stanley Kunitz. CP-KunSC

Fitz-Eustace's Song. Sir Walter Scott. SP-ScotW *Fr.* Marmion.

Fitz-Greene Halleck. John Greenleaf Whittier. CP-WhitJ

Five. Robert Graves. CP-GravR

Five A.M. in the Pinewoods. Mary Oliver. SP-OlivM

Five Accounts of a Monogamous Man. William Meredith. SP-MereW

Five AM. William Stafford. SP-StafWW

Five Americans. E. E. Cummings. CP-CummE

Five-and-twenty years have gone. In Memory of Alfred Pollexfen. William Butler Yeats. CP-YeatW

Five beringed fingers of Creation. Five. Robert Graves. CP-GravR

Five breaths pray in me: sun moon. Thomas Merton. CP-MertT

Five brick panels, three small windows, six lions' heads with. Backside of the Academy, The. Muriel Rukeyser. CP-RukeM

Five Carlins—A Ballad—Tune, Chevy Chase, The. Robert Burns. CP-BurnR

Five Cent Balloons. Carl Sandburg. CP-SandC

Five circus clowns dying this year, morning newspapers told their lives. Legends. Carl Sandburg. CP-SandC

Five-Day Week, The. Grace Paley. CP-PalGC

Five-day week was set like a firecracker, The. Five-Day Week, The. Grace Paley. CP-PalGC

5 / derbies-with-men-in-them smoke Helmar. E. E. Cummings. CP-CummE

Five Elephants. Rita Dove. SP-DoveR

Five Enemies, The. Chuang Tzu. CP-MertT

Five English Poets. Dante Gabriel Rossetti.
   John Keats. CW-RossD
   Percy Bysshe Shelley. CW-RossD
   Samuel Taylor Coleridge. CW-RossD
   Thomas Chatterton. CW-RossD
   William Blake. CW-RossD

Five Epigrams. James Vincent Cunningham.
   "Bride loved old words, and found her pleasure marred." CP-CunnJ
   Epitaph for Someone or Other. CP-CunnJ
   Lip. CP-CunnJ

515 Madison Avenue. Rhapsody. Frank O'Hara. SP-OharF

Five-Finger Exercises. T. S. Eliot. CP-ElioT

Five Flights Up. Elizabeth Bishop. CP-BishE

Five geese deploy mysteriously. Bas-Relief. Carl Sandburg. CP-SandC

Five hours, (and who can do it less in?). Lady's Dressing Room, The. Jonathan Swift. CP-SwifJ

Five hundred years in the wake of the Hegira. Unending Rose, The. Jorge Luis Borges. SP-BorgJ, *tr.* by Alastair Reid

Five Interior Landscapes. Olga Broumas. SP-BrouO

Five kings ruled o'er the Amorite. Ballad of the Battle of Gibeon, The. G. K. Chesterton. CP-ChesG

Five Ladies' Answer to the Beau, with the Wig and Wings at His Head, The. Thomas Sheridan. CP-SherT

Five lines, not four. And keep the song. Tanck's Prolegomenon. Hayden Carruth. CP-CarHS *Fr.* Songs About What Comes Down: The Complete Works of Mr. Septic Tanck.

Five little roses spoke. Public Letter to Emily Dickinson. Carl Sandburg. CP-SandC

Five lone clangs from the house-clock nigh. Shiver, The. Thomas Hardy. CP-HardT

Five men pull straws. Fragging. Yusef Komunyakaa. CP-KomuY

Five months ago the stream did flow. Change Upon Change. Elizabeth Barrett Browning. CP-BroEB

Five Nocturnes. Robert Frost. CP-FrosR

Five O'Clock, Beacon Hill. Adrienne Rich. CP-RicAE

Five O'Clock in the Morning. Raymond Carver. CP-CarvR

Five o'clock prairie sunset is a strong man going to sleep after a long, The. Rusty Crimson. Carl Sandburg. CP-SandC

Five old bells, The. Weeknight Service. D. H. Lawrence. CP-LawrD

Five Old Favorites. James Merrill. SP-MerrJ

Five or four whippoorwhills. Nature Note, A. Robert Frost. CP-FrosR

Five Peaks turn to dust, The. Han-shan. CP-ColdM, *tr.* by Red Pine

Five people were sitting on the balcony. Summer Night in the King David Hotel. Yehuda Amichai. SP-AmicYL, *tr.* by Benjamin Harshav *and* Barbara Harshav

Five planets and a brilliant young moon. Moon and Five Planets. Robinson Jeffers. CP-JefR3

5:00 p.m. Federico García Lorca. CP-GarcF, *tr.* by Jerome Rothenberg *Fr.* Summer Hours.

Five Poems about Poetry. George Oppen. CP-OppGN

Five Poems for Dolls. Margaret Atwood. SP-AtwM2

Five Poems for Grandmothers. Margaret Atwood. SP-AtwM2

Five Poems from Mexico. Denise Levertov. SP-LeveDP

Five Preludes For Buffalo's Own Forest Lawn. John Logan. CP-LogaJ

Five quid for the sloth. At a Loss. Heather McHugh. SP-McHuH

Five rings light your approach across. Father out Walking on the Lawn, A. Rita Dove. SP-DoveR

Five / Senses gone, The. Ozymandias. George Oppen. CP-OppGN

Five sessions of God willing lethal x. Santorini: Stopping the Leak. James Merrill. SP-MerrJ

Five soldiers fixed by Mathew Brady's eye. Looking into History. Richard Wilbur. CP-WilbR

Five Songs. W. H. Auden. CP-AudeW

Five Songs. W. H. Auden. CP-AudeW

Five Students, The. Thomas Hardy. CP-HardT

Five summer days, five summer nights. Blue-Fly, The. Robert Graves. CP-GravR

5:30 A.M. Adrienne Rich. CP-RicAE; SP-RicA1; SP-RicA2

Five Threes (Fast Bike). Heather McHugh. SP-McHuH

Five Towns on the B. and O. Carl Sandburg. CP-SandC

Five Virgins, The. Thomas Merton. CP-MertT

5 Ways of Saying the Same Thing. Andrei Codrescu. SP-CodrA

Five windows light the cavern'd Man; thro' one he breathes the air. Europe; A Prophecy. William Blake. CP-BlakW

Five Women Bathing in Moonlight. Richard Wilbur. CP-WilbR

Five years ago I planted a buttonwood slip. Money. A. R. Ammons. CP-AmmoA

Five years have passed [or past]; five summers, with the length. Lines Composed a Few Miles above Tintern Abbey on Revisiting the Banks of the Wye During a Tour, July 13, 1798. William Wordsworth. CP-WorW1

Five years of cringing child small. Child, The. Richard Eberhart. CP-EberR

Five Years Old. James Tate. SP-TateJ

Five young men, canteen. Acapulco Canyon: Two Kodachromes. John Logan. CP-LogaJ

Fix. Heather McHugh. SP-McHuH

Fix this pothook of beauty on this palette. Serena III. Samuel Beckett. CP-BeckS

Fix your eyes on any chance object. For instance. Brotherhood in Pain. Robert Penn Warren. CP-WarrR

Fixers. William Stafford. SP-StafWW

Fizzle. A. K. Ramanujan. CP-RamaA

Fl / a / tt / ene / d d. E. E. Cummings. CP-CummE

Flabbergasting of the True & False Basilisk, The. Robert Stock. SP-StocR

Flag, The. Rainer Maria Rilke. CP-RilkFr, *tr.* by A. Poulin, Jr. *Fr.* Orchards.

Flag, The. Richard Eberhart. CP-EberR

Flag moves through a disgusting landscape, and our patois drowns out the drum, The. Democracy. Arthur Rimbaud. CP-RimbA, *tr.* by Martin Sorrell

Flag of Summer. May Swenson. SP-SwenM

Flags. Gwendolyn Brooks. SP-BrooG
   (Love Note II: Flags.) SP-BrooG

Flags are up again along the coast, The. Coast of Maine. Richard Eberhart. CP-EberR

Flags of the Pacific. Wedding of the Rose and the Lotus, The. Nicholas Vachel Lindsay. CP-LindV

Flags of war like storm-birds fly, The. Battle Autumn of 1862, The. John Greenleaf Whittier. CP-WhitJ

Flags Vex a Dying Face. Emily Dickinson. CP-DickE

Flags were put in mothballs, The. That arrogance—he said. Spinelessly. Yannis Ritsos. SP-RitsY, *tr.* by N. C. Germanacos

Flailed from the heart of water in a bow. Ballade for the Duke of Orléans. Richard Wilbur. CP-WilbR

Flake the Wind exasperate, The. Emily Dickinson. CP-DickE

Flakes pour to the black dead. In the Camp There Was One Alive. Randall Jarrell. CP-JarrR

Flame. Charles Tomlinson. CP-TomlC

Flame, A. Adam Zagajewski. SP-ZagaA, *tr.* by Clare Cavanagh

Flame at my footfall, Parnassus! Apollo. Apollo and the Fates. Robert Browning. CP-BroR2

Flame blue wisps in the west. October Paint. Carl Sandburg. CP-SandC

Flame crept up the prtrait line by line, The. Photograph, The. Thomas Hardy. CP-HardT

Flame from each finger, A. I Am A Light You Could Read By. Marge Piercy. SP-PierM

Flame guttered, flared impossibly high, The. Dazzle of Darkness. Robert Graves. CP-GravR

Flame in the pit, flame. Last Judgement. Charles Tomlinson. CP-TomlC

Flame of a Candle, The. Howard Nemerov. CP-NemeH

Flame of California. California Poppy. Gabriela Mistral. SP-MistG, *tr.* by Maria Giachetti [or Jacketti]

Flame-red moon, the harvest moon, The. Harvest Moon, The. Ted Hughes. SP-HughTN

Flamenco Vignettes. Federico García Lorca. CP-GarcF, *tr.* by Cola Franzen *and* Christopher Maurer

Flames of a blasted escape. Long Enough. Thomas Merton. CP-MertT

Flamey monster—plumage and blossoms, A. Son, A. Denise Levertov. SP-LeveDL

Flaming Heart, The. Richard Crashaw. CP-CrasR

Flaming sighs that boil within my breast, The. Sir Thomas Wyatt. CP-WyatT

Flamingo pink on the chimney stacks. Fanny Howe. SP-HoweF *Fr.* Robeson Street.

Flammonde. Edwin Arlington Robinson. CP-RobiE

Flanders. Carl Sandburg. CP-SandC

Flanders, the name of a place, a country of people. Flanders. Carl Sandburg. CP-SandC

Flanking the place, / a cypress. At Sant' Antimo. Charles Tomlinson. CP-TomlC; SP-TomlC

Flapper. D. H. Lawrence. CP-LawrD

Flapper, The. Allen Tate. CP-TateA

Flapper Vote. D. H. Lawrence. CP-LawrD

Flash Back. Allen Ginsberg. CP-GinsA

Flash, The. James Dickey. CP-DickJ

Flash Crimson. Carl Sandburg. CP-SandC

Flashback. Ai. SP-Ai

Flashboat, The. Jane Cooper. CP-CoopJ

Flashes. James Schuyler. CP-SchuJ

Flashing Cliff, A. Muriel Rukeyser. CP-RukeM

Flashlights, their / palaver. Paul Celan. SP-CelaP, *tr. by* John Felstiner

Flat. C. K. Williams. CP-WillC; SP-WillC

Flat as to an eagle's eye. Nuptials of Attila, The. George Meredith. CP-MerG1

Flat, eventless afternoon. To a Fish Head Found on the Beach Near Málaga. Philip Levine. SP-LeviP

Flat-Foot's Song. D. H. Lawrence. CP-LawrD

Flat gray banana store front, The. Unintentional Paint. Carl Sandburg. CP-SandC

Flat Lands. Carl Sandburg. CP-SandC

Flat Suburbs, S.W., in the Morning. D. H. Lawrence. CP-LawrD

Flat Waters of the West in Kansas. Carl Sandburg. CP-SandC

Flat with variations. Not. Delft. Rita Dove. SP-DoveR

Flatness is all. The sunfish lives in it. Post-Therapy Room. William Dickey. SP-DickW

Flatted Fifths. Langston Hughes. CP-HughL; CP-HughL3

Flattened shape / the first shape, The. Andrew Lord Poems. James Schuyler. CP-SchuJ

Flattered at having no. Anglican Lady, An. Donald Davie. CP-DaviDC

Flattered with promise of escape. Thoughts on the Seasons. William Wordsworth. CP-WorW2

Flatterie. Robert Herrick. CP-HerrR

Flattery. William Carlos Williams. CP-WilW2

Flattery has been infrequent, The. Monday Morning. James Vincent Cunningham. CP-CunnJ

Flatting Mill, The. William Cowper. CP-CowpW

Flaubert in Egypt. Robert Penn Warren. CP-WarrR

Flaubert wanted to write a novel. Style. Howard Nemerov. CP-NemeH

Flaubert's Early Prose. Robert Creeley. SP-CreeR

Flavio Gonzales, seventy-two, made jackhammer. Moon Is a Diamond, The. Arthur Sze. SP-SzeA

Flavius—that delicate lass—to Catullus. Catullus. *See* Your most recent acquisition, Flavius

Flavius to Postumia. James Laughlin. CP-LaugJ

Flavor like wild honey begins, A. Looking for Gold. William Stafford. SP-StafWW

Flaw, The. Robert Lowell. SP-LoweR

Flaw in Paganism, The. Dorothy Parker. CP-ParkD

"Flawless" is the word, no doubt, for this third of May. Hourglass. Josephine Jacobsen. CP-JacoJ

Flax, chicory, scabious. Flowers of Sophia. Denise Levertov. SP-LeveDS

Flayed Crow in the Hall of Judgement, A. Ted Hughes. SP-HughTN

Flea, The. John Donne. CP-DonnJ; MW-DonnJ

Flea is carrying a bag of diseases, A. Flea's Carrying Words, A. W. S. Merwin. SP-MerwW

Flea's Carrying Words, A. W. S. Merwin. SP-MerwW

Fleas, too, / have fled, The. C. K. Williams. CP-WillC

Flèche d'Or. James Merrill. SP-MerrJ

Fleck of sky you are. Mother to Babe. George Meredith. CP-MerG1

Fleckings, The. John Updike. CP-UpdiJ

Flecknoe, an English Priest at Rome. Andrew Marvell. CP-MarvA

Fled are the frosts, and now the fields appear[e]. Farewell Frost; or, Welcome the Spring. Robert Herrick. CP-HerrR

Fled are those times, when, in harmonious strains. Truth in Poetry. George Crabbe. SP-CrabG *Fr.* Village, The.

Fledgling, The. Edna St. Vincent Millay. CP-MillE

Fledglings. William Meredith. SP-MereW

Fle[e] fro[m] the pres[s] [*or* prees] and dwelle with so[o]th[e][ ]fastnesse. Balade of Bon Conseill. Geoffrey Chaucer. CP-ChauG

Flee from this Love, you lovers; flee the flame! Michelangelo Buonarroti. CP-Miche, *tr. by* John Frederick Nims

Flee into some forgotten night and be. Tryst, The. Walter De la Mare. CP-DeLaW

Flee on Your Donkey. Anne Sexton. CP-SextA; SP-SextA

Flee to the Mountains. Jones Very. CP-VeryJ

Fleeing from short-haired mad executives. Two Climbs. W. H. Auden. CP-AudeW

Fleet Astronomer can bore, The. Vanity [*or* Vanitie] (1). George Herbert. CP-HerbG

Fleet ships encountering on the high seas. Good Ships. John Crowe Ransom. SP-RansJ

Fleet Visit. W. H. Auden. CP-AudeW

Fleeting, The. Walter De la Mare. CP-DeLaW

Fleeting years are ever bearing. Eheu! fugaces, Posthume, Posthume, Labuntur anni. Jones Very. CP-VeryJ

Fleg. Charles Bukowski. SP-BukC2

Fleming Helphenstine. Edwin Arlington Robinson. CP-RobiE

Flemish style, late 17th century. First Icon with Gun, The. Andrei Codrescu. SP-CodrA

Flesh. Robert Creeley. CP-CreeR

Flesh, a woman's heavenly flesh. Clay. "Rubén Dario." SP-DariR, *tr. by* Alberto Acereda *and* Will Derusha

Flesh and Blood. Adrienne Rich. CP-RicAE

Flesh and the Spirit, The. Anne Bradstreet. CP-BradA

Flesh bears early fruit; most eat of it, The. Flesh, The. Jones Very. CP-VeryJ

Flesh covers the bone, The. Alone with Everybody. Charles Bukowski. SP-BukC1

Flesh is sad, alas, and there's nothing but words!, The. Sea Breeze. Stéphane Mallarmé. CP-MallS, *tr. by* Henry Weinfield

Flesh, of a sudden, gone nameless in music, flesh. Old Nigger on One-Mule Cart Encountered Late at Night When Driving Home from Party in the Back Country. Robert Penn Warren. CP-WarrR

Flesh of our flesh—bone of our bone. Burial Anthem. Christina Georgina Rossetti. CP-RosC3

Flesh of the house is heavy sea-orphaned stone, the imagination of, The. Winged Rock. Robinson Jeffers. CP-JefR2

Flesh, The. Jones Very. CP-VeryJ

Fleshing-out the Season. Yusef Komunyakaa. CP-KomuY

Flesh's / signals. Robert Creeley. CP-CreeR

Fleuves et océans. Samuel Beckett. CP-BeckS

Flicker / of *this* light / on consciousness—a. Christmas: May 10, 1970. Robert Creeley. CP-CreeR

Flicker with a broken neck, A. On Addy Road. May Swenson. SP-SwenM

Flickering / in the buildings. Rock Flow, River Mix. Muriel Rukeyser. CP-RukeM

Flickering Mind. Denise Levertov. SP-LeveDS

Flickering shades. Hunt by Night, The. Derek Mahon. CP-MahoD

Flies. Donald Hall. CP-HallD

Flies. Galway Kinnell. SP-KinnGN

Flies. W. S. Merwin. SP-MerwW

Flight. Langston Hughes. CP-HughL; CP-HughL1; CP-HughL2 *Fr.* Three Songs about Lynching.

Flight. Primo Levi. CP-LeviP, *tr. by* Ruth Feldman

Flight. Robert Lowell. SP-LoweR

Flight. Czeslaw Milosz. CP-MiloC; CP-MiloCN, *tr. by* John Carpenter *and* Bogdana Carpenter

Flight. George Oppen. CP-OppGN

Flight. Anne Sexton. CP-SextA

Flight. James Tate. SP-TateJ

Flight. C. K. Williams. CP-WillC

Flight, The. Rudyard Kipling. CP-KiplR

Flight, The. Walter De la Mare. CP-DeLaW

Flight, The. W. S. Merwin. SP-MerwWF

Flight, The. Charles Tomlinson. CP-TomlC

Flight, The. Jones Very. CP-VeryJ

Flight into Egypt, The. W. H. Auden. CP-AudeW *Fr.* For the Time Being; a Christmas Oratorio.

Flight into Egypt, The. Thomas Merton. CP-MertT

Flight of Apollo, The. Stanley Kunitz. CP-KunSC

Flight of flaming hair at the extreme, The. Stéphane Mallarmé. CP-MallS, *tr. by* Henry Weinfield

Flight of Lin Hui, The. Chuang Tzu. CP-MertT

Flight of six heavy-motored bombing-planes, A. Great Sunset, The. Robinson Jeffers. CP-JefR2

Flight of Swans. Robinson Jeffers. CP-JefR2

Flight of the Duchess, The. Robert Browning. CP-BroR1

Flight of the Duchess, The. Robert Browning. CP-BroR1

Flight of the Heart. Louis MacNeice. CP-MacNL

Flight of the Reader, The. Billy Collins. SP-CollB

Flight 162. George Oppen. CP-OppGN

Flight Path, The. Seamus Heaney.
  "Following fro the record, in the light." SP-HeanSO

Flight to the City. William Carlos Williams. CP-WilW1

Flightily falling words like yellow. Idle Talk. Louis MacNeice. CP-MacNL

Fling him amongst the cobbles of the street. Assassin, The. James Whitcomb
  Riley. CP-RileJ

Fling out your banners, your honors be bringing. Emancipation. Paul Laurence
  Dunbar. CP-DunbP

Fling your red scarf faster and faster, dancer. Mask. Carl Sandburg. CP-SandC

Flint. Christina Georgina Rossetti. CP-RosC2

Flint and Steel. Thomas McGrath. SP-McGrT

Flint-skinned, bone-hued. Hickory Grove, The. Amy Clampitt. CP-ClamA

Flintlike, her feet struck. Hardcastle Crags. Sylvia Plath. CP-PlatS

Flippancies. Richard Wilbur. CP-WilbR

Flirt. John Updike. CP-UpdiJ

Flirtation. Rita Dove. SP-DoveR

Flirt's Tragedy, The. Thomas Hardy. CP-HardT

Float / ing / ly) / i / (in Khoury's warm). E. E. Cummings. CP-CummE

Floatfloafloflf / lloloa. E. E. Cummings. CP-CummE

Floating. James Laughlin. CP-LaugJ

Floating. Kenneth Rexroth. CP-RexrK

Floating Baby Paintings. Thomas Lux. SP-LuxT

Floating Bridges. Federico García Lorca. CP-GarcF, *tr. by* Jerome Rothenberg
  Fr. In the Garden of the Lunar Grapefruits.

Floating cloud follows the sun, The. To Li Po. Tu Fu. CP-WilW2

Floating feather, too, can sketch your image, A. Day and Night. Eugenio
  Montale. CP-MontE, *tr. by* Jonathan Galassi

Floating Free. James Laughlin. CP-LaugJ

Floating of a leaf that fell, The. Golden Leaf, The. Kathleen Jessie Raine. SP-
  RainK

Flock, The. Derek Walcott. CP-WalcD

Flock of Sheep Near the Airport, A. Yehuda Amichai. SP-AmicY, *tr. by* Chana
  Bloch

Flock of sheep that leisurely pass by, A. To Sleep. William Wordsworth. CP-
  WorW1

Flock of timid sheep, A. Shih-te. CP-ColdM, *tr. by* Red Pine

Flocks feed by darkness with a noise of whispers. Carol: "Flocks feed by
  darkness with a noise of whispers." Thomas Merton. CP-MertT

Flood, The. Elizabeth Bishop. CP-BishE

Flood, The. Robert Frost. CP-FrosR

Flood, The. Charles Tomlinson. CP-TomlC; SP-TomlC

Flood, The. Jones Very. CP-VeryJ

Flood at the International Writer's Workshop. Bogomil Gjuzel. CP-KizeC, *tr. by*
  Carolyn Kizer

Flood, if he has for him and his a bit. Upon Flood, Or a Thankfull Man. Robert
  Herrick. CP-HerrR

Flood-Tide below me! I see you face to face! Crossing Brooklyn Ferry. Walt
  Whitman. CP-WhitW

Flood with reed-grown slime banks, till I be past. Elegy 3.5: "Flood with reed-
  grown slime banks, till I be past." Ovid. CP-MarlC *Fr.* Elegies.

Floodcrest of afternoon passes, The. Three. A. R. Ammons. CP-AmmoA

Flooded Meadows. Thom Gunn. CP-GunnT

Flooded, the soul pours out. Michelangelo Buonarroti. CP-Miche, *tr. by* John
  Frederick Nims

Floodplain river is wide, The. Han-shan. CP-ColdM, *tr. by* Red Pine

Floods, The. Rudyard Kipling. CP-KiplR

Floor. C. K. Williams. CP-WillC; SP-WillC

Floor / of the temple, The. Trance. "H. D." CP-DoolH

Floor Plans. Yusef Komunyakaa. CP-KomuY

Floral Decorations for Bananas. Wallace Stevens. CP-StevW; CP-StevWP

Floral Teaching. Christina Georgina Rossetti. CP-RosC3

Florence. Aleksandr Aleksandrovich Blok. SP-BlokA, *tr. by* Peter France *and*
  Jon Stallworthy

Florence. Robert Lowell. SP-LoweR

Florence, Bologna, Parma, Modena. Italy and the World. Elizabeth Barrett
  Browning. CP-BroEB

Florentine Ingratitude. William Blake. CP-BlakW

Florentine Madrigals. Eugenio Montale. CP-MontE, *tr. by* Jonathan Galassi

Florentines. Geoffrey Hill. CP-HillG

Floretty's Musical Contribution. James Whitcomb Riley. CP-RileJ *Fr.* Child-
  World, A.

Florida. Lorine Niedecker. CP-NiedL

Florida. Elizabeth Bishop. CP-BishE

Florida means land of flowers. Ballad of Harry Moore. Langston Hughes. CP-
  HughL; CP-HughL3

Florida Night, A. Paul Laurence Dunbar. CP-DunbP

Florida Road Workers. Langston Hughes. CP-HughL1
  (Hey, Buddy! / Look at me!) CP-HughL; CP-HughL2; CP-HughL3

Floris in Italy. Gerard Manley Hopkins. CP-HopkG

Florist Rose, The. Robert Graves. CP-GravR

Florist was told, cyclamen or azalea, The. Lines to Accompany Flowers for Eve.
  Carolyn Kizer. CP-KizeC

Florists Wears Knee-Breeches, The. Wallace Stevens. CP-StevWP

Floss won't save you from an Abyss. Emily Dickinson. CP-DickE

Flossie put the velvet pansies. Modest Achievement, The. William Carlos
  Williams. CP-WilW2

Flotsam. Langston Hughes. CP-HughL; CP-HughL3

Flotsam. Walter De la Mare. CP-DeLaW

Flotsam and jetsam / are gentlemen poeds. E. E. Cummings. CP-CummE; SP-
  CummE

Flounder. Robert Lowell. SP-LoweR

Flour. Gabriela Mistral. SP-MistG, *tr. by* Maria Giachetti [*or* Jacketti]

Flour is luminous and soft, the mother of abundance. Flour. Gabriela Mistral.
  SP-MistG, *tr. by* Maria Giachetti [*or* Jacketti]

Flourish. Joseph Brodsky. CP-BrodJ

Flourishing vine, whose kindling clusters glow. Fragment: The Vine-Shroud.
  Percy Bysshe Shelley. CP-ShelP

Flow down, cold rivulet, to the sea. Farewell, A: "Flow down, cold rivulet, to
  the sea." Alfred Tennyson. CP-TennA

Flow, Flow, Flow. Stevie Smith. CP-SmitS

Flow, flow pure tears that from cold fountains run. Marya Alexandrovna
  Zaturenska. SP-ZatuM *Fr.* Fountains of Rome, The.

Flow, flow the waves hated. Illusions. Ralph Waldo Emerson. CP-EmerR

Flow Gently, Sweet Afton. Robert Burns. CP-BurnR
  (Afton Water.) CP-BurnR

Flow of Memories, The. Jorge Luis Borges. SP-BorgJ, *tr. by* Charles Tomlinson

Flow of Thought. Richard Eberhart. CP-EberR

Flow was toward the land, The. Soul. Richard Eberhart. CP-EberR

Flow, water, the blue water. All Is Safe. Kenneth Patchen. CP-PatcK

Flower. Federico García Lorca. CP-GarcF, *tr. by* Alan S. Trueblood *Fr.* Moon
  Songs.

Flower. Paul Celan. SP-CelaP, *tr. by* John Felstiner

Flower Arrangements. Howard Nemerov. CP-NemeH

Flower, The. Robert Creeley. CP-CreeR

Flower, The. Robert Creeley. CP-CreeR

Flower, The. George Herbert. CP-HerbG

Flower, The. Carolyn Kizer. CP-KizeC

Flower, The. Walter De la Mare. CP-DeLaW

Flower, The. William Carlos Williams. CP-WilW1

Flower, The. William Carlos Williams. CP-WilW2

Flower-Arranging Summer, A. May Sarton. SP-SartM

Flower asked: "Will my scent, / Perhaps, survive me?", The. Meditation before
  an Ancient Poem. Pablo Antonio Cuadra. CP-MertT

Flower beds, The. City Talk. Lorine Niedecker. CP-NiedL

Flower Boat, The. Robert Frost. CP-FrosR

Flower Dump. Theodore Roethke. CP-RoetT

Flower / fallen / she saw it, The. Loving Dexterity, The. William Carlos
  Williams. CP-WilW2

Flower from "to flow," the One who Flows, The. Hymn of Pan the Flower, The.
  Andrei Codrescu. SP-CodrA

Flower Garden at Coleorton Hall, Leicestershire, A. William Wordsworth. CP-
  WorW2

Flower-Gathering. Robert Frost. CP-FrosR

Flower Grower in Aquarius. Alan Dugan. CP-DugaA

Flower grows, The. Charles Olson. CP-OlsoC

Flower Herding on Mount Monadnock. Galway Kinnell. SP-KinnGN

Flower—I never fancied, jewel—I profess you! Magical Nature. Robert
  Browning. CP-BroR2

Flower in a Letter, A. Elizabeth Barrett Browning. CP-BroEB

Flower in the Crannied Wall. Alfred Tennyson. CP-TennA

Flower in the glass peanut bottle formerly in the kitchen crooked to take.
  Transcription of Organ Music. Allen Ginsberg. CP-GinsA

Flower is red, or yellow, as the case may be, The. Agreeing. Miller Williams.
  CP-WillM

Flower it blaws, it fades, it fa's, The. Lovely Polly Stewart. Robert Burns. CP-
  BurnR

Flower keeps it's appointment. Emily Dickinson. SP-DickE

Flower, memory—. Kathleen Jessie Raine. SP-RainK

Flower must not blame the Bee, The. Emily Dickinson. CP-DickE

Flower of capital is small and white large and grey-green in a storm its petals
  sing, The. Michael Palmer. SP-PalmM

Flower of dawn, The. Echo. Federico García Lorca. CP-GarcF, *tr. by* Alan S.
  Trueblood *Fr.* Love.

Flower of Mending, The. Nicholas Vachel Lindsay. CP-LindV

Flower of the Fruit, The. Alfonso Cortes. CP-MertT

Flower of the Ruins, The. George Meredith. CP-MerG1

Flower Parry. Olga Broumas. SP-BrouO

Flower Path, The. Arthur Sze. SP-SzeA

Flower Show. Louis MacNeice. CP-MacNL

Flower Sutra, The. Kenneth Rexroth. CP-RexrK

Flower that repeats, The. Eugenio Montale. CP-MontE, tr. by Jonathan Galassi

Flower that smiles today, The. Mutability. Percy Bysshe Shelley. CP-ShelP

Flower unfolds its dawning cup, The. Song: "Flower unfolds its dawning cup, The." George Meredith. CP-MerG1

Flower was offered [or offerd] to me, A. My Pretty Rose-Tree. William Blake. CP-BlakW Fr. Songs of Experience.

Flower will not trouble her, it has so small a Foot, A. Emily Dickinson. CP-DickE

Flower-wreathed with all unfading calumnies. To the Jesuits. G. K. Chesterton. CP-ChesG

Flowerbeds of amaranth as far as. Arthur Rimbaud. CP-RimbA, tr. by Martin Sorrell

Flowering Aloe, The. Robert Graves. CP-GravR

Flowering balls! Poem: "Flowering balls!" Alan Dugan. CP-DugaA

Flowering breaker detonates its surf, The. Origins. Derek Walcott. CP-WalcD

Flowering Death. John Ashbery. SP-AshbJ

Flowering of the oak blurs, The. Hirbeţ Sayid, Yehuda Amichai. SP-AmicYL, tr. by Benjamin Harshav and Barbara Harshav

Flowering of the Rod, The. "H. D." CP-DoolH

Flowering Plum. Louise Glück. SP-GlucL

Flowering Quince. John Ciardi. CP-CiarJ

Flowering quince bush, The. Quince Bush, The. A. R. Ammons. CP-AmmoA

Flowering stomach / scroll of leaf. Yellow Pitcher Plant. Thom Gunn. CP-GunnT

Flowering Urn, The. Laura Riding Jackson. CP-RidiL

Flowerlike / animal perfume, The. Eros. Denise Levertov. SP-LeveDP

Flowers. Robert Creeley. CP-CreeR

Flowers. D. H. Lawrence. CP-LawrD

Flowers. Robert Pinsky. CP-PinsR

Flowers. Arthur Rimbaud. CP-RimbA, tr. by Martin Sorrell

Flowers, The. Rudyard Kipling. CP-KiplR

Flowers, The. Stéphane Mallarmé. CP-MallS, tr. by Henry Weinfield

Flowers achieve their own floweriness and it is a miracle. Flowers and Men. D. H. Lawrence. CP-LawrD

Flowers Alone, The. William Carlos Williams. CP-WilW1

Flowers and Men. D. H. Lawrence. CP-LawrD

Flowers Appear on the Earth, The. Christina Georgina Rossetti. CP-RosC2

Flowers are happy in summer. Autumn Thought. Langston Hughes. CP-HughL

Flowers are yours, The. Rosebush in an Unlikely Garden, A. William Carlos Williams. CP-WilW2

Flowers by the Sea. William Carlos Williams. CP-WilW1

Flowers by the Sea. William Carlos Williams. CP-WilW1

Flowers can be cousins of the stars. There Are Different Gardens. Carl Sandburg. CP-SandC

Flowers for My Date. Clarence Major. SP-MajoC

Flowers hast thou in thyself, and foliage. Sonnet: To his Lady Joan, of Florence. Guido Cavalcanti. CW-RossD, tr. by Dante Gabriel Rossetti

Flowers I pass have eyes that look at me, The. To the Pure All Things Are Pure. Jones Very. CP-VeryJ

Flowers in a room are prettier than the seed's lust outside. Yehuda Amichai. SP-AmicYL, tr. by Benjamin Harshav and Barbara Harshav

Flowers in the Interval. Louis MacNeice. CP-MacNL

Flowers in Winter. John Greenleaf Whittier. CP-WhitJ

Flowers! My friend, be delighted with what you like; but with. Delighted with Bluepink. Kenneth Patchen. CP-PatcK

Flowers of air / With lilac defining air. Air. Muriel Rukeyser. CP-RukeM

Flowers of Sophia. Denise Levertov. SP-LeveDS

Flowers of Spring had faded from my sight, The. To the Misses Williams, On Seeing Their Beautiful Paintings of Wild Flowers. Jones Very. CP-VeryJ

Flowers of Spring have faded fast, The. Hymn: Reflections at the Close of the Year. Jones Very. CP-VeryJ

Flowers of the field, The. Hawthorn Hath a Deathly Smell, The. Walter De la Mare. CP-DeLaW

Flowers of the willow-herb are wool. Seed-Time. George Meredith. CP-MerG1

Flowers preach to us if we will hear. Consider the Lilies of the Field. Christina Georgina Rossetti. CP-RosC1

Flowers remind of jewels. Song: Three Rings for Her. Robert Graves. CP-GravR

Flowers Tell Months. Carl Sandburg. CP-SandC

Flowers that a friend brings twice a week, The. Flower Arrangements. Howard Nemerov. CP-NemeH

Flowers that bloom in sun and shade / And glitter in the dew, The. Patience of Hope. Christina Georgina Rossetti. CP-RosC2

Flowers through the window. Nantucket. William Carlos Williams. CP-WilW1

Flowers to the House. Kenneth Patchen. CP-PatcK

Flower's Tragedy, The. Thomas Hardy. CP-HardT

Flowers—Well—if anybody. Emily Dickinson. CP-DickE

Flowers White and Beautiful, as Were Most Becoming. Constantine P. Cavafy. CP-CavaC, tr. by Theoharis Constantine Theoharis

Flowers with the ragged names. Companions. Archibald MacLeish. CP-MacLA

Flowing edge to edge. Winds, The. William Carlos Williams. CP-WilW1 Fr. Folded Skyscraper, A.

Flowing of the River, The. Marya Alexandrovna Zaturenska. SP-ZatuM

Flowing River, A. William Carlos Williams. CP-WilW2

Flows between roof & roof. Pueblo. Federico García Lorca. CP-GarcF, tr. by Jerome Rothenberg Fr. Shadow.

Floyd O'Brien, Teagardens Charlie & Jack. Who Cares, Long as It's B-Flat. Hayden Carruth. CP-CarHS

Fluffy Stuff, The. May Swenson. SP-SwenM

Flumen Tenebrarum. Richard Wilbur. CP-WilbR

Flung / far down, / as the / gull rises. Gull. Charles Tomlinson. CP-TomlC

Flung from demonic wombs. Gary Snyder. CP-SnydG Fr. Myths and Texts.

Flurry. John Updike. CP-UpdiJ

Flush or Faunus. Elizabeth Barrett Browning. CP-BroEB

Flush pink runner of the sun, The. Yellow Evening Star. Carl Sandburg. CP-SandC

Flute, The. Jelaluddin Rumi. CP-EmerR

Flute Music. Charles Tomlinson. CP-TomlC

Flute-Music, with an Accompaniment. Robert Browning. CP-BroR2

Flute of the Lonely, The. Nicholas Vachel Lindsay. CP-LindV

Flute of water . . . green deep and hearing, The. Crowded Net, The. Kenneth Patchen. CP-PatcK

Flute Overheard, A. Kenneth Rexroth. CP-RexrK

Flute-Player, The. Yannis Ritsos. SP-RitsY, tr. by Gwendolyn MacEwen and Nikos Tsingos

Flute Song. "H. D." CP-DoolH

Flutes for Dancing. Jelaluddin Rumi. SP-Rumi, tr. by Coleman Barks

Flutesong willow winding weather. World War. Richard Eberhart. CP-EberR

Flutter of blue pigeon's wings, The. Pigeon. Carl Sandburg. CP-SandC

Fluttered Wings. Christina Georgina Rossetti. CP-RosC2

Fluttering spread thy purple pinions. Love Song in the Modern Taste, A. Jonathan Swift. CP-SwifJ

Fluttering strips of paper strung on cord. Voyage. Denise Levertov. SP-LeveDL

Flux. Richard Eberhart. CP-EberR

Flux. Eugenio Montale. CP-MontE, tr. by Jonathan Galassi

Flux. Carl Sandburg. CP-SandC

Flux abalze flog a new. Phlox. Louis Zukofsky. CP-ZukLS

Flux cause. Samuel Beckett. CP-BeckS

Fly. Federico García Lorca. CP-GarcF, tr. by Christopher Maurer

Fly. W. S. Merwin. SP-MerwW

Fly. John Updike. CP-UpdiJ

Fly, The. William Blake. See Songs of Experience

Fly, The. Joseph Brodsky. CP-BrodJ, tr. by Jane Miller

Fly, The. Galway Kinnell. SP-KinnGN

Fly, The. Primo Levi. CP-LeviP, tr. by Ruth Feldman

Fly, The. Ogden Nash. CP-NashO

Fly, The. Karl Shapiro. SP-ShapK

Fly against the window pane, The. Captivity of the Fly. Archibald MacLeish. CP-MacLA

Fly Away, Fly Away. Christina Georgina Rossetti. CP-RosC2

Fly down, Death: call me. Madboy's Song. Muriel Rukeyser. CP-RukeM

Fly envious Time, till thou run out thy race. On Time. John Milton. CP-MiltJ

Fly hence Pale Care, noe more remember. Charroll Presented to Dr. Williams Bp. of Lincolne as a Newyears Guift, A. Robert Herrick. CP-HerrR

Fly me not, though I be gray. Upon His Gray Haires. Robert Herrick. CP-HerrR

Fly Me to the Moon. Miller Williams. CP-WillM

Fly not from him whose silent misery. To His Mistress Retiring in Affection. Thomas Carew. CP-CareT

Fly on black water stands, A. Black Water. Wyatt Prunty. SP-PrunW

Fly sleeps on the field of a green curtain, A. Flies. Donald Hall. CP-HallD

Fly, some kind Harbinger, to Grasmere-dale! William Wordsworth. CP-WorW1

Fly, some kind Spirit, fly to Grasmere Vale! William Wordsworth. See Fly, some kind Harbinger, to Grasmere-dale!

Fly That Flew into My Mistress'[s] Eye, A. Thomas Carew. CP-CareT

Fly to my Mistresse, pretty pilfring Bee. Present: or, The Bag of the Bee, The. Robert Herrick. CP-HerrR

Flycatcher, small, species not identified, is perched, A. Sunset Scrupulously Observed. Robert Penn Warren. CP-WarrR

Flyer's Fall. Wallace Stevens. CP-StevW; CP-StevWP

Flying Above California. Thom Gunn. CP-GunnT

Flying at Night. Wyatt Prunty. SP-PrunW

Flying at night, above the clouds, all earthmarks spurned. Star, The. Wendell Berry. CP-BerrW

Flying away to Milan / I look down and back at Paris. Plan du Centre de Paris à Vol D'Oiseau. Lawrence Ferlinghetti. SP-FerlL

Flying Crooked. Robert Graves. CP-GravR

Flying Dutchman, The. Edwin Arlington Robinson. CP-RobiE

Flying Elegy. Allen Ginsberg. CP-GinsA

Flying Fish. Carl Sandburg. CP-SandC

Flying Home from Utah. May Swenson. SP-SwenM

Flying House, and the May Queen Eternal, The. Nicholas Vachel Lindsay. CP-LindV

Flying Inside Your Own Body. Margaret Atwood. SP-AtwM2

Flying into a strange town, being met at the. On and Off the Road. Charles Bukowski. SP-BukC3

Flying Islands of the Night, The. James Whitcomb Riley. CP-RileJ

'Flying mare'—that / Throw in wrestling, The. Wrestlers on the Vase, The. Charles Tomlinson. CP-TomlC

Flying Noises. Thomas Lux. SP-LuxT

Flying pigeon hit me on a fall day, A. 851. Alan Dugan. CP-DugaA

Flying Red Horse, The. Muriel Rukeyser. CP-RukeM

Flying south-west—say Washington to Albuquerque. Sight and Flight. Charles Tomlinson. CP-TomlC

Flying to Hanoi. Muriel Rukeyser. CP-RukeM

Flying word from here and there, A. Master, The. Edwin Arlington Robinson. CP-RobiE

Flyting of Dumbar [or Dunbar] and Kennedie [or Kennedy], The. William Dunbar. CP-DunbW

Foal of generous breed along the plains, The. Horse, The. William Wordsworth. CP-WorW1

Foam lips / waters / in following folds. Flight, The. Charles Tomlinson. CP-TomlC

Focherty. Hugh MacDiarmid. SP-MacDH

Focus. Adrienne Rich. CP-RicAE; SP-RicA1; SP-RicA2

Fodder. Seamus Heaney. SP-HeanSO

Foe, The. Jones Very. CP-VeryJ

Foemineos dea quae nigro sub Limine manes. Umbra. Thomas Campion. CP-CampT

Fog. Amy Clampitt. CP-ClamA

Fog. Langston Hughes. CP-HughL; CP-HughL1

Fog. Robinson Jeffers. CP-JefR1

Fog. Walter De la Mare. CP-DeLaW

Fog. Kenneth Patchen. CP-PatcK

Fog. A. K. Ramanujan. CP-RamaA

Fog. Carl Sandburg. CP-SandC

Fog. Henry David Thoreau. CP-ThorH

Fog all day, skim. At Easterly. Amy Clampitt. CP-ClamA

Fog, and orchid sun. Signs. Charles Olson. CP-OlsoC

Fog, as it enters the lowland, is smoothing away, The. In December. Charles Tomlinson. CP-TomlC

Fog blows, The. Mind's Notice, The. Charles Olson. CP-OlsoC

Fog burns off and the crowd mingles promiscuously, The. At the Barriers. Thom Gunn. CP-GunnT

Fog comes, The. Fog. Carl Sandburg. CP-SandC

Fog dark morning I wait here. Three Mornings. Philip Whalen. SP-WhalP

Fog drifts slowly down the hill, The. Night Piece, The. Thom Gunn. CP-GunnT

Fog Envelops the Animals. James Dickey. CP-DickJ

Fog erases Boston's. Poor. Old. China. Man. William Corbett. SP-CorbW

Fog fills the little square. La Vie en Rose. Kenneth Rexroth. CP-RexrK

Fog Galleon. Yusef Komunyakaa. SP-KomuY

Fog grays the skyline. Fanny Howe. SP-HoweF Fr. Vineyard, The.

Fog in the morning here. Where We Are. William Stafford. SP-StafWW

Fog is departing, let it go. Odor, The. To Artemis. Hayden Carruth. CP-CarHS

Fog, now, and a bell. On the Ferry. Wallace Stevens. CP-StevWP

Fog Numbers. Carl Sandburg. CP-SandC

Fog over the base: the beams ranging. Front, A. Randall Jarrell. CP-JarrR

Fog Over the Sea and the Sun Going Down. Kenneth Patchen. CP-PatcK

Fog Portrait. Carl Sandburg. CP-SandC

Fog puffed from crusted snow, rain sputters. Medium, The. Theodore Weiss. SP-WeisT

Fog / stammers everywhere, The. Girl in the Fog, The. John Logan. CP-LogaJ

Fog-thick morning. Lorine Niedecker. SP-NiedL

Fogged hill-scene on an enormous continent, A. Hunger. Adrienne Rich. SP-RicA2

Foggy Street. Andrey Andreievich Voznesensky. CP-WilbR

Foghorn in Horror. Muriel Rukeyser. CP-RukeM

Foil, The. George Herbert. CP-HerbG

Fold now thine armes; and hang the head. To Myrrha Hard-Hearted. Robert Herrick. CP-HerrR

Fold the little waxen hands. Harlie. James Whitcomb Riley. CP-RileJ

Folded Skyscraper, A. William Carlos Williams.
    Hemmed-in Males. CP-WilW1
    Winds, The. CP-WilW1

Folders, papers, proofs, maps. Artists' Letters. Thomas Kinsella. CP-KinsT

Folding away my tools with the dead parts of. Bring Down the Beams. Charles Bukowski. SP-BukC2

Folding His *USA Today* He Makes His Point in the Blue Star Café. Miller Williams. CP-WillM

Foliage Tour, The. Wyatt Prunty. SP-PrunW

Folk Art. W. S. Merwin. SP-MerwW

Folk Singer of the Thirties, A. James Dickey. CP-DickJ

Folk Singer, The. David Ignatow. SP-IgnaD

Folk Song. Dorothy Parker. CP-ParkD

Folk Song, A: "Hitch up honey for the / market race all." Robert Creeley. CP-CreeR

Folk Tune. Joseph Brodsky. CP-BrodJ

Folk Tune. Dorothy Parker. CP-ParkD

Folk Tune. Richard Wilbur. CP-WilbR

Folk Wisdom. Thomas Kinsella. CP-KinsT

Folk Wisdom. James Laughlin. CP-LaugJ

Folkestone Limerick. Robert Browning. CP-BroR2

Folks ain't got no right to censuah othah [or utah] folks about dey habits. Accountability. Paul Laurence Dunbar. CP-DunbP

Folks at Lonesomeville. James Whitcomb Riley. CP-RileJ

Folks built that barn, your great grandfather, and them, The. Mona Van Duyn. SP-VanDM

Folks has be'n to town, and Sahry. Canary at the Farm, A. James Whitcomb Riley. CP-RileJ

Folks, I come up North. Evenin' Air Blues. Langston Hughes. CP-HughL; CP-HughL2

Folks, I'm telling you. Advice. Langston Hughes. CP-HughL; CP-HughL3

Folks in town, I reckon, thinks. At "The Literary" James Whitcomb Riley. CP-RileJ

Folks is talkin' 'bout de money. Real Question, The. Paul Laurence Dunbar. CP-DunbP

Folks, this is of the Jonah Man. Coon Showman. Clarence Major. SP-MajoC

Folks up here at Rossville got up a Lectur' Course. Rossville Lectur' Course, The. James Whitcomb Riley. CP-RileJ

Folks, we'd have zero'd in to a big break-thru. Personal Packaging, Inc. Robert Graves. CP-GravR

Folks with no titles in front of their names, The. In Explanation of Our Times. Langston Hughes. CP-HughL; CP-HughL3

Folktale. Ted Hughes. SP-HughTN

Follen. John Greenleaf Whittier. CP-WhitJ

Follies. Carl Sandburg. CP-SandC

Follies of Adam, The. Theodore Roethke. CP-RoetT

Follow a shadow [or shaddow], it still flies you. Song. That Women Are But Men's Shadows. Ben Jonson. CP-JonsB; SP-JonsB

Follow its lazy main street lounging. Hawthorne. Robert Lowell. SP-LoweR

Follow me, follow me. Will o' the Wisp. George Meredith. CP-MerG1

Follow Me 'Ome. Rudyard Kipling. CP-KiplR

"Follow the Drinking Gourd." Robert Creeley. CP-CreeR

Follow the train full of bodies. Judge Every One with Perfect Calm. Alice Walker. CP-WalkA

Follow Thy Fair Sun[ne] [Unhappy Shadow]. Thomas Campion. CP-CampT
    (Followe thy faire sunne unhappy shaddowe.) CP-CampT

Follow to the deep wood's weeds. Fragment: "Follow to the deep wood's weeds." Percy Bysshe Shelley. CP-ShelP

Follow wise Orion. Emily Dickinson. CP-DickE

Followe thy faire sunne unhappy shaddowe. Thomas Campion. *See* Follow Thy Fair Sun[ne] [Unhappy Shadow]

Followed by garrulous hunters, the soft children grovel. All the Bright Foam of Talk. Kenneth Patchen. CP-PatcK

Follower. Seamus Heaney. SP-HeanSO

Following day was overcast, each street, The. Pity. Richard Wilbur. CP-WilbR

Following fro the record, in the light. Seamus Heaney. SP-HeanSO Fr. Flight Path, The.

Following is about the dangers, The. Song about a Donkey, A. Jelaluddin Rumi. SP-Rumi, *tr. by* Coleman Barks

Following the Formulas of Ancient Greco-Syrian Magicians. Constantine P. Cavafy. CP-CavaC, *tr. by* Theoharis Constantine Theoharis

Folly of Being Comforted, The. William Butler Yeats. CP-YeatW

Folly of Clowns. Kenneth Patchen. CP-PatcK

Folly on Royal Street before the Raw Face of God. Robert Penn Warren. CP-WarrR

Fond credos, plaster ecstasies! Stranger, The. Adrienne Rich. CP-RicAE

Fond Farewell, A. William Carlos Williams. CP-WilW2

Fond man, that canst believe [or beleeve] her blood. Celia Bleeding, to the Surgeon. Thomas Carew. CP-CareT

Fond man, that hop'st to catch that face. To the Painter. Thomas Carew. CP-CareT

Fond scenes, which delighted my youthful existence. Exile's Departure, The. John Greenleaf Whittier. CP-WhitJ

Fond woman, which wouldst [or would'st] have thy husband die. Jealousy [or Jealousie]. John Donne. MW-DonnJ *Fr.* Elegies.

Fond words have oft been spoken to thee, sleep! To Sleep. William Wordsworth. CP-WorW1

Fond youth! who dream'st that hoarded gold. From Menander. Menander. CP-CowpW, *tr. by* William Cowper

Fondling only to throttle the nuzzling moment. Restaurant Car. Louis MacNeice. CP-MacNL

Fone sayes, those mighty whiskers he do's weare. Upon Fone a School-master. Epigram. Robert Herrick. CP-HerrR

Font of Type, A. Walt Whitman. CP-WhitW

Fontaine, Je Ne Boirai Pas De Ton Eau! Edna St. Vincent Millay. CP-MillE

Fontenelle. Howard Nemerov. CP-NemeH

Food. Andrei Codrescu. SP-CodrA

Food. Josephine Jacobsen. CP-JacoJ

Food. Anne Sexton. CP-SextA; SP-SextA

Food. John Updike. CP-UpdiJ

Food Chain, The. Maxine W. Kumin. SP-KumiM

Food for Thought; or, Death Is Physical. Clarence Major. SP-MajoC

Food Notes. John Ciardi. CP-CiarJ

Food of Love. Carolyn Kizer. CP-KizeC

Food of the Dead. Robert Graves. CP-GravR

Food of the North. D. H. Lawrence. CP-LawrD

Food on the walls of the dark tombs, The. Réchauffé. Louis MacNeice. CP-MacNL

Food Sack, The. Jelaluddin Rumi. SP-Rumi, *tr. by* Coleman Barks

Fool, The. Hugh MacDiarmid. SP-MacDH

Fool, The. Charles Olson. CP-OlsoC

Fool, The. Stevie Smith. CP-SmitS

Fool by the Roadside, The. William Butler Yeats. CP-YeatW

Fool I was to sleep at noon, A. Daughter of Eve, A. Christina Georgina Rossetti. CP-RosC1

Fool, if to keep thy wife thou hast no need. Elegy 2.19: "Fool, if to keep thy wife thou hast no need." Ovid. CP-MarlC *Fr.* Elegies.

Fool, / put your adventures. Hero. William Carlos Williams. CP-WilW1

Fool there was and he made his prayer, A. Vampire, The. Rudyard Kipling. CP-KiplR

Fool-Youngens. James Whitcomb Riley. CP-RileJ

Fooles are they, who never know. Best To Be Merry. Robert Herrick. CP-HerrR

Foolhearted mindreader. Beg Song. Yusef Komunyakaa. CP-KomuY

Foolin' wid de Seasons. Paul Laurence Dunbar. CP-DunbP

Foolish About Windows. Carl Sandburg. CP-SandC

Foolish Enemy's Face Tells All, The. Shmuel HaNagid. SP-HaNaS, *tr. by* Peter Cole

Foolish Heart, The. Countee Cullen. CP-CullC

Foolish poet wonders, The. Poet Hin, The. Stevie Smith. CP-SmitS

Foolish queen of fairyland, The. Crickets on a Strike. Nicholas Vachel Lindsay. CP-LindV

Foolish Wing, The. John Ciardi. CP-CiarJ

Foolishnesse. Robert Herrick. CP-HerrR

Fools. Ben Jonson. CP-JonsB *Fr.* Volpone.

Fools. Robert Graves. CP-GravR

Fool's Paradise. Charles Simic. SP-SimiCE

Fool's Song, The. Walter De la Mare. CP-DeLaW

Fool's Song, The. William Carlos Williams. CP-WilW1

Fools! That when things of high import concern. On the late Disgraceful Scene in Congress. Jones Very. CP-VeryJ

Fools, they are the only nation. Fools. Ben Jonson. CP-JonsB *Fr.* Volpone.

Foot/feet / rain/tulip. April Showers Bring Rain? Philip Whalen. SP-WhalP

Foot is growing old, The. Real-Life Story. Dan Pagis. SP-PagiD

Foot-Note, A. William Carlos Williams. CP-WilW1

Foot of death has printed on my chest, The. Shudder [, The]. Donald Hall. CP-HallD

Foot-Washing, The. A. R. Ammons. CP-AmmoA

Football at Slack. Ted Hughes. SP-HughTN

Football rush of him, and that country knowledge, The. George Chapman—The Iliad. Ivor Gurney. SP-GurnI

Football with white eyebrows the, A. E. E. Cummings. CP-CummE

Footfalling. Laura Riding Jackson. CP-RidiL

Footlights cannot improve the grave. Emily Dickinson. SP-DickE

Footling. Paul Muldoon. CP-MuldP

Footnote. James Schuyler. CP-SchuJ

Footnote, A. Stephen Spender. CP-SpenS

Footnote on the Invention of Small Pleasures. Miller Williams. CP-WillM

Footnote to Howl. Allen Ginsberg. CP-GinsA; SP-GinsA

Footnote to Weather Forecasts, A. Joseph Brodsky. CP-BrodJ

Footnotes to "The Autobiography of Bertrand Russell" Mona Van Duyn. SP-VanDM

Footprint and eye fringe. All Wise. Louis Zukofsky. CP-ZukLS

Footprint of a bird in sand brought your face, The. Bird Footprint. Carl Sandburg. CP-SandC

Footprints. Dan Pagis. SP-PagiD, *tr. by* Stephen Mitchell

Footprints on the Glacier. W. S. Merwin. SP-MerwW

Footprints that met in the sand were erased. At the Beach. Yehuda Amichai. SP-AmicY, *tr. by* Chana Bloch

Footsteps of the Eumenides, The. Constantine P. Cavafy. CP-CavaC, *tr. by* Theoharis Constantine Theoharis

Footsteps, The. Constantine P. Cavafy. CP-CavaC, *tr. by* Theoharis Constantine Theoharis

For a Berry Voice. Ezra Pound. CP-PoEar

For a Birthday. Thom Gunn. CP-GunnT

For a Boy Born in Wartime. Jane Cooper. CP-CoopJ

For a Bus on Its Side and the Man Inside It. Robert Creeley. CP-CreeR

For a Child. Peter Blue Cloud. SP-BlueP

For a Child. Denise Levertov. SP-LeveDL

For a Child. Marya Alexandròvna Zaturenska. SP-ZatuM

For a College Yearbook. James Vincent Cunningham. CP-CunnJ

For a Coming Extinction. W. S. Merwin. SP-MerwW

For a Critic Who Tries to Write Poems. Thomas McGrath. SP-McGrT

For a Daughter Gone Away. William Stafford. SP-StafWW

For a Dead Citizen. Allen Tate. CP-TateA

For a Dead Lady. Edwin Arlington Robinson. CP-RobiE

For a Dog-killed Doe. Peter Blue Cloud. SP-BlueP

For a Fatherless Son. Sylvia Plath. CP-PlatS

For a Favorite Grand-Daughter. Dorothy Parker. CP-ParkD

For a Friend. Robert Creeley. CP-CreeR

For a Friend. Robert Creeley. CP-CreeR

For a Friend. David Ignatow. SP-IgnaD

For a Friend Who Thinks Himself Urbane. Robert Penn Warren. CP-WarrR

For a Girl I Know about to be a Woman. Miller Williams. CP-WillM

For a Godchild. Charles Tomlinson. SP-TomlC

For a Good Dog. Ogden Nash. CP-NashO

For a good hour I have been singing lays. Plight of the Troubadour. Billy Collins. SP-CollB

For a Good Man. Heather McHugh. SP-McHuH

For A Granddaughter. Charles Tomlinson.

    Jessica Learned to Kiss. SP-TomlC

    On The Terrace. SP-TomlC

    To Be Read Later On. SP-TomlC

    To My Daughter. SP-TomlC

For a Heracles in his fighting ire there is never the glory that follows. Labourer, The. George Meredith. CP-MerG2

For a hundred years the pulse of time. Liberty. James Whitcomb Riley. CP-RileJ

For a kiss or two, confesse. Bucolick betwixt Two: Lacon and Thyrsis, A. Robert Herrick. CP-HerrR

For a Lady I Know. Countee Cullen. CP-CullC *Fr.* Four Epitaphs.

For a Lady of Whom I Speak. Charles Olson. CP-OlsoC

For a Lady Who Must Write Verse. Dorothy Parker. CP-ParkD

For a Lamb. Richard Eberhart. CP-EberR

For a Literary Survey. Dan Pagis. SP-PagiD, *tr. by* Stephen Mitchell

For a long day and a night we read the names. Reading the Names of the Vietnam War Dead. Thomas McGrath. SP-McGrT

For a long time I used to get up early. Bird's-Eye View of the Tool and Die Co. John Ashbery. SP-AshbJ

For a long time some of us. Current, The. W. S. Merwin. SP-MerwW

For a long time under the covers. Witch, The. Primo Levi. CP-LeviP, *tr. by* Ruth Feldman *and* Brian Swann

For a Lost Child. William Stafford. SP-StafW; SP-StafWW

For a Lost Girl. Alan Dugan. CP-DugaA

For a Low Voice. William Carlos Williams. CP-WilW2

For a Man Gone to Stuttgart Who Left an Automobile Behind Him. Charles Olson. CP-OlsoC

For a man to come out of the sea, they. Evil. Charles Olson. CP-OlsoC

For a Market-Clock. Samuel Taylor Coleridge. CP-ColeS

For a Marriage. Louise Bogan. CP-BogaL

For a Mercy Received. Christina Georgina Rossetti. CP-RosC3

For a Mexican Painter. Muriel Rukeyser. CP-RukeM

For a Moment. D. H. Lawrence. CP-LawrD

For a moment pause. Mound, The. Thomas Hardy. CP-HardT

For a month now, wandering over the Sierras. Climbing Milestone Mountain, August 22, 1937. Kenneth Rexroth. CP-RexrK

For a Mouthy Woman. Countee Cullen. CP-CullC

For a mud ball dropped in water. Shih-te. CP-ColdM, tr. by Red Pine

For a Muse Meant. Robert Duncan. SP-DuncR

For a night when sleep eludes you, I have. Better Than Counting Sheep. Robert Penn Warren. CP-WarrR

For a Pessimist. Countee Cullen. CP-CullC

For a Picture of Saint Dorothea. Gerard Manley Hopkins. CP-HopkG

For a Picture Where a Queen Laments over the Tomb of a Slain Knight. Thomas Carew. CP-CareT

For a Play. Ezra Pound. CP-PoEar

For a Poet. Countee Cullen. CP-CullC

For a reliable guide in my vocation. Michelangelo Buonarroti. CP-Miche, tr. by John Frederick Nims

For a Russian Poet. Adrienne Rich. CP-RicAE; SP-RicA2

For a Sad God. Heather McHugh. SP-McHuH

For a Sad Lady. Dorothy Parker. CP-ParkD

For a safe haven, for escape at last. Michelangelo Buonarroti. CP-Miche, tr. by John Frederick Nims

For a Screaming Lady. Robert Creeley. CP-CreeR

For a season there must be pain. Widower, The. Rudyard Kipling. CP-KiplR

For a Seat in the Groves of Coleorton. William Wordsworth. CP-WorW1

For a Self-Possessed Friend. Robert Penn Warren. CP-WarrR

For a Sister. Adrienne Rich. SP-RicA2

For a Song of the Languagers. Robert Duncan. SP-DuncR

For a Stone Girl at Sanchi. Gary Snyder. CP-SnydG

For a Time and Place. James Dickey. CP-DickJ

For a time it is part of the machinery. Death and the Lovers. May Sarton. SP-SartM

For a Version of I Ching. Jorge Luis Borges. SP-BorgJ, tr. by Eric McHenry

For a Very Old Man, on the Death of His Wife. Jane Cooper. CP-CoopJ

For a War Memorial. G. K. Chesterton. CP-ChesG

For a week now our bodies have whispered. Sestina: "For a week now our bodies have whispered." Marilyn Hacker. SP-HackM

For a while I've been meaning to tell you to sleep. Mutual Lullaby, A. Yehuda Amichai. SP-AmicY, tr. by Chana Bloch

For a while my mother was a believer in Coué. To My Friend Who Rhymes with Peace. Carolyn Kizer. CP-KizeC

For a while today, the rafts almost float side by side. Gilded Man, The. Ai. SP-Ai

For a woman named Gorrel. Poor Gorrel. Kenneth Patchen. CP-PatcK

For a Woman with Child. James Vincent Cunningham. CP-CunnJ

For a woman's face remembered as a spot of quick light on the flat land. Remembered Women. Carl Sandburg. CP-SandC

For a wound from the searing arrows Love lets fly. Michelangelo Buonarroti. CP-Miche, tr. by John Frederick Nims

For a year he'd collect. Milkman and His Son, The. Thomas Lux. SP-LuxT

For a Young Artist. Robert Earl Hayden. CP-HaydR

For Ace. Peter Blue Cloud. SP-BlueP

For Adolf Eichmann. Primo Levi. CP-LeviP, tr. by Ruth Feldman, Ruth Feldman and Brian Swann and Brian Swann

For Advent. Christina Georgina Rossetti. CP-RosC3

For ages, on our river borders. First Flowers, The. John Greenleaf Whittier. CP-WhitJ

For Air Heroes. William Meredith. SP-MereW

For Al—. Charles Bukowski. SP-BukC1

For Albert Saijo. Philip Whalen. SP-WhalP

For Alexander there was no Far East. Worlds. Richard Wilbur. CP-WilbR

For All. Christina Georgina Rossetti. CP-RosC2

For All. Gary Snyder. CP-SnydG

For All Friends. David Ignatow. SP-IgnaD

For all his vehemence & hydraulic opinions. Heroes, The. John Berryman. CP-BerrJ

For all night sins, with others' wives, unknown. On Old Colt. Ben Jonson. CP-JonsB; SP-JonsB

For All Our Great-Grandchildren. Miller Williams. CP-WillM

For all our workes, a recompence is sure. Satisfaction for Sufferings. Robert Herrick. CP-HerrR

For All That. D. H. Lawrence. CP-LawrD

For All the Grief. Walter De la Mare. CP-DeLaW

For all they said, / I could not see the waterfall. Waterfall, The. Mary Oliver. SP-OlivM

For all thy many courtesies to me. To his Faithfull Friend, Master John Crofts, Cup-bearer to the King. Robert Herrick. CP-HerrR

For All We Have and Are [1914]. Rudyard Kipling. CP-KiplR

For All Who Ever Sent Lace Valentines. Nicholas Vachel Lindsay. CP-LindV

For Allen. Robert Creeley. CP-CreeR

For Allen, on His 60th Birthday. Philip Whalen. SP-WhalP

For Ammonis, Who at Died at 29, in 610. Constantine P. Cavafy. CP-CavaC, tr. by Theoharis Constantine Theoharis

For an Album. Eugenio Montale. CP-MontE, tr. by Jonathan Galassi

For "An Allegorical Dance of Women" by Andrea Mantegna. Dante Gabriel Rossetti. CW-RossD

For An Amorous Lady. Theodore Roethke. CP-RoetT

For an Anarchist. Countee Cullen. CP-CullC

For an Anniversary. Robert Creeley. CP-CreeR

For An Annunciation, Early German. Dante Gabriel Rossetti. CW-RossD

For an Atheist. Countee Cullen. CP-CullC

For an Autumn Festival. John Greenleaf Whittier. CP-WhitJ

For an End. Helen Pinkerton. CP-PinkH

For an Evolutionist and His Opponent. Countee Cullen. CP-CullC

For an Exchange of Rings. Donald Hall. CP-HallD

For an "Homage to Rimbaud" Eugenio Montale. CP-MontE, tr. by Jonathan Galassi

For an image of life and death. Han-shan. CP-ColdM, tr. by Red Pine

For an Indian Screen. Langston Hughes. CP-HughL; CP-HughL1

For an Obligate Parasite. Alan Dugan. CP-DugaA

For an Old Woman in a Wig. Wallace Stevens. CP-StevWP

For an Oxford don, doomed during term to sit. Alice. Amy Clampitt. CP-ClamA

For an Unknown Lady. Dorothy Parker. CP-ParkD

For Anne Gregory. William Butler Yeats. CP-YeatW

For Annie. Edgar Allan Poe. CP-PoeEd

For "Antrim" read "Armagh" Errata. Paul Muldoon. CP-MuldP

For Any Member of the Security Police. Josephine Jacobsen. CP-JacoJ

For any ruffian of the sky. E. E. Cummings. CP-CummE

For any save a lover. George Meredith. CP-MerG2

For Anybody. Robert Creeley. CP-CreeR

For Arthur Okamura. Robert Creeley. CP-CreeR

For Arvia. Edwin Arlington Robinson. CP-RobiE

For as the baby springs out like a starfish into her million light. Tenth Psalm. Anne Sexton. SP-SextA Fr. O Ye Tongues.

For asking, why is there something. Childhood of Parmenides, The. Charles Simic. SP-SimiC; SP-SimiCE

For authorities whose hopes. Paper Nautilus, The. Marianne Craig Moore. CP-MoorM

For awhile I thought I had gotten. Cripple in the Subway, The. Louise Glück. SP-GlucL

For beauty, say an ash-fork staked in peat. Nerthus. Seamus Heaney. SP-HeanSO

For being comely, consonant, and free. To His Brother in Law Master John Wingfield. Robert Herrick. CP-HerrR

For Benny. Robert Creeley. SP-CreeR

For Benny and Sabina. Robert Creeley. CP-CreeR

For best work. Lorine Niedecker. CP-NiedL

For Bet. Denise Levertov. SP-LeveDS

For Betsy and Tom. Robert Creeley. CP-CreeR

For Billy Holt. Ted Hughes. SP-HughTN

For Bob Dash. James Schuyler. CP-SchuJ

For boys in love with maps and coloured prints. Travellers. Charles Baudelaire. CP-BaudC, tr. by Walter Martin

For brave comportment, wit without offence. To His Honoured and Most Ingenious Friend Mr. Charles Cotton. Robert Herrick. CP-HerrR

For Brother Antoninus. Philip Whalen. SP-WhalP

For C.W.B. Elizabeth Bishop. CP-BishE

For centuries abiding hidden. Mimiambi of Herodas, The. Constantine P. Cavafy. CP-CavaC, tr. by Theoharis Constantine Theoharis

For centuries only painters, poets and sculptors. Aging Actress Sees Herself a Starlet on the Late Show, The. Miller Williams. CP-WillM

For centuries sadhus live and die. Circumambulating Arunachala. Gary Snyder. CP-SnydG

For certain minutes at the least. Demon and Beast. William Butler Yeats. CP-YeatW

For certain ones what was written may come true. Seamus Heaney. SP-HeanSO Fr. Squarings.

For Cheryl. Robert Creeley. SP-CreeR

For Children When They Grow Up. C. K. Williams. CP-WillC

For Chile, 1977. Denise Levertov. SP-LeveDL

For Chuck Hinman. Robert Creeley. CP-CreeR

For civill, cleane, and circumcised wit. To His Honoured Friend, Sir John Mynts. Robert Herrick. CP-HerrR

For clarity, for insight. Sebastian's Mirror. Heather McHugh. SP-McHuH

For Clark Coolidge. Philip Whalen. SP-WhalP

For cosmos, which has too much to live up to. Garland for Christopher Smart, A. Mona Van Duyn. SP-VanDM

For Creely's Ear. Allen Ginsberg. CP-GinsA

For Cy Twombly Faced with His First Chicago & N.Y. Shows. Charles Olson. CP-OlsoC

For Danny. Grace Paley. CP-PalGC

For Danton. Charles Tomlinson. CP-TomlC; SP-TomlC

For Daughters of Magdalen. Countee Cullen. CP-CullC

For days he has dumped a trail of tuna blood. Great White Shark, The. Arthur Sze. SP-SzeA

For days I have wakened and felt immediately. Messenger, The. Thomas Kinsella. CP-KinsT

For days neglected. Robert Creeley. CP-CreeR

For days the good old bitch had been dying, her back. Another Dog's Death. John Updike. CP-UpdiJ

For days the house is dark and slightly cold. Domestic of the Outer Banks. Wyatt Prunty. SP-PrunW

For Dead Mimes. Langston Hughes. CP-HughL; CP-HughL2

For Death—or rather. Emily Dickinson. CP-DickE

For deathless powers to verse belong. Ralph Waldo Emerson. CP-EmerR

For Deliverance from a Fever. Anne Bradstreet. CP-BradA

For Doreen. A Voice from the Garden. Donald Davie. CP-DaviDC

For Dudley. Richard Wilbur. CP-WilbR

For E. McC ("Gone ere the tang of earth"). Ezra Pound. CP-PoEar

For E. McC ("Gone while your tastes were keen to you"). Ezra Pound. CP-PoEar

For Each. Christina Georgina Rossetti. CP-RosC2

For each ecstatic instant. Emily Dickinson. CP-DickE

For each of us there is a place. Day Trees Were About to Bloom, The. Philip Whalen. SP-WhalP

For Each of You. Audre Lorde. SP-LordA

For each one Body, that i'th earth is sowne. Resurrection, Possible, and Probable, The. Robert Herrick. CP-HerrR

For Ebbe. Robert Creeley. CP-CreeR

For Edgar Bowers. Helen Pinkerton. CP-PinkH

For Eleanor and Bill Monahan. William Carlos Williams. CP-WilW2

For Eleanor Boylan Talking with God. Anne Sexton. CP-SextA; SP-SextA

For Elektra. Marilyn Hacker. SP-HackM

For Eli Jacobson. Kenneth Rexroth. CP-RexrK

For Ellen. Richard Wilbur. CP-WilbR

For Eric. Paul Celan. SP-CelaP, tr. by John Felstiner

For Ethel Rosenberg. Adrienne Rich. SP-RicA1; SP-RicA2

For Eugene McCarthy. Robert Lowell. SP-LoweR

For Euthanasia and Pain-Killing Drugs. Alan Dugan. CP-DugaA

For Ever. Robert Graves. CP-GravR

For ever and ever. Overture. Thomas Kinsella. CP-KinsT

For-ever Morning. Laura Riding Jackson. CP-RidiL

For every Bird a Nest. Emily Dickinson. CP-DickE

For every god. Ralph Waldo Emerson. CP-EmerR

For Every Heart. Olga Broumas. SP-BrouO

For every hour that thou wilt spare me now. Love's Usury. John Donne. CP-DonnJ; MW-DonnJ

For Every Last Batch When the Next One Comes Along. William Dickey. SP-DickW

For every living creature on this earth. Petrarch. CP-Petra, tr. by J. G. Nichols

For every man in a rage there are always. Statistics. Yehuda Amichai. SP-AmicY, tr. by Chana Bloch

For every parcel I stoop down to seize. Armful, The. Robert Frost. CP-FrosR

For every tiny town or place. To Hilaire Belloc. G. K. Chesterton. CP-ChesG

For exactly sixty seconds riding to work. One of Those Rare Occurrences on a City Bus. Miller Williams. CP-WillM

For Example. Gary Snyder. CP-SnydG

For Exhibition. Lorine Niedecker. CP-NiedL

For Fear. Robert Creeley. CP-CreeR

For fear strangers might intrude upon us. Fortunate Child. Robert Graves. CP-GravR

For February 14th. Marianne Craig Moore. CP-MoorM

For fifteen winter days. Ralph Waldo Emerson. CP-EmerR

For fifty thousand years man has been dreaming of powers. Unnatural Powers. Robinson Jeffers. CP-JefR3

For fifty years I've drifted. Watching the Waves. Sam Hamill. SP-HamiS

For five years the swallows did not build. Swallows Return, The. Richard Eberhart. CP-EberR

For Floss. Denise Levertov. SP-LeveDP

For fortunes favours you your riches bring. Mr Stothard to Mr Cromek. William Blake. CP-BlakW

For Fran. Philip Levine. SP-LeviP

For Fred Carpenter Who Died in His Sleep. Miller Williams. CP-WillM

For Friendship. Robert Creeley. CP-CreeR

For/From Lew. Gary Snyder. CP-SnydG

For Fun. Muriel Rukeyser. CP-RukeM

For G.B.S., Old. William Carlos Williams. CP-WilW2

For Gabriela Münter. Adam Zagajewski. SP-ZagaA, tr. by Clare Cavanagh

For Gail, When I Was Five. C. K. Williams. CP-WillC; SP-WillC

For G. H. Esq. Robert Burns. CP-BurnR

For gear your typewriter and an old rugby boot. Homage to Malcolm Lowry. Derek Mahon. CP-MahoD

For Genius made his cabin wide. Ralph Waldo Emerson. CP-EmerR

For George (I). Grace Paley. CP-PalGC

For George (II). Grace Paley. CP-PalGC

For George Santayana. Robert Lowell. SP-LoweR

For God, our God, is a gallant foe. Ballad for Gloom. Ezra Pound. CP-PoEar

For God to send a son into the world. During the Hymn Before the Christmas Sermon the Mind of the Young Preacher Wanders Again. Miller Williams. CP-WillM

For God While Sleeping. Anne Sexton. CP-SextA

"For God's sake, help!" the drowning seaman cries. "Tuesday night, the schooner Weaver, of Glen Creek, N.J., went to pieces near Sandy Hook, and her entire crew were lost."—Transcript, March 22d. Jones Very. CP-VeryJ

For God's sake, let us be men. Let Us Be Men. D. H. Lawrence. CP-LawrD

For God's sake [or Godsake] hold your tongue, and let me love. Canonization, The. John Donne. CP-DonnJ; MW-DonnJ

For Grace, after a Party. Frank O'Hara. SP-OharF

For Greater Accuracy. Yannis Ritsos. SP-RitsY, tr. by Kimon Friar

For Guillaume Apollinaire. William Meredith. SP-MereW

For H.P. Christina Georgina Rossetti. CP-RosC3

For half an hour, through a magnifying glass. Eclipse. Ted Hughes. SP-HughTN

For having left the birds that left me. Poem: "For having left the birds that left me." James Dickey. CP-DickJ

For healthful indigence in vain they pray. Virgil. CP-JohnS Fr. Aeneid [or Eneados or Aeneis], The.

For heaven's sake, dear Cory. Santayana's. Lorine Niedecker. CP-NiedL

For Helen. Robert Creeley. CP-CreeR

For Helen Keller. Countee Cullen. CP-CullC

For Helen the ornamental saps conspired in the virgin shades. Fairy. Arthur Rimbaud. CP-RimbA, tr. by Martin Sorrell

For her size the moor hen. Wild Eggs. James Schuyler. CP-SchuJ

For her to whom the thousand stares below. Tight-Rope Construction Surrounded by a Thousand Sonnets. Robert Stock. SP-StocR

For him alone life's worse than worst. E. E. Cummings. CP-CummE

For Him I Sing. Walt Whitman. CP-WhitW

For him the cosmos was a pearl, hell. About the Pseudo St. Dionysius. Alan Dugan. CP-DugaA

For him who struck thy foreign string. Lady to Her Guitar, The. Emily Jane Brontë. CP-BronE

For his constant dwelling place has Hafiz. Hafiz. CP-EmerR Fr. Odes.

For His Father. William Meredith. SP-MereW

For his o'erarching and last lesson the greybeard sufi. Persian Lesson, A. Walt Whitman. CP-WhitW

For his portrait of the poet now in the Tate in London. Reclining Position, The. James Laughlin. CP-LaugJ

For hours he gazed at the statue's severed hand—only one hand. Meaning of Art, The. Yannis Ritsos. SP-RitsY, tr. by Kimon Friar and Kostas Myrsiades

For hours / they float in the distance. Field near Linden, Alabama. Mary Oliver. SP-OlivM

For How Long. Dan Pagis. SP-PagiD, tr. by Stephen Mitchell

For I am an orphan with two death masks on the mantel. Fourth Psalm. Anne Sexton. SP-SextA Fr. O Ye Tongues.

For I am rightful fellow of their band. Mentors. Gwendolyn Brooks. SP-BrooG

For I can snore like a bullhorn. After Making Love We Hear Footsteps. Galway Kinnell. SP-KinnGN

For I was a gaunt, grave councilor. La Fraisne. Ezra Pound. CP-PoEar

For I will consider the graces of this woman. Jubilate Sutra. Sam Hamill. SP-HamiS

For Instance. John Ciardi. CP-CiarJ

For instance you walk in and faint. Mozart Chemisier. Frank O'Hara. SP-OharF

For Irving. Robert Creeley. CP-CreeR

For it did come to that. And a Man Went Out Alone. Kenneth Patchen. CP-PatcK

For Italico Brass. Ezra Pound. CP-PoEar

For J. William Fulbright on the Day of His Death. Miller Williams. CP-WillM

For James Dean. Frank O'Hara. SP-OharF

For Jan. Grace Paley. CP-PalGC

For Jan as the End Draws Near. Carolyn Kizer. CP-KizeC

For Jan, in Bar Maria. Carolyn Kizer. CP-KizeC

For Jan Lebenstein. Czeslaw Milosz. CP-MiloC; CP-MiloCN, tr. by Robert Hass

For Jane Myers. Louise Glück. SP-GlucL

For Jean Migrenne. Marilyn Hacker. SP-HackM

For Jeriann's Hands. Marge Piercy. SP-PierM

For Joe Pernice. William Corbett. SP-CorbW

For Joel. Robert Creeley. CP-CreeR

For John Berryman. David Ignatow. SP-IgnaD

For John Chamberlain. Robert Creeley. SP-CreeR

For John Chappell. Gary Snyder. CP-SnydG

For John Clare. John Ashbery. SP-AshbJ

For John Duff. Robert Creeley. SP-CreeR

For John F. Kennedy; His Inauguration. Robert Frost. CP-FrosR

For John Keats, Apostle of Beauty. Countee Cullen. CP-CullC *Fr.* Four Epitaphs.

For John, Who Begs Me Not to Enquire Further. Anne Sexton. CP-SextA; SP-SextA

For Johnny Pole on the Forgotten Beach. Anne Sexton. CP-SextA

For Jordan With Love the Eighth Year of the Slaughter: A Minuet for Army Boots and Orchestra. Miller Williams. CP-WillM

For Joseph Conrad. Countee Cullen. CP-CullC

For joy & beauty planted it. Ralph Waldo Emerson. CP-EmerR

For Judith. John Ciardi. CP-CiarJ

For Julia in Nebraska. Adrienne Rich. SP-RicA2

For just a moment, O Swan, I will link my longings. "Rubén Dario." SP-DariR, *tr. by* Alberto Acereda *and* Will Derusha

For K.J., Leaving and Coming Back. Marilyn Hacker. SP-HackM

For K. R. on Her Sixtieth Birthday. Richard Wilbur. CP-WilbR

For Kayle Boyle. Muriel Rukeyser. CP-RukeM

For Kazuko. Rita Dove. SP-DoveR

For King, for Robert Kennedy. Words in the Mourning Time. Robert Earl Hayden. CP-HaydR

For L.G.: Unseen for Twenty Years. Adrienne Rich. SP-RicA2

For lack of Knowledge do my people die! My People are destroyed for lack of Knowledge.—Hosea 4:6. Jones Very. CP-VeryJ

For largest Woman's Heart I knew. Emily Dickinson. CP-DickE

For Leopoldo Lugones. Jorge Luis Borges. SP-BorgJ, *tr. by* Ken Krabbenhoft

For Leslie. Robert Creeley. CP-CreeR

For let the impediment be what it may. Fragment: "For let the impediment be what it may." William Wordsworth. CP-WorW1

For Lew Welch in a Snowfall. Gary Snyder. CP-SnydG

For Lewis, to Say It. Robert Creeley. CP-CreeR

For Life I Had Never Cared Greatly. Thomas Hardy. CP-HardT

For Lisa. Alan Dugan. CP-DugaA

For long my life left hers. It went. Memorial for My Mother, A. William Stafford. SP-StafWW

For long the cruel wish I knew. Coquette, and After, The. Thomas Hardy. CP-HardT

For Lords or kings I dinna mourn. Elegy on the Year 1788. Robert Burns. CP-BurnR

For losing her love all would I profane. Kenneth Patchen. CP-PatcK

For Love. Robert Creeley. CP-CreeR

For love—I would. Warning, The. Robert Creeley. CP-CreeR

For love we all go. People, the People, The. George Oppen. CP-OppGN

For Lucifer, that old athlete. Ralph Waldo Emerson. CP-EmerR

For Lucinda, Robert, and Karyn. Miller Williams. CP-WillM

For Lucy, on the Twelfth Month. Miller Williams. CP-WillM

For Lyra yet shall be the pole. Ralph Waldo Emerson. CP-EmerR

For M. Adam Zagajewski. SP-ZagaA, *tr. by* Clare Cavanagh

For Mac Hammond. Charles Olson. CP-OlsoC

For many years now—being a smalltime dreamer & an easygoing guy. Meditations & Allegories of Water. Federico García Lorca. CP-GarcF, *tr. by* Jerome Rothenberg

For Marg So She Could Fuck Again. Andrei Codrescu. SP-CodrA

For Marisol. Robert Creeley. CP-CreeR

For Martin. Robert Creeley. CP-CreeR

For Masturbation. Alan Dugan. CP-DugaA

For me a perfectly ordinary. Routine Day Sonnet. A. K. Ramanujan. CP-RamaA

For me, my friend, if not that tears did tremble. Fragment: To a Friend Released from Prison. Percy Bysshe Shelley. CP-ShelP

For me, the naked and the nude. Naked and the Nude, The. Robert Graves. CP-GravR

For me the tragedy's most important act is the sixth. Theatre Impressions. Wisława Szymborska. SP-SzymW, *tr. by* Stanislaw Barańczak *and* Clare Cavanagh

For me those steps of flamenco. When You Danced. James Laughlin. CP-LaugJ

For me will you fashion acts each year. Victory Over Seville, The. Shmuel HaNagid. SP-HaNaS, *tr. by* Peter Cole

For Medgar Evers. David Ignatow. SP-IgnaD

For Mélisande / flower-child of the forest. Mélisande. Charles Tomlinson. CP-TomlC

For Memory. Adrienne Rich. SP-RicA1; SP-RicA2

For Memory. Muriel Rukeyser. CP-RukeM

For Mercedes in Her Flight. Federico García Lorca. CP-GarcF, *tr. by* Christopher Maurer

For Mercy of Death. Ivor Gurney. SP-GurnI

For Mike and Jeannie: Resisters Fifteen Years Later. Grace Paley. CP-PalGC

For Milarepa, In Ruse, on Rice Paper. Norman Dubie. CP-DubiN

For Miller Williams. John Ciardi. CP-CiarJ

For Miriam. Kenneth Patchen. CP-PatcK

For Miriam. Kenneth Patchen. CP-PatcK

For Miriam. Kenneth Patchen. CP-PatcK

For Miriam. Kenneth Patchen. CP-PatcK

For Miriam. Kenneth Patchen. CP-PatcK

For Miriam. Charles Tomlinson. CP-TomlC; SP-TomlC

For Mr. Death Who Stands with His Door Open. Anne Sexton. CP-SextA; SP-SextA

For Monique. Rainer Maria Rilke. CP-RilkFr, *tr. by* A. Poulin, Jr.

For months my hand had been sealed off. Touch, The. Anne Sexton. CP-SextA

For more than five thousand years. At the Jewish New Year. Adrienne Rich. CP-RicAE; SP-RicA2

For Mother on Father's Day. James Tate. SP-TateJ

For My Birthday. Yehuda Amichai. SP-AmicY, *tr. by* Stephen Mitchell

For My Brother: Reported Missing In Action, 1943. Thomas Merton. CP-MertT

For My Contemporaries. James Vincent Cunningham. CP-CunnJ

For my dagger is bathed in the blood of the brave. Dialogue, A. Percy Bysshe Shelley. CP-ShelP

For My Daughter. David Ignatow. SP-IgnaD

For My Daughter. Carolyn Kizer. CP-KizeC

For My Daughter. Grace Paley. CP-PalGC

For My Daughter in Reply to a Question. David Ignatow. SP-IgnaD

For My Daughter When She Can Read. Thomas Lux. SP-LuxT

For My Eighty-eighth Birthday. Czeslaw Milosz. CP-MiloCN, *tr. by* Robert Hass

For my embalming, Julia, do but this. His Embalming to Julia. Robert Herrick. CP-HerrR

For My Father. Christopher Logue. SP-LoguC

For My Father. Philip Whalen. SP-WhalP

For My Friend. Charles Olson. CP-OlsoC

For My Friend Who Planted a Tree for His Daughter Jane. Grace Paley. CP-PalGC

For My Funeral. A. E. Housman. CP-HousA

For My Grandmother. Countee Cullen. CP-CullC *Fr.* Four Epitaphs.

For My Great-Grandfather: A Message Long Overdue. Maxine W. Kumin. SP-KumiM

For My Lover, Returning to His Wife. Anne Sexton. CP-SextA; SP-SextA

For My Mother. Yehuda Amichai. SP-AmicYL, *tr. by* Benjamin Harshav *and* Barbara Harshav

For My Mother. Louise Glück. SP-GlucL

For My Mother: Genevieve Jules Creeley. Robert Creeley. CP-CreeR

For My Mother Ill. David Ignatow. SP-IgnaD

For My Mother in Her First Illness, from a Window Overlooking Notre Dame. Jane Cooper. CP-CoopJ

For my neighbour Ile not know. Safety To Look to Ones Selfe. Robert Herrick. CP-HerrR

For My Nephew Going to Bed. John Ciardi. CP-CiarJ

For my part. Northwood Path. Louise Glück. SP-GlucL

For my part, I never care. Lips Tongueless[e]. Robert Herrick. CP-HerrR

For My Singing Sister. Audre Lorde. SP-LordA

For my sins I live in the city of New York. Whitman in Black. Ted Berrigan. SP-BerrT

For My Sister Molly Who in the Fifties. Alice Walker. CP-WalkA

For My Son. Muriel Rukeyser. CP-RukeM

For My Son John. John Ciardi. CP-CiarJ

For My Son Noah, Ten Years Old. Robert Bly. SP-BlyR

For My Young Friends Who Are Afraid. William Stafford. SP-StafW; SP-StafWW

For Myra, John L., and Benn. John Ciardi. CP-CiarJ

For Myra out of the Album. John Ciardi. CP-CiarJ

For Myself. Countee Cullen. CP-CullC

For nations vague as weed. Nothing to Be Said. Philip Larkin. CP-LarkP

For Nature true & like in every place. Ralph Waldo Emerson. CP-EmerR

For Nikolai, Many Thousand Miles Away. Denise Levertov. SP-LeveDL

For No Clear Reason. Robert Creeley. CP-CreeR

For Noel. Gabriela Mistral. SP-MistG, *tr. by* Maria Giachetti [*or* Jacketti]

For not the brave, or wise, or great. Pindar. CP-JohnS *Fr.* Pythian Odes.

For Nothing. Gary Snyder. CP-SnydG

For Now. David Ignatow. SP-IgnaD

For Now. W. S. Merwin. SP-MerwW

For Oh, her lanely nights are lang. Robert Burns. *See* How lang and dreary is the night

For old New England. Seeking. James Schuyler. CP-SchuJ

For once she gets to go with big Cousin Beatie. Speak, Memory! Mona Van Duyn. SP-VanDM

For Once, Then, Something. Robert Frost. CP-FrosR

For one bright moment, heavenly goddess! shine. Philis's Reply to the Answer in Our Last by the Gentleman in the Navy. Phillis Wheatley. CP-WheaP

For One Moment. David Ignatow. SP-IgnaD

For One Sake. Christina Georgina Rossetti. CP-RosC3

For one so rarely tun'd to fit all parts. To the Most Accomplisht Gentleman, Master Edward Norgate, Clark of the Signet to His Majesty. Robert Herrick. CP-HerrR

For one, the amaryllis and the rose. Vers Démodé. Dorothy Parker. CP-ParkD

For one throb of the artery. Meditation in Time of War, A. William Butler Yeats. CP-YeatW

For one who has failed, one brought low. Constantine P. Cavafy. CP-CavaC, *tr. by* Theoharis Constantine Theoharis

For one who watches with too little rest. Sacred Heart. Thom Gunn. CP-GunnT

For Orford and for Waldegrave. Lord Byron. CP-Byron

For "Our Lady of the Rocks" by Leonardo da Vinci. Dante Gabriel Rossetti. CW-RossD

For Our Party Last Night. William Stafford. SP-StafWW

For our white and our excellent nights—for the nights of swift running. Rudyard Kipling. CP-KiplR *Fr.* Second Jungle Book, The.

For over forty years I'd paid it atlas homage. Hammerfest. W. H. Auden. CP-AudeW

For Pao-Chin, a Boatman on the Yellow Sea, Edna St. Vincent Millay. CP-MillE

For Paolo and Andy. Michael Palmer. SP-PalmM

For Papa. Hayden Carruth. CP-CarHS

For papers I think I need, we bump off. On the Way Home From Nowhere, New Year's Eve. Miller Williams. CP-WillM

For parents, the only way. Way of Pain, The. Wendell Berry. CP-BerrW

For Paul Laurence Dunbar. Countee Cullen. CP-CullC *Fr.* Four Epitaphs.

For pearls, plunge in the sea. *Unknown.* CP-EmerR

For Pen ("Last day of year"). Robert Creeley. SP-CreeR

For Pen ("Reading, in the chair"). Robert Creeley. SP-CreeR

For Pen ("Thinking out / of the heart"). Robert Creeley. SP-CreeR

For pity's sake. Pity's Sake. Archibald MacLeish. CP-MacLA

For prodigal read generous. E. E. Cummings. CP-CummE

For Proust. James Merrill. SP-MerrJ

For pungent scents all matter is porous. Perfume-flask, The. Charles Baudelaire. CP-BaudC, *tr. by* Walter Martin

For punishment in warre, it will suffice. Clemency. Robert Herrick. CP-HerrR

For Queen Victoria's Birthday. Walt Whitman. CP-WhitW

For R.C.B. Dorothy Parker. CP-ParkD

For Rainer Gerhardt. Robert Creeley. CP-CreeR

For Randall Jarrell, 1914–1965. Norman Dubie. CP-DubiN

For Rebecca, for Whom Nothing Has Been Written Page after Page. Miller Williams. CP-WillM

For Rene Ricard. Robert Creeley. SP-CreeR

For Reuben, at Twelve Months. Miller Williams. CP-WillM

For Richard Wilbur. James Dickey. CP-DickJ

For Righteousness' Sake. John Greenleaf Whittier. CP-WhitJ

For R. A. Esq. Robert Burns. CP-BurnR

For Robert Bhain Campbell. James Dickey. CP-DickJ

For Robert Frost. Galway Kinnell. SP-KinnGN

For Robert Frost, in the Autumn, in Vermont. Howard Nemerov. CP-NemeH

For Robert Kennedy Nineteen Twenty-Five to Sixty-Eight. Robert Lowell. SP-LoweR

For Robert, Son of Man. Miller Williams. CP-WillM

For ropes of pearle, first Madam Ursly showes. Upon Madam Ursly. Robert Herrick. CP-HerrR

For Rosaline's Album. Christina Georgina Rossetti. CP-RosC3

For round / or of. For Exhibition. Lorine Niedecker. CP-NiedL

For "Ruggiero and Angelica" by Ingres. Dante Gabriel Rossetti. CW-RossD

For Russell and Rowena Jelliffe. Langston Hughes. CP-HughL; CP-HughL3

For safety on the expedition. Ballad of Johnny, The. May Sarton. SP-SartM

For Sale. Robert Lowell. SP-LoweR

For sale: by order of the remaining heirs. Sale. Theodore Roethke. CP-RoetT

For sale what the Jews have not sold, what neither nobility nor crime has tasted. Sales. Arthur Rimbaud. CP-RimbA, *tr. by* Martin Sorrell

For Salome. Langston Hughes. CP-HughL; CP-HughL1

For Sappho/After Sappho. Carolyn Kizer. CP-KizeC

For Sappho, Back. Charles Olson. CP-OlsoC; SP-OlsoC

For Saying That It Won't Matter. W. S. Merwin. SP-MerwW

For seasons the walled meadow. September Plowing. W. S. Merwin. SP-MerwWF

For second course, last night, a Custard came. Custard, The. Robert Herrick. CP-HerrR

For security against robbers who snatch purses, rifle luggage, and crack safes. Cracking the Safe. Chuang Tzu. CP-MertT

For Selma Gubin's Umbrellas. Louis Zukofsky. CP-ZukLS

For Semra, with Martial Vigor. Raymond Carver. CP-CarvR

For seven days it rained that June. Wash. John Updike. CP-UpdiJ

For seven years at school I named. Song of the Dead Soldier, The. Christopher Logue. SP-LoguC

For several blocks to any. Lauds. James McMichael. SP-McMiJ

For several days I have been under. Jail Journal. Derek Mahon. CP-MahoD

For several weeks I have been reading. Expression. Thom Gunn. CP-GunnT

For shame! / Let Folly and Knavery. On Johnson's Opinion of Hampden. Robert Burns. CP-BurnR

For shamefast harm of great and hateful need. Sir Thomas Wyatt. CP-WyatT

For Sharon, As Soon As She Wants It. Robert Stock. SP-StocR

For Shoshana Rihn—Pat Swinton. Marge Piercy. SP-PierM

For Sidney Bechet. Philip Larkin. CP-LarkP

For Signs. Thom Gunn. CP-GunnT

For simple pleasure, he beheld. Saturday Night at the Chiropodist's. Wallace Stevens. CP-StevWP

For Sir W. Trumbull. Alexander Pope. CP-PopeA

For sixty years I have been forgetful. Music, The. Jelaluddin Rumi. SP-Rumi, *tr. by* Coleman Barks

For so many weeks now everything. Cuckoo. Rainer Maria Rilke. CP-RilkFr, *tr. by* A. Poulin, Jr.

For some / it is stone. Garden of Delight, The. Lucille Clifton. SP-ClifL

For some semitropical reason. Tarantulas on the Lifebuoy. Thomas Lux. SP-LuxT

"For Some Weeks." Robert Creeley. CP-CreeR

For some weeks / now, caught in my. "For Some Weeks." Robert Creeley. CP-CreeR

For Somebody's Marriage. Robert Creeley. CP-CreeR

For something out of sight. Summons, The. James Dickey. CP-DickJ

For sometimes over the fields astride. Political Poem, A. George Oppen. CP-OppGN

For sport my *Julia* threw a Lace. Silken Snake, The. Robert Herrick. CP-HerrR

For Spring, by Sandro Botticelli, in the Accademia of Florence. Dante Gabriel Rossetti. CW-RossD

For Strong Women. Marge Piercy. SP-PierM

For such a theme (atrocities) you find. Method. For Ronald Gaskell. Donald Davie. CP-DaviDC

For, suckling her baby and glimpsing on the wall. Trajectory of a Scream. Robert Stock. SP-StocR

For suffering the bitter weather of his wars. Theodore Weiss. SP-WeisT *Fr.* Storeroom, The.

For sun and moon and radio. Lorine Niedecker. CP-NiedL

For Sunday's play he never makes excuse. Lout, The: "For Sunday's play he never makes excuse." John Clare. SP-ClarJ

For surely the flower, as Williams. Excursus of Reassurance in Begonia Time, An. Hayden Carruth. CP-CarHS

For ten years I have been rooted in these hills. Gestalt at Sixty. May Sarton. SP-SartM

For Tess. Raymond Carver. CP-CarvR

For that a man is a mark. Ralph Waldo Emerson. CP-EmerR

For that free Grace bringing us past great risks. John Berryman. *See* For that free Grace bringing us past terrible risks

For that free Grace bringing us past terrible risks. Minnesota Thanksgiving. John Berryman. CP-BerrJ

For that I have forgot the world these days. Sonnet: "For that I have forgot the world these days." E. E. Cummings. CP-CummE

For that I never knew you, I only learned to dread you. St. Roach. Muriel Rukeyser. CP-RukeM

For that it is love and covers us. Love I. Charles Olson. CP-OlsoC

For that moment we had been the others. Bang. Paul Muldoon. CP-MuldP

For that whole year I was in the weight of myself. My Seasonal Body. Clarence Major. SP-MajoC

For that you never acknowledged me, I acknowledge. Desdichada. Muriel Rukeyser. CP-RukeM

For the angels who inhabit this town. Locked Doors. Anne Sexton. CP-SextA

For the Anniversary of My Death. W. S. Merwin. SP-MerwW

For the Anniversary of my Mother's Death. Archibald MacLeish. CP-MacLA

For the Author's Father. Robert Burns. CP-BurnR

For the Blind. Denise Levertov. SP-LeveDL

For the Boy Who Was Dodger Point Lookout Fifteen Years Ago. Gary Snyder. CP-SnydG

For the bumps bangs and scratches of. Auto Mobile. A. R. Ammons. CP-AmmoA

For the Children. Gary Snyder. CP-SnydG

For the children is the challenge of the giant. Chorus for a Play. G. K. Chesterton. CP-ChesG

For the Chinese Actress, Gardenia Chang. Kenneth Rexroth. CP-RexrK

For the Chinese New Year and for Bill Berkson. Frank O'Hara. SP-OharF

For the comprehension of Suffering. Emily Dickinson. SP-DickE

For the Conjunction of Two Planets. Adrienne Rich. CP-RicAE; SP-RicA2

For the Dead. Adrienne Rich. SP-RicA1; SP-RicA2

For the Death of Vince Lombardi. James Dickey. CP-DickJ

For the discipline nothing had changed. The mood was still. Lament Upon the Waters, The. John Ashbery. SP-AshbJ

For the Duration. Ted Hughes. SP-HughTN

For the Egyptian Coin Today, Arden, Thank You. Raymond Carver. CP-CarvR

For the eyes of the children. Sorrow Song. Lucille Clifton. SP-ClifL

For the fairest maid in Hampton. Changeling, The. John Greenleaf Whittier. CP-WhitJ

For the Felling of an Elm in the Harvard Yard. Adrienne Rich. CP-RicAE

For the First Time. James Laughlin. CP-LaugJ

For the first time he sees light. Birth. Czeslaw Milosz. CP-MiloC; CP-MiloCN, tr. by Peter Dale Scott

For the first time the only. Rescue. James Tate. SP-TateJ

For the first time today. Willkie—Stopless Falling through Air. Muriel Rukeyser. CP-RukeM

For the first twenty years [or yeares], since yesterday. Computation, The. John Donne. CP-DonnJ; MW-DonnJ

For the Future. Wendell Berry. CP-BerrW

For the gladness here where the sun is shining at evening on the weeds at. Our Prayer of Thanks. Carl Sandburg. CP-SandC

For the Graduation. Robert Creeley. CP-CreeR

For the Graduation. Robert Creeley. CP-CreeR

For the Graduation: Bolinas, 1972. Robert Creeley. CP-CreeR

For the Grave of a Peace-Loving Man. Hans Magnus Enzensberger. SP-EnzeH, tr. by Hans Magnus Enzensberger, Michael Hamburger and Michael Hamburger

For the Grave of Posterity. W. S. Merwin. SP-MerwW

For the Heroes Are Dipped in Scarlet. D. H. Lawrence. CP-LawrD

For the Hog Killing. Wendell Berry. CP-BerrW

For The Holy Family, by Michelangelo, in the National Gallery. Dante Gabriel Rossetti. CW-RossD

For the Hour of Prime. Richard Crashaw. CP-CrasR

For the huge. Whirl Wind Must, The. George Oppen. CP-OppGN

For the hundred years of human life. Han-shan. CP-ColdM, tr. by Red Pine

For the lands and for these passionate days and for myself. Return of the Heroes, The. Walt Whitman. CP-WhitW

For the last time, for this or perhaps. Last Walk of Season. Robert Penn Warren. CP-WarrR

For the Last Wolverine. James Dickey. CP-DickJ

For the Madrid Road. Randall Jarrell. CP-JarrR

For the Man Who Fails. Paul Laurence Dunbar. CP-DunbP

For the Marriage of Faustus and Helen. Hart Crane. CP-CranH

For the Marsh's Birthday. James Wright. CP-WrigJ

For the Mother of My Mother's Mother. Kenneth Patchen. CP-PatcK

For the Negro Nurse there's been no easy way. Where Service Is Needed. Langston Hughes. CP-HughL; CP-HughL3

For the New Railway Station in Rome. Richard Wilbur. CP-WilbR

For the New Year. Robert Creeley. CP-CreeR

For the New Year, 1981. Denise Levertov. SP-LeveDL

For the Nightly Ascent of the Hunter Orion over a Forest Clearing. James Dickey. CP-DickJ

For the Old Year. William Corbett. SP-CorbW

For the past. Dedications / Pledges / Commitments. William Stafford. SP-StafWW

For the pleasures of the many. Variations, Calypso and Fugue on a Theme of Ella Wheeler Wilcox. John Ashbery. SP-AshbJ

For the Prince in Exile. Tu Fu. CP-KizeC, tr. by Carolyn Kizer

For the Rebuilding of a House. Wendell Berry. CP-BerrW

For the Record. Raymond Carver. CP-CarvR

For the Record. Adrienne Rich. SP-RicA2

For the Recorder of Suicides. Jane Cooper. CP-CoopJ

For the Restoration of My Dear Husband from a Burning Ague. Anne Bradstreet. CP-BradA

For the Running of the New York City Marathon. James Dickey. CP-DickJ

For the Sailors' Fair. Jones Very. CP-VeryJ

For the Sake o' Somebody. Robert Burns. See Somebody

For the sake of guilty conscience, and the heart that ticks the time. George Mullen's Confession. James Whitcomb Riley. CP-RileJ

For the sake of him who showed. Outsong in the Jungle. Rudyard Kipling. CP-KiplR Fr. Second Jungle Book, The.

For the sake of some things. Rosemary. Edna St. Vincent Millay. CP-MillE

For the sake of the record. Customs Collector's Report, The. Stanley Kunitz. CP-KunSC

For the sake of voyaging—heedlessly. Stéphane Mallarmé. CP-MallS, tr. by Henry Weinfield

For the scaffold spreads its gray flower. Devotion, A. Kenneth Patchen. CP-PatcK

For the Seasons. Marya Alexandrovna Zaturenska. SP-ZatuM

For the second time in a year this lady with the white hands is brought. White Hands. Carl Sandburg. CP-SandC

For the seven lakes, and by no man these verses. Canto 49: "For the seven lakes, and by no man these verses." Ezra Pound. SP-PounE Fr. Cantos.

For the Sexes the Gates of Paradise. William Blake. See Gates of Paradise, The

For the Shop. Constantine P. Cavafy. CP-CavaC, tr. by Theoharis Constantine Theoharis

For the Spanish Poet Miguel Hernandez. Thomas Merton. CP-MertT

For the Spot Where the Hermitage Stood on St Herbert's Island, Derwent-Water. William Wordsworth. CP-WorW1; MW-WorW

For the Squadron. Howard Nemerov. CP-NemeH

For the Student Strikers. Richard Wilbur. CP-WilbR

For the sugar, for the mule, those candles too. Michelangelo Buonarroti. CP-Miche, tr. by John Frederick Nims

For the sweet sake of inscapes. Since You Asked Me. Mona Van Duyn. SP-VanDM

For the Time Being; a Christmas Oratorio. W. H. Auden. CP-AudeW
     Flight into Egypt, The. CP-AudeW

For the Triumph of the Arts. Ezra Pound. CP-PoEar

For the Union Dead. Robert Lowell. SP-LoweR

For the Unknown Enemy. William Stafford. SP-StafWW

For the Visitors' Book. Kathleen Jessie Raine. SP-RainK

For the Walking Dead. Yusef Komunyakaa. CP-KomuY

For the West. Gary Snyder. CP-SnydG

For 'The Wine of Circe' by Edward Burne Jones. Dante Gabriel Rossetti. CW-RossD

For the wrongs that women do. Nun's Song. William Carlos Williams. CP-WilW2

For the Year of the Insane. Anne Sexton. CP-SextA; SP-SextA

For the Young Who Want To. Marge Piercy. SP-PierM

For thee I drop the tender tear. Elegy: "For thee I drop the tender tear." Annis Boudinot Stockton. CP-StocA

For thee the Muse shall twine a wreath. To Amanda—Who Was Obliging Enough to Delight Her Friend with Singing Every Evening Two Songs Which She Was Very Fond Off. Annis Boudinot Stockton. CP-StocA

For their descent, / dancing round my desk. Blessed Be the Muses. Allen Ginsberg. CP-GinsA

For Theodore Roosevelt. Paul Laurence Dunbar. CP-DunbP

For There's Bishop's Teign. John Keats. CP-KeatJ

For these of old the trader. A. E. Housman. CP-HousA

For they are dead. Respect for the Dead. Laura Riding Jackson. CP-RidiL

For thine is the kingdom. Lord's Prayer. D. H. Lawrence. CP-LawrD

For Thine Own Sake, O My God. Christina Georgina Rossetti. CP-RosC2

For things we never mention. Broken Men, The. Rudyard Kipling. CP-KiplR

For thirst of power that Heaven disowns. Ode on the Installation of His Royal Highness Prince Albert as Chancellor of the University of Cambridge, July, 1847. William Wordsworth. CP-WorW2

For thirty yeares, Tubbs has been proud and poor. Upon Tubbs. Robert Herrick. CP-HerrR

For this—accepted Breath. Emily Dickinson. CP-DickE

For This Christmas. James Whitcomb Riley. CP-RileJ

For this my mother wrapped me warm. Fulfilment. Dorothy Parker. CP-ParkD

For this present, hard. Woodnotes I ("For this present, hard"). Ralph Waldo Emerson. CP-EmerR

For this your mother sweated in the cold. To Jesus on His Birthday. Edna St. Vincent Millay. CP-MillE

For Thom Gunn. Andrei Codrescu. SP-CodrA

For Thomas Hardy. Jane Cooper. CP-CoopJ

For thon demgeorne dreorigne oft. Hayden Carruth. CP-CarHS Fr. Bloomingdale Papers, The.

For those little stabs of pain. Anginal Equivalent, An. James Laughlin. CP-LaugJ

For Those my unbaptized Rhymes [or Rhimes]. His Prayer for Absolution. Robert Herrick. CP-HerrR

For those this mausoleum is erected. Ambrose Bierce. SP-BierA

For Those Who Have Not Eaten the Apple. Josephine Jacobsen. CP-JacoJ

For those who worship Thee there is no death. Trees of Life, The. Jones Very. CP-VeryJ

For those who'll take my place. Rockets, The. David Ignatow. SP-IgnaD

For Those Whom the Gods Love Less. Denise Levertov. SP-LeveDS

For though the eaves [or Caves] were rabitted [or rabbeted or rabbited]. For though the eaves were rabbeted. Henry David Thoreau. CP-ThorH

For thought & not praise. Terminus. Ralph Waldo Emerson. CP-EmerR

For three insane things evil, and for four. Amos. John Berryman. CP-BerrJ

For three score years my wandering feet have strayed. Vision of Rabbi Ben Issac, The. James Whitcomb Riley. CP-RileJ

For three years at evening. Sleeping Brute, The. William Carlos Williams. CP-WilW2

For three years, out of key with his time. Hugh Selwyn Mauberley (Life and Contacts). Ezra Pound. SP-PounE

For to Admire. Rudyard Kipling. CP-KiplR

For to love her for her looks lovely. Sir Thomas Wyatt. CP-WyatT

For Tom. Robert Creeley. CP-CreeR

For truth I may this sentence tell. Good Death, A. Robert Herrick. CP-HerrR

For two days I have dug around a rock. Rock. Miller Williams. CP-WillM

For Two Lovers in the Year 2075 in the Canadian Woods. William Meredith. SP-MereW

For two rewards, & nought beside. Ibn-i-Yamin. CP-EmerR

For two who. For Two Who Slipped Away Almost Entirely. Alice Walker. CP-WalkA

For Two Who Slipped Away Almost Entirely. Alice Walker. CP-WalkA (Dedication.) CP-WalkA

For two years I had observed this impeccable Mycennienne profile. Chommoda. Ezra Pound. CP-PoEar

For Una. Robinson Jeffers. CP-JefR3

For us like any other fugitive. Another Time. W. H. Auden. CP-AudeW

For us, these little books contain. From a Vagabond. Wallace Stevens. CP-StevWP

For Us Two, Reader Dear. Walt Whitman. CP-WhitW

For Us, Who Dare Not Dare. Maya Angelou. SP-AngeM

For us who, from the moment. Address to the Beasts. W. H. Auden. CP-AudeW

For Victor Jara. Miller Williams. CP-WillM

For Viola: De Gustibus. William Carlos Williams. CP-WilW1

For W.C.W. Robert Creeley. CP-CreeR

For W. H. Auden. Richard Wilbur. CP-WilbR

For W———, Who Commanded Well. Howard Nemerov. CP-NemeH

For Walter Chappell. Robert Creeley. CP-CreeR

For want of [or I] will in woe I plain. Sir Thomas Wyatt. CP-WyatT

For Warmth Alone, for Shelter Only. Edna St. Vincent Millay. CP-MillE

For wars his life and half a world away. Lullaby, A: "For wars his life and half a world away." Randall Jarrell. CP-JarrR

For W.C.W. Robert Creeley. CP-CreeR

For we are all His offspring, why deny. Brethren, The. Jones Very. CP-VeryJ

For we are old / And the earth passion dyeth. In Tempore Senectutis ("For we are old / And the earth passion dyeth"). Ezra Pound. CP-PoEar

For we be the beaten wands. Prometheus. Ezra Pound. CP-PoEar

For we have gone a curious way from there. William Dickey. SP-DickW Fr. Part Song, With Concert of Recorders.

For We Walk by Faith, Not by Sight. Jones Very. CP-VeryJ

For well Thou knowest, O God most wise, On Lucian Oldershaw, Who Introduced Him to Frances. G. K. Chesterton. CP-ChesG

For what are we to think? But that Philo. Simple Philo of Alexandria. Norman Dubie. CP-DubiN

For what emperor / Was this bowl of Earth designed? Bowl. Wallace Stevens. CP-StevWP

For what it's worth, the last panther in Massachusetts. Panther, The. Paul Muldoon. CP-MuldP

For what need I of book or priest. Ralph Waldo Emerson. CP-EmerR

For what we owe to other days. Exit. Edwin Arlington Robinson. CP-RobiE

For whatever did it—the cider. Cure at Porlock, A. Amy Clampitt. CP-ClamA

For whatever is let go. May Song. Wendell Berry. CP-BerrW

For whatever, it could / be done, simply. Chance, The. Robert Creeley. CP-CreeR

For when they meet, the tensile air. Paradigm, The. Allen Tate. CP-TateA

For whom the possessed sea littered, on both shores. Requiem for the Plantagenet Kings. Geoffrey Hill. CP-HillG

For whose adornment the mouths. Kenneth Patchen. CP-PatcK

For Wilfred Owen. Josephine Jacobsen. CP-JacoJ

For William Carlos Williams. Galway Kinnell. SP-KinnGN

For X. Denise Levertov. SP-LeveDL

For Yaedi. David Ignatow. SP-IgnaD

For years and years he fretted; he undressed. Known Consequences. Yannis Ritsos. SP-RitsY, tr. by Kimon Friar

For years he had been staring at. Metamorphoses at a College for Women. Eleanor Wilner. SP-WilnE

For years he had not seen his native place. Vagrant at the Church Door, The. Jones Very. CP-VeryJ

For years I explored the pharmacopoeia. On the Threshold of His Greatness, the Poet Comes Down With a Sore Throat. Howard Nemerov. CP-NemeH

For years I fantasized pain. Beauty and the Beast. Olga Broumas. SP-BrouO

For years I thought I knew, at the bottom of the dream. Meeting, The. Louise Bogan. CP-BogaL

For years I tried to conceal from the villagers that I wrote poetry. Shameful Profession, The. James Laughlin. CP-LaugJ

For years it was land working me, oil fields. 3 A.M. Kitchen: My Father Talking. Tess Gallagher. SP-GallT

For years the dead. Change, The. Denise Levertov. SP-LeveDS

For years the old Italians have been dying. Old Italians Dying, The. Lawrence Ferlinghetti. SP-FerlL

For years we've had a little dog. Two Dogs Have I. Ogden Nash. CP-NashO

For years, when things got tough, they looked to the day. Something to Believe In. Miller Williams. CP-WillM

For You. Ted Berrigan. SP-BerrT

For You. Robert Creeley. CP-CreeR

For You. Carl Sandburg. CP-SandC

For You. Adam Zagajewski. SP-ZagaA, tr. by Clare Cavanagh

For you and I are bathed in silence. We Must Be Slow. Kenneth Patchen. CP-PatcK

For you, fear. Fear. A. K. Ramanujan. CP-RamaA

For you, I could forget the gay. James Whitcomb Riley. CP-RileJ

For you I have emptied the meaning. Louis Zukofsky. CP-ZukLS

For You O Democracy. Walt Whitman. CP-WhitW

For you, or of you? It can't be. Why Don't You Write for Me? John Ciardi. CP-CiarJ

For you, Pygmalion, no silver bought. Sonnet for Pygmalion. Tennessee Williams. CP-WillT

For you, sweetheart, I'll ride back down. For You, Sweetheart, I'll Sell Plutonium Reactors. Yusef Komunyakaa. CP-KomuY

For You, Sweetheart, I'll Sell Plutonium Reactors. Yusef Komunyakaa. CP-KomuY

For you there ought. For Leslie. Robert Creeley. CP-CreeR

For you, who whirled with horse and hound. To Enid the Huntress. G. K. Chesterton. CP-ChesG

For Your Fear. David Ignatow. SP-IgnaD

For your love given. Hayden Carruth. CP-CarHS Fr. Clay Hill Anthology, The.

For Ysolt. The Triad of Dawn. Ezra Pound. CP-PoEar

For Zadkine. Louis Zukofsky. CP-ZukLS

Forage Sestina. Marilyn Hacker. SP-HackM

Foraminiferal millennia. Undersea. A. R. Ammons. CP-AmmoA

Forbear to tempt me, Prowl, I will not show. To Prowl the Plagiary. Ben Jonson. CP-JonsB; SP-JonsB

Forbearance. Samuel Taylor Coleridge. CP-ColeS

Forbearance. Ralph Waldo Emerson. CP-EmerR

Forbearance. Jones Very. CP-VeryJ

Forbears, The. W. S. Merwin. SP-MerwW

Forbidden Banns, The. Thomas Hardy. CP-HardT

Forbidden Fruit a flavor has. Emily Dickinson. CP-DickE

Forbidden Ground. Yannis Ritsos. SP-RitsY, tr. by Andonis Decavalles

Forbidden Things. Alice Walker. CP-WalkA

Forbidden Words. Robert Graves. CP-GravR

Forbore the ant hill, shunned to tread. Ralph Waldo Emerson. CP-EmerR

Forc'd from home, and all its pleasures. Negro's Complaint, The. William Cowper. CP-CowpW

Force and His Master. George Meredith. CP-MerG2

Force-feeding swans—let me tell. Farmers. Thomas Lux. SP-LuxT

Force is my lot and not pink-clustered. Examination of the Hero in a Time of War. Wallace Stevens. CP-StevW; CP-StevWP

Force, just here, rolls up. Low Tide at Schoodic. Amy Clampitt. CP-ClamA

Force of Eloquence, The. Thomas Kinsella. CP-KinsT

Force of Friendship, The. Jelaluddin Rumi. SP-Rumi, tr. by Coleman Barks

Force of Habit, The. Hans Magnus Enzensberger. SP-EnzeH, tr. by Michael Hamburger

Force of Prayer, The; or, The Founding of Bolton Priory; A Tradition. William Wordsworth. CP-WorW1

Force of reason, who shut up the shrill. Athena. Amy Clampitt. CP-ClamA

Force that pulses, The. That Force. Adam Zagajewski. SP-ZagaA, tr. by Renata Gorczynski

Force that through the green fuse drives the flower, The. Dylan Thomas. CP-ThomD

Forced as I was, I ran a race with death. Track. Richard Eberhart. CP-EberR

Forced Recruit, The. Elizabeth Barrett Browning. CP-BroEB

Forced yellow spring before crenated. Forsythia. Louis Zukofsky. CP-ZukLS

Forces, the Will & the Weather. Wallace Stevens. CP-StevW; CP-StevWP

Forcibly I try to make the night supply me. Fingerprints. Jaroslav Seifert. SP-SeifJ, tr. by Ewald Osers

Forcing House. Theodore Roethke. CP-RoetT

Ford Madox Ford. Robert Lowell. SP-LoweR

Ford Manor. Derek Mahon. CP-MahoD

Ford o' Kabul River. Rudyard Kipling. CP-KiplR

Foreboding. Raymond Carver. CP-CarvR

Foreboding. Walter De la Mare. CP-DeLaW

Foreboding. Walter De la Mare. CP-DeLaW

Foreboding, The. Robert Graves. CP-GravR

Forecast. Yehuda Amichai. SP-AmicYL, tr. by Benjamin Harshav and Barbara Harshav

Forecast. D. H. Lawrence. CP-LawrD

Foreclosure. Lorine Niedecker. CP-NiedL

Forefinger of stone, dreamed by a sculptor, points to the sky, The. Slants at Buffalo, New York. Carl Sandburg. CP-SandC

Foregoing Subject Resumed, The. William Wordsworth. CP-WorW2

Foreguarded and unfevered and serene. Sage, The. Edwin Arlington Robinson. CP-RobiE

Forehead on forearm, eyes unfocused. Hellenic Triptych. Sam Hamill. SP-HamiS

Foreign. William Carlos Williams. CP-WilW1

Foreign Affairs. Stanley Kunitz. CP-KunSC

Foreign hands and feet that tear my window shades, The. Wrong Number. Charles Bukowski. SP-BukC2

Foreign Lands, The. Josephine Jacobsen. CP-JacoJ

Foreign Missions in Battle Array. Nicholas Vachel Lindsay. CP-LindV

Foreign voice woman. Huckleberry Woman. W. S. Merwin. SP-MerwW

Foreign Woman, The. Gabriela Mistral. SP-MistG, tr. by Maria Giachetti [or Jacketti]

Foreigner. Olga Broumas. SP-BrouO

Foreigners are people somewhere else. Goody for Our Side and Your Side Too. Ogden Nash. CP-NashO

Foreknown. The victor / sees the disaster through and through. Letters: March 1969. Adrienne Rich. CP-RicAE; SP-RicA2

Foremost of false philosophies. Sea, False Philosophy. Laura Riding Jackson. CP-RidiL

Forerunners. Ralph Waldo Emerson. CP-EmerR

Forerunners. Muriel Rukeyser. CP-RukeM

Forerunners, The. George Herbert. CP-HerbG

Foreseeing typographical errors. Bitterness of Children, The. Thomas Lux. SP-LuxT

Foreseen for so many years: these evils, this monstrous violence. May-June, 1940. Robinson Jeffers. CP-JefR3

Foresight. William Wordsworth. CP-WorW1

Foresight and Patience. George Meredith. CP-MerG1

Forest. May Swenson. SP-SwenM

Forest Birds. Charles Simic. SP-SimiC; SP-SimiCE

Forest Fire. Wyatt Prunty. SP-PrunW

Forest Greeting, The. Paul Laurence Dunbar. CP-DunbP

Forest History. George Meredith. CP-MerG1

Forest huge of ancient Caledon, The. Suggested by a View from an Eminence in Inglewood Forest. William Wordsworth. CP-WorW2

Forest is multitude. Kathleen Jessie Raine. SP-RainK

Forest Murmurs. Eduard Friedrich Mörike. CP-JarrR, tr. by Randall Jarrell

Forest of Arden. Marya Alexandrovna Zaturenska. SP-ZatuM

Forest of Europe. Derek Walcott. CP-WalcD

Forest of pine darkness. Shadows, A. Chase in Spring, The. Hayden Carruth. CP-CarHS

Forest Thought, A. Robert Browning. CP-BroR2

Forests. Walter De la Mare. CP-DeLaW

Forests are branches of a tree lying down. Flying Home from Utah. May Swenson. SP-SwenM

Forests of Lithuania, The. Donald Davie. CP-DaviDC

Forever. Raymond Carver. CP-CarvR

Forever. Paul Laurence Dunbar. CP-DunbP

Forever. David Ignatow. SP-IgnaD

Forever at His side to walk. Emily Dickinson. CP-DickE

Forever at war news I am. Mary Sheffield. James Dickey. CP-DickJ

Forever honored be the Tree. Emily Dickinson. CP-DickE

Forever in my dream & in my morning thought. Henry David Thoreau. CP-ThorH

Forever—is composed of Nows. Emily Dickinson. CP-DickE

Forever, it comes from the head. / Where does it end? Venom. James Dickey. CP-DickJ

Forever nameless / Forever unknown. Belief. D. H. Lawrence. CP-LawrD

Forever O'Clock. Robert Penn Warren. CP-WarrR

Forever over now, forever, forever gone. Cameo, The. Edna St. Vincent Millay. CP-MillE

Forever revealing the wheel. Saint Catherine. Rainer Maria Rilke. CP-RilkFr, tr. by A. Poulin, Jr.

Forevermore. Jones Very. CP-VeryJ

Forewarned of madness. Halls of Bedlam, The. Robert Graves. CP-GravR

Foreword. W. S. Merwin. SP-MerwW

Forge, The. Seamus Heaney. SP-HeanSO

Forge, and a Scythe, A. Raymond Carver. CP-CarvR

Forged Passport. Yannis Ritsos. SP-RitsY, tr. by Kimon Friar

Forger, The. Derek Mahon. CP-MahoD

Forget. D. H. Lawrence. CP-LawrD

Forget. Czeslaw Milosz. CP-MiloCN, tr. by Jessica Fisher and Bozena Gilewska

Forget all experiences involving wincing. Young Girls, The. Raymond Carver. CP-CarvR

Forget Fez. Arthur Sze. SP-SzeA

Forget! Forget it to know it. It sings! Memory Forgotten. Robert Penn Warren. CP-WarrR

Forget Me Not. Christina Georgina Rossetti. CP-RosC3

Forget not yet the tried intent. Steadfastness. Sir Thomas Wyatt. CP-WyatT

Forget the foolishness with which I vexed you. Superstition. Robert Graves. CP-GravR

Forget! The lady with the Amulet. Emily Dickinson. CP-DickE

Forget the rest: my heart is true. Leap, The. Robert Graves. CP-GravR

Forget the suffering. Forget. Czeslaw Milosz. CP-MiloCN, tr. by Jessica Fisher and Bozena Gilewska

Forget the tube of bark. Very Tree. Stanley Kunitz. CP-KunSC

Forget understanding. There will be none. Some Figures for Who Must Speak. John Ciardi. CP-CiarJ

Forget What Did. Philip Larkin. CP-LarkP

Forgetful thou to manhood's years had'st grown. On reading the Memorial of John White Browne. Jones Very. CP-VeryJ

Forgetfulness. Billy Collins. SP-CollB

Forgetfulness. Hart Crane. CP-CranH

Forgetting I am alive, the tent comes over me. Jewel, The. James Dickey. CP-DickJ

Forgetting someone is like. Yehuda Amichai. SP-AmicY, tr. by Chana Bloch

Forgetting someone is like. Yehuda Amichai. SP-AmicYL, tr. by Benjamin Harshav and Barbara Harshav

Forgetting sounds that we no longer hear. Suburbans, The. Carolyn Kizer. CP-KizeC

Forgive me, father! Remembrances of Senility. Arthur Rimbaud. CP-RimbA

Forgive me Father! for to Thee I stand. Forgiveness. Jones Very. CP-VeryJ

Forgive Me, Forgive Me. Stevie Smith. CP-SmitS

Forgive me. I was a schemer like many of those who steal by human habitations at night. Not This Way. Czeslaw Milosz. CP-MiloC; CP-MiloCN, tr. by Lillian Vallee

Forgive me if, forgetful now and again. This Book is for Harriette. Robert Stock. SP-StocR

Forgive me if I come too much. Emily Dickinson. SP-DickE

Forgive Me If My Praises. Alice Walker. CP-WalkA

Forgive me, love, if I withdraw awhile. Her Brief Withdrawal. Robert Graves. CP-GravR

Forgive me, my delight. To Tanya at Christmas. Wendell Berry. CP-BerrW

Forgive Me My Trespasses. Jones Very. CP-VeryJ

Forgive me, soldier. Please. Yusef Komunyakaa. CP-KomuY

Forgive, O Lord, my little jokes on Thee. Robert Frost. CP-FrosR

Forgive The Man Who Sinned Against You. Shmuel HaNagid. SP-HaNaS, tr. by Peter Cole

Forgive the weasel his tooth. Guru, The. A. K. Ramanujan. CP-RamaA

Forgive this singsong, / It's just my spring song. Eternal Vernal, or, In All My Dreams My Fair Face Beams, The. Ogden Nash. CP-NashO

Forgive us you, whose pageant flames. Apology ("Forgive us you, whose pageant flames"). G. K. Chesterton. CP-ChesG

Forgive what I give you. Though nightmare and cinders. To Mary. Louis MacNeice. CP-MacNL

Forgiven Past, The. Laura Riding Jackson. CP-RidiL

Forgiveness. Walter De la Mare. CP-DeLaW

Forgiveness. Jones Very. CP-VeryJ

Forgiveness. Alice Walker. CP-WalkA

Forgiveness. John Greenleaf Whittier. CP-WhitJ

Forgiveness, A. Robert Browning. CP-BroR2

Forgot! Stevie Smith. CP-SmitS

Forgotten Girlhood. Laura Riding Jackson. CP-RidiL

Forgotten Miniature, A. Thomas Hardy. CP-HardT

Forgotten Rock, The. Richard Eberhart. CP-EberR

Forgotten Wars. Carl Sandburg. CP-SandC

Fork. Charles Simic. SP-SimiC; SP-SimiCE

Fork in the garden, the widow digging, A. Widow of the Beast of Ingolstadt, The. Norman Dubie. CP-DubiN

Forlorn indeed Hope on these shores. Killala. Donald Davie. CP-DaviDC

Forlorn, my love, no comfort near. English Song. Robert Burns. CP-BurnR

Forlorn Sea, The. Stevie Smith. CP-SmitS

Form. James Dickey. CP-DickJ

Form. Heather McHugh. SP-McHuH

Form, The. John Berryman. CP-BerrJ

Form and Theory of Poetry. Miller Williams. CP-WillM

Form imposes, structure allows— / the slow destruction of form. Sitting at Dusk in the Back Yard after the Mondrian Retrospective. Charles Wright. SP-WrigCN

Form of Adaptation, A. Robert Creeley. CP-CreeR

Form of Christ cut from dark wood, the pale, A. Sonnet: "Form of Christ cut from dark wood, the pale, A." Howard Nemerov. CP-NemeH

Form of Pity, A. Robert Stock. SP-StocR

Form of the grasses against, The. Total Parts of a World, The. Robert Creeley. CP-CreeR

Form of Women, A. Robert Creeley. CP-CreeR

Form upon the quilted, A. Threshold. Denise Levertov. SP-LeveDP

Formal as minuet or sonnet. Mystery Story. Howard Nemerov. CP-NemeH

Formal, blooded stallion, the Arabian, The. On an Old Advertisement and After a Photograph by Alfred Stieglitz. Alan Dugan. CP-DugaA

Formal Design, A. William Carlos Williams. CP-WilW2

Formal Elegy. John Berryman. CP-BerrJ

Formal, informal, by a country's cast. Homage to Edward Thomas. Derek Walcott. CP-WalcD

Formalities, The. John Ciardi. CP-CiarJ

Formative Mastership. Richard Eberhart. CP-EberR

Former Age, The. Geoffrey Chaucer. CP-ChauG

Former Attachment, A. Robert Graves. CP-GravR

Former four now ending their discourse, The. Of the Four Humors in Man's Constitution. Anne Bradstreet. CP-BradA

Former gave with eloquent characters, The. In the French Translation of Lucan by Monsieur De Brebeuf Are These Verses: Lib 3. Lucan. CP-MarvA *Fr.* Civil War [Bellum Civile] *or* Pharsalia.

Formerly a Slave. Herman Melville. SP-MelvH

Formianus's whore, / long-nosed. Carmen 41. Catullus. CP-ZukLS *Fr.* Carmina.

Formosa. Muriel Rukeyser. CP-RukeM

Forms and colors of my dreams have changed, The. New England, 1967. Jorge Luis Borges. SP-BorgJ, *tr.* by Stephen Kessler

Forms of Knowledge, The. Kenneth Patchen. CP-PatcK

Forms of Love, The. George Oppen. CP-OppGN

Forms of the Human. Richard Eberhart. CP-EberR

Forms' passage as. Robert Creeley. CP-CreeR

Forms, qualities, lives, humanity, language, thoughts. Germs. Walt Whitman. CP-WhitW

Formula. Langston Hughes. CP-HughL; CP-HughL1

Formulas of recognition, The. Several Love-Stories. Laura Riding Jackson. CP-RidiL

Formulation that, The. Square. A. R. Ammons. CP-AmmoA

Fornicator. A New Song. The. Robert Burns. CP-BurnR

Forsaken and Forlorn. D. H. Lawrence. CP-LawrD

Forsaken Girl, The. Eduard Friedrich Mörike. CP-JarrR, *tr. by* Randall Jarrell

Forsaken Harvest Field, The. Jones Very. CP-VeryJ

Forsaken Merman, The. Matthew Arnold. SP-ArnoM

Forsaken, The. William Wordsworth. CP-WorW1

Forsythia. Louis Zukofsky. CP-ZukLS

Fort Collins Remembered. Robert Creeley. SP-CreeR

Forte Dei Marmi. D. H. Lawrence. CP-LawrD

Forth from a Jutting Ridge, Around Whose Base. William Wordsworth. CP-WorW2

Forth from ages thick in mystery. Sine Prole. Thomas Hardy. CP-HardT

Forth from the glaring heat. By the Passeyr. George Meredith. CP-MerG2

Forth from the hand. At a Rest Stop in Ohio. Amy Clampitt. CP-ClamA

Forth rushed from Envy sprung and Self-conceit. Protest against the Ballot. William Wordsworth. CP-WorW2

Forth went the candid man. Stephen Crane. CP-CranS

Forthwith readily swathing her head in a sheeny fine linen. Helen on the Skaian Gates. Homer. CP-MerG2 *Fr.* Iliad, The.

Forties Flick. John Ashbery. SP-AshbJ

Fortification, A. Margaret Atwood. SP-AtwM1

Fortitude incarnate. Emily Dickinson. CP-DickE

Fortitude of the North, The. Herman Melville. SP-MelvH

Fortress, The. Louise Glück. SP-GlucL

Fortress, The. Anne Sexton. CP-SextA; SP-SextA

Fortù, fortù, my beloved one. Englishman in Italy, The. Robert Browning. CP-BroR1

Fortunate Child. Robert Graves. CP-GravR

Fortunate desecrate Nature, The. Melancholy Hours. Constantine P. Cavafy. CP-CavaC, *tr. by* Theoharis Constantine Theoharis

Fortunate land, that Egypt, where / From time to time the phoenix comes. Fact of the Matter, The. Hayden Carruth. CP-CarHS

Fortunate man it is not too late. Woodthrush, The. William Carlos Williams. CP-WilW2

Fortunate sheer a mile's upmost. Lily-of-the-Valley Fortunei. Louis Zukofsky. CP-ZukLS

Fortunate Traveller, The. Derek Walcott. CP-WalcD

Fortunatus. Ezra Pound. CP-PoEar

Fortune. Geoffrey Chaucer. CP-ChauG

Fortune. Robert Herrick. CP-HerrR

Fortune and Glory may be lost and woone. To the Most High and Mighty Prince Charles. Thomas Campion. CP-CampT

Fortune and Hope! I've made my port. Prudentius. CP-EmerR

Fortune did never favour one. Fortune Favours. Robert Herrick. CP-HerrR

Fortune doth frown. Sir Thomas Wyatt. CP-WyatT

Fortune Favours. Robert Herrick. CP-HerrR

Fortune favours the Brave, old Proverbs say. Mr Cromek to Mr Stothard. William Blake. CP-BlakW

Fortune! I thank thee: gentle Goddess! thanks! Verses Written at Bath on Finding the Heel of a Shoe. William Cowper. CP-CowpW

Fortune, Nature, Love. Sir Philip Sidney. SP-SidnP *Fr.* Arcadia.

Fortune, Nature, Love, long have contended about me. Fortune, Nature, Love. Sir Philip Sidney. SP-SidnP *Fr.* Arcadia.

Fortune no higher Project can devise. Discord Not Disadvantageous. Robert Herrick. CP-HerrR

Fortune Teller Blues. Langston Hughes. CP-HughL; CP-HughL1

Fortune teller looked in my hand. Madam and the Fortune Teller. Langston Hughes. CP-HughL; CP-HughL2

Fortune Teller, The. Howard Nemerov. CP-NemeH

Fortune, what aileth thee. Sir Thomas Wyatt. CP-WyatT

Fortune's a blind profuser of her own. Fortune. Robert Herrick. CP-HerrR

Fortune's Mist. Richard Eberhart. CP-EberR

Forty Augusts—aye, and several more—ago. Voice of Things, The. Thomas Hardy. CP-HardT

Forty cards have taken the place of life. Truco. Jorge Luis Borges. SP-BorgJ, *tr. by* Alastair Reid

Forty feet long sixty feet high hotel. Heat. Allen Ginsberg. CP-GinsA

45 Mercy Street. Anne Sexton. CP-SextA

44th Birthday Evening, at Harris's. Ted Berrigan. SP-BerrT

49th and 5th, December 13. Josephine Jacobsen. CP-JacoJ

40 odd year old Para 10, A. Birth, The. William Carlos Williams. CP-WilW2

Forty-odd years ago—. Anniversaries. Thomas McGrath. SP-McGrT

Forty springs back, I recall. Opportunity, The. Thomas Hardy. CP-HardT

Forty-two years ago (to me if to no one else. Star-Gazer. Louis MacNeice. CP-MacNL

Forty Years. Wendell Berry. CP-BerrW

Forty years back, when much had place. George Meredith (1828-1909). Thomas Hardy. CP-HardT

Forty Years On. W. H. Auden. CP-AudeW

Forward rush by the lamp in the gloom, A. Contretemps, The. Thomas Hardy. CP-HardT

Forward she leans, with hollowing back, stock-still. Io. Gerard Manley Hopkins. CP-HopkG

Forward! You must. Keep. Hayden Carruth. CP-CarHS *Fr.* Clay Hill Anthology, The.

Forward Youth that would appear, The. Horatian Ode upon Cromwell's Return from Ireland, An. Andrew Marvell. CP-MarvA

Fossil Flower, The. Jones Very. CP-VeryJ

Fossil, fuchsia, mantis, man. Theme and Variation. Robert Earl Hayden. CP-HaydR

Fossil shells, far inland; a god; bones. Unresolved. Denise Levertov. SP-LeveDL

Fossil Unwound. Joseph Brodsky. CP-BrodJ

Foss'io regina / Tu re saresti. Christina Georgina Rossetti. CP-RosC3

Foster child of ragweed. Unnatural Deaths. Yusef Komunyakaa. CP-KomuY

Foster-Mother's Tale, The. Samuel Taylor Coleridge. CP-ColeS

Foster the Light. Dylan Thomas. CP-ThomD

Fosterling. Seamus Heaney. SP-HeanSO

Foul Babylon has overstepped the mark. Petrarch. CP-Petra, *tr. by* J. G. Nichols

Foul is she and ill-favoured, set askew. Babylon the Great. Christina Georgina Rossetti. CP-RosC2

Foul weather sighs old time. Azalea. Louis Zukofsky. CP-ZukLS

Foulest brute that stinks below. Clad All in Brown. Jonathan Swift. CP-SwifJ

Found. Dante Gabriel Rossetti. CW-RossD

Found a family, build a state. Fragments of a Lost Gnostic Poem of the Twelfth [*or* 12th] Century. Herman Melville. SP-MelvH

Found in a Notebook. William Corbett. SP-CorbW

Found in a Storm. William Stafford. SP-StafW; SP-StafWW

Found myself wondering / if i had entered. Yeti Poet Returns to His Village to Tell His Story, The. Lucille Clifton. SP-ClifL

Foundations of American Industry, The. Donald Hall. CP-HallD

Founded on rock and facing the night-fouled sea. Beacon, The. Richard Wilbur. CP-WilbR

Founder, The. George Oppen. CP-OppGN

Founder of the Feast, The. Robert Browning. CP-BroR2

Founderous wilding weeds endear paradise. Weeds. Louis Zukofsky. CP-ZukLS

Foundling, A. Margaret Atwood. SP-AtwM1

Foundlings in the Yukon. A. K. Ramanujan. CP-RamaA

Foundry of the dead, the dead invisible hammer. Ghost Hammer, The. Robert Pinsky. CP-PinsR

Fount of Tears, The. Paul Laurence Dunbar. CP-DunbP

Fountain. Federico García Lorca. CP-GarcF, *tr. by* Jerome Rothenberg *Fr.* Secrets.

Fountain. Charles Tomlinson. SP-TomlC

Fountain, The. Rainer Maria Rilke. CP-RilkFr, *tr. by* A. Poulin, Jr. *Fr.* Orchards.

Fountain, The. Donald Davie. CP-DaviDC

Fountain, The. Denise Levertov. SP-LeveDP

Fountain, The. W. S. Merwin. SP-MerwWF

Fountain, The. John Greenleaf Whittier. CP-WhitJ

Fountain, The. William Wordsworth. CP-WorW1; MW-WorW

Fountain, a Bottle, a Donkey's Ears and Some Books, A. Robert Frost. CP-FrosR

Fountain flows, but where the bowl, The. Broken Bowl, The. Jones Very. CP-VeryJ

Fountain—from four blocks away—can look like ice, A. Gate Is Prouti, The. Charles Olson. CP-OlsoC

Fountain in its source, The. Living Water. Jeanne Marie Bouvier de la Motte-Guyon. CP-CowpW

Fountain of Arethusa, The. Donald Davie. CP-DaviDC

Fountain of Blood. Charles Baudelaire. CP-BaudC, *tr. by* Walter Martin

Fountain of Cyanë, The. Donald Davie. CP-DaviDC

Fountain of our sweetest, quick to spring, A. J. C. M. George Meredith. CP-MerG1

Fountain of sorrow, dwelling-place of wrath. Petrarch. CP-Petra, *tr. by* J. G. Nichols

Fountain Piece. May Swenson. SP-SwenM

Fountains are dry and the roses over, The. Manor Garden, The. Sylvia Plath. CP-PlatS

Fountains mingle with the river, The. Love's Philosophy. Percy Bysshe Shelley. CP-ShelP

Fountains of Rome, The. Marya Alexandrovna Zaturenska.
"Flow, flow pure tears that from cold fountains run." SP-ZatuM

Four. Robert Creeley. CP-CreeR

Four, The. D. H. Lawrence. CP-LawrD

Four a.m. in summertime. Lovely Morning Thought. Arthur Rimbaud. CP-RimbA, *tr. by* Martin Sorrell

Four Ages of Man, The. William Butler Yeats. CP-YeatW

Four Ages, The. William Cowper. CP-CowpW

Four Ages, The. Howard Nemerov. CP-NemeH

4 AM Blues. Allen Ginsberg. SP-GinsA

4 a.m. freight comes pounding and shaking through the fall night, The. Don't You Hear that Whistle Blowin'. Denise Levertov. SP-LeveDL

4:00 A.M. on the Terrace. John Ciardi. CP-CiarJ

Four Angels, The. Rudyard Kipling. CP-KiplR

Four Archangels, so the legends tell, The. Legend of Mirth, The. Rudyard Kipling. CP-KiplR

Four Auguries. Margaret Atwood. SP-AtwM1

Four Ballads in Yellow. Federico García Lorca. CP-GarcF, *tr. by* Jerome Rothenberg

Four be the things I am wiser to know. Inventory. Dorothy Parker. CP-ParkD

Four Beginnings / for Kyra. Olga Broumas. SP-BrouO

Four billion people on this earth. Large Number, A. Wisława Szymborska. SP-SzymW, *tr. by* Stanislaw Barańczak *and* Clare Cavanagh

Four billion people on this earth. Large Number, A. Wisława Szymborska. SP-SzymWM, *tr. by* Joanna Trzeciak

Four boards of the coffin lid, The. After Death. Algernon Charles Swinburne. SP-SwinA

Four bright steel crosses. Detroit Grease Shop Poem. Philip Levine. SP-LeviP

Four Brothers, The. Carl Sandburg. CP-SandC

Four climbed High-Stoy from Ivelwards. Under High-Stoy Hill. Thomas Hardy. CP-HardT

Four close but several trees, each green, none equal. Democrats. Donald Davie. CP-DaviDC

Four Dancers at an Irish Wedding. Tess Gallagher. SP-GallT

Four days with you, my father three months dead. Stream, The. Mona Van Duyn. SP-VanDM

Four Elements, The. Anne Bradstreet. CP-BradA

Four Epitaphs. Countee Cullen.
For a Lady I Know. CP-CullC
For John Keats, Apostle of Beauty. CP-CullC
For My Grandmother. CP-CullC

For Paul Laurence Dunbar. CP-CullC

Four Exposures. Richard Eberhart. CP-EberR

Four-faced clocks on market-towers school the town. On a Delhi Sundial. A. K. Ramanujan. CP-RamaA

Four-Feet. Rudyard Kipling. CP-KiplR

Four Fiery Steed Impatient of the Rein. William Wordsworth. CP-WorW2

Four-footed at dawn, in the daytime tall. Oedipus and the Enigma. Jorge Luis Borges. SP-BorgJ, *tr. by* Alan S. Trueblood

Four Footprints. Thomas Hardy. CP-HardT

Four for Sir John Davies. Theodore Roethke. CP-RoetT

Four ghosts now walk the Russian forests, girls. Marya Alexandrovna Zaturenska. SP-ZatuM

Four Good Things. James McMichael. SP-McMiJ

Four Haiku. Allen Ginsberg. CP-GinsA

403 Blues. Langston Hughes. CP-HughL; CP-HughL2

400-Meter Freestyle. Maxine W. Kumin. SP-KumiM

Four hundred years ago a tangled waste. Columbian Ode. Paul Laurence Dunbar. CP-DunbP

Four in a Family. Muriel Rukeyser. CP-RukeM

Four in the Morning. Thomas Hardy. CP-HardT

Four Inscriptions for the Sundial of a Lost Race of Polyphemus. Robert Stock. SP-StocR

Four Kantian Lyrics. Charles Tomlinson. CP-TomlC

Four Lakes' Days. Richard Eberhart. CP-EberR

Four little girls. Birmingham Sunday. Langston Hughes. CP-HughL; CP-HughL3

Four maner of folkis ar evill to pleis. William Dunbar. CP-DunbW

Four Medieval Latin Poems. *Various authors.* CP-MacNL

Four men got in discussion. Each one said. Metamorphosis. Chuang Tzu. CP-MertT

Four Motions for the Pea Vines. A. R. Ammons. CP-AmmoA

Four nights after the moon's full. Grunion Run. Robert Stock. SP-StocR

Four-o'clock. Louis Zukofsky. CP-ZukLS

Four o'clock this afternoon. Cortège. Edwin Arlington Robinson. CP-RobiE

Four of the generations are taking tea. On The Terrace. Charles Tomlinson. SP-TomlC *Fr.* For A Granddaughter.

Four of us lived off half an acre. Gen. Rodimstev's Story / (Stalingrad). Lorine Niedecker. CP-NiedL

Four of us sitting around that afternoon, The. Slippers. Raymond Carver. CP-CarvR

Four or five dumb upstarts. Han-shan. CP-ColdM, *tr. by* Red Pine

4 Other Countries. Louis Zukofsky. CP-ZukLS

Four pelicans went over the house. Pelicans. Robinson Jeffers. CP-JefR1

Four Poems. Elizabeth Bishop. CP-BishE

Four Poems. James Schuyler. CP-SchuJ

Four Poems after Rilke. Heather McHugh. SP-McHuH

Four Poems for Robin. Gary Snyder. CP-SnydG

Four Poems Regarding the Endurance of Poets. Geoffrey Hill. CP-HillG

Four Points, The. Rudyard Kipling. CP-KiplR *Fr.* Muse among the Motors, The.

Four pomegranate trees. Brief Madrigal. Federico García Lorca. CP-GarcF, *tr. by* Alan S. Trueblood *Fr.* Love.

Four Preludes on Playthings of the Wind. Carl Sandburg. CP-SandC

Four Quartets. T. S. Eliot. CP-ElioT

Four Quartz Crystal Clocks. Marianne Craig Moore. CP-MoorM

Four Resurrections in the Valley of the Ghosts. Yehuda Amichai. SP-AmicYL, *tr. by* Benjamin Harshav *and* Barbara Harshav

Four-room shack aspiring high. Robert Frost. CP-FrosR

Four Sambas. *Unknown.* CP-BishE

Four seasons fill the measure of the year. Human Seasons, The. John Keats. CP-KeatJ

Four Seasons in American Woods. Robert Bly.
"Spring has come; I look up and see." SP-BlyR

Four Seasons of the Year, The. Anne Bradstreet. CP-BradA

Four Short Pieces. Grace Paley. CP-PalGC

462-0614. Charles Bukowski. SP-BukC1

Four skin heads stand in the streetlight rain chatting under an umbrella. American Sentences. Allen Ginsberg. SP-GinsA

Four Small Elegies. Margaret Atwood. SP-AtwM2

Four Small Windows. Jaroslav Seifert. SP-SeifJ, *tr. by* Ewald Osers

4 Sniffs & I'm High. Aether. Allen Ginsberg. CP-GinsA

Four Songs, by Way of Chorus To a Play. Thomas Carew. CP-CareT

Four songs that follow now, The. Fernando Pessoa. SP-PessF *Fr.* Keeper of Sheep, The.

Four Songs the Night Nurse Sang. Robert Duncan. SP-DuncR

Four Sonnets. Howard Nemerov. CP-NemeH

Four Steichen Prints. Carl Sandburg. CP-SandC

Four sweaters are woven upon me. Springer Mountain. James Dickey. CP-DickJ

Four Sweet Months, The. Robert Herrick. CP-HerrR

(Succession of the Foure Sweet Months, The.) CP-HerrR

Four synagogues are entrenched together. Yehuda Amichai. SP-AmicY, *tr. by* Chana Bloch *Fr.* Songs of Zion the Beautiful.

Four talked about the pine tree. One defined it by genus, species, and variety. Conversation. Dan Pagis. SP-PagiD, *tr. by* Stephen Mitchell

4:30 A.M. Charles Bukowski. SP-BukC2

Four-thirty in the morning. Fragment of New York, 1929. Richard Eberhart. CP-EberR

Four III. E. E. Cummings. CP-CummE; SP-CummE

Four Trees—upon a solitary Acre. Emily Dickinson. CP-DickE

Four waitresses (one a lovely eagle). Caffè Dante in New York—1. Yehuda Amichai. SP-AmicYL, *tr. by* Benjamin Harshav *and* Barbara Harshav

Four waitresses talking in the tongue. Caffè Dante in New York—2. Yehuda Amichai. SP-AmicYL, *tr. by* Benjamin Harshav *and* Barbara Harshav

Four walls can hold. Walls. Langston Hughes. CP-HughL; CP-HughL2

Four Walls of My Room, The. Constantine P. Cavafy. CP-CavaC, *tr. by* Theoharis Constantine Theoharis

Four Ways of Knowledge. Robert Bly. SP-BlyR

Four Winter Flies. Wyatt Prunty. SP PrunW

Four years ago I met your death here. Letter from Chicago. May Sarton. SP-SartM

Four Years Later. Robert Creeley. SP-CreeR

Four years my father fought their wars in vain. Yehuda Amichai. SP-AmicYL *Fr.* Here We Loved.

Four[e] Monarchies, The. Anne Bradstreet. CP-BradA

Foure Teeth thou had'st that ranck'd in goodly state. Out of Martiall. Martial. CP-CrasR

Four[e] Things Make Us Happy Here. Robert Herrick. CP-HerrR

Fourfold Aspect, The. Elizabeth Barrett Browning. CP-BroEB

Fourteen. Marilyn Hacker. SP-HackM

Fourteen, a sonneteer thy praises sings. Sonnet upon Sonnets, A. Robert Burns. CP-BurnR

Fourteen centuries fall away, The. Shadow and the Light, The. John Greenleaf Whittier. CP-WhitJ

Fourteen people have been known to come again. One came. Little Novel, A. Gertrude Stein. CP-SteiG

Fourteen-year-old, why must you giggle and dote. Conventionalist, The. Stevie Smith. CP-SmitS

Fourth. Hayden Carruth. CP-CarHS

Fourth Act. Robinson Jeffers. CP-JefR3

Fourth Caprice in Montparnasse. T. S. Eliot. SP-ElioT

Fourth David, The. Eleanor Wilner. SP-WilnE

Fourth Elegy. The Refugees. Muriel Rukeyser. CP-RukeM

Fourth Floor, Dawn, Up All Night Writing Letters. Allen Ginsberg. CP-GinsA; SP-GinsA

Fourth Grade, The. Thomas Lux. SP-LuxT

Fourth Limick. Ogden Nash. CP-NashO

4th May Morning. Christina Georgina Rossetti. CP-RosC3

Fourth of July. Ted Hughes. CP-HughTN

4th of July. William Carlos Williams. CP-WilW1

Fourth of July. A stillness across the morning like. After Rereading Robert Graves, I Go Outside to Get My Head Together. Charles Wright. SP-WrigCN

Fourth of July in Maine. Robert Lowell. SP-LoweR

Fourth of July Night. Carl Sandburg. CP-SandC

Fourth of July, The. Howard Nemerov. CP-NemeH

Fourth of July, The. Richard Wilbur. CP-WilbR

Fourth of July Thought. Langston Hughes. CP-HughL; CP-HughL3

Fourth of October, 1963, The. Philip Whalen. SP-WhalP

Fourth Page. Federico García Lorca. CP-GarcF, *tr. by* Jerome Rothenberg *Fr.* White Album.

Fourth Psalm. Anne Sexton. SP-SextA *Fr.* O Ye Tongues.

Fourth Psalm: The Cerements. W. S. Merwin. SP-MerwW

Fourth Song, The. Thomas Carew. CP-CareT *Fr.* Carew's Masque.

Fous qui disiez. Samuel Beckett. CP-BeckS

Foutains of Aix. May Swenson. SP-SwenM

Fowls speak and sing, settling for the night, The. Winter Nightfall. Wendell Berry. CP-BerrW

Fowre Hymnes. Edmund Spenser. CP-Spens

Fox. Lucille Clifton. SP-ClifL

Fox, The. Philip Levine. SP-LeviP

Fox, The. Paul Muldoon. CP-MuldP

Fox, The. Kenneth Patchen. CP-PatcK

Fox, The. Charles Tomlinson. CP-TomlC

Fox and the Bird, The. Jones Very. CP-VeryJ

Fox and the Grapes, The. Marianne Craig Moore. CP-MoorM *Fr.* Fables of La Fontaine.

Fox Blood. James Dickey. CP-DickJ

Fox came every evening to my door, The. Telling Our Stories. Lucille Clifton. SP-ClifL

Fox Gallery, The. Charles Tomlinson. CP-TomlC; SP-TomlC

Fox-Hunting. Rudyard Kipling. CP-KiplR

Fox / is so quiet, The. Snowshoe Hare, The. Mary Oliver. SP-OlivM

Fox lifts his head from the feathers, The. Ghost Story, A. Randall Jarrell. CP-JarrR

Fox of Gascon, though some say of Norman descent, A. Fox and the Grapes, The. Marianne Craig Moore. CP-MoorM *Fr.* Fables of La Fontaine.

Fox, the owl, the spider, and the mole, The. William Blake. CP-BlakW

Fox was crossing the, A. Failure of Communication in the Animal Kingdom, A. James Laughlin. CP-LaugJ

Fox Who Watched for the Midnight Sun, The. Norman Dubie. CP-DubiN

Foxes and pheasants adorn. Pouilly-Fuissé. Arthur Sze. SP-SzeA

Foxes' Moon. Charles Tomlinson. CP-TomlC

Foxfur. Robert Lowell. SP-LoweR

Foxgloves. Carl Sandburg. CP-SandC

Foxtail Pine. Gary Snyder. CP-SnydG

Fra Lippo Lippi. Robert Browning. CP-BroR1; SP-BroR

Fractal Song. Michael Palmer. SP-PalmM

Frae Anither Window in Thrums. Hugh MacDiarmid.
    "Gin but the oor 'ud chop and set me free." SP-MacDH
    "Here in the hauf licht hoo I've grown!" SP-MacDH
    "Here in the hauf licht waitin' till the clock." SP-MacDH
    "I'm weary o' the shapes mere chance can thraw." SP-MacDH
    "That's the condition o't or near." SP-MacDH

Frae the friends and Land I love. Robert Burns. CP-BurnR

Fragging. Yusef Komunyakaa. CP-KomuY

Fragile! Charles Bukowski. SP-BukC2

Fragile Vial, The. Jelaluddin Rumi. SP-Rumi, *tr. by* Coleman Barks

Fragment. Christopher Logue. SP-LoguC

Fragment 40: "Keep love and he wings." "H. D." CP-DoolH

Fragment 41: "Am I blind alas." "H. D." CP-DoolH

Fragment 68: "I envy you your chance of death." "H. D." CP-DoolH (Envy.) CP-DoolH

Fragment 113: "Not honey, / not the plunder of the bee." "H. D." CP-DoolH

Fragment, A. Robert Burns. *See* Green Grow[s] the Rashes

Fragment, A: "And the Woods, with gnarled and cruel." G. K. Chesterton. CP-ChesG

Fragment, A: "Could I remount the river of my years." Lord Byron. CP-Byron

Fragment, A: "Dreadful burden of our sins we feel, The." John Greenleaf Whittier. CP-WhitJ

Fragment, A: "On the street I am met with constant hostility." Robert Creeley. CP-CreeR

Fragment, A: "One night as I did wander." Robert Burns. CP-BurnR

Fragment: A Roman's Chamber. Percy Bysshe Shelley. CP-ShelP

Fragment: A Serpent-Face. Percy Bysshe Shelley. CP-ShelP

Fragment: A Somersetshire Tragedy. William Wordsworth. CP-WorW1

Fragment: A Tale Untold. Percy Bysshe Shelley. CP-ShelP

Fragment: A Wanderer. Percy Bysshe Shelley. CP-ShelP

Fragment, A: "When first I came to Stewart Kyle." Robert Burns. CP-BurnR

Fragment, A: "When *Guilford* good our Pilot stood." Robert Burns. CP-BurnR

Fragment, A: "When, to their airy hall, my fathers' voice." Lord Byron. CP-Byron

Fragment: "Alas! this is not what I thought life was." Percy Bysshe Shelley. CP-ShelP

Fragment: "All one winter, in every crowded hall." Denise Levertov. SP-LeveDL

Fragment: "Altho' my bed were in yon muir." Robert Burns. CP-BurnR

Fragment: Amor Aeternus. Percy Bysshe Shelley. CP-ShelP

Fragment: "And that I walk thus proudly crowned withal." Percy Bysshe Shelley. CP-ShelP

Fragment: Apostrophe to Silence. Percy Bysshe Shelley. CP-ShelP

Fragment: "Are you shaken, are you stirred." Robert Graves. CP-GravR

Fragment: "As bronze may be much beautified." Wilfred Owen. CP-OwenW

Fragment: "As for him who." William Carlos Williams. CP-WilW2

Fragment: "At last I entered a long dark gallery." Thomas Hardy. CP-HardT

Fragment: Beauty's Halo. Percy Bysshe Shelley. CP-ShelP

Fragment: "Cramped in that funnelled hole, they watched the dawn." Wilfred Owen. CP-OwenW

Fragment: Death in Life. Percy Bysshe Shelley. CP-ShelP

Fragment—Epistle from Esopus to Maria. Robert Burns. CP-BurnR

Fragment: "Faint white pillars that seem to fade." Edwin Arlington Robinson. CP-RobiE

Fragment: "Follow to the deep wood's weeds." Percy Bysshe Shelley. CP-ShelP

Fragment: "For let the impediment be what it may." William Wordsworth. CP-WorW1

Fragment from Correspondence. Howard Nemerov. CP-NemeH

Fragment from Dante. G. K. Chesterton. CP-ChesG

Fragment from Dove Cottage Manuscript 44 (I). William Wordsworth. CP-WorW1

Fragment from May. Philip Larkin. CP-LarkP

Fragment from the "Monk of Athos" Lord Byron. CP-Byron

Fragment from the Wandering Jew. Percy Bysshe Shelley. CP-ShelP

Fragment: "Gentle story of two lovers young, A." Percy Bysshe Shelley. CP-ShelP

Fragment: "Great Spirit whom the sea of boundless thought." Percy Bysshe Shelley. CP-ShelP

Fragment: "He came to him in the extasy of pray'r." William Cowper. CP-CowpW

Fragment: "Her flowing locks, the raven's wing." Robert Burns. CP-BurnR

Fragment: Home. Percy Bysshe Shelley. CP-ShelP

Fragment: "I faint, I perish with my love! I grow." Percy Bysshe Shelley. CP-ShelP

Fragment: "I saw his round mouth's crimson deepen as it fell." Wilfred Owen. CP-OwenW

Fragment: "I stood upon a heaven-cleaving turret." Percy Bysshe Shelley. CP-ShelP

Fragment: "I would not be a king—enough." Percy Bysshe Shelley. CP-ShelP

Fragment: Igniculus Desiderii. Percy Bysshe Shelley. CP-ShelP

Fragment in Correction of D. H. Lawrence. G. K. Chesterton. CP-ChesG

Fragment: "In vain did Time and Nature." William Wordsworth. CP-WorW1

Fragment: "Is it that in some brighter sphere." Percy Bysshe Shelley. CP-ShelP

Fragment, Janu'ry 1786. Annis Boudinot Stockton. CP-StocA

Fragment: Life Rounded with Sleep. Percy Bysshe Shelley. CP-ShelP

Fragment: Love the Universe To-day. Percy Bysshe Shelley. CP-ShelP

Fragment: Love's Tender Atmosphere. Percy Bysshe Shelley. CP-ShelP

Fragment: May the Limner. Percy Bysshe Shelley. CP-ShelP

Fragment: "Methought I was a billow in the crowd." Percy Bysshe Shelley. CP-ShelP

Fragment: Milton's Spirit. Percy Bysshe Shelley. CP-ShelP

Fragment: Music and Sweet Poetry. Percy Bysshe Shelley. CP-ShelP

Fragment: "My God, Bill, what have you done?" William Carlos Williams. CP-WilW2

Fragment: "My head is wild with weeping for a grief." Percy Bysshe Shelley. CP-ShelP

Fragment 1956. Allen Ginsberg. CP-GinsA

Fragment: "Not one corner of a foreign field." Wilfred Owen. CP-OwenW

Fragment: "Now health forsakes that angel face." Robert Burns. CP-BurnR

Fragment: "O thou immortal deity." Percy Bysshe Shelley. CP-ShelP

Fragment: "O'er the raised earth the gales of evening sigh." Samuel Taylor Coleridge. CP-ColeS

Fragment of a Bas Relief. John Ciardi. CP-CiarJ

Fragment of a Ghost Story. Percy Bysshe Shelley. CP-ShelP

Fragment of a "Gothic" Tale. William Wordsworth. CP-WorW1

Fragment of a Letter. Jaroslav Seifert. SP-SeifJ, *tr.* by Ewald Osers

Fragment of a Lost Poem. Robert Graves. CP-GravR

Fragment of a Meditation. Allen Tate. CP-TateA

Fragment of a Satire on Satire. Percy Bysshe Shelley. CP-ShelP

Fragment of a Sonnet: Farewell to North Devon. Percy Bysshe Shelley. CP-ShelP

Fragment of a Sonnet: To Harriet. Percy Bysshe Shelley. CP-ShelP

Fragment of an Ancient Tablet. Ted Hughes. SP-HughTN

Fragment of an Epistle to Thomas Moore. Lord Byron. CP-Byron

Fragment of an Intended Poem on Milton, Written in the Copy of *Paradise Lost* Which Belonged to Wordsworth at Cambridge. William Wordsworth. CP-WorW1

Fragment of an Ode to Maia Written on May Day, 1818. John Keats. CP-KeatJ
(Ode to May. Fragment.) CP-KeatJ

Fragment of Anything You Like, A. Gerard Manley Hopkins. CP-HopkG

Fragment of *Brutus*, an Epic. Alexander Pope. CP-PopeA

Fragment of New York, 1929. Richard Eberhart. CP-EberR

Fragment of the "Castle Builder" John Keats. CP-KeatJ

Fragment of the Elegy on the Death of Adonis. Bion. CP-ShelP *Fr.* Lament for Adonis.

Fragment of weak flesh that circles round, A. Plan of Self-Subjection, A. Thom Gunn. CP-GunnT

Fragment: Omens. Percy Bysshe Shelley. CP-ShelP

Fragment—on Glenriddel's Fox Breaking His Chain, A. Robert Burns. CP-BurnR

Fragment on Hearing the Account of Mrs Ramseys Death. Annis Boudinot Stockton. CP-StocA

Fragment on Keats. Percy Bysshe Shelley. CP-ShelP

Fragment on the British Museum. Alan Dugan. CP-DugaA

Fragment on the Death of a Minester. Annis Boudinot Stockton. CP-StocA

Fragment: "Once more the man stood, saying 'A cottage-door'." G. K. Chesterton. CP-ChesG

Fragment: Pater Omnipotens. Percy Bysshe Shelley. CP-ShelP

Fragment: Rain. Percy Bysshe Shelley. CP-ShelP

Fragment: Rain. Percy Bysshe Shelley. CP-ShelP

Fragment: Redundance. William Wordsworth. CP-WorW1

Fragment: Rome and Nature. Percy Bysshe Shelley. CP-ShelP

Fragment: "Rude wind is singing, The." Percy Bysshe Shelley. CP-ShelP

Fragment: Satan Broken Loose. Percy Bysshe Shelley. CP-ShelP

Fragment: "Such hope, as is the sick despair of good." Percy Bysshe Shelley. CP-ShelP

Fragment: Sufficient Unto the Day. Percy Bysshe Shelley. CP-ShelP

Fragment: The Baker's Cart. William Wordsworth. CP-WorW1

Fragment: The Deserts of Dim Sleep. Percy Bysshe Shelley. CP-ShelP

Fragment: The False Laurel and the True. Percy Bysshe Shelley. CP-ShelP

Fragment: The Lady of the South. Percy Bysshe Shelley. CP-ShelP

Fragment: The Lake's Margin. Percy Bysshe Shelley. CP-ShelP

Fragment: The Names II. Allen Ginsberg. CP-GinsA

Fragment: The Sepulchre of Memory. Percy Bysshe Shelley. CP-ShelP

Fragment: The Vine-Shroud. Percy Bysshe Shelley. CP-ShelP

Fragment: "There pipes the woodlark, and the song[-]thrush there." Thomas Gray. CP-GrayT
(Couplet about Birds.) CP-GrayT

Fragment 36 [*or* Thirty-Six]: "I know not what to do." "H. D." CP-DoolH

Fragment: Thoughts Come and Go in Solitude. Percy Bysshe Shelley. CP-ShelP

Fragment: To a Friend Released from Prison. Percy Bysshe Shelley. CP-ShelP

Fragment: To Byron. Percy Bysshe Shelley. CP-ShelP

Fragment: To Italy. Percy Bysshe Shelley. CP-ShelP

Fragment: To Music, A. Percy Bysshe Shelley. CP-ShelP

Fragment: To One Singing. Percy Bysshe Shelley. CP-ShelP

Fragment: "To the laboratory then I went. What little." John Ciardi. CP-CiarJ

Fragment: To the Mind of Man. Percy Bysshe Shelley. CP-ShelP

Fragment: To the Moon. Percy Bysshe Shelley. CP-ShelP

Fragment: To the People of England. Percy Bysshe Shelley. CP-ShelP

Fragment to W. C. W.'s Romance. William Carlos Williams. CP-PoEar, *tr.* by Ezra Pound

Fragment: "Unrisen splendour of the brightest sun." Percy Bysshe Shelley. CP-ShelP

Fragment: "Viewless and invisible Consequence, The." Percy Bysshe Shelley. CP-ShelP

Fragment: "Wake the serpent not—lest he." Percy Bysshe Shelley. CP-ShelP

Fragment: Wedded Souls. Percy Bysshe Shelley. CP-ShelP

Fragment: "What men gain fairly—that they should possess." Percy Bysshe Shelley. CP-ShelP

Fragment: "When a lover clasps his fairest." Percy Bysshe Shelley. CP-ShelP

Fragment: "When soft winds and sunny skies." Percy Bysshe Shelley. CP-ShelP

Fragment, Which Was Meant for the Beginning of an Elegy on the Late Miss Burnet of Monboddo, A. Robert Burns. CP-BurnR

Fragment: "Who can know more deeply than I your loneliness there?" Hayden Carruth. CP-CarHS

Fragment: "Why should we set these hearts of ours above." Dorothy Parker. CP-ParkD

Fragment: "Why, why tell thy lover." Robert Burns. CP-BurnR

Fragment: Wine of the Fairies. Percy Bysshe Shelley. CP-ShelP

Fragment: "Witness thou / The dear companion of my lonely walk." William Wordsworth. CP-WorW1

Fragment Written Shortly after the Marriage of Miss Chaworth. Lord Byron. CP-Byron

Fragment: "Ye gentle visitations of calm thought." Percy Bysshe Shelley. CP-ShelP

Fragment: "Yet once again" William Wordsworth. *See* Voice of the Derwent, The

Fragment: Zephyrus the Awakener. Percy Bysshe Shelley. CP-ShelP

Fragmentary Blue. Robert Frost. CP-FrosR

Fragmenti. Ezra Pound. CP-PoEar

Fragments. Gerard Manley Hopkins. CP-HopkG

Fragments. Gerard Manley Hopkins. CP-HopkG

Fragments. Gerard Manley Hopkins. CP-HopkG

Fragments. Gerard Manley Hopkins. CP-HopkG

Fragments. Gerard Manley Hopkins. CP-HopkG

Fragments. Rainer Maria Rilke.
"After a day of practical rain." CP-RilkFr, *tr.* by A. Poulin, Jr.
"Ah, sudden lover, we have simply." CP-RilkFr, *tr.* by A. Poulin, Jr.
"All condemns us to be part." CP-RilkFr, *tr.* by A. Poulin, Jr.
"All infatuated with the future, I contemplate the skies." CP-RilkFr, *tr.* by A. Poulin, Jr.
"All that was divine remains divine." CP-RilkFr, *tr.* by A. Poulin, Jr.
"And beauty becomes ever more difficult." CP-RilkFr, *tr.* by A. Poulin, Jr.

"And yet life's secret is in us." CP-RilkFr, *tr.* by A. Poulin, Jr.

"Are we the only ones to have received." CP-RilkFr, *tr.* by A. Poulin, Jr.

"At least let it be." CP-RilkFr, *tr.* by A. Poulin, Jr.

"At night, back upstairs." CP-RilkFr, *tr.* by A. Poulin, Jr.

"By sheer dint of prayer he makes himself an archangel." CP-RilkFr, *tr.* by A. Poulin, Jr.

"Capitals in bloom with Corinthian acanthus." CP-RilkFr, *tr.* by A. Poulin, Jr.

"Come admire this hour turning silver." CP-RilkFr, *tr.* by A. Poulin, Jr.

"Day is uncertain, night is ephemeral." CP-RilkFr, *tr.* by A. Poulin, Jr.

"Did the long goodbyes of dying water lilies." CP-RilkFr, *tr.* by A. Poulin, Jr.

"Divinity of the sleep of cats." CP-RilkFr, *tr.* by A. Poulin, Jr.

"Enormous and strong monks who from their place." CP-RilkFr, *tr.* by A. Poulin, Jr.

"Gods: those obstinates who live, The." CP-RilkFr, *tr.* by A. Poulin, Jr.

"How the night made her uncertain." CP-RilkFr, *tr.* by A. Poulin, Jr.

"How to make you linger more, lovely summer." CP-RilkFr, *tr.* by A. Poulin, Jr.

"If death were something evil, we'd be surrounded." CP-RilkFr, *tr.* by A. Poulin, Jr.

"If for just one day we knew." CP-RilkFr, *tr.* by A. Poulin, Jr.

"Instead of this life in which we remain." CP-RilkFr, *tr.* by A. Poulin, Jr.

"Is it the flight of God." CP-RilkFr, *tr.* by A. Poulin, Jr.

"King: a man who for a moment." CP-RilkFr, *tr.* by A. Poulin, Jr.

"Let us not name what was the past." CP-RilkFr, *tr.* by A. Poulin, Jr.

"Let your absence be the latest shape." CP-RilkFr, *tr.* by A. Poulin, Jr.

"Let's not be obstinate, for all reveals." CP-RilkFr, *tr.* by A. Poulin, Jr.

"Love, I know, is a loss." CP-RilkFr, *tr.* by A. Poulin, Jr.

"Monk locks himself up so that his god, The." CP-RilkFr, *tr.* by A. Poulin, Jr.

"Multiple song that carries to our ears." CP-RilkFr, *tr.* by A. Poulin, Jr.

"My heart, we must abdicate this waiting." CP-RilkFr, *tr.* by A. Poulin, Jr.

"No, I want no more: no." CP-RilkFr, *tr.* by A. Poulin, Jr.

"Now and then some animals stops you." CP-RilkFr, *tr.* by A. Poulin, Jr.

"Oh life lived since who knows when!" CP-RilkFr, *tr.* by A. Poulin, Jr.

"Oh moment, inconceivable to all." CP-RilkFr, *tr.* by A. Poulin, Jr.

"Onrushing spring, Oh secret will." CP-RilkFr, *tr.* by A. Poulin, Jr.

"Perhaps I'll find my lover." CP-RilkFr, *tr.* by A. Poulin, Jr.

"Profound lover rising from the earth." CP-RilkFr, *tr.* by A. Poulin, Jr.

"See how night opens for you its arms of space." CP-RilkFr, *tr.* by A. Poulin, Jr.

"Some slowness across the day." CP-RilkFr, *tr.* by A. Poulin, Jr.

"Star of our absent ones, O listless mirror." CP-RilkFr, *tr.* by A. Poulin, Jr.

"Stranger, don't forget to say goodbye." CP-RilkFr, *tr.* by A. Poulin, Jr.

"Sudden loss can be cruel, but that other, A." CP-RilkFr, *tr.* by A. Poulin, Jr.

"Suddenly I recall a place." CP-RilkFr, *tr.* by A. Poulin, Jr.

"We have made a new surface of the earth." CP-RilkFr, *tr.* by A. Poulin, Jr.

"We'd want a little mercy, a little." CP-RilkFr, *tr.* by A. Poulin, Jr.

"What stranger passion." CP-RilkFr, *tr.* by A. Poulin, Jr.

"When all I wanted was to sing." CP-RilkFr, *tr.* by A. Poulin, Jr.

"Why is our soul sometimes so weary." CP-RilkFr, *tr.* by A. Poulin, Jr.

"Will those who praise things go to paradise." CP-RilkFr, *tr.* by A. Poulin, Jr.

"Wind of what memory, from what life did the wind, The." CP-RilkFr, *tr.* by A. Poulin, Jr.

"You, all of you who know how to bless." CP-RilkFr, *tr.* by A. Poulin, Jr.

"You have the tender advantage over us." CP-RilkFr, *tr.* by A. Poulin, Jr.

Fragments According to the Gospel. Arthur Rimbaud. CP-RimbA, *tr.* by Martin Sorrell

see also Epipsychidion. Percy Bysshe Shelley. CP-ShelP

Fragments: "Decorous, and forbearing further correction" Robert Creeley. CP-CreeR

Fragments: Drafts, Mostly or All for a Poem on a Heroic Theme. William Wordsworth. CP-WorW1

Fragments for "The Harvest Home" and "The Doe" George Meredith. CP-MerG2

Fragments from an Apocryphal Gospal. Jorge Luis Borges. SP-BorgJ, *tr.* by Stephen Kessler

Fragments [*or* Poems] from Italy. John Ciardi. CP-CiarJ

Fragments from the Alfoxden Note-Book (II). William Wordsworth. CP-WorW1

Fragments from the Alfoxden Note-Book (III). William Wordsworth. CP-WorW1

Fragments from the Alfoxden Notebook (I). William Wordsworth. CP-WorW1

Fragments from the "Christabel" Note-book. William Wordsworth. CP-WorW1

Fragments: "Locke sank into a swoon." William Butler Yeats. CP-YeatW

Fragments of a Liquidation. Susan Howe. SP-HoweS

Fragments of a Lost Gnostic Poem of the Twelfth [*or* 12th] Century. Herman Melville. SP-MelvH

Fragments of an Elegy. Dan Pagis. SP-PagiD, *tr.* by Stephen Mitchell

Fragments of an Unfinished Drama. Percy Bysshe Shelley. CP-ShelP

Fragments on St. Winefred. Gerard Manley Hopkins. CP-HopkG

Fragments Supposed to Be Parts of Otho. Percy Bysshe Shelley. CP-ShelP

Fragments, The. Jones Very. CP-VeryJ

Fragments: "There was a jolly tinker came across the sea." T. S. Eliot. SP-ElioT

Fragments: "Whispers / Of springtime." Langston Hughes. CP-HughL; CP-HughL2

Fragments Written for Hellas. Percy Bysshe Shelley. CP-ShelP

Fragonard. Ogden Nash. CP-NashO

Fragonard, / Your spiral women. George Oppen. CP-OppGN

Fragrance is, The. Of Mathilde. Charles Olson. CP-OlsoC

Fragrance lingered in his room, perhaps, A. Final Hour. Yannis Ritsos. SP-RitsY, *tr.* by Kimon Friar

Fragrance of Life, Odor of Death. Denise Levertov. SP-LeveDL

Fragrance of the teapot, The. Kenneth Rexroth. CP-RexrK

Fragrant sag of fruit distinctly grouped, A. E. E. Cummings. CP-CummE

Frail as the leaves that quiver on the sprays. Homer. CP-JohnS *Fr.* Iliad, The.

Frail creatures are we all! To be the best. Humility the Mother of Charity. Samuel Taylor Coleridge. CP-ColeS

Frail woman there and childhood's tender years. At Sea ("Frail woman there and childhood's tender years"). Jones Very. CP-VeryJ

Frailty. George Herbert. CP-HerbG

Frailty, Thy Name Is a Misnomer. Ogden Nash. CP-NashO

Fram Pharos I have seen her white. Song from "Cleopatra" John Berryman. CP-BerrJ

Frame. Adrienne Rich. SP-RicA2

Frame, The. Charles Baudelaire. CP-BaudC, *tr.* by Walter Martin *Fr.* Phantom, A.

Frame defines a work of art, A. Frame, The. Charles Baudelaire. CP-BaudC, *tr.* by Walter Martin *Fr.* Phantom, A.

Frame within frame, the evolving conversation. Dancers Exercising. Amy Clampitt. CP-ClamA

Framed by our window, skaters, winding. Gothic Tale, A. Theodore Weiss. SP-WeisT

Framed in her phoenix fire-screen, Edna Ward. Cottage Street, 1953. Richard Wilbur. CP-WilbR

France. George Meredith. CP-MerG1

"Ah, what a dawn of splendour, when her sowers." CP-MerG1

"Behold, the Gods are with her, and are known." CP-MerG1

"Ever invoking fire from heaven, the fire." CP-MerG1

"Henceforth of her the Gods are known." CP-MerG1

"Look not for spreading boughs." CP-MerG1

"O she that made the brave appeal." CP-MerG1

"Swift fall the blows, and men upbraid." CP-MerG1

"They are with her now, and in her ears, and known." CP-MerG1

"We look for her that sunlike stood." CP-MerG1

France. Ambrose Bierce. SP-BierA

France. Rudyard Kipling. CP-KiplR

France: An Ode. Samuel Taylor Coleridge. CP-ColeS; MW-ColeS

France has victory, England yet firm shall stay. Possessions. Diana Gurney. SP-GurnI

France! How shall we call her belle again? La Belle, La Douce, La Grande. Countee Cullen. CP-CullC

France is no longer. Visit (1). George Oppen. CP-OppGN

France of the poujadiste! Right Wing Sympathies. Donald Davie. CP-DaviDC

France, one of the great modes of the human mind and heart. Letter to Pierre Emmanuel. Kathleen Jessie Raine. SP-RainK

France, The. 18th Year of These States. Walt Whitman. CP-WhitW

Frances (A Fragment) ("'Twixt Bedford Park and Westminster"). G. K. Chesterton. CP-ChesG

Frances ("Dearest, whatever others see"). G. K. Chesterton. CP-ChesG

Frances ("God made thee mightily, my love"). G. K. Chesterton. CP-ChesG

Francesca. Ezra Pound. CP-PoEar

Francesca da Rimini. Dante Alighieri. CW-RossD *Fr.* Divina Commedia.

Francesca in Winter. Stevie Smith. CP-SmitS

Francesca of Rimini. Dante Alighieri. CP-Byron *Fr.* Divina Commedia.

Francisco, I'll Bring You Red Carnations. Philip Levine. SP-LeviP

Francisco on his shelf. Santo. James Merrill. SP-MerrJ

Franck ne'r wore silk she sweares; but I reply. Upon Franck. Robert Herrick. CP-HerrR

Franck wo'd go scoure her teeth; and setting to't. Upon Franck. Robert Herrick. CP-HerrR

François Villon Forgotten. Carl Sandburg. CP-SandC

Frank Courtship, The. George Crabbe. SP-CrabG *Fr.* Tales.

Frank O'Hara. Ted Berrigan. SP-BerrT

Frankfurt, September. Paul Celan. SP-CelaP, *tr.* by John Felstiner

Frankie's Trade. Rudyard Kipling. CP-KiplR

Frankincense, The. Robert Herrick. CP-HerrR

Franklin Square. William Carlos Williams. CP-WilW2

Frankly, I Don't Care. Thomas Lux. SP-LuxT

Frankly, I don't care if the billionaire is getting divorced. Frankly, I Don't Care. Thomas Lux. SP-LuxT

Frank's Poem. Yusef Komunyakaa. CP-KomuY

Frantic elk climb from the valleys to escape the flies, The. On the Elk, Unwitnessed. Alan Dugan. CP-DugaA

Frantic throb of the train, The. Train at Night, A. D. H. Lawrence. CP-LawrD

Franz, a Goose. May Sarton. SP-SartM

Franz Liszt eloped with Countess Marie d'Agoult. Music. Raymond Carver. CP-CarvR

Franz Schubert: A Press Conference. Adam Zagajewski. SP-ZagaA, *tr. by* Renata Gorczynski

Fratello Mio, Zephyrus. Ezra Pound. CP-PoEar

Frater Ave Atque Vale. Alfred Tennyson. CP-TennA

Fraternal Rage, the guilty Thebes alarms. Publius Papinius Statius. CP-PopeA *Fr.* Thebais [*or* Thebaid].

Fratricide, The. John Greenleaf Whittier. CP-WhitJ

Frau Bauman, Frau Schmidt, and Frau Schwartze. Theodore Roethke. CP-RoetT

Frau Doktor, / Mama Brundig. Frog Prince, The. Anne Sexton. CP-SextA; SP-SextA

Fräulein Reads Instructive Rhymes. Maxine W. Kumin. SP-KumiM

Freak but moist flower, A. Love Plant, The. Anne Sexton. CP-SextA

Freaks of Fashion. Christina Georgina Rossetti. CP-RosC2

Fred. Miller Williams. CP-WillM

Fred and the Holy Grail. William Dickey. SP-DickW

Fred Astaire. William Corbett. SP-CorbW

Fred Astaire. It's all in the name. Fred. Single. Fred Astaire. William Corbett. SP-CorbW

"Fred, where is north?" West-Running Brook. Robert Frost. CP-FrosR

Freddy. Stevie Smith. CP-SmitS

Frederick Alexander Pott. Time's Fool. John Updike. CP-UpdiJ

Frederick Douglass. Paul Laurence Dunbar. CP-DunbP

Frederick Douglass. Robert Earl Hayden. CP-HaydR

Frederick Douglass: 1817–1895. Langston Hughes. CP-HughL; CP-HughL3

Fredome, honour and nobilnes. William Dunbar. CP-DunbW

Free, The. W. S. Merwin. SP-MerwW

Free bird leaps / on the back of the wind, A. Caged Bird. Maya Angelou. SP-AngeM

Free breath breathes in Nature, A. Walk in the Pastures, A. Jones Very. CP-VeryJ

Free evening fades, outside the windows fastened with decorative iron grilles, The. Evening in the Sanitarium. Louise Bogan. CP-BogaL

Free Fantasia: Tiger Flowers. Robert Earl Hayden. CP-HaydR

Free from the proud, the pompous, and the vain. To My Worthy Friend, Mr. T.B. One of the People Called Quakers. Christopher Smart. SP-SmarC

Free heart, that singest to-day. Calls on the Heart. Elizabeth Barrett Browning. CP-BroEB

Free Love: A Sonnet. G. K. Chesterton. CP-ChesG

Free Man. Langston Hughes. CP-HughL; CP-HughL2

Free man, you'll always love the open sea! Man and Sea. Charles Baudelaire. CP-BaudC, *tr. by* Walter Martin

Free of memory and hope. Remorse for Any Death. Jorge Luis Borges. SP-BorgJ, *tr. by* W. S. Merwin

Free One, A. W. H. Auden. *See* Watch Any Day

Free thyself from wo. Hafiz. CP-EmerR *Fr.* Odes.

FREE / To the World. Man! Archibald MacLeish. SP-MacLA

Free to travel, he still couldn't be shown how lucky. David Walker (1785–1830). Rita Dove. SP-DoveR

Free Variation on a Translation from Greek. Alan Dugan. CP-DugaA

Free Welcome. Robert Herrick. CP-HerrR

Free! while in the cathedral at Seville. Heaven. John Berryman. SP-BerrJ

Free Will. D. H. Lawrence. CP-LawrD

Freed dove flew to the Rajah's tower, The. Dove of Dacca, The. Rudyard Kipling. CP-KiplR

Freed from Another Context. Eleanor Wilner. SP-WilnE

Freed Islands, The. John Greenleaf Whittier. CP-WhitJ

Freed the Fret of Thinking. Thomas Hardy. CP-HardT

Freedmen of the Mississippi Valley, The. Jones Very. CP-VeryJ

Freedom. Ambrose Bierce. SP-BierA *Fr.* Devil's Dictionary, The.

Freedom. Ralph Waldo Emerson. CP-EmerR

Freedom. Denise Levertov. SP-LeveDL

Freedom. William Stafford. SP-StafWW

Freedom a fortress firm shall stand. Ode to Freedom. Jones Very. CP-VeryJ

Freedom and Discipline. Hayden Carruth. CP-CarHS

Freedom and Union. Jones Very. CP-VeryJ

Freedom, as every schoolboy knows. Freedom. Ambrose Bierce. SP-BierA *Fr.* Devil's Dictionary, The.

Freedom as Experience. Thomas Merton. CP-MertT

Freedom, farewell! Or so the soldiers say. Port of Embarkation. Randall Jarrell. CP-JarrR

Freedom ("Freedom will not come"). Langston Hughes. CP-HughL; CP-HughL3 (Democracy.) CP-HughL2

Freedom in Brazil. John Greenleaf Whittier. CP-WhitJ

Freedom in love? It has been questioned. Think. Sonnet: "Freedom in love? It has been questioned. Think." Hayden Carruth. CP-CarHS *Fr.* Sonnets.

Freedom is a Habit. Carl Sandburg. CP-SandC

Freedom / Is just frosting. Frosting. Langston Hughes. CP-HughL; CP-HughL3

Freedom is not following a river. Freedom. William Stafford. SP-StafWW

Freedom Machine, The. Dan Pagis. SP-PagiD, *tr. by* Stephen Mitchell

Freedom National, Slavery Sectional. Jones Very. CP-VeryJ

Freedom, New Hampshire. Galway Kinnell. SP-KinnGN

Freedom of Expression. William Stafford. SP-StafWW

Freedom of Saturday afternoons, The. Sunstruck. Ted Hughes. SP-HughTN

Freedom of the Moon, The. Robert Frost. CP-FrosR

Freedom of the wholly mad, The. Phenomenology of Anger, The. Adrienne Rich. SP-RicA1; SP-RicA2

Freedom Seeker. Langston Hughes. CP-HughL; CP-HughL1

Freedom ("Some folks think / By burning books"). Langston Hughes. CP-HughL; CP-HughL2

Freedom ("Some folks think / By burning churches"). Langston Hughes. CP-HughL; CP-HughL3

Freedom: The Unmolested Eagle of Myself. Charles Bukowski. SP-BukC2

Freedom Train. Langston Hughes. CP-HughL; CP-HughL3

Freedom will not come. Freedom ("Freedom will not come"). Langston Hughes. CP-HughL; CP-HughL3

Freedom's Plow. Langston Hughes. CP-HughL; CP-HughL2

Freehold. Robert Graves. CP-GravR

Freeing of the Dust, The. Denise Levertov. SP-LeveDL; SP-LeveDS

Freely Espousing. James Schuyler. CP-SchuJ

Freewheeling down the escarpment past the unpassing horse. Cyclist, The. Louis MacNeice. CP-MacNL

Freezeburn forms whirlpools and bearfur has curve. Curve. Heather McHugh. SP-McHuH

Freezing. William Meredith. SP-MereW

Freezing convict wanted, The. Thanksgiving for My Father, A. William Stafford. SP-StafW

Freezing Rain. Charles Wright. SP-WrigCN

Freighter, gay with rust, The. Jews at Haifa. Randall Jarrell. CP-JarrR

Frémont Campaign Song, A. John Greenleaf Whittier. CP-WhitJ

French, The. James Laughlin. CP-LaugJ

French and the Spanish Guerrillas, The. William Wordsworth. CP-WorW1

French Army in Russia 1812–1813, The. William Wordsworth. CP-WorW2

French blue morning. Poem: "French blue morning." William Corbett. SP-CorbW

French Distichs. Samuel Johnson. CP-JohnS

French for April Fool's. Michael Palmer. SP-PalmM

French Hill. Hayden Carruth. CP-CarHS

French is easy. Chacun à Son Berlitz. Ogden Nash. CP-NashO

French Revolution as It Appeared to Enthusiasts at Its Commencement. Reprinted from "The Friend" William Wordsworth. CP-WorW1

French Revolution, The. William Blake. CP-BlakW

French Wars, The. Rudyard Kipling. CP-KiplR

Frenzy. Clarence Major. SP-MajoC

Frenzy. Anne Sexton. CP-SextA; SP-SextA

Frequency of images of the moon, The. Study of Images 2. Wallace Stevens. CP-StevW; CP-StevWP

Frequent guest of hunger and cold, A. Han-shan. CP-ColdM, *tr. by* Red Pine

Frequently the woods are pink. Emily Dickinson. CP-DickE

Frequently when the night. Apparition, The. John Berryman. CP-BerrJ

Frequently, while I watch people playing chess. Pawn, The. Constantine P. Cavafy. CP-CavaC, *tr. by* Theoharis Constantine Theoharis

Fresco: Departure for an Imperialist War. Thomas McGrath. SP-McGrT

Fresh, A Memory ("Fresh, A"). Robert Creeley. SP-CreeR

Fresh Air. Kenneth Koch. SP-KochK

Fresh as the day, and new as are the hours. Song of Welcome to King Charles, A. Ben Jonson. CP-JonsB

Fresh Cheese and Cream. Robert Herrick. CP-HerrR

Fresh, flowery hill, so full of shade, so green. Petrarch. CP-Petra, *tr. by* J. G. Nichols

Fresh from the dewy hill, the merry year. Song: "Fresh from the dewy hill, the merry year." William Blake. CP-BlakW

Fresh from the knife and coming to. Louis MacNeice. CP-MacNL *Fr.* Jigsaws.

Fresh hair flickered at her brows, The. Gladstone. G. K. Chesterton. CP-ChesG

Fresh morning gusts have blown away all fear. To a Young Lady Who Sent Me a Laurel Crown. John Keats. CP-KeatJ

Fresh Paint. Theodore Weiss. SP-WeisT

"Fresh Paint?" I took that sign. Fresh Paint. Theodore Weiss. SP-WeisT

Fresh Spring has come with flower and leaf to warn. George Meredith. CP-MerG2

Fresh strewings [or strowings] allow. Peter-penny, The. Robert Herrick. CP-HerrR

Fresh Water. D. H. Lawrence. CP-LawrD

Freshet, The. Henry David Thoreau. CP-ThorH

Freshly, gaily, the rivulet flows. Shout to the Sheperds, A. Ralph Waldo Emerson. CP-EmerR

Freshman Blues. John Berryman. CP-BerrJ

Freshman Sonnet: Success. John Ciardi. CP-CiarJ

Freshness, The. Jelaluddin Rumi. SP-Rumi, tr. by Coleman Barks

Fret not thyself because of evildoers. Psalm 37: "Fret not thyself because of evildoers." Bible, O.T. CP-WyatT Fr. Psalms.

Fretful and sick, you ask. William Dickey. SP-DickW Fr. At Your Old House.

Fretful and sick, you long. William Dickey. SP-DickW Fr. At Your Old House.

Friar had said his paternosters duly, The. Necrological. John Crowe Ransom. SP-RansJ

Friar uxorious! George Meredith. CP-MerG2

Friary at Blossom, Prologue & Instructions, The. Norman Dubie. CP-DubiN

Friday Afternoon. James Whitcomb Riley. CP-RileJ

Friday arrives with all its attendant ecstasies. Called Back. Charles Wright. SP-WrigC

Friday first's the day appointed. To Dr. John MacKenzie. Robert Burns. CP-BurnR

Friday, Good Friday, which. Charles Olson. CP-OlsoC

Friday Lunchbreak. Gregory Orr. SP-OrrG

Friday Night. Robert Graves. CP-GravR

Friday Night. Robert Graves. CP-GravR

Friday Night in the Royal Station. Philip Larkin. CP-LarkP

Friday the Thirteenth. Allen Ginsberg. CP-GinsA

Friday's Child. W. H. Auden. CP-AudeW

Fridge, The. Paul Muldoon. CP-MuldP

Friend. Robert Creeley. SP-CreeR

Friend. Sam Hamill. SP-HamiS

Friend, The. Robert Creeley. CP-CreeR

Friend, The. Charles Olson. CP-OlsoC

Friend, The. Marge Piercy. SP-PierM

Friend, The. Stevie Smith. SP-SmitS

Friend, The. Henry David Thoreau. CP-ThorH

Friend, The. Miller Williams. CP-WillM

Friend Anguish reveals is, The. Emily Dickinson. SP-DickE

Friend by enemy I call you out. To Others than You. Dylan Thomas. CP-ThomD

Friend, call it bad karma if you're. Tanck's Song About the Jinx. Hayden Carruth. CP-CarHS Fr. Songs About What Comes Down: The Complete Works of Mr. Septic Tank.

Friend comes into my body, The. Jelaluddin Rumi. SP-Rumi, tr. by Coleman Barks

Friend, Ego's a bastard. Eleemosynary. Yusef Komunyakaa. CP-KomuY

Furius, with no key to service, no key. Catullus. See Friend Furius, / "who has no slaves & no money"

Friend Furius, / "who has no slaves & no money" Carmen 23. Catullus. CP-ZukLS Fr. Carmina.

Friend, / get up and listen. Landscape with Two Graves and an Assyrian Dog. Federico García Lorca. CP-GarcF, tr. by Greg Simon and Steven F. White

Friend has come by after twenty years, A. Hello. I'll Bet You Don't Know Who This Is. Miller Williams. CP-WillM

Friend I can trust is the one who will let me have my death, The. Ghazal. Adrienne Rich. CP-RicAE

Friend I commend to thee the narrow way. Then They That Feared the Lord Spake Often One to Another. Christina Georgina Rossetti. CP-RosC3

Friend, I well know that you know how to polish. Guido Orlandi. CP-CavaG, tr. by Marc Cirigliano

Friend in a tipi in the, A. Two Fawns That Didn't See the Light This Spring. Gary Snyder. CP-SnydG

Friend is a / solemnity, A. Emily Dickinson. SP-DickE

Friend is he, who, hunted as a foe, A. Nuru'ddin Abdu 'R-Rahman Jami. CP-EmerR

Friend, Lover, Husband, Sister, Brother! Exile, An. Samuel Taylor Coleridge. CP-ColeS

Friend o' the Poet, tired and leal. Poem: "Friend o' the Poet, tired and leal." Robert Burns. CP-BurnR

Friend of a wayward hour, you came. James Whitcomb Riley. CP-RileJ

Friend of hours when no on remains. Rainer Maria Rilke. CP-RilkFr, tr. by A. Poulin, Jr. Fr. Roses, The.

Friend of mine! whose lot was cast. Remembrance. John Greenleaf Whittier. CP-WhitJ

Friend of my earliest youth. To the Judge. James Whitcomb Riley. CP-RileJ

Friend of my many years! Legacy, A. John Greenleaf Whittier. CP-WhitJ

Friend of my soul! as with moist eye. Follen. John Greenleaf Whittier. CP-WhitJ

Friend of my winter, yesterday's friend. Winter. Pablo Neruda. SP-NeruP

Friend of my youth! when young we roved. To the Earl of Clare. Lord Byron. CP-Byron

Friend of the Fourth Decade, The. James Merrill. SP-MerrJ

Friend of the slave, and friend of all mankind. John Woolman. Jones Very. CP-VeryJ

Friend of the Slave, and yet the friend of all. Daniel Neall. John Greenleaf Whittier. CP-WhitJ

Friend of the wise! and teacher of the good! To William Wordsworth. Samuel Taylor Coleridge. CP-ColeS; MW-ColeS

Friend, on This Scaffold Thomas More Lies Dead. James Vincent Cunningham. CP-CunnJ

Friend, our closeness is this. Jelaluddin Rumi. SP-Rumi, tr. by Coleman Barks

Friend remarks to the Prophet, "Why is it" Deliberation. Jelaluddin Rumi. SP-Rumi, tr. by Coleman Barks

Friend Revisited, A. Donald Hall. CP-HallD

Friend Rundle fell with grievous bump. Epigram, An: "Friend Rundle fell with grievous bump." Jonathan Swift. CP-SwifJ

Friend saw the rooms, A. Boy's Room. George Oppen. CP-OppGN

Friend Says of Job. Robert Creeley. SP-CreeR

Friend, then, whatever has become of us. Rhetoric. Marilyn Hacker. SP-HackM

Friend (this is an imaginary letter). Marilyn Hacker. SP-HackM Fr. Separations.

Friend, thou beholdest the lightning? Who has the charge of it. Song in the Desert, A. Rudyard Kipling. CP-KiplR

Friend, well I know thou knowest well to bear. Prolonged Sonnet: He finds fault with the Conceits of the foregoing Sonnet. Guido Orlandi. CW-RossD, tr. by Dante Gabriel Rossetti

Friend, when the thundercloud is low. George Meredith. CP-MerG2

Friend who wild from Wisdom's way, The. To Mr. S. McKenzie. Robert Burns. CP-BurnR

Friend, with regard to this same hare. To the Rev. Mr. Powell. Christopher Smart. SP-SmarC

Friend, your white beard sweeps the ground. Stephen Crane. CP-CranS

Friendless. John Berryman. CP-BerrJ

Friendless and faint, with martyred steps and slow. Calvary. Edwin Arlington Robinson. CP-RobiE

Friendless in Clare, except Brian Boydell. Friendless. John Berryman. CP-BerrJ

Friendly Advice to a Lot of Young Men. Charles Bukowski. SP-BukC2

Friendly are meadows when the sun's gone in. Ivor Gurney. CP-GurnI

Friendly in a Friendly Way. Langston Hughes. CP-HughL

Friendly Touch, The. Ogden Nash. CP-NashO

Friends. John Ashbery. SP-AshbJ

Friends. G. K. Chesterton. CP-ChesG

Friends. John Ciardi. CP-CiarJ

Friends. A. E. Housman. CP-HousA

Friends. William Stafford. SP-StafWW

Friends. C. K. Williams. CP-WillC

Friends. William Butler Yeats. CP-YeatW

Friends, The. Robert Creeley. CP-CreeR

Friends, The. Shmuel HaNagid. SP-HaNaS

Friends, The. Rudyard Kipling. CP-KiplR

Friends, A Fence Surrounds Us. Shmuel HaNagid. SP-HaNaS, tr. by Peter Cole

Friends, a fence surrounds us. Friends, A Fence Surrounds Us. Shmuel HaNagid. SP-HaNaS, tr. by Peter Cole

Friends are nations in themselves. Emily Dickinson. SP-DickE

Friends Beyond. Thomas Hardy. CP-HardT

Friend's Burial, The. John Greenleaf Whittier. CP-WhitJ

Friends, Farewell. William Stafford. SP-StafWW

Friends, I commend to you the narrow way. Thy Friend and Thy Father's Friend Forget Not. Christina Georgina Rossetti. CP-RosC2

Friends I made have slipped and strayed, The. Leal, The. Dorothy Parker. CP-ParkD

Friend's Illness, A. William Butler Yeats. CP-YeatW

Friends make / the most of it. For Tom. Robert Creeley. CP-CreeR

Friends making off ahead of time. In Loving Memory of the Late Author of Dream Songs. William Meredith. SP-MereW

Friends, my heart is half aweary. Old Times Were the Best, The. James Whitcomb Riley. CP-RileJ

Friends of an Xmas ago. 1991. William Corbett. SP-CorbW

Friends of faces unknown and a land. Only a Curl. Elizabeth Barrett Browning. CP-BroEB

Friends of the River Trent. Stevie Smith. CP-SmitS

Friend's Song, A. Marya Alexandrovna Zaturenska. SP-ZatuM

Friends— / They cannot help. Henry David Thoreau. CP-ThorH

Friends to me are frozen wine. Ralph Waldo Emerson. CP-EmerR

Friends warned of moose that. Moose Wallow, The. Robert Earl Hayden. CP-

HaydR

Friends, when I think of how we talked and bored and bawled and banged. J.D.C. Unhung, The. G. K. Chesterton. CP-ChesG

Friends who come to see you, The. Sleep. James Schuyler. CP-SchuJ

Friendship. William Cowper. CP-CowpW

Friendship. Ralph Waldo Emerson. CP-EmerR

Friendship. Hafiz. CP-EmerR

Friendship. Henry David Thoreau. CP-ThorH

Friendship. Henry David Thoreau. CP-ThorH

Friendship. Jones Very. CP-VeryJ

Friendship agony! words came to me. Postscript, A. Hart Crane. CP-CranH

Friendship Greetings. Philip Whalen. SP-WhalP

Friendship ("I think awhile of Love, and while I think"). Henry David Thoreau. CP-ThorH

Friendship on Visit. Laura Riding Jackson. CP-RidiL

Friendship, peculiar Gift of Heav'n. Ode on Friendship, An. Samuel Johnson. CP-JohnS

Friendship: To J. M. S. Jones Very. CP-VeryJ

Friendship, when a friend meant a helping sword. No Resurrection. Robinson Jeffers. CP-JefR2

Frieze. Federico García Lorca. CP-GarcF, *tr. by* Alan S. Trueblood *Fr.* Theories.

Frigate Pelican, The. Marianne Craig Moore. CP-MoorM

Fright in the Dining Room. Federico García Lorca. CP-GarcF, *tr. by* Alan S. Trueblood *Fr.* Eros with a Cane.

Frightened at the slant of the writing, I looked up. At This Point on the Page. William Stafford. SP-StafWW

Frightened Bird, The. James Laughlin. CP-LaugJ

Frightened fearful afraid. Age. Grace Paley. CP-PalGC

Frightened Man, The. Louise Bogan. CP-BogaL

Frightened Men. Robert Graves. CP-GravR

Frightening the blood in its tunnel. Sunstroke. Ted Hughes. SP-HughTN

Frigid and sweet Her parting Face. Emily Dickinson. CP-DickE

Frigid roses to survive. Fan, A; of Méry Laurent. Stéphane Mallarmé. CP-MallS, *tr. by* Henry Weinfield

Fringed Gentian. Emily Dickinson. CP-DickE

Friskers, or, Gods and Men. Stevie Smith. CP-SmitS

Frisky Lamb, A. Christina Georgina Rossetti. CP-RosC2

Fritillary, The. John Updike. CP-UpdiJ

Frivolous Blind Death Child. James Tate. SP-TateJ

Frivolous can call me frivolous, The. Byzantine Gentleman, in Exile, Composing Verses, A. Constantine P. Cavafy. CP-CavaC, *tr. by* Theoharis Constantine Theoharis

Frivolous Conversation, A. Czeslaw Milosz. CP-MiloC; CP-MiloCN, *tr. by* Lillian Vallee

Frock. James Schuyler. CP-SchuJ

Frock coat and the snowy cuff, The. Portrait of the Engineer, A. Thomas Kinsella. CP-KinsT

Froebel be hanged! And Pestalozzi—pooh! To Miss Gage. Wallace Stevens. CP-StevWP

Frog, The. Paul Muldoon. CP-MuldP

Frog, The. James Whitcomb Riley. CP-RileJ

Frog and the Golden Ball, The. Robert Graves. CP-GravR

Frog Autumn. Sylvia Plath. CP-PlatS

Frog, first to strike his chord, The. Eugenio Montale. CP-MontE, *tr. by* Jonathan Galassi

Frog noise / suddenly stops. Lorine Niedecker. CP-NiedL

Frog Pond, The. Galway Kinnell. SP-KinnGN

Frog Prince, The. Anne Sexton. CP-SextA; SP-SextA

Frog Prince, The. Stevie Smith. CP-SmitS

Frog Songs. Carl Sandburg. CP-SandC

Frog, that Naked Creature, The. May Sarton. SP-SartM

Frogs Eat Butterflies. Snakes Eat Frogs. Hogs Eat Snakes. Men Eat Hogs. Wallace Stevens. CP-StevW; CP-StevWP

Frogs' eggs in globular clusters. Tommy's Pond. John Ciardi. CP-CiarJ

Frog's Fate, A. Christina Georgina Rossetti. CP-RosC3

Frogs of Bikini, The. Hans Magnus Enzensberger. SP-EnzeH

Frogs of expectation leaped out of me and came back, The. Yehuda Amichai. SP-AmicYL *Fr.* At Right Angles.

Frolic, A. Paul Laurence Dunbar. CP-DunbP

Frolic[k], A. Robert Herrick. CP-HerrR

Frollick Virgins once these were. How Pansies or Hearts-Ease Came First. Robert Herrick. CP-HerrR

From 112. Ezra Pound. *See* Cantos

From a Balloon. James Whitcomb Riley. CP-RileJ

From a beautiful mouth. Yannis Ritsos. SP-RitsY *Fr.* First Series.

From a Book. William Carlos Williams. CP-WilW1

From a Bus Window in Central Ohio, Just before a Thunder Shower. James Wright. CP-WrigJ

From a Chapter on Literature. Adrienne Rich. CP-RicAE

From a Clinic Waiting Room. Amy Clampitt. CP-ClamA

From a College Window. D. H. Lawrence. CP-LawrD

From a distance, he dims the lamp, moves chairs. Almost a Conjuror. Yannis Ritsos. SP-RitsY, *tr. by* Kimon Friar

From a documentary on marsupials I learn. Nurture. Maxine W. Kumin. SP-KumiM

From a Dream. David Ignatow. SP-IgnaD

From a duck's egg, a duck. Doubtless his relative Scamander. Homer. SP-LoguC *Fr.* Iliad, The.

From a D— W— in the N. C. Emily Jane Brontë. *See* Death Scene, A

From a Dungeon Wall in the Southern College. Emily Jane Brontë. CP-BronE

From a far mountain creeping down. Ralph Waldo Emerson. CP-EmerR

From a friend's friend I taste friendship. Dirge: "From a friend's friend I taste friendship." Stevie Smith. CP-SmitS

From a golden tier—among the silk ropes, grey gauzes, green velvets, and crystal discs. Flowers. Arthur Rimbaud. CP-RimbA, *tr. by* Martin Sorrell

From a / highway below a face. View of a Lake. William Carlos Williams. CP-WilW1

From a Junk. Wallace Stevens. CP-StevWP

From a Letter from Lesbia. Dorothy Parker. CP-ParkD

From a libation cup. Shang Cup. Louis Zukofsky. CP-ZukLS

From a lineage of Protestant ministers. Yesterdays. Jorge Luis Borges. SP-BorgJ, *tr. by* Stephen Kessler

From a lofty mountain peak. Han-shan. CP-ColdM, *tr. by* Red Pine

From a Long Way Out of Pah-Gatzin-Kay. Thomas McGrath. SP-McGrT

From a magician's midnight sleeve. Late Air. Elizabeth Bishop. CP-BishE

From a Manhattan Tomb. Ogden Nash. CP-NashO

From a Milkweed Pod. Robert Frost. CP-FrosR
(Pod of the Milkweed.) CP-FrosR

From a Notebook. James Merrill. SP-MerrJ

From a parrot-heavy and speech-forsaken island. Epilogue to Robinson Crusoe. Dan Pagis. SP-PagiD, *tr. by* Stephen Mitchell

From a Photograph. George Oppen. CP-OppGN

From a Phrase of Simone Weil's and Some Words of Hegel's. George Oppen. CP-OppGN

From a place in the kingdom of France. Cloisters, The. Jorge Luis Borges. SP-BorgJ, *tr. by* W. S. Merwin

From a Plane. Denise Levertov. SP-LeveDL

From a Play. William Carlos Williams. CP-WilW2

From a Play: Publisher's Song. Muriel Rukeyser. CP-RukeM

From a Record of Disappointment. Howard Nemerov. CP-NemeH

From a Schuylkill in mid-earth there came emerging. Completely New Set of Objects, A. Wallace Stevens. CP-StevW; CP-StevWP

From a Series. W. S. Merwin. SP-MerwW

From a single grain they have multiplied. Crows. Mary Oliver. SP-OlivM

From a Survivor. Adrienne Rich. SP-RicA1; SP-RicA2

From a Swiss Lake. Eugenio Montale. CP-MontE, *tr. by* Jonathan Galassi

From a tavern fight, where he was wounded. In a Town of Osroini. Constantine P. Cavafy. CP-CavaC, *tr. by* Theoharis Constantine Theoharis

From A to Z. Theodore Weiss. SP-WeisT

From a Tower. Eugenio Montale. CP-MontE, *tr. by* Jonathan Galassi

From a Train Window. Edna St. Vincent Millay. CP-MillE

From a Trilogy of Birds. Andrei Codrescu. SP-CodrA

From a Vagabond. Wallace Stevens. CP-StevWP

From a Very Little Sphinx. Edna St. Vincent Millay. CP-MillE

From a view to a kill in pursuit. Leicestershire. Donald Davie. CP-DaviDC

From a Window. William Carlos Williams. CP-WilW2

From a Winter Journal. Marya Alexandrovna Zaturenska. SP-ZatuM

From a woman's dream of being. Written in Water. Amy Clampitt. CP-ClamA

From Above. John Updike. CP-UpdiJ

From above the green mist. Horizon. Federico García Lorca. CP-GarcF, *tr. by* Jerome Rothenberg *Fr.* Six Songs at Nightfall.

From Adam's Diary. John Ciardi. CP-CiarJ

From air seen fathom-deep. Island in the Works. James Merrill. SP-MerrJ

From all I did and all I said. Hidden Things. Constantine P. Cavafy. CP-CavaC, *tr. by* Theoharis Constantine Theoharis

From all the generations of past roses. Rose and Milton, A. Jorge Luis Borges. SP-BorgJ, *tr. by* Alastair Reid

From all the Jails the Boys and Girls. Emily Dickinson. CP-DickE

From all the rest I single you out, having a message for you. To One Shortly to Die. Walt Whitman. CP-WhitW

From all the spaces between times. Yehuda Amichai. SP-AmicYL, *tr. by* Benjamin Harshav *and* Barbara Harshav

From Alton Bay to Sandwich Dome. Wood Giant, The. John Greenleaf Whittier. CP-WhitJ

From America comes the little huming-bird. Vermont Apollinaire. William Corbett. SP-CorbW

From an Artist's House. Carolyn Kizer. CP-KizeC

From an Asian Tent. Thom Gunn. CP-GunnT

From an empty sky. Object in a Setting. Charles Tomlinson. CP-TomlC

From an Old House in America. Adrienne Rich. SP-RicA1; SP-RicA2

From Anacreon. Lord Byron. CP-Byron

From Anacreon. Lord Byron. CP-Byron

From announcements in the paper and on bulletin boards. Lost Objects. Yehuda Amichai. SP-AmicY, *tr. by* Chana Bloch

From Another Sore Fit. Anne Bradstreet. CP-BradA

From any event intervals radiate in. Fundamental Disagreement with Two Contemporaries. Kenneth Rexroth. CP-RexrK

From any hedgerow, any copse. Gerard Manley Hopkins. CP-HopkG

From bar to bar, from curb to curb I run. Cupid and Venus. Mark Alexander Boyd. CP-KizeC, *tr. by* Carolyn Kizer

From barren coldness birds. Games Two. Richard Wilbur. CP-WilbR

From behind he takes her waist. First Dances. Frank O'Hara. SP-OharF

From behind my eyes. Perspective. Federico García Lorca. CP-GarcF, *tr. by* Jerome Rothenberg *Fr.* In the Garden of the Lunar Grapefruits.

From Below. James Whitcomb Riley. CP-RileJ

From below, the waist-thick pine. Yggdrasill. Paul Muldoon. CP-MuldP

From beneath two arching brows. Michelangelo Buonarroti. CP-Miche, *tr. by* John Frederick Nims

From "Bird Conversations." Farid-uddin Attar. CP-EmerR

From blackhearted water colder. Castles and Distances. Richard Wilbur. CP-WilbR

From Blank to Blank. Emily Dickinson. CP-DickE

From boat to boat the bridge makes long its strand. For Italico Brass. Ezra Pound. CP-PoEar

From broken sleep I rose, from dream as clear as truth. Dream Message. Marya Alexandrovna Zaturenska. SP-ZatuM

From Brooklyn Heights one sees the bay. With a Photograph to Zell, Now Bound for Spain. Hart Crane. CP-CranH

From Brooklyn, over the Brooklyn Bridge, on this fine morning. Invitation to Miss Marianne Moore. Elizabeth Bishop. CP-BishE

From Cádiz to Gibraltar. Night Song of the Andalusian Sailors. Federico García Lorca. CP-GarcF, *tr. by* Christopher Maurer

From Canto 115: "Scientists are in terror, The." Ezra Pound. CP-PoCan *Fr.* Cantos.

From Chebar. Ezra Pound. CP-PoEar

From child to youth; from youth to arduous man. Heart of the Night, The. Dante Gabriel Rossetti. CW-RossD *Fr.* House of Life, The.

From Christ to Gandhi. Wealth. Langston Hughes. CP-HughL; CP-HughL2

From Clee to heaven the beacon burns. 1887. A. E. Housman. CP-HousA

From clutch of clock and calendar now fled. Michelangelo Buonarroti. CP-Miche, *tr. by* John Frederick Nims

From Cocoon forth a Butterfly. Emily Dickinson. CP-DickE

From commissures of daylight. Marriage Portion, The. Adrienne Rich. CP-RicAE

From Cratetos. William Blake. CP-BlakW

From Croatia my home to Moelling no pay. European Travel / (Nazi New Order). Lorine Niedecker. CP-NiedL

From dark abodes to fair etherial light. On the Death of a Young Lady of Five Years of Age. Phillis Wheatley. CP-WheaP

From dates we can never count. Wharf, The. W. S. Merwin. SP-MerwW

From Dawn to Noon. Dante Gabriel Rossetti. CW-RossD *Fr.* House of Life, The.

From death and dark oblivion (near the Same). Mind of the Frontispiece to a Book, The. Ben Jonson. CP-JonsB

From Delphi to Camden—little Hoosier towns. James Whitcomb Riley. CP-RileJ

From depth of sinn and from a diepe dispaire. Psalm 130. De profundis clamavi. Bible, *O.T.* CP-WyatT, *tr. by* Sir Thomas Wyatt *Fr.* Psalms.

From depth to height, from height to loftier height. Resurgam. Christina Georgina Rossetti. CP-RosC2

From Disaster. George Oppen. CP-OppGN

From disorder (a chaos). Descent. William Carlos Williams. CP-WilW2

From distance that drew me closer it seemed I could hear. Death Embrace, The. Tennessee Williams. CP-WillT

From distant regions, Fortune sends. Revolution at Market Hill, The. Jonathan Swift. CP-SwifJ

From Dr. Swift to Dr. Sheridan. Jonathan Swift. CP-SwifJ

From Dread in the Eyes of Horses. Tess Gallagher. SP-GallT

From dreams I wake to real woe. Lyric Ode, A.—Feb. 28. Annis Boudinot Stockton. CP-StocA

From early dawn until the flush of noon. Christina Georgina Rossetti. CP-RosC3

From east and west across the horizon's edge. Old Age's Ship & Crafty Death's. Walt Whitman. CP-WhitW

From easterly crepuscular arrivals. English Revenant, An. Donald Davie. CP-DaviD

From empty windows / Voice of dead eyes. Rafael Alberti. CP-MertT *Fr.* Roman Nocturnes.

From epigram to epic is the course. Strange Metamorphosis of Poets. Howard Nemerov. CP-NemeH

From every folly vain. Real Anthem, The. G. K. Chesterton. CP-ChesG

From every quarter of your land. Ave Imperatrix! Rudyard Kipling. CP-KiplR

From everywhere else (Ceylon, Orinoco, Valdivia). Island (XX), The. Pablo Neruda. SP-NeruP *Fr.* Separate Rose, The.

From eyes of my beloved one, come burning. Michelangelo Buonarroti. CP-Miche, *tr. by* John Frederick Nims

From fabrication springs the spiral stair. Princess and the Goblins, The. Sylvia Plath. CP-PlatS

From fall to spring the russet acorn. Holidays. Ralph Waldo Emerson. CP-EmerR

From famine, pestilence and persecution. Canadian Pacific. Derek Mahon. CP-MahoD

From far and near / He drew the scattered ciphers. Arthur Hugh Clough. SP-ClouA

From Far Dakota's Cañons (June 25, 1876). Walt Whitman. CP-WhitW

From Far, from Eve and Morning. A. E. Housman. CP-HousA

From far, from eve and morning. From Far, from Eve and Morning. A. E. Housman. CP-HousA

From far out in the center of the naked lake. Loon's Cry, The. Robert Bly. SP-BlyR

From Father to Son. Rainer Maria Rilke. CP-RilkFr, *tr. by* A. Poulin, Jr.

From feather-stuffed bolsters of cloud. Cold Spring Harbor. Derek Walcott. CP-WalcD

From Frodmer's Drama "The Friends" Ralph Waldo Emerson. CP-EmerR

From gold to gray. Eve of Election, The. John Greenleaf Whittier. CP-WhitJ

From golden showers of the ancient skies. Flowers, The. Stéphane Mallarmé. CP-MallS, *tr. by* Henry Weinfield

From Great Consciousness vision Harlem 1948 buildings standing in Eternity. Who. Allen Ginsberg. CP-GinsA

From grief I cherished to a rueful laugh. Michelangelo Buonarroti. CP-Miche, *tr. by* John Frederick Nims

From Hafiz. Hafiz. CP-EmerR *Fr.* Odes.

From half past ten he'd been at the coffeehouse. Two Young Men, 23 to 24 Years Old. Constantine P. Cavafy. CP-CavaC, *tr. by* Theoharis Constantine Theoharis

From harmony, from heavenly [*or* heav'nly] harmony. Song for St Cecilia's Day, 1687, A. John Dryden. SP-DrydJ

From heaven it ventured forth, there must return. Michelangelo Buonarroti. CP-Miche, *tr. by* John Frederick Nims

From heaven my beauty, flawless and divine. Michelangelo Buonarroti. CP-Miche, *tr. by* John Frederick Nims

From Heine. Heinrich Heine. CP-BogaL, *tr. by* Louise Bogan

From Her in the Country. Thomas Hardy. CP-HardT

From her perch of beauty. Avec Merci, Mother. Maya Angelou. SP-AngeM

From Heraclitus. Alan Dugan. CP-DugaA

From here on, all of us will be living. 8/8/68: i. Adrienne Rich. CP-RicAE *Fr.* Ghazals: Homage to Ghalib.

From here, the quay, one looks above to mark. Harbour Bridge, The. Thomas Hardy. CP-HardT

From here through tunnelled gloom the track. Railway Junction, The. Walter De la Mare. CP-DeLaW

From high to higher forces. Ralph Waldo Emerson. CP-EmerR

From him did forty million serfs, endow'd. Czar Alexander the Second. Dante Gabriel Rossetti. CW-RossD

From his brimstone bed at break of day. Devil's Thoughts, The. Samuel Taylor Coleridge. CP-ColeS

From his slim Palace in the Dust. Emily Dickinson. CP-DickE

From his small village near the outskirts. 31 B.C. in Alexandria. Constantine P. Cavafy. CP-CavaC, *tr. by* Theoharis Constantine Theoharis

From House to Home. Christina Georgina Rossetti. CP-RosC1

From Ibn Jemin. Ibn-i-Yamin. CP-EmerR

From ink, from pen in hand we see outflow. Michelangelo Buonarroti. CP-Miche, *tr. by* John Frederick Nims

From Iron. Robert Frost. CP-FrosR

From Jehovah's Witnesses stopped by the house the other morning. Bible Lady, The. James Laughlin. CP-LaugJ

From Jerusalem to the Sea and Back. Yehuda Amichai. SP-AmicYL, *tr. by* Benjamin Harshav *and* Barbara Harshav

From Julianus. Emperor Julian. CP-CowpW

From Kansas City, the. Elegy Before the Time. William Dickey. SP-DickW

From labours through the night, outworn. George Meredith. CP-MerG2

From lamplight and an aged leaf. George Meredith. CP-MerG2

From Later to Earlier. Laura Riding Jackson. CP-RidiL

From leaf to leaf in silence. Ascension Day, 1964. W. H. Auden. CP-AudeW

From loud sound and still chance. Baroque Comment. Louise Bogan. CP-BogaL

From love one takes. Necessity, The. Denise Levertov. SP-LeveDP

From loveliest eyes, and from the visage which. Petrarch. CP-Petra, *tr. by* J. G. Nichols

From lovely clear and polished living ice. Petrarch. CP-Petra, *tr.* by J. G. Nichols

From Love's First Fever to Her Plague. Dylan Thomas. CP-ThomD

From low to high doth dissolution climb. Mutability. William Wordsworth. MW-WorW *Fr.* Ecclesiastical Sonnets.

From Man You Came and to Man You Shall Return. Yehuda Amichai. SP-AmicYL, *tr.* by Benjamin Harshav *and* Barbara Harshav

From Manhattan, a glittering shambles. My Cousin Muriel. Amy Clampitt. CP-ClamA

From many boats. Arrival, The. W. S. Merwin. SP-MerwWF

From me my Silvia ranne away. Song upon Silvia, A. Robert Herrick. CP-HerrR

From meander to meander, year by year. Gulls of Settimo, The. Primo Levi. CP-LeviP, *tr.* by Ruth Feldman

From Memory. Adam Zagajewski. SP-ZagaA, *tr.* by Clare Cavanagh

From Menander. Menander. CP-CowpW, *tr.* by William Cowper

From Mestastasio. Christina Georgina Rossetti. CP-RosC3

From Mexico, where people drink. Three Conquistadors, The. G. K. Chesterton. CP-ChesG

From Molepolole and Morogoro. Reflexions on the Seizure of the Suez, and on a Proposal to Line the Banks of That Canal with Billboard Advertisements. Howard Nemerov. CP-NemeH

From Montauk Point. Walt Whitman. CP-WhitW

From Morning-Glory to Petersburg. Adrienne Rich. CP-RicAE; SP-RicA2

From my ancestors the Gauls I have inherited pale blue eyes. Bad Blood. Arthur Rimbaud. CP-RimbA, *tr.* by Martin Sorrell

From my bed I see. Lorine Niedecker. CP-NiedL

From My Dentist's Window. Czeslaw Milosz. CP-MiloCN, *tr.* by Robert Hass

From My Diary. Stephen Spender. CP-SpenS

From My Diary, July 1914. Wilfred Owen. CP-OwenW

From my great-grandmother on. Escape, The. James Dickey. CP-DickJ

From My High Love. Kenneth Patchen. CP-PatcK

From my high love I look at that poor world there. From My High Love. Kenneth Patchen. CP-PatcK

From my journal, March Eight, Nineteen Sixty-nine: Garnie's whisper to me, while we were. Many of Our Waters: Variaitons on a Poem by a Black Child. James Wright. CP-WrigJ

From My Last Years. Walt Whitman. CP-WhitW

From my mother's sleep I fell into the State. Death of the Ball Turret Gunner, The. Randall Jarrell. CP-JarrR

From My Much Honored Friend at Heldelville. Patrick Delany. CP-SherT

From my neat desk I ran. Secretary's Story, The. James Laughlin. CP-LaugJ

From My Notes for a Series of Lectures on Murder. Stevie Smith. CP-SmitS

From my rented attic with no earth. Landowners. Sylvia Plath. CP-PlatS

From my room I hear. Interior ("From my room I hear"). Federico García Lorca. CP-GarcF, *tr.* by Jerome Rothenberg *Fr.* Water Jets.

From my shadow. Salutation, A. Federico García Lorca. CP-GarcF, *tr.* by Jerome Rothenberg

From my villa on the hill I long looked down. Fernando Pessoa. SP-PessF *Fr.* Inscriptions.

From my wife and household and fields. Air and Fire. Wendell Berry. CP-BerrW

From my window. Granada 1850. Federico García Lorca. CP-GarcF, *tr.* by Alan S. Trueblood *Fr.* Love.

From My Window. C. K. Williams. CP-WillC; SP-WillC

From narrow provinces. Moose, The. Elizabeth Bishop. CP-BishE

From Nature's beginning. Ralph Waldo Emerson. CP-EmerR

From near the sea, like Whitman my great predecessor, I call. Ode: Salute to the French Negro Poets. Frank O'Hara. SP-OharF

From night rocks, above an ocean alive with yellow kelp. Dream of Three Sisters, A. Norman Dubie. CP-DubiN

From nine o'clock till morning light. Nightingale, The. Gerard Manley Hopkins. CP-HopkG

From noise of scare-fires rest ye free. Bellman, The. Robert Herrick. CP-HerrR

From Now On. C. K. Williams. CP-WillC

From old Fort Walla Walla and the Klickitats. In the Oregon Country. William Stafford. SP-StafW; SP-StafWW

From Omar Chiam. Omar Khayyám. CP-EmerR

From one all loveliness and all allure. Michelangelo Buonarroti. CP-Miche, *tr.* by John Frederick Nims

From one to two. To My Valentines. Louis Zukofsky. CP-ZukLS

From our evening fireside now. Emily Jane Brontë. CP-BronE

From our very high window at the Sheraton. Sonnet: "From our very high window at the Sheraton." Hayden Carruth. CP-CarHS *Fr.* Sonnets.

From Out Here. Federico García Lorca. CP-GarcF, *tr.* by Jerome Rothenberg

From out its large estate. Hymn: "From out its large estate." Jones Very. CP-VeryJ

From out the midst of Europe in alarms. Congress of Peace at Brussels, The. Jones Very. CP-VeryJ

From pain and peril, by land and main. Captain's Well, The. John Greenleaf Whittier. CP-WhitJ

From Paumanok Starting I Fly Like a Bird. Walt Whitman. CP-WhitW

From Pent-up Aching Rivers. Walt Whitman. CP-WhitW

From Perugia. John Greenleaf Whittier. CP-WhitJ

From Pico & the Women: A Life. Robert Creeley. CP-CreeR

From plane of light to plane, wings dipping through. Evening Hawk. Robert Penn Warren. CP-WarrR

From Plane to Plane. Robert Frost. CP-FrosR

From pleasure of the bed. Chambermaid's Second Song, The. William Butler Yeats. CP-YeatW

From powdery Palmyre, the tireless wind. Waters, The. Richard Wilbur. CP-WilbR

From pride, guile, hate, greed, melancholy. Incurable. Ambrose Bierce. SP-BierA

From purest wells of English undefiled. James Russell Lowell. John Greenleaf Whittier. CP-WhitJ

From right to left, and to and fro. Maze, The. Vincent Bourne. CP-CowpW

From Rome, for More Public Fountains in New York City. Alan Dugan. CP-DugaA

From sand he pours himself into deep water. Life of the Otter, The. Thom Gunn. CP-GunnT

From sandy volcanoes. D-Day 1989. William Corbett. SP-CorbW

From Sappho to myself, consider the fate of women. One. Carolyn Kizer. CP-KizeC *Fr.* Pro Femina.

From scalp to sole, all muscles in slow motion. Bodybuilders' Contest. Wisława Szymborska. SP-SzymW, *tr.* by Stanisław Barańczak *and* Clare Cavanagh

From scars where kestrels hover. Missing. W. H. Auden. CP-AudeW

From Sea Cliff, March. May Swenson. SP-SwenM

From Selma. Langston Hughes. CP-HughL; CP-HughL2

From shade to shade our neighbor mows. Memorial Day. Wyatt Prunty. SP-PrunW

From shelving cliff-darkness, green arch and nave. Place, The. Robert Penn Warren. CP-WarrR

From silence to silence. Breaks. A. R. Ammons. CP-AmmoA

From sleep, before first light. Phaedra in the Farm House. Thom Gunn. CP-GunnT

From solitary flowerstalk some fingers. Snow-Wreath. Louis Zukofsky. CP-ZukLS

From something in the trees. For the New Year. Robert Creeley. CP-CreeR

From somewhere underneath my window. Household Spirits. Thomas Kinsella. CP-KinsT

From Spain to Alabama. Langston Hughes. CP-HughL; CP-HughL2

From Spain to the Hydaspes in the East. Petrarch. CP-Petra, *tr.* by J. G. Nichols

From spiralling ecstatically this. E. E. Cummings. CP-CummE

From Spring Days to Winter. Oscar Wilde. CP-WildO

From Stephen's Green I turned my feet. Open Court. Thomas Kinsella. CP-KinsT

From Stirling Castle we had seen. Yarrow Unvisited [1803]. William Wordsworth. CP-WorW1; MW-WorW

From Strength to Strength. Paul Muldoon. CP-MuldP

From summer and the wheel-shaped city. Washington Cathedral. Karl Shapiro. SP-ShapK

From Sunset to Star Rise. Christina Georgina Rossetti. CP-RosC1

From Syria. Peire Bremon. CP-PoEar, *tr.* by Ezra Pound

From Talcahuano comes. Talcahuano. Gabriela Mistral. SP-MistG, *tr.* by Maria Giachetti [*or* Jacketti]

From tall rooms, largesse of peonies. Winter Burial, A. Amy Clampitt. CP-ClamA

From ten to five we whacked the waves. Bath after Sailing. John Updike. CP-UpdiJ

From Thallus the pederast. Carmen 25. Catullus. CP-ZukLS *Fr.* Carmina.

From that day[e] thee Hart strokes [*or* strokys]. Sums. Donald Hall. CP-HallD

From the alley's gloom and chill. Marilyn Marilyn. Dorothy Parker. CP-ParkD

From the Antique. Christina Georgina Rossetti. CP-RosC3

From the Arabic: An Imitation. Percy Bysshe Shelley. CP-ShelP

From the archaic ships the green and red. Mathilde in Normandy. Adrienne Rich. CP-RicAE

From the back of the room, the bed, only a pallor spread. Rainer Maria Rilke. CP-RilkFr, *tr.* by A. Poulin, Jr. *Fr.* Windows, The.

From the bad eye and early morning. Lost Souls. Charles Wright. SP-WrigC

From the balcony of the Thetford Hill. Choir Singing, The. Grace Paley. CP-PalGC

From the balcony we see a town we see a lake we see walkers along the shore. Six Illustrations. Michael Palmer. SP-PalmM

From the bare planks the reflected sun lights up. Nest of Vampires. James Fenton. SP-FentJ

From the Beginning. David Ignatow. SP-IgnaD

From the beginning life holds death in me. Original Sin. Helen Pinkerton. CP-PinkH

From the beginning, SIN. There Was a Youth Whose Name Was Thomas Granger. Charles Olson. CP-OlsoC

From "The Birth of Venus," Song. William Carlos Williams. CP-WilW1

From the Book of Esther I Filtered the Sediment. Yehuda Amichai. SP-AmicY, *tr. by* Chana Bloch

From the book of Esther I filtered the sediment. From the Book of Esther I Filtered the Sediment. Yehuda Amichai. SP-AmicY, *tr. by* Chana Bloch

From the boy's identification. Myself, Rousseau, a Few Others. William Meredith. SP-MereW

From the bray of gray donkeys. Fanny Howe. SP-HoweF *Fr.* O'Clock.

From the breach to the iron explosion. Pablo Neruda. SP-NeruP *Fr.* Skystones.

From the Bunkers. Sam Hamill. SP-HamiS

From the Canton of Expectation. Seamus Heaney. SP-HeanSO

From the center of the Sea of Tranquility. Planet, The. Josephine Jacobsen. CP-JacoJ

From the Childhood of Jesus. Robert Pinsky. CP-PinsR

From the Chronicles of the Town of Pornic. Czeslaw Milosz. CP-MiloC; CP-MiloCN, *tr. by* Lillian Vallee

From the Cliffs: Noon. Dante Gabriel Rossetti. CW-RossD

From the closed garden. Hymen. "H. D." CP-DoolH

From the cognoscenti. E. E. Cummings. CP-CummE

From the contamination / Of laudation. Arthur Hugh Clough. SP-ClouA

From the Coptic. Stevie Smith. CP-SmitS

From the Corpse Woodpiles, from the Ashes. Robert Earl Hayden. CP-HaydR

From the Country to the City. Elizabeth Bishop. CP-BishE

From the County Lunatic Asylum. Stevie Smith. CP-SmitS

From the Crest. Wendell Berry. CP-BerrW

From the cry of children on the floors of stations beyond time. Spirit of the Laws, The. Czeslaw Milosz. CP-MiloC; CP-MiloCN, *tr. by* John Carpenter *and* Bogdana Carpenter

From the Cupola. James Merrill. SP-MerrJ

From the Dark Chambers of Dejection Freed. William Wordsworth. CP-WorW2

From the dark / fragmentations. Muse. A. R. Ammons. CP-AmmoA

From the dark side, feet first, breech birth, the fighter falls. Paratrooper. Mona Van Duyn. SP-VanDM

From the Dark Tower. Countee Cullen. CP-CullC

From the dark yard by the sheepbarn the cock crowed. Henyard Round, The. Donald Hall. CP-HallD

From the date that the doors of his prep-school close. Waster, The. Rudyard Kipling. CP-KiplR

From the Desk of the Laureate: For Immediate Release. Howard Nemerov. CP-NemeH

From the Diary of John Manningham of the Middle Temple. Sir Walter Ralegh. CP-RaleW

From the Distance. Wendell Berry. CP-BerrW

From the dithyramb to the root of the sea. Search. Pablo Neruda. SP-NeruP

From the drama of horror and despair. Gesture, The. Richard Eberhart. CP-EberR

From the Drawer. Constantine P. Cavafy. CP-CavaC, *tr. by* Theoharis Constantine Theoharis

From the dress-box's plashing tis–. Catch, The. Richard Wilbur. CP-WilbR

From the Duck-Pond to the Carousel. Muriel Rukeyser. CP-RukeM

From the dull confines of the drooping West. His Return to London. Robert Herrick. CP-HerrR

From the Earth, and from thy bloud, O heaven, they came. Sir Walter Ralegh. CP-RaleW

From the East, Light. Raymond Carver. CP-CarvR

From the edge of the bare reef in the afternoon. Tidal Lagoon. W. S. Merwin. SP-MerwWF

From the edge of the drained beaver swamp. Winter Dreams. Robert Penn Warren. CP-WarrR

From the Embassy. Robert Graves. CP-GravR

From the famous Peak of Derby. Ben Jonson. CP-JonsB *Fr.* Gypsies Metamorphosed, The.

From the Fantasy all the way to the Page. Ships, The. Constantine P. Cavafy. CP-CavaC, *tr. by* Theoharis Constantine Theoharis

From the first / abstraction. Purpose. Rae Armantrout. SP-ArmaA

From the first it had been like a. Bronzeville Mother Loiters in Mississippi, A. Meanwhile, a Mississippi Mother Burns Bacon. Gwendolyn Brooks. SP-BrooG

From the first whimper to the expiring sigh. Michelangelo Buonarroti. CP-Miche, *tr. by* John Frederick Nims

From the forests and highlands. Hymn of Pan. Percy Bysshe Shelley. CP-ShelP

From the French. Lord Byron. CP-Byron

From the French. Lord Byron. CP-Byron

From the French (1). Stevie Smith. CP-SmitS

From the French (2). Stevie Smith. CP-SmitS

From the Frick. The weather. Back. James Schuyler. CP-SchuJ

From the Friendly Local Press. George Oppen. CP-OppGN

From the Frontier of Writing. Seamus Heaney. SP-HeanSO

From the Garden. Anne Sexton. CP-SextA

From the great, imperial city. Abolition of Serfdom in Russia, The. Jones Very. CP-VeryJ

From the Greek. Stevie Smith. CP-SmitS

From the Greek Anthology. Alan Dugan. CP-DugaA

From the green Amesbury hill which bears the name. Bay of Seven Islands, The. John Greenleaf Whittier. CP-WhitJ

From the Headboard of a Grave in Paraguay. James Whitcomb Riley. CP-RileJ

From the heart of this dark, evacuated campus. Books. Billy Collins. SP-CollB

From the heart of Waumbek Methma. Mary Garvin. John Greenleaf Whittier. CP-WhitJ

From the heel / Of a half loaf. Austerities. Charles Simic. SP-SimiC; SP-SimiCE

From the high senate of the gods, to you. Coelum Britannicum. Thomas Carew. CP-CareT *Fr.* Carew's Masque.

From the Highest Camp. Thom Gunn. CP-GunnT

From the highest window of my house. Fernando Pessoa. SP-PessF *Fr.* Keeper of Sheep, The.

From the hills of home forth looking, far beneath the tent-like span. Garrison of Cape Ann, The. John Greenleaf Whittier. CP-WhitJ

From the hodge porridge. Farmer's Wife, The. Anne Sexton. CP-SextA

From the Hole. James Tate. SP-TateJ

From the houses of American engineers. In Haiti [or Haitian Suite]. Gregory Orr. SP-OrrG

From the Inca. Charles Olson. CP-OlsoC

From the indigo straits to Ossian's seas, on the orange-pink sand. Metropolitan. Arthur Rimbaud. CP-RimbA, *tr. by* Martin Sorrell

From the inlet. Help. A. R. Ammons. CP-AmmoA

From the Inside. Paul Éluard. CP-WilW2

From the Italian. Stevie Smith. CP-SmitS

From the Japanese. Louise Glück. SP-GlucL

From the Journal Concerning My Father. Jane Cooper. CP-CoopJ

From the last hill that looks on thy once holy dome. On the Day of the Destruction of Jerusalem by Titus. Lord Byron. CP-Byron

From the Legend of St. Clement. Thomas Merton. CP-MertT

From the Lives of Things. Adam Zagajewski. SP-ZagaA, *tr. by* Renata Gorczynski, Benjamin Ivry *and* C. K. Williams

From the Lookout Rock. Richard Wilbur. CP-WilbR

From the low eighteenth-century window—its thicknesses. Kapuzinerberg (Salzburg). Pierre Jean Jouve. CP-BogaL

From the low palace of old father Ocean. Song: "From the low palace of old father Ocean." John Dryden. CP-DryJ2 *Fr.* Albion and Albanius.

From the McMichaels'. Four Good Things. James McMichael. SP-McMiJ

From the Misery of Don Joost. Wallace Stevens. CP-StevW; CP-StevWP

From the moment you were born. Anniversary. Eugenio Montale. CP-MontE, *tr. by* Jonathan Galassi

From the Motorway. Charles Tomlinson. CP-TomlC

From the new Babylon where shame is dead. Petrarch. CP-Petra, *tr. by* J. G. Nichols

From the New World. Donald Davie. CP-DaviDC

"From the next ." James Schuyler. CP-SchuJ

From the north the wands the long. Banishment in Winter. W. S. Merwin. SP-MerwW

From the Observatory. David Ignatow. SP-IgnaD

From the official hurry on the top floor. On Hat: On Vertical Mobility as a Concept. Alan Dugan. CP-DugaA

From the open market with its tangy smell. If Blood Were Not as Powerful as It Is. Tess Gallagher. SP-GallT

From the Original Draft of the Poem to William Shelley. Percy Bysshe Shelley. CP-ShelP

From the orphanage Al came to. Orphanage Boy. Robert Penn Warren. CP-WarrR

From the outset. Theresa's Friends. Robert Creeley. SP-CreeR

From the Outside. Paul Éluard. CP-WilW2

From the outthrust ledge of sea-cliff you. Question at Cliff-Thrust. Robert Penn Warren. CP-WarrR

From the Packet of Anacharsis. Wallace Stevens. CP-StevW; CP-StevWP

From the Paris Commune to the Kronstadt Rebellion. Kenneth Rexroth. CP-RexrK

From the Past and Unavailing. Pilot, The. Edwin Arlington Robinson. CP-RobiE

From the Persian (1). *Unknown.* CP-RexrK, *tr. by* Kenneth Rexroth

From the Persian (2). Kenneth Rexroth. CP-RexrK

From the Persian of Hafiz. Hafiz. CP-EmerR

From the place where we are right. Place Where We Are Right, The. Yehuda Amichai. SP-AmicY, *tr. by* Stephen Mitchell

From the porch at dusk I watched. Before Dark. Wendell Berry. CP-BerrW

From the Porch at Runnymede. Paul Laurence Dunbar. CP-DunbP

From the Prison House. Adrienne Rich. SP-RicA2

From the private ease of Mother's womb. Baby Song. Thom Gunn. CP-GunnT

Fr. Three Songs.

From the Prometheus Vinctus of Aeschylus. Lord Byron. CP-Byron

From the quarters of the compass. Carmen 42. Catullus. CP-ZukLS *Fr.* Carmina.

From the racked substance of the earth comes the plant and. Of Cruelty. Ivor Gurney. SP-GurnI

From the Republic of Conscience. Seamus Heaney. SP-HeanSO

From the Rising of the Sun. Czeslaw Milosz. CP-MiloC; CP-MiloCN

From the Roof. Denise Levertov. SP-LeveDP

From the Rooftop. Arthur Sze. SP-SzeA

From the Saddle. Ezra Pound. CP-PoEar

From the salt age, yes from the salt age. Old snapshot from Venice 1952. Robert Lowell. SP-LoweR

From the School of the Renowned Philosopher. Constantine P. Cavafy. CP-CavaC, *tr. by* Theoharis Constantine Theoharis

From the Scroll of Esther, I filtered out the sediment. Yehuda Amichai. SP-AmicYL, *tr. by* Benjamin Harshav *and* Barbara Harshav

From the sea came a hand. Two Hands. Anne Sexton. CP-SextA

From the sea, this sea. Unforgiven. Sam Hamill. SP-HamiS

From the Second Chapter of a Verse History of the World. Thomas Merton. CP-MertT

From the sermons in stone and the cymbals. Apology for Clowns, An. G. K. Chesterton. CP-ChesG

FROM THE SHADOWS OF THE QUARTER. Is It True? Langston Hughes. CP-HughL; CP-HughL3

FROM THE SHADOWS OF THE QUARTER. Ask Your Mama. Langston Hughes. CP-HughL; CP-HughL3

From the Ship. Constantine P. Cavafy. CP-CavaC, *tr. by* Theoharis Constantine Theoharis

From the Shore. Carl Sandburg. CP-SandC

From the shrivelling gray. Disclosure, The. Denise Levertov. SP-LeveDP; SP-LeveDS

From the sky in the form of snow. November. William Stafford. SP-StafWW

From the slow march and muffled drum. King's Soliloquy, A. Thomas Hardy. CP-HardT

From *The Song of Ullikummi*. Charles Olson. CP-OlsoC

From the speaker's place of speech there's nothing. No Page (Unturned). Michael Palmer. SP-PalmM

From the start, the forces were unequal: Satan a grand seigneur in Heaven. Homily. Dan Pagis. SP-PagiD, *tr. by* Stephen Mitchell

From the stores of eldest Matter. Ralph Waldo Emerson. CP-EmerR

From the tawny light. Everything That Acts Is Actual. Denise Levertov. SP-LeveDS

From the Temple to your home. Connubii Flores, or the Well-Wishes at Weddings. Robert Herrick. CP-HerrR

From the Theater Lobby. Alan Dugan. CP-DugaA

From the throat he can rally strength. Remembering. Muriel Rukeyser. CP-RukeM

From the time he knew. Growing a Ghost. Howard Nemerov. CP-NemeH

From the time of the early radishes. Weeds. Carl Sandburg. CP-SandC

From the top of. Pine River. Gary Snyder. CP-SnydG

From *The Touchstone of Truth*. Ben Jonson. CP-JonsB

From the Train. Eugenio Montale. CP-MontE, *tr. by* Jonathan Galassi

From the Train, Eastward. Denise Levertov. SP-LeveDL

From the train window. Brief Visit to Venice. Clarence Major. SP-MajoC

From the train window at daybreak. At Daybreak. Adam Zagajewski. SP-ZagaA, *tr. by* Renata Gorczynski, Renata Gorczynski, Benjamin Ivry *and* C. K. Williams

From the very first coming down. Letter, The. W. H. Auden. CP-AudeW

From the wash the laundress sends. A. E. Housman. CP-HousA

From the Wave. Thom Gunn. CP-GunnT

From the well-springs of Hudson, the sea-cliffs of Maine. Quaker Alumni, The. John Greenleaf Whittier. CP-WhitJ

From the west comes Harold, with a bitter smile. Harold. David Ignatow. SP-IgnaD

From the western shore of oceans on the world. Whorls. William Meredith. SP-MereW

From the wheel and the drift of Things. Prayer of Miriam Cohen, The. Rudyard Kipling. CP-KiplR

From the white-blossom'd sloe, my dear Chloris requested. On Chloris Requesting Me to Give Her a Spray of a Sloe-Thorn in Full Blossom. Robert Burns. CP-BurnR

From the window I see her bend to the roses. Cherish. Raymond Carver. CP-CarvR

From the Wood of the Old Wives' Fables. Mortal Answers, The. G. K. Chesterton. CP-ChesG

From the years. Things Kept. William Dickey. SP-DickW

From thee, ELIZA, I must go. Song: "From thee, ELIZA, I must go." Robert Burns. CP-BurnR

From their grave lion-mouths, oracles. Oracles. Kathleen Jessie Raine. SP-RainK

From thence his way the Trojan hero bent. Nisus and Euryalus ("From thence his way the Trojan hero bent"). Virgil. CP-DryJ2, *tr. by* John Dryden *Fr.* Aeneid (Dryden translation).

From thence our kinde hard-hearted is, enduring paine and care. Ovid. CP-RaleW *Fr.* Metamorphoses.

From these drear solitudes and frowzy Cells. Fragment—Epistle from Esopus to Maria. Robert Burns. CP-BurnR

From these high [*or* hie] hill[e]s as when a spring doth fall. Comparison of Love to a Streame Falling from the Alpes. Sir Thomas Wyatt. CP-WyatT

From these wild rocks I look to-day. Laurels, The. John Greenleaf Whittier. CP-WhitJ

From thirty years back my grandmother with us boys. Housekeeping. Donald Davie. CP-DaviDC

From this bleeding hand of mine. Bleeding Hand: or, The Sprig of Eglantine Given to a Maid, The. Robert Herrick. CP-HerrR

From this deep chasm, where quivering sunbeams play. William Wordsworth. CP-WorW2 *Fr.* River Duddon [A Series of Sonnets], The.

From this distance thinking toward you. George Oppen. CP-OppGN

From this emblem what variance your motto evinces. Ich Dien. Lord Byron. CP-Byron

From This Far. Derek Walcott. CP-WalcD

From this hospital bed. Injury, The. William Carlos Williams. CP-WilW2

From this Midland scene—glum slagheaps. George Eliot Country. Amy Clampitt. CP-ClamA

From this new culture of the air we finally see. Ode to Gaea. W. H. Auden. CP-AudeW

From this the muse rich consolation draws. On the Death of General Wooster. Phillis Wheatley. CP-WheaP

From thorny wilds a Monster came. Self-Love and Truth Incompatible. Jeanne Marie Bouvier de la Motte- Guyon. CP-CowpW

From thought to thought, along each mountain top. Petrarch. CP-Petra, *tr. by* J. G. Nichols

From thought to thought, from hill to hill love doth me lead. Sir Thomas Wyatt. CP-WyatT

From thy far sources 'mid mountains airily climbing. Arthur Hugh Clough. SP-ClouA

From thy worth and weight the stars gravitate. To the Shah, from Enweri. "Anvari." CP-EmerR

From Time. James Dickey. CP-DickJ

From time to time, let us be allowed. To Mimi Romanelli. Rainer Maria Rilke. CP-RilkFr, *tr. by* A. Poulin, Jr.

From too much love of living. Beginners. Denise Levertov. SP-LeveDL; SP-LeveDS

From trapeze to. Acrobat, The. Wisława Szymborska. SP-SzymW, *tr. by* Stanislaw Barańczak *and* Clare Cavanagh

From trivia of froth and pollen. Cromlech, The. Louis MacNeice. CP-MacNL

From Trollope's Journal. Elizabeth Bishop. CP-BishE

From 20,000 Feet. Heather McHugh. SP-McHuH

From twig to twig the spider weaves. Outer and Inner. George Meredith. CP-MerG1

From under crunch of my man's boot. Ode for Ted. Sylvia Plath. CP-PlatS

From under wide wings of blackest velvet. Visitant. Denise Levertov. SP-LeveDL

From up here in the crow's nest. Jesus Dies. Anne Sexton. CP-SextA; SP-SextA

From Up-State. George Oppen. CP-OppGN

From us, of course, you want gristly bones. Talking to Dogs. W. H. Auden. CP-AudeW

From Us She wandered now a Year. Emily Dickinson. CP-DickE

From vague regions of sleep I come again. Kathleen Jessie Raine. SP-RainK

From Venus born, thy beauty shows. Pethox the Great. Jonathan Swift. CP-SwifJ

From Victor Hugo. Thomas Hardy. CP-HardT

From Vienna it's picture postcard all the way. At Auden's Grave. Karl Shapiro. SP-ShapK

From Water-Tower Hill to the brick prison. Point Shirley. Sylvia Plath. CP-PlatS

From what circle of heaven, from what idea. Petrarch. CP-Petra, *tr. by* J. G. Nichols

From what dog's dish or crocodile's rotten. Song: "From what dog's dish or crocodile's rotten." Ted Hughes. SP-HughTN *Fr.* Bawdry Embraced.

From what hardened hands / the tool comes to us. Gift, The. Pablo Neruda. SP-NeruP

From what these eyes, my lady, see of you. Michelangelo Buonarroti. CP-Miche, *tr. by* John Frederick Nims

From whence cometh song? Song: "From whence cometh song?" Theodore Roethke. CP-RoetT

From Where? A. K. Ramanujan. CP-RamaA

From where do poems come? Crucibles of Love. Robert Graves. CP-GravR

From where I lingered in a lull in March. Evening in a Sugar Orchard. Robert Frost. CP-FrosR

From where she stood the air she craved. Two Who Croseed a Line (She

Crosses). Countee Cullen. CP-CullC

From where you triumphed in me, Love, right here. Michelangelo Buonarroti. CP-Miche, *tr. by* John Frederick Nims

From Wherever I Am. Robert Stock. SP-StocR

From whom did you inherit your dark hair. Maryam. Ingeborg Bachmann. CP-KizeC, *tr. by* Carolyn Kizer

From wisedome Fortune differs farre. Sir Walter Ralegh. CP-RaleW

From word to word th' ambiguous sense is played. Claudian. CP-SherT, *tr. by* Thomas Sheridan

From Wynyard's Gap the livelong day. Trampwoman's Tragedy, A. Thomas Hardy. CP-HardT

From Yellow Lake: An Interval. Mona Van Duyn. SP-VanDM

From Yorktown's ruins, ranked and still. Yorktown. John Greenleaf Whittier. CP-WhitJ

Frondes Agrestes. Charles Tomlinson. CP-TomlC; SP-TomlC

Fronleichnam. D. H. Lawrence. CP-LawrD

Front, A. Randall Jarrell. CP-JarrR

Front Door Soliloquy. Robert Graves. CP-GravR

Front lawn is littered with young men, The. Aging Female Poet Sits on the Balcony. Margaret Atwood. SP-AtwM2

Front Lines. Gary Snyder. CP-SnydG

Front Page. Federico García Lorca. CP-GarcF, *tr. by* Jerome Rothenberg *Fr.* Palimpsests.

Frontal Lobe Postscript. Yusef Komunyakaa. CP-KomuY

Frontenac. Donald Davie. CP-DavID C

Frontier, The. James Wright. CP-WrigJ

Frontispiece. John Ashbery. SP-AshbJ

Frontispiece. Yusef Komunyakaa. CP-KomuY

Frost. Arthur Sze. SP-SzeA

Frost. Charles Tomlinson. CP-TomlC

Frost. John Updike. CP-UpdiJ

Frost, The. Jones Very. CP-VeryJ

Frost at Midnight. Samuel Taylor Coleridge. CP-ColeS; MW-ColeS

Frost covered this decades ago. Splitting Wood. Billy Collins. SP-CollB

Frost Flowers. D. H. Lawrence. CP-LawrD

Frost has settled down upon the trees, The. Winter in the Boulevard. D. H. Lawrence. CP-LawrD

Frost is out amid our open fields, The. Frost, The. Jones Very. CP-VeryJ

Frost-locked all the winter. Spring. Christina Georgina Rossetti. CP-RosC1

Frost of Death was on the Pane, The. Emily Dickinson. CP-DickE

Frost on the windowpanes; the sick. Eugenio Montale. CP-MontE, *tr. by* Jonathan Galassi

Frost performs its secret ministry, The. Frost at Midnight. Samuel Taylor Coleridge. CP-ColeS; MW-ColeS

Frost-rime edges blades of grass. Kathleen Jessie Raine. SP-RainK

Frost Spirit, The. John Greenleaf Whittier. CP-WhitJ

Frost upon small rain—the ebony lacquered avenue. Arterial. Rudyard Kipling. CP-KiplR *Fr.* Muse among the Motors, The.

Frost was never seen, The. Emily Dickinson. CP-DickE

Frost will come out under the stars, The. Writing on a Fallen Leaf, The. W. S. Merwin. SP-MerwW

Frosting. Langston Hughes. CP-HughL; CP-HughL3

Frosty Night, A. Robert Graves. CP-GravR

Froth. Richard Eberhart. CP-EberR

Frown there like Cressy or like Agincourt. Landscape: Wheatfields. Thomas Merton. CP-MertT

Frowned the Laird on the Lord: "So, red-handed I catch thee?" Muckle-Mouth Meg. Robert Browning. CP-BroR2

Frowns are on every Muse's face. On Seeing a Needlecase in the Form of a Harp; the Work of E.M.S. William Wordsworth. CP-WorW2

Frozen City, The. Howard Nemerov. CP-NemeH

Frozen-faced, by the stripped trees. Cold. Pablo Neruda. SP-NeruP

Frozen Food Section. Charles Bukowski. SP-BukC3

Frozen Greenhouse, The. Thomas Hardy. CP-HardT

Frozen Heart, The. Robert Herrick. CP-HerrR

Frozen in a grimace, all cavernous threat. Tiger Skull. Charles Tomlinson. CP-TomlC

Frozen Lake, The. Stevie Smith. CP-SmitS

Frozen moon wheels in the sky, The. Uncertain Solitude. Federico García Lorca. CP-GarcF, *tr. by* Christopher Maurer

Frozen Motion. Wisława Szymborska. SP-SzymW, *tr. by* Stanislaw Barańczak *and* Clare Cavanagh

Frozen rain of the first November days, The. Without Notice Beforehand. Carl Sandburg. CP-SandC

Frozen Ship, The. Jones Very. CP-VeryJ

Frozen sleepy pause, The. Interrupted Concert, The. Federico García Lorca. SP-GarcF, *tr. by* W. S. Merwin

Frozen Zone; or, Julia Disdainful, The. Robert Herrick. CP-HerrR

Fruit. Gabriela Mistral. SP-MistG, *tr. by* Maria Giachetti [*or* Jacketti]

Fruit. Adam Zagajewski. SP-ZagaA, *tr. by* Renata Gorczynski, Benjamin Ivry *and* C. K. Williams

Fruit, The. Jones Very. SP-VeryJ

Fruit, The. William Carlos Williams. CP-WilW2

Fruit flies lift off the bowl of brown pears. Looking up from Two Renaissance Paintings to the Massacre at Tiananmen Square. Norman Dubie. CP-DubiN

Fruit, for sculpture. Charles Tomlinson. CP-TomlC

Fruit-Gift, The. John Greenleaf Whittier. CP-WhitJ

Fruit is small, and often served, The. Ume: *Plum*. Eleanor Wilner. SP-WilnE

Fruit machines and pin tables. Yours Next. Louis MacNeice. CP-MacNL

Fruit of all the service that I serve, The. Sir Thomas Wyatt. CP-WyatT

Fruit of the Flower. Countee Cullen. CP-CullC

Fruit-Piece, A. James Whitcomb Riley. CP-RileJ

Fruit Plucker, The. Samuel Taylor Coleridge. CP-ColeS

Fruit rolled by all day, The. Pickle Belt. Theodore Roethke. CP-RoetT

Fruitful woman, A. My Dream About Falling. Lucille Clifton. SP-ClifL

Frustration. Dorothy Parker. CP-ParkD

Fry's Cocoa! The word / means food of the gods. Adverts. James Schuyler. CP-SchuJ

Fu' de peace o' my eachin' heels, set down. Itching Heels. Paul Laurence Dunbar. CP-DunbP

Fu I loved the high cloud and the hill. Epitaphs: "Fu I loved the high cloud and the hill." Ezra Pound. SP-PounE

Fuck. Charles Bukowski. SP-BukC1

Fuck Communism / it's red white and blue. Tambourine Life. Ted Berrigan. SP-BerrT

Fuck the Astronauts. James Tate. SP-TateJ

Fucked the Mountain. From *The Song of Ullikummi*. Charles Olson. CP-OlsoC

Fucker, you might at least send me a couple of your. . . . American Express, Athens, Greece. Charles Bukowski. SP-BukC2

Fugitive. Thomas Merton. CP-MertT

Fugitive firs and larches for a moment. Advocates. Robert Graves. CP-GravR

Fugitive Kind, The. Tennessee Williams.

Not a Soul; Blanket Roll Blues. CP-WillT

Fugitive Slaves, The. Jones Very. CP-VeryJ

Fugitive's Ride, The. Stevie Smith. CP-SmitS

Fugitives, The. Rainer Maria Rilke. CP-RilkFr, *tr. by* A. Poulin, Jr.

Fugitives, The. Percy Bysshe Shelley. CP-ShelP

Fugue. Howard Nemerov. CP-NemeH

Fuite d'Enfance. Stevie Smith. CP-SmitS

Fulfillment. Langston Hughes. CP-HughL; CP-HughL2

Fulfillment. Dorothy Parker. CP-ParkD

Fulfillment. Yannis Ritsos. SP-RitsY, *tr. by* Thanasis Maskaleris

Fulfillment. Marya Alexandrovna Zaturenska. SP-ZatuM

Fulfillment of their lawless pleasure, The. Their Origin. Constantine P. Cavafy. CP-CavaC, *tr. by* Theoharis Constantine Theoharis

Fulfilment. Paul Laurence Dunbar. CP-DunbP

Full cloves / Of your buttocks, the convex, The. Shallot, A. Richard Wilbur. CP-WilbR

Full Fathom Five. Sylvia Plath. CP-PlatS

Full fed Rose on meals of Tint, A. Emily Dickinson. CP-DickE

Full Harvest, A. James Whitcomb Riley. CP-RileJ

Full in the hand, heavy. September Afternoon at Four o'Clock. Marge Piercy. SP-PierM

Full Irish breakfast, A. Fanny Howe. SP-HoweF *Fr.* O'Clock.

Full Life. D. H. Lawrence. CP-LawrD

Full Life, The. James Laughlin. CP-LaugJ

Full many a dreary hour have I passed. To My Brother George. John Keats. CP-KeatJ

Full Moon. Federico García Lorca. CP-GarcF, *tr. by* Jerome Rothenberg *Fr.* Sublunar Cantos.

Full Moon. Robert Graves. CP-GravR

Full Moon. Robert Earl Hayden. CP-HaydR

Full Moon. William Carlos Williams. CP-WilW1

Full Moon and Little Frieda. Ted Hughes. SP-HughTN

Full moon and the whispering leaves. Autumn Morning. Peter Blue Cloud. SP-BlueP

Full moon, as she tipped the hill, rising, The. Common Place. Charles Olson. CP-OlsoC

Full moon easterly rising, furious, The. Love Story, A. Robert Graves. CP-GravR

Full moon. Everyone in silhouette. Night Launch. Maxine W. Kumin. SP-KumiM

Full moon illuminated large initial for letter M. Appalachian Book of the Dead 3, The. Charles Wright. SP-WrigCN

Full moon is partly hidden by cloud, The. Fable of the War, A. Howard Nemerov. CP-NemeH

Full moon is so fierce that I can count the, The. Europa. Derek Walcott. CP-WalcD

Full moon is the Shield of faith, The. Shield of Faith, The. Nicholas Vachel Lindsay. CP-LindV

Full moon over the shopping mall. Spring Fashions. Allen Ginsberg. CP-GinsA; SP-GinsA

Full moon, the eighth of March; clouds. Paesaggio Notturno. Charles Wright. SP-WrigCN

Full moon was shining upon the broad sea, The. Shy Man, The. Theodore Roethke. CP-RoetT

Full Moonlight in Spring. W. S. Merwin. SP-MerwW

Full moon's sharp. Tropic Ritual. Denise Levertov. SP-LeveDL

Full nine years old my cellar stows. Ode 4.11: To Phyllis. Horace. SP-SmarC *Fr.* Odes.

Full of her long white arms and milky skin. Equilibrists, The. John Crowe Ransom. SP-RansJ

Full of Joy Do Not Know; They Need Not, The. Richard Eberhart. CP-EberR

Full of Life Now. Walt Whitman. CP-WhitW

Full of passion and giggles. Young Poet, A. Frank O'Hara. SP-OharF

Full of rebellion, I would die. Nature. George Herbert. CP-HerbG

Full of scars / & fast asleep. Air. Federico García Lorca. CP-GarcF, *tr. by* Jerome Rothenberg *Fr.* Palimpsests.

Full of that indescribable delight. Petrarch. CP-Petra, *tr. by* J. G. Nichols

Full of that strong desire which sunders me. Petrarch. CP-Petra, *tr. by* J. G. Nichols

Full of thy glory am I. Song. George Meredith. CP-MerG2

Full of wickedness, I—of many a smutch'd deed reminiscent—of worse deeds capable. Of Many a Smutch'd Deed Reminiscent. Walt Whitman. CP-WhitW

Full oft I mvse and hes in thocht. William Dunbar. CP-DunbW

Full-orbed moon with unchanged ray, The. Moon, The. Henry David Thoreau. CP-ThorH

Full Professor, A. Howard Nemerov. CP-NemeH

FULL SPEED ASTERN). E. E. Cummings. CP-CummE

Full-tailed stallion rears, A. Martyrdom of St. Eulalia. Federico García Lorca. CP-GarcF, *tr. by* Will Kirkland

Full thirty foot she towered from waterline to rail. Three-Decker, The. Rudyard Kipling. CP-KiplR

Full thirty frosts since thou wert young. Upon a Venerable Rival. William Cowper. CP-CowpW

Full twenty years and more our labouring stage. Prologue. John Dryden. CP-DryJ2 *Fr.* Albion and Albanius.

Full week I'd been on the road, feet, A. At the Green Inn, Five P.M. Arthur Rimbaud. CP-RimbA, *tr. by* Martin Sorrell

Full Well I Know. Stevie Smith. CP-SmitS

Full well it may be seen. Sir Thomas Wyatt. CP-WyatT

Full well thou knowest I love thee dear. Song. Robert Burns. CP-BurnR

Full well thou knowest, song, what grace I mean. Ballata, Fragment. Ezra Pound. CP-PoEar

Fullness of love sleeps in us like a sea. George Meredith. CP-MerG2

Fully occupied with growing—that's. Métier of Blossoming, The. Denise Levertov. SP-LeveDS

Fulness of the Gentiles, The. Jones Very. CP-VeryJ

Fumes from all kinds, The. Coming Down Cleveland Avenue. James Tate. SP-TateJ

Function of Blizzard. Robert Penn Warren. CP-WarrR

Functioning total then, The. Death, Judgment, Heaven, Hell. Kenneth Rexroth. CP-RexrK

Fund Appeal. Grace Paley. CP-PalGC

Fundamental characteristic of matter, The. Logician's Nocturne, The. John Ciardi. CP-CiarJ

Fundamental Disagreement with Two Contemporaries. Kenneth Rexroth. CP-RexrK

Fundamental Project of Technology, The. Galway Kinnell. SP-KinnGN

Fundamental question about revolution, The. Facing the Way. Alice Walker. CP-WalkA

Fundamentals, The. Yannis Ritsos. SP-RitsY, *tr. by* N. C. Germanacos

Funebrial Reflection. Ogden Nash. CP-NashO

Funeral. Langston Hughes. CP-HughL; CP-HughL2

Funeral. Rainer Maria Rilke. CP-RilkFr, *tr. by* A. Poulin, Jr.

Funeral. Wisława Szymborska. SP-SzymW, *tr. by* Stanisław Barańczak *and* Clare Cavanagh

Funeral. Miller Williams. CP-WillM

Funeral Bell, The. Henry David Thoreau. CP-ThorH

Funeral Elegy upon that Pattern and Patron of Virtue, A. John Norton. CP-BradA

Funeral Music. Geoffrey Hill. CP-HillG

Funeral of Bobò, The. Joseph Brodsky. CP-BrodJ; CP-WilbR, *tr. by* Richard Wilbur

Funeral of Sarpedon, The ("Heart of Zeus is filled with grief, The"). Constantine P. Cavafy. CP-CavaC, *tr. by* Theoharis Constantine Theoharis

Funeral of Sarpedon, The ("Zeus grieves mightily. Patroklos"). Constantine P. Cavafy. CP-CavaC, *tr. by* Theoharis Constantine Theoharis

Funeral Oration for a Mouse. Alan Dugan. CP-DugaA

Funeral paths are hung with snow, The. Night-Time in the Cemetery. Stevie Smith. CP-SmitS

Funeral Poem on the Death of C. E. an Infant of Twelve Months, A. Phillis Wheatley. CP-WheaP

(Poem on the Death of Charles Eliot Aged 12 Months, A [variant 2].) CP-WheaP

Funeral procession swinging empty belts, The. Next, The. W. S. Merwin. SP-MerwW

Funeral Rites. Seamus Heaney. SP-HeanSO

Funeral, The. Norman Dubie. CP-DubiN

Funeral Tree of the Sokokis. John Greenleaf Whittier. CP-WhitJ

Funeral under My Window. Jaroslav Seifert. SP-SeifJ, *tr. by* Ewald Osers

Funeral[1] Rites of the Rose, The. Robert Herrick. CP-HerrR

Funeral[1] stone, A. To Laurels. Robert Herrick. CP-HerrR

Funeral[1], The. John Donne. CP-DonnJ; MW-DonnJ

Funerals, The. Wyatt Prunty. SP-PrunW

Funerals, The. Jones Very. CP-VeryJ

Funereal Toast. Stéphane Mallarmé. CP-MallS, *tr. by* Henry Weinfield

Funky barn, black hills approaching Fulton. Allen Ginsberg. SP-GinsA *Fr.* Kansas City to Saint Louis.

Funky blues / Keen toed shoes. Country Lover. Maya Angelou. SP-AngeM

Funnel. Anne Sexton. CP-SextA

Funniest thing in the world, I know, The. James Whitcomb Riley. CP-RileJ

Funny. Charles Bukowski. SP-BukC3

Funny. Robert Creeley. CP-CreeR

Funny Death. Allen Ginsberg. CP-GinsA

Funny Little Fellow, The. James Whitcomb Riley. CP-RileJ

Funny thing about a chair, A. Chair, The. Theodore Roethke. CP-RoetT

Funny this den of Five Shades. Han-shan. CP-ColdM, *tr. by* Red Pine

Funny—to be a Century. Emily Dickinson. CP-DickE

Fur came near, night inside it. Little Gift, A. Wendell Phillips Stafford. SP-StafWW

Fur the color of mud, the smooth loper. Berry Feast, A. Gary Snyder. CP-SnydG

Furies, The. Anne Sexton. CP-SextA

Fury of Beautiful Bones, The. SP-SextA

Fury of Cocks, The. SP-SextA

Fury of Cooks, The. SP-SextA

Fury of Guitars and Sopranos, The. SP-SextA

Fury of Sunrises, The. SP-SextA

Fury of Sunsets, The. SP-SextA

Furies, The. May Sarton. SP-SartM

Furies, The. Stephen Spender. CP-SpenS

Furious Frenchman comes with his clarions and his drums, The. Bellocose. G. K. Chesterton. CP-ChesG

Furious gun in his raging ire, The. Sir Thomas Wyatt. CP-WyatT

Furious prisoner of the womb, The. Argument, An. Of the Passion of Christ. Thomas Merton. CP-MertT

Furious Voyage, The. Robert Graves. CP-GravR

Furius, Aurelius: comities—Catullus. Catullus. *See* Furius, Aurelius, friends of my youth

Furius, Aurelius, friends of my youth. Carmen 11. Catullus. CP-ZukLS *Fr.* Carmina.

Furius, "Little Villa" has no nod for Auster. Catullus. *See* Your cottage, Furius, sheltered

Furl of fresh-leaved dogrose down, The. Gerard Manley Hopkins. CP-HopkG

Furnace, The. Thomas Kinsella. CP-KinsT

Furnished and clean, this room does not betray. Succession. Howard Nemerov. CP-NemeH

Furnished rooms, flats, a hayloft. He Has Lived in Many Houses. Thomas Lux. SP-LuxT

Furniture. D. H. Lawrence. CP-LawrD

Furniture Mover. Charles Simic. SP-SimiC; SP-SimiCE

Furniture of a Woman's Mind, The. Jonathan Swift. CP-SwifJ

Furniture, The. John Updike. CP-UpdiJ

Furred sons of the blue wolf slant-eyed rode from the east. Ashes Ashes All Fall Down. Robert Stock. SP-StocR

'Furrow' is inexact: / no ship could be. On Water. Charles Tomlinson. CP-TomlC; SP-TomlC

Furry blond wheatfield in. From the Train, Eastward. Denise Levertov. SP-LeveDL

Further Advantages of Learning. Kenneth Rexroth. CP-RexrK

Further Adventures of Charles Simic. Charles Simic. SP-SimiCE

Further Arrivals. Margaret Atwood. SP-AtwM1

Further Details. Laura Riding Jackson. CP-RidiL

Further in Summer than the Birds. Emily Dickinson. CP-DickE

Further Note to Clark. Lucille Clifton. SP-ClifL

Further Notice. Philip Whalen. SP-WhalP

Further-off people are the smaller. Grandparents, The. Perspectives. Louis MacNeice. CP-MacNL

Further On. A. R. Ammons. CP-AmmoA

Further Passages from *The Kind of Poetry I Want*. Hugh MacDiarmid.
"Greatest poets undergo a kind of crisis in their art, The." SP-MacDH
"Poetry like a lance at rest, A." SP-MacDH
"Poetry like the barrel of a gun, A." SP-MacDH

Further Proposal, A. Allen Ginsberg. CP-GinsA

Further Reasons Why Poets Do Not Tell the Truth. Hans Magnus Enzensberger. SP-EnzeH

Further Reflection on Parsley. Ogden Nash. CP-NashO

"Further Than." Louis Zukofsky. CP-ZukLS

Furtive the hedgerow cat. Eyeing the World. Wyatt Prunty. SP-PrunW

Furtively sounding / In the high. It Is Big Inside a Man. Kenneth Patchen. CP-PatcK

Fury and counter fury! The volcano! Catastrophic Birth. William Carlos Williams. CP-WilW2

Fury of Aerial Bombardment, The. Richard Eberhart. CP-EberR

Fury of Beautiful Bones, The. Anne Sexton. SP-SextA *Fr.* Furies, The.

Fury of Cocks, The. Anne Sexton. SP-SextA *Fr.* Furies, The.

Fury of Cooks, The. Anne Sexton. SP-SextA *Fr.* Furies, The.

Fury of Guitars and Sopranos, The. Anne Sexton. SP-SextA *Fr.* Furies, The.

Fury of Sunrises, The. Anne Sexton. SP-SextA *Fr.* Furies, The.

Fury of Sunsets, The. Anne Sexton. SP-SextA *Fr.* Furies, The.

Fusion. George Meredith. CP-MerG2

Fust and His Friends. Robert Browning. CP-BroR2

Futile of me to offer you my hand. Last Prince of the East. Langston Hughes. CP-HughL; CP-HughL3

Futile Petition. Stéphane Mallarmé. CP-MallS, *tr.* by Henry Weinfield

Futility. Walter De la Mare. CP-DeLaW

Futility. Wilfred Owen. CP-OwenW

Futter or rest, every soul. Shmuel HaNagid. SP-HaNaS, *tr.* by Peter Cole

Future. Joseph Brodsky. CP-BrodJ *Fr.* Shorts.

Future days stand before us. Candles. Constantine P. Cavafy. CP-CavaC, *tr.* by Theoharis Constantine Theoharis

Future in Miniature. Marya Alexandrovna Zaturenska. SP-ZatuM

Future—never spoke, The. Emily Dickinson. CP-DickE

Future of religion lies in the mystery of touch, The. Future Religion. D. H. Lawrence. CP-LawrD

Future Relationships. D. H. Lawrence. CP-LawrD

Future Religion. D. H. Lawrence. CP-LawrD

Future rose and held vein. Useless Song. Federico García Lorca. SP-GarcF, *tr.* by W. S. Merwin

Future State of the Wicked and Its Duration, The. Jones Very. CP-VeryJ

Future States. D. H. Lawrence. CP-LawrD

Future sucks, The. Hustings, The. Charles Olson. CP-OlsoC

Future, The. Ralph Waldo Emerson. CP-EmerR

Future, The. David Ignatow. SP-IgnaD

Future, The. Gabriela Mistral. SP-MistG, *tr.* by Maria Giachetti [*or* Jacketti]

Future, The: time's excuse. Rainer Maria Rilke. CP-RilkFr, *tr.* by A. Poulin, Jr.

Future War. D. H. Lawrence. CP-LawrD

Future weighs down on me, The. Blue Anchor, The. Jane Cooper. CP-CoopJ

Futurity. Elizabeth Barrett Browning. CP-BroEB

Fuzon, on a chariot iron-wing'd. Book of Ahania, The. William Blake. CP-BlakW

Fuzzed snow browning in lastyear's haystubble, the pasture's winter-starved moss. Thaw. Hayden Carruth. CP-CarHS

Fuzzy fellow, without feet, A. Caterpillar. Emily Dickinson. CP-DickE

Fuzzy-Wuzzy. Rudyard Kipling. CP-KiplR

Fy let us a' to K[IRKUDBRIGHT]. Election, The: A New Song. Robert Burns. CP-BurnR *Fr.* Heron Ballads, 1795, The.

Fyodor. Allen Ginsberg. CP-GinsA; SP-GinsA

G

G, also inevitably, is for GNU. John Ciardi. CP-CiarJ

G. M. B. Donald Davie. CP-DaviDC

G / ra / D / ua / lLy &. E. E. Cummings. CP-CummE

G. S. Reading Poesy at Princeton. Allen Ginsberg. CP-GinsA

Gabriel. Adrienne Rich. CP-RicAE

Gabriel, from heaven's king. Angelus Ad Virginem. Gerard Manley Hopkins. CP-HopkG

Gabriel Preil, the Grand Duke of New York. Grand Duke of New York, The. Dan Pagis. SP-PagiD, *tr.* by Stephen Mitchell

Gacela of Desperate Love. Federico García Lorca. SP-GarcF, *tr.* by W. S. Merwin

Gacela of the Bitter Root. Federico García Lorca. SP-GarcF, *tr.* by Edwin Honig

Gacela of the Dark Death. Federico García Lorca. SP-GarcF, *tr.* by J. L. Gili *and* Stephen Spender

Gacela of the Dead Child. Federico García Lorca. SP-GarcF, *tr.* by Edwin Honig

Gacela of the Flight. Federico García Lorca. SP-GarcF, *tr.* by J. L. Gili *and* Stephen Spender

Gacela of the Morning Market. Federico García Lorca. SP-GarcF, *tr.* by J. L. Gili *and* Stephen Spender

Gacela of the Terrible Presence. Federico García Lorca. SP-GarcF, *tr.* by W. S. Merwin

Gacela of Unforeseen Love. Federico García Lorca. SP-GarcF, *tr.* by W. S. Merwin

Gagarin says, in ecstasy. Heel & Toe to the End. William Carlos Williams. CP-WilW2

Gaia, first-born daughter of Chaos. Lithuania, after Fifty-two Years. Czeslaw Milosz. CP-MiloCN, *tr.* by Robert Hass

Gaily bedight. Eldorado. Edgar Allan Poe. CP-PoeEd

Gain. A. R. Ammons. CP-AmmoA

Gain and Gettings. Robert Herrick. CP-HerrR

Gainst Fate no counsell can prevaile. Ovid. CP-RaleW *Fr.* Tristium.

Gairmscoile. Hugh MacDiarmid. SP-MacDH

Gal; many a thing I've seen her lift without strain or hurry of. Sturdy Legs, That. Kenneth Patchen. CP-PatcK

Gala, holding on. Zinnias. Robert Earl Hayden. CP-HaydR

Galahad, Knight Who Perished. Nicholas Vachel Lindsay. CP-LindV

Galahad . . . soldier that perished . . . ages ago. Galahad, Knight Who Perished. Nicholas Vachel Lindsay. CP-LindV

Galán. Archibald MacLeish. CP-MacLA

Galatea. Ovid. CP-MahoD, *tr.* by Derek Mahon *Fr.* Metamorphoses.

Galatea Encore. Joseph Brodsky. CP-BrodJ

Gale in April. Robinson Jeffers. CP-JefR1

Galiano Coast: Four Entrances. Margaret Atwood. SP-AtwM2

Galilee Shore. Allen Ginsberg. CP-GinsA

Galileo and the Laws. John Ciardi. CP-CiarJ

Galileo thought he saw. Galileo and the Laws. John Ciardi. CP-CiarJ

Galla Water. Robert Burns. CP-BurnR

Gallant Chateau. Wallace Stevens. CP-StevW; CP-StevWP

Gallant Weaver, The. Robert Burns. CP-BurnR

Gallant Youth, who may have gained, The. Yarrow Revisited. William Wordsworth. CP-WorW2; MW-WorW

Gallants, our business is to let you know. Prologue to the Farce of *Punch Turned Schoolmaster*. Thomas Sheridan. CP-SherT

Gallant's Song. Thomas Hardy. CP-HardT

Gallery of sacred pictures manifold. Book, The. John Greenleaf Whittier. CP-WhitJ

Gallery, The. Andrew Marvell. CP-MarvA

Gallery Walk: Fifteen Italian Drawings 1780–1890. John Logan. CP-LogaJ

Galley-Slave, The. Rudyard Kipling. CP-KiplR

Galley, The. Petrarch. CP-WyatT, *tr.* by Sir Thomas Wyatt *Fr.* Sonnets to Laura.

Galliass, The. Walter De la Mare. CP-DeLaW

Gallio's Song. Rudyard Kipling. CP-KiplR

Galloping Cat, The. Stevie Smith. CP-SmitS

Galloping collection of boards, The. Somewhere. Robert Creeley. CP-CreeR

Galloping Green: May 1962. Thomas Kinsella. CP-KinsT *Fr.* Selected Life, A.

Galloping horses / Of the departed century. Early Morning. Czeslaw Milosz. CP-MiloC; CP-MiloCN, *tr.* by Robert Hass

Galloway Tam. Robert Burns. CP-BurnR

Gallows Etiquette. Charles Simic. SP-SimiC; SP-SimiCE

Gallows, The. John Greenleaf Whittier. CP-WhitJ

Gallowstree drops, The. Jesus Unborn. Anne Sexton. CP-SextA; SP-SextA

Gallup Swill-Hole, A; or, Cantina Blues. Clarence Major. SP-MajoC

Gallus ha' but brothers: bro one's lady slip's make so young she's. Catullus. *See* Gallus's brothers possess / one, the most attractive of wives

Gallus's brothers possess / one, the most attractive of wives. Carmen 78. Catullus. CP-ZukLS *Fr.* Carmina.

Galoots. Carl Sandburg. CP-SandC

Galoots, you hairy, hankering. Galoots. Carl Sandburg. CP-SandC

Gal's Cry for a Dying Lover. Langston Hughes. CP-HughL; CP-HughL1

Galway Jack, Dublin Moira, wild swans. Inchiquin Lake, Penobscot Bay. Richard Eberhart. CP-EberR

Gamble everything for love. Jelaluddin Rumi. SP-Rumi, *tr.* by Coleman Barks

Gamblers, The. Nicholas Vachel Lindsay. CP-LindV

Gambling. Kenneth Rexroth. CP-RexrK

Gambling at Reno. William Dickey. SP-DickW

Gambling in Stateline, Nevada. James Wright. CP-WrigJ

Gambling Phoenix, The. Andrei Codrescu. SP-CodrA

Gambol and song and jubilee are done. Valedictory Poem. Ralph Waldo Emerson. CP-EmerR

Game, A. Andrei Codrescu. SP-CodrA

Game, The. Louise Glück. SP-GlucL

Game, The. Stanley Kunitz. CP-KunSC

Game, The. Charles Simic. SP-SimiC; SP-SimiCE

Game, The. C. K. Williams. SP-WillC

Game after Supper. Margaret Atwood. SP-AtwM1

Game at Salzburg, A. Randall Jarrell. CP-JarrR

Game of Ball, A. Muriel Rukeyser. CP-RukeM

Game of Darts at the Chesterfield Arms, A. Muriel Rukeyser. CP-RukeM

Game of Monopoly in Chavannes. Maxine W. Kumin. SP-KumiM

Game of Moons, A. Federico García Lorca. CP-GarcF, *tr. by* Jerome Rothenberg *Fr.* Barrage of Firework Poems on the Occasion of the Poet's Birthday.

Game of the Thunderbolt Goddesses, The. Robert Stock. SP-StocR

Gamecock. James Dickey. CP-DickJ

Games. Federico García Lorca.

  "Orange and lemon." CP-GarcF, *tr. by* Alan S. Trueblood

  "People were leaving." CP-GarcF, *tr. by* Alan S. Trueblood

  Song of the Fairy. CP-GarcF, *tr. by* Alan S. Trueblood

  Songs of the Riverbank. CP-GarcF, *tr. by* Alan S. Trueblood

  Street of the Mute, The. CP-GarcF, *tr. by* Alan S. Trueblood

  To Irene García. CP-GarcF, *tr. by* Alan S. Trueblood

  Tree of Song. CP-GarcF, *tr. by* Alan S. Trueblood

  Whispered to a Girl. CP-GarcF, *tr. by* Alan S. Trueblood

Games. Yehuda Amichai. SP-AmicYL, *tr. by* Benjamin Harshav *and* Barbara Harshav

Games of cards are such that they create women. Partiti Sunt Vestimenta Mea Miserunt Sortem Contra Me ad Incarte Cla a Filii a Eniol Liebee Braya Braguesca et Belzebuth. Andrei Codrescu. SP-CodrA

Games of Chance. Charles Baudelaire. CP-BaudC, *tr. by* Walter Martin

Games One. Richard Wilbur. CP-WilbR

Games Two. Richard Wilbur. CP-WilbR

Gamut. Louis Zukofsky. CP-ZukLS

Gamut, The. Maya Angelou. SP-AngeM

Gander, The. Ogden Nash. CP-NashO

Gandhi Is Fasting. Langston Hughes. CP-HughL; CP-HughL3

Gandhi's Gun (and Brecht's Vow). Denise Levertov. SP-LeveDS *Fr.* Staying Alive.

Gane is the day and mirk's the night. Then Guidwife Count the Lawin. Robert Burns. CP-BurnR

Gang of labourers on the piled wet timber, A. Morning Work. D. H. Lawrence. CP-LawrD

Ganges, The. Norman Dubie. CP-DubiN

Gangster. Robert Creeley. CP-CreeR

Gangsters. Langston Hughes. CP-HughL; CP-HughL2

Gangsters of the world, The. Gangsters. Langston Hughes. CP-HughL; CP-HughL2

Gangway or Curtain Up! Then forth. Sailing Orders. Louis MacNeice. CP-MacNL

Gannets. Mary Oliver. SP-OlivM

Gap, The. Charles Tomlinson. CP-TomlC

Gap, The. C. K. Williams. *See* Dream of Mind, A: The Gap

Gap in the White, The. Thomas Hardy. CP-HardT

Gap where the quarry is keeps moving away, The. Quarry, The. Charles Tomlinson. CP-TomlC

Gape, gape, gorlin'. Ex Vermibus. Hugh MacDiarmid. SP-MacDH

Garage in Co. Cork, A. Derek Mahon. CP-MahoD

Garden. Federico García Lorca. CP-GarcF, *tr. by* Jerome Rothenberg *Fr.* Water Jets.

Garden. A. R. Ammons. CP-AmmoA

Garden. "H. D." CP-DoolH

Garden. Langston Hughes. CP-HughL

  (Poem.) CP-HughL1

Garden. John Greenleaf Whittier. CP-WhitJ

Garden, The. Federico García Lorca. CP-GarcF, *tr. by* Jerome Rothenberg *Fr.* In the Garden of the Lunar Grapefruits.

Garden, The. Rae Armantrout. SP-ArmaA

Garden, The. Raymond Carver. CP-CarvR

Garden, The. Louise Glück. SP-GlucL

Garden, The. Robert Graves. CP-GravR

Garden, The. Ivor Gurney. SP-GurnI

Garden, The. Thomas Lux. SP-LuxT

Garden, The. Andrew Marvell. CP-MarvA

Garden, The. Eugenio Montale. CP-MontE, *tr. by* Jonathan Galassi

Garden, The. Robert Pinsky. CP-PinsR

Garden, The. Alexander Pope. CP-PopeA

Garden, The. Ezra Pound. SP-PounE

Garden, The. Edwin Arlington Robinson. CP-RobiE

Garden, The. Jones Very. CP-VeryJ

Garden, The. Robert Penn Warren. CP-WarrR

Garden, The. Philip Whalen. SP-WhalP

Garden Abstract. Hart Crane. CP-CranH

Garden alley with statues of hardened mud, A. Footnote to Weather Forecasts, A. Joseph Brodsky. CP-BrodJ

Garden at Cliveden, The. Marya Alexandrovna Zaturenska. SP-ZatuM

Garden at St. John's, The. May Swenson. SP-SwenM

Garden called Gethsemane, The. Gethsemane. Rudyard Kipling. CP-KiplR

Garden Fancies. Robert Browning. CP-BroR1

Garden flew round with the angel, The. Pleasures of Merely Circulating, The. Wallace Stevens. CP-StevW; CP-StevWP

Garden gate is opened, The. Simplicity. Jorge Luis Borges. SP-BorgJ, *tr. by* Stephen Kessler

Garden God, The. Richard Eberhart. CP-EberR

Garden Idyl, A. George Meredith. CP-MerG1

Garden in a garden; a green spot, A. On Keats, 18 January, 1948 (Eve of St Agnes). Christina Georgina Rossetti. CP-RosC3

Garden in Umber; or The Garden of the Brownhaired Girls. Federico García Lorca.

  Acacia. CP-GarcF, *tr. by* Jerome Rothenberg

  Encounter ("María del Reposo, / again I encounter"). CP-GarcF, *tr. by* Jerome Rothenberg

  "Lemongrove. / Flash / in my dream." CP-GarcF, *tr. by* Jerome Rothenberg

  Portico ("Water / taps its silver"). CP-GarcF, *tr. by* Jerome Rothenberg

Garden is dark green and the king, The. Dispute, The. Clarence Major. SP-MajoC

Garden of Boccaccio, The. Samuel Taylor Coleridge. CP-ColeS

Garden of Childhood, The. May Sarton. SP-SartM

Garden of Delight, The. Lucille Clifton. SP-ClifL

Garden of Delights, The. James Laughlin. CP-LaugJ

Garden of Earthly Delights, The. Czeslaw Milosz. CP-MiloC; CP-MiloCN, *tr. by* Robert Hass

Garden of Earthly Delights, The: Hell. Czeslaw Milosz. CP-MiloCN, *tr. by* Robert Hass

Garden of Epicurus, The. George Meredith. CP-MerG1

Garden of Eros, The. Oscar Wilde. CP-WildO

Garden of Love, The. William Blake. CP-BlakW *Fr.* Songs of Experience.

Garden of Metrodorus, The. Herman Melville. SP-MelvH

Garden of mouthings, A. Purple, scarlet-speckled, black. Beekeeper's Daughter, The. Sylvia Plath. CP-PlatS

Garden of the Gods, The. Thom Gunn. CP-GunnT

Garden of the Virgin, The. G. K. Chesterton. CP-ChesG

Garden Party, The. Donald Davie. CP-DaviDC

Garden Seat, The. Thomas Hardy. CP-HardT

Garden-Spot. Dorothy Parker. CP-ParkD

Garden State. Allen Ginsberg. CP-GinsA

Garden, the rose hedges, the crisp-cut privet, The. Leaves from the Book of Dorothy Wordsworth. Marya Alexandrovna Zaturenska. SP-ZatuM

Garden Wall, The. Denise Levertov. SP-LeveDP

Garden—was it real or was it dream?, The. Adam Cast Forth. Jorge Luis Borges. SP-BorgJ, *tr. by* Alastair Reid

Garden Waters. Robert Penn Warren. CP-WarrR

Garden Wireless. Carl Sandburg. CP-SandC

Gardener. Robert Graves. CP-GravR

Gardener. Czeslaw Milosz. CP-MiloCN, *tr. by* Brian Glazer *and* Martin Sabiniewicz

Gardener in Haying-Time, The. Edna St. Vincent Millay. CP-MillE

Gardener to His God, The. Mona Van Duyn. SP-VanDM

Gardener wi' His Paddle—or, The Gardener's March, The. Robert Burns. CP-BurnR

Gardens No Emblems. Donald Davie. CP-DaviDC

Gardens of Alcinous, The. Homer. CP-PopeA, *tr. by* Alexander Pope *Fr.* Odyssey.

Gardens of Buckingham Palace, The. I Remember Sir Alfred. Paul Muldoon. CP-MuldP

Gardens of the Savoy, The. Donald Davie. CP-DaviDC

Gardens of Zuñi, The. W. S. Merwin. SP-MerwW

Gare du Midi. W. H. Auden. CP-AudeW

Gargoyle. Carl Sandburg. CP-SandC

Gargoyle's Song for the Warming Trend. Alan Dugan. CP-DugaA

Garibaldi. Elizabeth Barrett Browning. CP-BroEB

Garibaldi. John Greenleaf Whittier. CP-WhitJ

Garish room—oil-lamped; a stove's warm blaze, A. Of a Son. Walter De la Mare. CP-DeLaW

Garland for Christopher Smart, A. Mona Van Duyn. SP-VanDM

Garland for Ivor Gurney, A. Donald Davie. CP-DaviDC

Garland for Ronsard, A. Donald Davie. CP-DaviDC

Garland for Thomas Eakins, A. Charles Tomlinson. CP-TomlC; SP-TomlC

Garland for You. Robert Penn Warren. CP-WarrR

Garland on the Wrist, A. Jaroslav Seifert. SP-SeifJ, tr. by Ewald Osers

Garland [or Ghyrlond] of the Blessèd Virgin Mary [or Marie], The. Ben Jonson. CP-JonsB

Garland was wound out of blackening leaves in the region of Akra, A. Song in the Wilderness, A. Paul Celan. SP-CelaP, tr. by John Felstiner

Garlands for Queens, may be. Emily Dickinson. CP-DickE

Garment. Langston Hughes. CP-HughL

Garments. Constantine P. Cavafy. CP-CavaC, tr. by Theoharis Constantine Theoharis

Garnie, I wish I was a seagull. Poem by Garnie Braxton, A. James Wright. CP-WrigJ

Garret, The. Paul Laurence Dunbar. CP-DunbP

Garret, The. Ezra Pound. SP-PounE

Garrison. John Greenleaf Whittier. CP-WhitJ

Garrison, The. W. H. Auden. CP-AudeW

Garrison of Cape Ann, The. John Greenleaf Whittier. CP-WhitJ

Gary allow me. Namaste. Olga Broumas. SP-BrouO

Gas fire, The. Persian, The. Stevie Smith. CP-SmitS

Gas or Novocain. Kenneth Rexroth. CP-RexrK

Gas Station, The. C. K. Williams. CP-WillC; SP-WillC

Gash in the azure. Bolt from the Blue. Gregory Orr. SP-OrrG

Gasman Invites the Skyscrapers to Dance. Marge Piercy. SP-PierM

Gasoline makes game scarce. Written on the Stub of the First Paycheck. William Stafford. SP-StafW Fr. Move to California, The.

Gasp-glory of gold light of dawn on gold maple. Glimpses of Seasons. Robert Penn Warren. CP-WarrR

Gassing the woodchucks didn't turn out right. Woodchucks. Maxine W. Kumin. SP-KumiM

Gat ye me, O gat ye me. Lass of Ecclefechan, The. Robert Burns. CP-BurnR

Gate City Breakdown. Charles Wright. SP-WrigC

Gate-crashing ghost, aggressive. Loneliness. W. H. Auden. CP-AudeW

Gate creaked in the dusk, The. The trampled grass. St Godnait's Graveyard, Ballyvourney: That Evening. Thomas Kinsella. CP-KinsT Fr. Selected Life, A.

Gate Is Prouti, The. Charles Olson. CP-OlsoC

Gate of Everywhere, The. G. K. Chesterton. CP-ChesG

Gate posts where the drive begins, The. Patronage. Heather McHugh. SP-McHuH

Gate, The. Charles Tomlinson. CP-TomlC

Gates, The. Muriel Rukeyser. CP-RukeM

Gates clanged and they walked you into jail, The. Conscientious Objector, The. Karl Shapiro. SP-ShapK

Gates have closed to the rotted park, The. American Painting, with Rain. Eleanor Wilner. SP-WilnE

Gates of grammar closed behind him, The. On the Death of a Poet. Czeslaw Milosz. CP-MiloCN, tr. by Robert Hass

Gates of Paradise, The. William Blake. CP-BlakW

(For the Sexes the Gates of Paradise.) CP-BlakW

Gates of the Arsenal, The. Czeslaw Milosz. CP-MiloC; CP-MiloCN, tr. by Robert Hass

Gateway, Grove, / and Dover say. Rack of Paperbacks, A. John Updike. CP-UpdiJ

Gateway, The. Robert Graves. CP-GravR

Gather a body to me. Telesphere, The. Charles Olson. SP-OlsoC Fr. Maximus Poems, The.

Gather all the old, rip and sew. Hand Crocheted Rug. Lorine Niedecker. CP-NiedL

Gather around thee treasures bright. Religion. Jones Very. CP-VeryJ

Gather, O gather, / Foeman and friend in love and peace! Cancelled Stanza. Percy Bysshe Shelley. CP-ShelP

Gather out of star-dust. Dream Dust. Langston Hughes. CP-HughL; CP-HughL2; CP-HughL3

Gather quickly. Bouquet. Langston Hughes. CP-HughL; CP-HughL3

Gather the heart! The leaves. Autumn. James Vincent Cunningham. CP-CunnJ

Gather the stars if you wish it so. Stars, Songs, Faces. Carl Sandburg. CP-SandC

Gather up in the arms of your pity. Prayer ("Gather up / In the arms of your pity"). Langston Hughes. CP-HughL; CP-HughL2

Gather while you may. Rose. Kathleen Jessie Raine. SP-RainK

Gather ye rose-buds while ye may. To the Virgins, to Make Much of Time. Robert Herrick. CP-HerrR

Gather young men as the twilight gathers. Carmen 62. Catullus. CP-ZukLS Fr. Carmina.

Gathered at the time of thanks; and the harvest. Family Reunion. Hayden Carruth. CP-CarHS

Gathered in inter-admiration. When the Five Prominent Poets. Josephine Jacobsen. CP-JacoJ

Gathered into the Earth. Emily Dickinson. CP-DickE

Gathering, The. Wendell Berry. CP-BerrW

Gathering, The. Josephine Jacobsen. CP-JacoJ

Gathering Apricots. Czeslaw Milosz. CP-MiloCN, tr. by Robert Hass

Gathering Leaves. Robert Frost. CP-FrosR

Gathering lotuses we called to each other. Han-shan. CP-ColdM, tr. by Red Pine

Gathering Mushrooms. Paul Muldoon. CP-MuldP

Gathering the Bones Together. Gregory Orr. SP-OrrG

Gathering Wood. Philip Larkin. CP-LarkP

Gaudy space capsule. Sleeping Pill. Hans Magnus Enzensberger. SP-EnzeH

Gauge. Langston Hughes. CP-HughL; CP-HughL3

Gauley Bridge. Muriel Rukeyser. CP-RukeM

Gauley Bridge is a good town for Negroes, they let us stand. George Robinson: Blues. Muriel Rukeyser. CP-RukeM

Gaunt kept house with her child for the old man. Montana Fifty Years Ago. James Vincent Cunningham. CP-CunnJ

Gaunt, my hope, horse-wise. Min Schleppner. William Carlos Williams. CP-WilW1

Gaurus pretends to Cato's fame. Martial. CP-JohnS Fr. Epigrams.

Gautama in the Deer Park at Benares. Kenneth Patchen. CP-PatcK

Gave me things I. Swallow the Lake. Clarence Major. SP-MajoC

Gawaine, aware again of Lancelot. Lancelot. Edwin Arlington Robinson. CP-RobiE

Gawaine, Gawaine, what look ye for to see. Merlin. Edwin Arlington Robinson. CP-RobiE

Gay Chaps at the Bar. Gwendolyn Brooks. SP-BrooG Fr. Gay Chaps at the Bar.

Gay go up and gay go down. Bells and Queen Victoria, The. Rudyard Kipling. CP-KiplR

"Gay" is the captivating cognomen of a Young Woman of cambridge, mass. E. E. Cummings. CP-CummE

Gay little devils. Nocturne for the Drums. Langston Hughes. CP-HughL; CP-HughL1

Gay ore gook con candlelows. Bearded Iris. Louis Zukofsky. CP-ZukLS

Gayest of Bright Flowers, The. William Carlos Williams. CP-WilW1

Gaza. Jane Cooper. CP-CoopJ

Gazelle Calf, The. D. H. Lawrence. CP-LawrD

Gazelle, I killed you. Ode to a Drum. Yusef Komunyakaa. CP-KomuY

Gazelle, The. Shmuel HaNagid. SP-HaNaS, tr. by Peter Cole

Gazing Grain, The. John Ashbery. SP-AshbJ

Gazing, listless, from his book. Scholar Dreaming, The. Jones Very. CP-VeryJ

Gazing on some higher sphere. On Seeing the Portrait of Helen Ruthven Waterston. Jones Very. CP-VeryJ

Gazing thro' her chamber window. Reflection. Christina Georgina Rossetti. CP-RosC3

Gazing through the / night and its stars. Shmuel HaNagid. SP-HaNaS, tr. by Peter Cole

Gedale's Song. Primo Levi. CP-LeviP, tr. by Ruth Feldman

Gee, I know / a lovely girl. Person. Robert Creeley. CP-CreeR

Gee i like to think of dead it means nearer because deeper firmer. E. E. Cummings. CP-CummE

Geese and brant, their wingbeat. Over the North Jetty. William Stafford. SP-StafW

Geese Going South. Charles Tomlinson. SP-TomlC

Gehazi. Rudyard Kipling. CP-KiplR

Gellius, / hearing his uncle anathematise the mere mention. Carmen 74. Catullus. CP-ZukLS Fr. Carmina.

Gellius how he'd rare at pot true uncle objurgate soul array. Catullus. See Gellius, / hearing his uncle anathematise the mere mention

Gellius is thin. / So? Carmen 89. Catullus. CP-ZukLS Fr. Carmina.

Gellius is thin why yes: kiddin'? quite a bonny mater. Catullus. See Gellius is thin. / So?

Gemini. Robert Creeley. CP-CreeR

Gemini. Louise Glück. SP-GlucL

Gemini. Audre Lorde. SP-LordA

Gemini. Richard Wilbur. CP-WilbR

Gemona-del-Friuli, 1961–1976. Donald Davie. CP-DaviDC

Gems and jewels let them heap. In a Garret. Herman Melville. SP-MelvH

Gen. Gary Snyder. CP-SnydG

Gen. Rodimstev's Story / (Stalingrad). Lorine Niedecker. CP-NiedL

Gene sat on a rock, dangling our map. Route of the Táin, The. Thomas Kinsella. CP-KinsT

Genealogical Reflection. Ogden Nash. CP-NashO

Genealogy. Yusef Komunyakaa. CP-KomuY

Genealogy. Robert Penn Warren. CP-WarrR

General Assembly and Church of the Firstborn, The. Christina Georgina Rossetti. CP-RosC2

General 'eard the firin' on the flank, The. Stellenbosch. Rudyard Kipling. CP-KiplR

General George Armstrong Custer: My Life in the Theater. Ai. SP-Ai

General Joubert. Rudyard Kipling. CP-KiplR

General Lew Wallace. James Whitcomb Riley. CP-RileJ

General Martinet Gem Coughed A-hem, and A-hem, and A-hem. Motet. Louis Zukofsky. CP-ZukLS

General Prothalamion for Wartimes. Alan Dugan. CP-DugaA

General Prothalamion in Populous Times. Alan Dugan. CP-DugaA

General Quiroga Rides to His Death in a Carriage. Jorge Luis Borges. SP-BorgJ, tr. by Alastair Reid

General Review of the Sex Situation. Dorothy Parker. CP-ParkD

General Song of Humanity, The. Lawrence Ferlinghetti. SP-FerlL

General Summary, A. Rudyard Kipling. CP-KiplR

General William Booth Enters into Heaven. Nicholas Vachel Lindsay. CP-LindV

Generalization of Distrust. Yannis Ritsos. SP-RitsY, tr. by N. C. Germanacos

Generally, reading palms or handwriting or faces. Model, The. W. H. Auden. CP-AudeW

Generals came to the president, The. Connections: Vermont Vietnam (II). Grace Paley. CP-PalGC

General's men sit at the door, The. Her eyes. Confession. Norman Dubie. CP-DubiN

Generation. Rae Armantrout. SP-ArmaA

Generation. Audre Lorde. SP-LordA

Generation Before, The. Robert Pinsky. CP-PinsR

Generation Gap. John Ciardi. CP-CiarJ

Generation of Drivers. George Oppen. CP-OppGN

Generation, The. Adam Zagajewski. SP-ZagaA, tr. by Renata Gorczynski

Generation II. Audre Lorde. SP-LordA

Generations. Ivor Gurney. SP-GurnI

Generations. Rachel Korn. CP-KizeC, tr. by Carolyn Kizer

Generations, The. James Laughlin. CP-LaugJ

Generations / and the solace, The. Till Other Voices Wake Us. George Oppen. CP-OppGN

Generations of Men, The. Robert Frost. CP-FrosR

Generic College. John Updike. CP-UpdiJ

Generic Vision, 1991. Eleanor Wilner. SP-WilnE

Generous Days, The. Stephen Spender. CP-SpenS

Genesis. Ambrose Bierce. SP-BierA

Genesis. Geoffrey Hill. CP-HillG

Genesis. Nicholas Vachel Lindsay. CP-LindV

Genesis. Louis MacNeice. CP-MacNL

Genesis. Theodore Roethke. CP-RoetT

Genesis. William Carlos Williams. CP-WilW1

Genesis tells us of Jubal and Jabal. Efforts of Affection. Marianne Craig Moore. CP-MoorM

Genesis Text for Larry Levis, Who Died Alone, A. Norman Dubie. CP-DubiN

Geneva Restored. Charles Tomlinson. CP-TomlC

Genevieve. Samuel Taylor Coleridge. MW-ColeS Fr. Effusions.

Genevieve / what are you seeing. MemorialII. Audre Lorde. SP-LordA

Genial poets, pink-faced. Goodbye to Tolerance. Denise Levertov. SP-LeveDL

Genial spark the poet felt, The. Ralph Waldo Emerson. CP-EmerR

Genie. Arthur Rimbaud. CP-RimbA, tr. by Martin Sorrell

Genitrix Laesa. Thomas Hardy. CP-HardT

Genius. Philip Levine. SP-LeviP

Genius, The. William Carlos Williams. CP-WilW2

Genius Child. Langston Hughes. CP-HughL; CP-HughL2

Genius in Beauty. Dante Gabriel Rossetti. CW-RossD Fr. House of Life, The.

Genius is the ignition of affection. Emily Dickinson. SP-DickE

Genius mixt too strong a cup, The. Dreamers, The. Robert Duncan. SP-DuncR

Genius of Raphael! if thy wings. Jewish Family (in a Small Valley Opposite St Goar, upon the Rhine), A. William Wordsworth. CP-WorW2

Genius of th' Augustan age, The. On the Author of Letters on Literature. William Cowper. CP-CowpW

Genius of the Crowd, The. Charles Bukowski. SP-BukC2

Genius! Thou gift of Heaven! thou light divine! Edward Shore. George Crabbe. SP-CrabG Fr. Tales.

Genius / totality under partial control. When Lightning Struck, 1. Andrei Codrescu. SP-CodrA

Genoa and the Mediterranean. Thomas Hardy. CP-HardT

Genoan, glory of Italy, Columbus thou sure light. Christophori Columbi Tumulus. Hippolytus Capilupus. CP-PoEar, tr. by Ezra Pound

Genocide doesn't only mean bombs. Vietnam Addenda. Audre Lorde. SP-LordA

Gentian has a parched Corolla, The. Emily Dickinson. CP-DickE

Gentian weaves her fringes, The. Emily Dickinson. CP-DickE

Gentile or Jew or simply a man. Luke 23. Jorge Luis Borges. SP-BorgJ, tr. by Mark Strand

Gentilesse. Geoffrey Chaucer. CP-ChauG

Gentle, The. Theodore Roethke. CP-RoetT

"Gentle and Giving" and Other Sayings. Kenneth Patchen. CP-PatcK

Gentle and mild as is the summers Breeze. Acrostic for Georgeana Cuthbert. Annis Boudinot Stockton. CP-StocA

Gentle and smiling as before. Wheel, The. Robert Earl Hayden. CP-HaydR

Gentle breeze that, through fresh greenery, The. Petrarch. CP-Petra, tr. by J. G. Nichols

Gentle curves along the ivy. Rainer Maria Rilke. CP-RilkFr, tr. by A. Poulin, Jr. Fr. Valaisian Quatrains, The.

Gentle Earthquake, A. Peter Blue Cloud. SP-BlueP

Gentle, gentle river / Hurrying along. Rose, The. Christina Georgina Rossetti. CP-RosC3

Gentle knights, / Know some measure of your nights. Ben Jonson. CP-JonsB Fr. Oberon, the Fairy Prince.

Gentle Love, be not dismayed. Ben Jonson. CP-JonsB Fr. Love Freed from Ignorance and Folly.

Gentle Man, The. William Carlos Williams. CP-WilW1

Gentle Negress, The. William Carlos Williams. CP-WilW2

Gentle Pilgrim, rest thy feet. Godmersham The Temple of Delight. Henry Thomas Austen. CP-AustJ

Gentle Pincher, cock thy tail. George Knight to His Dog Pincher. George Knight. CP-AustJ

Gentle poet pauses, The. Poet, The. Rainer Maria Rilke. CP-RilkFr, tr. by A. Poulin, Jr.

Gentle quince blossoms open, The. Quince. W. S. Merwin. SP-MerwW

Gentle Reader. Josephine Jacobsen. CP-JacoJ

Gentle Reader browsing on his tomb, The. Epigraph for a Condemned Book. Charles Baudelaire. CP-BaudC, tr. by Walter Martin

Gentle Rejoinder, The. William Carlos Williams. CP-WilW2

Gentle river, gentle river. Voyagers Song. Henry David Thoreau. CP-ThorH

Gentle River, in her Cupid's honor, The. Psyche and Pan. Elizabeth Barrett Browning. CP-BroEB

Gentle shepheard satte beside a springe, The. December. Edmund Spenser. CP-Spens Fr. Shepheardes [or Shepeards or Shepherd's] Calender, The.

Gentle Snorer, The. Mona Van Duyn. SP-VanDM

Gentle snowman. End of Winter, The. Dan Pagis. SP-PagiD, tr. by Stephen Mitchell

Gentle Spring has charmed the earth. Ralph Waldo Emerson. CP-EmerR

Gentle story of two lovers young, A. Fragment: "Gentle story of two lovers young, A." Percy Bysshe Shelley. CP-ShelP

Gentle tongue lapping, A. Ocean. Czeslaw Milosz. CP-MiloC; CP-MiloCN, tr. by Peter Dale Scott

Gentle Weight Lifter, The. David Ignatow. SP-IgnaD

Gentle wind blows in from the water, A. Great Birds, The. Kenneth Patchen. CP-PatcK

Gentleman and the Bastard, The. Charles Bukowski. SP-BukC3

Gentleman from the second, The. Dance on the Staircase, The. Rainer Maria Rilke. CP-RilkFr, tr. by A. Poulin, Jr.

Gentleman of Shalott, The. Elizabeth Bishop. CP-BishE

Gentleman, The. Robert Graves. CP-GravR

Gentleman, The. D. H. Lawrence. CP-LawrD

Gentlemanly gentleman, as mild as May, A. Coffee with the Meal. Ogden Nash. CP-NashO

Gentleman's coming, A. Catching Ballet of the Wedding Clothes, The. Thomas Hardy. CP-HardT

Gentleman's Epitaph on Himself and a Lady, Who Were Buried Together, A. Thomas Hardy. CP-HardT

Gentleman's Second-Hand Suit, A. Thomas Hardy. CP-HardT

Gentlemen, I Address You Publicly. Kenneth Rexroth. CP-RexrK

Gentlemen, I give you the British Empire. Scram, Lion! Ogden Nash. CP-NashO

Gentlemen Prefer Blondes. G. K. Chesterton. CP-ChesG

Gentlemen-Rankers. Rudyard Kipling. CP-KiplR

Gentlemen who have got to be classics and are now old with beards, The. Letter to the Academy. Langston Hughes. CP-HughL; CP-HughL1

Gentleness and starvation tame. Lady with a Falcon. May Sarton. SP-SartM

Gentleness for my dog, A. Red Front, The. Louis Aragon. CP-CummE

Gentleness of Death, The. George Meredith. CP-MerG2

Gentleness of rain was in the wind, The. Fragment: Rain. Percy Bysshe Shelley. CP-ShelP

Gentlenesse. Robert Herrick. CP-HerrR

Gentlest Lady, The. Dorothy Parker. CP-ParkD

Gentlest Poet, with free thoughts endowed, The. Suggested by a Picture of the Bird of Paradise. William Wordsworth. CP-WorW2

Gentlest Shade that walked Elysian plains, The. Departure from the Vale of Grasmere. August, 1803. William Wordsworth. CP-WorW1

Gently Bent to Ease Us. Norman Dubie. CP-DubiN

Gently I took that which ungently came. Forbearance. Samuel Taylor Coleridge. CP-ColeS

Gently, my lambs, move gently. Far West. Czeslaw Milosz. CP-MiloC; CP-MiloCN, *tr. by* Robert Hass

Gently the women have spread me naked on linen. Laying-Out of Lazarus. Robert Stock. SP-StocR

Gentyl redar, haif at me non dispyte. Exclamatioun to the Redar, Tuycheyng the Wryttyng of Vulgare and Maternall Language, Ane. Sir David Lyndsay. SP-LyndD *Fr.* Dialog betwix Experience and ane Courteour, Ane.

Geographer. Marilyn Hacker. SP-HackM

Geographic Origins. Yannis Ritsos. SP-RitsY *Fr.* Monovasia.

Geographical Knowledge. Thomas Hardy. CP-HardT

Geography. Kenneth Koch. SP-KochK

Geography comes to an end. Sacred Heart 2. Thomas Merton. CP-MertT

Geography Lesson, The. Paul Muldoon. CP-MuldP

Geography of Lograire, The. Thomas Merton. CP-MertT

Geography of this Time. Archibald MacLeish. CP-MacLA

Geography of Time, The. Miller Williams. CP-WillM

Geology set this story down so long ago. In the Rif Mountains. William Meredith. SP-MereW

Geometric form, seated, erect, A. On an Early Cycladic Harpist (2500 B.C.) in the Archaeological Museum in Athens. Helen Pinkerton. CP-PinkH

Geometry. Rita Dove. SP-DoveR

Geometry tells us how to tell. Manifold Usefulness of an Education, The. Miller Williams. CP-WillM

Geordie [An Old Ballad]. *Unknown.* CP-BurnR

George A. Carr. James Whitcomb Riley. CP-RileJ

George Chapman—The Iliad. Ivor Gurney. SP-GurnI

George Crabbe. Edwin Arlington Robinson. CP-RobiE

George Eliot Country. Amy Clampitt. CP-ClamA

George hadn't gone down to the canyon mouth for a whole week and so. Resurrection. Robinson Jeffers. CP-JefR2

George Knight to His Dog Pincher. George Knight. CP-AustJ

George L. Stearns. John Greenleaf Whittier. CP-WhitJ

George Mensch's cattle. Return. Raymond Carver. CP-CarvR

George Meredith (1828–1909). Thomas Hardy. CP-HardT

George Mullen's Confession. James Whitcomb Riley. CP-RileJ

George Nim-Dan-Dean, Esq. to Mr. Sheridan. Jonathan Swift. CP-SwifJ

George Nim-Dan-Dean's Invitation to Mr. Thomas Sheridan. Jonathan Swift. CP-SwifJ

George Perry here is stiff and stark. Ambrose Bierce. SP-BierA

George Robinson: Blues. Muriel Rukeyser. CP-RukeM

George Seferis in Sonora. Sam Hamill. SP-HamiS

George Sterling. Robinson Jeffers. CP-JefR1

George Sterling's Death. Robinson Jeffers. CP-JefR1

George Trakl Journal. Charles Wright. SP WrigC

George Washington. Louis Zukofsky. CP-ZukLS

George Washington Brige. John Ciardi. CP-CiarJ

Georges Seurat: Factory. Adam Zagajewski. SP-ZagaA, *tr. by* Clare Cavanagh

Georgia Beach. Margaret Atwood. SP-AtwM2

Georgia Dusk. Langston Hughes. CP-HughL; CP-HughL3

Georgia Song, A. Maya Angelou. SP-AngeM

Georgics. Virgil.

  Georgics 4.

  "And the cloven waters like a chasm of mountains." CP-ShelP, *tr. by* Percy Bysshe Shelley

  "Even so bewails, the poplar groves among." CP-WorW2, *tr. by* William Wordsworth

  "On vent'rous wing in quest of praise I go." CP-JohnS

  Orpheus and Eurydice. CP-WorW1

  Out of Virgil, in the Praise of the Spring. CP-CrasR

Geotheos. Ambrose Bierce. SP-BierA

Geraldine. Emily Jane Brontë. CP-BronE

Geraldine, the moon is shining. Song By Julius Brenzaida To G. S. Emily Jane Brontë. CP-BronE

Geranium. Rainer Maria Rilke. CP-RilkFr, *tr. by* A. Poulin, Jr.

Geranium and the begonia, The. High Culture. Amy Clampitt. CP-ClamA

Geranium, exploding. Geranium. Rainer Maria Rilke. CP-RilkFr, *tr. by* A. Poulin, Jr.

Geranium, The. Theodore Roethke. CP-RoetT

Gerd sits spindle-shanked in her dark tent. Crystal Gazer. Sylvia Plath. CP-PlatS

Gerda. Carolyn Kizer. CP-KizeC

Gerda in the Aerie. Marilyn Hacker. SP-HackM

Germ, The. Ogden Nash. CP-NashO

Germ-Destroyer, A. Rudyard Kipling. *Fr.* Plain Tales from the Hills.

German-French Campaign, 1870–1871, The. Christina Georgina Rossetti. CP-RosC1

German Girls, The! The German Girls! Archibald MacLeish. CP-MacLA

German Lairdie, The. Robert Burns. CP-BurnR

German Requiem, A. James Fenton. SP-FentJ

  "Doctor Gliedschirm, skin specialist, surgeries 14–16 hours or by appointment." SP-FentJ

Germans Are Lunatics, The. Randall Jarrell. CP-JarrR

Germans on the Heights of Hochheim, The. William Wordsworth. CP-WorW2

Germans, she said, were sometimes independent. Middlesex. Donald Davie. CP-DaviDC

Germs. Walt Whitman. CP-WhitW

Gerontion. T. S. Eliot. CP-ElioT

  (Gerousia.) SP-ElioT

Gerousios Oinos. Robert Browning. CP-BroR2

Gerry's Jazz. Yusef Komunyakaa. SP-KomuY

Gerti's Carnival. Eugenio Montale. CP-MontE, *tr. by* Jonathan Galassi

Gertrude's Prayer. Rudyard Kipling. CP-KiplR

Gestalt at Sixty. May Sarton. SP-SartM

Gesture, The. Robert Creeley. CP-CreeR

Gesture, The. Richard Eberhart. CP-EberR

Gesture, The. Josephine Jacobsen. CP-JacoJ

Gesture by a Lady with an Assumed Name, A. James Wright. CP-WrigJ

Gesture she makes / to rise, The. Gesture, The. Robert Creeley. CP-CreeR

Gesture toward an Unfound Renaissance, A. William Stafford. SP-StafWW

Gestures. Rainer Maria Rilke. CP-RilkFr, *tr. by* A. Poulin, Jr

Get a load. Lorine Niedecker. CP-NiedL

Get gone, thou most uncomfortable ghost! To an Importunate Ghost. James Whitcomb Riley. CP-RileJ

Get Hence Foule Griefe. Sir Philip Sidney. SP-SidnP *Fr.* Arcadia.

Get hence foul[e] grief[e], the canker of the mind[e]. Get Hence Foule Griefe. Sir Philip Sidney. SP-SidnP *Fr.* Arcadia.

Get it anyway. Robert Creeley. CP-CreeR

Get out of here get. Deathfear. James Laughlin. CP-LaugJ

Get Out of Town. Thomas McGrath. SP-McGrT

Get out the lunch-box of your dreams. Jim Crow Car. Langston Hughes. CP-HughL; CP-HughL3

Get Somebody Else. Paul Laurence Dunbar. CP-DunbP

  (Too Busy.) CP-DunbP

Get the gasworks in a poem. David Ignatow. SP-IgnaD

Get thee back neglected friends. To a Jilted Swain. James Whitcomb Riley. CP-RileJ

Get thee behind me. Even as, heavy-curled. Retro me, Sathana! Dante Gabriel Rossetti. CW-RossD *Fr.* House of Life, The.

Get up, get up for shame! the blooming morn[e]. Corinna's Going a-Maying. Robert Herrick. CP-HerrR

Get Up off That Old Jive. Langston Hughes. CP-HughL; CP-HughL3

Get up thou lazy lump thou log get up. Lament of a Slug-a-Bed's Wife. Stevie Smith. CP-SmitS

Get used to it then. Successions. Pablo Neruda. SP-NeruP

Get ye up from the wrath of God's terrible day! Cities of the Plain, The. John Greenleaf Whittier. CP-WhitJ

Get your own clothes if you're cold. Han-shan. CP-ColdM, *tr. by* Red Pine

Gethsemane. Rudyard Kipling. CP-KiplR

Gethsemani, KY. Ernesto Cardenal.

  "Dog barks far out, A." CP-MertT

  "Every evening the L & N." CP-MertT

  "I do not know who is out in the snow." CP-MertT

  "I turned out the light to see the snow." CP-MertT

  Like Empty Beer Cans. CP-MertT, *tr. by* Thomas Merton

  "Like the flights of ducks." CP-MertT

  "Long freight train / Wakes me in my cell, The." CP-MertT

  "Sound of passing cars, (if a car comes), The." CP-MertT

  "Spring has come with its smell of Nicaragua." CP-MertT

  "That auto horn sounds familiar." CP-MertT

  "When the first signs go on." CP-MertT

  "Zinc roofs in the moonlight, The." CP-MertT

Gethsemene and Cana. Emily Dickinson. SP-DickE

Gets made up of 5.3 billion little pictures (sacks, thousands). Big Picture, The. Thomas Lux. SP-LuxT

Getting a grip on the leash. Goodbye, A. Mona Van Duyn. SP-VanDM

Getting Dressed. Gregory Orr. SP-OrrG

Getting dressed, in the mirror. Public Bath, The. Gary Snyder. CP-SnydG

Getting in the Wood. Gary Snyder. CP-SnydG

Getting It Wrong Again. Sam Hamill. SP-HamiS

Getting Paid. James Laughlin. CP-LaugJ

Getting the Message. Miller Williams. CP-WillM

Getting There. Andrei Codrescu. SP-CodrA

Getting There. Sylvia Plath. CP-PlatS

Getting Through. Maxine W. Kumin. SP-KumiM

Getting through with the world. Approach to a City. William Carlos Williams. CP-WilW2

Getting Up Ahead of Someone (Sun). Frank O'Hara. SP-OharF

Getting Up Late. Robert Bly. SP-BlyR

Getting Warm. Rae Armantrout. SP-ArmaA

Geysers, The. Thom Gunn. CP-GunnT

G. F. Died 1954, Aged 27. William Dickey. SP-DickW

Ghalib Decides to Be Reticent. William Stafford. SP-StafWW

Ghaselle. Hafiz. CP-EmerR

Ghazal. Adrienne Rich. CP-RicAE

Ghazal V. Adrienne Rich. SP-RicA2 *Fr.* Shooting Script.

Ghazal of Dark Death. Federico García Lorca. CP-GarcF, *tr. by* Catherine Brown *Fr.* Ghazals.

Ghazal of Desperate Love. Federico García Lorca. CP-GarcF, *tr. by* Catherine Brown *Fr.* Ghazals.

Ghazal of Love Unforeseen. Federico García Lorca. CP-GarcF, *tr. by* Catherine Brown *Fr.* Ghazals.

Ghazal of Marvelous Love. Federico García Lorca. CP-GarcF, *tr. by* Catherine Brown *Fr.* Ghazals.

Ghazal of the Bitter Root. Federico García Lorca. CP-GarcF, *tr. by* Catherine Brown *Fr.* Ghazals.

Ghazal of the Dead Child. Federico García Lorca. CP-GarcF, *tr. by* Catherine Brown *Fr.* Ghazals.

Ghazal of the Flight. Federico García Lorca. CP-GarcF, *tr. by* Catherine Brown *Fr.* Ghazals.

Ghazal of the Hundred-Year-Old Love. Federico García Lorca. CP-GarcF, *tr. by* Catherine Brown *Fr.* Ghazals.

Ghazal of the Love That Hides from Sight. Federico García Lorca. CP-GarcF, *tr. by* Catherine Brown *Fr.* Ghazals.

Ghazal of the Market in the Morning. Federico García Lorca. CP-GarcF, *tr. by* Christopher Maurer

Ghazal of the Memory of Love. Federico García Lorca. CP-GarcF, *tr. by* Catherine Brown *Fr.* Ghazals.

Ghazal of the Terrible Presence. Federico García Lorca. CP-GarcF, *tr. by* Catherine Brown *Fr.* Ghazals.

Ghazals. Federico García Lorca.

    Ghazal of Dark Death. CP-GarcF, *tr. by* Catherine Brown

    Ghazal of Desperate Love. CP-GarcF, *tr. by* Catherine Brown

    Ghazal of Love Unforeseen. CP-GarcF, *tr. by* Catherine Brown

    Ghazal of Marvelous Love. CP-GarcF, *tr. by* Catherine Brown

    Ghazal of the Bitter Root. CP-GarcF, *tr. by* Catherine Brown

    Ghazal of the Dead Child. CP-GarcF, *tr. by* Catherine Brown

    Ghazal of the Flight. CP-GarcF, *tr. by* Catherine Brown

    Ghazal of the Hundred-Year-Old Love. CP-GarcF, *tr. by* Catherine Brown

    Ghazal of the Love That Hides from Sight. CP-GarcF, *tr. by* Catherine Brown

    Ghazal of the Memory of Love. CP-GarcF, *tr. by* Catherine Brown

    Ghazal of the Terrible Presence. CP-GarcF, *tr. by* Catherine Brown

Ghazals: Homage to Ghalib. Adrienne Rich. SP-RicA2

    8/8/68: i. CP-RicAE

    8/8/68: ii. CP-RicAE

    8/1/68. CP-RicAE

    August fourth nineteen sixty eight. CP-RicAE

    7/14/68: i. CP-RicAE

    7/14/68: i. CP-RicAE

    July seventeenth nineteen sixty eight. CP-RicAE

    7/16/68: i. CP-RicAE

    7/16/68: ii. CP-RicAE

    7/13/68. CP-RicAE

    7/12/68. CP-RicAE

    7/26/68: i. CP-RicAE

    7/26/68: ii. CP-RicAE

Ghiberti's great door keeps his Adam immured. Invisible Golden Sections. Robert Stock. SP-StocR

Ghost. Norman Dubie. CP-DubiN

Ghost. Robinson Jeffers. CP-JefR3

Ghost, The. Walter De la Mare. CP-DeLaW

Ghost, The. Heather McHugh. SP-McHuH

Ghost, The. Propertius. SP-LoweR, *tr. by* Robert Lowell

Ghost, The. Jones Very. CP-VeryJ

Ghost, The. James Wright. CP-WrigJ

Ghost, a Real Ghost, A. Randall Jarrell. CP-JarrR

Ghost Chant, et alii. Yusef Komunyakaa. CP-KomuY

Ghost Crabs. Ted Hughes. SP-HughTN

Ghost-grey the fall of night. Robin, A. Walter De la Mare. CP-DeLaW

Ghost Hammer, The. Robert Pinsky. CP-PinsR

Ghost House. Robert Frost. CP-FrosR

Ghost is someone: death has left a hole, A. Ghost, The. Propertius. SP-LoweR, *tr. by* Robert Lowell

Ghost May Come, A. Allen Ginsberg. CP-GinsA

Ghost of a Chance. Adrienne Rich. CP-RicAE; SP-RicA1; SP-RicA2

Ghost of Abel, The. William Blake. CP-BlakW

Ghost of His Wife Comes to Tell Him How It Is, The. Miller Williams. CP-WillM

Ghost of Ninon would be sorry now, The. Veteran Sirens. Edwin Arlington Robinson. CP-RobiE

Ghost of Roger Casement, The. William Butler Yeats. CP-YeatW

Ghost of the Buffaloes, The. Nicholas Vachel Lindsay. *See* Ghosts of the Buffaloes, The

Ghost of the Past, The. Thomas Hardy. CP-HardT

Ghost of Ware, The. Stevie Smith. CP-SmitS

Ghost rose when the waves rose, A. Faith Upon the Waters. Laura Riding Jackson. CP-RidiL

Ghost said nothing that added to our knowledge, The. Ash Manor. James Tate. SP-TateJ

Ghost Story, A. Randall Jarrell. CP-JarrR

Ghost Video. Yusef Komunyakaa. CP-KomuY

Ghosts. Countee Cullen. CP-CullC

Ghosts. Derek Mahon. CP-MahoD

Ghosts. Mary Oliver. SP-OlivM

Ghosts. Anne Sexton. CP-SextA

Ghosts. Miller Williams. CP-WillM

Ghosts as Cocoons. Wallace Stevens. CP-StevW; CP-StevWP

Ghosts in England. Robinson Jeffers. CP-JefR2

Ghosts in Love. Nicholas Vachel Lindsay. CP-LindV

Ghost's Leavetaking, The. Sylvia Plath. CP-PlatS

Ghosts Listen to Orpheus Sing, The. Gregory Orr. SP-OrrG

Ghosts of all my lovely sins. Rainy Night. Dorothy Parker. CP-ParkD

Ghosts of all too solid flesh. Ghosts of 1619. Langston Hughes. CP-HughL; CP-HughL3

Ghosts of 1619. Langston Hughes. CP-HughL; CP-HughL3

Ghosts of the Buffaloes, The. Nicholas Vachel Lindsay. CP-LindV

    (Ghost of the Buffaloes, The.) CP-LindV

Ghosts of the House, The. William Meredith. SP-MereW

Ghosts on the Northern Land of Ur. Norman Dubie. CP-DubiN

Ghost's Petition, The. Christina Georgina Rossetti. CP-RosC1

Ghosts share us with the past & future. Jungle Surrender. Yusef Komunyakaa. CP-KomuY

Ghosts there must be with me in this old house. Solitude. Walter De la Mare. CP-DeLaW

Ghouls of Candlemas, The. Andrei Codrescu. SP-CodrA

Gi' me a reefer, Lawd. Wrong Door, The. William Carlos Williams. CP-WilW2

Giacometti. Richard Wilbur. CP-WilbR

Gianni, Guido greets. Guido Cavalcanti. CP-CavaG, *tr. by* Marc Cirigliano

Giant fall of a jungle ceiba, The. Antaeus. Robert Stock. SP-StocR

Giant in the Garden. May Sarton. SP-SartM

Giant Mirror, The. Federico García Lorca. CP-GarcF, *tr. by* Jerome Rothenberg *Fr.* Mirror Suite.

Giant Norway spruce from Podunk, its lower branches bound, The. December. James Schuyler. CP-SchuJ

Giant Red Woman. Clarence Major. SP-MajoC

Giant Sequoias. Philip Whalen. SP-WhalP

Giant Weapon, The. Kenneth Rexroth. CP-RexrK

Giant whispering and coughing from. Broadcast. Philip Larkin. CP-LarkP

Giant with an ox's head, A. Spelling Lesson, A. G. K. Chesterton. CP-ChesG

Giant Yea, The. Theodore Weiss. SP-WeisT

Giantess, The. Charles Baudelaire. SP-ShapK

Giantess, The. Charles Baudelaire. CP-BaudC, *tr. by* Walter Martin

Giantess, The. Richard Eberhart. CP-EberR

Giants, The. Jones Very. CP-VeryJ

Giants did advance their wicked hand, The. Sir Walter Ralegh. CP-RaleW

Giant's Ring, The. Robinson Jeffers. CP-JefR2

Giants, they who walked the earth of old, The. Giants, The. Jones Very. CP-VeryJ

Giaour, The. Lord Byron. CP-Byron

Giaour and the Pacha, The. Richard Wilbur. CP-WilbR

Gibbous moon hangs out of the twilight, A. Yew-Tree on the Downs, The. D. H. Lawrence. CP-LawrD

Gibbs. Muriel Rukeyser. CP-RukeM

Gic to Har. Kenneth Rexroth. CP-RexrK

Giddiness. George Herbert. CP-HerbG

Gie the Lass her Fairin'. Robert Burns. CP-BurnR

Gif Ye Wol Stonden Hardie Wight. John Keats. CP-KeatJ

Giffen's Debt. Rudyard Kipling. CP-KiplR

Gift. "H. D." CP-DoolH

Gift. W. S. Merwin. SP-MerwW

Gift. Czeslaw Milosz. CP-CarvR; CP-MiloC; CP-MiloCN

Gift. Grace Paley.

Gift. Muriel Rukeyser. CP-RukeM

Gift. Alice Walker. CP-WalkA

Gift, The. Charles Bukowski. SP-BukC2

Gift, The. Raymond Carver. CP-CarvR

Gift, The. John Ciardi. CP-CiarJ

Gift, The. Robert Creeley. CP-CreeR

Gift, The. "H. D." CP-DoolH

Gift, The. Louise Glück. SP-GlucL

Gift, The. Carolyn Kizer. CP-KizeC

Gift, The. John Logan. CP-LogaJ

Gift, The. Pablo Neruda. SP-NeruP

Gift, The. Gregory Orr. SP-OrrG

Gift, The. Helen Pinkerton. CP-PinkH

Gift, The. William Stafford. SP-StafWW

Gift, The. Jones Very. CP-VeryJ

Gift, The. William Carlos Williams. CP-WilW2

Gift, The. C. K. Williams. SP-WillC

Gift for a Believer. Philip Levine. SP-LeviP

Gift from the cold and silent Past! Norsemen, The. John Greenleaf Whittier. CP-WhitJ

Gift Horse. Yusef Komunyakaa. CP-KomuY

Gift is small, The. Lines for a Gift. Robert Browning. CP-BroR2

Gift of another day! Gift, The. Carolyn Kizer. CP-KizeC

Gift of God, The. Edwin Arlington Robinson. CP-RobiE

Gift of Gravity, The. Wendell Berry. CP-BerrW

Gift of Great Value, A. Robert Creeley. CP-CreeR

Gift of Harun Al-Rashid, The. William Butler Yeats. CP-YeatW

Gift of Light, A. Marge Piercy. SP-PierM

Gift of neither Heaven nor Earth, The. Emily Dickinson. SP-DickE

Gift of Prophecy Lost, The. Miller Williams. CP-WillM

Gift of Sight. Robert Graves. CP-GravR

Gift of Stone. Peter Blue Cloud. SP-BlueP

Gift of the Poem. Stéphane Mallarmé. CP-MallS, *tr. by* Henry Weinfield

Gift of the Sea, The. Rudyard Kipling. CP-KiplR

Gift of Tongues, The. Sam Hamill. SP-HamiS

Gift of Tritemius, The. John Greenleaf Whittier. CP-WhitJ

Gift of Water, The. Jelaluddin Rumi. SP-Rumi, *tr. by* Coleman Barks

Gift Outright, The. Robert Frost. CP-FrosR

Gift-Poem. Muriel Rukeyser. CP-RukeM

Gift: The Gifted. George Oppen. CP-OppGN

Gift was never named, The. We lived and a hot light created stood in its sphere. With Trumpets and Zithers. Czeslaw Milosz. CP-MiloC; CP-MiloCN

Gifted, and loved and praised. Luther A. Todd. James Whitcomb Riley. CP-RileJ

Gifts. Robert Creeley. SP-CreeR

Gifts. Langston Hughes. CP-HughL2

Gifts Accompaniment, A. Alan Dugan. CP-DugaA

Gifts of God, The. Jones Very. CP-VeryJ

Gifts of Love. Yehuda Amichai. SP-AmicY, *tr. by* Chana Bloch

Gifts of Love. Yehuda Amichai. SP-AmicYL, *tr. by* Benjamin Harshav *and* Barbara Harshav

Gifts of one who loved me. Motto to "Gifts." Ralph Waldo Emerson. CP-EmerR

Gifts of Percussion. Andrei Codrescu. SP-CodrA

Gifts of Rain. Seamus Heaney. SP-HeanSO

Gifts, The. Richard Wilbur. CP-WilbR

Gig at Big Al's. Heather McHugh. SP-McHuH

Gigantic Grandfather. Karl Heinrich Marx. Hans Magnus Enzensberger. SP-EnzeH, *tr. by* Michael Hamburger

Gigantic tree, / with its lianas, fishes. Fishermen. Federico García Lorca. CP-GarcF, *tr. by* Jerome Rothenberg *Fr.* Six Songs at Nightfall.

Gigantomachia. Wallace Stevens. CP-StevW; CP-StevWP

Gigolo. Sylvia Plath. CP-PlatS

Gila Bend. James Dickey. CP-DickJ

Gilbert had sailed to India's shore. Vampirine Fair, The. Thomas Hardy. CP-HardT

Gilded Man, The. Ai. SP-Ai

Gilded phaloi of the crocuses, The. Coitus. Ezra Pound. SP-PounE

Giles Corey of the Salem Farms. Henry Wadsworth Longfellow. SP-LongH

Gilgamesh Was Very Lascivious. A. R. Ammons. CP-AmmoA

Gillis van Conninxloo, Landscape. Panel, 65 x 119 cm. Hans Magnus Enzensberger. SP-EnzeH

Gimme six-bits' worth o' ticket. Six-Bits Blues. Langston Hughes. CP-HughL;

CP-HughL2

Gimme $25.00 / and the change. Request. Langston Hughes. CP-HughL; CP-HughL3

Gin but the oor 'ud chop and set me free. Hugh MacDiarmid. SP-MacDH *Fr.* Frae Anither Window in Thrums.

Gina, I saw you walk. Apparition, An. Donald Davie. CP-DaviDC

Ginevra. Percy Bysshe Shelley. CP-ShelP

Ginkakuji Michi. Philip Whalen. SP-WhalP

Ginkgo, cottonwood, pin oak, sweet gum, tulip tree. Shapes of Leaves, The. Arthur Sze. SP-SzeA

Ginkgoes in Fall. Howard Nemerov. CP-NemeH

Ginoine Ar-tickle, The. James Whitcomb Riley. CP-RileJ

Ginsberg? Charles Bukowski. SP-BukC3

Ginza Samba. Robert Pinsky. CP-PinsR

Giordano, verily thy Pencil's skill. To Lucca Giordano. William Wordsworth. CP-WorW2

Giorgio Morandi and the Talking Eternity Blues. Charles Wright. SP-WrigCN

Giorgione's *Tempest*. Robert Stock. SP-StocR

Giorno dei Morti. D. H. Lawrence. CP-LawrD

Giovanni Diodati. Charles Tomlinson. CP-TomlC

Giovanni's *Rape of the Sabine Women* at Wildenstein's. George Oppen. CP-OppGN

Gipsies. Derek Mahon. CP-MahoD

Gipsies: "Gipsies seek wide sheltering woods again, The." John Clare. SP-ClarJ

Gipsies: "Snow falls deep; the forest lies alone, The." John Clare. SP-ClarJ

Gipsy. D. H. Lawrence. CP-LawrD

Gipsy Trail, The. Rudyard Kipling. CP-KiplR

Gipsy Vans. Rudyard Kipling. CP-KiplR *Fr.* Debits and Credits.

Giraffe, The. Gabriela Mistral. SP-MistG, *tr. by* Maria Giachetti [*or* Jacketti]

Girandole, The. Charles Baudelaire. CP-BaudC, *tr. by* Walter Martin

Girl. Langston Hughes. CP-HughL; CP-HughL2

Girl, A. Ezra Pound. CP-PoEar

Girl, The. William Carlos Williams. CP-WilW1; CP-WilW2

Girl alone in the wood's, The. Party Piece. Paul Muldoon. CP-MuldP

Girl and Baby Florist Sidewalk Pram Nineteen Seventy Something. Kenneth Koch. SP-KochK

Girl and Horse, 1928. Margaret Atwood. SP-AtwM1

Girl and Scarecrow. Marya Alexandrovna Zaturenska. SP-ZatuM

Girl at the Play. Muriel Rukeyser. CP-RukeM

Girl being chosen stood in her naked room, The. Mortal Girl. Muriel Rukeyser. CP-RukeM

Girl Child. Peter Blue Cloud. SP-BlueP

Girl-Child of Pompeii, The. Primo Levi. CP-LeviP, *tr. by* Ruth Feldman

Girl Child so quiet and watchful. Little Fawn. Peter Blue Cloud. SP-BlueP

Girl do you think. Excavation of Troy. Archibald MacLeish. CP-MacLA

Girl Dreams that She Is Giselle, The. Randall Jarrell. CP-JarrR

Girl goes dancing there, The. Sweet Dancer. William Butler Yeats. CP-YeatW

Girl Goes Out in the Morning Like a Knight, A. Yehuda Amichai. SP-AmicYL, *tr. by* Benjamin Harshav *and* Barbara Harshav

Girl grown woman fire mother of fire. Waterlily Fire. Muriel Rukeyser. CP-RukeM

Girl Guides. G. K. Chesterton. CP-ChesG

Girl in a Cage. Carl Sandburg. CP-SandC

Girl in a Library. Marya Alexandrovna Zaturenska. SP-ZatuM

Girl in a Library, A. Randall Jarrell. CP-JarrR

Girl in a Nightgown. Wallace Stevens. CP-StevW; CP-StevWP

Girl in a Window, A. James Wright. CP-WrigJ

Girl in the bikini, my / wife, the lady—she sits on, The. Obscene Poem, An. Robert Creeley. CP-CreeR

Girl in the Fog, The. John Logan. CP-LogaJ

Girl in the front row who had no mother. At Liberty School. William Stafford. SP-StafWW

Girl in the lobby reading a leather-bound book, The. In the Lobby of the Hotel del Mayo. Raymond Carver. CP-CarvR

Girl in the sand, The. Nude Kneeling in Sand. John Logan. CP-LogaJ

Girl in the tea shop, The. Tea Shop, The. Ezra Pound. SP-PounE

Girl in White. Marge Piercy. SP-PierM

Girl is running, A. *Don't* tell me. Anti-Short Story. Rae Armantrout. SP-ArmaA

Girl lies down on the hill, The. Pastoral: "Girl lies down on the hill, The." William Meredith. SP-MereW

Girl minding the store, The. Sinew. Raymond Carver. CP-CarvR

Girl moves across my brow, The. First Anniversary. Federico García Lorca. CP-GarcF, *tr. by* Alan S. Trueblood *Fr.* Moon Songs.

Girl of Cadiz, The. Lord Byron. CP-Byron

Girl on a Swing. Thomas Kinsella. CP-KinsT

Girl on the Bus Stop Bench, The. Charles Bukowski. SP-BukC1

Girl on the swing, The. On the Swing. Federico García Lorca. CP-GarcF, *tr. by*

Jerome Rothenberg *Fr.* Fairs.

Girl pushes a bicycle through tall grass, A. Country Matters. Raymond Carver. CP-CarvR

Girl Takes Her Place Among the Mothers, The. Marya Alexandrovna Zaturenska. SP-ZatuM

Girl this evening regrets her surrender with tears, A. Somewhere. Howard Nemerov. CP-NemeH

Girl Walking into a Shadow, A. James Wright. CP-WrigJ

Girl was riding a horse, The. Riders. Clarence Major. SP-MajoC

Girl was singing in the choir with fervo[u]r, A. Aleksandr Aleksandrovich Blok. SP-BlokA, *tr. by* Peter France *and* Jon Stallworthy

Girl Who Died #1, The. Alice Walker. CP-WalkA

Girl Who Died #2, The. Alice Walker. CP-WalkA

Girl Who Has Drowned Herself Speaks, A. Stephen Spender. CP-SpenS

Girl who, in 1971, when I was living by myself, painfully lonely, bereft, depressed, A. Shame. C. K. Williams. SP-WillC

Girl who mounted in the omnibus, The. Paysage Triste. T. S. Eliot. SP-ElioT

Girl who used to sing in the choir, The. Back Home. William Stafford. SP-StafWW

Girl whose arms are leaves, The. Yellow Tree Peony, The. William Carlos Williams. CP-WilW2

Girl whose cheeks are covered with paint, A. Biological Reflection. Ogden Nash. CP-NashO

Girl with all that raising, A. Ballad of the Girl Whose Name Is Mud. Langston Hughes. CP-HughL; CP-HughL2

Girl with 'Cello. May Sarton. SP-SartM

Girl with Eighteen Nightgowns, The. Gregory Orr. SP-OrrG

Girl with the burning golden eyes. To Gloriana. Nicholas Vachel Lindsay. CP-LindV

Girls. Charles Bukowski. SP-BukC3

Girls! Stevie Smith. CP-SmitS

Girls, The. Christopher Logue. SP-LoguC

Girls and Boys. G. K. Chesterton. CP-ChesG

Girls are coming home in their cars, The. Girls Coming Home. Charles Bukowski. SP-BukC1

Girls as Windmills. James Laughlin. CP-LaugJ

Girls at the Green Hotel, The. Charles Bukowski. SP-BukC1

Girls buck the wind in the grooves toward work. Morning Half-Life Blues, The. Marge Piercy. SP-PierM

Girls Coming Home. Charles Bukowski. SP-BukC1

Girls Fighting, Broadway. Karl Shapiro. SP-ShapK

Girls from Nowhere. Charles Bukowski. SP-BukC3

Girl's Garden, A. Robert Frost. CP-FrosR

Girls in Pantyhose. Charles Bukowski. SP-BukC1

Girls in the Poolroom, The. Paul Muldoon. CP-MuldP

Girls Next Door, The. Thom Gunn. CP-GunnT

Girls of the breeze, The. Earth ("Girls of the breeze, The"). Federico García Lorca. CP-GarcF, *tr. by* Jerome Rothenberg *Fr.* In the Garden of the Lunar Grapefruits.

Girls of the breeze, The. Frieze. Federico García Lorca. CP-GarcF, *tr. by* Alan S. Trueblood *Fr.* Theories.

Girls on the Bridge. Derek Mahon. CP-MahoD

Girls, protected by gold wire from the gaze, The. And You Know. John Ashbery. SP-AshbJ

Girl's Ring, A. E. E. Cummings. CP-CummE

Girl's Song. Louise Bogan. CP-BogaL

Girl's Song. William Butler Yeats. CP-YeatW

Girl's Spare Chorus, The. Christopher Logue. SP-LoguC *Fr.* Lily-White Boys, The.

Girls that have loved me. Song: "Girls that have loved me." Tennessee Williams. CP-WillT

Girls wake, stretch, and pad up to the door, The. Apartment Cats. Thom Gunn. CP-GunnT

Girls with eyes of wicks of lights, The. Oracle, The. Thomas Merton. CP-MertT

Girt in dark growths, yet glimmering with one star. Sleepless Dreams. Dante Gabriel Rossetti. CW-RossD *Fr.* House of Life, The.

Gislebertus' Eve. John Berryman. CP-BerrJ

Gist. Andrei Codrescu. SP-CodrA

Giunts is the biggest mens they air. Truly Marvelous, The. James Whitcomb Riley. CP-RileJ

Give a man his. Wait for Me. Robert Creeley. CP-CreeR

Give All to Love. Ralph Waldo Emerson. CP-EmerR

Give and it shall be given unto you. Spiritual Debtors. Jones Very. CP-VeryJ

Give and Take. William Meredith. SP-MereW

Give, ask for nothing, hope for nothing. Expect Nothing. Robert Graves. CP-GravR

Give back the heart that I gave. Triolet: "Give back the heart that I gave." Dorothy Parker. CP-ParkD

Give back to my eyes their flow, O spring, O river. Michelangelo Buonarroti. CP-Miche, *tr. by* John Frederick Nims

Give beauty all her right. Beauty Is Not Bound. Thomas Campion. CP-CampT

Give ear, O Shepherd of Israel, thou that leadest Joseph like a flock. Psalm 80: "Give ear, O Shepherd of Israel, thou that leadest Joseph like a flock." Bible, *O.T.* CP-MiltJ *Fr.* Psalms.

Give ear to my words, O Lord, consider my meditation. Psalm 5: "Give ear to my words, O Lord, consider my meditation." Bible, *O.T.* CP-MiltJ *Fr.* Psalms.

Give end unto thy pastimes, Love. Ben Jonson. CP-JonsB *Fr.* Love Restored.

Give him the darkest inch your shelf allows. George Crabbe. Edwin Arlington Robinson. CP-RobiE

Give honour unto Luke Evangelist. Old and New Art (St Luke the Painter). Dante Gabriel Rossetti. CW-RossD *Fr.* House of Life, The.

Give house-roome to the best; 'Tis never known. Choose for the Best. Robert Herrick. CP-HerrR

Give, if thou canst, an Almes; if not, afford. Almes. Robert Herrick. CP-HerrR

Give It to the Wind. Thomas Lux. SP-LuxT

Give it what name you choose. Comparative Iconography. Hayden Carruth. CP-CarHS

Give little Anguish. Emily Dickinson. CP-DickE

Give Lucinda pearl nor stone. To the New Year [For the Countess of Carlisle]. Thomas Carew. CP-CareT

Give me a Cell. His Wish to Privacie. Robert Herrick. CP-HerrR

Give me a golden pen, and let me lean. On Leaving Some Friends at an Early Hour. John Keats. CP-KeatJ

Give me a hidden eddy. Han-shan. CP-ColdM, *tr. by* Red Pine

Give me a land of boughs in leaf. A. E. Housman. CP-HousA

Give me a man that is not dull. His Desire. Robert Herrick. CP-HerrR

Give me a reason why men call. Upon Punchin. Robert Herrick. CP-HerrR

Give me a rose, cool-petaled, virgin white. Rondeau: "Give me a rose, cool-petaled, virgin white." Dorothy Parker. CP-ParkD

Give Me a Sponge. D. H. Lawrence. CP-LawrD

Give me a thrill, says the reader. Fiction and the Reading Public. Philip Larkin. CP-LarkP

Give me all mountains. All Mountains. "H. D." CP-DoolH

Give me an eye, that manly deeds. Jones Very. CP-VeryJ

Give me another life, and I'll be singing. To My Daughter. Joseph Brodsky. CP-BrodJ

Give me Honours: what are these. Honours Are Hindrances. Robert Herrick. CP-HerrR

Give me hunger / O you gods that sit and give. At a Window. Carl Sandburg. CP-SandC

Give me just a second before you start. Excuse Me. Miller Williams. CP-WillM

Give me more love or more disdain. Mediocrity in Love Rejected. Thomas Carew. CP-CareT

Give me my Scallop[-]shell of quiet. Passionate Man[']s Pilgrimage, The. Sir Walter Ralegh. CP-RaleW

Give me no days more brilliant than I know. Content. Paul Laurence Dunbar. CP-DunbP

Give me, O Father! to thy throne access. Boethius. CP-JohnS *Fr.* Consolation of Philosophy, The ("De Consolacione Philosophie").

Give me one kiss. To Dianeme. Robert Herrick. CP-HerrR

Give me some luck, sweet Peg. To Peg. Robert Stock. SP-StocR

Give me that man that dares bestride. His Cavalier. Robert Herrick. CP-HerrR

Give me the baby to hold, my dear. James Whitcomb Riley. CP-RileJ

Give me the food that satisfies a Guest. Kisses. Robert Herrick. CP-HerrR

Give me the lowest place: not that I dare. Lowest Place, The. Christina Georgina Rossetti. CP-RosC1

Give me the moon at my feet. Prayer: "Give me the moon at my feet." D. H. Lawrence. CP-LawrD

Give me the names for things, just give me their real names. Writing Life, The. Charles Wright. SP-WrigCN

Give Me the Splendid Silent Sun. Walt Whitman. CP-WhitW

Give me truths / For I am weary of the surfaces. Blight. Ralph Waldo Emerson. CP-EmerR

Give me wine, and give me meate. To Sir Clipseby Crew. Robert Herrick. CP-HerrR

Give Me Women, Wine, and Snuff. John Keats. CP-KeatJ

Give me your anathema. Whiffletree. Carl Sandburg. CP-SandC

Give me your hand. Conceit, A. Maya Angelou. SP-AngeM

Give me your hand old Revolutionary. Centenarian's Story, The. Walt Whitman. CP-WhitW

Give me your patience, sister, while I frame. Acrostic. John Keats. CP-KeatJ

Give me your poppies. Choros Sequence. "H. D." CP-DoolH

Give over seeking bastard joy. Exhortation. Louise Bogan. CP-BogaL

Give pensions to the Learned Pig. William Blake. CP-BlakW

Give place all ye that doth rejoice. Sir Thomas Wyatt. CP-WyatT

Give them my regards when you go to the school reunion. More of a Corpse than a Woman. Muriel Rukeyser. CP-RukeM

Give to barrows, trays, and pans. Art. Ralph Waldo Emerson. CP-EmerR

Give unto all, lest he, whom thou deni'st. Almes. Robert Herrick. CP-HerrR

Give Us. Primo Levi. CP-LeviP, *tr. by* Ruth Feldman

Give us a peace equal to the war. Give Us Our Peace. Langston Hughes. CP-HughL; CP-HughL2

Give us back, Oh give us back. Cry of the Masses. D. H. Lawrence. CP-LawrD

Give Us Gods. D. H. Lawrence. CP-LawrD

Give Us Our Peace. Langston Hughes. CP-HughL; CP-HughL2

Give us something to destroy. Give Us. Primo Levi. CP-LeviP, *tr. by* Ruth Feldman

Give us the grace to be men. Thus Far So Nobly Advanced. Kenneth Patchen. CP-PatcK

Give Us the Thebaïd. D. H. Lawrence. CP-LawrD

Give Want her welcome if she comes; we find. Poverty and Riches. Robert Herrick. CP-HerrR

Give way, and be ye ravished by the sun. To Marygolds. Robert Herrick. CP-HerrR

Give way, give way, now, now my Charles shines here. To the King. Robert Herrick. CP-HerrR

Give way, give way ye Gates, and win. Wassaile, The. Robert Herrick. CP-HerrR

Give Way, Ye Gates. Theodore Roethke. CP-RoetT

Give you a lantern. Kenneth Patchen. CP-PatcK

Give Your Heart to the Hawks. Robinson Jeffers. CP-JefR2

Give Your Wish Light. Robinson Jeffers. CP-JefR2

Given a godchild. For a Godchild. Charles Tomlinson. SP-TomlC

Given Grace, A. Charles Tomlinson. CP-TomlC; SP-TomlC

Given in Marriage unto Thee. Emily Dickinson. CP-DickE

Given Note, The. Seamus Heaney. SP-HeanSO

Giving and Taking. John Greenleaf Whittier. CP-WhitJ

Giving It Up. C. K. Williams. CP-WillC; SP-WillC

Giving me things. Gifts. Robert Creeley. SP-CreeR

Giving of the Torah, The. Yehuda Amichai. SP-AmicYL, *tr. by* Benjamin Harshav *and* Barbara Harshav

Giving oneself to the dentist or doctor who is a good one. Kind of Act Of, The. Robert Creeley. CP-CreeR

Gizmos and jeremiads aside, God. Meaning Business. Heather McHugh. SP-McHuH

Glacial Marks on Our Hills, The. Jones Very. CP-VeryJ

Glacier Country. Peter Blue Cloud. SP-BlueP

Glacier, The. Primo Levi. CP-LeviP, *tr. by* Ruth Feldman *and* Brian Swann

Glacier, The. Louis MacNeice. CP-MacNL

Glacier, The. Charles Tomlinson. CP-TomlC

Glad. W. H. Auden. CP-AudeW *Fr.* Three Posthumous Poems.

Glad at the Cold (1955). Alan Dugan. CP-DugaA

Glad Christmas Day once more has come. With Best Wishes. Dorothy Parker. CP-ParkD

Glad I wake with morning light. Morning Hymn for a Little Child. Jones Very. CP-VeryJ

Glad morning, coming, The. Lyric: "Glad morning, coming, The." Tennessee Williams. CP-WillT

Glad old house of lichened stonework. To a Well-Named Dwelling. Thomas Hardy. CP-HardT

Glad Sight Wherever New with Old. William Wordsworth. CP-WorW2

Glad they were there. Louis Zukofsky. CP-ZukLS

Glad time is at his point arrived. Epithalamion: "Glad time is at his point arrived." Ben Jonson. CP-JonsB *Fr.* Masque of Hymen.

Glade on a bench of the mountain, A. Have You Ever Eaten Stars? Robert Penn Warren. CP-WarrR

Gladeth, ye foules, of the morrowe gray. Complaint of Mars, The. Geoffrey Chaucer. CP-ChauG

Gladethe, thoue queyne of Scottis regioun. William Dunbar. CP-DunbW

Gladiators, The. Stanley Kunitz. CP-KunSC

Gladly I would be again. High Summer. Kathleen Jessie Raine. SP-RainK

Gladness. James Whitcomb Riley. CP-RileJ

Gladness of Death. D. H. Lawrence. CP-LawrD

Gladstone. G. K. Chesterton. CP-ChesG

Gladstone Street. Charles Tomlinson. CP-TomlC; SP-TomlC

Glamour. James Whitcomb Riley. CP-RileJ

Glamour of the end attic, the smell of old, The. Perdita. Louis MacNeice. CP-MacNL

Glamoured the road, the day, and him and her. Walk, The. Seamus Heaney. SP-HeanSO

Glance, The. George Herbert. CP-HerbG

Glance, The. Walter De la Mare. CP-DeLaW

Glance—and instantly the small meek flower, A. Pot Of Musk, A. Walter De la Mare. CP-DeLaW

Glance drops here like a hawk falling, The. Morwenna's Cliff. Charles Tomlinson. CP-TomlC

Glance from the Bridge, A. Richard Wilbur. CP-WilbR

Glances. William Stafford. SP-StafWW

Glancing by chance at my unusual pallor. Petrarch. CP-Petra, *tr. by* J. G. Nichols

Glancing over my shoulder at the past. Schoolsville. Billy Collins. SP-CollB

Glanders. Paul Muldoon. CP-MuldP

Glanmore Revisited. Seamus Heaney.
  Cot, The. SP-HeanSO
  Lustral Sonnet. SP-HeanSO
  Scrabble. SP-HeanSO
  Skylight, The. SP-HeanSO

Glanmore Sonnets. Seamus Heaney. SP-HeanSO

Glaphira 3. Donald Davie. CP-DaviDC

Glare from the brass horn makes sun-brown satin fit smoothly the girl by the window, The. Fancy Another Day Gone. Lorine Niedecker. CP-NiedL

Glare goes down, The. The metal of a molten pane. Glass Grain. Charles Tomlinson. CP-TomlC; SP-TomlC

Glasco had none, but now some teeth has got. Upon Glasco. Epig. Robert Herrick. CP-HerrR

Glasgow, 1960. Hugh MacDiarmid. SP-MacDH

Glass. A. R. Ammons. CP-AmmoA

Glass. W. S. Merwin. SP-MerwW

Glass, The. Carolyn Kizer. CP-KizeC

Glass, air, ice, light. Waiting on the Corners. Donald Hall. CP-HallD

Glass / and wide seaview. Art Center. Lorine Niedecker. CP-NiedL

Glass Ark, The. Yusef Komunyakaa. CP-KomuY

Glass Darkly, A. Miller Williams. CP-WillM

Glass Dialectic. Howard Nemerov. CP-NemeH

Glass Face in the Rain, A. William Stafford. SP-StafWW

Glass Falling. Louis MacNeice. CP-MacNL

Glass gauds from Murano. Death in Venice. Charles Tomlinson. CP-TomlC

Glass Grain. Charles Tomlinson. CP-TomlC; SP-TomlC

Glass has been falling all the afternoon, The. Storm Warnings. Adrienne Rich. CP-RicAE; SP-RicA1; SP-RicA2

Glass House Canticle. Carl Sandburg. CP-SandC

Glass in a Liverpool drawing room cracked across, A. Nineteen-Seventeen. Donald Davie. CP-DaviDC

Glass is going down, The. The sun. Glass Falling. Louis MacNeice. CP-MacNL

Glass of Pure Water, The. Hugh MacDiarmid. SP-MacDH

Glass of Water, A. May Sarton. SP-SartM

Glass of Water, The. Wallace Stevens. CP-StevW; CP-StevWP

Glass of wine, the book, A. Recipe for Contemplation. William Corbett. SP-CorbW

Glass Orchard. Raissa Maritain. CP-MertT

Glass, out of deep[e] and out of desperate [*or* desp'rate] want. Upon Glass: Epigram. Robert Herrick. CP-HerrR

Glass Poem. Karl Shapiro. CP-ShapK

Glass stems of the clouds are breaking, The. Spring. W. S. Merwin. SP-MerwW

Glass was the Street—in tinsel Peril. Emily Dickinson. CP-DickE

Glasses. John Updike. CP-UpdiJ

Glassy Harbor, The. James Tate. SP-TateJ

Glassy water, glassy water. Translation of the Beginning of *Rio Verde*. Samuel Johnson. CP-JohnS

Glastonbury Thorn, The. George Meredith. CP-MerG2

Glazed mind layed in a, A). E. E. Cummings. CP-CummE

Glazed surface of the world, dusk, The. To My Father. Robert Pinsky. CP-PinsR

Glazier, The. Stéphane Mallarmé. CP-MallS, *tr. by* Henry Weinfield *Fr.* Street Songs.

Glazunoviana. John Ashbery. SP-AshbJ

Gleam of an heroic Act, The. Emily Dickinson. CP-DickE

Gleaming above the bewildered human herd. Jinx, The. Stéphane Mallarmé. CP-MallS, *tr. by* Henry Weinfield

Gleaner (Suggested by a Picture), The. William Wordsworth. CP-WorW2

Gleaning. Randall Jarrell. CP-JarrR

Glee. George Meredith. CP-MerG2

Glee—The great storm is over. Emily Dickinson. CP-DickE

Glen-Almain; or, the Narrow Glen. William Wordsworth. CP-WorW1; MW-WorW

Glen of Silence, The. Hugh MacDiarmid. SP-MacDH

Glencoe. G. K. Chesterton. CP-ChesG

Gleneden's Dream. Emily Jane Brontë. CP-BronE

Glengormley. Derek Mahon. CP-MahoD

Gli Scafari. Charles Tomlinson. CP-TomlC

Glide gentle streams, and beare. Teare Sent to Her from Stanes, The. Robert Herrick. CP-HerrR

Glide gently, thus for ever glide. Remembrance of Collins, Composed upon the

Thames near Richmond. William Wordsworth. CP-WorW1

Gliding o'er All. Walt Whitman. CP-WhitW

Glimmer. Carl Sandburg. CP-SandC

Glimmer of the limes, sun-heavy, sleeping, The. From a College Window. D. H. Lawrence. CP-LawrD

Glimmer'd along the square-cut steep. Gerard Manley Hopkins. CP-HopkG

Glimmering dusk above the moist plough and the. Ivor Gurney. SP-GurnI

Glimpse, A. Walt Whitman. CP-WhitW

Glimpse, The. Thomas Hardy. CP-HardT

Glimpse, The. George Herbert. CP-HerbG

Glimpse, The. Walter De la Mare. CP-DeLaW

Glimpse of Main Event. Heather McHugh. SP-McHuH

Glimpse of Pan, A. James Whitcomb Riley. CP-RileJ

Glimpse of the Ice. W. S. Merwin. SP-MerwW

Glimpse of the Waterer. Robert Bly. SP-BlyR

Glimpse through an interstice caught, A. Glimpse, A. Walt Whitman. CP-WhitW

Glimpses. D. H. Lawrence. CP-LawrD

Glimpses of Eden for the tired mind. Rest. Wallace Stevens. CP-StevWP

Glimpses of Seasons. Robert Penn Warren. CP-WarrR

Glistening field has survived its battles, The. Near York. Charles Tomlinson. CP-TomlC

Glitter of grey. What Harbinger? Denise Levertov. SP-LeveDS

Glitter of Nausicaä's. Homer in Basic. Kenneth Rexroth. CP-RexrK

Glitter of particles, A. Soajo. Charles Tomlinson. SP-TomlC *Fr.* Portugeuse Pieces.

Glittering rises in flocks, The. Approaches, The. W. S. Merwin. SP-MerwW

Globe in [North] Carolina, The. Derek Mahon. CP-MahoD

Globe of Gneiss. Robert Penn Warren. CP-WarrR

Gloire de Dijon. D. H. Lawrence. CP-LawrD

Gloom in my mind: I leaned. On a May Night. Charles Tomlinson. CP-TomlC

Gloom that breathes upon me with these airs, The. Dark Day, A. Dante Gabriel Rossetti. CW-RossD *Fr.* House of Life, The.

Gloomy December. Robert Burns. CP-BurnR

Gloomy grammarians in golden gowns. On [or Of] the Manner of Addressing Clouds. Wallace Stevens. CP-StevW; CP-StevWP

Gloomy hulls, in armour [or armor] grim, The. *Temeraire,* The. Herman Melville. SP-MelvH

Gloomy Lady. Charles Bukowski. SP-BukC1

Gloomy night is gath'ring fast, The. Song: "Gloomy night is gath'ring fast, The." Robert Burns. CP-BurnR

Gloria in Excelsis, The. Saint Ambrose. CP-MertT

Gloria in Profundis. G. K. Chesterton. CP-ChesG

Gloria Mundi. Walter De la Mare. CP-DeLaW

Gloria's Clues. Yusef Komunyakaa. CP-KomuY

Glorie. Robert Herrick. CP-HerrR

Glories, The. Rudyard Kipling. CP-KiplR

Glorious people vibrated again, A. Ode to Liberty. Percy Bysshe Shelley. CP-ShelP

Glorious pourtraict of that angels face, The. Sonnet 17. Edmund Spenser. CP-Spens *Fr.* Amoretti.

Glorious summer day! Clump of hot rocks! Question of Personnel, The. Andrei Codrescu. SP-CodrA

Glorious vision hovers o'er his soul, A. Tasso and Leonora. Christina Georgina Rossetti. CP-RosC3

Glory. Robert Herrick. CP-HerrR

Glory. Yusef Komunyakaa. CP-KomuY

Glory. D. H. Lawrence. CP-LawrD

Glory. Stéphane Mallarmé. CP-MallS, *tr. by* Henry Weinfield

Glory, The. John Ciardi. CP-CiarJ

Glory and loveliness have passed away. To Leigh Hunt, Esq. John Keats. CP-KeatJ

Glory be to God for dappled things. Pied Beauty. Gerard Manley Hopkins. CP-HopkG

Glory be to the Graces! Psalme or Hymne to the Graces, A. Robert Herrick. CP-HerrR

Glory! Hallelujah [or Halleluiah]! / The dawn's a-comin'! Prayer Meeting. Langston Hughes. CP-HughL; CP-HughL1

Glory is a flame off exploit, so we say. In Honour of St. Alphonsus Rodriguez. Gerard Manley Hopkins. CP-HopkG

Glory is fallen out of, The. E. E. Cummings. CP-CummE

Glory is that bright tragic thing. Emily Dickinson. CP-DickE

Glory / is the second child. Yannis Ritsos. SP-RitsY *Fr.* Paper Poems 1.

Glory no ther thing is (Tullie sayes). Glory. Robert Herrick. CP-HerrR

Glory of Darkness. D. H. Lawrence. CP-LawrD

(It is dark.) CP-LawrD

Glory of evening was spread through the west, The. Convict, The. William Wordsworth. CP-WorW1

Glory of expanded noon. Eugenio Montale. CP-MontE, *tr. by* Jonathan Galassi

Glory of the Garden, The. Rudyard Kipling. CP-KiplR

Glory of the Ptolemies, The. Constantine P. Cavafy. CP-CavaC, *tr. by* Theoharis Constantine Theoharis

Glory to God Alone. Jeanne Marie Bouvier de la Motte Guyon. CP-CowpW, *tr. by* William Cowper

Glory to God in the highest. Gloria in Excelsis, The. Saint Ambrose. CP-MertT

Glory Trumpeter, The. Derek Walcott. CP-WalcD

Glory! Until yesterday I didn't know it in its indisputable essence. Glory. Stéphane Mallarmé. CP-MallS, *tr. by* Henry Weinfield

Gloss, A. Charles Olson. CP-OlsoC

Gloss on the Sin of Ixion. Thomas Merton. CP-MertT

Glossina morsitans bit rich Aunt Betsy, A. *Glossina Morsitans,* or, the Tsetse. Ogden Nash. CP-NashO

Glossina Morsitans, or, the Tsetse. Ogden Nash. CP-NashO

Gloucestershire. Donald Davie. CP-DaviDC

Glove, The. Ben Jonson. CP-JonsB *Fr.* Cynthia's Revels.

Glove, The. Robert Browning. CP-BroR1

Glove, The. Raissa Maritain. CP-MertT

Glow of my campfire is dark red and flameless, The. Toward an Organic Philosophy. Kenneth Rexroth. CP-RexrK

Glow Worm. Thomas Lux. SP-LuxT

Glow-worm, The. Vincent Bourne. CP-CowpW

Glowing is her Bonnet. Emily Dickinson. CP-DickE

Glukupikron. Gregory Orr. SP-OrrG

Glutton, The. Sylvia Plath. CP-PlatS

Glutton, The. Jones Very. CP-VeryJ

Gluttony, sleep, swans-down of idleness. Petrarch. CP-Petra, *tr. by* J. G. Nichols

Gnädiges Fräulein. Stevie Smith. CP-SmitS

Gnarled avenues the years have mapped. Poem, The: "Gnarled avenues the years have mapped." Wyatt Prunty. SP-PrunW

Gnat on My Paper. Richard Eberhart. CP-EberR

Gnat-Psalm. Ted Hughes. SP-HughTN

Gnats. Richard Eberhart. CP-EberR

Gnats inside the Wind. Jelaluddin Rumi. SP-Rumi, *tr. by* Coleman Barks

Gnawing the highway's edges, its black mouth. Swamp, The. Derek Walcott. CP-WalcD

Gnome. Samuel Beckett. CP-BeckS

Gnomes. Howard Nemerov. CP-NemeH

Gnomes / astride their secrets, The. In the Woods. Federico García Lorca. CP-GarcF, *tr. by* Jerome Rothenberg *Fr.* Newton.

Gnomic Verses. William Blake. CP-BlakW

Gnomic Verses. Ezra Pound. CP-PoEar

Gnomons. Richard Wilbur. CP-WilbR

Gnostic at the Zoo, The. Wyatt Prunty. SP-PrunW

Gnostology. Sam Hamill. SP-HamiS

Gnothi Seauton. James Vincent Cunningham. CP-CunnJ

Γνωθι Σεαυτον. Ralph Waldo Emerson. CP-EmerR

Gnothi seauton!—and is this the prime. Self-Knowledge. Samuel Taylor Coleridge. CP-ColeS; MW-ColeS

Gnothi Seauton (Post Lexicon Anglicanum Auctum et Emendatum). Samuel Johnson. CP-JohnS

Gnu, The. Theodore Roethke. CP-RoetT

Go. Ai. SP-Ai

Go ahead stockpile rhino horn. Han-shan. CP-ColdM, *tr. by* Red Pine

Go and ask Robin to bring the girls over. Vision by Sweetwater. John Crowe Ransom. SP-RansJ

Go and catch a falling star. Song: "Go and catch a falling star." John Donne. CP-DonnJ; MW-DonnJ

Go as Played in the Best Circles; or Rotten Axe-Handle. Robert Stock. SP-StocR

Go Ask the Dead. Thomas McGrath. SP-McGrT

Go away from me—do! I am tired of you! End, An. James Whitcomb Riley. CP-RileJ

Go away. Leave the high winds of May. Crossing the Ohio when Poppies Bloom in Ashtabula. Carl Sandburg. CP-SandC

Go Back to Antique Ages, if Thine Eyes. William Wordsworth. CP-WorW2

Go back to Egypt and the Greeks. Mad Gleam, A. Allen Ginsberg. CP-GinsA

Go boldly forth, and feast on being's banquet. Ralph Waldo Emerson. CP-EmerR

Go book. Envoy from d'Aubigné. W. S. Merwin. SP-MerwW

Go, burning sighs, unto the frozen heart. Sir Thomas Wyatt. CP-WyatT

Go deeper than love, for the soul has greater depths. Know Deeply, Know Thyself More Deeply. D. H. Lawrence. CP-LawrD

Go down obscurely. Be of Good Cheer. Robert Creeley. SP-CreeR

Go down the left. Space Travel. A. R. Ammons. CP-AmmoA

Go! fair Example of untainted youth. Epitaph on the Monument of the Honourable Robert Digby, and of his Sister Mary, erected by their Father the Lord Digby, in the Church of Sherborne in Dorsetshire, 1727. Alexander Pope. CP-PopeA

Go, faithful Portrait! and where long hath knelt. To the Author's Portrait. William Wordsworth. CP-WorW2

Go fetch to me a pint o' [or of] wine. Silver Tassie, The. Robert Burns. CP-BurnR

Go Fishing. Ted Hughes. SP-HughTN

Go, fool, and hatch of the air. Green Man, The. Charles Olson. CP-OlsoC

Go foolish thoughts, and join the throng. Arthur Hugh Clough. SP-ClouA

Go, for they call you, Shepherd, from the hill. Scholar Gypsy, The. Matthew Arnold. SP-ArnoM

Go from me. I am one of those who spoil. L'Invitation. Ezra Pound. CP-PoEar

Go from me, summer friends, and tarry not. From Sunset to Star Rise. Christina Georgina Rossetti. CP-RosC1

Go Get the Goodly Squab. Sylvia Plath. CP-PlatS

Go hang yourself, you old M.D.! Common Cold, The. Ogden Nash. CP-NashO

Go hence, and with this parting kisse. Parting Verse, or Charge to His Supposed Wife when He Travelled, The. Robert Herrick. CP-HerrR

Go home, stupid. Ultimatum: Kid to Kid. Langston Hughes. CP-HughL; CP-HughL3

Go I must along my ways. Second Oldest Story, The. Dorothy Parker. CP-ParkD

Go I must; when I am gone. To His Tomb-Maker. Robert Herrick. CP-HerrR

Go if thou wilt ambrosial Flower. Ralph Waldo Emerson. CP-EmerR

Go in Green. Gertrude Stein. CP-SteiG

Go in Manhattan. I Heard Brew Moore Say, One Day. Ted Berrigan. SP-BerrT

Go in Peace. Christina Georgina Rossetti. CP-RosC2

Go in peace my Beloved; tho' never again. Young Men Aye Were Fickle Found since Summer Trees Were Leafy. Christina Georgina Rossetti. CP-RosC3

Go inside a stone. Stone. Charles Simic. SP-SimiC; SP-SimiCE

Go, intercept some fountain in the vein. Upon the Death of the Lord Hastings. Andrew Marvell. CP-MarvA

Go into the garden. Ralph Waldo Emerson. CP-EmerR

Go little book, go little fable. Author ad Librum. Ben Jonson. CP-JonsB; SP-JonsB

Go, little book. If anybody asks. Envoi: "Go, little book. If anybody asks." William Meredith. SP-MereW

Go, little book, / To him who, on a lute with horns of pearl. With a Copy of 'A House of Pomegranates'. Oscar Wilde. CP-WildO

Go look for beauty where you least. More than a Fool's Song. Countee Cullen. CP-CullC

Go / Make a Bridge. Charles Olson. CP-OlsoC

Go, my sad rhymes, until you reach the stone. Petrarch. CP-Petra, tr. by J. G. Nichols

Go, my songs, seek your praise from the young and from the intolerant. Ité. Ezra Pound. SP-PounE

Go, my warm sighs, and melt her frozen heart. Petrarch. CP-Petra, tr. by J. G. Nichols

Go not too near a House of Rose. Emily Dickinson. CP-DickE

Go not, young cloud, too boldly through the sky. Quatrain: "Go not, young cloud, too boldly through the sky." Wallace Stevens. CP-StevWP

Go on brave Hopton, to effectuate that. To the Lord Hopton, on His Fight in Cornwall. Robert Herrick. CP-HerrR

Go on, cedar that away. All Your Seals Broken? Never. Paul Celan. SP-CelaP, tr. by John Felstiner

Go on, high ship, since now, upon the shore. Farewell to Florida. Wallace Stevens. CP-StevW; CP-StevWP

Go on out but come back in. Fanny Howe. SP-HoweF Fr. O'Clock.

Go on, sweet bird, and soothe my care. Revision for Clarinda. Robert Burns. CP-BurnR

Go out into Nature and plant trees. Ralph Waldo Emerson. CP-EmerR

Go pretty [or prettie] child and bear[e] this flower. To His Saviour, a Child; a Present, by a Child. Robert Herrick. CP-HerrR

Go Read Your Book! James Whitcomb Riley. CP-RileJ

Go, roads, to the four quarters of our quiet distance. Evening of the Visitation, The. Thomas Merton. CP-MertT

Go Round. Gary Snyder. CP-SnydG

Go slow, my soul, to feed thyself. Emily Dickinson. CP-DickE

Go slow, they say. Langston Hughes. CP-HughL; CP-HughL3

Go, Soul [or Goe soule], the body's [or bodies] guest. Lie, The. Sir Walter Ralegh. CP-RaleW

Go, speed the stars of thought. Intellect. Ralph Waldo Emerson. CP-EmerR

Go, stalk the red dear o'er the heather. Rudyard Kipling. CP-KiplR Fr. Plain Tales from the Hills.

Go talk with those who are rumored to be unlike you. For the Student Strikers. Richard Wilbur. CP-WilbR

Go tell Amynta, gentle swain. Song: "Go tell Amynta, gentle swain." John Dryden. CP-DryJ2; SP-DrydJ

"Go tell it." What a Message. Emily Dickinson. CP-DickE

Go tell the earth to shake. Earthquake. Thomas Merton. CP-MertT

Go—thou art all unfit to share. On a Mischievous Bull. William Cowper. CP-CowpW

Go thou gentle whispering wind. Prayer to the Wind, A. Thomas Carew. CP-CareT

Go thy great way! Emily Dickinson. CP-DickE

Go to sleep—though of course you will not. Goodnight, A. William Carlos Williams. CP-WilW1

Go to the ant, you sluggard, and go. Cycle, The. Dan Pagis. SP-PagiD, tr. by Stephen Mitchell

Go to the depths of willing. American Hakluyt. Richard Eberhart. CP-EberR

Go / to the other / shore. Blue Bottle, The. May Swenson. SP-SwenM

Go to the Shine That's on a Tree. Richard Eberhart. CP-EberR

Go to the Wall. Christopher Logue. SP-LoguC Fr. Lily-White Boys, The.

Go to the western gate, Luke Havergal. Luke Havergal. Edwin Arlington Robinson. CP-RobiE

Go to Tibet. / Ride a camel. Friendly Advice to a Lot of Young Men. Charles Bukowski. SP-BukC2

Go traveling with us! Emily Dickinson. CP-DickE

Go tuneful bird, forbear to soar. Presenting a *Lark*. Alexander Pope. CP-PopeA

Go, wash thyself in Jordan—go, wash thee and be clean! Naaman's Song. Rudyard Kipling. CP-KiplR

Go West Young Man. James Laughlin. CP-LaugJ

Go where you will. No Fixed Place. Alice Walker. CP-WalkA

Go, Winter! Go thy ways! We want again. James Whitcomb Riley. CP-RileJ

Go wooe young Charles no more to looke. To His Muse. Robert Herrick. CP-HerrR

Goal in sight, The! Look up and sing, / Set faces full against the light. Christina Georgina Rossetti. CP-RosC2

Goal of Intellectual Man, The. Richard Eberhart. CP-EberR

Goalposts were imaginary lines. Touch. Yusef Komunyakaa. CP-KomuY

Goat and Amalthea. Laura Riding Jackson. CP-RidiL

Goat, The. William Carlos Williams. CP-WilW2

Goats and Monkeys. Derek Walcott. CP-WalcD

Goats go past the back of the house like dry leaves in the dawn. She-Goat. D. H. Lawrence. CP-LawrD

Goatsucker. Sylvia Plath. CP-PlatS

Gob Music. Theodore Roethke. CP-RoetT

Goblets all are broken, The. Have Patience. Christina Georgina Rossetti. CP-RosC3

Goblin Market. Christina Georgina Rossetti. CP-RosC1

Goblins, The. Sir John Suckling. CP-SuckJ

God. G. K. Chesterton. CP-ChesG

God. John Ciardi. CP-CiarJ

God. E. E. Cummings. CP-CummE

God. Robert Herrick. CP-HerrR

God. Langston Hughes. CP-HughL; CP-HughL1

God. D. H. Lawrence. CP-LawrD

God. Miller Williams. CP-WillM

God, A. Ted Hughes. SP-HughTN

God, The. "H. D." CP-DoolH

God, The. Ted Hughes. SP-HughTN

God, A Poem. James Fenton. SP-FentJ

God and all angels sing the world to sleep. Men That Are Falling, The. Wallace Stevens. CP-StevW; CP-StevWP

God, and Lord. Robert Herrick. CP-HerrR

God and Man. Richard Eberhart. CP-EberR

God and man. Stevie Smith. CP-SmitS

God and the Devil. Stevie Smith. CP-SmitS

God and the devil still are wrangling. For a Mouthy Woman. Countee Cullen. CP-CullC

God and the Holy Ghost. D. H. Lawrence. CP-LawrD

God, and the King. Robert Herrick. CP-HerrR

God answers with my doom! I am annulled. Reply, The. Allen Ginsberg. CP-GinsA

God, as He is most Holy knowne. God Is One. Robert Herrick. CP-HerrR

God, as He's potent, so He's likewise known. Gods Bounty. Robert Herrick. CP-HerrR

God, awful and powerful beyond the sky's acre. At the End of the War. Richard Eberhart. CP-EberR

God banish from your house. Benediction. Stanley Kunitz. CP-KunSC

God be praised that made. Garland for Ivor Gurney, A. Donald Davie. CP-DaviDC

God be with thee, gladsome Ocean! On Revisiting the Sea-Shore, after Long Absence. Samuel Taylor Coleridge. CP-ColeS

God be with thee, my beloved,—God be with thee! Valediction, A: "God be with thee, my beloved,—God be with thee!" Elizabeth Barrett Browning. CP-BroEB

God Bless America! James Laughlin. CP-LaugJ

God bless New Hampshire! from her granite peaks. New Hampshire. John Greenleaf Whittier. CP-WhitJ

God bless the little Island! Song: "God bless the little Island!" George Meredith. CP-MerG2

God bless ye, brothers! in the fight. To the Reformers of England. John Greenleaf Whittier. CP-WhitJ

God bought man here with his hearts blood expense. Gods Price, and Mans Price. Robert Herrick. CP-HerrR

God called the nearest angels who dwell with Him above. Two Angels, The. John Greenleaf Whittier. CP-WhitJ

God called the Prophet Muhammad *Muzzammil*. One Who Wraps Himself. Jelaluddin Rumi. SP-Rumi, *tr. by* Coleman Barks

God came to a man, A. Stephen Crane. CP-CranS

God can do all things, save but what are known. His Power. Robert Herrick. CP-HerrR

God can't be wrathfull; but we may conclude. Gods Anger. Robert Herrick. CP-HerrR

God careth for the smallest seed. New Body, The. Jones Very. CP-VeryJ

God co'd [*or* could] have made all rich, or all men poor[e]. Riches and Poverty. Robert Herrick. CP-HerrR

God created alcohol. Io Baccho! William Carlos Williams. CP-WilW2

God did forbid the Israelites, to bring. Ass[e], The. Robert Herrick. CP-HerrR

God doth embrace the good with love; & gaines. Pittie, and Punishment. Robert Herrick. CP-HerrR

God doth not promise here to man, that He. Gods Time Must End Our Trouble. Robert Herrick. CP-HerrR

God dreamed—the suns sprang flaming into place. Creation. Ambrose Bierce. SP-BierA

God fashioned the ship of the world carefully. Stephen Crane. CP-CranS

God-Forgotten. Thomas Hardy. CP-HardT

God Forsakes Antony, The. Constantine P. Cavafy. CP-CavaC, *tr. by* Theoharis Constantine Theoharis

God from a Cloud to Spender spoke. Airs of Palestine, No. 2. T. S. Eliot. SP-ElioT

God from our eyes all teares hereafter wipes. Teares. Robert Herrick. CP-HerrR

God Full of Mercy. Yehuda Amichai. SP-AmicYL, *tr. by* Benjamin Harshav *and* Barbara Harshav

God-Full-of-Mercy, the prayer for the dead. God Full of Mercy. Yehuda Amichai. SP-AmicYL, *tr. by* Benjamin Harshav *and* Barbara Harshav

God gave a Loaf to every Bird. Emily Dickinson. CP-DickE

God gave all men all earth to love. Sussex. Rudyard Kipling. CP-KiplR

God gets up in the morning. Carl Sandburg. God Is No Gentleman. CP-SandC

God, give us a long winter. Flame, A. Adam Zagajewski. SP-ZagaA, *tr. by* Clare Cavanagh

God give you pardon from gratitude. Song: "God give you pardon from gratitude." Robert Creeley. CP-CreeR

God gives not onely corne, for need. To God. Robert Herrick. CP-HerrR

God gives to none so absolute an Ease. Ease. Robert Herrick. CP-HerrR

God gloats upon Her stunning flesh. Upon. E. E. Cummings. CP-CummE

God grant a blessing on this tower and cottage. Prayer on Going into My House. William Butler Yeats. CP-YeatW

God guard me from those thoughts men think. Prayer for Old Age, A. William Butler Yeats. CP-YeatW

God guided my hand. Vita. William Stafford. SP-StafWW

God had but one Son free from sin; but none. Correction. Robert Herrick. CP-HerrR

God had called us, and we came. Blue-Flag in the Bog, The. Edna St. Vincent Millay. CP-MillE

God has a brown voice. For Eleanor Boylan Talking with God. Anne Sexton. CP-SextA; SP-SextA

God has a Right Hand, but is quite bereft. Right Hand, The. Robert Herrick. CP-HerrR

God Has a Twofold Part. Robert Herrick. CP-HerrR

God has foure keyes, which He reserves alone. Gods Keyes. Robert Herrick. CP-HerrR

God has given us a dark wine so potent that. Many Wines, The. Jelaluddin Rumi. SP-Rumi, *tr. by* Coleman Barks

God has his plans, and what if we. To the Memory of Mary Young. Paul Laurence Dunbar. CP-DunbP

God has his whips here to a twofold end. Whips. Robert Herrick. CP-HerrR

God Has Pity on Kindergarten Children. Yehuda Amichai. SP-AmicY, *tr. by* Stephen Mitchell

God hates the Duall Number; being known. Number of Two, The. Robert Herrick. CP-HerrR

God hath put me here. Dawn Song, A. Ezra Pound. CP-PoEar

God hath this world for many made; 'tis true. This, and the Next World. Robert Herrick. CP-HerrR

God hath two wings, which He doth ever move. Mercy and Love. Robert Herrick. CP-HerrR

God having a hemorrhage. Caribbean Sunset. Langston Hughes. CP-HughL; CP-HughL1

God He refuseth no man; but makes way. Free Welcome. Robert Herrick. CP-HerrR

God He rejects all prayers that are sleight. Prayers Must Have Poise. Robert Herrick. CP-HerrR

God Heares Us. Robert Herrick. CP-HerrR

God heares us when we pray, but yet defers. Gods Gifts Not Soon[e] Granted. Robert Herrick. CP-HerrR

God help that country where informers thrive! Black Day, The. Archibald MacLeish. CP-MacLA

God help the fingernails. On Fingernails in Bloody Times. Alan Dugan. CP-DugaA

God help us on a day. Grace for Thursday. Alan Dugan. CP-DugaA

God hides from man the reck'ning Day, that He. Judgment-Day, The. Robert Herrick. CP-HerrR

God Hides His People. Jeanne Marie Bouvier de la Motte Guyon. CP-CowpW, *tr. by* William Cowper

God i had forgotten how. New York—Albany. Lawrence Ferlinghetti. SP-FerlL

God, I know nothing, my sense is all nonsense. Grace, A. Donald Hall. CP-HallD

God, I need a job because I need money. Prayer: "God, I need a job because I need money." Alan Dugan. CP-DugaA

God in Heaven, forgive my death, it lies. Death in the Rose Garden. Stevie Smith. CP-SmitS

God, in His infinite wisdom. Acceptance. Langston Hughes. CP-HughL; CP-HughL3

God in His own Day will be then severe. Sin Severely Punisht. Robert Herrick. CP-HerrR

God in his wisdom made the fly. Fly, The. Ogden Nash. CP-NashO

God in the great assembly stands. Bible, *O.T. See* God standeth in the congregation of the mighty

God, in the *holy Tongue*, they call. God. Robert Herrick. CP-HerrR

God in wrath, A. Stephen Crane. CP-CranS

God is a distant—stately Lover. Emily Dickinson. CP-DickE

God is above the sphere of our esteem. What God Is. Robert Herrick. CP-HerrR

God is all fore-part; for, we never see. Upon God. Robert Herrick. CP-HerrR

God is all-present to what e'er we do. Gods Presence. Robert Herrick. CP-HerrR

God is all-sufferance here; here He doth show. To God. Robert Herrick. CP-HerrR

God is already ahead and waiting: the future is full. Fanny Howe. SP-HoweF *Fr.* In the Spirit There Are No Accidents.

God Is Born. D. H. Lawrence. CP-LawrD

God is good but. Notes. Thomas Kinsella. CP-KinsT

God is Good. It Is a Beautiful Night. Wallace Stevens. CP-StevW; CP-StevWP

God is great: through the tangle of scorns. Reparation. G. K. Chesterton. CP-ChesG

God, is His Name of Nature; but that word. God, and Lord. Robert Herrick. CP-HerrR

God is indeed a jealous God. Emily Dickinson. CP-DickE

God is indeed a jealous God. Emily Dickinson. CP-DickE

God is *Jehovah* cal'd; which name of His. Another. Robert Herrick. CP-HerrR

God is more here, then in another place. God. Robert Herrick. CP-HerrR

God Is No Gentleman. Carl Sandburg. CP-SandC

God is not offered to the senses. December Journal. Charles Wright. SP-WrigC

God is not on[e]ly merciful, to call. Calling, and Correcting. Robert Herrick. CP-HerrR

God is not only [*or* onely] said to be. Upon God. Robert Herrick. CP-HerrR

God is older than the sun and moon. Maximus. D. H. Lawrence. CP-LawrD

God Is One. Robert Herrick. CP-HerrR

God Is Our Hope and Strength. Christina Georgina Rossetti. CP-RosC2

God is simpler than you are. For Children when They Grow Up. C. K. Williams. CP-WillC

God is so potent, as His Power can. Gods Power. Robert Herrick. CP-HerrR

God is the great urge that has not yet found a body. Body of God, The. D. H. Lawrence. CP-LawrD

God is then said for to descend, when He. Gods Descent. Robert Herrick. CP-HerrR

God, Jack of all trades. Praying to Big Jack. Anne Sexton. CP-SextA

God knows how our neighbor managed to breed. Sow. Sylvia Plath. CP-PlatS

God knows I would not blame you, dear. Invisible, The. G. K. Chesterton. CP-ChesG

God knows / We have our troubles, too. High to Low. Langston Hughes. CP-HughL; CP-HughL3

God knows who first thought up. Struggle with the Angel. Jaroslav Seifert. SP-SeifJ, *tr. by* Ewald Osers

God lay dead in Heaven. Stephen Crane. CP-CranS

God loads, and unloads, (thus His work begins). Loading and Unloading. Robert Herrick. CP-HerrR

God loafs around heaven. Earth, The. Anne Sexton. CP-SextA; SP-SextA

God love you now, if no one else will ever. Ode for the American Dead in

Korea. Thomas McGrath. SP-McGrT

God Maddens Him Whom 'Tis His Will to Lose. Lord Byron. CP-Byron

God made a little Gentian. Fringed Gentian. Emily Dickinson. CP-DickE

God made no act without a cause. Emily Dickinson. CP-DickE

God made the wicked grocer. Song against Grocers, The. G. K. Chesterton. CP-ChesG

God made thee mightily, my love. Frances ("God made thee mightily, my love"). G. K. Chesterton. CP-ChesG

God made you very carefully. To My Lady. G. K. Chesterton. CP-ChesG

God make me the poet of simplicity. My Prayer. E. E. Cummings. CP-CummE

God makes not good men wantons, but doth bring. Good Men Afflicted Most. Robert Herrick. CP-HerrR

God maketh the birds his care. Cherry Birds, The. Jones Very. CP-VeryJ

God-Monger, The. Anne Sexton. CP-SextA; SP-SextA

God, naměd Love, whose fount Thou art. Supplication for Love, A. Elizabeth Barrett Browning. CP-BroEB

God Neither Known nor Loved by the World. Jeanne Marie Bouvier de la Motte Guyon. CP-CowpW, tr. by William Cowper

God n'ere afflicts us more then our desert. Affliction. Robert Herrick. CP-HerrR

God Not Afar Off. Jones Very. CP-VeryJ

God Not to Be Comprehended. Robert Herrick. CP-HerrR

God of being demoralized, The. Distraction. Howard Nemerov. CP-NemeH

God of day rolls his car up the slopes, The. Guido's Aurora. Henry David Thoreau. CP-ThorH

God of Details, The. Boris Leonidovich Pasternak. CP-DaviDC, tr. by Donald Davie

God of Fair Beginnings, The, Song of Diego Valdez, The. Rudyard Kipling. CP-KiplR

God of Love—ah, benedicite!, The. Cuckoo and the Nightingale, The. William Wordsworth. CP-WorW1

God of love my Shepherd is, The. Twenty-third Psalm, The. George Herbert. CP-HerbG

God of my father discovered at midnight. Oya. Audre Lorde. SP-LordA

God of our fathers, known of old. Recessional. Rudyard Kipling. CP-KiplR

God of the golden bow. Ode to Apollo. John Keats. CP-KeatJ

God of the Living, The. G. K. Chesterton. CP-ChesG

God of the Meridian. John Keats. CP-KeatJ

God of the people. Dodona. "H. D." CP-DoolH

God of the right, arise. To Miss Mary Britton. Paul Laurence Dunbar. CP-DunbP

God of the river leans, The. Observance. Wendell Berry. CP-BerrW

God of This World, The. Howard Nemerov. CP-NemeH

God of Visions. Emily Jane Brontë. CP-BronE
   (Plead for Me.) CP-BronE

God of your fathers, known of old. Post-Recessional. G. K. Chesterton. CP-ChesG

God on our Youth bestowes but little ease. Youth, and Age. Robert Herrick. CP-HerrR

God, only God is eternal. Moth and Rust. D. H. Lawrence. CP-LawrD

God only knew how Saadi dined. Ralph Waldo Emerson. CP-EmerR

God only knows what he'd been doing. Painting or sewing? Parish. Norman Dubie. CP-DubiN

God pardons those, who do through frailty sin. Pardon. Robert Herrick. CP-HerrR

God permits industrious Angels. Emily Dickinson. CP-DickE

God pity me whom (god distinctly has). E. E. Cummings. CP-CummE

God prosper, speed, and save. New National Anthem, A. Percy Bysshe Shelley. CP-ShelP

God Reigns. Paul Laurence Dunbar. CP-DunbP

God Rest Ye Merry, Gentlemen. Derek Walcott. CP-WalcD

God rest you, merry gentlemen. Happy Xmas, A ("God rest you, merry gentlemen"). G. K. Chesterton. CP-ChesG

God rest you merry gentlemen. Christmas Carol, A: "God rest you merry gentlemen." G. K. Chesterton. CP-ChesG

God rest you, merry Innocents. Carol for Children, A. Ogden Nash. CP-NashO

God rest you, peaceful gentlemen, let nothing you dismay. Russia to the Pacifists. Rudyard Kipling. CP-KiplR

God said, Let there be light; and there was light. At the Sun-Rise in 1848. Dante Gabriel Rossetti. CW-RossD

God said: "Let there be Man," and from the clay. Genesis. Ambrose Bierce. SP-BierA

God Said "They Did Not Hear." Thomas Merton. CP-MertT

God Saves the King. Donald Davie. CP-DaviDC

God scourgeth some severely, some He spares. No Escaping the Scourging. Robert Herrick. CP-HerrR

God seems much more friendly. Emily Dickinson. SP-DickE

God shook thy roundness in His finger's cup. D. H. Lawrence. See Who shook thy roundness in his finger's cup?

God slumbers in a back alley. Christian Country, A. Langston Hughes. CP-

HughL; CP-HughL1

God snaps your picture—don't look away. Archival Print, An. William Stafford. SP-StafW; SP-StafWW

God Sparing in Scourging. Robert Herrick. CP-HerrR

God Speaks. Stevie Smith. CP-SmitS

God standeth in the congregation of the mighty. Psalm 82: "God standeth in the congregation of the mighty." Bible, O.T. CP-MiltJ Fr. Psalms.

God still rewards us more then our desert. God Sparing in Scourging. Robert Herrick. CP-HerrR

God strengthen me to bear myself. Who Shall Deliver Me? Christina Georgina Rossetti. CP-RosC1

God strikes His Church, But 'tis to this intent. Persecutions Purifie. Robert Herrick. CP-HerrR

God suffers not His Saints, and Servants deere. Paine and Pleasure. Robert Herrick. CP-HerrR

God tackled and pistol-whipped me till I wept. Adam in Extremis. Robert Stock. SP-StocR

God takes care of it for. Right to Die. William Stafford. SP-StafWW

God Takes Pity on Kindergarten Children. Yehuda Amichai. SP-AmicYL, tr. by Benjamin Harshav and Barbara Harshav

God! that mad'st her well regard her. Dieu Qu'il la Fait. Charles, Duc d' Orléans. CP-PoEar, tr. by Ezra Pound

God the Creator, with a pulseless hand. Measure, The. Elizabeth Barrett Browning. CP-BroEB

God the Drinker. Stevie Smith. CP-SmitS

God the Eater. Stevie Smith. CP-SmitS

God, the Eternal! Infinite! All-wise! Cain: A Mystery. Lord Byron. CP-Byron

God the Lord save Massachusetts. Ralph Waldo Emerson. CP-EmerR

God then confounds mans face, when He not hears. Confusion of Face. Robert Herrick. CP-HerrR

God,Thine the hand that doth extend. E. E. Cummings. CP-CummE

God, this mud. Fear's habit. Water Buffalo. Yusef Komunyakaa. CP-KomuY

God, though to Thee our psalm we raise. Nondum. Gerard Manley Hopkins. CP-HopkG

God to Be First Served. Robert Herrick. CP-HerrR

God to Hungry Child. Langston Hughes. CP-HughL; CP-HughL1

God! to my little meale and oyle. To God. Robert Herrick. CP-HerrR

God took a crayon in his hand. Cul-de-Sac. Allen Tate. CP-TateA

God tried to teach Crow how to talk. Crow's First Lesson. Ted Hughes. SP-HughTN

God turne us every drem to goode! House of Fame, The. Geoffrey Chaucer. CP-ChauG

God Victimized. Robert Stock. SP-StocR

God went out of me. Sickness unto Death, The. Anne Sexton. CP-SextA

God when for sin He makes His Children smart. God Has a Twofold Part. Robert Herrick. CP-HerrR

God when He takes my goods and chattels hence. Upon God. Robert Herrick. CP-HerrR

God when He's angry here with any one. Gods Anger without Affection. Robert Herrick. CP-HerrR

God, whether by unconscious instinct, or waking, or in a dream, I do. What Odd Expedients. Robinson Jeffers. CP-JefR3

God, who me gives a will for to repent. To God. Robert Herrick. CP-HerrR

God, who with the thunders and great voices. Heaven and Earth. Elizabeth Barrett Browning. CP-BroEB

God, whom a soldier of the line of Atreus, The. Poem of the Fourth Element. Jorge Luis Borges. SP-BorgJ, tr. by Alastair Reid

God, who's in Heav'n, will hear from thence. God Heares Us. Robert Herrick. CP-HerrR

God will have all or none; serve Him, or fall. Neutrality Loathsome. Robert Herrick. CP-HerrR

God Wills It. Gabriela Mistral. SP-MistG, tr. by Maria Giachetti [or Jacketti]

God with honour hang your head. At the Wedding March. Gerard Manley Hopkins. CP-HopkG

God Works in a Mysterious Way. Gwendolyn Brooks. SP-BrooG

God would not let the spheric Lights accost. Hugh Stuart Boyd [His Blindness]. Elizabeth Barrett Browning. CP-BroEB

God, you could grow to love it, God-fearing, God. Ecclesiastes. Derek Mahon. CP-MahoD

Godchildren. William Meredith. SP-MereW

Goddamned animals might know more than we do about some things, The. Ribbons. C. K. Williams. CP-WillC

Goddess. Philip Whalen. SP-WhalP

Goddess, The. Rainer Maria Rilke. CP-RilkFr, tr. by A. Poulin, Jr. Fr. Orchards.

Goddess, The. Thom Gunn. CP-GunnT

Goddess, The. James Laughlin. CP-LaugJ

Goddess of health whose all inspiring charm. On the Birth Day of the Revd Doctor Witherspoon, 1788. Annis Boudinot Stockton. CP-StocA

Goddess of Liberty! O thou. Invocation. Ambrose Bierce. SP-BierA

Goddess of pleasure, where thy golden car? Pleasure ("Goddess of pleasure, where thy golden car?"). Jones Very. CP-VeryJ

Goddess of the murmuring courts. Nicotine. Ezra Pound. CP-PoEar

Goddess, on this blanched morning your mercy. Faded Offering. Rainer Maria Rilke. CP-RilkFr, *tr.* by A. Poulin, Jr.

Goddess stands in front of her cave, The. In Anselm Hollo's Poems. Ted Berrigan. SP-BerrT

Goddess, with a siren's grace, A. Orlie Wilde. James Whitcomb Riley. CP-RileJ

Goddesse, I begin an Art. Vow to Minerva, A. Robert Herrick. CP-HerrR

Goddesse, I do love a girle. Short Hymne to Venus, A. Robert Herrick. CP-HerrR

Goddesse of Youth, and Lady of the Spring. To the Queene. Robert Herrick. CP-HerrR

Godfather. Louis MacNeice. CP-MacNL

Godfather Death. Anne Sexton. CP-SextA

Godfather Returns to Color TV, The. Amy Clampitt. CP-ClamA

Godfrey of Boulogne. Henry David Thoreau. CP-ThorH

Godhead as Lynx, The. May Sarton. SP-SartM

Godhead, I adore thee fast in hiding; thou. S. Thomae Aquinatis Rhythmus ad SS. Sacramentum. Gerard Manley Hopkins. CP-HopkG

Godhulivela. Hayden Carruth. CP-CarHS

Godiva County, Montana. William Stafford. SP-StafWW

Godlike the man who. Carmen 51. Catullus. CP-ZukLS *Fr.* Carmina.

Godly Girzie. Robert Burns. CP-BurnR

Godmersham the Temple of Delight. Henry Thomas Austen. CP-AustJ

Godmother. Dorothy Parker. CP-ParkD

Godolphin School was large and cool. Lines to the Air of "Godolphin Horne" G. K. Chesterton. CP-ChesG

Gods. Hayden Carruth. CP-CarHS

Gods. Langston Hughes. CP-HughL; CP-HughL1

God's. David Ignatow. SP-IgnaD

Gods. D. H. Lawrence. CP-LawrD

Gods. Anne Sexton. CP-SextA

Gods. Walt Whitman. CP-WhitW

Gods, The. D. H. Lawrence. CP-LawrD

Gods, The. W. S. Merwin. SP-MerwW

God's Acre. A. E. Housman. CP-HousA

God's Acre. Christina Georgina Rossetti. CP-RosC2

God's acre was her garden-spot, she said. Garden-Spot. Dorothy Parker. CP-ParkD

Gods, angels, men, months, rivers, wind. Of the Genders of Nouns. Thomas Sheridan. CP-SherT

Gods Anger. Robert Herrick. CP-HerrR

Gods Anger without Affection. Robert Herrick. CP-HerrR

God's angry with the world again. Electrical Storm. Robert Earl Hayden. CP-HaydR

Gods are always being forgotten; and if tonight we've remembered Poseidon, The. Memorial Service at Poros. Yannis Ritsos. SP-RitsY, *tr.* by N. C. Germanacos

Gods are dead: no longer do we bring, The. Santa Decca. Oscar Wilde. CP-WildO

Gods are less, The. Hidden Singer, The. Wendell Berry. CP-BerrW

Gods are never the same but remain the same body, The. Olga Broumas. SP-BrouO *Fr.* Black Holes, Black Stockings.

Gods are too airy: feathery as the snow, The. Skier and the Mountain, The. Richard Eberhart. CP-EberR

God's Backside. Anne Sexton. CP-SextA

Gods Blessing. Robert Herrick. CP-HerrR

Gods boundlesse mercy is (to sinfull man). Gods Mercy. Robert Herrick. CP-HerrR

Gods Bounty. Robert Herrick. CP-HerrR

God's child in Christ adopted—Christ my all. My Baptismal Birthday [or Birth-Day]. Samuel Taylor Coleridge. CP-ColeS

Gods Come and Go, Prayers Remain Forever. Yehuda Amichai. SP-AmicYL, *tr.* by Benjamin Harshav *and* Barbara Harshav

Gods Commands. Robert Herrick. CP-HerrR

God's counsel còlumnar-severe. Margaret Clitheroe. Gerard Manley Hopkins. CP-HopkG

Gods Descent. Robert Herrick. CP-HerrR

Gods do not die, The. The faith. Memory. Constantine P. Cavafy. CP-CavaC, *tr.* by Theoharis Constantine Theoharis

Gods Dwelling. Robert Herrick. CP-HerrR

God's Education. Thomas Hardy. CP-HardT

God's evident, and may be said to be. Gods Presence. Robert Herrick. CP-HerrR

God's Funeral. Thomas Hardy. CP-HardT

Gods Gifts Not Soon[e] Granted. Robert Herrick. CP-HerrR

God's Glory and my country's shame. Black Christ, The. Countee Cullen. CP-CullC

God's goose, neck neatly wrung, is being plucked. Function of Blizzard. Robert Penn Warren. CP-WarrR

Gods Grace. Robert Herrick. CP-HerrR

God's Grandeur. Gerard Manley Hopkins. CP-HopkG

Gods grant us this one, The. Fernando Pessoa. SP-PessF, *tr.* by Susan M. Brown *and* Edwin Honig

God's Hand in the World. Yehuda Amichai. SP-AmicY, *tr.* by Stephen Mitchell

God's Hand in the World. Yehuda Amichai. SP-AmicYL, *tr.* by Benjamin Harshav *and* Barbara Harshav

God's hand is in the world. God's Hand in the World. Yehuda Amichai. SP-AmicY, *tr.* by Stephen Mitchell

Gods Hands. Robert Herrick. CP-HerrR

God's Host. Jones Very. CP-VeryJ

Gods Keyes. Robert Herrick. CP-HerrR

God's Little Mountain. Geoffrey Hill. CP-HillG

God's love and peace be with thee, where. Benedicite. John Greenleaf Whittier. CP-WhitJ

God's love is busy with the trees. Frontal Lobe Postscript. Yusef Komunyakaa. CP-KomuY

Gods Mercy. Robert Herrick. CP-HerrR

God's Mercy. James Whitcomb Riley. CP-RileJ

Gods Mirth, Mans Mourning. Robert Herrick. CP-HerrR

Gods of Hellas, gods of Hellas. Dead Pan, The. Elizabeth Barrett Browning. CP-BroEB

Gods of old are silent on their shore, The. Aristomenes. Lord Byron. CP-Byron

Gods of the Copybook Headings, The. Rudyard Kipling. CP-KiplR

Gods of the sea. Hermonax. "H. D." CP-DoolH

Gods of Washington, D.C, The. Richard Eberhart. CP-EberR

Gods Pardon. Robert Herrick. CP-HerrR

Gods Power. Robert Herrick. CP-HerrR

Gods Prescience makes none sinfull; but th'offence. Prescience. Robert Herrick. CP-HerrR

Gods Presence. Robert Herrick. CP-HerrR

God's present ev'ry where; but most of all. Gods Presence. Robert Herrick. CP-HerrR

Gods Price, and Mans Price. Robert Herrick. CP-HerrR

Gods Providence. Robert Herrick. CP-HerrR

Gods Prt. Robert Herrick. CP-HerrR

Gods require the thighes, The. Smell of the Sacrifice, The. Robert Herrick. CP-HerrR

God's Residence. Emily Dickinson. CP-DickE

Gods Rod doth watch while men do sleep; & then. Rod, The. Robert Herrick. CP-HerrR

God's said our hearts to harden them. Hardning of Hearts. Robert Herrick. CP-HerrR

God's said to dwell there, wheresoever He. Gods Dwelling. Robert Herrick. CP-HerrR

God's said to leave this place, and for to come. Another of God. Robert Herrick. CP-HerrR

God's Spies. Susan Howe. SP-HoweS

Gods that are wiser than Learning, The. Rector's Memory, A. Rudyard Kipling. CP-KiplR

Gods! The Gods!, The. D. H. Lawrence. CP-LawrD

Gods: those obstinates who live, The. Rainer Maria Rilke. CP-RilkFr, *tr.* by A. Poulin, Jr. *Fr.* Fragments.

Gods Time Must End Our Trouble. Robert Herrick. CP-HerrR

Gods to Kings the Judgement give to sway, The. Obedience in Subjects. Robert Herrick. CP-HerrR

God's undivided, One in Persons Three. To God. Robert Herrick. CP-HerrR

Gods walk in the breath of the woods, The. Ralph Waldo Emerson. CP-EmerR

Gods were jealous, The. Jealous Gods, The. James Laughlin. CP-LaugJ

God's World. Edna St. Vincent Millay. CP-MillE

God's worship to no temple is confined. Primitive Worship. Jones Very. CP-VeryJ

Gods | Children. May Swenson. SP-SwenM

Godspeed. Dorothy Parker. CP-ParkD

Godspeed. John Greenleaf Whittier. CP-WhitJ

Goe, happy Rose, and, enterwove. To the Rose; a Song. Robert Herrick. CP-HerrR

Goe hence away, and in thy parting know. Upon Parting. Robert Herrick. CP-HerrR

Goe now; and with some dar[e]ing drugg. Temperance or the Cheap Physitian upon the Translation of Lessius. Richard Crashaw. CP-CrasR

Go[e], perjured [or perjur'd] man, and if thou e'er [or ere] return. Curse. A Song, The. Robert Herrick. CP-HerrR

Go[e], smiling soul[e]s, your new-built cages break[e]. To the Infant Martyrs. Richard Crashaw. CP-CrasR

Goe thou forth my booke, though late. To His Booke. Robert Herrick. CP-HerrR

Goes by below. Sun Cab, A. James Schuyler. CP-SchuJ

Goes the world now, it will with thee goe hard. Once Poore, Still Penurious. Robert Herrick. CP-HerrR

Goethe and Pose. D. H. Lawrence. CP-LawrD

Goethe in Weimar sleeps, and Greece. Memorial Verses. Matthew Arnold. SP-ArnoM

Goethe, they say, was a great poet, Pindar, perhaps, was a great poet. Robinson Jeffers. CP-JefR3

Goethe's last words were "Mehr Licht." Last Words. James Laughlin. CP-LaugJ

Goffle brook of a May day. Spring is Here Again, Sir. William Carlos Williams. CP-WilW2

Gog. Ted Hughes. SP-HughTN

Goin' Back. Paul Laurence Dunbar. CP-DunbP

Goin' down the [or de] road, Lawd. Bound No'th Blues. Langston Hughes. CP-HughL; CP-HughL1

Goin' Home. Paul Laurence Dunbar. CP-DunbP

Goin' to the Fair. James Whitcomb Riley. CP-RileJ

Going. Robert Creeley. CP-CreeR

Going. Richard Eberhart. CP-EberR

Going. Philip Larkin. CP-LarkP

Going. W. S. Merwin. SP-MerwWF

Going. James Schuyler. CP-SchuJ

Going. Miller Williams. CP-WillM

Going abruptly into a starry night. Starlight. William Meredith. SP-MereW

Going and Staying. Thomas Hardy. CP HardT

Going Away. Howard Nemerov. CP-NemeH

Going Back. D. H. Lawrence. CP-LawrD

Going Back to the River. Marilyn Hacker. SP-HackM

Going backward / All of me and some. In the Pocket. James Dickey. CP-DickJ

Going Backward Going Forward. Richard Eberhart. CP-EberR

Going Deaf. Miller Williams. CP-WillM

Going Down. David Ignatow. SP-IgnaD

Going for grapes with. Continuum: a Love Poem. Maxine W. Kumin. SP-KumiM

Going for Water. Robert Frost. CP-FrosR

Going from a world we know, The. Emily Dickinson. CP-DickE

Going from Battle to Battle. Charles Olson. CP-OlsoC

Going from the Green Window. W. S. Merwin. SP-MerwWF

Going, Going. Philip Larkin. CP-LarkP

Going Gone. Anne Sexton. CP-SextA

Going his rounds one day in Ispahan. Melon-Seller, The. Robert Browning. CP-BroR2

Going Home. Robert Creeley. SP-CreeR

Going Home. Derek Mahon. CP-MahoD

Going Home. Wisława Szymborska. SP-SzymW, tr. by Stanislaw Barańczak and Clare Cavanagh

Going home by lamplight across Boston Common. Revivalist in Boston, A. Adrienne Rich. CP-RicAE

Going In. Marge Piercy. SP-PierM

Going of the Battery, The. Thomas Hardy. CP-HardT

Going of the glade-boat, The. Load of Sugar-Cane, The. Wallace Stevens. CP-StevW; CP-StevWP

Going Out. Gregory Orr. SP-OrrG

Going Out at Dawn. Ivor Gurney. SP-GurnI

Going out naked in the August fog. Boy and Education. Alan Dugan. CP-DugaA

Going Somewhere. Walt Whitman. CP-WhitW

Going, The. Thomas Hardy. CP-HardT

Going through me, the roman sun. Via Appia. James Dickey. CP-DickJ

Going to Bed. Robert Creeley. CP-CreeR

Going to bed / And when we have done. She Had Concealed Him in a Deep Dark Cave. Kenneth Patchen. CP-PatcK

Going to Chicago. Allen Ginsberg. CP-GinsA

Going to Heaven! Emily Dickinson. CP-DickE

Going—to—Her! Emily Dickinson. CP-DickE

Going to Him! Happy letter! Emily Dickinson. CP-DickE

Going to Horse Flats. Robinson Jeffers. CP-JefR2

Going to Italy. Donald Davie. CP-DaviDC

Going to Maine. Richard Eberhart. CP-EberR

Going to the Bakery. Elizabeth Bishop. CP-BishE

Going to the desert. Extremities. Rae Armantrout. SP-ArmaA

Going to the Dogs. John Ciardi. CP-CiarJ

Going to Walden. Mary Oliver. SP-OlivM

Going Too Far. Robert Stock. SP-StocR

Going up for the assault that morning. Walt. Ted Hughes. SP-HughTN

Going up or coming down. Colorado. Mona Van Duyn. SP-VanDM

Going up through the hill called the vineyard. Vineyard, The. W. S. Merwin. SP-MerwWF

Going west. Wagons. A. R. Ammons. CP-AmmoA

Going West. Robert Penn Warren. CP-WarrR

Goiter it seems I got from this backward craning, A. Michelangelo Buonarroti. CP-Miche, tr. by John Frederick Nims

Gold. Donald Hall. CP-HallD

Gold. Walter De la Mare. CP-DeLaW

Gold. Paul Muldoon. CP-MuldP

Gold and Frankincense. Robert Herrick. CP-HerrR

Gold and iron are good. Politics. Ralph Waldo Emerson. CP-EmerR

Gold and Malachite. Robert Graves. CP-GravR

Gold and pearls, and blossoms, white and red, The. Petrarch. CP-Petra, tr. by J. G. Nichols

Gold and Silver Fishes in a Vase. William Wordsworth. CP-WorW2

Gold beard combd down like chinese fire gold hair braided at skull-nape. G. S. Reading Poesy at Princeton. Allen Ginsberg. CP-GinsA

Gold, before Goodnesse. Robert Herrick. CP-HerrR

Gold buttons in the garden today. Flowers Tell Months. Carl Sandburg. CP-SandC

Gold Cloud. Robert Graves. CP-GravR

Gold-colored skin of my Lebanese friends, The. Trip to Four or Five Towns, A. John Logan. CP-LogaJ

Gold dung and urinous straw from the horse garages. Midsummer: XXX. Derek Walcott. CP-WalcD Fr. Midsummer.

Gold dust of your voice, The. Letter to Bob Kaufman. Yusef Komunyakaa. CP-KomuY

Gold fringe on the purpling hem, A. Sunset on the Bearcamp. John Greenleaf Whittier. CP-WhitJ

Gold Hair: A Story of Pornic. Robert Browning. CP-BroR1; SP-BroR

Gold Hesperidee, The. Robert Frost. CP-FrosR

Gold I have none, but I present my need. To God, His Good Will. Robert Herrick. CP-HerrR

Gold is for the mistress—silver for the maid. Cold Iron. Rudyard Kipling. CP-KiplR

Gold is not autumn's privilege. Wearing of the Green, The. Donald Davie. CP-DaviDC

Gold I've none, for use or show. Lyric[k] for Legacies. Robert Herrick. CP-HerrR

Gold Key, The. Anne Sexton. CP-SextA

Gold Leaf. Muriel Rukeyser. CP-RukeM

Gold leaf fell. Fall, The. Heather McHugh. SP-McHuH

Gold leaves, The. Sacre de Printemps. Tennessee Williams. CP-WillT

Gold like a half-slice of orange. August Moon. Robert Penn Warren. CP-WarrR

Gold moth did not love him, The. Fire-Caught. Langston Hughes. CP-HughL; CP-HughL1

Gold Mouths Cry. Sylvia Plath. CP-PlatS

Gold Mud. Carl Sandburg. CP-SandC

Gold of a ripe oat straw, gold of a southwest moon. Falltime. Carl Sandburg. CP-SandC

Gold of her promise, The. America. Maya Angelou. SP-AngeM

Gold of that Land Is Good, The. Christina Georgina Rossetti. CP-RosC2

Gold of the Tigers, The. Jorge Luis Borges. SP-BorgJ, tr. by Alastair Reid

Gold on Mule. Thomas Lux. SP-LuxT

Gold on Oak Leaves. George Oppen. CP-OppGN

Gold or iv'ry's not intended. Ode 2.18: "Gold or iv'ry's not intended." Horace. SP-SmarC, tr. by Christopher Smart Fr. Odes.

Gold Pocket Watch, A. Charles Bukowski. SP-BukC1

Gold said her golden. Gold on Oak Leaves. George Oppen. CP-OppGN

Gold serves for Tribute to the King. Gold and Frankincense. Robert Herrick. CP-HerrR

Gold, with an innermost speck. Street Lamps. D. H. Lawrence. CP-LawrD

Golden Age, The. W. H. Auden. CP-AudeW Fr. Man of La Mancha.

Golden Age, The. Ambrose Bierce. SP-BierA

Golden Anchor. Robert Graves. CP-GravR

Golden Apollo, that thro' heaven wide. Imitation of Spen[s]er, An. William Blake. CP-BlakW

Golden blood of the sun, The. Blood of the Sun. Kenneth Patchen. CP-PatcK

Golden Bough, The. Virgil. SP-HeanSO Fr. Aeneid [or Eneados or Aeneis], The.

Golden dawn and trembling dusk find our brig lying off the coast opposite that villa and its outbuildings. Promontory. Arthur Rimbaud. CP-RimbA, tr. by Martin Sorrell

Golden Day, A. Paul Laurence Dunbar. CP-DunbP

Golden Fleece, The. Yannis Ritsos. SP-RitsY, tr. by Kimon Friar and Karelisa Hartigan

Golden flie one shew'd to me, A. Upon a Flie. Robert Herrick. CP-HerrR

Golden gates of Sleep unbar, The. Bridal Song, A: "Golden gates of Sleep unbar, The." Percy Bysshe Shelley. CP-ShelP

Golden girl, The. Casida of the Golden Girl. Federico García Lorca. SP-GarcF, tr. by W. S. Merwin

Golden girl / bathed in the water, The. Qasida of the Golden Girl. Federico García Lorca. CP-GarcF, tr. by Catherine Brown *Fr.* Qasidas.

Golden girl / in a golden gown. College Formal: Renaissance Casino. Langston Hughes. CP-HughL; CP-HughL3

Golden Glories. Christina Georgina Rossetti. CP-RosC2

Golden-haired Ally whose name is one with mine. To Alfred Tennyson, My Grandson. Alfred Tennyson. CP-TennA

Golden-hairèd Bacchus did espouse, The. Bacchus and Ariadne. Hesiod. CP-BroEB *Fr.* Theogony.

Golden haired, lily white / Will you pluck me lilies. Rivals. Christina Georgina Rossetti. CP-RosC3

Golden haired, lily white, / Will you pluck me lilies? As Cold Water to a Thirsty Soul, so Is Good News from a Far Country. Christina Georgina Rossetti. CP-RosC2

Golden Hills of Hell, The. Robert Penn Warren. CP-WarrR

Golden Hind went bowling, The. Patriotic Song, A. G. K. Chesterton. CP-ChesG

Golden Holly. Christina Georgina Rossetti. CP-RosC3

Golden Khan, The. Game of the Thunderbolt Goddesses, The. Robert Stock. SP-StocR

Golden Leaf, The. Kathleen Jessie Raine. SP-RainK

Golden maples had not yet begun their work, The. Leaves Apples. Grace Paley. CP-PalGC

Golden Mean, The. A. R. Ammons. CP-AmmoA

Golden Mirror, The. Marya Alexandrovna Zaturenska. SP-ZatuM

Golden Net, The. William Blake. CP-BlakW

Golden one is gone from the banquets, The. Epigram: "Golden one is gone from the banquets, The." "H. D." CP-DoolH

Golden particles, The. Sands of the Well. Denise Levertov. SP-LeveDS

Golden photon white on granulated red. Sunshine on Sandstone. John Updike. CP-UpdiJ

Golden robe, yet will she wear, A. Dante Gabriel Rossetti. CW-RossD

Golden rose the house, in the portal I saw. Apparuit. Ezra Pound. CP-PoEar; SP-PounE

Golden roses of the glorious mysteries, The. Party Question, A. G. K. Chesterton. CP-ChesG

Golden Section. Kenneth Rexroth. CP-RexrK

Golden Sestina, The. Pico della Mirandola. CP-PoEar, tr. by Ezra Pound

Golden sheep are feeding, and, The. To a Very Slow Air. Philip Larkin. CP-LarkP

Golden Silences. Christina Georgina Rossetti. CP-RosC2

Golden to itself it lay. Chrysalis. Laura Riding Jackson. CP-RidiL

Golden tortoise walks across the carpet, The. "Rubén Dario." SP-DariR, tr. by Alberto Acereda *and* Will Derusha

Golden Wedding, A. James Whitcomb Riley. CP-RileJ

Golden Wedding of Longwood, The. John Greenleaf Whittier. CP-WhitJ

Golden Whales of California. Nicholas Vachel Lindsay. CP-LindV

Golden-winged Angel stood, A. Fragment: Satan Broken Loose. Percy Bysshe Shelley. CP-ShelP

Golden-winged, silver-winged. Paradise: In a Symbol. Christina Georgina Rossetti. CP-RosC3

Golden Woman in a Silver Mirror, A. Wallace Stevens. CP-StevW; CP-StevWP

Golden Year, The. Alfred Tennyson. CP-TennA

Goldenrod. Mary Oliver. SP-OlivM

Goldenrod. Grace Paley.

Goldfinches. Mary Oliver. SP-OlivM

Goldfish. Charles Bukowski. SP-BukC2

Goldfish. Howard Nemerov. CP-NemeH

Goldfish (Essence of Summer Magazines). T. S. Eliot. SP-EliotT

Goldie Goodwin. James Whitcomb Riley. CP-RileJ

Golding from green, gorgeous the mountain. Vision under the October Mountain: A Love Poem. Robert Penn Warren. CP-WarrR

Goldoni. Robert Browning. CP-BroR2

Goldrush, The. Andrei Codrescu. SP-CodrA

Goldwing Moth. Carl Sandburg. CP-SandC

Goldwing moth is between the scissors and the ink bottle on the desk, A. Goldwing Moth. Carl Sandburg. CP-SandC

Goldyn [*or* Golden] Targe, The. William Dunbar. CP-DunbW

Golem, The. Jorge Luis Borges. SP-BorgJ, tr. by Alan S. Trueblood

Golfers. John Updike. CP-UpdiJ

Goliath. Walter De la Mare. CP-DeLaW

Goliath. Jones Very. CP-VeryJ

Goliath of Gath. Phillis Wheatley. CP-WheaP

Golly, How Truth Will Out. Ogden Nash. CP-NashO

(Goma / Homa) / I have raised pure flames. To Fire. Gary Snyder. CP-SnydG

Gombrowicz died; Americans walked on the Moon. 1969. Adam Zagajewski. SP-ZagaA, tr. by Clare Cavanagh

GON splashes-sink. E. E. Cummings. CP-CummE

Gondola that glides, The. Eugenio Montale. CP-MontE, tr. by Jonathan Galassi

Gondolier handed you a rose, The. Venice. Raymond Carver. CP-CarvR

Gone. Paul Muldoon. CP-MuldP

Gone. Carl Sandburg. CP-SandC

Gone. John Greenleaf Whittier. CP-WhitJ

Gone: and to an undisclosed region. Golden Anchor. Robert Graves. CP-GravR

Gone are the drab monosyllabic days. Tilth. Robert Graves. CP-GravR

Gone are the flowers, which bloomed so sweet and fair. On Some Eternals from a Friend's Garden. Jones Very. CP-VeryJ

Gone are the lovers under the bush. Later Autumn, The. Thomas Hardy. CP-HardT

Gone Away. Denise Levertov. SP-LeveDP

Gone Away Blues. Thomas McGrath. SP-McGrT

Gone bare the fields now, and the starlings gather. Change, The. Ivor Gurney. SP-GurnI

Gone Before. Christina Georgina Rossetti. CP-RosC3

Gone before us, O our brother. Lines on the Death of S. Oliver Torrey. John Greenleaf Whittier. CP-WhitJ

Gone Boy. Langston Hughes. CP-HughL; CP-HughL3

Gone ere the tang of earth. For E. McC ("Gone ere the tang of earth"). Ezra Pound. CP-PoEar

Gone—faded out of the story, the sea-faring friend I remember? Pasa Thalassa Thalassa. Edwin Arlington Robinson. CP-RobiE

Gone for Ever. Christina Georgina Rossetti. CP-RosC1

Gone, gone again is Summer the lovely. Song: "Gone, gone again is Summer the lovely." Edna St. Vincent Millay. CP-MillE

Gone, gone,—sold and gone. Farewell, The: "Gone, gone,—sold and gone." John Greenleaf Whittier. CP-WhitJ

Gone hath the Spring, with all its flowers. Autumn Thoughts. John Greenleaf Whittier. CP-WhitJ

Gone, I say and walk from church. Truth the Dead Know, The. Anne Sexton. CP-SextA; SP-SextA

Gone in good sooth you are: not even in dream. Edna St. Vincent Millay. CP-MillE

Gone, inner and outer. Jelaluddin Rumi. SP-Rumi, tr. by Coleman Barks

Gone into night are all the eyes from every intersection. Street with a Pink Corner Store. Jorge Luis Borges. SP-BorgJ, tr. by Stephen Kessler

Gone Ladies. François Villon. SP-LoguC, tr. by Christopher Logue

Gone now the baby's nurse. Home after Three Months away. Robert Lowell. SP-LoweR

Gone she is a long, long way. Upon a Maid. Robert Herrick. CP-HerrR

Gone silence down lowered sun. Lowellville Cemetery: Twilight. Kenneth Patchen. CP-PatcK

Gone the scab of ice that kept it snug. Spring Uncovered. May Swenson. SP-SwenM

Gone the three ancient ladies. Frau Bauman, Frau Schmidt, and Frau Schwartze. Theodore Roethke. CP-RoetT

Gone to his rest / Bright little Bouby! Christina Georgina Rossetti. CP-RosC3

Gone to thy Heavenly Father's rest! To the Memory of Thomas Shipley. John Greenleaf Whittier. CP-WhitJ

Gone under now, the sun you loved to greet. Michelangelo Buonarroti. CP-Miche, tr. by John Frederick Nims

Gone were but the Winter. Spring Quiet. Christina Georgina Rossetti. CP-RosC1 *Fr.* Spring Fancies.

Gone while your tastes were keen to you. For E. McC ("Gone while your tastes were keen to you"). Ezra Pound. CP-PoEar

Gonfalon Raised Tonight, The. Charles Olson. CP-OlsoC

Gong. Rainer Maria Rilke. CP-RilkFr, tr. by A. Poulin, Jr.

Gong of Time, The. Carl Sandburg. CP-SandC

Goo'-by, Jinks, I got to hump. Delinquent, The. Paul Laurence Dunbar. CP-DunbP

Goo-dmore-ning(en / ter)nize-aday(most). E. E. Cummings. CP-CummE

Goo Girl. Theodore Roethke. CP-RoetT

Good, and Bad. Robert Herrick. CP-HerrR

Good and Bad Weather. Constantine P. Cavafy. CP-CavaC, tr. by Theoharis Constantine Theoharis

Good, and great God, can I not think[e] of thee. To Heaven. Ben Jonson. CP-JonsB; SP-JonsB

Good and great God! How should [*or* sho'd] I fear[e]. No Coming to God without Christ. Robert Herrick. CP-HerrR

Good are attracted by Mens perceptions, The. Motto to the Songs of Innocence & of Experience. William Blake. CP-BlakW

Good at maps and vistas, poor. Arch, The. Charles Tomlinson. CP-TomlC

Good Author, The. Carolyn Kizer. CP-KizeC

Good Bluffers. Langston Hughes. CP-HughL; CP-HughL3

Good-By, A. James Whitcomb Riley. CP-RileJ

Good-by and Keep Cold. Robert Frost. CP-FrosR

Good-by er Howdy-do. James Whitcomb Riley. CP-RileJ

Good-by is a loose word, a yellow ribbon. Different Kinds of Good-by. Carl Sandburg. CP-SandC

Good-By, my friend! Good-By, A. James Whitcomb Riley. CP-RileJ

Good-by now to the streets and the clash of wheels and locking hubs. Teamster's Farewell, A. Carl Sandburg. CP-SandC

Good-by, Old Year. James Whitcomb Riley. CP-RileJ

Good-By, Old Year, You Oaf or Why Don't They Pay the Bonus. Ogden Nash. CP-NashO

Good-by to you whom I shall see tomorrow. Stepping Backward. Adrienne Rich. CP-RicAE; SP-RicA2

Good-bye. Ralph Waldo Emerson. CP-EmerR

Good-bye. Walter De la Mare. CP-DeLaW

Good-bye. Wyatt Prunty. SP-PrunW

"Good-bye," I said to my conscience. Conscience and Remorse. Paul Laurence Dunbar. CP-DunbP

Good-Bye My Fancy. Walt Whitman. CP-WhitW

Good-Bye, My Fancy! Walt Whitman. CP-WhitW

Good-bye, proud world! I'm going home. Good-bye. Ralph Waldo Emerson. CP-EmerR

Good-Bye to the Mezzogiorno. W. H. Auden. CP-AudeW

Good-bye Twilight. Hugh MacDiarmid.
   "Back to the great music, Scottish Gaels. Too long." SP-MacDH

Good-bye, Wendover; Good-bye, Mountain Home. Randall Jarrell. CP-JarrR

Good cause have I to sing and vapour. To Dean Swift. Jonathan Swift. CP-SwifJ

Good Charles the springs adorer. Ralph Waldo Emerson. CP-EmerR

Good Christians, Robert Herrick. CP-HerrR

Good Company. Walter De la Mare. CP-DeLaW

Good Comrade, The. Ludwig Uhland. CP-MerG2

Good Counsel to a Young Maid. Thomas Carew. CP-CareT

Good creatures, do you love your lives. I Counsel You Beware. A. E. Housman. CP-HousA

Good day, *Mitrillo*. [*Mirt.*] And to you no lesse. Pastorall Upon the Birth of Prince Charles, A. Robert Herrick. CP-HerrR

Good deal of superciliousness, A. Platitudinous Reflection. Ogden Nash. CP-NashO

Good Death, A. Robert Herrick. CP-HerrR

Good Dream. Louis MacNeice. CP-MacNL

Good duds, good-bye. Before I shut. On Sending Home My Civilian Clothes. John Ciardi. CP-CiarJ

Good enough place I guess, A. Logistics. James Laughlin. CP-LaugJ

Good enough: so I never returned. I no longer grieve. Star. Pablo Neruda. SP-NeruP

Good evening. At the feet of the king, my Lord. Overseas Prayer. John Berryman. CP-BerrJ

Good evening, Charlie. Yes, I know. You rise. Christmas Greeting, A. James Wright. CP-WrigJ

Good evening, daddy! Boogie: 1 a.m. Langston Hughes. CP-HughL; CP-HughL3

Good Father!.It was eve in middle June. Peasant's Confession, The. Thomas Hardy. CP-HardT

Good Father John O'Hart. Ballad of Father O'Hart, The. William Butler Yeats. CP-YeatW

Good Fight, The. Thomas Kinsella. CP-KinsT

Good for You, Gavin. Philip Larkin. CP-LarkP

Good Fortune. Chuang Tzu. CP-MertT

Good Fortune of Pigeons, The. Josephine Jacobsen. CP-JacoJ

Good Fortune, when I hailed her recently. Epigram: "Good Fortune, when I hailed her recently." James Vincent Cunningham. CP-CunnJ

Good Friday. Amy Clampitt. CP-ClamA

Good Friday. George Herbert. CP-HerbG

Good Friday. Helen Pinkerton. CP-PinkH

Good Friday. Christina Georgina Rossetti. CP-RosC1, CP-RosC2

Good Friday crowd went, The. Monologue for the Good Friday Christ. John Logan. CP-LogaJ

Good Friday Evening. Christina Georgina Rossetti. CP-RosC2

Good Friday in the Tunnels of the Métro. Adam Zagajewski. SP-ZagaA, *tr. by* Renata Gorczynski

Good Friday Morning. Christina Georgina Rossetti. CP-RosC2

Good Friday, 1971. Driving Westward. Paul Muldoon. CP-MuldP

Good Friday: Rex Tragicus, or, Christ Going to His Cross[e]. Robert Herrick. CP-HerrR

Good Friday [*or* Goodfriday], 1613. Riding Westward. John Donne. CP-DonnJ; MW-DonnJ

Good Friday was the day. Martyr, The. Herman Melville. SP-MelvH

Good friend, from my province what is there to say? On Being Asked to Write a Poem for the Centenary of the Civil War. Maxine W. Kumin. SP-KumiM

Good friend, / it is a long afternoon. Hunter's Moon—Eating the Bear. Mary Oliver. SP-OlivM

Good Gift, The. Jones Very. CP-VeryJ

Good gray [*or* grey] guardians of art, The. Museum Piece. Richard Wilbur. CP-WilbR

Good Great Man, The. Samuel Taylor Coleridge. CP-ColeS

Good Grocer (An Apology), The. G. K. Chesterton. CP-ChesG

Good Ground, The. Jones Very. CP-VeryJ

Good Heart, that ownest all! Lover's Petition. Ralph Waldo Emerson. CP-EmerR

Good Hours. Robert Frost. CP-FrosR

Good house, and ground whereon, A. Salt Garden, The. Howard Nemerov. CP-NemeH

Good how can we trust?, The. Henry David Thoreau. CP-ThorH

Good hunting!—aye, good hunting. Forest Greeting, The. Paul Laurence Dunbar. CP-DunbP

Good Husband, A. Robert Herrick. CP-HerrR

Good Husbands Make Unhappy Wives. D. H. Lawrence. CP-LawrD

Good is what goes on the road of Nature. Hafiz. CP-EmerR *Fr.* Odes.

Good Joe. Yusef Komunyakaa. CP-KomuY

Good Jonathan, I've read your ditty. Perlegi Versus Versos, Jonathan Bone, Tersos. Thomas Sheridan. CP-SherT, *tr. by* Robert Hogan

Good king pities Elsa, The. Lohengrin. Constantine P. Cavafy. CP-CavaC, *tr. by* Theoharis Constantine Theoharis

Good King Wenceslas looked out. Happy Xmas, A ("Good King Wenceslas looked out"). G. K. Chesterton. CP-ChesG

Good Kosciusko, thy great name alone. To Kosciusko. John Keats. CP-KeatJ

Good Life, The. Charles Bukowski. SP-BukC1

Good Lord, today / I scarce find breath to say. Christina Georgina Rossetti. CP-RosC2

Good Loser, The. Charles Bukowski. SP-BukC1

Good luck is slow to reach me, always late. Petrarch. CP-Petra, *tr. by* J. G. Nichols

Good Luck Not Lasting. Robert Herrick. CP-HerrR

Good man, A. Likeness. Adrienne Rich. CP-RicAE

Good Man, A. James Whitcomb Riley. CP-RileJ

Good Man, Bad Woman. Wallace Stevens. CP-StevWP

Good Man Has No Shape, The. Wallace Stevens. CP-StevW; CP-StevWP

Good Man in a Bad Time, A. Archibald MacLeish. CP-MacLA

Good man never dies, A. Good Man, A. James Whitcomb Riley. CP-RileJ

Good Man, The. Mona Van Duyn. SP-VanDM

Good Manners at Meat. Robert Herrick. CP-HerrR

Good many times I've come down among you, A. Low Voice, Out Loud. James Dickey. CP-DickJ

Good Martha / you back into town like a tug. Martha as the Angel Gabriel. Marge Piercy. SP-PierM

Good meal can somewhat repair, A. After-Dinner Remarks. Philip Larkin. CP-LarkP

Good Memory, A. Yusef Komunyakaa. CP-KomuY

Good Men Afflicted Most. Robert Herrick. CP-HerrR

Good men, shew, if you can tell. Thomas Campion. CP-CampT

Good Mirrors Are Not Cheap. Audre Lorde. SP-LordA

Good Morning. Andrei Codrescu. SP-CodrA

Good Morning. James Schuyler. CP-SchuJ

Good Morning, America. Carl Sandburg. CP-SandC

Good morning, daddy! Langston Hughes. CP-HughL; CP-HughL3 *Fr.* Lenox Avenue Mural.

Good morning, daddy! Dream Boogie. Langston Hughes. CP-HughL; CP-HughL3

Good Morning—Midnight. Emily Dickinson. CP-DickE

Good Morning Revolution. Langston Hughes. CP-HughL; CP-HughL1

"Good-morning," says the Fine Brisk Man in the mirror. Dialogue. John Ciardi. CP-CiarJ

Good Morning, Stalingrad. Langston Hughes. CP-HughL; CP-HughL2

Good-Morrow, The. John Donne. CP-DonnJ; MW-DonnJ

Good morrow to the day so fair. Mad Maid's Song, The. Robert Herrick. CP-HerrR

Good Mother: Out. C. K. Williams. SP-WillC

Good News. G. K. Chesterton. CP-ChesG
   (Between a meadow and a cloud that sped.) CP-ChesG

Good News and Gospel. Philip Whalen. SP-WhalP

Good news: but if you ask me what it is, I know not. Xmas Day. G. K. Chesterton. CP-ChesG

Good-Night. Paul Laurence Dunbar. CP-DunbP

Good-night. Seamus Heaney. SP-HeanSO

Good Night. Thomas Kinsella. CP-KinsT

Good Night. Czeslaw Milosz. CP-MiloCN, *tr. by* Robert Hass

Good Night. Carl Sandburg. CP-SandC

Good-Night. Percy Bysshe Shelley. CP-ShelP

Good Night. William Carlos Williams. CP-WilW1

Good night, because we must. Emily Dickinson. CP-DickE

Good-night; ensured release. Parta Quies. A. E. Housman. CP-HousA

Good-night, my love, for I have dreamed of thee. Absence. Paul Laurence Dunbar. CP-DunbP

Good-Night, or Blessing, The. Robert Herrick. CP-HerrR

Good night! the gossips cry; Good night! Carol of Jack Frost, A. George Meredith. CP-MerG2

Good Night to the Old Gods. Robert Graves. CP-GravR

Good Night! Which put the Candle out? Emily Dickinson. CP-DickE

Good Night, Willie Lee, I'll See You in the Morning. Alice Walker. CP-WalkA

Good of the Chaplain to enter Lone Bay. Billy in the Darbies. Herman Melville. SP-MelvH *Fr.* Billy Budd, Foretopman.

Good, Old-fashioned People, The. James Whitcomb Riley. CP-RileJ

"Good old times"—all times when old are good, The. Age of Bronze, The. Lord Byron. CP-Byron

Good One, A. Charles Bukowski. SP-BukC1

Good Parent's Garden of Vision, A. Ogden Nash. CP-NashO

Good Plays Are Scarce. Lord Byron. CP-Byron

Good Precepts, or Counsell. Robert Herrick. CP-HerrR

Good Precepts we must firmly hold. Precepts. Robert Herrick. CP-HerrR

Good Princes must be pray'd for: for the bad. Duty to Tyrants. Robert Herrick CP-HerrR

Good Resolution, The. Mona Van Duyn. SP-VanDM

Good Rich Man, The. G. K. Chesterton. CP-ChesG

Good Riddance, but Now What? Ogden Nash. CP-NashO

Good Saint Patrick, in his day, The. Paging Saint Patrick. Dorothy Parker. CP-ParkD

Good Samaritan, The. Jones Very. CP-VeryJ

Good Servant, The. Richard Wilbur. CP-WilbR

Good Shepherd, The: Atlanta, 1981. Ai. SP-Ai

Good Shepherd, The. Christina Georgina Rossetti. CP-RosC2

Good Ships. John Crowe Ransom. SP-RansJ

Good Silence, The. Robert Bly. SP-BlyR

Good snow the sky black, The. Wolf, A. Paul Éluard. CP-WilW2

Good Son, A. Miller Williams. CP-WillM

Good soul, my mother holds my daughter. Three Views of a Mother. John Ciardi. CP-CiarJ

Good speed, for I this day. To the Lark. Robert Herrick. CP-HerrR

Good Spirit, The. Andrei Codrescu. SP-CodrA

Good Students Tend, The. Shmuel HaNagid. SP-HaNaS, *tr. by* Peter Cole

Good Taste. Christopher Logue. SP-LoguC

Good, The. Jones Very. CP-VeryJ

Good thing about the younger generations, The. Young Are Not Mean in Material Things, The. D. H. Lawrence. CP-LawrD

Good thing I'm in a dark room eating rocks. Good Thing when I See One, A. Andrei Codrescu. SP-CodrA

Good Thing when I See One, A. Andrei Codrescu. SP-CodrA

Good things, that come of course, far less[e] do[e] please. Casualties. Robert Herrick. CP-HerrR

Good things will happen. As Pippa Lilted. William Stafford. SP-StafWW

Good Time, A. Yehuda Amichai. SP-AmicYL, *tr. by* Benjamin Harshav *and* Barbara Harshav

Good Time Girl. Charles Bukowski. SP-BukC3

Good time to meet a new, A. Good Time, A. Yehuda Amichai. SP-AmicYL, *tr. by* Benjamin Harshav *and* Barbara Harshav

Good times are always mutual. Emily Dickinson. SP-DickE

Good, to forgive. Robert Browning. CP-BroR2

Good to hide, and hear 'em hunt! Emily Dickinson. CP-DickE

Good we must love, and must hate ill. Community. John Donne. CP-DonnJ; MW-DonnJ

Good weather / is like / good women—. Cows in Art Class. Charles Bukowski. SP-BukC2

Good while after, on the upstairs east sleeping porch he used for a studio, A. After Joe Was at the Island. James Schuyler. CP-SchuJ

Good Will of a Flower, The. Emily Dickinson. CP-DickE

Good Woman Feeling Bad, A. Maya Angelou. SP-AngeM

Goodby Betty,don't remember me. E. E. Cummings. CP-CummE

Goodbye. Charles Bukowski. SP-BukC3

Goodbye. Robert Creeley. CP-CreeR

Goodbye. Philip Levine. SP-LeviP

Goodbye. Robert Penn Warren. CP-WarrR

Goodbye, A. Mona Van Duyn. SP-VanDM

"Goodbye!" called the stockholders as the ship pulled out from. Cruise, The. Muriel Rukeyser. CP-RukeM

Goodbye, children: the bad Good Knight. Romance of the Escaped Children. Alan Dugan. CP-DugaA

Goodbye Christ. Langston Hughes. CP-HughL; CP-HughL1

Goodbye, Goldeneye. May Swenson. SP-SwenM

Goodbye, Göteborg. John Updike. CP-UpdiJ

Goodbye Harry I must have you by me for a time. Wedding Photograph, The.

Stevie Smith. CP-SmitS

Goodbye Hemingway goodbye Celine (you died on the same day). Goodbye. Charles Bukowski. SP-BukC3

Goodbye in fear, goodbye in sorrow. Christina Georgina Rossetti. CP-RosC2

Goodbye, Post Office Square. Fanny Howe. SP-HoweF

Goodbye red moon. Moonset, Gloucester, December 1, 1957, 1:58 A.M. Charles Olson. CP-OlsoC; SP-OlsoC

Goodbye to London. Louis MacNeice. CP-MacNL

Goodbye to Serpents. James Dickey. CP-DickJ

Goodbye to the Poetry of Calcium. James Wright. CP-WrigJ

Goodbye to Tolerance. Denise Levertov. SP-LeveDL

Goodbye, Winter, / The days are getting longer. Prognosis. Louis MacNeice. CP-MacNL

Goodbyes, Still More Goodbyes. Rainer Maria Rilke. CP-RilkFr, *tr. by* A. Poulin, Jr.

Goodman sat beside his door, The. Exiles, The. John Greenleaf Whittier. CP-WhitJ

Goodmorning with Light. John Ciardi. CP-CiarJ

Goodnesse of His God, The. Robert Herrick. CP-HerrR

Goodnight. John Ciardi. CP-CiarJ

Goodnight. D. H. Lawrence. CP-LawrD

Goodnight. Stevie Smith. CP-SmitS

Goodnight. May Swenson. SP-SwenM

Goodnight, A. William Carlos Williams. CP-WilW1

Goods. Wendell Berry. CP-BerrW

Goodtime Jesus. James Tate. SP-TateJ

Goody Blake and Harry Gill. William Wordsworth. CP-WorW1; MW-WorW

Goody for Our Side and Your Side Too. Ogden Nash. CP-NashO

Goodyere, I am [or I'm] glad and grateful to report. To Sir Henry Goodyere. Ben Jonson. CP-JonsB; SP-JonsB

Goofing Again. Gary Snyder. CP-SnydG

Goose Fish, The. Howard Nemerov. CP-NemeH

Goose-Girl, The. Edna St. Vincent Millay. CP-MillE

Goose Pond's imaginable snows. Stanley Kunitz. CP-KunSC

Gooseberry Fool. Amy Clampitt. CP-ClamA

Gooseflesh Abbey. Robert Graves. CP-GravR

Go(perpe)go / (tu)to(al). E. E. Cummings. CP-CummE

Gorbunov and Gorchakov. Joseph Brodsky. CP-BrodJ, *tr. by* Harry Thomas

Gordale. William Wordsworth. CP-WorW2

Gordon, Jim, / Life and Limb. George Meredith. CP-MerG2

Gordon of Khartoum. George Meredith. CP-MerG1

Gorge, The. Robert Graves. CP-GravR

Gorge, The. Charles Tomlinson. CP-TomlC

Gorgeous landscape embroidered green. Prose Poem. Rainer Maria Rilke. CP-RilkFr, *tr. by* A. Poulin, Jr.

Gorgeous Surfaces. Thomas Lux. SP-LuxT

Gorgon Mask. Robert Graves. CP-GravR

Gorilla mask got put away, The. On Halloween. Alan Dugan. CP-DugaA

Goring, The. Sylvia Plath. CP-PlatS

Gorselight, yellow, the slopes. Matière de Bretagne. Paul Celan. SP-CelaP, *tr. by* John Felstiner

Gospel. Rita Dove. SP-DoveR

Gospel Cha-Cha. Langston Hughes. CP-HughL; CP-HughL3

Gospel Hour. Charles Simic. SP-SimiCE

Gospel Noble Truths. Allen Ginsberg. CP-GinsA; SP-GinsA

Gospel of Beauty, A. Nicholas Vachel Lindsay. CP-LindV

Gospel the Reconciling Power, The. Jones Very. CP-VeryJ

Gossamers, The. Charles Tomlinson. CP-TomlC

Gossips, The. William Carlos Williams. CP-WilW2

Gossips agreed all was wrong with poor Sally! Falling of Sally, The. George Meredith. CP-MerG2

Got it down so tight the hinges squeaked. Take It. Charles Bukowski. SP-BukC3

Got Me Home, the Light Snow Gives the Air, Falling. Charles Olson. SP-OlsoC *Fr.* Maximus Poems, The.

Got up on a cool morning. Leaned out a window. Just Thinking. William Stafford. SP-StafWW

Gothic Candor. William Carlos Williams. CP-WilW2

Gothic looks solemn, The. On Oxford. John Keats. CP-KeatJ

Gothic Tale, A. Theodore Weiss. SP-WeisT

Gothic, The. Adam Zagajewski. SP-ZagaA, *tr. by* Renata Gorczynski, Benjamin Ivry *and* C. K. Williams

Goths, The. William Carlos Williams. CP-WillT

Goths, Vandals, Huns, Isaurian mountaineers. Cuirassiers of the Frontier, The. Robert Graves. CP-GravR

Gotta hold your nose. Metric Figure. William Carlos Williams. CP-WilW2

Gourd, The. Paul Laurence Dunbar. CP-DunbP

Governess, The. Stevie Smith. CP-SmitS

Governing the country from a kitchen sink. Ruler, A. A. K. Ramanujan. CP-RamaA

Government. Carl Sandburg. CP-SandC

Government—I heard about the Government and I went out to find, The. Government. Carl Sandburg. CP-SandC

Government men said Don't plant wheat, The. Lorine Niedecker. CP-NiedL

Government of your body, sweet, The. United States, The. William Carlos Williams. CP-WilW2

Government that died long ago once decided, A. Oleander. Yehuda Amichai. SP-AmicYL, tr. by Benjamin Harshav and Barbara Harshav

Governor, A. Split Mind, The. Denise Levertov. SP-LeveDL

Governor came to visit in the mountains, The. He Shot Arrows, but Not at Birds Perching. Gary Snyder. CP-SnydG

Governor Fires Dean. Langston Hughes. CP-HughL; CP-HughL3

Governor it was proclaimed this time, A. Generations of Men, The. Robert Frost. CP-FrosR

Goya & the Sleep of Reason. Lawrence Ferlinghetti. SP-FerlL

Goya's "Two Old People Eating Soup." Mona Van Duyn. SP-VanDM

Gr / eyhaire / d(m), A. E. E. Cummings. CP-CummE

Gr-r-r—there go, my heart's abhorrence! Soliloquy of the Spanish Cloister. Robert Browning. CP-BroR1; SP-BroR

Grace. Rae Armantrout. SP-ArmaA

Grace. Wendell Berry. CP-BerrW

Grace. Olga Broumas. SP-BrouO

Grace. Ralph Waldo Emerson. CP-EmerR

Grace. George Herbert. CP-HerbG

Grace. Laura Riding Jackson. CP-RidiL

Grace. John Logan. CP-LogaJ

Grace. William Meredith. SP-MereW

Grace. Gabriela Mistral. SP-MistG, tr. by Maria Giachetti [or Jacketti]

Grace. James Tate. SP-TateJ

Grace. Richard Wilbur. CP-WilbR

Grace, A. G. K. Chesterton. CP-ChesG

Grace, A. Donald Hall. CP-HallD

Grace Abounding. A. R. Ammons. CP-AmmoA

Grace Abounding. William Stafford. SP-StafWW

Grace after Meat. Robert Burns. CP-BurnR

Grace and Love. George Meredith. CP-MerG1

Grace at Kirkudbright. Robert Burns. CP-BurnR
  (Burns Grace at Kirkudbright.) CP-BurnR

Grace, Beauty, and Caprice. Manners. Ralph Waldo Emerson. CP-EmerR

Grace before Dinner, Extempore, A. Robert Burns. CP-BurnR

Grace before Song. Ezra Pound. CP-PoEar

Grace Darling. William Wordsworth. CP-WorW2

Grace-face: hot-pot. Readie Pome. William Carlos Williams. CP-WilW1

Grace for a Child. Robert Herrick. CP-HerrR
  (Another Grace for a Child.) CP-HerrR

Grace for Children, A. Robert Herrick. CP-HerrR
  (Graces for Children.) CP-HerrR

Grace for Thursday. Alan Dugan. CP-DugaA

Grace in the Fore Street. Donald Davie. CP-DaviDC

Grace is the focal point. Bar Giamaica, 1959-60. Charles Wright. SP-WrigC

Grace—Myself—might not obtain, The. Emily Dickinson. CP-DickE

Grace-Note, The. Denise Levertov. SP-LeveDP

Grace Notes. Robert Graves. CP-GravR

Grace to be born and live as variously as possible. Sonnet LV: "Grace to be born and live as variously as possible." Ted Berrigan. SP-BerrT Fr. Sonnets, The.

Grace to Be Said at the Supermarket. Howard Nemerov. CP-NemeH

Grace to Be Said before Committee Meetings. Howard Nemerov. CP-NemeH

Graceful Bastion, The. William Carlos Williams. CP-WilW2

Graceful Exit, A. James Laughlin. CP-LaugJ

Graceful in name and in thyself, our river. To G. G. John Greenleaf Whittier. CP-WhitJ

Graceful son of Pan! Around your head crowned with little flowers and berries. Antique. Arthur Rimbaud. CP-RimbA, tr. by Martin Sorrell

Gracefullest leaper, the dappled fox-cub. Young Reynard. George Meredith. CP-MerG1

Graceland. Carl Sandburg. CP-SandC

Graces————at the Globe Tavern. Robert Burns. CP-BurnR

Graces denied to almost everyone. Petrarch. CP-Petra, tr. by J. G. Nichols

Graces for Children. Robert Herrick. See Grace for Children, A

Grace's House. Thomas Merton. CP-MertT

Graces, yes—and the airs! To airs and graces, The. Yorkshire. Donald Davie. CP-DaviDC

Gracie, thou art a man of worth. On Mr. James Gracie. Robert Burns. CP-BurnR

Gracie wuz allus a careless tot. Diverted Tragedy, A. James Whitcomb Riley. CP-RileJ

Gracious gods, The. To Empty the Mind. Charles Olson. CP-OlsoC

Gracious Goodness. Marge Piercy. SP-PierM

Gracious Living. James Laughlin. CP-LaugJ

Gracious Moonlight. Dante Gabriel Rossetti. CW-RossD Fr. House of Life, The.

Gracious Spirit sings as it comes, A. Desolation. Wendell Berry. CP-BerrW

Grackle, The. Ogden Nash. CP-NashO

Grackles, Goodbye. Robert Penn Warren. CP-WarrR

Grackles sing avant the spring, The. Snow and Stars. Wallace Stevens. CP-StevW; CP-StevWP

Gradations. Yannis Ritsos. SP-RitsY, tr. by Kimon Friar

Gradations of Black. John Updike. CP-UpdiJ

Grade surmounted, we were riding high, The. Figure in the Doorway, The. Robert Frost. CP-FrosR

Gradual Clearing. Amy Clampitt. CP-ClamA

Gradual numbness spreads through streets and homes, A. Meditation. Charles Baudelaire. CP-BaudC, tr. by Walter Martin

Gradualism. Kenneth Rexroth. CP-RexrK

Gradually in gardens. Journey of the Snowmen. Howard Nemerov. CP-NemeH

Gradually it is. At the Home for Unwed Mothers. James Dickey. CP-DickJ

Gradually Stripped Bare. Yannis Ritsos. SP-RitsY, tr. by Kimon Friar and Kostas Myrsiades

Graduate, The. Robert Lowell. SP-LoweR

Graduates in Economics. Black Trout, The. Eugenio Montale. CP-MontE, tr. by Jonathan Galassi

Graduation. Langston Hughes. CP-HughL; CP-HughL2

Gradus ad Parnassum. Muriel Rukeyser. CP-RukeM

Graecinus (well I wot) thou told'st me once. Elegy 2.10: "Graecinus (well I wot) thou told'st me once." Ovid. CP-MarlC, tr. by Christopher Marlowe Fr. Elegies.

Graffiti from the Gare Saint-Manqué. Marilyn Hacker. SP-HackM

Graffiti 12th Cubicle Men's Room Syracuse Airport. Allen Ginsberg. CP-GinsA

Graii, sive magis iuvat vetustum. Ad Graios. Thomas Campion. CP-CampT

Grammar. Andrei Codrescu. SP-CodrA

Grammar, A. Andrei Codrescu. SP-CodrA

Grammar Lesson. Stanley Kunitz. CP-KunSC

Grammarian's Funeral, A. Robert Browning. CP-BroR1; SP-BroR

Grampa's Choice. James Whitcomb Riley. CP-RileJ

Grampa's got his old age pension. Lorine Niedecker. CP-NiedL

Gramsci's Ashes. Pier Paolo Pasolini.
  "There's nothing May-like in this toxic air." CP-MahoD

Gran freddo è infuori, e dentro è freddo un poco. Christina Georgina Rossetti. CP-RosC3

Granada 1850. Federico García Lorca. CP-GarcF, tr. by Alan S. Trueblood Fr. Love.

Granary Floor, The. Jelaluddin Rumi. SP-Rumi, tr. by Coleman Barks

Grand Central Station. Muriel Rukeyser. CP-RukeM

Grand Central, with Soldiers, in Early Morning. Howard Nemerov. CP-NemeH

Grand Design, The. Philip Whalen. SP-WhalP

Grand Duke of New York, The. Dan Pagis. SP-PagiD, tr. by Stephen Mitchell

Grand Duo. James Schuyler. CP-SchuJ

Grand Galop. John Ashbery. SP-AshbJ

Grand Haven is in Michigan, and in possession, too. Artemus of Michigan, The. James Whitcomb Riley. CP-RileJ

Grand hotels, dancing girls, The. Hop o' My Thumb. John Ashbery. SP-AshbJ

Grand Illusion. Norman Dubie. CP-DubiN

Grand Is the Seen. Walt Whitman. CP-WhitW

Grand Palace of Versailles, The. Kenneth Patchen. CP-PatcK

Grand Procession of Priests and Laymen. Constantine P. Cavafy. CP-CavaC, tr. by Theoharis Constantine Theoharis

Grand Question Debated, The. Jonathan Swift. CP-SwifJ

Grand rough old Martin Luther. Twins, The. Robert Browning. CP-BroR1

Grand time when the words, The. Diction. Robert Creeley. CP-CreeR

Grandchild. Maxine W. Kumin. SP-KumiM

Granddaughter. Robinson Jeffers. CP-JefR3

Grande Passion. Dorothy Parker. CP-ParkD

Grandfather. Derek Mahon. CP-MahoD

Grandfather / advised me. Poet's Work. Lorine Niedecker. CP-NiedL

Grandfather and grandfather's uncle stand looking at the harbor. Destroyers. Carl Sandburg. CP-SandC

Grandfather Bridgeman. George Meredith. CP-MerG1

Grandfather-Father Poem, The. Charles Olson. CP-OlsoC

Grandfather Gabriel rode up to town. Genealogy. Robert Penn Warren. CP-WarrR

Grandfather Said It. Dorothy Parker. CP-ParkD

Grandfather says that. Upstate New York. James Laughlin. CP-LaugJ

Grandfather, sleepless in a room upstairs. John Berryman. CP-BerrJ Fr. Black Book, The.

Grandfather Squeers. James Whitcomb Riley. CP-RileJ

Grandfather, Your Wound. Anne Sexton. CP-SextA

Grandfather's Last Letter, A. Norman Dubie. CP-DubiN

Grandfather's Railroad. John Logan. CP-LogaJ

Grandior et primis fatis post terga relictis. In Obitum Hen. Mag. Brit. Principis. Thomas Campion. CP-CampT

Grandma Marie Potts. Peter Blue Cloud. SP-BlueP

Grandma sleeps with / my sick. Medicine. Alice Walker. CP-WalkA

Grandmas are all coming down like f-101's like gulls, The. What Did the Man Do with the Clouds? C. K. Williams. CP-WillC

Grandmother. Norman Dubie. CP-DubiN

Grandmother, The. Wendell Berry. CP-BerrW

Grandmother after that late eclipse. Grandmother Dead in the Aeroplane. John Logan. CP-LogaJ

Grandmother Dead in the Aeroplane. John Logan. CP-LogaJ

Grandmother in Heaven. Philip Levine. SP-LeviP

Grandmother in the Garden. Louise Glück. SP-GlucL

Grandmothers. Adrienne Rich. SP-RicA2

Grandmothers, mothers, aunts and sisters dear. Epilogue to *Julius Caesar*, The. Thomas Sheridan. CP-SherT

Grandmother's version. Death in Search of a Comfortable Metaphor. A. K. Ramanujan. CP-RamaA

Grandmothers who wring the necks. Classic Ballroom Dances. Charles Simic. SP-SimiC; SP-SimiCE

Grandpa masquerades as an ordinary sugar merchant. Sugarduke. Dan Pagis. SP-PagiD, *tr. by* Stephen Mitchell

Grandparents. Robert Lowell. SP-LoweR

Grandparents. Stephen Spender. CP-SpenS

Grandpa's Stories. Langston Hughes. CP-HughL

Grange, The. Stevie Smith. CP-SmitS

Granite. John Updike. CP-UpdiJ

Granite and Cypress. Robinson Jeffers. CP-JefR1

Granite and Grass. Donald Hall. CP-HallD

Granite and marble, / women and men. Homage to Paul Mellon, I. M. Pei, Their Gallery, and Washington City. William Meredith. SP-MereW

Granite and Steel. Marianne Craig Moore. CP-MoorM

Granite and Wineglass. Jelaluddin Rumi. SP-Rumi, *tr. by* Coleman Barks

Granite-colored gulls unlocked, The. 1938. Yusef Komunyakaa. CP-KomuY

Granny, / tell me again in the dark. Lines to a Granny. A. K. Ramanujan. CP-RamaA

Granny's come to our house. James Whitcomb Riley. CP-RileJ

Granny's gone a-visitin'. Opportunity. Paul Laurence Dunbar. CP-DunbP

Grant. James Whitcomb Riley. CP-RileJ

Grant, The. Raymond Carver. CP-CarvR

Grant had a sledgehammer pounding and pounding and Lee had a sledge. Hammers Pounding. Carl Sandburg. CP-SandC

Grant me forever of thy word to hear. Priest, The. Jones Very. CP-VeryJ

Grant me the muse, ye Gods! whose humble flight. In a Letter to C. P. William Cowper. CP-CowpW

Grant Park. Langston Hughes. CP-HughL; CP-HughL1

Grant Park: August 28, 1968. Allen Ginsberg. CP-GinsA

Grant us, O Lord, that patience and that faith. Lord, It Is Good for Us to Be Here. Christina Georgina Rossetti. CP-RosC2

Grant us such grace that we may work Thy Will. Christina Georgina Rossetti. CP-RosC2

Granta—A Medley. Lord Byron. CP-Byron

Granted that what we summon is absurd. President and Poet. Donald Hall. CP-HallD

Granted the all / saving our young kiss only. E. E. Cummings. CP-CummE

Granted, we die for good. Table Talk. Wallace Stevens. CP-StevWP

Grant's Tomb Revisited. Karl Shapiro. SP-ShapK

Grape. Ambrose Bierce. SP-BierA

Grape conserve from the red Caco vine. Gift of Light, A. Marge Piercy. SP-PierM

Grape-Hyacinth. Louis Zukofsky. CP-ZukLS

Grape Sherbet. Rita Dove. SP-DoveR

Grape-treader Time. Resolution. Robert Penn Warren. CP-WarrR

Grapes. D. H. Lawrence. CP-LawrD

Grapes grow up a difficult and. Cornucopia, The. Arthur Sze. SP-SzeA

Grapes were big and fresh, The. Emily Dickinson. SP-DickE

Grapevine, The. John Ashbery. SP-AshbJ

Graph. William Carlos Williams. CP-WilW2

Graph for Action. William Carlos Williams. CP-WilW1

Graphic of the Petenera. Federico García Lorca. CP-GarcF, *tr. by* Cola Franzen, Christopher Maurer *and* Robert Nasatir

Grappling in the Central Blue. Maxine W. Kumin. SP-KumiM

Grasmere. Amy Clampitt. CP-ClamA

Grass. James Merrill. SP-MerrJ

Grass. Carl Sandburg. CP-SandC

Grass and Children. G. K. Chesterton. CP-ChesG

Grass Beginning July. W. S. Merwin. SP-MerwWF

Grass below the willow, The. Grandmother in the Garden. Louise Glück. SP-GlucL

Grass bends low, the pregnant trees, The. Singing in the Rain. Countee Cullen. CP-CullC

Grass between the tombs is intensely green, The. Abode. Czeslaw Milosz. CP-MiloCN, *tr. by* Robert Hass

Grass-blade is not without, The. Ted Hughes. SP-HughTN

Grass clutches at the dark dirt with finger holds. Grassroots. Carl Sandburg. CP-SandC

Grass commence a-comin'. Spring Fever. Paul Laurence Dunbar. CP-DunbP

Grass from Two Years. Robert Bly. SP-BlyR

Grass-green and aspen-green. Variables of Green. Robert Graves. CP-GravR

Grass grows out of every sidewalk crack. Summer Afternoon an Old Man Gives Some Thought to the Central Questions, A. Miller Williams. CP-WillM

Grass is green, The. Oh Grateful Colours, Bright Looks! Stevie Smith. SP-SmitS

Grass is half-covered with snow, The. Snowfall in the Afternoon. Robert Bly. SP-BlyR

Grass is in seed, The. The young birds are flying. Ghosts as Cocoons. Wallace Stevens. CP-StevW; CP-StevWP

Grass is very green, my friend, The. Unison, A. William Carlos Williams. CP-WilW2

Grass miracles have kept me down all autumn, The. A. R. Ammons. CP-AmmoA

Grass resurrects to mask, to strangle. Distant Fury of Battle, The. Geoffrey Hill. CP-HillG

Grass shakes. / Smoke streaks, no, The. Growing Dark. James Schuyler. CP-SchuJ

Grass so little has to do, The. Grass, The. Emily Dickinson. CP-DickE

Grass that was moving found all shades of brown. Little Girl by the Fence at School, The. William Stafford. SP-StafWW

Grass, The. Emily Dickinson. CP-DickE

Grass Widow. Paul Muldoon. CP-MuldP

Grass yellow hill. Carmel Valley. Allen Ginsberg. CP-GinsA

Grasse: The Olive Trees. Richard Wilbur. CP-WilbR

Grasses. Amy Clampitt. CP-ClamA

Grasses. Thom Gunn. CP-GunnT

Grasses, The. Jelaluddin Rumi. SP-Rumi, *tr. by* Coleman Barks

Grassflower. Louis Zukofsky. CP-ZukLS

Grasshopper, A. Richard Wilbur. CP-WilbR

Grasshopper and the Ant, The. Jean de La Fontaine. CP-WilbR (Grasshopper, having sung her song.) CP-WilbR

Grasshopper, having sung her song. Jean de La Fontaine. *See* Until fall, a grasshopper / Chose to chirr

Grasshopper Is a Burden. D. H. Lawrence. CP-LawrD

Grasshopper, the grasshopper, The. Explanation of the Grasshopper, An. Nicholas Vachel Lindsay. CP-LindV

Grasshoppers. John Clare. SP-ClarJ

Grasshoppers Are Very Intelligent. Ogden Nash. CP-NashO

Grasshoppers go in many a thrumming spring. Grasshoppers. John Clare. SP-ClarJ

Grassroots. Carl Sandburg. CP-SandC

Grassy Sound. A. R. Ammons. CP-AmmoA

Grate, The. Robert Stock. SP-StocR

Grateful change! Favonius, and the spring, A. Ode 1.4: "Grateful change! Favonius, and the spring, A." Horace. SP-SmarC, *tr. by* Christopher Smart *Fr.* Odes.

Grateful for a breeze. Wind Makes Up, A. George Oppen. CP-OppGN

Grateful is Sleep, my life in stone bound fast. Michelangelo Buonarroti. CP-WorW1

Gratefulness. George Herbert. CP-HerbG

Gratitude. William Cowper. CP-CowpW

Gratitude. Louise Glück. SP-GlucL

Gratitude and Love to God. Jeanne Marie Bouvier de la Motte Guyon. CP-CowpW, *tr. by* William Cowper

Gratitude for a Nightmare. Robert Graves. CP-GravR

Gratitude—is not the mention. Emily Dickinson. CP-DickE

Gratitude is the timid wealth. Emily Dickinson. SP-DickE

Gratitude to Mother Earth, sailing through night and day. Prayer for the Great Family. Gary Snyder. CP-SnydG

Gratitude to the Unknown Instructors. William Butler Yeats. CP-YeatW

Grauballe Man, The. Seamus Heaney. SP-HeanSO

Grave. Rainer Maria Rilke. CP-RilkFr, *tr. by* A. Poulin, Jr. *Fr.* Affectionate Taxes to France.

Grave, A. Marianne Craig Moore. CP-MoorM

Grave, A. James Schuyler. CP-SchuJ

Grave by a Holm-Oak. Stevie Smith. CP-SmitS

Grave by the Lake, The. John Greenleaf Whittier. CP-WhitJ

Grave Dean of St. Patrick's, how comes it to pass. Dean to Himself on St. Cecilia's Day, The. Jonathan Swift. CP-SwifJ

Grave *Jonas Kindred*, Sibyl Kindred's sire. Frank Courtship, The. George Crabbe. SP-CrabG *Fr.* Tales.

Grave my little cottage is, The. Emily Dickinson. CP-DickE

Grave needed a stone marker, The. Pricing. David Ignatow. SP-IgnaD

Grave of Alexander Hamilton is in Trinity yard, The. Trinity Place. Carl Sandburg. CP-SandC

Grave of Arthur, The. G. K. Chesterton. CP-ChesG

Grave of Keats, The. Oscar Wilde. CP-WildO

Grave of Shelley, The. Oscar Wilde. CP-WildO

Grave of Signor Casanova, The. Jaroslav Seifert. SP-SeifJ, *tr. by* Ewald Osers

Grave of the Hundred Dead, The. Rudyard Kipling. CP-KiplR

Grave Piece. Richard Eberhart. CP-EberR

Grave the Well, The. Donald Hall. CP-HallD

Grave, to the will. Barcelona: February 13, 1977. Robert Creeley. SP-CreeR

Grave-worm revels now, The. Death. Christina Georgina Rossetti. CP-RosC3

Grave Yard. Langston Hughes. CP-HughL; CP-HughL2

Gravel Walks, The. Seamus Heaney. SP-HeanSO

Gravelly Run. A. R. Ammons. CP-AmmoA

Graven Thoughts. Sir Philip Sidney. SP-SidnP *Fr.* Arcadia.

Graves. Rainer Maria Rilke. CP-RilkFr, *tr. by* A. Poulin, Jr.

Graves. Carl Sandburg. CP-SandC

Graves in Jerusalem are the openings, The. Yehuda Amichai. SP-AmicY, *tr. by* Chana Bloch *Fr.* Songs of Zion the Beautiful.

Graves of Our Ancestors, The. Yannis Ritsos. SP-RitsY, *tr. by* Kimon Friar *and* Karelisa Hartigan

Graves, The. Lorine Niedecker. CP-NiedL *Fr.* Element Mother, The.

Graveside. James Tate. SP-TateJ

Gravestone upon the Floor in the Cloisters of Worcester Cathedral, A. William Wordsworth. CP-WorW2

Graveyard being what he called his face, The. Shaving the Graveyard. Thomas Lux. SP-LuxT

Graveyard by the Sea. Thomas Lux. SP-LuxT

Graveyard is the, The. Boarding House. Langston Hughes. CP-HughL; CP-HughL2

Graveyard of Dead Creeds, The. Thomas Hardy. CP-HardT

Gravity. Charles Simic. SP-SimiC; SP-SimiCE

Gravy. Raymond Carver. CP-CarvR

Gray. Constantine P. Cavafy. CP-CavaC, *tr. by* Theoharis Constantine Theoharis

Gray. Alice Walker. CP-WalkA

Gray-blue shadows lift. Starlight Scope Myopia. Yusef Komunyakaa. CP-KomuY

Gray Brother, The. Sir Walter Scott. SP-ScotW

Gray clouds blot sunglare, mountains float west, plane. Over Denver Again. Allen Ginsberg. CP-GinsA

Gray dawn on the mountain top, The. Day. Paul Laurence Dunbar. CP-DunbP

Gray Day. James Schuyler. CP-SchuJ

Gray earth peeping through snow. To P. L., 1916–1937. Philip Levine. SP-LeviP

Gray-eyed huntress in whose hair. Hymn to Artemis, the Destroyer. Marya Alexandrovna Zaturenska. SP-ZatuM

Gray Eyes. Tess Gallagher. SP-GallT

Gray Fox, The. Gregory Orr. SP-OrrG

Gray fox, female, nine pounds three ounces, A. "One Should Not Talk to a Skilled Hunter about What Is Forbidden by the Buddha" Gary Snyder. CP-SnydG

Gray Graeae, The. Classical Optical. John Updike. CP-UpdiJ

Gray, Intermittently Blue, Eyed Hero. James Schuyler. CP-SchuJ

Gray is the palace where she dwells. My Lady of Castle Grand. Paul Laurence Dunbar. CP-DunbP

Gray maidservant lets me in, A. Matinees. James Merrill. SP-MerrJ

Gray of Dawn, The. A tremor slight. Empty Stirrups. Herman Melville. SP-MelvH *Fr.* Clarel: A Poem and Pilgrimage in the Holy Land.

Gray of the sea, and the gray of the sky, The. Her Thought and His. Paul Laurence Dunbar. CP-DunbP

Gray prinked with rose. High-School Lawn, The. Thomas Hardy. CP-HardT

Gray Room. Wallace Stevens. CP-StevWP

Gray searcher of the upper air. Mount Agiochook. John Greenleaf Whittier. CP-WhitJ

Gray smoke rose from the morning ground. Actual Vision of Morning's Extrusion. Alan Dugan. CP-DugaA

Gray Spring Morning, A. John Ciardi. CP-CiarJ

Gray steel, cloud-shadow-stained. Watch the Lights Fade. Robinson Jeffers. CP-JefR3

Gray Stones and Gray Pigeons. Wallace Stevens. CP-StevW; CP-StevWP

Gray Weather. Robinson Jeffers. CP-JefR2

Gray whale / Now that we are sending you to The End. For a Coming Extinction. W. S. Merwin. SP-MerwW

Gray whales are going south: I see their fountains, The. Ocean. Robinson Jeffers. CP-JefR3

Grayish cloud flows fast, The. To Myself, in an Album. Adam Zagajewski. SP-ZagaA, *tr. by* Renata Gorczynski, Benjamin Ivry *and* C. K. Williams

Gray's Apocrypha. Mona Van Duyn. SP-VanDM

Grazia Deledda, Young. Donald Davie. CP-DaviDC

Grazing Locomotives. Archibald MacLeish. CP-MacLA

Great Advances in Vanity. Thomas Lux. SP-LuxT

Great advantage of being alive, The. E. E. Cummings. CP-CummE; SP-CummE

Great Alexander sailing was from his true course turned. Speaking Tree, The. Muriel Rukeyser. CP-RukeM

Great and glorious thing it is, A. Arithmetic on the Frontier. Rudyard Kipling. CP-KiplR

Great and Small. Chuang Tzu. CP-MertT

Great are the Hittites. Concerning My Neighbors, the Hittites. Charles Simic. SP-SimiC; SP-SimiCE

Great Are the Myths. Walt Whitman. CP-WhitW

Great automobile turns slowly in, A. Dazzling Burden, The. Kenneth Patchen. CP-PatcK

Great beauty scattering its brilliant flame. Michelangelo Buonarroti. CP-Miche, *tr. by* John Frederick Nims

Great Beethoven, you trouble me this watchful night. Quartet in F Major. William Meredith. SP-MereW

Great bird landed here, A. Heptonstall Old Church. Ted Hughes. SP-HughTN

Great Birds, The. Kenneth Patchen. CP-PatcK

Great Blue Heron, The. Carolyn Kizer. CP-KizeC

Great blue mountain! Ghost. Mount Kearsarge. Donald Hall. CP-HallD

Great Boast, Small Rost. Robert Herrick. CP-HerrR

Great bridge didn't lead to you, The. Wind on the Crescent. Eugenio Montale. CP-MontE, *tr. by* Jonathan Galassi

Great, bright portal. Cliff Temple, The. "H. D." CP-DoolH

Great Caesar! Condescend. Emily Dickinson. CP-DickE

Great Calm: Questions and Answers. Yehuda Amichai. SP-AmicYL, *tr. by* Benjamin Harshav *and* Barbara Harshav

Great Carbuncle, The. Sylvia Plath. CP-PlatS

Great carnal mountains crouching in the cloud. Sunset. E. E. Cummings. CP-CummE

Great Charles, among the holy gifts of grace. Epigram, An. To K[ing] Charles for a[n] Hundred Pounds He Sent Me in My Sickness. 1629. Ben Jonson. CP-JonsB

Great church institutions, The. From Up-State. George Oppen. CP-OppGN

Great Cities seldom[e] rest: If there be none. Peace Not Permanent. Robert Herrick. CP-HerrR

Great cold shoulders bared, The. McKane's Falls. James Merrill. SP-MerrJ

Great command will never be obsolete, The. Know Thyself. D. H. Lawrence. CP-LawrD

Great Contemporary Discoveries. Archibald MacLeish. CP-MacLA

Great cracked shadow of the Sierra Nevada, The. Gambling in Stateline, Nevada. James Wright. CP-WrigJ

Great cry and little wool—is now become. Prologue Spoke by Mr. Elrington at the Theatre-Royal on Saturday the First of April, A. Thomas Sheridan. CP-SherT

Great Dante stands in Florence, looking down. E. E. Cummings. CP-CummE

Great dark bodies, the mountains. North Rim, The. May Swenson. SP-SwenM

Great dawn-color rose widening the petals around her gold eye, A. Shears, The. Robinson Jeffers. CP-JefR3

Great Day, The. William Butler Yeats. CP-YeatW

Great Day in the Cows' House. Donald Hall. CP-HallD

Great dream stinks like a whale gone aground, The. Why the Soup Tastes Like the *Daily News*. Marge Piercy. SP-PierM

Great-enough both accepts and subdues; the great frame takes all creatures. Phenomena. Robinson Jeffers. CP-JefR1

Great events are about to happen. Day of Foreboding. Stanley Kunitz. CP-KunSC

Great Explorer, The. James Whitcomb Riley. CP-RileJ

Great Explosion, The. Robinson Jeffers. CP-JefR3

Great Facts of Christ's History, The. Jones Very. CP-VeryJ

Great fatigue like that of horses. Yehuda Amichai. SP-AmicYL, *tr. by* Benjamin Harshav *and* Barbara Harshav

Great Feast at the Home of Sosibios, A. Constantine P. Cavafy. CP-CavaC, *tr. by* Theoharis Constantine Theoharis

Great Figure, The. William Carlos Williams. CP-WilW1

Great fish plunges in the dark, A. From a Junk. Wallace Stevens. CP-StevWP

Great fish that vomited out Jonah, The. Tidings. Dan Pagis. SP-PagiD, *tr. by* Stephen Mitchell

Great folks are of a finer mould. Epigram on Scolding, An. Jonathan Swift. CP-

SwifJ

Great Friend. Henry David Thoreau. CP-ThorH

Great friend, The. Friend, The. Henry David Thoreau. CP-ThorH

Great Garret, or 100 Wheels, The. James McMichael. SP-McMiJ

Great geometrical winter constellations, The. Requiem for the Spanish Dead. Kenneth Rexroth. CP-RexrK

Great Giambattista Marino did not die that afternoon, nor the next, The. Yellow Rose, A. Jorge Luis Borges. SP-BorgJ, *tr.* by Ken Krabbenhoft

Great glimmering wagons rumble across this sky. Lenada. Kenneth Patchen. CP-PatcK

Great, gnarled fingers of roots, The. Fallen Oak, A. Peter Blue Cloud. SP-BlueP

Great God I ask thee for no meaner pelf. Henry David Thoreau. CP-ThorH

Great God Pan, The. James Whitcomb Riley. CP-RileJ

Great God, that bowest sky and star. Hymn for the Church Militant, A. G. K. Chesterton. CP-ChesG

Great gods are blind or pretend to be, The. Laughter. W. S. Merwin. SP-MerwW

Great gold apples of night, The. People. D. H. Lawrence. CP-LawrD

"Great, good and just" was once applied. To His Grace the Archbishop of Dublin. Jonathan Swift. CP-SwifJ

Great, good, just, kind and loving God. God. E. E. Cummings. CP-CummE

Great-Grandmother, The. Robert Graves. CP-GravR

Great gray *gaviota*, The. Baja Beatitudes. Lawrence Ferlinghetti. SP-FerlL

Great green ships. Azores. John Updike. CP-UpdiJ

Great Grief, Great Glory. Robert Herrick. CP-HerrR

Great-Heart. Rudyard Kipling. CP-KiplR

Great High Feasts on the Birthdays of Little Men. Robert Stock. SP-StocR

Great Hope fell, A. Emily Dickinson. CP-DickE

Great Horned Owl, The. Clarence Major. SP-MajoC

Great Horned Owl, The. Charles Simic. SP-SimiC; SP-SimiCE

Great Hungers feed themselves. Emily Dickinson. SP-DickE

Great Hunt, The. Carl Sandburg. SP-SandC

Great Indulgent Heart. Rainer Maria Rilke. CP-RilkFr

Great Infirmities. Charles Simic. SP-SimiC; SP-SimiCE

Great is the task, and worthy such a Muse. To Mr Dryden, on His Poem Called *Religio Laici. Unknown*. CP-DryJ2

Great Jove, to whose almighty throne. From the Prometheus Vinctus of Aeschylus. Lord Byron. CP-Byron

Great Knowledge. Chuang Tzu. CP-MertT

Great lonely hills. Big Sur. Langston Hughes. CP-HughL; CP-HughL2

Great Lord Archibald, The. G. K. Chesterton. CP-ChesG

Great Maladies, Long Medicines. Robert Herrick. CP-HerrR

Great / man / is / gone, A. E. E. Cummings. CP-CummE

Great Man's House, A. Wisława Szymborska. SP-SzymWM, *tr.* by Joanna Trzeciak

Great Men. Robinson Jeffers. CP-JefR3

Great men by small meanes oft are overthrown. Losse from the Heat. Robert Herrick. CP-HerrR

Great Men & Fools do often me Inspire. William Blake. CP-BlakW

Great men have been among us; hands that penned. William Wordsworth. CP-WorW1; MW-WorW

Great Men of Former Times, The. Thomas Merton. CP-MertT

Great mercy, my lady, as likely as great pain. Michelangelo Buonarroti. CP-Miche, *tr.* by John Frederick Nims

Great Michelangelo, with age grown bleak. Michelangelo's Kiss. Dante Gabriel Rossetti. CW-RossD *Fr.* House of Life, The.

Great mob that knows no fear. Revolution. Langston Hughes. CP-HughL; CP-HughL1

Great mother has no face, The. Palaeolithic Fertility Fetish, A. Wisława Szymborska. SP-SzymW, *tr.* by Stanislaw Barańczak *and* Clare Cavanagh

Great mounds of salt on the beach of Eve, The. In Praise of Salt. Gabriela Mistral. SP-MistG, *tr.* by Maria Giachetti [*or* Jacketti]

Great Mullen. William Carlos Williams. CP-WilW1

Great Muse, that from this hall absent for long. Invocation to the Muses. Edna St. Vincent Millay. CP-MillE

Great Newspaper Editor to His Subordinate, The. D. H. Lawrence. CP-LawrD

Great Night, The. Randall Jarrell. CP-JarrR

Great one, austere. Prayer before Work. May Sarton. SP-SartM

Great open, The. Waking Who Knows. George Oppen. CP-OppGN

Great or small below, / Great or small above. Ye That Fear Him, Both Small and Great. Christina Georgina Rossetti. CP-RosC2

Great Overdog, The. Canis Major. Robert Frost. CP-FrosR

Great Pardon, The. Rainer Maria Rilke. CP-RilkFr, *tr.* by A. Poulin, Jr.

Great peace in Europe! Order reigns. Peace of Europe, The. John Greenleaf Whittier. CP-WhitJ

Great poets are not in the language but in business because what poet can make, The. Poetry Paper. Andrei Codrescu. SP-CodrA

Great poets fire the world with fagots big. Humility. Ambrose Bierce. SP-BierA

Great Praises. Richard Eberhart. CP-EberR

Great Prayer. Alfonso Cortes. CP-MertT, *tr.* by Thomas Merton

Great Principles Are Thrown Down by Time. Richard Eberhart. CP-EberR

Great Proud Wagon Wheels Go On, The. Carl Sandburg. CP-SandC

Great pulsation passed. Glass lay around me, The. Rejoice in the Abyss. Stephen Spender. CP-SpenS

Great Sadness, The. Federico García Lorca. CP-GarcF, *tr.* by Jerome Rothenberg *Fr.* Night (Suite for Piano and Poet's Voice).

Great Sadnesses, The. Kenneth Patchen. CP-PatcK

Great Scarf of Birds, The. John Updike. CP-UpdiJ

Great Sea has no limit, The. Han-shan. CP-ColdM, *tr.* by Red Pine

Great sir, than Phoebus more divine. Palinodia. Thomas Sheridan. CP-SherT

Great-Sledmakers, The. Kenneth Patchen. CP-PatcK

Great snowy owl, A. Emblem. Richard Eberhart. CP-EberR

Great Society, Mark X, The. Howard Nemerov. CP-NemeH

Great song ceased, The. Moment in Eternity, A. Hugh MacDiarmid. SP-MacDH

Great sorrow and regret overcame them on their separation. Before Time Could Change Them. Constantine P. Cavafy. CP-CavaC, *tr.* by Theoharis Constantine Theoharis

Great speakers held their microphone to their mouths. Yehuda Amichai. SP-AmicYL *Fr.* At Right Angles.

Great Spirit whom the sea of boundless thought. Fragment: "Great Spirit whom the sea of boundless thought." Percy Bysshe Shelley. CP-ShelP

Great Spirits Now on Earth. John Keats. CP-KeatJ

Great Spirits Supervive. Robert Herrick. CP-HerrR

Great Square Has No Corners, A. Arthur Sze. SP-SzeA

Great starfish was hauled up by a point, The. Starfish, The. Josephine Jacobsen. CP-JacoJ

Great starry night showing its bare claws, A. Midnight. Yannis Ritsos. SP-RitsY, *tr.* by Athan Anagnostopoulos

Great steam-station full of folk, A. Eternal Heart, The. G. K. Chesterton. CP-ChesG

Great stories matter. Childish. Robert Creeley. SP-CreeR

Great Streets of silence led away. Emily Dickinson. CP-DickE

Great Sunset, The. Robinson Jeffers. CP-JefR2

Great tarry wings splatter grayly up out of the blinding glare of. Family Portrait. Kenneth Patchen. CP-PatcK

Great Things. Thomas Hardy. CP-HardT

Great Thoughts and Noble Feelings. Wyatt Prunty. SP-PrunW

Great Toby is dead, The. Lament for Toby, a French Poodle. May Sarton. SP-SartM

Great toy-maker, light-bringer, patient, A. Edison. Robinson Jeffers. CP-JefR2

Great Tranquillity, A: Questions and Answers. Yehuda Amichai. SP-AmicY, *tr.* by Chana Bloch

Great Unaffected Vampires and the Moon. Stevie Smith. CP-SmitS

Great Uncle Beefheart. Rita Dove. SP-DoveR

Great Vine left its glory to reign as Forest King, The. Maundy Thursday. Christina Georgina Rossetti. CP-RosC2

Great voice that calls us in the wind of dawn. Tree Ceremonies. Edna St. Vincent Millay. CP-MillE

Great Wagon, A. Jelaluddin Rumi. SP-Rumi, *tr.* by Coleman Barks

Great wave of youth, ere you be spent. Sew the Flags Together. Nicholas Vachel Lindsay. CP-LindV

Great Wave, The. Denise Levertov. SP-LeveDL

Great wedge of snow geese wafted over, A. Snow Geese at Jamaica Bay, The. May Swenson. SP-SwenM

Great Western Plains, The. Hart Crane. CP-CranH

Great White Shark, The. Arthur Sze. SP-SzeA

Great work laid upon his twoscore years. Thomas Starr King. John Greenleaf Whittier. CP-WhitJ

Great wrong I doe, I can it not deny. Sonnet 33. Edmund Spenser. CP-Spens *Fr.* Amoretti.

Great year and place, A. France, the 18th Year of These States. Walt Whitman. CP-WhitW

Greater Grand Rapids Lover, The. Marge Piercy. SP-PierM

Greater Grandeur. Robinson Jeffers. CP-JefR3

Greater is the depth of sadness. Henry David Thoreau. CP-ThorH

Greater is to lesser. Scornful or Fond Infinity. Laura Riding Jackson. CP-RidiL

Greater light is set, my love; our fitful lamp, The. World Whose Sun Retreats before the Brave, A. Kenneth Patchen. CP-PatcK

Greater Love. Wilfred Owen. CP-OwenW

Greater than memory of Achilles or Ulysses. Wallabout Martyrs, The. Walt Whitman. CP-WhitW

Greater tribute than the Temple's height, A. Widow, The. Jones Very. CP-VeryJ

Greatest Desire of All, The. Yehuda Amichai. SP-AmicYL, *tr.* by Benjamin Harshav *and* Barbara Harshav

Greatest Desire, The. Yehuda Amichai. SP-AmicY, *tr.* by Chana Bloch

Greatest error ever erred, The. Oh, Shucks, Ma'am, I Mean Excuse Me. Ogden Nash. CP-NashO

Greatest monarch may be stabbed by night, The. To a Friend Who Had Been Much Abused in Many Inveterate Libels. Jonathan Swift. CP-SwifJ

Greatest of These Is Charity, The. Christina Georgina Rossetti. CP-RosC2

Greatest plumber, The. Nursery Rhyme. Lorine Niedecker. CP-NiedL

Greatest poets undergo a kind of crisis in their art, The. Hugh MacDiarmid. SP-MacDH *Fr.* Further Passages from *The Kind of Poetry I Want.*

Greatest saint of all is she, The. To a Tolerant Mother. G. K. Chesterton. CP-ChesG

Greatgrandfather / under wild flowers sons. I Visit / the Graves. Lorine Niedecker. CP-NiedL

Greatness. Warmth, and human insight. Music. Chromium-Plated Hat, A. Inlaid with Scenes from Siegfried. Howard Nemerov. CP-NemeH

Grecian Windflower. Louis Zukofsky. CP-ZukLS

Greece. Henry David Thoreau. CP-ThorH

Greed. Ai. SP-Ai

Greed. C. K. Williams. SP-WillC

Greedy man who piles up wealth, A. Han-shan. CP-ColdM, *tr. by* Red Pine

Greedy the people, The. E. E. Cummings. CP-CummE

Greek, The. Charles Bukowski. SP-BukC1

Greek Architecture. Herman Melville. SP-MelvH

Greek Cart-Drivers. Yannis Ritsos. SP-RitsY, *tr. by* Kimon Friar

Greek Epigram. Ezra Pound. CP-PoEar

Greek from Ancient Times. Constantine P. Cavafy. CP-CavaC, *tr. by* Theoharis Constantine Theoharis

Greek guide, The. Absence of Slaves, An. Josephine Jacobsen. CP-JacoJ

Greek Masonry. Herman Melville. SP-MelvH

Greek National Anthem, The. Rudyard Kipling. *See* Ode to Liberty

Greek Portrait. Czeslaw Milosz. CP-MiloC; CP-MiloCN, *tr. by* Peter Dale Scott

Greek Rose, if he men called the Greek. To Rhoda, otherwise called Rohda. G. K. Chesterton. CP-ChesG

Greek Wind, The. Josephine Jacobsen. CP-JacoJ

Greek Women, The. Thomas Merton. CP-MertT

Greeks Are Coming!, The. D. H. Lawrence. CP-LawrD

Greeks mounted on needle points. Junk Dawn, NYC. Andrei Codrescu. SP-CodrA

Greeks said: Never to be born is best, The. Best. Gregory Orr. SP-OrrG

Greeks were wrong who said our eyes have rays, The. Lamarck Elaborated. Richard Wilbur. CP-WilbR

Green. Charles Bukowski. SP-BukC3

Green. Amy Clampitt. CP-ClamA

Green. D. H. Lawrence. CP-LawrD

Green, The. Thomas Lux. SP-LuxT

Green abundance. Magnanimity. Thomas Kinsella. CP-KinsT

Green air, children sat under trees with the old. Grant Park: August 28, 1968. Allen Ginsberg. CP-GinsA

Green and silent spot, amid the hills, A. Fears in Solitude [Written in April, 1798, during the Alarm of an Invasion]. Samuel Taylor Coleridge. CP-ColeS; MW-ColeS

Green and White. Wendell Berry. CP-BerrW

Green and yellow parrot, The. Parrot, The. Gabriela Mistral. SP-MistG, *tr. by* Maria Giachetti [*or* Jacketti]

Green Automobile, The. Allen Ginsberg. CP-GinsA; SP-GinsA

Green bearded Arthur with his men still blinking from underground wars. Fall '66. Thomas Merton. CP-MertT

Green below and the blue above!, The. Life at the Lake. James Whitcomb Riley. CP-RileJ

Green-blue ground, The. On Gay Wallpaper. William Carlos Williams. CP-WilW1

Green branch barren. Cheating Mirror, The. Federico García Lorca. CP-GarcF, *tr. by* Alan S. Trueblood *Fr.* Songs to End With.

Green Buddhas / On the fruit stand. Watermelons. Charles Simic. SP-SimiC; SP-SimiCE

Green bug sleeps in the white lily car, The. Small Homes. Carl Sandburg. CP-SandC

Green Castle, The. Robert Graves. CP-GravR

Green Connection, The. Eleanor Wilner. SP-WilnE

Green Cornfield, A. Christina Georgina Rossetti. CP-RosC1

Green Door, The. James Schuyler. CP-SchuJ

Green Ears. Jelaluddin Rumi. SP-Rumi, *tr. by* Coleman Barks

Green Eyes. William Carlos Williams. CP-WilW2

Green eyes from under cornsheaf curls. Garland for Ronsard, A. Donald Davie. CP-DaviDC

Green Fields and Running Brooks. James Whitcomb Riley. CP-RileJ

Green fields were beginning, The. And the tall, white. In a Marine Light near Sequim, Washington. Raymond Carver. CP-CarvR

Green fingers / holding the hillside. Holding On. Philip Levine. SP-LeviP

Green Fires, The. Kenneth Patchen. CP-PatcK

Green going through the jungle of those years. Poem: "Green going through the jungle of those years." Muriel Rukeyser. CP-RukeM

Green-gold, the garden leans into the room. Townhouse Interior with Cat. Amy Clampitt. CP-ClamA

Green Gown. Paul Muldoon. CP-MuldP

Green grass grows where'er it wills, The. Soul's Freedom, The. Jones Very. CP-VeryJ

Green grass is bowing, The. To Ellen, at the South. Ralph Waldo Emerson. CP-EmerR

Green Grass of Old Ireland, The. James Whitcomb Riley. CP-RileJ

Green Grow the Rashes [A Fragment]. Robert Burns. CP-BurnR

Green Grow[s] the Rashes. Robert Burns. CP-BurnR (Fragment, A.) CP-BurnR

Green, how much I want you green. Somnambule Ballad. Federico García Lorca. SP-GarcF, *tr. by* J. L. Gili *and* Stephen Spender

Green I want you green. Sleepwalking Ballad. Federico García Lorca. CP-GarcF, *tr. by* Christopher Maurer

Green in light are the hills, and a calm wind flowing. Reawakening, The. Walter De la Mare. CP-DeLaW

Green is the night, green kindled and apparelled. Candle a Saint, The. Wallace Stevens. CP-StevW; CP-StevWP

Green lamp flares on the table, The. This Life. Rita Dove. SP-DoveR

Green lawn / a picket fence. Once. Alice Walker. CP-WalkA

Green leaf that will outlast the winter. Louis Zukofsky. CP-ZukLS

Green Leaves. G. K. Chesterton. CP-ChesG

Green leaves on a grey tree. LOVE 6: Winter. A. K. Ramanujan. CP-RamaA

Green level of lily leaves, A. To Paint a Water Lily. Ted Hughes. SP-HughTN

Green limb hangs in the crotch, A. Gary Snyder. CP-SnydG *Fr.* Myths and Texts.

Green Limits. Muriel Rukeyser. CP-RukeM

Green Linnet, The. William Wordsworth. CP-WorW1 (May is come again:—how sweet, The.) MW-WorW

Green lizard, if it darts, The. Eugenio Montale. CP-MontE, *tr. by* Jonathan Galassi

Green Man, The. Charles Olson. CP-OlsoC

Green Mansions. Miller Williams. CP-WillM

Green Memory. Langston Hughes. CP-HughL; CP-HughL3

Green Mistletoe! / Oh, I remember now. Winter. Walter De la Mare. CP-DeLaW

Green moon blaze. Camargue. Kenneth Rexroth. CP-RexrK

Green morning of indolence one hedge beyond, A. Morning in the Park. John Ciardi. CP-CiarJ

Green Mountain Idyl. Hayden Carruth. CP-CarHS

Green Notebook, The. Jane Cooper. CP-CoopJ

Green plant grows, The. Louis Zukofsky. CP-ZukLS

Green Plant, The. Wallace Stevens. CP-StevW; CP-StevWP

Green points on the shrub. Elegy for D. H. Lawrence, An. William Carlos Williams. CP-WilW1

Green Quinces. Charles Tomlinson. CP-TomlC

Green Red Brown and White. May Swenson. SP-SwenM

Green River. Donald Davie. CP-DaviDC

Green Rock, Winthrop Bay. Sylvia Plath. CP-PlatS

Green rustlings, more-than-regal charities. Royal Palm. Hart Crane. CP-CranH

Green-Sailed Vessel, The. Robert Graves. CP-GravR

Green-shadowed people sit, or walk in rings. Spring. Philip Larkin. CP-LarkP

Green Shelf, The. Donald Hall. CP-HallD

Green silk, or a shot silk, blue. Green River. Donald Davie. CP-DaviDC

Green skeletons of fish, they swim across the pale. Windowscape. Louis MacNeice. CP-MacNL

Green Slates. Thomas Hardy. CP-HardT

Green Sleeves [and Tartan Ties]. Robert Burns. CP-BurnR

Green sludge of a riverbank. One Volume Missing. Rita Dove. SP-DoveR

Green Snake, when I hung you round my neck. To the Snake. Denise Levertov. SP-LeveDS

Green sound intact. Bacchus. Federico García Lorca. CP-GarcF, *tr. by* Alan S. Trueblood *Fr.* Three Portraits with Shading.

Green sprout the grasses. I Have a Message unto Thee. Christina Georgina Rossetti. CP-RosC3

Green stalks rustle. Island City. W. S. Merwin. SP-MerwWF

Green star Sirius. Winter Dawn. D. H. Lawrence. CP-LawrD

Green upright rope. Old-Fashioned Lightning Rod. John Updike. CP-UpdiJ

Green Valentine Blues. Allen Ginsberg. CP-GinsA; SP-GinsA

Green water of lagoons. From a Plane. Denise Levertov. SP-LeveDL

Green Water Tower. W. S. Merwin. SP-MerwWF

Green Ways. Stanley Kunitz. CP-KunSC

Green Wolf, The. Ted Hughes. SP-HughTN

Green Woods of Unrest, The. Robert Graves. CP-GravR

Green young leaves. A cuckoo. Echo. Linnaeus. Czeslaw Milosz. CP-MiloCN, *tr. by* Robert Hass

Greendoon's Song. Robert Creeley. CP-CreeR

Greenhouse is my summer seat, The. Faithful Friend, The. William Cowper. CP-CowpW

Greenhouse, The. Adam Zagajewski. SP-ZagaA, *tr. by* Clare Cavanagh

Greenness Taller than Gods, A. Yusef Komunyakaa. CP-KomuY

GrEEn's d / an / cing on hollow was. E. E. Cummings. CP-CummE

Green's the predominant color here. Prospect. Robert Creeley. SP-CreeR

Greensweet breathing, A. Cow, The. John Ciardi. CP-CiarJ

Greenwich Avenue. James Schuyler. CP-SchuJ

Greenwich Time 11:16 P.M. August 5 1945. New Dawn. Robert Penn Warren. CP-WarrR

Greeting. Rae Armantrout. SP-ArmaA

Greeting. May Sarton. SP-SartM

Greeting. John Greenleaf Whittier. CP-WhitJ

Greeting, A. John Greenleaf Whittier. CP-WhitJ

Greeting, and thanks, from this sick place, A. Apostle of Hope. Thomas Kinsella. CP-KinsT

Greeting Card. Robert Creeley. SP-CreeR

Greeting for Old Age. William Carlos Williams. CP-WilW2

Greeting of the company throughout, The. Pathos of Applause, The. James Whitcomb Riley. CP-RileJ *Fr.* Child-World, A.

Greeting, The. Charles Tomlinson. CP-TomlC

Greeting the dawn, / A shift of rubber workers presses down. Porphyro in Akron. Hart Crane. CP-CranH

Greeting to the Vietnamese Delegates to the U.N. Denise Levertov. SP-LeveDL

Greeting to you both in hearty wise. Sir Thomas Wyatt. CP-WyatT

Greetings from the Chateau. James Schuyler. CP-SchuJ

Greetings to all from the pine-scented woods! Letter to Robert Benchley; Roughing It in the Country at the Birches, Maine. Dorothy Parker. CP-ParkD

Gregory Corso's Story. Allen Ginsberg. CP-GinsA

Grenadier. A. E. Housman. CP-HousA

Greta. Derek Mahon. CP-MahoD

Gretel in Darkness. Louise Glück. SP-GlucL

Grew hair for fun. Ike. Rita Dove. SP-DoveR

Grey and boiling street, A. Stephen Crane. CP-CranS

Grey apparitions at verandah ends. Verandah. Derek Walcott. CP-WalcD

Grey August. Denise Levertov. SP-LeveDL

Grey crystal skies. A bizarre pattern of bridges, some straight, some curved. Bridges, The. Arthur Rimbaud. CP-RimbA, *tr. by* Martin Sorrell

Grey day for the Show, but cars jam the narrow lanes. Show Saturday. Philip Larkin. CP-LarkP

Grey English road hissed emptily under the tires, The. Derek Walcott. CP-WalcD *Fr.* Midsummer.

Grey Evening. D. H. Lawrence. CP-LawrD

Grey eyes watchful and a lightened hand, The. To Natty Bumppo. Thom Gunn. CP-GunnT

Grey gaunt days dividing us in twain, The. Minute before Meeting, The. Thomas Hardy. CP-HardT

Grey girl who had not been singing stopped, The. New Year's Eve. John Berryman. CP-BerrJ

Grey haunted eyes, absent-mindedly glaring. Face in the Mirror, The. Robert Graves. CP-GravR

Grey horse, Death, in profile bears the young Titus, The. Polish Rider, The. Derek Walcott. CP-WalcD

Grey hungry men are loading. In Darmstadt. James Laughlin. CP-LaugJ

Grey Monk, The. William Blake. CP-BlakW

Grey Ones, The. Louis MacNeice. CP-MacNL

Grey Rock, The. William Butler Yeats. CP-YeatW

Grey [*or* gray] sea and the long black land, The. Meeting at Night. Robert Browning. CP-BroR1; SP-BroR

Grey Sparrow Addresses the Mind's Ear. Denise Levertov. SP-LeveDP

Grey summer. Flute Overheard, A. Kenneth Rexroth. CP-RexrK

Grey water tanks in grey mist. Bayonne Turnpike to Tuscarora. Allen Ginsberg. CP-GinsA

Grey with all honours of age! but fresh-featured and ruddy. Poetry of Chaucer, The. George Meredith. CP-MerG1

Greyday. Maya Angelou. SP-AngeM

Greyness Is All. Louis MacNeice. CP-MacNL

Grief. Wendell Berry. CP-BerrW

Grief. Elizabeth Barrett Browning. CP-BroEB

Grief. Raymond Carver. CP-CarvR

Grief. Lucille Clifton. SP-ClifL

Grief. George Herbert. CP-HerbG

Grief. Langston Hughes. CP-HughL; CP-HughL2

Grief. D. H. Lawrence. CP-LawrD

Grief. Denise Levertov. SP-LeveDL

Grief. Paul Muldoon. CP-MuldP

Grief. Robert Stock. SP-StocR

Grief. Jones Very. CP-VeryJ

Grief Ago, A. Dylan Thomas. CP-ThomD

Grief-chewers enter, their shoes hard on the marble, The. Office of the Dead. Thomas Kinsella. CP-KinsT

Grief Engrossed. Thomas Carew. CP-CareT

Grief for a generation—all. Dakota, The. Amy Clampitt. CP-ClamA

Grief, have I denied thee? Lamentation, A. Denise Levertov. SP-LeveDP; SP-LeveDS

Grief is a Mouse. Emily Dickinson. CP-DickE

Grief is this quiet room we shared. Husband. Wyatt Prunty. SP-PrunW

Grief may have thought it was grief. They Were Welcome to Their Belief. Robert Frost. CP-FrosR

Grief now hath pacified her face. Widow, The. Walter De la Mare. CP-DeLaW

Grief of an Heir, The. William Cowper. CP-CowpW

Grief of Cafeterias, The. John Updike. CP-UpdiJ

Grief of the coyote seems to make, The. Arizona Midnight. Robert Penn Warren. CP-WarrR

Grief of wonder at her fate. Emily Dickinson. SP-DickE

Grief sate upon a rock and sighed one day. Claim, The. Elizabeth Barrett Browning. CP-BroEB

Grief sinks and sinks. Dwellers at the Hermitage. Denise Levertov. SP-LeveDL

Grief-tailed fish, / Sunday-eye in walking shorts. I Write This upon the Last Drink's Hammer. Charles Bukowski. SP-BukC2

Grief that is grief and properly so hight. Edna St. Vincent Millay. CP-MillE

Grief Thief of Time. Dylan Thomas. CP-ThomD

Grief, thou hast lost an ever ready friend. William Wordsworth. CP-WorW1

Griefe. Robert Herrick. CP-HerrR

Griefes. Robert Herrick. CP-HerrR

Griefs / Marking indelibly our later loves. Wedding Presents. Muriel Rukeyser. CP-RukeM

Grieg Being Dead. Carl Sandburg. CP-SandC

Grievance, A. Paul Laurence Dunbar. CP-DunbP

Grievances. William Meredith. SP-MereW

Grieve for the loveless, spiritless, faceless men. Dead Hand. Robert Graves. CP-GravR

Grieve not for happy Claudius, he is dead. Epitaph: "Grieve not for happy Claudius, he is dead." Edna St. Vincent Millay. CP-MillE

Grieve not, my Celia, but with haste. To His Mistress. Thomas Carew. CP-CareT

Grieve Not the Holy Spirit, Etc. George Herbert. CP-HerbG

(Ephesians 4:30. Grieve not the Holy Spirit, etc.) CP-HerbG

Griggsby's Station. James Whitcomb Riley. CP-RileJ

Grim Grizzle. Robert Burns. CP-BurnR

Grim monarch! see, deprived [*or* depriv'd] of vital breath. To a Lady on the Death of Her Husband. Phillis Wheatley. CP-WheaP

Grim New Englanders stand around, The. Once More, O Ye. Richard Eberhart. CP-EberR

Grim Skeleton. Allen Ginsberg. CP-GinsA

Grim Skeleton come back and put me out of Action. Grim Skeleton. Allen Ginsberg. CP-GinsA

Grim Town in a Steep Valley. Thomas Lux. SP-LuxT

Grin and Bear Left. Ogden Nash. CP-NashO

Grin without a / face(a look), A. E. E. Cummings. CP-CummE

Grindstone, The. Robert Frost. CP-FrosR

Grinning monster out side the system. Charles Olson. CP-OlsoC

Grip of the ice is gone now, The. Wind Sings Welcome in Early Spring, The. Carl Sandburg. CP-SandC

Grip of winter tightening, its thinned, The. Flock, The. Derek Walcott. CP-WalcD

Gripping Serial. Donald Davie. CP-DaviDC

Gripus. John Keats. CP-KeatJ

Grisaille. Rainer Maria Rilke. CP-RilkFr, *tr. by* A. Poulin, Jr.

Gristly bare-bone fingers. Song of the Sturdy Snails, The. Nicholas Vachel Lindsay. CP-LindV

Gristmill. Yusef Komunyakaa. CP-KomuY

Grit / of things, The. Song: "Grit / of things, The." Robert Creeley. CP-CreeR

Grizzled Athenian ordered to hemlock, The. Anecdote of Hemlock for Two Athenians. Carl Sandburg. CP-SandC

Grizzled doorman lets the doctors' wives, The. Marilyn Hacker. SP-HackM *Fr.* Taking Notice.

Groan then, groan. Stoic. D. H. Lawrence. CP-LawrD

Grocery. Charles Simic. SP-SimiC; SP-SimiCE

Grocery Store. Langston Hughes. CP-HughL

Groin, come of age, his state sold out of hand. On Groin. Ben Jonson. CP-JonsB; SP-JonsB

Groom Falconer. Norman Dubie. CP-DubiN

Groom Kisses the Bride and the Mind of the Young Preacher Wanders Again, The. Miller Williams. CP-WillM

Grooving clam shell. Wave. Gary Snyder. CP-SnydG

Groping back to bed after a piss. Sad Steps. Philip Larkin. CP-LarkP

Gross, Coarse, Hideous. D. H. Lawrence. CP-LawrD

Grosse Fuge. Ted Hughes. SP-HughTN

Grotesque. William Carlos Williams. CP-WilW1

Grotesques. Robert Graves. CP-GravR

Grottamare. Lawrence Ferlinghetti. SP-FerlL

Grotus and Coventina. Seamus Heaney. SP-HeanSO

Ground Cries Out, The. Jelaluddin Rumi. SP-Rumi, *tr.* by Coleman Barks

Ground fog blurring the dogwood. Notes on the State of Virginia. Amy Clampitt. CP-ClamA

Ground-Mist, The. Denise Levertov. SP-LeveDP

Ground seems almost stolid, The. Some Echo. Robert Creeley. SP-CreeR

Ground Tide. A. R. Ammons. CP-AmmoA

Ground / under a maple-tree. Sigil. "H. D." CP-DoolH

Ground Zero [December 1982]. William Stafford. SP-StafWW

Ground Zero [June 1982]. William Stafford. SP-StafWW

Grounded here, carrying a daily cross. Some Relations. A. K. Ramanujan. CP-RamaA

Groundhog, The. Richard Eberhart. CP-EberR

Groundhog on the mountain did not run, The. Incommunicado. Sylvia Plath. CP-PlatS

Groundhog Revisiting, The. Richard Eberhart. CP-EberR

Group of girls play in fading light, A. Han-shan. CP-ColdM, *tr.* by Red Pine

Group of little children with their ways and chatter flow in, A. After the Argument. Walt Whitman. CP-WhitW

Grouse Pouts Are Come In. Thomas Sheridan. CP-SherT

Grouse pouts, / Fine trouts. Thomas Sheridan. CP-SherT

Grove, The. Octavio Paz. CP-BishE, *tr.* by Elizabeth Bishop

Grove, forest, jungle—a thickening motion. Village, Town, City—Highway, Road, Path. A. R. Ammons. CP-AmmoA

Grove kept us dry, The. Mediation, A. R. Ammons. CP-AmmoA

Grove of deep sycamores drifts into the Hudson, A. Night before Thanksgiving, The. Norman Dubie. CP-DubiN

Groves are down, The. Gary Snyder. CP-SnydG *Fr.* Myths and Texts.

Grow angry, sweetheart, if you must, with me. Ugly Secret, The. Robert Graves. CP-GravR

Grow for two ends, it matters not at all. Rosemarie Branch, The. Robert Herrick. CP-HerrR

Grow not too high, grow not too far from home. Edna St. Vincent Millay. CP-MillE

Grow old along with me! Rabbi Ben Ezra. Robert Browning. CP-BroR1

Grow plumpe, leane Death; his Holinesse a feast. Upon the Gunpowder Treason. Richard Crashaw. CP-CrasR

Grow up in Beauty, as thou do'st begin. On Tomasin Parsons. Robert Herrick. CP-HerrR

Grower of trees, the gardener, the man born to farming, The. Man Born to Farming, The. Wendell Berry. CP-BerrW

Growin' Gray. Paul Laurence Dunbar. CP-DunbP

Growing. Kenneth Rexroth. CP-RexrK

Growing a Ghost. Howard Nemerov. CP-NemeH

Growing and Changing. Philip Whalen. SP-WhalP

Growing Dark. James Schuyler. CP-SchuJ

Growing idleness of summer grass, The. Lesson for This Sunday, A. Derek Walcott. CP-WalcD

Growing in the vale / By the uplands hilly. Christina Georgina Rossetti. CP-RosC2

Growing need to be moving around it to see it, The. View of the Brooklyn Bridge, A. William Meredith. SP-MereW

Growing Old. Matthew Arnold. SP-ArnoM

Growing Old. Rainer Maria Rilke. CP-RilkFr, *tr.* by A. Poulin, Jr.

Growing Old Again. Allen Ginsberg. CP-GinsA

Growing old in shabby clothes. Rummage. Hayden Carruth. CP-CarHS

Growing Pains. Robert Graves. CP-GravR

Growing Up. William Stafford. SP-StafWW

Growing Up Askew. Mona Van Duyn. SP-VanDM

Growing weather; enough rain. Satisfactions of the Mad Farmer, The. Wendell Berry. CP-BerrW

Growler, A. Ambrose Bierce. SP-BierA

Growling of the constellations, you said, The. Orion over Farne. Charles Tomlinson. SP-TomlC

Grown and Flown. Christina Georgina Rossetti. CP-RosC1

Grown Cold. Christina Georgina Rossetti. CP-RosC3

Grown Men at Touch. Wyatt Prunty. SP-PrunW

Grown old in courts, thou art not surely one. Translations from Metastasio. Pietro Metastasio. CP-JohnS *Fr.* Adriano in Syria.

Grown old in Love from Seven till Seven times Seven. William Blake. CP-BlakW

Grown old in Rhyme, 'twere barbarous to discard. Prologue Design'd for Mr. Durfy's Last Play. Alexander Pope. CP-PopeA

Grown son's tears in a restaurant mix their salt, A. Elegy: "Grown son's tears in a restaurant mix their salt, A." A. K. Ramanujan. CP-RamaA

Grown tired of this rank summer's wealth. Fall of the Leaf, The ("Grown tired of this rank summer's wealth"). Henry David Thoreau. CP-ThorH

Grown too big for his skin. Fable for When There's No Way Out. May Swenson. SP-SwenM

Grown-up. Edna St. Vincent Millay. CP-MillE

Grown-Up, The. Randall Jarrell. CP-JarrR

Grown-Ups, The. Donald Hall. CP-HallD

Grown used to New York weather. Thank You, Fog. W. H. Auden. CP-AudeW

Grows till it is not what but which. Web One Weaves of Italy, The. Marianne Craig Moore. CP-MoorM

Growth. Laura Riding Jackson. CP-RidiL

Growth (Harriet). Robert Lowell. SP-LoweR

Growth in May. Thomas Hardy. CP-HardT

Growth of a Poet. Denise Levertov. SP-LeveDL

Growth of "Lorraine," The. Edwin Arlington Robinson. CP-RobiE

Growth of Man—like Growth of Nature. Emily Dickinson. CP-DickE

Groynes, for his fleshly *Burglary* of late. Upon Groynes. Robert Herrick. CP-HerrR

Grub-white mulberries redden among leaves. Moonrise. Sylvia Plath. CP-PlatS

Grubs loves his Wife and Children, while that they. Upon Grubs. Robert Herrick. CP-HerrR

Grudge of the Old, The. D. H. Lawrence. CP-LawrD

Grudge on who list, this is my lot. Sir Thomas Wyatt. CP-WyatT

Grudging Respect. Donald Davie. CP-DaviDC

Grudgings turnes bread to stones, when to the Poore. Upon Grudgings. Robert Herrick. CP-HerrR

Gruffly growled the wind on Toller downland broad and bare. Homecoming, The. Thomas Hardy. CP-HardT

Grundy and Hoagland and all the rest who ganged. Dropout. William Stafford. SP-StafWW

Grunion Run. Robert Stock. SP-StocR

Gryll eates, but ne're sayes grace; to speak the troth. Upon Gryll. Robert Herrick. CP-HerrR

Guaranteed Antique. Carl Sandburg. CP-SandC

Guard has a right to despair. He stands by God, The. In Galleries. Randall Jarrell. CP-JarrR

Guard the knowledge. Desert as Garden of Paradise, The. Adrienne Rich. SP-RicA1

Guard yourself from the terrible empty light of space, the bottomless. Quia Absurdum. Robinson Jeffers. CP-JefR3

Guardian Angel. Gabriela Mistral. SP-MistG, *tr.* by Maria Giachetti [*or* Jacketti]

Guardian-Angel, The. Robert Browning. CP-BroR1

Guardian of long-distance conduits in the desert?, A. Study of Loneliness. Czeslaw Milosz. CP-MiloC; CP-MiloCN, *tr.* by Lillian Vallee

Guardian of the Books, The. Jorge Luis Borges. SP-BorgJ, *tr.* by Charles Tomlinson

Guardians. W. S. Merwin. SP-MerwWF

Guardians, The. Geoffrey Hill. CP-HillG

Guards. D. H. Lawrence. CP-LawrD

Guards cried out incomprehensibly, The. Castle. Adam Zagajewski. SP-ZagaA, *tr.* by Clare Cavanagh

Guards sleep they breathe uneven, The. Pathological Case in Pliny, A. John Logan. CP-LogaJ

Guardsmen, The. Federico García Lorca. CP-GarcF, *tr.* by Jerome Rothenberg *Fr.* Seaside Prints.

Guatemala, Nicaragua, Salvador. Yannis Ritsos. SP-RitsY *Fr.* Second Series.

Guatemala: 1964. C. K. Williams. SP-WillC

Gubbinal. Wallace Stevens. CP-StevW; CP-StevWP

Gubbs call's his children Kitlings: and wo'd bound. Upon Gubbs. Robert Herrick. CP-HerrR

Gude pity me, because I'm little. Adam A———'s Prayer. Robert Burns. CP-BurnR

Gude Wallace. Robert Burns. CP-BurnR

Gudeen to You Kimmer. Robert Burns. CP-BurnR

Gudewife, The. James Whitcomb Riley. CP-RileJ

Gudique is the chastening. Compline. James McMichael. SP-McMiJ

Guelder Roses. D. H. Lawrence. CP-LawrD

Guess 'at Billy hain't got back. Rivals, The; or the Showman's Ruse. James Whitcomb Riley. CP-RileJ

Guess what smells so . . . You didn't guess. Winter's Tale, The. Randall Jarrell. CP-JarrR

Guesse cuts his shooes, and limping, goes about. Upon Guesse. Robert Herrick. CP-HerrR

Guesses. Christina Georgina Rossetti. CP-RosC3

Guest, A. Ambrose Bierce. SP-BierA

Guest, A. May Sarton. SP-SartM

Guest, The. Wendell Berry. CP-BerrW

Guest, The. Charles Simic. SP-SimiCE

Guest, The. Jones Very. CP-VeryJ

Guest am I to have. Emily Dickinson. CP-DickE

Guest at Thanksgiving said And you've got, A. Green Water Tower. W. S. Merwin. SP-MerwWF

Guest departs, The. After the Guest. Gregory Orr. SP-OrrG

Guest House, The. Jelaluddin Rumi. SP-Rumi, *tr. by* Coleman Barks

Guest is gold and crimson, The. Emily Dickinson. CP-DickE

Guest Room. George Oppen. CP-OppGN

Guest, still drunk, sprawls in my bed, The. After the Party. Meng Hao Jan. CP-WilW2

Guests in their summer colors have fled, The. Last Picnic, The. Stanley Kunitz. CP-KunSC

Guests, The. Louis Zukofsky. CP-ZukLS

Guid Ale Keeps the Heart Aboon. Robert Burns. CP-BurnR

Guid-mornin to your MAJESTY. Dream, A. Robert Burns. CP-BurnR

Guid New-year I wish thee, Maggie!, A. Auld Farmer's New-Year-Morning Salutation to His Auld Mare, Maggie, on Giving Her the Accustomed Ripp of Corn to Hansel in the New-Year, The. Robert Burns. CP-BurnR

Guid speed an' furder to you Johny. Third Epistle to J. Lapraik. Robert Burns. CP-BurnR

Guide. A. R. Ammons. CP-AmmoA

Guide, The. Ted Hughes. SP-HughTN

Guide, The. James Whitcomb Riley. CP-RileJ

Guide for Survivors. Josephine Jacobsen. CP-JacoJ

Guide to Poetry, A. John Ciardi. CP-CiarJ

Guide to the Ruins. Howard Nemerov. CP-NemeH

Guide to the Stone Age, The. James Tate. SP-TateJ

Guidebooks play deception, The; oceans are. Itinerary. Adrienne Rich. CP-RicAE

Guiding hand raised, A. When Asked to Lie Down on the Altar. Eleanor Wilner. SP-WilnE

Guiding Lights, The. Charles Baudelaire. CP-BaudC, *tr. by* Walter Martin

Guido, i' vorrei che tu e Lapo ed io. Robert Creeley. CP-CreeR

Guido, I wish that Lapo, thou, and I. Sonnet: He imagines a pleasant Voyage for Guido, Lapo Gianni, and himself, with their three Ladies. Dante Alighieri. CW-RossD, *tr. by* Dante Gabriel Rossetti

Guido, I would like that you and Lapo and I. Dante Alighieri. CP-CavaG, *tr. by* Marc Cirigliano

Guido / I would that you me & Lapo. Guido, i' vorrei che tu e Lapo ed io. Robert Creeley. CP-CreeR

Guido Invites You Thus. Ezra Pound. CP-PoEar

Guido's Aurora. Henry David Thoreau. CP-ThorH

Guido's Aurora. Jones Very. CP-VeryJ

Guiffre's Nightmusic. Thomas McGrath. SP-McGrT

Guillaume de Lorris Belated. Ezra Pound. CP-PoEar

Guillaume de Machault (1300–1377) Ballade: Plourès, dames. Louis Zukofsky. CP-ZukLS

Guilt and Sorrow; or Incidents upon Salisbury Plain. William Wordsworth. CP-WorW1

Guilt is the cause of more disauders. E. E. Cummings. CP-CummE

Guilt of man does not defer the sun, The. 1935. Kenneth Patchen. CP-PatcK

Guilt said the bony man. Song of Another Tribe, A. Muriel Rukeyser. CP-RukeM

Guilt unavowed is guilt in its extreme. Error Pursued. Helen Pinkerton. CP-PinkH

Guiltless Inconstant, The. Sir John Suckling. CP-CareT; CP-SuckJ

Guilty, be wise; and though thou know'st the crimes. To Person Guilty ("Guilty, be wise; and though thou know'st the crimes"). Ben Jonson. CP-JonsB; SP-JonsB

Guilty, because I bad[e] you late be wise. To Person Guilty ("Guilty, because I bad[e] you late be wise"). Ben Jonson. CP-JonsB

Guinevere. James Whitcomb Riley. CP-RileJ

Guinevere at Her Fireside. Dorothy Parker. CP-ParkD

Guiney-pigs is awful cute. James Whitcomb Riley. CP-RileJ

Guise and disguise, the mirroring and masquerades. Venice Revisited. Amy Clampitt. CP-ClamA

Guitar Recitativos. A. R. Ammons. CP-AmmoA

Gulelme gente Perciorum ab inclita. Ad nobiliss. virum Gul. Percium. Thomas Campion. CP-CampT

Gules and cement dust. A matte tacky blood. Damson. Seamus Heaney. SP-HeanSO

Gulf, The. D. H. Lawrence. CP-LawrD

Gulf, The. Derek Walcott. CP-WalcD

Gulf between us and the brutes, The. Louis MacNeice. CP-MacNL *Fr.* Jigsaws.

Gulf of Maine, The. Charles Olson. SP-OlsoC *Fr.* Maximus Poems, The.

Gulf of seven and fifty years, The. Reunion, The. John Greenleaf Whittier. CP-WhitJ

Gulkana, The. Ted.Hughes. SP-HughTN

Gull. Anne Sexton. CP-SextA

Gull. Charles Tomlinson. CP-TomlC

Gull rides on the ripples of a dream, A. Walk in Late Summer, A. Theodore Roethke. CP-RoetT

Gull shall whistle in his wake, the blind wave break in fire, The. Voortrekker, The. Rudyard Kipling. CP-KiplR

Gull, up close, A. Seagulls. John Updike. CP-UpdiJ

Gulled. Richard Eberhart. CP-EberR

Gullies as deep as halls held these surveyors. Muriel Rukeyser. CP-RukeM

Gulliver. Sylvia Plath. CP-PlatS

Gulls. Robert Earl Hayden. CP-HaydR

Gulls. James Schuyler. CP-SchuJ

Gulls. William Carlos Williams. CP-WilW1

Gulls, The. Howard Nemerov. CP-NemeH

Gulls are out at the Old Head, The. Birdlife. Derek Mahon. CP-MahoD

Gulls escorted us. From time to time. Sonnet from the Voyage. Yehuda Amichai. SP-AmicY, *tr. by* Stephen Mitchell

Gulls flock in to feed from the waste. From the Motorway. Charles Tomlinson. CP-TomlC

Gulls fly in close formation becoming a patch of sail, The. Scrivener's Roses, The. Norman Dubie. CP-DubiN

Gull's image and the gull, The. Before March. Archibald MacLeish. CP-MacLA

Gulls in Wyoming, Utah, flow the plows. Orders. John Ciardi. CP-CiarJ

Gulls Land and Cease to Be. John Ciardi. CP-CiarJ

Gulls / loudly insist on indefensible rights. Gulls. James Schuyler. CP-SchuJ

Gulls of Settimo, The. Primo Levi. CP-LeviP, *tr. by* Ruth Feldman

Gulls on the grass / and the odor of live worms / and worms dead on the walk. Conqueror. Charles Olson. CP-OlsoC

Gulls over a rotting hull. Louis Zukofsky. CP-ZukLS

Gully of green, a laughing river, A. Asleep in the Valley. Paul Verlaine. CP-RimbA, *tr. by* Martin Sorrell

Gum-Gatherer, The. Robert Frost. CP-FrosR

Gum wrappers with nothing, Coors can. Gutters of Jackson: Cache Street North. William Stafford. SP-StafWW

Gun full swing the swimmer catapults and cracks, The. 400-Meter Freestyle. Maxine W. Kumin. SP-KumiM

Gunga Din. Rudyard Kipling. CP-KiplR

Gunman and the Débutante, The. Dorothy Parker. CP-ParkD

Gunnar Thorgilsson (1816–1879). Jorge Luis Borges. SP-BorgJ, *tr. by* Hoyt Rogers

Gunner. Randall Jarrell. CP-JarrR

Gunny sacks and bushels in rows standing in the courtyard. Esteem. Yannis Ritsos. SP-RitsY, *tr. by* Kostas Myrsiades

Guns at the camp (I hear them suddenly). Guns of Fort Knox, The. Thomas Merton. CP-MertT

Guns from the sea open against us:. Dawn Bombardment. Robert Graves. CP-GravR

Guns / Long, steel guns. Iron. Carl Sandburg. CP-SandC

Guns of Fort Knox, The. Thomas Merton. CP-MertT

Guns on the battle lines have pounded now a year between Brussels and. Salvage. Carl Sandburg. CP-SandC

Guns salute, and crowds and pigeons fly. Village Improvement Parade, The. Nicholas Vachel Lindsay. CP-LindV

Gunsight. Theodore Weiss. SP-WeisT

Guppy, The. Ogden Nash. CP-NashO

Gurney, Hampton, Cradock Newton, last. Cradock Newton: From an Epitaph. Charles Tomlinson. CP-TomlC

Guru. Charles Bukowski. SP-BukC1

Guru. Allen Ginsberg. CP-GinsA; SP-GinsA

Guru, The. A. K. Ramanujan. CP-RamaA

Guru Blues. Allen Ginsberg. SP-GinsA

Guru Om. Allen Ginsberg. CP-GinsA

Gust blustering, and the March rain. This. Wyatt Prunty. SP-PrunW

Gust of night rain lightly, A. Mystery (Oaxaca, Mexico), A. Denise Levertov. SP-LeveDL

Gust that lifted the bitter scent, The. Other Lines. Eugenio Montale. CP-MontE, *tr. by* Jonathan Galassi

Gustatory Achievement, A. James Whitcomb Riley. CP-RileJ

Gut eats all day and lechers all the night. On Gut. Ben Jonson. CP-JonsB; SP-JonsB

Gutters of Jackson: Cache Street North. William Stafford. SP-StafWW

Guttersnipe and the albatross, The. Drifting Off. Seamus Heaney. SP-HeanSO *Fr.* Sweeney Redivivus.

Guttural Muse, The. Seamus Heaney. SP-HeanSO

Guy. Ralph Waldo Emerson. CP-EmerR

Guy I Know on 47th and Cottage, A. Clarence Major. SP-MajoC

Guy in the front court can't, The. Greek, The. Charles Bukowski. SP-BukC1

Guyana. Derek Walcott. CP-WalcD

Guys who own, The. What I Think. Langston Hughes. CP-HughL; CP-HughL3

Gwin, King of Norway. William Blake. CP-BlakW

Gyges['] ring they bear[e] about them still, A. Lovers How They Come and Part. Robert Herrick. CP-HerrR

Gypsies. Langston Hughes. CP-HughL

Gypsies. William Wordsworth. CP-WorW1

Gypsies are picture-book people. Gypsies. Langston Hughes. CP-HughL

Gypsies carry sacks of walnuts out of the groves, The. Coleridge Crossing the Plain of Jars [1833]. Norman Dubie. CP-DubiN

Gypsies Metamorphosed, The. Ben Jonson.
  Dinner for the Devil. CP-JonsB
  Faery Beam upon You, The. CP-JonsB
  "From the famous Peak of Derby." CP-JonsB
  Song: "To the old, long life and treasure." CP-JonsB

Gypsies Near Del Mar, The. Charles Bukowski. SP-BukC2

Gypsy. Carl Sandburg. CP-SandC

Gypsy gazes into her crystal ball, The. Feet Nailed to the Floor. Yusef Komunyakaa. CP-KomuY

Gypsy Man. Langston Hughes. CP-HughL; CP-HughL1

Gypsy Melodies. Langston Hughes. CP-HughL; CP-HughL2

Gypsy Mother. Carl Sandburg. CP-SandC

Gypsy, new bawd, is turned physician. On Gypsy. Ben Jonson. CP-JonsB; SP-JonsB

Gypsy Nun, The. Federico García Lorca. CP-GarcF, tr. by Will Kirkland

Gyrates & shakes / like crazy. Ruby Disc, The. Federico García Lorca. CP-GarcF, tr. by Jerome Rothenberg Fr. Barrage of Firework Poems on the Occasion of the Poet's Birthday.

Gyres, The. William Butler Yeats. CP-YeatW

Gyroscope. Howard Nemerov. CP-NemeH

Gyroscope, The. Muriel Rukeyser. CP-RukeM

H

H. Robert Graves. CP-GravR

H. Arthur Rimbaud. CP-RimbA, tr. by Martin Sorrell

H. A. and A. S. Emily Jane Brontë. CP-BronE

H. D. Donald Davie. CP-DaviDC

H is, reluctantly, for HUMAN, a word. John Ciardi. CP-CiarJ

H may be N for those who speak. H. Robert Graves. CP-GravR

H. T. Louis Zukofsky. CP-ZukLS

H. W. in Hibernia Belligeranti. John Donne. CP-DonnJ; MW-DonnJ

Ha ha ha! the sun is shining! Nothing but Nature. Ogden Nash. CP-NashO

Ha! My dear! I'm back again. In Bohemia. James Whitcomb Riley. CP-RileJ

Ha! Original Sin! Ogden Nash. CP-NashO

Ha' we lost the goodliest fere o' all. Ballad of the Goodly Fere. Ezra Pound. CP-PoEar; SP-PounE

Ha! whare ye gaun, ye crowlin' [or crowlan] ferlie! To a Louse [On Seeing One on a Lady's Bonnet at Church]. Robert Burns. CP-BurnR

Habeas Corpus. Kenneth Rexroth. CP-RexrK

Habit I can't break, caring, A. In Memoriam P. W. Jr. 1921–1980. Maxine W. Kumin. SP-KumiM

Habit of Perfection, The. Gerard Manley Hopkins. CP-HopkG

Habitation. Margaret Atwood. SP-AtwM1

Habits. W. S. Merwin. SP-MerwW

Habits, The. Louis MacNeice. CP-MacNL

Hacienda. Charles Tomlinson. CP-TomlC

Hacker School House, The. Jones Very. CP-VeryJ

Hackney'd in business, wearied at that oar. Retirement. William Cowper. CP-CowpW

Had a harelip—Joney had. Joney. James Whitcomb Riley. CP-RileJ

Had but the light come just a little nearer. Petrarch. CP-Petra, tr. by J. G. Nichols

Had Fortune parted us / Fortune is blind. Christina Georgina Rossetti. CP-RosC3

Had God but made me a religious man. Common Saw, A. Howard Nemerov. CP-NemeH

Had he and I but met. Man He Killed, The. Thomas Hardy. CP-HardT

Had I a cave on some wild, distant shore. Song: "Had I a cave on some wild, distant shore." Robert Burns. CP-BurnR

Had I a man's fair form, then might my sighs. To ———: "Had I a man's fair form, then might my sighs" John Keats. CP-KeatJ

Had I a pleasure you had not. Emily Dickinson. SP-DickE

Had I a Song. Ivor Gurney. SP-GurnI

Had I been the seventh son of a seventh son. Cure for Warts, The. Paul

Muldoon. CP-MuldP

Had I believed those words would turn out dear. Petrarch. CP-Petra, tr. by J. G. Nichols

Had I but lived a hundred years ago. At Lulworth Cove a Century Back. Thomas Hardy. CP-HardT

Had I but plenty of money, money enough and to spare. Up at a Villa—Down in the City. Robert Browning. CP-BroR1; SP-BroR

Had I but the torrent's might. Death of Hoel, The. Thomas Gray. CP-GrayT

Had I know it then, really known. This Gray Age. Theodore Weiss. SP-WeisT

Had I known that the first was the last. Emily Dickinson. CP-DickE

Had I known that the heart. Prescience. Maya Angelou. SP-AngeM

Had I known that you were going. To One Who Might Have Borne a Message. Edna St. Vincent Millay. CP-MillE

"Had I my will," the shrill wind sang. Che Farò Senza Euridice. Randall Jarrell. CP-JarrR

Had I not been frail and half broken inside. In a Parish. Czeslaw Milosz. CP-MiloCN, tr. by Robert Hass

Had I not loved. For an End. Helen Pinkerton. CP-PinkH

Had I not seen the Sun. Emily Dickinson. CP-DickE

Had I not This, or This, I said. Emily Dickinson. CP-DickE

Had I presumed to hope. Emily Dickinson. CP-DickE

Had I ten thousand mouths and tongues. Upon the Author. Patrick Delany. CP-SherT

Had I the heavens' embroidered cloths, He Wishes for the Cloths of Heaven. William Butler Yeats. CP-YeatW

Had I the world for my enemy. Sadi. CP-EmerR

Had I the Wyte She Bade Me. Robert Burns. CP-BurnR

Had I, when young, been leery of the glow. Michelangelo Buonarroti. CP-Miche, tr. by John Frederick Nims

Had I wist that now I wot. Sir Thomas Wyatt. CP-WyatT

Had it to do / all over again. Detachment, Wisdom and Compassion. Philip Whalen. SP-WhalP

Had Lucan hid the truth to please the time. To the Translator of Lucan [or Lucan's Pharsalia, 1614]. Sir Walter Ralegh. CP-RaleW

Had not / thought / of it . . . . Thinking. Robert Creeley. CP-CreeR

Had old Hippocrates, or Galen. Ben Jonson. CP-JonsB Fr. Volpone.

Had the gods loved me I had lain. Exile. Walter De la Mare. CP-DeLaW

Had the ham bone, had the lentils. Mud Soup. Carolyn Kizer. CP-KizeC

Had there been falsehood in my breast. Emily Jane Brontë. CP-BronE

Had these eyes never seen you. Adieu. Walter De la Mare. CP-DeLaW

Had this effulgence disappeared. Composed upon an Evening of Extraordinary Splendour and Beauty. William Wordsworth. CP-WorW2; MW-WorW

Had this fair figure which this frame displays. On Seeing a Portrait of Mrs Montagu. Samuel Johnson. CP-JohnS

Had this one Day not been. Emily Dickinson. CP-DickE

Had those that dwell in error foul. Ben Jonson. CP-JonsB Fr. Masque of Beauty, The.

Had, too! She "Displains" It. James Whitcomb Riley. CP-RileJ

Had we but World enough and Time. To His Coy Mistress. Andrew Marvell. CP-MarvA

Had we known the Ton she bore. Emily Dickinson. CP-DickE

Had we less to say to those we love. Emily Dickinson. SP-DickE

Had we our senses. Emily Dickinson. CP-DickE

Had you an Hour unengrossed. Emily Dickinson. SP-DickE

Had you died when we were together. Fire, The. Louise Glück. SP-GlucL

Had you the eyes of a goat. Disappointment, The. Robert Creeley. CP-CreeR

Had You Wept. Thomas Hardy. CP-HardT

Hada is light, Estela is harmony. Three Sisters, The. Alfonso Cortes. CP-MertT

Hadda be flashing like the Daily Double. Hadda Be Playing on the Jukebox. Allen Ginsberg. CP-GinsA

Hadda Be Playing on the Jukebox. Allen Ginsberg. CP-GinsA

Haddington Masque, The. Ben Jonson.
  Epithalamion: "Up, youths and virgins, up, and praise." CP-JonsB

Hadera. Yehuda Amichai. SP-AmicYL, tr. by Benjamin Harshav and Barbara Harshav

Hadn't I been / aching, for you. Distance. Robert Creeley. CP-CreeR

Hadramauti. Rudyard Kipling. CP-KiplR Fr. Plain Tales from the Hills.

Hadrian's Address to His Soul When Dying. Emperor Hadrian.
  Adrian's Address to His Soul When Dying. CP-Byron

Hadst thou lived in days of old. To [Mary Frogley]. John Keats. CP-KeatJ

'Hadvantageous' breathes Arrius heavily. Carmen 84. Catullus. CP-ZukLS Fr. Carmina.

Haec Fabula Docet. Robert Frost. CP-FrosR

Haec te jubent salvere, quod possunt, loca. Gerard Manley Hopkins. CP-HopkG

Haecceity. James Vincent Cunningham. CP-CunnJ

Hafiz since on the world. Hafiz. CP-EmerR Fr. Odes.

Hafiz thou art from Eternity. Hafiz. CP-EmerR Fr. Odes.

Hag. Heather McHugh. SP-McHuH

Hag, The. Robert Herrick. CP-HerrR

Hag is astride, The. Hag, The. Robert Herrick. CP-HerrR

Hag-Ridden. Robert Graves. CP-GravR

Hag Riding. Lucille Clifton. SP-ClifL

Hagar repudiated. Gillis van Conninxloo, Landscape. Panel, 65 x 119 cm. Hans Magnus Enzensberger. SP-EnzeH

Haggard woman with a hacking cough and a deathless love whispers, The. Cups of Coffee. Carl Sandburg. CP-SandC

Haggling over fish and meat. Han-shan. CP-ColdM, tr. by Red Pine

Hagia Sophia. Thomas Merton. CP-MertT

Haglets, The. Herman Melville. SP-MelvH

Haiku: "You are the bright bird." Robert Stock. SP-StocR

Haiku, for Gary Snyder. Philip Whalen. SP-WhalP

Haiku for Mike. Philip Whalen. SP-WhalP

Hail and beware the dead who will talk life until you are blue. Newly Discovered "Homeric" Hymn, A. Charles Olson. CP-OlsoC; SP-OlsoC

Hail Bard triumphant! Whose poetic fire. To My Worthy Friend T S——, D. D. on His Incomparable Translation of and Notes on Persius. Unknown. CP-SherT

Hail Bishop Valentine, whose day this is. Epithalamion, or Marriage Song on the Lady Elizabeth and Count Palatine Being Married on St. Valentine's Day, An. John Donne. CP-DonnJ; MW-DonnJ

Hail brother dawn that casteth light. Battle Dawn. Ezra Pound. CP-PoEar

Hail candid, gen'rous man, whoe'er thou art. To the Visitant, from a Circle of Ladies, on Reading His Paper. No. 3, in the Pennsylvania Chronicle. Annis Boudinot Stockton. CP-StocA

Hail, Common Sense! most rare of all! George Meredith. CP-MerG2

Hail early harbinger of Spring! Snow Drop, The. Jones Very. CP-VeryJ

Hail Energeia! hail, my native tongue. Christopher Smart. SP-SmarC

Hail, future friend, whose present I. Bathtub Thoughts. W. H. Auden. CP-AudeW

Hail, garden of confident hope! God's Acre. Christina Georgina Rossetti. CP-RosC2

Hail goes / dancing, The. C. K. Williams. CP-WillC

Hail, happy day, when smiling like the morn. To the Right Honourable William, Earl of Dartmouth, His Majesty's Principal Secretary of State for North America. Phillis Wheatley. CP-WheaP

Hail, happy genius of this ancient pile! Lord Bacon's Birthday. Ben Jonson. CP-JonsB

Hail, happy little animal. Imitation of Anacreon's Grasshopper, Applied to Mr. T. S., Commonly Known by the Name of Skeleton, An. Unknown. CP-SherT

Hail, happy saint, on thine [or thy] immortal throne. On the Death of the Rev. Mr. George Whitefield [1770]. Phillis Wheatley. CP-WheaP

Hail, heavenly gift! within the human breast. Benevolence. John Greenleaf Whittier. CP-WhitJ

Hail heavenly pensive solitude. Ode to Solitude Inscribed to Mrs Boudinot, An. Annis Boudinot Stockton. CP-StocA

Hail heav'nly harp, where Memnon's skill is shewn. Inscriptions on an Aeolian Harp. Christopher Smart. SP-SmarC

Hail! Ho! Sea-Song from the Shore, A. James Whitcomb Riley. CP-RileJ

Hail, horrors, hail! ye ever gloomy bowers. Hymn to Ignorance. Thomas Gray. CP-GrayT

Hail, human compound quadrifarious! To George Nim-Dan-Dean, Esq. upon His Incomparable Verses, &c. of August 2d, 1721. Thomas Sheridan. CP-SherT

Hail, Love of Country! noble flame. Hymn: Sung at the Celebration of the Fourth of July, in Salem, 1854. Jones Very. CP-VeryJ

Hail[!] lovely flower, first honour of the year! On a Daffodil, the First Flower the Author Had Seen That Year. Samuel Johnson. CP-JohnS

Hail Mary, full of grace, it once was said. Epigram to the Queen, then Lying In, An. 1630. Ben Jonson. CP-JonsB

Hail Mary, thou blessed among women, generations shall rise up to greet. Ave Maria. G. K. Chesterton. CP-ChesG

Hail Michael Agnolo! my soul lay slain. Redivivus. Ezra Pound. CP-PoEar

Hail, most high, most humble one! O Gloriosa Domina. Richard Crashaw. CP-CrasR

Hail native Language, that by sinews weak. At a Vacation Exercise [in the Col[l]e[d]ge[, Part Latin, Part English]. John Milton. CP-MiltJ

Hail, noble face of noble friend! Christina Georgina Rossetti. CP-RosC3

Hail noble fruit!—by Homer sung. Grape. Ambrose Bierce. SP-BierA

Hail, orient Conqueror of Gloomy Night! Ode: The Morning of the Day Appointed for a General Thanksgiving. January 18, 1816. William Wordsworth. CP-WorW2

Hail, peerless Pun! thou last and best. Pun, The. Ambrose Bierce. SP-BierA

Hail, Poesie! thou nymph reserv'd! Sketch. Robert Burns. CP-BurnR

Hail requiem of departed time. To the Clock. Ralph Waldo Emerson. CP-EmerR

Hail sacred spring, whose fruitful stream. River, The. Alexander Pope. CP-PopeA

Hail, sister springs! Weeper, The. Richard Crashaw. CP-CrasR

Hail, thairm-inspirin, rattlin Willie! Epistle to Captn Willm Logan at Park. Robert Burns. CP-BurnR

Hail the tree's meadow. Madrigal for 3 Voices, A. Louis Zukofsky. CP-ZukLS

Hail the vagina. Joseph Brodsky. CP-BrodJ Fr. Shorts.

Hail to posterity! Pennsylvania Pilgrim, The. John Greenleaf Whittier. CP-WhitJ

Hail to the Chief Who in Triumph Advances. Sir Walter Scott. SP-ScotW Fr. Lady of the Lake, The.

Hail to the fields—with Dwellings sprinkled o'er. Open Prospect. William Wordsworth. CP-WorW2 Fr. River Duddon [A Series of Sonnets], The.

Hail to the man who upward strives. On Ignaz Moscheles. Robert Browning. CP-BroR2

Hail to the sage who, from his native store. From My Much Honored Friend at Heldelville. Patrick Delany. CP-SherT

Hail to the Sons of Roosevelt. Nicholas Vachel Lindsay. CP-LindV

Hail to thee, blithe Spirit! To a Skylark. Percy Bysshe Shelley. CP-ShelP

Hail to thee, Cambria; for the unfettered wind. On Leaving London for Wales. Percy Bysshe Shelley. CP-ShelP

Hail to thee, with all good cheer! Whittier—at Newburyport. James Whitcomb Riley. CP-RileJ

Hail, Twilight, sovereign of one peaceful hour! William Wordsworth. CP-WorW1

Hail, venerable Night! Translation of a Greek Ode on Astronomy. Samuel Taylor Coleridge. CP-ColeS

Hail, wond'rous Being, who in pow'r supreme. On the Eternity of the Supreme Being. Christopher Smart. SP-SmarC

Hail wonrous being who in power supreme. Christopher Smart. CP-StocA Fr. On the Eternity of the Supreme Being.

Hail, ye hills and heaths of Ecclefechan! Terse Verse. Robert Browning. CP-BroR2

Hail, Zaragoza! If with unwet eye. William Wordsworth. CP-WorW1

Haile holy, and all-honour'd Tomb. To His Saviours Sepulcher: His Devotion. Robert Herrick. CP-HerrR

Hailstones. Seamus Heaney. SP-HeanSO

Hailstones falling like sharp blue sky chips. Crazy Horse Monument. Peter Blue Cloud. SP-BlueP

Hailstones puncture the ground. Tenant Farmer, The. Ai. SP-Ai

Hailstorm in May. Gerard Manley Hopkins. CP-HopkG

Hain't you see my Mandy Lou. Plantation Portrait, A. Paul Laurence Dunbar. CP-DunbP

Hair. David Ignatow. SP-IgnaD

Hair slicked back as if. Child's Play. Yusef Komunyakaa. CP-KomuY

Hair, wax, rouge, honey, teeth, you buy. On a Battered Beauty. Unknown. CP-CowpW

Hair your a brook. E. E. Cummings. CP-CummE

Haircut. Karl Shapiro. SP-ShapK

Haircut, A. Raymond Carver. CP-CarvR

Hairless and worse than leathery, the skin. Corrib. An Emblem. Donald Davie. CP-DaviDC

Hairline Fracture, A. Amy Clampitt. CP-ClamA

Hairs turn gold upon my thigh, The. Value of Gold, The. Thom Gunn. CP-GunnT

Hairy full stern face, The. Attila. Kenneth Patchen. CP-PatcK

Hairy was here. News from the Cabin. May Swenson. SP-SwenM

Haitian Cadavers. Thomas Lux. SP-LuxT

Hal o' the Draft. Rudyard Kipling. Fr. Puck of Pook's Hill.

Halation. Carolyn Kizer. CP-KizeC

Halbert and Hob. Robert Browning. CP-BroR2

Halcyon. "H. D." CP-DoolH

Halcyon Days. Walt Whitman. CP-WhitW

Hale [or Hail], sterne superne, hale [or hail], in eterne. Ballat [or Ballad] of Our Lady[, Ane]. William Dunbar. CP-DunbW

Half a league, half a league. Charge of the Light Brigade, The. Alfred Tennyson. CP-TennA

Half a moon is flaming in the south. Daybreak. William Carlos Williams. CP-WilW1

Half a year after war's end, Roosevelt and Hitler dead, Stalin tired. Greater Grandeur. Robinson Jeffers. CP-JefR3

Half a year, then a year and a half, then. Harriet. Robert Lowell. SP-LoweR

Half across the world from me. Hearthside. Dorothy Parker. CP-ParkD

Half an Hour. Constantine P. Cavafy. CP-CavaC, tr. by Theoharis Constantine Theoharis

Half an hour ago. Death of Assia G., The. Yehuda Amichai. SP-AmicYL, tr. by Benjamin Harshav and Barbara Harshav

Half-asleep on the back deck, / low wasp-hum of power mower. Appalachian Book of the Dead 5, The. Charles Wright. SP-WrigCN

Half asleep on the cold grass. For a Stone Girl at Sanchi. Gary Snyder. CP-SnydG

Half asleep on top of this bleak landscape. Hunter. Raymond Carver. CP-CarvR

Half awake in my Sunday nap. Three Green Windows. Anne Sexton. CP-SextA

Half-Ballad of Waterval. Rudyard Kipling. CP-KiplR

Half-bent Man. Richard Eberhart. CP-EberR

Half-Blind, The. D. H. Lawrence. CP-LawrD

Half circle's come before we know. Italian Morning. Louise Bogan. CP-BogaL

Half close your eyelids, loosen your hair. He Thinks of Those Who Have Spoken Evil of His Beloved. William Butler Yeats. CP-YeatW

"Half-cracked" to Higginson, living. I Am in Danger—Sir. Adrienne Rich. CP-RicAE; SP-RicA1; SP-RicA2

Half Dead. Christina Georgina Rossetti. CP-RosC2

Half-Dead Black Cherry Tree across the Road from My Childhood House, A. Gregory Orr. SP-OrrG

Half death, The. In Prague. Paul Celan. SP-CelaP, tr. by John Felstiner

Half-dollar in the hand of a gypsy, A. Fame if Not Fortune. Carl Sandburg. CP-SandC

Half drunk. Shit Time. Charles Bukowski. SP-BukC1

Half February. Charles Wright. SP-WrigCN

Half-Finished Letter, The. Robert Graves. CP-GravR

Half hidden by trees, the sheer roof of the barn. Barn, The. Stephen Spender. CP-SpenS

Half-hidden in a graveyard. Stranger, The. Walter De la Mare. CP-DeLaW

Half-hidden in the dying light's caress. Damned Women ("Half-hidden in the dying light's caress"). Charles Baudelaire. CP-BaudC, tr. by Walter Martin

Half hour for coffee, and at night, A. James Vincent Cunningham. CP-CunnJ

Half in Monet's colors, headlong into this light. Poplars, The. Yusef Komunyakaa. CP-KomuY

Half-light, appalled, blinked when I said. Sharing It with Angels. Robert Stock. SP-StocR

Half Moon. Federico García Lorca. SP-GarcF, tr. by W. S. Merwin

Half Moon. Federico García Lorca. CP-GarcF, tr. by Jerome Rothenberg Fr. Backwaters.

Half moon, a fermata, The. Interrupted Concert, The. Federico García Lorca. CP-GarcF, tr. by Catherine Brown

Half Moon in a High Wind. Carl Sandburg. CP-SandC

Half Moon Shows a Face of Plaintive Sweetness, The. Christina Georgina Rossetti. CP-RosC2

Half-moon westers low, my love, The. So Sound You Sleep. A. E. Housman. CP-HousA

Half my friends are dead. Sea Canes. Derek Walcott. CP-WalcD

Half my life ago. Signs. W. S. Merwin. SP-MerwW

Half of my life is gone, and I have let. Mezzo Cammin. Henry Wadsworth Longfellow. SP-LongH

Half of my youth I watched the soldiers. Corporal, The. Thom Gunn. CP-GunnT

Half of the fellow father as he doubles. My World Is Pyramid. Dylan Thomas. CP-ThomD

Half of the round. Round of the Rainbow. Gabriela Mistral. SP-MistG, tr. by Maria Giachetti [or Jacketti]

Half-opened, my door gave onto a long road. Unmapped Road. Robert Stock. SP-StocR

Half Past Home. Marge Piercy. SP-PierM

Half past twelve. The time has passed quickly. Since Nine o'Clock. Constantine P. Cavafy. CP-CavaC, tr. by Theoharis Constantine Theoharis

Half pear, cool, A. Fruit, for Sculpture. Charles Tomlinson. CP-TomlC

Half-Sized Violin. Yehuda Amichai. SP-AmicY, tr. by Chana Bloch

Half squatter, half tenant (no rent). Manuelzinho. Elizabeth Bishop. CP-BishE

Half-starved goat followed the man, The. He Is Guarded by Crowds and Shackled with Formalities. Kenneth Patchen. CP-PatcK

Half-stripped trees, The. Approach of Winter. William Carlos Williams. CP-WilW1

Half the night sky deep cloud. Warm Pastures. W. S. Merwin. SP-MerwWF

Half the People in the World. Yehuda Amichai. SP-AmicY, tr. by Stephen Mitchell

Half the People of the World. Yehuda Amichai. SP-AmicYL, tr. by Benjamin Harshav and Barbara Harshav

Half Truth from Cape Town. Louis MacNeice. CP-MacNL

"Half was not told me," said Sheba's Queen, The. She Came from the Uttermost Part of the Earth. Christina Georgina Rossetti. CP-RosC2

Half Way. W. H. Auden. CP-AudeW

Half Way. Carl Sandburg. CP-SandC

Half-way, for one commandment broken. A. E. Housman. CP-HousA

Half-way House, The. Gerard Manley Hopkins. CP-HopkG

Half-wild, I hear a wolf. Existences. William Stafford. SP-StafWW

Halfnaked children / met us singing for coins. Kodachromes of the Island. Robert Earl Hayden. CP-HaydR

Halfway. A. R. Ammons. CP-AmmoA

Halfway. Maxine W. Kumin. SP-KumiM

Halfway. Adrienne Rich. CP-RicAE; SP-RicA2

Halfway across a bridge one night. Swerve, The. William Stafford. SP-StafWW

Halfway between the rain and Washington. My Fifth Trip to Washington Ended

in Northeast Delaware. Audre Lorde. SP-LordA

Halfway down the gorge. Feud, The. Federico García Lorca. CP-GarcF, tr. by Christopher Maurer

Halfway up from the little harbor of sardine boats. Net-Menders, The. Sylvia Plath. CP-PlatS

Halfway up the Cinder Hill. Cinder Hill. Tennessee Williams. CP-WillT

Halfworld, The. William Carlos Williams. CP-WilW1

Halibut, The. Arthur Sze. SP-SzeA

Hall, A. Czeslaw Milosz. CP-MiloCN, tr. by Robert Hass

Hall Five. Hayden Carruth. CP-CarHS Fr. Bloomingdale Papers, The.

Hallaj said what he said and went to the origin. Jelaluddin Rumi. SP-Rumi, tr. by Coleman Barks

Hallelujah! kneel and sing / Praises to the heav'nly king. Bible, O.T. See Praise ye the Lord. Praise ye the Lord from the heavens

Halley's Comet. Stanley Kunitz. CP-KunSC

Halley's Comet. Jaroslav Seifert. SP-SeifJ, tr. by Ewald Osers

Hallow Eve with Spaces for Ghosts. Marge Piercy. SP-PierM

Hallowed be thy Name. Jones Very. CP-VeryJ

Halloween. Robert Burns. CP-BurnR

Halloween Parade, The. Amy Clampitt. CP-ClamA

Halloween, the Late Fifties. Yusef Komunyakaa. CP-KomuY

Hallowing of Pain, The. Emily Dickinson. CP-DickE

Halls of Bedlam, The. Robert Graves. CP-GravR

Halsted Street Car. Carl Sandburg. CP-SandC

Halt, The. Kathleen Jessie Raine. SP-RainK

Halted against the shade of a last hill. Spring Offensive. Wilfred Owen. CP-OwenW

Halves. C. K. Williams. CP-WillC; SP-WillC

Hamadiya, memory of bliss. The forties. Yehuda Amichai. SP-AmicYL, tr. by Benjamin Harshav and Barbara Harshav

Hamadiya, memory of pleasures. The forties. Yehuda Amichai. SP-AmicY, tr. by Chana Bloch

Hamatreya. Ralph Waldo Emerson. CP-EmerR

Hamburg, 1929. Stephen Spender. CP-SpenS

Hamelin Town's in Brunswick. Pied Piper of Hamelin, The. Robert Browning. CP-BroR1; SP-BroR

Hamid Ramouz (1818–1906). Raymond Carver. CP-CarvR

Hamilton Hotel. Robert Creeley. SP-CreeR

Hamilton, if he rides you down, remember. On the Way. Edwin Arlington Robinson. CP-RobiE

Hamlen Brook. Richard Wilbur. CP-WilbR

Hamlet. Nicholas Vachel Lindsay. CP-LindV

Hamlet. Walter De la Mare. CP-DeLaW

Hamlet Father, The. Richard Eberhart. CP-EberR

Hamlet of A. Macleish. Archibald MacLeish. CP-MacLA

Hamlin Garland rose up from the Oklahoma powwow and declared with spirit. Money Musk. James Schuyler. CP-SchuJ

Hammer, nail, and board I go, pounding. Stick Builder. Wyatt Prunty. SP-PrunW

Hammer struck my nail, instead of nail, The. Almanac. May Swenson. SP-SwenM

Hammer, The. Carl Sandburg. CP-SandC

Hammerfest. W. H. Auden. CP-AudeW

Hammering of the nails, The. Yannis Ritsos. SP-RitsY Fr. Paper Poems 2.

Hammers pound there above. Along Galeana Street. Octavio Paz. CP-BishE, tr. by Elizabeth Bishop

Hammers Pounding. Carl Sandburg. CP-SandC

Hammond Organ lubricates the air, The. Widow, The. Miller Williams. CP-WillM

Hampshire. Donald Davie. CP-DaviDC

Hampstead; the Horse Chestnut Trees. Thom Gunn. CP-GunnT

Hampton Beach. John Greenleaf Whittier. CP-WhitJ

Hanch, since he (lately) did interre his wife. Upon Hanch a Schoolmaster. Robert Herrick. CP-HerrR

Hand. Robinson Jeffers. CP-JefR3

Hand. Robert Stock. SP-StocR

Hand, The. Richard Eberhart. CP-EberR

Hand, The: "Brightness Falls from the Air" Gregory Orr. SP-OrrG

Hand a shade of moonlight on the pillow, The. Non Ti Fidar. Louis Zukofsky. CP-ZukLS

Hand and Foot, The [or Hand and the Foot, The]. Jones Very. CP-VeryJ

Hand and the Shadow, The. Richard Eberhart. CP-EberR

Hand and Tongue, The. Robert Herrick. CP-HerrR

Hand appears, A. In the Book. William Stafford. SP-StafWW

Hand as a Being, The. Wallace Stevens. CP-StevW; CP-StevWP

Hand at Callow Hill Farm, The. Charles Tomlinson. CP-TomlC; SP-TomlC

Hand between the candle and the wall, The. Poem with Rhythms. Wallace Stevens. CP-StevW; CP-StevWP

Hand Crocheted Rug. Lorine Niedecker. CP-NiedL

Hand Games. Marge Piercy. SP-PierM

Hand gold / glass holds flower under water dome bright. Imagination of the Taj Mahal. Philip Whalen. SP-WhalP

Hand / holding on to this. Maintenant. Charles Tomlinson. CP-TomlC

Hand in hand, we ran through the Autumn forest. Oh Look—I Can Do It Too. Dorothy Parker. CP-ParkD

Hand is risen from the earth, The. Familiar, The. Wendell Berry. CP-BerrW

Hand made a number, A. 2 8 3 2 5 6 7 4 5 4 9. Pablo Neruda. SP-NeruP

Hand Me Down My Old School Sliding Pads, or, There's a Hint of Strawberry Leaves in the Air. Ogden Nash. CP-NashO

Hand-me-down, The. Wyatt Prunty. SP-PrunW

Hand-Me-Downs. Grace Paley. CP-PalGC

Hand-Mirror, A. Walt Whitman. CP-WhitW

Hand of Art here torpid lies, The. Epitaph on William Hogarth, An. Samuel Johnson. CP-JohnS

Hand of man. Stonecarver's Poem, The. Denise Levertov. SP-LeveDP; SP-LeveDS

Hand of Snapshots, A. Louis MacNeice. CP-MacNL

Hand of Solo, A. Thomas Kinsella. CP-KinsT

Hand over hand and over the backs. Enemy the Wind, The. Thomas Lux. SP-LuxT

Hand penetrated an abyss of shadow, The. Hand and the Shadow, The. Richard Eberhart. CP-EberR

Hand That Signed the Paper, The. Dylan Thomas. CP-ThomD

Hand Trick, The. James Laughlin. CP-LaugJ

Handclap. Muriel Rukeyser. CP-RukeM

Handed Down. Amy Clampitt. CP-ClamA

Handfuls. Carl Sandburg. CP-SandC

Handing Down, The. Wendell Berry. CP-BerrW

Handkerchiefs of Khaibar Khan, The. John Updike. CP-UpdiJ

Hands. W. H. Auden. CP-AudeW

Hands. Robinson Jeffers. CP-JefR2

Hands. Archibald MacLeish. CP-MacLA

Hands. Yannis Ritsos. SP-RitsY, tr. by Edmund Keeley

Hands, The. Erich Arendt. CP-MuldP, tr. by Paul Muldoon

Hands, The. Robert Creeley. CP-CreeR

Hands, The. W. S. Merwin. SP-MerwW

Hands and Eyes. Louis MacNeice. CP-MacNL

Hands, do what you're bid. Balloon of the Mind, The. William Butler Yeats. CP-YeatW

Hands explore tentatively, The. Feel of Hands, The. Thom Gunn. CP-GunnT

Hands filled with tenderness. Solitude. Rainer Maria Rilke. CP-RilkFr, tr. by A. Poulin, Jr.

Hands, hard and veined all over. Orders for the Day. Theodore Roethke. CP-RoetT

Hands must touch and handle many things, The. New Man, The. Jones Very. CP-VeryJ

Hands of God, The. D. H. Lawrence. CP-LawrD

Hands of Jeanne-Marie, The. Arthur Rimbaud. CP-RimbA, tr. by Martin Sorrell

Hands of the Betrothed, The. D. H. Lawrence. CP-LawrD

Hands of the Blindman, The. Tess Gallagher. SP-GallT

Hands of the clock go 'round, The. Working Day, The. Kenneth Rexroth. CP-RexrK

Hands of Venus, The. Jaroslav Seifert. SP-SeifJ, tr. by George Gibian

Hands off! thou tithe-fat plunderer! play. Elliott. John Greenleaf Whittier. CP-WhitJ

Handshake, the Entrance, The. John Berryman. CP-BerrJ

Handsome and clever and he went cruising. E. E. Cummings. CP-CummE

Handsome and self-absorbed young man, The. True Love at Last. D. H. Lawrence. CP-LawrD

Handsome fullgrown child, he seems, A. Fellow Passengers. Denise Levertov. SP-LeveDL

Handsome Heart, The. Gerard Manley Hopkins. CP-HopkG
  (But tell me, child, your choice, your fancy; what to buy.) CP-HopkG

Handsome is the peasant sprawling under the shadow of the plane tree. Summer Sorrow. Yannis Ritsos. SP-RitsY, tr. by Kimon Friar

Handsome men wearing red ties walk past my window. Love. Grace Paley. CP-PalGC

Handsome, sea-born lads on gravel roads. Encounters. Yannis Ritsos. SP-RitsY, tr. by Kostas Myrsiades

Handy Mole who plied no shovel, A. Christina Georgina Rossetti. CP-RosC3

Hang-Glider's Daughter, The. Marilyn Hacker. SP-HackM

Hang it all, Ezra Pound, there is only the one sestina. Sestina: "Hang it all, Ezra Pound, there is only the one sestina." Donald Hall. CP-HallD

Hang it all, Robert Browning. Canto 2: "Hang it all, Robert Browning." Ezra Pound. SP-PounE Fr. Cantos.

Hang up brave tapestries. Wallace Stevens. CP-StevWP

Hang up Hooks, and shears [or Sheers] to scare. Another Charme for Stables. Robert Herrick. CP-HerrR

Hang up those dull, and envious fools. Another. In Defense of Their Inconstancy [or Inconstancie]. A Song. Ben Jonson. CP-JonsB

Hanged / if n / y in a real hot spell. E. E. Cummings. CP-CummE

Hanged Man, The. Kenneth Rexroth. CP-RexrK

Hanged man on the gallows, The. Randall Jarrell. CP-JarrR

Hanged Men Dance. Arthur Rimbaud. CP-RimbA, tr. by Martin Sorrell

Hanging around the house each day. Mailman as Cancer Patient, The. Raymond Carver. CP-CarvR

Hanging from the beam. Portent, The. Herman Melville. SP-MelvH

Hanging Man, The. Sylvia Plath. CP-PlatS

Hanging of the Mouse, The. Elizabeth Bishop. CP-BishE

Hangman. Ai. SP-Ai

Hangman, The. Anne Sexton. CP-SextA

Hangman at Home, The. Carl Sandburg. CP-SandC

Hangman points out, The. Articulation & Class. Yusef Komunyakaa. CP-KomuY

Hangman's Great Hands, The. Kenneth Patchen. CP-PatcK

Hangman's Oak. Edna St. Vincent Millay. CP-MillE

Hangover and Sick Leave. Charles Bukowski. SP-BukC2

Hangs by a thread. Two Riddles. Charles Simic. SP-SimiC; SP-SimiCE

Hangs heavy / down into trees: dawn. Haze. James Schuyler. CP-SchuJ

Hannibal. Robert Frost. CP-FrosR

Hannibal won indeed, yet failed to take. Petrarch. CP-Petra, tr. by J. G. Nichols

Hanoi Hannah. Yusef Komunyakaa. CP-KomuY

Hanoi Market, The. Yusef Komunyakaa. CP-KomuY

Hanoverian silverware, this jug. On Generous Lines. Donald Davie. CP-DaviDC

Hans Euler. Johann Gabriel Seidl. CP-MerG2

Hans, there are moments when the whole mind. Dedication: "Hans, there are moments when the whole mind." James Merrill. SP-MerrJ

Hansel and Gretel. Anne Sexton. CP-SextA

Hansome you are, and Proper you will be. To the Most Comely and Proper M. Elizabeth Finch. Robert Herrick. CP-HerrR

Hanusevich wants Nina. But why? Why? Mister Hanusevich. Czeslaw Milosz. CP-MiloCN, tr. by Robert Hass

Hap. Thomas Hardy. CP-HardT

Hap happeth oft unlooked for. Sir Thomas Wyatt. CP-WyatT

Hapax. Kenneth Rexroth. CP-RexrK

Happen. How Everything Happens (Based on a Study of the Wave). May Swenson. SP-SwenM

Happen you come on your own. Seven Sides and Seven Syllables. Edouard J. Maunick. CP-KizeC, tr. by Carolyn Kizer

Happenings Elsewhere. Czeslaw Milosz. CP-MiloCN, tr. by Robert Hass

Happens Every Day. W. S. Merwin. SP-MerwWF

Happenstance. Rita Dove. SP-DoveR

Happenstance, / a storyline between the surf's. Continuo, The. Olga Broumas. SP-BrouO

Happenstance reveals its tricks. Séance. Wisława Szymborska. SP-SzymW, tr. by Stanislaw Barańczak and Clare Cavanagh

Happiest Day, the Happiest Hour, The. Edgar Allan Poe. CP-PoeEd

Happily I had a sight. Vow to Venus, A. Robert Herrick. CP-HerrR

Happiness. Jorge Luis Borges. SP-BorgJ, tr. by Stephen Kessler

Happiness. Raymond Carver. CP-CarvR

Happiness. John Ciardi. CP-CiarJ

Happiness. Louise Glück. SP-GlucL

Happiness. Yusef Komunyakaa. CP-KomuY

Happiness. Czeslaw Milosz. CP-MiloC; CP-MiloCN, tr. by Richard Lourie

Happiness. Mary Oliver. SP-OlivM

Happiness. Wilfred Owen. CP-OwenW

Happiness. Grace Paley.

Happiness. Carl Sandburg. CP-SandC

Happiness. Stevie Smith. CP-SmitS

Happiness achieved, for you. Eugenio Montale. CP-MontE, tr. by Jonathan Galassi

Happiness in Cornwall. Raymond Carver. CP-CarvR

Happiness Makes Up in Height for What It Lacks in Length. Robert Frost. CP-FrosR

Happiness of youth, The. Year 1934, The. Jaroslav Seifert. SP-SeifJ, tr. by Ewald Osers

"Happiness" without a cause, The. Emily Dickinson. SP-DickE

Happinesse. Robert Herrick. CP-HerrR

Happinesse to Hospitalitie, or a Hearty Wish to Good House-Keeping. Robert Herrick. CP-HerrR

Happy and sad, together and yet sole. Petrarch. CP-Petra, tr. by J. G. Nichols

Happy are men who yet before they are killed. Insensibility. Wilfred Owen. CP-OwenW

Happy are the mad for they are able. To the Mad Poets. Richard Eberhart. CP-

EberR

Happy are those who have never tasted evil. Sophocles. CP-SpenS *Fr.* Antigone.

Happy Cat, The. Randall Jarrell. CP-JarrR

Happy Encounter, The. Walter De la Mare. CP-DeLaW

Happy End. Charles Simic. SP-SimiC; SP-SimiCE

Happy Ending. W. H. Auden. CP-AudeW

Happy Ending of Mr. Train, The. Ogden Nash. CP-NashO

Happy Families. Louis MacNeice. CP-MacNL

Happy-Go-Lucky's Wolf Skull Dream Mask. Yusef Komunyakaa. CP-KomuY

Happy, happy glowing fire! Song of Four Faeries. John Keats. CP-KeatJ

Happy he to whom fortune gives two beauties. Carmina Gemina. James Laughlin. CP-LaugJ

Happy he whose eyes have view'd. Boethius. CP-JohnS *Fr.* Consolation of Philosophy, The ("De Consolacione Philosophie").

Happy Home, The. Samuel Taylor Coleridge. CP-ColeS

Happy Husband, The. Samuel Taylor Coleridge. CP-ColeS

Happy in sleep, content to lie around. Petrarch. CP-Petra, *tr. by* J. G. Nichols

Happy in the sparkling green. Lament of Catherine Howard, Fifth Queen of Henry VIII. Marya Alexandrovna Zaturenska. SP-ZatuM

Happy is England! I Could be Content. John Keats. CP-KeatJ

Happy is he, that from all business clear. Praises of a Country Life, The. Horace. CP-JonsB; SP-JonsB, *tr. by* Ben Jonson *Fr.* Epodes.

Happy Life of a Country Parson, The. Alexander Pope. CP-PopeA

Happy lip—breaks sudden, A. Emily Dickinson. CP-DickE

Happy Little Cripple, The. James Whitcomb Riley. CP-RileJ

Happy love, this. Robert Creeley. CP-CreeR

Happy Man, The. Robert Creeley. CP-CreeR

Happy Marriage, The. Archibald MacLeish.
"And he had used love's dream of love before." CP-MacLA
"Beauty is that Medusa's head." CP-MacLA
"Beside her in the dark the chime." CP-MacLA
"But she was both,—she was both loved and love." CP-MacLA
"First I will tell you something of these two." CP-MacLA
"He had used love or lust or what's between." CP-MacLA
"He leans against the window-sill." CP-MacLA
"Here, O wanderer, here is the hill and the harbor." CP-MacLA
"Humid air precipitates, The." CP-MacLA
"Love is the way that lovers never know." CP-MacLA
"No doubt he'd once had eyes to see." CP-MacLA
"O hide your eyes." CP-MacLA
"Passing her in the day he had but dared." CP-MacLA
"She was herself, not his, not anything." CP-MacLA
"They say they are one flesh." CP-MacLA
"Things he had loved because he knew them lost." CP-MacLA
"This was not love but love's true negative." CP-MacLA
"Throwing a careless pebble in the lake." CP-MacLA
"Under an elm tree where the river reaches." CP-MacLA
"Well, he was drunk. That much was clear." CP-MacLA
"White of her Colonial, The." CP-MacLA
"Whom do you love, she said, when you look out." CP-MacLA

Happy me! o happy sheepe! Bible, *O.T. See* Lord is my shepherd; I shall not want, The

Happy Men and Women. Rainer Maria Rilke. CP-RilkFr, *tr. by* A. Poulin, Jr.

Happy New Year. Lorine Niedecker. CP-NiedL

Happy on Heimaey. Hugh MacDiarmid. SP-MacDH

Happy people die whole, they are all dissolved in a moment, they have had what they wanted. Post Mortem. Robinson Jeffers. CP-JefR1

Happy Poets, The. James Laughlin. CP-LaugJ

Happy schoolchildren. Spring Song. Federico García Lorca. CP-GarcF, *tr. by* Catherine Brown

Happy season of my early prime, The. Petrarch. CP-Petra, *tr. by* J. G. Nichols

Happy Solitude—Unhappy Men. Jeanne Marie Bouvier de la Motte Guyon. CP-CowpW, *tr. by* William Cowper

Happy songster! perch'd above. On the Grasshopper. *Unknown.* CP-CowpW

Happy the feeling from the bosom thrown. Sonnet: To———. William Wordsworth. CP-WorW2

Happy the Man. Joachim Du Bellay. CP-WilbR

Happy the man who has made harbor. Landing. Primo Levi. CP-LeviP, *tr. by* Ruth Feldman *and* Brian Swann

Happy the man who, journeying far and wide. Happy the Man. Joachim Du Bellay. CP-WilbR

Happy the man who, like Ulysses, goodly ways. Sonnet from the Book of Regrets. Joachim Du Bellay. CP-StevWP, *tr. by* Wallace Stevens

Happy the man who loves what / he has and worked for it also. Puritan Ethos, The. Robert Creeley. CP-CreeR

Happy the man whose wish and care. Ode on Solitude. Alexander Pope. CP-PopeA

Happy Three, The. Theodore Roethke. CP-RoetT

Happy time. Each walled town was a big family which fear kept together. At the Gates of Aerea. René Char. CP-MertT

Happy to have these fish! Catch, The. Raymond Carver. CP-CarvR

Happy Townland, The. William Butler Yeats. CP-YeatW

Happy verses! that were prest. To Ethelinda. Christopher Smart. SP-SmarC

Happy, who like Ulysses or that lord. Heureux Qui, comme Ulysse, a Fait un Beau Voyage. Joachim Du Bellay. CP-ChesG, *tr. by* G. K. Chesterton

Happy Xmas, A. G. K. Chesterton. CP-ChesG

Happy Xmas, A ("God rest you, merry gentlemen"). G. K. Chesterton. CP-ChesG

Happy Xmas, A ("Good King Wenceslas looked out"). G. K. Chesterton. CP-ChesG

Happy Xmas, A ("Observe the Convalescent Child"). G. K. Chesterton. CP-ChesG

Happy Xmas, A ("There came to Rhoda's Christmas feast"). G. K. Chesterton. CP-ChesG

Happy Xmas, A ("This Infant used to howl and yell"). G. K. Chesterton. CP-ChesG

Happy Xmas, A ("Upon me and my mackintosh"). G. K. Chesterton. CP-ChesG

Happy young friends, sit by me. How the Robin Came. John Greenleaf Whittier. CP-WhitJ

Happy youth! that shalt possess[e]. To My Cousin (C. R.) Marrying My Lady (A.). Thomas Carew. CP-CareT

Happy's that man, to whom God gives. None Truly Happy Here. Robert Herrick. CP-HerrR

Harbingers are come. See, see their mark, The. Forerunners, The. George Herbert. CP-HerbG

Harbor, The. Carl Sandburg. CP-WilbR

Harbour, The. Derek Walcott. CP-WalcD

Harbour Bridge, The. Thomas Hardy. CP-HardT

Hard. Heather McHugh. SP-McHuH

Hard are the two first staires unto a Crowne. Beginning, Difficult. Robert Herrick. CP-HerrR

Hard as hurdle arms, with a broth of goldish flue. Harry Ploughman. Gerard Manley Hopkins. CP-HopkG

Hard-Boiled Conservatives. D. H. Lawrence. CP-LawrD

Hard-boiled egg cupped by the marble cold, A. Lines for the Winter Recess. Joseph Brodsky. CP-BrodJ

Hard, chilly colors. Conquest. William Carlos Williams. CP-WilW1

Hard cold fire of the northerner, The. Belfast. Louis MacNeice. CP-MacNL

Hard Core of Beauty, The. William Carlos Williams. CP-WilW2

Hard Daddy. Langston Hughes. CP-HughL; CP-HughL1

Hard Death, A. May Sarton. SP-SartM

Hard Facts. Robert Stock. SP-StocR

Hard. Hard. As she-cat whelped in desert mountains. Carmen 60. Catullus. CP-ZukLS *Fr.* Carmina.

Hard, hard to learn—. Crystal Maze, A. William Carlos Williams. CP-WilW1

Hard heart of the weathervane. Fallen Weathervane, The. Federico García Lorca. CP-GarcF, *tr. by* Catherine Brown

Hard hook-finger clutching down to the bottom, The. Creature Has a Purpose, The. Thomas Lux. SP-LuxT

Hard is it to persuade the public mind of its plain duty & true interest. Ralph Waldo Emerson. CP-EmerR

Hard is my pillow. Princess Recalls Her One Adventure, The. Edna St. Vincent Millay. CP-MillE

Hard is the doubt, and difficult to deeme. Book 4, Canto 9. Edmund Spenser. CP-Spens *Fr.* Faerie Queene, The.

Hard is the life when naked and unhouzed. Salisbury Plain. William Wordsworth. MW-WorW

Hard journey—yes, A. Hayden Carruth. CP-CarHS *Fr.* Clay Hill Anthology, The.

Hard Listener, The. William Carlos Williams. CP-WilW1; CP-WilW2

Hard Love Rock. Audre Lorde. SP-LordA

Hard Love Rock II. Audre Lorde. SP-LordA

Hard Luck. Langston Hughes. CP-HughL; CP-HughL1

Hard men, red-eyed. Sharm A-Sheikh. Yehuda Amichai. SP-AmicYL, *tr. by* Benjamin Harshav *and* Barbara Harshav

Hard-on Death. Alan Dugan. CP-DugaA

Hard Part, The. C. K. Williams. CP-WillC

Hard rain pummels the Avenida da Liberdade. Historical Romance. Sam Hamill. SP-HamiS

Hard sand breaks, The. Hermes of the Ways. "H. D." CP-DoolH

Hard seeds of hate I planted. Blight. Edna St. Vincent Millay. CP-MillE

Hard Structure of the World, The. Richard Eberhart. CP-EberR

Hard task! exclaim the undisciplined, to lean. At Bologna, in Remembrance of the Late Insurrections, 1837, Continued: "Hard task! exclaim the undisciplined, to lean." William Wordsworth. CP-WorW2

Hard Times. William Carlos Williams. CP-WilW2

Hard times loom in Texas. 1931. Yusef Komunyakaa. CP-KomuY

Hard to Be Moving among Them. Aleksandr Aleksandrovich Blok. SP-BlokA, tr. by Peter France and Jon Stallworthy

Hard to believe. Now. Robert Creeley. SP-CreeR

Hard to Translate. James Laughlin. CP-LaugJ

Hard Up. Yusef Komunyakaa. CP-KomuY

Hard up for better lays with. Civics. A. R. Ammons. CP-AmmoA

Hard water (water-). Afica. Charles Olson. CP-OlsoC

Hard Way, The. Robert Lowell. SP-LoweR

Hard Weather. George Meredith. CP-MerG1

Hard white land, The. Returning the Borrowed Road. Yusef Komunyakaa. CP-KomuY

Hardcastle Crags. Sylvia Plath. CP-PlatS

Harden now thy tyred hart, with more than flinty rage. Catullus. See Break off / fallen Catullus

Hardening into Print. Richard Eberhart. CP-EberR

Harder lesson, to learn continence, A. Book 2, Canto 6. Edmund Spenser. CP-Spens Fr. Faerie Queene, The.

Harder perhaps than a newengland bed. E. E. Cummings. CP-CummE

Hardest headlands / Gravel down, The. La Rose des Vents. Richard Wilbur. CP-WilbR

Hardly a day passes I don't think of him. Robert Schumann. Mary Oliver. SP-OlivM

Hardly a one but here he is improved. After the Match. Donald Davie. CP-DaviDC

Hardly anything flies north these days. September Drift. A. R. Ammons. CP-AmmoA

Hardly ever, now, has a human face. Human Face, The. D. H. Lawrence. CP-LawrD

Hardness of Light, The. Donald Davie. CP-DaviDC

Hardning of Hearts. Robert Herrick. CP-HerrR

Hardon Blues. Allen Ginsberg. SP-GinsA

Hardship Put upon Ladies, The. Jonathan Swift. CP-SwifJ

Hardweed Path Going. A. R. Ammons. CP-AmmoA

Hardy Garden, The. Edna St. Vincent Millay. CP-MillE

Hardy Perennial. Richard Eberhart. CP-EberR

Hardy, thy brain is valiant, 'tis confessed. To Brain-Hardy. Ben Jonson. CP-JonsB; SP-JonsB

Hare, A. Walter De la Mare. CP-DeLaW

Hare in the Data Processing Centre, A. Hans Magnus Enzensberger. SP-EnzeH

Hare, The. Ted Hughes. SP-HughTN

Hark, All You Ladies [That Do Sleep]. Thomas Campion. CP-CampT (Canto Primo.) CP-CampT

Hark—hark—from out the thickest fog. Shrike, The. Henry David Thoreau. CP-ThorH

Hark! hark! I think I hear the horn. Hunting Song, A. Unknown, sometimes at. to Thomas Sheridan. CP-SherT

Hark! Hark! / The dogs do bark! Hibiscus and Salvia Flowers. D. H. Lawrence. CP-LawrD

Hark hark the lark, no it is not a lark, it is a robin singing like a lark. Who Called That Robin a Piccolo Player? Ogden Nash. CP-NashO

Hark, hearer, hear what I do; lend a thought now, make believe. Epithalamion: "Hark, hearer, hear what I do; lend a thought now, make believe." Gerard Manley Hopkins. CP-HopkG

Hark, how my Celia, with the choice. Celia Singing. Thomas Carew. CP-CareT

Hark, how the birds do sing. Man's Medley. George Herbert. CP-HerbG

Hark how the Mower Damon sung. Damon the Mower. Andrew Marvell. CP-MarvA

Hark in the Dusk! D. H. Lawrence. CP-LawrD

Hark, Martha! some one knocks without; go, let him in, I pray! Hans Euler. Johann Gabriel Seidl. CP-MerG2

Hark, plaintful ghosts! Infernal furies, hark. Sir Philip Sidney. SP-SidnP Fr. Arcadia.

Hark, some wild trumpeter, some strange musician. Mystic Trumpeter, The. Walt Whitman. CP-WhitW

Hark! the Alleluias of the great salvation. Christina Georgina Rossetti. CP-RosC2

Hark, the mavis' evening sang. Ca' the Yowes [to the Knowes]. Robert Burns. CP-BurnR

Hark! the owlet flaps his wings. Fragment: Omens. Percy Bysshe Shelley. CP-ShelP

Hark! 'Tis the Thrush, Undaunted, Undeprest. William Wordsworth. CP-WorW2

Hark to the locusts in their shrill armadas. I Happen to Know. Ogden Nash. CP-NashO

Hark to the song of greeting! the tall trees. Summer. Christina Georgina Rossetti. CP-RosC3

Hark to the whimper of the sea-gull. Sea-Gull, The. Ogden Nash. CP-NashO

Hark what, now loud, now low, the pining flute complains. Flute, The. Jelaluddin Rumi. CP-EmerR

Harke, al[l] you ladies that do sleep [or doo sleepe]. Thomas Campion. See Hark, All You Ladies [That Do Sleep]

Harke shee is called, the parting houre is come. Hymn in the Assumption. Richard Crashaw. CP-CrasR

Harlem ("Here on the edge of hell"). Langston Hughes. CP-HughL; CP-HughL3 (Puzzled.) CP-HughL2

Harlem ("What happens to a dream deferred?"). Langston Hughes. CP-HughL; CP-HughL3 Fr. Lenox Avenue Mural.

Harlem Dance Hall. Langston Hughes. CP-HughL; CP-HughL2

Harlem Hopscotch. Maya Angelou. SP-AngeM

Harlem / Knows a song. Harlem Night. Langston Hughes. CP-HughL; CP-HughL2

Harlem Night. Langston Hughes. CP-HughL; CP-HughL2

Harlem Night Club. Langston Hughes. CP-HughL; CP-HughL1

Harlem Night Song. Langston Hughes. CP-HughL; CP-HughL1

Harlem / Sent him home. Deceased. Langston Hughes. CP-HughL; CP-HughL2

Harlem Sweeties. Langston Hughes. CP-HughL; CP-HughL2

Harlequin. Federico García Lorca. CP-GarcF, tr. by Alan S. Trueblood Fr. Theories.

Harlequin speaks by the moon's light. Variations on a theme. Josephine Jacobsen. CP-JacoJ

Harley, the nation's great support. Horace, Epistle VII, Book I: Imitated and Addressed to the Earl of Oxford. Jonathan Swift. CP-SwifJ

Harley's Swans. Raymond Carver. CP-CarvR

Harlie. James Whitcomb Riley. CP-RileJ

Harlot squatted, The. Jesus Raises Up the Harlot. Anne Sexton. CP-SextA; SP-SextA

Harlot's House, The. Oscar Wilde. CP-WildO

Harm. C. K. Williams. SP-WillC

Harm of Years is on him, The. Emily Dickinson. CP-DickE

Harmless Streets. Tess Gallagher. SP-GallT

Harmodius and Aristogeiton. Kenneth Rexroth. CP-RexrK

Harmonica Humdrums. Carl Sandburg. CP-SandC

Harmonies. Thomas Kinsella. CP-KinsT

Harmonious first and last. Bits and Pieces. Donald Davie. CP-DaviDC

Harmony. Federico García Lorca. CP-GarcF, tr. by Jerome Rothenberg Fr. Newton.

Harmony of colours, features, grace, The. Epitaph on the Lady S.: Wife of Sir W. S. Thomas Carew. CP-CareT

Harnessed and zipped on a bright. Hazard's Optimism. William Meredith. SP-MereW

Harold. David Ignatow. SP-IgnaD

Harold, are you asleep? Harold's Leap. Stevie Smith. CP-SmitS

Harold's Leap. Stevie Smith. CP-SmitS

Harold's Song. Sir Walter Scott. See Lay of the Last Minstrel, The

Harp at Nature's advent strung, The. Worship of Nature, The. John Greenleaf Whittier. CP-WhitJ

Harp has fallen from the master's hand, The. Bryant. James Whitcomb Riley. CP-RileJ

Harp of Aengus, The. William Butler Yeats. CP-YeatW

Harp of the minstrel has never a tone, The. James Whitcomb Riley. CP-RileJ

Harp of the North, Farewell! The Hills Grow Dark. Sir Walter Scott. SP-ScotW Fr. Lady of the Lake, The.

Harp of Wales, The. Tennessee Williams. CP-WillT

Harp of wild and dream-like strain. Emily Jane Brontë. CP-BronE

Harp Song of the Dane Women. Rudyard Kipling. CP-KiplR Fr. Puck of Pook's Hill.

Harp, The. Ralph Waldo Emerson. CP-EmerR

Harp the Monarch Minstrel Swept, The. Lord Byron. CP-Byron

Harper had grown old, The. His voice was choked sounding. Omar and the Old Poet. Jelaluddin Rumi. SP-Rumi, tr. by Coleman Barks

Harper, The. James Whitcomb Riley. CP-RileJ

Harps. Clarence Major. SP-MajoC

Harps in Heaven. Nicholas Vachel Lindsay. CP-LindV

Harps the harps, The. Silence before Harvest, The. W. S. Merwin. SP-MerwW

Harried / earth is swept, The. Wind Increases, The. William Carlos Williams. CP-WilW1

Harriet. Robert Lowell. SP-LoweR

Harriet Beecher Stowe. Paul Laurence Dunbar. CP-DunbP

Harriet! To see such Circumspection. To Harriet. Lord Byron. CP-Byron

Harriet's Dream. Robert Lowell. SP-LoweR

Harrison loves my country too. Case for Jefferson, A. Robert Frost. CP-FrosR

Harrison Street Court. Carl Sandburg. CP-SandC

Harrow, The. Donald Davie. CP-DaviDC

Harrowed by These Apprehensions He Resolved to Commit Himself to the Mercy of the Storm. Kenneth Patchen. CP-PatcK

Harry. Robert Creeley. CP-CreeR

Harry has written / all he knows. Names. Robert Creeley. CP-CreeR

Harry of Hereford, Lancaster, and Derby. School Play, The. James Merrill. SP-MerrJ

Harry, our King in England, from London town is gone. King Henry VII. And the Shipwrights. Rudyard Kipling. CP-KiplR

Harry Ploughman. Gerard Manley Hopkins. CP-HopkG

Harry Semen. Hugh MacDiarmid. SP-MacDH

Harry, whose tuneful[l] and well-measured [or well-measur'd] song. To Mr. H. Lawes on His Airs. John Milton. CP-MiltJ

Harsh Climate. Charles Simic. SP-SimiC; SP-SimiCE

Harsh Country, The. Theodore Roethke. CP-RoetT

Harsh Judgment, The. Stanley Kunitz. CP-KunSC

Harsh-voiced it was, and shrill and high. Old Hand-Organ, The. James Whitcomb Riley. CP-RileJ

Harsh World That Lashest Me. Countee Cullen. CP-CullC

Harsk, Harsk. Carl Sandburg. CP-SandC

Harsk, harsk, the wind blows tonight. Harsk, Harsk. Carl Sandburg. CP-SandC

Hart Crane. Robert Creeley. CP-CreeR

Hart Crane 2. Robert Creeley. CP-CreeR

Hart-Leap Well. William Wordsworth. CP-WorW1; MW-WorW

Hart's-Horn Tree, near Penrith. William Wordsworth. CP-WorW2

Harum-scarum haze on the Pollock streets / The fleet drifts in on an angry tidal wave. Lines for Lauren Owen. Ted Berrigan. SP-BerrT Fr. Sonnets, The.

Harum-scarum haze on the Pollock streets / Where Snow White sleeps among the silent dwarfs. Ted Berrigan. SP-BerrT Fr. Sonnets, The.

Harun Omar and Master Hafiz. Puella Mea. E. E. Cummings. CP-CummE

Harvard Stadium. Richard Eberhart. CP-EbcrR

Harvard, Yale, don't have problems getting bodies. Haitian Cadavers. Thomas Lux. SP-LuxT

Harvest. Carl Sandburg. CP-SandC

Harvest. Charles Tomlinson. SP-TomlC

Harvest, The ("Plant it springs it rears its drooping head, The"). Jones Very. CP-VeryJ

Harvest, The ("They love me not, who at my table eat"). Jones Very. CP-VeryJ

Harvest approaches with its bustling day. August. John Clare. SP-ClarJ Fr. Shepherd's [or Shepheards] Calendar, The.

Harvest Bow, The. Seamus Heaney. SP-HeanSO

Harvest Festival: at Ozleworth. Charles Tomlinson. CP-TomlC

Harvest Home. John Dryden. SP-DrydJ Fr. King Arthur.

Harvest Home, A. Howard Nemerov. CP-NemeH

Harvest Moon, The. Ted Hughes. SP-HughTN

Harvest of learning I have reaped. Kathleen Jessie Raine. SP-RainK

Harvest of the Void. Yannis Ritsos. SP-RitsY, tr. by Minas Savvas

Harvest shall flourish in wintry weather, The. Merlins Prophecy. William Blake. CP-BlakW

Harvest Sunset. Carl Sandburg. CP-SandC

Harvest-Supper, The. Thomas Hardy. CP-HardT

Harvests. Dan Pagis. SP-PagiD, tr. by Stephen Mitchell

Harvests with abundance fill the land, The. National Thanksgiving, The. Jones Very. CP-VeryJ

Has All. Emily Dickinson. SP-DickE

Has Anybody Seen My Noumenon? Ogden Nash. CP-NashO

Has anybody seen the great Sea Serpent? Song of the Great Sea Serpent, The. G. K. Chesterton. CP-ChesG

Has anyone ever earned the respect of sand? On Organization. Andrei Codrescu. SP-CodrA

Has auld Kilmarnock [or K*********] seen the Deil? Tam Samson's Elegy. Robert Burns. CP-BurnR

Has bath and shave. Homecoming. Derek Mahon. CP-MahoD

Has been designed by the master. House of Light, The. James Laughlin. CP-LaugJ

Has-Been, The. Carl Sandburg. CP-SandC

Has he not led us into these waste seas. Shadowy Waters, The. William Butler Yeats. CP-YeatW

Has it been only two years. Lost Tribe, The. Paul Muldoon. CP-MuldP

Has its wonders too which. Sorrow. James Laughlin. CP-LaugJ

Has Nature a new sympathy with man. Change in the Seasons. Jones Very. CP-VeryJ

Has no one said those daring. Two Years Later. William Butler Yeats. CP-YeatW

Has not altered. Spenser's Ireland. Marianne Craig Moore. CP-MoorM

Has not yet been cut. Stone, The. Ted Hughes. SP-HughTN

Has she forgotten? On this very May. James Whitcomb Riley. CP-RileJ

Has spread its wings. Owl of Minerva, The. James Laughlin. CP-LaugJ

Has the sum. Louis Zukofsky. CP-ZukLS

Has thine enemy slandered thy house. Hafiz. CP-EmerR Fr. Odes.

Has Your Soul Sipped? Wilfred Owen. CP-OwenW

Haschish, The. John Greenleaf Whittier. CP-WhitJ

Hasn't the sky? Returned from moving the other. Clepsydra. John Ashbery. SP-AshbJ

Hast Du Dich Verirrt? Stevie Smith. CP-SmitS

Hast ever seen a man. Epigramme: "Hast ever seen a man." William Carlos Williams. CP-WilW1

Hast Never Come to Thee an Hour. Walt Whitman. CP-WhitW

Hast thou a charm to stay the morning-star. Hymn before Sunrise, in the Vale of Chamouni. Samuel Taylor Coleridge. CP-ColeS; MW-ColeS

Hast thou a friend? Thou hast indeed. On a True Friend. Unknown. CP-CowpW

Hast thou attempted greatnesse? then go on. Regression Spoiles Resolution. Robert Herrick. CP-HerrR

Hast thou begun an act? ne're then give o're. Perseverance. Robert Herrick. CP-HerrR

Hast thou but faith thou shalt the mountain bid. Faith ("Hast thou but faith thou shalt the mountain bid"). Jones Very. CP-VeryJ

Hast thou ever heard the voice of nature. Jones Very. CP-VeryJ

Hast thou from the caves of Golconda a gem. On Receiving a Curious Shell, and a Copy of Verses, from the Same Ladies. John Keats. CP-KeatJ

Hast— / thou hast drunken. Benedicta. Paul Celan. SP-CelaP, tr. by John Felstiner

Hast thou named all the birds without a gun? Forbearance. Ralph Waldo Emerson. CP-EmerR

Hast thou not seen, officious with delight. Pedro Calderón de la Barca. CP-ShelP Fr. Cisma de Inglaterra.

Hast thou stolen aught from hunger, or in thirst. Unrevealed, The. Jones Very. CP-VeryJ

Hast thou then nought wiser to bring. Catechism, The. Walter De la Mare. CP-DeLaW

Haste Hurtfull. Robert Herrick. CP-HerrR

Haste is unhappy: what we Rashly do. Haste Hurtfull. Robert Herrick. CP-HerrR

Haste thee harsh verse as fast as thy lame measure. To Mr T. W ("Haste thee harsh verse as fast as thy lame measure"). John Donne. CP-DonnJ; MW-DonnJ

Hasten slowly, the sundial said. Mox Note. Heather McHugh. SP-McHuH

Hasten to your own gun, to your own star, to your own tribe. But the Images of His Former Dreams Still Haunted Him. Kenneth Patchen. CP-PatcK

Hastening years fall slow, The. Christmas. Laura Riding Jackson. CP-RidiL

Hastily Adam our driver swallowed a curse in the darkness. Bother, The. Rudyard Kipling. CP-KiplR Fr. Muse among the Motors, The.

Hastings! I knew thee young, and of a mind. To Warren Hastings. William Cowper. CP-CowpW

Hat on the table, The. Headdress. Rita Dove. SP-DoveR

Hat Salesman and a Capable Ruler, A. Chuang Tzu. CP-MertT

Hat, The. Raymond Carver. CP-CarvR

Hat, The. Stevie Smith. CP-SmitS

Hatband, The. Thomas Hardy. CP-HardT

Hatchery's old bachelor, Henry Manley, The. Food Chain, The. Maxine W. Kumin. SP-KumiM

Hate. Charles Olson. CP-OlsoC

Hate. Carl Sandburg. CP-SandC

Hate blows a bubble of despair into. E. E. Cummings. CP-CummE; SP-CummE

Hate is only one of many responses. Poem: "Hate is only one of many responses." Frank O'Hara. SP-OharF

Hate makes my head light. Against a Dark Field. Heather McHugh. SP-McHuH

Hate-Song, A. Percy Bysshe Shelley. CP-ShelP

Hate the people of this village. People of the Other Village, The. Thomas Lux. SP-LuxT

Hate whom ye list for I care not. Sir Thomas Wyatt. CP-WyatT

Hateful are those false themes of speculation. Sonnet: "Hateful are those false themes of speculation." George Meredith. CP-MerG2

Hateful cure with hate to heal, A. Sir Philip Sidney. SP-SidnP Fr. Arcadia.

Hateful destinies cloud the eye. Han-shan. CP-ColdM, tr. by Red Pine

Hater he came and sat by a ditch, A. Hate-Song, A. Percy Bysshe Shelley. CP-ShelP

Hath aged winter, fleg'd with feathered raine. Elegy upon the Death of Mr. Stanninow Fellow of Queenes Colledge. Richard Crashaw. CP-CrasR

Hath onely Anger an Omnipotence. Upon the Asse That Bore Our Saviour. Richard Crashaw. CP-CrasR

Hath the Rain a Father? Or Who Hath Begotten the Drops of Dew? Job 38:28. Jones Very. CP-VeryJ

Hating myself, the more I run away. Michelangelo Buonarroti. CP-Miche, tr. by John Frederick Nims

Hatred. Frank O'Hara. SP-OharF

Hatred. Wisława Szymborska. SP-SzymW, tr. by Stanisław Barańczak and Clare Cavanagh

Hatred. Wisława Szymborska. SP-SzymWM, tr. by Marek Lugowski and Joanna Trzeciak

Hatred and vengeance, my eternal portion. Lines Written during a Period of Insanity. William Cowper. CP-CowpW

Hatred of Men with Black Hair. Robert Bly. SP-BlyR

(I hear spokesmen praising Tshombe, and the Portuguese.) SP-BlyR

Hatred of the Old River. Richard Eberhart. CP-EberR

Hats. Carl Sandburg. CP-SandC

Hats. James Schuyler. CP-SchuJ

Hats, The. Gregory Orr. SP-OrrG

Hats are hungry, The. Hats, The. Gregory Orr. SP-OrrG

Hats are innocent, bathed, The. Degas: *The Milliner's Shop*. Adam Zagajewski. SP-ZagaA, *tr. by* Clare Cavanagh

Hats, where do you belong? Hats. Carl Sandburg. CP-SandC

Hattie Bloom. Mary Oliver. SP-OlivM

Hatton's "God of War." George Meredith. CP-MerG2

Haughty Snail-King, The. Nicholas Vachel Lindsay. CP-LindV

Haughty wind tormenting the flag. Flag, The. Rainer Maria Rilke. CP-RilkFr, *tr. by* A. Poulin, Jr. *Fr.* Orchards.

Haul your paper ships on the seared. Eugenio Montale. CP-MontE, *tr. by* Jonathan Galassi

Haunched like a faun, he hooed. Faun. Sylvia Plath. CP-PlatS

Haunted. Walter De la Mare. CP-DeLaW

Haunted Country. Robinson Jeffers. CP-JefR1

Haunted House, The. Robert Graves. CP-GravR

Haunted Landscape. John Ashbery. SP-AshbJ

Haunted Oak, The. Paul Laurence Dunbar. CP-DunbP

Haunted of Beauty, like the marvelous youth. Artist of the Beautiful, An. John Greenleaf Whittier. CP-WhitJ

Haunted Palace, The. Edgar Allan Poe. CP-PoeEd

Haunted Tree, The; To———. William Wordsworth. CP-WorW2

Haunter, The. Thomas Hardy. CP-HardT

Haunting face of poverty, The. Grant Park. Langston Hughes. CP-HughL; CP-HughL1

Haunting Fingers. Thomas Hardy. CP-HardT

Haunting Poe's Baltimore. Allen Ginsberg. CP-GinsA

Haunts. Carl Sandburg. CP-SandC

Haunts me the lugubrious shape. Half-bent Man. Richard Eberhart. CP-EberR

Haunts of my youth farewell! A while I leave. Jones Very. CP-VeryJ

Havana Dreams. Langston Hughes. CP-HughL; CP-HughL2

Havana 1953. Allen Ginsberg. CP-GinsA

Havana Rose. Hart Crane. CP-CranH

Havdalah. Paul Celan. SP-CelaP, *tr. by* John Felstiner

Have a Genuine American Horror-&-Mist on the Rocks. John Berryman. CP-BerrJ

Have a Good Time. W. H. Auden. CP-AudeW

Have a Seat behind the Potted Palm, Sir. Ogden Nash. CP-NashO

Have another helping of blue snow. Bleeding Gums. James Schuyler. CP-SchuJ

Have any like Myself. Emily Dickinson. CP-DickE

Have arrived at this interrogatory. Advertisement. Laura Riding Jackson. CP-RidiL

Have but one God: thy knees were sore. New Decalogue, The. Ambrose Bierce. SP-BierA

Have compassion for everyone you meet. Compassion. Miller Williams. CP-WillM

Have dead men long to wait?— / There is a certain term. What Good Shall My Life Do Me? Christina Georgina Rossetti. CP-RosC2

Have Done With It. D. H. Lawrence. CP-LawrD

Have ever you harked to the jackass wild. Wild Jackass, The. Ogden Nash. CP-NashO

Have fáir fallen, O fáir, fáir have fállen, so déar. Henry Purcell. Gerard Manley Hopkins. CP-HopkG

Have, have ye no regard, all ye. His Saviour[']s Words, Going to the Cross[e]. Robert Herrick. CP-HerrR

Have I a hundred years since or. Jean Sans Terre Leads the Caravan. Iwan Goll. CP-WilW2

Have I broken the smaller tabernacles, O Lord? Broken Tabernacles. Carl Sandburg. CP-SandC

Have I no weapon-word for thee—some message brief and fierce? To the Pending Year. Walt Whitman. CP-WhitW

Have I not blessed [*or* blest] thee? Then go forth; nor fear. To His Book[e]. Robert Herrick. CP-HerrR

Have I not striven, my God, and watched and prayed? Christina Georgina Rossetti. CP-RosC2

Have I not voyaged, friend beloved, with thee. In Quest. John Greenleaf Whittier. CP-WhitJ

Have I seen her? Portrait of a Young Man with a Bad Heart. William Carlos Williams. CP-WilW1

Have I told any man to be a liar for my sake? Questionnaire. Carl Sandburg. CP-SandC

Have Me. Carl Sandburg. CP-SandC

Have me in the blue and the sun. Have Me. Carl Sandburg. CP-SandC

Have men beheld the graces dance. Ben Jonson. CP-JonsB *Fr. Love Restored.*

Have mercy, Lord! Sinner. Langston Hughes. CP-HughL; CP-HughL1

Have mercy, Thou my God; mercy, my God. Out of the Deep. Christina Georgina Rossetti. CP-RosC3

Have mercy upon me, O God, according to thy lovingkindness. Psalm 51: "Have mercy upon me, O God, according to thy lovingkindness." Bible, *O.T.* CP-WyatT *Fr.* Psalms.

Have no wide fears for Earth. Earth. Laura Riding Jackson. CP-RidiL

Have Patience. Christina Georgina Rossetti. CP-RosC3

Have patience, my weary lady. 12 July 1980. Primo Levi. CP-LeviP, *tr. by* Ruth Feldman

Have speciall care, that valiant povertie. Sir Walter Ralegh. CP-RaleW

Have the angels turned discreet! Rainer Maria Rilke. CP-RilkFr, *tr. by* A. Poulin, Jr. *Fr.* Orchards.

"Have, then, thy wish!" He whistled shrill. Ambuscade, The. Sir Walter Scott. SP-ScotW *Fr.* Lady of the Lake, The.

Have unknown words ever sprung to your lips. Demon of Analogy, The. Stéphane Mallarmé. CP-MallS, *tr. by* Henry Weinfield

Have we not gathered here because. Amnesia People. James Tate. SP-TateJ

Have we now not spent three years waiting. Three Years Waiting. Robert Graves. CP-GravR

Have ye beheld (with much delight). Upon the Nipples of Julia's Breast. Robert Herrick. CP-HerrR

Have ye heard of our hunting, o'er mountain and glen. Hunters of Men, The. John Greenleaf Whittier. CP-WhitJ

Have ye no work for a man to do. Henry David Thoreau. CP-ThorH

Have ye seen the caterpillar. Ralph Waldo Emerson. CP-EmerR

Have ye seen the tusky boar. Caradoc. Thomas Gray. CP-GrayT

Have you any old clothes to sell? Old Clothes Man, The. Stanley Kunitz. CP-KunSC

Have you bought a suit at Spand and Spitz? Consider the Lapel, Sir. Ogden Nash. CP-NashO

Have you built your ship of death, oh have you? Ship of Death, The. D. H. Lawrence. CP-LawrD

Have you dug the spill. Harlem Sweeties. Langston Hughes. CP-HughL; CP-HughL2

Have you ever been in a room. Insomnia. Charles Bukowski. SP-BukC2

Have you ever clung to the cliffside while. Questions You Must Learn to Live Past. Robert Penn Warren. CP-WarrR

Have you ever done this with another man. Question of Time, A. Miller Williams. CP-WillM

Have You Ever Eaten Stars? Robert Penn Warren. CP-WarrR

Have you ever forgotten. On the Post Office. Kenneth Rexroth. CP-RexrK

Have you ever heard the rain at night. Rain Spirit Passing. Denise Levertov. SP-LeveDL

Have you ever lost your early start on a six-hundred-mile trip and. I Want a Drink of Water, but Not from the Thermos. Ogden Nash. CP-NashO

Have you ever made a just man? Stephen Crane. CP-CranS

Have you ever noticed how, the. Valuta. Kenneth Rexroth. CP-RexrK

Have you ever seen. Hayden Carruth. CP-CarHS *Fr.* Clay Hill Anthology, The.

Have you ever seen / anything / in your life. Sun, The. Mary Oliver. SP-OlivM

Have you ever walked along a road. Walk, A. G. K. Chesterton. CP-ChesG

Have You Forgotten? Christina Georgina Rossetti. CP-RosC3

Have you forgotten what we were like then. Animals. Frank O'Hara. SP-OharF

Have you got a Brook in your little heart. Emily Dickinson. CP-DickE

Have you heard about Mr. Bratuscha? Cannibal Bratuscha. Muriel Rukeyser. CP-RukeM

Have you heard how I helped the wise. How I Helped the Wise. Shmuel HaNagid. SP-HaNaS, *tr. by* Peter Cole

Have you heard the one about. Alabama 9/15/63. Lucille Clifton. SP-ClifL

Have You Killed Your Man for Today? Kenneth Patchen. CP-PatcK

Have you learn'd lessons only of those who admired you, and were tender with you, and stood aside for you? Stronger Lessons. Walt Whitman. CP-WhitW

Have you listened for the things I have left out? Unsaid. A. R. Ammons. CP-AmmoA

Have you news of my boy Jack? My Boy Jack. Rudyard Kipling. CP-KiplR

Have you no Bananas, simple townsmen all. Song of Bananas, A. Rudyard Kipling. CP-KiplR

Have you not heard the song. Song That Sounds like This, The. James Fenton. SP-FentJ

Have you not noted, in some family. Birth-Bond, The. Dante Gabriel Rossetti. CW-RossD *Fr.* House of Life, The.

Have you not read. Despite and Still. Robert Graves. CP-GravR

Have you not seen in saffron drest, *the Sun*. Impromptu on Reading the Several Motions Made against Mr. Hamilton. Annis Boudinot Stockton. CP-StocA

Have you noticed? Ghosts. Mary Oliver. SP-OlivM

Have you read the biography of Mr. Schwellenbach? You can miss. Strange Case of the Cautious Motorist, The. Ogden Nash. CP-NashO

Have you seen men handed refusals. Carl Sandburg. CP-SandC *Fr.* People, Yes, The.

Have you seen my memory. To Be Sung while Still Looking. W. S. Merwin. SP-

MerwW
Have You Seen This Movie? Allen Ginsberg. CP-GinsA
Have you seen those who build out of instinct. Builders. Yannis Ritsos. SP-RitsY, *tr. by* Kimon Friar
Have you time for a story. Charity Overcoming Envy. Marianne Craig Moore. CP-MoorM
Have you, too, known how tempting pain can be. Curious Man's Dream, A. Charles Baudelaire. CP-BaudC, *tr. by* Walter Martin
Have You Tried Staying Awake? or, They'll Find a Way to Stop That, Too. Ogden Nash. CP-NashO
Haverhill. John Greenleaf Whittier. CP-WhitJ
Having a Coke with You. Frank O'Hara. SP-OharF
Having a wheel and four legs of its own. Grindstone, The. Robert Frost. CP-FrosR
Having abdicated with comparative ease. Half Way. W. H. Auden. CP-AudeW
Having Arrived by Bike at Battery Park. Grace Paley. CP-PalGC
Having avantbiographed the world. En Passant. Andrei Codrescu. SP-CodrA
Having Been Asked "What is a Man?" I Answer. Philip Levine. SP-LeviP
Having been in this place, I will leave it. Identity and Argument for Prayer. Robert Penn Warren. CP-WarrR
Having Been Interstellar. A. R. Ammons. CP-AmmoA
Having been mellow & wonderful so many years. For Allen, on His 60th Birthday. Philip Whalen. SP-WhalP
Having Been Near. Kenneth Patchen. CP-PatcK
Having been tenant long to a rich Lord. Redemption. George Herbert. CP-HerbG
Having bitten on life like a sharp apple. Aubade. "Having bitten on life like a sharp apple." Louis MacNeice. CP-MacNL
Having breakfast in the kitchen. Here I Am. James Laughlin. CP-LaugJ
Having come to this place. This Place in the Ways. Muriel Rukeyser. CP-RukeM
Having crowded once onto the threshold of mortality. Divinities. W. S. Merwin. SP-MerwW
Having crowed the seed. Conception. Galway Kinnell. SP-KinnGN
Having descried the nation. Charles Olson. SP-OlsoC *Fr.* Maximus Poems, The.
Having died / one is at great advantage. Spring Song. William Carlos Williams. CP-WilW1
Having Eaten of the Tree of Knowledge. Eleanor Wilner. SP-WilnE
Having eaten their mackerel, drunk their milk. Sign, The. Randall Jarrell. CP-JarrR
Having Eaten Two Pillows. Alice Walker. CP-WalkA
Having Failed. James Laughlin. CP-LaugJ
Having fed impalpably on the ineluctable. Seeing Is Deceiving. Richard Eberhart. CP-EberR
Having finished the Blue-plate Special. In Schrafft's. W. H. Auden. CP-AudeW
Having given great offence by writing in Prose. Blakes Apology for His Catalogue. William Blake. CP-BlakW
Having Grown Up in Shade of Church and State. Philip Larkin. CP LarkP
Having heard the instruction. One Modern Poet. Carl Sandburg. CP-SandC
Having in the mind thought. Goat, The. William Carlos Williams. CP-WilW2
Having inherited a vigorous mind. My Descendants. William Butler Yeats. CP-YeatW *Fr.* Meditations in Time of Civil War.
Having invented a new Holocaust. U. S. 1946 King's X. Robert Frost. CP-FrosR
Having known robins on the window sill. Old Age. Langston Hughes. CP-HughL; CP-HughL3
Having lately taken up residence. Prism. James Merrill. SP-MerrJ
Having left the great mean city, I make. Goodbye to London. Louis MacNeice. CP-MacNL
Having looked long at two gardens rows. Corn and Beans. Carl Sandburg. CP-SandC
Having Lost My Sons, I Confront the Wreckage of the Moon: Christmas, 1960. James Wright. CP-WrigJ
Having lost the woman I loved. Ho-Hum Again. Hayden Carruth. CP-CarHS
Having Lunch at Brasenose. Amy Clampitt. CP-ClamA
Having met the protozoic. Traces of Living Things. Lorine Niedecker. CP-NiedL
Having mislaid it, and then. Way of a World, The. Charles Tomlinson. CP-TomlC; SP-TomlC
Having misread the house, What. Question, The. Charles Tomlinson. CP-TomlC
Having, my friend, your letter here in hand. Michelangelo Buonarroti. CP-Miche, *tr. by* John Frederick Nims
Having no ear, I hear. Donald Davie. CP-DaviDC
Having once put his hand into the ground. Current, The. Wendell Berry. CP-BerrW
Having planted our little Northern Spy at the wrong season. "I've Never Seen Such a Real Hard Time Before": Three-Part Invention. Hayden Carruth. CP-CarHS
Having planted / that seven-mile plot. Beans. Maxine W. Kumin. SP-KumiM
Having reached perfection. Perfection. Alice Walker. CP-WalkA
Having read the promise of the hedgerow. Sketch of the Great Dejection, A. Thom Gunn. CP-GunnT

Having returned sorrowing from his funeral. Epitaph of Antiochus, King of Kommagini. Constantine P. Cavafy. CP-CavaC, *tr. by* Theoharis Constantine Theoharis
Having roughed up the waters. Lithuanian Nocturne. Joseph Brodsky. CP-BrodJ
Having so rich a treasury, so fine a hoard. Daisy, The. Marya Alexandrovna Zaturenska. SP-ZatuM
Having spent the night in a sewer of precognition. Apotheosis of Tins, The. Derek Mahon. CP-MahoD
Having split up the chaparral. Wide Land, The. A. R. Ammons. CP-AmmoA
Having survived my fill of wrestling at the ford. Jacob Agonistes. Robert Stock. SP-StocR
Having thought all his life. Question Mark. Richard Eberhart. CP-EberR
Having to— / what do I think. Robert Creeley. CP-CreeR
Having used every subterfuge. Renewal, A. James Merrill. SP-MerrJ
Having, with bold Horatius, stamped her feet. Bold Horatius. Wilfred Owen. CP-OwenW
Having witnessed much contempt extant. Julian, Seeing Contempt. Constantine P. Cavafy. CP-CavaC, *tr. by* Theoharis Constantine Theoharis
Haw Lantern, The. Seamus Heaney. SP-HeanSO
Hawaii Dantesca. Charles Wright. SP-WrigC
Hawarden. George Meredith. CP-MerG1
Hawk. John Ciardi. CP-CiarJ
Hawk. Mary Oliver. SP-OlivM
Hawk, The. Robert Bly. SP-BlyR
Hawk, The. William Butler Yeats. CP-YeatW
Hawk or shrike has done this deed. Whimper of Sympathy. George Meredith. CP-MerG1
Hawk Roosting. Ted Hughes. SP-HughTN
Hawk sweeps down from his aerie, The. Hawk, The. Robert Bly. SP-BlyR
Hawks. Charles Tomlinson. CP-TomlC; SP-TomlC
Hawk's Cry in Autumn, The. Joseph Brodsky. CP-BrodJ, *tr. by* Joseph Brodsky *and* Alan Myers
Hawk's Shadow. Louise Glück. SP-GlucL
Hawkshead and Dachau in a Christmas Glass. Donald Davie. CP-DaviDC
Hawkweed, The. Edna St. Vincent Millay. CP-MillE
Hawley's Leaving Town. Charles Bukowski. SP-BukC1
Haworth Churchyard. Matthew Arnold.
    "Turn we next to the dead." SP-ArnoM
Hawthorn Hath a Deathly Smell, The. Walter De la Mare. CP-DeLaW
Hawthorn in Trent Vale, The. Charles Tomlinson. SP-TomlC
Hawthorne. Henry Wadsworth Longfellow. SP-LongH
Hawthorne. Robert Lowell. SP-LoweR
Hay. Paul Muldoon. CP-MuldP
Hay. Charles Tomlinson. CP-TomlC; SP-TomlC
Hay for the Horses. Gary Snyder. CP-SnydG
Hay-time when the Boston forecast. New England Weather. Archibald MacLeish. CP-MacLA
Haycutters. William Stafford. SP-StafWW
Haydn, Opus 76, Number 5. Yehuda Amichai. SP-AmicYL, *tr. by* Benjamin Harshav *and* Barbara Harshav
Haydon! forgive me that I cannot speak. To B. R. Haydon, with a Sonnet Written on Seeing the Elgin Marbles. John Keats. CP-KeatJ
Haydon! let worthier judges praise the skill. To B. R. Haydon, on Seeing His Picture of Napoleon Buonaparte on the Island of St Helena. William Wordsworth. CP-WorW2
Hayfoot; strawfoot; the illiterate seasons. Wessex Guidebook. Louis MacNeice. CP-MacNL
Haying. William Corbett. SP-CorbW
Haying. Wyatt Prunty. SP-PrunW
Haying before Storm. Muriel Rukeyser. CP-RukeM
Hayley, thy tenderness fraternal shown. To Hayley. William Cowper. CP-CowpW
Haymaking. May Swenson. SP-SwenM
Hays Says Ray Lies. Sin City, D.C. John Updike. CP-UpdiJ
Haystack, The. Richard Eberhart. CP-EberR
Haystacks burned to black moss, The. Brueghel. Arthur Sze. SP-SzeA
Hazard Faces a Sunday in the Decline. William Meredith. SP-MereW
Hazardous Occupations. Carl Sandburg. CP-SandC
Hazard's friend Elliot is homosexual. Prodigious. Wholesome. William Meredith. SP-MereW
Hazard's Optimism. William Meredith. SP-MereW
Haze. Carl Sandburg. CP-SandC
Haze. James Schuyler. CP-SchuJ
Haze. Henry David Thoreau.
Haze, char, and the weather of All Souls'. In the Elegy Season. Richard Wilbur. CP-WilbR
Haze Gold. Carl Sandburg. CP-SandC
Haze of gold, the Occident lights up, A. Baruch Spinoza. Jorge Luis Borges. SP-

BorgJ, *tr.* by Willis Barnstone

Haze of noon wanned silver-grey, The. Sotto Voce. Walter De la Mare. CP-DeLaW

Hazel Blossoms. John Greenleaf Whittier. CP-WhitJ

Hazel Grove, The. Robert Graves. CP-GravR

Hazel stealth. A trickle in the culvert. Settings. Seamus Heaney. SP-HeanSO *Fr.* Squarings.

Hazel Stick for Catherine Ann, A. Seamus Heaney. SP-HeanSO

Hazlitt. Ivor Gurney. SP-GurnI

Hazlitt, also, tea-drinker and joyous walker. Hazlitt. Ivor Gurney. SP-GurnI

Hazy Day in the Composition. Clarence Major. SP-MajoC

He. Federico García Lorca. CP-GarcF, *tr.* by Jerome Rothenberg *Fr.* In the Forest of Clocks.

He. John Ashbery. SP-AshbJ

He. Randall Jarrell. CP-JarrR

He. Stanley Kunitz. CP-KunSC

He. Howard Nemerov. CP-NemeH

He, a grave poet, fell in love with her. Beatrice and Dante. Robert Graves. CP-GravR

He a recreant; in me a true knight thou dub'st, and. Rhyming Exercises. Robert Browning. CP-BroR2

He Abjures Love. Thomas Hardy. CP-HardT

He acts, in splendor and in darkness. Adam Zagajewski. SP-ZagaA, *tr.* by Renata Gorczynski

He always searched, without reason, without need. Forbidden Ground. Yannis Ritsos. SP-RitsY, *tr.* by Andonis Decavalles

He and I. Dante Gabriel Rossetti. CW-RossD *Fr.* House of Life, The.

He and I. James Whitcomb Riley. CP-RileJ

He and I—he says—do two jobs totally similar in their dissimilarity. Tricks. Yannis Ritsos. SP-RitsY, *tr.* by N. C. Germanacos

He and I sought together. Heliodora. "H. D." CP-DoolH

He and She. Christina Georgina Rossetti. CP-RosC2

He and She. William Butler Yeats. CP-YeatW

He / and she, A. Pair, A. May Swenson. SP-SwenM

He and the wind. Goodnight. May Swenson. SP-SwenM

He angled the bright shield. Baroque Image. May Sarton. SP-SartM

He arises. Oriane / the lurcher wants. Red Brick and Brown Stone. James Schuyler. CP-SchuJ

He arose early, the morning tinged with excitement. One More. Raymond Carver. CP-CarvR

He as o / ld as who stag, A. E. E. Cummings. CP-CummE

He ascended and descended the stairs. Little by little. Stairs, The. Yannis Ritsos. SP-RitsY, *tr.* by N. C. Germanacos

He Asked about the Quality. Constantine P. Cavafy. CP-CavaC, *tr.* by Theoharis Constantine Theoharis

He asked: Will man obsolesce. Could You Be Right. Lorine Niedecker. CP-NiedL

He ate and drank the precious Words. Emily Dickinson. CP-DickE

He ate his bread. He drank water. He didn't eat. Multidimensional. Yannis Ritsos. SP-RitsY, *tr.* by Kostas Myrsiades

He avoided the empty millyards. Under the Viaduct, 1932. Rita Dove. SP-DoveR

He bad / o he bad / He make a honky. Pusher, The. Maya Angelou. SP-AngeM

He began the poem at the kitchen table. Account, An. Raymond Carver. CP-CarvR

He begins with charcoal and outlines. Taoist Painter, The. Arthur Sze. SP-SzeA

He bends his travel-tarnished feet. Supplanter, The. Thomas Hardy. CP-HardT

He bent his head upon his breast. Garibaldi. Elizabeth Barrett Browning. CP-BroEB

He Bids His Beloved Be at Peace. William Butler Yeats. *See* Michael Robartes Bids His Beloved Be at Peace

He blinks he sighs. King in Funeral Procession, A. Stevie Smith. CP-SmitS

He bore an agony whereof the name / Hath turned his fellows pale. St. Bartholomew. Christina Georgina Rossetti. CP-RosC2

He bore the name of William Brown. William Brown. James Whitcomb Riley. CP-RileJ

He bows and extracts from his pockets a live rabbit, a tiger cub. Juggler, The. David Ignatow. SP-IgnaD

He breaks as the river knots about their knees. His Dream of Flood: And Eden. Muriel Rukeyser. CP-RukeM

He breaks the silence. Artist. George Oppen. CP-OppGN

He brings me cast-off innertubes. It's a Smallworld. Kenneth Patchen. CP-PatcK

He built four houses. Lorine Niedecker. CP-NiedL

He buried his wife, who'd died in. Lightning Speed of the Past, The. Raymond Carver. CP-CarvR

He called her in from me and shut the door. James Whitcomb Riley. CP-RileJ

He called home every once in a while. Good Son, A. Miller Williams. CP-WillM

He called hydrangeas purple. And they were. Anecdote of the Abnormal.

Wallace Stevens. CP-StevWP

He came by, wanting to speak with me on a downtown street. Fernando Pessoa. SP-PessF, *tr.* by Susan M. Brown *and* Edwin Honig

He came from the far north I can name the country. Briefcase, The. W. S. Merwin. SP-MerwWF

He came home. Said nothing. Going Home. Wisława Szymborska. SP-SzymW, *tr.* by Stanislaw Barańczak *and* Clare Cavanagh

He came / in flowing robes. Armah: October 12, 1990. Alice Walker. CP-WalkA

He came into the café where they always went together. Flowers White and Beautiful, as Were Most Becoming. Constantine P. Cavafy. CP-CavaC, *tr.* by Theoharis Constantine Theoharis

He came out of the womb running. Long-Distance Runner, The. James Laughlin. CP-LaugJ

He came to him in the extasy of pray'r. Fragment: "He came to him in the extasy of pray'r." William Cowper. CP-CowpW

He came to read. There are. Constantine P. Cavafy. CP-CavaC, *tr.* by Theoharis Constantine Theoharis

He came to the door one night wet thin beaten and. History of a Tough Motherfucker, The. Charles Bukowski. SP-BukC3

He can find no rest among us. Rainer Maria Rilke. CP-RilkFr, *tr.* by A. Poulin, Jr.

He can say, I am / watching a boat tug. Problem, The. Robert Creeley. CP-CreeR

He Cannot Deny Himself. Christina Georgina Rossetti. CP-RosC2

He cannot move the furniture. Ear, The. Robert Creeley. CP-CreeR

He can't be more than twenty-two years old. Next Table, The. Constantine P. Cavafy. CP-CavaC, *tr.* by Theoharis Constantine Theoharis

He carried me out of the lamplight. Thomas Kinsella. CP-KinsT

He carries / His own strength. Young Sailor. Langston Hughes. CP-HughL; CP-HughL1

He cast off all his golden robes. In Memoriam: William Cannastra, 1922–1950. Allen Ginsberg. CP-GinsA

He changes shirts. Yannis Ritsos. SP-RitsY *Fr.* So?

He chases his tail. Analysand. Stevie Smith. CP-SmitS

He clasps the crag with crookèd hands. Eagle, The. Alfred Tennyson. CP-TennA

He climbed hard. Reward. A. R. Ammons. CP-AmmoA

He climbed to his feet in the cold light, and began. Poet Egan O'Rahilly, Homesick in Old Age, The. Egan O'Rahilly. CP-KinsT, *tr.* by Thomas Kinsella

He climbed to the top. Fergus Falling. Galway Kinnell. SP-KinnGN

He clutched the shallow drum. Selected Life, A. Thomas Kinsella. CP-KinsT

He clutched the shallow drum. Galloping Green: May 1962. Thomas Kinsella. CP-KinsT *Fr.* Selected Life, A.

He coils so close around his double-bass. Double Bass. Robert Graves. CP-GravR

He comes along the street, singing. To Go By Singing. Wendell Berry. CP-BerrW

He comes at dead of night, when all asleep. Watcher, The. Jones Very. CP-VeryJ

He comes,—he comes,—the Frost Spirit comes! You may trace his footsteps now. Frost Spirit, The. John Greenleaf Whittier. CP-WhitJ

He comes toward me. Returning (1975). Yusef Komunyakaa. CP-KomuY

He comes toward me with lashless eyes. Upon Meeting Don L. Lee, in a Dream. Rita Dove. SP-DoveR

He Cometh in Sweet Sense. James Whitcomb Riley. CP-RileJ

He concentrated, as he ought. JVC. Thom Gunn. CP-GunnT

He continued to consult her for her beauty. Popular Songs. John Ashbery. SP-AshbJ

He could be just one more erstwhile aristocrat lightfooting it. Chateaubriand on the Niagara Frontier, 1791. Gregory Orr. SP-OrrG

He could condense cerulean ether. Ralph Waldo Emerson. CP-EmerR

He could have killed more than he could have fed. Epitaph for a Tyrant. Joseph Brodsky. CP-BrodJ *Fr.* Shorts.

He could not die when trees were green. Dying Child, The. John Clare. SP-ClarJ

He could remember that in the past, seven months ago. Hole, The. Donald Hall. CP-HallD

He couldn't get the puck into the net. Hog. Charles Bukowski. SP-BukC3

He coveted her portrait. Moon Is a Painter, The. Nicholas Vachel Lindsay. CP-LindV

He cracked almonds. Yannis Ritsos. SP-RitsY *Fr.* So?

He crawls to the edge of the foaming creek. Meeting the Mountains. Gary Snyder. CP-SnydG

He cuts down the lakes so they appear straight. He. John Ashbery. SP-AshbJ

He danced in feathers, with paint across his nose. Learning About the Indians. Mary Oliver. SP-OlivM

He danced with tall grass. We Never Know. Yusef Komunyakaa. CP-KomuY

He dances to that music in the wood. Andean Flute, The. Derek Mahon. CP-MahoD

He de dark. George Oppen. CP-OppGN

He describes a city that apparently never was. Seven Lines of Equal Length. Michael Palmer. SP-PalmM

He describes eagle feathers with his hands. Empty Words. Arthur Sze. SP-SzeA

He Did It to Please His Mother. James Laughlin. CP-LaugJ

He Did Not Know Me. Thomas Hardy. CP-HardT

He did not know she had risen out of cinders. Folktale. Ted Hughes. SP-HughTN

He did not pretend. Exile. Louise Glück. SP-GlucL

He did not wear his scarlet coat. Ballad of Reading Gaol, The. Oscar Wilde. CP-WildO

He didn't deny it. Curly Blue Buppo, The. Kenneth Patchen. CP-PatcK

He didn't know, King Kleomenis, he didn't dare. In Sparta. Constantine P. Cavafy. CP-CavaC, *tr. by* Theoharis Constantine Theoharis

He didn't want to do it with skill. Lion & Honeycomb. Howard Nemerov. CP-NemeH

He Died at Dawn. Federico García Lorca. SP-GarcF, *tr. by* Greville Texidor

He died for me: what can I offer Him? Not Yours but You. Christina Georgina Rossetti. CP-RosC3

He died in December. He must descend. Epilogue: "He died in December. He must descend." John Berryman. CP-BerrJ

He "Digesteth Ilarde Yron." Marianne Craig Moore. CP-MoorM

He Digs, He Dug, He Has Dug. Ogden Nash. CP-NashO

He dines alone surrounded by reflections. Witch Doctor. Robert Earl Hayden. CP-HaydR

He disagrees with Simone de Beauvoir. His Plans for Old Age. William Meredith. SP-MereW

He disappeared in the dead of winter. In Memory of W. B. Yeats. W. H. Auden. CP-AudeW

He discovers himself on an old airfield. Old Pilot, The. Donald Hall. CP-HallD

Ile does not have to feel because he thinks. E. E. Cummings. CP-CummE

He does not think that I haunt here nightly. Haunter, The. Thomas Hardy. CP-HardT

He doesn't know what she wants or why she stays. Jonathan Seduced. Miller Williams. CP-WillM

He drags his bare feet. Sakyamuni Coming Out from the Mountain. Allen Ginsberg. CP-GinsA

He drank strong waters and his speech was coarse. Rudyard Kipling. CP-KiplR *Fr.* Plain Tales from the Hills.

He Dreamed His Death. James Laughlin. CP-LaugJ

He Dreams of Being Warm. Amy Clampitt. CP-ClamA

He drives onto the grassy shoulder and unfastens. Earth Walk. William Meredith. SP-MereW

He drives, she mostly sleeps; when she's awake, they quarrel, and now, in a violet dusk. Travelers. C. K. Williams. SP-WillC

He dropped, [—]more sullenly than wearily. Dead-Beat, The. Wilfred Owen. CP-OwenW

He drums the piano wood. Shakespeare Say. Rita Dove. SP-DoveR

He dwelt in himself. Master, The. Seamus Heaney. SP-HeanSO *Fr.* Sweeney Redivivus.

He eats (a moment's stoppage to his song). Tramp, The. John Clare. SP-ClarJ

He entered the hall. There was little light. He scrutinized. Wax Dummies. Yannis Ritsos. SP-RitsY, *tr. by* Andonis Decavalles

He faced his canvas (as a seer whose ken). Art and Love. James Whitcomb Riley. CP-RileJ

He fared from Bethany to Jerusalem. Miracle, The. Donald Davie. CP-DaviDC

He Fears His Good Fortune. Thomas Hardy. CP-HardT

He feeds me with His manna every day. Soliloquy of One of the Spies Left in the Wilderness, A. Gerard Manley Hopkins. CP-HopkG

He feels a breeze rise from. Conversation of Old Men, The. Thom Gunn. CP-GunnT

He feels small as he awakens. Awakening, The. Robert Creeley. CP-CreeR

He finished the picture yesterday noon. Now. Picture of a Young Man, Twenty-three, Done by His Friend of the Same Age, an Amateur. Constantine P. Cavafy. CP-CavaC, *tr. by* Theoharis Constantine Theoharis

He fished the black deep. Chimney Sweep. Lorine Niedecker. CP-NiedL

He flies so high. Look, Look. Stevie Smith. CP-SmitS

He Follows Himself. Thomas Hardy. CP-HardT

He forgo—and I—remembered. Emily Dickinson. CP-DickE

He fought like those Who've nought to lose. Emily Dickinson. CP-DickE

He found my Being—set it up. Emily Dickinson. CP-DickE

He fumbles at your Soul. Emily Dickinson. CP-DickE

He gave away his Life. Emily Dickinson. CP-DickE

He gave the Fascisti salute. Clarence Major. SP-MajoC

He gave the solid rail a hateful kick. Egg and the Machine, The. Robert Frost. CP-FrosR

He gave up fine cordials and. Compendium. Rita Dove. SP-DoveR

He gazed and gazed and gazed and gazed. Rhyme for a Child Viewing a Naked Venus in a Painting [of "The Judgement of Paris"]. Robert Browning. CP-BroR2

He gazed at the morning through the windowpanes. He felt with precision. Incense. Yannis Ritsos. SP-RitsY, *tr. by* Edmund Keeley

He Gives His Beloved Certain Rhymes. William Butler Yeats. CP-YeatW

He gives to the chief the head of an enemy. Ball, A. Czeslaw Milosz. CP-MiloCN, *tr. by* Robert Hass

He glides, descending. Great Horned Owl, The. Clarence Major. SP-MajoC

He glides so swiftly. Snake. Langston Hughes. CP-HughL; CP-HughL2

He Glimpses a Nobler Vision. Miller Williams. CP-WillM

He-Goat. D. H. Lawrence. CP-LawrD

He goes regularly to the taverna. 25th Year of His Life, The. Constantine P. Cavafy. CP-CavaC, *tr. by* Theoharis Constantine Theoharis

He grew up by the sea. Adam. William Carlos Williams. CP-WilW1

He had a back office in his older brother's. Remembering an Account Executive. Alan Dugan. CP-DugaA

He had a devil's look; and no rain. Painter at Xyochtl. Josephine Jacobsen. CP-JacoJ

He had a long white streak. At Master McGrath's Grave. Paul Muldoon. CP-MuldP

He Had a Quality of Growth. Muriel Rukeyser. CP-RukeM

He liad asked for immortal life. Thetis. "H. D." CP-DoolH

He had been stuttering, by the edge. Hart Crane. Robert Creeley. CP-CreeR

He had bowed down to drunkenness. Disenthralled, The. John Greenleaf Whittier. CP-WhitJ

He had come nearly half a thousand miles. Strayed Village, The. Adrienne Rich. CP-RicAE

He had devirginated my friend Nan. Days of 1959. Marilyn Hacker. SP-HackM

Ile had done for her all that a man could. I Will Write. Robert Graves. CP-GravR

He had driven half the night. Hay for the Horses. Gary Snyder. CP-SnydG

He had had it told to him on the sward. Another Chain Letter. John Ashbery. SP-AshbJ

He Had His Dream. Paul Laurence Dunbar. CP-DunbP

He had his home, posthumous, in the town of New Haven. Beinecke Library. Czeslaw Milosz. CP-MiloCN, *tr. by* Robert Hass

He had loved her. You Wouldn't Say They Didn't Get Along Exactly. Miller Williams. CP-WillM

He had never dwelled on the pleasures of memory. Maker, The ("He had never dwelled on the pleasures of memory"). Jorge Luis Borges. SP-BorgJ, *tr. by* Ken Krabbenhoft

He had no arguments, yet always insisted on the same position. Roughly Square. Yannis Ritsos. SP-RitsY, *tr. by* N. C. Germanacos

He had no past and he certainly. Pity Ascending with the Fog. James Tate. SP-TateJ

He had not looked. During the Eichmann Trial. Denise Levertov. SP-LeveDP

He had nothing to say. He fed the mutes, wrote on his empty cigarette box. After a Settlement of Debts. Yannis Ritsos. SP-RitsY, *tr. by* Kimon Friar *and* Kostas Myrsiades

He had the gift of being pitiless. War Criminal. Donald Davie. CP-DaviDC

He had toiled away for a weary while. Toil. James Whitcomb Riley. CP-RileJ

He had used love or lust or what's between. Archibald MacLeish. CP-MacLA *Fr.* Happy Marriage, The.

He had walked so far to find her. Die Heimat. James Laughlin. CP-LaugJ

He halted in the wind, and—what was that. Boundless Moment, A. Robert Frost. CP-FrosR

He hammered a nail on the wall. He had nothing. Nocturnal Episode. Yannis Ritsos. SP-RitsY, *tr. by* Kimon Friar

He hands / down the gift. Gift, The. Robert Creeley. CP-CreeR

He Has Beaten about the Bush Long Enough. William Carlos Williams. CP-WilW2

He has been / Many places. Old Sailor. Langston Hughes. CP-HughL; CP-HughL2

He has blown in from the badlands. Vaquero. Paul Muldoon. CP-MuldP

He has come to the conclusion. Need, The. David Ignatow. SP-IgnaD

He has done the work of a true man. George L. Stearns. John Greenleaf Whittier. CP-WhitJ

He has gone over to new flowers in a garden. Groundhog Revisiting, The. Richard Eberhart. CP-EberR

He has had his Future. Emily Dickinson. SP-DickE

He has hid his face, and he's gone! Dirge: "He has hid his face, and he's gone!" George Meredith. CP-MerG2

He has just cornered and skewered. Why We Are Going Back to Paradise Island. Marilyn Hacker. SP-HackM

He Has Lived in Many Houses. Thomas Lux. SP-LuxT

He has many a car and chuffer. Peace of Petrol, The. G. K. Chesterton. CP-ChesG

He has never killed anyone. No. Employee, The. Hans Magnus Enzensberger. SP-EnzeH, *tr. by* Michael Hamburger

He has on. Late for Summer Weather. William Carlos Williams. CP-WilW1

He has only to pass by a tree moodily walking head down. Fiend, The. James Dickey. CP-DickJ

He has stamped the clay with his hostile. Cup with a Jaguar for the Drinking of

Health. Pablo Antonio Cuadra. CP-MertT

He has two antennae. Gnat on My Paper. Richard Eberhart. CP-EberR

He has woven rose-vines. C33. Hart Crane. CP-CranH

He hasn't gone to work. Poem Circling Hamtramck, Michigan, All Night in Search of You, The. Philip Levine. SP-LeviP

He hasn't taken his eyes off you since we walked in, although you seem not to notice particularly. Silence, The. C. K. Williams. SP-WillC

He hath abolished the old drouth. Gerard Manley Hopkins. CP-HopkG

He hath wrong'd his queen, but still he is her lord. Sardanapalus. Lord Byron. CP-Byron

He heard that in Derryscollop there is a tree. February. Paul Muldoon. CP-MuldP

He heard the centuries tick slowly. Pivot, The. Stanley Kunitz. CP-KunSC

He heard the coughing tiger in the night. Edna St. Vincent Millay. CP-MillE *Fr.* Epitaph for the Race of Man.

He hears lithe trees and last leaves swatting the glass. TV Off. Ted Hughes. SP-HughTN

He Hears that His Beloved Has Become Engaged. Philip Larkin. CP-LarkP

He Hears the Cry of the Sedge. William Butler Yeats. CP-YeatW

He hears the whir of the battledrum. Conqueror, The. James Whitcomb Riley. CP-RileJ

He Held Radical Light. A. R. Ammons. CP-AmmoA

He held the drum up. Earth and Creation. Peter Blue Cloud. SP-BlueP

He hie fie finger / speak in simple sound. Man, The. Robert Creeley. CP-CreeR

He holds a volume open in his hands. Boy with Book of Knowledge. Howard Nemerov. CP-NemeH

He holds conversation sacred. World Book Salesman, The. Raymond Carver. CP-CarvR

He holds him from desire, all but stops his breathing lest. What Magic Drum? William Butler Yeats. CP-YeatW

He hopes his arm is strong as the gods'. Poet, The. Richard Eberhart. CP-EberR

He hopped boxcars to Chitown. Testimony. Yusef Komunyakaa. CP-KomuY

He hung up his coat on the clothes rack in the corridor. Need of Proof. Yannis Ritsos. SP-RitsY, *tr. by* Kimon Friar

He, hunger-stung, hard to slake. Glutton, The. Sylvia Plath. CP-PlatS

He / in the dark stall, no day now for him, to paw. Charles Olson. CP-OlsoC

He Inadvertently Cures His Love-Pains. Thomas Hardy. CP-HardT

He is a bad man. He says this in French. Man Takes His Daughter, Age Five, to a Public Execution by Guillotine, Paris, 1857, A. Thomas Lux. SP-LuxT

He is a Cock would. William Blake. CP-BlakW

He is a delicate flower indeed. Sorrows of Smindyrides, The. James Laughlin. CP-LaugJ

He is a good workman. 2 Propositions and 3 Proof. Charles Olson. CP-OlsoC

He is a tower unleaning. But how he'll break. John Crowe Ransom. *See* He is a tower unleaning. But how will he not break

He is a tower unleaning. But how will he not break. Vaunting Oak. John Crowe Ransom. SP-RansJ

He is affection and the present since he has opened the house to frothy winter. Genie. Arthur Rimbaud. CP-RimbA, *tr. by* Martin Sorrell

He is alive, this morning. Emily Dickinson. CP-DickE

He is amazed how hard it is to die. Day in the Death, A. Miller Williams. CP-WillM

He Is An. Kenneth Patchen. CP-PatcK

He is breaking the nets in his wildness for the real. Muriel Rukeyser. CP-RukeM

He is busy destroying the landscape with lightning bolts. Fred and the Holy Grail. William Dickey. SP-DickW

He is divested of the diverse world. Blind Man, The. Jorge Luis Borges. SP-BorgJ, *tr. by* Alastair Reid

He is earthed to his girl, one hand fastened. Aran. Derek Mahon. CP-MahoD

He is forever trapped. Audre Lorde. *See* Pity for him who suffers from his waste

He is gone, loaded with years and honors! Death of Lafayette. Jones Very. CP-VeryJ

He is gone on the mountain. Coronach. Sir Walter Scott. SP-ScotW *Fr.* Lady of the Lake, The.

He Is Guarded by Crowds and Shackled with Formalities. Kenneth Patchen. CP-PatcK

He is here, come down to look for you. Eurydice. Margaret Atwood. SP-AtwM2

He is here, Urania's son. Epithalamium: "He is here, Urania's son." A. E. Housman. CP-HousA

He is Huitzilopochtli. Second Song of Huitzilopochtli. D. H. Lawrence. CP-LawrD

He is, I should say, on a level. Sappho. CP-CunnJ, *tr. by* James Vincent Cunningham

He is in his room sulked shut. The small. Boy. John Ciardi. CP-CiarJ

He is just plain drunk. I Am a Sioux Brave, He Said in Minneapolis. James Wright. CP-WrigJ

"He is my friend," I said. My Friend. James Whitcomb Riley. CP-RileJ

He is no fugitive—escaped, escaping. Escapist—Never. Robert Frost. CP-FrosR

He is no more dead than Finland herself is dead. Tapiola. William Carlos Williams. CP-WilW2

He is no one I really know. Piccola Commedia. Richard Wilbur. CP-WilbR

He is not as young as he used to be. With a groan. Apocalypse. Umbrian Master, about 1490. Hans Magnus Enzensberger. SP-EnzeH

He is not de[a]d that sometime [*or* somtyme] hath a fall. Sir Thomas Wyatt. CP-WyatT

He is not here, the old sun. No Possum, No Sop, No Taters. Wallace Stevens. CP-StevW; CP-StevWP

He is not the last one. Small Blue Heron, The. James Wright. CP-WrigJ

He is one of / The human machines. Solipsist. Stephen Spender. CP-SpenS

He is quick, thinking in clear images. In Broken Images. Robert Graves. CP-GravR

He is quite captive to the Lady of the Well-Spring. Lady of the Well-Spring, The. Stevie Smith. CP-SmitS

He is running, lifting a little the skirt of his winter cloak. Philology. Czeslaw Milosz. CP-MiloCN, *tr. by* Robert Hass

He is said to have been the last Red Man. Vanishing Red, The. Robert Frost. CP-FrosR

He is scared of the frankness of women. Young Man Travelling, A. Denise Levertov. SP-LeveDL

He is stark mad, who ever says. Broken Heart, The. John Donne. CP-DonnJ; MW-DonnJ

He is that fallen lance that lies as hurled. Soldier, A. Robert Frost. CP-FrosR

He is the Devil. He whores Nature. Love is a word in his Mouth. He has no Mouth. Charles Olson. CP-OlsoC

He is the final builder of the total building. Sketch of the Ultimate Politician. Wallace Stevens. CP-StevW; CP-StevWP

He is the morning's poet. To Bliss Carman. James Whitcomb Riley. CP-RileJ

He is there, somewhere. Enemy, The. Thomas McGrath. SP-McGrT

He is thinking of everyone. Age ("He is thinking of everyone"). Robert Creeley. SP-CreeR

He is thinking of us. Prisoner, The. Charles Simic. SP-SimiC; SP-SimiCE

He is to weet a melancholy carle. Portrait, A. John Keats. CP-KeatJ

He is wearing my grandfather's hat. My Dream about God. Lucille Clifton. SP-ClifL

He is wintering out. Servant Boy. Seamus Heaney. SP-HeanSO

He is wisest who has the most caution. Debris. Walt Whitman. CP-WhitW

He isn't looking at anything. Doveglion. E. E. Cummings. CP-CummE

He journeyed through America. Rover Come Home, The. Thomas Hardy. CP-HardT

He kept a grog shop, this fur trader killer? Du Bay. Lorine Niedecker. CP-NiedL

He kicked the world, and lunging long ago. Horse, The. James Wright. CP-WrigJ

He kisses me! Ah, now, at last. Songs Tuneless. James Whitcomb Riley. CP-RileJ

He knew he had another thirty years. Quantum Theory Made Simple. Miller Williams. CP-WillM

He knew he was. Reaching. Raymond Carver. CP-CarvR

He knew he would say it. But could he believe it again? Mornings on Bourbon Street. Tennessee Williams. CP-WillT

He knew that he was a spirit without a foyer. Local Objects. Wallace Stevens. CP-StevWP

He knocked, and I beheld him at the door. Alma Mater. Edwin Arlington Robinson. CP-RobiE

He knows he will be hurt. Night Piece. Louise Glück. SP-GlucL

He knows how few people get to be. Liberal Imagination, The. Miller Williams. CP-WillM

He knows no change who knows the true. Henry David Thoreau. CP-ThorH

He knows that when he has to go to sleep. Man Who Stays Up Late, The. Miller Williams. CP-WillM

He knows / the hunger, walking. Hunger. Robert Creeley. CP-CreeR

He knows there are those who say you can never know. Jonathan Confronts the Question. Miller Williams. CP-WillM

He knows what it signifies, lifting the veil. Groom Kisses the Bride and the Mind of the Young Preacher Wanders Again, The. Miller Williams. CP-WillM

He lay awake with a harassed air. Conversation at Dawn, A. Thomas Hardy. CP-HardT

He lay down in this field to rest. Large White Rock Called "The Sleeping Angel," A. Gregory Orr. SP-OrrG

He leads me into much that is sorrow. Poor Child with the Hooked Hands, The. Kenneth Patchen. CP-PatcK

He leads: we hear our Seaman's call. Trafalgar Day. George Meredith. CP-MerG2

He leaned against a lamp-post, lost. Lounger, A. James Whitcomb Riley. CP-RileJ

He leans against the window-sill. Archibald MacLeish. CP-MacLA *Fr.* Happy Marriage, The.

He leans over—well. Let's Say. Yusef Komunyakaa. CP-KomuY

He leaped. With none to hinder. Empedocles. George Meredith. CP-MerG1

He learns what love can do and what it can't do. Fly Me to the Moon. Miller Williams. CP-WillM

He left himself on my doorstep. Foundling, A. Margaret Atwood. SP-AtwM1

He left his dust, by all the myriad tread. St. Francis Xavier. G. K. Chesterton. CP-ChesG

He left his pickaxe by the wall and said. Farmer. Yannis Ritsos. SP-RitsY, *tr. by* Kimon Friar

He left me for a foreign land. Last Words. James Whitcomb Riley. CP-RileJ

He left the office where he'd been taken on. He Asked about the Quality. Constantine P. Cavafy. CP-CavaC, *tr. by* Theoharis Constantine Theoharis

"He left two sons," they say. Yehuda Amichai. SP-AmicYL, *tr. by* Benjamin Harshav *and* Barbara Harshav

He lets her pick the color. Nothing Down. Rita Dove. SP-DoveR

He licks the last chocolate ice cream. Sweet Things. Thom Gunn. CP-GunnT

He lies alone in his bed. Long Night, The. James Laughlin. CP-LaugJ

He: Life is an old / casino in the park. I. Hayden Carruth. CP-CarHS *Fr* Clay Hill Anthology, The.

He lifts the white skiff up onto the beach. It is Easter. Not the Cuckold's Dream. Norman Dubie. CP-DubiN

He liked to joke and all of his jokes were practical. Sunday Night at Grandfather's. Rita Dove. SP-DoveR

He listened at the porch that day. Year's Spinning, A. Elizabeth Barrett Browning. CP-BroEB

He listens to a punk rock group. New Wave. Arthur Sze. SP-SzeA

He lived—childhood summers. Lorine Niedecker. CP-NiedL

He lived / from his second year. Garland for Thomas Eakins, A. Charles Tomlinson. CP-TomlC; SP-TomlC

He lived in a double-wide and drove a truck. Affair, The. Miller Williams. CP-WillM

He lived in a small farm-house. Refusal to Mourn, A. Derek Mahon. CP-MahoD

He lived on the wings of storm. Memoir of a Proud Boy. Carl Sandburg. CP-SandC

He lived the Life of Ambush. Emily Dickinson. CP-DickE

He lives among a dog. Child, The. Donald Hall. CP-HallD

He Lives in a Box. James Laughlin. CP-LaugJ

He lives in a house with a swimming pool. About My Very Tortured Friend, Peter. Charles Bukowski. SP-BukC2

He lives not who can refuse me. Ralph Waldo Emerson. CP-EmerR

He lives who lives to God alone. On a Similar Occasion for the Year 1793. William Cowper. CP-CowpW

He-lizard is crying, The. Lizard Is Crying, The. Federico García Lorca. SP-GarcF, *tr. by* J. L. Gili *and* Stephen Spender

He locked the door, looked behind him distrustfully. Suspect, The. Yannis Ritsos. SP-RitsY, *tr. by* Kimon Friar

He lolls in the supermarket. Portrait of a House Detective. Hans Magnus Enzensberger. SP-EnzeH, *tr. by* Michael Hamburger

He looked at me, bestowing beauty. Drinking Wine. Wisława Szymborska. SP-SzymWM, *tr. by* Joanna Trzeciak

He looked at me with eyes I thought. A. E. Housman. CP-HousA

He looks. Looks. Looks in rapture. Man in Majesty. Randall Jarrell. CP-JarrR

He looks over the laborious drafts. Poet of the Thirteenth Century, A. Jorge Luis Borges. SP-BorgJ, *tr. by* Alan S. Trueblood

He loomed above the others when he walked. Emanuel Swedenborg. Jorge Luis Borges. SP-BorgJ, *tr. by* Willis Barnstone

He loved her and she loved him. Lovesong: "He loved her and she loved him." Ted Hughes. SP-HughTN

He loved her, and through many years. Then and Now. Paul Laurence Dunbar. CP-DunbP

He loved the way her fingers loved the ground. Midas and Wife. Mona Van Duyn. SP-VanDM

He loved to watch & wake. Ralph Waldo Emerson. CP-EmerR

He loved you and you lay upon His breast. Saint John. Kenneth Rexroth. CP-RexrK

He loveth not! he knows not God! Hymn: "He loveth not! he knows not God!" Jones Very. CP-VeryJ

He makes the Lame to walk we all agree. On the Venetian Painter. William Blake. CP-BlakW

He marked the pattern of the sky. "H. D." Doolittle. CP-DoolH *Fr* Electra-Orestes.

He might be slow and something feckless first. Gerard Manley Hopkins. CP-HopkG

He motions me over with a question. Kidnap[p]er. Tess Gallagher. SP-GallT

He Mourns for the Change That Has Come upon Him and His Beloved, and Longs for the End of the World. William Butler Yeats. *See* Mongan Laments the Change That Has Come upon Him and His Beloved

He moved in light. Lorine Niedecker. CP-NiedL

He moves straight before him, legs moving lightly. David Ignatow. SP-IgnaD

He must have been just as old in. Ballad of Mister Dutcher and the Last Lynching in Gupton. Robert Penn Warren. CP-WarrR

He must have / Droll fancies sometimes cross his quiet thoughts. Ralph Waldo Emerson. CP-EmerR

He needs the antiseptic of the sunlight: neither. Stranger, The. Kenneth Patchen. CP-PatcK

He Never Expected Much. Thomas Hardy. CP-HardT

He never felt twice the same about the flecked river. This Solitude of Cataracts. Wallace Stevens. CP-StevW; CP-StevWP

He never listened while friends talked. Chicago English Afternoon. Ted Berrigan. SP-BerrT

He never made the dive—not while I watched. Springboard, The. Louis MacNeice. CP-MacNL

He never spoke a word to me. Simon the Cyrenian Speaks. Countee Cullen. CP-CullC

He never was a silly little boy. Ph.D. Langston Hughes. CP-HughL; CP-HughL1

He no longer loved things, words, or birds that had become. Unfamiliar Instrument. Yannis Ritsos. SP-RitsY, *tr. by* Andonis Decavalles

He numbed my heart, he stole away my truth. Purification. Robert Graves. CP-GravR

He, of his gentleness. In the Wilderness. Robert Graves. CP-GravR

He offers, between planes. Conversation with a Fireman from Brooklyn. Tess Gallagher. SP-GallT

He often gazes on the air. Agnostic, An. Stevie Smith. CP-SmitS

He often would ask us. Choirmaster's Burial, The. Thomas Hardy. CP-HardT

He, on whose natal hour you glance. Ode 4,3; To Melpomene. Horace. SP-SmarC *Fr*. Odes.

He outstripped Time with but a Bout. Emily Dickinson. CP-DickE

He paces the blue rug. It is the end of summer. On Looking at *La Grande Jatte*, the Czar Wept Anew. Frank O'Hara. SP-OharF

He painted the mountain over and over again. Dearest Reader. Michael Palmer. SP-PalmM

He parted a beard where his mouth might be. Generation Gap. John Ciardi. CP-CiarJ

He parts Himself—like Leaves. Emily Dickinson. CP-DickE

He passed away with morning light. My Dear Brother Washington. Jones Very. CP-VeryJ

He passed by with another woman. Ballad: "He passed by with another woman." Gabriela Mistral. SP-MistG, *tr. by* Maria Giachetti [*or* Jacketti]

He passed her only once in a crowded street. Portraits of Three Ladies. Robert Penn Warren. CP-WarrR

He passed in the very battle-smoke. Lord Roberts. Rudyard Kipling. CP-KiplR

He passes down the churchyard track. Sexton at Longpuddle, The. Thomas Hardy. CP-HardT

He paused on the sill of a door ajar. Newcomer's Wife, The. Thomas Hardy. CP-HardT

He picks up crystal buttons from the ocean floor. Growth of a Poet. Denise Levertov. SP-LeveDL

He picks up what he thinks is. My Father: October 1942. William Stafford. SP-StafW; SP-StafWW

He pitied them, himself deserving pity. Heraclitus. Czeslaw Milosz. CP-MiloC; CP-MiloCN, *tr. by* Richard Lourie

He placed his hands on the floor; he stood upside down; not merely. Acrobatics. Yannis Ritsos. SP-RitsY, *tr. by* Kostas Myrsiades

He placed the fish on the chair. Condensation. Yannis Ritsos. SP-RitsY, *tr. by* Kostas Myrsiades

He placed the paper box on the table quietly. Liturgical. Yannis Ritsos. SP-RitsY, *tr. by* Kimon Friar *and* Kostas Myrsiades

He planted, years ago, before his door. On the Mountain Ash Tree: In front of the house of the late Capt. Robert W. Gould. Jones Very. CP-VeryJ

He play'd his wings as though for flight. Love Preparing to Fly. Gerard Manley Hopkins. CP-HopkG

He played jacks with me. Rocker, The. Donald Hall. CP-HallD

He plodded away through drifts of i / ce. Pythagorean Silence. Susan Howe. SP-HoweS

He preached upon "Breadth" till it argued him narrow. Emily Dickinson. CP-DickE

He Prefers Her Earthly. Thomas Hardy. CP-HardT

He pressed his face against the bars. Monkey House, The. Yusef Komunyakaa. CP-KomuY

He presses the eight o'clock dew with short sharp paces. Mexican Peacock, The. Josephine Jacobsen. CP-JacoJ

He pulled off on the shoulder, less to lend. Funeral. Miller Williams. CP-WillM

He pushes behind the words. Waiting ("He pushes behind the words"). Robert Creeley. CP-CreeR

He put on his shoes, his gloves, his cap. Ultimate Innocence. Yannis Ritsos. SP-RitsY, *tr. by* Kimon Friar *and* Kostas Myrsiades

He put the Belt around my life. Emily Dickinson. CP-DickE

He puts four dimes into the slot. Vending Machine. Hans Magnus Enzensberger. SP-EnzeH

He puts the poem by, to say. Old School-Chum, The. James Whitcomb Riley. CP-RileJ

He ran the course and as he ran he grew. Innocence. Thom Gunn. CP-GunnT

He reads in a book, he reads in a book. Triennial, The. Jones Very. CP-VeryJ

He recalled the young newboys, in winter, in the subway station. New Pretexts. Yannis Ritsos. SP-RitsY, *tr. by* Minas Savvas

He remained silent on many things. My Father's Birthday. Kathleen Jessie Raine. SP-RainK

He Remembereth that We Are Dust. Adrienne Rich. CP-RicAE

He Remembers Forgotten Beauty. William Butler Yeats. CP-YeatW

He replied to his own question, and with the unmannered. Meditation on John Constable, A. Charles Tomlinson. CP-TomlC; SP-TomlC

He Reproves the Curlew. William Butler Yeats. CP-YeatW

He Resigns. John Berryman. CP-BerrJ

He Resolves to Say No More. Thomas Hardy. CP-HardT

He resteth: weep not! Resurrection Eve. Christina Georgina Rossetti. CP-RosC3

He rests at last, as on the mother-breast. Rest, The. James Whitcomb Riley. CP-RileJ

He Revisits His First School. Thomas Hardy. CP-HardT

He rides at their head. College Colonel, The. Herman Melville. SP-MelvH

He rises and begins to round. Lark Ascending, The. George Meredith. CP-MerG1

He rises he stretches he liquefies he is hammered again. Squeal. Allen Ginsberg. CP-GinsA

He rode across like a cavalier. Two Who Crossed a Line. Countee Cullen. CP-CullC

He rode into town upon a wild-eyed mountain horse. Yellowjacket. Peter Blue Cloud. SP-BlueP

He rose up on his dying bed. Hope ("He rose up on his dying bed"). Langston Hughes. CP-HughL; CP-HughL3

He runs before the wise men: he. He. Stanley Kunitz. CP-KunSC

He runs his eyes out idly, sliding. Tower, The. Randall Jarrell. CP-JarrR

He runs in his sleep, snaps, leaps up, without. Midnight. John Ciardi. CP-CiarJ

He Said. A. R. Ammons. CP-AmmoA

He Said. Alice Walker. CP-WalkA

He said: "Awake my soul, and with the sun." Barthélémon at Vauxhall. Thomas Hardy. CP-HardT

He Said Come. Alice Walker. CP-WalkA

He said: "Even solitude is a correlation." Reverse Side. Yannis Ritsos. SP-RitsY, *tr. by* Kimon Friar

He said: "Form cannot be contrived nor imposed." On Form. Yannis Ritsos. SP-RitsY, *tr. by* Kimon Friar

He said he would be back and we'd drink wine together. Waiting for Icarus. Muriel Rukeyser. CP-RukeM

He said he'd knocked against a wall, or that he'd fallen. Bandaged Shoulder, The. Constantine P. Cavafy. CP-CavaC, *tr. by* Theoharis Constantine Theoharis

He said: Here is my soul. Gift. Alice Walker. CP-WalkA

He said / I am mud. Upright. A. R. Ammons. CP-AmmoA

He said: I believe in poetry, in love, in death. Last Will and Testament. Yannis Ritsos. SP-RitsY, *tr. by* N. C. Germanacos

He said: "I do not know you." He Did Not Know Me. Thomas Hardy. CP-HardT

He said: I want you to be happy. He Said. Alice Walker. CP-WalkA

He said, I'm just out of hospital. R. A. F. "H. D." CP-DoolH

He said it doesn't look good. What the Doctor Said. Raymond Carver. CP-CarvR

He said: It is God's way. William McKinley. James Whitcomb Riley. CP-RileJ

He said no word of her to us. Nor We of Her to Him. Stevie Smith. CP-SmitS

He said that he was God. Fool, The. Hugh MacDiarmid. SP-MacDH

He said: "The birds go against the wind." Courage or Ignorance. Yannis Ritsos. SP-RitsY, *tr. by* Thanasis Maskaleris

He said: this universe is very clever. T. S. Eliot. SP-ElioT

He said to me: You don't trust me! Emotional Friend, The. D. H. Lawrence. CP-LawrD

He said to me: Your life will be so much the poorer. Refused Friendship. D. H. Lawrence. CP-LawrD

He said, turning, unconscious of. Gangster. Robert Creeley. CP-CreeR

He sailed o'er the weltery watery miles. Great Explorer, The. James Whitcomb Riley. CP-RileJ

He sang, and, in her heart, the sound. Wallace Stevens. CP-StevWP

He sang / How the swan blanched forever. Owl's Song. Ted Hughes. SP-HughTN

He sang of life, serenely sweet. Poet, The. Paul Laurence Dunbar. CP-DunbP

He sat down with his arms. For the First Time. James Laughlin. CP-LaugJ

He sat for days in a stranger's field, always planning. Ascent. Yannis Ritsos. SP-RitsY, *tr. by* Kimon Friar

He sat in a wheeled chair, waiting for dark. Disabled. Wilfred Owen. CP-OwenW

He sat in an enamel tub with a black. Mercy Seat, The. Norman Dubie. CP-DubiN

He sat in the shade of trees at moonrise. In the Time of False Messiahs. Norman Dubie. CP-DubiN

He sat upon the rolling deck. Sailor. Langston Hughes. CP-HughL; CP-HughL1

He sate, no stiller stands a rock. Arthur Hugh Clough. SP-ClouA

He saw a fire dancer take two flambeaus. Impossible Iambics. Carl Sandburg. CP-SandC

He saw a laughing girl. Emily Dickinson. Richard Eberhart. CP-EberR

He saw her from the bottom of the stairs. Home Burial. Robert Frost. CP-FrosR

He saw her: that is, he labored. Gloss on the Sin of Ixion. Thomas Merton. CP-MertT

He saw the clouds from the park bench. Laugh, The. Yannis Ritsos. SP-RitsY, *tr. by* Kostas Myrsiades

He saw the portrait of his enemy, offered. Enemy's Portrait, The. Thomas Hardy. CP-HardT

He saw them tasked with heavy burthens all. Compassion. Jones Very. CP-VeryJ

He saw them tasked with heavy burthens all. Christ's Compassion. Jones Very. CP-VeryJ

He sayeth there is no sin, and all his sin. Modern Manichee, The. G. K. Chesterton. CP-ChesG

He says he doesn't feel like working today. My Erotic Double. John Ashbery. SP-AshbJ

He says that religious thought and all our nerviness. Religious Man, A. Stevie Smith. CP-SmitS

He says the waves in the ship's wake. Leaving Forever. Denise Levertov. SP-LeveDP

He says this red as dust, eyes a literal self among selves and picks the coffee up. Notes for Echo Lake 1. Michael Palmer. SP-PalmM

He scanned it—staggered. Emily Dickinson. CP-DickE

He scribbles some in prose and verse. Dilettante, The: A Modern Type. Paul Laurence Dunbar. CP-DunbP

He seemed so strange to me, every way. Little Fat Doctor, The. James Whitcomb Riley. CP-RileJ

He sees the fields that still belong to him. John Kantakuzinos Triumphs. Constantine P. Cavafy. CP-CavaC, *tr. by* Theoharis Constantine Theoharis

He sees the world as a boisterous place. John and Jane. Thomas Hardy. CP-HardT

He seized me by the waist and kissed my throat. Charleston in the Eighteen-Sixties. Adrienne Rich. CP-RicAE; SP-RicA2

He set out and kept hunting. Hunter, The. Frank O'Hara. SP-OharF

He shakes the dust from off his feet. Battle of Murfreesboro. Allen Tate. CP-TateA

He Shall Go No More Out. Christina Georgina Rossetti. CP-RosC2

He shall sleep unscathed of thieves. Out of Nazareth. James Whitcomb Riley. CP-RileJ

He-she bends at the mirrored waist. False Portrait. Michael Palmer. SP-PalmM

He Shot Arrows, but Not at Birds Perching. Gary Snyder. CP-SnydG

He shoves the .38. Cage Walker, The. Yusef Komunyakaa. CP-KomuY

He shuffles, and his face is white and lazy. Clam Man. Mary Oliver. SP-OlivM

He Shuts His Eyes for the Layman's Long Prayer about Lust and the Mind of the Young Preacher Wanders Again. Miller Williams. CP-WillM

He sighed with relief. He had the job. He was safe. Schoolmaster. Philip Larkin. CP-LarkP

He sings: and his song is heard. One with a Song. James Whitcomb Riley. CP-RileJ

He sits before me now, reptilian, cold. Old Man Drunk. James Wright. CP-WrigJ

He sits crouched in a hole. Eyeball Television. Yusef Komunyakaa. CP-KomuY

He sits in the room alone, imagines a storm. Professor. Miller Williams. CP-WillM

He sits on a hill. Jaime. Langston Hughes. CP-HughL; CP-HughL2

He / sits on the bridge. Yannis Ritsos. SP-RitsY *Fr.* So?

He sits there. Not to Worry. Charles Bukowski. SP-BukC3

He slashed the briars, shovelled up grey silt. Undine. Seamus Heaney. SP-HeanSO

He sleeps on the top of a mast. Unbeliever, The. Elizabeth Bishop. CP-BishE

He slept on his hands. Sleeping. Raymond Carver. CP-CarvR

He smelled bad and was red-eyed with the miseries. Portrait from the Infantry. Alan Dugan. CP-DugaA

He smiles in a mirror, shrinking the whole. Meeting. Ted Hughes. SP-HughTN

He smiles to see His children, born to sin. God of This World, The. Howard Nemerov. CP-NemeH

"He smokes—and that's enough," says Ma. While Cigarettes to Ashes Turn. James Whitcomb Riley. CP-RileJ

He sold rotten barley at a high price. Alexandrian Merchant. Constantine P. Cavafy. CP-CavaC, *tr. by* Theoharis Constantine Theoharis

He sought the music of the distant spheres. Quatrain: "He sought the music of the distant spheres." Wallace Stevens. CP-StevWP

He speaks of eating three hot meals a day. Courtesies of the Interregnum. Thom Gunn. CP-GunnT

He Speaks to His Arguing Friends and to Himself. Miller Williams. CP-WillM

He speaks to the sea. Apparition. Tennessee Williams. CP-WillT

He spends lots of time in that all-night movie. That One. Philip Whalen. SP-WhalP

He spoke with a studied indifference, gazing at his fingernails. Night after night—he said. Imitation of an Imitation. Yannis Ritsos. SP-RitsY, tr. by Kimon Friar and Kostas Myrsiades

He spreads pale lids to make the mirror jump. Translated from Silence. Robert Stock. SP-StocR

He, standing hushed, a pace or two apart. A. E. Housman. CP-HousA

He stands at the marble table. He persists. Unacceptable, The. Yannis Ritsos. SP-RitsY, tr. by N. C. Germanacos

He stands, filling the doorway. Risen, The. Ted Hughes. SP-HughTN

He stands there sleek and calm. Fourth David, The. Eleanor Wilner. SP-WilnE

He stands with his forefeet on the drum. Two Performing Elephants. D. H. Lawrence. CP-LawrD

He stares upward at a monstrous face. Pietà, Rhenish, 14th C., the Cloisters, The. Mona Van Duyn. SP-VanDM

He startles awake. His eyes are full of white light. Hermit Wakes to Bird Sounds, The. Maxine W. Kumin. SP-KumiM

He starts awake in the city. Orion believing. Muriel Rukeyser. CP-RukeM

He stayed a student of Ammonias Sakkas for two years. From the School of the Renowned Philosopher. Constantine P. Cavafy. CP-CavaC, tr. by Theoharis Constantine Theoharis

He stepped out of bed at night. Truncated Bird, The. Richard Eberhart. CP-EberR

He steps around a gate of bushes. Cold Water. Donald Hall. CP-HallD

He stirs, beginning to awake. Field Hospital, A. Randall Jarrell. CP-JarrR

He stood, a point / on a sheet of green paper. Progressive Insanities of a Pioneer. Margaret Atwood. SP-AtwM1

He stood against the stove. Mearl Blankenship. Muriel Rukeyser. CP-RukeM

He stood among a crowd at Drumahair [or Dromahair]. Man Who Dreamed of Faeryland, The. William Butler Yeats. CP-YeatW

He stood, and heard the steeple. Eight o'Clock. A. E. Housman. CP-HousA

He stood before the throne. Ghosts Listen to Orpheus Sing, The. Gregory Orr. SP-OrrG

He stood behind the rock to undress. He couldn't be seen. Adolescent. Yannis Ritsos. SP-RitsY, tr. by Athan Anagnostopoulos

He stood beside the station rail. Goin' Back. Paul Laurence Dunbar. CP-DunbP

He stood in a green stand of corn. Accident. Norman Dubie. CP-DubiN

He stood on the brow of the well-known hill. Fratricide, The. John Greenleaf Whittier. CP-WhitJ

He stopped at the bend of the cobbled road under the extinguished lamplight. Coins. Yannis Ritsos. SP-RitsY Fr. Monovasia.

He stops his wife in the street. Shapely. David Ignatow. SP-IgnaD

He strained my faith. Emily Dickinson. CP-DickE

He strolled from one end of the beach to the other, his entire body glowing. Summer. Yannis Ritsos. SP-RitsY, tr. by Kimon Friar

He suspects that the seasons. Set of Seasons, A. Donald Hall. CP-HallD

He swears every now and then to start a better life. Constantine P. Cavafy. CP-CavaC, tr. by Theoharis Constantine Theoharis

He swings his lamp into a hovel. Lamp Carrier, The. Yusef Komunyakaa. CP-KomuY

He takes clay, molds the face, the body. Craftsman, The. Yannis Ritsos. SP-RitsY, tr. by Kimon Friar

He talked of Africa. Companion—North-East Dug-Out. Ivor Gurney. SP-GurnI

He Tells a Valley Full of Lovers. William Butler Yeats. CP-YeatW

He tells me in Bangkok he's robbed. Baby Villon. Philip Levine. SP-LeviP

He Tells of the Perfect Beauty. William Butler Yeats. CP-YeatW

He tells you when you've got on too much lipstick. Perfect Husband, The. Ogden Nash. CP-NashO

He thanked his parents for keeping still. Upriver Incident, The. Paul Muldoon. CP-MuldP

He thanks God daily. Profile. W. H. Auden. CP-AudeW

He that ascended in a cloud, shall come. Clouds. Robert Herrick. CP-HerrR

He that cannot choose but love. Self Love. John Donne. CP-DonnJ

He that dwelleth in the secret place of the most High. Psalm 91: "He that dwelleth in the secret place of the most High." Bible, O.T. CP-PopeA Fr. Psalms.

He that fears death, or mourns it, in the just. Of Death. Ben Jonson. CP-JonsB; SP-JonsB

He that hath a Gospel. Disciple, The. Rudyard Kipling. CP-KiplR

He that hes gold and grit riches. William Dunbar. CP-DunbW

He that imposes an oath, makes it. Unknown, sometimes at. to Thomas Sheridan. CP-SherT

He that ingenious art did first descry. In the French Translation of Lucan by Monsieur De Brebeuf Are These Verses: Lib 3. Lucan. CP-MarvA Fr. Civil War [Bellum Civile] or Pharsalia.

He that is hurt seeks help: sin is the wound. Eucharist, The. Robert Herrick. CP-HerrR

He that is Lord of all the realms of light. Canzone: Of Angels. Ezra Pound. CP-PoEar

He that is one. Trinity Sunday. George Herbert. CP-HerbG

He that is robbed and smiles. Emily Dickinson. SP-DickE

He that is weary, let him sit. Employment: "He that is weary, let him sit." George Herbert. CP-HerbG

He that loves a rosy cheek. Disdain Returned. Thomas Carew. CP-CareT

He that may sin, sins least; Leave to transgresse. More Potent, Lesse Peccant. Robert Herrick. CP-HerrR

He that should search all glories of the gown. Epigram on Sir Edward Coke, when He Was Lord Chief Justice of England, An. Ben Jonson. CP-JonsB

He that will live of all cares dispossest. Suspicion Makes Secure. Robert Herrick. CP-HerrR

He that will not love must be. Not to Love. Robert Herrick. CP-HerrR

He that would move another man to laughter. Martial. CP-SherT, tr. by Thomas Sheridan

He thinks / always things. Out of Sight. Robert Creeley. CP-CreeR

He thinks he wouldn't have thought for all those miles. 71 South. Miller Williams. CP-WillM

He Thinks of His Past Greatness when a Part of the Constellations of Heaven. William Butler Yeats. CP-YeatW

He Thinks of Those Who Have Spoken Evil of His Beloved. William Butler Yeats. CP-YeatW

He thinks of when he is dead and how it will be. Jonathan at Lenox. Miller Williams. CP-WillM

He thought he kept the universe alone. Most of It, The. Robert Frost. CP-FrosR

He thought he saw the Unicorn, the horned and holy horse. Apology for a Letter Unposted, An. G. K. Chesterton. CP-ChesG

He Thought of Mad Ellen's Ravings and of the Wretched Skeleton on the Rock. Kenneth Patchen. CP-PatcK

He thrives on deserts: his hands are stones, his tongue a thistle. Azazel. Robert Stock. SP-StocR

He, through the eyes of the first marauder. To a Girl Who Knew What Side Her Bread Was Buttered On. Audre Lorde. SP-LordA

He throws his arms around. Making Out with the Dream-Shredding Machine. Yusef Komunyakaa. CP-KomuY

He told a homely tale. Emily Dickinson. CP-DickE

He Told His Life Story to Mrs. Courtly. Stevie Smith. CP-SmitS (Autumn.) CP-SmitS

He told me he had all the gas on. Suicide. Charles Bukowski. SP-BukC2

He told me he loved me. Broken Heart, The. Stevie Smith. CP-SmitS

He told me he was well-to-do. Concerning a Jackass. Charles Baudelaire. CP-BaudC, tr. by Walter Martin

He told us we were free to choose. Friday's Child. W. H. Auden. CP-AudeW

He toned the sprightly beam of morning. Marchioness of Brinvilliers, The. Herman Melville. SP-MelvH

He too has eaten well—. Lizard, The. Theodore Roethke. CP-RoetT

He too has flitted from his secret nest. Pang More Sharp than All, The. Samuel Taylor Coleridge. CP-ColeS; MW-ColeS

He Too Was a Light Sleeper Once. A. K. Ramanujan. CP-RamaA

He took a frayed hat from his head. Peace on Earth. Edwin Arlington Robinson. CP-RobiE

He took a room in a port city with a fellow. To Begin With. Raymond Carver. CP-CarvR

He took all his money. Ballad of the Miser. Langston Hughes. CP-HughL; CP-HughL1

He took her, trembling. Anniversaries. Thomas Kinsella. CP-KinsT

He took it seriously. Rozewicz. Czeslaw Milosz. CP-MiloCN, tr. by Robert Hass

He touched me, so I live to know. Emily Dickinson. CP-DickE

He touches me in the nocturnal dew. Obsession, The. Frédéric Mistral. SP-MistG, tr. by Maria Giachetti [or Jacketti]

He tramped in the fading light. Monk, The. Thomas Kinsella. CP-KinsT

He traveled, traveled in the human climate. Explorer. Josephine Jacobsen. CP-JacoJ

He travels three hundred miles to New York. Traveler. Grace Paley. CP-PalGC

He treads on edges of being where the drop. Charles Olson. CP-OlsoC

He tried to speak; he faltered. Proletarian Speaker, A. Yannis Ritsos. SP-RitsY, tr. by Minas Savvas

He trod in dream upon the brim. Death's Ostracism. Stevie Smith. CP-SmitS

He trusted death when it said "I am the end!" Mourner Betrayed. Josephine Jacobsen. CP-JacoJ

He turned and. Moment. A. R. Ammons. CP-AmmoA

He turned cruel. Absorbed in his own cruelty. Muriel Rukeyser. CP-RukeM

He turned the key in the door. Statues, The. Yannis Ritsos. SP-RitsY, tr. by Minas Savvas

He turns through the lucid stars of a lit city. Muriel Rukeyser. CP-RukeM

He unlocked his dark room with hesitation. Conqueror, The. Yannis Ritsos. SP-RitsY, tr. by Kimon Friar

He, unto whom thou art so partial. Martial, Lib. I. Epig. I. Lord Byron. CP-

Byron

He used to frighten me in the nights of childhood. Man in the Moon, The. Billy Collins. SP-CollB

He used to pass, well-trimmed and brushed. Passer-By, The. Thomas Hardy. CP-HardT

He waited in the sadness of the sun's intention. Sun, The. Donald Hall. CP-HallD

He waits, and it is not without. Lover, The. Frank O'Hara. SP-OharF

He wakes up to the noise of ravens in the spruce trees. From the Rooftop. Arthur Sze. SP-SzeA

He walked—loped—the bridge. LZ. Lorine Niedecker. CP-NiedL

He walked around dictating. Memories of a Boss in an Ad Agency. Alan Dugan. CP-DugaA

He walked the streets of great New York. Ralph Waldo Emerson. CP-EmerR

He walks ahead. Dog's Theology, The. Yusef Komunyakaa. CP-KomuY

He walks in the rain. He's in no hurry at all. In the Rain. Yannis Ritsos. SP-RitsY, tr. by Kostas Myrsiades

He walks out of the village. The road. Village in East Anglia, A. Donald Hall. CP-HallD

He walks up to my Volks. Fear. Charles Bukowski. SP-BukC1

He wandered down the mountain grade. Idiot Boy, The. Rudyard Kipling. CP-KiplR Fr. Muse among the Motors, The.

He wandering far along the lonely main. Orpheus and Eurydice. Virgil. CP-WorW1 Fr. Georgics.

He Wanders. Grace Paley. CP-PalGC

He wanders, like a day-appearing dream. Fragment: A Wanderer. Percy Bysshe Shelley. CP-ShelP

He wanted so much to have it perfectly right. First Date. Miller Williams. CP-WillM

He wants to be. Self-Portrait. Robert Creeley. SP-CreeR

He wants to be an Indian. Yellow. Robert Creeley. CP-CreeR

He wants to go north. His life has become. Old Prof. William Stafford. SP-StafWW

He wants to go somewhere he hasn't been. She Prays for Her Husband, the Good Pastor, Lying on His Deathbed at Last. Miller Williams. CP-WillM

He Was. Richard Wilbur. CP-WilbR

He was a cold-hearted Saxon. Fanny Howe. SP-HoweF Fr. O'Clock.

He was a Dreamer of the Days. Mr. Hammond's Parable. James Whitcomb Riley. CP-RileJ Fr. Child-World, A.

He was a farmboy who had drowned that Wednesday. Revelation 20:11–15. Norman Dubie. CP-DubiN

He was a Grecian lad, who coming home. Charmides. Oscar Wilde. CP-WildO

He was a man made a bank. Friend, The. Charles Olson. CP-OlsoC

He was a man of his time and of its distresses and he rode. August. Hayden Carruth. CP-CarHS

He was a messy sort of person. Reading the Obituary Page in *The Times*. James Laughlin. CP-LaugJ

He was a poet who wrote clever verses. Confirmation. Paul Laurence Dunbar. CP-DunbP

He was a shepherd of the Arcadian mood. Richard. Gerard Manley Hopkins. CP-HopkG

He was a soldier in the army. Casualty. Langston Hughes. CP-HughL; CP-HughL3

He was a young guy with surrealist connections. Epitaph (2): "He was a young guy with surrealist connections." Andrei Codrescu. SP-CodrA

He Was Acquainted with Grief. Jones Very. CP-VeryJ

He was all in;—what use to him were glories now?—enough. Achilles after Death. Yannis Ritsos. SP-RitsY, tr. by N. C. Germanacos

He Was Alone (as in Reality) upon His Humble Bed. Kenneth Patchen. CP-PatcK

He was always hunting for the *mot juste*. Lament for a Master of Style. Dan Pagis. SP-PagiD, tr. by Stephen Mitchell

He was always surrounded by the sea of his elders. Herman Melville. Jorge Luis Borges. SP-BorgJ, tr. by Stephen Kessler

He was always there. Weatherman. Miller Williams. CP-WillM

He was at Naples writing letters home. Esthétique du Mal. Wallace Stevens. CP-StevV; CP-StevWP

He was believed by his peers to be an important poet. Days of 1986. Carolyn Kizer. CP-KizeC

He was born far inland in a little town. Mr. Dodd's Son. Robert Penn Warren. CP-WarrR

He was born in Deutschland, as you would suspect. Progress of Faust, The. Karl Shapiro. SP-ShapK

He was born in Dublin, but two years later. Biography of the Author, A: A Cento. Charles Tomlinson. CP-TomlC

He was born to wonder about numbers. Number Man. Carl Sandburg. CP-SandC

He was caressing the back and shoulders. Across the Room. David Ignatow. SP-IgnaD

He was facing phantasma when the bell rang. Dinner Bell in the Woods. Wallace Stevens. CP-StevWP

He was found by the Bureau of Statistics to be. Unknown Citizen, The. W. H. Auden. CP-AudeW

He was fully debased. A sexual drift in him. Days of 1896. Constantine P. Cavafy. CP-CavaC, tr. by Theoharis Constantine Theoharis

He was generally liked in Alexandria. Prince from Western Libya, A. Constantine P. Cavafy. CP-CavaC, tr. by Theoharis Constantine Theoharis

He was in charge of something large. Epitaph to a Tyrant. Joseph Brodsky. CP-BrodJ Fr. Shorts.

He was in Cincinnati, she in Burlington. Couple, A. Carl Sandburg. CP-SandC

He was jes' a plain, ever'-day, all-round kind of a jour. Jim. James Whitcomb Riley. CP-RileJ

He was just a. One for the Old Boy. Charles Bukowski. SP-BukC3

He was leaning by a face. Mismet. Thomas Hardy. CP-HardT

He was measuring his gestures, his expressions, his words. Calculated Behavior. Yannis Ritsos. SP-RitsY, tr. by Minas Savvas

He was my host—he was my guest. Emily Dickinson. CP-DickE

He was naked in water. Country Bath. Josephine Jacobsen. CP-JacoJ

He was never above the mêlée. After a Change of Régime. Donald Davie. CP-DaviDC

He was never the same, they said, after that. Prize, The. Raymond Carver. CP-CarvR

He was no longer my father. Mirror, The. Michael Davitt. CP-MuldP, tr. by Paul Muldoon

He was not armed like those of eastern clime. Soldier of the Cross, The. Jones Very. CP-VeryJ

He was not bad, as emperors go, not really. Two Pieces after Suetonius. Robert Penn Warren. CP-WarrR

He was not changed. His friends around the grave. Lazarus Not Raised. Thom Gunn. CP-GunnT

He was one of those first butterflies. Few Easter Eggs, A. Rainer Maria Rilke. CP-RilkFr, tr. by A. Poulin, Jr.

He was ploughing his single furrow. Merman, The. Paul Muldoon. CP-MuldP

He was standing at the far end of the street. Doxology. Yannis Ritsos. SP-RitsY, tr. by Kimon Friar

He was talking so fast I. James Laughlin. CP-LaugJ Fr. America I Love You.

He was the finest of our happy men. For a Dead Citizen. Allen Tate. CP-TateA

He was the man—Pope Sixtus, that Fifth, that swineherd's son. Bean-Feast, The. Robert Browning. CP-BroR2

He was the only poet of his small nation. Persons. Czeslaw Milosz. CP-MiloCN, tr. by Robert Hass

He was the son of a much wronged, penniless sailor. Days of 1909, '10 and '11. Constantine P. Cavafy. CP-CavaC, tr. by Theoharis Constantine Theoharis

He was the surveyor of his own ice-world. Order of Service, An. Geoffrey Hill. CP-HillG

He was the youngest son of a strange brood. Otto. Theodore Roethke. CP-RoetT

He was there as the yachts went by. Maine Roustabout, A. Richard Eberhart. CP-EberR

He was there in my room. Caged Bird, The. May Sarton. SP-SartM

He was there / with his crown of. Tower. Federico García Lorca. CP-GarcF, tr. by Jerome Rothenberg Fr. In the Forest of the Lunar Grapefruits.

He was very beautiful. Master, The. "H. D." CP-DoolH

He was very much the less attractive of the two: heavyset, part punk, part L.L. Bean. Love: Wrath. C. K. Williams. SP-WillC

He was very old. but his spirit held. King, A. Adam Zagajewski. SP-ZagaA, tr. by Clare Cavanagh

He was warned aginst the *womern*. On a Splendud Match. James Whitcomb Riley. CP-RileJ

He was weak, and I was strong—then. Emily Dickinson. CP-DickE

He was wise, / they said, / in being dead. Message, The. Robert Creeley. CP-CreeR

He wastes time walking and telling the air, "I am superior even to the wind." Sketch of a Poet. Carl Sandburg. CP-SandC

He wears in his heart. Two Sailors on the Beach. Federico García Lorca. SP-GarcF, tr. by Donald Jenks

He went by sleep that drowsy route. Emily Dickinson. CP-DickE

He went out to their glorious. Summons, The. James Laughlin. CP-LaugJ

He went to being called a Colored man. Calling of Names, The. Maya Angelou. SP-AngeM

He went up under the gray leaves. Olive Garden, The. Randall Jarrell. CP-JarrR

He where the great sun looks his last. George Meredith. CP-MerG2

He whitewashed the house. Yannis Ritsos. SP-RitsY Fr. Paper Poems 1.

He who beguiles both time and death together. Michelangelo Buonarroti. CP-Miche, tr. by John Frederick Nims

He who beneath thy shelt'ring wing resides. Bible, *O.T. See* He that dwelleth in the secret place of the most High

He-who-came-forth was. Son, The. Denise Levertov. SP-LeveDP

He who commends the vanquisht, speaks the Power. Credit of the Conquerer, The. Robert Herrick. CP-HerrR

He Who Depends on the Princes. Shmuel HaNagid. SP-HaNaS, *tr.* by Peter Cole

He who died was, in truth, remarkable. Evaluation. Yannis Ritsos. SP-RitsY, *tr.* by Kimon Friar

He who disappeared inexplicably one afternoon (perhaps). Real Hands. Yannis Ritsos. SP-RitsY, *tr.* by Kimon Friar *and* Kostas Myrsiades

He who had gone a beast. John Chrysostom. Richard Wilbur. CP-WilbR

He who has a thousand friends has not a friend to spare. Make Friends. Omar Khayyám. CP-EmerR

He who has looked upon Earth. Day of the Daughter of Hades, The. George Meredith. CP-MerG1

He, who has suffer'd Ship-wrack, feares to saile. Ship-Wrack. Robert Herrick. CP-HerrR

He who in Himself believes. Emily Dickinson. CP-DickE

He, Who, in His Abandoned Infancy, Spoke of Jesus, Caesar, Those Who Beg, and Hell. Charles Olson. CP-OlsoC

He, who in Thessaly was all too keen. Petrarch. CP-Petra, *tr.* by J. G. Nichols

He who is adamant to live his life. Petrarch. CP-Petra, *tr.* by J. G. Nichols

He who is ridden by a conscience. Reflection of the Fallibility of Nemesis. Ogden Nash. CP-NashO

He Who Lingers at the Court of the King. Shmuel HaNagid. SP-HaNaS, *tr.* by Peter Cole

He Who made all there is, made every part. Michelangelo Buonarroti. CP-Miche, *tr.* by John Frederick Nims

He, who navigated with success. Death of a Young Son by Drowning. Margaret Atwood. SP-AtwM1

He who of Rankine [*or* R--k-n] sang, lies stiff and dead, Lines on the Author's Death. Robert Burns. CP-BurnR

He who proposes. On a Proposed Celebration of Ezra Pound. Donald Davie. CP-DaviDC

He Who reveals His providence and art. Petrarch. CP-Petra, *tr.* by J. G. Nichols

He who rules men lives in confusion. Empty Boat, The. Chuang Tzu. CP-MertT

He who saw everything, of him learn, o my land, learn. Bigmans II. Charles Olson. CP-OlsoC

He who sits from day to day. On a Similar Occasion for the Year 1790. William Cowper. CP-CowpW

He who sublime in epic numbers roll'd. Translation of the Epitaph on Virgil and Tibullus. Lord Byron. CP-Byron

He who wears Blacks, and mournes not for the Dead. False Mourning. Robert Herrick. CP-HerrR

He whom God had thus preferred. Ralph Waldo Emerson. CP-EmerR

He whom the dread of want ensnares. Ode 3.24: "He whom the dread of want ensnares." Horace. CP-JohnS *Fr.* Odes.

He whose heart. He Whose Heart in His Heart. Shmuel HaNagid. SP-HaNaS, *tr.* by Peter Cole

He Whose Heart in His Heart. Shmuel HaNagid. SP-HaNaS, *tr.* by Peter Cole

He whose law is within himself. Inner Law, The. Chuang Tzu. CP-MertT

He Will Come to My Funeral with a White Flower. Arthur Sze. SP-SzeA

He will love you presently. To a Much Too Unfortunate Lady. Dorothy Parker. CP-ParkD

He will not answer now. He will go down. Biography. John Ciardi. CP-CiarJ

He will watch the hawk with an indifferent eye. Icarus. Stephen Spender. CP-SpenS

He Wishes for the Cloths of Heaven. William Butler Yeats. CP-YeatW

He Wishes His Beloved Were Dead. William Butler Yeats. CP-YeatW

He with body waged a fight. Four Ages of Man, The. William Butler Yeats. CP-YeatW

He with the Beating Wings. Lawrence Ferlinghetti. SP-FerlL

He with whom I ran hand in hand. Woman Meets an Old Lover, A. Denise Levertov. SP-LeveDL

He withdrew from our company little by little, as though he were somewhat sad. Unacceptable Man, The. Yannis Ritsos. SP-RitsY, *tr.* by Kimon Friar

He woke in his usual room, decided. Good Dream. Louis MacNeice. CP-MacNL

He won her Classic races, at the start. Last Fistful, The. Robert Graves. CP-GravR

He Wonders about Himself. Thomas Hardy. CP-HardT

He wooed her first in an atmosphere. Test of Love, A. James Whitcomb Riley. CP-RileJ

He wore his coffin for a hat. For a Pessimist. Countee Cullen. CP-CullC

He wore the burnt-cork moustache and coonskin cap. Portrait. Alan Dugan. CP-DuganA

He worried every morning about the earth [*or* bomb]. He Glimpses a Nobler Vision. Miller Williams. CP-WillM

He would live against sentences. Symmetrical Poem: They Were Afraid of Death. Michael Palmer. SP-PalmM

He would always return to the same themes. One and one—he kept repeating. For Greater Accuracy. Yannis Ritsos. SP-RitsY, *tr.* by Kimon Friar

He would assume a seeing into the word, whoever was there to look. Notes for Echo Lake 2. Michael Palmer. SP-PalmM

He would declare and could himself believe. Never Again Would Birds' Song

Be the Same. Robert Frost. CP-FrosR

He would do as he had done in other states. Muriel Rukeyser. CP-RukeM

He would drink by himself. Casualty. Seamus Heaney. SP-HeanSO

He would have holiday—outworn, in sooth. Paths of Peace, The. James Whitcomb Riley. CP-RileJ

He would like not to kill. He would like. Robber Bridegroom, The. Margaret Atwood. SP-AtwM2

He would live against sentences. Notes for Echo Lake 10. Michael Palmer. SP-PalmM

He would not stay for me; and who can wonder? A. E. Housman. CP-HousA

He would / vacation in a mountain boarding house, he would. In Broad Daylight. Wisława Szymborska. SP-SzymW, *tr.* by Stanisław Barańczak *and* Clare Cavanagh

He would write a message to her. Curious Romance, A. James Laughlin. CP-LaugJ

He wrapped them up carefully, neatly. For the Shop. Constantine P. Cavafy. CP-CavaC, *tr.* by Theoharis Constantine Theoharis

He writes: Let us bear. Days, The: Spring. Adrienne Rich. CP-RicAE

He writes to the editors. Old Buddy, An. Charles Bukowski. SP-BukC3

He Wrote the History Book. Marianne Craig Moore. CP-MoorM

He wrote *The I and the It*. On the Death of a German Philosopher. Stevie Smith. CP-SmitS

Head. Carl Sandburg. CP-SandC

Head, A. James Schuyler. CP-SchuJ

Head a ray helix good morning. Sprengeri. Louis Zukofsky. CP-ZukLS

Head above the Fog, The. Thomas Hardy. CP-HardT

Head against White. Margaret Atwood. SP-AtwM1

Head-Aim, The. James Dickey. CP-DickJ

Head-Ake, The. Robert Herrick. CP-HerrR

Head alone shows you in the prodigious act. Perseus. Sylvia Plath. CP-PlatS

Head and hands of murdered Cicero, The. Tiber, Nile, and Thames. Dante Gabriel Rossetti. CW-RossD

Head Byzantine or from, The. Resting Figure. Denise Levertov. SP-LeveDP

Head: egg of all, The. Right Thinking Man. Marge Piercy. SP-PierM

Head fast / in out as dead. Dread Nay. Samuel Beckett. CP-BeckS

Head first, face down, into Mercator's world. For a Boy Born in Wartime. Jane Cooper. CP-CoopJ

Head Hewn with an Axe. Charles Tomlinson. CP-TomlC; SP-TomlC

Head Lines. Louis Zukofsky. CP-ZukLS

Head of. A. Robert Creeley. CP-CreeR

Head of Bran the Blest, The. George Meredith. CP-MerG1

Head of cheese raised by wolves, A. Wild Cheese, The. James Tate. SP-TateJ

Head of Lincoln looks down from the wall, The. Lincoln Theatre. Langston Hughes. CP-HughL; CP-HughL2

Head of Medusa. Marya Alexandrovna Zaturenska. SP-ZatuM

Head of the District, The. Rudyard Kipling. *Fr.* Life's Handicap.

Head of the German Shepherd I have now, The. Going to the Dogs. John Ciardi. CP-CiarJ

Head of the Virgin Mary, The. Jaroslav Seifert. SP-SeifJ, *tr.* by Ewald Osers

Head of Wisdom, The. Randall Jarrell. CP-JarrR

Head or Tail—which does he lack?, A. Hippo, The. Theodore Roethke. CP-RoetT

Head, The. Czeslaw Milosz. CP-MiloCN, *tr.* by Robert Hass

Head thrusts in as for the view, A. All Revelation. Robert Frost. CP-FrosR

Head to limp head, the sunk-eyed wounded scanned. Smile, Smile, Smile. Wilfred Owen. CP-OwenW

Headache. Wallace Stevens. CP-StevWP

Headdress. Rita Dove. SP-DoveR

Headed back home from Harold's, we came down. Ground Tide. A. R. Ammons. CP-AmmoA

Heading for Nandi. John Updike. CP-UpdiJ

Heading North, straw hat. Jiving. Rita Dove. SP-DoveR

Heading south, above. Daughter (2), A. Denise Levertov. SP-LeveDL

Headland, The. Charles Tomlinson. SP-TomlC

Headland towers over ocean, The. California. George Oppen. CP-OppGN

Headless fountains / running loose. Preponderance, The. William Meredith. SP-MereW

Headless in East Berlin, no goddess. Archaic Figure. Amy Clampitt. CP-ClamA

Headless man walks, lives, a. Sun. Michael Palmer. SP-PalmM

Headless squirrel, some blood, A. Day Begins, A. Denise Levertov. SP-LeveDP

Headlights fading out at dawn, The. New Day, A. Philip Levine. SP-LeviP

Heads. James Dickey. CP-DickJ

Heads, impenetrable / And the slow bulk, The. Oxen: Ploughing at Fiesole. Charles Tomlinson. CP-TomlC; SP-TomlC

Heads in the Women's Ward. Philip Larkin. CP-LarkP

Heads up to the sky. Juggler's Thought. Robert Creeley. CP-CreeR

Heal the soul, O still-featured host. Progress to a View of Life. Kenneth Patchen. CP-PatcK

Healall. William Carlos Williams. CP-WilW1

Healed. Dorothy Parker. CP-ParkD

Healed Heart shows its shallow scar, The. Emily Dickinson. CP-DickE

Healer, The. Charles Simic. SP-SimiC; SP-SimiCE

Healer, The. John Greenleaf Whittier. CP-WhitJ

Healing. D. H. Lawrence. CP-LawrD

Health. Robert Herrick. CP-HerrR

Health-Food Diner, The. Maya Angelou. SP-AngeM

Health is everything, health is all. Bathing Resort. D. H. Lawrence. CP-LawrD

Health is no other (as the learned hold). Health. Robert Herrick. CP-HerrR

Health is the first good lent to men. Four[e] Things Make Us Happy Here. Robert Herrick. CP-HerrR

Health of Body Dependent on the Soul. Jones Very. CP-VeryJ

Health of Captains, The. John Ciardi. CP-CiarJ

Health of captains is the sex of war, The. Health of Captains, The. John Ciardi. CP-CiarJ

Health to the Maxwells' veteran Chief! To Terraughty, on His Birth-Day. Robert Burns. CP-BurnR

Healthy Spot, A. W. H. Auden. CP-AudeW

Heaney, one can get word-perfect at. Summer Lightning. Donald Davie. CP-DaviDC

Heap not on this mound. Epitaph: "Heap not on this mound." Edna St. Vincent Millay. CP-MillE *Fr.* Memorial to D. C.

Heap of Broken Images, A. Lawrence Ferlinghetti. SP-FerlL

Heap we these coppered hulls. Voyage. Archibald MacLeish. CP-MacLA

Hear dat rum'lin' in de sky! Plantation Hymn. James Whitcomb Riley. CP-RileJ

Hear, her. Songs of Degrees. Louis Zukofsky. CP-ZukLS

Hear it tease question will. Crocus. Louis Zukofsky. CP-ZukLS

Hear, Land o' Cakes, and brither Scots. On the Late Captain Grose's Peregrinations thro' Scotland, Collecting the Antiquities of That King. Robert Burns. CP-BurnR

Hear, Lord, the song of praise and pray'r. Hymn for the Sunday School at Olney. William Cowper. CP-CowpW

Hear Me. Philip Levine. SP-LeviP

Hear me [*or* Heare mee], O God! Hymn[e] to God the Father, A. Ben Jonson. CP-JonsB

Hear me when I call, O God of my righteousness. Psalm 4: "Hear me when I call, O God of my righteousness." Bible, *O.T.* CP-MiltJ *Fr.* Psalms.

Hear me, whom I betrayed. Envoi: "Hear me, whom I betrayed." James Vincent Cunningham. CP-CunnJ

Hear, my belovéd, an old Milesian story! Catullian Hendecasyllables. Samuel Taylor Coleridge. CP-ColeS

Hear my prayer my father. Charles Olson. CP-OlsoC

Hear my prayer, O Lord, and let my cry come unto thee. Psalm 102: "Hear my prayer, O Lord, and let my cry come unto thee." Bible, *O.T.* CP-WyatT *Fr.* Psalms.

Hear my prayer, O Lord, give ear to my supplications. Psalm 143: "Hear my prayer, O Lord, give ear to my supplications." Bible, *O.T.* CP-WyatT *Fr.* Psalms.

Hear my prayer, O Lord, hear my request. Bible, *O.T. See* Hear my prayer, O Lord, give ear to my supplications

Hear my rigamarole. Reflex, A. Robert Frost. CP-FrosR

Hear now a curious dream I dreamed last night. My Dream. Christina Georgina Rossetti. CP-RosC1

Hear now the mission of good wine. George Meredith. CP-MerG2

Hear now the Song of the Dead—in the North by the torn berg-edges. Song of the Dead, The. Rudyard Kipling. CP-KiplR

Hear, sweet spirit, hear the spell. Invocation, An: "Hear, sweet spirit, hear the spell." Samuel Taylor Coleridge. CP-ColeS *Fr.* Remorse.

Hear the beautiful tinny voices of the trumpets. Hearing. Kenneth Koch. SP-KochK

Hear the bellow. Arthur Rimbaud. CP-RimbA, *tr. by* Martin Sorrell

Hear the sledges with the bells. Bells, The. Edgar Allan Poe. CP-PoeEd

Hear then the pride & knowledge of a Sailor. William Blake. CP-BlakW *Fr.* Island in the Moon, An.

Hear this, and tremble, all. Upon My Lord Chief Justice's Election of My Lady Anne Wentworth [*or* A. W.] for His Mistress. Thomas Carew. CP-CareT

Hear what a dead man said to me. What a Dead Man Said. James Whitcomb Riley. CP-RileJ

Hear what British Merlin sung. Motto to "Considerations by the Way." Ralph Waldo Emerson. CP-EmerR

Hear what the glass will tell thee. Hafiz. CP-EmerR *Fr.* Odes.

Hear what the mournful linnets say. Christina Georgina Rossetti. CP-RosC2

Hear / where her snow-grave is. Lorine Niedecker. CP-NiedL

Heard and Seen. W. H. Auden. CP-AudeW

Heard by a Girl. Louise Bogan. CP-BogaL

Heard de owl a hootin'. Gal's Cry for a Dying Lover. Langston Hughes. CP-HughL; CP-HughL1

Heard in a Violent Ward. Theodore Roethke. CP-RoetT

Heard say that four times four is eight. Footnote, A. Stephen Spender. CP-SpenS

Heard ye o' the tree o' France. Tree of Liberty, The. Robert Burns. CP-BurnR

Heard'st thou yon universal cry. Destruction of the Bastile. Samuel Taylor Coleridge. CP-ColeS

Hear[e] ye Virgins, and I'll [*or* Ile] teach. To Virgins. Robert Herrick. CP-HerrR

Hearing. Kenneth Koch. SP-KochK

Hearing. W. S. Merwin. SP-MerwWF

Hearing. Yannis Ritsos. SP-RitsY, *tr. by* Kostas Myrsiades

Hearing a car pass—. Sound. Robert Creeley. CP-CreeR

Hearing a white saint rave. On the Plethora of Dryads. Sylvia Plath. CP-PlatS

Hearing from some how the Sierra answers. Frontenac. Donald Davie. CP-DaviDC

Hearing of harvests rotting in the valleys. Paysage Moralisé. W. H. Auden. CP-AudeW

Hearing of you, I never lost a brother. Stepping Outside. Tess Gallagher. SP-GallT

Hearing offstage the taps filling the bath. Schizophrene. Louis MacNeice. CP-MacNL

Hearing one saga, we enact the next. Remembering the 'Thirties. Donald Davie. CP-DaviDC

Hearing Russian Spoken. Donald Davie. CP-DaviDC

Hearing shingle explode, seeing it skip. Crow on the Beach. Ted Hughes. SP-HughTN

Hearing the flute call. Two, The. Ivor Gurney. SP-GurnI

Hearing the hawk squeal in the high sky. Rabbit, The. Edna St. Vincent Millay. CP-MillE

Hearing the thunder of the intransitive weirs. Arthur Rimbaud. CP-MahoD *Fr.* Drunken Boat [*or* Barge], The.

Hearing the Wind at Night. May Swenson. SP-SwenM

Hearing Your Words, and Not a Word among Them. Edna St. Vincent Millay. CP-MillE

Hearing your words, and not a word among them. Hearing Your Words, and Not a Word among Them. Edna St. Vincent Millay. CP-MillE

Hearken, hearken! / Rapid river carrieth, The. Sounds. Elizabeth Barrett Browning. CP-BroEB

Hearken, landsmen, hearken, seamen. Land of Biscay, The. A. E. Housman. CP-HousA

Hearken!—now the hermit bee. Quiet Enemy, The. Walter De la Mare. CP-DeLaW

Hearken, O dear, now strikes the hour we die. Life. Walter De la Mare. CP-DeLaW

Hearken, thou craggy ocean pyramid! To Ailsa Rock. John Keats. CP-KeatJ

Hearken! Tiny, clear, discrete. Clavichord. Walter De la Mare. CP-DeLaW

Hearken! 'Tis news I cry! News. Walter De la Mare. CP-DeLaW

Hears't thou, my soul, what serious things. Dies Irae. Thomas of Celano. CP-CrasR, *tr. by* Richard Crashaw

Hearst thou, sweet spirit, thou hast heard before. Ralph Waldo Emerson. CP-EmerR

Heart. Langston Hughes. CP-HughL; CP-HughL2

Heart. Gregory Orr. SP-OrrG

Heart, The. Robert Herrick. CP-HerrR

Heart, The. W. S. Merwin. SP-MerwWF

Heart, The. Jones Very. CP-VeryJ

Heart and service to you proffered, The. Sir Thomas Wyatt. CP-WyatT

Heart asks Pleasure—first, The. Emily Dickinson. CP-DickE

Heart Attack in Bad Air. Alan Dugan. CP-DugaA

Heart Beats. Donald Davie. CP-DaviDC

Heart beats in its little red drum, The. Sleep. Charles Simic. SP-SimiCE

Heart Believes with Blows. Olga Broumas. SP-BrouO

Heart can think of no devotion, The. Devotion. Robert Frost. CP-FrosR

Heart has many Doors, The. Emily Dickinson. CP-DickE

Heart has narrow Banks, The. Emily Dickinson. CP-DickE

Heart has need of some deceit, The. Only the Polished Skeleton. Countee Cullen. CP-CullC

Heart, have no pity on this house of bone. Edna St. Vincent Millay. CP-MillE

Heart, heart, heart . . . yes, I know thee! Meaning of Life, The. Kenneth Patchen. CP-PatcK

Heart holds hidden, The. Heart Holds Hidden Knowledge, The. Shmuel HaNagid. SP-HaNaS, *tr. by* Peter Cole

Heart, in the ardor of Whose holy day. Transformation, The: For the Sacred Heart. Thomas Merton. CP-MertT

Heart is a clock, The. Charles Olson. CP-OlsoC; SP-OlsoC

Heart Is a Corrupt Stage Director, The. Yehuda Amichai. SP-AmicYL, *tr. by* Benjamin Harshav *and* Barbara Harshav

Heart is colder than the eye is, The. Still Life on a Matchbox Lid. Charles Wright. SP-WrigCN

Heart is the Capital of the Mind, The. Emily Dickinson. CP-DickE

Heart is the only workman, The. Emily Dickinson. SP-DickE

Heart Knoweth Its Own Bitterness, The. Christina Georgina Rossetti. CP-RosC2 (Whatsoever Is Right, That Shall Ye Receive.) CP-RosC2

Heart Knoweth Its Own Bitterness, The. Christina Georgina Rossetti. CP-RosC3

Heart may live a lifetime in an hour, The. Time. George Meredith. CP-MerG2

Heart mine, art mine, whose embraces. Canzon: "Heart mine, art mine, whose embraces." Ezra Pound. CP-PoEar

Heart, my heart, what will you do? Flight of the Heart. Louis MacNeice. CP-MacNL

Heart, not so heavy as mine. Emily Dickinson. CP-DickE

Heart of Autumn. Robert Penn Warren. CP-WarrR

Heart of God. Nicholas Vachel Lindsay. CP-LindV

Heart of Harlem, The. Langston Hughes. CP-HughL; CP-HughL2

Heart of Man, The. D. H. Lawrence. CP-LawrD

Heart of my heart, the day is chill. Misty Day, A. Paul Laurence Dunbar. CP-DunbP

Heart of the Backlog. Robert Penn Warren. CP-WarrR

Heart of the Night, The. Dante Gabriel Rossetti. CW-RossD Fr. House of Life, The.

Heart of the Southland, heed me pleading now. To the South. Paul Laurence Dunbar. CP-DunbP

Heart of the Woman, The. William Butler Yeats. CP-YeatW

Heart of Zeus is filled with grief, The. Funeral of Sarpedon, The ("Heart of Zeus is filled with grief, The"). Constantine P. Cavafy. CP-CavaC, tr. by Theoharis Constantine Theoharis

Heart once broken is a heart no more, The. Edna St. Vincent Millay. CP-MillE

Heart oppressed [or oppress'd] with desperate thought. Sir Thomas Wyatt. CP-WyatT

Heart-sick of his journey was the Wanderer. Journey, The. Walter De la Mare. CP-DeLaW

Heart Test with an Echo Chamber. Margaret Atwood. SP-AtwM2

Heart that resembles a cave, A. Guide to the Stone Age, The. James Tate. SP-TateJ

Heart time, those. Cologne, at the Station. Paul Celan. SP-CelaP, tr. by John Felstiner

Heart to Heart Talk with My Liver. John Logan. CP-LoganJ

Heart Unbroken and the Courage Free, The. Kenneth Rexroth. CP-RexrK

Heart us invisbly thyme time. Louis Zukofsky. CP-ZukLS

Heart wants what it wants, The. Emily Dickinson. SP-DickE

Heart warm as Summer, fresh as Spring. Lady Isabella. Christina Georgina Rossetti. CP-RosC3

Heart! We [or Heart, we] will forget him! Emily Dickinson. CP-DickE

Heart, with what lonely fears you ached. Leda. Robert Graves. CP-GravR

Heartbeat trembling. Refusing Silence. Tess Gallagher. SP-GallT

Hearted Americans are. Kind-, The. James Laughlin. CP-LaugJ

Hearth, The. Robert Graves. CP-GravR

Hearth Eternal, The. Nicholas Vachel Lindsay. CP-LindV

Hearthside. Dorothy Parker. CP-ParkD

Heartily heartily / Nothing be false. Ralph Waldo Emerson. CP-EmerR

Heartily heartily sing. Ralph Waldo Emerson. CP-EmerR

Heartland Music. Clarence Major. SP-MajoC

Heartmoss, The. Robert Pinsky. CP-PinsR

Hearts, The. Robert Pinsky. CP-PinsR

Hearts' and Flowers'. Archibald MacLeish. CP-MacLA

Hearts and Flowers or What I Know about Bolivar Black. Ogden Nash. CP-NashO

Heart's Chill Between. Christina Georgina Rossetti. CP-RosC3

Heart's Compass. Dante Gabriel Rossetti. CW-RossD Fr. House of Life, The.

Heart's Ease. Louis Zukofsky. CP-ZukLS

Heart's Garden, the Garden's Heart, The. Kenneth Rexroth. CP-RexrK

Heart's Graveyard Shift, The. Yusef Komunyakaa. CP-KomuY

Heart's grief like sharp arrows. To Yehosef, His Son. Shmuel HaNagid. SP-HaNaS, tr. by Peter Cole

Heart's Haven. Dante Gabriel Rossetti. CW-RossD Fr. House of Life, The.

Heart's Hope. Dante Gabriel Rossetti. CW-RossD Fr. House of Life, The.

Hearts I lift out of snow, The. On Valentine's Day to Friends. Louis Zukofsky. CP-ZukLS

Hearts in Amherst ache tonight, The. Emily Dickinson. SP-DickE

Heart's Limbo. Carolyn Kizer. CP-KizeC

Heart's Music. Thomas Campion. CP-CampT

Heart's Noise. Rainer Maria Rilke. CP-RilkFr, tr. by A. Poulin, Jr.

Hearts-of-Gold. Herman Melville. SP-MelvH

Hearts of Gold. Ogden Nash. CP-NashO

Hearts that never lean, must fall, The. Emily Dickinson. SP-DickE

Heartsease heart's ease love-in-idleness viola. Heart's Ease. Louis Zukofsky. CP-ZukLS

Heartsease I found, where Love-lies-bleeding / Empurpled all the ground. Balm in Gilead. Christina Georgina Rossetti. CP-RosC2

Heartsease in my garden bed, / With sweetwilliam white and red. Christina

Georgina Rossetti. CP-RosC2

Heartstring. Blessed wood. Copacetic Mingus. Yusef Komunyakaa. CP-KomuY

Heat. A. R. Ammons. CP-AmmoA

Heat. Allen Ginsberg. CP-GinsA

Heat-blaze, white dazzle: and white is the dust. Day Dr. Knox Did It, The. Robert Penn Warren. CP-WarrR

Heat / counts us together, The. Paul Celan. SP-CelaP, tr. by John Felstiner

Heat-Lightning. James Whitcomb Riley. CP-RileJ Fr. Child-World, A.

Heat Lightning. Robert Penn Warren. CP-WarrR

Heat-lightning at the outset. Parades of 1949, The. Eugenio Montale. CP-MontE, tr. by Jonathan Galassi

Heat lightning prowls, pranks the mountain horizon like. Heat Lightning. Robert Penn Warren. CP-WarrR

Heat Wave Breaks. Robert Penn Warren. CP-WarrR

Heated Minutes, The. Louis MacNeice. CP-MacNL

Heathen doth believe in Christ, The. Lines to Pope. Jonathan Swift. CP-SwifJ

Heather and Calendulas. James Schuyler. CP-SchuJ

Heather and holly. Bites and Kisses. Robert Graves. CP-GravR

Heather and kesh and turf stacks reappear. Seamus Heaney. SP-HeanSO Fr. Squarings.

Heather was blooming, the meadows were mawn, The. Hunting Song. Robert Burns. CP-BurnR

Heatstroke. James Tate. SP-TateJ

Heatwave. John Ciardi. CP-CiarJ

Heave the anchor short! Sail Out for Good, Eidólon Yacht! Walt Whitman. CP-WhitW

Heaven. John Berryman. CP-BerrJ

Heaven. Lucille Clifton. SP-ClifL

Heaven. Robert Graves. CP-GravR

Heaven. George Herbert. CP-HerbG

Heaven. Robert Herrick. CP-HerrR

Heaven. Langston Hughes. CP-HughL; CP-HughL2 (Reprise.) CP-HughL2

Heaven. Philip Levine. SP-LeviP

Heaven. Christina Georgina Rossetti. CP-RosC3

Heaven and earth. Visitation. Ai. SP-Ai

Heaven and Earth. Elizabeth Barrett Browning. CP-BroEB

Heaven and Earth. Lord Byron. CP-Byron

Heaven and Earth. Kenneth Patchen. CP-PatcK

Heaven and earth, and all that hear me plain. Protest, A. Sir Thomas Wyatt. CP-WyatT

Heaven and Earth one forme did beare. Sir Walter Ralegh. CP-RaleW

Heaven as Anus. Maxine W. Kumin. SP-KumiM

"Heaven bless the babe!" they said. Humoresque. Edna St. Vincent Millay. CP-MillE

Heaven has been my nation-state. Fanny Howe. SP-HoweF Fr. Q.

"Heaven" has different Signs—to me. Emily Dickinson. CP-DickE

Heaven-Haven. Gerard Manley Hopkins. CP-HopkG

Heaven help the man who wastes the full moon. Avigliana. Primo Levi. CP-LeviP, tr. by Ruth Feldman and Brian Swann

Heaven help you, messenger, if you lie to your old sovereign. Huayna Capac. Primo Levi. CP-LeviP, tr. by Ruth Feldman

Heaven ("I don't want"). Robert Creeley. CP-CreeR

Heaven ("If life were easy"). Robert Creeley. SP-CreeR

Heaven is boundlessly high. Han-shan. CP-ColdM, tr. by Red Pine

Heaven is but a little way. Emily Dickinson. SP-DickE

Heaven is full of definite stars. Homestead Called Damascus, The. Kenneth Rexroth. CP-RexrK

Heaven Is Heaven. Christina Georgina Rossetti. CP-RosC2

Heaven Is Not Far. Christina Georgina Rossetti. CP-RosC2 (Yet a Little While.) CP-RosC2

Heaven is not given for our good works here. Heaven. Robert Herrick. CP-HerrR

Heaven is so far of the Mind. Emily Dickinson. CP-DickE

Heaven is / The place where. Heaven. Langston Hughes. CP-HughL; CP-HughL2

"Heaven"—is what I cannot reach! Emily Dickinson. CP-DickE

Heaven now not strives, alone, our breasts to fill. Panegyre, on the Happy Entrance of James, Our Sovreign, to His First High Session of Parliament in This Kingdom, the 19 of March, 1603, A. Ben Jonson. CP-JonsB

Heaven of Animals, The. James Dickey. CP-DickJ

Heaven overarches earth and sea. Christina Georgina Rossetti. CP-RosC3

Heaven preserve the Lord's anointed. Hero, The. G. K. Chesterton. CP-ChesG

Heaven, the earth, and all the liquid mayne, The. Anchises to Aeneas. Virgil. CP-RaleW Fr. Aeneid [or Eneados or Aeneis], The.

Heaven vests for Each, The. Emily Dickinson. CP-DickE

Heaven / was only half as far that night. 21. Lawrence Ferlinghetti. SP-FerlL

Heaven will not be as good as Earth. Emily Dickinson. SP-DickE

Heaven won't have to do with its multitudes. Saints, The. Robert Creeley. CP-CreeR

Heavenborn Helen, Sparta's queen. Troy Town. Dante Gabriel Rossetti. CW-RossD

Heavenly Archer, bend thy bow. Dust to Dust. Walter De la Mare. CP-DeLaW

Heavenly breeze that breathes throughout the green, The. Petrarch. CP-Petra, tr. by J. G. Nichols

Heavenly Circuit; Berenice's Hair, The. Veronica's Napkin. William Butler Yeats. CP-YeatW

Heavenly City, The. Stevie Smith. CP-SmitS

"Heavenly Father"—take to thee. Emily Dickinson. CP-DickE

Heavenly Grass. Tennessee Williams. CP-WillT

Heavenly Rest, The. Jones Very. CP-VeryJ

Heavens are lying like wreaths, The. Last Song, A. Hugh MacDiarmid. SP-MacDH

Heavens are shaken, The! not the solid earth. Yet Once More. Jones Very. CP-VeryJ

Heaven's Carriage. Gabriela Mistral. SP-MistG, tr. by Maria Giachetti [or Jacketti]

Heaven's chimes are slow, but sure to strike at last. Christina Georgina Rossetti. CP-RosC2

Heaven's glory shone where he was laid. Emily Jane Brontë. CP-BronE

Heavens sway at his touch, The. There Is One Who Watches. Kenneth Patchen. CP-PatcK

Heaviest of Flowers, the Head. Philip Larkin. CP-LarkP

Heaviest snow in years. Two Kinds of Cause. Wyatt Prunty. SP-PrunW

Heaviness May Endure for a Night, but Joy Cometh in the Morning. Christina Georgina Rossetti. CP-RosC2

Heavy and Light. Carl Sandburg. CP-SandC

Heavy and yellow with the clay wrack from the flooded valley. Robinson Jeffers. CP-JefR3

Heavy blue chain, The. Ralph Waldo Emerson. CP-EmerR

Heavy coins roll down hallways. Slot-o-Topia. Andrei Codrescu. SP-CodrA

Heavy crow, the jay and daw, The. Dawn in Threshing Time. Robert Bly. SP-BlyR

Heavy Date. W. H. Auden. CP-AudeW

Heavy Dead, The. Rainer Maria Rilke. CP-RilkFr, tr. by A. Poulin, Jr.

Heavy hangs the raindrop. Two Children, The. Emily Jane Brontë. CP-BronE

Heavy heart, if ever heart was heavy, A. Christina Georgina Rossetti. CP-RosC2

Heavy / Heavy / Hangs. Boobus Hierophante. Philip Whalen. CP-WhalP

Heavy, heavy, heavy, hand and heart. Tenebrae. Denise Levertov. SP-LeveDS

Heavy old man in his bed at night, The. Call of the Wild, The. Gary Snyder. CP-SnydG

Heavy Sermon!, A—Sure the error's great. Impromptu on Hearing a Sermon by the Rev. T. R.—Pronounced "Heavy." Robert Browning. CP-BroR2

Heavy Surf, A. Pablo Neruda. SP-NeruP

Heavy umbrellas / aren't worth their weight, The. Crocus Night. James Schuyler. CP-SchuJ

Heavy white rooves. Stillness. William Carlos Williams. CP-WilW1

Heavy with the herd, like our forefathers in the Bible, so. State of Affairs. Yehuda Amichai. SP-AmicYL, tr. by Benjamin Harshav and Barbara Harshav

Heavy Women. Sylvia Plath. CP-PlatS

Heber. Stevie Smith. CP-SmitS

Hebrew Nation did not write it, The. William Blake. CP-BlakW

Hebrew writing and Arabic writing go from east to west. Temporary Poem of My Time. Yehuda Amichai. SP-AmicYL, tr. by Benjamin Harshav and Barbara Harshav

Hebrides. Archibald MacLeish. CP-MacLA

Hebrides, The. Louis MacNeice. CP-MacNL

Hectate. George Meredith. CP-MerG2

Hector and Andromache. Homer. CP-BroEB Fr. Iliad, The.

Hector (for example) is dead. So also. Baron Baedeker Blew His Nose and, Sighing, Departed, The. Howard Nemerov. CP-NemeH

Hector in the Garden. Elizabeth Barrett Browning. CP-BroEB

Hector spake to them thus, & the Trojans cheered with applauses. Night Watch of the Trojans before Troy. Homer. CP-MerG2 Fr. Iliad, The.

Hector, this heard without a moment's stay. Translation of Part of the Dialogue between Hector and Andromach; from the Sixth Book of Homer's Iliad (VI 390–502). Homer. CP-JohnS Fr. Iliad, The.

Hecuba. Euripides.
  "O fair wind blowing from the sea!" CP-WildO
  Sea-Choros. CP-DoolH

He'd been a clod, he knew, yes, always aiming toward his vision of the good life, always acting on it. Alzheimer's: The Husband. C. K. Williams. SP-WillC

He'd been fighting it for years. Frozen Food Section. Charles Bukowski. SP-BukC3

He'd felt uneasy these last days, as though he were a sentry who'd deserted. Return of a Deserter. Yannis Ritsos. SP-RitsY, tr. by John Stathatos

He'd have given me rolling lands. Choice, The. Dorothy Parker. CP-ParkD

He'd like the edge. Beside Her to Lie. Robert Creeley. SP-CreeR

He'd never—though he say the failing. Jonathan Happy. Miller Williams. CP-WillM

Hedge Life. James Dickey. CP-DickJ

Hedge of Hemlocks, The. Edna St. Vincent Millay. CP-MillE

Hedge of Rubber Trees. A. Amy Clampitt. CP-ClamA

Hedgehog. Paul Muldoon. CP-MuldP

Hedgehog, The. John Clare. SP-ClarJ

Hedgehog hides beneath the rotten hedge, The. Hedgehog, The. John Clare. SP-ClarJ

Hedger. Ivor Gurney. SP-GurnI

Hedgerows. Charles Tomlinson. CP-TomlC

Hedges. Ivor Gurney. SP-GurnI

Hedges in Winter. Paul Muldoon. CP-MuldP

Hee-balou, my sweet, wee Donald. Highland Balou, The. Robert Burns. CP-BurnR

Heed not the darkness and the rain. Our Ship Comes Home! G. K. Chesterton. CP-ChesG

Heel and toe, heel and toe. Dance, The. Paul Laurence Dunbar. CP-DunbP

Heel & Toe to the End. William Carlos Williams. CP-WilW2

Heels. Raymond Carver. CP-CarvR

Hee's dead: Oh what harsh musicks there. Upon the Death of a Friend. Richard Crashaw. CP-CrasR

Heh! Walk her round. Heave, ah, heave her short again! Anchor Song. Rudyard Kipling. CP-KiplR

"Heigh, boys!" cried Grandfather Bridgeman, "it's time before dinner to-day" Grandfather Bridgeman. George Meredith. CP-MerG1

Heigh-ho! Babyhood! Tell me where you linger! Babyhood. James Whitcomb Riley. CP-RileJ

Heigh-ho on a Winter Afternoon. Donald Davie. CP-DaviDC

Heigh me! brazen of front, thou glutton for plunder, now can one. Invective of Achilles, The. Homer. CP-MerG1 Fr. Iliad, The.

Heigh-O! our jolly tilts at New World song! Old Hec's Idolatry. James Whitcomb Riley. CP-RileJ

"Heigho!" yawned one day King Francis. Glove, The. Robert Browning. CP-BroR1

Height. A. R. Ammons. CP-AmmoA

Height of Man, The. Richard Eberhart. CP-EberR

Heights, Depths, Silence, Unceasing Sound of the Surf. Denise Levertov. SP-LeveDL

Heights of Macchu Picchu, III, The. Pablo Neruda. CP-WrigJ

Heights, The. Louis Zukofsky. CP-ZukLS

Heine Journal, A. Carolyn Kizer.
  Apostate, The. CP-KizeC
  Old Gods, The. CP-KizeC
  Tying One On in Vienna. CP-KizeC

Heine, Too, Lived in Germany. Kenneth Patchen. CP-PatcK

Heine's mother was a monster. Century Piece for Poor Heine, A. John Logan. CP-LogaJ

Heir Apparent, The. Theodore Weiss. SP-WeisT

Heir being born, was in his tender age, The. To My Honoured Friend, Master Thomas May, upon His Comedy The Heir. Thomas Carew. CP-CareT

Heir endis the Prologe. And beginnis the Mater. Sir David Lyndsay. SP-LyndD Fr. Dialog betwix Experience and ane Courteour, Ane.

Heir to the office of a man not dead. Miltonic Sonnet for Mr. Johnson on His Refusal of Peter Hurd's Official Portrait, A. Richard Wilbur. CP-WilbR

Heiress and Architect. Thomas Hardy. CP-HardT

Heirloom. Kathleen Jessie Raine. SP-RainK

Heirs of the Ages, The. G. K. Chesterton. CP-ChesG

Heisenberg, Schrodinger, and Dirac. Quanta. Richard Eberhart. CP-EberR

Hel——am does truly wit command. Jonathan Swift. CP-SherT Fr. Letter from Dean Swift to Dean Smedley, A.

Hélas. Robert Creeley. CP-CreeR

Hélas! Oscar Wilde. CP-WildO

Hélas! Or Christus fails. Hélas. Robert Creeley. CP-CreeR

Held between wars / my lifetime. Käthe Kollwitz. Muriel Rukeyser. CP-RukeM

Held Breath, A. James Schuyler. CP-SchuJ

Held like this, to draw in milk. Jelaluddin Rumi. SP-Rumi, tr. by Coleman Barks

Held on the slightest of bamboo poles. Ode to the Chinese Paper Snake. Richard Eberhart. CP-EberR

Helen. E. E. Cummings. CP-CummE

Helen. "H. D." CP-DoolH

Helen. Yannis Ritsos. SP-RitsY, tr. by Gwendolyn MacEwen and Nikos Tsingos

Helen. Paul Valéry. CP-WilbR, tr. by Richard Wilbur

Helen. C. K. Williams. SP-WillC

Helen All Alone. Rudyard Kipling. CP-KiplR

Helen, did Homer never see. Ode, An: "Helen, did Homer never see." Ben Jonson. CP-JonsB; SP-JonsB

Helen Grey. Christina Georgina Rossetti. CP-RosC3

Helen Groves. Olga Broumas. SP-BrouO

Helen, had I known yesterday. Release. D. H. Lawrence. CP-LawrD

Helen Keller. Langston Hughes. CP-HughL; CP-HughL1

Helen of Troy had a wandering glance. Words of Comfort to Be Scratched on a Mirror. Dorothy Parker. CP-ParkD

Helen on the Skaian Gates. Homer. CP-MerG2 *Fr.* Iliad, The.

Helen, thy beauty is to me. To Helen. Edgar Allan Poe. CP-PoeEd

Helena brought me / hang their heads. Lilacs. James Schuyler. CP-SchuJ

Helena Morley. Donald Davie. CP-DaviDC

Helene. Czeslaw Milosz. CP-MiloCN, *tr. by* Robert Hass

Helene's Religion. Czeslaw Milosz. CP-MiloCN, *tr. by* Robert Hass

Helen's Burning. Laura Riding Jackson. CP-RidiL

Helen's Faces. Laura Riding Jackson. CP-RidiL

Helen's House. Yannis Ritsos. SP-RitsY, *tr. by* Kimon Friar

Helen's Rape. Thom Gunn. CP-GunnT

Helen's Tower. Robert Browning. CP-BroR2

Helga. Carl Sandburg. CP-SandC

Helian. Georg Trakl. CP-LogaJ, *tr. by* John Logan

Heliodora. "H. D." CP-DoolH

Helios. "H. D." CP-DoolH

Helios and Athene. "H. D." CP-DoolH

Helios makes all things right. Helios. "H. D." CP-DoolH

Heliotrope sprouts from your shoes, brother. Blue Suede Shoes. Ai. SP-Ai

Heliotrope's fragrant breath, The. To Thee, My Darling. Ambrose Bierce. SP-BierA

Hell. W. H. Auden. CP-AudeW

Hell. Robert Graves. CP-GravR

Hell. Robert Herrick. CP-HerrR

He'll bring you trouble with talk like dreams. Shmuel HaNagid. SP-HaNaS, *tr. by* Peter Cole

He'll Come Out for Sure. Dan Pagis. SP-PagiD, *tr. by* Stephen Mitchell

Hell cried "My name is Legion"; and heaven then. Quotation, A. G. K. Chesterton. CP-ChesG

Hell Fire. Robert Herrick. CP-HerrR

Hell Gate. A. E. Housman. CP-HousA

Hell has no fury like women's fury. Scorned. Maenad. Olga Broumas. SP-BrouO

He'll hie me, par *is* he? the God divide her. Catullus. *See* Godlike the man who

Hell Is Graduated. Max Jacob. SP-BishE

Hell is neither here nor there. Hell. W. H. Auden. CP-AudeW

Hell is no other, but a soundlesse pit. Hell. Robert Herrick. CP-HerrR

Hell is the place where whipping-cheer abounds. Hell. Robert Herrick. CP-HerrR

Hell on the Wabash. Carl Sandburg. CP-SandC

Hell Poem, The. John Berryman. CP-BerrJ

Hell, they'll never let him in. Let Me In! Kenneth Patchen. CP-PatcK

Hellas. Percy Bysshe Shelley. CP-ShelP

Hellenic Triptych. Sam Hamill. SP-HamiS

Hellenistics. Robinson Jeffers. CP-JefR2

Hello. John Berryman. CP-BerrJ

Hello. Robert Creeley. CP-CreeR

Hello. David Ignatow. SP-IgnaD

Hello. Miller Williams. CP-WillM

Hello, drug addict, can you become a poem of perfect form? Hello. David Ignatow. SP-IgnaD

Hello eternal life in the light. Fanny Howe. SP-HoweF *Fr.* O'Clock.

Hello, Hello Henry. Maxine W. Kumin. SP-KumiM

Hello, hello, what I wanted to tell you was. Historical Disquisitions. Philip Whalen. SP-WhalP

Hello. I'll Bet You Don't Know Who This Is. Miller Williams. CP-WillM

Hello is what a mirror says. E. E. Cummings. CP-CummE

Hello, Jamaica! Broadcast to the West Indies. Langston Hughes. CP-HughL; CP-HughL2

Hello, Mister Jack. Light on the Subject. Yusef Komunyakaa. SP-KomuY

Hello NBC, this is London speaking. Un Bel di Vedremo. Kenneth Rexroth. CP-RexrK

Hello, ole man, you're a-gittin' gray. Growin' Gray. Paul Laurence Dunbar. CP-DunbP

Hello, sailor boy. Port Town. Langston Hughes. CP-HughL; CP-HughL1

Hel*lo* there, Biscuit! You're a better-looking broad. Hello. John Berryman. CP-BerrJ

Hello to you, lady / who will not stay with me. Irishman's Lament on the Approaching Winter, An. Robert Creeley. CP-CreeR

Hello up There. Marge Piercy. SP-PierM

Hello, Willie Shoemaker. Charles Bukowski. SP-BukC2

Hello! winged seed flying. Winged Seed. Rainer Maria Rilke. CP-RilkFr, *tr. by* A. Poulin, Jr.

Hello young sailor. / You are betrayed and. Martial Choreograph. Maya Angelou. SP-AngeM

Hells and Heavens. Carl Sandburg. CP-SandC

Hell's Prayer. Ivor Gurney. SP-GurnI

Hellvellyn. Sir Walter Scott. SP-ScotW

Helmet of Goliath, The. Robert Duncan. SP-DuncR

Helmet, The. Philip Levine. SP-LeviP

Helmsman, The. "H. D." CP-DoolH

Helmsman, The; an Ode. James Vincent Cunningham. CP-CunnJ

Helmsmen, The. W. S. Merwin. SP-MerwWF

Helmut. Stephen Spender. CP-SpenS

Heloise. Ted Berrigan. SP-BerrT

Help. A. R. Ammons. CP-AmmoA

Help. Jones Very. CP-VeryJ

Help. John Greenleaf Whittier. CP-WhitJ

Help for a patriot distressed, a spotless spirit hurt. Cleared. Rudyard Kipling. CP-KiplR

Help for the Memory of the Grand Independent, A; A New Song. William Wordsworth. CP-WorW2

Help heaven up out. Robert Creeley. SP-CreeR

Help, help all tongues to celebrate this wonder. Ben Jonson. CP-JonsB *Fr.* Masque of Queens, The.

Help! Help! they want to burn my pictures. Auto-Da-Fé. D. H. Lawrence. CP-LawrD

Help, Lord; for the godly man ceaseth. Psalm 12: "Help, Lord; for the godly man ceaseth." Bible, *O.T.* SP-SidnP *Fr.* Psalms.

Help me in Christ to learn to do Thy will. Will, The. Jones Very. CP-VeryJ

Help me, Julia, for to pray. To Julia. Robert Herrick. CP-HerrR

Help Me, Venus, You Who Led Me On. Charles Olson. CP-OlsoC

Help of the Spirit, The. Jones Very. CP-VeryJ

Help the hearts so submissive and soft. Prayer of One Not Indifferent Enough. Rainer Maria Rilke. CP-RilkFr, *tr. by* A. Poulin, Jr. *Fr.* Affectionate Taxes to France.

Help Wanted. Charles Simic. SP-SimiC; SP-SimiCE

Help[e] me! help[e] me! now I call. To His Mistress[es]. Robert Herrick. CP-HerrR

Help[e] me to seek [*or* seke] for I lost it there. Sir Thomas Wyatt. CP-WyatT

Helping her with her knots. Sailing. Clarence Major. SP-MajoC

Helplessly besieging: it is dim. Snow Thickets. James Dickey. CP-DickJ

Helpmeet for Him, A. Christina Georgina Rossetti. CP-RosC2

Helter Skelter. Jonathan Swift. CP-SwifJ

Helves surling out of eakspeasies per(reel)hapsingly. E. E. Cummings. CP-CummE

Hemingway. Archibald MacLeish. CP-MacLA

Hemlock and Cedar. Carl Sandburg. CP-SandC

Hemmed by loud seas. Birdham. Amy Clampitt. CP-ClamA

Hemmed in by the prim. Balms. Amy Clampitt. CP-ClamA

Hemmed-in Males. William Carlos Williams. CP-WilW1 *Fr.* Folded Skyscraper, A.

Hemorrhage, The. Stanley Kunitz. CP-KunSC

Hemp . . . / A stick. Gauge. Langston Hughes. CP-HughL; CP-HughL3

Hen, The. Ted Hughes. SP-HughTN

Hen Flower, The. Galway Kinnell. SP-KinnGN

Hen Woman. Thomas Kinsella. CP-KinsT

Hence a blessed soule is fled. Upon a Maide. Robert Herrick. CP-HerrR

Hence, avaunt, ('tis holy ground). Ode for Music. Thomas Gray. CP-GrayT

Hence Burgundy, Claret, and Port. John Keats. CP-KeatJ

Hence, hence, profane; soft silence let us have. Dirge upon the Death of the Right Valiant Lord, Bernard Stuart, A. Robert Herrick. CP-HerrR

Hence, hence prophane, and none appeare. Another New-Yeeres Gift, or Song for the Circumcision. Robert Herrick. CP-HerrR

Hence loathèd Melancholy. L'Allegro. John Milton. CP-MiltJ

Hence my epistle—skim the deep—fly o'er. John Milton. *See* Quickly, my letter, run through the boundless deep

Hence sensual gross desires. Il Mystico. Gerard Manley Hopkins. CP-HopkG

Hence, soul-dissolving Harmony. Ode on the Ottery and Tiverton Church Music. Samuel Taylor Coleridge. CP-ColeS

Hence that fantastic wantonness of woe. Addressed to a Young Man of Fortune. Samuel Taylor Coleridge. CP-ColeS

Hence they have born my Lord: Behold! the Stone. His Coming to the Sepulcher. Robert Herrick. CP-HerrR

Hence vain deluding joy[e]s. Il Penseroso. John Milton. CP-MiltJ

Hence, vain intruder, haste away. To My Rival. Thomas Carew. CP-CareT

Henceforth, from the Mind. Louise Bogan. CP-BogaL

Henceforth of her the Gods are known. George Meredith. CP-MerG1 *Fr.* France.

Henchman, The. John Greenleaf Whittier. CP-WhitJ

Hendecasyllabics. Algernon Charles Swinburne. SP-SwinA

Hendecasyllabics. Alfred Tennyson. CP-TennA

Hendecasyllables. Stevie Smith. CP-SmitS

Hengist Wants Men (A.D. 449). Jorge Luis Borges. SP-BorgJ, *tr. by* Alastair Reid

Henley Regatta. Thomas Hardy. CP-HardT

Henpeck'd Husband, The. Robert Burns. CP-BurnR

Henriette. D. H. Lawrence. CP-LawrD

Henry and Mary. Robert Graves. CP-GravR

Henry by Night. John Berryman. CP-BerrJ

Henry Chard. G. K. Chesterton. CP-ChesG

Henry Hardiman. Christina Georgina Rossetti. CP-RosC3

Henry Hudson. Robert Stock. SP-StocR

Henry Irving. James Whitcomb Riley. CP-RileJ

Henry Manley Blues, The. Maxine W. Kumin. SP-KumiM

Henry Manley Looks Back. Maxine W. Kumin. SP-KumiM

Henry Manley's house, unpainted for. Henry Manley Blues, The. Maxine W. Kumin. SP-KumiM

Henry of England could pray or roister. Ballad of Henry, Bridegroom. Josephine Jacobsen. CP-JacoJ

Henry Purcell. Gerard Manley Hopkins. CP-HopkG

Henry Thoreau is lost in the Maine woods. True Story of God, A. Norman Dubie. CP-DubiN

Henry W. Grady. James Whitcomb Riley. CP-RileJ

Henry was a young king. Henry and Mary. Robert Graves. CP-GravR

Henry's nocturnal habits were the terror of his women. Henry by Night. John Berryman. CP-BerrJ

Henyard Round, The. Donald Hall. CP-HallD

Hepatica in Winter, The. Jones Very. CP-VeryJ

Heptonstall. Ted Hughes. SP-HughTN

Heptonstall Old Church. Ted Hughes. SP-HughTN

Her advent was not hailed with shouts. Impromptu Lines to Greet Marie Bancroft. Robert Browning. CP-BroR2

Her ankles are watches. George Oppen. CP-OppGN

Her Anxiety. William Butler Yeats. CP-YeatW

Her Apotheosis. Thomas Hardy. CP-HardT

Her arms around me—child. From a Photograph. George Oppen. CP-OppGN

Her arms semaphore fat triangles. Momma Welfare Roll. Maya Angelou. SP-AngeM

Her attachment may differ from yours in degree. Love and Friendship Opposite. Samuel Taylor Coleridge. CP-ColeS

Her Beautiful Eyes. James Whitcomb Riley. CP-RileJ

Her Beautiful Hands. James Whitcomb Riley. CP-RileJ

Her Beauty. Robert Graves. CP-GravR

Her beauty, which we talk of. Helen's Burning. Laura Riding Jackson. CP-RidiL

Her beauty's alive in heaven! I believe her. Michelangelo Buonarroti. CP-Miche, *tr. by* John Frederick Nims

Her Bed. Robert Herrick. CP-HerrR

Her big basket. Three Poems for Joanne. Gary Snyder. CP-SnydG

Her body is not so white as. Queen-Anne's-Lace. William Carlos Williams. CP-WilW1

Her Body Is Private. Eleanor Wilner. SP-WilnE

Her boudoir is ornamented with. Incense. Kenneth Rexroth. CP-RexrK

Her brain is an attic where things. Attic, The. Raymond Carver. CP-CarvR

Her breast is cold; her hands how faint and wan! Virtue. Walter De la Mare. CP-DeLaW

Her breast is fit for pearls. Emily Dickinson. CP-DickE

Her breasts / Naked, the soft. Zulu Girl, The. George Oppen. CP-OppGN

Her Brief Withdrawal. Robert Graves. CP-GravR

Her brilliance consists in colors. She can sink her teeth. Alice's Brilliance. Andrei Codrescu. SP-CodrA

Her brown falcon perches above the sink. Exiles. Marilyn Hacker. SP-HackM

Her careful distinct sex whose sharp lips comb. E. E. Cummings. CP-CummE

Her chair drawn to the door. Laundress, The. Thomas Kinsella. CP-KinsT

Her Choice. James Whitcomb Riley. CP-RileJ

Her clitoris / the size of a Romanian pepper. Memoria Voraciae Simplex. Andrei Codrescu. SP-CodrA

Her Confession. Thomas Hardy. CP-HardT

Her counsel was accepted: the times are grave. Lady Luncheon Club. Maya Angelou. SP-AngeM

Her cunt lifts on a / velvet couch, red. Irish. Robert Creeley. CP-CreeR

Her Daddie forbad, her Minnie forbad. Jumpin John. Robert Burns. CP-BurnR

Her dark brown face. Young Prostitute. Langston Hughes. CP-HughL; CP-HughL1

Her Dead Brother. Robert Lowell. SP-LoweR

Her Death and After. Thomas Hardy. CP-HardT

Her Definition. Thomas Hardy. CP-HardT

Her Delight. Denise Levertov. SP-LeveDL

Her Destiny. Denise Levertov. SP-LeveDL

Her diary soared above her house. Susan Howe. SP-HoweS

Her Dilemma. Thomas Hardy. CP-HardT

Her Dream. William Butler Yeats. CP-YeatW

Her Dream, Half Remembered. Charles Olson. CP-OlsoC

Her dying feels to me. Emily Dickinson. SP-DickE

Her Eyes. John Crowe Ransom. SP-RansJ

Her Eyes. Edwin Arlington Robinson. CP-RobiE

Her eyes are like the putrid sores of infants. Mais L'Amour Infini Me Montera dans L'Âme. Richard Eberhart. CP-EberR

Her Eyes Are Wild. William Wordsworth. CP-WorW1

Her eyes flood lickes his feets faire staine. Luke 7; She Began to Wash His Feet with Teares and Wipe Them with the Haires of Her Head. Bible, *N.T.* CP-CrasR, *tr. by* Richard Crashaw *Fr.* St. Luke.

Her Eyes Had. Hart Crane. CP-CranH

Her eyes the glow-worm[e] lend thee. Night-Piece, to Julia, The. Robert Herrick. CP-HerrR

Her face has made my life most proud and glad. Sonnet: Of His Lady's Face. Jacopo da Lentino. CW-RossD, *tr. by* Dante Gabriel Rossetti

Her face like a rain-beaten stone on the day she rolled off. Elegy: "Her face like a rain-beaten stone on the day she rolled off." Theodore Roethke. CP-RoetT

Her face the Book of—Love Delights in—Praises. Louis Zukofsky. CP-ZukLS

Her face was in a bed of hair. Emily Dickinson. CP-DickE

Her face was like an opening rose. Last Look, The. Christina Georgina Rossetti. CP-RosC3

Her fate seizes her and brings her. Her First Calf. Wendell Berry. CP-BerrW

Her Father. Thomas Hardy. CP-HardT

Her father. Spirit of '76. William Carlos Williams. CP-WilW1

Her father was a policeman who went fishing summer Sundays and. Two Women and Their Fathers. Carl Sandburg. CP-SandC

Her father's brother rapes her! Fountain of Cyanë, The. Donald Davie. CP-DaviDC

Her fayre inflaming eyes. Thomas Campion. CP-CampT

Her final Summer was it. Emily Dickinson. CP-DickE

Her fingers toyed absently with her rings. Sensationist Poem, A. Fernando Pessoa. SP-PessF

Her fingertips touch his. Rendezvous. Yusef Komunyakaa. CP-KomuY

Her First Calf. Wendell Berry. CP-BerrW

Her / flesh / Came / at. E. E. Cummings. CP-CummE

Her flowing locks, the raven's wing. Fragment: "Her flowing locks, the raven's wing." Robert Burns. CP-BurnR

Her footsteps were a season's coming. Lyric: "Her footsteps were a season's coming." Tennessee Williams. CP-WillT

Her fur new-licked, the whitetail fawn. Beauty and the Beast. Eleanor Wilner. SP-WilnE

Her furrowed heart, her brittle life, her mind. Dactyls. Olga Broumas. SP-BrouO

Her Gifts. Dante Gabriel Rossetti. CW-RossD *Fr.* House of Life, The.

Her gnarled, brown fingers. Pomo Basketmaker. Peter Blue Cloud. SP-BlueP

Her golden hair was blowing in the breeze. Petrarch. CP-Petra, *tr. by* J. G. Nichols

Her Grace is all she has. Emily Dickinson. CP-DickE

Her grace is not of any part. Unwithered Garland, The. Stanley Kunitz. CP-KunSC

Her Grave. Mary Oliver. SP-OlivM

Her great adventure ended. S-sss-ss-sh! Langston Hughes. CP-HughL; CP-HughL2

Her Hair. Charles Baudelaire. CP-BaudC, *tr. by* Walter Martin

Her Hair. James Whitcomb Riley. CP-RileJ

Her hair fallen over her eyes, her mouth. Without a Mirror Now. Yannis Ritsos. SP-RitsY, *tr. by* Kimon Friar *and* Kostas Myrsiades

Her hair is a brilliant red, and her voice like a bumblebee's hum. My Best Girl. Paul Laurence Dunbar. CP-DunbP

Her hair is as a floating fire. Portrait, A ("Her hair is as a floating fire"). G. K. Chesterton. CP-ChesG

Her hair was made of poisonous snakes. Perverse Explanation for Mutilated Statuary. Alan Dugan. CP-DugaA

Her hair was, oh, so dense a blur. Ylladmar. James Whitcomb Riley. CP-RileJ

Her hair was tawny with gold, her eyes with purple were dark. Court Lady, A. Elizabeth Barrett Browning. CP-BroEB

Her hands intend no harm. Portrait. Philip Larkin. CP-LarkP

Her hard heart and her will to cruelty. Petrarch. CP-Petra, *tr. by* J. G. Nichols

Her Haunting-Ground. Thomas Hardy. CP-HardT

Her Head on the Pillow. Tennessee Williams. CP-WillT

Her heart knew naught of sorrow. Our Little Girl. James Whitcomb Riley. CP-RileJ

Her heart that loved me once is rottenness. Two Thoughts of Death. Christina

Georgina Rossetti. CP-RosC3

Her heart was a delicate silver lyre. Under the April Rain. Tennessee Williams. CP-WillT

Her heart was in her throat. God's Spies. Susan Howe. SP-HoweS

Her high heels sounded nearer. Madonna. Thomas Kinsella. CP-KinsT

Her house loomed at the end of a Berkshire lane. Not at Home. Robert Graves. CP-GravR

Her house loooked cold from the foggy lea. In Her Precincts. Thomas Hardy. CP-HardT

Her Husband. Ted Hughes. SP-HughTN

Her imaginary playmate was a grown-up. Cinderella. Randall Jarrell. CP-JarrR

Her Immortality. Thomas Hardy. CP-HardT

Her inevitable complaint or accusation. Semi-Detached. Robert Graves. CP-GravR

Her Initials. Thomas Hardy. CP-HardT

Her Irish maids could never spoon out mush. Mary Winslow. Robert Lowell. SP-LoweR

Her & It. John Berryman. CP-BerrJ

Her ivory hands on the ivory keys. In the Gold Room: A Harmony. Oscar Wilde. CP-WildO

Her jaw wagging. His Daughter. William Carlos Williams. CP-WilW2

Her Judgement. Denise Levertov. SP-LeveDL

Her Kind. Anne Sexton. CP-SextA; SP-SextA

Her Lament. Denise Levertov. SP-LeveDL

Her— last Poems.' Emily Dickinson. CP-DickE

Her Late Husband. Thomas Hardy. CP-HardT

Her laugh was not in the middle of her face quite. Countenance, A. Thomas Hardy. CP-HardT

Her laughter was infectious; so, some found. Ecstasies of Dialectic, The. Howard Nemerov. CP-NemeH

Her Legs. Robert Herrick. CP-HerrR

Her Letters. James Laughlin. CP-LaugJ

Her Light Guitar. James Whitcomb Riley. CP-RileJ

Her liquid look as dark. Slow Motion. Amy Clampitt. CP-ClamA

Her little Parasol to lift. Emily Dickinson. CP-DickE

Her Lonesomeness. James Whitcomb Riley. CP-RileJ

Her long quiet hands. Mary. George Oppen. CP-OppGN

Her Longing. Theodore Roethke. CP-RoetT

Her loss is as something beautiful in air. Loss. Richard Eberhart. CP-EberR

Her Losses make our Gains ashamed. Emily Dickinson. CP-DickE

Her Love-Birds. Thomas Hardy. CP-HardT

Her lute hangs shadowed in the apple-tree. Sea-Spell, A. Dante Gabriel Rossetti. CW-RossD

Her Majesty never shall be my exalter. Epigram on the Hermitage at Richmond. Jonathan Swift. CP-SwifJ

Her Majesty's Servants. Rudyard Kipling. Fr. Jungle Book, The.

Her Management. May Swenson. SP-SwenM

Her milk don't seem to. Detail. William Carlos Williams. CP-WilW2

Her mind lives in a quiet room. Interior. Dorothy Parker. CP-ParkD

Her Monologue of Dark Crepe with Edges of Light. Norman Dubie. CP-DubiN

Her Monument, the Image Cut Thereon. Giacomo Leopardi. CP-PoEar, tr. by Ezra Pound

Her mouth is empty. Monument Rescue Dim. Philip Whalen. SP-WhalP

Her Nightmare. Denise Levertov. SP-LeveDL

Her of your name, whose fair inheritance. To Mrs Magdalen Herbert: Of St. Mary Magdalen. John Donne. CP-DonnJ; MW-DonnJ

Her Only Pilot the Soft Breeze, the Boat. William Wordsworth. CP-WorW2

Her parents and her dolls destroyed. Belsen, Day of Liberation. Robert Earl Hayden. CP-HaydR

Her pen drops eloquence as sweet. On a Letter of Miss Fanshawe. William Cowper. CP-CowpW

Her Pet. Thom Gunn. CP-GunnT

Her Poet-Brother. James Whitcomb Riley. CP-RileJ

Her polka-dot dress—that's all I know of her. Polka-dot Dress, A. Czeslaw Milosz. CP-MiloCN, tr. by Robert Hass

Her Praise. William Butler Yeats. CP-YeatW

Her Prayer. Denise Levertov. SP-LeveDL

Her pretty feet. Upon Her Feet. Robert Herrick. CP-HerrR

Her prime of life—cut down too soon. Gerard Manley Hopkins. CP-HopkG

Her pure nails on high displaying their onyx. Stéphane Mallarmé. CP-MallS, tr. by Henry Weinfield

Her red dress & hat. South Carolina Morning. Yusef Komunyakaa. CP-KomuY

Her reluctances are sweeter. Emily Dickinson. SP-DickE

Her Reply. James Laughlin. CP-LaugJ

Her Reproach. Thomas Hardy. CP-HardT

Her Reticence. Theodore Roethke. CP-RoetT

Her Room. Kathleen Jessie Raine. SP-RainK

"Her room," you'd say—and wonder why you'd called it. Sketch for a Portrait of Mme. G———M———. Archibald MacLeish. CP-MacLA

Her rosie cheekes, her ever smiling eyes. Thomas Campion. CP-CampT

Her sacred body bear: the tenement. At the Funeral. George Meredith. CP-MerG2

Her Sadness. Denise Levertov. SP-LeveDL

Her Second Husband Hears Her Story. Thomas Hardy. CP-HardT

Her Secret. Thomas Hardy. CP-HardT

Her Secret. Denise Levertov. SP-LeveDL

Her Seed; It Shall Bruise Thy Head. Christina Georgina Rossetti. CP-RosC2

Her Sister. Denise Levertov. SP-LeveDL

Her skin / covered me, illuminated. Charles Olson. CP-OlsoC

Her sleeping head with its great gelid mass. Perseus. Robert Earl Hayden. CP-HaydR

Her Smile of Cheer and Voice of Song. James Whitcomb Riley. CP-RileJ

Her smile was shaped like other smiles. Emily Dickinson. CP-DickE

Her son, albeit the Muse's livery. Orson of the Muse, An. George Meredith. CP-MerG1

Her Song. Thomas Hardy. CP-HardT

Her soul was bred by a throne, and fed. Nature's Remorses. Elizabeth Barrett Browning. CP-BroEB

Her sovereign People. Emily Dickinson. CP-DickE

Her spirit rose to such a height. Emily Dickinson. CP-DickE

Her Strong Enchantments Failing. A. E. Housman. CP-HousA

Her strong enchantments failing. Her Strong Enchantments Failing. A. E. Housman. CP-HousA

Her Sweet Deceit. James Laughlin. CP-LaugJ

Her Sweet turn to leave the Homestead. Emily Dickinson. CP-DickE

Her sweet Weight on my Heart at Night. Emily Dickinson. CP-DickE

Her Talents . . . Of. Kenneth Patchen. CP-PatcK

Her Task. Denise Levertov. SP-LeveDL

Her tawny eyes are onyx of thoughtlessness. Hands of the Betrothed, The. D. H. Lawrence. CP-LawrD

Her teacher's certainty it must be Mabel. Maple. Robert Frost. CP-FrosR

Her teeth are as white as the meat of an apple. Fascination. Langston Hughes. CP-HughL; CP-HughL1

Her Telepathic-Station transmits thought-waves. Circe. W. H. Auden. CP-AudeW

Her Temple. Thomas Hardy. CP-HardT

Her terrace was the sand. Infanta Marina. Wallace Stevens. CP-StevW; CP-StevWP

Her thot's tho' they are older. Emily Dickinson. SP-DickE

Her, Though. Miller Williams. CP-WillM

Her Thought and His. Paul Laurence Dunbar. CP-DunbP

Her Thoughts. Samuel Taylor Coleridge. CP-ColeS

Her Time. Theodore Roethke. CP-RoetT

Her title. I refused. Poem for Me Mother. William Corbett. SP-CorbW

Her Triumph. William Butler Yeats. CP-YeatW

Her trousers are red; she wears a coatee. George Meredith. CP-MerG2

Her Valentine. James Whitcomb Riley. CP-RileJ

Her Vision. Denise Levertov. SP-LeveDL

Her Vision in the Wood. William Butler Yeats. CP-YeatW

Her voice. Bobbie ("Her voice"). Robert Creeley. SP-CreeR

Her Voice. Oscar Wilde. CP-WildO

Her voice did quiver as we parted. On Fanny Godwin. Percy Bysshe Shelley. CP-ShelP

Her voice is a magnet into which flows. Eyes of a Blind Man. Edwin Rolfe. CP-CareT

Her voice, that scooped me out of the games of the others. Remedies, Maladies, Reasons. Mona Van Duyn. SP-VanDM

Her Waiting Face. James Whitcomb Riley. CP-RileJ

Her whole life is an Epigram smack smooth & neatly pend. William Blake. CP-BlakW

Her will to come on one Greek, archaic, nearly. Study of a House with Garden Attached. Robert Stock. SP-StocR

Her Words. Theodore Roethke. CP-RoetT

Her words curled before him in spirals. Gallup Swill-Hole, A; or, Cantina Blues. Clarence Major. SP-MajoC

Her Wrath. Theodore Roethke. CP-RoetT

Her young employers, having got in late. Summer Morning, A. Richard Wilbur. CP-WilbR

Her-zie. Stevie Smith. CP-SmitS

Hera, Hung from the Sky. Carolyn Kizer. CP-KizeC

Heraclitus. Czeslaw Milosz. CP-MiloC; CP-MiloCN, tr. by Richard Lourie

Heraclitus on Rivers. Derek Mahon. CP-MahoD

Herakles. Robert Browning. CP-BroR2

Herakles. C. K. Williams. SP-WillC

Heralds of the Spring, The. Jones Very. CP-VeryJ

Herba Santa. Herman Melville. SP-MelvH

Herbal Tea. Yehuda Amichai. SP-AmicYL, *tr. by* Benjamin Harshav *and* Barbara Harshav

Herbalist's Rose, The. Pablo Neruda. SP-NeruP

Herbals. Federico García Lorca. CP-GarcF, *tr. by* Jerome Rothenberg

Herbs, garlic, / cheese, please let me in! Fury of Cooks, The. Anne Sexton. SP-SextA *Fr.* Furies, The.

Herculasses, a feminine fauna. Rubens' Women. Wisława Szymborska. SP-SzymWM, *tr. by* Joanna Trzeciak

Hercules and Antaeus. Seamus Heaney. SP-HeanSO

Hercules at Nemea. Robert Graves. CP-GravR

Hercules, Deianira, Nessus. C. K. Williams. SP-WillC

Hercules Furens. Seneca.

    "Capricious fortune ever joys." CP-JohnS

    "O! save ye Gods, omnipotent and kind." CP-JohnS

Hercules, his muscles useless now. Recovery. Eleanor Wilner. SP-WilnE

Herd is standing on the hill, The. Cows Waiting at the Pasture Gate, The. Jones Very. CP-VeryJ

Herd of wild helicopters scuds in the night. Engines. Ron Silliman. SP-ArmaA

Herd, The. Robert Creeley. CP-CreeR

Herds, The. W. S. Merwin. SP-MerwW

Herds of the deer wander—their heads like wands. Fanny Howe. SP-HoweF *Fr.* O'Clock.

Here. Rae Armantrout. SP-ArmaA

Here. Andrei Codrescu. SP-CodrA

Here ("Here is"). Robert Creeley. CP-CreeR

Here ("Little earth, water"). Robert Creeley. CP-CreeR

Here ("No one / else in the room"). Robert Creeley. CP-CreeR

Here ("Past time—those"). Robert Creeley. CP-CreeR

Here ("Since I can't"). Robert Creeley. SP-CreeR

Here ("Sounds like ball"). Robert Creeley. SP-CreeR

Here ("What / has happened"). Robert Creeley. CP-CreeR

Here. Philip Larkin. CP-LarkP

Here. Gregory Orr. SP-OrrG

Here. Grace Paley. CP-PalGC

Here. Arthur Sze. SP-SzeA

Here a little child I stand. Grace for a Child. Robert Herrick. CP-HerrR

Here a pretty Baby lies. Upon a Child. Robert Herrick. CP-HerrR

Here a snail on a wet leaf shivers and dreams of spring. Here. Arthur Sze. SP-SzeA

Here a solemn[e] fast keep[e]. Epitaph upon a Virgin, An. Robert Herrick. CP-HerrR

Here, a Sunday, when light. Proensa. Charles Olson. CP-OlsoC

Here, above, / cracks in the buildings are filled with battered moonlight. Man-Moth, The. Elizabeth Bishop. CP-BishE

Here Again ("After we / were all"). Robert Creeley. CP-CreeR

Here Again ("No sadness"). Robert Creeley. SP-CreeR

Here, again. A smell of dying in the milk-pale carton. Pouring Milk Away. Muriel Rukeyser. CP-RukeM

Here again, / shifting days. Robert Creeley. SP-CreeR

Here, all sings the life of yesterday. Rainer Maria Rilke. CP-RilkFr, *tr. by* A. Poulin, Jr. *Fr.* Valaisian Quatrains, The.

Here alone by the logs in my chamber. Flirt's Tragedy, The. Thomas Hardy. CP-HardT

Here am I with my head held high! Sister Johnson Marches. Langston Hughes. CP-HughL; CP-HughL1

Here among silent lakes and dripping pines. Yaddo Letter, The. Derek Mahon. CP-MahoD

Here among tables lit with bottled tapers. Kursaal at Interlaken, The. Adrienne Rich. CP-RicAE

Here among them the americans this baffling. [American Journal]. Robert Earl Hayden. CP-HaydR

Here & Now. A. R. Ammons. CP-AmmoA

Here and Now, The. Theodore Weiss. SP-WeisT

Here and There. William Meredith. SP-MereW

Here and there in the searing beam. Deer among Cattle. James Dickey. CP-DickJ

Here are all the captivities, the cells are as real. Schoolchildren. W. H. Auden. CP-AudeW

Here are consoling pieties. Elegy: "Here are consoling pieties." Gregory Orr. SP-OrrG

Here, are five letters in this blessed name. Garland [*or* Ghyrlond] of the Blessèd Virgin Mary [*or* Marie], The. Ben Jonson. CP-JonsB

Here are five simple facts no sub. POEM(or "the divine right of majorities, that illegitimate offspring of the divine right of kings" Homer Lea). E. E. Cummings. CP-CummE

Here Are My Black Clothes. Louise Glück. SP-GlucL

Here are plates but no appetite. Museum. Wisława Szymborska. SP-SzymW, *tr. by* Stanislaw Barańczak *and* Clare Cavanagh

Here are shapes form'd fit for heaven. Second Song, The. Thomas Carew. CP-CareT *Fr.* Carew's Masque.

Here are some pretty things picked for you. Risks and Possibilities. A. R. Ammons. CP-AmmoA

Here are the fireworks. The men who conspired and labored. Pearl Harbor. Robinson Jeffers. CP-JefR3

Here are the long fields involiate of thought. Notes for a Poem. Muriel Rukeyser. CP-RukeM

Here are the miracle-signs you want: that. Acts of Helpessness. Jelaluddin Rumi. SP-Rumi, *tr. by* Coleman Barks

Here are the perfect / fans of the scallops. Whelks. Mary Oliver. SP-OlivM

Here are the red flags. Moscow. Langston Hughes. CP-HughL; CP-HughL1

Here are the skies, the planets seven. A. E. Housman. CP-HousA

Here are the tracks upon the sand. Four Footprints. Thomas Hardy. CP-HardT

Here are two half-grown black cats perched on a. Walking beside the Kamogawa, Remembering Nansen and Fudo and Gary's Poem. Philip Whalen. SP-WhalP

Here are two pupils. On Looking into the Eyes of a Demon Lover. Sylvia Plath. CP-PlatS

Here at right of the entrance this bronze head. Bronze Head, A. William Butler Yeats. CP-YeatW

Here at the atomic Crack-end of Time XX Century. Methedrine Vision in Hollywood, A. Allen Ginsberg. CP-GinsA

Here at the foot of Mount Gilboa we met. 1978 Reunion of Palmach Veterans at Ma-ayan Harod. Yehuda Amichai. SP-AmicY, *tr. by* Chana Bloch

Here at the height of passion. As Lovers Do. Hugh MacDiarmid. SP-MacDH

Here at the level of leaves supposedly for good. Sustainment. James Dickey. CP-DickJ

Here at the seashore they use the clouds over & over. Rhode Island. William Meredith. SP-MereW

Here at the shore of Ashkelon we arrived at. Shore of Ashkelon, The. Yehuda Amichai. SP-AmicY, *tr. by* Chana Bloch

Here at the Super Duper, in a glass tank. Lobsters. Howard Nemerov. CP-NemeH

Here at the Vespasian-Carlton, it's just one. Boom! Howard Nemerov. CP-NemeH

Here Awa' There Awa' [Here awa', there awa' wandering, Willie]. Robert Burns. CP-BurnR

Here before me, snake-head. Cormorant, A. Ted Hughes. SP-HughTN

Here behold, and likewise lo. Life's Valentines. Dorothy Parker. CP-ParkD

Here brewer Gabriel's fire's extinct. On Gabriel Richardson. Robert Burns. CP-BurnR

Here by the baring bough. Autumn in King's Hintock Park. Thomas Hardy. CP-HardT

Here, by the Latin sea. Eheu! "Rubén Dario." SP-DariR, *tr. by* Alberto Acereda *and* Will Derusha

Here by the moorway you returned. Your Last Drive. Thomas Hardy. CP-HardT

Here chimes no clock, no pedant calendar. Seashore. Ralph Waldo Emerson. CP-EmerR

Here come I, old April Fool. April Fool. Louis MacNeice. CP-MacNL

Here come I to my own again. Prodigal Son, The. Rudyard Kipling. CP-KiplR *Fr.* Kim.

Here come real stars to fill the upper skies. Fireflies in the Garden. Robert Frost. CP-FrosR

Here come the capybaras on their bikes. Wild Ones[, The]. James Fenton. SP-FentJ *Fr.* Wild Life Studies.

Here come the line-gang pioneering by. Line-Gang, The. Robert Frost. CP-FrosR

Here Come the Saints. Thom Gunn. CP-GunnT

Here comes man the master. Man the Master. Thomas Merton. CP-MertT

Here comes the fishhead singing. Most, The. Charles Bukowski. SP-BukC1

Here comes the man! He's talking a lot. Wrong Train. Ted Berrigan. SP-BerrT

Here comes the shadow not looking where it is going. Sire. W. S. Merwin. SP-MerwW

Here cursing swearing Burton lies. Epitaph on Mr. Burton. Robert Burns. CP-BurnR

Here dies another day. Evening. G. K. Chesterton. CP-ChesG

Here dock and tare. In the Grave No Flower. Edna St. Vincent Millay. CP-MillE

Here down my wearied [*or* wearyed] limbs I'll [*or* Ile] lay. On Himself[e]. Robert Herrick. CP-HerrR

Here even now I see a place. Shadow Realm. Hans Magnus Enzensberger. SP-EnzeH, *tr. by* Michael Hamburger

Here Everything Is Still Floating. John Ashbery. SP-AshbJ

Here few signs distinguish dawns from nights. Prisoner's Dream, The. Eugenio Montale. CP-MontE, *tr. by* Jonathan Galassi

Here first the duties of to-day, the lessons of the concrete. United States to Old World Critics, The. Walt Whitman. CP-WhitW

Here Follow Certain Other Verses, as Charms to Unlock the Mystery of the *Crudities*. Ben Jonson. CP-JonsB

Here Follows Some Verses upon the Burning of Our House [July 10th, 1666.

Copied Out of a Loose Paper]. Anne Bradstreet. CP-BradA

Here, foremost in the dang'rous paths of fame. Epitaph on Sir William Williams. Thomas Gray. CP-GrayT

Here four of you got mischances to plague you. Upon Four Dismal Stories in the Doctor's Letter. Jonathan Swift. CP-SwifJ

Here *Francis Ch[artre]s* lies—Be civil! *see also* Epitaph on the Count of Mirandula. Alexander Pope. CP-PopeA

Here, free from a riot's hated noise. Inscription for a Moss-House. William Cowper. CP-CowpW

Here, freed from pain, secure from misery, lies. Epitaph on a Child. Thomas Gray. CP-GrayT

Here from the corridor of an English train. Wild Sky, The. Adrienne Rich. CP-RicAE

Here from the field's edge we survey. Highway: Michigan. Theodore Roethke. CP-RoetT

Here further up the mountain slope. Birthplace, The. Robert Frost. CP-FrosR

Here goes a man of seventy-four. Seventy-four and Twenty. Thomas Hardy. CP-HardT

Here green is king again. Vermont. John Updike. CP-UpdiJ

Here gunned he homeward in the birdy breast. Young Hunter, The. Richard Eberhart. CP-EberR

Here hand was still on her sword-hilt, the spur was still on her heel. Young Queen, The. Rudyard Kipling. CP-KiplR

Here has my salient faith annealed me. Key West. Hart Crane. CP-CranH

Here have I been these one and twenty years. Arthur Hugh Clough. SP-ClouA

Here he comes. For Lucy, on the Twelth Month. Miller Williams. CP-WillM

Here lie is of course. It was his best. Rastignac at 45. Thom Gunn. CP-GunnT

Here, here I live. His Almes. Robert Herrick. CP-HerrR

Here, here I live with what my board. His Content in the Country. Robert Herrick. CP-HerrR

Here Hitler had his first success, disguised. Munich. John Updike. CP-UpdiJ

Here *Hobson* lies amongst his many betters. Hobsons Epitaph. John Milton. CP-MiltJ

Here I Am. Charles Bukowski. SP-BukC3

Here I Am. James Laughlin. CP-LaugJ

Here I am, an old man in a dry month. Gerontion. T. S. Eliot. CP-ElioT

Here I am at 8:08 p.m. indefinable ample rhythmic frame. Red Shift. Ted Berrigan. SP-BerrT

Here I am at my desk. The. Pleasant Thought from Whitehead, A. Frank O'Hara. SP-OharF

Here I am / at the toilet bowl. David Ignatow. SP-IgnaD

Here I am, Cassandra. Soliloquy for Cassandra. Wisława Szymborska. SP-SzymW, *tr. by* Stanisław Barańczak *and* Clare Cavanagh

Here I am, digging worms behind the chickenhouse. Digging Worms. Robert Bly. SP-BlyR

Here I am in the garden laughing. Here. Grace Paley. CP-PalGC

Here i am, naked. Charles Olson. CP-OlsoC

Here I am not the Kleon famous in Alexandria. Tomb of Ignatios, The. Constantine P. Cavafy. CP-CavaC, *tr. by* Theoharis Constantine Theoharis

Here I am, walking along your eyelid again. In There. C. K. Williams. CP-WillC

Here I am, with mike in hand, shooting down the rapids. David Ignatow. SP-IgnaD

Here I am / with one foot on a floating platform. Falling-Down Song, The. Yusef Komunyakaa. CP-KomuY

Here I am yours, and here, and here. Song: "Here I am yours, and here, and here." Jane Cooper. CP-CoopJ

Here I come! Little Song on Housing. Langston Hughes. CP-HughL; CP-HughL3

Here I heard the snorting of hogs trying to re-enter the underearth. Road between Here and There, The. Galway Kinnell. SP-KinnGN

Here I lie, Iasis. The young man. Tomb of Iasis, The. Constantine P. Cavafy. CP-CavaC, *tr. by* Theoharis Constantine Theoharis

Here I myself [*or* my selfe] might likewise die. Poetry Perpetuates the Poet. Robert Herrick. CP-HerrR

Here I set with a bitter old thought. Seven Moments of Love; An Un-Sonnet Sequence in Blues. Langston Hughes. CP-HughL; CP-HughL2

Here I sit, reading the Stoic. Gas or Novocain. Kenneth Rexroth. CP-RexrK

Here I sit with my belly full. Success. Langston Hughes. CP-HughL1

Here I sit / With my shoes mismated. Bad Morning. Langston Hughes. CP-HughL; CP-HughL2

Here, if Forlorn. Ivor Gurney. SP-GurnI

Here I'll be. Clean Old Man. Charles Bukowski. SP-BukC1

Here I'm gazing, wide awake. Inscription for a Sketch. Robert Browning. CP-BroR2

Here I'm thought dead. Alive, I comforted. Michelangelo Buonarroti. CP-Miche, *tr. by* John Frederick Nims

Here in a cage the dollars come down. Girl in a Cage. Carl Sandburg. CP-SandC

Here in a place where much. Autopsy. Miller Williams. CP-WillM

Here in a Rocky Cup. Edna St. Vincent Millay. CP-MillE

Here in America. Stone and Flower. Kenneth Rexroth. CP-RexrK

Here in bed behind a brick wall. David Ignatow. SP-IgnaD

Here in caterpillar country. Hornworm: Summer Reverie. Stanley Kunitz. CP-KunSC

Here in dawn's routine. Christmas. A. K. Ramanujan. CP-RamaA

Here, in front of the summer hotel. Kite, The. Anne Sexton. CP-SextA

Here in my drive in the rain. Pulling Back. Miller Williams. CP-WillM

Here in my head, the home that is left for you. Burning the Letters. Randall Jarrell. CP-JarrR

Here in my heart I am Helen. Song of One of the Girls. Dorothy Parker. CP-ParkD

Here in my workroom, in its listlessness. For Robert Kennedy Nineteen Twenty-Five to Sixty-Eight. Robert Lowell. SP-LoweR

Here in Nantucket does the tiny soul. Phenomenal Survivals of Death in Nantucket. Louise Glück. SP-GlucL

Here in our aging district the wood pigeon lives with us. All Morning. Theodore Roethke. CP-RoetT

Here, in our familiar streets, the day. Last Man, The. Eleanor Wilner. SP-WilnE

Here in our room. Illuminator, The. Eleanor Wilner. SP-WilnE

Here in surprising chaos, doubly sweet. Pere Bouhours' Fountain Made Muddy by the Translator. *Unknown.* CP-SherT, *tr. by* Thomas Sheridan

Here in the great cemetery. Francisco, I'll Bring You Red Carnations. Philip Levine. SP-LeviP

Here in the hauf licht hoo I've grown! Hugh MacDiarmid. SP-MacDH *Fr.* Frae Anither Window in Thrums.

Here in the hauf licht waitin' till the clock. Hugh MacDiarmid. SP-MacDH *Fr.* Frae Anither Window in Thrums.

Here in the mountain woods. To Antonio Machado. Denise Levertov. SP-LeveDS

Here in the north, a cold gray morning. Here and There. William Meredith. SP-MereW

Here in the olive grove. Olive Grove, The. May Sarton. SP-SartM

Here, / in the room of my life. Room of My Life, The. Anne Sexton. CP-SextA

Here, in the summer city. William Dickey. SP-DickW *Fr.* In the Dreaming.

Here in the thrust-green. Remnant Water. James Dickey. CP-DickJ

Here in the twilight the translucent hands. Spinoza. Jorge Luis Borges. SP-BorgJ, *tr. by* Willis Barnstone

Here in the window beaming across. Love Watches a Window. Thomas Hardy. CP-HardT

Here, in the withered arbor, like the arrested wind. Statue and Birds. Louise Bogan. CP-BogaL

Here / in the wombed room. Zorro Man, A. Maya Angelou. SP-AngeM

Here in this carload. Written in Pencil in the Sealed Railway-Car. Dan Pagis. SP-PagiD, *tr. by* Stephen Mitchell

Here in this corner, ladies and gentlemen. Wrestling Match, The. Robert Penn Warren. CP-WarrR

Here in This Spring. Dylan Thomas. CP-ThomD

Here in this valley of discreet academies. Above the Oxbow. Sylvia Plath. CP-PlatS

Here in this wadi we lived during the war. Ruhama. Yehuda Amichai. SP-AmicY, *tr. by* Chana Bloch

Here is. Here ("Here is"). Robert Creeley. CP-CreeR

Here is a box for you. Model towards a Theory of Cognition. Hans Magnus Enzensberger. SP-EnzeH

Here is a child who presses his head to the ground. Windows, The. W. S. Merwin. SP-MerwWF

Here is a coast; here is a harbor. Arrival at Santos. Elizabeth Bishop. CP-BishE

Here is a face that says half-past seven the same way whether a murder or. Clocks. Carl Sandburg. CP-SandC

Here is a fat animal, a bear. Self-Portrait as a Bear. Donald Hall. CP-HallD

Here is a glass of water from my well. Glass of Water, A. May Sarton. SP-SartM

Here is a head with a blur of horizons. Head. Carl Sandburg. CP-SandC

Here is a horse to tame. Verses on Games. Rudyard Kipling. CP-KiplR

Here is a Jolly Good Fellow. Once More by the Potomac. Joseph Brodsky. CP-BrodJ

Here is a room with heavy-footed chairs. Nature of an Action, The. Thom Gunn. CP-GunnT

Here is a story shall stir you! Stand up, Greeks dead and gone. Echetlos. Robert Browning. CP-BroR2

Here is a symbol in which. Rock and Hawk. Robinson Jeffers. CP-JefR2

Here is a thing that happened. Like wild beasts whelped, for den. Halbert and Hob. Robert Browning. CP-BroR2

Here is a wound that never will heal, I know. Edna St. Vincent Millay. CP-MillE

Here is dust remembers it was a rose. Dust. Carl Sandburg. CP-SandC

Here is fresh matter, poet. Church and State. William Butler Yeats. CP-YeatW

Here is how I sum it up. Perfect Joy. Chuang Tzu. CP-MertT

Here is its mark left, thumbnail of enigma. Death of a Voice. Boris Leonidovich Pasternak. CP-DaviDC, *tr. by* Donald Davie

Here is Joe Blow the poet. On Being Asked for a Peace Poem. Howard Nemerov. CP-NemeH

Here is little Effie's Head. E. E. Cummings. CP-CummE; SP-CummE

"Here is nothing new nor aught unproven," say the Trumpets. Old Issue, The. Rudyard Kipling. CP-KiplR

Here is one leaf already gone from green. First Leaf, The. Howard Nemerov. CP-NemeH

Here is ouzo (she said) to try you. Ouzo Unclouded. Robert Graves. CP-GravR

Here is poor Villon's final word. Ballade to End With, A. François Villon. CP-WilbR, tr. by Richard Wilbur

Here is that sleeping place. Grave Yard. Langston Hughes. CP-HughL; CP-HughL2

Here is the ample place. Mediterranean. May Sarton. SP-SartM

Here is the ancient floor. Self-Unseeing, The. Thomas Hardy. CP-HardT

Here is the bronze youth. Charioteer 1970. Yannis Ritsos. SP-RitsY, tr. by N. C. Germanacos

Here is the doctor, an abstracted lover. Death by Aesthetics. Mona Van Duyn. SP-VanDM

Here is the endless / wet thick / cosmos, the center. Crossing the Swamp. Mary Oliver. SP-OlivM

Here is the fern's frond, unfurling a gesture. Fern. Ted Hughes. SP-HughTN

Here is the girl's head like an exhumed gourd. Strange Fruit. Seamus Heaney. SP-HeanSO

Here is the glen, and here the bower. Banks of Cree. Robert Burns. CP-BurnR

Here is the little earthworm-eater. Frenzy. Clarence Major. SP-MajoC

Here is the man of the islands. Poem: "Here is the man of the islands." Thomas Merton. CP-MertT

Here is the man who fancies Arab ponies. Man in the Wind, The. Thomas Merton. CP-MertT

Here is the ocean,this is moonlight:say. E. E. Cummings. CP-CummE

Here is the place; right over the hill. Telling the Bees. John Greenleaf Whittier. CP-WhitJ

Here is the playhouse of weather-faded white. Playhouse, The. May Swenson. SP-SwenM

Here is the poem I was going to write. Poem I Didn't Write, The. Raymond Carver. CP-CarvR

Here is the pond, here sky, and the long grasses. Composition. May Sarton. SP-SartM

Here is the shadow of truth, for only the shadow is true. Way to Love God, A. Robert Penn Warren. CP-WarrR

Here is the skull of a man: a man's thoughts and emotions. De Rerum Virtute. Robinson Jeffers. CP-JefR3

Here is the sweet punk priest. Working the Block. Eleanor Wilner. SP-WilnE

Here is the threshold of holiness in the dust of the road. Tomb Cover of Imam Riza. Unknown. CP-MertT

Here is the trapdoor. Lullaby. Christopher Logue. SP-LoguC

Here is the world's end. When our fathers forded the first river in Asia we crossed the world's end. Torch-Bearers' Race, The. Robinson Jeffers. CP-JefR1

Here is your frozen city cut into marble cubes. View from the Hill. Joseph Brodsky. CP-BrodJ, tr. by Alan Myers

Here is your parents' dwelling with its curtained windows telling. Dawn after the Dance, The. Thomas Hardy. CP-HardT

Here it begins: the worm of love breeding. Hearth, The. Robert Graves. CP-GravR

Here it comes again, imagination of myself. International Date Line, Monday/Monday 27:XI:67. Philip Whalen. SP-WhalP

Here it gives the laws for fishing thru the ice. Lorine Niedecker. CP-NiedL

Here / it is. Locus. A. R. Ammons. CP-AmmoA

Here it is: a thousand miles. Travels of a Vigilante, The. Andrei Codrescu. SP-CodrA

Here it is bright, by the rusty water, nowhere. Here. Lachesis Lapponica. Hans Magnus Enzensberger. SP-EnzeH, tr. by Michael Hamburger

Here it is hanging in the sun. Gentleman's Second-Hand Suit, A. Thomas Hardy. CP-HardT

Here it is, near the house. Right in the Trail. Gary Snyder. CP-SnydG

Here it is spring again. Late Singer, The. William Carlos Williams. CP-WilW1

Here Johnson lies—a sage by all allow'd. Epitaph on Dr. Johnson. William Cowper. CP-CowpW

Here lakeshore modulated to a cove. Two Poets by the Lake. Carolyn Kizer. CP-KizeC

Here let the Church her holy mission prove. Jones Very. CP-VeryJ

Here let thy clemency, Persephone, hold firm. Prayer for His Lady's Life. Propertius. CP-PoEar, tr. by Ezra Pound

Here lie Ciardi's pearly bones. Elegy Just in Case. John Ciardi. CP-CiarJ

Here lie Willie Michie's [or M—hie's] banes. Epitaph on a Schoolmaster. Robert Burns. CP-BurnR

Here lies a lady. Day was her double pain. Billie Holiday. Hayden Carruth. CP-CarHS

Here lies a man. And here, a girl. They live. Memorial. Robert Pinsky. CP-PinsR

Here lies a mock Marquis whose titles were shamm'd. Epitaph Extempore, on a Person Nicknamed the Marquis, Who Desired Burns to Write One on Him. Robert Burns. CP-BurnR

Here lies a most beautiful lady. Epitaph, An: "Here lies a most beautiful lady." Walter De la Mare. CP-DeLaW

Here lies a poet who would not write. Voice from the Tomb (1). Stevie Smith. CP-SmitS

Here lies a round Woman, who thought *mighty odd*. Epitaph (of By-Words). Alexander Pope. CP-PopeA

Here lies a Scots mile of a chiel. Epitaph for J. H. Writer in Ayr. Robert Burns. CP-BurnR

Here lies a Virgin, and as sweet. Upon his Kinswoman Mrs. M. S. Robert Herrick. CP-HerrR

Here lies / A worthy matron of unspotted life. Epitaph on my Dear and Ever Honored Mother Mrs. Dorothy Dudley. Anne Bradstreet. CP-BradA

Here lies an honest man. Epitaph: "Here lies an honest man." Henry David Thoreau. CP-ThorH

Here lies Boghead among the dead. Epitaph on James Grieve, Laird of Boghead. Robert Burns. CP-BurnR

Here lies Hobinall, our Pastor while ere. Epitaph on the Earl of Salisbury. *Unknown, sometimes at. to* Sir Walter Ralegh. CP-RaleW

Here lies honest John. Impromptu Epitaph on the Grave Digger of Princeton—1769. Annis Boudinot Stockton. CP-StocA

Here lies in earth a root of H-ll. Epitaph on D——— C———. Robert Burns. CP-BurnR

Here lies J-hn B-shby, *honest man!* Epitaph on J-hn B-shby. Robert Burns. CP-BurnR

Here lies John Trot, the Friend of all mankind. Another [Epitaph]: "Here lies John Trot, the Friend of all mankind." William Blake. CP-BlakW

Here lies Johnny Pidgeon. Epitaph on John Dove [Innkeeper, Mauchline]. Robert Burns. CP-BurnR

Here lies Jonson [or lyes Johnson] with the rest. Upon Ben Jo[h]nson. Robert Herrick. CP-HerrR

Here lies 'mang ither useless matters. On an Innkeeper in Tarbolton. Robert Burns. CP-BurnR

Here lies my wife. Eternal peace. Epigram: "Here lies my wife. Eternal peace." James Vincent Cunningham. CP-CunnJ

Here lies New Critic who would fox us. Epigram: "Here lies New Critic who would fox us." James Vincent Cunningham. CP-CunnJ

Here lies nipped in this narrow cyst. Epitaph for G. K. Chesterton. Thomas Hardy. CP-HardT

Here lies old *Hobson*, Death hath broke his girt. On the University Carrier Who Sick'n'd [or Sickened] in the Time of His Vacancy [, Being Forbid to go to London, by Reason of the Plague]. John Milton. CP-MiltJ

Here lies one, who never drew. Epitaph, An: "Here lies one, who never drew." William Cowper. CP-CowpW

Here lies our freind who having promis-ed. Epitaph: "Here lies our freind who having promis-ed." Jane Austen. CP-AustJ

Here lies the body of this world. Ep[itaph] on the World. Henry David Thoreau. CP-ThorH

Here lies the last of Deacon Fitch. Ambrose Bierce. SP-BierA

Here lies [or lyes] the noble warrior [or Warryor] that never blunted sword. Epitaph on the Earl of Leicester [or Leceister]. Sir Walter Ralegh. CP-RaleW

Here lies—the world. Ep on a Good Man. Henry David Thoreau. CP-ThorH

Here lies to each her parents' ruth. On My First Daughter. Ben Jonson. CP-JonsB; SP-JonsB

Here lies, whom hound did ne'er pursue. Epitaph on a Hare. William Cowper. CP-CowpW

Here lieth one who did most truly prove. Another on the Same. John Milton. CP-MiltJ

Here lieth One whose name was writ on water. Fragment on Keats. Percy Bysshe Shelley. CP-ShelP

Here, like Arion, our Coriat doth draw. Here Follow Certain Other Verses, as Charms to Unlock the Mystery of the *Crudities*. Ben Jonson. CP-JonsB

Here, long ere kings to battle rode. English Downs. Walter De la Mare. CP-DeLaW

Here luxury's the common lot. The light. Grasse: The Olive Trees. Richard Wilbur. CP-WilbR

Here lyes Squire Hugh———ye harlot crew. Epitaph for H——— L———, Esq., of L———. Robert Burns. CP-BurnR

Here meet together the prefiguring day. Passover in the Holy Family, The. Dante Gabriel Rossetti. CW-RossD

Here might have been the thinking of mountains. Kenneth Patchen. CP-PatcK

Here my assurance drops away. I lose. With a Telescope Rod on Cowiche Creek. Raymond Carver. CP-CarvR

Here, my dear friend, is a new book for you. see also Epipsychidion. Percy Bysshe Shelley. CP-ShelP

Here, my God, / is my heart. Prologue: "Here, my God, / is my heart." Federico

García Lorca. CP-GarcF, *tr.* by Catherine Brown

Here no dreams touch me to colour. Depths, The. Ivor Gurney. SP-GurnI

Here, no woman, nor man besides. Man in a Room. William Carlos Williams. CP-WilW1

Here, O wanderer, here is the hill and the harbor. Archibald MacLeish. CP-MacLA *Fr.* Happy Marriage, The.

Here, on our native soil, we breathe once more. Composed in the Valley near Dover, on the Day of Landing. William Wordsworth. CP-WorW1

Here on our rocks the marks we see. Glacial Marks on Our Hills, The. Jones Very. CP-VeryJ

Here on the dreary beach I sit alone. Elegy on the Death of Mrs Dickinson. The Event Was Communicated at the Sea Shore. Annis Boudinot Stockton. CP-StocA

Here on the edge of hell. Harlem ("Here on the edge of hell"). Langston Hughes. CP-HughL; CP-HughL3

Here, on the farthest point of the peninsula. Of Politics, & Art. Norman Dubie. CP-DubiN

Here on the rim, cringing. Place, A: Fragments. Margaret Atwood. SP-AtwM1

Here, on the wall. Men. Robert Creeley. SP-CreeR

Here on the warm strand, where a turquoise light. Seasons' Difference, The. William Meredith. SP-MereW

Here once again the memorable lips, unique and like yours. My Whole Life. Jorge Luis Borges. SP-BorgJ, *tr.* by W. S. Merwin

Here once engaged the stranger's view. On Revisiting Harrow. Lord Byron. CP-Byron

Here, our possessions are cut. Highest Altitude. Margaret Atwood. SP-AtwM1

Here pasture ends— / this girl and boy. E. E. Cummings. CP-CummE

Here pause: the poet claims at least this praise. 1811. William Wordsworth. CP-WorW1

Here pollen's cornmeal. Last Words. William Corbett. SP-CorbW

Here redbuds like momentary trees. Locus. Robert Earl Hayden. CP-HaydR

Here rests a Woman, good without pretence. Epitaph on Mrs. Corbet, Who Died of a Cancer in Her Breast. Alexander Pope. CP-PopeA

Here rests a writer, great but not immense. Loring Pickering. Ambrose Bierce. SP-BierA

Here, Romans owned the need—to give. Harvest Festival: At Ozleworth. Charles Tomlinson. CP-TomlC

Here Salomon's body reposes. Ambrose Bierce. SP-BierA

Here she comes / the Queen of Moons! Pictures of Philippa. Donald Hall. CP-HallD

Here she is, you cowards! Pile out onto station platforms! Parisian Orgy, or Paris Filling Up Again. Arthur Rimbaud. CP-RimbA, *tr.* by Martin Sorrell

Here she lies, a pretty bud. Upon a Child That Died [*or* Dyed]. Robert Herrick. CP-HerrR

Here she lies [*or* lyes] (in Bed of Spice). Upon a Maid[e]. Robert Herrick. CP-HerrR

Here Sleeps. Walter De la Mare. CP-DeLaW

Here soft hills touch the sea. North of San Francisco. Yehuda Amichai. SP-AmicYL, *tr.* by Benjamin Harshav and Barbara Harshav

Here something stubborn comes. Seed Leaves. Richard Wilbur. CP-WilbR

Here Sowter **** in Death does sleep. On a Celebrated Ruling Elder. Robert Burns. CP-BurnR

Here space, time, peace are given a habitation. These Pure Arches. May Sarton. SP-SartM

Here Stanford lies, who thought it odd. Ambrose Bierce. SP-BierA

Here stood an Oak, that long had borne affixed. Hart's-Horn Tree, near Penrith. William Wordsworth. CP-WorW2

Here take my Picture, though I bid farewell. His Picture. John Donne. MW-DonnJ *Fr.* Elegies.

Here, take this gift. To a Certain Cantatrice. Walt Whitman. CP-WhitW

Here tame boys fly down the long light of halls. To a Visiting Poet in a College Dormitory. Carolyn Kizer. CP-KizeC

Here Tantalus in water seek[e]s for water, and doth miss[e]. Ovid. CP-RaleW *Fr.* Amores.

Here the earth is surrounded. Rainer Maria Rilke. CP-RilkFr, *tr.* by A. Poulin, Jr. *Fr.* Valaisian Quatrains, The.

Here the earth tells her story. Rainer Maria Rilke. CP-RilkFr, *tr.* by A. Poulin, Jr. *Fr.* Valaisian Quatrains, The.

Here the face turns. Apple Garths of Avalon, The. Kenneth Rexroth. CP-RexrK

Here, the foregound of the other. Freed from Another Context. Eleanor Wilner. SP-WilnE

Here the Frailest Leaves of Me. Walt Whitman. CP-WhitW

Here the grass grows. Concert of Fishes, A. Wallace Stevens. CP-StevWP

Here the hangman stops his cart. Carpenter's Son, The. A. E. Housman. CP-HousA

Here the huge moth. Twilight. Wallace Stevens. CP-StevWP

Here the human past is dim and feeble and alien to us. Haunted Country. Robinson Jeffers. CP-JefR1

Here the image of a child on a hill. Michael Palmer. SP-PalmM

Here the jack-hammer jabs into the ocean. Colloquy in Black Rock. Robert Lowell. SP-LoweR

Here the round laughter, up-tossed. Swimmer and Fish Group. Tennessee Williams. CP-WillT

Here the sky is clear and deep. Meeting-Place. Dorothy Parker. CP-ParkD

Here the soft hills touch the ocean. North of San Francisco. Yehuda Amichai. SP-AmicY, *tr.* by Chana Bloch

Here the swans' wings stretch. Images of Little Compton, Rhode Island. James Tate. SP-TateJ

Here then is where the wolf of summer lay. Hollow, A. W. S. Merwin. SP-MerwW

Here then / She lies / Her hair a scroll along. One. Stephen Spender. CP-SpenS

Here there are armored snails. 2. Comment on 1. Alan Dugan. CP-DugaA

Here There Are Three of Us Driving South in This Expensive Car. William Dickey. SP-DickW

Here there is death. But even here, they say. Dead Village, The. Edwin Arlington Robinson. CP RobiE

Here they all come to die. Country of a Thousand Years of Peace, The. James Merrill. SP-MerrJ

Here they are common as pebbles. Tree. Presences. Josephine Jacobsen. CP-JacoJ

Here they are. The soft eyes open. Heaven of Animals, The. James Dickey. CP-DickJ

Here they come / grey and beastly. End, The. Charles Bukowski. SP-BukC2

Here they lie, still and cat-like. Clothes. Hans Magnus Enzensberger. SP-EnzeH

Here they stand, a living tree next to a dead one. Orchard. Yehuda Amichai. SP-AmicY, *tr.* by Chana Bloch

Here, time concurring (and it does). Epitaph: "Here, time concurring (and it does)." John Ciardi. CP-CiarJ

Here too. Here as at the other edge. Texas. Jorge Luis Borges. SP-BorgJ, *tr.* by Mark Strand

Here, under the kites the children float. Yehuda Amichai. SP-AmicYL, *tr.* by Benjamin Harshav and Barbara Harshav

Here under the radiant rays of the sun. Facing the Chair. Hugh MacDiarmid. SP-MacDH

Here, underneath the kites that the children are flying. Yehuda Amichai. SP-AmicY, *tr.* by Stephen Mitchell

Here upon the prairie. Prairie Battlements, The. Nicholas Vachel Lindsay. CP-LindV

Here Usually Comes the Bride. Ogden Nash. CP-NashO

Here / walls are cool / and coolness is. Chaconne for Unaccompanied Violin. Charles Tomlinson. CP-TomlC

Here was I with my arm and heart. Too Late. Robert Browning. CP-BroR1

Here was my relation with the woman who lived all last autumn and winter day and night. Thirst. C. K. Williams. SP-WillC

Here was the sound of water falling only. Owl, The. Robert Penn Warren. CP-WarrR

Here we are all, by day; by night we are [*or* w'are] hurled. Dream[e]s. Robert Herrick. CP-HerrR

Here we are in Merry Madness Hall. Merry Madness Hall. James Laughlin. CP-LaugJ

Here we are, naked lovers. Openness. Wisława Szymborska. SP-SzymWM, *tr.* by Joanna Trzeciak

Here we are on the other side. Helene. Czeslaw Milosz. CP-MiloCN, *tr.* by Robert Hass

Here we are, picking the first fern-shoots. Song of the Bowmen of Shu. Ezra Pound. SP-PounE

Here we are: the Bowl, the thousands. Nursery Rhyme, A. Randall Jarrell. CP-JarrR

Here we broached the Christmas barrel. House of Hospitalities, The. Thomas Hardy. CP-HardT

Here we go in a flung festoon. Road-Song of the *Bandar-Log*. Rudyard Kipling. CP-KiplR *Fr.* Jungle Book, The.

Here We Go Quietly Nuts in May. Ogden Nash. CP-NashO

Here we have thirst. Egyptian Pulled Glass Bottle in the Shape of a Fish, An. Marianne Craig Moore. CP-MoorM

Here we have watched ten thousand. View from Rosehill Cemetery: Vicksburg. Alice Walker. CP-WalkA

Here We Loved. Yehuda Amichai.

　"At night, as in a tomb, a pyramid." SP-AmicYL

　"Birds return without a rhyme or reason, The." SP-AmicYL

　"Doves sit on shoulder and on window sill." SP-AmicYL

　"Four years my father fought their wars in vain." SP-AmicYL

　"Lips of the dead naively whispered words." SP-AmicYL

　"Thoughts came in to him—a convoy run, The." SP-AmicYL

Here we securely live, and eate. Ode to Sir Clipsebie Crew, An. Robert Herrick. CP-HerrR

Here: wear this spectacle bra. It is the fashion. Issue of Life, An. Howard Nemerov. CP-NemeH

Here, where a ruin wants to be. In the Jerusalem Mountains. Yehuda Amichai. SP-AmicYL, *tr.* by Benjamin Harshav *and* Barbara Harshav

Here, where I dwell, I waste to skin and bone. By the Waters of Babylon. B.C. 570. Christina Georgina Rossetti. CP-RosC1

Here where I once stayed. Han-shan. CP-ColdM, *tr.* by Red Pine

Here, where my fresh-turned furrows run. Settler, The. Rudyard Kipling. CP-KiplR

Here, where, of havoc tired and rash undoing. At Furness Abbey. William Wordsworth. CP-WorW2

Here where of old was heard. Ours. James Whitcomb Riley. CP-RileJ

Here, where our fathers homeless came. English Sparrows. Jones Very. CP-VeryJ

Here, where our Lord once laid his Head. Upon the Sepulchre of our Lord. Richard Crashaw. CP-CrasR

Here, where the Daisies fit my Head. Emily Dickinson. CP-DickE

Here where the golden apples grow. Interlude ("Here where the golden apples grow"). G. K. Chesterton. CP-ChesG

Here where the insidious cricket. Fiesole Window. Eugenio Montale. CP-MontE, *tr.* by Jonathan Galassi

Here where the laurel grows. On Mount Muhraka. Yehuda Amichai. SP-AmicY, *tr.* by Chana Bloch

Here, where the rose opens. Anacreon's Grave. Johann Wolfgang von Goethe. CP-WrigJ

Here, where the Scotish Muse immortal lives. To Miss Graham of Fintray. Robert Burns. CP-BurnR

Here where the wayward stream. Old-Timer, An. James Whitcomb Riley. CP-RileJ

Here, where Vespasian's legions struck the sands. Embarcation. Thomas Hardy. CP-HardT

Here where we are, wrapped in the afternoon. Obligations. Jane Cooper. CP-CoopJ

Here, while the loom of Winter weaves. Memory, A. John Greenleaf Whittier. CP-WhitJ

Here, with my knee upon thy stone. Emily Jane Brontë. CP-BronE

Here, Withers, rest! thou bravest, gentlest mind. Epitaph on General Henry Withers, in Westminster-Abbey, 1729. Alexander Pope. CP-PopeA

Here without question is the bird-torn design. I Am with the Roots of Flowers. Charles Bukowski. SP-BukC2

Here writ was the World's History by his hand. Raleigh's Cell in the Tower. Dante Gabriel Rossetti. CW-RossD

Here Yet Be Dragons. Lucille Clifton. SP-ClifL

Here you stay / Night and day. To a Tree in London. Thomas Hardy. CP-HardT

Here you watch the Bard's Career. To Dorothy Collins from G. K. Chesterton. G. K. Chesterton. CP-ChesG

Hereabouts the signs are good. Midsummer. Thomas Kinsella. CP-KinsT

Hereafter, I will pick no Rose. Emily Dickinson. SP-DickE

Hereafter! O we need not waste. Hereafter, The. James Whitcomb Riley. CP-RileJ

Hereafter, The. Constantine P. Cavafy. CP-CavaC, *tr.* by Theoharis Constantine Theoharis

Hereafter, The. James Whitcomb Riley. CP-RileJ

Heredity. Thomas Hardy. CP-HardT

Herefordshire. Donald Davie. CP-DaviDC

Herein a Blossom lies. Emily Dickinson. CP-DickE

Herein are blown from out the South. Southern Singer, A. James Whitcomb Riley. CP-RileJ

Here's, a bottle and an honest friend. Robert Burns. CP-BurnR

Here's a fine bag of meat. Bags of Meat. Thomas Hardy. CP-HardT

Here's a girl from a dangerous town. Belfast Tune. Joseph Brodsky. CP-BrodJ

Here's a good rule of thumb. Reflection on Ingenuity. Ogden Nash. CP-NashO

Here's a Happy New Year! But with Reason. Lord Byron. CP-Byron

Here's a Health to Ane I Lo'e Dear. Robert Burns. CP-BurnR

Here's a Health to Them That's Awa'. Robert Burns. CP-BurnR

Here's a little mouse)and. Four III. E. E. Cummings. CP-CummE; SP-CummE

Here's a man who falls hard asleep. Man Asleep in a Child's Bed. Thomas Lux. SP-LuxT

Here's a message for the faithful. Han-shan. CP-ColdM, *tr.* by Red Pine

Here's a poem for you young lords. Han-shan. CP-ColdM, *tr.* by Red Pine

Here's a question for us. Help me. From a Window. William Carlos Williams. CP-WilW2

Here's a seed. Food. Beggar's Song. Gregory Orr. SP-OrrG

Here's a tin cup. Tin Cup. Gregory Orr. SP-OrrG

Here's a verse about rabbits. Rabbits, The. Ogden Nash. CP-NashO

Here's a Woman of the Town. Extempore Elegy, An. Samuel Johnson. CP-JohnS

Here's about sunshine and the sun. Letter to Man's Reasonable Soul. Laura Riding Jackson. CP-RidiL

Here's all at an end between us, or I'll never taste sack again. Marrèd Drives of Windsor, The. Rudyard Kipling. CP-KiplR *Fr.* Muse among the Motors, The.

Here's "anguish" and over. Shaky Spectrum. Gregory Orr. SP-OrrG

Here's first a gloveless hand warm from my pocket. To a Moth Seen in Winter. Robert Frost. CP-FrosR

Here's good health, friends. Progression. Lorine Niedecker. CP-NiedL

Here's green, here's the tree. Here. Gregory Orr. SP-OrrG

Here's His Health in Water. Robert Burns. CP-BurnR

Here's his ragged "roundabout." Little Coat, The. James Whitcomb Riley. CP-RileJ

Here's Holy Willie's sair worn clay. Epitaph on Holy Willie. Robert Burns. CP-BurnR

Here's mist and wild wind on the sandy. Return, The. Eugenio Montale. CP-MontE, *tr.* by Jonathan Galassi

Here's my case. Of old I used to love him. Fears and Scruples. Robert Browning. CP-BroR2

Here's no more news, than virtue, I may as well. To Sir Henry Wotton ("Here's no more news, than virtue, I may as well"). John Donne. CP-DonnJ; MW-DonnJ

Here's one in whom Nature feared—faint at such vying. Cardinal Bembo's Epitaph on Raphael. Thomas Hardy. CP-HardT

Here's one more dead man, boxed, nosegayed. Elegy for Sam. John Ciardi. CP-CiarJ

Here's s / omething round(& so). E. E. Cummings. CP-CummE

Here's some advice for meat-eating people. Han-shan. CP-ColdM, *tr.* by Red Pine

Here's that old drunk, already mellow. Fall. Mona Van Duyn. SP-VanDM

Here's the cave where Sorrow dwells. Stratagem, The. Walter De la Mare. CP-DeLaW

Here's the church. Waiting for a Bus "en Frente de la Iglesia." Robert Creeley. SP-CreeR

Here's the huge Brockhaus encyclopedia. On Acquiring an Encyclopedia. Jorge Luis Borges. SP-BorgJ, *tr.* by Alan S. Trueblood

Here's the mould of a musical bird long passed from light. In a Museum. Thomas Hardy. CP-HardT

Here's the pub they conked. Heroes of Waterloo. Yusef Komunyakaa. CP-KomuY

Here's to Adhering. Maya Angelou. SP-AngeM

Here's to Eddie. Thanks. Robert Creeley. SP-CreeR

Here's to Her Who Long. Lord Byron. CP-Byron

Here's to opening and upward,to leaf and to sap. E. E. Cummings. CP-CummE; SP-CummE

Here's to Samuel Greenberg. Thomas Lux. SP-LuxT

Here's to the emperor's peasants! Old Lady's Old Men! Arthur Rimbaud. CP-RimbA, *tr.* by Martin Sorrell

Here's to the Spirit of Fire. Nicholas Vachel Lindsay. CP-LindV

Here's to thy health, my bonie lass. Robert Burns. CP-BurnR

Here's where I started / running from a little bee. Or. C. K. Williams. CP-WillC

Here's your mom, here's your dad. Song of Welcome. Joseph Brodsky. CP-BrodJ

Heresy. Walter De la Mare. CP-DeLaW

Heretic's Tragedy, The. Robert Browning. CP-BroR1

Hereto I come to view a voiceless ghost. After a Journey. Thomas Hardy. CP-HardT

Hereunder Jacob Schmidt who, man and bones. Immortal Helix. Archibald MacLeish. CP-MacLA

Herewith I send you my heart. Triolets: "Herewith I send you my heart." Dorothy Parker. CP-ParkD

Heriot's Ford. Rudyard Kipling. CP-KiplR *Fr.* Light That Failed, The.

Heritage. Countee Cullen. CP-CullC

Heritage of Wonder, The. G. K. Chesterton. CP-ChesG

Heritage, The. Rudyard Kipling. CP-KiplR

Herma, seal with wax and string. Florentine Madrigals. Eugenio Montale. CP-MontE, *tr.* by Jonathan Galassi

Herman Melville. W. H. Auden. CP-AudeW

Herman Melville. Jorge Luis Borges. SP-BorgJ, *tr.* by Stephen Kessler

Hermaphroditic Telephones, The. William Carlos Williams. CP-WilW1

Hermes and Mr Shaw. Donald Davie. CP-DaviDC

Hermes, god. Prayer to Hermes. Robert Creeley. SP-CreeR

Hermes it was. Hermes with wingèd heels. Getting the Message. Miller Williams. CP-WillM

Hermes of the Ways. "H. D." CP-DoolH

Hermes Rising. Sam Hamill. SP-HamiS

Hermes Trismegistus / is patron of alchemists. Tribute to the Angels. "H. D." CP-DoolH

Hermetic Poem. Stanley Kunitz. CP-KunSC

Hermione. Ralph Waldo Emerson. CP-EmerR

Hermit at Outermost House, The. Sylvia Plath. CP-PlatS

Hermit Crab, The. Mary Oliver. SP-OlivM

Hermit Hoar. Samuel Johnson. CP-JohnS

   (Lines on Thomas Warton's Poems.) CP-JohnS

Hermit Meets the Skunk, The. Maxine W. Kumin. SP-KumiM

Hermit of Hudson Pond, The. Mona Van Duyn. SP-VanDM

Hermit of the Thebaid, The. John Greenleaf Whittier. CP-WhitJ

Hermit (or if 'chance you hold), A. Moralizer Corrected, The. William Cowper. CP-CowpW

Hermit Picks Berries, The. Maxine W. Kumin. SP-KumiM

Hermit Prays, The. Maxine W. Kumin. SP-KumiM

Hermit, The. Seamus Heaney. SP-HeanSO *Fr.* Sweeney Redivivus.

Hermit Thrush, A. Amy Clampitt. CP-ClamA

Hermit Wakes to Bird Sounds, The. Maxine W. Kumin. SP-KumiM

Hermitage. Wisława Szymborska. SP-SzymW, *tr.* by Stanislaw Barańczak *and* Clare Cavanagh

Hermitage at the Center, The. Wallace Stevens. CP-StevW; CP-StevWP

Hermit's dog skitters home, The. Hermit Meets the Skunk, The. Maxine W. Kumin. SP-KumiM

Hermit's heart is heavy, A. Han-shan. CP-ColdM, *tr.* by Red Pine

Hermocratia nam'd—save only me. On Hermocratia. *Unknown.* CP-CowpW

Hermonax. "H. D." CP-DoolH

Hernani. George Meredith. CP-MerG1

Hero. William Corbett. SP-CorbW

Hero. Robert Creeley. CP-CreeR

Hero. William Carlos Williams. CP-WilW1

Hero, The. Marianne Craig Moore. CP-MoorM *Fr.* Part of a Novel, Part of a Poem, Part of a Play.

Hero, The. G. K. Chesterton. CP-ChesG

Hero, The. Robert Creeley. CP-CreeR

Hero, The. Robert Graves. CP-GravR

Hero, The. Henry David Thoreau. CP-ThorH

Hero, The. John Greenleaf Whittier. CP-WhitJ

Hero and Leander. Christopher Marlowe. CP-MarlC

Hero and Leander. John Donne. CP-DonnJ; MW-DonnJ

Hero as liberator. There is also. At the Western Ocean's Edge. Thomas Kinsella. CP-KinsT

Hero Comes Home in His Hamper, and Is Exhibited at the World's Fair, The. Howard Nemerov. CP-NemeH

Hero—International Brigade. Langston Hughes. CP-HughL; CP-HughL3

Hero of moment is no bigger than a bean, The. Childhood of the Hero. Kenneth Patchen. CP-PatcK

Hero of phantasies and catcher of chills. Poetaster. Theodore Roethke. CP-RoetT

Hero Sandwiches. Charles Tomlinson. CP-TomlC

Hero Speech. Muriel Rukeyser. CP-RukeM

Hero with Girl and Gorgon. Howard Nemerov. CP-NemeH

Hérodiade. Stéphane Mallarmé. CP-MallS, *tr.* by Henry Weinfield

Herodion, Apelles, Amplias. Three Taverns, The. Edwin Arlington Robinson. CP-RobiE

Herodis Attikos. Constantine P. Cavafy. CP-CavaC, *tr.* by Theoharis Constantine Theoharis

Herodotus Reports. James Laughlin. CP-LaughJ

Herod's Lament for Mariamne. Lord Byron. CP-Byron

Heroes. Robert Creeley. CP-CreeR

Heroes, and Kings! your distance keep. Epitaph for One Who Would Not Be Buried in Westminster Abbey. Alexander Pope. CP-PopeA

Heroes of Childhood, The. Thomas McGrath. SP-McGrT

Heroes of Waterloo. Yusef Komunyakaa. CP-KomuY

Heroes paused upon the plain, The. Byrnies, The. Thom Gunn. CP-GunnT

Heroes, The. John Berryman. CP-BerrJ

Heroic Sculpture. Frank O'Hara. SP-OharF

Heroic stars spending themselves, The. Epic Stars, The. Robinson Jeffers. CP-JefR3

Heroides. Ovid.

    "Strong Ilion thou shalt see with walls and towers high." CP-RaleW

    "Succeeding years thy early frame destroy." CP-JohnS

Heroine, The. William Dickey. SP-DickW

Heroine in ass-skin. WHITE FOOLSCAP / Book of Cordelia. Susan Howe. SP-HoweS

Heroine of the Academy, A. Donald Davie. CP-DaviDC

Heroines. Adrienne Rich. SP-RicA2

Heroism. William Cowper. CP-CowpW

Heroism. Ralph Waldo Emerson. CP-EmerR

Heron, The. Wendell Berry. CP-BerrW

Heron, The. Theodore Roethke. CP-RoetT

Heron Ballads, 1795, The. Robert Burns.

    Buy Braw Troggin. An Excellent New Song. CP-BurnR

    Election: A New Song, The. CP-BurnR

    Johnie B———'s Lament. CP-BurnR

    "Wham will we send to London town." CP-BurnR

Heron-billed pale cattle-birds, The. At Algeciras—a Meditation upon Death.

William Butler Yeats. CP-YeatW

Heron warps its neck, a broken pick, The. Mills of the Kavanaughs, The. Robert Lowell. SP-LoweR

Hero's Lamp. Dante Gabriel Rossetti. CW-RossD *Fr.* House of Life, The.

Herr Weiser!—Threescore years and ten. James Whitcomb Riley. CP-RileJ

Hers was the last authentic rape. Helen's Rape. Thom Gunn. CP-GunnT

Herself a Rose Who Bore the Rose. Christina Georgina Rossetti. CP-RosC2

Hertfordshire. Donald Davie. CP-DaviDC

Hervé Riel. Robert Browning. CP-BroR2

Hes a Blockhead who wants a proof of what he Cant Percieve. William Blake. CP-BlakW

He's a Critic—damn his eyes! Singular Effects of Malediction. G. K. Chesterton. CP-ChesG *Fr.* Thought and Reflections.

He's a sad sack. So's he. Jottings, not so Random. Donald Davie. CP-DaviDC

He's an old man. Spent, hunched over. Very Seldom. Constantine P. Cavafy. CP-CavaC, *tr.* by Theoharis Constantine Theoharis

He's been wading deeper into the accident area. Blue Spill. James Tate. SP-TateJ

He's dead / the dog won't have to. Death. William Carlos Williams. CP-WilW1

He's gone, and all our plans. To His Love. Ivor Gurney. SP-GurnI

He's here again. Is this hunger I smell, something like wildflowers and afterbirth tangled in sage? Dream Animal. Yusef Komunyakaa. CP-KomuY

He's in class teaching. Now. David Ignatow. SP-IgnaD

He's jes' a great, big, awk'ard, hulkin'. My Henry. James Whitcomb Riley. CP-RileJ

He's just an ordinary guy. Just an Ordinary Guy. Langston Hughes. CP-HughL

He's King of Mirth that slyly cheats our sense. Lucan. CP-SherT, *tr.* by Thomas Sheridan

He's lost him utterly. And now he seeks. Desperation. Constantine P. Cavafy. CP-CavaC, *tr.* by Theoharis Constantine Theoharis

He's lost his old daring, his nerve. Battle of Magnesia, The. Constantine P. Cavafy. CP-CavaC, *tr.* by Theoharis Constantine Theoharis

He's lying in poor water, a yard or so depth of poor safety. October Salmon[, An]. Ted Hughes. SP-HughTN

He's never been pointed to first for anything. Sissy, The. Miller Williams. CP-WillM

He's not sure how to get the jack on—he must have recently bought the car, although it's ancient. Reading: Winter. C. K. Williams. SP-WillC

He's one of those men who want to do everything by themselves. Man's Household, A. Wisława Szymborska. SP-SzymWM, *tr.* by Joanna Trzeciak

He's out stuck in a bird's craw. Maitreya the Future Buddha. Gary Snyder. CP-SnydG *Fr.* Myths and Texts.

He's tucked his feet into corduroy scuffs. Recovery. Rita Dove. SP-DoveR

He's wedded to his theory, they say. By Mrs. Hopley. Gerard Manley Hopkins. CP-HopkG

Hesitate, cease to exist, glitter again. Thomas Kinsella. CP-KinsT

Hesitate to Call. Louise Glück. SP-GlucL

Hesitating Veteran, The. Ambrose Bierce. SP-BierA

Hesitation, The. Charles Tomlinson. CP-TomlC

Hesitations Outside the Door. Margaret Atwood. SP-AtwM1

Hesperia the Gr[a]ecians call the place. Virgil. CP-RaleW *Fr.* Aeneid [*or* Eneados *or* Aeneis], The.

Hester Johnson (STELLA) was baptized on the 20th March 1680–1. Fragments of a Liquidation. Susan Howe. SP-HoweS

Heu non maturo mihi fato, dulcis Huissi. In obitum Iacobi Huissii. Thomas Campion. CP-CampT

Heu! Quam Remotus. William Cowper. CP-CowpW

Heureux Qui, comme Ulysse, A Fait un Beau Voyage. Joachim Du Bellay. CP-ChesG, *tr.* by G. K. Chesterton

Hex, The. Anne Sexton. CP-SextA

Hexahedrons of wood and glass. Objects & Apparitions. Octavio Paz. CP-BishE, *tr.* by Elizabeth Bishop

Hexameters. Samuel Taylor Coleridge. CP-ColeS

Hey. Robert Creeley. CP-CreeR

Hey! Langston Hughes. CP-HughL; CP-HughL1

Hey, Basho, you there! Hayden Carruth. CP-CarHS *Fr.* Clay Hill Anthology, The.

"Hey, Bud! *O* Bud!" rang out a gleeful call. Loehrs and the Hammonds, The. James Whitcomb Riley. CP-RileJ *Fr.* Child-World, A.

Hey, Buddy! / Look at me! Langston Hughes. *See* I'm makin' a road

Hey Ca' thro'. Robert Burns. CP-BurnR

Hey! / Can I have some more. Detail. William Carlos Williams. CP-WilW2

Hey, Ezra, Listen to This. Charles Bukowski. SP-BukC3

Hey for a Lass wi' a Tocher. Robert Burns. CP-BurnR

    (Then hey, for a lass wi' a tocher, then hey, for a lass wi' a tocher.) CP-BurnR

Hey! Hey! Langston Hughes. CP-HughL; CP-HughL1

Hey-Hey Blues. Langston Hughes. CP-HughL; CP-HughL2

Hey, hey, daddio. November Jeans Song. Hayden Carruth. CP-CarHS

Hey! Hey! / That's what the. Blues Fantasy. Langston Hughes. CP-HughL; CP-

HughL1

Hey man! Somebody yells down to me through my broken / window. Somebody Always Breaking My Dainty Solitude. Charles Bukowski. SP-BukC2

Hey! Mister Bloodhound Boss. False Leads. Yusef Komunyakaa. CP-KomuY

Hey music and / me. My Dream About Being White. Lucille Clifton. SP-ClifL

Hey! my little Yellowbird. Yellowbird, The. James Whitcomb Riley. CP-RileJ

Hey Ninetto, remember that dream. One of the Many Epilogs. Pier Paolo Pasolini. SP-PasoP, *tr.* by Norman MacAfee *and* Luciano Martinengo

Hey ninny neigh! Shakespeare in Harlem. Langston Hughes. CP-HughL; CP-HughL2

Hey, Old Midsummer! are you here again. Old Friend, An. James Whitcomb Riley. CP-RileJ

Hey Red! William Carlos Williams. CP-WilW2

Hey, said my friend, I want you to meet. Twins. Charles Bukowski. SP-BukC1

Hey the dusty Miller. Dusty Miller. Robert Burns. CP-BurnR

Hey there, you in the macadam suit! Mr. U.S. Highway #1. Just outside Tombstone. Kenneth Patchen. CP-PatcK

Hey Tuti Tatey. Robert Burns. CP-BurnR

Hey you followers of the Way. Han-shan. CP-ColdM, *tr.* by Red Pine

Hey you people who leave home. Han-shan. CP-ColdM, *tr.* by Red Pine

Hi and whoop-hooray, boys! On the Sunny Side. James Whitcomb Riley. CP-RileJ

Hi-Ho the Ambulance-O. Ogden Nash. CP-NashO

Hi, Hot-and-Humid. Lorine Niedecker. CP-NiedL

Hi, Kuh, / those / gold'n bees / are I's. I's (Pronounced *Eyes*). Louis Zukofsky. CP-ZukLS

Hi, open up a dozen. At the Bar. William Carlos Williams. CP-WilW1

Hi! The creator too is blind. Negation. Wallace Stevens. CP-StevW; CP-StevWP

Hi There! Robert Creeley. CP-CreeR

Hiatus. Louis MacNeice. CP-MacNL

Hiawatha's Childhood. Henry Wadsworth Longfellow. SP-LongH *Fr.* Song of Hiawatha, The.

Hiawatha's Fasting. Henry Wadsworth Longfellow. SP-LongH *Fr.* Song of Hiawatha, The.

Hibernaculum. A. R. Ammons. CP-AmmoA

Hibiscus and Salvia Flowers. D. H. Lawrence. CP-LawrD

Hibiscus on the Sleeping Shores. Wallace Stevens. CP-StevW; CP-StevWP

Hic etiam jacet. Epitaphium Alterum. William Cowper. CP-CowpW

Hic Jacet. William Carlos Williams. CP-WilW1

Hic sinu fessum caput hospitali. Epitaphium. Percy Bysshe Shelley. CP-ShelP

Hickory-dickory-dock. Nursery Rhymes. Robert Penn Warren. CP-WarrR

Hickory Grove, The. Amy Clampitt. CP-ClamA

Hid by the august foliage and fruit of the grape vine. To a Chameleon. Marianne Craig Moore. CP-MoorM

Hidden behind his smile of brotherly regard. Mid-Twentieth-Century Portrait. Czeslaw Milosz. CP-MiloC; CP-MiloCN, *tr.* by Jan Darowski

Hidden by old age awhile. Meeting. William Butler Yeats. CP-YeatW

Hidden Door. Lawrence Ferlinghetti. SP-FerlL

Hidden from the darkness of our mortal sight. Antipas. Christina Georgina Rossetti. CP-RosC2

Hidden Garden, The. Robert Graves. CP-GravR

Hidden Ice. Louis MacNeice. CP-MacNL

Hidden in the study at dusk. Point of Departure. Dan Pagis. SP-PagiD, *tr.* by Stephen Mitchell

Hidden in this heaven-harbor. Clairvaux. Thomas Merton. CP-MertT

Hidden Law, The. W. H. Auden. CP-AudeW

Hidden Monsters at the Mount Auburn Cemetery. A Found Poem. Denise Levertov. SP-LeveDL

Hidden, oh hidden. Song for the Rainy Season. Elizabeth Bishop. CP-BishE

Hidden Singer, The. Wendell Berry. CP-BerrW

Hidden Things. Constantine P. Cavafy. CP-CavaC, *tr.* by Theoharis Constantine Theoharis

Hidden under the heron's wing. T. S. Eliot. SP-EliotT

Hide and Seek. Thom Gunn. CP-GunnT

Hide in cesspools, sleep well. Qualifications of Survivors. Alan Dugan. CP-DugaA

Hide in the hollow trunk. Oracle. Seamus Heaney. SP-HeanSO

Hide not, sweetest Love, a sight so pleasing. Thomas Campion. CP-CampT

Hide & Seek. Howard Nemerov. CP-NemeH

Hide the name away in the Secret. Fanny Howe. SP-HoweF *Fr.* Introduction to the World.

Hide thou thy face in clouds and mysteries. Love of God. G. K. Chesterton. CP-ChesG

Hideousness of the inland spine of Cornwall!, The. Short Run to Camborne. Donald Davie. CP-DaviDC

Hiding in the church of an abandoned stone. Confession to J. Edgar Hoover. James Wright. CP-WrigJ

Hiding Our Love. Emperor Wu of Han. CP-KizeC, *tr.* by Carolyn Kizer

Hieroglyphic. Hart Crane. CP-CranH

Hieroglyphica. Wallace Stevens. CP-StevWP

Hieros Gamos. Kathleen Jessie Raine. SP-RainK

High above Plymouth, not so high. Among Artisans' Houses. Donald Davie. CP-DaviDC

High above us a chain of white buckets. End of Summer. W. S. Merwin. SP-MerwW

High & Low. A. R. Ammons. CP-AmmoA

High and smaller goes the moon, she is small and very far from me. Pang of Reminiscence, A. D. H. Lawrence. CP-LawrD

High-beam light swung, The. Nocturne: "High-beam light swung, The." Yusef Komunyakaa. CP-KomuY

High bliss is only for a higher state. Farewell Lines. William Wordsworth. CP-WorW2

High Bridge above the Tagus River at Toledo, The. William Carlos Williams. CP-WilW2

High ceilingd and the double mirrors, the. Bubbs Creek Haircut. Gary Snyder. CP-SnydG

High-class families, The. Dullness in February: Japan. Gary Snyder. CP-SnydG

High climbs June's wild rose. Wild Rose, The. George Meredith. CP-MerG2

High Culture. Amy Clampitt. CP-ClamA

High deck, A. Blue skies overhead. White distance. Flashboat, The. Jane Cooper. CP-CoopJ

High deeds, O Germans, are to come from you! Prophecy February, 1807, A. William Wordsworth. CP-WorW1

High-dwelling 'bove the people here. Prelude: Over the Ognisanti. Ezra Pound. CP-PoEar

High Fidelity. Thom Gunn. CP-GunnT

High-fiving in Charlottesville. Appalachian Book of the Dead 4, The. Charles Wright. SP-WrigCN

High fog, white sky. Fennel. Thom Gunn. CP-GunnT

High Frequency. Marge Piercy. SP-PierM

High from the earth I heard a bird. Emily Dickinson. CP-DickE

High grace, the dower of queens; and therewithal. Her Gifts. Dante Gabriel Rossetti. CW-RossD *Fr.* House of Life, The.

High heart, O Hafiz! though not thine. Hafiz. CP-EmerR *Fr.* Odes.

High-Hearts, The. John Updike. CP-UpdiJ

"High heavenly priest of the White Lake" is now, The. Portrait of the Artist with Li Po. Charles Wright. SP-WrigC

High Hills, The. Ivor Gurney. SP-GurnI

High horses of the sea broke their white riders. How Yesterday Looked. Carl Sandburg. CP-SandC

High in Hollywood Hills a door opens. Poem: "High in Hollywood Hills a door opens." James Tate. SP-TateJ

High in the air these placid mountains or. Clouds ("High in the air these placid mountains or"). Jorge Luis Borges. SP-BorgJ, *tr.* by Willis Barnstone

High in the alpine. Sinking Stone, The. James Laughlin. CP-LaugJ

High in the breathless Hall the Minstrel sate. Song at the Feast of Brougham Castle upon the Restoration of Lord Clifford, the Shepherd, to the Estates and Honours of His Ancestors. William Wordsworth. CP-WorW1

High in the dome, suspended, of Hell, sad triumph, behold us! Ixion. Robert Browning. CP-BroR2

High in the jacaranda shines the gilded thread. 90th Year, The. Denise Levertov. SP-LeveDL; SP-LeveDS

High in the midst, surrounded by his peers. Thoughts Suggested by a College Examination. Lord Byron. CP-Byron

High in the mountain pass, tucked in a crevice. American Sublime, The: Robert Penn Warren. Eleanor Wilner. SP-WilnE

High is our calling, Friend!—Creative Art. To B. R. Haydon. William Wordsworth. CP-WorW2; MW-WorW

High Jinx. Heather McHugh. SP-McHuH

High, lovely, light. Lorine Niedecker. CP-NiedL

High Master and the Abbot of Fulham, the. G. K. Chesterton. CP-ChesG

High Moments. Carl Sandburg. CP-SandC

High mounted on an Ant *Nanus* the tall. On Nanus Mounted on an Ant. Ausonius. CP-CrasR

High nave, in a place of ships, The. At Saint Mary's Church. Charles Tomlinson. CP-TomlC

High near the heart of the mountain there is a cavern. Survivor. Thomas Kinsella. CP-KinsT

High Noon. Amy Clampitt. CP-ClamA

High Noon at Los Alamos. Eleanor Wilner. SP-WilnE

High noon has me pitchblack, so in hope out. Sext. John Berryman. CP-BerrJ

High noon. White sun flashes on the Michigan Avenue asphalt. Drum. In a Breath. Carl Sandburg. CP-SandC

High o'er a flood, which boils and foams below. Bridge of Time, The. Jones Very. CP-VeryJ

High o'er the silver rocks I roved. Beauty and Moonlight. William Wordsworth. CP-WorW1

High on a broad unfertile tract of forest-skirted Down. Norman Boy, The. William Wordsworth. CP-WorW2

High on a slope in New Guinea. Man in the Dead Machine, The. Donald Hall. CP-HallD

High on his figured couch beyond the waves. Theseus and Ariadne. Robert Graves. CP-GravR

High on his stockroom ladder like a dunce. Playboy. Richard Wilbur. CP-WilbR

High on Laughing Gas. Laughing Gas. Allen Ginsberg. CP-GinsA

High on Sadness. Yusef Komunyakaa. CP-KomuY

High on the summit. Tankas. Jorge Luis Borges. SP-BorgJ, tr. by Alastair Reid

High on the wall that holds Jerusalem. Sonnet: "High on the wall that holds Jerusalem." G. K. Chesterton. CP-ChesG

High ones, Berryman said, die, die, die, The. March 4th. Anne Sexton. CP-SextA

High over the deep. Near Zermatt: The Drahtseilbahn. James Laughlin. CP-LaugJ

High over the graves of our comrades, banked. Leaflet (Two). Kenneth Patchen. CP-PatcK

High over the October wood the Lion. Lion, The. Thomas Merton. CP-MertT

High Pasture, The. Donald Hall. CP-HallD

High plane for whom the winds incline. Airman's Virtue. William Meredith. SP-MereW

High Priests of telescopes and cyclotrons, The. Ode to Terminus. W. H. Auden. CP-AudeW

High Provence. Kenneth Rexroth. CP-RexrK

High Quality Information. Gary Snyder. CP-SnydG

High rides the moon. Nocturnes from the Window. Federico García Lorca. CP-GarcF, tr. by Alan S. Trueblood

High-Rise of the New World, The. Charles Bukowski. SP-BukC2

High Road, The. Thomas Kinsella. CP-KinsT

High-School Lawn, The. Thomas Hardy. CP-HardT

High-spirited friend. Ode, An: "High-spirited friend." Ben Jonson. CP-JonsB; SP-JonsB

High state and honours to others impart. Song: "High state and honours to others impart." John Dryden. CP-DryJ2

High stratosphere winds with their juvenile whistle. Future. Joseph Brodsky. CP-BrodJ Fr. Shorts.

High Summer. Kathleen Jessie Raine. SP-RainK

High Summer. Charles Tomlinson. CP-TomlC

High Surreal. A. R. Ammons. CP-AmmoA

High Talk. William Butler Yeats. CP-YeatW

High Tension Lines across a Landscape. John Ciardi. CP-CiarJ

High-tension on Low-pressure Non-accomplishment Blues. Philip Whalen. SP-WhalP

High the vancs of Shrewsbury gleam. Welsh Marches, The. A. E. Housman. CP-HousA

High to Low. Langston Hughes. CP-HughL; CP-HughL3

High-Toned Old Christian Woman, A. Wallace Stevens. CP-StevW; CP-StcvWP

High up on the mountain. Four Ballads in Yellow. Federico García Lorca. CP-GarcF, tr. by Jerome Rothenberg

High up on the patio window, centered exactly. Impact. Karl Shapiro. SP-ShapK

High walls / pale brick like Babylon. Church, The. W. S. Merwin. SP-MerwW

High Water. W. S. Merwin. SP-MerwWF

High waving heather, 'neath stormy blasts bending. 'High waving heather.' Emily Jane Brontë. CP-BronE

High wind blows, A. Air for the Witness of a Departure. Christopher Logue. SP-LoguC

High Windows. Philip Larkin. CP-LarkP

High wooded hill near Florence, an April, A. In Memory: Stuart Egnal. Wendell Berry. CP-BerrW

Higher Arguments in Favor of Discipline Derived from the Speech Before the Council of the Universal State in 2068. Czeslaw Milosz. CP-MiloC; CP-MiloCN, tr. by Robert Hass

Higher than gulls' nests, higher than children go. Rock Climbing. Jane Cooper. CP-CoopJ

Higher than the handsomest hotel. Building, The. Philip Larkin. CP-LarkP

Higher thought than fills the narrow mind, A. E Pluribus Unum. Jones Very. CP-VeryJ

Higher Unity, The. G. K. Chesterton. CP-ChesG

Highest Altitude. Margaret Atwood. SP-AtwM1

Highest Good, The. James Whitcomb Riley. CP-RileJ

Highgate Cemetery. Amy Clampitt. CP-ClamA

Highland Balou, The. Robert Burns. CP-BurnR

Highland Broach, The. William Wordsworth. CP-WorW2

Highland Harry Back Again. Robert Burns. CP-BurnR

Highland Hut. William Wordsworth. CP-WorW2

Highland Laddie. Robert Burns. CP-BurnR

Highland Lassie O. Robert Burns. CP-BurnR

Highland Mary. Robert Burns. CP-BurnR

Highland Widow's Lament, The. Robert Burns. CP-BurnR

Highlander Once Fought a Frenchman at Margate, A. Thomas Sheridan. CP-SherT

Highmindedness, a jealousy for good. Addressed to Haydon. John Keats. CP-KeatJ

Highway cuts through, The. Fanny Howe. SP-HoweF Fr. Sea-Garden, The.

Highway ended, The. 7 Years from Somewhere. Philip Levine. SP-LeviP

Highway is full of big cars, The. Come, And Be My Baby. Maya Angelou. SP-AngeM

Highway: Michigan. Theodore Roethke. CP-RoetT

Highway 99E from Chico. Raymond Carver. CP-CarvR

Highway 66. James Laughlin. CP-LaugJ

Highway Stripper. A. K. Ramanujan. CP-RamaA

Hik-Tee-Dik. James Whitcomb Riley. CP-RileJ

Hiking on the Coast Range. Kenneth Rexroth. CP-RexrK

Hiking out to Ratcliff. Pagan Saturday. John Logan. CP-LogaJ

Hilarious God. Lawrence Ferlinghetti. SP-FerlL

Hilda. John Crowe Ransom. SP-RansJ

Hilda's Morning and Evening Dose of Rhyme. George Meredith. CP-MerG2

Hill. Louis Zukofsky. CP-ZukLS

Hill, The. Robert Creeley. CP-CreeR

Hill, The. Yannis Ritsos. SP-RitsY, tr. by Kimon Friar

Hill, The. Charles Tomlinson. CP-TomlC

Hill blue among the leaves in summer. Cheap Blue. Carl Sandburg. CP-SandC

Hill (breeder) of Helicon. Carmen 61. Catullus. CP-ZukLS Fr. Carmina.

Hill Dream of Youth, Thirty Years Later. Richard Eberhart. CP-EberR

Hill Field, The. Donald Davie. CP-DaviDC

Hill Has Something to Say, The. Rita Dove. SP-DoveR

—Hill / Heaven and every field, are still. Gerard Manley Hopkins. CP-HopkG

Hill of Beans, A. Rita Dove. SP-DoveR

Hill of the white skull in the summer moon, The. Three Hills Look Different in the Moonshine. Carl Sandburg. CP-SandC

Hill pasture, an open place among the trees, The. In This World. Wendell Berry. CP-BerrW

Hill-sides are dark. In the Woods. George Meredith. CP-MerG2

Hill Summit, The. Dante Gabriel Rossetti. CW-RossD Fr. House of Life, The.

Hill-top schloss, The. Legend. Charles Tomlinson. CP-TomlC

Hill-Top, The. John Greenleaf Whittier. CP-WhitJ

Hill Walk. Charles Tomlinson. CP-TomlC; SP-TomlC

Hill Wife, The. Robert Frost. CP-FrosR

Hillcrest. Edwin Arlington Robinson. CP-RobiE

Hillocky alpine rosy bells name. Alpine Rosy Bells. Louis Zukofsky. CP-ZukLS

Hills, The. D. H. Lawrence. CP-LawrD

Hills, The. George Oppen. CP-OppGN

Hills are grey elephants. Sing, Mister, Sing. Charles Olson. CP-OlsoC

Hills are tipped with sunshine, while I walk / In shadows dim and cold. Christina Georgina Rossetti. CP-RosC2

Hills behind, The. One Year. Gary Snyder. CP-SnydG

Hills chime with thrush. E. E. Cummings. CP-CummE

Hills erect their Purple Heads, The. Emily Dickinson. CP-DickE

Hills haven the last cloud. However white. From. First Moment of Autumn Recognized. Robert Penn Warren. CP-WarrR

Hills in Purple syllables, The. Emily Dickinson. CP-DickE

Hills in Their Recumbent Postures, The. Philip Larkin. CP-LarkP

Hills / like poets put on, The. E. E. Cummings. CP-CummE

Hills my brothers & I created, The. Believing in Iron. Yusef Komunyakaa. CP-KomuY

Hills of Annesley! bleak and barren. Fragment Written Shortly after the Marriage of Miss Chaworth. Lord Byron. CP-Byron

Hills of May, The. Robert Graves. CP-GravR

Hills on which I left myself behind, The. Petrarch. CP-Petra, tr. by J. G. Nichols

Hills step off into whiteness, The. Sheep in Fog. Sylvia Plath. CP-PlatS

Hills uncap their tops, The. Life and Death at Sunrise. Thomas Hardy. CP-HardT

Hills Whence. The. Ezra Pound. CP-PoEar

Hillside Thaw, A. Robert Frost. CP-FrosR

Hilltops seen through rain and cloud. Chinese England. Christopher Logue. SP-LoguC

Him with His Tail in His Mouth. D. H. Lawrence. CP-LawrD

Himmaleh was known to stoop, The. Emily Dickinson. CP-DickE

Himself it was who wrote. Astræa. Ralph Waldo Emerson. CP-EmerR

Hind and the Panther, The. John Dryden.
  "Swallow, privileged above the rest, The." SP-DrydJ

Hindoo Converts: On the Domestic Trials of Hindoo Converts. Report of Unitarian Mission in India. Jones Very. CP-VeryJ

HINDOO, THE: He Doesn't Hurt a Fly or a Spider Either. A. K. Ramanujan. CP-RamaA

HINDOO, THE: He Reads His GITA and Is Calm at All Events. A. K. Ramanujan. CP-RamaA

HINDOO, THE: The Only Risk. A. K. Ramanujan. CP-RamaA

Hindu to His Body, A. A. K. Ramanujan. CP-RamaA

Hinge Picture. Susan Howe. SP-HoweSE

Hint from the Mountains for Certain Political Pretenders. William Wordsworth. CP-WorW2

Hint of Spring, A. James Whitcomb Riley. CP-RileJ

Hints. Yannis Ritsos. SP-RitsY, tr. by Kimon Friar

Hints for the Fancy. William Wordsworth. CP-WorW2 Fr. River Duddon [A Series of Sonnets], The.

Hints from Horace. Lord Byron. CP-Byron

Hip boots / Deep in the blues. Not Else—But. Langston Hughes. CP-HughL; CP-HughL3

Hippety hoppety down. Nathaniel Hawthorne. Robert Creeley. CP-CreeR

Hippie Hop. A. R. Ammons. CP-AmmoA

Hippo, The. Theodore Roethke. CP-RoetT

Hippocrene. Amy Clampitt. CP-ClamA

Hippolytus. Euripides.

　Chorus of Troizenian Women. CP-DoolH

　Chorus sing of escape, The. CP-DoolH

　"Daemon initiate, spirit." CP-DoolH

　"Lift my head, help me up." CP-DoolH

　"Men you strike." CP-DoolH

　"No more, O my spirit." CP-DoolH

　"O Spirit, / spark by spark." CP-DoolH

Hippolytus. Seneca.

　"Not faster in the summer's ray." CP-JohnS

Hippolytus Temporizes. "H. D." CP-DoolH

Hippopotamus, The. T. S. Eliot. CP-ElioT

Hippopotamus, The. Ogden Nash. CP-NashO

Hippy-Mo. Stevie Smith. CP-SmitS

Hips lOOsest OOping shoulders blonde& pastoral hair,strong. E. E. Cummings. CP-CummE

Hiram Powers' "Greek Slave." Elizabeth Barrett Browning. CP-BroEB

Hirbet Sayid. Yehuda Amichai. SP-AmicYL, tr. by Benjamin Harshav and Barbara Harshav

Hired Man and Floretty, The. James Whitcomb Riley. CP-RileJ Fr. Child-World, A.

Hired Man's Dog-Story, The. James Whitcomb Riley. CP-RileJ

Hired Man's Faith in Children, The. James Whitcomb Riley. CP-RileJ

Hired Man's supper, which he sat before, The. Hired Man and Floretty, The. James Whitcomb Riley. CP-RileJ Fr. Child-World, A.

His Age, Dedicated to His Peculiar Friend, Master John Wickes, under the Name of Posthumus. Robert Herrick. CP-HerrR

His Almes. Robert Herrick. CP-HerrR

His amiable face a little pale. In the Street. Constantine P. Cavafy. CP-CavaC, tr. by Theoharis Constantine Theoharis

His Answer to a Friend. Robert Herrick. CP-HerrR

His Answer to a Question. Robert Herrick. CP-HerrR

His Anthem, to Christ on the Crosse. Robert Herrick. CP-HerrR

His Apologies. Rudyard Kipling. CP-KiplR

His appearances are incalculable. Gratitude for a Nightmare. Robert Graves. CP-GravR

His are the generous days that balance. Generous Days, The. Stephen Spender. CP-SpenS

His arm slept. Dream-wounded and a former. To Robert E. Symmes 1933 for a gift of resemblances. Michael Palmer. SP-PalmM

His armour glittered in the [ ]. Fragments: Drafts, Mostly or All for a Poem on a Heroic Theme. William Wordsworth. CP-WorW1

His arms and legs were wholly literate. Rickshaw-Wallah, The. A. K. Ramanujan. CP-RamaA

His attitude towards woman is the basic point. Hugh MacDiarmid. SP-MacDH Fr. Cornish Heroic Song for Valda Trevlyn.

His awful skin. Bat. Anne Sexton. CP-SextA

His Banner over Me Was Love. Christina Georgina Rossetti. CP-RosC2

His Bargain. William Butler Yeats. CP-YeatW

His Bathrobe Pockets Stuffed with Notes. Raymond Carver. CP-CarvR

His beak could open a bottle. Little Owl Who Lives in the Orchard. Mary Oliver. SP-OlivM

His beautiful eyes! I hardly saw them, only. Michelangelo Buonarroti. CP-Miche, tr. by John Frederick Nims

His behavior was all one gesture to drive away the big fly. Bloodletting. Yannis Ritsos. SP-RitsY, tr. by Kimon Friar and Kostas Myrsiades

His Bill an Auger is. Emily Dickinson. CP-DickE

His Bill is clasped—his Eye forsook. Emily Dickinson. CP-DickE

His blood, Stravinsky used to say. Fizzle. A. K. Ramanujan. CP-RamaA

His bought arms Mong' not liked; for his first day. On Mongrel Esquire. Ben Jonson. CP-JonsB; SP-JonsB

His brain simplified itself. My Father at 89. Grace Paley. CP-PalGC

His Brother's Illness. Shmuel HaNagid. SP-HaNaS

His Carpets Flowered. Lorine Niedecker. CP-NiedL

His case is typical. Christopher Logue. SP-LoguC

His Cavalier. Robert Herrick. CP-HerrR

His Chance in Life. Rudyard Kipling. Fr. Plain Tales from the Hills.

His Change. Robert Herrick. CP-HerrR

His Charge to Julia at His Death. Robert Herrick. CP-HerrR

His Cheek is his Biographer. Emily Dickinson. CP-DickE

His chosen comrades thought at school. What Then? William Butler Yeats. CP-YeatW

His Christmas Sled. James Whitcomb Riley. CP-RileJ

His clock stopped watching. Time X. James Tate. SP-TateJ

His clothes, his elegance, his ease. Digby D'Avigdor. G. K. Chesterton. CP-ChesG

His coat resembles the snow. Polar Bear, The. William Carlos Williams. CP-WilW2

His Comfort. Robert Herrick. CP-HerrR

His Coming to the Sepulcher. Robert Herrick. CP-HerrR

His companions fell asleep over the ropes at the stern. Choice. Yannis Ritsos. SP-RitsY, tr. by Kimon Friar

His Confession. Robert Herrick. CP-HerrR

His Confidence. William Butler Yeats. CP-YeatW

His Content in the Country. Robert Herrick. CP-HerrR

His corpse owre a' the city lies. Dead Liebknecht, The. Hugh MacDiarmid. SP-MacDH

His Country. Thomas Hardy. CP-HardT

His Covenant or Protestation to Julia. Robert Herrick. CP-HerrR

His Creed. Robert Herrick. CP-HerrR

His Daughter. William Carlos Williams. CP-WilW2

His Death from Cancer. William Dickey. SP-DickW

His Desire. Robert Herrick. CP-HerrR

His Dream. Sir John Suckling. CP-SuckJ

His Dream. William Butler Yeats. CP-YeatW

His Dream of Flood: And Eden. Muriel Rukeyser. CP-RukeM

His Dream: The Black Tree / Thirst. Gregory Orr. SP-OrrG

His Dream[e]. Robert Herrick. CP-HerrR

His Ejaculation to God. Robert Herrick. CP-HerrR

His Embalming to Julia. Robert Herrick. CP-HerrR

His End and His Beginning. Jorge Luis Borges. SP-BorgJ, tr. by Alexander Coleman

His enemy, the universe, surrounds him nightly with stars. Bird Killer, The. Wendell Berry. CP-BerrW

His errand took him to the brink of Ragnorok. Perseus. Amy Clampitt. CP-ClamA

His Excellency. W. H. Auden. CP-AudeW

His eyes are always turned inward. Distinct Motion. Yannis Ritsos. SP-RitsY, tr. by Kostas Myrsiades

His eyes are darker than he knows. Narcissus. May Sarton. SP-SartM

His eyes are moss-green. LOVE 1: What She Said. A. K. Ramanujan. CP-RamaA

His eyes are quickened so with grief. Lost Love. Robert Graves. CP-GravR

His eyes, expressionless and fixed—he affected blindness. In a patched. Mutual Concessions. Yannis Ritsos. SP-RitsY, tr. by Andonis Decavalles

His eyes shallow and empty, the magician. Magician, The. Rainer Maria Rilke. CP-RilkFr, tr. by A. Poulin, Jr.

His eyes shine like an expensive car. Standing Close to Greatness. Miller Williams. CP-WillM

His face was charged with beauty as a cloud. Storm. Wilfred Owen. CP-OwenW

His face was like a snake's—wrinkled and loose. Fragment: A Serpent-Face. Percy Bysshe Shelley. CP-ShelP

His faces crack . . . if mine could crack and breathe! Rembrandt. Robert Lowell. SP-LoweR

His faithful love his pious zeal. Fragment on the Death of a Minester. Annis Boudinot Stockton. CP-StocA

His Farewell [or Fare-well] to Sack. Robert Herrick. CP-HerrR

His father gave him a box of truisms. Truisms, The. Louis MacNeice. CP-MacNL

His father is lost and away. Muriel Rukeyser. CP-RukeM

His father's clothes embarrass him. Hand-me-down, The. Wyatt Prunty. SP-PrunW

His father's sense, his mother's grace. On the Birth of John William Rizzo Hoppner. Lord Byron. CP-Byron

His Feet are shod with Gauze. Emily Dickinson. CP-DickE

His fingernails are black. Apprenticeship. Yusef Komunyakaa. CP-KomuY

His fingers hesitate over. Dream of Games, A. Josephine Jacobsen. CP-JacoJ

His fingers wake, and flutter; up the bed. Conscious. Wilfred Owen. CP-OwenW

His Foreboding. Theodore Roethke. CP-RoetT

His former wife called while he was in the south. Offending Eel, The. Raymond Carver. CP-CarvR

His foundation is in the holy mountains. Psalm 87: "His foundation is in the holy mountains." Bible, O.T. CP-MiltJ *Fr.* Psalms.

His gay words, words of delight. Muriel Rukeyser. CP-RukeM

His Glasses. Yannis Ritsos. SP-RitsY, *tr. by* Kimon Friar

His glazed lips / moved slower. Sound Lag. Arthur Sze. SP-SzeA

His Grace! impossible! what dead! Satirical Elegy on the Death of a Late Famous General, A. Jonathan Swift. CP-SwifJ

His Grace's Answer to Jonathan. Jonathan Swift. CP-SwifJ

His Grange. Robert Herrick. CP-HerrR

His Grange, or Private Wealth. Robert Herrick. CP-HerrR

His Grief. Gregory Orr. SP-OrrG

His hand changed in the kitchen. In a Court. Hart Crane. CP-CranH

His Hands Have Five Knives Each. Alan Dugan. CP-DugaA

His hands were warm and small and knowlegeable. August Night, An. Seamus Heaney. SP-HeanSO

His Head is Full of Faces. Muriel Rukeyser. CP RukeM

His head split in four parts. Promenade. David Ignatow. SP-IgnaD

His Heart. Thomas Hardy. CP-HardT

His Heart of Constant Youth. James Whitcomb Riley. CP-RileJ

His Heart was darker then the starless night. Emily Dickinson. CP-DickE

His high-boned, young face is so brown. White Pass Ski Patrol. John Logan. CP-LogaJ

His holy / slowly. Darwin. Lorine Niedecker. CP NiedL

His "Hoosier poems" Riley says he writes. Literary Method, A. Ambrose Bierce. SP-BierA

His Hope or Sheet-Anchor. Robert Herrick. CP-HerrR

His hopes, each one of them, turned out wrong! Of Dimitrios Sotir (162–150 B.C.). Constantine P. Cavafy. CP-CavaC, *tr. by* Theoharis Constantine Theoharis

His hour of birth he rolled. Lives of the Poet, The. John Logan. CP-LogaJ

His house / in the branches of. Charles Olson. CP-OlsoC

His Immortality. Thomas Hardy. CP-HardT

His instant thought the Poet spoke. Ralph Waldo Emerson. CP-EmerR

His job is honest and simple: keeping. Thomas Lux. SP-LuxT

His kidney floats in a bowl. I Have Got to Stop Loving You. So I Have Killed My Black Goat. Ai. SP-Ai

His kisses airbrush over her. Cinderella at Big Sur. Yusef Komunyakaa. CP-KomuY

His Lachrimae or Mirth, Turn'd to Mourning. Robert Herrick. CP-HerrR

His Lady queen of woods to meet. Youthful Quest, The. George Meredith. CP-MerG1

His Lament. Gregory Orr. SP-OrrG

His Lamp. Yannis Ritsos. SP-RitsY, *tr. by* Kimon Friar

His Lamp toward Daybreak. Yannis Ritsos. SP-RitsY, *tr. by* Kimon Friar

His land may burst the galling chain. Emily Jane Brontë. CP-BronE

His Last Picture. James Whitcomb Riley. CP-RileJ

His Last Request to Julia. Robert Herrick. CP-HerrR

His last train home is Purgatory in reverse. Drunkard, The. Louis MacNeice. CP-MacNL

His laurels fresh from song and lay. Our Autocrat. John Greenleaf Whittier. CP-WhitJ

His learning truly lifted Hafiz to Heaven. Hafiz. CP-EmerR *Fr.* Odes.

His legs are pillars of marble. Bride's Song, The. John Logan. CP-LogaJ *Fr.* Epilogue, Songs of the Spouses, Complaint of Love.

His lens misses her. Miracles. Arthur Sze. SP-SzeA

His Letanie, to the Holy Spirit. Robert Herrick.

His life gave yours rich reason for thanksgiving. Michelangelo Buonarroti. CP-Miche, *tr. by* John Frederick Nims

His life is in the body of the living. Soul and Body of John Brown, The. Muriel Rukeyser. CP-RukeM

His Life was so shy and his tastes so unknown. Emily Dickinson. SP-DickE

His little Hearse like Figure. Emily Dickinson. CP-DickE

His little trills and chirpings were his best. Tombstones in the Starlight. Dorothy Parker. CP-ParkD

His Losse. Robert Herrick. CP-HerrR

His Love of Home. James Whitcomb Riley. CP-RileJ

His lungs heaving all day in a sulphur mist. Black Money. Tess Gallagher. SP-GallT

His mangy buttocks levered high. Evangelists, The. Robert Stock. SP-StocR

His Manner of Returning. Tennessee Williams. CP-WillT

His Mansion in the Pool. Emily Dickinson. CP-DickE

His Meditation upon Death. Robert Herrick. CP-HerrR

His memories lived in the place. Praise, A. Wendell Berry. CP-BerrW

His memory was shaped by forgetting. Snow Man, The. Louis MacNeice. CP-MacNL

His mind is like a great peak. Han-shan.

His Mind like Fabrics of the East. Emily Dickinson. CP-DickE

His mind of man, a secret makes. Emily Dickinson. CP-DickE

His Misery in a Mistresse. Robert Herrick. CP-HerrR

His Mistris to Him at His Farwell. Robert Herrick. CP-HerrR

His Modest Apology for Knocking Out a News-Boy's Teeth, Who Told Him His Works Would Not Sell. Thomas Sheridan. CP-SherT

His Mother. James Whitcomb Riley. CP-RileJ

His mother would sigh. Life & Times of Billy Boy, The. Yusef Komunyakaa. CP-KomuY

His Mother's Service to Our Lady. François Villon. CW-RossD, *tr. by* Dante Gabriel Rossetti

His Mother's Way. James Whitcomb Riley. CP-RileJ

His Name. David Ignatow. SP-IgnaD

His name is Legion, and with a red eye. Armistice. Howard Nemerov. CP-NemeH

His name was Tug. Hers, Margo. Margo. Raymond Carver. CP-CarvR

His number is zero, or twenty-one. Fool, The. Charles Olson. CP-OlsoC

His Offering, with the Rest, at the Sepulcher. Robert Herrick. CP-HerrR

His old age fell on years of abundant harvest. Felicitous Life, A. Czeslaw Milosz. CP-MiloC; CP-MiloCN, *tr. by* Lillian Vallee

His oriental heresies. Emily Dickinson. CP-DickE

His Own Epitaph. Robert Herrick. CP-HerrR

His Own Face Hidden. Carl Sandburg. CP SandC

His own fair countenance, his kingly forehead. Inward Light. Samuel Taylor Coleridge. CP-ColeS

His pads furring the scarp's rime. Snow-Leopard, The. Randall Jarrell. CP-JarrR

His paintings grew darker every year. Artist, The. Stanley Kunitz. CP-KunSC

His Parting from Mistress Dorothy Keneday. Robert Herrick. CP-HerrR

His Pa's Romance. James Whitcomb Riley. CP-RileJ

His Petition. Robert Herrick. CP-HerrR

His Phoenix. William Butler Yeats. CP-YeatW

His Picture. John Donne. MW-DonnJ *Fr.* Elegies.

His piercing pince-nez. Some dim frieze. Sonnet I: "His piercing pince-nez. Some dim frieze." Ted Berrigan. SP-BerrT *Fr.* Sonnets, The.

His place, as he sat and as he thought, was not. Quiet Normal Life, A. Wallace Stevens. CP-StevW; CP-StevWP

His Plans for Old Age. William Meredith. SP-MereW

His Poetry His Pillar. Robert Herrick. CP-HerrR

His Power. Robert Herrick. CP-HerrR

His Prayer for Absolution. Robert Herrick. CP-HerrR

His Prayer to Ben Jonson. Robert Herrick. CP-HerrR

His Protestation to Perilla. Robert Herrick. CP-HerrR

His Recantation. Robert Herrick. CP-HerrR

His Request to Julia. Robert Herrick. CP-HerrR

His Return to London. Robert Herrick. CP-HerrR

His Reward. Sir Thomas Wyatt. CP-WyatT

His Room. James Whitcomb Riley. CP-RileJ

His room was big and clean. View from His Room. Clarence Major. SP-MajoC

His Rooms in College. Thom Gunn. CP-GunnT

His Sailing from Julia. Robert Herrick. CP-HerrR

His sandals, left on the sand, warping in the sun. Messenger. Yannis Ritsos. SP-RitsY, *tr. by* Kimon Friar

His Saviour['|s Words, Going to the Cross[e]. Robert Herrick. CP-HerrR

His Shield. Marianne Craig Moore. CP-MoorM

His Shining Helmet; Its Horsehair Crest. Tess Gallagher. SP-GallT

His Shirt. Rita Dove. SP-DoveR

His simple truths did Andrew glean. Oak and the Broom, The; A Pastoral. William Wordsworth. CP-WorW1; MW-WorW

His sin was to speak first. Origen. Thomas Merton. CP-MertT

His soul curdled. John J. Maya Angelou. SP-AngeM

His Soul fared forth (as from the deep home-grove). Samuel Taylor Coleridge. Dante Gabriel Rossetti. CW-RossD *Fr.* Five English Poets.

His Spine Curved Just Enough. Thomas Lux. SP-LuxT

His spots are the joy of the Leopard: his horns are the Buffalo's pride. Rudyard Kipling. CP-KiplR *Fr.* Jungle Book, The.

His stalk the dark delphinium. Edna St. Vincent Millay. CP-MillE

His Students. William Meredith. SP-MereW

His sweet moist eye missed nothing—the vague guerilla. Alexander. Robert Lowell. SP-LoweR

His tears fell from his veins. Writer, The. Muriel Rukeyser. CP-RukeM

His Tears to Thamesis [or Thamasis]. Robert Herrick. CP-HerrR

His theme / over and over. Williams: An Essay. Denise Levertov. SP-LeveDL; SP-LeveDS

His themes? Ah yes he had themes. Donald Davie. CP-DaviDC

His tongue was framed to music. Motto to "Power." Ralph Waldo Emerson. CP-EmerR

His topic, the Character of Dimaratos. Dimaratos. Constantine P. Cavafy. CP-CavaC, *tr. by* Theoharis Constantine Theoharis

His two aspects are open and shut. Han-shan. CP-ColdM, *tr. by* Red Pine

His unlidded eyes a wish. Eclogue at Daybreak. Yusef Komunyakaa. CP-KomuY

His valor passed beyond the Andes. Sepulchral Inscription. Jorge Luis Borges. SP-BorgJ, *tr. by* Robert Fitzgerald

His vest of fifty pockets. Parrot Asylum, The. Yusef Komunyakaa. CP-KomuY

His Vigil. James Whitcomb Riley. CP-RileJ

His Visitor. Thomas Hardy. CP-HardT

His voice decrepit was with Joy. Emily Dickinson. CP-DickE

His Weaknesse in Woes. Robert Herrick. CP-HerrR

His Wedded Wife. Rudyard Kipling. *Fr.* Plain Tales from the Hills.

His Wife at Bellevue. Marilyn Hacker. SP-HackM *Fr.* Navigators, The.

His wife died, and he grew old. Happiness in Cornwall. Raymond Carver. CP-CarvR

His wife. Forty years he painted her. Bonnard's Nudes. Raymond Carver. CP-CarvR

His wife worked and bought his. Big John of Echo Park. Charles Bukowski. SP-BukC3

His Winding-Sheet. Robert Herrick. CP-HerrR

His Wish. Robert Herrick. CP-HerrR

His Wish to God. Robert Herrick. CP-HerrR

His Wish to Privacie. Robert Herrick. CP-HerrR

His Words to Christ, Going to the Cross. Robert Herrick. CP-HerrR

His words were magic and his heart was true. Uncle Ananias. Edwin Arlington Robinson. CP-RobiE

Hispaniola. Amy Clampitt. CP-ClamA

Hist, but a word, fair and soft! Master Hugues of Saxe-Gotha. Robert Browning. CP-BroR1

Hist whist / little ghostthings. E. E. Cummings. CP-CummE

Historians may scorn the close engagement. Tomorrow's Envy of Today. Robert Graves. CP-GravR

Historic be the survey of our kind. Society. George Meredith. CP-MerG1

Historic Evening. Arthur Rimbaud. CP-RimbA, *tr. by* Martin Sorrell

Historic Pun. George Oppen. CP-OppGN

Historic weariness had spread over the afternoon, A. Therapy. Yannis Ritsos. SP-RitsY, *tr. by* Kimon Friar

Historical Choice. Robinson Jeffers. CP-JefR3

Historical Disquisitions. Philip Whalen. SP-WhalP

Historical Epitaphs. Allen Tate. CP-TateA

Historical Process. Hans Magnus Enzensberger. SP-EnzeH, *tr. by* Michael Hamburger

Historical Romance. Sam Hamill. SP-HamiS

History. Wendell Berry. CP-BerrW

History. Ralph Waldo Emerson.
"I am owner of the sphere." CP-EmerR
Mottoes to "History." CP-EmerR

History. Yehuda Amichai. SP-AmicY, *tr. by* Chana Bloch

History. Andrei Codrescu. SP-CodrA

History. Langston Hughes. CP-HughL; CP-HughL1; CP-HughL3

History. D. H. Lawrence. CP-LawrD

History. Robert Lowell. SP-LoweR

History. Thomas McGrath. SP-McGrT

History. Paul Muldoon. CP-MuldP

History. A. K. Ramanujan. CP-RamaA

History. Charles Simic. SP-SimiC; SP-SimiCE

History. Charles Tomlinson. CP-TomlC

History. Jones Very. CP-VeryJ

History. Robert Penn Warren. CP-WarrR

History. William Carlos Williams. CP-WilW1

History. C. K. Williams. SP-WillC

History as Poetry. Geoffrey Hill. CP-HillG

History bless me. Relevant Is Different Points on the Circle. Audre Lorde. SP-LordA

History Book. Charles Simic. SP-SimiC; SP-SimiCE

History Books. Thomas Lux. SP-LuxT

History Display. William Stafford. SP-StafWW

History during Nocturnal Snowfall. Robert Penn Warren. CP-WarrR

History falls like rain. For Shoshana Rihn—Pat Swinton. Marge Piercy. SP-PierM

History has to live with what was here. History. Robert Lowell. SP-LoweR

History has tongues / Has angels has guns. Exiles, The. Stephen Spender. CP-SpenS

History in a Minor Key. Kenneth Patchen. CP-PatcK

History is a dialogue between. Tower of Babel. Thomas Merton. CP-MertT

History Is a Throne and a Gate. Kenneth Patchen. CP-PatcK

History Lesson. Maxine W. Kumin. SP-KumiM

History Lessons. Yusef Komunyakaa. CP-KomuY

History melts my houses. Love and its Doors and Windows. Muriel Rukeyser. CP-RukeM

History, not wanted yet. Cowper's 'Yardley Oak': A Continuation. Donald Davie. CP-DaviDC

History of a Literary Movement. Howard Nemerov. CP-NemeH

History of a Malady. Charles Tomlinson. CP-TomlC

History of a Tough Motherfucker, The. Charles Bukowski. SP-BukC3

History of Alchemy. W. S. Merwin. SP-MerwW

History of an Hour, The. Thomas Hardy. CP-HardT

History of Hair from World War II to the Present. Howard Nemerov. CP-NemeH

History of Love, A. William Carlos Williams. CP-WilW2

History of melancholia, The. Melancholia. Charles Bukowski. SP-BukC1

History of My Heart. Robert Pinsky. CP-PinsR

History of my stupidity would fill many volumes, The. Account. Czeslaw Milosz. CP-MiloC; CP-MiloCN, *tr. by* Robert Pinsky

History of Science, The. W. H. Auden. CP-AudeW

History of Solitude, A. Adam Zagajewski. SP-ZagaA, *tr. by* Renata Gorczynski, Benjamin Ivry *and* C. K. Williams

History of strangers in their dreams, The. Desire Is a World by Night. John Berryman. CP-BerrJ

History of the cosmos, The. God Is Born. D. H. Lawrence. CP-LawrD

History of the Fall. Robert Graves. CP-GravR

History of the Growth of Heaven, The ("As a funny monk one is never sure where"). Andrei Codrescu. SP-CodrA

History of the Growth of Heaven, The (""*Tout ce qui existe est situé*" said max jacob and one day my situation"). Andrei Codrescu. SP-CodrA

History of the Moon, The. William Dickey. SP-DickW

History of the Night. Jorge Luis Borges. SP-BorgJ, *tr. by* Charles Tomlinson

History of the Twentieth Century (A Roadshow). Joseph Brodsky. CP-BrodJ

History of the World: a TV Docu-Drama. Lawrence Ferlinghetti. SP-FerlL

History of Truth, The. W. H. Auden. CP-AudeW

History of Vanbrug's House, The. Jonathan Swift. CP-SwifJ

History of Weather, A. Billy Collins. SP-CollB

History & prophecy are alike. Ralph Waldo Emerson. CP-EmerR

History repeats her lessons; oft in vain! On the Neglect of the Study of History. Jones Very. CP-VeryJ

History Teacher, The. Billy Collins. SP-CollB

History that thou hast never known, The. History. Jones Very. CP-VeryJ

History's can / can only be filled. November 6, 1984. Andrei Codrescu. SP-CodrA

History's long page. Prelude to Our Age. Langston Hughes. CP-HughL; CP-HughL3

"History's Wings Beating," They Used to Say. Yehuda Amichai. SP-AmicYL, *tr. by* Benjamin Harshav *and* Barbara Harshav

Histrion. Ezra Pound. CP-PoEar

Hit me! Jab me! Third Degree. Langston Hughes. CP-HughL; CP-HughL2; CP-HughL3

Hitch up honey for the / market race all. Folk Song, A: "Hitch up honey for the / market race all." Robert Creeley. CP-CreeR

Hitch Your Wagon to a Star. Allen Tate. CP-TateA

Hitchhiker, The. Ai. SP-Ai

Hitchhiker, The. James Laughlin. CP-LaugJ

Hitching into Frisco. Thom Gunn. CP-GunnT *Fr.* Three Songs.

Hither, Blanche! 'Tis you and I. Montaigne and His Kitten. Herman Melville. SP-MelvH

Hither, come hither, my little foot-page. Little Foot-Page, The. George Meredith. CP-MerG2

Hither, Hither, Love. John Keats. CP-KeatJ

Hitler had fingertips of apprehension. Attila, Hitler. Robert Lowell. SP-LoweR

Hitler, housepainter who painted Warsaw. Report, A. A. K. Ramanujan. CP-RamaA

Hitler Spring, The. Eugenio Montale. CP-MontE, *tr. by* Jonathan Galassi

Hitler's First Photograph. Wisława Szymborska. SP-SzymW, *tr. by* Stanislaw Barańczak *and* Clare Cavanagh

Hits and Runs. Carl Sandburg. CP-SandC

Hit's been drizzlin' an' been sprinklin'. Drizzle. Paul Laurence Dunbar. CP-DunbP

Hive at Gettysburg, The. John Greenleaf Whittier. CP-WhitJ

Hive-sized creams are on the chestnut tree. Fanny Howe. SP-HoweF *Fr.* O'Clock.

Hive, The. Hart Crane. CP-CranH

Hive the honey-bee has found, The. Bee Hive, The. Jones Very. CP-VeryJ

Hiway Poesy: L.A.–Albuquerque–Texas–Witchita. Allen Ginsberg. CP-GinsA

Ho—all to the borders! Vermonters, come down. Song of the Vermonters, 1779, The. John Greenleaf Whittier. CP-WhitJ

Ho! but the darkness was densely black! Out of the Dark and the Dearth. James

Whitcomb Riley. CP-RileJ

Ho! did ye hear of Mordameer. Romaunt of King Mordameer, The. James Whitcomb Riley. CP-RileJ

Ho, everyone that thirsteth. A. E. Housman. CP-HousA

Ho, Giant! This is I! Bean-Stalk, The. Edna St. Vincent Millay. CP-MillE

Ho! green fields and running brooks! Green Fields and Running Brooks. James Whitcomb Riley. CP-RileJ

Ho! ho! thou jolly god, with kinkèd lips. To the Wine-God Merlus. James Whitcomb Riley. CP-RileJ

Ho! ho! Ye Scholar recketh not how lean. Ye Scholar. James Whitcomb Riley. CP-RileJ

Ho-Hum Again. Hayden Carruth. CP-CarHS

Ho! I'm going back where. Our Boyhood Haunts. James Whitcomb Riley. CP-RileJ

Ho! in the dawn. Side by Side. Adrienne Rich. CP-RicAE

Ho! it's come, kids, come! Billy and His Drum. James Whitcomb Riley. CP-RileJ

Ho, Moeris! whither [or whether] on thy way so fast? Eclogue 9: Lycidas and Moeris. Virgil. CP-DryJ2, tr. by John Dryden Fr. Eclogues.

Ho! my little maiden. Twintorette, A. James Whitcomb Riley. CP-RileJ

Ho! the old Snow-Man. Uncle Mart's Poem. James Whitcomb Riley. CP-RileJ Fr. Child-World, A.

Ho! thou who seekest late and long. Sentence of John L. Brown, The. John Greenleaf Whittier. CP-WhitJ

Ho, Varlet! My Two Cents' Worth of Penny Postcard! Ogden Nash. CP-NashO

Ho! we are loose. Hear how they shout. From a Balloon. James Whitcomb Riley. CP-RileJ

Ho! workers of the old time styled. Shoemakers, The. John Greenleaf Whittier. CP-WhitJ

Hoar-frost crumbles in the sun, The. Endless Anxiety. D. H. Lawrence. CP-LawrD

Hoarded Joy. Dante Gabriel Rossetti. CW-RossD Fr. House of Life, The.

Hoarder, The. Anne Sexton. CP-SextA

Hobby Lobby, The. Jane Cooper. CP-CoopJ

Hobo Bird. Peter Blue Cloud. SP-BlueP

Hobo Voluntary, A. James Whitcomb Riley. CP-RileJ

Hobsons Epitaph. John Milton. CP-MiltJ

Hock-Cart, or Harvest Home, The. Robert Herrick. CP-HerrR

Hockey Poem, The. Robert Bly. SP-BlyR

Hoe scrapes earth as fine in grain as sand, The. Ivor Gurney. SP-GurnI

Hoeing. John Updike. CP-UpdiJ

Hoeing the bean field here are the dragonfly's wings. Dragonfly, The. W. S. Merwin. SP-MerwW

Hofer. William Wordsworth. CP-WorW1

Hog. Charles Bukowski. SP-BukC3

Hog. Anne Sexton. CP-SextA

Hog has a place i'th'Kitchen, and his share. Upon Hog. Robert Herrick. CP-HerrR

Hog Heaven. C. K. Williams. CP-WillC; SP-WillC

Hogh Conspiratorial Persons. Carl Sandburg. CP-SandC

Hogpen, deciduous growth, etc. Rites, The. Robert Creeley. CP-CreeR

Hohensalzburg: Fantastic Variations on a Theme of Romantic Character. Randall Jarrell. CP-JarrR

Hoist up and I could lean over, A. Bull Moses, The. Ted Hughes. SP-HughTN

Hojoki. Kenneth Rexroth. CP-RexrK

Hokku. E. E. Cummings. CP-CummE

Hokum. Hugh MacDiarmid. SP-MacDH

Hokusai on the Trent. Charles Tomlinson. CP-TomlC

Hokusai's portrait of himself. His Own Face Hidden. Carl Sandburg. CP-SandC

Holbein's More, my patron saint as a convert. Sir Thomas More. Robert Lowell. SP-LoweR

Holcomb, Kansas. William Stafford. SP-StafWW

Hold a glass of pure water to the eye of the sun! Glass of Pure Water, The. Hugh MacDiarmid. SP-MacDH

Hold, are you mad? you damned [or damn'd] confounded dog. Epilogue to Tyrannic[k] Love. John Dryden. SP-DrydJ Fr. Tyrannic Love.

Hold Back! D. H. Lawrence. CP-LawrD

Hold down the skylines now with your themes. Carl Sandburg. CP-SandC Fr. People, Yes, The.

Hold fast to dreams. Dreams. Langston Hughes. CP-HughL; CP-HughL1

Hold Hard, These Ancient Minutes in the Cuckoo's Month. Dylan Thomas. CP-ThomD

Hold it in a high wind. The fender curving over the. Supplication to the Muses on a Trying Day. Hart Crane. CP-CranH

Hold it up sternly—see this it sends back, (who is it? is it you?). Hand-Mirror, A. Walt Whitman. CP-WhitW

Hold Me. Philip Levine. SP-LeviP

Hold my hand, Auntie, Auntie. British Workman and the Government, The. D.

H. Lawrence. CP-LawrD

Hold of the Maker, not the made. Ralph Waldo Emerson. CP-EmerR

'Hold on,' she said, 'I'll just run out and get him.' Call, A. Seamus Heaney. SP-HeanSO

Hold thy tongue, death! Kenneth Patchen. CP-PatcK

Hold-up. Louis MacNeice. CP-MacNL

Holdfast, The. George Herbert. CP-HerbG

Holding / for one / instant this / moment—. Two. Robert Creeley. CP-CreeR

Holding On. A. R. Ammons. CP-AmmoA

Holding On. Philip Levine. SP-LeviP

Holding onto myself by the hand. Other, The. James Dickey. CP-DickJ

Holding Out. Jane Cooper. CP-CoopJ

Holding Out. Adrienne Rich. CP-RicAE; SP-RicA2

Holding the Mirror Up to Nature. Howard Nemerov. CP-NemeH

Holds that cat dander. Folk Wisdom. James Laughlin. CP-LaugJ

Hole, The. Robert Creeley. CP-CreeR

Hole, The. Donald Hall. CP-HallD

Hole Filler. Heather McHugh. SP-McHuH

Hole in the Floor, A. Richard Wilbur. CP-WilbR

Holes. James Laughlin. CP-LaugJ

Holiday. Denise Levertov. SP-LeveDL

Holiday. Alan Dugan. CP-DugaA

Holiday. Adrienne Rich. CP-RicAE

Holiday, The. Hans Magnus Enzensberger. SP-EnzeH, tr. by Hans Magnus Enzensberger and Michael Hamburger

Holiday: / every / yard or, A. C. K. Williams. CP-WillC

Holiday in Reality. Wallace Stevens. CP-StevW; CP-StevWP

Holiday Inn: Surrounded by Someone Else's Reunion He Comes to Terms. Miller Williams. CP-WillM

Holiday mourners, we are name-engravers on stones. In the Old City. Yehuda Amichai. SP-AmicYL, tr. by Benjamin Harshav and Barbara Harshav

Holidays. Ralph Waldo Emerson. CP-EmerR

Holidays. George Meredith. CP-MerG2

Holidays / travel on wheels. Merry-go-round. Federico García Lorca. CP-GarcF, tr. by Alan S. Trueblood Fr. Theories.

Holie man, Job, ground of patience, The. Testament of Squyer Meldrum, The. Sir David Lyndsay. SP-LyndD

Holiness[e] on the head. Aaron. George Herbert. CP-HerbG

Holland, that scarce deserves the name of land. Character of Holland, The. Andrew Marvell. CP-MarvA

Hollow, A. W. S. Merwin. SP-MerwW

Hollow Hill, The. Kathleen Jessie Raine. SP-RainK

Hollow homestead of life. In the venthole. Paul Celan. SP-CelaP, tr. by John Felstiner

Hollow Men, The. T. S. Eliot. CP-ElioT

Hollow rang the house when I knocked at the door. Turned Down. D. H. Lawrence. CP-LawrD

Hollow-Sounding and Mysterious. Christina Georgina Rossetti. CP-RosC2

Hollow Tree, A. Robert Bly. SP-BlyR

Hollow Walnut, The. Gabriela Mistral. SP-MistG, tr. by Maria Giachetti [or Jacketti]

Hollows round His eager Eyes, The. Emily Dickinson. CP-DickE

Holly. Seamus Heaney. SP-HeanSO Fr. Sweeney Redivivus.

Holly. A. R. Ammons. CP-AmmoA

Hollybush flowers, The. Holly. A. R. Ammons. CP-AmmoA

Holy Baptism (1). George Herbert. CP-HerbG

Holy Baptism (2). George Herbert. CP-HerbG

Holy Child's Song, The. Thomas Merton. CP-MertT

Holy City, New Jerusalem, The. Christina Georgina Rossetti. CP-RosC2

H[oly] Communion, The. George Herbert. CP-HerbG

Holy Communion, The. George Herbert. CP-HerbG

Holy Communion: the City. Thomas Merton. CP-MertT

Holy-Cross Day. Robert Browning. CP-BroR1

Holy Fair, The. Robert Burns. CP-BurnR

Holy Family. Muriel Rukeyser. CP-RukeM

Holy Ghost. Rainer Maria Rilke. CP-RilkFr, tr. by A. Poulin, Jr.

Holy Ghost Asketh for Us with Mourning and Weeping Unspeakable, The. Charles Wright. SP-WrigCN

Holy Ghost on the Nod over the Body of Bliss. Allen Ginsberg. CP-GinsA

Holy Grail, The. Andrei Codrescu. SP-CodrA

Holy haloes / Ring me round. Lord, in My Heart. Maya Angelou. SP-AngeM

Holy! Holy! Holy! Holy! Holy! Holy! Holy! Holy! Holy! Holy! Holy! Holy! Holy! Holy! Footnote to Howl. Allen Ginsberg. CP-GinsA; SP-GinsA

Holy Innocent gone home, A. Michael F. M. Rossetti. Christina Georgina Rossetti. CP-RosC3

Holy Innocents. Christina Georgina Rossetti. CP-RosC3

Holy Innocents. Christina Georgina Rossetti. CP-RosC2

Holy Innocents, The. Robert Lowell. SP-LoweR

Holy Isles, The. Kathleen Jessie Raine. SP-RainK

Holy Land, The. Jones Very. CP-VeryJ

Holy Land, The. John Greenleaf Whittier. CP-WhitJ

Holy of Holies, The. G. K. Chesterton. CP-ChesG

Holy of Holies, The. Jones Very. CP-VeryJ

Holy one called, The. Fanny Howe. SP-HoweF *Fr.* Quietist, The.

Holy Rivers, The. James Laughlin. CP-LaugJ

Holy-Rood come forth and shield. Old Wives Prayer, The. Robert Herrick. CP-HerrR

Holy Sacrament of the Altar, The. Thomas Merton. CP-MertT

Holy Saturday in Paris. Adam Zagajewski. SP-ZagaA, *tr. by* Clare Cavanagh

Holy Saturday night. Easter. Charles Olson. CP-OlsoC

Holy Satyr. "H. D." CP-DoolH

Holy Scriptures (1), The. George Herbert. CP-HerbG

Holy Scriptures (2), The. George Herbert. CP-HerbG

Holy Sonnets. John Donne. CP-DonnJ; MW-DonnJ

Holy Sonnets. Helen Pinkerton. CP-PinkH

Holy Spring. Dylan Thomas. CP-ThomD

Holy the untouched mothers. Offertory. Olga Broumas. SP-BrouO

Holy Thursday. Geoffrey Hill. CP-HillG

Holy Thursday. Paul Muldoon. CP-MuldP

Holy Thursday. Charles Wright. SP-WrigC

Holy Thursday [2]. William Blake. CP-BlakW *Fr.* Songs of Experience.

Holy Tulzie, The. Robert Burns. CP-BurnR

Holy War, The. Rudyard Kipling. CP-KiplR

Holy Water come and bring. Spell, The. Robert Herrick. CP-HerrR

Holy waters hither bring. To Julia. Robert Herrick. CP-HerrR

Holy Week. Once more the full moon. Hapax. Kenneth Rexroth. CP-RexrK

Holy Willie's Prayer. Robert Burns. CP-BurnR

Holy Writ. Robert Penn Warren. CP-WarrR

Holyhead. September 25, 1727. Jonathan Swift. CP-SwifJ

Homage. William Carlos Williams. CP-WilW1

Homage. Louis Zukofsky. CP-ZukLS

Homage: "Even a Dawn too numb." Stéphane Mallarmé. CP-MallS, *tr. by* Henry Weinfield

Homage: "Silence already funereal spreads a pall, The." Stéphane Mallarmé. CP-MallS, *tr. by* Henry Weinfield

Homage to a Government. Philip Larkin. CP-LarkP

Homage to a Rake-Hell. William Meredith. SP-MereW

Homage to Binsey Poplars. Maxine W. Kumin. SP-KumiM

Homage to Bly & Lorca. In London. Robert Creeley. CP-CreeR

Homage to Cesare Pavese. Charles Wright. SP-WrigC

Homage to Chekhov. Joseph Brodsky. CP-BrodJ, *tr. by* Jonathan Aaron

Homage to Christina Rossetti. John Logan. CP-LogaJ

Homage to Christina Rossetti. Marya Alexandrovna Zaturenska. SP-ZatuM

Homage to Claude Lorrain. Charles Wright. SP-WrigC

Homage to Clichés. Louis MacNeice. CP-MacNL

Homage to Clio. W. H. Auden. CP-AudeW

Homage to Diana. Sir Walter Ralegh. CP-RaleW

Homage to Edward Thomas. Derek Walcott. CP-WalcD

Homage to Emerson, On Night Flight to New York. Robert Penn Warren. CP-WarrR

Homage to George Whitefield. Donald Davie. CP-DaviDC

Homage to Girolamo Marcello. Joseph Brodsky. CP-BrodJ

Homage to Gödel. Hans Magnus Enzensberger. SP-EnzeH

Homage to Hart Crane. Philip Whalen. SP-WhalP

Homage to Herman Melville. John Logan. CP-LogaJ

Homage to John Cowper Powys. Stevie Smith. CP-SmitS

Homage to John L. Stephens. Donald Davie. CP-DaviDC

Homage to John Lyly and Frankie Newton. Hayden Carruth. CP-CarHS

Homage to John Muir. John Logan. CP-LogaJ

Homage to John the Baptist. John Logan. CP-LogaJ

Homage to Literature. Muriel Rukeyser. CP-RukeM

Homage to Lucretius. Philip Whalen. SP-WhalP

Homage to Malcolm Lowry. Derek Mahon. CP-MahoD

Homage to Mistress Bradstreet. John Berryman. CP-BerrJ

Homage to Paul Cézanne. Charles Wright. SP-WrigC

Homage to Paul Mellon, I. M. Pei, Their Gallery, and Washington City. William Meredith. SP-MereW

Homage to Paul Robeson. Robert Earl Hayden. CP-HaydR

Homage to Philip K. Dick. Norman Dubie. CP-DubiN

Homage to Rainer Maria Rilke. John Logan. CP-LogaJ

Homage to Rodin. Philip Whalen. SP-WhalP

Homage to St. Patrick, García Lorca, & the Itinerant Grocer. Philip Whalen. SP-WhalP

Homage to Sextus Propertius. Ezra Pound. SP-PounE

Homage to the Empress of the Blues. Robert Earl Hayden. CP-HaydR

Homage to the North. Richard Eberhart. CP-EberR

Homage to Theodore Dreiser. Robert Penn Warren. CP-WarrR

Homage to Trakl. Sam Hamill. SP-HamiS

Homage to Wilfrid Scawen Blunt. Ezra Pound. CP-PoEar

Homage to William Cowper. Donald Davie. CP-DaviDC

Homage to William Seward Burroughs. Philip Whalen. SP-WhalP

Homage to Wren. Louis MacNeice. CP-MacNL

Homage to Yalta. Joseph Brodsky. CP-BrodJ, *tr. by* Barry Rubin

Homage Vajracarya. Allen Ginsberg. SP-GinsA

Home. Robert Creeley. CP-CreeR

Home. George Herbert. CP-HerbG

Home. Robinson Jeffers. CP-JefR1

Home, The ("Love builds for us a bower"). Jones Very. CP-VeryJ

Home, The ("See! from yon low-roofed cottage shines a light"). Jones Very. CP-VeryJ

Home, The ("Supper o'er, with books, or converse sweet, The"). Jones Very. CP-VeryJ

Home After Three Months Away. Robert Lowell. SP-LoweR

Home Again. James Whitcomb Riley. CP-RileJ

Home Again. Wallace Stevens. CP-StevWP

Home Again. Wallace Stevens. CP-StevWP

Home Ag'in. James Whitcomb Riley. CP-RileJ

Home agin, an' home to stay. Bein' Back Home. Paul Laurence Dunbar. CP-DunbP

Home and Heaven. Jones Very. CP-VeryJ

Home, and I've. Marilyn Hacker. SP-HackM

Home at Grasmere. William Wordsworth. CP-WorW1 *Fr.* Recluse, The.

Home at Grasmere. William Wordsworth. MW-WorW

Home at Night. James Whitcomb Riley. CP-RileJ

Home Ballad, The. John Berryman. CP-BerrJ

Home Burial. Robert Frost. CP-FrosR

Home by different ways. Yet all. End Is Not Yet, The. Christina Georgina Rossetti. CP-RosC2

Home-Coming, The. Robert Graves. CP-GravR

Home-Coming of the Bride, The. John Greenleaf Whittier. CP-WhitJ

Home Federal. Rae Armantrout. SP-ArmaA

Home Fires. Carl Sandburg. CP-SandC

Home-Folks!—Well, that-air name, to me. James Whitcomb Riley. CP-RileJ

Home for a visit, you brought me. Bangkok Gang, The. Maxine W. Kumin. SP-KumiM

Home for Thanksgiving. W. S. Merwin. SP-MerwW

Home for the aged opens its windows in May, The. Next Door. Richard Wilbur. CP-WilbR

Home for the Holidays. Howard Nemerov. CP-NemeH

Home for the night on my ten years' workbed. Sleepless. Robert Lowell. SP-LoweR

Home from Guatemala, back at the Waldorf. Arrival at the Waldorf. Wallace Stevens. CP-StevW; CP-StevWP

Home Home Home. Lawrence Ferlinghetti. SP-FerlL

Home, home, / Wild birds home! Spell to Bring Lost Creatures Home. Kathleen Jessie Raine. SP-RainK

Home in Dark Grass, A. Robert Bly. SP-BlyR

Home is my Bethlehem. January 19th. Anne Sexton. CP-SextA

Home is so far from Home. Emily Dickinson. *See* Home itself is far from home

Home Is So Sad. Philip Larkin. CP-LarkP

Home is the riddle of the wise. Emily Dickinson. SP-DickE

Home is the sailor, home from sea. R. L. S. A. E. Housman. CP-HousA

Home itself is far from home. Emily Dickinson. SP-DickE

Home late, one lamp turned low. At Our House. William Stafford. SP-StafW; SP-StafWW

Home Longings. Paul Laurence Dunbar. CP-DunbP

Home-Made Fairy Tale, A. James Whitcomb Riley. CP-RileJ

Home-made Riddles. James Whitcomb Riley. CP-RileJ

Home means that / when the certainly. E. E. Cummings. CP-CummE

Home Movies. Olga Broumas. SP-BrouO

Home Movies. John Updike. CP-UpdiJ

Home of my youth! Where first my lot was cast. Jones Very. CP-VeryJ

Home Olga. Samuel Beckett. CP-BeckS

Home on Rue du Bourg-Tibourg. Clarence Major. SP-MajoC

Home-Sick. Samuel Taylor Coleridge. CP-ColeS

Home State. William Stafford. SP-StafWW

Home Thoughts. Carl Sandburg. CP-SandC

Home-Thoughts, from Abroad. Robert Browning. CP-BroR1; SP-BroR

Home-Thoughts, from the Sea. Robert Browning. CP-BroR1

Home-Voyage, The. James Whitcomb Riley. CP-RileJ

Homebody, The. Dorothy Parker. CP-ParkD

Homecoming. Hayden Carruth. CP-CarHS

Homecoming. Paul Celan. CP-PinsR, *tr. by* Robert Pinsky

Homecoming. Christian J. Van Geel. CP-RicAE

Homecoming. Langston Hughes. CP-HughL; CP-HughL2

Homecoming. Derek Mahon. CP-MahoD

Homecoming. William Stafford. SP-StafWW

Homecoming. Jay Wright. SP-WrigJ

Homecoming, A. Wendell Berry. CP-BerrW

Homecoming, The. Thomas Hardy. CP-HardT

Homecoming: Anse La Raye. Derek Walcott. CP-WalcD

Homecoming—Massachusetts. John Ciardi. CP-CiarJ

Homecoming Singer, The. Jay Wright. SP-WrigJ

Homecomings. Pablo Neruda. SP-NeruP

Homefires. William Corbett. SP-CorbW

Homeland. Amy Clampitt. CP-ClamA

Homeland. W. S. Merwin SP-MerwW

Homeland ("Trees laid out"). Federico García Lorca. CP-GarcF, *tr. by* Jerome Rothenberg *Fr.* Water Suite.

Homeland ("Water jets in dreams"). Federico García Lorca. CP-GarcF, *tr. by* Jerome Rothenberg *Fr.* Water Jets.

Homeless. Samuel Taylor Coleridge. CP-ColeS

Homeless, The. Charles Simic. SP-SimiCE

Homeless people I know, The. Han-shan. CP ColdM, *tr. by* Red Pine

Homeless Wind, The. Jones Very. CP-VeryJ

Homely little woman with big hands, A. One Angel. James Whitcomb Riley. CP-RileJ

Homely War, The. Marge Piercy. SP-PierM

Homeowners unite. Firebombing, The. James Dickey. CP-DickJ

Homer, A.D. 1982. Amy Clampitt. CP-ClamA

Homer da Vinci. Part, The. Denise Levertov. SP-LeveDP

Homer in Basic. Kenneth Rexroth. CP-RexrK

Homer was a ventriloquist. Uncle. James Tate. SP-TateJ

Homeric Hexameter, The. Samuel Taylor Coleridge. CP-ColeS

Homeric Hymns. *Unknown.*

  Homer's Hymn to the Sun. CP-ShelP, *tr. by* Percy Bysshe Shelley

  Homer's Hymn to Venus. CP-ShelP, *tr. by* Percy Bysshe Shelley

  Hymn to Athena.

    (Homer's Hymn to Minerva.) CP-ShelP

  Hymn to Castor and Pollux.

    (Homer's Hymn to Castor and Pollux.) CP-ShelP

  Hymn to Earth the Mother of All.

    (Homer's Hymn to the Earth: Mother of All.) CP-ShelP

  Hymn to Mercury [*or* Hermes]. CP-ShelP, *tr. by* Percy Bysshe Shelley

  Hymn to Selene.

    (Homer's Hymn to the Moon.) CP-ShelP

Homer's Hymn to Castor and Pollux. *Unknown. See* Homeric Hymns

Homer's Hymn to Minerva. *Unknown. See* Homeric Hymns

Homer's Hymn to the Earth: Mother of All. *Unknown. See* Homeric Hymns

Homer's Hymn to the Moon. *Unknown. See* Homeric Hymns

Homer's Hymn to the Sun. *Unknown.* CP-ShelP, *tr. by* Percy Bysshe Shelley *Fr.* Homeric Hymns.

Homer's Hymn to Venus. *Unknown.* CP-ShelP, *tr. by* Percy Bysshe Shelley *Fr.* Homeric Hymns.

Homesick. Walter De la Mare. CP-DeLaW

Homesick. Marge Piercy. SP-PierM

Homesick Blues. Langston Hughes. CP-HughL; CP-HughL1

Homestead, The. John Greenleaf Whittier. CP-WhitJ

Homestead Called Damascus, The. Kenneth Rexroth. CP-RexrK

Hometown after a War. John Ciardi. CP-CiarJ

Hometown Piece for Messrs. Alston and Reese. Marianne Craig Moore. CP-MoorM

Homework. Mona Van Duyn. SP-VanDM

Homework. Allen Ginsberg. CP-GinsA; SP-GinsA

Homewreck. Karl Shapiro. SP-ShapK

Homily. Dan Pagis. SP-PagiD, *tr. by* Stephen Mitchell

Homily. Allen Tate. CP-TateA

Homing swallow vainly seeks her loft. Dead of Lidice, The. Jaroslav Seifert. SP-SeifJ, *tr. by* Ewald Osers

Hominy and Rain. Raymond Carver. CP-CarvR

Homo Ludens: On an Argument with an Actor. Alan Dugan. CP-DugaA

Homo Sum, Nihil Humani—. Arthur Hugh Clough. SP-ClouA

Homunculus. Louise Bogan. CP-BogaL

Homunculus et La Belle Etoile. Wallace Stevens. CP-StevW; CP-StevWP

Honest Confrontation. Yannis Ritsos. SP-RitsY, *tr. by* Kimon Friar

Honest Description of Myself with a Glass of Whiskey at an Airport, Let Us Say, in Minneapolis, An. Czeslaw Milosz. CP-MiloCN, *tr. by* Robert Hass

Honest lover whosoever. Song: "Honest lover whosoever." Sir John Suckling. CP-SuckJ

Honest man here lies at rest, An. Epitaph on My Own Friend, and My Father's Friend, Wm Muir in Tarbolton Miln. Robert Burns. CP-BurnR

Honest morning blesses the Sun's beauty. Blessed Sun. Robert Graves. CP-GravR

Honest Tear, An. Emily Dickinson. CP-DickE

Honesty. Yannis Ritsos. SP-RitsY, *tr. by* Kimon Friar

Honesty. Sir Thomas Wyatt. CP-WyatT

Honesty. Louis Zukofsky. CP-ZukLS

Honesty can't be encouraged in individuals. It must. Andrei Codrescu. SP-CodrA

Honey and Salt. Carl Sandburg. CP-SandC

Honey babe, / You braid your hair too tight. Langston Hughes. CP-HughL; CP-HughL2

Honcy Bee, The. Ted Hughes. SP-HughTN

Honey, darling, baby . . . but no endearments. Sonnet: "Honey, darling, baby . . . but no endearments." Hayden Carruth. CP-CarHS *Fr.* Sonnets.

Honey Dripper. Clarence Major. SP-MajoC

Honey Dripping from the Comb. James Whitcomb Riley. CP-RileJ

Honey-flowers to the honey-comb. Chimes. Dante Gabriel Rossetti. CW-RossD

Honey from silkworms who can gather. Lines to a Critic. Percy Bysshe Shelley. CP ShelP

Honey I'd split your kindling. Green Mountain Idyl. Hayden Carruth. CP-CarHS

Honey of man is, The. Second Didactic Poem. Denise Levertov. SP-LeveDP; SP-LeveDS

Honey you went so far to seek, The. Emily Dickinson. SP-DickE

Honeybee struggles in gardensnipder web. Duerden's Garage, Stinson Beach. Philip Whalen. SP-WhalP

Honeymoon. D. H. Lawrence. *See* Excursion Train

Honeymoon. Jaroslav Seifert. SP-SeifJ, *tr. by* Ewald Osers

Honeymoon Time at an Inn. Thomas Hardy. CP-HardT

Honeysuckle. William Stafford. SP-StafWW

Honeysuckle. Louis Zukofsky. CP-ZukLS

Honeysuckle, The. Dante Gabriel Rossetti. CW-RossD

Honeysuckle hanging her fangs. Night Arrival of Sea-Trout. Ted Hughes. SP-HughTN

Hong Kong—Last Words. Robert Creeley. SP-CreeR

Hong Kong Window. Robert Creeley. SP-CreeR

Honky Tonk in Cleveland, Ohio. Carl Sandburg. CP-SandC

Honolulu and Back. John Logan. CP-LogaJ

Honor a going thing, goldfinch, corporation, tree. Mechanism. A. R. Ammons. CP-AmmoA

Honor Among Scamps. Nicholas Vachel Lindsay. CP-LindV

Honor bright o muse. Ralph Waldo Emerson. CP-EmerR

Honor is saved by the national will. Peace in Our Time. Howard Nemerov. CP-NemeH

Honor / of being human, The. For the Graduation. Robert Creeley. CP-CreeR

Honor the maggot. Catalyst. A. R. Ammons. CP-AmmoA

Honor to those who in their life. Thermopylae. Constantine P. Cavafy. CP-CavaC, *tr. by* Theoharis Constantine Theoharis

Honorable citizen's son—chiefly, a good-looking, An. Theater of Sidon (400 A.D.). Constantine P. Cavafy. CP-CavaC, *tr. by* Theoharis Constantine Theoharis

Honour and magnify this man of men. Alfred the Great. Stevie Smith. CP-SmitS

Honour corruption villainy holiness. E. E. Cummings. CP-CummE

Honour is so sublime perfection. To the Countess of Bedford ("Honour is so sublime perfection"). John Donne. CP-DonnJ; MW-DonnJ

Honour thy parents; but good manners call. God to Be First Served. Robert Herrick. CP-HerrR

Honour to you who sit! Hymne to the Muses, An. Robert Herrick. CP-HerrR

Honours Are Hindrances. Robert Herrick. CP-HerrR

Hony-Combe, The. Robert Herrick. CP-HerrR

Hood. C. K. Williams. CP-WillC; SP-WillC

Hooded Flame. Robert Graves. CP-GravR

Hooded Night. Robinson Jeffers. CP-JefR2

Hoodlums. Carl Sandburg. CP-SandC

Hoodoo, The. James Whitcomb Riley. CP-RileJ

Hoof Dusk. Carl Sandburg. CP-SandC

Hoof-marks on the dead wildcat, The. Cruelty. Ai. SP-Ai

Hook, The. Theodore Weiss. SP-WeisT

Hook-nosed was I, loose-lipped; greed fixed its gaze. Isaac Meek. Walter De la Mare. CP-DeLaW

Hook of adrenaline shoves, The. Anger against Beasts. Wendell Berry. CP-BerrW

Hooks. C. K. Williams. SP-WillC

Hooks of a Corset, The. Czeslaw Milosz. CP-MiloC; CP-MiloCN, *tr.* by Robert Hass

Hooper was ninety. One September dawn. Squire Hooper. Thomas Hardy. CP-HardT

Hoopoe, happy bird maligned. Eugenio Montale. CP-MontE, *tr. by* Jonathan Galassi

Hoopoe Tells Us How, The. Robert Graves. CP-GravR

Hoosier Calendar, A. James Whitcomb Riley. CP-RileJ

Hoosier Folk-Child—all unsung, The. James Whitcomb Riley. CP-RileJ

Hoosier in Exile—a toast, The. James Whitcomb Riley. CP-RileJ

Hoosier Spring-Poetry. James Whitcomb Riley. CP-RileJ

Hoot!—daur ye shaw ye're face again. Drunkard to His Bottle, The. John Greenleaf Whittier. CP-WhitJ

Hoot Owls. Richard Eberhart. CP-EberR

Hoover, Edgar J. Ai. SP-Ai

Hoover Trismegistus. Ai. SP-Ai

Hooves, The. Josephine Jacobsen. CP-JacoJ

Hop hop, thump thump. Dedicated Dancing Bull and the Water Maid, The. Stevie Smith. CP-SmitS

Hop o' My Thumb. John Ashbery. SP-AshbJ

Hop-o'-my-thumb and little Jack Horner. Christina Georgina Rossetti. CP-RosC2

Hop press. Lorine Niedecker. CP-NiedL

Hop Scotch. Andrei Codrescu. SP-CodrA

Hop, Skip, and Jump. Gary Snyder. CP-SnydG

Hop-Toad, The. Richard Eberhart. CP-EberR

Hop-toad jumped away, missing the blade, The. Hop-Toad, The. Richard Eberhart. CP-EberR

Hope. William Cowper. CP-CowpW

Hope. Emily Jane Brontë. CP-BronE

Hope. Raymond Carver. CP-CarvR

Hope. Paul Laurence Dunbar. CP-DunbP

Hope. George Herbert. CP-HerbG

Hope ("He rose up on his dying bed"). Langston Hughes. CP-HughL; CP-HughL3

Hope ("Sometimes when I'm lonely"). Langston Hughes. CP-HughL; CP-HughL2

Hope. Randall Jarrell. CP-JarrR

Hope. Howard Nemerov. CP-NemeH

Hope. Jones Very. CP-VeryJ

Hope. Robert Penn Warren. CP-WarrR

Hope, The. David Ignatow. SP-IgnaD

Hope against Pollution, A. Alan Dugan. CP-DugaA

Hope and Joy. Christina Georgina Rossetti. CP-RosC2

Hope and Time. Samuel Taylor Coleridge. CP-ColeS

Hope and Tranquillity. Samuel Taylor Coleridge. CP-ColeS

Hope, bending o'er me one time, snowed the flakes. James Whitcomb Riley. CP-RileJ

Hope Carol, A. Christina Georgina Rossetti. CP-RosC2

!Hope / faith! / !life / love! E. E. Cummings. CP-CummE

Hope for Harlem. Langston Hughes. CP-HughL; CP-HughL3

Hope Heartens. Robert Herrick. CP-HerrR

Hope holds to Christ. Gerard Manley Hopkins. CP-HopkG

Hope I dreamed of was a dream, The. Mirage. Christina Georgina Rossetti. CP-RosC1

Hope in Grief. Christina Georgina Rossetti. CP-RosC3

Hope is a knave befools us evermore. Nicolas-Sébastien Roch Chamfort. CP-BeckS

Hope is a strange invention. Emily Dickinson. CP-DickE

Hope is a subtle Glutton. Emily Dickinson. CP-DickE

Hope is like a harebell trembling from its birth. Comparisons. Christina Georgina Rossetti. CP-RosC2

Hope is Not for the Wise. Robinson Jeffers. CP-JefR2

Hope is the counterpoise of fear / While night enthralls us here. Christina Georgina Rossetti. CP-RosC2

"Hope" is the thing with feathers. Emily Dickinson. CP-DickE

Hope it was that tutored me. Post-Graduate. Dorothy Parker. CP-ParkD

Hope, like the short-liv'd ray that gleams awhile. William Cowper. CP-CowpW

Hope new born one pleasant morn. Dead Hope. Christina Georgina Rossetti. CP-RosC1

Hope, not Love, twangles her single string. Poor Others. Robert Graves. CP-GravR

Hope of even seeing you again, The. Eugenio Montale. CP-MontE, *tr. by* Jonathan Galassi

Hope of the Year, The. G. K. Chesterton. CP-ChesG

Hope Overtaken. Dante Gabriel Rossetti. CW-RossD *Fr.* House of Life, The.

Hope rules a land for ever green. Wishing-Gate, The. William Wordsworth. CP-WorW2

Hope Springs. James Laughlin. CP-LaugJ

Hope that you may understand! Realists, The. William Butler Yeats. CP-YeatW

Hope was but a timid friend. Hope. Emily Jane Brontë. CP-BronE

Hope Well and Have Well: or, Faire after Foule Weather. Robert Herrick. CP-HerrR

Hope, whose weak[e] being ruined [*or* ruin'd] is. Against Hope. Abraham Cowley. CP-CrasR *Fr.* Mistress, The.

Hope, wreathed with roses. Euphrasy. Walter De la Mare. CP-DeLaW

Hopeful each morning I arise. Song Before Breakfast. Ogden Nash. CP-NashO

Hopeless and Felons. Thomas Merton. CP-MertT

Hopeless Case, A. Christina Georgina Rossetti. CP-RosC3

Hopelessly wound round with the cords of streets. Hamburg, 1929. Stephen Spender. CP-SpenS

Hope's Okay. A. R. Ammons. CP-AmmoA

Hopes, that swell in youthful breasts. Love's Rose. Percy Bysshe Shelley. CP-ShelP

Hopewell Haiku. Paul Muldoon. CP-MuldP

Hoping Against Hope. Christina Georgina Rossetti. CP-RosC3 (If.) CP-RosC3

Hoping my face shows the pleasure I felt, I'm. Tone. Rae Armantrout. SP-ArmaA

Hopping frog, hop here and be seen. Christina Georgina Rossetti. CP-RosC2

Horace, Book I, Ode XIV. Jonathan Swift. CP-SwifJ

Horace, Epistle VII, Book I: Imitated and Addressed to the Earl of Oxford. Jonathan Swift. CP-SwifJ

Horace in Athens. Constantine P. Cavafy. CP-CavaC, *tr. by* Theoharis Constantine Theoharis

Horace, Lib. 2, Sat. 6. Jonathan Swift. CP-SwifJ

Horace: Odi Profanum Volgus Et Arceo. Horace. *See* Odes

Horace of course is not. Wombwell on Strike. Donald Davie. CP-DaviDC

Horace, of the Art of Poetry. Horace. CP-JonsB

Horace: Persicos Odi, Puer, Apparatus. Horace. *See* Odes

Horace to Leuconoë. Edwin Arlington Robinson. CP-RobiE

Horae Canonicae. W. H. Auden. CP-AudeW

Horae Canonicae. Donald Davie. CP-DaviDC

Horatian Epode to the Duchess of Malfi. Allen Tate. CP-TateA

Horatian Notion, An. Thomas Lux. SP-LuxT

Horatian Ode upon Cromwell's Return from Ireland, An. Andrew Marvell. CP-MarvA

Horatians, The. W. H. Auden. CP-AudeW

Horatio took me to the cliff. Hamlet. Nicholas Vachel Lindsay. CP-LindV

Horizon. Federico García Lorca. CP-GarcF, *tr. by* Jerome Rothenberg *Fr.* Six Songs at Nightfall.

Horizon. Robert Graves. CP-GravR

Horizon of islands shifting. Outer Banks, The. Muriel Rukeyser. CP-RukeM

Horizon to horizon, lies outspread. Flower, The. Walter De la Mare. CP-DeLaW

Horizons ring me like faggots, The. Wuthering Heights. Sylvia Plath. CP-PlatS

Horn of Egremont Castle, The. William Wordsworth. CP-WorW1

Horn of Plenty. Langston Hughes. CP-HughL; CP-HughL3

Horne sells to others teeth; but has not one. Upon Horne. Robert Herrick. CP-HerrR

Horned owl / stops his meditations. Pool, The. Federico García Lorca. CP-GarcF, *tr. by* Jerome Rothenberg *Fr.* Mirror Suite.

Horned Purple. William Carlos Williams. CP-WilW1

Horned Rampion, The. Amy Clampitt. CP-ClamA

Hornet. Donald Davie. CP-DaviDC

Hornet. Anne Sexton. CP-SextA; SP-SextA

Hornet as if, The. Trouble Making Trouble. A. R. Ammons. CP-AmmoA

Hornet, thou hast thy wife dressed, for the stall. To Hornet. Ben Jonson. CP-JonsB; SP-JonsB

Hornets by the Sill. Richard Eberhart. CP-EberR

Horns crowding toward us. Dream 3: Night Bear Which Frightened Cattle. Margaret Atwood. SP-AtwM1

Horns of the Morning, The. Philip Larkin. CP-LarkP

Hornworm: Autumn Lamentation. Stanley Kunitz. CP-KunSC

Hornworm: Summer Reverie. Stanley Kunitz. CP-KunSC

Horny Dilemma. Kenneth Rexroth. CP-RexrK

Horologikos. Hayden Carruth. CP-CarHS

Horoscope. James Vincent Cunningham. CP-CunnJ

Horrible History of Jones, The. G. K. Chesterton. CP-ChesG

"Horrible Incredible Lies" : Keith Lampe Spontaneously. Philip Whalen. SP-WhalP

Horrible of hue, hideous to behold. Sir Thomas Wyatt. CP-WyatT

Horrible Religious Error, A. Ted Hughes. SP-HughTN

Horror came / When I was in my mother's womb, The. After an Old Song. Kenneth Patchen. CP-PatcK

Horrors of the personal, revealed, The. Rooms in Bloomsbury. Marilyn Hacker. SP-HackM

Hors crâne seul dedans. Samuel Beckett. CP-BeckS

Horse. Louise Glück. SP-GlucL

Horse. Anne Sexton. CP-SextA

Horse. May Swenson. SP-SwenM

Horse, The. Philip Levine. SP-LeviP

Horse, The. W. S. Merwin. SP-MerwWF

Horse, The. William Carlos Williams. CP-WilW2

Horse, The. William Wordsworth. CP-WorW1

Horse, The. James Wright. CP-WrigJ

Horse beneath me seemed, The. Ride, The. Richard Wilbur. CP-WilbR

Horse Chestnut Tree, The. Richard Eberhart. CP-EberR

Horse-Chestnut Trees and Roses. James Schuyler. CP-SchuJ

Horse could gallop over our bridge that minnows, A. Believer. William Stafford. SP-StafWW

Horse-drawn rocket, A. From the Hole. James Tate. SP-TateJ

Horse Face. Arthur Sze. SP-SzeA

Horse Fiddle. Carl Sandburg. CP-SandC

Horse gets into me, its mane. Hag. Heather McHugh. SP-McHuH

Horse-headed clouds, flags. Fog Galleon. Yusef Komunyakaa. CP-KomuY

Horse, hello. Lorine Niedecker. CP-NiedL

Horse in a Field. Walter De la Mare. CP-DeLaW
(To K. M.) CP-DeLaW

Horse in the Drugstore, The. Tess Gallagher. SP-GallT

Horse is shivering flies off its ribs, grazing, A. Oration: Half-Moon in Vermont. Norman Dubie. CP-DubiN

Horse is white, The. Or it. Saving the Appearances. Charles Tomlinson. CP-TomlC

Horse moves, The. Horse, The. William Carlos Williams. CP-WilW2

Horse of Desire, The. Robert Bly. SP-BlyR

Horse on Fire. Charles Bukowski. SP-BukC2

Horse, our poor creature, we treat as if elemental. Equestrian Sestina. Donald Davie. CP-DaviDC

Horse Power. Andrei Codrescu. SP-CodrA

Horse Show, The. William Carlos Williams. CP-WilW2

Horseback. Carolyn Kizer. CP-KizeC

Horseback on Sunday morning. Wild Geese, The. Wendell Berry. CP-BerrW

Horseman high-alone as an eagle on the spur of the mountain over. Coast-Road, The. Robinson Jeffers. CP-JefR2

Horsemeat. Charles Bukowski. SP-BukC3

Horsemen on the Sands, The. Jones Very. CP-VeryJ

Horses. Wendell Berry. CP-BerrW

Horses. W. S. Merwin. SP-MerwW

Horses. Paul Muldoon. CP-MuldP

Horses. Gregory Orr. SP-OrrG

Horses, The. Jorge Guillén. CP-WilbR

Horses, The. Ted Hughes. SP-HughTN

Horses Aboard. Thomas Hardy. CP-HardT

Horses and Men in the Rain. Carl Sandburg. CP-SandC

Horses and Prisoners. James Dickey. CP-DickJ

Horses, black-lidded mouths peeled back. Florentines. Geoffrey Hill. CP-HillG

Horses face out over the world, The. Shadows and Spring Flowers. Kenneth Patchen. CP-PatcK

Horses imagined by a boy, The. Wild Horses, The. Wyatt Prunty. SP-PrunW

Horses in horsecloths stand in a row. Horses Aboard. Thomas Hardy. CP-HardT

Horse's name was Remorse, The. Remorse. Carl Sandburg. CP-SandC

Horses of Achilles, The. Homer. CP-MerG1 Fr. Iliad, The.

Horses of Achilles, The. Constantine P. Cavafy. CP-CavaC, tr. by Theoharis Constantine Theoharis

Horses of the sea; remember, The. On a Horse Carved in Wood. Donald Hall. CP-HallD

Horses of the Sea, The. Christina Georgina Rossetti. CP-RosC2

Horses out of their brains bored all, The. Flying Noises. Thomas Lux. SP-LuxT

Horses running. Communion. Charles Bukowski. SP-BukC1

Horseshoe, The. James Tate. SP-TateJ

Horseshoe crabs, which are not crabs at all. Successful Species, A. John Ciardi. CP-CiarJ

Hortatory Address to the Greeks. Saint Justin Martyr.
"Then marking this my sacred speech, but truly lend." CP-RaleW

Hortus. Andrew Marvell. CP-MarvA

Hosanna! God be prais'd. Bible, O.T. See Praise ye the Lord. Sing unto the Lord a new song

Hosanna! praise the Lord, and bless. Bible, O.T. See Praise ye the Lord. Praise God in his sanctuary

Hospital. Walter De la Mare. CP-DeLaW

Hospital. Karl Shapiro. SP-ShapK

Hospital, and the father's room, where light. Daughter. James Dickey. CP-DickJ

Hospital barber, for instance, The. Whispers in the Next Room. Charles Simic. SP-SimiC

Hospital barber next door, The. Whispers. Charles Simic. SP-SimiCE

Hospital Barge at Cérisy. Wilfred Owen. CP-OwenW

Hospital Kitchen. Lorine Niedecker. CP-NiedL

Hospital racket, nurses' iron smiles. Hell Poem, The. John Berryman. CP-BerrJ

Hospital, The: it wasn't her idea. Darlene's Hospital. John Ashbery. SP-AshbJ

Hospital Visits. Philip Larkin. CP-LarkP

Hospital Window. Allen Ginsberg. CP-GinsA

Hospital Window, The. James Dickey. CP-DickJ

Hospitality of Lagides, The. Constantine P. Cavafy. CP-CavaC, tr. by Theoharis Constantine Theoharis

Hospitality to Words. Laura Riding Jackson. CP-RidiL

Hoss, The. James Whitcomb Riley. CP-RileJ

Hoss he is a splendud beast, The. Hoss, The. James Whitcomb Riley. CP-RileJ

Host. Olga Broumas. SP-BrouO

Host, The. William Carlos Williams. CP-WilW2

Host, he says that all is well, The. Fear. Hart Crane. CP-CranH

Host is riding from Knocknarea, The. Hosting of the Sidhe, The. William Butler Yeats. CP-YeatW

Host of the Air, The. William Butler Yeats. CP-YeatW

Hostage, The. Stevie Smith. CP-SmitS

Hostage, The. Robert Stock. SP-StocR

Hostage, The. Theodore Weiss. SP-WeisT

Hostess, in pink satin and blond hair, The. Delicacies, The. William Carlos Williams. CP-WilW1

Hostile Philharmonic Orchestra, The. James Tate. SP-TateJ

Hostile Sun, The. D. H. Lawrence. CP-LawrD

Hosting of the Sidhe, The. William Butler Yeats. CP-YeatW

Hosts. A. R. Ammons. CP-AmmoA

Hosts, The. W. S. Merwin. SP-MerwWF

Hosts of the glittering fay return, The. Kingdom of Jerusalem, The. Robert Duncan. SP-DuncR

Hot beautiful furless animals. Adultery. Thom Gunn. CP-GunnT

Hot gold runs a winding stream on the inside of a green bowl. Crucible. Carl Sandburg. CP-SandC

Hot Hands. Donald Davie. CP-DaviDC

Hot night makes us keep our bedroom windows open, The. To Speak of Woe That Is in Marriage. Robert Lowell. SP-LoweR

Hot shallows and seas we bring our blood from, The. Fourth of July. Ted Hughes. SP-HughTN

Hot Springs Infernal in the Human Beast. Philip Whalen. SP-WhalP

Hot summer day / on the River Road. Connections: Vermont Vietnam (I). Grace Paley. CP-PalGC

Hot summer has exhausted her intent. Two Quatrains for First Frost. Richard Wilbur. CP-WilbR

Hot Water. John Updike. CP-UpdiJ

Hot weather? Yes; but really not. At Ninety in the Shade. James Whitcomb Riley. CP-RileJ

Hotblood on Friday. Thom Gunn. CP-GunnT

Hotel Breakfast. Archibald MacLeish. CP-MacLA

Hotel de Dream. Jane Cooper. CP-CoopJ

Hotel de l'Univers et Portugal. James Merrill. SP-MerrJ

Hotel François Ier. Gertrude Stein. CP-SteiG

Hotel in whose ledgers departures are more prominent than arrivals, A. Dutch Mistress. Joseph Brodsky. CP-BrodJ

Hotel Lobby. Robert Creeley. SP-CreeR

Hotel Merlin. Robert Creeley. SP-CreeR

Hotel Normandie Pool, The. Derek Walcott. CP-WalcD

Hotel St. Louis, New York City, Fall 1969. Gregory Orr. SP-OrrG

Hotel Steinplatz, Berlin, December 25 (1966). Charles Olson. SP-OlsoC Fr. Maximus Poems, The.

Hôtel Transylvanie. Frank O'Hara. SP-OharF

Hotels, hospitals, jails. Private Intrigue of Melancholy, The. James Tate. SP-TateJ

Hothouses' offerings, costly and rare, The. Woodland Song. Dorothy Parker. CP-ParkD

Hound of Ulster, The. Stevie Smith. CP-SmitS

Hound Voice. William Butler Yeats. CP-YeatW

Hounded Lovers, The. William Carlos Williams. CP-WilW2

Hounding Mercy. C. K. Williams. CP-WillC

Hounds pass here? The. At Wynard's Gap. Thomas Hardy. CP-HardT

Hour after sunset, Venus hangs, An. Cold Fire, A. Sam Hamill. SP-HamiS

Hour ago the lulling twilight leant, An. Earthquake, The. James Whitcomb Riley. CP-RileJ

Hour, An. Czeslaw Milosz. CP-MiloC; CP-MiloCN, tr. by Lillian Vallee

Hour, The. Norman Dubie. CP-DubiN

Hour, The. Jones Very. CP-VeryJ

Hour and the Ghost, The. Christina Georgina Rossetti. CP-RosC1

Hour before Dawn, The. William Butler Yeats. CP-YeatW

Hour before the dawn, An. Fetching Her. Thomas Hardy. CP-HardT

Hour before the Dawn, The. James Whitcomb Riley. CP-RileJ

Hour before the Dawn, The. Jones Very. CP-VeryJ

Hour-bell sounds, and I must go, The. William Wordsworth. CP-WorW1

Hour by hour the storm deepened. He read. Mountain Cabin, The. Hayden Carruth. CP-CarHS

Hour comes, An. Memory of the Loss of Wings. W. S. Merwin. SP-MerwW

Hour for books, those enthralling friends, An. Emily Dickinson. SP-DickE

Hour glares narrowly at five, An. Dead Season. Michael Palmer. SP-PalmM

Hour-Glass [or Houre-Glasse], The. Ben Jonson. CP-JonsB; SP-JonsB

Hour Glass, The. James Laughlin. CP-LaugJ

Hour-Glass, The. Walter De la Mare. CP-DeLaW

Hour-glass whispers to the lion's roar, The. Our Bias. W. H. Auden. CP-AudeW

Hour is a Sea, An. Emily Dickinson. CP-DickE

Hour of evening—supper hour, for my neighbors—quietness, The. Charles Olson. SP-OlsoC *Fr.* Maximus Poems, The.

Hour of Grace, An. Yehuda Amichai. SP-AmicYL, *tr. by* Benjamin Harshav *and* Barbara Harshav

Hour of Grace, The. Yehuda Amichai. SP-AmicY, *tr. by* Chana Bloch

Hour of noon is fully come, The. Feast, The. Jones Very. CP-VeryJ

Hour of Song. Yannis Ritsos. SP-RitsY, *tr. by* Kimon Friar

Hour of Stars. Federico García Lorca. CP-GarcF, *tr. by* Catherine Brown

Hour of the Angel, The. Rudyard Kipling. CP-KiplR *Fr.* Land and Sea Tales.

Hour pings like a bird hatched from a bell, The. Letter from an Empty House. John Ciardi. CP-CiarJ

Hour was taken, An. Sleep Contravened. Laura Riding Jackson. CP-RidiL

Hour When We Shall Meet Again, The. Samuel Taylor Coleridge. CP-ColeS

Hour which might have been yet might not be, The. Stillborn Love. Dante Gabriel Rossetti. CW-RossD *Fr.* House of Life, The.

Hourglass. Josephine Jacobsen. CP-JacoJ

Hourglass. James Merrill. SP-MerrJ

Hourglass, The. Jorge Luis Borges. SP-BorgJ, *tr. by* Alastair Reid

Hours, The. Norman Dubie. CP-DubiN

Hours, The. Jones Very. CP-VeryJ

Hours brown, The. LOVE 3: What He Said, Remembering. A. K. Ramanujan. CP-RamaA

Hours Continuing Long. Walt Whitman. CP-WhitW

Hours have tumbled their leaden, monotonous sands, The. Rondeau of a Conscientious Objector. D. H. Lawrence. CP-LawrD

Hours have Wings. Emily Dickinson. SP-DickE

Hours, Maycolor, cool. Eye, Open, An. Paul Celan. SP-CelaP, *tr. by* John Felstiner

Hours rise up putting off stars and it is, The. Impression. E. E. Cummings. CP-CummE

House. Robert Browning. CP-BroR2; SP-BroR

House. Carl Sandburg. CP-SandC

House, The ("Mas-Soñer / Restaurat—Any"). Robert Creeley. SP-CreeR

House, The ("Mud put / upon mud"). Robert Creeley. CP-CreeR

House, The. Ralph Waldo Emerson. CP-EmerR

House, The. Heather McHugh. SP-McHuH

House, The. James Merrill. SP-MerrJ

House, The. Mary Oliver. SP-OlivM

House, The. Charles Olson. CP-OlsoC

House, The. Anne Sexton. CP-SextA

House, The. Jones Very. CP-VeryJ

House, The. William Carlos Williams. CP-WilW1

House, The. Adam Zagajewski. SP-ZagaA, *tr. by* Clare Cavanagh

House, and a Dead Man In It. Kenneth Patchen. CP-PatcK

House and hollow; village and valley-side. Winter Encounters. Charles Tomlinson. CP-TomlC; SP-TomlC

House at the Cascades, The. Adrienne Rich. CP-RicAE; SP-RicA2

House behind This One, The. Raymond Carver. CP-CarvR

House by the Sea. Eugenio Montale. CP-MontE, *tr. by* Jonathan Galassi

House can be haunted by those who were never there, A. Selva Oscura. Louis MacNeice. CP-MacNL

House Dog's Grave, The. Robinson Jeffers. CP-JefR3

House-dust mite (*Dermatophagoides farinae*), A. Mites. John Updike. CP-UpdiJ

House Fly, The. James Merrill. SP-MerrJ

House-fronts flare, The. Chiaroscuro. Wallace Stevens. CP-StevWP

House Growing, The. John Updike. CP-UpdiJ

House Guest. Elizabeth Bishop. CP-BishE

House had gone to bring again, The. Need of Being Versed in Country Things, The. Robert Frost. CP-FrosR

House has rotten places: cellar walls, A. Rats. John Updike. CP-UpdiJ

House.———House, and / a dead man in it. House, and a Dead Man In It. Kenneth Patchen. CP-PatcK

House, house, go away, you're looking. Paint 'Til You Faint. James Tate. SP-TateJ

House in Taos, A. Langston Hughes. CP-HughL; CP-HughL2

House in the Quarry, The. Charles Tomlinson. SP-TomlC

House in the Vacant Lot, The. Miller Williams. CP-WillM

House in the Wood, The. Randall Jarrell. CP-JarrR

House in the World. Langston Hughes. CP-HughL; CP-HughL1

House in Winter, The. May Sarton. SP-SartM

House is bleak and cold, The. Everything Comes. Thomas Hardy. CP-HardT

House is filled, The. The last heartthrob. Near the Ocean. Robert Lowell. SP-LoweR

House is named of night. Pale maidens sing, The. Two Poems. Howard Nemerov. CP-NemeH

House is silent, it is late at night, I am alone, The. Forsaken and Forlorn. D. H. Lawrence. CP-LawrD

House is so quiet now, The. Vacuum, The. Howard Nemerov. CP-NemeH

House like a man all lean and coughing, A. Even Numbers. Carl Sandburg. CP-SandC

House-martin. Donald Davie. CP-DaviDC

House my earthly parent left, The. Cottage, The. Jones Very. CP-VeryJ

House Not Made with Hands, Eternal in the Heavens, The. Jones Very. CP-VeryJ

House of Caiphas, The. Thomas Merton. CP-MertT

House of cards / Is neat and small, A. Christina Georgina Rossetti. CP-RosC2

House of Christmas, The. G. K. Chesterton. CP-ChesG

House of Clouds, The. Elizabeth Barrett Browning. CP-BroEB

House of Fame, The. Geoffrey Chaucer. CP-ChauG

House of Fire. Theodore Weiss. SP-WeisT

House of Friends, The. Walt Whitman. CP-WhitW

House of Hospitalities, The. Thomas Hardy. CP-HardT

House of Life, The. Dante Gabriel Rossetti.

  Ardour and Memory. CW-RossD

  Autumn Idleness. CW-RossD

  Barren Spring. CW-RossD

  Beauty's Pageant. CW-RossD

  Birth-Bond, The. CW-RossD

  Body's Beauty. CW-RossD

  Bridal Birth. CW-RossD

  Broken Music. CW-RossD

  Choice, The ("Eat thou and drink; to-morrow thou shalt die"). CW-RossD

  Choice, The ("Think thou and act; to-morrow thou shalt die"). CW-RossD

  Choice, The ("Watch thou and fear; to-morrow thou shalt die"). CW-RossD

  Cloud and Wind. CW-RossD

  Dark Day, A. CW-RossD

  Dark Glass, The. CW-RossD

  Day of Love, A. CW-RossD

  Death-in-Love. CW-RossD

  Death's Songsters. CW-RossD

  Equal Troth. CW-RossD

  Farewell to the Glen. CW-RossD

  From Dawn to Noon. CW-RossD

  Genius in Beauty. CW-RossD

  Gracious Moonlight. CW-RossD

  He and I. CW-RossD

  Heart of the Night, The. CW-RossD

  Heart's Compass. CW-RossD

  Heart's Haven. CW-RossD

  Heart's Hope. CW-RossD

  Her Gifts. CW-RossD

  Hero's Lamp. CW-RossD

  Hill Summit, The. CW-RossD

  Hoarded Joy. CW-RossD

  Hope Overtaken. CW-RossD

  Inclusiveness. CW-RossD

  Kiss, The. CW-RossD

  Known in Vain. CW-RossD

  Lamp's Shrine, The. CW-RossD

  Landmark, The. CW-RossD

  Last Fire. CW-RossD

  Life-in-Love. CW-RossD

  Life the Beloved. CW-RossD

  "Lost days of my life until to-day, The." CW-RossD

  Lost on Both Sides. CW-RossD

  Love and Hope. CW-RossD

Love Enthroned. CW-RossD

Love-Letter, The. CW-RossD

Love-Moon, The. CW-RossD

Love-Sweetness. CW-RossD

Lovers' Walk, The. CW-RossD

Love's Baubles. CW-RossD

Love's Fatality. CW-RossD

Love's Last Gift. CW-RossD

Love's Lovers. CW-RossD

Love's Testament. CW-RossD

Lovesight. CW-RossD

Memorial Thresholds. CW-RossD

Michelangelo's Kiss. CW-RossD

Mid-Rapture. CW-RossD

Monochord, The. CW-RossD

Moonstar, The. CW-RossD

Morrow's Message, The. CW-RossD

Newborn Death ("And thou, O Life, the lady of all bliss"). CW-RossD

Newborn Death ("To-day Death seems to me an infant child"). CW-RossD

Nuptial Sleep. CW-RossD

Old and New Art (Not as These). CW-RossD

Old and New Art (St Luke the Painter). CW-RossD

Old and New Art (The Husbandmen). CW-RossD

One Hope, The. CW-RossD

Parted Love. CW-RossD

Passion and Worship. CW-RossD

Portrait, The. CW-RossD

Pride of Youth. CW-RossD

Retro me, Sathana! CW-RossD

Secret Parting. CW-RossD

Severed Selves. CW-RossD

Silent Noon. CW-RossD

Sleepless Dreams. CW-RossD

Song-Throe, The. CW-RossD

Sonnet, A: "Sonnet is a moment's monument, A." CW-RossD

Soul-Light. CW-RossD

Soul's Beauty. CW-RossD

Soul's Sphere, The. CW-RossD

Stillborn Love. CW-RossD

Sun's Shame, The ("As some true chief of men, bowed down with stress"). CW-RossD

Sun's Shame, The ("Beholding youth and hope in mockery caught"). CW-RossD

Superscription, A. CW-RossD

Supreme Surrender. CW-RossD

Through Death to Love. CW-RossD

Transfigured Life. CW-RossD

Trees of the Garden, The. CW-RossD

True Woman (Her Heaven). CW-RossD

True Woman (Her Love). CW-RossD

True Woman (Herself). CW-RossD

Vain Virtues. CW-RossD

Vase of Life, The. CW-RossD

Venus Victrix. CW-RossD

Willowwood ("And now Love sang: but his was such a song"). CW-RossD

Willowwood ("I sat with Love upon a woodside well"). CW-RossD

Willowwood ("O ye, all ye that walk in Willowwood"). CW-RossD

Willowwood ("So sang he: and as meeting rose and rose"). CW-RossD

Winged Hours. CW-RossD

Without Her. CW-RossD

Youth's Antiphony. CW-RossD

Youth's Spring-Tribute. CW-RossD

House of Light, The. James Laughlin. CP-LaugJ

House of Mercy, A. Stevie Smith. CP-SmitS

House of Mourning Written by Mr Scott, The. John Keats. CP-KeatJ

House of Music, A. Kathleen Jessie Raine. SP-RainK

House of Over-Dew, The. Stevie Smith. CP-SmitS

House of Prayer, The. Shmuel HaNagid. SP-HaNaS, tr. by Peter Cole

House of Silence, The. Thomas Hardy. CP-HardT

House of Snow, A. Yusef Komunyakaa. CP-KomuY

House of Splendour, The. Ezra Pound. SP-PounE Fr. Und Drang.

House of the Customs Men, The. Eugenio Montale. CP-MontE, tr. by Jonathan Galassi

House on a Cliff. Louis MacNeice. CP-MacNL

House on Bishop Street, The. Rita Dove. SP-DoveR

House on the Edge of the Serious Wood, The. Philip Larkin. CP-LarkP

House on the Hill, The. Edwin Arlington Robinson. CP-RobiE

House rocked and shouted all night, The. From the East, Light. Raymond Carver. CP-CarvR

House sits at one end of a two-acre trapezoid, The. Where I Live. Billy Collins. SP-CollB

House Slave, The. Rita Dove. SP-DoveR

House-snake dwells here still, The. Closed World, The. Denise Levertov. SP-LeveDP; SP-LeveDS

House: Some Instructions. Grace Paley. CP-PalGC

House that holds me, household that I hold dear. Ten-Day Leave. William Meredith. SP-MereW

House to the West, A. W. S. Merwin. SP-MerwWF

House-Top, The. Herman Melville. SP-MelvH

House / two floors. Foreigner. Olga Broumas. SP-BrouO

House unoccupied for years, The. When the newlyweds leased it. Old House, The. Yannis Ritsos. SP-RitsY, tr. by Kostas Myrsiades

House upon the Height, A. Emily Dickinson. CP-DickE

House was Dutch, The. Judge and the Bird, The. Louis Zukofsky. CP-ZukLS

House Was Quiet and the World Was Calm, The. Wallace Stevens. CP-StevW; CP-StevWP

House was shaken by a rising wind, The. Brainstorm. Howard Nemerov. CP-NemeH

House we built gradually, The. Small Cabin, The. Margaret Atwood. SP-AtwM1

House with a Garden. Constantine P. Cavafy. CP-CavaC, tr. by Theoharis Constantine Theoharis

House with a History, A. Thomas Hardy. CP-HardT

House with 7 or 8 people, A. Good Life, The. Charles Bukowski. SP-BukC1

Houseboat Days. John Ashbery. SP-AshbJ

Housed (A Report on a Visiting Dog). William Meredith. SP-MereW

Household. Heather McHugh. SP-McHuH

Household, A. W. H. Auden. CP-AudeW

Household, The. Robert Duncan. SP-DuncR Fr. Dante Études.

Household Spirits. Thomas Kinsella. CP-KinsT

Household to provide shelter, The. Household, The. Robert Duncan. SP-DuncR Fr. Dante Études.

Householder, The. Robert Browning. CP-BroR2

Householder issuing to the street, The. Vulcan. George Oppen. CP-OppGN

Housekeeper, The. Robert Frost. CP-FrosR

Housekeeping. Donald Davie. CP-DaviDC

Houseless Dead, The. D. H. Lawrence. CP-LawrD

Houses, The. Rudyard Kipling. CP-KiplR

Houses, The. W. S. Merwin. SP-MerwWF

Houses, an embassy, the hospital. Days of 1964. James Merrill. SP-MerrJ

Houses and cafés the quarter, The. In the Same Space. Constantine P. Cavafy. CP-CavaC, tr. by Theoharis Constantine Theoharis

Houses and trees are bare. Birds. Same as Always. Yannis Ritsos. SP-RitsY, tr. by Kostas Myrsiades

Houses are haunted, The. Disillusionment of Ten O'Clock. Wallace Stevens. CP-StevW; CP-StevWP

Houses fade in a melt of mist, The. Parliament Hill in the Evening. D. H. Lawrence. CP-LawrD

Houses haunt me. February 11th. Anne Sexton. CP-SextA

Houses have dropped their bricks, The. On Plumbing after an Air Raid. Alan Dugan. CP-DugaA

Houses in / the ring. Circle, The. Robert Creeley. CP-CreeR

"Houses"—so the wise men tell me. Emily Dickinson. CP-DickE

Houses— / the dark side silhouetted. Night. William Carlos Williams. CP-WilW1

Houses, waves, clouds, and shadows. View of Delft, A. Adam Zagajewski. SP-ZagaA

Housewife. Anne Sexton. CP-SextA; SP-SextA

Housing. Grace Paley. CP-PalGC

Housing conditions: number of galaxy and star. End of the Questionnaire. Dan Pagis. SP-PagiD, tr. by Stephen Mitchell

Housman came, savage recluse. Cambridgeshire. Donald Davie. CP-DaviDC

Housman was perfectly right. Shock, A. W. H. Auden. CP-AudeW

Houston, 6 P.M. Adam Zagajewski. SP-ZagaA, tr. by Clare Cavanagh

Houstonia, The. Jones Very. CP-VeryJ

Houynhnm's Holiday. Robert Stock. SP-StocR

Hovenweep. Kenneth Patchen. CP-PatcK

How. Philip Larkin. CP-LarkP

How a Little Girl Danced. Nicholas Vachel Lindsay. CP-LindV

How a Little Girl Sang. Nicholas Vachel Lindsay. CP-LindV

How about an oak leaf. Poem: "How about an oak leaf." James Schuyler. CP-SchuJ

How About It, Dixie. Langston Hughes. CP-HughL; CP-HughL2

How about that? As I stepped outside, the doe and her twin fawns. Three Deer, Mount Rose, August 1995. Paul Muldoon. CP-MuldP

How agreeable it is not to be touring Italy this summer. Consolation. Billy Collins. SP-CollB

How all is one way wrought! Gerard Manley Hopkins. CP-HopkG

How am I bound to Two! God, who doth give. God, and the King. Robert Herrick. CP-HerrR

How am I ravisht! When I do but see. On Julia's Picture. Robert Herrick. CP-HerrR

How amiable are thy tabernacles, O Lord of hosts! Psalm 84: "How amiable are thy tabernacles, O Lord of hosts!" Bible, *O.T.* CP-MiltJ *Fr.* Psalms.

How Annandale Went Out. Edwin Arlington Robinson. CP-RobiE

How Are They Bandied Up and Down by Fate. *Unknown, sometimes at. to* Thomas Sheridan. CP-SherT

How are you harry the. Drums, The. Robert Creeley. CP-CreeR

How art thou named? In search of what strange land. To the Torrent at the Devil's Bridge, North Wales, 1824. William Wordsworth. CP-WorW2; MW-WorW

How Bacchus Comforts Ariadne. Nonnus. CP-BroEB *Fr.* Dionysiaca.

How Bacchus Finds Ariadne Sleeping. Nonnus. CP-BroEB *Fr.* Dionysiaca.

How Bad It Is to Say. William Carlos Williams. CP-WilW2

How Beastly the Bourgeois Is. D. H. Lawrence. CP-LawrD

How beautiful I was! Everything I see. To Serve as an Epitaph for the Beautiful Madame B. Rainer Maria Rilke. CP-RilkFr, *tr. by* A. Poulin, Jr.

How beautiful it was, that one bright day. Hawthorne. Henry Wadsworth Longfellow. SP-LongH

How beautiful the Earth is still. Anticipation. Emily Jane Brontë. CP-BronE

How Beautiful the Queen of Night, on High. William Wordsworth. CP-WorW2

How beautiful the sight. On the Sudden Snow. Jones Very. CP-VeryJ

How beautiful the sight of woods still fair. October ("How beautiful the sight of woods still fair"). Jones Very. CP-VeryJ

How beautiful to think. Fellatio. John Updike. CP-UpdiJ

How beautiful when up a lofty height. Widow on Windmere Side, The. William Wordsworth. CP-WorW2

"How beautifully it falls," you said. Leaf, The. Kathleen Jessie Raine. SP-RainK

How, best of kings, dost thou a scepter bear[e]! To King James ("How, best of kings, dost thou a scepter bear[e]!"). Ben Jonson. CP-JonsB; SP-JonsB

How, beyond all foresight. Against Portraits. Charles Tomlinson. CP-TomlC

How big and white the night is! Rebuked. D. H. Lawrence. CP-LawrD

How big of breast our Mother Gaea laughed. Cageing of Ares, The. George Meredith. CP-MerG1

How bitter and how sweet on winter nights. Cracked Bell, The. Charles Baudelaire. CP-BaudC, *tr. by* Walter Martin

How bland and sweet the greeting of this breeze. Chalkley Hall. John Greenleaf Whittier. CP-WhitJ

How blessed is he, who for his country dies. To the Earl of Oxford, Late Lord Treasurer. Jonathan Swift. CP-SwifJ

How blessed is he who leads a country life. To My Honoured [*or* Honour'd] Kinsman, John Driden [of Chesterton in the County of Huntingdon, Esquire]. John Dryden. SP-DrydJ

How blessed the tears of him who still weeps on. Mourner, The. Jones Very. CP-VeryJ

How blessed the tears of those, who still weep on. "Blessed are they that mourn: for they shall be comforted." Math. 5:4. Jones Very. CP-VeryJ

How blest art thou, canst love the country [*or* countrey], Wroth. To Sir Robert Wroth. Ben Jonson. CP-JonsB; SP-JonsB

How blest is her lot to set by his side. Impromptu on Seeing a Very Agreeable Gentleman and Lady, Particular Friends Conversing Together. Annis Boudinot Stockton. CP-StocA

How blest the land that counts among. Statesmen, The. Ambrose Bierce. SP-BierA

How blest the soul to whom indulgent heaven. Annis Boudinot Stockton. CP-StocA

How blest the youth whom Fate ordains. William Cowper. CP-CowpW

How blest the youth whom Genius deigns to guide. Addressed to a Student of Divinity. Annis Boudinot Stockton. CP-StocA

How blest to meet my dear Lucinda here! Peace, a Pastoral Dialogue.—Part the Second. Annis Boudinot Stockton. CP-StocA

How Blind! Walter De la Mare. CP-DeLaW

How Blind and Bright. Laura Riding Jackson. CP-RidiL

How blind is he who, powerless to discern. Ambrose Bierce. SP-BierA

How bold it is, this fine young love we bear. Dorothy Parker. CP-ParkD

How bright you'll find young people. Lorine Niedecker. CP-NiedL

How brittle are the Piers. Emily Dickinson. CP-DickE

How broad-minded were Nature and My Parents. Contrast, A. W. H. Auden. CP-AudeW

How calmly does the orange branch. Tennessee Williams. CP-WillT *Fr.* Night of the Iguana, The.

How calmly we walk. To My Older Brother. Adam Zagajewski. SP-ZagaA, *tr. by* Clare Cavanagh

How came pride in Man. William Blake. CP-BlakW

How came this modest lily fair. Nodding Meadow Lily, The. Jones Very. CP-VeryJ

How came this ranger. Chambermaid's First Song, The. William Butler Yeats. CP-YeatW

How came you in Hob's pound to cool. New Song to the Tune of "Whare Hae Ye Been a' Day, My Boy Tammy O? Courting O' a Young Thing, Just Come Frae Her Mammie O?" Lord Byron. CP-Byron

How can anyone know that a whale. Shore, The. W. S. Merwin. SP-MerwWF

How can I care whether you sigh for me. Song: How Can I Care? Robert Graves. CP-GravR

How can I choose but love, and follow her. Another on Her. Robert Herrick. CP-HerrR

How Can I Finish What You Have Begun? Thomas Sheridan. CP-SherT

How can I help thy Husbands copying Me. To Nancy F[laxman]. William Blake. CP-BlakW

How can I persuade today that it's. This Day of This Month of This Year of This. W. S. Merwin. SP-MerwW

How can I recognize again. Rainer Maria Rilke. CP-RilkFr, *tr. by* A. Poulin, Jr. *Fr.* Orchards.

How can I regret my life. Signal, The. David Ignatow. SP-IgnaD

How Can I Speak for Her. Jane Cooper. CP-CoopJ

How can I teach you when your blue. D. H. Lawrence. CP-LawrD *Fr.* Schoolmaster [A], The.

How can I thank you B, for your ear, your mind, your affection? Inn at Kirchstetten, The. James Laughlin. CP-LaugJ

How can I, that girl standing there. Politics. William Butler Yeats. CP-YeatW

How can I think what thoughts. Candle, Lamp & Firefly. Tess Gallagher. SP-GallT

How can it be, as long experience shows. Michelangelo Buonarroti. CP-MahoD, *tr. by* Derek Mahon

How can love heal. Safe Subjects. Yusef Komunyakaa. CP-KomuY

How can my friend expect the chearful lay. Epistle to a Friend Who Urg'd to Have Some Poetry Sent Her in the Year 1759, in the Winter, An. Annis Boudinot Stockton. CP-StocA

How can my poor heart be glad. On the Seas and Far Away. Robert Burns. CP-BurnR

How can one man, how can all men, / How can we be like St. Paul. Every One That Is Perfect Shall Be as His Master. Christina Georgina Rossetti. CP-RosC2

How can one write about Bosnia. Bosnia. A. K. Ramanujan. CP-RamaA

How can there be a difference between twice once and twice twice once. With a Wife. Gertrude Stein. CP-SteiG

How can they write or paint. Observations in a Cornish Teashop. Kenneth Rexroth. CP-RexrK

How can we endure? Dow Jones: Down. Charles Bukowski. SP-BukC2

How can we own a thing that travels. Water. Wyatt Prunty. SP-PrunW

How can we tell a paper bird. Paper Cranes. Thomas Merton. CP-MertT

How can we thank each other. Emily Dickinson. SP-DickE

How can we upward go. Help of the Spirit, The. Jones Very. CP-VeryJ

How can you be quite so uncouth? After sharing. Ode to the Diencephalon. W. H. Auden. CP-AudeW

How can you forget me? Low to High. Langston Hughes. CP-HughL; CP-HughL3

How can you / Shake a fist at tyranny. Dixie Man to Uncle Sam. Langston Hughes. CP-HughL; CP-HughL3

How! Canst thou see the basket, wherein lay. Moses in Infancy. Jones Very. CP-VeryJ

How carefully, fastidiously. To a Dead Drunk. James Wright. CP-WrigJ

How carelessly you wore your beauty! Epitaph for a Careless Beauty. Marya Alexandrovna Zaturenska. SP-ZatuM

How cast down is the mind that took to my Lesbia, culprit. Catullus. *See* Reason blinded by sin, Lesbia

How certain / days filter themselves through. It Is 70 Degrees in Late November. Opening a Window, You Nearly Know. Heather McHugh. SP-McHuH

How changed is here each spot man makes or fills! Thyrsis. Matthew Arnold. SP-ArnoM

How charming the sticky sweat. Tears and Recriminations. Philip Whalen. SP-WhalP

How clean these shallows. Labrador. William Carlos Williams. CP-WilW2

How clear, how keen, how marvellously bright. November 1 [1815]. William Wordsworth. CP-WorW2

How clear, how lovely bright. A. E. Housman. CP-HousA

How Clear She Shines! Emily Jane Brontë. CP-BronE

How closely these long years have bound us. Love Charms. Robert Graves. CP-GravR

How Clowns Go. Adam Zagajewski. SP-ZagaA, *tr. by* Clare Cavanagh

How co'd Luke Smeaton weare a shoe, or boot. Upon Smeaton. Robert Herrick. CP-HerrR

How cold is that bosom which folly once fired. Monody on Maria. Robert Burns. CP-BurnR

How Come? David Ignatow. SP-IgnaD

How come a thickish tree. View, A. James Schuyler. CP-SchuJ

How Come He Got Canned at the Ribbon Factory. Allen Ginsberg. CP-GinsA

How come nobody is being bombed today? All Quiet. David Ignatow. SP-IgnaD

How Come the Dead? Jones Very. CP-VeryJ

How come the dead? we anxious ask. How Come the Dead? Jones Very. CP-VeryJ

How come to town she was, tied bright and prim. On a Photograph of My Mother at Seventeen. Miller Williams. CP-WillM

How come when grandpa is teaching the little boy. Ashes Ashes We All Fall Down. C. K. Williams. CP-WillC

How Come You're Not Unlisted? Charles Bukowski. SP-BukC1

How comes it, Flora, that, whenever we. Queen of Hearts, The. Christina Georgina Rossetti. CP-RosC1

How comes it, gentlemen, that nowadays. Prologue: "How comes it, gentlemen, that nowadays." Thomas Southerne. CP-DryJ2 *Fr.* Disappointment, The.

How comes it that, at even-tide. To the Companions. Rudyard Kipling. CP-KiplR *Fr.* Debits and Credits.

How could I be aware. At Mayfair Lodgings. Thomas Hardy. CP-HardT

How could I have come so far? Poem: "How could I have come so far?" Thomas McGrath. SP-McGrT

How could I have told you except to tell you? Coming Out. Miller Williams. CP-WillM

How could I know. Dance Called David, The. Theodore Weiss. SP-WeisT

How could I, since it's so. Michelangelo Buonarroti. CP-Miche, *tr. by* John Frederick Nims

How could nothing turn so gold? Message at Sunset for Bishop Berkeley. Heather McHugh. SP-McHuH

How could those artists paint. Narrative. George Oppen. CP-OppGN

How could you be so happy, now some thousand years. Note to Wang Wei. John Berryman. CP-BerrJ

How could you, Gay, disgrace the muses' train. To Mr. Gay. Jonathan Swift. CP-SwifJ

How could you hear him. Glass Ark, The. Yusef Komunyakaa. CP-KomuY

How Could You Loathe. Shmuel HaNagid. SP-HaNaS, *tr. by* Peter Cole

How countlessly they congregate. Stars. Robert Frost. CP-FrosR

How courteous is the Japanese. Japanese, The. Ogden Nash. CP-NashO

How credible, the room which you evoke. Advice from the Muse. Richard Wilbur. CP-WilbR

How cruel are the Parents. Altered from an Old English Song. Robert Burns. CP-BurnR

How Cruel Is the Story of Eve. Stevie Smith. CP-SmitS

How dare one say it? Unexpress'd, The. Walt Whitman. CP-WhitW

How dare the robins sing. Emily Dickinson. CP-DickE

How dark and single,where he ends,the earth. E. E. Cummings. CP-CummE

How daur ye ca' me "Howlet-face" Keekin' Glass, The. Robert Burns. CP-BurnR

How dear the sky has been above this place! Place de la Bastille, Paris. Dante Gabriel Rossetti. CW-RossD

How dear to my heart are the scenes of my childhood. Old-fashioned Bible, The. James Whitcomb Riley. CP-RileJ

How defenceless a sleeper is at night! November Rain. Jaroslav Seifert. SP-SeifJ, *tr. by* Ewald Osers

How destitute is he. Emily Dickinson. CP-DickE

How did a banner begin? Let's assume there was something whole. Yehuda Amichai. SP-AmicYL, *tr. by* Benjamin Harshav *and* Barbara Harshav

How did a great Red-tailed Hawk. Dead by the Side of the Road, The. Gary Snyder. CP-SnydG

How did I bear it—how could I possibly as a child. Edna St. Vincent Millay. CP-MillE

How did it happen? Murder. Federico García Lorca. CP-GarcF, *tr. by* Greg Simon *and* Steven F. White

How did midsummer come so soon. Solstice. Louis MacNeice. CP-MacNL

How did Saint Sebastian die? San Sebastiano de Sodoma. Tennessee Williams. CP-WillT

How did this story end? Ten Dollars Reward. James Laughlin. CP-LaugJ

How did you decide to translate me. Translation, A. James Laughlin. CP-LaugJ

How Did You Ever Live Without It? A Peppermill with a Light. Miller Williams. CP-WillM

How Did You Rest, Last Night? James Whitcomb Riley. CP-RileJ

How died Melissa none dares shape in words. Periander. George Meredith. CP-MerG1

How different, in the midst of snow, the great school rises red! School on the Outskirts. D. H. Lawrence. CP-LawrD

"How disappeared he?" Ask the newt and toad. Brownie, The. William Wordsworth. CP-WorW2

How Distant. Philip Larkin. CP-LarkP

How do I feel today? I feel as unfit as an unfiddle. They Won't Believe, on New Year's Eve, that New Year's Day Will Come What May. Ogden Nash. CP-NashO

How do I know it was a fox? Blue Teal's Mother. James Wright. CP-WrigJ

How do I know what Order brings. Song of the Dynamo. Rudyard Kipling. CP-KiplR

How do I love on summer nights. Written in Aspin Castle. Emily Jane Brontë. CP-BronE

How do I say. On Not Writing a Love Poem. Miller Williams. CP-WillM

How do the days press on, and lay. Flight, The. Walter De la Mare. CP-DeLaW

How Do They Get Your Number? Charles Bukowski. SP-BukC3

How do they know. Each Summer's Swallows. John Updike. CP-UpdiJ

How do we cut for the deal? Bridge Fiend, The. Dorothy Parker. CP-ParkD

How do we know, by the bank-high river. Last Lap, The. Rudyard Kipling. CP-KiplR *Fr.* Land and Sea Tales.

How do we know where we are going? Perpetual Migration, The. Marge Piercy. SP-PierM

How Do You Do, Dr Berryman, Sir? John Berryman. CP-BerrJ

How do you know that the pilgrim track. Year's Awakening, The. Thomas Hardy. CP-HardT

How do you know what effigy of self. Letter to the Inventors of a Tradition, A. Kenneth Patchen. CP-PatcK

How do you like the music of Adolph. Fantasy. Frank O'Hara. SP-OharF

How do you masterbate in Greek. P.S. Olga Broumas. SP-BrouO

How Do You Say Ha-Ha in French. Ogden Nash. CP-NashO

How Do You See? Stevie Smith. CP-SmitS

How do you see out of a sub? Seeing out of the Sub. Andrei Codrescu. SP-CodrA

How do you spell change. Audre Lorde. *See* How do you spell change brother like frayed slogan underwear

How do you spell change brother like frayed slogan underwear. New York City 1970. Audre Lorde. SP-LordA

How does a part of the world leave the world? Enough Words? Jelaluddin Rumi. SP-Rumi, *tr. by* Coleman Barks

How does a person get to be a capable liar? Golly, How Truth Will Out. Ogden Nash. CP-NashO

How Does It Look? James Laughlin. CP-LaugJ

How does one stand. American Sublime, The. Wallace Stevens. CP-StevW; CP-StevWP

How Does the Man Look Who's Right. Adam Zagajewski. SP-ZagaA, *tr. by* Clare Cavanagh

How does the pot pray. Utensil. A. R. Ammons. CP-AmmoA

How does the true man of Tao. Wholeness. Chuang Tzu. CP-MertT

How drearily in College hall. Ralph Waldo Emerson. CP-EmerR

How Dulcenia del Toboso Is Like the Left Wing of a Bird. Nicholas Vachel Lindsay. CP-LindV

How dull and dead are books, that cannot show. To the Right Honourable, Philip, Earle of Pembroke, and Montgomerie. Robert Herrick. CP-HerrR

How dull the age when ladies must express. Satire on the Fashionable Pompoons Worn by the Ladies in the Year 1753. by a Gentleman, A; Answered by a Young Lady of Sixteen. Annis Boudinot Stockton. CP-StocA

How [*or* Followis How] Dumbar wes Desyrd to be ane Freir. William Dunbar. CP-DunbW

How eagerly you fought, defeated soul. Desire for Oblivion. Charles Baudelaire. CP-BaudC, *tr. by* Walter Martin

How easily the ripe grain. Widow, The. W. S. Merwin. SP-MerwW

How eas'ly wert thou chained. Thomas Campion. CP-CampT

How eloquent are eyes! Eyes: A Fragment. Percy Bysshe Shelley. CP-ShelP

How Else. David Ignatow. SP-IgnaD

How enduring, how we need durability. At Dawn. Czeslaw Milosz. CP-MiloC; CP-MiloCN, *tr. by* Robert Hass

How Everything Happens (Based on a Study of the Wave). May Swenson. SP-SwenM

How exactly good it is. Cold, The. Wendell Berry. CP-BerrW

How faint the horn sounds in the mountain passes. May Sarton. SP-SartM *Fr.* To the Living.

How Faith Comes. Jones Very. CP-VeryJ

How Far Can You Press a Poet? Stevie Smith. CP-SmitS

How far civilization is from procuring the enjoyments. Interrupted Performance, An. Stéphane Mallarmé. CP-MallS, *tr. by* Henry Weinfield

How far friends are! They forget you. Friends. William Stafford. SP-StafWW

How far from us. Charles Tomlinson. CP-TomlC; SP-TomlC

How far hast thou travelled? Though many thy years. Distant, The. Jones Very. CP-VeryJ

How far is it? Getting There. Sylvia Plath. CP-PlatS

How far is it to Heaven? Emily Dickinson. CP-DickE

How far is St. Helena from a little child at play? St. Helena Lullaby, A. Rudyard Kipling. CP-KiplR

How far / Must that star descend. Star of Bethlehem. Kathleen Jessie Raine. SP-RainK

How far off are those years, mine and not mine. In Milan. Czeslaw Milosz. CP-

MiloC; CP-MiloCN, tr. by Robert Hass

How fares it with you, Mrs. Cooper my bride? Sea-Widow, The. Stevie Smith. CP-SmitS

How fervent-strong and heaven-deep the blue. Blue Flower, The. Marya Alexandrovna Zaturenska. SP-ZatuM

How fever'd is the man who cannot look. On Fame ("How fever'd is the man who cannot look"). John Keats. CP-KeatJ Fr. Two Sonnets on Fame.

How few can be of grandeure sure! New Year's Gift for the Dean of St. Patrick's Given Him at Quilca, 1723/24, A. Thomas Sheridan. CP-SherT

How few, of all the hearts that loved. E.W. to A.G.A. Emily Jane Brontë. CP-BronE

How few the reapers in life's whitening fields! Reapers Are the Angels, The. Jones Very. CP-VeryJ

How fierce was I, when I did see. Upon Julia['s] Washing Herself in the River. Robert Herrick. CP-HerrR

How firm Eternity must look. Emily Dickinson. CP-DickE

How fit our well-rank'd Feasts doe follow. Upon the Powder Day. Richard Crashaw. CP-CrasR

How fits his Umber Coat. Emily Dickinson. CP-DickE

How fleet—how indiscreet an one. Emily Dickinson. CP-DickE

How Fortunate. James Laughlin. CP-LaugJ

How fortunate that instant when there came. Petrarch. CP-Petra, tr. by J. G. Nichols

How fortunate the Grave. Emily Dickinson. CP-DickE

How fortunate the tree that is scarcely aware. What Gets You. "Rubén Dario." SP-DariR, tr. by Alberto Acereda and Will Derusha

How fortunate to bear two small breasts. Breasts. Rainer Maria Rilke. CP-RilkFr, tr. by A. Poulin, Jr.

How freely do the flowers their wealth bestow. Sensibility to the Beauty and Fragrance of Flowers. Jones Very. CP-VeryJ

How fresh, O[h] Lord, how sweet and clean. Flower, The. George Herbert. CP-HerbG

How funny, she beat him, she. Grazia Deledda, Young. Donald Davie. CP-DaviDC

How funny you are today New York. Steps. Frank O'Hara. SP-OharF

How generous is that himself the sun. E. E. Cummings. CP-CummE

How glamourous the Sun looks, heading west. Last Rays of the Romantic Sun. Charles Baudelaire. CP-BaudC, tr. by Walter Martin

How God Was Made. Kenneth Patchen. CP-PatcK

How gold their hair was. Nightingale Road. Denise Levertov. SP-LeveDL

How golden bright from earth and heaven. Emily Jane Brontë. CP-BronE

How good his Lava Bed. Emily Dickinson. CP-DickE

How good it is, the hollow reed—giving us the marvellous sounds. Flute-Player, The. Yannis Ritsos. SP-RitsY, tr. by Gwendolyn MacEwen and Nikos Tsingos

How good it is to feel the joy at last. Night. David Ignatow. SP-IgnaD

How good of Mrs. Metz! The blur. Snapshots. John Updike. CP-UpdiJ

How goodly are your tents, Jacob. Even when there are no. Yehuda Amichai. SP-AmicYL, tr. by Benjamin Harshav and Barbara Harshav

How gorgeous that shock of red lilies, and larkspur cleaving. Twofold. D. H. Lawrence. CP-LawrD

How gray and hard the brown feet of the wretched of the earth. Wealth of the Destitute, The. Denise Levertov. SP-LeveDL

How great is little man! / Sun, moon, and stars respond to him. Christina Georgina Rossetti. CP-RosC2

How Great My Grief. Thomas Hardy. CP-HardT

How grimly do petunias look. Tennessee Williams. CP-WillT Fr. Case of the Crushed Petunias, The: A Lyrical Fantasy.

How happy are the new-born race. Testimony of Divine Adoption, The. Jeanne Marie Bouvier de la Motte- Guyon. CP-CowpW

How happy I was if I could forget. Emily Dickinson. CP-DickE

How happy I was the day I told the young Blandina of mauve-legged giraffes. Analysis of a Theme. Wallace Stevens. CP-StevW; CP-StevWP

How happy in his low degree. Epode 2: "How happy in his low degree." Horace. CP-DryJ2 Fr. Epodes.

How happy is the little Stone. Emily Dickinson. CP-DickE

How happy the lover. Song: "How happy the lover." John Dryden. SP-DrydJ Fr. King Arthur.

How happy were the subject if he knew. Epigram. To our Great and Good K[ing] Charles on his Anniversary Day, An. 1629. Ben Jonson. CP-JonsB

How hard for a dead man to pretend to be. Dances of Death. Aleksandr Aleksandrovich Blok. SP-BlokA, tr. by Peter France and Jon Stallworthy

How hard it is for me, who live. Marriage. Wendell Berry. CP-BerrW

How Hard It Is to Keep from Being King When It's in You and in the Situation. Robert Frost. CP-FrosR

How hard it is, we say. Clothes Maketh the Man. Theodore Weiss. SP-WeisT

How hard the truth of words like these to feel. Blessed are they that mourn: for they shall be comforted. Jones Very. CP-VeryJ

How hard they try! Death. Federico García Lorca. CP-GarcF, tr. by Greg Simon

and Steven F. White

How has New England's romance fled. Extract from "A New England Legend." John Greenleaf Whittier. CP-WhitJ

How Has the Way Been Found? William Carlos Williams. CP-WilW1

How hasten? hearten? O morning star and. Letter on Liberty, A. Kenneth Patchen. CP-PatcK

How have I wandered here to this vaulted room. Next Morning. D. H. Lawrence. CP-LawrD

How he sleepeth, having drunken. Child Asleep, A. Elizabeth Barrett Browning. CP-BroEB

How he survived them they could never understand. Diaspora. W. H. Auden. CP-AudeW

How He Would Drinke His Wine. Robert Herrick. CP-HerrR

How healthily their feet upon the floor. Edna St. Vincent Millay. CP-MillE

How Heav'n in Scorn of human Arrogance. Samuel Johnson. CP-JohnS Fr. Irene.

How heavy is it? Fifteen tons? Thirty? More? Globe of Gneiss. Robert Penn Warren. CP-WarrR

How heavy the heart is now, and every heart. Again at Waldheim. Kenneth Rexroth. CP-RexrK

How High the Moon. Adam Zagajewski. SP-ZagaA, tr. by Clare Cavanagh

How high they build hospitals! How. Philip Larkin. CP-LarkP

How high Thou art! our songs can own. Mediator, The. Elizabeth Barrett Browning. CP-BroEB

How His Soule Came Ensnared. Robert Herrick. CP-HerrR

How hollow heart and full. Nicolas-Sébastien Roch Chamfort. CP-BeckS

How horrible late Spring is, with the full death of the frozen tight bulbs. Wooden Spring. Muriel Rukeyser. CP-RukeM

"How, how," he said. "Friend Chang," I said. Chinese Nightingale, The. Nicholas Vachel Lindsay. CP-LindV

How Human Nature dotes. Emily Dickinson. CP-DickE

How Humble We Were before This. C. K. Williams. CP-WillC

How I Can Lie to You. Maya Angelou. SP-AngeM

How I do[e] love thee, Beaumont, and thy Muse. To Francis Beaumont. Ben Jonson. CP-JonsB; SP-JonsB

How I Got Started. Charles Bukowski. SP-BukC3

How I hate myself, this body which is me. Eloi, Eloi, Lama Sabachthani? D. H. Lawrence. CP-LawrD

How I Helped the Wise. Shmuel HaNagid. SP-HaNaS, tr. by Peter Cole

How I lived, ere my human life began. Rephan. Robert Browning. CP-BroR2

How I long to pull the old man in. Dark Night, A. Gregory Orr. SP-OrrG

How I loved one like you when I was little!—. Slug. Theodore Roethke. CP-RoetT

How I miss my father. Poem at Thirty-nine. Alice Walker. CP-WalkA

How I remember cleaning that strange picture! Collector Cleans His Picture, The. Thomas Hardy. CP-HardT

How I See Things. Yusef Komunyakaa. CP-KomuY

How I was caught. Missed Train, The. Thomas Hardy. CP-HardT

How I woke to the color-tone. Remembering. Denise Levertov. SP-LeveDP

How ill doth he deserve a lover's name. Eternity of Love Protested. Thomas Carew. CP-CareT

How impossible it is. T. E. Lawrence. Lorine Niedecker. CP-NiedL

How in all wonder Columbus got over. Arthur Hugh Clough. SP-ClouA

How, in the first place, did. Torn Shades. Thomas Lux. SP-LuxT

How, in the inmost soul. Thoughts and Desires. Jones Very. CP-VeryJ

How, indeed? For some do die without it. How Did You Ever Live Without It? A Peppermill with a Light. Miller Williams. CP-WillM

How innocent of me and my dark pain. Edna St. Vincent Millay. CP-MillE

How innocent we lie among. Edna St. Vincent Millay. CP-MillE

How intelligent he looks! Changing Diapers. Gary Snyder. CP-SnydG

How is it, Gellius. Carmen 80. Catullus. CP-ZukLS Fr. Carmina.

How is it never the same. Woodsmoke at 70. Hayden Carruth. CP-CarHS

How is it she lies here. His Lament. Gregory Orr. SP-OrrG

How is it some of us don't believe. Kingdom of Stinking Wishes, The. C. K. Williams. CP-WillC

How is it, tell me, that this new self can be—. Sonnet: "How is it, tell me, that this new self can be—" Hayden Carruth. CP-CarHS Fr. Sonnets.

How is it that my saints from Voragine. Colloquy with a Polish Aunt. Wallace Stevens. CP-StevW; CP-StevWP

How Is My Sun. Sir Philip Sidney. SP-SidnP Fr. Arcadia.

How is my sun, whose beams are shining bright. How Is My Sun. Sir Philip Sidney. SP-SidnP Fr. Arcadia.

How is the word made flesh made steel made shit. Sewerplant Grows In Harlem Or I'm a Stranger Here Myself. Audre Lorde. SP-LordA

How It Began. William Stafford. SP-StafWW

How it came to an end! Coming of the End, The. Thomas Hardy. CP-HardT

How it feels to be touching. We Become New. Marge Piercy. SP-PierM

How It Goes On. Maxine W. Kumin. SP-KumiM

How It Happened. James Whitcomb Riley. CP-RileJ

How it hung / In the electrical loom. Remembering Teheran. Ted Hughes. SP-HughTN

How It Is. Richard Eberhart. CP-EberR

How It Is. Maxine W. Kumin. SP-KumiM

How It Is. William Stafford. SP-StafW; SP-StafWW

How It Is with Family. William Stafford. SP-StafWW

How It Passes. Carolyn Kizer. CP-KizeC

How it rained. We Field-Women. Thomas Hardy. CP-HardT

How it reminds me of that day! Photograph, The. Stephen Spender. CP-SpenS

How it should be in heaven I know, for I was there. Czeslaw Milosz. CP-MiloC; CP-MiloCN, tr. by Robert Hass

How It Started. Robert Graves. CP-GravR

How It Strikes a Contemporary. Robert Browning. CP-BroR1; SP-BroR

How It Was. Czeslaw Milosz. CP-MiloC; CP-MiloCN, tr. by Lillian Vallee

How It's Born in Us to Understand That There Are Two Sides to Every Question. Miller Williams. CP-WillM

How Jimsey O'Roon and Peter Stack, Coal Miners, Came to Be Put in the Ferbettville (Pa.) Jail Early One Saturday Night. Kenneth Patchen. CP-PatcK

How John Quit the Farm. James Whitcomb Riley. CP-RileJ

How Johnny Appleseed Walked Alone in the Jungles of Heaven. Nicholas Vachel Lindsay. CP-LindV

How joyfully it shows, the garland there. Michelangelo Buonarroti. CP-Miche, tr. by John Frederick Nims

How joyously the young sea-mew. Sea-Mew, The. Elizabeth Barrett Browning. CP-BroEB

How kind, how secret[ly], [now] the sun. Garden, The. Robert Penn Warren. CP-WarrR

How know I that it looms lovely that land I have never seen. That Where I Am, There Ye May Be Also. Christina Georgina Rossetti. CP-RosC2

How know it from a Summer's Day? Emily Dickinson. CP-DickE

How lang and dreary is the night. Robert Burns. CP-BurnR

How large that thrush looks on the bare thorn-tree! Winter. Dante Gabriel Rossetti. CW-RossD

How large was Alexander, father, Lawyer and Child. James Whitcomb Riley. CP-RileJ

How leaky are the borders of man-made states! Psalm: "How leaky are the borders of man-made states!" Wisława Szymborska. SP-SzymWM, tr. by Joanna Trzeciak

How Lewisburg, Pa., Escaped the Avenging Angel. Hayden Carruth. CP-CarHS

How Liberty, girl, can it be by thee nam'd? To the Beautiful Miss Eliza J———n, on Her Principles of Liberty and Equality. Robert Burns. CP-BurnR

How life and death in Thee. To Our Blessed Lord upon the Choice of His Sepulchre. Richard Crashaw. CP-CrasR

How light the heavy world becomes, when with transparent waters. Song of the Traveller, The. Thomas Merton. CP-MertT

How, like a blessing, falls the rain. Blessing of Rain, The. Jones Very. CP-VeryJ

How like a column, Radcliffe, left alone. To Sir John Radcliffe. Ben Jonson. CP-JonsB; SP-JonsB

How like a golden dreame you met and parted. To the Most Illustrious and Mighty Fredericke the Fift, Count Palantine of the Rhein. Thomas Campion. CP-CampT

How, like a virgin! Presence, dost thou rise. Mt. Shasta: A Painting, by H. O. Young. Jones Very. CP-VeryJ

How Lillies Came White. Robert Herrick. CP-HerrR

How little curious is man. Henry David Thoreau. CP-ThorH

How little does history manage to tell! Lesson in History. Robert Penn Warren. CP-WarrR

How little seen, and little understood. Ambition. George Meredith. CP-MerG2

How lonesome the Wind must feel Nights. Emily Dickinson. CP-DickE

How lonesome to be an Article! Emily Dickinson. SP-DickE

How Long Has This Been Going On? Oh, Quite Long. Ogden Nash. CP-NashO

How long have I been here? I can't recall. Bird in the Laurel's Song, The. Eleanor Wilner. SP-WilnE

How long have I meditated, O Prince. Meditation. Wallace Stevens. CP-StevWP

How long / Is a song? / O Lord / How long? Screen with the Face with the Voice, The. Ogden Nash. CP-NashO

How Long Is the Night? Stanley Kunitz. CP-KunSC

How long it takes to learn a simple thing. Endor. Howard Nemerov. CP-NemeH

How long I've waited, I can't count. Fanny Howe. SP-HoweF Fr. Lines Out to Silence.

How long, Perenna, wilt thou see. To Perenna. Robert Herrick. CP-HerrR

How long she waited for her executioner! Head of Medusa. Marya Alexandrovna Zaturenska. SP-ZatuM

How Long We Wait. Thomas Merton. CP-MertT

How long will ye round me be roaring. Address to the Ocean. William Wordsworth. CP-WorW1

How long will you remain? The midnight hour. Emily Jane Brontë. CP-BronE

How long would a rhinoceros last. Pablo Neruda. SP-NeruP Fr. Question Book.

How loud the storm sounds round the Hall! Emily Jane Brontë. CP-BronE

How Love came in, I do not know. Of Love. A Sonnet. Robert Herrick. CP-HerrR

How love whom we see not, and cannot see. Love Needing a Visible Object. Jones Very. CP-VeryJ

How lovely all that glitters. Four Songs the Night Nurse Sang. Robert Duncan. SP-DuncR

How lovely are her feet. Epilogue, Songs of the Spouses, Complaint of Love. John Logan. CP-LogaJ

How lovely are her feet. Bridegroom's Song, The. John Logan. CP-LogaJ Fr. Epilogue, Songs of the Spouses, Complaint of Love.

How lovely are thy dwellings fair! Bible, O.T. See How amiable are thy tabernacles, O Lord of hosts!

How lovely in the warm September days. Paradise. Jones Very. CP-VeryJ

How lovely the elder brother's. Brothers. Gerard Manley Hopkins. CP-HopkG

How low when angels fall their black descent. Promise in Disturbance, The. George Meredith. CP-MerG1

How Lucy Backslid. Paul Laurence Dunbar. CP-DunbP

How luscious is the dripping. Emily Dickinson. SP-DickE

How mad would he have to be to say, "He beheld." In a Bad Time. Wallace Stevens. CP-StevW; CP-StevWP

How many ancient sages. Han-shan. CP-ColdM, tr. by Red Pine

How many authors are my first! Christina Georgina Rossetti. CP-RosC3

'How Many Bards Gild the Lapses of Time!' John Keats. CP-KeatJ

How many between East and West. To Miss Creuzé. William Cowper. CP-CowpW

How many big events to shake the earth. Future, The. Ralph Waldo Emerson. CP-EmerR

How many bullets does it take. Death in Yorkville. Langston Hughes. CP-HughL; CP-HughL3

How many constants should there be? Native. Rae Armantrout. SP-ArmaA

How many cowgirls did the. Nothing That's Lovely Can My Love Escape. James Laughlin. CP-LaugJ

How many dawns, chill from his rippling rest. Bridge, The. Hart Crane. CP-CranH

How many falls have I spent on Cold Mountain. Han-shan. CP-ColdM, tr. by Red Pine

How many feet ran with sunlight, water, and air? Garden Wireless. Carl Sandburg. CP-SandC

How many Flowers fail in Wood. Emily Dickinson. CP-DickE

How many gifted pens have penned. Compliments of a Friend. Ogden Nash. CP-NashO

How many guys are sitting at their kitchen tables. Ray. Hayden Carruth. CP-CarHS

How many lives were torn apart. Philip Levine. SP-LeviP Fr. Poem with No Ending, A.

How many million stars there be. At Night. G. K. Chesterton. CP-ChesG

How many moments must(amazing each). E. E. Cummings. CP-CummE

How many more this morning are there dead of. Morning Sun. Howard Nemerov. CP-NemeH

How Many Nights. Galway Kinnell. SP-KinnGN

How many of my selves are dead? Dead Selves. James Whitcomb Riley. CP-RileJ

How many of the body's health complain. Soul-Sickness. Jones Very. CP-VeryJ

How many of those I knew. Elegiac Calculation. Wisława Szymborska. SP-SzymW, tr. by Stanislaw Barańczak and Clare Cavanagh

How many people have thought to keep a whatnot. Whatnot, The. John Logan. CP-LogaJ

How many schemes may die. Emily Dickinson. CP-DickE

How many Scientists have written. Shark, The. Ogden Nash. CP-NashO

How Many Seconds in a Minute? Christina Georgina Rossetti. CP-RosC2

How many secret nooks in copse or glen. Beds of Grainne and Diarmuid, The. Robert Graves. CP-GravR

How many strange secrets. Rainer Maria Rilke. CP-RilkFr, tr. by A. Poulin, Jr. Fr. Orchards.

How many things alike! The horseman and the plain. Mexico. Jorge Luis Borges. SP-BorgJ, tr. by Stephen Kessler

How many things there are in common life. Superfluities. Jones Very. CP-VeryJ

How many Tientai people. Han-shan. CP-ColdM, tr. by Red Pine

How many times already Love has said. Petrarch. CP-Petra, tr. by J. G. Nichols

How many times, Death. O All Down within the Pretty Meadow. Kenneth Patchen. CP-PatcK

How many times does a man wait for another man. To Die, to Be Torn. Yehuda Amichai. SP-AmicYL, tr. by Benjamin Harshav and Barbara Harshav

How many times has a verse come to my mind. Hunt for the Kingfisher, The. Jaroslav Seifert. SP-SeifJ, tr. by Ewald Osers

How many times have I come here. Looking at Pictures. Charles Wright. SP-

WrigC

How many times, like lotus lilies risen. Lotus and Frost. D. H. Lawrence. CP-LawrD

How many times that grim old phrase. Go Read Your Book! James Whitcomb Riley. CP-RileJ

How many times these low feet staggered. Emily Dickinson. CP-DickE

How many turn back toward dreams and magic, how many children. Thebaid. Robinson Jeffers. CP-JefR2

How many years we've circled round this date. Talk, The. Gregory Orr. SP-OrrG

How Marigolds Came Yellow. Robert Herrick. CP-HerrR

How Mary Grew. John Greenleaf Whittier. CP-WhitJ

How may a lover draw two bows at once. Circus Ring. Robert Graves. CP-GravR

How most unnatural-seeming, yet how proper. Sirocco at Deyá. Robert Graves. CP-GravR

How motionless they stand on moving stairs. Escalator. Adam Zagajewski. SP-ZagaA, tr. by Clare Cavanagh

How Much? Carl Sandburg. CP-SandC

How Much Can It Hurt? Philip Levine. SP-LeviP

How much death works. Eyes Fastened with Pins. Charles Simic. SP-SimiC; SP-SimiCE

How much do writers make? she said. For Semra, with Martial Vigor. Raymond Carver. CP-CarvR

How much do you love me, a million bushels? How Much? Carl Sandburg. CP-SandC

How much dust settles. Dust. Primo Levi. CP-LeviP, tr. by Ruth Feldman

How Much Earth. Philip Levine. SP-LeviP

How much, egregious *Moore*, are we. To Mr. John Moore, Author of the Celebrated Worm-Powder. Alexander Pope. CP-PopeA

How much havoc this woman spills. Mothers. Margaret Atwood. SP-AtwM2

How much I disapprove of it! Revolving Meditation. Stanley Kunitz. CP-KunSC

How much I envy you, gluttonous ground. Petrarch. CP-Petra, tr. by J. G. Nichols

How much less torment to breathe out my soul. Michelangelo Buonarroti. CP-Miche, tr. by John Frederick Nims

How Much Longer Will I Be Able to Inhabit the Divine Sepulcher. John Ashbery. SP-AshbJ

How much of Source escapes with thee. Emily Dickinson. CP-DickE

How much, Preventing God! how much I owe. Grace. Ralph Waldo Emerson. CP-EmerR

How much shall I love her? Echo-Elf Answers, The. Thomas Hardy. CP-HardT

How much the present moment means. Emily Dickinson. CP-DickE

How much there is within this rich abode. Miser, The. Jones Very. CP-VeryJ

How much there was had escaped him. Thief's Journal, The. Charles Tomlinson. CP-TomlC

How Much Time. Yehuda Amichai. SP-AmicYL, tr. by Benjamin Harshav and Barbara Harshav

How my city has grown! Air. Louis Zukofsky. CP-ZukLS

How, my dear Mary,—are you critic-bitten. Witch of Atlas, The. Percy Bysshe Shelley. CP-ShelP

How My Fever Left. James Wright. CP-WrigJ

How my own hills / and how Gloucester Harbor suddenly. Got Me Home, the Light Snow Gives the Air, Falling. Charles Olson. SP-OlsoC Fr. Maximus Poems, The.

How Naked, How Without a Wall. Edna St. Vincent Millay. CP-MillE

How near this suffering Summer. Emily Dickinson. SP-DickE

How News must feel when travelling. Emily Dickinson. CP-DickE

How nice it is to be superior! To Be Superior. D. H. Lawrence. CP-LawrD

How nice it is to slink the streets at night. Suburb. Stevie Smith. CP-SmitS

How noteless Men, and Pleiads, stand. Emily Dickinson. CP-DickE

How Now, O, Brightener. Wallace Stevens. CP-StevWP

How Now, Sirrah? Oh, Anyhow. Ogden Nash. CP-NashO

How Now We Talk. Laura Riding Jackson. CP-RidiL

How of his fate, the Pilgrims' soldier-guide. Camel-Driver, A. Robert Browning. CP-BroR2

How oft by passion, or by interest led. Looking Before and After. Jones Very. CP-VeryJ

How oft have I, my dear [or dere] and cruel[l] foe. Petrarch. CP-WyatT

How oft, with homesick hearts, their fancy flies. Longing. Jones Very. CP-VeryJ

How often did she make such quiet, one wonders. On Gari Melchers's *Writing* (1905) in the Los Angeles County Museum of Art. Helen Pinkerton. CP-PinkH

How often do I come to this retreat. Petrarch. CP-Petra, tr. by J. G. Nichols

How often have I carried our family word. Quoof. Paul Muldoon. CP-MuldP

How often have I said before. Loving True, Flying Blind. Robert Graves. CP-GravR

How often I have said. Life Encompassed. Donald Davie. CP-DaviDC

How often must I shake my bells and kiss. Death of Artists, The. Charles Baudelaire. CP-BaudC, tr. by Walter Martin

How often must we. Reverses. Maya Angelou. SP-AngeM

How often pass we by the works of God. Moss and Its Teachings, The. Jones Very. CP-VeryJ

How often, these hours, have I heard the monotonous crool of a dove. Dove, The. Walter De la Mare. CP-DeLaW

How often we forget all time, when lone. Stanzas: "How often we forget all time, when lone." Edgar Allan Poe. CP-PoeEd

How often we sit weeping—you. Voice from the Chorus, A. Aleksandr Aleksandrovich Blok. SP-BlokA, tr. by Peter France and Jon Stallworthy

How Old the World Is! Kenneth Patchen. CP-PatcK

How, on a dare, he would dive where the stream. Brave Child, The. Gregory Orr. SP-OrrG

How One Chose. Christina Georgina Rossetti. CP-RosC3

How painful I would find it. Jaroslav Seifert. SP-SeifJ, tr. by Ewald Osers

How Pansies or Hearts-Ease Came First. Robert Herrick. CP-HerrR

How parched, how marrow-dust dry. Thirst of Turtles, The. Thomas Lux. SP-LuxT

How patient man is in his time! The day. Clock in the Tower of the Church, The. Randall Jarrell. CP-JarrR

How pensively the Moon slides by tonight. Melancholy Moon, The. Charles Baudelaire. CP-BaudC, tr. by Walter Martin

How pitiful is her sleep. In Memory of Kathleen. Kenneth Patchen. CP-PatcK

How pleasant the banks of the clear-winding Devon. Banks of the Devon, The. Robert Burns. CP-BurnR

How pleasant to sit on the beach. Pretty Halcyon Days. Ogden Nash. CP-NashO

How pleased I am to submit to your example. Ardent Country. Rainer Maria Rilke. CP-RilkFr, tr. by A. Poulin, Jr.

How Poems Are Made: A Discredited View. Alice Walker. CP-WalkA

How Poetry Comes to Me. Gary Snyder. CP-SnydG

How precious Thought and Speech are! Emily Dickinson. SP-DickE

How Primroses Came Green. Robert Herrick. CP-HerrR

How profitless the relics that we cull. Roman Antiquities. William Wordsworth. CP-WorW2

How pure the hearts of lovers as they walk. Prothalamion. May Sarton. SP-SartM

How quick the change from joy to woe. Written after Leaving Her at New Burns. William Cowper. CP-CowpW

How quick upon the eye and mind. Standley's Grove. Jones Very. CP-VeryJ

How quickly the postures shift. On Your Own. Tess Gallagher. SP-GallT

How quiet / It is in this sick room. Sick Room. Langston Hughes. CP-HughL; CP-HughL1

How quiet sleep the silent waves! North River. Jones Very. CP-VeryJ

How quiet the diversion stands. Plural of "Jack-in-the-Box," The. John Ashbery. SP-AshbJ

How rare to be born a human being! Gary Snyder. CP-SnydG Fr. Myths and Texts.

How red the roses were. Places. Marya Alexandrovna Zaturenska. SP-ZatuM

How rich a man is, all desire to know. Gold, before Goodnesse. Robert Herrick. CP-HerrR

How rich and pleasing thou, my Julia, art. To Julia. Robert Herrick. CP-HerrR

How Rich That Forehead's Calm Expanse! William Wordsworth. CP-WorW2

How richly glows the water's breast. Lines Written While Sailing in a Boat at Evening. William Wordsworth. CP-WorW1

How Roses Came Red. Robert Herrick. CP-HerrR

How ruthless are the gentle. Emily Dickinson. CP-DickE

How sad the furniture in a lone man's room. Lone Man's Night, A. Yannis Ritsos. SP-RitsY, tr. by Kimon Friar

How Samson Bore Away the Gates of Gaza. Nicholas Vachel Lindsay. CP-LindV

How sayest thou we must be born again. Man's Need of a Spiritual Birth. Jones Very. CP-VeryJ

How seldom, friend, a good, great man inherits. Good Great Man, The. Samuel Taylor Coleridge. CP-ColeS

How / ses humble. E. E. Cummings. CP-CummE

How shall I know, unless I go. To the Not Impossible Him. Edna St. Vincent Millay. CP-MillE

How shall I know when the end of things is coming? Sign, A. Walter De la Mare. CP-DeLaW

How shall I light. Poem, The ("How shall I light"). George Oppen. CP-OppGN

How shall I wail, that wasn't meant for weeping? Convalescent. Dorothy Parker. CP-ParkD

How Shall I Woo Thee. Paul Laurence Dunbar. CP-DunbP

How Shall My Animal. Dylan Thomas. CP-ThomD

How shall she know the worship we would do her? Song for the Women, The. Rudyard Kipling. CP-KiplR

How shall the wine be drunk, or the woman known? Voice from under the Table, A. Richard Wilbur. CP-WilbR

How shall we tell. Chrysanthemum, The. William Carlos Williams. CP-WilW2

How shalt thou give account to God, O man. Man's Accountability. Jones Very.

CP-VeryJ

How she held up the horses' heads. Woman Driving, A. Thomas Hardy. CP-HardT

How she let her long hair down over her shoulders, making a love. O Best of All Nights, Return and Return Again. James Laughlin. CP-LaugJ

How She Went to Ireland. Thomas Hardy. CP-HardT

How she would have loved. Lament: "How she would have loved." Thomas Hardy. CP-HardT

How short their lives were then, but how crammed! Mary Coldwell. Jane Cooper. CP-CoopJ

How should I / Be so pleasant. Betrayal. Sir Thomas Wyatt. CP-WyatT

How should I not be glad to contemplate. Everything Is Going to Be All Right. Derek Mahon. CP-MahoD

How should I praise thee, Lord! how should my r[h]ymes. Temper (1), The. George Herbert. CP-HerbG

How should I your true love know. Old Song Ended, An. Dante Gabriel Rossetti. CW-RossD

How should the dreamer, on those slow. Clouds. Charles Tomlinson. CP-TomlC

How should the world be luckier if this house. Upon a House Shaken by the Land Agitation. William Butler Yeats. CP-YeatW

How sick I am! Marijuana Notation. Allen Ginsberg. CP-GinsA; SP-GinsA

How sick—to wait—in any place—but thine. Emily Dickinson. CP-DickE

How silent are the things of heaven. Kenneth Patchen. CP-PatcK

How simple was the relationship between the sexes in the days. It's about Time. Ogden Nash. CP-NashO

How simply / for another. Song: "How simply / for another." Robert Creeley. CP-CreeR

How sits this city, late most populous. Lamentations of Jeremy, for the Most Part According to Tremeullius, John Donne. CP-DonnJ

How Sleep the Brave. Walter De la Mare. CP-DeLaW

How slight a thing may set one's fancy drifting. Honey Dripping from the Comb. James Whitcomb Riley. CP-RileJ

How slow the Wind. Emily Dickinson. CP-DickE

How Slowly Time Lengthens. Stevie Smith. CP-SmitS

How small the furniture of bliss! Emily Dickinson. SP-DickE

How small the news was. Some Good News. Charles Olson. SP-OlsoC Fr. Maximus Poems, The.

How small the stars are tonight, bandannaed by moonlight. Star Turn 2. Charles Wright. SP-WrigCN

How smartly the quarters of the hour march by. Copying Architecture in an Old Minster. Thomas Hardy. CP-HardT

How smiled the land of France. To a Friend. John Greenleaf Whittier. CP-WhitJ

How smiles he at a generation ranked. Spirit of Shakespeare: Continued, The. George Meredith. CP-MerG1

How soft a Caterpillar steps—. Caterpillar. Emily Dickinson. CP-DickE

How soft this Prison is. Emily Dickinson. CP-DickE

How Solemn as One by One. Walt Whitman. CP-WhitW

How solemn! sweeping this dense black tide! Mississippi at Midnight, The. Walt Whitman. CP-WhitW

How soon doth man decay! Mortification. George Herbert. CP-HerbG

How Soon the Servant Sun. Dylan Thomas. CP-ThomD

How soon we come to road's end. Apologia Pro Vita Sua. Charles Wright. SP-WrigCN

How sowld I rewill me or quhat wyis. William Dunbar. CP-DunbW

How spacious must be the Heart. Emily Dickinson. SP-DickE

How speak to stone when stone and grief are mute to me? Verses After Which the Mourning Statue is Presumed to Speak. Robert Stock. SP-StocR

How Springs Came First. Robert Herrick. CP-HerrR

How steep the stairs within Kings' houses are. At Verona. Oscar Wilde. CP-WildO

How still, how happy! These [or Those] are words. Emily Jane Brontë. CP-BronE

How still, / How strangely still. Sea Calm. Langston Hughes. CP-HughL; CP-HughL1

How still the Bells in Steeples stand. Emily Dickinson. CP-DickE

How Still the Hawk. Charles Tomlinson. CP-TomlC; SP-TomlC

How strange!—but, first of all, the little fact. With Charles Avison. Robert Browning. CP-BroR2

How strange it is to awake. Three Poems for the New Year [2]. Charles Wright. SP-WrigC Fr. Three Poems for the New Year.

How strange it seems! These Hebrews in their graves. Jewish Cemetery at Newport, The. Henry Wadsworth Longfellow. SP-LongH

How strange it was to hear the furniture being moved around in the apartment upstairs! Magic of Numbers, The. Kenneth Koch. SP-KochK

How strange it would be if some women came forward and said. Sun-Women. D. H. Lawrence. CP-LawrD

How strange life is! How incomprehensible! As if I returned from it. After Traveling. Czeslaw Milosz. CP-MiloCN, tr. by Robert Hass

How strange that Nature does not knock. Emily Dickinson. SP-DickE

How strange the thought, that in the very light. City of God, The. Jones Very. CP-VeryJ

How strange to be gone in a minute? A man. Final Sonnet, A. Ted Berrigan. SP-BerrT Fr. Sonnets, The.

How strange to be gone in a minute / Bearden is dead Gallup is dead Margie is dead. Ted Berrigan. SP-BerrT Fr. Sonnets, The.

How strange to greet, this frosty morn. Flowers in Winter. John Greenleaf Whittier. CP-WhitJ

How strange to think of giving up all ambition! Watering the Horse. Robert Bly. SP-BlyR

How strangely crows the Gallic cock. New Era the Army of the Future the Egg of an Army, The. George Meredith. CP-MerG2

How strangely this world wags! Now what distressed. Petrarch. CP-Petra, tr. by J. G. Nichols

How stript and bare is every bush and tree. Soul's Preparation for Adversity, The. Jones Very. CP-VeryJ

How stupid the shoe felt in my hand! Shoe, The. William Corbett. SP-CorbW

How Sweet I Roamed [or Roam'd] from Field to Field. William Blake. CP-BlakW

(Song.) CP-BlakW

How sweet in sleep to pass the careless hours. Tibullus. CP-JohnS, tr. by Samuel Johnson Fr. Elegies.

How sweet is the shepherd's sweet life! Masque of Plenty, The. Rudyard Kipling. CP-KiplR

How sweet it is to find an asphodel. Wallace Stevens. CP-StevWP

How sweet it is to sit and read the tales. Fragment: Music and Sweet Poetry. Percy Bysshe Shelley. CP-ShelP

How sweet it is, when mother Fancy rocks. William Wordsworth. CP-WorW1; MW-WorW

How sweet on sunny afternoons. Pastorals. George Meredith. CP-MerG1

How sweet that he rose in the morning. Emily Dickinson. SP-DickE

How sweet the birds of Avondale. Avondale. Stevie Smith. CP-SmitS

How sweet the "Life that now is." Emily Dickinson. SP-DickE

How sweet the memory of a friend. Friendship. Jones Very. CP-VeryJ

How sweet the music sounded. Old Memory, An. Paul Laurence Dunbar. CP-DunbP

How sweet the silent backward tracings! Memories. Walt Whitman. CP-WhitW

How sweet the sound in the city an hour before sunrise. English Sparrows. Edna St. Vincent Millay. CP-MillE

How sweet the walk along the woody steep. At the Isle of Wight. 1793. William Wordsworth. CP-WorW1

How sweet, when crimson colours dart. Alcaeus to Sappho. William Wordsworth. CP-WorW1

How sweetly came the holy psalms. Memory of Burns, The. John Greenleaf Whittier. CP-WhitJ

How sweetly doth My Master sound! My Master! Odour, The. (2 Corinthians 2). George Herbert. CP-HerbG

How sweetly on the wood-girt town. Pentucket. John Greenleaf Whittier. CP-WhitJ

How sweetly shines through azure skies. Oscar of Alva. Lord Byron. CP-Byron

How swiftly they cease to be. To the Nieuport Scout. Geoffrey Hill. CP-HillG

How tall the buildings were as I began. Untilted. John Ashbery. SP-AshbJ

How that fact of. Robert Creeley. CP-CreeR

How the arrogant iris would wither and fade. Lyric. Dorothy Parker. CP-ParkD

How the Camel Got His Hump. Rudyard Kipling. Fr. Just-So Stories.

How the children have changed! Rapt, we stare. Home Movies. John Updike. CP-UpdiJ

How the days went. Now That I Am Forever with Child. Audre Lorde. SP-LordA

How the Earth turns round under the Sun I know. Ballad of the Enamord Image, The. Robert Duncan. SP-DuncR

How the elements solidify! Event. Sylvia Plath. CP-PlatS

How the Elephant Got His Hump. Miller Williams. CP-WillM

How the evenings are drawing in. Silence Full of Sleighbells. Jaroslav Seifert. SP-SeifJ, tr. by Ewald Osers

How the Fear Came. Rudyard Kipling. Fr. Second Jungle Book, The.

How the Friends Met. James Tate. SP-TateJ

How the Leopard Got His Spots. Rudyard Kipling. Fr. Just-So Stories.

How the Lover Perisheth in His Delight, As the Fly in the Fire. Petrarch. CP-WyatT, tr. by Sir Thomas Wyatt Fr. Sonnets to Laura.

How the night made her uncertain. Rainer Maria Rilke. CP-RilkFr, tr. by A. Poulin, Jr. Fr. Fragments.

How the old Mountains drip with Sunset. Emily Dickinson. CP-DickE

How the Real Bible Is Written. William Stafford. SP-StafWW

How the Rhinoceros Got His Skin. Rudyard Kipling. Fr. Just-So Stories.

How the River Ninfa Runs through the Ruined Town Beneath the Lime Quarry. Archibald MacLeish. CP-MacLA

How the Robin Came. John Greenleaf Whittier. CP-WhitJ

How the shrimp fisherman's daughter did a handstand against the schoolyard fence. Class. Jane Cooper. CP-CoopJ

How the Wall-Flower Came First, and Why So Called. Robert Herrick. CP-HerrR

How the Waters closed above Him. Emily Dickinson. CP-DickE

How the Whale Got his Throat. Rudyard Kipling. *Fr.* Just-So Stories.

How the Women Went from Dover. John Greenleaf Whittier. CP-WhitJ

How the young attempt / and are broken. Generation. Audre Lorde. SP-LordA

How the zebra died in the mouth. For Now. David Ignatow. SP-IgnaD

How these must be larded down with im-. Inscription for a Temple of Cloacina. Robert Stock. SP-StocR

How These Words Happened. William Stafford. SP-StafW; SP-StafWW

How they are provided for upon the earth, (appearing at intervals). Beginners. Walt Whitman. CP-WhitW

How They Brought the Good News from Ghent to Aix. Robert Browning. CP-BroR1; SP-BroR

How They Hunt the Quck Red Fox. Robert Stock. SP-StocR

How Thin a Blanket. Langston Hughes. CP-HughL; CP-HughL1

How thin and sharp is the moon tonight! Winter Moon. Langston Hughes. CP-HughL; CP-HughL1

How Things Change. Charles Olson. CP-OlsoC

How this tart fable instructs. Virgin in a Tree. Sylvia Plath. CP-PlatS

How this uncouth enchanted. E. E. Cummings. CP-CummE

How, through what tube, mechanism. Passage. A. R. Ammons. CP-AmmoA

How time reverses. For My Contemporaries. James Vincent Cunningham. CP-CunnJ

How times change, old friend. Old Worshipper, The. William Carlos Williams. CP-WilW1

How / tinily / of / squir(two be). E. E. Cummings. CP-CummE

How tired I am! I sink down all alone. Out-worn Sappho, An. James Whitcomb Riley. CP-RileJ

How Tit'rus you supine and careless laid. Translation of Virgil: Pastoral I. Virgil. CP-JohnS *Fr.* Pastorals.

How To. Hayden Carruth. CP-CarHS

How To. Dan Pagis. SP-PagiD, *tr. by* Stephen Mitchell

How to Be a Great Writer. Charles Bukowski. SP-BukC1

How to Be Married without a Spouse, or, Mr. Kipling, What Have You Done with Mr. Hauksbee? Ogden Nash. CP-NashO

How to Be Old. May Swenson. SP-SwenM

How to Be Successful & Happy Without Anybody Else Finding Out About It. Philip Whalen. SP-WhalP

How to Be Uncle Sam. John Updike. CP-UpdiJ

How to do it from the beginning. Let Me Tell You. Miller Williams. CP-WillM

How to Enter a Big City. Thomas Merton. CP-MertT

How to fit. Problem, The. William Carlos Williams. CP-WilW2

How to Get in the Best Magazines. Eleanor Wilner. SP-WilnE

How to Harry a Husband, or, Is That Accessory Really Necessary? Ogden Nash. CP-NashO

How to keep—is there ány any, is there none such, nowhere known. Leaden Echo and the Golden Echo, The. Gerard Manley Hopkins. CP-HopkG

How to Know Love from Deceit. William Blake. CP-BlakW

How to live. Clock. Robert Creeley. SP-CreeR

How to Live. What to Do. Wallace Stevens. CP-StevW; CP-StevWP

How to make you linger more, lovely summer. Rainer Maria Rilke. CP-RilkFr, *tr. by* A. Poulin, Jr. *Fr.* Fragments.

How to Play Championship Tennis. Paul Muldoon. CP-MuldP

How to prove. Yannis Ritsos. SP-RitsY *Fr.* Paper Poems 3.

How to Regain Your Soul. William Stafford. SP-StafW

How to remove oneself from oneself. Dying. Pablo Neruda. SP-NeruP

How to repair my shattered ranks. Emily Dickinson. SP-DickE

How to Sleep. Philip Larkin. CP-LarkP

How to speak with the dead. In Memoriam Thomas Hardy. Charles Tomlinson. CP-TomlC

How to Stop Smoking. Miller Williams. CP-WillM

How to Survive Nuclear War. Maxine W. Kumin. SP-KumiM

How to Tell a Love Story. Robert Penn Warren. CP-WarrR

How to Tell a Story (My Method) (Most of the Time). Grace Paley. CP-PalGC

How to tell it all? Referring to what chronicles? Six Lectures in Verse. Czeslaw Milosz. CP-MiloC; CP-MiloCN, *tr. by* Leonard Nathan

How To Tell One Country from Another. Margaret Atwood. SP-AtwM2

How to the invisible. Elementary Cosmogony. Charles Simic. SP-SimiC; SP-SimiCE

How ugly, those elderly specimens. Czeslaw Milosz. CP-MiloC; CP-MiloCN, *tr. by* Renata Gorczynski *and* Robert Hass

How unattainable life is, it only reveals. Fruit. Adam Zagajewski. SP-ZagaA, *tr. by* Renata Gorczynski, Benjamin Ivry *and* C. K. Williams

How unlike you. Plaster, The. W. S. Merwin. SP-MerwW

How vain and dull this common world must seem. Phèdre. Oscar Wilde. CP-

WildO

How vainly lovers marvel, all. Lover's Garden, A. Allen Ginsberg. CP-GinsA

How vainly men themselves amaze. Garden, The. Andrew Marvell. CP-MarvA

How vast is the chastisement of Beauty. Emily Dickinson. SP-DickE

How very hard it is to be. Easter-Day. Robert Browning. CP-BroR1

How very sweet indeed the prayers I'd say. Michelangelo Buonarroti. CP-Miche, *tr. by* John Frederick Nims

How Violets Came Blue. Robert Herrick. CP-HerrR

How warm the light! From the glowing bay. Happiness. Czeslaw Milosz. CP-MiloC; CP-MiloCN, *tr. by* Richard Lourie

How warm this woodland wild Recess! Recollections of Love. Samuel Taylor Coleridge. CP-ColeS

How was he first aware he would never walk again? Muriel Rukeyser. CP-RukeM

How was it possible, I a father. Lost Childhood. David Ignatow. SP-IgnaD

How was my spirit torn in twain. Lines on a Cricket Match. G. K. Chesterton. CP-ChesG

How was this I did not see. Faded Face, The. Thomas Hardy. CP-HardT

How Water Began to Play. Ted Hughes. SP-HughTN

How We Are Spared. W. S. Merwin. SP-MerwW

How We Danced. Anne Sexton. SP-SextA *Fr.* Death of the Fathers, The.

How We Did It. Muriel Rukeyser. CP-RukeM

How we happened to be both human. To a Loveless Lover. Laura Riding Jackson. CP-RidiL

How We Heard the Name. Alan Dugan. CP-DugaA

How We Learn. Josephine Jacobsen. CP-JacoJ

How we loved them. Bicycles and the Apex, The. George Oppen. CP-OppGN

How we made them sleep and purified them. Chant to Be Used in Processions around a Site with Furnaces. Thomas Merton. CP-MertT

How We May By Chance Pronounce the Unsuspected Residence of a Ghost. Miller Williams. CP-WillM

How welcome death would be. Welcome Death. D. H. Lawrence. CP-LawrD

How well contented in this private Grange. His Grange. Robert Herrick. CP-HerrR

How well, fair crown of your fair sex, might he. To Mary, Lady Wroth ("How well, fair crown of your fair sex, might he"). Ben Jonson. CP-JonsB; SP-JonsB

How well her name an *Army* doth present. Anagram. George Herbert. CP-HerbG

How well I have repressed the dream of death I had after the war when I was nine in Newark. Dream, The. C. K. Williams. SP-WillC

How well I knew Her not. Emily Dickinson. CP-DickE

How well I know, how clearly I see. EAMD. Philip Whalen. SP-WhalP

How well I know what I mean to do. By the Fire-Side. Robert Browning. CP-BroR1

How well this man unfolded to our view. J.F.B. Ambrose Bierce. SP-BierA

How well you served me above ground. Spirit's Song. Louise Bogan. CP-BogaL

How well, you, you resemble! You or You. Laura Riding Jackson. CP-RidiL

How we're carpet-making. His Carpets Flowered. Lorine Niedecker. CP-NiedL

How white how calm the hours are. This Man Was Your Brother. Kenneth Patchen. CP-PatcK

How white my father looked in the water. Sunset Water. W. S. Merwin. SP-MerwWF

How white the gulls. Lorine Niedecker. CP-NiedL

How will he hear the bell at school. Mutterings Over the Crib of a Deaf Child. James Wright. CP-WrigJ

How will you catch these clues at the moment of waking. Clues. Muriel Rukeyser. CP-RukeM

How Wisdom and Folly meet, mix and unite. Sketch. Inscribed to the Rt. Hon. Ch. J. Fox Esq. Robert Burns. CP-BurnR

How wise age is—. Robert Creeley. CP-CreeR

How wise am I to have instructed the butler to instruct the first. I Do, I Will, I Have. Ogden Nash. CP-NashO

How wisely Nature did decree. Eyes and Tears. Andrew Marvell. CP-MarvA

How wonderful is Death. Daemon of the World, The; A Fragment. Percy Bysshe Shelley. CP-ShelP

How wonderful, Tomasito! Celebration. Thomas McGrath. SP-McGrT

How would it be, then, if I showed you. Coyote's Song. William Dickey. SP-DickW

How would Willie like to go. Land of Thus-and-So, The. James Whitcomb Riley. CP-RileJ

How would you have her? En Promenade des Anglais. Clarence Major. SP-MajoC

How Yesterday Looked. Carl Sandburg. CP-SandC

How you buy a factory. Nucleus. A. R. Ammons. CP-AmmoA

How you shine from the inside. In the Wet. Marge Piercy. SP-PierM

How young and fresh I am tonight. Ben Jonson. CP-JonsB *Fr.* Mercury Vindicated.

How young and unassuming. Rogers Group, A. Robert Frost. CP-FrosR

Howard at Atlanta. John Greenleaf Whittier. CP-WhitJ

Howdy. Andrei Codrescu. SP-CodrA

Howdy, Honey, Howdy! Paul Laurence Dunbar. CP-DunbP

Howdy, Mister Hop-Toad! Glad to see you out! Mister Hop-Toad. James Whitcomb Riley. CP-RileJ

Howe'er the brightness may amaze. Ben Jonson. CP-JonsB *Fr.* News from the New World.

However artfully you transformed yourself. Ample Garden, The. Robert Graves. CP-GravR

However just and anxious I have been. Standing Ground, A. Wendell Berry. CP-BerrW

However legendary, / The stone is still a stone. Diamond Cutters, The. Adrienne Rich. CP-RicAE; SP-RicA1; SP-RicA2

However that principle of reason. Shapes and Intensities of This Man, This Confucius, The. Kenneth Patchen. CP-PatcK

However the image enters. Afterimages. Audre Lorde. SP-LordA

However you stem Nature. Emily Dickinson. SP-DickE

Howl. Allen Ginsberg. CP-GinsA; SP-GinsA

Howle not you Ghosts & furies while I sing. Orpheus and Pluto. Robert Herrick. CP-HerrR

Howling of Wolves, The. Ted Hughes. SP-HughTN

Howres for the Hours of Matines, The. Richard Crashaw. CP-CrasR

How's a man to write a sonnet, can you tell. Poet and the Baby, The. Paul Laurence Dunbar. CP-DunbP

Hrishikesa, destroyer of Titans, ogres and canailles. Thomas Merton. CP-MertT

Huayna Capac. Primo Levi. CP-LeviP, *tr. by* Ruth Feldman

Hubbub of the Hall of Languages, our Babel, The. Sonnet: "Hubbub of the Hall of Languages, our Babel, The." Hayden Carruth. CP-CarHS *Fr.* Sonnets.

Huckleberry Woman. W. S. Merwin. SP-MerwW

Hucksters haggle in the mart, The. For a War Memorial. G. K. Chesterton. CP-ChesG

Huddle of Need, A. John Berryman. CP-BerrJ

Hudor / HUDOR et Pax. Canto 83: "Hudor / HUDOR et Pax." Ezra Pound. SP-PounE *Fr.* Cantos.

Hudson Ferry. James Schuyler. CP-SchuJ

Hudson Letter, The. Derek Mahon. CP-MahoD

Hue and Cry of John Lewars, The. Robert Burns. CP-BurnR

Hue and Cry, The. James Shirley. *See* Love's Hue and Cry

Hueless Love, The. George Meredith. CP-MerG1

Hues of a Cloud. Yannis Ritsos. SP-RitsY, *tr. by* Kimon Friar *and* Kostas Myrsiades

Hug, The. Tess Gallagher. SP-GallT

Hug, The. Thom Gunn. CP-GunnT

Hug, The. Paul Muldoon. CP-MuldP

Huge are the canna in the dreams of. Anecdote of Canna. Wallace Stevens. CP-StevW; CP-StevWP

Huge dog, Broderick, and, The. Messengers, The. Robert Creeley. CP-CreeR

Huge Ear Rings. Charles Bukowski. SP-BukC1

Huge figure drags a body riddled, A. Generic Vision, 1991. Eleanor Wilner. SP-WilnE

Huge figure kneeling, The. Strange, Moving Lights of People Handle Holinesses Unknown, The. Kenneth Patchen. CP-PatcK

Huge frostbank of the North, The. November: Indian Summer. Hayden Carruth. CP-CarHS

Huge head tosses on the roof of the village, A. How Old the World Is! Kenneth Patchen. CP-PatcK

Huge old female on the drum, The. On the Drum. D. H. Lawrence. CP-LawrD

Huge purple elephant came out of my crayons, The. Present, The. John Logan. CP-LogaJ

Huge upon the hazy plain. Grazing Locomotives. Archibald MacLeish. CP-MacLA

Huge white poplar half fills the prison garden, A. Threads: Rosa Luxemburg from Prison. Jane Cooper. CP-CoopJ

Huge wound in my head began to heal, The. Wound, The. Thom Gunn. CP-GunnT

Hugerl, for a decade now. Glad. W. H. Auden. CP-AudeW *Fr.* Three Posthumous Poems.

Hugh Selwyn Mauberley (Life and Contacts). Ezra Pound. SP-PounE

Hugh Stuart Boyd [His Blindness]. Elizabeth Barrett Browning. CP-BroEB

Hugh Stuart Boyd [His Death, 1848]. Elizabeth Barrett Browning. CP-BroEB

Hugh Stuart Boyd [Legacies]. Elizabeth Barrett Browning. CP-BroEB

Hughie Graham. Robert Burns. CP-BurnR

Hughley Steeple. A. E. Housman. CP-HousA

Hugy spider stooping through the door, The. Some Oddities. Donald Hall. CP-HallD

Hui Tzu said to Chang Tzu. Useless, The. Chuang Tzu. CP-MertT

Hui Tzu said to Chuang: / I have a big tree. Useless Tree, The. Chuang Tzu. CP-MertT

Hui Tzu was Prime Minister of Liang. Owl and Phoenix. Chuang Tzu. CP-MertT

Huitzilopochtli Gives the Black Blade of Death. D. H. Lawrence. CP-LawrD

Huitzilopochtli's Watch. D. H. Lawrence. CP-LawrD

Hula-Hula. William Carlos Williams. CP-WilW1

Huleikat—The Third Poem about Dicky. Yehuda Amichai. SP-AmicY, *tr. by* Chana Bloch

Hulk grown monumental with refusal. Atlas Immobilized. Amy Clampitt. CP-ClamA

Hulk, The. W. S. Merwin. SP-MerwW

Hulk, three masted once, three stubbed now, A. Benefits of an Education, The. John Ciardi. CP-CiarJ

Hum Bom! Allen Ginsberg. CP-GinsA

Hum drum, sauce for a cony. Ben Jonson. CP-JonsB *Fr.* Christmas His Masque.

Hum of the bees in the pear-tree bloom, The. She Was a Good Little Wife. D. H. Lawrence. CP-LawrD

Human Abstract, The. William Blake. CP-BlakW *Fr.* Songs of Experience.

Human Affection. Stevie Smith. CP-SmitS

Human all key mog knee this pecks it loom in a moon the. Catullus. *See* Who scans the bright machinery of the skies

Human Arrangement. Wallace Stevens. CP-StevW; CP-StevWP

Human, Avian, Vegetable, Blood. Kenneth Rexroth. CP-RexrK

Human Being Is a Lonely Creature, The. Richard Eberhart. CP-EberR

Human being—walking. Denise Levertov. SP-LeveDL

Human bodies are different from each other. Yehuda Amichai. SP-AmicYL, *tr. by* Benjamin Harshav *and* Barbara Harshav

Human body is not the world, and yet it is, The. Body Language. Charles Wright. SP-WrigCN

Human Communion. Traces, The. Robert Duncan. SP-DuncR

Human condition is not pain only, The. Body. Czeslaw Milosz. CP-MiloCN, *tr. by* Robert Hass

Human Condition, The. Howard Nemerov. CP-NemeH

Human cunt, like the eye, dilates, The. Tryst. Olga Broumas. SP-BrouO

Human Face, The. D. H. Lawrence. CP-LawrD

Human face becoming locked insect face. Richard Hunt's "Arachne." Robert Earl Hayden. CP-HaydR

Human Fly, A. Czeslaw Milosz. CP-MiloCN, *tr. by* Robert Hass

Human Frailty. William Cowper. CP-CowpW

Human Honesty. Jelaluddin Rumi. SP-Rumi, *tr. by* Coleman Barks

Human Image, The. William Blake. CP-BlakW

Human is a thing, The. Fanny Howe. SP-HoweF *Fr.* Sea-Garden, The.

Human labour! the explosion which illuminates my abyss from time to time. Lightning. Arthur Rimbaud. CP-RimbA, *tr. by* Martin Sorrell

Human Life; on the Denial of Immortality. Samuel Taylor Coleridge. CP-ColeS

Human Life's Mystery. Elizabeth Barrett Browning. CP-BroEB

Human nature is a bird. Human Nature: or Marconi Memories. G. K. Chesterton. CP-ChesG

Human Nature: or Marconi Memories. G. K. Chesterton. CP-ChesG

Human reason is beautiful and invincible. Incantation. Czeslaw Milosz. CP-MiloC; CP-MiloCN; CP-PinsR, *tr. by* Robert Pinsky

Human Sacrifice, The. John Greenleaf Whittier. CP-WhitJ

Human Seasons, The. John Keats. CP-KeatJ

Human Song. Robert Creeley. CP-CreeR

Human soul was threshed out like maize in the endless, The. Heights of Macchu Picchu, III, The. Pablo Neruda. CP-WrigJ

Human spirits saw I on a day, The. Questioning Spirit, The. Arthur Hugh Clough. SP-ClouA

Human, step not into the Middle / of the Road! Roto: How the Bourgeoisie Dream. Andrei Codrescu. SP-CodrA

Human Things. Howard Nemerov. CP-NemeH

Human Touch Misunderstood, A. Andrei Codrescu. SP-CodrA

Human Tree, The. G. K. Chesterton. CP-ChesG

Human will is free, ultimately, to choose one of two things, The. Free Will. D. H. Lawrence. CP-LawrD

Humane Materialist at the Burning of a Heretic, A. Stevie Smith. CP-SmitS

Humanist, The. Richard Eberhart. CP-EberR

Humanist, The. Geoffrey Hill. CP-HillG

Humanist's Tragedy, The. Robinson Jeffers. CP-JefR1

Humanitad. Oscar Wilde. CP-WildO

Humanities Building, The. Karl Shapiro. SP-ShapK

Humanities Course. John Updike. CP-UpdiJ

Humanity. Walter De la Mare. CP-DeLaW

Humanity. William Wordsworth. CP-WorW2

Humanity, delighting to behold. French Army in Russia 1812–1813, The. William Wordsworth. CP-WorW2

Humanity i love you. E. E. Cummings. CP-CummE; SP-CummE

Humanity laments, and still will weep. Humanity Mourning for Her Children Slain in War. Jones Very. CP-VeryJ

Humanity Mourning for Her Children Slain in War. Jones Very. CP-VeryJ

Humanity Needs Pruning. D. H. Lawrence. CP-LawrD

Humanity ("O'er the night-black city gazing, broken by the blaze and spark"). G. K. Chesterton. CP-ChesG

Humanity ("Poet, pallid and perverse, A"). G. K. Chesterton. CP-ChesG

Humanly Speaking. Donald Davie. CP-DaviDC

Humble, The. Jones Very. CP-VeryJ

Humble-Bee, The. Ralph Waldo Emerson. CP-EmerR

Humble in victory, chivalrous in defeat. 1930's. Robert Lowell. SP-LoweR

Humble living does not diminish. It fills. Jelaluddin Rumi. SP-Rumi, *tr.* by Coleman Barks

Humble one(gifted with / illimitable joy). E. E. Cummings. CP-CummE

Humble Petition of Bruar Water to the Noble Duke of Athole, The. Robert Burns. CP-BurnR

Humble Petition of Poor Ben to the Best of Monarchs, Masters, Men, King Charles, The. Ben Jonson. CP-JonsB

Humble Petition of Rd Buller & W. Goodenough, The. Mrs. Austen. CP-AustJ

Humble Petition of Stella's Friends, The. Thomas Sheridan. CP-SherT

Humble Singer, A. James Whitcomb Riley. CP-RileJ

Humble we must be, if to Heaven we go. Humility. Robert Herrick. CP-HerrR

Humbly—but without caution in unbridled vigor of faith: acceptful. Court of First Appeal. Kenneth Patchen. CP-PatcK

Humbly I bow my shoulders, bear the yoke. Michelangelo Buonarroti. CP-Miche, *tr.* by John Frederick Nims

Humdrum. Carl Sandburg. CP-SandC

Humid air precipitates, The. Archibald MacLeish. CP-MacLA *Fr.* Happy Marriage, The.

Humiliation. D. H. Lawrence. CP-LawrD

Humility. Ambrose Bierce. SP-BierA

Humility. Robert Browning. CP-BroR2

Humility. George Herbert. CP-HerbG

Humility. Robert Herrick. CP-HerrR

Humility. D. H. Lawrence. CP-LawrD

Humility. Jones Very. CP-VeryJ

Humility Mongers. D. H. Lawrence. CP-LawrD

Humility the Mother of Charity. Samuel Taylor Coleridge. CP-ColeS

Humming a Tune for an Old Lady in West Virginia. James Wright. CP-WrigJ

Humming-Bird. D. H. Lawrence. CP-LawrD

Humming bird darning the trumpet vine, A. 11:02 A.M. The Bird Disappeared. John Ciardi. CP-CiarJ

Humming-Bird, The. Jones Very. CP-VeryJ

Humming Bird, The. Jones Very. CP-VeryJ

Humming Birds and Orioles, The. Emily Dickinson. SP-DickE

Hummingbird. Raymond Carver. CP-CarvR

Hummingbird, A. Emily Dickinson. CP-DickE

Hummingbird make yr mark he said and then something about. Thank God for Alleys. Charles Bukowski. SP-BukC2

Hummingbird Pauses at the Trumpet Vine. Mary Oliver. SP-OlivM

Hummingbird thrum . . . she's not there. Listening for Jane. William Corbett. SP-CorbW

Hummingbird Woman. Carl Sandburg. CP-SandC

Hummingbirds. Norman Dubie. CP-DubiN

Hummingbird's rainbow, The. Nothing Big. Yusef Komunyakaa. CP-KomuY

Humoresque. Edna St. Vincent Millay. CP-MillE

Humouresque. T. S. Eliot. SP-ElioT

Hump, The. Rudyard Kipling. CP-KiplR *Fr.* Just-So Stories.

Humpbacks. Mary Oliver. SP-OlivM

Humped, half-subterranean, The. Paumanok. Amy Clampitt. CP-ClamA

Humpty Dumpty. May Sarton. SP-SartM

Hun turned sculptor spoke, A. Sculptures in Hungary. Donald Davie. CP-DaviDC

Hunchback in the Park, The. Dylan Thomas. CP-ThomD

Hunchback in the park with halo of pigeons, The. Emblems of Exile. Thomas McGrath. SP-McGrT

Hunchback on the corner, with gum and shoelaces, The. Pursuit. Robert Penn Warren. CP-WarrR

Hunched in the dark beneath his mother's heart. Origin of Laughter, The. John Updike. CP-UpdiJ

Hunched over hard white bread. Lifer. Sam Hamill. SP-HamiS

Hunched over your pages. Russian Lesson. Theodore Weiss. SP-WeisT

Huncks ha's no money (he do's sweare, or say). Upon Huncks: Epigram. Robert Herrick. CP-HerrR

Hundred, a thousand to one; even so, A. In the Round Tower at Jhansi, June 8, 1857. Christina Georgina Rossetti. CP-RosC1

Hundred and forty thousand warriors of Mithridates Ponticus, A. Cappadocia. Joseph Brodsky. CP-BrodJ, *tr.* by Paul Graves

Hundred beached, A. On an Industrial Ruin. Andrei Codrescu. SP-CodrA

Hundred Collars, A. Robert Frost. CP-FrosR

Hundred-foot trees produced by Heaven. Han-shan. CP-ColdM, *tr.* by Red Pine

Hundred mares, all white! their manes, A. Mares of the Camargue, The. Frédéric Mistral. CP-MerG1, *tr.* by George Meredith *Fr.* Mirèio.

Hundred million cars running out of gasoline. Yes and It's Hopeless. Allen Ginsberg. CP-GinsA

Hundred Nights, A. Maxine W. Kumin. SP-KumiM

Hundred Times Nothing, A. Jaroslav Seifert. SP-SeifJ, *tr.* by Ewald Osers

Hundred-year-old servants, The. Devotions. Charles Simic. SP-SimiCE

Hundred years ago I made a book, A. Michael Palmer. SP-PalmM

Hundred years have passed, and he, The. October 21, 1905. George Meredith. CP-MerG2

Hundred years I slept beneath a thorn, A. Traveller, The. Kathleen Jessie Raine. SP-RainK

Hundred Years Since, A. Thomas Hardy. CP-HardT

Hundreds of birds are singing in the square. Marché aux Oiseaux. Richard Wilbur. CP-WilbR

Hundreds of flies. Elegy: "Hundreds of flies." Ai. SP-Ai

Hundreds of leaves inside our dreams also quiver, The. Olga Broumas. SP-BrouO *Fr.* Black Holes, Black Stockings.

Hung from a foot, I walk upon my head. Eight Riddles from Symphosius. Richard Wilbur. CP-WilbR

Hung there in the thermal. Vultures. Margaret Atwood. SP-AtwM2

Hung up there in the sky. Looking at the Stars. Richard Eberhart. CP-EberR

Hung Wu Vase, The. Robert Graves. CP-GravR

Hungarian Air. George Meredith. CP-MerG2

Hungarian Horse-Herd, The. Karl Beck. CP-MerG2

Hunger. Robert Creeley. CP-CreeR

Hunger. Countee Cullen. CP-CullC

Hunger. Robert Herrick. CP-HerrR

Hunger. Derek Mahon.

Hunger. Adrienne Rich. SP-RicA2

Hunger. William Stafford. SP-StafWW

Hunger and Cold. Carl Sandburg. CP-SandC

Hunger, and sultry heat, and nipping blast. French and the Spanish Guerrillas, The. William Wordsworth. CP-WorW1

Hunger long gone holds little heroic. Hunger and Cold. Carl Sandburg. CP-SandC

Hunger / of Mountains / spoke. Cries From Chiapas. Muriel Rukeyser. CP-RukeM

Hunger stalks the mess. Mess-room by Night. Arthur Rimbaud. CP-RimbA, *tr.* by Martin Sorrell

Hunger / with wonder. Alliance. Lorine Niedecker. CP-NiedL

Hungerfield. Robinson Jeffers. CP-JefR3

Hungry and Laughing Men. Carl Sandburg. CP-SandC

Hungry cancer will not let him rest, A. Thorn Forever in the Breast, A. Countee Cullen. CP-CullC

Hungry child, / I didn't make this world for you. God to Hungry Child. Langston Hughes. CP-HughL; CP-HughL1

Hungry for music with a desperate hunger. Written for a Musician. Nicholas Vachel Lindsay. CP-LindV

Hungry winter, this winter. To Hell with It. Frank O'Hara. SP-OharF

Hunkered down, nerve-numb. (Trauma) Storm. Gregory Orr. SP-OrrG

Hunt by Night, The. Derek Mahon. CP-MahoD

Hunt for the Kingfisher, The. Jaroslav Seifert. SP-SeifJ, *tr.* by Ewald Osers

Hunt in the Black Forest, A. Randall Jarrell. CP-JarrR

Hunt, Its Chant, A. Peter Blue Cloud. SP-BlueP

Hunted by friends who think that life is play. In the Immaculate Conception Church. Nicholas Vachel Lindsay. CP-LindV

Hunted City, The. Kenneth Patchen. CP-PatcK

Hunter. Federico García Lorca. CP-GarcF, *tr.* by Alan S. Trueblood *Fr.* Theories.

Hunter. Raymond Carver. CP-CarvR

Hunter Boy of Hazelwood. Hunter Boy, The. James Whitcomb Riley. CP-RileJ

Hunter, The. Walter De la Mare. CP-DeLaW

Hunter, The. Ogden Nash. CP-NashO

Hunter, The. Frank O'Hara. SP-OharF

Hunter, The. Kenneth Patchen. CP-PatcK

Hunter, The. William Carlos Williams. CP-WilW1

Hunter Boy, The. James Whitcomb Riley. CP-RileJ

Hunters. Yannis Ritsos. SP-RitsY, *tr.* by John Stathatos

Hunters are back / from beating the winter's face, The. Woman Thing, The. Audre Lorde. SP-LordA

Hunter's Moon—Eating the Bear. Mary Oliver. SP-OlivM

Hunters of Men, The. John Greenleaf Whittier. CP-WhitJ

Hunters' shack will do, The. Holding Out. Adrienne Rich. CP-RicAE; SP-RicA2

Hunting. Gary Snyder. *Fr.* Myths and Texts.

Hunting Civil War Relics at Nimblewill Creek. James Dickey. CP-DickJ

Hunting Dog, The. James Laughlin. CP-LaugJ

Hunting for the truly human. Humanist, The. Richard Eberhart. CP-EberR

Hunting Manual. Eleanor Wilner. SP-WilnE

Hunting of the Dragon, The. G. K. Chesterton. CP-ChesG

Hunting Pheasants in a Cornfield. Robert Bly. SP-BlyR

Hunting Season. W. H. Auden. CP-AudeW

Hunting season: / Once every year, the Deer catch human beings. They. Long Hair. Gary Snyder. CP-SnydG

Hunting Song. Samuel Taylor Coleridge. CP-ColeS; MW-ColeS *Fr.* Zapolya.

Hunting Song. Robert Burns. CP-BurnR

Hunting Song. Paul Laurence Dunbar. CP-DunbP

Hunting Song. Sir Walter Scott. SP-ScotW

Hunting Song, A. *Unknown, sometimes at. to* Thomas Sheridan. CP-SherT

Hunting-Song of the Seeonee Pack. Rudyard Kipling. CP-KiplR *Fr.* Jungle Book, The.

Hunting the Phoenix. Denise Levertov. SP-LeveDS

Huntingdonshire. Donald Davie. CP-DaviDC

Huntington sleeps in a house six feet long. Southern Pacific. Carl Sandburg. CP-SandC

Huntress. "H. D." CP-DoolH

Huntsman, What Quarry? Edna St. Vincent Millay. CP-MillE

Huon of Bordeaux. Robert Duncan. SP-DuncR

Hurdle of water, and O these waters are cold. Formal Elegy. John Berryman. CP-BerrJ

Hurly-burly: taking on whatever is about to get off, up the. Extremes and Moderations. A. R. Ammons. CP-AmmoA

Hurra, hurra, away they go. Sleigh Ride. Jones Very. CP-VeryJ

Hurrah for revolution and more cannon-shot! Great Day, The. William Butler Yeats. CP-YeatW

Hurrah for the next. On Hearing About the Death of Mitzi Mayfair. Miller Williams. CP-WillM

Hurrah! the seaward breezes. Fishermen, The. John Greenleaf Whittier. CP-WhitJ

Hurrahing in Harvest. Gerard Manley Hopkins. CP-HopkG

Hurray! Hurry! / Come through the keyhole. Starvation. Maya Angelou. SP-AngeM

Hurree Chunder Mookerjee, pride of Bow Bazar. What Happened. Rudyard Kipling. CP-KiplR

Hurricane. Archibald MacLeish. CP-MacLA

Hurricane, The. Hart Crane. CP-CranH

Hurricane, The. William Carlos Williams. CP-WilW2

Hurricane and Charlotte Mew, The. Amy Clampitt. CP-ClamA

Hurricane Andrew. Peter Blue Cloud. SP-BlueP

Hurricane at Sea, A. May Swenson. SP-SwenM

Hurricane Can Cast, A. Heather McHugh. SP-McHuH

Hurricane Season. Charles Simic. SP-SimiC; SP-SimiCE

Hurried Meeting, A. Thomas Hardy. CP-HardT

Hurried, running water—forgetful water. Rainer Maria Rilke. CP-RilkFr, *tr. by* A. Poulin, Jr. *Fr.* Orchards.

Hurry, Godfather death. Godfather Death. Anne Sexton. CP-SextA

Hurry! Hurry! Montalban: Near the Ancient Fort. Clarence Major. SP-MajoC

Hurry of bell-notes, A. Station Island. Seamus Heaney. SP-HeanSO

Hurry to bless the hands that play. Players Ask for a Blessing on the Psalteries and on Themselves, The. William Butler Yeats. CP-YeatW

Hurry Up Please It's Time. Anne Sexton. CP-SextA

Hurry, worry, unwary. Old Amusement Park. Marianne Craig Moore. CP-MoorM

Hurrying to catch my Comet. Naturally the Foundation Will Bear Your Expenses. Philip Larkin. CP-LarkP

Hurt. Langston Hughes. CP-HughL; CP-HughL1

Hurt Hawks. Robinson Jeffers. CP-JefR1

Hurt No Living Thing. Christina Georgina Rossetti. CP-RosC2

Hurt was the Nation with a mighty wound. Lincoln. Paul Laurence Dunbar. CP-DunbP

Hurucan. Derek Walcott. CP-WalcD

Husam, / tell about the visions of Daquqi. Visions of Daquqi, The. Jelaluddin Rumi. SP-Rumi, *tr. by* Coleman Barks

Husam demands that we begin Book 5. Muhammad and the Huge Eater. Jelaluddin Rumi. SP-Rumi, *tr. by* Coleman Barks

Husband. Wyatt Prunty. SP-PrunW

Husband. Miller Williams. CP-WillM

Husband and Wife. Christina Georgina Rossetti. CP-RosC3

Husband and wife had planned it for a long time, The. Trying. Miller Williams. CP-WillM

Husband has the nearest acres, The. Ralph Waldo Emerson. CP-EmerR

Husband, husband, cease your strife. English Song. Robert Burns. CP-BurnR

Husband is a man who two minutes after his head touches the, A. Trouble with Women Is Men, The. Ogden Nash. CP-NashO

Husband, / last night I dreamt. Where It Was at Back Then. Anne Sexton. CP-

SextA; SP-SextA

Husband of the widow care for her, The. Our Widowed Queen. Christina Georgina Rossetti. CP-RosC3

Husband stands at door of flat. How to Harry a Husband, or, Is That Accessory Really Necessary? Ogden Nash. CP-NashO

Husband was cutting his toenails, The. The wife was preparing his bags. Separation. Yannis Ritsos. SP-RitsY, *tr. by* Kimon Friar

Husbandman doth still go out to hire, The. "Agriculture the Source of Individual and of National Prosperity."—Anne Pratt. Jones Very. CP-VeryJ

Husbandman, The. Jones Very. CP-VeryJ

Husbands; A Hymn of Hate. Dorothy Parker. CP-ParkD

Husbands are things that wives have to get used to putting up with. What Almost Every Woman Knows Sooner or Later. Ogden Nash. CP-NashO

Husband's View, The. Thomas Hardy. CP-HardT

Hush, Here They Come. Ogden Nash. CP-NashO

Hush! hush! list, heart of mine, and hearken low! My Night. James Whitcomb Riley. CP-RileJ

Hush, hush! tread softly! hush, hush my dear. Song: "Hush, hush! tread softly! hush, hush my dear." John Keats. CP-KeatJ

Hush is over all the teeming lists, A. Frederick Douglass. Paul Laurence Dunbar. CP-DunbP

Hush) / noones / are coming. E. E. Cummings. CP-CummE

Hush then / why do you cry? Why Does She Weep? D. H. Lawrence. CP-LawrD

Hush, thrush! / Hush, missen-thrush, I listen. Elegy in April and September. Wilfred Owen. CP-OwenW

Hush! ye clamorous Cares! be mute! To the Rev. W. J. Hort. Samuel Taylor Coleridge. CP-ColeS

Hushaby baby, on a tree top. Broadcasting to the G.B.P. D. H. Lawrence. CP-LawrD

Hushaby, hushaby, dark one at my knee. Negro Mother's Lullaby, A. Countee Cullen. CP-CullC

Hush'd are the winds, and still the evening gloom. On the Death of a Young Lady. Lord Byron. CP-Byron

Hushed now the sweet consoling tongue. On a Fly-Leaf of Longfellow's Poems. John Greenleaf Whittier. CP-WhitJ

Hushed to the crushing cloud. Stéphane Mallarmé. CP-MallS, *tr. by* Henry Weinfield

Huskers, The. John Greenleaf Whittier. CP-WhitJ

Husks, rags and bones, waste paper, excrement. Hell. Robert Graves. CP-GravR

Hustings, The. Charles Olson. CP-OlsoC

Hustings, The. Charles Olson. CP-OlsoC

Hustle, The. Charles Bukowski. SP-BukC3

Hut. Robert Pinsky. CP-PinsR

Hut of the man alone, The. Donald Hall. CP-HallD

Hutch. Anne Sexton. CP-SextA

Huts at Esquimaux, The. Norman Dubie. CP-DubiN

Huzza! Hodgson, we are going. Lines to Mr Hodgson. Lord Byron. CP-Byron

Hyacinth. "H. D." CP-DoolH

Hyacinth. Louise Glück. SP-GlucL

Hyacinth. Edna St. Vincent Millay. CP-MillE

Hyacinth. Louis Zukofsky. CP-ZukLS

Hyacinth, The. Kathleen Jessie Raine. SP-RainK

Hyænas [*or* Hyenas]. The. Rudyard Kipling. CP-KiplR

Hyde Park at Night, before the War. D. H. Lawrence. CP-LawrD

Hydra, The. W. S. Merwin. SP-MerwW

Hydrangea / pink cheeked nods its head, The. Lesson, The. William Carlos Williams. CP-WilW2

Hydraulics. William Meredith. SP-MereW

Hyeah come Cæsar Higgins. Jealous. Paul Laurence Dunbar. CP-DunbP

Hyeah dat singin' in de medders. When Sam'l Sings. Paul Laurence Dunbar. CP-DunbP

Hyla Brook. Robert Frost. CP-FrosR

Hymb of Faith, A. James Whitcomb Riley. CP-RileJ

Hymen. "H. D." CP-DoolH

Hymen, O Hymen king. Cassandra. "H. D." CP-DoolH

Hymeneal Song, on the Nuptials of the Lady Ann Wentworth and the Lord Lovelace, An. Thomas Carew. CP-CareT

Hymeneal[1] Dialogue, An. Thomas Carew. CP-CareT

Hymn: "Amidst the pastures green." Jones Very. CP-VeryJ

Hymn: "As by the quickening breath of Spring." Jones Very. CP-VeryJ

Hymn: "At morn—at noon—at twilight dim." Edgar Allan Poe. CP-PoeEd

Hymn: "From out its large estate." Jones Very. CP-VeryJ

Hymn: "He loveth not! he knows not God!" Jones Very. CP-VeryJ

Hymn: "I know if I find you I will have to leave the earth." A. R. Ammons. CP-AmmoA

Hymn: "I well remember / A time when." Alice Walker. CP-WalkA

Hymn: "In the shock of mighty armies." Jones Very. CP-VeryJ

Hymn: "No hyacinthine imagination can express this clock of meat bleakly pining." Allen Ginsberg. CP-GinsA

Hymn: "Not tears alone for natural grief." Jones Very. CP-VeryJ

Hymn: "O Holy Father! just and true." John Greenleaf Whittier. CP-WhitJ

Hymn: "O li'l lamb out in de col'." Paul Laurence Dunbar. CP-DunbP

Hymn: "O the bitter shame and sorrow." Christina Georgina Rossetti. CP-RosC3

Hymn: "O Thou, whose presence went before." John Greenleaf Whittier. CP-WhitJ

Hymn: "Our voices with our hearts we lift." Jones Very. CP-VeryJ

Hymn: "Room, room, make room for the bouncing belly." Ben Jonson. CP-JonsB *Fr.* Pleasure Reconciled to Virtue.

Hymn: "There is no one between you and me." Czeslaw Milosz. CP-MiloC; CP-MiloCN

Hymn: "Thou who keepst us each together." Jones Very. CP-VeryJ

Hymn: "Though few, with noble purpose came." Jones Very. CP-VeryJ

Hymn: "To Love and to the lovely eyes." Charles Baudelaire. CP-BaudC, *tr. by* Walter Martin

Hymn: "To the God Who reigns on high." Christina Georgina Rossetti. CP-RosC3

Hymn: "When storms arise." Paul Laurence Dunbar. CP-DunbP

Hymn 2: "So when the year had come full round." A. R. Ammons. CP-AmmoA

Hymn 3: "As a fragile and lovely flower unfolds its gleaming." Marc Antony Flaminius. CP-PoEar, *tr. by* Ezra Pound

Hymn 3: "In the hour of extreme." A. R. Ammons. CP-AmmoA

Hymn 4: "I hold you responsible for." A. R. Ammons. CP-AmmoA

Hymn 5: "Assure us you side with order: throw." A. R. Ammons. CP-AmmoA

Hymn, A: "Lead gently, Lord, and slow." Paul Laurence Dunbar. CP-DunbP

Hymn, A: "O God of earth and altar." G. K. Chesterton. CP-ChesG

Hymn, The: "Come we shepheards whose blest Sight." Richard Crashaw. *See* In the Holy Nativity of Our Lord God

Hymn Among the Ruins. Octavio Paz. CP-WilW2, *tr. by* William Carlos Williams

Hymn before Action. Rudyard Kipling. CP-KiplR

Hymn before Sunrise, in the Vale of Chamouni. Samuel Taylor Coleridge. CP-ColeS; MW-ColeS

Hymn: Christ's Invitation in the Apocalypse. Jones Very. CP-VeryJ

Hymn Directed Somewhere Toward the Pantheon. Robert Stock. SP-StocR

Hymn Exultant. James Whitcomb Riley. CP-RileJ

Hymn for Christmas Day, A. Christina Georgina Rossetti. CP-RosC3

Hymn for Independence Day, A. So distant. Yehuda Amichai. SP-AmicYL, *tr. by* Benjamin Harshav *and* Barbara Harshav

Hymn for New Year's Day. Richard Crashaw. CP-CrasR

Hymn for the Celebration of Emancipation at Newburyport. John Greenleaf Whittier. CP-WhitJ

Hymn for the Church Militant, A. G. K. Chesterton. CP-ChesG

Hymn for the Dead. Sir Walter Scott. SP-ScotW *Fr.* Lay of the Last Minstrel, The.

Hymn for the Feast of Duns Scotus. Thomas Merton. CP-MertT

Hymn for the House of Worship at Georgetown. John Greenleaf Whittier. CP-WhitJ

Hymn for the Opening of Plymouth Church. John Greenleaf Whittier. CP-WhitJ

Hymn for the Opening of Thomas Starr King's House of Worship. John Greenleaf Whittier. CP-WhitJ

Hymn for the Sunday School at Olney. William Cowper. CP-CowpW

Hymn from a Watermelon Pavilion. Wallace Stevens. CP-StevW; CP-StevWP

Hymn: Home. Jones Very. CP-VeryJ

Hymn: I Am the Way. Jones Very. CP-VeryJ

Hymn in Adversity. James Vincent Cunningham. CP-CunnJ

Hymn in Drought. Jones Very. CP-VeryJ

Hymn in Praise of Neptune, A. Thomas Campion. CP-CampT
  (Hymne in Praise of Neptune, A.) CP-CampT

Hymn in the Assumption. Richard Crashaw. CP-CrasR

Hymn in the Glorious Epiphanie. Richard Crashaw. *See* In the Glorious Epiphanie of Our Lord God

Hymn: Nature's Sympathy with Freedom. Jones Very. CP-VeryJ

Hymn: Nevertheless, when the Son of Man cometh, shall he find faith on the earth? Luke 18:8. Jones Very. CP-VeryJ

Hymn of Breaking Strain. Rudyard Kipling. CP-KiplR

Hymn of Not Much Praise for New York City. Thomas Merton. CP-MertT

Hymn of Pan. Percy Bysshe Shelley. CP-ShelP

Hymn of Pan the Flower, The. Andrei Codrescu. SP-CodrA

Hymn of the Children. John Greenleaf Whittier. CP-WhitJ

Hymn of the Dunkers. John Greenleaf Whittier. CP-WhitJ

Hymn of the I.D.K., The. G. K. Chesterton. CP-ChesG

Hymn of the Poor, The. G. K. Chesterton. CP-ChesG

Hymn of the Triumphant Airman. Rudyard Kipling. CP-KiplR

Hymn on the Logos: The Light Still Shining in the Darkness. Jones Very. CP-VeryJ

Hymn: Our Country's Dead. Jones Very. CP-VeryJ

Hymn: Prayer for the Gift of the Holy Spirit. Jones Very. CP-VeryJ

Hymn: Reflections at the Close of the Year. Jones Very. CP-VeryJ

Hymn: So also will God, through Jesus, bring with him them who sleep. Jones Very. CP-VeryJ

Hymn Sung at Christmas by the Scholars of St. Helena's Island, S.C. John Greenleaf Whittier. CP-WhitJ

Hymn: Sung at the Celebration of the Fourth of July, in Salem, 1854. Jones Very. CP-VeryJ

Hymn[:] Sung at the Completion of the Concord Monument, April 19, 1836. Ralph Waldo Emerson. *See* Concord Hymn

Hymn: Sung at the Dedication of Plummer Hall, Salem, Oct. 6, 1857. Jones Very. CP-VeryJ

Hymn, Sung at the Dedication of the New Stone Church of the North Society in Salem June 22d, 1836. Jones Very. CP-VeryJ

Hymn: Sung at the Dedication of the Peabody Academy of Science, Aug. 18, 1869. Jones Very. CP-VeryJ

Hymn: Sung at the Eulogy on Abraham Lincoln June 1st 1865. Jones Very. CP-VeryJ

Hymn, Sung at the Fiftieth Anniversary of the Essex Historical Society, Salem. April 21, 1871. Jones Very. CP-VeryJ

Hymn Sung at the Second Church, Boston, at the Ordination of Rev. Chandler Robbins. Ralph Waldo Emerson. CP-EmerR

Hymn, Sung at the Thompson Jubilee, at Barre, Jan. 12, 1854. Jones Very. CP-VeryJ

Hymn: Sung at the Unitarian Festival, in Faneuil Hall, May 26th 1863. Jones Very. CP-VeryJ

Hymn: The Cause of Peace. Jones Very. CP-VeryJ

Hymn: The Dew. Jones Very. CP-VeryJ

Hymn: The Efficacy of a Mother's Prayer. Jones Very. CP-VeryJ

Hymn: The Forms of Nature, and the Unity of Their Origin. Jones Very. CP-VeryJ

Hymn: The Good Fight. Jones Very. CP-VeryJ

Hymn: The Light of Life. Jones Very. CP-VeryJ

Hymn: The New Life of Humanity. Jones Very. CP-VeryJ

Hymn: The Promise of the Spirit. Jones Very. CP-VeryJ

Hymn: The Rest of the Righteous. Jones Very. CP-VeryJ

Hymn: The Spirit Itself Maketh Intercession for Us. Jones Very. CP-VeryJ

Hymn: The Spiritual Body. Jones Very. CP-VeryJ

Hymn: The Way of the Righteous Easy. Jones Very. CP-VeryJ

Hymn: The Word Before All Things. Jones Very. CP-VeryJ

Hymn to a Masseuse. Yehuda Amichai. SP-AmicYL, *tr. by* Benjamin Harshav *and* Barbara Harshav

Hymn to a Trench Gun. Kenneth Patchen. CP-PatcK

Hymn to Adversity. Thomas Gray. CP-GrayT

Hymn to Artemis, the Destroyer. Marya Alexandrovna Zaturenska. SP-ZatuM

Hymn to Athena. *Unknown. Fr.* Homeric Hymns.

Hymn to Beauty. Charles Baudelaire. CP-BaudC, *tr. by* Walter Martin

Hymn to Castor and Pollux. *Unknown. Fr.* Homeric Hymns.

Hymn to Colour. George Meredith. CP-MerG1

Hymn to Commerce. Thomas Merton. CP-MertT
  (Dreaming Trader, The.) CP-MertT

Hymn[e] to Cynthia. Ben Jonson. CP-JonsB; SP-JonsB *Fr.* Cynthia's Revels.

Hymn to Earth the Mother of All. *Unknown. Fr.* Homeric Hymns.

Hymn to Eros. Denise Levertov. SP-LeveDP

Hymn[e] to God My God, In My Sickness[e], A. John Donne. CP-DonnJ; MW-DonnJ

Hymn to Humanity, An. Phillis Wheatley. CP-WheaP ·
  (Lo! for this dark terrestrial Dome.) CP-WheaP

Hymn to Ignorance. Thomas Gray. CP-GrayT

Hymn to Intellectual Beauty. Percy Bysshe Shelley. CP-ShelP

Hymn to Life. James Schuyler. CP-SchuJ

Hymn to Love Ended. William Carlos Williams. CP-WilW1

Hymn to Mercury [*or* Hermes]. *Unknown.* CP-ShelP, *tr. by* Percy Bysshe Shelley *Fr.* Homeric Hymns.

Hymn to Nothingness. D. H. Lawrence. CP-LawrD

Hymn to Physical Pain. Rudyard Kipling. CP-KiplR

Hymn to Priapus. D. H. Lawrence. CP-LawrD

Hymn to Proserpine. Charles Olson. CP-OlsoC

Hymn to Selene. *Unknown. Fr.* Homeric Hymns.

Hymn to Summer. Yehuda Amichai. SP-AmicYL, *tr. by* Benjamin Harshav *and* Barbara Harshav

Hymn to the Earth. Samuel Taylor Coleridge. CP-ColeS

Hymn to the Evening, An. Phillis Wheatley. CP-WheaP

Hymn to the Living. Jones Very. CP-VeryJ

Hymn to the Lovely Couple Varda and Schimmel. Yehuda Amichai. SP-AmicYL, *tr. by* Benjamin Harshav *and* Barbara Harshav

Hymn to the Morning, An. Phillis Wheatley. CP-WheaP

Hymn to the Name and Hono[u]r of the Admirable Saint[e] Teresa, A. Richard Crashaw. CP-CrasR

Hymn to the Saints, and to Marquis Hamilton, An. John Donne. CP-DonnJ; MW-DonnJ

Hymn to the Seal. Stevie Smith. CP-SmitS

Hymn to the Supreme Being. Christopher Smart. SP-SmarC

Hymn to the Virgin. Elizabeth Bishop. CP-BishE

Hymn to the Word. Charles Olson. CP-OlsoC

Hymn to These Newly Abbreviated States. John Updike. CP-UpdiJ (ZIP Code Ode.) CP-UpdiJ

Hymn: Waiting for Christ. Jones Very. CP-VeryJ

Hymn Written in the Year 1753, A. Annis Boudinot Stockton. CP-StocA

Hymne in Praise of Neptune, A. Thomas Campion. *See* Hymn in Praise of Neptune, A

Hymne of the Nativity, Sung by the Shepheards, A. Richard Crashaw. CP-CrasR

Hymn[e] on the Nativity [*or* Nativitie] of My Saviour, A. Ben Jonson. CP-JonsB

Hymn[e] to Bacchus, A. Robert Herrick. CP-HerrR

Hymne to Bacchus, A. Robert Herrick. CP-HerrR

Hymn[e] to Christ, at the Author's Last Going into Germany, A. John Donne. CP-DonnJ; MW-DonnJ

Hymne to Cupid, An. Robert Herrick. CP-HerrR

Hymn[e] to God the Father, A. John Donne. CP-DonnJ; MW-DonnJ

Hymn[e] to God the Father, A. Ben Jonson. CP-JonsB

Hymne to Juno, An. Robert Herrick. CP-HerrR

Hymne to Love, An. Robert Herrick. CP-HerrR

Hymne to Sir Clipseby Crew, A. Robert Herrick. CP-HerrR

Hymne to the Graces, A. Robert Herrick. CP-HerrR

Hymne, to the Lares, A. Robert Herrick. CP-HerrR

Hymne to the Muses, A. Robert Herrick. CP-HerrR

Hymne to the Muses, An. Robert Herrick. CP-HerrR

Hymne to Venus, and Cupid, A. Robert Herrick. CP-HerrR

Hymnos Aymnos. Arthur Hugh Clough. SP-ClouA

Hymns. Callimachus.
On Pallas Bathing, from a Hymn of Callimachus. CP-CowpW

Hymns and Spiritual Songs for the Fasts and Festivals of the Church of England. Christopher Smart. SP-SmarC

Hymns for the Amusement of Children. Christopher Smart. SP-SmarC

Hymns from the French of Lamartine. John Greenleaf Whittier. CP-WhitJ

Hymns of the Brahmo Somaj. John Greenleaf Whittier. CP-WhitJ

Hymns to Our Lady of Chartres. Geoffrey Hill. CP-HillG

Hymnus Ad Patrem Sinensis. Philip Whalen. SP-WhalP

Hyperbole! can you not rise. Prose. Stéphane Mallarmé. CP-MallS, *tr.* by Henry Weinfield

Hyperion. John Keats. CP-KeatJ

Hyphens. Donald Davie. CP-DaviDC

Hyphens. Charles Tomlinson. CP-TomlC

Hypnos on Ida. Homer. CP-MerG1 *Fr.* Iliad, The.

Hypochondriac Logic. Donald Davie. CP-DaviDC

Hypochondriacs / Spend the winter at the bottom of Florida and the summer on top of the Adirondriacs. Oh to Be Odd! Ogden Nash. CP-NashO

Hypocrite Auteur. Archibald MacLeish. CP-MacLA

Hypocrite Swift. Louise Bogan. CP-BogaL

Hypocrite women, how seldom we speak. Denise Levertov. SP-LeveDP; SP-LeveDS

Hypothesis of resurrection, The. After Enduring. Czeslaw Milosz. CP-MiloCN, *tr.* by Robert Hass

Hysteria. T. S. Eliot. CP-ElioT

I

I. Federico García Lorca. CP-GarcF, *tr.* by Jerome Rothenberg *Fr.* Narcissus.

I. Jorge Luis Borges. SP-BorgJ, *tr.* by Alastair Reid

I. Robert Creeley. CP-CreeR

I a Dirge will pen for thee. To Perenna. Robert Herrick. CP-HerrR

I, a princess, king-descended, decked with jewels, gilded, drest. Royal Princess, A. Christina Georgina Rossetti. CP-RosC1

I, a writer, at one time hipped on. Raindrops on a Briar. William Carlos Williams. CP-WilW2

I abdicate my daily self that bled. Vita Nuova. Stanley Kunitz. CP-KunSC

I abhor the slimy [*or* slimie] kiss [*or* kisse]. Kisses Loathesome. Robert Herrick. CP-HerrR

I abide and abide and better abide. Sir Thomas Wyatt. CP-WyatT

I accuse. Judgments. William Stafford. SP-StafWW

I admire the Bishops of the Church of England. Bishops of the Church of England, The. Stevie Smith. CP-SmitS

I admire the roughness and brutality of the sea. Recognition. Richard Eberhart.

CP-EberR

I admire the solitary power. Sacred Place. Rainer Maria Rilke. CP-RilkFr, *tr.* by A. Poulin, Jr.

I admit the briar. First Confession, A. William Butler Yeats. CP-YeatW

I adore a sleepwalker with Héloïe's soul. Ite, Missa Est. "Rubén Dario." SP-DariR, *tr.* by Alberto Acereda *and* Will Derusha

I adore you. I love you. Kannon. Sam Hamill. SP-HamiS

I adored her and she giggled and I adored her. On the Poet as a Damned Poor Thing. John Ciardi. CP-CiarJ

I adorned. Gifts of Love. Yehuda Amichai. SP-AmicYL, *tr.* by Benjamin Harshav *and* Barbara Harshav

I advance and extend my hand. In the Ballet. James Laughlin. CP-LaugJ

I advise the monks I meet. Shih-te. CP-ColdM, *tr.* by Red Pine

I advise you, Eurydice, not to follow me. Orpheus. James Laughlin. CP-LaugJ

I advocate a semi-revolution. Semi-Revolution, A. Robert Frost. CP-FrosR

I agree that something. Excerpt from an Argument with Enthusiasts, Concerning Inspiration. Heather McHugh. SP-McHuH

I ain't a-goin' to cry no more, no more! Almost beyond Endurance. James Whitcomb Riley. CP-RileJ

I ain't gonna mistreat ma. Evil Woman. Langston Hughes. CP-HughL; CP-HughL1

I ain't got no body. Amherst to Easthampton. James Tate. SP-TateJ

I ain't, ner don't p'tend to be. My Philosofy. James Whitcomb Riley. CP-RileJ

I all-creation sing my song of praise. "All Thy Works Praise Thee, O Lord": A Processional of Creation. Christina Georgina Rossetti. CP-RosC2

I almost love you. I've wanted to be you. Gerda in the Aerie. Marilyn Hacker. SP-HackM

I Almost Remember. Maya Angelou. SP-AngeM

I almost squashed a tarantula on the road. Early Autumn. Arthur Sze. SP-SzeA

I almost trust myself to know. Amnesia. Adrienne Rich. SP-RicA2

I alone, solemn land. Three, The. James Dickey. CP-DickJ

I, Alphonso, live and learn. Alphonso of Castile. Ralph Waldo Emerson. CP-EmerR

I always admire a beautiful woman. Rehearsal, The. Stevie Smith. CP-SmitS

I always felt like a bird blown through the world. Stripping and Putting On. May Swenson. SP-SwenM

I always have many flowers. Heatstroke. James Tate. SP-TateJ

I always ran Home to Awe when a child. Emily Dickinson. SP-DickE

I always remember your beautiful flowers. Pad, Pad. Stevie Smith. CP-SmitS

I always return to this place. Kenneth Patchen. CP-PatcK

I always saw, I always said. Red Dress, The. Dorothy Parker. CP-ParkD

I always say I won't go back to the mountains. Sourdough Mountain Lookout. Philip Whalen. SP-WhalP

I Always Say There's No Place Like New York in the Summer, or, That Cottage Small by a Waterfall Was Snapped Up Last February. Ogden Nash. CP-NashO

I always take my judgement from a Fool. Cromek Speaks. William Blake. CP-BlakW

I always think of a coffin's quiet. Poem for a Poet, A. Audre Lorde. SP-LordA

I always thought if I could just. Place Where Things Got. Heather McHugh. SP-McHuH

I always thought she was white, I thought she was an Indian. Clementene. Jane Cooper. CP-CoopJ

I always wanted to ball. Dead Now. Charles Bukowski. SP-BukC1

I always was, in my soul and in my head. Spaniard. "Rubén Dario." SP-DariR, *tr.* by Alberto Acereda *and* Will Derusha

I Am. Jorge Luis Borges. SP-BorgJ, *tr.* by Alastair Reid

I Am. G. K. Chesterton. CP-ChesG

I Am. John Clare. SP-ClarJ

I Am. David Ignatow. CP-IgnaD

I Am. Stevie Smith. CP-SmitS

I am a barber, and I'd have you know. Barber, A. Sir John Suckling. CP-SuckJ

I am a beggar always. E. E. Cummings. CP-CummE

I am a black Pierrot. Black Pierrot, A. Langston Hughes. CP-HughL; CP-HughL1

I am a child who receives First Communion in Wilno and afterwards drinks cocoa served by zealous Catholic ladies. Capri. Czeslaw Milosz. CP-MiloCN, *tr.* by Robert Hass

I am a copper wire slung in the air. Under a Telephone Pole. Carl Sandburg. CP-SandC

I am a cross and the idea. To My Heart. Andrei Codrescu. SP-CodrA

I am a democrat in so far as I love the free sun in men. Democracy. D. H. Lawrence. CP-LawrD

I am a displaced person. My Heart Has Reopened to You. Alice Walker. CP-WalkA

I am a frog. Frog Prince, The. Stevie Smith. CP-SmitS

I am a gentleman in a dustcoat trying. Piazza Piece. John Crowe Ransom. SP-RansJ

I Am a Girl Who Loves to Shoot. Stevie Smith. CP-SmitS

I am a goddess of the ambrosial courts. Artemis Prologizes. Robert Browning. CP-BroR1

I am a grave poetic hen. Statement of Being. Ezra Pound. CP-PoEar

I am a hoodlum, you are a hoodlum, we and all of us are a world of. Hoodlums. Carl Sandburg. CP-SandC

I am a hunter of sounds and a collector. Song of the Nightingale, The. Jaroslav Seifert. SP-SeifJ, tr. by Ewald Osers

I am a keeper of the law. Verses: "I am a keeper of the law." Robert Burns. CP-BurnR

I am a King, / Or an Emperor rather. Christina Georgina Rossetti. CP-RosC2

I Am A Light You Could Read By. Marge Piercy. SP-PierM

I am a little church(no great cathedral). E. E. Cummings. CP-CummE

I am a lonely Troll after my gala night. Troll's Courtship. Louis MacNeice. CP-MacNL

I am a man and do not know why I was born. I can tell you the facts. Wait. David Ignatow. SP-IgnaD

I am a man of face like another is "a man." Face Portrait. Andrei Codrescu. SP-CodrA

I am a man of war and might. Soldier, A. Sir John Suckling. CP-SuckJ

I am a man with no ambitions. Advantages of Learning, The. Kenneth Rexroth. CP-RexrK

I am a man's head hunched in the road. Jasper Texas 1998. Lucille Clifton. SP-ClifL

I am a miner. The light burns blue. Nick and the Candlestick. Sylvia Plath. CP-PlatS

I am a monarch of all I survey. Alexander Selkirk. William Cowper. CP-CowpW

I am a moody woman. Moody. Alice Walker. CP-WalkA

I Am a Most Fleshly Man. Robert Duncan. SP-DuncR

I am a Negro. Negro. Langston Hughes. CP-HughL

I am a painter. Jingle on the Times, A. Thomas Hardy. CP-HardT

I am a panther shut up and bellowing in. Report Upon the Consumption of Myself, A. Charles Bukowski. SP-BukC2

I am a parcel of vain strivings tied. Sic Vita. Henry David Thoreau. CP-ThorH

I am a peaceful mastodon at rest! clump! clump! Night of a Faun. Andrei Codrescu. SP-CodrA

I am a poor prophet. Like a poor boy with only. Yehuda Amichai. SP-AmicYL, tr. by Benjamin Harshav and Barbara Harshav

I Am a Preposterous Beetle. James Laughlin. CP-LaugJ

I am a profound man sitting in a park. Redemption. Richard Eberhart. CP-EberR

I am a sewer. Gargoyle's Song for the Warming Trend. Alan Dugan. CP-DugaA

I am a shepherd of those sheep. Nuit Blanche. Edna St. Vincent Millay. CP-MillE

I Am a Sioux Brave, He Said in Minneapolis. James Wright. CP-WrigJ

I am a spirit now. After that death. Revenant, The. William Meredith. SP-MereW

I am a star dwelling on high. Song of the Star, The. Christina Georgina Rossetti. CP-RosC3

I am a tarsier and a tarsier's son. Tarsier. Wisława Szymborska. SP-SzymW, tr. by Stanisław Barańczak and Clare Cavanagh

I am a trombone. By the chinaberry tree. New Orleans. Hayden Carruth. CP-CarHS

I Am a Victim of Telephone. Allen Ginsberg. CP-GinsA; SP-GinsA

I am a vision looking for a way out of. Saturnian Dilemma. Andrei Codrescu. SP-CodrA

I am a woman lying on a leaf. Deep Analysis. Philip Larkin. CP-LarkP

I am a writer. From a Play. William Carlos Williams. CP-WilW2

I am about to close the refrigerator after removing a package of meat. Account in the Present Tense of How It all Happened, An. David Ignatow. SP-IgnaD

I am afraid. Wedding Day. Seamus Heaney. SP-HeanSO

I am afraid for you a little, for your sense of shame; I feel you are accustomed to ordinary evil. Bishop Tutu's Visit to the White House: 1984. C. K. Williams. SP-WillC

I am afraid / of dead leaves. Nocturne: "I am afraid / of dead leaves." Federico García Lorca. CP-GarcF, tr. by Catherine Brown

I am afraid of nature. Fear. Grace Paley. CP-PalGC

I am afraid these verses will not please you, but. Percy Bysshe Shelley. See If I esteemed you less, Envy would kill

I am afraid to own a Body. Emily Dickinson. CP-DickE

I am alive at night. Moon Song, Woman Song. Anne Sexton. CP-SextA

I am alive—I guess. Emily Dickinson. CP-DickE

I am all bent to glean the golden ore. Madrigal: To his Lady Selvaggia Vergiolesi; likening his Love to a search for Gold. Cino da Pistoia. CW-RossD, tr. by Dante Gabriel Rossetti

I am alone here in my own mind. January 24th. Anne Sexton. CP-SextA; SP-SextA

I am alone in my banishment. Song: "Forever." George Meredith. CP-MerG2

I am alone. Sad is my solitude. Ralph Waldo Emerson. CP-EmerR

I am alone tonight. Report of Health. John Updike. CP-UpdiJ

I am already a singing flower. Singing Flower, The. "Shu Ting." CP-KizeC, tr.

by Carolyn Kizer and Y. H. Zhao

I am already quite scarce. For years. Last Ones, The. Dan Pagis. SP-PagiD, tr. by Stephen Mitchell

I am an ancient reluctant conscript. Old Timers. Carl Sandburg. CP-SandC

I am an architect in Vienna. Michael Palmer. SP-PalmM

I Am an Atheist Who Says His Prayers. Karl Shapiro. SP-ShapK

I am an ephemeral and none too discontented citizen of a metropolis thought to be modern. City. Arthur Rimbaud. CP-RimbA, tr. by Martin Sorrell

I am an exile from my home; heavily. Ralph Waldo Emerson. CP-EmerR

I am an inconvenient woman. Nuisance, The. Marge Piercy. SP-PierM

I am an indicated other. Laura Riding Jackson. CP-RidiL

I am an old and solitary man. Aeschylus' Soliloquy. Robert Browning. CP-BroR2

I am approaching. Past dry. Loot. Thom Gunn. CP-GunnT

I am as a spirit who has dwelt. Fragment: Wedded Souls. Percy Bysshe Shelley. CP-ShelP

I am as brisk. Three Undated Fragments. John Keats. CP-KeatJ

I am as I am and so will I be. Sir Thomas Wyatt. CP-WyatT

I am as yet / a storm of zero force. Wind From Variable Directions. Dan Pagis. SP-PagiD, tr. by Stephen Mitchell

I am ashamed—I hide. Emily Dickinson. CP-DickE

I am asked why I do not. In the Glass of Fashion. Howard Nemerov. CP-NemeH

I Am Aware. James Laughlin. CP-LaugJ

I am becalmed in a deep sea. Look! Stevie Smith. CP-SmitS

I am become a stranger to my dreams. Dream. Kathleen Jessie Raine. SP-RainK

I Am Big and Fat. Yehuda Amichai. SP-AmicYL, tr. by Benjamin Harshav and Barbara Harshav

I am blind. Blind. Langston Hughes. CP-HughL; CP-HughL2

I am blind, you out there. That is a curse. Blind Man's Song, The. Randall Jarrell. CP-JarrR

I am bone lonely. Idea of the Good, The. James Wright. CP-WrigJ

I am born at home. Birthday Poem. Maxine W. Kumin. SP-KumiM

I am bound, I am bound, for a distant shore. Henry David Thoreau. CP-ThorH

I am bringing a little Granite Book. Emily Dickinson. SP-DickE

I am brother to the tree. David Ignatow. SP-IgnaD

"I am but clay," the sinner plead. Distinction. Paul Laurence Dunbar. CP-DunbP

I am buying presents for everyone. Night before Christmas, The. Howard Nemerov. CP-NemeH

I am careful in my work and love it. Painted. Constantine P. Cavafy. CP-CavaC, tr. by Theoharis Constantine Theoharis

I Am Cassander Come Down From the Sky. Samuel Johnson. CP-JohnS

(Translation from a Pantomime Version of Benserade's Ballet de Cassandre.) CP-JohnS

I am caught in the body of a fish. Thinking. David Ignatow. SP-IgnaD

I am commited. Commitment, A. Richard Eberhart. CP-EberR

I am confirm'd a woman can. Verses: "I am confirm'd a woman can." Sir John Suckling. CP-SuckJ

I am dancing on the silver beach. Drunken Charlie. Robinson Jeffers. CP-JefR3

I am dazed and bewildered with living. Ballad from April, A. James Whitcomb Riley. CP-RileJ

I am dead, to be sure. Small Fig Tree, A. Donald Hall. CP-HallD

I am divorcing Daddy—Dybbuk! Dybbuk! Divorce, Thy Name Is Woman. Anne Sexton. CP-SextA; SP-SextA

I am done with apologies. If contrariness is my. Contrariness of the Mad Farmer, The. Wendell Berry. CP-BerrW

I Am Dreaming of a White Christmas: The Natural History of a Vision. Robert Penn Warren. CP-WarrR

I am dressed in my big shoes and wrinkled socks. X-Ray Waiting Room in the Hospital, The. Randall Jarrell. CP-JarrR

I am driving down Wilton Avenue. Sex. Charles Bukowski. SP-BukC1

I am driving; it is dusk; Minnesota. Driving toward the Lac Qui Parle River. Robert Bly. SP-BlyR

I am drunk with the honey wine. Fragment: Wine of the Fairies. Percy Bysshe Shelley. CP-ShelP

I am dust particles in sunlight. Say I Am You. Jelaluddin Rumi. SP-Rumi, tr. by Coleman Barks

I am dying Egypt dying. Death of Mr. Mounsel. Stevie Smith. CP-SmitS

I am exceedingly green: chillgreen. Twelve Faces of the Emerald. Dan Pagis. SP-PagiD, tr. by Stephen Mitchell

I am Fake Saint. Blame the Thought, Cling to the Bummer. Allen Ginsberg. CP-GinsA

I am falling into the abyss. Night at the Opera, A. James Laughlin. CP-LaugJ

I am fifty-two years old. Untitled: "I am fifty-two years old." Kenneth Rexroth. CP-RexrK

I am filled with you. Jelaluddin Rumi. SP-Rumi, tr. by Coleman Barks

I am five. Venus's-flytraps. Yusef Komunyakaa. CP-KomuY

I am five. Son to Father to Son. A. K. Ramanujan. CP-RamaA

I am fond of the Swallow—I learn from her flight. Swallow, The. Jeanne Marie

Bouvier de la Motte- Guyon. CP-CowpW

I am for sleeping and forgetting. Requiescam. Countee Cullen. CP-CullC

I am forgetting Louie the buoyant. Louie. Thomas Hardy. CP-HardT

I am Freed. César Vallejo. CP-WrigJ

I am frightened by the sorrow. In the Face of Hatred. James Wright. CP-WrigJ

I am frightened Master, quivering with fear. Misericordia. William Carlos Williams. CP-WilW1

I Am Full of Previous Experience. Ogden Nash. CP-NashO

I am Gilgamesh. Tomorrow. Charles Olson. CP-OlsoC

I am glad God saw Death. Junk Man, The. Carl Sandburg. CP-SandC

I am glad, I think, my happy mother died. Memory of England. Edna St. Vincent Millay. CP-MillE

I am glad you are in the open Air. Emily Dickinson. SP-DickE

I am God— / Without one friend. God. Langston Hughes. CP-HughL; CP-HughL1

I am going backward in a home movie. Deaths of the Uncles, The. Maxine W. Kumin. SP-KumiM

I am going on a long trip. Prologue: "I am going on a long trip." Federico García Lorca. CP-GarcF, tr. by Jerome Rothenberg Fr. In the Forest of the Lunar Grapefruits.

I am going on with my beautiful procession. In Your Body All Bodies Lie. Kenneth Patchen. CP-PatcK

I am going to have my dinner. Song: "I am going to have my dinner." Jane Austen. CP-AustJ

I am going to leave a child in an empty room. Future, The. David Ignatow. SP-IgnaD

I am going to rip myself down the middle into two pieces. Halves. C. K. Williams. CP-WillC; SP-WillC

I am going to try a comedy like that. Comedy like That, A. Gertrude Stein. CP-SteiG

I am going to utter a tree,Noboby. E. E. Cummings. CP-CummE

I am hard to disgust. Mercifully. Marianne Craig Moore. CP-MoorM

I Am He That Aches with Love. Walt Whitman. CP-WhitW

I am he who knows himself no less vain. I Am. Jorge Luis Borges. SP-BorgJ, tr. by Alastair Reid

I am heaping the bones of the old mother. To the House. Robinson Jeffers. CP-JefR1

I am hearing the shape of the rain. In the Mountain Tent. James Dickey. CP-DickJ

I am Hectate Queen of Hags. Hectate. George Meredith. CP-MerG2

I Am Held by My Fear of Death. Robert Creeley. CP-CreeR

I am here myself; as though this heave of effort. Rose of All the World, D. H. Lawrence. CP-LawrD

I am here to time, you see. Duel, The. Thomas Hardy. CP-HardT

I am hiding beside you to tell you. Reading *Genesis* to a Blind Child. James Dickey. CP-DickJ

I am holy, while I stand. To Silvia. Robert Herrick. CP-HerrR

I am home eating a heart A very slow. Opium for Archie Anderson. Andrei Codrescu. SP-CodrA

I am homesick after mine own kind. In Durance. Ezra Pound. CP-PoEar

I am Huitzilopochtli. First Song of Huitzilopochtli. D. H. Lawrence. CP-LawrD

I am I, old Father Fisheye that begat the ocean, the worm at my own ear, the serpent turning around a tree. End, The. Allen Ginsberg. CP-GinsA; SP-GinsA

I am in a cliff-hollow, surrounded by fossils and furry. Sitting on Some Rocks in Shaw Cove. Robert Bly. SP-BlyR

I Am in a Novel. D. H. Lawrence. CP-LawrD

I am in a painting by Camille Pissarro. Returning to Paris with Pissarro. Lawrence Ferlinghetti. SP-FerlL

I am in a room. Dream and Reality. John Updike. CP-UpdiJ

I Am in Danger—Sir. Adrienne Rich. CP-RicAE; SP-RicA1; SP-RicA2

I am in God what I am. Sum. "Rubén Dario". SP-DariR, tr. by Alberto Acereda and Will Derusha

I am in love with a pig. Adonis. David Ignatow. SP-IgnaD

I am in love with him to whom a hyacinth is dearer. Hyacinth. Edna St. Vincent Millay. CP-MillE

I am in mourning. Natural Star. Alice Walker. CP-WalkA

I am in need of music that would flow. Sonnet: "I am in need of music that would flow." Elizabeth Bishop. CP-BishE

I am in Rome, Vatican bells tolling. Apartment with a View, An. John Ciardi. CP-CiarJ

I am in the old room across from the synagogue. Old Room, The. W. S. Merwin. SP-MerwW

I am indeed the personage you know. Forgiveness, A. Robert Browning. CP-BroR2

I am indifferent again, I am obsessed by indifference. Worried by it. Opening Paths. David Ignatow. SP-IgnaD

I am just going outside and may be some time. Antarctica. Derek Mahon. CP-MahoD

I am just two and two, I am warm, I am cold. Riddle: "I am just two and two, I am warm, I am cold." William Cowper. CP-CowpW

I am King of the Universe. Proclamation. Allen Ginsberg. SP-GinsA

I am kneading my bread Winnie Mandela. Evening News, The. Audre Lorde. SP-LordA

I am Lagides, king. In perfect possession. Glory of the Ptolemies, The. Constantine P. Cavafy. CP-CavaC, tr. by Theoharis Constantine Theoharis

I am laughing by the brook with her. Dream Is—Which?, The. Thomas Hardy. CP-HardT

I am leading a quiet life. Autobiography. Lawrence Ferlinghetti. SP-FerlL

I am leaving earth with little knowledge of it. Permanence. David Ignatow. SP-IgnaD

I am like a leaf that knows its limits. Yehuda Amichai. SP-AmicYL, tr. by Benjamin Harshav and Barbara Harshav

I Am like a Rose. D. H. Lawrence. CP-LawrD

I am like a slip of comet. Gerard Manley Hopkins. CP-HopkG

I am listening here in Rome. Song for the Ragged Schools of London, A. Elizabeth Barrett Browning. CP-BroEB

I am living more alone now than I did. Last Chapter, The. Walter De la Mare. CP-DeLaW

I am looking at trees. Trees. W. S. Merwin. SP-MerwWF

I am looking for a past. Journey, The. David Ignatow. SP-IgnaD

I am looking for Love. Has he passed this way. Quest, The. James Whitcomb Riley. CP-RileJ

I am Lot's pillar, caught in turning. Columns and Caryatids. Carolyn Kizer. CP-KizeC

I am made all things to all men. At His Execution. Rudyard Kipling. CP-KiplR

I am making a Cartoon of a Woman. She is the Poeple. She is the Great. Cartoon. Carl Sandburg. CP-SandC

I am married and would like to fuck someone else. Graffiti 12th Cubicle Men's Room Syracuse Airport. Allen Ginsberg. CP-GinsA

I am Mfu, not a bit romantic, a water spirit. Slave Trade, The: View from the Middle Passage. Clarence Major. SP-MajoC

I am Miles, I did not die. Last Turn of the Screw, The. Stevie Smith. CP-SmitS

I am mourning a murder; one I have done. In Mourning for Betrayal. Robert Bly. SP-BlyR

I am my mammie's ae bairn. I'm Owre [or O'er] Young to Marry Yet. Robert Burns. CP-BurnR

I am my verified and proper self. Serenade in a Drugstore. John Ciardi. CP-CiarJ

I am myself at last; now I achieve. I Am like a Rose. D. H. Lawrence. CP-LawrD

I Am Nailed to a Bar with Liquor. Aleksandr Aleksandrovich Blok. SP-BlokA, tr. by Peter France and Jon Stallworthy

I am no Homers Hero You all know. William Blake. CP-BlakW

I am no more than a secretary of the invisible thing. Secretaries. Czeslaw Milosz. CP-MiloC; CP-MiloCN, tr. by Robert Hass

I am no priests of crooks nor creeds. Religion. Paul Laurence Dunbar. CP-DunbP

I am no shepherd of a child's surmises. Montana Pastoral. James Vincent Cunningham. CP-CunnJ

I am no trumpet, but a reed. Reed, A. Elizabeth Barrett Browning. CP-BroEB

I Am Not a Camera. W. H. Auden. CP-AudeW

I am not a mechanism, an assembly of various sections. Healing. D. H. Lawrence. CP-LawrD

I am not a painter, I am a poet. Why I Am Not a Painter. Frank O'Hara. SP-OharF

'I am not as these are,' the poet saith. Old and New Art (Not as These). Dante Gabriel Rossetti. CW-RossD Fr. House of Life, The.

I am not ashamed of this. I Remember. Laura Riding Jackson. CP-RidiL

I am not black in my mind. Ralph Waldo Emerson. CP-EmerR

I am not dead, I have only become inhuman. Inscription for a Gravestone. Robinson Jeffers. CP-JefR2

I Am Not Even Dust. Jorge Luis Borges. SP-BorgJ, tr. by Eric McHenry

I am not fond of Oliver Montrose. Nevertheless. Ogden Nash. CP-NashO

I am not God's little lamb. Little Boy Sick. Stevie Smith. CP-SmitS

I am not lazy. Frenzy. Anne Sexton. CP-SextA; SP-SextA

I am not looking for your jugular. Threat, The. Andrei Codrescu. SP-CodrA

I am not one who much or oft delight. Personal Talk. William Wordsworth. CP-WorW1; MW-WorW

I am not prone to moralize. Natural Perversities. James Whitcomb Riley. CP-RileJ

I am not resigned to the shutting away of loving hearts in the hard ground. Dirge Without Music. Edna St. Vincent Millay. CP-MillE

I am not sure I would always fight for my life. What Would You Fight For? D. H. Lawrence. CP-LawrD

I am not the one who once spoke with you. (Overheard at the) Maykovsky Station. Michael Palmer. SP-PalmM

I am not the same man. Lazarus ("I am not the same man"). Lucille Clifton. SP-ClifL

I am not treacherous, callous, jealous, superstitious. Face, A. Marianne Craig Moore. CP-MoorM

I am not well civilized, really alien here: trust me not. Trap, The. Robinson Jeffers. CP-JefR2

I am not willing you should go. To S. M. Edna St. Vincent Millay. CP-MillE

I am not yet born; O hear me. Prayer Before Birth. Louis MacNeice. CP-MacNL

I am now about to make a remark that I suppose most parents will. Our Child Doesn't Know Anything. Ogden Nash. CP-NashO

I am now utterly translated into Macedonian, after two days and nights, nonstop in Skopje. Translation. Carolyn Kizer. CP-KizeC

I am of all bereft. Plunder, The. Robert Herrick. CP-HerrR

I Am of Ireland. William Butler Yeats. CP-YeatW

I am of the family of the universe, and with all of us together. In No Way. David Ignatow. SP-IgnaD

I am old. Epitaph: "I am old." Christopher Logue. SP-LoguC

I am old. Fire Spirit. William Carlos Williams. CP-WilW1

I am old and in the ordinary course of nature shall die soon, but the. Birth and Death. Robinson Jeffers. CP-JefR3

I am old, stony-faced, and hard. Edgar Lee Masters. Richard Eberhart. CP-EberR

I am on the run. I have lost my shoes. Dream, A. Hans Magnus Enzensberger. SP-EnzeH

I am oppressed by all the room taken up by the dead. Farmer Among the Tombs, The. Wendell Berry. CP-BerrW

I am oppressed, I am oppressed, I am oppressed—. Eurydice. Robert Graves. CP-GravR

I am out alone on the road. On the Road. D. H. Lawrence. CP-LawrD

I am owner of the sphere. Ralph Waldo Emerson. CP-EmerR *Fr.* History.

I am pale with sick desire. I Will Lift Up Mine Eyes unto the Hills. Christina Georgina Rossetti. CP-RosC1

I am part of the load. Milk of Millennia, The. Jelaluddin Rumi. SP-Rumi, *tr. by* Coleman Barks

I am piled up so high. Allegorical Seduction. Yusef Komunyakaa. CP-KomuY

"I am playing my oldest tunes," declared she. Last Performance, The. Thomas Hardy. CP-HardT

I am poor brother Lippo, by your leave! Fra Lippo Lippi. Robert Browning. CP-BroR1; SP-BroR

I am pure loneliness. Unloved, The. Kathleen Jessie Raine. SP-RainK

I am put high over all others in the city today. Killers. Carl Sandburg. CP-SandC

I am Raftery, hesitant and confused. Derek Mahon. CP-MahoD

I am ready and ever will be. Sir Thomas Wyatt. CP-WyatT

I am reft to the innermost heart. Direadh III. Hugh MacDiarmid. SP-MacDH

I am riding on a limited express, one of the crack trains of the nation. Limited. Carl Sandburg. CP-SandC

I am saying goodbye to the trees. Going Home. Derek Mahon. CP-MahoD

"I am self-evident," the mirror said. Critic. Howard Nemerov. CP-NemeH

I am sending back the key. Bluebeard. Sylvia Plath. CP-PlatS

I am seventy-four years old and suddenly all my strength. Robinson Jeffers. CP-JefR3

I am sick and tired of the river, the stars. Night Dampness. Raymond Carver. CP-CarvR

I am sick, because I have given myself away. Sick. D. H. Lawrence. CP-LawrD

I am sick of people's cerebral emotions. Cerebral Emotions. D. H. Lawrence. CP-LawrD

I am sick with the Time's buying sickness. Lorine Niedecker. CP-NiedL

I am silver and exact. I have no preconceptions. Mirror. Sylvia Plath. CP-PlatS

I am singing to you. Killers. Carl Sandburg. CP-SandC

I AM SINGLE AND I AM JUST. Photo Genic. Olga Broumas. SP-BrouO

I am sitting across the table. Sunday at the State Hospital. David Ignatow. SP-IgnaD

I am sitting at a table in the mall drinking coffee while. Skaters, The. Charles Bukowski. SP-BukC3

I am sitting in the clubhouse. Ginsberg? Charles Bukowski. SP-BukC3

I am sitting on the / edge of the impartial. Margaret Atwood. SP-AtwM1

I am sitting quietly on the verandah, an instrument. No Rest for the Gambler. James Tate. SP-TateJ

I am Sive-like, and can hold. Upon Himselfe. Robert Herrick. CP-HerrR

I am slow as the world. I am very patient. Three Women. Sylvia Plath. CP-PlatS

I Am Small and of No Reputation. Christina Georgina Rossetti. CP-RosC2

I am so delighted. Moon. James Wright. CP-WrigJ

I am so glad and very. E. E. Cummings. CP-CummE

I am so glad to be moving. Moving Out Or the End of Cooperative Living. Audre Lorde. SP-LordA

I am so small I can barely be seen. Jelaluddin Rumi. SP-Rumi, *tr. by* Coleman Barks

I Am So Small You Can Hardly See Me. Charles Olson. CP-OlsoC

I am so swift to seize affronts. Song of Cosmopolitan Courage, A. G. K. Chesterton. CP-ChesG

I am so thankful I have seen. On Sight. Alice Walker. CP-WalkA

I am so tired of waiting. Tired. Langston Hughes. CP-HughL; CP-HughL1

I am so weary and so heavy laden. Petrarch. CP-Petra, *tr. by* J. G. Nichols

I am sober and industrious. To a Poet. Frank O'Hara. SP-OharF

I am soiled with the repetition of your loves and hatreds. Soft Toy. Thomas Kinsella. CP-KinsT

I am some man come out of some strange place. Configuration. Richard Eberhart. CP-EberR

I am someone who boots myself from bed. Rainy 4th. Marge Piercy. SP-PierM

I am sorry you need Health. Emily Dickinson. SP-DickE

I am sowing wild oats. Wild Oats. Robert Penn Warren. CP-WarrR

I am speechlessly grateful for a friend. Emily Dickinson. SP-DickE

I am spinning. Fierceness of Female, The. Anne Sexton. CP-SextA

I am standing on a disused iron bridge. Iron Bridge, The. Billy Collins. SP-CollB

I am standing on one foot. At the Battery. Grace Paley. CP-PalGC

I am standing smong the coal black. Will, The. James Merrill. SP-MerrJ

I am stopped from hoping what I have hoped before. Concerning Agnes. Thomas Hardy. CP-HardT

I am strange here and often I am still trying. Evening. W. S. Merwin. SP-MerwW

I am stretched out under the lean-to. Promises, Promises. Paul Muldoon. CP-MuldP

I am stuck with a snarl. Man with the Hot Nose, The. Charles Bukowski. SP-BukC2

I am studying music now with the jays. Emily Dickinson. SP-DickE

I am summoned from my bed. White Shroud. Allen Ginsberg. SP-GinsA

I am supposed to apologize. Mustered into the Avant-Garde. Donald Davie. CP-DaviDC

I am supposed to say. And Don't Think I Won't Be Waiting. Audre Lorde. SP-LordA

I am sure I feel as Noah did. Emily Dickinson. SP-DickE

I am sure now. Glimpse of the Ice. W. S. Merwin. SP-MerwW

I am sure that if anybody into the condition of humanity cares to probe. Little Miss Muffet Sat on a Prophet—and Quite Right, Too! Ogden Nash. CP-NashO

I am surprised to see. Letter Written on a Ferry While Crossing Long Island Sound. Anne Sexton. CP-SextA; SP-SextA

I am surrounded by the pieces of this huge. Prose Poem. James Tate. SP-TateJ

I am taking a walk about 2:30 p.m. Promenade. Charles Bukowski. SP-BukC3

I am that Adam who, with Snake for guest. Exile, The. Walter De la Mare. CP-DeLaW

I am that Dido which thou here do'st see. Ausonius. CP-RaleW

I am that Persephone. Persephone. Stevie Smith. CP-SmitS

I am that vile worm of Satan. Assassin, The. Richard Eberhart. CP-EberR

I am the absurd lunatic. Il Pastor Fido. James Laughlin. CP-LaugJ

I am the American heartbreak. American Heartbreak. Langston Hughes. CP-HughL; CP-HughL3

I am the Arranger of Inanities. Job Description, A. James Laughlin. CP-LaugJ

I am the Autumnal sun. Henry David Thoreau. CP-ThorH

I Am the Bitter Name. C. K. Williams. CP-WillC; SP-WillC

I Am the Bread of Life. Jones Very. CP-VeryJ

I Am the Door [or Doore]. Richard Crashaw. CP-CrasR

I am the falcon of the spirit world. Soul, The. Jelaluddin Rumi. CP-EmerR

I am the family face. Heredity. Thomas Hardy. CP-HardT

I am the father of no country. Narrative, A. George Oppen. CP-OppGN

I am the figure of a Jewish father with a sack on his back, returning. Yehuda Amichai. SP-AmicYL, *tr. by* Benjamin Harshav *and* Barbara Harshav

I am the First and Last declare my Word. Apostle, The. Jones Very. CP-VeryJ

I am the ghost of Shadwell Stair. Shadwell Stair. Wilfred Owen. CP-OwenW

I am The Great White Way of the city. Poems Done on a Late Night Car. Carl Sandburg. CP-SandC

I am the hounds. High Pasture, The. Donald Hall. CP-HallD

I am the hunted king. Robin Song. Ted Hughes. SP-HughTN

I am the land of their fathers. Recall, The. Rudyard Kipling. CP-KiplR

I am the Lieutenant Colonel of the Civil Guard. Scene of the Lieutenant Colonel of the Civil Guard. Federico García Lorca. CP-GarcF, *tr. by* Christopher Maurer

I Am the Light of the World. Jones Very. CP-VeryJ

I am the lightness that I know. Love Poem, A: "I am the lightness that I know." Richard Eberhart. CP-EberR

I am the little Irish boy. Henry David Thoreau. CP-ThorH

I am the Living Quetzalcoatl. Living Quetzalcoatl, The. D. H. Lawrence. CP-LawrD

I am the love killer. Killing the Love. Anne Sexton. CP-SextA

I am the magical mouse. Magical Mouse, The. Kenneth Patchen. CP-PatcK

I am the Metoposcoper. James Laughlin. CP-LaugJ

I am the mist, the impalpable mist. Mist, The. Carl Sandburg. CP-SandC

I askéd a thief to steal me a peach. Angel, The. William Blake. CP-BlakW

I asked a Whig the other night. Upon the Horrid Plot Discovered by Harlequin the Bishop of Rochester's French Dog. Jonathan Swift. CP-SwifJ

I asked / did this happen before you moved to New York or. One of the Softer Sorrows of Age. Grace Paley. CP-PalGC

I asked her, "Is Aladdin's lamp." Sorceress!, The. Nicholas Vachel Lindsay. CP-LindV

I asked if I should pray. Mohini Chatterjee. William Butler Yeats. CP-YeatW

I asked no other thing. Emily Dickinson. CP-DickE

I asked no quarter and I gave none. Old Fashioned American Business Man, An. Richard Eberhart. CP-EberR

I asked of Time to tell me where was Love. Love. Jones Very. CP-VeryJ

I asked of your face. God, The. "H. D." CP-DoolH

I asked [or askd] my Dear Friend, Orator Prigg. Orator Prigg. William Blake. CP-BlakW

I asked [or ask't] thee oft what poets thou hast read. Upon the Same. Robert Herrick. CP-HerrR

I asked professors who teach the meaning of life to tell me what is happiness. Happiness. Carl Sandburg. CP-SandC

I asked the doctor who had pronounced me dead. Credo ("I asked the doctor who had pronounced me dead"). John Ciardi. CP-CiarJ

I asked the Lord: "Sire, is this true." Dream Question, A. Thomas Hardy. CP-HardT

I asked the Mayor of Gary about the 12-hour day and the 7-day week. Mayor of Gary, The. Carl Sandburg. CP-SandC

I asked you, baby. Maybe. Langston Hughes. CP-HughL; CP-HughL3

I askt my Lucia but a kisse. Upon Lucia. Robert Herrick. CP-HerrR

I assume a Buddha-like expression in the mirror. I Am. David Ignatow. SP-IgnaD

I Assume the World Is Curious About Me. A. R. Ammons. CP-AmmoA

I ate my fill of a whale that died. Natural Theology. Rudyard Kipling. CP-KiplR

I ate pancakes one night in a Pancake House. Player Piano, The. Randall Jarrell. CP-JarrR

I attempted to concentrate. Allen Ginsberg. CP-GinsA

I attended school and I liked the place. Values in Use. Marianne Craig Moore. CP-MoorM

I attended the burial of all my rosy feelings. Transaction. A. R. Ammons. CP-AmmoA

I awoke happy, the house. Revelation, The. William Carlos Williams. CP-WilW1

I awoke in profuse sweat, arms aching. Hag-Ridden. Robert Graves. CP-GravR

I awoke in the midsummer not-to-call night, in the white and the walk of the morning. Moonrise. Gerard Manley Hopkins. CP-HopkG

I Awoke with the Room Cold. Marge Piercy. SP-PierM

I bade, because the wick and oil are spent. Living Beauty, The. William Butler Yeats. CP-YeatW

I balance myself carefully. Wish: Metamorphosis to Heraldic Emblem. Margaret Atwood. SP-AtwM1

I banged it out. Stone and Flower Series. Charles Olson. CP-OlsoC

I batter the wheel of heaven. Hafiz. CP-EmerR Fr. Odes.

I bear a basket lined with grass. For a Picture of Saint Dorothea. Gerard Manley Hopkins. CP-HopkG

I bear a basket lined with grass. Lines for a Picture of St. Dorothea. Gerard Manley Hopkins. CP-HopkG

I bear a basket lined with grass. St. Dorothea. Gerard Manley Hopkins. CP-HopkG

I bear dis cross dis many a mile. Chant of the Cross-bearing Child, The. James Whitcomb Riley. CP-RileJ

I bear in youth the sad infirmities. Written in Sickness. Ralph Waldo Emerson. CP-EmerR

I bear the prints of my ascended Lord. Redeemed, The. Jones Very. CP-VeryJ

I been t'inkin' 'bout de preachah; whut he said de othah night. Philosophy. Paul Laurence Dunbar. CP-DunbP

I Beg You Come Back & Be Cheerful. Allen Ginsberg. CP-GinsA

"I beg you to note," said a Man to a Goose. Political Economy. Ambrose Bierce. SP-BierA

I began in Ohio. Stages on a Journey Westward. James Wright. CP-WrigJ

I began to be followed by a voice saying. Song in a Year of Catastrophe. Wendell Berry. CP-BerrW

I begged my love to wait a bit. All I Tell You From My Heart. Robert Graves. CP-GravR

I beginne to waine in sight. Upon His Eye-Sight Failing Him. Robert Herrick. CP-HerrR

I, Being Born A Woman. Edna St. Vincent Millay. CP-MillE

I, being born a woman and distressed. I, Being Born A Woman. Edna St. Vincent Millay. CP-MillE

I believe all childern's good. Hired Man's Faith in Children, The. James Whitcomb Riley. CP-RileJ

I believe in stillness. Blessing Myself. David Ignatow. SP-IgnaD

I believe in the great discovery. Discovery. Wisława Szymborska. SP-SzymW, tr. by Stanisław Barańczak and Clare Cavanagh

I believe in the Hereafter. Appetites for the material. Hereafter, The. Constantine P. Cavafy. CP-CavaC, tr. by Theoharis Constantine Theoharis

I believe in the increasing of life: whatever. Escape, The. Ivor Gurney. SP-GurnI

I Believe in You. Charles Olson. CP-OlsoC

I believe it to be true. First of May. Langston Hughes. CP-HughL; CP-HughL2

I believe my apprenticeship. Pro Nobis. George Oppen. CP-OppGN

I believe my favorite country's German. Deutsch durch Freud. Randall Jarrell. CP-JarrR

I believe my old lady's. What? So Soon! Langston Hughes. CP-HughL; CP-HughL3

I believe that a young woman. Irkalla's White Caves. Kenneth Patchen. CP-PatcK

I believe you did not have a happy life. Bitterness, A. Mary Oliver. SP-OlivM

I believed in those plains. Radio Horse, The. Paul Muldoon. CP-MuldP

I' b'en a-kindo' "musin'," as the feller says, and I'm. Romancin'. James Whitcomb Riley. CP-RileJ

I be'n down in ole Kentucky. After a Visit. Paul Laurence Dunbar. CP-DunbP

I' be'n down to the Capital at Washington, D.C. Down to the Capital. James Whitcomb Riley. CP-RileJ

I bend over an old hollow cottonwood stump. Hollow Tree, A. Robert Bly. SP-BlyR

I bend over the woman. Country Midwife, The: A Day. Ai. SP-Ai

I bend to the ground. Noon. Philip Levine. SP-LeviP

I bent in the deep of night. Pedigree, The. Thomas Hardy. CP-HardT

I bet with every Wind that blew. Emily Dickinson. CP-DickE

I betook myself to Italy right after the harvest. 1913. Czeslaw Milosz. CP-MiloC; CP-MiloCN, tr. by Robert Hass

I bid thee weep but mourn not at thy lot. Grief. Jones Very. CP-VeryJ

I bid you cast out pity. At a Deathbed in the Year Two Thousand. Adrienne Rich. CP-RicAE

I bind the sinew tight. First Brother. Peter Blue Cloud. SP-BlueP

I bless thee, O Father of Heaven & Earth, that ever I saw Flaxman's face. To John Flaxman, 12 September 1800. William Blake. CP-BlakW

I bless[e] thee, Lord, because I GROW. Paradise. George Herbert. CP-HerbG

I bore a daughter flower-fair. Sunday Morning Tragedy, A. Thomas Hardy. CP-HardT

I bore with thee long weary days and nights. Love of Christ Which Passeth Knowledge, The. Christina Georgina Rossetti. CP-RosC1

I bought a carpet. Day Went Dark, The. A. K. Ramanujan. CP-RamaA

I bought a dishmop. Youth and Beauty. William Carlos Williams. CP-WilW1

I bought a new. William Carlos Williams. CP-WilW1 Fr. Paterson.

I bought my wife a stane o' lint. Weary Pund o' Tow, The. Robert Burns. CP-BurnR

I bought the river from an old man. Anna Karenina and the Love-sick River. Kenneth Patchen. CP-PatcK

I bow down to the great goiter of Verdun. Verdun. Robert Lowell. SP-LoweR

I brace my knee against. Horses. Gregory Orr. SP-OrrG

I braced the drum to my arm, a flat drum, and began to play. Dream-Drumming. Muriel Rukeyser. CP-RukeM

I brake thy Bracelet 'gainst my will. Bracelet of Pearle: To Silvia, The. Robert Herrick. CP-HerrR

I breathe, sweet Gib [or Ghib], the temperate air of Wrest. To my Friend G.N. from Wrest. Thomas Carew. CP-CareT

I breathe the air you have breathed. Kathleen Jessie Raine. SP-RainK

I breathe to you. Spring Equinox Full Moon. W. S. Merwin. SP-MerwWF

I breathed enough to take the Trick. Emily Dickinson. CP-DickE

I bring an unaccustomed wine. Emily Dickinson. CP-DickE

I bring fresh showers for the thirsting flowers. Cloud, The. Percy Bysshe Shelley. CP-ShelP

I bring myself back from the streets that open like long. Home for Thanksgiving. W. S. Merwin. SP-MerwW

I bring to countryside my father's sense. Poem for My Father. Charles Tomlinson. CP-TomlC; SP-TomlC

I bring ye little noisy crew! Dirge: "I bring ye little noisy crew!" William Wordsworth. MW-WorW

I bring ye love. Quest. What will love do? Upon Love, by Way of Question and Answer. Robert Herrick. CP-HerrR

I bring you now these flowers. Elegy for Maria Alves. Joaquim Cardozo. CP-BishE

I bring you the child of an Idumaean night. Gift of the Poem. Stéphane Mallarmé. CP-MallS, tr. by Henry Weinfield

I bring you the spoils, my nation. Epilogue: "I bring you the spoils, my nation." Ezra Pound. CP-PoEar

I bring you with reverent hands. Poet to His Beloved, A. William Butler Yeats. CP-YeatW

I Broke a Sheaf of Light. A. R. Ammons. CP-AmmoA

I broke my [or ma] heart this mornin'. Cora. Langston Hughes. CP-HughL; CP-HughL1

I brought a book to make the time pass. On a Trailways Bus a Man Who Holds His Head Strangely Speaks to the Seat Behind Him. Miller Williams. CP-WillM

I brought my children to the mound. Anniversaries of War. Yehuda Amichai. SP-AmicYL, *tr. by* Benjamin Harshav *and* Barbara Harshav

I build a house, but in this 'twill appear. House, The. Jones Very. CP-VeryJ

I build a tottering pillar of my blood. Siege, The. Tennessee Williams. CP-WillT

I built her a tower when I was young. For Una. Robinson Jeffers. CP-JefR3

I built my soul a lordly pleasurehouse. Palace of Art, The. Alfred Tennyson. CP-TennA

I buried a skunk in the garden. Dead Skunk. Richard Eberhart. CP-EberR

I buried Mama in her wedding dress. She Didn't Even Wave. Ai. SP-Ai

I buried my first womern. My First Womern. James Whitcomb Riley. CP-RileJ

I burn, I burn; and beg of you. To Dewes. A Song. Robert Herrick. CP-HerrR

I Burn Money. Ogden Nash. CP-NashO

I burn[e], and cruel[l] you, in vain[e]. To My Mistress [*or* Mistris], I Burning in Love. Thomas Carew. CP-CareT

I burned and burned. But one day I turned. Still Another View of Grace. A. K. Ramanujan. CP-RamaA

I burned my life, that I might find. Alchemist, The. Louise Bogan. CP-BogaL

I busied myself to find a sure. Misconception. Thomas Hardy. CP-HardT

"I busy too," the little boy. World to Do, A. Theodore Weiss. SP-WeisT

I buy what I buy from the candyman. Sugar. Olga Broumas. SP-BrouO

I cain't git used to city ways. Uncle Dan'l in Town over Sunday. James Whitcomb Riley. CP-RileJ

I Call and I Call. Robert Herrick. CP-HerrR

I call her beautiful;—she says. Ralph Waldo Emerson. CP-EmerR

I call no goddess to inspire my strains. To Mr. Graham of Fintry, On Being Appointed to My Excise Division. Robert Burns. CP-BurnR

I call on those that call me son. Are You Content. William Butler Yeats. CP-YeatW

I call out a sceret name, the name. Making Light of It. Philip Levine. SP-LeviP

I call the old time back: I bring my lay. Mabel Martin. John Greenleaf Whittier. CP-WhitJ

I called her across the room. Woman, The. Robert Creeley. CP-CreeR

I called him *Comfort*. Anne Sexton. SP-SextA *Fr.* Letters to Dr. Y.

I called him to come in. Evening. James Wright. CP-WrigJ

I called the wind and it. Raft. A. R. Ammons. CP-AmmoA

I called through your door. Jelaluddin Rumi. SP-Rumi, *tr. by* Coleman Barks

I came among you in a time of hunger. Song of Autobiography, The. Christopher Logue. SP-LoguC

I came an errand one cloud-blowing evening. Census-Taker, The. Robert Frost. CP-FrosR

I came back from Cape Cod. White. James Schuyler. CP-SchuJ

I came back from Texas. Texas. Czeslaw Milosz. CP-MiloCN, *tr. by* Robert Hass

I came back from the depths of the sea. Another One. Pablo Neruda. SP-NeruP

I came back into my own house. How Things Change. Charles Olson. CP-OlsoC

I came before the water. Mussel Hunter at Rock Harbor. Sylvia Plath. CP-PlatS

I came far. Dancer, The. "H. D." CP-DoolH

I came from very far away. Crow's Song, The. Primo Levi. CP-LeviP, *tr. by* Ruth Feldman *and* Brian Swann

I came here on purpose. 5th Position. Philip Whalen. SP-WhalP

I came home and found a lion in my living room. Lion for Real, The. Allen Ginsberg. CP-GinsA; SP-GinsA

I came home from the movies with nothing on my mind. 345 W. 15th St. Allen Ginsberg. CP-GinsA

I Came in a Dark Woods Upon. A. R. Ammons. CP-AmmoA

I came in from the roar. Metropolitan Museum. Langston Hughes. CP-HughL; CP-HughL3

I came out on the wrong. Attempted Rescue, The. Alan Dugan. CP-DugaA

I came out to the barn lot. Adze, The. Wendell Berry. CP-BerrW

I came to a bounty of black lustre. Good Memory, A. Yusef Komunyakaa. CP-KomuY

I came to a great door. Beast, The. Theodore Roethke. CP-RoetT

I came to a meadow. Pastoral: "I came to a meadow." Charles Simic. SP-SimiC; SP-SimiCE

I came to buy a smile—today. Emily Dickinson. CP-DickE

I came to cast a fire into the earth. Hindoo Converts: On the Domestic Trials of Hindoo Converts. Report of Unitarian Mission in India. Jones Very. CP-VeryJ

I came to my senses with a pencil in my hand. All Landscape Is Abstract, and Tends to Repeat Itself. Charles Wright. SP-WrigCN

I came to the house. It was dark. If We Are to Know Where We Live. Kenneth Patchen. CP-PatcK

I came to their white terror first. Release Time. Audre Lorde. SP-LordA

I came too late to the hills: they were swept bare. Wilderness, The. Kathleen Jessie Raine. SP-RainK

I Came Upon a Plateau. A. R. Ammons. CP-AmmoA

I came upon it in a dream. Dream. Stevie Smith. CP-SmitS

I came upon two wasps. Language as an Escape from the Discrete. Josephine Jacobsen. CP-JacoJ

I came with some trepidation to your vernissage. Arthur's Party. Carolyn Kizer. CP-KizeC

I can almost see it. Elegy: "I can almost see it." Thom Gunn. CP-GunnT

I can be stopped. Maudit. George Oppen. CP-OppGN

I can but name thee, and methinks I call. To His Honoured Kinsman Sir William Soame. Robert Herrick. CP-HerrR

I can call up old ghosts, and they will come. Old Ghosts. Stevie Smith. CP-SmitS

I can change my- / self more easily. She Considers Evading Him. Margaret Atwood. SP-AtwM1

I can easily believe that I. Dear Joe. James Schuyler. CP-SchuJ

I can feel she has got out of bed. Rapture. Galway Kinnell. SP-KinnGN

I can feel the tug. Punishment. Seamus Heaney. SP-HeanSO

I Can Hardly Wait for the Sandman. Ogden Nash. CP-NashO

I can HEY on water. Hey-Hey Blues. Langston Hughes. CP-HughL; CP-HughL2

I can imagine, in some otherworld. Humming-Bird. D. H. Lawrence. CP-LawrD

I can just see from the attic window. Gray Spring Morning, A. John Ciardi. CP-CiarJ

I can lay down that history. Action. Denise Levertov. SP-LeveDS

I can look at your forehead. I am the Metoposcoper. James Laughlin. CP-LaugJ

I can love both fair[e] and brown[e]. Indifferent, The. John Donne. CP-DonnJ, MW-DonnJ

I can make out the rigging of a schooner. North Haven. Elizabeth Bishop. CP-BishE

"I" can never be a great man, An. Trigorin. Stephen Spender. CP-SpenS

I can not bow to woo thee. Summons, The. Ezra Pound. CP-PoEar

I can not say, and I will not say. Away. James Whitcomb Riley. CP-RileJ

I Can Only Stay for Fifteen Minutes. Miller Williams. CP-WillM

I can see by their mark how high the waters reached. Elegy on the Lost Child, The. Yehuda Amichai. SP-AmicY, *tr. by* Stephen Mitchell

I can see down there. Slave Song. Langston Hughes. CP-HughL; CP-HughL2

I can see in the night. Well. Charles Olson. CP-OlsoC

I can see the toweres. Evelyn G. of Christminster. Thomas Hardy. CP-HardT

I can see them standing politely on the wide pages. First Reader. Billy Collins. SP-CollB

I can see you. Not Now. Robert Creeley. CP-CreeR

I can see your daughter walking down streets of love. Dear Toni Instead of a Letter of Congratulation. Audre Lorde. SP-LordA

I can see your house, babe. Curious. Langston Hughes. CP-HughL; CP-HughL2

I can sense it coming from far, too, Maman, the tide. Derek Walcott. CP-WalcD *Fr.* Midsummer.

I can stay awake all night, if need be. Zoo Keeper's Wife. Sylvia Plath. CP-PlatS

I can still hear her. How My Fever Left. James Wright. CP-WrigJ

I can still sing. Epilogue to the Opera of Dead on Arrival. Yusef Komunyakaa. CP-KomuY

I can support it no longer. Flower Herding on Mount Monadnock. Galway Kinnell. SP-KinnGN

I can taste the tin of the sky—the real tin thing. Waking in Winter. Sylvia Plath. CP-PlatS

I can tell you what I need is. Devising. A. R. Ammons. CP-AmmoA

I can tell you what I need is. Emplacement. A. R. Ammons. CP-AmmoA

I can tell you what I need is a good periodontist. Renovating. A. R. Ammons. CP-AmmoA

I can tell you what I need is for. Positions. A. R. Ammons. CP-AmmoA

I can tell you what I need is one of those. Alternatives. A. R. Ammons. CP-AmmoA

I can tell you what I need, what I need. Reassessing. A. R. Ammons. CP-AmmoA

I can think of William of Orange. Centaurs, The. Paul Muldoon. CP-MuldP

I Can Wade Grief. Emily Dickinson. CP-DickE

I can write no stately proem. To My Wife: With a Copy of My Poems. Oscar Wilde. CP-WildO

I cannot be ashamed. Emily Dickinson. CP-DickE

I cannot bring my muse to drop her vies. Epigram to My Jovial Good Friend Mr Robert Dover, on His Great Instauration of His Hunting and Dancing at Cotswold, An. Ben Jonson. CP-JonsB

I cannot but remember. When the Year Grows Old. Edna St. Vincent Millay. CP-MillE

I cannot but think that we live in a bad age. Dean of St. Patrick's to Thomas Sheridan, The. Jonathan Swift. CP-SwifJ

I cannot buy it—'tis not sold. Emily Dickinson. CP-DickE

I Cannot Command You. James Laughlin. CP-LaugJ

I cannot conjecture a form of space. Emily Dickinson. SP-DickE

I cannot count the pebbles in the brook. Eternities. G. K. Chesterton. CP-ChesG

I cannot count the years. Vittoria's *Italia* Song. George Meredith. CP-MerG2

I choose the road from here to there. Walks. W. H. Auden. CP-AudeW

I Chop Some Parsley While Listening to Art Blakey's Version of "Three Blind Mice." Billy Collins. SP-CollB

I chopped down the house that you had been saving to live in next summer. Variations on a Theme by William Carlos Williams. Kenneth Koch. SP-KochK

I chose a secluded place to live. Han-shan. CP-ColdM, *tr. by* Red Pine

I chose among others, proud and glorious. Sonnets of Death 5. Gabriela Mistral. SP-MistG, *tr. by* Maria Giachetti [*or* Jacketti]

I chose the bed down-stairs by the sea-window for a good death-bed. Bed by the Window, The. Robinson Jeffers. CP-JefR2

I circle your nest tonight. Jelaluddin Rumi. SP-Rumi, *tr. by* Coleman Barks

I circled on leather paws. Return, The. Theodore Roethke. CP-RoetT

I claim no tide can wrest from us. We Mutually Pledge to Each Other. Kenneth Patchen. CP-PatcK

I classed, appraising once. Loved Once. Elizabeth Barrett Browning. CP-BroEB

I cleared the trees about my cabin, all. Tract. Paul Muldoon. CP-MuldP

I climb down the bank of Rock Island, Illinois. Dried Sturgeon, The. Robert Bly. SP-BlyR

I climb the steps to my room. Beyond impasse. Clarence Major. SP-MajoC

I climb to the tower-top and lean upon broken stone. I See Phantoms of Hatred and of the Heart's Fullness and of the Coming Emptiness. William Butler Yeats. CP-YeatW *Fr.* Meditations in Time of Civil War.

I climb'd [*or* climbed] the dark brow of the mighty Hellvellyn. Hellvellyn. Sir Walter Scott. SP-ScotW

I climbed out, tired of waiting. Drinking from a Helmet. James Dickey. CP-DickJ

I climbed through woods in the hour-before-dawn dark. Horses, The. Ted Hughes. SP-HughTN

I climbed to the crest. Wound, The. Thomas Hardy. CP-HardT

I climbed to your high village through the snow. For Miriam. Charles Tomlinson. CP-TomlC; SP-TomlC

I cling to the spar. Et Faim Sallir les Loups des Boys. Ezra Pound. CP-PoEar

I close my eyes and the smell of your brown. Exotic Scent. Charles Baudelaire. CP-BaudC, *tr. by* Walter Martin

I close my eyes like a good little boy at night in bed. David Ignatow. SP-IgnaD

I close my overgrown door in vain. Han-shan. CP-ColdM, *tr. by* Red Pine

I close the book I am reading in which. Marianne, My Mother, and Me. Maxine W. Kumin. SP-KumiM

I closed and drew for my love's sake. Tarrant Moss. Rudyard Kipling. CP-KiplR *Fr.* Plain Tales from the Hills.

I closed my ears with stinging bugs. Elegy for a Puritan Conscience. Alan Dugan. CP-DugaA

I co'd but see thee yesterday. To Dianeme. Robert Herrick. CP-HerrR

I co'd never love indeed. Upon Himselfe. Robert Herrick. CP-HerrR

I coft a stane o' haslock woo. Cardin o't, The. Robert Burns. CP-BurnR

I come across from Mellstock while the moon wastes weaker. His Visitor. Thomas Hardy. CP-HardT

I come back. Attempted Departure. James Dickey. CP-DickJ

I Come Back from a Journey. Pablo Neruda. SP-NeruP

I come back from the belly of the whale. Jonah. May Sarton. SP-SartM

I come back to the cottage in. Only Years. Kenneth Rexroth. CP-RexrK

I come back to the geography of it. Maximus, to Gloucester, Letter 27. Charles Olson. SP-OlsoC *Fr.* Maximus Poems, The.

I come back to the old river. Hatred of the Old River. Richard Eberhart. CP-EberR

I come back to your youth, my Nana. Walking in Paris. Anne Sexton. CP-SextA; SP-SextA

I Come Before Dawn. Jelaluddin Rumi. SP-Rumi, *tr. by* Coleman Barks

I come down from the gold mountains. Summer Doorway. W. S. Merwin. SP-MerwWF

I come from around Beja. Written in a Book Abandoned on the Trip. Fernando Pessoa. SP-PessF, *tr. by* Susan M. Brown *and* Edwin Honig

I come from Castlepatrick, and me heart is on me sleeve. Me Heart. G. K. Chesterton. CP-ChesG

I come from England into France. Cantilena Politica-Jocunda Facta Post Principis Discessum In Hispaniam. Sir John Suckling. CP-SuckJ

I come from Tu Ling, an unimportant man. Testament. Tu Fu. CP-KizeC, *tr. by* Carolyn Kizer

I come into my dim bedroom. Stunt Flier, The. John Updike. CP-UpdiJ

I come into the room The room stands waiting. Breaking Open. Muriel Rukeyser. CP-RukeM

I come not to ravish your body, O beast. Anguish. Stéphane Mallarmé. CP-MallS, *tr. by* Henry Weinfield

I come on the debt again this day in November. Debt, A. W. S. Merwin. SP-MerwW

I come out on the open highway. Autumn Freedom. Aleksandr Aleksandrovich Blok. SP-BlokA, *tr. by* Peter France *and* Jon Stallworthy

I come the rushing wind that shook the place. Promise, The ("I come the rushing

wind that shook the place"). Jones Very. CP-VeryJ

I come to it again. To What Listens. Wendell Berry. CP-BerrW

I come to look at the cherryblossoms. Japane Tea Garden Golden Gate Park in Spring. Philip Whalen. SP-WhalP

I come to the fear of love. Fear of Love, The. Wendell Berry. CP-BerrW

I come to thee by daytime constantly. Sonnet: He rebukes Dante for his way of Life, after the death of Beatrice. Guido Cavalcanti. CW-RossD, *tr. by* Dante Gabriel Rossetti

I come unto thee thru the hidden ways. Roundel: "I come unto thee thru the hidden ways." Joachim Du Bellay. CP-PoEar, *tr. by* Ezra Pound

I come up to a break. Beachhead. Derek Walcott. CP-WalcD

I come upon it suddenly, alone. Country Pathway, A. James Whitcomb Riley. CP-RileJ

I come, ye little noisy Crew. Address to the Scholars of the Village School of—1798. William Wordsworth. CP-WorW1

I commend you to George Washington Hill. Instructions. Carl Sandburg. CP-SandC

I complain like the flute. Banks. Max Jacob. CP-BishE

I complain to the wind, our life's but a minute. Funeral under My Window. Jaroslav Seifert. SP-SeifJ, *tr. by* Ewald Osers

I concentrate. / My books hypnotize each other. February 20th. Anne Sexton. CP-SextA

I confess I cannot guess. Two Early Poems. Tennessee Williams. CP-WillT

I confess that I love him. Emily Dickinson. SP-DickE

I conquer the world with a cough. I Have Spoken. David Ignatow. SP-IgnaD

I conquered. Far barbarians hear my name. Fernando Pessoa. SP PessF *Fr.* Inscriptions.

I consign to the ship of the rose. Herbalist's Rose, The. Pablo Neruda. SP-NeruP

I cough a lot (sinus?) so I. Getting Up Ahead of Someone (Sun). Frank O'Hara. SP-OharF

I could be well content, allow'd the use. Four Ages, The. William Cowper. CP-CowpW

I could begin with that grave form, "Here lies." To the Memory of That Most Honoured Lady Jane, Eldest Daughter to Cuthbert, Lord Ogle: and Countess of Shrewsbury. Ben Jonson. CP-JonsB

I Could Believe. Philip Levine. SP-LeviP

I could bring You Jewels—had I a mind to. Emily Dickinson. CP-DickE

I could carry a little boat out. Kah Tai Purgatorio. Sam Hamill. SP-HamiS

I could climb a mountain / for a view. For Anybody. Robert Creeley. CP-CreeR

I could come to believe. I Could Believe. Philip Levine. SP-LeviP

I could cry for roses, thinking of you. They Met Young. Carl Sandburg. CP-SandC

I could die—to know. Emily Dickinson. CP-DickE

I could digest the white slick watery mash. Cafeteria in Boston. Thom Gunn. CP-GunnT

I could draw its map by heart. Amor Loci. W. H. Auden. CP-AudeW

I Could Give All to Time. Robert Frost. CP-FrosR

I could have painted pictures like that youth's. Pictor Ignotus. Robert Browning. CP-BroR1

I could have plowed the slim forty and back eighty. Elegy for Moral Self-Assurance and Country Virtue, An. John Ciardi. CP-CiarJ

I Could Have Rested. A. K. Ramanujan. CP-RamaA

I could have rested. I Could Have Rested. A. K. Ramanujan. CP-RamaA

I could have told much by the way. Kathleen Jessie Raine. SP-RainK

I could hear a gown-skirt rustling. On a Heath. Thomas Hardy. CP-HardT

I Could Let Tom Go—But What about the Children. Stevie Smith. CP-SmitS

I could look at. Joy. Robert Creeley. CP-CreeR

I could look at you a long time. Face. Adrienne Rich. CP-RicAE

I could love you. Offering and Rebuff. Carl Sandburg. CP-SandC

I could never have come to the present without you. Different Stars, The. W. S. Merwin. SP-MerwW

I could not bring this splendid world nor any trading beast. Lines Written in Recapitulation. Edna St. Vincent Millay. CP-MillE

I could not draw a map of it, this road. Return, The. Charles Tomlinson. SP-TomlC

I could not drink it, Sweet. Emily Dickinson. CP-DickE

I could not live here, though I must and do. Low Lands. Donald Davie. CP-DaviDC

I could not prove the Years had feet. Emily Dickinson. CP-DickE

I could not think of thee as pieced rot. Fernando Pessoa. SP-PessF *Fr.* 35 Sonnets.

I could not weigh myself, Myself. Emily Dickinson. SP-DickE

I could replace. Earth Psalm. Denise Levertov. SP-LeveDP

I could say it's the happiest period of my life. Ongoing Story, The. John Ashbery. SP-AshbJ

I could say the day began / behind the Sierras. Wednesday. Philip Levine. SP-LeviP

I could see God once when I believed telling. One Wet Iota. John Ciardi. CP-CiarJ

I could suffice for Him, I knew. Emily Dickinson. CP-DickE

I Could Take. Hayden Carruth. CP-CarHS

I could take the Harlem night. Juke Box Love Song. Langston Hughes. CP-HughL; CP-HughL3

I could tell you. Impasse. Langston Hughes. CP-HughL; CP-HughL3

I could wish you all, who love. To All Young Men That Love. Robert Herrick. CP-HerrR

I couldn't paint, my voice cracked. Twenty-Year-Old Soldiers. Adam Zagajewski. SP-ZagaA, tr. by Clare Cavanagh

I couldn't take my eyes off. At an Intersection. Thom Gunn. CP-GunnT

I couldn't tell fact from fiction. Senses of Insecurity. Maya Angelou. SP-AngeM

I Counsel You Beware. A. E. Housman. CP-HousA

I count the dismal time by months and years. Prisoner, The. Elizabeth Barrett Browning. CP-BroEB

I counted trip flares. Combat Pay for Jody. Yusef Komunyakaa. CP-KomuY

I cradle my four-year-old daughter. Mississippi Winter III. Alice Walker. CP-WalkA

I crave, dear Lord. Ike Walton's Prayer. James Whitcomb Riley. CP-RileJ

I crawle, I creep; my *Christ*, I come. To Christ. Robert Herrick. CP-HerrR

I creature being mad. Poem of Margery Kempe. A. Howard Nemerov. CP-NemeH

I cried at Pity—not at Pain. Emily Dickinson. CP-DickE

I cried over beautiful things knowing no beautiful thing lasts. Autumn Movement. Carl Sandburg. CP-SandC

I cried when the moon was murmuring to the birds. Withering of the Boughs, The. William Butler Yeats. CP-YeatW

I cross till I am weary. Emily Dickinson. CP-DickE

I crossed a barren waste of blighted land. My Beatrice. Charles Baudelaire. CP-BaudC, tr. by Walter Martin

I crossed sand-hills. Chorus of the Women of Chalkis. Euripides. CP-DoolH Fr. Iphigenia [or Iphigeneia] in Aulis.

I crossed the dreary moor. Incipient Madness. William Wordsworth. CP-WorW1

I crossed the stream. Crossing Place. W. S. Merwin. SP-MerwWF

I crossed through a souk where the butchers. Market, The. Shmuel HaNagid. SP-HaNaS, tr. by Peter Cole

I crouch naked at the wound's edge. Singing the Pain Back into the Wound. Gregory Orr. SP-OrrG

I cry I cry. No Categories! Stevie Smith. CP-SmitS

I Cry, Love! Love! Theodore Roethke. CP-RoetT

I Cry Your Mercy, Pity, Love—Ay, Love! John Keats. CP-KeatJ

I cuffed you into shape. I molded you. Robber Woman, The. Marilyn Hacker. SP-HackM

I curse paradox. Curse in Free Verse, A. G. K. Chesterton. CP-ChesG

I cut a new thread on it this morning. Tooling Up. A. R. Ammons. CP-AmmoA

I cut a staff in a churchyard copse. Modern Elfland. G. K. Chesterton. CP-ChesG

I cut it in two and give the child. Star-Apple. Robert Stock. SP-StocR

I cut the middle fingernail of the middle. Like a Flower in the Rain. Charles Bukowski. SP-BukC2

I cut the sentence. Song of a Camera. Thom Gunn. CP-GunnT

I dance in circles holding. Wedding Ring Dance, The. Anne Sexton. CP-SextA

I dance on all the mountains. This Poem Is for Deer. Gary Snyder. CP-SnydG Fr. Myths and Texts.

I Dare Do All. D. H. Lawrence. CP-LawrD

I dare interpret: Adonai of rescue. Unknowable? Perhaps Not Altogether. John Berryman. CP-BerrJ

I dare not ask a kiss[e]. To Electra. Robert Herrick. CP-HerrR

I deal in wisdom, not in dry desire. Supper with Lindsay. Theodore Roethke. CP-RoetT

I deal with farmers, things like dips and feed. Livings. Philip Larkin. CP-LarkP

I deamt that people from the Land of Chimes. On the Belgian Expatriation. Thomas Hardy. CP-HardT

I deem that God is not disquieted. Legend Glorified, The. James Whitcomb Riley. CP-RileJ

I deemed thy garments, O my Hope, were grey. Hope Overtaken. Dante Gabriel Rossetti. CW-RossD Fr. House of Life, The.

I demand that they give me a bed. My Secret. James Laughlin. CP-LaugJ

I deplore this vulgar place. Han-shan. CP-ColdM, tr. by Red Pine

I desire to hold in my heart. Lines for an Unknown Lover. John Logan. CP-LogaJ

I determined to find out whose it was. Rival, The. Thomas Hardy. CP-HardT

I did but dream. I never knew. Clear Vision, The. John Greenleaf Whittier. CP-WhitJ

I did but taste a little of the honey with the. John Logan. CP-LogaJ Fr. Monologues of the Son of Saul.

I did not buy you the tiara. False Witness. Ai. SP-Ai

I did not chide him, tho' I knew. Heart's Chill Between. Christina Georgina Rossetti. CP-RosC3

I did not expect to live in such an unusual moment. Oeconomia Divina. Czeslaw Milosz. CP-MiloC; CP-MiloCN

I did not expect you. Letter, The. Robert Creeley. CP-CreeR

I did not have exactly a way of life. Lines: "I did not have exactly a way of life." John Ciardi. CP-CiarJ

I did not know Love had settled down on me. Love Comes Late. D. H. Lawrence. CP-LawrD

I did not know that life could be so sweet. Awakening, The. Paul Laurence Dunbar. CP-DunbP

I did not know / that the Mexicans. Brave Bull. Charles Bukowski. SP-BukC2

I did not know you when you came in there. William Dickey. SP-DickW Fr. Part Song, With Concert of Recorders.

I did not look upon her eyes. Penumbra. Dante Gabriel Rossetti. CW-RossD

I did not lose my heart in summer's even. A. E. Housman. CP-HousA

I did not meet him in the gleaming years. George Sterling. Robinson Jeffers. CP-JefR1

I did not plow her darkness. So She Said. James Wright. CP-WrigJ

I did not reach Thee. Emily Dickinson. CP-DickE

I did not really realize how much. Power of Poesy, The. James Laughlin. CP-LaugJ

I did not see thy shadow fall. Legend of Good Women, The. G. K. Chesterton. CP-ChesG

I did not see you even when I went. Holy Sonnets. Helen Pinkerton. CP-PinkH

I did not sleep; 'twas noon of day. Lines by Claudia. Emily Jane Brontë. CP-BronE

I did not tell you to open the window. For a Friend. David Ignatow. SP-IgnaD

I did not think that I should find them there. Clerks, The. Edwin Arlington Robinson. CP-RobiE

I did not think to see them once again. Hieros Gamos. Kathleen Jessie Raine. SP-RainK

I did not want to be dependent on autumn. When I Was Asked How I Could Leave Vermont in the Middle of October. Grace Paley. CP-PalGC

I did not want to grow, but quick-fingered memories. Tower, The. Dan Pagis. SP-PagiD, tr. by Stephen Mitchell

I did the dragon's will until you came. Her Triumph. William Butler Yeats. CP-YeatW

I didn't always think Penelope. Ambition. Eleanor Wilner. SP-WilnE

I didn't find them again, ever—those lost so fast. Days of 1903. Constantine P. Cavafy. CP-CavaC, tr. by Theoharis Constantine Theoharis

I didn't get much sleep last night. Underwear. Lawrence Ferlinghetti. SP-FerlL

I didn't have to buy the acid. Blue Hog, A. Norman Dubie. CP-DubiN

I didn't just read the Bible, I lived it. Charisma. Ai. SP-Ai

I didn't know the burly old man who lived in a small house like ours down the block in Newark. Secrets. C. K. Williams. SP-WillC

I didn't make you know how glad I was. Servant to Servants, A. Robert Frost. CP-FrosR

I didn't notice. Invention of Nothing. Charles Simic. SP-SimiC; SP-SimiCE

I Didn't Say a Word, or, Who Called That Piccolo Player a Father? Ogden Nash. CP-NashO

I didn't say mass this morning. Priest's Confession, The. Ai. SP-Ai

I didn't / want / to hurt you. Pieces. Robert Creeley. CP-CreeR

I didn't want to use it at first. Fishing Pole of the Drowned Man, The. Raymond Carver. CP-CarvR

I didn't write Etsuko. Nothing but Color. Ai. SP-Ai

I die; but when the grave shall press. Lines: "I die; but when the grave shall press." Emily Jane Brontë. CP-BronE

I die I die the Mother said. Grey Monk, The. William Blake. CP-BlakW

I die, no matter what I do I die. Sestina: "I die, no matter what I do I die." Richard Eberhart. CP-EberR

I died and called for you. In Dream. David Ignatow. SP-IgnaD

I died for Beauty—but was scarce. Emily Dickinson. CP-DickE

I died for lack of company. Voice from the Tomb (4). Stevie Smith. CP-SmitS

I died with the first blow and was buried. Autobiography. Dan Pagis. SP-PagiD, tr. by Stephen Mitchell

I dig my foot into the stubborn grass. His Death from Cancer. William Dickey. SP-DickW

I dined at Natorp's yester-eve. Last Poem. Robert Browning. CP-BroR2

I dip the oar and lean. Shoals Returning, The. Thomas Kinsella. CP-KinsT

I discover in myself. August, 1968. Donald Davie. CP-DaviDC

I dislikt but even now. Upon Himself. Robert Herrick. CP-HerrR

I do believe, and yet, in grief. Chapel of the Hermits, The. John Greenleaf Whittier. CP-WhitJ

I do believe, if you were made of stone. Michelangelo Buonarroti. CP-Miche, tr. by John Frederick Nims

I do believe that die I must. His Creed. Robert Herrick. CP-HerrR

I do but ask that you be always fair. Edna St. Vincent Millay. CP-MillE

I do confess thou art sae fair. Robert Burns. CP-BurnR

I Do, I Will, I Have. Ogden Nash. CP-NashO

I do, Lord, I do. Therefore I am. After You Die You Don't Give a Piddling Damn. Miller Williams. CP-WillM

I do no cry, beloved, neither curse. Unpardonable Sin, The. G. K. Chesterton.

CP-ChesG

I do not always understand what you say. Poem: "I do not always understand what you say." James Schuyler. CP-SchuJ

I do not ask for mercy for understanding for peace. I Do Not Speak. Stevie Smith. CP-SmitS

I do not ask you for presents rare. Christmas, 1921. Dorothy Parker. CP-ParkD

I do not bring you health, or cold. To His Wife, in Her Illness. G. K. Chesterton. CP-ChesG

I do not care for Bolivar Black. Hearts and Flowers or What I Know about Bolivar Black. Ogden Nash. CP-NashO

I do not choose to dream; there cometh on me. In the Old Age of the Soul. Ezra Pound. CP-PoEar

I do not claim to put an end to anything. Poetry Ends with Me. Nicanor Parra. CP-MertT

I do not count the day. What the Grecian Earns. Kenneth Patchen. CP-PatcK

I do not count the hours I spend. Waldeinsamkeit. Ralph Waldo Emerson. CP-EmerR

I do not doubt you. In Due Form. Laura Riding Jackson. CP-RidiL

I do not fear my thoughts will die. Henry David Thoreau. CP-ThorH

I do not feel spring's windy ingress. Scarf of June, The. Richard Eberhart. CP-EberR

I do not hate you. White Ones, The. Langston Hughes. CP-HughL; CP-HughL1

I do not have a fiddle so. Gob Music. Theodore Roethke. CP-RoetT

I do not intend the people I know to believe me. Inscription for Richard Eberhard, An. John Ciardi. CP-CiarJ

I do not know, alas, where I should turn. Petrarch. CP-Petra, tr. by J. G. Nichols

I do not know more than the Sea tells me. Achilles' Song. Robert Duncan. SP-DuncR

I do not know what face is looking back. Blind Man, A. Jorge Luis Borges. SP-BorgJ, tr. by Alastair Reid

I do not know what we say. I know that your poems. Epistle to Léon-Paul Fargue. Archibald MacLeish. CP-MacLA

I do not know where I will be in July. Fractal Song. Michael Palmer. SP-PalmM

I do not know whether it is possible to present. Bowl of Blood, The. Robinson Jeffers. CP-JefR3

I do not know who is out in the snow. Ernesto Cardenal. CP-MertT Fr. Gethsemani, KY.

I do not like my state of mind. Symptom Recital. Dorothy Parker. CP-ParkD

I do not like the winter wind. It's Never Fair Weather. Ogden Nash. CP-NashO

I do not look for holy saints to guide me on my way. Pilgrim's Way, A. Rudyard Kipling. CP-KiplR

I Do Not Look for Love That Is a Dream. Christina Georgina Rossetti. CP-RosC3

   (Lady Montrevor.) CP-RosC3

I do not love my Empire's foes. Piet. Rudyard Kipling. CP-KiplR

I do not love, nor can it be. Of Love. Robert Herrick. CP-HerrR

I do not love thee, Isabel, and yet thou art most fair! Isabel. John Greenleaf Whittier. CP-WhitJ

I do not love to wed. Poet Loves a Mistress, but Not to Marry, The. Robert Herrick. CP-HerrR

I do not mean the symbol. Woman Who Could Not Live With Her Faulty Heart, The. Margaret Atwood. CP-AtwM2

I do not move my hands any longer. I do not. Still, A. Andrei Codrescu. SP-CodrA

I do not need thy food, but thou dost mine. My Meat and Drink. Jones Very. CP-VeryJ

I do not see the hills around. Rambler, The. Thomas Hardy. CP-HardT

I do not sit and sigh for wealth untold. Fulfillment. Dorothy Parker. CP-ParkD

I Do Not Speak. Stevie Smith. CP-SmitS

I do not speak of what's yours. End of Owls, The. Hans Magnus Enzensberger. SP-EnzeH, tr. by Michael Hamburger

I do not think that I ought to appear in public. Intimations. Tennessee Williams. CP-WillT

I Do Not Understand. Czeslaw Milosz. CP-MiloCN, tr. by Robert Hass

I do not want a plain box, I want a sarcophagus. Last Words. Sylvia Plath. CP-PlatS

I do not want to be reflective any more. Wolves. Louis MacNeice. CP-MacNL

I do not want to be who I am. Petty luck. I Am Not Even Dust. Jorge Luis Borges. SP-BorgJ, tr. by Eric McHenry

I do not weep, I would not weep. A.S. to G.S. Emily Jane Brontë. CP-BronE

I do not wish to win your vow. Maiden's Pledge, A. Thomas Hardy. CP-HardT

I do not wonder, stones. Chartres. Archibald MacLeish. CP-MacLA

I do remember some things. Manna. James Tate. SP-TateJ

I Do Set My Bow in the Cloud. Christina Georgina Rossetti. CP-RosC3

I do tricks in order to know. With My Crowbar Key. William Stafford. SP-StafWW

I do. / Victim. / Sales. Study Nature. Gertrude Stein. CP-SteiG

I do what Simon says. Simon. Josephine Jacobsen. CP-JacoJ

I do[e] but name thee Pembroke, and I find. To William, Earl[e] of Pembroke.

Ben Jonson. CP-JonsB; SP-JonsB

I doe love I know not what. No Luck in Love. Robert Herrick. CP-HerrR

I done got 'uligion, honey, an' I's happy ez a king. Temptation. Paul Laurence Dunbar. CP-DunbP

I don't always see you clearly. Garden of Delights, The. James Laughlin. CP-LaugJ

I don't ask the Foreign Legion. On Working White Liberals. Maya Angelou. SP-AngeM

I don't beat the walls with my fists. Madness. Charles Bukowski. SP-BukC1

I don't begrudge the spring. Parting with a View. Wisława Szymborska. SP-SzymWM, tr. by Joanna Trzeciak

I don't believe in 'ristercrats. My Sort o' Man. Paul Laurence Dunbar. CP-DunbP

I don't believe the sleepers in this house. Cabin in the Clearing, A. Robert Frost. CP-FrosR

I don't belive in ashes; some of the others do. Veteran. Fanny Howe. SP-HoweF

I don't blame the kettle drums—they are hungry. Blizzard Notes. Carl Sandburg. CP-SandC

I don't care whether I am beautiful to you. One Woman to All Women. D. H. Lawrence. CP-LawrD

I don't dare start thinking in the morning. Blues at Dawn. Langston Hughes. CP-HughL; CP-HughL3

I don't get tired of you. Don't grow weary. Thirsty Fish, A. Jelaluddin Rumi. SP-Rumi, tr. by Coleman Barks

I don't give a damn. Croon. Langston Hughes. CP-HughL; CP-HughL3

I don't hate you lately. Robert Creeley. CP-CreeR

I don't know. Gonfalon Raised Tonight, The. Charles Olson. CP-OlsoC

I don't know about the cold. Poem (I Can't Speak for the Wind). James Tate. SP-TateJ

I don't know as I get what D.H. Lawrence is driving at. Poem: "I don't know as I get what D.H. Lawrence is driving at." Frank O'Hara. SP-OharF

I don't know exactly how long ago Hector was a pup. Nature Knows Best. Ogden Nash. CP-NashO

I don't know how he came. Osawatomie. Carl Sandburg. CP-SandC

I don't know / how late it is. I'm writing. Essential Resources. Adrienne Rich. SP-RicA2

I don't know how many bottles of beer. Beer. Charles Bukowski. SP-BukC1

I don't know how to kiss. Burning Mystery of Anna in 1951, The. Kenneth Koch. SP-KochK

I don't know if I helped him up. Transport of Slaves from Maryland to Mississippi, The. Rita Dove. SP-DoveR

I don't know if I shall have a share in the World to Come. My Children. Yehuda Amichai. SP-AmicYL, tr. by Benjamin Harshav and Barbara Harshav

I don't know / if I'll be able to visit. Request for Blanca, A. Gabriela Mistral. SP-MistG, tr. by Maria Giachetti [or Jacketti]

I don't know if you doubt it. Poem V (F) W. Frank O'Hara. SP-OharF

I don't know, it was raining and I had fallen down. Parts of an Opera, Parts of a Guitar, Part of Nowhere. Charles Bukowski. SP-BukC2

I don't know somehow it seems sufficient. Gravelly Run. A. R. Ammons. CP-AmmoA

I don't know the names of flowers. Rhodes. Raymond Carver. CP-CarvR

I don't know what bee balm is. To Go. Heather McHugh. SP-McHuH

I don't know what day or year of their secret cycle this blazing golden afternoon might be. Dominion: Depression. C. K. Williams. SP-WillC

I don't know what her name is, for you see we've never met. Lady in Back, The. Dorothy Parker. CP-ParkD

I don't know what is good or bad for me hereabout. Yehuda Amichai. SP-AmicYL Fr. At Right Angles.

I don't know what the hell happened all that summer. Recovery. John Berryman. CP-BerrJ

I Don't Know Where She Is Wandering Tonight. James Laughlin. CP-LaugJ

I don't know whether you know what's new in juvenile literature. Fee Fi Ho Hum, No Wonder Baby Sucks Her Thumb. Ogden Nash. CP-NashO

I don't know which to mourn. Both have died on me, my wife and my car. That's the Sum of It. David Ignatow. SP-IgnaD

I don't know why. Puzzlement. Langston Hughes. CP-HughL; CP-HughL3

I don't know why or how. Leaf from Mr. Dyer's Woods, A. Hayden Carruth. CP-CarrHS

I don't know why the moth. Green, The. Thomas Lux. SP-LuxT

I don't know why they turn the irrigation. Bus Stopped in Fields of Misdemeanor, The. Norman Dubie. CP-DubiN

I don't like diamonds. Voracities and Verities Sometimes Are Interacting. Marianne Craig Moore. CP-MoorM

I don't like the government where I live. Capitol Air. Allen Ginsberg. CP-GinsA; SP-GinsA

I don't mean, just like that, to put down. Maximus, to Gloucester. Charles Olson. SP-OlsoC Fr. Maximus Poems, The.

I don't mind dying. As Befits a Man. Langston Hughes. CP-HughL; CP-HughL3

I don't mind eels. Eel, The. Ogden Nash. CP-NashO

I don't mind the human race. Discrimination. Kenneth Rexroth. CP-RexrK

I don't move. Spectacles. Heather McHugh. SP-McHuH

I Don't Need a Bedsheet with Slits for Eyes to Kill You In. Charles Bukowski. SP-BukC2

I don't need no sleepin' medecine. What, No Sheep? Ogden Nash. CP-NashO

I don't remember anything of then, down there around the magnolias. Ode to Michael Goldberg ('s Birth and Other Births). Frank O'Hara. SP-OharF

I don't remember exactly when Budberg died, it was either two years ago or three. Magic Mountain, A. Czeslaw Milosz. CP-MiloC; CP-MiloCN, tr. by Lillian Vallee

I don't reproach the spring. Parting with a View. Wisława Szymborska. SP-SzymW, tr. by Stanislaw Barańczak and Clare Cavanagh

I don't see your head. To Frantz Fanon. Adrienne Rich. CP-RicAE

I don't show my work to anybody, I am quite alone. Monkhood. John Berryman. CP-BerrJ

I don't suppose that he will be able to build these fires much longer. Part of a Hero. Tennessee Williams. CP-WillT

I don't think we shall. Centenarian, The. William Carlos Williams. CP-WilW1

I don't travel on planes. Unwinged Ones, The. Ogden Nash. CP-NashO

I don't understand by what perversity. Shelf Is a Ledge, A. Gregory Orr. SP-OrrG

I don't understand it all and I am. Ode to Plurality. Adam Zagajewski. SP-ZagaA, tr. by Renata Gorczynski

I don't usually try to listen / in on conversations but. Social Note. James Laughlin. CP-LaugJ

I don't want. Heaven ("I don't want"). Robert Creeley. CP-CreeR

I don't want real narcisi—nor do I like. Artificial Flowers. Constantine P. Cavafy. CP-CavaC, tr. by Theoharis Constantine Theoharis

I don't want the sincere gifts. Fernando Pessoa. SP-PessF, tr. by Susan M. Brown and Edwin Honig

I don't want to be classed among the pedantics. Grin and Bear Left. Ogden Nash. CP-NashO

I don't want to leave. Lunch and After. Robert Creeley. SP-CreeR

I don't want to speak of your sky. Read the Signs. Clarence Major. SP-MajoC

I Don't Want to Startle You but They Are Going to Kill Most of Us. Kenneth Patchen. CP-PatcK

I don't wish you were one. Never Land. Yusef Komunyakaa. CP-KomuY

I doubt if you knew. Rescue, The. John Logan. CP-LogaJ

I doubt if you'll remember (we were younger then). Cenotaph for Two Butterflies. Robert Stock. SP-StocR

I doubt I'll get silk stockings out. Lorine Niedecker. CP-NiedL

I doubt it not—then more, far more. Shakespeare-Bacon's Cipher. Walt Whitman. CP-WhitW

I doubt not God is good, well-meaning, kind. Yet Do I Marvel. Countee Cullen. CP-CullC

I drank at every vine. Feast. Edna St. Vincent Millay. CP-MillE

I drank cool water from the fountain. Raisin, The. Donald Hall. CP-HallD

I drank musty ale at the Illinois Athletic Club with the millionaire. Fellow Citizens. Carl Sandburg. CP-SandC

I draw near to the roof's edge. Play Again. David Ignatow. SP-IgnaD

I dreaded that first Robin, so. Emily Dickinson. CP-DickE

I dream a world where man. Langston Hughes. CP-HughL; CP-HughL2

I dream about father every night. Emily Dickinson. SP-DickE

I dream an inescapable dream. Dream, The. Wendell Berry. CP-BerrW

I dream awake in the uptown morning. Elegy 2: "I dream awake in the uptown morning." John Ciardi. CP-CiarJ

I dream I am flying above the city. Question, The. David Ignatow. SP-IgnaD

I dream I am lying in the mud on my back and staring up into the sky. David Ignatow. SP-IgnaD

I dream I hurl a spear into the body of my love. David Ignatow. SP-IgnaD

I Dream I'm the Death of Orpheus. Adrienne Rich. CP-RicAE; SP-RicA1; SP-RicA2

I dream my love goes riding out. Song for a Dancer. Kenneth Rexroth. CP-RexrK

I dream of a blitz-war of sweating teenagers. Note. Andrei Codrescu. SP-CodrA

I dream of a red-rose tree. Women and Roses. Robert Browning. CP-BroR1

I dream of language as the sun. While I live. David Ignatow. SP-IgnaD

I dream of poems like the bread-knife. Hugh MacDiarmid. SP-MacDH Fr. Kind of Poetry I Want, The.

I dream of the drums. Drums. Langston Hughes. CP-HughL; CP-HughL3

I dream that the dearest I ever knew. Bereft, She Thinks She Dreams. Thomas Hardy. CP-HardT

I dream that you are kisses Allah sent. Rose-Lady, The. James Whitcomb Riley. CP-RileJ

I dream the sea, that sea, surrounding me. Alexander Selkirk. Jorge Luis Borges. SP-BorgJ, tr. by Stephen Kessler

I dream'd I lay where flowers were springing. Robert Burns. CP-BurnR

I Dream'd in a Dream. Walt Whitman. CP-WhitW

I dreamed a dream: I dreamt that I espied. Arthur Hugh Clough. SP-ClouA

I dreamed a dream of heaven, white as frost. Mirror of Madmen, The. G. K. Chesterton. CP-ChesG

I dreamed a dream: seven fat, fleshy girls. Yehuda Amichai. SP-AmicYL, tr. by Benjamin Harshav and Barbara Harshav

I dreamed and did not seek: today I seek. Yet A Little While. Christina Georgina Rossetti. CP-RosC2

I dreamed as in my bed I lay. Her Dream. William Butler Yeats. CP-YeatW

I dreamed I already loved you. Three Poems with Yevtushenko. James Dickey. CP-DickJ

I dreamed I called you on the telephone. For the Dead. Adrienne Rich. SP-RicA1; SP-RicA2

I dreamed I dwelled in a homeless place. New Stanzas for Amazing Grace. Allen Ginsberg. SP-GinsA

I Dreamed I Got a Letter from Ezra Pound. Alan Dugan. CP-DugaA

I Dreamed I Moved among the Elysian Fields. Edna St. Vincent Millay. CP-MillE

I dreamed I moved among the Elysian fields. I Dreamed I Moved among the Elysian Fields. Edna St. Vincent Millay. CP-MillE

I dreamed I stood upon a hill, and, lo! Christian. Ambrose Bierce. SP-BierA

I dreamed I was a spider. Dream, A. James Whitcomb Riley. CP-RileJ

I dreamed I was among the conquerors. Sonnet: "I dreamed I was among the conquerors." E. E. Cummings. CP-CummE

I dreamed, Justine, we chanced on one another. Apparition, The. Charles Tomlinson. CP-TomlC

I dreamed kind Jesus fouled the big-gun gears. Soldier's Dream. Wilfred Owen. CP-OwenW

I dreamed my father flicked. Father. A. R. Ammons. CP-AmmoA

I dreamed my friend got up and walked. Elegy for Robert Winner. Thomas Lux. SP-LuxT

I Dreamed My Genesis. Dylan Thomas. CP-ThomD

I dreamed myself of their people, I am of their people. Populist. George Oppen. CP-OppGN

I dreamed of a tiger, wounded. Two Pendants: For the Ears. William Carlos Williams. CP-WilW2

I dreamed of an instrument of political torture. Another Dollar. C. K. Williams. CP-WillC

I Dreamed of an Out-Thrust Arm of Land. Philip Larkin. CP-LarkP

I dreamed one man stood against a thousand. Graves. Carl Sandburg. CP-SandC

I dreamed one night that I was in Northern France in one. Dream, The. George Oppen. CP-OppGN

I dreamed [or dream'd] that, as I wandered [or wander'd] by the way. Question, The. Percy Bysshe Shelley. CP-ShelP

I dreamed [or dream'd] this mortal part of mine. Vine, The. Robert Herrick. CP-HerrR

I dreamed that dead, and meditating. Weed, The. Elizabeth Bishop. CP-BishE

I dreamed that I stood in a valley, and amid sighs. He Tells a Valley Full of Lovers. William Butler Yeats. CP-YeatW

I dreamed that I was dead, as all men do. But Only Mine. James Wright. CP-WrigJ

I dreamed that I was old: in stale declension. Stanley Kunitz. CP-KunSC

I dreamed that loving me he would love on. Zara. Christina Georgina Rossetti. CP-RosC3

I dreamed that Milton's spirit rose, and took. Fragment: Milton's Spirit. Percy Bysshe Shelley. CP-ShelP

I dreamed that one had died in a strange place. Dream of Death, A. William Butler Yeats. CP-YeatW

I dreamed the play was real. Doll's "Arabian Nights," A. Nicholas Vachel Lindsay. CP-LindV

I dreamed there was once held a feast. Gerousios Oinos. Robert Browning. CP-BroR2

I dreamed [or dream'd] we both were in bed. Vision to Electra, The. Robert Herrick. CP-HerrR

I Dreamt a Dream—What can it mean? Angel, The. William Blake. CP-BlakW Fr. Songs of Experience.

I dreamt all night such glad painful exultant dreams. Dream of What Is Missing, A. Robert Bly. SP-BlyR

I dreamt her sensual proportions. Death of Venus, The. Robert Creeley. CP-CreeR

I dreamt I caught a little owl. Christina Georgina Rossetti. CP-RosC2

I dreamt. I saw three ladies in a tree. Three Ladies, The. Robert Creeley. CP-CreeR

I dreamt last night. For No Clear Reason. Robert Creeley. CP-CreeR

I dreamt, last night, of your stone cabinet, Porte de l'Enfer. Parallax Monograph for Rodin, The. Norman Dubie. CP-DubiN

I Dreamt, last night, Thou didst transfuse. His Dream[e]. Robert Herrick. CP-HerrR

I dreamt of a seal. Seal. Anne Sexton. CP-SextA

I dreamt the roses one time went. Parliament of Roses to Julia, The. Robert Herrick. CP-HerrR

I dreamt Tolstoi was mad and running away. Diamond Persona, The. Norman

Dubie. CP-DubiN

I drew solitude over me, on the lone shore. Prelude: "I drew solitude over me, on the lone shore." Robinson Jeffers. CP-JefR1

I drew the letter out, while gleamed. Sun on the Letter, The. Thomas Hardy. CP-HardT

I drink the juice of fruit. In the Room. Yehuda Amichai. SP-AmicYL, *tr. by* Benjamin Harshav *and* Barbara Harshav

I drink wine from two glasses. Paul Celan. SP-CelaP, *tr. by* John Felstiner

I drip, drip here. Sundial on a Wet Day, The. Thomas Hardy. CP-HardT

I drive Eastward. The ethics of return. James Vincent Cunningham. CP-CunnJ

I drive my car / through a valley. Countryside. Charles Bukowski. SP-BukC2

I drive my car to supermarket. Superman. John Updike. CP-UpdiJ

I drive Westward. Tumble and loco weed. J. V. Cunningham. CP-CunnJ

I dropped my pen; and listened to the Wind. Sonnet: Composed While the Author Was Engaged in Writing a Tract Occasioned by the Convention of Cintra. William Wordsworth. CP-WorW1

I dropped to depth. Birth and Death. Richard Eberhart. CP-EberR

I drove a day and a night. Eastport. Heather McHugh. SP-McHuH

I drove north, lost. Wyoming. Clarence Major. SP-MajoC

I drove out to the airport / on a blue sunny day. Airplane Blues. Allen Ginsberg. SP-GinsA

I drove up to the graveyard, which. Soul Longs to Return Whence It Came, The. Richard Eberhart. CP-EberR

I dug and dug amongst the snow. Christina Georgina Rossetti. CP-RosC2

I dunno yer highfalutin' words, but here's th' way it seems. Poem in the American Manner. Dorothy Parker. CP-ParkD

I dwell alone—I dwell alone, alone. Autumn. Christina Georgina Rossetti. CP-RosC1

I dwell amid the city ever. Soul's Travelling, The. Elizabeth Barrett Browning. CP-BroEB

I dwell in a lonely house I know. Ghost House. Robert Frost. CP-FrosR

I dwell in Possibility. Emily Dickinson. CP-DickE

I dwelled in Hell on earth to write this rhyme. Two Sonnets. Allen Ginsberg. CP-GinsA

I dwelt alone. Eulalie—A Song. Edgar Allan Poe. CP-PoeEd

I dwelt in the shade of a city. Gentleman's Epitaph on Himself and a Lady, Who Were Buried Together, A. Thomas Hardy. CP-HardT

I eat oatmeal for breakfast. Oatmeal. Galway Kinnell. SP-KinnGN

I eat these. Appetite. Maxine W. Kumin. SP-KumiM

I employ the blind mandolin player. Music, A. Wendell Berry. CP-BerrW

I enjoy the simple path. Han-shan. CP-ColdM, *tr. by* Red Pine

I enter. Stillness and Vertigo. Clarence Major. SP-MajoC

I enter a daisy-and-buttercup land. Growth in May. Thomas Hardy. CP-HardT

I enter the city's sinuous folds. Little Old Women, The. Charles Baudelaire. CP-BaudC, *tr. by* Walter Martin

I Enter the Dark Church Slowly. Aleksandr Aleksandrovich Blok. SP-BlokA, *tr. by* Peter France *and* Jon Stallworthy

I enter the waiting room in a station. Wanderer, A. Adam Zagajewski. SP-ZagaA, *tr. by* Renata Gorczynski

I enter thy garden of roses. Translation of the Romaic Song *Mpeno mes to periboli, Horaiotate Haide, k. t. l.* Lord Byron. CP-Byron

I entered at the top of my voice. I forget the song. Acclimatization. W. S. Merwin. SP-MerwW

I entered the cave of the amethysts. Pablo Neruda. SP-NeruP *Fr.* Skystones.

I entered the forest / of clocks. Federico García Lorca. CP-GarcF, *tr. by* Jerome Rothenberg *Fr.* In the Forest of Clocks.

I entered weary of my woes. Rose, The. John Crowe Ransom. SP-RansJ

I envy seas—whereon He rides. Emily Dickinson. CP-DickE

I envy you your chance of death. Fragment 68: "I envy you your chance of death." "H. D." CP-DoolH

I escaped once and don't remember what god it was from, what test. Yehuda Amichai. SP-AmicY *Fr.* In a Right Angle: A Cycle of Quatrains.

I—even I—am he who knoweth the roads. Aegupton. Ezra Pound. CP-PoEar

I evoke / the Corinthian capital. Contemplation. Federico García Lorca. CP-GarcF, *tr. by* Jerome Rothenberg *Fr.* Seaside Prints.

I exchange nervous glances. Seeds. Raymond Carver. CP-CarvR

I exhibit here the well-known failure of. Hero Comes Home in His Hamper, and Is Exhibited at the World's Fair, The. Howard Nemerov. CP-NemeH

I exist without the dignity of stone. Tomorrow. David Ignatow. SP-IgnaD

I existed before my mind realized me. Two Selves, The. David Ignatow. SP-IgnaD

I expand my heart so that. Dawn. Gabriela Mistral. SP-MistG, *tr. by* Maria Giachetti [*or* Jacketti]

I expected to be greeted by one of the figures. Pleasures of This Gentle Day. Kenneth Patchen. CP-PatcK

I explain the silvered passing of a ship at night. Stephen Crane. CP-CranS

I Ezra the dying. Whose Timeless Reach. A. R. Ammons. CP-AmmoA

I face impossible feats at your command. Pride of Love. Robert Graves. CP-GravR

I faced the star maker, the candy butcher. Mystic Moment. James Tate. SP-TateJ

I failed to draw a map and you followed it perfectly. Lens. Michael Palmer. SP-PalmM

I fain would sing of Cadmus king. Transcriptions from the "Anacreontea." Robert Browning. CP-BroR2

I faint, I perish with my love! I grow. Fragment: "I faint, I perish with my love! I grow." Percy Bysshe Shelley. CP-ShelP

I fall asleep, and dream I am working in the fields. Dream of a Brother, A. Robert Bly. SP-BlyR

I fall asleep these days too easily. Dozing on the Lawn. Archibald MacLeish. CP-MacLA

I Fall into It Without Trying. Charles Bukowski. SP-BukC3

I fancy the good fairies dressed in white. Christina Georgina Rossetti. CP-RosC3

I farm a pasture where the boulders lie. Of the Stones of the Place. Robert Frost. CP-FrosR

I fasted for some forty days on bread and buttermilk. Pilgrim, The. William Butler Yeats. CP-YeatW

I fear a Man of frugal Speech. Emily Dickinson. CP-DickE

I fear from my misfortune. Guido Cavalcanti. CP-CavaG, *tr. by* Marc Cirigliano

I fear my conscience because it makes me lie. Symptoms. Robert Lowell. SP-LoweR

I fear the ladies and. Rencontres Funestes. Stevie Smith. CP-SmitS

I fear this war. Lorine Niedecker. CP-NiedL

I fear thy kisses, gentle maiden. To ———: "I fear thy kisses, gentle maiden." Percy Bysshe Shelley. CP-ShelP

I fear to draw the wing of the sparrow. Written Next to a Blue Flower. Pablo Antonio Cuadra. CP-MertT

I fear we think too lightly of. Emily Dickinson. SP-DickE

I fear you have much happiness. Emily Dickinson. SP-DickE

I feard the fury [*or* roughness] of my wind. William Blake. CP-BlakW

I fear[e] no Earthly Powers. On Himselfe. Robert Herrick. CP-HerrR

I feared that the future, now already dwindling. 1972. Jorge Luis Borges. SP-BorgJ, *tr. by* Alastair Reid

I feared these present years. On Being Twenty-Six. Philip Larkin. CP-LarkP

I fearing trite things. Nous N'osons Plus Chanter les Roses. Constantine P. Cavafy. CP-CavaC, *tr. by* Theoharis Constantine Theoharis

I fed on you, and with you, many a year. Michelangelo Buonarroti. CP-Miche, *tr. by* John Frederick Nims

I feed a flame within, which so torments me. Song: "I feed a flame within, which so torments me." John Dryden. SP-DrydJ *Fr.* Secret Love; or, The Maiden Queen.

I fee'd a man at Martinmass. Can Ye Labor Lea. Robert Burns. CP-BurnR

I feed my mind on such a noble food. Petrarch. CP-Petra, *tr. by* J. G. Nichols

I feel a mortal isolation. Every Lovely Limb's a Desolation. Stevie Smith. CP-SmitS

I feel absolute reverence to nobody and to nothing human. Absolute Reverence. D. H. Lawrence. CP-LawrD

I feel all right. Now. White Rose. César Vallejo. CP-WrigJ

I feel an apparition. Instant of Clearness. Jean Le Roy. CP-StevWP, *tr. by* Wallace Stevens

I feel as if I am at a dead. Allen Ginsberg. CP-GinsA

I feel congruity, feel colleagueship. Relations. John Berryman. CP-BerrJ

I Feel Drunk All the Time. Kenneth Patchen. CP-PatcK

I feel funny today. Picnic Cantata, A. James Schuyler. CP-SchuJ

I feel, if aught I ought to rhyme. Autographic. James Whitcomb Riley. CP-RileJ

I feel ill. What can the matter be? Come, Death (2). Stevie Smith. CP-SmitS

I feel illimitable essence. Undercliff Evening. Richard Eberhart. CP-EberR

I Feel Just Fine in My Pants. Yehuda Amichai. SP-AmicY, *tr. by* Chana Bloch

I feel like dancin', baby. Sunday by the Combination. Langston Hughes. CP-HughL; CP-HughL3

I feel like the end. Fanny Howe. SP-HoweF *Fr.* O'Clock.

I feel like the ground, astonished. Ground Cries Out, The. Jelaluddin Rumi. SP-Rumi, *tr. by* Coleman Barks

I feel my face being bitten by the tides. Knowledge that Comes through Experience, The. Jane Cooper. CP-CoopJ

I feel my heart melt. Dusk. Gabriela Mistral. SP-MistG, *tr. by* Maria Giachetti [*or* Jacketti]

I feel sure you will be pleased. Spiel. A. R. Ammons. CP-AmmoA

I feel terribly strong today. Beginning of April, The. C. K. Williams. CP-WillC; SP-WillC

I feel the ancient breeze, see with delight. Petrarch. CP-Petra, *tr. by* J. G. Nichols

I feel the bitter rain of tears distilled. Petrarch. CP-Petra, *tr. by* J. G. Nichols

I feel the caress of my own fingers. Gentle Man, The. William Carlos Williams. CP-WilW1

I feel the city grow wild with desire fertile. Fanny Howe. SP-HoweF *Fr.* In the Spirit There Are No Accidents.

I feel the onward rush of spring once more. Sonnets for the Spring (A Sequence). Tennessee Williams. CP-WillT

I fell asleep and dreamed that I. Oneiromancy. Ambrose Bierce. SP-BierA

I fell away toward death. Flower Grower in Aquarius. Alan Dugan. CP-DugaA

I fell from the bouncing tailgate to roll in traffic. Elegy 1: "I fell from the bouncing tailgate to roll in traffic." John Ciardi. CP-CiarJ

I fell in love at my first evening party. Dream of Frances Speedwell, A. Robert Graves. CP-GravR

I fell in love with a girl. Her & It. John Berryman. CP-BerrJ

I fell in love with Major Spruce. Progression. Stevie Smith. CP-SmitS

I fell in the battle of Ashdod. Since Then. Yehuda Amichai. SP-AmicYL, tr. by Benjamin Harshav and Barbara Harshav

I Fellowed Sleep. Dylan Thomas. CP-ThomD

I felt a Cleaving in my Mind. Emily Dickinson. CP-DickE

I Felt a Funeral in My Brain. Emily Dickinson. CP-DickE

I felt a strange fear when the war-talk. For the Duration. Ted Hughes. SP-HughTN

I felt both pleasure and a shiver. River, The. Gregory Orr. SP-OrrG

I felt life coming on. Listing. Richard Eberhart. CP-EberR

I felt my life with both my hands. I Took My Power in My Hand. Emily Dickinson. CP-DickE

I felt the chill of the meadow underfoot. Quest of the Purple-Fringed, The. Robert Frost. CP-FrosR

I felt the lurch and halt of her heart. Lightning. D. H. Lawrence. CP-LawrD

I felt, under my old breasts, this April day. Kathleen Jessie Raine. SP-RainK

I fight with the tools of the mind. Ways and Means. Richard Eberhart. CP-EberR

I figured you as nude between. Apostrophe to Vincentine, The. Wallace Stevens. CP-StevW; CP-StevWP

I find, after all these years, I am a believer. Ars Poetica 2. Charles Wright. SP-WrigCN

I find an old deserted nest. Empty Nest, An. James Whitcomb Riley. CP-RileJ

I find it very difficult to enthuse. Everybody Tells Me Everything. Ogden Nash. CP-NashO

I find it written of SIMONIDES. William Wordsworth. CP-WorW1

I find no peace and all my war[r] is done. Description of the Contrarious Passions in a Lover. Petrarch. CP-WyatT, tr. by Sir Thomas Wyatt Fr. Sonnets to Laura.

I find no peace, yet have no war in hand. Petrarch. CP-Petra, tr. by J. G. Nichols

I find no record of one in. Can There Be a Female Bodhissatva? James Laughlin. CP-LaugJ

I find nothing to say. Inditing a Good Matter. Donald Davie. CP-DaviDC

I finish the Times. Shut eyes. My head. Commuter's Entry in a Connecticut Diary. Robert Penn Warren. CP-WarrR

I finished my wine. Night on a Visa Card. Charles Bukowski. SP-BukC3

I first discovered what was killing these men. Absalom. Muriel Rukeyser. CP-RukeM

I first tasted under Apollo's lips. Evadne. "H. D." CP-DoolH

I fished alone that languid autumn evening. Evening. Raymond Carver. CP-CarvR

I fit for them. Emily Dickinson. CP-DickE

I fix[e] mine eye on thine, and there. Witchcraft by a Picture. John Donne. CP-DonnJ; MW-DonnJ

I flash-glimpsed in the headlights—the high moment. Coming Down through Somerset. Ted Hughes. SP-HughTN

I Float Between the Spheres. James Laughlin. CP-LaugJ

I fly a black kite on a long string. Dangerous Games. Carolyn Kizer. CP-KizeC

I fly on wings of fancy up to heaven. Petrarch. CP-Petra, tr. by J. G. Nichols

I followed Christ, and vainly hoped on earth. Christ Abiding Forever. Jones Very. CP-VeryJ

I followed deadpan rivers down and down. Drunken Boat. Arthur Rimbaud. CP-RimbA, tr. by Martin Sorrell

I followed my Duke ere I was a lover. Sir Richard's Song. Rudyard Kipling. CP-KiplR Fr. Puck of Pook's Hill.

I followed the narrow cliffside trail half way up the mountain. Deer Lay Down Their Bones, The. Robinson Jeffers. CP-JefR3

I followed Thee, my God, I followed Thee / To see the end. Christina Georgina Rossetti. CP-RosC2

I for whom the world is a clear stream. In San Marco, Venezia. William Carlos Williams. CP-WilW1

I forgot that your light foot. Useless Vigil, The. Gabriela Mistral. SP-MistG, tr. by Maria Giachetti [or Jacketti]

I forgot / to send a card to Jennie. Madam's Christmas (or Merry Christmas Everybody). Langston Hughes. CP-HughL

I found a dimpled spider, fat and white. Design. Robert Frost. CP-FrosR

I found a loose cement slab outside the icecream store. Best Way to Get Famous Is to Run Away, The. Charles Bukowski. SP-BukC2

I found a pigeon's skull on the machair. Perfect. Hugh MacDiarmid. SP-MacDH

I found a shepherdess in a grove. Guido Cavalcanti. CP-CavaG, tr. by Marc Cirigliano

I found a torrent falling in a glen. Torrent, The. Edwin Arlington Robinson. CP-RobiE

I found a / weed. Reflective. A. R. Ammons. CP-AmmoA

I found an appeasable place. Battleground. Robert Stock. SP-StocR

I found an old book on animals. Yehuda Amichai. SP-AmicYL Fr. Elegies on the War Dead.

I found far culled from fragrant field and grove. Stranger's Gift, The. Jones Very. CP-VeryJ

I Found Her Out There. Thomas Hardy. CP-HardT

I found in dreams a place of wind and flowers. Ballad of Life, A. Algernon Charles Swinburne. SP-SwinA

I found it flaming in the scarlet rose. Wallace Stevens. CP-StevWP

I found Love in a certain place. In a Certain Place. Christina Georgina Rossetti. CP-RosC3

I found me in a great surging space. Masked Face, The. Thomas Hardy. CP-HardT

I found my father. Cockfighter's Daughter, The. Ai. SP-Ai

I found myself at the conceptual tomb. Notes. John Ciardi. CP-CiarJ

I found myself inside a massive concrete shell. Trade, The. Gary Snyder. CP-SnydG

I found out where the smell was coming from. On a Skunked Fox. Alan Dugan. CP-DugaA

I found that consciouness itself betrays. Convalescence. James Vincent Cunningham. CP-CunnJ

I found that ivory image there. Crazy Jane Grown Old Looks at the Dancers. William Butler Yeats. CP-YeatW

I found the words to every thought. Emily Dickinson. CP-DickE

I found them blind I taught how to see. On Flaxman and Stothard. William Blake. CP-BlakW

I found them blind, I taught them how to see. William Blake. CP-BlakW

I found them there. Report from the angel of eden. Lucille Clifton. SP-ClifL

I found this jawbone at the sea's edge. Relic. Ted Hughes. SP-HughTN

I found upon our neighboring hills. May Flower, The. Jones Very. CP-VeryJ

I found you and I lost you. Golden Day, A. Paul Laurence Dunbar. CP-DunbP

I found you on a rainy morning. Nansen. Gary Snyder. CP-SnydG

I free your forehead of the ice. Eugenio Montale. CP-MontE, tr. by Jonathan Galassi

I freeze, I freeze, and nothing dwels. Frozen Heart, The. Robert Herrick. CP-HerrR

I gaed a waefu' gate, yestreen. Blue-Eyed Lassie, The. Robert Burns. CP-BurnR

I gaed up to Dunne. Robin Shure in Hairst. Robert Burns. CP-BurnR

I gained it so. Emily Dickinson. CP-DickE

I gaped, admitted, at some of what we did. Massive Retaliation. John Ciardi. CP-CiarJ

I gat your letter, winsome Willie. To William Simpson, Ochiltree. Robert Burns. CP-BurnR

I gather thyme upon the sunny hills. Immalee. Christina Georgina Rossetti. CP-RosC3

I Gave a Sweet Smell. Christina Georgina Rossetti. CP-RosC2

I Gave Away That Kid. Grace Paley. CP-PalGC

I gave away that kid like [or kidlike] he was an old button. I Gave Away That Kid. Grace Paley. CP-PalGC

I gave myself to Him—. Emily Dickinson. CP-DickE

I gave our difference 10,000 miles. Letter from an Island. John Ciardi. CP-CiarJ

I gave them to you. Gifts of Love. Yehuda Amichai. SP-AmicY, tr. by Chana Bloch

I gave to Hope a watch of mine: but he. Hope. George Herbert. CP-HerbG

I gave up Art because. Retraction. Alan Dugan. CP-DugaA

I gave you sorrow to hang on your wall. Nails, The. W. S. Merwin. SP-MerwW

I gaze at you. Tattooed Man, The. Robert Earl Hayden. CP-HaydR

I gaze through a telescope at the Orion Nebula. Before Completion. Arthur Sze. SP-SzeA

I gazed afar from the rocky hill. Sight of the Ocean, The. Jones Very. CP-VeryJ

I gazed upon the cloudless moon. Emily Jane Brontë. CP-BronE

I gazed upon the silent burial-ground. Sonnet: "I gazed upon the silent burial-ground." Jones Very. CP-VeryJ

I gazed upon thy face—and beating life. Beauty. Jones Very. CP-VeryJ

I gazed within thine earnest eyes. Emily Jane Brontë. CP-BronE

I Genitori Perduti. Lawrence Ferlinghetti. SP-FerlL

I get many phonecalls now. 462-0614. Charles Bukowski. SP-BukC1

I get more and more mimeo chapbooks in the mail. Note to the Boys in the Back Room, A. Charles Bukowski. SP-BukC3

I get, surprisingly, a sense of space. To Londoners. Donald Davie. CP-DaviDC

I get too many. Good One, A. Charles Bukowski. SP-BukC1

I get up late and ask what has to be done today. Getting Up Late. Robert Bly. SP-BlyR

I give the undertakers permission to haul my body. Testament. Carl Sandburg. CP-SandC

I give thee joy!—I know to thee. Naples. John Greenleaf Whittier. CP-WhitJ

I give this island green in the green sea. Island, The. Marya Alexandrovna Zaturenska. SP-ZatuM

I give you now Professor Twist. Purist, The. Ogden Nash. CP-NashO

I give you the cosmos, freely the whole works. Scriptsmith. Carl Sandburg. CP-SandC

I give you the end of a golden string. William Blake. CP-BlakW *Fr.* Jerusalem.

I give you the rain, its long hollow. Around You, Your House. William Stafford. SP-StafWW

I give you the wretched sympathy stone. Eolith. A. R. Ammons. CP-AmmoA

I glanced at her and took my glasses. When I Met My Muse. William Stafford. SP-StafWW

I glanced in as I walked past. Man in the Chair, The. Galway Kinnell. SP-KinnGN

I glimpsed a woman's muslined form. On Stinsford Hill at Midnight. Thomas Hardy. CP-HardT

I go a road / among the upturned. In the Underworld. Muriel Rukeyser. CP-RukeM

I go in mourning for those years of mine. Petrarch. CP-Petra, *tr.* by J. G. Nichols

I go in under foliage. In Rain. Wendell Berry. CP-BerrW

I go indoors, and shut the window. Fernando Pessoa. SP-PessF *Fr.* Keeper of Sheep, The.

I go into the men's room Springfield bus station. Love Nut, The. Lawrence Ferlinghetti. SP-FerlL

I go not on a pilgrimage. Holy Land, The. Jones Very. CP-VeryJ

I go on listening, but I cannot hear. Petrarch. CP-Petra, *tr.* by J. G. Nichols

I Go Out of the House for the First Time. Miller Williams. CP-WillM

I go through hollyhocks. Las Trampas U. S. A. Charles Tomlinson. CP-TomlC; SP-TomlC

I go to concert, party, ball. My Rival. Rudyard Kipling. CP-KiplR

I go to my desk to write a letter. Second Month It's Not Itemized, The. Ogden Nash. CP-NashO

I go to pick her up. Huge Ear Rings. Charles Bukowski. SP-BukC1

I go to sleep on one beach. Quiet Nights. Raymond Carver. CP-CarvR

I go to the door often. Indigo Bunting, The. Robert Bly. SP-BlyR

I go to the movies. Madam and the Movies. Langston Hughes. CP-HughL; CP-HughL2

I go to this window. E. E. Cummings. CP-CummE

I go to Town. Song: "I go to Town." Jane Austen. CP-AustJ

I got a job now. Elevator Boy. Langston Hughes. CP-HughL; CP-HughL1

I got a seat down front and started. Bad Action. Charles Bukowski. SP-BukC3

I got bored with watching the stage. At the Theater. Constantine P. Cavafy. CP-CavaC, *tr.* by Theoharis Constantine Theoharis

I got drunk your house. Lotus Sutra, Naturalized, The. Philip Whalen. SP-WhalP

I got his ashes, she said, and I took them. Ashes. Charles Bukowski. SP-BukC1

I got my hair cut. Poem: "I got my hair cut." James Schuyler. CP-SchuJ

I got my tubes tied on the coast. Landscape with Driver. Olga Broumas. SP-BrouO

I got no patience with blues at all! Dos't o' Blues, A. James Whitcomb Riley. CP-RileJ

I got one good look. Coon Song. A. R. Ammons. CP-AmmoA

I got sleepy while driving and pulled in under a tree at the side of the road. Name, The. Tomas Tranströmer. CP-CarvR, *tr.* by Robert Bly

I got so I could take his name. Emily Dickinson. CP-DickE

I got that title out of a book in school. Thanatopsis. Miller Williams. CP-WillM

I Got the Fat Poet into a Corner. Kenneth Patchen. CP-PatcK

I got there by dusk. Opening the Door of a Barn I Thought Was Empty on New Year's Eve. Robert Bly. SP-BlyR

I got there on time. Tell Them Was Here. James Tate. SP-TateJ

I got those sad old weary blues. Too Blue. Langston Hughes. CP-HughL; CP-HughL2

I got tired of writing the wrong stories. Journalist Buys a Pig Farm, The. Miller Williams. CP-WillM

I' got to face Mother to-day, fer a fact! James Whitcomb Riley. CP-RileJ

I got to leave this town. Lonesome Place. Langston Hughes. CP-HughL; CP-HughL1

I got to *thinkin'* of her—both her parunts dead and gone. How It Happened. James Whitcomb Riley. CP-RileJ

I got up in the night. Riverman, The. Elizabeth Bishop. CP-BishE

I gotta / buy me a new. Après le Bain. William Carlos Williams. CP-WilW2

I grant you: peace is desirable. Peace. William Carlos Williams. CP-WilW1

I grew a rose once more to please mine eyes. Fulfilment. Paul Laurence Dunbar. CP-DunbP

I grew a rose within a garden fair. Promise. Paul Laurence Dunbar. CP-DunbP

I grew up bent over. Prodigy. Charles Simic. SP-SimiC; SP-SimiCE

I grew up in Paterson New Jersey and was. Allen Ginsberg. SP-GinsA *Fr.* Reading Bai Juyi.

I grieve and grieve for what I have done. At Shag's Heath. Thomas Hardy. CP-HardT

I grieve not, Courtling, thou art started up. To Courtling. Ben Jonson. CP-JonsB; SP-JonsB

I grieve that better souls than mine. Ralph Waldo Emerson. CP-EmerR

I grieved for Buonoparté, with a vain. 1801. William Wordsworth. CP-WorW1; MW-WorW

I grizzle the embers of our onetime life. Randall Jarrell 2. Robert Lowell. SP-LoweR

I groped for him before I knew. Emily Dickinson. CP-DickE

I grow not old not tall smiling. Working for Profit. Andrei Codrescu. SP-CodrA

I grow old, but I know that Science some. James Vincent Cunningham. CP-CunnJ

I grow old, old. Little Red Riding Hood. Olga Broumas. SP-BrouO

I grow old under an intensity. Mirror. James Merrill. CP-MerrJ

I grow so weary: is it death. Yawn, A. Christina Georgina Rossetti. CP-RosC3

I grow so weary, someway, of all things. Lost Thrill, The. James Whitcomb Riley. CP-RileJ

I guard the children in the schoolyard. Yehuda Amichai. SP-AmicY, *tr.* by Chana Bloch

I guess all I'm trying to say is I saw Crazy Horse die for. You Can Start the Poetry Now, Or: News from Crazy Horse. Thomas McGrath. SP-McGrT

I guess DEMOCRACY'S meant to be. Song after Lynching. Langston Hughes. CP-HughL; CP-HughL3

I guess I am just an old fogey. I Remember Yule. Ogden Nash. CP-NashO

I guess I like it there. It's Warm Under Your Thumb. James Laughlin. CP-LaugJ

I guess it is farewell to grammatical compunction. Oafishness Sells Good, Like an Advertisement Should. Ogden Nash. CP-NashO

I guess there is a garden named. Mirror Perilous, The. Alan Dugan. CP-DugaA

I guessed the letter. Thrush. Paul Muldoon. CP MuldP

I ha' seen them 'mid the clouds on the heather. White Stag, The. Ezra Pound. CP-PoEar; SP-PounE

I had a barrel organ and I cranked its distant tones. Organ. Alfonso Cortes. CP-MertT

I had a daily Bliss. Emily Dickinson. CP-DickE

I had a Donkey, that was all right. Donkey, The. Theodore Roethke. CP-RoetT

I had a dove and the sweet dove died. Song: "I had a dove and the sweet dove died." John Keats. CP-KeatJ

I had a dream. Nightmare Boogie. Langston Hughes. CP-HughL; CP-HughL3

I Had a Dream. Stevie Smith. CP-SmitS

I had a dream. A wondrous thing. Spring and Death. Gerard Manley Hopkins. CP-HopkG

I had a dream I was a bird. Avondall. Stevie Smith. CP-SmitS

I had a dream of nourishment. Dream of Nourishment, A. Stevie Smith. CP-SmitS

I had a dream once of dancing with a tiger. As it took. Dream, A. John Ciardi. CP-CiarJ

I had a dream three walls stood up wherein a raven bird. Anger's Freeing Power. Stevie Smith. CP-SmitS

I had a dream, which was not all a dream. Darkness. Lord Byron. CP-Byron

I had a gal, / She was driving alone. Announcement. Langston Hughes. CP-HughL; CP-HughL2

I had a gardener. I had him until haying-time. Gardener in Haying-Time, The. Edna St. Vincent Millay. CP-MillE

I had a gift once that I then refused. Gift, The. Helen Pinkerton. CP-PinkH

I had a girl's fancies. Song: "I had a girl's fancies." Ivor Gurney. SP-GurnI

I had a guinea golden. Emily Dickinson. CP-DickE

"I had a holiday once," said the woman. Expectation and Experience. Thomas Hardy. CP-HardT

I had a little Sorrow. Penitent, The. Edna St. Vincent Millay. CP-MillE

I had a love in soft south land. Love from The North. Christina Georgina Rossetti. CP-RosC1

I had a lover. Let us say we were married, owned. Field. Olga Broumas. SP-BrouO

I had a misfortune in September. Detail. William Carlos Williams. CP-WilW2

I had a picture by him—a print, I think—on my bedroom wall. Homage to Claude Lorrain. Charles Wright. SP-WrigC

I had a sweet bird. Hippy-Mo. Stevie Smith. CP-SmitS

I had a vision when the night was late. Vision of Sin, The. Alfred Tennyson. CP-TennA

I had as lief be embraced by the porter at the hotel. Two Figures in Dense Violet Night. Wallace Stevens. CP-StevW; CP-StevWP

I had been here before. Tax Inspector, The. Charles Tomlinson. SP-TomlC

I had been his fool. Cuchulain. William Carlos Williams. CP-WilW2

I had been hungry, all the Years. Emily Dickinson. CP-DickE

I had been meaning to work through lunch. Trifle, A. Paul Muldoon. CP-MuldP

I had been reading what you have written of your idleness. La Flor. William Carlos Williams. CP-WilW1

I had brainphotos. Reminiscence. Yusef Komunyakaa. CP-KomuY

I had come all the way here from the sea. And Bees of Paradise. Hart Crane. CP-CranH

I had come to the house, in a cave of trees. Medusa. Louise Bogan. CP-BogaL

I had eight birds hatcht [*or* hatched] in one nest. In Reference to Her Children,

23 June, 1659. Anne Bradstreet. CP-BradA

I had exploded, a bombcloud, lob-headed, my huge. Crow Wakes. Ted Hughes. SP-HughTN

I had fed the fire and stirred it, till the sparkles in delight. Das Krist Kindel. James Whitcomb Riley. CP-RileJ

I had finished my dinner. Easy Decision, An. Kenneth Patchen. CP-PatcK

I had for my winter evening walk. Good Hours. Robert Frost. CP-FrosR

I had forgotten about the quail that live. Away. Raymond Carver. CP-CarvR

I had forgotten how the frogs must sound. Assault. Edna St. Vincent Millay. CP-MillE

I had gone broke, and got set to come back. Epigram: "I had gone broke, and got set to come back." James Vincent Cunningham. CP-CunnJ

I had gone to a frieghtyard auction of sealed crates. Crate of Sterling Loving Cups, A. John Ciardi. CP-CiarJ

I had grasped God's garment in the void. Suspended. Denise Levertov. SP-LeveDS

I had grown invisible as a city sparrow. Some Collisions Bring Luck. Marge Piercy. SP-PierM

I had grown weary of him; of his breath. Thou Shalt Not Kill. G. K. Chesterton. CP-ChesG

I had had / a beetle. Charles Olson. CP-OlsoC

I had heard / before, of an. Mr. Brodsky. Charles Tomlinson. CP-TomlC; SP-TomlC

I had hold of the comet's mane. Comet of Prophecy, The. Nicholas Vachel Lindsay. CP-LindV

I Had Hope When Violence Was Ceas't. Geoffrey Hill. CP-HillG

I had hoped to express more. Emily Dickinson. SP-DickE

I had just won $115 from the headshakers and. I Am Visited by an Editor and a Poet. Charles Bukowski. SP-BukC2

I had long known the diverse tastes of the wood. Gift of Sight. Robert Graves. CP-GravR

I had ma clothes cleaned. Dressed Up. Langston Hughes. CP-HughL; CP-HughL1

I had no Cause to be awake. Emily Dickinson. CP-DickE

I Had No Idea It Was So Late. Ogden Nash. CP-NashO

I had no right to talk of you that way. To Robert Lowell. Czeslaw Milosz. CP-MiloCN, tr. by Robert Hass

I had no time to Hate. Emily Dickinson. CP-DickE

I had not known before. Forever. Paul Laurence Dunbar. CP-DunbP

I had not minded—Walls. Emily Dickinson. CP-DickE

I had not much thought of mercy. Lasting Seasons, The. Kenneth Patchen. CP-PatcK

I had nothing to do with it. I was not here. Centenary Note: Inscribed to Little Crow, Leader of the Sioux Rebellion in Minnesota, 1862, A. James Wright. CP-WrigJ

I had over-prepared the event. Villanelle: The Psychological Hour. Ezra Pound. SP-PounE

I had read a long time. All afternoon. Reader, The. Randall Jarrell. CP-JarrR

I had rowed for a long time, with a clean, sweeping, drowsy motion. White Water Lily, The. Stéphane Mallarmé. CP-MallS, tr. by Henry Weinfield

I had said improbable. I. Names. Hayden Carruth. CP-CarHS

I had seen a tree before. Tree, The. Charles Tomlinson. CP-TomlC

I had seen, as dawn was breaking. La Nuit Blanche. Rudyard Kipling. CP-KiplR

I had seen her. Salomé. Yusef Komunyakaa. CP-KomuY

I had some cards printed. Madam's Calling Cards. Langston Hughes. CP-HughL; CP-HughL2

I had some friends—but I dreamed that they were dead. Friends, The. Rudyard Kipling. CP-KiplR

I had some things that I called mine. Emily Dickinson. CP-DickE

I had the Glory—that will do. Emily Dickinson. CP-DickE

I had this room in front on DeLongpre. Strangest Sight You Ever Did See—, The. Charles Bukowski. SP-BukC1

I had this thought a while ago. Words. William Butler Yeats. CP-YeatW

I had to assure myself. Screech-Owl. Donald Davie. CP-DaviDC

I had to drive to Palos Verdes to do some business at the. Sweater. Charles Bukowski. SP-BukC3

I had to kick their law into their teeth in order to save them. "Negro" Hero. Gwendolyn Brooks. SP-BrooG

I had to take a shit. Lovely Couple, A. Charles Bukowski. SP-BukC1

I had to unship the mast or we would have been over, & in, to. Mast, The. Charles Olson. CP-OlsoC

I had two husbands. Madam and Her Might-Have-Been. Langston Hughes. CP-HughL; CP-HughL2

I had walked since dawn and lay down to rest on a bare hillside. Vulture. Robinson Jeffers. CP-JefR3

I had wanted a quiet testament. Song, A: "I had wanted a quiet testament." Robert Creeley. CP-CreeR

I had withdrawn in forest, and my song. Dream Pang, A. Robert Frost. CP-FrosR

I had worked my charms on her. Problems About the Other Woman. Charles Bukowski. SP-BukC1

I had you for a servant, once, Dick Brome. To My Old Faithful Servant: And (by His Continued Virtue) My Loving Friend: The Author of this Work, M[r] Rich[ard] Brome. Ben Jonson. CP-JonsB

I hadn't seen him in twelve years. Friend, The. Miller Williams. CP-WillM

I Hae a Wife o' My Ain. Robert Burns. CP-BurnR

I hae been at Crookieden. Bonie Laddie, Highland Laddie. Robert Burns. CP-BurnR

I hail thee, Nessmuk, for the lofty tone. Nessmuk. James Whitcomb Riley. CP-RileJ

I Hain't no hand at tellin' tales. Squire Hawkins's Story. James Whitcomb Riley. CP-RileJ

I hang by my heels from the sky. Hera, Hung from the Sky. Carolyn Kizer. CP-KizeC

I hang from the horn of the crescent moon. Ballad of the Sun's Hunting. Ezra Pound. CP-PoEar

I hang my head. Delicate Riders, The. James Tate. SP-TateJ

I hang on by. Charles Olson. CP-OlsoC

I hang the cloth water bag from the door mirror. Driving across the American Desert and Thinking of the Sahara. John Ciardi. CP-CiarJ

I Happen To Know. Ogden Nash. CP-NashO

I hardly hear the curlew cry. Baile and Aillinn. William Butler Yeats. CP-YeatW

I hardly slept across the North Atlantic. London. John Berryman. CP-BerrJ

I hardly suppose I know anybody who wouldn't rather be a success than a failure. Kindly Unhitch That Star, Buddy. Ogden Nash. CP-NashO

I has hyeahd o' people dancin' an' I's hyeahd o' people singin'. Whistling Sam. Paul Laurence Dunbar. CP-DunbP

I hate Actors. Actors; A Hate Song. Dorothy Parker. CP-ParkD

I hate Actresses. Actresses; A Hate Song. Dorothy Parker. CP-ParkD

I hate and I love. And if you ask me how. Carmen 85. Catullus. CP-ZukLS Fr. Carmina.

I hate and love her. If you ask me why. Catullus. CP-CunnJ, tr. by James Vincent Cunningham

I hate Bohemians. Bohemians; A Hate Song. Dorothy Parker. CP-ParkD

I hate Books. Books; A Hymn of Hate. Dorothy Parker. CP-ParkD

I hate Bores. Bores; A Hymn of Hate. Dorothy Parker. CP-ParkD

I hate College Boys. College Boys; A Hymn of Hate. Dorothy Parker. CP-ParkD

I hate / everything that moves faster than my body because. &. Andrei Codrescu. SP-CodrA

I hate Husbands. Husbands; A Hymn of Hate. Dorothy Parker. CP-ParkD

I Hate Love. James Laughlin. CP-LaugJ

I hate men. Men; A Hate Song. Dorothy Parker. CP-ParkD

I hate movies. Movies; A Hymn of Hate. Dorothy Parker. CP-ParkD

I hate my verses, every line, every word. Love the Wild Swan. Robinson Jeffers. CP-JefR2

I hate Parties. Parties; A Hymn of Hate. Dorothy Parker. CP-ParkD

I hate photographs. About Photography. Andrei Codrescu. SP-CodrA

I hate reading about dead men knowing. Saturday. C. K. Williams. CP-WillC

I hate Relatives. Relatives; A Hate Song. Dorothy Parker. CP-ParkD

I hate Slackers. Slackers; A Hate Song. Dorothy Parker. CP-ParkD

I hate Summer Resorts. Summer Resorts; A Hymn of Hate. Dorothy Parker. CP-ParkD

I hate that Andrew Jones: he'll breed. Andrew Jones. William Wordsworth. CP-WorW1

I hate the Drama. Drama, The; A Hymn of Hate. Dorothy Parker. CP-ParkD

I hate the Office. Our Office; An Intimate Glimpse of Vanity Fair—En Famille A Hate Song. Dorothy Parker. CP-ParkD

I hate the very noise of troublous man. Love and Solitude. John Clare. SP-ClarJ

I hate the Younger Set. Younger Set, The; A Hymn of Hate. Dorothy Parker. CP-ParkD

I HATE THIS GIRL. Stevie Smith. CP-SmitS

I hate this yoke; for the world's sake here put it on. Perfect Marriage, The. Nicholas Vachel Lindsay. CP-LindV

I hate to die this way with the quiet. Cabaret Girl Dies on Welfare Island. Langston Hughes. CP-HughL; CP-HughL2

"I hate to lose something." / then she bent her head. No Loser, No Weeper. Maya Angelou. SP-AngeM

I hate Wives. Wives; A Hymn of Hate. Dorothy Parker. CP-ParkD

I hate Women. Women; A Hate Song. Dorothy Parker. CP-ParkD

I hated thee, fallen tyrant! I did groan. Feelings of a Republican on the Fall of Bonaparte. Percy Bysshe Shelley. CP-ShelP

I hauled down lifeless mattresses to sidewalk refuse-piles. Rain-Wet Asphalt Heat, Garbage Curbed Cans Overflowing. Allen Ginsberg. CP-GinsA; SP-GinsA

I have a bag with a silver dollar in it. Dollar Air. Andrei Codrescu. SP-CodrA

I have a bird in my head and a pig in my stomach. Alive for an Instant. Kenneth Koch. SP-KochK

I have a Bird in spring. Emily Dickinson. CP-DickE

I have a bone to pick with Fate. Lines on Facing Forty. Ogden Nash. CP-NashO

I have a boy of five years old. Anecdote for Fathers. William Wordsworth. CP-WorW1; MW-WorW

I have a burial ground in me where I place the bodies. Reading the Headlines. David Ignatow. SP-IgnaD

I have a child in limbo. In Limbo. David Ignatow. SP-IgnaD

I have a coat. Han-shan. CP-ColdM, tr. by Red Pine

I have a country but no town. Talking Myself to Sleep at One More Hilton. John Ciardi. CP-CiarJ

I have a deep identity. Red Jacket's Grave. James Wright. CP-WrigJ

I have a delicious problem. Giant Red Woman. Clarence Major. SP-MajoC

I have a dream—a dreadful dream. Mother's Son, The. Rudyard Kipling. CP-KiplR

I have a dream of where (when I grow old). To France. Countee Cullen. CP-CullC

I have a fantasy that a small idea. Fantasy of a Small Idea. Richard Eberhart. CP-EberR

I have a fifth of therapy. Interview with Doctor Drink. James Vincent Cunningham. CP-CunnJ

I have a foolishness here which is lamp-like. New Poem. Charles Olson. CP-OlsoC

I have a foreboding . . . I'm oppressed. Foreboding. Raymond Carver. CP-CarvR

I have a friend. Black March. Stevie Smith. CP-SmitS

I have a friend. Gray. Alice Walker. CP-WalkA

I have a friend in ghostland. Coast-Nightmare, A. Christina Georgina Rossetti. CP-RosC3

I have a friend named Mr. Sherman who is far from dodderin'. Sic Semper Mr. Sherman's Temper, or Kindly Place Your Order in English. Ogden Nash. CP-NashO

I have a friend who would give a price for those long fingers all of one length. Snakes, Mongooses, Snake-Charmers, and the Like. Marianne Craig Moore. CP-MoorM

I have a friend whose hair is like time: dark. Time. Thomas Lux. SP-LuxT

I have a funny daddy. My Daddy. Ogden Nash. CP-NashO

I have a happy nature. Mother. Stevie Smith. CP-SmitS

I have a hat, but not to wear. Riddle of the Conjurer, The. G. K. Chesterton. CP-ChesG

I have a hope that's like a star. George Meredith. CP-MerG2

I have a job with a tiny salary of 80 crowns, and. Kafka's Watch. Raymond Carver. CP-CarvR

I have a King, who does not speak. Emily Dickinson. CP-DickE

I have a leaden, thou a shaft of gold. To Cupid. Robert Herrick. CP-HerrR

I have a little dog. Please Pass the Biscuit. Ogden Nash. CP-NashO

I have a little husband / And he is gone to sea. Christina Georgina Rossetti. CP-RosC2

I have a little . . . not fame, call it reputation—for writing verses. Old Wolf My Father, The. James Wright. CP-JefR3

I have a Love I love too well. Sacrilege, The. Thomas Hardy. CP-Hard1

I Have a Message unto Thee. Christina Georgina Rossetti. CP-RosC3

I have a name, a little name. Pet-Name, The. Elizabeth Barrett Browning. CP-BroEB

I have a number and my name is dumb. On a Line from Julian. Carolyn Kizer. CP-KizeC

I have a pack of letters. Inventory of Goodbyes, The. Anne Sexton. CP-SextA

I have a photograph here. Father, the Cavalier. Donald Davie. CP-DaviDC

I have a place to come to. My Place. David Ignatow. SP-IgnaD

I have a Poll parrot, / And Poll is my doll. Christina Georgina Rossetti. CP-RosC2

I have a rendezvous with Life. Life's Rendezvous. Countee Cullen. CP-CullC

I have a room of my own. Mother and Jack and the Rain. Anne Sexton. CP-SextA

I have a saying, "the tough ones always come." One to the Breastplate. Charles Bukowski. SP-BukC1

I have a single cave. Han-shan. CP-ColdM, tr. by Red Pine

I have a small grain of hope. For the New Year, 1981. Denise Levertov. SP-LeveDL

I have a smiling face, she said. Mask, The. Elizabeth Barrett Browning. CP-BroEB

I have a superstition of destiny. Those poets who have. Any Way But Back. George Oppen. CP-OppGN

I have a terrible age and I part. Hatred. Frank O'Hara. SP-OharF

I have a terrible cold. Fernando Pessoa. SP-PessF, tr. by Susan M. Brown and Edwin Honig

"I have a thousand men," said he. Rudyard Kipling. CP-KiplR Fr. Light That Failed, The.

I have a thousand times, dear enemy. Petrarch. CP-Petra, tr. by J. G. Nichols

I have a tree in my arm. Maze. Richard Eberhart. CP-EberR

I have a vast traumatic eye. Tennessee Williams. CP-WillT Fr. Moise and the World of Reason.

I have abandoned the dream kitchens for a low fire. Mayo Tao, The. Derek Mahon. CP-MahoD

I have abhorred the wars and despised the liars, laughed at the frightened. We Are Those People. Robinson Jeffers. CP-JefR3

I have, alas, no taste. Taste. John Updike. CP-UpdiJ

I have allowed myself. For Masturbation. Alan Dugan. CP-DugaA

I have almost nailed my left thumb to the 2 x 4 brace that holds the deck together. Deck, The. Yusef Komunyakaa. CP-KomuY

I have already come to the verge of. Unborn Child, An. Derek Mahon. CP-MahoD

I have always aspired to a more spacious form. Ars Poetica? Czeslaw Milosz. CP-MiloC; CP-MiloCN, tr. by Lillian Vallee

I have always wanted brook trout. Looking for Work 2. Raymond Carver. CP-CarvR

I have an abiding bliss. Riches. Gabriela Mistral. SP-MistG, tr. by Maria Giachetti [or Jacketti]

I have an arrow that can find its mark. Ralph Waldo Emerson. CP-EmerR

I have an invention. Patent Pending. James Laughlin. CP-LaugJ

I have answers to all of your questions. My name is the word for wall, my head is buried in that wall. Michael Palmer. SP-PalmM

I have appropriated the windy twittering of aspen leaves. Plunder. A. R. Ammons. CP-AmmoA

I have backed up / into my silence. Fanny Howe. SP-HoweF Fr. O'Clock.

I have become a gate. Lot's Wife. Howard Nemerov. CP-NemeH

I have been a lover. Sir Thomas Wyatt. CP-Wyat1

I have been a seeker. Star Seeker. Langston Hughes. CP-HughL; CP HughL1

I have been alone for two days, and still everything is cloudy. Falling Asleep. Robert Bly. SP-BlyR

I have been altered like a suit. À Face. Andrei Codrescu. SP-CodrA

I have been an ability—a machine—up to. Charles Olson. SP-OlsoC Fr. Maximus Poems, The.

I have been assaulted by the moths. Goat and Amalthea. Laura Riding Jackson. CP-RidiL

I have been brought out of day. Consignee. A. R. Ammons. CP-AmmoA

I have been cruel to a fat pigeon. Fly. W. S. Merwin. SP-MerwW

I have been defeated and dragged down by pain. Kissing and Horrid Strife. D. H. Lawrence. CP-LawrD

I have been, faithfully, to the thirty-nine birthplaces of Beethoven. Tying One On in Vienna. Carolyn Kizer. CP-KizeC Fr. Heine Journal, A.

I have been given my charge to keep. Fairies' Siege, The. Rudyard Kipling. CP-KiplR Fr. Kim.

I have been heavy and much selecting. I saw a star which. Lifting Belly. Gertrude Stein. CP-SteiG

I have been here before. City. W. S. Merwin. SP-MerwWF

I have been here. Dispersed in meditation. Agnosco Veteris Vestigia Flammae. James Vincent Cunningham. CP-CunnJ

I have been here in the Moon light. Fragment from Dove Cottage Manuscript 44 (I). William Wordsworth. CP-WorW1

I have been horrified before all mirrors. Mirrors. Jorge Luis Borges. SP-BorgJ, tr. by Alastair Reid

I have been idly leafing through the Book of Proverbs and the Book of Deuteronomy. Woman Pulls the Wires. Ogden Nash. CP-NashO

I have been in Pennsylvania. Pennsylvania. Carl Sandburg. CP-SandC

I have been in the meadows all the day. Irreparableness. Elizabeth Barrett Browning. CP-BroEB

I have been in this garden of unripe fruit. First Love. Hugh MacDiarmid. SP-MacDH

I have been instructed by your sacred Majesty to examine the histories. What to Think When It Rains Blood. Thomas Merton. CP-MertT

I have been insulted in St Peter's. Epigram: "I have been insulted in St Peter's." George Oppen. CP-OppGN

I have been nowhere else where I could see. Petrarch. CP-Petra, tr. by J. G. Nichols

I have been one acquainted with the night. Acquainted with the Night. Robert Frost. CP-FrosR

I have been saying what I have to say. Don't. C. K. Williams. CP-WillC

I have been seeking. Stokely Malcolm Me. Langston Hughes. CP-HughL; CP-HughL3

I have been shown a myriad slopes and more. Petrarch. CP-Petra, tr. by J. G. Nichols

I have been so innerly proud, and so long alone. Humiliation. D. H. Lawrence. CP-LawrD

I have been spared another day. Poem of Thanks, A. Wendell Berry. CP-BerrW

I have been the dawn's summer lord. Arthur Rimbaud.

I have been thinking. Lilies. Mary Oliver. SP-OlivM

I have been thinking of the victims bound. Prisoners of Naples, The. John Greenleaf Whittier. CP-WhitJ

I have been throughout the world sleuthing. Libation. A. R. Ammons. CP-AmmoA

I have been to a fair alone. Coin, The. W. S. Merwin. SP-MerwWF

I have been to Tientai. Feng-kan. CP-ColdM, *tr. by* Red Pine

I have been told, and have been glad to hear. Barmecide Feast. John Ciardi. CP-CiarJ

I have been treading on leaves all day until I am autumn-tired. Leaf-Treader, A. Robert Frost. CP-FrosR

I have been urged by earnest violins. Music. Wilfred Owen. CP-OwenW

I have been wanton, and too bold I feare. His Last Request to Julia. Robert Herrick. CP-HerrR

I have been warned. It is more than thirty years since I wrote. But I Am Growing Old and Indolent. Robinson Jeffers. CP-JefR3

I have been watching crows and now it is dark. New Moon in November. W. S. Merwin. SP-MerwW

I have been watching the war map slammed up for advertising in front of the newspaper office. Buttons. Carl Sandburg. CP-SandC

I have been young, and now am old. Saw I Never the Righteous Forsaken. Donald Davie. CP-DaviDC

I have begun my freedom and it hurts. Stability before Departure. Alan Dugan. CP-DugaA

I have beholde two louers in a night. Mr. Robert Hericke His Farwell unto Poetrie. Robert Herrick. CP-HerrR

I have braved, for want of wild beasts, steel cages. May 24, 1980. Joseph Brodsky. CP-BrodJ, *tr. by* Joseph Brodsky

I have brought back a good message from the land of 102°. Fever. John Updike. CP-UpdiJ

I have but one rose in the world. Christina Georgina Rossetti. CP-RosC2

I have by now my sixteenth year of sighs. Petrarch. CP-Petra, *tr. by* J. G. Nichols

I Have Called You. Thomas Merton. CP-MertT

I have carried my pillow to the windowsill. Summer near the River. Carolyn Kizer. CP-KizeC

I have caught a glimpse of the seamless garment. In the Slums of Glasgow. Hugh MacDiarmid. SP-MacDH

I have climbed a long way. Ascent. W. S. Merwin. SP-MerwW

I have closed my ears, I refuse. No! Kenneth Rexroth. CP-RexrK

I have closed off my balcony. Qasida of the Weeping. Federico García Lorca. CP-GarcF, *tr. by* Catherine Brown *Fr.* Qasidas.

I have come all this way. Ways of Day. Robert Penn Warren. CP-WarrR

I have come back to ancient shores where it is always now. Return, The. Kathleen Jessie Raine. SP-RainK

I have come far enough. Form of Women, A. Robert Creeley. CP-CreeR

I have come forth alive from the land of purple and poison and glamour. Crusader Returns from Captivity, The. G. K. Chesterton. CP-ChesG

I have come home. Fortune and Hope, goodbye! *Unknown.* CP-CunnJ, *tr. by* J. V. Cunningham

I have come to the church and chancel. She Revisits Alone the Church of Her Marriage. Thomas Hardy. CP-HardT

I have come to the house of God. Irreverent Thoughts. D. H. Lawrence. CP-LawrD

I have come with wingéd step, stick in hand, hound at heel. Brothers. Thomas Kinsella. CP-KinsT

I have committed many errors. Visit, The. William Carlos Williams. CP-WilW2

I have committed the worst sin of all. Remorse. Jorge Luis Borges. SP-BorgJ, *tr. by* Willis Barnstone

I have compassion on the carpeting. Lines Given with a Penwiper. Christina Georgina Rossetti. CP-RosC3

I have considered [*or* consider'd] it, and find[e]. Reprisal[l], The. George Herbert. CP-HerbG

I have crossed the dunes with their whistling bent. Shore Woman. Seamus Heaney. SP-HeanSO

I have cut bamboo. Paul Celan. SP-CelaP, *tr. by* John Felstiner

I have dead people, buried in the air. Yehuda Amichai. SP-AmicYL, *tr. by* Benjamin Harshav *and* Barbara Harshav

I have desired, and I have been desired. Soeur Louise De La Miséricorde. Christina Georgina Rossetti. CP-RosC2

I have desired to go. Heaven-Haven. Gerard Manley Hopkins. CP-HopkG

I have distracted time. Distraction. James Vincent Cunningham. CP-CunnJ

I have done all I could. Tree and the Lady, The. Thomas Hardy. CP-HardT

I have done all, you have done all. Benedictory. Laura Riding Jackson. CP-RidiL

I have done it again. Lady Lazarus. Sylvia Plath. CP-PlatS

I have done mostly what most men do. Four-Feet. Rudyard Kipling. CP-KiplR

I have done one braver thing. Undertaking, The. John Donne. CP-DonnJ; MW-DonnJ

I have done so little. Poet to Bigot. Langston Hughes. CP-HughL; CP-HughL3

I have done with hope. Christina Georgina Rossetti. CP-RosC3

I have drawn my hands away. Meditation. Hart Crane. CP-CranH

I have dreamt it again: standing suddenly still. Wormwood. Thomas Kinsella. CP-KinsT

I have drunk ale from the Country of the Young. He Thinks of His Past Greatness When a Part of the Constellations of Heaven. William Butler Yeats. CP-YeatW

I have eaten. This Is Just to Say. William Carlos Williams. CP-WilW1

I have eaten your bread and salt. Prelude to "Departmental Ditties." Rudyard Kipling. CP-KiplR

I have escaped from the two-acre rolled garden. If It Would All Please Hurry. James Tate. SP-TateJ .

I have escaped in the dream; I was in danger, at peril, at immediate, furious, frightening risk. History. C. K. Williams. SP-WillC

I have experienc'd / The worst, the World can wreak on me; the worst. Despair. Samuel Taylor Coleridge. CP-ColeS

I have felt darkness lead me by the hand. Suicide. Allen Tate. CP-TateA

I have felt like a troubled Top. Emily Dickinson. SP-DickE

I have felt the lithe wind. Ezra Pound. CP-PoEar

I have fetched the tears up out of the little wells. Punisher, The. D. H. Lawrence. CP-LawrD

"I have finished another year," said God. New Year's Eve. Thomas Hardy. CP-HardT

I have finished my combat with the sun. From the Misery of Don Joost. Wallace Stevens. CP-StevWP

I Have Five Things to Say. Jelaluddin Rumi. SP-Rumi, *tr. by* Coleman Barks

I have food for my children in the cart. I Can't Understand! I Can't Understand! Kenneth Patchen. CP-PatcK

I Have Fought a Good Fight. Christina Georgina Rossetti. CP-RosC3

I have found a nobler love. Ralph Waldo Emerson. CP-EmerR

I have found a place of loneliness. Elysium. D. H. Lawrence. CP-LawrD

I have found my figures. I Have Met the Enemy and I Am Theirs. Alan Dugan. CP-DugaA

I have found what pleases my friend's chubby, rosy, gloriously shining-eyed year-old daughter. Gift, The. C. K. Williams. CP-WillC; SP-WillC

I have found what you are like. E. E. Cummings. CP-CummE

I have gone out, a possessed witch. Her Kind. Anne Sexton. CP-SextA; SP-SextA

I have gone past all those times when the poets. In Memory of Leopardi. James Wright. CP-WrigJ

I have got into the slow train. In the Stopping Train. Donald Davie. CP-DaviDC

I Have Got to Stop Loving You. So I Have Killed My Black Goat. Ai. SP-Ai

I have gret wonder, be this lyght. Book of the Duchesse, The. Geoffrey Chaucer. CP-ChauG

I have grown a marsh dweller. Sumerian. A. R. Ammons. CP-AmmoA

I have had enough. Sheltered Garden. "H. D." CP-DoolH

I have had my dream—like others. Thursday. William Carlos Williams. CP-WilW1

I have had my time dressed up as something else. False Youth: Two Seasons. James Dickey. CP-DickJ

I have had to learn the simplest things. Maximus, to Himself. Charles Olson. SP-OlsoC *Fr.* Maximus Poems, The.

I have had to write this down. Love Poem to Be Read to an Illiterate Friend. Tess Gallagher. SP-GallT

I Have Heard. James Laughlin. CP-LaugJ

I have heard a wee wind searching. Motif. Ezra Pound. CP-PoEar

I have heard all day the voices. Winds. Kathleen Jessie Raine. SP-RainK

I have heard it said. To the Muse. Denise Levertov. SP-LeveDP

I have heard of fish. Sun, The. Anne Sexton. CP-SextA

I have heard of reasons manifold. Reason for Love's Blindness. Samuel Taylor Coleridge. CP-ColeS

I have heard on Mount Tientai. Han-shan. CP-ColdM, *tr. by* Red Pine

I have heard that hysterical women say. Lapis Lazuli. William Butler Yeats. CP-YeatW

I have heard the dread song I had not heard. Tanto e Amara. Charles Olson. CP-OlsoC

I have heard the pigeons of the Seven Woods. In the Seven Woods. William Butler Yeats. CP-YeatW

I have heard the self's stir. Noon. James Vincent Cunningham. CP-CunnJ

I have heard the sunset song of the birches. Stephen Crane. CP-CranS

I have heard the yap of the fairy dog / P'ti'cru. "It Is a Shame"—with Apologies to the Modern Celtic School. Ezra Pound. CP-PoEar

I have heard them as I lie. Dark Mutinous Shannon Waves, The. James Laughlin. CP-LaugJ

I Have Increased Power. Allen Ginsberg. CP-GinsA

I have instructed you to follow me. Jesus to His Disciples. Edna St. Vincent Millay. CP-MillE

I have invented new worlds. I have dreamed. Birth of the Sun, The. Pablo Antonio Cuadra. CP-MertT, *tr. by* Thomas Merton

I have it in my heart to serve God so. Sonnet: Of [*or* To] his Lady in Heaven. Jacopo da Lentino. CW-RossD, *tr. by* Dante Gabriel Rossetti

I Have It on Good Authority. Ogden Nash. CP-NashO

I have jest about decided. Old Winters on the Farm. James Whitcomb Riley. CP-

RileJ

I have just come down from my father. Hospital Window, The. James Dickey. CP-DickJ

I have just returned from a foreign tour. My Trip Daorba. Ogden Nash. CP-NashO

I have kept all, not one is thrown away, not one given to the ragman, not. Films. Carl Sandburg. CP-SandC

I have killed our lives together. Divorce. Anne Sexton. CP-SextA

I have known. Which Reminds Me. A. K. Ramanujan. CP-RamaA

I have known all the storms that roll. Skald's Death. Hugh MacDiarmid. SP-MacDH

I have known the hissing assemblies. Thomas Kinsella. CP-KinsT

I have known the inexorable sadness of pencils. Dolor. Theodore Roethke. CP-RoetT

I have labored for her love. Love Poem, A: "I have labored for her love." John Ciardi. CP-CiarJ

I have laid out the singer. Memento ("I have laid out the singer"). Federico García Lorca. CP-GarcF, tr. by Jerome Rothenberg Fr. Epitaph for a Bird.

I have lain in bed all day. Farewell, Foolish Objects. Charles Bukowski. SP-BukC2

I have learned not to worry about love. New Face. Alice Walker. CP-WalkA

I have learned this winter that, yes. 1971. Alice Walker. CP-WalkA

I have lighted the candles, Mary. Kenneth Patchen. CP-PatcK

I have lived and followed my fate without flinching, followed it gladly. Dido's Farewell to Aeneas. Stevie Smith. CP-SmitS

I have lived at Cold Mountain. Gary Snyder. CP-SnydG

I have lived in a single landscape. Every tone. At Stoke. Charles Tomlinson. CP-TomlC; SP-TomlC

I Have Lived in England. Charles Bukowski. SP-BukC2

I have lived on the lip. Jelaluddin Rumi. SP-Rumi, tr. by Coleman Barks

I have lived so long with the rhetoricians. Wallace Stevens. CP-StevWP

I Have Lived with Shades. Thomas Hardy. CP-HardT

I have lives in many half-worlds myself . . . and so I know you. Flying Fish. Carl Sandburg. CP-SandC

I have long been a Lunatic on Bulbs. Emily Dickinson. SP-DickE

I have long desired to shine. Horny Dilemma. Kenneth Rexroth. CP-RexrK

I Have Longed to Move Away. Dylan Thomas. CP-ThomD

I have looked at them long. To the Romantic Traditionists. Allen Tate. CP-TateA

I have looked for you at the familiar center. Penelope. Norman Dubie. CP-DubiN

I have looked upon thee—and I have loved thee. E. E. Cummings. CP-CummE

I have lost, and lately, these. Upon the Loss[e] of His Mistresses. Robert Herrick. CP-HerrR

I have lost myself in the sea many times. Gacela of the Flight. Federico García Lorca. SP-GarcF, tr. by J. L. Gili and Stephen Spender

I have lost the wood, the heath. Avowal, The. Richard Wilbur. CP-WilbR

I have love / And a child. Losses. Carl Sandburg. CP-SandC

I have loved always, and I do love still. Petrarch. CP-Petra, tr. by J. G. Nichols

I have loved,let us see if that's all. E. E. Cummings. CP-CummE

I have loved my land yet hailed it as a stranger. Heritage of Wonder, The. G. K. Chesterton. CP-ChesG

I have loved you for long long years Ellen. Song: "I have loved you for long long years Ellen." Christina Georgina Rossetti. CP-RosC3

I have made for you a song. To Thomas Atkins. Rudyard Kipling. CP-KiplR

I have made the incantatory. Calling Collect. Josephine Jacobsen. CP-JacoJ

I have many prayers to say. Ah, Muriel! D. H. Lawrence. CP-LawrD

I Have Met the Enemy and I Am Theirs. Alan Dugan. CP-DugaA

I have met them at close of day. Easter 1916. William Butler Yeats. CP-YeatW

I have millions of gathas. Shih-te. CP-ColdM, tr. by Red Pine

I have my Laurel Chaplet on my head. To Sir George Parrie, Doctor of the Civill Law. Robert Herrick. CP-HerrR

I have my piety too, which could. Epitaph on Master Vincent Corbet[t], An. Ben Jonson. CP-JonsB

I have never been. Sconset. Charles Tomlinson. CP-TomlC

I have never been fishing on the Susquehanna. Fishing on the Susquehanna in July. Billy Collins. SP-CollB

I have never beheld you, O pawky Scot. Who Taught Caddies to Count? or A Burnt Golfer Fears the Child. Ogden Nash. CP-NashO

I have never / clearly given to you. Woman, The. Robert Creeley. CP-CreeR

I have never lived on the reservation. Lines Written in Dejection, Oklahoma. Gregory Orr. SP-OrrG

I have never seen a. One Jay at a Time. John Ciardi. CP-CiarJ

I have never seen a cicada, but nothing so pollutes. Walking the Dog: A Diatribe. Mona Van Duyn. SP-VanDM

I have never seen "Volcanoes." Emily Dickinson. CP-DickE

I have news to tell you, do you hear, Nerone. Guido Cavalcanti. CP-CavaG, tr. by Marc Cirigliano

I have no answer, time or will, to answer those. Mechanical Heart, The. Kenneth

Patchen. CP-PatcK

I have no Brother—they who meet me now. Thy Brother's Blood. Jones Very. CP-VeryJ

I have no brothers & no peers. Ralph Waldo Emerson. CP-EmerR

I have no cause, and God has not confessed. Old Man Confesses, An. John Ciardi. CP-CiarJ

I have no desire any more. Desire Goes Down into the Sea. D. H. Lawrence. CP-LawrD

I have no doubt that it is very important and so are you. Very Very Important. Carl Sandburg. CP-SandC

I have no fancy for that ancient cant. Right to Die, The. Paul Laurence Dunbar. CP-DunbP

I have no happiness in dreaming of Brycelinde. Under the Moon. William Butler Yeats. CP-YeatW

I have no head for tunes. Rather Foolish Sentiment, A. A. K. Ramanujan. CP-RamaA

I have no heart, she cries. I am driving her madder. Epona. Paul Muldoon. CP-MuldP

I have no hoarded treasure. Hafiz. CP-EmerR Fr. Odes.

I have no Life but this. Emily Dickinson. CP-DickE

"I have no master," said the Blind Boy. Blind Boy, The. Walter De la Mare. CP-DeLaW

I have no name for the nameless thing. Nameless Thing. Robert Penn Warren. CP-WarrR

I Have No Place to Take Thee. Kenneth Patchen. CP-PatcK

I have no program for. Hippie Hop. A. R. Ammons. CP-AmmoA

I have no respect for you. No Respect. Stevie Smith. CP-SmitS

I have no store. Canzonet. Oscar Wilde. CP-WildO

I have no wine of Gaza, nor Falerna wine. Sir Walter Ralegh. CP-RaleW

I have no wit, no words, no tears. Better Resurrection, A. Christina Georgina Rossetti. CP-RosC1

I have not felt, o'er seas of sand. Holy Land, The. John Greenleaf Whittier. CP-WhitJ

I have not lain with beauty all my life. Lawrence Ferlinghetti. SP-FerlL

I have not lived the flesh has hedged me in. Spring ("I have not lived the flesh has hedged me in"). Jones Very. CP-VeryJ

I have not loved thee much my heart is poor. Effort. Jones Very. CP-VeryJ

I have not loved you in the noblest way. Sonnet: "I have not loved you in the noblest way." Countee Cullen. CP-CullC

I have not seen you lay your veil apart. Petrarch. CP-Petra, tr. by J. G. Nichols

I have not slept for a week. Death of the Race Car Driver, The. Norman Dubie. CP-DubiN

I have not so much emulated the birds that musically sing. To Soar in Freedom and in Fullness of Power. Walt Whitman. CP-WhitW

I have not sought Thee, I have not found Thee. Love Is Stronger than Death. Christina Georgina Rossetti. CP-RosC2

I have not told my garden yet. Secret, The. Emily Dickinson. CP-DickE

I have not written my poem. Experiment That Failed, The. John Logan. CP-LogaJ

I have nothing new to ask of you. Another Year Come. W. S. Merwin. SP-MerwW

I have nothing to give you but these days. Geographer. Marilyn Hacker. SP-HackM

I have nothing to say about the war. Yehuda Amichai. SP-AmicYL Fr. Poems of the Land of Zion and Jerusalem.

I have nothing to say about the war, nothing. Yehuda Amichai. SP-AmicY, tr. by Chana Bloch Fr. Songs of Zion the Beautiful.

I have nothing to say about the way the sky tilts. Three Poems for the New Year [1]. Charles Wright. SP-WrigC Fr. Three Poems for the New Year.

I have noticed that people who talk a lot about loyalty. Talk of Loyalty. D. H. Lawrence. CP-LawrD

I have often been lost on the sea. Ghazal of the Flight. Federico García Lorca. CP-GarcF, tr. by Catherine Brown Fr. Ghazals.

I have only one enemy. I'll never know how he managed to enter my house. Leaves of the Cypress, The. Jorge Luis Borges. SP-BorgJ, tr. by Alan S. Trueblood

I have opened the window to warm my hands on the sill. Dreams Old and Nascent. D. H. Lawrence. CP-LawrD

I have opened the windows to warm my hands on the sill. Dreams Old and Nascent: Old. D. H. Lawrence. CP-LawrD

I have phrases and whole pages memorized. Jelaluddin Rumi. SP-Rumi, tr. by Coleman Barks

'I have' poem, The. Oak Openings. Donald Davie. CP-DaviDC

I have prayed Love, and yet again I pray. Petrarch. CP-Petra, tr. by J. G. Nichols

I have ransacked the encyclopedia. Old-Fashioned Requited Love. Carl Sandburg. CP-SandC

I have reached a time when words no longer help. For a Birthday. Thom Gunn. CP-GunnT

I have reached, alas, the long shadow. Sestina: "I have reached, alas, the long shadow." Dante Alighieri. CP-SchuJ, tr. by James Schuyler

I hear on the radio that Anastasio Somoza. Axis, The. Arthur Sze. SP-SzeA

I hear Robert offed himself. Tanck's Song About Dying Young. Hayden Carruth. CP-CarHS *Fr.* Songs About What Comes Down: The Complete Works of Mr. Septic Tanck.

I hear something coming. Breathing. James Tate. SP-TateJ

I hear spokesmen praising Tshombe, and the Portuguese. Robert Bly. *See* Hatred of Men with Black Hair

I hear that maiden still. Maid of Keinton Mandeville, The. Thomas Hardy. CP-HardT

I hear, the axe has flowered. Paul Celan. SP-CelaP, *tr. by* John Felstiner

I hear the bell-rope sawing. Drawing Details in an Old Church. Thomas Hardy. CP-HardT

I hear the piano playing. Strange House, The. Thomas Hardy. CP-HardT

I hear the Shadowy Horses, their long manes a-shake. Michael Robartes Bids His Beloved Be at Peace. William Butler Yeats. CP-YeatW

I hear the sunset ambulances surround. California Petrarchan. Karl Shapiro. SP-ShapK

I hear the weather. Lorine Niedecker. CP-NiedL

I hear the world reciting. Courage to Be New, The. Robert Frost. CP-FrosR

I hear them outside. I Have Shit Stains in My Underwear Too. Charles Bukowski. SP-BukC1

I hear you again, mosquito hymn of summer! Eclogue 5: Summer. Joseph Brodsky. CP-BrodJ, *tr. by* George L. Kline

I hear you were. How I See Things. Yusef Komunyakaa. CP-KomuY

I Heard. Lorine Niedecker. CP-NiedL

I heard a child's voice. Old Youth. Langston Hughes. CP-HughL; CP-HughL1

I heard a dying man. Dying Man, The. Theodore Roethke. CP-RoetT

I heard a Fly buzz—when I died. Emily Dickinson. CP-DickE

I Heard a Hermit Speak. Adrienne Rich. CP-RicAE

I heard a little chicken chirp. Thomas Earp. D. H. Lawrence. CP-LawrD

I heard a little child beneath the stars. Universe, The. Walter De la Mare. CP-DeLaW

I heard a maid on a godolphin's back. To a Poetess. G. K. Chesterton. CP-ChesG

I heard a pouting siren. Roll On, Thou Deep and Dark Blue Copy Writer—Roll! Ogden Nash. CP-NashO

I heard a radio-parrot, an ordinary newscaster. Ordinary Newscaster, An. Robinson Jeffers. CP-JefR3

I heard a small sad sound. To-Be-Forgotten, The. Thomas Hardy. CP-HardT

I heard a song that the fairies sang. Chosen. G. K. Chesterton. CP-ChesG

I heard a thousand blended notes. Lines Written in Early Spring. William Wordsworth. CP-WorW1; MW-WorW

I heard a voice from Etna's side. Mad Monk, The. Samuel Taylor Coleridge. CP-ColeS; CP-WorW1

I heard a woman's lips. Harrison Street Court. Carl Sandburg. CP-SandC

I Heard (Alas! 'Twas Only in a Dream). William Wordsworth. CP-WorW2

I heard an Angel singing. William Blake. CP-BlakW

I heard an elf go whistling by. Behind Stowe. Elizabeth Bishop. CP-BishE

I heard, as if I had no Ear. Emily Dickinson. CP-DickE

I Heard Brew Moore Say, One Day. Ted Berrigan. SP-BerrT

I Heard Her Say. D. H. Lawrence. CP-LawrD

I Heard Immanuel Singing. Nicholas Vachel Lindsay. CP-LindV

I heard it first while screwing a blonde. Bee's 5th. Charles Bukowski. SP-BukC1

I heard it said, there is. Paul Celan. SP-CelaP, *tr. by* John Felstiner

I heard it told that once when Persia. Fernando Pessoa. SP-PessF, *tr. by* Susan M. Brown *and* Edwin Honig

I heard my heart screeching like a subway train. Hard Love Rock. Audre Lorde. SP-LordA

I heard my son burst out of his room. Rightful One, The. David Ignatow. SP-IgnaD

I heard new words prayed at cows. Cleric, The. Seamus Heaney. SP-HeanSO *Fr.* Sweeney Redivivus.

I heard of those eternal pains. Chorus: "I heard of those eternal pains." Sophocles. CP-SherT *Fr.* Philoctetes.

I heard one who said: "Verily." Cassandra. Edwin Arlington Robinson. CP-RobiE

I heard or seemed to hear the chiding Sea. Sea-Shore. Ralph Waldo Emerson. CP-EmerR

I heard that you ask'd for something to prove this puzzle the New World. To Foreign Lands. Walt Whitman. CP-WhitW

I heard that you were dead, Edgar, and wept. For Edgar Bowers. Helen Pinkerton. CP-PinkH

I heard the bells at midnight. Song of the New Year. James Whitcomb Riley. CP-RileJ

I heard the front door close. After a Death. Gregory Orr. SP-OrrG

I heard the Indian Agent say. Old man's lazy, The. Peter Blue Cloud. SP-BlueP

I heard the old, old men say. Old Men Admiring Themselves in the Water, The. William Butler Yeats. CP-YeatW

I heard the ship pass by. You were late. Cardplayers. Yannis Ritsos. SP-RitsY, *tr.*

by Kostas Myrsiades

I heard the sound of the wild, heaving sea. New Sea, The. Jones Very. CP-VeryJ

I heard the sparrows shouting "Eat, eat." In the Night Fields. W. S. Merwin. SP-MerwW

I heard the train's shrill whistle call. Rendition, The. John Greenleaf Whittier. CP-WhitJ

I heard the virgins sigh, I saw the sleek[e]. Obsequies to the Lady Anne Hay. Thomas Carew. CP-CareT

I heard the wind coming. Hearing the Wind at Night. May Swenson. SP-SwenM

I heard thee laugh. Stephen Crane. CP-CranS

I heard them marching the leaf-wet roads of my head. Derek Walcott. CP-WalcD *Fr.* Midsummer.

I heard thy fate without a tear. Stanzas: "I heard thy fate without a tear." Lord Byron. CP-Byron

I heard two workers say, "This chaos." Idiom of the Hero. Wallace Stevens. CP-StevW; CP-StevWP

I heard ye co'd coole heat; and came. To Springs and Fountains. Robert Herrick. CP-HerrR

I Heard You Solemn-Sweet Pipes of the Organ. Walt Whitman. CP-WhitW

I heed not that my earthly lot. To ———: "I heed not that my earthly lot." Edgar Allan Poe. CP-PoeEd

I held a Jewel in my fingers. Emily Dickinson. CP-DickE

I held a poor opinion of myself. My Ghost. Robert Graves. CP-GravR

I held Europe in my hand. Yonder. Richard Eberhart. CP-EberR

I held it in my hands while he told the story. Book, The. Miller Williams. CP-WillM

I held Love's head while it did ake. Upon Love. Robert Herrick. CP-HerrR

I held my breath for years, for fear. Ghost, The. Heather McHugh. SP-McHuH

I held my heart so far from harm. Kidnaped. Paul Laurence Dunbar. CP-DunbP

I held the briefcase at arm's length from me. Briefcase, The. Paul Muldoon. CP-MuldP

I held you / through all your shifts. Eventual Proteus. Margaret Atwood. SP-AtwM1

I hesitate which word to take. Emily Dickinson. SP-DickE

I hide behind simple things that you may find me. Meaning of Simplicity, The. Yannis Ritsos. SP-RitsY, *tr. by* Kimon Friar

I hide myself within my flower. Emily Dickinson. CP-DickE

I hiked yesterday to the summit. Han-shan. CP-ColdM, *tr. by* Red Pine

I hired a carpenter. Death King, The. Anne Sexton. CP-SextA

I hoed and trenched and weeded. A. E. Housman. CP-HousA

I hold a key in my hand. Key, The. Muriel Rukeyser. CP-RukeM

I hold a pair of scissors over my head and open and close the blades. Scissors. David Ignatow. SP-IgnaD

I hold in my hand this cup. Hermit Prays, The. Maxine W. Kumin. SP-KumiM

I hold it, Sir, my bounden duty. To Mr Gavin Hamilton, Mauchline. Robert Burns. CP-BurnR

I hold my honey and I store my bread. My Dreams, My Works Must Wait Till after Hell. Gwendolyn Brooks. SP-BrooG

I hold not with the fatalist creed. Ultimatum. Countee Cullen. CP-CullC

I hold that the true age of wisdom is when. Uncle Sidney's Views. James Whitcomb Riley. CP-RileJ

I hold you responsible for. Hymn 4: "I hold you responsible for." A. R. Ammons. CP-AmmoA

I hold your trembling hand tonight—and yet. Dearth. James Whitcomb Riley. CP-RileJ

I honor those who try. Jelaluddin Rumi. SP-Rumi, *tr. by* Coleman Barks

I hook my fingers into the old tennis court fence. Of What Is Past. C. K. Williams. CP-WillC; SP-WillC

I hope I'm, Mark, The. A. R. Ammons. CP-AmmoA

I hope, my Anna, you'll believe. Mrs. Austen. CP-AustJ

I hope my child'll [or chile'll]. Lament over Love. Langston Hughes. CP-HughL; CP-HughL1

I hope my good old asshole holds out. Sphincter. Allen Ginsberg. SP-GinsA

I hope that in my eldering age I'm not becoming noticeably querulous. Is This Seat Taken? Yes, or, My Neck Is Sticking In. Ogden Nash. CP-NashO

I hope that you are well. Emily Dickinson. SP-DickE

I hope they never get a rope on you, weather. Weather. May Swenson. SP-SwenM

I hope you are joyful frequently. Emily Dickinson. SP-DickE

I hope you may not go. Emily Dickinson. SP-DickE

I hope you may sometime be. Emily Dickinson. SP-DickE

I hope your rambles have been sweet. Emily Dickinson. SP-DickE

I humm'd an air of sweet Mozart. George Meredith. CP-MerG2

I hung my verses in the wind. Test, The. Ralph Waldo Emerson. CP-EmerR

I, Hypocrite Harry, that Hamburg hand-kisser. Apostate, The. Carolyn Kizer. CP-KizeC *Fr.* Heine Journal, A.

"I," I mused, "yes, I," and turned to the fenestrations of the night. Wonderful World. James Schuyler. CP-SchuJ

I?/ I walk alone. Soliloquy of the Solipsist. Sylvia Plath. CP-PlatS

I identify with the wooden shed in my neighbor's backyard. David Ignatow. SP-IgnaD

I idle stand that I may find employ. Idler, The. Jones Very. CP-VeryJ

I idly cut a parsley stalk. On a Midsummer Eve. Thomas Hardy. CP-HardT

I imagine him still with heavy brow. Beethoven's Death Mask. Stephen Spender. CP-SpenS

I imagine this [or the] midnight moment's forest. Thought-Fox, The. Ted Hughes. SP-HughTN

I, in disgust with the living, having read. Edna St. Vincent Millay. CP-MillE

I, in My Intricate Image. Dylan Thomas. CP-ThomD

I inhabited the wake of a long wave. Wave, The. W. S. Merwin. SP-MerwW

I innocently meant to go away. I mentioned digestion. I heard it. Painted Lace. Gertrude Stein. CP-SteiG

I invited Mozart to dinner. Dinner, The. Gregory Orr. SP-OrrG

I is a statue of white-hot metal. Sad Song. Philip Whalen. SP-WhalP

I is, naturally enough, any author. John Ciardi. CP-CiarJ

I is the director of three letters and not the dead director. Left Unfinished Sixteen Times. Michael Palmer. SP-PalmM

I is the total black. Audre Lorde. See I / is the total black

I / is the total black. Coal. Audre Lorde. SP-LordA

I, Ishmael, hunted him, but now no more. Melvilliana. Helen Pinkerton. CP-PinkH

I journey not whence nor whither. Song for Ditherers. Ogden Nash. CP-NashO

I journeyed from my native spot. His Country. Thomas Hardy. CP-HardT

I joy, dear[e] Mother, when I view. British Church, The. George Herbert. CP-HerbG

I joy in grief, and do detest all joys. Corona. Sir Philip Sidney. SP-SidnP Fr. Arcadia.

I jump between the cat. Charmed. Yusef Komunyakaa. CP-KomuY

I jump with terror seeing him. Modes of Pleasure. Thom Gunn. CP-GunnT

I just got here myself and I feel like hell. Rituals. Miller Williams. CP-WillM

I just had the old Dodge in the shop. Eternity Blues. Hayden Carruth. CP-CarHS

I just passed. Charles Olson. CP-OlsoC

I just saw two boys. Details for Paterson. William Carlos Williams. CP-WilW2

I keep finding this letter. Bread and Butter. W. S. Merwin. SP-MerwW

I keep hearing cars demons ghosts. In the Night. Philip Whalen. SP-WhalP

I keep my diamond necklace in a pond of sparkling water for invisibility. Fabergé. James Schuyler. CP-SchuJ

I keep my pledge. Emily Dickinson. CP-DickE

I keep on dying again. Lesson, The. Maya Angelou. SP-AngeM

I keep practicing death. Practice. Charles Bukowski. SP-BukC2

I keep putting the empties out back but. Conversation in a Cheap Room. Charles Bukowski. SP-BukC2

I keep six honest serving-men. Rudyard Kipling. CP-KiplR Fr. Just-So Stories.

I keep so many deaths in reserve. Coming Back. Pablo Neruda. SP-NeruP

I keep thinking it will be outside. Stolen. Charles Bukowski. SP-BukC1

I keep thinking of young Dostoyevsky, caught reading forbidden books, talking about unlawful topics. Trick, The. Gregory Orr. SP-OrrG

"I Keep to Myself Such Measures." Robert Creeley. CP-CreeR

I keep trying to live as if this world were heaven. Love Love Love Again. Philip Whalen. SP-WhalP

I keep winning now. Revolution, A. Philip Whalen. SP-WhalP

I keep your old snaps in my bottom drawer. Old Snaps, The. Derek Mahon. CP-MahoD

I ken these islands each inhabited. Harry Semen. Hugh MacDiarmid. SP-MacDH

I kept searching for you in the stars. 11 February 1946. Primo Levi. CP-LeviP, tr. by Ruth Feldman and Brian Swann

I kept the whiskey in the caves. Kate Whiskey. Paul Muldoon. CP-MuldP

I killed a bee on the Street of Scissors. Michael Palmer. SP-PalmM

I Killed a Fly. David Ignatow. SP-IgnaD

I killed someone. Other, The. Gabriela Mistral. SP-MistG, tr. by Maria Giachetti [or Jacketti]

I kin hump my back and take the rain. Fall-Crick View of the Earthquake, A. James Whitcomb Riley. CP-RileJ

I kind of like the playful porpoise. Porpoise, The. Ogden Nash. CP-NashO

I kiss the hem of my fate, as my father would kiss the side. Yehuda Amichai. SP-AmicY Fr. In a Right Angle: A Cycle of Quatrains.

I kissed them in fancy as I came. Two Lips. Thomas Hardy. CP-HardT

I kissed you, bride and lost, and went. Loser, The. Adrienne Rich. CP-RicAE; SP-RicA2

I kissed you in the dead of dark. Accusation, The. James Wright. CP-WrigJ

I Kneel. Charles Bukowski. SP-BukC2

I kneel down to peer into a culvert. Kneeling Down to Look [or Peer] into a Culvert. Robert Bly. SP-BlyR

I knelt down / at the edge of the water. Alligator Poem. Mary Oliver. SP-OlivM

I knew a Bird that would sing as firm. Emily Dickinson. SP-DickE

I knew a clean man. Lorine Niedecker. CP-NiedL

I Knew a Lady. Thomas Hardy. CP-HardT

I knew a man by sight. Henry David Thoreau. CP-ThorH

"I knew a real man once," says Agatha in the slendor of a shagbark. Plaster. Carl Sandburg. CP-SandC

I Knew A Woman. Theodore Roethke. CP-RoetT

I knew a youth named Henry Chard. Henry Chard. G. K. Chesterton. CP-ChesG

I knew already, Love, our human ploys. Petrarch. CP-Petra, tr. by J. G. Nichols

I knew her for a little ghost. Little Ghost, The. Edna St. Vincent Millay. CP-MillE

I knew I looked into the blazing throne. Grate, The. Robert Stock. SP-StocR

I Knew I'd Sing. Heather McHugh. SP-McHuH

I knew it was going to end badly. Oxymoronic Hospital Blues. Alan Dugan. CP-DugaA

I knew more surely than the name of my train, The Crescent. Impressions Through a Pennsy Window. Tennessee Williams. CP-WillT

I knew not 'twas so dire a crime. Song By J. Brenzaida To G.S. Emily Jane Brontë. CP-BronE

I knew—so much heaven opened up my eyes. Petrarch. CP-Petra, tr. by J. G. Nichols

I knew that I had gained. Emily Dickinson. CP-DickE

I knew the General only by name of course. I Don't Want to Startle You but They Are Going to Kill Most of Us. Kenneth Patchen. SP-PatcK

I knew where they were. People. Robert Creeley. CP-CreeR

I knew you forever and you were always old. Some Foreign Letters. Anne Sexton. CP-SextA; SP-SextA

I knew you once so well I know you still. Old Poems. Randall Jarrell. CP-JarrR

I knock at the door of the rock. Conversation with a Rock. Wisława Szymborska. SP-SzymWM, tr. by Joanna Trzeciak

I knock at the stone's front door. Conversation with a Stone. Wisława Szymborska. SP-SzymW, tr. by Stanislaw Barańczak and Clare Cavanagh

I knock, but knock in vain; there is no call. Guest, The. Jones Very. CP-VeryJ

I knocked upon thy door ajar. In Vain. Walter De la Mare. CP-DeLaW

I Know. John Berryman. CP-BerrJ

I know a baby, such a baby,— / Round blue eyes and cheeks of pink. Christina Georgina Rossetti. CP-RosC2

I know a bitch who amuses herself making messes. Ermine, The. James Laughlin. CP-LaugJ

I know a friend, very strong and good. He is the best friend in the world. List, A. G. K. Chesterton. CP-ChesG

I know a girl who is in Paris, France. Absence Makes the Heart Grow Heart Trouble. Ogden Nash. CP-NashO

I know a guy, 63.5 years old. Tanck's Song About the Younger Generation. Hayden Carruth. CP-CarHS Fr. Songs About What Comes Down: The Complete Works of Mr. Septic Tank.

I know a Jew fish crier down on Maxwell Street. Fish Crier. Carl Sandburg. CP-SandC

I know a little restaurant. Try It Suns. and Hols.; It's Closed Then. Ogden Nash. CP-NashO

I Know a Man. Yehuda Amichai. SP-AmicY, tr. by Chana Bloch

I Know a Man. Robert Creeley. CP-CreeR

I know a man. Sand-Man, The. Paul Laurence Dunbar. CP-DunbP

I know a man named Mr. Nagle. I Know Exactly Who Dropped the Overalls in Mrs. Murphy's Chowder. Ogden Nash. CP-NashO

I know a Mount, the gracious Sun perceives. Rudel to the Lady of Tripoli. Robert Browning. CP-BroR1

I know a noble Englishman. Noble Englishman, The. D. H. Lawrence. CP-LawrD

I Know a Noble Englishman. D. H. Lawrence. See Noble Englishman, The

I know a place where all is real. Interjection #3: I Know a Place Where All Is Real. Robert Penn Warren. CP-WarrR

I know a place where Summer strives. Emily Dickinson. CP-DickE

I know a pool where nightshade preens. Crazed. Walter De la Mare. CP-DeLaW

I know a ray of sun (of God?) can still. Eugenio Montale. CP-MontE, tr. by Jonathan Galassi

I know a renegade hotel. Traveler's Rest. Ogden Nash. CP-NashO

I know a seraph who has golden eyes. Alone in the Wind, on the Prairie. Nicholas Vachel Lindsay. CP-LindV

I know a woman. One for Old Snaggle-Tooth. Charles Bukowski. SP-BukC1

I know all about the Sphinx. Sphinx, The. James Whitcomb Riley. CP-RileJ

I Know All This When Gipsy Fiddles Cry. Nicholas Vachel Lindsay. CP-LindV

I know, although when looks meet. Crazy Jane and Jack the Journeyman. William Butler Yeats. CP-YeatW

I know an aged Man constrained to dwell. William Wordsworth. CP-WorW2; MW-WorW

I know an ice handler who wears a flannel shirt. Ice Handler. Carl Sandburg. CP-SandC

I know an island, pale in the green sea. Marya Alexandrovna Zaturenska. SP-ZatuM

I know better. Family Tree. Yusef Komunyakaa. CP-KomuY

I know but little of Little Ones. Emily Dickinson. SP-DickE

I know but will not tell. Elegy: "I know but will not tell." Alan Dugan. CP-DugaA

I Know Exactly Who Dropped the Overalls in Mrs. Murphy's Chowder. Ogden Nash. CP-NashO

I know God doesn't need my pity. For a Sad God. Heather McHugh. SP-McHuH

I know hands that leapt from childhood to old age. Span. W. S. Merwin. SP-MerwW

I know him, February's thrush. Thrush in February, The. George Meredith. CP-MerG1

I Know How Every Poet. James Laughlin. CP-LaugJ

I know how high the flooding waters came. Elegy on the Lost Child. Yehuda Amichai. SP-AmicYL, tr. by Benjamin Harshav and Barbara Harshav

I know how I have learned to hate. I've turned on trees and animals. My Enemies. David Ignatow. SP-IgnaD

I know I am but summer to your heart. Edna St. Vincent Millay. CP-MillE

I know I am noble with the nobility of the sun. Noble. D. H. Lawrence. CP-LawrD

I know I am nothing. Nullus. D. H. Lawrence. CP-LawrD

I know I am / The Negro Problem. Dinner Guest: Me. Langston Hughes. CP-HughL; CP-HughL3

I know I change / have changed. Daguerreotype Taken in Old Age. Margaret Atwood. SP-AtwM1

I know I have been happiest at your side. Dorothy Parker. CP-ParkD

I know, I know—though the evidence. Blow, West Wind. Robert Penn Warren. CP-WarrR

I know I might have lived in such a way. Fontaine, Je Ne Boirai Pas De Ton Eau! Edna St. Vincent Millay. CP-MillE

I Know, I Remember, But How Can I Help You. Hayden Carruth. CP-CarHS

I know if I find you I will have to leave the earth, Hymn: "I know if I find you I will have to leave the earth." A. R. Ammons. CP-AmmoA

"I know I'm not the first," I said one night. Muse of the Evening. Miller Williams. CP-WillM

I know it is dark; and though I have lain. Ode to the Rain, An. Samuel Taylor Coleridge. CP-ColeS

I know it is my sin[ne] which locks thine ear[e]s. Church-Lock and Key. George Herbert. CP-HerbG

I know little or nothing of the Borges. Borges, The. Jorge Luis Borges. SP-BorgJ, tr. by Alastair Reid

I know lives, I could miss. Emily Dickinson. CP-DickE

I know lots of men who are in love and lots of men who are. I Never Even Suggested It. Ogden Nash. CP-NashO

I know my love is true. Ballad: "I know my love is true." Paul Laurence Dunbar. CP-DunbP

I know my mind and I have made my choice. Edna St. Vincent Millay. CP-MillE

I know my time, which is obscure, silent and brief. Night-Flowering Cactus. Thomas Merton. CP-MertT

I know no greater delight than the sheer delight of being alone. Delight of Being Alone. D. H. Lawrence. CP-LawrD

I know not, Dante, in what refuge dwells. Sonnet: He answers the foregoing Sonnet, and prays Dante, in the name of Beatrice, to continue his great Poem. Cino da Pistoia. CW-RossD, tr. by Dante Gabriel Rossetti

I know not how it falls on me. Emily Jane Brontë. CP-BronE

I know not how it is—it seems. My Day of Life. Ambrose Bierce. SP-BierA

I know not how it may be with others. Old Furniture. Thomas Hardy. CP-HardT

I know not how to thank you. Emily Dickinson. SP-DickE

I know not if it was a dream. I viewed. Passing Show, The. Ambrose Bierce. SP-BierA

I know not in Whose hands are laid. Necessitarian, The. Rudyard Kipling. CP-KiplR

I know not, Time and Space so intervene. Countess, The. John Greenleaf Whittier. CP-WhitJ

I know not what to do. Fragment 36 [or Thirty-Six]: "I know not what to do." "H. D." CP-DoolH

I know not where my heavy sighs to hide. Sir Thomas Wyatt. CP-WyatT

I know / nothing anymore. C. K. Williams. CP-WillC; SP-WillC

I know now how a man whose blood is hot. Sonnet: "I know now how a man whose blood is hot." Countee Cullen. CP-CullC

I know now / That Notre Dame is in Paris. I Thought It Was Tangiers I Wanted. Langston Hughes. CP-HughL; CP-HughL1

I know of people in the Grave. Emily Dickinson. CP-DickE

I know one German. Why Not? James Laughlin. CP-LaugJ

I know only the bare rocks of today. Prelude, A: "I know only the bare rocks of today." William Carlos Williams. CP-WilW1

I know salt marshes that move along like one big. Audacity of the Lower Gods. Yusef Komunyakaa. CP-KomuY

I know, Sister, that solitude. To a Severe Nun. Thomas Merton. CP-MertT

I know so much. Spleen. Frank O'Hara. SP-OharF

I know some lonely Houses off the Road. Emily Dickinson. CP-DickE

I know Suspense, it steps so terse. Emily Dickinson. CP-DickE

I know that a little verse is a versicle but I don't know if a little phrase is a phrasical. From a Manhattan Tomb. Ogden Nash. SP-NashO

I know that behind these walls is the city, over these rooftops. Foghorn in Horror. Muriel Rukeyser. CP-RukeM

I know that He exists. Emily Dickinson. CP-DickE

I know that honour is. War Poet. Ivor Gurney. SP-GurnI

I know that I shall meet my fate. Irish Airman Foresees His Death, An. William Butler Yeats. CP-YeatW

I know that my profile will be serene. Sonnet: "I know that my profile will be serene." Federico García Lorca. CP-GarcF, tr. by Christopher Maurer

I know that my redeemer liveth because. Notes from a Lenten Bar. Josephine Jacobsen. CP-JacoJ

I know that never with a tranquil mind. Petrarch. CP-Petra, tr. by J. G. Nichols

I know that silence will greet me, but still. Pursuit. Wisława Szymborska. SP-SzymWM, tr. by Joanna Trzeciak

I know that some night. We Will Taste the Islands and the Sea. Charles Bukowski. SP-BukC1

I know that there are those who say, "Why don't you sing now" In Autumn ("I know that there are those who say, 'Why don't you sing now'"). "Rubén Dario." SP-DariR, tr. by Alberto Acereda and Will Derusha

I know that they're all modest. Four Walls of My Room, The. Constantine P. Cavafy. CP-CavaC, tr. by Theoharis Constantine Theoharis

I know that tonight the wind is sighing. M.A. Written on the Dungeon Wall. Emily Jane Brontë. CP-BronE

I know that what Nietzsche said is true. Reflection. Ezra Pound. CP-PoEar

I know that you have tried, dear friend. For a Friend Who Thinks Himself Urbane. Robert Penn Warren. CP-WarrR

I know that you will die / before I do. Keep. Margaret Atwood. SP-AtwM2

I know the appointed hour. Ralph Waldo Emerson. CP-EmerR

I know the bottom, she says. I know it with my great tap root. Elm. Sylvia Plath. CP-PlatS

I know the face of Falsehood and her tongue. Edna St. Vincent Millay. CP-MillE

I know the moment when a raw grimace. Eugenio Montale. CP-MontE, tr. by Jonathan Galassi

I know the [or a] thing that's most uncommon. On a Certain Lady at Court. Alexander Pope. CP-PopeA

I know the way[e]s of learning; both the head. Pearl, The. Matth. 13:45. George Herbert. CP-HerbG

I know the world where land and water meet. Fisher's Son, The. Henry David Thoreau. CP-ThorH

I know them at their worst, when by the shore. Gulls, The. Howard Nemerov. CP-NemeH

I know there are some fools that care. Deformed Mistress, The. Sir John Suckling. CP-SuckJ

I know / there is. Come Prima. A. R. Ammons. CP-AmmoA

I know there is a country where we go. Hayden Carruth. CP-CarHS Fr. Bloomingdale Papers, The.

I know there shall dawn a day. Reverie. Robert Browning. CP-BroR2

I know this happiness. Of Being. Denise Levertov. SP-LeveDS

I know this perilous love-lane. Hafiz. CP-EmerR Fr. Odes.

I know / this rose is only. Rose for Janet, A. Charles Tomlinson. SP-TomlC

I know 'tis but a Dream, yet feel more anguish. Night-Mare Death in Life, The. Samuel Taylor Coleridge. CP-ColeS

I know to bore you with tales. It's Indelicate. James Laughlin. CP-LaugJ

I know to whom I write. Here, I am sure. Epistle to Master John Selden, An. Ben Jonson. CP-JonsB; SP-JonsB

I know two women / and the one. Wife, The. Robert Creeley. CP-CreeR

I know very little. Hangover and Sick Leave. Charles Bukowski. SP-BukC2

I know very well, goddess, she is not beautiful. Calypso's Island. Archibald MacLeish. CP-MacLA

I know well. Ted Hughes. SP-HughTN

I know what it means not to return. Sunset at Fossoli. Primo Levi. CP-LeviP, tr. by Ruth Feldman and Brian Swann

I know what my heart is like. Ebb. Edna St. Vincent Millay. CP-MillE

I know what the caged bird feels, alas! Sympathy. Paul Laurence Dunbar. CP-DunbP

I know what you'd say. Soup ("I know what you'd say"). Robert Creeley. SP-CreeR

I know where lurk. Fear. Walter De la Mare. CP-DeLaW

I know where Wells grow—Droughtless Wells. Emily Dickinson. CP-DickE

I know why the yellow forsythia. Spring Song. Edna St. Vincent Millay. CP-MillE

I know: you are glycerine. Any Husband to Any Wife. Adrienne Rich. CP-RicAE

I know you love me, baby. Guitar Recitativos. A. R. Ammons. CP-AmmoA

I Know You Not. Christina Georgina Rossetti. CP-RosC3

I know, you told me. Death and the Good Citizen. A. K. Ramanujan. CP-RamaA

I know you would have known the names. Garden of the Virgin, The. G. K. Chesterton. CP-ChesG

I know you would. You will hail the huge release. Sonnet with the Compliments of the Season. G. K. Chesterton. CP-ChesG

I know you, you're the one bent over low. Paul Celan. SP-CelaP, *tr.* by John Felstiner

I Know You'll Like Them. Ogden Nash. CP-NashO

I know your moral sources, prig. Neoclassicist, A. Kenneth Rexroth. CP-RexrK

I labored in vain reciting the Three Histories. Han-shan. CP-ColdM, *tr. by* Red Pine

I lafs und sings, und shumps aroundt. Lager Beer. Paul Laurence Dunbar. CP-DunbP

I laid beside thy gate, am Lazarus. Son, Remember. Christina Georgina Rossetti. CP-RosC2

I laid me down upon a bank. William Blake. CP-BlakW

I laid my inventory at the hand. Even In The Grave. Walter De la Mare. CP-DeLaW

I lang hae thought, my youthfu' friend. Epistle to a Young Friend. Robert Burns. CP-BurnR

I late the Roman youth's loud prayse and pride. Alexias. Richard Crashaw. CP-CrasR

I lately fri'd, but now behold. Upon Himselfe. Robert Herrick. CP-HerrR

I laughed. Calvus. I laughed today. Carmen 53. Catullus. CP-ZukLS *Fr.* Carmina.

I lay at the edge of a well. Underground Stream, The. James Dickey. CP-DickJ

I lay beneath the stars of another sky. For M. Adam Zagajewski. SP-ZagaA, *tr. by* Clare Cavanagh

I lay down for a nap. But every time I closed my eyes. All Her Life. Raymond Carver. CP-CarvR

I lay down in my grave. Elegy: "I lay down in my grave." Maya Angelou. SP-AngeM

I lay down to rest. Love Comes. Allen Ginsberg. SP-GinsA

I lay in my bed and fiddled. In the Small Hours. Thomas Hardy. CP-HardT

I lay in silence, dead. A woman came. Another Way. Ambrose Bierce. SP-BierA

I Lay Love on My Knee. Allen Ginsberg. CP-GinsA

I lay me down and slumber. A. E. Housman. CP-HousA

I lay my branch of laurel down. To Lord Thurlow. Lord Byron. CP-Byron

I lay waiting. Bog Queen. Seamus Heaney. SP-HeanSO

I lead a life unpleasant, nothing glad. Sir Thomas Wyatt. CP-WyatT

I lean over the balcony of the minaret. Mosque in Jaffa, The. Raymond Carver. CP-CarvR

I leaned to hear your song. Poem for Kathleen Ferrier. James Wright. CP-WrigJ

I leant [*or* leaned] upon a coppice gate. Darkling Thrush, The. Thomas Hardy. CP-HardT

I learned a world from each. Allen Ginsberg. CP-GinsA

I learned—at least—what Home could be. Emily Dickinson. CP-DickE

I Learned That Her Name Was Proverb. Denise Levertov. SP-LeveDS

I learned to live with my despair. Against the Poetry of Philip Larkin. Czeslaw Milosz. CP-MiloCN, *tr. by* Robert Hass

I leave no tracks so my live loves. Death of Thelma Sayles. Lucille Clifton. SP-ClifL

I leave the book, I leave the wine. Ralph Waldo Emerson. CP-EmerR

I leave the drink and cigarette. Where. Heather McHugh. SP-McHuH

I leave you in your garden. To Yvor Winters, 1955. Thom Gunn. CP-GunnT

I leave you these, good daughters and honest son. For Lucinda, Robert, and Karyn. Miller Williams. CP-WillM

I left my baby in Forest A. Wartime. Lorine Niedecker. CP-NiedL

I left my dreamy page & sallied forth. Ralph Waldo Emerson. CP-EmerR

I left my room at last, I walked. Monster, The. Thom Gunn. CP-GunnT

I left the Evening Land by the will of the night. Yehuda Amichai. SP-AmicYL *Fr.* Poems of the Land of Zion and Jerusalem.

I left the road where a stile entered the wood. Thomas Kinsella. CP-KinsT

I left the shutter open, the camera. Olympic Rain Forest. Jane Cooper. CP-CoopJ

I left you in the morning. Flower-Gathering. Robert Frost. CP-FrosR

I let it go for the fact of it fast as it will. Reading the Newspaper on Microfilm. Miller Williams. CP-WillM

I let myself be carried along by every breeze. I Am a Preposterous Beetle. James Laughlin. CP-LaugJ

I let myself in at the kitchen door. Housekeeper, The. Robert Frost. CP-FrosR

I let the smoke out of the windows. Complex Autumnal. Carolyn Kizer. CP-KizeC

I let them whip and fuck me. Attitude. Olga Broumas. SP-BrouU

I lie and imagine a first light gleam in the bay. Achill. Derek Mahon. CP-MahoD

I lie and live. Stealer, The. Thom Gunn. CP-GunnT

I lie down and spread my legs and arms. O Sleepless Night. James Schuyler. CP-SchuJ

I lie dreaming 'neath the moon. Pierrot. Wallace Stevens. CP-StevWP

I lie for a long time on my left side and my right side. Dead Color. Charles Wright. SP-WrigC

I lie here thinking of you. Love Song: "I lie here thinking of you." William Carlos Williams. CP-WilW1

I lie in the bath and contemplate the toilet-paper. From a Play: Publisher's Song. Muriel Rukeyser. CP-RukeM

I lie low-coiled in a nest of dreams. Bells Jangled. James Whitcomb Riley. CP-RileJ

I lie on my daughter's body. Detective, The. Ai. SP-Ai

I lie on my hospital bed. With the World in My Blood Stream. Thomas Merton. CP-MertT

I lift mine eyes, and see / Thee, tender Lord, in pain upon the tree. Palm Sunday. Christina Georgina Rossetti. CP-RosC2

I lift mine eyes to see: earth vanisheth. Christina Georgina Rossetti. CP-RosC2

I lift the boy's body. Good Shepherd, The: Atlanta, 1981. Ai. SP-Ai

I lift the lid to my box of Phantoms. Emily Dickinson. CP-DickE

I lift the small brown mouse. Encounter. Mary Oliver. SP-OlivM

I lift up mine eyes unto the hills. Hills, The. D. H. Lawrence. CP-LawrD

I lifted a glass to get the waiter's attention. How We May By Chance Pronounce the Unsuspected Residence of a Ghost. Miller Williams. CP-WillM

I light up the grids. Fanny Howe. SP-HoweF *Fr.* Q.

I like a church; I like a cowl. Problem, The. Ralph Waldo Emerson. CP-EmerR

I like a look of Agony. Emily Dickinson. CP-DickE

I like fun—and I like jokes. Thoughts on a Pore Joke. James Whitcomb Riley. CP-RileJ

I like it back here. Ars Poetica. Charles Wright. SP-WrigC

I like it when. My Weariness of Epic Proportions. Charles Simic. SP-SimiC; SP-SimiCE

I like it when my friend has lovers, their happy moans. For Every Heart. Olga Broumas. SP-BrouO

I like me yet dot leedle chile. Mr. Silberberg. James Whitcomb Riley. CP-RileJ

I like my body when it is with your. E. E. Cummings. CP-CummE; SP-CummE

I like my picture to be in the box. Her Reply. James Laughlin. CP-LaugJ

I like not that dainty-cut raiment, those earrings of pearl. Daughter Returns, A. Thomas Hardy. CP-HardT

I like people quite well. People. D. H. Lawrence. CP-LawrD

I like relativity and quantum theories. Relativity. D. H. Lawrence. CP-LawrD

I like rust on a nail. And the Same Words. David Ignatow. SP-IgnaD

I like that poem, Win. There's a green world in it. To W. T. Scott. John Ciardi. CP-CiarJ

I like the crush here. What Virginia Said. Charles Tomlinson. CP-TomlC

I like the paintings by the Venetian painters. Floating Baby Paintings. Thomas Lux. SP-LuxT

I like the rich—the way. Rich, The. Charles Tomlinson. CP-TomlC

I like the sidewalks of an American city. Agave in the West. Donald Davie. CP-DaviDC

I like the way, in winter, cars. Short Days, The. John Updike. CP-UpdiJ

I like to beat people up. Ted Berrigan. SP-BerrT *Fr.* Sonnets, The.

I like to find. Pleasures. Denise Levertov. SP-LeveDS

I like to get off with people. Conviction IV. Stevie Smith. CP-SmitS

I like to hear of wealth and gold. Common Things. Paul Laurence Dunbar. CP-DunbP

I Like to Play with Him. Stevie Smith. CP-SmitS

I like to see doctors cough. On the Subject of Doctors. James Tate. SP-TateJ

I like to see him drink the gash. God the Drinker. Stevie Smith. CP-SmitS

I like to see, when I am low. Mediterranean Song. Richard Eberhart. CP-EberR

I like to stray into the. Maze, The. James Laughlin. CP-LaugJ

I like to think about that great French critic and historian, Hippolyte Adolphe Taine. If Me Scholars, Let Him Go. Ogden Nash. CP-NashO

I Like to Think of You. James Laughlin. CP-LaugJ

I like / to think that on. E. E. Cummings. CP-CummE

I like to toss him up and down. My Cats. Stevie Smith. CP-SmitS

I like to watch the clouds roll by. Cherub, The. Ogden Nash. CP-NashO

I Like You. James Laughlin. CP-LaugJ

I like you with nothing. Are you. Sky. William Stafford. SP-StafWW

I Like Your Collyrium. Thomas Sheridan. CP-SherT

I liked it coming out of that expensive. Some of My Readers. Charles Bukowski. SP-BukC3

I liked the bellows operated by rope. Blacksmith Shop. Czeslaw Milosz. CP-MiloCN, *tr. by* Robert Hass

I liked your velvet yoni, Annalena, long voyages in the delta of your legs. Annalena. Czeslaw Milosz. CP-MiloC; CP-MiloCN, *tr. by* Robert Hass

I likes a woman. Preference. Langston Hughes. CP-HughL; CP-HughL3

I lingered through the night to break of day. Her Definition. Thomas Hardy. CP-HardT

I 'listed at home for a lancer. Lancer. A. E. Housman. CP-HousA

I listen for the sounds of cannon, cries. On Lookout Mountain. Robert Earl Hayden. CP-HaydR

I listen to the holy antheming. St. Andrew's Church. Christina Georgina

Rossetti. CP-RosC3

I listen to the stillness of you. Listening. D. H. Lawrence. CP-LawrD

I lit upon the graveyard of dead creeds. Graveyard of Dead Creeds, The. Thomas Hardy. CP-HardT

I Live Admiring the Sky. David Ignatow. SP-IgnaD

I live among ideal men. Ralph Waldo Emerson. CP-EmerR

I live at the top of old West Chop. Martha's Vineyard. Ogden Nash. CP-NashO

I live but in the present, where art thou? Today. Jones Very. CP-VeryJ

I live for sinning, for the self that dies. Michelangelo Buonarroti. CP-Miche, *tr. by* John Frederick Nims

I live here on this harsh and lonely cliff. Dirge, A. Derek Mahon. CP-MahoD

I live here: "Wessex" is my name. Popular Personage at Home, A. Thomas Hardy. CP-HardT

I live in a bodiless loft. Loft. A. R. Ammons. CP-AmmoA

I live in a middle class neighborhood of an unfashionable. Sad Poem, A. Charles Bukowski. SP-BukC3

I live in a place without limits. Shih-te. CP-ColdM, *tr. by* Red Pine

I live in an age of varied powers and knowledge. Blessing, A ("I live in an age of varied powers and knowledge"). G. K. Chesterton. CP-ChesG

I live in an apartment, sink leaks thru the walls. New York Blues. Allen Ginsberg. SP-GinsA

I live in an orchard. Confetti of bruised petals. Postcard from the Garden. Marge Piercy. SP-PierM

I live in my wooden legs and O. Where I Live in This Honorable House of the Laurel Tree. Anne Sexton. CP-SextA

I live in the countryside. Han-shan. CP-ColdM, *tr. by* Red Pine

I Live in Three Worlds. James Laughlin. CP-LaugJ

I live inside of a machine. On Being a Householder. Alan Dugan. CP-DugaA

I live life seated, like an angel in a barber's chair. Evening Prayers. Arthur Rimbaud. CP-RimbA, *tr. by* Martin Sorrell

I live now inside an abandoned love, like a guest. Yehuda Amichai. SP-AmicYL *Fr.* At Right Angles.

I live on a park bench. Park Bench. Langston Hughes. CP-HughL; CP-HughL1

I live on the water. Winding Up. Derek Walcott. CP-WalcD

I live only here, between your eyes and you. To Be Written on the Mirror in Whitewash. Elizabeth Bishop. CP-BishE

"I live, therefore I love," said the Excerpt-Lifter. Evening of the Private Eye, An. John Ciardi. CP-CiarJ

I live underneath / the light of day. Charles Olson. SP-OlsoC *Fr.* Maximus Poems, The.

I Live Up Here. W. S. Merwin. SP-MerwW

I live where Frost lived. Hayden Carruth. CP-CarHS *Fr.* Clay Hill Anthology, The.

I live with Him—I see His face. Emily Dickinson. CP-DickE

I Live with My Contradictions. David Ignatow. SP-IgnaD

I lived an age that could not be. Afternoon in the Park, An. John Ciardi. CP-CiarJ

I lived in a dry well. Wells. Donald Hall. CP-HallD

I lived in the first century of world wars. Poem: "I lived in the first century of world wars." Muriel Rukeyser. CP-RukeM

I lived no-color. In a gray room I talked. No Color Man. Donald Hall. CP-HallD

I lived on a back street where. Ambassador, The. Pablo Neruda. SP-NeruP

I lived on Dread. Emily Dickinson. CP-DickE

I lived with Mr. Punch, they said my name was Judy. Variations. Randall Jarrell. CP-JarrR

I loathe, O Lord, this life below. Complaint on the Miseries of Life, A. James Thomson. CP-ThomD

I long for joy, O Lord, I long for gold / I long for all Thou profferest to me. Gold of that Land is Good, The. Christina Georgina Rossetti. CP-RosC2

I long for some, even. Interruptions. James Tate. SP-TateJ

I long for the black ink. Florence. Robert Lowell. SP-LoweR

I long for the desolate valleys. Lot's Wife. Stevie Smith. CP-SmitS

I long not now, a little while at least. Protest. Countee Cullen. CP-CullC

I long to talk[e] with some old lover's ghost. Love's Deity [*or* Deitie]. John Donne. CP-DonnJ; MW-DonnJ

I longed for companionship rather. In the Night. Stevie Smith. CP-SmitS

I longed to kill you once, when I was young. Devotions. James Wright. CP-WrigJ

I longed to love a full-boughed beech. Ivy-Wife, The. Thomas Hardy. CP-HardT

I longed to visit the eastern cliff. Han-shan. CP-ColdM, *tr. by* Red Pine

I look a long way back. Stratford on Avon. Donald Davie. CP-DaviDC

I look at my hand and see. May Swenson. SP-SwenM

I look at the bottle, when mournful I feel. Bottle of Aspirins, The. Stevie Smith. CP-SmitS

I look at the crisp golden-threaded hair. Canzone: His Portrait of his Lady, Angiola of Verona. Fazio degli Uberti. CW-RossD, *tr. by* Dante Gabriel Rossetti

I look at the Greek-derived design that nourished my infancy — this. Hellenistics. Robinson Jeffers. CP-JefR2

I look at the nephew. Slow Waker. Thom Gunn. CP-GunnT

I look at the pins on the hillside. Sequence 1944-6. Louis Zukofsky. CP-ZukLS

I look at the rock and the house. Stories. Donald Hall. CP-HallD

I look at the swaling sunset. In Trouble and Shame. D. H. Lawrence. CP-LawrD

I look back to you, and cherish what I wanted. Searching. Robert Lowell. SP-LoweR

I Look for the Lord. Christina Georgina Rossetti. CP-RosC3

I look for the way. Poetics. A. R. Ammons. CP-AmmoA

I Look in Her Face. Thomas Hardy. CP-HardT

I look in the glass. Repentance of Lady T, The. Stevie Smith. CP-SmitS

I look in the mirror. Ghost of Ware, The. Stevie Smith. CP-SmitS

I Look into My Glass. Thomas Hardy. CP-HardT

I look on the specious electrical light. Rhyme About an Electrical Advertising Sign, A. Nicholas Vachel Lindsay. CP-LindV

I look onto an alley here. Day for Anne Frank, A. C. K. Williams. CP-WillC; SP-WillC

I look out at the back yard — *l / sur le motif*, as Paul Cèzanne would say. Back Yard Boogie Woogie. Charles Wright. SP-WrigCN

I look out into the Yonder. Last Call. Langston Hughes. CP-HughL; CP-HughL3

I look out of these two holes, or I run. Where He's Staying Now. William Meredith. SP-MereW

I look out over the sterile snow. World Breaking Apart. Louise Glück. SP-GlucL

I look out the window. Poona Train Window. A. K. Ramanujan. CP-RamaA

I look round the cluttered. Selves. Thom Gunn. CP-GunnT

I Look to the North. Robert Burns. CP-BurnR

I look up and see. Late Harvest. James Tate. SP-TateJ

I look up and see them starting. My Work. Raymond Carver. CP-CarvR

I look up at the cliffs. Canyon Wren, The. Gary Snyder. CP-SnydG

I look up from the book. When I Read John Wieners's Selected Poems. William Corbett. SP-CorbW

I look up, you are standing. Margaret Atwood. SP-AtwM1

I look upon the map that hangs by me. Place on the Map, The. Thomas Hardy. CP-HardT

I look'd for my poet—he came not! George Meredith. CP-MerG2

I looked after the carving while it was executing at the prison. Hidden Monsters at the Mount Auburn Cemetery. A Found Poem. Denise Levertov. SP-LeveDL

I looked and I saw. Who but the Lord? Langston Hughes. CP-HughL; CP-HughL3

I looked and saw your eyes. Three Shadows. Dante Gabriel Rossetti. CW-RossD

I looked and saw your life. Spellbound. Marya Alexandrovna Zaturenska. SP-ZatuM

I looked and thought, "All is too gray and cold." Aberdeen. Thomas Hardy. CP-HardT

I looked around in the unknown year, aware that few are those who come from so far. Year, The. Czeslaw Milosz. CP-MiloC; CP-MiloCN, *tr. by* Richard Lourie

I looked at that face, dumbfounded. The lights of *métro* stations flew by. Esse. Czeslaw Milosz. CP-MiloC; CP-MiloCN, *tr. by* Robert Pinsky

I looked at their black faces. Negro Ghetto. Langston Hughes. CP-HughL; CP-HughL1

I Looked Back. Thomas Hardy. CP-HardT

I looked down 31st Street. Midnight Chippie's Lament. Langston Hughes. CP-HughL; CP-HughL2

I looked for that which is not, nor can be. Pause of Thought, A. Christina Georgina Rossetti. CP-RosC1 *Fr.* Three Stages.

I looked from the book of the story of men. George Meredith. CP-MerG2

I looked grotesque, covered with lice and strange purple roses. Waking. James Tate. SP-TateJ

I looked here; / I looked there. Stephen Crane. CP-CranS

I looked in my heart while the wild swans went over. Wild Swans. Edna St. Vincent Millay. CP-MillE

I looked into the eyes of Robert Frost. Worldly Failure. Richard Eberhart. CP-EberR

I looked into the room a moment ago. Loafing. Raymond Carver. CP-CarvR

I looked into your eyes. Madrigal: "I looked into your eyes." Federico García Lorca. CP-GarcF, *tr. by* Catherine Brown

I looked long and long at my mother's miniature. Roma II. Charles Wright. SP-WrigC

I looked out the window at dawn and saw a young apple tree translucent in brightness. Window. Czeslaw Milosz. CP-MiloC; CP-MiloCN, *tr. by* Lillian Vallee

I looked to find a man who walked with God. Enoch. Jones Very. CP-VeryJ

I looked to find Spring's early flowers. Lament of the Flowers, The. Jones Very. CP-VeryJ

I looked to the west. Blade, The. Charles Tomlinson. SP-TomlC

I looked up and saw. Charles Olson. SP-OlsoC *Fr.* Maximus Poems, The.

I Looked Up from My Writing. Thomas Hardy. CP-HardT

I, Lord, Thy foolish sinner low and small. Christina Georgina Rossetti. CP-

RosC2

I lose faith in my left hand. Heart's Graveyard Shift, The. Yusef Komunyakaa. CP-KomuY

I lost a few goddesses on my way from south to north. Speech at the Lost and Found, A. Wisława Szymborska. SP-SzymWM, tr. by Joanna Trzeciak

I lost a World—the other day! Emily Dickinson. CP-DickE

I Lost My Identity Card. Yehuda Amichai. SP-AmicY, tr. by Chana Bloch

I lost you to water, summer. Lorine Niedecker. CP-NiedL

I Love. Stevie Smith. CP-SmitS

I love a careless streamlet. Henry David Thoreau. CP-ThorH

I love a man who is not worth / my love. Did This Happen to Your Mother? Did Your Sister Throw Up a Lot? Alice Walker. CP-WalkA

I love a rock, for holding. Fast. Heather McHugh. SP-McHuH

I love, and he loves me again. Nymph's Passion, A. Ben Jonson. CP-JonsB

I love and love not: Lord, it breaks my heart. Dost Thou Not Care? Christina Georgina Rossetti. CP-RosC1

I love at quiet eventide. Evening Walk, An. Jones Very. CP-VeryJ

I love breasts, hard. Breasts. Charles Simic. SP-SimiC; SP-SimiCE

I love creeks and the music they make. Where Water Comes Together with Other Water. Raymond Carver. CP-CarvR

I love crystal fringe on a dance frock. Frock. James Schuyler. CP-SchuJ

I love him, I love him, ran the patter of her lips. Circle of Doors. Carl Sandburg. CP-SandC

I love him, she said. LOVE 4: What He Said, to His Daughter. A. K. Ramanujan. CP-RamaA

I love how it swells. Anodyne. Yusef Komunyakaa. CP-KomuY

'I love', I heard you say. Paris in Sixty-Nine. Charles Tomlinson. SP-TomlC

I love life, I love life so dearly, I could almost die. Life and the Human Consciousness. D. H. Lawrence. CP-LawrD

I love little Heber. Heber. Stevie Smith. CP-SmitS

I love, loved, and so doth she. Sir Thomas Wyatt. CP-WyatT

I love Meng-fu-tsu. To Meng Hao-Jan. Li Po. CP-WilW2

I love my beautiful hat more than anything. Hat, The. Stevie Smith. CP-SmitS

I Love My Jean. Robert Burns. See Of A' the Airts [the Wind Can Blaw]

I love my little son, and yet when he was ill. Two Parents, The. Hugh MacDiarmid. SP-MacDH

I Love My Love in Secret. Robert Burns. CP-BurnR

I love my neighbour. Love Thy Neighbour. D. H. Lawrence. CP-LawrD

I love my own Humans and their friends. Her Judgement. Denise Levertov. SP-LeveDL

I love my work and my children. God. Ovid in the Third Reich. Geoffrey Hill. CP-HillG

I love Nowhere where the factories die of malnutrition. Nebraska. Karl Shapiro. SP-ShapK

I love one, and he loveth me. Novice, The. Christina Georgina Rossetti. CP-RosC3

I love the beginning, always a promise. Years of Loss, The. David Ignatow. SP-IgnaD

I love the bird that appears. Omen, An. David Ignatow. SP-IgnaD

I love the church—its standards bearing cherubim. In Church. Constantine P. Cavafy. CP-CavaC, tr. by Theoharis Constantine Theoharis

I love the dear old ballads best. Songs. Paul Laurence Dunbar. CP-DunbP

I love the faces pallid. "Rubén Dario." CP-DariR, tr. by Alberto Acereda and Will Derusha

I love the jocund dance. Song: "I love the jocund dance." William Blake. CP-BlakW

I love the joys of the mountains. Han-shan. CP-ColdM, tr. by Red Pine

I love the light, when first its beams. Song: I Love the Light. Jones Very. CP-VeryJ

"I love the Lord," is still the strain. Love Increased by Suffering. Jeanne Marie Bouvier de la Motte- Guyon. CP-CowpW

I love the old melodious lays. Proem: "I love the old melodious lays." John Greenleaf Whittier. CP-WhitJ

I love the only day that I was born. Self-Centered. David Ignatow. SP-IgnaD

I love the poor, weak words. Homage to Rainer Maria Rilke. John Logan. CP-LogaJ

I love the sound of the bone against the plate. Osso Buco. Billy Collins. SP-CollB

I love the things I never had. Things. Gabriela Mistral. SP-MistG, tr. by Maria Giachetti [or Jacketti]

I love the thought of his anger. Artist, An. Seamus Heaney. SP-HeanSO Fr. Sweeney Redivivus.

I love the Turkana tribesman who gave me his cane. To Kenya Tribesmen, the Turkana. Richard Eberhart. CP-EberR

I Love the Way. James Laughlin. CP-LaugJ

I love the way Janie Crawford. Janie Crawford. Alice Walker. CP-WalkA

I love the way the evening sun goes down. Looking across Laguna Canyon at Dusk, West-by-Northwest. Charles Wright. SP-WrigCN

I love the way the heel of my hand feels. Untitled Poem: "I love the way the

heel of my hand feels." Alan Dugan. CP-DugaA

I love the way you dance, your nonchalance. Love of Artifice, The. Charles Baudelaire. CP-BaudC

I love thee, Baby! for thine own sweet sake. To Ianthe. Percy Bysshe Shelley. CP-ShelP

I love thee, love thee, Giulio. Parting Lovers. Elizabeth Barrett Browning. CP-BroEB

I love thee when thy swelling buds appear. Tree, The ("I love thee when thy swelling buds appear"). Jones Very. CP-VeryJ

I Love Therefore I Am I Suffer But I'm Alive. James Laughlin. CP-LaugJ

I love these people in their tall house. Yehuda Amichai. SP-AmicYL, tr. by Benjamin Harshav and Barbara Harshav

I love those former winters that still weren't meant for sports. Winter. Rainer Maria Rilke. CP-RilkFr, tr. by A. Poulin, Jr.

I love thy music, mellow bell. Ralph Waldo Emerson. CP-EmerR

I love to go out in late September. Blackberry Eating. Galway Kinnell. SP-KinnGN

I love to hear the cock crow in. Cock-a-Doo. Stevie Smith. CP-SmitS

I love to lie down weary. Sleep. Wendell Berry. CP-BerrW

I love to rise in a summer morn. School-Boy, The. William Blake. CP-BlakW Fr. Songs of Experience.

I love to see boards lying on the ground in early spring. Old Boards. Robert Bly. SP-BlyR

I love to see the big white moon. My Loves. Langston Hughes. CP-HughL; CP-HughL1

I love to see the man, a long-lived child. Manhood. Henry David Thoreau. CP-ThorH

I love to see the summer beaming forth. Sonnet: "I love to see the summer beaming forth." John Clare. SP-ClarJ

I Love to See You. James Laughlin. CP-LaugJ

I love to sit on the green hill's side. Nature ("I love to sit on the green hill's side"). Jones Very. CP-VeryJ

I love to stay in bed. Summer Morning. Charles Simic. SP-SimiC; SP-SimiCE

I love to toy with the Platonic notion. Boeotian. Robert Frost. CP-FrosR

I love to wake to the coo coo of the mourning dove. Meditation on Song and Structure. Charles Wright. SP-WrigCN

I love to walk. Discharged Soldier, The. William Wordsworth. MW-WorW

I love to watch the shadows undermine. Promise in a Pair of Eyes, The. Charles Baudelaire. CP-BaudC, tr. by Walter Martin

I love upon a stormy night. William Wordsworth. CP-WorW1

I love when you take over. Lumens. Olga Broumas. SP-BrouO

I Love You. Robert Creeley. SP-CreeR

I love you and it makes me rather dull. Villanelle: Late Summer. Marilyn Hacker. SP-HackM

I love you and you know it—this at least. Christina Georgina Rossetti. CP-RosC3

I love you as a sheriff searches for a walnut. To You. Kenneth Koch. SP-KochK

I love you first because your face is fair. V-Letter. Karl Shapiro. SP-ShapK

I love you / for your little,startled,thoughtless ways. E. E. Cummings. CP-CummE

I love you much(most beautiful darling). E. E. Cummings. CP-CummE

I love you, my plain pine box. First Coffin Poem. David Ignatow. SP-IgnaD

I love you, rotten. Medlars and Sorb-Apples. D. H. Lawrence. CP-LawrD

I love you so . . . .Gone? Who will swear you wouldn't. For Eugene McCarthy. Robert Lowell. SP-LoweR

I love you so much with this curiously alive and lonely body. Cry Going Out over Pastures, The. Robert Bly. SP-BlyR

I Love You Sweatheart. Thomas Lux. SP-LuxT

I love you, sweet: how can you ever learn. Youth's Antiphony. Dante Gabriel Rossetti. CW-RossD Fr. House of Life, The.

I love you. That is all I wanted to say. All I Wanted to Say. Robert Stock. SP-StocR

I love you . . . What if you are daughter to a humble fisherman. Beizades to His Beloved. Constantine P. Cavafy. CP-CavaC, tr. by Theoharis Constantine Theoharis

I love your faces I saw the many years. Red Son, The. Carl Sandburg. CP-SandC

I loved a shadow long ago. Familiar, The. Marya Alexandrovna Zaturenska. SP-ZatuM

I loved—alas! our life is love. see also Scene from "Tasso." Percy Bysshe Shelley. CP-ShelP

I loved bar room fights. My Friend. Charles Bukowski. SP-BukC3

I loved my friend. Poem: "I loved my friend." Langston Hughes. CP-HughL; CP-HughL1

I loved my love from green of Spring. Grown and Flown. Christina Georgina Rossetti. CP-RosC1

I loved thee ere I loved a woman, Love. To Art. Dante Gabriel Rossetti. CW-RossD

I loved Theotormon. Visions of the Daughters of Albion. William Blake. CP-

BlakW

I loved you, Leslie, long ago. Sappho. CP-RexrK, *tr.* by Kenneth Rexroth

I loved you, too. There was no use. I had no time. Randall Jarrell. CP-JarrR

I.M. to I.G. Emily Jane Brontë. CP-BronE

I made a fire; being tired. Burning the Letters. Sylvia Plath. CP-PlatS

I Made a Mistake. Charles Bukowski. SP-BukC1

I made a posy [*or* posie], while the day ran by. Life. George Herbert. CP-HerbG

I made an opening. Planting Crocuses. Wendell Berry. CP-BerrW

I made love to myself. Allen Ginsberg. CP-GinsA

I made Man with too many faults. Yet I love him. God Speaks. Stevie Smith. CP-SmitS

I made my eyes an entryway for poison. Michelangelo Buonarroti. CP-Miche, *tr.* by John Frederick Nims

I made my song a coat. Coat, A. William Butler Yeats. CP-YeatW

I made myself an expert in farewells. Tristia. Osip Emilevich Mandelstam. CP-KunSC, *tr.* by Stanley Kunitz

I made no sound, at all, like the wintering. Revelations. Norman Dubie. CP-DubiN

I made slow Riches but my Gain. Emily Dickinson. CP-DickE

I maister Andro Kennedy. Testament of [Mr.] Andro Kennedy, The. William Dunbar. CP-DunbW

I make a pact with you, Walt Whitman. Pact, A. Ezra Pound. SP-PounE

I make a simple assertion. Working with Tools. A. R. Ammons. CP-AmmoA

I make a trip to each clock in the apartment. Paris, 7 A.M. Elizabeth Bishop. CP-BishE

I make a Y. La Ultima Carta: A Young Wife Writes to Her Husband in the Mountains. Miller Williams. CP-WillM

I make His Crescent fill or lack. Emily Dickinson. CP-DickE

I make my children promises. Teacher. Audre Lorde. SP-LordA

I make my head, as I used to. Paper Bag, A. Margaret Atwood. SP-AtwM2

I make no haste to have my Numbers read. Glorie. Robert Herrick. CP-HerrR

I make the old sign. Ad Castitatem. Louise Bogan. CP-BogaL

I Make This in a Warring Absence. Dylan Thomas. CP-ThomD

I make ye an offer. Offer, The. Henry David Thoreau. CP-ThorH

I manage to forget, distracted purchases or friends. Out of Mind. Olga Broumas. SP-BrouO

I many times thought Peace had come. Emily Dickinson. CP-DickE

I marched [*or* march'd] three miles through scorching sand. Verses Spoken Extempore by Dean Swift on His Curate's Complaint of Hard Duty. Jonathan Swift. CP-SwifJ

I mark the months in liveries dank and dry. Sign-Seeker, A. Thomas Hardy. CP-HardT

I mark the summer's swift decline. Henry David Thoreau. CP-ThorH

I marked all kindred Powers the heart finds fair. Love Enthroned. Dante Gabriel Rossetti. CW-RossD *Fr.* House of Life, The.

I marked her ruined hues. Amabel. Thomas Hardy. CP-HardT

I marked when the weather changed. Night in November, A. Thomas Hardy. CP-HardT

I marked where lovely Venus and her court. Venus's Looking-Glass. Christina Georgina Rossetti. CP-RosC1

I married. Lorine Niedecker. CP-NiedL

I married in my youth a wife. James Vincent Cunningham. CP-CunnJ

I married the Earl of Egremont. Castle, The. Stevie Smith. CP-SmitS

I marvel at the incessant labor of pelicans. Pelicans. Czeslaw Milosz. CP-MiloCN, *tr.* by Robert Hass

I marvel how Nature could ever find space. Character, A. William Wordsworth. CP-WorW1; MW-WorW

I marvel not Bassanio was so bold. Portia. Oscar Wilde. CP-WildO

I maun hae a wife, whatsoe'er she be. Broom Besoms ["I maun hae a wife, whatsoe'er she be"]. Robert Burns. CP-BurnR

I may be oversusceptible to news. Roger Clay's Proposal. James Merrill. SP-MerrJ

I may be smelly and I may be old. River God, The. Stevie Smith. CP-SmitS

I may even be. Power and Light. James Dickey. CP-DickJ

I may have no more to say to my left arm. Mutterings. John Ciardi. CP-CiarJ

I May, I Might, I Must. Marianne Craig Moore. CP-MoorM

I may never see the Vatican or Troy. Fanny Howe. SP-HoweF *Fr.* Lines Out to Silence.

I may practice divination with the bones. Axolotl. Arthur Sze. SP-SzeA

I may sing; but minstrel's singing. Stanzas: "I may sing; but minstrel's singing." Elizabeth Barrett Browning. CP-BroEB

I Mean, No. Charles Olson. CP-OlsoC

I mean not to defend the scapes of any. Elegy 2.4: "I mean not to defend the scapes of any." Ovid. CP-MarlC *Fr.* Elegies.

I mean / the fiddleheads have forced their babies. May 10th. Maxine W. Kumin. SP-KumiM *Fr.* Joppa Diary.

I mean to build a hall anon. Spell of the Rose, The. Thomas Hardy. CP-HardT

I meant to find Her when I came. Emily Dickinson. CP-DickE

I meant to have but modest needs. Emily Dickinson. CP-DickE

I meant to see. Melancholy. William Corbett. SP-CorbW

I measure every Grief I meet. Emily Dickinson. CP-DickE

I measure years by days and days by hours. Subjectivity. Helen Pinkerton. CP-PinkH

I meditate upon a swallow's flight. Coole Park, 1929. William Butler Yeats. CP-YeatW

I meet her on the street. Talk of Fortune. W. S. Merwin. SP-MerwWF

I meet you in an evil time. Eclogue for Christmas, An. Louis MacNeice. CP-MacNL

I / (meet)t(touch). E. E. Cummings. CP-CummE

I, Mencius, Pupil of the Master. Charles Olson. CP-OlsoC

I mentioned my demon to a friend. Demon. Anne Sexton. CP-SextA

I met a brilliant scholar once. Han-shan. CP-ColdM, *tr.* by Red Pine

I met a fellow in whose hand. Tax-Free Encounter. John Updike. CP-UpdiJ

I met a girl from Derrygarve. New Song, A. Seamus Heaney. SP-HeanSO

I met a girl to the east. Han-shan. CP-ColdM, *tr.* by Red Pine

I met a guy I used to know, who said. Ozymandias II. Howard Nemerov. CP-NemeH

I met a King this afternoon! Emily Dickinson. CP-DickE

I met a lady from the South who said. New Hampshire. Robert Frost. CP-FrosR

I met a Lady Poet. Impeccable Conception. Maya Angelou. SP-AngeM

I Met a Man. Thomas Hardy. CP-HardT

I met a man the other day. Counselor, The. Dorothy Parker. CP-ParkD

I met a man under the moon. E. E. Cummings. CP-CummE

I met a master of demolition. Certain Paralipomena to an Unbegun Epic. Robert Stock. SP-StocR

I met a ragged man. Song, The: "I met a ragged man." Theodore Roethke. CP-RoetT

I met a seer. Stephen Crane. CP-CranS

I met a seer. Eidolons. Walt Whitman. CP-WhitW

I met a traveler [*or* traveller] from an antique land. Ozymandias. Percy Bysshe Shelley. CP-ShelP

I met a traveller from the holy desert. Prophet. Thomas Merton. CP-MertT

I met, among the amber tamarinds. To a Creole Lady. Charles Baudelaire. CP-BaudC, *tr.* by Walter Martin

I met ayont the cairney. Empty Vessel. Hugh MacDiarmid. SP-MacDH

I met Death—he was a sportsman—on Cole's. Cole's Island. Charles Olson. SP-OlsoC *Fr.* Maximus Poems, The.

I met Einstein in a dream. Xmas Gift. Allen Ginsberg. CP-GinsA; SP-GinsA

I met her as a blossom on a stem. Dream, The. Theodore Roethke. CP-RoetT

I met her, as we had privily planned. Her Father. Thomas Hardy. CP-HardT

I met her in the summertime. There were red flowers in the lanes. Not If He Has Any Sense, He Won't Be Back. Kenneth Patchen. CP-PatcK

I met him, as one meets a ghost or two. Old Trails. Edwin Arlington Robinson. CP-RobiE

I met him in the street. Man in the Street, The. D. H. Lawrence. CP-LawrD

I met him quite by accident. Love-Letters, The. Thomas Hardy. CP-HardT

I met, in a close City square. Linnet-Hawker, The. George Meredith. CP-MerG2

I met Ivan in a marvelous foxfur coat. Foxfur. Robert Lowell. SP-LoweR

I met Louisa in the shade. Louisa [After Accompanying Her on a Mountain Excursion]. William Wordsworth. CP-WorW1; MW-WorW

I met my Angel last night on Cinvat Bridge. Charles Olson. CP-OlsoC

I met my mates in the morning (and oh, but I am old!). Lukannon. Rudyard Kipling. CP-KiplR *Fr.* Jungle Book, The.

I met the Bishop on the road. Crazy Jane Talks with the Bishop. William Butler Yeats. CP-YeatW

I met you first—ah, when did I first meet you? Apostrophe to an Old Psalm Tune. Thomas Hardy. CP-HardT

I met You on Your way to death. Encounter. Langston Hughes. CP-HughL; CP-HughL3

I met you the first time ever in latitudes you'd call foreign. Vertumnus. Joseph Brodsky. CP-BrodJ

I met your husband in a bookshop. Madman of the South Side. Clarence Major. SP-MajoC

I might as well be another guest. Marriage of Strongbow and Aoife, The. Paul Muldoon. CP-MuldP

I might as well begin by saying how much I like the title. Workshop. Billy Collins. SP-CollB

I might by no means surmise. Sir Thomas Wyatt. CP-WyatT

I mind as 'ow the night afore that show. Chances, The. Wilfred Owen. CP-OwenW

I mind it weel in early date. Answer, The [To the Guidwife of Wauchope-House]. Robert Burns. CP-BurnR

I mind me how when first I looked at her. Medusa. Countee Cullen. CP-CullC

I mind me in the days departed. Deserted Garden, The. Elizabeth Barrett Browning. CP-BroEB

I mind when my first wife died. Hugh MacDiarmid. SP-MacDH *Fr.* Ode to All

Rebels.

I misremembered. He went down on all fours. Seamus Heaney. SP-HeanSO *Fr.* Squarings.

I miss my volley; walking back to serve. Northern Snows, The. Randall Jarrell. CP-JarrR

I miss that red clay, Lawd, I. Red Clay Blues. Langston Hughes. CP-HughL; CP-HughL1

I miss the long swing. Long Swing, The. Richard Eberhart. CP-EberR

I miss the polished brass, the powerful black horses. On the Road to Woodlawn. Theodore Roethke. CP-RoetT

I miss you in the dawn, of gradual flowering lights. Longing. E. E. Cummings. CP-CummE

I Missed His Book, but I Read His Name. John Updike. CP-UpdiJ

I missed one night, but the next I went. Second Night, The. Thomas Hardy. CP-HardT

I mist my end, and lost my way. Ode 1.24: "I mist my end, and lost my way." Horace. CP-JohnS *Fr.* Odes.

I mock thee not, though I by thee am mocked. To Flaxman. William Blake. CP-BlakW

I model myself after someone I made up at ten walking. Model Work. Andrei Codrescu. SP-CodrA

I mourn Adonis dead—loveliest Adonis. Fragment of the Elegy on the Death of Adonis. Bion. CP-ShelP *Fr.* Lament for Adonis.

I mourn for Adonis—the Loves are lamenting. Lament for Adonis. Bion. CP-BroEB, *tr. by* Elizabeth Barrett Browning

I mourn no more my vanished years. My Psalm. John Greenleaf Whittier. CP-WhitJ

I mourn upon this battle-field. In Memoriam. Ralph Waldo Emerson. CP-EmerR

I move my hand over. Poem of Night. Galway Kinnell. SP-KinnGN

I Move that We Adjourn the Meeting. Nicanor Parra. *See* Manifesto

I Move the Meeting Be Adjourned. Nicanor Parra. HoPM, *tr. by* Miller Williams *Fr.* Manifesto.

I moved like a double agent among the big concepts. England's Difficulty. Seamus Heaney. SP-HeanSO

I Muriel stood at the altar-table. Don Baty, the Draft Resister. Muriel Rukeyser. CP-RukeM

I murmur not though hard the lot. Jones Very. CP-VeryJ

I muse to-day, in a listless way. What the Wind Said. James Whitcomb Riley. CP-RileJ

I must believe some miracles still be. To Mrs Phillip Sidney. Ben Jonson. CP-JonsB; SP-JonsB

I must complain, yet doe enjoy my Love. Thomas Campion. CP-CampT

I must confess that I was somewhat warm. My Modest Apology for Knocking Out a News-Boy's Teeth, Who Told Him His Works Would Not Sell. Thomas Sheridan. CP-SherT

I must confess, when I did part from you. To My Lady E.C. at Her Going Out of England. Sir John Suckling. CP-SuckJ

I must direct these lines so full of sorrow. Petrarch. CP-Petra, *tr. by* J. G. Nichols

I must go on, till in my tearful line. Cross, The ("I must go on, till in my tearful line"). Jones Very. CP-VeryJ

I must go walk the woods so wild. Sir Thomas Wyatt. CP-WyatT

I must have been dozing in the tub. Soap-Pig, The. Paul Muldoon. CP-MuldP

I must have misunderstood something. Overpopulation. Lawrence Ferlinghetti. SP-FerlL

I must hunt down the prize. Gerard Manley Hopkins. CP-HopkG

I must love the questions. Reassurance. Alice Walker. CP-WalkA

I must not borrow light. Ralph Waldo Emerson. CP-EmerR

I must not die of pity; I must live. Edna St. Vincent Millay. CP-MillE

I must / Not trust. Anacreontike. Robert Herrick. CP-HerrR

I must say I never liked. Boy Wearing a Dead Man's Clothes. Yusef Komunyakaa. CP-KomuY

I must say / Yes, sir. Porter. Langston Hughes. CP-HughL; CP-HughL1

I must tell you. Young Sycamore. William Carlos Williams. CP-WilW1

I Must Tell You about My Novel. Ogden Nash. CP-NashO

I must think many stones till I have my true home. Yehuda Amichai. SP-AmicYL *Fr.* At Right Angles.

I must think suddenly of matters too difficult for a bear of little brain. Christoper Robin. Czeslaw Milosz. CP-MiloCN, *tr. by* Robert Hass

I must train myself to no longer exist. God's. David Ignatow. SP-IgnaD

I must, Varus, tell you. Carmen 22. Catullus. CP-ZukLS *Fr.* Carmina.

I myself saw furious with blood. Aeneas at Washington. Allen Tate. CP-TateA

I need a mouth as wide as the sky. Fragile Vial, The. Jelaluddin Rumi. SP-Rumi, *tr. by* Coleman Barks

I need everything else. If You're So Smart, Why Ain't You Rich? Philip Whalen. SP-WhalP

I Need, I Need. Theodore Roethke. CP-RoetT

I need no assurances, I am a man who is pre-occupied of his own soul. Assurances. Walt Whitman. CP-WhitW

I need not ask thee, for my sake. Lines on a Fly-Leaf. John Greenleaf Whittier.

CP-WhitJ

I Need Not Go. Thomas Hardy. CP-HardT

I need not say I love you yet. Epithalamium Argentum. G. K. Chesterton. CP-ChesG

I need to walk down a sidewalk. Truce. Charles Bukowski. SP-BukC3

I needle April into letting go. Fix. Heather McHugh. SP-McHuH

I never barked when out of season. On a Dog of Lord Eglinton's. Robert Burns. CP-BurnR

I never cared for Life: Life cared for me. Epitaph: "I never cared for Life: Life cared for me." Thomas Hardy. CP-HardT

I never dared be radical when young. Ten Mills. Robert Frost. CP-FrosR

I never did eat, yet I'm still at a feast. Enigma. *Unknown, sometimes at. to* Thomas Sheridan. CP-SherT

I never dreamt you would die. Keen. Eibhlín Ní Chonaill. CP-MuldP, *tr. by* Paul Muldoon

I Never Even Suggested It. Ogden Nash. CP-NashO

I never felt at Home—Below. Emily Dickinson. CP-DickE

I / never / guessed any / thing(even a). E. E. Cummings. CP-CummE

I Never Had Any Other Desire So Strong. Kenneth Patchen. CP-PatcK

I never had you, nor will I have you. Half an Hour. Constantine P. Cavafy. CP-CavaC, *tr. by* Theoharis Constantine Theoharis

I never happened to contrast. Two Leading Lights. Robert Frost. CP-FrosR

I never have been able to determine. Error, An. Ambrose Bierce. SP-BierA

I never hear that one is dead. Emily Dickinson. CP-DickE

I never hear the word "escape." Emily Dickinson. CP-DickE

I never kept sheep. Fernando Pessoa. SP-PessF, *tr. by* Susan M. Brown *and* Edwin Honig *Fr.* Keeper of Sheep, The.

I never knew a broken Heart. Emily Dickinson. SP-DickE

I never knew a soul who ever took a licking. Poem in a Straight Line. Fernando Pessoa. SP-PessF, *tr. by* Susan M. Brown *and* Edwin Honig

I never knew but one. Ralph Waldo Emerson. CP-EmerR

I never knew I could bear pain. PAIN: Trying to Find a Metaphor. A. K. Ramanujan. CP-RamaA

I never knew the road. Sirens, The. Richard Wilbur. CP-WilbR

I never knew there was so much blood. Experience of Blood. James Laughlin. CP-LaugJ

I never know what people mean when they complain of loneliness. Loneliness. D. H. Lawrence. CP-LawrD

I never learned the trick of snaps, got sick. Lyricist's Lament, The. Heather McHugh. SP-McHuH

I never learned to swim. In shallow waters. Sport. Dan Pagis. SP-PagiD, *tr. by* Stephen Mitchell

I never learnt to attract, you see. Sad Heart, The. Stevie Smith. CP-SmitS

I never lost as much but twice. Emily Dickinson. CP-DickE

I never may turn the loop of a road. Temps Perdu. Dorothy Parker. CP-ParkD

I never met a single. Prestige. D. H. Lawrence. CP-LawrD

I never pass that inn "The Ring of Bells." Whaler's Wife, The. Thomas Hardy. CP-HardT

I never played for you. You'd have thrown. For the Death of Vince Lombardi. James Dickey. CP-DickJ

I never remember holding a full drink. Party Politics. Philip Larkin. CP-LarkP

I never said I loved you, John. No, Thank You, John. Christina Georgina Rossetti. CP-RosC1

I never saw a Moor. Emily Dickinson. CP-DickE

I never saw a wild thing. Self-Pity. D. H. Lawrence. CP-LawrD

I never saw my father old. Celebration for George Sarton, A. May Sarton. SP-SartM

I never saw the man whom you describe. Foster-Mother's Tale, The. Samuel Taylor Coleridge. CP-ColeS

I never see red very well. Visit to Bill Merwin at His Hawaiian Home, A. John Logan. CP-LogaJ

I never see that prettiest thing. Cherry White. Dorothy Parker. CP-ParkD

I never shall furgit that night when father hitched up Dobbin. Spellin'-Bee, The. Paul Laurence Dunbar. CP-DunbP

I never slept late in the morning. Bach Concerto, A. Jaroslav Seifert. SP-SeifJ, *tr. by* Ewald Osers

I never stooped so low, as they. Negative Love. John Donne. CP-DonnJ; MW-DonnJ

I never then noticed the rather sausage-like trotters. Old Flame. Robert Penn Warren. CP-WarrR

I never thought that heav'n would lose its blue. Absence. Dorothy Parker. CP-ParkD

I never thought we'd end up. Rural Delivery. Charles Simic. SP-SimiC; SP-SimiCE

I never told the buried gold. Emily Dickinson. CP-DickE

I never understood hop scotch. all the. Hop Scotch. Andrei Codrescu. SP-CodrA

I never used to think that my heart. Guido Cavalcanti. CP-CavaG, *tr. by* Marc Cirigliano

I never warmed to them. Scribes, The. Seamus Heaney. SP-HeanSO *Fr.* Sweeney

Redivivus.

"I never was in Hadera" is like. Hadera. Yehuda Amichai. SP-AmicYL, *tr. by* Benjamin Harshav *and* Barbara Harshav

I never wear dark shades. Dark Shades. Charles Bukowski. SP-BukC1

I never went out of my country. Hafiz. CP-EmerR, *tr. by* Ralph Waldo Emerson *Fr.* Odes.

I—"Next Poet?" No, my hearties. At the "Mermaid." Robert Browning. CP-BroR2

I no longer want to feel with you. David Ignatow. SP-IgnaD

I nodded at the sun. Friendly in a Friendly Way. Langston Hughes. CP-HughL

I nodded. The books agree. Drowsing over *The Arabian Nights*. Thomas Kinsella. CP-KinsT

I note the moods and feelings men betray. Sancti Dominici Pallium. Samuel Taylor Coleridge. CP-ColeS

I notice where Death has been introduced. Emily Dickinson. SP-DickE

I noticed People disappeared. Emily Dickinson. CP-DickE

I now think[e], Love is rather deaf[e], than blind. My Picture Left in Scotland. Ben Jonson. CP-JonsB; SP-JonsB

I nurs'd love where he lay. I Lay Love on My Knee. Allen Ginsberg. CP-GinsA

I nursed it in my bosom while it lived. Memory. Christina Georgina Rossetti. CP-RosC1

I objurgate the centipede. Centipede, The. Ogden Nash. CP-NashO

I observe, as I hold my lonely course. Very Unclubbable Man, The. Ogden Nash. CP-NashO

I observe: "Our sentimental friend the moon!" Conversation Galante. T. S. Eliot. CP-ElioT; SP-ElioT

I offer to this ground. Libation. Lucille Clifton. SP-ClifL

I often believe that nothing can be lost. Fanny Howe. SP-HoweF *Fr.* O'Clock.

I often find that I forget. This One Rhymes. James Laughlin. CP-LaugJ

I often live in the Institute of the Impossible. Institute of the Impossible. Robert Penn Warren. CP-WarrR

I often passed the village. Emily Dickinson. CP-DickE

I often see flowers from a passing car. Passing Glimpse, A. Robert Frost. CP-FrosR

I often tried in vain to find. New Simile for the Ladies, A. Thomas Sheridan. CP-SherT

I often wish I was a grass. Emily Dickinson. SP-DickE

I often wished that I had clear. Horace, Lib. 2, Sat. 6. Jonathan Swift. CP-SwifJ

I often wonder how. Emily Dickinson. SP-DickE

I often wonder why on earth. To My Dog. Dorothy Parker. CP-ParkD

I, on your wedding days, funerals, holidays. Artist, The. Aleksandr Aleksandrovich Blok. SP-BlokA, *tr. by* Peter France *and* Jon Stallworthy

I once bought a toy rabbit. Look, The. Charles Bukowski. SP-BukC2

I once dreamt that Cézanne lectured on the circumnavigation of a pear. Clouds of Magellan (Aphorisms of Mr. Canon Aspirin), The. Norman Dubie. CP-DubiN

I once fled, I don't recall from what God, for what wish. Yehuda Amichai. SP-AmicYL *Fr.* At Right Angles.

I once gave my daughters, separately, two conch shells. Derek Walcott. CP-WalcD *Fr.* Midsummer.

I once had a cow that jumped over the moon. Lines Written in Dejection on the Eve of Great Success. Robert Frost. CP-FrosR

I once knew a foolish man. Han-shan. CP-ColdM, *tr. by* Red Pine

I once looked on a young green tree. Shadow Wood. Tennessee Williams. SP-WillT

I once thought it could be resolved like this. Hour of Grace, An. Yehuda Amichai. SP-AmicYL, *tr. by* Benjamin Harshav *and* Barbara Harshav

I once wrote a letter as follows. Invoice, The. Robert Creeley. CP-CreeR

I, one day abashed. Transfiguration: Natura Naturans. Robert Stock. SP-StocR

I, one thing, as relation to one thing. Canto 111, Notes for: "I, one thing, as relation to one thing." Ezra Pound. CP-PoCan *Fr.* Cantos.

I Only Am Escaped Alone to Tell Thee. Howard Nemerov. CP-NemeH

I only ask the gods to grant me. Fernando Pessoa. SP-PessF, *tr. by* Susan M. Brown *and* Edwin Honig

I only have two hands. Jungle, The. Raymond Carver. CP-CarvR

I only knew one poet in my life. How It Strikes a Contemporary. Robert Browning. CP-BroR1; SP-BroR

I only looked for pain and grief. William Wordsworth. MW-WorW

I only regret the days wasted in no pain. Penance. C. K. Williams. CP-WillC

I only write about the dead. Line Four. Adam Zagajewski. SP-ZagaA, *tr. by* Clare Cavanagh

I open a tree. Splitting Wood at Six Above. Maxine W. Kumin. SP-KumiM

I open my journal, write a few. Words Rising. Robert Bly. SP-BlyR

I open the door, return to the familiar mercy. Widower's Monologue. Alí Chumacero. CP-WilW2

I opened my shutter at sunrise. Death of Regret, The. Thomas Hardy. CP-HardT

I opened the door so my last look. One More Brevity. Robert Frost. CP-FrosR

I opened the old spiral notebook to see what I'd been. Egress. Raymond Carver. CP-CarvR

I order you to operate. I was not made to suffer. So Going Around Cities. Ted Berrigan. SP-BerrT

I ordered this, this clean wood box. Arrival of the Bee Box, The. Sylvia Plath. CP-PlatS

I, Ovid, poet of my wantonness. Elegy 2.1: "I, Ovid, poet of my wantonness." Ovid. CP-MarlC, *tr. by* Christopher Marlowe *Fr.* Elegies.

I owe a lot / to those I do not love. Thank-You Note, A. Wisława Szymborska. SP-SzymWM, *tr. by* Joanna Trzeciak

I owe so much. Thank-You Note. Wisława Szymborska. SP-SzymW, *tr. by* Stanislaw Barańczak *and* Clare Cavanagh

I owe you an explanation. Amenities, The. Heather McHugh. SP-McHuH

I own I am shock'd at the purchase of slaves. Pity for Poor Africans. William Cowper. CP-CowpW

I own the ticks on a horse. Seahorse. Charles Bukowski. SP-BukC2

I own 'tis not my bread and butter. Mad Mullinix and Timothy. Jonathan Swift. CP-SwifJ

I owned a slope full of stones. Stones, The. Wendell Berry. CP-BerrW

I pace along, the rain-shafts riddling me. Wet Night, A. Thomas Hardy. CP-HardT

I paid the woman what she asked and followed her down to the water-side. Come Little Birds. Robinson Jeffers. CP-JefR3

I paid this one's fare all the way from Houston. Waving and Waving Goodbye. Charles Bukowski. SP-BukC1

I paint my nails gold. Goldrush, The. Andrei Codrescu. SP-CodrA

I Paint so ill, my peece had need to bee. With a Picture Sent to a Friend. Richard Crashaw. CP-CrasR

I painted on the roof of a skyscraper. People Who Must. Carl Sandburg. CP-SandC

I pant for the music which is divine. Music. Percy Bysshe Shelley. CP-ShelP

I park my old maroon Ford in the field outside El Reno. Antihero, The. Ai. SP-Ai

I park the car half in the ditch and switch off and sit. Stealing Trout on a May Morning. Ted Hughes. SP-HughTN

I part the out thrusting branches. Woods. Wendell Berry. CP-BerrW

I pass enough savages on the street. Daemons. John Ciardi. CP-CiarJ

I pass your home in a slow vermilion dawn. Confusion. Kenneth Rexroth. CP-RexrK

I passed along the water's edge below the humid trees. Indian upon God, The [*or* An]. William Butler Yeats. CP-YeatW

I passed between the bell and the glass. 49th and 5th, December 13. Josephine Jacobsen. CP-JacoJ

I passed by an imposing house with a sign saying. Language School. Yehuda Amichai. SP-AmicYL, *tr. by* Benjamin Harshav *and* Barbara Harshav

I passed the lodge and avenue. Widow Betrothed, The. Thomas Hardy. CP-HardT

I passed you many times as I went down the cliff walk. Mediterranean. Thomas McGrath. SP-McGrT

I paused on the threshold, I turned to the sky. Emily Jane Brontë. CP-BronE

I paused to read a letter of hers. Read by Moonlight. Thomas Hardy. CP-HardT

I pay—in Satin Cash. Emily Dickinson. CP-DickE

I peeled bits o strews and I got switches too. John Clare. *See* I peeled bits of straw and I got switches too

I peeled bits of straw and I got switches too. Song: "I peeled bits of straw and I got switches too." John Clare. SP-ClarJ

I peered within, and saw a world of sin. Escape to the Mountain. Christina Georgina Rossetti. CP-RosC2

I peopled the dark park with gowns. Naked Eye of the Aunt, The. Wallace Stevens. CP-StevWP

I pick up a loaded pen and twiddle it. Pastime. James Schuyler. CP-SchuJ

I pick up my life. One-Way Ticket. Langston Hughes. CP-HughL; CP-HughL2

I picked myself up from the dust again. Spring Song. A. R. Ammons. CP-AmmoA

I picked up a leaf. Les Étiquettes Jaunes. Frank O'Hara. SP-OharF

I pitched in the Tower, not yet struck. Part of a Tarot Fortune. Robert Stock. SP-StocR

I pitched my day's leazings in Crimmercrock Lane. Dark-Eyed Gentleman, The. Thomas Hardy. CP-HardT

I pitied you. To ———. "Shu Ting." CP-KizeC, *tr. by* Carolyn Kizer *and* Y. H. Zhao

I place an off'ring at thy shrine. Perfect Sacrifice, The. Jeanne Marie Bouvier de la Motte Guyon. CP-CowpW, *tr. by* William Cowper

I place my hand before my beard with awe. Waking in New York. Allen Ginsberg. CP-GinsA

I place thee as a watchman on a tower. Watchman, The. Jones Very. CP-VeryJ

I placed a jar in Tennessee. Anecdote of the Jar. Wallace Stevens. CP-StevW; CP-StevWP

I plaid with Love, as with the fire. Upon Love. Robert Herrick. CP-HerrR

I plainly see, good Mr. Dean. Quilca House to the Dean. Henry Brooke. CP-SherT

I plant a tree whose leaf. Romaunt of Margret, The. Elizabeth Barrett Browning. CP-BroEB

I planted a hand / And there came up a palm. Christina Georgina Rossetti. CP-RosC2

I planted a young tree when I was young. Dumb Friend, A. Christina Georgina Rossetti. CP-RosC3

I planted lupine and nasturtiums. Lupine. Arthur Sze. SP-SzeA

I play at Riches—to appease. Emily Dickinson. CP-DickE

I play it cool / And dig all jive. Motto. Langston Hughes. CP-HughL; CP-HughL3

I play my old sweet airs. Lost Love. Thomas Hardy. CP-HardT

I play your furies back to me at night. High Fidelity. Thom Gunn. CP-GunnT

I playact the three monkeys. Touch-up Man. Yusef Komunyakaa. CP-KomuY

I pledge allegiance to the old. Double Agent. Heather McHugh. SP-McHuH

I plod and peer amid mean sounds and shapes. Triumph of Man, The ("I plod and peer amid mean sounds and shapes"). G. K. Chesterton. CP-ChesG

I plodded to Fairmile Hill-top, where. Dear, The. Thomas Hardy. CP-HardT

I plucked a honeysuckle where. Honeysuckle, The. Dante Gabriel Rossetti. CW-RossD

I plucked pink blossoms from mine apple tree. Apple Gathering, An. Christina Georgina Rossetti. CP-RosC1

I plunged into my. Chaparral. Federico García Lorca. CP-GarcF, *tr. by* Jerome Rothenbury *Fr.* In the Forest of Clocks.

I pour a coating of salt on the table. Design. Billy Collins. SP-CollB

I praise those ancient Chinamen. Hymnus Ad Patrem Sinensis. Philip Whalen. SP-WhalP

I praised the myrtle and the rose. Charity. Christina Georgina Rossetti. CP-RosC3

I pray! My little body and whole span. Supplication of the Black Aberdeen. Rudyard Kipling. CP-KiplR

I pray that the great world's flowering stay as it is. Gardener to His God, The. Mona Van Duyn. SP-VanDM

I pray thee, Dante, shouldst thou meet with Love. Sonnet: He mistrusts the Love of Lapo Gianni. Guido Cavalcanti. CW-RossD, *tr. by* Dante Gabriel Rossetti

I pray there where is the old-time wig. Ballade of the Pink Parasol. Wallace Stevens. CP-StevWP

I pray to the Divine Mother of God. Poet Prays to the Virgin for Help, The. Federico García Lorca. CP-GarcF, *tr. by* Greg Simon *and* Steven F. White

I pray you, do not use this thing. What Redress. James Whitcomb Riley. CP-RileJ

I pray you if you love me, bear my joy. Edna St. Vincent Millay. CP-MillE

I pray you not, Leuconoë, to pore. Horace to Leuconoë. Edwin Arlington Robinson. CP-RobiE

I pray you who speak of suffering. Guido Cavalcanti. CP-CavaG, *tr. by* Marc Cirigliano

I prayed, at first, a little Girl. Emily Dickinson. CP-DickE

I Prayed, Thy Kingdom Come. Jones Very. CP-VeryJ

I prayed, Thy kingdom come! For Winter long. I Prayed, Thy Kingdom Come. Jones Very. CP-VeryJ

I press[e] not to the choir [*or* quire], nor dare I greet. To My Worthy Friend Master George Sands [*or* Sandys], on His Translation of the Psalms. Thomas Carew. CP-CareT

I prest my Julia's lips, and in the kisse. Love Palpable. Robert Herrick. CP-HerrR

I prithee send me back my heart. Song: "I prithee send me back my heart." Sir John Suckling. CP-SuckJ

I prithee spare me, gentle boy. Song: "I prithee spare me, gentle boy." Sir John Suckling. CP-SuckJ

I, proclaiming that there is. Dancer at Cruachan and Cro-Patrick, The. William Butler Yeats. CP-YeatW

I promise nothing: friends will part. A. E. Housman. CP-HousA

I promise you these days and an understanding. Tourist Death. Archibald MacLeish. CP-MacLA

I promised once if I got hold of. Written in a Copy of Swift's Poems, for Wayne Burns. James Wright. CP-WrigJ

I prop up my face and go out, avoiding the sunlight. Aging Female Poet on Laundry Day. Margaret Atwood. SP-AtwM2

I propose to you. Statue, The. Robert Creeley. CP-CreeR

I protest against the manner of these ruins. O Howling Cells. Kenneth Patchen. CP-PatcK

I prove a theorem and the house expands. Geometry. Rita Dove. SP-DoveR

I pull a knife but it is to protest. Murderer, The. David Ignatow. SP-IgnaD

I pull it down while glancing through. Venetian Blind. Thom Gunn. CP-GunnT

I pulled him back. Another Day. Paul in the Mountains of Fantasy. Paul Tells His Adventure. Muriel Rukeyser. CP-RukeM

I pulled the street up as you suggested. Something for Easter. Robert Creeley. CP-CreeR

I pursue a form that my style does not find. "Rubén Dario." SP-DariR, *tr. by* Alberto Acereda *and* Will Derusha

I put by the half-written poem. Lost Kiss, The. James Whitcomb Riley. CP-RileJ

I put my book face down. August 14, 1961. Hayden Carruth. CP-CarHS

I put my hat upon my head. Second Stanza, A. Donald Hall. CP-HallD

I put my hat upon my head. Ballad: "I put my hat upon my head." Samuel Johnson. CP-JohnS

I Put My Mouth. Philip Larkin. CP-LarkP

I put my nickel. Midnight Raffle. Langston Hughes. CP-HughL; CP-HughL2

I put on my travelling clothes. Travelling to the Capital. Gary Snyder. CP-SnydG

I put those things there.—See them burn. Song of the Demented Priest, The. John Berryman. CP-BerrJ

I quarrel not with Destiny. Best Is Good Enough, The. James Whitcomb Riley. CP-RileJ

I quartered the troops for the night in a fortress. Shmuel HaNagid. SP-HaNaS, *tr. by* Peter Cole

I raise only robins on my farm. Emily Dickinson. SP-DickE

I raised my gun. Es War Einmal. Stevie Smith. CP-SmitS

I raised myself in thought to where I found. Petrarch. CP-Petra, *tr. by* J. G. Nichols

I rake no coffined clay, nor publish wide. Ralph Waldo Emerson. CP-EmerR

I ran beneath the shade of shining leaves. Petrarch. CP-Petra, *tr. by* J. G. Nichols

I ran into Foley six months ago in a dubbing suite in Los Angeles. Key, The. Paul Muldoon. CP-MuldP

I ran through the snow like a young Czarevitch! Poem: "I ran through the snow like a young Czarevitch!" Frank O'Hara. SP-OharF

I ransack'd, for a theme of song. Annus Memorabilis, 1789. William Cowper. CP-CowpW

I ranted to the knave and fool. Remorse for Intemperate Speech. William Butler Yeats. CP-YeatW

I reach beyond the laboratory brain. The brass. American Scene, An. Norman Dubie. CP-DubiN

I reach for a piece of wood. It turns into a lute. Jelaluddin Rumi. SP-Rumi, *tr. by* Coleman Barks

I reach for the awkward shotgun not to disarm. Dreams of Suicide. William Meredith. SP-MereW

I reach the marble-streeted town. Marble-Streeted Town, The. Thomas Hardy. CP-HardT

I reached Cold Mountain and all cares stopped. Han-shan. CP-ColdM, *tr. by* Red Pine

I reached the Alps; the soul within me burned. Sonnet on Approaching Italy. Oscar Wilde. CP-WildO

I reached up into the top of the closet. I Made a Mistake. Charles Bukowski. SP-BukC1

I read a Chinese poem. Chinese Poem. Adam Zagajewski. SP-ZagaA, *tr. by* Clare Cavanagh

I read a novel by a friend of mine. I Am in a Novel. D. H. Lawrence. CP-LawrD

I read almost with envy my contemporaries' verse. Separation. Adam Zagajewski. SP-ZagaA, *tr. by* Clare Cavanagh

I read, before my eyelids dropt their shade. Dream of Fair Women, A. Alfred Tennyson. CP-TennA

I read how Quixote in his random ride. Parable. Richard Wilbur. CP-WilbR

I read in a tattered book about Sheik Bedreddin. Thought about Sheik Bedreddin, A. John Ciardi. CP-CiarJ

I read in the papers about the / Freedom Train. Freedom Train. Langston Hughes. CP-HughL; CP-HughL3

I read it quickly: all the old clichés. Time and the Thing-in-Itself in a Textbook. Randall Jarrell. CP-JarrR

I read last Saturday in the. My Groupie. Charles Bukowski. SP-BukC1

I read my sentence—steadily. Emily Dickinson. CP-DickE

I read of battles, and my faith grows weak. Faith in Time of War. Jones Very. CP-VeryJ

I read on the porch of a palace bold. Ibn-i-Yamin. CP-EmerR

I read poems on Poland written. Poems on Poland. Adam Zagajewski. SP-ZagaA, *tr. by* Renata Gorczynski

I Read the "Christabel." Lord Byron. CP-Byron

I read your name when you were strange to me. To an Actress. Thomas Hardy. CP-HardT

I realize as I. Survival of the Fittest. Kenneth Rexroth. CP-RexrK

I really believe He's here all over this room. Facts & Issues, The. John Berryman. CP-BerrJ

I really believed, that first great day when, awed. Michelangelo Buonarroti. CP-Miche, *tr. by* John Frederick Nims

I really did believe I would go on. Petrarch. CP-Petra, *tr. by* J. G. Nichols

I reason, Earth is short. Emily Dickinson. CP-DickE

I recall the days of my youth. Han-shan. CP-ColdM, *tr. by* Red Pine

I recall the gestures. Refreshment. Gabriela Mistral. SP-MistG, *tr. by* Maria Giachetti [*or* Jacketti]

I recall the places I've been. Han-shan. CP-ColdM, *tr. by* Red Pine

I recall twenty years ago. Han-shan. CP-ColdM, *tr. by* Red Pine

I received in mail offer beautiful certificate National Conference Synagogue Youth. Junk Mail. Allen Ginsberg. CP-GinsA

I recently hiked to a temple in the clouds. Han-shan. CP-ColdM, *tr. by* Red Pine

I reckon they must have. Southern Negro Speaks. Langston Hughes. CP-HughL; CP-HughL2

I reckon—when I count at all. Emily Dickinson. CP-DickE

I recognize it, but where from, this park: sugar and ice. Central Park, Twilight. Dan Pagis. SP-PagiD, *tr. by* Stephen Mitchell

I recognize the quiet and the charm. Dutch Interior. May Sarton. SP-SartM

I reenter a day in a late summer. Philip Levine. SP-LeviP *Fr.* Poem with No Ending, A.

I reflect on my son's crying. Waiting in the Children's Hospital. Clarence Major. SP-MajoC

I refuse to name the gods, because they have no name. Name the Gods! D. H. Lawrence. CP-LawrD

I regret that before people can be reformed they have to be sinners. Piano Tuner, Untune Me That Tune. Ogden Nash. CP-NashO

I remark that this beach has been used too. much Too. originally. E. E. Cummings. CP-CummE

I Remember. Laura Riding Jackson. CP-RidiL

I Remember. Anne Sexton. CP-SextA; SP-SextA

I Remember. Stevie Smith. CP-SmitS

I remember a fight / In a snow fall. Larry. James Wright. CP-WrigJ

I remember a house where all were good. In the Valley of the Elwy. Gerard Manley Hopkins. CP-HopkG

I remember a square of New York's Hudson River glinting. Time of the Missile. George Oppen. CP-OppGN

I remember black winter waters. New Hampshire Again. Carl Sandburg. CP-SandC

I remember going out there. Black Coat. Ted Hughes. SP-HughTN

I remember here by the fire. Fire Dreams. Carl Sandburg. CP-SandC

I remember him falling beside me. Litany, A: "I remember him falling beside me." Gregory Orr. SP-OrrG

I remember how I would say, "I will gather." October. W. S. Merwin. SP-MerwW

I remember how, long ago, I found. Crystals like Blood. Hugh MacDiarmid. SP-MacDH

I Remember, I Remember. Philip Larkin. CP-LarkP

I remember, I remember. Race-Memory. G. K. Chesterton. CP-ChesG

I remember, long ago. Fair Bedfellow, The. George Meredith. CP-MerG2

I remember Miss Olivia Branton, which. Miss Olivia Branton. John Ciardi. CP-CiarJ

I remember my littlest one in a field. One Morning. John Ciardi. CP-CiarJ

I remember once I ran after you and tagged the fluttering shirt of you in. Shirt. Carl Sandburg. CP-SandC

I remember one death in my boyhood. Of John Davidson. Hugh MacDiarmid. SP-MacDH

I Remember Sir Alfred. Paul Muldoon. CP-MuldP

I remember summers. Jimmy Hoffa's Odyssey. Ai. SP-Ai

I remember the Chillicothe ball players grappling the Rock. Hits and Runs. Carl Sandburg. CP-SandC

I remember the cloud on its blue bicycle. Daffodil Poem. Gregory Orr. SP-OrrG

I remember the crossing tender's geranium border. Reminder, The. Theodore Roethke. CP-RoetT

I remember the evening. Swarming Bees, The. James Laughlin. CP-LaugJ

I remember the forehead born. Uncle. Philip Levine. SP-LeviP

I Remember the House That Was. John Ciardi. CP-CiarJ

I remember the leaves were falling. Emily Dickinson. SP-DickE

I remember the moth that flew in. Old Lines. Eugenio Montale. CP-MontE, *tr. by* Jonathan Galassi

I remember the neckcurls, limp and damp as tendrils. Elegy for Jane. Theodore Roethke. CP-RoetT

I remember the new-dropped colts in the time when I was a boy. Used Up. Thomas McGrath. SP-McGrT

I remember the puddles and tensions, I see. Tragedy's Greatest Hits. James Tate. SP-TateJ

I remember the quick, nervous bird of your love. Paradelle for Susan. Billy Collins. SP-CollB

I remember the rain. How Much Time. Yehuda Amichai. SP-AmicYL, *tr. by* Benjamin Harshav *and* Barbara Harshav

I remember the Roman Emperor, one of the cruellest of them. Exeat. Stevie Smith. CP-SmitS

I remember the scarlet setts. In Chopin's Garden. Donald Davie. CP-DaviDC

I remember the synagogue at Amsterdam. Sometimes. James Schuyler. CP-SchuJ

I remember the terraces down from Portland Road. I Remember the House That Was. John Ciardi. CP-CiarJ

I remember the United States of America. Box Comes Home, A. John Ciardi. CP-CiarJ

I remember this woman who sat for years. Field of Vision. Seamus Heaney. SP-HeanSO

I remember watching / from the porch of a cottage. Sea, The. Donald Hall. CP-HallD

I remember we used to meet. Roses and Rue. Oscar Wilde. CP-WildO

I remember when I learned he was dead. Remembering Walter. Miller Williams. CP-WillM

I remember when I wrote The Circus. Circus, The. Kenneth Koch. SP-KochK

I remember your coming as serious sweetness. Emily Dickinson. SP-DickE

I Remember Yule. Ogden Nash. CP-NashO

I remind myself at that time of Plato's uterus. Two Organs. John Berryman. CP-BerrJ

I renounce the blindness of the magazines. Prayer to Escape from the Market Place, A. James Wright. CP-WrigJ

I represent *The Morning Shout*. We hear you are dying. Interview 2, The. David Ignatow. SP-IgnaD

I resemble everyone. Self-Portrait. A. K. Ramanujan. CP-RamaA

I reserve the triangle. Drawing the Triangle. Charles Simic. SP-SimiC; SP-SimiCE

I resign. Poems of Resigning. Yehuda Amichai. SP-AmicYL, *tr. by* Benjamin Harshav *and* Barbara Harshav

I resolved it, I. Some Place. Robert Creeley. CP-CreeR

I retired to the edge of a forest. Han-shan. CP-ColdM, *tr. by* Red Pine

I return from the wide open spaces. Smalltown, South India. A. K. Ramanujan. CP-RamaA

I return late / on a wintry road: the beam. . . . Or Traveller's Joy. Charles Tomlinson. CP-TomlC

I return to my limbs with the first. Paw, The. W. S. Merwin. SP-MerwW

I returned to a long strand. North. Seamus Heaney. SP-HeanSO

I rickollect the little tad, back, years and years ago. Preacher's Boy, The. James Whitcomb Riley. CP-RileJ

I ride a great horse climbing. One Night. W. S. Merwin. SP-MerwWF

I ride through Queens. Invitation to Madison County, An. Jay Wright. SP-WrigJ

I rise, gentlemen, it is the pleasant hour. Meaning of Death, The. Allen Tate. CP-TateA

I rise in the dawn, and I kneel and blow. Song of the Old Mother, The. William Butler Yeats. CP-YeatW

I rise out of my depths with my language. Jabberers. Carl Sandburg. CP-SandC

I Ritu a Verse o Na Molli o Mi Ne. Thomas Sheridan. CP-SherT

I Rob My Breast. Hart Crane. CP-CranH

I robbed the Woods. Emily Dickinson. CP-DickE

I rock high in the oak—secure, big branches. Little Rooms. William Stafford. SP-StafWW

I rode one evening with Count Maddalo. Percy Bysshe Shelley. CP-ShelP *Fr.* Julian and Maddalo; A Conversation.

I rode the tail of a comet into the world. Hoover Trismegistus. Ai. SP-Ai

I Rode With My Darling. Stevie Smith. CP-SmitS

I Rose and Went to Rou'tor Town. Thomas Hardy. CP-HardT

I rose at night, and visited. Unborn, The. Thomas Hardy. CP-HardT

I rose at the dead of night. Chilly Night, A. Christina Georgina Rossetti. CP-RosC3

I rose—because He sank. Emily Dickinson. CP-DickE

I rose from marsh mud. Lorine Niedecker. CP-NiedL

I rose from stiffening. Lazarus. Lucille Clifton. SP-ClifL

I Rose Up as My Custom Is. Thomas Hardy. CP-HardT

I rose up at the dawn of day. William Blake. CP-BlakW

I rose up in the world, Ooray! Rise in the World, A. D. H. Lawrence. CP-LawrD

I rose while yet the cattle, heat-opprest [*or* oppressed]. Journey Renewed. William Wordsworth. CP-WorW2 *Fr.* River Duddon [A Series of Sonnets], The.

I rose with my own human might. Mortesto. George Meredith. CP-MerG2

I rowed: the dimpled tide was at the turn. Singing Lovers. Thomas Hardy. CP-HardT

I rub my head and find a turtle shell. Neo-Classical Urn, The. Robert Lowell. SP-LoweR

I Rubens am a Statesman & a Saint. William Blake. CP-BlakW

I run along the road, I run. Orphan, The. Rainer Maria Rilke. CP-RilkFr, *tr. by* A. Poulin, Jr.

I run, cried the fox, in circles. Cried the Fox. Tennessee Williams. CP-WillT

I run my fingers over a photo. Le Xuan, Beautiful Spring. Yusef Komunyakaa. CP-KomuY

I run you through the projector. When I'm Missing You. James Laughlin. CP-LaugJ

I rushed to my brother who was. On the Death of Isaac, His Brother. Shmuel HaNagid. SP-HaNaS

I sacrifice to God the Beefe, which you adore. Sir Walter Ralegh. CP-RaleW

I Said. "H. D." CP-DoolH

I said: "Afternoon." Crazy Boy, The. Federico García Lorca. CP-GarcF, *tr. by* Alan S. Trueblood *Fr.* Back of the World.

I said: "Afternoon." Little Mad Boy, The. Federico García Lorca. SP-GarcF, *tr. by* W. S. Merwin

I said "All's over"—& I made my. Christina Georgina Rossetti. CP-RosC3

I Said and Sang Her Excellence. Thomas Hardy. CP-HardT

I said: dark voyage, I am deeply wounded. Photograph of a Lighthouse Through Fog. Tess Gallagher. SP-GallT

I said darkling you said sparkling. As a Real House. Michael Palmer. SP-PalmM

I said fate plays a game without a score. I Sit by the Window. Joseph Brodsky. CP-BrodJ, *tr. by* Howard Moss

I said,—for Love was laggard, oh, Love was slow to come. Indifference. Edna St. Vincent Millay. CP-MillE

I said, I believe. Madam and the Crime Wave. Langston Hughes. CP-HughL; CP-HughL3

I said: I cannot tell you. Instant of Our Parting, The. Alice Walker. CP-WalkA

I said, "I do not fear the." Sadi. CP-RexrK, *tr. by* Kenneth Rexroth

I said I stood upon thy grave. Arisen at Last. John Greenleaf Whittier. CP-WhitJ

I said I will find what is lowly. Still. A. R. Ammons. CP-AmmoA

I said I will shake myself out of my clothes. Mormon Question, The. Ambrose Bierce. SP-BierA

I said in my youth. Primer, The. Josephine Jacobsen. CP-JacoJ

I said in the beginning, did I not? Edna St. Vincent Millay. CP-MillE

I said: Mighty men have encamped against me. Defensio in Extremis. John Berryman. CP-BerrJ

I said / Mr. Schafer. Dominion. A. R. Ammons. CP-AmmoA

I said: 'Nay, pluck not,—let the first fruit be.' Hoarded Joy. Dante Gabriel Rossetti. CW-RossD *Fr.* House of Life, The.

I said: / Now will the poets sing. Scottsboro, Too, Is Worth Its Song. Countee Cullen. CP-CullC

I said: "O let me sing the praise." He Inadvertently Cures His Love-Pains. Thomas Hardy. CP-HardT

I said of laughter: it is vain. Testimony, A. Christina Georgina Rossetti. CP-RosC1

I said of old when darkness brooded long. Creation, The. Jones Very. CP-VeryJ

I said our lives are improvisation and it sounded. Improvisation. Thom Gunn. CP-GunnT

I said out of sleeping. Second Song. Louise Bogan. CP-BogaL

I said, seeing how the winter gale increased. Edna St. Vincent Millay. CP-MillE

I said so little. So Little. Czeslaw Milosz. CP-MiloC; CP-MiloCN, *tr. by* Lillian Vallee

I said the people come inside. Acts of God. Heather McHugh. SP-McHuH

I said, the summer garden I planted. Living Alone (3). Denise Levertov. SP-LeveDL; SP-LeveDS

I said, / "the town bird." In the Rain. "H. D." CP-DoolH

I said—Then, dearest, since 'tis so. Last Ride Together, The. Robert Browning. CP-BroR1

I said: This is a beautiful fresh rose. Once for All. (Margaret). Christina Georgina Rossetti. CP-RosC1

I said to heaven that glowed above. Hafiz. *Fr.* Odes.

I said to her tears: "I am fallible and hungry." Plea, A. John Ciardi. CP-CiarJ

I said to It: "We grasp not what you meant." Inquiry, An. Thomas Hardy. CP-HardT

I Said to Love. Thomas Hardy. CP-HardT

I said to my baby. Same in Blues. Langston Hughes. CP-HughL *Fr.* Lenox Avenue Mural.

I said to my head, Write somethng. Lorine Niedecker. CP-NiedL

I said to myself almost in prayer. Trial Run, A. Robert Frost. CP-FrosR

I said to myself: 'That's enough.' Thirty-ninth Psalm, Adapted, The. Donald Davie. CP-DaviDC

I Said to Poetry. Alice Walker. CP-WalkA

I said to Poetry: "I'm finished." I Said to Poetry. Alice Walker. CP-WalkA

I said to the East wind. Hafiz. CP-EmerR *Fr.* Odes.

I said to the stone, "Am I standing all right?" Poet as Eagle Scout, The. Howard Nemerov. CP-NemeH

I said to the watcher at the gate. Signal from the House, The. Stanley Kunitz. CP-KunSC

I said within myself: I am a fool. Christina Georgina Rossetti. CP-RosC3

I sailed a little shallop. Path in the Sky, The. Nicholas Vachel Lindsay. CP-LindV

I sailed too long over that monstered ocean. Sinbad. Allen Tate. CP-TateA

I sailed up a river with a pleasant wind. Henry David Thoreau. CP-ThorH

I salute the section of our lordly Sunday journals which is entitled. One Man's Meed Is Another Man's Overemphasis. Ogden Nash. CP-NashO

I saluted a nobody. Chicago Poet. Carl Sandburg. CP-SandC

I Sang. Carl Sandburg. CP-SandC

I sang a canto in a canton. Country Words. Wallace Stevens. CP-StevW; CP-StevWP

I sang an idle song of happy youth. Wallace Stevens. CP-StevWP

I sang in the sun. Race Relations. Carolyn Kizer. CP-KizeC

I sang once: now I weep; and I take pleasure. Petrarch. CP-Petra, *tr. by* J. G. Nichols

I sang that song on Sunday. Her Song. Thomas Hardy. CP-HardT

I sang to you and the moon. I Sang. Carl Sandburg. CP-SandC

I sat all morning in the college sick bay. Mid-Term Break. Seamus Heaney. SP-HeanSO

I sat at dinner in my prime. At the Dinner-Table. Thomas Hardy. CP-HardT

I sat beneath a willow tree, / Where water falls and calls. In the Willow Shade. Christina Georgina Rossetti. CP-RosC2

I sat by a stream in a. Classic. A. R. Ammons. CP-AmmoA

I sat down. Round. A. R. Ammons. CP-AmmoA

I sat down. Pause of the Clock. Federico García Lorca. SP-GarcF, *tr. by* Stanley Read

I sat down / in a clearing in time. Clock Echo. Federico García Lorca. CP-GarcF, *tr. by* Jerome Rothenberg *Fr.* In the Forest of Clocks.

I sat in a café in San Francisco. Name of the Place "Trieste," The. Yehuda Amichai. SP-AmicYL, *tr. by* Benjamin Harshav *and* Barbara Harshav

I Sat in the Happiness. Yehuda Amichai. SP-AmicYL, *tr. by* Benjamin Harshav *and* Barbara Harshav

I sat in the Muses' hall at the mid of the day. Rome: The Vatican: Sala delle Muse. Thomas Hardy. CP-HardT

I sat in the playground where I played as a child. Half-Sized Violin. Yehuda Amichai. SP-AmicY, *tr. by* Chana Bloch

I sat. It was all past. Just the Same. Thomas Hardy. CP-HardT

I sat on cushioned otter-skin. Madness of King Goll, The. William Butler Yeats. CP-YeatW

I sat on the Dogana's steps. Canto 3: "I sat on the Dogana's steps." Ezra Pound. SP-PounE *Fr.* Cantos.

I sat on the edge of the bed. Ave Atque Vale. James Laughlin. CP-LaugJ

I sat on the eve-lit weir. Before My Friend Arrived. Thomas Hardy. CP-HardT

I sat on the wide sidewalk of Café Willheim in Ramatayim. Wonderful Baker, The. Yehuda Amichai. SP-AmicYL, *tr. by* Benjamin Harshav *and* Barbara Harshav

I sat one sprinkling day upon the lea. Childhood among the Ferns. Thomas Hardy. CP-HardT

I sat there singing her. Songs. Langston Hughes. CP-HughL; CP-HughL2

I sat up in bed and pondered what I'd learned. China Bronchitis. Allen Ginsberg. SP-GinsA *Fr.* Reading Bai Juyi.

I sat upon the ground. Ralph Waldo Emerson. CP-EmerR

I sat with a dynamiter at supper in a German saloon eating steak and. Dynamiter. Carl Sandburg. CP-SandC

I sat with Love upon a woodside well. Willowwood ("I sat with Love upon a woodside well"). Dante Gabriel Rossetti. CW-RossD *Fr.* House of Life, The.

I Save Your Coat, But You Lose It Later. Tess Gallagher. SP-GallT

I saved a chipmunk from a cat. Vastness and Indifference of the World, The. Richard Eberhart. CP-EberR

I saw a bird alone, / In its nest it sat alone. Let Patience Have Her Perfect Work. Christina Georgina Rossetti. CP-RosC3

I saw a bird pasted to muck. Small Elegy. John Ciardi. CP-CiarJ

I saw a bunch of flowers, and Time. Bunch of Flowers, The. Jones Very. CP-VeryJ

I saw a Cherry weep, and why? Weeping Cherry, The. Robert Herrick. CP-HerrR

I saw a child, whose eyes had never drank. Jones Very. CP-VeryJ

I saw a cottage in the sky. Friends. John Ashbery. SP-AshbJ

I saw a dead man's finer part. His Immortality. Thomas Hardy. CP-HardT

I saw a delicate flower had grown up two feet high. Henry David Thoreau. CP-ThorH

I saw a famous man eating soup. Soup. Carl Sandburg. CP-SandC

I saw a fantastic description of a monk's cell. This monk made wine. Monk, The. Andrei Codrescu. SP-CodrA

I saw a fly [*or* Flie] within a Bead[e]. Amber Bead, The. Robert Herrick. CP-HerrR

I saw a high window struck blind. Note Slipped Under a Door. Charles Simic. SP-SimiC; SP-SimiCE

I saw a lady; on each side a lover. Petrarch. CP-Petra, *tr. by* J. G. Nichols

I saw a lady underneath green laurel. Petrarch. CP-Petra, *tr. by* J. G. Nichols

I saw a leaf flying the direction opposite the ground, but there was no wind. David Ignatow. SP-IgnaD

I saw a man—and envied him beside. Plain Sermons. James Whitcomb Riley. CP-RileJ

I saw a man pursuing the horizon. Stephen Crane. CP-CranS

I saw a man wearing a skullcap embroidered. Same Embroidery, the Same Pattern, The. Yehuda Amichai. SP-AmicYL, *tr. by* Benjamin Harshav *and* Barbara Harshav

I saw a modern girl and understood. Modern Girl, A. Yehuda Amichai. SP-AmicYL, *tr. by* Benjamin Harshav *and* Barbara Harshav

I saw a mongoose this morning ripple down the scarp. Foreign Lands, The.

Josephine Jacobsen. CP-JacoJ

I saw a Monk of Charlemaine. Monk, The. William Blake. CP-BlakW *Fr.* Jerusalem.

I saw a mouth jeering. Gargoyle. Carl Sandburg. CP-SandC

I saw a picture of Rilke. Portrait of Rilke. Richard Eberhart. CP-EberR

I saw a proud, mysterious cat. Mysterious Cat, The. Nicholas Vachel Lindsay. CP-LindV

I saw a querulous old man, the tobacconist of Eighth Street. Tobacconist of Eighth Street, The. Richard Eberhart. CP-EberR

I saw a regiment of soldiers shuffling and stumbling. Robinson Jeffers. CP-JefR3

I saw a rose, in bloom, but sad. Fading Rose, The. Thomas Hardy. CP-HardT

I saw a Saint.—How canst thou tell that he. Embertide. Christina Georgina Rossetti. CP-RosC2

I saw a Ship of martial build. Berg, The. Herman Melville. SP-MelvH

I saw a slowly-stepping train. God's Funeral. Thomas Hardy. CP-HardT

I saw a staring virgin stand. Two Songs from a Play. William Butler Yeats. CP-YeatW *Fr.* Resurrection, The.

I saw a telegram handed a two hundred pound man at a desk. And the. Telegram. Carl Sandburg. CP-SandC

I saw a vision of the morning age. Snail, The. G. K. Chesterton. CP-ChesG

I saw a war yet none the trumpet blew. War, The. Jones Very. CP-VeryJ

I saw a white dove in a tree. Morgenlied. Tennessee Williams. CP-WillT

I saw a woman getting out of a car. Memphis, 2 P.M. [or 2:00 P.M.]. Miller Williams. CP-WillM

I saw a worm, with many a fold. Worm, The. Jones Very. CP-VeryJ

I saw a young snake glide. Snake. Theodore Roethke. CP-RoetT

I saw about her spotless wrist. Upon a Black Twist, Rounding the Arm of the Countess of Carlisle. Robert Herrick. CP-HerrR

I saw again in a dream the other night. Two Girls. Howard Nemerov. CP-NemeH

I saw again the spirits on a day. Bethesda: A Sequel. Arthur Hugh Clough. SP-ClouA

I saw amid the sunshine and the dews. God. G. K. Chesterton. CP-ChesG

I saw an aged Beggar in my walk. Old Cumberland Beggar, The. William Wordsworth. CP-WorW1; MW-WorW

I saw an ocean liner in the desert, its crew leaning over the railing. Ship, The. David Ignatow. SP-IgnaD

I saw an old man. In his youth. Family. Yehuda Amichai. SP-AmicYL, *tr. by* Benjamin Harshav *and* Barbara Harshav

I saw an old man like a child. Behind. G. K. Chesterton. CP-ChesG

I saw angelic qualities on earth. Petrarch. CP-Petra, *tr. by* J. G. Nichols

I saw, as in a dream sublime. Occultation of Orion, The. Henry Wadsworth Longfellow. SP-LongH

I saw brown Corrib lean upon his urn. On Sutton Strand. Donald Davie. CP-DaviDC

I saw by looking in his eyes. Wandering Jew, The. Edwin Arlington Robinson. CP-RobiE

I saw clay jars covered with barnacles. At the Maritime Museum. Yehuda Amichai. SP-AmicY, *tr. by* Chana Bloch

I Saw Eternity. Louise Bogan. CP-BogaL

I saw, from under Him, the beginning. Charles Olson. CP-OlsoC

I saw her as something in my inner eye. Statue of Liberty. Richard Eberhart. CP-EberR

I saw her at the hilltop. Landscape with Mantra. Olga Broumas. SP-BrouO

I Saw Her First. James Laughlin. CP-LaugJ

I saw her, out past the first. His Dream: The Black Tree / Thirst. Gregory Orr. SP-OrrG

I saw her; she was lovely. Song: "I saw her; she was lovely." Christina Georgina Rossetti. CP-RosC3

I saw her when I was in the left lane. Girl on the Bus Stop Bench, The. Charles Bukowski. SP-BukC1

I saw him forging link by link his chain. Slave, The. Jones Very. CP-VeryJ

I saw him—he said—with my own eyes; he was hanging one meter high. Undressing of the Hanged Man, The. Yannis Ritsos. SP-RitsY, *tr. by* Kimon Friar *and* Kostas Myrsiades

I saw him / in a dry place / on a hot day. Water Snake. Mary Oliver. SP-OlivM

I saw him pass as the new day dawned. Youth Who Carried a Light, The. Thomas Hardy. CP-HardT

I saw him steal the light away. God's Education. Thomas Hardy. CP-HardT

I saw his round mouth's crimson deepen as it fell. Fragment: "I saw his round mouth's crimson deepen as it fell." Wilfred Owen. CP-OwenW

I Saw in Louisiana a Live-Oak Growing. Walt Whitman. CP-WhitW

I saw in the street on a summer evening. Gods Come and Go, Prayers Remain Forever. Yehuda Amichai. SP-AmicYL, *tr. by* Benjamin Harshav *and* Barbara Harshav

I saw it as driving snow, the spume. Chance. Charles Tomlinson. SP-TomlC

I saw it—pink and white—revealed. Thought in Two Moods, A. Thomas Hardy. CP-HardT

I saw it, the mystical beast in the shadows. Mystical Beast in the Shadows, The.

Richard Eberhart. CP-EberR

I saw Love in eyes. Guido Cavalcanti. CP-CavaG, *tr. by* Marc Cirigliano

I saw Man, the man-hunter. Man, the Man-Hunter. Carl Sandburg. CP-SandC

I saw many today. Homeless, The. Charles Simic. SP-SimiCE

I saw my toes the other day. In Extremis. John Updike. CP-UpdiJ

I saw myself in your eyes. Little Backwater. Federico García Lorca. CP-GarcF, *tr. by* Jerome Rothenberg *Fr.* Backwaters.

I saw no Way. The Heavens were stitched. Emily Dickinson. CP-DickE

I saw nothing at that moment. Halley's Comet. Jaroslav Seifert. SP-SeifJ, *tr. by* Ewald Osers

I Saw Old General at Bay. Walt Whitman. CP-WhitW

I saw old Idleness, fat, with great cheeks. Idleness. Walter De la Mare. CP-DeLaW

I saw on earth another light. Light from Within, The. Jones Very. CP-VeryJ

I saw on the slant hill a putrid lamb. For a Lamb. Richard Eberhart. CP-EberR

I saw one born, yet he was of the dead. Still-Born, The. Jones Very. CP-VeryJ

I saw past the door, today. Mictlantecuhtli. Charles Tomlinson. CP-TomlC

I saw St. Francis by a stream. Voice of St. Francis of Assisi, The. Nicholas Vachel Lindsay. CP-LindV

I saw some trees by the river. Han-shan. CP-ColdM, *tr. by* Red Pine

I saw, strange sight! the children sat at meat. Children, The. Jones Very. CP-VeryJ

I saw sweet Poetry turn troubled eyes. Happy Encounter, The. Walter De la Mare. CP DeLaW

I saw that the Flake was on it. Emily Dickinson. CP-DickE

I saw that the shanty town had grown over the graves and that the crowd lived among the memorials. Lines for Translation into Any Language. James Fenton. SP-FentJ

I saw the best minds of my generation destroyed by madness, starving hysterical naked. Howl. Allen Ginsberg. CP-GinsA; SP-GinsA

I saw the city, 'twas not built by hands. New Jerusalem, The ("I saw the city, 'twas not built by hands"). Jones Very. CP-VeryJ

I saw the civil sun drying earth's tears. Thaw, The. Henry David Thoreau. CP-ThorH

I saw the dwellings of the Just. Dwellings of the Just, The. Jones Very. CP-VeryJ

I saw the first pear. Orchard. "H. D." CP-DoolH

I saw the full body of the wind, he said, its full body. Wind's Body, The. Yannis Ritsos. SP-RitsY, *tr. by* Kimon Friar

I saw the ghostly lady fleeting. Story I Have Told, The. Stevie Smith. CP-SmitS

I saw the hawk ride updraft in the sunset over Wyoming. Mortal Limit. Robert Penn Warren. CP-WarrR

I saw the Jays this Morning. Emily Dickinson. SP-DickE

I saw the laboratory animals: throat-bandaged dogs cowering in cages, still. Memoir. Robinson Jeffers. CP-JefR2

I saw the locust fall upon the leaf. Modus Vivendi. Tennessee Williams. CP-WillT

I saw the midlands. Kisses in the Train. D. H. Lawrence. CP-LawrD

I saw the old Chinese men standing. Some Painful Butterflies Pass Through. Tess Gallagher. SP-GallT

I saw the sailor dead at sea. Virgin and Martyr. Howard Nemerov. CP-NemeH

I saw the Sibyl at Cumæ. Petronius Arbiter. CW-RossD, *tr. by* Dante Gabriel Rossetti *Fr.* Satyricon.

I saw the sky descending, black and white. Where the Rainbow Ends. Robert Lowell. SP-LoweR

I saw the sky was lit. Moon New-Risen. D. H. Lawrence. CP-LawrD

I saw the Sphinx on the sands of Egypt. Sphinx. Richard Eberhart. CP-EberR

I saw the spiders marching through the air. Mr. Edwards and the Spider. Robert Lowell. SP-LoweR

I saw the spot where our first parents dwelt. Garden, The. Jones Very. CP-VeryJ

I saw the two starlings. Maneuver [or Manoeuvre], The. William Carlos Williams. CP-WilW2

I saw the virtues sitting hand in hand. Humility. George Herbert. CP-HerbG

I saw the water flow. Yannis Ritsos. SP-RitsY *Fr.* Paper Poems 3.

I saw the wind within her. Emily Dickinson. CP-DickE

I saw thee, child, one summer's day. Emily Jane Brontë. CP-BronE

I saw thee on thy bridal day. To ———: "I saw thee on thy bridal day." Edgar Allan Poe. CP-PoeEd

I saw thee once—once only—years ago. To Helen. Edgar Allan Poe. CP-PoeEd

I Saw Thee Weep. Lord Byron. CP-Byron

I saw their lives curl upward like a wave. Bacchus and Ariadne; 2nd Debate between the Body and Soul. T. S. Eliot. SP-ElioT

I saw them—he said—the two burglars behind the grilles. Eyewitness. Yannis Ritsos. SP-RitsY, *tr. by* Kimon Friar *and* Kostas Myrsiades

I saw them last night in a box at the play. In a Box. James Whitcomb Riley. CP-RileJ

I saw them often when they drove to Lyons. Couple, The. Tennessee Williams. CP-WillT

I saw three ships go sailing by. North Ship, The. Philip Larkin. CP-LarkP

I saw—twas in a dream, the other night. Montefiore. Ambrose Bierce. SP-BierA

I saw twelve ladies sailing at their ease. Petrarch. CP-Petra, *tr.* by J. G. Nichols

I saw two trees embracing. All That Time. May Swenson. SP-SwenM

I saw wild domes and bowers. Angel and the Clown, The. Nicholas Vachel Lindsay. CP-LindV

I saw you arise from your bed, I saw your door open. All Is Well with the Child. Marya Alexandrovna Zaturenska. SP-ZatuM

I saw you last night in the gathering. Jelaluddin Rumi. SP-Rumi, *tr.* by Coleman Barks

I saw you once, Medusa; we were alone. Muse as Medusa, The. May Sarton. SP-SartM

I saw young Spring leap over the hills. George Meredith. CP-MerG2

I saw your hands. Audre Lorde. *See* I saw / Your hands on my lips like blind needles

I saw / Your hands on my lips like blind needles. Pirouette. Audre Lorde. SP-LordA

I saw your shoulder swell and pitch. Erinna to Sappho. James Wright. CP-WrigJ

I say, I am quite done. Let Zeus Record. "H. D." CP-DoolH

I Say, "I'll Seek Her." Thomas Hardy. CP-HardT

I say, instead of the white man. Five Preludes For Buffalo's Own Forest Lawn. John Logan. CP-LogaJ

I say it; low she lay as one in dreams. Crystal, The. G. K. Chesterton. CP-ChesG

I say myself. Disclaimer of the Person. Laura Riding Jackson. CP-RidiL

I say no more for Clavering. Clavering. Edwin Arlington Robinson. CP-RobiE

I say no world. E. E. Cummings. CP-CummE; SP-CummE

I say now, Fernando, that on that day. Hibiscus on the Sleeping Shores. Wallace Stevens. CP-StevW; SP-StevWP

I say, "She was as good as fair!" Inconstant, The. Thomas Hardy. CP-HardT

I say, that but for black Foakes'-day. George Meredith. CP-MerG2

I say that Roger Casement. Roger Casement. William Butler Yeats. CP-YeatW

I say this evening we'll [*or* we'd] all get drunk. William Blake. CP-BlakW *Fr.* Island in the Moon, An.

I say to the lead. Poem without a Title. Charles Simic. SP-SimiC; SP-SimiCE

I scanned her picture, dreaming. Song from Heine. Thomas Hardy. CP-HardT

I scarce believe [*or* beleeve] my love to be so pure. Love's Growth. John Donne. CP-DonnJ; MW-DonnJ

I search in vain your childlike face to see. Young Girl, A. Walter De la Mare. CP-DeLaW

I searched all morning. Wokanmagulli. Yusef Komunyakaa. CP-KomuY

I searched the meadow far around. Solitary Gentian, The. Jones Very. CP-VeryJ

I see a bird of five colors. Han-shan. CP-ColdM, *tr.* by Red Pine

I see a camel in my mind. Exercise for Professor X, An. Wallace Stevens. CP-StevWP

I see a fair young couple in a wood. Time and Sentiment. George Meredith. CP-MerG1

I see a fresh-cheeked figure. She Would Welcome Old Tribulations. Thomas Hardy. CP-HardT

I See a Girl Dragged by the Wrists. Philip Larkin. CP-LarkP

I see a man with a whistle between his lips. "Woods" at Midnight, The. Andrei Codrescu. SP-CodrA

I see a woman with wings. Freedom Seeker. Langston Hughes. CP-HughL; CP-HughL1

I see all, am all, all. Childhood. Kathleen Jessie Raine. SP-RainK

I see an empty place at the table. No Need. Raymond Carver. CP-CarvR

I see around me tombstones grey. Emily Jane Brontë. CP-BronE

I see before me now a traveling army halting. Bivouac on a Mountain Side. Walt Whitman. CP-WhitW

I see birds below me with massive shoulders. Woman Bewildered, The. Robert Bly. SP-BlyR

I see by the papers / What seems mighty funny to me. Explain It, Please. Langston Hughes. CP-HughL; CP-HughL3

I see by the papers / Where Governor Talmadge get real mad. Governor Fires Dean. Langston Hughes. CP-HughL; CP-HughL3

I see by the papers / Where Mitchell's won his case. Mitchell Case, The. Langston Hughes. CP-HughL; CP-HughL3

I see by the papers / Where the NAACP. NAACP. Langston Hughes. CP-HughL; CP-HughL2

I see Captain Holm. Captain Holm. May Swenson. SP-SwenM

I see from the paper that Florrie Forde is dead. Death of an Actress. Louis MacNeice. CP-MacNL

"I see herrin'."—I hear the glad cry. With the Herring Fishers. Hugh MacDiarmid. SP-MacDH

I see him moving, in his legendary fleece. Buffalo Coat, The. Thomas McGrath. SP-McGrT

I see him old, trapped in a burly house. Pauper, A. Allen Tate. CP-TateA

I see hundreds of dogs. Han-shan. CP-ColdM, *tr.* by Red Pine

I see in you the estuary that enlarges and spreads itself. To Old Age. Walt Whitman. CP-WhitW

I see it in my Lady's eyes. Guido Cavalcanti. CP-CavaG, *tr.* by Marc Cirigliano

I see it out there like a small. It. A. K. Ramanujan. CP-RamaA

I see Mrs. Garret opening the glass doors of the tomb. Dream & Excursus, Arlington Massachusetts. Philip Whalen. SP-WhalP

I see my father. First Principles. Jay Wright. SP-WrigJ

I See My Friend Everywhere. Grace Paley. CP-PalGC

I see my kind protector come. Disappointment, an Ode 1756 to Mr Stockton, The. Annis Boudinot Stockton. CP-StocA

I see, my noble lady. Petrarch. CP-Petra, *tr.* by J. G. Nichols

I see my plaint with open ears. Sir Thomas Wyatt. CP-WyatT

I see my Scotland now, a puzzle. Vision of Scotland, A. Hugh MacDiarmid. SP-MacDH

I see now all the things I shall not do. Doggerel for My Seventieth Birthday, A. Charles Tomlinson. SP-TomlC

I see now I see. Resurrection. Margaret Atwood. SP-AtwM1

I see people chanting sutras. Han-shan. CP-ColdM, *tr.* by Red Pine

I see people everywhere. Han-shan. CP-ColdM, *tr.* by Red Pine

I See Phantoms of Hatred and of the Heart's Fullness and of the Coming Emptiness. William Butler Yeats. CP-YeatW *Fr.* Meditations in Time of Civil War.

I see so clearly now my similar years. Edna St. Vincent Millay. CP-MillE

I see someone deceiving others. Han-shan. CP-ColdM, *tr.* by Red Pine

I see someone short on sense. Shih-te. CP-ColdM, *tr.* by Red Pine

I see, spread out and waving in the breeze. Petrarch. CP-Petra, *tr.* by J. G. Nichols

I See That All Things Come to an End. Christina Georgina Rossetti. CP-RosC2

I see that chance hath chosen me. Sir Thomas Wyatt. CP-WyatT

I see that there it is on the beach. It is. Memorial Service for the Invasion Beach Where the Vacation in the Flesh Is Over. Alan Dugan. CP-DugaA

I see the blue, the green, the golden and the red. Angelus. Kathleen Jessie Raine. SP-RainK

I See the Boys of Summer. Dylan Thomas. CP-ThomD

I see the change from that that was. Sir Thomas Wyatt. CP-WyatT

I see the child playing in the corn. Rest of the Flight, The. Flemish, 1521. Hans Magnus Enzensberger. SP-EnzeH

I see the ghost of a perished day. Procession of Dead Days, A. Thomas Hardy. CP-HardT

I see the grass shake in the sun for leagues on either hand. Prairie, The. Rudyard Kipling. CP-KiplR

I see the hand in which the sun rises. Third Psalm: The September Vision. W. S. Merwin. SP-MerwW

I see the horses and the sad streets. Eye, The. Allen Tate. CP-TateA

I see the low black wherry. House-martin. Donald Davie. CP-DaviDC

I see the oak's bride in the oak's grasp. Ted Hughes. SP-HughTN

I see the sleeping babe nestling the breast of its mother. Mother and Babe. Walt Whitman. CP-WhitW

I see the tree think it will turn. Autumn. James Dickey. CP-DickJ

I see the Yellow River. Han-shan. CP-ColdM, *tr.* by Red Pine

I see thee better—in the Dark. Emily Dickinson. CP-DickE

I see thee clearer for the Grave. Emily Dickinson. CP-DickE

I see them as an ancient print. Wise and Foolish Virgins, The. Rainer Maria Rilke. CP-RilkFr, *tr.* by A. Poulin, Jr.

I see them crowd on crowd they walk the earth. Dead, The. Jones Very. CP-VeryJ

I see them lying sheeted in their graves. Tennessee Williams. CP-WillT

I see them spreading o'er the land. Plagues of Egypt, The. Jones Very. CP-VeryJ

I see these winds, these are the tops of trees. These Winds. Robert Lowell. SP-LoweR

I see Tientai summit. Han-shan. CP-ColdM, *tr.* by Red Pine

I see two eyes like two children. Wind, The. Rainer Maria Rilke. CP-RilkFr, *tr.* by A. Poulin, Jr.

I see what's past and what's. With My Third Eye. James Laughlin. CP-LaugJ

I see you, Aunt Bernice. I Love You. Robert Creeley. SP-CreeR

I see You / Brown-skinned, / Neat Afro. Thank You, Lord. Maya Angelou. SP-AngeM

I see you, centered. Lullaby: "I see you, centered." Olga Broumas. SP-BrouO

I see you, child, standing above the river. Leaving Water Hyacinths. Jane Cooper. CP-CoopJ

I see you cruel, you find me less than fair. On a Line from Sophocles. Carolyn Kizer. CP-KizeC

I see you drinking at a fountain with tiny. Almost Made Up Poem, An. Charles Bukowski. SP-BukC1

I see you flashing in the night and try to catch you. Firefly, The. James Laughlin. CP-LaugJ

I see you fugitive, stumbling across the prarie. Margaret Atwood. SP-AtwM1

I see you, rose, half-open book. Rainer Maria Rilke. CP-RilkFr, *tr.* by A. Poulin, Jr. *Fr.* Roses, The.

I see you scraping carrots by the stove. Dear Silent Ghost. Tennessee Williams. CP-WillT

I see you standing out from the mind's roadstead. Battlewagon. William Meredith. SP-MereW

I see you strangling. In Memory of a Spanish Poet. James Wright. CP-WrigJ

I seek among the living & I seek. Christina Georgina Rossetti. CP-RosC3

I seek not what his soul desires. Two Races. Rudyard Kipling. CP-KiplR

I Seek Salvation. Aleksandr Aleksandrovich Blok. SP-BlokA, *tr. by* Peter France *and* Jon Stallworthy

I seek the place of Macaroons. Macaroons. G. K. Chesterton. CP-ChesG

I seek the Present Time. Henry David Thoreau. CP-ThorH

I seem to hear that messenger once more. Petrarch. CP-Petra, *tr. by* J. G. Nichols

I seem to see enormous peristyles. Previous Existence. Charles Baudelaire. CP-BaudC, *tr. by* Walter Martin

I seemed to be drawn. Death of Fred Clifton, The. Lucille Clifton. SP-ClifL

I seik [*or* seek] about[e] this warld onstable [*or* world unstable]. William Dunbar. CP-DunbW

I seize in a central knot. George Meredith. CP-MerG2

I seldom see / A kangaroo. Not Often. Langston Hughes. CP-HughL

I sell myths not poems. With each poem goes a little myth. De Natura Rerum. Andrei Codrescu. SP-CodrA

I send, I send here my supremest kiss. His Tears to Thamesis [*or* Thamasis]. Robert Herrick. CP-HerrR

I send my heart up to thee, all my heart. In a Gondola. Robert Browning. CP-BroR1

I send my messages ahead of me. Poet and Person. Denise Levertov. SP-LeveDL; SP-LeveDS

I send this at nine / To know will you dine. Thomas Sheridan. CP-SherT

I send Two Sunsets. Emily Dickinson. CP-DickE

I send you a decrepit flower. Emily Dickinson. CP-DickE

I send you here a list of all. Mrs. Austen. CP-AustJ

I send you here a sort of allegory. To — With the Following Poem. Alfred Tennyson. CP-TennA

I sense Your coming. One year follows another. Aleksandr Aleksandrovich Blok. SP-BlokA, *tr. by* Peter France *and* Jon Stallworthy

I sensed my spirits flagging day by day. Petrarch. CP-Petra, *tr. by* J. G. Nichols

I Sent a Mental to My Love. Kenneth Patchen. CP-PatcK

I sent a message to my dear. Miracles, The. Rudyard Kipling. CP-KiplR

I sent my love to the showers. Marfa. James Tate. SP-TateJ

I Sent Thee Late. Louis Zukofsky. CP-ZukLS

I serve you not, if you I follow. Etienne de la Boéce. Ralph Waldo Emerson. CP-EmerR

I set forth one misted white day of June. On the Great Atlantic Rainway. Kenneth Koch. SP-KochK

I set out from the Port of Acapulco on the twenty-third of March. Drake in the Southern Sea. Ernesto Cardenal. CP-MertT

I settled at Cold Mountain long ago. Gary Snyder. CP-SnydG

I shake an absolute around the world. What Gives. Richard Eberhart. CP-EberR

I Shake My Fist at a Tree. David Ignatow. SP-IgnaD

I shall be glad to be silent, Mother, and hear you speak. White Thought, The. Stevie Smith. CP-SmitS

I shall be in the Shenandoah some day. Shenandoah Journey. Carl Sandburg. CP-SandC

I shall be still stronger. I Want to Sleep. Jorge Guillén. CP-WrigJ, *tr. by* James Wright

I shall be the last to come into the word. Abstract of Knowledge, The / The First Test. Jay Wright. SP-WrigJ

I shall be with you when hollow faces. Loyalty Is the Life You Are. Kenneth Patchen. CP-PatcK

I shall begin with a rose for courage. Poem of Flight, The. Philip Levine. SP-LeviP

I shall build me a house where the larkspur blooms. Vision. Robert Penn Warren. CP-WarrR

I shall come back without fanfaronade. Dorothy Parker. CP-ParkD

I shall cry God to give me a broken foot. Flash Crimson. Carl Sandburg. CP-SandC

I shall die, but that is all that I shall do for Death. Conscientious Objector. Edna St. Vincent Millay. CP-MillE

I shall die in Paris, in a rainstorm. Black Stone on Top of a White Stone. César Vallejo. CP-MertT

I shall expect / you in to dine. Carmen 13. Catullus. CP-ZukLS, *tr. by* Louis Zukofsky *Fr.* Carmina.

I shall foot it. Road and the End, The. Carl Sandburg. CP-SandC

I shall forget you presently, my dear. Edna St. Vincent Millay. CP-MillE

I shall go back. Edna St. Vincent Millay. CP-MillE

I shall go back again to the bleak shore. I shall go back. Edna St. Vincent Millay. CP-MillE

I shall / go down. River. A. R. Ammons. CP-AmmoA

I shall go from my sickbed to heaven. Hafiz. CP-EmerR, *tr. by* Ralph Waldo Emerson *Fr.* Odes.

I shall grieve, I grieve, I am grieving. Lament on the Eve of Parting. Ogden Nash. CP-NashO

I shall have to pee out the window, says the translation. Festung, Salzburg, The.

Maxine W. Kumin. SP-KumiM

I shall imagine life. E. E. Cummings. CP-CummE

I shall keep singing! Emily Dickinson. CP-DickE

I shall know better next time than to drink with any but certified. Prose Take-Out, Portland, 13:ix:58. Philip Whalen. SP-WhalP

I shall know why—when Time is over. Emily Dickinson. CP-DickE

I Shall Laugh Purely. Robinson Jeffers. CP-JefR3

I shall never forget the wind. North Wind: Portrush. Derek Mahon. CP-MahoD

I shall never forget you, Broadway. Broadway. Carl Sandburg. CP-SandC

I shall never get out of this! There are two of me now. In Plaster. Sylvia Plath. CP-PlatS

I shall never get you put together entirely. Colossus, The. Sylvia Plath. CP-PlatS

I shall not ask Jean Jacques Rousseau. Pairing Time Anticipated. William Cowper. CP-CowpW

I shall not die for you. A. E. Housman. CP-HousA

I shall not murmur if at last. Emily Dickinson. CP-DickE

I shall not see—and don't I know 'em? Song in the Worst Possible Taste. Dorothy Parker. CP-ParkD

I shall not see the end of this unweaving. May Sarton. SP-SartM *Fr.* Divorce of Lovers, A.

I shall not sing a May song. Crazy Woman, The. Gwendolyn Brooks. SP-BrooG

I shall not soon forget. Still Life. Thom Gunn. CP-GunnT

I shall not soon forget that sight. Raphael. John Greenleaf Whittier. CP-WhitJ

I shall rot here, with those whom in their day. In Death Divided. Thomas Hardy. CP-HardT

I shall tread, another year. Paths. Dorothy Parker. CP-ParkD

I shall vote Labour because. Christopher Logue. SP-LoguC

I shall watch your passage from Crutch to Cane. Emily Dickinson. SP-DickE

I shall write of the old men I knew. In These Dissenting Times. Alice Walker. CP-WalkA

I shiver, Spirit fierce and bold. At the Grave of Burns (1803, Seven Years After His Death). William Wordsworth. CP-WorW1

I shot my friend to save my country's life. Body Politic, The. Donald Hall. CP-HallD

I should always have known; those who sang from the river. Hohensalzburg: Fantastic Variations on a Theme of Romantic Character. Randall Jarrell. CP-JarrR

I should be content. Content. David Ignatow. SP-IgnaD

I should be someplace else! Not to Choose. Alan Dugan. CP-DugaA

I should—but anyone can and. 4:00 A.M. on the Terrace. John Ciardi. CP-CiarJ

I should have been delighted there to hear. Cold Divinities, The. James Wright. CP-WrigJ

I should have been too glad, I see. Emily Dickinson. CP-DickE

I should have begun with this: the sky. Sky. Wisława Szymborska. SP-SzymW, *tr. by* Stanisław Barańczak *and* Clare Cavanagh

I should have deem'd it one effort vain. On Receiving Heyne's Virgil. William Cowper. CP-CowpW

I should have had my macadam. Tight. A. R. Ammons. CP-AmmoA

I should have known if you gave me flowers. Then Came Flowers. Rita Dove. SP-DoveR

I should have something to say of/to this. On Meeting Miss B. John Ciardi. CP-CiarJ

I should have thought. At Baia. "H. D." CP-DoolH

I should have to be. Flowers Alone, The. William Carlos Williams. CP-WilW1

I should like, Fortunatus, to live in a city where a riv-. Plato Elaborated. Joseph Brodsky. CP-BrodJ, *tr. by* George L. Kline

I should like to come upon. Hula-Hula. William Carlos Williams. CP-WilW1

I should like to see that country's tiles, bedrooms. Keeping Their World Large. Marianne Craig Moore. CP-MoorM

I should not dare to be so sad. Emily Dickinson. CP-DickE

I should not dare to leave my friend. Emily Dickinson. CP-DickE

I should not have shown in the flesh. He Revisits His First School. Thomas Hardy. CP-HardT

I should relate sometime how I changed. No More. Czeslaw Milosz. CP-MiloC; CP-MiloCN, *tr. by* Tony Milosz

I should walk maniacal. Old Question. Richard Eberhart. CP-EberR

I shouldered a kind of manhood. Funeral Rites. Seamus Heaney. SP-HeanSO

I shouldn't have been surprised. Engagement. A. K. Ramanujan. CP-RamaA

I showed her Heights she never saw. Emily Dickinson. CP-DickE

I shut myself away from nothing. Everything allowed, I went. I Went. Constantine P. Cavafy. CP-CavaC, *tr. by* Theoharis Constantine Theoharis

I shut myself in with my soul. Dante Gabriel Rossetti. CW-RossD

I sigh at day-dawn, and I sigh. Sappho. Christina Georgina Rossetti. CP-RosC3

I sigh, fair injur'd stranger! for thy fate. On a Late Connubial Rupture in High Life. Samuel Taylor Coleridge. CP-ColeS

I sigh for the heavenly country. Heavenly City, The. Stevie Smith. CP-SmitS

I sigh when I see learned men. Shih-te. CP-ColdM, *tr. by* Red Pine

I sigh when I see worldly people. Shih-te. CP-ColdM, *tr. by* Red Pine

I sing a subject sung by no man. Wonderful Man, Part the Third. *Unknown, sometimes at. to* Thomas Sheridan. CP-SherT

I sing not of the Drapier's [*or* draper's] praise, nor yet of William Wood. Excellent New Song upon His Grace Our Good Lord Archbishop of Dublin, An. Jonathan Swift. CP-SwifJ

I sing of a journey to Clifton. Distressed Travellers, The. William Cowper. CP-CowpW

I sing of a Whistle, a Whistle of worth. Whistle. A Ballad, The. Robert Burns. CP-BurnR

I sing of autumn and the falling fruit. Ship of Death. D. H. Lawrence. CP-LawrD

I sing of brooks, of blossom[e]s, birds, and bowers. Argument of His Book, The. Robert Herrick. CP-HerrR

I sing of Cornwall. Hugh MacDiarmid. SP-MacDH *Fr.* Cornish Heroic Song for Valda Trevlyn.

I sing of deadly dolorous debate. Muiopotmos: or The Fate of the Butterflie. Edmund Spenser. CP-Spens

I sing of Morrisville. Song of the Two Crows. Hayden Carruth. CP-CarHS

I Sing of Olaf Glad and Big. E. E. Cummings. CP-CummE; SP-CummE

I sing of the prodigal race. One Hand in Space. Tennessee Williams. CP-WillT

I sing the birth, was born[e] to-night. Hymn[e] on the Nativity [*or* Nativitie] of My Saviour, A. Ben Jonson. CP-JonsB

I Sing the Body Electric. Walt Whitman. CP-WhitW

I sing the body electric. I Sing the Body Electric. Walt Whitman. CP-WhitW

I sing the gaudy to-day and cosmopolite civilization. Redondillas, or Something of That Sort. Ezra Pound. CP-PoEar

I sing the NAME which None can say. To the Name above Every Name, the Name of Jesus, a Hymn. Richard Crashaw. CP-CrasR

I sing the song of the sleeping wife. Sing Song. Robert Creeley. CP-CreeR

I sing the tree is a heron. Merce of Egypt. Charles Olson. CP-OlsoC; SP-OlsoC

I sing them spiraling in flame. For Air Heroes. William Meredith. SP-MereW

I sing thy praise Iacchus. Hymne to Bacchus, A. Robert Herrick. CP-HerrR

I sing to use the Waiting. Emily Dickinson. CP-DickE

I sing what was lost and dread what was won. What Was Lost. William Butler Yeats. CP-YeatW

I sink back upon the ground, expecting to die. A voice speaks out of my ear. David Ignatow. SP-IgnaD

I sit a queen, and am no widow, and shall see no sorrow. Christina Georgina Rossetti. CP-RosC3

I sit a throne upon the times. Let's Majeste. Maya Angelou. SP-AngeM

I sit all day outside a bank. He. Randall Jarrell. CP-JarrR

I Sit Alone. Walter De la Mare. CP-DeLaW

I sit among the green shady valleys oft. Christina Georgina Rossetti. CP-RosC3

I Sit and Look Out. Walt Whitman. CP-WhitW

I sit and watch the winding way. Funerals, The. Jones Very. CP-VeryJ

I sit at my desk. Joseph Brodsky. CP-BrodJ *Fr.* Shorts.

I sit at my desk. Love Poems of Marichiko, The. Kenneth Rexroth. CP-RexrK

I sit because the Dadaists screamed on Mirror Street. Why I Meditate. Allen Ginsberg. SP-GinsA

I sit beside two women, kitty-corner. Jasmine. Yusef Komunyakaa. SP-KomuY

I Sit by the Window. Joseph Brodsky. CP-BrodJ, *tr. by* Howard Moss

I Sit Down to Type. James Schuyler. CP-SchuJ

I sit dreaming. I've brought. I've Brought to Art. Constantine P. Cavafy. CP-CavaC, *tr. by* Theoharis Constantine Theoharis

I sit for hours staring at my own right hand. January 10, 1973. Alice Walker. CP-WalkA

I sit here, doing nothing, alone, worn out by long winter. Mary Bly. James Wright. CP-WrigJ

I sit here eating milk-toast in my lap-robe. Money. Randall Jarrell. CP-JarrR

I sit here in these stocks. In Weatherbury Stocks. Thomas Hardy. CP-HardT

I sit here on a Sunday. Plantation a Beginning, A. Charles Olson. SP-OlsoC *Fr.* Maximus Poems, The.

I sit high on this bridge in Laventille. Spoiler's Return, The. Derek Walcott. CP-WalcD

I sit in a café in the afternoon hours. Like the Streams in the Negev. Yehuda Amichai. SP-AmicYL, *tr. by* Benjamin Harshav *and* Barbara Harshav

I sit in a chair and read the newspapers. Smoke. Carl Sandburg. CP-SandC

I sit in a waiting room with bridegrooms. Late Marriage. Yehuda Amichai. SP-AmicY, *tr. by* Chana Bloch

I sit in an office at 244 Madison Avenue. Spring Comes to Murray Hill. Ogden Nash. CP-NashO

I sit in my own house. Lorine Niedecker. CP-NiedL

I sit in my room. C. K. Williams. CP-WillC; SP-WillC

I sit in my window with a tommy gun across my knees. I Never Had Any Other Desire So Strong. Kenneth Patchen. CP-PatcK

I sit in sun. Mays Landing. A. R. Ammons. CP-AmmoA

I sit in the dusk. I am all alone. Tableau at Twilight. Ogden Nash. CP-NashO

I sit in the study. Pavilion. Billy Collins. SP-CollB

I sit in the top of the wood, my eyes closed. Hawk Roosting. Ted Hughes. SP-HughTN

I sit in the waiting room with bridegrooms many years. Late Marriage. Yehuda Amichai. SP-AmicYL, *tr. by* Benjamin Harshav *and* Barbara Harshav

I sit looking at my features. Looking Head On. Richard Eberhart. CP-EberR

I sit looking dumbly at this stuffed red devil on my desk. I am in. Valentine Gift, A. Charles Bukowski. SP-BukC3

I sit musing, ten minutes from the Jap. Letter for Marian, A. Thomas McGrath. SP-McGrT

I sit not here the noble horse to see. Elegy 3.2: "I sit not here the noble horse to see." Ovid. CP-MarlC *Fr.* Elegies.

I sit on the tracks. Success Comes to Cow Creek. James Tate. SP-TateJ

I sit on top of a boulder. Han-shan. CP-ColdM, *tr. by* Red Pine

I sit secreted in the dark. Swift Completion of Their Appointed Rounds, The. Robert Stock. SP-StocR

I sit, sit listening; my lashes droop. Bad Music, The. Randall Jarrell. CP-JarrR

I sit under Rand MacNally's. Westering. Seamus Heaney. SP-HeanSO

I sit upon the old sea wall. On the Sea Wall. Paul Laurence Dunbar. CP-DunbP

I sit within my room and joy to find. Presence, The. Jones Very. CP-VeryJ

I sit within the room where thou once sat. Jonathan Huntington Bright. Jones Very. CP-VeryJ

I slapped him a third time. Nude Pictures. Yusef Komunyakaa. CP-KomuY

I sleep a lot and read St. Thomas Aquinas. Czeslaw Milosz. CP-MiloC; CP-MiloCN

I sleep, I sleep. Sleeping Beauty. Olga Broumas. SP-BrouO

I sleep. If I dream, I do not know on waking. Fernando Pessoa. SP-PessF, *tr. by* Susan M. Brown *and* Edwin Honig

I sleep in my girl's bed all day long. Morning of the Dying Gigolo, The. Alan Dugan. CP-DugaA

I sleep so that in the silence. David Ignatow. SP-IgnaD

I sleep so you will be alive. Dream of Mourning, The. Louise Glück. SP-GlucL

I slept a few minutes ago. In the Cold House. James Wright. CP-WrigJ

I slept across the front of the clock. Watcher's Regret, A. Thomas Hardy. CP-HardT

I slept last night. December 2nd. Anne Sexton. SP-SextA *Fr.* Eighteen Days without You.

I slept, when Venus enter'd: to my bed. By Moschus. Moschus. CP-CowpW, *tr. by* William Cowper

I slept with Buddha—dog-eyes. Backgammon. Olga Broumas. SP-BrouO

I slide my face along to the mirror. Looking-glass. Denise Levertov. SP-LeveDP

I slumbered with your poems on my breast. To E.T. Robert Frost. CP-FrosR

I smell a smell of death. July, 1964. Donald Davie. CP-DaviDC

I smell upon this twisted. Of Mothers. A. K. Ramanujan. CP-RamaA

I smoke a cigarette. Support for My Breathing. Yehuda Amichai. SP-AmicYL, *tr. by* Benjamin Harshav *and* Barbara Harshav

I Smoke My Pipe. James Whitcomb Riley. CP-RileJ

I snap the book shut. February. Alternate sky. It's Turtles All the Way Down. Charles Wright. SP-WrigCN

I snuggle down under the electric blanket. Christmas Morning. Howard Nemerov. CP-NemeH

I so admired you then. Ending. Alice Walker. CP-WalkA

I so loved once, when Death came by I hid. Rival, The. James Whitcomb Riley. CP-RileJ

I sold you playthings, very little more. Letter to an Old Love. Tennessee Williams. CP-WillT

I sometimes drop it, for a Quick. Emily Dickinson. CP-DickE

I sometimes fear that I shall never view. John Updike. *See* I sometimes think that I shall never view

I sometimes fear the younger generation will be deprived. Hoeing. John Updike. CP-UpdiJ

I Sometimes Think. Thomas Hardy. CP-HardT

I sometimes think of those pale, perfect faces. One Remains, The. Wilfred Owen. CP-OwenW

I sometimes think that I shall never view. Déjà, Indeed. John Updike. CP-UpdiJ

I sometimes write about the 30's because. John Dillinger Marches On. Charles Bukowski. SP-BukC3

I soothed and pitied thee: and for thy lips. Farewell, A. Niccolò Tommaseo. CW-RossD, *tr. by* Dante Gabriel Rossetti

I sought a theme and sought for it in vain. Circus Animals' Desertion, The. William Butler Yeats. CP-YeatW

I sought my home;—an earthly guide. Hymn: Home. Jones Very. CP-VeryJ

I sought of Thee my promised wife. Bride, The. Jones Very. CP-VeryJ

I sought the flowers, but o'er them lay. Song: "I sought the flowers, but o'er them lay." Jones Very. CP-VeryJ

I speak in the name of the black millions. New Song, A. Langston Hughes. CP-HughL; CP-HughL1

I speak in you the word that gave you birth. Charge, The. Jones Very. CP-VeryJ

I speak not, I trace not, I breathe not thy name. Stanzas for Music. Lord Byron. CP-Byron

I speak of love that comes to mind. Eastern Ballad, An. Allen Ginsberg. CP-

GinsA

I speak this poem now with grave and level voice. Immortal Autumn. Archibald MacLeish. CP-MacLA

I speak to the unbeautiful of this bird. Peacock, The. James Merrill. SP-MerrJ

I speak to you as a friend speaks. Conversations in Crisis. Audre Lorde. SP-LordA

I speak to you, my son. Farewell: "I speak to you, my son." Czeslaw Milosz. CP-MiloC; CP-MiloCN, tr. by Renata Gorczynski and Robert Hass

I speak two languages. I've learnt one of them in a trance, for no reason at all. Bi-lingual. Andrei Codrescu. SP-CodrA

I spent a night turning in bed. Whip, The. Robert Creeley. CP-CreeR

I spent last night in the nursery of a house in Pennsylvania. Ontario. Paul Muldoon. CP-MuldP

I spent my money. Lorine Niedecker. CP-NiedL

I spent the day. Zone. A. R. Ammons. CP-AmmoA

I spent the night after my mother died. Autumn 1980. Marilyn Hacker. SP-HackM

I spent with her. Bearing Mercy. A. R. Ammons. CP-AmmoA

I spent years, on and off, in academe. Possible, The. Raymond Carver. CP-CarvR

I spoke to thee. E. E. Cummings. CP-CummE

I s'pose it takes a feller 'at's be'n. Rabbit. James Whitcomb Riley. CP-RileJ

I spot the hills. Theme in Yellow. Carl Sandburg. CP-SandC

I sprang to the stirrup, and Joris, and he. How They Brought the Good News from Ghent to Aix. Robert Browning. CP-BroR1; SP-BroR

I spread a scanty board too late. Greeting. John Greenleaf Whittier. CP-WhitJ

I spread my gorgeous sail. Ralph Waldo Emerson. CP-EmerR

I spring joy out of my rib cage. Incidence of Flight. Richard Eberhart. CP-EberR

I spur my horse past ruins. Han-shan. CP-ColdM, tr. by Red Pine

I Spy, or, The Depravity of Privacy. Ogden Nash. CP-NashO

I squeezed up the last stair to the room in the roof. Unfinished Poem. Philip Larkin. CP-LarkP

I stalked a cougar once in a lost box-canyon. Cougar, The. Raymond Carver. CP-CarvR

I stand above the city's rush and din. From the Porch at Runnymede. Paul Laurence Dunbar. CP-DunbP

I stand alone, nor tho' my Heart should break. Loss. Samuel Taylor Coleridge. CP-ColeS

I stand and listen, head bowed. Self-Employed. David Ignatow. SP-IgnaD

I stand and watch for minutes by the pond. This, That, & the Other. Howard Nemerov. CP-NemeH

I stand as on some mighty eagle's beak. From Montauk Point. Walt Whitman. CP-WhitW

I stand at the front of the chariot. Chariot, The. Philip Whalen. SP-WhalP

I stand before the sea. Consecrating Mother, The. Anne Sexton. CP-SextA; SP-SextA

I stand beside the window here. Old Story, The. Paul Laurence Dunbar. CP-DunbP

I stand by the river where both of us stood. That Day. Elizabeth Barrett Browning. CP-BroEB

I stand here in the sight of everyone a man full of sense. Pretty Redhead, The. Guillaume Apollinaire. CP-WrigJ

I stand I fall. Does No Love Last? Stevie Smith. CP-SmitS

I stand in the ring. Red Shoes, The. Anne Sexton. CP-SextA

I stand most humbly. Wisdom. Langston Hughes. CP-HughL; CP-HughL2

I stand near Soberanes Creek, on the knoll over the sea, west of the road. I. Theory of Truth. Robinson Jeffers. CP-JefR2

I stand on slenderness all fresh and fair. Cut Flower, A. Karl Shapiro. SP-ShapK

I stand on the first step under the torn mouths of hours. Patience Is When You Stop Waiting. C. K. Williams. CP-WillC

I stand on the ledge where rock runs into the river. Wreck of the Thresher, The (Lost at Sea, April 10, 1963). William Meredith. SP-MereW

I stand on the mark beside the shore. Runaway Slave at Pilgrim's Point, The. Elizabeth Barrett Browning. CP-BroEB

I stand up, and this one of me. Jelaluddín Rumi. SP-Rumi, tr. by Coleman Barks

I stand upon a hill and see. Map of the City, A. Thom Gunn. CP-GunnT

I stand upon the hills to-night. Night-Song. Wallace Stevens. CP-StevWP

I stand with standing stones. All the Earth, All the Air. Theodore Roethke. CP-RoetT

I stare at the day as though I had suckled it. First Winter. Pablo Neruda. SP-NeruP

I stare at the stars. Nocturne: "I stare at the stars." Federico García Lorca. CP-GarcF, tr. by Jerome Rothenberg Fr. Seaside Prints.

I start out for a walk at last after weeks at the desk. After Long Busyness. Robert Bly. SP-BlyR

I started picking up the stones. Apologia pro Vita Sua. A. R. Ammons. CP-AmmoA

I stay; / But it isn't as if. Empty Threat, An. Robert Frost. CP-FrosR

I step from the door with a shiver. Study in Gray, A. Ambrose Bierce. SP-BierA

I step out onto the porch a few minutes. Dawn Walk and Prayer. Thomas Lux. SP-LuxT

I stepped from Plank to Plank. Emily Dickinson. CP-DickE

I stepped it, perch by perch. Land. Seamus Heaney. SP-HeanSO

I still balk at my preference for rhyme. Marilyn Hacker. SP-HackM Fr. Separations.

I still have some money. In Terror of Hospital Bills. James Wright. CP-WrigJ

I stirred wet sand and gathered myself. Sweeney Redivivus. Seamus Heaney. SP-HeanSO Fr. Sweeney Redivivus.

I stole forth dimly in the dripping pause. Moon Compasses. Robert Frost. CP-FrosR

I stole them from a Bee. Emily Dickinson. CP-DickE

I stomp about these rooms in an old overcoat. Sketch for an Aesthetic Project. Jay Wright. SP-WrigJ

I stood above the sown and generous sea. Morality of Poetry, The. James Wright. CP-WrigJ

I stood among my sheep. Skaters, The. Randall Jarrell. CP-JarrR

I stood and heard the steps of the city. Song (3). Wendell Berry. CP-BerrW

I stood at 6 a.m. on the wharf. Someone's Blood. Rita Dove. SP-DoveR

I stood at the gate of the cot. Change in Recurrence. George Meredith. CP-MerG1

I stood beside the grave of him who blazed. Churchill's Grave. Lord Byron. CP-Byron

I stood between them. Making Strange. Seamus Heaney. SP-HeanSO

I stood by the shore at the death of day. Wind and the Sea, The. Paul Laurence Dunbar. CP-DunbP

I stood by the unvintageable sea. Vita Nuova. Oscar Wilde. CP-WildO

I stood by weeping. Only Believe. Christina Georgina Rossetti. CP-RosC3

I stood in Luttrell's Glen. Ash saplings tossed. Lead. Thomas Kinsella. CP-KinsT

I stood in silence before a dark picture. Canvas. Adam Zagajewski. SP-ZagaA, tr. by Renata Gorczynski, Benjamin Ivry and C. K. Williams

I stood inside myself. Self-Portrait at Twenty. Gregory Orr. SP-OrrG

I stood knee-deep in the sea. Venus When Young Choosing Death. Stevie Smith. CP-SmitS

I stood musing in a black world. Stephen Crane. CP-CranS

I stood on a dark summit, among dark summits. Cock-Crows. Ted Hughes. SP-HughTN

I stood on Brocken's sovran [or sovereign] height, and saw. Lines Written in the Album at Elbingerode, in the Har[t]z Forest. Samuel Taylor Coleridge. CP-ColeS; MW-ColeS

I stood on the reed bank. Fishing for Eel Totems. Margaret Atwood. SP-AtwM1

I stood once more in that garden. Dream 1: the Bush Garden. Margaret Atwood. SP-AtwM1

I stood still and was a tree amid the wood. Tree, The. Ezra Pound. SP-PounE

I stood there on a bridge and watched the moonbeams varnish the smirking crocodiles. Responsible Romance, The. James Tate. SP-TateJ

I Stood Tip-Toe upon a Little Hill. John Keats. CP-KeatJ

I stood upon a heaven-cleaving turret. Fragment: "I stood upon a heaven-cleaving turret." Percy Bysshe Shelley. CP-ShelP

I stood upon a high place. Stephen Crane. CP-CranS

I stood upon a highway. Stephen Crane. CP-CranS

I stood upon a hill. The setting sun. Vision of Doom, A. Ambrose Bierce. SP-BierA

I stood where Love in brimming armfuls bore. Love's Baubles. Dante Gabriel Rossetti. CW-RossD Fr. House of Life, The.

I stood within the City disinterred. Ode to Naples. Percy Bysshe Shelley. CP-ShelP

I stop my car at the signal. Beautiful Young Girl Walking Past the Graveyard—, The. Charles Bukowski. SP-BukC1

I stop on. Woodsroad, The. A. R. Ammons. CP-AmmoA

I stopped the car. Blueflags. William Carlos Williams. CP-WilW1

I stopped to pick up the bagel. Bagel, The. David Ignatow. SP-IgnaD

I straightened my back from turmut-hoeing. Turmut-Hoeing. Ivor Gurney. SP-GurnI

I strayed, all alone, where the Autumn. Rose in October, A. James Whitcomb Riley. CP-RileJ

I strode along my beaches like a sea. Wallace Stevens. CP-StevWP

I strolled across. Waking, The. Theodore Roethke. CP-RoetT

I Struck a Diminished Seventh. A. R. Ammons. CP-AmmoA

I struck the board, and cried [or cry'd], No more. Collar, The. George Herbert. CP-HerbG

I studied it and it taught me nothing. Wisdom. Thomas Merton. CP-MertT

I study out a dark similitude. Swan, The. Theodore Roethke. CP-RoetT

I study the lives on a leaf: the little. Minimal, The. Theodore Roethke. CP-RoetT

I Suddenly Became Conscious That This Thing Was Looking at Me Intently. Kenneth Patchen. CP-PatcK

I sued the News—yet feared—the News. Emily Dickinson. CP-DickE

I suffer from ire, it's electric. Fanny Howe. SP-HoweF Fr. O'Clock.

I suffer fruitless anguish day by day. Vicissitudes Experienced in the Christian Life, The. Jeanne Marie Bouvier de la Motte Guyon. CP-CowpW, *tr. by* William Cowper

I suffer racking pain all day, and desire death so. For Mercy of Death. Ivor Gurney. SP-GurnI

I suffered bitter longings in the tranquil night. Venus. "Rubén Dario." SP-DariR, *tr. by* Alberto Acereda *and* Will Derusha

I suggest that this day be made holy. Kenneth Patchen. CP-PatcK

I summon to the winding ancient stair. Dialogue of Self and Soul, A. William Butler Yeats. CP-YeatW

I summoned Christopher Columbus. Navigator. Charles Simic. SP-SimiC

I suppose France this morning is as white as here. Behind the Line. Ivor Gurney. SP-GurnI

I suppose it's raining in some Spanish town. Weather Report. Charles Bukowski. SP-BukC1

I suppose like any other boy. Bee, The. Charles Bukowski. SP-BukC1

I suppose tarts are called tarts because they're tart. Tarts. D. H. Lawrence. CP-LawrD

I suppose that plumbers' children know more about plumbing than. There's Nothing Like Instinct, Fortunately. Ogden Nash. CP-NashO

I suppose that we were shocked. Fourth Grade, The. Thomas Lux. SP-LuxT

I suppose the time will come. Emily Dickinson. CP-DickE

I suppose there is nothing. Easter Greeting. Lorine Niedecker. CP-NiedL

I suppose you never heard of Ben's first meeting with Shady Rovers. Ben's Last Fight. Thomas Merton. CP-MertT

I swam alone far away. Yehuda Amichai. SP-AmicYL *Fr.* Poems on the Shore of Caesarea.

I swayed upon the gaudy stern. His Dream. William Butler Yeats. CP-YeatW

I swear affective life is water. Well. Heather McHugh. SP-McHuH

I swear to the Lord. Black Man Speaks, The. Langston Hughes. CP-HughL; CP-HughL2

I swept underneath and got him. Dagwood and Blondie. Charles Bukowski. SP-BukC3

I swung a switchman's lantern. Playthings. Yusef Komunyakaa. CP-KomuY

I, Sylvia, tell you, my piglets. Her Delight. Denise Levertov. SP-LeveDL

I Take a Certain Pride. James Laughlin. CP-LaugJ

I take a jewel from a junk-shop tray. Nothing. James Fenton. SP-FentJ

I take advantage of breakfast time. Soda Fountains. Nicanor Parra. CP-MertT

I take as my theme "The Independent Woman" Two. Carolyn Kizer. CP-KizeC *Fr.* Pro Femina.

I Take Back All My Kisses. James Tate. SP-TateJ

I take it back. Corrigenda. Yusef Komunyakaa. CP-KomuY

I take my bike. Oregon Landscape with Lost Lover. Olga Broumas. SP-BrouO

I take my dreams. Dreamer. Langston Hughes. CP-HughL; CP-HughL1

I take no virtue of this as I finger the hand gun. Suicide Note. Richard Eberhart. CP-EberR

I take the road that bears leaves in the mountains. Dream Again, The. W. S. Merwin. SP-MerwW

I take the taxi to Newport and study the wrinkles in the. Very. Charles Bukowski. SP-BukC2

I take your hand. I want to touch your eyes. Blind Girl. Jane Cooper. CP-CoopJ

I tarry in days shaped like the high staired street. Birthday Memorial to Seventh Street, A. Audre Lorde. SP-LordA

I Taste a Liquor Never Brewed. Emily Dickinson. CP-DickE

I teach in a high school. Wrong Kind of Insurance, The. John Ashbery. SP-AshbJ

I tell my love in rhyme. Song: "I tell my love in rhyme." Wendell Berry. CP-BerrW

I tell my secret? No indeed, not I. Winter: My Secret. Christina Georgina Rossetti. CP-RosC1

I tell the birds you can stop now. Alba. James Laughlin. CP-LaugJ

I tell the maple it's unwise—though. Lonely Splendor. A. R. Ammons. CP-AmmoA

I tell thee, Dick, where I have been. Ballad[e] [upon a Wedding], A. Sir John Suckling. CP-SuckJ

I tell thee, fellow, whoe'er thou be. Sir John Suckling's Answer. Sir John Suckling. CP-SuckJ

I tell them where the wind comes from. People with Proud Chins. Carl Sandburg. CP-SandC

I tell this tale, which is strictly true. Truthful Song, The. Rudyard Kipling. CP-KiplR

I tell you, Chickadee. S M. Alice Walker. CP-WalkA

I Tell You For Several Years of My Madness I Heard the Voice of Lilith Singing in the Trees of Chicago. Hayden Carruth. CP-CarHS

I tell you, hopeless grief is passionless. Grief. Elizabeth Barrett Browning. CP-BroEB

I tell you that I see her still. I Only Am Escaped Alone to Tell Thee. Howard Nemerov. CP-NemeH

I tell you what I'd ruther do. My Ruthers. James Whitcomb Riley. CP-RileJ

I tend my flowers for thee. Emily Dickinson. CP-DickE

I tend to suppose the part I know least. Cumberland. Donald Davie. CP-DaviDC

I test my bath before I sit. Samson Agonistes. Ogden Nash. CP-NashO

I tetter I dangle I jingle. Composition. Philip Whalen. SP-WhalP

I thank God Mother Cabrini's. Cycle for Mother Cabrini, A. John Logan. CP-LogaJ

I thank thee, Father, that the night is near. Night. Jones Very. CP-VeryJ

I thank thee, O Lord, for the stones in the street. Thank-You. G. K. Chesterton. CP-ChesG

I Thank You God. E. E. Cummings. CP-CummE; SP-CummE

I thank You God for most this amazing. I Thank You God. E. E. Cummings. CP-CummE; SP-CummE

I that have been a lover, and could show it. Sonnet to the Noble Lady, the Lady Mary Wroth, A. Ben Jonson. CP-JonsB

I that in heill [*or* health] wes [*or* was] and gladnes[s] [*or* gladiness]. Lament for the Makaris [*or* Makars *or* Makers]. William Dunbar. CP-DunbW

I, the alleged culprit, have a case. Swine Who's Eclipsed Me, The. Clarence Major. SP-MajoC

I, the city mouse, have traveled from a long ways away. Something Similar. John Ashbery. SP-AshbJ

I' the how-dumb-deid o' the cauld hairst nicht. Eemis-Stane, The. Hugh MacDiarmid. SP-MacDH

I, the man with the red scarf. Gipsy. D. H. Lawrence. CP-LawrD

I, the performer / in the tense arena, glittered. Speeches for Dr Frankenstein. Margaret Atwood. SP-AtwM1

I the poet Gary Snyder. Poem Left in Sourdough Mountain Lookout. Gary Snyder. CP-SnydG

I, the poet Robert Stock. First Last Will & Testament. Robert Stock. SP-StocR

I, the poet William Yeats. To Be Carved on a Stone at Thoor Ballylee. William Butler Yeats. CP-YeatW

I the roses love in the gardens of Adonis. Fernando Pessoa. SP-PessF, *tr. by* Susan M. Brown *and* Edwin Honig

I therefore pray thee, Renny dear. Ballad: "I therefore pray thee, Renny dear." Samuel Johnson. CP-JohnS

I Think. James Schuyler. CP-SchuJ

I think a lot about. Three-Penny Opera, The. Frank O'Hara. SP-OharF

I think a lot about you, Ed. To Ed Sissman. John Updike. CP-UpdiJ

I think about things that might have been and never were. Things That Might Have Been. Jorge Luis Borges. SP-BorgJ, *tr. by* Hoyt Rogers

I think about you now, Andromache. Swan, The. Charles Baudelaire. CP-BaudC, *tr. by* Walter Martin

I think about you / till you're naked. High on Sadness. Yusef Komunyakaa. CP-KomuY

I think all this is somewhere in myself. Room, The. W. S. Merwin. SP-MerwW

I think an impulse stronger than my mind. Mood. Countee Cullen. CP-CullC

I think and think, and in my thoughts I feel. Petrarch. CP-Petra, *tr. by* J. G. Nichols

I think and think; yet still I fail. Veil, The. Walter De la Mare. CP-DeLaW

I think awhile of Love, and while I think. Friendship ("I think awhile of Love, and while I think"). Henry David Thoreau. CP-ThorH

I think back on your smile, and for me it's a clear pool. Eugenio Montale. CP-MontE, *tr. by* Jonathan Galassi

I think continually of the differences. Sonnet: "I think continually of the differences." Hayden Carruth. CP-CarHS *Fr.* Sonnets.

I Think Continually of Those Who Were Truly Great. Stephen Spender. CP-SpenS

(Truly Great, The.) CP-SpenS

I think I can offer this / simple remedy for a part. Modest Proposal, A. James Laughlin. CP-LaugJ

I think I grow tensions. Flower, The. Robert Creeley. CP-CreeR

I think I have never been so exalted. Aux Imagistes. William Carlos Williams. CP-WilW1

I think I hear beyond the walls. Window in the Slums, A. Wallace Stevens. CP-StevWP

I think I learned much about writing when. Hey, Ezra, Listen to This. Charles Bukowski. SP-BukC3

I think I must have lived. Fox, The. Philip Levine. SP-LeviP

I think I should have loved you presently. Edna St. Vincent Millay. CP-MillE

I think I was cold in the womb. Forbears, The. W. S. Merwin. SP-MerwW

I think I was enchanted. Emily Dickinson. CP-DickE

I think I will learn some beautiful language, useless for commercial. Intention to Escape from Him. Edna St. Vincent Millay. CP-MillE

I think, in connection with this weeping elm. Camperdown Elm, The. Marianne Craig Moore. CP-MoorM

I think, indeed know well, some crushing sin. Michelangelo Buonarroti. CP-Miche, *tr. by* John Frederick Nims

I think it better that in times like these. On Being Asked for a War Poem. William Butler Yeats. CP-YeatW

I think it may be, so. Michelangelo Buonarroti. CP-Miche, *tr. by* John Frederick

Nims

I think it sad to have a friend. Emily Dickinson. SP-DickE

I think just how my shape will rise. Emily Dickinson. CP-DickE

I think most people are relieved the first time they actually know someone who goes crazy. Cave, The. C. K. Williams. CP-WillC; SP-WillC

I think my days are numbered. Numbered. Langston Hughes. CP-HughL; CP-HughL3

I think my grandfather knew. Grandfather's Railroad. John Logan. CP-LogaJ

I think, no matter where you stray. But Not Forgotten. Dorothy Parker. CP-ParkD

I think now how we biked toward the sand. Way a Child Might Believe, The. Olga Broumas. SP-BrouO

I think now it is better to love no one. Here Are My Black Clothes. Louise Glück. SP-GlucL

I think of a coffin's quiet. Audre Lorde. *See* I always think of a coffin's quiet

I think of a man on foot. Thomas Bewick. Thom Gunn. CP-GunnT

I think of a tiger. The fading light [*or* half-light] enhances. Other Tiger, The. Jorge Luis Borges. SP-BorgJ, *tr. by* Alastair Reid

I think of all the toughs through history. Lines for a Book. Thom Gunn. CP-GunnT

I think of Amundsen, enormously bit. On the Eyes of an SS Officer. Richard Wilbur. CP-WilbR

I think of an early Christian. Concerto. Eleanor Wilner. SP-WilnE

I think of automobiles parked in a. When I Think of Myself Dead. Charles Bukowski. SP-DukC1

I think of Balzac in his nightcap after. Balzac. Raymond Carver. CP-CarvR

I think of her. Nelly Myers. A. R. Ammons. CP-AmmoA

I think of Issa, a man of few words. Night Journal. Charles Wright. SP-WrigC

I think of that old woman in the song. Ghost, a Real Ghost, A. Randall Jarrell. CP-JarrR

I think of the Celts as rather a whining lady. Celts, The. Stevie Smith. CP-SmitS

I think of the saints I have known, and lift up mine eyes. So Great a Cloud of Witnesses. Christina Georgina Rossetti. CP-RosC2

I think of the slope where the rabbits fed. Background and the Figure, The. Thomas Hardy. CP-HardT

I think of the stark and puritanical sky. Poem of Quantity. Jorge Luis Borges. SP-BorgJ, *tr. by* Alastair Reid

I think of us lying asleep. Thief, The. Wendell Berry. CP-BerrW

I think of you. Now That I Am in Madrid and Can Think. Frank O'Hara. SP-OharF

I think of you as a great king, cold and austere. To Death. Robinson Jeffers. CP-JefR3

I THINK OF YOU as of rebellion's self. New Poet, The. Tennessee Williams. CP-WillT

I think of your blind odor. In a Town for Which I Know No Name. James Tate. SP-TateJ

I think that I shall never know. Fairly Sad Tale, A. Dorothy Parker. CP-ParkD

I think that I shall never see. Song of the Open Road. Ogden Nash. CP-NashO

I think that look of Christ might seem to say. Meaning of the Look, The. Elizabeth Barrett Browning. CP-BroEB

I think that someone will remember us in another time. Yard Work. Charles Wright. SP-WrigCN

I think that the Root of the Wind is Water. Emily Dickinson. CP-DickE

I think that though the clouds be dark. After While. Paul Laurence Dunbar. CP-DunbP

I think that we should never freeze / Such lively assets as our cheese. Chee$e. Thomas Merton. CP-MertT

I think that you could only pity me. Balto; The Lead Dog of the Team that Brough Antitoxin to Nome. Dorothy Parker. CP-ParkD

I think the dead are tender. Shall we kiss? She. Theodore Roethke. CP-RoetT

I think the deaths of domestic animals. Animals. Miller Williams. CP-WillM

I think the deed was richer than the dying. Last Full Measure of Devotion, The. Kenneth Patchen. CP-PatcK

I think the Hemlock likes to stand. Emily Dickinson. CP-DickE

I think the loathed minutes one by one. Moments. Ivor Gurney. SP-GurnI

I think the longest Hour of all. Emily Dickinson. CP-DickE

I think the strange, the crazed, the queer. Tennessee Williams. CP-WillT

I think these empty pews are not deserted. St. Philip's Church in Antigua. Archibald MacLeish. CP-MacLA

I think these houses are the ghosts. Old Street. Kenneth Rexroth. CP-RexrK

I think this was a dream, and yet we saw. Swans, The. May Sarton. SP-SartM

I think, though I don't believe it, you were my airhole. To Daddy. Robert Lowell. SP-LoweR

I think to compose a sonnet. Apology, The. Robert Creeley. CP-CreeR

I think to Live—may be a Bliss. Emily Dickinson. CP-DickE

I think we are too ready with complaint. Cheerfulness Taught by Reason. Elizabeth Barrett Browning. CP-BroEB

I think when Judas' mother heard. Judas Iscariot. Countee Cullen. CP-CullC

I think you are in love with more. Brother of the Unknown Ancient Man. James

Tate. SP-TateJ

"I think you like." E. E. Cummings. CP-CummE

I thocht lang quhill sum lord come hame. William Dunbar. CP-DunbW

I thought a germ of Consciousness. Aerolite, The. Thomas Hardy. CP-HardT

I thought about his death for so many hours. Wires of the Night, The. Billy Collins. SP-CollB

I thought: all this is only preparation. Mistake, A. Czeslaw Milosz. CP-MiloC; CP-MiloCN, *tr. by* Renata Gorczynski *and* Robert Hass

I thought (and before it was too late). Song on the Dread of a Chill Spring. John Logan. CP-LogaJ

I thought and thought of thy crass clanging town. From Her in the Country. Thomas Hardy. CP-HardT

I thought as I lay on my bed one night, I am only a passing cloud. Passing Cloud, The. Stevie Smith. CP-SmitS

I thought, as I wiped my eyes on the corner of my apron. Ancient Gesture, An. Edna St. Vincent Millay. CP-MillE

I thought because I had looked into your eyes. Star, The. Kathleen Jessie Raine. SP-RainK

I thought he was dumb. Tortoise Shout. D. H. Lawrence. CP-LawrD

I thought he was torturing another patient. Suffering Ophthalmologist, The. Alan Dugan. CP-DugaA

I thought I could leave my habitation for the summer. Stealth and Subtleties of Growth. Richard Eberhart. CP-EberR

I thought I knew something. Epithalamion for Tyler. James Tate. SP-TateJ

I thought I was going to the poets, but I am going to the. Flying to Hanoi. Muriel Rukeyser. CP-RukeM

I thought I was so tough. Tamer and Hawk. Thom Gunn. CP-GunnT

I thought I would / sit down at one of those park department tables. Having Arrived by Bike at Battery Park. Grace Paley. CP-PalGC

I thought I'd say a thing to please myself. Damn You, Jim D., You Woke Me Up. John Berryman. CP-BerrJ

I thought it was an empty doorway. Woman from the River. W. S. Merwin. SP-MerwW

I Thought It Was Tangiers I Wanted. Langston Hughes. CP-HughL; CP-HughL1

I thought it would last my time. Going, Going. Philip Larkin. CP-LarkP

I Thought, My Heart. Thomas Hardy. CP-HardT

I thought my wings were fledged for such a flight. Petrarch. CP-Petra, *tr. by* J. G. Nichols

I thought no more was needed. Song, A: "I thought no more was needed." William Butler Yeats. CP-YeatW

I thought of a house where the stones seemed suddenly changed. Lo! A Child Is Born. Hugh MacDiarmid. SP-MacDH

I thought of Alun Lewis. Dylan Thomas, and Now Matthew Mead—as He Himself, "To Edward Thomas." Charles Olson. CP-OlsoC

I thought of Christopher Columbus. Navigator. Charles Simic. SP-SimiCE

I thought of happiness, how it is woven. Work of Happiness, The. May Sarton. SP-SartM

I thought of her as the wishing tree that died. Wishing Tree, The. Seamus Heaney. SP-HeanSO

I thought of killing myself because I am only a bricklayer and you a. Bricklayer Love. Carl Sandburg. CP-SandC

I thought of myself as happily sitting someplace quietly. War Poem for Diane di Prima. Philip Whalen. SP-WhalP

I thought of offering you apothegms. Put Off the Wedding Five Times and Nobody Comes to It. Carl Sandburg. CP-SandC

I thought of Thee, my partner and my guide. After-Thought. William Wordsworth. CP-WorW2 *Fr.* River Duddon [A Series of Sonnets], The.

I thought of you. Lament: "I thought of you." Gregory Orr. SP-OrrG

I thought of you tonight, *a leanbh*, lying there in your long barrow. Incantata. Paul Muldoon. CP-MuldP

I thought of your beauty, and this arrow. Arrow, The. William Butler Yeats. CP-YeatW

I thought once, that your hillshapes swam and swayed. Van Gogh. Charles Tomlinson. CP-TomlC

I thought she was a liberated woman. Pretrial Hearing. Alan Dugan. CP-DugaA

I thought Silver must have snaked logs. Silver. A. R. Ammons. CP-AmmoA

I thought that being a Poem one's self. Emily Dickinson. SP-DickE

I thought that I would like to see. Next! Ogden Nash. CP-NashO

I thought that if I were broken enough. Revelation, The. Robert Creeley. CP-CreeR

I Thought That Knowledge Alone Would Suffice. Walt Whitman. CP-WhitW

I thought that nature was enough. Emily Dickinson. CP-DickE

I thought that the north. In April. Charles Tomlinson. CP-TomlC

I thought that you would have written: my birthday came and went. Complaint, A. Gerard Manley Hopkins. CP-HopkG

I thought the deacon liked me, yit. Sister Jones's Confession. James Whitcomb Riley. CP-RileJ

I thought the earth / remembered me, she. Sleeping in the Forest. Mary Oliver. SP-OlivM

I thought the Train would never come. Emily Dickinson. CP-DickE

I thought they'd be strangers aroun' me. Curate's Kindness, The. Thomas Hardy. CP-HardT

I thought to be for ever separate. Sonnet: He rebukes Cino for Fickleness. Dante Alighieri. CW-RossD, *tr.* by Dante Gabriel Rossetti

I thought to hear him speak. Nossis. "H. D." CP-DoolH

I thought to shun the Loneliness. Emily Dickinson. SP-DickE

I thought you a fire. At Moonrise and Onwards. Thomas Hardy. CP-HardT

I thought your approbation Fame. Emily Dickinson. SP-DickE

I thought your face as lovely. Demonstration. Kenneth Patchen. CP-PatcK

"I thought your search was over,"—"So I thought." Discovery, A. Christina Georgina Rossetti. CP-RosC3

I threat'ned [*or* threatened] to observe the strict decree. Holdfast, The. George Herbert. CP-HerbG

I threw a snowball across the backyard. Listen. Miller Williams. CP-WillM

I threw a stick. The dog. Between. John Ciardi. CP-CiarJ

I threw a stone into a cavern deep. Mind the Greatest Mystery, The. Jones Very. CP-VeryJ

I thrust my heart, in danger of decay. Heart's Limbo. Carolyn Kizer. CP-KizeC

I thumb pages, thinking onion. What Counts. Yusef Komunyakaa. CP-KomuY

I tie a second necktie over the first. Double Vision. Robert Lowell. SP-LoweR

I tie my Hat—I crease my Shawl. Emily Dickinson. CP-DickE

I tiptoed into her sleep. Mirru. Kenneth Patchen. CP-PatcK

I to my garden went. Ralph Waldo Emerson. CP-EmerR

I to my perils. A. E. Housman. CP-HousA

I toiled on, but thou. Christina Georgina Rossetti. CP-RosC3

I told a lie once in a verse. I said. To Bhain Campbell. John Berryman. CP-BerrJ

I told her that my mother would make. Kibali-Ituri. Kenneth Patchen. CP-PatcK

I told her then in bed. All the Casualties. Charles Bukowski. SP-BukC3

I told her when I left one day. In the Night She Came. Thomas Hardy. CP-HardT

I told him about the galleries upstairs. Dangerous Painters, The. Tennessee Williams. CP-WillT

I told him: The time has come, I must be gone. Animal Trainer, The. John Berryman. CP-BerrJ

I told my brothers I heard. Songs for My Father. Yusef Komunyakaa. CP-KomuY

I told my love I told my love. William Blake. CP-BlakW

"I Told Myself": Bobbie Spontaneously. Philip Whalen. SP-WhalP

I told myself that I wasn't going to get high today. "I Told Myself": Bobbie Spontaneously. Philip Whalen. SP-WhalP

I Told You It Would Be So—And You Didn't Believe. Yehuda Amichai. SP-AmicYL, *tr.* by Benjamin Harshav *and* Barbara Harshav

I too a sister had! too cruel Death! On Seeing a Youth Affectionately Welcomed by a Sister. Samuel Taylor Coleridge. CP-ColeS

I, too. born on the other side, alongside. Reverse. Andrei Codrescu. SP-CodrA

I, too, dislike it. / Reading it, however, with a perfect contempt for it, one discovers in. Marianne Craig Moore. *See* I, too, dislike it: there are things that are important beyond all this fiddle

I, too, dislike it: there are things that are important beyond all this fiddle. Poetry: "I, too, dislike it: there are things that are important beyond all this fiddle." Marianne Craig Moore. CP-MoorM

I too have a garret of old playthings. Upstairs. Carl Sandburg. CP-SandC

I too have been drawn in. Adolescence. David Ignatow. SP-IgnaD

I, Too, Have Been to the Huntington. James Vincent Cunningham. CP-CunnJ

I too have dreamed of dark titanic roses. Sonnets in Summer Heat. G. K. Chesterton. CP-ChesG

I, too, have felt the fire of being burn. On Leonard Baskin's Etching *Benevolent Angel*. Helen Pinkerton. CP-PinkH

I too have had my dreams: ay, known indeed. Sen Artysty; or, The Artist's Dream. Oscar Wilde. CP-WildO

I too have taken the god into my mouth. Eating Snake. Margaret Atwood. SP-AtwM2

I, too, have trailed my father's spirit. Immrama. Paul Muldoon. CP-MuldP

I too, like all the apes in the neighborhood. Readiness, The. Dan Pagis. SP-PagiL, *tr.* by Stephen Mitchell

I too on Corpus Christi Day. Garland on the Wrist, A. Jaroslav Seifert. SP-SeifJ, *tr.* by Ewald Osers

I, too, once hoped to have a hoopoe. Pooem. John Updike. CP-UpdiJ

I, too, once lived in a city whose cornices used to court. In Italy. Joseph Brodsky. CP-BrodJ

I, too, saw God through mud. Apologia Pro Poemate Meo. Wilfred Owen. CP-OwenW

I, too, sing America. Langston Hughes. CP-HughL

I too was born out of a lion's mouth. Let Heroes Account to Love. Alan Dugan. CP-DugaA

I too will wait with thee returning spring. Tree, The ("I too will wait with thee returning spring"). Jones Very. CP-VeryJ

I took a shortcut through blood. Back in the World. Ai. SP-Ai

I took a tree for a guide—I mean. Tree. Charles Tomlinson. CP-TomlC

I took a walk on the railroad track. Walk, A. Raymond Carver. CP-CarvR

I took another day. Postponement of Self. Laura Riding Jackson. CP-RidiL

I took away three pictures. Sandhill People. Carl Sandburg. CP-SandC

I took her and I flattened her. Joys of Science, The. G. K. Chesterton. CP-ChesG

I took my cousin to Prettyboy Dam. Poems for My Cousin. Josephine Jacobsen. CP-JacoJ

I took my heart in my hand. Twice. Christina Georgina Rossetti. CP-RosC1

I took my life and threw it on the skip. Skip, The. James Fenton. SP-FentJ

I took my likely schizophrenia in hand. One More Time. A. R. Ammons. CP-AmmoA

I took my Power in my Hand. Emily Dickinson. CP-DickE

I took my two friends with me to find. Suflah Spring in the Judean Mountains. Yehuda Amichai. SP-AmicYL, *tr.* by Benjamin Harshav *and* Barbara Harshav

I took one Draught of Life. Emily Dickinson. CP-DickE

I took orders, made my trail. Fever. Yusef Komunyakaa. CP-KomuY

I took the test. Circles. Robert Creeley. SP-CreeR

I tore it open, by one end, & found. My Special Fate. John Berryman. CP-BerrJ

I tore thee—thou who looked so sweet. Torn Flower, The. Jones Very. CP-VeryJ

I tore your letter into strips. Torn Letter, The. Thomas Hardy. CP-HardT

I toss off my clothes. Lonesome Blues. Federico García Lorca. CP-GarcF, *tr.* by Jerome Rothenberg *Fr.* Blue River.

I touch you in the night, whose gift was you. Science of the Night, The. Stanley Kunitz. CP-KunSC

I towered far, and lo! I stood within. God-Forgotten. Thomas Hardy. CP-HardT

I traced a circle on the ground. Circle, The. Fernando Pessoa. SP-PessF

I traced the Circus whose grey stones incline. In the Old Theatre, Fiesole. Thomas Hardy. CP-HardT

I Travel as a Phantom Now. Thomas Hardy. CP-HardT

I travel on by barren farms. Wind's Prophecy, The. Thomas Hardy. CP-HardT

I travelled [*or* travel'd] thro' a land of men. Mental Traveller, The. William Blake. CP-BlakW

I travelled to where in her lifetime. They Would Not Come. Thomas Hardy. CP-HardT

I traversed a dominion. Mute Opinion. Thomas Hardy. CP-HardT

I tread the dark and my steps are silent. Brightness as a Poignant Light. David Ignatow. SP-IgnaD

I tried all night to sleep. Fragile! Charles Bukowski. SP-BukC2

I tried each thing, only some were immortal and free. As One Put Drunk into the Packet-Boat. John Ashbery. SP-AshbJ

I tried it standing up. End of a Short Affair, The. Charles Bukowski. SP-BukC1

I tried to help. Suffering catfish, I tried! Tanck's Song About Pride. Hayden Carruth. CP-CarHS *Fr.* Songs About What Comes Down: The Complete Works of Mr. Septic Tank.

I tried to put a bird in a cage. Fool's Song, The. William Carlos Williams. CP-WilW1

I tried to think a lonelier Thing. Emily Dickinson. CP-DickE

I tried to think of some way. Least Figure, The. Jelaluddin Rumi. SP-Rumi, *tr.* by Coleman Barks

I trod a foreign path, dears. Voice from the Tomb (2). Stevie Smith. CP-SmitS

I trust I am not a spoil sport, but there is one thing I deplore. Party Next Door, The. Ogden Nash. CP-NashO

I trust none of them. Only my existence. For a Sister. Adrienne Rich. SP-RicA2

I trust this sweet May Morning. Emily Dickinson. SP-DickE

I trust you may have the dearest summer. Emily Dickinson. SP-DickE

I try to hide in Proust. No-Good Blues. Yusef Komunyakaa. CP-KomuY

I try to take them where they want to go. Showing Late Symptoms She First Tries to Fix Herself in the Minds of Her Children. Miller Williams. CP-WillM

I turn myself into a sack. Travel[l]ing. Charles Simic. SP-SimiC

I turn myself into an acrobat to please them. I'm Not Lucky with Girls. James Laughlin. CP-LaugJ

I turn round. Lady's First Song, The. William Butler Yeats. CP-YeatW

I turned from side to side, from image to image, to put you down. Poem in Prose. Louise Bogan. CP-BogaL

I turned—heaven knows we women turn too much. Lady Geraldine's Hardship. Rudyard Kipling. CP-KiplR *Fr.* Muse among the Motors, The.

I turned in. WCW. A. R. Ammons. CP-AmmoA

I turned out the light to see the snow. Ernesto Cardenal. CP-MertT *Fr.* Gethsemani, KY.

I twined a net; I drove a stake; laid a glittering bait. Captive, The. Walter De la Mare. CP-DeLaW

I type at a window that faces the street. New Place, The. Charles Bukowski. SP-BukC2

I understand her well because I too practice love. Etymology. Olga Broumas. SP-BrouO

I understand myself. And Step. David Ignatow. SP-IgnaD

I understand / reading the modern philosophers. Uh, Philosophy. A. R. Ammons.

CP-AmmoA

I understand Xerxes' command to wield the whips. Massacre, The. Olga Broumas. SP-BrouO

I understand you're writing your autobiography. Threatening Letter. Carolyn Kizer. CP-KizeC

I unearthed / what seemed like the jawbone of an ass. Bone. Charles Tomlinson. CP-TomlC

I use the knife. Ralph Waldo Emerson. CP-EmerR

I used to be bothered by death. Death's Chicken, Named Amelia. Alan Dugan. CP-DugaA

I used to be good friends with God, but He. God. John Ciardi. CP-CiarJ

I used to be shy. Jelaluddin Rumi. SP-Rumi, *tr. by* Coleman Barks

I used to beg for roses in the garden of love. Narcissus 2. Alan Dugan. CP-DugaA

I used to enjoy the night-time. Untitled Poem: "I used to enjoy the night-time." Alan Dugan. CP-DugaA

I used to feel like fossil pollen. Life Story, A. Clarence Major. SP-MajoC

I used to get up, in the tent. Place of the Skull, The. James Dickey CP-DickJ

I used to hate to ride the Long Island Railroad trains. On the Long Island Railroad System. Alan Dugan. CP-DugaA

I used to have tricks, dodges, a whole sackful. Porcupine Meditation. Margaret Atwood. SP-AtwM2

I used to imagine him. Stanley Kunitz. Mary Oliver. SP-OlivM

I used to imagine we were a fine two-headed. Alive. Hayden Carruth. CP-CarHS

I used to know a breadwinner named Mr. Purefoy. There'll Always Be a War between the Sexes, or, A Woman Can Be Sometimes Pleased, but Never Satisfied. Ogden Nash. CP-NashO

I used to press tools in the Texas oil fields. Muriel Rukeyser. CP-RukeM

I used to see her in the door. Paul. James Wright. CP-WrigJ

I used to spend 3 days a week. Girls. Charles Bukowski. SP-BukC3

I used to stray far from the fountainhead. Petrarch. CP-Petra, *tr. by* J. G. Nichols

I used to take the back off. I'm Getting Back to Where I Was. Charles Bukowski. SP-BukC1

I used to take the blame, but now excuse. Petrarch. CP-Petra, *tr. by* J. G. Nichols

I used to think it could be solved this way. Hour of Grace, The. Yehuda Amichai. SP-AmicY, *tr. by* Chana Bloch

I used to think that life wouldn't always be wounded. Man Lives Here, A. Kenneth Patchen. CP-PatcK

I used to think that obstacles to love. During an Absence. Thom Gunn. CP-GunnT

I used to think that the animals. On a Desolation of the Animals at Night. Alan Dugan. CP-DugaA

I used to think, when the corn was blowing. Life Transcendent. Nicholas Vachel Lindsay. CP-LindV

I used to walk quickly. On Walking Slowly after an Accident. Stevie Smith. CP-SmitS

I used to want buyers for my words. No Flag. Jelaluddin Rumi. SP-Rumi, *tr. by* Coleman Barks

I used to watch it on the ledge. Crippling, The. Marge Piercy. SP-PierM

I used to wonder / About living and dying. Border Line. Langston Hughes. CP-HughL; CP-HughL2

I used to write in the café sometimes. Marsyas. James Merrill. SP-MerrJ

I usually live in seclusion. Han-shan. CP-ColdM, *tr. by* Red Pine

I view, in the flying time. Faces of Girls Looking at Themselves in the River. Pablo Antonio Cuadra. CP-MertT, *tr. by* Thomas Merton

I Visit Brooklyn with a Queen in Mind. Andrei Codrescu. SP-CodrA

I Visit / the Graves. Lorine Niedecker. CP-NiedL

I visited Père Lachaise to look for the remains of Apollinaire. At Apollinaire's Grave. Allen Ginsberg. CP-GinsA

I wade through wheat up to my belly. Shooting. Raymond Carver. CP-CarvR

I waded, deepening, into the dark water. River, The. Raymond Carver. CP-CarvR

I Wait. Ezra Pound. CP-PoEar

I wait and watch: before my eyes. Waiting, The. John Greenleaf Whittier. CP-WhitJ

I wait beside the fount. Wooden Mirror, The. John Logan. CP-LogaJ

I wait for the holiday crowd to clear the beach. Walking across the Atlantic. Billy Collins. SP-CollB

I Wait in the White Rain. Charles Bukowski. SP-BukC2

I wait ouside the Beacon Hotel. Doppelgängers. Yusef Komunyakaa. CP-KomuY

I Waited. Theodore Roethke. CP-RoetT

I waited at home all the while they were boating together. Two Wives, The. Thomas Hardy. CP-HardT

I waited long but now my joy is great. Husbandman, The. Jones Very. CP-VeryJ

I waited today for a freight train to pass. 'Boes. Carl Sandburg. CP-SandC

I waited too long. In a Boat Shed. Robert Creeley. CP-CreeR

I Wake and Feel the Fell of Dark, Not Day. Gerard Manley Hopkins. CP-HopkG

I wake and feel the fell of dark, not day. I Wake and Feel the Fell of Dark, Not Day. Gerard Manley Hopkins. CP-HopkG

I wake and find myself in the woods, far from the castle. Night Frogs. Robert Bly. SP-BlyR

I wake, but before I know it it is done. Aging. Randall Jarrell. CP-JarrR

I wake earlier, now that the birds have come. No Voyage. Mary Oliver. SP-OlivM

I wake from dreams and turning. A. E. Housman. CP-HousA

I wake in a dark flat. Afterlives. Derek Mahon. CP-MahoD

I wake in the early dawn and my hand has fallen asleep. Praises IV. Thomas McGrath. SP-McGrT

I wake in the night. Middle of the Way. Galway Kinnell. SP-KinnGN

I wake in the night with such uncertain gladness. Girl Takes Her Place Among the Mothers, The. Marya Alexandrovna Zaturenska. SP-ZatuM

I wake now to find myself this long alone. Sick. Robert Lowell. SP-LoweR

I wake, sweating, reach for your rosary and drop it. Ravine, The. Ai. SP-Ai

I wake to sleep, and take my waking slow. Waking, The. Theodore Roethke. CP-RoetT

I wake to sounds. Drawing from Life. Clarence Major. SP-MajoC

I wake to the sound of a soft, low patter. Night Rain. Countee Cullen. CP-CullC

I wake to the sound of horses' hooves clacking. Leaving My Daughter's House. Maxine W. Kumin. SP-KumiM

I wake up cold, I who. Man With Night Sweats, The. Thom Gunn. CP-GunnT

I waked, and sat out the watch, the night. Night, The. Charles Olson. CP-OlsoC

I waked at midmost in the night. Dream, A. Allen Ginsberg. CP-GinsA

I, wakeful for the skylark voice in men. To Cardinal Manning. George Meredith. CP-MerG1

I waken and / lean and look out. Stepping Backward. Hayden Carruth. CP-CarHS

I walk, alone and troubled, desert places. Petrarch. CP-Petra, *tr. by* J. G. Nichols

I walk along the length of a stone-and-gravel garden. Archipelago. Arthur Sze. SP-SzeA

I walk and I rest while the eyes of my dead. Choir, The. Olga Broumas. SP-BrouO

I walk around town with my baby. Distraction Fit, A. Philip Whalen. SP-WhalP

I walk before no man, a hawk in his fist. Verses Made in Swift's Sleep. Jonathan Swift. CP-SwifJ

I Walk before No Man (Composed While Asleep). Jonathan Swift. *See* Verses Made in Swift's Sleep

I walk [*or* walked] beside the prisoners to the road. Camp in the Prussian Forest, A. Randall Jarrell. CP-JarrR

I walk in nature still alone. Great Friend. Henry David Thoreau. CP-ThorH

I Walk in the Old Street. Louis Zukofsky. CP-ZukLS

I walk in the old street. I Walk in the Old Street. Louis Zukofsky. CP-ZukLS

I walk on my cliff above the Pacific Ocean and feel the tides. Robinson Jeffers. CP-JefR3

I walk on the cold mountain above the city. New Year, The. Kenneth Rexroth. CP-RexrK

I walk the floor, read, watch a cop-show, drink. Her Pet. Thom Gunn. CP-GunnT

I walk the path that. Tennessee Williams. CP-WillT

I walk the streets and though not meanly drest. Poor, The. Jones Very. CP-VeryJ

I walk those corridors by torchlight. Those Corridors. Czeslaw Milosz. CP-MiloC; CP-MiloCN, *tr. by* Robert Pinsky

I walk through the long schoolroom questioning. Among School Children. William Butler Yeats. CP-YeatW

I walk / Unwind with activity of legs. Ted Hughes. SP-HughTN *Fr.* Seven Dungeon Songs.

I walk uphill through the snow. Carrying Food Home in Winter. Margaret Atwood. SP-AtwM1

I walked a hangover like my death down. Letter to Donald Fall. Alan Dugan. CP-DugaA

I walked abroad in Easter Park. Conviction (ii). Stevie Smith. CP-SmitS

I walked abroad in [*or* on] a snowy day. Soft Snow. William Blake. CP-BlakW

I walked all over the zoo and the park. Stranger in Town. Langston Hughes. CP-HughL; CP-HughL2

I walked alone and thinking. Sinner's Rue. A. E. Housman. CP-HousA

I walked among the seven woods of Coole. William Butler Yeats. CP-YeatW

I walked among the streets of an old city and the streets were as lean as the. Streets Too Old. Carl Sandburg. CP-SandC

I walked away with your face. Providence. Yusef Komunyakaa. CP-KomuY

I walked de streets till. Out of Work. Langston Hughes. CP-HughL; CP-HughL2

I walked down alone Sunday after church. Pea Brush. Robert Frost. CP-FrosR

I walked / from Chicago to Big Bull Falls (Wausau). Lorine Niedecker. CP-NiedL

I walked in a desert. Stephen Crane. CP-CranS

I walked in loamy Wessex lanes, afar. Pity of It, The. Thomas Hardy. CP-HardT

I walked into a loge in the Teatro Melisso. Pound at Spoleto. Lawrence Ferlinghetti. SP-FerlL

I walked into the cocktail party. In Society. Allen Ginsberg. CP-GinsA; SP-GinsA

I walked on the banks of the tincan banana dock and sat down under the huge shade. Sunflower Sutra. Allen Ginsberg. CP-GinsA; SP-GinsA

I walked on the ocean beach. Ocean's Treasures. Jones Very. CP-VeryJ

I walked out, before. Che Di Lor Suona Su Nella Tua Vita. Louis Zukofsky. CP-ZukLS

I walked out on the lamp shadowed concrete at midnight May Day passing a dark'd barfront. Manhattan May Day Midnight. Allen Ginsberg. CP-GinsA; SP-GinsA

I Walked Out to the Graveyard to See the Dead. Richard Eberhart. CP-EberR

I walked outside & the bomb'd. Everybody's Fantasy. Allen Ginsberg. SP-GinsA Fr. Nagasaki Days.

I Walked over the Grave of Henry James. Richard Eberhart. CP-EberR

I Walked Past a House Where I Lived Once. Yehuda Amichai. SP-AmicY, tr. by Chana Bloch

I walked the boulevard. E. E. Cummings. CP-CummE

I walked the grove where rest the mortal forms. Walk in Harmony Grove, A. Jones Very. CP-VeryJ

I walked the streets of a market town. Son's Portrait, The. Thomas Hardy. CP-HardT

I walked the unwalked garden of rose-beds. Fable of the Rhododendron Stealers. Sylvia Plath. CP-PlatS

I Walked Through the Medieval Town. Adam Zagajewski. SP-ZagaA, tr. by Clare Cavanagh

I walked to the edge of you, looked over. History Is a Throne and a Gate. Kenneth Patchen. CP-PatcK

I walked upon a vacant shore. —And Return. Dorothy Parker. CP-ParkD

I walked, when love was gone. Breath of Air, A. James Wright. CP-WrigJ

I wallow in the wineshops and brothels. In the Wineshops. Constantine P. Cavafy. CP-CavaC, tr. by Theoharis Constantine Theoharis

I wander all night in my vision. Sleepers, The. Walt Whitman. CP-WhitW

I wander by the edge. He Hears the Cry of the Sedge. William Butler Yeats. CP-YeatW

I wander down on Clinton street south of Polk. Clinton South of Polk. Carl Sandburg. CP-SandC

I wander through [or thro'] each chartered [or charter'd] street. London. William Blake. CP-BlakW Fr. Songs of Experience.

I Wandered [or Wander'd] Lonely as a Cloud. William Wordsworth. CP-WorW1; MW-WorW

I wandered lonely where the pinetrees made. Trailing Arbutus, The. John Greenleaf Whittier. CP-WhitJ

I wandered through Scoglietto's far retreat. Sonnet Written in Holy Week at Genoa. Oscar Wilde. CP-WildO

I wandered to a crude coast. Discovery, The. Thomas Hardy. CP-HardT

I wandered to the surfy marge. Sea Knell. John Updike. CP-UpdiJ

I want a bedroom near the sky, an astrologer's cave. Landscape (After Baudelaire). John Ashbery. SP-AshbJ

I Want a Drink of Water, but Not from the Thermos. Ogden Nash. CP-NashO

I want a squirrel-foil for my martin pole. Imagined Land, The. A. R. Ammons. CP-AmmoA

"I want," he says again, through his tears, in this unfamiliar voice, again, "I want, I want." Good Mother: Out. C. K. Williams. SP-WillC

I Want, I Want. Sylvia Plath. CP-PlatS

"I want"—it pleaded—All its life. Emily Dickinson. CP-DickE

I want just one lesson, and it's yours. Fountain, The. Rainer Maria Rilke. CP-RilkFr, tr. by A. Poulin, Jr. Fr. Orchards.

I want, like a little boat, to be isolate. Laguna Dantesca. Charles Wright. SP-WrigC

I want mother's milk. Food. Anne Sexton. CP-SextA; SP-SextA

I want no easy light to lift my eyes. There's a Train Leaving Soon. Kenneth Patchen. CP-PatcK

I want no tricks in speaking of this man. Adolf Eichmann. Hayden Carruth. CP-CarHS

I want no wonder's cloud or church to wake me. Note for a Diary. Kenneth Patchen. CP-PatcK

I want nothing else, only a hand. Qasida of the Impossible Hand. Federico García Lorca. CP-GarcF, tr. by Catherine Brown Fr. Qasidas.

I want something suited to my special needs. Needs. A. R. Ammons. CP-AmmoA

I want that height and prospect such as music. Movements. Charles Tomlinson. CP-TomlC

I want the cries of my geese. Prelude, A. Charles Tomlinson. CP-TomlC

I want the fluffy stuff to keep coming down. Fluffy Stuff, The. May Swenson. SP-SwenM

I want the jailed / light to awaken: I want. Pablo Neruda. SP-NeruP Fr. Skystones.

I want the scissors to be sharp. Vade Mecum. Billy Collins. SP-CollB

I want the water reft from its bed. Gacela of the Terrible Presence. Federico García Lorca. SP-GarcF, tr. by W. S. Merwin

I want there to be no channel for the water. Ghazal of the Terrible Presence. Federico García Lorca. CP-GarcF, tr. by Catherine Brown Fr. Ghazals.

I want to apologize. Getting Through. Maxine W. Kumin. SP-KumiM

I want to be. Last of the Fire Kings, The. Derek Mahon. CP-MahoD

I want to be a Soldier! Boy Patriot, The. James Whitcomb Riley. CP-RileJ

I want to Be Buried. David Ignatow. SP-IgnaD

I Want to be Echopractic. James Laughlin. CP-LaugJ

I want to be known as the most brilliant man in America. Ego Confession. Allen Ginsberg. CP-GinsA; SP-GinsA

I want to be neither a poet. Interior ("I want to be neither a poet"). Federico García Lorca. CP-GarcF, tr. by Alan S. Trueblood Fr. Eros with a Cane.

I want to be the publisher of a vicious illuminated newspaper. New Gazette, The. Andrei Codrescu. SP-CodrA

I want to be where Fordie is. Incognito. William Carlos Williams. CP-WilW2

I want to be with you. Telling. Alice Walker. CP-WalkA

I want to be your pinkie. Le Désert de l'Amour. Stevie Smith. CP-SmitS

I Want to Breathe. James Laughlin. CP-LaugJ

I want to clean the lover of the dead warrior. For Marg So She Could Fuck Again. Andrei Codrescu. SP-CodrA

I want to compare a cloud. 26 January 1949. Yannis Ritsos. SP-RitsY Fr. Exile's Journals 2.

I Want to Confuse the Bible. Yehuda Amichai. SP-AmicYL, tr. by Benjamin Harshav and Barbara Harshav

I want to cry my pain, and I tell you. Poet Tells the Truth, The. Federico García Lorca. CP-GarcF, tr. by Angela Jaffray

I Want to Die in My Own Bed. Yehuda Amichai. SP-AmicYL, tr. by Benjamin Harshav and Barbara Harshav

I want to dig a ditch in fertile earth. Carefree Corpse, The. Charles Baudelaire. CP-BaudC, tr. by Walter Martin

I want to do a complaint now. Which is to say. Sonnet: "I want to do a complaint now. Which is to say." Hayden Carruth. CP-CarHS Fr. Sonnets.

I want to express my anguish in verses that tell. Nocturne: "I want to express my anguish in verses that tell." "Rubén Dario." SP-DariR, tr. by Alberto Acereda and Will Derusha

I want to forget everything. Eye Witness. Yusef Komunyakaa. CP-KomuY

I want to fuck you. Robert Creeley. CP-CreeR

I want to get off. Hong Kong—Last Words. Robert Creeley. SP-CreeR

I want to get up early one more morning. At Least. Raymond Carver. CP-CarvR

I want to go back to childhood. Oxbow. Federico García Lorca. CP-GarcF, tr. by Jerome Rothenberg Fr. Return, The.

I want to go down to the well. Casida of the Boy Wounded by the Water. Federico García Lorca. SP-GarcF, tr. by Edwin Honig

I want to go down to the well. Qasida of One Wounded by Water. Federico García Lorca. CP-GarcF, tr. by Catherine Brown Fr. Qasidas.

I want to go out to the woodlands green. Wanderlust. Dorothy Parker. CP-ParkD

I want to go under the sea in a diving-bell. Diving Bell, The. Tennessee Williams. CP-WillT

I Want to Go Wandering. Nicholas Vachel Lindsay. CP-LindV

I want to help you. Friends, The. Robert Creeley. CP-CreeR

I want to hold you close like a lute. Jelaluddin Rumi. SP-Rumi, tr. by Coleman Barks

I want to lay down. Catching Cold. Robert Creeley. SP-CreeR

I want to live, live to distraction. Aleksandr Aleksandrovich Blok. SP-BlokA, tr. by Peter France and Jon Stallworthy

I want to praise one I love. Praise. Robert Penn Warren. CP-WarrR

I want to read and nap. August. William Corbett. SP-CorbW

I want to ride once more on. Before I Die. James Laughlin. CP-LaugJ

I want to say it, and I will. Song Discordant. James Whitcomb Riley. CP-RileJ

I want to say words that flame. Egypt That Doesn't Exist, An. Jelaluddin Rumi. SP-Rumi, tr. by Coleman Barks

I WANT TO SEE MY MOTHER MOTHER. Ride, Red, Ride. Langston Hughes. CP-HughL; CP-HughL3

I want to see the old country before I die. L'Enfant Prodigue. Philip Whalen. SP-WhalP

I want to see you as the blue flower. Blue Flower, The. James Laughlin. CP-LaugJ

I want to show you these rose clouds in the night. Maybe, Someday. Yannis Ritsos. SP-RitsY, tr. by Edmund Keeley

I want to sing something—but this is all. Scrawl, A. James Whitcomb Riley. CP-RileJ

I Want to Sleep. Jorge Guillén. CP-WrigJ, tr. by James Wright

I want to sleep the dream of the apples. Gacela of the Dark Death. Federico García Lorca. SP-GarcF, tr. by J. L. Gili and Stephen Spender

I want to sleep the sleep of apples. Ghazal of Dark Death. Federico García Lorca. CP-GarcF, tr. by Catherine Brown Fr. Ghazals.

I want to speak in my voice! Suicide Blues. Muriel Rukeyser. CP-RukeM

I want to speak to you. Marriage 2, The. Denise Levertov. SP-LeveDS

I want to tear you apart. On Inter-Relatedness in the Universe. Alan Dugan. CP-DugaA

I want to tell you a. Returning Home. John Ciardi. CP-CiarJ

I want to tell you 'bout that woman. Only Woman Blues. Langston Hughes. CP-

HughL; CP-HughL2

I want to touch something sensational. *Zzzzzzzzzzzz*. Andrei Codrescu. SP-CodrA

I want to touch you. Touching. James Laughlin. CP-LaugJ

I want to write a sonnet stonier. Irritated Office, The. Carlos Drummond de Andrade. SP-StocR, *tr.* by Robert Stock

I want to write down the life. More about Poems. Andrei Codrescu. SP-CodrA

I want you, spider: walker-on-the-ceiling. Spiders Wanting. Thomas Lux. SP-LuxT

I want you to plunge into my life. Deep Pool, The. James Laughlin. CP-LaugJ

I wanted a man's face looking into the jaws and throat of life. Aztec Mask. Carl Sandburg. CP-SandC

I wanted so ably. World, The. Robert Creeley. CP-CreeR

I wanted the plums, but I waited. Thinking about Being Called Simple by a Critic. William Stafford. SP-StafWW

I wanted to be more human. Forms of the Human. Richard Eberhart. CP-EberR

I wanted to be sure to reach you. To the Harbormaster. Frank O'Hara. SP-OharF

I wanted to bring her a chalice. For My Daughter. Grace Paley. CP-PalGC

I wanted to give him some gift. To Evan. Richard Eberhart. CP-EberR

I wanted / to know all the bones of your spine, all. What She Could Not Tell Him. Denise Levertov. SP-LeveDL

I wanted to marry, but father said, "No." Orphaned Old Maid, The. Thomas Hardy. CP-HardT

I wanted to take up room. What a strange dream! I wanted to take up as much room as I could. Room. C. K. Williams. SP-WillC

I wanted to tell the truth. Vipera Berus. Czeslaw Milosz. CP-MiloCN, *tr.* by Robert Hass

I wanted wisdom, yet the indifferent glance. False Solomon's Seal. Howard Nemerov. CP-NemeH

I wanted you / without virtue—. Again. Robert Creeley. CP-CreeR

I was a beautiful plant. Stroke, The. Stevie Smith. CP-SmitS

I was a boy then. Man. Langston Hughes. CP-HughL; CP-HughL2

I was a boy when I heard three red words a thousand Frenchmen. Threes. Carl Sandburg. CP-SandC

I was a cottage maiden. Cousin Kate. Christina Georgina Rossetti. CP-RosC1

I was a frenetic wretch of a man. Making It. Charles Bukowski. SP-BukC3

I was a god and self-enchanted. Dream, A. May Swenson. SP-SwenM

I was a good child. Katy Did. James Wright. CP-WrigJ

I was a groveling creature once. Lively Hope, and Gracious Fear. William Cowper. CP-CowpW *Fr.* Olney Hymns.

I was a leopard caught by a demented. Visit to the Island of Lost Souls. Gregory Orr. SP-OrrG

I was a lookout posted and forgotten. In the Beech. Seamus Heaney. SP-HeanSO *Fr.* Sweeney Redivivus.

I was a man so skinny light travelled with a. Remembrance of My Forgotten Skinniness. Andrei Codrescu. SP-CodrA

I was a peeping Tom wandering the earth. Voyeur. Czeslaw Milosz. CP-MiloCN, *tr.* by Robert Hass

I was a Phoebe—nothing more. Emily Dickinson. CP-DickE

I was a pretty baby. Amoebaean for Daddy. Maya Angelou. SP-AngeM

I was a red man one time. Lament for Dark Peoples. Langston Hughes. CP-HughL; CP-HughL1

I was a slow developer. Too Late. Charles Bukowski. SP-BukC3

I was a soldier who slept in the bed. Metempsychosis. "Rubén Dario." SP-DariR, *tr.* by Alberto Acereda *and* Will Derusha

"I Was a Stranger and Ye Took Me in." John Greenleaf Whittier. CP-WhitJ

I was a young guy in Los Angeles. Training for Kid Aztec. Charles Bukowski. SP-BukC3

I Was Afraid of Dying. James Wright. CP-WrigJ

I was alone once, waiting. For the Marsh's Birthday. James Wright. CP-WrigJ

I was always a thoughtful youngster. Northumberland House. Stevie Smith. CP-SmitS

I was always afraid. Drive Home, The. W. S. Merwin. SP-MerwWF

I was an ice baby. Death Baby, The. Anne Sexton. CP-SextA; SP-SextA

I was angry with my friend. Poison Tree, A. William Blake. CP-BlakW *Fr.* Songs of Experience.

I was asking for something specific and perfect for my city. Mannahatta. Walt Whitman. CP-WhitW

I was at peace until you came. Remonstrance, The. Walter De la Mare. CP-DeLaW

I was awakened from a dream. Daughter. John Updike. CP-UpdiJ

I was better with the sounds of the sea. Hugh MacDiarmid. SP-MacDH *Fr.* War with England, The.

I was born and grew up in the Baltic marshland. Part of Speech, A. Joseph Brodsky. CP-BrodJ, *tr.* by Daniel Weissbort

I was born during the night sea-journey. December 23, 1926. Robert Bly. SP-BlyR

I was born here. New Yorkers. Langston Hughes. CP-HughL; CP-HughL3

I was born in a city of wild cherries. Presence. Adam Zagajewski. SP-ZagaA, *tr.*

by Renata Gorczynski, Benjamin Ivry *and* C. K. Williams

I was born in Belfast between the mountain and the gantries. Carrickfergus. Louis MacNeice. CP-MacNL

"I was born in Indiany," says a stranger, lank and slim. Like His Mother Used to Make. James Whitcomb Riley. CP-RileJ

I Was Born in Lucerne. Philip Levine. SP-LeviP

I was born in 1924. If I were a violin my age. 1924. Yehuda Amichai. SP-AmicY, *tr.* by Chana Bloch

I was born in 1924. If I were a violin my age. 1924. Yehuda Amichai. SP-AmicYL, *tr.* by Benjamin Harshav *and* Barbara Harshav

I was born in the month of the bull. Brooding Likeness. Louise Glück. SP-GlucL

I was born in Wyoming, Cody is my home town. Stool Pigeon Blues. Allen Ginsberg. CP-GinsA

I was born on a street named Joy. Lines on His Birthday. John Logan. CP-LogaJ

I was born on the prairie and the milk of its wheat, the red of its clover. Prairie. Carl Sandburg. CP-SandC

I Was Born to Hustle Roses Down the Avenues of the Dead. Charles Bukowski. SP-BukC2

I was born upon thy bank, river. Henry David Thoreau. CP-ThorH

I was born when she was thirty-eight. Mother. Marilyn Hacker. SP-HackM

I was born with a knife. Like Any Other Man. Gregory Orr. SP-OrrG

I was buried near this dyke [*or* Dike]. Epitaph, An: "I was buried near this dyke [*or* Dike]." William Blake. CP-BlakW

I was but a half-grown boy. Genesis. Nicholas Vachel Lindsay. CP-LindV

I was but what you'd brush. Seven Strophes. Joseph Brodsky. CP-BrodJ, *tr.* by Paul Graves

I was coming off an affair that had gone badly. Numb Your Ass and Your Brain and Your Heart—. Charles Bukowski. SP-BukC1

I was conceived in the summer of Nineteen Eighteen. True Confessional. Lawrence Ferlinghetti. SP-FerlL

I was considering how. E. E. Cummings. CP-CummE

I was consumed by so much hate. Man I Am, A. Stevie Smith. CP-SmitS

I was coral first. Reincarnations. "Rubén Dario." SP-DariR, *tr.* by Alberto Acereda *and* Will Derusha

I was dead and i wanted peace. Grammar, A. Andrei Codrescu. SP-CodrA

I was dead, then alive. Sublime Generosity. Jelaluddin Rumi. SP-Rumi, *tr.* by Coleman Barks

I was deep in thoughts of Love when I found. Guido Cavalcanti. CP-CavaG, *tr.* by Marc Cirigliano

I was down by the mill at last. Ants, The. Charles Bukowski. SP-BukC2

I was drunk and they. Star, The. Charles Bukowski. SP-BukC3

I was fairly and squarely behind the eight. Immram. Paul Muldoon. CP-MuldP

I was falling asleep in my chair. How to Be Successful & Happy Without Anybody Else Finding Out About It. Philip Whalen. SP-WhalP

I was foolish about windows. Foolish About Windows. Carl Sandburg. CP-SandC

I was for Union—you, ag'in' it. Thoughts on the Late War. James Whitcomb Riley. CP-RileJ

I was, for years and years now, wounded, killed. Michelangelo Buonarroti. CP-Miche, *tr.* by John Frederick Nims

I was foretold, your rebel[l] sex. Deposition from Love, A. Thomas Carew. CP-CareT

I was fortunate enough to have. Lives of the Poets. Mona Van Duyn. SP-VanDM

I was four but I turned four hundred maybe. Seamus Heaney. SP-HeanSO *Fr.* Squarings.

I was full of sadness, and I was sitting silent with no companion. Elegy 3: On the Death of the Bishop of Winchester. John Milton. CP-CowpW; CP-MiltJ

I was given my bedding, and a bunk. Meaningless Institution, A. Allen Ginsberg. CP-GinsA

I was going along a dusty highroad. Mountain Talk. A. R. Ammons. CP-AmmoA

I was going to make something of it. Testimony. Richard Eberhart. CP-EberR

I was going to say something. Ancestor. Thomas Kinsella. CP-KinsT

I was going to write a poem. Poet's Occasional Alternative, The. Grace Paley. CP-PalGC

I was happy, with fate favoring, to abide. Michelangelo Buonarroti. CP-Miche, *tr.* by John Frederick Nims

I was haunted for several days in a row by an imaginary pair of almost identical Siren voices. Bleakness, Farewell. Philip Whalen. SP-WhalP

I was heavy-laden, grieving. Give and it shall be given unto you. Spiritual Debtors. Jones Very. CP-VeryJ

I was here alone. Seraph. William Carlos Williams. CP-WilW1

I was here before, a long time ago. Lines Composed over Three Thousand Miles from Tintern Abbey. Billy Collins. SP-CollB

I was high on tea in my fo'c'sle near the forepeak hatch listening to the stars. Battleship Newsreel. Allen Ginsberg. CP-GinsA

I was hungry, and Thou feddest me. Because He First Loved Us. Christina Georgina Rossetti. CP-RosC2

I was. / I had been. Monday, Wednesday, and Friday. Federico García Lorca.

CP-GarcF, *tr.* by Alan S. Trueblood *Fr.* Moon Songs.

I was ill, lying on my bed of old papers. Secret Garden, The. Rita Dove. SP-DoveR

I was in a mood for disaster. Diary Entry. John Ciardi. CP-CiarJ

I was in Mannheim when my agent phoned me. Krutz. Charles Bukowski. SP-BukC3

I was in Prague looking for Vladimir Holan's house. September. Adam Zagajewski. SP-ZagaA, *tr.* by Clare Cavanagh

I was in the darkness. Stephen Crane. CP-CranS

I was in the days of peace. Airman Considers His Power, An. Richard Eberhart. CP-EberR

I was in the fields. Three Songs. Gregory Orr. SP-OrrG

I was just walking about. Astrological Conundrums. Ted Hughes. SP-HughTN

I was kind to all my masters. True Sympathy; or, Prevention of Cruelty to Teachers. G. K. Chesterton. CP-ChesG

I was kissed once. Kiss, The. Alice Walker. CP-WalkA

I was leaving my fifty-eighth year. 1994. Lucille Clifton. SP-ClifL

I was Leda's intimate, and slave. Leda's Handmaiden. Eleanor Wilner. SP-WilnE

I was listening to Gregorian chants. Quick Poem, A. Adam Zagajewski. SP-ZagaA, *tr.* by Clare Cavanagh

I was living underground. At Eleusis. James Laughlin. CP-LaugJ

I was lookin' for a sandwich, Judge. Brief Encounter. Langston Hughes. CP-HughL; CP-HughL2

I Was Looking a Long While. Walt Whitman. CP-WhitW

I was looking at the prickly pears. The beautiful aged woman. White. Yannis Ritsos. SP-RitsY *Fr.* Monovasia.

I was looking for a way out of a lifetime's consolations. Adrienne Rich. SP-RicA2 *Fr.* Shooting Script.

I was Lord of Cities very sumptuously builded. Song of Seven Cities, The. Rudyard Kipling. CP-KiplR

I was made erect and lone. Henry David Thoreau. CP-ThorH

I was making my way home late one night. Aisling. Paul Muldoon. CP-MuldP

I was micro-tagging Chinook salmon. Chinook. Paul Muldoon. CP-MuldP

I was moving down the bank. Gregory Orr. SP-OrrG

I was named after my daddy, Vern. Greed. Ai. SP-Ai

I was nearsighted and had to get up close. Fields, The. Raymond Carver. CP-CarvR

I was never impressed, when they presented. Tiger at the Movie-Show. Donald Davie. CP-DaviDC

I was never so upset. Robert Creeley. CP-CreeR

I was nine years old. Luck. Raymond Carver. CP-CarvR

I Was Not He. Thomas Hardy. CP-HardT

I was not; now I am—a few days hence. Mystery, The. Paul Laurence Dunbar. CP-DunbP

I was not on the parapets at Cretae. After Teacups. Robert Penn Warren. CP-WarrR

I was not pure. Dead Priestess Speaks, A. "H. D." CP-DoolH

I was not sleeping nor awake. It was. John Ciardi. CP-CiarJ

I was not willing. Whispered to a Girl. Federico García Lorca. CP-GarcF, *tr.* by Alan S. Trueblood *Fr.* Games.

I was of late a barren plant. On the Reed. *Unknown.* CP-CowpW

I was on my high. Thorn Merchant's Mistress, The. Yusef Komunyakaa. CP-KomuY

I was on the corner. Somewhere. Yusef Komunyakaa. CP-KomuY

I was once a part. Three Songs. Louise Bogan. CP-BogaL

I was once the snake woman. Snake Woman. Margaret Atwood. SP-AtwM2

I was one / among 2000 million. Singles. Christopher Logue. SP-LoguC

I was only the girl under the stairs. Big House, The. Paul Muldoon. CP-MuldP

I was out last night. Miser, The. Mona Van Duyn. SP-VanDM

I was out of your Church for 43 years, my Dear. Back. John Berryman. CP-BerrJ

I was painting the. Churchill's Death. Lorine Niedecker. CP-NiedL

I was Pickup from the first. Shih-te. CP-ColdM, *tr.* by Red Pine

I was playing records on Sunday. Records. Robert Lowell. SP-LoweR

I was pouring a drink when the night-monotony. Vertical Man. Thomas Kinsella. CP-KinsT

I was raised in the suburbs where spite is the child of love. Love Song: Class Analysis. Alan Dugan. CP-DugaA

I was raised / on the shore. Memphis. Lucille Clifton. SP-ClifL

I was reading *The English Patient* by. Translation. Grace Paley. CP-PalGC

I was reading the novel. His Shining Helmet; Its Horsehair Crest. Tess Gallagher. SP-GallT

I was ready long before this day. Jonah on His Deathbed. Miller Williams. CP-WillM

I was returning from the drylands. Down below a river valley trembled. Border. Federico García Lorca. CP-GarcF, *tr.* by Jerome Rothenberg

I was rooting through tea-chest after tea-chest. Tea. Paul Muldoon. CP-MuldP

I was seduced by innocence. Odysseus on Hermes. Thom Gunn. CP-GunnT

I was sent in to see her. Tear. Thomas Kinsella. CP-KinsT

I was setting on the hen-house steps. Crowing Hen Blues. Langston Hughes. CP-HughL; CP-HughL2

I was setting out from my house. Dragonfly-Mother, The. Denise Levertov. SP-LeveDL; SP-LeveDS

I was seventy-seven, come August. Little Old Lady in Lavender Silk, The. Dorothy Parker. CP-ParkD

I was shacked with a. Who in the Hell is Tom Jones? Charles Bukowski. SP-BukC1

I Was Sick and in Prison. Jones Very. CP-VeryJ

I was sick of my wits. Fanny Howe. SP-HoweF *Fr.* Q.

I was sitting in a Third-Class carriage; an old priest. Arthur Rimbaud. CP-RimbA, *tr.* by Martin Sorrell

I was sitting in mcsoreley's. outside it was New York and beauti- / fully snowing. E. E. Cummings. CP-CummE

I was sitting, / She was knitting. She, I, and They. Thomas Hardy. CP-HardT

I was sitting there. I knew it was her. Metaphysical Town Hall and Bookshop, The. Philip Whalen. SP-WhalP

I was sleeping in Madison, Anthony Bradbury's spare room. Milkers Broken Up. Donald Hall. CP-HallD

I was so blest by sheer good luck and Love. Petrarch. CP-Petra, *tr.* by J. G. Nichols

I Was So Full. Stevie Smith. CP-SmitS

I was so poor in the past. Han-shan. CP-ColdM, *tr.* by Red Pine

I was so sick last night I. Morning After. Langston Hughes. CP-HughL; CP-HughL2

I was spading a flower bed while the old dog. Knowing Bitches. John Ciardi. CP-CiarJ

I was standing in for myself, my own stunt double. Between Takes. Paul Muldoon. CP-MuldP

I was standing outside this cocktail bar, see, on the Nile. To Fuzzy. James Tate. SP-TateJ

I was stretched out on the earth so that a wild geranium. Charles Olson. CP-OlsoC

I was strolling sorrowfully. Trees' Counselling, The. Christina Georgina Rossetti. CP-RosC3

I was strolling under the tents of trees. Anecdote of Rain. Adam Zagajewski. SP-ZagaA, *tr.* by Renata Gorczynski, Benjamin Ivry *and* C. K. Williams

I was supposed to wake. Dreams. Robert Creeley. SP-CreeR

I was sure, my worthy friend, that you would understand. Philoctetes; The Ultimate Mask. Yannis Ritsos. SP-RitsY, *tr.* by Peter Bien

I was talcuming my windshield. Toward Saint Looey. James Tate. SP-TateJ

I was talking one day. Angel of Grace. Stevie Smith. CP-SmitS

I was talking to older. Still Too Young. Robert Creeley. SP-CreeR

I was talking to the Baroness in the Green Room. Michael Palmer. SP-PalmM

I was the first of fools. Dreaming Fool. Carl Sandburg. CP-SandC

I was / the girl of the chain letter. Love Song: "I was / the girl of the chain letter." Anne Sexton. CP-SextA

I Was the Midmost. Thomas Hardy. CP-HardT

I Was the Moon. Yehuda Amichai. SP-AmicYL, *tr.* by Benjamin Harshav *and* Barbara Harshav

I was the Nazis' padre, you might say. Three Pastors in Berlin. Donald Davie. CP-DaviDC

I was the only man in the world. On a Fallen Statue Forbidden to the Women at Pompeii. Alan Dugan. CP-DugaA

I was the slightest in the House. Emily Dickinson. CP-DickE

I was the staunchest of our fleet. Derelict, The. Rudyard Kipling. CP-KiplR

I was the whole summer remembering. Waters, The. W. S. Merwin. SP-MerwWF

I was there—by the curtains. Peeping Tom. Walter De la Mare. CP-DeLaW

I was thinking, Mother, of that poor old horse. Reserved. Walter De la Mare. CP-DeLaW

I was thinking of a son. Menstruation at Forty. Anne Sexton. CP-SextA; SP-SextA

I was thinking, while I was working on my income tax. On the Edge. May Swenson. SP-SwenM

I was three-ish. Right Arm, The. Paul Muldoon. CP-MuldP

I was thy Neighbour once, thou rugged Pile! Elegiac Stanzas Suggested by a Picture of Peele Castle, in a Storm, Painted by Sir George Beaumont. William Wordsworth. CP-WorW1; MW-WorW

I was tired of being a woman. Consorting with Angels. Anne Sexton. CP-SextA; SP-SextA

I was trying to figure out. Communion. Langston Hughes. CP-HughL; CP-HughL2

I was twelve when my father gave me this .22. Merle Bascom's .22. Donald Hall. CP-HallD

I was upon the high and blessed mound. Sonnet: Of the grave of Selvaggia, on the Monte della Sambuca. Cino da Pistoia. CW-RossD, *tr.* by Dante Gabriel Rossetti

I was very well pleased with what I knowed. Brookland Road. Rudyard Kipling. CP-KiplR

I Was Waiting for My Girl and Her Steps Were Absent. Yehuda Amichai. SP-AmicYL, tr. by Benjamin Harshav and Barbara Harshav

I was walking behind Elliot Carter. Poem for Elliot Carter on His 90th Birthday. Alan Dugan. CP-DugaA

I was walking down by the old / Santee. Second Carolina Said-Song. A. R. Ammons. CP-AmmoA

I was walking in a dark valley. Returning. Wendell Berry. CP-BerrW

I was walking my garden. Silent Visit. Robert Graves. CP-GravR

I was walking near the hotel in the evening. Southern Dawn. Pier Paolo Pasolini. SP-PasoP, tr. by Norman MacAfee and Luciano Martinengo

I was watching a building wall being knocked. Prose Poem. Alan Dugan. CP-DugaA

I was weaned from the curse of Adam. Yehuda Amichai. SP-AmicYL, tr. by Benjamin Harshav and Barbara Harshav

I was welcomed here—clear gold. Settling. Denise Levertov. SP-LeveDS

I was with you in all the loneliness. Emily Dickinson. SP-DickE

I was wondering about the gods. Gods of Washington, D.C, The. Richard Eberhart. CP-EberR

I was wrapped in black. Us. Anne Sexton. CP-SextA; SP-SextA

I was writing a trentesei for the boat-people. Apology for a Lost Classicism, An. John Ciardi. CP-CiarJ

I washd them out & washd them in. Washer Womans Song, The. William Blake. CP-BlakW

I washed lobster and stale gin. Love Song for K. Owyne. Anne Sexton. CP-SextA

I wasn't getting anywhere. Impressionist. Heather McHugh. SP-McHuH

I Wasn't In This Poem. Adam Zagajewski. SP-ZagaA, tr. by Clare Cavanagh

I watch a man soldering positive and negative speaker. Solderer, The. Arthur Sze. SP-SzeA

I watch, and long have watched, with calm regret. William Wordsworth. CP-WorW2

I watch him with his Christmas sled. His Christmas Sled. James Whitcomb Riley. CP-RileJ

I watch myself aging in your yes. Aging Together. Clarence Major. SP-MajoC

I watch the filthy light seep through. Hear Me. Philip Levine. SP-LeviP

I watch the Indians dancing to help the young corn at Taos pueblo. The old men squat in a ring. New Mexican Mountain. Robinson Jeffers. CP-JefR2

I watch the Tagus in such a way. Beyond God. Fernando Pessoa. SP-PessF, tr. by Susan M. Brown and Edwin Honig

I watch you throw salt on the path. Throwing Salt on a Path. Arthur Sze. SP-SzeA

I watch you where the wren will wake. Our Tree of Opposites. Wyatt Prunty. SP-PrunW

I watch'd thee when the foe was at our side. Love and Death. Lord Byron. CP-Byron

I Watched a Blackbird. Thomas Hardy. CP-HardT

I watched a rosebud very long. Symbols. Christina Georgina Rossetti. CP-RosC1

I watched an armory combing its bronze bricks. Poem: "I watched an armory combing its bronze bricks." Frank O'Hara. CP-OharF

I watched her face to see which way. Emily Dickinson. CP-DickE

I watched men at Angola. Sugar. Yusef Komunyakaa. CP-KomuY

I watched my father's friends. Makings. Gary Snyder. CP-SnydG

I watched the Moon around the House. Emily Dickinson. CP-DickE

I watched the seeds come down this afternoon. At a Country Hotel. Howard Nemerov. CP-NemeH

I watched the solitary flight. Crow's Flight. Peter Blue Cloud. SP-BlueP

I watched them from the window, the children at their play. Thoughts of Home. Arthur Hugh Clough. SP-ClouA

I watched, upon a vase's rim. Round, The. Walter De la Mare. CP-DeLaW

I wayfared at the nadir of the sun. Murmurs in the Gloom. Thomas Hardy. CP-HardT

I wear my life loosely around me. Loose Gown, A. David Ignatow. SP-IgnaD

I wear no badge; no tinsel star. Ralph Waldo Emerson. CP-EmerR

I wear them. They help me. But I. Glasses. John Updike. CP-UpdiJ

I wear your fragrant memory, like a spray of mignonette. Rosemary ("I wear your fragrant memory, like a spray of mignonette"). Dorothy Parker. CP-ParkD

I wear your smile upon my lips. Mornings Innocent. May Swenson. SP-SwenM

I weary of my life / Thro' the long sultry day. Of My Life. Christina Georgina Rossetti. CP-RosC3

I weave for the Lamp of Evening. Emily Dickinson. SP-DickE

I weep all day; and in the night-time, when. Petrarch. CP-Petra, tr. by J. G. Nichols

I weep for Adonais—he is dead! Adonais; An Elegy on the Death of John Keats. Percy Bysshe Shelley. CP-ShelP

I Weep, Fountain of Jazer. Charles Olson. CP-OlsoC

I weep, I burn—burn up!—my heart thereby. Michelangelo Buonarroti. CP-Miche, tr. by John Frederick Nims

I well remember / A time when. Hymn: "I well remember / A time when." Alice Walker. CP-WalkA

I Went. Constantine P. Cavafy. CP-CavaC, tr. by Theoharis Constantine Theoharis

I Went. Pablo Neruda. SP-NeruP

I went and stood outside myself. At a Seaside Town in 1869. Thomas Hardy. CP-HardT

I went back in the alley. Homecoming. Langston Hughes. CP-HughL; CP-HughL2

I went by footpath and by stile. Paying Calls. Thomas Hardy. CP-HardT

I went by star and planet shine. Well-Beloved, The. Thomas Hardy. CP-HardT

I went by the Druid stone. Shadow on the Stone, The. Thomas Hardy. CP-HardT

I went disguised in it, pronouncing it with a soft church-Latin. Incertus. Seamus Heaney. SP-HeanSO

I went down by Cascadilla. Cascadilla Falls. A. R. Ammons. CP-AmmoA

I went down / Into the cavern. All the Way Down. Thomas Merton. CP-MertT

I Went Down into the Desert. Nicholas Vachel Lindsay. See I Went Down into the Desert to Meet Elijah

I Went Down into the Desert to Meet Elijah. Nicholas Vachel Lindsay. CP-LindV

(I Went Down into the Desert.) CP-LindV

I went down not long ago. Tecumseh. Mary Oliver. SP-OlivM

I went down the road. Ballad of the Sinner. Langston Hughes. CP-HughL; CP-HughL2

I went down to the corner. Lonesome Corner. Langston Hughes. CP-HughL, CP-HughL2

I went down to the river. Life Is Fine. Langston Hughes. CP-HughL; CP-HughL2

I went for a walk over the dunes again this morning. Corsons Inlet. A. R. Ammons. CP-AmmoA

I went from enclosed Jerusalem toward the open sea. From Jerusalem to the Sea and Back. Yehuda Amichai. SP-AmicYL, tr. by Benjamin Harshav and Barbara Harshav

I went in the forest to look for a sign. Green Valentine Blues. Allen Ginsberg. CP-GinsA; SP-GinsA

I went into a public-'ouse to get a pint o' beer. Tommy. Rudyard Kipling. CP-KiplR

I went / into / his. Tom's Attempt to Seduce Big Brother Steve. James Schuyler. CP-SchuJ

I went into my parlor. Irate Songster, The. Kenneth Patchen. CP-PatcK

I went into the deserts of dim sleep—, Fragment: The Deserts of Dim Sleep. Percy Bysshe Shelley. CP-ShelP

I went into the dim wood. Winter Melody. Wallace Stevens. CP-StevWP

I Went Into the Maverick Bar. Gary Snyder. CP-SnydG

I went into the wood one day. Fairy Story. Stevie Smith. CP-SmitS

I went on a journey in order to acquaint myself with my province. Road-side Dog. Czeslaw Milosz. CP-MiloCN, tr. by Robert Hass

I went out alone. Girl's Song. William Butler Yeats. CP-YeatW

I went out for a minute and. After Reading Two Towns in Provence. Raymond Carver. CP-CarvR

I went out / from the news of your illness. Three Poems for James Wright. Mary Oliver. SP-OlivM

I went out in the naked light. Kathleen Jessie Raine. SP-RainK

I went out of the house to smoke. A thousand. Thomas Merton and the Winter Marsh. Norman Dubie. CP-DubiN

I went out on. Saying. A. R. Ammons. CP-AmmoA

I went out to cut a last batch of zinnias this. Equinox. A. R. Ammons. CP-AmmoA

I went out to the hazel wood. Song Of Wandering Aengus, The. William Butler Yeats. CP-YeatW

I Went Out to the Sun. A. R. Ammons. CP-AmmoA

I went out walking. On Mother's Day. Grace Paley. CP-PalGC

I went to a museum. Joseph Brodsky. CP-BrodJ Fr. Shorts.

I went to a party / out in Hollywood. Here's to Adhering. Maya Angelou. SP-AngeM

I went to Chicago. Poor Girl's Ruination. Langston Hughes. CP-HughL

I went to de gypsy. Fortune Teller Blues. Langston Hughes. CP-HughL; CP-HughL1

I went to Egypt to escape. Cuban Doctor, The. Wallace Stevens. CP-StevW; CP-StevWP

I went to Heaven. Emily Dickinson. CP-DickE

I went to his fortieth birthday. Wystan Auden. James Schuyler. CP-SchuJ

I went to look for Joy. Joy. Langston Hughes. CP-HughL; CP-HughL1

I went to ma daddy. Hard Daddy. Langston Hughes. CP-HughL; CP-HughL1

I went to New York and went to the poet's address. And Then I Headed on Back Home. Miller Williams. CP-WillM

I went to San Francisco. Trip: San Francisco. Langston Hughes. CP-HughL

I Went to See Irving Babbitt. Richard Eberhart. CP-EberR

I went to thank Her. Emily Dickinson. CP-DickE

I went to the bird. What the Bird with the Human Head Knew. Anne Sexton. CP-SextA

I went to the cupboard, I opened the door. Song: Not There. Randall Jarrell. CP-JarrR

I went to the field to break. Unsteady Yellow. Tess Gallagher. SP-GallT

I went to the Garden of Love. Garden of Love, The. William Blake. CP-BlakW *Fr.* Songs of Experience.

I went to the Gypsy's. Ballad of the Gypsy. Langston Hughes. CP-HughL; CP-HughL2

I went to the house of Everyman. Everyman. Tennessee Williams. CP-WillT

I went to the opera and God was not there. Faustus and I. Anne Sexton. CP-SextA

I went to the physician to complain. Bursting Rapture. Robert Frost. CP-FrosR

I went to turn the grass once after one. Tuft of Flowers, The. Robert Frost. CP-FrosR

I went to visit several thousand gold buddhas. Dharma Youth League, The. Philip Whalen. SP-WhalP

I went to war once, I'm not sure for what. To a Staffordshireman, from a Devon Villa. Donald Davie. CP-DaviDC

I went under cover of night. Nicodemus. Howard Nemerov. CP-NemeH

I went up the hill / At moonrise. Despairing Man Draws a Serpent, The. Pablo Antonio Cuadra. CP-MertT

I went walkin' / By the blue bayou. Blue Bayou. Langston Hughes. CP-HughL; CP-HughL2

I went walking (said the girl). Septentrion. René Char. CP-MertT

I went way back and asked the old. Origin. Howard Nemerov. CP-NemeH

I went with Anger at my heel. Butcher's Dozen. Thomas Kinsella. CP-KinsT

I went with two ladies. 56 Year Old Poem, A. Charles Bukowski. SP-BukC1

I wept, but now I sing: my living sun. Petrarch. CP-Petra, *tr. by* J. G. Nichols

I, when you notice. Apple, The. Shmuel HaNagid. SP-HaNaS, *tr. by* Peter Cole

I, which that am the sorwefulleste man. Complaynt d'Amours. Geoffrey Chaucer. CP-ChauG

I whispered, 'I am too young.' Brown Penny. William Butler Yeats. CP-YeatW

I whispered to the holly. Trees. Ted Hughes. SP-HughTN

I who am singing these lines today. Enigmas, The. Jorge Luis Borges. SP-BorgJ, *tr. by* John Updike

I, who had been erased. Departure from the Bush. Margaret Atwood. SP-AtwM1

I who have favour'd many, come to be. To the Most Learned, Wise, and Arch-Antiquary, M. John Selden. Robert Herrick. CP-HerrR

I who picked up the neat. Eleanor's Letters. Donald Hall. CP-HallD

I who speak to you am old as the world. Autobiography. Primo Levi. CP-LeviP, *tr. by* Ruth Feldman

I will accept thy will to do and be. Bruised Reed Shall He Not Break, A. Christina Georgina Rossetti. CP-RosC1

I will and yet I may not. Ballad of Will, The. Sir Thomas Wyatt. CP-WyatT

I Will Arise. Christina Georgina Rossetti. CP-RosC2

I Will Arise and Go Now. Ogden Nash. CP-NashO

I will arise and go now, and go to Innisfree. Lake-Isle of Innisfree, The. William Butler Yeats. CP-YeatW

I will be drunk and down with wine. Hafiz. CP-EmerR *Fr.* Odes.

I will be earth you be the flower. May Swenson. SP-SwenM

I will be happy if but for once. Dubiety. Robert Browning. CP-BroR2

I will be / M o ving in the Street of her. E. E. Cummings. CP-CummE

I will be short, and having quickly hurl'd. To M. Leonard Willan His Peculiar Friend. Robert Herrick. CP-HerrR

I will be the gladdest thing. Afternoon on a Hill. Edna St. Vincent Millay. CP-MillE

I will begin again in May, describing weather, how. Notes Toward a Spring Offensive. Alan Dugan. CP-DugaA

I will bring you big things. Wooing, A. Langston Hughes. CP-HughL; CP-HughL1

I will bring you great harps in Heaven. Harps in Heaven. Nicholas Vachel Lindsay. CP-LindV

I will build you a house. Tou Wan Speaks to Her Husband Liu Sheng. Rita Dove. SP-DoveR

I will climb thirty steps to my room. Ugly Sister. Philip Larkin. CP-LarkP

I Will Come and Heal Him. Christina Georgina Rossetti. CP-RosC2

I will confesse. Hymne to Love, An. Robert Herrick. CP-HerrR

I will consider the outnumbering dead. Merlin. Geoffrey Hill. CP-HillG

I will cultivate within. E. E. Cummings. CP-CummE

I will die in Paris, on a day the rain's been coming down hard. Testimony. César Vallejo. CP-MuldP, *tr. by* Paul Muldoon

I will enforce it that after supper you speak about dusk. President of the Holding Company, The. Lorine Niedecker. CP-NiedL

I will enjoy thee now my Celia, come. Rapture, A. Thomas Carew. CP-CareT

I will forgive you everything. Nature and Free Animals. Stevie Smith. CP-SmitS

I will get a new string for my fiddle. Merrymaking in Question, A. Thomas Hardy. CP-HardT

I will get me up unto the hills. Hills Whence, The. Ezra Pound. CP-PoEar

I will give you all my keys. Tease. D. H. Lawrence. CP-LawrD

I will go back to that silent evening. That Silent Evening. Galway Kinnell. SP-KinnGN

I will grieve alone. In Response to a Rumor that the Oldest Whorehouse in Wheeling, West Virginia, Has Been Condemned. James Wright. CP-WrigJ

I will haunt these States. Vow, A. Allen Ginsberg. CP-GinsA

I will have to accept women. This Form of Life Needs Sex. Allen Ginsberg. CP-GinsA; SP-GinsA

I will have to begin to remember you. Yehuda Amichai. SP-AmicYL, *tr. by* Benjamin Harshav *and* Barbara Harshav

I will keep you and bring hands to hold you against a great hunger. Mascots. Carl Sandburg. CP-SandC

I will let loose against you the fleet-footed vines. Mowgli's Song Against People. Rudyard Kipling. CP-KiplR *Fr.* Second Jungle Book, The.

I will lie down in autumn. May Swenson. SP-SwenM

I Will Lift Up Mine Eyes unto the Hills. Christina Georgina Rossetti. CP-RosC1; CP-RosC2; CP-RosC3

(Chiefest among Ten Thousand, The.) CP-RosC3

I will love thee, O Lord, my strength. Psalm 18: "I will love thee, O Lord, my strength." Bible, *O.T.* SP-SmarC *Fr.* Psalms.

I will marry this clump of flowers. Kadava Kumbis Devise a Way to Marry for Love, The. Rita Dove. SP-DoveR

I will name it anything I will name you this. French for April Fool's. Michael Palmer. SP-PalmM

I will never be only a Lesbian. Marilyn Hacker. SP-HackM *Fr.* Taking Notice.

I will never leave you darling. Starling, The. Stevie Smith. CP-SmitS

I will no longer kiss. On Himselfe. Robert Herrick. CP-HerrR

I Will Not Be Your Sickness. Marge Piercy. SP-PierM

I will not build on yonder mount. Dean's Reasons for Not Building at Drapier's Hill, The. Jonathan Swift. CP-SwifJ

I will not call it Spring for me. Seasons, The. Jones Very. CP-VeryJ

I WILL NOT CARE FOR TIME. FORBIDDING ME. Time Hinder Not Me; His Arms Reach Here and There. Muriel Rukeyser. CP-RukeM

I Will Not Dare to Ask One Question. Richard Eberhart. CP-EberR

I will not faint, but trust in God. In Patience. Christina Georgina Rossetti. CP-RosC3

I will not go when she calls. This Word Love. Raymond Carver. CP-CarvR

I will not grace you with a name . . . Even "you," however modest the convention: not here. One of the Muses. C. K. Williams. CP-WillC

I will not hesitate to speak the word. Ralph Waldo Emerson. CP-EmerR

I will not kill my father. Oedipus Reformed. David Ignatow. SP-IgnaD

I will not lie and say I grieve. Cushing. Robert Stock. SP-StocR

I will not live out of me. Ralph Waldo Emerson. CP-EmerR

I will not look upon the lands you own. My Sheep. Jones Very. CP-VeryJ

I will not love one minute more, I swear. Love Turned to Hatred. Sir John Suckling. CP-SuckJ

I will not think of her in her coffin. Virgin, The. Richard Eberhart. CP-EberR

I will now sing a song for you, Miss Lorence. Another Day (I will now sing). Muriel Rukeyser. CP-RukeM

I will now step over the soft velvet rope. Brooklyn Museum of Art, The. Billy Collins. SP-CollB

I will obey the strictest law of love. Henry David Thoreau. CP-ThorH

I will paint her as I see her. Portrait, A. Elizabeth Barrett Browning. CP-BroEB

I will pass from his mind. Images ("I will pass from his mind"). A. K. Ramanujan. CP-RamaA

I will put Chaos into fourteen lines. Edna St. Vincent Millay. CP-MillE

I will read a few of these to see if they exist. Theory of the Flower, The. Michael Palmer. SP-PalmM

I will read ashes for you, if you ask me. Fire Pages. Carl Sandburg. CP-SandC

I will remember well. To the Dead Owner of a Gym. Thom Gunn. CP-GunnT

I will remember what I was. I am sick of rope and chain—. Elephant, The. Rudyard Kipling. CP-KiplR *Fr.* Jungle Book, The.

I will rise / from my troth. Wine Bowl. "H. D." CP-DoolH

I Will Sing a Joyous Song. William Carlos Williams. CP-WilW1

I will sing you a song of Los. the Eternal Prophet. Song of Los, The. William Blake. CP-BlakW

I Will Sing You One-O. Robert Frost. CP-FrosR

I will speak about women of letters, for I'm in the racket. Three. Carolyn Kizer. CP-KizeC *Fr.* Pro Femina.

I will take your heart. To Artina. Langston Hughes. CP-HughL; CP-HughL3

I will teach you my townspeople. Tract. William Carlos Williams. CP-WilW1

I will teach you to become American, my students. Notes for a Lecture. David Ignatow. SP-IgnaD

I will tell you what he told me. Berryman. W. S. Merwin. SP-MerwWF

I will tell you what Joseph of Arimathea. William Blake. CP-BlakW

I will tell you when they met. One Day. Christina Georgina Rossetti. CP-RosC1

I will turn very dark. Cabala. May Swenson. SP-SwenM

I will wade out. E. E. Cummings. CP-CummE

I will wait here in the fields. Stay Home. Wendell Berry. CP-BerrW

I will walk, if I must. Be Like Me. David Ignatow. SP-IgnaD

I will win you away from every earth, from every sky. Marina Ivanovna Tsvetayeva. CP-BrodJ, *tr. by* Joseph Brodsky

I Will Write. Robert Graves. CP-GravR

I will write you a letter. I Think. James Schuyler. CP-SchuJ

I, William Lyon Mackenzie King. Visions of Mackenzie King, The. John Updike. CP-UpdiJ

I Wish. Stevie Smith. CP-SmitS

I Wish a God Were Possible. David Ignatow. SP-IgnaD

I wish de day was neah at han'. Goin' Home. Paul Laurence Dunbar. CP-DunbP

I wish for you that when you wake. Aubade: "I wish for you that when you wake." Donald Davie. CP-DaviDC

I wish I could appear at will in your thoughts. Wishes. Andrei Codrescu. SP-CodrA

I wish I could teach you how ugly. On Flunking a Nice Boy out of School. John Ciardi. CP-CiarJ

I wish I had been at Rodmell. Virginia Woolf. James Schuyler. CP-SchuJ

I Wish I Knew a Woman. D. H. Lawrence. CP-LawrD

I wish I knew what you wanted. Blocked Road, The. Jelaluddin Rumi. SP-Rumi, *tr. by* Coleman Barks

I wish I might say one liquid word. Emily Dickinson. SP-DickE

I wish I understood the beauty. Three in Transition. David Ignatow. SP IgnaD

I wish I was a gentleman. True Democracy. D. H. Lawrence CP-LawrD

I wish I were a Girl Oulde. Wish, A. G. K. Chesterton. CP-ChesG

I wish I were a jelly fish. Triolet: "I wish I were a jelly fish." G. K. Chesterton. CP-ChesG

I wish I were a little bird. Christina Georgina Rossetti. CP-RosC3

I wish I were a Thibetan monk. Away from It All. Ogden Nash. CP-NashO

I wish I'd want what I don't want, Lord, at all. Michelangelo Buonarroti. CP-Miche, *tr. by* John Frederick Nims

I wish it were over the terrible pain. Introspective. Christina Georgina Rossetti. CP-RosC3

I wish it were spring in the world. Craving for Spring. D. H. Lawrence. CP-LawrD

I wish it were the nineteen-fifties. Nostalgia for Edith Sitwell. Richard Eberhart. CP-EberR

I wish my mother could see me now, with a fence-post under my arm. M. I. Rudyard Kipling. CP-KiplR

I wish not to lie here. Iona: the Graves of the Kings. Robinson Jeffers. CP-JefR2

I wish one could be sure the suffering. Emily Dickinson. SP-DickE

I wish that when you died last May. May and Death. Robert Browning. CP-BroR1

I wish the bell saved you. Once the Dream Begins. Yusef Komunyakaa. CP-KomuY

I wish the long ship Argo had never passed that perilous channel between the Symplegades. Medea. Euripides. CP-JefR3, *tr. by* Robinson Jeffers

I wish the rent. Little Lyric (*Of Great Importance*). Langston Hughes. CP-HughL

I wish them cramps. Wishes for Sons. Lucille Clifton. SP-ClifL

I wish they'd wrap that rug around me. Model, The. Jaroslav Seifert. SP-SeifJ, *tr. by* Ewald Osers

I wish thy lot, now bad, still worse my friend. To a Friend in Distress. William Cowper. CP-CowpW

I wish to God I never saw you, Mag. Mag. Carl Sandburg. CP-SandC

I wish to own only the warmth. Thief. Alice Walker. CP-WalkA

I wish to see it never. Concerning His Old Home. Thomas Hardy. CP-HardT

I wish to sing no more as once I did. Petrarch. CP-Petra, *tr. by* J. G. Nichols

I wish to tune my quivering lyre. From Anacreon. Lord Byron. CP-Byron

I wish we once were wedded,—then I must be true. Look on This Picture and on This. Christina Georgina Rossetti. CP-RosC3

I wish you were a pleasant wren. Child's Talk in April. Christina Georgina Rossetti. CP-RosC1

I wish you were here, dear. Song, A: "I wish you were here, dear." Joseph Brodsky. CP-BrodJ

I wish your body were in the grave. Song of Sour Grapes, A. Countee Cullen. CP-CullC

I Wish Your Reverence Were Here to *Hear* the Trumpets. Thomas Sheridan. CP-SherT

I wish'd the world a blindness. George Meredith. CP-MerG2

I wished for death often. Above Everything. David Ignatow. SP-IgnaD

I wist not that I had the pow'r to sing. Question, A. Paul Laurence Dunbar. CP-DunbP

I with a Housemaid once was curst. Charade: "I with a Housemaid once was curst." Henry Thomas Austen. CP-AustJ

I with foolish mind and heedless zeal formerly. John Milton. CP-MiltJ

I, with legs crossed along the daylight, watch. Prelude: "I, with legs crossed along the daylight, watch." Derek Walcott. CP-WalcD

I woke from a dream of verbs. NOW. Grace Paley. CP-PalGC

I woke from a first-day-of-snow dream. Dream on the Night of First Snow, A. Robert Bly. SP-BlyR

I woke in the night and heard the wind, and it blowing half a gale. Edna St. Vincent Millay. CP-MillE

I woke / Just about daybreak, and fell back. Poems to a Brown Cricket. James Wright. CP-WrigJ

I woke to a shout: 'I am Alpha and Omega.' Gog. Ted Hughes. SP-HughTN

I woke up feeling wiped out. God knows. Phenomenon, The. Raymond Carver. CP-CarvR

I woke up in the dark. After *The Little Mariner*. Olga Broumas. SP-BrouO

I woke up this mornin'. Sylvester's Dying Bed. Langston Hughes. CP-HughL; CP-HughL2

I woke up tousled, one strap falling. Little Poems. John Updike. CP-UpdiJ

I woke up with a spot of blood. Scratch, The. Raymond Carver. CP-CarvR

I wokr in Florida, late and lazy, my sill. Yet Not to Listen to That Sung Nothing. John Ciardi. CP-CiarJ

I wonder about the trees. Sound of Trees, The. Robert Frost. CP-FrosR

I wonder, by my troth, what thou and I. Good-Morrow, The. John Donne. CP-DonnJ; MW-DonnJ

I wonder, can the night go by. Excursion Train. D. H. Lawrence. CP-LawrD

I wonder do you feel today. Two in the Campagna. Robert Browning. CP-BroR1; SP-BroR

I wonder, have I lived a skeleton's life. First Warmth. Wallace Stevens. CP-StevWP

I wonder how it feels. Aspiration. Langston Hughes. CP-HughL; CP-HughL2

I wonder how many old men last winter. Minneapolis Poem, The. James Wright. CP-WrigJ

I wonder if sometimes in the dusk. Stephen Crane. CP-CranS

I wonder if the sap is stirring yet. First Spring Day, The. Christina Georgina Rossetti. CP-RosC1

I wonder if they sleep better here. Graveyard by the Sea. Thomas Lux. SP-LuxT

I wonder if with you, as it is with me. After Many Days. D. H. Lawrence. CP-LawrD

I wonder what I should do now. Looking Over the Acreage. A. R. Ammons. CP-AmmoA

I wonder what Spanish poets would say about this. Cicada Blue. Charles Wright. SP-WrigCN

I wonder what they called. Spray. Carl Sandburg. CP-SandC

I wonder what to mean by *sanctuary*, if a real or. Triphammer Bridge. A. R. Ammons. CP-AmmoA

I wonder whether one expects. Thomas Kinsella. CP-KinsT

I wonder whether the Girls are mad. William Bond. William Blake. CP-BlakW

I wonder whether two trees standing side by side really need each other. Life They Lead, The. David Ignatow. SP-IgnaD

I wonder why Proust should have thought. Phèdre. Stevie Smith. CP-SmitS

I wondered about their things. Were they large or small? Huddle of Need, A. John Berryman. CP-BerrJ

I wondered ever too what my fate would be. Search, The. John Berryman. CP-BerrJ

I wondered what had. They. Robert Creeley. CP-CreeR

I won't be able to complain. Living Sky. Federico García Lorca. CP-GarcF, *tr. by* Greg Simon *and* Steven F. White

I won't be able to write from the grave. Fanny Howe. SP-HoweF *Fr.* O'Clock.

I won't be at this boring poetry reading / again! Ann Arbor Song. Ted Berrigan. SP-BerrT

I won't crawl into. Under House Arrest. Yusef Komunyakaa. CP-KomuY

I won't go with you. I want to stay with Grandpa! My Last Afternoon with Uncle Devereux Winslow. Robert Lowell. SP-LoweR

I won't look at her. Work. Yusef Komunyakaa. CP-KomuY

I work all day, and get half-drunk at night. Aubade: "I work all day, and get half-drunk at night." Philip Larkin. CP-LarkP

I work all day, / Said Simple John. Pierrot. Langston Hughes. CP-HughL; CP-HughL1

I work to drive the awe away. Emily Dickinson. SP-DickE

I worked for a woman. Madam and Her Madam. Langston Hughes. CP-HughL; CP-HughL2

I worked for chaff and earning Wheat. Emily Dickinson. CP-DickE

I Worked No Wile to Meet You. Thomas Hardy. CP-HardT

I works all day. Workin' Man. Langston Hughes. CP-HughL; CP-HughL1

I worship the greatest first. Hippolytus Temporizes. "H. D." CP-DoolH

I would adorn the day and give it voice. Day Unto Day Uttereth Speech. Jones Very. CP-VeryJ

I would at this late hour little as may be. Compline. John Berryman. CP-BerrJ

I would bathe myself in strangeness. Plunge. Ezra Pound. CP-PoEar

I would be buried beside my parents. Sky. David Ignatow. SP-IgnaD

I would be happy in the knowledge. Paul Muldoon. CP-MuldP *Fr.* Last Poems.

I would be ignorant as the dawn. Dawn, The. William Butler Yeats. CP-YeatW

I would be married, but I'd[e] have no wife. On Marriage. Richard Crashaw. CP-CrasR

I would be meek as He who bore his cross. Meek, The. Jones Very. CP-VeryJ

I would be one with the dark, dark earth. Traveller-Heart, The. Nicholas Vachel Lindsay. CP-LindV

I would be simple again. Disillusion. Langston Hughes. CP-HughL; CP-HughL1

I would be the bounding deer. Song: "I would be the bounding deer." George Meredith. CP-MerG2

I would beat out your face in brass. Face. Carl Sandburg. CP-SandC

I would begin by explaining. Poem for D. H. Lawrence. Robert Creeley. CP-CreeR

I would build a cloudy House. House of Clouds, The. Elizabeth Barrett Browning. CP-BroEB

I would call Attila on his little horse. Attila. D. H. Lawrence. CP-LawrD

I would come in a shirt of hair. Love Song of St. Sebastian, The. T. S. Eliot. SP-EliotT

I would distil a cup. Emily Dickinson. CP-DickE

I would enfold you in my. Like the Octopus. James Laughlin. CP-LaugJ

I would go home o go home to the rough. Powers, The. George Oppen. CP-OppGN

I would have each couple turn. Dance, The. Wendell Berry. CP-BerrW

I would have gone; God bade me stay. Weary in Well-Doing. Christina Georgina Rossetti. CP-RosC1

I would have it, were I bold. Paul Muldoon. CP-MuldP *Fr.* Last Poems.

I would have touched the heavenly key. Emily Jane Brontë. CP-BronE

I would hope fo the children of West Ham. Wish, A. Ivor Gurney. SP-GurnI

I would I had a flower-boy! Plaint of the Poet in an Ignorant Age. Carolyn Kizer. CP-KizeC

I Would I Were a Careless Child. Lord Byron. CP-Byron

I would I were the drop of rain. Song: "I would I were the drop of rain." George Meredith. CP-MerG1

I would I were with Jean. George Meredith. CP-MerG2

I would lie low, the ground on which men tread. Earth, The. Jones Very. CP-VeryJ

I would like a few men to be at peace with. Compari. D. H. Lawrence. CP-LawrD

I would like my last poem thus. My Last Poem. Manuel Bandeira. CP-BishE

I would like my love to die. Poem: "I would like my love to die." Samuel Beckett. CP-BeckS

I would like to be a sinner. It Gives Me Pause. Langston Hughes. CP-HughL; CP-HughL2

I would like to be a white man, wouldn't you? Song of Adoration. Langston Hughes. CP-HughL; CP-HughL3

I would like to believe in something. 25 February 1944. Primo Levi. CP-LeviP, *tr. by* Ruth Feldman *and* Brian Swann

I would like to sleep with deer. Moral Poem Freely Accepted from Sappho, A. James Wright. CP-WrigJ

I would like to speak of this memory. Far Off. Constantine P. Cavafy. CP-CavaC, *tr. by* Theoharis Constantine Theoharis

I would like to throw a net over these moments when i find myself. Les Fleurs du Cinéma. Andrei Codrescu. SP-CodrA

I would like to watch a movie tonight. Movies, The. Billy Collins. SP-CollB

I would like to watch you sleeping. Variation on the Word *Sleep*. Margaret Atwood. SP-AtwM2

I would liken you. Ardella. Langston Hughes. CP-HughL; CP-HughL1

I would live all my life in nonchalance and insouciance. Introspective Reflection. Ogden Nash. CP-NashO

I would lose myself. Song in Brown. Federico García Lorca. CP-GarcF, *tr. by* Jerome Rothenberg *Fr.* Fairs.

I would love to kiss you. Jelaluddin Rumi. SP-Rumi, *tr. by* Coleman Barks

I would make this all as single as a song. To William Carlos Williams. Richard Eberhart. CP-EberR

I would never have thought I would be born here. Crossroads of the World Etc., The. W. S. Merwin. CP-MerwW

I would not be a king—enough. Fragment: "I would not be a king—enough." Percy Bysshe Shelley. CP-ShelP

I would not breathe, when blows thy mighty wind. Spirit, The. Jones Very. CP-VeryJ

I would not call my love a red, red rose. Sonnet. Sam Hamill. SP-HamiS

"I Would Not Change For Thine." William Carlos Williams. CP-WilW2

I would not despoil this page. Flow of Thought. Richard Eberhart. CP-EberR

I would not if I could undo my past. They Desire a Better Country. Christina Georgina Rossetti. CP-RosC1

I would not paint—a picture. Emily Dickinson. CP-DickE

I would not rest till work came from my hand. Ivor Gurney. SP-GurnI

I would not sin, in this half-playful strain. Tent on the Beach, The. John Greenleaf Whittier. CP-WhitJ

I would not study Nature's lore. Nature a Living Teacher. Jones Very. CP-VeryJ

I would not tarry, Look! the things before. Things Before, The. Jones Very. CP-VeryJ

I would not trace the hackneyed phrase. Lines for an Album. James Whitcomb Riley. CP-RileJ

I would not wish to sit. Between Two Prisoners. James Dickey. CP-DickJ

I would purify my own idyllic verse. Landscape. Charles Baudelaire. CP-BaudC, *tr. by* Walter Martin

I would rather look down. From a Book. William Carlos Williams. CP-WilW1

I would rather sit still in a state of peace on a stone. Choice. D. H. Lawrence. CP-LawrD

I would say to all parents. Education. G. K. Chesterton. CP-ChesG

I would shake off the lethargy of this our time. Revolt. Ezra Pound. CP-PoEar

I would take you. Meeting Her in Chapultepec. Jay Wright. SP-WrigJ

I would that folk forgot me quite. Tess's Lament. Thomas Hardy. CP-HardT

I would that we were, my beloved, white birds on the foam of the sea! White Birds, The. William Butler Yeats. CP-YeatW

I would the gift I offer here. Dedication: "I would the gift I offer here." John Greenleaf Whittier. CP-WhitJ

I would the saints could hear our prayers! Divine and Human Pleading. Christina Georgina Rossetti. CP-RosC3

I would to God I were quenched and fed. Anguish, The. Edna St. Vincent Millay. CP-MillE

I would to God, that mine old age might have. His Wish to God. Robert Herrick. CP-HerrR

I would wear it. Langston Hughes. *See* Wear it / Like a banner

I would weigh out my love with nicest care. Fragments, The. Jones Very. CP-VeryJ

I would write poems of love of such a kind. Petrarch. CP-Petra, *tr. by* J. G. Nichols

I wouldn't / embarrass you. Song: "I wouldn't / embarrass you." Robert Creeley. CP-CreeR

I wouldn't have known if I didn't stay home. Night in a World, A. Heather McHugh. SP-McHuH

I wouldn't if I could, Love, check the urge. Michelangelo Buonarroti. CP-Miche, *tr. by* John Frederick Nims

I wouldn't know how rare they come these days. Recognition, A. May Sarton. SP-SartM

I wouldn't like to upset the universe. Unresolved Burdens. Primo Levi. CP-LeviP, *tr. by* Ruth Feldman

I wouldn't much object, if I were black. Negro Cemetery Next to a White One, A. Howard Nemerov. CP-NemeH

I wouldn't say it was a particularly low time, it was. Overhead Mirrors. Charles Bukowski. SP-BukC3

I wound myself in a white cocoon of singing. Dragonfly, The. Edna St. Vincent Millay. CP-MillE

I write for antiquity. Enemy Number One. Carl Sandburg. CP-SandC

I write from the denser enclave of the stricken. From a Clinic Waiting Room. Amy Clampitt. CP-ClamA

I write in the midst of Sweet-Peas. Emily Dickinson. SP-DickE

I write my name as one. Autograph, An. John Greenleaf Whittier. CP-WhitJ

I write now in English and now in Scots. Caledonian Antisyzygy, The. Hugh MacDiarmid. SP-MacDH

I write only to say this. James Vincent Cunningham. CP-CunnJ

I write the lips of the moon upon her shoulders. In a temple of. Not Many Kingdoms Left. Kenneth Patchen. CP-PatcK

I write the Rascal thanks till he & I. On H[ayley] the Pick Thank. William Blake. CP-BlakW

I Write This Upon the Last Drink's Hammer. Charles Bukowski. SP-BukC2

I write to capture the meaningless as it were an animal in the thickets. David Ignatow. SP-IgnaD

I write what I know on one side of the paper. Paper II. Carl Sandburg. CP-SandC

I write you in my need. Please write. James Vincent Cunningham. CP-CunnJ

I write you this out of another province. Letter from the Land of Sinners. Adrienne Rich. CP-RicAE; SP-RicA2

I wrote a poem on the mist. Last Answers. Carl Sandburg. CP-SandC

I wrote stubbornly into the evening. Nexus. Rita Dove. SP-DoveR

I wrote the president. Rite, The. John Ciardi. CP-CiarJ

I wrote 2 letters & a postcard. Philip Whalen. SP-WhalP

I Years had been from Home. Emily Dickinson. CP-DickE

I Yield to My Learned Brother or Is There a Candlestick Maker in the House? Ogden Nash. CP-NashO

"I yield you my whole heart, Countess," said he. Question of Marriage, A. Thomas Hardy. CP-HardT

Ia Drang Valley. Yusef Komunyakaa. CP-KomuY

Iago. Walter De la Mare. CP-DeLaW

Iago. Robert Graves. CP-GravR

Iago learned from that old witch, his mother. Iago. Robert Graves. CP-GravR

Ibis. Norman Dubie. CP-DubiN

Ibn Gabirol. Yehuda Amichai. SP-AmicYL, *tr. by* Benjamin Harshav *and* Barbara Harshav

Ibn Gabirol. Yehuda Amichai. SP-AmicY, *tr. by* Stephen Mitchell

Ibycus of Samos. Robert Graves. CP-GravR

Icarium Mare. Richard Wilbur. CP-WilbR

Icarus. Stephen Spender. CP-SpenS

(Airman.) CP-SpenS

Ice. Ai. SP-Ai

Ice. Robert Lowell. SP-LoweR

Ice. Mary Oliver. SP-OlivM

Ice. Stephen Spender. CP-SpenS

Ice age is here, The. Attention. Adrienne Rich. CP-RicAE; SP-RicA2

Ice-Blue Wind, The. Tennessee Williams. CP-WillT

Ice-cold passion. Poem to a Dead Soldier. Langston Hughes. CP-HughL; CP-HughL1

Ice Cream. Robert Creeley. CP-CreeR

Ice Cream at Blauenberg. Charles Tomlinson. CP-TomlC

Ice-Cream Wars, The. John Ashbery. SP-AshbJ

Ice, Eden. Paul Celan. SP-CelaP, *tr. by* John Felstiner

Ice-Fishing. William Stafford. SP-StafWW

Ice Floe. Arthur Sze. SP-SzeA

Ice from the wings, a rattle against metal. All right, come down. Muriel Rukeyser. CP-RukeM

Ice-gate over the land, a shock of closure. Muriel Rukeyser. CP-RukeM

Ice Handler. Carl Sandburg. CP-SandC

Ice not / wet not. Blue. Robert Creeley. CP-CreeR

Ice on the Highway. Thomas Hardy. CP-HardT

Ice / on the minnow bucket. Autumn. Lorine Niedecker. CP-NiedL

Ice Shall Cover Nineveh. Kenneth Rexroth. CP-RexrK

Ice Skin, The. James Dickey. CP-DickJ

Ice Storm. Robert Earl Hayden. CP-HaydR

Ice-Storm, The. Robert Pinsky. CP-PinsR

Iceberg, The. Randall Jarrell. CP-JarrR

Icebergs. Louis MacNeice. CP-MacNL

Icebergs italicize the Sea. Emily Dickinson. SP-DickE

Iced over soon; it's nothing; we're used to sickness. Ice. Robert Lowell. SP-LoweR

Iced stones in a nice hotel. Fanny Howe. SP-HoweF *Fr.* O'Clock.

Iced with a vanilla. Meeting of Cultures, A. Donald Davie. CP-DaviDC

Icehouse in Summer, The. Howard Nemerov. CP-NemeH

Iceland. Jorge Luis Borges. SP-BorgJ, *tr. by* Hoyt Rogers

Iceland. Louis MacNeice. CP-MacNL

Iceland of the seas. Iceland. Jorge Luis Borges. SP-BorgJ, *tr. by* Hoyt Rogers

Iceland Revisited. W. H. Auden. CP-AudeW

Ich Dien. Lord Byron. CP-Byron

Ichabod[!] John Greenleaf Whittier. CP-WhitJ

Ichetucknee. Richard Eberhart. CP-EberR

Ichneumons are fond of little ichneumons. Some of My Best Friends Are Children. Ogden Nash. CP-NashO

Icicles. Robert Pinsky. CP-PinsR

Icon. Marge Piercy. SP-PierM

Iconia. George Meredith. CP-MerG2

Icos. Charles Tomlinson. CP-TomlC

Icosasphere, The. Marianne Craig Moore. CP-MoorM

Icta fenestra Euri flatu stridebat, avarus. Avarus et Plutus. John Gay. CP-CowpW

ICU: Space/Time in the Waiting Room. Miller Williams. CP-WillM

Icy evil that struck his father down, The. El-Hajj Malik El-Shabazz. Robert Earl Hayden. CP-HaydR

ID. Heather McHugh. SP-McHuH

I'd almost know, the nights I snuck in late. Fifteen to Eighteen. Marilyn Hacker. SP-HackM

I'd be a dainty contained cool. If I Were a Bird. Lorine Niedecker. CP-NiedL

I'd curse if the sun left these shores! Michael and Christine. Arthur Rimbaud. CP-RimbA, *tr. by* Martin Sorrell

I'd Die for You. Robert Graves. CP-GravR

I'd feel lost as Lorca. Uncertainty in Blue. Yusef Komunyakaa. CP-KomuY

I'd feel the more secure. Michelangelo Buonarroti. CP-Miche, *tr. by* John Frederick Nims

I'd forgotten and / how could I ever. C. K. Williams. CP-WillC

I'd give anything if only my life were an oxcart. Fernando Pessoa. SP-PessF *Fr.* Keeper of Sheep, The.

I'd give everything I own for that fawn. Fawn, The. Shmuel HaNagid. SP-HaNaS, *tr. by* Peter Cole

I'd give everything I own for that gazelle. Gazelle, The. Shmuel HaNagid. SP-HaNaS, *tr. by* Peter Cole

I'd have the silence like a heavy chock. Zip! Donald Davie. CP-DaviDC

I'd have you t' know, George, Dan, Dean, 'nd Nim. Copy of a Copy of Verses

from Thomas Sheridan, Clerk, to George Nim-Dan-Dean, Esq., A. Thomas Sheridan. CP-SherT

I'd have you to know, as sure as you're Dean. Letter from Dr. Sheridan to Dr. Swift, A. Thomas Sheridan. CP-SherT

I'd intended to place it on a wall in my room. From the Drawer. Constantine P. Cavafy. CP-CavaC, *tr. by* Theoharis Constantine Theoharis

I'd just heard that day. Minor Sacrifice, A. A. K. Ramanujan. CP-RamaA

I'd like every girl in the world to have a poem of her own. Yours. C. K. Williams. CP-WillC; SP-WillC

I'd like to be able to say a good word for parsley, but I can't. Parsley for Vice-President! Ogden Nash. CP-NashO

I'd like to be cheerful, she said. All day. Small Confession. Yannis Ritsos. SP-RitsY, *tr. by* Kimon Friar

I'd Like to Be Putty. James Laughlin. CP-LaugJ

I'd like to die like this. Crossing on Staten Island Ferry. Kenneth Patchen. CP-PatcK

I'd like to have a country house. House with a Garden. Constantine P. Cavafy. CP-CavaC, *tr. by* Theoharis Constantine Theoharis

I'd like to have a word. Book of Lies, The. James Tate. SP-TateJ

I'd like to live on Tulip Street. Passaic, N.J. William Carlos Williams. CP-WilW2

I'd like to / Pull. Intelligent Sheepman and the New Cars, The. William Carlos Williams. CP-WilW2

I'd like to see it once. Gravity. Charles Simic. SP-SimiC; SP-SimiCE

I'd pictured your poem like the king's daughter. Critique, The. Shmuel HaNagid. SP-HaNaS, *tr. by* Peter Cole

I'd rather be Muriel. Not to Be Printed, Not to Be Said, Not to Be Thought. Muriel Rukeyser. CP-RukeM

I'd rather read an account. Song: "I'd rather read an account." William Carlos Williams. CP-WilW2

I'd rather recollect a setting. Emily Dickinson. CP-DickE

I'd ride a cock horse to Banbury Cross. Absentees, The. Ogden Nash. CP-NashO

I'd seen / their hoofprints in the deep. Five A.M. in the Pinewoods. Mary Oliver. SP-OlivM

I'd speak if I wasn't afraid of inhaling. Fanny Howe. SP-HoweF *Fr.* Introduction to the World.

I'd Suck Bitter Poison From The Viper's Mouth. Shmuel HaNagid. SP-HaNaS, *tr. by* Peter Cole

I'd tell them to have an unhappy love. Now, If You Were Teaching Creative Writing, He Asked, What Would You Tell Them? Charles Bukowski. SP-BukC1

I'd think "wonder / if" if. E. E. Cummings. CP-CummE

"I'd Understand Yer Poemes Better," Writes the Lady Editor from San Francisco, "If I Knowed What the Words Mean." Robert Stock. SP-StocR

I'd want her eyes to fill with wonder. Kenneth Patchen. CP-PatcK

Idea. Czeslaw Milosz. CP-MiloC; CP-MiloCN, *tr. by* Robert Hass

Idea. Howard Nemerov. CP-NemeH

Idea blazes in darkness, a lonely star. Idea. Howard Nemerov. CP-NemeH

Idea of Flying, The. Donald Hall. CP-HallD

Idea of justice may be precious, An. Ode: "Idea of justice may be precious, An." Frank O'Hara. SP-OharF

Idea of Order at Key West, The. Wallace Stevens. CP-StevW; CP-StevWP

Idea of the Good, The. James Wright. CP-WrigJ

Idea of Trust, The. Thom Gunn. CP-GunnT

Idea ran about the world, An. Return, The. Muriel Rukeyser. CP-RukeM

Ideal, The. Charles Baudelaire. CP-BaudC, *tr. by* Walter Martin

Ideal and loved voices. Voices. Constantine P. Cavafy. CP-CavaC, *tr. by* Theoharis Constantine Theoharis

Ideal and the Real, The. Richard Eberhart. CP-EberR

Ideal Landscape. Adrienne Rich. CP-RicAE; SP-RicA2

Idealism. Ralph Waldo Emerson. CP-EmerR

Ideally, you should be in your own. American Living Room, The: A Tract. William Meredith. SP-MereW

Ideals are like the stars. Teacher. Langston Hughes. CP-HughL; CP-HughL1

Ideals are the Fairy Oil. Emily Dickinson. CP-DickE

Ideas hit like / planks hitting water. Some skim. Hayden Carruth. CP-CarHS *Fr.* Clay Hill Anthology, The.

Idem 1. Michael Palmer. SP-PalmM

Idem 2. Michael Palmer. SP-PalmM

Idem 4. Michael Palmer. SP-PalmM

Idem 3. Michael Palmer. SP-PalmM

Identical, electrifying Eyes. Living Torch, The. Charles Baudelaire. CP-BaudC, *tr. by* Walter Martin

Identities. Paul Muldoon. CP-MuldP

Identities. William Stafford. SP-StafWW

Identities become confused. Penates. Tennessee Williams. CP-WillT

Identity. A. R. Ammons. CP-AmmoA

Identity and Argument for Prayer. Robert Penn Warren. CP-WarrR

Identity Check. Hans Magnus Enzensberger. SP-EnzeH

Identity, known or unknown, survives. Indecision. Helen Pinkerton. CP-PinkH

Identity of opposites had linked us, The. Pact, The. Robert Graves. CP-GravR

Identity, that spectator. James Vincent Cunningham. CP-CunnJ

Ideogram. William Meredith. SP-MereW

Ides of March, The. Constantine P. Cavafy. CP-CavaC, *tr.* by Theoharis Constantine Theoharis

Ides of March, The. Richard Eberhart. CP-EberR

Idiom of the Hero. Wallace Stevens. CP-StevW; CP-StevWP

Idiomatic. Billy Collins. SP-CollB

Idiot. Allen Tate. CP-TateA

Idiot, An. James Whitcomb Riley. CP-RileJ

Idiot, The. Hart Crane. CP-CranH

Idiot, The. Yannis Ritsos. SP-RitsY, *tr.* by Kimon Friar

Idiot bird leaps out and drunken leans, The. Doomsday. Sylvia Plath. CP-PlatS

Idiot Boy, The. Rudyard Kipling. CP-KiplR *Fr.* Muse among the Motors, The.

Idiot Boy, The. William Wordsworth. CP-WorW1; MW-WorW

Idiot greens the meadows with his eyes, The. Idiot. Allen Tate. CP-TateA

Idiot, last night, I prayed thee but forbear. To Groom Idiot. Ben Jonson. CP-JonsB; SP-JonsB

Idiotic and Politic. Jay Wright. SP-WrigJ

Idle boys the Sunday never heed, The. Young Rabbits. John Clare. SP-ClarJ

Idle dayseye, the laborious wheel, The. . Richard Wilbur. CP-WilbR

Idle I called on an eminent monk. Han-shan. CP-ColdM, *tr.* by Red Pine

Idle I sat—my book upon my knee. Dream, A. Walter De la Mare. CP-DeLaW

Idle man, An. Sometimes he feels like crying. Bitter Knowledge. Yannis Ritsos. SP-RitsY, *tr.* by Kostas Myrsiades

Idle Shepherd-Boys, The; or, Dungeon-Ghyll Force. A Pastoral. William Wordsworth. CP-WorW1; MW-WorW

Idle Talk. Louis MacNeice. CP-MacNL

Idleness. Walter De la Mare. CP-DeLaW

Idleness gilds an encompassing giantess. Giantess, The. Richard Eberhart. CP-EberR

Idler, The. Jones Very. CP-VeryJ

Idling through the mean space dozing. Choice. A. R. Ammons. CP-AmmoA

Idol, The. Arsehole Sonnet. Arthur Rimbaud. CP-RimbA, *tr.* by Martin Sorrell

Idol of Sarapis, The. Clement of Alexandria. CP-MertT *Fr.* Diatribe Against the Old Gods.

Idolatry. G. K. Chesterton. CP-ChesG

Idrigill. Charles Tomlinson. CP-TomlC

Idris—Ilyas: two names / One star, one prophet. Lubnan. Thomas Merton. CP-MertT

Idyl. Dorothy Parker. CP-ParkD

Idyl: "In a valley late bees with whining gold." Allen Tate. CP-TateA

Idyl: "They say to me, 'There is'." William Carlos Williams. CP-WilW1

Idyl: "Wine of the grey sky." William Carlos Williams. CP-WilW1

Idyl for Glaucus, An. Ezra Pound. CP-PoEar

Idyll 3: Amaryllis. Theocritus. CP-DryJ2 *Fr.* Idylls.

Idyll 18: The Epithalamium of Helen and Menelaus. Theocritus. CP-DryJ2 *Fr.* Idylls.

Idyll 23: The Despairing Lover. Theocritus. CP-DryJ2 *Fr.* Idylls.

Idyll 27: Daphnis. Theocritus. CP-DryJ2 *Fr.* Idylls.

Idyll, An: "Tea is made; the red fogs shut round the house but the gas burns." G. K. Chesterton. CP-ChesG

Idyll: "As a horn of the high moon veers in clear skies over Main Street." Giorgio Bassani. CP-DaviDC, *tr.* by Donald Davie

Idyll: "Door: / PER L'UNIVERSO / is what it says, A." Charles Tomlinson. CP-TomlC; SP-TomlC

Idyll: "Now as from maple to elm the flittermice skitter and twirl." Theodore Roethke. CP-RoetT

Idyll of Ascension. Alan Dugan. CP-DugaA

Idyll: "You wanted me to tell you." Federico García Lorca. CP-GarcF, *tr.* by Alan S. Trueblood *Fr.* Love.

Idylls. Theocritus.

   Cyclops, The. CP-BroEB

   Idyll 3: Amaryllis. CP-DryJ2

   Idyll 18: The Epithalamium of Helen and Menelaus. CP-DryJ2

   Idyll 23: The Despairing Lover. CP-DryJ2

   Idyll 27: Daphnis. CP-DryJ2

Idylls of the King. Alfred Tennyson. CP-TennA

Iernë's eyes were glazed and dim. Emily Jane Brontë. CP-BronE

If. Robert Creeley. SP-CreeR

If. E. E. Cummings. CP-CummE

If. Paul Laurence Dunbar. CP-DunbP

If—. Rudyard Kipling. CP-KiplR

If. Czeslaw Milosz. CP-MiloCN, *tr.* by Robert Hass

If. Christina Georgina Rossetti. *See* Hoping Against Hope

If. Robert Penn Warren. CP-WarrR

If a cheerfulest Elephantangelchild should sit. E. E. Cummings. CP-CummE; SP-CummE

If a city / takes its rhythms. St. Louis Out of Time. Audre Lorde. SP-LordA

If a cuckoo comes into the village. Way It Is, The. Charles Simic. SP-SimiC

If a god, Love, can't you do. Michelangelo Buonarroti. CP-Miche, *tr.* by John Frederick Nims

If a joyous heart makes beautiful the face. Michelangelo Buonarroti. CP-Miche, *tr.* by John Frederick Nims

If a life could own another life. Identities. William Stafford. SP-StafWW

If a man can say of his life or. Mind's Games, The. William Carlos Williams. CP-WilW2

If a man stands by a pin oak emptying. Ghost. Norman Dubie. CP-DubiN

If a man steps on a stranger's foot. Apologies. Chuang Tzu. CP-MertT

If a Man who Turnips cries. Turnip Vendor, The. Samuel Johnson. CP-JohnS

If a man with a shovel came down the road. Diggers, The. W. S. Merwin. SP-MerwW

If a mouse could fly, / Or if a crow could swim. Christina Georgina Rossetti. CP-RosC2

If a Phoenincian born I am, what then? Sir Walter Ralegh. CP-RaleW

If a pig wore a wig. If a Pig Wore a Wig. Christina Georgina Rossetti. CP-RosC2

If a Poem Can Be Headed into Its Proper Current. Kenneth Patchen. CP-PatcK

If a Poet. James Laughlin. CP-LaugJ

If a rock on the slope. Impulse. A. R. Ammons. CP-AmmoA

If a stranger asked me. Four Small Windows. Jaroslav Seifert. SP-SeifJ, *tr.* by Ewald Osers

If a stranger passed the tent of Hóseyn, he cried "A churl's!" Muléykeh. Robert Browning. CP-BroR2

If Accusation onely can draw blood. Accusation. Robert Herrick. CP-HerrR

If Actually Dead. Constantine P. Cavafy. CP-CavaC, *tr.* by Theoharis Constantine Theoharis

If, after attaining Buddhahood, anyone in my land. Amitabha's Vow. Gary Snyder. CP-SnydG *Fr.* Myths and Texts.

If, after I die, they want to write my biography. Fernando Pessoa. SP-PessF, *tr.* by Susan M. Brown *and* Edwin Honig

If after rude and boisterous seas. Plaudite, or End of Life, The. Robert Herrick. CP-HerrR

If all a top physicist knows. After Reading a Child's Guide to Modern Physics. W. H. Auden. CP-AudeW

"If all example is from nature," I. Down Narrow Stairs from a Thin Eye. John Ciardi. CP-CiarJ

If all his mourning friends unselfishly. Noblest Service, The. James Whitcomb Riley. CP-RileJ

If all rivers are sweet. Pablo Neruda. SP-NeruP *Fr.* Question Book.

If all the gentlest-hearted friends I know. Apprehension, An. Elizabeth Barrett Browning. CP-BroEB

If all the grief and woe and bitterness. Planh for the Young English King. Bertrans de Born. CP-PoEar; SP-PounE, *tr.* by Ezra Pound

If all the griefs I am to have. Emily Dickinson. CP-DickE

If all the sky were full of stars. Babe Unborn, The. G. K. Chesterton. CP-ChesG

If all the tears you shed so lavishly. To Marjorie Rambeau; In "Daddy's Gone A-Hunting." Dorothy Parker. CP-ParkD

If all the world and love were young. Nymph's [*or* Nimphs] Reply to the Shepherd [*or* Sheepheard], The. Sir Walter Ralegh. CP-MarlC; CP-RaleW

If all these Cupids now were blind. Ben Jonson. CP-JonsB *Fr.* Masque of Beauty, The.

If all this world had no original[l]. Lucretius. CP-RaleW *Fr.* De Rerum Natura (On the Nature of Things).

If all those females who so passionately loved. Film Passion. D. H. Lawrence. CP-LawrD

If all transgressions here should have their pay. Gods Providence. Robert Herrick. CP-HerrR

If all were rain and never sun. Christina Georgina Rossetti. CP-RosC2

If all you boast of your great art be true. To Alchemists. Ben Jonson. CP-JonsB; SP-JonsB

If amorous faith in heart unfeigned. Sir Thomas Wyatt. CP-WyatT

If an expert does not have some problem to vex him, he is unhappy! Active Life. Chuang Tzu. CP-MertT

If an old board laid out in a field. Praising Dark Places. Yusef Komunyakaa. CP-KomuY

If an unfeigning heart, and amorous faith. Petrarch. CP-Petra, *tr.* by J. G. Nichols

If, antique hateful bird. Raven, The. Adrienne Rich. CP-RicAE

If any day a promised play. At a Rehearsal of One of J.M.B.'s Plays. Thomas Hardy. CP-HardT

If any duck in any brook. Sonatina to Hans Christian. Wallace Stevens. CP-StevW; CP-StevWP

If any God should say. Rebirth. Rudyard Kipling. CP-KiplR

If any hath the heart to kill. Thomas Campion. CP-CampT

If any in an island cradle curled. In Memoriam P. D. G. K. Chesterton. CP-ChesG

If any line I write's a hobbler. Letter from a Cobbler in Patrick's Street to Jet Black, A. Thomas Sheridan. CP-SherT

If any man can better rules impart. Horace. CP-SherT *Fr.* Epistles.

If any man drew near. Woman Homer Sung, A. William Butler Yeats. CP-YeatW

If any of those old proverbs, lord, make sense. Michelangelo Buonarroti. CP-Miche, *tr. by* John Frederick Nims

If any sink, assure that this, now standing. Emily Dickinson. CP-DickE

If any thing delight me for to print. To God. Robert Herrick. CP-HerrR

If anybody says conversation in our day is as good as it was in. Let's Not Play Lotto, Let's Just Talk. Ogden Nash. CP-NashO

If Anybody's Friend be Dead. Emily Dickinson. CP-DickE

If anybody's friend be dead. If Anybody's Friend be Dead. Emily Dickinson. CP-DickE

If anyone asks you. Like This. Jelaluddin Rumi. SP-Rumi, *tr. by* Coleman Barks

If anything should put an end to This. Planners, The. Robert Frost. CP-FrosR

If Anything Will Level with You Water Will. A. R. Ammons. CP-AmmoA

If as a flower [*or* flowre] doth spread and die. Employment (1). George Herbert. CP-HerbG

If, as mine is, thy life a slumber be. To Mr R. W ("If, as mine is, thy life a slumber be"). John Donne. CP-DonnJ; MW-DonnJ

If, as the Greek maintains in the *Cratylus*. Golem, The. Jorge Luis Borges. SP-BorgJ, *tr. by* Alan S. Trueblood

If as the windfels and waters here below. Storm, The. George Herbert. CP-HerbG

If, as their ends, their fruits were so, the same. On Bawds and Usurers. Ben Jonson. CP-JonsB; SP-JonsB

If, as they say, some dust thrown in my eyes. Dust in the Eyes. Robert Frost. CP-FrosR

If asked if I would want to be. Gestures. Rainer Maria Rilke. CP-RilkFr, *tr. by* A. Poulin, Jr.

If at times I say that flowers smile. Fernando Pessoa. SP-PessF *Fr.* Keeper of Sheep, The.

If at your coming princes disappear. Comets and Princes. Samuel Johnson. CP-JohnS

If Auntie doesn't love me. Working Man, The. D. H. Lawrence. CP-LawrD

If being mortised with a dream. E. E. Cummings. CP-CummE

If black were truly black not grey. Greyness Is All. Louis MacNeice. CP-MacNL

If Blame be my side—forfeit Me. Emily Dickinson. CP-DickE

If Blood Were Not as Powerful as It Is. Tess Gallagher. SP-GallT

If Braccio's beauty, phoenix-like, could be. Michelangelo Buonarroti. CP-Miche, *tr. by* John Frederick Nims

If bright the sun, he tarries. Ralph Waldo Emerson. CP-EmerR

If Brother Francis pardoned Brother Flea. Broad Minded Bishop Rebukes the Verminous St. Francis, A. G. K. Chesterton. CP-ChesG

If but some vengeful god would call to me. Hap. Thomas Hardy. CP-HardT

If but that honoured branch which turns away. Petrarch. CP-Petra, *tr. by* J. G. Nichols

If but these thoughts that hurt. Petrarch. CP-Petra, *tr. by* J. G. Nichols

If but this reticent house would speak. Old House, The. Marya Alexandrovna Zaturenska. SP-ZatuM

If by Dull Rhymes Our English Must Be Chained. John Keats. CP-KeatJ

If, by general consent, it should be decided. Carmen 108. Catullus. CP-ZukLS *Fr.* Carmina.

If by its heaven-sent power the mind conceives. Michelangelo Buonarroti. CP-Miche, *tr. by* John Frederick Nims

If calendars are made of square holes, something. January 1, 1973. John Ciardi. CP-CiarJ

If, Calvus, effects of grief. Carmen 96. Catullus. CP-ZukLS *Fr.* Carmina.

If chance assigned [*or* assign'd]. Sir Thomas Wyatt. CP-WyatT

If "compression is the first grace of style." To a Snail. Marianne Craig Moore. CP-MoorM

If, Cornelius, we entrust our secrets. Carmen 102. Catullus. CP-ZukLS *Fr.* Carmina.

If Croesus over Halys goe. Sir Walter Ralegh. CP-RaleW

If curses be the wage of love. Ralph Waldo Emerson. CP-EmerR

If Cynthia Be a Queen. Sir Walter Ralegh. CP-RaleW

(If Synthia Be a Queene, a Princes, and Supreame.) CP-RaleW

If dead, we cease to be; if total gloom. Human Life; on the Denial of Immortality. Samuel Taylor Coleridge. CP-ColeS

If, deare Anthea, my hard fate it be. To Anthea. Robert Herrick. CP-HerrR

If, dearest "Dismal," you for once can dine. Toland's Invitation to Dismal to Dine with the Calves' Head Club. Jonathan Swift. CP-SwifJ

If death comes in July, they'll put me down. Reviewing the Summer and Winter Calender of the Next Life. Maxine W. Kumin. SP-KumiM

If death has buried here, hardly in leaf. Michelangelo Buonarroti. CP-Miche, *tr. by* John Frederick Nims

If Death should claim me for her own to-day. Love-Song: "If Death should claim me for her own to-day." Paul Laurence Dunbar. CP-DunbP

If death were something evil, we'd be surrounded. Rainer Maria Rilke. CP-RilkFr, *tr. by* A. Poulin, Jr. *Fr.* Fragments.

If distance lends enchantment to the view. Eight Years After. Donald Davie. CP-DaviDC

If distraught shall be the word or not. Memorandum. Kenneth Rexroth. CP-RexrK

If down here I chance to die. Ballade of Burial, A. Rudyard Kipling. CP-KiplR

If dreaming really were a kind of truce. Dream. Jorge Luis Borges. SP-BorgJ, *tr. by* Alastair Reid

If each of them wasn't a prig. Drum-Majors in the Labor Day Parade, The. Wallace Stevens. CP-StevWP

If e'er our minds be ill at ease. Travelling. Henry David Thoreau. CP-ThorH

If Ever. Robert Penn Warren. CP-WarrR

If ever against this easy blue and silver. Interruption. Robert Graves. CP-GravR

If ever anyone anywhere, Lesbia, is looking. Carmen 107. Catullus. CP-ZukLS *Fr.* Carmina.

If ever anyone / was deservedly plagued by a goat under his armpits. Carmen 71. Catullus. CP-ZukLS *Fr.* Carmina.

If ever had a covenant been sought. Last Covenant, The. Laura Riding Jackson. CP-RidiL

If ever I am old, and all alone. On the Night of a Friend's Wedding. Edwin Arlington Robinson. CP-RobiE

If ever I had dreamed of my dead name. To My Friend (With an Identity Disc). Wilfred Owen. CP OwenW

If ever I render back your heart. Song for a Slight Voice. Louise Bogan. CP-BogaL

If ever I walk to church to wed. Satin Shoes, The. Thomas Hardy. CP-HardT

If ever joy leave. Face at the Casement, The. Thomas Hardy. CP-HardT

If ever man might him avaunt. Sir Thomas Wyatt. CP-WyatT

If ever Pitty were acquainted. Another on [Mr. Herrys]. Richard Crashaw. CP-CrasR

If ever the lid gets off my head. Emily Dickinson. CP-DickE

If ever there was a beginning. Let There Be Light! D. H. Lawrence. CP LawrD

If Ever There Was One. Miller Williams. CP-WillM

If ever two were one, then surely we. To My Dear and Loving Husband. Anne Bradstreet. CP-BradA

If ever wit or genius shown. Impromptu Epigram upon Being Asked to Accompany Three or Four Very Fine Girls with Some Gentleman in a Rural Walk. Annis Boudinot Stockton. CP-StocA

If ever you come where once it happened. If Ever. Robert Penn Warren. CP-WarrR

If ever you meet a rhinoceros. Replies to Challenges to Rhyme. Robert Browning. CP-BroR2

If Every Person There Is But One. Miller Williams. CP-WillM

If every second squandered while I sat. 151st Psalm, The. Robert Stock. SP-StocR

If everything happens that can't be done. E. E. Cummings. CP-CummE; SP-CummE

If evocations of past kindness shed. Carmen 76. Catullus. CP-ZukLS *Fr.* Carmina.

If external action is effete. Past Is the Present, The. Marianne Craig Moore. CP-MoorM

If Eyes Can See. A. K. Ramanujan. CP-RamaA

If fancy [*or* fansy] would favour. Sir Thomas Wyatt. CP-WyatT

If fate should seal my Death to-morrow. Egotism. A Letter to J.T. Becher. Lord Byron. CP-Byron

If felt and heard, (unseen) thou dost me please. Upon Deb. Robert Herrick. CP-HerrR

If fire can melt down steel and shatter flint. Michelangelo Buonarroti. CP-Miche, *tr. by* John Frederick Nims

If fire, so quick to char. Michelangelo Buonarroti. CP-Miche, *tr. by* John Frederick Nims

If for just one day we knew. Rainer Maria Rilke. CP-RilkFr, *tr. by* A. Poulin, Jr. *Fr.* Fragments.

If for Silver, or for Gold. Lord Byron. CP-Byron

If for thyself thou wilt not watch thy whore. Elegy 2.19: "If for thyself thou wilt not watch thy whore." Ovid. CP-DryJ2 *Fr.* Elegies.

If forgiveness comes / it will be gradual. William Dickey. SP-DickW *Fr.* In The Dreaming.

If freckles were lovely, and day was night. If. E. E. Cummings. CP-CummE

If from the earth we came, it was an earth. Anatomy of Monotony. Wallace Stevens. CP-StevWP; CP-StevWP

If from the public way you turn your steps. Michael [A Pastoral Poem]. William Wordsworth. CP-WorW1; MW-WorW

If from your price ye will not swerve. Henry David Thoreau. CP-ThorH

If Fun Is Fun, Isn't That Enough? Ogden Nash. CP-NashO

If gibbets, axes, confiscations, chains. Fragment of a Satire on Satire. Percy Bysshe Shelley. CP-ShelP

If Gideon's fleece, which drench'd with dew he found. To a Young Friend. William Cowper. CP-CowpW

If God compel thee to this destiny. Thought for a Lonely Death-Bed, A. Elizabeth Barrett Browning. CP-BroEB

If God has any voice it is the wind. Wind. John Updike. CP-UpdiJ

If God has been good enough to give you a poet. Let Them Alone. Robinson Jeffers. CP-JefR3

If God incarnated himself in man, died and rose from the dead. Either-Or. Czeslaw Milosz. CP-MiloCN, *tr.* by Robert Hass

If grief come early. First or Last. Thomas Hardy. CP-HardT

If Grief Could Burn Out. Philip Larkin. CP-LarkP

If grief dismiss me not to them that rest. Sonnet: "If grief dismiss me not to them that rest." Petrarch. CP-WorW1

If grief for grief can touch thee. Emily Jane Brontë. CP-BronE

If groves are choirs and sanctuaried fanes. Children of Darkness. Richard Wilbur. CP-WilbR

If Hands Could Free You, Heart. Philip Larkin. CP-LarkP

If Hanson Baldwin got a bullet in his brain, outrage. Chicago to Salt Lake by Air. Allen Ginsberg. CP-GinsA

If hap it must, that I must see thee lye. To His Book[e]. Robert Herrick. CP-HerrR

If happiness were. Robert Creeley. SP-CreeR

If he asks, "Is now the time?", it is not the time. Is Now the Time? Robert Graves. CP-GravR

If he could solve the riddle. Sphinx. Robert Earl Hayden. CP-HaydR

If He dissolve—then—there is nothing—more. Emily Dickinson. CP-DickE

If he go apart. Ralph Waldo Emerson. CP-EmerR

If he goes rowing in the park tho he may row so well that. Preface, A: "If he goes rowing in the park tho he may row so well that." George Oppen. CP-OppGN

If he is of constant depth. Lorine Niedecker. CP-NiedL

If—he says—I placed the bird in the green cage. Simple Honesty. Yannis Ritsos. SP-RitsY, *tr.* by Kostas Myrsiades

If He Scholars, Let Him Go. Ogden Nash. CP-NashO

If he should live a thousand years. Woman's Trust, A. Thomas Hardy. CP-HardT

If He were living—dare I ask. Emily Dickinson. CP-DickE

If he will be heaven after death. Prelude to Objects. Wallace Stevens. CP-StevW

If he would come to-day, to-day, to-day. Hoping Against Hope. Christina Georgina Rossetti. CP-RosC3

If heaven were to do again. Peaceful Shepherd, The. Robert Frost. CP-FrosR

If help there is not, but the Muse. Arthur Hugh Clough. SP-ClouA

If here the imaginative Greek had lived. Evergreen, The. Jones Very. CP-VeryJ

If he's not peewee wafted. Adirondack Summer. Lorine Niedecker. CP-NiedL

If his bright eyes are closed and laid to rest. Michelangelo Buonarroti. CP-MicheJ, *tr.* by John Frederick Nims

If hope grew on a bush, / And joy grew on a tree. Hope and Joy. Christina Georgina Rossetti. CP-RosC2

If hours be years the twain are blest. At a Hasty Wedding. Thomas Hardy. CP-HardT

If I am not mistaken. Final Examination. Dan Pagis. SP-PagiD, *tr.* by Stephen Mitchell

If I am poor it is that I am proud. Poverty. Henry David Thoreau. CP-ThorH

If I am really walking with ordinary habit. Waiting Head, The. Anne Sexton. CP-SextA

If I ask Pity not to be. Guido Cavalcanti. CP-CavaG, *tr.* by Marc Cirigliano

If i believe / in death be sure. E. E. Cummings. CP-CummE

If I can / remember anything, it. For Helen. Robert Creeley. CP-CreeR

If I can say yes I. Birds on the Morning of Going, The. W. S. Merwin. SP-MerwW

If I can stop one Heart from breaking. Emily Dickinson. CP-DickE

If I cannot ascend to Paradise. If. Czeslaw Milosz. CP-MiloCN, *tr.* by Robert Hass

If I cannot love myself, can you? Flight. Robert Lowell. SP-LoweR

If I can't hope then to hell with it. Entre Nous. Robert Creeley. CP-CreeR

If I choose remorse. Kathleen Jessie Raine. SP-RainK

If I could at last tell you what is in me. This. Czeslaw Milosz. CP-MiloCN, *tr.* by Robert Hass

If I Could Be Like Wallace Stevens. William Stafford. SP-StafW; SP-StafWW

If I could begin anything. Words Written Near a Candle. Tess Gallagher. SP-GallT

If I could blame it all on the weather. Earth Falls Down, The. Anne Sexton. CP-SextA

If I could bribe them by a Rose. Emily Dickinson. CP-DickE

If I could but abide. Wish for Unconsciousness, A. Thomas Hardy. CP-HardT

If I Could But Forget. Paul Laurence Dunbar. CP-DunbP

If I / could count the silence. Song: "If I / could count the silence." William Carlos Williams. CP-WilW2

If I could get. Later ("If I could get"). Robert Creeley. SP-CreeR

If I could have. Moriturus. Edna St. Vincent Millay. CP-MillE

If I could have chosen another time to be. Longing, The. Miller Williams. CP-WillM

If I could have put you in my heart. End, The. D. H. Lawrence. CP-LawrD

If I could hope by dying to be rid. Petrarch. CP-Petra, *tr.* by J. G. Nichols

If I could I would sing you to sleep. Variation on "To Say to Go to Sleep," A. Randall Jarrell. CP-JarrR

If I could keep her. Another Old Woman. William Carlos Williams. CP-WilW2

If I could lay hold. Before the Concert. Charles Tomlinson. SP-TomlC

If I could let you go as trees let go. May Sarton. SP-SartM *Fr.* Autumn Sonnets, The.

'If I Could Only Live at the Pitch That Is near Madness.' Richard Eberhart. CP-EberR

If I could put my woods in song. My Garden. Ralph Waldo Emerson. CP-EmerR

If I could send him only. Her Reticence. Theodore Roethke. CP-RoetT

If I could set the moon upon. Encyclopædia, The. Nicholas Vachel Lindsay. CP-LindV

If I Could Sing. G. K. Chesterton. CP-ChesG

If I could sing as you can sing. If I Could Sing. G. K. Chesterton. CP-ChesG

If I could take a bite of the whole earth. Fernando Pessoa. SP-PessF *Fr.* Keeper of Sheep, The.

If I could tell how glad I was. Emily Dickinson. CP-DickE

If I Could Tell You. W. H. Auden. CP-AudeW

If I could write a poem without meaning. Meaningless Poem. Richard Eberhart. CP-EberR

If I could write: Summer waits your coming. Letter, Unposted. Muriel Rukeyser. CP-RukeM

If I cried out in anger against music. Death by Drums. Robert Graves. CP-GravR

If I dare write to You, my Lord, who are. To the Right Honourable Edward Earle of Dorset. Robert Herrick. CP-HerrR

If I dared to write you, borrowed. Orchard, The. Rainer Maria Rilke. CP-RilkFr, *tr.* by A. Poulin, Jr. *Fr.* Orchards.

If I did love a cyclops. Sunflower. Federico García Lorca. CP-GarcF, *tr.* by Jerome Rothenberg *Fr.* Barrage of Firework Poems on the Occasion of the Poet's Birthday.

If I die. Farewell: "If I die." Federico García Lorca. SP-GarcF, *tr.* by W. S. Merwin

If I Die Before I Wake. Thomas Lux. SP-LuxT

If I die before I wake. If I Die Before I Wake. Thomas Lux. SP-LuxT

"If I die first," my old chum paused to say. Old Chums. James Whitcomb Riley. CP-RileJ

If I die, / leave the balcony open. Leave-taking. Federico García Lorca. CP-GarcF, *tr.* by Alan S. Trueblood *Fr.* Back of the World.

If I die solvent—die, that is to say. Edna St. Vincent Millay. CP-MillE

If I die today, which statistically speaking. Sonnet: "If I die today, which statistically speaking." Hayden Carruth. CP-CarHS *Fr.* Sonnets.

If I do not know where He is. Circulations of the Song. Robert Duncan. SP-DuncR

If I do not sin, she said, you shall not. Venus Over the Desert. William Carlos Williams. CP-WilW2

If I don't drive around the park. Observation. Dorothy Parker. CP-ParkD

If I don't go there. Nomad Songs. W. S. Merwin. SP-MerwW

If I don't love you I. Scorpio. Ted Berrigan. SP-BerrT

If I eer Grow to a Mans Estate. William Blake. CP-BlakW

If I entreat this lady that all grace. Sonnet: To a Friend who does not pity his Love. Guido Cavalcanti. CW-RossD, *tr.* by Dante Gabriel Rossetti

If I envy anyone it must be. Answers. Mary Oliver. SP-OlivM

If I esteemed you less, Envy would kill. Sonnet to Byron. Percy Bysshe Shelley. CP-ShelP

If I ever go back to Baltimore. Memory. G. K. Chesterton. CP-ChesG

If I ever hit for a dollar. Numbers. Langston Hughes. CP-HughL; CP-HughL3

If I freely may discover. Song: "If I freely may discover." Ben Jonson. CP-JonsB *Fr.* Poetaster, The.

If I grow bitterly. Scrub. Edna St. Vincent Millay. CP-MillE

If I had a Green Automobile. Green Automobile, The. Allen Ginsberg. CP-GinsA; SP-GinsA

If I had a heart of gold. Vari-Colored Song. Langston Hughes. CP-HughL; CP-HughL3

If I had a million lives to live. Humdrum. Carl Sandburg. CP-SandC

If I had a shiny gun. Frustration. Dorothy Parker. CP-ParkD

If I had been a heathen. Song of the Strange Ascetic, The. G. K. Chesterton. CP-ChesG

If I Had but Two Little Wings. Samuel Taylor Coleridge. CP-ColeS (Something Childish, but Very Natural.) CP-ColeS

If I Had Children. May Swenson. SP-SwenM

If I had children, might name. If I Had Children. May Swenson. SP-SwenM

If I had erased my life there. Mississippi Winter I. Alice Walker. CP-WalkA

If I had lingered longer in the cave. Petrarch. CP-Petra, *tr.* by J. G. Nichols

If I had my way, dear. Robert Creeley. SP-CreeR

If I had said out passions as they were. Cadenza on Garnette. John Berryman. CP-BerrJ

If I had some small change. *If*-ing. Langston Hughes. CP-HughL; CP-HughL2

If I had, uncut, the fingernails. Pruned Roses, The. William Dickey. SP-DickW

If I Had Words. Christina Georgina Rossetti. CP-RosC3

If I have been born. Dwarf in the Woods. Mona Van Duyn. SP-VanDM

If I have complained I hope I have done with it. Gods, The. W. S. Merwin. SP-MerwW

If I have given you delight. Appeal, The. Rudyard Kipling. CP-KiplR

If I Have Made, My Lady. E. E. Cummings. CP-CummE; SP-CummE

If i have made, my lady, intricate. If I Have Made, My Lady. E. E. Cummings. CP-CummE; SP-CummE

If I have plaid the Truant, or have here. To God. Robert Herrick. CP-HerrR

If I have seemed more prompt to censure wrong. To Charles Sumner. John Greenleaf Whittier. CP-WhitJ

If I have taken the common clay. Rudyard Kipling. CP-KiplR *Fr.* Light That Failed, The.

If I have to choose between the bourgeois and the bolshevist. Choice of Evils. D. H. Lawrence. CP-LawrD

If I hope, I pine; if I feare, I faint and die. Thomas Campion *and* Philip Rosseter. CP-CampT

If I just had a piano. Testimonial. Langston Hughes. CP-HughL; CP-HughL3

If I kiss[e] Anthea's bre[a]st. Love Perfumes All Parts. Robert Herrick. CP-HerrR

If I Knew What Poets Know. James Whitcomb Riley. CP-RileJ

If I Lie Down. Stevie Smith. CP-SmitS

If I, like Solomon. O To Be A Dragon. Marianne Craig Moore. CP-MoorM

If I lived in sight of the lake. Matter of Locality, A. Paul Laurence Dunbar. CP-DunbP

If I love thee, I am thine. Wallace Stevens. CP-StevWP

If i love You. E. E. Cummings. CP-CummE; SP-CummE

If I love you. To the Oak. "Shu Ting." CP-KizeC, *tr. by* Carolyn Kizer *and* Y. H. Zhao

If I lye unburied Sir. To the Passenger. Robert Herrick. CP-HerrR

If I make the lashes dark. Before the World Was Made. William Butler Yeats. CP-YeatW

If I may have it, when it's dead. Emily Dickinson. CP-DickE

If I might have at mine own will. Sir Thomas Wyatt. CP-WyatT

If I might only love my God and die! If Only. Christina Georgina Rossetti. CP-RosC1

If I might see another Spring. Another Spring. Christina Georgina Rossetti. CP-RosC1

If I might see his face to-day! Blind Girl, The. James Whitcomb Riley. CP-RileJ

If I might take a weight of bronze. Red Roses for Bronze. "H. D." CP-DoolH

If I mix a vegetable and moral metaphor. Endive. Thomas Lux. SP-LuxT

If I must of my Senses lose. Prayer: "If I must of my Senses lose." Theodore Roethke. CP-RoetT

If I must speak—though really I'm quite ashamed to say it. Noun Verse. Caroline Mary Craven Austen. CP-AustJ

If i / or anybody don't. E. E. Cummings. CP-CummE; SP-CummE

If I order a sandwich and get a plate of ham and eggs instead. Diner, The. David Ignatow. SP-IgnaD

If I really believe in the gods. She Asks Me. James Laughlin. CP-LaugJ

If I rest for a moment near The Equestrian. Music. Frank O'Hara. SP-OharF

If I said it, may I be held to scorn. Petrarch. CP-Petra, *tr. by* J. G. Nichols

If I saw you liked that dull unhappy boy. Road Map, The. Thom Gunn. CP-GunnT

If I say I have heard voices. Pastoral: "If I say I have heard voices." William Carlos Williams. CP-WilW1

If I set the sun beside the moon. Comparisons. G. K. Chesterton. CP-ChesG

If I Should. Lucille Clifton. SP-ClifL

If I should cast off this tattered coat. Stephen Crane. CP-CranS

If I should cease to bring a Rose. Emily Dickinson. CP-DickE

If I should die. Emily Dickinson. CP-DickE

If I should ever say "my heart is in my home." Christina Georgina Rossetti. CP-RosC2

If I should labor through daylight and dark. Philosophy. Dorothy Parker. CP-ParkD

If I should learn, in some quite casual way. Edna St. Vincent Millay. CP-MillE

If I should need to name, O Western World, your powerfulest scene and show. Election Day, November, 1884. Walt Whitman. CP-WhitW

If I should pamphleteer twenty years against royalists. To the Ghost of John Milton. Carl Sandburg. CP-SandC

If I should pass the tomb of Jonah. Losers. Carl Sandburg. CP-SandC

If I should riffle a pack. Orvieto. The King of Clubs. Donald Davie. CP-DaviDC

If I should sing. Love Song for Antonia. Langston Hughes. CP-HughL; CP-HughL1

If i should sleep with a lady called death. E. E. Cummings. CP-CummE

If I shouldn't be alive. Emily Dickinson. CP-DickE

If I suffer at this. Meek Have Inherited, The. Charles Bukowski. SP-BukC1

If I Take the Wings of the Morning. Donald Davie. CP-DaviDC

If I talk to things. Pastoral 2: "If I talk to things." William Carlos Williams. CP-WilW1

If I think at all of the broken-down hearse. Grief. Paul Muldoon. CP-MuldP

If I think of a horse wandering about sleeplessly. Night. Robert Bly. SP-BlyR

If I told you I used to know the circular truth. Eagles. James Dickey. CP-DickJ

If I told you that the old woman. These Streets. Philip Levine. SP-LeviP

If I urge my kinde desires. Thomas Campion *and* Philip Rosseter. CP-CampT

If I walk in Autumn's even. Stanza: "If I walk in Autumn's even." Percy Bysshe Shelley. CP-ShelP

If I was a member of the Church of Rome. Church, The. D. H. Lawrence. CP-LawrD

If I was a sea-lion. Declaration. Langston Hughes. CP-HughL; CP-HughL2

If I Were a Bird. Lorine Niedecker. CP-NiedL

If I were a fish I should. Thought and Reflections. G. K. Chesterton. CP-ChesG

If I were a king and did not know it. Tauler. James Fenton. SP-FentJ

If I Were a Queen. Christina Georgina Rossetti. CP-RosC2

If I were called in. Water. Philip Larkin. CP-LarkP

If I Were Certain. Faiz Ahmad Faiz. CP-KizeC, *tr. by* Carolyn Kizer

If I were certain, O my dear companion. If I Were Certain. Faiz Ahmad Faiz. CP-KizeC, *tr. by* Carolyn Kizer

If I were doing my Laundry I'd wash my dirty Iran. Homework. Allen Ginsberg. CP-GinsA; SP-GinsA

If I were hanged on the highest hill. Mother o' Mine. Rudyard Kipling. CP-KiplR *Fr.* Light That Failed, The.

If I were in the belly of the whale. Two Hatreds of Action. Alan Dugan. CP-DugaA

If I were in the middle of the Atlantic. Drowning (I). Grace Paley. CP-PalGC

If I were in the place of young poets. Counsels. Czeslaw Milosz. CP-MiloC; CP-MiloCN

If I were mild, and I were sweet. Dilemma. Dorothy Parker. CP-ParkD

If I were one worthy of Love. Guido Cavalcanti. CP-CavaG, *tr. by* Marc Cirigliano

If I were out of love. Conspiracy of Two against the World. Alan Dugan. CP-DugaA

If I were Sophocles, brave with truth. Kaire. Richard Eberhart. CP-EberR

If I were still that man, worthy to love. Sonnet: Guido answers the foregoing Sonnet, speaking with shame of his changed Love. Guido Cavalcanti. CW-RossD, *tr. by* Dante Gabriel Rossetti

If I were thou, O butterfly. Wisdom Unapplied. Elizabeth Barrett Browning. CP-BroEB

If I were Tickled by the Rub of Love. Dylan Thomas. CP-ThomD

If I were to walk this way. Wood Road, The. Edna St. Vincent Millay. CP-MillE

If I were well-to-do. Birthday. D. H. Lawrence. CP-LawrD

If I were you. Kate's. Robert Creeley. CP-CreeR

If I would wish, for truth, and not for show. To the Same [Benjamin Rudyerd] ("If I would wish, for truth, and not for show"). Ben Jonson. CP-JonsB; SP-JonsB

If I write any more, it will make my poor muse sick. To Dr. Sheridan. Jonathan Swift. CP-SwifJ

If I write not to you. Letter in Verse. William Cowper. CP-CowpW

If I Yes. Olga Broumas. SP-BrouO

If icebergs were warm below the water. Icebergs. Louis MacNeice. CP-MacNL

If I'd known enough. Lesson, The. Rainer Maria Rilke. CP-RilkFr, *tr. by* A. Poulin, Jr.

If I'm dead and don't know it. Pablo Neruda. SP-NeruP *Fr.* Question Book.

If I'm lost—now. Emily Dickinson. CP-DickE

If I'm lucky, I'll be wired every whichway. My Death. Raymond Carver. CP-CarvR

If I'm more alive because love burns and chars me. Michelangelo Buonarroti. CP-Miche, *tr. by* John Frederick Nims

If I'm to believe my eyes now, your response. Michelangelo Buonarroti. CP-Miche, *tr. by* John Frederick Nims

If, in an odd angle of the hutment. Eighth Air Force. Randall Jarrell. CP-JarrR

If in beginning twilight of winter will stand. E. E. Cummings. CP-CummE

If in his garden all night fell the stream. Garden Waters. Robert Penn Warren. CP-WarrR

If in his study he hath so much care. Antiquary. John Donne. CP-DonnJ; MW-DonnJ

If in that Syrian garden, ages slain. Easter Hymn. A. E. Housman. CP-HousA

If, in the Foggy Aleutians. Edna St. Vincent Millay. CP-MillE

If in the future. Sitting Alone at Sunrise: Problems in the Space-Time Continuum. Miller Williams. CP-WillM

If in the latter. Epitaph for Liberal Poets. Louis MacNeice. CP-MacNL

If, in the light of things, you fade. Star. Derek Walcott. CP-WalcD

If, in the month of dark December. Written After Swimming from Sestos to Abydos. Lord Byron. CP-Byron

If, in the silent mind of One all-pure. In Utrumque Paratus. Matthew Arnold. SP-ArnoM

If in the white Basilica of St George. St George's Basilica. Jaroslav Seifert. SP-SeifJ, *tr. by* Ewald Osers

If in the world there be more woe. Disdain. Sir Thomas Wyatt. CP-WyatT

If in the years to come you should recall. Edna St. Vincent Millay. CP-MillE

If, in this fourteenth year of all my sighs. Petrarch. CP-Petra, *tr. by* J. G. Nichols

If, in Your name, some image comes to mind. Michelangelo Buonarroti. CP-Miche, *tr. by* John Frederick Nims

If indeed we were allowed to choose. One Version of Events. Wisława Szymborska. SP-SzymWM, *tr. by* Joanna Trzeciak

If, into this evening as the grass receives the dew. Kathleen Jessie Raine. SP-RainK

If It All Went Up in Smoke. George Oppen. CP-OppGN

If it be so that I forsake thee. Sir Thomas Wyatt. CP-WyatT

If it be very strange and sorrowful. Sonnet Autumnal. Wilfred Owen. CP-OwenW

If it chance your eye offend you. A. E. Housman. CP-HousA

If it could be, to revive my life once more. Michelangelo Buonarroti. CP-Miche, *tr. by* John Frederick Nims

If it ever is. Invitation, The. Robert Creeley. CP-CreeR

If it falls flat / I'm used to it. Yet. Kid, The. Robert Creeley. CP-CreeR

If it form the one landscape that we, the inconstant ones. In Praise of Limestone. W. H. Auden. CP-AudeW

If it had no pencil. Emily Dickinson. CP-DickE

If it hadn't been for the desert and laughter and music. Three Kings, The. Adam Zagajewski. SP-ZagaA, *tr. by* Clare Cavanagh

If it is a question of him or me. My Enemy. D. H. Lawrence. CP-LawrD

If it is a world without a genius. In the Element of Antagonisms. Wallace Stevens. CP-StevW; CP-StevWP

If it is True What the Prophets write. William Blake. CP-BlakW

If it is unpermissible, in fact fatal. To a Giraffe. Marianne Craig Moore. CP-MoorM

If it isn't the birds / covered with ash. Blind Panorama of New York. Federico García Lorca. CP-GarcF, *tr. by* Greg Simon *and* Steven F. White

If it shine or if it rain. New Love, The. Dorothy Parker. CP-ParkD

If it should rain—(the sneezy moon). Edna St. Vincent Millay. CP-MillE

If it was treason it was so well handled that it. Absence of a Noble Presence, The. John Ashbery. SP-AshbJ

If it were done, twere well it were done quickly. Artist's Model. Robert Lowell. SP-LoweR

(If it were evening on a dead man's watch). Blues for Jimmy. Thomas McGrath. SP-McGrT

If it were mine, you'd see every value. Guido Cavalcanti. CP-CavaG, *tr. by* Marc Cirigliano

If it were not for all those foolish kisses. Honeymoon. Jaroslav Seifert. SP-SeifJ, *tr. by* Ewald Osers

If it were not for England, who would bear. Servitude. Ivor Gurney. SP-GurnI

If It Were Not for You. Hayden Carruth. CP-CarHS

If it were only still! Pastoral: "If it were only still!" Edna St. Vincent Millay. CP-MillE

If it were set anywhere else but so. Pride of Head. Laura Riding Jackson. CP-RidiL

If it weren't for you Mr Jukebox with yr aluminum belly roaring & thirty teeth eating dirty drx. Seabattle of Salamis Took Place off Perama. Allen Ginsberg. CP-GinsA

If It Would All Please Hurry. James Tate. SP-TateJ

If it's a God who tears us down, let us obey! Judgments. Rainer Maria Rilke. CP-RilkFr, *tr. by* A. Poulin, Jr.

If it's chariots or sandals. Traveler, A. Denise Levertov. SP-LeveDS

If It's Ever Spring Again. Thomas Hardy. CP-HardT

If it's invented it will be used. Tool. W. S. Merwin. SP-MerwW

If it's raining and you're sitting behind a shade with. I Don't Need a Bedsheet with Slits for Eyes to Kill You In. Charles Bukowski. SP-BukC2

If, jetting, I committed the noble fault. My Heat. Frank O'Hara. SP-OharF

If John marries Mary, and Mary alone. Impromptu ["If John marries Mary, and Mary alone"]. William Cowper. CP-CowpW

If Jupiter and Saturn meet. Conjunctions. William Butler Yeats. CP-YeatW

If just for once the swing of cause and effect. Variation and Reflection on a Theme by Rilke. Denise Levertov. SP-LeveDS

If Kings and kingdomes, once dstiracted be. Warre. Robert Herrick. CP-HerrR

If learned darkness from our searched world. E. E. Cummings. CP-CummE

If leaves aren't what you're wanting. Michelangelo Buonarroti. CP-Miche, *tr. by* John Frederick Nims

If life were but a dream, my love. If. Paul Laurence Dunbar. CP-DunbP

If life were easy. Heaven ("If life were easy"). Robert Creeley. SP-CreeR

If little labour, little are our gaines. No Paines, No Gaines. Robert Herrick. CP-HerrR

If longings for the immortal, which exalt. Michelangelo Buonarroti. CP-Miche, *tr. by* John Frederick Nims

If Love be dead. Love's Burial-Place. Samuel Taylor Coleridge. CP-ColeS

If Love does not bring better thoughts to bear. Petrarch. CP-Petra, *tr. by* J. G. Nichols

If love is not worth loving, then life is not worth living. Christina Georgina Rossetti. CP-RosC2

If Love loves truth, then women do[e] not love. Thomas Campion. CP-CampT

If Luther's day expand to Darwin's year. Epilogue: "If Luther's day expand to Darwin's year." Herman Melville. SP-MelvH *Fr.* Clarel: A Poem and Pilgrimage in the Holy Land.

If man might know. Ei Men Een Mathein. Sir John Suckling. CP-SuckJ

If man only looks to man, and no-one sees beyond. False Democracy and Real. D. H. Lawrence. CP-LawrD

If Margie Polite. Ballad of Margie Polite, The. Langston Hughes. CP-HughL; CP-HughL2

If Mary came would Mary. Penitent Considers Another Coming of Mary, A. Gwendolyn Brooks. SP-BrooG

If Maudie doesn't love us. Clydesider. D. H. Lawrence. CP-LawrD

If meat the gods give, I the steam. Steam in Sacrifice. Robert Herrick. CP-HerrR

If men, and times were now. Ode: "If men, and times were now." Ben Jonson. CP-JonsB; SP-JonsB

If Men can say that beauty dyes. Upon a Comely, and Curious Maide. Robert Herrick. CP-HerrR

If men get name, for some one virtue: then. To Sir Edward Herbert. Ben Jonson. CP-JonsB; SP-JonsB

If men only fought outwards into the world. Female Coercion. D. H. Lawrence. CP-LawrD

If men should arise and return to the noise and time of the tourney. Mediaevalism. G. K. Chesterton. CP-ChesG

If Men will act like a maid smiling over a Churn. William Blake. CP-BlakW

If Michael, leader of God's host. Rose of Peace, The. William Butler Yeats. CP-YeatW

If mine eyes can speak to do hearty errand. Sapphics. Sir Philip Sidney. SP-SidnP *Fr.* Arcadia.

If 'Miss Moore's (birds) squeal, shuffle, lose their food.' Cultural Triumph, A. George Oppen. CP-OppGN

If Mr. Bright retiring does not please. Counterblast on Penny Trumpet. Christina Georgina Rossetti. CP-RosC3

If modest Youth, with cool Reflection crown'd. Epitaph on Edmund Duke of Buckingham, Who Died in the Nineteenth Year of His Age, 1735. Alexander Pope. CP-PopeA

If money I lack. Placard for a Poll Bearing an Old Shirt. William Wordsworth. CP-WorW2

If money made the mind more sane. Stanzas: Written at Night in Radio City. Allen Ginsberg. CP-GinsA

If 'mongst my many Poems, I can see. To Cedars. Robert Herrick. CP-HerrR

If more than once, as annals tell. Timoleon. Herman Melville. SP-MelvH

If, Mother and Daddy, you were to visit us. Returning. Robert Lowell. SP-LoweR

If mouth could open its cliff. Ted Hughes. SP-HughTN *Fr.* Seven Dungeon Songs.

If music be the muses' paragon. Heart Beats. Donald Davie. CP-DaviDC

If my Bark sink. Emily Dickinson. CP-DickE

If My Belly Aches. Yehuda Amichai. SP-AmicYL, *tr. by* Benjamin Harshav *and* Barbara Harshav

If My Darling. Philip Larkin. CP-LarkP

If my darling should depart. Hafiz. CP-EmerR *Fr.* Odes.

If, my friend, you would have said of Mary so. Guido Orlandi. CP-CavaG, *tr. by* Marc Cirigliano

If My Head Hurt a Hair's Foot. Dylan Thomas. CP-ThomD

If, my irrepressible Calvus, I didn't. Carmen 14. Catullus. CP-ZukLS *Fr.* Carmina.

If my manner of song disturbs the dead the living. Worst Poems Make the Best "Poems," The. Andrei Codrescu. SP-CodrA

If my parents and your parents. Almost a Love Poem. Yehuda Amichai. SP-AmicYL, *tr. by* Benjamin Harshav *and* Barbara Harshav

If my parents and yours. Almost a Love Poem. Yehuda Amichai. SP-AmicY, *tr. by* Chana Bloch

If my pen hand were snapped by a Broadway truck. After Whitman & Reznikoff. Allen Ginsberg. CP-GinsA

If, my religion safe, I durst embrace. To Sir Henry [*or* Henrie] Savile [upon His Translation of Tacitus]. Ben Jonson. CP-JonsB; SP-JonsB

If my rough hammer shapes the obdurate stone. Michelangelo Buonarroti. CP-Miche, *tr. by* John Frederick Nims

If my words are not saying what you would say. Babbling Child, A. Jelaluddin Rumi. SP-Rumi, *tr. by* Coleman Barks

If Nature do deny. Painting Sometimes Permitted. Robert Herrick. CP-HerrR

If nature, for a favo[u]rite child. Matthew. William Wordsworth. CP-WorW1;

MW-WorW

If nature now deferred to death, dejected. Michelangelo Buonarroti. CP-Miche, *tr.* by John Frederick Nims

If Nature smiles—the Mother must. Emily Dickinson. CP-DickE

If neither brass, nor marble, can withstand. Power of Time, The. Jonathan Swift. CP-SwifJ

If neither Love nor Death blights this endeavour. Petrarch. CP-Petra, *tr.* by J. G. Nichols

If night's mostness(and whom did merely day / close). E. E. Cummings. CP-CummE

If night's the harder. This World. Robert Creeley. SP-CreeR

If nine times you your bridegroom[e] kiss[e]. Tithe [*or* Tythe]: To the Bride, The. Robert Herrick. CP-HerrR

If No Cuckoo Sings. Robert Graves. CP-GravR

If no one moved on order, she would kill. My Mother Was a Soldier. William Stafford. SP-StafWW

If no one moved on order, she would kill—. My Mother Was a Soldier. William Stafford. SP-StafW

If noisy Tom should in the senate prate. On Noisy Tom. Jonathan Swift. CP-SwifJ

If not by all that his friends boast. Carmen 54. Catullus. CP-ZukLS *Fr.* Carmina.

If not for the existence of Earth, would there be a Hell? Garden of Earthly Delights, The: Hell. Czeslaw Milosz. CP-MiloCN, *tr.* by Robert Hass

If not, why should the willow bend? It bends. Willow. James Merrill. SP-MerrJ

If not with hope of life, / Begin with fear of death. Christina Georgina Rossetti. CP-RosC2

If now, in the middle of my life, I think, Yehuda Amichai. SP-AmicYL, *tr.* by Benjamin Harshav *and* Barbara Harshav

If now is not the time more. How Now We Talk. Laura Riding Jackson. CP-RidiL

If objects are of two kinds—those. Prose Poem. Charles Tomlinson. CP-TomlC; SP-TomlC

If obligated by so great a favor. Michelangelo Buonarroti. CP-Miche, *tr.* by John Frederick Nims

If, of meaner happiness. Passage from Mary Barker's *Lines Addressed to a Noble Lord* (His Lordship Will Know Why). William Wordsworth. CP-WorW2

If old Bacchus were the speaker. Wine of Cyprus. Elizabeth Barrett Browning. CP-BroEB

If, on a dark and gloomy night. Burial, A. Charles Baudelaire. CP-BaudC, *tr.* by Walter Martin

If on any warm day when you ramble around. Lizard, The. Thomas Hardy. CP-HardT

If on me too came once the mood. Unwritten. G. K. Chesterton. CP-ChesG

If on the tally-board of wasted days, Sonnet: "If on the tally-board of wasted days." Ezra Pound. CP-PoEar

If once a year / the house of the dead. De Sole. Charles Tomlinson. CP-TomlC

If once we dreamed love had a tongue. Love's Voice. Robert Penn Warren. CP-WarrR

If one could have that little head of hers. Face, A. Robert Browning. CP-BroR1

If one could tell one's heart. Jaroslav Seifert. SP-SeifJ, *tr.* by Ewald Osers

If one had stumbled on these. Parkway. George Oppen. CP-OppGN

If / one night / I write. Sickness, The. Charles Bukowski. SP-BukC3

If one should tell them what's clearly seen. Crumbs or the Loaf. Robinson Jeffers. CP-JefR2

If one takes trouble to explain. James Vincent Cunningham. CP-CunnJ

If one's heart is broken twenty times a day. Daily—Old Tale. Ivor Gurney. SP-GurnI

If Only. Christina Georgina Rossetti. CP-RosC1

If only a maniac possessed it, he. On a Pocketknife. On Carrying. Alan Dugan. CP-DugaA

If only birds of sudden white. Wallace Stevens. CP-StevWP

If only I could cleave myself from the water table. Water. Yusef Komunyakaa. CP-KomuY

If only Mercy befriended my desires. Guido Cavalcanti. CP-CavaG, *tr.* by Marc Cirigliano

If only my friend. Lorine Niedecker. CP-NiedL

If only something would happen! Dialogue *En Route*. Sylvia Plath. CP-PlatS

If only the phantom would stop reappearing! Faust. John Ashbery. SP-AshbJ

If only the rose wished to tell us. Rose. Rainer Maria Rilke. CP-RilkFr, *tr.* by A. Poulin, Jr.

If only they hadn't shown that cruel mercy. Girl Who Has Drowned Herself Speaks, A. Stephen Spender. CP-SpenS

If only we weren't so small next to the stars. Cellophane. C. K. Williams. CP-WillC

If others are wothy accept them. Han-shan. CP-ColdM, *tr.* by Red Pine

If our father were alive. Letter from Gussie, A. W. S. Merwin. SP-MerwW

If our very thirst for longer life bids fair. Michelangelo Buonarroti. CP-Miche, *tr.* by John Frederick Nims

If pain for peace prepares. Emily Dickinson. CP-DickE

If, passenger, thou canst but read. Epitaph, on Henry L[ord] La-ware. To the Passer-By, An. Ben Jonson. CP-JonsB

If Pegasus will let *thee* ride him. Mathematical Problem, A. Samuel Taylor Coleridge. CP-ColeS

If Plato, haunted by an eternal past. Hostage, The. Robert Stock. SP-StocR

If pleasures come be happy. Han-shan. CP-ColdM, *tr.* by Red Pine

If Poetry Were Not a Morality. Tess Gallagher. SP-GallT

If poets are evidence, let's begin with the fact. For Myra, John L., and Benn. John Ciardi. CP-CiarJ

If Polyclitus studied earnestly. Petrarch. CP-Petra, *tr.* by J. G. Nichols

If pure devotion, passion without stain. Michelangelo Buonarroti. CP-Miche, *tr.* by John Frederick Nims

If reading verse be your delight. To the Rev. William Bull. William Cowper. CP-CowpW

If recollecting were forgetting. Emily Dickinson. CP-DickE

If right desire takes wing. Michelangelo Buonarroti. CP-Miche, *tr.* by John Frederick Nims

If Rome so great, and in her wisest age. To Edward Alleyn. Ben Jonson. CP-JonsB; SP-JonsB

If roses had not faded. Emily Dickinson. CP-DickE

If rustic Phidyle her prayer renews. Ode 3.23: "If rustic Phidyle her prayer renews." Horace. CP-JohnS *Fr.* Odes.

If Sackville, all that have the power to do[e]. Epistle to Sir Edward Sackville, now Earl of Dorset, An. Ben Jonson. CP-JonsB

If seasons all were summers. Farm-Woman's Winter, The. Thomas Hardy. CP-HardT

If seventy were young / and death uncommon. E. E. Cummings. CP-CummE

If shame can on a soldier's vein-swollen front. King Stephen. A Fragment of a Tragedy. John Keats. CP-KeatJ

If she didn't sing the day. Nightbird. Yusef Komunyakaa. CP-KomuY

If she forsake me, I must die. Thomas Campion *and* Philip Rosseter. CP-CampT

If she had been beautiful, even. Of a Woman, Dead Young. Dorothy Parker. CP-ParkD

If she had been the Mistletoe. Emily Dickinson. CP-DickE

If she rejoices in my tears, and you. Michelangelo Buonarroti. CP-Miche, *tr.* by John Frederick Nims

If she waits late at night. Persuasion, A. Hart Crane. CP-CranH

If she would come to me here. Dog-Tired. D. H. Lawrence. CP-LawrD

If sixteen shadows flapping on the line. Times Worsen, The. Randall Jarrell. CP-JarrR

If snakes were blue, it was the kind of day. Robert Penn Warren. CP-WarrR

If so he a toad be laid. Charme, or an Allay for Love, A. Robert Herrick. CP-HerrR

If So Hap May Be. Carl Sandburg. CP-SandC

If some confectioner were willing. Assorted Chocolates. Ogden Nash. CP-NashO

If someone is pleased to boast. Outlaw of the Lowest Planet, The. Kenneth Patchen. CP-PatcK

If someone were to ask me. Song from an Intermezzo. Jaroslav Seifert. SP-SeifJ, *tr.* by Ewald Osers

If Sometimes in the Haunts of Men. Lord Byron. CP-Byron

If sorrow makes one beautiful (it's said). Michelangelo Buonarroti. CP-Miche, *tr.* by John Frederick Nims

If souls are immortal, as they tell us. Stephanos Skilitsis. Constantine P. Cavafy. CP-CavaC, *tr.* by Theoharis Constantine Theoharis

If stars dropped out of heaven, / And if flowers took their place. Christina Georgina Rossetti. CP-RosC2

If Still Your Orchards Bear. Edna St. Vincent Millay. CP-MillE

If strange things happen where she is. On Portents. Robert Graves. CP-GravR

If suddenly you walk on grass turned stone. Torso. Joseph Brodsky. CP-BrodJ, *tr.* by Howard Moss

If sunset clouds could grow on trees. Mystery, The. G. K. Chesterton. CP-ChesG

If Synthia Be a Queene, a Princes, and Supreame. Sir Walter Ralegh. *See* If Cynthia Be a Queen

If that attractive look of hers can kill. Petrarch. CP-Petra, *tr.* by J. G. Nichols

If That High World. Lord Byron. CP-Byron

If that my Fate has now fulfill'd my yeere. On Himselfe. Robert Herrick. CP-HerrR

If that thou hast the gift of strength, then know. Burden of Strength, The. George Meredith. CP-MerG1

If that we thus are guilty doth appear. Thesis and Antithesis. Arthur Hugh Clough. SP-ClouA

If that's how it is / then that's how it. Well All Right. James Laughlin. CP-LaugJ

If that's water you wash your hands in. Cannot Sweeten. Christina Georgina Rossetti. CP-RosC3

If the alphabet should die. Pirouette. Federico García Lorca. CP-GarcF, *tr.* by Jerome Rothenberg *Fr.* Capriccios.

If the anguish of others helped one with one's own. Emily Dickinson. SP-DickE

If the autumn would. Winter Is Another Country. Archibald MacLeish. CP-MacLA

If the beloved is everywhere. Jelaluddin Rumi. SP-Rumi, *tr. by* Coleman Barks

If the Birds Knew. John Ashbery. SP-AshbJ

If the blues would let me. Miss Blues'es Child. Langston Hughes. CP-HughL; CP-HughL3

If the city has roots, they are in filth. Source, The. George Oppen. CP-OppGN

If the clock had stopped in 1936. Mother and Father 1. Robert Lowell. SP-LoweR

If the distrait verdure cleave not to the branch. Croesus in Autumn. Robert Penn Warren. CP-WarrR

If the foolish, call them "flowers." Emily Dickinson. CP-DickE

If the future is mighty as the past. Emily Dickinson. SP-DickE

If the great outside system—species and stars—proceeds. Across Space and Time. Charles Olson. CP-OlsoC

If the / green / opens. E. E. Cummings. CP-CummE

If the half moon stamp of a sacred hoof showed Cadmus. John Logan. CP-LogaJ *Fr.* Monologues of the Son of Saul.

If the houses in Wyeth's Christina's dream. My Grandfather's Wake. Paul Muldoon. CP-MuldP

If the kept secrets of our finished lives. Vision of Good Secrets, A. William Meredith. SP-MereW

If the Led Striker call it a strike. American, An. Rudyard Kipling. CP-KiplR

If the Lovestar grows most big. E. E. Cummings. CP-CummE

If the Man who Turneps cries. Samuel Johnson. *See* If a Man who Turnips cries

If the moon came from heaven, / Talking all the way. Christina Georgina Rossetti. CP-RosC2

If the moon smiled, she would resemble you. Rival, The. Sylvia Plath. CP-PlatS

If the mountain by which this valley's closed. Petrarch. CP-Petra, *tr. by* J. G. Nichols

If the muse were mine to tempt it. Colored Soldiers, The. Paul Laurence Dunbar. CP-DunbP

If the oriole calls like last year. South Wind Says So, The. Carl Sandburg. CP-SandC

If the pain is greater. Written to Music. Kenneth Rexroth. CP-RexrK

If the poem is a trajectory. Poem as Trajectory, The. Richard Eberhart. CP-EberR

If the poetry of X was music. Creations of Sound, The. Wallace Stevens. CP-StevW; CP-StevWP

If the pool were still. Peace of Mind. Kathleen Jessie Raine. SP-RainK

If the quick spirits in your eye. Persuasions to Enjoy. Thomas Carew. CP-CareT

If the red slayer think he slays. Brahma. Ralph Waldo Emerson. CP-EmerR

If the robot can recognise the clean flame of life. Real Democracy. D. H. Lawrence. CP-LawrD

If the Romans hadn't boasted about their victory. I Feel Just Fine in My Pants. Yehuda Amichai. SP-AmicY, *tr. by* Chana Bloch

If the soul, in truth, from body once set free. Michelangelo Buonarroti. CP-Miche, *tr. by* John Frederick Nims

If the soul returns, that last. Michelangelo Buonarroti. CP-Miche, *tr. by* John Frederick Nims

If the stars fell; night's nameless dreams. Joseph. G. K. Chesterton. CP-ChesG

If the sun could tell us half / That he hears and sees. Christina Georgina Rossetti. CP-RosC2

If the tongue keeps nothing from you. To Pia Di Valmarana. Rainer Maria Rilke. CP-RilkFr, *tr. by* A. Poulin, Jr.

If the universe is this gaol where now. Richard Coeur-de-Lion. Louis Aragon. CP-MacNL

If the vicar you treat. Receipt for a Pudding, A. Mrs. Austen. CP-AustJ

If the water forms. Poem, A: "If the water forms." Robert Creeley. CP-CreeR

If the water were clear enough. King of the River. Stanley Kunitz. CP-KunSC

If the whole weight of what we think and feel. Retirement. William Wordsworth. CP-WorW2

If the wicked gods were willing. Possibility, A. Ambrose Bierce. SP-BierA

If the wind touches your cheek. Give It to the Wind. Thomas Lux. SP-LuxT

If the work be not direct. Bible, *O.T. See* Except the Lord build the house

If there are angels. Slapstick. Wisława Szymborska. SP-SzymW, *tr. by* Stanisław Barańczak *and* Clare Cavanagh

If there are any heavens my mother will (all by herself) have. E. E. Cummings. CP-CummE; SP-CummE

If there are any wives present who wish to irritate their husbands. Don't Wait, Hit Me Now! Ogden Nash. CP-NashO

If there are intelligent beings. It Came to Pass on a Planet Third from a Minor Sun in a Solar System Out on the Edge of One of the Galaxies. Miller Williams. CP-WillM

If there be a power of sweetness, let it lie. Blackberry Winter. John Crowe Ransom. SP-RansJ

If there be truth in what you sing. On Reading Dr. Young's Satires. Jonathan Swift. CP-SwifJ

If there ever was a spoiled darling. Blood and Sand. Kenneth Rexroth. CP-RexrK

If there had been but three of you. In Memoriam M. D. G. K. Chesterton. CP-ChesG

If there had been only. Buddha in the Woodpile, A. Lawrence Ferlinghetti. SP-FerlL

If there has been no spiritual change of kind. Mutations. Louis MacNeice. CP-MacNL

If there is a man white as marble. Metaphor as Degeneration. Wallace Stevens. CP-StevW; CP-StevWP

If there is a river. Poem in Praise of Menstruation. Lucille Clifton. SP-ClifL

If there is a witness to my little life. Stephen Crane. CP-CranS

If there is an outside out there. On Finding the Tree of Life. Alan Dugan. CP-DugaA

If there is only enough time in the final. Dancing toward Bethlehem. Billy Collins. SP-CollB

If there must be a god in the house, must be. Less and Less Human, O Savage Spirit. Wallace Stevens. CP-StevW; CP-StevWP

If there was a broken whispering by night. Parting at Dawn. John Crowe Ransom. SP-RansJ

If There Was Any Justice. Alice Walker. CP-WalkA

If there was just this. Without Form. Adam Zagajewski. SP-ZagaA, *tr. by* Renata Gorczynski, Benjamin Ivry *and* C. K. Williams

If there were balm in Gilead, I would go. Czecho-Slovakia. Edna St. Vincent Millay. CP-MillE

If there were in my kalendar. Conjecture. Thomas Hardy. CP-HardT

If there were not an utter and absolute dark. End, The Beginning, The. D. H. Lawrence. CP-LawrD

If there's a god of amphetamine, he's also the god of wrecked lives. Gregory Orr. SP-OrrG

If these are letters, they will have to be misread. August fourth nineteen sixty eight. Adrienne Rich. CP-RicAE *Fr.* Ghazals: Homage to Ghalib.

If these brief Records, by the Muses' art. To ———: "If these brief Records, by the Muses' art." William Wordsworth. CP-WorW2

If These Can't Keep Your Ladies Quiet. Thomas Sheridan. CP-SherT

If these dried hearts indeed forget. Pagans, The. G. K. Chesterton. CP-ChesG

If Thetis and the Morn their sons did wail. Elegy 3.8: "If Thetis and the Morn their sons did wail." Ovid. CP-MarlC *Fr.* Elegies.

If They Come in the Night. Marge Piercy. SP-PierM

If they want me to be a mystic, fine. I'm a mystic. Fernando Pessoa. SP-PessF *Fr.* Keeper of Sheep, The.

If they've compared you. Eugenio Montale. CP-MontE, *tr. by* Jonathan Galassi

If thieves got your bags at Istanbul. Tale of a Later Leander. John Logan. CP-LogaJ

If this be night, break softly, blessed day. To the Morn. Wallace Stevens. CP-StevWP

If this continues the children. He Wanders. Grace Paley. CP-PalGC

If this country is a bastard. Request. Maya Angelou. SP-AngeM

If This Great World of Joy and Pain. William Wordsworth. CP-WorW2

If this importunate heart trouble your peace. Lover Asks Forgiveness because of His Many Moods. William Butler Yeats. CP-YeatW

If this is death, it is not hard to bear. Vittoria Concluding the Opera of "Camilla." George Meredith. CP-MerG2

If this is "fading." Emily Dickinson. CP-DickE

If this is the way it is, we must live through it. If. Robert Penn Warren. CP-WarrR

If this uncertain age in which we dwell. Lesson for Today, The. Robert Frost. CP-FrosR

If those I loved were lost. Emily Dickinson. CP-DickE

If "Those People" Like You. Alice Walker. CP-WalkA

If thou art balked, O Freedom. House of Friends, The. Walt Whitman. CP-WhitW

If thou art sorrowful, hide thy face! George Meredith. CP-MerG2

If thou art sweet as they are sad. Thule. Walter De la Mare. CP-DeLaW

If thou aske me (Deare) wherefore. To Mistresse Dorothy Parsons. Robert Herrick. CP-HerrR

If thou be dead, forgive and thou shalt live. Christina Georgina Rossetti. CP-RosC2

If Thou beest taken, God forbid. Another, to His Saviour. Robert Herrick. CP-HerrR

If thou be'st ice, I do admire. Miracle, The. Sir John Suckling. CP-SuckJ

If thou canst bear. Γνωθι Σεαυτον. Ralph Waldo Emerson. CP-EmerR

If thou chance for to find. To My Successor. George Herbert. CP-HerbG

If thou dislik'st the piece thou light'st on first. To the Sour[e] Reader. Robert Herrick. CP-HerrR

If thou hast found an honie-combe. Hony-Combe, The. Robert Herrick. CP-HerrR

If thou in the dear love of some one Friend. For the Spot Where the Hermitage Stood on St Herbert's Island, Derwent-Water. William Wordsworth. CP-WorW1; MW-WorW

If thou indeed derive thy light from Heaven. William Wordsworth. CP-WorW1

If thou longst so much to learne (sweet boy) what 'tis to love. Thomas Campion. CP-CampT

If Thou Sayest, Behold, We Knew It Not. Christina Georgina Rossetti. CP-RosC2

If thou wert here, these tears were tears of light! Day-Dream, The. Samuel Taylor Coleridge. CP-ColeS

If thou wilt but stand by my ear. Inspiration. Henry David Thoreau. CP-ThorH

If thou wilt mighty be, flee from the rage. Sir Thomas Wyatt. CP-WyatT

If thou wouldst know the virtues of mankind. Epigram on William, Lord Burl[eigh], Lo[rd] High Treasurer of England, An. Ben Jonson. CP-JonsB

If thought can reach to Heaven. Rabbi's Song, The. Rudyard Kipling. CP-KiplR

If thro' the sea of night which here surrounds me. Anchored. Paul Laurence Dunbar. CP-DunbP

If, through our eyes, the heart's seen in the face. Michelangelo Buonarroti. CP-Miche, tr. by John Frederick Nims

If thy body pine. Ralph Waldo Emerson. CP-EmerR

If thy darling favor thee. Hafiz. CP-EmerR Fr. Odes.

If time is only another dimension, then all that dies. Hungerfield. Robinson Jeffers. CP-JeffR3

If tired of trees I seek again mankind. Vantage Point, The. Robert Frost. CP-FrosR

If to a woman's head a painter would. Horace, of the Art of Poetry. Horace. CP-JonsB

If to admire were to commend, my praise. To Mr Joshua Sylvester. Ben Jonson. CP-JonsB; SP-JonsB

If to be left were to be left alone. Edna St. Vincent Millay. CP-MillE

If to dance the hotel ballroom. 1975. Thom Gunn. CP-GunnT

If to grow old in Heaven is to grow young. True Woman (Her Heaven). Dante Gabriel Rossetti. CW-RossD Fr. House of Life, The.

If to my mind, great lord, I had a state. To the Right Honourable, the Lord Treasurer of England. An Epigram. Ben Jonson. CP-JonsB

If, to rejoice, you crave our tears and woe. Michelangelo Buonarroti. CP-Miche, tr. by John Frederick Nims

If to Tradition faith be due. Highland Broach, The. William Wordsworth. CP-WorW2

If to write, rewrite, and write again. Arthur Hugh Clough. SP-ClouA

If today, I follow death. Mourning Grace. Maya Angelou. SP-AngeM

If trees were tall and grasses short. By the Babe Unborn. G. K. Chesterton. CP-ChesG

If true (and it is) that with body's final breath. Michelangelo Buonarroti. CP-Miche, tr. by John Frederick Nims

If truth in hearts that perish. A. E. Housman. CP-HousA

If 'twere fair to suppose. Suppose. Paul Laurence Dunbar. CP-DunbP

If two hours' dying steals a hundred years. Michelangelo Buonarroti. CP-Miche, tr. by John Frederick Nims

If underneath the water. Peter Grump. Christina Georgina Rossetti. CP-RosC3

If up's the word;and a world grows greener. E. E. Cummings. CP-CummE

If vases curious to behold. To Doctor Smith on His Birth Day March 16th, 92. Annis Boudinot Stockton. CP-StocA

If Virgil and Homer had but seen that sun. Petrarch. CP-Petra, tr. by J. G. Nichols

If virtuous love can merit a reward. Petrarch. CP-Petra, tr. by J. G. Nichols

If, vulnerable from early youth, a heart. Michelangelo Buonarroti. CP-Miche, tr. by John Frederick Nims

If waker care, if sudden [or sodayne] pale colo[u]r. Sir Thomas Wyatt. CP-WyatT

If warre, or want shall make me grow so poore. His Petition. Robert Herrick. CP-HerrR

If wars were won by feasting. Dutch in the Medway, The. Rudyard Kipling. CP-KiplR

If we all go, seeing we all were made. Serial Murderer Says Something to the Priest, The. Miller Williams. CP-WillM

If we are leaves that fall upon the ground. Wallace Stevens. CP-StevWP

If we are to exist. Dying. Robert Creeley. CP-CreeR

If We Are to Know Where We Live. Kenneth Patchen. CP-PatcK

If we ask you to gleam through the tears. Kisses, Can You Come Back like Ghosts? Carl Sandburg. CP-SandC

If we constrain the eyes' easy response. Michelangelo Buonarroti. CP-Miche, tr. by John Frederick Nims

If we could be brought to the surface. David Ignatow. SP-IgnaD

If we could find a way to turn the wind toward home. Conditional Riff. Eleanor Wilner. SP-WilnE

If we could get the hang of it entirely. Entirely. Louis MacNeice. CP-MacNL

If we could reverse the world to what it changed. Outlivers (Harriet and Elizabeth). Robert Lowell. SP-LoweR

If we could see below. Foil, The. George Herbert. CP-HerbG

If we go back to where. But. Robert Creeley. CP-CreeR

If we had been given names to love. Bird-Window-Flying. Tess Gallagher. SP-GallT

If we happen to choke up on history, none too soon. Serious Case, A. Mona Van Duyn. SP-VanDM

If we meet a gorilla. We Must Be Polite. Carl Sandburg. CP-SandC

If we must live again, not us; we might. Seals. Robert Lowell. SP-LoweR

If we rally at all, today, instead of keeping stark asunder. Rallying-Point. D. H. Lawrence. CP-LawrD

If we see better through tiny. American Gothic. William Stafford. SP-StafWW

If we shall live, we live. Meeting. Christina Georgina Rossetti. CP-RosC3

If we sing a god, that god. Rainer Maria Rilke. CP-RilkFr, tr. by A. Poulin, Jr. Fr. Orchards.

If We Take All Gold. Louise Bogan. CP-BogaL

If we talk, we're too tired to make love; if we. Marilyn Hacker. SP-HackM Fr. Taking Notice.

If we two clung to a sad sea-crag. Lines Inscribed for Mr. Thomas Hutchinson. G. K. Chesterton. CP-ChesG

If we were as ferries and lived only a summer, how lovely to sleep without contact. Olga Broumas. SP-BrouO Fr. Black Holes, Black Stockings.

If we were such and so, the same as these. Purple Martins. Carl Sandburg. CP-SandC

If we'd been allowed to choose. One Version of Events. Wisława Szymborska. SP-SzymW, tr. by Stanislaw Barańczak and Clare Cavanagh

If well the Dice runne, lets applaud the cast. Good Luck Not Lasting. Robert Herrick. CP-HerrR

If well thou hast begun, goe on fore-right. End, The. Robert Herrick. CP-HerrR

If we're sometimes so amazed. Rainer Maria Rilke. CP-RilkFr, tr. by A. Poulin, Jr. Fr. Roses, The.

If What we could—were what we would. Emily Dickinson. CP-DickE

If when Don Cupid's dart. Love's Offence. Sir John Suckling. CP-SuckJ

If, when it caught my eye first, I'd been bolder. Michelangelo Buonarroti. CP-Miche, tr. by John Frederick Nims

If when my wife is sleeping. Danse Russe. William Carlos Williams. CP-WilW1

If, when Simone laboured to depict. Petrarch. CP-Petra, tr. by J. G. Nichols

If when the sun at noon displays. Beautiful Mistress, A. Thomas Carew. CP-CareT

If when these Lyricks (Cesar) You shall heare. To the King. Robert Herrick. CP-HerrR

If, while I lived, a someone, eyes on me. Michelangelo Buonarroti. CP-Miche, tr. by John Frederick Nims

If, whittler and dumper, gross carver. Arc Inside and Out, The. A. R. Ammons. CP-AmmoA

If wholsome Diet can re-cure a man. Diet. Robert Herrick. CP-HerrR

If wild my breast and sore my pride. Rhyme against Living. Dorothy Parker. CP-ParkD

If wishes would carry me over the land. Ralph Waldo Emerson. CP-EmerR

If with complaint the pain might be expressed. Sir Thomas Wyatt. CP-WyatT

If with my burning hands I could melt. Its Summer Night. Rainer Maria Rilke. CP-RilkFr, tr. by A. Poulin, Jr.

If within tonight's erect. E. E. Cummings. CP-CummE

If Wordsworth, a boy, reached out. Rather like a Dream. Robert Penn Warren. CP-WarrR

If wounds in clothes, Cuts calls his rags, 'tis cleere. Upon Cuts. Robert Herrick. CP-HerrR

If wrecked upon the Shoal of Thought. Emily Dickinson. CP-DickE

If ye fear[e] to be affrighted. Charm, A. Robert Herrick. CP-HerrR

If ye gae up to yon hill-tap. Tarbolton Lasses, The. Robert Burns. CP-BurnR

If ye will with Mab find grace. Fairies, The. Robert Herrick. CP-HerrR

If yellow betokens infidelity. Injudicious Gardening. Marianne Craig Moore. CP-MoorM

If yet I have not all thy love. Lovers' Infiniteness[e]. John Donne. CP-DonnJ; MW-DonnJ

If You. Robert Creeley. CP-CreeR

If you and i awakening. E. E. Cummings. CP-CummE

If you and I could change to beasts, what beast should either be? White Witchcraft. Robert Browning. CP-BroR2

If you appear in the fire. Your Flight. Eugenio Montale. CP-MontE, tr. by Jonathan Galassi

If You Are a Man. D. H. Lawrence. CP-LawrD

If you are a man. How to Stop Smoking. Miller Williams. CP-WillM

If you are become an eternal idea. To Giacomo Leopardi in the Sky. Charles Wright. SP-WrigC

If you are Black and for me. To a Suitor. Maya Angelou. SP-AngeM

If you are happy, I will give you an apple. Covenant. Tennessee Williams. CP-WillT

If you are one of the truly elect. Theodotos. Constantine P. Cavafy. CP-CavaC, tr. by Theoharis Constantine Theoharis

If You Are Only Flirting. James Laughlin. CP-LaugJ

If you, by showing signs of your unease. Petrarch. CP-Petra, tr. by J. G. Nichols

If you call poetry a song. Jaroslav Seifert. SP-SeifJ, tr. by Ewald Osers

If you can come to no conclusion about death whatever. New Entrepreneurial

Plan. Nelle Richmond Eberhart. CP-EberR

If you can explain the / secret of the avalanche. Avalanche, The. James Laughlin. CP-LaugJ

If you can keep your head when all about you. If—. Rudyard Kipling. CP-KiplR

If you can't eat you got to. E. E. Cummings. CP-CummE

If you come as softly. Memorial I. Audre Lorde. SP-LordA

If you could see, fair brother, how dead beat. Prolonged Sonnet: When the Troops Were Returning from Milan. Niccolò degli Albizzi. CW-RossD, tr. by Dante Gabriel Rossetti

If you could sit with me beside the sea to-day. Longing. Paul Laurence Dunbar. CP-DunbP

If you could take the day by the hand. Day, The. W. S. Merwin. SP-MerwW

If You Could Write One Great Poem, What Would You Want It to Be About? Robert Pinsky. CP-PinsR

If you danced from midnight. Twelve Dancing Princesses, The. Anne Sexton. CP-SextA

If you don't go you don't go. Ceremonial. Richard Eberhart. CP-EberR

If you don't have the power to pay back the cruel. Shmuel HaNagid. SP-HaNaS, tr. by Peter Cole

If you don't know DOC SIFERS I'll jes' argy, here and now. Rubáiyát of Doc Sifers. James Whitcomb Riley. CP-RileJ

If you don't know the kind of person I am. Ritual to Read to Each Other, A. William Stafford. SP-StafW; SP-StafWW

If you fight guerrilla warfare in a green skirt. 1st Avenue Basics. Andrei Codrescu. SP-CodrA

If you from spoil of th' old world's farthest end. Cales and Guiana. John Donne. CP-DonnJ; MW-DonnJ

If you get enough money. Sayings of Henry Stephens. Carl Sandburg. CP-SandC

If you had asked. Strands. Yusef Komunyakaa. CP-KomuY

If you had come away with me. April. William Carlos Williams. CP-WilW1

If You Had Known. Thomas Hardy. CP-HardT

If you happen upon my love. Love Message. D. H. Lawrence. CP-LawrD

If you have a house. House: Some Instructions. Grace Paley. CP-PalGC

If you have ceased. Kathleen Jessie Raine. SP-RainK

If you have formed [or formd] a Circle to go into. To God. William Blake. CP-BlakW

If you have lips and forests. For Two Lovers in the Year 2075 in the Canadian Woods. William Meredith. SP-MereW

If you have not read the Slavic poets. To Robinson Jeffers. Czeslaw Milosz. CP-MiloC; CP-MiloCN, tr. by Richard Lourie

If you have picked your lawn of leaves and snails. Sonnet: "If you have picked your lawn of leaves and snails." G. K. Chesterton. CP-ChesG

If you have revisited the town, thin Shade. To a Shade. William Butler Yeats. CP-YeatW

If you have taken this rubble for my past. Delta. Adrienne Rich. SP-RicA1

If you have to die. Fanny Howe. SP-HoweF Fr. Introduction to the World.

If you ignore the possibilities of art. For a Low Voice. William Carlos Williams. CP-WilW2

If you keep command of yourself. Nightpiece. Robinson Jeffers. CP-JefR3

If You Leave a Long-Loved Friend. Shmuel HaNagid. SP-HaNaS, tr. by Peter Cole

If you like my poems let them. E. E. Cummings. CP-CummE

If you live along with all the other people. Worm Either Way. D. H. Lawrence. CP-LawrD

If you look at your succession of desires. Muriel Rukeyser. CP-RukeM

If you make a revolution, make it for fun. Sane Revolution, A. D. H. Lawrence. CP-LawrD

If you mean to Please Every body you will. English Encouragement of Art Cromeks Opinions Put Into Rhyme. William Blake. CP-BlakW

If you mess up, run to the west. Fanny Howe. SP-HoweF Fr. O'Clock.

If you must leave the shores of mind. Discoverer. A. R. Ammons. CP-AmmoA

If you never came with a pigeon rainbow purple. Sumach and Birds. Carl Sandburg. CP-SandC

If you never do anything for anyone else. Immoral Proposition, The. Robert Creeley. CP-CreeR

If you never heard of Hunchley, I would say in his behalf. Thanksgiving Day at Hunchley's. James Whitcomb Riley. CP-RileJ

If you or I should die. Five Accounts of a Monogamous Man. William Meredith. SP-MereW

If you play a Game of Chance know before you begin. William Blake. CP-BlakW

If you press me for the legend. Legend of the Chippewa Spring and Minnehaha, the Indian Maiden. Ezra Pound. CP-PoEar

If you put in enough hours in bars, sooner or later you get to hear every imaginable kind of bullshit. Bob. C. K. Williams. CP-WillC; SP-WillC

"If you raise canary birds," my grandfather said to me. Summer Night. James Tate. SP-TateJ

If you rattle along like your mistress's tongue. Extempore Pinned to a Lady's Coach. Robert Burns. CP-BurnR

If you refuse me once and think again. Song: "If you refuse me once and think again." Sir John Suckling. CP-SuckJ

If you say this was made for friend Dan, you belie it. On the Same. Thomas Sheridan. CP-SherT

If you see a child that shivers when it hears. Sonnet: "If you see a child that shivers when it hears." Hayden Carruth. CP-CarHS Fr. Sonnets.

If you see Love, Dante. Guido Cavalcanti. CP-CavaG, tr. by Marc Cirigliano

If you seek a heavenly light. Song: If You Seek. Thomas Merton. CP-MertT

If you shame a man for the flaws he shows you. Shmuel HaNagid. SP-HaNaS, tr. by Peter Cole

If you should break your beauteous nose. Grande Passion. Dorothy Parker. CP-ParkD

If You Should Go. Countee Cullen. CP-CullC

If you should look for this place after a handful of lifetimes. Tor House. Robinson Jeffers. CP-JefR1

If you should rise from Nowhere up to Somewhere. Fear of God, The. Robert Frost. CP-FrosR

If you should sail for Trebizond, or die. Immortals, The. Dorothy Parker. CP-ParkD

If you speak to me, some night. Gifts, The. Richard Wilbur. CP-WilbR

If you stop to find out what your wages will be. Mary's Son. Rudyard Kipling. CP-KiplR

If You Talk the Talk, You Better Walk the Walk. Charles Wright. SP-WrigCN

If you taste tears too often, inquisitive tongue. Reprimand, The. Elizabeth Bishop. CP-BishE

If you, that have grown old, were the first dead. New Faces, The. William Butler Yeats. CP-YeatW

If you trap the moment before its ripe. William Blake. CP-BlakW

If you wake at midnight and hear a horse's feet. Smuggler's Song, A. Rudyard Kipling. CP-KiplR Fr. Puck of Pook's Hill.

If you wander far enough. Oh No. Robert Creeley. CP-CreeR

If you want justice. Demon Justice. D. H. Lawrence. CP-LawrD

If you want me again under your yoke. Petrarch. CP-Petra, tr. by J. G. Nichols

If you want my apartment, sleep in it. Rent. Jane Cooper. CP-CoopJ

If you want to come after me for any reason. Route with No Number. W. S. Merwin. SP-MerwW

If you want to get a glimpse of future possibilities. Signs of the Times. D. H. Lawrence. CP-LawrD

If you want to have sex, you've got to trust. Sex and Trust. D. H. Lawrence. CP-LawrD

If you want to kill yourself, how come you don't want to kill yourself. Fernando Pessoa. SP-PessF, tr. by Susan M. Brown and Edwin Honig

If you want to know yourself. Know Thyself, and That Thou Art Mortal. D. H. Lawrence. CP-LawrD

If you want to learn how to meditate. Do the Meditation Rock. Allen Ginsberg. SP-GinsA

If you want to say no say. Lighthouses, The. George Oppen. CP-OppGN

If you want to see that nothing is left. Nocturne of Emptied Space. Federico García Lorca. CP-GarcF, tr. by Greg Simon and Steven F. White

If you want what visible reality. Jelaluddin Rumi. SP-Rumi, tr. by Coleman Barks

If you were alive, Art. Pepper. Yusef Komunyakaa. CP-KomuY

If you were coming in the Fall. Emily Dickinson. CP-DickE

If you were drowning, I'd come to the rescue. Love Song: "If you were drowning, I'd come to the rescue." Joseph Brodsky. CP-BrodJ

If you were exchanged in the cradle and. Story That Could Be True, A. William Stafford. SP-StafW; SP-StafWW

If you were sealed inside a box. Rhythm Method. Yusef Komunyakaa. CP-KomuY

If you were to stop and ask me. Conductor of Nothing, The. Philip Levine. SP-LeviP

If you were too dumb the life before. Han-shan. CP-ColdM, tr. by Red Pine

If you were twenty-seven. Heaven. Philip Levine. SP-LeviP

If you will choose the portrait. As to a Frontispiece. Laura Riding Jackson. CP-RidiL

If you will go down into yourself, under your surface personality. Primal Passions, The. D. H. Lawrence. CP-LawrD

If You Will Let Me Sing. "H. D." CP-DoolH

If you will sit in the chair of the flower it will bear you. Inadequate Orderly Simplification, The. But the Three Natural Units. And Only Arbitrary Constants. Charles Olson. CP-OlsoC

If you will tell me why the fen. I May, I Might, I Must. Marianne Craig Moore. CP-MoorM

If you wonder who stays happy. Shih-te. CP-ColdM, tr. by Red Pine

If you work a body of water and a body of woman. Monologue of a Commercial Fisherman. Alan Dugan. CP-DugaA

If You Would. Langston Hughes. CP-HughL; CP-HughL3

If You Would Disappear at Sea. James Tate. SP-TateJ

If you would go down to the dead. La Chute II. Charles Olson. CP-OlsoC

If you would guess, fond man, the secret. Help Me, Venus, You Who Led Me On. Charles Olson. CP-OlsoC

If you would happy company win. Titmouse. Walter De la Mare. CP-DeLaW

If you would have my heart love on. To Madame du Châtelet. Voltaire. CP-WilbR

If you would increase increase your essence. Han-shan. CP-ColdM, tr. by Red Pine

If you would love happily. Advice to Aurelius. James Laughlin. CP-LaugJ

If you would run. For the Running of the New York City Marathon. James Dickey. CP-DickJ

If you would seek a friend among men. Stephen Crane. CP-CranS

If you'll busk you as a bride. Boy Johnny. Christina Georgina Rossetti. CP-RosC2

If your gaze takes in. Gregory Orr. SP-OrrG

If your hair was brown. If. Robert Creeley. SP-CreeR

If your Nerve, deny you. Emily Dickinson. CP-DickE

If your reputation. Snob. Langston Hughes. CP-HughL; CP-HughL2

If your tired unspeaking head. Homily. Allen Tate. CP-TateA

If your wheel gets snared in tangled. Gerti's Carnival. Eugenio Montale. CP-MontE, tr. by Jonathan Galassi

If you're at your wits' end concerning love. Umbrella from Piccadilly, An. Jaroslav Seifert. SP-SeifJ, tr. by Ewald Osers

If You're Finding The Good At Fault. Shmuel HaNagid. SP-HaNaS, tr. by Peter Cole

If You're Going to Have One. Robert Creeley. SP-CreeR

If you're great enough. Shame on You. Langston Hughes. CP-HughL; CP-HughL3

If you're in Dublin, she said that time. Staircase, A. Hans Magnus Enzensberger. SP-EnzeH, tr. by Michael Hamburger

If you're off to Philadelphia in the morning. Philadelphia. Rudyard Kipling. CP-KiplR

If You're So Smart, Why Ain't You Rich? Philip Whalen. SP-WhalP

If you're still and never speak. Han-shan. CP-ColdM, tr. by Red Pine

If you've ever been in a car. Stun. James Schuyler. CP-SchuJ

If you've ever stole a pheasant-egg be'ind the keeper's back. Loot. Rudyard Kipling. CP-KiplR

If you've forgotten me forever, Mercy. Guido Cavalcanti. CP-CavaG, tr. by Marc Cirigliano

If you've noticed that people have been acting. Leaflet. Grace Paley. CP-PalGC

If Zeus chose us a King of the flowers in his mirth. Song of the Rose. Sappho. CP-BroEB

If(among / silent skies). E. E. Cummings. CP-CummE

If-ing. Langston Hughes. CP-HughL; CP-HughL2

If(touched by love's own secret)we,like homing. E. E. Cummings. CP-CummE; SP-CummE

If(you are i why certainly). E. E. Cummings. CP-CummE

Iglits and His Wife. Carl Sandburg. CP-SandC

Iglits' wife spoke of her own novel, of a Norwegian's novel and came. Iglits and His Wife. Carl Sandburg. CP-SandC

Igni Natura Renovatur Integra (Nature Is Completely Renewed by Fire). Andrei Codrescu. SP-CodrA

Ignoble Procession, The. D. H. Lawrence. CP-LawrD

Ignominy to receive, The. Emily Dickinson. SP-DickE

Ignorance. Philip Larkin. CP-LarkP

Ignorance a Sunset, An. Emily Dickinson. CP-DickE

Ignorance came in stones of gold. Medley. Carl Sandburg. CP-SandC

Ignorance, error, cupidity, and sin. To the Reader. Charles Baudelaire. CP-KunSC, tr. by Stanley Kunitz

Ignorant pronounce it Frood, The. On Professor Freud. G. K. Chesterton. CP-ChesG

Ignorant two, we glide. On Minding One's Own Business. James Wright. CP-WrigJ

Ignotum spatiari horto, dicumbere mensis. Ad Reverendum Patrem Fratrem Thomam Burke O.P. Collegium S. Beunonis Invisentem. Gerard Manley Hopkins. CP-HopkG

Ignu. Allen Ginsberg. CP-GinsA; SP-GinsA

Igor Stravinsky. Charles Olson. CP-OlsoC

Ike. Rita Dove. SP-DoveR

Ike Walton's Prayer. James Whitcomb Riley. CP-RileJ

IKEY(GOLDBERG)'S WORTH I'M. E. E. Cummings. CP-CummE

Ikon: The Harrowing of Hell. Denise Levertov. SP-LeveDS

Il etait une petite fille de dix ans. Si Peu Séduisante. Stevie Smith. CP-SmitS

Il Mystico. Gerard Manley Hopkins. CP-HopkG

Il Pastor Fido. James Laughlin. CP-LaugJ

Il Penseroso. John Milton. CP-MiltJ

Il Piccolo Rifiuto. Louis MacNeice. CP-MacNL

Il Rosseggiar Dell'Oriente Canzoniere. Christina Georgina Rossetti. CP-RosC3

Il y a Cent Ans. George Meredith. CP-MerG2

Il y avait cinq vierges. Les Cinq Vierges. Thomas Merton. CP-MertT

I'le come, I'le creep, (though Thou dost threat). To God. Robert Herrick. CP-HerrR

Ile dote noe more, nor shall mine eyes. Sonnet, A: "Ile dote noe more, nor shall mine eyes." Robert Herrick. CP-HerrR

Ile get me hence. Of Love. Robert Herrick. CP-HerrR

I'le hope no more. To His Deere God. Robert Herrick. CP-HerrR

Ile sing no more, nor will I longer write. On Himselfe. Robert Herrick. CP-HerrR

I'le to thee a Simnell bring. To Dianeme; a Ceremonie in Glocester. Robert Herrick. CP-HerrR

Ilford Rose Book. James Schuyler. CP-SchuJ

Iliad, The. Homer.

    Achilles over the Trench. CP-MerG2, tr. by George Meredith

    Agamemnon in the Fight. CP-MerG1, tr. by George Meredith

    Assembly of the Achaians. CP-MerG2, tr. by George Meredith

    "Bibber besotted, with scowl of a cur, having heart of a deer, thou!" CP-MerG1, tr. by George Meredith

    Clash in Arms of the Achaians and Trojans. CP-MerG1, tr. by George Meredith

    Episode of Sarpedon, The. CP-PopeA, tr. by Alexander Pope

    "Frail as the leaves that quiver on the sprays." CP-JohnS, tr. by Samuel Johnson

    "From a duck's egg, a duck. Doubtless his relative Scamander." SP-LoguC, tr. by Christopher Logue

    Hector and Andromache. CP-BroEB, tr. by Elizabeth Barrett Browning

    Helen on the Skaian Gates. CP-MerG2, tr. by George Meredith

    Horses of Achilles, The. CP-MerG1, tr. by George Meredith

    Hypnos on Ida. CP-MerG1, tr. by George Meredith

    Invective of Achilles, The. CP-MerG1, tr. by George Meredith

    Marshalling of the Achaians. CP-MerG1, tr. by George Meredith

    Night Watch of the Trojans before Troy. CP-MerG2, tr. by George Meredith

    Nourishment before Battle. CP-MerG2, tr. by George Meredith

    Odysseus Encircled. CP-MerG2, tr. by George Meredith

    Paris and Diomedes. CP-MerG1, tr. by George Meredith

    Shield of Achilles, The. CP-MerG2, tr. by George Meredith

    Translation of Part of the Dialogue Between Hector and Andromach; from the Sixth Book of Homer's *Iliad* (VI 390–502). CP-JohnS, tr. by Samuel Johnson

    Vengeance of Apollo, The. CP-MerG2, tr. by George Meredith

    "Work'd into sudden rage by wintry show'rs." CP-JohnS, tr. by Samuel Johnson

I'll always / look that way. Women. Robert Creeley. SP-CreeR

I'll Ay[e] Ca' in by Yon Town. Robert Burns. CP-BurnR

I'll be in my own room, upstairs. Nightmare of the Suburbs, A. Jane Cooper. CP-CoopJ

I'll be saying goodbye. Saying Goodbye. Federico García Lorca. CP-GarcF, tr. by Jerome Rothenberg Fr. Return, The.

I'll bet you think the room was empty. Suicide's Room, The. Wisława Szymborska. SP-SzymW, tr. by Stanisław Barańczak *and* Clare Cavanagh

I'll call it the daring. Wild Anemone, The. James Laughlin. CP-LaugJ

I'll clutch—and clutch. Emily Dickinson. CP-DickE

I'll come when thou art saddest. Emily Jane Brontë. CP-BronE

I'll dabble in specifics in my bath. Marilyn Hacker. SP-HackM Fr. Separations.

I'll do what the raids suggest. Boy, A. John Ashbery. SP-AshbJ

I'll [or I'le] do [or doe] my best to win, when'ere I wooe. Zeal Required in Love. Robert Herrick. CP-HerrR

I'll Eat My Split-Level Turkey in the Breezeway. Ogden Nash. CP-NashO

Ill fared it now with his poor wife, I ween. Fragment: A Somersetshire Tragedy. William Wordsworth. CP-WorW1

Ill fares the land, to hastening ills of prey. Judgment of England, The. G. K. Chesterton. CP-ChesG

Ill-fated Genius! Heaven-taught Fergusson. Robert Burns. CP-BurnR

Ill-fated hand that sent the cruel dart. On Hearing that General Warren Was Killed on Bunker-Hill, on the 17th of June 1775. Annis Boudinot Stockton. CP-StocA

Ill-fated Heart! and can it be. On a Cornelian Heart Which Was Broken. Lord Byron. CP-Byron

I'll gaze no more on her bewitching face. Murdering Beauty. Thomas Carew. CP-CareT

I'll Get One Tomorrow. Ogden Nash. CP-NashO

I'll go and sit down a few minutes with my soul. Hello. Of the United States. Charles Olson. CP-OlsoC

I'll go into the bedroom silently and lie down between the bridegroom and the bride. Love Poem on Theme by Whitman. Allen Ginsberg. CP-GinsA; SP-GinsA

Ill Government. Robert Herrick. CP-HerrR

I'll haunt this town, though gone the maids and men. Dream of All the Springfield Writers, The. Nicholas Vachel Lindsay. CP-LindV

I'll Have Your Heart. Stevie Smith. CP-SmitS

I'll join you in your sleep. For My Mother Ill. David Ignatow. SP-IgnaD

I'll keep a little tavern. Tavern. Edna St. Vincent Millay. CP-MillE

I'll know no more;—the heart is torn. Sir Eustace Grey. George Crabbe. SP-CrabG

I'll Mak You Be Fain to Follow Me. Robert Burns. CP-BurnR

I'll make it; but it may take me. O, Thou Opening, O. Theodore Roethke. CP-RoetT

I'll miss the small birds that come. Birds, The. Robert Creeley. CP-CreeR

I'll need new strings to sing your praise. In Praise of My Françoise. Charles Baudelaire. CP-BaudC, *tr. by* Walter Martin

I'll never get to where I'm going! Everything in Order. Thomas McGrath. SP-McGrT

I'll not mis-spend in praise the narrow room. To My Worthy Friend, Master Davenant Upon His Excellent Play, *The Just Italian.* Thomas Carew. CP-CareT

I'll not offend thee with a vain tear more. To the Same [Sir John Roe]. Ben Jonson. CP-JonsB; SP-JonsB

I'll not weep that thou art going to leave me. Stanzas: "I'll not weep that thou art going to leave me." Emily Jane Brontë. CP-BronE

I'll not wish you the death. No My Dear. James Laughlin. CP-LaugJ

I'll not write again. After. Robert Creeley. SP-CreeR

I'll [*or* Ile] come to thee in all those shapes. To Electra. Robert Herrick. CP-HerrR

I'll [*or* Ile] write, because I'll [*or* Ile] give. To Critic[k]s. Robert Herrick. CP-HerrR

I'll [*or* Il'e] write no more of Love; but now repent. On Himselfe. Robert Herrick. CP-HerrR

I'll pay and bow out. Fanny Howe. SP-HoweF *Fr.* Introduction to the World.

Ill Penserosa, an Ode. Annis Boudinot Stockton. CP-StocA

I'll put this in my diary. Turkey in the Straw. William Carlos Williams. CP-WilW2

I'll restore this old church for our marriage. Church and the Wedding, The. Thomas Hardy. CP-HardT

I'll say she's handsome, by all laws. Faithful Wilson. Thomas Hardy. CP-HardT

I'll send the feather from my Hat! Emily Dickinson. CP-DickE

I'll send these ducks of Aylesbury. Song to an Old Tune. G. K. Chesterton. CP-ChesG

I'll shake the bees. Shepherd, The. "H. D." CP-DoolH

I'll show you a fawn who'll wound. Shmuel HaNagid. SP-HaNaS, *tr. by* Peter Cole

I'll stick with the transparent little man. Earth and Moon. Federico García Lorca. CP-GarcF, *tr. by* Greg Simon *and* Steven F. White

I'll surely be thought a dullard in talent, art. Michelangelo Buonarroti. CP-Miche, *tr. by* John Frederick Nims

I'll Take the High Road Commission. Ogden Nash. CP-NashO

I'll tell my deaf mother on you! Fall on the floor. Punk Rock Your My Big Crybaby. Allen Ginsberg. CP-GinsA; SP-GinsA

I'll tell thee now (dear Love) what thou shalt do. Valediction, A: of the Book. John Donne. CP-DonnJ; MW-DonnJ

I'll tell you a dream i had once i was away up in the sky Blue,everything. E. E. Cummings. CP-CummE

I'll tell you a story in majolica. Mother Pomegranate. Gabriela Mistral. SP-MistG, *tr. by* Maria Giachetti [*or* Jacketti]

I'll tell you a tale of a Wife. Song: "I'll tell you a tale of a Wife." Robert Burns. CP-BurnR

I'll tell you a thing or two. Han-shan. CP-ColdM, *tr. by* Red Pine

I'll tell you how the Sun rose. Emily Dickinson. CP-DickE

I'll tell you what I don't want: an affair. Marilyn Hacker. SP-HackM *Fr.* Taking Notice.

I'll tell you what it was. I thought about those. In Nashville, Standing in the Wooden Circle Sawed Out from the Old Ryman Stage, the Picker has a vision. Miller Williams. CP-WillM

I'll tell you what to do. Defense. William Carlos Williams. CP-WilW2

I'll tell you who will end in Hell. Another Monday. Primo Levi. CP-LeviP, *tr. by* Ruth Feldman *and* Brian Swann

I'll walk awhile, maybe as high as the tree line. Elegy for My Brother. Norman Dubie. CP-DubiN

I'll watch that mailbox as if it were an ikon of some religious order. Trough. David Ignatow. SP-IgnaD

Ill wind is stalking, An. Temper of Time. Sylvia Plath. CP-PlatS

Ill wind with a Samsonite suitcase, An. Chance. Ai. SP-Ai

I'll Write Their Number Down When We Get Home. Ogden Nash. CP-NashO

I'll Write While I Have Half an Eye in My Head. Thomas Sheridan. CP-SherT

Illegal Aliens. Grace Paley. CP-PalGC

Illegal ditch riders of the previous night, The. Homage to Philip K. Dick. Norman Dubie. CP-DubiN

Illegitimate Things. William Carlos Williams. CP-WilW2

Illic Jacet. A. E. Housman. CP-HousA

Illicitly, Mr. Mahoney roams. Mr. Mahoney. Josephine Jacobsen. CP-JacoJ

Illileo, the moonlight seemed lost across the vales. James Whitcomb Riley. CP-RileJ

Illinois Farmer. Carl Sandburg. CP-SandC

Illiterate, The. William Meredith. SP-MereW

Illness. Boris Leonidovich Pasternak.
  "At dusk you appear, a school-girl still." SP-WeisT, *tr. by* Theodore Weiss

Illness, An. Robert Creeley. CP-CreeR

Illness of Kleitos, The. Constantine P. Cavafy. CP-CavaC, *tr. by* Theoharis Constantine Theoharis

Ills I sorrow at, The. Any Human to Another. Countee Cullen. CP-CullC

Illumination, The. Stanley Kunitz. CP-KunSC

Illuminations. Louise Glück. SP-GlucL

Illuminator, The. Eleanor Wilner. SP-WilnE

Illusion. Aleksandr Aleksandrovich Blok. SP-BlokA, *tr. by* Peter France *and* Jon Stallworthy

Illusion. Kenneth Rexroth. CP-RexrK

Illusion, An. David Ignatow. SP-IgnaD

Illusion and delusion are that real. James Vincent Cunningham. CP-CunnJ

Illusion of Eternity, The. Richard Eberhart. CP-EberR

Illusion works impenetrable. Maia. Ralph Waldo Emerson. CP-EmerR

Illusions. Ralph Waldo Emerson. CP-EmerR
  (Motto to "Illusions.") CP-EmerR

Illusions like the tints of pearl. Ralph Waldo Emerson. CP-EmerR

Illuster Lodouick, of France most cristin king. William Dunbar. CP-DunbW

Illustrated Books and Newspapers. William Wordsworth. CP-WorW2

Illustration. John Ashbery. SP-AshbJ

Illustration. Donald Hall. CP-HallD

Illustration[—a Footnote], The. Denise Levertov. SP-LeveDP

Illustration / is nothing to you without the application, The. To a Steam Roller. Marianne Craig Moore. CP-MoorM

Illustrative Lines. Robert Duncan. SP-DuncR

Illustrious Ancestors. Denise Levertov. SP-LeveDS

Illustrious man! who doth to heaven appeal. Kossuth. Jones Very. CP-VeryJ

Illustrious tree. Yannis Ritsos. SP-RitsY *Fr.* So?

Illustrissimo, Potentissimoque Principi, *Federico* Quinto, Rheni Comiti Palatino, Duci Bavariae, &c. Thomas Campion. CP-CampT

Illustrissimo Viro Domino Lanceloto Josepho de Maniban Grammatomanti [To That Renowned Man Lord Lancelot Joseph de Maniban Graphologist]. Andrew Marvell. CP-MarvA

Illyrian woodlands, echoing falls. To E.L., on His Travels in Greece. Alfred Tennyson. CP-TennA

Ils ont vu les Pays-Bas, ils rentrent à Terre Haute. Lune de Miel. T. S. Eliot. CP-ElioT; SP-ElioT

I'm a bad, bad man. Bad Man. Langston Hughes. CP-HughL; CP-HughL1

I'm a bone roller. Addendum. Yusef Komunyakaa. CP-KomuY

I'm a bow, my dual kiss, Ipsithilla. Catullus. *See* Call me to you / at siesta

I'm a Depressed Poem. David Ignatow. SP-IgnaD

I'm a-feelin' ruther sad. Home Ag'in. James Whitcomb Riley. CP-RileJ

I'm a frogman. Naked by the water. Margaret's Speech. Norman Dubie. CP-DubiN

I'm a keeper of sheep. Fernando Pessoa. SP-PessF *Fr.* Keeper of Sheep, The.

I'm a lofty lovely woman. Lady in the Furs, The. Thomas Hardy. CP-HardT

I'm a long way from that place. What Is and Is Not. C. K. Williams. CP-WillC

I'm a Pleasure to Shop for. Ogden Nash. CP-NashO

I'm a riddle in nine syllables. Metaphors. Sylvia Plath. CP-PlatS

I'm a Runaway. Fernando Pessoa. SP-PessF, *tr. by* Susan M. Brown *and* Edwin Honig

I'm a sharecropper. Lorine Niedecker. CP-NiedL

I'm a tranquillizer. Advertisement. Wisława Szymborska. SP-SzymW, *tr. by* Stanislaw Barańczak *and* Clare Cavanagh

I'm a traveller in a strange country. Allen Ginsberg. SP-GinsA *Fr.* Reading Bai Juyi.

I'm about to go shopping. Song: "I'm about to go shopping." James Schuyler. CP-SchuJ

I'm afraid of needles. Old. Anne Sexton. CP-SextA; SP-SextA

I'm alive to prove the existence of death in me too. Between Shade and Sun. David Ignatow. SP-IgnaD

I'm all alone; I can't organise anyone. Comfort for Communists. G. K. Chesterton. CP-ChesG

I'm all alone in this world, she said. 50–50. Langston Hughes. CP-HughL; CP-HughL2

I'm almost / done, the hour. Echo ("I'm almost / done, the hour"). Robert Creeley. CP-CreeR

I'm alone in the house. Absent Good Girl, Life of My Mind. Alan Dugan. CP-DugaA

I'm angry with time because. Hour Glass, The. James Laughlin. CP-LaugJ

I'm / asking / you dear to. E. E. Cummings. CP-CummE

I'm at a table with Canadians. First Night at Sea. John Berryman. CP-BerrJ

I'm beginning to know myself. I don't exist. Fernando Pessoa. SP-PessF, tr. by Susan M. Brown and Edwin Honig

I'm being punished this time for crying. Jetsam. C. K. Williams. CP-WillC

I'm big. 6 Foot Goddess, The. Charles Bukowski. SP-BukC1

I'm bin a-visitun 'bout a week. Home Again. James Whitcomb Riley. CP-RileJ

I'm call'd Will Whistle by a throng. Will Whistle. George Meredith. CP-MerG2

I'm careful with my dreams of death. Andrei Codrescu. SP-CodrA

I'm caught by Love within a harsh embrace. Petrarch. CP-Petra, tr. by J. G. Nichols

I'm ceded—I've stopped being Theirs. Emily Dickinson. CP-DickE

I'm coming back / for my wings. Federico García Lorca. CP-GarcF, tr. by Jerome Rothenberg Fr. Return, The.

I'm conscious of your being. Rainer Maria Rilke. CP-RilkFr, tr. by A. Poulin, Jr. Fr. Roses, The.

I'm contented you should stay. Henry David Thoreau. CP-ThorH

I'm crying all the time now. Tears. Allen Ginsberg. CP-GinsA

I'm dearer dead than ever I was, before. Michelangelo Buonarroti. CP-Miche, tr. by John Frederick Nims

I'm dearer to me, much more, than ever I was. Michelangelo Buonarroti. CP-Miche, tr. by John Frederick Nims

I'm death's forever, who, that one forlorn. Michelangelo Buonarroti. CP-Miche, tr. by John Frederick Nims

I'm deep in trouble. Moan. Langston Hughes. CP-HughL; CP-HughL1

I'm doing you a wrong and well I know it. Letter to Dante. John Ciardi CP-CiarJ

I'm doomed here at Saint Isidore. On the Old Roman Road. Clarence Major. SP-MajoC

I'm dreaming of an ancient king. His crown. Nightmare. Jorge Luis Borges. SP-BorgJ, tr. by Willis Barnstone

I'm dreaming the My Lai soldier again. Anne Sexton. SP-SextA Fr. Letters to Dr. Y.

I'm 'ere in a ticky ulster an' a broken billycock 'at. Back to the Army Again. Rudyard Kipling. CP-KiplR

I'm Fed Up with My Life. James Laughlin. CP-LaugJ

I'm free from thee; and thou no more shalt heare. To Love. Robert Herrick. CP-HerrR

I'm Getting Back to Where I Was. Charles Bukowski. SP-BukC1

I'm getting better but Mendelssohn was right. Schumann Adds Trombones to His Second Symphony After Mendelssohn Conducts the First Performance. Miller Williams. CP-WillM

I'm getting tired of not wearing underwear. F. (Missive & Walk) I. #53. Frank O'Hara. SP-OharF

I'm gittin' old—I know. Mother. James Whitcomb Riley. CP-RileJ

I'm glad it didn't offend me. Otherwise. John Ashbery. SP-AshbJ

I'm glad when my boots sink. Swamp Songs. Gregory Orr. SP-OrrG

I'm glad when they arrive. Scarlet. Charles Bukowski. SP-BukC1

I'm glad you're not plump. Real Bones. James Laughlin. CP-LaugJ

I'm going down to Puerto Rico. Vomit Express. Allen Ginsberg. SP-GinsA

I'm going out and get something. Riot Act, April 29, 1992. Ai. SP-Ai

I'm going out to clean the pasture spring. Pasture, The. Robert Frost. CP-FrosR

I'm going to beat. Winner, The. Robert Creeley. SP-CreeR

I'm going to get. Winter Solstice. Charles Olson. CP-OlsoC

I'm going to lie down next to you. Chorus for One Voice. Charles Simic. SP-SimiC; SP-SimiCE

I'm going to murder you with love. Food of Love. Carolyn Kizer. CP-KizeC

I'm going to pull my stinking wagon. Refuse Man, The. David Ignatow. SP-IgnaD

I'm going to roll up. Jack's Blues. Robert Creeley. CP-CreeR

I'm going to swim for my life. All Havens Astern. Charles Olson. CP-OlsoC

I'm going to write a novel, hey. Ode, An: "I'm going to write a novel, hey." John Updike. CP-UpdiJ

I'm gonna wake up some mornin'. So Tired Blues. Langston Hughes. CP-HughL; CP-HughL3

I'm gonna walk to the [or de] graveyard. Young Gal's Blues. Langston Hughes. CP-HughL; CP-HughL1

I'm growing much fonder of Barlow. Barlow. Stevie Smith. CP-SmitS

I'm guided in the darkest night. Henry David Thoreau. CP-ThorH

I'm happiest when most away. Emily Jane Brontë. CP-BronE

I'm happy, Kerouac, your madman Allen's. Malest Cornifici Tuo Catullo. Allen Ginsberg. CP-GinsA; SP-GinsA

I'm having a real day of it. Anxiety. Frank O'Hara. SP-OharF

I'm having a sunbath on the rug. Last Day. May Swenson. SP-SwenM

I'm here to recreate. Here. Rae Armantrout. SP-ArmaA

I'm here to say you've given earth your all. Michelangelo Buonarroti. CP-Miche, tr. by John Frederick Nims

I'm home again, my dear old Room. His Room. James Whitcomb Riley. CP-RileJ

I'm hurrying to an urgent appointment. Moment at the Louvre, A. Dan Pagis. SP-PagiD, tr. by Stephen Mitchell

I'm in a state of translation like a pregnant. Invitation to a Molecular Feast. Andrei Codrescu. SP-CodrA

I'm in Great Trouble. Yehuda Amichai. SP-AmicYL, tr. by Benjamin Harshav and Barbara Harshav

I'm in New York covered by a layer of soap foam. How Come? David Ignatow. SP-IgnaD

I'm in the house because. Untitled Poem: "I'm in the house because." Alan Dugan. CP-DugaA

I'm jealous of your life. What. To a Colleague. From the Country. Alan Dugan. CP-DugaA

I'm Jewish because love my family matzoh ball soup. Yiddishe Kopf. Allen Ginsberg. SP-GinsA

I'm just an untutored traveling man. Have a Seat behind the Potted Palm, Sir. Ogden Nash. CP-NashO

I'm just in love with all these three. Three-Part Song, A. Rudyard Kipling. CP-KiplR Fr. Puck of Pook's Hill.

I'm laughing, but being very quiet about it. Small Song. James Dickey. CP-DickJ

I'm leaving, Im leaving. Do not detain me. Displeased Viewer, A. Constantine P. Cavafy. CP-CavaC, tr. by Theoharis Constantine Theoharis

I'm leaving you, I won't touch you anymore. Tirade for the Next-to-Last Act. Nina Cassian. CP-KizeC, tr. by Carolyn Kizer

I'm like a backward berry Calendar Watchers, or, What's So Wonderful about Being a Patriarch, The. Ogden Nash. CP-NashO

I'm living in Battersea, July. Old-Fashioned Air. Ted Berrigan. SP-BerrT

I'm longing again. White Negress. Yehuda Amichai. SP-AmicYL, tr. by Benjamin Harshav and Barbara Harshav

I'm looking at the lemon tree I planted. Pace Like That, A. Yehuda Amichai. SP-AmicY, tr. by Chana Bloch

I'm looking for a house. House in the World. Langston Hughes. CP-HughL; CP-HughL1

I'm looking for the idea of order. Discussion, A. David Ignatow. SP-IgnaD

I'm looking out of the window. Invention of a Garden, The. Jay Wright. SP-WrigJ

I'm makin' a road. Florida Road Workers. Langston Hughes. CP-HughL1

I'm modal, how are you, Nicolas of Cusa? 2nd Musical Form, for Dave Young, A. Charles Olson. CP-OlsoC

I'm mooring my rowboat. Rowing Endeth, The. Anne Sexton. CP-SextA; SP-SextA

I'm more medicine. John Says. Yusef Komunyakaa. CP-KomuY

I'm no good for you and you. John Ciardi. CP-CiarJ

I'm no photophil who burns. Stark Bewölkt. W. H. Auden. CP-AudeW

I'm Nobody! Who are you? Emily Dickinson. CP-DickE

I'm not a-workin' now! Symptoms. James Whitcomb Riley. CP-RileJ

I'm not alone. Henry David Thoreau. CP-ThorH

I'm not going anywhere. Reverie. Gregory Orr. SP-OrrG

I'm not going to cry all the time. My Heart. Frank O'Hara. SP-OharF

I'm not here. Halcyon. "H. D." CP-DoolH

I'm Not Lucky with Girls. James Laughlin. CP-LaugJ

I'm Not Saying This Right. Jelaluddin Rumi. SP-Rumi, tr. by Coleman Barks

I'm not sure of the sea. Bomb (II). Pablo Neruda. SP-NeruP

I'm not the man she claims. But. Author of Her Misfortune, The. Raymond Carver. CP-CarvR

I'm nothing. / I'll always be nothing. Tobacco Shop. Fernando Pessoa. SP-PessF, tr. by Susan M. Brown and Edwin Honig

I'm now arrived—thanks to the gods! Epigram on Rough Roads. Robert Burns. CP-BurnR

I'm now tending a son's hearth. Old Man. Kenneth Patchen. CP-PatcK

I'm on a stair going down. From a Dream. David Ignatow. SP-IgnaD

I'm on my way to the doctor to get the result of chest X-rays because I coughed blood. Philadelphia: 1978. C. K. Williams. SP-WillC

I'm on my way to work. Flashback. Ai. SP-Ai

I'm on the ledge / outside your hotel bedroom. Paparazzi, The. Ai. SP-Ai

I'm one o' these cur'ous kind o' chaps. Tradin' Joe. James Whitcomb Riley. CP-RileJ

I'm only a wartime working girl. Swing-Song. Louis MacNeice. CP-MacNL

I'm on'y thist a' idiot. Idiot, An. James Whitcomb Riley. CP-RileJ

I'm out of matches. Something. Charles Bukowski. SP-BukC1

I'm Owre [or O'er] Young to Marry Yet. Robert Burns. CP-BurnR

I'm packaged in here like the pulp in fruit. Michelangelo Buonarroti. CP-Miche, tr. by John Frederick Nims

I'm persistent as the pink locust. Pink Locust, The. William Carlos Williams. CP-WilW2

I'm poor alas and I'm sick. Han-shan. CP-ColdM, tr. by Red Pine

"I'm pregnant," I wrote to her in delight. 1973. Marilyn Hacker. SP-HackM

I'm reading that new thing of Locke's. Any Porch. Dorothy Parker. CP-ParkD

I'm ready to climb into the shower. That Kind of Thing. Tess Gallagher. SP-

WorW2

Imagination of Necessity, The. Andrei Codrescu. SP-CodrA

Imagination of the Taj Mahal. Philip Whalen. SP-WhalP

Imagination's Pride, The. Walter De la Mare. CP-DeLaW

Imaginative Life, The. Geoffrey Hill. CP-HillG

Imagine a crowded war-time street. White Feather. John Berryman. CP-BerrJ

Imagine a day begun in Le Bon Café. World's Prose, The. Adam Zagajewski. SP-ZagaA, tr. by Clare Cavanagh

Imagine a king-of-the-wheel. Han-shan. CP-ColdM, tr. by Red Pine

Imagine a young man, alone, without anyone. Aspens. Raymond Carver. CP-CarvR

Imagine an empty house—a mansion, vast. Hot Water. John Updike. CP-UpdiJ

Imagine bird bones. Hayden Carruth. CP-CarHS Fr. Clay Hill Anthology, The.

Imagine David, how a single. Salute to Donald Davie. Eleanor Wilner. SP-WilnE

Imagine father that you had a brother were. Landscape with Next of Kin. Olga Broumas. SP-BrouO

Imagine having forever nowhere to go. Loving You Is Something to Do. John Ciardi. CP-CiarJ

Imagine him too tall and too wide. Imagining Bear. Lucille Clifton SP-ClifL

Imagine it, a Sophocles complete. Fire at Alexandria, The. Theodore Weiss. SP-WeisT

Imagine or remember how the road at last led us. Nocturne Militaire. Thomas McGrath. SP-McGrT

Imagine si ceci. Samuel Beckett. CP-BeckS

Imagine that any mind ever *thought* a red geranium! Red Geranium and Godly Mignonette. D. H. Lawrence. CP-LawrD

Imagine that the fast life of a bird. Branches of Water or Desire, The. Alan Dugan. CP-DugaA

Imagine that war is over, that peace has resumed its reign. New Life. Joseph Brodsky. CP-BrodJ, tr. by David MacFadyen

Imagine the time the particle you are. Bowl, A. Jelaluddin Rumi. SP-Rumi, tr. by Coleman Barks

Imagine! / They are afraid of you. Langston Hughes. CP-HughL; CP-HughL3

Imagine what it must have been to have existence. Think—! D. H. Lawrence. CP-LawrD

Imagine yourself in a country, poor. Story of the Road, The. Christopher Logue. SP-LoguC

Imagine yourself, / in the suit of lights. Sense of Comedy, The: 1. Jay Wright. SP-WrigJ

Imagined Land, The. A. R. Ammons. CP-AmmoA

Imagining Bear. Lucille Clifton. SP-ClifL

Imagining How It Would Be to Be Dead. Richard Eberhart. CP-EberR

Imagining in Writing. Robert Duncan. SP-DuncR

Imaginings. Thomas Hardy. CP-HardT

Imago. Amy Clampitt. CP-ClamA

Imago. Wallace Stevens. CP-StevW; CP-StevWP

Imbecile, The. Wilfred Owen. CP-OwenW

Imbecile Night. Charles Bukowski. SP-BukC2

Imber Nocturnus. Elizabeth Bishop. CP-BishE

Imberbi, si cui, Laurentia nubere vovit. In Laurentiam. Thomas Campion. CP-CampT

Imbued / with the light. Charles Olson. SP-OlsoC Fr. Maximus Poems, The. (Im)c-a-t(mo). E. E. Cummings. CP-CummE

Imenos. Constantine P. Cavafy. CP-CavaC, tr. by Theoharis Constantine Theoharis

Imerro. Ezra Pound. See O Atthis

Imitated From the Arpa Evangelica: Page 121. Christina Georgina Rossetti. CP-RosC3

Imitated from the Japanese. William Butler Yeats. CP-YeatW

Imitation of an Imitation. Yannis Ritsos. SP-RitsY, tr. by Kimon Friar and Kostas Myrsiades

Imitation of Anacreon's Grasshopper, Applied to Mr. T. S., Commonly Known by the Name of Skeleton, An. Unknown. CP-SherT

Imitation of Chaucer. Alexander Pope. CP-PopeA

Imitation of Horace; Carmina 1.6. Robert Stock. SP-StocR

Imitation of Juvenal — Satire VIII. William Wordsworth. CP-WorW1

Imitation of Pope: A Compliment to the Ladies. William Blake. See Compliment to the Ladies, A

Imitation of Sidney: To Stella. (Miss B?). Wallace Stevens. CP-StevWP

Imitation of Spenser. John Keats. CP-KeatJ

Imitation of Spen[s]er, An. William Blake. CP-BlakW

Imitation of Tibullus. Lord Byron. CP-Byron

Imitations of Drowning. Anne Sexton. CP-SextA

Imitations of the Chinese. Kenneth Rexroth. CP-RexrK

Immaculate / December garden, An. Last Days of the Miser. Charles Tomlinson. CP-TomlC

Immalee. Christina Georgina Rossetti. CP-RosC3

Immanence. Robert Penn Warren. CP-WarrR

Immense head emerged slowly, An. Head, The. Czeslaw Milosz. CP-MiloCN, tr. by Robert Hass

Immense hope, and forbearance, The. Spring Day. John Ashbery. SP-AshbJ

Immigrant Story, The. Grace Paley. CP-PalGC

Immigrants. Robert Frost. CP-FrosR

Immigrants, The. Margaret Atwood. SP-AtwM1

Imminent is a immutable, The. For a Version of I Ching. Jorge Luis Borges. SP-BorgJ, tr. by Eric McHenry

Imminent Seventies, The. Robert Graves. CP-GravR

Immobilizing the Boundless. Yannis Ritsos. SP-RitsY, tr. by Kostas Myrsiades

Immolated. Herman Melville. SP-MelvH

Immolatus. Yusef Komunyakaa. CP-KomuY

Immoral Man. D. H. Lawrence. CP-LawrD

Immoral Proposition, The. Robert Creeley. CP-CreeR

Immoralist, The. Norman Dubie. CP-DubiN

Immorality. D. H. Lawrence. CP-LawrD

Immorality, An. Ezra Pound. CP-PoEar

Immortal. William Carlos Williams. CP-WilW1

Immortal, The. Jones Very. CP-VeryJ

Immortal Autumn. Archibald MacLeish. CP-MacLA

Immortal Ennui, that hath driven men. Thersites: On the Surviving Zeus. Ezra Pound. CP-PoEar

Immortal Heat, O let thy greater flame. Love (2). George Herbert. CP-HerbG

Immortal Helix. Archibald MacLeish. CP-MacLA

Immortal is an ample word. Emily Dickinson. CP-DickE

Immortal Longings. Robert Pinsky. CP-PinsR

Immortal Longings. Before Surgery. Donald Davie. CP-DaviDC

Immortal Love, author of this great frame. Love (1). George Herbert. CP-HerbG

Immortal Love, forever full. Our Master. John Greenleaf Whittier. CP-WhitJ

Immortal Part, The. A. E. Housman. CP-HousA

Immortal Prankster. Charles Simic. SP-SimiCE

Immortality. Adam Zagajewski. SP-ZagaA, tr. by Clare Cavanagh

Immortality of Flowers, The. Emily Dickinson. SP-DickE

Immortality of the soul, The. Animula. Robinson Jeffers. CP-JefR3

Immortality Over the Dakotas. Robert Penn Warren. CP-WarrR

Immortality she gave, The. Emily Dickinson. CP-DickE

Immortal[l] clothing I put on. Transfiguration, The. Robert Herrick. CP-HerrR

Immortals. James Dickey. CP-DickJ

Immortals, The. Dorothy Parker. CP-ParkD

Immortals, The. James Tate. SP-TateJ

Immram. Paul Muldoon. CP-MuldP

Immrama. Paul Muldoon. CP-MuldP

"Immurata" Sister, An. Christina Georgina Rossetti. CP-RosC2

Immured in Bothwell's towers, at times the Brave. Bothwell Castle. William Wordsworth. CP-WorW2

Immured in Heaven! Emily Dickinson. CP-DickE

Imogen. Walter De la Mare. CP-DeLaW

Imp Within, The. Walter De la Mare. CP-DeLaW

Impact. Karl Shapiro. SP-ShapK

Impact of a dollar upon the heart, The. Stephen Crane. CP-CranS

Impalpabilities, The. Charles Tomlinson. CP-TomlC

Imparitie doth ever discord bring. Meane, The. Robert Herrick. CP-HerrR

Impartial Law enrolled a name, The. My Name and I. Robert Graves. CP-GravR

Impasse. Langston Hughes. CP-HughL; CP-HughL3

Impasse. Carl Sandburg. CP-SandC

Impassioned as I am. Michelangelo Buonarroti. CP-Miche, tr. by John Frederick Nims

Impasto of what is past, The. Travels. Denise Levertov. SP-LeveDP

Impatience. Jones Very. CP-VeryJ

Impatiens. Louis Zukofsky. CP-ZukLS

Impatiens impatience luckless wit touch-me-not. Impatiens. Louis Zukofsky. CP-ZukLS

Impatient all the foggy day for night. Fever. Thom Gunn. CP-GunnT

Impatient as we were for all of them to join us. Bungalows, The. John Ashbery. SP-AshbJ

Impatient with cripples, foreigners, children. Il Piccolo Rifiuto. Louis MacNeice. CP-MacNL

Impeccable Conception. Maya Angelou. SP-AngeM

Imperante Augusto Natus Est. Robert Browning. CP-BroR2

Imperator Victus. Hart Crane. CP-CranH

Imperceptively the world became haunted by her white dress. White Dress, The. Marya Alexandrovna Zaturenska. SP-ZatuM

Impercipient, The. Thomas Hardy. CP-HardT

Imperfect, The. Marya Alexandrovna Zaturenska. SP-ZatuM

Imperfect Lover, The. Nicanor Parra. CP-MertT

Imperial bird, who wont to soar. On an Eagle Confined in a College-Court. Christopher Smart. SP-SmarC

Imperial by the People's will. Ode to H.I.M. Napoleon 3d. George Meredith. CP-MerG2

Imperial consort of the Fairy-king, The. Wild Duck's Nest, The. William Wordsworth. CP-WorW2

Imperial Rescript, An. Rudyard Kipling. CP-KiplR

Imperial Song for Warmth. Alan Dugan. CP-DugaA

Imperial Stature, the colossal stride, The. Recollection of the Portrait of King Henry Eighth, Trinity Lodge, Cambridge. William Wordsworth. CP-WorW2

Imperiously ringing, "&Ngr;α τα πον&mgr;ε." Chimes for Yahya. James Merrill. SP-MerrJ

Imperishable creatures. Furnace, The. Thomas Kinsella. CP-KinsT

Impermanence. G. K. Chesterton. CP-ChesG

Imperturbable miller's man, The. Miller's Man, The. Robert Graves. CP-GravR

Impetuous Resolve, An. James Whitcomb Riley. CP-RileJ

Impingement Sydrome. Thomas Lux. SP-LuxT

Implications. Carl Sandburg. CP-SandC

Implies that some therefore. All Do Not All Things Well. Thom Gunn. CP-GunnT

Imploring Mecca / to achieve. Be-Bop Boys. Langston Hughes. CP-HughL; CP-HughL3

Implosions. Adrienne Rich. CP-RicAE; SP-RicA1; SP-RicA2

Impomptu, on Mrs. W. Riddell's Birthday, 4th Novr. 1793. Robert Burns. CP-BurnR

Imponderous Night, The. Yannis Ritsos. SP-RitsY, tr. by Kimon Friar

Import, of body a hostess at lunch to my friend a representative, The. Woman's Nipples Is the Rose of the World, A. Charles Olson. CP-OlsoC

Importance of Being Toothless, The. Chuang Tzu. CP-MertT

Importance of Dictionaries, The. James Laughlin. CP-LaugJ

Importance of Elsewhere, The. Philip Larkin. CP-LarkP

Importance of Gourdcrafting, The. Jelaluddin Rumi. SP-Rumi, tr. by Coleman Barks

Importance of its hat to a form becomes, The. Pastor Caballero, The. Wallace Stevens. CP-StevW; CP-StevWP

Importance of Silence, The. James Laughlin. CP-LaugJ

Importation of Landscapes. Alan Dugan. CP-DugaA

Imported Days. Andrei Codrescu. SP-CodrA

Importer, An. Robert Frost. CP-FrosR

Importunate for attention. Bowing the Head. Donald Davie. CP-DaviDC

Importunately / inopportune. Benedictus. Donald Davie. CP-DaviDC

Importuned through the mails, accosted over the telephone. Cave Canem. Edna St. Vincent Millay. CP-MillE

Impossibilities to His Friend. Robert Herrick. CP-HerrR

Impossibility, like Wine. Emily Dickinson. CP-DickE

Impossible, The. Robert Graves. CP-GravR

Impossible, The. Arthur Rimbaud. CP-RimbA, tr. by Martin Sorrell

Impossible Day, The. Robert Graves. CP-GravR

Impossible Iambics. Carl Sandburg. CP-SandC

Impossible Indispensability of the Ars Poetica, The. Hayden Carruth. CP-CarHS

Impossible Marriage, The. Donald Hall. CP-HallD

Impossible, rightly, to define these / conditions of. For Rainer Gerhardt. Robert Creeley. CP-CreeR

Impossible to Tell. Robert Pinsky. CP-PinsR

Impossibly / motivated by midnight. E. E. Cummings. CP-CummE

Impresario of neediness. Carmen 21. Catullus. CP-ZukLS Fr. Carmina.

Impression. E. E. Cummings. CP-CummE

Impression de Voyage. Oscar Wilde. CP-WildO

Impression du Matin. Oscar Wilde. CP-WildO

Impression: Fog Off the Coast of Dorset. Edna St. Vincent Millay. CP-MillE

Impression: Le Réveillon. Oscar Wilde. CP-WildO

Impressionist. Heather McHugh. SP-McHuH

Impressions ("Lily's withered chalice falls, The"). Oscar Wilde. CP-WildO

Impressions ("Sea is flecked with bars of grey, The"). Oscar Wilde. CP-WildO

Impressions / bribe or threaten. Creation, The. Rae Armantrout. SP-ArmaA

Impressions of the New Mexico Legislature. Arthur Sze. SP-SzeA

Impressions Through a Pennsy Window. Tennessee Williams. CP-WillT

Imprimis he was "broke." Thereafter left. Giffen's Debt. Rudyard Kipling. CP-KiplR

Imprimis, there's a table blotted. Faithful Inventory of the Furniture Belonging to —— Room in T. C. D., A. Unknown, sometimes at. to Thomas Sheridan. CP-SherT

Imprisoned in these wires of rain, I watch. Return to D'Ennery; Rain. Derek Walcott. CP-WalcD

Improbable Truth. Denise Levertov. SP-LeveDL

Impromptu. Lord Byron. CP-Byron

Impromptu ["If John marries Mary, and Mary alone"]. William Cowper. CP-CowpW

Impromptu ["So I have seen the maids in vain"]. William Cowper. CP-CowpW

Impromptu. Thomas Gray. CP-GrayT

Impromptu Epigram upon Being Asked to Accompany Three or Four Very Fine Girls with Some Gentleman in a Rural Walk. Annis Boudinot Stockton. CP-StocA

Impromptu Epitaph on the Grave Digger of Princeton—1769. Annis Boudinot Stockton. CP-StocA

Impromptu Fairy-Tale, An. James Whitcomb Riley. CP-RileJ

Impromptu, in Reply to a Friend. Lord Byron. CP-Byron

Impromptu Lines to Greet Marie Bancroft. Robert Browning. CP-BroR2

Impromptu Ode before Day on the 24th of Dec, Christmas Morning, An. Annis Boudinot Stockton. CP-StocA

Impromptu on Hearing a Sermon by the Rev. T. R—Pronounced "Heavy." Robert Browning. CP-BroR2

Impromptu on Hearing that a Print of the Guliteene with Our Beloved Presidents Figure under It Was Executed in Mr Genets Family—under His Sanction. Annis Boudinot Stockton. CP-StocA

Impromptu on Parting from Elizabeth MacFadden, An. Unknown, sometimes at. to Thomas Sheridan. CP-SherT

Impromptu on Reading the Several Motions Made against Mr. Hamilton. Annis Boudinot Stockton. CP-StocA

Impromptu on Richard Wagner. Robert Browning. CP-BroR2

Impromptu on Roller Skates, An. James Whitcomb Riley. CP-RileJ

Impromptu on Seeing a Very Agreeable Gentleman and Lady, Particular Friends Conversing Together. Annis Boudinot Stockton. CP-StocA

Impromptu on the Morning of my Sons Weding Day Which Was Ushered in by a Fall of Snow and Soon after Cleared by a Very Bright Sun. Annis Boudinot Stockton. CP-StocA

Impromptu on Winter. John Clare. SP-ClarJ

Impromptu: The Suckers. William Carlos Williams. CP-WilW1

Impromptu to Lady Winchelsea. Alexander Pope. CP-PopeA

Impromptu with a Breeze. Robert Stock. SP-StocR

Impromptu Written with a Pencil in a Chinese Temple in the Garden of Mr Elisha Boudinot. Annis Boudinot Stockton. CP-StocA

Improved Farm Land. Carl Sandburg. CP-SandC

Improvisation. Thom Gunn. CP-GunnT

Improvisation for a Southern Night. John Ciardi. CP-CiarJ

Improvisatore, The. Samuel Taylor Coleridge. CP-ColeS; MW-ColeS

Impudent Love has perched astride. Cupid & Skull. Charles Baudelaire. CP-BaudC, tr. by Walter Martin

Impulse. A. R. Ammons. CP-AmmoA

Impulse. D. H. Lawrence. CP-LawrD

Impulses of youth, again, The. Aleksandr Aleksandrovich Blok. SP-BlokA, tr. by Peter France and Jon Stallworthy

Imra'u 'l-Qays. Jelaluddin Rumi. SP-Rumi, tr. by Coleman Barks

Imra'u 'l-Qays, King of the Arabs. Imra'u 'l-Qays. Jelaluddin Rumi. SP-Rumi, tr. by Coleman Barks

In a Back Alley. Carl Sandburg. CP-SandC

In a Bad Time. Wallace Stevens. CP-StevW; CP-StevWP

In a Balcony. Robert Browning. CP-BroR1

In a barren land I wander. Lead Me to the Rock That Is Higher Than I. Jones Very. CP-VeryJ

In a between world, a world of amber. Spring Sunshine. Louis MacNeice. CP-MacNL

In a big city, on the boulevards, early. The raising of jalousies and marquees. Hooks of a Corset, The. Czeslaw Milosz. CP-MiloC; CP-MiloCN, tr. by Robert Hass

In a Bird Sanctuary. Richard Wilbur. CP-WilbR

In a blazing sunset. Clarence Major. SP-MajoC

In a blue bar at the crossroads, before you turn. Liberator, The. Derek Walcott. CP-WalcD

In a Boat. D. H. Lawrence. CP-LawrD

In a boat down a fast-running creek. Jelaluddin Rumi. SP-Rumi, tr. by Coleman Barks

In a Boat Shed. Robert Creeley. CP-CreeR

In a bookshelf at the dark living room's end. Illustration. Donald Hall. CP-HallD

In a bookstore I accidentally ended up at the section on Tao, or. Treatise on Emptiness. Adam Zagajewski. SP-ZagaA, tr. by Clare Cavanagh

In a bookstore on the East Side. Burning Oneself In. Adrienne Rich. SP-RicA2

In a borrowed field they dig in their feet. Women's Tug of War at Lough Arrow. Tess Gallagher. SP-GallT

In a Box. James Whitcomb Riley. CP-RileJ

In a Breath. Carl Sandburg. CP-SandC

In a broad, grassy field. Yellow Violets, The. Jones Very. CP-VeryJ

In a broken / mirror you might. Point, The. Hayden Carruth. CP-CarHS

In a Brooklyn Park. Charles Tomlinson. CP-TomlC

In a Buggy at Dusk. Czeslaw Milosz. CP-MiloC; CP-MiloCN, tr. by Robert Hass

In a Bye-Canal. Herman Melville. SP-MelvH

In a cage of light, the splendid creatures. Ballet, The. William Meredith. SP-MereW

In a car Gray smoke over Elmira. Flash Back. Allen Ginsberg. CP-GinsA

In a Cathedral City. Thomas Hardy. CP-HardT

In a cave somewhere they carved an animal. They Carved an Animal. William Stafford. SP-StafWW

In a Certain Place. Christina Georgina Rossetti. CP-RosC3

In a cerulean ruckus. Yellow Dog Café. Yusef Komunyakaa. CP-KomuY

In a Church of Padua. Herman Melville. SP-MelvH

In a Churchyard. James Schuyler. CP-SchuJ

In a Churchyard. Richard Wilbur. CP-WilbR

In a City. Czeslaw Milosz. CP-MiloCN, tr. by Robert Hass

In a city garden an espaliered tree. Rus in Urbe. William Meredith. SP-MereW

In a Clearing. W. S. Merwin. SP-MerwW

In a cleft that's christened Alt. Man and the Echo. William Butler Yeats. CP-YeatW

In a coffee house at 3 a.m. My Son and I. Philip Levine. SP-LeviP

In a cold night. Blood. James Dickey. CP-DickJ

In a concussion, / the mind severs the pain. Shooting Star. Arthur Sze. SP-SzeA

In a Copy of Yeats' Poems. William Meredith. SP-MereW

In a Corner. William Stafford. SP-StafWW

In a corner of a parlor-car. En Route to Southampton. James Schuyler. CP-SchuJ

In a Corner of the Sky. Federico García Lorca. CP-GarcF, tr. by Jerome Rothenberg Fr. Night (Suite for Piano and Poet's Voice).

In a country without saints or shrines. Springs, The. Wendell Berry. CP-BerrW

In a Court. Hart Crane. CP-CranH

In a cove reaching back between ridges. Persimmons, The. Gary Snyder. CP-SnydG

In a crash my head hit the pavement. Put These in Your Pipe. William Stafford. SP-StafWW

In a Crowd. Wallace Stevens. CP-StevWP

In a Crumbling. Kenneth Patchen. CP-PatcK

In a Dark House. Muriel Rukeyser. CP-RukeM

In a Dark Time. Theodore Roethke. CP-RoetT

In a dark time, the eye begins to see. In a Dark Time. Theodore Roethke. CP-RoetT

In a day we pass from the Northern Lights. Flounder. Robert Lowell. SP-LoweR

In a dead tree. Horse, The. W. S. Merwin. SP-MerwWF

In a deep, in a dark wood, somewhere north of Loch Lomond. Capercaillies. Paul Muldoon. CP-MuldP

In a deep thought of you and concentration. Terraced Valley, The. Robert Graves. CP-GravR

In a dense wood, a drear wood. Bitter Waters. Walter De la Mare. CP-DeLaW

In a detachment cool as the glint of light. On Looking East to the Sea with a Sunset behind Me. John Ciardi. CP-CiarJ

In a dim corner of my room for longer than my fancy thinks. Sphinx, The. Oscar Wilde. CP-WildO

In a Disused Graveyard. Robert Frost. CP-FrosR

In a Dream 1. David Ignatow. SP-IgnaD

In a Dream 2. David Ignatow. SP-IgnaD

In a dream I meet. Meeting, A. Wendell Berry. CP-BerrW

In a dream I returned to the river of bees. River of Bees, The. W. S. Merwin. SP-MerwW

In a dream I was in a tunnel struggling. Dream, The. Richard Eberhart. CP-EberR

In a dream I'm no longer in love. I breathe deeply this sense of freedom. On Freedom. David Ignatow. SP-IgnaD

In a dream within a dream I dreamt a dream. Rough Song of Animals Dying. Lawrence Ferlinghetti. SP-FerlL

In a Dreame, Love bad me go. Upon Love. Robert Herrick. CP-HerrR

In a dusty square hemmed by pink stucco. Married Walk in a Hot Place, A. Marge Piercy. SP-PierM

In a English Garden. Paul Laurence Dunbar. CP-DunbP

In a Eweleaze near Weatherbury. Thomas Hardy. CP-HardT

In a far-away northern county in the placid pastoral region. Ox-Tamer, The. Walt Whitman. CP-WhitW

In a far-distant land they dwell. Lotus-Eaters: Ulysses to Penelope, The. Christina Georgina Rossetti. CP-RosC3

In a far far land where men are men. Snow King, The. Rita Dove. SP-DoveR

In a fashionable suburb of Santa Barbara. In Montecito. Randall Jarrell. CP-JarrR

In a ferny byway. Alarm, The. Thomas Hardy. CP-HardT

In a few days now when two memories meet. James Vincent Cunningham. CP-CunnJ

In a fine country, in a sunny country. Short Story. Edna St. Vincent Millay. CP-MillE

In a foreign country you must love. Yehuda Amichai. SP-AmicYL, tr. by Benjamin Harshav and Barbara Harshav

In a Former Resort after Many Years. Thomas Hardy. CP-HardT

In a fourfold silence the music. Two Deliberate Exercises. William Carlos Williams. CP-WilW2

In a fright-wig / that is his own hair. Performances. William Dickey. SP-DickW

In a Garden. Wallace Stevens. CP-StevWP

In a garden I once heard. Eternal Window, An. Yehuda Amichai. SP-AmicY, tr. by Chana Bloch

In a garden where the whitethorn spreads her leaves. Alba Innominata. Unknown. CP-PoEar, tr. by Ezra Pound

In a Garret. Herman Melville. SP-MelvH

In a gigantic pot du chambre, scrolled. Rustication. Adrienne Rich. CP-RicAE

In a Glass of Cider. Robert Frost. CP-FrosR

In a Gondola. Robert Browning. CP-BroR1

In a Gradually Moving Car Somewhere in Calcutta. Miller Williams. CP-WillM

In a grayish sky / a cloud even more gray. Negative. Wisława Szymborska. SP-SzymWM, tr. by Joanna Trzeciak

In a Greek Orthodox Church near Daphne. Raymond Carver. CP-CarvR

In a Green Night. Derek Walcott. CP-WalcD

In a hand like a bowl. Restored, The. Theodore Roethke. CP-RoetT

In a Hard Intellectual Light. Richard Eberhart. CP-EberR

In a hard intellectual light / I will kill all delight. In a Hard Intellectual Light. Richard Eberhart. CP-EberR

In a heavy time I dogged myself. He Follows Himself. Thomas Hardy. CP-HardT

In a high wind. Hands and Eyes. Louis MacNeice. CP-MacNL

In a hole-in-a-wall on Halsted Street sits a gypsy woman. Gypsy Mother. Carl Sandburg. CP-SandC

In a Hospital Garden. Randall Jarrell. CP-JarrR

In a house between the sunrise and the sunset. Crown of Woman, The. G. K. Chesterton. CP-ChesG

In a house he remembers in the Howlong valley. Old Hokusai Print. Carl Sandburg. CP-SandC

In a Hudson Valley. Apple-Maggot Fly, The. Clarence Major. SP-MajoC

In a hundred places in North Dakota. Something Is Dying Here. Thomas McGrath. SP-McGrT

In a hut of mud and fire. Gautama in the Deer Park at Benares. Kenneth Patchen. CP-PatcK

In a Jar. Czeslaw Milosz. CP-MiloC; CP-MiloCN, tr. by Robert Hass

In a jeweler's shop I saw a man beating. Thin Strips. Carl Sandburg. CP-SandC

In a land that the sand overlays—the ways to her gates are untrod. City of Brass, The. Rudyard Kipling. CP-KiplR

In a large box or in a bureau of highly valued ebony I will place and. Garments. Constantine P. Cavafy. CP-CavaC, tr. by Theoharis Constantine Theoharis

In a Large Greek Colony, 200 B.C. Constantine P. Cavafy. CP-CavaC, tr. by Theoharis Constantine Theoharis

In a late Impressionist dream I am riding in an open touring-car with a. Late Impressionist Dream. Lawrence Ferlinghetti. SP-FerlL

In a leap year the date of your death gets closer. Yehuda Amichai. SP-AmicY, tr. by Chana Bloch

In a Letter to C.P. William Cowper. CP-CowpW

In a Letter to the Same [C. P.]. William Cowper. CP-CowpW

In a Library. Walter De la Mare. CP-DeLaW

In a limpidity of silences. Limpidity of Silences. Kenneth Patchen. CP-PatcK

In a little bar on the Gulf Coast. Christmas Poem, A. Miller Williams. CP-WillM

In a little, half-built street, where red and white villas. After School. D. H. Lawrence. CP-LawrD

In a little house keep I pictures suspended, it is not a fix'd house. My Picture-Gallery. Walt Whitman. CP-WhitW

In a little house pictures I keep, many pictures hanging suspended—It is not a fixed house. Earlier vers. of My Picture-Gallery. Walt Whitman. CP-WhitW

In a little off-water. Precursors. A. R. Ammons. CP-AmmoA

In a little patch of ground beside. Hominy and Rain. Raymond Carver. CP-CarvR

In a little side street. Living Theatre, The. Lawrence Ferlinghetti. SP-FerlL

In a London Flat. Thomas Hardy. CP-HardT

In a lonely place. Stephen Crane. CP-CranS

In a long appendix of unexhausted. Appendix to the "Religion": A Light. Pier Paolo Pasolini. SP-PasoP, tr. by Norman MacAfee and Luciano Martinengo

In a manmade lake at first light. Jungle Clearance Ceylon. Louis MacNeice. CP-MacNL

In a Marine Light near Sequim, Washington. Raymond Carver. CP-CarvR

In a middle of a room. E. E. Cummings. CP-CummE

In a minute the doctor will find out what is wrong. Utopian Journey, A. Randall Jarrell. CP-JarrR

In a minute, two inches of rain stream through my dry. Bosworth Field. Robert Lowell. SP-LoweR

In a moment exaggeration. Portrait by Holbein. May Sarton. SP-SartM

In a Moonlit Hermit's Cabin. Allen Ginsberg. CP-GinsA

In a morning coat. Benjamin Banneker Helps to Build a City. Jay Wright. SP-WrigJ

In a Motel on Lake Erie. James Tate. SP-TateJ

In a Museum. Thomas Hardy. CP-HardT

In a Myrtle [*or* Mirtle] Shade. William Blake. CP-BlakW
(To a lovely mirtle bound.) CP-BlakW

In a national magazine of repute. 10 Lions and the End of the World. Charles Bukowski. SP-BukC2

In a nearby town. Ass's Song, The. Christopher Logue. SP-LoguC

In a Neighborhood of Murder. Charles Bukowski. SP-BukC1

In a Notebook. James Fenton. SP-FentJ

In a Parish. Czeslaw Milosz. CP-MiloCN, *tr. by* Robert Hass

In a photograph now left to me. Depression, the War, and Gypsy Rose Lee, The. Wyatt Prunty. SP-PrunW

In a Poem. Robert Frost. CP-FrosR

In a pyloned desert where the scorpion reigns. Red Stains. Allen Tate. CP-TateA

In a Right Angle: A Cycle of Quatrains. Yehuda Amichai.
"Along the summer, along the sandy shoreline." SP-AmicY, *tr. by* Stephen Mitchell
"Driver asked, The. We answered, All the way." SP-AmicY, *tr. by* Stephen Mitchell
"I escaped once and don't remember what god it was from, what test." SP-AmicY, *tr. by* Stephen Mitchell
"I kiss the hem of my fate, as my father would kiss the side." SP-AmicY, *tr. by* Stephen Mitchell
"In the right angle between a dead man and his mourner I'll start." SP-AmicY, *tr. by* Stephen Mitchell
"In the sands of prayer my father saw angels' traces." SP-AmicY, *tr. by* Stephen Mitchell
"Like torn shirts that my mother couldn't mend." SP-AmicY, *tr. by* Stephen Mitchell
"My love writes commentaries on me, like the rabbis explaining the Bible." SP-AmicY, *tr. by* Stephen Mitchell
"Two hopes away from the battle, I had a vision of peace." SP-AmicY, *tr. by* Stephen Mitchell
"Young soldier lies in the springtime, cut off from his name, A." SP-AmicY, *tr. by* Stephen Mitchell

In a robot-democracy, nobody is willing to serve. Robot-Democracy. D. H. Lawrence. CP-LawrD

In a Roman tram, where the famous Roman mob. Thief, The. Stanley Kunitz. CP-KunSC

In a room on West Tenth Street in June. Fate. Kenneth Koch. SP-KochK

In a Room with Picassos. Jane Cooper. CP-CoopJ

In a rundown tenement. Healer, The. Charles Simic. SP-SimiC; SP-SimiCE

In a semicircle we toed the line chalked round the master's desk. Wanderer, The. Seamus Heaney. SP-HeanSO

In a shoe box stuffed in an old nylon stocking. Meadow Mouse, The. Theodore Roethke. CP-RoetT

In a short time we shall have cleared the gazebo. Vacant Possession, A. James Fenton. SP-FentJ

In a shower of tears I sped my fears. And the Clouds Return after the Rain. Stevie Smith. CP-SmitS

In a small and lonely cabin out of noisy traffic's way. Voice of the Banjo, The. Paul Laurence Dunbar. CP-DunbP

In a small black town, your town. Greenhouse, The. Adam Zagajewski. SP-ZagaA, *tr. by* Clare Cavanagh

In a small town in the mountains they tell of a man. Story, The. Miller Williams. CP-WillM

In a soft-complexioned sky. Plighted Promise. Dante Gabriel Rossetti. CW-RossD

In a solitude of the sea. Convergence of the Twain, The. Thomas Hardy. CP-HardT

In a Spanish Tram-Car. D. H. Lawrence. CP-LawrD

In a stable of boats I lie still. Lifeguard, The. James Dickey. CP-DickJ

In a Station of the Metro. Ezra Pound. SP-PounE

In a Strange House. Stanley Kunitz. CP-KunSC

In a summer forest, when the profuse season. Muriel Rukeyser. CP-RukeM

In a tangle of cliffs I chose a place. Gary Snyder. CP-SnydG

In a tavern by the wobbly splendor of the sea. Table 2. Czeslaw Milosz. CP-MiloC; CP-MiloCN, *tr. by* Robert Hass

In a thousand years, if there's History. Ecologue. Allen Ginsberg. CP-GinsA

In a Time. Maya Angelou. SP-AngeM

In a time that breaks. To Think of the Life of a Man. Wendell Berry. CP-BerrW

In a tissue-thin monotone of blue-grey buds. Spring Strains. William Carlos Williams. CP-WilW1

In a Town for Which I Know No Name. James Tate. SP-TateJ

In a Town of Osroini. Constantine P. Cavafy. CP-CavaC, *tr. by* Theoharis Constantine Theoharis

In a Township of Asia Minor. Constantine P. Cavafy. CP-CavaC, *tr. by* Theoharis Constantine Theoharis

In a tree at the edge of the clearing. On Falling Asleep to Birdsong. William Meredith. SP-MereW

In a Troubled Key. Langston Hughes. CP-HughL; CP-HughL2

In a Vale. Robert Frost. CP-FrosR

In a valley late bees with whining gold. Idyl: "In a valley late bees with whining gold." Allen Tate. CP-TateA

In a Vermont bedroom closet. Record Stride, A. Robert Frost. CP-FrosR

In a very short, black velvet skirt. Czech Refugee in London, A. Yehuda Amichai. SP-AmicYL, *tr. by* Benjamin Harshav *and* Barbara Harshav

In a vicious world—to love virtue. Marianne Moore. E. E. Cummings. CP-CummE

In a Viennese Cemetery. James Wright. CP-WrigJ

In a Waiting-Room. Thomas Hardy. CP-HardT

In a war where every second counts. Making Love in Poetry. Lawrence Ferlinghetti. SP-FerlL

In a weird, forlorn voice. President Slumming, The. James Tate. SP-TateJ

In a while they rose and went out aimlessly riding. Merlin Enthralled. Richard Wilbur. CP-WilbR

In a Whispering Gallery. Thomas Hardy. CP-HardT

In a wife I would desire. William Blake. CP-BlakW

In a Wood. Thomas Hardy. CP-HardT
(Pale beech and pine so blue.) CP-HardT

In a workplace torn by a union. Fanny Howe. SP-HoweF *Fr.* Vineyard, The.

In a World of Taking, the Mistake. Heather McHugh. SP-McHuH

In a World too full of Beauty for Peace. Emily Dickinson. SP-DickE

In a world where no one knows for sure. Wanderer Awaiting Preferment, The. William Stafford. SP-StafWW

In a Year. Robert Browning. CP-BroR1; SP-BroR

In a year the nightingales were said to be so loud. Kingfisher, The. Amy Clampitt. CP-ClamA

In a Yiddish eating place on Rivington Street . . . faces . . . coffee. Home Fires. Carl Sandburg. CP-SandC

In Abeyance. Denise Levertov. SP-LeveDP

In Abraham Lincoln's city. Knucks. Carl Sandburg. CP-SandC

In Absence of the Tree. Clarence Major. SP-MajoC

In Abundance. Wisława Szymborska. SP-SzymWM, *tr. by* Joanna Trzeciak

In Adams fall. Henry David Thoreau. CP-ThorH

In advanced age, my health worsening, I woke up in the middle of the night. Awakened. Czeslaw Milosz. CP-MiloCN, *tr. by* Robert Hass

In aerobatics, white, red, speckled & spectacular. Chickens in San Francisco. William Dickey. SP-DickW

In aeternum I was once determed. Sir Thomas Wyatt. CP-WyatT

In Africa the wine is cheap, and it is. Certain Slant of Sunlight, A. Ted Berrigan. SP-BerrT

In Africa, when river beds. Lung Fish, The. John Ciardi. CP-CiarJ

In after Time. Richard Eberhart. CP-EberR

In After-Time, a Sage of Mickle Lore. John Keats. CP-KeatJ

In ages past ere wisdom's height. God Reigns. Paul Laurence Dunbar. CP-DunbP

In agony saying: "The last night of his life." Double Dialogue: *Homage to Robert Frost.* Muriel Rukeyser. CP-RukeM

In air heavy. Two Worlds. Raymond Carver. CP-CarvR

In Aix. Grace Paley. CP-PalGC

In Alicante they bowl the barrels. Alicante Lullaby. Sylvia Plath. CP-PlatS

In all creation, only man cowers and is afraid of life. Cowards. D. H. Lawrence. CP-LawrD

In all of Greater Grand Rapids you. Greater Grand Rapids Lover, The. Marge Piercy. SP-PierM

In all our daily war of words. George Meredith. CP-MerG2

In all our high designments, 'twill appeare. First Marrs or Makes, The. Robert Herrick. CP-HerrR

In all respects unready for a fall. Original Aversions. William Meredith. SP-MereW

In all the cities of this year. King's Mountain. Muriel Rukeyser. CP-RukeM

In all the good Greek of Plato. Survey of Literature. John Crowe Ransom. SP-RansJ

In all the teeth Death turned over. Unfinished Book of Kings. W. S. Merwin. SP-MerwW

In all those stories the hero. Heroes. Robert Creeley. CP-CreeR

IN) all those who got. E. E. Cummings. CP-CummE

In all thy need, be thou possest. Good Precepts, or Counsell. Robert Herrick. CP-HerrR

In Allusion to Various Recent Histories and Notices of the French Revolution. William Wordsworth. CP-WorW2

In Allusion to Various Recent Histories and Notices of the French Revolution, Concluded. William Wordsworth. CP-WorW2

In Allusion to Various Recent Histories and Notices of the French Revolution, Continued. William Wordsworth. CP-WorW2

In Amaze / Lost, I gaze. To Quinbus Flestrin the Man-Mountain, a Lilliputian Ode. Alexander Pope. CP-PopeA

"In America," began / the lecturer, "everyone must have a." Student, The. Marianne Craig Moore. CP-MoorM

In Amorem Divinum. Richard Crashaw. CP-CrasR

In an Act of Pity. Robert Creeley. CP-CreeR

In an afternoon bright with / September, or in an old dissension. This Song. Hayden Carruth. CP-CarHS

In An Artist's Studio. Christina Georgina Rossetti. CP-RosC3

In an Automotive Store. Charles Olson. CP-OlsoC

In an ebony bed adorned. Footsteps, The. Constantine P. Cavafy. CP-CavaC, tr. by Theoharis Constantine Theoharis

In an empty and small room, just four walls. Chandelier. Constantine P. Cavafy. CP-CavaC, tr. by Theoharis Constantine Theoharis

In an Empty Room. Jaroslav Seifert. SP-SeifJ, tr. by Ewald Osers

In an envelope marked. Personal. Langston Hughes. CP-HughL; CP-HughL2

In an old book—close to a hundred years old. Constantine P. Cavafy. CP-CavaC, tr. by Theoharis Constantine Theoharis

In an old master's landscape. Landscape. Wisława Szymborska. SP-SzymWM, tr. by Joanna Trzeciak

In an olive dress / The amoreuse. Come Dance in Baronies. René Char. CP-MertT

In an owl cry, night became real night. Bridge Begins in the Trees, A. William Stafford. SP-StafWW

In an upper room at midnight. Love Feast, The. W. H. Auden. CP-AudeW

In Ancient Times. David Ignatow. SP-IgnaD

In ancient times, as story tells. Baucis and Philemon. Jonathan Swift. CP-SwifJ

In ancient times the wise were able. Answer to Dr. Delany's Fable of the Pheasant and the Lark, An. Jonathan Swift. CP-SwifJ

In and Come In. Archibald MacLeish. CP-MacLA

In and out of the shy, limp leaves of the grape arbor. Remembering Spello, Sitting Outside in Prampolini's Garden. Charles Wright. SP-WrigCN

In and out the bushes, up the ivy. Chipmunk's Day, The. Randall Jarrell. CP-JarrR

In anguish of my heart replete with woes. Upon Some Distemper of Body. Anne Bradstreet. CP-BradA

In Another Country. James Laughlin. CP-LaugJ

In another country, black poplars shake themselves over a pond. North Country, The. D. H. Lawrence. CP-LawrD

In another life in a convent I. With God. Olga Broumas. SP-BrouO

In Another Manner. Federico García Lorca. CP-GarcF, tr. by Alan S. Trueblood Fr. Songs to End With.

In Another Mode. Federico García Lorca. SP-GarcF, tr. by Lysander Kemp

In Another Town. Miller Williams. CP-WillM

In Anselm Hollo's Poems. Ted Berrigan. SP-BerrT

In Answer of an Elegiacal[l] Letter, Upon the Death of the King of Sweden [from Aurelian Townsend, Inviting Me to Write on That Subject]. Thomas Carew. CP-CareT

In Answer to One Who Affirmed of a Well Known Character Here, Dr B———, That There Was Falsehood in His Very Looks. Robert Burns. See Parson's Looks, The

In Answer to Your Silly Question. Alice Walker. CP-WalkA

In antient Time, as Story tells. Jonathan Swift. See In ancient times, as story tells

In Antioch we were perplexed on hearing. In the Districts Surrounding Antioch. Constantine P. Cavafy. CP-CavaC, tr. by Theoharis Constantine Theoharis

In April. Wallace Stevens. CP-StevWP

In April. Charles Tomlinson. CP-TomlC

In April, in April. Well-Worn Story, A. Dorothy Parker. CP-ParkD

In April, in Princeton. Maxine W. Kumin. SP-KumiM

In April the lake water is clear. Late Spring. Meng Hao Jan. CP-WilW2

In April the Morgan was bred. I was chased away. Spring. Mary Oliver. SP-OlivM

In April / the ponds / open / like black blossoms. Blossom. Mary Oliver. SP-OlivM

In April, thirteen centuries ago. Gnomons. Richard Wilbur. CP-WilbR

In April when I see all through. From Syria. Peire Bremon. CP-PoEar, tr. by Ezra Pound

In April, when our land last died. Mysterious Song in the Spring of the Year, A. Thomas Merton. CP-MertT

In April when silkworms are small. Han-shan. CP-ColdM, tr. by Red Pine

In April, when the yellow whin. Ballad of Chaldon Down, The. Edna St. Vincent Millay. CP-MillE

In Arden. Charles Tomlinson. CP-TomlC; SP-TomlC

In art / in art / the image. Dream of Politics, A. George Oppen. CP-OppGN

In atmosphere almost too heavenly. Delusion?—No! Robert Penn Warren. CP-WarrR

In Attica. Stephen Spender. CP-SpenS

In August. Paul Laurence Dunbar. CP-DunbP

In Authorem. Ben Jonson. CP-JonsB

In Autumn ("I know that there are those who say, 'Why don't you sing now'"). "Rubén Dario." SP-DariR, tr. by Alberto Acereda and Will Derusha

In Autumn ("In the pallid afternoons"). "Rubén Dario." SP-DariR, tr. by Alberto Acereda and Will Derusha

In Autumn. W. S. Merwin. SP-MerwW

In autumn in this same life. Passage. W. S. Merwin. SP-MerwWF

In back deep the jewel. From a Phrase of Simone Weil's and Some Words of Hegel's. George Oppen. CP-OppGN

In Back of the Real. Allen Ginsberg. CP-GinsA; SP-GinsA

In Bacon see the culminating prime. Novum Organum. Ambrose Bierce. SP-BierA

In Baghdad, Dreaming of Cairo: In Cairo, Dreaming of Baghdad. Jelaluddin Rumi. SP-Rumi, tr. by Coleman Barks

In balance, the moon and dawn cast equal light and shadows. Dawn. Peter Blue Cloud. SP-BlueP

In balmy / iconic / prague. Smell of Lebanon, The. Alice Walker. CP-WalkA

In Barnum. Thomas Campion. CP-CampT

In Battailes what disasters fall. Blame. Robert Herrick. CP-HerrR

In battles of no renown. Defeated, The. A. E. Housman. CP-HousA

In Bayreuth once. Mary Desti's Ass. Frank O'Hara. SP-OharF

In Bed. Kenneth Koch. SP-KochK

In bed, dull man[?]. Upon My Lord Brohall's Wedding. Sir John Suckling. CP-SuckJ

In bed I muse on Tenier's [or Teniers'] boors. Bench of Boors, The. Herman Melville. SP-MelvH

In bed on my green purple pink. Journal Night Thoughts. Allen Ginsberg. CP-GinsA

In bed we laugh, in bed we cry. Translation of Lines by Benserade. Isaac de Benserade. CP-JohnS, tr. by Samuel Johnson

In Benidorm there are melons. Fiesta Melons. Sylvia Plath. CP-PlatS

In Berkeley. Robert Pinsky. CP-PinsR

In Bethlehem. Christus Natus Est. Countee Cullen. CP-CullC

In Bethlehem on a Christmas night. On a Christmas Night. Langston Hughes. CP-HughL; CP-HughL3

In Between Stories. Jelaluddin Rumi. SP-Rumi, tr. by Coleman Barks

In between the route marks. I'll Take the High Road Commission. Ogden Nash. CP-NashO

In birds is our stolen being. from summer to summer. From a Trilogy of Birds. Andrei Codrescu. SP-CodrA

In Birmingham among my own. Speech Reported, A. G. K. Chesterton. CP-ChesG

In Black Despair. Czeslaw Milosz. CP-MiloCN, tr. by Robert Hass

In Blackwater Woods. Mary Oliver. SP-OlivM

In blazing driftwood / the green keeps showing at the same place. Plumet Basilisk, The. Marianne Craig Moore. CP-MoorM

In Blood's Domaine. Robert Duncan. SP-DuncR Fr. Passages.

In blue / confusion. Last Light. Federico García Lorca. CP-GarcF, tr. by Jerome Rothenberg Fr. Six Songs at Nightfall.

In Bohemia. James Whitcomb Riley. CP-RileJ

In books the various scenes of life he drew. Satire 2.1: "In books the various scenes of life he drew." Horace. CP-JohnS Fr. Satires.

In bounding youth the night & train. Hafiz. CP-EmerR Fr. Odes.

In breath where kingdoms hide. Moment Again. William Stafford. SP-StafWW

In Brest near the flaming rings. Afternoon with Circus and Citadel. Paul Celan. SP-CelaP, tr. by John Felstiner

In Bretonem. Thomas Campion. CP-CampT

In brilliant gas light. Good Night. William Carlos Williams. CP-WilW1

In Britain's Isle, no matter where. Long Story, A. Thomas Gray. CP-GrayT

In Broad Daylight. Wisława Szymborska. SP-SzymW, tr. by Stanisław Barańczak and Clare Cavanagh

In broad daylight it starts to get dark with breathless. August Rain. Joseph Brodsky. CP-BrodJ

In Broken Images. Robert Graves. CP-GravR

In Brueghel's great picture, The Kermess. Dance, The. William Carlos Williams. CP-WilW2

In Bruges town is many a street. Incident at Bruges. William Wordsworth. MW-WorW Fr. Memorials of a Tour of the Continent; 1820.

In Buckinghamshire hedgerows. Icosasphere, The. Marianne Craig Moore. CP-MoorM

In burning summer I saw a season of betrayal. Sixth Elegy. River Elegy. Muriel Rukeyser. CP-RukeM

In Business Don't Get Involved. Shmuel HaNagid. SP-HaNaS, tr. by Peter Cole

In buzzing clusters out they swarm. Midwives, The. Hans Magnus Enzensberger. SP-EnzeH, tr. by Michael Hamburger

In Cabin'd Ships at Sea. Walt Whitman. CP-WhitW

In California. Donald Davie. CP-DaviDC

In calm and cool and silence, once again. First-Day Thoughts. John Greenleaf Whittier. CP-WhitJ

In Cambrum. Thomas Campion. CP-CampT

In Camp. William Stafford. SP-StafW; SP-StafWW

In Canaan's Happy Land. Stevie Smith. CP-SmitS

In Canada, a sense. Continent. Denise Levertov. SP-LeveDL

In Carrowdore Churchyard. Derek Mahon. CP-MahoD

In case of this. Subject-Cases: The Background of a Detective Story. Gertrude Stein. CP-SteiG

In Casterbridge there stood a noble pile. Man, A. Thomas Hardy. CP-HardT

In caves emptied of their workers, turning. Angels at Hamburg, The. Randall Jarrell. CP-JarrR

In celebration of Mitos. Charles Olson. CP-OlsoC

In Celebration of My Uterus. Anne Sexton. CP-SextA; SP-SextA

In Celia's face a question did arise. Lips and Eyes. Thomas Carew. CP-CareT, tr. by Thomas Carew

In Central Park we talked of our own cowardice. 7/14/68: i. Adrienne Rich. CP-RicAE Fr. Ghazals: Homage to Ghalib.

In Chains. William Carlos Williams. CP-WilW2

In Chicago it blows. Take Care. A. K. Ramanujan. CP-RamaA

In Childbed. Thomas Hardy. CP-HardT

In childish days! O memory. Jack-in-the-Box. James Whitcomb Riley. CP-RileJ

In Chile after the earthquake. People Boxes, The. James Laughlin. CP-LaugJ

In Chopin's Garden. Donald Davie. CP-DaviDC

In Chota Nagpur and Bengal. Tree Marriage. William Meredith. SP-MereW

In Church. Constantine P. Cavafy. CP-CavaC, tr. by Theoharis Constantine Theoharis

In Church. D. H. Lawrence. CP-LawrD

In Cicatrices Domini Jesu. Richard Crashaw. CP-CrasR

In Claremont woods we wandered once. George Meredith. CP-MerG2

In Clarke County, the story goes, the family name. Virginia Reel. Charles Wright. SP-WrigC

In clear March wind, some weeks before he died. Mary on the Death of Joachim. Robert Stock. SP-StocR

In cloudy quiet of the day. Spectre, The. Walter De la Mare. CP-DeLaW

In Cnidus born, the consort I became. By Heraclides. Unknown. CP-CowpW, tr. by William Cowper

In cock-wattle sunset or grey. Nostalgia. Louis MacNeice. CP-MacNL

In cold blood, I cannot feel goddesses in the summer evening. Cold Blood. D. H. Lawrence. CP-LawrD

In cold gray. Song Sung, A. Federico García Lorca. SP-GarcF Fr. Songs of Childhood.

In Cold Hell, in Thicket. Charles Olson. CP-OlsoC; SP-OlsoC

In comin by the brig o' Dye. Theniel Menzies' Bony Mary. Robert Burns. CP-BurnR

In Commendation of George Gascoigne's Steel Glass. Sir Walter Ralegh. CP-RaleW

(Walter Rawley [or Ralegh or Rawely] of the Middle Temple, in Commendation of the Steel[e] Glass[e].) CP-RaleW

In Common. Czeslaw Milosz. CP-MiloCN, tr. by Robert Hass

In Connecticut. Charles Tomlinson. CP-TomlC

In constancy content with one man, there. Carmen 111. Catullus. CP-ZukLS Fr. Carmina.

In controversial foul impureness. Arthur Hugh Clough. SP-ClouA

In controversy with facile tongue. Controversy. Ambrose Bierce. SP-BierA

In cooking petits pois, or lesser peas. Reflections on the Vernacular. Ogden Nash. CP-NashO

In coos a pigeon's measuring. Sultry Dawn. Theodore Weiss. SP-WeisT

In Copeman's ear this truth let Echo tell. Thanks for a Gift of Pheasants. William Cowper. CP-CowpW

In countless upward-striving waves. Nominalist and Realist. Ralph Waldo Emerson. CP-EmerR

In Country Sleep. Dylan Thomas. CP-ThomD

In court to serve, decked with fresh array. Courtier's Life, The. Sir Thomas Wyatt. CP-WyatT

In craters in the west other suns went down. Water of the Suns, The. W. S. Merwin. SP-MerwW

In Crispinum. Thomas Campion. CP-CampT

In-curve scooped out and necklaced with light. Bridge Through My Window. Audre Lorde. SP-LordA

In danger, the holothurain cuts itself in two. Autotomy. Wisława Szymborska. SP-SzymW, tr. by Stanislaw Barańczak and Clare Cavanagh

In dark, climbing up. Then down-riding the sand sluice. Youthful Truth-Seeker, Half-Naked, at Night, Running down Beach South of San Francisco. Robert Penn Warren. CP-WarrR

In darkness we cannot see. After Restless Night. Robert Penn Warren. CP-WarrR

In darkroom of your eye the moonly mind. Sonnet to Satan. Sylvia Plath. CP-PlatS

In Darmstadt. James Laughlin. CP-LaugJ

In Daybreak / Tower. Sea with Two Stars, The. Federico García Lorca. CP-GarcF, tr. by Jerome Rothenberg Fr. Seaside Prints.

In days of old. Fairy Story. Donald Davie. CP-DaviDC

In days of yore, tis said, the swimming alder. Henry David Thoreau. CP-ThorH

In days to come—whatever ache. James Whitcomb Riley. CP-RileJ

In days when men found joy in war. Sick Battle-God, The. Thomas Hardy. CP-HardT

In de dead of night I sometimes. Old Cabin, The. Paul Laurence Dunbar. CP-DunbP

In dead of winter. Approximations. Robert Earl Hayden. CP-HaydR

In Dear Detail, by Ideal Light. William Stafford. SP-StafWW

In death alone is what consoles; and life. Death to the Poor. Charles Baudelaire. CP-CullC

In Death, Cannot Reach What Is Most Near. Allen Ginsberg. CP-GinsA

In Death Divided. Thomas Hardy. CP-HardT

In December. Ivor Gurney. SP-GurnI

In December. Charles Tomlinson. CP-TomlC

In December the stubble nearly is. In December. Ivor Gurney. SP-GurnI

In December's slaughterhouse. After the Heart's Interrogation. Yusef Komunyakaa. CP-KomuY

In deep winter the sea roams. Hayden Carruth. CP-CarHS Fr. Bloomingdale Papers, The.

In Deepest Summer. Grace Paley. CP-PalGC

In Defence of Metaphysics. Charles Tomlinson. CP-TomlC

In Den'-shire Kerzie Lusk (when he was dead). Upon Luske. Robert Herrick. CP-HerrR

In despite of its eyes. Cuckoo's First Nocturne. Federico García Lorca. CP-GarcF, tr. by Jerome Rothenberg Fr. Cúckoo-Cuckoo-Cuckóo.

In desp'rate cases, all, or most are known. Most Words, Lesse Workes. Robert Herrick. CP-HerrR

In desultory walk through orchard grounds. Prelude, Prefixed to the Volume Entitled "Poems Chiefly of Early and Late Years." William Wordsworth. CP-WorW2

In Dickens, sure, philosophy was lacking. Reflections on Reading a Life of Dickens. Robert Browning. CP-BroR2

In Disgrace. Walter De la Mare. CP-DeLaW

In Disguise. Robert Graves. CP-GravR

In distant countries have I been. Last of the Flock, The. William Wordsworth. CP-WorW1

In distant countries I have been. William Wordsworth. See In distant countries have I been

In Distrust of Merits. Marianne Craig Moore. CP-MoorM

In doggerel and stout let me honour this country. Western Landscape. Louis MacNeice. CP-MacNL

In doing justice, God shall then be known. Judgement Day, The. Robert Herrick. CP-HerrR

In doubtful breast whilst motherly Pity. Sir Thomas Wyatt. CP-WyatT

In doubtful state I weep, at times I sing. Petrarch. CP-Petra, tr. by J. G. Nichols

In Dream. David Ignatow. SP-IgnaD

In Dream Time. Thomas McGrath. SP-McGrT

In dreaming you have power. Perennial. Olga Broumas. SP-BrouO

In dreams a dark château. Dark Château, The. Walter De la Mare. CP-DeLaW

In dreams (Coleridge writes), images take the shape of the effects we believe they cause. Ragnarök. Jorge Luis Borges. SP-BorgJ, tr. by Ken Krabbenhoft

In dreams I crossed a barren land. Ballade of Broken Flutes. Edwin Arlington Robinson. CP-RobiE

In dreams I was a ship, and sail'd the boundless seas. Ship Ahoy! Walt Whitman. CP-WhitW

In dreams / the same bad dream goes on. House, The. Anne Sexton. CP-SextA

In Dream's Wake. Ts'un Hsu Li. CP-WilW2

In dreamy woods, what forms abound. Ralph Waldo Emerson. CP-EmerR

In Drear-nighted December. John Keats. CP-KeatJ

In Duc Ninh a village of 1,654 households. Two Villages. Grace Paley. CP-PalGC

In Due Form. Laura Riding Jackson. CP-RidiL

In due observance of an ancient rite. William Wordsworth. CP-WorW1

In Due Season. W. H. Auden. CP-AudeW

In dungeons dark I cannot sing. Emily Jane Brontë. CP-BronE

In Durance. Ezra Pound. CP-PoEar

In each man's heart that doth begin. Love's World. Sir John Suckling. CP-SuckJ

In each world they may put us. Do Not Die. W. S. Merwin. SP-MerwW

In Eandem Reginae Sueciae Transmissam [To Christina, Queen of Sweden]. Andrew Marvell. CP-MarvA

In Earliest Morning. James Schuyler. CP-SchuJ

In early April the trees. Lesson. Carl Sandburg. CP-SandC

In early August among the spruce. 8/12/70. James Schuyler. CP-SchuJ

In Early Autumn. Thomas McGrath. SP-McGrT

In early snow. Road. W. S. Merwin. SP-MerwWF

In early spring, so much like a late autumn. Mud Season. May Sarton. SP-SartM

In Ebon Box, when years have flown. Emily Dickinson. CP-DickE

In Eden it was never winter, the ground. Candied. Eleanor Wilner. SP-WilnE

In Eden palm and open-handed pine. Problem from Milton, A. Richard Wilbur. CP-WilbR

In-edger: Rembrandt. Paul Celan. SP-CelaP, *tr.* by John Felstiner

In Edinburgh town they've made a law. Act Sederunt of the Session—A Scots Ballad. Robert Burns. CP-BurnR

In Effigiem Oliveri Cromwell [On a Portrait of Oliver Cromwell]. Andrew Marvell. CP-MarvA

In Egypt. Paul Celan. SP-CelaP, *tr.* by John Felstiner

In Egypt's Land. James Laughlin. CP-LaugJ

In 1861, George Hew sailed in a rowboat. Network, The. Arthur Sze. SP-SzeA

In 1863 whole towns. On Seeing a Photograph by Mathew Brady. Miller Williams. CP-WillM

In Emanuel's Nightmare: Another Coming of Christ. Gwendolyn Brooks. SP-BrooG

In England. Joseph Brodsky. CP-BrodJ, *tr.* by Alan Myers

In English the poetics became meubles—furniture. Later Note on Letter #15, A. Charles Olson. SP-OlsoC *Fr.* Maximus Poems, The.

In English, we're in trouble. Trouble with "In," The. Heather McHugh. SP-McHuH

In envy's carriage there's a witness. Fanny Howe. SP-HoweF *Fr.* O'Clock.

In eosdem. Thomas Campion. CP-CampT

In Epitaphium. Ezra Pound. CP-PoEar

In Epitaphium Eius. Ezra Pound. CP-PoEar

In Error. Rudyard Kipling. *Fr.* Plain Tales from the Hills.

In Europe they grow a new bean while here. Lorine Niedecker. CP-NiedL

In Evening Air, Theodore Roethke. CP-RoetT

In evening purples, the kings. House, The. Heather McHugh. SP-McHuH

In every bone. Space, The. George Oppen. CP-OppGN

In every heart there is a coward and a procrastinator. Kookaburras, The. Mary Oliver. SP-OlivM

In every part of every living thing. Lake Superior. Lorine Niedecker. CP-NiedL

In every room, encircled by a name. Thanksgiving. Louise Glück. SP-GlucL

In every room rubber bands turn up loose. Numbered Apartment. W. S. Merwin. SP-MerwWF

In every soul is born some thought of God. Intuitions of the Soul, The. Jones Very. CP-VeryJ

In every town and village. Where We Belong, A Duet. Maya Angelou. SP-AngeM

In everything I see, the meaning's plain. Michelangelo Buonarroti. CP-Miche, *tr.* by John Frederick Nims

In ev'ry town, where Thamis rolls his tyde. Alley, The. Alexander Pope. CP-PopeA

In Excelsis. Anne Sexton. CP-SextA; SP-SextA

In Exitum Cuiusdam. Ezra Pound. CP-PoEar

In Explanation of Our Times. Langston Hughes. CP-HughL; CP-HughL3

In extended observation of the ways and works of man. Et Dona Ferentes. Rudyard Kipling. CP-KiplR

In Extremis. John Updike. CP-UpdiJ

In Extremis *in Hardy, Arkansas.* Miller Williams. CP-WillM

In fable all things hold discourse. Aye and No: A Fable. Jonathan Swift. CP-SwifJ

In Fact I Love That Fawn. Shmuel HaNagid. SP-HaNaS, *tr.* by Peter Cole

In fairyland the little boys. Dangerous Little Boy Fairies, The. Nicholas Vachel Lindsay. CP-LindV

In faith I not [well] what to say. Sir Thomas Wyatt. CP-WyatT

In Faiths and Food and Books and Friends. Glories, The. Rudyard Kipling. CP-KiplR

In fall and whiskey weather when. Variation on a Theme by Stevens. Alan Dugan. CP-DugaA

In fall the fields are poisonous but fair. Autumn Crocuses. Guillaume Apollinaire. SP-MereW, *tr.* by William Meredith

In falling the dream was broken. Wrested from Mirrors. Nicolas Calas. CP-WilW2

In falling Timbers buried. Emily Dickinson. CP-DickE

In famous poems by the sage Han Shan. Squarings. Seamus Heaney. SP-HeanSO *Fr.* Squarings.

In fancy, always, at thy desk, thrown wide. To My Good Master. James Whitcomb Riley. CP-RileJ

In far Australia's middle region lies. Stony Desert of Life, The. Jones Very. CP-VeryJ

In far Esthonian solitudes. Forest Thought, A. Robert Browning. CP-BroR2

In far Tibet / There live a lama. I Will Arise and Go Now. Ogden Nash. CP-NashO

In Fargo, North Dakota, a man. To Flood Stage Again. James Wright. CP-WrigJ

In Farsistan the violet spreads. Exile, The. Khvaju of Kerman. CP-EmerR

In Favor of a Free Public Library System. Alan Dugan. CP-DugaA

In Favor of One's Time. Frank O'Hara. SP-OharF

In fear and trembling, I think I would fulfill my life. Task, A. Czeslaw Milosz. CP-MiloC; CP-MiloCN, *tr.* by Czeslaw Milosz

In Fear and Valor. William Stafford. SP-StafWW

In Fear of Harvests. James Wright. CP-WrigJ

In fear of the rich mouth. Frightened Man, The. Louise Bogan. CP-BogaL

In Fervent Praise of Picnics. James Whitcomb Riley. CP-RileJ

In fits and starts around. Squirrels Mating. John Updike. CP-UpdiJ

In five-score summers! All new eyes. 1967. Thomas Hardy. CP-HardT

In flat America, in Chicago. Visiting a Dead Man on a Summer Day. Marge Piercy. SP-PierM

In Former Songs. Walt Whitman. CP-WhitW

In fourteen hundred and ninety-two. Look What You Did, Christopher! Ogden Nash. CP-NashO

In frames as large as rooms that face all ways. Essential Beauty. Philip Larkin. CP-LarkP

In France. Grace Paley. CP-PalGC

In Front of a Candle. Paul Celan. SP-CelaP, *tr.* by John Felstiner

In Front of Casa Marcello. Joseph Brodsky. CP-BrodJ

In front of me on my desk. January Night. Kenneth Rexroth. CP-RexrK

In front of mc, thc palings of a fencc. For Signs. Thom Gunn. CP-GunnT

In front of the big window, they're digging a pit in the street. Caffè Dante in New York—3. Yehuda Amichai. SP-AmicYL, *tr.* by Benjamin Harshav *and* Barbara Harshav

In front of the cathedral hovered a mumbling nobody:its greenish fumbling. After Seeing French Funeral. E. E. Cummings. CP-CummE

In Front of the Landscape. Thomas Hardy. CP-HardT

In front of the mighty washing machine. Small Lady, The. Stevie Smith. CP-SmitS

In front of the sombre mountains. On the Balcony. D. H. Lawrence. CP-LawrD

In front of you, long tables leading down to the sun. Vegetarians, The. John Ashbery. SP-AshbJ

In front of your house i. E. E. Cummings. CP-CummE

In front the awful Alpine track. Stanzas in Memory of the Author of "Obermann." Matthew Arnold. SP-ArnoM

In Fur. William Stafford. SP-StafW

In futurity / I prophetic see. Little Girl Lost, The. William Blake. CP-BlakW *Fr.* Songs of Experience.

In futurity / I prophetic see. Little Girl Lost, The. William Blake. CP-BlakW *Fr.* Songs of Innocence.

In Galleries. Randall Jarrell. CP-JarrR

In gentlest worship has he bowed. The Naturalist, The. James Whitcomb Riley. CP-RileJ

In giving me a subject as big as the world. Not a Pot to Piss In. Andrei Codrescu. SP-CodrA

In glistening shot-silk she seems to wind. Charles Baudelaire. CP-BaudC, *tr.* by Walter Martin

In God there's nothing, but 'tis known to be. God. Robert Herrick. CP-HerrR

In Gods Commands, ne're ask the reason why. Gods Commands. Robert Herrick. CP-HerrR

In going from room to room in the dark. Door in the Dark, The. Robert Frost. CP-FrosR

In Golden Gate Park that day. Lawrence Ferlinghetti. SP-FerlL

In gorgeous robes befitting the occasion. Council, The. W. H. Auden. CP-AudeW

In Goya's greatest scenes we seem to see. Lawrence Ferlinghetti. SP-FerlL

In grappled ships around The Victory. Last Three from Trafalgar, The. Dante Gabriel Rossetti. CW-RossD

In gray, battle-scarred Leningrad. Enemy, The. Alice Walker. CP-WalkA

In grayish doubt and black despair. In Black Despair. Czeslaw Milosz. CP-MiloCN, *tr.* by Robert Hass

In great contrast to the nightingale's preeminent voice. Nightingales. Paul Muldoon. CP-MuldP

In greenwoods once these relics must have known. Driftwood. Richard Wilbur. CP-WilbR

In grimy winter dusk / We slowed for a concrete platform. Stop. Richard Wilbur. CP-WilbR

In Hac Spe Vivo. James Laughlin. CP-LaugJ

In Hades, Orpheus. Muriel Rukeyser. CP-RukeM

In Haiti [or Haitian Suite]. Gregory Orr. SP-OrrG

In Half Darkness. James Laughlin. CP-LaugJ

In half-sleep felt an arm go round me. Laocoön Dream Recorded in Diary Dated 1943. May Swenson. SP-SwenM

In hammamet did camping queers et al). E. E. Cummings. CP-CummE

In Hanoi 1969. Grace Paley. CP-PalGC

In Harbor. William Carlos Williams. CP-WilW1

In Hardcastle Crags, that echoey museum. Leaf Mould. Ted Hughes. SP-HughTN

In Hardwood Groves. Robert Frost. CP-FrosR

In Harmony with Nature. Matthew Arnold. SP-ArnoM

In harmony would you excel. Cantata, A. Jonathan Swift. CP-SwifJ

In Harvard Square. W. E. B. DuBois at Harvard. Jay Wright. SP-WrigJ

In Havana in 1948 I ate fried dog. Salts and Oils. Philip Levine. SP-LeviP

In Havenpool Harbour the ebb was strong. Mongrel, The. Thomas Hardy. CP-HardT

In Healey's Palace I was sitting. E. E. Cummings. CP-CummE

In hearts like thine ne'er may I hold a place. Answer to ——'s Professions of Affection. Lord Byron. CP-Byron

In Heaven a spirit doth dwell. Israfel. Edgar Allan Poe. CP-PoeEd

In heaven-high musings and many. Strength of Fate, The. Euripides. CP-HousA, *tr. by* A. E. Housman *Fr.* Alcestis.

In Heaven, if not on earth. Celestial Circus, The. Nicholas Vachel Lindsay. CP-LindV

In Heaven, / Some little blades of grass. Stephen Crane. CP-CranS

In heaven that our planets. Is It Written. James Laughlin. CP-LaugJ

In heaven, too. Heard in a Violent Ward. Theodore Roethke. CP-RoetT

In heavenly realms of hellas dwelt. E. E. Cummings. CP-CummE

In heavens eternal court it was decreed. On the Death of Mr. Snider Murder'd by Richardson. Phillis Wheatley. CP-WheaP

In Hell with Virg and Dan. Carolyn Kizer. CP-KizeC

In Her Burning. Muriel Rukeyser. CP-RukeM

In her gnarled sleep it. Cherry Tree, The. Thom Gunn. CP-GunnT

In Her Praise. Robert Graves. CP-GravR

In Her Precincts. Thomas Hardy. CP-HardT

In her room at the prow of the house. Writer, The. Richard Wilbur. CP-WilbR

In her, two enemies were brought together. Petrarch. CP-Petra, *tr. by* J. G. Nichols

In Heraclitus' River. Wisława Szymborska. SP-SzymWM, *tr. by* Joanna Trzeciak

In here, caught by the storm. How the rain beats. Missing the Bo in the Henhouse. Hayden Carruth. CP-CarHS

In hintertime Praxiteles. Lawrence Ferlinghetti. SP-FerlL

In his dream zealous. Bad Night, A. W. H. Auden. CP-AudeW

In his early days he was quite surprised. Sweet Hussy, The. Thomas Hardy. CP-HardT

In his fur the animal rode, and in his fur he strove. It Filled My Heart with Love. Stevie Smith. CP-SmitS

In his head. Whole Half, The. A. R. Ammons. CP-AmmoA

In his heart he brought back. Two Sailors Ashore. Federico García Lorca. CP-GarcF, *tr. by* Alan S. Trueblood *Fr.* Songs to End With.

In his iron land lives an old man of renown. Walt Whitman. "Rubén Dario." SP-DariR, *tr. by* Alberto Acereda *and* Will Derusha

In his last phase when hardly bothering. Autolycus. Louis MacNeice. CP-MacNL

In his little bed in the. Child, The. James Laughlin. CP-LaugJ

In his packet Anacharsis found the lines. From the Packet of Anacharsis. Wallace Stevens. CP-StevW; CP-StevWP

In his perpetual cycle Time, rolling back. Elegy 5: On the Coming of Spring. John Milton. CP-CowpW; CP-MiltJ

In his prayer sands, my father saw traces of angels in heaven's gates. Yehuda Amichai. SP-AmicYL *Fr.* At Right Angles.

In his school of "The Fiddle and Bow." Preface to "Bob Taylor's Birthday." Nicholas Vachel Lindsay. CP-LindV

In his tenth July some instinct. For Johnny Pole on the Forgotten Beach. Anne Sexton. CP-SextA

In hollows of the land. Ground-Mist, The. Denise Levertov. SP-LeveDP

In Hollywood with the Zuni God of War. Clarence Major. SP-MajoC

In holy meetings, there a man may be. Crowd and Company, The. Robert Herrick. CP-HerrR

In homes all green, but cold in death. Our Martyred Soldiers. Paul Laurence Dunbar. CP-DunbP

In honest Bacon's ingle-neuk. To William Stewart. Robert Burns. CP-BurnR

In Honor of David Anderson Brooks, My Father. Gwendolyn Brooks. SP-BrooG

In Honor of Du Bartas, 1641. Anne Bradstreet. CP-BradA

In Honour of St. Alphonsus Rodriguez. Gerard Manley Hopkins. CP-HopkG

In Honour of that High and Mighty Princess Queen Elizabeth of Happy Memory. Anne Bradstreet. CP-BradA

In Honour of the Author by *Tho: Campion* Doctor in Physicke. To the Reader. Thomas Campion. CP-CampT

In Horologium. Percy Bysshe Shelley. CP-ShelP

In horror the God-thrown lie. Kenneth Patchen. CP-PatcK

In hospital where windows meet. Lady of Quality, A. Thomas Kinsella. CP-KinsT

In how many of the miserable little life dramas I play out in my mind am I unforgivable. Conscience. C. K. Williams. SP-WillC

In Hurricane Canyon. William Stafford. SP-StafWW

In Hydaspia, by Howzen. Oak Leaves Are Hands. Wallace Stevens. CP-StevW; CP-StevWP

In idle August, while the sea soft. Schooner Flight, The. Derek Walcott. CP-WalcD

In ignorance of the source, our want. Song (1). Wendell Berry. CP-BerrW

In Illo Tempore. Seamus Heaney. SP-HeanSO *Fr.* Sweeney Redivivus.

In Ilopongo Prison. Women's Prison, The: El Salvador / The Ballad of Visiting Day. Grace Paley. CP-PalGC

In India in their lives they happen. Ways to Live. William Stafford. SP-StafWW

In innocence, and nothing much to remember. Distance Between, The: Picnic of Old Friends. Robert Penn Warren. CP-WarrR

In innocence I said. James Vincent Cunningham. CP-CunnJ

In Isolation. Josephine Jacobsen. SP-JacoJ

In Italy. Joseph Brodsky. CP-BrodJ

In its color, shade and shine. Wraith of Summer-Time, A. James Whitcomb Riley. CP-RileJ

In its deep little gorge my brook swells big. Weather Report. Robert Penn Warren. CP-WarrR

In its terrible and tragic depth. To Speak a Flower. Rainer Maria Rilke. CP-RilkFr, *tr. by* A. Poulin, Jr.

In Jack-O'-Lantern's Weather. Tennessee Williams. CP-WillT

In Jakarta, / among the vendors. Acid. Mary Oliver. SP-OlivM

In January. James Schuyler. CP-SchuJ

In January everything freezes. One Third of a Calendar. Ogden Nash. CP-NashO

In January, shed twigs of hemlock. Runes, Blurs, Sap Rising. Amy Clampitt. CP-ClamA

In January the dawn comes late. Ein Kitzbuehler Tag (1947). James Laughlin. CP-LaugJ

In Jinotega women greeted us. Dance in Jinotega, The. Grace Paley. CP-PalGC

In Joe Brainard's collage its white arrow. Ted Berrigan. SP-BerrT *Fr.* Sonnets, The.

In Judgment of the Leaf. Kenneth Patchen. CP-PatcK

In July / No goodbye. Christina Georgina Rossetti. CP-RosC3

In June, above Pontrèmoli, high in the Lunigiana. In the Valley of the Magra. Charles Wright. SP-WrigCN

In June, amid the golden fields. Groundhog, The. Richard Eberhart. CP-EberR

In June, in the Kyborg Castle, in the canton. Wake Up. Raymond Carver. CP-CarvR

In June the bush we call. Victors, The. Denise Levertov. SP-LeveDP

In June two oaks fell. Ethnobotany. Gary Snyder. CP-SnydG

In June, which is still June here, but once removed. June: Dutch Harbor. William Meredith. SP-MereW

In junior high school. Big Max. Charles Bukowski. SP-BukC1

In just a minute we will say goodbye. Time Is an Inclusion Series Said McTaggart. Kenneth Rexroth. CP-RexrK

In Just-. E. E. Cummings. CP-CummE; SP-CummE

In keeping with its custom, the sun. Where Can They Have Gone? Jorge Luis Borges. SP-BorgJ, *tr. by* Eric McHenry

In keeping with universal saloon practice. Bar Time. Billy Collins. SP-CollB

In Key West, poinciana trees bloom flamboyant red. Papa's House, Son's Room. John Logan. CP-LogaJ

In Köhln [Köln], a town of monks and bones. Cologne. Samuel Taylor Coleridge. CP-ColeS

In Krakow it rained, the stone arcades and cobbles. Unseen, The. Robert Pinsky. CP-PinsR

In La Mancha he mopeth. Rusty Man, The. Herman Melville. SP-MelvH

In lands I never saw—they say. Emily Dickinson. CP-DickE

In language warm as could be breath'd or penn'd. On Receiving Hayley's Picture. William Cowper. CP-CowpW

In last night's dream who put into my hand. Dream-flowers. Kathleen Jessie Raine. SP-RainK

In late afternoon. Bricks and Sleep. Clarence Major. SP-MajoC

In late afternoon, when the light. Evensong. John Ciardi. CP-CiarJ

In late summer the wild geese. August Hail. James Vincent Cunningham. CP-CunnJ

In late winter / I sometimes glimpse bits of steam. Bear, The. Galway Kinnell. SP-KinnGN

In later days, remembering this I shall certainly go mad. Returning to the Country for a Brief Visit. Allen Ginsberg. CP-GinsA

In Laughter. Ted Hughes. SP-HughTN

In Laurentiam. Thomas Campion. CP-CampT

In law an infant and in years a boy. Damaetas. Lord Byron. CP-Byron

In Legationem Domini Oliveri St John ad Provincias Foederatas [On the Embassy of Lord Oliver St John to the United Provinces]. Andrew Marvell. CP-MarvA

In Leonardo's light. Lorine Niedecker. CP-NiedL

In Lieu. Louis MacNeice. CP-MacNL

In Lieu of the Lyre. Marianne Craig Moore. CP-MoorM

In life we could seldom meet. Visit. Tu Fu. CP-WilW2

In Life's Red Sea with faith I plant my feet. Mare Rubrum. Paul Laurence Dunbar. CP-DunbP

In Ligonem. Thomas Campion. CP-CampT

In lilac trained on the colonnade's archway, what. Hornet. Donald Davie. CP-DaviDC

In Limbo. David Ignatow. SP-IgnaD

In Limbo. Richard Wilbur. CP-WilbR

In line at lunch I cross my fork and spoon. Objector. William Stafford. SP-StafW; SP-StafWW

In line of what my folks say in Montgomery. Brotherly Love. Langston Hughes. CP-HughL; CP-HughL3

In lions' lair of sand. Poems to a Girl on the Seashore. Yehuda Amichai. SP-AmicYL, *tr.* by Benjamin Harshav *and* Barbara Harshav

In Lisbon. Charles Tomlinson. SP-TomlC *Fr.* Portugeuse Pieces.

In Little Rock the people bear. Chicago *Defender* Sends a Man to Little Rock, The. Gwendolyn Brooks. SP-BrooG

In London. Robert Creeley. CP-CreeR

In Longfellow's Library. Charles Tomlinson. CP-TomlC

In Los Angelos the cars are flowing. Late Wonders. W. S. Merwin. SP-MerwWF

In love it may be dangerous. Elusive Time. James Laughlin. CP-LaugJ

In Love with You. Kenneth Koch. SP-KochK

In lovelier and crueller flesh than yours. Michelangelo Buonarroti. CP-Miche, *tr.* by John Frederick Nims

In Love's name you are charged: oh, fly [*or* charged hereby]. Love's Hue and Cry. James Shirley. CP-CareT

In Loving Memory of the Late Author of *Dream Songs*. William Meredith. SP-MereW

In Lowestoft a boat was laid. Lowestoft Boat, The. Rudyard Kipling. CP-KiplR

In Loyang so many girls. Han-shan. CP-ColdM, *tr.* by Red Pine

In Lycium et Clytham. Thomas Campion. CP-CampT

In Maceio. Tess Gallagher. SP-GallT

In Madurai. River, A. A. K. Ramanujan. CP-RamaA

In Magpies Hollow thorns. Magpies. Yusef Komunyakaa. CP-KomuY

In Magritte's painting *Les Amants* a man and woman are kissing. Les Amants. James Laughlin. CP-LaugJ

In making Marjorie god hurried. E. E. Cummings. CP-CummE

In Malaga. Federico García Lorca. SP-GarcF, *tr.* by Ben Belitt

In Málaga. Federico García Lorca. CP-GarcF, *tr.* by Alan S. Trueblood *Fr.* Eros with a Cane.

In man, ambition is the common'st thing. Ambition. Robert Herrick. CP-HerrR

In many and reportless places. Emily Dickinson. CP-DickE

In many forms we try. Bohemian Hymn, The. Ralph Waldo Emerson. CP-EmerR

In many houses the cry has a window. Cry, The. W. S. Merwin. SP-MerwW

In many ways does the full heart reveal. Eros aei lalethros hetairos. Samuel Taylor Coleridge. CP-ColeS

In March. Charles Tomlinson. CP-TomlC

In March I travelled. A. K. Ramanujan. CP-RamaA

In March the dust of Tartary has swept over the capital. Knight, The. Li Po. CP-WilW2

In March, the farmer's month. Black Buttercups. Amy Clampitt. CP-ClamA

In march the soldiers. Kolo. Joseph Brodsky. CP-BrodJ

In March / you go off to the moon. First Page. Federico García Lorca. CP-GarcF, *tr.* by Jerome Rothenberg *Fr.* White Album.

In March's black boat. St. Francis Einstein of the Daffodils. William Carlos Williams. CP-WilW1

In Marion, the honey locust trees are falling. Two Poems about President Harding. James Wright. CP-WrigJ

In Mauchline there dwells six proper young Belles. Song: "In Mauchline there dwells six proper young Belles." Robert Burns. CP-BurnR

In May. Paul Laurence Dunbar. CP-DunbP

In May. Adam Zagajewski. SP-ZagaA, *tr.* by Renata Gorczynski

In May, approaching the city, I. Ritualists, The. William Carlos Williams. CP-WilW2

In May as that Aurora did vpspring. William Dunbar. CP-DunbW

In May my heart was breaking. Autumn Valentine. Dorothy Parker. CP-ParkD

In May, was it, Ophelia drowned? Tanck's Song About His Unicameral Mind. Hayden Carruth. CP-CarHS *Fr.* Songs About What Comes Down: The Complete Works of Mr. Septic Tank.

In May, when sea-winds pierced our solitudes. Rhodora, The [On Being Asked Whence Is the Flower]. Ralph Waldo Emerson. CP-EmerR

In Me. David Ignatow. SP-IgnaD

In me there is a rage to defy. Rage. Alice Walker. CP-WalkA

In me there's only death; my life's in you. Michelangelo Buonarroti. CP-Miche, *tr.* by John Frederick Nims

In measured verse I'll now rehearse. Jane Austen. CP-AustJ

In Medias Res. William Stafford. SP-StafWW

In Melleam. Thomas Campion. CP-CampT

In Memoriam. Ambrose Bierce. SP-BierA

In Memoriam. Joseph Brodsky. CP-BrodJ

In Memoriam. Hayden Carruth. CP-CarHS

In Memoriam. Ralph Waldo Emerson. CP-EmerR

In Memoriam. Federico García Lorca. CP-GarcF, *tr.* by Catherine Brown

In Memoriam. John Updike. CP-UpdiJ

In Memoriam A. H. H. Alfred Tennyson. CP-TennA

In Memoriam: Aurelius Battaglia, and against His Tragic Sense of Life. Alan Dugan. CP-DugaA

In Memoriam Charles Reznikoff. George Oppen. CP-OppGN

In Memoriam: Donald Mark Fall. Alan Dugan. CP-DugaA

In Memoriam Felis Felis. John Updike. CP-UpdiJ

In Memoriam Francis Ledwidge. Seamus Heaney. SP-HeanSO

In Memoriam James Joyce. Hugh MacDiarmid.
  "All dreams of "imperialism" must be exorcised." SP-MacDH
  "And all this here, everything I write, of course." SP-MacDH
  "So, like him, we cry *'l'honneur des hommes: Saint Langage.'*" SP-MacDH

In Memoriam M. D. G. K. Chesterton. CP-ChesG

In Memoriam (1914–1953). John Berryman. CP-BerrJ

In Memoriam P. D. G. K. Chesterton. CP-ChesG

In Memoriam P. W. Jr. 1921–1980. Maxine W. Kumin. SP-KumiM

In Memoriam Paul Éluard. Paul Celan. SP-CelaP, *tr.* by John Felstiner

In Memoriam Stratton Christensen. William Meredith. SP-MereW

In Memoriam Thomas Hardy. Charles Tomlinson. CP-TomlC

In Memoriam. Unfinished. For Robert Barlow. 1950. Alan Dugan. CP-DugaA

In Memoriam: William Cannastra, 1922–1950. Allen Ginsberg. CP-GinsA

In Memory. Thomas Kinsella. CP-KinsT

In Memory. John Greenleaf Whittier. CP-WhitJ

In memory I see a youth. Haystack, The. Richard Eberhart. CP-EberR

In Memory of a Child. Nicholas Vachel Lindsay. CP-LindV

In Memory of a Spanish Poet. James Wright. CP-WrigJ

In Memory of Alfred Pollexfen. William Butler Yeats. CP-YeatW

In Memory of Arthur Winslow. Robert Lowell.
  Death from Cancer. SP-LoweR

In Memory of Boris Pasternak. Denise Levertov. SP-LeveDP

In Memory of Clifford Brown. Joseph Brodsky. CP-BrodJ

In Memory of Donald A. Stauffer. William Meredith. SP-MereW

In Memory of Ernst Toller. W. H. Auden. CP-AudeW

In Memory of Eva Gore-Booth and Con Markievicz. William Butler Yeats. CP-YeatW

In Memory of George Oppen. Charles Tomlinson. SP-TomlC

In Memory of Jane Fraser [*or* Frazer]. Geoffrey Hill. CP-HillG

In Memory of John Thorton. William Cowper. CP-CowpW

In Memory of Kathleen. Kenneth Patchen. CP-PatcK

In Memory of Leopardi. James Wright. CP-WrigJ

In Memory of Major Robert Gregory. William Butler Yeats. CP-YeatW

In Memory of Muriel Rukeyser. Denise Levertov. SP-LeveDL

In Memory of My Dear Grandchild Anne Bradstreet Who Deceased June 20, 1669, Being Three Years and Seven Months Old. Anne Bradstreet. CP-BradA

In Memory of My Dear Grandchild Elizabeth Bradstreet Who Deceased August, 1665, Being a Year and Half Old. Anne Bradstreet. CP-BradA

In Memory of My Feelings. Frank O'Hara. SP-OharF

In Memory of My Friend, Joyce Kilmer, Poet and Soldier. Nicholas Vachel Lindsay. CP-LindV

In Memory of Robert Frost. William Meredith. SP-MereW

In Memory of Sigmund Freud. W. H. Auden. CP-AudeW

In Memory of the Horse David, Who Ate One of my Poems. James Wright. CP-WrigJ

In Memory of the Spanish Poet Federico Garcia Lorca. Thomas Merton. CP-MertT

In Memory of W. B. Yeats. W. H. Auden. CP-AudeW

In Memory: Stuart Egnal. Wendell Berry. CP-BerrW

In Mexico the little mixed herds come home in the evening. Recovery. Mona Van Duyn. SP-VanDM

In Michoacán. Charles Tomlinson. CP-TomlC

In mid-advance. To Gather Something. Yehuda Amichai. SP-AmicYL, *tr.* by Benjamin Harshav *and* Barbara Harshav

In mid-August, in the second year. Wolf Knife. Donald Hall. CP-HallD

In mid-March in the heart of. Mocking Birds. Kenneth Rexroth. CP-RexrK

In Midas' Country. Sylvia Plath. SP-PlatS

In middle age an evil thing. Archduchess Anne. George Meredith. CP-MerG1

In midmost Ind, beside Hydaspes cool. Cap and Bells; or, The Jealousies, The. John Keats. CP-KeatJ

In midnight sleep of many a face of anguish. Old War-Dreams. Walt Whitman. CP-WhitW

In midnights of November. A. E. Housman. CP-HousA

In Midsummer Quiet. Charles Simic. SP-SimiC; SP-SimiCE

In Milan. Czeslaw Milosz. CP-MiloC; CP-MiloCN, *tr.* by Robert Hass

In Mind. Denise Levertov. SP-LeveDP; SP-LeveDS

In minds emptied of memory like mine, no myth is lost. Gambling Phoenix, The. Andrei Codrescu. SP-CodrA

In Montecito. Randall Jarrell. CP-JarrR

In Montpelier this morning. In Montpelier, Vermont. Grace Paley. CP-PalGC

In Montpelier, Vermont. Grace Paley. CP-PalGC

In moonlight lies. Lorine Niedecker. CP-NiedL

In Morachum. Thomas Campion. CP-CampT

In Morte De. Ezra Pound. CP-PoEar

In most self-portraits it is the face that dominates. Candle Hat. Billy Collins. SP-CollB

In Motion. Federico García Lorca. CP-GarcF, *tr. by* Jerome Rothenberg *Fr.* Return, The.

In Mourning for Betrayal. Robert Bly. SP-BlyR

In mourning wise since daily I increase. Sir Thomas Wyatt. CP-WyatT

In movies I prefer something unpretentious, like "Marty." What's in a Name? Here's What's in a Name, or, I Wonder What Became of John and Mary. Ogden Nash. CP-NashO

In moving-slow he has no Peer. Sloth, The. Theodore Roethke. CP-RoetT

In Murray, Kentucky, I lay once. Self-Portait. Charles Wright. SP-WrigC

In Music. Czeslaw Milosz. CP-MiloCN, *tr. by* Robert Hass

In music we are sick lovers. Music. Andrei Codrescu. SP-CodrA

In my Autumn garden I was fain. October Garden, An. Christina Georgina Rossetti. CP-RosC2

In my bachelor days, no parent I. Good Parent's Garden of Vision, A. Ogden Nash. CP-NashO

In my beginning was the memory, somehow. After Jonah. Hart Crane. CP-CranH

In my cellar the poisoned mice, thirsty to death. Mouse Sex. John Updike. CP-UpdiJ

In My Childhood. Yehuda Amichai. SP-AmicYL, *tr. by* Benjamin Harshav *and* Barbara Harshav

In my childhood I awoke to my mother's voice. David Ignatow. SP-IgnaD

In my childhood trees were green. Autobiography. Louis MacNeice. CP-MacNL

In my childhood when I first. Reflecting Trees of Being and Not Being, The. Kenneth Rexroth. CP-RexrK

In my cottage near the Styx. Charon. Christina Georgina Rossetti. CP-RosC3

In my country. Statement. Rae Armantrout. SP-ArmaA

In my cradle and then driving. My Life. William Stafford. SP-StafWW

In My Craft or Sullen Art. Dylan Thomas. CP-ThomD

In my dark moments. Loophole. Fernando Pessoa. SP-PessF, *tr. by* Susan M. Brown *and* Edwin Honig

In my distress I sought the Lord. From Another Sore Fit. Anne Bradstreet. CP-BradA

In my dream. Author of the Jesus Papers Speaks, The. Anne Sexton. CP-SextA; SP-SextA

In my dream. 45 Mercy Street. Anne Sexton. CP-SextA

In my dream, children. Jerusalem. Adrienne Rich. CP-RicAE; SP-RicA2

In my dream I know I see my father Saul a king. John Logan. CP-LogaJ *Fr.* Monologues of the Son of Saul.

In my dream, methought I trod. My Dream. John Greenleaf Whittier. CP-WhitJ

In my dream, my belly is yellow, panels. Serpent, The. Robert Lowell. SP-LoweR

In my dreams. Sex and/or Love. Charles Bukowski. SP-BukC3

In My Dreams. Stevie Smith. CP-SmitS

In my dreams / I paint like Vermeer van Delft. In Praise of Dreams. Wisława Szymborska. SP-SzymW, *tr. by* Stanislaw Barańczak *and* Clare Cavanagh

In My End Is My Beginning. Chuang Tzu. CP-MertT, *tr. by* Thomas Merton

In my ending is my meaning. Night of Destiny, The. Thomas Merton. CP-MertT

In my family. People in My Family. Grace Paley. CP-PalGC

In my Father's bedroom. Father's Bedroom. Robert Lowell. SP-LoweR

In my favorite one. Fable: "In my favorite one." Charles Simic. SP-SimiCE

In my first dark before the world began. And Thy Mother. John Ciardi. CP-CiarJ

In my first that he may not be tardy & late. Charade: "In my first that he may not be tardy & late." James Austen. CP-AustJ

In my first thirty years of life. Gary Snyder. CP-SnydG

In My Garden. Ralph Waldo Emerson. CP-EmerR

In my garden three ways meet. In My Garden. Ralph Waldo Emerson. CP-EmerR

In my gay room, bare as a barn. Eine Kleine Nachtmusik. Randall Jarrell. CP-JarrR

In my great silence and my small scream, I inspire. And This Is Your Glory. Yehuda Amichai. SP-AmicYL, *tr. by* Benjamin Harshav *and* Barbara Harshav

In my hand I hold. Stone Crock, The. William Carlos Williams. CP-WilW2

In my head I am. Walking. Robert Creeley. CP-CreeR

In my head the juxtapositions. Vsion of Labor, A: 1931. William Carlos Williams. CP-WilW2

In my heart a phoenix flame. Song: A Phoenix Flame. Robert Graves. CP-GravR

In my house the walls are not true. Breaking Child, The. Wyatt Prunty. SP-PrunW

In my imagination I was the pivot of a fresh beginning. Adrienne Rich. SP-RicA2 *Fr.* Shooting Script.

In my line of paperwork. Autumn Burning, An. Wendell Berry. CP-BerrW

In my loamy nook. Milestone by the Rabbit-Burrow, The. Thomas Hardy. CP-HardT

In my mind, a curved tool. Frank's Poem. Yusef Komunyakaa. CP-KomuY

In my mind a lilac begins to leaf. X Ray. Arthur Sze. SP-SzeA

In My Mind's Eye a Temple, Like a Cloud. William Wordsworth. CP-WorW2

In my old age I decided to visit places where I wandered long ago in my early youth. Return. Czeslaw Milosz. CP-MiloCN, *tr. by* Robert Hass

In My Own Shire. A. E. Housman. CP-HousA

In my own shire, if I was sad. In My Own Shire. A. E. Housman. CP-HousA

In my paintings for they are present. Ted Berrigan. SP-BerrT *Fr.* Sonnets, The.

In my room at the Hotel Continentàl. Buenos Aires. Robert Lowell. SP-LoweR

In my room, the world is beyond my understanding. Of the Surface of Things. Wallace Stevens. CP-StevW; CP-StevWP

In my sage moments I can say. Come Not; Yet Come! Thomas Hardy. CP-HardT

In my serpentine researches. Olympus. John Berryman. CP-BerrJ

In my sixties I wll buy a hat. Visit Home, A. William Stafford. SP-StafWW

In My Solitary Hours in My Dear Husband His Absence. Anne Bradstreet. CP-BradA

In my stone eyes I see. What Riddle Asked the Sphinx. Archibald MacLeish. CP-MacLA

In my unlikeliest dream, my dead are with me again, companions again, in an ordinary way. Covenant, The. C. K. Williams. SP-WillC

In My Worst Dreams. Yehuda Amichai. SP-AmicYL, *tr. by* Benjamin Harshav *and* Barbara Harshav

In Nashville, Standing in the Wooden Circle Sawed Out from the Old Ryman Stage, the Picker has a vision. Miller Williams. CP-WillM

In Nature There Is Neither Right nor Left nor Wrong. Randall Jarrell. CP-JarrR

In nature's paid discernment. Poet, The. Ivor Gurney. SP-GurnI

In Nature's pieces still I see. Divine Mistress, A. Thomas Carew. CP-CareT

In Neglect. Robert Frost. CP-FrosR

In Nervam. Thomas Campion. CP-CampT

In New York beautiful girls can become more beautiful by going. Brief Guide to New York, A. Ogden Nash. CP-NashO

In New York, it is said. Place (Any Place) to Transcend All Places, A. William Carlos Williams. CP-WilW2

In Nine Sleep Valley. James Merrill. SP-MerrJ

In 1945, when the keepers cried *kaput*. Gift, The. John Ciardi. CP-CiarJ

In 1946 there was my mother inside whom. History. Andrei Codrescu. SP-CodrA

In nineteen hundred / *Jeunes filles* wondered. Reflection on the Passage of Time, Its Inevitability and Its Quirks. Ogden Nash. CP-NashO

In nineteen-nine a fire swept our coast hills. Cawdor. Robinson Jeffers. CP-JefR1

In 1935, the year I was born. Chinese Journal. Charles Wright. SP-WrigC

In nineteen-thirty-four we [I] spent July. 1934. Donald Hall. CP-HallD

In 1929. Stephen Spender. CP-SpenS

In nineteen twenty-seven, in the spring. Laura Riding Jackson. CP-RidiL

In Nishapur did Khaibar Khan. Handkerchiefs of Khaibar Khan, The. John Updike. CP-UpdiJ

In No Direction. Robert Graves. CP-GravR

In No Way. David Ignatow. SP-IgnaD

In Noah's ark / I did sing. Old Cuckoo's Song, The. Federico García Lorca. CP-GarcF, *tr. by* Jerome Rothenberg *Fr.* Cúckoo-Cuckoo-Cuckóo.

In Northern seas there roams a fish called K'un. P'eng That Was a K'un, The. Chuang Tzu. CP-GravR, *tr. by* Robert Graves

In northwest Worcestershire / in eighteen-sixty. Witley Court. James Schuyler. CP-SchuJ

In Nottingham. D. H. Lawrence. CP-LawrD

In Nottingham county there lives at Swan Green. Epigram on an Old Lady Who Had Some Curious Notions Respecting the Soul. Lord Byron. CP-Byron

In Nottingham, that dismal town. Nottingham's New University. D. H. Lawrence. CP-LawrD

In November, in the days to remember the dead. St. Malachy. Thomas Merton. CP-MertT

In Numbers, and but these few. Ode on the Birth of Our Saviour, An. Robert Herrick. CP-HerrR

In obitum Gual. Devoreux fratris clariss. Comitus Essexiae. Thomas Campion. CP-CampT

In Obitum Hen. Mag. Brit. Principis. Thomas Campion. CP-CampT, *acc. by English translation*

In obitum Iacobi Huissii. Thomas Campion. CP-CampT

In October. G. K. Chesterton. CP-ChesG

In October. Charles Tomlinson. CP-TomlC

In October of the year. Ox Cart Man. Donald Hall. CP-HallD

In, of all places, Tashkent. Two Widows in Tashkent. Donald Davie. CP-DaviDC

In Ohio. James Wright. CP-WrigJ

In Ohio we did not have boats, we had horses. Bailing the Boat. Mary Oliver. SP-OlivM

In Oklahoma, / Bonnie and Josie. Life Is Motion. Wallace Stevens. CP-StevW; CP-StevWP

In old days / driving through soft waters. Carmen 64. Catullus. CP-ZukLS *Fr.* Carmina.

In old King George's June. Sports without Blood—a Letter to Dylan Thomas (1948). Thomas Merton. CP-MertT

In old-world nursery vacant now of children. Juliet's Nurse. Walter De la Mare. CP-DeLaW

In olden days there dwelt a piper's son. Piper's Son, The. James Whitcomb Riley. CP-RileJ

In One. Paul Celan. SP-CelaP, *tr.* by John Felstiner

In one age or other, if not in this. Charles Olson. CP-OlsoC

In one day of mankind are all the days. James Joyce. Jorge Luis Borges. SP-BorgJ, *tr.* by Stephen Kessler

In one dread night our city saw, and sigh'd. Address. Lord Byron. CP-Byron

In one hand / I hold tragedy. Jester, The. Langston Hughes. CP-HughL; CP-HughL1

In one of the Assyrian wars. Wading at Wellfleet. Elizabeth Bishop. CP-BishE

In one of the creations. Robin. W. S. Merwin. SP-MerwWF

In one of the dreams men tell how they woke. Dreamers, The. W. S. Merwin. SP-MerwW

In One of the Retreats of Morning. W. S. Merwin. SP-MerwW

In one who felt as once he felt. On Finding a Fan. Lord Byron. CP-Byron

In one window. Under Black Leaves. W. S. Merwin. SP-MerwW

In Order to. Kenneth Patchen. CP-PatcK

In order to be able to live. Money. Raymond Carver. CP-CarvR

In order to perfect all readers, Wall, Cave, and Pillar Statements, after Asōka. Alan Dugan. CP-DugaA

In our cabin we eat breaded oysters and fries. Marriage. Raymond Carver. CP-CarvR

In our city markets. Poem on Particulars, A. A. K. Ramanujan. CP-RamaA

In our eyes the roads. Eyes. Federico García Lorca. CP-GarcF, *tr.* by Jerome Rothenberg *Fr.* Mirror Suite.

In our houses, the snow keeps us. Snowheart. Tess Gallagher. SP-GallT

In our Museum galleries. Burden of Nineveh, The. Dante Gabriel Rossetti. CW-RossD

In our period, they say there is free speech. In Our Time. Muriel Rukeyser. CP-RukeM

In Our Time. Muriel Rukeyser. CP-RukeM

In Our Town. "H. D." CP-DoolH

In & Out. John Berryman. CP-BerrJ

In out of this shower. William Corbett. SP-CorbW

In painted plumes superbly drest. Parrot, The. Vincent Bourne. CP-CowpW

In Pandarum. Thomas Campion. CP-CampT

In paper sacks the customers carry away millions of tons of goods daily. Carl Sandburg. CP-SandC *Fr.* People, Yes, The.

In paradise I poised my foot above the boat and said. Father. James Wright. CP-WrigJ

In Paris in a loud dark winter. Lawrence Ferlinghetti. SP-FerlL

In Paris, on a day that stayed morning until dusk. Clochard. Wisława Szymborska. SP-SzymW, *tr.* by Stanislaw Barańczak *and* Clare Cavanagh

In Paris once, just as the waiter. Coq au Vin. John Ciardi. CP-CiarJ

In parody / of a grade-B film, our private. Bitterness. Olga Broumas. SP-BrouO

In Part from Moschus's Lament for Bion. William Wordsworth. SP-WorW1

In part to get one epoch's details right. Kaisarion. Constantine P. Cavafy. CP-CavaC, *tr.* by Theoharis Constantine Theoharis

In particular one man. Drum World, The. Charles Olson. CP-OlsoC

In Pascal's endless queue. Second Sight. A. K. Ramanujan. CP-RamaA

In passage along an endless, eventless pavement. Endless Pavement. Robert Graves. CP-GravR

In passing with my mind. Right of Way, The. William Carlos Williams. CP-WilW1

In pasture where the leaf and wood. Quest, The. James Wright. CP-WrigJ

In Paths Untrodden. Walt Whitman. CP-WhitW

In Patience. Christina Georgina Rossetti. CP-RosC3

In Paul's Room. John Ciardi. CP-CiarJ

In Peace. John Greenleaf Whittier. CP-WhitJ

In peace tomorrow, when your slack hands weigh. 1945: The Death of the Gods. Randall Jarrell. CP-JarrR

In people, nothing is clear. They knot together. History of the Moon, The. William Dickey. SP-DickW

In Perspective. Robert Graves. CP-GravR

In Piam Memoriam. Geoffrey Hill. CP-HillG

In picture, they which truly understand. To the Author. Ben Jonson. CP-JonsB

In pink fingers of magnolia. Journey, The. Czeslaw Milosz. CP-MiloC; CP-MiloCN, *tr.* by Robert Hass

In pious times ere priest-craft did begin. Absalom and Achitophel. John Dryden. SP-DrydJ

In Piranezi's rarer prints. Prelusive. Herman Melville. SP-MelvH *Fr.* Clarel: A Poem and Pilgrimage in the Holy Land.

In Piso's suite / are empty pockets. Carmen 28. Catullus. CP-ZukLS *Fr.* Carmina.

In Pity as We Kiss and Lie. John Ciardi. CP-CiarJ

In Pity First to Human Kind. Elizabeth MacFadden. CP-SherT

In pity to the emptying town. Jonathan Swift. CP-SwifJ

In Place of a Curse. John Ciardi. CP-CiarJ

In place of scutcheons, that should deck thy hearse. On Sir John Roe ("In place of scutcheons, that should deck thy hearse"). Ben Jonson. CP-JonsB; SP-JonsB

In place of you. Midnight 2. David Ignatow. SP-IgnaD

In places like / Selma, Alabama. From Selma. Langston Hughes. CP-HughL; CP-HughL2

In placid hours well-pleased we dream. Art. Herman Melville. SP-MelvH

In Plaster. Sylvia Plath. CP-PlatS

In Pliny, *Phoenice*. Phoenicians. Island of Summer. Robert Penn Warren. CP-WarrR

In pools / along the wide terraces of shards of shale. Cape Elizabeth: A Photograph. John Logan. CP-LogaJ

In Portsmouth, New Hampshire, plugged with morphia. Messiah, The. Louis MacNeice. CP-MacNL

In Prague. Paul Celan. SP-CelaP, *tr.* by John Felstiner

In Praise of $(C_{10}H_9O_5)x$. John Updike. CP-UpdiJ

In Praise of Cities. Thom Gunn. CP-GunnT

In Praise of Darkness. Jorge Luis Borges. SP-BorgJ, *tr.* by Hoyt Rogers

In Praise of Dreams. Wisława Szymborska. SP-SzymW, *tr.* by Stanislaw Barańczak *and* Clare Cavanagh

In Praise of Feeling Bad about Yourself. Wisława Szymborska. SP-SzymW, *tr.* by Stanislaw Barańczak *and* Clare Cavanagh

In Praise of Gold. Gabriela Mistral. SP-MistG, *tr.* by Maria Giachetti [*or* Jacketti]

In Praise of His Mistress. Thomas Carew. CP-CareT

In Praise of Johnny Appleseed. Nicholas Vachel Lindsay. CP-LindV

In Praise of Limestone. W. H. Auden. CP-AudeW

In Praise of My Françoise. Charles Baudelaire. CP-BaudC, *tr.* by Walter Martin

In Praise of My Sister. Wisława Szymborska. SP-SzymW, *tr.* by Stanislaw Barańczak *and* Clare Cavanagh

In Praise of Necessity. Thomas McGrath. SP-McGrT

In Praise of Pain. Heather McHugh. SP-McHuH

In Praise of Prairie. Theodore Roethke. CP-RoetT

In Praise of Salt. Gabriela Mistral. SP-MistG, *tr.* by Maria Giachetti [*or* Jacketti]

In Praise of Small Towns. Gabriela Mistral. SP-MistG, *tr.* by Maria Giachetti [*or* Jacketti]

In Praise of Songs That Die. Nicholas Vachel Lindsay. CP-LindV

In Praise of Stones. Gabriela Mistral. SP-MistG, *tr.* by Maria Giachetti [*or* Jacketti]

In Praise of the Author, Mistress Anne Bradstreet, Virtue's True and Lively Pattern. *Unknown.* CP-BradA

In Praise of the New Russian Writers. Andrei Codrescu. SP-CodrA

In Prais[e] of Women [*or* Wemen]. William Dunbar. CP-DunbW

In Praise of Women. Robert Herrick. CP-HerrR

In Prayer the Lips ne're act the winning part. Heart, The. Robert Herrick. CP-HerrR

In Prisons of Established Craze. Richard Eberhart. CP-EberR

In private she mourns not the late-lamented. Martial. CP-CunnJ, *tr.* by James Vincent Cunningham

In Procession. Robert Graves. CP-GravR

In Progress. Christina Georgina Rossetti. CP-RosC3

In Progress you have little faith, say you. Progress. George Meredith. CP-MerG1

In Protocreation. Stevie Smith. CP-SmitS

In purest song one plays the constant fool. Infirmity. Theodore Roethke. CP-RoetT

In Qazwin, they have a custom of tattooing themselves. Tattooing in Qazwin. Jelaluddin Rumi. SP-Rumi, *tr.* by Coleman Barks

In Quest. John Greenleaf Whittier. CP-WhitJ

In Question. Denise Levertov. SP-LeveDS

In rags mysterious as these. Emily Dickinson. CP-DickE

In Railway Halls. Stephen Spender. CP-SpenS

In Rain. Wendell Berry. CP-BerrW

In rain like this what you want is an open barn door. It Is Teeming. C. K. Williams. CP-WillC

In Rainy September. Robert Bly. SP-BlyR

In reality the barn wasn't clean, ninety men. Trakl. Norman Dubie. CP-DubiN

In Reference to Her Children, 23 June, 1659. Anne Bradstreet. CP-BradA

In Remembrance of Joseph Sturge. John Greenleaf Whittier. CP-WhitJ

In Response to a Question. William Stafford. SP-StafWW

In Response to a Rumor that the Oldest Whorehouse in Wheeling, West

Virginia, Has Been Condemned. James Wright. CP-WrigJ

In restaurants we argue. They Eat Out. Margaret Atwood. SP-AtwM1

In resurrection is it awfuller. Christina Georgina Rossetti. CP-RosC3

In Retrospect. Maya Angelou. SP-AngeM

In rivers north of the future. Paul Celan. SP-CelaP, *tr.* by John Felstiner

In Rivum a Mola Stoana Lichfeldiæ Diffluentem. Samuel Johnson. CP-JohnS

In Rome on the Campo dei Fiori. Campo dei Fiori. Czeslaw Milosz. CP-MiloC; CP-MiloCN, *tr.* by David Brooks *and* Louis Iribarne

In ruck and quibble of courtfolk. Queen's Complaint, The. Sylvia Plath. CP-PlatS

In Russia. Hayden Carruth. CP-CarHS

In S. Winefridam. Gerard Manley Hopkins. CP-HopkG

In Sabbath quiet, a street. Grace-Note, The. Denise Levertov. SP-LeveDP

In Saginaw, in Saginaw. Saginaw Song, The. Theodore Roethke. CP-RoetT

In St. Paul's a While Ago. Thomas Hardy. CP-HardT

In Salem. Czeslaw Milosz. CP-MiloC; CP-MiloCN, *tr.* by Robert Hass

In Salute again. Clarence Major. SP-MajoC

In Samaria, many people have shown their faith in him. Fragments According to the Gospel. Arthur Rimbaud. CP-RimbA, *tr.* by Martin Sorrell

In San Marco, Venezia. William Carlos Williams. CP-WilW1

In San Salvador (I). Grace Paley. CP-PalGC

In San Salvador (II). Grace Paley. CP-PalGC

In Sanct Androis on Witsoun Monnunday. Justing Betwix James Watsoun and Jhone Barbour, The. Sir David Lyndsay. SP-LyndD

In Sannium. Thomas Campion. CP-CampT

In Santa Maria del Popolo. Thom Gunn. CP-GunnT

In scarecrow patches and tatters, face. Rag Man, The. Robert Earl Hayden. CP-HaydR

In scenery I like flat country. Passing Remark. William Stafford. SP-StafW; SP-StafWW

In School and at the University. Federico García Lorca. CP-GarcF, *tr.* by Alan S. Trueblood *Fr.* Love.

In School-Days. John Greenleaf Whittier. CP-WhitJ

In Schrafft's. W. H. Auden. CP-AudeW

In Scotland's realm, where trees are few. Tale, A: "In Scotland's realm, where trees are few." William Cowper. CP-CowpW

In scudding cloud on high steep meadows shed. Good News. G. K. Chesterton. CP-ChesG

In se. Thomas Campion. CP-CampT

In sea-cold Lyonesse. Šunk Lyonesse. Walter De la Mare. CP-DeLaW

In seas and stones and painful lore of weeds. Apocalypse ("In seas and stones and painful lore of weeds"). G. K. Chesterton. CP-ChesG

In secreit place this hyndir [*or* hindir] nycht [*or* nicht]. William Dunbar. CP-DunbW

In secret place where once I stood. Flesh and the Spirit, The. Anne Bradstreet. CP-BradA

In secret / the out's in—. Robert Creeley. CP-CreeR

In Seditionem Horrendum. William Cowper. CP-CowpW

In seemly burial, love may not rest. Sonnet: "In seemly burial, love may not rest." Dorothy Parker. CP-ParkD

In se'enteen hunder'n [*or* hunder an'] forty-nine. On Andrew Turner. Robert Burns. CP-BurnR

In Senahar, my first born sleeps. Sadi. CP-EmerR

In sepia, I draw a face and hands. Pentimento. Arthur Sze. SP-SzeA

In settling the property question between them. Property Question, The. D. H. Lawrence. CP-LawrD

In shade of death's sad TREE. Sancta Maria Dolorum. Richard Crashaw. CP-CrasR

In shadings of an obscure punishment. Kenneth Patchen. CP-PatcK

In Shadow. Hart Crane. CP-CranH

In Shame and Humiliation. James Wright. CP-WrigJ

In shapes that grow organic and bizarre. Air Show. John Updike. CP-UpdiJ

In sheer amazement, Love and I together. Petrarch. CP-Petra, *tr.* by J. G. Nichols

In Sherborne Abbey. Thomas Hardy. CP-HardT

In ships all over the world. English, The. Langston Hughes. CP-HughL; CP-HughL1

In short, convince you that however wise. Fragment of the "Castle Builder." John Keats. CP-KeatJ

In short, she is not enough. Bella. Rainer Maria Rilke. CP-RilkFr, *tr.* by A. Poulin, Jr.

In Sickness. Jonathan Swift. CP-SwifJ

In Sickness and in Health. W. H. Auden. CP-AudeW

In Sickness Like Sleep. Thomas McGrath. SP-McGrT

In Silence. Thomas Merton. CP-MertT

In silence the heart raves. It utters words. True Love. Robert Penn Warren. CP-WarrR

In silent barren Synod met. Stanzas on Some Skulls in Beauly Abbey, Near Inverness. John Keats. CP-KeatJ

In silent corridors of death. T. S. Eliot. SP-ElioT

In silent gaze the tuneful choir among. Stanzas to Mr. Bentley. Thomas Gray. CP-GrayT

In silent night when rest I took. Here Follows Some Verses upon the Burning of Our House [July 10th, 1666. Copied Out of a Loose Paper]. Anne Bradstreet. CP-BradA

In simmer when the hay was mawn. Country Lassie. Robert Burns. CP-BurnR

In Singapore, in the airport. Singapore. Mary Oliver. SP-OlivM

In Sisterly Fashion. William Carlos Williams. CP-WilW2

In Sixteen Hundred Sixty-eight. Poem Delivered to the Reverend Doctor Swift, Dean of St. Patrick's, Dublin, by a Young Nobleman, November 30, 1725, Being the Dean's Birthday, A. Thomas Sheridan. CP-SherT

In skilful gathering ruffled hairs in order. Elegy 1.11: "In skilful gathering ruffled hairs in order." Ovid. CP-MarlC *Fr.* Elegies.

In sky and wave the white clouds swam. Maids of Attitash, The. John Greenleaf Whittier. CP-WhitJ

In Sleep. Eugenio Montale. CP-MontE, *tr.* by Jonathan Galassi

In sleep I am not, I am gone. Sleep and Waking. D. H. Lawrence. CP-LawrD

In sleep where all that's past goes on. Alba (1952). Louis Zukofsky. CP-ZukLS

In snow thou comest. Emily Dickinson. CP-DickE

In sober mornings, do[e] not thou rehe[a]rse. When He Would Have His Verses Read. Robert Herrick. CP-HerrR

In Society. Allen Ginsberg. CP-GinsA; SP-GinsA

In softness, languor, bloom and growth. Then Shall Perceive. Walt Whitman. CP-WhitW

In some countries laughter. Place of Laughter, The. Theodore Weiss. SP-WeisT

In Some Doubt but Willingly. John Ciardi. CP-CiarJ

In some strange place. Her Waiting Face. James Whitcomb Riley. CP-RileJ

In some suburban cellar. Rat Rises, A. Charles Bukowski. SP-BukC2

In some summers there is so much fruit. Growing Old. Rainer Maria Rilke. CP-RilkFr, *tr.* by A. Poulin, Jr.

In some, the man they made. Dreams About Clothes. James Merrill. SP-MerrJ

In some unused lagoon, some nameless bay. Dismantled Ship, The. Walt Whitman. CP-WhitW

In some village, tucked away among ravines of rolling green. Color of a House, The. Tennessee Williams. CP-WillT

In Sparta. Constantine P. Cavafy. CP-CavaC, *tr.* by Theoharis Constantine Theoharis

In Spayn. Sir Thomas Wyatt. CP-WyatT

In / s p i r e d / the aspirate. For a Muse Meant. Robert Duncan. SP-DuncR

In spite of a Sunday idleness, selling and buying continued. Morning in Salerno 4. Yannis Ritsos. SP-RitsY, *tr.* by Kostas Myrsiades

In spite of all. Her Body Is Private. Eleanor Wilner. SP-WilnE

In Spite of Death. Countee Cullen. CP-CullC

In spite of everything. E. E. Cummings. CP-CummE; SP-CummE

In spite of her sniffle. Sniffle, The. Ogden Nash. CP-NashO

In spite of Pope, in spite of Gay. Pastoral Dialogue between Richmond Lodge and Marble Hill, A. Jonathan Swift. CP-SwifJ

In Spring. "Rubén Dario." SP-DariR, *tr.* by Alberto Acereda *and* Will Derusha

In / Spring comes(no- / one). E. E. Cummings. CP-CummE

In spring from the black branches of the flowering plum tree. Flowering Plum. Louise Glück. SP-GlucL

In spring if there are dogs they will bark. Ballade of Sayings. W. S. Merwin. SP-MerwW

In spring looking at a. Art, The. William Carlos Williams. CP-WilW2

In Spring, no doubt I prefer the drinking-place. Arthur Rimbaud. CP-RimbA, *tr.* by Martin Sorrell

In spring of youth it was my lot. Lake: To———, The. Edgar Allan Poe. CP-PoeEd

In spring the blue azures bow down. Spring Azures. Mary Oliver. SP-OlivM

In spring when the ego arose from the genitals. Sixteen Lines on Marching. Alan Dugan. CP-DugaA

In spring, when the green gits back in the trees. When the Green Gits Back in the Trees. James Whitcomb Riley. CP-RileJ

In spring women flaunt their looks. Han-shan. CP-ColdM, *tr.* by Red Pine

In spring you sleep and never know when the morn comes. Meng Hao Jan. CP-WilW2

In Springtime. Rudyard Kipling. CP-KiplR

In springtime when the leaves are young. Seasons. Christina Georgina Rossetti. CP-RosC3

In St. Peter's Basilica in the City of Rome. Notes from the Agent on Earth: How to be Human. Miller Williams. CP-WillM

In State. James Whitcomb Riley. CP-RileJ

In storms of half-light, in a separate, dim. Another Comedy. John Ciardi. CP-CiarJ

In strange cities, there's an unexpected joy. Adam Zagajewski. SP-ZagaA, *tr.* by Renata Gorczynski, Benjamin Ivry *and* C. K. Williams

In Strasbourg in 1349. A. R. Ammons. CP-AmmoA

In Stratis Viarum I. Arthur Hugh Clough. *See* In the Great Metropolis

In Stratis Viarum II. Arthur Hugh Clough. SP-ClouA

In Stratis Viarum III. Arthur Hugh Clough. SP-ClouA

In Stratis Viarum IV. Arthur Hugh Clough. SP-ClouA

In such a night as this. Memorandum Book. Primo Levi. CP-LeviP, *tr. by* Ruth Feldman

In such a tremendous window. For Richard Wilbur. James Dickey. CP-DickJ

In such an armor he may rise and raid. Bronzeville Man with a Belt in the Back. Gwendolyn Brooks. SP-BrooG

In such servility! and all so boring! Michelangelo Buonarroti. CP-Miche, *tr. by* John Frederick Nims

In Suffolk they are no longer there. Hedgerows. Charles Tomlinson. CP-TomlC

In Summer. "Rubén Dario." SP-DariR, *tr. by* Alberto Acereda *and* Will Derusha

In Summer. Paul Laurence Dunbar. CP-DunbP

In Summer. Denise Levertov. SP-LeveDL

In summer. North Wind. W. S. Merwin. SP-MerwWF

In summer, above a mountain stream scented with willows. Summer's Fullness. Adam Zagajewski. SP-ZagaA, *tr. by* Clare Cavanagh

In Summer Time. Paul Laurence Dunbar. CP-DunbP

In summer's heat[e] and mid-time of the day. Elegy 1.5: "In summer's heat[e] and mid-time of the day." Ovid. CP-MarlC, *tr. by* Christopher Marlowe *Fr.* Elegies.

In summertime on Bredon. Bredon Hill. A. E. Housman. CP-HousA

In sun and snow; peacefully, in slumbers. Bridgehead Photograph. Dan Pagis. SP-PagiD, *tr. by* Stephen Mitchell

In sun-whetted / morning. Gulls. Robert Earl Hayden. CP-HaydR

In sunless air, under pines. Child's Park Stones. Sylvia Plath. CP-PlatS

In sunlight now, after the weeks it rained. Flooded Meadows. Thom Gunn. CP-GunnT

In sun's / slow rising. Morning (8:10 AM). Robert Creeley. SP-CreeR

In Swimming-Time. James Whitcomb Riley. CP-RileJ

In Switzerland. Raymond Carver. CP-CarvR

In Szetejnie. Czeslaw Milosz. CP-MiloCN, *tr. by* Robert Hass

In "taking charge of your possessions when you saw them" you became a golden jay. To the Peacock of France. Marianne Craig Moore. CP-MoorM

In Tall Grass. Carl Sandburg. CP-SandC

In Tara's Halls. William Butler Yeats. CP-YeatW

In Tarbolton, ye ken, there are proper young men. Ronalds of the Bennals, The. Robert Burns. CP-BurnR

In tema e in pena addio. Christina Georgina Rossetti. CP-RosC3

In tempest and storm blackness of darkness for ever. Where Their Worm Dieth Not, and the Fire Is Not Quenched. Christina Georgina Rossetti. CP-RosC2

In Tempore Senectutis ("For we are old / And the earth passion dyeth"). Ezra Pound. CP-PoEar

In Tempore Senectutis ("When I am old / I will not have you look apart"). Ezra Pound. CP-PoEar

In Tenebris. Thomas Hardy. CP-HardT

In Tennessee once the campfire glowed. Youthful Picnic Long Ago: Sad Ballad on Box. Robert Penn Warren. CP-WarrR

In Terror of Hospital Bills. James Wright. CP-WrigJ

In Thai Binh (Peace) Province. Denise Levertov. SP-LeveDL

In Thankful Acknowledgement for the Letters I Received from My Husband Out Of England. Anne Bradstreet. CP-BradA

In Thankful[l] Remembrance for My Dear Husband['] s Safe Arrival[l]. Anne Bradstreet. CP-BradA

In that ago when being was believing. History of Truth, The. W. H. Auden. CP-AudeW

In that bad year and city of your birth. To the New World. Randall Jarrell. CP-JarrR

In that bad year, in a city to have now no name. Answer to Prayer. Robert Penn Warren. CP-WarrR

In that black forest, where, when day is done. Cry of a Lost Soul, The. John Greenleaf Whittier. CP-WhitJ

In that building, long and low. Ropewalk, The. Henry Wadsworth Longfellow. SP-LongH

In that 'corridor of garments.' Byzantium. Charles Tomlinson. CP-TomlC

In That Country. Ezra Pound. CP-PoEar

In that country he was an officer of cavalry. Incarnated. Czeslaw Milosz. CP-MiloCN, *tr. by* Robert Hass

In that country the animals. Animals in That Country, The. Margaret Atwood. SP-AtwM1

In that dark year an angry rain came down. Rain of Blood, The. Adrienne Rich. CP-RicAE

In that far land, and time, near the castrated drawbridge where. Star-Fall. Robert Penn Warren. CP-WarrR

In that hotel my life. Illumination, The. Stanley Kunitz. CP-KunSC

In that hour I have seen. Lantern and a Shadow, A. Kenneth Rexroth. CP-RexrK

In that I loved you, Love, I worshipped you. To Eros. Wilfred Owen. CP-OwenW

In that instant. Image from Beckett, An. Derek Mahon. CP-MahoD

In that library in Almagro Sur. Two Cathedrals, The. Jorge Luis Borges. SP-BorgJ, *tr. by* Stephen Kessler

In that November off Tehuantepec. Sea Surface Full of Clouds. Wallace Stevens. CP-StevW; CP-StevWP

In that oblivious, concentrated, fiercely fetal decontraction peculiar to the lost. Park, The. C. K. Williams. SP-WillC

In that old house of many generations. First Travels of Max. John Crowe Ransom. SP-RansJ

In that part of the book of my memory before the which is little that can be read. La Vita Nuova. Dante Alighieri. CW-RossD, *tr. by* Dante Gabriel Rossetti

In that part of the book of my memory before which little could be read. Dante's Vita Nuova. Dante Alighieri. CP-EmerR, *tr. by* Ralph Waldo Emerson

In that place. Song under Tears. Federico García Lorca. CP-GarcF, *tr. by* Jerome Rothenberg *Fr.* Moments of Song.

In that place, shepherd, all the men are dead. Eclogue of the Liberal and the Poet. Allen Tate. CP-TateA

In that Poussin the clouds are like golden tea. Poussin. Louis MacNeice. CP-MacNL

In that rich burial ground where the levelled dead. Dream, The. Marya Alexandrovna Zaturenska. SP-ZatuM

In that situation, all the signs were right: scars. Sorcerer's Daughter, The. Louise Bogan. CP-BogaL

In that slick and new-fangled coach we go slam-banging. Last Night Train. Robert Penn Warren. CP-WarrR

In that soft season, when descending show'rs. Temple of Fame, The. Alexander Pope. CP-PopeA

In that stage of psychosexual development called latency, when not that much, at least supposedly. Child Psychology. C. K. Williams. SP-WillC

In that world we weary to attain, / Love's furled banner floats at large unfurled. His Banner over Me Was Love. Christina Georgina Rossetti. CP-RosC2

In the Absence of Bliss. Maxine W. Kumin. SP-KumiM

In the Afternoon. James Whitcomb Riley. CP-RileJ

In the afternoon I wander away through. Through the Junipers. William Stafford. SP-StafWW

In the afternoon I watched. Happiness. Mary Oliver. SP-OlivM

In the afternoon we carried rocks. Fast work. 12 November 1948. Yannis Ritsos. SP-RitsY *Fr.* Exile's Journals 1.

In the air your root stays on, there. Paul Celan. SP-CelaP, *tr. by* John Felstiner

In the All-Verbs Navaho World. William Stafford. SP-StafWW

In the almond—what stands in the almond? Mandorla. Paul Celan. SP-CelaP, *tr. by* John Felstiner

In the ancient Christian ages, while a dreamy faith and wonder. St. Francis of Assisi. G. K. Chesterton. CP-ChesG

In the animal eye I saw. Rainer Maria Rilke. CP-RilkFr, *tr. by* A. Poulin, Jr. *Fr.* Orchards.

In the April rain I climbed up to drink. Meditation in the Spring Rain. Wendell Berry. CP-BerrW

In the Arc of Your Mallet. Jelaluddin Rumi. SP-Rumi, *tr. by* Coleman Barks

In the Arden Apartments. Night before the Night before Christmas, The. Randall Jarrell. CP-JarrR

In the Armpit of the Hill. Clarence Major. SP-MajoC

In the Audience. John Ciardi. CP-CiarJ

In the autumn brilliance. Air of November. Denise Levertov. SP-LeveDP

In the autumnal blue. Elegy: For Robert Lowell. Joseph Brodsky. CP-BrodJ

In the Aztec design God crowds. Ultimate Problems. William Stafford. SP-StafW; SP-StafWW

In the back of the closet what. My Old Gray Sweater. James Laughlin. CP-LaugJ

In the background a saint walks a path. Story Sassetta Paints, A. Gregory Orr. SP-OrrG

In the Background of Silence. Yusef Komunyakaa. CP-KomuY

In the bad old days a bewigged country Squire. Wigs and Beards. Robert Graves. CP-GravR

In the bad old days it was not so bad. Managers, The. W. H. Auden. CP-AudeW

In the Baggage Room at Greyhound. Allen Ginsberg. CP-GinsA

In the Balance. G. K. Chesterton. CP-ChesG

In the Balance. Charles Tomlinson. CP-TomlC

In the Ballet. James Laughlin. CP-LaugJ

In the bare trees old husks make new designs. Aigeltinger. William Carlos Williams. CP-WilW2

In the basement of the waxworks the old guard puts on his. Fire at the Waxworks, The. Randall Jarrell. CP-JarrR

In the Beach House. Anne Sexton. CP-SextA; SP-SextA

In the Beauty Created by Others. Adam Zagajewski. SP-ZagaA, *tr. by* Renata Gorczynski

In the Beck. Kathleen Jessie Raine. SP-RainK

In the bedchamber window, near the glass. Flower's Tragedy, The. Thomas Hardy. CP-HardT

In the bedroom, the woman with the black dog. Inertia. Yannis Ritsos. SP-RitsY, *tr. by* Kostas Myrsiades

In the Beech. Seamus Heaney. SP-HeanSO *Fr.* Sweeney Redivivus.

In the Beginning. Laura Riding Jackson. CP-RidiL

In the Beginning. Primo Levi. CP-LeviP, *tr. by* Ruth Feldman *and* Brian Swann

In the Beginning. Dylan Thomas. CP-ThomD

In the beginning and in the end the only decent. Plain Speaking. Louis MacNeice. CP-MacNL

In the beginning God began. Miller Williams. CP-WillM

In the beginning life was good to me. Widow's Song, The. Randall Jarrell. CP-JarrR

In the Beginning of Beginnings was Void of Void, the Nameless. In My End Is My Beginning. Chuang Tzu. CP-MertT, *tr. by* Thomas Merton

In the beginning that unbroken breath. Logos. Miller Williams. CP-WillM

In the beginning was Love. Song of Songs, The. G. K. Chesterton. CP-ChesG

In the beginning was order, a uniform. Creation According to Ovid. Robert Pinsky. CP-PinsR

In the beginning was Scream. Lineage. Ted Hughes. SP-HughTN

In the beginning was the Word next God. Morgante Maggiore, The. Luigi Pulci. CP-Byron, *tr. by* Byron

In the best season of our earthly span. Petrarch. CP-Petra, *tr. by* J. G. Nichols

In the big maple / behind the willow. Scarlet Tanager. James Schuyler. CP-SchuJ

In the black moon. Song of the Rider (1860). Federico García Lorca. SP-GarcF, *tr. by* J. L. Gili *and* Stephen Spender

In the Black Museum. Howard Nemerov. CP-NemeH

In the black winter morning. Bereft. Thomas Hardy. CP-HardT

In the bleak mid-winter. Christmas Carol, A: "In the bleak mid-winter." Christina Georgina Rossetti. CP-RosC1

In the bleak time look for no cooperation. Doubling the Nerve. A. R. Ammons. CP-AmmoA

In the blizzard's heart. Kazuko's Vision. Eleanor Wilner. SP-WilnE

In the blue hour. Citizen Dreaming, The. Thomas McGrath. SP-McGrT

In the blue hubbub of the same-through-wealth sky. Geography. Kenneth Koch. SP-KochK

In the blue night. Pine Tree Tops. Gary Snyder. CP-SnydG

In the Bodies of Words. May Swenson. SP-SwenM

In the Book. William Stafford. SP-StafWW

In the Borghese Gardens. Charles Tomlinson. SP-TomlC

In the Boston Public Library on Boylston Street, where all the bums come in stinking from the cold. Critic, The. C. K. Williams. SP-WillC

In the *Boston Sunday Herald* just three lines. To an American Poet Just Dead. Richard Wilbur. CP-WilbR

In the bowels of the earth resides a very ancient Giant. Pelasgian Image. Constantine P. Cavafy. CP-CavaC, *tr. by* Theoharis Constantine Theoharis

In the bowers of the rising moon. To a Nightingale. George Meredith. CP-MerG2

In the box of paperclips on my desk. I Love to See You. James Laughlin. CP-LaugJ

In the bran-new pulpit the bishop stands. Whispered at the Church-Opening. Thomas Hardy. CP-HardT

In the branches of / the great plane tree. Cardinal, A. James Schuyler. CP-SchuJ

In the bright season when He, most high Jove. Golden Sestina, The. Pico della Mirandola. CP-PoEar, *tr. by* Ezra Pound

In the British Museum. Thomas Hardy. CP-HardT

In the brutal nights we used to dream. Reveille. Primo Levi. CP-LeviP, *tr. by* Ruth Feldman *and* Brian Swann

In the Bulrush. Rita Dove. SP-DoveR

In the Bus. Grace Paley. CP-PalGC

In the bush country of Jamaica. Mendicant Order, A. Tennessee Williams. CP-WillT

In the busy streets, domains of trade. Henry David Thoreau. CP-ThorH

In the cab there was a song. Open Fire Near a Shed. Tess Gallagher. SP-GallT

In the cabin. Here we have love. Voyage. George Oppen. CP-OppGN

In the Cage. Robert Lowell. SP-LoweR

In the cage of the Siberian snow fox. Freedom Machine, The. Dan Pagis. SP-PagiD, *tr. by* Stephen Mitchell

In the calm black stream where stars sleep. Ophelia. Arthur Rimbaud. CP-RimbA, *tr. by* Martin Sorrell

In the Camp There Was One Alive. Randall Jarrell. CP-JarrR

In the canoe wilderness branches wait for winter. Representing Far Places. William Stafford. SP-StafWW

In the Carolinas. Wallace Stevens. CP-StevW; CP-StevWP

In the cave mouth I stopped. Gregory Orr. SP-OrrG

In the cave which wild weeds cover. Fragment: A Roman's Chamber. Percy Bysshe Shelley. CP-ShelP

In the cave with a long-ago flare. Painters. Muriel Rukeyser. CP-RukeM

In the Cemetery. Constantine P. Cavafy. CP-CavaC, *tr. by* Theoharis Constantine Theoharis

In the cemetery of Childhood. Cemetery of Childhood. Joaquim Cardozo. CP-BishE

In the Central Park Zoo, just past the ants. Zoo Bats. John Updike. CP-UpdiJ

In the chapel where I could praise. Icon. Marge Piercy. SP-PierM

In the Children's Hospital. Hugh MacDiarmid. SP-MacDH

In the Child's Night. James Dickey. CP-DickJ

In the chill rains of the early winter I hear something—. All the Dead Soldiers. Thomas McGrath. SP-McGrT

In the Chill— / what is nameless but the Source, the Cause. Radiance in a Dark Wood, The. Kenneth Patchen. CP-PatcK

In the choir the boys are singing the hymn. In Church. D. H. Lawrence. CP-LawrD

In the circus tent of a hurricane. Circus in Three Rings. Sylvia Plath. CP-PlatS

In the Cities. D. H. Lawrence. CP-LawrD

In the city of fire the eyes. Pens, The. W. S. Merwin. SP-MerwW

In the city set upon slime and loam. Who Goes Home? G. K. Chesterton. CP-ChesG

In the city that ruled me. Street Has Changed, The. Randall Jarrell. CP-JarrR

In the city, under the saw-toothed leaves of an oak. Straw Hat. Rita Dove. SP-DoveR

In the clean, anodyne. Nostalgia for India. May Sarton. SP-SartM

In the clear atmosphere. Wild Birds, The. Randall Jarrell. CP-JarrR

In the clear dark lake a lady dived. George Meredith. CP-MerG2

In the Clear Season of Grapes. Wallace Stevens. CP-StevW; CP-StevWP

In the cold, cold parlor. First Death in Nova Scotia. Elizabeth Bishop. CP-BishE

In the Cold House. James Wright. CP-WrigJ

In the Cold Kingdom. Mona Van Duyn. SP-VanDM

In the cold light of morning she was looking rather queer. Gnädiges Fräulein. Stevie Smith. CP-SmitS

In the cold morning the rested street stands up. Perimeters. Allen Tate. CP-TateA

In the cold season, in a locality accustomed to heat more than. Star of the Nativity. Joseph Brodsky. CP-BrodJ

In the cold shed sharpening saws. Sixth-Month Song in the Foothills. Gary Snyder. CP-SnydG

In the cold spring night. Smelt Fishing. Robert Earl Hayden. CP-HaydR

In the Colonial Luncheonette on Sixth Street they know everything there is to know, the shits. Regulars, The. C. K. Williams. CP-WillC; SP-WillC

In the Commercial Gardens. Howard Nemerov. CP-NemeH

In the common mind a corked bottle. Lines on Receiving *The Dial's* Award: 1927. William Carlos Williams. CP-WilW1

In the concrete cells of the hatchery. Winter Trout. James Dickey. CP-DickJ

In the Constellations. "Rubén Dario." SP-DariR, *tr. by* Alberto Acereda *and* Will Derusha

In the constellations Pythagoras used to read. In the Constellations. "Rubén Dario." SP-DariR, *tr. by* Alberto Acereda *and* Will Derusha

In the cool of the night time. Interior. Carl Sandburg. CP-SandC

In the Corridor. James Whitcomb Riley. CP-RileJ

In the country of eight hundred different kinds. Your Country. Andrei Codrescu. SP-CodrA

In the course of a meditation. Meditation, A. A. K. Ramanujan. CP-RamaA

In the court- / yard at midnight, at. La Noche. Robert Creeley. CP-CreeR

In the Courtyard of Secret Life. Kenneth Patchen. CP-PatcK

In the courtyard of the Brera. Nausea. William Meredith. SP-MereW

In the creative generations there is often. Brothers in the Craft. Thomas Kinsella. CP-KinsT

In the crept hours on our street. Move to California, The. William Stafford. SP-StafWW

In the Crevice of Time. Josephine Jacobsen. CP-JacoJ

In the damp park, no larger than a stamp. Banyan Tree, Old Year's Night, The. Derek Walcott. CP-WalcD

In the Dark. D. H. Lawrence. CP-LawrD

In the Dark. James Whitcomb Riley. CP-RileJ

In the dark. Black Jewel, The. W. S. Merwin. SP-MerwWF

In the dark / Before the tall. Night Song. Langston Hughes. CP-HughL; CP-HughL2

In the Dark House. Stanley Kunitz. CP-KunSC

In the dark I step out of bed. Ontology, An. David Ignatow. SP-IgnaD

In the dark kitchen the electric icebox rustles. Mission, The. Robert Penn Warren. CP-WarrR

In the dark night of the skull. Brain. Dan Pagis. SP-PagiD, *tr. by* Stephen Mitchell

In the Dark None Dainty. Robert Herrick. CP-HerrR

In the dark of the moon. Rider's Song (1860). Federico García Lorca. CP-GarcF, *tr. by* Alan S. Trueblood *Fr.* Andalusian Songs.

In the dark of the moon, in flying snow, in the dead of winter. February 2, 1968. Wendell Berry. CP-BerrW

In the dark of this cloud-laden even. Calvary, The. G. K. Chesterton. CP-ChesG

In the dark original water. Sphere. A. R. Ammons. CP-AmmoA

In the dark they fell a-crying. Irish Wake. Langston Hughes. CP-HughL; CP-HughL1

In the dark tie-up seven huge Holsteins. Great Day in the Cows' House. Donald Hall. CP-HallD

In the dark with an old song. Trappers. C. K. Williams. CP-WillC

In the dawn-dirty light, in the biggest snow of the year. Roe-Deer. Ted Hughes. SP-HughTN

In the dawn light these white girders. Bridge, The. Gregory Orr. SP-OrrG

In the dawn of a sumptuous November. November. Stevie Smith. CP-SmitS

In the Day of His Espousals. Christina Georgina Rossetti. CP-RosC2

In the day of the mustering of thine army. Church Militant. Donald Davie. CP-DaviDC

In the day's mirror. Reflections. Yusef Komunyakaa. CP-KomuY

In the Days of Crinoline. Thomas Hardy. CP-HardT

In the days of lace-ruffles, perukes and brocade. Brown Bess. Rudyard Kipling. CP-KiplR

In the days of my youth. Typical Optical. John Updike. CP-UpdiJ

In the Days of Prismatic Color. Marianne Craig Moore. CP-MoorM

In the days of the broken cubes of Picasso. Cubes. Langston Hughes. CP-HughL; CP-HughL1

In the days of the cockade and the brass pistol. Carl Sandburg. CP-SandC Fr. People, Yes, The.

In the days when everyone said. Meantime. Heather McHugh. SP-McHuH

In the days when life seemed a dream. Grave of Signor Casanova, The. Jaroslav Seifert. SP-SeifJ, tr. by Ewald Osers

In the days when twenty fellows. Effusions of a School-Patriarch, The. Arthur Hugh Clough. SP-ClouA

In the daytime, when she moved about me. Rudyard Kipling. CP-KiplR Fr. Plain Tales from the Hills.

In the dead hour of the afternoon. Image of Man as a Gardener after Two World Wars. John Ciardi. CP-CiarJ

In the dead of January, while snow fell. Deleted Passage. Amy Clampitt. CP-ClamA

In the Dead of the Night. Norman Dubie. CP-DubiN

In the deep armchair, the boy sits motionless. Limits of Physics, The. Dan Pagis. SP-PagiD, tr. by Stephen Mitchell

In the Deep Channel. William Stafford. SP-StafW; SP-StafWW

In the deep fall, terror increases. Home in Dark Grass, A. Robert Bly. SP-BlyR

In the deep heart of man a poet dwells. Ralph Waldo Emerson. CP-EmerR

In the Deep Museum. Anne Sexton. CP-SextA; SP-SextA

In the deep night of the universe. Break of Day. Jorge Luis Borges. SP-BorgJ, tr. by Stephen Kessler

In the deep reaches of the night. Ancient Ballet, An. Thomas Kinsella. CP-KinsT

In the Defense Department there is a shop. Heaven as Anus. Maxine W. Kumin. SP-KumiM

In the denouement of the beautiful storm. Pigeons, The. Karl Shapiro. SP-ShapK

In the Department store. T. S. Eliot. SP-ElioT

In the depth and rustle of midnight, how do you know. Whatever You Now Are. Robert Penn Warren. CP-WarrR

In the depths of the Greyhound Terminal. In the Baggage Room at Greyhound. Allen Ginsberg. CP-GinsA

In the desert. Stephen Crane. CP-CranS

In the Desert. Herman Melville. SP-MelvH

In the desert a. Self-Portrait. A. R. Ammons. CP-AmmoA

In the desert midnight I said. Driving Through. A. R. Ammons. CP-AmmoA

In the desert of Itabira. Travelling in the Family. Carlos Drummond de Andrade. CP-BishE

In the deserted, moon-blanched [or moon-blanch'd] street. Summer Night, A. Matthew Arnold. SP-ArnoM

In the dim summer night they were leaning alone. From Below. James Whitcomb Riley. CP-RileJ

In the distant past I can see. White Night. Boris Leonidovich Pasternak. CP-MahoD, tr. by Derek Mahon

In the Districts Surrounding Antioch. Constantine P. Cavafy. CP-CavaC, tr. by Theoharis Constantine Theoharis

In the Dock. Walter De la Mare. CP-DeLaW

In the dome of my sires as the clear moonbeam falls. Newstead Abbey. Lord Byron. CP-Byron

In the door, / Long legged, tall. Blood from the Stone. George Oppen. CP-OppGN

In the doorway of the bar. Le Seul Malheur Est que Je ne Sais pas Lire. Archibald MacLeish. CP-MacLA

In the dour ages. Lesson in Vengeance, A. Sylvia Plath. CP-PlatS

In the dream. Stand-Ins, The. Anne Sexton. CP-SextA

In the dream I enter the house. Bone-Flower Elegy. Robert Earl Hayden. CP-HaydR

In the dream of death where I listen, the voices of the dream keep diminishing, fading away. To Listen. C. K. Williams. SP-WillC

In the dream of foxes. Dream of Foxes, A. Lucille Clifton. SP-ClifL

In The Dreaming. William Dickey. SP-DickW

"At Maganosc / in the stone bedroom." SP-DickW

"Here, in the summer city." SP-DickW

"If forgiveness comes / it will be gradual." SP-DickW

"In the dreaming / we walk through the streets of Oxford." SP-DickW

"Thinking of me / think of what was." SP-DickW

"We meet, eating, smoking." SP-DickW

In the dreaming / we walk through the streets of Oxford. William Dickey. SP-DickW Fr. In The Dreaming.

In the Dry. George Meredith. CP-MerG2

In the dull and gloomy village where he works. Constantine P. Cavafy. CP-CavaC, tr. by Theoharis Constantine Theoharis

In the dumbest movie they can play it on us with a sunrise and a passage of adagio Vivaldi. Nostalgia. C. K. Williams. SP-WillC

In the dungeon-crypts, idly did I stray. Prisoner, The. Emily Jane Brontë. CP-BronE

In the dusk of the evening. Old Mountain Road. Charles Simic. SP-SimiC; SP-SimiCE

In the dusk of the river, the wind. Porch over the River, The. Wendell Berry. CP-BerrW

In the dust are my father's beautiful hands. At Night. Richard Eberhart. CP-EberR

In the early evening, as now, a man is bending. Poem: "In the early evening, as now, a man is bending." Louise Glück. SP-GlucL

In the early evening rain. Tryst, The. James Tate. SP-TateJ

In the early morning hour. Sunrise Ruby, The. Jelaluddin Rumi. SP-Rumi, tr. by Coleman Barks

In the early morning, past the shut houses. Scroppo's Dog. May Swenson. SP-SwenM

In the early winter dusk the broken city dark. City Dark, The. Robert Pinsky. CP-PinsR

In the earth, the earth, thou shalt be laid. Warning and Reply. Emily Jane Brontë. CP-BronE

In the East fames are won. Henry David Thoreau. CP-ThorH

In the east the morning comes. Dirge for a Soldier. Paul Laurence Dunbar. CP-DunhP

In the eaves of the barn. Knowledge of Old Towns, The. Kenneth Patchen. CP-PatcK

In the eel-thin belly of the Metro Swearingen. Long Approach, The. Maxine W. Kumin. SP-KumiM

In the eighties of the twentieth century, in Rome, via Condotti. Caffé Greco. Czeslaw Milosz. CP-MiloC; CP-MiloCN, tr. by Robert Hass

In the Elegy Season. Richard Wilbur. CP-WilbR

In the Element of Antagonisms. Wallace Stevens. CP-StevW; CP-StevWP

In the Empire in question, the Cartographer's Art reached such a degree of Perfection. Museum. Jorge Luis Borges. SP-BorgJ, tr. by Ken Krabbenhoft

In the emplacements of the wood. Automaton, The. Randall Jarrell. CP-JarrR

In the empty lot—a place. Wild, The. Wendell Berry. CP-BerrW

In the empty sleeping noon. Goddess, The. Rainer Maria Rilke. CP-RilkFr, tr. by A. Poulin, Jr. Fr. Orchards.

In the empty square, an orphan wind. Orphan Wind. Rainer Maria Rilke. CP-RilkFr, tr. by A. Poulin, Jr.

In the encyclopedia. Fact ("In the encyclopedia"). Kenneth Rexroth. CP-RexrK

In the Encyclopedias, No Room for Osip Mandelstam. Adam Zagajewski. SP-ZagaA, tr. by Renata Gorczynski

In the encyclopedias once again no room for. In the Encyclopedias, No Room for Osip Mandelstam. Adam Zagajewski. SP-ZagaA, tr. by Renata Gorczynski

In the end, afraid of the poems and the many cigarettes. Midnight Stroll. Yannis Ritsos. SP-RitsY, tr. by Kimon Friar and Kostas Myrsiades

In the end, we too will be winds from beyond the rim. Yehuda Amichai. SP-AmicYL Fr. At Right Angles.

In the end you are weary of this ancient world. Zone. Guillaume Apollinaire. CP-BeckS, tr. by Samuel Beckett

In the Estuary. Charles Tomlinson. CP-TomlC

In the eternal dream-time. Sueño Real. Lawrence Ferlinghetti. SP-FerlL

In the Evening. Constantine P. Cavafy. CP-CavaC, tr. by Theoharis Constantine Theoharis

In the Evening. G. K. Chesterton. CP-ChesG

In the Evening. Thomas Hardy. CP-HardT

In the evening. Another Night in the Ruins. Galway Kinnell. SP-KinnGN

In the evening. Beggars and Kings. W. S. Merwin. SP-MerwW

In the Evening. Adrienne Rich. CP-RicAE; SP-RicA2

In the Evening. James Whitcomb Riley. CP-RileJ

In the evening, just before. Mary and the Seasons. Kenneth Rexroth. CP-RexrK

In the evening of a brightly. Greenwich Avenue. James Schuyler. CP-SchuJ

In the evening of our days. In the Evening. James Whitcomb Riley. CP-RileJ

In the evening there is a sunset sonata comes to the cities. Good Morning, America. Carl Sandburg. CP-SandC

In the evening there were flocks of nighthawks. September 2, 1969. Wendell Berry. CP-BerrW

In the evening we came back. Light Left On, A. May Sarton. SP-SartM

In the evening, when the world knew he was dead. In the Evening. Thomas Hardy. CP-HardT

In the evenings / what it was the soft tap tap. What Did She Know, When Did She Know It. Lucille Clifton. SP-ClifL

In the Evil Days. John Greenleaf Whittier. CP-WhitJ

In the Face of Hatred. James Wright. CP-WrigJ

In the fact that in my verses. I Take a Certain Pride. James Laughlin. CP-LaugJ

In the fair land o'erwatched by Ischia's mountains. In Remembrance of Joseph Sturge. John Greenleaf Whittier. CP-WhitJ

In the Fall. Robert Creeley. CP-CreeR

In the far South the sun of autumn is passing. Like Decorations in a Nigger Cemetery. Wallace Stevens. CP-StevW; CP-StevWP

In the farmyard the white moon of autumn shines. Rats, The. Georg Trakl. CP-WrigJ

In the featherbeds of grander times. Not Quite So Soon. Charles Bukowski. SP-BukC2

In the Field. Richard Wilbur. CP-WilbR

In the field, a. For a Child. Denise Levertov. SP-LeveDL

In the field is a house. Inside. Heather McHugh. SP-McHuH

In the field the air writhes, a heat-pocket. Halfway. Adrienne Rich. CP-RicAE; SP-RicA2

In the field, two horses. Winter. Philip Larkin. CP-LarkP

In the fields, the silos open their mouths. Hangman. Ai. SP-Ai

In the fields / we let them have. Goldfinches. Mary Oliver. SP-OlivM

In the fifth grade. Birthday on the Acropolis. May Sarton. SP-SartM

In the 51st State. Ted Berrigan. SP-BerrT

In the films they fall into bed. Nowadays. James Laughlin. CP-LaugJ

In the films when the couples kiss. Kissing. James Laughlin. CP-LaugJ

In the fine cataracts of falling mountain water. Skeleton for Mr. Paul in Paradise, A. Norman Dubie. CP-DubiN

In the fine print of her face. My Beloved. Charles Simic. SP-SimiCE

In the first. Three Dreams. A. K. Ramanujan. CP-RamaA

In the first canto of the final canticle. Hand as a Being, The. Wallace Stevens. CP-StevW; CP-StevWP

In the first chamber of the heart. Heart, The. W. S. Merwin. SP-MerwWF

In the first display. Note, A. Wisława Szymborska. SP-SzymWM, tr. by Joanna Trzeciak

In the first hours of darkness. Summer Night on the Stone Barrens. W. S. Merwin. SP-MerwWF

In the First Page of an Album by One Whose Handwriting Is Wretchedly Bad. William Wordsworth. CP-WorW2

In the first ruder age, when love was wild. Love's Force. Thomas Carew. CP-CareT

In the First Stanza. Carolyn Kizer. CP-KizeC

In the first taxi he was alone tra-la. Taxis, The. Louis MacNeice. CP-MacNL

In the first world we know there is only the present. Sir. Miller Williams. CP-WillM

In the first year of the first war called the *World*. Soldier, The. Randall Jarrell. CP-JarrR

In the first years, when your hair. Early Pompeian. Derek Walcott. CP-WalcD

In the flame of the flickering fire. My Soul. Stevie Smith. CP-SmitS

In the flashes and black shadows. Hunter, The. William Carlos Williams. CP-WilW1

In the fog a farmer with a hobbled leg. Autumn. Guillaume Apollinaire. SP-MereW, tr. by William Meredith

In the fog, lemon trees hang their lanterns. Yannis Ritsos. SP-RitsY Fr. First Series.

In the foliage, verdant jewel-case splashed with gold. Faun's Head. Arthur Rimbaud. CP-RimbA, tr. by Martin Sorrell

'In the footsteps of the walking air.' Kenneth Patchen. CP-PatcK

In the Ford plant. Foundations of American Industry, The. Donald Hall. CP-HallD

In the foreground we see time and life. Cézanne's Ports. Allen Ginsberg. CP-GinsA

In the forenoon's restful quiet. When the Old Man Smokes. Paul Laurence Dunbar. CP-DunbP

In the Forest. Alan Dugan. CP-DugaA

In the Forest. Oscar Wilde. CP-WildO

In the Forest of Clocks. Federico García Lorca.
Chaparral. CP-GarcF, tr. by Jerome Rothenberg
Clock Echo. CP-GarcF, tr. by Jerome Rothenberg
First/Last Meditation. CP-GarcF, tr. by Jerome Rothenberg
He. CP-GarcF, tr. by Jerome Rothenberg
"I entered the forest / of clocks." CP-GarcF, tr. by Jerome Rothenberg
"One . . . two . . . three." CP-GarcF, tr. by Jerome Rothenberg
Overview. CP-GarcF, tr. by Jerome Rothenberg
Sphinx Hour, The. CP-GarcF, tr. by Jerome Rothenberg

In the Forest of the Lunar Grapefruits. Federico García Lorca.
Prologue: "I am going on a long trip." CP-GarcF, tr. by Jerome Rothenberg
Reflections. CP-GarcF, tr. by Jerome Rothenberg
Situation. CP-GarcF, tr. by Jerome Rothenberg
Three Disillusioning Witches, The. CP-GarcF, tr. by Jerome Rothenberg
Tower. CP-GarcF, tr. by Jerome Rothenberg

In the forgotten woods, when somber winter glowers. Sonnet: "In the forgotten woods, when somber winter glowers." Stéphane Mallarmé. CP-MallS, tr. by Henry Weinfield

In the French Translation of Lucan by Monsieur De Brebeuf Are These Verses: Lib 3. Lucan. CP-MarvA Fr. Civil War [Bellum Civile] or Pharsalia.

In the Full Severity of Mercy. Yehuda Amichai. SP-AmicY, tr. by Stephen Mitchell

In the full sun. In the fruitfall season. Children's Orchard, The. Muriel Rukeyser. CP-RukeM

In the Fullness of Time. Charles Tomlinson. CP-TomlC; SP-TomlC

In the Garden. Richard Eberhart. CP-EberR

In the Garden. Thomas Hardy. CP-HardT

In the Garden. David Ignatow. SP-IgnaD

In the Garden. Walter De la Mare. CP-DeLaW

In the Garden at Swainston. Alfred Tennyson. CP-TennA

In the Garden, at the White Table. Yehuda Amichai. SP-AmicY, tr. by Chana Bloch

In the garden, at the white table. Yehuda Amichai. SP-AmicYL, tr. by Benjamin Harshav and Barbara Harshav

In the garden of earth a square of water. Shalimar Gardens. Carolyn Kizer. CP-KizeC

In the Garden of the Lunar Grapefruits. Federico García Lorca.
Avenue. CP-GarcF, tr. by Jerome Rothenberg
Dune. CP-GarcF, tr. by Jerome Rothenberg
Earth ("Girls of the breeze, The"). CP-GarcF, tr. by Jerome Rothenberg
Encounter ("Sun flower. / River flower"). CP-GarcF, tr. by Jerome Rothenberg
Engravings of the Garden. CP-GarcF, tr. by Jerome Rothenberg
Floating Bridges. CP-GarcF, tr. by Jerome Rothenberg
Garden, The. CP-GarcF, tr. by Jerome Rothenberg
Little Song of the Unborn Child. CP-GarcF, tr. by Jerome Rothenberg
Moments of the Garden. CP-GarcF, tr. by Jerome Rothenberg
Moonbow. CP-GarcF, tr. by Jerome Rothenberg
Parenthesis. CP-GarcF, tr. by Jerome Rothenberg
Pergola. CP-GarcF, tr. by Jerome Rothenberg
Perspective. CP-GarcF, tr. by Jerome Rothenberg
Portico ("Clang clang / The air, having been killed"). CP-GarcF, tr. by Jerome Rothenberg
Prologue: "I have taken leave of the friends I love the most & have set out on a short dramatic journey." CP-GarcF, tr. by Jerome Rothenberg
Sky. CP-GarcF, tr. by Jerome Rothenberg
Song of the Motionless Gardener. CP-GarcF, tr. by Jerome Rothenberg
Song of the Seven-Hearted Boy. CP-GarcF, tr. by Jerome Rothenberg
Wake Up/Ring Out. CP-GarcF, tr. by Jerome Rothenberg
White Satyr. CP-GarcF, tr. by Jerome Rothenberg
White Smell. CP-GarcF, tr. by Jerome Rothenberg

In the garden, small laughter from years ago. Garden, The. Raymond Carver. CP-CarvR

In the garden. Sun / on the river. We Walk. James Schuyler. CP-SchuJ

In the garden that seems an abyss. Butterfly. Nicanor Parra. CP-MertT

In the ghostly virgin forests. G. K. Chesterton. CP-ChesG Fr. Vision of Edens, A.

In the glad spring when leaves were green. From Spring Days to Winter. Oscar Wilde. CP-WildO

In the Glass of Fashion. Howard Nemerov. CP-NemeH

In the glittering collection of paste diamonds one in particular ranks very high. Oh, Stop Being Thankful All over the Place. Ogden Nash. CP-NashO

In the Glorious Epiphanie of Our Lord God. Richard Crashaw. CP-CrasR (Hymn in the Glorious Epiphanie.) CP-CrasR

In the gold mouth of a flower. Another Spring. Denise Levertov. SP-LeveDP

In the Gold Room: A Harmony. Oscar Wilde. CP-WildO

In the golden afternoon, or in. June, 1968. Jorge Luis Borges. SP-BorgJ, tr. by Hoyt Rogers

In the golden noon-shine. Summer-Time and Winter-Time. James Whitcomb Riley. CP-RileJ

In the Golden Triangle Café, I see two waitresses tiptoe and reach for plates and teapots. Ghost Video. Yusef Komunyakaa. CP-KomuY

In the Gonzaga Palace in Mantua. Endless Mirrors, The. James Laughlin. CP-LaugJ

In the Gorge. W. S. Merwin. SP-MerwW

In the Grace of Wit, of Tongue and Face. Sir Walter Ralegh. CP-RaleW

In the grassplot's center was a bed of red roses. Cul de Sac. Josephine Jacobsen. CP-JacoJ

In the Grave No Flower. Edna St. Vincent Millay. CP-MillE

In the graveyard, in the graveyard. English Visitor, The. Stevie Smith. CP-SmitS

In the gray / the griffon bird. Song Sung. Federico García Lorca. CP-GarcF, tr. by Alan S. Trueblood Fr. Songs for Children.

In the great circle, dancing in. Our Children, Coming of Age. Wendell Berry. CP-BerrW

In the great City rear'd, my fancy rude. Hope and Time. Samuel Taylor Coleridge. CP-ColeS

In the Great Hall where Lady Ann by firelight after dining alone. Revolution, The. Donald Hall. CP-HallD

In the Great Metropolis. Arthur Hugh Clough. SP-ClouA
  (In Stratis Viarum I.) SP-ClouA

In the great place the great house is gone from in the sun. Slave Quarters. James Dickey. CP-DickJ

In the great silence of my favorite month. All Hallows' Eve. Czeslaw Milosz. CP-MiloC; CP-MiloCN, tr. by Leonard Nathan

In the great snowfall before the bomb. Lorine Niedecker. CP-NiedL

In the green morning. Ditty of First Desire. Federico García Lorca. CP-GarcF, tr. by Alan S. Trueblood Fr. Love.

In the greenest growth of the Maytime. Interlude, An. Algernon Charles Swinburne. SP-SwinA

In the greenest of our valleys. Haunted Palace, The. Edgar Allan Poe. CP-PoeEd

In the Greenhouse. Eugenio Montale. CP-MontE, tr. by Jonathan Galassi

In the grove / young poplars are dancing. To Irene García. Federico García Lorca. CP-GarcF, tr. by Alan S. Trueblood Fr. Games.

In the gutter / boys who try Up-Beat. Langston Hughes. CP-HughL; CP-HughL3

In the Hall of Mirrors. James Merrill. SP-MerrJ

In the hall of the Hofbräuhaus. At the German Writers Conference in Munich. Rita Dove. SP-DoveR

In the hard brightness of that winter day. Page from a Tale. Wallace Stevens. CP-StevW; CP-StevWP

In the heart of June, love. James Whitcomb Riley. CP-RileJ

In the Heart of the Beast. C. K. Williams. CP-WillC

In the heart of the night. Two Houses, The. Thomas Hardy. CP-HardT

In the heart of the queen anne's lace, a knot of blood. Knot, The. Adrienne Rich. CP-RicAE; SP-RicA2

In the heavy earth the miner. Gourd, The. Paul Laurence Dunbar. CP-DunbP

In the heroic days when Ferdinand. Theologian's Tale: Torquemada, The. Henry Wadsworth Longfellow. SP-LongH Fr. Tales of a Wayside Inn.

In the hetaera Leah's room. Horace in Athens. Constantine P. Cavafy. CP-CavaC, tr. by Theoharis Constantine Theoharis

In the hexameter rises the fountain's silvery column. Ovidian Elegiac Metre, The. Samuel Taylor Coleridge. CP-ColeS

In the heydays of 'forty-five. For George Santayana. Robert Lowell. SP-LoweR

In the hickory scent. Smokehouse, The. Yusef Komunyakaa. CP-KomuY

In the hidden garden. Clarence Major. SP-MajoC

In the high seat, before-dawn dark. Why Log Truck Drivers Rise Earlier Than Students of Zen. Gary Snyder. CP-SnydG

In the Hill at Newgrange. Robinson Jeffers. CP-JefR2

In the hills ahead a pain is moving its light. Late Night in Autumn. W. S. Merwin. SP-MerwW

In the Hills South of Capernaum, Port. Charles Olson. CP-OlsoC

In the Holy Nativity of Our Lord God. Richard Crashaw. CP-CrasR
  (Hymn, The.) CP-CrasR

In the Home Stretch. Robert Frost. CP-FrosR

In the hope of ease to come. Sufferance. Robert Herrick. CP-HerrR

In the Hospital for Tests. Mona Van Duyn. SP-VanDM

In the hospital, in the impartial beauty of sunlight. Périsprit. Olga Broumas. SP-BrouO

In the hospitals and jails. Worst and the Best, The. Charles Bukowski. SP-BukC1

In the hospitals I've been in. Bedpans. Charles Bukowski. SP-BukC1

In the hot high summer I came. Hayden Carruth. CP-CarHS Fr. Bloomingdale Papers, The.

In the hot street at noon I saw him. St. Thomas Didymus. Denise Levertov. SP-LeveDS

In the hot sun and dazzle of grass. Deaf-Mutes at the Ballgame. Josephine Jacobsen. CP-JacoJ

In the hour of extreme. Hymn 3: "In the hour of extreme." A. R. Ammons. CP-AmmoA

In the hour that has no friends. Lark. W. S. Merwin. SP-MerwW

In the house of. Robert Creeley. CP-CreeR

In the House of Suddhoo. Rudyard Kipling. Fr. Plain Tales from the Hills.

In the House of the Dying. Jane Cooper. CP-CoopJ

In the House of the Rising Sun. Gary Snyder. CP-SnydG

In the House of the Soul. Constantine P. Cavafy. CP-CavaC, tr. by Theoharis Constantine Theoharis

In the house / of the vine-grower. Rhenish Winter. Charles Tomlinson. CP-TomlC

In the huge, wide-open, sleeping eye of the mountain. Bear, The. Ted Hughes. SP-HughTN

In the human cities, never again to. Despisals. Muriel Rukeyser. CP-RukeM

In the humans' house. Her Secret. Denise Levertov. SP-LeveDL

In the ice-filled chaos before the end of creation. Beginning, The. Dan Pagis. SP-PagiD

In the Immaculate Conception Church. Nicholas Vachel Lindsay. CP-LindV

In the "immaculately neat" cabin it is calm and warm. Hermit of Hudson Pond, The. Mona Van Duyn. SP-VanDM

IN THE / IN THE QUARTER / IN THE QUARTER OF THE NEGROES. Cultural Exchange ("IN THE / IN THE QUARTER / IN THE QUARTER OF THE NEGROES"). Langston Hughes. CP-HughL; CP-HughL3

In the infinity of white. Juan Ramón Jiménez. Federico García Lorca. CP-GarcF, tr. by Alan S. Trueblood Fr. Three Portraits with Shading.

In the inmost fieriest circle. G. K. Chesterton. CP-ChesG Fr. Vision of Edens, A.

In the Intensity of Final Light. Charles Tomlinson. CP-TomlC

In the irruptive mode. Belligerence. Andrei Codrescu. SP-CodrA

In the Japanese. Grey Sparrow Addresses the Mind's Ear. Denise Levertov. SP-LeveDP

In the Jerusalem Mountains. Yehuda Amichai. SP-AmicYL, tr. by Benjamin Harshav and Barbara Harshav

In the Jewish Cemetery in Prague. On Ethnic Definitions. Eleanor Wilner. SP-WilnE

In the Johannesburg mines. Johannesburg Mines. Langston Hughes. CP-HughL; CP-HughL1

In the jolly winters. Old Man's Nursery Rhyme. James Whitcomb Riley. CP-RileJ

In the July sun they were leading me to the Prado. Garden of Earthly Delights, The. Czeslaw Milosz. CP-MiloC; CP-MiloCN, tr. by Robert Hass

In the Keyfood Market on Broadway. Keyfoods. Audre Lorde. SP-LordA

In the kingdom of Poesy Hafiz waves like a banner. Hafiz. CP-EmerR Fr. Odes.

In the Kingdom of the Past, the Brown-Eyed Man is King. Charles Wright. SP-WrigCN

In the kingdom of the sea. Guardsmen, The. Federico García Lorca. CP-GarcF, tr. by Jerome Rothenberg Fr. Seaside Prints.

In the Kitchen of the Old House. Donald Hall. See In the Old House

In the kitchen of the old house, late. In the Old House. Donald Hall. CP-HallD

In the Labor Camp of Good Intentions. Yusef Komunyakaa. CP-KomuY

In the Laboratory. Dan Pagis. SP-PagiD, tr. by Stephen Mitchell

In the laboratory waiting room. Through a Glass Eye, Lightly. Carolyn Kizer. CP-KizeC

In the Lake District. Joseph Brodsky. CP-BrodJ, tr. by George L. Kline

In the land of the peacocks, the prince thereof. Anecdote of the Prince of Peacocks ("In the land of the peacocks, the prince thereof"). Wallace Stevens. CP-StevWP

In the land of turkeys in turkey weather. Dance of the Macabre Mice. Wallace Stevens. CP-StevW; CP-StevWP

In the Lane. Christina Georgina Rossetti. CP-RosC3

In the last Battle that Arthur fought, the most Beautiful was one. Verse from the Advertisement to Blake's Exhibition of Paintings, 1809. William Blake. CP-BlakW

In the last bus last night that dead musician. Exile of Music. Muriel Rukeyser. CP-RukeM

In the last, far field [half-buried in barberry bushes, red-fruited]. Dead Horse in Field. Robert Penn Warren. CP-WarrR

In the Last Few Moments Came the Old German Cleaning Woman. Jane Cooper. CP-CoopJ

In the last hour of night, a zebra racing dawn. Muriel Rukeyser. CP-RukeM

In the last room in our house. Recognition. Dan Pagis. SP-PagiD, tr. by Stephen Mitchell

In the last sad watches of night. Between Moon and Moon. Robert Graves. CP-GravR

In the last storm, when hawks. Epitaph Ending in And, The. William Stafford. SP-StafWW

In the late day shining cobwebs trailed from my fingers. Autumn Evening. W. S. Merwin. SP-MerwWF

In the late night listening from bed. Thinking for Berky. William Stafford. SP-StafW; SP-StafWW

In the Life of Dust. W. S. Merwin. SP-MerwW

In the Likeness of a Grasshopper. Ted Hughes. SP-HughTN

In the list of one thousand false addresses. Poem: "In the list of one thousand false addresses." Thomas McGrath. SP-McGrT

In the little mountain town of Urbino. Traveling. John Logan. CP-LogaJ

In the little movie. Calder's Hands. John Updike. CP-UpdiJ

In the little woodlets. Chinese Garden. Federico García Lorca. CP-GarcF, tr. by Jerome Rothenberg Fr. Barrage of Firework Poems on the Occasion of the Poet's Birthday.

In the living room Walter Cronkite. Trying to Sleep Late on a Saturday Morning in November. Raymond Carver. CP-CarvR

In the livingroom you are someplace else like a cat. Concerning the Mathematician. Marge Piercy. SP-PierM

In the loam we sleep. Loam. Carl Sandburg. CP-SandC

In the Lobby of the Hotel del Mayo. Raymond Carver. CP-CarvR

In the lodges of the perishable souls. Shakspere. Gerard Manley Hopkins. CP-HopkG

In the lone tent, waiting for victory. Queen Henrietta Maria. Oscar Wilde. CP-WildO

In the long nights our room was closed off and. Yehuda Amichai. SP-AmicY, tr. by Stephen Mitchell Fr. We Loved Here.

In the long shadow of Mr. Clark's woods. Beef. Grace Paley. CP-PalGC

In the long, sleepless watches of the night. Cross of Snow, The. Henry Wadsworth Longfellow. SP-LongH

In the lot through which lovers took a short-cut. Yehuda Amichai. SP-AmicY, tr. by Chana Bloch Fr. Songs of Zion the Beautiful.

In the lower left-hand corner. Imaginary Happening, London, An. Lawrence Ferlinghetti. SP-FerlL

In the Lupanar at Pompeii. James Dickey. CP-DickJ

In the Lyme-Light. G. K. Chesterton. CP-ChesG

In the M5 Restaurant. Ted Hughes. SP-HughTN

In the magic the Homer dusk. Dortmunder. Samuel Beckett. CP-BeckS

In the magnolia's. In the Park. Eugenio Montale. CP-MontE, tr. by Jonathan Galassi

In the Mail. Robert Lowell. SP-LoweR

In the main[e] sea the i[s]le of Cre[e]te doth lie. Virgil. CP-RaleW Fr. Aeneid [or Eneados or Aeneis], The.

In the Marble Quarry. James Dickey. CP-DickJ

In the Marquee. Thomas Hardy. CP-HardT

In the mating of trees. Planting Trees. Wendell Berry. CP-BerrW

In the Matter of One Compass. Rudyard Kipling. CP-KiplR

In the May breeze. Elegy: "In the May breeze." M. Safdar Mir. CP-KizeC, tr. by Carolyn Kizer

In the Meadow. Dorothy Parker. CP-ParkD

In the meadow this afternoon, I fetch. Meadow, The. Raymond Carver. CP-CarvR

In the meadow—what in the meadow? Christina Georgina Rossetti. CP-RosC2

In the Memory of Andrée Rexroth. Kenneth Rexroth. CP-RexrK

In the Men's Room(s). Marge Piercy. SP-PierM

In the metropolis of hooligans. Stare of the Man from the Provinces, The. Howard Nemerov. CP-NemeH

In the middle distance. Tree and the Cloud, The. Donald Hall. CP-HallD

In the middle / of a bite of. C. K. Williams. CP-WillC; SP-WillC

In the middle of life I found myself. Curriculum Vitae. Robert Stock. SP-StocR

In the middle of the long friendship, five. William Meredith. SP-MereW

In the middle of the night. In Childbed. Thomas Hardy. CP-HardT

In the middle of the night. Talking in the Night. Jelaluddin Rumi. SP-Rumi, tr. by Coleman Barks

In the middle of the night you have opened your eyes. Hermes Rising. Sam Hamill. SP-HamiS

In the Middle of the Road. Carlos Drummond de Andrade. CP-BishE, tr. by Elizabeth Bishop

In the [or de] middle of the [or de] winter. Midwinter Blues. Langston Hughes. CP-HughL; CP-HughL1

In the middle of this century we turned to each other. Yehuda Amichai. SP-AmicY, tr. by Stephen Mitchell

In the middle of this century we turned to each other. Yehuda Amichai. SP-AmicYL, tr. by Benjamin Harshav and Barbara Harshav

In the midmost glee of the Christmas. Lewis D. Hayes. James Whitcomb Riley. CP-RileJ

In the midst of a deafening roar, svelte. Passing Glance, A. Charles Baudelaire. CP-BaudC, tr. by Walter Martin

In the midst of the battle I turned. On Reading Omar Khayyam. Nicholas Vachel Lindsay. CP-LindV

In the midst of the poplar that stands by our door. Bluebirds, The. Henry David Thoreau. CP-ThorH

In the midst of things. Louis Zukofsky. CP-ZukLS

In the Midwest of Willa Cather. For Julia in Nebraska. Adrienne Rich. SP-RicA2

In the mind of the kiss occurs a thought so rich. Sonnet: "In the mind of the kiss occurs a thought so rich." Hayden Carruth. CP-CarHS Fr. Sonnets.

In the Mind's Eye. Thomas Hardy. CP-HardT

In the mind's eye. On the Bank Street Pier. Grace Paley. CP-PalGC

In the minister's morning sermon. Minister's Daughter, The. John Greenleaf Whittier. CP-WhitJ

In the Mirror. Yusef Komunyakaa. CP-KomuY

In the Missouri Ozarks. Mona Van Duyn. SP-VanDM

In the mist of the moon I saw you, / O, Nanette. Langston Hughes. CP-HughL; CP-HughL1

In the Month of Athyr. Constantine P. Cavafy. CP-CavaC, tr. by Theoharis Constantine Theoharis

In the month of her death, she is standing by the windowframe. Ein Leben. Dan Pagis. SP-PagiD, tr. by Stephen Mitchell

In the Month of May. Robert Bly. SP-BlyR

In the month of May, when the sun turns, it strikes the house. Honesty. Yannis Ritsos. SP-RitsY, tr. by Kimon Friar

In the month of the long decline of roses. Hendecasyllabics. Algernon Charles Swinburne. SP-SwinA

In the month when the Kamchatka bugbane. Going. James Schuyler. CP-SchuJ

In the moon as Phebus stood over his oriental Gardening. William Blake. CP-BlakW Fr. Island in the Moon, An.

In the Moon / Of Frost in the Tepees. Year of the Sloes, for Ishi, The. Paul Muldoon. CP-MuldP

In the moonlight / I met Berserk. Anecdote of the Prince of Peacocks ("In the moonlight / I met Berserk"). Wallace Stevens. CP-StevW; CP-StevWP

In the moonlight under a shag-bark hickory tree. Shag-Bark Hickory. Carl Sandburg. CP-SandC

In the Morning. Paul Laurence Dunbar. CP-DunbP

In the Morning. Kenneth Koch. SP-KochK

In the morning. Yannis Ritsos. SP-RitsY Fr. So?

In the morning, a Sunday morning, shadows of sea and adumbrants of. Chords. Carl Sandburg. CP-SandC

In the morning eyes of the brown-eyed Susans. Field People. Carl Sandburg. CP-SandC

In the morning I lie partly propped up. Way I Write, The. William Stafford. SP-StafWW

In the morning, I pull on. Getting Dressed. Gregory Orr. SP-OrrG

In the morning I watched her rise. Her Head on the Pillow. Tennessee Williams. CP-WillT

In the morning in the blue snow. Annual Gaiety. Wallace Stevens. CP-StevWP

In the morning, in the morning. A. E. Housman. CP-HousA

In the morning / it shuffles, unhurried. Certain Sharpness in the Morning Air, A. Mary Oliver. SP-OlivM

In the morning it was still night and the lights were on. Yehuda Amichai. SP-AmicY, tr. by Chana Bloch

In the morning the city / Spreads its wings. City. Langston Hughes. CP-HughL

In the morning, / The jack-rabbit sang to the Arkansaw. Jack-Rabbit, The. Wallace Stevens. CP-StevW; CP-StevWP

In the morning / the room is sharp with mirrors. Knife & the Bread, The. Olga Broumas. SP-BrouO

In the morning when I found History. Lesson, The. Billy Collins. SP-CollB

In the morning when ye rise. Another. Robert Herrick. CP-HerrR

In the mornings especially, in the greenhouses. Bell Jar, The. Hans Magnus Enzensberger. SP-EnzeH, tr. by Michael Hamburger

In the Mountain Tent. James Dickey. CP-DickJ

In the Mountains. Robert Penn Warren. CP-WarrR

In the mountains. Guests, The. Louis Zukofsky. CP-ZukLS

In the mountains it's cold. Gary Snyder. CP-SnydG

In the mountains, on the map's edge, where the grass is brash and. Georges Seurat: Factory. Adam Zagajewski. SP-ZagaA, tr. by Clare Cavanagh

In the / mouth—a. Robert Creeley. CP-CreeR

In the multiple encounter. Rainer Maria Rilke. CP-RilkFr, tr. by A. Poulin, Jr. Fr. Orchards.

In the Museum at Teheran. James Laughlin. CP-LaugJ

In the mustardseed sun. Poem on His Birthday. Dylan Thomas. CP-ThomD

In the mytic eastern forest. G. K. Chesterton. CP-ChesG Fr. Vision of Edens, A.

In the Name of the Empress of India, make way. Overland Mail, The. Rudyard Kipling. CP-KiplR

In the Name of Virtue. Alfred Percival Graves. CP-GravR

In the nap there are numerous doors, boudoirs, a talking hall. Six Naps in One Day. Donald Hall. CP-HallD

In the narcotic and act / of omniscience. For Martin. Robert Creeley. CP-CreeR

In the natural year come two thanksgivings. Sabbath of Mutual Respect, The. Marge Piercy. SP-PierM

In the need that bows us thus, / America! America. James Whitcomb Riley. CP-RileJ

IN THE NEGROES OF THE QUARTER. Jazztet Muted. Langston Hughes. CP-HughL; CP-HughL3

In the Neolithic Age. Rudyard Kipling. CP-KiplR

In the net of moon. Capriccio ("In the net of moon"). Federico García Lorca. CP-GarcF, tr. by Jerome Rothenberg Fr. Sublunar Cantos.

In the never, still arriving, I find you. Dwingelo. Gerrit Achterberg. CP-RicAE

In the New Garden. Walt Whitman. CP-WhitW

In the newspaper office—who are the spooks? Palladiums. Carl Sandburg. CP-SandC

In the next chair in the barber- / shop this morning the director. Ars Gratia Artis. James Laughlin. CP-LaugJ

In the next life. C. K. Williams. CP-WillC; SP-WillC

In the night. Stephen Crane. CP-CranS

In the Night. Carolyn Kizer. CP-KizeC

In the Night. James Whitcomb Riley. CP-RileJ

In the Night. Stevie Smith. CP-SmitS

In the Night. Philip Whalen. SP-WhalP

In the Night Desert. William Stafford. SP-StafW; SP-StafWW

In the Night Fields. W. S. Merwin. SP-MerwW

In the night fouled the nets. Shark Meat. Gary Snyder. CP-SnydG

In the night, my Lord Jesus. Terror. Constantine P. Cavafy. CP-CavaC, tr. by Theoharis Constantine Theoharis

In the Night She Came. Thomas Hardy. CP-HardT

In the Night the Sound Woke Us. Muriel Rukeyser. CP-RukeM

In the night the white skin. Boil. John Updike. CP-UpdiJ

In the night, when the sea-winds take the city in their arms. Night Movement—New York. Carl Sandburg. CP-SandC

In the night's dream of day. Vron Woods (North Wales), The. Denise Levertov. SP-LeveDL

In the night's rising cool. Late August. William Corbett. SP-CorbW

In the nighttime of fair autumn weather. By an Open Window. Constantine P. Cavafy. CP-CavaC, tr. by Theoharis Constantine Theoharis

In the North. Adrienne Rich. CP-RicAE

In the northern hemisphere. Kangaroo. D. H. Lawrence. CP-LawrD

In the oblivion of cards. Solitaire under the Oaks. Wallace Stevens. CP-StevWP

In the Old Age of the Soul. Ezra Pound. CP-PoEar

In the old brownstone on W. 35th. Reading of Rex Stout, A. Mona Van Duyn. SP-VanDM

In the Old City. Yehuda Amichai. SP-AmicY, tr. by Chana Bloch

In the Old City. Yehuda Amichai. SP-AmicYL, tr. by Benjamin Harshav and Barbara Harshav

In the Old Country, then, two ladies and two boys. Mona Van Duyn. SP-VanDM

In the old days (a custom laid aside). Abraham Davenport. John Greenleaf Whittier. CP-WhitJ

In the old days autumn would clang a gong. Bronze Sounding, The. Ivor Gurney. SP-GurnI

In the old days either the plaintiff or the defendant won or lost. Poem: "In the old days either the plaintiff or the defendant won or lost." Alan Dugan. CP-DugaA

In the old days with married women's stockings. Libertine, The. Louis MacNeice. CP-MacNL

In the old deep sing-song of the sea. Old Deep Sing-Song. Carl Sandburg. CP-SandC

In the Old Garden. Yannis Ritsos. SP-RitsY, tr. by N. C. Germanacos

In the old Hebrew myth the lion's frame. Hive at Gettysburg, The. John Greenleaf Whittier. CP-WhitJ

In the Old House. Donald Hall. CP-HallD

(In the Kitchen of the Old House.) CP-HallD

In the old master's landscape. Landscape. Wisława Szymborska. SP-SzymW, tr. by Stanislaw Barańczak and Clare Cavanagh

In the Old Neighborhood. Rita Dove. SP-DoveR

In the old neighborhood, each funeral parlor. Teach Us to Number Our Days. Rita Dove. SP-DoveR

In the old paintings, the ones with silken oils. Trümmerfrauen. Eleanor Wilner. SP-WilnE

In the old photograph. Journalist, The. Ai. SP-Ai

In the old, scratched, cheap wood of the typing stand. Dreamwood. Adrienne Rich. SP-RicA1

In the old Scripture I have often read. Lip Labour. Robert Herrick. CP-HerrR

In the "Old South." John Greenleaf Whittier. CP-WhitJ

In the Old Theatre, Fiesole. Thomas Hardy. CP-HardT

In the old time when September's stubble gleamed. Ivor Gurney. SP-GurnI

In the old wars drum of hoofs and the beat of shod feet. Wars. Carl Sandburg. CP-SandC

In the one state of ours that is a shire. To the Right Person. Robert Frost. CP-FrosR

In The Orchard. Algernon Charles Swinburne. SP-SwinA

In the Orchard-Days, when you. Robins' Other Name, The. James Whitcomb Riley. CP-RileJ

In the orchidaceous light of evening. Hope. Robert Penn Warren. CP-WarrR

In the Oregon Country. William Stafford. SP-StafW; SP-StafWW

In the other 'eighties, a hundred midsummers gone. Derek Walcott. CP-WalcD Fr. Midsummer.

In the outskirts of the village. Sycamores, The. John Greenleaf Whittier. CP-WhitJ

In the palace of Heaven God's holy angels were touching and fondling one another. Jesus and Isolt. Robert Pinsky. CP-PinsR

In the pallid afternoons. In Autumn. "Rubén Dario." SP-DariR, tr. by Alberto Acereda and Will Derusha

In the pantry the dear dense cheeses, Cheddars and harsh. O Cheese. Donald Hall. CP-HallD

In the Parc de Saint-Cloud, birds sang. Cruel. Adam Zagajewski. SP-ZagaA, tr.

by Renata Gorczynski, Benjamin Ivry and C. K. Williams

In the parched path. Old Lizard, The. Federico García Lorca. SP-GarcF, tr. by Lysander Kemp

In the Park. Maxine W. Kumin. SP-KumiM

In the Park. Eugenio Montale. CP-MontE, tr. by Jonathan Galassi

In the Park. Stevie Smith. CP-SmitS

In the Park at Caserta. Eugenio Montale. CP-MontE, tr. by Jonathan Galassi

In the Pass. W. S. Merwin. SP-MerwWF

In the past, we had faith in invisible. Adam Zagajewski. SP-ZagaA, tr. by Renata Gorczynski

In the pathway of the sun. Penelope. Dorothy Parker. CP-ParkD

In the Pea Patch. Maxine W. Kumin. SP-KumiM

In the Person of a Lady To Her Inconstant Servant. Thomas Carew. CP-CareT

In the Person of Womankind [A Song Apologetic]. Ben Jonson. CP-JonsB

In the photograph of my grandfather Kunat when he was six. My Grandfather Sigismund Kunat. Czeslaw Milosz. CP-MiloCN, tr. by Robert Hass

In the picture soldiers. 1937. Lorine Niedecker. CP-NiedL

In the place called Swords on the Irish road. Song of Swords, A. G. K. Chesterton. CP-ChesG

In the place of the west. Coming of Quetzalcoatl, The. D. H. Lawrence. CP-LawrD

In the place that is my own place, whose earth. Sycamore, The. Wendell Berry. CP-BerrW

In the place where I never was. Place Where I Never Was, The. Yehuda Amichai. SP-AmicYL, tr. by Benjamin Harshav and Barbara Harshav

In the planetarium of an apple tree. From Adam's Diary. John Ciardi. CP-CiarJ

In the play Amy didn't want to be. First Grade. William Stafford. SP-StafW; SP-StafWW

In the pleasant orchard-closes. Lost Bower, The. Elizabeth Barrett Browning. CP-BroEB

In the Pocket. James Dickey. CP-DickJ

In the poem. Probity. George Oppen. CP-OppGN

In the poem's opening words. Evaluation of an Unwritten Poem. Wisława Szymborska. SP-SzymW, tr. by Stanislaw Barańczak and Clare Cavanagh

In the pond in the park. Water Picture. May Swenson. SP-SwenM

In the Port. Constantine P. Cavafy. CP-CavaC, tr. by Theoharis Constantine Theoharis

In the prebirth of the evening. Cherry Blossoms at Evening. William Carlos Williams. CP-WilW2

In the premortuary tomb. Time Beneath, The. Laura Riding Jackson. CP-RidiL

In the Pride of His Youth. Rudyard Kipling. Fr. Plain Tales from the Hills.

In the prologue to her Alexiad. Anna Komnina. Constantine P. Cavafy. CP-CavaC, tr. by Theoharis Constantine Theoharis

In the Public Garden. Marianne Craig Moore. CP-MoorM

In the purple light, heavy with redwood, the slopes drop seaward. Apology for Bad Dreams. Robinson Jeffers. CP-JefR1

IN THE QUARTER OF THE NEGROES / BELGIUM SHADOW[S] LEOPOLD. Shades of Pigmeat. Langston Hughes. CP-HughL; CP-HughL3

In the Quarter of the Negroes / Where the doors are doors of paper. Cultural Exchange ("In the Quarter of the Negroes / Where the doors are doors of paper"). Langston Hughes. CP-HughL3

IN THE QUARTER OF THE NEGROES / WHERE THE PALMS AND COCONUTS. Gospel Cha-Cha. Langston Hughes. CP-HughL; CP-HughL3

IN THE QUARTER OF THE NEGROES / WHERE TO SNOW NOW ACCLIMATED. Ode to Dinah. Langston Hughes. CP-HughL; CP-HughL3

In the quick fresh season. Song for a Season. Marya Alexandrovna Zaturenska. SP-ZatuM

In the quiet spaces between equinoctial gales. Just before Fall. James Schuyler. CP-SchuJ

In the quiet waters. Fafnir and the Knights. Stevie Smith. CP-SmitS

In the Rain. "H. D." CP-DoolH

In the Rain. Eugenio Montale. CP-MontE, tr. by Jonathan Galassi

In the Rain. Yannis Ritsos. SP-RitsY, tr. by Kostas Myrsiades

In the Rain and the Sun. Thomas Merton. CP-MertT

In the rain- / darkness, the sunset. E. E. Cummings. CP-CummE

In the rain, the lonesome. Banner Bearer, The. William Carlos Williams. CP-WilW2

In the rain, the naked old father is dancing, he will get wet. Natural History. Robert Penn Warren. CP-WarrR

In the ranks of the Austrian you found him. Forced Recruit, The. Elizabeth Barrett Browning. CP-BroEB

In the reading room in the New York Public Library. Reading Room, The New York Public Library. Richard Eberhart. CP-EberR

In the Realm of the Ignition. James Tate. SP-TateJ

In the rectory garden on his evening walk. Dialogue between Ghost and Priest. Sylvia Plath. CP-PlatS

In the Red Mountains. W. S. Merwin. SP-MerwWF

In the reptile-car, past. Paul Celan. SP-CelaP, tr. by John Felstiner

In the Rich Farmer's Field. John Ciardi. CP-CiarJ

In the Rif Mountains. William Meredith. SP-MereW

In the right angle between a dead man and his mourner I'll start. Yehuda Amichai. SP-AmicY *Fr.* In a Right Angle: A Cycle of Quatrains.

In the Ringwood. Thomas Kinsella. CP-KinsT

In the riprap, / in the cool caves. Mussels. Mary Oliver. SP-OlivM

In the Romanesque church round stones. Moment. Adam Zagajewski. SP-ZagaA, *tr. by* Clare Cavanagh

In the Room. Yehuda Amichai. SP-AmicYL, *tr. by* Benjamin Harshav *and* Barbara Harshav

In the room, our old room, barred with moonlight. Summer Night, A. Randall Jarrell. CP-JarrR

In the Root Cellar. Maxine W. Kumin. SP-KumiM

In the rose garden in the park. Another Year. William Carlos Williams. CP-WilW2

In the Round. James Schuyler. CP-SchuJ

In the Round. Theodore Weiss. SP-WeisT

In the Round Tower at Jhansi, June 8, 1857. Christina Georgina Rossetti. CP-RosC1

In the royal decree that Alexios Komninos. Anna Dalassini. Constantine P. Cavafy. CP-CavaC, *tr. by* Theoharis Constantine Theoharis

In the Salzkammergut. James Laughlin. CP-LaugJ

In the, same in (when qualm?) thick wee poetry, putrid Victi. Catullus. *See* Same can be said of you, Victius, The

In the same place, when Nature wore. H.A. and A.S. Emily Jane Brontë. CP-BronE

In the Same Space. Constantine P. Cavafy. CP-CavaC, *tr. by* Theoharis Constantine Theoharis

In the sands of prayer my father saw angels' traces. Yehuda Amichai. SP-AmicY *Fr.* In a Right Angle: A Cycle of Quatrains.

In the Sap. George Meredith. CP-MerG2

In the 'Sconset Bus. William Carlos Williams. CP-WilW1

In the sea, Biscayne, there prinks. Homunculus et La Belle Etoile. Wallace Stevens. CP-StevW; CP-StevWP

In the sea rocks, / in the stone pockets. Starfish. Mary Oliver. SP-OlivM

In the sealed cars of freight trains. Still. Wisława Szymborska. SP-SzymWM, *tr. by* Joanna Trzeciak

In the season of late August star-fall. Amazing Grace in the Back Country. Robert Penn Warren. CP-WarrR

In the secret heart all men are free. Secret Heart, The. Richard Eberhart. CP-EberR

In the semi-darkness white buildings loom, not fully. Sunrise Over Cassis. Adam Zagajewski. SP-ZagaA, *tr. by* Clare Cavanagh

In the separate histories. Pretty Blue Apron. James McMichael. SP-McMiJ

In the Servants' Quarters. Thomas Hardy. CP-HardT

In the Seven Woods. William Butler Yeats. CP-YeatW

In the Seventies. Thomas Hardy. CP-HardT

In the shabby train no seat is vacant. Refugees, The. Randall Jarrell. CP-JarrR

In the shade. City Garden in April, A. May Swenson. SP-SwenM

In the Shadow of the Palace. Carl Sandburg. CP-SandC

In the shadow of the second world. Legend for a Little Child. Kenneth Patchen. CP-PatcK

In the shadows at the clearing's. Gregory Orr. SP-OrrG

In the shaft graves, butterflies. Mycenae. Donald Hall. CP-HallD

In the Shenandoah Valley, one rider gray and one rider blue, and the sun. Shenandoah. Carl Sandburg. CP-SandC

In the shimmering countries that exude the summer. Manuscript Found in a Book of Joseph Conrad. Jorge Luis Borges. SP-BorgJ, *tr. by* Alastair Reid

In the shock of mighty armies. Hymn: "In the shock of mighty armies." Jones Very. CP-VeryJ

In the shows of the round Ox. Song: In the Shows of the Round Ox. Thomas Merton. CP-MertT

In the Shreve High football stadium. Autumn Begins in Martins Ferry, Ohio. James Wright. CP-WrigJ

In the shut drawer, even now, they rave and grieve. Packet of Letters. Louise Bogan. CP-BogaL

In the silence of flowers is found a sacred love. Flower of the Fruit, The. Alfonso Cortes. CP-MertT

In the silence of my heart. Communion. Paul Laurence Dunbar. CP-DunbP

In the silence of the garret. Old Things. Tennessee Williams. CP-WillT

In the silence that prolongs the span. Black Jackets. Thom Gunn. CP-GunnT

In the silent hour of even. Water Spirit's Song, The. Christina Georgina Rossetti. CP-RosC3

In the Skagit Valley, cherries. February Awakening. John Logan. CP-LogaJ

In the sky above the quarry, scored at dawn. Punta del Mesco. Eugenio Montale. CP-MontE, *tr. by* Jonathan Galassi

In the sky of men the bread of stars seemed to me shadowy and hardened. Fighters. René Char. CP-MertT

In the skylight it's Sunday. Reading Rorty and Paul Celan One Morning in Early June. Charles Wright. SP-WrigCN

In the slaughterhouse of love, they kill. Jelaluddin Rumi. SP-Rumi, *tr. by* Coleman Barks

In the Sleep of Reason. Thomas McGrath. SP-McGrT

In the slow world of dream. Memory. Theodore Roethke. CP-RoetT

In the slump between rounds he looks. Glimpse of Main Event. Heather McHugh. SP-McHuH

In the Slums of Glasgow. Hugh MacDiarmid. SP-MacDH

In the small beauty of the forest. Psalm: "In the small beauty of the forest." George Oppen. CP-OppGN

In the small bright square. Man and Woman in Camera and Out. A. K. Ramanujan. CP-RamaA

In the Small Hours. Thomas Hardy. CP-HardT

In the small territory and time. Sandpipers. Howard Nemerov. CP-NemeH

In the Smoking-Car. Richard Wilbur. CP-WilbR

In the Snow. James Laughlin. CP-LaugJ

In the snow light. Snow Light, The. May Sarton. SP-SartM

In the solemn days of old, The. Calef in Boston. John Greenleaf Whittier. CP-WhitJ

In the Sound of Mull. William Wordsworth. CP-WorW2

In the South. James Whitcomb Riley. CP-RileJ

In the Spirit There Are No Accidents. Fanny Howe.
　"Constant X, The." SP-HoweF
　"First disappointment, The." SP-HoweF
　"God is already ahead and waiting: the future is full." SP-HoweF
　"I feel the city grow wild with desire fertile." SP-HoweF
　"Indivisible heavens, The." SP-HoweF
　"It was a night to be left alone." SP-HoweF
　"Sister Poverty, welcome to my cloister." SP-HoweF
　"Some patios won't allow the shadow of a maid." SP-HoweF
　"Son the One who was also called Sun." SP-HoweF

In the spring of the year, in the spring of the year. Spring and the Fall, The. Edna St. Vincent Millay. CP-MillE

In the spring thaw. Winter Roads. Thomas McGrath. SP-McGrT

In the springs of your eyes. Praise of Distance. Paul Celan. SP-CelaP, *tr. by* John Felstiner

In the square room. Hands of the Blindman, The. Tess Gallagher. SP-GallT

In the staring darkness. Gerard Manley Hopkins. CP-HopkG

In the steep street where the sea hangs over the houses. In the Lyme-Light. G. K. Chesterton. CP-ChesG

In the stilled place that once was a road going down. Sowing. Wendell Berry. CP-BerrW

In the Stopping Train. Donald Davie. CP-DaviDC

In the story of Patroclus. Triumph of Achilles, The. Louise Glück. SP-GlucL

In the Street. Constantine P. Cavafy. CP-CavaC, *tr. by* Theoharis Constantine Theoharis

In the Street. Thomas Hardy. CP-HardT

In the street, a long-tailed horse. Martyrdom of Saint Eulalia, The. Federico García Lorca. SP-GarcF, *tr. by* A. L. Lloyd

In the street outside a school. Bees, The. Audre Lorde. SP-LordA

In the street, stars collide. Muse of Midnight. Gregory Orr. SP-OrrG

In the street two children sharpen. East Bronx. David Ignatow. SP-IgnaD

In the streets of the city: there is my love. Allegiance. René Char. CP-MertT

In the Studio. Charles Tomlinson. CP-TomlC

In the stupors before sleep. It Is for the Waking Man to Tell His Dreams. John Ciardi. CP-CiarJ

In the Style of Filippo De Pisis, on Sending Him This Book. Eugenio Montale. CP-MontE, *tr. by* Jonathan Galassi

In the suburbs, in the town. Motto to "New England Reformers." Ralph Waldo Emerson. CP-EmerR

In the suburbs of the ganglia. Provocation of the Dream, The. Marge Piercy. SP-PierM

In the summer I live so. Winter Saint. A. R. Ammons. CP-AmmoA

In the summer, in a big park among the trees, I saw. Changes, Mistakes, Loves. Yehuda Amichai. SP-AmicYL, *tr. by* Benjamin Harshav *and* Barbara Harshav

In the summer, nations come to one another. Yehuda Amichai. SP-AmicYL *Fr.* Poems of the Land of Zion and Jerusalem.

In the summer, when the Archduke dies. Sarajevo. Howard Nemerov. CP-NemeH

In the summer whole peoples visit one another. Yehuda Amichai. SP-AmicY, *tr. by* Chana Bloch *Fr.* Songs of Zion the Beautiful.

In the Sun. Wallace Stevens. CP-StevWP

In the sun-drenched. City of Salt, The. Gregory Orr. SP-OrrG

In the sun, while there, below, over the bay. Gathering Apricots. Czeslaw Milosz. CP-MiloCN, *tr. by* Robert Hass

In the sunbaked path. Old Lizard, The. Federico García Lorca. CP-GarcF, *tr. by* Catherine Brown

In the Supermarket. Andrei Codrescu. SP-CodrA

In the sweet shire of Cardigan. Simon Lee, the Old Huntsman; with an incident in which he was concerned. William Wordsworth. CP-WorW1; MW-WorW

In the sweet solitude of this calm place. Pedro Calderón de la Barca. CP-ShelP *Fr.* Magico Prodigioso.

In the sylvan section of the old zoo. Fanny Howe. SP-HoweF *Fr.* Robeson Street.

In the tall grass, a mauve rose. Rainer Maria Rilke. CP-RilkFr, *tr.* by A. Poulin, Jr. *Fr.* Valaisian Quatrains, The.

In the Tank. Thom Gunn. CP-GunnT

In the technician's thicket. Laboratory, The. Randall Jarrell. CP-JarrR

In the Tents of Akbar. Paul Laurence Dunbar. CP-DunbP

In the theatre / The actors play the rituals of their parts. Furies, The. Stephen Spender. CP-SpenS

In the theosophy of light. Suchness. Kenneth Rexroth. CP-RexrK

In the thick of a teeming snowfall. Afterflakes. Robert Frost. CP-FrosR

In the thin classroom, where your face. Elegy in the Classroom. Anne Sexton. CP-SextA

In the thin cold town where I was born, I hauled and groaned. Paperboys, The. John Logan. CP-LogaJ

In the third-class seat sat the journeying boy. Midnight on the Great Western. Thomas Hardy. CP-HardT

In the thirtieth year of life. James Vincent Cunningham. CP-CunnJ

In the time of early love. George Meredith. CP-MerG2

In the Time of False Messiahs. Norman Dubie. CP-DubiN

In the Time of the Blossoms. W. S. Merwin. SP-MerwW

In the time of the scorpion we first came. Chorale for the Seasons. Marya Alexandrovna Zaturenska. SP-ZatuM

In the top and front of a bus, eager to meet his fate. Figure of Eight. Louis MacNeice. CP-MacNL

In the town where I was born. Eagle Rock. Alice Walker. CP-WalkA

In the town where the hero was born you may. Pietà. Wisława Szymborska. SP-SzymW, *tr.* by Stanisław Barańczak *and* Clare Cavanagh

In the town's graveyard the oldest plot now frees itself. Meadow, The. Wendell Berry. CP-BerrW

In the trailer next to this one. Louise. Raymond Carver. CP-CarvR

In the Train. James Laughlin. CP-LaugJ

In the transcendence. Lorine Niedecker. CP-NiedL

In the Tree House at Night. James Dickey. CP-DickJ

In the trees, in the crowns of the trees, under rich. Adam Zagajewski. SP-ZagaA, *tr.* by Renata Gorczynski

In the Trenches with Robert Graves. Raymond Carver. CP-CarvR

In the trough of the emergency. Ballad Written in a Hospital. Eugenio Montale. CP-MontE, *tr.* by Jonathan Galassi

In the tunnel of woods, as the road. Last Things. William Meredith. SP-MereW

In the turbulent beauty. South Wind. Ralph Waldo Emerson. CP-EmerR

In the Turret. Herman Melville. SP-MelvH

In the turret's great glass dome, the apparition, death. Siegfried. Randall Jarrell. CP-JarrR

In the twenties, I would visit Dachau often with my brother. Audabe of the Singer and Saboteur, Marie Triste. Norman Dubie. CP-DubiN

In the Underworld. Muriel Rukeyser. CP-RukeM

In the unreason of a rainy midnight. Night Train, The. Thomas Merton. CP-MertT

In the usual iconography of the temple or the local Wok. Shoveling Snow with Buddha. Billy Collins. SP-CollB

In the Valley of Cauteretz. Alfred Tennyson. CP-TennA

In the Valley of the Elwy. Gerard Manley Hopkins. CP-HopkG

In the Valley of the Magra. Charles Wright. SP-WrigCN

In the Valley of Waters. Lord Byron. CP-Byron

In the Vanities. Theatrical Reflection. Ogden Nash. CP-NashO

In the Vaulted Way. Thomas Hardy. CP-HardT

In the Vestry. Robert Graves. CP-GravR

In the victim's room. Fatigue of Objects, The. Thomas McGrath. SP-McGrT

In the village it must be a clear night with the light of a red. Everlastings, The. Norman Dubie. CP-DubiN

In the village of the dead. First Shaman Song. Gary Snyder. CP-SnydG *Fr.* Myths and Texts.

In the Waiting Room. Elizabeth Bishop. CP-BishE

In the Wake of Home. Adrienne Rich. SP-RicA1; SP-RicA2

In the walled off swimming-pool the water is perfectly flat. Pleasure Seas. Elizabeth Bishop. CP-BishE

In the war where many men fell. Horses and Prisoners. James Dickey. CP-DickJ

In the Ward. Charles Tomlinson. CP-TomlC

In the Ward: The Sacred Wood. Randall Jarrell. CP-JarrR

In the warm classroom, they give off heat. His Students. William Meredith. SP-MereW

In the way that the most of the wind. Wind and Tree. Paul Muldoon. CP-MuldP

In the way you went you were important. Memorial: Son Bret, A. William

Stafford. SP-StafW; SP-StafWW

In the weed of summer comes this green sprout why. Questions Are Remarks. Wallace Stevens. CP-StevW; CP-StevWP

In the well-fed cage-sound of diesels. Them, Crying. James Dickey. CP-DickJ

In the Welsh town of Laugharne across the way from the Brown. Elegy for Dylan Thomas. John Logan. CP-LogaJ

In the West of the country where I was. Ballad of the Sixties. May Sarton. SP-SartM

In the Wet. Marge Piercy. SP-PierM

In the white egg. Yannis Ritsos. SP-RitsY *Fr.* Second Series.

In the White Giant's Thigh. Dylan Thomas. CP-ThomD

In the white morning, where is the enchanted room of the night before? Married in June. D. H. Lawrence. CP-LawrD

In the white painted dark lobby. Awakening, The. Ivor Gurney. SP-GurnI

In the white pasture of the sun. Fruit. Gabriela Mistral. SP-MistG, *tr.* by Maria Giachetti [*or* Jacketti]

In the White Sky. William Stafford. SP-StafW

In the wild October night-time, when the wind raved round the land. Night of Trafalgar, The. Thomas Hardy. CP-HardT *Fr.* Dynasts, The.

In the Wilderness. Robert Graves. CP-GravR

In the Willow Shade. Christina Georgina Rossetti. CP-RosC2

In the willows along the river at Pleasure Bay. At Pleasure Bay. Robert Pinsky. CP-PinsR

In the Wind My Rescue Is. A. R. Ammons. CP-AmmoA

In the windbreaker's pocket you find. Vaporetto. Adam Zagajewski. SP-ZagaA, *tr.* by Constantine P. Cavafy

In the Wineshop of Chinling. Li Po. CP-WilW2

In the Wineshops. Constantine P. Cavafy. CP-CavaC, *tr.* by Theoharis Constantine Theoharis

In the Winter of My Thirty-eighth Year. W. S. Merwin. SP-MerwW

In the winter walking on my. Trapped. Charles Bukowski. SP-BukC1

In the wood of Wallow. Ass, The. Stevie Smith. CP-SmitS

In the Woods. Federico García Lorca. CP-GarcF, *tr.* by Jerome Rothenberg *Fr.* Newton.

In the Woods. David Ignatow. SP-IgnaD

In the Woods. George Meredith. CP-MerG2

In the Woods. Adrienne Rich. CP-RicAE; SP-RicA1; SP-RicA2

In the woods as I did walk. Stranger, The. Walter De la Mare. CP-DeLaW

In the woods as the trees fade in the dusk. Hope, The. David Ignatow. SP-IgnaD

In the woods I came on an old friend fishing. Finding a Teacher. W. S. Merwin. SP-MerwW

In the Woods of Rydal. William Wordsworth. CP-WorW2

In the world are millions and millions of men, and each man. Angel and Stone. Howard Nemerov. CP-NemeH

In the world of mules. Mules, The. Ogden Nash. CP-NashO

In the Yard. May Swenson. SP-SwenM

In the yard, by the house of boxes. Stalag Luft. Randall Jarrell. CP-JarrR

In the year 1945 an Original Child was born. Original Child Bomb. Thomas Merton. CP-MertT

In the Year of Many Conversions and the Private Soul. John Ciardi. CP-CiarJ

In The Year of Pompey's First Consulate, Cinna. Carmen 113. Catullus. CP-ZukLS *Fr.* Carmina.

In the year since Jesus died for men. Siege of Corinth, The. Lord Byron. CP-Byron

In the Year 200 B.C. Constantine P. Cavafy. CP-CavaC, *tr.* by Theoharis Constantine Theoharis

In the Year 2020. Raymond Carver. CP-CarvR

In the years to come they will say. Falling Leaves and Early Snow. Kenneth Rexroth. CP-RexrK

In the yellow church he saw himself. Harps. Clarence Major. SP-MajoC

In the yellow light, an old man. "Between the Clock and the Bed." Donald Hall. CP-HallD

In the yellow mists of morning. G. K. Chesterton. CP-ChesG *Fr.* Vision of Edens, A.

In the yellow / tower. Graphic of the Petenera. Federico García Lorca. CP-GarcF, *tr.* by Cola Franzen, Christopher Maurer *and* Robert Nasatir

In the Yukon the other day. Foundlings in the Yukon. A. K. Ramanujan. CP-RamaA

In the zero of the night, in the lipping hour. Approach to Thebes, The. Stanley Kunitz. CP-KunSC

In the Zoo. A. K. Ramanujan. CP-RamaA

In thee, I fondly hoped to clasp. To D———. Lord Byron. CP-Byron

In their aged, ruined bodies. Old Men's Souls, The. Constantine P. Cavafy. CP-CavaC, *tr.* by Theoharis Constantine Theoharis

In their congealed light. Through Binoculars. Charles Tomlinson. CP-TomlC

In their conventicles. Elect, The. Donald Davie. CP-DaviDC

In their deepest caverns of limestone. Threshold, The. Rudyard Kipling. CP-KiplR

In their faint photographs. Jean Rhys. Derek Walcott. CP-WalcD

In their own way, by their own lights. Meditations for a Savage Child. Adrienne Rich. SP-RicA2

In them days / they won't hardly no way to know if. First Carolina Said-Song. A. R. Ammons. CP-AmmoA

In Themclam Virginem. Gerard Manley Hopkins. CP-HopkG

In There. C. K. Williams. CP-WillC

In these Danish paintings. Air and Light, The. William Corbett. SP-CorbW

In these dark rooms, where I go. Windows, The. Constantine P. Cavafy. CP-CavaC, *tr.* by Theoharis Constantine Theoharis

In these days when we are living on the rim of a crater. Listen to the Linotype. Ogden Nash. CP-NashO

IN these deep solitudes and awful cells. Eloisa to Abelard. Alexander Pope. CP-PopeA

In These Dissenting Times. Alice Walker. CP-WalkA

In These Fair Vales Hath Many a Tree. William Wordsworth. CP-WorW2

In these gay thoughts the Loves and Graces shine. Epistle to Miss Blount, with the Works of Voiture. Alexander Pope. CP-PopeA

In these hands, the cities; in my weather, the armies. Have You Killed Your Man for Today? Kenneth Patchen. CP-PatcK

In these hills even the oil rigs. Huleikat—The Third Poem about Dicky. Yehuda Amichai. SP-AmicY, *tr.* by Chana Bloch

In these low hills, lives that were meant to endure. Kibbutz Gevaram. Yehuda Amichai. SP-AmicY, *tr.* by Chana Bloch

In these red London labyrinths. Browning Resolves to Be a Poet. Jorge Luis Borges. SP-BorgJ, *tr.* by Alastair Reid

In these sad hours, a prey to ceaseless pain. R.S.S. Written in a Fit of Illness. William Cowper. CP-CowpW

In these stern times of ours, when crimson strife. Prologue: "In these stern times of ours, when crimson strife." Thomas Hardy. CP-HardT *Fr.* Dynasts, The.

In these two seperate rooms we sit. June. Thom Gunn. CP-GunnT

In things a moderation keep[e]. Moderation. Robert Herrick. CP-HerrR

In This Age of Hard Trying, Nonchalance Is Good and. Marianne Craig Moore. CP-MoorM

In this artfully carved sepulcher. Tomb of Evrion. Constantine P. Cavafy. CP-CavaC, *tr.* by Theoharis Constantine Theoharis

In this attractive desolation. Towards Tucson. James Vincent Cunningham. CP-CunnJ

In this beloved marble view. On the Bust of Helen by Canova. Lord Byron. CP-Byron

In This Beloved Marble View. Lord Byron. *See* On the Bust of Helen by Canova

In this book the pretty pictures. Inscribed in a Copy of "The Ballad of the White Horse" G. K. Chesterton. CP-ChesG

In this café Durruti. Midget, The. Philip Levine. SP-LeviP

In this camera shot. Blue Bug. Marianne Craig Moore. CP-MoorM

In this country of grapes. Mediterranean, The. Charles Tomlinson. CP-TomlC; SP-TomlC

In this country there is neither measure nor balance. Two Campers in Cloud Country. Sylvia Plath. CP-PlatS

In this dark-grained news photograph, whose glare. Che. Derek Walcott. CP-WalcD

In this day and age Lord. Loss. C. K. Williams. CP-WillC; SP-WillC

In This Dream. Grace Paley. CP-PalGC

In this dream I do not exist. This I know since it is my dream. David Ignatow. SP-IgnaD

In this dream that dogs me I am part. Traumerai. Philip Larkin. CP-LarkP

In this dream the typewriter. In This Dream. Grace Paley. CP-PalGC

In this dry, stubble field. Excavation, The. Gregory Orr. SP-OrrG

In this evening room there is no stir, no fuss. Evening Indoors. Louis MacNeice. CP-MacNL

In this fair niche above the unslumbering sea. Singer Asleep, A. Thomas Hardy. CP-HardT

In this fairly temperate clime. Man Bites Dog-Days. Ogden Nash. CP-NashO

In this field / Where the small animals ran from a brush fire. Brush Fire. James Wright. CP-WrigJ

In this foolish world, there is nothing more numerous. Very Funny, Very Funny. Ogden Nash. CP-NashO

In this great city now the haunt. True Story, A. Christina Georgina Rossetti. CP-RosC3

In this her thirty-seventh year, the Italy. Margaret Fuller, 1847. Amy Clampitt. CP-ClamA

In this hopeless & wasting love of mine. Carmen 91. Catullus. CP-ZukLS *Fr.* Carmina.

In this image of my friend's studio. Chariot. Stanley Kunitz. CP-KunSC

In this land, Rilke's country if you will. At Muzot. May Sarton. SP-SartM

In this life of neglect, is there anything desired. Rainer Maria Rilke. CP-RilkFr

In this little Urn[e] is laid. Upon Prue [or Prew], His Maid. Robert Herrick. CP-HerrR

In this little vault she lyes. Upon a Wife That Dyed Mad with Jealousie. Robert Herrick. CP-HerrR

In this long room, upon each western pane. Colophon. Adrienne Rich. CP-RicAE

In this long routine "Push Hands." Annals of *Tai Chi*: "Push Hands." William Stafford. SP-StafWW

In this mimic form of a matron in years. Denner's Old Woman. Vincent Bourne. CP-CowpW

In this misfortune Kings doe most excell. Bad Wages for Good Service. Robert Herrick. CP-HerrR

In this moist season. Mushrooms. Margaret Atwood. SP-AtwM2

In this motel where I was told to wait. Human Condition, The. Howard Nemerov. CP-NemeH

In this motionless sun, no leaf now moves, the stream. Heat Wave Breaks. Robert Penn Warren. CP-WarrR

In this museum is a replica of "Little Boy" and "Fat Man." Los Alamos Museum, The. Arthur Sze. SP-SzeA

In this my green world. What There Is. Kenneth Patchen. CP-PatcK

In this, my last poem about my father. Cherish the Ladies. Paul Muldoon. CP-MuldP

In this new shade of Death, the show. Spheral Change. Dante Gabriel Rossetti. CW-RossD

In this obscene photograph covertly. So. Constantine P. Cavafy. CP-CavaC, *tr.* by Theoharis Constantine Theoharis

In this old garden, fair, I walk to-day. In a English Garden. Paul Laurence Dunbar. CP-DunbP

In this one sheet, how much for thought profound. Newspaper, The. Jones Very. CP-VeryJ

In this place of helmets and tar. On Being Asked to Leave a Place of Honor for One of Comfort, Preferably in the Northern Suburbs. Alice Walker. CP-WalkA

In this place of shafts, I hope. Emily Dickinson. SP-DickE

In this place the light makes us despair. This pitiless month. Summer in the City. Yannis Ritsos. SP-RitsY, *tr.* by Kimon Friar

In this pond of placid water. Pond, The. Edna St. Vincent Millay. CP-MillE

In this roadstead I have ridden. Departure, The. Henry David Thoreau. CP-ThorH

In this short Life. Emily Dickinson. CP-DickE

In this silvery now of living alone. Living Alone (1). Denise Levertov. SP-LeveDL; SP-LeveDS

In this single world. Fellow Soul, Sound Hunting to Thy Immeasurable Heart. Kenneth Patchen. CP-PatcK

In this small shell. This Cryptic Bone. Tennessee Williams. CP-WillT

In this sombre garden close. Monk's Walk, The. Paul Laurence Dunbar. CP-DunbP

In this sour world, o summerwind. Ralph Waldo Emerson. CP-EmerR

In this squalid, dirty dooryard. Pear Tree, The. Edna St. Vincent Millay. CP-MillE

In this still place, remote from men. Glen-Almain; or, the Narrow Glen. William Wordsworth. CP-WorW1; MW-WorW

In this strange land, this uncouth clime. Epistle to Hugh Parker. Robert Burns. CP-BurnR

In this stucco house there is nothing but air. Night Watch. Rita Dove. SP-DoveR

In this summer month, two separate men were lost. Woods, The. Josephine Jacobsen. CP-JacoJ

In this suspense of ours before the fall. Annunciation. May Sarton. SP-SartM

In this, the City of my Discontent. Springfield Magical. Nicholas Vachel Lindsay. CP-LindV

In this town the shops are all the same. Trouble with the Times, The. Thomas McGrath. SP-McGrT

In this unyielding, even. Stone Walls: at Chew Magna. Charles Tomlinson. CP-TomlC

In this valley, where many waters. Yehuda Amichai. SP-AmicYL, *tr.* by Benjamin Harshav *and* Barbara Harshav

In this village is a house. Han-shan. CP-ColdM, *tr.* by Red Pine

In this woman the earth speaks. Earth and Fire. Wendell Berry. CP-BerrW

In This World. Wendell Berry. CP-BerrW

In this world of. Spouts. William Carlos Williams. CP-WilW1

In this world, (the *Isle of Dreames*). White Island. Robert Herrick. CP-HerrR

In this yard, barnyard / I dig with a shovel. Digging. Margaret Atwood. SP-AtwM1

In those cold regions which no summers cheer. Prologue to His Royal Highness. John Dryden. CP-DryJ2

In Those Days. Randall Jarrell. CP-JarrR

In those days, in a place where dentists thrive. In the Lake District. Joseph Brodsky. CP-BrodJ, *tr.* by George L. Kline

In Those Days, in This Time. Yehuda Amichai. SP-AmicYL, *tr.* by Benjamin Harshav *and* Barbara Harshav

In those days the oatfields. Stacking the Straw. Amy Clampitt. CP-ClamA

In those days we were going places. But that Sunday. Union Street: San

Francisco, Summer 1975. Raymond Carver. CP-CarvR
In those days when we were. Your Eyes. James Laughlin. CP-LaugJ
In those far years of inertia. Aleksandr Aleksandrovich Blok. SP-BlokA *Fr.* Retribution.
In those first years I came down. Frog Pond, The. Galway Kinnell. SP-KinnGN
In those reaches of the night when your thoughts. Mein Kampf. William Stafford. SP-StafWW
In Three Days. Robert Browning. CP-BroR1
In thy holiday of life. Hafiz. CP-EmerR *Fr.* Odes.
In thy long Paradise of Light. Emily Dickinson. CP-DickE
In thy western halls of gold. Ode to Apollo. John Keats. CP-KeatJ
In Tilbury Town did Old King Cole. Old King Cole. Edwin Arlington Robinson. CP-RobiE
In Time. Robert Graves. CP-GravR
In time a timeless act. Good Friday. Helen Pinkerton. CP-PinkH
In time all undertakings are made good. In Time. Robert Graves. CP-GravR
In time and measure perfect moves. Dupont's Round Fight. Herman Melville. SP-MelvH
In Time Like Air. May Sarton. SP-SartM
In time like lenses, magnified and calm. Saipan. John Ciardi. CP-CiarJ
In Time of Absence. Robert Graves. CP-GravR
In Time of Carnival. Adrienne Rich. CP-RicAE
In Time of Cloudburst. Robert Frost. CP-FrosR
In time of daffodils(who know. E. E. Cummings. CP-CummE
In time of life, I grac't ye with my Verse. To Flowers. Robert Herrick. CP-HerrR
In Time of Plague. Thom Gunn. CP-GunnT
In Time of Silver Rain. Langston Hughes. CP-HughL; CP-HughL2
In Time of "The Breaking of Nations." Thomas Hardy. CP-HardT
In Time of Wars and Tumults. Thomas Hardy. CP-HardT
In time, these people all will know each other. Reflexion of a Novelist. Howard Nemerov. CP-NemeH
In time's a noble mercy of proportion. E. E. Cummings. CP-CummE
In Time's concatenation and. Mortmain. Robert Penn Warren. CP-WarrR
In times of old, when time was young. Vanbrug's House. Jonathan Swift. CP-SwifJ
In times of peace and good government. Free Variation on a Translation from Greek. Alan Dugan. CP-DugaA
In times of stormy weather. Strange Hurt. Langston Hughes. CP-HughL; CP-HughL2
In Times When Nothing Stood. Philip Larkin. CP-LarkP
In to thir dirk and drublie day[i]s. William Dunbar. CP-DunbW
In Tobey Woods. Hayden Carruth. CP-CarHS
In today's mail a poem. Sparks. Denise Levertov. SP-LeveDP
In tombs of gold and lapis lazuli. Oil and Blood. William Butler Yeats. CP-YeatW
In touching gently like a golden finger. Visible and Invisible. Helen Pinkerton. CP-PinkH
In Town. Wallace Stevens. CP-StevWP
In trance and dream of old, God's prophet saw. Garibaldi. John Greenleaf Whittier. CP-WhitJ
In Trance At A Distance. Robert Graves. CP-GravR
In Transformation of an Imago. Robert Stock. SP-StocR
In Transit. W. H. Auden. CP-AudeW
In trees still dripping night some nameless birds. Morning in a New Land. Mary Oliver. SP-OlivM
In Trouble and Shame. D. H. Lawrence. CP-LawrD
In Truth and Honour's name—AMEN. Libel Summons. Robert Burns. CP-BurnR
In truth your fair eyes, my lady. Sonnet 5: "In truth your fair eyes, my lady." John Milton. CP-CowpW; CP-MiltJ
In 200 miles. Speed. May Swenson. SP-SwenM
In twos and threes, they have not far to roam. Six o'clock in Princes Street. Wilfred Owen. CP-OwenW
In Uganda an Early King. Alice Walker. CP-WalkA
In Umbria: A Snapshot. Amy Clampitt. CP-ClamA
In Upperville, the upper crust. Upon Learning That a Town Exists in Virginia Called Upperville. John Updike. CP-UpdiJ
In using there are always two. Song of the Fucked Duck. Marge Piercy. SP-PierM
In Utrumque Paratus. Matthew Arnold. SP-ArnoM
In Vain. Walter De la Mare. CP-DeLaW
In vain anigh the windows high. Absent Friends. G. K. Chesterton. CP-ChesG
In vain did Time and Nature toil to throw. Fragment: "In vain did Time and Nature." William Wordsworth. CP-WorW1
In vain do we reach for wind-blown cobwebs. Cry of the Spectres, The. Jaroslav Seifert. SP-SeifJ, *tr. by* Ewald Osers
In vain have I striven. Praise of Ysolt. Ezra Pound. CP-PoEar
In vain have I striven. Vana. Ezra Pound. CP-PoEar
In vain I see the morning rise. Poet's Delay, The. Henry David Thoreau. CP-

ThorH
In Vain, Mine Eyes. Sir Philip Sidney. SP-SidnP *Fr.* Arcadia.
In vain, mine eyes, you labour to amend. In Vain, Mine Eyes. Sir Philip Sidney. SP-SidnP *Fr.* Arcadia.
In vain our labours are, whatsoe're they be. Gods Blessing. Robert Herrick. CP-HerrR
In vain to live from age to age. Lines Written for Miss Patty More. William Cowper. CP-CowpW
In vain to me the smiling [*or* smileing] Mornings shine. Sonnet [on the Death of Mr. Richard West]. Thomas Gray. CP-GrayT
In vain would Prudence, with decorous sneer. Passion's Cry. Robert Burns. CP-BurnR
In vain ye woo me to your harmless joys. Love Faithful in the Absence of the Beloved. Jeanne Marie Bouvier de la Motte- Guyon. CP-CowpW
In vain you boast poetic names of yore. Impromptu to Lady Winchelsea. Alexander Pope. CP-PopeA
In vaine I seeke and sew to her for grace. Sonnet 20. Edmund Spenser. CP-Spens *Fr.* Amoretti.
In valleys green and still. A. E. Housman. CP-HousA
In vaulted place where shadows flit. In a Church of Padua. Herman Melville. SP-MelvH
In Verdi Square. Charles Tomlinson. CP-TomlC
In vestibules the doormen. Lament for Doormen. Charles Tomlinson. CP-TomlC
In vice most vicius he excellis. William Dunbar. CP-DunbW
In Vienna there are ten little girls. Little Viennese Waltz. Federico García Lorca. CP-GarcF, *tr. by* Greg Simon *and* Steven F. White
In view of the fading animals. They Are Hostile Nations. Margaret Atwood. SP-AtwM1
In vinum solui cupis Aufilena quod haurit. In Barnum. Thomas Campion. CP-CampT
In Vision I Roamed. Thomas Hardy. CP-HardT
In visions of the dark night. Dream, A. Edgar Allan Poe. CP-PoeEd
In Waking. Robert Duncan. SP-DuncR
In Walden wood the chickadee. Ralph Waldo Emerson. CP-EmerR
In Wales at Laugharne at last I stand beside. Belated Palinode for Dylan Thomas. Lawrence Ferlinghetti. SP-FerlL
In Walked Bud with a Palette. Clarence Major. SP-MajoC
In walks the Emperor, dressed as Mars. Tale, A. Joseph Brodsky. CP-BrodJ
In Warm Rooms, Before a Blue Light. Maxine W. Kumin. SP-KumiM
In Warsaw. Czeslaw Milosz. CP-MiloC; CP-MiloCN, *tr. by* Robert Hass *and* Madeline Levine
In water-heavy nights behind grandmother's porch. Adolescence—I. Rita Dove. SP-DoveR
In wayes to greatnesse, think on this. Ambition. Robert Herrick. CP-HerrR
In weariness and painfulness St. Paul. Christina Georgina Rossetti. CP-RosC2
In Weatherbury Stocks. Thomas Hardy. CP-HardT
In western fields of corn and northern timber lands. Jungheimer's. Carl Sandburg. CP-SandC
In westerns the man who saddles up at night. Pity and Fear. Miller Williams. CP-WillM
In Westminster's royal halls. Curse of the Charter-Breakers, The. John Greenleaf Whittier. CP-WhitJ
In wet green midspring, midnight and the wind. Mrs. Walpurga. Muriel Rukeyser. CP-RukeM
In what at least. 18 West 11th Street. James Merrill. SP-MerrJ
In what hat, from what epoch. Anka. Czeslaw Milosz. CP-MiloC; CP-MiloCN, *tr. by* Robert Hass
In what torn[e] ship soever I embark[e]. Hymn[e] to Christ, at the Author's Last Going into Germany, A. John Donne. CP-DonnJ; MW-DonnJ
In Which Roosevelt Is Compared to Saul. Nicholas Vachel Lindsay. CP-LindV
In Which the Poet Is Ashamed but Pleased. Ogden Nash. CP-NashO
In white plaster, a neighing fellow. Houynhnm's Holiday. Robert Stock. SP-StocR
In whiteout, with its. World at Large, The. James McMichael. SP-McMiJ
In Whom We Live and Move and Have Our Being. Denise Levertov. SP-LeveDS
In whomsoe'er, since Poesy began. On Burns. Dante Gabriel Rossetti. CW-RossD
In whose heart it / burns. Epigon. Charles Olson. CP-OlsoC
In wild October when the low hills lie. Two States of Prayer. Thomas Merton. CP-MertT
In wilful riches I have found poverty. Sir Thomas Wyatt. CP-WyatT
In wingbar light. Making. A. R. Ammons. CP-AmmoA
In winter a crow flew at my head. Admonitor: A Pearl for Arrogance. Alan Dugan. CP-DugaA
In winter in Diamantina. Helena Morley. Donald Davie. CP-DaviDC
In Winter in my Room. Emily Dickinson. CP-DickE
In winter, in the dark hours, when others. How These Words Happened. William Stafford. SP-StafW; SP-StafWW

In winter in the woods alone. Robert Frost. CP-FrosR

In winter it darkens the moment lunch is over. Eclogue 4: Winter. Joseph Brodsky. CP-BrodJ, *tr.* by Joseph Brodsky

In winter the beach is empty. Georgia Beach. Margaret Atwood. SP-AtwM2

In winter the house, which sits on rock. Gesture, The. Josephine Jacobsen. CP-JacoJ

In winter two kinds of fields on the hills. Prosser. Raymond Carver. CP-CarvR

In Winter, we'll travel in a small pink coach. Winter Dream. Arthur Rimbaud. CP-RimbA, *tr.* by Martin Sorrell

In Winter Woods. Charles Tomlinson. CP-TomlC

In Wiro language. Charles Olson. CP-OlsoC

In Wiry Winter. James Schuyler. CP-SchuJ

In Wisconsin or Texas or Alabama some boys are playing war, and the two sides are the North and the South. Note for a Fantastic Story. Jorge Luis Borges. SP-BorgJ, *tr.* by Stephen Kessler

In wood and wild, ye warbling throng. On the Death of Echo, a Lap-Dog. Robert Burns. CP-BurnR

In woods where many rivers run. Lawrence Ferlinghetti. SP-FerlL

In Worcester, Massachusetts. In the Waiting Room. Elizabeth Bishop. CP-BishE

In world, world / of terror. Whisper, The. Denise Levertov. SP-LeveDP

In Xanadu did Kubla Khan. Kubla Khan: or, A Vision in a Dream. Samuel Taylor Coleridge. CP-ColeS; MW-ColeS

In years defaced and lost. Spot, A. Thomas Hardy. CP-HardT

In you flowers and greenery. Guido Cavalcanti. CP-CavaG, *tr.* by Marc Cirigliano

In Your Body All Bodies Lie. Kenneth Patchen. CP-PatcK

In your empty pocket an ancient coin, forgotten. Hints. Yannis Ritsos. SP-RitsY, *tr.* by Kimon Friar

In your eyes, the serpent. Federico García Lorca. CP-GarcF, *tr.* by Christopher Maurer

In your first book of poems, printed. Silent Man, The. Carolyn Kizer. CP-KizeC

In your garden the damned. Sphinx Hour, The. Federico García Lorca. CP-GarcF, *tr.* by Jerome Rothenberg *Fr.* In the Forest of Clocks.

In your ghost, Dick King, in your phantom vowels I read. Dick King. Thomas Kinsella. CP-KinsT

In your hands you must. I'd Like to Be Putty. James Laughlin. CP-LaugJ

In your honor, a man presents a sea bass. Arthur Sze. SP-SzeA

In your indignation what mercy appears. Epigram, An: "In your indignation what mercy appears." Jonathan Swift. CP-SwifJ

In your light I learn how to love. Jelaluddin Rumi. SP-Rumi, *tr.* by Coleman Barks

In your minds you jump from doors. Writer's Prologue to a Play in Verse. William Carlos Williams. CP-WilW2

In your next letter I wish you'd say. Letter to N.Y. Elizabeth Bishop. CP-BishE

In Your Own Words Without Lying Tell Something of Your Background With Particular Attention to Anything Relating to the Position For Which You Are Applying. Press Down. Miller Williams. CP-WillM

In your sleep you talked. Fever. Norman Dubie. CP-DubiN

In your time, there have been those who spoke clearly. Muriel Rukeyser. CP-RukeM

In youth, before I waxed old. Epigrams. Edmund Spenser. CP-Spens *Fr.* Amoretti.

In youth from rock to rock I went. To the Daisy ("In youth from rock to rock I went"). William Wordsworth. CP-WorW1; MW-WorW

In youth he wrought, with eyes ablur. Wife-Blessed, The. James Whitcomb Riley. CP-RileJ

In youth I thought I could live without pleasure as the stones live their. Pleasures. Robinson Jeffers. CP-JefR3

In youth, it was a way I had. Indian Summer. Dorothy Parker. CP-ParkD

In youth we dream of death. Hardy Perennial. Richard Eberhart. CP-EberR

In Zululand the huts are round. Zulus Live in Land without a Square. John Updike. CP-UpdiJ

Inadequate Orderly Simplification, The. But the Three Natural Units. And Only Arbitrary Constants. Charles Olson. CP-OlsoC

INAMORATAS, with an approbation. Sundays of Satin-Legs Smith, The. Gwendolyn Brooks. SP-BrooG

Inapprehensiveness. Robert Browning. CP-BroR2

Inaudible consonant inaudible vowel. Silent Journal. Charles Wright. SP-WrigC

Inauguration Day: January 1953. Robert Lowell. SP-LoweR

Inauspiciously. Ambrose Bierce. SP-BierA

Incalculably old. Crystal, The. Robert Graves. CP-GravR

Incantata. Paul Muldoon. CP-MuldP

Incantation. Walter De la Mare. CP-DeLaW

Incantation. Czeslaw Milosz. CP-MiloC; CP-MiloCN; CP-PinsR, *tr.* by Robert Pinsky

Incantation. Eugenio Montale. CP-MontE, *tr.* by Jonathan Galassi

Incantation. May Swenson. SP-SwenM

Incarcerate me in yourself. Emily Dickinson. SP-DickE

Incarnate Devil. Dylan Thomas. CP-ThomD

Incarnated. Czeslaw Milosz. CP-MiloCN, *tr.* by Robert Hass

Incarnation. Kenneth Rexroth. CP-RexrK

Incarnation, The. Jones Very. CP-VeryJ

Incarnations. Laura Riding Jackson. CP-RidiL

Inca's Daughter, The. Walt Whitman. CP-WhitW

Incense. Peter Blue Cloud. SP-BlueP

Incense. Nicholas Vachel Lindsay. CP-LindV

Incense. Kenneth Rexroth. CP-RexrK

Incense. Yannis Ritsos. SP-RitsY, *tr.* by Edmund Keeley

Incense and splendor haunt me as I go. Johnny Appleseed Speaks of Great Cities in the Future. Nicholas Vachel Lindsay. CP-LindV

Incense Bearers, The. Ivor Gurney. SP-GurnI

Incense of the Lucky Virgin. Robert Earl Hayden. CP-HaydR

Incense under Horse Heaven Hills. Northwest Passage. Allen Ginsberg. CP-GinsA

Incertus. Seamus Heaney. SP-HeanSO

Incessantly a restive devil frets. Ruin. Charles Baudelaire. CP-BaudC, *tr.* by Walter Martin

Inches. C. K. Williams. CP-WillC

Inchiquin Lake, Penobscot Bay. Richard Eberhart. CP-EberR

Incidence of Flight. Richard Eberhart. CP-EberR

Incident. John Ciardi. CP-CiarJ

Incident. Countee Cullen. CP-CullC

Incident. William Stafford. SP-StafWW

Incident, An. Arthur Hugh Clough. SP-ClouA

Incident, An. Louis Zukofsky. CP-ZukLS

Incident at Bruges. William Wordsworth. MW-WorW *Fr.* Memorials of a Tour of the Continent; 1820.

Incident Characteristic of a Favourite Dog. William Wordsworth. CP-WorW1

Incident in the Life of a Prophet, An. Thomas McGrath. SP-McGrT

Incident of May. Hayden Carruth. CP-CarHS

Incident of the French Camp. Robert Browning. CP-BroR1

Incident on a Journey. Thom Gunn. CP-GunnT

Incidents of love, The. Emily Dickinson. CP-DickE

Incipience. Adrienne Rich. SP-RicA2

Incipient Madness. William Wordsworth. CP-WorW1

Incipit Thomas Campianus Medicinae Doctor. In Peragrantissimi, Itinerosissimi, Montiscandentissimique Peditis, Thomae Coryati, viginti-hebdomadarium Diarium, sex pedibus gradiens, partim vero claudicans, Encomiasticon. Thomas Campion. CP-CampT

Inclusiveness. Dante Gabriel Rossetti. CW-RossD *Fr.* House of Life, The.

Incognito. William Carlos Williams. CP-WilW2

Incoherent rushing of the train, The. Way-Station. Archibald MacLeish. CP-MacLA

Incommunicado. Sylvia Plath. CP-PlatS

Incomparable Harriot, loveliest fair. To Miss H—— with Some Music. Christopher Smart. SP-SmarC

Incomparable Light, The. Richard Eberhart. CP-EberR

Incomplete Latin Version of "In all things beautiful" by Robert Bridges. Robert Bridges. CP-HopkG

Inconceivably solemn! Emily Dickinson. CP-DickE

Inconsistent, The. Thomas Hardy. CP-HardT

Incorporeal Ruler. Adam Zagajewski. SP-ZagaA, *tr.* by Renata Gorczynski, Benjamin Ivry *and* C. K. Williams

Incorrigible Dirigible, The. Hayden Carruth. CP-CarHS

Incredible Activities in the Eyrie. Robert Stock. SP-StocR

Incredible never surprises us, The. Emily Dickinson. SP-DickE

Incredible the Lodging. Emily Dickinson. SP-DickE

Incredibly worn, the cafeteria of the fur workers and the. Amalgamated, The. George Oppen. CP-OppGN

Increment. A. R. Ammons. CP-AmmoA

Incunabula, 1958. Charles Olson. CP-OlsoC

Incurable. Ambrose Bierce. SP-BierA

Incurable. Dorothy Parker. CP-ParkD

Indecent Assumption, the Slaughter Songs, The. Andrei Codrescu. SP-CodrA

Indecision. Helen Pinkerton. CP-PinkH

Indeed my Fidelia now you are mounted. Epigram to Fidelia. Annis Boudinot Stockton. CP-StocA

"Indeed," said the proconsul, closing the book, "this." Rest I Will Tell to Those Below in Hades, The. Constantine P. Cavafy. CP-CavaC, *tr.* by Theoharis Constantine Theoharis

Indefinable idol's invisible to the mind, The. Image. A. R. Ammons. CP-AmmoA

Indelicate is he who loathes. Epidermal Macabre. Theodore Roethke. CP-RoetT

Independence. Henry David Thoreau. CP-ThorH

Independence Day. Wendell Berry. CP-BerrW

Independence Day. Allen Ginsberg. CP-GinsA

Indestructible Girl spun on a wheel, The. Carney Elegy. Josephine Jacobsen. CP-JacoJ

Index, a Mountain. Carolyn Kizer. CP-KizeC

Indian, The. Randall Jarrell. CP-JarrR

Indian calls! Grant him a place of rest, The. Indian's Petition, The. Jones Very. CP-VeryJ

Indian Cave Jerry Ramsey Found, The. William Stafford. SP-StafWW

Indian Caves in the Dry Country. William Stafford. SP-StafW; SP-StafWW

Indian Emperor, The. John Dryden.
 (Song.) SP-DrydJ

Indian Image. Constantine P. Cavafy. CP-CavaC, *tr. by* Theoharis Constantine Theoharis

Indian king Arjuna, humane and mild, The. Eternity. Constantine P. Cavafy. CP-CavaC, *tr. by* Theoharis Constantine Theoharis

Indian Market in Mexico, An. Randall Jarrell. CP-JarrR

Indian Pipe. Richard Eberhart. CP-EberR

Indian Princess, The. Pet Deer, The. James Tate. SP-TateJ

Indian Relics. Jones Very. CP-VeryJ

Indian Remains. Jones Very. CP-VeryJ

Indian River. Wallace Stevens. CP-StevW; CP-StevWP

Indian saw the butterfly, The. Cahokia. Carl Sandburg. CP-SandC

Indian Serenade. Eugenio Montale. CP-MontE, *tr. by* Jonathan Galassi

Indian Serenade, The. Percy Bysshe Shelley. CP-ShelP

Indian Summer. Emily Dickinson. CP-DickE

Indian Summer. Norman Dubie. CP-DubiN

Indian Summer. Gregory Orr. SP-OrrG

Indian Summer. Dorothy Parker. CP-ParkD

Indian Summer 2. Charles Wright. SP-WrigCN

Indian Summer at Land's End. Stanley Kunitz. CP-KunSC

Indian Summer Day on the Prairie, An. Nicholas Vachel Lindsay. CP-LindV

Indian Summer in Princeton. Yehuda Amichai. SP-AmicYL, *tr. by* Benjamin Harshav *and* Barbara Harshav

Indian summer is Jewish summer. Indian Summer in Princeton. Yehuda Amichai. SP-AmicYL, *tr. by* Benjamin Harshav *and* Barbara Harshav

Indian-summer-sun / With crimson feathers whips away the mists. October-November. Hart Crane. CP-CranH

Indian to His Love, The. William Butler Yeats. CP-YeatW

Indian trinity and my son an Etchimin. Charles Olson. CP-OlsoC

Indian Undertaker, The. James Tate. SP-TateJ

Indian upon God, The [*or* An]. William Butler Yeats. CP-YeatW

Indian Village. Louis MacNeice. CP-MacNL

Indiana. James Whitcomb Riley. CP-RileJ

Indianapolis. John Updike. CP-UpdiJ

Indians, Robert Creeley. CP-CreeR

Indians' Belief in a Future State, The. Jones Very. CP-VeryJ

Indians on Alcatraz, The. Paul Muldoon. CP-MuldP

Indian's Petition, The. Jones Very. CP-VeryJ

Indian's Retort, The. Jones Very. CP-VeryJ

Indians were born, The. Quechuan Song. Gabriela Mistral. SP-MistG, *tr. by* Maria Giachetti [*or* Jacketti]

Indications. Yannis Ritsos. SP-RitsY, *tr. by* Kimon Friar *and* Kostas Myrsiades

Indifference. Edna St. Vincent Millay. CP-MillE

Indifference of the Heavens, The. Samuel Taylor Coleridge. CP-ColeS

Indifferent rivers, The. Almanac. Primo Levi. CP-LeviP, *tr. by* Ruth Feldman

Indifferent, The. John Donne. CP-DonnJ; MW-DonnJ

Indifferent to the indifference that conceived her. In Praise of Cities. Thom Gunn. CP-GunnT

Indigestion of the Vampire, The. W. S. Merwin. SP-MerwW

Indignant at the fumbling wits, the obscure spite. Paudeen. William Butler Yeats. CP-YeatW

Indignant Bard composed this furious ode, The. Devonshire Road, A. Samuel Taylor Coleridge. CP-ColeS

Indignation of a High-Minded Spaniard 1810. William Wordsworth. CP-WorW1

Indigo Bunting, The. Robert Bly. SP-BlyR

Indigo Glass in the Grass, The. Wallace Stevens. CP-StevWP

Indigo, mottle of purple and amber, ink. Littoral. Louis MacNeice. CP-MacNL

Indiscriminately. Yannis Ritsos. SP-RitsY, *tr. by* N. C. Germanacos

Inditing a Good Matter. Donald Davie. CP-DaviDC

Individual spider web, An. Identity. A. R. Ammons. CP-AmmoA

Individualist Speaks, The. Louis MacNeice. CP-MacNL

Individualist, The. Ogden Nash. CP-NashO

Indivisible heavens, The. Fanny Howe. SP-HoweF *Fr.* In the Spirit There Are No Accidents.

Indo-European vision said clouds, The. When One Age Goes with It Suddenly Its Errors Evaporate. Charles Olson. CP-OlsoC

Indolent youth, / Drawn by everything in turn. From the French (1). Stevie Smith. CP-SmitS

Indomitably must. Little Air 2. Stéphane Mallarmé. CP-MallS, *tr. by* Henry Weinfield

Indonesia. Mary Oliver. SP-OlivM

Indoor Sports. Louis MacNeice. CP-MacNL

Indoor winter white begonia fibril. White Begonia. Louis Zukofsky. CP-ZukLS

Indoors the tang of a tiny oil lamp. Outdoors. House on a Cliff. Louis MacNeice. CP-MacNL

Indra, perhaps, is the god to invoke. Killing the Grubs. Eleanor Wilner. SP-WilnE

Indulge no more may we. End of the Episode, The. Thomas Hardy. CP-HardT

Indulgent muse! my grov'ling mind inspire. To a Lady on Her Coming to North-America with Her Son, for the Recovery of Her Health. Phillis Wheatley. CP-WheaP

Indulgent, or candid, or uncommon reader. Conversation with the Devil, A. Randall Jarrell. CP-JarrR

Industrial Archaeology. James Schuyler. CP-SchuJ

Industrious / mineral resources, domestic. Paul Celan. SP-CelaP, *tr. by* John Felstiner

Ineffable, The. Richard Eberhart. CP-EberR

Inelligible this / world. Everything doubled. Paul Celan. SP-CelaP, *tr. by* John Felstiner

Inert and in the twilight . . . Peace is not hers. Bored to Choresis. Allen Tate. CP-TateA

Inert in his chair. Drugged. Walter De la Mare. CP-DeLaW

Inert Perfection. Edna St. Vincent Millay. CP-MillE

Inertia. Yannis Ritsos. SP-RitsY, *tr. by* Kostas Myrsiades

Inevitable Frontier. Robert Penn Warren. CP-WarrR

Inevitables. Yannis Ritsos. SP-RitsY, *tr. by* Andonis Decavalles

Inevitably. Yannis Ritsos. SP-RitsY, *tr. by* N. C. Germanacos

Inexhaustible, delicate, as if. Lair. Robert Pinsky. CP-PinsR

Inexhaustible, The. Yannis Ritsos. SP-RitsY *Fr.* Wavering Scales, The.

Infancy. Carlos Drummond de Andrade. CP-BishE, *tr. by* Elizabeth Bishop

Infancy and Age. George Meredith. CP-MerG2

Infant. Stevie Smith. CP-SmitS

Infant M— M—, The. William Wordsworth. CP-WorW2

Infant Sorrow. William Blake. CP-BlakW *Fr.* Songs of Experience.

Infanta Marina. Wallace Stevens. CP-StevW; CP-StevWP

Infantile Language, The. James Laughlin. CP-LaugJ

Infatuate Britons, will you still proclaim. Lines Written on 29 May / The Anniversary of the Restoration of Charles the 2nd. John Keats. CP-KeatJ

Infelice. Stevie Smith. CP-SmitS

Inference. Miller Williams. CP-WillM

Inference of Mexico, An. Robert Earl Hayden. CP-HaydR

Inferential. Edwin Arlington Robinson. CP-RobiE

Inferential Knowledge, The. Emily Dickinson. SP-DickE

Infernale. Wallace Stevens. CP-StevWP

Inferno 5, 129. Jorge Luis Borges. SP-BorgJ, *tr. by* Alan S. Trueblood

Inferno: Canto 1. Dante Alighieri. *Fr.* Divina Commedia.

Inferno in a bacteria could be covered up, The. Letter to Ezra Pound. Andrei Codrescu. SP-CodrA

Inferno of God is not in need of, The. Of Heaven and Hell. Jorge Luis Borges. SP-BorgJ, *tr. by* Alastair Reid

Infinite a sudden Guest, The. Emily Dickinson. CP-DickE

"Infinite Beauty"—of which you speak, The. Emily Dickinson. SP-DickE

Infinite Horses, The. Silvina Ocampo. CP-WilW2

Infinite jukethrob smoke & swallow to dis. E. E. Cummings. CP-CummE

Infinite Portugal, June eleventh, nineteen hundred and fifteen. Salutation to Walt Whitman. Fernando Pessoa. SP-PessF, *tr. by* Susan M. Brown *and* Edwin Honig

Infinite Reason, The. Archibald MacLeish. CP-MacLA

Infinitely at ease. Rainer Maria Rilke. CP-RilkFr, *tr. by* A. Poulin, Jr. *Fr.* Roses, The.

Infinite's being so wide, The. Triple Bronze. Robert Frost. CP-FrosR

Infinitive. Joseph Brodsky. CP-BrodJ

Infirmity. Theodore Roethke. CP-RoetT

Inflation. Heather McHugh. SP-McHuH

Inflections of joy. The inflections of, The. Bonfire. Tess Gallagher. SP-GallT

Influence of Channing, The. Jones Very. CP-VeryJ

Influence of Natural Objects [in Calling Forth and Strengthening the Imagination in Boyhood and Early Youth]. William Wordsworth. CP-WorW1 *Fr.* Prelude, The; Growth of a Poet's Mind [1850 vers.].

Influence of Puritanism. Jones Very. CP-VeryJ

Influence of the Night on Faith and Imagination, The. Jones Very. CP-VeryJ

Influential Writers. William Stafford. SP-StafWW

Information. David Ignatow. SP-IgnaD

Information. Dan Pagis. SP-PagiD, *tr. by* Stephen Mitchell

Informative Object, An. William Carlos Williams. CP-WilW2

Infralapsarian. Ambrose Bierce. SP-BierA

Infrequently, dreams are heavenly. David Dancing. Donald Davie. CP-DaviDC

Infusion Room, The. Jane Cooper. CP-CoopJ

Ingathering. Carolyn Kizer. CP-KizeC

Ingenium Nobis Ipsa Puella Facit. James Laughlin. CP-LaugJ

Ingenuities of Debt, The. Robert Frost. CP-FrosR

Ingenuity too astonishing, An. Sun Underfoot Among the Sundews, The. Amy Clampitt. CP-ClamA

Ingrateful[l] Beauty Threatened. Thomas Carew. CP-CareT

Inheritance. Charles Simic. SP-SimiC; SP-SimiCE

Inheritance, The. D. H. Lawrence. CP-LawrD

Inheritance, The. Thomas McGrath. SP-McGrT

Inheritances. Marilyn Hacker. SP-HackM

Inherited Estate, The. Thom Gunn. CP-GunnT

Inheriting the Earth: Quail. William Stafford. SP-StafWW

Inheritor. Czeslaw Milosz. CP-MiloCN, tr. by Robert Hass

Inheritors. Tennessee Williams. CP-WillT

Inhuman man! curse on thy barb'rous art. On Seeing a Wounded Hare Limp by Me, Which a Fellow Had Just Shot At. Robert Burns. CP-BurnR

Iniquity of the Fathers upon the Children, The. Christina Georgina Rossetti. CP-RosC1

Inishbofin on a Sunday morning. Seeing Things. Seamus Heaney. SP-HeanSO

Initial. Pablo Neruda. SP-NeruP

Initial, Dæmonic, and Celestial Love. Ralph Waldo Emerson. CP-EmerR

Initials on Aspens. Yusef Komunyakaa. CP-KomuY

Initiate, The. W. S. Merwin. SP-MerwW

Initiation. Czeslaw Milosz. CP-MiloC; CP-MiloCN, tr. by Robert Hass

Initiation, The. James Tate. SP-TateJ

Initiation Degrees. D. H. Lawrence. CP-LawrD

Initium. Federico García Lorca. CP-GarcF, tr. by Jerome Rothenberg Fr. Mirror Suite.

Injian Ocean sets an' smiles, The. For to Admire. Rudyard Kipling. CP-KiplR

Injudicious Gardening. Marianne Craig Moore. CP-MoorM

Injure yourself, you injure me. Injuries. Robert Graves. CP-GravR

Injured? Unenviable? Comforters, The. George Oppen. CP-OppGN

Injuries. Robert Graves. CP-GravR

Injury, The. William Carlos Williams. CP-WilW2

Ink, fire, quintuple mirrors. Personal Devil, The. Robert Pinsky. CP-PinsR

Ink-Sack. Robinson Jeffers. CP-JefR3

Inked-in / nerve endings. Fanny Howe. SP-HoweF Fr. O'Clock.

Inkidoo and the Queen of Babel. Robert Graves. CP-GravR

Inkling only, whisper in the bones, An. Dowser, The. Louis MacNeice. CP-MacNL

Inkwell, The. Constantine P. Cavafy. CP-CavaC, tr. by Theoharis Constantine Theoharis

Inland. Edna St. Vincent Millay. CP-MillE

Inland Lighthouse, The. James McMichael. SP-McMiJ

Inland, within a hollow Vale, I stood. Near Dover, September 1802. William Wordsworth. CP-WorW1; MW-WorW

Inlet. George Oppen. CP-OppGN

Inlet, The. Louise Glück. SP-GlucL

Inmate of a mountain-dwelling. To—, on Her First Ascent to the Summit of Helvellyn. William Wordsworth. CP-WorW2

Inmates put an acetylene torch to another inmate's face. Written the Day I Was to Begin a Residency at the State Penitentiary. Arthur Sze. SP-SzeA

Inn Album, The. Robert Browning. CP-BroR2

Inn at Kirchstetten, The. James Laughlin. CP-LaugJ

Inn / Kyoto. Robert Creeley. SP-CreeR

Innate Helium. Robert Frost. CP-FrosR

Inner Law, The. Chuang Tzu. CP-MertT

Inner Life of the Septic Tank, The. James Laughlin. CP-LaugJ

Inner Man, The. Charles Simic. SP-SimiC; SP-SimiCE

Inner not outer, without gnash of teeth. Martyr, A. Christina Georgina Rossetti. CP-RosC2

Inner Source, The. Andrei Codrescu. SP-CodrA

Innerly / UningstrolL / (stamens & pistil). E. E. Cummings. CP-CummE

Innings. C. K. Williams. CP-WillC

Innocence. Olga Broumas. SP-BrouO

Innocence. Thom Gunn. CP-GunnT

Innocence? / In a sense. Life, A. Howard Nemerov. CP-NemeH

Innocence! Innocence is the condition of heaven. Woodpecker, The. William Carlos Williams. CP-WilW2

Innocence is the children's country, these. Giant in the Garden. May Sarton. SP-SartM

Innocence, The. Robert Creeley. CP-CreeR

Innocent England. D. H. Lawrence. CP-LawrD

Innocent eyes not ours / Are made to look on flowers. All Things Wait upon Thee. Christina Georgina Rossetti. CP-RosC2

Innocent locomotive, The. East Coocoo. William Carlos Williams. CP-WilW2

Innocent paper, whom too cruell hand. Sonnet 48. Edmund Spenser. CP-Spens Fr. Amoretti.

Innocent Thief, The. Vincent Bourne. CP-CowpW

Innocent to innocent. James Vincent Cunningham. CP-CunnJ

Innocents, The. Josephine Jacobsen. CP-JacoJ

Innocents, The. Adrienne Rich. CP-RicAE

Innocents tug blindly at the yielding, The. Essay on the Human Will, An. Randall Jarrell. CP-JarrR

Innumerable and unnameable, foreign flowers. Hill Walk. Charles Tomlinson. CP-TomlC; SP-TomlC

Innumerable Christ, The. Hugh MacDiarmid. SP-MacDH

Inquest. Robert Stock. SP-StocR

Inquire what consciousness is made of. Anatomy of Migraine, An. Amy Clampitt. CP-ClamA

Inquiry. Federico García Lorca. CP-GarcF, tr. by Catherine Brown

Inquiry, An. Thomas Hardy. CP-HardT

Inquisitors, The. Robinson Jeffers. CP-JefR3

In's Tusc'lanes, Tullie doth confesse. Foolishnesse. Robert Herrick. CP-HerrR

Insane Always Loved Me, The. Charles Bukowski. SP-BukC1

Insane and the invalids increase, The. 19 May 1950. Yannis Ritsos. SP-RitsY Fr. Exile's Journals 3.

Insant on Crowded Street. Robert Penn Warren. CP-WarrR

Inscribed in a Copy of "Greybeards at Play." G. K. Chesterton. CP-ChesG

Inscribed in a Copy of "The Ballad of the White Horse." G. K. Chesterton. CP-ChesG

Inscribed in a Copy of "The Return of Don Quixote." G. K. Chesterton. CP-ChesG

Inscribed on a Prayer Wheel and Spun. William Stafford. SP-StafWW

Inscribenda Luparae [To Be Written on the Louvre]. Andrew Marvell. CP-MarvA

Inscription, The. Thomas Hardy. CP-HardT

Inscription, The: "While yet Rolfe's foot in stirrup stood." Herman Melville. SP-MelvH Fr. Clarel: A Poem and Pilgrimage in the Holy Land.

Inscription: "Eagle, stooping from yon snow-blown peaks, The." John Greenleaf Whittier. CP-WhitJ

Inscription: "To them who crossed the flood." Herman Melville. SP-MelvH

Inscription Facing Western Sea. W. S. Merwin. SP-MerwW

Inscription for a Burned Bridge. W. S. Merwin. SP-MerwW

Inscription for a Bust of Homer. William Cowper. CP-CowpW

Inscription for a Fountain on a Heath. Samuel Taylor Coleridge. CP-ColeS; MW-ColeS

Inscription for a Gravestone. Robinson Jeffers. CP-JefR2

Inscription for a Monument. Wallace Stevens. CP-StevWP

Inscription for a Monument in Crossthwaite Curch, in the Vale of Keswick. William Wordsworth. CP-WorW2

Inscription for a Moss-House. William Cowper. CP-CowpW

Inscription for a Seat by a Roadside, Half Way up a Steep Hill, Facing the South. William Wordsworth. CP-WorW1

Inscription for a Seat by the Pathway Side Ascending to Windy Brow. William Wordsworth. CP-WorW1

Inscription for a Sketch. Robert Browning. CP-BroR2

Inscription for a Stone. William Cowper. CP-CowpW

Inscription for a Temple of Cloacina. Robert Stock. SP-StocR

Inscription for an Hermitage. William Cowper. CP-CowpW

Inscription for Rhoda Bastable. G. K. Chesterton. CP-ChesG

Inscription for Richard Eberhard, An. John Ciardi. CP-CiarJ

Inscription for the Ceiling of a Bedroom. Dorothy Parker. CP-ParkD

Inscription for the Moss-Hut at Dove Cottage. William Wordsworth. CP-WorW1

Inscription for the Tank. James Wright. CP-WrigJ

Inscription for the Tomb of Hamilton. William Cowper. CP-CowpW

Inscription in "Poems and Ballads." G. K. Chesterton. CP-ChesG

Inscription on a Goblet. Robert Burns. CP-BurnR

Inscription on a Rock at Rydal Mount. William Wordsworth. CP-WorW2

Inscription on a Well in Memory of the Martyrs of the War. Ralph Waldo Emerson. CP-EmerR

Inscription on Any Tomb. Jorge Luis Borges. SP-BorgJ, tr. by W. S. Merwin

Inscription on the Monument of a Newfoundland Dog. Lord Byron. CP-Byron

Inscriptions. Fernando Pessoa.

  "From my villa on the hill I long looked down." SP-PessF

  "I conquered. Far barbarians hear my name." SP-PessF

  "Life lived us, not we life. We, as bees sip." SP-PessF

  "Not Cecrops kept my bees. My olives bore." SP-PessF

  "Some were as love loved, some as prizes prized." SP-PessF

  "There is a silence where the town was old." SP-PessF

  "This covers me, that erst had the blue sky." SP-PessF

  "Work is done, The. The hammer is laid down." SP-PessF

Inscriptions. John Greenleaf Whittier. CP-WhitJ

Inscriptions for a Peal of Eight Bells. Thomas Hardy. CP-HardT

Inscriptions on an Aeolian Harp. Christopher Smart. SP-SmarC
(Salve, quae fingis proprio modulamine carmen.) SP-SmarC

Inscriptions Supposed to Be Found in and near a Hermit's Cell; 1818. William
Wordsworth. CP-WorW2

Inscrutability. Jay Wright. SP-WrigJ

Inscrutable when I speak. Inscrutability. Jay Wright. SP-WrigJ

Insect beads crawl on the warm soil. To Autumn. Thomas Kinsella. CP-KinsT

Insect clings, The. Be–all. Gregory Orr. SP-OrrG

Insect world appealed to Fabre, The. Creeps and Crawls. Ogden Nash. CP-
NashO

Insectivora. Ambrose Bierce. SP-BierA

Insensibility. Wilfred Owen. CP-OwenW

Inside. Heather McHugh. SP-McHuH

Inside. Pablo Neruda. SP-NeruP

Inside a cave in a narrow canyon near Tassajara. Hands. Robinson Jeffers. CP-
JefR2

Inside, a hundred doors by which to leave. Harsh Judgment, The. Stanley
Kunitz. CP-KunSC

Inside and Outside. Allen Tate. CP-TateA

Inside Chance, The. Marge Piercy. SP-PierM

Inside Chapultepec Castle. Jay Wright. SP-WrigJ

Inside his Cantos like a pal- / ace ten times larger than Ver-. Some of Us Come
to Live. James Laughlin. CP-LaugJ

Inside, his soul could not be outside too. Michelangelo Buonarroti. CP Miche, tr.
by John Frederick Nims

Inside I am on fire. Imagine, though, coming up to City Hall. Of That Fire.
David Ignatow. SP-IgnaD

Inside Jade Hall is a curtain of pearls. Han-shan. CP-ColdM, tr. by Red Pine

Inside many of us. Rumpelstiltskin. Anne Sexton. CP-SextA

Inside me a hundred beings. Send the Chaperones Away. Jelaluddin Rumi. SP-
Rumi, tr. by Coleman Barks

Inside Me Is the Peace of an Egg. David Ignatow. SP-IgnaD

Inside, my darling wife. Happy Three, The. Theodore Roethke. CP-RoetT

Inside my father's close. My Father's Close. Unknown. CW-RossD, tr. by Dante
Gabriel Rossetti

Inside or out, the key is pain. It holds. Hospital. Karl Shapiro. SP-ShapK

Inside Out. Rae Armantrout. SP-ArmaA

Inside-Outside Game, The. Thom Gunn. CP-GunnT

Inside Stuff. Philip Whalen. SP-WhalP

Inside that loving country girl. Bernardo da Bologna. CP-CavaG, tr. by Marc
Cirigliano

Inside / that mud-hive, that gas-sponge. Lilies Break Open Over the Dark Water,
The. Mary Oliver. SP-OlivM

Inside the Apple. Yehuda Amichai. SP-AmicY, tr. by Chana Bloch

Inside the brand-new museum. Poem Without an End. Yehuda Amichai. SP-
AmicY, tr. by Chana Bloch

Inside, the church lights up today's rain. Fernando Pessoa. SP-PessF Fr. Oblique
Rain.

Inside the City Walls. Norman Dubie. CP-DubiN

Inside the crate, dark. Scattered Words for Emily Dickinson. Jane Cooper. CP-
CoopJ

Inside the gloom / Of a garret room. T. S. Eliot. SP-ElioT

Inside the old chair. Trap, The. James Tate. SP-TateJ

Inside the River. James Dickey. CP-DickJ

Inside the Rust. Yannis Ritsos. SP-RitsY Fr. Monovasia.

Inside the silver body. Immortal Longings. Robert Pinsky. CP-PinsR

Inside the snug house, blue willow-ware. Cove, The. Amy Clampitt. CP-ClamA

Inside the Storm. Boris Leonidovich Pasternak. SP-WeisT, tr. by Theodore Weiss

Inside the teepee that admits. Encounter in August. Maxine W. Kumin. SP-
KumiM

Inside the veins there are navies setting forth. Waking from Sleep. Robert Bly.
SP-BlyR

Inside this new love, die. Quietness. Jelaluddin Rumi. SP-Rumi, tr. by Coleman
Barks

Inside this pencil. Unwritten, The. W. S. Merwin. SP-MerwW

Inside us there is a listener who listens for what we say. Watcher, The. Robert
Bly. SP-BlyR

Inside water, a waterwheel turns. Jelaluddin Rumi. SP-Rumi, tr. by Coleman
Barks and John Moyne

Insight. Mona Van Duyn. SP-VanDM

Insignificant Elephants. W. H. Auden. CP-AudeW

Insinuations. Yusef Komunyakaa. CP-KomuY

Insist there be a voice, then listen. Treading Water. Philip Whalen. SP-WhalP

Insistence being of its nature. Wind. Charles Tomlinson. CP-TomlC

Insistence of Things, The. Charles Tomlinson. CP-TomlC

Insistent resolution like, The. When the Berry Bush Dies I'll Swim Down the

Green River with My Hair on Fire. Charles Bukowski. SP-BukC2

Insistent / this yearning / toward. Robert Creeley. CP-CreeR

Insolent Storm Strikes at the Skull. Sylvia Plath. CP-PlatS

Insomnia. Elizabeth Bishop. CP-BishE

Insomnia. Charles Bukowski. SP-BukC2

Insomnia. Billy Collins. SP-CollB

Insomnia. Wyatt Prunty. SP-PrunW

Insomnia. Dante Gabriel Rossetti. CW-RossD

Insomnia the Gem of the Ocean. John Updike. CP-UpdiJ

Insomniac. Maya Angelou. SP-AngeM

Insomniac. Sylvia Plath. CP-PlatS

Insomniac of a Zen-Garden Fruit. Olga Broumas. SP-BrouO

Insomniac since four, hearing this narrow. Nearing Forty. Derek Walcott. CP-
WalcD

Insomniac Sleeps Well for Once and, The. Hayden Carruth. CP-CarHS

Insomniac's Bird. Josephine Jacobsen. CP-JacoJ

Insomniacs, The. Adrienne Rich. CP-RicAE

Inspecting eye / shows cold, The. Crow. Charles Tomlinson. CP-TomlC

Inspection. Wilfred Owen. CP-OwenW

Inspector of stairs is on the stairs, The. Walk-up. W. S. Merwin. SP-MerwW

Inspiration. Paul Laurence Dunbar. CP-DunbP

Inspiration. Henry David Thoreau. CP-ThorH

Inspiration caught from dubious hues, An. Later Alexandrian, A. George
Meredith. CP-MerG1

Inspired evil and the inspired good, The. Irony as Nursery. Andrei Codrescu. SP
CodrA

Inspired we must forget our books. Ralph Waldo Emerson. CP-EmerR

Inspiring music's thrilling sound, The. Emily Jane Brontë. CP-BronE

Instance, The. Charles Tomlinson. CP-TomlC

Instances. John Ciardi. CP-CiarJ

Instances of Communication. Josephine Jacobsen. CP-JacoJ

Instans Tyrannus. Robert Browning. CP-BroR1

Instant coffee with slightly sour cream. Poem: "Instant coffee with slightly
sour cream." Frank O'Hara. SP-OharF

Instant milk and then I saw. Money Is the Roost of All Eagles. Philip Whalen.
SP-WhalP

Instant of Clearness. Jean Le Roy. CP-StevWP, tr. by Wallace Stevens

Instant of low white clouds before the rising of the moon, An. Evening. Czeslaw
Milosz. CP-MiloCN, tr. by Robert Hass

Instant of Our Parting, The. Alice Walker. CP-WalkA

Instant sprang at me, a winter instant, An. At Fourth and Main in Liberal,
Kansas, 1932. William Stafford. SP-StafWW

Instant, The. Jorge Luis Borges. SP-BorgJ, tr. by Alastair Reid

Instant, The. Denise Levertov. SP-LeveDS

Instantly they are about me, presences. Descent Into Hades. Kathleen Jessie
Raine. SP-RainK

Instead of a Farewell. A. K. Ramanujan. CP-RamaA

Instead of a Love Poem. Yehuda Amichai. SP-AmicYL, tr. by Benjamin Harshav
and Barbara Harshav

Instead of a song, boys, I'll give you a toast. Toast, A. Robert Burns. CP-BurnR

Instead of an Essay. Charles Tomlinson. CP-TomlC

Instead of angels, give us aero. Unguent. Heather McHugh. SP-McHuH

Instead of gazing at the sea. Going to the Bakery. Elizabeth Bishop. CP-BishE

Instead of Orient pearls, of Jet. Carkanet, The. Robert Herrick. CP-HerrR

Instead of pearls—a wrought clasp. Gift, The. "H. D." CP-DoolH

Instead of shaded here. On a Row of Cabins / Next My Home. Lorine
Niedecker. CP-NiedL

Instead of singing Hallelujah, a curtain. Greatest Desire, The. Yehuda Amichai.
SP-AmicY, tr. by Chana Bloch

Instead of singing hallelujah, a curtain waves in an open window. Greatest
Desire of All, The. Yehuda Amichai. SP-AmicYL, tr. by Benjamin Harshav
and Barbara Harshav

Instead of / the flower of the hawthorn. Franklin Square. William Carlos
Williams. CP-WilW2

Instead of this life in which we remain. Rainer Maria Rilke. CP-RilkFr, tr. by A.
Poulin, Jr. Fr. Fragments.

Instead of throwing them away. Old Pair of Shoes, An. Kenneth Patchen. CP-
PatcK

Instead of Words. Yehuda Amichai. SP-AmicY, tr. by Chana Bloch

Instead of Words. Yehuda Amichai. SP-AmicYL, tr. by Benjamin Harshav and
Barbara Harshav

Instep-shaped landscape, the shade of a jackboot, with nothing moving, The.
Centaurs 4. Joseph Brodsky. CP-BrodJ

Instigator of the ruin— / Whichsoever thou mayst be. Cry of the Homeless.
Thomas Hardy. CP-HardT

Instinct. C. K. Williams. SP-WillC

Institute of Defectology. Thomas Lux. SP-LuxT

Institute of the Impossible. Robert Penn Warren. CP-WarrR

Institutions of society, The. Mermaid Emerging. Robert Lowell. SP-LoweR

Instruct me now, what love will do. Of Love. Robert Herrick. CP-HerrR

Instruction. Olga Broumas. SP-BrouO

Instruction booklet on a certain effect, An. Light. Louis Zukofsky. CP-ZukLS

Instruction Manual, The. John Ashbery. SP-AshbJ

Instructions. Carl Sandburg. CP-SandC

Instructions for Angels. Kenneth Patchen. CP-PatcK

Instructions for Building Straw Huts. Yusef Komunyakaa. CP-KomuY

Instructions for Crossing the Border. Dan Pagis. SP-PagiD, *tr.* by Stephen Mitchell

Instructions for Her Voyage. Yehuda Amichai. SP-AmicYL, *tr.* by Benjamin Harshav *and* Barbara Harshav

Instructions for Use of This Toy. Howard Nemerov. CP-NemeH

Instructions to Any Painter for a "Coronation of Inés de Castro." Robert Stock. SP-StocR

Instructions to Four Walls. W. S. Merwin. SP-MerwW

Instructions to Painters by Wang Wei, Eighth Century. Eleanor Wilner. SP-WilnE

Instructions to the Double. Tess Gallagher. SP-GallT

Instructions to the Orphic Adept. Robert Graves. CP-GravR

Instructor said, The. Theme for English B. Langston Hughes. CP-HughL; CP-HughL3

Instructor, The. Rudyard Kipling. CP-KiplR

Insu nli gh t / o / verand. E. E. Cummings. CP-CummE

Insufficiency. Yannis Ritsos. SP-RitsY *Fr.* Wavering Scales, The.

Insufficiency. Elizabeth Barrett Browning. CP-BroEB

Insufficient Blue. Yusef Komunyakaa. CP-KomuY

Insult, The. C. K. Williams. SP-WillC

Insulting chance ne'er call'd with louder voice. Seneca. CP-JohnS *Fr.* Troades.

Insurance man. Madam and the Insurance Man. Langston Hughes. CP-HughL; CP-HughL2

Insusceptibles, The. Adrienne Rich. CP-RicAE

Intact as concave. Organon. Kenneth Rexroth. CP-RexrK

Integrity. Adrienne Rich. SP-RicA1; SP-RicA2

Intellect. Ralph Waldo Emerson. CP-EmerR

(Motto to "Intellect.") CP-EmerR

Intellect Cannot Measure the Divine, The. Aleksandr Aleksandrovich Blok. SP-BlokA, *tr.* by Peter France *and* Jon Stallworthy

Intellect / Gravely broods apart on joy. Ralph Waldo Emerson. CP-EmerR

Intellect of man is forced to choose, The. Choice, The. William Butler Yeats. CP-YeatW

Intellectual, The. Karl Shapiro. SP-ShapK

Intellectual Detachment. Allen Tate. CP-TateA

Intellectual Englishman shrank away from the bedside, The. Oh, If Only. Stevie Smith. CP-SmitS

Intellectual Limitations. James Whitcomb Riley. CP-RileJ

Intellectuals. Robinson Jeffers. CP-JefR2

Intelligence does help, sometimes. Bindweed. John Updike. CP-UpdiJ

Intelligence illuminates his face. On Rembrandt's Etching of Joseph Telling His Dream (1636). Helen Pinkerton. CP-PinkH

Intelligent companion, / Talented—yes, and blind—but can. Door, The. Jane Cooper. CP-CoopJ

Intelligent Prayer. Laura Riding Jackson. CP-RidiL

Intelligent Sheepman and the New Cars, The. William Carlos Williams. CP-WilW2

Intended Angle of Vision Is from My Kitchen, The. Charles Olson. CP-OlsoC

Intended for Sir Isaac Newton. Alexander Pope. CP-PopeA

(Epitaph Intended for Sir Isaac Newton, in Westminster Abbey.) CP-PopeA

Intense and terrible beauty, how has our race with the frail naked nerves. Gale in April. Robinson Jeffers. CP-JefR1

Intense and terrible, I think, must be the loneliness. Edna St. Vincent Millay. CP-MillE

Intense pressure of the earth, The. Fern, Coal, Diamond. Arthur Sze. SP-SzeA

Intensification of compassion; extraordinary; incalculable. Unanswering Correspondences, The. Kenneth Patchen. CP-PatcK

Intent gets blocked by noise. Hand Games. Marge Piercy. SP-PierM

Intent in the / night in the. Cowshed Blues, The. Hayden Carruth. CP-CarHS

Intent on Gathering Wool from Hedge and Brake. William Wordsworth. CP-WorW2

Intent wind that plays tonight, The. English Horn. Eugenio Montale. CP-MontE, *tr.* by Jonathan Galassi

Intention. Andrei Codrescu. SP-CodrA

Intention to Escape from Him. Edna St. Vincent Millay. CP-MillE

Inter marmoreas Leonorae pendula colles. In Horologium. Percy Bysshe Shelley. CP-ShelP

Inter-Office Memorandum. Ogden Nash. CP-NashO

Interalienation of their hearts. Perfectionists. Robert Graves. CP-GravR

Interchanges. Yannis Ritsos. SP-RitsY, *tr.* by Kimon Friar

Interdiction, The. James Laughlin. CP-LaugJ

Interest grows not knowing dahlia. Dahlia. Louis Zukofsky. CP-ZukLS

"Interesting, but futile," said his diary. Writer, A. Philip Larkin. CP-LarkP

Interests of a black man in a cellar, The. Black Tambourine. Hart Crane. CP-CranH

Interests of 1926. William Carlos Williams. CP-WilW1

Interference. A. R. Ammons. CP-AmmoA

Interim. Edna St. Vincent Millay. CP-MillE

Interior. Hart Crane. CP-CranH

Interior. Dorothy Parker. CP-ParkD

Interior. Carl Sandburg. CP-SandC

Interior ("From my room I hear"). Federico García Lorca. CP-GarcF, *tr.* by Jerome Rothenberg *Fr.* Water Jets.

Interior ("I want to be neither a poet"). Federico García Lorca. CP-GarcF, *tr.* by Alan S. Trueblood *Fr.* Eros with a Cane.

Interior of the Pocket, The. Tennessee Williams. CP-WillT

Interior Portrait. Rainer Maria Rilke. CP-RilkFr, *tr.* by A. Poulin, Jr. *Fr.* Orchards.

Interior (With Jane). Frank O'Hara. SP-OharF

Interiors. Howard Nemerov. CP-NemeH

Interjection #1: The Need For Re-evaluation. Robert Penn Warren. CP-WarrR

Interjection #2: Caveat. Robert Penn Warren. CP-WarrR

Interjection #3: I Know a Place Where All Is Real. Robert Penn Warren. CP-WarrR

Interjection #4: Bad Year, Bad War: A New Year's Card, 1969. Robert Penn Warren. CP-WarrR

Interjection #5: Solipsism and Theology. Robert Penn Warren. CP-WarrR

Interjection #6: What You Sometimes Feel on Your Face at Night. Robert Penn Warren. CP-WarrR

Interjection #7: Remarks of Soul to Body. Robert Penn Warren.

Interjection #8: Or, Sometimes, Night. Robert Penn Warren. CP-WarrR

Interloper, The. Thomas Hardy. CP-HardT

Interlude ("Here where the golden apples grow"). G. K. Chesterton. CP-ChesG

Interlude ("There sunken in deep woods they sang their song"). G. K. Chesterton. CP-ChesG

Interlude. Theodore Roethke. CP-RoetT

Interlude. Charles Simic. SP-SimiC; SP-SimiCE

Interlude, An. Walter De la Mare. CP-DeLaW

Interlude, An. Algernon Charles Swinburne. SP-SwinA

Interlude, The. Karl Shapiro. SP-ShapK

Interlude: in a Bar. T. S. Eliot. SP-ElioT

Interlude in London. T. S. Eliot. SP-ElioT

Interlude: Time's Mischief. Thomas Kinsella. CP-KinsT

Interludium. Hart Crane. CP-CranH

Interlunar. Margaret Atwood. SP-AtwM2

Intermezzo. Thomas Kinsella. CP-KinsT

Intermingled, / There come in wild revelling strains. Stephen Crane. CP-CranS

Intermittent Light, An. Wyatt Prunty. SP-PrunW

"Internal and External Forms." Donald Hall. CP-HallD

Internal Harmony. George Meredith. CP-MerG1

Internal Injuries. Robert Penn Warren. CP-WarrR

Internal Migration: On Being on Tour. Alan Dugan. CP-DugaA

International Date Line, Monday/Monday 27:XI:67. Philip Whalen. SP-WhalP

International Exhibition at Philadelphia, The. Jones Very. CP-VeryJ

International Women's Day I hitch. Banner. Olga Broumas. SP-BrouO

Interne at Provident. Langston Hughes. CP-HughL; CP-HughL2

Interpolation. Robert Burns. CP-BurnR

Interpolation Sounds. Walt Whitman. CP-WhitW

Interpret not God's ways, unless his light. Interpreting God's Ways. Jones Very. CP-VeryJ

Interpretation of High Finance. Robert Stock. SP-StocR

Interpreter of Silence, The. Marya Alexandrovna Zaturenska. SP-ZatuM

Interpreting God's Ways. Jones Very. CP-VeryJ

Interpreting Nature. Jones Very. CP-VeryJ

Interrogate the Stones. Archibald MacLeish. CP-MacLA

Interrogation. Josephine Jacobsen. CP-JacoJ

Interrogation of the Man of Many Hearts, The. Anne Sexton. CP-SextA

Interrogation II. C. K. Williams. SP-WillC

Interrupted Concert, The. Federico García Lorca. SP-GarcF, *tr.* by W. S. Merwin

Interrupted Concert, The. Federico García Lorca. CP-GarcF, *tr.* by Catherine Brown

Interrupted Performance, An. Stéphane Mallarmé. CP-MallS, *tr.* by Henry Weinfield

Interrupted, The. Josephine Jacobsen. CP-JacoJ

Interruption. Constantine P. Cavafy. CP-CavaC, *tr.* by Theoharis Constantine Theoharis

Interruption. Robert Graves. CP-GravR

Interruption, An. John Ciardi. CP-CiarJ

Interruptions. James Tate. SP-TateJ

Interstitial Office. John Berryman. CP-BerrJ

Interval. A. R. Ammons. CP-AmmoA

Interval. Fernando Pessoa. SP-PessF, *tr. by* Susan M. Brown *and* Edwin Honig

Interval, An: the view across the fields. View of Merton College, A. Adrienne Rich. CP-RicAE

Intervals. Robert Creeley. CP-CreeR

Intervals in a Busy Life. Donald Davie. CP-DaviDC

Intervals / so frank. Mystery of Deep Candor, The. Denise Levertov. SP-LeveDS

Intervention of the Gods, The. Constantine P. Cavafy. CP-CavaC, *tr. by* Theoharis Constantine Theoharis

Interview. Raymond Carver. CP-CarvR

Interview. Dorothy Parker. CP-ParkD

Interview, An. Howard Nemerov. CP-NemeH

Interview 2, The. David Ignatow. SP-IgnaD

Interview, The. Robert Creeley. CP-CreeR

Interview in Midsummer. Marya Alexandrovna Zaturenska. SP-ZatuM

Interview is acres. Emily Dickinson. SP-DickE

Interview with a Child. Wisława Szymborska. SP-SzymWM, *tr. by* Joanna Trzeciak

Interview with a Policeman. Ai. SP-Ai

Interview with Doctor Drink. James Vincent Cunningham. CP-CunnJ

Interviewed by a Guggenheim Recipient. Charles Bukowski. SP-BukC2

Inthe,exquisite; / morning sure lyHer eye s exactly sit,ata little roundtable. E. E. Cummings. CP-CummE

In the *Las Meninas* of Velázquez, subjects are not the subject. Prose for the Children of Aborted Revolution. Robert Stock. SP-StocR

Intimate Guest, The. Kenneth Patchen. CP-PatcK

Intimates. D. H. Lawrence. CP-LawrD

Intimation. Denise Levertov. SP-LeveDL

Intimation of Immortality. Stevie Smith. CP-SmitS

Intimations. Tennessee Williams. CP-WillT

Intimations of Mortality. Louis MacNeice. CP-MacNL

Intimidations of an Autobiography. James Tate. SP-TateJ

Into a gentle wildness and confusion. Sea Side. Robert Graves. CP-GravR

Into a truly / curving form. E. E. Cummings. CP-CummE

Into another mission / Circling my exposed continent. Kenneth Patchen. CP-PatcK

Into any little room. Sleep Song. Carl Sandburg. CP-SandC

Into any sound important. Boom Town. William Stafford. SP-StafWW

Into birdsong I'd called out en route. Visit to the Painter Vladimír Komárek, A. Jaroslav Seifert. SP-SeifJ, *tr. by* Ewald Osers

Into Distance. Charles Tomlinson. CP-TomlC

Into Each Life. James Laughlin. CP-LaugJ

Into exile with only a few shirts. Cloak, The. Robert Graves. CP-GravR

Into Her Lying Down Head. Dylan Thomas. CP-ThomD

Into her mother's bedroom to wash the ballooning body. Jessie Mitchell's Mother. Gwendolyn Brooks. SP-BrooG

Into love and out again. Theory. Dorothy Parker. CP-ParkD

Into Mexico. Mona Van Duyn. SP-VanDM

Into my empty head there come. Morning Swim. Maxine W. Kumin. SP-KumiM

Into my heart an air that kills. Yon Far Country. A. E. Housman. CP-HousA

Into My Own. Robert Frost. CP-FrosR

Into Summer. Theodore Weiss. SP-WeisT

Into that park I sawe appeir. Heir endis the Prologe. And beginnis the Mater. Sir David Lyndsay. SP-LyndD *Fr.* Dialog betwix Experience and ane Courteour, Ane.

Into the Ark. Wisława Szymborska. SP-SzymW, *tr. by* Stanisław Barańczak *and* Clare Cavanagh

Into the blue river hills. Sunset from Omaha Hotel Window. Carl Sandburg. CP-SandC

Into the closed air of the slow. Ted Berrigan. SP-BerrT *Fr.* Sonnets, The.

Into the Distance. Paul Celan. SP-CelaP, *tr. by* John Felstiner

Into the Dusk-Charged Air. John Ashbery. SP-AshbJ

Into the flame Godmother put her hand. David's Night in Veliès. James Merrill. SP-MerrJ

Into the Flats, thru Cleveland's. Cleveland, the Flats. Allen Ginsberg. CP-GinsA

Into the forest again. Traveller, The. Robert Creeley. CP-CreeR

Into the forest I went walking—to get lost. Fanny Howe. SP-HoweF *Fr.* O'Clock.

Into the golden vessel of great song. Edna St. Vincent Millay. CP-MillE

Into the Grand Canyon of the Colorado. Enthusiast Is a Devotee Is a Rooter, or, Mr. Hemingway, Meet Mr. Stengel, An. Ogden Nash. CP-NashO

Into the grooves. Paul Celan. SP-CelaP, *tr. by* John Felstiner

Into the gulf and the pit of the dark night, the cold night, there is a man. John Ericsson Day Memorial, 1918. Carl Sandburg. CP-SandC

Into the Interior. Denise Levertov. SP-LeveDP

Into the Known. Tess Gallagher. SP-GallT

Into the laps / of black celebrities. Mellow. Langston Hughes. CP-HughL; CP-HughL3

Into the lower right / Square of the window frame. Sketch, A. Richard Wilbur. CP-WilbR

Into the mirrored room, her eyes glazed and remote. Mirrored Room, The. Marya Alexandrovna Zaturenska. SP-ZatuM

Into the moonlit midnight. Aardvark, The. Christopher Logue. SP-LoguC

Into the night. Inland Lighthouse, The. James McMichael. SP-McMiJ

Into the night, into the blanket of night. Slabs of the Sunburnt West. Carl Sandburg. CP-SandC

Into the pool at 5 AM to freshen. Ferrini—I. Charles Olson. CP-OlsoC

Into the sacred precincts come the savage sages. Relation of Art and Life, A. Howard Nemerov. CP-NemeH

Into the shadow-white chamber silts the white. Two Wives. D. H. Lawrence. CP-LawrD

Into the Shandy Westerness. Kenneth Rexroth. CP-RexrK

Into the slain tons of needles. On the Coosawattee. James Dickey. CP-DickJ

Into the smiting / sky tense. E. E. Cummings. CP-CummE

Into the Stone. James Dickey. CP-DickJ

Into the strenuous briefness. E. E. Cummings. CP-CummE

Into the the the air far. Into the opposites. Muriel Rukeyser. CP-RukeM

Into the Tree. Czeslaw Milosz. CP-MiloC; CP-MiloCN, *tr. by* Robert Hass

Into the Twilight. William Butler Yeats. CP-YeatW

Into this narrow vault I came when young. Sanders Theater. Richard Eberhart. CP-EberR

Into what fictive worlds can imagination. Horatians, The. W. H. Auden. CP-AudeW

Into what pattern, into what music have the spheres whirled us. Kathleen Jessie Raine. SP-RainK

Into your outstretched hands come pouring. Song: Come, Enjoy Your Sunday! Robert Graves. CP-GravR

Intra Sepulchrum. Thomas Hardy. CP-HardT

Intrepid sons of Albion! not by you. Occasioned by the Battle of Waterloo (the Last Six Lines Intended for an Inscription) February, 1816. William Wordsworth. CP-WorW2

Intricacies of a devious mind. Princess Di. James Schuyler. CP-SchuJ

Intricate and untraceable. Web. Denise Levertov. SP-LeveDS

Intricate intrigues were her. Cynthia in California. James Laughlin. CP-LaugJ

Intrigue. Stephen Crane. CP-CranS

Intrigue taunts my / heart like a pennant. Curse, A. Shmuel HaNagid. SP-HaNaS, *tr. by* Peter Cole

Introduce me first as a man. Unnatural State of the Unicorn. Yusef Komunyakaa. CP-KomuY

Introducing the Fathers. Maxine W. Kumin. SP-KumiM

Introduction: "Hear the voice of the Bard!" William Blake. CP-BlakW *Fr.* Songs of Experience.

Introduction—Childhood and School-Time. William Wordsworth. *Fr.* Prelude, The; Growth of a Poet's Mind [1850 vers.].

Introduction, The. Andrei Codrescu. SP-CodrA

Introduction, The. Louis MacNeice. CP-MacNL

Introduction, The. Ogden Nash. CP-NashO

Introduction to Poetry. Billy Collins. SP-CollB

Introduction to Some Poems, An. William Stafford. SP-StafWW

Introduction to the Second Book of Poems. Aleksandr Aleksandrovich Blok. SP-BlokA, *tr. by* Peter France *and* Jon Stallworthy

Introduction to the Telephone. Alan Dugan. CP-DugaA

Introduction to the World. Fanny Howe.

"Come, tinkers, among droves of acorn trees." SP-HoweF

"Concentrate on the top of the mast, father." SP-HoweF

"Hide the name away in the Secret." SP-HoweF

"I am the people never so alone." SP-HoweF

"I'd speak if I wasn't afraid of inhaling." SP-HoweF

"If you have to die." SP-HoweF

"I'll pay and bow out." SP-HoweF

"Sea at last lies over this place, The." SP-HoweF

"Sea mist surprises my heavy eyes." SP-HoweF

"Small birds puff their chests and feathers." SP-HoweF

"There is nothing I hear as well as my name." SP-HoweF

"When mirth sways like a mast." SP-HoweF

Introspection. T. S. Eliot. SP-ElioT

Introspective. Christina Georgina Rossetti. CP-RosC3

Introspective Reflection. Ogden Nash. CP-NashO

Intruder, An. May Sarton. SP-SartM

Intruder, The. Carolyn Kizer. CP-KizeC

Intruding. Marge Piercy. SP-PierM

Intrusiveness of flowers. Emily Dickinson. SP-DickE

Intuitions of the Soul, The. Jones Very. CP-VeryJ

Inundatio Oxoniana. Gerard Manley Hopkins. CP-HopkG

Inundation of the Spring, The. Emily Dickinson. CP-DickE

Inundation, says the fable, An. On the Words "Brother Protestants and Fellow Christians." Jonathan Swift. CP-SwifJ

Invaders, The. Marya Alexandrovna Zaturenska. SP-ZatuM

Invading nightmare, spinning up through sleep. Three Black Women. Muriel Rukeyser. CP-RukeM

Invalid girl asked, An. Those Who Do Not Dance. Gabriela Mistral. SP-MistG, tr. by Maria Giachetti [or Jacketti]

Invalid's Day, An. Yannis Ritsos. SP-RitsY, tr. by Kimon Friar

Invariably when wine redeems the sight. Wine Menagerie, The. Hart Crane. CP-CranH

Invasion. Robinson Jeffers. CP-JefR3

Invasion of Sleep Walkers, The. John Ciardi. CP-CiarJ

Invective against Swans. Wallace Stevens. CP-StevW; CP-StevWP

Invective of Achilles, The. Homer. CP-MerG1 Fr. Iliad, The.

Inventing a story with grass. Birth, A. James Dickey. CP-DickJ

Invention of a Garden, The. Jay Wright. SP-WrigJ

Invention of Nothing. Charles Simic. SP-SimiC; SP-SimiCE

Invention of the Center. Yannis Ritsos. SP-RitsY, tr. by Andonis Decavalles

Invention sleeps within a skull. Death Piece. Theodore Roethke. CP-RoetT

Inventor, The. Rudyard Kipling. CP-KiplR Fr. Muse among the Motors, The.

Inventory. Dorothy Parker. CP-ParkD

Inventory of Goodbyes, The. Anne Sexton. CP-SextA

Inventory, The. Robert Burns. CP-BurnR

Invern. Ezra Pound. CP-PoEar

Inversely, as the Square of Their Distances Apart. Kenneth Rexroth. CP-RexrK

Inversion Factor. Robert Stock. SP-StocR

Inversnaid. Gerard Manley Hopkins. CP-HopkG

Investigation. Gregory Orr. SP-OrrG

Investigation of Certain Interesting Questions. Kenneth Patchen. CP-PatcK

Investment, The. Robert Frost. CP-FrosR

Invictus. Dorothy Parker. CP-ParkD

Invideat quamvis sua verba Latina Britannis. In Ligonem. Thomas Campion. CP-CampT

Invincibility. Frank O'Hara. SP-OharF

Inviolable Maiden, The. James Laughlin. CP-LaugJ

Invisible almost shines, The. Rainer Maria Rilke. CP-RilkFr, tr. by A. Poulin, Jr. Fr. Valaisian Quatrains, The.

Invisible angel confined. Hinge Picture. Susan Howe. SP-HoweSE

Invisible bird flies over, An. Where Are We? Jelaluddin Rumi. SP-Rumi, tr. by Coleman Barks

Invisible chariots, The. Isle of Patmos. Carl Sandburg. CP-SandC

Invisible Glory. Yannis Ritsos. SP-RitsY, tr. by Kimon Friar

Invisible Golden Sections. Robert Stock. SP-StocR

Invisible gulls with human voices cry in the sea-cloud. Fog. Robinson Jeffers. CP-JefR1

Invisible, The. G. K. Chesterton. CP-ChesG

Invitation. William Carlos Williams. CP-WilW1

Invitation, An. Thom Gunn. CP-GunnT

Invitation, The. Robert Creeley. CP-CreeR

Invitation, The. George Herbert. CP-HerbG

Invitation, The. Robert Herrick. CP-HerrR

Invitation, The. Thomas Sheridan. CP-SherT

Invitation, The ("Stay where thou art, thou need'st not further go"). Jones Very. CP-VeryJ

Invitation, The ("There is no sound but thou dost hear my voice"). Jones Very. CP-VeryJ

Invitation Declined, An. G. K. Chesterton. CP-ChesG

Invitation Ode to a Young Lady in New York from Her Friend in the Country—New Brunswick May the 22d 1753, An. Annis Boudinot Stockton. CP-StocA

Invitation to a Molecular Feast. Andrei Codrescu. SP-CodrA

Invitation to a Voyage. Charles Baudelaire. CP-BaudC, tr. by Walter Martin

Invitation to Bristol. Robert Graves. CP-GravR

Invitation to Dinner, from Doctor Sheridan to Doctor Swift, An. Thomas Sheridan. CP-SherT

Invitation to Love. Paul Laurence Dunbar. CP-DunbP

Invitation to Madison County, An. Jay Wright. SP-WrigJ

Invitation to Miss Marianne Moore. Elizabeth Bishop. CP-BishE

Invitation to the Country. George Meredith. CP-MerG1

Invitation to the Redbreast. Vincent Bourne. CP-CowpW

Invitation to the Robin. Jones Very. CP-VeryJ

Inviting a Friend to Supper. Ben Jonson. CP-JonsB; SP-JonsB

Invocation. Ambrose Bierce. SP-BierA

Invocation: "Burning fire shakes in the night, The." Walter De la Mare. CP-DeLaW

Invocation: "Come out of the dark earth." May Sarton. SP-SartM

Invocation: "Day hanging by its feet with a hole, The." W. S. Merwin. SP-MerwW

Invocation: "Dirt and stone, if I may know you as you know yourselves." David Ignatow. SP-IgnaD

Invocation: "Dolphin plunge, fountain play." Louis MacNeice. CP-MacNL

Invocation: "Harp of the North! that mouldering long hast hung." Sir Walter Scott. SP-ScotW Fr. Lady of the Lake, The.

Invocation: "Senator Smoot (Republican, Ut.)." Ogden Nash. CP-NashO

Invocation: "Sweet mother, sweet muscle." Thomas Kinsella. CP-KinsT

Invocation: "Through Thy clear spaces, Lord, of old." John Greenleaf Whittier. CP-WhitJ

Invocation, An: "Hear, sweet spirit, hear the spell." Samuel Taylor Coleridge. CP-ColeS Fr. Remorse.

Invocation, An: "Sweet sleep, with mellow palms trailed listlessly." James Whitcomb Riley. CP-RileJ

Invocation, The: "Ye juster Powers of Love and Fate." Sir John Suckling. CP-SuckJ

Invocation and Conclusion. William Carlos Williams. CP-WilW1

Invocation for "The Map of the Universe" Nicholas Vachel Lindsay. CP-LindV

Invocation to Joyce. Jorge Luis Borges. SP-BorgJ, tr. by Charles Tomlinson

Invocation to Kali, The. May Sarton. SP-SartM

Invocation to Misery. Percy Bysshe Shelley. CP-ShelP

Invocation to St. Lucy, An. Thomas Merton. CP-MertT

Invocation to the Earth; February, 1816. William Wordsworth. CP-WorW2

Invocation to the Moon. D. H. Lawrence. CP-LawrD

Invocation to the Muses. Edna St. Vincent Millay. CP-MillE

Invocation to the Social Muse. Archibald MacLeish. CP-MacLA

Invoice, The. Robert Creeley. CP-CreeR

Involv'd in Clouds of Wo, *Maria* mourns. Elegy, To Miss. Mary Moorhead, on the Death of Her Father, The Rev. Mr. John Moorhead, An. Phillis Wheatley. CP-WheaP

Involved. A. R. Ammons. CP-AmmoA

Inward coky assertiveness of the Spaniard seems to say, The. Spanish Privilege. D. H. Lawrence. CP-LawrD

Inward Direction. Jones Very. CP-VeryJ

Inward Light. Samuel Taylor Coleridge. CP-ColeS

Inward Morning, The. Henry David Thoreau. CP-ThorH

Inward parcels / Outward parcels. Kandy Express. Thomas Merton. CP-MertT

Inward Phenomena. Jones Very. CP-VeryJ

Inwardly centered like a child. Sawyer's Rage against Trees Noble as Horses, A. Alan Dugan. CP-DugaA

Inwardly fired with vehement wrath. Confession of Bishop Golias, The. The Archpoet. CP-CunnJ, tr. by James Vincent Cunningham

Io. Olga Broumas. SP-BrouO

Io. Gerard Manley Hopkins. CP-HopkG

Io Baccho! William Carlos Williams. CP-WilW2

Io no piangeva. Sam Hamill. SP-HamiS

Io venni luogo d'ogni luce muto. Canto 14: "Io venni luogo d'ogni luce muto." Ezra Pound. SP-PounE Fr. Cantos.

Iola, Kansas. Amy Clampitt. CP-ClamA

Ion. Euripides.

   "Birds from Parnassus, / swift." CP-DoolH

Iona: the Graves of the Kings. Robinson Jeffers. CP-JefR2

Ione. Paul Laurence Dunbar. CP-DunbP

Ionian. Constantine P. Cavafy. CP-CavaC, tr. by Theoharis Constantine Theoharis

Iopas's Song. Sir Thomas Wyatt. CP-WyatT

Iota Subscript. Robert Frost. CP-FrosR

Iowa. Donald Davie. CP-DaviDC

Iowa. John Updike. CP-UpdiJ

Iowa Summer. Raymond Carver. CP-CarvR

Iphigenia [or Iphigeneia] in Aulis. Euripides.

   "And Pergamos, / City of the Phrygians." CP-DoolH, tr. by "H.D."

   "Burnished-head / By burnished-head." CP-DoolH, tr. by "H.D."

   Chorus of the Women of Chalkis. CP-DoolH, tr. by "H.D."

   "Crowd of the Greek force, The." CP-DoolH, tr. by "H.D."

   "It is not for me, the day." CP-DoolH, tr. by "H.D."

   "Now sing, O slight girls." CP-DoolH, tr. by "H.D."

   "Paris came to Ida." CP-DoolH, tr. by "H.D."

Iphigenia: Politics. Thomas Merton. CP-MertT

Iphigenia, Setting the Record Straight. Eleanor Wilner. SP-WilnE

Ipse Dixit. James Laughlin. CP-LaugJ

Irate Songster, The. Kenneth Patchen. CP-PatcK

Ireland. George Meredith. CP-MerG2

Ireland. Paul Muldoon. CP-MuldP

Ireland. Jonathan Swift. CP-SwifJ

Ireland is now our royal care. Apollo's Edict. Jonathan Swift. CP-SwifJ

Ireland was better in its dream. Mockery Against the Irish Censorship. Alan Dugan. CP-DugaA

Irene. Samuel Johnson.

"Aginst the Head which Innocence secures." CP-JohnS

"Ambition is the Stamp impress'd by Heav'n." CP-JohnS

"Aspasia, yet pursue the sacred Theme." CP-JohnS

"At my Command yon' Iron Gates unfold." CP-JohnS

"How Heav'n in Scorn of human Arrogance." CP-JohnS

"Sons of *Greece*, The." CP-JohnS

"Unhappy Lot of all that shine in Courts." CP-JohnS

"What Plagues, what Tortures are in store for thee." CP-JohnS

"Ye glitt'ring Train! whom Lace and Velvet bless." CP-JohnS

Irene ducks and runs amuck, The. George Meredith. CP-MerG2

Iride swordblade road *dutch purple*. Dutch White Iris. Louis Zukofsky. CP-ZukLS

Iris. Eugenio Montale. CP-MontE, *tr. by* Jonathan Galassi

Iris. Muriel Rukeyser. CP-RukeM

Iris by Night. Robert Frost. CP-FrosR

Iris-Eaters, The. Muriel Rukeyser. CP-RukeM

Iris hazel, pupils, The. Wanderer, A. Denise Levertov. SP-LeveDL

Irish. Robert Creeley. CP-CreeR

Irish Airman Foresees His Death, An. William Butler Yeats. CP-YeatW

Irish and the Italians own the place, The. Enemies of the Angels, The. John Berryman. CP-BerrJ

Irish Avatar, The. Lord Byron. CP-Byron

Irish Cliffs of Moher, The. Wallace Stevens. CP-StevW; CP-StevWP

Irish Guards, The. Rudyard Kipling. CP-KiplR

Irish Headland, An. Robinson Jeffers. CP-JefR2

Irish Masque, The. Ben Jonson.

"Bow both your heads at once, and hearts." CP-JonsB

"So breaks the sun earth's rugged chains." CP-JonsB

Irish nightingale, The. Serenades. Seamus Heaney. SP-HeanSO

Irish Wake. Langston Hughes. CP-HughL; CP-HughL1

Irishman's Lament on the Approaching Winter, An. Robert Creeley. CP-CreeR

Irkalla's White Caves. Kenneth Patchen. CP-PatcK

Iron. Jane Cooper. CP-CoopJ

Iron. Carl Sandburg. CP-SandC

Iron. Adam Zagajewski. SP-ZagaA, *tr. by* Renata Gorczynski

Iron Bridge, The. Billy Collins. SP-CollB

Iron cape of the Law, the gray, The. Memoir. Robert Pinsky. CP-PinsR

Iron Characters, The. Howard Nemerov. CP-NemcH

Iron Coin, The. Jorge Luis Borges. SP-BorgJ, *tr. by* Eric McHenry

Iron growing in the dark. Fist. Philip Levine. SP-LeviP

Iron Hans. Anne Sexton. CP-SextA

Iron Horse. Allen Ginsberg. CP-GinsA

"And ninety-nine soldiers piled on the train at Amarillo." SP-GinsA

Iron Horse, The. James Whitcomb Riley. CP-RileJ

Iron Horse is rusting, The. End of the Line, The. Thomas McGrath. SP-McGrT

Iron is the winter, locked upon the south. Tennessee Williams. CP-WillT

Iron Landscapes (and the Statue of Liberty). Thom Gunn. CP-GunnT

Iron Mike. Charles Bukowski. SP-BukC1

Iron Palace. Robert Graves. CP-GravR

Iron rails run into the sun, The. Slow Program. Carl Sandburg. CP-SandC

Iron Ring, The. Quoit, The. W. S. Merwin. SP-MerwWF

Iron rusts, and bronze has its green sickness; while flint, the hard stones. Stone Axe, The. Robinson Jeffers. CP-JefR2

Iron scallops border the path, barely. Earliest Spring. Denise Levertov. SP-LeveDL

Iron though / that, fired to the utmost, can be loving. Theodore Weiss. SP-WeisT *Fr.* Storeroom, The.

Ironist, The. Donald Davie. CP-DaviDC

Ironmonger's Shop, The. Hans Magnus Enzensberger. SP-EnzeH

Irony as Nursery. Andrei Codrescu. SP-CodrA

Irreconcilabilia. Thomas Lux. SP-LuxT

Irrefutable, beautifully smug. Heavy Women. Sylvia Plath. CP-PlatS

Irregular Ode, An. Philip Whalen. SP-WhalP

Irregular rattle (shutters) and, An. Master of the Golden Glow, The. James Schuyler. CP-SchuJ

Irrelevance characterizes the behavior of our puppy. Kind of Music, A. Mona Van Duyn. SP-VanDM

Irreparable, The. Charles Baudelaire. CP-BaudC, *tr. by* Walter Martin

Irreparableness. Elizabeth Barrett Browning. CP-BroEB

Irreproachable ladies firmly lewd. E. E. Cummings. CP-CummE

Irresolute, pausing on a doubtful journey. It Rolls On. Kenneth Rexroth. CP-RexrK

Irreverent Thoughts. D. H. Lawrence. CP-LawrD

Irrevocable, The. Walter De la Mare. CP-DeLaW

Irritability unnatural. Arthur Hugh Clough. SP-ClouA

Irritated and sometimes utterly through. Extravagant Love. Wyatt Prunty. SP-PrunW

Irritated Office, The. Carlos Drummond de Andrade. SP-StocR, *tr. by* Robert Stock

Irwin Street. Thomas Kinsella. CP-KinsT

Iry and Billy and Jo. James Whitcomb Riley. CP-RileJ

Is a black shambling bear. Earth Is a Living Thing, The. Lucille Clifton. SP-ClifL

Is a condition. New England. William Carlos Williams. CP-WilW1

I's a-gittin' weary of de way dat people do. Faith. Paul Laurence Dunbar. CP-DunbP

Is a mental object. Symmetry of Thought, A. A. R. Ammons. CP-AmmoA

Is a monstrance / the blue dogs bay. Moon Is the Number 18, The. Charles Olson. CP-OlsoC; SP-OlsoC

Is a nice month to be / born, don't you agree. November. James Schuyler. CP-SchuJ

Is a noble task (whatever the / feminists may say) it insures. Care and Feeding of a Poet, The. James Laughlin. CP-LaugJ

Is a pleasure to at least. Junk Mail. James Laughlin. CP-LaugJ

Is a question of mutual being. In the Memory of Andrée Rexroth. Kenneth Rexroth. CP-RexrK

Is a thinking a / choosing. Image. George Oppen. CP-OppGN

Is a useful and versatile instrument for lovers. Cardiac Autoscope, The. James Laughlin. CP-LaugJ

Is a wonderful world. Word Thrum, The. Grace Paley. CP-PalGC

Is a word with unfortunate con- / notations but I readily confess. Obsession. James Laughlin. CP-LaugJ

Is all peace a dove's peace? Pablo Neruda. SP-NeruP *Fr.* Question Book.

Is all there is left of it which walked. Streak of Blood That Once Was a Tiny Red Spider, A. Thomas Lux. SP-LuxT

I's always been a workin' girl. Black Gal. Langston Hughes. CP-HughL; CP-HughL1

Is an enchanted thing. Mind Is an Enchanting Thing, The. Marianne Craig Moore. CP-MoorM

Is an odd infinitive, in which. To Have To. Heather McHugh. SP-McHuH

Is any grieved or tired? Yea, by God's Will. Mid-Lent. Christina Georgina Rossetti. CP-RosC2

Is anything sadder than a train. Monday. Primo Levi. CP-LeviP, *tr. by* Ruth Feldman *and* Brian Swann

Is Bliss then, such Abyss. Emily Dickinson. CP DickE

I's boun' to see my gal to-night. On the Road. Paul Laurence Dunbar. CP-DunbP

Is Death miles away from this house. My Number. Billy Collins. SP-CollB

Is done now with bright thinness of upper air. Weight. Foolish Wing, The. John Ciardi. CP-CiarJ

Is even more fun than going to San Sebastian, Irún, Hendaye, Biarritz, Bayonne. Having a Coke with You. Frank O'Hara. SP-OharF

Is far out, umbilically extravagant. Key West. Richard Eberhart. CP-EberR

I's feelin kin o' lonesome in my little room to-night. To the Eastern Shore. Paul Laurence Dunbar. CP-DunbP

Is 4 always 4 for everybody? Pablo Neruda. SP-NeruP *Fr.* Question Book.

Is Germany's bestiality, in detail. Mirrors, The. William Carlos Williams. CP-WilW2

Is Heaven a Physician? Emily Dickinson. CP-DickE

Is Helena's birthday: / she isn't getting any. Tomorrow. James Schuyler. CP-SchuJ

IS / Here's a dragonfly. Haiku, for Gary Snyder. Philip Whalen. SP-WhalP

Is his own master he doesn't. Maker of Dreams, The. James Laughlin. CP-LaugJ

Is his sweet wife too faint to remember. Emily Dickinson. SP-DickE

Is hovering in the air, there, in the highest. All the Wide Grin of Him. Eleanor Wilner. SP-WilnE

Is Immortality a bane. Emily Dickinson. CP-DickE

Is is too late to touch you, Dear? Emily Dickinson. CP-DickE

Is is true, dear Sue? Emily Dickinson. CP-DickE

Is it a joyous expanse of Year. Emily Dickinson. SP-DickE

Is it a myth? And if so, what does it tell us about ourselves? Seventeen Questions about KING KONG. Jane Cooper. CP-CoopJ

Is it a reed that's shaken by the wind. Calais, August, 1802. William Wordsworth. CP-WorW1; MW-WorW

Is it any better in Heaven, my friend Ford. To Ford Madox Ford in Heaven. William Carlos Williams. CP-WilW2

Is it bad to have come here. Gallant Chateau. Wallace Stevens. CP-StevW; CP-StevWP

Is / it / because there struts a distinct silver lady. E. E. Cummings. CP-CummE

Is it dirty. Song: "Is it dirty." Frank O'Hara. SP-OharF

Is it for a swarm of dawns, for a few. On an Unwritten Letter. Eugenio Montale. CP-MontE, *tr. by* Jonathan Galassi

Is it for naught that where the tired crowds see. Town of American Visions, The. Nicholas Vachel Lindsay. CP-LindV

Is it for Satan's, God's, or Nature's uses. New Weapons in the Old War. Howard Nemerov. CP-NemeH

Is It Happy? Stevie Smith. CP-SmitS

Is it her nature, or is it her will. Sonnet 41. Edmund Spenser. CP-Spens *Fr.* Amoretti.

Is it in the anthracite face of a coal miner. Unnamable River, The. Arthur Sze. SP-SzeA

Is it Intellect that the Patriot means. Emily Dickinson. SP-DickE

Is it less than your brilliance, Ishtar. To Ishtar. Richard Wilbur. CP-WilbR

Is it my clothes, my way of walking. Disembarking at Quebec. Margaret Atwood. SP-AtwM1

Is it not by his high superfluousness we know. Excesses of God, The. Robinson Jeffers. CP-JefR1

Is it not interesting to see. Thoughts about the Christian Doctrine of Eternal Hell. Stevie Smith. CP-SmitS

Is It Now Or For Always. Philip Larkin. CP-LarkP

Is it only Cotswold that holds the glamour. That Centre of Old. Ivor Gurney. SP-GurnI

Is it possible. George Washington. Louis Zukofsky. CP-ZukLS

Is it possible. Maiden without Hands, The. Anne Sexton. CP-SextA

Is it really a revolution, though? Lunch with Pancho Villa. Paul Muldoon. CP-MuldP

Is it St. Peter's or St. Paul's this dome. Cumuli. May Swenson. SP-SwenM

Is it salt that strafes or hail? It slays. Eugenio Montale. CP-MontE, *tr. by* Jonathan Galassi

Is it so hard for men to stand by themselves. Intellectuals. Robinson Jeffers. CP-JefR2

Is it that in some brighter sphere. Fragment: "Is it that in some brighter sphere." Percy Bysshe Shelley. CP-ShelP

Is it that you feel not our dying? Hymn to a Trench Gun. Kenneth Patchen. CP-PatcK

Is it the cut glass. Photograph, The: A Lynching. Lucille Clifton. SP-ClifL

Is it the end of the world to. Occidit brevis lux. James Laughlin. CP-LaugJ

Is it the Eternal Triune, is it He. Wandering Jew's Soliloquy, The. Percy Bysshe Shelley. CP-ShelP

Is it the flight of God. Rainer Maria Rilke. CP-RilkFr, *tr. by* A. Poulin, Jr. *Fr.* Fragments.

Is it the martins or katydids? In State. James Whitcomb Riley. CP-RileJ

Is it the palm, the cocoa-palm. Palm-Tree, The. John Greenleaf Whittier. CP-WhitJ

Is it this sky's vast vault or ocean's sound. Monochord, The. Dante Gabriel Rossetti. CW-RossD *Fr.* House of Life, The.

Is it thy will that I should wax and wane. Apologia. Oscar Wilde. CP-WildO

Is it to love to muse the live long day. Question, upon Being Told in Jest by Mr Stockton that He Was Not Loved Much, The. Annis Boudinot Stockton. CP-StocA

Is it tommorrow yet? To the Jewish People. Kenneth Patchen. CP-PatcK

Is It True? Langston Hughes. CP-HughL; CP-HughL3

Is It True? Anne Sexton. CP-SextA

Is it true that amber contains. Pablo Neruda. SP-NeruP *Fr.* Question Book.

Is it true the ribs can tell. Kind of Love, Some Say, A. Maya Angelou. SP-AngeM

Is it Ulysses that approaches from the east. World as Meditation, The. Wallace Stevens. CP-StevW; CP-StevWP

Is It Well with The Child? Christina Georgina Rossetti. CP-RosC2

Is It Wise? Stevie Smith. CP-SmitS

Is it worth while, dear, now. Long Plighted. Thomas Hardy. CP-HardT

Is It Written. James Laughlin. CP-LaugJ

Is Jove immortal / So is Cerberus at his portal. Ralph Waldo Emerson. CP-EmerR

Is life strife, is it the long combat? Battle of Life. D. H. Lawrence. CP-LawrD

Is like the sieve of the Danaïdes. Cask of Hate, The. Charles Baudelaire. CP-BaudC, *tr. by* Walter Martin

Is love so prone to change and rot. Bed of Forget-Me-Nots, A. Christina Georgina Rossetti. CP-RosC3

Is made up of reservoirs. Hard Structure of the World, The. Richard Eberhart. CP-EberR

Is melting an old frost moon. Dawn's Rose. Ted Hughes. SP-HughTN *Fr.* Crow.

Is memory most of miseries miserable. Memory. Dante Gabriel Rossetti. CW-RossD

Is merry glory. Langston Hughes. Gwendolyn Brooks. SP-BrooG

Is much as before. Night. Afterward. James Schuyler. CP-SchuJ

Is murther no sin? or a sin so cheape. To Pontius Washing His Blood-Stained Hands. Richard Crashaw. CP-CrasR

Is my concern. That's this moment. Overthrow of One o'Clock at Night, The. Muriel Rukeyser. CP-RukeM

Is my heart / your heart? Confusion ("Is my heart / your heart?"). Federico

García Lorca. CP-GarcF, *tr. by* Jerome Rothenberg *Fr.* Mirror Suite.

Is my team ploughing. A. E. Housman. CP-HousA

Is my team plowing? A. E. Housman. CP-HousA

Is not an absent friend as mysterious. Emily Dickinson. SP-DickE

Is not moveable / though your block might be getting worse. Status of the Monk, The. Andrei Codrescu. SP-CodrA

Is / Not. Margaret Atwood. SP-AtwM1

Is not silent, it is a speaking. Voice You Hear When You Read Silently, The. Thomas Lux. SP-LuxT

Is not the distinction of Affection. Emily Dickinson. SP-DickE

Is not the messenger return'd? Marino Faliero, Doge of Venice. Lord Byron. CP-Byron

Is not thilke same a goteheard prowde. July. Edmund Spenser. CP-Spens *Fr.* Shepheardes [*or* Shepeards *or* Shepherd's] Calender, The.

Is not thilke the mery moneth of May. May. Edmund Spenser. CP-Spens *Fr.* Shepheardes [*or* Shepeards *or* Shepherd's] Calender, The.

Is not this house a harp whose living chords. Poem, Spoken Before the ΦBK Society, August, 1834. Ralph Waldo Emerson. CP-EmerR

Is not thy sacred hunger of science. To Mr B. B. John Donne. CP-DonnJ; MW-DonnJ

Is not to-day enough? Why do I peer. Fragment: Sufficient Unto the Day. Percy Bysshe Shelley. CP-ShelP

Is Now the Time? Robert Graves. CP-GravR

Is our Charles Simic afraid of death? Further Adventures of Charles Simic. Charles Simic. SP-SimiCE

Is pink and many-petalled: / it rests on the rim. Rose of Marion, The. James Schuyler. CP-SchuJ

I's (Pronounced *Eyes*). Louis Zukofsky. CP-ZukLS

Is reform needed? is it through you? To a Pupil. Walt Whitman. CP-WhitW

Is ripeness all and what's in the howling storm? Storm. Robert Stock. SP-StocR

Is she the star of one that is away? Fireside Reverie. George Meredith. CP-MerG2

Is small and stamped, / MADE IN ITALY. This Notebook. James Schuyler. CP-SchuJ

Is some such word / as the chord. Propriety. Marianne Craig Moore. CP-MoorM

Is speaking it pelts. Then and Now. James Laughlin. CP-LaugJ

Is such a touching child. Nature. John Updike. CP-UpdiJ

Is superficially / The same as a hotel, grand and de luxe. Fragment from Correspondence. Howard Nemerov. CP-NemeH

Is that an attitude for a flower, to stand. Hyacinth. Louise Glück. SP-GlucL

Is that dance slowing in the mind of man. Four for Sir John Davies. Theodore Roethke. CP-RoetT

Is that Philosophy, which doth declare. Search for the Truth Not Vain, The. Jones Very. CP-VeryJ

Is that the moon. Dream-Confused. D. H. Lawrence. CP-LawrD

Is That What You Are. W. S. Merwin. SP-MerwW

Is that when we. Tragedy of Time, The. James Laughlin. CP-LaugJ

Is the absolute road to. Highway 66. James Laughlin. CP-LaugJ

Is the basketball coach a homosexual lemon manufacturer? It is suspected by O'Ryan in his submarine. Aus Einer Kindheit. Kenneth Koch. SP-KochK

Is the body's way. Coming. Heather McHugh. SP-McHuH

Is the governor falling. Brassiere Factory, The. Kenneth Koch. SP-KochK

Is the grandson / of Thomas L. Creeley, who acquired. I. Robert Creeley. CP-CreeR

Is the Moon Tired? Christina Georgina Rossetti. CP-RosC2

Is the pace of nature slow? Ralph Waldo Emerson. CP-EmerR

Is the Pacific Sea my home? Or is. John Donne in California. Amy Clampitt. CP-ClamA

Is the slim tall. Sandra. Charles Bukowski. SP-BukC1

Is the soul solid, like iron? Some Questions You Might Ask. Mary Oliver. SP-OlivM

Is the stair here? Abyss, The. Theodore Roethke. CP-RoetT

Is the stern old story shattered. Vision of Edens, A. G. K. Chesterton. CP-ChesG

Is the sun a miner, a thief, a gambler. June Ghazal. Arthur Sze. SP-SzeA

Is the way Donald Schwartz went. Way to Go, The. William Corbett. SP-CorbW

Is the way that you treat me. Three Skirmishes in the Endless Battle. James Laughlin. CP-LaugJ

Is then no nook of English ground secure. On the Projected Kendal and Windermere Railway. William Wordsworth. CP-WorW2

Is There a Danger. James Laughlin. CP-LaugJ

Is There a Difference between Men and Women. Grace Paley. CP-PalGC

Is there a flower(whom). E. E. Cummings. CP-CummE

Is there a hope, that man would thankful be. To Esmé, Lord Aubigny. Ben Jonson. CP-JonsB; SP-JonsB

Is there a power that can sustain and cheer. William Wordsworth. CP-WorW1

Is there a self or not. Han-shan. CP-ColdM, *tr. by* Red Pine

Is there a sharp edge? Lulu Morose. Wallace Stevens. CP-StevWP

Is there a whim-inspir'd fool. Bard's Epitaph, A. Robert Burns. CP-BurnR

Is there an aftertaste of life in these graves? Cemetary. Rainer Maria Rilke. CP-RilkFr, *tr. by* A. Poulin, Jr.

Is There Any Easy Road to Freedom? Carl Sandburg. CP-SandC

Is there any frustration like that of these. Shmuel HaNagid. SP-HaNaS, *tr. by* Peter Cole

"Is there anybody there?" said the Traveler. Listeners, The. Walter De la Mare. CP-DeLaW

Is there anything crazier in this life. Pablo Neruda. SP-NeruP *Fr.* Question Book.

Is there for feckless poverty. To Hulme (T. E.) and Fitzgerald (A Certain). Ezra Pound. CP-PoEar

Is there, or do enthusiasts dream. To Mrs Powel, an Ode. Annis Boudinot Stockton. CP-StocA

Is there poise for the stumbling and fallen. Miracle at Sea, The. Shmuel HaNagid. SP-HaNaS, *tr. by* Peter Cole

Is, they are hoarse. Thing about Crows, The. Josephine Jacobsen. CP-JacoJ

Is this a fast, to keep. To Keep a True Lent. Robert Herrick. CP-HerrR

Is this a holy thing to see. Holy Thursday [2]. William Blake. CP-BlakW *Fr.* Songs of Experience.

Is this a life, to break thy sleep? Paranæticall, or Advisive Verse, to His Friend, M. John Wicks. Robert Herrick. CP-HerrR

Is this a sentence passed upon us both. Sentence, The. Robert Graves. CP-GravR

Is this all life is then. Everything. Gregory Orr. SP-OrrG

Is this fame then what it is to be. On Stuffing a Goose. Theodore Weiss. SP-WeisT

Is This Feeling about the West Real? William Stafford. SP-StafWW

Is this man turning angel as he stares. Messenger, The. Thom Gunn. CP-GunnT

Is this really me? Of course not, for Time. Interjection #1: The Need For Re-evaluation. Robert Penn Warren. CP-WarrR

Is This Seat Taken? Yes, or, My Neck Is Sticking In. Ogden Nash. CP-NashO

Is this Sir Philip Sidney, this loud clown. Knight in Disguise, The. Nicholas Vachel Lindsay. CP-LindV

Is this that Name as ointment poured forth. King of Kings and Lord of Lords. Christina Georgina Rossetti. CP-RosC2

Is this the bliss for which you've tried to live? At the End of the Rainbow. John Updike. CP-UpdiJ

Is this the end? is there no end but this? / Yea, none beside. Standing Afar Off for the Fear of Her Torment. Christina Georgina Rossetti. CP-RosC2

Is this the Face that thrills with awe. Descent from the Cross, The. Christina Georgina Rossetti. CP-RosC2

Is this the God of Gods, the one I heard about. Holy Ghost on the Nod over the Body of Bliss. Allen Ginsberg. CP-GinsA

Is this the Hope that opens and shuts. Emily Dickinson. SP-DickE

Is this the land our fathers loved. Stanzas for the Times. John Greenleaf Whittier. CP-WhitJ

Is this the moment? / No, not yet. Linen. James Schuyler. CP-SchuJ

Is this the mouth of truth. Mouth of truth, The. Lawrence Ferlinghetti. SP-FerlL

Is this the nest in which my phoenix put. Petrarch. CP-Petra, *tr. by* J. G. Nichols

Is this the night the world must burn like Troy? Like Ilium. Thomas Merton. CP-MertT

Is this the sir, who, some waste wife to win. To Sir Luckless Woo-All. Ben Jonson. CP-JonsB; SP-JonsB

Is this thy plighted, fond regard. Can You Leave Me Thus, My Katy. Robert Burns. CP-BurnR

Is this thy voice whose treble notes of fear. To a Southern Statesman. John Greenleaf Whittier. CP-WhitJ

Is Time on my hands? Yes it is, it is on my hands and my face and. Thoughts Thought While Waiting for a Pronouncement from a Doctor, an Editor, a Big Executive, the Department of Internal Revenue or Any Other Momentous Pronouncer. Ogden Nash. CP-NashO

Is to become a footnote. My Ambition. James Laughlin. CP-LaugJ

Is too much with me daylong and / in my dreams my mind is invaded. *Non-World, The.* James Laughlin. CP-LaugJ

Is trying to find a way to get out of town. Man Who Believes in Five, The. Miller Williams. CP-WillM

Is what I wanted to write. Little Uncomplicated Hymn, A. Anne Sexton. CP-SextA

Is where you find it. Maestria. Howard Nemerov. CP-NemeH

Is Wisdom a Lot of Language? Carl Sandburg. CP-SandC

Is without world. Howling of Wolves, The. Ted Hughes. SP-HughTN

Is worked this way. Release the striking arm. Instructions for Use of This Toy. Howard Nemerov. CP-NemeH

Is your hate, then, of such measure? Translations from Heine. Heinrich Heine. CP-PoEar, *tr. by* Ezra Pound

Is Zelot pure? he is: ye see he weares. Upon Zelot. Robert Herrick. CP-HerrR

Isaac and Archibald. Edwin Arlington Robinson. CP-RobiE

Isaac Leybush Peretz. Moyshe-Leyb Halpern. CP-PinsR, *tr. by* Robert Pinsky

Isaac Meek. Walter De la Mare. CP-DeLaW

Isabel. John Greenleaf Whittier. CP-WhitJ

Isabella of Austria. John Greenleaf Whittier. CP-WhitJ

Isabella; or, The Pot of Basil. John Keats. CP-KeatJ

Isaiah 63. 1–8. Phillis Wheatley. CP-WheaP

Isaiah, the country-boy, marched against the jazz. Babylon, Babylon, Babylon the Great. Nicholas Vachel Lindsay. CP-LindV

Ischia. W. H. Auden. CP-AudeW

Ischia in October. Joseph Brodsky. CP-BrodJ

Iseult of Brittany. Matthew Arnold. SP-ArnoM *Fr.* Tristram and Iseult.

Iseult of Brittany. Dorothy Parker. CP-ParkD

Isidora. Christina Georgina Rossetti. CP-RosC3

Isis Speaks. Denise Levertov. SP-LeveDL

Island ("Between two rivers"). Langston Hughes. CP-HughL; CP-HughL3 *Fr.* Lenox Avenue Mural.

Island ("Wave of sorrow"). Langston Hughes. CP-HughL; CP-HughL2

Island. W. S. Merwin. SP-MerwWF

Island. Czeslaw Milosz. CP-MiloC; CP-MiloCN, *tr. by* Lillian Vallee

Island, An. Elizabeth Barrett Browning. CP-BroEB

Island, An. Edwin Arlington Robinson. CP-RobiE

Island, The. Lord Byron. CP-Byron

Island, The. James Dickey. CP-DickJ

Island, The. Randall Jarrell. CP-JarrR

Island, The. Louis MacNeice. CP-MacNL

Island, The. Marya Alexandrovna Zaturenska. SP-ZatuM

Island (7), The. Pablo Neruda. SP-NeruP *Fr.* Separate Rose, The.

Island (8), The. Pablo Neruda. SP-NeruP *Fr.* Separate Rose, The.

Island (12), The. Pablo Neruda. SP-NeruP *Fr.* Separate Rose, The.

Island (17), The. Pablo Neruda. SP-NeruP *Fr.* Separate Rose, The.

Island (20), The. Pablo Neruda. SP-NeruP *Fr.* Separate Rose, The.

Island cast, An. After the Calamitous Convoy (July 1942). Donald Davie. CP-DaviDC

Island Cemetery, An. W. H. Auden. CP-AudeW

Island City. W. S. Merwin. SP-MerwWF

Island doesn't stink, The. Syllables. Heather McHugh. SP-McHuH

Island dreams under the dawn, The. Indian to His Love, The. William Butler Yeats. CP-YeatW

Island-end here is. Ocean City. A. R. Ammons. CP-AmmoA

Island Funeral. Hugh MacDiarmid. SP-MacDH

Island Galaxy, An. John Ciardi. CP-CiarJ

Island high as our inland hills. Two Preludes for La Push. John Logan. CP-LogaJ

Island in the Harbor, An. W. S. Merwin. SP-MerwW

Island in the Moon, An. William Blake.
  Chapter Six.
    "Ah said Sipsop, I only wish Jack [*Hunter*] Tearguts had." CP-BlakW
    "Crowned king, A." CP-BlakW
    "Hear then the pride & knowledge of a Sailor." CP-BlakW
    "I say this evening we'll [*or* we'd] all get drunk." CP-BlakW
    "In the moon as Phebus stood over his oriental Gardening." CP-BlakW
    "O I say you Joe." CP-BlakW
    "Phebe drest like beauties Queen." CP-BlakW
    "Then the Cynic sung." CP-BlakW
    "Upon a holy thursday their innocent faces clean." CP-BlakW

Island in the Works. James Merrill. SP-MerrJ

Island Is Memorable to Us, The. Tennessee Williams. CP-WillT

Island of Puerto Rico. Caribbean Sea. Gabriela Mistral. SP-MistG, *tr. by* Maria Giachetti [*or* Jacketti]

Island of Summer. Robert Penn Warren. CP-WarrR

Island Quarry. Hart Crane. CP-CranH

Island Sun. John Updike. CP-UpdiJ

Island where all becomes clear. Utopia. Wisława Szymborska. SP-SzymW, *tr. by* Stanislaw Barańczak *and* Clare Cavanagh

Island, you mustn't say, had only rocks and scrub pine, The. Pennacesse Leper Colony for Women, Cape Cod, The: 1922. Norman Dubie. CP-DubiN

Islanded, my wife turned on the radio for news of home. On an Island. John Updike. CP-UpdiJ

Islander, The. Louise Glück. SP-GlucL

Islanders, The. Rudyard Kipling. CP-KiplR

Islands. W. S. Merwin. SP-MerwWF

Islands. Muriel Rukeyser. CP-RukeM

Islands. Derek Walcott. CP-WalcD

Islands, The. "H. D." CP-DoolH

Islands, The. Robert Earl Hayden. CP-HaydR

Islands, The. Randall Jarrell. CP-JarrR

Islands and towers I visited in the dreams. Adam Zagajewski. SP-ZagaA, *tr. by* Renata Gorczynski, Benjamin Ivry *and* C. K. Williams

Islandward, nearby the dead ones. Paul Celan. SP-CelaP, *tr. by* John Felstiner

Isle, The. Percy Bysshe Shelley. CP-ShelP

Isle of Patmos. Carl Sandburg. CP-SandC

Isle of Portland, The. A. E. Housman. CP-HousA

Isle of Wight, The. Amy Clampitt. CP-ClamA

Isled in the midnight air. Moth, The. Walter De la Mare. CP-DeLaW

Isle's Enchantress, The. Robert Browning. CP-BroR2

Isles of Jessamy, The. Christopher Logue. SP-LoguC

Islet the Dachs. George Meredith. CP-MerG1

Isn't it good she asked (as). Rhyme. James Laughlin. CP-LaugJ

Isn't it nice (Diane Keaton). Snowdrops 1987. John Updike. CP-UpdiJ

Isn't it plain the sheets of moss, except that. Landscape. Mary Oliver. SP-OlivM

Isn't it sad that our eyes close? Rainer Maria Rilke. CP-RilkFr, *tr. by* A. Poulin, Jr. *Fr.* Orchards.

Isn't That a Dainty Dish? No! Ogden Nash. CP-NashO

Isn't very tall, 4 ft. Man Inside the Chipmunk Suit, The. Thomas Lux. SP-LuxT

Isobel's Child. Elizabeth Barrett Browning. CP-BroEB

Isolate city spread alongside water. Bridge for the Living. Philip Larkin. CP-LarkP

Isolation is populous, it has many voices. Interpreter of Silence, The. Marya Alexandrovna Zaturenska. SP-ZatuM

Isolation: To Marguerite. Matthew Arnold. SP-ArnoM *Fr.* Switzerland.

Israel. Karl Shapiro. SP-ShapK

Israel's Lament. Samuel Taylor Coleridge. CP-ColeS

Israfel. Edgar Allan Poe. CP-PoeEd

Issue, Mood. Charles Olson. CP-OlsoC

Issue of Life, An. Howard Nemerov. CP-NemeH

Issues from the Hand of God. Charles Olson. CP-OlsoC

Issues from the hand of God, the simple soul. Animula. T. S. Eliot. CP-ElioT

Istanbul is a terminal city. Food. Andrei Codrescu. SP-CodrA

Istanbul. 21 March. I woke today. Thousand and Second Night, The. James Merrill. SP-MerrJ

It. A. K. Ramanujan. CP-RamaA

It. Gary Snyder. CP-SnydG

It ain't a woman. Da Boyg. Charles Olson. CP-OlsoC

It all begins with fear of *mana*. Comp. Religion. John Updike. CP-UpdiJ

It all depends on how fast you're going. Homage to Lucretius. Philip Whalen. SP-WhalP

It all started with the maps. Hanging in the living room, the hall. From the Journal Concerning My Father. Jane Cooper. CP-CoopJ

It always felt to me—a wrong. Emily Dickinson. CP-DickE

It appears that it was all a misunderstanding. This World. Czeslaw Milosz. CP-MiloCN, *tr. by* Robert Hass

It arose with him as a joke. Joke Gold. Carl Sandburg. CP-SandC

It baffles the foreigner like an idiom. Drug Store. Karl Shapiro. SP-ShapK

It beats love because there aren't any. Sweet Music. Charles Bukowski. SP-BukC1

It began with A—years before in a room. Robert Schumann, Or: Musical Genius Begins with Affliction. Rita Dove. SP-DoveR

It began with begging. Fire Thief, The. Anne Sexton. CP-SextA

It began with light lute music. My Daughter's Wedding. John Logan. CP-LogaJ

It begins in indolence. Vocation: A Life: *Suite Based on Four Words from Willa Cather*. Jane Cooper. CP-CoopJ

It begins when you smell a funny smell. Seaside Serenade. Ogden Nash. CP-NashO

It begins with closed eyes. Night Room Composition. Peter Blue Cloud. SP-BlueP

It begins with my dog, now dead, who all his long life. Retrieval System, The. Maxine W. Kumin. SP-KumiM

It begins with one or two soldiers. Truce. Paul Muldoon. CP-MuldP

It beguiles— / This little Odyssey. Battle-Scene. Sylvia Plath. CP-PlatS

It being in this life forbidden to move. Death-Wish, The. Louis MacNeice. CP-MacNL

It bends far over Yell'ham Plain. Comet at Yell'ham, The. Thomas Hardy. CP-HardT

It Bids Pretty Fair. Robert Frost. CP-FrosR

It bloomed and dropt, a Single Noon. Emily Dickinson. CP-DickE

It bloweth where it listeth hark the sound. So is every one who is born of the spirit. Jones Very. CP-VeryJ

It Breaks. Marge Piercy. SP-PierM

It brightens up into the branches. George Oppen. CP-OppGN

It burneth yet, alas, my heart's desire. Sir Thomas Wyatt. CP-WyatT

It burns in the void. World, The. Kathleen Jessie Raine. SP-RainK

It came about that there was no way of passing. Pursuit of Happiness, The. John Ashbery. SP-AshbJ

It came at last, a letter of true love. Love Letter, The. Robert Graves. CP-GravR

It came at last but prompter Death. Emily Dickinson. CP-DickE

It came bone-time. The metric of ten thousand. Mr. & Mrs. John Ciardi. CP-CiarJ

It came down to this: that merely naming the creatures. Channel 13. James Merrill. SP-MerrJ

It came his turn to beg. Emily Dickinson. CP-DickE

It came into my mind that no one had painted. At Lascaux. William Stafford. SP-StafWW

It came to me on the Nile my passport lied. Beni Hasan. Louis MacNeice. CP-MacNL

It came to me that all this time. Days and Nights. Kenneth Koch. SP-KochK

It Came to Pass on a Planet Third from a Minor Sun in a Solar System Out on the Edge of One of the Galaxies. Miller Williams. CP-WillM

It can be done. The seal of frost. Working Outdoors in Winter. John Updike. CP-UpdiJ

It Can Happen. James Laughlin. CP-LaugJ

It cannot be. Where is that mighty joy. Temper (2), The. George Herbert. CP-HerbG

It can't be "Summer"! Emily Dickinson. CP-DickE

It can't be the passing of time that casts. RIP. James Wright. CP-WrigJ

It can't take a joke. On Death, without Exaggeration. Wisława Szymborska. SP-SzymW, *tr. by* Stanislaw Barańczak *and* Clare Cavanagh

It can't tell a joke. On Death, without Exaggeration. Wisława Szymborska. SP-SzymWM, *tr. by* Joanna Trzeciak

It ceased to hurt me, though so slow. Emily Dickinson. CP-DickE

It chanced that while the pious troops of France. Dream of Pio Nono, The. John Greenleaf Whittier. CP-WhitJ

It chaunced me on day beside the shore. Ruines of Time, The. Edmund Spenser. CP-Spens

It circled, hung, and circled. I watched it come. Hawk. John Ciardi. CP-CiarJ

It comes about that the drifting of these curtains. Curtains in the House of the Metaphysician, The. Wallace Stevens. CP-StevW; CP-StevWP

It comes blundering over the. How Poetry Comes to Me. Gary Snyder. CP-SnydG

It comes in black. Telephone, The. Maya Angelou. SP-AngeM

It comes oozing. Evil Eye, The. Anne Sexton. CP-SextA

It Comes to a Standstill. Adam Zagajewski. SP-ZagaA

It comes up out of the darkness, and it returns. Beyond the Pleasure Principle. Howard Nemerov. CP-NemeH

It comforts the Criminal little to know. Emily Dickinson. SP-DickE

It commonly sings. Xmas. Robert Creeley. CP-CreeR

It consoles the happy Sorrow of Autumn. Emily Dickinson. SP-DickE

It corners the sun and caroms one. Prism. Howard Nemerov. CP-NemeH

It costs me never a stab or squirm. Thought for a Sunshiny Morning. Dorothy Parker. CP-ParkD

It could be a jaw-bone. Viking Dublin: Trial Pieces. Seamus Heaney. SP-HeanSO

It could be, Christopher, from your leafed-in house. To Isherwood Dying. Thom Gunn. CP-GunnT

It could be that you are driving by. Gap, The. Charles Tomlinson. CP-TomlC

It could happen any time, tornado. Yes. William Stafford. SP-StafWW

It could have been the grassiest of places. Desert Wasn't Loved Enough said Reich, The. Grace Paley. CP-PalGC

It could have happened. Could Have. Wisława Szymborska. SP-SzymW, *tr. by* Stanislaw Barańczak *and* Clare Cavanagh

It darkened; I was cold. Princess Wakes in the Wood, The. Randall Jarrell. CP-JarrR

It darted across the pond. Catch, The. Stanley Kunitz. CP-KunSC

It Depends on Whose Science. Kenneth Patchen. CP-PatcK

It depends who's talking if you're a 'Sabine.' Carmen 44. Catullus. CP-ZukLS *Fr.* Carmina.

It Did. Robert Lowell. SP-LoweR

It did not surprise me. Emily Dickinson. CP-DickE

It didn't come all at once, it didn't come easy. Her, Though. Miller Williams. CP-WillM

It didn't happen that way. Zone of Silence. Czeslaw Milosz. CP-MiloCN, *tr. by* Robert Hass

It died in its sleep. Death of a Lawn Mower. David Ignatow. SP-IgnaD

It discovers by night. Poem, The: "It discovers by night." Donald Hall. CP-HallD

It does amaze me, when the clicking hour. Floris in Italy. Gerard Manley Hopkins. CP-HopkG

It does for the time of man to walk here. S.P.Q.R. A Letter from Rome. John Ciardi. CP-CiarJ

It Does Me Good. James Laughlin. CP-LaugJ

It does my heart with deepest sorrow fill. Complaint, The. Jones Very. CP-VeryJ

It does no good to speak of the big, blue bush. Study of Images 1. Wallace Stevens. CP-StevW; CP-StevWP

It does not bother me if outside. Good and Bad Weather. Constantine P. Cavafy. CP-CavaC, *tr. by* Theoharis Constantine Theoharis

It does not come round in hundreds of thousands of years. Déjà Vu. Louis MacNeice. CP-MacNL

It Does Not Follow, but When in the Street. A. K. Ramanujan. CP-RamaA

It does not impress me that I have. Will. Alice Walker. CP-WalkA

It does not know it glitters. What Does It Mean. Czeslaw Milosz. CP-MiloC; CP-MiloCN

It does not know / its name. It sits. Corner, The. Donald Hall. CP-HallD

It don't sound so terrible—quite—as it did. Emily Dickinson. CP-DickE

It dreams in the deepest sleep, it remembers the storm last month or it feels the far storm. Ocean. Robinson Jeffers. CP-JefR1

It Dropped So Low in My Regard. Emily Dickinson. CP-DickE

It eats into the brain. Tour Guide. Yusef Komunyakaa. CP-KomuY

It Exists. Yannis Ritsos. SP-RitsY, tr. by Kostas Myrsiades

It faces west, and round the back and sides. Domicilium. Thomas Hardy. CP-HardT

It falleth like a stick. My Love. Robert Creeley. CP-CreeR

It falls me here to write of Chastity, Book 3. Edmund Spenser. CP-Spens Fr. Faerie Queene, The.

It falls onto my page like rain. Poem: "It falls onto my page like rain." Charles Tomlinson. CP-TomlC

It falls to an idiot to talk wisely. Way It Is, The. Laura Riding Jackson. CP-RidiL

It feels a shame to be Alive. Emily Dickinson. CP-DickE

It feels things. Later ("It feels things"). Robert Creeley. SP-CreeR

It fell in the ancient periods. Uriel. Ralph Waldo Emerson. CP-EmerR

It Fell on a Summer's [or Sommers] Day [or Daie]. Thomas Campion. CP-CampT

It felt like the zero in brook ice. Funeral, The. Norman Dubie. CP-DubiN

It Figures. Ogden Nash. CP-NashO

It Filled My Heart with Love. Stevie Smith. CP-SmitS

It fills me with elation. We Would Refer You to Our Service Department, If We Had One. Ogden Nash. CP-NashO

It finds the park first, and the trees. Flood, The. Elizabeth Bishop. CP-BishE

It fits not only him that makes a book. To the Worthy Author on The Husband. Ben Jonson. CP-JonsB

It flatters and deceives thy view. To Demosthenis. Unknown. CP-CowpW

It flows out of mystery into mystery: there is no beginning—. Robinson Jeffers. CP-JefR3

It follows now you are to prove. Ben Jonson. CP-JonsB Fr. Pleasure Reconciled to Virtue.

It fortifies my soul to know. With Whom Is No Variableness, Neither Shadow of Turning. Arthur Hugh Clough. SP-ClouA

It froze in Paris last night and a rag doll. Matins. John Ciardi. CP-CiarJ

It gave itself into your hand. Syllable Pain, The. Paul Celan. SP-CelaP, tr. by John Felstiner

It Gives Me Pause. Langston Hughes. CP-HughL; CP-HughL2

It goes, all inside itself. It keeps touching. Machine. John Ciardi. CP-CiarJ

It got beyond all orders an' it got beyond all 'ope. That Day. Rudyard Kipling. CP-KiplR

It got to cost $1,000,000 to kill an Indian. Nerves Are Staves, and When the Tears Come There Is Voice, The. Charles Olson. CP-OlsoC

It grew in the black mud. Rice. Mary Oliver. SP-OlivM

It had been badly shot. Widgeon. Seamus Heaney. SP-HeanSO

It had no dignity before. Harlem Dance Hall. Langston Hughes. CP-HughL; CP-HughL2

It had to be, of course, a rock. Rock-Old Dogma, The. William Carlos Williams. CP-WilW2

It hain't no use to grumble and complane [or complain]. Wet-Weather Talk. James Whitcomb Riley. CP-RileJ

It hangs from heaven to earth. Tapestry. Charles Simic. SP-SimiC; SP-SimiCE

It hangs from the edges of your mouth. Confession. Gabriela Mistral. SP-MistG, tr. by Maria Giachetti [or Jacketti]

It happened, halfway through the nineteen hundreds. Architecture of the American Mind. Miller Williams. CP-WillM

It happened not far away. Clonfeacle. Paul Muldoon. CP-MuldP

It happened once, before the duller. Green Slates. Thomas Hardy. CP-HardT

It happened so fast. Fenya was in the straight. Pastoral: "It happened so fast. Fenya was in the straight." Norman Dubie. CP-DubiN

It happened that my uncle liked to take my hand in his. Triptych, Middle Panel Burning. Thomas Lux. SP-LuxT

It happened this month, in this country. Cherries. Pablo Neruda. SP-NeruP

It happened thus: my slab, though new. Bad Dreams IV. Robert Browning. CP-BroR2

It happened when they came to find our brother. Image of True Lovers' Death, The. Thomas Merton. CP-MertT

It happens. Will it go on? Paralytic. Sylvia Plath. CP-PlatS

It has a bronze covering inlaid with silver. My Heart. Billy Collins. SP-CollB

It has / a life of its own however long it. Pilate. W. S. Merwin. SP-MerwW

It has an edge, or many edges. Berlin in Ruins. Thom Gunn. CP-GunnT

It has been a long journey. Edge of the River, The. Thomas McGrath. SP-McGrT

It has been a long time. Orphan, The. Thomas McGrath. SP-McGrT

It has been raining now since. Rain Downriver. Philip Levine. SP-LeviP

It Has Been Read by All. Laura Riding Jackson. CP-RidiL

It has been snowing. Past nidnight, drunk on purple wine, you leave. Winter Night, A. Georg Trakl. CP-WrigJ

It has been uppermost in my mind to write about my clothes. Love of a Coat, The. Andrei Codrescu. SP-CodrA

It has been well said that quietness. Dog's Best Friend Is His Illiteracy, A. Ogden Nash. CP-NashO

It has come to this: I'm sitting under a tree. No Title Required. Wisława Szymborska. SP-SzymW, tr. by Stanislaw Barańczak and Clare Cavanagh

It has grown late, my friends. Leavetaking. Primo Levi. CP-LeviP, tr. by Ruth Feldman and Brian Swann

It has happened. In Fear of Harvests. James Wright. CP-WrigJ

It has happened suddenly. Je Suis une Table. Donald Hall. CP-HallD

It has nothing to do with the warmth of moonset. Anima Poeta: A Christmas Entry for the Suicide, Mayakovsky. Norman Dubie. CP-DubiN

It has taken me decades to realize. How I Got Started. Charles Bukowski. SP-BukC3

It has to be the end of the day. Surf-Casting. W. S. Merwin. SP-MerwW

It hath been questioned, Michael, if I be. Vision of Ben Jonson, on the Muses of His Friend M. Drayton, The. Ben Jonson. CP-JonsB

It hath been said of old that plays are feasts. To the Reader of Master William Davenant's Play [The Wits]. Thomas Carew. CP-CareT

It huddled there. Laventille. Derek Walcott. CP-WalcD

It if isn't fun, don't do it. Sad Advice. Robert Creeley. SP-CreeR

It is a beauteous evening, calm and free. William Wordsworth. CP-WorW1; MW-WorW

It is a beauteous morning but the air turns sick. Tornado Warning. Karl Shapiro. SP-ShapK

It is a big question to pose so early in the morning. Idiomatic. Billy Collins. SP-CollB

It is a broken country. Wild Orchard. William Carlos Williams. CP-WilW1

It is a certain satisfaction to overlook a cemetary. On First Opening the Lyric Year. William Carlos Williams. CP-WilW1

It is a chilly god, a god of shades. Ouija. Sylvia Plath. CP-PlatS

It is a classic picture. Classic Picture. William Carlos Williams. CP-WilW2

It is a clearing deep in a forest: overhanging boughs. Johnson's Cabinet Watched by Ants. Robert Bly. SP-BlyR

It is a common fancy that trees are somehow conscious and. Thought of Trees, The. Howard Nemerov. CP-NemeH

It is a cramped little state with no foreign policy. Shame. Richard Wilbur. CP-WilbR

It is a day of the earth's renewing without any man's doing or help. Rain. Wendell Berry. CP-BerrW

It is a fearful thing to fall into the hands of the living God. Hands of God, The. D. H. Lawrence. CP-LawrD

"It is a foolish thing," said I. Tolerance. Thomas Hardy. CP-HardT

It is a formal and deserted garden. Out of Time. Stevie Smith. CP-SmitS

It Is a German Honeymoon. Kenneth Rexroth. CP-RexrK

It is a God-damned lie to say that these. Another Epitaph on an Army of Mercenaries. Hugh MacDiarmid. SP-MacDH

It is a good thing. Baskets. Louise Glück. SP-GlucL

It is a green globe like a vegetable light bulb. Avocado. John Logan. CP-LogaJ

It is a hard thing to say that when I first saw. For Zadkine. Louis Zukofsky. CP-ZukLS

It is a hollow garden, under the cloud. Winter Swan. Louise Bogan. CP-BogaL

It is a human universe: & I. Ted Berrigan. SP-BerrT Fr. Sonnets, The.

It is a hundred years since your shy feet. La Salette. Thomas Merton. CP-MertT

It is a kind of chalky russet. Sandstone Keepsake. Seamus Heaney. SP-HeanSO

It is a land with neither night nor day. Cobwebs. Christina Georgina Rossetti. CP-RosC3

It is a lie—their Priests, their Pope. Confessional, The. Robert Browning. CP-BroR1

It Is a Living Coral. William Carlos Williams. CP-WilW1

It is a lonesome Glee. Emily Dickinson. CP-DickE

It is a long way from there to here. Seated Figure. Sam Hamill. SP-HamiS

It is a lost road into the air. Airstrip in Essex, 1960, An. Donald Hall. CP-HallD

It is a maxim of much weight. William Cowper. CP-CowpW

It is a misery, beloved friends, and my last wish. Rituals of Departure. Thomas Kinsella. CP-KinsT

It is a multiple million eyed monster. Lysergic Acid. Allen Ginsberg. CP-GinsA

It is a nation of nothing but poetry. Charles Olson. CP-OlsoC

It is a noble country where we dwell. Our Country. Henry David Thoreau. CP-ThorH

It is a Pilgrim village; heavy rain is falling. Pilgrim Fish Heads. Robert Bly. SP-BlyR

It is a pity the shock-waves. Robinson Jeffers. CP-JefR3

It is a place where poets crowned may feel the heart's decaying. Cowper's Grave. Elizabeth Barrett Browning. CP-BroEB

It is a poet's privilege and fate. Darien. Robert Graves. CP-GravR

It is a posture for two multiplied. Butterandeggs. William Carlos Williams. CP-WilW1

It is a Presbyterian. Long Search, The. John Logan. CP-LogaJ

It is a quality of air, a temperate sharpness. At Holwell Farm. Charles Tomlinson. CP-TomlC; SP-TomlC

It is a real one—no more symbolic. Castle, The. Charles Tomlinson. CP-TomlC

It is a real place. Henry David Thoreau. CP-ThorH

It is a satisfaction. Portrait of a Woman at Her Bath. William Carlos Williams. CP-WilW2

It is a sea but is it music. All This Strangeness. George Oppen. CP-OppGN

"It Is a Shame"—with Apologies to the Modern Celtic School. Ezra Pound. CP-PoEar

It Is a Small Plant. William Carlos Williams. CP-WilW1

It is a special moment every year. Head of the Virgin Mary, The. Jaroslav Seifert. SP-SeifJ, tr. by Ewald Osers

It is a Spring Afternooon. Anne Sexton. CP-SextA; SP-SextA

It is a storm strid night, winds footing swift. Night-Time in Mid-Fall. Thomas Hardy. CP-HardT

It is a stubble field, where a black rain is falling. De Profundis. Georg Trakl. CP-WrigJ, tr. by James Wright

It is a Suffering, to have a sea. Emily Dickinson. SP-DickE

It is a summer evening. Lullaby: "It is a summer evening." Anne Sexton. CP-SextA; SP-SextA

It is a various tribute you command. To Edmund Clarence Stedman. James Whitcomb Riley. CP-RileJ

It is a waste of time to hate a mirror. Good Mirrors are Not Cheap. Audre Lorde. SP-LordA

It is a willow when summer is over. Willow Poem. William Carlos Williams. CP-WilW1

It is a winter's tale. Winter's Tale, A. Dylan Thomas. CP-ThomD

It is a wonder foam is so beautiful. Spray. D. H. Lawrence. CP-LawrD

It is a year of strategy. Clairvaux Prison. Thomas Merton. CP-MertT

It is all a rhythm. Rhythm, The. Robert Creeley. CP-CreeR

It is all here. Shad-Blow Tree, The. Louise Glück. SP-GlucL

It is all much worse than I dreamed. Child in the Great Wood. Muriel Rukeyser. CP-RukeM

It is all right. All they do. To the Muse. James Wright. CP-WrigJ

It is all to clear that order wasn't our invention. Pot-au-feu. Mona Van Duyn. SP-VanDM

It is almost dawn. Elegy: "It is almost dawn." Sam Hamill. SP-HamiS

It is almost polio season. The girls. Ars Poetica. Norman Dubie. CP-DubiN

It Is Almost the Year Two Thousand. Robert Frost. CP-FrosR

It is almost unbearably harmonious. Good Man, The. Mona Van Duyn. SP-VanDM

It is already late, my sister. Dreams. Randall Jarrell. CP-JarrR

It is already six. From the steeple. Mausoleum, The. Charles Tomlinson. CP-TomlC

It is always a temptation to an armed and agile nation. Dane-Geld. Rudyard Kipling. CP-KiplR

It is always best, of course. Object Lesson. Charles Bukowski. SP-BukC2

It is always there. Food. John Updike. CP-UpdiJ

It is an accurate nose. Nose. Donald Hall. CP-HallD

It is an age. Giving It Up. C. K. Williams. CP-WillC; SP-WillC

It is an ancient Mariner. Rime of the Ancient Mariner, The. Samuel Taylor Coleridge. CP-ColeS; MW-ColeS

It is an ancyent Marinere. Samuel Taylor Coleridge. See It is an ancient Mariner

It is an honorable Thought. Emily Dickinson. CP-DickE

It is an hour that makes the dust your escort. On a Journey. Paul Celan. SP-CelaP, tr. by John Felstiner

It is an illusion that we were ever alive. Rock, The. Wallace Stevens. CP-StevW; CP-StevWP

It is an orange / animal. High-Rise of the New World, The. Charles Bukowski. SP-BukC2

It is ancient, it is spongy. Limbic System. Hans Magnus Enzensberger. SP-EnzeH

It is, and is not, I am sane enough. Sub Mare. Ezra Pound. CP-PoEar

It is Anguish I long conceal from you. Emily Dickinson. SP-DickE

It is appropriate that time be measured. Hourglass, The. Jorge Luis Borges. SP-BorgJ, tr. by Alastair Reid

It is as if a silver chord. To a Dead Friend. Paul Laurence Dunbar. CP-DunbP

It is as one imagined it: an English garden. English Garden in Austria, An. Randall Jarrell. CP-JarrR

It is as simple as it can be. What I Want to Say. Mona Van Duyn. SP-VanDM

It is as though three forms move on a road. To Whom It May Concern. Kenneth Patchen. CP-PatcK

It is as true as Caesar's name was Kaiser. Equalizer, An. Robert Frost. CP-FrosR

It is as well that you should know. Some Revelations of Journalism. G. K. Chesterton. CP-ChesG

It Is At Moments After I Have Dreamed. E. E. Cummings. CP-CummE

It is at moments after i have dreamed. It Is At Moments After I Have Dreamed. E. E. Cummings. CP-CummE

It Is at Times. Robert Creeley. CP-CreeR

It is August moonlight in the tall plantation. Hurried Meeting, A. Thomas Hardy. CP-HardT

It is August. Your father is walking you. 1940. William Stafford. SP-StafW; SP-StafWW

It is autumn and there are no flowers in this desert garden. Near and the Far, The. Charles Tomlinson. CP-TomlC

It is autumn but early. No crow cries from the dry woods. Woodcut. Thomas McGrath. SP-McGrT

It is autumn still, but at three in the morning. October Week-End. Robinson Jeffers. CP-JefR2

It is bad enough crying for children. C. K. Williams. See It's bad enough crying for children

It is because of the savage mystery. Matador. Richard Eberhart. CP-EberR

It is beginning oh. Robert Earl Hayden. CP-HaydR Fr. Snow Lamp, The.

It is better in the long run to possess an abscess or a tumor. Don't Grin, or You'll Have to Bear It. Ogden Nash. CP-NashO

It is better this year. If the Birds Knew. John Ashbery. SP-AshbJ

It Is Better To Go into Heaven with One Eye. Richard Crashaw. CP-CrasR

It Is Big Inside a Man. Kenneth Patchen. CP-PatcK

It is bitter to praise God in misfortune. Before Majesty. Czeslaw Milosz. CP-MiloC; CP-MiloCN, tr. by Robert Hass

It is blue-butterfly day here in spring. Blue-Butterfly Day. Robert Frost. CP-FrosR

It is borne in upon me that pain. Human Being Is a Lonely Creature, The. Richard Eberhart. CP-EberR

It is carried beyond itself a little way. End in Spring, An. W. S. Merwin. SP-MerwW

It is certain that who his mind. Hafiz. CP-EmerR Fr. Odes.

It is certainly the mystical hour of day. Solace. Richard Eberhart. CP-EberR

It is cold here. Moths, The. W. S. Merwin. SP-MerwW

It is cold in my refrigerator. Lean and Hungry Look, A. Howard Nemerov. CP-NemeH

It is cold. / The bitter of the winter. Winter Weather. Carl Sandburg. CP-SandC

It is cold. The white moon. Cold Night, The. William Carlos Williams. CP-WilW1

It is colder now. Epistle to Be Left in the Earth. Archibald MacLeish. CP-MacLA

It is common knowledge to every schoolboy and even every Bachelor of Arts. Portrait of the Artist as a Prematurely Old Man. Ogden Nash. CP-NashO

It is conceit that kills us. Conceit. D. H. Lawrence. CP-LawrD

It is contagious as a dance. Franz, a Goose. May Sarton. SP-SartM

It is curious I cannot feel it yet. Beautiful Captive, The. Robinson Jeffers. CP-JefR3

It is curious that I should have spoken of Raël. Desire & the Object. Wallace Stevens. CP-StevWP

It is curious, too, that though the modern man in the street. Robot Feelings. D. H. Lawrence. CP-LawrD

It Is Dangerous to Read Newspapers. Margaret Atwood. SP-AtwM1

It is dark. D. H. Lawrence. See Blue and dark

It is dark as a cave. Clock-Winder, The. Thomas Hardy. CP-HardT

It is dark in the sky. Looking Across. Thomas Hardy. CP-HardT

It is dead. Find it. Emily Dickinson. CP-DickE

It is deep twilight, my wife. Organization Men in Affluent Society. Kenneth Rexroth. CP-RexrR

It is delicate that each Mind is itself. Emily Dickinson. SP-DickE

It is difficult to read. The page is dark. Phosphor Reading by His Own Light. Wallace Stevens. CP-StevW; CP-StevWP

It is difficult to separate the tapestry. Tapestry. John Ashbery. SP-AshbJ

It is done! Laus Deo! John Greenleaf Whittier. CP-WhitJ

It is done by us all, as God disposes, from. Excrement Poem, The. Maxine W. Kumin. SP-KumiM

It is early afternoon. Your Face on the Dog's Neck. Anne Sexton. CP-SextA; SP-SextA

It is easier to look behind at a pain. Emily Dickinson. SP-DickE

It is easy, often, and natural even. In Trance At A Distance. Robert Graves. CP-GravR

It is easy to be young. (Everybody is). How to Be Old. May Swenson. SP-SwenM

It is easy to work when the soul is at play. Emily Dickinson. CP-DickE

"It is enough, enough," one said. Books In the Running Brooks. Christina Georgina Rossetti. CP-RosC3

It is equal to living in a tragic land. Dry Loaf. Wallace Stevens. CP-StevW; CP-StevWP

It is evening. One bat dances. Soul, A. Randall Jarrell. CP-JarrR

It is far to Assisi. Mental Hospital Garden, The. William Carlos Williams. CP-WilW2

It Is Finished. Christina Georgina Rossetti. CP-RosC2

It Is for the Waking Man to Tell His Dreams. John Ciardi. CP-CiarJ

It Is for Us the Living. Kenneth Patchen. CP-PatcK

It is Friday, a usual day. Gift for a Believer. Philip Levine. SP-LeviP

It is full summer now, the heart of June. Garden of Eros, The. Oscar Wilde. CP-WildO

It is full Winter now: the trees are bare. Humanitad. Oscar Wilde. CP-WildO

It is funny—strange—to see the young. Robert Creeley. CP-CreeR

It is funny,you will be dead some day. E. E. Cummings. CP-CummE

It is getting dark and time he drew to a house. Willful Homing. Robert Frost. CP-FrosR

It is good for strength not to be merciful. To a Young Artist. Robinson Jeffers. CP-JefR1

It is good to be last not first, / Pending the present distress. Lent. Christina Georgina Rossetti. CP-RosC2

It is good, when leaving a place. Seeking the Chosen. James Dickey. CP-DickJ

It is green, it is made of willow. Day-Bed, The. Richard Eberhart. CP-EberR

It is half winter, half spring. In Excelsis. Anne Sexton. CP-SextA; SP-SextA

It is hard going to the door. Door, The. Robert Creeley. CP-CreeR

It is hard sometimes to drag ourselves. Love of Morning, The. Denise Levertov. SP-LeveDS

It is hard to be a man. Falcon Woman, The. Robert Graves. CP-GravR

It is hard to guess tales from the sight of a thing. Coin, The. Ivor Gurney. SP-GurnI

It is hard to hear the north wind again. Region November, The. Wallace Stevens. CP-StevWP

It is hard to know the logic of mere recollection. Upwardness. Robert Penn Warren. CP-WarrR

It is hard to remain human on a day. Times, The. Lucille Clifton. SP-ClifL

It is heart-rending to know a kiss. David Ignatow. SP-IgnaD

It is here, the long Awaited bleap-blast light that Speaks one red tongue like Politician, but happy its own govt. Television Was a Baby Crawling toward That Deathchamber. Allen Ginsberg. CP-GinsA

It is I, O Azure, come from the caves below. Helen. Paul Valéry. CP-WilbR, tr. by Richard Wilbur

It is I, Odysseus—Eplenor. Eplenor. Archibald MacLeish. CP-MacLA

It is, I think, a robin tinkling away. This Moving Meaninglessness. John Ciardi. CP-CiarJ

It is impossible. The Uncertainty Principle. Prothalamion of Quantum Mechanics and Astrophysics against the Text "Philosophia Biou Kubernetes" (Philosophy the Guide of Life). Alan Dugan. CP-DugaA

It is impossible to know by your letter whether the wine is to be. From Dr. Swift to Dr. Sheridan. Jonathan Swift. CP-SwifJ

It is impossible to see anything. Inversely, as the Square of Their Distances Apart. Kenneth Rexroth. CP-RexrK

It is in captivity. Bull, The. William Carlos Williams. CP-WilW1

It is in the minds. Light Shall Not Enter. William Carlos Williams. CP-WilW2

It is in the sky—the new moon is looking at me. Little New Moon, The. Gabriela Mistral. SP-MistG, tr. by Maria Giachetti [or Jacketti]

It is in the small things we see it. Courage. Anne Sexton. CP-SextA

It is in us they burn. Kathleen Jessie Raine. SP-RainK

It is Isis the mystery. Don Juan. D. H. Lawrence. CP-LawrD

It is June, it is June. Andraitx—Pomegranate Flowers. D. H. Lawrence. CP-LawrD

It is just getting dark as the rain stops. New York Scene: May 1958. John Logan. CP-LogaJ

It is just what they would do eventually. Prudence Caution and Foresight: A Story of Avignon. Gertrude Stein. CP-SteiG

It is known. She Steals Birds. George Oppen. CP-OppGN

It is late at night, cold and damp. Gic to Har. Kenneth Rexroth. CP-RexrK

It is late autumn, the end of Indian summer. Heart Unbroken and the Courage Free, The. Kenneth Rexroth. CP-RexrK

It is late December; I walk through the pasture. Out Picking up Corn. Robert Bly. SP-BlyR

It is late. the train. Birthday 1999. Lucille Clifton. SP-ClifL

It is life in slow motion. Wait, The. Rainer Maria Rilke. CP-RilkFr, tr. by A. Poulin, Jr.

It is light and dark a book lay on the table beside the sun are moon and. Alogon. Michael Palmer. SP-PalmM

It is like a monster come to dinner. Saturday Afternoon. Robert Creeley. CP-CreeR

It is like tanks come through Hungary and. Spain Sits Like a Hidden Flower in My Coffeepot. Charles Bukowski. SP-BukC2

It is like this perhaps. In Sickness Like Sleep. Thomas McGrath. SP-McGrT

It is likely enough that lions and scorpions. Ante Mortem. Robinson Jeffers. CP-JefR1

It is low tide. Fog. I have climbed down the cliffs from Pierce Ranch to the tide

pools. Starfish, The. Robert Bly. SP-BlyR

It is March and black dust falls out of the books. W. S. Merwin. SP-MerwW

It is May: 'A bad winter.' Providence. Charles Tomlinson. CP-TomlC

It is May on every hand. Bird Song. William Carlos Williams. CP-WilW2

It Is Much. Carl Sandburg. CP-SandC

It is my dream to have you here with me. Voice from the Farm, A. James Whitcomb Riley. CP-RileJ

It is my responsibility. My Problem. Rae Armantrout. SP-ArmaA

It is myself. To a Dog Injured in the Street. William Carlos Williams. CP-WilW2

It is na, Jean, thy bonie face. Robert Burns. CP-BurnR

It is near Toussaints, the living and the dead will say. Ivor Gurney. SP-GurnI

It is never enough to know what you want. Wish to Be Believed, The. Mona Van Duyn. SP-VanDM

It is never the cost of the gift. Triolet: "It is never the cost of the gift." Dorothy Parker. CP-ParkD

It is night and your plane is now. Prisoner of Childhood, The. James Laughlin. CP-LaugJ

It is night for the last time. Letters, The. Louise Glück. SP-GlucL

It is night. You are asleep. And beautiful tears. Ted Berrigan. SP-BerrT Fr. Sonnets, The.

It is 1939. Album. Lucille Clifton. SP-ClifL

It is no gift I tender. A. E. Housman. CP-HousA

It is no longer necessary to sleep. Man Walking and Singing, A. Wendell Berry. CP-BerrW

It is no longer night. But there is a sameness. Tone Poem, A. John Ashbery. SP-AshbJ

It is no night to drown in. Lorelei. Sylvia Plath. CP-PlatS

It is no spirit who from heaven hath flown. William Wordsworth. CP-WorW1; MW-WorW

It is no wonder that new lovers run. Poem: "It is no wonder that new lovers run." Alan Dugan. CP-DugaA

It is not a turtle. Dead Heart, The. Anne Sexton. CP-SextA

It is not bad. Let them play. Bloody Sire, The. Robinson Jeffers. CP-JefR3

It is not because we are going—. When We Say Goodbye. Thomas McGrath. SP-McGrT

It is not blasphemy to hope that Heaven. To Harriet. Percy Bysshe Shelley. CP-ShelP

It is not dead. It is simply weighty with wisdom. Robert Penn Warren. CP-WarrR

It is not death, O Christ, to die for Thee: / Nor is that silence of a silent land. Christina Georgina Rossetti. CP-RosC2

"It is not death that harrows us," they lipped. Spectres That Grieve. Thomas Hardy. CP-HardT

It is not difficult to come here. Thinking Rock. Kenneth Patchen. CP-PatcK

It is not difficult to kill. From My Notes for a Series of Lectures on Murder. Stevie Smith. CP-SmitS

It is not easy for an eye to see. Aeneas Underground. Robert Stock. SP-StocR

It is not easy to die, O it is not easy. Difficult Death. D. H. Lawrence. CP-LawrD

It is not easy to fall out of the hands of the livng God. Abysmal Immortality. D. H. Lawrence. CP-LawrD

It is not enough to be willing to come out of the dark. Two Motions. A. R. Ammons. CP-AmmoA

It is not far to my place. Visit. A. R. Ammons. CP-AmmoA

It is not for earthly bread, Annie. Annie. Christina Georgina Rossetti. CP-RosC3

It is not for her even brow. Song: "It is not for her even brow." Christina Georgina Rossetti. CP-RosC3

It is not for me, the day. Euripides. CP-DoolH Fr. Iphigenia [or Iphigeneia] in Aulis.

It is not four years ago. Proffered Love Rejected. Sir John Suckling. CP-SuckJ

It is not in the books. Three Movements, The. Donald Hall. CP-HallD

It is not Lake Michigan's lapping waves. Chicago. Langston Hughes. CP-HughL; CP-HughL3

It is not life being short. Winter Landscape near Ely, A. Donald Davie. CP-DaviDC

It is not life upon Thy gifts to live. Life. Jones Very. CP-VeryJ

It is not long since, here among all these folk. Frost Flowers. D. H. Lawrence. CP-LawrD

It is not magic now, the world. Alone. 1964. Jorge Luis Borges. SP-BorgJ, tr. by Alastair Reid

It is not music, though one has tried music. Words in a Certain Appropriate Mode. Hayden Carruth. CP-CarHS

It is not my habit. Dear Fox. Lucille Clifton. SP-ClifL

It is not 1937 for long. A clump of ash trees and a walk. Grand Illusion. Norman Dubie. CP-DubiN

It is not now I learn. Song: "It is not now I learn." Louise Bogan. CP-BogaL

It is not only the ant that walks on the carpenter's board alone. "Out of the Rolling Ocean, the Crowd." Robert Bly. SP-BlyR

It is not only the present that is at stake. Statement by Willkie after Returning from England. Muriel Rukeyser. CP-RukeM

It is not pride, it is not shame. Emily Jane Brontë. CP-BronE

It is not sad, or I would laugh. Laura Riding Jackson. CP-RidiL

It is not sleep itself but dreams we miss. Dawn Chorus, The. Derek Mahon. CP-MahoD

It is not so much trying to keep alive. Prisoner at a Desk. May Sarton. SP-SartM

It is not spring. The furnace. It's SPRing AgAIN! Charles Olson. CP-OlsoC

It Is Not That It Came to Nothing, Emiliano. Miller Williams. CP-WillM

It is not the still weight. Jungle, The. William Carlos Williams. CP-WilW1

It is not the tilted buildings or the blind alleys. Jealousy. Billy Collins. SP-CollB

It is not to be thought of that the Flood. William Wordsworth. CP-WorW1; MW-WorW

It is not true that we are just meat. On the Inequality of Men. Czeslaw Milosz. CP-MiloCN, tr. by Robert Hass

It is not weariness. Burden. Langston Hughes. CP-HughL; CP-HughL2

It Is Not Well for Man to Be Alone. G. K. Chesterton. CP-ChesG

It is not what they built. It is what they knocked down. German Requiem, A. James Fenton. SP-FentJ

It is not what they intend. Fear of Angels, The. May Sarton. SP-SartM

It is not yet the grey and frosty time. After the Night Office—Gethsemani Abbey. Thomas Merton. CP-MertT

It is not you that moves. It is the dark. Immortality Over the Dakotas. Robert Penn Warren. CP-WarrR

It is nothing till it takes. To See the Light. Heather McHugh. SP-McHuH

It is November nineteen ninety-two. Matisse at the Modern, Magritte at the Met. Lawrence Ferlinghetti. SP-FerlL

It is obvious that the three brown dogs, on the beach. Dogs, The. Josephine Jacobsen. CP-JacoJ

It is odd, again, about the young. Young Want to Be Just, The. D. H. Lawrence. CP-LawrD

It is of Realms unratified. Emily Dickinson. SP-DickE

It is old school custom to pretend to be sad. Trenta-Sei of the Pleasure We Take in the Early Death of Keats, A. John Ciardi. CP-CiarJ

It is one of Oriane's "difficult" evenings, and she has hidden herself. Encounter at the Casino, Aix-les-Bains. James Laughlin. CP-LaugJ

It is only after. Finally that Blue Receding Sphere. John Ciardi. CP-CiarJ

It is only immoral. Immorality. D. H. Lawrence. CP-LawrD

It is only that this warmth and movement are like. Woman in Sunshine, The. Wallace Stevens. CP-StevW; CP-StevWP

It is over now, with no more need. In the Vestry. Robert Graves. CP-GravR

It is over the horrible pain. Martyr, A. Christina Georgina Rossetti. CP-RosC3

It is over. What is over? Amen. Christina Georgina Rossetti. CP-RosC1

It is patent to the eye that cannot face the sun. Plurality. Louis MacNeice. CP-MacNL

It is people at the edge who say. Sayings from the Northern Ice. William Stafford. SP-StafW; SP-StafWW

It is portentous, and a thing of state. Abraham Lincoln Walks at Midnight. Nicholas Vachel Lindsay. CP-LindV

It is posed and it is posed. Add This to Rhetoric. Wallace Stevens. CP-StevW; CP-StevWP

It is possible—I found out near the top of Sauk Mountain. Walking. Philip Whalen. SP-WhalP

It is possible, in words, to speak. Enough. Robert Creeley. CP-CreeR

It is possible that a change may come. Hugh MacDiarmid. SP-MacDH Fr. England Is Our Enemy.

It is possible that most individual and international social and economic collisions. Are You a Snodgrass? Ogden Nash. CP-NashO

It is possible that to seem—it is to be. Description without Place. Wallace Stevens. CP-StevW; CP-StevWP

It is possible to be struck by a meteor. Picnic, Lightning. Billy Collins. SP-CollB

It is quick it is far it is over it is. New Ribbon. Thomas Merton. CP-MertT

It is quite easy to appear modern. Word on the Quick and Modern Poem-Makers, A. Charles Bukowski. SP-BukC2

It is raining. Self-Portrait 2. William Carlos Williams. CP-WilW1

It is raining hard, too hard for us to go down to Paestum. Can Language Be Taught with the Fingertips? James Laughlin. CP-LaugJ

It is raining. The child is waiting. Dublin Suite: Homage to James Joyce. John Logan. CP-LogaJ

It is remarkable but it is no less painful for that, how rarely. O What a Revolution! Kenneth Patchen. CP-PatcK

It is right in there. Peril of Hope. Robert Frost. CP-FrosR

It is sad that so many of worth. While Drawing in a Churchyard. Thomas Hardy. CP-HardT

It is sad to be. Mayor, The. Yehuda Amichai. SP-AmicYL, tr. by Benjamin Harshav and Barbara Harshav

It is said that he laughs at himself. Alzheimer's Disease. Donald Davie. CP-DaviDC

It is said that man is gulled but I. Gulled. Richard Eberhart. CP-EberR

It is September and the wry corn rattles. Motto on the Sundial, The. Kenneth Rexroth. CP-RexrK

It is seven years now that we first loved. Scared Child, The. Robert Graves. CP-GravR

It Is 70 Degrees in Late November. Opening a Window, You Nearly Know. Heather McHugh. SP-McHuH

It is she alone that matters. Bouquet of Belle Scavoir. Wallace Stevens. CP-StevW; CP-StevWP

It is sin it is sin it is a. Voices, The. James Laughlin. CP-LaugJ

It is small and no more visible than a cricket. Self, The. Adam Zagajewski. SP-ZagaA, tr. by Renata Gorczynski

It is snowing and death bugs me. Oh. Anne Sexton. CP-SextA

It is so long since my heart has been with yours. E. E. Cummings. CP-CummE

It is so peaceful at last. Good Night. Thomas Kinsella. CP-KinsT

It is so peaceful on the ceiling! Sleeping on the Ceiling. Elizabeth Bishop. CP-BishE

It is so rare and new a thing to see. To His Much Honoured the Lord Lepington upon His Translation of Malvezzi, His "Romulus" and "Tarquin." Sir John Suckling. CP-SuckJ

It is solemn to remember. Emily Dickinson. SP-DickE

It is solstice. Dragon in the Clouds, A. Sam Hamill. SP-HamiS

It is some school, brick, green, a sleepy hill. Officers' Prison Camp Seen from a Troop-Train, An. Randall Jarrell. CP-JarrR

It is some time since I have been. Hill, The. Robert Creeley. CP-CreeR

It is someone's deserted private beach. Shore Piece. John Ciardi. CP-CiarJ

It is someone's mimicry, the clockworks. Water Slide Along the Beach. Wyatt Prunty. SP-PrunW

It is something to face the sun and know you are free. Clean Hands. Carl Sandburg. CP-SandC

It is spring. Interests of 1926. William Carlos Williams. CP-WilW1

It is spring, full moon in a cloudless sky. Leaf, A. Sam Hamill. SP-HamiS

It is spring once more in the Coast Range. Yin and Yang. Kenneth Rexroth. CP-RexrK

It is still as distinct as Paradise. Emily Dickinson. SP-DickE

It is stormy, and raindrops cling like silver bees to the panes. Discipline. D. H. Lawrence. CP-LawrD

It is strange that I should want. Prisoners. "H. D." CP-DoolH

It is strange to think of the Annas, the Vronskys, the Pierres, all the Tolstoyan lot wiped out. Fate and the Younger Generation. D. H. Lawrence. CP-LawrD

'It is such a beautiful day I had to write you a letter.' Thoughts of a Young Girl. John Ashbery. SP-AshbJ

It is sufficient if we pray. His Wish. Robert Herrick. CP-HerrR

It is summer, winter, any. Birds and Flowers. William Carlos Williams. CP-WilW1

It is summertime. L'Homme et La Bête. Philip Levine. SP-LeviP

It is Sunday, day of roughhousing. We are let out in the woods. Kentucky, 1833. Rita Dove. SP-DoveR

It is supernal what a youth can take. Down & Back. John Berryman. CP-BerrJ

It is taught that the soul. Atman, The. James Laughlin. CP-LaugJ

It Is Teeming. C. K. Williams. CP-WillC

It is ten years, now, since we rowed to Children's Island. Babysitters, The. Sylvia Plath. CP-PlatS

It is the afternoon hour. Summit. Gabriela Mistral. SP-MistG, tr. by Maria Giachetti [or Jacketti]

It is the bird of burial. Oh Stubborn Race of Cadmus' Seed. Stevie Smith. CP-SmitS

It is the blond Mediterraneans you know the ones with Norman. Blond Mediterraneans, The. Tennessee Williams. CP-WillT

It is the cause the cause, still, it is (and she, still). Cause, the Cause, The. Charles Olson. CP-OlsoC

It is the continuous welling up from the earth. Ichetucknee. Richard Eberhart. CP-EberR

It is the daily love, grass high. Healall. William Carlos Williams. CP-WilW1

It is the dark of the moon. Doubled Mirrors. Kenneth Rexroth. CP-RexrK

It is the day when all the sons of God. Hellas. Percy Bysshe Shelley. CP-ShelP

It is the end of the grape. Song at the Winepresses, A. Kenneth Rexroth. CP-RexrK

It is the evening. Nativity Poem. Louise Glück. SP-GlucL

It is the fashion now to wave aside. Edna St. Vincent Millay. CP-MillE

It is the first day of the world. Venetian Blind, The. Randall Jarrell. CP-JarrR

It is the first mild day of March. To My Sister. William Wordsworth. CP-WorW1

It is the fish tank room—the small room. Fish Tank Room, The. Josephine Jacobsen. CP-JacoJ

It is the greatness of Thy love, dear Lord, that we would celebrate. Passiontide. Christina Georgina Rossetti. CP-RosC2

It is the hour of indecision. From a Record of Disappointment. Howard Nemerov. CP-NemeH

It is the hour when from the boughs. Parisina. Lord Byron. CP-Byron

It is the kind of raw and changeable afternoon. Travel Advisory for a Night Shift. Alan Dugan. CP-DugaA

It is the kind of spring morning—candid sunlight. History of Weather, A. Billy Collins. SP-CollB

It is the little brown hour of twilight. In the Evening. G. K. Chesterton. CP-ChesG

It is the May-tme now. Spinners. Marya Alexandrovna Zaturenska. SP-ZatuM

It is the Meek that Valor wear. Emily Dickinson. SP-DickE

It is the mind experiencing its pleasure. Orgasm. David Ignatow. SP-IgnaD

It is the moon that disappears. Guru. Allen Ginsberg. CP-GinsA; SP-GinsA

It is the nature of poets. Poets. James Laughlin. CP-LaugJ

It is the Old Man through the sleeping town. Fall Again, The. Howard Nemerov. CP-NemeH

It is the one in homespun. Woman, The. Denise Levertov. SP-LeveDL; SP-LeveDS

It is the opposite or so of the friendly gossip from upstairs who stops by every other evening. End of Drought. C. K. Williams. SP-WillC

It is the picnic with Ruth in the spring. Picnic, The. John Logan. CP-LogaJ

It is the poem, yes. Work, for the Day Is Coming. Muriel Rukeyser. CP-RukeM

It is the responsibility of society to let the poet be a poet. Responsibility. Grace Paley. CP-PalGC

It is the same everywhere for me. Always the Same. Langston Hughes. CP-HughL; CP-HughL1

It Is the Same Place Always Once Again. John Ciardi. CP-CiarJ

It Is the Season. Josephine Jacobsen. CP-JacoJ

It is the sense / of things that we must include. Impalpabilities, The. Charles Tomlinson. CP-TomlC

It is the sink of the afternoon. Sowing. Audre Lorde. SP-LordA

It is the sinking of things. Rain. James Wright. CP-WrigJ

It Is the Sinner's Dust-Tongued Bell. Dylan Thomas. CP-ThomD

It is the sixth year of the war in China. Muriel Rukeyser. CP-RukeM

It is the sound of lions lapping. Bush. Josephine Jacobsen. CP-JacoJ

It is the staling music of memory. Dance, The. Thomas Kinsella. CP-KinsT

It is the test of us. It plumbs us. Three Sorts of Violence, The. William Meredith. SP-MereW

It is the truth, not a fairytale. Guardian Angel. Gabriela Mistral. SP-MistG, tr. by Maria Giachetti [or Jacketti]

It is the unregarded congruence. History. Charles Tomlinson. CP-TomlC

It is the very bewitching hour of eight. Hendecasyllables. Stevie Smith. CP-SmitS

It is the whales that drive. Fish. William Carlos Williams. CP-WilW1

It is the wish. Eight Poems on Portraits of the Foot. John Logan. CP-LogaJ

It is the word *pejorative* that hurts. Sailing after Lunch. Wallace Stevens. CP-StevW; CP-StevWP

It is the young fresh rainy leaf. George Meredith. CP-MerG2

It Is There. Muriel Rukeyser. CP-RukeM

It is there, above him, beyond, behind. Being, The. James Dickey. CP-DickJ

It is this that you get for being so far-sighted. Not so many years. Road to the Past, The. Edna St. Vincent Millay. CP-MillE

It Is This Way with Men. C. K. Williams. CP-WillC; SP-WillC

It is time for all the heroes to go home. Allegiances. William Stafford. SP-StafW; SP-StafWW

It is time for applause. My hands rest. My Hands. William Stafford. SP-StafW

It is time for bed. The cups and saucers are gathered. Before Sleep. Thomas Kinsella. CP-KinsT

It is time for the others to come. Magus, The. James Dickey. CP-DickJ

It is time I came back to my real life. Return. May Sarton. SP-SartM

It is time I got out. Fragment. Christopher Logue. SP-LoguC

It is time men took their thoughts off women. Love as an Escape. D. H. Lawrence. CP-LawrD

It is time that beats in the breast and it is time. Pure Good of Theory, The. Wallace Stevens. CP-StevW; CP-StevWP

It is time the big bird with the angry neck. Phoenix, The. May Sarton. SP-SartM

It is time to be old. Terminus. Ralph Waldo Emerson. CP-EmerR

It is time to break a house. Divorced, Husband Demolishes House. John Ciardi. CP-CiarJ

It is time to drive in the hills. Day in Late October, A. Mona Van Duyn. SP-VanDM

It is to make a fill, not find a land. Toward a Definition of Marriage. Mona Van Duyn. SP-VanDM

It is too easy not to like. J, My Good Friend (Another Foolish Innocent). Alice Walker. CP-WalkA

It is too late for the ambiguous thrush. Ultimate Song. Richard Eberhart. CP-EberR

It is too late to call thee now. Emily Jane Brontë. CP-BronE

It is too simple to turn to the sound. Cold before the Moonrise, The. W. S. Merwin. SP-MerwW

It Is True. Federico García Lorca. SP-GarcF, tr. by Harriet de Onís

It is true, Martin Heidegger, as you have written. Envelope, The. Maxine W. Kumin. SP-KumiM

It is true, our tribe is similar to the bees. Woe! Czeslaw Milosz. CP-MiloCN, tr. by Robert Hass

It is true, that even in the best-run state. Murder of William Remington, The. Howard Nemerov. CP-NemeH

It is true that half the glory is gone. Salvage. Robinson Jeffers. CP-JefR3

It is true that, older than man and ages to outlast him, the Pacific surf. Gray Weather. Robinson Jeffers. CP-JefR2

It is true that the rivers went nosing like swine. Frogs Eat Butterflies. Snakes Eat Frogs. Hogs Eat Snakes. Men Eat Hogs. Wallace Stevens. CP-StevW; CP-StevWP

It is true that you say the gods are more use to you than fairies. Choice, The. Ezra Pound. CP-PoEar

It is 12:10 in New York and I am wondering. Adieu to Norman, Bon Jour to Joan and Jean-Paul. Frank O'Hara. SP-OharF

It is 12:20 in New York a Friday. Day Lady Died, The. Frank O'Hara. SP-OharF

It is twenty years. Piper, The. W. S. Merwin. SP-MerwW

It is useless, good woman, useless: the spark fails me. Death of Franco of Cologne, The: His Prophecy of Beethoven. William Carlos Williams. CP-WilW1

"It is vain to say, that this is the country of the 'white man.' It is the country of man." Charles Sumner. Jones Very. CP-VeryJ

It is very hard to understand that. Treading More Water. Philip Whalen. SP-WhalP

It is very meritorious to work very hard in a garden. What Does She See When She Shuts Her Eyes. Gertrude Stein. CP-SteiG

It is very wrong that you were ill. Emily Dickinson. SP-DickE

It is war. They put us on a train and. How It Is. William Stafford. SP-StafW; SP-StafWW

It is we who are liars. Liars. Langston Hughes. CP-HughL; CP-HughL1

It is well to be disciplined in all the social usages. Behaviour. D. H. Lawrence. CP-LawrD

It is well to remember, to celebrate and remember. Wreath for Alexandra Molostvova, A. Tennessee Williams. CP-WillT

It is what he does not know. On a Squirrel Crossing the Road in Autumn, in New England. Richard Eberhart. CP-EberR

It is what I never quite understood. Testament, A. Richard Eberhart. CP-EberR

It is what we both knew in the sunlight of a restaurant's garden. Circus Ringmaster's Apology to God, The. Norman Dubie. CP-DubiN

It is when I have thought of the universe. Walking After Supper. Miller Williams. CP-WillM

It is wild country here. Eve Thinking. Lucille Clifton. SP-ClifL

It is winter a moon in the afternoon. E. E. Cummings. CP-CummE

It is winter, the soon dark annoys me. Ivor Gurney. SP-GurnI

It is winter. We have ransacked. Winter. Charles Tomlinson. CP-TomlC

It is with a strange malice. Weeping Burgher, The. Wallace Stevens. CP-StevW; CP-StevWP

It is with the poet as with a guinea worm. To a Friend and Fellow Poet. Hugh MacDiarmid. SP-MacDH

It is wonderful to die amidst the pleasures I have known. Without Recrimination. David Ignatow. SP-IgnaD

It is worth it to get. Drifting. James Dickey. CP-DickJ

It is written in the Book of Usable Minutes. Train Rising Out of the Sea. John Ashbery. SP-AshbJ

It is yes with a lyre, ax and shovel. Letter from Paul. Lorine Niedecker. CP-NiedL

It is You have borne the shame and sorrow. Last Words to Muriel. D. H. Lawrence. CP-LawrD

It is you who have made light crawl. Lazarus to the Assembled. James Dickey. CP-DickJ

It is your afternoon that I lived. Unknown Woman's Afternoon. Rainer Maria Rilke. CP-RilkFr, tr. by A. Poulin, Jr.

It is yourself you seek. Man Alone. Louise Bogan. CP-BogaL

It isna fair to my wife and weans. Hokum. Hugh MacDiarmid. SP-MacDH

It isn't easy running through the halls. Nice Place, A. Charles Bukowski. SP-BukC2

It isn't fair, to me, when you're away. Rondeau: "It isn't fair, to me, when you're away." Dorothy Parker. CP-ParkD

It isn't just spying that turns me on. Ode to Curiosity. Andrei Codrescu. SP-CodrA

It isn't May-like, this impure air. Ashes of Gramsci, The. Pier Paolo Pasolini. SP-PasoP, tr. by Norman MacAfee and Luciano Martinengo

It isn't my word but my mother's. Charles Olson. CP-OlsoC

It isn't supposed to happen. Snow in May. Marge Piercy. SP-PierM

It isn't that the blossoms fall, Ezra. Slow News from Our Place. William Stafford. SP-StafWW

It isn't the body. Inner Man, The. Charles Simic. SP-SimiC; SP-SimiCE

It isn't very far as highways lie. Going to Walden. Mary Oliver. SP-OlivM

It! It! / That's what the unknown bird said. Forest Birds. Charles Simic. SP-SimiC; SP-SimiCE

It keeps eternal whisperings around. On the Sea. John Keats. CP-KeatJ

It keeps out everything! It goes. Umbrella, The. Donald Hall. CP-HallD

It kept treading air, as if it were a ghost with claims on us. Visitant. Seamus Heaney. SP-HeanSO

It kissed us, soft, to cut our throats, this coast. Not to Live. John Berryman. CP-BerrJ

It knew no lapse, nor Diminution. Emily Dickinson. CP-DickE

It knew no Medicine. Emily Dickinson. CP-DickE

It lay in my palm soft and trembled. Lorena. Lucille Clifton. SP-ClifL

It leaves me plunged in gloom and pain—yet dear. Michelangelo Buonarroti. CP-Miche, tr. by John Frederick Nims

It lies on its side in the grassy Mall. Vietnam Memorial. Karl Shapiro. SP-ShapK

It lieth, gazing on the midnight sky. On the Medusa of Leonardo da Vinci in the Florentine Gallery. Percy Bysshe Shelley. CP-ShelP

It little profits that an idle king. Ulysses. Alfred Tennyson. CP-TennA

It looked like a clump of small dusty nettles. Mint. Seamus Heaney. SP-HeanSO

It looks easy to win but watch out. Poem Seen as a Shell Game, The. James Laughlin. CP-LaugJ

It looks like there's. Vespers. Paul Muldoon. CP-MuldP

It looks like to me. Little Green Tree. Langston Hughes. CP-HughL; CP-HughL2

It looks like we are the Last Unmarried. Country & Western II. Marilyn Hacker. SP-HackM

It makes me weary when I realise. Petrarch. CP-Petra, tr. by J. G. Nichols

It makes no difference abroad. Emily Dickinson. CP-DickE

It makes so little difference, at so much more. Long and Sluggish Lines. Wallace Stevens. CP-StevW; CP-StevWP

It may be good like it who list. Sir Thomas Wyatt. CP-WyatT

It may be grubs / and worms and. Roads. Robert Creeley. CP-CreeR

It may be misery not to sing at all. Life's Tragedy. Paul Laurence Dunbar. CP-DunbP

It may be the sea-moving moon. Near Darien. James Dickey. CP-DickJ

It may be we are in the last days. Time. Amy Clampitt. CP-ClamA

It may have been she came to show you. Emily Dickinson. SP-DickE

It may have been the pride in me for aught. Corridor, The. Edwin Arlington Robinson. CP-RobiE

It may indeed be phantasy [or fantasy], when I. To Nature. Samuel Taylor Coleridge. CP-ColeS

It may not always be so; and i say. E. E. Cummings. CP-CummE; SP-CummE

It may not cover all theodicy. Zander on God. Howard Nemerov. CP-NemeH

It might be lonelier. Emily Dickinson. CP-DickE

It might be that horses would be useful. Fence Posts. Gary Snyder. CP-SnydG

It mounts at sea, a concave wall. From the Wave. Thom Gunn. CP-GunnT

It must be nice to be a sheep. Shearing Time. Langston Hughes. CP-HughL

It Must Be the Milk. Ogden Nash. CP-NashO

It Must Be the Monk in Me. Thomas Lux. SP-LuxT

It must come as leaves. Black Hen, The. A. K. Ramanujan. CP-RamaA

It must have been a profound and a serene communion. Parker River, The. Richard Eberhart. CP-EberR

It must have been as if he had come. Emily Dickinson. SP-DickE

It must have been yesterday. Evil Morning. Langston Hughes. CP-HughL; CP-HughL2

It must have recesses. There is a great charm in a room broken up. Architecture, The. Robert Duncan. SP-DuncR Fr. Passages.

It must make a great difference, having friends. Catullus on Friendship. Donald Davie. CP-DaviDC

It nearly cancels my fear of death, my dearest said. Cremation. Robinson Jeffers. CP-JefR3

It needs there to be no one. Looking Out from Ferrara. Giorgio Bassani. CP-DaviDC, tr. by Donald Davie

It needs there to be no one. Boyhood Misremembered. Donald Davie. CP-DaviDC

It Never Looks Like Summer. Thomas Hardy. CP-HardT

It never was known that circular letters. To Mr. Sheridan, upon His Verse, Written in Circles. Jonathan Swift. CP-SwifJ

It nods and curtseys and recovers. A. E. Housman. CP-HousA

It occurred to me there are no. Grassy Sound. A. R. Ammons. CP-AmmoA

It occurs at a time of stillness when you're alone and there's that. His Manner of Returning. Tennessee Williams. CP-WillT

It occurs to me now. Lesson, The. Charles Simic. SP-SimiC; SP-SimiCE

It once might have been, once only. Youth and Art. Robert Browning. CP-BroR1; SP-BroR

It ought to be lovely to be old. Beautiful Old Age. D. H. Lawrence. CP-LawrD

It perished with beautiful reluctance. Emily Dickinson. SP-DickE

It pleads through dogwood. Leper's Bell, The. Yusef Komunyakaa. CP-KomuY

It pleased her to step in front and sit. Figure in the Scene, The. Thomas Hardy. CP-HardT

It Pleases. Gary Snyder. CP-SnydG

It pusheth us out before it, out, and to the side. Dry Ode, The. Charles Olson. CP-OlsoC

It quit raining and I could spend some time on the beach turning over pebbles. 3 Days Ago. Philip Whalen. SP-WhalP

It rained when it should have snowed. Holly. Seamus Heaney. SP-HeanSO Fr. Sweeney Redivivus.

It rains in Santiago. Madrigal to the City of Santiago. Federico García Lorca. SP-GarcF, tr. by Norman Thomas Di Giovanni

It rains on the roofs. Sottoportico San Zaccaria. Kenneth Rexroth. CP-RexrK

It really must / be Nice,never to. E. E. Cummings. CP-CummE

It requires great love of it deeply to read. Scotland. Hugh MacDiarmid. SP-MacDH

It resembles a green tin coffin. Venus Emerging. Arthur Rimbaud. CP-RimbA, tr. by Martin Sorrell

It rests me to be among beautiful women. Tame Cat. Ezra Pound. SP-PounE

It rises—passes—on our South. Emily Dickinson. CP-DickE

It Rolls On. Kenneth Rexroth. CP-RexrK

It rules out use. Porcelain Bowl. Louise Glück. SP-GlucL

It runs ahead. And now. Barometer, The. Charles Tomlinson. CP-TomlC

It said "Come home, here is an end, a goal." Woodrow Wilson. Robinson Jeffers. CP-JefR1

It sat between my husband and my children. Seele im Raum. Randall Jarrell. CP-JarrR

It says in the science section. Bless You, Mr President. James Laughlin. CP-LaugJ

It seemed a curious place to rest one's body and take one's ease. Road Up. Stevie Smith. SP-SmitS

It seemed as if the house would fall upon its knees. Demolition Report. Jaroslav Seifert. SP-SeifJ, tr. by Ewald Osers

It seemed at first like a piece of luck. Camouflage. Amy Clampitt. CP-ClamA

It seemed at the time like a slow road and a late afternoon. Tree. Muriel Rukeyser. CP-RukeM

It seemed I was a mite of sediment. In a Glass of Cider. Robert Frost. CP-FrosR

It seemed infinity to him. Odyssey. Tennessee Williams. CP-WillT

It seemed simple to make nothing from. Balcony, The. Eugenio Montale. CP-MontE, tr. by Jonathan Galassi

It seemed that out of battle I escaped. Strange Meeting. Wilfred Owen. CP-OwenW

It seemed to see that. Piteous Sight, A. James Laughlin. CP-LaugJ

It seemed, when I was a child, as if you could just reach back and rummage in the 19th century. Past, The. Jane Cooper. CP-CoopJ

It seems a day. Nutting. William Wordsworth. CP-WorW1; MW-WorW

It seems an easy thing / Mayhap one day to sing. Then Shall Ye Shout. Christina Georgina Rossetti. CP-RosC2

It seems as if . . . or did the actual chance. With Christopher Smart. Robert Browning. CP-BroR2

It seems each honest man has got. Serpent's Tooth, The. Charles Baudelaire. CP-BaudC, tr. by Walter Martin

It seems, Love, out you've flung. Michelangelo Buonarroti. CP-Miche, tr. by John Frederick Nims

It seems now far off and foolish, a memory. Lot Later. Howard Nemerov. CP-NemeH

It seems these poets have nothing. Reading an Anthology of Chinese Poems of the Sung Dynasty, I Pause to Admire the Length and Clarity of Their Titles. Billy Collins. SP-CollB

It seems to be DARK all the time. Despair. John Berryman. CP-BerrJ

It seems to be the trouble, everyone. Sonnet: "It seems to be the trouble, everyone." Howard Nemerov. CP-NemeH

It seems to me that for five thousand years at least. Triumph. D. H. Lawrence. CP-LawrD

It seems to me that if you must be sociable it is better to go and see. Suppose I Darken Your Door. Ogden Nash. CP-NashO

It shakes whenever you try—the tree by the door. Network. William Stafford. SP-StafWW

It sheds a shy solemnity. Interior. Hart Crane. CP-CranH

It should have all the repose, fixedness. Model for an Object in Y Space. Robert Stock. SP-StocR

It should have all the speed, tenacity. Model for an Object in X Space. Robert Stock. SP-StocR

It should not exist. On Poetry, upon the Occasion of Many Telephone Calls after Zbigniew Herbert's Death. Czeslaw Milosz. CP-MiloCN, tr. by Robert Hass

It shuffled round and round a concrete log. Charlie. Thomas Kinsella. CP-KinsT

It sifts from Leaden Sieves. Snow, The. Emily Dickinson. CP-DickE

It sings, it sings. Song of the Wind, The. Aleksandr Aleksandrovich Blok. SP-BlokA, tr. by Peter France and Jon Stallworthy

It sits lopsided. Nazi Doll, The. Yusef Komunyakaa. CP-KomuY

It smells of sea and earth, of things dying and newly born. Hanoi Market, The.

Yusef Komunyakaa. CP-KomuY

It snowed in spring on earth so dry and warm. Our Singing Strength. Robert Frost. CP-FrosR

It sounded as if the Streets were running. Storm. Emily Dickinson. CP-DickE

It sounds unconvincing to say *When I was young*. In the Winter of My Thirty-eighth Year. W. S. Merwin. SP-MerwW

It speaks, it moves. La Belle Dame de Tous les Jours. William Carlos Williams. CP-WilW1

It sprang up out of him in the dark. Poet's Thoughts, A. Thomas Hardy. CP-HardT

It spreads, the campaign—carried on. Carnegie Hall: Rescued. Marianne Craig Moore. CP-MoorM

It stands amidst the beauty of the Spring. Dead Elm, The. Jones Very. CP-VeryJ

It stands 'mid other trees dry-barked. Withered Tree, The. Jones Very. CP-VeryJ

It started just now with a hummingbird. Migration of Birds. Gary Snyder. CP-SnydG

It started, unexpectedly of course. How It Started. Robert Graves. CP-GravR

It started when Bill's chip let on to. E. E. Cummings. CP-CummE

It starts like this. Morning at Great Pond. Mary Oliver. SP-OlivM

It starts, somehow, in the hot damp. Barn Fire. Thomas Lux. SP-LuxT

It starts with the clothes-prop man. Thirties Revisited, The. Maxine W. Kumin. SP-KumiM

It Still Happens Now. William Stafford. SP-StafWW

It still makes sense. Song, The: "It still makes sense." Robert Creeley. CP-CreeR

It stills, incites, infatuates. Emily Dickinson. SP-DickE

It stinks. It stinks and it stinks and it stinks and it stinks. Hog Heaven. C. K. Williams. CP-WillC; SP-WillC

It stole along so stealthy. Emily Dickinson. CP-DickE

It struck me—every Day. Emily Dickinson. CP-DickE

It suits me not to hold my peace. Little Air (Martial). Stéphane Mallarmé. CP-MallS, *tr. by* Henry Weinfield

It takes a fast car. Lost Parents. Lawrence Ferlinghetti. SP-FerlL

It takes a heap o' pluggin' t' make a classic sell. Publius Vergilius Maro, the Madison Avenue Hick. John Updike. CP-UpdiJ

It takes a philosopher or fool. Ralph Waldo Emerson. CP-EmerR

It takes a whole house to put a child to bed. For My Nephew Going to Bed. John Ciardi. CP-CiarJ

It takes all sorts of in- and outdoor schooling. Robert Frost. CP-FrosR

It Takes Few Kinds. Kenneth Patchen. CP-PatcK

It takes joy to listen and it is inspiring being listened to. Andrei Codrescu. SP-CodrA

It takes so long to look down. Two Times. Robert Creeley. CP-CreeR

It Took Four Flowerboats to Convoy My Father's Black. John Ciardi. CP-CiarJ

It took that pause to make him realize. Time Out. Robert Frost. CP-FrosR

It tossed—and tossed. Emily Dickinson. CP-DickE

It tossed its head at the wooing breeze. Rose, The. James Whitcomb Riley. CP-RileJ

It troubled me as once I was. Emily Dickinson. CP-DickE

It turns on its axis. Dialogue. Charles Tomlinson. CP-TomlC

It Turns Over. Kenneth Rexroth. CP-RexrK

It used to be, farms. Garden State. Allen Ginsberg. CP-GinsA

It used to be only Sunday afternoons. Watching Football on TV. Howard Nemerov. CP-NemeH

It was a beauty that I saw. Ben Jonson. CP-JonsB; SP-JonsB *Fr.* New Inn, The.

It was a big house, bleak. Order to View. Louis MacNeice. CP-MacNL

It Was a Bomby Evening. Kenneth Patchen. CP-PatcK

It was a bright and cheerful afternoon. Summer and Winter. Percy Bysshe Shelley. CP-ShelP

It was a coat worth keeping even with. I Save Your Coat, But You Lose It Later. Tess Gallagher. SP-GallT

It was a cynical babe. Infant. Stevie Smith. CP-SmitS

It was a day that licked envelope flaps. Love Sonnet: Believing Part of Almost All I Say. John Ciardi. CP-CiarJ

It was a dream and shouldn't I bother about a dream? Songe d'Athalie. Stevie Smith. CP-SmitS

It was a dream and you were walking through a field of hosannas. Abstract. Sam Hamill. SP-HamiS

It was a dream delivered the epilogue. Epilogue, The: "It was a dream delivered the epilogue." Charles Tomlinson. CP-TomlC; SP-TomlC

It was a face which darkness could kill. Lawrence Ferlinghetti. SP-FerlL

It was a flower. First Love. Denise Levertov. SP-LeveDS

It was a' for our rightfu' king. Robert Burns. CP-BurnR

It was a gentle air, with leisurely turns. "Rubén Dario." SP-DariR, *tr. by* Alberto Acereda *and* Will Derusha

It was a glorious morning. The sun was shining brightly and. Such Diamonds. Raymond Carver. CP-CarvR

It was a goodly co. E. E. Cummings. CP-CummE

It was a Grave, yet bore no Stone. Emily Dickinson. CP-DickE

It was a graveyard scene. The crescent moon. Great Unaffected Vampires and the Moon. Stevie Smith. CP-SmitS

It was a gray landscape, houses small. Elegy: "It was a gray landscape, houses small." Adam Zagajewski. SP-ZagaA, *tr. by* Clare Cavanagh

It was a hard thing to undo this knot. At a Welsh Waterfall. Gerard Manley Hopkins. CP-HopkG

It was a house of female habitation. House of Mercy, A. Stevie Smith. CP-SmitS

It was a human face in my oblivion. Oblivion. Stevie Smith. CP-SmitS

It was a jeweled tapestry. Unstrung. Eleanor Wilner. SP-WilnE

It was a Jolly Miller lived on the River Dee. Jolly Miller, The. James Whitcomb Riley. CP-RileJ

It was a kind and northern face. Praise for an Urn. Hart Crane. CP-CranH

It was a land where the wingéd mind. For Chile, 1977. Denise Levertov. SP-LeveDL

It was a language of water, light and air. Marl Pits, The. Charles Tomlinson. CP-TomlC; SP-TomlC

It was a little captive cat. Singing Cat, The. Stevie Smith. CP-SmitS

It was a little dead man. Little Dead Man, The. James Whitcomb Riley. CP-RileJ

It was a long fall, that particular. Closing Ceremonies for the Bicentennial. Eleanor Wilner. SP-WilnE

It was a long time. None of It Was. Clarence Major. SP-MajoC

It was a long time ago. As I Grew Older. Langston Hughes. CP-HughL; CP-HughL1

It was a Maine lobster town. Water. Robert Lowell. SP-LoweR

It was a man of many parts, A. Man of Many Parts, A. James Whitcomb Riley. CP-RileJ

It was a matter of life and death. Two Comments on "Death's Chicken, Named Amelia." Alan Dugan. CP-DugaA

It was a mile of greenest grass. Occasional Yarrow, The. Stevie Smith. CP-SmitS

It was a *moral* end for which they fought. On the Final Submission of the Tyrolese. William Wordsworth. CP-WorW1

It was a most unfriendly part. Journal of a Modern Lady, The. Jonathan Swift. CP-SwifJ

It was a night like all the others. Empty. Listening. Raymond Carver. CP-CarvR

It was a night to be left alone. Fanny Howe. SP-HoweF *Fr.* In the Spirit There Are No Accidents.

It was a place. Story, A. Charles Olson. CP-OlsoC

It was a place of force. Rabbit Catcher, The. Sylvia Plath. CP-PlatS

It was a pure white cloud that hung there. Landing. Eleanor Wilner. SP-WilnE

It was a quiet seeming Day. Emily Dickinson. CP-DickE

It was a quiet way—. Emily Dickinson. CP-DickE

It was a rainy summer, you remember. Sonnets of Two Summers. Robert Penn Warren. CP-WarrR

It was a riverside meadow, lush, from before the hay harvest. Meadow, A. Czeslaw Milosz. CP-MiloCN, *tr. by* Robert Hass

It was a sampling of humanity in transit. Airport. Ruth Feldman. CP-LeviP

It was a sixteen-inch ling cod that the eagle. Eagles. Raymond Carver. CP-CarvR

It was a slender British bird. British Song, A. Stevie Smith. CP-SmitS

It was a small canyon, very small. Coyote Creek. Norman Dubie. CP-DubiN

It was a steep hill that you went down, calling back to me. Descent. Tennessee Williams. CP-WillT

It was a stew of a night. The power failed. Conversation with Leonardo, A. John Ciardi. CP-CiarJ

It was a time to find a new world: who was sent forth? Columbus, that is. Real and Half Real. Robinson Jeffers. CP-JefR3

It was a useless thing to do with the morning. Buffalo Clouds over the Maestro Hoon. Norman Dubie. CP-DubiN

It was a very little while and they had gone in. Hotel François Ier. Gertrude Stein. CP-SteiG

It was a violent time. Wheels, racks, and fires. Mirror for Poets, A. Thom Gunn. CP-GunnT

It was a waning crescent. July Dawn. Louise Bogan. CP-BogaL

It was a weekday afternoon, around three. Scotland. Billy Collins. SP-CollB

It was a wet wan hour in spring. King's Experiment, The. Thomas Hardy. CP-HardT

It was about the deep of night. Ballad of Christmas, A. Walter De la Mare. CP-DeLaW

It was after war; Edward Thomas had fallen at Arras. Mangel-Bury, The. Ivor Gurney. SP-GurnI

It was agreed we would not mount by those. Jacob's Ladder. Donald Davie. CP-DaviDC

It was Aisling who first soft-talked my penis tip between her legs. Little Black Book, The. Paul Muldoon. CP-MuldP

It was all an appropriate if nervous afternoon. Joy. William Dickey. SP-DickW

It was all predictable, and just as well. Filling Night with the Name: Funeral as Local Color. Robert Penn Warren. CP-WarrR

It was all so different from what she'd expected. At Thirty-Three. Hans Magnus Enzensberger. SP-EnzeH, *tr. by* Hans Magnus Enzensberger *and* Michael

Hamburger

It was all the clods at once become. Earth Dweller. William Stafford. SP-StafW; SP-StafWW

It Was All Very Tidy. Robert Graves. CP-GravR

It was also my violent heart that broke. Break, The. Anne Sexton. CP-SextA

It was always fiercer, brighter, gentler than could be told. Yet Unsayable, The. Robert Graves. CP-GravR

It was always November there. The farms. Chateau Hardware, The. John Ashbery. SP-AshbJ

It was among ferns I learned about eternity. Ferns. Robert Bly. SP-BlyR

It was amusing on that antique grass. Recorders in Italy. Adrienne Rich. CP-RicAE

It was an April morning: fresh and clear. William Wordsworth. CP-WorW1; MW-WorW

It was an artless *Bandar* and he danced upon a pine. Divided Destinies. Rudyard Kipling. CP-KiplR

It was an August evening and, in snowy garments clad. Municipal. Rudyard Kipling. CP-KiplR

It was an English ladye bright. Song of Albert Graeme. Sir Walter Scott. SP-ScotW *Fr.* Lay of the Last Minstrel, The.

It was an epoch of heroes. Parable, A. Louise Glück. SP-GlucL

It was an icy day. Complete Destruction. William Carlos Williams. CP-WilW1

It was, and still my care is. Hymne, to the Lares, A. Robert Herrick. CP-HerrR

It was as if I woke. Looking in a Mirror. Margaret Atwood. SP-AtwM1

It was, as if the Heaven. Moonlight Night. Joseph, Freiherr von Eichendorff. CP-MerG2

It was as if thunder took form upon. Woman Looking at a Vase of Flowers. Wallace Stevens. CP-StevW; CP-StevWP

It was as near invisible. So Slight. Laura Riding Jackson. CP-RidiL

It was as though you struggled against. Letter. Robert Earl Hayden. CP-HaydR

It was as though you were a man in a wheelchair. Seated Figure. Louise Glück. SP-GlucL

It was at first your great. Bone. Thom Gunn. CP-GunnT

It was at the town convention. "Chronic Kicker," The. Paul Laurence Dunbar. CP-DunbP

It was at the very date to which we have come. Anniversary, An. Thomas Hardy. CP-HardT

It was autumn. Foreign troops. November 1918. Jaroslav Seifert. SP-SeifJ, *tr. by* Ewald Osers

It was awful. Martha and Joe had not seen one another since. Hostile Philharmonic Orchestra, The. James Tate. SP-TateJ

It Was Being. Kenneth Patchen. CP-PatcK

It was better when we were. For My Mother. Louise Glück. SP-GlucL

It was born in perhaps the Holland Tunnel. Love in a Bus. Thomas McGrath. SP-McGrT

It was but a little thing. Peace-Offering, The. Thomas Hardy. CP-HardT

It was by fate that I found her. Air Flower, The. Gabriela Mistral. SP-MistG, *tr. by* Maria Giachetti [*or* Jacketti]

"It was Cavalcante," my Mother said, "killed you Father." Elegy 3, Cavalcante. John Ciardi. CP-CiarJ

It was Chrismus Eve, I mind hit fu' a mighty gloomy day. Chrismus on the Plantation. Paul Laurence Dunbar. CP-DunbP

It was cold and windy, scarcely the day. End of March, The. Elizabeth Bishop. CP-BishE

It was Crow, with beak and belly. White Corn Sister. Peter Blue Cloud. SP-BlueP

It was Easter as I walked in the public gardens. 1929. W. H. Auden. CP-AudeW

It was easy enough. Circe. "H. D." CP-DoolH

It was far in the sameness of the wood. Demiurge's Laugh, The. Robert Frost. CP-FrosR

It was first marching, hardly we had settled yet. First March. Ivor Gurney. SP-GurnI

It was given to me by the Gods. Emily Dickinson. CP-DickE

It was going to rain. Smile, The. James Merrill. SP-MerrJ

It was good getting lost. Eclogue: "It was good getting lost." Eugenio Montale. CP-MontE, *tr. by* Jonathan Galassi

It was good going along with the sun. Good Friday, 1971. Driving Westward. Paul Muldoon. CP-MuldP

It was good of my father, whom I hated at times. Robinson Jeffers. CP-JefR3

It was good. You found your America. It was worth all. Letter to Mother. John Ciardi. CP-CiarJ

It was gray. Goya's "Two Old People Eating Soup." Mona Van Duyn. SP-VanDM

It was held in God's great temple. Concert, The. Paul Laurence Dunbar. CP-DunbP

It was in October, a favorite season. Elegy for a Nature Poet. Howard Nemerov. CP-NemeH

It was in sweet Senegal that my foes did me enthrall. Slave's Lament, The. Robert Burns. CP-BurnR

It was in the earth only. Yellow Afternoon. Wallace Stevens. CP-StevW; CP-StevWP

It was in the empty house. Empty House. Langston Hughes. CP-HughL; HughL1

It was in the fields. The trees grew still. Jeanne d'Arc. Louise Glück. SP-GlucL

It was in the Spring. Ballad of Mary's Son. Langston Hughes. CP-HughL; CP-HughL3

It was in winter. Steeples, spires. Fortunate Traveller, The. Derek Walcott. CP-WalcD

It was Isaiah Bunter. Higher Unity, The. G. K. Chesterton. CP-ChesG

It was John the Baptist, son to Zechariah. Birth of a Goddess. Robert Graves. CP-GravR

It was just a very. Pixy People, The. James Whitcomb Riley. CP-RileJ

It was just children playing in the sand. Just Children. Adam Zagajewski. SP-ZagaA, *tr. by* Clare Cavanagh

It was late in mild October, and the long autumnal rain. Huskers, The. John Greenleaf Whittier. CP-WhitJ

It was late in September when you took me. Metaphysical Garden, The. May Sarton. SP-SartM

It was like everything else, like everything. Iris-Eaters, The. Muriel Rukeyser. CP-RukeM

It was like listening to the record of a symphony before you knew anything at all about the music. First Desires. C. K. Williams. SP-WillC

It was like passing a boundary to dive. Lot of People Bathing in a Stream, A. Wallace Stevens. CP-StevW; CP-StevWP

It was like the moon, the open before us. Cave Painting. William Stafford. SP-StafWW

It was like this, like the biting. Local Train. Eugenio Montale. CP-MontE, *tr. by* Jonathan Galassi

It was Lilith the wife of Adam. Eden Bower. Dante Gabriel Rossetti. CW-RossD

It was lingering summer. For My Daughter. Carolyn Kizer. CP-KizeC

It was long before the national performance. For Fun. Muriel Rukeyser. CP-RukeM

It was long I lay. I Will Sing You One-O. Robert Frost. CP-FrosR

It was lying near my back porch. Traveling Through the Yard. Rae Armantrout. SP-ArmaA

It was many and many a year ago. Annabel Lee. Edgar Allan Poe. CP-PoeEd

It was May before my. Eyesight. A. R. Ammons. CP-AmmoA

It was me here. Though. And whether this. At the Inn. John Ashbery. SP-AshbJ

It was more sleepwalk than spasm. First Flight, The. Seamus Heaney. SP-HeanSO *Fr.* Sweeney Redivivus.

It was much easier to be a genius in the twenties, there were. Last Generation, The. Charles Bukowski. SP-BukC3

It was much later in his life he rose. Gibbs. Muriel Rukeyser. CP-RukeM

It was much stronger than they said. Noisier. F.O.M. Muriel Rukeyser. CP-RukeM

It was much—that far and ill. Emily Dickinson. SP-DickE

It was my bridal night I remember. I Remember. Stevie Smith. CP-SmitS

It was my choice, it was no chance. Sir Thomas Wyatt. CP-WyatT

It was my day to study. Field, The. Heather McHugh. SP-McHuH

It was my first time in a bubble bed and I was full of apprehension. Bubble Bed, The. James Laughlin. CP-LaugJ

It was my love and grief which drove my tongue. Petrarch. CP-Petra, *tr. by* J. G. Nichols

It was my thirtieth year to heaven. Poem in October. Dylan Thomas. CP-ThomD

It was near evening, the room was cold. Oath, The. Allen Tate. CP-TateA

It was near last century's ending. In the Marquee. Thomas Hardy. CP-HardT

It was nearly morning when the giant. Reason for Skylarks, The. Kenneth Patchen. CP-PatcK

It was necessary at the time that the sun. For Our Party Last Night. William Stafford. SP-StafWW

It was needless to say 'twas a glorious day. McFeeters' Fourth. James Whitcomb Riley. CP-RileJ

It was never the air. Over Timberline. Josephine Jacobsen. CP-JacoJ

It was never there and already it's vanishing. Before That. W. S. Merwin. SP-MerwW

It was new about eighteen-sixty. Dates: Penkhull New Road. Charles Tomlinson. CP-TomlC

It was night, and on the mountains. Emily Jane Brontë. CP-BronE

It was no accident Marpessa preferred Ida to Apollo. Marpessa's Selection. Yannis Ritsos. SP-RitsY, *tr. by* N. C. Germanacos

It was no costume jewellery I sent. With a Gift of Rings. Robert Graves. CP-GravR

It was not a heart, beating. Night Shift. Sylvia Plath. CP-PlatS

It was not a part of their blood. Beginnings, The. Rudyard Kipling. CP-KiplR

It was not as if he didn't try. Great Uncle Beefheart. Rita Dove. SP-DoveR

It was not Death, for I stood up. Emily Dickinson. CP-DickE

It was not dying: everybody died. Losses. Randall Jarrell. CP-JarrR

It was not given me to linger at this lake. Poems of Spring in the Appalachian

Mountains. Yehuda Amichai. SP-AmicYL, *tr. by* Benjamin Harshav *and* Barbara Harshav

It was not God that told us. We knew. Le Secret Humain. Archibald MacLeish. CP-MacLA

It was not he who broke their compact. Broken Compact. Robert Graves. CP-GravR

It was not I who begot you. It was the dead. To the Son. Jorge Luis Borges. SP-BorgJ, *tr. by* Alastair Reid

It was not in the open fight. Rudyard Kipling. CP-KiplR *Fr.* Plain Tales from the Hills.

It was not only those that came of themselves. Usefulness of Art, The. Yannis Ritsos. SP-RitsY, *tr. by* Kimon Friar

It was not Saint—it was too large. Emily Dickinson. CP-DickE

It was not the Five Mississippi Blind Boys. Sunday Morning with the Sensational Nightingales. Billy Collins. SP-CollB

It was not the words, nor the melody. Grace Notes. Robert Graves. CP-GravR

It was not warning that our fathers lacked. Changing Chimes. Christina Georgina Rossetti. CP-RosC2

It was not what you bore with you, Woman. Without, Not within Her. Thomas Hardy. CP-HardT

It was not you I came to please. Dissemblers, The. Thomas Hardy. CP-HardT

It was October. It was the Depression. Money. Tale of Time. Robert Penn Warren. CP-WarrR

It was on a winter's day, as cold, as clear. Sunderland. Howard Nemerov. CP-NemeH

It was on the old Paterson and. Period Piece. 1834. William Carlos Williams. CP-WilW2

It was one of those clear,sharp,mistless days. Eagle, The. E. E. Cummings. CP-CummE

It was one of those [kind of] days. Same Tits. James Tate. SP-TateJ

It was one of those evenings when the clouds. Ancient History. Adam Zagajewski. SP-ZagaA, *tr. by* Clare Cavanagh

It was only a bird call at evening, unidentified. Some Quiet, Plain Poems. Robert Penn Warren. CP-WarrR

It was only important. Moss of His Skin, The. Anne Sexton. CP-SextA; SP-SextA

It was our war-ship *Clampherdown*. Ballad of the *Clampherdown*, The. Rudyard Kipling. CP-KiplR

It was outside a place. Fight, The. William Carlos Williams. CP-WilW2

It was patience / protecting the soul as clothing the body. Expedient, An—Leonardo da Vinci's—and a Query. Marianne Craig Moore. CP-MoorM

It Was Raining in the capital. John Ashbery. SP-AshbJ

It was roses, roses, all the way. Patriot, The [An Old Story], Robert Browning. CP-BroR1; SP-BroR

It was rumored on the block. Figure Motioned with Its Mangled Hand Toward the Wall Behind It, The. Kenneth Patchen. CP-PatcK

It was said of Herodotus the Liar. On Herodotus. Alan Dugan. CP-DugaA

It was 7 or 8 years ago. Lady Poet, The. Charles Bukowski. SP-BukC3

It was so cold last night the water in the barrel grew a sod. Twice. Paul Muldoon. CP-MuldP

It was so delicious to see you. Emily Dickinson. SP-DickE

It was some Spirit, Sheridan! that breath'd. To Richard Brinsley Sheridan, Esq. Samuel Taylor Coleridge. CP-ColeS *Fr.* Effusions.

It was something flawless. Mt. Fuji and the Martial Arts. Eleanor Wilner. SP-WilnE

It was something to see that their white was different. Holiday in Reality. Wallace Stevens. CP-StevW; CP-StevWP

It was sometime near one at night. To Abide. Constantine P. Cavafy. CP-CavaC, *tr. by* Theoharis Constantine Theoharis

It was such a pretty little donkey. Donkey, The. Stevie Smith. CP-SmitS

It was sudden. Sea Fog, The. Josephine Jacobsen. CP-JacoJ

It was summer on the north coast. Cloistered. Sam Hamill. SP-HamiS

It was summer. We were there. And THERE WAS NO. Ted Berrigan. SP-BerrT *Fr.* Sonnets, The.

It was supposed to be better than the rest, our twentieth century. Turn of the Century, The. Wisława Szymborska. SP-SzymWM, *tr. by* Joanna Trzeciak

It was taken some time ago. This Is a Photograph of Me. Margaret Atwood. SP-AtwM1

It was that lonely day, folks. Crossing. Langston Hughes. CP-HughL; CP-HughL2

It was the charming month of May. Chloe. Robert Burns. CP-BurnR

It was the day Apollo's rays turned pale. Petrarch. CP-Petra, *tr. by* J. G. Nichols

It was the dingiest bird. Robin Redbreast. Stanley Kunitz. CP-KunSC

It was the first snow in memory, and. Saints of Negativity, The. Norman Dubie. CP-DubiN

It Was the First Time. James Laughlin. CP-LaugJ

It was the first Wednesday of a scarcity of candles. Psalm 23. Norman Dubie. CP-DubiN

It was the form of the thing, the unmanaged. Man Feeding Pigeons. Amy Clampitt. CP-ClamA

It was the Great Alexander. Alexander. Walter De la Mare. CP-DeLaW

It was the hour when night makes the mountains lament. Rainbow. Max Jacob. CP-BishE

It was the mighty Engine Drain, the Engine Drain, the Engine Drain. Engine Drain, The. Stevie Smith. CP-SmitS

It was the month in which the righteous Maide. Prosopopoia: or Mother Hubberds Tale. Edmund Spenser. CP-Spens

It was the morn. Shape of the Coroner, The. Wallace Stevens. CP-StevWP

It was the night of the flood first took away. Flood, The. Charles Tomlinson. CP-TomlC; SP-TomlC

It was the noise that drew me first. Being as I Was, How Could I Help. Eleanor Wilner. SP-WilnE

It was the place to go in nineteen-thirty. Gladstone Street. Charles Tomlinson. CP-TomlC; SP-TomlC

It was the privation, the thorns, the stones, the well. Inside the Rust. Yannis Ritsos. SP-RitsY *Fr.* Monovasia.

It was the schooner *Hesperus*. Wreck of the *Hesperus*, The. Henry Wadsworth Longfellow. SP-LongH

It was the season, when through all the land. Birds of Killingworth, The (The Poet's Tale). Henry Wadsworth Longfellow. SP-LongH *Fr.* Tales of a Wayside Inn.

It was the Sung Dynasty. Dream. Norman Dubie. CP-DubiN

It was the twilight of the iguana. Some Beasts. Pablo Neruda. CP-WrigJ, *tr by* James Wright

It was the voice I had before. Double Poem of Lake Eden. Federico García Lorca. CP-GarcF, *tr. by* Greg Simon *and* Steven F. White

It was the War. Soldier Dear to Us, A. Stevie Smith. CP-SmitS

It was the way. Enduring Love. Denise Levertov. SP-LeveDS

It was the west wind caught her up, as. Ring of, The. Charles Olson. CP-OlsoC; SP-OlsoC

It was the year. Jesus Awake. Anne Sexton. CP-SextA; SP-SextA

It was the year the ICONDIC. Ballad of the Icondic. John Ciardi. CP-CiarJ

It was then that carrying brief cases. Brief Cases. David Ignatow. SP-IgnaD

It was there, but I said I coudln't be true in daylight. Short Thoughts for Long Nights. Robert Penn Warren. CP-WarrR

It was thy noble soul and high desert. To the Hon.ble Commodore Hood on His Pardoning a Deserter. Phillis Wheatley. CP-WheaP

It was to our interest to be quiet. Though I Had Much More To Say. Kenneth Patchen. CP-PatcK

It was to this, then, that your life was a tender prelude. Graves. Rainer Maria Rilke. CP-RilkFr, *tr. by* A. Poulin, Jr.

It was too good to be changed. Remembrance. James Laughlin. CP-LaugJ

It was too late for Man. Emily Dickinson. CP-DickE

It was too simple and too right. Four Dancers at an Irish Wedding. Tess Gallagher. SP-GallT

It was upon a Lammas night. Rigs o' Barley, The. Robert Burns. CP-BurnR

It was warm and cold. In the Forest. Alan Dugan. CP-DugaA

It was when he began to see fields. Comedy. Charles Tomlinson. CP-TomlC

It was when I said. On the Road Home. Wallace Stevens. CP-StevW; CP-StevWP

It was when / Whirls of thick waters laved me. Something that Saved Him, The. Thomas Hardy. CP-HardT

It was where the wooden bridge. Dora Markus. Eugenio Montale. CP-MontE, *tr. by* Jonathan Galassi

It Was Winter. Czeslaw Milosz. CP-MiloC; CP-MiloCN, *tr. by* Renata Gorczynski, Robert Hass *and* Robert Pinsky

It was winter and late at night, an hour or two before the first. Night Visit. Tennessee Williams. CP-WillT

"It was wrong to do this," said the angel. Stephen Crane. CP-CranS

It was yesterday morning. Little Old Letter. Langston Hughes. CP-HughL; CP-HughL2

It was your birthday, we had drunk and dined. Hug, The. Thom Gunn. CP-GunnT

It was your smell that, for a day after, I carried with me. Anniversary, The. William Dickey. SP-DickW

It was your way, my dear. Without Ceremony. Thomas Hardy. CP-HardT

It wasn't Ernest; it wasn't Scott—. Song for the Squeeze-Box. Theodore Roethke. CP-RoetT

It wasn't in the cards. Radio Again, The. Philip Whalen. SP-WhalP

It wasn't ringworm he. New York. Thom Gunn. CP-GunnT

It wasn't safe to stay in Saint-Brieuc. Days of 1944: Three Friends. Marilyn Hacker. SP-HackM

It wasn't the earth that swallowed them. Was it the air? Vanished, The. Hans Magnus Enzensberger. SP-EnzeH, *tr. by* Rita Dove *and* Fred Viebahn

It wasn't your crippled rhythm. Woman Makes Peace with Her Faulty Heart, The. Margaret Atwood. SP-AtwM2

It well may be, so vehement my sighing. Michelangelo Buonarroti. CP-Miche, *tr. by* John Frederick Nims

It went many years. Lockless Door, The. Robert Frost. CP-FrosR

It whizzed and whistled along the blurred. Song of the Bullet. James Whitcomb Riley. CP-RileJ

It will always happen—the death of a friend. Genesis Text for Larry Levis, Who Died Alone, A. Norman Dubie. CP-DubiN

It will be cloudy. There will be rain. Forecast. Yehuda Amichai. SP-AmicYL, tr. by Benjamin Harshav and Barbara Harshav

It will be coming toward Earth, and. We Interrupt to Bring You. William Stafford. SP-StafWW

It will be looked for, book[e], when some but see. To My Book. Ben Jonson. CP-JonsB; SP-JonsB

It will be much better when. When Dead. Thomas Hardy. CP-HardT

It will be Summer—eventually. Emily Dickinson. CP-DickE

It will not be necessary for you to look very far for the boy. Interior of the Pocket, The. Tennessee Williams. CP-WillT

It will not be simple, it will not be long. Final Notations. Adrienne Rich. SP-RicA1

It will not help, my heart. Duplicity in Prayer. Donald Davie. CP-DaviDC

It will not shine again. Emily Jane Brontë. CP-BronE

It will not stay! the robe so pearly white. April Snow, The. Jones Very. CP-VeryJ

It won't stand up to the light. Zodiac, The. Donald Davie. CP-DaviDC

It would be easier. Albuquerque Graveyard, The. Jay Wright. SP-WrigJ

It would be more decorous not to live. To live is not decorous. City of My Youth. Czeslaw Milosz. CP-MiloCN, tr. by Robert Hass

It would be nice. Enemy. Langston Hughes. CP-HughL; CP-HughL2

It would be nice if you. Suggestion, A. James Laughlin. CP-LaugJ

It would be nice to die at the typer instead of with my. Suggestion for an Arrangement. Charles Bukowski. SP-BukC3

It would be too bad if Jesus. Bible Belt. Langston Hughes. CP-HughL; CP-HughL3

It would be wonderful to be quiet now. Inches. C. K. Williams. CP-WillC

It would be wrong to let one man. Thomas Merton. CP-MertT

It would have been because. Kingship. Donald Davie. CP-DaviDC

It Would Have Been Quicker to Walk, or, Don't Tell Me We're There Already. Ogden Nash. CP-NashO

It would have delighted Bishop Berkeley by. TV. Howard Nemerov. CP-NemeH

It would have starved a Gnat. Emily Dickinson. CP-DickE

It would help if no one ever mentioned. Merci Beaucoup. William Stafford. SP-StafWW

It would never be Common—more—I said. Emily Dickinson. CP-DickE

It would not know if it were spurned. Emily Dickinson. CP-DickE

It would take a voice from the Bible or a verse from Walt Whitman. To Roosevelt. "Rubén Dario." SP-DariR, tr. by Alberto Acereda and Will Derusha

It would take more than that to banish. Bus along St Clair: December, A. Margaret Atwood. SP-AtwM1

It wounded well—one time and. War Wound, The. James Dickey. CP-DickJ

It yawns at me the cavernous gulf. Litany: "It yawns at me the cavernous gulf." Thomas Merton. CP-MertT

Italia. Oscar Wilde. CP-WildO

Italia, Io Ti Saluto! Christina Georgina Rossetti. CP-RosC2

Italia! thou art fallen, though with sheen. Italia. Oscar Wilde. CP-WildO

Italian Days. Charles Wright. SP-WrigC

Italian Garden. May Sarton. SP-SartM

Italian Garden, The. William Carlos Williams. CP-WilW2

Italian in England, The. Robert Browning. CP-BroR1

Italian in Hackensack got mad, An. Why There Is No Class Solidarity in America I Read It In The Times. Aug. 2, 1987. Alan Dugan. CP-DugaA

Italian Kittens, The. Carolyn Kizer. CP-KizeC

Italian Morning. Louise Bogan. CP-BogaL

Italian Music in Dakota. Walt Whitman. CP-WhitW

Italian prisoners of war still haunted. Huntingdonshire. Donald Davie. CP-DaviDC

Italy. George Meredith. CP-MerG2

Italy. John Greenleaf Whittier. CP-WhitJ

Italy and the World. Elizabeth Barrett Browning. CP-BroEB

Italy breaking her bones for bread. How the River Ninfa Runs through the Ruined Town Beneath the Lime Quarry. Archibald MacLeish. CP-MacLA

Itch, Come and Gone. Charles Bukowski. SP-BukC2

Itching Heels. Paul Laurence Dunbar. CP-DunbP

Itchy with time in the dogday summer stew. Poem for My Thirty-ninth Birthday. John Ciardi. CP-CiarJ

Ité. Ezra Pound. SP-PounE

Ite, Missa Est. "Rubén Dario." SP-DariR, tr. by Alberto Acereda and Will Derusha

Ite procul tetrici, moneo, procul ite severi. Elegeia I (1595). Thomas Campion. CP-CampT

Item. E. E. Cummings. CP-CummE

Item. William Carlos Williams. CP-WilW1

Item:is / Clumsily with of. E. E. Cummings. CP-CummE

Items of Identification. Yannis Ritsos. SP-RitsY Fr. Monovasia.

Ithaca. Constantine P. Cavafy. CP-CavaC, tr. by Theoharis Constantine Theoharis

Ithaca: Little Summer in Winter. Olga Broumas. SP-BrouO

Ithaca, N.Y. A. R. Ammons. CP-AmmoA

Ithers seek they kenna what. Jockey Fou and Jenny Fain. Robert Burns. CP-BurnR

Itinerary. James McMichael. SP-McMiJ

Itinerary. Adrienne Rich. CP-RicAE

Itinerary of an Obsession. Maxine W. Kumin. SP-KumiM

It)It will it. E. E. Cummings. CP-CummE

It's a cold cold piece of meat. Winter River. Thomas Lux. SP-LuxT

"It's a Cold Night," Said Coney to Coney. Josephine Jacobsen. CP-JacoJ

It's a dark drama, this; and yet I know the house, and date. Mock Wife, The. Thomas Hardy. CP-HardT

It's a Grand Parade It Will Be, Modern Design. Ogden Nash. CP-NashO

It's a great pleasure to. Many Happy Returns. Ted Berrigan. SP-BerrT

It's a habit of yours to walk slowly. Bismillah. Jelaluddin Rumi. SP-Rumi, tr. by Coleman Barks

It's a hot day: / not so hot. Overcast, Hot. James Schuyler. CP-SchuJ

It's a jazz affair, drum crashes and cornet razzes. Honky Tonk in Cleveland, Ohio. Carl Sandburg. CP-SandC

It's a lean car . . . a long-legged dog of a car . . . a gray-ghost eagle. Portrait of a Motorcar. Carl Sandburg. CP-SandC

It's a little Walden. You All Know the Story of the Other Woman. Anne Sexton. CP-SextA; SP-SextA

It's a mystery to see me—a man o' fifty-four. Farmer Whipple—Bachelor. James Whitcomb Riley. CP-RileJ

It's a purty hard world you find, my child. Our Queer Old World. James Whitcomb Riley. CP-RileJ

It's a question of bright stars. Dogwood Blossoms. Peter Blue Cloud. SP-BlueP

It's a room I dream about. February 4th. Anne Sexton. CP-SextA

It's a Smallworld. Kenneth Patchen. CP-PatcK

It's a spring morning; sun pours in the window. Erotic Philosophers, The. Carolyn Kizer. CP-KizeC Fr. Pro Femina.

It's a strange courage. El Hombre. William Carlos Williams. CP-WilW1

It's a summertime night. Birds. Clarence Major. SP-MajoC

It's a Sunday kind / of Sunday, the first. Up. James Schuyler. CP-SchuJ

It's a tiny noise. Sensitive Ears. James Tate. SP-TateJ

It's a weary life, it is. From the Antique. Christina Georgina Rossetti. CP-RosC3

It's a wide dresser carved in old, dark oak. Dresser, The. Arthur Rimbaud. CP-RimbA, tr. by Martin Sorrell

It's a year almost that I have not seen her. Bird Song, A. Christina Georgina Rossetti. CP-RosC1

It's about Time. Ogden Nash. CP-NashO

It's abstract nouns, among the myths of mind. Metaphysical Automobile, The. Howard Nemerov. CP-NemeH

It's afternoon when he takes off. Scale. Raymond Carver. CP-CarvR

It's all a farce,—these tales they tell. Merry Autumn. Paul Laurence Dunbar. CP-DunbP

It's all about tithing now. Old Man Leaves His Church for the Last Time, An. Miller Williams. CP-WillM

It's all back up in there. Stolen and Abandoned. Philip Whalen. SP-WhalP

It's all come down to me sitting under a tree. No Title Required. Wisława Szymborska. SP-SzymWM, tr. by Joanna Trzeciak

It's all different from what you think, from what I think. Paul Celan. SP-CelaP, tr. by John Felstiner

It's all I have to bring today. Emily Dickinson. CP-DickE

It's all in / the sound. A song. Poem, The: "It's all in / the sound. A song." William Carlos Williams. CP-WilW2

It's all put away now. I don't want to drag it out again. Native Speech. Philip Whalen. SP-WhalP

It's all right for them to make a stinking mess of everything. Don't Wash Your Hair in the Streetcar, Nora Dear. Kenneth Patchen. CP-PatcK

It's all right. Things slow down. Some light. Five Interior Landscapes. Olga Broumas. SP-BrouO

It's all so pitiful, really, the little photographs. In the Kingdom of the Past, the Brown-Eyed Man is King. Charles Wright. SP-WrigCN

It's already too much when we must say: I love. To Jean-Louis Vandoyer. Rainer Maria Rilke. CP-RilkFr, tr. by A. Poulin, Jr.

It's always there. My back's. Cell, The. Louise Glück. SP-GlucL

It's amazing all / this motion going. Spaceship. A. R. Ammons. CP-AmmoA

It's an earth song. Earth Song. Langston Hughes. CP-HughL; CP-HughL2

It's around / the corner. For Arthur Okamura. Robert Creeley. CP-CreeR

It's as fake as Zuni. In Hollywood with the Zuni God of War. Clarence Major. SP-MajoC

It's as if they're glued together. Summer Heaven, Angels, Heaven. Alan Dugan.

CP-DugaA

It's August and I have not. Drinking While Driving. Raymond Carver. CP-CarvR

It's bad enough crying for children. Ten Below. C. K. Williams. CP-WillC; SP-WillC

Its balmy lips the infant blest. Epitaph on an Infant. Samuel Taylor Coleridge. CP-ColeS

It's barely October, but almost. Friend. Sam Hamill. SP-HamiS

It's because I saw you. Rainer Maria Rilke. CP-RilkFr, tr. by A. Poulin, Jr. Fr. Windows, The.

It's because you are so young. Being Old. Langston Hughes. CP-HughL; CP-HughL1

It's Because Your Heart Is Pure, Honey. Kenneth Patchen. CP-PatcK

It's been four years now, come October five. She Talks to Her Sister, Briefly By on the Way to West Memphis. Miller Williams. CP-WillM

It's been going on a long time. Way of Life, A. Howard Nemerov. CP-NemeH

It's been like this every morning. Early Fix. Andrei Codrescu. SP-CodrA

It's before my opium fix that my soul is sick. Opium Eater. Fernando Pessoa. SP-PessF, tr. by Susan M. Brown and Edwin Honig

It's best. Probable Truth. Robert Creeley. SP-CreeR

It's best, when watching the surprising levitations. Pictures at an Exhibition. Norman Dubie. CP-DubiN

"It's called God," he said. Carmel: Point Lobos. John Logan. CP-LogaJ

It's Chairley Burke's in town, b'ys! Chairley Burke's in Town. James Whitcomb Riley. CP-RileJ

It's coming—the postponeless Creature. Emily Dickinson. CP-DickE

Its Course. Raymond Carver. CP-CarvR

It's crazy to think one could describe them. Essay on Psychiatrists. Robert Pinsky. CP-PinsR

Its crisp sheets, unfolded. Letter from Costa Brava. Charles Tomlinson. CP-TomlC

It's cutting into me on its bareback with talons lifted. Savoy. Frank O'Hara. SP-OharF

It's dark in this wood, soft mocker. Praise to the End! Theodore Roethke. CP-RoetT

It's day again, the fourth day. Clearing. A. R. Ammons. CP-AmmoA

It's deep summer east of the Blue Ridge. China Mail. Charles Wright. SP-WrigCN

Its door opens near. It's a shrine. Poetry. William Stafford. SP-StafWW

It's easy to invent a Life. Emily Dickinson. CP-DickE

It's easy to oblige you / when you say your whole. Unanswerable Question, The. James Laughlin. CP-LaugJ

It's easy to talk. Rondeau: "It's easy to talk." Hans Magnus Enzensberger. SP-EnzeH, tr. by Michael Hamburger

It's easy to walk out of Hell. But there. Sermon Notes. John Ciardi. CP-CiarJ

It's easy to write when you've nothing to write about. Good for You, Gavin. Philip Larkin. CP-LarkP

It's 8:54 a.m. in Brooklyn it's the 28th [or 26th] of July [and]. Personal Poem #9. Ted Berrigan. SP-BerrT Fr. Sonnets, The.

It's either this or bobcat hunting. Grant, The. Raymond Carver. CP-CarvR

It's Either You Fight or You Die. D. H. Lawrence. CP-LawrD

It's enough that on a balcony. Rainer Maria Rilke. CP-RilkFr, tr. by A. Poulin, Jr. Fr. Windows, The.

It's evening and the orchestra of winds. Emily Dickinson. SP-DickE

It's everybody's fault but me. "Drive All Blames into One." Allen Ginsberg. CP-GinsA

It's falling, Mother, snow in the Ukraine. Winter. Paul Celan. SP-CelaP, tr. by John Felstiner

It's farewell to the drawing-room's mannerly cry. Danse Macabre. W. H. Auden. CP-AudeW

It's fitting, on my forty-fifth. Giorgione's Tempest. Robert Stock. SP-StocR

It's for you whose name's better omitted—since for them it's no arduous task. To a Friend: In Memoriam. Joseph Brodsky. CP-BrodJ

Its former green is blue and thin. Garden Seat, The. Thomas Hardy. CP-HardT

It's forty in the shade to-day, the spouting eaves declare. Pan in Vermont. Rudyard Kipling. CP-KiplR

It's fragrant news, to know they pine. Emily Dickinson. SP-DickE

It's frail, this spring snow, it's pot cheese. Late Snow. Maxine W. Kumin. SP-KumiM

It's funny early spring weather, mild and washy. 3/23/66. James Schuyler. CP-SchuJ

It's funny, Howard, I never thought I'd be. Eros to Howard Nemerov. Mona Van Duyn. SP-VanDM

It's getting dark. But don't turn on the light. Nocturnal Divertimento. Jaroslav Seifert. SP-SeifJ, tr. by Ewald Osers

It's going on now. Note: The Sea Grinds Things Up. Alan Dugan. CP-DugaA

It's going to be the sunny side. Walking to Work. Frank O'Hara. SP-OharF

It's going to come out all right—do you know? Caboose Thoughts. Carl Sandburg. CP-SandC

It's good to be a burglar once in a while. They Call It "Grumus Merdae." Alan Dugan. CP-DugaA

It's good to live near the water. Asia. Raymond Carver. CP-CarvR

It's *Got* to Be. James Whitcomb Riley. CP-RileJ

It's Got to This. Charles Olson. CP-OlsoC

It's Greek glasses I want. Views and Spectacles. Theodore Weiss. SP-WeisT

It's hard to see but think of a sea. Louis Zukofsky. CP-ZukLS

It's Hard to Think the Brain. Miller Williams. CP-WillM

It's Heart That Discerns. Shmuel HaNagid. SP-HaNaS, tr. by Peter Cole

It's heavy to drag, this big sack of what. William Stafford. SP-StafWW

Its hinges rustless. Heart. Gregory Orr. SP-OrrG

It's horrible, being run over by a bus. Shells. C. K. Williams. CP-WillC

It's hot to-day. The bees is buzzin'. Summer Pastoral, A. Paul Laurence Dunbar. CP-DunbP

Its Hour with itself. Emily Dickinson. CP-DickE

It's Important. Ted Berrigan. SP-BerrT

It's in the heart of the grape. Baby Picture. Anne Sexton. CP-SextA

It's Indelicate. James Laughlin. CP-LaugJ

It's jolly / odd what pops into. E. E. Cummings. CP-CummE

It's June and summer's height. 6/21. Adrienne Rich. SP-RicA1

It's just a humble broom, too stiff. Broom, The. Arthur Rimbaud. CP-RimbA, tr. by Martin Sorrell

It's just like a coffin's. E. E. Cummings. CP-CummE

It's late for the world. L'Acceleration de l'Histoire. Czeslaw Milosz. CP-MiloC; CP-MiloCN, tr. by Robert Hass

It's late September now. Fall Creek. A. R. Ammons. CP-AmmoA

It's late when I try to sleep, resting. Voyages, The. Gregory Orr. SP-OrrG

It's like being a winner at an all-night poker game. Portrait of a Local Politician. Alan Dugan. CP-DugaA

It's like being German. Being Southern. Jane Cooper. CP-CoopJ

It's like him, surely, this small. From the Ship. Constantine P. Cavafy. CP-CavaC, tr. by Theoharis Constantine Theoharis

It's like the Light. Emily Dickinson. CP-DickE

Its little Ether Hood. Emily Dickinson. CP-DickE

It's little I care what path I take. Departure. Edna St. Vincent Millay. CP-MillE

It's lonesome—sorto' lonesome,—it's a *Sund'y-day*, to me. Decoration Day on the Place. James Whitcomb Riley. CP-RileJ

"It's love," they say. You touch. Choosing a Dog. William Stafford. SP-StafWW

It's lucky to hear the flutes for dancing. Flutes for Dancing. Jelaluddin Rumi. SP-Rumi, tr. by Coleman Barks

It's made of everything, slow. Sandy's Sunday Best. Ted Berrigan. SP-BerrT

It's many a penny you'll pay to go. George Meredith. CP-MerG2

It's March. James Laughlin. CP-LaugJ

It's midnight, the house silent. Midnight. David Ignatow. SP-IgnaD

It's mighty good to git back to the old town, shore. Old Band, The. James Whitcomb Riley. CP-RileJ

It's more than a hundred years now. He Thought of Mad Ellen's Ravings and of the Wretched Skeleton on the Rock. Kenneth Patchen. CP-PatcK

It's moughty tiahsome layin' 'roun'. W'en I Gits Home. Paul Laurence Dunbar. CP-DunbP

It's music you've never heard. Anne Sexton. SP-SextA Fr. Letters to Dr. Y.

It's my delight to recite. Happy Poets, The. James Laughlin. CP-LaugJ

It's my job to burn the papers. At Our House. James Laughlin. CP-LaugJ

It's my lunch hour, so I go. Step Away from Them, A. Frank O'Hara. SP-OharF

It's My Town! Kenneth Patchen. CP-PatcK

It's natural the Boys should whoop it up for. Moon Landing. W. H. Auden. CP-AudeW

It's Never Fair Weather. Ogden Nash. CP-NashO

It's night and Tom / comes in and says. Suddenly. James Schuyler. CP-SchuJ

It's 1974 again, and he's back once more. Smirking. On an Old Photograph of My Son. Raymond Carver. CP-CarvR

It's no coincidence / this is a used. Tricks With Mirrors. Margaret Atwood. SP-AtwM1

It's no go the merry-go-round [or merrygoround], it's no go the rickshaw. Bagpipe Music. Louis MacNeice. CP-MacNL

It's No Good! D. H. Lawrence. CP-LawrD

It's no good my dear. So There! D. H. Lawrence. CP-LawrD

It's not a virtue either, really, this. Not a Sin. Heather McHugh. SP-McHuH

It's Not Cold Here. Eleanor Wilner. SP-WilnE

It's not difficult. Writing in the Dark. Denise Levertov. SP-LeveDL

It's not enough, if it doesn't come from you. Michelangelo Buonarroti. CP-Miche, tr. by John Frederick Nims

It's not enough / That doom shall find us whole of hate. Letter to the Liberals, A. Kenneth Patchen. CP-PatcK

It's not enough to mourn. Bombings in Dixie. Langston Hughes. CP-HughL; CP-HughL3

It's not for us to give this soul to God. At the Christening of an Infant the Mind of the Young Preacher Wanders Again. Miller Williams. CP-WillM

It's not good to be complete. Blaise Pascal Lip-syncs the Void. Charles Wright. SP-WrigCN

It's not like other bridges. Bridge, A. Primo Levi. CP-LeviP, *tr.* by Ruth Feldman

It's not my office, after all; it's yours. Senator Explains a Vote, The. Miller Williams. CP-WillM

It's not solely the dance. Revelation at Cap Ferrat. Clarence Major. SP-MajoC

It's not that I can't. Holiday. Denise Levertov. SP-LeveDL

It's not that I'm out of touch. Suicide Note. Jane Cooper. CP-CoopJ

It's not that the Muse feels like clamming up. Folk Tune. Joseph Brodsky. CP-BrodJ

It's not the case, though some might wish it so. Orchard Trees, January. Richard Wilbur. CP-WilbR

It's not the color blue, it's the color cold. In Memory of Clifford Brown. Joseph Brodsky. CP-BrodJ

It's Not / the Erotic. Charles Olson. CP-OlsoC

It's Not the Heat So Much as the Humidity. James Tate. SP-TateJ

It's not the kind of thing that ought to happen; so. Not in the Headlines. William Stafford. SP-StafWW

It's not the only poem—are you asleep now. For You. Adam Zagajewski. SP-ZagaA, *tr.* by Clare Cavanagh

It's not the provinces, exactly, though. Postcard from Provincetown. Heather McHugh. SP-McHuH

It's not the tunes, although as I get older. About Opera. William Meredith. SP-MereW

It's not the white powder cauliflower of still-distant moons. Shadows at Boxford, The. Norman Dubie. CP-DubiN

It's Not Who Lived Here. Charles Bukowski. SP-BukC2

It's not wise to go walking in the ruin. Letter to Wystan Hugh Auden, A. Kenneth Rexroth. CP-RexrK

It's Not You I Miss. David Ignatow. SP-IgnaD

It's not you in particular. See. David Ignatow. SP-IgnaD

It's Nothing to Laugh About. Charles Bukowski. SP-BukC2

It's now the hour / for being sincere. Evening ("It's now the hour / for being sincere"). Federico García Lorca. CP-GarcF, *tr.* by Jerome Rothenberg

It's obscene, the way you have a girl's voice. Provincetown *Totentanz.* Alan Dugan. CP-DugaA

It's odd enough to be alive with others. Brother. Robert Graves. CP-GravR

It's oh in Paradise that I fain would be. Saints and Angels. Christina Georgina Rossetti. CP-RosC1

It's opium we need not truth. Manifesto. Andrei Codrescu. SP-CodrA

It's out there ahead of me. Can I Catch Up with the Future? James Laughlin. CP-LaugJ

It's over a(see just). E. E. Cummings. CP-CummE

It's over now. I watch. C. K. Williams. CP-WillC

It's over now; I've known it all. Emily Jane Brontë. CP-BronE

Its piers less black for sunny smiles above. Good Servant, The. Richard Wilbur. CP-WilbR

It's pleasant to board the ferry in the sunscape. Déjeuner sur l'herbe. Tu Fu. CP-KizeC, *tr.* by Carolyn Kizer

"It's queer," she said, "I see the light." Maid-Servant at the Inn, The. Dorothy Parker. CP-ParkD

Its quick soft silver bell beating, beating. Auto Wreck. Karl Shapiro. SP-ShapK

It's quite true we live / in a kind of rural twilight. Concerning Necessity. Hayden Carruth. CP-CarHS

It's raining on black coal and warm wet ashes. Two Lorries. Seamus Heaney. SP-HeanSO

It's raining. There is silence, since the rain itself. Fernando Pessoa. SP-PessF, *tr.* by Susan M. Brown *and* Edwin Honig

It's rather sad we can only meet people. Posthumous Letter to Gilbert White. W. H. Auden. CP-AudeW

It's rickety down to the dark. Cellar Stairs. Thomas Lux. SP-LuxT

Its roots are bristling in the air. Tree, The. Thomas Hardy. CP-HardT

It's sad to be / the mayor of Jerusalem. Mayor. Yehuda Amichai. SP-AmicY, *tr.* by Stephen Mitchell

It's said by the thoughtful masters that to know death. Sonnet: "It's said by the thoughtful masters that to know death." Hayden Carruth. CP-CarHS *Fr.* Sonnets.

It's Saturday afternoon at the edge of the world. Laguna Blues. Charles Wright. SP-WrigC

Its shutters closed, the white house. Summer Day. Rainer Maria Rilke. CP-RilkFr, *tr.* by A. Poulin, Jr.

Its skin tough and unpliable as scar, the pulp out of focus, weak, granular, powdery, blank. Modern, The. C. K. Williams. SP-WillC

It's / snowing defective. Self-Pity Is a Kind of Lying, Too. James Schuyler. CP-SchuJ

It's snowing on the unpedimented lions. On ventilator hoods. April and Its Forsythia. James Schuyler. CP-SchuJ

It's Snug to Be Smug. Ogden Nash. CP-NashO

It's so beautiful, life, goddamn death. Thing Was Moving, The. Charles Olson.

CP-OlsoC; SP-OlsoC

It's / so damn sweet when Anybody. E. E. Cummings. CP-CummE

It's so hard to say in a son's words. Prayer to My Mother. Pier Paolo Pasolini. SP-PasoP, *tr.* by Norman MacAfee *and* Luciano Martinengo

It's so pure in the cemetery. Not Like That. Adrienne Rich. CP-RicAE

It's somewhere, somewhere, thought beats stupidly. Cicero, the Sacrificial Killing. Robert Lowell. SP-LoweR

It's SPRing AgAIN! Charles Olson. CP-OlsoC

It's still the same, Charles. Postcard to Baudelaire. Thomas Lux. SP-LuxT

It's still you, lemon and laburnum. Lemon and Laburnum. Rainer Maria Rilke. CP-RilkFr, *tr.* by A. Poulin, Jr.

Its storming color-load. Hurricane Can Cast, A. Heather McHugh. SP-McHuH

It's strange what the past brings back. Driving through Tennessee. Charles Wright. SP-WrigC

It's such a / Bore. Ennui. Langston Hughes. CP-HughL; CP-HughL2

It's such a little thing to weep. Life's Trades. Emily Dickinson. CP-DickE

Its Summer Night. Rainer Maria Rilke. CP-RilkFr, *tr.* by A. Poulin, Jr.

It's that we must consent. Rainer Maria Rilke. CP-RilkFr, *tr.* by A. Poulin, Jr. *Fr.* Orchards.

It's the anarchy of poverty. Poor, The. William Carlos Williams. CP-WilW1

It's the curiousest thing in creation. Old Played-out Song, A. James Whitcomb Riley. CP-RileJ

It's the endless landscape, it's a bell. Rainer Maria Rilke. CP-RilkFr, *tr.* by A. Poulin, Jr. *Fr.* Orchards.

It's the fact. Trees Eat Sunshine. John Updike. CP-UpdiJ

It's the fourteenth of August, and I'm too hot. Banishment. Tu Fu. CP-KizeC, *tr.* by Carolyn Kizer

It's the greyness said greendoon. Greendoon's Song. Robert Creeley. CP-CreeR

It's the immemorial feelings. Goods. Wendell Berry. CP-BerrW

It's the Little Towns I Like. Thomas Lux. SP-LuxT

It's the lost, the hidden. Autobiographia Illiteraria. Theodore Weiss. SP-WeisT

It's the ocean of western steel. West Wind. Kenneth Koch. SP-KochK

It's the old rule that drunks have to argue. New Rule, The. Jelaluddin Rumi. SP-Rumi, *tr.* by Coleman Barks *and* Robert Bly

It's the poor first light of morning. Obscure, The. Norman Dubie. CP-DubiN

It's the same as before. This Then—. Charles Bukowski. SP-BukC1

It's the same if it's. Sphere. Federico García Lorca. CP-GarcF, *tr.* by Jerome Rothenberg *Fr.* Suite.

It's the scale. Robert Creeley. SP-CreeR

It's the scene where Hector, reluctant. Tableau Vivant. Gregory Orr. SP-OrrG

It's the Way You Play the Game. Charles Bukowski. SP-BukC1

It's this crazy weather we've been having. Crazy Weather. John Ashbery. SP-AshbJ

It's this way: the tree has to be pruned. How Else. David Ignatow. SP-IgnaD

It's thoughts—and just One Heart. Emily Dickinson. CP-DickE

Its Time. James McMichael. SP-McMiJ

It's time again. / Tear up the violets. Earth's Holocaust. James Schuyler. CP-SchuJ

It's time I told you why. HINDOO, THE: He Doesn't Hurt a Fly or a Spider Either. A. K. Ramanujan. CP-RamaA

It's time to put fertilizer on the grass again. Notes from a Suburban Heart. Mona Van Duyn. SP-VanDM

It's time you learned something. Roses. Rita Dove. SP-DoveR

It's too late now to put a curse on you—wish you. To My Daughter. Raymond Carver. CP-CarvR

It's too much: this hard work—. Night Work. Thomas McGrath. SP-McGrT

It's too wrestling at the beach the sand. Colloque Sentimental. Frank O'Hara. SP-OharF

It's True. Federico García Lorca. CP-GarcF, *tr.* by Alan S. Trueblood *Fr.* Andalusian Songs.

It's True. Grace Paley. CP-PalGC

It's true I got caught in / the world. Allen Ginsberg. SP-GinsA *Fr.* After Lalon.

It's true Mattie Lee. Unidentified Flying Object. Robert Earl Hayden. CP-HaydR

It's true, then. "?!" "Shu Ting." CP-KizeC, *tr.* by Carolyn Kizer *and* Y. H. Zhao

It's true. When a crazy woman. Unnatural Unselection. Hayden Carruth. CP-CarHS

It's Turtles All the Way Down. Charles Wright. SP-WrigCN

Its up wi' the Sutors o Selkirk. Sutors o' Selkirk. Robert Burns. CP-BurnR

It's useless to think of myself in medieval terms. Thing, A. Andrei Codrescu. SP-CodrA

It's Venice, late August, outside after lunch, and Hart. Portrait of the Artist with Hart Crane. Charles Wright. SP-WrigC

It's very cold, Catherine is bundled in a coat, a poncho on the top of that, high boots, gloves. Snow: II. C. K. Williams. SP-WillC

It's very late; sick to his stomach. Squatting Down. Arthur Rimbaud. CP-RimbA, *tr.* by Martin Sorrell

It's Warm Under Your Thumb. James Laughlin. CP-LaugJ

It's well enough to work there. In Town. Wallace Stevens. CP-StevWP

It's what the kids nowadays call weed. And it drifts. Stupid. Raymond Carver. CP-CarvR

Its windows flashing to the sky. Preacher, The. John Greenleaf Whittier. CP-WhitJ

It's wise to know one's self enough to share. Origami. Miller Williams. CP-WillM

It's wonderful how I jog. Animals Are Passing from Our Lives. Philip Levine. SP-LeviP

It's written in marble in golden letters. Great Man's House, A. Wisława Szymborska. SP-SzymWM, tr. by Joanna Trzeciak

Its yellow floodtide cresting at the bend. Near Capua. Eugenio Montale. CP-MontE, tr. by Jonathan Galassi

It's you who in you is preparing. Rainer Maria Rilke. CP-RilkFr, tr. by A. Poulin, Jr. Fr. Roses, The.

Itylus. Algernon Charles Swinburne. SP-SwinA

Itzhak's Last Kit Bag. Yehuda Amichai. SP-AmicYL, tr. by Benjamin Harshav and Barbara Harshav

Iuventius, / were I allowed. Carmen 48. Catullus. CP-Byron; CP-ZukLS Fr. Carmina.

Iva asks me for stories of her father's. Inheritances. Marilyn Hacker. SP-HackM

Ivàn Ivànovitch. Robert Browning. CP-BroR2

Ivana. Robert Lowell. SP-LoweR

Ivanhoe. Sir Walter Scott.
  Rebecca's Hymn. SP-ScotW

Iva's Birthday Poem. Marilyn Hacker. SP-HackM

Iva's Pantoum. Marilyn Hacker. SP-HackM

I've a Friend, over the sea. Time's Revenges. Robert Browning. CP-BroR1

I've a head like a concertina, I've a tongue like a buttonstick. Cells. Rudyard Kipling. CP-KiplR

I've a humble little motto. Keep A-Pluggin' Away. Paul Laurence Dunbar. CP-DunbP

I've a pain in my head. Jane Austen. CP-AustJ

I've allus held—till jest of late. Rhymes of Ironquill, The. James Whitcomb Riley. CP-RileJ

I've already been weaned from the curse of Adam, the First Man. Yehuda Amichai. SP-AmicY, tr. by Chana Bloch

I've always been a faithful man. After Many Days. Paul Laurence Dunbar. CP-DunbP

I've always had trouble with. $$$$$$. Charles Bukowski. SP-BukC1

I've always liked the view from my mother-in-law's house at night. Looking West from Laguna Beach at Night. Charles Wright. SP-WrigCN

I've always looked for joy as a pretext to write. Why Write. Andrei Codrescu. SP-CodrA

I've always loved friends of the Way. Han-shan. CP-ColdM, tr. by Red Pine

I've always thought Polonius a dry. Lines to His Son on Reaching Adolescence. John Logan. CP-LogaJ

I've always wanted a gig. Prevalent At One Time. Marianne Craig Moore. CP-MoorM

I've always wanted brook trout. Looking for Work 1. Raymond Carver. CP-CarvR

I've been away from poetry. Lorine Niedecker. CP-NiedL

I've been drunk in front of cracked bathroom mirrors. Green. Charles Bukowski. SP-BukC3

I've been free. To My Pres- / sure Pump. Lorine Niedecker. CP-NiedL

I've been going right on, page by page. Errand, The. Anne Sexton. CP-SextA

I've been here before, dreaming myself. Confluence. Yusef Komunyakaa. CP-KomuY

I've been here fur many days. Home Longings. Paul Laurence Dunbar. CP-DunbP

I've been list'nin' to them lawyers. Lawyers' Ways, The. Paul Laurence Dunbar. CP-DunbP

I've been outside to see the countryside. On Cabin Fever, On Boredom in the Countryside. Alan Dugan. CP-DugaA

I've been reproached for everything save the weather. Taps. Joseph Brodsky. CP-BrodJ

I've [or I] been scar[r]ed and battered. Still Here. Langston Hughes. CP-HughL; CP-HughL2; CP-HughL3

I've been thinking it through, as I play here to-night, to play never again. Chapel-Organist, The. Thomas Hardy. CP-HardT

I've been thinking—mean, cogitating. Avec Ardeur. Marianne Craig Moore. CP-MoorM

I've been trying for hours to figure out who I was reminded of by the welterweight fighter. Combat. C. K. Williams. CP-WillC; SP-WillC

I've been trying, my darling, to explain. Train, The. Paul Muldoon. CP-MuldP

I've been wandering in the greenwoods. Emily Jane Brontë. CP-BronE

I've been watchin' of 'em, parson. Deacon Jones' Grievance. Paul Laurence Dunbar. CP-DunbP

I've be'n thinkin' back, of late. Thinkin' Back. James Whitcomb Riley. CP-RileJ

I've Brought to Art. Constantine P. Cavafy. CP-CavaC, tr. by Theoharis Constantine Theoharis

I've changed my ways a little; I cannot now. House Dog's Grave, The. Robinson Jeffers. CP-JefR3

I've closed myself up, now I'm like. Yehuda Amichai. SP-AmicY, tr. by Chana Bloch Fr. Songs of Zion the Beautiful.

I've closed your eyes. Fragments of an Elegy. Dan Pagis. SP-PagiD, tr. by Stephen Mitchell

I've come back so slowly. Beginning Again. Jay Wright. SP-WrigJ

I've come by, she says, to tell you. Eat Your Heart Out. Charles Bukowski. SP-BukC1

I've come down a lot on the tree of terror. Fall, The. A. R. Ammons. CP-AmmoA

I've come to ask you if there isn't a. E. E. Cummings. CP-CummE

I've come to give you fruit from out my orchard. Crossed Apple, The. Louise Bogan. CP-BogaL

I've died, but you are still living! March. Jane Cooper. CP-CoopJ

I've dropped my Brain—My Soul is numb. Emily Dickinson. CP-DickE

I've eaten handfuls of fire. Back Then. Yusef Komunyakaa. CP-KomuY

I've even heard of surviving. Compensations. A. K. Ramanujan. CP-RamaA

I've fond anticipation of a day. Uses of Poetry, The. William Carlos Williams. CP-WilW1

I've found the dainty malice out. Ralph Waldo Emerson. CP-EmerR

I've gathered the women like talismans, one, Calypso. Olga Broumas. SP-BrouO

I've gazed so long, so much on beauty. Constantine P. Cavafy. CP-CavaC, tr. by Theoharis Constantine Theoharis

I've got a stubborn goose whose gut's. Rhyme. Sylvia Plath. CP-PlatS

I've got an arrow here. Emily Dickinson. CP-DickE

I've got the children to tend. Woman Work. Maya Angelou. SP-AngeM

I've got to get out of the sun. Vulture Peak: Gridhakuta Hill. Allen Ginsberg. CP-GinsA

I've got two / hundred / dollars. Ballad of the Brown Girl. Alice Walker. CP-WalkA

I've got what I was after. America! Philip Whalen. SP-WhalP

I've grown very hairy all over my body. Yehuda Amichai. SP-AmicY, tr. by Chana Bloch

I've had enough of the mug they've given me. I'm Fed Up with My Life. James Laughlin. CP-LaugJ

I've had my eye on you. San Francisco Streets. Thom Gunn. CP-GunnT

I've heard an Organ talk, sometimes. Emily Dickinson. CP-DickE

I've heard it argued in some quarters. Lull. Paul Muldoon. CP-MuldP

I've heard my neighbor's pump at night. Henry David Thoreau. CP-ThorH

I've heard the tempest howl along the plain. Elegiack Ode on the 28th Day of February 1782, An. The Anniversary of Mr. Stockton's Death. Annis Boudinot Stockton. CP-StocA

I've hit bottom, nearly homeless and penniless. They Might Have Bothered. Constantine P. Cavafy. CP-CavaC, tr. by Theoharis Constantine Theoharis

I've journeyed 'roun' consid'able. Possum Trot. Paul Laurence Dunbar. CP-DunbP

I've known a Heaven, like a Tent. Emily Dickinson. CP-DickE

I've known ere now an interfering branch. Axe-Helve, The. Robert Frost. CP-FrosR

I've known rivers. Negro Speaks of Rivers, The. Langston Hughes. CP-HughL; CP-HughL1

I've launched my inkpots a the fiend, but he. J. Robert Stock. SP-StocR

I've lived at Cold Mountain—how many autumns. Gary Snyder. CP-SnydG

I've lost place, / coming here. Berlin: First Night & Early Morning. Robert Creeley. CP-CreeR

"I've made it," she said, "I've come." Chicago. Charles Bukowski. SP-BukC1

I've mastered the great craft of separation. Tristia. Osip Emilevich Mandelstam. CP-BrodJ, tr. by Joseph Brodsky

I've never bet on a so-called horse. Turns in a Worm's Lane. Ogden Nash. CP-NashO

I've never gone to Donaghadee. Donaghadee. Thomas Hardy. CP-HardT

I've never sailed the Amazon. Rudyard Kipling. CP-KiplR Fr. Just-So Stories.

I've never seen a field on fire, a field. Zero at the Bone. Eleanor Wilner. SP-WilnE

"I've Never Seen Such a Real Hard Time Before": Three-Part Invention. Hayden Carruth. CP-CarHS

I've never seen such exigence. Certain Pretexts. Robert Stock. SP-StocR

I've never seen the sun rise in such glory. Petrarch. CP-Petra, tr. by J. G. Nichols

I've never written poems for you, have I. For X. Denise Levertov. SP-LeveDL

I've none to tell me to but Thee. Emily Dickinson. CP-DickE

I've nothing else—to bring, You know. Emily Dickinson. CP-DickE

I've often made clothes. Miss Green's Reply. Mrs. Austen. CP-AustJ

I've often wish'd that I had clear. Sixth Satire of the Second Book of Horace Imitated, The. Alexander Pope. CP-PopeA

I've often wondered why she laughed. Edges. Allen Tate. CP-TateA

I've paid for your sickest fancies; I've humoured your crackedest whim. *Mary Gloster*, The. Rudyard Kipling. CP-KiplR

I've paid thee what I promised; that's not all:. To His Peculiar Friend Master Thomas Shapcott, Lawyer. Robert Herrick. CP-HerrR

I've played cool. Jumping Bad Blues. Yusef Komunyakaa. CP-KomuY

I've promised that I will not care about things. Untitled Poem: "I've promised that I will not care about things." Alan Dugan. CP-DugaA

I've pulled up to the doorway / of *Then*. Afterwards ("I've pulled up to the doorway / of *Then*"). Federico García Lorca. CP-GarcF, *tr. by* Jerome Rothenberg

I've put Miss Hopper upon the train. Polterguest, My Polterguest. Ogden Nash. CP-NashO

I've read all the books but one. Kathleen Jessie Raine. SP-RainK

I've read that Luther said (it's come to me). Author to the Reader, The. Randall Jarrell. CP-JarrR

I've read your poem, lady, and admire. Another to Mrs. Anne Bradstreet, Author of this Poem. *Unknown*. CP-BradA

I've run so far in one circle I'm visible now. Take, 25:iii:59. Philip Whalen. SP-WhalP

I've said before that every craftsman. Craftsmanship and Emptiness. Jelaluddin Rumi. SP-Rumi, *tr. by* Coleman Barks

I've said: I wouldn't ever. Apology. Adrienne Rich. CP-RicAE

I've sat on the park benches in Paris. Park Benching. Langston Hughes. CP-HughL; CP-HughL1

Ive searched my faculties around. Henry David Thoreau. CP-ThorH

I've seen a Dying Eye. Emily Dickinson. CP-DickE

I've seen one in a fairground. Bearded Woman, by Ribera, The. Paul Muldoon. CP-MuldP

"I've seen people in front of." After the Reading. Charles Bukowski. SP-BukC1

I've seen that face before. Oswald Incognito & Astral Travels. Ai. SP-Ai

I've seen the Atlantic. Joseph Brodsky. CP-BrodJ *Fr.* Shorts.

I've seen the waterdipper. From a Tower. Eugenio Montale. CP-MontE, *tr. by* Jonathan Galassi

I've seen them: the fixers. Little Devils. Pablo Neruda. SP-NeruP

I've seen this dell in July's shine. Farewell To Alexandria, A. Emily Jane Brontë. CP-BronE

I've Seen Too Many Glazed-Eyed Bums Sitting under a Bridge Drinking Cheap Wine. Charles Bukowski. SP-BukC1

Ive seen ye, sisters, on the mountain-side. Henry David Thoreau. CP-ThorH

I've sent to the ladies this morning to warn 'em. Invitation to Dinner, from Doctor Sheridan to Doctor Swift, An. Thomas Sheridan. CP-SherT

I've taken my fun where I've found it. Ladies, The. Rudyard Kipling. CP-KiplR

I've thought a power on men and things. As My Uncle Ust to Say. James Whitcomb Riley. CP-RileJ

I've traveled this road thirty years. Road, The. Tennessee Williams. CP-WillT

I've tried the new moon tilted in the air. Freedom of the Moon, The. Robert Frost. CP-FrosR

I've tried to seal it in. Knot, The. Stanley Kunitz. CP-KunSC

I've used up all my film on bombed hospitals. In Thai Binh (Peace) Province. Denise Levertov. SP-LeveDL

I've walked every walkable bridge. Boast. Alan Dugan. CP-DugaA

I've Wanted to Write My Way into Paradise. David Ignatow. SP-IgnaD

I've wasted my time this morning, and I'm deeply ashamed. Trestle, The. Raymond Carver. CP-CarvR

I've watched them mother, and I know. Fiammetta Breaks Her Peace. Rita Dove. SP-DoveR

I've watched you now a full half-hour. To a Butterfly ("I've watched you now a full half-hour"). William Wordsworth. CP-WorW1; MW-WorW

I've worked here all my life. Christopher Logue. SP-LoguC

I've written many words in my life. Words of evasion or honesty. Writers. Dan Pagis. SP-PagiD, *tr. by* Stephen Mitchell

I've yoked together my large silence and my small outcry. And That Is Your Glory. Yehuda Amichai. SP-AmicY, *tr. by* Stephen Mitchell

I've zeroed an altimeter on the floor. Measurements. John Ciardi. CP-CiarJ

Ives. Richard Eberhart. CP-EberR

Ives. Muriel Rukeyser. CP-RukeM

Ivory Fragment. Rainer Maria Rilke. CP-RilkFr, *tr. by* A. Poulin, Jr. *Fr.* Orchards.

Ivory gods, The. Gods. Langston Hughes. CP-HughL; CP-HughL1

Ivory performing rose, The. E. E. Cummings. CP-CummE

Ivory Tower, The. John Ashbery. SP-AshbJ

Ivory Tower, The. Allen Tate. CP-TateA

Ivy Crown, The. William Carlos Williams. CP-WilW2

Ivy is trembling in the hammock, The. Poem: "Ivy is trembling in the hammock, The." Frank O'Hara. SP-OharF

Ivy-Wife, The. Thomas Hardy. CP-HardT

Ixion. Robert Browning. CP-BroR2

Izhab-O-Rasai (Expression and Reach). N. M. Rashid. CP-KizeC, *tr. by* Carolyn Kizer

J

J. Robert Stock. SP-StocR

J. C. M. George Meredith. CP-MerG1

J Car. The. Thom Gunn. CP-GunnT

J.D.C.: Chaunt of the Junior Debating Club. G. K. Chesterton. CP-ChesG

J.D.C.: Ode; On the Second Annual Assembly of the Junior Debating Club, 1900. G. K. Chesterton. CP-ChesG

J.D.C., The. G. K. Chesterton. CP-ChesG

J.D.C., The: A Celebration. G. K. Chesterton. CP-ChesG

J.D.C., The: A Reunion. G. K. Chesterton. CP-ChesG

J.D.C. Unhung, The. G. K. Chesterton. CP-ChesG

J.F.B. Ambrose Bierce. SP-BierA

J is, splendidly, for JOHN, my. John Ciardi. CP-CiarJ

J might be made sit up for a jade of hope (and exile, don't you know). Home Olga. Samuel Beckett. CP-BeckS

J, My Good Friend (Another Foolish Innocent). Alice Walker. CP-WalkA

J.P. Donleavy's Dublin. Derek Mahon.

Ja, we had it hard. Mona Van Duyn. SP-VanDM

Jabberers. Carl Sandburg. CP-SandC

Jabowsky's place is on a side street and only the rain washes the dusty three balls. Three Balls. Carl Sandburg. CP-SandC

Jack. Randall Jarrell. CP-JarrR

Jack. Carl Sandburg. CP-SandC

Jack and Jill. James Vincent Cunningham. CP-CunnJ

Jack and Jill. Robert Herrick. CP-HerrR

Jack and Joan. Thomas Campion. CP-CampT
   (*Jacke* and *Jone*, they thinke no ill.) CP-CampT

Jack and Joan they think no ill. Jack and Joan. Thomas Campion. CP-CampT

Jack Baker / rises when / the steeple. Valley of Morning. Donald Hall. CP-HallD

Jack Barrett went to Quetta. Story of Uriah, The. Rudyard Kipling. CP-KiplR

Jack Frost at Bedtime. Paul Laurence Dunbar. CP-DunbP

Jack & Harry. George Meredith. CP-MerG2

Jack, if you got to be a rounder. Street Song. Langston Hughes. CP-HughL; CP-HughL3

Jack-in-the-Box. James Whitcomb Riley. CP-RileJ

Jack-Knife. Charles Bukowski. SP-BukC3

Jack London and O. Henry. Carl Sandburg. CP-SandC

Jack of Hearts, The. Lawrence Ferlinghetti. SP-FerlL

Jack-Off of the Graveyard Shift, The. Alan Dugan. CP-DugaA

Jack, oh big Jack. Surgeon, The. Anne Sexton. CP-SextA

Jack-Rabbit, The. Wallace Stevens. CP-StevW; CP-StevWP

Jack Roy. Herman Melville. SP-MelvH

Jack Ruby on Ice. Ai. SP-Ai

Jack Straw's Castle. Thom Gunn. CP-GunnT

Jack the Giant-Killer. James Whitcomb Riley. CP-RileJ

Jack was a swarthy, swaggering son-of-a-gun. Jack. Carl Sandburg. CP-SandC

Jack with the Sun, is twenty-one. Atlas. George Meredith. CP-MerG2

Jackdaw, The. Vincent Bourne. CP-CowpW

Jacke and *Jone*, they thinke no ill. Thomas Campion. *See* Jack and Joan they think no ill

Jacket of her chalk-stripe suit, The. Earthquake, The. Paul Muldoon. CP-MuldP

Jacket, The. Rudyard Kipling. CP-KiplR

Jack's Blues. Robert Creeley. CP-CreeR

Jack's Letter. John Crowe Ransom. SP-RansJ

Jack's white horse(up). E. E. Cummings. CP-CummE

Jacob Agonistes. Robert Stock. SP-StocR

Jacob and the Angel. Yehuda Amichai. SP-AmicY, *tr. by* Stephen Mitchell

Jacob, double-tongued with Rachel and farmy Leah. Rachel and Leah. Robert Stock. SP-StocR

Jacob Gods Beggar was; and so we wait. Beggars. Robert Herrick. CP-HerrR

Jacob Wrestling with the Angel. Jones Very. CP-VeryJ

Jacob's Ladder. Donald Davie. CP-DaviDC

Jacob's Ladder, The. Denise Levertov. SP-LeveDP; SP-LeveDS

Jacob's Well. Jones Very. CP-VeryJ

Jade. Louis Zukofsky. CP-ZukLS

Jade pendants chime before the dawn audience. Imitations of the Chinese. Kenneth Rexroth. CP-RexrK

Jade— / Stone of the side. Purdah. Sylvia Plath. CP-PlatS

Jagg'd mountain peaks and skies ice-green. Breughel's Winter. Walter De la Mare. CP-DeLaW

Jaguar, The. Ted Hughes. SP-HughTN

Jaguar king sent to my eyes, The. Eye Is a Dog Howling in the Distance, The. Pablo Antonio Cuadra. CP-MertT

Jaguar Myth, The. Pablo Antonio Cuadra. CP-MertT

Jail Journal. Derek Mahon. CP-MahoD

Jailer, The. Sylvia Plath. CP-PlatS

Jaime. Langston Hughes. CP-HughL; CP-HughL2

Jain Bird Hospital in Delhi, The. William Meredith. SP-MereW

Jake Balokowsky, my biographer. Posterity. Philip Larkin. CP-LarkP

Jake Flower, The. Clarence Major. SP-MajoC

Jake hates / all the girls(the). E. E. Cummings. CP-CummE

Jam Session. Langston Hughes. CP-HughL; CP-HughL3

Jam Trap, The. Charles Tomlinson. CP-TomlC

James. W. S. Merwin. SP-MerwWF

James A. Wright, my difficult older brother. Elevens. Marilyn Hacker. SP-HackM

James Brydges and the Dean had long been friends. Dean and the Duke, The. Jonathan Swift. CP-SwifJ

James Dean. Ai. SP-Ai

James derided the Purgatorial fire of the soul. On the Same ["James derided the Purgatorial fire of the soul"]. John Milton. CP-MiltJ

James Honeyman. W. H. Auden. CP-AudeW

James, it is snowing here. It is November. Letter to James Stephens, A. May Sarton. SP-SartM

James Joyce. Jorge Luis Borges. SP-BorgJ, tr. by Stephen Kessler

James Lee's Wife. Robert Browning. CP-BroR1; SP-BroR

James My Namesake. James Laughlin. CP-LaugJ

James Russell Lowell. Ralph Waldo Emerson. CP-EmerR

James Russell Lowell. John Greenleaf Whittier. CP-WhitJ

James I. Rudyard Kipling. CP-KiplR

James Whitcomb Riley. Paul Laurence Dunbar. CP-DunbP

Jamesian. Thom Gunn. CP GunnT

Jamestown. Randall Jarrell. CP-JarrR

Jamie Come Try Me. Robert Burns. CP-BurnR

Jammed standing in the. In the Train. James Laughlin. CP-LaugJ

Jan Kubelik. Carl Sandburg. CP-SandC

Jan, the Son of Thomas. Carl Sandburg. CP-SandC

Jan van Hogspeuw staggers to the door. Card-Players, The. Philip Larkin. CP-LarkP

Jane Austen Beecher Stowe De Rouse. Mare's Nest, The. Rudyard Kipling. CP-KiplR

Jane Awake. Frank O'Hara. SP-OharF

Jane awoke Ralph so gently on one morning. Morning. John Crowe Ransom. SP-RansJ

JANE SNEED BEGAN IT: My poor John, alas. Eclogue: "JANE SNEED BEGAN IT: My poor John, alas." John Crowe Ransom. SP-RansJ

Jane went to Paradise. Jane's Marriage. Rudyard Kipling. CP-KiplR Fr. Debits and Credits.

Jane's Marriage. Rudyard Kipling. CP-KiplR Fr. Debits and Credits.

Janet Waking. John Crowe Ransom. SP-RansJ

Janey Pettibone's the best. Prospective Glimpse, A. James Whitcomb Riley. CP-RileJ

Jangle Bells. Ogden Nash. CP-NashO

Jangle of the jeering crows, The. Black Humor. Archibald MacLeish. CP-MacLA

Jangling Yarn, A. James Tate. SP-TateJ

Janie Crawford. Alice Walker. CP-WalkA

Janis Joplin's Dead: Long Live Pearl. James Schuyler. CP-SchuJ

Januaries, Nature greets our eyes. Brazil, January 1, 1502. Elizabeth Bishop. CP-BishE

January. Donald Davie. CP-DaviDC

January. William Carlos Williams. CP-WilW1

January: A Winters Day. John Clare. SP-ClarJ Fr. Shepherd's [or Shepheards] Calendar, The.

January and May, or the Merchant's Tale. Geoffrey Chaucer. CP-PopeA Fr. Canterbury Tales, The.

January cold desolate; / February all dripping wet. Months, The. Christina Georgina Rossetti. CP-RosC2

January First. Octavio Paz. CP-BishE

January 1st. Anne Sexton. CP-SextA

January 1, 1973. John Ciardi. CP-CiarJ

January Night. Kenneth Rexroth. CP-RexrK

January Night, A. Thomas Hardy. CP-HardT

January 1904. Constantine P. Cavafy. CP-CavaC, tr. by Theoharis Constantine Theoharis

January 1938. Randall Jarrell. CP-JarrR

January 19th. Anne Sexton. CP-SextA

January not June. Then why the scent. Garden at Cliveden, The. Marya Alexandrovna Zaturenska. SP-ZatuM

January 2, 1978. John Ciardi. CP-CiarJ

January sunshine; frozen, denuding translucency. Month of Cleansing. Yannis Ritsos. SP-RitsY, tr. by Kimon Friar

January 10, 1973. Alice Walker. CP-WalkA

January! The beginning! Moon and Stars. William Carlos Williams. CP-WilW2

January!/ The beginning of all things! Invocation and Conclusion. William Carlos Williams. CP-WilW1

January, / the dragon maple sunk in its bones. Journal of the Year of the Ox, A. Charles Wright. SP-WrigC

January? / The month is dumb. Sermon of the Twelve Acknowledgements, The. Anne Sexton. CP-SextA

January 25th. Maxine W. Kumin. SP-KumiM Fr. Joppa Diary.

January 24th. Anne Sexton. CP-SextA; SP-SextA

January's fist / unclenches. Modes of Being. Denise Levertov. SP-LeveDL

Jap Miller down at Martinsville's the blamedest feller yit! James Whitcomb Riley. CP-RileJ

Japan. Billy Collins. SP-CollB

Japan invades. Far Eastern vines. Kudzu. James Dickey. CP-DickJ

Japanese, The. Ogden Nash. CP-NashO

Japanese Prints. May Sarton. SP-SartM

Japanese River Tales. Ted Hughes. SP-HughTN

Japanese soldier, A. Narrow Road to the Deep North, The. Paul Muldoon. CP-MuldP

Japanese Tea Garden Golden Gate Park in Spring. Philip Whalen. SP-WhalP

Japanese Wife, The. Charles Bukowski. SP-BukC2

Japonica. Louise Glück. SP-GlucL

Jar of Nations, The. A. E. Housman. CP-HousA

Jargon-Jingle. James Whitcomb Riley. CP-RileJ

Jarred. / The oars creaked in their locks. Li Po. Arthur Sze. SP-SzeA

Jas Jargon. Charles Olson. CP-OlsoC

Jasmine. Yehuda Amichai. SP-AmicY, tr. by Chana Bloch

Jasmine. Shmuel HaNagid. SP-HaNaS, tr. by Peter Cole

Jasmine. Yusef Komunyakaa. CP-KomuY

Jasmine came upon us, as always, from behind, The. Jasmine. Yehuda Amichai. SP-AmicY, tr. by Chana Bloch

Jasmine flower and bull beheaded. Qasida of the Dream in Open Air. Federico García Lorca. CP-GarcF, tr. by Catherine Brown Fr. Qasidas.

Jasmine's Beautiful Thoughts Underneath the Willow. Wallace Stevens. CP-StevW; CP-StevWP

Jasmine's Beautiful Thoughts Underneath the Willow. Wallace Stevens. CP-StevW; CP-StevWP

Jason, that cunning old soldier. Jason's Grave in Jerusalem. Dan Pagis. SP-PagiD, tr. by Stephen Mitchell

Jason, the valiant prince of Greece. Mr. Jason Hassard, a Woolen Draper in Dublin. Jonathan Swift. CP-SwifJ

Jason Visits His Gypsy. Jay Wright. SP-WrigJ

Jason's Grave in Jerusalem. Dan Pagis. SP-PagiD, tr. by Stephen Mitchell

Jasper Texas 1998. Lucille Clifton. SP-ClifL

Jaunt. Louis Zukofsky. CP-ZukLS

Jaunty crop-haired graying, The. Poem about People. Robert Pinsky. CP-PinsR

Jaunty style of Arnold Bennett's 'Card', The. Staffordshire. Donald Davie. CP-DaviDC

Jaweh and Allah Battle. Allen Ginsberg. CP-GinsA; SP-GinsA

Jaweh with Atom Bomb. Jaweh and Allah Battle. Allen Ginsberg. CP-GinsA; SP-GinsA

Jaws. Robert Creeley. SP-CreeR

Jaws. Carl Sandburg. CP-SandC

Jay his Castanet has struck, The. Emily Dickinson. CP-DickE

Jay slants into a dogwood cloud, then out, A. Last Rites. John Ciardi. CP-CiarJ

Jaybird he's my favorite, The. Jaybird, The. James Whitcomb Riley. CP-RileJ

Jaybird, The. James Whitcomb Riley. CP-RileJ

Jazz, The. G. K. Chesterton. CP-ChesG

Jazz Band in a Parisian Cabaret. Langston Hughes. CP-HughL; CP-HughL1

Jazz Fantasia. Carl Sandburg. CP-SandC

Jazz Girl. Langston Hughes. CP-HughL; CP-HughL3

Jazz? / Remember that song. Jazz Girl. Langston Hughes. CP-HughL; CP-HughL3

Jazzonia. Langston Hughes. CP-HughL; CP-HughL1

Jazztet Muted. Langston Hughes. CP-HughL; CP-HughL3

Je Crois En L'Amour. Thomas Merton. CP-MertT

Je suis au bout de mon Latin. I don't know what more. Family Council of the Yakovlevs, The. James Laughlin. CP-LaugJ

Je suis ce cours de sable qui glisse. Samuel Beckett. CP-BeckS

Je Suis une Table. Donald Hall. CP-HallD

Je T'adore. Thomas Kinsella. CP-KinsT

Je Vois dans le Hasard Tous les Biens Que J'espere. Robert Creeley. CP-CreeR

Je voudrais que mon amour meure. Samuel Beckett. CP-BeckS

Jealous. Paul Laurence Dunbar. CP-DunbP

Jealous, and with Love o'erflowing. Love Pure and Fervent. Jeanne Marie Bouvier de la Motte- Guyon. CP-CowpW

Jealous girls these sometimes were. How Marigolds Came Yellow. Robert Herrick. CP-HerrR

Jealous Gods, The. James Laughlin. CP-LaugJ

Jealous Lovers, The. Donald Hall. CP-HallD

Jealous Man, A. Robert Graves. CP-GravR

Jealousy. G. K. Chesterton. CP-ChesG

Jealousy. Billy Collins. SP-CollB

Jealousy [or Jealousie]. John Donne. MW-DonnJ *Fr.* Elegies.

Jealousy. D. H. Lawrence. CP-LawrD

Jealousy runs only skin deep. Drowning Another Peasant Inquisition. Andrei Codrescu. SP-CodrA

Jealousy. Whispered weather reports. Errors. John Ashbery. SP-AshbJ

Jean, death comes close to us all. Child Bearers, The. Anne Sexton. CP-SextA

Jean Rhys. Derek Walcott. CP-WalcD

Jean Sans Terre at the Final Port. Iwan Goll. CP-WilW2

Jean Sans Terre Circles the Earth Seven Times. Iwan Goll. CP-WilW2

Jean Sans Terre Discovers the West Pole. Iwan Goll. CP-WilW2

Jean Sans Terre Leads the Caravan. Iwan Goll. CP-WilW2

Jean Sans Terre Reviews the Fathers. Iwan Goll. CP-WilW2

Jeanne d'Arc. Louise Glück. SP-GlucL

Jeanne-Marie has strong hands. Hands of Jeanne-Marie, The. Arthur Rimbaud. CP-RimbA, *tr.* by Martin Sorrell

Jean's TV. Raymond Carver. CP-CarvR

Jed is breathlessly, deliriously happy because he's just been deftly ambushed and gunned down. War. C. K. Williams. SP-WillC

Jed says: How come I'm afraid to climb on the jungle game when even the littler kids aren't? Body, The. C. K. Williams. SP-WillC

Jedge is good at argyin'. Local Politician from Away Back, A. James Whitcomb Riley. CP-RileJ

Jefferson and Adams. Lorine Niedecker. CP-NiedL

Jefferson: I was confident. Jefferson and Adams. Lorine Niedecker. CP-NiedL

Jefferson spoke of freedom but he held slaves. Secrets of American Civilization. Muriel Rukeyser. CP-RukeM

JEHOVAH. Robert Herrick. CP-HerrR

Jehovah buried,Satan dead. E. E. Cummings. CP-CummE; SP-CummE

Jehovah to my words give ear. Bible, *O.T. See* Give ear to my words, O Lord, consider my meditation

Jehu. Louis MacNeice. CP-MacNL

Jelaludin Muhammed Akbar, Guardian of Mankind. Akbar's Bridge. Rudyard Kipling. CP-KiplR

Jelka Revisited. James Tate. SP-TateJ

Jelka's profile decorates the doorway to my secret architecture. Jelka Revisited. James Tate. SP-TateJ

Jelly Jelly. James Schuyler. CP-SchuJ

Jellyfish, A. Marianne Craig Moore. CP-MoorM

Jellyfish, The. Ogden Nash. CP-NashO

Jemez. Charles Tomlinson. CP-TomlC

Jemez / Indians mention the Los Ojos bar, The. Olive Night. Arthur Sze. SP-SzeA

Jennie—my Jennie Humphrey. Emily Dickinson. SP-DickE

Jenny. Dante Gabriel Rossetti. CW-RossD

Jenny and Me were engaged, you see. Pink Dominoes. Rudyard Kipling. CP-KiplR

Jenny sits up i' the laft. Brose and Butter. Robert Burns. CP-BurnR

Jenny Wren. Walter De la Mare. CP-DeLaW

Jephson, thou man of men, to whose loved name. To Sir William Jephson. Ben Jonson. CP-JonsB; SP-JonsB

Jephtha's Daughter. Lord Byron. CP-Byron

Jerboa, The. Marianne Craig Moore. CP-MoorM

Jeremiad. Norman Dubie. CP-DubiN

Jeremiah 15th Ch. 10 V. Robert Burns. CP-BurnR

Jericho. Louis MacNeice. CP-MacNL

Jermiah at Miminagish. William Stafford. SP-StafWW

Jerome. Randall Jarrell. CP-JarrR

Jerome had lived alone for thirty years. Hut of the man alone, The. Donald Hall. CP-HallD

Jerónimo's House. Elizabeth Bishop. CP-BishE

Jersey Cedars. A. R. Ammons. CP-AmmoA

Jersey hills / to grandfather's house, The. Over the Hills. James Schuyler. CP-SchuJ

Jersey Lyric. William Carlos Williams. CP-WilW2

Jerusalem. William Blake. CP-BlakW

  Epigraph.

  "I give you the end of a golden string." CP-BlakW

  Monk, The. CP-BlakW

Jerusalem. Yehuda Amichai. SP-AmicY, *tr.* by Stephen Mitchell

Jerusalem. Adrienne Rich. CP-RicAE; SP-RicA2

Jerusalem 1967. Yehuda Amichai. SP-AmicYL, *tr.* by Benjamin Harshav *and* Barbara Harshav

Jerusalem Ecology. Yehuda Amichai. SP-AmicYL, *tr.* by Benjamin Harshav *and* Barbara Harshav

Jerusalem in the week of the marriage of. Hymn to the Lovely Couple Varda and Schimmel. Yehuda Amichai. SP-AmicYL, *tr.* by Benjamin Harshav *and* Barbara Harshav

Jerusalem is built of gold, / Of crystal, pearl, and gem. Holy City, New Jerusalem, The. Christina Georgina Rossetti. CP-RosC2

Jerusalem is full of Jews used up in history. Jerusalem Is Full of Used Jews. Yehuda Amichai. SP-AmicYL, *tr.* by Benjamin Harshav *and* Barbara Harshav

Jerusalem Is Full of Used Jews. Yehuda Amichai. SP-AmicYL, *tr.* by Benjamin Harshav *and* Barbara Harshav

Jerusalem is full of used Jews, worn out by history. Yehuda Amichai. SP-AmicY, *tr.* by Chana Bloch

Jerusalem, 1985. Yehuda Amichai. SP-AmicY, *tr.* by Chana Bloch

Jerusalem 1985. Yehuda Amichai. SP-AmicYL, *tr.* by Benjamin Harshav *and* Barbara Harshav

Jerusalem, 1967. Yehuda Amichai. SP-AmicY, *tr.* by Stephen Mitchell

Jerusalem of fire / And gold and pearl and gem. Christina Georgina Rossetti. CP-RosC2

Jerusalem the cradle city that rocks me. Yehuda Amichai. SP-AmicYL, *tr.* by Benjamin Harshav *and* Barbara Harshav

Jerusalem's a place where everyone remembers. Yehuda Amichai. SP-AmicY, *tr.* by Chana Bloch *Fr.* Songs of Zion the Beautiful.

Jerusalem's Suicide Attempts. Yehuda Amichai. SP-AmicYL, *tr.* by Benjamin Harshav *and* Barbara Harshav

Jes' a little bit o' feller—I remember still. Who Santy Claus Wuz. James Whitcomb Riley. CP-RileJ

Jes' lak toddy wahms you thoo'. Dely. Paul Laurence Dunbar. CP-DunbP

Jess and Jill are pretty girls. Ring Posy, A. Christina Georgina Rossetti. CP-RosC1

Jessamine shows like a star, The. Queen Rose. Christina Georgina Rossetti. CP-RosC3

Jesse James and his brother Frank. Lorine Niedecker. CP-NiedL

Jessica Learned to Kiss. Charles Tomlinson. SP-TomlC *Fr.* For A Granddaughter.

Jessie—A New Scots Song. Robert Burns. CP-BurnR

Jessie Cameron. Christina Georgina Rossetti. CP-RosC1

Jessie, Jessie Cameron. Jessie Cameron. Christina Georgina Rossetti. CP-RosC1

Jessie Mitchell's Mother. Gwendolyn Brooks. SP-BrooG

Jest Frank Reed's his *real* name—though. Ringworm Frank. James Whitcomb Riley. CP-RileJ

Jest rain and snow! and rain again! First Bluebird, The. James Whitcomb Riley. CP-RileJ

Jester, The. Langston Hughes. CP-HughL; CP-HughL1

Jester, The. Rudyard Kipling. CP-KiplR

Jester walked in the garden, The. Cap and Bells, The. William Butler Yeats. CP-YeatW

Jesu. George Herbert. CP-HerbG

Jesu Dulcis Memoria. Gerard Manley Hopkins. CP-HopkG

JESU is in my heart, his sacred name. Jesu. George Herbert. CP-HerbG

Jesu, no more, it is full tide. On the Bleeding Wounds of Our Crucified Lord. Richard Crashaw. CP-CrasR

Jesu that dost in Mary dwell. Oratio Patris Condren: O Jesu Vivens in Maria. Gerard Manley Hopkins. CP-HopkG

Jesuit Graves. Charles Wright. SP-WrigCN

Jesuits in North America, The. Donald Davie. CP-DaviDC

Jesus alone:—if thus it were to me. Christina Georgina Rossetti. CP-RosC3

Jesus and His Mother. Thom Gunn. CP-GunnT

Jesus and Isolt. Robert Pinsky. CP-PinsR

Jesus Asleep. Anne Sexton. CP-SextA; SP-SextA

Jesus Awake. Anne Sexton. CP-SextA; SP-SextA

Jesus Cooks. Anne Sexton. CP-SextA; SP-SextA

Jesus Dies. Anne Sexton. CP-SextA; SP-SextA

Jesus, do I love Thee? Ash Wednesday. Christina Georgina Rossetti. CP-RosC3

Jesus emptied the devils of one man into forty hogs and the hogs took. Always the Mob. Carl Sandburg. CP-SandC

Jesús, Estrella, Esperanza, Mercy. Middle Passage. Robert Earl Hayden. CP-HaydR

Jesus' Farewell. D. H. Lawrence. CP-LawrD

Jesus got up one day a little later than usual. Goodtime Jesus. James Tate. SP-TateJ

Jesus had gone far up the dark slope, when he looked back. Quetzalcoatl Looks Down on Mexico. D. H. Lawrence. CP-LawrD

Jesus, incomparable forgiver of trespasses. Spes. "Rubén Dario." SP-DariR, *tr.* by Alberto Acereda *and* Will Derusha

Jesus Infection, The. Maxine W. Kumin. SP-KumiM

Jesus is with me. Jesus Infection, The. Maxine W. Kumin. SP-KumiM

Jesus it's beautiful! I Feel Drunk All the Time. Kenneth Patchen. CP-PatcK

Jesus, Lord God from all eternity, / Whom love of us brought down to shame. Name of Jesus, The. Christina Georgina Rossetti. CP-RosC2

Jesus loved the sunsets on Galilee. Epistle: "Jesus loved the sunsets on Galilee." Carl Sandburg. CP-SandC

Jesus on the Lean Donkey. Jelaluddin Rumi. SP-Rumi, *tr.* by Coleman Barks

Jesus Raises Up the Harlot. Anne Sexton. CP-SextA; SP-SextA

Jesus saw Lazarus. Jesus Summons Forth. Anne Sexton. CP-SextA; SP-SextA

Jesus saw the multitudes were hungry. Jesus Cooks. Anne Sexton. CP-SextA; SP-SextA

Jesus slept as still as a toy. Jesus Asleep. Anne Sexton. CP-SextA; SP-SextA

Jesus Suckles. Anne Sexton. CP-SextA; SP-SextA

Jesus Summons Forth. Anne Sexton. CP-SextA; SP-SextA

"Jesus, The." Langston Hughes. CP-HughL; CP-HughL3

Jesus, the Actor, Plays the Holy ghost. Anne Sexton. CP-SextA; SP-SextA

Jesus! thy Crucifix. Emily Dickinson. CP-DickE

Jesus thy Servant is resign'd. Hymn Written in the Year 1753, A. Annis Boudinot Stockton. CP-StocA

Jesus to cast one thought upon. Jesu Dulcis Memoria. Gerard Manley Hopkins. CP-HopkG

Jesus to His Disciples. Edna St. Vincent Millay. CP-MillE

Jesus Unborn. Anne Sexton. CP-SextA; SP-SextA

Jesus Walking. Anne Sexton. CP-SextA

Jet Ring Sent, A. John Donne. CP-DonnJ; MW-DonnJ

J'étais confus à cet instant. Sincèrement. Robert Graves. CP-GravR

Jetsam. C. K. Williams. CP-WillC

Jetty, Dover, The. Muriel Rukeyser CP-RukeM

Jeune Fille, The. D. H. Lawrence. CP-LawrD

Jew, The. Jones Very. CP-VeryJ

Jew did not go to his synagogue, The. Winter Bells. Wallace Stevens. CP-StevW; CP-StevWP

Jew Is Angry with His Friend Who Does Not Believe in Circumcision, A. Stevie Smith. CP-SmitS

Jewel Lotus Harp. Olga Broumas. SP-BrouO

Jewel Stairs' Grievance, The. Li Po. SP-PounE, *tr.* by Ezra Pound

Jewel, The. James Dickey. CP-DickJ

Jewel, The. James Wright. CP-WrigJ

Jeweled entrails of pomegranates, The. Last Feast of Belshazzar, The. Langston Hughes. CP-HughL; CP-HughL1

Jewelled steps are already quite white with dew, The. Jewel Stairs' Grievance, The. Li Po. SP-PounE, *tr.* by Ezra Pound

Jewels. Charles Baudelaire. CP-BaudC, *tr.* by Walter Martin

Jewels and After. Laura Riding Jackson. CP-RidiL

Jewels here lie heaped for you. Song: Basket of Blossom. Robert Graves. CP-GravR

Jewels of Indoor Glass. Alan Dugan. CP-DugaA

Jewes their beds, and offices of ease, The. North and South. Robert Herrick. CP-HerrR

Jewes, when they built Houses (I have read), The. Observation. Robert Herrick. CP-HerrR

Jewess was happy, The. Resemblance, The. William Carlos Williams. CP-WilW2

Jewish atheist stubborn as Freud, A. Memory of My Friend, A. Howard Nemerov. CP-NemeH

Jewish Cemetery. Federico García Lorca. CP-GarcF, *tr.* by Greg Simon *and* Steven F. White

Jewish Cemetery at Newport, The. Henry Wadsworth Longfellow. SP-LongH

Jewish Family (in a Small Valley Opposite St Goar, upon the Rhine), A. William Wordsworth. CP-WorW2

Jewish Graveyards, Italy. Philip Levine. SP-LeviP

Jews, The. Yehuda Amichai. SP-AmicYL, *tr.* by Benjamin Harshav *and* Barbara Harshav

Jews, The. George Herbert. CP-HerbG

Jews are like photos in a display window, The. Jews, The. Yehuda Amichai. SP-AmicYL, *tr.* by Benjamin Harshav *and* Barbara Harshav

Jews at Haifa. Randall Jarrell. CP-JarrR

Jews: / Groceries / Suits, The. Likewise. Langston Hughes. CP-HughL; CP-HughL3

Jews in the Land of Israel. Yehuda Amichai. SP-AmicY, *tr.* by Chana Bloch

Jews in the Land of Israel. Yehuda Amichai. SP-AmicYL, *tr.* by Benjamin Harshav *and* Barbara Harshav

Jews of various religions meet. Good Friday in the Tunnels of the Métro. Adam Zagajewski. SP-ZagaA, *tr.* by Renata Gorczynski

Jezreel. Thomas Hardy. CP-HardT

Jigsaws. Louis MacNeice. CP-MacNL

"Although we say we disbelieve." CP-MacNL

"Fresh from the knife and coming to." CP-MacNL

"Gulf between us and the brutes, The." CP-MacNL

"What ghosts of cuckoo-spit and dew." CP-MacNL

Jilted. Paul Laurence Dunbar. CP-DunbP

Jilted. Sylvia Plath. CP-PlatS

Jim. James Whitcomb Riley. CP-RileJ

Jim Crow Car. Langston Hughes. CP-HughL; CP-HughL3

Jim Crow's Last Stand. Langston Hughes. CP-HughL; CP-HughL2

Jim Poor's his name. Lorine Niedecker. CP-NiedL

Jim Wright, who was a good poet and my friend, died two or three years ago. Not Transhistorical Death, or at Least Not Quite. Hayden Carruth. CP-CarHS

Jimmall Ring, or True-Love-Knot, The. Robert Herrick. CP-HerrR

Jimmie's got a goil. E. E. Cummings. CP-CummE

Jimmy Berman Rag. Allen Ginsberg. SP-GinsA

Jimmy, go / To the store, please. Grocery Store. Langston Hughes. CP-HughL

Jimmy Hoffa's Odyssey. Ai. SP-Ai

Jimmy Schuyler's heart. This Morning After. William Corbett. SP-CorbW

Jimmy Wimbledon listened a first week in June. Young Bullfrogs. Carl Sandburg. CP-SandC

Jimson weed / has nothing to do. Magnetized. Arthur Sze. SP-SzeA

Jingle. William Carlos Williams. CP WilW2

Jingle on the Times, A. Thomas Hardy. CP-HardT

Jingling the Cookery. Andrei Codrescu. SP-CodrA

Jingo and the Minstrel, The. Nicholas Vachel Lindsay. CP-LindV

Jinx, The. Stéphane Mallarmé. CP-MallS, *tr.* by Henry Weinfield

Jitney. Langston Hughes. CP-HughL; CP-HughL2

Jittery, missing their cues. Around Pastor Bonhoeffer. Stanley Kunitz. CP-KunSC

Jittoku, Buddhist Mystic—15th Century. Jane Cooper. CP-CoopJ

Jiving. Rita Dove. SP-DoveR

Jo Jo's Fireworks—Next Exit. James Tate. SP-TateJ

Joan. G. K. Chesterton. CP-ChesG

Joan and Darby. Robert Graves. CP-GravR

Joan, Joan, can you be. To the Maid of Orleans. Edna St. Vincent Millay. CP-MillE

Joannes jacet hic Mirandula—cætera norunt. Epitaph on the Count of Mirandula. Alexander Pope. CP-PopeA

Job Description, A. James Laughlin. CP-LaugJ

Job the Rejected. Edwin Arlington Robinson. CP-RobiE

Job Work. James Whitcomb Riley. CP-RileJ

Job's Problems. Thomas Lux. SP-LuxT

Job's Wife, a Twentieth-Century Casting Script. Eleanor Wilner. SP-WilnE

Job's wife, bereft, without. Job's Wife, a Twentieth-Century Casting Script. Eleanor Wilner. SP-WilnE

Jobson's Amen. Rudyard Kipling. CP KiplR

Jochanan Hakkadosh. Robert Browning. CP-BroR2

Jock of Hazeldean. Sir Walter Scott. SP-ScotW

Jockey Fou and Jenny Fain. Robert Burns. CP-BurnR

Jockeys at Hialeah, The. Tennessee Williams. CP-WillT

Jockey's Ta'en the Parting Kiss. Robert Burns. CP-BurnR

Joe Blow has decided. Archetype Poem, The. Allen Ginsberg. CP-GinsA; SP-GinsA

Joe Brainard. William Corbett. SP-CorbW

Joe, Gus, Sham. Changes; or, Reveries at a Window Overlooking a Country Road, with Two Women Talking Blues in the Kitchen. Yusef Komunyakaa. CP-KomuY

Joe Hill Listens to the Praying. Kenneth Patchen. CP-PatcK

Joe, little serpentine white boy. Song for These Crusaders, A. Donald Davie. CP-DaviDC

Joe Louis ("Joe Louis is a man"). Langston Hughes. CP-HughL; CP-HughL3

Joe Louis ("They worshipped Joe"). Langston Hughes. CP-HughL; CP-HughL3

Joe Louis is a man. Joe Louis ("Joe Louis is a man"). Langston Hughes. CP-HughL3

Joe with a wooden leg comes home. John Ciardi. CP-CiarJ

Joe's Corner. William Stafford. SP-StafWW

Joe's Jacket. Frank O'Hara. SP-OharF

Joey, you're behind shades. In the Mirror. Yusef Komunyakaa. CP-KomuY

Jog-Trot Pair, A. Thomas Hardy. CP-HardT

Joggin' Erlong. Paul Laurence Dunbar. CP-DunbP

Johann. Alice Walker. CP-WalkA

Johannes Agricola in Meditation. Robert Browning. CP-BroR1; SP-BroR

Johannesburg Mines. Langston Hughes. CP-HughL; CP-HughL1

John. Jones Very. CP-VeryJ

John I:14. Jorge Luis Borges. SP-BorgJ, *tr.* by Willis Barnstone

John 3; But Men Loved Darknesse Rather than Light. Bible, *N.T.* CP-CrasR, *tr.* by Richard Crashaw *Fr.* St. John.

John 15; Upon Our Lords Last Comfortable Discourse with His Disciples. Bible, *N.T.* CP-CrasR *Fr.* St. John.

John 16; Verily I Say unto You, Yee Shall Weep and Lament. Bible, *N.T.* CP-CrasR *Fr.* St. John.

John Adams is our man. Three Americans. Lorine Niedecker. CP-NiedL

John Adams lies here, of the parish of Southwell. Epitaph on John Adams, of Southwell. Lord Byron. CP-Byron

John Alden and Percilly. James Whitcomb Riley. CP-RileJ

John and Anne. William Meredith. SP-MereW

John And I. Laura Riding Jackson. CP-RidiL

John and I have decided. Menu, The. Robert Creeley. CP-CreeR

John and Jane. Thomas Hardy. CP-HardT

John Anderson my jo, John / When we were first acquent. Robert Burns. CP-BurnR

John Barleycorn [a Ballad]. Robert Burns. CP-BurnR

John berryman asked me to write a poem about roosters. Poem with Capital Letters, A. Jane Cooper. CP-CoopJ

John Boyle O'Reilly. Paul Laurence Dunbar. CP-DunbP

John Boyle O'Reilly. James Whitcomb Riley. CP-RileJ

John Brown. Robert Earl Hayden. CP-HaydR

John Brown. James Whitcomb Riley. CP-RileJ

John Brown. Edwin Arlington Robinson. CP-RobiE

John Brown's body under the morning stars. Old Osawatomie. Carl Sandburg. CP-SandC

John Burke. Charles Olson. SP-OlsoC *Fr.* Maximus Poems, The.

John Button Birthday. Frank O'Hara. SP-OharF

John Chapman. Richard Wilbur. CP-WilbR

John Chrysostom. Richard Wilbur. CP-WilbR

John Come Kiss Me Now. Robert Burns. CP-BurnR

John Dillinger Marches On. Charles Bukowski. SP-BukC3

John Donne in California. Amy Clampitt. CP-ClamA

John Dryden. Hayden Carruth. CP-CarHS

John Endicott. Henry Wadsworth Longfellow. SP-LongH

John Ericsson Day Memorial, 1918. Carl Sandburg. CP-SandC

John Evereldown. Edwin Arlington Robinson. CP-RobiE

John Finley. Richard Eberhart. CP-EberR

John Fleming walked in the house his cousin left him. Beau of the Dead. Donald Hall. CP-HallD

John Fowles's book, *The French Lieutenant's Woman.* Dorset. Donald Davie. CP-DaviDC

John Gilpin. William Cowper. CP-CowpW

John Gorham. Edwin Arlington Robinson. CP-RobiE

John Grubby, who was short and stout. New Freethinker, The. G. K. Chesterton. CP-ChesG

John J. Maya Angelou. SP-AngeM

John Jameson, my jo John! John Tarkington Jameson. James Whitcomb Riley. CP-RileJ

John, John of Ottenhaw! George Meredith. CP-MerG2

John Kantakuzinos Triumphs. Constantine P. Cavafy. CP-CavaC, *tr. by* Theoharis Constantine Theoharis

John Keats. Dante Gabriel Rossetti. CW-RossD *Fr.* Five English Poets.

John Kinsella's Lament for Mrs. Mary Moore. William Butler Yeats. CP-YeatW

John L. Sullivan, the Strong Boy of Boston. Nicholas Vachel Lindsay. CP-LindV

John Lackland. George Meredith. CP-MerG1

John Landless leads his landless folk. Jean Sans Terre Discovers the West Pole. Iwan Goll. CP-WilW2

John Landless sailing on a helmless boat. Jean Sans Terre at the Final Port. Iwan Goll. CP-WilW2

John Ledyard. Richard Eberhart. CP-EberR

John Lennon in the Porto Santo Stefano. Lawrence Ferlinghetti. SP-FerlL

John Littlehouse the redhead was a large ruddy man. Blacksmith's Serenade, The. Nicholas Vachel Lindsay. CP-LindV

John Maclean (1879-1923). Hugh MacDiarmid. SP-MacDH

John Marr. Herman Melville. SP-MelvH

John Maydew or The Allotment. Charles Tomlinson. CP-TomlC; SP-TomlC

John McKeen, in his rusty dress. James Whitcomb Riley. CP-RileJ

John Milton. Allen Tate. CP-TateA

John Muir on Mt. Ritter. Gary Snyder. CP-SnydG *Fr.* Myths and Texts.

John of Tours is back with peace. *Unknown.* CW-RossD, *tr. by* Dante Gabriel Rossetti

John, oh John. St John. D. H. Lawrence. CP-LawrD

John Says. Yusef Komunyakaa. CP-KomuY

John Tarkington Jameson. James Whitcomb Riley. CP-RileJ

John the Baptist spoke in the great. Homage to John the Baptist. John Logan. CP-LogaJ

John the Cat. Catpig, The. Denise Levertov. SP-LeveDL

John the tailor had gone racing up the stairs in back of his store and because he was so frightened. Crime. C. K. Williams. SP-WillC

John Underhill. John Greenleaf Whittier. CP-WhitJ

John Walsh. James Whitcomb Riley. CP-RileJ

John Woolman. Jones Very. CP-VeryJ

Johnie B———'s Lament. Robert Burns. CP-BurnR *Fr.* Heron Ballads, 1795, The.

Johnie Blunt. Robert Burns. CP-BurnR

Johnie Cope. Robert Burns. CP-BurnR

Johnny. Christina Georgina Rossetti. CP-RosC2

Johnny Appleseed Speaks of Great Cities in the Future. Nicholas Vachel Lindsay. CP-LindV

Johnny Appleseed Speaks of the Appleblossom Amaranth That Will Come to This City. Nicholas Vachel Lindsay. CP-LindV

Johnny Appleseed's Hymn to the Sun. Nicholas Vachel Lindsay. CP-LindV

Johnny Appleseed's Ship Comes In. Nicholas Vachel Lindsay. CP-LindV

Johnny Appleseed's Wife from the Palace of Eve. Nicholas Vachel Lindsay. CP-LindV

Johnny Appleseed's Wife of the Mind. Nicholas Vachel Lindsay. CP-LindV

Johnny had a golden head / Like a golden mop in blow. Johnny. Christina Georgina Rossetti. CP-RosC2

Johnny, since to-day is. Many Happy Returns. W. H. Auden. CP-AudeW

Johnny Spain's White Heifer. Hayden Carruth. CP-CarHS

Johnny Speaks. Paul Laurence Dunbar. CP-DunbP

John's Birches. Robert Penn Warren. CP-WarrR

Johnson's Boy. James Whitcomb Riley. CP-RileJ

Johnson's Cabinet Watched by Ants. Robert Bly. SP-BlyR

Johnson's pentameters, nailed by the solid *ictus.* Northumberland. Donald Davie. CP-DaviDC

Join water, wade in underbeing. Go Fishing. Ted Hughes. SP-HughTN

Joinery. Olga Broumas. SP-BrouO

Joint. James Schuyler. CP-SchuJ

Joints were none that mortar sealed. Greek Masonry. Herman Melville. SP-MelvH

Joinville and Louis IX. Robert Lowell. SP-LoweR

Joinville and Louis the Ninth. Joinville and Louis IX. Robert Lowell. SP-LoweR

Joke, The. Robert Creeley. CP-CreeR

Joke about Don Pedro on Horseback. Federico García Lorca. CP-GarcF, *tr. by* Will Kirkland

Joke county, smallest in England. Rutland. Donald Davie. CP-DaviDC

Joke Gold. Carl Sandburg. CP-SandC

Jokes, repartees, and laugh, and pun polite. Petronius Arbiter. CP-SherT, *tr. by* Thomas Sheridan

Jokes, the feuds, the puns, the punishments, The. Louis Sonnet, A. Muriel Rukeyser. CP-RukeM

Joliet. Carl Sandburg. CP-SandC

Jolly and Jillie, bite and scratch all day. Upon Jolly and Jilly. Robert Herrick. CP-HerrR

Jolly Beggars, The. Robert Burns. CP-BurnR

(Love and Libery—A Cantata.) CP-BurnR

Jolly boys of St. Kevin's, St. Patrick's, Donore. Yahoo's Overthrow, The. Jonathan Swift. CP-SwifJ

Jolly Gauger, The. Robert Burns. CP-BurnR

Jolly Greene Giant, The. John Updike. CP-UpdiJ

Jolly-hearted old Josh Billings. Josh Billings. James Whitcomb Riley. CP-RileJ

Jolly Miller, The. James Whitcomb Riley. CP-RileJ

Jolly Young Carpenter, The. George Meredith. CP-MerG2

Jonah. Randall Jarrell. CP-JarrR

Jonah. May Sarton. SP-SartM

Jonah made his living. Making a Living. Anne Sexton. CP-SextA

Jonah on His Deathbed. Miller Williams. CP-WillM

Jonathan Aging. Miller Williams. CP-WillM

Jonathan at Last. Miller Williams. CP-WillM

Jonathan Confronts the Question. Miller Williams. CP-WillM

Jonathan doesn't know how to tell a lie. Jonathan's Secret. Miller Williams. CP-WillM

Jonathan Edwards. Jorge Luis Borges. SP-BorgJ, *tr. by* Alan S. Trueblood

Jonathan Edwards in Western Massachusetts. Robert Lowell. SP-LoweR

Jonathan Entertaining. Miller Williams. CP-WillM

Jonathan feels like a character out of Dickens. Jonathan Aging. Miller Williams. CP-WillM

Jonathan Happy. Miller Williams. CP-WillM

Jonathan has invited all his friends. Jonathan Entertaining. Miller Williams. CP-WillM

Jonathan Huntington Bright. Jones Very. CP-VeryJ

Jonathan in Awe. Miller Williams. CP-WillM

Jonathan in Mourning. Miller Williams. CP-WillM

Jonathan Jukes is full of health. Tell It to the Eskimos or Tell it to the Esquimaux. Ogden Nash. CP-NashO

Jonathan Losing. Miller Williams. CP-WillM

Jonathan Seduced. Miller Williams. CP-WillM

Jonathan Swift / Had the gift. Lines on a Drawing of a Monument to Swift's Grandfather. Alexander Pope. CP-PopeA

Jonathan, the last of the giant tortoises. Signs and Portents. Stanley Kunitz. CP-KunSC

Jonathan walking, careful of every crack. Jonathan in Awe. Miller Williams. CP-WillM

Jonathan's Secret. Miller Williams. CP-WillM

Jone is a wench that's painted. Upon Jone and Jane. Robert Herrick. CP-HerrR

Jone wo'd go tel her haires; and well she might. On Jone. Robert Herrick. CP-HerrR

Jones! as from Calais southward you and I. Composed near Calais, on the Road Leading to Ardres, August 7, 1802. William Wordsworth. CP-WorW1

Jones had a dog; it had a chain. Horrible History of Jones, The. G. K. Chesterton. CP-ChesG

Jones! when from Calais southward you and I. To a Friend, Composed near Calais, on the Road Leading to Ardres, August 7, 1802. William Wordsworth. MW-WorW

Jonestown: More eyes for *Jadwiga's Dream*. Yusef Komunyakaa. CP-KomuY

Joney. James Whitcomb Riley. CP-RileJ

Jonnel, this is for you—my river-saint-named. For My Son John. John Ciardi. CP-CiarJ

Joppa Diary. Maxine W. Kumin.

     January 25th. SP-KumiM

     June 15th. SP-KumiM

     May 10th. SP-KumiM

     September 22nd. SP-KumiM

Jordan (1). George Herbert. CP-HerbG

Jordan (2). George Herbert. CP-HerbG

Joree sang. What does he sing? He says, The. What the Joree Said, The Joree Being Only a Bird. Robert Penn Warren. CP-WarrR *Fr.* Prognosis: A Short Story, the End of Which You Will Know Soon Enough.

Joseph. G. K. Chesterton. CP-ChesG

Joseph and Mary. Robert Graves. CP-GravR

Josepha. George Meredith. CP-MerG2

Joseph's Coat. George Herbert. CP-HerbG

Josh Billings. James Whitcomb Riley. CP-RileJ

Joshua Battus's Spepeech to the Paparliament. Thomas Sheridan. CP-SherT

Joshua on Eighth Avenue. John Ciardi. CP-CiarJ

Joshua Tree. A. R. Ammons. CP-AmmoA

Jottings, not so Random. Donald Davie. CP-DaviDC

Jouga. Wallace Stevens. CP-StevW; CP-StevWP

Journal. Edna St. Vincent Millay. CP-MillE

Journal Entry (April 1969, Villa Serbelloni). William Meredith. SP-MereW

Journal Entry (With the Udalls, June 1968). William Meredith. SP-MereW

Journal for My Daughter. Stanley Kunitz. CP-KunSC

Journal in Cephalonia. Lord Byron. CP-Byron

Journal Night Thoughts. Allen Ginsberg. CP-GinsA

Journal of a Modern Lady, The. Jonathan Swift. CP-SwifJ

Journal of English Days, A. Charles Wright. SP-WrigC

Journal of One Significant Landscape, A. Charles Wright. SP-WrigC

Journal of Southern Rivers, A. Charles Wright. SP-WrigC

Journal of the Year of the Ox, A. Charles Wright. SP-WrigC

Journal of Three Questions, A. Charles Wright. SP-WrigC

Journal of True Confessions, A. Charles Wright. SP-WrigC

Journalist, The. Ai. SP-Ai

Journalist Buys a Pig Farm, The. Miller Williams. CP-WillM

Journey. Federico García Lorca. CP-GarcF, *tr. by* Jerome Rothenberg *Fr.* Secrets.

Journey. Edna St. Vincent Millay. CP-MillE

Journey, A. William Stafford. SP-StafWW

Journey, The. Walter De la Mare. CP-DeLaW

Journey, The. Sam Hamill. SP-HamiS

Journey, The. David Ignatow. SP-IgnaD

Journey, The. Czeslaw Milosz. CP-MiloC; CP-MiloCN, *tr. by* Robert Hass

Journey, The. Mary Oliver. SP-OlivM

Journey, The. Gregory Orr. SP-OrrG

Journey, The. Kathleen Jessie Raine. SP-RainK

Journey, The. Charles Tomlinson. CP-TomlC

Journey, The. Jones Very. CP-VeryJ

Journey ends between the black spiders and the white spiders, The. Mondo Henbane. Charles Wright. SP-WrigCN

Journey ends here, The. House by the Sea. Eugenio Montale. CP-MontE, *tr. by* Jonathan Galassi

Journey Home. Archibald MacLeish. CP-MacLA

Journey of the Magi. T. S. Eliot. CP-ElioT

Journey of the Snowmen. Howard Nemerov. CP-NemeH

Journey Renewed. William Wordsworth. CP-WorW2 *Fr.* River Duddon [A Series of Sonnets], The.

Journey to a Known Place. Hayden Carruth. CP-CarHL

Journey to Cracow, A. Paul Muldoon. CP-MuldP

Journey to Iceland. W. H. Auden. CP-AudeW

Journey to the Interior. Margaret Atwood. SP-AtwM1

Journey toward Poetry. May Sarton. SP-SartM

Journeying over many seas and through many countries. Carmen 101. Catullus. CP-ZukLS *Fr.* Carmina.

Journeyings. Denise Levertov. SP-LeveDL

Jove and Caesar were never so moved—the one. Petrarch. CP-Petra, *tr. by* J. G. Nichols

Jove call'd before him t'other Day. Verses Occasioned by an & c. at the End of Mr. D'Urfy's Name in the Title to One of His Plays. Alexander Pope. CP-PopeA

Jove may afford us thousands of reliefs. Griefes. Robert Herrick. CP-HerrR

Joy. Robert Creeley. CP-CreeR

Joy. William Dickey. SP-DickW

Joy. Hans Magnus Enzensberger. SP-EnzeH

Joy. Langston Hughes. CP-HughL; CP-HughL1

Joy. Robinson Jeffers. CP-JefR1

Joy. Denise Levertov. SP-LeveDP; SP-LeveDS

Joy. Carl Sandburg. CP-SandC

Joy ("Joy Thou giv'st no man can take away, The"). Jones Very. CP-VeryJ

Joy ("Thou hast a moon for every cloudy night"). Jones Very. CP-VeryJ

Joy—a beginning. Anguish, ardor. Relearning the Alphabet. Denise Levertov. SP-LeveDS

Joy and Agony of Improvisation, The. Hayden Carruth. CP-CarHS

Joy and balm of my life, the memory of those hours. Pleasure in the Flesh. Constantine P. Cavafy. CP-CavaC, *tr. by* Theoharis Constantine Theoharis

Joy at Sudden Disappointment. Jelaluddin Rumi. SP-Rumi, *tr. by* Coleman Barks

Joy, did I [*or* I did] lock thee up; but some bad man. Bunch of Grapes, The. George Herbert. CP-HerbG

Joy Had I Known. Fanny Howe.

     "Nothing in life is so exciting." SP-HoweF

     "Outside snow decays the country." SP-HoweF

     "There's a lot of the West." SP-HoweF

Joy has no parents. No joy ever. You Can Rely on Him. Yehuda Amichai. SP-AmicY, *tr. by* Chana Bloch

Joy in Martyrdom. Jeanne Marie Bouvier de la Motte- Guyon. CP-CowpW

Joy is a trick in the air. Birth-Dues. Robinson Jeffers. CP-JefR1

Joy is but sorrow, / While we know. Christina Georgina Rossetti. CP-RosC2

Joy is fleet, / Sorrow slow. George Meredith. CP-MerG1

Joy! Joy! Joy! that on my quiet day. Variation on a Polish Folk Song. Marya Alexandrovna Zaturenska. SP-ZatuM

Joy of Fishes, The. Chuang Tzu. CP-MertT

Joy of my life! you tell me this. Carmen 109. Catullus. CP-ZukLS *Fr.* Carmina.

Joy of Saints, like incense turned to fire, The. Christina Georgina Rossetti. CP-RosC2

Joy of the Cross, The. Jeanne Marie Bouvier de la Motte- Guyon. CP-CowpW

Joy of the moment turns suddenly, The. Elegy for the Living. Adam Zagajewski. SP-ZagaA, *tr. by* Renata Gorczynski, Benjamin Ivry *and* C. K. Williams

Joy of wax teeth, The. Hallow Eve with Spaces for Ghosts. Marge Piercy. SP-PierM

Joy of Writing, The. Wisława Szymborska. SP-SzymW, *tr. by* Stanisław Barańczak *and* Clare Cavanagh

Joy of Writing, The. Wisława Szymborska. SP-SzymWM, *tr. by* Joanna Trzeciak

Joy, Shipmate, Joy! Walt Whitman. CP-WhitW

Joy so short alas, the pain so near, The. Sir Thomas Wyatt. CP-WyatT

Joy stayed with me a night. Light of Love. Dorothy Parker. CP-ParkD

Joy that has no stem nor core, The. Emily Dickinson. CP-DickE

Joy, the, 'well . . . *joyfulness* of.' Joy. Denise Levertov. SP-LeveDP; SP-LeveDS

Joy Thou giv'st no man can take away, The. Joy ("Joy Thou giv'st no man can take away, The"). Jones Very. CP-VeryJ

Joy to have merited the Pain. Emily Dickinson. CP-DickE

Joy we most revere, The. Emily Dickinson. SP-DickE

Joy . . . weaving two violet petals for a coat lapel. Brass Keys. Carl Sandburg. CP-SandC

Joyce was afraid of thunder. Volcano. Derek Walcott. CP-WalcD

Joyful / And woful. Song: "Joyful / And woful." Johann Wolfgang von Goethe. CP-MerG2

Joyful lady, sing! / And I will lurk here listening. To a Lady Playing and Singing in the Morning. Thomas Hardy. CP-HardT

Joyful my run through dark parks in the fall. Run, A. Czeslaw Milosz. CP-MiloCN, *tr. by* Tony Milosz

Joyful spirit to the world, A. International Exhibition at Philadelphia, The. Jones Very. CP-VeryJ

Joyful your complete fearless and pure love. E. E. Cummings. CP-CummE

Joyfull Spring did ever last, The. Ovid. CP-RaleW *Fr.* Metamorphoses.

Joyfull The transporting news will Chear, The. On Hearing of the Out Powering of the Divine Spirit in Nassau Hall, Feb 24 1757. Annis Boudinot Stockton. CP-StocA

Joys faces friends / feet terrors fate. E. E. Cummings. CP-CummE

Joys have no parents. Not a single joy. You Can Rely on Him. Yehuda Amichai. SP-AmicYL, *tr. by* Benjamin Harshav *and* Barbara Harshav

Joys of Memory. Thomas Hardy. CP-HardT

Joys of Science, The. G. K. Chesterton. CP-ChesG

Juan Ramón Jiménez. Federico García Lorca. CP-GarcF, *tr. by* Alan S. Trueblood *Fr.* Three Portraits with Shading.

Juanita Tinsley. Muriel Rukeyser. CP-RukeM

Juan's Song. Louise Bogan. CP-BogaL

Juan's Twilight Dance. Marge Piercy. SP-PierM

Jubal and Tubal Cain. Rudyard Kipling. CP-KiplR

Jubal sang of the Wrath of God. Jubal and Tubal Cain. Rudyard Kipling. CP-KiplR

Jubilación. Charles Tomlinson. SP-TomlC

Jubilate. Thomas Hardy. CP-HardT

Jubilate Agno. Christopher Smart. SP-SmarC

Jubilate Sutra. Sam Hamill. SP-HamiS

Jubilee of a Magazine, The. Thomas Hardy. CP-HardT

Jubilee Singers, The. John Greenleaf Whittier. CP-WhitJ

Jubilemus omnes una Deo nostro qui creavit omnia. *Unknown.* CP-MertT

Jubilo. Allen Tate. CP-TateA

Judas. James Dickey. CP-DickJ

Judas. Jonathan Swift. CP-SwifJ

Judas Iscariot. Countee Cullen. CP-CullC

Judex Jocosus. Ambrose Bierce. SP-BierA

Judex Judicatus. Ambrose Bierce. SP-BierA

Judge a Moth by the Beauty of Its Candle. Jelaluddin Rumi. SP-Rumi, *tr. by* Coleman Barks

Judge and the Bird, The. Louis Zukofsky. CP-ZukLS

Judge Armstrong, when the poor have sought your aid. Judex Judicatus. Ambrose Bierce. SP-BierA

Judge Every One with Perfect Calm. Alice Walker. CP-WalkA

Judge his favour timely then extends, The. Another to Him. Ben Jonson. CP-JonsB

Judge is like the Owl, The. Emily Dickinson. CP-DickE

Judge mildly the tasked world; and disincline. World's Advance, The. George Meredith. CP-MerG1

Judge Not. Theodore Roethke. CP-RoetT

Judge Not According to the Appearance. Christina Georgina Rossetti. CP-RosC2

Judge Nothing before the Time. Christina Georgina Rossetti. CP-RosC2

Judge removed, though he's no more My Lord, The. Prologue to *Don Sebastian.* John Dryden. SP-DrydJ *Fr.* Don Sebastian.

Judge Shafter, you're an aged man, I know. Growler, A. Ambrose Bierce. SP-BierA

Judge William Hastie. Langston Hughes. CP-HughL; CP-HughL3

Judgement. George Herbert. CP-HerbG

Judgement Day, The. Robert Herrick. CP-HerrR

Judgement occurs, but is not. Three Beyond. Donald Davie. CP-DaviDC

Judgement of Paris. Robert Graves. CP-GravR

Judges have chains in their sleeves, The. Bread at Midnight. W. S. Merwin. SP-MerwW

Judges of the Secret Court, The. James Laughlin. CP-LaugJ

Judges, The. Robert Graves. CP-GravR

Judgment. Eleanor Wilner. SP-WilnE

Judgment, The. Laura Riding Jackson. CP-RidiL

Judgment Day. Langston Hughes. CP-HughL; CP-HughL1

Judgment Day. Ogden Nash. CP-NashO

Judgment-Day, The. Robert Herrick. CP-HerrR

Judgment is justest. Emily Dickinson. CP-DickE

Judgment is prepared, The. Judgment, The. Laura Riding Jackson. CP-RidiL

Judgment of England, The. G. K. Chesterton. CP-ChesG

Judgment of Paris, The. W. S. Merwin. SP-MerwW

Judgment of the Poets, The. William Cowper. CP-CowpW

Judgments. Rainer Maria Rilke. CP-RilkFr, *tr. by* A. Poulin, Jr.

Judgments. William Stafford. SP-StafWW

Judith. James Whitcomb Riley. CP-RileJ

Judith. Muriel Rukeyser. CP-RukeM

Judith at the Tent of Holofernes. John Greenleaf Whittier. CP-WhitJ

Judith has cast her old-skin, and got new. Upon Judith. Robert Herrick. CP-HerrR

Judith of Bethulia. John Crowe Ransom. SP-RansJ

Judy Sugden! Judy, I made you caper. Barnsley and District. Donald Davie. CP-DaviDC

Jug. Carl Sandburg. CP-SandC

Juggler. Richard Wilbur. CP-WilbR

Juggler, The. John Donne. *See* Manliness

Juggler, The. David Ignatow. SP-IgnaD

Juggler at *Heaven's Gate*, The. Raymond Carver. CP-CarvR

Juggler's Hat her Country is, The. Emily Dickinson. CP-DickE

Jugglers keep six bottles in the air. Hazardous Occupations. Carl Sandburg. CP-SandC

Juggler's Song, The. Rudyard Kipling. CP-KiplR *Fr.* Kim.

Juggler's Thought. Robert Creeley. CP-CreeR

Juggling Jerry. George Meredith. CP-MerG1

Jugum Improbum. Robert Graves. CP-GravR

Juice Joint: Northern City. Langston Hughes. CP-HughL; CP-HughL2

Juke Box Love Song. Langston Hughes. CP-HughL; CP-HughL3

Julia and I did lately sit. Cherry-Pit. Robert Herrick. CP-HerrR

Julia, I bring. Ring Presented to Julia, A. Robert Herrick. CP-HerrR

Julia, if I chance to die. His Request to Julia. Robert Herrick. CP-HerrR

Julia was carelesse, and withall. Upon Julia's Fall. Robert Herrick. CP-HerrR

Julia, when thy Herrick dies. To Julia. Robert Herrick. CP-HerrR

Julian [A Fragment]. Lord Byron. CP-Byron

Julian and Maddalo; A Conversation. Percy Bysshe Shelley. CP-ShelP

Julian and the Antiochians. Constantine P. Cavafy. CP-CavaC, *tr. by* Theoharis Constantine Theoharis

Julian at the Mysteries. Constantine P. Cavafy. CP-CavaC, *tr. by* Theoharis Constantine Theoharis

Julian in Nicomedia. Constantine P. Cavafy. CP-CavaC, *tr. by* Theoharis Constantine Theoharis

Julian M. and A.G. Rochelle. Emily Jane Brontë. CP-BronE

Julian, Seeing Contempt. Constantine P. Cavafy. CP-CavaC, *tr. by* Theoharis Constantine Theoharis

Julian the Apostate. Thom Gunn. CP-GunnT

Julian, there are vast gaps we call black holes. Showings, The: Lady Julian of Norwich, 1342-1416. Denise Levertov. SP-LeveDS

Julia's Churching, or Purification. Robert Herrick. CP-HerrR

Julia's Petticoat. Robert Herrick. CP-HerrR

Julie-Jane. Thomas Hardy. CP-HardT

Juliet. Langston Hughes. CP-HughL
   (There are wonder.) CP-HughL2

Juliet's Garden. Charles Tomlinson. CP-TomlC

Juliet's Nurse. Walter De la Mare. CP-DeLaW

Julio hernadez does not lie here. Epitaph (1): "Julio hernadez does not lie here." Andrei Codrescu. SP-CodrA

Julius Caesar, when false Ptolemy. Petrarch. CP-Petra, *tr. by* J. G. Nichols

July. Seamus Heaney. SP-HeanSO

July. George Meredith. CP-MerG1

July. Edmund Spenser. CP-Spens *Fr.* Shepheardes [*or* Shepeards *or* Shepherd's] Calender, The.

July. John Updike. CP-UpdiJ

July, Against Hunger. Maxine W. Kumin. SP-KumiM

July Dawn. Louise Bogan. CP-BogaL

July 8 or July 9 the eighth surely, certainly / 1976 that I know. Morning of the Poem, The. James Schuyler. CP-SchuJ

July: Fargo Street. Robert Creeley. SP-CreeR

7/14/68: i. Adrienne Rich. CP-RicAE *Fr.* Ghazals: Homage to Ghalib.

July Fourth by the Ocean. Robinson Jeffers. CP-JefR1

July in Washington. Robert Lowell. SP-LoweR

July Is Over and There's Very Little Trace. Frank O'Hara. SP-OharF

July Morning. Robert Bly. SP-BlyR

July Mountain. Wallace Stevens. CP-StevWP

July, 1964. Donald Davie. CP-DaviDC

July 1968. Denise Levertov. SP-LeveDS

July, 1773. Wendell Berry. CP-BerrW

July seventeenth nineteen sixty eight. Adrienne Rich. CP-RicAE *Fr.* Ghazals: Homage to Ghalib.

7/16/68: i. Adrienne Rich. CP-RicAE *Fr.* Ghazals: Homage to Ghalib.

7/16/68: ii. Adrienne Rich. CP-RicAE *Fr.* Ghazals: Homage to Ghalib.

7/13/68. Adrienne Rich. CP-RicAE *Fr.* Ghazals: Homage to Ghalib.

7/12/68. Adrienne Rich. CP-RicAE *Fr.* Ghazals: Homage to Ghalib.

7/26/68: i. Adrienne Rich. CP-RicAE *Fr.* Ghazals: Homage to Ghalib.

7/26/68: II. Adrienne Rich. CP-RicAE *Fr.* Ghazals: Homage to Ghalib.

July, waxwings. Lorine Niedecker. CP-NiedL

July's Farewell. Arthur Hugh Clough. SP-ClouA

Jumbled iceberg hills, away to the North. Gulkana, The. Ted Hughes. SP-HughTN

Jumbo. Stevie Smith. CP-SmitS

Jumbo. Wallace Stevens. CP-StevW; CP-StevWP

Jump stone hand leaf shadow sun. Fire, The. Robert Duncan. SP-DuncR *Fr.* Passages.

Jump-to-Glory Jane. George Meredith. CP-MerG1

Jumpin John. Robert Burns. CP-BurnR

Jumping Bad Blues. Yusef Komunyakaa. CP-KomuY

Jumping from the certain earth, the river so. Transfer, The. Richard Eberhart. CP-EberR

Juncos. William Stafford. SP-StafWW

Junction. W. S. Merwin. SP-MerwWF

Junction, on a Warm Afternoon, The. Howard Nemerov. CP-NemeH

Junction-Station—Pilot Knob. Christmas along the Wires. James Whitcomb Riley. CP-RileJ

June. Thom Gunn. CP-GunnT

June. James Whitcomb Riley. CP-RileJ

June. Carl Sandburg. CP-SandC

June. James Schuyler. CP-SchuJ

June. Edmund Spenser. CP-Spens *Fr.* Shepheardes [*or* Shepeards *or* Shepherd's] Calender, The.

June at Woodruff. James Whitcomb Riley. CP-RileJ

June Bracken and Heather. Alfred Tennyson. CP-TennA

June Bug. Anne Sexton. CP-SextA

June day dawns, the joy-winds rush, The. Clover. Herman Melville. SP-MelvH

June: Dutch Harbor. William Meredith. SP-MereW

June, 1820. William Wordsworth. CP-WorW2

June 15th. Maxine W. Kumin. SP-KumiM *Fr.* Joppa Diary.

June Ghazal. Arthur Sze. SP-SzeA

June is the floodtide of green. Cod Summer. Marge Piercy. SP-PierM

June Leaves and Autumn. Thomas Hardy. CP-HardT

June Light. Richard Wilbur. CP-WilbR

June means weddings in everyone's lexicon. Here Usually Comes the Bride. Ogden Nash. CP-NashO

June 9. William Carlos Williams. CP-WilW2

June, 1968. Jorge Luis Borges. SP-BorgJ, *tr. by* Hoyt Rogers

June on the Merrimac. John Greenleaf Whittier. CP-WhitJ

June Rain. W. S. Merwin. SP-MerwWF

June 6, 1970. Robert Creeley. CP-CreeR

June 30, 1974. James Schuyler. CP-SchuJ

June Thunder. Louis MacNeice. CP-MacNL

June Twenty, *Three Days After*. Miller Williams. CP-WillM

June was not over. Another Way of Love. Robert Browning. CP-BroR1

June's edge. The sun. Solstice. Louise Glück. SP-GlucL

Junes were free and full, driving through tiny, The. June Thunder. Louis MacNeice. CP-MacNL

Jungheimer's. Carl Sandburg. CP-SandC

Jungle, The. Raymond Carver. CP-CarvR

Jungle, The. William Carlos Williams. CP-WilW1

Jungle Book, The. Rudyard Kipling.
    Her Majesty's Servants.
       Parade-Song of the Camp Animals. CP-KiplR
    Kaa's Hunting.
       "His spots are the joy of the Leopard: his horns are the Buffalo's pride." CP-KiplR
       Road-Song of the *Bandar-Log*. CP-KiplR
    Mowgli's Brothers.
       Hunting-Song of the Seeonee Pack. CP-KiplR
       "Now Chil the Kite brings home the night." CP-KiplR
    Rikki-Tikki-Tavi.
       "At the hole where he went in." CP-KiplR
       Darzee's Chaunt. CP-KiplR
    Toomai of the Elephants.
       Elephant, The. CP-KiplR
       Shiv and the Grasshopper. CP-KiplR
    White Seal, The.
       Lukannon. CP-KiplR
       Seal Lullaby. CP-KiplR
       "You mustn't swim till you're six weeks old." CP-KiplR

Jungle Clearance Ceylon. Louis MacNeice. CP-MacNL

Jungle Husband, The. Stevie Smith. CP-SmitS

Jungle Knot. A. R. Ammons. CP-AmmoA

Jungle Surrender. Yusef Komunyakaa. CP-KomuY

Junior Addict. Langston Hughes. CP-HughL; CP-HughL3

Junior High School Concert: Salle Rossini. C. K. Williams. SP-WillC

Juniper / fires burn in the crisp night. Arthur Sze. SP-SzeA

Junk. Richard Wilbur. CP-WilbR

Junk and the Dhow, The. Rudyard Kipling. CP-KiplR *Fr.* Land and Sea Tales.

Junk Collector, The. James Laughlin. CP-LaugJ

Junk Dawn, NYC. Andrei Codrescu. SP-CodrA

Junk-Heap at Murano. Muriel Rukeyser. CP-RukeM

Junk Mail. Allen Ginsberg. CP-GinsA

Junk Mail. James Laughlin. CP-LaugJ

Junk mail. A gun for a dollar. Andrei Codrescu. SP-CodrA

Junk Man, The. Carl Sandburg. CP-SandC

Junkie Monkey Reel. Maya Angelou. SP-AngeM

Junkies. Charles Bukowski. SP-BukC1

Junta was jubilant around the mortised fountain, The. Nine Black Poppies for Chac. Norman Dubie. CP-DubiN

Jupiter as the Evening Star. Jones Very. CP-VeryJ

Jury's the *mot juste* under our ground rules. On Being a Member of the Jury for a Poetry Prize. Howard Nemerov. CP-NemeH

Jus Primae Noctis. Robert Graves. CP-GravR

Jusque dans la caverne ciel et sol. Samuel Beckett. CP-BeckS

Just, The. Jorge Luis Borges. SP-BorgJ, *tr. by* Alastair Reid

Just, The. Jones Very. CP-VeryJ

Just a few of the roses we gathered from the Isar. Roses on the Breakfast Table. D. H. Lawrence. CP-LawrD

Just a herd of Negroes. Share-Croppers. Langston Hughes. CP-HughL; CP-HughL2

Just a rainy day or two. Souvenir. Edna St. Vincent Millay. CP-MillE

Just a short time ago I sat with him. At The Canoe Club. Richard Eberhart. CP-EberR

Just after the sun. Vegetable King, The. James Dickey. CP-DickJ

Just an Ordinary Guy. Langston Hughes. CP-HughL

Just and fit actions, Ptolemy (he saith). Lucan. CP-JonsB, *tr. by* Ben Jonson *Fr.* Civil War [Bellum Civile] *or* Pharsalia.

Just Anger, A. Marge Piercy. SP-PierM

Just Another Apotheosis. Robert Stock. SP-StocR

Just as a flame, by wind and weather flailed. Michelangelo Buonarroti. CP-Miche, *tr. by* John Frederick Nims

Just as a moth, enamoured of the light. Petrarch. CP-Petra, *tr. by* J. G. Nichols

Just as He spoke it from his Hands. Emily Dickinson. CP-DickE

Just as he was falling asleep, standing upright in the garden with his back against a tree. Lack of Will Power. Yannis Ritsos. SP-RitsY, *tr. by* Kimon Friar *and* Kostas Myrsiades

Just as his dream foretold, he met them all. Misunderstanding, A. W. H. Auden. CP-AudeW

Just as I used to say. Lawrence Ferlinghetti. SP-FerlL

Just as my fingers on these keys. Peter Quince at the Clavier. Wallace Stevens. CP-StevW; CP-StevWP

Just as of old! The world rolls on an on. James Whitcomb Riley. CP-RileJ

Just as of old,—with fearless foot. Onward Trail, The. James Whitcomb Riley. CP-RileJ

Just as on maps. To Marie Laurencin. Rainer Maria Rilke. CP RilkFr, *tr. by* A. Poulin, Jr,

Just as the iron. Fall 1970. William Corbett. SP-CorbW

Just as the master's drawing hoards. To Miss Nicola B. Rainer Maria Rilke. CP-RilkFr, *tr. by* A. Poulin, Jr.

Just as the plane was ready to. That Other World. James Laughlin. CP-LaugJ

Just as the trumpets' ringing tempest once toppled. Trumpets. Rainer Maria Rilke. CP-RilkFr

Just as the world was ending. Hurricane Season. Charles Simic. SP-SimiC; SP-SimiCE

Just as those final words were penned, the sun broke out in power. Poet's Dream, The. William Wordsworth. CP-WorW2

Just as those who gaze get higher than those who climb. Glacier, The. Louis MacNeice. CP-MacNL

Just as you cannot not be lovely here. Michelangelo Buonarroti. CP-Miche, *tr. by* John Frederick Nims

Just at the corner of the wall. Two Soldiers, The. Thomas Hardy. CP-HardT

Just because I loves you. Reasons Why. Langston Hughes. CP-HughL; CP-HughL1

Just Before April Came. Carl Sandburg. CP-SandC

Just before dawn she sighed and held him. Jacob and the Angel. Yehuda Amichai. SP-AmicY, *tr. by* Stephen Mitchell

Just before Fall. James Schuyler. CP-SchuJ

Just before she died. Lorine Niedecker. CP-NiedL

Just before sunlight. At the Screen Door. Yusef Komunyakaa. SP-KomuY

Just before the curtain falls in the river. Performance. Ted Hughes. SP-HughTN

Just before the high time of autumn. Proud Torsos. Carl Sandburg. CP-SandC

Just Beyond my reaching. Slave Coffle. Maya Angelou. SP-AngeM

Just Children. Adam Zagajewski. SP-ZagaA, *tr. by* Clare Cavanagh

Just comb your hair. Excerpts from a Father's Wisdom. A. K. Ramanujan. CP-RamaA

Just drifting on together. He and I. James Whitcomb Riley. CP-RileJ

Just-Finishing Candle, A. Jelaluddin Rumi. SP-Rumi, *tr. by* Coleman Barks

Just for a handful of silver he left us. Lost Leader, The. Robert Browning. CP-BroR1; SP-BroR

Just for a Time. Maya Angelou. SP-AngeM

Just for this afternoon. In the Realm of the Ignition. James Tate. SP-TateJ

Just friend, you are my only friend. Song: Just Friends. Robert Graves. CP-GravR

Just Friends. Robert Creeley. CP-CreeR

Just full of springs the world was in Illinois. Mona Van Duyn. SP-VanDM

Just God! and these are they. Clerical Oppressors. John Greenleaf Whittier. CP-WhitJ

"Just how much are you worth?" Xerxes asks Pythius, reputedly the richest man in Lydia. Allies: According to Herodotus. C. K. Williams. SP-WillC

Just imagine yourself seated on a shadowy terrace. That Reminds Me. Ogden Nash. CP-NashO

Just Inside the Vigil of Christmas. Charles Olson. CP-OlsoC

Just junk / is what it amounts to. Moral, The. William Carlos Williams. CP-WilW2

Just Keep Quiet and Nobody Will Notice. Ogden Nash. CP-NashO

Just let a man into your house. Girl's Spare Chorus, The. Christopher Logue. SP-LoguC *Fr.* Lily-White Boys, The.

Just lift me to the window while the British boys march by. Loyal Soldier, The. George Meredith. CP-MerG2

Just like a shadow in an empty room. Songs We Know Best, The. John Ashbery. SP-AshbJ

Just Like Job. Maya Angelou. SP-AngeM

Just look, Manetto, at that wry-mouth'd minx. Sonnet: Of an ill-favoured Lady. Guido Cavalcanti. CW-RossD, *tr.* by Dante Gabriel Rossetti

Just lost, when I was saved! Called Back. Emily Dickinson. CP-DickE

Just Made Perfect, The. Henry David Thoreau. CP-ThorH

Just Man. Heather McHugh. SP-McHuH

Just Man, A. Robert Herrick. CP-HerrR

Just man followed then his angel guide, The. Lot's Wife. Anna Andreyevna Akhmatova. CP-WilbR, *tr.* by Richard Wilbur

Just Man stood upright on firm hips, The. Arthur Rimbaud. CP-RimbA, *tr.* by Martin Sorrell

Just man's like a Rock that turnes the wroth, A. Just Man, A. Robert Herrick. CP-HerrR

Just north of the Yaak River, one man sits bolt upright. Mount Caribou at Night. Charles Wright. SP-WrigC

Just now at five. To Say It. Robert Creeley. SP-CreeR

Just o'er the stony wall. Azalea Swamp. Jones Very. CP-VeryJ

Just off the highway to Rochester, Minnesota. Blessing, A. James Wright. CP-WrigJ

Just Once. Anne Sexton. CP-SextA; SP-SextA

Just once I knew what life was for. Just Once. Anne Sexton. CP-SextA; SP-SextA

Just Once! Oh least Request! Emily Dickinson. CP-DickE

Just outside Tombstone. Kenneth Patchen. CP-PatcK

Just Right. C. K. Williams. CP-WillC

Just Shall Live by Faith, The. Jones Very. CP-VeryJ

'Just shall live by faith' the Prophet cried, The. Just Shall Live by Faith, The. Jones Very. CP-VeryJ

Just so—Jesus—raps. Emily Dickinson. CP-DickE

Just-So Stories. Rudyard Kipling.

  Beginning of the Armadilloes, The.

    "I've never sailed the Amazon." CP-KiplR

  Butterfly That Stamped, The.

    Butterfly that Stamped, The. CP-KiplR

  Cat That Walked by Himself, The.

    "Pussy can sit by the fire and sing." CP-KiplR

  Crab That Played with the Sea, The.

    "China-going P. & O.'s." CP-KiplR

  Elephant's Child, The.

    "I keep six honest serving-men." CP-KiplR

  How the Camel Got His Hump.

    Hump, The. CP-KiplR

  How the Leopard Got His Spots.

    "I am the Most Wise Baviaan, saying in most wise tones." CP-KiplR

  How the Rhinoceros Got His Skin.

    "This Uninhabited Island." CP-KiplR

  How the Whale Got his Throat.

    Fifty North and Forty West. CP-KiplR

  Merrow Down. CP-KiplR

  Sing-Song of Old Man Kangaroo, The.

    "This is the mouth-filling song of the race that was run by a Boomer." CP-KiplR

Just so that each stark. Crows. Charles Simic. SP-SimiC; SP-SimiCE

Just so you shouldn't have to ask again. What Kind of a Guy Was He? Howard Nemerov. CP-NemeH

Just take a look at the servants of the idols. Priests of the Old Gods, The. Clement of Alexandria. CP-MertT *Fr.* Diatribe Against the Old Gods.

Just the airiest, fairiest slip of a thing. Discouraging Model, A. James Whitcomb Riley. CP-RileJ

Just the kind of a guy who. Key West. Charles Olson. CP-OlsoC

Just the ordinary days, please. Notes for the Program. William Stafford. SP-StafWW

Just the Same. Thomas Hardy. CP-HardT

Just the thought of them makes your jawbone ache. Relatives. John Updike. CP-UpdiJ

Just there, in a corner of the whin-field. Our Lady of Ardboe. Paul Muldoon. CP-MuldP

Just think of it, and you. Thought of Night. Heather McHugh. SP-McHuH

Just think: / the Peat-Bog Soldier of Masada. Paul Celan. SP-CelaP, *tr.* by John Felstiner

Just Thinking. William Stafford. SP-StafWW

Just thinking of you—such is your power. To Anna Akhmátova. Boris Leonidovich Pasternak. SP-WeisT, *tr.* by Theodore Weiss

Just to Be Good. James Whitcomb Riley. CP-RileJ

Just to hear / the bell of the Vela. Ghazal of the Love That Hides from Sight. Federico García Lorca. CP-GarcF, *tr.* by Catherine Brown *Fr.* Ghazals.

Just to keep the heart's simple given beat. HINDOO, THE: The Only Risk. A. K. Ramanujan. CP-RamaA

Just trees and the smell. I Went. Pablo Neruda. SP-NeruP

Just Vengeance Claims Thy Soul for Rights Invaded? William Wordsworth. CP-WorW2

Just Walking Around. John Ashbery. SP-AshbJ

Just when he had given up thinking. March into Russia, The. Raymond Carver. CP-CarvR

Just when I imagined I had conquered nostalgia so odious. Letter to Maxine Sullivan. Hayden Carruth. CP-CarHS

Just when I'm lost in adoration of you. Michelangelo Buonarroti. CP-Miche, *tr.* by John Frederick Nims

Just Whistle a Bit. Paul Laurence Dunbar. CP-DunbP

Just why I picked so wretched a morn. Just Another Apotheosis. Robert Stock. SP-StocR

Just why should it invariably happen. Awakening, The. Robert Graves. CP-GravR

Just Wrap It Up, and I'll Throw It Away Later. Ogden Nash. CP-NashO

Just yesterday afternoon I heard a man. Way of the Conventicle of the Trees, The. Hayden Carruth. CP-CarHS

Just You Wait! Donald Davie. CP-DaviDC

Justice. Paul Laurence Dunbar. CP-DunbP

Justice. Langston Hughes. CP-HughL; CP-HughL1; CP-HughL3

Justice. Rudyard Kipling. CP-KiplR

Justice Denied in Massachusetts. Edna St. Vincent Millay. CP-MillE

Justice hath heaved a sword to plunge in Albion's breast. Prologue to King John. William Blake. CP-BlakW

Justice (1). George Herbert. CP-HerbG

Justice (2). George Herbert. CP-HerbG

Justice's Tale, The. Rudyard Kipling. CP-KiplR *Fr.* Muse among the Motors, The.

Justification by Faith. Jones Very. CP-VeryJ

Justification of blood and rock is. Freedom: The Unmolested Eagle of Myself. Charles Bukowski. SP-BukC2

Justin. Thom Gunn. CP-GunnT

Justing Betwix James Watsoun and Jhone Barbour, The. Sir David Lyndsay. SP-LyndD

Justly our dearest Saviour may abhorre us. Christs Suffering. Robert Herrick. CP-HerrR

Justus Quidem Tu Es, Domine. Gerard Manley Hopkins. *See* Thou Art Indeed Just, Lord

Juvenilia. Adrienne Rich. CP-RicAE; SP-RicA2

JVC. Thom Gunn. CP-GunnT

K

K. McB. William Carlos Williams. CP-WilW1

K, The. Charles Olson. CP-OlsoC

K with quick laughter, honey skin and hair. Brise Marine. Derek Walcott. CP-WalcD

Kaa's Hunting. Rudyard Kipling. *Fr.* Jungle Book, The.

Kabul town's by Kabul river. Ford o' Kabul River. Rudyard Kipling. CP-KiplR

Kadava Kumbis Devise a Way to Marry for Love, The. Rita Dove. SP-DoveR

Kaddish. Allen Ginsberg. CP-GinsA; SP-GinsA

Kaddish. David Ignatow. SP-IgnaD

Kafka. Ted Hughes. SP-HughTN *Fr.* Boom.

Kafka's Watch. Raymond Carver. CP-CarvR

Kah Tai Purgatorio. Sam Hamill. SP-HamiS

Kai, Today. Gary Snyder. CP-SnydG

Kai twists / rubs "bellybutton." Egg, The. Gary Snyder. CP-SnydG

Kaire. Richard Eberhart. CP-EberR

Kairos and Logos. W. H. Auden. CP-AudeW

Kaisarion. Constantine P. Cavafy. CP-CavaC, *tr. by* Theoharis Constantine Theoharis

Kaiseki. Arthur Sze. SP-SzeA

Kalamazoo. Nicholas Vachel Lindsay. CP-LindV

Kalashnikov. Thomas Lux. SP-LuxT

Kali. Sam Hamill. SP-HamiS

Kali Ma tottering up steps to shelter tin roof, feeling her way to curb. Describe: The Rain on Dasaswamedh Ghat. Allen Ginsberg. CP-GinsA; SP-GinsA

Kallundborg Church. John Greenleaf Whittier. CP-WhitJ

Kallyope Yell, The. Nicholas Vachel Lindsay. CP-LindV

Kandy Express. Thomas Merton. CP-MertT

Kangaroo. D. H. Lawrence. CP-LawrD

Kangaroo, The. Ogden Nash. CP-NashO

Kannon. Sam Hamill. SP-HamiS

Kansas. Nicholas Vachel Lindsay. CP-LindV

Kansas City to Saint Louis. Allen Ginsberg. CP-GinsA
   "Funky barn, black hills approaching Fulton." SP-GinsA

Kansas Emigrants, The. John Greenleaf Whittier. CP-WhitJ

Kansas! Kansas! Shuddering at last! Allen Ginsberg. SP-GinsA *Fr.* Wichita Vortex Sutra.

Kansas Lessons. Carl Sandburg. CP-SandC

Kant saw them as the two eternal sources of awe. Starry Heavens, the Moral Law, The. John Ciardi. CP-CiarJ

Kapuzinerberg (Salzburg). Pierre Jean Jouve. CP-BogaL

Karamojongs. Alice Walker. CP-WalkA

Karenge Ya Marenge. Countee Cullen. CP-CullC

Karl Heinrich Marx. Hans Magnus Enzensberger. SP-EnzeH, *tr. by* Michael Hamburger

Karl Marx, cold mark that you are. Yehuda Amichai. SP-AmicYL, *tr. by* Benjamin Harshav *and* Barbara Harshav

Karl Onyx. George Meredith. CP-MerG2

Karma. Walter De la Mare. CP-DeLaW

Karshish, the picker-up of learning's crumbs. Epistle Containing the Strange Medical Experience of Karshish, the Arab Physician, An. Robert Browning. CP-BroR1; SP-BroR

Kate Whiskey. Paul Muldoon. CP-MuldP

Kate's. Robert Creeley. CP-CreeR

Katharine Anne. Lorine Niedecker. CP-NiedL

Käthe Kollwitz. Muriel Rukeyser. CP-RukeM

Kathleen. John Greenleaf Whittier. CP-WhitJ

Kathleen Mavourneen. James Whitcomb Riley. CP-RileJ

Kathleen ni Houlihan. Celtic Fringe, The. Stevie Smith. CP-SmitS

Katie at the Pool. Derek Mahon. CP-MahoD

Katic is making / velvet roses: next. Velvet Roses. James Schuyler. CP-SchuJ

Katy Did. James Wright. CP-WrigJ

Katydids, The. James Whitcomb Riley. CP-RileJ

Katy-dids at Ephrata return, The. Memorandum. Wallace Stevens. CP-StevWP

Kavafis wears a dark, striped suit. He is seated. Photograph of Kavafis, A. Sam Hamill. SP-HamiS

Kavyria. Donald Davie. CP-DaviDC

Kaya, my gentle. Her Sister. Denise Levertov. SP-LeveDL

Kayak on the black water. Kayaking at Night on Tomales Bay. Arthur Sze. SP-SzeA

Kayaking at Night on Tomales Bay. Arthur Sze. SP-SzeA

Kayser! to whom, as to a second self. To the Young Artist. Samuel Taylor Coleridge. CP-ColeS

Kazia. Czeslaw Milosz. CP-MiloCN, *tr. by* Robert Hass

Kazuko's Vision. Eleanor Wilner. SP-WilnE

KE 6-8018. Anne Sexton. CP-SextA

Keats, and Kirk White, David Gray and the rest of you. Meredith Nicholson. James Whitcomb Riley. CP-RileJ

Keats at Highgate. Thom Gunn. CP-GunnT

Keekin' Glass, The. Robert Burns. CP-BurnR

Keen. Eibhlín Ní Chonaill. CP-MuldP, *tr. by* Paul Muldoon

Keen. Edna St. Vincent Millay. CP-MillE

Keen and lovely man moved as in a dance. Lorine Niedecker. CP-NiedL

Keen as an eagle whose flight towards the dim empyréan. Poetry of Southey, The. George Meredith. CP-MerG1

Keen, Fitful Gusts Are Whispering Here and There. John Keats. CP-KeatJ

Keen stars were twinkling, The. To Jane: The keen stars were twinkling. Percy Bysshe Shelley. CP-ShelP

Keep. Margaret Atwood. SP-AtwM2

Keep A-Pluggin' Away. Paul Laurence Dunbar. CP-DunbP

Keep a red heart of memories. Haze. Carl Sandburg. CP-SandC

Keep a Song Up on de Way. Paul Laurence Dunbar. CP-DunbP

Keep away, son, these lakes are salt. These flowers. Advice to a Young Prophet.

Thomas Merton. CP-MertT

Keep ever on your eagle flight. To the High-Flyers. Johann Gabriel Seidl. CP-MerG2

Keep for the Young the impassioned smile. To Enterprise. William Wordsworth. CP-WorW2

Keep from me all that I might comprehend! Keep Hidden from Me. Rachel Korn. CP-KizeC, *tr. by* Carolyn Kizer

Keep Hidden from Me. Rachel Korn. CP-KizeC, *tr. by* Carolyn Kizer

Keep Innocency. Walter De la Mare. CP-DeLaW

Keep It. C. K. Williams. CP-WillC

Keep It Up. D. H. Lawrence. CP-LawrD

Keep love and he wings. Fragment 40: "Keep love and he wings." "H. D." CP-DoolH

Keep love for youth, and violets for the spring. Autumn Violets. Christina Georgina Rossetti. CP-RosC1

Keep not thou silence, O God. Psalm 83: "Keep not thou silence, O God." Bible, O.T. CP-MiltJ *Fr.* Psalms.

Keep off when I worship Siva. Mythologies 3. A. K. Ramanujan. CP-RamaA

Keep the quick eyes hid in the mind! Fancy. James Vincent Cunningham. CP-CunnJ

Keep this flower to remember me by. High Moments. Carl Sandburg. CP-SandC

Keep walking, though there's no place to get to. Jelaluddin Rumi. SP-Rumi, *tr. by* Coleman Barks

Keeper, / Is silent is living in the air not, The. Two Poems of Going Home. James Dickey. CP-DickJ

Keeper of Sheep, The. Fernando Pessoa.
   "And there are poets who are artists." SP-PessF
   "At night I suddenly waken." SP-PessF
   "Four songs that follow now, The." SP-PessF
   "From the highest window of my house." SP-PessF
   "I go indoors, and shut the window." SP-PessF
   "I never kept sheep." SP-PessF
   "I'd give anything if only my life were an oxcart." SP-PessF
   "If at times I say that flowers smile." SP-PessF
   "If I could take a bite of the whole earth." SP-PessF
   "If they want me to be a mystic, fine. I'm a mystic." SP-PessF
   "I'm a keeper of sheep." SP-PessF
   "Moonlight behind the tall branches, The." SP-PessF
   "My glance is clear like a sunflower." SP-PessF
   "On a terribly clear day." SP-PessF
   "Once at mid-day in late spring." SP-PessF
   "One way or another." SP-PessF
   "Only Nature is divine, and she's not divine." SP-PessF
   "Rather the flight of the bird passing and leaving no trace." SP-PessF
   "Rhymes mean nothing to me. Only rarely." SP-PessF
   "To think of God is to disobey God." SP-PessF
   "Today I read nearly two pages." SP-PessF

Keeper of the Vigil. Yusef Komunyakaa. CP-KomuY

Keeping. John Ciardi. CP-CiarJ

Keeping a Journal. William Stafford. SP-StafWW

Keeping Cool. Hans Magnus Enzensberger. SP-EnzeH

Keeping Going. Seamus Heaney. SP-HeanSO

Keeping Informed in D.C. Howard Nemerov. CP-NemeH

Keeping the City. Anne Sexton. CP-SextA

Keeping Their World Large. Marianne Craig Moore. CP-MoorM

Keeping your mind wide-open. Shih-te. CP-ColdM, *tr. by* Red Pine

Keepsake. Eugenio Montale. CP-MontE, *tr. by* Jonathan Galassi

Keepsake, The. Samuel Taylor Coleridge. CP-ColeS

Keepsake Boxes. Carl Sandburg. CP-SandC

Keepsakes. William Stafford. SP-StafWW

Keller Gegen Dom. William Carlos Williams. CP-WilW1

Kellomäki. Joseph Brodsky. CP-BrodJ

Kellyburnbraes. Robert Burns. CP-BurnR

Kelly's kept an unlicensed bull, well away. Outlaw, The. Seamus Heaney. SP-HeanSO

Kemble, thou cur'st my unbelief. On Seeing Mrs. Kemble in Yarico. Robert Burns. CP-BurnR

Ken ye ought o' Captain Grose? Robert Burns. CP-BurnR

Ken Ye What Meg o' the Mill Has Gotten. Robert Burns. CP-BurnR

Kendal . . . Shap Fell! Is that in Westmorland? Westmorland. Donald Davie. CP-DaviDC

Keng Sang Chu. Chuang Tzu. CP-MertT

Keng's Disciple. Chuang Tzu. CP-MertT

Kennedy's Inauguration. Robert Bly. SP-BlyR

Kenners' Cat, The. James Laughlin. CP-LaugJ

Kenneths. John Updike. CP-UpdiJ

Kenoza Lake. John Greenleaf Whittier. CP-WhitJ

Kensington Church Walk, St. Mary Abbots. Journal of English Days, A. Charles Wright. SP-WrigC

Kensington Notebook, A. Derek Mahon. CP-MahoD

Kent. Donald Davie. CP-DaviDC

Kentucky, 1833. Rita Dove. SP-DoveR

Kentucky Mountain Farm. Robert Penn Warren. CP-WarrR

Kentucky River Junction. Wendell Berry. CP-BerrW

Kentucky water, clear springs: a boy fleeing. Swimmers, The. Allen Tate. CP-TateA

Keokea. Arthur Sze. SP-SzeA

Kepler. Lorine Niedecker. CP-NiedL *Fr.* Element Mother, The.

Keppel, returning from afar. Trail of Admiral Keppel, The. William Cowper. CP-CowpW

Kept. Louise Bogan. CP-BogaL

Kept up by relays of generations young. Jack Roy. Herman Melville. SP-MelvH

Kernel escaped from the nut uncracked, The. Miracle, The. George Meredith. CP-MerG2

Kettle changes its note, The. Unknown, The. Denise Levertov. SP-LeveDP

Kettle descants in a cosy drone, The. Satires of Circumstance in Fifteen Glimpses. Thomas Hardy. CP-HardT

Kettle Song. Ivor Gurney. SP-GurnI

Kevin, Kevin Rooney, is it you? Re-Acquaintance. Hayden Carruth. CP-CarHS

Key, A. The door. Open. Tom. James Schuyler. CP-SchuJ

Key, The. Paul Muldoon. CP-MuldP

Key, The. Adrienne Rich. CP-RicAE

Key, The. Muriel Rukeyser. CP-RukeM

Key and bar, key and bar. Love's Castle. Paul Laurence Dunbar. CP-DunbP

Key-Note, The. Christina Georgina Rossetti. CP-RosC2

Key of C— an interlude for Marvin. William Stafford. SP-StafWW

Key of Water, The. Octavio Paz. CP-BishE, *tr.* by Elizabeth Bishop

Key-reist, I am fed and sick unto death with this. Sonnet: "Key-reist, I am fed and sick unto death with this." Hayden Carruth. CP-CarHS *Fr.* Sonnets.

Key West. Hart Crane. CP-CranH

Key West. Richard Eberhart. CP-EberR

Key West. Charles Olson. CP-OlsoC

Keyfoods. Audre Lorde. SP-LordA

Keys of Morning, The. Walter De la Mare. CP-DeLaW

Khan came from Bokhara town, The. Khan's Devil, The. John Greenleaf Whittier. CP-WhitJ

Khan's Devil, The. John Greenleaf Whittier. CP-WhitJ

Khing, the master carver, made a bell stand. Woodcarver, The. Chuang Tzu. CP-MertT

Khrushchev is coming on the right day! Poem: "Khrushchev is coming on the right day!" Frank O'Hara. SP-OharF

Kibali-Ituri. Kenneth Patchen. CP-PatcK

Kibbutz Gevaram. Yehuda Amichai. SP-AmicY, *tr.* by Chana Bloch

Kibbutz Gvar-'Am. Yehuda Amichai. SP-AmicYL, *tr.* by Benjamin Harshav *and* Barbara Harshav

Kick at the rock, Sam Johnson, break your bones. Epistemology. Richard Wilbur. CP-WilbR

Kick / of the foot against . . . , The. Robert Creeley. CP-CreeR

Kick Up the Fire, and Let the Flames Break Loose. Philip Larkin. CP-LarkP

Kicking his mother until she let go of his soul. Mundus et Infans. W. H. Auden. CP-AudeW

Kicking the Leaves. Donald Hall. CP-HallD

Kicks. Howard Nemerov. CP-NemeH

Kid ("Kid left / out back waits, The"). Robert Creeley. CP-CreeR

Kid ("Smaller, no recall"). Robert Creeley. SP-CreeR

Kid, The. Ai. SP-Ai

Kid, The. William Blake. CP-BlakW

Kid, The. Robert Creeley. CP-CreeR

Kid found its loose pages, A. History Book. Charles Simic. SP-SimiC; SP-SimiCE

Kid in the Park. Langston Hughes. CP-HughL; CP-HughL2

Kid left / out back waits, The. Kid ("Kid left / out back waits, The"). Robert Creeley. CP-CreeR

Kid Sleepy. Langston Hughes. CP-HughL; CP-HughL2

Kidnaped. Paul Laurence Dunbar. CP-DunbP

Kidnapped. Rudyard Kipling. *Fr.* Plain Tales from the Hills.

Kidnap[p]er. Tess Gallagher. SP-GallT

Kid's been crying. Mommy. Robert Creeley. SP-CreeR

Kids in School with Me, The. Langston Hughes. CP-HughL

Kids of Kyoto. For Benny. Robert Creeley. SP-CreeR

Kids / Seoul. Robert Creeley. SP-CreeR

Kids walking beach. Robert Creeley. CP-CreeR

Kids went off to school, The. Oddly Lovely Day Alone, An. John Updike. CP-UpdiJ

Kids Who Die. Langston Hughes. CP-HughL; CP-HughL1

Kierkegaard / cripple and a Dane, A. Die Neuen Heiligen. John Updike. CP-UpdiJ

Kierkegaard on Hegel. Adam Zagajewski. SP-ZagaA, *tr.* by Renata Gorczynski

Kierkegaard said of Hegel: He reminds me of someone. Kierkegaard on Hegel. Adam Zagajewski. SP-ZagaA, *tr.* by Renata Gorczynski

Kike is the most dangerous, A. E. E. Cummings. CP-CummE

Kiki. Robert Creeley. CP-CreeR

Kill, The. Donald Hall. CP-HallD

Kill me not every [or ev'ry] day. Affliction: "Kill me not every [or ev'ry] day." George Herbert. CP-HerbG

Kill Money. D. H. Lawrence. CP-LawrD

Kill of loose-voiced reason, The. Continual Ministry of Thy Anger, The. Kenneth Patchen. CP-PatcK

Kill your Balm—and its Odors bless you. Emily Dickinson. CP-DickE

Killala. Donald Davie. CP-DaviDC

Killed, the sand. Dry Time. Heather McHugh. SP-McHuH

Killer, A. Charles Bukowski. SP-BukC1

Killer, The. Richard Eberhart. CP-EberR

Killer Snails, The. James Fenton. SP-FentJ

Killers. Carl Sandburg. CP-SandC

Killers. Alice Walker. CP-WalkA

Killiecrankie. Robert Burns. CP-BurnR

Killing Floor. Ai. SP-Ai

Killing is not evil. Murder. D. H. Lawrence. CP-LawrD

Killing summer heat wraps up the city, A. Poem for Women in Rage, A. Audre Lorde. SP-LordA

Killing the Calves. Robert Earl Hayden. CP-HaydR

Killing the Grubs. Eleanor Wilner. SP-WilnE

Killing the Love. Anne Sexton. CP-SextA

Killing the Spring. Anne Sexton. CP-SextA

Killings continue, each second, The. City Psalm. Denise Levertov. SP-LeveDP

K********* Wabsters, fidge an' claw. Ordination, The. Robert Burns. CP-BurnR

Kim. Rudyard Kipling.
  Fairies' Siege, The. CP-KiplR
  Juggler's Song, The. CP-KiplR
  Prayer, The: "My brother kneels, so saith Kabir." CP-KiplR
  Prodigal Son, The. CP-KiplR
  Two-Sided Man, The. CP-KiplR
  "Unto whose use the pregnant suns are poised." CP-KiplR
  Wishing-Caps, The. CP-KiplR

Kimon, Son of Learchos, Age 22, Student of Greek Literature (in Kyrini). Constantine P. Cavafy. CP-CavaC, *tr.* by Theoharis Constantine Theoharis

Kimono, The. James Merrill. SP-MerrJ

Kimos, son of Menedoros, a young Greek-Italian. On an Italian Shore. Constantine P. Cavafy. CP-CavaC, *tr.* by Theoharis Constantine Theoharis

Kin. Maya Angelou. SP-AngeM

Kin. W. S. Merwin. SP-MerwW

Kin. Charles Olson. CP-OlsoC

Kin. Carl Sandburg. CP-SandC

Kin. C. K. Williams. SP-WillC

Kin: quiet grasses. Above. Deborah as Scion. James Dickey. CP-DickJ

Kin to Sorrow. Edna St. Vincent Millay. CP-MillE

Kinaesthesia. Richard Eberhart. CP-EberR

Kind. A. R. Ammons. CP-AmmoA

Kind-, The. James Laughlin. CP-LaugJ

Kind Are Her Answers. Thomas Campion. CP-CampT
  (Kinde are her answeres.) CP-CampT

Kind Ghosts, The. Wilfred Owen. CP-OwenW

Kind & holy were the words. Ralph Waldo Emerson. CP-EmerR

Kind is his mouth and smiling are his eyes. Chaucer. E. E. Cummings. CP-CummE

Kind, kind, milk in the mind. Stars in Your Name. Olga Broumas. SP-BrouO

Kind kinderpark. Bears and Waterfalls. May Sarton. SP-SartM

Kind of, A. Sunbather, to Herself, The. Raymond Carver. CP-CarvR

Kind of a man for you and me, The! Our Kind of a Man. James Whitcomb Riley. CP-RileJ

Kind of Act Of, The. Robert Creeley. CP-CreeR

Kind of an Ode to Duty. Ogden Nash. CP-NashO

Kind of empty in the way it sees everything, the earth gets to its feet. For John Clare. John Ashbery. SP-AshbJ

Kind of Ethics, A. Thom Gunn. CP-GunnT

Kind of Garden, A: A Poem for My Sister. George Oppen. CP-OppGN

Kind of Lecture on a Dull Day When There Isn't Even a Fly Around to Kill, A. Charles Bukowski. SP-BukC2

Kind of Love, Some Say, A. Maya Angelou. SP-AngeM

Kind of monkey or pine-lemur, A. Monkey Puzzle, The. Marianne Craig Moore. CP-MoorM

Kind of Music, A. Mona Van Duyn. SP-VanDM

Kind of Poetry I Want, The. Hugh MacDiarmid.
  "Ah, sweetheart, what a pool! Broad, deep, strong, silent, and sedate!" SP-MacDH
  "And a poetry in which as in a film." SP-MacDH
  "And thus a poetry which fully understands." SP-MacDH
  "I dream of poems like the bread-knife." SP-MacDH
  "Poetry full of *cynghanedd*, and hair-trigger relationships, A." SP-MacDH
  "Poetry in which all connections will constantly render such services, A." SP-MacDH
  "Poetry like the character of Indian culture, A." SP-MacDH
  "Poetry like the hope of achieving ere very long." SP-MacDH
  "Poetry of such an integration as cannot be effected." SP-MacDH
  "Poetry that goes all the way, A." SP-MacDH
  "Poetry that never for a moment forgets, A." SP-MacDH
  "Poetry the quality of which, A." SP-MacDH

Kind of Poor. Heather McHugh. SP-McHuH

Kind of rain we knew is a thing of the past, The. Kinsale. Derek Mahon. CP-MahoD

Kind of Scorn, A. Nicholas Vachel Lindsay. CP-LindV

Kind of upended cas- / ket with roller skates, A. He Lives in a Box. James Laughlin. CP-LaugJ

Kind of wooden Boston, crowding toward, A. Charleston. John Updike. CP-UpdiJ

Kind old man—the mild old man, The. James Whitcomb Riley. CP-RileJ

Kind pity [or Kinde pitty] chokes my spleen[e]; brave scorn forbids. Satire 3 [Religion]. John Donne. MW-DonnJ *Fr.* Satires.

Kind Reader! take your choice to cry or laugh. Substitute for an Epitaph. Lord Byron. CP-Byron

Kind Sir, I've read your paper through. To a Gentleman Who Had Sent Him a News-Paper, and Offered to Continue It Free of Expense. Robert Burns. CP-BurnR

Kind Sir: These Woods. Anne Sexton. CP-SextA; SP-SextA

Kind Sir: This is an old game. Kind Sir: These Woods. Anne Sexton. CP-SextA; SP-SextA

Kind solace in a dying hour! Tamerlane. Edgar Allan Poe. CP-PoeEd

Kind Words. Jones Very. CP-VeryJ

Kind) / YM&WC / (of sort of). E. E. Cummings. CP-CummE; SP-CummE

Kinde are her answeres. Thomas Campion. *See* Kind Are Her Answers

Kinde in unkindnesse, when will you relent. Thomas Campion *and* Philip Rosseter. CP-CampT

Kindergarten children first come forth, The. May Day Dancing, The. Howard Nemerov. CP-NemeH

Kindest of traps, The. Day Marked with a Small White Stone, A. Charles Simic. SP-SimiC; SP-SimiCE

Kindle the Christmas Brand, and then. Ceremonies for Candlemasse Day, The. Robert Herrick. CP-HerrR

Kindly fortune that made me once so happy. Petrarch. CP-Petra, *tr. by* J. G. Nichols

Kindly I envy thy song's [or songs] perfection. To Mr R. W ("Kindly I envy thy song's [or songs] perfection"). John Donne. CP-DonnJ; MW-DonnJ

Kindly to others, to itself unkind. Michelangelo Buonarroti. CP-Miche, *tr. by* John Frederick Nims

Kindly Unhitch That Star, Buddy. Ogden Nash. CP-NashO

Kindly Widow Lady, who lived upon a hill, A. Ballad of the Clairvoyant Widow. Theodore Roethke. CP-RoetT

Kindness. Denise Levertov. SP-LeveDL

Kindness. Sylvia Plath. CP-PlatS

Kindness, A. William Dickey. SP-DickW

Kindness glides about my house. Kindness. Sylvia Plath. CP-PlatS

Kindred forgets Thee. Love. George Meredith. CP-MerG2

King, A. Adam Zagajewski. SP-ZagaA, *tr. by* Clare Cavanagh

King, The. Shmuel HaNagid. SP-HaNaS, *tr. by* Peter Cole

King, The. Rudyard Kipling. CP-KiplR

King, The. James Whitcomb Riley. CP-RileJ

King!, The. William Carlos Williams. CP-WilW2

King: a man who for a moment. Rainer Maria Rilke. CP-RilkFr, *tr. by* A. Poulin, Jr. *Fr.* Fragments.

King and No King. William Butler Yeats. CP-YeatW

King and No King, A. Robert Herrick. CP-HerrR

"King and Queen." Donald Hall. CP-HallD

King and queen will stand to the child, The. Royal Sponsors. Thomas Hardy. CP-HardT

King and the Handmaiden and the Doctor, The. Jelaluddin Rumi. SP-Rumi, *tr. by* Coleman Barks

King and the Sea, The. Rudyard Kipling. CP-KiplR

King Arthur. John Dryden.
  Harvest Home. SP-DrydJ
   (Song by Comus and Three Peasants, A.) SP-DrydJ
  Song: "How happy the lover." SP-DrydJ
  Song of Venus. SP-DrydJ
   (Song.) SP-DrydJ

King Arthur on Mount Badon. Ballad of King Arthur, The. G. K. Chesterton. CP-ChesG

King Arthur rode in another world. Blue from Heaven, The. Stevie Smith. CP-SmitS

King Arthur's Men Have Come Again. Nicholas Vachel Lindsay. CP-LindV

King Claudius. Constantine P. Cavafy. CP-CavaC, *tr. by* Theoharis Constantine Theoharis

King David Dances. John Berryman. CP-BerrJ

King Dimitrios. Constantine P. Cavafy. CP-CavaC, *tr. by* Theoharis Constantine Theoharis

King Dives he was walking in his garden all alone. Song of the Wheels, The. G. K. Chesterton. CP-ChesG

King Edward the Third. William Blake. CP-BlakW

King Eochaid came at sundown to a wood. Two Kings, The. William Butler Yeats. CP-YeatW

King—estranged from his loving Queen, A. Speeding of the King's Spite, The. James Whitcomb Riley. CP-RileJ

King Hamlet's Ghost. Stevie Smith. CP-SmitS

King Harald's Trance. George Meredith. CP-MerG1

King has called for priest and cup, The. Last Rhyme of True Thomas, The. Rudyard Kipling. CP-KiplR

King Henry VII. And the Shipwrights. Rudyard Kipling. CP-KiplR

King. If farmers make my land secure. Ralph Waldo Emerson. CP-EmerR

King in Funeral Procession, A. Stevie Smith. CP-SmitS

King is Dead, The. Paul Laurence Dunbar. CP-DunbP

King John's Castle. Thomas Kinsella. CP-KinsT

King Julius left the south country. Song: "King Julius left the south country." Emily Jane Brontë. CP-BronE

King Leer. Ogden Nash. CP-NashO

King Marsilius of Saragossa. Death of Count Roland. Robert Lowell. SP-LoweR

King of Beasts, The. Robinson Jeffers. CP-JefR3

King of Bores, The. Ambrose Bierce. SP-BierA

King of Glory [or Glorie], King of Peace, / I will love thee. Praise (2). George Herbert. CP-HerbG

King of Glory [or Glorie], King of Peace, / With the one make war[re] to cease. L'Envoy. George Herbert. CP-HerbG

King of Harlem, The. Federico García Lorca. SP-GarcF, *tr. by* J. L. Gili *and* Stephen Spender

King of Harlem, The. Federico García Lorca. CP-GarcF, *tr. by* Greg Simon *and* Steven F. White

King of Hearts a broadsword bears, The. Song: Sword and Rose. Robert Graves. CP-GravR

King of Ice, The. A. R. Ammons. CP-AmmoA

King of Kings and Lord of Lords. Christina Georgina Rossetti. CP-RosC2

King of Oo-Rinktum-Jing, The. James Whitcomb Riley. CP-RileJ

King of rock 'n' roll, The. Painkillers. Thom Gunn. CP-GunnT

King of Sweden, The. William Wordsworth. CP-WorW1

King of the Ditchbacks, The. Seamus Heaney. SP-HeanSO

King of the Earthworms, The. Gregory Orr. SP-OrrG

King of the River. Stanley Kunitz. CP-KunSC

King of the Wood / King of the Dead. Charles Olson. CP-OlsoC

King of Tirmid, The. Dalqak's Message. Jelaluddin Rumi. SP-Rumi, *tr. by* Coleman Barks

King of us all, we cried to thee, cried to thee. King Victor Emanuel Entering Florence, April, 1860. Elizabeth Barrett Browning. CP-BroEB

King of Yellow Butterflies, The. Nicholas Vachel Lindsay. CP-LindV

King Philip. Jones Very. CP-VeryJ

King Popiel. Czeslaw Milosz. CP-MiloC; CP-MiloCN

King Prajadhipok his cataract. Rape of the Cataract, The. Richard Eberhart. CP-EberR

King said to his son, The: "Enough of this!" How Hard It Is to Keep from Being King When It's in You and in the Situation. Robert Frost. CP-FrosR

King Solomon and the Ants. John Greenleaf Whittier. CP-WhitJ

King Solomon drew merchantmen. Merchantmen, The. Rudyard Kipling. CP-KiplR

King Solomon: my master and the imbeciles. Thomas Merton. CP-MertT

King Stephen. A Fragment of a Tragedy. John Keats. CP-KeatJ

King Victor Emanuel Entering Florence, April, 1860. Elizabeth Barrett Browning. CP-BroEB

King Volmer and Elsie. John Greenleaf Whittier. CP-WhitJ

King was on his throne, The. Vision of Belshazzar, The. Lord Byron. CP-Byron

Kingdom, The. Rudyard Kipling. CP-KiplR *Fr.* Naulahka, The.

Kingdom of air, of lightly looming air, The. Attention Makes Infinity. Richard Wilbur. CP-WilbR

Kingdom of God Is Within You, The. Jones Very. CP-VeryJ

Kingdom of Heaven, The. G. K. Chesterton. CP-ChesG

Kingdom of Heaven: In Its Growth and Coming a Mystery, The. Jones Very. CP-VeryJ

Kingdom of Jerusalem, The. Robert Duncan. SP-DuncR

Kingdom of Number is all boundaries, The. Numbers and Faces. W. H. Auden. CP-AudeW

Kingdom of Stinking Wishes, The. C. K. Williams. CP-WillC

Kingdom of the Truth, The. Jones Very. CP-VeryJ

Kingdom, The. Louis MacNeice. CP-MacNL

Kingdoms of Heaven. Denise Levertov. SP-LeveDP

Kingfisher, The. Amy Clampitt. CP-ClamA

Kingfishers, The. Charles Olson. CP-OlsoC; SP-OlsoC

Kingfisher's Boxing Gloves, The. James Fenton. SP-FentJ

Kingly Man, The. Chuang Tzu. CP-MertT

Kingry's Mill. James Whitcomb Riley. CP-RileJ

Kings. Robert Herrick. CP-HerrR

Kings and Tyrants. Robert Herrick. CP-HerrR

King's Ankus, The. Rudyard Kipling. *Fr.* Second Jungle Book, The.

Kings Are Gone, The. Charles Bukowski. SP-BukC2

King's Arm Chair, The. Jones Very. CP-VeryJ

King's Bowman, The. James Laughlin. CP-LaugJ

King's Cliffe, in the evening: that Northampton stone. Northamptonshire. Donald Davie. CP-DaviDC

King's Cross Station. G. K. Chesterton. CP-ChesG

King's Daughter is all glorious within, The. She Shall Be Brought unto the King. Christina Georgina Rossetti. CP-RosC2

King's Experiment, The. Thomas Hardy. CP-HardT

King's fickleness, The. King, The. Shmuel HaNagid. SP-HaNaS, *tr. by* Peter Cole

King's Gift, The. Elizabeth Barrett Browning. CP-BroEB

King's Job, The. Rudyard Kipling. CP-KiplR

King's Missive, The. John Greenleaf Whittier. CP-WhitJ

King's most humble servant, I, The. Answer to an Invitation. Robert Burns. CP-BurnR

King's Mountain. Charles Olson. CP-OlsoC

King's Mountain. Muriel Rukeyser. CP-RukeM

Kings must be dauntlese: Subjects will contemne. Upon Kings. Robert Herrick. CP-HerrR

Kings must not oft be seen by publike eyes. Distance Betters Dignities. Robert Herrick. CP-HerrR

Kings must not only cherish up the good. Clemency in Kings. Robert Herrick. CP-HerrR

Kings must not use the Axe for each offence. Patience in Princes. Robert Herrick. CP-HerrR

King's Pilgrimage, The. Rudyard Kipling. CP-KiplR

Kings, queens of Judah, patriarchs, prophets, saints. On the Jamb-Statues of the Portail Royal (1150) on Chartres Cathedral. Helen Pinkerton. CP-PinkH

King's rage, stone-maned, out front. Paul Celan. SP-CelaP, *tr. by* John Felstiner

King's Soliloquy, A. Thomas Hardy. CP-HardT

King's Task, The. Rudyard Kipling. CP-KiplR

King's Tragedy, The. Dante Gabriel Rossetti. CW-RossD

King's way behind the false door, The. Paul Celan. SP-CelaP, *tr. by* John Felstiner

Kings who slept in the caves are awake and out, The. National Gallery, The. Louis MacNeice. CP-MacNL

Kingship. Donald Davie. CP-DaviDC

Kinned by hieroglyphic. Kinship. Seamus Heaney. SP-HeanSO

Kinsale. Derek Mahon. CP-MahoD

Kinship. Seamus Heaney. SP-HeanSO

Kinsman. John Greenleaf Whittier. CP-WhitJ

Kinsman belov'd, and as a son, by me! To John Johnson. William Cowper. CP-CowpW

Kipling's Vermont. Ogden Nash. CP-NashO

Kirilov on a Skyscraper. Randall Jarrell. CP-JarrR

Kirk of Scotland's Garland—a New Song, The. Robert Burns. *See* Kirk's Alarm, The

KIRK OF ULPHA to the pilgrim's eye, The. William Wordsworth. CP-WorW2 *Fr.* River Duddon [A Series of Sonnets], The.

Kirk's Alarm, The. Robert Burns. CP-BurnR

(Kirk of Scotland's Garland—a New Song, The.) CP-BurnR

Kisiabaton. Gary Snyder. CP-SnydG

Kiss, A. Thomas Hardy. CP-HardT

Kiss, A. D. H. Lawrence. CP-LawrD

"Kiss, The." Donald Hall. CP-HallD

Kiss, The. James Laughlin. CP-LaugJ

Kiss, The. Dante Gabriel Rossetti. CW-RossD *Fr.* House of Life, The.

Kiss, The. Anne Sexton. CP-SextA

Kiss, The. Alice Walker. CP-WalkA

Kiss, and a clasp, and an eye to eye, A. George Meredith. CP-MerG2

Kiss Ass. Allen Ginsberg. CP-GinsA; SP-GinsA

Kiss at Bayreuth, The. Thom Gunn. CP-GunnT

Kiss brings pain, A. Not Without Knowledge. Tennessee Williams. CP-WillT

Kiss, dear maid! thy lip has left, The. On Parting. Lord Byron. CP-Byron

Kiss had been given and taken, The. Last Time, The. Thomas Hardy. CP-HardT

Kiss, lovely Celia, and be kind. Love's Courtship. Thomas Carew. CP-CareT

Kiss me and comfort my heart. Beggar's Valentine, The. Nicholas Vachel Lindsay. CP-LindV

Kiss me, Miami, thou most constant one. To the Miami. Paul Laurence Dunbar. CP-DunbP

Kiss to the Bride, A. Walt Whitman. CP-WhitW

Kissass is the Part of Peace. Kiss Ass. Allen Ginsberg. CP-GinsA; SP-GinsA

Kiss[e], A. Robert Herrick. CP-HerrR

Kisse, The. Robert Herrick. CP-HerrR

Kiss[e] me, sweet: the wary [or warie] lover. To the Same [Celia]. Ben Jonson. CP-JonsB; SP-JonsB, *tr. by* Ben Jonson *Fr.* Volpone.

Kisses. Thomas Campion. CP-CampT

(Canto Tertio.) CP-CampT

Kisses. Robert Herrick. CP-HerrR

Kisses and poetry you endured. Yannis Ritsos. SP-RitsY *Fr.* First Series.

Kisses, Can You Come Back Like Ghosts? Carl Sandburg. CP-SandC

Kisses Forgotten. Carl Sandburg. CP-SandC

Kisses in the Train. D. H. Lawrence. CP-LawrD

Kisses Loathesome. Robert Herrick. CP-HerrR

Kissing. James Laughlin. CP-LaugJ

Kissing and Bussing. Robert Herrick. CP-HerrR

Kissing and Horrid Strife. D. H. Lawrence. CP-LawrD

Kissing and Telling. Paul Muldoon. CP-MuldP

Kissing Helena. Plato. CP-ShelP, *tr. by* Percy Bysshe Shelley

Kissing Her Hair. Algernon Charles Swinburne. SP-SwinA (Rondel.) SP-SwinA

Kissing Seat, The. Paul Muldoon. CP-MuldP

Kissing the Rod. James Whitcomb Riley. CP-RileJ

Kissing the Toad. Galway Kinnell. SP-KinnGN

Kissing Usurie. Robert Herrick. CP-HerrR

Kitchen. Robert Creeley. CP-CreeR

Kitchen, The. Raymond Carver. CP-CarvR

Kitchen Chair Poem #4. Clarence Major. SP-MajoC

Kitchen Chair Poem #5. Clarence Major. SP-MajoC

Kitchen chair speaks to the bread knife, The. Love Letter to Hans Christian Andersen. Carl Sandburg. CP-SandC

Kitchen Chimney, The. Robert Frost. CP-FrosR

Kitchen Door Blues. Tennessee Williams. CP-WillT

Kitchen is its readiness, The. This Winter Day. Maya Angelou. SP-AngeM

Kitchener's School. Rudyard Kipling. CP-KiplR

Kitchens would grow bright, The. Shapes and Shadows. Derek Mahon. CP-MahoD

Kite, The. Aleksandr Aleksandrovich Blok. SP-BlokA, *tr. by* Peter France *and* Jon Stallworthy

Kite, The. Wyatt Prunty. SP-PrunW

Kite, The. Anne Sexton. CP-SextA

Kite for Michael and Christopher, A. Seamus Heaney. SP-HeanSO

Kites. Donald Davie. CP-DaviDC

Kitten, The. Ogden Nash. CP-NashO

Kitten and [the] Falling Leaves, The. William Wordsworth. CP-WorW1

Kitten can, A. Where Knock Is Open Wide. Theodore Roethke. CP-RoetT

Kitten! Kitten! grown woman! Mama. William Carlos Williams. CP-WilW2

Kitty-Cat Bird, The. Theodore Roethke. CP-RoetT

Kitty Hawk. Robert Frost. CP-FrosR

Kitty Hawk is a Caesar among monuments. Structure of the Plane, The. Muriel Rukeyser. CP-RukeM

"Kitty" sixteen,5'1",white,prostitute. E. E. Cummings. CP-CummE

Kitville. Frank O'Hara. SP-OharF

Kiver up yo' haid, my little lady. Lullaby: "Kiver up yo' haid, my little lady." Paul Laurence Dunbar. CP-DunbP

Kleitos, a likable young man. Illness of Kleitos, The. Constantine P. Cavafy. CP-CavaC, *tr. by* Theoharis Constantine Theoharis

Klimt and Schiele Confront the Cunt. John Updike. CP-UpdiJ

Klockius. John Donne. CP-DonnJ; MW-DonnJ

Klockius so deeply hath sworn[e] [or vowed], ne'er more to come. Klockius. John Donne. CP-DonnJ; MW-DonnJ

Klondike, The. Edwin Arlington Robinson. CP-RobiE

KMnO$_4$ in Grandfather's Shaving Class. A. K. Ramanujan. CP-RamaA

Knave of darkness, limber in the leaves, The. Death for the Dark Stranger. Thomas McGrath. SP-McGrT

Knave of Hearts, The. Donald Davie. CP-DaviDC

Knave who scampered through the needle's eye, A. Favorite, The. Theodore Roethke. CP-RoetT

Knee-deep in June. James Whitcomb Riley. CP-RileJ

Knee Song. Anne Sexton. CP-SextA

Kneel down, fair Love, and fill thyself with tears. Ballad of Death, A. Algernon Charles Swinburne. SP-SwinA

Kneeling at the Pipes. Marge Piercy. SP-PierM

Kneeling Down to Look [or Peer] into a Culvert. Robert Bly. SP-BlyR

Kneeling stones, stones falling in cavalcades, and those never wanting to fall. In Praise of Stones. Gabriela Mistral. SP-MistG, tr. by Maria Giachetti [or Jacketti]

Kneeling with Herrick. James Whitcomb Riley. CP-RileJ

Knees / Of this proud woman / are bone, The. Cadenza. Carl Sandburg. CP-SandC

Knell, The. George Herbert. CP-HerbG

Kneller, by Heav'n and not a Master taught. Epitaph on Sir Godfrey Kneller, in Westminster-Abbey, 1723. Alexander Pope. CP-PopeA

Knew'st thou, one moneth wo'd take thy life away. Teares, and Laughter. Robert Herrick. CP-HerrR

Knife. Charles Simic. SP-SimiC; SP-SimiCE

Knife & the Bread, The. Olga Broumas. SP-BrouO

Knife at the Jugular. Arthur Sze. SP-SzeA

Knife blade of cold air keeps prying, A. Upstate. Derek Walcott. CP-WalcD

Knife-edge / days and shimmering nights. Corona, The. Arthur Sze. SP-SzeA

Knife, the priest, the heifer, The. Fragment of a Bas Relief. John Ciardi. CP-CiarJ

Knight, The. Paul Laurence Dunbar. CP-DunbP

Knight, The. Li Po. CP-WilW2

Knight, The. Adrienne Rich. CP-RicAE; SP-RicA1; SP-RicA2

Knight, a true sister-love. After Schiller. Thomas Hardy. CP-HardT

Knight came home from the quest, The. Quest, The. Rudyard Kipling. CP-KiplR

Knight, Death, and the Devil, The. Randall Jarrell. CP-JarrR

Knight had ridden down from Wensley Moor, The. Hart-Leap Well. William Wordsworth. CP-WorW1; MW-WorW

Knight in Disguise, The. Nicholas Vachel Lindsay. CP-LindV

Knight of gallant deeds, A. Romaunt of the Page, The. Elizabeth Barrett Browning. CP-BroEB

Knight of St. John, The. John Greenleaf Whittier. CP-WhitJ

Knight rides into the noon, A. Knight, The. Adrienne Rich. CP-RicAE; SP-RicA1; SP-RicA2

Knightly Rider of the Knee. Rider of the Knee, The. James Whitcomb Riley. CP-RileJ

Knights mine, all that be in hall. Masque of Queen Bersabe, The. Algernon Charles Swinburne. SP-SwinA

Knights of the Joyous Venture, The. Rudyard Kipling. Fr. Puck of Pook's Hill.

Knights of the White Camellia & Deacons of Defense. Yusef Komunyakaa. CP-KomuY

Knight's Tomb, The. Samuel Taylor Coleridge. CP-ColeS; MW-ColeS

Knit the mosquitoes together. Recipe for Sleep. James Tate. SP-TateJ

Knobs and Levers. Robert Graves. CP-GravR

Knock. James Dickey. CP-DickJ

Knock is at her door, but she is weak, A. Dead. Paul Laurence Dunbar. CP-DunbP

Knock, Knock. Ai. SP-Ai

Knock, knock! / Who's there? Federico García Lorca. CP-GarcF, tr. by Christopher Maurer

Knock off that hincty blowing, you Megarians. Little Old Funky Homeric Blues for Herm, A. Hayden Carruth. CP-CarHS

Knock the / light-wedges away. Paul Celan. SP-CelaP, tr. by John Felstiner

Knock with tremor. Emily Dickinson. CP-DickE

Knocking. Yannis Ritsos. SP-RitsY, tr. by Kimon Friar

Knokke. Robert Creeley. CP-CreeR

Knot, The. Stanley Kunitz. CP-KunSC

Knot, The. Adrienne Rich. CP-RicAE; SP-RicA2

Knot, The. C. K. Williams. SP-WillC

Knot in my gut's, The. Plexus. A. R. Ammons. CP-AmmoA

Knot which first my heart did strain, The. Sir Thomas Wyatt. CP-WyatT

Knothole in Spent Time, A. John Ciardi. CP-CiarJ

Know-All. D. H. Lawrence. CP-LawrD

Know all men by these presents, Death the tamer. Elegy on the Much Lamented Death of Mr. Demar, the Famous Rich Usurer [or Man], An. Patrick Delany. CP-SherT; CP-SwifJ

Know Celia, (since thou art so proud,). Ingrateful[l] Beauty Threatened. Thomas Carew. CP-CareT

Know Deeply, Know Thyself More Deeply. D. H. Lawrence. CP-LawrD

Know he who tills this lonely field. Ralph Waldo Emerson. CP-EmerR

Know of the limbs that embroidered with dust. Shmuel HaNagid. SP-HaNaS, tr. by Peter Cole

Know, that I would accounted be. To Ireland in the Coming Times. William Butler Yeats. CP-YeatW

Know the pinetrees. Know the orange dryness of sickness. Runes, The. Denise Levertov. SP-LeveDP

Know the world by heart. Theory of Poetry. Archibald MacLeish. CP-MacLA

Know this, my brethren, Heaven is clear. Song of the Old Guard, The. Rudyard Kipling. CP-KiplR

Know this, O King! that if thou shalt destroy. Philosopher and the King, The. William Cowper. CP-CowpW

Know thou, O stranger to the fame. For R. A. Esq. Robert Burns. CP-BurnR

Know Thyself. D. H. Lawrence. CP-LawrD

Know Thyself, and That Thou Art Mortal. D. H. Lawrence. CP-LawrD

Know Thyself: Suggested by Hearing Dr. A. E. Miller's Lectures on the Human Body. Jones Very. CP-VeryJ

Know when to speake; for many times it brings. Caution in Councell. Robert Herrick. CP-HerrR

Know ye the land where the cypress and myrtle. Bride of Abydos, The. Lord Byron. CP-Byron

Know you fair[e], on what you look[e]? On Mr. G. Herberts Booke, The Temple. Richard Crashaw. CP-CrasR

Know you the low pervading breeze. Twilight Music. George Meredith. CP-MerGI

Know you, winds that blow your course. Alice. Paul Laurence Dunbar. CP-DunbP

Knowest thou what ambition gains. Ambitione inani pectus caret. Jones Very. CP-VeryJ

Knowing again / that nothing / has been spoken. War Comes into my Room, The. Muriel Rukeyser. CP-RukeM

Knowing All Ways, Including the Transposition of Continents. Charles Olson. CP-OlsoC

Knowing Bitches. John Ciardi. CP-CiarJ

Knowing that nothing is in it. Sprinter at Forty, The. James Dickey. CP-DickJ

Knowing the dead, and how some are disposed. Two Formal Elegies. Geoffrey Hill. CP-HillG

Knowing the Enemy. Eleanor Wilner. SP-WilnE

Knowing the shape of the country. Knowing the midway to. Fifth Elegy. A Turning Wind. Muriel Rukeyser. CP-RukeM

Knowing the Unknown. Denise Levertov. SP-LeveDL

Knowing the voices of the country, gathering. Ives. Muriel Rukeyser. CP-RukeM

Knowing what. On a Theme by Lawrence, Hearing Purcell. Robert Creeley. SP-CreeR

Knowing what even scholars have surmised. That the Sestina Is What it is Despite What it is Not. Robert Stock. SP-StocR

Knowing what it bore. Leaving, A. Thomas Hardy. CP-HardT

Knowingly, knowing what secret, but. Insant on Crowded Street. Robert Penn Warren. CP-WarrR

Knowledge. Louise Bogan. CP-BogaL

Knowledge. Robert Herrick. See Science in God

Knowledge. David Ignatow. SP-IgnaD

Knowledge. James Laughlin. CP-LaugJ

Knowledge. Howard Nemerov. CP-NemeH

Knowledge and Truth. Jones Very. CP-VeryJ

"Knowledge deposed, then!"—groaned whom that most grieved. Pillar at Sebzevar, A. Robert Browning. CP-BroR2

Knowledge is not like truth, of heavenly birth. Knowledge and Truth. Jones Very. CP-VeryJ

Knowledge my nakedness. Muriel Rukeyser. CP-RukeM

Knowledge not of sorrow, you were, The. George Oppen. CP-OppGN

Knowledge of history fetches, A. Love and the Times. Donald Davie. CP-DaviDC

Knowledge of Old Towns, The. Kenneth Patchen. CP-PatcK

Knowledge of the Ambiguous. Yannis Ritsos. SP-RitsY, tr. by Kimon Friar

Knowledge that Comes through Experience, The. Jane Cooper. CP-CoopJ

Knowledge wandered north. When Knowledge Went North. Chuang Tzu. CP-MertT

Known color gown mountain laurel. Mountain Laurel. Louis Zukofsky. CP-ZukLS

Known Consequences. Yannis Ritsos. SP-RitsY, tr. by Kimon Friar

Known for its repertory lineages. Blood. Wyatt Prunty. SP-PrunW

Known Had I. Thomas Hardy. CP-HardT

Known in Vain. Dante Gabriel Rossetti. CW-RossD Fr. House of Life, The.

Known love standing in deep grove. Still Afternoon Light. W. S. Merwin. SP-MerwW

Known Soldier, The. Kenneth Patchen. CP-PatcK

Knows he who tills this lonely field. Dirge: "Knows he who tills this lonely field." Ralph Waldo Emerson. CP-EmerR

Knows how to forget! Emily Dickinson. CP-DickE

Know'st thou not at the fall of the leaf. Autumn Song. Dante Gabriel Rossetti. CW-RossD

Know'st thou, O slave-cursed land! Mithridates at Chios. John Greenleaf Whittier. CP-WhitJ

Know'st thou the land where the pale citrons grow. Mignon's Song. Johann Wolfgang von Goethe. CP-ColeS

Know'st thou the life of a single flower. Life of the Flower, The. Jones Very. CP-VeryJ

Knowst thou the luck the friends face to see. Hafiz. CP-EmerR *Fr.* Odes.

Know'st thou this, Souldier? 'tis a much chang'd plant, which yet. Upon the Thornes Taken Downe from Our Lords Head Bloody. Richard Crashaw. CP-CrasR

Knucks. Carl Sandburg. CP-SandC

Koan for Two Minutes of Intensive Meditation. Robert Stock. SP-StocR

Kodachromes of the Island. Robert Earl Hayden. CP-HaydR

Kodiak Poem, A. William Meredith. SP-MereW

Koenig of the River. Derek Walcott. CP-WalcD

Kolo. Joseph Brodsky. CP-BrodJ

Komboloi. James Merrill. SP-MerrJ

Komm Schöpfer Geist I bellow as Herr Beer. Whitsunday in Kirchstetten. W. H. Auden. CP-AudeW

Kookaburras, The. Mary Oliver. SP-OlivM

"Kookoorookoo! kookoorookoo!" / Crows the cock before the morn. Christina Georgina Rossetti. CP-RosC2

Kore. Robert Creeley. CP-CreeR

Kore. W. S. Merwin. SP-MerwWF

Kore. Kathleen Jessie Raine. SP-RainK

Korean Mums. James Schuyler. CP-SchuJ

Korean slang. Robert Creeley. SP-CreeR

Korean Woman Seated by a Wall, A. William Meredith. SP-MereW

Kosmos. Yusef Komunyakaa. CP-KomuY

Kosmos. Walt Whitman. CP-WhitW

Kossuth. Jones Very. CP-VeryJ

Kossuth. John Greenleaf Whittier. CP-WhitJ

Kostas Tympakianákis. James Merrill. SP-MerrJ

Kraken, The. Alfred Tennyson. CP-TennA

Kral Majales. Allen Ginsberg. CP-GinsA; SP-GinsA

Kralupy is not a pretty town. Bombing of the Town of Kralupy, The. Jaroslav Seifert. SP-SeifJ, *tr.* by Ewald Osers

Kratisikleia did not deign to let. Come, O King of the Lacedaimonians. Constantine P. Cavafy. CP-CavaC, *tr.* by Theoharis Constantine Theoharis

Kreisler. Carl Sandburg. CP-SandC

Kreutzer Sonata. Ted Hughes. SP-HughTN

Kruger. G. K. Chesterton. CP-ChesG

Krutz. Charles Bukowski. SP-BukC3

Ku Klux. Langston Hughes. CP-HughL; CP-HughL2; CP-HughL3

Kubla Khan: or, A Vision in a Dream. Samuel Taylor Coleridge. CP-ColeS; MW-ColeS

Kudzu. James Dickey. CP-DickJ

Kudzu Dormant. Amy Clampitt. CP-ClamA

Kumrads die because they're told). E. E. Cummings. CP-CummE; SP-CummE

Kung walked / by the dynastic temple. Canto 13: "Kung walked / by the dynastic temple." Ezra Pound. SP-PounE *Fr.* Cantos.

Kung Wen Hsien saw a maimed official. Man with One Foot and the Marsh Pheasant, The. Chuang Tzu. CP-MertT

Kursaal at Interlaken, The. Adrienne Rich. CP-RicAE

Kušiwoqqób. Gary Snyder. CP-SnydG

Kusta ben Luka is my name, I write. Gift of Harun Al-Rashid, The. William Butler Yeats. CP-YeatW

"Kwakwha." / "Askwali." Parallax. Arthur Sze. SP-SzeA

KWANNON, (*sine qua non*). Sanjusangendo. Philip Whalen. SP-WhalP

Kwashiorkor; Marasmus. Thomas Lux. SP-LuxT

Kyoto. Robert Creeley. SP-CreeR

Kyoto Born in Spring Song. Gary Snyder. CP-SnydG

Kyoto: March. Gary Snyder. CP-SnydG

Kyrie Eleison, O wild lynx! Godhead as Lynx, The. May Sarton. SP-SartM

L

L.A. John Updike. CP-UpdiJ

L. A. Rams in those years had, The. Gentleman and the Bastard, The. Charles Bukowski. SP-BukC3

L.E.L.'s Last Question. Elizabeth Barrett Browning. CP-BroEB

L M F B R. Gary Snyder. CP-SnydG

L of G. Walt Whitman. CP-WhitW

L. of G.'s Purport. Walt Whitman. CP-WhitW

L. Z ("Acre of music, An"). Lorine Niedecker. CP-NiedL

La Bella Donna della Mia Mente. Oscar Wilde. CP-WildO

La Bella Mano. Dante Gabriel Rossetti. CW-RossD

La Belle au Bois Dormant. Randall Jarrell. CP-JarrR

La Belle Dame de Tous les Jours. William Carlos Williams. CP-WilW1

La Belle Dame sans Merci [A Ballad]. John Keats. CP-KeatJ

La Belle Époque. Czeslaw Milosz. CP-MiloC; CP-MiloCN, *tr.* by Robert Hass

La Belle, La Douce, La Grande. Countee Cullen. CP-CullC

La Chute. Charles Olson. CP-OlsoC; SP-OlsoC

La Chute II. Charles Olson. CP-OlsoC

La Chute III. Charles Olson. CP-OlsoC

La Clemenza di Tito. Pietro Metastasio. Translations from Metastasio. CP-JohnS

La Comparsa en Oriente. Thomas Merton. CP-MertT

La Conca. Robert Creeley. SP-CreeR

La Crosse at Ninety Miles an Hour. Richard Eberhart. CP-EberR

La Figlia Che Piange. T. S. Eliot. CP-ElioT

La Flor. William Carlos Williams. CP-WilW1

La Foce. Archibald MacLeish. CP-MacLA

La Fontaine de Vaucluse. Marilyn Hacker. "Azure striation swirls beyond the stones." SP-HackM

La Force. Louise Glück. SP-GlucL

La Fraisne. Ezra Pound. CP-PoEar

La Gorgue. Ivor Gurney. SP-GurnI

La Gretchen de Nos Jours (I). Stevie Smith. CP-SmitS

La Gretchen de Nos Jours (II). Stevie Smith. CP-SmitS

La Jeunesse Blanche. Constantine P. Cavafy. CP-CavaC, *tr.* by Theoharis Constantine Theoharis

La-la! The cat is in the violets. Mandolin and Liqueurs. Wallace Stevens. CP-StevWP

L(a / le / af / fa / ll / s). E. E. Cummings. CP-CummE

La Lune, A. William Carlos Williams. CP-WilW1

La Mejicana. Robert Graves. CP-GravR

La Mouche. Samuel Beckett. CP-BeckS

La Noche. Robert Creeley. CP-CreeR

La Nuit Blanche. Rudyard Kipling. CP-KiplR (Much—discerning Public hold, A.) CP-KiplR

La nuit venue où l'âme allait. Samuel Beckett. CP-BeckS

La Nuvoletta. Dante Alighieri. CP-PoEar, *tr.* by Ezra Pound

La Pampa. Norman Dubie. CP-DubiN

La petite vie, a young man called it later, it had been the last thing offered. Historic Pun. George Oppen. CP-OppGN

La Pia. Dante Alighieri. CW-RossD *Fr.* Divina Commedia.

"*La Pologne? La Pologne?* Isn't it terribly cold there?" she asked. Vocabulary. Wisława Szymborska. SP-SzymW, *tr.* by Stanislaw Barańczak *and* Clare Cavanagh

La Préface. Charles Olson. CP-OlsoC

La Prisonnière. Thom Gunn. CP-GunnT

La Regina Avrillouse. Ezra Pound. CP-PoEar

La Revanche. Lord Byron. CP-Byron

La rosa china il volto rosseggiato. Christina Georgina Rossetti. CP-RosC3

La Rose des Vents. Richard Wilbur. CP-WilbR

La Saisiaz. Robert Browning. CP-BroR2

La Salette. Thomas Merton. CP-MertT

La Speakerine de Putney. Stevie Smith. CP-SmitS

La Torre. Charles Olson. CP-OlsoC

La Tristesse. James Laughlin. CP-LaugJ

La Ultima Carta: A Young Wife Writes to Her Husband in the Mountains. Miller Williams. CP-WillM

La Vie en Rose. Kenneth Rexroth. CP-RexrK

La Vita Nuova. Dante Alighieri. CW-RossD, *tr.* by Dante Gabriel Rossetti

La Vita Nuova. Dante Alighieri. "What Mary is when she a little smiles." CP-ShelP, *tr.* by Percy Bysshe Shelley

L'Abécédérien de la lubricité. James Laughlin. CP-LaugJ

Labor. Heather McHugh. SP-McHuH

Labor and Rest. Jones Very. CP-VeryJ

Labor Day. Louise Glück. SP-GlucL

Labor Day. James Schuyler. CP-SchuJ

Labor Day. Philip Whalen. SP-WhalP

Labor might fatigue. Emily Dickinson. SP-DickE

Labor Storm. Langston Hughes. CP-HughL; CP-HughL2

Labor to breathe that younger, rawer air:, The. Bobby Delano. Robert Lowell. SP-LoweR

Laboratory, The. Randall Jarrell. CP-JarrR

Laboratory, The (Ancien Régime). Robert Browning. CP-BroR1

Laborer, The. Jones Very. CP-VeryJ

Laborers, The. Jones Very. CP-VeryJ

Laborie, Choiseul, Vieuxfort, Dennery. Sainte Lucie. Derek Walcott. CP-WalcD

Labors of Hercules, The. Marianne Craig Moore. CP-MoorM

Labour. Robert Herrick. CP-HerrR

Labour Battalion. D. H. Lawrence. CP-LawrD

Labourer, The. George Meredith. CP-MerG2

Labourer's Noon-Day Hymn, The. William Wordsworth. CP-WorW2

Labourers pedalling at ease. Bann Clay. Seamus Heaney. SP-HeanSO

Labrador. William Carlos Williams. CP-WilW2

Labyrinth. Eleanor Wilner. SP-WilnE

Labyrinth, The. Jorge Luis Borges. SP-BorgJ, *tr.* by Stephen Kessler

Labyrinth has vanished, The. Vanished also. Elegy for a Park. Jorge Luis Borges. SP-BorgJ, *tr.* by Alastair Reid

Labyrinths, symbols, all the tricks of language. Baltasar Gracián. Jorge Luis Borges. SP-BorgJ, *tr.* by Alastair Reid

Lac into Seal. A. K. Ramanujan. CP-RamaA

L'Accélération de l'Histoire. Czeslaw Milosz. CP-MiloC; CP-MiloCN, *tr.* by Robert Hass

Lace cushions were considered by a tall. Le Travail Rajeunit. Marilyn Hacker. SP-HackM

Lace sweeps itself aside. Stéphane Mallarmé. CP-MallS, *tr.* by Henry Weinfield

Laced gaiter, A. George Oppen. CP-OppGN

Lacedemonian Instruction. William Blake. CP-BlakW

Lachesis. Kathleen Jessie Raine. SP-RainK

Lachesis Lapponica. Hans Magnus Enzensberger. SP-EnzeII, *tr.* by Michael Hamburger

Lachin y Gair. Lord Byron. CP-Byron

Lachrimae; or Seven Tears Figured in Seven Passionate Pavans. Geoffrey Hill. CP-HillG

Lachrymae Christi. Hart Crane. CP-CranH

Lack. Robert Graves. CP-GravR

Lack Love. Allen Ginsberg. CP-GinsA

Lack of Repose, The. Wallace Stevens. CP-StevW; CP-StevWP

Lack of Will Power. Yannis Ritsos. SP-RitsY, *tr.* by Kimon Friar *and* Kostas Myrsiades

Lackawanna. W. S. Merwin. SP-MerwW

Lackawanna Twilight. Carl Sandburg. CP-SandC

Lacking Factor, A. Ambrose Bierce. SP-BierA

Lacking Sense, The. Thomas Hardy. CP-HardT

Lacoste. Charles Tomlinson. CP-TomlC

Lad and a maid at a curve in the stream, A. Stephen Crane. CP-CranS

Lad came to the door at night, The. True Lover, The. A. E. Housman. CP-HousA

Lad changed to a shrub in spring, A. Transformations. Jaroslav Seifert. SP-SeifJ, *tr.* by Ewald Osers

Lad of Athens, faithful be. Emily Dickinson. CP-DickE

Lad was going blank, The. Suicide. Federico García Lorca. CP-GarcF, *tr.* by Alan S. Trueblood *Fr.* Back of the World.

Ladakh Buddhess Biker. Lawrence Ferlinghetti. SP-FerlL

Ladder, The. Kenneth Patchen. CP-PatcK

Ladder, flag, and amplifier. Corner Meeting. Langston Hughes. CP-HughL; CP-HughL3

Ladder horned against moonlight. Days of 1935. James Merrill. SP-MerrJ

Laddies by the banks o' Nith, The. Robert Burns. CP-BurnR

Ladie [*or* Lady], that in the prime of earliest youth. Sonnet 9: "Ladie [*or* Lady], that in the prime of earliest youth." John Milton. CP-MiltJ

Ladies, The. Rudyard Kipling. CP-KiplR

Ladies and gentlemen and the gay! History of the Twentieth Century (A Roadshow). Joseph Brodsky. CP-BrodJ

Ladies and Gentlemen: / I am going to ask just one question. I Move the Meeting Be Adjourned. Nicanor Parra. *Fr.* Manifesto.

Ladies and gentlemen this little girl. E. E. Cummings. CP-CummE

Ladies and gentlemen, you have made most remarkable. W. H. Auden. *See* Progress you have made is very remarkable, The

Ladies! And likewise Gentlemen! Suite for All Clown's Day. Josephine Jacobsen. CP-JacoJ

Ladies, fly from love's smooth tale. Conquest by Flight. Thomas Carew. CP-CareT

Ladies, I crave your indulgence for. Young Laundryman, The. William Carlos Williams. CP-WilW1

Ladies! (I hope there's none behind to hear). Prologue: "Ladies! (I hope there's none behind to hear)." Nathaniel Lee. CP-DryJ2 *Fr.* Princess of Cleves, The.

Ladies in my life, serially sexed, The. Lights of Love, The. James Vincent Cunningham. CP-CunnJ

Ladies in red capes and golden bracelets, The. Greek Women, The. Thomas Merton. CP-MertT

Ladies, ladies! what you offer. Conventional Ballad. William Carlos Williams. CP-WilW2

Ladies men admire, I've heard, The. Interview. Dorothy Parker. CP-ParkD

Ladies of the garden club, The. Correction: *Eve* Delved and *Adam* Span. Ogden Nash. CP-NashO

Ladies, on whom my attentions have waited. Triumph of Bullshit, The. T. S. Eliot. SP-ElioT

Ladies, our Master chose a dreadful play. Prologue to *Julius Caesar*, as It Was Acted at Madam Violante's Booth, Dec. the 15th, 1732, by Some of the Young Gentlemen in Dr. Sheridan's School, A. Thomas Sheridan. CP-SherT

Ladies who are interested in Assyrian art, The. Afternoon. T. S. Eliot. SP-ElioT

Ladies who ask me to portray my love. Portrait of Her Lover. Gaspara Stampa. SP-ZatuM, *tr.* by Marya Alexandrovna Zaturenska

Ladies who in chains of wedlock. Preaching from a Spanish Ballad, A. George Meredith. CP-MerG1

Lads in Their Hundreds, The. A. E. Housman. CP-HousA

Lads in their hundreds to Ludlow come in for the fair, The. Lads in Their Hundreds, The. A. E. Housman. CP-HousA

Lads of the Village, The. Stevie Smith. CP-SmitS

Lady. Ted Berrigan. SP-BerrT

Lady. Hayden Carruth. CP-CarHS

Lady! a Pen (perhaps with thy regard). Lines Written in the Album of the Countess of Lonsdale. William Wordsworth. CP-WorW2

Lady, accept a birth-day thought—haply an idle gift and token. For Queen Victoria's Birthday. Walt Whitman. CP-WhitW

Lady, accept the box a hero wore. Napoleon's Snuff-Box. Lord Byron. CP-Byron

Lady Acheson Weary of the Dean. Jonathan Swift. CP-SwifJ

Lady and the Bear, The. Theodore Roethke. CP-RoetT

Lady and the Earthenware Head, The. Sylvia Plath. CP-PlatS

Lady and the Painter, The. Robert Browning. CP-BroR2

Lady and the Unicorn, The. May Sarton. SP-SartM

Lady, Anemone. Tennessee Williams. CP-WillT

Lady asks me, A. Lady Bird. Robert Creeley. CP-CreeR

Lady Asks Me, A. James Laughlin. CP-LaugJ

Lady asks me, A / I speak in season. Canto 36: "Lady asks me, A / I speak in season." Ezra Pound. SP-PounE *Fr.* Cantos.

Lady Barbara; or, The Ghost. George Crabbe. SP-CrabG *Fr.* Tales of the Hall.

Lady Bates. Randall Jarrell. CP-JarrR

Lady Bird. Robert Creeley. CP-CreeR

Lady C. M, The. George Meredith. CP-MerG1

Lady came to a Bear by a Stream, A. Lady and the Bear, The. Theodore Roethke. CP-RoetT

Lady Cochrane. Donald Davie. CP-DaviDC

Lady dying of diabetes, A. Thought Revolved, A. Wallace Stevens. CP-StevW; CP-StevWP

Lady, farewell, whom[e] I in silence serve. Poem Put into My Lady Laiton's Pocket, A. Sir Walter Ralegh. CP-RaleW

Lady feeds Her little Bird, The. Emily Dickinson. CP-DickE

Lady from near Rising Sun, A. It Figures. Ogden Nash. CP-NashO

Lady gave me a gift she had not, A. Sir Thomas Wyatt. CP-WyatT

Lady Geraldine's Courtship. Elizabeth Barrett Browning. CP-BroEB

Lady Geraldine's Hardship. Rudyard Kipling. CP-KiplR *Fr.* Muse among the Motors, The.

Lady Hope should look ridiculous, and she does, The. Hope. Howard Nemerov. CP-NemeH

Lady, I cannot act, though I admire. Tramp's Refusal, The. Nicholas Vachel Lindsay. CP-LindV

Lady, I have read your verse on. To Elspeth. Dorothy Parker. CP-ParkD

Lady I intreate yow weare. Upon a Cherrystone Sent to the Tip of the Lady Jemmonia Walgraves Eare. Robert Herrick. CP-HerrR

Lady I know disapproves of the vulgarization of Christmas, A. I'll Eat My Split-Level Turkey in the Breezeway. Ogden Nash. CP-NashO

Lady / i pray to what is unimaginable. E. E. Cummings. CP-CummE

Lady! I rifled a Parnassian Cave. To the Lady Mary Lowther. William Wordsworth. CP-WorW2

Lady, I thank thee for thy loveliness. Moonstar, The. Dante Gabriel Rossetti. CW-RossD *Fr.* House of Life, The.

Lady,i will touch you with my mind. E. E. Cummings. CP-CummE

Lady! if for the cold and cloudy clime. Prophecy of Dante, The. Lord Byron. CP-Byron

Lady, if you'd slumber sound. For an Unknown Lady. Dorothy Parker. CP-ParkD

Lady in Back, The. Dorothy Parker. CP-ParkD

Lady in Black. Robert Creeley. CP-CreeR

Lady in Cabaret. Langston Hughes. CP-HughL; CP-HughL1

Lady in her silver, The. Caravan. John Berryman. CP-BerrJ

Lady in pink sits on her porch, A. Mother and Son. Charles Bukowski. SP-BukC2

Lady in red, she in the chile con carne red, The. Dancer. Carl Sandburg. CP-SandC

Lady in the Furs, The. Thomas Hardy. CP-HardT

Lady in the Leopard Coat. Lorine Niedecker. CP-NiedL

Lady in the Single, The. Louise Glück. SP-GlucL

Lady! in whose heroic port. Ode to a Lady Whose Lover Was Killed by a Ball, Which at the Same Time Shivered a Portrait next His Heart. Lord Byron. CP-Byron

Lady, in your Palace Hall. Emily Jane Brontë. CP-BronE

Lady Isabella. Christina Georgina Rossetti. CP-RosC3

Lady! It cannot be, but that thine eyes. John Milton. *See* In truth your fair eyes, my lady

Lady, lady, never start. Lady's Reward, The. Dorothy Parker. CP-ParkD

Lady, lady, should you meet. Social Note. Dorothy Parker. CP-ParkD

Lady Lazarus. Sylvia Plath. CP-PlatS

Lady, look up and laugh, at least. Spring Song, A. G. K. Chesterton. CP-ChesG

Lady Lost. John Crowe Ransom. SP-RansJ

  (This morning, flew up the lane.) SP-RansJ

Lady Love. Paul Éluard. CP-BeckS, *tr. by* Samuel Beckett

Lady, lovely lady. Vain and Careless. Robert Graves. CP-GravR

Lady Luncheon Club. Maya Angelou. SP-AngeM

Lady Mary Villiers lies, The. Epitaph on the Lady Mary Villiers. Thomas Carew. CP-CareT

Lady Montrevor. Christina Georgina Rossetti. *See* I Do Not Look for Love That Is a Dream

Lady Moon. / (Did someone shatter the quicksilver?). Reflection. Federico García Lorca. CP-GarcF, *tr. by* Jerome Rothenberg *Fr.* Mirror Suite.

Lady much more radiant than the sun, A. Petrarch. CP-Petra, *tr. by* J. G. Nichols

Lady, of anonymous flesh and face. New York: 5 March 1957. James Vincent Cunningham. CP-CunnJ

Lady of dusk-wood fastnesses. First Praise. William Carlos Williams. CP-WilW1

Lady of Forebodings, The. Thomas Hardy. CP-HardT

Lady of Heaven and earth, and therewithal. His Mother's Service to Our Lady. François Villon. CW-RossD, *tr. by* Dante Gabriel Rossetti

Lady of Heaven, the mother glorified. Sonnet: To the Blessed Virgin Mary. Fra Guittone d'Arezzo. CW-RossD, *tr. by* Dante Gabriel Rossetti

Lady of light, I would admit a dream. Buried Lake, The. Allen Tate. CP-TateA

Lady of May, The. Sir Philip Sidney.

  "Come, *Espilus*, come now declare thy skill." SP-SidnP

  "*Silvanus* long in love, and long in vain." SP-SidnP

  "To one whose state is raised over all." SP-SidnP

Lady of Quality, A. Thomas Kinsella. CP-KinsT

Lady of rich allure. La Regina Avrillouse. Ezra Pound. CP-PoEar

Lady of Shalott, The. Alfred Tennyson. CP-TennA

Lady of Shalott, Her Mirror Broken, The. William Dickey. SP-DickW

Lady of Silence. E. E. Cummings. CP-CummE

Lady of the Lake, The. Sir Walter Scott.

  Allan-Bane's Lament. SP-ScotW

  Ambuscade, The. SP-ScotW

  Chase, The.

  Invocation: "Harp of the North! that mouldering long hast hung." SP-ScotW

  Coronach. SP-ScotW

  Ellen's Song. SP-ScotW

  Fiery Cross, The. SP-ScotW

  Hail to the Chief Who in Triumph Advances. SP-ScotW

  (Boat Song.) SP-ScotW

  Harp of the North, Farewell! The Hills Grow Dark. SP-ScotW

  (Farewell.) SP-ScotW

  Lay of the Imprisoned Huntsman. SP-ScotW

  Ride to Stirling, The. SP-ScotW

  Trossachs, The. SP-ScotW

Lady of the Pearls, The. Alexandre Dumas.

  Trossachs, The. SP-ScotW

Lady of the porcelain department, The. In the Department Store. T. S. Eliot. SP-ElioT

Lady of the Well-Spring, The. Stevie Smith. CP-SmitS

Lady on a Balcony, A. Randall Jarrell. CP-JarrR

Lady Onlie. Robert Burns. CP-BurnR

Lady Painter, The. Andrei Codrescu. SP-CodrA

Lady Poet, The. Charles Bukowski. SP-BukC3

Lady, pretty lady, delicate and sweet. To a Lady. Dorothy Parker. CP-ParkD

Lady red amid the Hill, A. Emily Dickinson. *See* Lady red—amid the Hill, A

Lady red—amid the Hill, A. Emily Dickinson. CP-DickE

Lady, Rescued from Death by a Knight, Who in the Instant Leaves Her, Complains Thus, A. Thomas Carew. CP-CareT

Lady, reserved by the heav'ns to do pastors' company honour. Sir Philip Sidney.

SP-SidnP *Fr.* Arcadia.

Lady "Rogue" Singleton. Stevie Smith. CP-SmitS

Lady sent me Macaroons, A. Macaroons: An Ode. G. K. Chesterton. CP-ChesG

Lady, since your footstep. E. E. Cummings. CP-CummE

Lady speaks, The. William Carlos Williams. CP-WilW2

Lady Spring / is exquisitely dressed. Gabriela Mistral. SP-MistG, *tr. by* Maria Giachetti [*or* Jacketti]

Lady, the night is falling and the dark. To the Immaculate Virgin, on a Winter Night. Thomas Merton. CP-MertT

Lady! the songs of Spring were in the grove. To Lady Beaumont. William Wordsworth. CP-WorW1

Lady they calls me, Lady, and they always has. Lady. Hayden Carruth. CP-CarHS

Lady Thinks She Is Thirty, A. Ogden Nash. CP-NashO

Lady three chairs, The. Reading. William Corbett. SP-CorbW

Lady thus address'd her spouse, The. Mutual Forbearance. William Cowper. CP-CowpW

Lady, to Death we're doom'd, our crime the same! Alla Sua Amica. Samuel Taylor Coleridge. CP-ColeS

Lady to Her Guitar, The. Emily Jane Brontë. CP-BronE

Lady Vi. Thomas Hardy. CP-HardT

Lady was sitting at a table at dinner, The. Hand, The. Richard Eberhart. CP-EberR

Lady[,] Weeping at the Crossroads. W. H. Auden. CP-AudeW

Lady, what are you laughing at? Is it the joke. Grown-Ups, The. Donald Hall. CP-HallD

Lady / who burns without being burnt or trying. Sonnet: "Lady / who burns without being burnt or trying." Stéphane Mallarmé. CP-MallS, *tr. by* Henry Weinfield

Lady, who now with our Original. Petrarch. CP-Petra, *tr. by* J. G. Nichols

Lady Whom You Here Behold, The. William Wordsworth. CP-WorW2

Lady Wife. D. H. Lawrence. CP-LawrD

Lady will you come with me into. E. E. Cummings. CP-CummE

Lady, wise as well as fair, A. Apology to the Lady Carteret, An. Jonathan Swift. CP-SwifJ

Lady with a Falcon. May Sarton. SP-SartM

Lady with No One at All, The. Tennessee Williams. CP-WillT

Lady you have written me a letter. E. E. Cummings. CP-CummE

Lady, your room is lousy with flowers. Leaving Early. Sylvia Plath. CP-PlatS

Lady's Boogie. Langston Hughes. CP-HughL; CP-HughL3

Lady's Dressing Room, The. Jonathan Swift. CP-SwifJ

Lady's First Song, The. William Butler Yeats. CP-YeatW

Lady's Lament, The. Dante Gabriel Rossetti. CW-RossD

Lady's Reward, The. Dorothy Parker. CP-ParkD

Lady's Second Song, The. William Butler Yeats. CP-YeatW

Lady's Song, The. John Dryden. SP-DrydJ

Lady's Third Song, The. William Butler Yeats. CP-YeatW

Lady's "Yes," The. Elizabeth Barrett Browning. CP-BroEB

Læstrygonians, The. William Dickey. SP-DickW

Lag. Paul Muldoon. CP-MuldP

Lag, The. Adrienne Rich. CP-RicAE

Lager Beer. Paul Laurence Dunbar. CP-DunbP

Laggardly adventurer, The. Hands of Venus, The. Jaroslav Seifert. SP-SeifJ, *tr. by* George Gibian

Lagoon. Joseph Brodsky. CP-BrodJ, *tr. by* Anthony Hecht

Laguipière, the Emperor's cook. Emperor's Cook, The. Josephine Jacobsen. CP-JacoJ

Laguna Blues. Charles Wright. SP-WrigC

Laguna Dantesca. Charles Wright. SP-WrigC

Laid in unconsecrated ground, a scandal. Highgate Cemetery. Amy Clampitt. CP-ClamA

Laid out for dead, let thy last kindness be. To Robin Redbreast. Robert Herrick. CP-HerrR

Laid Up. Primo Levi. CP-LeviP, *tr. by* Ruth Feldman

Lain in Nature—so suffice us. Emily Dickinson. CP-DickE

Lair. Robert Pinsky. CP-PinsR

Lais. "H. D." CP-DoolH

Lak of Stedfastnesse. Geoffrey Chaucer. CP-ChauG

Lake. Czeslaw Milosz. CP-MiloCN, *tr. by* Martin Sabiniewicz *and* Jennifer Scappettone

Lake, The. Matthew Arnold. SP-ArnoM *Fr.* Switzerland.

Lake, The. Ted Hughes. SP-HughTN

Lake, The. Raissa Maritain. CP-MertT

Lake, The. W. S. Merwin. SP-MerwW

Lake Chelan. William Stafford. SP-StafWW

Lake full of glass houses, The. Lake, The. Raissa Maritain. CP-MertT

Lake House, The. Wyatt Prunty. SP-PrunW

Lake in the head, A. Dream, The. Robert Creeley. CP-CreeR

Lake in the Park, The. Louis MacNeice. CP-MacNL

Lake is deserted now, The. Dispossessed, The. Thomas Kinsella. CP-KinsT

Lake is known as West Branch Pond, The. Ballad of Blossom, The. Mona Van Duyn. SP-VanDM

Lake is thine, The. To the Evening Star over Grasmere Water. William Wordsworth. CP-WorW1

Lake Isle, The. Ezra Pound. SP-PounE

Lake-Isle of Innisfree, The. William Butler Yeats. CP-YeatW

Lake like glass, like space, The. Leaving Yannina. Amy Clampitt. CP-ClamA

Lake Michigan Morning. Carl Sandburg. CP-SandC

Lake Road. William Corbett. SP-CorbW

Lake Scene, A. May Swenson. SP-SwenM

Lake sunken among, A. Woman Skating. Margaret Atwood. SP-AtwM1

Lake Superior. Lorine Niedecker. CP-NiedL

Lake supports some kind of bathysphere, The. Paul Klee: *They're Biting*. Paul Muldoon. CP-MuldP

Lake: To———, The. Edgar Allan Poe. CP-PoeEd

Lake was filled with wax, The. Frivolous Blind Death Child. James Tate. SP-TateJ

Lake water lifted a little and fell, The. Crab Orchard Sanctuary, Late October. Thomas Kinsella. CP-KinsT

Lake's dark breast, The. Rising of the Storm, The. Paul Laurence Dunbar. CP-DunbP

Lakes of Värmland. James Dickey. CP-DickJ

Lakes where the sunsheen is mystic with splendour and softness. Poetry of Spenser, The. George Meredith. CP-MerG1

Lakeside, The. John Greenleaf Whittier. CP-WhitJ

Lalage! Charles Olson. CP-OlsoC

Lalage's coming: / Where is she now, O? Timing Her. Thomas Hardy. CP-HardT

L'Allegro. John Milton. CP-MiltJ

Lama, The. Ogden Nash. CP-NashO

Lamarck Elaborated. Richard Wilbur. CP-WilbR

Lamb, The. John Ciardi. CP-CiarJ

Lamb, The. Theodore Roethke. CP-RoetT

Lamb could not get born, A. Ice wind. February 17th. Ted Hughes. SP-HughTN

Lamb dead, dead lamb. Death Bereaves Our Common Mother Nature Grieves for My Dead Brother. Stevie Smith. CP-SmitS

Lamb just says, I AM!, The. Lamb, The. Theodore Roethke. CP-RoetT

Lambent cobblestones refract the blue, The. Next to the *Café Chaos*. Olga Broumas. SP-BrouO

Lambs at Play. Christina Georgina Rossetti. CP-RosC2

Lambs don't fight being itinerant. Fanny Howe. SP-HoweF *Fr.* Q.

Lambs of Grasmere, 1860, The. Christina Georgina Rossetti. CP-RosC1

Lambs that learn to walk in snow. First Sight. Philip Larkin. CP-LarkP

Lame Beggar, A. John Donne. CP-DonnJ; MW-DonnJ

Lame Boy and the Fairy, The. Nicholas Vachel Lindsay. CP-LindV

Lame boy / Met a fairy, A. Lame Boy and the Fairy, The. Nicholas Vachel Lindsay. CP-LindV

Lame Goat, The. Jelaluddin Rumi. SP-Rumi, *tr. by* Coleman Barks

Lame horse moves, A. Night Ride. Jay Wright. SP-WrigJ

Lament: "All is far." Randall Jarrell. CP-JarrR

Lament: "All morning I have been reading poems." Eleanor Wilner. SP-WilnE

Lament: "How she would have loved." Thomas Hardy. CP-HardT

Lament: "I thought of you." Gregory Orr. SP-OrrG

Lament: "Let me pick / olives in the moonlight." Arthur Sze. SP-SzeA

Lament: "Listen, children: / Your father is dead." Edna St. Vincent Millay. CP-MillE

Lament: "Nashe's old queens who bartered young and fair." Richard Wilbur. CP-WilbR

Lament: "Now let all lovely things embark." Countee Cullen. CP-CullC

Lament: "Someone is dead." Anne Sexton. CP-SextA; SP-SextA

Lament: "Sting of bees took away my father, The." Sylvia Plath. CP-PlatS

Lament: "Too limpid streets have grown narrow, The." Tennessee Williams. CP-WillT

Lament: "What face, in the water." William Carlos Williams. CP-WilW2

Lament: "When I was a windy boy and a bit." Dylan Thomas. CP-ThomD

Lament: "Your dying was a difficult enterprise." Thom Gunn. CP-GunnT

Lament, A: "Circle is broken, one seat is forsaken, The." John Greenleaf Whittier. CP-WhitJ

Lament, A: "O world! O life! O time!" Percy Bysshe Shelley. CP-ShelP

Lament for a Master of Style. Dan Pagis. SP-PagiD, *tr. by* Stephen Mitchell

Lament for Adonis. Bion.
     Fragment of the Elegy on the Death of Adonis. CP-ShelP

Lament for Adonis. Bion. CP-BroEB, *tr. by* Elizabeth Barrett Browning

Lament for Bion. Moschus.
     "Ye Dorian woods and waves, lament aloud." CP-ShelP

Lament for Cellists and Jacqueline DuPré. Alan Dugan. CP-DugaA

Lament, for Cocoa. John Updike. CP-UpdiJ

Lament for Dark Peoples. Langston Hughes. CP-HughL; CP-HughL1

Lament for Doormen. Charles Tomlinson. CP-TomlC

Lament for Ignacio Sánchez Mejías. Federico García Lorca. SP-GarcF, *tr. by* J. L. Gili *and* Stephen Spender

Lament for Ignacio Sánchez Mejías. Federico García Lorca. CP-GarcF, *tr. by* Galway Kinnell

Lament for James, Earl of Glencairn. Robert Burns. CP-BurnR

Lament for Javier Heraud. Thomas Merton. CP-MertT

Lament for Misenus. John Logan. CP-LogaJ

Lament for My Brother on a Hayrake. James Wright. CP-WrigJ

Lament for Pablo Neruda. Thomas McGrath. SP-McGrT

Lament for Pasiphaë. Robert Graves. CP-GravR

Lament for the Makaris [*or* Makars *or* Makers]. William Dunbar. CP-DunbW

Lament for the Makers. Robert Pinsky. CP-PinsR

Lament for the Makers of Songs. Kenneth Patchen. CP-PatcK

Lament for the Moths. Tennessee Williams. CP-WillT

Lament for the Two Brothers Slain by Each Other's Hand. Aeschylus. CP-HousA *Fr.* Seven against Thebes, The.

Lament for Toby, a French Poodle. May Sarton. SP-SartM

Lament 'im Mauchline husbands a'. Epitaph on a Wag in Mauchline. Robert Burns. CP-BurnR

Lament in rhyme, lament in prose. Poor Mailie's Elegy. Robert Burns. CP-BurnR

Lament in Spring. John Logan. CP-LogaJ

Lament my loss[e], my labo[u]r, and my pain [*or* payne]. Sir Thomas Wyatt. CP-WyatT

Lament not, o Hafiz, the distribution. Hafiz. CP-EmerR *Fr.* Odes.

Lament, o graces of Venus, and Cupids. Catullus. *See* Who loves beauty / veil her statues

Lament. Occasioned by the Unfortunate Issue of a Friend's Amour, The. Robert Burns. CP-BurnR

Lament of a Graying Woman. Cho Wen-chun. CP-WilW2

Lament of a Maiden for the Warrior's Death. Pablo Antonio Cuadra. CP-MertT

Lament of a New England Mother, The. Richard Eberhart. CP-EberR

Lament of a Slug-a-Bed's Wife. Stevie Smith. CP-SmitS

Lament of a Vanquished Beau, The. Langston Hughes. CP-HughL

Lament of Catherine Howard, Fifth Queen of Henry VIII. Marya Alexandrovna Zaturenska. SP-ZatuM

Lament of Mary Queen of Scots on the Approach of Spring. Robert Burns. CP-BurnR

Lament of Mary Queen of Scots on the Eve of a New Year. William Wordsworth. CP-WorW2

Lament of Professor Turbojet, The. James Laughlin. CP-LaugJ

Lament of Tasso, The. Lord Byron. CP-Byron

Lament of the Border Cattle Thief, The. Rudyard Kipling. CP-KiplR

Lament of the Children of Israel in Rome. Randall Jarrell. CP-JarrR

Lament of the Flowers, The. Jones Very. CP-VeryJ

Lament of the Frontier Guard. Li Po. SP-PounE, *tr. by* Ezra Pound

Lament of the Looking-Glass, The. Thomas Hardy. CP-HardT

Lament of the Valkyrie, The. Eleanor Wilner. SP-WilnE

Lament on the Eve of Parting. Ogden Nash. CP-NashO

Lament over Love. Langston Hughes. CP-HughL; CP-HughL1

Lament upon the Waters, The. John Ashbery. SP-AshbJ

Lamentation, A. Thomas Campion. CP-CampT

Lamentation, A. Denise Levertov. SP-LeveDP; SP-LeveDS

Lamentation of Glumdalclitch for the Loss of Grildrig, The. Alexander Pope. CP-PopeA

Lamentation of the Old Pensioner, The. William Butler Yeats. CP-YeatW

Lamentations. Norman Dubie. CP-DubiN

Lamentations. Louise Glück. SP-GlucL

Lamentations of Jeremy, for the Most Part According to Tremeullius. John Donne. CP-DonnJ

Laments of an Icarus, The. Charles Baudelaire. CP-BaudC, *tr. by* Walter Martin

Lamia. John Keats. CP-KeatJ

Lamia in Love. Robert Graves. CP-GravR

L'Amitié est l'Amour sans Ailes. Lord Byron. CP-Byron

Lamp, The. Robert Herrick. CP-HerrR

Lamp, The. Charles Olson. CP-OlsoC; SP-OlsoC

Lamp burns sure—within, The. Emily Dickinson. CP-DickE

Lamp Carrier, The. Yusef Komunyakaa. CP-KomuY

Lamp is calm and convenient; he prefers it, The. His Lamp. Yannis Ritsos. SP-RitsY, *tr. by* Kimon Friar

Lamp must be replenish'd [*or* replenished], but even then, The. Manfred. Lord Byron. CP-Byron

Lamp of day, with ill-presaging glare, The. On the Death of Sir J. Hunter Blair.

Robert Burns. CP-BurnR

Lamp Post, The. G. K. Chesterton. CP-ChesG

Lampblack of the mirror shows, The. Earrings, The. Eugenio Montale. CP-MontE, *tr. by* Jonathan Galassi

Lamped in a postered arch, her settecento name. Dorabella's Naples Watercolor. James Schuyler. CP-SchuJ

Lampfall. Derek Walcott. CP-WalcD

Lamplight. John Updike. CP-UpdiJ

Lamplighter: 1914. Stanley Kunitz. CP-KunSC

Lamps, The. Mary Oliver. SP-OlivM

Lamps are on: terrestrial galaxies, The. Night Ride. Charles Tomlinson. CP-TomlC

Lamp's Shrine, The. Dante Gabriel Rossetti. CW-RossD *Fr.* House of Life, The.

L'An Trentiesme de Mon Eage. Archibald MacLeish. CP-MacLA

Lana. Hayden Carruth. CP-CarHS

Lancashire. Donald Davie. CP-DaviDC

Lancaster bore him—such a little town. Hundred Collars, A. Robert Frost. CP-FrosR

Lancelot. Edwin Arlington Robinson. CP-RobiE

Lancer. A. E. Housman. CP-HousA

Land. Seamus Heaney. SP-HeanSO

Land. Jones Very. CP-VeryJ

Land, The. Rudyard Kipling. CP-KiplR

Land and Sea Tales. Rudyard Kipling.
   Counting-Out Song, A. CP-KiplR
   Departure, A. CP-KiplR
   Hour of the Angel, The. CP-KiplR
   Junk and the Dhow, The. CP-KiplR
   Last Lap, The. CP-KiplR
   Master-Cook, The. CP-KiplR
   Nurses, The. CP-KiplR
   Preface, A: "To all to whom this little book may come." CP-KiplR

Land is an ark, full of things waiting, The. Wet Time, A. Wendell Berry. CP-BerrW

Land is plowed up, The. Inside is outside. North of Beer Sheba. Yehuda Amichai. SP-AmicYL, *tr. by* Benjamin Harshav *and* Barbara Harshav

Land is rich where'er we go, The. Brotherhood. George Meredith. CP-MerG2

Land knows where the clouds come from and whence the hot wind, The. Yehuda Amichai. SP-AmicYL, *tr. by* Benjamin Harshav *and* Barbara Harshav

Land lies in water; it is shadowed green. Map, The. Elizabeth Bishop. CP-BishE

Land o' Used to Be, The. Paul Laurence Dunbar. CP-DunbP

Land of Biscay, The. A. E. Housman. CP-HousA

Land of Dreams, The. William Blake. CP-BlakW

Land of four o'clocks is here, The. Lorine Niedecker. CP-NiedL

Land of leaning ice, A. North Labrador. Hart Crane. CP-CranH

Land of Little Sticks, 1945. James Tate. SP-TateJ

Land of Loss, The. Thomas Kinsella. CP-KinsT

Land of Our Birth. Rudyard Kipling. CP-KiplR *Fr.* Puck of Pook's Hill.

Land of the Winding Waters, Wallowa, The. Chief Joseph of the Nez Perce. Robert Penn Warren. CP-WarrR

Land of Thus-and-So, The. James Whitcomb Riley. CP-RileJ

Land of Used-to-Be, The. James Whitcomb Riley. CP-RileJ

Land of Whipperginny, The. Robert Graves. CP-GravR

Land O'Lakes, Wisc. Allen Ginsberg. CP-GinsA

Land O'Lakes, Wisconsin: Vajrayana Seminary. Allen Ginsberg. CP-GinsA

Land outside, and the night is the enemy's, The. House, The. Charles Olson. CP-OlsoC

Land runs in a flat strip of jungle along the coast, The. Coastal Strip. George Oppen. CP-OppGN

Land that, from the rule of kings, The. Bartholdi Statue, The. John Greenleaf Whittier. CP-WhitJ

Land that has no song, The. Trimountain. Ralph Waldo Emerson. CP-EmerR

Land / Wants me to come back, The. Dustbowl. Langston Hughes. CP-HughL; CP-HughL2

Land was all electric, The. Ralph Waldo Emerson. CP-EmerR

Land was ours before we were the land's, The. Gift Outright, The. Robert Frost. CP-FrosR

Land was overmuch like scenery, The. Beowulf. Richard Wilbur. CP-WilbR

Land was pale with famine, The. Dole of Jarl Thorkell, The. John Greenleaf Whittier. CP-WhitJ

Land we from our fathers had in trust, The. Feelings of the Tyrolese. William Wordsworth. CP-WorW1

Land where I was born sits by the seas, The. Francesca of Rimini. Dante Alighieri. CP-Byron *Fr.* Divina Commedia.

Land-Worker. D. H. Lawrence. CP-LawrD *Fr.* Bits.

Landau, The. Rudyard Kipling. CP-KiplR *Fr.* Muse among the Motors, The.

Landcrab I. Margaret Atwood. SP-AtwM2

Landcrab II. Margaret Atwood. SP-AtwM2

Landed Fish. Marge Piercy. SP-PierM

Landfall. Alan Dugan. CP-DugaA

Landfall, The. Thomas Merton. CP-MertT

Landfall among Friends. Donald Davie. CP-DaviDC

Landfall, Grenada. Derek Walcott. CP-WalcD

Landing. Primo Levi. CP-LeviP, *tr. by* Ruth Feldman *and* Brian Swann

Landing. Eleanor Wilner. SP-WilnE

Landing, The. Charles Tomlinson. CP-TomlC

Landing, The. Jones Very. CP-VeryJ

Landing / At four o'clock in the morning. Approach—Calcutta, The. May Sarton. SP-SartM

Landing in the Rain at La Guardia. John Updike. CP-UpdiJ

Landing on the Moon. May Swenson. SP-SwenM

Landings had gone wrong; white silk, The. Bailing Out—A Poem for the 1970s. Eleanor Wilner. SP-WilnE

Landlady, The. Margaret Atwood. SP-AtwM1

Landlady count the lawin. Hey Tuti Tatey. Robert Burns. CP-BurnR

Landlady's Daughter, The. Ludwig Uhland. CP-MerG2

Landlady's wearing her OLD WOMAN costume, The. Garden, The. Philip Whalen. SP-WhalP

Landlord, landlord, / My roof has sprung a leak. Ballad of the Landlord. Langston Hughes. CP-HughL; CP-HughL2; CP-HughL3

Landlord walks up and down the hall, The. Breakout. Charles Bukowski. SP-BukC2

Landlord's hammer in the yard. Passing On. Adrienne Rich. CP-RicAE

Landlord's Tale: Paul Revere's Ride, The. Henry Wadsworth Longfellow. *See* Tales of a Wayside Inn

Landmark, The. Dante Gabriel Rossetti. CW-RossD *Fr.* House of Life, The.

Landmarks, The. John Greenleaf Whittier. CP-WhitJ

Landor, not that I doubt your word. Unnatural Love. Allen Tate. CP-TateA

Landowners. Sylvia Plath. CP-PlatS

Land's End. Archibald MacLeish. CP-MacLA

Land's end. And sound and river come. Point, The. Robert Earl Hayden. CP-HaydR

Landscape. Charles Baudelaire. CP-BaudC, *tr. by* Walter Martin

Landscape. Paul Celan. SP-CelaP, *tr. by* John Felstiner

Landscape. Thomas Merton. CP-MertT

Landscape ("By mistake the evening"). Federico García Lorca. CP-GarcF, *tr. by* Alan S. Trueblood *Fr.* Songs for Children.

Landscape. Mary Oliver. SP-OlivM

Landscape. Dorothy Parker. CP-ParkD

Landscape. Octavio Paz. CP-TomlC, *tr. by* Charles Tomlinson

Landscape. Carl Sandburg. CP-SandC

Landscape. Wisława Szymborska. SP-SzymW, *tr. by* Stanislaw Barańczak *and* Clare Cavanagh

Landscape. Wisława Szymborska. SP-SzymWM, *tr. by* Joanna Trzeciak

Landscape, The. November. W. S. Merwin. SP-MerwWF

Landscape (After Baudelaire). John Ashbery. SP-AshbJ

Landscape and Figure. Thomas Kinsella. CP-KinsT

Landscape as a Nude. Archibald MacLeish. CP-MacLA

Landscape as Metaphor, Landscape as Fate and a Happy Life. Charles Wright. SP-WrigCN

Landscape Finally with Human Figure. Josephine Jacobsen. CP-JacoJ

Landscape for the Disappeared. Yusef Komunyakaa. CP-KomuY

Landscape Including Three States of the Union. Carl Sandburg. CP-SandC

Landscape lacked nothing except glorification, The. View, The. Czeslaw Milosz. CP-MiloC; CP-MiloCN, *tr. by* Lillian Vallee

Landscape, liked the awed face of a child, The. Shower, The. James Whitcomb Riley. CP-RileJ

Landscape minus Song. Federico García Lorca. CP-GarcF, *tr. by* Jerome Rothenberg *Fr.* Moments of Song.

Landscape near an Aerodrome, The. Stephen Spender. CP-SpenS

Landscape of a Pissing Multitude. Federico García Lorca. CP-GarcF, *tr. by* Greg Simon *and* Steven F. White

Landscape of a Vomiting Multitude. Federico García Lorca. CP-GarcF, *tr. by* Greg Simon *and* Steven F. White

Landscape of love, The. Erotic Epigrams. John Updike. CP-UpdiJ

Landscape of the Star. Adrienne Rich. CP-RicAE

Landscape Seen with the Nose. Federico García Lorca. CP-GarcF, *tr. by* Jerome Rothenberg *Fr.* Suite.

Landscape stopped halfway. Rainer Maria Rilke. CP-RilkFr, *tr. by* A. Poulin, Jr. *Fr.* Valaisian Quatrains, The.

Landscape (the landscape!) again: Gloucester, The. Librarian, The. Charles Olson. CP-OlsoC; SP-OlsoC

Landscape: Wheatfields. Thomas Merton. CP-MertT

Landscape where I lie, The. Song for a Lyre. Louise Bogan. CP-BogaL

Landscape Winter. Anne Sexton. CP-SextA

Landscape with Angels. Olga Broumas. SP-BrouO

Landscape with Boat. Wallace Stevens. CP-StevW; CP-StevWP

Landscape with Crutches, A. Charles Simic. SP-SimiC; SP-SimiCE

Landscape with Driver. Olga Broumas. SP-BrouO

Landscape with Figures. A. R. Ammons. CP-AmmoA

Landscape with Figures. Howard Nemerov. CP-NemeH

Landscape with Leaves and Figure. Olga Broumas. SP-BrouO

Landscape with Mantra. Olga Broumas. SP-BrouO

Landscape with Next of Kin. Olga Broumas. SP-BrouO

Landscape with Poets. Olga Broumas. SP-BrouO

Landscape with Seated Figure and Olive Trees. Charles Wright. SP-WrigC

Landscape with Two Graves and an Assyrian Dog. Federico García Lorca. CP-GarcF, tr. by Greg Simon and Steven F. White

Landscape with urn beings. Paul Celan. SP-CelaP, tr. by John Felstiner

Landscape with Wave Approaching. Muriel Rukeyser. CP-RukeM

Landscape, without Color. Charles Olson. CP-OlsoC

Landscape without Touch. Olga Broumas. SP-BrouO

Landscapes. T. S. Eliot. CP-ElioT

Landscape's got / a century of cobwebs. Old Melancholy. Federico García Lorca. CP-GarcF, tr. by Jerome Rothenberg

Landscapes of My Name. John Ciardi. CP-CiarJ

Landscapes reverence the Frost. Emily Dickinson. SP-DickE

Lane of Yellow led the eye, A. Emily Dickinson. CP-DickE

Lane painted true color, and drew. "Enthusiasm.", An. Charles Olson. CP-OlsoC

Lang hae we parted been. Lassie Lie near Me. Robert Burns. CP-BurnR

Lang heff I maed of ladyes quhytt. William Dunbar. CP-DunbW

Langston Hughes. Gwendolyn Brooks. SP-BrooG

Langston Hughes. Yusef Komunyakaa. CP-KomuY

Language, The. Robert Creeley. CP-CreeR

Language among the clashing winds, The. Violence, The. David Ignatow. SP-IgnaD

Language as an Escape from the Discrete. Josephine Jacobsen. CP-JacoJ

Language as city: Wittgenstein. Images for Godard. Adrienne Rich. CP-RicAE

Language Barrier. Robert Penn Warren. CP-WarrR

Language ends in the tongue's clay pit. Poet's Words, The. John Ciardi. CP-CiarJ

Language Journal. Charles Wright. SP-WrigC

Language Lesson 1976. Heather McHugh. SP-McHuH

Language of Flowers, Etc, The. Hayden Carruth. CP-CarHS

Language of invasion, cloth of grief. Shiva and Parvati Hiding in the Rain. Robert Pinsky. CP-PinsR

Language of Love. Rae Armantrout. SP-ArmaA

Language of Moss. Josephine Jacobsen. CP-JacoJ

Language of New York, A. George Oppen. CP-OppGN

Language of the Country. Hans Magnus Enzensberger. SP-EnzeH, tr. by Michael Hamburger

Language of the Seasons. Robert Graves. CP-GravR

Language School. Yehuda Amichai. SP-AmicYL, tr. by Benjamin Harshav and Barbara Harshav

Language thou art too narrow, and too weak. Elegy upon the Death of Mistress Boulstred, An. John Donne. CP-DonnJ; MW-DonnJ

Language was almost impossible in those days. Poem: "Language was almost impossible in those days." James Tate. SP-TateJ

Language wasn't any. Inflation. Heather McHugh. SP-McHuH

Languages. Carl Sandburg. CP-SandC

Langue d'Oc. Ezra Pound.

Alba ("When the nightingale to his mate"). SP-PounE

Languedocienne. Marilyn Hacker. SP-HackM

Languid atmosphere, a lazy breeze, A. Summer Afternoon, A. James Whitcomb Riley. CP-RileJ

Languidly month by month. Change of Life. D. H. Lawrence. CP-LawrD

Lanis that you loved is not here, Markos, The. Tomb of Lanis, The. Constantine P. Cavafy. CP-CavaC, tr. by Theoharis Constantine Theoharis

Lansing Bad Penny Come Again Blues, The. Marge Piercy. SP-PierM

Lantern, The. W. S. Merwin. SP-MerwW

Lantern and a Shadow, A. Kenneth Rexroth. CP-RexrK

Lantern-light from deeper in the barn, A. Fear, The. Robert Frost. CP-FrosR

Lantern Out of Doors, The. Gerard Manley Hopkins. CP-HopkG

Lanternslides grinding out B-flat minor, The. Lunch. Kenneth Koch. SP-KochK

Lao Tan lay dead / Chin Shih attended the wake. Lao Tzu's Wake. Chuang Tzu. CP-MertT

Lao Tsze. Kenneth Patchen. CP-PatcK

Lao Tzu's Wake. Chuang Tzu. CP-MertT

Laocoön. Richard Eberhart. CP-EberR

Laocoön Dream Recorded in Diary Dated 1943. May Swenson. SP-SwenM

Laocoön Is the Name of the Figure. Marge Piercy. SP-PierM

Laodamia. William Wordsworth. CP-WorW2

Lapis Lazuli. William Butler Yeats. CP-YeatW

Lappo I leave behind and Dante too. Guido Invites You Thus. Ezra Pound. CP-PoEar

Lapse, The. Paul Laurence Dunbar. CP-DunbP

Lapse of Memory, A. A. K. Ramanujan. CP-RamaA

Lapse of time and rivers is the same, The. Comparison, A. William Cowper. CP-CowpW

Lara. Lord Byron. CP-Byron

L'ara sul rostro / 20 years of the dream. Ezra Pound. See And the sun high over horizon hidden in cloud bank

Larches. Ivor Gurney. SP-GurnI

Larches are most fitting small red hills. Larches. Ivor Gurney. SP-GurnI

Large Bad Picture. Elizabeth Bishop. CP-BishE

Large blinding sunflowers in deserted gardens. Sunflowers. Yannis Ritsos. SP-RitsY, tr. by Athan Anagnostopoulos

Large Bounds Doe but Bury Us. Robert Herrick. CP-HerrR

Large Cool Store, The. Philip Larkin. CP-LarkP

Large finger-like leaves of an Hawaiian fern. Czeslaw Milosz. CP-MiloCN, tr. by Robert Hass

Large gut, this was the vision, A. Nature. May Swenson. SP-SwenM

Large is gone—well, it, The. Autumn Song. A. R. Ammons. CP-AmmoA

Large kitchen is almost dark, The. Acolyte, The. Denise Levertov. SP-LeveDL

Large lady laboriously climbs, The. Dream of a Large Lady. Carolyn Kizer. CP-KizeC

Large leaved day grows rapidly, The. Red Fern, The. Wallace Stevens. CP-StevW; CP-StevWP

Large man rowing in a white tub, A. Bellevue Exchange. Norman Dubie. CP-DubiN

Large marquee said, Welcome Family Winston, The. Holiday Inn: Surrounded by Someone Else's Reunion He Comes to Terms. Miller Williams. CP-WillM

Large Number, A. Wisława Szymborska. SP-SzymW, tr. by Stanislaw Barańczak and Clare Cavanagh

Large Number, A. Wisława Szymborska. SP-SzymWM, tr. by Joanna Trzeciak

Large Opera Singer, The. James Laughlin. CP-LaugJ

Large Red Man Reading. Wallace Stevens. CP-StevW; CP-StevWP

Large shark roam our shore—he said. Ethography. Yannis Ritsos. SP-RitsY, tr. by Kostas Myrsiades

Large White Rock Called "The Sleeping Angel," A. Gregory Orr. SP-OrrG

Largess, The. Richard Eberhart. CP-EberR

Largesse. Paul Muldoon. CP-MuldP

Largest Fire ever known, The. Emily Dickinson. CP-DickE

Lark. Olga Broumas. SP-BrouO

Lark. W. S. Merwin. SP-MerwW

Lark, The. Gabriela Mistral. SP-MistG, tr. by Maria Giachetti [or Jacketti]

Lark Ascending, The. George Meredith. CP-MerG1

Lark begins to go up. Skylarks. Ted Hughes. SP-HughTN

Lark has no tree, The. He with the Beating Wings. Lawrence Ferlinghetti. SP-FerlL

Lark is silent in his nest, The. Good-Night. Paul Laurence Dunbar. CP-DunbP

Lark will make her hymn to God, The. Rudyard Kipling. CP-KiplR Fr. Light That Failed, The.

Larks, this year, The. Lesson, The. Charles Tomlinson. CP-TomlC

Larr's Portion, and the Poets Part. Robert Herrick. CP-HerrR

Larry. James Wright. CP-WrigJ

Larry Noolan's New Year. James Whitcomb Riley. CP-RileJ

L'Art. Ezra Pound. CP-PoEar

Las' July—and, I persume. Way It Wuz, The. James Whitcomb Riley. CP-RileJ

Las' time 'at Uncle Sidney come. Boy's Candidate, The. James Whitcomb Riley. CP-RileJ

Las Trampas U.S.A. Charles Tomlinson. CP-TomlC; SP-TomlC

Las Vegas: Verses Improvised for El Dorado H.S. Newspaper. Allen Ginsberg. CP-GinsA

Lasalle. Donald Davie. CP-DaviDC

Lasciviousnesse. Robert Herrick. CP-HerrR

Laser. A. R. Ammons. CP-AmmoA

Lashes of white light. Peace. Adrienne Rich. CP-RicAE

Lass of Aughrim, The. Paul Muldoon. CP-MuldP

Lass of Ecclefechan, The. Robert Burns. CP-BurnR

Lass That Made the Bed for Me, The. Robert Burns. CP-BurnR

(Bonie Lass Made the Bed to Me, The.) CP-BurnR

Lassie, lend me your braw hemp-heckle. Bob o' Dumblane, The. Robert Burns. CP-BurnR

Lassie Lie near Me. Robert Burns. CP-BurnR

Lassie wi' the Lintwhite Locks. Robert Burns. CP-BurnR

Lassitudes of Contemplation, The. Emily Dickinson. CP-DickE

Last, The. Thomas Kinsella. CP-KinsT

Last, The. Jones Very. CP-VeryJ

Last, The. C. K. Williams. CP-WillC

Last All Saints' holy-day, even now gone by. Sonnet: Of Beatrice de' Portinari, on All Saints' Day. Dante Alighieri. CW-RossD, *tr. by* Dante Gabriel Rossetti

Last Answer, The. Christina Georgina Rossetti. CP-RosC3

Last Answers. Carl Sandburg. CP-SandC

Last Arrow, The. Walter De la Mare. CP-DeLaW

Last as first the question rings. Last Chorus. Thomas Hardy. CP-HardT *Fr.* Dynasts, The.

Last before America. Louis MacNeice. CP-MacNL

Last Call. Langston Hughes. CP-HughL; CP-HughL3

Last Caress, The. James Laughlin. CP-LaugJ

Last Chantey, The. Rudyard Kipling. CP-KiplR

Last Chapter, The. Walter De la Mare. CP-DeLaW

Last Chorus. Thomas Hardy. CP-HardT *Fr.* Dynasts, The.

Last Chris'mus, little Benny. Some Christmas Youngsters. James Whitcomb Riley. CP-RileJ

Last Christmas Was a Year Ago. James Whitcomb Riley. CP-RileJ

Last Chrysanthemum, The. Thomas Hardy. CP-HardT

Last cigarette / a companion, A. Louis Zukofsky. CP-ZukLS

Last Class, The. William Stafford. SP-StafWW

Last Coachload, The. Walter De la Mare. CP-DeLaW

Last Complaint, The. Christina Georgina Rossetti. CP-RosC3

Last Confession, A. Dante Gabriel Rossetti. CW-RossD

Last Confession, A. William Butler Yeats. CP-YeatW

Last Conservative, The. Robinson Jeffers. CP-JefR3

Last Contention, The. George Meredith. CP-MerG1

Last Covenant, The. Laura Riding Jackson. CP-RidiL

Last Day. Margaret Atwood. SP-AtwM2

Last Day. May Swenson. SP-SwenM

Last Day and the First, The. Theodore Weiss. SP-WeisT

Last day of year. For Pen ("Last day of year"). Robert Creeley. SP-CreeR

Last Days. Mary Oliver. SP-OlivM

Last Days at Teddington. Thom Gunn. CP-GunnT

Last Days of Alice. Allen Tate. CP-TateA

Last Days of April, The. James Tate. SP-TateJ

Last days of summer are, The. Heart Is a Corrupt Stage Director, The. Yehuda Amichai. SP-AmicYL, *tr. by* Benjamin Harshav *and* Barbara Harshav

Last Days of the Miser. Charles Tomlinson. CP-TomlC

Last Deaths, The. C. K. Williams. CP-WillC; SP-WillC

Last Decision, The. Maya Angelou. SP-AngeM

Last Department, The. Rudyard Kipling. CP-KiplR

Last Droplets. Walt Whitman. CP-WhitW

Last Eve of Summer, The. John Greenleaf Whittier. CP-WhitJ

Last evening I gave you the parable. My Father on Passover Eve. Yehuda Amichai. SP-AmicYL, *tr. by* Benjamin Harshav *and* Barbara Harshav

Last evening the moon rose above this rock. How to Live. What to Do. Wallace Stevens. CP-StevW; CP-StevWP

Last event, The. In Memory of Muriel Rukeyser. Denise Levertov. SP-LeveDL

Last Farewell, The. Edward Bliss Emerson. CP-EmerR

Last Feast of Belshazzar, The. Langston Hughes. CP-HughL; CP-HughL1

Last Fellows. Laura Riding Jackson. CP-RidiL

Last Fire. Dante Gabriel Rossetti. CW-RossD *Fr.* House of Life, The.

Last Fistful, The. Robert Graves. CP-GravR

Last flame / sole leaf, A. Elemental. Charles Tomlinson. CP-TomlC

Last Friday, in the big light of last Friday night. Reality Is an Activity of the Most August Imagination. Wallace Stevens. CP-StevWP

Last Full Measure of Devotion, The. Kenneth Patchen. CP-PatcK

Last Generation, The. Charles Bukowski. SP-BukC3

Last Gods. Galway Kinnell. SP-KinnGN

Last Hero, The. G. K. Chesterton. CP-ChesG

Last Hill in a Vista. Louise Bogan. CP-BogaL

Last Hours. D. H. Lawrence. CP-LawrD

Last Instructions to a Painter, The. Andrew Marvell. CP-MarvA

Last Invocation, The. Walt Whitman. CP-WhitW

Last Journal. Charles Wright. SP-WrigC

Last Journey, A. Thomas Hardy. CP-HardT

Last Judgement. Charles Tomlinson. CP-TomlC

Last Lap, The. Rudyard Kipling. CP-KiplR *Fr.* Land and Sea Tales.

Last Laugh. Robert Penn Warren. CP-WarrR

Last Laugh, The. Wilfred Owen. CP-OwenW

Last Leaf, The. Thomas Hardy. CP-HardT

Last leaves fell like notes from a piano, The. Forest of Europe. Derek Walcott. CP-WalcD

Last Lesson of the Afternoon. D. H. Lawrence. CP-LawrD

Last Letters, The. Theodore Weiss. SP-WeisT

Last Light. Federico García Lorca. CP-GarcF, *tr. by* Jerome Rothenberg *Fr.* Six Songs at Nightfall.

Last Light. Charles Baudelaire. CP-BaudC, *tr. by* Walter Martin

Last Look, The. Christina Georgina Rossetti. CP-RosC3

Last Look round St. Martin's Fair. Thomas Hardy. CP-HardT

Last Looks at the Lilacs. Wallace Stevens. CP-StevW; CP-StevWP

Last love, / proper in conclusion, A. Recovery. Maya Angelou. SP-AngeM

Last Love-Word. Thomas Hardy. CP-HardT

Last Man Living, The. Langston Hughes. CP-HughL; CP-HughL3

Last Man, The. Eleanor Wilner. SP-WilnE

Last Masquerade, The. G. K. Chesterton. CP-ChesG

Last May a braw wooer cam down the lang glen. Scotish Ballad. Robert Burns. CP-BurnR

Last Meeting. Robert Penn Warren. CP-WarrR

Last Metaphor, The. Robert Penn Warren. CP-WarrR

Last Mile, The. Robert Creeley. SP-CreeR

Last Month. John Ashbery. SP-AshbJ

Last month in your little Roman house, The. On the Death of Keats; Lines for Those Who Drown Twice. John Logan. CP-LogaJ

Last Mornings in California. James Merrill. SP-MerrJ

Last Mowing, The. Robert Frost. CP-FrosR

Last Night. Christina Georgina Rossetti. CP-RosC3

Last night a baby gargled in the throes. Widow in Wintertime, A. Carolyn Kizer. CP-KizeC

Last night a January wind was ripping at the shingles over our house and. Manitoba Childe Roland. Carl Sandburg. CP-SandC

Last night a thief came to me. Thief in the Night. D. H. Lawrence. CP-LawrD

Last night, alone, 3000 miles away from the one. Party, The. Raymond Carver. CP-CarvR

Last Night—and This. James Whitcomb Riley. CP-RileJ

Last night as I lay gazing with shut eyes. Henry David Thoreau. CP-ThorH

Last night at black midnight I woke with a cry. Ghosts of the Buffaloes, The. Nicholas Vachel Lindsay. CP-LindV

Last night at my daughter's, near Blaine. Energy. Raymond Carver. CP-CarvR

Last night, before I came to bear. Angel, The. James Wright. CP-WrigJ

Last night, first frost of sudden fall. Gathering, The. Josephine Jacobsen. CP-JacoJ

"Last night," he said, "I slept well." Dream, The. Sylvia Plath. CP-PlatS

Last night—how deep the darkness was! Last Night—and This. James Whitcomb Riley. CP-RileJ

Last night I crossed the river. Not a Soul; Blanket Roll Blues. Tennessee Williams. CP-WillT *Fr.* Fugitive Kind, The.

Last night, I don't know if from habit or intent. Sonnet: "Last night, I don't know if from habit or intent." Hayden Carruth. CP-CarHS *Fr.* Sonnets.

Last night I dreamed. Night-Apple, The. Allen Ginsberg. CP-GinsA

Last night I dreamed I ran through the streets of New York. October 1973. Carolyn Kizer. CP-KizeC

Last night, I dreamed of America. More. Ai. SP-Ai

Last night I dreamed we were in Venice. Song of Invisible Boundaries. Louise Glück. SP-GlucL *Fr.* Marathon.

Last night I dreamt. Dream. Langston Hughes. CP-HughL; CP-HughL2

Last night I dreamt a priest came to me. Poem for Dr Pratt, a Lady Pathologist. Raymond Carver. CP-CarvR

Last night I dreamt I went home. Han-shan. CP-ColdM, *tr. by* Red Pine

Last night I drew up mine Account. Summe, and the Satisfaction, The. Robert Herrick. CP-HerrR

Last night I dropped in at the Con- / cord—out on Erie? You. Lana. Hayden Carruth. CP-CarHS

Last night I fled until I came. Light. Allen Tate. CP-TateA

Last night I lay upon my bed and would have slept. After a Visit. Countee Cullen. CP-CullC

Last night I met you in my sister's house. Stelae, The. Adrienne Rich. CP-RicAE; SP-RicA2

Last night I saw you in my sleep. Bad Dreams I. Robert Browning. CP-BroR2

Last night I seemed in your embrace. Kathleen Jessie Raine. SP-RainK

Last night I thought of Torri del Benaco again. Lost Bodies. Charles Wright. SP-WrigC

Last night I woke in fright: you were not there. Without a Counterpart. Thom Gunn. CP-GunnT

Last Night in Calcutta. Allen Ginsberg. CP-GinsA

Last night, in some lost mood of meditation. Old, Old Wish, The. James Whitcomb Riley. CP-RileJ

Last night / in the fields. White Flowers. Mary Oliver. SP-OlivM

Last night it was neither an- / ticipated nor anything spectacu-. He Dreamed His Death. James Laughlin. CP-LaugJ

Last night, just as the tints of autumn's sky. Fruit-Gift, The. John Greenleaf Whittier. CP-WhitJ

Last night my color-blind chain-smoking father. My Father's Neckties. Maxine W. Kumin. SP-KumiM

Last night my mind limped. Gain. A. R. Ammons. CP-AmmoA

Last night my teacher taught me the lesson of poverty. I Have Such a Teacher. Jelaluddin Rumi. SP-Rumi, tr. by Coleman Barks

Last night, reading the Anthology. Harmodius and Aristogeiton. Kenneth Rexroth. CP-RexrK

Last night returning from my twilight walk. Ballad of Past Meridian, A. George Meredith. CP-MerG1

Last Night that She Lived, The. Emily Dickinson. CP-DickE

Last night the cold wind and the rain blew. Sunday at the End of Summer. Howard Nemerov. CP-NemeH

Last night the geese came back. Two Kinds of Deliverance. Mary Oliver. SP-OlivM

Last night the trash barrel. Lorine Niedecker. CP-NiedL

Last night there was / a lunar eclipse: the. Moon. James Schuyler. CP-SchuJ

Last night thou didst invite me home to eat[e]. Upon Showbread [or Shewbread]: Epigram. Robert Herrick. CP-HerrR

Last Night Train. Robert Penn Warren. CP-WarrR

Last night we sat with the stereopticon. Readings of History. Adrienne Rich CP-RicAE

Last night you came into my. Frightened Bird, The. James Laughlin. CP-LaugJ

Last night you would not come. Love Poem: "Last night you would not come." John Logan. CP-LogaJ

Last night you wrote on the wall: Revolution is poetry. 7/26/68: i. Adrienne Rich. CP-RicAE Fr. Ghazals: Homage to Ghalib.

Last night your watchdog barked all night. Unstamped Letter in Our Rural Letter Box, An. Robert Frost. CP-FrosR

Last night's dreams disappear. Washing My Face. Gregory Orr. SP-OrrG

Last night's stars and last night's wind. Under the Nine Trees in January. Charles Wright. SP-WrigCN

Last night's thunderstorm's. Rectitude. A. R. Ammons. CP-AmmoA

Last Nocturne. Federico García Lorca. CP-GarcF, tr. by Jerome Rothenberg Fr. Cúckoo-Cuckoo-Cuckóo.

Last Ode, The. Rudyard Kipling. CP-KiplR Fr. Debits and Credits.

Last of last words spoken is Good-bye, The. Good-bye. Walter De la Mare. CP-DeLaW

Last of Night, The. Charles Tomlinson. CP-TomlC

Last of Summer is Delight, The. Emily Dickinson. CP-DickE

Last of the Book, The. Ivor Gurney. SP-GurnI

Last of the Fire Kings, The. Derek Mahon. CP-MahoD

Last of the 1st/5th Lancashire Fusiliers, The. Ted Hughes. SP-HughTN

Last of the Flock, The. William Wordsworth. CP-WorW1
   (In distant countries I have been.) MW-WorW

Last of the Light Brigade, The. Rudyard Kipling. CP-KiplR

Last of the Princes, The. A. K. Ramanujan. CP-RamaA

Last One, The. W. S. Merwin. SP-MerwW

Last Ones, The. Dan Pagis. SP-PagiD, tr. by Stephen Mitchell

Last page, The Appalachian Book of the Dead, / full moon. Appalachian Book of the Dead 6, The. Charles Wright. SP-WrigCN

Last party before I left was in an old, run-down apartment house, The. Flight. C. K. Williams. CP-WillC

Last People. W. S. Merwin. SP-MerwW

Last Performance, The. Thomas Hardy. CP-HardT

Last Person to Speak His Language Is Dying, The. Miller Williams. CP-WillM

Last Picnic, The. Stanley Kunitz. CP-KunSC

Last Poem. Ted Berrigan. SP-BerrT

Last Poem. Robert Browning. CP-BroR2

Last Poem, A. Robert Graves. CP-GravR

Last Poem, Snow Tree. Norman Dubie. CP-DubiN

Last Poem to Be Written, The. James Laughlin. CP-LaugJ

Last Poems. Paul Muldoon.
   "I would be happy in the knowledge." CP-MuldP
   "I would have it, were I bold." CP-MuldP
   "Not that I care who's sleeping with whom." CP-MuldP
   "Ours would be a worldly wisdom, heaven-sent." CP-MuldP

Last Post sounded. After the War. Thomas Hardy. CP-HardT

Last Prince of the East. Langston Hughes. CP-HughL; CP-HughL3

Last Quatrain of the Ballad of Emmett Till, The. Gwendolyn Brooks. SP-BrooG

Last Question, The. Dorothy Parker. CP-ParkD

Last Rays of the Romantic Sun. Charles Baudelaire. CP-BaudC, tr. by Walter Martin

Last Rhyme of True Thomas, The. Rudyard Kipling. CP-KiplR

Last Ride Together, The. Robert Browning. CP-BroR1

Last Rites. John Ciardi. CP-CiarJ

Last Rites. Christina Georgina Rossetti. CP-RosC2

Last short-cut along Croaghmarhin's base, A. Love. Thomas Kinsella. CP-KinsT

Last Signal, The. Thomas Hardy. CP-HardT

Last silk-floating thought has gone from the dandelion stem, The. Repulsed. D. H. Lawrence. CP-LawrD

Last Song. Adrienne Rich. CP-RicAE

Last Song, A. Hugh MacDiarmid. SP-MacDH

Last Song of Lucifer, The. Nicholas Vachel Lindsay. CP-LindV

Last Speech and Dying Words of Daniel Jackson, The. Thomas Sheridan. CP-SherT

Last Statement for a Last Oracle. Alan Dugan. CP-DugaA

Last step taken found your heft, The. To a Thinker. Robert Frost. CP-FrosR

Last Step, The. Philip Levine. SP-LeviP

Last, Stone, a little yet. Epitaph, An: "Last, Stone, a little yet." Walter De la Mare. CP-DeLaW

Last Stroke Strike Sure, The. Robert Herrick. CP-HerrR

Last summer a tiny spider wove. Brief History (June–December 1994). Peter Blue Cloud. SP-BlueP

Last sunbeam, The. Dirge for Two Veterans. Walt Whitman. CP-WhitW

Last Supper. Venetian, Sixteenth Century. Hans Magnus Enzensberger. SP-EnzeH

Last Suttee, The. Rudyard Kipling. CP-KiplR

Last sweet night, The. Robert Creeley. CP-CreeR

Last tear turns, The. Song: Early Death of the Mother. Gregory Orr. SP-OrrG

Last Thanksgivin'-dinner we. Gustatory Achievement, A. James Whitcomb Riley. CP-RileJ

Last Things. William Meredith. SP-MereW

Last Three from Trafalgar, The. Dante Gabriel Rossetti. CW-RossD

Last Time, The. Marilyn Hacker. SP-HackM

Last Time, The. Thomas Hardy. CP-HardT

Last Time, The. Alice Walker. CP-WalkA

Last time I saw Donald Armstrong, The. Performance, The. James Dickey. CP-DickJ

Last time I talked to you in my head, The. Separate Lives. Marilyn Hacker. SP-HackM

Last time I went to see my child, The. To Bake the Bread of Yearning. Yehuda Amichai. SP-AmicY, tr. by Stephen Mitchell

Last time we met. Present for Tu Fu from Li Po, A. Li Po. CP-KizeC, tr. by Carolyn Kizer

Last Translation, The. Elizabeth Barrett Browning. CP-BroEB

Last Turn, The. William Carlos Williams. CP-WilW2

Last Turn of the Screw, The. Stevie Smith. CP-SmitS

Last twenty years were good for practically everybody, The. Transatlantic. Joseph Brodsky. CP-BrodJ

Last Visit to the Swimming Pool Soviets. Kenneth Rexroth. CP-RexrK

Last Walk in Autumn, The. John Greenleaf Whittier. CP-WhitJ

Last Walk of Season. Robert Penn Warren. CP-WarrR

Last waltz, The. Summer. Robert Creeley. SP-CreeR

Last week a doctor told me. Beauty I Would Suffer For. Marge Piercy. SP-PierM

Last Week in October. Thomas Hardy. CP-HardT

Last week—the Lord be praised for all His mercies. Letter from a Missionary of the Methodist Episcopal Church South, in Kansas, to a Distiguished Politician. John Greenleaf Whittier. CP-WhitJ

Last Will and Testament. Philip Larkin. CP-LarkP

Last Will and Testament. Yannis Ritsos. SP-RitsY, tr. by N. C. Germanacos

Last Wine, The. Tennessee Williams. CP-WillT

Last winter we were. Letter to Hitler, A. James Laughlin. CP-LaugJ

Last Word Is Captain, The. Yehuda Amichai. SP-AmicY, tr. by Benjamin Harshav and Barbara Harshav

Last Word Is the Captain, The. Yehuda Amichai. SP-AmicY, tr. by Chana Bloch

Last Word of a Bluebird, The. Robert Frost. CP-FrosR

Last word, the hasty swallow, The. Bogomil Gjuzel. CP-KizeC, tr. by Carolyn Kizer

Last Words. Emily Jane Brontë. See Song By J. Brenzaida To G.S

Last Words. William Corbett. SP-CorbW

Last Words. Stanley Kunitz. CP-KunSC

Last Words. James Laughlin. CP-LaugJ

Last Words. James Merrill. SP-MerrJ

Last Words. Sylvia Plath. CP-PlatS

Last Words. James Whitcomb Riley. CP-RileJ

Last Words. Theodore Roethke. CP-RoetT

Last Words of My English Grandmother, The. William Carlos Williams. CP-WilW1

Last Words of My Grandmother. William Carlos Williams. CP-WilW1

Last Words of St. Telemachus, The. Christina Georgina Rossetti. CP-RosC3

Last Words on Greece. Lord Byron. CP-Byron

Last Words to a Dumb Friend. Thomas Hardy. CP-HardT

Last Words to Miriam. D. H. Lawrence. CP-LawrD
   (Yours is the shame and sorrow.) CP-LawrD

Last Words to Muriel. D. H. Lawrence. CP-LawrD

Last World, A. John Ashbery. SP-AshbJ

Last year changed its seasons. In Retrospect. Maya Angelou. SP-AngeM

Last year, I admired wines. This. Burnt Kabob. Jelaluddin Rumi. SP-Rumi, *tr. by* Coleman Barks

Last year I called this world of gaingivings. At the War Office, London. Thomas Hardy. CP-HardT

Last year I used to ride the J CHURCH Line. J Car, The. Thom Gunn. CP-GunnT

Last year I was your friend, they fell, The. That Year. William Stafford. SP-StafWW

Last year of youth, The. Hayden Carruth. CP-CarHS *Fr.* Clay Hill Anthology, The.

Lasting Seasons, The. Kenneth Patchen. CP-PatcK

Lastingness. Czeslaw Milosz. CP-MiloCN, *tr. by* Robert Hass

Lastness. Galway Kinnell. SP-KinnGN

Lat. 10 Degrees North, Long. 45 Degrees West. Muriel Rukeyser. CP-RukeM

Latch lifting, an edged den of light, A. Good-night. Seamus Heaney. SP-HeanSO

Late. Louise Bogan. CP-BogaL

Late Abed. Archibald MacLeish. CP-MacLA

Late, about midday, after they've sold their produce. Greek Cart-Drivers. Yannis Ritsos. SP-RitsY, *tr. by* Kimon Friar

Late Afternoon, April 8, 1984. Raymond Carver. CP-CarvR

Late afternoon, autumn equinox. Natural History. Sam Hamill. SP-HamiS

Late afternoon light between peach trees. View from an Empty Chair. Tess Gallagher. SP-GallT

Late-afternoon rain stopped, The. The electric trolley. Trolley from Xochimilco, The. Norman Dubie. CP-DubiN

Late afternoon—the shadows lengthen. Fanny Howe. SP-HoweF *Fr.* O'Clock.

Late Air. Elizabeth Bishop. CP-BishE

Late and Deep. Paul Celan. SP-CelaP, *tr. by* John Felstiner

Late Anniversary, A. Donald Davie. CP-DaviDC

Late Answer, A. Philip Levine. SP-LeviP

Late April in January, seventy-some-odd degrees. Giorgio Morandi and the Talking Eternity Blues. Charles Wright. SP-WrigCN

Late Arrival. Marya Alexandrovna Zaturenska. SP-ZatuM

Late at night. Raid. Langston Hughes. CP-HughL; CP-HughL2

Late at Night. D. H. Lawrence. CP-LawrD

Late at Night ("Falling separate into the dark"). William Stafford. SP-StafWW

Late Aubade, A. Richard Wilbur. CP-WilbR

Late August. Margaret Atwood. SP-AtwM1

Late August. William Corbett. SP-CorbW

Late August. Marilyn Hacker. SP-HackM

Late August, given heavy rain and sun. Blackberry-Picking. Seamus Heaney. SP-HeanSO

Late August Letter. Marilyn Hacker. SP-HackM

Late Beethoven. Adam Zagajewski. SP-ZagaA, *tr. by* Renata Gorczynski

Late-blooming rose that the bitter. Rainer Maria Rilke. CP-RilkFr, *tr. by* A. Poulin, Jr. *Fr.* Roses, The.

Late Butterflies. Howard Nemerov. CP-NemeH

Late, by myself, in the boat of myself. Jelaluddin Rumi. SP-Rumi, *tr. by* Coleman Barks

Late Came the God. Rudyard Kipling. CP-KiplR *Fr.* Debits and Credits.

Late Comer, The. Robert Creeley. CP-CreeR

Late Corner. Langston Hughes. CP-HughL; CP-HughL3

Late crippled of an arm, and now a leg. To R***** G***** of F*****, Esq. Robert Burns. CP-BurnR

Late Days. Wyatt Prunty. SP-PrunW

Late Echo. John Ashbery. SP-AshbJ

Late Fall, Late Light. Wyatt Prunty. SP-PrunW

Late Feast. Adam Zagajewski. SP-ZagaA, *tr. by* Renata Gorczynski, Benjamin Ivry *and* C. K. Williams

Late February, five o'clock: the cantaloupe-colored light. Language Journal. Charles Wright. SP-WrigC

Late for Summer Weather. William Carlos Williams. CP-WilW1

Late Fragment. Raymond Carver. CP-CarvR

Late from your cocoon, miraculous. For an "Homage to Rimbaud." Eugenio Montale. CP-MontE, *tr. by* Jonathan Galassi

Late Half Moon. Kenneth Rexroth. CP-RexrK

Late Harvest. James Tate. SP-TateJ

Late hour, fattened with horn and tabor, The. Banquet, The. Robert Stock. SP-StocR

Late Hymn from the Myrrh-Mountain. Wallace Stevens. CP-StevW; CP-StevWP

Late I fell in the ecstasy. Gerard Manley Hopkins. CP-HopkG

Late Impressionist Dream. Lawrence Ferlinghetti. SP-FerlL

Late in my life, I come to you. Yehuda Amichai. SP-AmicYL, *tr. by* Benjamin Harshav *and* Barbara Harshav

Late in November, on a single night. Consent, The. Howard Nemerov. CP-NemeH

Late in the day the fog. Gradual Clearing. Amy Clampitt. CP-ClamA

Late in the night I pay. Awake at Night. Wendell Berry. CP-BerrW

Late in the night when I should be asleep. Gentle Reader. Josephine Jacobsen.

CP-JacoJ

Late in the winter came one day. Blossom Themes. Carl Sandburg. CP-SandC

Late January. John Updike. CP-UpdiJ

Late January / Snow is on everything. Waiting for the Paper to be Delivered. Miller Williams. CP-WillM

Late last night I / Set on my steps and cried. Langston Hughes. CP-HughL; CP-HughL2

Late Late Show. Howard Nemerov. CP-NemeH

Late light across a side porch where. Late Days. Wyatt Prunty. SP-PrunW

Late Marriage. Yehuda Amichai. SP-AmicY, *tr. by* Chana Bloch

Late Marriage. Yehuda Amichai. SP-AmicYL, *tr. by* Benjamin Harshav *and* Barbara Harshav

Late Moon. Robert Bly. SP-BlyR

Late Moon. Philip Levine. SP-LeviP

Late, my grandson! half the morning have I paced these sandy tracts. Locksley Hall Sixty Years After. Alfred Tennyson. CP-TennA

Late night / Coming back to Melbourne. Family, The. Kenneth Rexroth. CP-RexrK

Late Night in Autumn. W. S. Merwin. SP-MerwW

Late night on the porch, thinking. August First. Hayden Carruth. CP-CarHS

Late Night, San Francisco. Andrei Codrescu. SP-CodrA

Late Night with Fog and Horses. Raymond Carver. CP-CarvR

Late nights the world flooded our dark house. Atwater Kent. William Stafford. SP-StafWW

Late November in a Field. James Wright. CP-WrigJ

Late October. Maya Angelou. SP-AngeM

Late October Camping in the Sawtooths. Gary Snyder. CP-SnydG

Late on a breezy vernal eve. Barberry-Tree, The. Samuel Taylor Coleridge. CP-ColeS; CP-WorW1

Late on Christams Eve, in the street alone. Two Serenades. Thomas Hardy. CP-HardT

Late on Saturday morning I sat reading Hardy again. Gift of Prophecy Lost, The. Miller Williams. CP-WillM

Late one night she told me. Edward's Anecdote. Donald Hall. CP-HallD

Late peach yields a subtle musk, The. Coming of the Cold, The. Theodore Roethke. CP-RoetT

Late Peaches. John Ciardi. CP-CiarJ

Late Ripeness. Czeslaw Milosz. CP-MiloCN, *tr. by* Robert Hass

Late Romantic. A. R. Ammons. CP-AmmoA

Late Saturday afternoon in Charlottesville. / Columbus Day. Appalachian Book of the Dead 2, The. Charles Wright. SP-WrigCN

Late Show. Miller Williams. CP-WillM

Late Singer, The. William Carlos Williams. CP-WilW1

Late Snow. Louise Glück. SP-GlucL

Late Snow. Maxine W. Kumin. SP-KumiM

Late Snow. W. S. Merwin. SP-MerwWF

Late snow fell this early morning of spring. Love Is Like Sounds. Donald Hall. CP-HallD

Late Snow & Lumber Strike of the Summer of Fifty-four, The. Gary Snyder. CP-SnydG

Late Spring. "H. D." CP-DoolH

Late Spring. Meng Hao Jan. CP-WilW2

Late Stravinsky Listening to Late Beethoven. Stephen Spender. CP-SpenS

Late Subterfuge. Robert Penn Warren. CP-WarrR

Late Summer. Howard Nemerov. CP-NemeH

Late Summer. Edwin Arlington Robinson. CP-RobiE

Late summer, and at midnight. Guttural Muse, The. Seamus Heaney. SP-HeanSO

Late Summer at *Milgate*. Robert Lowell. SP-LoweR

Late summer's day, and my friend on the court, A. Migration. Raymond Carver. CP-CarvR

Late sun opening the book. Siesta in Xbalba. Allen Ginsberg. CP-GinsA

Late Sunday in Charlottesville. East of the Blue Ridge, Our Tombs Are in the Dove's Throat. Charles Wright. SP-WrigCN

Late sunlight breaking into the room. Rooms without Walls. Wyatt Prunty. SP-PrunW

Late, the time of humbling reconciliation. Reconciliation. Czeslaw Milosz. CP-MiloCN, *tr. by* Robert Hass

Late thou comest, little one. Hymn of the Poor, The. G. K. Chesterton. CP-ChesG

Late Train, The. Theodore Weiss. SP-WeisT

Late Walk, A. Robert Frost. CP-FrosR

Late War, The. D. H. Lawrence. CP-LawrD

Late wind failed; high on the hill, The. Fleeting, The. Walter De la Mare. CP-DeLaW

Late winter light. Winter Road, The. Jane Cooper. CP-CoopJ

Late Wonders. W. S. Merwin. SP-MerwWF

Lately, alas, I knew a gentle boy. Sympathy. Henry David Thoreau. CP-ThorH

Lately having escaped three-kinded death. Birth, A. Muriel Rukeyser. CP-

RukeM

Lately I've been eating a lot of pork. Plus. Raymond Carver. CP-CarvR

Lately I've seen myself. Old Age Echoes. Philip Whalen. SP-WhalP

Latent Desire, The. D. H. Lawrence. CP-LawrD

Later ("Drunks leaning on your arm"). Robert Creeley. SP-CreeR

Later ("If I could get"). Robert Creeley. SP-CreeR

Later ("It feels things"). Robert Creeley. SP-CreeR

Later ("Later than any time"). Robert Creeley. SP-CreeR

Later ("Shan't be winding"). Robert Creeley. SP-CreeR

Later, after the utter destruction of the Athenians at Aegospotámi, and a little later. After the Defeat. Yannis Ritsos. SP-RitsY, tr. by Kimon Friar and Karelisa Hartigan

Later Alexandrian, A. George Meredith. CP-MerG1

Later Autumn, The. Thomas Hardy. CP-HardT

Later he'll say Death stepped right up. Stroke, The. Rita Dove. SP-DoveR

Later I'll pull down the shade. Pictures of the People in the War. Louise Glück. SP-GlucL

Later in Belleville: Career. Margaret Atwood. SP-AtwM1

Later Life: A Double Sonnet of Sonnets. Christina Georgina Rossetti. CP-RosC2

Later man, one of the amorphous, A. Shakespeare in Vietnam. Robert Stock. SP-StocR

Later Note on Letter #15, A. Charles Olson. SP-OlsoC Fr. Maximus Poems, The.

Later or Sooner. Richard Eberhart. CP-EberR

Later Still. Philip Levine. SP-LeviP

Later than any time. Later ("Later than any time"). Robert Creeley. SP-CreeR

Later that week, when the reddish. Spring Floods. Gregory Orr. SP-OrrG

Later, the statues were totally hidden by the weeds. We couldn't tell. Signals. Yannis Ritsos. SP-RitsY, tr. by Gwendolyn MacEwen and Nikos Tsingos

Later when the gloated water. Thin Edge of Your Pride, The. Kenneth Rexroth. CP-RexrK

Latest creed that has to be believed, The. Concept Self-Conceived, A. Robert Frost. CP-FrosR

Latest Decalogue, The. Arthur Hugh Clough. SP-ClouA

Latest Face. Philip Larkin. CP-LarkP

Latest focus group research reveals, The. Market Discounts Love. James Laughlin. CP-LaugJ

Latest Freed Man, The. Wallace Stevens. CP-StevW; CP-StevWP

Latest sleeping on my pillow catches, The. One Night Stand. Charles Bukowski. SP-BukC2

Latesummer Blues. Kenneth Patchen. CP-PatcK

Lather as You Go. Ogden Nash. CP-NashO

Latin is now of equal use become. To Mr L. Maidwell on His New Method. John Dryden. CP-DryJ2

Latin sea! / palm trees. Mediterranean. Federico García Lorca. CP-GarcF, tr. by Jerome Rothenberg Fr. Palm Tree, The.

Latin winds of Majorca, The. In the Trenches with Robert Graves. Raymond Carver. CP-CarvR

Latitude, Longitude. George Oppen. CP-OppGN

Latley I saw a sight most quaint. Gross, Coarse, Hideous. D. H. Lawrence. CP-LawrD

Latter-Day Sinners. D. H. Lawrence. CP-LawrD

Latter Rain, The ("Latter rain,—it falls in anxious haste, The"). Jones Very. CP-VeryJ

Latter rain,—it falls in anxious haste, The. Latter Rain, The ("Latter rain,—it falls in anxious haste, The"). Jones Very. CP-VeryJ

Lattice of his back grows, the dolphin-arching, till. Ringling. Muriel Rukeyser. CP-RukeM

Lauda Sion Salvatorem. Richard Crashaw. CP-CrasR

Laudantes Decem Pulchritudinis Johannae Templi. Ezra Pound. CP-PoEar

Lauds. John Berryman. CP-BerrJ

Lauds. James McMichael. SP-McMiJ

Laugh, The. Robert Graves. CP-GravR

Laugh, The. Yannis Ritsos. SP-RitsY, tr. by Kostas Myrsiades

Laugh and Lie Downe. Robert Herrick. CP-HerrR

Laugh still, write always lovingly, for still. Heaven. Robert Graves. CP-GravR

Laugh your best, O blazoned forests. Lamp Post, The. G. K. Chesterton. CP-ChesG

Laughers. Langston Hughes. CP-HughL; CP-HughL1

Laughing. Robert Creeley. CP-CreeR

Laughing Blue Steel. Carl Sandburg. CP-SandC

Laughing Corn. Carl Sandburg. CP-SandC

Laughing Gas. Allen Ginsberg. CP-GinsA

Laughing Life cries at the feast. Christina Georgina Rossetti. CP-RosC2

Laughing, midst its yellow blooms. Woodwax, The. Jones Very. CP-VeryJ

Laughing Ones, The. Charles Olson. CP-OlsoC

Laughing Song. James Whitcomb Riley. CP-RileJ

Laughing to find / Anyone's blind. E. E. Cummings. CP-CummE

Laughing, with a TV's blue-static figures. When Loneliness Is a Man. Yusef
Komunyakaa. CP-KomuY

Laughing with ice. Midwinter. William Carlos Williams. CP-WilW2

Laughing young man and fiercest against sham. In Memoriam Stratton Christensen. William Meredith. SP-MereW

Laughter. G. K. Chesterton. CP-ChesG

Laughter. D. H. Lawrence. CP-LawrD

Laughter. W. S. Merwin. SP-MerwW

Laughter. James Whitcomb Riley. CP-RileJ

Laughter Holding Both His Sides. James Whitcomb Riley. CP-RileJ

Laughter is sacred, secret unalloyed. Secrecy. G. K. Chesterton. CP-ChesG

Laughter of sisters, mingling. Girls Next Door, The. Thom Gunn. CP-GunnT

Laughter of the Rain, The. James Whitcomb Riley. CP-RileJ

Launcelot in Hell. John Ciardi. CP-CiarJ

"Launch out into the deep," Christ spake of old. St. Peter. Christina Georgina Rossetti. CP-RosC2

Launched into an opposing wind, hangs. Atlantic, The. Charles Tomlinson. CP-TomlC; SP-TomlC

Launching themselves / beating silver. Running of the Grunion, The. Muriel Rukeyser. CP-RukeM

Laundress, The. Thomas Kinsella. CP-KinsT

Laundromat. Lorine Niedecker. CP-NiedL

Laundry Cellar, The. Yehuda Amichai. SP-AmicYL, tr. by Benjamin Harshav and Barbara Harshav

Laundry cellar in the big house, The. I love to. Laundry Cellar, The. Yehuda Amichai. SP-AmicYL, tr. by Benjamin Harshav and Barbara Harshav

Laura and Francisca. Laura Riding Jackson. CP-RidiL

LAURA, farewell my LAURA! Cantata, from Metastasio. William Wordsworth. CP-WorW1

L'aura, my breeze, so often breathes upon. Petrarch. CP-Petra, tr. by J. G. Nichols

L'aura, the gentle breeze that clears the hills. Petrarch. CP-Petra, tr. by J. G. Nichols

Laureate, The. Robert Graves. CP-GravR

Laurel and eucalyptus, dry sharp smells. Grasses. Thom Gunn. CP-GunnT

Laurel leafe which you this day doe weare, The. Sonnet 28. Edmund Spenser. CP-Spens Fr. Amoretti.

Laurelled soldier he; yet who could find, A. A.H., 1855–1912. Thomas Hardy. CP-HardT

Laurels. Eleanor Wilner. SP-WilnE

Laurels, The. John Greenleaf Whittier. CP-WhitJ

Laurels may flourish round the conqu'ror's tomb. Epitaph on Mrs. Higgins. William Cowper. CP-CowpW

Laurentides. Josephine Jacobsen. CP-JacoJ

Laus Deo! John Greenleaf Whittier. CP-WhitJ

Laus Veneris. Algernon Charles Swinburne. SP-SwinA

Lausanne: In Gibbon's Old Garden: 11–12 p.m. Thomas Hardy. CP-HardT

Lava. Adam Zagajewski. SP-ZagaA, tr. by Renata Gorczynski, Benjamin Ivry and C. K. Williams

Laval, Pomeret, Pétain. Lorine Niedecker. CP-NiedL

Lavender Cotton. Louis Zukofsky. CP-ZukLS

Lavender Lilies. Carl Sandburg. CP-SandC

Lavender lilies in Garfield Park lay lazy in the morning sun, The. Lavender Lilies. Carl Sandburg. CP-SandC

L'avenir de l'intelligence. T. S. Eliot (1928). Donald Davie. CP-DaviDC

Laventie. Ivor Gurney. SP-GurnI

Laventille. Derek Walcott. CP-WalcD

Lavinia and Amanda, a Pastoral. Annis Boudinot Stockton. CP-StocA

Law. Ambrose Bierce. SP-BierA

Law. Charles Olson. CP-OlsoC

Law, A. There Is Good News. Josephine Jacobsen. CP-JacoJ

Law like Love. W. H. Auden. CP-AudeW

Law of Poetry, The. George Oppen. CP-OppGN

Law of the Jungle, The. Rudyard Kipling. CP-KiplR Fr. Second Jungle Book, The.

Law of the Perverse, The. James Whitcomb Riley. CP-RileJ

Law, say the gardeners, is the sun. Law like Love. W. H. Auden. CP-AudeW

Law says you and I belong to each other, George, The. Two Strangers Breakfast. Carl Sandburg. CP-SandC

Law That Marries All Things, The. Wendell Berry. CP-BerrW

Law, The. The majesty of Law. "We are only." Eleusis. Eleanor Wilner. SP-WilnE

Law whereby my lady moves, The. My Lady's Law. Rudyard Kipling. CP-KiplR Fr. Naulahka, The.

Lawes. Robert Herrick. CP-HerrR

Lawn Bowlers, The. Josephine Jacobsen. CP-JacoJ

Lawne, The. Robert Herrick. CP-HerrR

Lawnmower's one of the babies I'd have, A. Lorine Niedecker. CP-NiedL

Lawrence of virtuous [or vertuous] Father virtuous [or vertuous] Son. To Mr.

Lawrence. John Milton. CP-MiltJ

Lawrence [Solomon]. G. K. Chesterton. CP-ChesG

Lawrence, with quiet face, scarce lit. Friends. G. K. Chesterton. CP-ChesG

Laws Can Say, The. Louis Zukofsky. CP-ZukLS

Laws for Creations. Walt Whitman. CP-WhitW

Laws of God, the laws of man, The. A. E. Housman. CP-HousA

Laws of the bronze gods, The. Cheap Rent. Carl Sandburg. CP-SandC

Lawsamassy, for heaven's sake! Lucy Lake. Ogden Nash. CP-NashO

Lawyer. Carl Sandburg. CP-SandC

Lawyer and Child. James Whitcomb Riley. CP-RileJ

Lawyers, Bob, know too much, The. Lawyers Know Too Much, The. Carl Sandburg. CP-SandC

Lawyers Know Too Much, The. Carl Sandburg. CP-SandC

Lawyers' Ways, The. Paul Laurence Dunbar. CP-DunbP

Lawzy! don't I rickollect. Waitin' fer the Cat to Die. James Whitcomb Riley. CP-RileJ

Laxare Fibulam. Robert Herrick. CP-HerrR

Lay away the story. Evensong. James Whitcomb Riley. CP-RileJ

Lay by the good a while; a resting field. Rest Refreshes. Robert Herrick. CP-HerrR

Lay down Lay down yr mountain Lay down God. Lay Down Yr Mountain. Allen Ginsberg. SP-GinsA

Lay down Lay down yr mountain Lay down God. Rolling Thunder Stones. Allen Ginsberg. CP-GinsA

Lay down these words. Riprap. Gary Snyder. CP-SnydG

Lay Down Yr Mountain. Allen Ginsberg. SP-GinsA

Lay in his grave for the dead man the words. In Memoriam Paul Éluard. Paul Celan. SP-CelaP, tr. by John Felstiner

Lay in the house mostly living. Madness. James Dickey. CP-DickJ

Lay me down beneaf de willers in de grass. Death Song[, A]. Paul Laurence Dunbar. CP-DunbP

"Lay me in a cushioned chair." Ballad of the Foxhunter, The. William Butler Yeats. CP-YeatW

Lay me on an anvil, O God. Prayers of Steel. Carl Sandburg. CP-SandC

Lay not thine hand upon me; let me go. Phaedra. Algernon Charles Swinburne. SP-SwinA

Lay of Old Time, A. John Greenleaf Whittier. CP-WhitJ

Lay of the Badde Wyf. Miller Williams. CP-WillM

Lay of the Brown Rosary, The. Elizabeth Barrett Browning. CP-BroEB

Lay of the Early Rose, A. Elizabeth Barrett Browning. CP-BroEB

Lay of the Imprisoned Huntsman. Sir Walter Scott. SP-ScotW Fr. Lady of the Lake, The.

Lay of the Last Minstrel, The. Sir Walter Scott.
    Bale-Fire, The. SP-ScotW
    Branksome Hall. SP-ScotW
    "Breathes there the [or a] Man with soul so dead." SP-ScotW
    Hymn for the Dead. SP-ScotW
    Melrose by Moonlight. SP-ScotW
    "O Caledonia! stern and wild." SP-ScotW
    Rosabelle. SP-ScotW
    (Harold's Song.) SP-ScotW
    Song of Albert Graeme. SP-ScotW

Lay this Laurel on the One. Emily Dickinson. CP-DickE

Lay Up for Yourselves Treasures in Heaven. Christina Georgina Rossetti. CP-RosC2

Lay your sleeping head, my love. Lullaby: "Lay your sleeping head, my love." W. H. Auden. CP-AudeW

Layer by layer, the dust of bitterness. Bangla Desh: 2. Faiz Ahmad Faiz. CP-KizeC, tr. by Carolyn Kizer

Layered bloom of hills and streams, The. Han-shan. CP-ColdM, tr. by Red Pine

Layers. James Laughlin. CP-LaugJ

Layers, The. Stanley Kunitz. CP-KunSC

Laying Down the Tower. Marge Piercy. SP-PierM

Laying-Out of Lazarus. Robert Stock. SP-StocR

Laying the Dust. Denise Levertov. SP-LeveDS

Layover. Charles Bukowski. SP-BukC2

Lazarus ("I am not the same man"). Lucille Clifton. SP-ClifL

Lazarus ("I rose from stiffening"). Lucille Clifton. SP-ClifL

Lazarus ("On the third day i contemplate"). Lucille Clifton. SP-ClifL

Lazarus. Edwin Arlington Robinson. CP-RobiE

Lazarus lay to see the body turn. Come Forth. James Wright. CP-WrigJ

Lazarus Not Raised. Thom Gunn. CP-GunnT

Lazarus to the Assembled. James Dickey. CP-DickJ

Lazy Day, A. Paul Laurence Dunbar. CP-DunbP

Lazy laughing languid Jenny. Jenny. Dante Gabriel Rossetti. CW-RossD

Lazy, laughing South, The. South, The. Langston Hughes. CP-HughL; CP-HughL1

Lazy Mist, The. Robert Burns. CP-BurnR

Le Christianisme. Wilfred Owen. CP-OwenW

Le conte de Beaumont carrying my daughter. White-Haired Girl. Archibald MacLeish. CP-MacLA

Le Désert de l'Amour. Stevie Smith. CP-SmitS

Le Directeur. T. S. Eliot. CP-ElioT

Le Fou. Robert Creeley. CP-CreeR

Le garçon délabré qui n'a rien à faire. Dans le Restaurant. T. S. Eliot. CP-ElioT; SP-ElioT

Le Jardin des Tuileries. Oscar Wilde. CP-WildO

Le Livre Est sur la Table. John Ashbery. SP-AshbJ

Le Majeur Ydow. Stevie Smith. CP-SmitS

Le Marais du Cygne. John Greenleaf Whittier. CP-WhitJ

Le Médecin Malgré Lui. William Carlos Williams. CP-WilW1

Le Monde regrets it must report. Exposé. John Updike. CP-UpdiJ

Le Monocle de Mon Oncle. Wallace Stevens. CP-StevW; CP-StevWP

Le Motif. Denise Levertov. SP-LeveDS

Le Musée Imaginaire. Charles Tomlinson. CP-TomlC

Le Petit Salvié. C. K. Williams. SP-WillC

Le Poète Contumace. Randall Jarrell. CP-JarrR

Le Revenant. Stevie Smith. CP-SmitS

Le Secret. Thomas Merton. CP-MertT

Le Secret Humain. Archibald MacLeish. CP-MacLA

Le Seul Malheur Est que Je ne Sais pas Lire. Archibald MacLeish. CP-MacLA

Le Singe qui swing. Stevie Smith. CP-SmitS

Le Travail Rajeunit. Marilyn Hacker. SP-HackM

Le Xuan, Beautiful Spring. Yusef Komunyakaa. CP-KomuY

Lea-Rig, The. Robert Burns. CP-BurnR

Lead. Thomas Kinsella. CP-KinsT

Lead gently, Lord, and slow. Hymn, A: "Lead gently, Lord, and slow." Paul Laurence Dunbar. CP-DunbP

Lead Me to the Rock That Is Higher than I. Jones Very. CP-VeryJ

Lead the black bull to slaughter, with the boar. Upon Master Walter Montagu's Return from Travel. Thomas Carew. CP-CareT

Leaden Echo and the Golden Echo, The. Gerard Manley Hopkins. CP-HopkG

Leaden-eyed, The. Nicholas Vachel Lindsay. CP-LindV

Leader, The. Charles Olson. CP-OlsoC

Leader, The. Stevie Smith. CP-SmitS

Leader and teacher, we whom you have taught. To William F. Bradbury. E. E. Cummings. CP-CummE

Leader of Fashion, A. Thomas Hardy. CP-HardT

Leaders of the Crowd, The. William Butler Yeats. CP-YeatW

Leaf, A. Sam Hamill. SP-HamiS

Leaf, A. David Ignatow. SP-IgnaD

Leaf, The. Giacomo Leopardi. CW-RossD, tr. by Dante Gabriel Rossetti

Leaf, The. Kathleen Jessie Raine. SP-RainK

Leaf and the Tree, The. Edna St. Vincent Millay. CP-MillE

Leaf, catching the sun, transmits it, A. Frondes Agrestes. Charles Tomlinson. CP-TomlC; SP-TomlC

Leaf-eater. Thomas Kinsella. CP-KinsT

Leaf fallen is, A. Event. A. R. Ammons. CP-AmmoA

Leaf falls in the night, A. The silence is audible. Imponderous Night, The. Yannis Ritsos. SP-RitsY, tr. by Kimon Friar

Leaf for Hand in Hand, A. Walt Whitman. CP-WhitW

Leaf from leaf Christ knows; / Himself the Lily and the Rose. Christina Georgina Rossetti. CP-RosC2

Leaf from Mr. Dyer's Woods, A. Hayden Carruth. CP-CarHS

Leaf-lace, a simple intricate design. Leaf-Lace Dress. Robert Lowell. SP-LoweR

Leaf-Lace Dress. Robert Lowell. SP-LoweR

Leaf lies shaking, A. Autumn 2. David Ignatow. SP-IgnaD

Leaf Mould. Ted Hughes. SP-HughTN

Leaf through discolored manuscripts. Hunting the Phoenix. Denise Levertov. SP-LeveDS

Leaf-Treader, A. Robert Frost. CP-FrosR

Leaf, treeless, A. Paul Celan. SP-CelaP, tr. by John Felstiner

Leaf-veined fire, The. Feuer-Nacht. Louise Bogan. CP-BogaL

Leaf with Berry. Josephine Jacobsen. CP-JacoJ

Leafbud straggles forth, The. Upper Broadway. Adrienne Rich. SP-RicA2

Leafless Dodder, Rabbit's Silk. Revolution of the Children. Archibald MacLeish. CP-MacLA

Leaflet. Grace Paley. CP-PalGC

Leaflet (One). Kenneth Patchen. CP-PatcK

Leaflet (Two). Kenneth Patchen. CP-PatcK

Leaflets. Adrienne Rich. CP-RicAE; SP-RicA2

Leaflets. Walt Whitman. CP-WhitW

Leaf's otherness, A. Egg-Head. Ted Hughes. SP-HughTN

Leafshade stirring on lichened bark. Culture and Anarchy. Adrienne Rich. SP-

RicA2

Leafy Angel, A. Andrei Codrescu. SP-CodrA

League gust strum ovally folium. Privet. Louis Zukofsky. CP-ZukLS

Leagues north, as fly the gull and auk. Palatine, The. John Greenleaf Whittier. CP-WhitJ

Leaky Tap after a Sister's Wedding, A. A. K. Ramanujan. CP-RamaA

Leal, The. Dorothy Parker. CP-ParkD

Lean and Hungry Look, A. Howard Nemerov. CP-NemeH

Lean and listen: lean and listen. Lilies of the Valley. G. K. Chesterton. CP-ChesG

Lean candles hunger in. E. E. Cummings. CP-CummE

Lean hands of wagon men, The. Windy City, The. Carl Sandburg. CP-SandC

Leanders Obsequies. Robert Herrick. CP-HerrR

Leaning her head upon my breast. Love's Representation. Sir John Suckling. CP-SuckJ

Leaning on my left hand. Incident, An. Louis Zukofsky. CP-ZukLS

Leaning on the gold. Mulch, The. Eleanor Wilner. SP-WilnE

Leaning on / the parapet stone. Well, The. Charles Tomlinson. CP-TomlC; SP-TomlC

Leaning / over the footbridge the Willamette. Landscape with Poets. Olga Broumas. SP-BrouO

Leans now the fair willow, dreaming. Willow, The. Walter De la Mare. CP-DeLaW

Leap, The. James Dickey. CP-DickJ

Leap, The. Robert Graves. CP-GravR

Leap before You Look. W. H. Auden. CP-AudeW

Leap-centuries, leap- / seconds, leap-. Paul Celan. SP-CelaP, tr. by John Felstiner

Leaping from Ambush. David Ignatow. SP-IgnaD

Leaping, leaping, leaping. Angel Food Dogs, The. Anne Sexton. CP-SextA

Leaping woman arrives in an ambulance of starlight, The. James Tate. SP-TateJ

Lear. William Carlos Williams. CP-WilW2

Lear Is Gay. Robert Earl Hayden. CP-HaydR

Learn about your inner self from those who know such things. Phrasing Must Change, The. Jelaluddin Rumi. SP-Rumi, tr. by Coleman Barks

Learn from Ali how to fight. Ali in Battle. Jelaluddin Rumi. SP-Rumi, tr. by Coleman Barks

Learn how to model before you learn to finish things. Lives of the Artists. Charles Wright. SP-WrigCN

Learn O man! the worth of time. Day Lily, The. Jones Very. CP-VeryJ

Learn this of me, where e'r thy Lot doth fall. Lots to Be Liked. Robert Herrick. CP-HerrR

Learn to submit to the laws of destiny. On the Death of the Vice-Chancellor, a Physician. John Milton. CP-CowpW; CP-MiltJ

Learn, ye nations of the earth. John Milton. See Learn to submit to the laws of destiny

Learned King fought, The. "O Flodden Field." Donald Hall. CP-HallD

Learned man came to me once, A. Stephen Crane. CP-CranS

Learned Men, The. Archibald MacLeish. CP-MacLA

Learners, The. Mona Van Duyn. SP-VanDM

Learners, The. Randall Jarrell. CP-JarrR

Learning. Robert Creeley. SP-CreeR

Learning. William Stafford. SP-StafWW

Learning. Miller Williams. CP-WillM

Learning about the Indians. Mary Oliver. SP-OlivM

Learning, Any Time. William Stafford. SP-StafWW

Learning by Doing. Howard Nemerov. CP-NemeH

Learning Experience. Marge Piercy. SP-PierM

Learning from a player piano. Player Piano, The. Wyatt Prunty. SP-PrunW

Learning from Barbara Deming. Grace Paley. CP-PalGC

Learning from Nature. Richard Eberhart. CP-EberR

Learning Russian. Miller Williams. CP-WillM

Learning the Bicycle. Wyatt Prunty. SP-PrunW

Learning the Trees. Howard Nemerov. CP-NemeH

Learning to Read. Miller Williams. CP-WillM

Leasing of September, The. John Ashbery. SP-AshbJ

Least Bee that brew. Emily Dickinson. CP-DickE

Least Figure, The. Jelaluddin Rumi. SP-Rumi, tr. by Coleman Barks

Least, if so I am; / If so, less than the least, The. I Am Small and of No Reputation. Christina Georgina Rossetti. CP-RosC2

Least little sound sets the coyotes walking, The. Outside. William Stafford. SP-StafWW

Least Rivers—docile to some sea. Emily Dickinson. CP-DickE

Leastlessly / out / of this. E. E. Cummings. CP-CummE

Leather fringes, The. Alabaster. Gary Snyder. CP-SnydG

Leather Leggings. Carl Sandburg. CP-SandC

Leave. Randall Jarrell. CP-JarrR

Leave April now, and autumn having. Reconciliation. Walter De la Mare. CP-DeLaW

Leave Cod, tobacco-like, burnt gums to take. To Sir Cod. Ben Jonson. CP-JonsB; SP-JonsB

'Leave colouring thy tresses,' I did cry. Elegy 1.14: "'Leave colouring thy tresses,' I did cry." Ovid. CP-MarlC Fr. Elegies.

Leave, Cytherea, Your Enchanted Isle. Lorenzo de' Medici. SP-ZatuM

Leave go my hands, let me catch breath and see. In the Orchard. Algernon Charles Swinburne. SP-SwinA

Leave him here in the fresh greening grasses and trees. At Crown Hill. James Whitcomb Riley. CP-RileJ

Leave, lady, in your glasse of christall clene. Sonnet 45. Edmund Spenser. CP-Spens Fr. Amoretti.

Leave me, Fear! thy throbs are base. Ralph Waldo Emerson. CP-EmerR

Leave Me O Love. Sir Philip Sidney. SP-SidnP

Leave me to my lonely pillow. Pattern. Dorothy Parker. CP-ParkD

Leave me, unhappy thoughts, leave me in peace! Petrarch. CP-Petra, tr. by J. G. Nichols

Leave now our streets, and in you plain behold. Alms-House and Trustees, The. George Crabbe. SP-CrabG Fr. Borough, The.

Leave now the beach, and even that perfect friendship. End of Season. Robert Penn Warren. CP-WarrR

Leave off! Leave off! Leave off! Sunset Verse, The. D. H. Lawrence. CP-LawrD

Leave off my sheep: it is no time to feed. Sir Philip Sidney. SP-SidnP Fr. Arcadia.

Leave prolonging thy distresse. Thomas Campion. CP-Camp1

Leave Sex Alone. D. H. Lawrence. CP-LawrD

Leave-taking. Federico García Lorca. CP-GarcF, tr. by Alan S. Trueblood Fr. Back of the World.

Leave-taking, A. James Laughlin. CP-LaugJ

Leave-Taking, A. James Whitcomb Riley. CP-RileJ

Leave-taking, A. Algernon Charles Swinburne. SP-SwinA

Leave the uproar: at a leap. Nature and Life. George Meredith. CP-MerG1

Leave your Coras. Draftees. Langston Hughes. CP-HughL; CP-HughL3

Leave your home behind, lad. Recruit, The. A. E. Housman. CP-HousA

Leaves. Ted Hughes. SP-HughTN

Leaves. Derek Mahon. CP-MahoD

Leaves and rain and the days of the year. Death-Parting, A. Dante Gabriel Rossetti. CW-RossD

Leaves Apples. Grace Paley. CP-PalGC

Leaves are eyes. Path. A. R. Ammons. CP-AmmoA

Leaves are greygreen. Lines: "Leaves are greygreen." William Carlos Williams. CP-WilW1

Leaves are piled thickly on the green tree, The. Pastoral Dialogue, A. Frank O'Hara. SP-OharF

Leaves are struck and dance, the bird is blown, The. To the New World. Randall Jarrell. CP-JarrR

Leaves Compared with Flowers. Robert Frost. CP-FrosR

Leaves embrace, The. Avenue of Poplars, The. William Carlos Williams. CP-WilW1

Leaves espaliered jade on our barn's loft window. Our Twentieth Wedding Anniversary (Elizabeth). Robert Lowell. SP-LoweR

Leaves fall, fall, The. To Betsy Steiger. Rainer Maria Rilke. CP-RilkFr, tr. by A. Poulin, Jr.

Leaves fall from my fingers, The. October. Charles Wright. SP-WrigC

Leaves fall from the trees. Fall in Connecticut. Yehuda Amichai. SP-AmicY, tr. by Chana Bloch

Leaves fritter / Teased edges. Single Most. Rae Armantrout. SP-ArmaA

Leaves from the Book of Dorothy Wordsworth. Marya Alexandrovna Zaturenska. SP-ZatuM

Leaves glowing in the sun, zealous hum of bumblebees. Hour, An. Czeslaw Milosz. CP-MiloC; CP-MiloCN, tr. by Lillian Vallee

Leaves / Murmuring by myriads in the shimmering trees. From My Diary, July 1914. Wilfred Owen. CP-OwenW

Leaves of a Dream Are the Leaves of an Onion, The. Arthur Sze. SP-SzeA

Leaves of autumn burning through the gray, The. Chorale for Autumn. Marya Alexandrovna Zaturenska. SP-ZatuM

Leaves of Grass, Flowers of Grass. D. H. Lawrence. CP-LawrD

Leaves of Nerves. Andrei Codrescu. SP-CodrA

Leaves of poplars pick Japanese prints against the west. Moonset. Carl Sandburg. CP-SandC

Leaves of the Cypress, The. Jorge Luis Borges. SP-BorgJ, tr. by Alan S. Trueblood

Leaves of the tree hide the sun, The. In Me. David Ignatow. SP-IgnaD

Leaves on the macadam make a noise, The. Hermitage at the Center, The. Wallace Stevens. CP-StevW; CP-StevWP

Leaves on the tree in front of my house—they live and die together, The. Separate Dead, The. David Ignatow. SP-IgnaD

Leaves That Rustled on This Oak-Crowned Hill, The. William Wordsworth. CP-WorW2

Leaves that shifted overhead all summer, The. Autumn Equinox. Adrienne Rich. CP-RicAE

Leaves That Talk. Anne Sexton. CP-SextA

Leaves, though little time they have to live, The. October Maples, Portland. Richard Wilbur. CP-WilbR

Leaves though thick are falling; one by one, The. Autumn Leaves. Jones Very. CP-VeryJ

Leaves throng thick above, The. Last Leaf, The. Thomas Hardy. CP-HardT

Leaves turn black when they have learned how to fly, The. Man with One Leaf in October Night. W. S. Merwin. SP-MerwW

Leaves were already on the trees, the fruit blossoms, The. With Janice. Kenneth Koch. SP-KochK

Leaves will fall again sometime and fill, The. Sunday Morning Apples. Hart Crane. CP-CranH

Leavetaking. Primo Levi. CP-LeviP, tr. by Ruth Feldman and Brian Swann

Leaving. Rae Armantrout. SP-ArmaA

Leaving. Richard Wilbur. CP-WilbR

Leaving, A. Thomas Hardy. CP-HardT

Leaving a Dove. Eugenio Montale. CP-MontE, tr. by Jonathan Galassi

Leaving an Island. Paul Muldoon. CP-MuldP

Leaving Barra. Louis MacNeice. CP-MacNL

Leaving Church Early. John Updike. CP-UpdiJ

Leaving Early. Sylvia Plath. CP-PlatS

Leaving—for the present—sunsets, bluebirds, pussywillows. Rhetoric for Danny Keough to Recite at the Bar, A. John Ciardi. CP-CiarJ

Leaving Forever. Denise Levertov. SP-LeveDP

Leaving Fox. Lucille Clifton. SP-ClifL

Leaving from Idlewild, whose agents. Flight 162. George Oppen. CP-OppGN

Leaving K.C. Mo. past Independence past Liberty. Kansas City to Saint Louis. Allen Ginsberg. CP-GinsA

Leaving L'Atelier—Aix-en-Provence. Kenneth Rexroth. CP-RexrK

Leaving Longboat Key. John Ciardi. CP-CiarJ

Leaving Monovasia. Yannis Ritsos. SP-RitsY Fr. Monovasia.

Leaving My Daughter's House. Maxine W. Kumin. SP-KumiM

Leaving New York, I looked back fourteen times. Muriel Rukeyser. CP-RukeM

Leaving the Asylum. Gregory Orr. SP-OrrG

Leaving the Cinema. Wisława Szymborska. SP-SzymWM, tr. by Joanna Trzeciak

Leaving the house each dawn I see the hawk. Workman. George Oppen. CP-OppGN

Leaving the Rest Unsaid. Robert Graves. CP-GravR

Leaving the splendid plaza and the esplanade—. Ah . . . to the Villages! Thomas McGrath. SP-McGrT

Leaving the white glow of filling stations. Strand at Lough Beg, The. Seamus Heaney. SP-HeanSO

Leaving Water Hyacinths. Jane Cooper. CP-CoopJ

Leaving Yannina. Amy Clampitt. CP-ClamA

Leavings. Seamus Heaney. SP-HeanSO

Lebensweisheitspielerei. Wallace Stevens. CP-StevW; CP-StevWP

Lector Aere Perennior. James Vincent Cunningham. CP-CunnJ

Lecture, A. Czeslaw Milosz. CP-MiloCN, tr. by Robert Hass

Lecture upon the Shadow, A. John Donne. CP-DonnJ; MW-DonnJ

Lecturer in Bookstore. Ogden Nash. CP-NashO

Leda. "H. D." CP-DoolH

Leda. Robert Graves. CP-GravR

Leda. D. H. Lawrence. CP-LawrD

Leda. Mona Van Duyn. SP-VanDM

Leda 1. Lucille Clifton. SP-ClifL

Leda 2. Lucille Clifton. SP-ClifL

Leda 3. Lucille Clifton. SP-ClifL

Leda and Her Swan. Olga Broumas. SP-BrouO

Leda and the Swan. William Butler Yeats. CP-YeatW

Leda Hidden. Kenneth Rexroth. CP-RexrK

Leda Reconsidered. Mona Van Duyn. SP-VanDM

Leda's Handmaiden. Eleanor Wilner. SP-WilnE

Lee O. Harris. James Whitcomb Riley. CP-RileJ

Leech boasts, he has a Pill, that can alone. Upon Leech. Robert Herrick. CP-HerrR

Leedle Dutch baby haff come ter town! James Whitcomb Riley. CP-RileJ

Leering across Pearl Street. Trouble. James Wright. CP-WrigJ

Lee's Lunch / Spaghetti. Brilliant Sad Sun. William Carlos Williams. CP-WilW1

Leeway. Hans Magnus Enzensberger. SP-EnzeH, tr. by Michael Hamburger

Leezie Lindsay. Robert Burns. CP-BurnR

Leffingwell. Edwin Arlington Robinson. CP-RobiE

Left. A. R. Ammons. CP-AmmoA

Left-alone grow-things wait, rustle-grass, click. In the All-Verbs Navaho World. William Stafford. SP-StafWW

Left by his friend to breakfast alone on the white. Edward Lear. W. H. Auden. CP-AudeW

Left by that father, who was known to few. Richard's Youth. George Crabbe. SP-CrabG Fr. Tales of the Hall.

Left by the ebbing tide of battle. Come On, Come Back. Stevie Smith. CP-SmitS

Left-Handed Cellist, The. Rita Dove. SP-DoveR

Left-Handed Letter to Dr. Sheridan, A. Jonathan Swift. CP-SwifJ

Left in immortal Youth. Emily Dickinson. CP-DickE

Left leg flung out, head cocked to the right. Poet. Karl Shapiro. SP-ShapK

Left lying in the grass. Bicycle Chain, A. John Updike. CP-UpdiJ

Left off the highway and. Waiting. Raymond Carver. CP-CarvR

Left out of vacation. Robert Lowell. SP-LoweR

Left Unfinished Sixteen Times. Michael Palmer. SP-PalmM

Left-wing poetry represents a rise in the price of bread. Hugh MacDiarmid. SP-MacDH Fr. England's Double Knavery.

Leg in a Plaster Cast, A. Muriel Rukeyser. CP-RukeM

Leg, The. Karl Shapiro. SP-ShapK

Legacy. Yusef Komunyakaa. CP-KomuY

Legacy, A. John Greenleaf Whittier. CP-WhitJ

Legacy [or Legacie], The. John Donne. CP-DonnJ; MW-DonnJ

Legacy of Herakleitos, The. Thomas Merton. CP-MertT

Legal children of a literary man, The. Relationships. Mona Van Duyn. SP-VanDM

Legal Reflection. Ogden Nash. CP-NashO

Legal Reform. Thom Gunn. CP-GunnT

Legate, I had the news last night—my cohort ordered home. Roman Centurion's Song, The. Rudyard Kipling. CP-KiplR

Legend. W. H. Auden. CP-AudeW

Legend. Hart Crane. CP-CranH

Legend. Louise Glück. SP-GlucL

Legend. Charles Tomlinson. CP-TomlC

Legend, A. Czeslaw Milosz. CP-MiloC; CP-MiloCN, tr. by Robert Hass

Legend, The. Tennessee Williams. CP-WillT

Legend for a Little Child. Kenneth Patchen. CP-PatcK

Legend Glorified, The. James Whitcomb Riley. CP-RileJ

Legend is bull's eye, part of a local scene, The. .22. John Ciardi. CP-CiarJ

Legend is whispered, The. Shapeshifter Poems. Lucille Clifton. SP-ClifL

Legend of Good Women, The. Geoffrey Chaucer. CP-ChauG

Legend of Good Women, The. G. K. Chesterton. CP-ChesG

Legend of Mirth, The. Rudyard Kipling. CP-KiplR

Legend of St. Hat, The. John Greenleaf Whittier. CP-WhitJ

Legend of the Chippewa Spring and Minnehaha, the Indian Maiden. Ezra Pound. CP-PoEar

Legend of the Dead Soldier, The. Bertolt Brecht. CP-MacNL

Legend of the Foreign Office, A. Rudyard Kipling. CP-KiplR (This is the reason why Rustum Beg.) CP-KiplR

Legend of the Lake, A. John Greenleaf Whittier. CP-WhitJ

Legend of the One-Eyed Man, The. Anne Sexton. CP-SextA; SP-SextA

Legend of the Pessimist, A. G. K. Chesterton. CP-ChesG

Legend of Truth, A. Rudyard Kipling. CP-KiplR Fr. Debits and Credits.

Legend of Viable Women, A. Richard Eberhart. CP-EberR

Legendary muscle that wants and grieves, The. Hearts, The. Robert Pinsky. CP-PinsR

Legendary Progress. Thomas McGrath. SP-McGrT

Legendary tree is upside down, The. That Tree. A. K. Ramanujan. CP-RamaA

Legende. Hart Crane. CP-CranH

Legends. Stephen Crane. CP-CranS

Legends. Carl Sandburg. CP-SandC

Legends of Evil, The. Rudyard Kipling. CP-KiplR

Leggett's Monument. John Greenleaf Whittier. CP-WhitJ

Legi operosum iamdudum, Camdene, volumen. Ad Guil. Camdenum. Thomas Campion. CP-CampT

Legs, The. Robert Graves. CP-GravR

Legs are gone and the hopes—the lava of outpouring, The. Empire of Coins, An. Charles Bukowski. SP-BukC2

Legs hold a torso away from the earth. Walking Man of Rodin, The. Carl Sandburg. CP-SandC

Legs of Lalage toss, and toss, and toss, The. Lalage! Charles Olson. CP-OlsoC

Leicestershire. Donald Davie. CP-DaviDC

Leipzig. Thomas Hardy. CP-HardT

L. E. L. Christina Georgina Rossetti. CP-RosC1

Lelloine. James Whitcomb Riley. CP-RileJ

Lelloine! Lelloine! Don't you hear me calling? Uncomforted. James Whitcomb Riley. CP-RileJ

Lemme kiss your face, lick your neck. Sweet Boy, Gimme Yr Ass. Allen Ginsberg. CP-GinsA

Lemme roll 'em, boy. Crap Game. Langston Hughes. CP-HughL; CP-HughL1

Lemon and Laburnum. Rainer Maria Rilke. CP-RilkFr, tr. by A. Poulin, Jr.

Lemon-house was being over-, The. In the Greenhouse. Eugenio Montale. CP-MontE, *tr. by* Jonathan Galassi

Lemon Trees. Philip Whalen. SP-WhalP

Lemonade. Raymond Carver. CP-CarvR

Lemongrove. / Flash / in my dream. Federico García Lorca. CP-GarcF, *tr. by* Jerome Rothenberg *Fr.* Garden in Umber; or The Garden of the Brownhaired Girls.

Lemons, The. Eugenio Montale. CP-MontE, *tr. by* Jonathan Galassi

Lemuel Shaw's Meditation. Helen Pinkerton. CP-PinkH

Lemuel's Blessing. W. S. Merwin. SP-MerwW

Lenada. Kenneth Patchen. CP-PatcK

Lend me an ear. To a Sea-Cliff. Thomas Hardy. CP-HardT

Lengthened shadow of my hand, The. Persephone Pauses. Carolyn Kizer. CP-KizeC

Lenin. Langston Hughes. CP-HughL; CP-HughL2

Lenin walks around the world. Lenin. Langston Hughes. CP-HughL; CP-HughL2

Lenitie. Robert Herrick. CP-HerrR

Lenore. Edgar Allan Poe. CP-PoeEd

Lenox Avenue Bar. Langston Hughes. CP-HughL; CP-HughL3

Lenox Avenue / by daylight. Dive. Langston Hughes. CP-HughL; CP-HughL3

Lenox Avenue: Midnight. Langston Hughes. CP-HughL; CP-HughL1

Lenox Avenue Mural. Langston Hughes.
　Comment on Curb. CP-HughL; CP-HughL3
　"Good morning, daddy!" CP-HughL; CP-HughL3
　Harlem ("What happens to a dream deferred?"). CP-HughL; CP-HughL3 (Dream Deferred.) CP-HughL3
　Island ("Between two rivers"). CP-HughL; CP-HughL3
　Letter ("Dear Mama, / Time I pay rent and get my food"). CP-HughL; CP-HughL3
　Same in Blues. CP-HughL

Lens. Michael Palmer. SP-PalmM

Lent. George Herbert. CP-HerbG

Lent. Thomas Merton. CP-MertT

Lent. Christina Georgina Rossetti. CP-RosC2

Lent in a Year of War. Thomas Merton. CP-MertT

Lent Lily, The. A. E. Housman. CP-HousA

Lenten. Olga Broumas. SP-BrouO

L'Envoi. Rudyard Kipling. CP-KiplR
　(When Earth's Last Picture Is Painted.) CP-KiplR

L'Envoi. Edwin Arlington Robinson. CP-RobiE

L'Envoi; Departmental Ditties. Rudyard Kipling. CP-KiplR

L'Envoy. George Herbert. CP-HerbG

Lenvoy de Chaucer a Bukton. Geoffrey Chaucer. CP-ChauG

Lenvoy de Chaucer a Scogan. Geoffrey Chaucer. CP-ChauG

"Leonainie!" angels missed her. To Leonainie. James Whitcomb Riley. CP-RileJ

Leonainic— Angels named her. James Whitcomb Riley. CP-RileJ

Leonardo Da Vinci's. Marianne Craig Moore. CP-MoorM

Leonids having fallen, The. Easy Lessons in Geophagy. Kenneth Rexroth. CP-RexrK

Leonora. Edwin Arlington Robinson. CP-RobiE

Leopard no more secret, A. Nocturne. Stanley Kunitz. CP-KunSC

Lepanto. G. K. Chesterton. CP-ChesG

Leper, The. Algernon Charles Swinburne. SP-SwinA

Leper is a Lazar or a Meazel, A. Rites for the Extrusion of a Leper. Thomas Merton. CP-MertT

Leper's Bell, The. Yusef Komunyakaa. CP-KomuY

L'Epreuve. Thom Gunn. CP-GunnT

Leprosie in Cloathes. Robert Herrick. CP-HerrR

Leprosie in Houses. Robert Herrick. CP-HerrR

Lepus Multis Amicus. John Gay. CP-CowpW

Lerici. Thom Gunn. CP-GunnT

Les Amants. James Laughlin. CP-LaugJ

Les Cinq Vierges. Thomas Merton. CP-MertT

Les Étiquettes Jaunes. Frank O'Hara. SP-OharF

Les Etoiles d'un Cirque. Tennessee Williams. CP-WillT

Les Fleurs du Cinéma. Andrei Codrescu. SP-CodrA

Les Luths. Frank O'Hara. SP-OharF

Les Millwin. Ezra Pound. SP-PounE

Les Noyades. Algernon Charles Swinburne. SP-SwinA

Les Plus Belles Pages. Wallace Stevens. CP-StevW; CP-StevWP

Les Saints Nouveaux. John Updike. CP-UpdiJ

Lesbia. Catullus. *See* Carmina

Lesbia forever on me rails. Catullus. *See* Lesbia loads me night & day with her curses

Lesbia is extraordinarily vindictive. Carmen 83. Catullus. CP-ZukLS *Fr.* Carmina.

Lesbia / live with me. Carmen 5. Catullus. CP-CampT; CP-ZukLS *Fr.* Carmina.

Lesbia loads me night & day with her curses. Carmen 92. Catullus. CP-ZukLS *Fr.* Carmina.

Lesbia may dicker simper maul or nag talk at whom, come. Catullus. *See* Lesbia loads me night & day with her curses

Lesbia (my price scent t'her hero) mauls and deplores me, '*dig it.*' Catullus. *See* Lesbia is extraordinarily vindictive

Lesbia, our Lesbia, the same old Lesbia. Carmen 58. Catullus. CP-ZukLS *Fr.* Carmina.

Lesbia says she'd rather marry me. Carmen 70. Catullus. CP-ZukLS *Fr.* Carmina.

Lesbia! since far from you I've ranged. To Lesbia. Lord Byron. CP-Byron

Lesbia's sparrow! / Lesbia's plaything. Carmen 2. Catullus. CP-ZukLS *Fr.* Carmina.

Lesbius has pooled her: kidney? whom Lesbia my—lit. Catullus. *See* They nickname Lesbia's brother 'pulcher'

Lesbos. Charles Baudelaire. CP-BaudC, *tr. by* Walter Martin

Lesbos. Sylvia Plath. CP-PlatS

L'Esprit de Géométrie et l'Esprit de Finesse. James Vincent Cunningham. CP-CunnJ

Less and Less Human, O Savage Spirit. Wallace Stevens. CP-StevW; CP-StevWP

Less than a score, the dregs of the last day. End of Camp Alamoosook. Robert Lowell. SP-LoweR

'Less you want your toes trod off you'd better get back at once. Rudyard Kipling. CP-KiplR

Lesse our sorrowes here and suffrings cease, The. Great Grief, Great Glory. Robert Herrick. CP-HerrR

Lesser proof than old Voltaire's, yet greater, A. Orange Buds by Mail from Florida. Walt Whitman. CP-WhitW

Lesson. Carl Sandburg. CP-SandC

Lesson, The. Maya Angelou. SP-AngeM

Lesson, The. W. H. Auden. CP-AudeW

Lesson, The. Billy Collins. SP-CollB

Lesson, The. Paul Laurence Dunbar. CP-DunbP

Lesson, The. Rudyard Kipling. CP-KiplR

Lesson, The. Stanley Kunitz. CP-KunSC

Lesson, The. Rainer Maria Rilke. CP-RilkFr, *tr. by* A. Poulin, Jr.

Lesson, The. Charles Simic. SP-SimiC; SP-SimiCE

Lesson, The. Charles Tomlinson. CP-TomlC

Lesson, The. William Carlos Williams. CP-WilW2

Lesson begins in a heated room, The. Several Measures for the Little Lost. Norman Dubie. CP-DubiN

Lesson for This Sunday, A. Derek Walcott. CP-WalcD

Lesson for Today, The. Robert Frost. CP-FrosR

Lesson in Geography, A. Kenneth Rexroth. CP-RexrK

Lesson in History. Robert Penn Warren. CP-WarrR

Lesson in Observation, A. Dan Pagis. SP-PagiD, *tr. by* Stephen Mitchell

Lesson in Vengeance, A. Sylvia Plath. CP-PlatS

Lesson of Grief, The. George Meredith. CP-MerG1

Lesson on the Twentieth Century, A. Miller Williams. CP-WillM

Lessons. Czeslaw Milosz. CP-MiloC; CP-MiloCN

Lessons. Walt Whitman. CP-WhitW

Lessons from the Gorse. Elizabeth Barrett Browning. CP-BroEB

Lessons in Hunger. Anne Sexton. CP-SextA

Lessons of History Unlearned, The. Jones Very. CP-VeryJ

L'Essor Saccadé. Wallace Stevens. CP-StevWP

Lest any doubt that we are glad that they were born Today. Emily Dickinson. CP-DickE

Lest it may more quarrels breed. Twelve Articles. Jonathan Swift. CP-SwifJ

Lest men suspect your tale to be untrue. Devil's Advice to Story-Tellers, The. Robert Graves. CP-GravR

Lest the fair cheeks begin their shrivelling. Homework. Mona Van Duyn. SP-VanDM

Lest they should come—is all my fear. Emily Dickinson. CP-DickE

Lest this be Heaven indeed. Emily Dickinson. CP-DickE

Lest you should think that verse shall die. Part of the Ninth Ode of Horace Imitated. Alexander Pope. CP-PopeA

Lest you should think this story true. Rudyard Kipling. *See* Now Jones had left his new-wed bride to keep his house in order

Let *a* be taken as. Project of Linear Inquiry, The. Michael Palmer. SP-PalmM

Let a joy keep you. Joy. Carl Sandburg. CP-SandC

Let a man alone in a cabin. Lament for Javier Heraud. Thomas Merton. CP-MertT

Let all chaste matrons, when they chance to see. Upon a Young Mother of Many Children. Robert Herrick. CP-HerrR

Let all the little poets be gathered together in classes. To School! Stevie Smith.

CP-SmitS

Let all the world in ev'ry corner sing / *My God and King*. Antiphon: "Let all the world in ev'ry corner sing / *My God and King*." George Herbert. CP-HerbG

Let all who will. Militant. Langston Hughes. CP-HughL; CP-HughL3

Let America Be America Again. Langston Hughes. CP-HughL; CP-HughL1

Let amicitia in her ample reign. On Friendship. Phillis Wheatley. CP-WheaP

Let another cross his way. Mortal Enemy. Dorothy Parker. CP-ParkD

Let Banister now lend his aid. William Cowper. CP-CowpW

Let but thy voice engender with the string. Upon Her Voice. Robert Herrick. CP-HerrR

Let *Cæsar* spread his conquests far. Horace. CP-JohnS

Let confusion be the design. Design for November. William Carlos Williams. CP-WilW2

Let crowned heads their laureats boast. Ode to Doctor Smith on His Birth Day March the 16th, 1791, An. Annis Boudinot Stockton. CP-StocA

Let darkness / Gather up its roses. Dare. Langston Hughes. CP-HughL; CP-HughL2

Let down the Bars, Oh Death. Emily Dickinson. CP-DickE

Let down you hair, dream-dark at night. Sanctuary. Tennessee Williams. CP-WillT

Let down your braids of hair, lady. Glimmer. Carl Sandburg. CP-SandC

Let Each Man Remember. Josephine Jacobsen. CP-JacoJ

Let Eagle bid the Tortoise sunward soar. Eagle and the Tortoise, The. Samuel Taylor Coleridge. CP-ColeS

Let Everything That Hath Breath Praise the Lord. Christina Georgina Rossetti. CP-RosC2

Let faire or foule my Mistresse be. Light Lightly Pleased. Robert Herrick. CP-HerrR

Let Fate or Insufficiency provide. To J.M. George Meredith. CP-MerG1

Let Folly smile, to view the names. To E———. Lord Byron. CP-Byron

Let fools great Cupid's yoke disdain. Song: The Willing Prisoner to His Mistress. Thomas Carew. CP-CareT

Let foreign [*or* forrain] nations of their language boast. Son[ne], The. George Herbert. CP-HerbG

Let God arise, let his enemies be scattered. Psalm 68: "Let God arise, let his enemies be scattered." Bible, *O.T.* SP-SmarC *Fr.* Psalms.

Let her be seen, a voice on a platform, heard. Ann Burlak. Muriel Rukeyser. CP-RukeM

Let her who walks in Paphos. Lais. "H. D." CP-DoolH

Let Heroes Account to Love. Alan Dugan. CP-DugaA

Let him answer as he will. Companion, The. Edwin Arlington Robinson. CP-RobiE

Let him be safe in sleep. Spell of Sleep. Kathleen Jessie Raine. SP-RainK

Let him rehearse the gifts reserved for age. Artifex in Extremis. Donald Davie. CP-DaviDC

Let him that will be free and keep his h[e]art from care. Thomas Campion *and* Philip Rosseter. CP-CampT

Let him, who from his tyrant mistress did. Elegy on the La: Pen: Sent to My Mistress Out of France, An. Thomas Carew. CP-CareT

Let him who may. To Be Recited to Flossie on Her Birthday. William Carlos Williams. CP-WilW2

Let History Be My Judge. W. H. Auden. CP-AudeW

Let hoary TIME's vast Bowels be the Grave. On the Frontispiece of Isaacsons Chronologie Explained. Richard Crashaw. CP-CrasR

Let it be alleys. Let it be a hall. Lovely Love, A. Gwendolyn Brooks. SP-BrooG

Let it be Rome's great Pope, adored. Ballade in Old French. François Villon. CP-WilbR

Let it be some sheets of music. Sonata Pathétique. Theodore Weiss. SP-WeisT

Let it go on; let the love of this hour be poured out till all the answers. Let Love Go On. Carl Sandburg. CP-SandC

Let it go—the. E. E. Cummings. CP-CummE; SP-CummE

Let it no longer be a forlorn[e] hope. On the Baptized Ethiopian. Richard Crashaw. CP-CrasR, *tr. by* Richard Crashaw

Let it stand / A stone guest. Aqueduct. Charles Tomlinson. CP-TomlC

Let Kate and Rose and sleepy Ned. Receipt to Frighten Away the Dean, A. Peter Murray. CP-SherT

Let Kings and Rulers, learn[e] this line from me. Strength to Support Soveraignty. Robert Herrick. CP-HerrR

Let kings command, and do[e] the best they may. Power in the People, The. Robert Herrick. CP-HerrR

Let klumps of Earth however glorified. Traveller through Infinity, The. Samuel Taylor Coleridge. CP-ColeS

Let Love Go On. Carl Sandburg. CP-SandC

Let man's soul[e] be a sphe[a]re, and then, in this. Good Friday [*or* Goodfriday], 1613. Riding Westward. John Donne. CP-DonnJ; MW-DonnJ

Let Me Be. Philip Levine. SP-LeviP

Let me be at the place of the castle. Psalm Concerning the Castle. Denise Levertov. SP-LeveDP

Let me be monosyllabic today, O Lord. Monosyllabic. Carl Sandburg. CP-SandC

Let me be my own fool. Counterpoint, A. Robert Creeley. CP-CreeR

Let me be to Thee as the circling bird. Gerard Manley Hopkins. CP-HopkG

Let me be warme; let me be fully fed. Love Kill'd by Lack. Robert Herrick. CP-HerrR

Let me be what I am, as Virgil cold. Elegy [*or* Elegie], An: "Let me be what I am, as Virgil cold." Ben Jonson. CP-JonsB; SP-JonsB

Let me be your baby, south wind. Baby Song of the Four Winds. Carl Sandburg. CP-SandC

Let me become dead eyed. Wise Men. Langston Hughes. CP-HughL; CP-HughL1

Let Me Begin Again. Philip Levine. SP-LeviP

Let Me Believe. Thomas Hardy. CP-HardT

Let me bow down before. Love's Altar. James Laughlin. CP-LaugJ

Let me celebrate you. I. Dialogue of Watching, A. Kenneth Rexroth. CP-RexrK

Let me close the eyes of my soul. Despair. Paul Laurence Dunbar. CP-DunbP

Let me come in where you sit weeping,—ay. Bereaved. James Whitcomb Riley. CP-RileJ

Let me come with you. What a moon tonight! Moonlight Sonata. Yannis Ritsos. SP-RitsY, *tr. by* Kimon Friar

Let Me Enjoy. Thomas Hardy. CP-HardT

Let me gaze, gaze forever. Camera. John Updike. CP-UpdiJ

Let me go where'er I will. Music. Ralph Waldo Emerson. CP-EmerR

Let me hip you to the streets. Letter to an Aspiring Junkie. Maya Angelou. SP-AngeM

Let Me In! Kenneth Patchen. CP-PatcK

Let Me in This Ae Night. Robert Burns. CP-BurnR

Let me know. Appetite. Stevie Smith. CP-SmitS

Let me look at what I was, before I die. Jamestown. Randall Jarrell. CP-JarrR

Let me my [*or* thy] properties explain. To Quilca. Jonathan Swift. CP-SherT; CP-SwifJ

Let me never weigh the handiwork. Reservation. Heather McHugh. SP-McHuH

Let me no more, my love, be what I've seemed to you. Sulpicia to Cerinthus. Tibullus. CP-TateA

Let me not forget at least. Aginst the Sky. William Carlos Williams. CP-WilW2

Let me not live, if I not love. On Himselfe. Robert Herrick. CP-HerrR

Let me not mar that perfect Dream. Emily Dickinson. CP-DickE

Let me not say it, let me not reveal. Green Ways. Stanley Kunitz. CP-KunSC

Let me not thirst with this Hock at my Lip. Emily Dickinson. CP-DickE

Let me pick / olives in the moonlight. Lament: "Let me pick / olives in the moonlight." Arthur Sze. SP-SzeA

Let me play to you tunes without measure or end. Bagpipe Music. Hugh MacDiarmid. SP-MacDH

Let me pour [*or* powre] forth. Valediction, A: of Weeping. John Donne. CP-DonnJ; MW-DonnJ

Let me put on record for posterity. Her Beauty. Robert Graves. CP-GravR

Let me say beginning I don't believe in Soul. Manifesto. Allen Ginsberg. CP-GinsA

Let me say (in anger) that since the day we were married. Crisis, The. Robert Creeley. CP-CreeR

Let me see. Dream Poems. Philip Whalen. SP-WhalP

Let me sleep this night away. Upon Himselfe Being Buried. Robert Herrick. CP-HerrR

Let me stop here. Let me too look at nature, briefly. Morning Sea. Constantine P. Cavafy. CP-CavaC

Let me tell you. June 30, 1974. James Schuyler. CP-SchuJ

Let Me Tell You. Miller Williams. CP-WillM

Let me tell you a little story. Miss Gee. W. H. Auden. CP-AudeW

Let me tell you, Mac, it's sure great. New Hartford. Hayden Carruth. CP-CarHS

Let me tell you of Aloysius Buck. Outcome of Mr. Buck's Superstition, The. Ogden Nash. CP-NashO

Let me tell you the story of how I began. Song: Lift-Boy. Robert Graves. CP-GravR

Let me walk through the fields of paper. Walk through the Notebooks, A. Denise Levertov. SP-LeveDP

Let me walk to you. Out. Robert Creeley. CP-CreeR

Let me write you a rune of a rhyme, Dave Field. Dave Field. James Whitcomb Riley. CP-RileJ

Let Memory Mountain remember instead of me. Yehuda Amichai. SP-AmicYL *Fr.* Poems of the Land of Zion and Jerusalem.

Let moderation on thy passions waite. Moderation. Robert Herrick. CP-HerrR

Let More Ambitious Poets Take the Heart. William Wordsworth. CP-WorW2

Let Mother Earth now deck herself in flowers. Epithalamium: "Let mother Earth." Sir Philip Sidney. SP-SidnP, *tr. by* Robert Hass *Fr.* Arcadia.

Let my first Knowing be of thee. Emily Dickinson. CP-DickE

Let my snow-tracks lead. Hayden Carruth. CP-CarHS *Fr.* Clay Hill Anthology, The.

Let no man ask thee of anything. Soothsay. Dante Gabriel Rossetti. CW-RossD

Let no one fear in the bewildering night. Adrogué. Jorge Luis Borges. SP-BorgJ, *tr. by* Alastair Reid

Let no one sing again of love or war. Black Stars, The. Primo Levi. CP-LeviP, *tr. by* Ruth Feldman *and* Brian Swann

Let not conceited sages laugh aloud. Ralph Waldo Emerson. CP-EmerR

Let not old age disgrace my high desire. Old Age. Sir Philip Sidney. SP-SidnP *Fr.* Arcadia.

Let not that Day Gods Friends and Servants scare. Doomes-Day. Robert Herrick. CP-HerrR

Let not the proud of heart condemn. Little Sonnet to Little Friends. Countee Cullen. CP-CullC

Let not the sad perplexity. Love Letter. Allen Ginsberg. CP-GinsA

Let not thy Tomb-stone er'e be laid by me. To Electra. Robert Herrick. CP-HerrR

Let not Woman e'er complain. Song: "Let not Woman e'er complain." Robert Burns. CP-BurnR

Let not young souls be smothered out before. Leaden-eyed, The. Nicholas Vachel Lindsay. CP-LindV

Let Observation with extensive View. Vanity of Human Wishes, The; The Tenth Satire of Juvenal Imitated. Samuel Johnson. CP-JohnS

Let other bards of angels sing. To ———: "Let other bards of angels sing." William Wordsworth. CP-WorW2; MW-WorW

Let other heroes boast their scars. Nature's Law. Robert Burns. CP-BurnR

Let other poets raise a fracas. Scotch Drink. Robert Burns. CP-BurnR

Let others look for Pearle and Gold. New-Yeeres Gift, The. Robert Herrick. CP-HerrR

Let others pray for the passenger pigeon. Elegy for the Giant Tortoises. Margaret Atwood. SP-AtwM1

Let others probe the mystery if they can. Right Thing, The. Theodore Roethke. CP-RoetT

Let others to the Printing Press[e] run fast. Posting to Printing. Robert Herrick. CP-HerrR

Let others with Parnassus swell their theme. Description of Mother Ludwell's Cave, A. Jonathan Swift. CP-SwifJ

Let out where two fears intersect, a point selected. In Transit. W. H. Auden. CP-AudeW

Let Patience Have Her Perfect Work. Christina Georgina Rossetti. CP-RosC2

Let Patience Have Her Perfect Work. Christina Georgina Rossetti. CP-RosC3

Let Persian meter modulate my verse. Rubaíyát. Jorge Luis Borges. SP-BorgJ, *tr. by* Charles Tomlinson

Let pride grow big, my rose, and let the clear[e]. On a Damask[e] Rose, Sticking upon a Lady's Breast. Thomas Carew. CP-CareT

Let some sad trumpeter stand. 'Back on Times Square, Dreaming of Times Square.' Allen Ginsberg. CP-GinsA

Let something else be / the question—. Robert Creeley. CP-CreeR

Let Something Good Be Said. James Whitcomb Riley. CP-RileJ

Let such pure hate still underprop. Friendship. Henry David Thoreau. CP-ThorH

Let that which stood in front go behind. Reversals. Walt Whitman. CP WhitW

Let the Air Circulate. Amy Clampitt. CP-ClamA

Let the bombs hang in air a moment. Taste, The. David Ignatow. SP-IgnaD

Let the boy try along this bayonet-blade. Arms and the Boy. Wilfred Owen. CP-OwenW

Let the Brothels of Paris be opened. William Blake. CP-BlakW

Let the chords commence and now. Milonga of Don Nicanor Paredes. Jorge Luis Borges. SP-BorgJ, *tr. by* Eric McHenry

Let the coin decide. Kings. Yehuda Amichai. SP-AmicYL, *tr. by* Benjamin Harshav *and* Barbara Harshav

Let the crows go by hawking their caw and caw. River Roads. Carl Sandburg. CP-SandC

Let the day glare: O memory, your tread. Ode to Fear. Allen Tate. CP-TateA

Let the Dead Bury their Dead. D. H. Lawrence. CP-LawrD

Let the downpour roil and toil! In Time of Cloudburst. Robert Frost. CP-FrosR

Let the end of all bathtubs. Watering Trough. Maxine W. Kumin. SP-KumiM

Let the foul Scene proceed. Marionettes, The. Walter De la Mare. CP-DeLaW

Let the god content himself with us. Rainer Maria Rilke. CP-RilkFr, *tr. by* A. Poulin, Jr. *Fr.* Orchards.

Let the loud men grow louder, weak weaker. We Hold These Truths to Be Self-Evident. Kenneth Patchen. CP-PatcK

Let the love-lorn lover cure insomnia. Sedative Reflection. Ogden Nash. CP-NashO

Let the lover be disgraceful, crazy. Jelaluddin Rumi. SP-Rumi *Fr.* Three Quatrains.

Let the memorial hill remember instead of me. Yehuda Amichai. SP-AmicY, *tr. by* Chana Bloch *Fr.* Songs of Zion the Beautiful.

Let the nickels and dimes explain. Carl Sandburg. CP-SandC *Fr.* People, Yes, The.

Let the old geezers jig on Penn. Mound Builders, The. Stanley Kunitz. CP-KunSC

Let the other boys from the village. Serenade: "Let the other boys from the village." Billy Collins. SP-CollB

Let the phantom love that enrolls the sparrow. Emily Dickinson. SP-DickE

Let the place of the solitaires. Place of the Solitaires, The. Wallace Stevens. CP-StevW; CP-StevWP

Let the Railsplitter Awake! Neruda's "Que dispierte el leñador." Allen Ginsberg. CP-GinsA

Let the rain kiss you. April Rain Song. Langston Hughes. CP-HughL

Let the reformers descend from the stands where they are forever brawling—let an idiot or insane person appear on each of the stands. Transpositions. Walt Whitman. CP-WhitW

Let the snake wait under. Sort of a Song, A. William Carlos Williams. CP-WilW2

Let the superstitious wife. Another. Robert Herrick. CP-HerrR

Let the Tight Lizard on the Wall. Richard Eberhart. CP-EberR

Let the weeks end as well they must. Green Woods of Unrest, The. Robert Graves. CP-GravR

Let the wind be a whirl of trumpets. Earth's Festival, The ("Let the wind be a whirl of trumpets"). G. K. Chesterton. CP-ChesG

Let Them Alone. Robinson Jeffers. CP-JeffR3

Let Them Ask Your Pardon. Carl Sandburg. CP-SandC

Let them fight it out, friend! things have gone too far. Before. Robert Browning. CP-BroR1

Let them give up the ghost, then there is nothing but dust. Put Not Your Trust in Princes. Donald Davie. CP-DaviDC

Let them go around on tiptoes. Working Principle, A. David Ignatow. SP-IgnaD

Let them not war in me. Triplex. "H. D." CP-DoolH

Let Them Rejoice in Their Beds. Christina Georgina Rossetti. CP-RosC2

Let Them Rejoice in Their Beds. Christina Georgina Rossetti. CP-RosC3

Let them return, saying you blush again for the great. Mango Tree, The. Hart Crane. CP-CranH

Let them stand still for the bullet, and stare the shooter in the eye. For the Hog Killing. Wendell Berry. CP-BerrW

Let them take to the air before. Untitled Poem: "Let them take to the air before." Alan Dugan. CP-DugaA

Let them who love their names. So Quictly the World. Eleanor Wilner. SP-WilnE

Let there be a God as large as a sunlamp to laugh his heat at you. First Psalm. Anne Sexton. SP-SextA *Fr.* O Ye Tongues.

Let there be hell again. Need For Hell, A. Laura Riding Jackson. CP-RidiL

Let There Be Light! D. H. Lawrence. CP-LawrD

"Let there be light!" God spake of old. Library, The. John Greenleaf Whittier. CP-WhitJ

Let there be Patrons, Patrons like to thee. To the Patron of Poets, M. End: Porter. Robert Herrick. CP-HerrR

Let there be ripeness, said the Lord. Their Mouths Full. David Ignatow. SP-IgnaD

Let there be treaties, bridges. Against Extremity. Charles Tomlinson. CP-TomlC; SP-TomlC

Let there stem (Gellius). Carmen 90. Catullus. CP-ZukLS *Fr.* Carmina.

Let these memorials of built stone—music's. Defense of the Islands. T. S. Eliot. CP-ElioT

Let this be scattered far and wide, laid low. Counter Mood. Countee Cullen. CP-CullC

Let those who pine in pride or in revenge. Marenghi. Percy Bysshe Shelley. CP-ShelP

Let those who will stride on their barren roads. Roadway, A. Paul Laurence Dunbar. CP-DunbP

Let those whom folly prompts to sneer. Phaedrus. CP-JohnS *Fr.* Fabulae.

Let those whose low delights to Earth are given. Faith, Hope, and Charity. Samuel Taylor Coleridge. CP-ColeS

Let thy wheel-barrow alone. To a Sexton. William Wordsworth. CP-WorW1; MW-WorW

Let us abandon then our gardens and go home. Justice Denied in Massachusetts. Edna St. Vincent Millay. CP-MillE

Let us admit it fairly, as a business people should. Lesson, The. Rudyard Kipling. CP-KiplR

Let us ask you a few questions, without rancor. For Any Member of the Security Police. Josephine Jacobsen. CP-JacoJ

Let us be circumspect, surrounded as we are. Two Voices. Edna St. Vincent Millay. CP-MillE

Let us be friends, said Walt. Communion 2. David Ignatow. SP-IgnaD

Let us be honest; the lady was not a harlot until she married a corporation. Soiled Dove. Carl Sandburg. CP-SandC

Let Us Be Men. D. H. Lawrence. CP-LawrD

Let us be thankful—not alone because. Thanksgiving. James Whitcomb Riley. CP-RileJ

Let us begin and carry up this corpse. Grammarian's Funeral, A. Robert Browning. CP-BroR1; SP-BroR

Let us begin to understand the argument. Ivory Tower, The. Allen Tate. CP-TateA

Let us call her Mrs. Mipping, but her name is legion. It Would Have Been Quicker to Walk, or, Don't Tell Me We're There Already. Ogden Nash. CP-NashO

Let us deceive ourselves a little. Secure. May Swenson. SP-SwenM

Let us do justice to the skink. Skink, The. Ogden Nash. CP-NashO

Let us forget praise and blame. Think. James Vincent Cunningham. CP-CunnJ

Let us forget that it is spring and celebrate the riderless will of five victims. Elegy for Five Old Ladies, An. Thomas Merton. CP-MertT

Let us forget. What matters it that we. James Whitcomb Riley. CP-RileJ

Let Us Gather at the River. Marge Piercy. SP-PierM

Let us give praise where praise is due. Brother Peter Considers Mulroy Drunk under the Rosebush. Josephine Jacobsen. CP-JacoJ

Let us go down, silent, to the bank of the ford. Nocturne of the Drowned Youth. Federico García Lorca. CP-GarcF, tr. by Catherine Brown

Let us go hence, my songs; she will not hear. Leave-taking, A. Algernon Charles Swinburne. SP-SwinA

Let us go now into the forest. Pine Forest. Gabriela Mistral. SP-MistG, tr. by Maria Giachetti [or Jacketti]

Let us go out of the fog, John, out of the filmy persistent drizzle on the. In the Shadow of the Palace. Carl Sandburg. CP-SandC

Let us go then, you and I. Love Song of J. Alfred Prufrock, The. T. S. Eliot. CP-ElioT

Let us go to the Animal Ball, disguised as bipeds! Animal Ball, The. Edna St. Vincent Millay. CP-MillE

Let Us Have Madness Openly. Kenneth Patchen. CP-PatcK

Let us inspect his masterwork at length. Mask, The. Charles Baudelaire. CP-BaudC, tr. by Walter Martin

Let us kill off youth. Comment on War. Langston Hughes. CP-HughL; CP-HughL1

Let us lie here in the disturbing grass. E. E. Cummings. CP-CummE

Let us listen to the confession of a companion in hell. First Delirium. The Foolish Virgin. The Infernal Bridegroom. Arthur Rimbaud. CP-RimbA, tr. by Martin Sorrell

Let us live in a lull of the long winter-winds. For C.W.B. Elizabeth Bishop. CP-BishE

Let us live, my Lesbia, and let us love each other. Catullus. CP-LaugJ, tr. by James Laughlin

Let us look into the matter of debt. First Payment Deferred. Ogden Nash. CP-NashO

Let us never forget—he said—the good lessons we have learned. Models, The. Yannis Ritsos. SP-RitsY, tr. by Kimon Friar

Let us never name that royal certitude. Unnamed Spell, The. Robert Graves. CP-GravR

Let us not live with Lear. Ripeness Is All. James Vincent Cunningham. CP-CunnJ

Let us not name what was the past. Rainer Maria Rilke. CP-RilkFr, tr. by A. Poulin, Jr. Fr. Fragments.

Let us not rash marble risk. Inscription on Any Tomb. Jorge Luis Borges. SP-BorgJ, tr. by W. S. Merwin

Let us not sit upon the ground. Elegy to Dispel Gloom, An. Lawrence Ferlinghetti. SP-FerlL

Let us not talk philosophy, drop it, Jeanne. Conversation with Jeanne. Czeslaw Milosz. CP-MiloCN Fr. Two Poems.

Let us not turn for this aside to die. At a Parting. Countee Cullen. CP-CullC

Let us now consider the ocean. Beginner's Guide to the Ocean, A. Ogden Nash. CP-NashO

"Let us now drink," I imagine patriot cry to patriot. Aftermath. Paul Muldoon. CP-MuldP

Let us now praise famous men. School Song, A. Rudyard Kipling. CP-KiplR

Let us now take time, and play. To Sappho. Robert Herrick. CP-HerrR

Let us off and search, and find a place. Recalcitrants, The. Thomas Hardy. CP-HardT

Let us pause, Love, to see her and her worth. Petrarch. CP-Petra, tr. by J. G. Nichols

Let Us play Yesterday. Emily Dickinson. CP-DickE

Let us praise death that turns pink cheeks to ashes. Praise for Death. Donald Hall. CP-HallD

Let us praise our Maker, with true passion extol Him. Anthem: "Let us praise our Maker, with true passion extol Him." W. H. Auden. CP-AudeW

Let us quit the leafy arbour. Longest Day; Addressed to My Daughter, The. William Wordsworth. CP-WorW2

Let us rejoice on our cots, for His nocturnal miracles. Lauds. John Berryman. CP-BerrJ

Let us rest ourselves a bit! Passing Hail, A. James Whitcomb Riley. CP-RileJ

Let us sing together to our God, Who made all things. Prose in Advent Time. Unknown. CP-MertT

Let Us Sing unto the Lord a New Song. Denise Levertov. SP-LeveDS Fr. Staying Alive.

Let us sit by the hissing steam radiator a winter's day, grey wind pattering. Horses and Men in the Rain. Carl Sandburg. CP-SandC

Let us sit now in the broad window. To Another. Kenneth Rexroth. CP-RexrK

Let us strip the desk for action—now we have a horse. Havana Rose. Hart Crane. CP-CranH

Let us suspect,chérie,this not very big. E. E. Cummings. CP-CummE

Let Us Talk, Let Us Laugh. D. H. Lawrence. CP-LawrD

Let us think of these. March. Archibald MacLeish. CP-MacLA

Let us (though late) at last (my Silvia) wed. To Silvia to Wed. Robert Herrick. CP-HerrR

(Let us tremble)a personal radiance sits. E. E. Cummings. CP-CummE

Let us twain walk aside from the rest. To You. Walt Whitman. CP-WhitW

Let us with a gladsom[e] mind. Psalm 136. John Milton. CP-MiltJ

Let Walton rejoice and be glad: it hath gained approval of Me. Walton-on-the-Naze. G. K. Chesterton. CP-ChesG

Let who will think of what they will. Lion and the Dog, The. Robert Creeley. CP-CreeR

Let wits contest. Posy [or Posie], The. George Herbert. CP-HerbG

Let you not say of me when I am old. Edna St. Vincent Millay. CP-MillE

Let your absence be the latest shape. Rainer Maria Rilke. CP-RilkFr, tr. by A. Poulin, Jr. Fr. Fragments.

Let your throat-song. Jelaluddin Rumi. SP-Rumi, tr. by Coleman Barks

Let yourself in by the leaf-yellow door. Beaver. Paul Muldoon. CP-MuldP

Let Zeus Record. "H. D." CP-DoolH

Letcher was Carted first about the streets. Upon Letcher: Epigram. Robert Herrick. CP-HerrR

Lethargic vs violence as alternatives of each other for los americanos, The. Anecdotes of the Late War. Charles Olson. CP-OlsoC

Lethe. Charles Baudelaire. CP-BaudC, tr. by Walter Martin

Lethe. "H. D." CP-DoolH

Lethe. Edna St. Vincent Millay. CP-MillE

"Lethe" in my flower. Emily Dickinson. CP-DickE

L'Etoile. Richard Wilbur. CP-WilbR

Let's All Hear It for Mildred Bailey! James Schuyler. CP-SchuJ

Let's assume you have neglected to write. How It Is with Family. William Stafford. SP-StafWW

Let's be jocund while we amy. End Decreed, An. Robert Herrick. CP-HerrR

Let's Be Merry. Christina Georgina Rossetti. CP-RosC2

Let's call for Hymen if agreed thou art. To Anthea. Robert Herrick. CP-HerrR

Let's contend no more, Love. Woman's Last Word, A. Robert Browning. CP-BroR1

Let's count the bodies over again. Counting Small-Boned Bodies. Robert Bly. SP-BlyR

Let's fall asleep. Far from people's. Lullaby 1957. Yehuda Amichai. SP-AmicYL, tr. by Benjamin Harshav and Barbara Harshav

Let's,from some loud unworld's most rightful wrong. E. E. Cummings. CP-CummE

Let's go—much as that dog goes. Overland to the Islands. Denise Levertov. SP-LeveDS

Let's go over to Lily's. Queen Is in the Parlor, The. Ogden Nash. CP-NashO

Let's go see old Abe. Lincoln Monument: Washington. Langston Hughes. CP-HughL; CP-HughL1

Let's leave, let's leave! See, the clouds. Rainer Maria Rilke. CP-RilkFr, tr. by A. Poulin, Jr.

Let's live in hast; use pleasures while we may. To Live Freely. Robert Herrick. CP-HerrR

Let's live suddenly without thinking. E. E. Cummings. CP-CummE

Let's live with that smal pittance that we have. Covetous Still Captives, The. Robert Herrick. CP-HerrR

Let's look at the face of tragedy. Let's see its creases. Portrait of Tragedy. Joseph Brodsky. CP-BrodJ

Let's love each other for what we are. Randall Jarrell. CP-JarrR

Let's Majeste. Maya Angelou. SP-AngeM

Let's not be obstinate, for all reveals. Rainer Maria Rilke. CP-RilkFr, tr. by A. Poulin, Jr. Fr. Fragments.

Let's Not Climb the Washington Monument Tonight. Ogden Nash. CP-NashO

Let's not do anything in par- / ticular let's not go anywhere. Still Pond No More Moving. James Laughlin. CP-LaugJ

Let's not have tea. White wine. Artemis. Olga Broumas. SP-BrouO

Let's Not Play Lotto, Let's Just Talk, Ogden Nash. CP-NashO

Let's not speak of you. Ineffable. Rainer Maria Rilke. CP-RilkFr, tr. by A. Poulin, Jr. Fr. Roses, The.

Lets now take our time. To Be Merry. Robert Herrick. CP-HerrR

Let's play a game. Lorine Niedecker. CP-NiedL

Let's pretend we are shepherds. Song: "Let's pretend we are shepherds." Rainer Maria Rilke. CP-RilkFr, tr. by A. Poulin, Jr.

Let's Roar, Your Honor. Dale R. Carver. CP-CarvR

Let's Say. Yusef Komunyakaa. CP-KomuY

Let's say it was September. Planetarium. Adam Zagajewski. SP-ZagaA, tr. by Clare Cavanagh

Let's see, how could you describe this to a listener? How can I describe this to our listeners? Idem 1. Michael Palmer. SP-PalmM

Let's see how we feel today. Expanded Composition, The. Clarence Major. SP-MajoC

Let's spin the bottle. Game, The. Stanley Kunitz. CP-KunSC

Let's start a magazine. E. E. Cummings. CP-CummE

Let's start again, says the Earth, start again. Springtime. Rainer Maria Rilke. CP-RilkFr, tr. by A. Poulin, Jr.

Let's stay by the lamp and say little. Rainer Maria Rilke. CP-RilkFr, tr. by A. Poulin, Jr. Fr. Affectionate Taxes to France.

Let's stay by the side of this dark road. Fugitives, The. Rainer Maria Rilke. CP-RilkFr, tr. by A. Poulin, Jr.

Let's step on daddy's head shout. Step on His Head. James Laughlin. CP-LaugJ

Let's stop a while, let's talk. Rainer Maria Rilke. CP-RilkFr, tr. by A. Poulin, Jr. Fr. Orchards.

Let's strive to be the best; the Gods, we know it. Parcell-gil't-Poetry. Robert Herrick. CP-HerrR

Let's take a walk. Spring. Kenneth Koch. SP-KochK

Let's take a walk, you. Poem: "Let's take a walk, you." Frank O'Hara. SP-OharF

Let's take / any. Place ("Let's take / any"). Robert Creeley. SP-CreeR

Let's talk of Judas for a while. Judas Iscariot. Countee Cullen. CP-CullC

Let's taste the trees, said chief. Work & the Labor, The. Andrei Codrescu. SP-CodrA

Let's throw it. Let's throw ice at her face, Another Day, For a Moment Slipping Back, Again the Unreal King. Muriel Rukeyser. CP-RukeM

Let's Wait. Pablo Neruda. SP-NeruP

Letsuzstayawayfromparades. O'Ryan 11-15. Charles Olson. CP-OlsoC

Letter. Wendell Berry. CP-BerrW

Letter. Raymond Carver. CP-CarvR

Letter. Robert Earl Hayden. CP-HaydR

Letter. Denise Levertov. SP-LeveDL

Letter. W. S. Merwin. SP-MerwW

Letter. Grace Paley. CP-PalGC

Letter. Wyatt Prunty. SP-PrunW

Letter, A. Yehuda Amichai. SP-AmicY, tr. by Chana Bloch

Letter, A. J. V. Cunningham. CP-CunnJ

Letter, A. James Dickey. CP-DickJ

Letter, A. Paul Laurence Dunbar. CP-DunbP

Letter, A. Grace Paley. CP-PalGC

Letter, A. Li Po. CP-WilW2

Letter, A. John Greenleaf Whittier. CP-WhitJ

Letter, The. W. H. Auden. CP-AudeW

Letter, The. Robert Creeley. CP-CreeR

Letter, The. Wilfred Owen. CP-OwenW

Letter always seemed to me, A. Emily Dickinson. SP-DickE

Letter ("Dear Mama, / Time I pay rent and get my food"). Langston Hughes. CP-HughL; CP-HughL3 Fr. Lenox Avenue Mural.

Letter for Marian, A. Thomas McGrath. SP-McGrT

Letter for Melville 1951. Charles Olson. CP-OlsoC

Letter for the End. Wyatt Prunty. SP-PrunW

Letter for Those Who Grew Up Together. John Ciardi. CP-CiarJ

Letter from a Cobbler in Patrick's Street to Jet Black, A. Thomas Sheridan. CP-SherT

Letter from a Coward to a Hero. Robert Penn Warren. CP-WarrR

Letter from a Death Bed. John Ciardi. CP-CiarJ

Letter from a flier, A. Ausonius, Epistle 7. Kenneth Rexroth. CP-RexrK

Letter from a Metaphysical Countryside. John Ciardi. CP-CiarJ

Letter from a Missionary of the Methodist Episcopal Church South, in Kansas, to a Distiguished Politician. John Greenleaf Whittier. CP-WhitJ

Letter from a Pander. John Ciardi. CP-CiarJ

Letter from a Reader. Adam Zagajewski. SP-ZagaA, tr. by Clare Cavanagh

Letter from a Rubber Raft. John Ciardi. CP-CiarJ

Letter from an Empty House. John Ciardi. CP-CiarJ

Letter from an Island. John Ciardi. CP-CiarJ

Letter from Brooklyn, A. Derek Walcott. CP-WalcD

Letter from Chicago. May Sarton. SP-SartM

Letter from Costa Brava. Charles Tomlinson. CP-TomlC

Letter from Dean Swift to Dean Smedley, A. Jonathan Swift. CP-SwifJ "Hel———am does truly wit command." CP-SherT

Letter from Dr. Sheridan to Dr. Swift, A. Thomas Sheridan. CP-SherT

Letter from Goose Creek: April. Marilyn Hacker. SP-HackM

Letter from Gussie, A. W. S. Merwin. SP-MerwW

Letter from Home, A. Mary Oliver. SP-OlivM

Letter from Ian. Lorine Niedecker. CP-NiedL

Letter from India. Louis MacNeice. CP-MacNL

Letter from Mexico (Vera Cruz, 10 February, 186–). Tristan Corbière. SP-MereW, tr. by William Meredith

Letter from our Man in Blossomtime. Louise Glück. SP-GlucL

Letter from Paul. Lorine Niedecker. CP-NiedL

Letter from Persephone. Margaret Atwood. SP-AtwM2

Letter from Phillis Wheatley, A. Robert Earl Hayden. CP-HaydR

Letter from Provence. Louise Glück. SP-GlucL

Letter from Spain. Langston Hughes. CP-HughL; CP-HughL1

Letter from the Land of Sinners. Adrienne Rich. CP-RicAE; SP-RicA2

Letter from the North. Charles Bukowski. SP-BukC2

Letter from the Pygmies, A. Theodore Weiss. SP-WeisT

Letter from Town: On a Grey Morning in March. D. H. Lawrence. CP-LawrD

Letter from Town: The Almond-Tree. D. H. Lawrence. CP-LawrD

Letter Homeward. John Ciardi. CP-CiarJ

Letter in my mailbox says you've made it, A. To the Girl Who Lives in a Tree. Audre Lorde. SP-LordA

Letter in November. Sylvia Plath. CP-PlatS

Letter in Verse. William Cowper. CP-CowpW

Letter is a joy of Earth, A. Emily Dickinson. CP-DickE

Letter is the heart's good-will in brief, A. Letter, A. J. V. Cunningham. CP-CunnJ

Letter of a Mother. Robert Penn Warren. CP-WarrR

Letter of Advice to the Reverend Dr. D-la-y, Humbly Proposed to the Consideration of a Certain Great Lord, A. Unknown, sometimes at. to Thomas Sheridan. CP-SherT

Letter of Advice to the Right Hon. John Earl of Orrery, A. Thomas Sheridan. CP-SherT

Letter of Poor Birds, The. Louis Zukofsky. CP-ZukLS

Letter of Recommendation, A. Yehuda Amichai. SP-AmicY, tr. by Chana Bloch

Letter on Liberty, A. Kenneth Patchen. CP-PatcK

Letter on the Use of Machine Guns at Weddings, A. Kenneth Patchen. CP-PatcK

Letter Poem #3. James Schuyler. CP-SchuJ

Letter Poem #2. James Schuyler. CP-SchuJ

Letter S. Carl Sandburg. CP-SandC

Letter to Tom Punsibi, Occasioned by Reading His Excellent Farce, Called Alexander's Overthrow, or, The Downfall of Babylon, A. Unknown. CP-SherT

Letter to a Friend. Robert Penn Warren. CP-WarrR

Letter to a Friend, A. James Whitcomb Riley. CP-RileJ

Letter to a Friend about Girls. Philip Larkin. CP-LarkP

Letter to a Friend: Who Is Nancy Daum? James Schuyler. CP-SchuJ

Letter to a Policemen in Kansas City, A. Kenneth Patchen. CP-PatcK

Letter to a Purist. Sylvia Plath. CP-PlatS

Letter to a Young Father in Exile. John Logan. CP-LogaJ

Letter to America, A. Thomas Merton. CP-MertT

Letter to an Archaeologist. Joseph Brodsky. CP-BrodJ

Letter to an Aspiring Junkie. Maya Angelou. SP-AngeM

Letter to an English Poet. Donald Hall. CP-HallD

Letter to an Old Love. Tennessee Williams. CP-WillT

Letter to Anne, A. Langston Hughes. CP-HughL; CP-HughL1

Letter to Any Friend, A. Laura Riding Jackson. CP-RidiL

Letter to be Disguised as a Gas Bill. Marge Piercy. SP-PierM

Letter to Bee. Emily Dickinson. CP-DickE

Letter to Bob Kaufman. Yusef Komunyakaa. CP-KomuY

Letter to Curtis Bradford, A. Donald Davie. CP-DaviDC

Letter to Dante. John Ciardi. CP-CiarJ

Letter to Doctor Ingelo, A. Andrew Marvell. CP-MarvA

Letter to Donald Fall. Alan Dugan. CP-DugaA

Letter to Eve. Alan Dugan. CP-DugaA

Letter to Ezra Pound. Andrei Codrescu. SP-CodrA

Letter to Graham and Anna. Louis MacNeice. CP-MacNL

Letter to Her. Robert Bly. SP-BlyR

Letter to Her Husband, Absent upon Public[k] Employment, A. Anne Bradstreet. CP-BradA

Letter to His Brother. John Berryman. CP-BerrJ

Letter to Hitler, A. James Laughlin. CP-LaugJ

Letter to James Stephens, A. May Sarton. SP-SartM

Letter to J———s T———t, Gl—nc———r. Robert Burns. CP-BurnR

Letter to John Fuller. James Fenton. SP-FentJ

Letter to John Logan from La Push. Sam Hamill. SP-HamiS

Letter to Lord Byron. W. H. Auden. CP-AudeW

Letter to Lucy Larcom. John Greenleaf Whittier. CP-WhitJ

Letter to Man's Reasonable Soul. Laura Riding Jackson. CP-RidiL

Letter to Marek about a Photograph, A. Denise Levertov. SP-LeveDL

Letter to Maria Gisborne. Percy Bysshe Shelley. CP-ShelP

Letter to Maxine Sullivan. Hayden Carruth. CP-CarHS

Letter to Mother. John Ciardi. CP-CiarJ

Letter to My Friends, A. Thomas Merton. CP-MertT

Letter to My Son. John Logan. CP-LogaJ

Letter to N.Y. Elizabeth Bishop. CP-BishE

Letter to Ogden Nash. Dorothy Parker. CP-ParkD

Letter to Pablo Antonio Cuadra Concerning Giants, A. Thomas Merton. CP-MertT

Letter to Pierre Emmanuel. Kathleen Jessie Raine. SP-RainK

Letter to Robert Benchley; Roughing It in the Country at the Birches, Maine. Dorothy Parker. CP-ParkD

Letter to Robert Hedin. Sam Hamill. SP-HamiS

Letter to Sara Hutchinson. Samuel Taylor Coleridge. CP-ColeS

Letter to the Academy. Langston Hughes. CP-HughL; CP-HughL1

Letter to the Countess of Denbigh. Richard Crashaw.

Letter to the Front. Muriel Rukeyser. CP-RukeM

Letter to the Heart. W. S. Merwin. SP-MerwW

Letter to the Inventors of a Tradition, A. Kenneth Patchen. CP-PatcK

Letter to the Lady Carey, and Mistress Essex Rich, from Amiens, A. John Donne. CP-DonnJ; MW-DonnJ

Letter to the Liberals, A. Kenneth Patchen. CP-PatcK

Letter to the Old Men. Kenneth Patchen. CP-PatcK

Letter to the Reverend Dr. Sheridan, A. Jonathan Swift. CP-SwifJ

Letter to the Young Men, A. Kenneth Patchen. CP-PatcK

Letter to Thomas Clark 22:VII:71 from Bolinas Where He Sat beside Me to Help to Write it, The. Philip Whalen. SP-WhalP

Letter to Those Who Are About to Die. Kenneth Patchen. CP-PatcK

Letter to Uehata. Charles Tomlinson. SP-TomlC

Letter to Virginia Johnson. John Ciardi. CP-CiarJ

Letter to William Kinter of Muhlenberg, A. Denise Levertov. SP-LeveDP

Letter to Wystan Hugh Auden, A. Kenneth Rexroth. CP-RexrK

Letter to Yvor Winters, A. Kenneth Rexroth. CP-RexrK

Letter, Unposted. Muriel Rukeyser. CP-RukeM

Letter Written by Sir H. G. and J. D. Alternis Vicibus, A. John Donne. CP-DonnJ; MW-DonnJ

Letter Written during a January Northeaster. Anne Sexton. CP-SextA

Letter Written on a Ferry while Crossing Long Island Sound. Anne Sexton. CP-SextA; SP-SextA

Letters. Jane Cooper. CP-CoopJ

Letters. Ralph Waldo Emerson. CP-EmerR

Letters, The. Louise Glück. SP-GlucL

Letters always just evade the hand, The. Mail Call. Randall Jarrell. CP-JarrR

Letters and the telegrams once sent, The. Stranger, The. Jorge Luis Borges. SP-BorgJ, tr. by Alastair Reid

Letters ask, The. Notes from India. May Sarton. SP-SartM

Letters come, the phone rings, you sit by your window. Holding Out. Jane Cooper. CP-CoopJ

Letters for the Dead. Philip Levine. SP-LeviP

Letters from a Father. Mona Van Duyn. SP-VanDM

Letters from Amherst. Charles Tomlinson. CP-TomlC

Letters from Jerusalem. Amy Clampitt. CP-ClamA

Letters from the Ming Dynasty. Joseph Brodsky. CP-BrodJ, tr. by Derek Walcott

Letters I never answered. New World. Adam Zagajewski. SP-ZagaA, tr. by Clare Cavanagh

Letters: March 1969. Adrienne Rich. CP-RicAE; SP-RicA2

Letters of the alphabet, The. Headache. Wallace Stevens. CP-StevWP

Letters of the Dead, The. Wisława Szymborska. SP-SzymW, tr. by Stanislaw Barańczak and Clare Cavanagh

Letters of the Jews as strict as flames, The. Alphabet, The. Karl Shapiro. SP-ShapK

Letters she left to clutter up the desk. Gesture by a Lady with an Assumed Name, A. James Wright. CP-WrigJ

Letters to a Roman Friend. Joseph Brodsky. CP-BrodJ, tr. by George L. Kline

Letters to Che: Canto Bilingue. Thomas Merton. CP-MertT

Letters to Dead Imagists. Carl Sandburg. CP-SandC

Letters to Dr. Y. Anne Sexton. CP-SextA

  "I called him *Comfort*." SP-SextA

  "I'm dreaming the My Lai soldier again." SP-SextA

  "It's music you've never heard." SP-SextA

  "What has it come to, Dr. Y." SP-SextA

Letter's Triumph, The. Thomas Hardy. CP-HardT

Letting go / in order to hold on. How Poems Are Made: A Discredited View. Alice Walker. CP-WalkA

Letting go, woman, is not as easy as pride. Blues / for J.C. Olga Broumas. SP-BrouO

Letting his wisdom be the whole of love. World and the Child, The. James Merrill. SP-MerrJ

Letting in the Jungle. Rudyard Kipling. *Fr.* Second Jungle Book, The.

Letting midnight / out on bail. Jam Session. Langston Hughes. CP-HughL; CP-HughL3

Letting the eye descend from reeking stack. Glance from the Bridge, A. Richard Wilbur. CP-WilbR

Letting You Go. William Stafford. SP-StafWW

Lettres d'un Soldat. Wallace Stevens. CP-StevWP

Level Light. William Stafford. SP-StafWW

Leveling of the water, its increase, The. Winter Rain, The. Wendell Berry. CP-BerrW

Levelled Churchyard, The. Thomas Hardy. CP-HardT

Leven. Robert Herrick. CP-HerrR

Leviathan. George Oppen. CP-OppGN

Leviora. Ezra Pound. CP-PoEar

Levitation. A. R. Ammons. CP-AmmoA

Levity. Donald Davie. CP-DaviDC

Lew Welch just turned up one day. For/From Lew. Gary Snyder. CP-SnydG

Lewis and Clark Overheard in Conversation. James Tate. SP-TateJ

Lewis D. Hayes. James Whitcomb Riley. CP-RileJ

Lewti. Samuel Taylor Coleridge. CP-ColeS

Lexicon ad finem longo luctamine tandem. Gnothi Seauton (Post Lexicon Anglicanum Auctum et Emendatum). Samuel Johnson. CP-JohnS

Lexington. John Greenleaf Whittier. CP-WhitJ

L'Homme et La Bête. Philip Levine. SP-LeviP

Li Bel Chasteus. Ezra Pound. CP-PoEar

Li Po. Charles Olson. CP-OlsoC

Li Po. Arthur Sze. SP-SzeA

Li Po who? "Everybody's Reading Li Po" Silkscreened on a Purple T-Shirt. Yusef Komunyakaa. CP-KomuY

Liadan and Curithir. Robert Graves. CP-GravR

Liaison. D. H. Lawrence. CP-LawrD

Liar, The. John Donne. CP-DonnJ; MW-DonnJ

Liar goes in fine clothes, A. Liars, The. Carl Sandburg. CP-SandC

Liars. Langston Hughes. CP-HughL; CP-HughL1

Liars, The. Carl Sandburg. CP-SandC

'Lias! 'Lias! Bless de Lawd! In the Morning. Paul Laurence Dunbar. CP-DunbP

Libation. A. R. Ammons. CP-AmmoA

Libation. Lucille Clifton. SP-ClifL

Libation. Denise Levertov. SP-LeveDL; SP-LeveDS

Libel on the Reverend Dr. Delany and His Excellency John, Lord Carteret. Jonathan Swift. CP-SwifJ

Libel Summons. Robert Burns. CP-BurnR

Liber, of all thy friends, thou sweetest care. Epigramma Martialis. Lib. VIII. lxxvii. The Same Translated. Ben Jonson. CP-JonsB

Liberal Imagination, The. Miller Williams. CP-WillM

Liberal Party, The. G. K. Chesterton. CP-ChesG

Liberation. Louise Glück. SP-GlucL

Liberator, The. Derek Walcott. CP-WalcD

Liberator Explodes, The. James Dickey. CP-DickJ

Libertad! Igualdad! Fraternidad! William Carlos Williams. CP-WilW1

Libertas & natale solum. Whitshed's Motto on His Coach. Jonathan Swift. CP-SwifJ

Libertatis Sacra Fames. Oscar Wilde. CP-WildO

Libertine, The. Louis MacNeice. CP-MacNL

Liberty. Charles Bukowski. SP-BukC1

Liberty. Robert Herrick. CP-HerrR

Liberty. Archibald MacLeish. CP-MacLA

Liberty. Fernando Pessoa. SP-PessF, tr. by Susan M. Brown and Edwin Honig

Liberty. James Whitcomb Riley. CP-RileJ

Liberty. Percy Bysshe Shelley. CP-ShelP

Liberty. Sir Thomas Wyatt. CP-WyatT

Liberty and Peace, a Poem. Phillis Wheatley. CP-WheaP

Liberty for the few. Fanny Howe. SP-HoweF *Fr.* Vineyard, The.

Liberty's Old Old Story. D. H. Lawrence. CP-LawrD

Librarian, The. Charles Olson. CP-OlsoC; SP-OlsoC

Libraries consumed by passionate eyes, The. Girl in a Library. Marya Alexandrovna Zaturenska. SP-ZatuM

Library, The. John Greenleaf Whittier. CP-WhitJ

Library Revisited, The. Theodore Weiss. SP-WeisT

Library Scene. Robert Pinsky. CP-PinsR

License plate was another state and year, The. Mecanic on Duty at All Times. Miller Williams. CP-WillM

License to Carry a Gun, The. Andrei Codrescu. SP-CodrA

Licentious Person, A. John Donne. CP-DonnJ; MW-DonnJ

Lichtenberg. Rudyard Kipling. CP-KiplR

Licked in the palm of my hand. Wild Blessings. Lucille Clifton. SP-ClifL

Lictor or heavy slave would wear it best. Julian the Apostate. Thom Gunn. CP-GunnT

Lictors bundl'd up their rods: beside, The. Cunctation in Correction. Robert Herrick. CP-HerrR

Lid, The. Charles Baudelaire. CP-BaudC, tr. by Walter Martin

Liddell and Scott. Thomas Hardy. CP-HardT

Liddell, the Oxford lexicographer. Fourth of July, The. Richard Wilbur. CP-WilbR

Lidless, lipless, opensocketed. Exit. Thomas Kinsella. CP-KinsT

Lie a-bed, / Sleepy head, / Shut up eyes, bo-peep. Christina Georgina Rossetti. CP-RosC2

Lie, adolescent weapon. Lies 1. Rainer Maria Rilke. CP-RilkFr, tr. by A. Poulin, Jr.

Lie down and rest—the fight is done. Rodric Lesley. 1830. Emily Jane Brontë. CP-BronE

Lie down upon your side. Process, The. May Swenson. SP-SwenM

Lie here, without a record of thy worth. Tribute to the Memory of the Same Dog. William Wordsworth. CP-WorW1

Lie in bed and watch the night. At Darragh's I. James Schuyler. CP-SchuJ

Lie of 10, or the Concept of Zero, The. Charles Olson. CP-OlsoC

Lie, plaything we shatter. Lies 2. Rainer Maria Rilke. CP-RilkFr, tr. by A. Poulin, Jr.

Lie shone in her face before she spoke it, The. Nike. James Merrill. SP-MerrJ

Lie still, be still, love, be thou not shaken. Song, the Brain-Coral. Muriel Rukeyser. CP-RukeM

Lie still, my restive heart, lie still. What Is That to Thee? Follow Thou Me. Christina Georgina Rossetti. CP-RosC2

Lie Still, Sleep Becalmed. Dylan Thomas. CP-ThomD

Lie, that we come from water, A. Landcrab I. Margaret Atwood. SP-AtwM2

Lie, The. Rudyard Kipling. Fr Naulahka, The.

Lie, The. Maya Angelou. SP-AngeM

Lie, The. Sir Walter Ralegh. CP-RaleW

Lie there, in sweat and dream, I do, and "there." What I See. Muriel Rukeyser. CP-RukeM

Liebe, meine liebe, I had not hoped. If It Were Not for You. Hayden Carruth. CP-CarHS

Liebestod. Dorothy Parker. CP-ParkD

Lied von Castelli. George Meredith. CP-MerG2

Lief Ericson crossed the sea. Lief the Lucky. Carl Sandburg. CP-SandC

Lief the Lucky. Carl Sandburg. CP-SandC

Lies. D. H. Lawrence. CP-LawrD

Lies 1. Rainer Maria Rilke. CP-RilkFr, tr. by A. Poulin, Jr.

Lies 2. Rainer Maria Rilke. CP-RilkFr, tr. by A. Poulin, Jr.

Lies 3. Rainer Maria Rilke. CP-RilkFr, tr. by A. Poulin, Jr.

Lies about Love. D. H. Lawrence. CP-LawrD

Lies of the Poem. Michael Palmer. SP-PalmM

Lieutenant governor sits in the center, The. Impressions of the New Mexico Legislature. Arthur Sze. SP-SzeA

Lieutenant ordered me to ask Abdhul, The. Sorrow of Obedience, The. John Ciardi. CP-CiarJ

Life. Yehuda Amichai. SP-AmicYL, tr. by Benjamin Harshav and Barbara Harshav

Life. Elizabeth Barrett Browning. CP-BroEB

Life. Samuel Taylor Coleridge. CP-ColeS

Life. Walter De la Mare. CP-DeLaW

Life. Paul Laurence Dunbar. CP-DunbP

Life. Ralph Waldo Emerson. CP-EmerR

Life. George Herbert. CP-HerbG

Life. Grace Paley. CP-PalGC

Life. Henry David Thoreau. CP-ThorH

Life. Jones Very. CP-VeryJ

Life. Walt Whitman. CP-WhitW

Life, A. Howard Nemerov. CP-NemeH

Life, A. Gregory Orr. SP-OrrG

Life, A. Sylvia Plath. CP-PlatS

Life, A. Yannis Ritsos. SP-RitsY, tr. by John Stathatos

Life, The. David Ignatow. SP-IgnaD

Life, The. James Wright. CP-WrigJ

Life, a Ritual, A. William Stafford. SP-StafWW

Life and Death. Richard Eberhart. CP-EberR

Life and Death. Christina Georgina Rossetti. CP-RosC1

Life and Death. Jones Very. CP-VeryJ

Life and Death. Walt Whitman. CP-WhitW

Life and Death and a Letter to My Mother beyond Them Both. Philip Whalen. SP-WhalP

Life, and Death, and Giants. Emily Dickinson. CP-DickE

Life and Death at Sunrise. Thomas Hardy. CP-HardT

Life and Death of the Cantata System, The. Alan Dugan. CP-DugaA

Life and Genuine Character of Dr Swift, The. Jonathan Swift. CP-SwifJ

Life and Letters. Adrienne Rich. CP-RicAE

Life and Love. Elizabeth Barrett Browning. CP-BroEB

Life and the Human Consciousness. D. H. Lawrence. CP-LawrD

Life & Times of Billy Boy, The. Yusef Komunyakaa. CP-KomuY

Life around Us, The. Denise Levertov. SP-LeveDS

Life as Visionary Spirit. Richard Eberhart. CP-EberR

Life at Bolinas. The Last of California. Philip Whalen. SP-WhalP

Life at the Lake. James Whitcomb Riley. CP-RileJ

Life at War. Denise Levertov. SP-LeveDP; SP-LeveDS

Life boosts herself rapidly at me. E. E. Cummings. CP-CummE

Life close to death. First Rain on a Burned Car, The. Yehuda Amichai. SP-AmicYL, tr. by Benjamin Harshav and Barbara Harshav

Life comes a-hurrying. For R.C.B. Dorothy Parker. CP-ParkD

Life Comparison. Alan Dugan. CP-DugaA

Life contracts and death is expected. Death of a Soldier, The. Wallace Stevens. CP-StevW; CP-StevWP

Life Cycle of Common Man. Howard Nemerov. CP-NemeH

Life deflowers itself / petal by petal. Deflowering. Lawrence Ferlinghetti. SP-FerlL

Life Doesn't Frighten Me. Maya Angelou. SP-AngeM

Life Encompassed. Donald Davie. CP-DaviDC

Life flies from us, and does not pause one hour. Petrarch. CP-Petra, tr. by J. G. Nichols

Life flows down to death; we cannot bind. "Immurata" Sister, An. Christina Georgina Rossetti. CP-RosC2

Life flows to death as rivers to the sea. James Vincent Cunningham. CP-CunnJ

Life / For him. Sport. Langston Hughes. CP-HughL; CP-HughL1

Life from the Litéless. Robinson Jeffers. CP-JefR2

Life goes on living. Manila. Robert Creeley. SP-CreeR

Life Hidden. Christina Georgina Rossetti. CP-RosC3

Life hurl my. E. E. Cummings. CP-CummE

Life I have led, The. In the 51st State. Ted Berrigan. SP-BerrT

Life in a Love. Robert Browning. CP-BroR1

Life in Death. Samuel Taylor Coleridge. CP-ColeS

Life in its brief episodes. Austere Poem. Richard Eberhart. CP-EberR

Life-in-Love. Dante Gabriel Rossetti. CW-RossD Fr. House of Life, The.

Life in the Boondocks. A. R. Ammons. CP-AmmoA

Life in the City: In Memoriam Edward Gibbon. Philip Whalen. SP-WhalP

Life in the Forest. Denise Levertov. SP-LeveDL

Life in the throat of my love leaps. Love Sleeping. May Swenson. SP-SwenM

Life is a summer's day. Henry David Thoreau. CP-ThorH

Life is death we're lengthy at. Emily Dickinson. SP-DickE

Life Is Fine. Langston Hughes. CP-HughL; CP-HughL2

Life is fleeting, joy is fleeting. Time of Waiting, The. Christina Georgina Rossetti. CP-RosC3

Life is for the living. Note in Music. Langston Hughes. CP-HughL; CP-HughL1

Life is funny. Peograms. Charles Olson. CP-OlsoC

Life is great / Men are small. Ralph Waldo Emerson. CP-EmerR

Life is just a bowl of cherries. Guaranteed Antique. Carl Sandburg. CP-SandC

Life is long in the desert. Wallace Stevens. CP-StevWP

Life is more true than reason will deceive. E. E. Cummings. CP-CummE

Life is most dear; and then, it seems to me. Petrarch. CP-Petra, tr. by J. G. Nichols

Life Is Motion. Wallace Stevens. CP-StevW; CP-StevWP

Life is not at all what you might think it to be. Some Words. John Ashbery. SP-AshbJ

Life is not sweet. One day it will be sweet. Life and Death. Christina Georgina Rossetti. CP-RosC1

Life is nothing without religion. Religion. D. H. Lawrence. CP-LawrD

Life is over and you are its. They, to Me. Donald Davie. CP-DaviDC

Life is random as a rolled pair of dice. Paradise. Gregory Orr. SP-OrrG

Life is so strong a vision. Emily Dickinson. SP-DickE

Life Is the Body's [or Bodies] Light. Robert Herrick. CP-HerrR

Life is the finest secret. Emily Dickinson. SP-DickE

Life is the story of a body, you say. Dialectic. Charles Tomlinson. CP-TomlC

Life Is Trying to Be Life. Ted Hughes. SP-HughTN

Life—is what we make it. Emily Dickinson. CP-DickE

Life is your privilege, not your belonging. Forty Years. Wendell Berry. CP-BerrW

Life itself like championship chess. Deep Chess. Lawrence Ferlinghetti. SP-FerlL

Life Laughs Onward. Thomas Hardy. CP-HardT

Life-Lesson, A. James Whitcomb Riley. CP-RileJ

Life lived us, not we life. We, as bees sip. Fernando Pessoa. SP-PessF Fr. Inscriptions.

Life longs to a perfection it never achieves. Supreme Authority of the Imagination, The. Richard Eberhart. CP-EberR

Life Moving More Rapidly than Hands Can Manage. William Dickey. SP-DickW

Life ne'er exulted in so rich a prize. Fragment, Which Was Meant for the Beginning of an Elegy on the Late Miss Burnet of Monboddo, A. Robert

Burns. CP-BurnR

Life of, The. Theodore Weiss. SP-WeisT

Life of Art, The. Denise Levertov. SP-LeveDS

Life of hope deferred too often is, A. Redeeming the Time. Christina Georgina Rossetti. CP-RosC2

Life of Literature, The. Philip Whalen. SP-WhalP

Life of my life, take not so soon thy flight. To His Dying Brother, Master William Herrick. Robert Herrick. CP-HerrR

Life of Others, The. Denise Levertov. SP-LeveDL; SP-LeveDS

Life of Poetry, The. James Tate. SP-TateJ

Life of Service, The. Donald Davie. CP-DaviDC

Life of the Dead, The. Laura Riding Jackson. CP-RidiL

Life of the Flower, The. Jones Very. CP-VeryJ

Life of the Otter, The. Thom Gunn. CP-GunnT

Life of the Party, The. Ogden Nash. CP-NashO

Life of the world depends on that he is, The. Wild Ducks, People and Distances. Wallace Stevens. CP-StevW; CP-StevWP

Life on a Battleship. Wallace Stevens. CP-StevWP

Life on earth. Mr. Pope. Thomas Lux. SP-LuxT

Life on Film of St. Theresa, The. Andrei Codrescu. SP-CodrA

Life out of Death. Christina Georgina Rossetti. CP-RosC3

Life pays no mind to dying lights. End of the Day, The. Charles Baudelaire. CP-BaudC, *tr. by* Walter Martin

Life relinquishing, by life relinquished. Burial, The. Archibald MacLeish. CP-MacLA

Life Sentence. Adam Zagajewski. SP-ZagaA

Life-Size Is Too Large. Laura Riding Jackson. CP-RidiL

Life sleeps in this tired old horse, but might. Few Snorts from a Wild One, A. William Stafford. SP-StafWW

Life spent seeking it, A. High Quality Information. Gary Snyder. CP-SnydG

Life stood on the top stair a moment. Resurgam. Allen Tate. CP-TateA

Life Story. Ai. SP-Ai

Life Story. Tennessee Williams. CP-WillT

Life Story, A. Clarence Major. SP-MajoC

Life taught me long ago. To Be a Poet. Jaroslav Seifert. SP-SeifJ, *tr. by* Ewald Osers

Life Term, A. James Whitcomb Riley. CP-RileJ

Life that breaks apart, The. Delta. Eugenio Montale. CP-MontE, *tr. by* Jonathan Galassi

Life that tied too tight escapes, The. Emily Dickinson. CP-DickE

Life that was born today / Must make no stay. Christina Georgina Rossetti. CP-RosC2

Life the Beloved. Dante Gabriel Rossetti. CW-RossD *Fr.* House of Life, The.

Life there was is, The. In Waking. Robert Duncan. SP-DuncR

Life They Lead, The. David Ignatow. SP-IgnaD

Life Transcendent. Nicholas Vachel Lindsay. CP-LindV

Life wakeful over all knew no gradation. Unity with Nature. Samuel Taylor Coleridge. CP-ColeS

Life was a mute wrenching of the heart. Outdoor Gallery, An. Thomas Kinsella. CP-KinsT

Life was mine full of the close concern, A. Love. Paul Laurence Dunbar. CP-DunbP

Life we have is very great, The. Emily Dickinson. CP-DickE

Life, were thy pains as are the pains of hell. Edna St. Vincent Millay. CP-MillE

Life with a Hole in It, The. Philip Larkin. CP-LarkP

Life with her weary eyes. Song: "Life with her weary eyes." Marya Alexandrovna Zaturenska. SP-ZatuM

Life with yon Lambs, like day, is just begun. Composed on a May Morning. William Wordsworth. CP-WorW2

Life Work. William Stafford. SP-StafWW

Life, you're beautiful (I say). Allegro Ma Non Troppo. Wisława Szymborska. SP-SzymW, *tr. by* Stanisław Barańczak *and* Clare Cavanagh

Lifeguard, The. James Dickey. CP-DickJ

Lifelike. Heather McHugh. SP-McHuH

Lifeline Train to Puerto Limón. Robert Stock. SP-StocR

Lifelong ago such days. Kathleen Jessie Raine. SP-RainK

Lifelong the way—. Binah. Kathleen Jessie Raine. SP-RainK

Lifelong to be / Seemed the fair colour of the time. Musical Box, The. Thomas Hardy. CP-HardT

Lifer. Sam Hamill. SP-HamiS

Lifers file into the hall, The. In the Cage. Robert Lowell. SP-LoweR

Life's a jail where men have common lot. Gamblers, The. Nicholas Vachel Lindsay. CP-LindV

Life's a many-dimensioned game of go. Go As Played in the Best Circles; Or Rotten Axe-Handle. Robert Stock. SP-StocR

Life's all getting and giving. Wishing-Caps, The. Rudyard Kipling. CP-KiplR *Fr.* Kim.

Life's bad on just a bit, but. Vivitur Parvo Malè, Sed Canebat. Thomas Sheridan. CP-SherT, *tr. by* Robert Hogan

Life's buried treasure's buried deeper still. Elderly Sex. John Updike. CP-UpdiJ

Life's final hours: brought there by many a year. Michelangelo Buonarroti. CP-Miche, *tr. by* John Frederick Nims

Life's Handicap. Rudyard Kipling.
  At the End of the Passage.
    "Sky is lead, and our faces are red, The." CP-KiplR
  Courting of Dinah Shadd, The.
    Private Ortheris's Song. CP-KiplR
  Head of the District, The.
    "There's a convict more in the Central Jail." CP-KiplR
  Man Who Was, The.
    "Earth gave up her dead that tide, The." CP-KiplR
  My New-Cut Ashlar. CP-KiplR
  Return of Imray, The.
    "Doors were wide, the story saith, The." CP-KiplR
  Without Benefit of Clergy.
    "Before my Spring I garnered Autumn's gain." CP-KiplR

Life's norm is lost: no doubt it is put away with Plato's. What of It? Robinson Jeffers. CP-JefR3

Life's Parallels, A. Christina Georgina Rossetti. CP-RosC2

Life's quick and brief; the more my days fly by. Michelangelo Buonarroti. CP-Miche, *tr. by* John Frederick Nims

Life's Rendezvous. Countee Cullen. CP-CullC

Life's Trades. Emily Dickinson. CP-DickE

Life's Tragedy. Paul Laurence Dunbar. CP-DunbP

Life's Valentines. Dorothy Parker. CP-ParkD

Life's Work. Maxine W. Kumin. SP-KumiM

Lifetime is for two. Emily Dickinson. SP-DickE

Liffey Hill, The. Thomas Kinsella. CP-KinsT

Lift again the stately emblem on the Bay State's rusted shield. Pine-Tree, The. John Greenleaf Whittier. CP-WhitJ

Lift it—with the Feathers. Emily Dickinson. CP-DickE

Lift me into heaven. Sufi Sam Christian. Robert Creeley. SP-CreeR

Lift my head, help me up. Euripides. CP-DoolH *Fr.* Hippolytus.

Lift through the Breaking Day. Philip Larkin. CP-LarkP

Lift to the spirit, when everything fell into place!, A. Cheshire. Donald Davie. CP-DaviDC

Lift up thine eyes to seek the invisible. Christina Georgina Rossetti. CP-RosC2

Lift up to heav'n, sad wretch, thy heavy spright. Thomas Campion. CP-CampT

Lift up your eyes on high. Erige Cor Tuum ad Me in Caelum. "H. D." CP-DoolH

Lift up your heads: in life, in death. To Them That Mourn. G. K. Chesterton. CP-ChesG

"Lift up your hearts." "We lift them up." Ah me! Sursum Corda. Christina Georgina Rossetti. CP-RosC2

Lift your flowers. Chicory and Daisies. William Carlos Williams. CP-WilW1

Lift your left hand. Sign Language. Clarence Major. SP-MajoC

Lifting Belly. Gertrude Stein. CP-SteiG

Lifting Illegal Nets by Flashlight. James Wright. CP-WrigJ

Lifting my coffee cup, I notice a caterpillar crawling. Caterpillar, A. Robert Bly. SP-BlyR

Lifts heavily / and cloud and sea. Sun, The. William Carlos Williams. CP-WilW1

Light. Rae Armantrout. SP-ArmaA

Light. Allen Tate. CP-TateA

Light. Louis Zukofsky. CP-ZukLS

Light, The. Paul Laurence Dunbar. CP-DunbP

Light, The. Lawrence Ferlinghetti. SP-FerlL

Light, The. Carolyn Kizer. CP-KizeC

Light, a form / shadow at the edge of the window, a, A. Medallion. Robert Creeley. CP-CreeR

Light, a glimmer outlines the crest of the mountain walls, A. Song of Labour, The. G. K. Chesterton. CP-ChesG

Light, a winged, & a holy thing, A. Poet at Forty, The. Howard Nemerov. CP-NemeH

Light again, and the one who brings light! Shreds of Steam. Jelaluddin Rumi. SP-Rumi, *tr. by* Coleman Barks

Light along the hills in the morning, The. Notice What This Poem Is Not Doing. William Stafford. SP-StafWW

Light and Moonbells. Carl Sandburg. CP-SandC

Light and Shadow. Hugh MacDiarmid. SP-MacDH

Light as a skiff, manoeuvrable. Wolfe Tone. Seamus Heaney. SP-HeanSO

Light at a window. Someone up. White Night. Adrienne Rich. SP-RicA2

Light Baggage. Alice Walker. CP-WalkA

Light beats upon me, The. Mid-day. "H. D." CP-DoolH

Light became her grace and dwelt among, The. Ballatetta. Ezra Pound. CP-PoEar

Light Becomes Darkness. William Carlos Williams. CP-WilW1

Light beyond compare is the light I saw, The. Incomparable Light, The. Richard Eberhart. CP-EberR

Light Blue Above. James Schuyler. CP-SchuJ

LIght blue above, darker below, lightly roughened by the stirring air. Light Blue Above. James Schuyler. CP-SchuJ

Light Breaks Where No Sun Shines. Dylan Thomas. CP-ThomD

Light Breather, A. Theodore Roethke. CP-RoetT

Light Brown. Charles Bukowski. SP-BukC1

Light burns through blood. Through Closed Eyes. Charles Tomlinson. CP-TomlC

Light by the barn that shines all night, The. William Stafford. SP-StafW; SP-StafWW

Light catches the sudden metal of the streams. Couplet. Charles Tomlinson. CP-TomlC

Light clarity avocado salad in the morning. Poem: "Light clarity avocado salad in the morning." Frank O'Hara. SP-OharF

Light colourless doth colour all things else. Truly the Light Is Sweet. Christina Georgina Rossetti. CP-RosC2

Light come from my head, A. Island, The. James Dickey. CP-DickJ

Light comes back with Columbine; she brings, The. Edna St. Vincent Millay. CP-MillE

Light Comes Brighter, The. Theodore Roethke. CP-RoetT

Light cursed falling in a singular block. E. E. Cummings. CP-CummE

Light enters and I remember who I am; he is there, The. Watcher, The. Jorge Luis Borges. SP-BorgJ, tr. by Alastair Reid

Light exists in Spring, A. Emily Dickinson. CP-DickE

Light eyes would have been more fortunate. Interview, The. Robert Creeley. CP-CreeR

Light fails, in crossing a river. Awaiting the Swimmer. James Dickey. CP-DickJ

Light falling on that filled will drives. Muriel Rukeyser. CP-RukeM

Light falls the rain-drop on the fallen leaf. Touch of Loving Hands, The. James Whitcomb Riley. CP-RileJ

Light flares from the tombstones. Poem: "Light flares from the tombstones." Thomas McGrath. SP-McGrT

Light flower leaves its little core, The. Changed Woman, The. Louise Bogan. CP-BogaL

Light flows our war of mocking words, and yet. Buried Life, The. Matthew Arnold. SP-ArnoM

Light foot hears you and the brightness begins, The. Poem Beginning with a Line by Pindar, A. Robert Duncan. SP-DuncR

Light from Above. Richard Eberhart. CP-EberR

Light from Canada. James Schuyler. CP-SchuJ

Light from the planet Venus, soon to set. Evening-Star. Louise Bogan. CP-BogaL

Light from Within, The. Jones Very. CP-VeryJ

Light going out in the forehead, A. Swimming by Night. James Merrill. SP-MerrJ

Light hearted, careless, shall I take my way. Loves Farewell. Henry David Thoreau. CP-ThorH

Light Hearted William. William Carlos Williams. CP-WilW1

Light human nature is too lightly tost. Discontent. Elizabeth Barrett Browning. CP-BroEB

Light, in its daylong play, refuses, The. Above the Rio Grande. Charles Tomlinson. SP-TomlC

Light in the Eyes, The. Miller Williams. CP-WillM

Light in the Locust Tree. Hayden Carruth. CP-CarHS

Light in the morning, The. Kitchen. Robert Creeley. CP-CreeR

Light in the window seemed perpetual, The. Room above the Square, The. Stephen Spender. CP-SpenS

Light into the olive entered. After Greece. James Merrill. SP-MerrJ

Light is like a spider, The. Tattoo. Wallace Stevens. CP-StevW; CP-StevWP

Light is our sorrow for it ends tomorrow. Whither the Tribes Go Up, Even the Tribes of the Lord. Christina Georgina Rossetti. CP-RosC2

Light is refracted at regular intervals on the wall, The. Indications. Yannis Ritsos. SP-RitsY, tr. by Kimon Friar and Kostas Myrsiades

Light Is Speech. Marianne Craig Moore. CP-MoorM

Light is sufficient to itself. Emily Dickinson. CP-DickE

Light Journal. Charles Wright. SP-WrigC

Light lay the earth on Billy's breast. On Capt. W——— R-dd-ck of C-rb—ton. Robert Burns. CP-BurnR

Light Left On, A. May Sarton. SP-SartM

Light lie the earth upon his dear dead heart. William F. Smith. Ambrose Bierce. SP-BierA

Light lies layered in the leaves, The. Song: "Light lies layered in the leaves, The." James Schuyler. CP-SchuJ

Light Lightly Pleased. Robert Herrick. CP-HerrR

Light Listened. Theodore Roethke. CP-RoetT

Light Love. Christina Georgina Rossetti. CP-RosC1

Light may be had for nothing. Little Candle. Carl Sandburg. CP-SandC

Light Music. Derek Mahon. CP-MahoD

Light now meets, The. Outside. Robert Creeley. SP-CreeR

Light of Day. George Oppen. CP-OppGN

Light of egg faces, lights of monkey skulls. Smoke Shapes. Carl Sandburg. CP-SandC

Light of evening, Lissadell, The. In Memory of Eva Gore-Booth and Con Markievicz. William Butler Yeats. CP-YeatW

Light of Freedom Necessary to National Progress, The. Jones Very. CP-VeryJ

Light of hyacinth illumines my hand, A. To Carmela Condón, Thanking Her for Some Dolls. Federico García Lorca. CP-GarcF, tr. by Christopher Maurer

Light of Lamps, The. Adam Zagajewski. SP-ZagaA, tr. by Renata Gorczynski, Benjamin Ivry and C. K. Williams

Light of Life, The. Stevie Smith. CP-SmitS

Light of Life! O blessed words, The. Hymn: The Light of Life. Jones Very. CP-VeryJ

Light of Light. Christina Georgina Rossetti. CP-RosC2

Light of Love. Dorothy Parker. CP-ParkD

Light of Love, The. James Whitcomb Riley. CP-RileJ

Light of the eyes in the house of the crow, The. Lost Month. W. S. Merwin. SP-MerwW

Light of the mind is poorer, The. Of Beginning Light. Charles Tomlinson. CP-TomlC; SP TomlC

Light of the moon on the white of the snow, The. Tinkle of Bells, A. James Whitcomb Riley. CP-RileJ

Light of the yellow flowers, The. Butter Colors. Carl Sandburg. CP-SandC

Light of the young, before you have grown old. To a Lady. G. K. Chesterton. CP-ChesG

Light off metal shaken. Rays of Dazzling Light. Czeslaw Milosz. CP-MiloCN, tr. by Jessica Fisher and Bozena Gilewska

Light on the leaves, The. Never Two Songs the Same. Carl Sandburg. CP-SandC

Light on the Pewter Dish, The. Kenneth Rexroth. CP-RexrK

Light on the Subject. Yusef Komunyakaa. CP-KomuY

Light Out), A. E. E. Cummings. CP-CummE; SP-CummE

Light passes, The. Evening. "H. D." CP-DoolH

Light plays like a radio in the iron tree. Poem: "Light plays like a radio in the iron tree." Thomas Merton. CP-MertT

Light Poem. Theodore Roethke. CP-RoetT

Light pulses through underground chambers. Noon. Adrienne Rich. CP-RicAE

Light rain stands / in little pools, A. Sparks. James Schuyler. CP-SchuJ

Light Shall Not Enter. William Carlos Williams. CP-WilW2

Light Snow-Fall after Frost, A. Thomas Hardy. CP-HardT

Light snow, like frost, has fallen during the night, A. On the Way to the Bus. Wallace Stevens. CP-StevWP

Light splashed this morning. Round, The. Stanley Kunitz. CP-KunSC

Light spreads darkly downwards from the high. Friday Night in the Royal Station. Philip Larkin. CP-LarkP

Light Switches. John Updike. CP-UpdiJ

Light takes new attribute. Projector. "H. D." CP-DoolH

Light That Failed, The. Rudyard Kipling.
  "And you may lead a thousand men." CP-KiplR
  Blue Roses. CP-KiplR
  Heriot's Ford. CP-KiplR
  "I have a thousand men," said he." CP-KiplR
  "If I have taken the common clay." CP-KiplR
  "Lark will make her hymn to God, The." CP-KiplR
  Mother o' Mine. CP-KiplR
  "So we settled it all when the storm was done." CP-KiplR
  "Then we brought the lances down—then the trumpets blew." CP-KiplR
  "There were three friends that buried the fourth." CP-KiplR
  "Wolf-cub at even lay hid in the corn, The." CP-KiplR
  "Yet at the last, ere our spearmen had found him." CP-KiplR

Light that fills thy house at morn, The. Gifts of God, The. Jones Very. CP-VeryJ

Light That Is Felt, The. John Greenleaf Whittier. CP-WhitJ

Light that rises on Jehosophat, The. Two Desert Fathers. Thomas Merton. CP-MertT

Light the first light of evening, as in a room. Final Soliloquy of the Interior Paramour. Wallace Stevens. CP-StevW; CP-StevWP

Light the sun withdraws the leaves replace, The. November. John Updike. CP-UpdiJ

Light, Time, Dark. Richard Eberhart. CP-EberR

Light up thy halls! 'Tis closing day. F. de Samara to A. G. A. Emily Jane Brontë. CP-BronE

Light, visibility of light. How Blind and Bright. Laura Riding Jackson. CP-RidiL

Light, warmth, and sprouting greenness, and o'er all. Pictures. John Greenleaf Whittier. CP-WhitJ

Light was calloused in the leaded panes of the college chapel. Cloistered.

Seamus Heaney. SP-HeanSO

Light was eerie, unreal. In our rush, The. Event at Konna, The. Kenneth Patchen. CP-PatcK

Light was gaunt and crawly, The. You May All Go Home Now. Kenneth Patchen. CP-PatcK

Light was on the golden sands, The. Paul Laurence Dunbar. CP-DunbP

Light weighs / light, to the hand. Two. Robert Creeley. CP-CreeR

Light wheels and comes in, The. Sunburst. Donald Davie. CP-DaviDC

Light will never open sightless eyes, The. Morning. Jones Very. CP-VeryJ

Light wind at Grand Prairie, drifting snow. Weather Report. William Stafford. SP-StafW; SP-StafWW

Light wind beyond the window, A. Lost and Found. Philip Levine. SP-LeviP

Light Within, The. James Schuyler. CP-SchuJ

Light Woman, A. Robert Browning. CP-BroR1

Light words forsook them. When Men Got to the Summit. Ted Hughes. SP-HughTN

Light words they were, and lightly, falsely said. Arthur Hugh Clough. SP-ClouA

Light You Give Off, The. Jelaluddin Rumi. SP-Rumi, *tr.* by Coleman Barks *and* John Moyne

Lighten, heavy hart, thy spright. Thomas Campion. CP-CampT

Lighten up, songbirds. Give me a break. Poem Not against Songbirds, A. Raymond Carver. CP-CarvR

Lightenings. Seamus Heaney. SP-HeanSO *Fr.* Squarings.

Lighter than light, blowing like air. Watchers, The. A. K. Ramanujan. SP-RamaA

Lighthouse, The. Charles Tomlinson. CP-TomlC; SP-TomlC

Lighthouse and a graveyard and gaunt pines, A. Point Pinos and Point Lobos. Robinson Jeffers. CP-JefR1

Lighthouse keeper's world is round, The. Round and Round. Thom Gunn. CP-GunnT

Lighthouses, The. George Oppen. CP-OppGN

Lighthouses the turning the turning. Gift: The Gifted. George Oppen. CP-OppGN

Lighting a spill late in the afternoon. Winter Talent, A. Donald Davie. CP-DaviDC

Lightly. David Ignatow. SP-IgnaD

Lightly Bound. Stevie Smith. CP-SmitS

Lightly, in the April mountains. Straight-Creek—Great Burn. Gary Snyder. CP-SnydG

Lightly, listlessly, my thoughts. Fernando Pessoa. SP-PessF, *tr.* by Susan M. Brown *and* Edwin Honig

Lightly, quickly, soft. Fernando Pessoa. SP-PessF, *tr.* by Susan M. Brown *and* Edwin Honig

Lightly stepped a yellow star. Emily Dickinson. CP-DickE

Lightness. Richard Wilbur. CP-WilbR

Lightnin' Blues. Rita Dove. SP-DoveR

Lightning. D. H. Lawrence. CP-LawrD

Lightning. Mary Oliver. SP-OlivM

Lightning. Arthur Rimbaud. CP-RimbA, *tr.* by Martin Sorrell

Lightning. Adam Zagajewski. SP-ZagaA, *tr.* by Renata Gorczynski

Lightning, The. John Berryman. CP-BerrJ

Lightning, The. May Swenson. SP-SwenM

Lightning dances down a naked. Lightshow. Yusef Komunyakaa. CP-KomuY

Lightning does not go out, The. It Turns Over. Kenneth Rexroth. CP-RexrK

Lightning enclosed by a vast ring of mirrors. Blackening Sky. Robert Graves. CP-GravR

Lightning-flashes of her lovely glance, The. Petrarch. CP-Petra, *tr.* by J. G. Nichols

Lightning inside the black cloud put slabs, The. Baptismal. Norman Dubie. CP-DubiN

Lightning is a yellow Fork, The. Emily Dickinson. CP-DickE

Lightning of a summer, The. Lady Bates. Randall Jarrell. CP-JarrR

Lightning playeth—all the while, The. Emily Dickinson. CP-DickE

Lightning Speed of the Past, The. Raymond Carver. CP-CarvR

Lightning Storm on Fuji. Howard Nemerov. CP-NemeH

Lightning waked me, The. It slid under. Lightning, The. May Swenson. SP-SwenM

Lights among Redwood. Thom Gunn. CP-GunnT

Lights are beginning to go out in the barracks, The. Absent with Official Leave. Randall Jarrell. CP-JarrR

Light's bright glimmer. Morning ("Light's bright glimmer"). Robert Creeley. SP-CreeR

Lights I Have Seen Before. Philip Levine. SP-LeviP

Lights in the Hallway, The. James Wright. CP-WrigJ

Lights in the Sky Are Stars, The. Kenneth Rexroth. CP-RexrK

Lights inside, The. Walking Basil. William Corbett. SP-CorbW

Lights, lifts. Lorine Niedecker. CP-NiedL

Light's lives lurch / a once world quickly from rises. E. E. Cummings. CP-CummE

Lights of Love, The. James Vincent Cunningham. CP-CunnJ

Lights or no lights. Books Men Die For. Carl Sandburg. CP-SandC

Lights out. Shades up. Girl in a Nightgown. Wallace Stevens. CP-StevW; CP-StevWP

Lights, paving—, The. George Oppen. CP-OppGN

Lights that blaze and promise, The. Tourist Eye. George Oppen. CP-OppGN

Lights that travel on her spectacles, The. Fernery, The. Hart Crane. CP-CranH

Lights up on the living. Bulletin from the Stadium, A. Thom Gunn. CP-GunnT

Lights were red, refused to change, The. Hold-up. Louis MacNeice. CP-MacNL

Lightshow. Yusef Komunyakaa. CP-KomuY

Lightweight poets are happier, The. Poetry and Games. Richard Eberhart. CP-EberR

Like. Heather McHugh. SP-McHuH

Like a bad suitor desperate and trembling. Fernando Pessoa. SP-PessF *Fr.* 35 Sonnets.

Like a benediction of blue. Short-timer's Calendar. Yusef Komunyakaa. CP-KomuY

Like a blind child is the loving heart. George Meredith. CP-MerG2

Like a Bulwark. Marianne Craig Moore. CP-MoorM

Like a cat haunting the familiar porch. Same Kiss after Many Years, The. Tess Gallagher. SP-GallT

Like a censer filled with desire. Elegy: "Like a censer filled with desire." Federico García Lorca. CP-GarcF, *tr.* by Catherine Brown

Like a challenge? Male, 45. Personals. Miller Williams. CP-WillM

Like a child the wise porpoise. Zoo, The. John Logan. CP-LogaJ

Like a cylindrical tank fresh silvered. To All Gentleness. William Carlos Williams. CP-WilW2

Like a downhill brakes-burned freight train. And Still It Comes. Thomas Lux. SP-LuxT

Like a drift of faded blossoms. Harper, The. James Whitcomb Riley. CP-RileJ

Like a dry fish flung inland far from shore. Lost Anchors. Edwin Arlington Robinson. CP-RobiE

Like a Fantasia. Eugenio Montale. CP-MontE, *tr.* by Jonathan Galassi

Like a first coat of whitewash when it's wet. Twelfth Morning; or What You Will. Elizabeth Bishop. CP-BishE

Like a flat sea. Population. George Oppen. CP-OppGN

Like a flood river whirled at rocky banks. Test of Manhood, The. George Meredith. CP-MerG1

Like a Flower in the Rain. Charles Bukowski. SP-BukC1

Like a foldout. Charles Olson. CP-OlsoC

Like a glass whose imprint. Strophes: "Like a glass whose imprint." Joseph Brodsky. CP-BrodJ, *tr.* by David McDuff

Like a glum cricket. Flight. James Tate. SP-TateJ

Like a grain of sand added to time. When You're Lost in Juarez, in the Rain, and It's Eastertime Too. Charles Wright. SP-WrigCN

Like a / grey / rock wanderin, A. E. E. Cummings. CP-CummE

Like a jeweled peacock he stirs all over. Moslems' Angel of Death, The. Thomas Merton. CP-MertT

Like a little bear twilight. E. E. Cummings. CP-CummE

Like a lizard in the sun, though not scuttling. Laureate, The. Robert Graves. CP-GravR

Like a lone Arab, old and blind. Love's Apparition and Evanishment. Samuel Taylor Coleridge. CP-ColeS

Like a mad lion, like a wild bull, like one. Race, The. Nuala Ni Dhomhnaill. CP-MahoD, *tr.* by Derek Mahon

Like a man committed to searching. Robert Creeley. CP-CreeR

Like a man on a stick on a sidewalk being peddled by a low pitchman. Jas Jargon. Charles Olson. CP-OlsoC

Like a Memoir of the Sun. Emily Dickinson. SP-DickE

Like a memory beyond death. Deeper than a Dream. Peter Blue Cloud. SP-BlueP

Like a Mourningless Child. Kenneth Patchen. CP-PatcK

Like a pile of gold that his breath. Saint. Frank O'Hara. SP-OharF

Like a Prayer. Yannis Ritsos. SP-RitsY, *tr.* by Kimon Friar *and* Kostas Myrsiades

Like a propped skull. Tutorial. Ted Hughes. SP-HughTN *Fr.* Boom.

Like a rainstorm, he said, the braided colors. Worsening Situation. John Ashbery. SP-AshbJ

Like a reed / but there are no reeds. So Slender. James Laughlin. CP-LaugJ

Like a river she was. Memory, The. Robert Creeley. CP-CreeR

Like a room, the clear stanza. Architecture, An. Wendell Berry. CP-BerrW

Like a sacred cow on the Ganges. Sheep to Slaughter. Sam Hamill. SP-HamiS

Like a sheep sweating inside. Fanny Howe. SP-HoweF *Fr.* O'Clock.

Like a shipwrecked Sailor tost. To — Upon the Birth of Her First-Born Child, March, 1833. William Wordsworth. CP-WorW2

Like a single drop of rain. Epiphany. A. R. Ammons. CP-AmmoA

Like a skein of loose silk blown against a wall. Garden, The. Ezra Pound. SP-PounE

Like a snake, my heart. New Heart. Federico García Lorca. CP-GarcF, *tr. by* Catherine Brown

Like a steel drum. Coming To. A. R. Ammons. CP-AmmoA

Like a tide it comes in. Arrival, The. Wendell Berry. CP-BerrW

Like a vein of hard coal, it was the strike. Gate City Breakdown. Charles Wright. SP-WrigC

Like a Vocation. W. H. Auden. CP-AudeW

Like a Wide Anvil From the Moon the Light. Thomas Lux. SP-LuxT

Like Aesop's fellow-slaves, O Mercury. Mercurius Gallo-Belgicus. John Donne. CP-DonnJ; MW-DonnJ

Like all his people he felt at home in the forest. Bearer, The. Hayden Carruth. CP-CarHS

Like an art-lover looking at the Mona Lisa in the Louvre. Political Reflection. Ogden Nash. CP-NashO

Like an / eddying willow leaf. Street Song. A. R. Ammons. CP-AmmoA

Like an immense white flower in a dream. Siren Music. Marya Alexandrovna Zaturenska. SP-ZatuM

Like an oarless boat through midnight's watery. Moon Clock. Donald Hall. CP-HallD

Like an old battle, youth is wild. Keep Innocency. Walter De la Mare. CP-DeLaW

Like an old windmill. For My Mother. Yehuda Amichai. SP-AmicYL, *tr. by* Benjamin Harshav *and* Barbara Harshav

Like Any Other Man. Gregory Orr. SP-OrrG

Like as a terrible fire feeds fast on a forest enormous. Marshalling of the Achaians. Homer. CP-MerG1 *Fr.* Iliad, The.

Like as the bird in the cage enclosed. Sir Thomas Wyatt. CP-WyatT

Like as the Dove. Sir Philip Sidney. SP-SidnP

Like as the dove which seeled-up doth fly. Like as the Dove. Sir Philip Sidney. SP-SidnP

Like As the Hart Desireth the Water Brooks. Christina Georgina Rossetti. CP-RosC2

Like as the Oak whose roots descend. Samuel Pepys. Rudyard Kipling. CP-KiplR

Like as the swan towards her death. Sir Thomas Wyatt. CP-WyatT

Like as the wind with raging blast. Sir Thomas Wyatt. CP-WyatT

Like bad credit. Betrayal. Raymond Carver. CP-CarvR

Like Brooms of Steel. Emily Dickinson. CP-DickE

Like bugs flying, beams flit around her. Theodore Weiss. SP-WeisT *Fr.* Storeroom, The.

Like burnt-out torches by a sick man's bed. Grave of Shelley, The. Oscar Wilde. CP-WildO

Like concentric waves / on the water. Madrigals: "Like concentric waves / on the water." Federico García Lorca. CP-GarcF, *tr. by* Jerome Rothenberg

Like Decorations in a Nigger Cemetery. Wallace Stevens. CP-StevW; CP-StevWP

Like deer (*rat-tat*) before we reach the clearing. Sonnet on Rare Animals. William Meredith. SP-MereW

Like dew the children beckon to the dry. Uninvited, The. Josephine Jacobsen. CP-JacoJ

Like divers, we ourselves must make the jump. Springboard, The. Adrienne Rich. CP-RicAE

Like diverse flowers, whose diverse beauties serve. Sir Philip Sidney. SP-SidnP *Fr.* Arcadia.

Like dogs in Mexico. As It Happens. Denise Levertov. SP-LeveDP

Like Empty Beer Cans. Ernesto Cardenal. CP-MertT, *tr. by* Thomas Merton *Fr.* Gethsemani, KY.

Like empty beer cans, like empty. Like Empty Beer Cans. Ernesto Cardenal. CP-MertT, *tr. by* Thomas Merton *Fr.* Gethsemani, KY.

Like Eyes that looked on Wastes. Emily Dickinson. CP-DickE

Like flowers sequestered from the sun. Lowest Room, The. Christina Georgina Rossetti. CP-RosC1

Like Flowers, that heard the news of Dews. Emily Dickinson. CP-DickE

Like gallant barque, with canvas spread. For the Sailors' Fair. Jones Very. CP-VeryJ

Like Henry VIII, Mohammed got religion. Robert Lowell. SP-LoweR

Like Henry the Eighth, Mohammed got religion. Like Henry VIII, Mohammed got religion. Robert Lowell. SP-LoweR

Like, *Her Cardboard Lover*. Thinness. James Schuyler. CP-SchuJ

Like her the Saints retire. Emily Dickinson. CP-DickE

Like high mountain climbers who set up a base in the valley at the foot of. Life. Yehuda Amichai. SP-AmicYL, *tr. by* Benjamin Harshav *and* Barbara Harshav

Like Him I Need the Past. James Laughlin. CP-LaugJ

Like His Mother Used to Make. James Whitcomb Riley. CP-RileJ

Like Ilium. Thomas Merton. CP-MertT

Like in the Brownie Books. Park ("Like in the Brownie Books"). Robert Creeley. SP-CreeR

Like labour-laden mooncolouds fain to flee. Through Death to Love. Dante Gabriel Rossetti. CW-RossD *Fr.* House of Life, The.

Like large dark / lazy / butterflies they sweep over. Vultures. Mary Oliver. SP-OlivM

Like Leonardo's idea. Map of Europe, A. Derek Walcott. CP-WalcD

Like light in matter, like diaphanous. Tears of the Sisters of Phaeton, The. Constantine P. Cavafy. CP-CavaC, *tr. by* Theoharis Constantine Theoharis

Like lines of verse REDBURN. Collected Poems of, The. Charles Olson. CP-OlsoC

Like liquid shadows. The ice is thin. Reflections. Charles Tomlinson. CP-TomlC

Like Little Birds. C. K. Williams. CP-WillC

Like little blackbirds in the street. Norther—Key West, A. Elizabeth Bishop. CP-BishE

Like Lorraine Ellison. James Schuyler. CP-SchuJ

Like Loves His Like. Robert Herrick. CP-HerrR

Like Magellan, let us find our islands. Magellan. Mary Oliver. SP-OlivM

Like mail order brides. Seedlings in the Mail. Marge Piercy. SP-PierM

Like Men and Women Shadows walk. Emily Dickinson. CP-DickE

Like Mighty Foot Lights—burned the Red. Emily Dickinson. CP-DickE

Like mine, the veins of these that slumber. A. E. Housman. CP-HousA

Like most godhouses this particular house. E. E. Cummings. CP-CummE

Like mourning women veiled to the feet. Distant Rainfall. Robinson Jeffers. CP-JefR2

Like my aunt timmie. Study the Masters. Lucille Clifton. SP-ClifL

Like Oedipus I am losing my sight. Legend of the One-Eyed Man, The. Anne Sexton. CP-SextA; SP-SextA

Like one that in a dream would fain arise. Arthur Hugh Clough. SP-ClouA

Like one who in her third widowhood [*or* widdowhood] doth profess[e]. To Mr. Roland Woodward. John Donne. CP-DonnJ; MW-DonnJ

Like Owls. Robert Graves. CP-GravR

Like Pattern, Like People. Robert Herrick. CP-HerrR

Like porches they trust their attachments. Rhododendrons. Tess Gallagher. SP-GallT

Like Princes crowned they bore them. Pageant of Elizabeth, A. Rudyard Kipling. CP-KiplR

Like Rain it sounded till it curved. Emily Dickinson. CP-DickE

Like ruminating cattle on the sand. Damned Women ("Like ruminating cattle on the sand"). Charles Baudelaire. CP-BaudC, *tr. by* Walter Martin

Like sea-washed sand upon the shore. On a Clean Book. Paul Laurence Dunbar. CP-DunbP

Like Shuttles Fleet the Clouds. Gerard Manley Hopkins. *See* Oxford Bells

Like shuttles fleet the clouds, and after. Oxford Bells. Gerard Manley Hopkins. CP-HopkG

Like skyscrapers with high windows staring down from the sun. Louis MacNeice. Stephen Spender. CP-SpenS

Like Snow. Robert Graves. CP-GravR

Like snow, white repetitions of the cold. Now I Can Go On and On. Eleanor Wilner. SP-WilnE

Like snows the camps on Southern hills. Armies of the Wilderness, The. Herman Melville. SP-MelvH

Like some lost part of a model kit. Dreambook Bestiary. Yusef Komunyakaa. CP-KomuY

Like Some Old fashioned Miracle. Emily Dickinson. CP-DickE

Like something washed up by the sea, something naked, invincible. Men (XVIII), The. Pablo Neruda. SP-NeruP *Fr.* Separate Rose, The.

Like souls that balance joy and pain. Sir Launcelot and Queen Guinevere. Alfred Tennyson. CP-TennA

Like stiff whipped cream in peaks and tufts above. New Pair, A. May Swenson. SP-SwenM

Like surveyors with their shiny, crystal. Blithewood. Theodore Weiss. SP-WeisT

Like that ancestral judge who bore his name. Samuel E. Sewall. John Greenleaf Whittier. CP-WhitJ

Like the blush upon the rose. Love's Pictures. Paul Laurence Dunbar. CP-DunbP

Like the conquistadors. Earthrise. Theodore Weiss. SP-WeisT

Like the embarrassed bull that woke up in a china shop. Early Winter, Long Island. Dan Pagis. SP-PagiD, *tr. by* Stephen Mitchell

Like the flesh of Venus is mud, every day is a good amount of time. Olga Broumas. SP-BrouO *Fr.* Black Holes, Black Stockings.

Like the flights of ducks. Ernesto Cardenal. CP-MertT *Fr.* Gethsemani, KY.

Like the foghorn that's all lung. Syrinx. Amy Clampitt. CP-ClamA

Like the ghost of a dear friend dead. Time Long Past. Percy Bysshe Shelley. CP-ShelP

Like the ghost of a woman from ruin. Fanny Howe. SP-HoweF *Fr.* Lines Out to Silence.

Like the Green Candles of Malintzi. D. H. Lawrence. CP-LawrD

Like the hills under dusk you. Love Song: "Like the hills under dusk you." A. R. Ammons. CP-AmmoA

Like the Inner Wall of a House. Yehuda Amichai. SP-AmicY, *tr. by* Chana Bloch

Like the magnificent stationary animal it is. Sonnet: "Like the magnificent stationary animal it is." Hayden Carruth. CP-CarHS *Fr.* Sonnets.

Like the Octopus. James Laughlin. CP-LaugJ

Like the scale of gold that lifts off from. Personae Separatae. Eugenio Montale. CP-MontE, *tr. by* Jonathan Galassi

Like the soldier, like the sailor, like the bib and tuck. Letter on the Use of Machine Guns at Weddings, A. Kenneth Patchen. CP-PatcK

Like the stars in commons blue. Field Asters. Herman Melville. SP-MelvH

Like the stench and smudge of the old dump-heap. Dream, Dump-Heap, and Civilization. Robert Penn Warren. CP-WarrR

Like the Streams in the Negev. Yehuda Amichai. SP-AmicYL, *tr. by* Benjamin Harshav *and* Barbara Harshav

Like the sun on February ice dazzling. Snow, Snow. Marge Piercy. SP-PierM

Like the sweet apple which reddens upon the topmost bough. One Girl. Sappho. CW-RossD, *tr. by* Dante Gabriel Rossetti

Like the Train's Beat. Philip Larkin. CP-LarkP

Like the vain curlings of the watery [*or* wat'ry] maze. First Anniversary of the Government under His Highness the Lord Protector, 1655, The. Andrew Marvell. CP-MarvA

Like They Say. Robert Creeley. CP-CreeR

Like This. Jelaluddin Rumi. SP-Rumi, *tr. by* Coleman Barks

Like This Together. Adrienne Rich. CP-RicAE; SP-RicA1; SP-RicA2

Like thosae infernall Deities which eate. Bad Princes Pill Their People. Robert Herrick. CP-HerrR

Like thoughts that flit across the mind. Humming Bird, The. Jones Very. CP-VeryJ

Like thousands, I took just pride and more than just. Reading Myself. Robert Lowell. SP-LoweR

Like Time's insidious wrinkle. Emily Dickinson. CP-DickE

Like to a Bride, come forth my Book, at last. To His Booke. Robert Herrick. CP-HerrR

Like to a fading flower in May. To the Memory of the Unfortunate Miss Burns 1791. Robert Burns. CP-BurnR

Like to a Hermit[e] Poor[e]. Sir Walter Ralegh. CP-RaleW

Like to a hermit[e] poor[e][,] in place obscure. Like to a Hermit[e] Poor[e]. Sir Walter Ralegh. CP-RaleW

Like to some deep-chested organ whose grand inspiration. Poetry of Milton, The. George Meredith. CP-MerG1

Like to the hand, that hath been used to play. Mr. Carew to His Friend. Thomas Carew. CP-CareT

Like to the Income must be our expence. Reverence to Riches. Robert Herrick. CP-HerrR

Like to these unme[a]surable montains [*or* mountayns]. Jacopo Sannazaro. CP-WyatT

Like torn shirts that my mother couldn't mend. Yehuda Amichai. SP-AmicY *Fr.* In a Right Angle: A Cycle of Quatrains.

Like Trains of Cars on Tracks of Plush. Bee, The. Emily Dickinson. CP-DickE

Like trumpets on a dry mountain, I blow. Landscapes of My Name. John Ciardi. CP-CiarJ

Like truthles[s] dream[e]s, so are my joys expired. Farewell to the Court. Sir Walter Ralegh. CP-RaleW

Like vaulters in the circus round. Ralph Waldo Emerson. CP-EmerR

Like watching rings extended in water. For You. Robert Creeley. CP-CreeR

Like well diggers. Inheritance, The. Thomas McGrath. SP-McGrT

Like will to like, each Creature loves his kinde. Like Loves His Like. Robert Herrick. CP-HerrR

Likeable excellent fellow, A. Han-shan. CP-ColdM, *tr. by* Red Pine

Passion. James Vincent Cunningham. CP-CunnJ

Likely as not a ruined head gasket. Image of the Engine. George Oppen. CP-OppGN

Likeness. Adrienne Rich. CP-RicAE

Likeness, A. Robert Browning. CP-BroR1; SP-BroR

Likeness has made them animal and shy. Twins, The. Karl Shapiro. SP-ShapK

Likewise. Langston Hughes. CP-HughL; CP-HughL3

Liking you, I want. To Kate Bluestein. William Corbett. SP-CorbW

Li'l' Gal. Paul Laurence Dunbar. CP-DunbP

Lilac. Louis Zukofsky. CP-ZukLS

Lilac is an ancient shrub, The. Emily Dickinson. CP-DickE

Lilac moon of the earth's backyard, The. May 31, 1961. Charles Olson. CP-OlsoC; SP-OlsoC

Lilac more grape than lavender. Runaway Pond. William Corbett. SP-CorbW

Lilac speaks without a voice: pure blue. Transformation. Richard Eberhart. CP-EberR

Lilacs. James Schuyler. CP-SchuJ

Lilacs, The. Richard Wilbur. CP-WilbR

Lilacs and the Roses, The. Louis Aragon. CP-MacNL, *tr. by* Louis MacNeice

Lilacs blossom just as sweet. Threnody: "Lilacs blossom just as sweet." Dorothy Parker. CP-ParkD

Lilacs wither in the Carolinas, The. In the Carolinas. Wallace Stevens. CP-StevW; CP-StevWP

Lilienthal said : I heard him saying words like these. Muriel Rukeyser. CP-RukeM

Lilies. Mary Oliver. SP-OlivM

Lilies. Arthur Rimbaud. CP-RimbA, *tr. by* Martin Sorrell

Lilies. Louis Zukofsky. CP-ZukLS

Lilies, The. Wendell Berry. CP-BerrW

Lilies are both pure and fair. Lovely Child, The. James Whitcomb Riley. CP-RileJ

Lilies Break Open over the Dark Water, The. Mary Oliver. SP-OlivM

Lilies in the Fire. D. H. Lawrence. CP-LawrD

Lilies of the Valley. G. K. Chesterton. CP-ChesG

Lilies of the Valley (The Tragedy of an Idealist). G. K. Chesterton. CP-ChesG

Lilies stand before her like a screen, The. For An Annunciation, Early German. Dante Gabriel Rossetti. CW-RossD

Lilies swaying, lillicrap, silver clyster-pumps! Lilies. Arthur Rimbaud. CP-RimbA, *tr. by* Martin Sorrell

Lilies white in the valley lay. Lilies of the Valley (The Tragedy of an Idealist). G. K. Chesterton. CP-ChesG

Lilies will languish; violets look ill. Sadness of Things for Sappho's Sickness, The. Robert Herrick. CP-HerrR

Lilith. Primo Levi. CP-LeviP, *tr. by* Ruth Feldman *and* Brian Swann

Lilith our second kinswoman. Lilith. Primo Levi. CP-LeviP, *tr. by* Ruth Feldman *and* Brian Swann

Lilly in a Christal, The. Robert Herrick. CP-HerrR

Lilt and a swing, A. At the Tavern. Paul Laurence Dunbar. CP-DunbP

Lily, The. William Blake. CP-BlakW *Fr.* Songs of Experience.

Lily, The. William Carlos Williams. CP-WilW1

Lily and the Rose, The. William Cowper. CP-CowpW

Lily at Noon, A. Donald Davie. CP-DaviDC

Lily, being white not red, The. Epilogue: "Lily, being white not red, The." Countee Cullen. CP-CullC

Lily Bloom, what ominous fallen crowfeathers of shadow. Living for Two. Denise Levertov. SP-LeveDL

Lily-girl, not made for this world's pain, A. Madonna Mia. Oscar Wilde. CP-WildO

Lily has a rose. E. E. Cummings. CP-CummE

Lily has a smooth stalk, / Will never hurt your hand, The. Christina Georgina Rossetti. CP-RosC2

Lily has an air, / And the snowdrop a grace, The. Christina Georgina Rossetti. CP-RosC2

Lily of the Valley, The. Paul Laurence Dunbar. CP-DunbP

Lily-of-the-Valley. Louis Zukofsky. CP-ZukLS

Lily-of-the-Valley Fortunei. Louis Zukofsky. CP-ZukLS

Lily, there isn't a thing you lack. Life of the Party, The. Ogden Nash. CP-NashO

Lily-White Boys, The. Christopher Logue.
    Chorale, The. SP-LoguC
    Girl's Spare Chorus, The. SP-LoguC
    Go to the Wall. SP-LoguC
    Song of Natural Capital, The. SP-LoguC
    Young Hero Sings a Song of Self-Understanding, A. SP-LoguC

Lily's withered chalice falls, The. Impressions ("Lily's withered chalice falls, The"). Oscar Wilde. CP-WildO

Lima was *limes,* limit. Ponte De Lima. Charles Tomlinson. SP-TomlC *Fr.* Portuguese Pieces.

Limb to limb, mouth to mouth. Winter Quiet. William Carlos Williams. CP-WilW1

Limbic System. Hans Magnus Enzensberger. SP-EnzeH

Limbo. Samuel Taylor Coleridge. CP-ColeS; MW-ColeS

Limbo. Seamus Heaney. SP-HeanSO

Limbo Culture. W. H. Auden. CP-AudeW

Limbo Dancer, The. Josephine Jacobsen. CP-JacoJ

Limbs are caught in each other, The. Clearing. Tess Gallagher. SP-GallT

Limbs of the giant spruce that leans, The. Stair, The. Charles Tomlinson. SP-TomlC

Limerick, A: "There was an old person of Lapland." G. K. Chesterton. CP-ChesG

Limestone and ceder. Indigo shadow. Why Boy Came to Lonely Place. Robert Penn Warren. CP-WarrR

Limestone, faulted with marble; the lengthening swell. Geneva Restored. Charles Tomlinson. CP-TomlC

Limit, The. A. R. Ammons. CP-AmmoA

Limit, The. Jorge Luis Borges. SP-BorgJ, *tr. by* Alan S. Trueblood

Limit of the song is this, The. Prelude: "Limit of the song is this, The." Michael Palmer. SP-PalmM

Limitations. Paul Laurence Dunbar. CP-DunbP

Limitations of Genius. James Whitcomb Riley. CP-RileJ *Fr.* Child-World, A.

Limited. Carl Sandburg. CP-SandC

Limited, The. Robert Penn Warren. CP-WarrR

Limited Achievement. Donald Davie. CP-DaviDC

Limited air drafts. Occurrences, The ("Limited air drafts"). George Oppen. CP-OppGN

Limits. Jorge Luis Borges. SP-BorgJ, *tr. by* Alastair Reid

Limits. Raymond Carver. CP-CarvR

Limits. Ralph Waldo Emerson. CP-EmerR

Limits. Federico García Lorca. CP-GarcF, *tr. by* Jerome Rothenberg *Fr.* Palm Tree, The.

Limits. Howard Nemerov. CP-NemeH

Limits have wintered me, The. Fanny Howe. SP-HoweF *Fr.* O'Clock.

Limits of Friendship, The. John Ciardi. CP-CiarJ

Limits of Physics, The. Dan Pagis. SP-PagiD, *tr. by* Stephen Mitchell

Limped out of the hot sky a hurt plane. Navy Field. William Meredith. SP-MereW

Limper, The. James Laughlin. CP-LaugJ

Limpidity of Silences. Kenneth Patchen. CP-PatcK

Lin Hui of Kia took to flight. Flight of Lin Hui, The. Chuang Tzu. CP-MertT

L'Incognita. Christina Georgina Rossetti. CP-RosC3

Lincoln. Paul Laurence Dunbar. CP-DunbP

Lincoln. James Whitcomb Riley. CP-RileJ

Lincoln Monument: Washington. Langston Hughes. CP-HughL; CP-HughL1

Lincoln Relics, The. Stanley Kunitz. CP-KunSC

Lincoln—The Boy. James Whitcomb Riley. CP-RileJ

Lincoln Theatre. Langston Hughes. CP-HughL; CP-HughL2

Lincoln University: 1954. Langston Hughes. CP-HughL; CP-HughL3

Lincolnshire. Donald Davie. CP-DaviDC

Linda, you are leaving. Mother and Daughter. Anne Sexton. CP-SextA; SP-SextA

Lindau. Eugenio Montale. CP-MontE, *tr. by* Jonathan Galassi

Linden Branch, The. Archibald MacLeish. CP-MacLA

Linden Trees, The. Archibald MacLeish. CP-MacLA

Lindenbloom. Amy Clampitt. CP-ClamA

Lindens. Adam Zagajewski. SP-ZagaA, *tr. by* Clare Cavanagh

L'Indifférent. Rainer Maria Rilke. CP-RilkFr, *tr. by* A. Poulin, Jr. *Fr.* Affectionate Taxes to France.

Lindsay mistakes the matter quite. Answer to "Paulus," The. Jonathan Swift. CP-SwifJ

Line. W. S. Merwin. SP-MerwWF

Line, The. Hayden Carruth. CP-CarHS

Line breaks and the guns go under, The. Song of Defeat, A. G. K. Chesterton. CP-ChesG

Line drawn straight from my heart to your heart, A. Lines for Myra to Grow To. John Ciardi. CP-CiarJ

Line Four. Adam Zagajewski. SP-ZagaA, *tr. by* Clare Cavanagh

Line-Gang, The. Robert Frost. CP-FrosR

Line in long array where they wind betwixt green islands, A. Cavalry Crossing a Ford. Walt Whitman. CP-WhitW

Line of dancing children on the shore, The. Eugenio Montale. CP-MontE, *tr. by* Jonathan Galassi

Line of eve o'er the moorland, A. George Meredith. CP-MerG2

Line of palm branch structures are along the beach, A. Story. George Oppen. CP-OppGN

Line of Trees. W. S. Merwin. SP-MerwWF

Line of Verse of Yeats, A. Richard Eberhart. CP-EberR

Line-storm clouds fly tattered and swift, The. Line-Storm Song, A. Robert Frost. CP-FrosR

Line-Storm Song, A. Robert Frost. CP-FrosR

Line that, The. Twelve Years. Paul Celan. SP-CelaP, *tr. by* John Felstiner

Lineage. Ted Hughes. SP-HughTN

Linear, encircled youth, The. On Alexander and Aristotle, on a Black-on-Red Greek Plate. Alan Dugan. CP-DugaA

Lined with light. April Light. May Swenson. SP-SwenM

Linen. James Schuyler. CP-SchuJ

Liner She's a Lady, The. Rudyard Kipling. CP-KiplR

Lines: "Before we part to alien thoughts and aims." Thomas Hardy. CP-HardT

Lines: "Cold earth slept below, The." Percy Bysshe Shelley. CP-ShelP

Lines: "Dear Becher, you tell me to mix with mankind." Lord Byron. CP-Byron

Lines: "Far away is the land of rest." Emily Jane Brontë. CP-BronE

Lines: "Far, far away, O ye." Percy Bysshe Shelley. CP-ShelP

Lines: "He who of Rankine [*or* R—k–n] sang, lies stiff and dead." Robert Burns. *See* Lines on the Author's Death

Lines: "I did not have exactly a way of life." John Ciardi. CP-CiarJ

Lines: "I die; but when the grave shall press." Emily Jane Brontë. CP-BronE

Lines: "Leaves are greygreen." William Carlos Williams. CP-WilW1

Lines: "Loud is the Vale! the Voice is up." William Wordsworth. CP-WorW1; MW-WorW

Lines: "Nay, Traveller." William Wordsworth. CP-WorW1; MW-WorW

Lines: "Portentous sound! mysteriously vast." James Whitcomb Riley. CP-RileJ

Lines: "Soft unclouded blue of air, The." Emily Jane Brontë. CP-BronE

Lines: "That time is dead for ever, child!" Percy Bysshe Shelley. CP-ShelP

Lines: "Thou little naked statuette." James Whitcomb Riley. CP-RileJ

Lines: "Unfelt, unheard, unseen." John Keats. CP-KeatJ

Lines: "We meet not as we parted." Percy Bysshe Shelley. CP-ShelP

Lines: "When the lamp is shattered [*or* shatter'd]." Percy Bysshe Shelley. CP-ShelP

Lines: "Who's this out there." A. K. Ramanujan. CP-RamaA

Lines: "You have seen a plough." Charles Tomlinson. CP-TomlC

Lines, The: "After the centers' naked files, the basic line." Randall Jarrell. CP-JarrR

Lines about Elias. Ted Hughes. SP-HughTN

Lines Addressed to a Young Lady. Lord Byron. CP-Byron

Lines Addressed to his Father on Making Him a Present of a Knife. James Edward Austen-Leigh. CP-AustJ

Lines Addressed to Mr. John Ranken. Robert Burns. CP-BurnR

Lines after Cummings. James Laughlin. CP-LaugJ

Lines after the Manner of Homer. William Cowper. CP-CowpW

Lines against a Loved American Poet after Hearing an Irish One's Nickman. John Logan. CP-LogaJ

Lines are straight and swift between the stars, The. Stars at Tallapoosa. Wallace Stevens. CP-StevW; CP-StevWP

Lines by Claudia. Emily Jane Brontë. CP-BronE

Lines by the Late Lord Tennyson (On Miss Spencer being transferred with her typewriter from the Study to the Dining Room). G. K. Chesterton. CP-ChesG

Lines & Circularities. Howard Nemerov. CP-NemeH

Lines Composed a Few Miles above Tintern Abbey on Revisiting the Banks of the Wye During a Tour, July 13, 1798. William Wordsworth. CP-WorW1
   (Lines Written a Few Miles above Tintern Abbey on Revisiting the Banks of the Wye During a Tour, July 13, 1798.) MW-WorW

Lines Composed in a Concert-Room. Samuel Taylor Coleridge. CP-ColeS

Lines Composed over Three Thousand Miles from Tintern Abbey. Billy Collins. SP-CollB

Lines Declining a Transatlantic Dinner Invitation. Marilyn Hacker. SP-HackM

Lines fer Isaac Bradwell, of Indanoplis, Ind., County-Seat of Marion. James Whitcomb Riley. CP-RileJ

Lines flying in, out: logarithmic. A. R. Ammons. CP-AmmoA

Lines for a Book. Thom Gunn. CP-GunnT

Lines for a Friend Who Left. John Logan. CP-LogaJ

Lines for a Gift. Robert Browning. CP-BroR2

Lines for a Grave-Stone. Edna St. Vincent Millay. CP-MillE

Lines for a Hospital. Countee Cullen. CP-CullC

Lines for a Memorial of Ashley Cowper. William Cowper. CP-CowpW

Lines for a Painting by Leighton. Robert Browning. CP-BroR2

Lines for a Picture of St Dorothea. Gerard Manley Hopkins. CP-HopkG

Lines for a Prologue. Archibald MacLeish. CP-MacLA

Lines for a Young Man Who Talked. John Logan. CP-LogaJ

Lines for a Young Wanderer in Mexico. John Logan. CP-LogaJ

Lines for an Album. James Whitcomb Riley. CP-RileJ

Lines for an Interment. Archibald MacLeish. CP-MacLA

Lines for an Old Man. T. S. Eliot. CP-ElioT

Lines for an Unknown Lover. John Logan. CP-LogaJ

Lines for His Son in Satin. John Logan. CP-LogaJ

Lines for Lauren Owen. Ted Berrigan. SP-BerrT *Fr.* Sonnets, The.

Lines for Michael in the Picture. John Logan. CP-LogaJ

Lines for My 55th Birthday. Thom Gunn. CP-GunnT

Lines for Myra to Grow To. John Ciardi. CP-CiarJ

Lines for the Jubilee Window. Robert Browning. CP-BroR2

Lines for the Painter Ota Janeček. Jaroslav Seifert. SP-SeifJ, *tr. by* Ewald Osers

Lines for the Tomb of Levi Lincoln Thaxter. Robert Browning. CP-BroR2

Lines for the Winter Recess. Joseph Brodsky. CP-BrodJ

Lines for Translation into Any Language. James Fenton. SP-FentJ

Lines from a Letter to a Young Clerical Friend. John Greenleaf Whittier. CP-WhitJ

Lines from Cadenus to Vanessa. Jonathan Swift. CP-SwifJ

Lines from the Testament. Pier Paolo Pasolini. SP-PasoP, *tr. by* Norman MacAfee *and* Luciano Martinengo

Lines Given with a Penwiper. Christina Georgina Rossetti. CP-RosC3

Lines Have Their Linings, and Bookes Their Buckram. Robert Herrick. CP-HerrR

Lines Impromptu on Miss Morgans Birth Day. Annis Boudinot Stockton. CP-StocA

Lines in a poem, long ones, short ones; each bound to its allotted end. Out of Line. Dan Pagis. SP-PagiD, *tr. by* Stephen Mitchell

Lines Indited with All the Depravity of Poverty. Ogden Nash. CP-NashO

Lines Inscribed for Mr. Thomas Hutchinson. G. K. Chesterton. CP-ChesG

Lines Inscribed in a Copy of His Poems Sent to the Queen for the Royal Library at Windsor. William Wordsworth. CP-WorW2

Lines Inscribed upon a Cup Formed from a Skull. Lord Byron. CP-Byron

Lines Lost among Trees. Billy Collins. SP-CollB

Lines Muttered in Sleep. Rita Dove. SP-DoveR

Line's not meant to lie there, longing, A. To God or Man. Heather McHugh. SP-McHuH

Lines of the young Temethos madly in love. Temethos, Antiochian; 400 A.D. Constantine P. Cavafy. CP-CavaC, tr. by Theoharis Constantine Theoharis

Lines of this new song are nothing, The. Louis Zukofsky. CP-ZukLS

Lines on a Carp. Gary Snyder. CP-SnydG

Lines on a Cricket Match. G. K. Chesterton. CP-ChesG

Lines on a Drawing of a Monument to Swift's Grandfather. Alexander Pope. CP-PopeA

Lines on a Fly-Leaf. John Greenleaf Whittier. CP-WhitJ

Lines on a Friend. Samuel Taylor Coleridge. CP-ColeS

Lines on a Portrait of a Lady. Samuel Taylor Coleridge. CP-ColeS

Lines on a Young Gentleman Who Died of the Yellow Fever at Princeton a Day or Two after He Fled from the City for Fear of It. Annis Boudinot Stockton. CP-StocA

Lines on a Young Lady's Photograph Album. Philip Larkin. CP-LarkP

Lines on Facing Forty. Ogden Nash. CP-NashO

Lines on Hearing of the Death of Doctor Franklin. Annis Boudinot Stockton. CP-StocA

Lines on Hearing that Lady Byron Was Ill. Lord Byron. CP-Byron

Lines on His Birthday. John Logan. CP-LogaJ

Lines on Leaving Appledore. John Greenleaf Whittier. CP-WhitJ

Lines on Locks (or Jail and the Erie Canal). John Logan. CP-LogaJ

Lines on Mount Auburn. Jones Very. CP-VeryJ

Lines on Reading the Death of Rev. Henry Ware, Jr. Jones Very. CP-VeryJ

Lines on Reading Too Many Poets. Dorothy Parker. CP-ParkD

Lines on Receiving *The Dial's* Award: 1927. William Carlos Williams. CP-WilW1

Lines on Seeing Mrs Elizabeth Witherspoon Put in the Grave. Annis Boudinot Stockton. CP-StocA

Lines on Stirling. Robert Burns. CP-BurnR

Lines on Swinburne. Robert Browning. CP-BroR2

Lines on the Author's Death. Robert Burns. CP-BurnR

(Lines.) CP-BurnR

Lines on the Death of Miss M. B. Farnham. Ralph Waldo Emerson. CP-EmerR

Lines on the Death of Mrs Hill Suppos'd to Be Spoken by Her Sister Mrs Clymer. Annis Boudinot Stockton. CP-StocA

Lines on the Death of Mrs Petit of Philadelphia. Annis Boudinot Stockton. CP-StocA

Lines on the Death of S. Oliver Torrey. John Greenleaf Whittier. CP-WhitJ

Lines on the Expected Invasion 1803. William Wordsworth. CP-WorW1

Lines on the Mermaid Tavern. John Keats. CP-KeatJ

Lines on the Old Danvers Burying Ground. Jones Very. CP-VeryJ

(Old Danvers Burying-Ground, The.) CP-VeryJ

Lines on the Portrait of a Celebrated Publisher. John Greenleaf Whittier. CP-WhitJ

Lines on the Winter Campaign, 1980. Joseph Brodsky. CP-BrodJ, tr. by Alan Myers

Lines on Thomas Warton's Poems. Samuel Johnson. *See* Hermit Hoar

Lines Out to Silence. Fanny Howe.

"Amber is a fossilized resin, yellow." SP-HoweF

"Blue river, icy sunk." SP-HoweF

"But if / never happened." SP-HoweF

"Dry is the word for a life of solitude." SP-HoweF

"How long I've waited, I can't count." SP-HoweF

"I may never see the Vatican or Troy." SP-HoweF

"Like the ghost of a woman from ruin." SP-HoweF

"No more cinders, the cellar water is iced over." SP-HoweF

"Snow be in this time with us as music." SP-HoweF

"Trailing the bill of a mallard." SP-HoweF

Lines Rhymed in a Letter Received (by J. H. R[eynolds]) from Oxford. John Keats. *See* On Oxford

Lines Sent to Sir John Whiteford, of Whiteford, Bart. with the Foregoing Poem. Robert Burns. CP-BurnR

Lines Suggested by a Portrait from the Pencil of F. Stone. William Wordsworth. CP-WorW2

Lines Suggested by Hearing the Beach, at F. Peabody's Mills, South Salem. December 21. 1833. Jones Very. CP-VeryJ

Lines Suggested by Seeing a Butterfly Sculptured upon a Tomb. Jones Very. CP-VeryJ

Lines Suggested by the Last Words of Berengarius. Samuel Taylor Coleridge. CP-ColeS; MW-ColeS

Lines *Supposed* to Have Been Sent to an Uncivil Dress Maker. Jane Austen. CP-AustJ

Lines That Could Have Been Written and Lost round about 1922. Jorge Luis Borges. SP-BorgJ, tr. by Charles Tomlinson

Lines to a Beautiful Spring in a Village. Samuel Taylor Coleridge. CP-ColeS

Lines to a Comic Author, on an Abusive Review. Samuel Taylor Coleridge. CP-ColeS

Lines to a Critic. Percy Bysshe Shelley. CP-ShelP

Lines to a Friend Visiting America. George Meredith. CP-MerG1

Lines to a Granny. A. K. Ramanujan. CP-RamaA

Lines to a Lady Weeping. Lord Byron. CP-Byron

Lines to a Movement in Mozart's E-Flat Symphony. Thomas Hardy. CP-HardT

Lines to a Poet. Josephine Jacobsen. CP-JacoJ

Lines to a Reviewer. Percy Bysshe Shelley. CP-ShelP

Lines to a Three-Name Lady. Ogden Nash. CP-NashO

Lines to a White Persian Sleeping. Robert Stock. SP-StocR

Lines to a World-famous Poet Who Failed to Complete a World-famous Poem; or, Come Clean, Mr. Guest! Ogden Nash. CP-NashO

Lines to a Young Lady Born before April Fools' Day. G. K. Chesterton. CP-ChesG

Lines to Accompany Flowers for Eve. Carolyn Kizer. CP-KizeC

Lines to an Old Pro-Boer Who Asked for a Contribution to a Peace Periodical. G. K. Chesterton. CP-ChesG

Lines to an Onsettled Young Man. James Whitcomb Riley. CP-RileJ

Lines to Be Embroidered on a Bib, or, The Child Is Father of the Man, but Not for Quite a While. Ogden Nash. CP-NashO

Lines to Be Mumbled at Ovington's. Ogden Nash. CP-NashO

Lines to Be Put into Latin. James Laughlin. CP-LaugJ

Lines to Be Scribbled on Somebody Else's Thirtieth Milestone. Ogden Nash. CP-NashO

Lines to Catherine. John Logan. CP-LogaJ

Lines to His Son on Reaching Adolescence. John Logan. CP-LogaJ

Lines to Mr Frost. John Berryman. CP-BerrJ

Lines to Mr Hodgson. Lord Byron. CP-Byron

Lines to My Brother from a Pavillion in His Garden. Annis Boudinot Stockton. CP-StocA

Lines to My Father. Countee Cullen. CP-CullC

Lines to My Grandfather. Christina Georgina Rossetti. CP-RosC3

Lines to ——— on the Death of His Friend. Jones Very. CP-VeryJ

Lines to Perfesser John Clark Ridpath. James Whitcomb Riley. CP-RileJ

Lines to Pope. Jonathan Swift. CP-SwifJ

Lines to the Air of "Godolphin Horne." G. K. Chesterton. CP-ChesG

Lines to the Memory of James Dow. Robert Browning. CP-BroR2

Lines to the Statue of Ferdinand Foch. G. K. Chesterton. CP-ChesG

Lines to Thomas Poole. Samuel Taylor Coleridge. CP-ColeS

Lines to Waterloo Station. G. K. Chesterton. CP-ChesG

Lines upon Delia and to the Chevaliers of the Cordon Bleu. Robert Stock. SP-StocR

Lines upon Leaving a Sanitarium. Theodore Roethke. CP-RoetT

Lines while Walking Home from a Party on Charles Street. John Ciardi. CP-CiarJ

Lines with a Pocket Book. Christopher Smart. SP-SmarC

Lines with Two Cockscombs. William Cowper. CP-CowpW

Lines Written a Few Miles above Tintern Abbey on Revisiting the Banks of the Wye during a Tour, July 13, 1798. William Wordsworth. *See* Lines Composed a Few Miles above Tintern Abbey on Revisiting the Banks of the Wye during a Tour, July 13, 1798

Lines Written after Reading Frank O'Hara's "A Step Away from Them." William Corbett. SP-CorbW

Lines Written among the Euganean Hills. Percy Bysshe Shelley. CP-ShelP

Lines Written as a School Exercise at Hawkshead, Anno Aetatis 14. William Wordsworth. CP-WorW1

Lines Written at a Small Distance from my House, and Sent by My Little Boy to the Person to Whom They Are Addressed. William Wordsworth. *See* To My Sister

Lines Written at Shurton Bars, near Bridgewater, September 1795, in Answer to a Letter from Bristol. Samuel Taylor Coleridge. MW-ColeS *Fr.* Poetical Epistles.

Lines Written at the King's Arms, Ross, Formerly the House of the "Man of Ross." Samuel Taylor Coleridge. CP-ColeS

Lines Written beneath a Picture. Lord Byron. CP-Byron

Lines Written beneath an Elm in the Churchyard of Harrow. Lord Byron. CP-Byron

Lines Written by Jane Austen for the Amusement of a Niece. Jane Austen. CP-AustJ

Lines Written during a Period of Insanity. William Cowper. CP-CowpW

Lines Written during the Castlereagh Administration. Percy Bysshe Shelley. CP-ShelP

Lines Written for Gene Kelly to Dance To. Carl Sandburg. CP-SandC

Lines Written for Miss Patty More. William Cowper. CP-CowpW

Lines Written in a Picture Book. G. K. Chesterton. CP-ChesG

Lines Written in an Album. John Greenleaf Whittier. CP-WhitJ

Lines Written in an Album, at Malta. Lord Byron. CP-Byron

Lines Written in an Asylum. Hayden Carruth. CP-CarHS

Lines Written in Dejection. G. K. Chesterton. CP-ChesG

Lines Written in Dejection. William Butler Yeats. CP-YeatW

Lines Written in Dejection, Oklahoma. Gregory Orr. SP-OrrG

Lines Written in Dejection on the Eve of Great Success. Robert Frost. CP-FrosR

Lines Written in Early Spring. William Wordsworth. CP-WorW1; MW-WorW

Lines Written in Oxford. G. K. Chesterton. CP-ChesG

Lines Written in Recapitulation. Edna St. Vincent Millay. CP-MillE

Lines Written in the Album at Elbingerode, in the Har[t]z Forest. Samuel Taylor Coleridge. CP-ColeS; MW-ColeS

Lines Written in the Album of the Countess of Lonsdale. William Wordsworth. CP-WorW2

Lines Written in the Bay of Lerici. Percy Bysshe Shelley. CP-ShelP

Lines Written in the Euganean Hills. Charles Tomlinson. CP-TomlC

Lines Written in the Fannie Farmer Cookbook. Elizabeth Bishop. CP-BishE

Lines Written in the Highlands after a Visit to Burns's Country. John Keats. CP-KeatJ

Lines Written in the Kirk of Lamington. Robert Burns. CP-BurnR

Lines Written in the Monthly Review. William Cowper. CP-CowpW

Lines Written in the Travellers' Book at Orchomenus. Lord Byron. CP-Byron

Lines Written on a Bank-Note. Robert Burns. CP-BurnR

Lines Written on a Blank Leaf in a Copy of the Author's Poem "The Excursion," upon Hearing of the Death of the Late Vicar of Kendal. William Wordsworth. CP-WorW2

Lines Written on a Blank Leaf of the "Pleasures of Memory." Lord Byron. CP-Byron

Lines Written on a Window, at the King's Arms Tavern, Dumfries. Robert Burns. CP-BurnR

Lines Written on a Window in the Episcopal Palace at Kilmore. Unknown, sometimes at. to Thomas Sheridan. CP-SherT

Lines Written on Hearing the News of the Death of Napoleon. Percy Bysshe Shelley. CP-ShelP

Lines, Written on Reading Stuart's Account of the Treatment of Slaves in Charleston. Jones Very. CP-VeryJ

Lines Written on the Windows of the Globe Tavern, Dumfries. Robert Burns. CP-BurnR

Lines Written on 29 May / The Anniversary of the Restoration of Charles the 2nd. John Keats. CP-KeatJ

Lines Written upon a Window-Shutter at Weston. William Cowper. CP-CowpW

Lines Written while Sailing in a Boat at Evening. William Wordsworth. CP-WorW1

Lingard and the Stars. Edwin Arlington Robinson. CP-RobiE

Lingering Last Drops. Walt Whitman. CP-WhitW

L'Inglese. John Ciardi. CP-CiarJ

Link between Barnum and Calas, The. Phoenix and the Tortoise, The. William Carlos Williams. CP-WilW2

Linked in the chain. Argumentum e Silentio. Paul Celan. SP-CelaP, tr. by John Felstiner

Linked Verses. Carolyn Kizer. CP-KizeC

Linkwood Road. Josephine Jacobsen. CP-JacoJ

Linnaeus. Czeslaw Milosz. CP-MiloCN, tr. by Robert Hass

Linnaeus in Lapland. Lorine Niedecker. CP-NiedL

Linnet, The. Walter De la Mare. CP-DeLaW

Linnet and the Jay, The. Unknown, sometimes at. to Thomas Sheridan. CP-SherT

Linnet-Hawker, The. George Meredith. CP-MerG2

Linnet in a gilded cage,— / A linnet on a bough, A. Christina Georgina Rossetti. CP-RosC2

Linnet's warble, sinking toward a close, The. By the Side of Rydal Mere. William Wordsworth. CP-WorW2

Linnit playes rarely on the Lute, we know. Upon Linnit. Robert Herrick. CP-HerrR

Linoleum. Tess Gallagher. SP-GallT

L'Invitation. Ezra Pound. CP-PoEar

L'Invitation au Voyage. Charles Baudelaire. CP-WilbR, tr. by Richard Wilbur

Linz (dpa)—A 13 year old schoolboy has killed himself. Munich Courier, The. James Laughlin. CP-LaugJ

Lion, The. Nicholas Vachel Lindsay. CP-LindV

Lion, The. Thomas Merton. CP-MertT

Lion, The. Ogden Nash. CP-NashO

Lion, The. William Carlos Williams. CP-WilW2

Lion and lioness are intractable, The. Letter to Eve. Alan Dugan. CP-DugaA

Lion and lioness, the mild. Assisi Fragments, The. Geoffrey Hill. CP-HillG

Lion and the Dog, The. Robert Creeley. CP-CreeR

Lion and the Rose, The. May Sarton. SP-SartM

Lion, awake, is out there, The. Lion under Maples. Josephine Jacobsen. CP-JacoJ

Lion dishonoured bids death come, The. Reversionary. Stevie Smith. CP-SmitS

Lion for Real, The. Allen Ginsberg. CP-GinsA; SP-GinsA

Lion-Gentle. Robert Graves. CP-GravR

Lion Grotto, The. Norman Dubie. CP-DubiN

Lion-heart, you prowl alone. Song: Crown of Stars. Robert Graves. CP-GravR

Lion & Honeycomb. Howard Nemerov. CP-NemeH

Lion in Love, The. Marianne Craig Moore. CP-MoorM Fr. Fables of La Fontaine.

Lion in the path, a lion, A. Song: Dream Warning. Robert Graves. CP-GravR

Lion is a kingly beast, The. Lion, The. Nicholas Vachel Lindsay. CP-LindV

Lion Lover. Robert Graves. CP-GravR

Lion::Mouse. A. R. Ammons. CP-AmmoA

Lion of St. Mark's upon the glass, The. Her Dead Brother. Robert Lowell. SP-LoweR

Lion sits within his cage, The. Zoo, The. Stevie Smith. CP-SmitS

Lion sunk by time's decay, A. Sick Lion and the Ass, The. Thomas Sheridan. CP-SherT

Lion under Maples. Josephine Jacobsen. CP-JacoJ

Lion upon the Floor, A. Charles Olson. CP-OlsoC

Lions, The. Robert Earl Hayden. CP-HaydR

Lions Copulating. Richard Eberhart. CP-EberR

Lions in Sweden. Wallace Stevens. CP-StevW; CP-StevWP

Lions of fire, The. Kenneth Patchen. CP-PatcK

Lions who ate the Christians on the sands of the arena, The. Sunt Leones. Stevie Smith. CP-SmitS

Lip. James Vincent Cunningham. CP-CunnJ Fr. Five Epigrams.

Lip Labour. Robert Herrick. CP-HerrR

Lip was a man who used his head. Lip. James Vincent Cunningham. CP-CunnJ Fr. Five Epigrams.

Lips and Eyes. Thomas Carew. CP-CareT, tr. by Thomas Carew

Lips and tongue. Hand of Solo, A. Thomas Kinsella. CP-KinsT

Lips half-willing in a doorway. Village in Late Summer. Carl Sandburg. CP-SandC

Lips of dead men whisper where they lie, The. Yehuda Amichai. SP-AmicY, tr. by Stephen Mitchell Fr. We Loved Here.

Lips of the dead naively whispered words. Yehuda Amichai. SP-AmicYL Fr. Here We Loved.

Lips Tongueless[e]. Robert Herrick. CP-HerrR

Liquor and love. World Narrowed to a Point, The. William Carlos Williams. CP-WilW2

Lis / -ten / you know what i mean when. E. E. Cummings. CP-CummE

Lisa, Leona, Loretta? Salt. Yusef Komunyakaa. CP-KomuY

Lisbon Revisited (1926). Fernando Pessoa. SP-PessF, tr. by Susan M. Brown and Edwin Honig

Lisbon Revisited (1923). Fernando Pessoa. SP-PessF, tr. by Susan M. Brown and Edwin Honig

Lisetta all' Amante. Christina Georgina Rossetti. CP-RosC3

Lisette and Eileen. Edwin Arlington Robinson. CP-RobiE

Lish, you rickollect that-air. Cuored o' Skeerin. James Whitcomb Riley. CP-RileJ

Lisp and wisp. Autumn Night. Lorine Niedecker. CP-NiedL

Lisper, The. James Whitcomb Riley. CP-RileJ

Lispeth. Rudyard Kipling. Fr. Plain Tales from the Hills.

Lisping in Numbers. James Whitcomb Riley. CP-RileJ

Lisping maid, The. Thoughts of Youth, The. James Whitcomb Riley. CP-RileJ

List, A. G. K. Chesterton. CP-ChesG

List of Famous Hats, The. James Tate. SP-TateJ

List! the bell-Sprite stuns my ears. Dirge Sung by a Minstrel. William Wordsworth. CP-WorW1

List the harp in window wailing. Aeolian Harp, The. Herman Melville. SP-MelvH

List, the winds of March are blowing. Sequel to To — Upon the Birth of Her First-Born Child, March, 1833. William Wordsworth. CP-WorW2

Listen. Hayden Carruth. CP-CarHS

Listen. Ogden Nash. CP-NashO

Listen. Alice Walker. CP-WalkA

Listen. Miller Williams. CP-WillM

Listen a while, the moon is a lovely woman, a lonely woman, lost in a. Night Stuff. Carl Sandburg. CP-SandC

Listen: about little Hendele. Song at the End, A. Jaroslav Seifert. SP-SeifJ, tr. by Ewald Osers

Listen, all of you, listen, all of you. To Dean Inge Lecturing on Origen. Stevie Smith. CP-SmitS

Listen! / All you beauty-makers. Call to Creation. Langston Hughes. CP-HughL; CP-HughL1

Listen, and I will tell you of a face. Christina Georgina Rossetti. CP-RosC3

Listen / beloved / i dreamed. E. E. Cummings. CP-CummE

Listen brother love you. Hard Love Rock II. Audre Lorde. SP-LordA

Listen, buds, it's March twenty-first. Spring Song. Ogden Nash. CP-NashO

Listen but once to the words written out by my hand. Short Summary. Louise Bogan. CP-BogaL

Listen carefully. / I'm meditating. C. K. Williams. CP-WillC; SP-WillC

Listen, children, if you'll only stop throwing peanuts and bananas. Let's Not Climb the Washington Monument Tonight. Ogden Nash. CP-NashO

Listen, children: / Your father is dead. Lament: "Listen, children: / Your father is dead." Edna St. Vincent Millay. CP-MillE

Listen, Christ, / You did alright in your day, I reckon. Goodbye Christ. Langston Hughes. CP-HughL; CP-HughL1

Listen! / Dear dream of utter aliveness. Demand. Langston Hughes. CP-HughL; CP-HughL1

Listen, Dugan, don't read. After a Poem by Carlos Drummond de Andrade Translated by Elizabeth Bishop as *Don't Kill Yourself*. Alan Dugan. CP-DugaA

Listen: from sleep's long pillow I arise. Last Words. Stanley Kunitz. CP-KunSC

Listen Here Blues. Langston Hughes. CP-HughL; CP-HughL1

Listen here. I've never played it safe. August 8th. Anne Sexton. CP-SextA

Listen here, Joe. Without Benefit of Declaration. Langston Hughes. CP-HughL; CP-HughL3

Listen here, / liver. Heart to Heart Talk With My Liver. John Logan. CP-LogaJ

Listen here, sistren and brethren, I am goddamn tired. Sociology of Toyotas and Jade Chrysanthemums, The. Hayden Carruth. CP-CarHS

Listen, I went to get a haircut, it was a perfectly good day. Big Bastard with a Sword. Charles Bukowski. SP-BukC2

Listen, Ianni. Sam Hamill. SP-HamiS

Listen! It's never sung like that! Listen! Fever. Hendrik de Vries. CP-RicAE

Listen, Kid Sleepy. Kid Sleepy. Langston Hughes. CP-HughL; CP-HughL2

Listen, listen, Mary mine. Passage of the Apennines. Percy Bysshe Shelley. CP-ShelP

Listen, maiden, to my strain. Serenade: "Listen, maiden, to my strain." Ambrose Bierce. SP-BierA

Listen motorists, and learn. Strange Case of Mr. Niobob's Transmogrification, The. Ogden Nash. CP-NashO

Listen my children and you. E. E. Cummings. CP-CummE

Listen my children, and you shall hear. Paul Revere's Ride [The Landlord's Tale]. Henry Wadsworth Longfellow. SP-LongH *Fr.* Tales of a Wayside Inn.

Listen natives of a dry place. Old Boast, The. W. S. Merwin. SP-MerwW

Listen, perhaps you will hear me, young man. Inheritor. Czeslaw Milosz. CP-MiloCN, *tr.* by Robert Hass

Listen, Saints. Thomas Merton. CP-MertT

Listen,—she hasn't stopped, she's not tired yet. She's unbearable. Orestes. Yannis Ritsos. SP-RitsY, *tr.* by Philip Pastras *and* George Pilitsis

Listen, / stop tanning yourself. Without Commercials. Alice Walker. CP-WalkA

Listen sweet Dove unto my song. Whitsunday. George Herbert. CP-HerbG

Listen, the hay-bells tinkle as the cart. Holy Innocents, The. Robert Lowell. SP-LoweR

Listen, the last stroke of death's noon has struck. Plague, The. Christina Georgina Rossetti. CP-RosC3

Listen! the sky! Vast conflagration! Midsummer Dawn. Archibald MacLeish. CP-MacLA

Listen: the wind in new leaves. For the Blind. Denise Levertov. SP-LeveDL

(Listen) / this a dog barks and. E. E. Cummings. CP-CummE

Listen—this is a faint station. Tuned in Late One Night. William Stafford. SP-StafWW

Listen to Gieseking playing a Berceuse. Berceuse. Amy Clampitt. CP-ClamA

Listen to me, angel tot. Thunder over the Nursery. Ogden Nash. CP-NashO

Listen to me, the poets laureate. Lemons, The. Eugenio Montale. CP-MontE, *tr.* by Jonathan Galassi

Listen to people laughing. Laughter. D. H. Lawrence. CP-LawrD

Listen to presences inside poems. Jelaluddin Rumi. SP-Rumi, *tr.* by Coleman Barks

Listen to the Band! D. H. Lawrence. CP-LawrD

Listen to the Linotype. Ogden Nash. CP-NashO

Listen to the poet Sanai. Children's Game, A. Jelaluddin Rumi. SP-Rumi, *tr.* by Coleman Barks

Listen to the story told by the reed. Reed Flute's Song, The. Jelaluddin Rumi. SP-Rumi, *tr.* by Coleman Barks

Listen to the tale of the sensitive car. Wrote This Last Night. Allen Ginsberg. CP-GinsA

Listen to the ticking of the old Great Clock. Altgeld. Carl Sandburg. CP-SandC

Listen to this, and hear the mystery inside. Snake-Catcher and the Frozen Snake, The. Jelaluddin Rumi. SP-Rumi, *tr.* by Coleman Barks

Listen to yo' prophets. Shout. Langston Hughes. CP-HughL; CP-HughL1

Listen! when your hair, like mine. From a Dungeon Wall in the Southern College. Emily Jane Brontë. CP-BronE

Listen, you morons great and small. Ballad of an Intellectual. E. E. Cummings.

CP-CummE

Listener, The. Stevie Smith. CP-SmitS

Listeners, The. Walter De la Mare. CP-DeLaW

Listening. Raymond Carver. CP-CarvR

Listening. D. H. Lawrence. CP-LawrD

Listening. Christina Georgina Rossetti. CP-RosC3

Listening. William Stafford. SP-StafW; SP-StafWW

Listening for Jane. William Corbett. SP-CorbW

Listening Landscape, The. Marya Alexandrovna Zaturenska. SP-ZatuM

Listening, listening; it is never still. Märchen, The. Randall Jarrell. CP-JarrR

Listening one day on the radio. Listener, The. Stevie Smith. CP-SmitS

Listening to a Broken Radio. Arthur Sze. SP-SzeA

Listening to Billy Graham. Accident: A Short Story. Miller Williams. CP-WillM

Listening to Bruckner on the radio. Defeat. Charles Bukowski. SP-BukC1

Listening to Distant Guns. Denise Levertov. SP-LeveDS

Listening to Foxhounds. James Dickey. CP-DickJ

Listening to Jefferson Airplane. Thom Gunn. CP-GunnT

Listening to the Köln Concert. Robert Bly. SP-BlyR

Listening to the Mourners. James Wright. CP-WrigJ

Listing. Richard Eberhart. CP-EberR

Listless beauty of the hour, The. History. D. H. Lawrence. CP-LawrD

Listless, / the heat rises—. Robert Creeley. CP-CreeR

Lit Instructor. William Stafford. SP-StafWW

Lit night glares like a day-glo strawberry, The. Godfather Returns to Color TV, The. Amy Clampitt. CP-ClamA

Lit room is blinding, The. This Is Mortal. David Ignatow. SP-IgnaD

Litanies to Satan. Charles Baudelaire. CP-BaudC, *tr.* by Walter Martin

Litany: "All holy souls / pray for us fellows." Thomas Merton. CP-MertT

Litany: "It yawns at me the cavernous gulf." Thomas Merton. CP-MertT

Litany: "Sing miserere / For the men who must die." Thomas Merton. CP-MertT

Litany. John Ashbery.

  "Some certified nut." SP-AshbJ

Litany, A: "Father of heaven, and him, by whom." John Donne. CP-DonnJ; MW-DonnJ

Litany, A: "I remember him falling beside me." Gregory Orr. SP-OrrG

Litany of the Dark People, The. Countee Cullen. CP-CullC

Litany of the Heroes. Nicholas Vachel Lindsay. CP-LindV

Literal. Heather McHugh. SP-McHuH

Literal Dream. Robert Penn Warren. CP-WarrR

Literal = The Abstract, The: A Demonstration. Eleanor Wilner. SP-WilnE

Literal Land, The. G. K. Chesterton. CP-ChesG

Literary Dublin. John Updike. CP-UpdiJ

Literary Life, The. Charles Bukowski. SP-BukC2

Literary Life in the Golden West. Philip Whalen. SP-WhalP

Literary Method, A. Ambrose Bierce. SP-BierA

Literary rats—says R.—that's us. R. Says. Adam Zagajewski. SP-ZagaA, *tr.* by Renata Gorczynski, Benjamin Ivry *and* C. K. Williams

Literary Reflection. Ogden Nash. CP-NashO

Literary Scene, The. Ogden Nash. CP-NashO

Literary Theorist. Helen Pinkerton. CP-PinkH

Literary World, The. Philip Larkin. CP-LarkP

Literate are ill-prepared for this, The. Stroke, The. Heather McHugh. SP-McHuH

Literate Farmer and the Planet Venus, The. Robert Frost. CP-FrosR

Literature is a phase of life. If one is afraid of it. Picking and Choosing. Marianne Craig Moore. CP-MoorM

Lithe-armed, and with satin-soft shoulders. Dolores. James Whitcomb Riley. CP-RileJ

Lithe girl, brown girl. Pablo Neruda. SP-LoguC, *tr.* by Christopher Logue *Fr.* Red Bird.

Lithesome, blithesome daughter mine. Rosalie. Ambrose Bierce. SP-BierA

Lithuania, after Fifty-two Years. Czeslaw Milosz. CP-MiloCN, *tr.* by Robert Hass

Lithuanian Divertissement. Joseph Brodsky. CP-BrodJ, *tr.* by Alan Myers

Lithuanian lithographer, A. Song of Paternal Care, A. John Updike. CP-UpdiJ

Lithuanian Nocturne. Joseph Brodsky. CP-BrodJ

Litter under the tree, The. Bone Poem. Mary Oliver. SP-OlivM

Little Air 1. Stéphane Mallarmé. CP-MallS, *tr.* by Henry Weinfield

Little Air 2. Stéphane Mallarmé. CP-MallS, *tr.* by Henry Weinfield

Little Air (Martial). Stéphane Mallarmé. CP-MallS, *tr.* by Henry Weinfield

Little airplanes of the heart, The. Sandinista Avioncitos. Lawrence Ferlinghetti. SP-FerlL

Little and Loud. Robert Herrick. CP-HerrR

Little Apocalypse; Hölderlin: 1770–1843. Geoffrey Hill. CP-HillG

Little arms ripped out. Honey Dripper. Clarence Major. SP-MajoC

Little ash, a painted rose, a name, A. After a Death. Charles Tomlinson. CP-TomlC; SP-TomlC

Little baby, you have wandered far away. Phantom, A. James Whitcomb Riley.

CP-RileJ

Little Backwater. Federico García Lorca. CP-GarcF, *tr. by* Jerome Rothenberg *Fr.* Backwaters.

Little bald old man, General Zhukov's cook, the very one, The. After the Fire. Raymond Carver. CP-CarvR

Little biplane that has the river-meadow for landing-field, The. Machine, The. Robinson Jeffers. CP-JefR1

Little bird has told me that today will appear, A. Song in July, A. Nicholas Vachel Lindsay. CP-LindV

Little bird sits in the nest and sings, The. Preparation. Paul Laurence Dunbar. CP-DunbP

Little bird, with plumage brown, A. Sparrow, The. Paul Laurence Dunbar. CP-DunbP

Little birds of the night. Stephen Crane. CP-CranS

Little birds sit on your shoulders. For Miriam. Kenneth Patchen. CP-PatcK

Little Black Book, The. Paul Muldoon. CP-MuldP

Little Black Heart of the Telephone. Robert Penn Warren. CP-WarrR

Little black thing among the snow, A. Chimney Sweeper, The. William Blake. CP-BlakW *Fr.* Songs of Experience.

Little Black Train, The. Kenneth Patchen. CP-PatcK

Little Blind Fish, thou art marvellous wise! Rudyard Kipling. CP-KiplR *Fr.* Plain Tales from the Hills.

Little blond boy, The. We Took the Town after a Heavy Bombing. Fernando Pessoa. SP-PessF, *tr. by* Susan M. Brown *and* Edwin Honig.

Little Blue-Fits has lost his wits. New Fiction, The. G. K. Chesterton. CP-ChesG

Little Bo-Peep has lost her Sheep. Nursery Rhymes No. 1. Property. G. K. Chesterton. CP-ChesG

Little boat at anchor, The. Fourth of July Night. Carl Sandburg. CP-SandC

Little Box from Olinalá, The. Gabriela Mistral. SP-MistG, *tr. by* Maria Giachetti [*or* Jacketti]

Little Boy and Lost Shoe. Robert Penn Warren. CP-WarrR

Little-Boy Brilliant. D. H. Lawrence. CP-LawrD

Little boy legged on through the dark. No Bell-Ringing. Thomas Hardy. CP-HardT

Little Boy Lost. Stevie Smith. CP-SmitS

Little Boy Lost, A. William Blake. CP-BlakW *Fr.* Songs of Experience.

Little-boy lover, The. For All Who Ever Sent Lace Valentines. Nicholas Vachel Lindsay. CP-LindV

Little boy once played so loud, A. Extremes. James Whitcomb Riley. CP-RileJ

Little Boy Sick. Stevie Smith. CP-SmitS

Little boy, The. Portrait, The. Dan Pagis. SP-PagiD, *tr. by* Stephen Mitchell

Little Boy, to show his might and power, The. Metamorphosis, The. Sir John Suckling. CP-SuckJ

Little boy was looking for his voice, The. Little Mute Boy, The. Federico García Lorca. SP-GarcF, *tr. by* W. S. Merwin

Little boy wears my mistakes, A. As I Grew Up Again. Audre Lorde. SP LordA

Little boy / who sticks a needle in his arm, The. Junior Addict. Langston Hughes. CP-HughL; CP-HughL3

Little boy / Will you stop. Hound of Ulster, The. Stevie Smith. CP-SmitS

Little bread, a crust, a crumb, A. Emily Dickinson. CP-DickE

Little bright yellow ones, The. Flowers. Robert Pinsky. CP-PinsR

Little brook! Little brook! Brook-Song, The. James Whitcomb Riley. CP-RileJ

Little Brown Baby. Paul Laurence Dunbar. CP-DunbP

Little brown face full of smiles. Liza May. Paul Laurence Dunbar. CP-DunbP

Little bunches of / grass pretend they are bushes. Stories from Kansas. William Stafford. SP-StafWW

Little Busch and Tommy Hays. Busch and Tommy. James Whitcomb Riley. CP-RileJ

Little by little it dawned on us that the row. Yarrow. Paul Muldoon. CP-MuldP

Little by little my gender drifts away. Apostrophe to a Dead Friend. Maxine W. Kumin. SP-KumiM

Little by little, things empty, like those large bones. Departures 3. Yannis Ritsos. SP-RitsY, *tr. by* N. C. Germanacos

Little by little, wean yourself. Wean Yourself. Jelaluddin Rumi. SP-Rumi, *tr. by* Coleman Barks

Little calls as they pass. Surrounded by Wild Turkeys. Gary Snyder. CP-SnydG

Little Candle. Carl Sandburg. CP-SandC

Little candy clock, The. Candy Wrapper and Toy. Federico García Lorca. CP-GarcF, *tr. by* Christopher Maurer

Little Cannibal's Bedtimesong. Kenneth Patchen. CP-PatcK

Little Cats. Langston Hughes. CP-HughL; CP-HughL3

Little child, A. Eternal Child, The. Kathleen Jessie Raine. SP-RainK

Little Child of Brightest Face. Stevie Smith. CP-SmitS

Little children have been fighting, The. I Am the Bitter Name. C. K. Williams. CP-WillC; SP-WillC

Little children you will all go. Song of Man Chipping an Arrowhead. W. S. Merwin. SP-MerwW

Little Christmas Basket, A. Paul Laurence Dunbar. CP-DunbP

Little cirque, horizon-wide, The. Evening. Walter De la Mare. CP-DeLaW

Little clover's on autumn lawns, A. Fanny Howe. SP-HoweF *Fr.* Q.

Little Coat, The. James Whitcomb Riley. CP-RileJ

Little Coat, The. Stephen Spender. CP-SpenS

Little colt—broncho, loaned to the farm, A. Broncho That Would Not Be Broken, The. Nicholas Vachel Lindsay. CP-LindV

Little cousin is dead, by foul subtraction, The. Dead Boy. John Crowe Ransom. SP-RansJ

Little Cousin Jasper, he. James Whitcomb Riley. CP-RileJ

Little cullud boys with beards. Flatted Fifths. Langston Hughes. CP-HughL; CP-HughL3

Little cullud boys / with fears. Tag. Langston Hughes. CP-HughL; CP-HughL3

Little dark baby. America. Langston Hughes. CP-HughL; CP-HughL1

Little Daughters of America, The. Stevie Smith. CP-SmitS

Little David. James Whitcomb Riley. CP-RileJ

Little Dead Man, The. James Whitcomb Riley. CP-RileJ

Little Devils. Pablo Neruda. SP-NeruP

Little Dick and the Clock. James Whitcomb Riley. CP-RileJ

Little Dog Laughs, The. James Laughlin. CP-LaugJ

Little Dog that wags his tail, A. Emily Dickinson. CP-DickE

Little Dog-Woggy, The. James Whitcomb Riley. CP-RileJ

Little Doncella, The. Federico García Lorca. CP-GarcF, *tr. by* Jerome Rothenberg *Fr.* Secrets.

Little dreaming by the way, A. Sum, The. Paul Laurence Dunbar. CP-DunbP

Little dreams / Of springtime. Slum Dreams. Langston Hughes. CP-HughL; CP-HughL3

Little drunk, / a little high, / about to go off, A. Saturday Night. James Schuyler. CP-SchuJ

Little earth, water. Here ("Little earth, water"). Robert Creeley. CP-CreeR

Little East of Jordan, A. Emily Dickinson. CP-DickE

Little Ellie sits alone. Romance of the Swan's Nest, The. Elizabeth Barrett Browning. CP-BroEB

Little Exercise. Elizabeth Bishop. CP-BishE

Little Fanfare for Felix Magowan. James Merrill. SP-MerrJ

Little Fat Doctor, The. James Whitcomb Riley. CP-RileJ

Little Fawn. Peter Blue Cloud. SP-BlueP

Little Feet. Ogden Nash. CP-NashO

Little fields of green and gold, The. Green Leaves. G. K. Chesterton. CP-ChesG

Little Fire in the Woods, The. Hayden Carruth. CP-CarHS

Little Fish. D. H. Lawrence. CP-LawrD

Little Flower grew in a lonely Vale, A. To Mrs Ann Flaxman. William Blake. CP-BlakW

Little flowers of yesterday, The. Autumn Note. Langston Hughes. CP-HughL; CP-HughL1

Little Fly. William Blake. CP-BlakW *Fr.* Songs of Experience.

Little fogs were gathered in every hollow. Country Wedding, The. Thomas Hardy. CP-HardT

Little Foot-Page, The. George Meredith. CP-MerG2

Little fox is still, The. Broadcast on Ethiopia. Langston Hughes. CP-HughL; CP-HughL1

Little Friend, The. Elizabeth Barrett Browning. CP-BroEB

Little frigidity allows the mind in, A. When Lightning Struck, 2. Andrei Codrescu. SP-CodrA

Little Fugue. Sylvia Plath. CP-PlatS

Little further, O my father, yet a little further, A. Wanderings of Cain, The. Samuel Taylor Coleridge. CP-ColeS

Little garden within, The. Emily Dickinson. SP-DickE

Little gay bonnets! so many. Watching Neighbors' Children. Kenneth Patchen. CP-PatcK

Little Georgie Tompers, he. Youthful Press, The. James Whitcomb Riley. CP-RileJ

Little Ghost, The. Edna St. Vincent Millay. CP-MillE

Little Gift, A. Wendell Phillips Stafford. SP-StafWW

Little girl, A. Christmas Star, The. Gabriela Mistral. SP-MistG, *tr. by* Maria Giachetti [*or* Jacketti]

Little Girl, Be Careful What You Say. Carl Sandburg. CP-SandC

Little Girl by the Fence at School, The. William Stafford. SP-StafWW

Little girl / Dreaming of a baby grand piano. To Be Somebody. Langston Hughes. CP-HughL; CP-HughL2

Little Girl Drowned in the Well. Federico García Lorca. CP-GarcF, *tr. by* Greg Simon *and* Steven F. White

Little Girl Found, The. William Blake. CP-BlakW *Fr.* Songs of Experience.

Little Girl Found, The. William Blake. CP-BlakW *Fr.* Songs of Innocence.

Little girl in white, gold-haired, A. Moral Dream. Alan Dugan. CP-DugaA

Little girl looks at a book with a picture of a cat, A. Portrait with a Cat, A. Czeslaw Milosz. CP-MiloC; CP-MiloCN, *tr. by* Robert Hass

Little Girl Lost, A. William Blake. CP-BlakW *Fr.* Songs of Experience.

Little Girl Lost, The. William Blake. CP-BlakW *Fr.* Songs of Experience.

Little Girl Lost, The. William Blake. CP-BlakW *Fr.* Songs of Innocence.

Little Girl, My String Bean, My Lovely Woman. Anne Sexton. CP-SextA; SP-SextA

Little Girl on Her Way to School, A. James Wright. CP-WrigJ

Little Girl Speakings. Maya Angelou. SP-AngeM

Little-Girl-Two-Little-Girls. James Whitcomb Riley. CP-RileJ

Little Girl Wakes Early. Robert Penn Warren. CP-WarrR

Little girl was given a new toy, A. Death Will Amuse Them. Kenneth Patchen. CP-PatcK

Little girl won't eat her sandwich, The. Blasting from Heaven. Philip Levine. SP-LeviP

Little Girls, The. Charles Bukowski. SP-BukC1

Little girls— / skinny, resigned. Moment in Troy, A. Wisława Szymborska. SP-SzymW, *tr. by* Stanislaw Barańczak *and* Clare Cavanagh

Little Girly-Girl, of you. James Whitcomb Riley. CP-RileJ

Little gold rooster. I. Federico García Lorca. CP-GarcF, *tr. by* Jerome Rothenberg *Fr.* Narcissus.

Little Good Fellows, The. Herman Melville. SP-MelvH

Little Gormley stole a purse. Moral Tales for the Young ("Little Gormley stole a purse"). Dorothy Parker. CP-ParkD

Little Green Tree. Langston Hughes. CP-HughL; CP-HughL2

"Little Haly! Little Haly!" cheeps the robin in the tree. On the Death of Little Mahala Ashcraft. James Whitcomb Riley. CP-RileJ

Little head against my shoulder. Sigh, The. Thomas Hardy. CP-HardT

Little Heartsong, A. James Laughlin. CP-LaugJ

Little hedgerow birds, The. Animal Tranquillity and Decay. William Wordsworth. CP-WorW1

Little hedge-row birds, The. Old Man Travelling [Animal Tranquillity and Decay, a Sketch]. William Wordsworth. MW-WorW

Little higher, A. By the Mango Trees. W. S. Merwin. SP-MerwWF

Little Hill, The. Edna St. Vincent Millay. CP-MillE

Little Horse. W. S. Merwin. SP-MerwW

Little Horse. Tennessee Williams. CP-WillT

Little horse is newlY, The. E. E. Cummings. CP-CummE

Little / house with, A. Picture, A. Robert Creeley. CP-CreeR

Little Infinite Poem. Federico García Lorca. CP-GarcF, *tr. by* Greg Simon *and* Steven F. White

Little ink more or less!, A. Stephen Crane. CP-CranS

Little inmate, full of mirth. Cricket, The. Vincent Bourne. CP-CowpW

Little islands out at sea, on the horizon. Greeks Are Coming!, The. D. H. Lawrence. CP-LawrD

Little Jack Horner. Nursery Rhymes No. 3. G. K. Chesterton. CP-ChesG

Little Jack Janitor. James Whitcomb Riley. CP-RileJ *Fr.* Child-World, A.

Little joe gould has lost his teeth and doesn't know where. E. E. Cummings. CP-CummE; SP-CummE

Little Johnts's Chris'mus. James Whitcomb Riley. CP-RileJ

Little Julie / Has grown quite tall. Delinquent. Langston Hughes. CP-HughL; CP-HughL3

Little ladies more / than dead exactly dance. E. E. Cummings. CP-CummE

Little Lady, The. James Whitcomb Riley. CP-RileJ

Little lady at de do'. Visitor, The. Paul Laurence Dunbar. CP-DunbP

Little Lamb, who lost thee?— / I myself, none other. Rejoice with Me. Christina Georgina Rossetti. CP-RosC2

Little Lame Boy's Views, A. James Whitcomb Riley. CP-RileJ

Little late rain, A. Sarah's Choice. Eleanor Wilner. SP-WilnE

Little less returned for him each spring, A. Anglais Mort à Florence. Wallace Stevens. CP-StevW; CP-StevWP

Little Litany, A. G. K. Chesterton. CP-ChesG

Little Lives of Earth and Form, The. Philip Larkin. CP-LarkP

Little Lucy Landman. Paul Laurence Dunbar. CP-DunbP

Little Lyric (*Of Great Importance*). Langston Hughes. CP-HughL

Little Mad Boy, The. Federico García Lorca. CP-GarcF, *tr. by* W. S. Merwin

Little Madness in the Spring, A. Emily Dickinson. CP-DickE

Little Maid-o'-Dreams, with your. James Whitcomb Riley. CP-RileJ

Little Man around the House. Yusef Komunyakaa. CP-KomuY

Little man at the, The. Getting Paid. James Laughlin. CP-LaugJ

Little man / (in a hurry). E. E. Cummings. CP-CummE

Little Man in the Tin-Shop, The. James Whitcomb Riley. CP-RileJ

Little Mandy and her Ma. Little Mandy's Christmas Tree. James Whitcomb Riley. CP-RileJ

Little Mandy's Christmas Tree. James Whitcomb Riley. CP-RileJ

Little Marjorie. James Whitcomb Riley. CP-RileJ

Little marsh-plant, yellow green, A. Sundew, The. Algernon Charles Swinburne. SP-SwinA

Little Mary Bell had a fairy in a nut. Long John Brown & Little Mary Bell. William Blake. CP-BlakW

Little Master Home-from-School. Father for a Fool, A. Stevie Smith. CP-SmitS

Little Mattie. Elizabeth Barrett Browning. CP-BroEB

Little Millwins attend the Russian Ballet, The. Les Millwin. Ezra Pound. SP-PounE

Little Miss Muffet Sat on a Prophet—and Quite Right, Too! Ogden Nash. CP-NashO

Little Mock-Man on the Stairs, The. James Whitcomb Riley. CP-RileJ

Little moon rode up a high corner, The. Clefs. Carl Sandburg. CP-SandC

Little More, The. James Dickey. CP-DickJ

Little mud, A. Just Man. Heather McHugh. SP-McHuH

Little Mute Boy, The. Federico García Lorca. SP-GarcF, *tr. by* W. S. Merwin

Little negro girl who lives across the alley, The. Easter: Sensations of April. T. S. Eliot. SP-ElioT

Little New Moon, The. Gabriela Mistral. SP-MistG, *tr. by* Maria Giachetti [*or* Jacketti]

Little Night Music, A. Charles Tomlinson. CP-TomlC

Little Novel, A. Gertrude Stein. CP-SteiG

Little Odyssey of Jason Quint, of Science, Doctor, The. Thomas McGrath. SP-McGrT

Little of what we have found, A. Beloved, Thomas Kinsella. CP-KinsT

Little oily fuzzbear. Sheep. Anne Sexton. CP-SextA

Little Old Funky Homeric Blues for Herm, A. Hayden Carruth. CP-CarHS

Little old house was out with a little new shed, The. Roadside Stand, A. Robert Frost. CP-FrosR

Little Old Lady in Lavender Silk, The. Dorothy Parker. CP-ParkD

Little Old Letter. Langston Hughes. CP-HughL; CP-HughL2

Little Old Poem That Nobody Reads, The. James Whitcomb Riley. CP-RileJ

Little Old Table, The. Thomas Hardy. CP-HardT

Little Old Women, The. Charles Baudelaire. CP-BaudC, *tr. by* Walter Martin

Little one-room schoolhouse among the redwoods, The. Loving Shepherdess, The. Robinson Jeffers. CP-JefR2

Little One, The. John Ciardi. CP-CiarJ

Little one, you have been buzzing in the books. On the Way. Carl Sandburg. CP-SandC

Little onward lend thy guiding hand, A. Samson Agonistes. John Milton. CP-MiltJ

LITTLE Onward Lend Thy Guiding Hand, A. William Wordsworth. CP-WorW2

Little Orphant Annie's come to our house to stay. James Whitcomb Riley. CP-RileJ

Little overflowing word, A. Emily Dickinson. CP-DickE

Little owl flew through the night, The. On the Adequacy of Landscape. Wallace Stevens. CP-StevW; CP-StevWP

Little Owl Who Lives in the Orchard. Mary Oliver. SP-OlivM

Little package of Ceylon, The. Emily Dickinson. SP-DickE

Little pansies by the road have turned, The. Meeting among the Mountains. D. H. Lawrence. CP-LawrD

Little Passion, The ("Of those ideas in his head"). T. S. Eliot. SP-ElioT *Fr.* Agony in the Garret, An.

Little Passion, The ("Upon those stifling August nights"). T. S. Eliot. SP-ElioT *Fr.* Agony in the Garret, An.

Little Peasant, The. Anne Sexton. CP-SextA

Little person, I lean in your eye, A. Pupil. Heather McHugh. SP-McHuH

Little pig goes to market, The. Nursery Rhyme. Charles Simic. SP-SimiC; SP-SimiCE

Little pilgrim there, The. Thoughts on the Run 4. Hans Magnus Enzensberger. SP-EnzeH, *tr. by* Rita Dove *and* Fred Viebahn

Little Pin, The: Fragment. George Oppen. CP-OppGN

Little places as / size of. Dimensions. Robert Creeley. CP-CreeR

Little places. / Corte stella. Clarence Major. SP-MajoC

Little plum / said the mother to her son. Hansel and Gretel. Anne Sexton. CP-SextA

Little Poem, A. Randall Jarrell. CP-JarrR

Little Poem, A. Miller Williams. CP-WillM

Little poem we will write unto our Cousin John, A. Emily Dickinson. SP-DickE

Little Poems. John Updike. CP-UpdiJ

Little poppies, little hell flames. Poppies in July. Sylvia Plath. CP-PlatS

Little porcelain angel. Rainer Maria Rilke. CP-RilkFr, *tr. by* A. Poulin, Jr. *Fr.* Orchards.

Little Priest of the Fen, The. Aleksandr Aleksandrovich Blok. SP-BlokA, *tr. by* Peter France *and* Jon Stallworthy

Little quids, the monstrous quids, The. Quids, The. Laura Riding Jackson. CP-RidiL

Little quietly outstanding uptown, A. Extirpation. Raymond Carver. CP-CarvR

Little ragamuffin, brat, a craving for Sen-Sen. With a Child All Day. James Tate. SP-TateJ

Little ragged girl, our ball-boy, A. Game at Salzburg, A. Randall Jarrell. CP-JarrR

Little Rapacity Greed was a glutton. Uncle Sidney's Rhymes. James Whitcomb Riley. CP-RileJ

Little Rapids, The. May Swenson. SP-SwenM

Little-Red-Apple Tree, The. James Whitcomb Riley. CP-RileJ

Little-red-apple Tree!, The. Little-Red-Apple Tree, The. James Whitcomb Riley. CP-RileJ

Little Red Riding Hood. Olga Broumas. SP-BrouO

Little river twittering in the twilight, The. Bei Hennef. D. H. Lawrence. CP-LawrD

Little Road—not made of Man, A. Emily Dickinson. CP-DickE

Little Robber Girl Considers the Wide World, The. Marilyn Hacker. SP-HackM

Little Robber Girl Gets On in the Wide World, The. Marilyn Hacker. SP-HackM

Little Rock. Clarence Major. SP-MajoC

Little Room, The. Raymond Carver. CP-CarvR

Little Rooms. William Stafford. SP-StafWW

Little Ruth. Yehuda Amichai. SP-AmicYL, tr. by Benjamin Harshav and Barbara Harshav

Little Saint best fits a little Shrine, A. Ternarie of Littles, upon a Pipkin of Jellie [or Jelly] Sent to a Lady, A. Robert Herrick. CP-HerrR

Little Salamander, The. Walter De la Mare. CP-DeLaW

Little Sallie, Little Sallie. Ballad of Little Sallie. Langston Hughes. CP-HughL; CP-HughL1

Little Sam Clemens, one night back in Hannibal, The. Last Laugh. Robert Penn Warren. CP-WarrR

Little sardines of the tin, The. Kruger. G. K. Chesterton. CP-ChesG

Little scavenger away. Flute Song. "H. D." CP-DoolH

Little Scraping, A. Robinson Jeffers. CP-JefR2

Little sentences I began, The. Emily Dickinson. SP-DickE

Little Shirt, The. C. K. Williams. CP-WillC

Little Shrub Growing By, A. Ben Jonson. CP-JonsB

Little silver rain-children were laughing in the street, The. Stayed No Longer in the Place than to Hire a Guide for the Next Stage. Kenneth Patchen. CP-PatcK

Little sister, not all Black. For My Singing Sister. Audre Lorde. SP-LordA

Little Sketch. Carl Sandburg. CP-SandC

Little Sleep's-Head Sprouting Hair in the Moonlight. Galway Kinnell. SP-KinnGN

Little slender lad, toad-headed. Ambrosia of Dionysus and Semele, The. Robert Graves. CP-GravR

Little snail, / Dreaming you go. Snail. Langston Hughes. CP-HughL; CP-HughL2

Little Snow was here and there, A. Emily Dickinson. CP-DickE

Little Song ("Carmencita loves Patrick"). Langston Hughes. CP-HughL

Little Song ("Lonely people"). Langston Hughes. CP-HughL; CP-HughL2

Little Song about Charity, A. Thomas McGrath. SP-McGrT

Little Song of the Unborn Child. Federico García Lorca. CP-GarcF, tr. by Jerome Rothenberg Fr. In the Garden of the Lunar Grapefruits.

Little Song on Housing. Langston Hughes. CP-HughL; CP-HughL3

Little Songs for Gaia. Gary Snyder. CP-SnydG

Little Sonnet to Little Friends. Countee Cullen. CP-CullC

Little soul so sleek and smiling. Animula, Vagula, Blandula. Stevie Smith. CP-SmitS

Little Southern colored child, A. Migration. Langston Hughes. CP-HughL; CP-HughL2

Little sparrows, The. Pastoral: "Little sparrows, The." William Carlos Williams. CP-WilW1

Little sport-fishing boat, A. Late Afternoon, April 8, 1984. Raymond Carver. CP-CarvR

Little Stanton. Federico García Lorca. CP-GarcF, tr. by Greg Simon and Steven F. White

Little Stone in the Middle of the Road, in Florida, A. Muriel Rukeyser. CP-RukeM

Little Tear Gland That Says, The. Charles Simic. SP-SimiC; SP-SimiCE

Little Testament. Eugenio Montale. CP-MontE, tr. by Jonathan Galassi

Little thanksgiving here. To labor, feed. On Breughel the Elder's *The Harvesters* (1565) in the Metropolitan Museum. Helen Pinkerton. CP-PinkH

Little things hide. Sometimes they. What Gets Away. William Stafford. SP-StafWW

Little things that no one needs. Bric-à-Brac. Dorothy Parker. CP-ParkD

Little thinks, in the field, yon red-cloaked clown. Each and All. Ralph Waldo Emerson. CP-EmerR

Little think'st thou, poor[e] flower. Blossom[e], The. John Donne. CP-DonnJ; MW-DonnJ

Little Tigers Everywhere. Charles Bukowski. SP-BukC1

Little Time—and Place. Robert Creeley. CP-CreeR

Little Tiny Kickshaw, The. James Whitcomb Riley. CP-RileJ

Little to do on a HOT night but swat at. Naked at 92 Degrees. Charles Bukowski. SP-BukC3

Little too abstract, a little too wise, A. Return. Robinson Jeffers. CP-JefR2

Little Tooth, A. Thomas Lux. SP-LuxT

Little Town, The. Tennessee Williams. CP-WillT

Little Town at Evening, The. D. H. Lawrence. CP-LawrD

Little Town o' Tailholt. The. James Whitcomb Riley. CP-RileJ

Little tree / little silent Christmas tree. E. E. Cummings. CP-CummE; SP-CummE

Little Turtle, The. Nicholas Vachel Lindsay. CP-LindV

Little Uncomplicated Hymn, A. Anne Sexton. CP-SextA

Little Vagabond, The. William Blake. CP-BlakW Fr. Songs of Experience.

Little Vesper, A. Jane Cooper. CP-CoopJ

Little Viennese Waltz. Federico García Lorca. CP-GarcF, tr. by Greg Simon and Steven F. White

Little Virgin, fitted out in white, The. Laurentides. Josephine Jacobsen. CP-JacoJ

Little voices of prairie dogs, The. Great Western Plains, The. Hart Crane. CP-CranH

Little Waltz. Adam Zagajewski. SP-ZagaA, tr. by Clare Cavanagh

Little / water, A. For Marisol. Robert Creeley. CP-CreeR

Little way ahead, A. Lantern, The. W. S. Merwin. SP-MerwW

Little Ways That Encourage Good Fortune, The. William Stafford. SP-StafWW

Little Whale Song. Ted Hughes. SP-HughTN

Little while a little love, A. Dante Gabriel Rossetti. CW-RossD

Little while, a little while, A. Emily Jane Brontë. CP-BronE

Little white-haired man moves off from where, The. Petrarch. CP-Petra, tr. by J. G. Nichols

Little White Hearse, The. James Whitcomb Riley. CP-RileJ

Little white love, your way you've taken. Now at Liberty. Dorothy Parker. CP-ParkD

Little White Rose, The. Hugh MacDiarmid. SP-MacDH

Little white-washed house we used to own, The. I Haven't Forgotten. Charles Baudelaire. CP-BaudC, tr. by Walter Martin

Little wild bird sometimes at my ear, A. Ballata: Of True and False Singing. Unknown. CW-RossD, tr. by Dante Gabriel Rossetti

Little Will comes naked to its world, The. Head of Wisdom, The. Randall Jarrell. CP-JarrR

Little Woman, The. James Whitcomb Riley. CP-RileJ

Little Word, Little White Bird. Carl Sandburg. CP-SandC

Little Words. Dorothy Parker. CP-ParkD

Little Wowser, The. D. H. Lawrence. CP-LawrD

Little wrists. So that Even a Lover. Louis Zukofsky. CP-ZukLS

Little you are; for Womans sake be proud. Little and Loud. Robert Herrick. CP-HerrR

Littleblood. Ted Hughes. SP-HughTN Fr. Crow.

Littlenesse No Cause of Leannesse. Robert Herrick. CP-HerrR

Littleton, N.H. Robert Creeley. CP-CreeR

Littleton Whale, The. Charles Tomlinson. CP-TomlC; SP-TomlC

Littoral. Louis MacNeice. CP-MacNL

Liturgical. Yannis Ritsos. SP-RitsY, tr. by Kimon Friar and Kostas Myrsiades

Liturgical / eighth day, The. Charles Olson. CP-OlsoC

Liturgy of Roses, A. Tennessee Williams. CP-WillT

Lityerses. Allen Tate. CP-TateA

Live. Heather McHugh. SP-McHuH

Live. Anne Sexton. CP-SextA; SP-SextA

Live all thy sweet life thro'. Summer Wish, A. Christina Georgina Rossetti. CP-RosC1

Live and clean forget from day to day. Nicolas-Sébastien Roch Chamfort. CP-BeckS

Live and Let Live. Langston Hughes. CP-HughL; CP-HughL3

Live by thy Muse thou shalt; when others die. On Himselfe. Robert Herrick. CP-HerrR

Live for myself. Weather, The. David Ignatow. SP-IgnaD

'Live-in-ease,' and then to wash. Livingshayes. Donald Davie. CP-DaviDC

Live Jesus, Live, and let it bee. Authors Motto, The. Richard Crashaw. CP-CrasR

"Live like the wind," he said, "unfettered." Wind Bloweth Where It Listeth, The. Countee Cullen. CP-CullC

Live, live with me, and thou shalt see. To Phyllis to Love and Live with Him. Robert Herrick. CP-HerrR

Live sparks rain from the central anvil. Red Shower, The. Robert Graves. CP-GravR

Live storm went through last night, The. Glad at the Cold (1955). Alan Dugan. CP-DugaA

Live thou gladly if so thou may. Sir Thomas Wyatt. CP-WyatT

Live with a thrifty, not a needy Fate. Expenses Exhaust. Robert Herrick. CP-HerrR

Live without making visits. Han-shan. CP-ColdM, tr. by Red Pine

Live, you say, in the present. Fernando Pessoa. SP-PessF, tr. by Susan M. Brown and Edwin Honig

Lived a woman wonderful. South Africa. Rudyard Kipling. CP-KiplR

Lived savage and simple, where teeth were tools. Dream after Nanook. May Swenson. SP-SwenM

Lived to see you throwing. Hesitate to Call. Louise Glück. SP-GlucL

Liveforever. Louis Zukofsky. CP-ZukLS

Lively and loathesome moe's respectably dead. E. E. Cummings. CP-CummE

Lively Hope, and Gracious Fear. William Cowper. CP-CowpW *Fr.* Olney Hymns.

Lively sparks that issue from those eyes, The. Sir Thomas Wyatt. CP-WyatT

Lively Watering Hole, A. Charles Baudelaire. CP-BaudC, *tr. by* Walter Martin

Liverpool Epistle, A. Donald Davie. CP-DaviDC

Lives. Lucille Clifton. SP-ClifL

Lives. Derek Mahon. CP-MahoD

Lives. Arthur Rimbaud. CP-RimbA, *tr. by* Martin Sorrell

Lives he in any other world. Emily Dickinson. CP-DickE

Lives in the woods. Last Visit to the Swimming Pool Soviets. Kenneth Rexroth. CP-RexrK

Lives of Gulls and Children, The. Howard Nemerov. CP-NemeH

Lives of the Artists. Charles Wright. SP-WrigCN

Lives of the Poet, The. John Logan. CP-LogaJ

Lives of the Poets. Mona Van Duyn. SP-VanDM

Lives of the Saints. Paul Muldoon. CP-MuldP

Lives of the Saints. Charles Wright. SP-WrigCN

Lives of the Swan. Kenneth Patchen. CP-PatcK

Live's on it. Dramatis Personae. Charles Olson. CP-OlsoC

Lives there a man with such base mettle. George Meredith. CP-MerG2

Livid lightnings flashed in the clouds, The. Stephen Crane. CP-CranS

Livid sky on London, A. Old Song, The. G. K. Chesterton. CP-ChesG

Livid to lurid switched the sky. Sky. Robert Penn Warren. CP-WarrR

Living. Denise Levertov. SP-LeveDP; SP-LeveDS

Living, A. D. H. Lawrence. CP-LawrD

Living a life. Man, A. Denise Levertov. SP-LeveDP

Living Alone. Hayden Carruth. CP-CarHS

Living Alone (1). Denise Levertov. SP-LeveDL; SP-LeveDS

Living Alone (2). Denise Levertov. SP-LeveDL; SP-LeveDS

Living Alone (3). Denise Levertov. SP-LeveDL; SP-LeveDS

Living Alone with Jesus. Maxine W. Kumin. SP-KumiM

Living among orchards, we are ruled. Language of the Seasons. Robert Graves. CP-GravR

Living backwards means only. Precognition. Margaret Atwood. SP-AtwM2

Living Beauty, The. William Butler Yeats. CP-YeatW

Living by the Red River. James Wright. CP-WrigJ

Living come with grassy tread, The. In a Disused Graveyard. Robert Frost. CP-FrosR

Living Dead, The. Charles Baudelaire. CP-BaudC, *tr. by* Walter Martin

Living for Two. Denise Levertov. SP-LeveDL

Living frame which sustains my soul, The. *See also* Ode to Heaven. Percy Bysshe Shelley. CP-ShelP

Living God, The. Jones Very. CP-VeryJ

Living Heaven thy prayers respect, The. Spiritual Laws. Ralph Waldo Emerson. CP-EmerR

Living in an apartment with a gelded cat. Typical Affair, A. Allen Ginsberg. CP-GinsA

Living in Sin. Adrienne Rich. SP-RicA1

Living in the earth-deposits of our history. Power. Adrienne Rich. SP-RicA1; SP-RicA2

Living in the Moment. Marilyn Hacker. SP-HackM

Living in the Open. Marge Piercy. SP-PierM

Living Memory. Adrienne Rich. SP-RicA1

Living mother-of-pearl of a salmon, The. Hazel Stick for Catherine Ann, A. Seamus Heaney. SP-HeanSO

Living on the Plains ("Carefully, sending leaves always toward the sun"). William Stafford. SP-StafWW

Living on the Plains ("That winter when this thought came—how the river"). William Stafford. SP-StafW; SP-StafWW

Living on the Surface. Miller Williams. SP-WillM

Living Pearl, A. Kenneth Rexroth. CP-RexrK

Living Quetzalcoatl, The. D. H. Lawrence. CP-LawrD

Living Room, A. Theodore Weiss. SP-WeisT

Living Sky. Federico García Lorca. CP-GarcF, *tr. by* Greg Simon *and* Steven F. White

Living someplace else is wrong. Spring Offensive of the Snail, The. Marge Piercy. SP-PierM

Living Statues. William Stafford. SP-StafWW

Living Tenderly. May Swenson. SP-SwenM

Living Theatre, The. Lawrence Ferlinghetti. SP-FerlL

Living Torch, The. Charles Baudelaire. CP-BaudC, *tr. by* Walter Martin

Living Water. Jeanne Marie Bouvier de la Motte- Guyon. CP-CowpW

Living while It May. Denise Levertov. SP-LeveDP

Living with a Wife. John Updike. CP-UpdiJ

Livings. Philip Larkin. CP-LarkP

Livingshayes. Donald Davie. CP-DaviDC

Liz-Town Humorist, A. James Whitcomb Riley. CP-RileJ

Liza May. Paul Laurence Dunbar. CP-DunbP

'Lizabuth-Ann on Bakin'-Day. James Whitcomb Riley. CP-RileJ

Lizard. D. H. Lawrence. CP-LawrD

Lizard, The. Thomas Hardy. CP-HardT

Lizard, The. Theodore Roethke. CP-RoetT

Lizard Is Crying, The. Federico García Lorca. SP-GarcF, *tr. by* J. L. Gili *and* Stephen Spender

Lizard, lover of heat, of high. Old Man to the Lizard, The. Archibald MacLeish. CP-MacLA

Lizard ran out on a rock and looked up, listening, A. Lizard. D. H. Lawrence. CP-LawrD

Lizard rusty as a leaf rubbed rough. Robert Lowell. SP-LoweR *Fr.* Mexico.

Lizard's iridescence, / the conch winged with mother-of-pearl, The. Earth. Pablo Neruda. SP-NeruP

Lizards leap aside and go panic-crashing. Expedition. Peter Blue Cloud. SP-BlueP

'Ll where in the world my eyes has bin. Train-Misser, The. James Whitcomb Riley. CP-RileJ

Llewellyn and the Tree. Edwin Arlington Robinson. CP-RobiE

Lo! A Child Is Born. Hugh MacDiarmid. SP-MacDH

Lo & behold. Yes, peat bogs. Landscape for the Disappeared. Yusef Komunyakaa. CP-KomuY

Lo, at its center one can find oneself. L.A. John Updike. CP-UpdiJ

Lo Christ returns! But where is love. Return of the Savior, The. Jones Very. CP-VeryJ

Lo, Collin, here the place whose pleasaunt syte. June. Edmund Spenser. CP-Spens *Fr.* Shepheardes [*or* Shepeards *or* Shepherd's] Calender, The.

Lo! Death has reared himself a throne. City in the Sea, The. Edgar Allan Poe. CP-PoeEd

Lo! for this dark terrestrial ball. Hymn to Humanity, An. Phillis Wheatley. CP-WheaP

Lo! for this dark terrestrial Dome. Phillis Wheatley. *See* Lo! for this dark terrestrial ball

Lo! Freedom comes. Th' prescient Muse foretold. Liberty and Peace, a Poem. Phillis Wheatley. CP-WheaP

Lo here I sit at Holyhead. Holyhead. September 25, 1727. Jonathan Swift. CP-SwifJ

Lo, here is God, and there is God. When Israel Came Out of Egypt. Arthur Hugh Clough. SP-ClouA

Lo here the faire *Chariclia!* in whom strove. Upon the Faire Ethiopian Sent to a Gentlewoman. Richard Crashaw. CP-CrasR

Lo, how I seek and sue to have. Sir Thomas Wyatt. CP-WyatT

Lo, I am dying! And to feel the King. Death. James Whitcomb Riley. CP-RileJ

Lo! I am she who makes the wheel to turn. Canzone: A Song of Fortune. Guido Cavalcanti. CW-RossD, *tr. by* Dante Gabriel Rossetti

Lo! I must tell a tale of chivalry. Specimen of an Induction to a Poem. John Keats. CP-KeatJ

Lo, Lord, Thou ridest! Hurricane, The. Hart Crane. CP-CranH

Lo: Masterman and Chesterton. Masterman and Chesterton. G. K. Chesterton. CP-ChesG

Lo now four other act upon the stage. Of the Four Ages of Man. Anne Bradstreet. CP-BradA

Lo! steadfast and serene. Old Man, The. James Whitcomb Riley. CP-RileJ

Lo! Swift to idiots bequeaths his store. On the Same. *Unknown, sometimes at. to* Thomas Sheridan. CP-SherT

Lo that the wood standeth drearily! Autumnus. Ezra Pound. CP-PoEar

Lo the leaves. To Be Closely Written on a Small Piece of Paper Which Folded into a Tight Lozenge Will Fit Any Girl's Locket. William Carlos Williams. CP-WilW1

Lo the twelfth year—the wedding-feast come round. After the German Subjugation of France, 1871. Dante Gabriel Rossetti. CW-RossD

Lo, the unbounded sea. Ship Starting, The. Walt Whitman. CP-WhitW

Lo! the Wild Cow of the Desert, her yeanling estrayed from her. Azrael's Count. Rudyard Kipling. CP-KiplR

Lo! thro' the dusky silence of the groves. Wish, A. Samuel Taylor Coleridge. CP-ColeS

Lo! 'tis a gala night. Conqueror Worm, The. Edgar Allan Poe. CP-PoeEd

Lo! very fair is she who knows the ways. Two Women, The. G. K. Chesterton. CP-ChesG

Lo, Victress on the Peaks. Walt Whitman. CP-WhitW

Lo! what is this that I make—sudden, supreme, unrehearsed. Beginner, The. Rudyard Kipling. CP-KiplR *Fr.* Muse among the Motors, The.

Lo, what it is to love! Sir Thomas Wyatt. CP-WyatT

Lo, what my country should have done (have raised). To William, Lord Mounteagle. Ben Jonson. CP-JonsB; SP-JonsB

Lo, whatever is at hand. All-kind Mother, The. James Whitcomb Riley. CP-RileJ

Lo! where from Heaven's high roof. Hafiz. CP-EmerR *Fr.* Odes.

Lo! Where She Stands Fixed in a Saint-like Trance. William Wordsworth. CP-WorW2

Lo! where the Moon along the sky. Night Thought, A. William Wordsworth. CP-WorW2

Lo! where the rosy-bosomed [*or* bosom'd] Hours. Ode on the Spring. Thomas Gray. CP-GrayT

Lo! where the silent marble weeps. Epitaph on Mrs Jane Clarke. Thomas Gray. CP-GrayT

Lo worms enjoy the seat of bliss. Epitaph: "Lo worms enjoy the seat of bliss." Robert Burns. CP-BurnR

Lo Yu Park. Tu Fu. CP-KizeC, *tr. by* Carolyn Kizer

Load of brushes and baskets and cradles and chairs, A. No Buyers [*or* No Buyers: A Street Scene]. Thomas Hardy. CP-HardT

Load of Sugar-Cane, The. Wallace Stevens. CP-StevW; CP-StevWP

Loaded like spoons. Slaveship[s]. Lucille Clifton. SP-ClifL

Loading and Unloading. Robert Herrick. CP-HerrR

Loaf of Time, A. May Swenson. SP-SwenM

Loafing. Raymond Carver. CP-CarvR

Loam. Carl Sandburg. CP-SandC

Loan, The. Muriel Rukeyser. CP-RukeM

Loaning, The. Seamus Heaney.
Aye. SP-HeanSO

Lobbed ball plops, then dribbles to the cup, The. Ford Madox Ford. Robert Lowell. SP-LoweR

Lobster. Anne Sexton. CP-SextA

Lobster-car, boat, or fishbasket. Ralph Waldo Emerson. CP-EmerR

Lobsters. Howard Nemerov. CP-NemeH

Local Genius, The. Amy Clampitt. CP-ClamA

Local Journal. Charles Wright. SP-WrigC

Local Legend. Robinson Jeffers. CP-JefR3

Local Matter, A. Theodore Weiss. SP-WeisT

Local Objects. Wallace Stevens. CP-StevWP

Local Politician from Away Back, A. James Whitcomb Riley. CP-RileJ

Local Snivels through the Field, The. Philip Larkin. CP-LarkP

Local Train. Eugenio Montale. CP-MontE, *tr. by* Jonathan Galassi

Localities. Carl Sandburg. CP-SandC

Locate I / love you some-. Language, The. Robert Creeley. CP-CreeR

Location. Jones Very. CP-VeryJ

Locations and Times. Walt Whitman. CP-WhitW

L'Occupation Obsédée. Lawrence Ferlinghetti. SP-FerlL

Loch Coruisk. Sir Walter Scott. SP-ScotW *Fr.* Lord of the Isles, The.

Lochinvar. Sir Walter Scott. SP-ScotW *Fr.* Marmion.

Lock, The. Robert Stock. SP-StocR

Lock Keeper, The. Ivor Gurney. SP-GurnI

Lock Up, Fair Lids. Sir Philip Sidney. SP-SidnP *Fr.* Arcadia.

Lock up, fair lids, the treasure of my heart. Lock Up, Fair Lids. Sir Philip Sidney. SP-SidnP *Fr.* Arcadia.

Lock up the church. Night Song for a Boy. Alan Dugan. CP-DugaA

Locke sank into a swoon. Fragments: "Locke sank into a swoon." William Butler Yeats. CP-YeatW

Locked arm in arm they cross the way. Tableau. Countee Cullen. CP-CullC

Locked Doors. Anne Sexton. CP-SextA

Locked in the dictionary on the table. Exasperations of a Novelist. Howard Nemerov. CP-NemeH

Locked Out. Robert Frost. CP-FrosR

Lockerbie. William Corbett. SP-CorbW

Lockerbie Fair. James Whitcomb Riley. CP-RileJ

Lockerbie Street. James Whitcomb Riley. CP-RileJ

Locket, The. Ted Hughes. SP-HughTN

Locking Yourself Out, Then Trying to Get Back In. Raymond Carver. CP-CarvR

Lockless Door, The. Robert Frost. CP-FrosR

Lockout. The seventh week. Men in the Square. Thanksgiving: Detroit. John Berryman. CP-BerrJ

Locks. Kenneth Koch. SP-KochK

Locksley Hall. Alfred Tennyson. CP-TennA

Locksley Hall Sixty Years After. Alfred Tennyson. CP-TennA

Locus. A. R. Ammons. CP-AmmoA

Locus. Robert Earl Hayden. CP-HaydR

Locust-Lovers, Attention! Ogden Nash. CP-NashO

Locust Songs. Geoffrey Hill. CP-HillG

Locust Tree in Flower, The. William Carlos Williams. CP-WilW1
(Among / the leaves.) CP-WilW1

Locusts have finished their ravage, The. Rainer Maria Rilke. CP-RilkFr, *tr. by* A. Poulin, Jr. *Fr.* Valaisian Quatrains, The.

Lodged. Robert Frost. CP-FrosR

Lodgepole / cone / seed waits for fire. Gary Snyder. CP-SnydG *Fr.* Myths and Texts.

Lodgepole Pine: the wonderful reproductive. Gary Snyder. CP-SnydG *Fr.* Myths and Texts.

Lodging-House Fuchsias, The. Thomas Hardy. CP-HardT

Lo[e] here a little volume, but great [*or* large] book[e]. Ode on a Prayer-Book. Richard Crashaw. CP-CrasR

Loe! I have made a Calender for every yeare. Edmund Spenser. CP-Spens *Fr.* Shepheardes [*or* Shepeards *or* Shepherd's] Calender, The.

Loe, when backe mine eye. Thomas Campion. CP-CampT

Loehrs and the Hammonds, The. James Whitcomb Riley. CP-RileJ *Fr.* Child-World, A.

Loft. A. R. Ammons. CP-AmmoA

Loft, out of the market place, A. Stable, The. Thomas Kinsella. CP-KinsT

Lofty in the Palais de Danse. Thom Gunn. CP-GunnT

Lofty pine, from high Mount Pelion raught, The. Elegy 2.11: "Lofty pine, from high Mount Pelion raught, The." Ovid. CP-MarlC *Fr.* Elegies.

Log. James Merrill. SP-MerrJ

Logbook of Judgments. Jay Wright. SP-WrigJ

Logeorge / lo / wellifitisn't eddy how's the boy. E. E. Cummings. CP-CummE

Loggerheads. D. H. Lawrence. CP-LawrD

Loggia circled by mouths of sleep, The. Diagram of Abandoned Mosque. Olga Broumas. SP-BrouO

Logging. Gary Snyder. *Fr.* Myths and Texts.

Logic. Robert Graves. CP-GravR

Logic. Charles Tomlinson. CP-TomlC

Logic and the Magic Flute. Marianne Craig Moore. CP-MoorM

Logic of Progress, The. G. K. Chesterton. CP-ChesG

Logical Conclusion, The. Ezra Pound. CP-PoEar

Logical pleasure of expectant mercy, The. Retrospective Forelook. Richard Eberhart. CP-EberR

Logical Vegetarian, The. G. K. Chesterton. CP-ChesG

Logician's Nocturne, The. John Ciardi. CP-CiarJ

Logistics. James Laughlin. CP-LaugJ

Logos. Robert Stock. SP-StocR

Logos. Miller Williams. CP-WillM

Logos Our Teacher, The. Clement of Alexandria. CP-MertT

Logs give back, in burning, solar fire, The. Energy: A Villanelle. John Updike. CP-UpdiJ

Logs on the Hearth. Thomas Hardy. CP-HardT

Lohengrin. Constantine P. Cavafy. CP-CavaC, *tr. by* Theoharis Constantine Theoharis

Loin Cloth. Carl Sandburg. CP-SandC

Loin de l'Être. Stevie Smith. CP-SmitS

Loitering with a vacant eye. A. E. Housman. CP-HousA

'Lola de Valence' by Manet. Charles Baudelaire. CP-BaudC, *tr. by* Walter Martin

Lola / sings *saetas*. Balcony. Federico García Lorca. SP-GarcF *Fr.* Poem of the Saeta.

Lollapalooza: 22 February. A. R. Ammons. CP-AmmoA

Lollipops of the Pomeranian Baroque. James Fenton. SP-FentJ
(Skies remind you of those mounds of custard, The.) SP-FentJ

Lollius. Rudyard Kipling. CP-KiplR

Lollocks. Robert Graves. CP-GravR

London. John Berryman. CP-BerrJ

London. William Blake. CP-BlakW *Fr.* Songs of Experience.

London. G. K. Chesterton. CP-ChesG

London. Ivor Gurney. SP-GurnI

London. Randall Jarrell. CP-JarrR

London: A Poem. Samuel Johnson. CP-JohnS

London air dims. Kathleen Jessie Raine. SP-RainK

London Bridge. Edwin Arlington Robinson. CP-RobiE

London by Lamplight. George Meredith. CP-MerG1

London / crossfigured / creeping with trams. Lawrence Ferlinghetti. SP-FerlL

London 1802. William Wordsworth. CP-WorW1; MW-WorW

London Inside and Outside. Amy Clampitt. CP-ClamA

London Mercury. D. H. Lawrence. CP-LawrD

London Rain. Louis MacNeice. CP-MacNL

London Stone. Rudyard Kipling. CP-KiplR

London / Used to wear her lights splendidly. Town in 1917. D. H. Lawrence. CP-LawrD

Lone Flower, hemmed in with snows and white as they. To a Snow-Drop. William Wordsworth. CP-WorW2

Lone Founts. Herman Melville. SP-MelvH

Lone gray bird, A. From the Shore. Carl Sandburg. CP-SandC

Lone Man's Night, A. Yannis Ritsos. SP-RitsY, *tr. by* Kimon Friar

Lone on the bleaky hills, the straying flocks. On the Death of the Late Lord President Dundas. Robert Burns. CP-BurnR

Lone Ranger, The. Donald Hall. CP-HallD

Lone streets inanimate, repetitive machine Crash cookie-cutting. Manhattan Thirties Flash. Allen Ginsberg. CP-GinsA

Lone Striker, A. Robert Frost. CP-FrosR

Lonedale Operator, The. John Ashbery. SP-AshbJ

Loneliness. W. H. Auden. CP-AudeW

Loneliness. Yusef Komunyakaa. CP-KomuY

Loneliness. D. H. Lawrence. CP-LawrD

Loneliness. Kenneth Rexroth. CP-RexrK

Loneliness[: An Outburst of Hexasyllables]. Hayden Carruth. CP-CarHS

Loneliness in Jersey City. Wallace Stevens. CP-StevW; CP-StevWP

Loneliness leapt in the mirrors, but all week. Departure's Girl-Friend. W. S. Merwin. SP-MerwW

Loneliness of Sundays grows, The. Their Week. W. S. Merwin. SP-MerwW

Loneliness / of the short-distance runner, The. Runner Artist, The. Dan Pagis. SP-PagiD, tr. by Stephen Mitchell

Loneliness One dare not sound, The. Emily Dickinson. CP-DickE

Loneliness terrific beats on my heart. Refugee. Langston Hughes. CP-HughL; CP-HughL2

Loneliness without rest! Ballad of One Doomed to Die. Federico García Lorca. SP-GarcF, tr. by Langston Hughes

Lonely as a dry and used orchard. Blackbirds Are Rough Today, The. Charles Bukowski. SP-BukC2

Lonely / As the wind. One. Langston Hughes. CP-HughL; CP-HughL2

Lonely at her window sitting. Emily Jane Brontë. CP-BronE

Lonely Days. Thomas Hardy. CP-HardT

Lonely he sat, the men were strange. Discontented Poet: A Masque, The. Ralph Waldo Emerson. CP-EmerR

Lonely heart, The. Ecce Sponsus. "H. D." CP-DoolH

Lonely her fate was. Lonely Days. Thomas Hardy. CP-HardT

Lonely in Ireland, since it was not home. Importance of Elsewhere, The. Philip Larkin. CP-LarkP

Lonely little question mark. Kid in the Park. Langston Hughes. CP-HughL; CP-HughL2

Lonely, Lonesome, Loney—O! D. H. Lawrence. CP-LawrD

Lonely Man, The. Randall Jarrell. CP-JarrR

Lonely Nocturne. Langston Hughes. CP-HughL; CP-HughL3

Lonely One, The. Paul Celan. SP-CelaP, tr. by John Felstiner

Lonely Particular. Alice Walker. CP-WalkA

Lonely people. Little Song ("Lonely people"). Langston Hughes. CP-HughL; CP-HughL2

Lonely people are marching, The. Keep It. C. K. Williams. CP-WillC

Lonely skyscrapers, deserted tombs of business risen. Gasman Invites the Skyscrapers to Dance. Marge Piercy. SP-PierM

Lonely Splendor. A. R. Ammons. CP-AmmoA

Lonely Street, The. William Carlos Williams. CP-WilW1

Lonely times of the soul, The. Helian. Georg Trakl. CP-LogaJ, tr. by John Logan

Lonely, White Fields. Mary Oliver. SP-OlivM

Lonely woman, not prompted. Woman with Umbrella. Lorine Niedecker. CP-NiedL

Loner. Robert Creeley. SP-CreeR

Lonesome. Paul Laurence Dunbar. CP-DunbP

Lonesome Blues. Federico García Lorca. CP-GarcF, tr. by Jerome Rothenberg Fr. Blue River.

Lonesome Boy Blues. Kenneth Patchen. CP-PatcK

Lonesome Corner. Langston Hughes. CP-HughL; CP-HughL2

Lonesome for they know not What, The. Emily Dickinson. CP-DickE

Lonesome Man. Tennessee Williams. CP-WillT

Lonesome Pine Special. Charles Wright. SP-WrigC

Lonesome Place. Langston Hughes. CP-HughL; CP-HughL1

Lonesome Valley. A. R. Ammons. CP-AmmoA

Long after Chamfort. Nicolas-Sébastien Roch Chamfort. CP-BeckS

Long after our departure. May Evening. Richard Eberhart. CP-EberR

Long after the days and seasons, and the creatures and countries. Barbaric. Arthur Rimbaud. CP-RimbA, tr. by Martin Sorrell

Long after the scheduled deaths of animals. Shoe Repairs. W. S. Merwin. SP-MerwW

Long after there were none of them alive. Recalled. Edwin Arlington Robinson. CP-RobiE

Long after you beat down the powerful hand. Girl at the Play. Muriel Rukeyser. CP-RukeM

Long after you have swung back. Losing Track. Denise Levertov. SP-LeveDP

Long Afternoons. Adam Zagajewski. SP-ZagaA, tr. by Clare Cavanagh

Long afterward, Oedipus, old and blinded, walked the. Myth. Muriel Rukeyser. CP-RukeM

Long afterwards. Judgment of Paris, The. W. S. Merwin. SP-MerwW

Long Ages Past. Wilfred Owen. CP-OwenW

Long Ago. Paul Laurence Dunbar. CP-DunbP

Long ago and long ago. Maiden-Song. Christina Georgina Rossetti. CP-RosC1

Long ago,between a dream and a dream. E. E. Cummings. CP-CummE

Long ago during Liang times. Han-shan. CP-ColdM, tr. by Red Pine

Long ago from radiant palace. Mourn'st Thou Now? Walter De la Mare. CP-DeLaW

Long ago I found a seed. Tree, The. Adrienne Rich. CP-RicAE

Long ago I learned how to sleep. Wind Song. Carl Sandburg. CP-SandC

Long ago I thought you young, bright daimon. Kathleen Jessie Raine. SP-RainK

Long ago on a night of danger and vigil. If They Come in the Night. Marge Piercy. SP-PierM

Long ago the world was finer. Golden Age, The. Ambrose Bierce. SP-BierA

Long ago was the then beginning to seem like now. Blue Sonata. John Ashbery. SP-AshbJ

Long Alley, The. Theodore Roethke. CP-RoetT

Long and dark the nights, dim and short the days. Vigil of the Presentation. Christina Georgina Rossetti. CP-RosC1

Long and Lazy [or Lazie]. Robert Herrick. CP-HerrR

Long and Sluggish Lines. Wallace Stevens. CP-StevW; CP-StevWP

Long Approach, The. Maxine W. Kumin. SP-KumiM

Long Banister Lane. Li Po. CP-WilW2

Long Barren. Christina Georgina Rossetti. CP-RosC1

Long before dawn has silvered the last star. Out of Sleep Awakened. Archibald MacLeish. CP-MacLA

Long before dawn your light. Chinese Nightingale. William Carlos Williams. CP-WilW1

Long before daybreak I started. For an Album. Eugenio Montale. CP-MontE, tr. by Jonathan Galassi

Long before he thought of his own death. My Dad's Wallet. Raymond Carver. CP-CarvR

Long before spring. Beginning. W. S. Merwin. SP-MerwW

Long before sun had toward the mountain dipped. Mediterranean Basin. Robert Penn Warren. CP-WarrR

Long Bells, The. C. K. Williams. CP-WillC

Long Boat, The. Stanley Kunitz. CP-KunSC

Long body of the water fills its hollow, The. Staring at the Sea on the Day of the Death of Another. May Swenson. SP-SwenM

Long Branch, New Jersey. Robert Pinsky. CP-PinsR

Long Branch Song, A. Robert Pinsky. CP-PinsR

Long buried, ancient men-at-arms. Two British Airmen. Thomas Merton. CP-MertT

Long cloud edged with streaming grey, The. Autumn Even-Song. George Meredith. CP-MerG1

Long days and changing weather. Division. Louise Bogan. CP-BogaL

Long Death, The. Marge Piercy. SP-PierM

Long, Disconsolate Lines. Jane Cooper. CP-CoopJ

Long Distance. Charles Olson. CP-OlsoC

Long Distance. William Stafford. SP-StafW; SP-StafWW

Long-Distance Runner, The. James Laughlin. CP-LaugJ

Long do we live upon the husks of corn. Bread from Heaven, The. Jones Very. CP-VeryJ

Long Door. Andrei Codrescu. SP-CodrA

Long-drawn bray of the ass, The. Ass, The. D. H. Lawrence. CP-LawrD

Long-eared beast, and a field-house for cattle, A. Probatur Aliter. Jonathan Swift. CP-SwifJ

Long Enough. Thomas Merton. CP-MertT

Long Enough. Long Enough. Muriel Rukeyser. CP-RukeM

Long enough to remember the girl. Atypical Affair, An. Allen Ginsberg. CP-GinsA

Long-expected one and twenty. Short Song of Congratulation, A [or To a Young Heir]. Samuel Johnson. CP-JohnS

Long-favoured England! be thou not misled. In Allusion to Various Recent Histories and Notices of the French Revolution, Concluded. William Wordsworth. CP-WorW2

Long Fingers. Allen Tate. CP-TateA

Long Finish. Paul Muldoon. CP-MuldP

Long for the evening, loathe the coming dawn. Petrarch. CP-Petra, tr. by J. G. Nichols

Long freight train / Wakes me in my cell, The. Ernesto Cardenal. CP-MertT Fr. Gethsemani, KY.

Long-gathering Old-end, I did fear thee wise. To Old-End Gatherer. Ben Jonson. CP-JonsB; SP-JonsB

Long gold nail from the Goldrush, A. West Is the Best and the Future Is Near, The. Andrei Codrescu. SP-CodrA

Long gone time ("Long gone time"). Robert Creeley. SP-CreeR

Long Goodbye. Thomas McGrath. SP-McGrT

Long Guns. Carl Sandburg. CP-SandC

Long had Christ's servant preached the word of truth. Poor Clergyman, The. Jones Very. CP-VeryJ

Long had I grieved at what I deemed abuse. Resignation. Paul Laurence Dunbar. CP-DunbP

Long Hair. Gary Snyder. CP-SnydG

Long have I borne much, mad thy faults me make. Elegy 3.10: "Long have I borne much, mad thy faults me make." Ovid. CP-MarlC *Fr.* Elegies.

Long have I framed weak phantasies of Thee. Agnosto Theo [To an Unknown God]. Thomas Hardy. CP-HardT

Long have I longed, till I am tired. Till Tomorrow. Christina Georgina Rossetti. CP-RosC2

Long have mine eies gaz'd with delight. Thomas Campion *and* Philip Rosseter. CP-CampT

Long Home, The. John Berryman. CP-BerrJ

Long Hot Summer. Archibald MacLeish. CP-MacLA

Long house— / the fox gallery you called, A. Fox Gallery, The. Charles Tomlinson. CP-TomlC; SP-TomlC

Long Hunter, The. Wendell Berry. CP-BerrW

Long I followed [*or* follow'd] happy guides. Forerunners. Ralph Waldo Emerson. CP-EmerR

Long I fought the driving lists. Prisoner. Dorothy Parker. CP-ParkD

Long Island Sound's. Meridian. Louise Glück. SP-GlucL

Long John Brown & Little Mary Bell. William Blake. CP-BlakW

Long lakes, flanked, The. Southwest of Buffalo. Donald Hall. CP-HallD

Long languishing in double malady. Sonnet 50. Edmund Spenser. CP-Spens *Fr.* Amoretti.

Long Last. Philip Larkin. CP-LarkP

Long-Legged Fly. William Butler Yeats. CP-YeatW

Long Life. Robert Herrick. CP-HerrR

Long life, My lord, an' health be yours. Address of Beelzebub. Robert Burns. CP-BurnR

Long life's a lovely thing to know. Exceeding All. James Whitcomb Riley. CP-RileJ

Long-lifes-day I've taken paines, A. Paines without Profit. Robert Herrick. CP-HerrR

Long Line of Doctors, A. Carolyn Kizer. CP-KizeC

Long lines of cliff breaking have left a chasm. Enoch Arden. Alfred Tennyson. CP-TennA

Long lines of coral light. Autumn. Wallace Stevens. CP-StevWP

Long Lion Days. Philip Larkin. CP-LarkP

Long Live the Spiderweb. Allen Ginsberg. CP-GinsA

Long Live the Weeds. Theodore Roethke. CP-RoetT

Long locks of late our Zelot Peason weares. Upon Peason. Robert Herrick. CP-HerrR

Long, Long Hence. Walt Whitman. CP-WhitW

Long long I lay in the sands. Vast Confusion, A. Lawrence Ferlinghetti. SP-FerlL

Long, long legs, The. From the Country to the City. Elizabeth Bishop. CP-BishE

Long—long Sleep—a famous—Sleep, A. Emily Dickinson. CP-DickE

Long long with wonder I thought you human. Ecce Homo. John Berryman. CP-BerrJ

Long Looked For. Christina Georgina Rossetti. CP-RosC3

Long Lookt for Comes at Last. Robert Herrick. CP-HerrR

Long love that in my thought doth harbo[u]r, The. Sir Thomas Wyatt. CP-WyatT

Long may live my lovely Hetty! Translation of Lines in Baretti's *Easy Phraseology*. Samuel Johnson. CP-JohnS

Long my heart has been. Joinery. Olga Broumas. SP-BrouO

Long Naked Walk of the Dead, The. C. K. Williams. CP-WillC

Long neglect has worn away. Emily Jane Brontë. CP-BronE

Long Night, The. James Laughlin. CP-LaugJ

Long night, the short sleep, and La Gorgue to wander, The. La Gorgue. Ivor Gurney. SP-GurnI

Long Novel, A. John Ashbery. SP-AshbJ

Long orange knife slits the darkness, A. Winter on the River. William Meredith. SP-MereW

Long over whatever edge. Edge, The ("Long over whatever edge"). Robert Creeley. SP-CreeR

Long Past Moncada. Muriel Rukeyser. CP-RukeM

Long Plighted. Thomas Hardy. CP-HardT

Long plung'd in sorrow, I resign. Joy of the Cross, The. Jeanne Marie Bouvier de la Motte Guyon. CP-CowpW, *tr. by* William Cowper

Long prostration has accustomed him, The. Paris, 1856. Jorge Luis Borges. SP-BorgJ, *tr. by* Willis Barnstone

Long Race, The. Edwin Arlington Robinson. CP-RobiE

Long River, The. Donald Hall. CP-HallD

Long road and a village, A. Holy Family. Muriel Rukeyser. CP-RukeM

Long Roots Moor Summer to Our Side of Earth. Philip Larkin. CP-LarkP

Long sea, how short-lasting, The. There Is No Land Yet. Laura Riding Jackson. CP-RidiL

Long Search, The. John Logan. CP-LogaJ

Long Shadow. John Updike. CP-UpdiJ

Long Shadow of Lincoln: A Litany, The. Carl Sandburg. CP-SandC

Long shines the thin light of the day to north-east. Early Spring Dawn. Ivor Gurney. SP-GurnI

Long sigh of the Frog, The. Emily Dickinson. CP-DickE

Long Sight in Age. Philip Larkin. CP-LarkP

Long since, a dream of heaven I had. Divine Compassion. John Greenleaf Whittier. CP-WhitJ

Long since, in sore distress, I heard one pray. Warrior's Prayer, The. Paul Laurence Dunbar. CP-DunbP

Long since, the flicker brushed with shameless wing. Sonnet: "Long since, the flicker brushed with shameless wing." E. E. Cummings. CP-CummE

Long since the time their wives had set for them to come. How Jimsey O'Roon and Peter Stack, Coal Miners, Came to Be Put in the Ferbettville (Pa.) Jail Early One Saturday Night. Kenneth Patchen. CP-PatcK

Long since the years. Message II. Allen Ginsberg. CP-GinsA

Long Story, A. Thomas Gray. CP GrayT

Long String, The. Jelaluddin Rumi. SP-Rumi, *tr. by* Coleman Barks

Long Summer. Robert Lowell. SP-LoweR

Long summer nights. Yannis Ritsos. SP-RitsY *Fr.* First Series.

Long Summers. Robert Lowell. SP-LoweR

Long sweep / of prairie to the mountains, A. Song: The Famous Vision of America. Hayden Carruth. CP-CarHS

Long Swing, The. Richard Eberhart. CP EberR

Long-tailed ponies go nosing the pine-lands. Parochial Theme. Wallace Stevens. CP-StevW; CP-StevWP

Long Term Suffering. Richard Eberhart. CP-EberR

Long time ago, we two set out. Vagrants. Paul Laurence Dunbar. CP-DunbP

Long time ago, when I was a child, A. Snow Globe, The. Howard Nemerov. CP-NemeH

Long time, many years, we've had these wars, A. On a Certain Engagement South of Seoul. Hayden Carruth. CP-CarHS

Long time no see. Stylist, The. William Carlos Williams. CP-WilW2

Long time since the last scream cut short, A. Rathlin. Derek Mahon. CP-MahoD

Long time you have been making the trip, A. Of Hartford in a Purple Light. Wallace Stevens. CP-StevW; CP-StevWP

'Long To'ds Night. Paul Laurence Dunbar. CP-DunbP

Long, Too Long America. Walt Whitman. CP-WhitW

Long Trail, The. Rudyard Kipling. *See* Envoi: "There's a whisper down the field where the year has shot her yield."

Long Trip. Langston Hughes. CP-HughL; CP-HughL1

Long Tunnel Ceiling, The. Ted Hughes. SP-HughTN

Long View from the Suburbs. Jane Cooper. CP-CoopJ

Long View: Negro. Langston Hughes. CP-HughL; CP-HughL3

Long waiting has by now so worn me out. Petrarch. CP-Petra, *tr. by* J. G. Nichols

Long wake continues, The. Initiation, The. James Tate. SP-TateJ

Long warned of many terrors more severe. Siege Perilous. Edwin Arlington Robinson. CP-RobiE

Long was the conflict, but now 'tis done. George Meredith. CP-MerG2

Long Way outside Yellowstone, A. Thomas McGrath. SP-McGrT

Long Way Round, The. Denise Levertov. SP-LeveDL

Long-while I sought to what I might compare. Sonnet 9. Edmund Spenser. CP-Spens *Fr.* Amoretti.

Long, white, summer cloud, like a cleared linen table, A. Derek Walcott. CP-WalcD *Fr.* Midsummer.

Long winter from home the gulls blew, A. To Lucasta, about That War. John Ciardi. CP-CiarJ

Long with us, now she leaves us; she has rest. Angela Burdett-Coutts. George Meredith. CP-MerG2

Long workroom, in a dead light, The. Back Lane, The. Thomas Kinsella. CP-KinsT

Long wound of the summer—, The. Poem: "Long wound of the summer—, The." Thomas McGrath. SP-McGrT

Long years ago, a funny man. Dead Joke and the Funny Man, The. James Whitcomb Riley. CP-RileJ

Long years ago, ere R—lls or R—ce. Curé, The. Rudyard Kipling. CP-KiplR

Long years ago, within a distant clime. Dream Song I. Paul Laurence Dunbar. CP-DunbP

Long Years apart can make no. Emily Dickinson. CP-DickE

Long years!—It tries the thrilling frame to bear. Lament of Tasso, The. Lord Byron. CP-Byron

Longa victa die, cum multo pulvere rerum. In Themclam Virginem. Gerard Manley Hopkins. CP-HopkG

Longbones. Paul Muldoon. CP-MuldP

Long[e] love that in my thought do[e]th [*or* I] harbour [*or* harber *or* harbar], The. LOVER FOR SHAMEFASTNESS HIDETH HIS DESIRE WITHIN HIS FAITHFUL HEART. Petrarch. CP-WyatT, *tr. by* Sir Thomas Wyatt *Fr.* Sonnets to Laura.

Longe nightes, whan every creature, The. Complaint unto His Lady, A. Geoffrey Chaucer. CP-ChauG

Longer ago than I had lived till then . . . . Anne Dick 2. 1936. Robert Lowell. SP-LoweR

Longer thred of life we spin, The. Long Life. Robert Herrick. CP-HerrR

Longer to muse. Sir Thomas Wyatt. CP-WyatT

Longer to trow ye. Sir Thomas Wyatt. CP-WyatT

Longer we are together, The. Ripening. Wendell Berry. CP-BerrW

Longer we stay here the harder, The. Soul, Geologically, A. Margaret Atwood. SP-AtwM1

Longest Day, The. George Meredith. CP-MerG1

Longest Day; Addressed to My Daughter, The. William Wordsworth. CP-WorW2

Longest day that God appoints, The. Emily Dickinson. CP-DickE

Longest Night, The. Marge Piercy. SP-PierM

Longfellow. James Whitcomb Riley. CP-RileJ

Longfellow's Love for the Children. James Whitcomb Riley. CP-RileJ

Longford Dawns. Ivor Gurney. SP-GurnI

Longing. E. E. Cummings. CP-CummE

Longing. Paul Laurence Dunbar. CP-DunbP

Longing. George Herbert. CP-HerbG

Longing. David Ignatow. SP-IgnaD

Longing. Jones Very. CP-VeryJ

Longing, The. Miller Williams. CP-WillM

Longing for Death because of Feebleness. Stevie Smith. CP-SmitS

Longing for the Spring, A. Jones Very. CP-VeryJ

Longing is like the Seed. Emily Dickinson. CP-DickE

Longing to Be Saved, The. Maxine W. Kumin. SP-KumiM

Longing to Be with Christ. William Cowper. CP-CowpW

Longitude 170° West, Latitude 35° North. Gary Snyder. CP-SnydG

Longships got this far. Then, The. For Billy Holt. Ted Hughes. SP-HughTN

Longshot. Charles Bukowski. SP-BukC1

Look. Robert Creeley. CP-CreeR

Look. Philip Levine. SP-LeviP

Look! Stevie Smith. CP-SmitS

Look, The. Elizabeth Barrett Browning. CP-BroEB

Look, The. Charles Bukowski. SP-BukC2

Look, a cypress tree. Hayden Carruth. CP-CarHS *Fr.* Clay Hill Anthology, The.

Look, a naked runner / A messenger. Messenger from the Horizon, A. Thomas Merton. CP-MertT

Look and remember. Look upon this sky. Travelogue for Exiles. Karl Shapiro. SP-ShapK

Look at Duke! Cotton Club, The. Clarence Major. SP-MajoC

Look at him / a withered man. Millionaire, The. Charles Bukowski. SP-BukC2

Look at it from this side. Yannis Ritsos. SP-RitsY *Fr.* Paper Poems 2.

Look at it hale, A. Pussy Willow. Louis Zukofsky. CP-ZukLS

Look at Jonah embarking from Joppa, deterred by. Tom Fool at Jamaica. Marianne Craig Moore. CP-MoorM

Look at Me! Look at Me! William Meredith. SP-MereW

Look at that hill, my sad heart, where we stood. Petrarch. CP-Petra, *tr. by* J. G. Nichols

Look at / that motherfucking smokestack. Blue Skies Motel. Robert Creeley. SP-CreeR

Look at that white cavalier. Dance of the Moon in Santiago. Federico García Lorca. CP-GarcF, *tr. by* Catherine Brown

Look at the fate of summer flowers. To ———: "Look at the fate of summer flowers." William Wordsworth. CP-WorW2

Look at the flower among the leaves. Han-shan. CP-ColdM, *tr. by* Red Pine

Look at the jasmine, whose branches are green. Jasmine. Shmuel HaNagid. SP-HaNaS, *tr. by* Peter Cole

Look at the little darlings in the corn! Fireflies in the Corn. D. H. Lawrence. CP-LawrD

Look at the nails on the wall. Think Also of Horseshoes. Miller Williams. CP-WillM

Look at the Night (Temple, Early '60's), A. Denise Levertov. SP-LeveDL

Look at the stars! look, look up at the skies! Starlight Night, The. Gerard Manley Hopkins. CP-HopkG

Look at the steady rifles, Joe. Joe Hill Listens to the Praying. Kenneth Patchen. CP-PatcK

Look at their faces. You know it all. Tenth Anniversary Photograph, 1952, A. Miller Williams. CP-WillM

Look at them blowing at these flowers! Girls and Boys. G. K. Chesterton. CP-ChesG

Look at them standing there in authority. Revolutionary, The. D. H. Lawrence. CP-LawrD

Look at this) / a 75 done. E. E. Cummings. CP-CummE

Look at this red pear. Indigestion of the Vampire, The. W. S. Merwin. SP-MerwW

Look away from me friend. War with Yadir, The. Shmuel HaNagid. SP-HaNaS, *tr. by* Peter Cole

Look Back. Gary Snyder. CP-SnydG

Look back, old Janus, and survey. New Year's Gift. To the King, A. Thomas Carew. CP-CareT

Look back on Time, with kindly eyes. Emily Dickinson. CP-DickE

Look, beloved child, into my eyes, see there. Message. Kathleen Jessie Raine. SP-RainK

Look Both Ways Crossing Streets. Tennessee Williams. CP-WillT

Look close. Lorine Niedecker. CP-NiedL

Look Closer. May Swenson. SP-SwenM

Look danger in the eye it vanishes. Ralph Waldo Emerson. CP-EmerR

Look Down Fair Moon. Walt Whitman. CP-WhitW

Look down out how pretty. Pretty. Louis Zukofsky. CP-ZukLS

Look down the long valley and there stands a mountain. Too Anxious for Rivers. Robert Frost. CP-FrosR

Look down. There is snow. On a Landscape by Li Ch'eng. Charles Tomlinson. CP-TomlC

Look, five blue eggs are gleaming there! William Wordsworth. *See* Behold, within the leafy shade

[*Look Flaxman & Stothard do*] old acquaintance well. William Blake. CP-BlakW

Look for My White Self. A. R. Ammons. CP-AmmoA

Look for the Silver Lining. Ogden Nash. CP-NashO

Look for us among those. Mandrakes. Thom Gunn. CP-GunnT

Look forward, truant, to your second childhood. Death Room, The. Robert Graves. CP-GravR

Look, friend, you don't know the half. Me. Sam and Poll Go Back to the City. Hayden Carruth. CP-CarHS

Look, friend, you got troubles? Like it's. Marge. Hayden Carruth. CP-CarHS

Look from your stillness as the light resumes. Request, The. Charles Tomlinson. CP-TomlC

Look hard at the world, they said. What I Remember the Writers Telling Me when I Was Young. William Meredith. SP-MereW

"Look!" he said, "all green!" but she. In Hades, Orpheus. Muriel Rukeyser. CP-RukeM

Look how crazy! Pan. Federico García Lorca. CP-GarcF, *tr. by* Jerome Rothenberg *Fr.* Secrets.

Look how our foule Dayes do exceed our faire. His Confession. Robert Herrick. CP-HerrR

Look how spry it still is. Hatred. Wisława Szymborska. SP-SzymWM, *tr. by* Marek Lugowski *and* Joanna Trzeciak

Look how the bittersweet with lazy muscle moves aside. Edna St. Vincent Millay. CP-MillE

Look, how the Rainbow doth appeare. Rainbow, The. Robert Herrick. CP-HerrR

Look hyeah, Molly, ain't it jolly. To Mary Church Terrell. Paul Laurence Dunbar. CP-DunbP

Look I have been had entered a room large or small had entered have been they wondered a door. Idem 4. Michael Palmer. SP-PalmM

Look, I strew beans. Bean-Stripe: also, Apple-Eating, A. Robert Browning. CP-BroR2

Look in my face; my name is Might-have-been. Superscription, A. Dante Gabriel Rossetti. CW-RossD *Fr.* House of Life, The.

Look, in the attic, the unentered room. Before the Carnival. Thom Gunn. CP-GunnT

Look! In the lilac bush! Critics on the Lawn. Archibald MacLeish. CP-MacLA

Look in the terrible mirror of the sky. Blanche McCarthy. Wallace Stevens. CP-StevWP

Look in this mirror, tell me what you see. Glass Dialectic. Howard Nemerov. CP-NemeH

Look, it's morning, and a little water gurgles in the tap. Morning Song. Alan Dugan. CP-DugaA

Look, Look. Stevie Smith. CP-SmitS

Look Look Look. Philip Whalen. SP-WhalP

Look, look where the mind can go. Staking Claim. A. R. Ammons. CP-AmmoA

Look, love / springs. Hi There! Robert Creeley. CP-CreeR

Look, man, look. Fish, Fish. Stevie Smith. CP-SmitS

Look, Mitterrand baby, your telegram. Simone Signoret. James Schuyler. CP-SchuJ

Look / my fingers,which. E. E. Cummings. CP-CummE

Look: no one ever promised for sure. Introduction to Some Poems, An. William Stafford. SP-StafWW

Look not for spreading boughs. George Meredith. CP-MerG1 *Fr.* France.

Look not in my eyes, for fear. A. E. Housman. CP-HousA

Look now on that Adventurer who hath paid. William Wordsworth. CP-WorW1

Look of thee, what is it like, The. Emily Dickinson. CP-DickE

Look on her face in a dream, The. Roses. Mary Oliver. SP-OlivM

Look on him! through his dungeon grate. Prisoner for Debt, The. John Greenleaf Whittier. CP-WhitJ

Look on myself, and thou shalt own at once. On the Engraver of His Pourtrait. William Cowper. CP-CowpW

Look on This Picture and on This. Christina Georgina Rossetti. CP-RosC3

Look one way and the sun is going down. Mockingbird, The. Randall Jarrell. CP-JarrR

Look-out, The. "H. D." CP-DoolH

Look out how you use proud words. Primer Lesson. Carl Sandburg. CP-SandC

Look out! there's that damned ape again. Word with You, A. Elizabeth Bishop. CP-BishE

Look round, brown moon, brown bird, as you rise to fly. God is Good. It Is a Beautiful Night. Wallace Stevens. CP-StevW; CP-StevWP

"Look!" she cried. Girl Who Died #1, The. Alice Walker. CP-WalkA

Look so neat an' sweet in all yer frills an' fancy pleatin'! Billy Goodin'. James Whitcomb Riley. CP-RileJ

Look soul. Animula. W. S. Merwin. SP-MerwW

Look, stranger, on this island now. On This Island. W. H. Auden. CP-AudeW

Look, the raft, a signal flying. Far Off-Shore. Herman Melville. SP-MelvH

Look, the trees / are turning / their own bodies. In Blackwater Woods. Mary Oliver. SP-OlivM

Look, the woods, the sky, our home. Lorine Niedecker. CP-NiedL

Look, there are two curves in the air: the air. Diagram. Robinson Jeffers. CP-JefR3

Look there at the star! Shepherd's Song at Christmas. Langston Hughes. CP-HughL

Look, there goes the young lady across the street. William Carlos Williams. CP-WilW2

"Look there," the star man says. Before our eye. As Long Ago As Far Away. May Swenson. SP-SwenM

Look there! The sunk road winding. Bonfires, The. W. H. Auden. CP-AudeW

Look there! What a wheaten. Hill Field, The. Donald Davie. CP-DaviDC

Look this figure half-hidden is not a book. Dear M ("Look this figure half-hidden is not a book"). Michael Palmer. SP-PalmM

Look: thoughts and dreams are weaving over us. Yehuda Amichai. SP-AmicY, tr. by Stephen Mitchell

Look, thoughts, and dreams weave above us. Yehuda Amichai. SP-AmicYL, tr. by Benjamin Harshav and Barbara Harshav

Look to me faith, and look to my faith, God. Elegy upon the Untimely Death of the Incomparable Prince Henry. John Donne. CP-DonnJ

Look to your muscle, look to your heart. Instructions to Any Painter for a "Coronation of Inés de Castro." Robert Stock. SP-StocR

Look up into the dome. Altitudes. Richard Wilbur. CP-WilbR

Look up, languishing Soul! Lo where the fair. Vexilla Regis. Richard Crashaw. CP-CrasR

Look up my dear at the dark. My Dear Love. Robinson Jeffers. CP-JefR3

Look up now at what's going on aloft—. Late Summer. Howard Nemerov. CP-NemeH

Look up, thou seed of envy, and still bring. On the Right Honourable and Virtuous Lord Weston, L[ord] High Treasurer of England, upon the Day He Was Made Earl of Portland, 17. Febr. 1632. To the Envious. Ben Jonson. CP-JonsB

Look upon Sapho's lip, and you will swear. Upon Sapho. Robert Herrick. CP-HerrR

Look westward over forever miles of wheat stubble. Prairie Harvest. Robert Penn Warren. CP-WarrR

Look What You Did, Christopher! Ogden Nash. CP-NashO

Look! Winter now in trembling haste. Spring ("Look! Winter now in trembling haste"). Jones Very. CP-VeryJ

Look with the ears, said Orazio Vecchi. Words for the Madrigalist. Charles Tomlinson. CP-TomlC

Look yonder at winding boy. Yonder. James Tate. SP-TateJ

Look, You Have Cast Out Love! Rudyard Kipling. CP-KiplR Fr. Plain Tales from the Hills.

Look, you have cast out Love! What Gods are these. Look, You Have Cast Out Love! Rudyard Kipling. CP-KiplR Fr. Plain Tales from the Hills.

Look You, I'll Go Pray. Nicholas Vachel Lindsay. CP-LindV

Look you, my simple friend, 'tis one of those. Arthur Hugh Clough. SP-ClouA

Look, your life, too, is becoming. Password. Adam Zagajewski. SP-ZagaA, tr. by Renata Gorczynski, Benjamin Ivry and C. K. Williams

Look, your longing swung from the trapeze. Circus. Adam Zagajewski. SP-ZagaA, tr. by Clare Cavanagh

Looke in my Book, and herein see. To a Friend. Robert Herrick. CP-HerrR

Looked back on happily, the ivy-hung. London Inside and Outside. Amy Clampitt. CP-ClamA

Looking. Gwendolyn Brooks. SP-BrooG

Looking. Muriel Rukeyser. CP-RukeM

Looking a Mad Dog Dead in the Eyes. Yusef Komunyakaa. CP-KomuY

Looking Across. Thomas Hardy. CP-HardT

Looking across Laguna Canyon at Dusk, West-by-Northwest. Charles Wright. SP-WrigCN

Looking across the Fields and Watching the Birds Fly. Wallace Stevens. CP-StevW; CP-StevWP

Looking across the line, the Grecian said. Eastern Question, The. Ambrose Bierce. SP-BierA

Looking across the River. William Stafford. SP-StafW; SP-StafWW

Looking Again at What I Looked at for Seventeen Years. Charles Wright. SP-WrigCN

Looking and Finding. A. K. Ramanujan. CP-RamaA

Looking as I've looked before, straight down the heart. Stranger, The. Adrienne Rich. SP-RicA1

Looking at a half-gray opal. Gray. Constantine P. Cavafy. CP-CavaC, tr. by Theoharis Constantine Theoharis

Looking at a Picture on an Anniversary. Thomas Hardy. CP-HardT

Looking at Each Other. Muriel Rukeyser. CP-RukeM

Looking at Images Reflected in the Showcase Plate Glass. Clarence Major. SP-MajoC

Looking at Pictures. Charles Wright. SP-WrigC

Looking at Quilts. Marge Piercy. SP-PierM

Looking at the Stars. Richard Eberhart. CP-EberR

Looking at Washington, Lee and Jefferson. Portraits. Ivor Gurney. SP-GurnI

Looking at Your Face. Galway Kinnell. SP-KinnGN

Looking Back. Thomas Hardy. CP-HardT

Looking Back. W. S. Merwin. SP-MerwW

Looking back along life's trodden way. Christina Georgina Rossetti. CP-RosC2

Looking back, I look. Round Time. Heather McHugh. SP-McHuH

Looking back in my mind I can see. Elementary Scene, The. Randall Jarrell. CP-JarrR

Looking back trying to decipher. Education of a Novelist. Adrienne Rich. SP-RicA2

Looking back 25 years I / imagine it simple. Simple. Hayden Carruth. CP-CarHS

Looking back, we cannot see. Traveling through Fog. Robert Earl Hayden. CP-HaydR

Looking Before and After. Jones Very. CP-VeryJ

Looking by chance in at the open window. Foreboding, The. Robert Graves. CP-GravR

Looking close in the evil mirror Crow saw. Crow's Vanity. Ted Hughes. SP-HughTN

Looking down at her. Paradox, The. Robert Creeley. CP-CreeR

Looking down into my father's / dead face. Good Night, Willie Lee, I'll See You in the Morning. Alice Walker. CP-WalkA

Looking East at Night. W. S. Merwin. SP-MerwW

Looking for a Cousin on a Swing. A. K. Ramanujan. CP-RamaA

Looking for a Sunset Bird in Winter. Robert Frost. CP-FrosR

Looking for a system, he finds a wife. Was it Vallejo who said. Looking and Finding. A. K. Ramanujan. CP-RamaA

Looking for a way. Robert Creeley. CP-CreeR

Looking for Choctaw. Yusef Komunyakaa. CP-KomuY

Looking for Gold. William Stafford. SP-StafWW

Looking for Mushrooms at Sunrise. W. S. Merwin. SP-MerwW

Looking for refuge. Han-shan. CP-ColdM, tr. by Red Pine

Looking for Someone. William Stafford. SP-StafWW

Looking for the centre these days. A. K. Ramanujan. CP-RamaA

Looking for Work 1. Raymond Carver. CP-CarvR

Looking for Work 2. Raymond Carver. CP-CarvR

Looking for you through the gray rain. William Stafford. SP-StafWW

Looking Forward. Christina Georgina Rossetti. CP-RosC3

Looking Forward to See Jane Real Soon. James Schuyler. CP-SchuJ

Looking forward to the spring. Before and after Summer. Thomas Hardy. CP-HardT

Looking Glass. Thom Gunn. CP-GunnT

Looking-glass. Denise Levertov. SP-LeveDP

Looking-Glass, A. Thomas Carew. CP-CareT

Looking Glass, The. Walter De la Mare. CP-DeLaW

Looking-Glass, The. Paul Laurence Dunbar. CP-DunbP

Looking Glass, The. Rudyard Kipling. CP-KiplR

Looking Head On. Richard Eberhart. CP-EberR

Looking in a Mirror. Margaret Atwood. SP-AtwM1

Looking in the mirrors at Macy's. Director of Alienation. Lawrence Ferlinghetti. SP-FerlL

Looking into History. Richard Wilbur. CP-WilbR

Looking into your eyes. Ndebele. Alice Walker. CP-WalkA

Looking Out. Robert Creeley. CP-CreeR

Looking Out from Ferrara. Giorgio Bassani. CP-DaviDC, tr. by Donald Davie

Looking out of the dark of the town. Letter, A. James Dickey. CP-DickJ

Looking out the window, across the room. True Story of What Happened, The. Miller Williams. CP-WillM

Looking out the window at the trees: For Yaedi. David Ignatow. SP-IgnaD2

Looking outside the Cabin Window, I Remember a Line by Li Po. Charles Wright. SP-WrigCN

Looking over my shoulder. Four Haiku. Allen Ginsberg. CP-GinsA

Looking over the Acreage. A. R. Ammons. CP-AmmoA

Looking Seaward. Samuel Taylor Coleridge. CP-ColeS

Looking through boxes. Toy Bone, The. Donald Hall. CP-HallD

Looking to the sea, it is a line. Innocence, The. Robert Creeley. CP-CreeR

Looking up at the stars, I know quite well. More Loving One, The. W. H. Auden. CP-AudeW

Looking up from Two Renaissance Paintings to the Massacre at Tiananmen Square. Norman Dubie. CP-DubiN

Looking up, of a sudden. Poem: "Looking up, of a sudden." William Carlos Williams. CP-WilW2

Looking upon my Venice and the stars. In That Country. Ezra Pound. CP-PoEar

Looking upon the light of those clear eyes. Petrarch. CP-Petra, tr. by J. G. Nichols

Looking West from Laguna Beach at Night. Charles Wright. SP-WrigCN

Looks. Thom Gunn. CP-GunnT

Looks from Money. Andrei Codrescu. SP-CodrA

Looks like a large. Solar Corona. May Swenson. SP-SwenM

Looks like what drives me crazy. Evil. Langston Hughes. CP-HughL; CP-HughL2

Looks thrown away on others. Michelangelo Buonarroti. CP-Miche, tr. by John Frederick Nims

Looky here, America. Beaumont to Detroit: 1943. Langston Hughes. CP-HughL; CP-HughL2

Looky here!—you fellers—you. Love's as Broad as Long. James Whitcomb Riley. CP-RileJ

Looming and phosphorescent against the dark. Cryopexy. Charles Wright. SP-WrigC

Loon Call, A. Richard Eberhart. CP-EberR

Loon on Forrester's Pond, The. Hayden Carruth. CP-CarHS

Loon's cry is a chortle from another world, A. Dream, A. Richard Eberhart. CP-EberR

Loon's Cry, The. Robert Bly. SP-BlyR

Loon's Cry, The. Howard Nemerov. CP-NemeH

Loop, A. Robert Creeley. CP-CreeR

Loophole. Fernando Pessoa. SP-PessF, tr. by Susan M. Brown and Edwin Honig

Looping off feline through the leisured air. Waterfall at Powerscourt, The. Donald Davie. CP-DaviDC

Loose Gown, A. David Ignatow. SP-IgnaD

Loose knot in a short rope, A. Lives of the Saints. Charles Wright. SP-WrigCN

Loose lips now. Against Confidences. Donald Davie. CP-DaviDC

Loose Mountain, A. Robert Frost. CP-FrosR

Loose no time nor youth but be. Song, A: "Loose no time nor youth but be." Robert Herrick. CP-HerrR

Loose Shutter, The. Robert Penn Warren. CP-WarrR

Loose the baleful lion, snap / The frosty bars down from his cage. Request for Offering. Richard Eberhart. CP-EberR

Loose the knots of the heart; never think on thy fate. Hafiz. CP-EmerR Fr. Odes.

Loot. Rudyard Kipling. CP-KiplR

Loot. Thom Gunn. CP-GunnT

Lorca. Richard Eberhart. CP-EberR

Lord and Master, to thine altar. Bible, O.T. See Unto thee, O Lord, do I lift up my soul

Lord Apollo, who has never died, The. Many Are Called. Edwin Arlington Robinson. CP-RobiE

Lord Archer, Death, whom sent you in your stead? Edna St. Vincent Millay. CP-MillE

Lord Babe, if Thou art He / We sought for patiently. Epiphany. Christina Georgina Rossetti. CP-RosC2

Lord Bacon. James Whitcomb Riley. CP-RileJ

Lord Bacon's Birthday. Ben Jonson. CP-JonsB

Lord Barrenstock. Stevie Smith. CP-SmitS

"Lord, being dark," I said, "I cannot bear." Shroud of Color, The. Countee Cullen. CP-CullC

Lord, but one wearies of flipping them. Light Switches. John Updike. CP-UpdiJ

Lord by thy sweet and saving sign. Compline. Richard Crashaw. CP-CrasR

Lord, by thy sweet and saving sign. Evensong. Richard Crashaw. CP-CrasR

Lord, by thy sweet and saving sign. For the Hour of Prime. Richard Crashaw. CP-CrasR

Lord, by thy sweet and saving sign. Howres for the Hours of Matines, The. Richard Crashaw. CP-CrasR

Lord, by what inconceivable dim road / Thou leadest man on footsore pilgrimage! Christina Georgina Rossetti. CP-RosC2

Lord, carry me.—Nay, but I grant thee strength. Christina Georgina Rossetti. CP-RosC2

Lord! cleanse thine inner temple, as of old. Purification of the Temple, The.

Jones Very. CP-VeryJ

Lord, comest Thou to me? Christina Georgina Rossetti. CP-RosC3

Lord, do not beat me. Another, to God. Robert Herrick. CP-HerrR

Lord, dost Thou look on me, and will not I. Christina Georgina Rossetti. CP-RosC2

Lord, give me blessed fear, / And much more blessed love. Perfect Love Casteth Out Fear. Christina Georgina Rossetti. CP-RosC2

Lord, give me grace / To take the lowest place. Sit Down in the Lowest Room. Christina Georgina Rossetti. CP-RosC2

Lord, give me love that I may love Thee much. Christina Georgina Rossetti. CP-RosC2

Lord God, bigger than the whole world, The. Ezekiel's Rabbit. William Dickey. SP-DickW

Lord God of heaven that with mercy dight. Grace before Song. Ezra Pound. CP-PoEar

Lord God of Hosts, most Holy and most High. Christina Georgina Rossetti. CP-RosC2

Lord God sat over space for a seat, The. Legend of the Pessimist. G. K. Chesterton. CP-ChesG

Lord God that dost me save and keep. Bible, O.T. See O God of my salvation

Lord, grant me grace to love Thee in my pain. Christina Georgina Rossetti. CP-RosC2

Lord, Grant Us Calm. Christina Georgina Rossetti. CP-RosC2

Lord, grant us eyes to see and ears to hear, / And souls to love and minds to understand. Christina Georgina Rossetti. CP-RosC2

Lord, grant us grace to mount by steps of grace. And Now Why Tarriest Thou? Christina Georgina Rossetti. CP-RosC2

Lord, grant us grace to rest upon Thy word. Christina Georgina Rossetti. CP-RosC2

Lord, grant us wills to trust Thee with such aim. As the Sparks Fly Upwards. Christina Georgina Rossetti. CP-RosC2

Lord Gregory. Robert Burns. CP-BurnR

Lord had a job for me, but I had so much to do, The. Get Somebody Else. Paul Laurence Dunbar. CP-DunbP

Lord, hast Thou so loved us, and will not we. Christina Georgina Rossetti. CP-RosC2

Lord, have mercy on my son: for he is lunatick. Opus Dei. John Berryman. CP-BerrJ

Lord, have mercy! what a day: what a merciful day. Lollapalooza: 22 February. A. R. Ammons. CP-AmmoA

Lord hear [or here] my prayer [or prayre] and let my cry[e] pass[e]. Bible, O.T. See Hear my prayer, O Lord, and let my cry come unto thee

Lord Heart, heal my right temple bang'd soft pain the bookshelf. On Illness. Allen Ginsberg. CP-GinsA

Lord, help, it is high time for me to call. Bible, O.T. See Help, Lord; for the godly man ceaseth

Lord help us! What strange foolish things are these men. Epilogue to the Sultan. James Austen. CP-AustJ

Lord, how are they increased that trouble me! Psalm 3: "Lord, how are they increased that trouble me!" Bible, O.T. CP-MiltJ Fr. Psalms.

Lord, how can man preach thy eternal[l] word? Windows, The. George Herbert. CP-HerbG

Lord, how couldst thou so much appease. Faith. George Herbert. CP-HerbG

Lord, how I am all ague, when I seek. Sinner, The. George Herbert. CP-HerbG

Lord, how is gamester changed! His hair close cut! On Reformed Gamester. Ben Jonson. CP-JonsB; SP-JonsB

Lord how many are my foes. Bible, O.T. See Lord, how are they increased that trouble me!

Lord, I am feeble and of mean account. Christina Georgina Rossetti. CP-RosC2

Lord, I am here.—But, child, I look for thee. Christina Georgina Rossetti. CP-RosC2

Lord, I am like to mistletoe. To God. Robert Herrick. CP-HerrR

Lord, I am waiting, weeping, watching for Thee. Of Him That Was Ready to Perish. Christina Georgina Rossetti. CP-RosC2

Lord, I believe, help Thou mine unbelief! / Lord, I repent, help mine impenitence. Cried Out with Tears. Christina Georgina Rossetti. CP-RosC2

Lord, I confess[e] my sin is great. Repentance. George Herbert. CP-HerbG

Lord, I confesse, that Thou alone art able. To His Saviour. Robert Herrick. CP-HerrR

Lord, I have loved Your sky. Astrometaphysical. Robert Frost. CP-FrosR

Lord, I love the habitation. Song of Mercy and Judgment, A. William Cowper. CP-CowpW

Lord, I will mean and speak thy praise. Praise (3). George Herbert. CP-HerbG

Lord, if I love Thee and Thou lovest me. Why? Christina Georgina Rossetti. CP-RosC2

Lord, if Thy word had been "Worship Me not." Worship God. Christina Georgina Rossetti. CP-RosC2

Lord, in My Heart. Maya Angelou. SP-AngeM

Lord, in my silence how do I despise. Frailty. George Herbert. CP-HerbG

Lord in the Air, the. James Dickey. CP-DickJ

Lord in thine anger do not reprehend me. Bible, *O.T. See* O Lord, rebuke me not in thine anger

Lord Is Good, The. Thomas Merton. CP-MertT

Lord is King, be the people, The. Curtains! Donald Davie. CP-DaviDC

Lord is my shepherd; I shall not want, The. Psalm 23: "Lord is my shepherd; I shall not want, The." Bible, *O.T.* CP-CrasR; SP-SidnP *Fr.* Psalms.

Lord, It Is Good for Us to Be Here. Christina Georgina Rossetti. CP-RosC2

Lord, it is quite possible that people, while praising you, were mistaken. Meditation. Czeslaw Milosz. CP-MiloCN, *tr. by* Robert Hass

Lord, it is time now. The winter. Poem, Slow to Come, on the Death of Cummings (1894–1962). John Logan. CP-LogaJ

Lord, it is time. Summer was very great. Ted Berrigan. SP-BerrT *Fr.* Sonnets, The.

Lord, it is time. The summer was so great. Rainer Maria Rilke. *See* Lord, it is time. The summer was too long

Lord, it is time. The summer was too long. Autumn Day. Rainer Maria Rilke. CP-SpcnS

Lord, it's time; the wine is already fermenting. After R.M. Rilke. Primo Levi. CP-LeviP, *tr. by* Ruth Feldman *and* Brian Swann

Lord Jesu, Thou art sweetness to my soul. Christina Georgina Rossetti. CP-RosC2

Lord Jesus Christ, grown faint upon the Cross. Good Friday. Christina Georgina Rossetti. CP-RosC2

Lord Jesus Christ, our Wisdom and our Rest. Whitsun Tuesday. Christina Georgina Rossetti. CP-RosC2

Lord Jesus, I Wonder. Robert Penn Warren. CP-WarrR

Lord Jesus, I wonder if I would recognize you. Lord Jesus, I Wonder. Robert Penn Warren. CP-WarrR

Lord Jesus, who would think that I am Thine? Christina Georgina Rossetti. CP-RosC2

Lord John Unalive(having a fortune of fifteengrand). E. E. Cummings. CP-CummE

Lord let me all I can wild cherry. Photovoltaic. Olga Broumas. SP-BrouO

Lord, let the angels praise thy name. Misery [*or* Miserie]. George Herbert. CP-HerbG

Lord Lilac thought it rather rotten. Shakespeare Memorial, The. G. K. Chesterton. CP-ChesG

Lord Lord I got the sickness blues, I must've done something wrong. Sickness Blues. Allen Ginsberg. CP-GinsA; SP-GinsA

Lord Love, to whom all hearts and minds are known. Petrarch. CP-Petra, *tr. by* J. G. Nichols

Lord Love, who holds the chief place in my mind. Petrarch. CP-Petra, *tr. by* J. G. Nichols

Lord Love, you see this lady full of scorn. Petrarch. CP-Petra, *tr. by* J. G. Nichols

Lord Lurch, C.B. (and now M.P.). Orator of the Opposition, The. G. K. Chesterton. CP-ChesG

Lord, make me coy and tender to offend. Unkindness. George Herbert. CP-HerbG

Lord, make me one with Thine own faithful ones. Christina Georgina Rossetti. CP-RosC2

Lord, make me pure: / Only the pure shall see Thee as Thou art. Christina Georgina Rossetti. CP-RosC2

Lord, make us all love all: that when we meet / Even myriads of earth's myriads at Thy Bar. Christina Georgina Rossetti. CP-RosC2

Lord might have spared us the harsh joke, The. On a Text: Jonah IV, xi. Howard Nemerov. CP-NemeH

Lord Mope. Stevie Smith. CP-SmitS

Lord, my first fruits present themselves to thee. Dedication, The: "Lord, my first fruits present themselves to thee." George Herbert. CP-HerbG

Lord my God to thee I flie / Save me and secure me under. Bible, *O.T. See* O Lord my God, in thee do I put my trust

Lord, my soul with pleasure springs. True Pleasures. William Cowper. CP-CowpW *Fr.* Olney Hymns.

Lord Myth. Norman Dubie. CP-DubiN

Lord, not you. Flickering Mind. Denise Levertov. SP-LeveDS

Lord of beauty enters the soul, The. You Sweep the Floor. Jelaluddin Rumi. SP-Rumi, *tr. by* Coleman Barks

Lord of each wave comes in. Inscription Facing Western Sea. W. S. Merwin. SP-MerwW

Lord of Elbë, on Elbë hill. A.G.A. to A.E. Emily Jane Brontë. CP-BronE

Lord of new arrivals. Prayers to Lord Murugan. A. K. Ramanujan. CP-RamaA

Lord of old has dealt in blood, The. George Meredith. CP-MerG2

Lord of the bow. In the Gorge. W. S. Merwin. SP-MerwW

Lord of the Isles, The. Sir Walter Scott.

    Autumn on Tweedside. SP-ScotW

    Brooch of Lorn, The. SP-ScotW

    Death of Argentine, The. SP-ScotW

    Loch Coruisk. SP-ScotW

    Voyage to Arran, The. SP-ScotW

Lord of the Morning Star. D. H. Lawrence. CP-LawrD

Lord of the vale! astounding Flood. Composed at Cora Linn in Sight of Wallace's Tower. William Wordsworth. CP-WorW2

Lord Pam in the church (could [*or* cou'd] you think it) kneeled [*or* kneel'd] down. Epigram: "Lord Pam in the church (could [*or* cou'd] you think it) kneeled [*or* kneel'd] down." Jonathan Swift. CP-SwifJ

Lord passed by! A mighty wind, The. Still Small Voice, The. Jones Very. CP-VeryJ

Lord, purge our eyes to see / Within the seed a tree. Judge Not According to the Appearance. Christina Georgina Rossetti. CP-RosC2

Lord, receive my prayer / Sweet as incense smoke. Evening Prayer. Thomas Merton. CP-MertT

Lord Roberts. Rudyard Kipling. CP-KiplR

Lord Ronald My Son. Robert Burns. CP-BurnR

Lord, Save Us, We Perish. Christina Georgina Rossetti. CP-RosC2

Lord Say-and-Seal. Stevie Smith. CP-SmitS

Lord Tennyson and Lord Melchett. D. H. Lawrence. CP-LawrD

Lord, the Lord my shepherd is, The. Bible, *O.T. See* Lord is my shepherd; I shall not want, The

Lord, the Roman hyacinths are blooming in bowls and. Song for Simeon, A. T. S. Eliot. CP-ElioT

Lord Thomas and Fair Margaret. Christina Georgina Rossetti. CP-RosC3

Lord, Thou art fulness, I am emptiness. Christina Georgina Rossetti. CP-RosC3

Lord, Thou art mine, and I am Thine. Clasping of Hands. George Herbert. CP-HerbG

Lord, thou hast been favourable unto thy land. Psalm 85: "Lord, thou hast been favourable unto thy land." Bible, *O.T.* CP-MiltJ; SP-SmarC *Fr.* Psalms.

Lord, Thou hast given me a cell. Thanksgiving to God for His House, A. Robert Herrick. CP-HerrR

Lord, Thou hast made this world below the shadow of a dream. McAndrew's Hymn. Rudyard Kipling. CP-KiplR

Lord, thou hast many a serving-man. Serving-Man, The. Jones Very. CP-VeryJ

Lord, to account who dares Thee call. On Commissary Goldie's Brains. Robert Burns. CP-BurnR

Lord, to Thine own grant watchful hearts and eyes. Vigil of St. Bartholomew. Christina Georgina Rossetti. CP-RosC2

Lord Walter's Wife. Elizabeth Barrett Browning. CP-BroEB

Lord, we are rivers running to Thy sea. Christina Georgina Rossetti. CP-RosC2

Lord, we look to once for all, The. Heretic's Tragedy, The. Robert Browning. CP-BroR1

Lord, what have I that I may offer Thee? Christina Georgina Rossetti. CP-RosC2

Lord, what have I to offer? sickening fear. Christina Georgina Rossetti. CP-RosC2

Lord, what is man? why should he cost[e] thee [*or* you]. C[h]aritas Nimia; or, The Dear[e] Bargain. Richard Crashaw. CP-CrasR

Lord, when my heart was whole I kept it back. Afterward He Repented, and Went. Christina Georgina Rossetti. CP-RosC2

Lord, when the clock strikes. Reader, The. Thomas Merton. CP-MertT

Lord, when the sense of Thy sweet grace. Song: "Lord, when the sense of Thy sweet grace." Richard Crashaw. CP-CrasR

Lord, when there is no escape, be my Defender. Be My Defender. Thomas Merton. CP-MertT

Lord, who createdst man in wealth and store. Easter Wings. George Herbert. CP-HerbG

Lord, who hast formed me out of mud. Trinity Sunday. George Herbert. CP-HerbG

Lord Whoever, thank you for this air. Poem in Thanks. Thomas Lux. SP-LuxT

Lord, whomsoever Thou shalt send to me, / Let that same be. Are They Not All Ministering Spirits? Christina Georgina Rossetti. CP-RosC2

Lord Will Happiness Divine, The. William Cowper. CP-CowpW *Fr.* Olney Hymns.

Lord, with what bounty and rare clemency. Ungratefulness. George Herbert. CP-HerbG

Lord, with what care hast thou begirt us round! Sin (1). George Herbert. CP-HerbG

Lord, with what glory [*or* glorie] wast thou served [*or* serv'd] of old. Sion. George Herbert. CP-HerbG

Lord, You may not recognize me. Gift, The. Louise Glück. SP-GlucL

Lord, you've sent both. Cancer Match, The. James Dickey. CP-DickJ

Lordly and Isolate Satyrs, The. Charles Olson. CP-OlsoC

Lords debate, the Commons brawl, The. George Meredith. CP-MerG2

Lord's lost Him His mockingbird. Mourning Poem for the Queen of Sunday. Robert Earl Hayden. CP-HaydR

Lords Mask[e], The. Thomas Campion.

    (Description, Speeches, and Songs, of the Lords Maske, Presented in the Banquetting-House on the Marriage Night of the High and Mightie Count Palatine, *and the Royally Descended the Ladie* ELISABETH.) CP-CampT

Stars Dance, The. CP-CampT

Lords of Life Are the Masters of Death, The. D. H. Lawrence. CP-LawrD

Lords of life, the lords of life, The. Experience. Ralph Waldo Emerson. CP-EmerR

Lord's Prayer. D. H. Lawrence. CP-LawrD

Lords Strand of Northumberland, The. Sir Walter Scott. SP-ScotW *Fr.* Marmion.

Lore. Howard Nemerov. CP-NemeH

Lorelei. James Merrill. SP-MerrJ

Lorelei. Sylvia Plath. CP-PlatS

Lorena. Lucille Clifton. SP-ClifL

Lorene—we thought she'd come home. But. Saint Matthew and All. William Stafford. SP-StafW; SP-StafWW

Loring Pickering. Ambrose Bierce. SP-BierA

Lorna the Second. Thomas Hardy. CP-HardT

Lorna! Yes, you are so sweet. Lorna the Second. Thomas Hardy. CP-HardT

Los Alamos Museum, The. Arthur Sze. SP-SzeA

Los Angeles back-yarding in its blue-eyed waters. Olympian, The. James Dickey. CP-DickJ

Los Guitaristas. Robert Creeley. CP-CreeR

Los Pobrecitos. Charles Tomlinson. CP-TomlC

Loser, The. Charles Bukowski. SP-BukC2

Loser, The. Adrienne Rich. CP-RicAE; SP-RicA2

Losers. Carl Sandburg. CP-SandC

Losing everytime I win, climbing. Snakes and Ladders. A. K. Ramanujan. CP-RamaA

Losing information he. Offset. A. R. Ammons. CP-AmmoA

Losing Track. Denise Levertov. SP-LeveDP

Losing Track of Language. Amy Clampitt. CP-ClamA

Losing yourself in thought, daydreaming. Georgy Vladimirovich Ivanov. SP-WeisT, *tr.* by Theodore Weiss

Loss. A. R. Ammons. CP-AmmoA

Loss. Samuel Taylor Coleridge. CP-ColeS

Loss. "H. D." CP-DoolH

Loss. Richard Eberhart. CP-EberR

Loss. Randall Jarrell. CP-JarrR

Loss. D. H. Lawrence. CP-LawrD

Loss. Rainer Maria Rilke. CP-RilkFr, *tr.* by A. Poulin, Jr.

Loss. C. K. Williams. CP-WillC; SP-WillC

Loss and Gain. Ralph Waldo Emerson. CP-EmerR

Loss is also clearance. All Clear. Marge Piercy. SP-PierM

Loss is small to lose such one, The. Sir Thomas Wyatt. CP-WyatT

Loss of one's temper in a room with absolutely nobody, The. Three Types of Loss. Andrei Codrescu. SP-CodrA

Loss, of Perhaps Love, in Our World of Contingency. Robert Penn Warren. CP-WarrR

Loss of something ever felt I, A. Emily Dickinson. CP-DickE

Loss of Sounds. Josephine Jacobsen. CP-JacoJ

Loss of the Eurydice, The. Gerard Manley Hopkins. CP-HopkG

Losse from the Heat. Robert Herrick. CP-HerrR

Losses. Randall Jarrell. CP-JarrR

Losses. Yusef Komunyakaa. CP-KomuY

Losses. Carl Sandburg. CP-SandC

Lost. Hayden Carruth. CP-CarHS

Lost. G. K. Chesterton. CP-ChesG

Lost. Carl Sandburg. CP-SandC

Lost, The. Richard Eberhart. CP-EberR

Lost, The ("Fairest day that ever yet has shone, The"). Jones Very. CP-VeryJ

Lost, The ("They wander, straggling sheep without a fold"). Jones Very. CP-VeryJ

Lost aboard the roll of Kodac. Exmoor. Amy Clampitt. CP-ClamA

Lost Acres. Robert Graves. CP-GravR

Lost Anchors. Edwin Arlington Robinson. CP-RobiE

Lost and Found. Philip Levine. SP-LeviP

Lost and stumbling across the window. Four Winter Flies. Wyatt Prunty. SP-PrunW

Lost as that ring that on my finger sparkles. For a Child. Marya Alexandrovna Zaturenska. SP-ZatuM

Lost Bodies. Charles Wright. SP-WrigC

Lost Bower, The. Elizabeth Barrett Browning. CP-BroEB

Lost Bride, The. Donald Davie. CP-DaviDC

Lost Childhood. David Ignatow. SP-IgnaD

Lost Children, The. Richard Eberhart. CP-EberR

Lost Children, The. Randall Jarrell. CP-JarrR

Lost Children, The. Gregory Orr. SP-OrrG

Lost Days. Stephen Spender. CP-SpenS

Lost days of my life until to-day, The. Dante Gabriel Rossetti. CW-RossD *Fr.* House of Life, The.

Lost Dream, A. Paul Laurence Dunbar. CP-DunbP

Lost Etc. Kenneth Rexroth. CP-RexrK

Lost Fish. Robert Lowell. SP-LoweR

Lost Follower, The. Robert Frost. CP-FrosR

Lost in Heaven. Robert Frost. CP-FrosR

Lost in Ladispoli. Miller Williams. CP-WillM

Lost in self, drowned; asphyxiated in ego. Glow Worm. Thomas Lux. SP-LuxT

Lost in summer, I worry about your silence. 95°. Jane Cooper. CP-CoopJ

Lost in the brush, bound by the other path. Quail, The. James Wright. CP-WrigJ

Lost in the Desert. Clarence Major. SP-MajoC

Lost in Translation. Carolyn Kizer. CP-KizeC

Lost in Translation. James Merrill. SP-MerrJ *Fr.* Book of Ephraim, The.

Lost Ingredient, The. Anne Sexton. CP-SextA; SP-SextA

Lost Jewel, A. Robert Graves. CP-GravR

Lost Kiss, The. James Whitcomb Riley. CP-RileJ

Lost Leader, The. Robert Browning. CP-BroR1; SP-BroR

Lost Legion, The. Rudyard Kipling. CP-KiplR

Lost Lie, The. Anne Sexton. CP-SextA

Lost Love. Robert Graves. CP-GravR

Lost Love. Thomas Hardy. CP-HardT

Lost Love, A. James Whitcomb Riley. CP-RileJ

Lost Love, The. Randall Jarrell. CP-JarrR

Lost Loves. Galway Kinnell. SP-KinnGN

Lost manor where I walk continually. Pier-Glass, The. Robert Graves. CP-GravR

Lost Mistress, The. Robert Browning. CP-BroR1

Lost Month. W. S. Merwin. SP-MerwW

Lost My Voice? Of Course. Alice Walker. CP-WalkA

Lost Nights. Rainer Maria Rilke. CP-RilkFr, *tr.* by A. Poulin, Jr.

Lost Objects. Yehuda Amichai. SP-AmicY, *tr.* by Chana Bloch

Lost Occasion, The. John Greenleaf Whittier. CP-WhitJ

Lost on Both Sides. Dante Gabriel Rossetti. CW-RossD *Fr.* House of Life, The.

Lost Paradise. Jaroslav Seifert. SP-SeifJ, *tr.* by Ewald Osers

Lost Parents. Lawrence Ferlinghetti. SP-FerlL

Lost Path, The. James Whitcomb Riley. CP-RileJ

Lost Pearl, The. Chuang Tzu. CP-MertT

Lost Pilot, The. James Tate. SP-TateJ

Lost Poem, A. Kenneth Patchen. CP-PatcK

Lost Pyx, The. Thomas Hardy. CP-HardT

Lost Romans, The. Muriel Rukeyser. CP-RukeM

Lost Secrets, The. James Laughlin. CP-LaugJ

Lost Sheep, The. Jones Very. CP-VeryJ

Lost Son, The. Theodore Roethke. CP-RoetT

Lost Souls. Charles Wright. SP-WrigC

Lost Speakers, The. Archibald MacLeish. CP-MacLA

Lost Statesman, The. John Greenleaf Whittier. CP-WhitJ

Lost storm in this temperate place, A. Cowan Bridge; At the Site of 'Lowood School.' Geoffrey Hill. CP-HillG

Lost, sweetheart, how our memories creep. Lines Written in an Asylum. Hayden Carruth. CP-CarHS

Lost Things. Rainer Maria Rilke. CP-RilkFr, *tr.* by A. Poulin, Jr.

Lost Thrill, The. James Whitcomb Riley. CP-RileJ

Lost to the world; lost to my selfe; alone. On Himselfe. Robert Herrick. CP-HerrR

Lost Tribe, The. Paul Muldoon. CP-MuldP

Lost Tune, The. Robert Lowell. SP-LoweR

Lost Wax. Yusef Komunyakaa. CP-KomuY

Lost with the sun in a chartreuse wood, afflicted. Towers of Silence, The. Eleanor Wilner. SP-WilnE

Lost World, A. Robert Graves. CP-GravR

Lost World, The. Randall Jarrell. CP-JarrR

Lot is vacant still, The. Randall Jarrell. CP-JarrR

Lot Later. Howard Nemerov. CP-NemeH

Lot of love is chosen, The. I learnt that much. Chosen. William Butler Yeats. CP-YeatW

Lot of men and armies stand to take, A. Letter to a Policemen in Kansas City, A. Kenneth Patchen. CP-PatcK

Lot of mouths and cocks, A. Under the World There's a Lot of Ass, a Lot of Cunt. Allen Ginsberg. CP-GinsA; SP-GinsA

Lot of People Bathing in a Stream, A. Wallace Stevens. CP-StevW; CP-StevWP

Loth to depart, but yet at last, each one. Parting Verse, the Feast There Ended, The. Robert Herrick. CP-HerrR

Lotophagi with their silly hands, The. Adonis in Summer. Kenneth Rexroth. CP-RexrK

Lotos-Eaters, The. Alfred Tennyson. *See* Lotus-Eaters, The

Lots of grapes this year. Yehuda Amichai. SP-AmicYL, *tr.* by Benjamin Harshav *and* Barbara Harshav

Lots of people are richer than me. Confession to Be Traced on a Birthday Cake.

Ogden Nash. CP-NashO

Lots of people who no longer love each other. Something Nice about Myself. Philip Whalen. SP-WhalP

Lots to Be Liked. Robert Herrick. CP-HerrR

Lot's Wife. Anna Andreyevna Akhmatova. CP-WilbR, *tr. by* Richard Wilbur

Lot's Wife. Howard Nemerov. CP-NemeH

Lot's Wife. Stevie Smith. CP-SmitS

Lot's Wife. Wisława Szymborska. SP-SzymW, *tr. by* Stanislaw Barańczak *and* Clare Cavanagh

Lot's wife, / married to chance. Epigraph: "Lot's wife, / married to chance." Robert Creeley. CP-CreeR

Lot's Wife 1988. Lucille Clifton. SP-ClifL

Lotus and Frost. D. H. Lawrence. CP-LawrD

Lotus-Bloom. Ezra Pound. CP-PoEar

Lotus-Eaters, The. Alfred Tennyson. CP-TennA
  (Lotos-Eaters, The.) CP-TennA

Lotus-Eaters: Ulysses to Penelope, The. Christina Georgina Rossetti. CP RosC3

Lotus Leaves. Oscar Wilde. CP-WildO

Lotus of toy china bells. Deutzia. Louis Zukofsky. CP-ZukLS

Lotus Sutra, Naturalized, The. Philip Whalen. SP-WhalP

Loud blaw the frosty breezes. Young Highland Rover, The. Robert Burns. CP-BurnR

Loud he sang the psalm of David! Slave Singing at Midnight, The. Henry Wadsworth Longfellow. CP-LongH

Loud is the Vale! the Voice is up. Lines: "Loud is the Vale! the Voice is up." William Wordsworth. CP-WorW1; MW-WorW

Loud on the bright-necked grass. Two for History. Kenneth Patchen. CP-PatcK

Loud sounds the clock. I sit at home. Shakespearean Cycle, A. Marya Alexandrovna Zaturenska. SP-ZatuM

Loud talk in the overlighted house. Ends. Robert Frost. CP-FrosR

Loud without the wind was roaring. Emily Jane Brontë. CP-BronE

Louder than gulls the little children scream. Beach, The. Robert Graves. CP-GravR

Loudest sound [*or* thing] in our car, The. Vacation Trip. William Stafford. SP-StafW; SP-StafWW

Loudest sound that burdens here the breeze, The. Cliffs. Henry David Thoreau. CP-ThorH

Loue in thy youth fayre Mayde bee wise. Advice to a Maid. Robert Herrick. CP-HerrR

Louella Wainie! where are you? James Whitcomb Riley. CP-RileJ

Lough Neagh Sequence, A. Seamus Heaney. SP-HeanSO

Lough waters, The. Relic of Memory. Seamus Heaney. SP-HeanSO

Lough will claim a victim every year. Lough Neagh Sequence, A. Seamus Heaney. SP-HeanSO

Louie. Thomas Hardy. CP-HardT

Louis MacNeice. Stephen Spender. CP-SpenS

Louis Napoleon. Oscar Wilde. CP-WildO

Louis Sonnet, A. Muriel Rukeyser. CP-RukeM

Louis XI. Robert Stock. SP-StocR

Louis, What Reck I by Thee. Robert Burns. CP-BurnR

Louisa [After Accompanying Her on a Mountain Excursion]. William Wordsworth. CP-WorW1; MW-WorW

Louise. Raymond Carver. CP-CarvR

Louise. Stevie Smith. CP-SmitS

Lounger, A. James Whitcomb Riley. CP-RileJ

Lourd on My Hert. Hugh MacDiarmid. SP-MacDH

Lourd on my hert as winter lies. Lourd on My Hert. Hugh MacDiarmid. SP-MacDH

Lousy times: nothing to steal and no one to steal from. MCMXCIV. Joseph Brodsky. CP-BrodJ

Lout, The: "For Sunday's play he never makes excuse." John Clare. SP-ClarJ

Lout, The: "No sort of learning ever hurts his head." John Clare. SP-ClarJ

Louvered lids, The. Three Poems on Aaron Siskind's Photographs. John Logan. CP-LogaJ

Lovable Babblers. Carl Sandburg. CP-SandC

Love. Elizabeth Barrett Browning. CP-BroEB

Love. Charles Bukowski. SP-BukC3

Love. G. K. Chesterton. CP-ChesG

Love. Samuel Taylor Coleridge. CP-ColeS; MW-ColeS

Love. Robert Creeley. CP-CreeR; SP-CreeR

Love. Paul Laurence Dunbar. CP-DunbP

Love. Federico García Lorca.
  "Against the green sky." CP-GarcF, *tr. by* Alan S. Trueblood
  Brief Madrigal. CP-GarcF, *tr. by* Alan S. Trueblood
  Ditty of First Desire. CP-GarcF, *tr. by* Alan S. Trueblood
  Echo. CP-GarcF, *tr. by* Alan S. Trueblood
  Granada 1850. CP-GarcF, *tr. by* Alan S. Trueblood

  Idyll: "You wanted me to tell you." CP-GarcF, *tr. by* Alan S. Trueblood
  In School and at the University. CP-GarcF, *tr. by* Alan S. Trueblood
  "Narcissus. / The smell of you." CP-GarcF, *tr. by* Alan S. Trueblood
  Prelude: "Poplar lanes move on, The." CP-GarcF, *tr. by* Alan S. Trueblood
  Sonnet: "Specter trailing restless silver, A." CP-GarcF, *tr. by* Alan S. Trueblood

Love. George Herbert. CP-HerbG

Love. Robert Herrick. CP-HerrR

Love. Langston Hughes. CP-HughL; CP-HughL2

Love. Thomas Kinsella. CP-KinsT

Love. Philip Larkin. CP-LarkP

Love. D. H. Lawrence. CP-LawrD

Love. George Meredith. CP-MerG2

Love. Charles Olson. CP-OlsoC

Love. Grace Paley. CP-PalGC

Love. Percy Bysshe Shelley. CP-ShelP

Love. Gary Snyder. CP-SnydG

Love. Henry David Thoreau. CP-ThorH

Love. Jones Very. CP-VeryJ

Love. William Carlos Williams. CP-WilW1

Love (1). George Herbert. CP-HerbG

Love I. Charles Olson. CP-OlsoC

LOVE 1: What She Said. A. K. Ramanujan. CP-RamaA

LOVE 2: What He Said, Groping. A. K. Ramanujan. CP-RamaA

Love (2). George Herbert. CP-HerbG

Love (3). George Herbert. CP-HerbG

LOVE 3: What He Said, Remembering. A. K. Ramanujan. CP-RamaA

LOVE 4: What He Said, to His Daughter. A. K. Ramanujan. CP-RamaA

LOVE 5. A. K. Ramanujan. CP-RamaA

LOVE 6: Winter. A. K. Ramanujan. CP-RamaA

Love, A. Constantine P. Cavafy. CP-CavaC, *tr. by* Theoharis Constantine Theoharis

Love a Life can show Below, The. Love a Life Can Show, The. Emily Dickinson. CP-DickE

Love a Life Can Show, The. Emily Dickinson. CP-DickE

Love Abused. William Cowper. CP-CowpW

Love after Love. Derek Walcott. CP-WalcD

Love Again. Philip Larkin. CP-LarkP

Love Again Blues. Langston Hughes. CP-HughL; CP-HughL2

Love against Death. Clarence Major. SP-MajoC

Love, all day there has been at the edge of my mind. Envoy: "Love, all day there has been at the edge of my mind." Wendell Berry. CP-BerrW

Love among the Manichees. William Dickey. SP-DickW

Love among the Ruins. Robert Browning. CP-BroR1; SP-BroR

Love among the Ruins. Richard Eberhart. CP-EberR

Love and a Question. Robert Frost. CP-FrosR

Love and Death. Lord Byron. CP-Byron

Love and Death. Christina Georgina Rossetti. CP-RosC3

Love and Death once ceased their strife. Explanation, The. Rudyard Kipling. CP-KiplR

Love and Debt Alike Troublesome. Sir John Suckling. CP-SuckJ

Love and forgetting might have carried them. Two Look at Two. Robert Frost. CP-FrosR

Love and Fortune and my mind, rememb'rer. Sir Thomas Wyatt. CP-WyatT

Love and Friendship. Emily Jane Brontë. CP-BronE

Love and Friendship Opposite. Samuel Taylor Coleridge. CP-ColeS

Love and Gold. Lord Byron. CP-Byron

Love and Grief. Paul Laurence Dunbar. CP-DunbP

Love and harmony combine. Song: "Love and harmony combine." William Blake. CP-BlakW

Love and Hope. Christina Georgina Rossetti. CP-RosC3

Love and Hope. Dante Gabriel Rossetti. CW-RossD *Fr.* House of Life, The.

Love and How It Becomes Important in Our Day to Day Lives. Miller Williams. CP-WillM

Love and its Doors and Windows. Muriel Rukeyser. CP-RukeM

Love and Jealousy. Sir Philip Sidney. SP-SidnP *Fr.* Arcadia.

Love and Law. Nicholas Vachel Lindsay. CP-LindV

Love and Libery—A Cantata. Robert Burns. *See* Jolly Beggars, The

Love and Money. Alan Dugan. CP-DugaA

Love and my selfe (beleeve me) on a day. Love's Play at Push-Pin. Robert Herrick. CP-HerrR

Love and Night. Robert Graves. CP-GravR

Love and Reason. Sir Philip Sidney. SP-SidnP *Fr.* Arcadia.

Love and Solitude. John Clare. SP-ClarJ

Love & the Documents. Andrei Codrescu. SP-CodrA

Love and the Graces evermore do wait. Potentates. Robert Herrick. CP-HerrR

Love and the Lady Lagia, Guido and I. Sonnet: On the Detection of a false

Friend. Guido Cavalcanti. CW-RossD, *tr.* by Dante Gabriel Rossetti

Love and the Times. Donald Davie. CP-DaviDC

Love and Thought. Ralph Waldo Emerson. CP-EmerR

Love, any devil else but you. Love's Exchange. John Donne. CP-DonnJ; MW-DonnJ

Love as an Escape. D. H. Lawrence. CP-LawrD

Love as Lovelessness. Robert Graves. CP-GravR

Love / Asks nought his brother cannot give. Ralph Waldo Emerson. CP-EmerR

Love at First Sight. Wisława Szymborska. SP-SzymW, *tr.* by Stanislaw Barańczak *and* Clare Cavanagh

Love at First Sight. Wisława Szymborska. SP-SzymWM, *tr.* by Joanna Trzeciak

"Love at first sight," some say, misnaming. At First Sight. Robert Graves. CP-GravR

Love at the lips was touch. To Earthward. Robert Frost. CP-FrosR

Love, at what distance mine! Fear. James Vincent Cunningham. CP-CunnJ

Love Attacked. Christina Georgina Rossetti. CP-RosC3

Love bade me aske a gift. On Love. Robert Herrick. CP-HerrR

Love bade me welcome: yet my soul drew back. Love (3). George Herbert. CP-HerbG

Love: Beginnnings. C. K. Williams. SP-WillC

Love beyond Keeping. Carl Sandburg. CP-SandC

Love beyond my maddest dreaming. Promise. Dorothy Parker. CP-ParkD

Love, brave vertue's younger brother. Love's Horoscope. Richard Crashaw. CP-CrasR

Love brought Me down: and cannot love make thee / Carol for joy to Me? Candlemas Dialogue, A. Christina Georgina Rossetti. CP-RosC2

Love brought me to a silent Grove. Upon Love. Robert Herrick. CP-HerrR

Love builds a nest on earth and waits for rest. Christina Georgina Rossetti. CP-RosC3

Love builds for us a bower. Home, The ("Love builds for us a bower"). Jones Very. CP-VeryJ

Love built a stately house; where *Fortune* came. World, The. George Herbert. CP-HerbG

Love by ambition. Too Dear, Too Vague. W. H. Auden. CP-AudeW

Love Calls Us to the Things of This World. Richard Wilbur. CP-WilbR

Love came down at Christmas, / Love all lovely, Love Divine. Christmastide. Christina Georgina Rossetti. CP-RosC2

Love came so late, so late. Late Arrival. Marya Alexandrovna Zaturenska. SP-ZatuM

Love came up to me. Love Replied. Allen Ginsberg. CP-GinsA; SP-GinsA

Love can do all but raise the Dead. Emily Dickinson. CP-DickE

Love Charm, The. William Carlos Williams. CP-WilW2

Love Charms. Robert Graves. CP-GravR

Love-Children. Robinson Jeffers. CP-JefR1

Love Comes. Allen Ginsberg. SP-GinsA

Love Comes Late. D. H. Lawrence. CP-LawrD

Love Comes Quietly. Robert Creeley. CP-CreeR

Love Crown. Paul Celan. CP-PinsR, *tr.* by Robert Pinsky

Love Defended. Christina Georgina Rossetti. CP-RosC3

Love Despoiled. Paul Laurence Dunbar. CP-DunbP

Love Dislikes Nothing. Robert Herrick. CP-HerrR

Love Dogs. Jelaluddin Rumi. SP-Rumi, *tr.* by Coleman Barks

Love doth so grace and dignify / That beggars treat as king with king. As a King, ...Unto the King. Christina Georgina Rossetti. CP-RosC2

Love Enthroned. Dante Gabriel Rossetti. CW-RossD *Fr.* House of Life, The.

Love Ephemeral. Christina Georgina Rossetti. CP-RosC3

Love Faithful in the Absence of the Beloved. Jeanne Marie Bouvier de la Motte Guyon. CP-CowpW, *tr.* by William Cowper

Love Feast, The. W. H. Auden. CP-AudeW

Love floods the tree of. Physics. Pablo Neruda. SP-NeruP

Love for a Hand. Karl Shapiro. SP-ShapK

Love for October, The. W. S. Merwin. SP-MerwWF

Love for One Orange, The. Randall Jarrell. CP-JarrR

Love forgive me if I wish you grief. Stephen Crane. CP-CranS

Love Forgiven. Allen Ginsberg. CP-GinsA; SP-GinsA

Love, Fortune, and my mind (hardly aware). Petrarch. CP-Petra, *tr.* by J. G. Nichols

Love Freed from Ignorance and Folly. Ben Jonson.

"Crown, a crown for Love's bright head, A." CP-JonsB

"Gentle Love, be not dismayed." CP-JonsB

"What just excuse had agèd Time." CP-JonsB

Love from the North. Christina Georgina Rossetti. CP-RosC1

Love Gifts. Robert Graves. CP-GravR

Love God, we rather may, than. From Pico & the Women: A Life. Robert Creeley. CP-CreeR

Love goddess, alas, grows frailer, The. Dying Goddess, The. Carolyn Kizer. CP-KizeC

Love had him fast but though he fought for breath. Meiosis. W. H. Auden. CP-AudeW

Love had revealed to me a tranquil harbour. Petrarch. CP-Petra, *tr.* by J. G. Nichols

Love has crept out of her sealéd heart. Flapper. D. H. Lawrence. CP-LawrD

Love has earth to which she clings. Bond and Free. Robert Frost. CP-FrosR

Love has gone a-rocketing. Wail. Dorothy Parker. CP-ParkD

Love has gone and left me and the days are all alike. Ashes of Life. Edna St. Vincent Millay. CP-MillE

Love has had his way with me. Burned Child, The. Dorothy Parker. CP-ParkD

Love has many joys. Her Sweet Deceit. James Laughlin. CP-LaugJ

Love has no other friends. Song: "Love has no other friends." Robert Creeley. SP-CreeR

Love has taken away my practices. Buoyancy. Jelaluddin Rumi. SP-Rumi, *tr.* by Coleman Barks

Love hath a name of Death. Christina Georgina Rossetti. CP-RosC3

Love hath again. Sir Thomas Wyatt. CP-WyatT

Love hath the wings of the butterfly. Love's Phases. Paul Laurence Dunbar. CP-DunbP

Love he that will; it best likes me. Another. Robert Herrick. CP-HerrR

Love, Hope, and Patience in Education. Samuel Taylor Coleridge. CP-ColeS

Love, Hope, Desire and Fear. Percy Bysshe Shelley. CP-ShelP

Love, I have broke. Upon Love. Robert Herrick. CP-HerrR

Love, I have sinned, and recognise my sin. Petrarch. CP-Petra, *tr.* by J. G. Nichols

Love, I know, is a loss. Rainer Maria Rilke. CP-RilkFr, *tr.* by A. Poulin, Jr. *Fr.* Fragments.

Love, I recant. His Recantation. Robert Herrick. CP-HerrR

Love, I shall perfect for you the child. Poem: "Love, I shall perfect for you the child." Seamus Heaney. SP-HeanSO

Love, I speak to your heart. Parted Presence. Dante Gabriel Rossetti. CW-RossD

Love I was shewn upon the mountain-side. Half-way House, The. Gerard Manley Hopkins. CP-HopkG

Love, if I weep it will not matter. Dream, The. Edna St. Vincent Millay. CP-MillE

Love! if Thy destined sacrifice am I. Acquiescence of Pure Love, The. Jeanne Marie Bouvier de la Motte Guyon. CP-CowpW, *tr.* by William Cowper

Love in a Bus. Thomas McGrath. SP-McGrT

Love in a Life. Robert Browning. CP-BroR1

Love in a showre of Blossomes came. Showre of Blossomes, The. Robert Herrick. CP-HerrR

Love in America. Marianne Craig Moore. CP-MoorM

Love in Barrenness. Robert Graves. CP-GravR

Love, in its separate being. Randall Jarrell. CP-JarrR

Love in Labrador. Carl Sandburg. CP-SandC

Love in the Asylum. Dylan Thomas. CP-ThomD

Love in the Museum. Adrienne Rich. CP-RicAE

Love in the Valley. George Meredith. CP-MerG1

　(Under yonder beech-tree standing on the green-sward.) CP-MerG1

Love in the Valley. Derek Walcott. CP-WalcD

Love / In whose rich honor. Song: Love in Whose Rich Honor. Muriel Rukeyser. CP-RukeM

Love in your eyes? No; life and death are there. Michelangelo Buonarroti. CP-Miche, *tr.* by John Frederick Nims

Love Increased by Suffering. Jeanne Marie Bouvier de la Motte Guyon. CP-CowpW, *tr.* by William Cowper

Love / Is a brown man's fist. Beale Street Love. Langston Hughes. CP-HughL; CP-HughL1

Love is a circle, and an Endlesse Sphere. Upon Love. Robert Herrick. CP-HerrR

Love is a circle that doth restless[e] move. Love What It Is. Robert Herrick. CP-HerrR

Love is a climate. Smaller Orchid, The. Amy Clampitt. CP-ClamA

Love Is a Deep and a Dark and a Lonely. Carl Sandburg. CP-SandC

Love Is a Dog from Hell. Charles Bukowski. SP-BukC1

Love is a door we shall open together. Moon Rondeau. Carl Sandburg. CP-SandC

Love is a game for only two to play at. Jus Primae Noctis. Robert Graves. CP-GravR

Love is a guess / that deepens. E. E. Cummings. CP-CummE

Love is a kind of warre; Hence those who feare. On Love. Robert Herrick. CP-HerrR

Love is a Leven, and a loving kisse. Leven. Robert Herrick. CP-HerrR

Love Is a Parallax. Sylvia Plath. CP-PlatS

Love Is a Piece of Paper Torn to Bits. Charles Bukowski. SP-BukC2

Love is a place. E. E. Cummings. CP-CummE

Love / Is a ripe plum. Love Song for Lucinda. Langston Hughes. CP-HughL; CP-HughL1

Love Is a School. James Laughlin. CP-LaugJ

Love Is a Sirrup. Robert Herrick. CP-HerrR

Love is a spring at which. E. E. Cummings. CP-CummE

Love Is a Star. Paul Laurence Dunbar. CP-DunbP

Love is a universal migraine. Symptoms of Love. Robert Graves. CP-GravR

Love is a wild wonder. Love. Langston Hughes. CP-HughL; CP-HughL2

Love is all happiness, love is all beauty. Christina Georgina Rossetti. CP-RosC3

"Love is all / Unsatisfied." Crazy Jane on the Day of Judgment. William Butler Yeats. CP-YeatW

Love is alone the worthy law of love: / All other laws have presupposed a taint. Quinquagesima. Christina Georgina Rossetti. CP-RosC2

Love is an illness still to be. Patient Lovers, The. Carolyn Kizer. CP-KizeC

Love—is anterior to Life. Emily Dickinson. CP-DickE

Love is blind, and a wanton. Ben Jonson. CP-JonsB Fr. Poetaster, The.

Love Is Cumulative. James Laughlin. CP-LaugJ

Love is done when Love's begun. Emily Dickinson. CP-DickE

"Love is enough," I read somewhere. To an Unknown Poet. Countee Cullen. CP-CullC

Love is finished again, like a profitable citrus season. Yehuda Amichai. SP-AmicY, tr. by Chana Bloch

Love, is it a cat with claws and wild mate screams. Little Word, Little White Bird. Carl Sandburg. CP-SandC

Love is like dew. Breath of a Rose. Langston Hughes. CP-HughL; CP-HughL2

Love Is like Sounds. Donald Hall. CP-HallD

Love is like the wild rose-briar. Love and Friendship. Emily Jane Bronte. CP-BronE

Love is like water or the air. Riposte. William Carlos Williams. CP-WilW1

Love is lost, nor can his Mother. Out of the Greeke Cupid's Cryer. Moschus. CP-CrasR, tr. by Richard Crashaw

Love is maintain'd by wealth; when all is spent. Adversity. Robert Herrick. CP-HerrR

Love is more thicker than forget. E. E. Cummings. CP-CummE; SP-CummE

Love is not a profession. Is / Not. Margaret Atwood. SP-AtwM1

"Love is not all: it is not meat nor drink." Edna St. Vincent Millay. CP-MillE

Love is not blind. I see with single eye. Edna St. Vincent Millay. CP-MillE

Love Is Not Concerned. Alice Walker. CP-WalkA

Love is not love demanding all, itself. Love's Way. Countee Cullen. CP-CullC

Love is not present now. Troilus. Charles Olson. CP-OlsoC

Love is not worth so much. Coda: "Love is not worth so much." James Tate. SP-TateJ

Love is sharper than stones or sticks. Ballade of Unfortunate Mammals. Dorothy Parker. CP-ParkD

Love is still Love, and doeth all things well. He Cannot Deny Himself. Christina Georgina Rossetti. CP-RosC2

"Love Is Strong as Death." Christina Georgina Rossetti. See Love Is Stronger than Death

Love Is Strong as Death. Christina Georgina Rossetti. CP-RosC2

Love Is Stronger than Death. Christina Georgina Rossetti. CP-RosC2 ("Love Is Strong as Death.") CP-RosC2

Love is sweet, and so are flowers. Love Ephemeral. Christina Georgina Rossetti. CP-RosC3

Love Is That Later Thing. Emily Dickinson. CP-DickE

Love—is that later Thing than Death. Love Is That Later Thing. Emily Dickinson. CP-DickE

Love is that one perfect labor. Emily Dickinson. SP-DickE

Love is the every only god. E. E. Cummings. CP-CummE; SP-CummE

Love is the key of life and death, / Of hidden heavenly mystery. Song for the Least of All Saints, A. Christina Georgina Rossetti. CP-RosC2

Love is the light of the world, my dear. Paul Laurence Dunbar. CP-DunbP

Love is the Lord whom I obey. Divine Love Endures No Rival. Jeanne Marie Bouvier de la Motte Guyon. CP-CowpW, tr. by William Cowper

Love is the master of the ring. Ring, The. Langston Hughes. CP-HughL; CP-HughL1

Love is the talk. Charles Olson. CP-OlsoC

Love is the way that lovers never know. Archibald MacLeish. CP-MacLA Fr. Happy Marriage, The.

Love is twain, it is not single. Love. William Carlos Williams. CP-WilW1

Love is winged for two. George Meredith. CP-MerG1

Love-Joy. George Herbert. CP-HerbG

Love kept me burning one-and-twenty years. Petrarch. CP-Petra, tr. by J. G. Nichols

Love Kill'd by Lack. Robert Herrick. CP-HerrR

Love kindle, / Death slay. Quenching the Red. Kathleen Jessie Raine. SP-RainK

Love, kindling in our hearts an ardent fire. Petrarch. CP-Petra, tr. by J. G. Nichols

Love, leave me like the light. If You Should Go. Countee Cullen. CP-CullC

Love, lend a hand to my afflicted mind. Petrarch. CP-Petra, tr. by J. G. Nichols

Love— / let it / Out, / open up. Robert Creeley. CP-CreeR

Love Letter. Allen Ginsberg. CP-GinsA

Love Letter. Sylvia Plath. CP-PlatS

Love Letter, A. Paul Laurence Dunbar. CP-DunbP

Love Letter, The. Robert Graves. CP-GravR

Love-Letter, The. Dante Gabriel Rossetti. CW-RossD Fr. House of Life, The.

Love Letter to Hans Christian Andersen. Carl Sandburg. CP-SandC

Love Letter Written in a Burning Building. Anne Sexton. CP-SextA

Love-Letters, The. Thomas Hardy. CP-HardT

Love Lies Bleeding. Christina Georgina Rossetti. CP-RosC1

Love Lies Bleeding. William Wordsworth. CP-WorW2

Love Lies Sleeping. Elizabeth Bishop. CP-BishE

Love, like a Beggar, came to me. Upon Cupid. Robert Herrick. CP-HerrR

Love, like a Gypsie, lately came. Upon Cupid. Robert Herrick. CP-HerrR

Love-Lily. Dante Gabriel Rossetti. CW-RossD

Love Lines. Olga Broumas. SP-BrouO

Love long delayed comes kindly, by fortune's favor. Michelangelo Buonarroti. CP-Miche, tr. by John Frederick Nims

Love long dormant showing itself. Palais des Arts. Louise Glück. SP-GlucL

Love-lorn Maid, at some far distant time, A. Tradition. William Wordsworth. CP-WorW2 Fr. River Duddon [A Series of Sonnets], The.

Love, love, a lily's my care. Words for the Wind. Theodore Roethke. CP-RoetT

Love love begets, then never be. To Electra. Love Looks for Love. Robert Herrick. CP-HerrR

Love, Love, cruel Love, long have you driven me. Nine Variations on Themes from Petrarch. Petrarch. SP-ZatuM, tr. by Marya Alexandrovna Zaturenska

Love Love Love Again. Philip Whalen. SP-WhalP

Love, love me now, because I place. To His Friend, Master J. Jincks. Robert Herrick. CP-HerrR

Love, Love, that having found a heart. What Sappho Would Have Said Had Her Leap Cured instead of Killing Her. Christina Georgina Rossetti. CP-RosC3

Love, Love, who once didst pass the Dardan portals. Aurora and Tithonus. Euripides. CP-BroEB Fr. Trojan Women, The.

Love loveth Thee, and wisdom loveth Thee. Christina Georgina Rossetti. CP-RosC2

Love makes me go where I had rather not. Petrarch. CP-Petra, tr. by J. G. Nichols

Love, Maybe. Audre Lorde. SP-LordA

Love Me! Stevie Smith. CP-SmitS

Love me and I'll think about it. For Your Fear. David Ignatow. SP-IgnaD

Love me as I love thee. O double sweet! Gerard Manley Hopkins. CP-HopkG

Love Me but Leave My Dog Alone. Ogden Nash. CP-NashO

Love me. I care not what the circling years. Love's Apotheosis. Paul Laurence Dunbar. CP-DunbP

Love me,—I love you / Love me, my baby. Lullaby: "Love me,—I love you / Love me, my baby." Christina Georgina Rossetti. CP-RosC2

Love me, let a little of this smile. Two Poems. Rainer Maria Rilke. CP-RilkFr, tr. by A. Poulin, Jr.

Love Me Little, Love Me Long. Robert Herrick. CP-HerrR

Love me, Love me, I cried to the rocks and the trees. Love Me! Stevie Smith. CP-SmitS

Love me no more, now let the god depart. Edna St. Vincent Millay. CP-MillE

Love Me or Not. Thomas Campion. CP-CampT

Love me or not, love her I must or die [or dye]. Love Me or Not. Thomas Campion. CP-CampT

Love me, Sweet, with all thou art. Man's Requirements, A. Elizabeth Barrett Browning. CP-BroEB

Love Message. D. H. Lawrence. CP-LawrD

Love met me at noonday. Stephen Crane. CP-CranS

Love-Moon, The. Dante Gabriel Rossetti. CW-RossD Fr. House of Life, The.

Love, Nature, and this lovely gentle soul. Petrarch. CP-Petra, tr. by J. G. Nichols

Love Needing a Visible Object. Jones Very. CP-VeryJ

Love never count your labour lost. Song: Sullen Moods. Robert Graves. CP-GravR

Love, never disavow our vow. Lion-Gentle. Robert Graves. CP-GravR

Love Note I: Surely. Gwendolyn Brooks. SP-BrooG

Love Note II: Flags. Gwendolyn Brooks. See Flags

Love now no more hath left him. Out of the Italian. Giovanni Giambattista. CP-CrasR, tr. by Richard Crashaw

Love Nut, The. Lawrence Ferlinghetti. SP-FerlL

Love of a Coat, The. Andrei Codrescu. SP-CodrA

Love of a mother for her child, The. Mother's Hearse, A. Stevie Smith. CP-SmitS

Love of a woman, The. Air: "The Love of a Woman." Robert Creeley. CP-CreeR

Love of Artifice, The. Charles Baudelaire. CP-BaudC

Love of Christ Which Passeth Knowledge, The. Christina Georgina Rossetti. CP-RosC1

Love of God. G. K. Chesterton. CP-ChesG

Love of God is love of self. Thesis and Counter-Thesis. Czeslaw Milosz. CP-

MiloC; CP-MiloCN

Love of God may be taught, The. Emily Dickinson. SP-DickE

Love of God the End of Life, The. Jeanne Marie Bouvier de la Motte- Guyon. CP-CowpW

Love of Jerusalem. Yehuda Amichai. SP-AmicYL, *tr. by* Benjamin Harshav *and* Barbara Harshav

Love of Lettuce, The. Marge Piercy. SP-PierM

Love of Morning, The. Denise Levertov. SP-LeveDS

Love of my heart, living death. Poet Asks His Love to Write Him, The. Federico García Lorca. CP-GarcF, *tr. by* Angela Jaffray

Love of old men is not worth a lot, The. Lines for My 55th Birthday. Thom Gunn. CP-GunnT

Love of the bone, The. Reunion. Charles Bukowski. SP-BukC2

Love of the Land. Yehuda Amichai. SP-AmicYL, *tr. by* Benjamin Harshav *and* Barbara Harshav

Love of the Woods. Johann N. Vogl. CP-MerG2

Love of the World Reproved, The. William Cowper. CP-CowpW

Love of What Is Not, The. Eleanor Wilner. SP-WilnE

Love of work. The blood singing. Work. Raymond Carver. CP-CarvR

Love on a day (wise poets tell). How Violets Came Blue. Robert Herrick. CP-HerrR

Love on the Farm. D. H. Lawrence. CP-LawrD

Love our so right. E. E. Cummings. CP-CummE; SP-CummE

Love & pain converge. Waratah. Yusef Komunyakaa. CP-KomuY

Love Palpable. Robert Herrick. CP-HerrR

Love-Passage, A. D. H. Lawrence. CP-LawrD

Love Perfumes All Parts. Robert Herrick. CP-HerrR

Love Plant, The. Anne Sexton. CP-SextA

Love Poem: "And while for the sake of sanity." Andrei Codrescu. SP-CodrA

Love Poem: "Black biplane crashes through [*or* into] the window, A [*or* The]." Gregory Orr. SP-OrrG

Love Poem: "Last night you would not come." John Logan. CP-LoganJ

Love Poem: "People use each other." Yehuda Amichai. SP-AmicYL, *tr. by* Benjamin Harshav *and* Barbara Harshav

Love Poem: "Six o'clock and / the sun rises." Miller Williams. CP-WillM

Love Poem: "Speek earth and bless me with what is richest." Audre Lorde. SP-LordA

Love Poem: "There is always something to be made of pain." Louise Glück. SP-GlucL

Love Poem: "What you give me is." Denise Levertov. SP-LeveDL; SP-LeveDS

Love Poem, A: "All the women." Charles Bukowski. SP-BukC3

Love Poem, A: "And they have to get it right. We just need." John Ashbery. SP-AshbJ

Love Poem, A: "Basic hatred / sometimes has a flower." William Carlos Williams. CP-WilW2

Love Poem, A: "I am the lightness that I know." Richard Eberhart. SP-EberR

Love Poem, A: "I have labored for her love." John Ciardi. CP-CiarJ

Love Poem for a Wife and Her Trees. A. K. Ramanujan. CP-RamaA

Love Poem for a Wife, 1. A. K. Ramanujan. CP-RamaA

Love Poem for a Wife, 2. A. K. Ramanujan. CP-RamaA

Love Poem for the Forty-Second Street Library. David Ignatow. SP-IgnaD

Love Poem in Twos and Threes. Robert Bly. SP-BlyR

Love Poem on Theme by Whitman. Allen Ginsberg. CP-GinsA; SP-GinsA

Love Poem to Be Read to an Illiterate Friend. Tess Gallagher. SP-GallT

Love Poem with Toast. Miller Williams. CP-WillM

Love-Poems: for Mairi MacInnes. Donald Davie. CP-DaviDC

Love Poems of Marichiko, The. Kenneth Rexroth. CP-RexrK

Love Preparing to Fly. Gerard Manley Hopkins. CP-HopkG

Love Pure and Fervent. Jeanne Marie Bouvier de la Motte- Guyon. CP-CowpW

Love, Reason, Hate, did once bespeak. Barley-Break, A. Sir John Suckling. CP-SuckJ

Love, receive Lais' glass, the famous whore. James Vincent Cunningham. CP-CunnJ

Love reckons by itself—alone. Emily Dickinson. CP-DickE

Love Recognized. Robert Penn Warren. CP-WarrR

Love Replied. Allen Ginsberg. CP-GinsA; SP-GinsA

Love requires / talk of itself. Alba, The. Charles Olson. CP-OlsoC

Love Restored. Ben Jonson.

    "Give end unto thy pastimes, Love." CP-JonsB

    "Have men beheld the graces dance." CP-JonsB

    "O how came Love, that is himself a fire." CP-JonsB

    "This motion was of love begot." CP-JonsB

Love Returned. Allen Ginsberg. CP-GinsA

Love returned with smiles. Love Returned. Allen Ginsberg. CP-GinsA

Love rose up between us. Two Palm Trees, The. Miguel Hernández. CP-MertT

Love said nay, while Hope kept saying / All his sweetest say. Now They Desire a Better Country. Christina Georgina Rossetti. CP-RosC2

Love, says the poet, has no reasons. Old Gray Couple (2), The. Archibald MacLeish. CP-MacLA

Love scorch'd my finger, but did spare. Upon Love. Robert Herrick. CP-HerrR

Love seeketh not Itself to please. Clod and the Pebble, The. William Blake. CP-BlakW *Fr.* Songs of Experience.

Love set me up to be his arrows' mark. Petrarch. CP-Petra, *tr. by* J. G. Nichols

Love set you going like a fat gold watch. Morning Song. Sylvia Plath. CP-PlatS

Love, should I fear death most for you or me? Cloud and Wind. Dante Gabriel Rossetti. CW-RossD *Fr.* House of Life, The.

Love should intend realities. Goodbye. John Ciardi.

Love-sick I am, and must endure. On Himselfe. Robert Herrick. CP-HerrR

Love-sick Lass, The. Hugh MacDiarmid. SP-MacDH

Love Sleeping. May Swenson. SP-SwenM

Love Song: "Daisies are broken." William Carlos Williams. CP-WilW1

Love Song: "I lie here thinking of you." William Carlos Williams. CP-WilW1

Love Song: "I was / the girl of the chain letter." Anne Sexton. CP-SextA

Love-Song: "If Death should claim me for her own to-day." Paul Laurence Dunbar. CP-DunbP

Love Song: "If you were drowning, I'd come to the rescue." Joseph Brodsky. CP-BrodJ

Love Song: "Like the hills under dusk you." A. R. Ammons. CP-AmmoA

Love Song: "My own dear love, he is strong and bold." Dorothy Parker. CP-ParkD

Love Song: "Oh, to fall easily, easily, easily in Love." Carolyn Kizer. CP-KizeC

Love Song: "Rings of birch bark." A. R. Ammons. CP-AmmoA

Love Song: "Suppose we two were cast away." Dorothy Parker. CP-ParkD

Love Song: "Sweep the house clean." William Carlos Williams. CP-WilW1

Love Song: "This is how it started: suddenly it felt." Yehuda Amichai. SP-AmicY, *tr. by* Chana Bloch

Love Song: "You have come between me and the terrifying presence." William Carlos Williams. CP-WilW1

Love Song: "Your beauty, which I lost sight of once." Denise Levertov. SP-LeveDP

Love Song, A: "Ah, love, my love is like a cry in the night." Paul Laurence Dunbar. CP-DunbP

Love Song, A: "Reject me not if I should say to you." D. H. Lawrence. CP-LawrD

Love Song: Class Analysis. Alan Dugan. CP-DugaA

Love Song: First Version, 1915, A. William Carlos Williams. CP-WilW1

Love Song for Antonia. Langston Hughes. CP-HughL; CP-HughL1

Love Song for K. Owyne. Anne Sexton. CP-SextA

Love Song for Lucinda. Langston Hughes. CP-HughL; CP-HughL1

Love Song: I and Thou. Alan Dugan. CP-DugaA

Love Song in the Modern Taste, A. Jonathan Swift. CP-SwifJ

Love Song of Har Dyal, The. Rudyard Kipling. CP-KiplR *Fr.* Plain Tales from the Hills.

Love Song of J. Alfred Prufrock, The. T. S. Eliot. CP-ElioT

    Love Song of J. Alfred Prufrock, Resumed, The. SP-ElioT

    Love Song of J. Alfred Prufrock, The (Prufrock among the Women). SP-ElioT Prufrock's Pervigilium. SP-ElioT

Love Song of St. Sebastian, The. T. S. Eliot. SP-ElioT

Love Song to a Morning. Jorge Guillén. CP-WrigJ

Love-Song to Eunoë. Ezra Pound. CP-PoEar

Love Songs in Age. Philip Larkin. CP-LarkP

Love Sonnet: Believing Part of Almost All I Say. John Ciardi. CP-CiarJ

Love spurs and at the same time reins me in. Petrarch. CP-Petra, *tr. by* J. G. Nichols

Love Storm. D. H. Lawrence. CP-LawrD

Love Story, A. Robert Graves. CP-GravR

Love strikes me again, that makes the legs give way. Sappho. CP-CunnJ, *tr. by* James Vincent Cunningham

Love, strong as Death, is dead. End, An. Christina Georgina Rossetti. CP-RosC1

Love-Sweetness. Dante Gabriel Rossetti. CW-RossD *Fr.* House of Life, The.

Love, that drained her, drained him she'd loved, though each. Turtle Dove, The. Geoffrey Hill. CP-HillG

Love that is dead and buried, yesterday. Love Lies Bleeding. Christina Georgina Rossetti. CP-RosC1

Love That Is Hereafter, The. Walt Whitman. CP-WhitW

Love the earth like a mole. Starting with Little Things. William Stafford. SP-StafWW

Love the Monopolist. Thomas Hardy. CP-HardT

Love, the Most Gen'rous Passion of the Mind. *Unknown, sometimes at. to* Thomas Sheridan. CP-SherT

Love the quick profit, the annual raise. Manifesto: the Mad Farmer Liberation Front. Wendell Berry. CP-BerrW

Love, the sole Goddess fit for swearing by. Friday Night. Robert Graves. CP-GravR

Love the Wild Swan. Robinson Jeffers. CP-JefR2

Love, the world. Letter in November. Sylvia Plath. CP-PlatS

Love, there have neccessarily been others. True Magic. Robert Graves. CP-GravR

Love they alone the joyful heart. George Meredith. CP-MerG2

Love / they say. *Barely* and *widely*. Louis Zukofsky. CP-ZukLS

Love, this is not the way. Prison Walls. Robert Graves. CP-GravR

Love, thou art absolute sole lord. Hymn to the Name and Hono[u]r of the Admirable Saint[e] Teresa, A. Richard Crashaw. CP-CrasR

Love Thou Art High. Emily Dickinson. CP-DickE

Love—thou art high. Love Thou Art High. Emily Dickinson. CP-DickE

Love thou thy dream. Song: "Love thou thy dream." Ezra Pound. CP-PoEar

Love, though for this you riddle me with darts. Edna St. Vincent Millay. CP-MillE

Love, though I sorrow, I shall never grieve. Hooded Flame. Robert Graves. CP-GravR

Love, through your spirit and mine what summer eve. Last Fire. Dante Gabriel Rossetti. CW-RossD *Fr.* House of Life, The.

Love Thy Neighbour. D. H. Lawrence. CP-LawrD

Love, to be love, must walk Thy way / And work Thy Will. Christina Georgina Rossetti. CP-RosC2

Love to faults is always blind. How to Know Love from Deceit. William Blake. CP-BlakW

Love, to give law unto his subject hearts. Prologue: "Love, to give law unto his subject hearts." Sir Thomas Wyatt. CP-WyatT *Fr.* Penitential Psalms.

Love to his singer held a glistening leaf. Love's Last Gift. Dante Gabriel Rossetti. CW-RossD *Fr.* House of Life, The.

Love to keep? There is no love to keep. Hungry and Laughing Men. Carl Sandburg. CP-SandC

Love Tree, The. Countee Cullen. CP-CullC

Love Turned to Hatred. Sir John Suckling. CP-SuckJ

Love Uncommanded. Eleanor Wilner. SP-WilnE

Love understands the mystery, whereof. Judge Nothing before the Time. Christina Georgina Rossetti. CP-RosC2

Love Unknown. George Herbert. CP-HerbG

Love used to carry a bow, you know. Change, The. Paul Laurence Dunbar. CP-DunbP

Love used to weep, and sometimes I did too. Petrarch. CP-Petra, *tr.* by J. G. Nichols

Love walked alone. Stephen Crane. CP-CranS

Love was—entire excellently steep. E. E. Cummings. CP-CummE

Love was perhaps a happy thing onetime. Petrarch. CP-Petra, *tr.* by J. G. Nichols

Love Watches a Window. Thomas Hardy. CP-HardT

Love, we are a small pond. We Are. Maxine W. Kumin. SP-KumiM

Love we had for one another is somewhere, The. David Ignatow. SP-IgnaD

Love, We Have Looked on Many Shows. G. K. Chesterton. CP-ChesG

Love, We Must Part Now. Philip Larkin. CP-LarkP

Love wears down to bare truth. Lack Love. Allen Ginsberg. CP-GinsA

Love What It Is. Robert Herrick. CP-HerrR

Love, when you lost your keepsake. St Antony of Padua. Robert Graves. CP-GravR

Love whets the dullest wittes, his plagues be such. Canto Quarto. Thomas Campion. CP-CampT

Love which comes without aspect, The. Emily Dickinson. SP-DickE

Love which is imprinted in my soul, The. Sir Philip Sidney. SP-SidnP *Fr.* Arcadia.

Love which is the most difficult mystery. Psyche with the Candle. Archibald MacLeish. CP-MacLA

Love which me so cruelly tormenteth, The. Sonnet 42. Edmund Spenser. CP-Spens *Fr.* Amoretti.

Love, while you were away there came to me. Wistful Lady, The. Thomas Hardy. CP-HardT

Love, who can promise so beguilingly. Petrarch. CP-Petra, *tr.* by J. G. Nichols

Love, who in good times kept me company. Petrarch. CP-Petra, *tr.* by J. G. Nichols

Love, whom I have loved too well. Isidora. Christina Georgina Rossetti. CP-RosC3

Love whom ye list and spare not. Sir Thomas Wyatt. CP-WyatT

Love, why have you led me here. Young Cordwainer, The. Robert Graves. CP-GravR

Love Winter when the Plant Says Nothing. Thomas Merton. CP-MertT

Love with his right hand opened my left side. Petrarch. CP-Petra, *tr.* by J. G. Nichols

Love within the lover's breast. Song: "Love within the lover's breast." George Meredith. CP-MerG1

Love without Hope. Robert Graves. CP-GravR

Love: Wrath. C. K. Williams. SP-WillC

Love, you are green only to grow yellow. Two Styles in Love. A. K. Ramanujan. CP-RamaA

Love you seek for, presupposes. Question and Answer. Elizabeth Barrett Browning. CP-BroEB

Love you that so long a. Return of Love, The. James Laughlin. CP-LaugJ

Love your rhythm and give rhythm to your actions. "Rubén Dario." SP-DariR, *tr.* by Alberto Acereda *and* Will Derusha

Love: Youth. C. K. Williams. SP-WillC

Loved feared hated. John Brown. Robert Earl Hayden. CP-HaydR

Loved I am, and yet complain[e] of Love. Complaint of Love. Sir Philip Sidney. SP-SidnP *Fr.* Arcadia.

Loved in the black weather . . . The. Cruelties of the Sportive Power. Kenneth Patchen. CP-PatcK

Loved Once. Elizabeth Barrett Browning. CP-BroEB

Loveliest flowers, though crooked in their border. Gardener. Robert Graves. CP-GravR

Loveliest of trees, the cherry now. A. E. Housman. CP-HousA

Loveliness, The. James Whitcomb Riley. CP-RileJ

Lovely Ad. William Carlos Williams. CP-WilW1

Lovely! all the essential parts. These Purists. William Carlos Williams. CP-WilW2

Lovely body gracefully is nodding, A. Something Amazing Just Happened. Ted Berrigan. SP-BerrT

Lovely Child, The. James Whitcomb Riley. CP-RileJ

Lovely city in a lovely land, / Whose citizens are lovely, and whose King, A. Beautiful for Situation. Christina Georgina Rossetti. CP-RosC2

Lovely Couple, A. Charles Bukowski. SP-BukC1

Lovely courier of the sky. Anacreon's Dove. Samuel Johnson. CP-JohnS

Lovely, dark, and lonely one. Song: "Lovely, dark, and lonely one." Langston Hughes. CP-HughL; CP-HughL1

Lovely Davies. Robert Burns. CP-BurnR

Lovely Face to sit by, A. Emily Dickinson. SP-DickE

Lovely flowers embarrass me, The. Emily Dickinson. SP-DickE

Lovely form there sate beside my bed, A. Phantom or Fact? Samuel Taylor Coleridge. CP-ColeS

Lovely house it was. We all thought so, A. Fat Lady, The. Hayden Carruth. CP-CarHS

Lovely Husband, The. James Whitcomb Riley. CP-RileJ

Lovely Lass o' Inverness, The. Robert Burns. CP-BurnR (Luvely Lass o' Inverness, The.) CP-BurnR

Lovely Love, A. Gwendolyn Brooks. SP-BrooG

Lovely Morning Thought. Arthur Rimbaud. CP-RimbA, *tr.* by Martin Sorrell

Lovely *obvious!*, The. The feet. Artist to Intellectual (Poet to Explainer). Denise Levertov. SP-LeveDL

Lovely Playthings. Ivor Gurney. SP-GurnI

Lovely Polly Stewart. Robert Burns. CP-BurnR

Lovely Shall Be Choosers, The. Robert Frost. CP-FrosR

Lovely, sleeping, lay in bed, The. Sleeper, The. Walter De la Mare. CP-DeLaW

Lovely Spring, / A brief sweet thing. Tempus Fugit. Christina Georgina Rossetti. CP-RosC2

Lovely was the night of May. Postillion, The. Nikolaus Lenau. CP-MerG2

Lovemusic. Carolyn Kizer. CP-KizeC

Lovenotes, a bra, lipstick. Wall, The. Yusef Komunyakaa. CP-KomuY

Lovepet, The. Ted Hughes. SP-HughTN

Lover. Yusef Komunyakaa. CP-KomuY

Lover, The. Robert Creeley. CP-CreeR

Lover, The. Frank O'Hara. SP-OharF

Lover and the Moon, The. Paul Laurence Dunbar. CP-DunbP

Lover as Fox. Muriel Rukeyser. SP-RukeM

Lover Asks Forgiveness because of His Many Moods. William Butler Yeats. CP-YeatW

Lover & child, a little sing. John Berryman. CP-BerrJ *Fr.* Black Book, The.

Lover divine and perfect Comrade. Gods. Walt Whitman. CP-WhitW

Lover For Shamefastness Hideth His Desire Within His Faithful Heart. Petrarch. CP-WyatT, *tr.* by Sir Thomas Wyatt *Fr.* Sonnets to Laura.

Lover, in melodious verses, The. No Sorrow Peculiar to the Sufferer. Vincent Bourne. CP-CowpW

Lover, in the Disguise of an Amazon, Is Dearly Beloved of His Mistress, A. Thomas Carew. CP-CareT

Lover Mourns for the Loss of Love, The. William Butler Yeats. CP-YeatW

Lover of palaces, muse of my heart. Mercenary Muse, The. Charles Baudelaire. CP-BaudC, *tr.* by Walter Martin

Lover Pleads with His Friend for Old Friends, The. William Butler Yeats. CP-YeatW

Lover said, "O Maiden, love me well," A. Man's Devotion. James Whitcomb Riley. CP-RileJ

Lover Showeth How He Is Forsaken of Such as He Sometime Enjoyed, The. Sir Thomas Wyatt. CP-WyatT

Lover Speaks to the Hearers of His Songs in Coming Days, The. William Butler Yeats. CP-YeatW

Lover Tells of the Rose in His Heart, The. William Butler Yeats. CP-YeatW

Lover to Mistress. Thomas Hardy. CP-HardT

Lover, upon an Accident Necessitating His Departure, Consults with Reason, A. Thomas Carew. CP-CareT

Lover was telling his beloved, A. Dying, Laughing. Jelaluddin Rumi. SP-Rumi, *tr.* by Coleman Barks

Lover whom duty called over the wave, A. Lover and the Moon, The. Paul Laurence Dunbar. CP-DunbP

Lovers, The. Josephine Jacobsen. CP-JacoJ

Lover's Appeal, The. Sir Thomas Wyatt. CP-WyatT

Lovers are happy. Secrecy. Robert Graves. CP-GravR

Lovers Are like Children. Adrienne Rich. CP-RicAE

Lover's Clock, The. Sir John Suckling. *See* Love's Clock

Lover's Complaint to His Mistress, A. Samuel Taylor Coleridge. CP-ColeS

Lover's death, how regular, The. Stark Major. Hart Crane. CP-CranH

Lovers everywhere are bringing babies into the world. Make Love Not War. Howard Nemerov. CP-NemeH

Lovers, forget your love. Wind and Window Flower. Robert Frost. CP-FrosR

Lover's Garden, A. Allen Ginsberg. CP-GinsA

Lovers How They Come and Part. Robert Herrick. CP-HerrR

Lovers in the act dispense. Thieves, The. Robert Graves. CP-GravR

Lovers in time of absence need not signal. In Time of Absence. Robert Graves. CP-GravR

Lovers in Winter. Robert Graves. CP-GravR

Lovers' Infiniteness[e]. John Donne. CP-DonnJ; MW-DonnJ

Lover's Lane. Paul Laurence Dunbar. CP-DunbP

Lovers lie in the shelter of night, the lovers, The. Lovers, The. Josephine Jacobsen. CP-JacoJ

Lovers' Litany, The. Rudyard Kipling. CP-KiplR

Lovers looked over the parapet-stone, The. Plena Timoris. Thomas Hardy. CP-HardT

Lovers love the boardwalk, the games of chance, The. What Why When How Who. Robert Pinsky. CP-PinsR

Lovers may come and go. "H. D." CP-DoolH *Fr.* Electra-Orestes.

Lover's Morning Salute to His Mistress, The. Robert Burns. CP-BurnR

Lovers, O lovers, listen to my call. Epilogue to the Adventures While Preaching the Gospel of Beauty. Nicholas Vachel Lindsay. CP-LindV

Lovers of God, sometimes a door opens. Sheba's Hesitation. Jelaluddin Rumi. SP-Rumi, *tr.* by Coleman Barks

Lovers of life on earth. Shmuel HaNagid. SP-HaNaS, *tr.* by Peter Cole

Lovers of the Poor, The. Gwendolyn Brooks. SP-BrooG

Lover's Petition. Ralph Waldo Emerson. CP-EmerR

Lovers' Quarrel, A. Robert Browning. CP-BroR1; SP-BroR

Lover's Quarrel, A. Sam Hamill. SP-HamiS

Lovers relentlessly contend to be. Stanley Kunitz. CP-KunSC

Lover's Return. Langston Hughes. CP-HughL; CP-HughL1; CP-HughL2

Lover's Song, The. William Butler Yeats. CP-YeatW

Lover's Stars, The. Gerard Manley Hopkins. CP-HopkG

Lovers that burn and learnéd scholars cold. Cats. Charles Baudelaire. CP-CullC

Lovers think they're looking for each other. There's Nothing Ahead. Jelaluddin Rumi. SP-Rumi, *tr.* by Coleman Barks *and* John Moyne

Lovers, those evening pilgrims. Jaroslav Seifert. SP-SeifJ, *tr.* by Ewald Osers

Lovers took within this ancient grove, The. Fancy and Tradition. William Wordsworth. CP-WorW2

Lovers' Walk, The. Dante Gabriel Rossetti. CW-RossD *Fr.* House of Life, The.

Lover's Wine. Charles Baudelaire. CP-BaudC, *tr.* by Walter Martin

Loversgrove lay / off to the lighthearted south. Scots Poem. John Berryman. CP-BerrJ

Love's a thing, (as I do heare). Upon Love. Robert Herrick. CP-HerrR

Love's absence is illusion,alias time. E. E. Cummings. CP-CummE

Love's Alchemy [*or* Alchemie]. John Donne. CP-DonnJ; MW-DonnJ

Love's Altar. James Laughlin. CP-LaugJ

Love's amorous spiritual glance. Guido Cavalcanti. CP-CavaG, *tr.* by Marc Cirigliano

Love's an old remembered song. Drunken Fiddler, The. Tennessee Williams. CP-WillT *Fr.* Night of the Iguana, The.

Love's Apotheosis. Paul Laurence Dunbar. CP-DunbP

Love's Apparition and Evanishment. Samuel Taylor Coleridge. CP-ColeS

Love's as Broad as Long. James Whitcomb Riley. CP-RileJ

Love's Baubles. Dante Gabriel Rossetti. CW-RossD *Fr.* House of Life, The.

Love's body and mouth lie down together. Fanny Howe. SP-HoweF *Fr.* Vineyard, The.

Love's Burial-Place. Samuel Taylor Coleridge. CP-ColeS

Love's Burning-Glass. Sir John Suckling. CP-SuckJ

Love's Castle. Paul Laurence Dunbar. CP-DunbP

Love's Chastening. Paul Laurence Dunbar. CP-DunbP

Love's Clock. Sir John Suckling. CP-SuckJ

(Lover's Clock, The.) CP-SuckJ

Love's Courtship. Thomas Carew. CP-CareT

Love's Deity [*or* Deitie]. John Donne. CP-DonnJ; MW-DonnJ

Love's Diet. John Donne. CP-DonnJ; MW-DonnJ

Love's doubts enrich my words; I stroke them out. Interlude: Time's Mischief. Thomas Kinsella. CP-KinsT

Love's Dozen. Jay Wright. SP-WrigJ

Love's Draft. Paul Laurence Dunbar. CP-DunbP

Love's Exchange. John Donne. CP-DonnJ; MW-DonnJ

Love's faint trace . . . . Robert Creeley. CP-CreeR

Loves Farewell. Henry David Thoreau. CP-ThorH

Love's Fatality. Dante Gabriel Rossetti. CW-RossD *Fr.* House of Life, The.

Love's fiery chariot, Delia, take. To a Lady, Persuading Her to a Car. Rudyard Kipling. CP-KiplR *Fr.* Muse among the Motors, The.

Love's Force. Thomas Carew. CP-CareT

Love's function is to fabricate unknownness. E. E. Cummings. CP-CummE; SP-CummE

Love's Growth. John Donne. CP-DonnJ; MW-DonnJ

Love's Horoscope. Richard Crashaw. CP-CrasR

Love's Hue and Cry. James Shirley. CP-CareT

(Hue and Cry, The.) CP-CareT

Love's Humility. Paul Laurence Dunbar. CP-DunbP

Love's Justification. Michelangelo Buonarroti. CP-WorW1, *tr.* by William Wordsworth

Love's Last Adieu. Lord Byron. CP-Byron

Love's Last Gift. Dante Gabriel Rossetti. CW-RossD *Fr.* House of Life, The.

Love's Loneliness. William Butler Yeats. CP-YeatW

Love's Lovers. Dante Gabriel Rossetti. CW-RossD *Fr.* House of Life, The.

Love's Nocturn. Dante Gabriel Rossetti. CW-RossD

Loves of Anat, I, The. Charles Olson. CP-OlsoC

Love's of it self, too sweet; the best of all. Another on Love. Robert Herrick. CP-HerrR

Loves of the Puppets. Richard Wilbur. CP-WilbR

Love's Offence. Sir John Suckling. CP-SuckJ

Love's Parable. Robert Penn Warren. CP-WarrR

Love's Phases. Paul Laurence Dunbar. CP-DunbP

Love's Philosophy. Percy Bysshe Shelley. CP-ShelP

Love's Pictures. Paul Laurence Dunbar. CP-DunbP

Love's Play at Push-Pin. Robert Herrick. CP-HerrR

Love's Progress. James Vincent Cunningham. CP-CunnJ

Love's Progress. John Donne. MW-DonnJ *Fr.* Elegies.

Love's Progress. Theodore Roethke. CP-RoetT

Love's Representation. Sir John Suckling. CP-SuckJ

Love's Rose. Percy Bysshe Shelley. CP-ShelP

Love's Sanctuary. Samuel Taylor Coleridge. CP-ColeS

Love's Seasons. Paul Laurence Dunbar. CP-DunbP

Love's Secret. William Blake. CP-BlakW

Love's Siege. Sir John Suckling. CP-SuckJ

(Siege, The.) CP-SuckJ

Love's stricken "why." Emily Dickinson. CP-DickE

Love's Testament. Dante Gabriel Rossetti. CW-RossD *Fr.* House of Life, The.

Love's the boy stood on the burning deck. Casabianca. Elizabeth Bishop. CP-BishE

Love's the i guess most only verb that lives. E. E. Cummings. CP-CummE

Love's Trappist. G. K. Chesterton. CP-ChesG

Love's Triumph through Callipolis. Ben Jonson. Euclia's Hymn. CP-JonsB

Love's Usury. John Donne. CP-DonnJ; MW-DonnJ

Love's Victorie. Mary Sidney, Countess of Montgomery Wroth. CP-WrotM

Love's Voice. Robert Penn Warren. CP-WarrR

Love's War. John Donne. MW-DonnJ *Fr.* Elegies.

Love's Way. Countee Cullen. CP-CullC

Love's World. Sir John Suckling. CP-SuckJ

Lovesight. Dante Gabriel Rossetti. CW-RossD *Fr.* House of Life, The.

Lovesong: "He loved her and she loved him." Ted Hughes. SP-HughTN

Loving and Beloved. Sir John Suckling. CP-SuckJ

Loving another, yet she married my father. Generations. Rachel Korn. CP-KizeC, *tr.* by Carolyn Kizer

Loving Cup, The. James Whitcomb Riley. CP-RileJ

Loving Dexterity, The. William Carlos Williams. CP-WilW2

Loving each other began this way: threading. Threading. Yehuda Amichai. SP-AmicY, *tr.* by Stephen Mitchell

Loving feels lonely in a violent world. Community. Marge Piercy. SP-PierM

Loving friend, the gift of one. To Flush, My Dog. Elizabeth Barrett Browning. CP-BroEB

Loving me with my shoes off. Barefoot. Anne Sexton. CP-SextA

Loving mind in this death-haunted body, The. Sonnet: "Loving mind in this death-haunted body, The." Hayden Carruth. CP-CarHS *Fr.* Sonnets.

Loving she is, and tractable, though wild. Characteristics of a Child Three Years Old. William Wordsworth. CP-WorW1; MW-WorW

Loving Shepherdess, The. Robinson Jeffers. CP-JefR2

Loving the Blest without Abode. Emily Dickinson. SP-DickE

Loving the Killer. Anne Sexton. CP-SextA; SP-SextA

Loving True, Flying Blind. Robert Graves. CP-GravR

Loving You Is Something to Do. John Ciardi. CP-CiarJ

Loving you less than life, a little less. Edna St. Vincent Millay. CP-MillE

Lovliest of Women! Could I gain. To My Burrissa. Annis Boudinot Stockton. CP-StocA

Low and brown barns thatched and repatched and tattered. Wife of Flanders, The. G. K. Chesterton. CP-ChesG

Low and mournful be the strain. Voluntaries. Ralph Waldo Emerson. CP-EmerR

Low at my problem bending. Emily Dickinson. CP-DickE

Low at the knee that bore her once. Emily Dickinson. SP-DickE

Low beating of the tom-toms, The. Danse Africaine. Langston Hughes. CP-HughL; CP-HughL1

Low-built houses of the poor, The. Look. Philip Levine. SP-LeviP

Low-cloudly it whistles, changing heads. Pine. James Dickey. CP-DickJ

Low dead Thunder muttered thro' the Night, A. Wish for Dreamful Sleep, A. Samuel Taylor Coleridge. CP-ColeS

Low December vault in June be up-lifted high. Ralph Waldo Emerson. CP-EmerR

Low eyelids that cloud like a prison. Our Lady of Wain. G. K. Chesterton. CP-ChesG

Low-fi scrapes the phrases from the strings, The. Two Hours. John Ciardi. CP-CiarJ

Low hidden in among the forest trees. Water-Color, A. James Whitcomb Riley. CP-RileJ

Low in the east, against a white, cold dawn. Christmas of 1888, The. John Greenleaf Whittier. CP-WhitJ

Low in the eastern sky. Henry David Thoreau. CP-ThorH

Low Lands. Donald Davie. CP-DaviDC

Low Sky, The. Robinson Jeffers. CP-JefR2

Low-Tide. Edna St. Vincent Millay. CP-MillE

Low Tide. Eugenio Montale. CP-MontE, *tr. by* Jonathan Galassi

Low Tide at Schoodic. Amy Clampitt. CP-ClamA

Low to High. Langston Hughes. CP-HughL; CP-HughL3

Low Voice, Out Loud. James Dickey. CP-DickJ

Low was our pretty Cot: our tallest rose. Reflections on Having Left a Place of Retirement. Samuel Taylor Coleridge. CP-ColeS; MW-ColeS

Low Water. Ted Hughes. SP-HughTN

Lowellville Cemetery: Twilight. Kenneth Patchen. CP-PatcK

Lower East Side. Allen Ginsberg. SP-GinsA *Fr.* After Whitman & Reznikoff.

Lower Field—Enniscorthy. Charles Olson. CP-OlsoC

Lower the flags. Special Bulletin. Langston Hughes. CP-HughL; CP-HughL3

Lowest Place, The. Christina Georgina Rossetti. CP-RosC1

Lowest place. Ah, Lord, how steep and high, The. Called to Be Saints. Christina Georgina Rossetti. CP-RosC2

Lowest Room, The. Christina Georgina Rossetti. CP-RosC1

Lowestoft Boat, The. Rudyard Kipling. CP-KiplR

Lowliest born of all the land, The. Wilson. John Greenleaf Whittier. CP-WhitJ

Lowly hill which overlooks a flat, A. Birchington Churchyard. Christina Georgina Rossetti. CP-RosC2

Loyal Brother, The. Thomas Southerne.
   Epilogue, The: "Virgin poet was served up today, A." CP-DryJ2
   Prologue, A: "Poets like lawful monarchs ruled the stage." CP-DryJ2

Loyal Scot, The. Andrew Marvell. CP-MarvA

Loyal Soldier, The. George Meredith. CP-MerG2

Loyal to the King. Christopher Logue. SP-LoguC

Loyalty Is the Life You Are. Kenneth Patchen. CP-PatcK

Lu Chi speaks of the heavenly arrow. Meditation on the *Wen-Fu*. Eleanor Wilner. SP-WilnE

Lubnan. Thomas Merton. CP-MertT

Lucent, the millpond mirrors September blue. Millpond Lost. Robert Penn Warren. CP-WarrR

Lucía Martínez. Federico García Lorca. CP-GarcF, *tr. by* Alan S. Trueblood *Fr.* Eros with a Cane.

Lucid at dusk the city lies revealed. Night Flight : New York. Muriel Rukeyser. CP-RukeM

Lucid winter, season of art serene. Renewal. Stéphane Mallarmé. CP-MallS, *tr. by* Henry Weinfield

Lucietta. A Fragment. Lord Byron. CP-Byron

Lucifer. D. H. Lawrence. CP-LawrD

Lucifer blazing in superb effigies. Bibliographers, The. Geoffrey Hill. CP-HillG

Lucifer Caditurus. Ezra Pound. CP-PoEar

Lucifer in Starlight. George Meredith. CP-MerG1

Lucifer in the Train. Adrienne Rich. CP-RicAE

Lucifer six-finger. Whispered to Lucifer. Lucille Clifton. SP-ClifL

Lucifer Speaks in His Own Voice. Lucille Clifton. SP-ClifL

Lucifer Understanding at Last. Lucille Clifton. SP-ClifL

Lucina schyning in silence of the nycht. William Dunbar. CP-DunbW

Lucinda and Aminta, a Pastoral, on the Capture of Lord Cornwallis and the British Army, by General Washington. Annis Boudinot Stockton. CP-StocA

Lucius Calpurnius Piso Cæsoninus. Carmen 47. Catullus. CP-ZukLS *Fr.* Carmina.

Luck. Charles Bukowski. SP-BukC1

Luck. Raymond Carver. CP-CarvR

Luck ("Sometimes a crumb falls"). Langston Hughes. CP-HughL

Luck ("Sometimes a few scraps fall"). Langston Hughes. CP-HughL2

Luck. Grace Paley. CP-PalGC

Luck is a star. Fireborn Are at Home in Fire, The. Carl Sandburg. CP-SandC

Luck is not chance. Emily Dickinson. CP-DickE

Luck to the craft that bears this name of mine. To a Cape Ann Schooner. John Greenleaf Whittier. CP-WhitJ

Luck, we've had it; our character the public's. It Did. Robert Lowell. SP-LoweR

Lucks, my fair falcon, and your fellows all. Sir Thomas Wyatt. CP-WyatT

Lucky. Gregory Orr. SP-OrrG

Lucky Little Britisher. D. H. Lawrence. CP-LawrD

Lucky means finding / Holes where. E. E. Cummings. CP-CummE

Lucrece and Nara. Laura Riding Jackson. CP-RidiL

Lucretius felt the change of the world in his time, the great republic riding to the height. Prescription of Painful Ends. Robinson Jeffers. CP-JefR3

Lucretius, 3, 1053–1076. Kenneth Rexroth. CP-RexrK

Lucretius versus the Lake Poets. Robert Frost. CP-FrosR

Lucubration. Richard Eberhart. CP-EberR

Lucy. Walter De la Mare. CP-DeLaW

Lucy. William Wordsworth. CP-WorW1
   "She dwelt among the untrodden ways." MW-WorW
   "Slumber did my spirit seal, A." MW-WorW
   "Strange fits of passion have I known." MW-WorW
   "Three years she grew in sun and shower." MW-WorW

Lucy done gone back on me. Jilted. Paul Laurence Dunbar. CP-DunbP

Lucy Gray; or, Solitude. William Wordsworth. CP-WorW1
   (Oft had I heard of Lucy Gray.) MW-WorW

Lucy Hooper. John Greenleaf Whittier. CP-WhitJ

Lucy Lake. Ogden Nash. CP-NashO

Lucy, whose day is in our darkest season. Invocation to St. Lucy, An. Thomas Merton. CP-MertT

Lucy, you brightness[e] of our sphere [*or* spheare], who are. To Lucy, Countess[e] of Bedford, with Mr. Donne's Satires [*or* Satyres]. Ben Jonson. CP-JonsB; SP-JonsB

Lueurs lisières. Samuel Beckett. CP-BeckS

Luftmenschen dream, the men who live on air. John Berryman. CP-BerrJ *Fr.* Black Book, The.

Luggs, by the Condemnation of the Bench. Upon Luggs. Robert Herrick. CP-HerrR

Lugubre e vagabondo in terra e in mare. Christina Georgina Rossetti. CP-RosC3

Lugubre for a child. Lorine Niedecker. CP-NiedL

Lugubrious, Salubrious Seaside, The. Louis MacNeice. CP-MacNL

Lugubrious Whing-Whang, The. James Whitcomb Riley. CP-RileJ

Lui et Elle. D. H. Lawrence. CP-LawrD

Luk at 'ere, ould baby,—who. Michael Flynn and the Baby. James Whitcomb Riley. CP-RileJ

Lukannon. Rudyard Kipling. CP-KiplR *Fr.* Jungle Book, The.

Luke 2; Quærit Jesum Suum Maria. Bible, *N.T.* CP-CrasR *Fr.* St. Luke.

Luke 7; She Began to Wash His Feet with Teares and Wipe Them with the Haires of Her Head. Bible, *N.T.* CP-CrasR, *tr. by* Richard Crashaw *Fr.* St. Luke.

Luke 10; And a Certaine Priest Comming That Way Looked on Him and Passed By. Bible, *N.T.* CP-CrasR *Fr.* St. Luke.

Luke 11; Blessed Be the Paps Which Thou Hast Sucked. Bible, *N.T. See* St. Luke

Luke 11; Upon the Dumbe Devill Cast Out, and the Slanderous Jewes Put to Silence. Bible, *N.T.* CP-CrasR *Fr.* St. Luke.

Luke 15; On the Prodigall. Bible, *N.T.* CP-CrasR *Fr.* St. Luke.

Luke 16; Dives *Asking a Drop.* Bible, *N.T.* CP-CrasR *Fr.* St. Luke.

Luke 23. Jorge Luis Borges. SP-BorgJ, *tr. by* Mark Strand

Luke Havergal. Edwin Arlington Robinson. CP-RobiE

Lull. Paul Muldoon. CP-MuldP

Lull. Theodore Roethke. CP-RoetT

Lullaby: "Bedtime's come fu' little boys." Paul Laurence Dunbar. CP-DunbP

Lullaby: "Beloved, may your sleep be sound." William Butler Yeats. CP-YeatW

Lullaby: "Birth I gave you in a desert." Joseph Brodsky. CP-BrodJ

Lullaby: "Din of work is subdued, The." W. H. Auden. CP-AudeW

Lullaby: "Here is the guillotine." Christopher Logue. SP-LoguC

Lullaby: "I see you, centered." Olga Broumas. SP-BrouO

Lullaby: "It is a summer evening." Anne Sexton. CP-SextA; SP-SextA

Lullaby: "Kiver up yo' haid, my little lady." Paul Laurence Dunbar. CP-DunbP

Lullaby: "Lay your sleeping head, my love." W. H. Auden. CP-AudeW

Lullaby: "Love me,—I love you / Love me, my baby." Christina Georgina Rossetti. CP-RosC2

Lullaby: "Maple strews the embers of its leaves, The." James Whitcomb Riley. CP-RileJ

Lullaby: "No sleep, not tonight. The window blazes. Adam Zagajewski. SP-ZagaA, tr. by Renata Gorczynski, Benjamin Ivry and C. K. Williams

Lullaby: "Ruin falls on blackening skies." Marya Alexandrovna Zaturenska. SP-ZatuM

Lullaby: "Sleep, pretty lady, the night is enfolding you." Dorothy Parker. CP-ParkD

Lullaby, A: "For wars his life and half a world away." Randall Jarrell. CP-JarrR

Lullaby, The: "Every poor fellow reminds me of my father." Laura Riding Jackson. CP-RidiL

Lullaby (For a Black Mother). Langston Hughes. CP-HughL; CP-HughL1

Lullaby for a Summer Recess. James Fenton. SP-FentJ

Lullaby for Now. Robert Stock. SP-StocR

Lullaby for the Cat. Elizabeth Bishop. CP-BishE

Lullaby in Death for Rosalía de Castro. Federico García Lorca. CP-GarcF, tr. by Catherine Brown

Lullaby 1957. Yehuda Amichai. SP-AmicYL, tr. by Benjamin Harshav and Barbara Harshav

Lullaby of Cape Cod. Joseph Brodsky. CP-BrodJ, tr. by Anthony Hecht

Lullaby, oh lullaby! / Flowers are closed and lambs are sleeping. Christina Georgina Rossetti. CP-RosC2

Lulled, at silence, the spent attack. Baggot Street Deserta. Thomas Kinsella. CP-KinsT

Lulled by stream-murmur and the afternoon's hypnosis. Summer Afternoon and Hypnosis. Robert Penn Warren. CP-WarrR

Lulls swears he is all heart, but you'l suppose. Upon Lulls. Robert Herrick. CP-HerrR

Lulu Gay. Wallace Stevens. CP-StevWP

Lulu Morose. Wallace Stevens. CP-StevWP

Lulu sang of barbarians before the eunuchs. Lulu Gay. Wallace Stevens. CP-StevWP

Lumber Yard Pools at Sunset. Carl Sandburg. CP-SandC

Lumbering chords that open, The. Scaffold, A. Amy Clampitt. CP-ClamA

Lumbermen, The. John Greenleaf Whittier. CP-WhitJ

Lumen / Ad revelationem gentium. Candlemas Procession, The. Thomas Merton. CP-MertT

Lumens. Olga Broumas. SP-BrouO

Luminescence thrusts aside the dark, A. On Rembrandt's Self-Portrait (1658) in the Frick Museum. Helen Pinkerton. CP-PinkH

Luminosity is an issue. Election. Andrei Codrescu. SP-CodrA

Luminous tendril of celestial wish. E. E. Cummings. CP-CummE; SP-CummE

Lumpectomy Eve. Lucille Clifton. SP-ClifL

Lumumba was black. Lumumba's Grave. Langston Hughes. CP-HughL; CP-HughL3

Lumumba's Grave. Langston Hughes. CP-HughL; CP-HughL3

Luna and Leopardi. Marya Alexandrovna Zaturenska. SP-ZatuM

Lunar Entrancement. Samuel Taylor Coleridge. CP-ColeS

Lunar Ironmongery. Jaroslav Seifert. SP-SeifJ, tr. by Ewald Osers

Lunar Paraphrase. Wallace Stevens. CP-StevW; CP-StevWP

Lunar Tides, The. Marya Alexandrovna Zaturenska. SP-ZatuM

Lunatic Witch-fires! Ghosts of Light and Motion! Wills of the Wisp, The. Samuel Taylor Coleridge. CP-ColeS

Lunch. Kenneth Koch. SP-KochK

Lunch and After. Robert Creeley. SP-CreeR

Lunch hour in flowery. Minor Tremor, A. Amy Clampitt. CP-ClamA

Lunch Wagon on Highway 57. Kenneth Patchen. CP-PatcK

Lunch with its divers. Wishes. Robert Creeley. SP-CreeR

Lunch with Pancho Villa. Paul Muldoon. CP-MuldP

Lune de Miel. T. S. Eliot. CP-ElioT; SP-ElioT

Lung Fish, The. John Ciardi. CP-CiarJ

Lungs (as some say) ne'r sets him down to eate. Upon Lungs. Robert Herrick. CP-HerrR

Lupes for the outside of his suit[e] has paid[e]. Upon Lupes. Robert Herrick. CP-HerrR

Lupine. Arthur Sze. SP-SzeA

Lure of Murder. Robert Graves. CP-GravR

Lured by the wall, and drawn. Poem about George Doty in the Death House, A. James Wright. CP-WrigJ

Lurking man in that half light, A. Seeing. Archibald MacLeish. CP-MacLA

Luscious and Sorrowful. Christina Georgina Rossetti. CP-RosC2

Lush summer lit the trees to green. June Leaves and Autumn. Thomas Hardy. CP-HardT

Lust goads, and Love goes with me as a guide. Petrarch. CP-Petra, tr. by J. G. Nichols

Lustra. Ezra Pound.
Rest, The. SP-PounE

Lustral Sonnet. Seamus Heaney. SP-HeanSO Fr. Glanmore Revisited.

Lustral sweat in its fine slow beads, The. Grave Piece. Richard Eberhart. CP-EberR

Lustrum for You, E.P., A. Charles Olson. CP-OlsoC

Lustspiel. William Carlos Williams. CP-WilW2

Lusus amicitia est, uni nisi dedita, ceu fit. Lepus Multis Amicus. John Gay. CP-CowpW

Lute and my skill with it came unasked from Apollo, The. Orpheus. William Meredith. SP-MereW

Lute in the Attic, The. Kenneth Patchen. CP-PatcK

Lute Music. Kenneth Rexroth. CP-RexrK

Lutea Allison. Sir John Suckling. CP-SuckJ

Luther. W. H. Auden. CP-AudeW

Luther A. Todd. James Whitcomb Riley. CP-RileJ

Luther Benson. James Whitcomb Riley. CP-RileJ

Luvely Lass o' Inverness, The. Robert Burns. See Lovely Lass o' Inverness, The

Luxuries ease, but when trouble comes. Shmuel HaNagid. SP-HaNaS, tr. by Peter Cole

Luxurious Man, to bring his Vice in use. Mower against Gardens, The. Andrew Marvell. CP-MarvA

Luxury. Yehuda Amichai. SP-AmicYL, tr. by Benjamin Harshav and Barbara Harshav

Luxury. Denise Levertov. SP-LeveDP

Luxury, A. Yehuda Amichai. SP-AmicY, tr. by Stephen Mitchell

Luxury in August. Philip Whalen. SP-WhalP

Luxury to apprehend, The. Emily Dickinson. CP-DickE

Luxury travel is something for which I pant. Change Here for Wichita Falls, or, Has Anybody Seen My Wanderlust? Ogden Nash. CP-NashO

Lycambes Talks to John. Allen Tate. CP-TateA

Lyceia. Robert Graves. CP-GravR

Lycidas. John Milton. CP-MiltJ

Lydia H. Sigourney. John Greenleaf Whittier. CP-WhitJ

Lydia, we know nothing. We are strangers. Fernando Pessoa. SP-PessF, tr. by Susan M. Brown and Edwin Honig

Lydia, when our Autumn comes. Fernando Pessoa. SP-PessF, tr. by Susan M. Brown and Edwin Honig

Lydians, lords of Hermus river. Atys. A. E. Housman. CP-HousA

Lyell's Hypothesis Again. Kenneth Rexroth. CP-RexrK

Lyf so short . . . , The. William Stafford. SP-StafWW

The lyf so short, the craft so long to lerne. Parlement of Foules, The. Geoffrey Chaucer. CP-ChauG

Lying. Richard Wilbur. CP-WilbR

Lying a-dying. / Have done with vain sighing. Is It Well with the Child? Christina Georgina Rossetti. CP-RosC2

Lying adying— / Such sweet things untasted. Young Death. Christina Georgina Rossetti. CP-RosC3

Lying and Looking. May Swenson. SP-SwenM

Lying at a Reverend Friend's House One Night, the Author Left the Following Verses in the Room Where He Slept. Robert Burns. CP-BurnR

Lying at home. Dust. James Dickey. CP-DickJ

Lying Awake. Thomas Hardy. CP-HardT

Lying between her legs. Knowledge. David Ignatow. SP-IgnaD

Lying between your sheets, I challenge. Death Grapple, The. Robert Graves. CP-GravR

Lying disembodied under the trees. Deliverance. Robert Graves. CP-GravR

Lying here among grass, am I dead am I sleeping. Among Grass. Muriel Rukeyser. CP-RukeM

Lying here, everything in me. Margaret Atwood. SP-AtwM1

Lying In. Olga Broumas. SP-BrouO

Lying in a Hammock at William Duffy's Farm in Pine Island, Minnesota. James Wright. CP-WrigJ

Lying in daylight, in the strong. Song: Lying in Daylight. Muriel Rukeyser. CP-RukeM

Lying in the mint. Eclogue: "Lying in the mint." Wallace Stevens. CP-StevWP

Lying in the moment, she climbs white snows. Wards, The. Muriel Rukeyser. CP-RukeM

Lying in the sun. Breathing Landscape. Muriel Rukeyser. CP-RukeM

Lying listless in the mosses. Dream of Long Ago, A. James Whitcomb Riley. CP-RileJ

Lying on the bed in the afternoon. Unlike Joubert. James Schuyler. CP-SchuJ

Lying on the highway. Everyone Dies in a Light Rain. Miller Williams. CP-WillM

Lying spying what men say of dead men. Laura Riding Jackson. CP-RidiL

Lying, thinking / Last night. Alone. Maya Angelou. SP-AngeM

Lying to a Child. Rainer Maria Rilke. CP-RilkFr

Lyke-Wake Song, A. Algernon Charles Swinburne. SP-SwinA

Lyme Regis Sed Sine Regina. G. K. Chesterton. CP-ChesG

Lynching Song. Langston Hughes. CP-HughL; CP-HughL1; CP-HughL2 *Fr.* Three Songs about Lynching.

Lynchings of Jesus, The. Muriel Rukeyser. CP-RukeM

Lynn Fontanne. Dorothy Parker. CP-ParkD

Lyonnesse. Sylvia Plath. CP-PlatS

Lyre at rest: / you fingered it awake, A. Archer, The. Charles Tomlinson. CP-TomlC

Lyre! Though Such Power Do in Thy Magic Live. William Wordsworth. CP-WorW2

Lyric: "Can it be again." Tennessee Williams. CP-WillT

Lyric: "Glad morning, coming, The." Tennessee Williams. CP-WillT

Lyric: "Her footsteps were a season's coming." Tennessee Williams. CP-WillT

Lyric: "How the arrogant iris would wither and fade." Dorothy Parker. CP-ParkD

Lyric, A: "My lady love lives far away." Paul Laurence Dunbar. CP-DunbP

Lyric Absolute, The. Richard Eberhart. CP-EberR

Lyric Ode, A.—Feb. 28. Annis Boudinot Stockton. CP-StocA

Lyric Poem. Yannis Ritsos. SP-RitsY, *tr. by* Athan Anagnostopoulos

Lyric to Mirth, A. Robert Herrick. CP-HerrR

Lyricist's Lament, The. Heather McHugh. SP-McHuH

Lyric[k] for Legacies. Robert Herrick. CP-HerrR

Lysergic Acid. Allen Ginsberg. CP-GinsA

Lytton Strachey, Also, Enters into Heaven. Wallace Stevens. CP-StevWP

LZ ("He walked—loped—the bridge"). Lorine Niedecker. CP-NiedL

LZ's. Lorine Niedecker. CP-NiedL

M

M. Philip Whalen. SP-WhalP

M.A. Written on the Dungeon Wall. Emily Jane Brontë. CP-BronE

M & K. James Laughlin. CP-LaugJ

M.B. William Carlos Williams. CP-WilW1

M-Day's Child Is Fair of Face. Muriel Rukeyser. CP-RukeM

M. Douglas to E.R. Gleneden. Emily Jane Brontë. CP-BronE

M.G. for the U.S. Emily Jane Brontë. CP-BronE

M. I. Rudyard Kipling. CP-KiplR

M is for MOTHERS, who are, above all. John Ciardi. CP-CiarJ

M. le professeur in prominent senility. My Neighbor in the Mirror. Louise Glück. SP-GlucL

M. M. George Meredith. CP-MerG1

M. quarrels with N., for M. wrote a book. On Madan's Answer to Newton. William Cowper. CP-CowpW

M., Singing. Louise Bogan. CP-BogaL

Ma. Paul Muldoon. CP-MuldP

Ma baby lives across de river. Wide River. Langston Hughes. CP-HughL; CP-HughL1

Ma Lord ain't no stuck-up man. Langston Hughes. CP-HughL; CP-HughL1

Ma Man. Langston Hughes. CP-HughL; CP-HughL1

Ma man's a gypsy. Gypsy Man. Langston Hughes. CP-HughL; CP-HughL1

Ma Provence. Kenneth Koch. SP-KochK

Ma put my Penny-Dog. Toy Penny-Dog, The. James Whitcomb Riley. CP-RileJ

Ma sweet good man has. Suicide. Langston Hughes. CP-HughL; CP-HughL1

Ma, What's a Banker? or, Hush, My Child. Ogden Nash. CP-NashO

Ma'am, you should see your house! Renovated Temple, The. Archibald MacLeish. CP-MacLA

Mabel. James Whitcomb Riley. CP-RileJ

Mabel Martin. John Greenleaf Whittier. CP-WhitJ

Mabel was married last week. Emily Writes Such a Good Letter. Stevie Smith. CP-SmitS

Mac Flecknoe [or, A Satire upon the True-Blue Protestant Poet T. S.]. John Dryden. SP-DrydJ

Macabre and golden the moon opened a slant of light. Feather Lights. Carl Sandburg. CP-SandC

Macarius and the Pony. Thomas Merton. CP-MertT

Macarius the Younger. Thomas Merton. CP-MertT

Macaroons. G. K. Chesterton. CP-ChesG

Macaroons: An Ode. G. K. Chesterton. CP-ChesG

Macbeth. Walter De la Mare. CP-DeLaW

MacDonough's Song. Rudyard Kipling. CP-KiplR

Macdougal Street. Edna St. Vincent Millay. CP-MillE

Macduff. Charles Tomlinson. CP-TomlC

Macer: A Character. Alexander Pope. CP-PopeA

Macha. Paul Muldoon. CP-MuldP

Macha, the Ice Age. Macha. Paul Muldoon. CP-MuldP

Machiavelli in Exile. Charles Tomlinson. CP-TomlC

Machine. John Ciardi. CP-CiarJ

Machine. Gun. Nest. Margaret Atwood. SP-AtwM2

Machine, The. Robinson Jeffers. CP-JefR1

Machine-Gun, The. Randall Jarrell. CP-JarrR

Machine stitched rivets ravel on a tree. Pilot in the Jungle, The. John Ciardi. CP-CiarJ

Machine will run on and on and on, The. On and On and On. D. H. Lawrence. CP-LawrD

Machineries of Shame. Donald Davie. CP-DaviDC

Machinery Doesn't Answer, Either, but You Aren't Married to It. Ogden Nash. CP-NashO

Macho Man. Charles Bukowski. SP-BukC3

Mackinnon's Boat. Charles Tomlinson. CP-TomlC

Macpherson's Farewell. Robert Burns. CP-BurnR

   (McPherson's Farewell.) CP-BurnR

Macrobian. Ambrose Bierce. SP-BierA

Mad as the Mist and Snow. William Butler Yeats. CP-YeatW

Mad contralto in room 503, The. Songbird, The. James Laughlin. CP-LaugJ

Mad Farmer in the City, The. Wendell Berry. CP-BerrW

Mad Farmer Manifesto: the First Amendment, The. Wendell Berry. CP-BerrW

Mad Farmer Revolution, The. Wendell Berry. CP-BerrW

Mad farmer, the thirsty one, The. Mad Farmer Revolution, The. Wendell Berry. CP-BerrW

Mad Farmer's Love Song, The. Wendell Berry. CP-BerrW

Mad Fight Song for William S. Carpenter, 1966, A. James Wright. CP-WrigJ

Mad girl with the staring eyes and long white fingers, The. Cassandra. Robinson Jeffers. CP-JefR3

Mad Gleam, A. Allen Ginsberg. CP-GinsA

Mad God, mad thought. Fanny Howe. SP-HoweF *Fr.* Quietist, The.

Mad have nightmares, The. When. Notes toward Time. Josephine Jacobsen. CP-JacoJ

Mad Judy. Thomas Hardy. CP-HardT

'Mad Laughter,' your sister—her grey perm. Old Oats. Ted Hughes. SP-HughTN

Mad Lover, The. James Whitcomb Riley. CP-RileJ

Mad Maid's Song, The. Robert Herrick. CP-HerrR

Mad Monk, The. Samuel Taylor Coleridge. CP-ColeS; CP-WorW1

   (Voice from the Side of Etna, The; or, the Mad Monk.) CP-WorW1

Mad Mullinix and Timothy. Jonathan Swift. CP-SwifJ

Mad Negro Soldier Confined at Munich, A. Robert Lowell. SP-LoweR

Mad old women, bolted from April's weather, The. April Asylum. Josephine Jacobsen. CP-JacoJ

Mad paper stay, and grudge not here to burn. To Mrs M. H. John Donne. CP-DonnJ; MW-DonnJ

Mad Scene, The. James Merrill. SP-MerrJ

Mad Song. William Blake. CP-BlakW

Madam, a stranger's purpose in these lays. Epistle to a Protestant Lady in France, An. William Cowper. CP-CowpW

Madam and Her Madam. Langston Hughes. CP-HughL; CP-HughL2

Madam and Her Might-Have-Been. Langston Hughes. CP-HughL; CP-HughL2

Madam and the Army. Langston Hughes. CP-HughL; CP-HughL2

Madam and the Census Man. Langston Hughes. CP-HughL; CP-HughL2

Madam and the Charity Child. Langston Hughes. CP-HughL; CP-HughL2

Madam and the Crime Wave. Langston Hughes. CP-HughL; CP-HughL3

Madam and the Fortune Teller. Langston Hughes. CP-HughL; CP-HughL2

Madam and the Insurance Man. Langston Hughes. CP-HughL; CP-HughL2

Madam and the Minister. Langston Hughes. CP-HughL; CP-HughL2

Madam and the Movies. Langston Hughes. CP-HughL; CP-HughL2

Madam and the Newsboy. Langston Hughes. CP-HughL; CP-HughL2

Madam and the Number Writer. Langston Hughes. CP-HughL; CP-HughL2

Madam and the Phone Bill. Langston Hughes. CP-HughL; CP-HughL2

Madam and the Rent Man. Langston Hughes. CP-HughL; CP-HughL2

Madam and the Wrong Visitor. Langston Hughes. CP-HughL; CP-HughL2

Madam could look in your hand. Ballad of the Fortune Teller. Langston Hughes. CP-HughL; CP-HughL2

Madam Death, I am writing to request. To. Adam Zagajewski. SP-ZagaA, *tr. by* Renata Gorczynski

Madam[e], had all antiquity [*or* antiquitie] been lost. To Mary, Lady Wroth ("Madam[e], had all antiquity [*or* antiquitie] been lost"). Ben Jonson. CP-JonsB; SP-JonsB

Madam / I have sold you. Christopher Logue. SP-LoguC

Madam, / I know your heart cannot so guilty be. Upon the Black Spots Worn, by My Lady D.E. Sir John Suckling. CP-SuckJ

Madam, I told you late how I repented. To Lucy, Countess of Bedford. Ben

Jonson. CP-JonsB; SP-JonsB

Madam, I you require. Sir Thomas Wyatt. CP-WyatT

Madam, / Man to God's image, Eve, to man's was made. To the Countess of Huntingdon ("Madam, / Man to God's image, Eve, to man's was made"). John Donne. CP-DonnJ; MW-DonnJ

Madam, men say you keep with dropping eyes. To the Countess of Anglesey. Thomas Carew. CP-CareT

Madam my action. Conversations. Thomas Merton. CP-MertT

Madam, / Reason is our soul's left hand, Faith her right. To the Countess of Bedford ("Madam, / Reason is our soul's left hand, Faith her right"). John Donne. CP-DonnJ; MW-DonnJ

Madam, / That I might make your cabinet my tomb. Epitaph on Himself. John Donne. CP-DonnJ; MW-DonnJ

Madam, twice through the Muses' Grove I walked. Upon Mrs. Anne Bradstreet, Her Poems, Etc. John Rogers. CP-BradA

Madam, / Whilst that, for which, all virtue now is sold. Epistle to Elizabeth, Countess of Rutland. Ben Jonson. CP-JonsB; SP-JonsB

Madam, / Wi' braw new branks in mickle pride. On Willie Chalmers. Robert Burns. CP-BurnR

Madam, withouten Many Words. Sir Thomas Wyatt. CP-WyatT

Madam, / You have refined me, and to worthiest things. To the Countess of Bedford ("Madam, / You have refined me, and to worthiest things"). John Donne. CP-DonnJ; MW-DonnJ

Madam, your men said thai wald ryd. William Dunbar. CP-DunbW

Madame Arrives in the Mail. Anne Sexton. CP-SextA

Madame de Lafayette, in her salon in the rue de Vaugirard, is telling her friend. As in Music / A Reprise / Across Time. James Laughlin. CP-LaugJ

Madame, for your[e] newefangelnesse. Against Women Unconstant [or A Ballade against Woman Inconstant]. Geoffrey Chaucer. CP-ChauG

Madam[e], / Here, where by all, all saints invoked are. Letter to the Lady Carey, and Mistress Essex Rich, from Amiens, A. John Donne. CP-DonnJ; MW-DonnJ

Madame, I have a confusion. Madame Arrives in the Mail. Anne Sexton. CP-SextA

Madame La Fleurie. Wallace Stevens. CP-StevW; CP-StevWP

Madame, ye be[e]n of al[le] beaute[e] shryne or shryne [or shrine]. To Rosamounde. Geoffrey Chaucer. CP-ChauG

Madam's Calling Cards. Langston Hughes. CP-HughL; CP-HughL2

Madam's Christmas (or Merry Christmas Everybody). Langston Hughes. CP-HughL

Madam's Past History. Langston Hughes. CP-HughL; CP-HughL2

Madboy's Song. Muriel Rukeyser. CP-RukeM

Maddened by Earth's wrong and evil. What the Voice Said. John Greenleaf Whittier. CP-WhitJ

Madder. C. K. Williams. CP-WillC

Made by Hand. Eleanor Wilner. SP-WilnE

Made me what I am. La Force. Louise Glück. SP-GlucL

Made of old rags of tongues. Snake. Anne Sexton. CP-SextA

Made to Order Smile, The. Paul Laurence Dunbar. CP-DunbP

Made worthy by excess of Love. Separation from Asra. Samuel Taylor Coleridge. CP-ColeS

Mademoiselle—goddess instead. Lion in Love, The. Marianne Craig Moore. CP-MoorM Fr. Fables of La Fontaine.

Mademoiselle Printemps, my sometimes instructress. À l'École Berlitz. John Updike. CP-UpdiJ

Madge. G. K. Chesterton. CP-ChesG

Madison and 42nd. Carl Sandburg. CP-SandC

Madly she came, and stood upon the lintel. Salem. Richard Eberhart. CP-EberR

Madman I have been calld Fool they call thee. William Blake. CP-BlakW

Madman of the South Side. Clarence Major. SP-MajoC

Madmen. Billy Collins. SP-CollB

Madness. Charles Bukowski. SP-BukC1

Madness. James Dickey. CP-DickJ

Madness. Allen Tate. CP-TateA

Madness, madness, / Madness from the gods! Skeptic, The. Ralph Waldo Emerson. CP-EmerR

Madness of Jean-Jacques Rousseau, The. Marya Alexandrovna Zaturenska.
 "Aging, forsaken, passionate, and unloved." SP-ZatuM
 "Who reads my book reads all my life." SP-ZatuM

Madness of King Goll, The. William Butler Yeats. CP-YeatW

Madoc: A Mystery. Paul Muldoon. CP-MuldP

Madonna. Thomas Kinsella. CP-KinsT

Madonna Mia. G. K. Chesterton. CP-ChesG

Madonna Mia. Oscar Wilde. CP-WildO

Madonna, mistress, let me now prepare. To a Madonna. Charles Baudelaire. CP-BaudC, tr. by Walter Martin

Madonna, wherefore hast thou sent to me. To Emilia Viviani. Percy Bysshe Shelley. CP-ShelP

Madonnas Touched Up with Goatees [or a Goatee]. Charles Simic. SP-SimiC;

SP-SimiCE

Madras, / 1965, and rain. Some Indian Uses of History on a Rainy Day. A. K. Ramanujan. CP-RamaA

Madrid [—1937]. Langston Hughes. CP-HughL; CP-HughL1

Madrid, May, 1977. Mona Van Duyn. SP-VanDM

Madrid, 1974. Mona Van Duyn. SP-VanDM

Madrigal: "I looked into your eyes." Federico García Lorca. CP-GarcF, tr. by Catherine Brown

Madrigal: "My kiss was a pomegranate." Federico García Lorca. CP-GarcF, tr. by Catherine Brown

Madrigal: "Oh Lucy of Granada!" Federico García Lorca. CP-GarcF, tr. by Jerome Rothenberg Fr. Palimpsests.

Madrigal: "She is the darkness where I wander." Howard Nemerov. CP-NemeH

Madrigal: "Since Tuck is faithless found, no more." George Meredith. CP-MerG2

Madrigal: "Today, I am dull, I am dull!" Tennessee Williams. CP-WillT

Madrigal: "Why dost thou haste away." Sir Philip Sidney. SP-SidnP Fr. Arcadia.

Madrigal, A: "Dream days of fond delight and hours." Paul Laurence Dunbar. CP-DunbP

Madrigal for the City of Santiago. Federico García Lorca. CP-GarcF, tr. by Catherine Brown

Madrigal for 3 Voices, A. Louis Zukofsky. CP-ZukLS

Madrigal: To His Lady Selvaggia Vergiolesi; Likening His Love to a Search for Gold. Cino da Pistoia. CW-RossD, tr. by Dante Gabriel Rossetti

Madrigal to the City of Santiago. Federico García Lorca. SP-GarcF, tr. by Norman Thomas Di Giovanni

Madrigale: "Clear is my love but shadowed." Ezra Pound. CP-PoEar

Madrigals: "Like concentric waves / on the water." Federico García Lorca. CP-GarcF, tr. by Jerome Rothenberg

Mae Marsh, Motion Picture Actress. Nicholas Vachel Lindsay. CP-LindV

Maecenas, of a race renown'd. Ode 1.1: To Maecenas: "Maecenas, of a race renown'd." Horace. SP-SmarC Fr. Odes.

Maecenas, you, beneath the myrtle shade. To Maecenas. Phillis Wheatley. CP-WheaP

Maedoc of the floating stone. St. Maedoc. Thomas Merton. CP-MertT

Maenad. Olga Broumas. SP-BrouO

Maerchen. Walter De la Mare. CP-DeLaW

Maestria. Howard Nemerov. CP-NemeH

Maestro di Tocar. Ezra Pound. CP-PoEar

Mag. Carl Sandburg. CP-SandC

Magdalene. Donald Davie. CP-DaviDC

Magellan. Mary Oliver. SP-OlivM

Magellan was x'ed here. Cebu. Robert Creeley. SP-CreeR

Magenta-colored clouds were gathering. Eugenio Montale. CP-MontE, tr. by Jonathan Galassi

Maggie a Lady. Christina Georgina Rossetti. CP-RosC1

Maggie and Milly and Molly and May. E. E. Cummings. CP-CummE

Maggie and milly and molly and may. Maggie and Milly and Molly and May. E. E. Cummings. CP-CummE

Magi. Sylvia Plath. CP-PlatS

Magi, The. Louise Glück. SP-GlucL

Magi, The. William Butler Yeats. CP-YeatW

Magic. Rita Dove. SP-DoveR

Magic. Denise Levertov. SP-LeveDL

Magic, as it electrifies. Emily Dickinson. SP-DickE

Magic Car, The. Kenneth Patchen. CP-PatcK

Magic Castle, The. Sir Walter Scott. SP-ScotW Fr. Bridal of Trierman, The.

Magic Curtain, The. Stanley Kunitz. CP-KunSC

Magic is tangled in a woman's hair. Snap-Comb Wilderness, The. Robert Graves. CP-GravR

Magic Morning, The. Stevie Smith. CP-SmitS

Magic Mountain, A. Czeslaw Milosz. CP-MiloC; CP-MiloCN, tr. by Lillian Vallee

Magic Mountain, The. William Stafford. SP-StafWW

Magic of Numbers, The. Kenneth Koch. SP-KochK

Magic Psalm. Allen Ginsberg. CP-GinsA; SP-GinsA

Magical Mouse, The. Kenneth Patchen. CP-PatcK

Magical Nature. Robert Browning. CP-BroR2

Magician, The. Rainer Maria Rilke. CP-RilkFr, tr. by A. Poulin, Jr.

Magician, appointed officer. Visions of Daniel. Robert Pinsky. CP-PinsR

Magician [Master]. "H. D." CP-DoolH

Magician's Retreat, The. Marianne Craig Moore. CP-MoorM

Magico Prodigioso. Pedro Calderón de la Barca.
 "In the sweet solitude of this calm place." CP-ShelP

Magistrate spoke / Said the future was going to be for the public, The. Public Affairs. Thomas Merton. CP-MertT

Magna est Veritas. Stevie Smith. CP-SmitS

Magnanimity. Thomas Kinsella. CP-KinsT

Magnetic Lady to Her Patient, The. Percy Bysshe Shelley. CP-ShelP

Magnetized. Arthur Sze. SP-SzeA

Magnets. Countee Cullen. CP-CullC

Magnificent Democracy. D. H. Lawrence. CP-LawrD

Magnificent willow, The. Flower. Federico García Lorca. CP-GarcF, *tr. by* Alan S. Trueblood *Fr.* Moon Songs.

Magnificent Words. Stevie Smith. CP-SmitS

Magnolia Flowers. Langston Hughes. CP-HughL; CP-HughL1

Magnolia Shoals. Sylvia Plath. CP-PlatS

Magnolia tree out window. Hamilton Hotel. Robert Creeley. SP-CreeR

Magnolias merge each to each, The. Day in the Sun, A. John Logan. CP-LogaJ

Magnolia's Shadow, The. Eugenio Montale. CP-MontE, *tr. by* Jonathan Galassi

Magot frequents those houses of good-cheere. Upon Magot a Frequenter of Ordinaries. Robert Herrick. CP-HerrR

Magpie and the bowerbird, its odd, The. Brought from Beyond. Amy Clampitt. CP-ClamA

Magpies. Yusef Komunyakaa. CP-KomuY

Magpie's Song. Gary Snyder. CP-SnydG

Magpiety. Czeslaw Milosz. CP-MiloC; CP-MiloCN, *tr. by* Peter Dale Scott

Magryme, The. William Dunbar. CP-DunbW

Magus, A. John Ciardi. CP-CiarJ

Magus, The. James Dickey. CP-DickJ

Mahabalipuram. Louis MacNeice. CP-MacNL

Mahavveray. Louis MacNeice. CP-MacNL

Mahayana. Philip Whalen. SP-WhalP

Mahomet. Samuel Taylor Coleridge. CP-ColeS

Maia. Ralph Waldo Emerson. CP-EmerR

Maia. Howard Nemerov. CP-NemeH

Maia was one, all gold, fire, and sapphire. Legend of Viable Women, A. Richard Eberhart. CP-EberR

Maid, The. *Unknown*. CP-WilW2, *tr. by* David Rafael Wang *and* William Carlos Williams

Maid is blest that will not hear, The. Version of the First Psalm, for the Use of a Young Lady, A. Alexander Pope. CP-PopeA

Maid of Athens, ere We Part. Lord Byron. CP-Byron

Maid of Keinton Mandeville, The. Thomas Hardy. CP-HardT

Maid of my love, sweet Genevieve! Genevieve. Samuel Taylor Coleridge. MW-ColeS *Fr.* Effusions.

Maid Quiet. William Butler Yeats. CP-YeatW

Maid-Servant at the Inn, The. Dorothy Parker. CP-ParkD

Maid whom now you court in vain, The. Ode 2.5: "Maid whom now you court in vain, The." Horace. CP-JohnS *Fr.* Odes.

Maiden, The. Robert Duncan. SP-DuncR

Maiden, The. Audre Lorde. SP-LordA

Maiden-Blush, The. Robert Herrick. CP-HerrR

Maiden caught me in the wild, The. Crystal Cabinet, The. William Blake. CP-BlakW

Maiden May. Christina Georgina Rossetti. CP-RosC2

Maiden May sat in her bower, / In her blush rose bower in flower. Maiden May. Christina Georgina Rossetti. CP-RosC2

Maiden Name. Philip Larkin. CP-LarkP

Maiden, quench the glare of sorrow. To Mary, Who Died in This Opinion. Percy Bysshe Shelley. CP-ShelP

Maiden-Song. Christina Georgina Rossetti. CP-RosC1

Maiden Speech of the Æolian Harp. Ralph Waldo Emerson. CP-EmerR

Maiden, that with sullen brow. To an Unfortunate Woman at the Theatre. Samuel Taylor Coleridge. CP-ColeS

Maiden wept and, as a comforter, A. Passion and Love. Paul Laurence Dunbar. CP-DunbP

Maiden with Orb and Planets. Howard Nemerov. CP-NemeH

Maiden! with the fair brown tresses. To ———: "Maiden! with the fair brown tresses." John Greenleaf Whittier. CP-WhitJ

Maiden without Hands, The. Anne Sexton. CP-SextA

Maidenly lake, fathomless lake. Lake. Czeslaw Milosz. CP-MiloCN, *tr. by* Martin Sabiniewicz *and* Jennifer Scappettone

Maidens, gather not the yew. Prologue to a Saga. Dorothy Parker. CP-ParkD

Maiden's Pledge, A. Thomas Hardy. CP-HardT

Maidens shall weep at merry morn. Summer Malison, The. Gerard Manley Hopkins. CP-HopkG

Maidens tell me I am old. Age Unfit for Love. Robert Herrick. CP-HerrR

Maid's Complaint, A. Thomas Campion. CP-CampT

(My Love Hath Vowd.) CP-CampT

Maids Nay's Are Nothing. Robert Herrick. CP-HerrR

Maids of Attitash, The. John Greenleaf Whittier. CP-WhitJ

Maid's Thought, The. Robinson Jeffers. CP-JefR1

Maid's Way, A. G. K. Chesterton. CP-ChesG

Mail. Andrei Codrescu. SP-CodrA

Mail, The. Raymond Carver. CP-CarvR

Mail box, the roadway, and the dump truck, The. Project, The. Richard Eberhart. CP-EberR

Mail Call. Randall Jarrell. CP-JarrR

Mailbox Whore San Francisco 1970, The. Operations of Desire, The. Andrei Codrescu. SP-CodrA

Maillol. Charles Tomlinson. CP-TomlC

Mailman, The. Gold hood. Crossing Borders. William Corbett. SP-CorbW

Mailman as Cancer Patient, The. Raymond Carver. CP-CarvR

Maimed, beggared, grey; seeking an alms; with nod. Bellerophon. George Meredith. CP-MerG1

Maimed Man, The. Allen Tate. CP-TateA

Main Regret, The. George Meredith. CP-MerG1

Main Street. Miller Williams. CP-WillM

Main Street / is deserted, the hills. Charles Olson. SP-OlsoC *Fr.* Maximus Poems, The.

Maine Roustabout, A. Richard Eberhart. CP-EberR

Maine Winter. Charles Tomlinson. CP-TomlC

Maintenant. Charles Tomlinson. CP-TomlC

Mais l'Amour Infini Me Montera dans l'Âme. Richard Eberhart. CP-EberR

Maisie. James Merrill. SP-MerrJ

Maitreya the Future Buddha. Gary Snyder. CP-SnydG *Fr.* Myths and Texts.

Majestic insects buzz through the sky. Journeyings. Denise Levertov. SP-LeveDL

Majesty of horns sweeps in the stagtide. In a Crumbling. Kenneth Patchen. CP-PatcK

Major faults in granite. Trio of Love Songs. Sylvia Plath. CP-PlatS

Major Hawkaby Cole Macroo. Major Macroo. Stevie Smith. CP-SmitS

Major is a fine cat. My Cat Major. Stevie Smith. CP-SmitS

Major Macroo. Stevie Smith. CP-SmitS

Major Patrick Ferguson. King's Mountain. Charles Olson. CP-OlsoC

Major progress is: in the act of embracing ourselves. Great Advances in Vanity. Thomas Lux. SP-LuxT

Major Road Ahead. Hugh MacDiarmid. SP-MacDH *Fr.* Battle Continues, The.

Major Work, A. William Meredith. SP-MereW

Make a garland of Leontynes and Lenas. Crowns and Garlands. Langston Hughes. CP-HughL; CP-HughL3

Make a motion. Virtu. A. R. Ammons. CP-AmmoA

Make and be eaten, the poet says. Muriel Rukeyser. CP-RukeM

Make Big Money at Home! Write Poems in Spare Time! Howard Nemerov. CP-NemeH

Make, for he loved thee well, our Merrimac. R. S. S., at Deer Island on the Merrimac. John Greenleaf Whittier. CP-WhitJ

Make Friends. Omar Khayyám. CP-EmerR

Make haste away, and let one be. To His Book[e]. Robert Herrick. CP-HerrR

Make it so simple a child. My Instructions. James Laughlin. CP-LaugJ

Make Love Not War. Howard Nemerov. CP-NemeH

Make, make me Thine, my gracious God. To God. Robert Herrick. CP-HerrR

Make me a heaven, and make me there. Eye, The. Robert Herrick. CP-HerrR

Make me a picture of the sun. Emily Dickinson. CP-DickE

Make me a song of all good things. Order for A Song, An. James Whitcomb Riley. CP-RileJ

Make me well, I said.——And the delighted touch. Panacea. Muriel Rukeyser. CP-RukeM

Make no mistake: if He rose at all. Seven Stanzas at Easter. John Updike. CP-UpdiJ

Make no mistake, you cannot take. Principle, The. David Ignatow. SP-IgnaD

"Make of yourself a light," / said the Buddha. Buddha's Last Instruction, The. Mary Oliver. SP-OlivM

Make Rundle bishop; fie, for shame! On Dr. Rundle. Jonathan Swift. CP-SwifJ

Make use of the things around you. Sunday Night. Raymond Carver. CP-CarvR

Make war songs out of these. Four Brothers, The. Carl Sandburg. CP-SandC

Make way, make way, give leave to rove. Little Good Fellows, The. Herman Melville. SP-MelvH

Maker, The. W. H. Auden. CP-AudeW

Maker, The ("He had never dwelled on the pleasures of memory"). Jorge Luis Borges. SP-BorgJ, *tr. by* Ken Krabbenhoft

Maker, The ("We are the river you spoke of, Heraclitus"). Jorge Luis Borges. SP-BorgJ, *tr. by* Stephen Kessler

Maker of Dreams, The. James Laughlin. CP-LaugJ

Maker of many mouths. E. E. Cummings. CP-CummE

Makers, The. A. R. Ammons. CP-AmmoA

Makers of History. W. H. Auden. CP-AudeW

Makes me feel sad. Ursa Major ("Makes me feel sad"). Federico García Lorca. CP-GarcF, *tr. by* Jerome Rothenberg *Fr.* Shadow.

Making. A. R. Ammons. CP-AmmoA

Making a fire. Walter De la Mare. CP-DeLaW

Making a form for you. Re C—. Robert Creeley. CP-CreeR

Making a Living. Anne Sexton. CP-SextA

Making a Love Poem. James Laughlin. CP-LaugJ

Making angels in the snow. Somewhere Else. Yusef Komunyakaa. CP-KomuY

Making Beasts. Gregory Orr. SP-OrrG

Making his advances. Tortoise Gallantry. D. H. Lawrence. CP-LawrD

Making It. Charles Bukowski. SP-BukC3

Making It. Theodore Weiss. SP-WeisT

Making it, making it. Thirst Song. Denise Levertov. SP-LeveDP

Making It New. Philip Levine. SP-LeviP

Making Light of It. Philip Levine. SP-LeviP

Making Love. William Dickey. SP-DickW

Making Love in Poetry. Lawrence Ferlinghetti. SP-FerlL

Making love in the sun, in the morning sun. Layover. Charles Bukowski. SP-BukC2

Making Out with the Dream-Shredding Machine. Yusef Komunyakaa. CP-KomuY

Making Peace. Denise Levertov. SP-LeveDS

Making Strange. Seamus Heaney. SP-HeanSO

Making the best and most of a visitation. Reflections on Deafness. Donald Davie. CP-DaviDC

Making the Jam without You. Maxine W. Kumin. SP-KumiM

Making the Move. Paul Muldoon. CP-MuldP

Making these word things to. Report from a Far Place. William Stafford. SP-StafWW

Making Waves. A. R. Ammons. CP-AmmoA

Makings. Gary Snyder. CP-SnydG

Malachy stamped the diving decks. Superiorities. Richard Wilbur. CP-WilbR

Malacoda. Samuel Beckett. CP-BeckS

Malade. D. H. Lawrence. CP-LawrD

Malady. Theodore Weiss. SP-WeisT

Malady smote the earth one year, A. Animals Sick of the Plague, The. Marianne Craig Moore. CP-MoorM *Fr.* Fables of La Fontaine.

Malarial, malodorous, papyrus-choked. Sudd as Metaphor, The. Thomas Lux. SP-LuxT

Malay took the Pearl, The. Emily Dickinson. CP-DickE

Malcolm. Alice Walker. CP-WalkA

Malcolm, I love thee more than women love. From Frodmer's Drama "The Friends." Ralph Waldo Emerson. CP-EmerR

Maldive Shark, The. Herman Melville. SP-MelvH

Male-throated under the shallow sea-fog. October Evening. Robinson Jeffers. CP-JefR1

Malebolge: Prince William Sound. Sam Hamill. SP-HamiS

Maledictus In Plebe Sit. James Laughlin. CP-LaugJ

Malest Cornifici Tuo Catullo. Allen Ginsberg. CP-GinsA; SP-GinsA

Malham Cove. William Wordsworth. CP-WorW2

Malheur à la malheureuse Tamise. Le Directeur. T. S. Eliot. CP-ElioT

Malheur before Dawn. William Stafford. SP-StafWW

Malice Domestic. Ogden Nash. CP-NashO

Malicorn, Malicorn, Malicorn, ho! Song: "Malicorn, Malicorn, Malicorn, ho!" Nathaniel Lee. CP-DryJ2 *Fr.* Duke of Guise, The.

Mallard ducks are down, The. Highway 99E from Chico. Raymond Carver. CP-CarvR

Mallarmé told Degas that poems. Importance of Dictionaries, The. James Laughlin. CP-LaugJ

Malleability / a precision, A. Portobello Carnival 1973. Charles Tomlinson. CP-TomlC

Malrin. Ezra Pound. CP-PoEar

Malrin, because of his jesting stood without, till all the guests. Malrin. Ezra Pound. CP-PoEar

Malvern Hill. Herman Melville. SP-MelvH

Mama. William Carlos Williams. CP-WilW2

Mama and Daughter. Langston Hughes. CP-HughL; CP-HughL2

Mama Elsie's ninety now. Little Man around the House. Yusef Komunyakaa. CP-KomuY

Mama, I found this soldier's cap. When the Armies Passed. Langston Hughes. CP-HughL; CP-HughL2

Mama, / I wish I were silver. Silly Song. Federico García Lorca. SP-GarcF, *tr. by* M. D. Herter Norton *and* Harriet de Onís

Mama Mary's counting them. Birds on a Powerline. Yusef Komunyakaa. CP-KomuY

Mama never forgets her birds. Emily Dickinson. CP-DickE

Mama, please brush off my coat. Mama and Daughter. Langston Hughes. CP-HughL; CP-HughL2

Mama / Remembers the four-leaf clover. Second Generation: New York. Langston Hughes. CP-HughL; CP-HughL2

Mamertinus on Rhetoric, A.D. 291. Donald Davie. CP-DaviDC

Mamie. Carl Sandburg. CP-SandC

Mamie beat her head against the bars of a little Indiana town and. Mamie. Carl Sandburg. CP-SandC

Mamma is a widow: There's only us three. Young Old Man, The. James Whitcomb Riley. CP-RileJ

Mammy. Langston Hughes. CP-HughL; CP-HughL1

Mammy Hums. Carl Sandburg. CP-SandC

Mammy's in de kitchen, an' de do' is shet. Curiosity. Paul Laurence Dunbar. CP-DunbP

Man. George Herbert. CP-HerbG

Man. Langston Hughes. CP-HughL; CP-HughL2

Man. Randall Jarrell. CP-JarrR

Man! Archibald MacLeish. CP-MacLA

Man, A. G. K. Chesterton. CP-ChesG

Man, A. Thomas Hardy. CP-HardT

Man, A. D. H. Lawrence. CP-LawrD

Man, A. Denise Levertov. SP-LeveDP

Man, The. Robert Creeley. CP-CreeR

Man, The. Charles Simic. SP-SimiC

Man: a flutter of pages. Plant and Phantom. Louis MacNeice. CP-MacNL

Man adrift on a slim spar, A. Stephen Crane. CP-CranS

Man against the Sky, The. Edwin Arlington Robinson. CP-RobiE

Man alive, that mournst thy lot. Lines for a Grave-Stone. Edna St. Vincent Millay. CP-MillE

Man all alone in an empty room, A. History. Yehuda Amichai. SP-AmicY, *tr. by* Chana Bloch

Man Alone. Louise Bogan. CP-BogaL

Man alone is immoral. Morality. D. H. Lawrence. CP-LawrD

Man, am I sick. Seven New Ways of Looking at the Moon. John Updike. CP-UpdiJ

Man and a Woman Arguing, A. Jelaluddin Rumi. SP-Rumi, *tr. by* Coleman Barks

Man and a Woman Might at This Moment, A. John Ciardi. CP-CiarJ

Man and a Woman Sit Near Each Other. Robert Bly. SP-BlyR

Man and Bat. D. H. Lawrence. CP-LawrD

Man and Bottle. Wallace Stevens. CP-StevW; CP-StevWP

Man and Boy. Seamus Heaney. SP-HeanSO

Man and Dog on an Early Winter Morning. Carl Sandburg. CP-SandC

Man and His Image, A. G. K. Chesterton. CP-ChesG

Man and Machine. D. H. Lawrence. CP-LawrD

Man and Nature. Elizabeth Barrett Browning. CP-BroEB

Man and Nature. Richard Eberhart. CP-EberR

Man and Nature. William Carlos Williams. CP-WilW1

Man and Sea. Charles Baudelaire. CP-BaudC, *tr. by* Walter Martin

Man and the Echo. William Butler Yeats. CP-YeatW

Man and the Lion. Josephine Jacobsen. CP-JacoJ

Man and the maid go side by side, The. Sunday Afternoon in Italy. D. H. Lawrence. CP-LawrD

Man and Wife. Robert Lowell. SP-LoweR

Man and Wife. Anne Sexton. CP-SextA

Man and Woman. Robert Lowell. SP-LoweR

Man and woman, A. Engraved. Denise Levertov. SP-LeveDL

Man and Woman in Camera and Out. A. K. Ramanujan. CP-RamaA

Man and woman lie on a white bed, A. Happiness. Louise Glück. SP-GlucL

"MAN" and "WOMAN," these are horrid words, they annoy me. Andrei Codrescu. SP-CodrA

Man applying gold leaf, A. Poem: "Man applying gold leaf, A." Alan Dugan. CP-DugaA

Man approaching his chair: / from that horizon, tonight as before. All Seated. Pablo Neruda. SP-NeruP

Man Asleep in a Child's Bed. Thomas Lux. SP-LuxT

Man at Play on the River, A. D. H. Lawrence. CP-LawrD

Man begins in zoology / He is the saddest animal. First Lesson about Man. Thomas Merton. CP-MertT

Man behind the book may not be man, The. Intellectual, The. Karl Shapiro. SP-ShapK

Man bent over his guitar, The. Man with the Blue Guitar, The. Wallace Stevens. CP-StevW; CP-StevWP

Man Bites Dog-Days. Ogden Nash. CP-NashO

Man Born on the Earth, A. G. K. Chesterton. CP-ChesG

Man Born to Farming, The. Wendell Berry. CP-BerrW

Man-brained and man-handed ground-ape, physically, The. Original Sin. Robinson Jeffers. CP-JefR3

Man builded a bugle for the storms to blow, A. Legends. Stephen Crane. CP-CranS

Man by the name of Bolus—(all 'at we'll ever know), A. James Whitcomb Riley. CP-RileJ

Man came slowly from the setting sun, A. Death of Cuchulain, The. William Butler Yeats. CP-YeatW

Man came to the pool of Bethesda, A. Pool of Bethesda. Carl Sandburg. CP-

SandC

Man Came Tuesday, A. John Ciardi. CP-CiarJ

Man can survive anything except not caring, A. Joshua on Eighth Avenue. John Ciardi. CP-CiarJ

Man can't fully live unless he dies and ceases to care, A. Full Life. D. H. Lawrence. CP-LawrD

Man Carrying Thing. Wallace Stevens. CP-StevW; CP-StevWP

Man Coming of Age. Robert Penn Warren. CP-WarrR

Man could be a god, A. Walking on the River Ice. Wendell Berry. CP-BerrW

Man could be granted to live a dozen lives, A. I Didn't Say a Word, or, Who Called That Piccolo Player a Father? Ogden Nash. CP-NashO

Man could never do, A. Miracle in Manila. Ai. SP-Ai

Man crossing the field was a Chief Rabbi, The. Yehuda Amichai. SP-AmicYL, *tr. by* Benjamin Harshav *and* Barbara Harshav

Man decided once to go steal truth, A. Refuge, Serpent-Riders. C. K. Williams. CP-WillC

Man descended from Pride, A. Han-shan. CP-ColdM, *tr. by* Red Pine

Man dies too soon, beside his works half planned. Doctors. Rudyard Kipling. CP-KiplR

Man-dirt and stomachs that the sea unloads; rockets. Eve of St. Agony, or the Middle Class Was Sitting on Its Fat. Kenneth Patchen. CP-PatcK

Man does not live by bread alone. Shooting Incident, The. Stevie Smith. CP-SmitS

Man Does, Woman Is. Robert Graves. CP-GravR

Man doesn't have time in his life, A. Man in His Life, A. Yehuda Amichai. SP-AmicY, *tr. by* Chana Bloch

Man dreams a great dream, A. In his dream he is covered with moss. Moss. Andrei Codrescu. SP-CodrA

Man driving the expensive car, The. Vision of Delight, The. Philip Whalen. SP-WhalP

Man existed for seventeen spidery years, A. Divorce. Miller Williams. CP-WillM

Man fades at the distant end of the street, A. Question: "Man fades at the distant end of the street, A." Yannis Ritsos. SP-RitsY, *tr. by* Minas Savvas

Man feared that he might find an assassin, A. Stephen Crane. CP-CranS

Man Feeding Pigeons. Amy Clampitt. CP-ClamA

Man Flammonde, from God knows where, The. Flammonde. Edwin Arlington Robinson. CP-RobiE

Man fought against beasts, and won. Gripping Serial. Donald Davie. CP-DaviDC

Man from a house not far who rode the train, A. Friends. John Ciardi. CP-CiarJ

Man from Ecuador beneath the Eiffel Tower, A. Jorge Carrera Andrade. CP-MertT

Man from Jehovah's, A. James Laughlin. CP-LaugJ *Fr.* America I Love You.

Man from the waste evolved. Wallace Stevens. CP-StevWP

Man-Giraffe. Robert Stock. SP-StocR

Man goes by with a woman, A. Leaping from Ambush. David Ignatow. SP-IgnaD

Man goes to Man! Cry the challenge though the Jungle! Rudyard Kipling. CP-KiplR *Fr.* Second Jungle Book, The.

Man growing old is going, A. Shalom. Denise Levertov. SP-LeveDP

Man hammers viciously / viciously like fucking, A. Nut, The. C. K. Williams. CP-WillC

Man has forgot his Origin; in vain. Origin of Man, The. Jones Very. CP-VeryJ

Man hauling coal in the street is stilled forever, A. Negative, The. Arthur Sze. SP-SzeA

Man He Killed, The. Thomas Hardy. CP-HardT

Man hung a sign above the town, A. Signs. Grace Paley. CP-PalGC

Man I Am, A. Stevie Smith. CP-SmitS

Man I praise that once in Tara's Halls, A. In Tara's Halls. William Butler Yeats. CP-YeatW

Man I saw in the forest, The. Dream 2: Brian the Still-Hunter. Margaret Atwood. SP-AtwM1

Man, I suck me tooth when I hear. Parang. Derek Walcott. CP-WalcD

Man / I think it is a man, A. My Dream about the Poet. Lucille Clifton. SP-ClifL

Man, if I said once, 'I know.' Islands, The. Randall Jarrell. CP-JarrR

Man I'm telling you about brought himself back alive, The. Zodiac, The. James Dickey. CP-DickJ

Man in a plane looks at the surface of land, A. Muriel Rukeyser. CP-RukeM

Man in a Room. William Carlos Williams. CP-WilW1

Man in a window? / When dead men sing. Songs. Thomas Merton. CP-MertT

Man in Black. Sylvia Plath. CP-PlatS

Man in Blue, A. James Schuyler. CP-SchuJ

Man in His Life, A. Yehuda Amichai. SP-AmicY, *tr. by* Chana Bloch

Man in his life has no time to have, A. Yehuda Amichai. SP-AmicYL, *tr. by* Benjamin Harshav *and* Barbara Harshav

Man, in life where-ever plac'd, The. First Psalm, The. Robert Burns. CP-BurnR

Man in Majesty. Randall Jarrell. CP-JarrR

Man in prison is called horse face, but does nothing, A. Horse Face. Arthur Sze. SP-SzeA

Man in Space. Billy Collins. SP-CollB

Man in terror of impotence, A. Ninth Symphony of Beethoven Understood at Last as a Sexual Message, The. Adrienne Rich. SP-RicA2

Man in the Bar Says He Has Something to Say, A. Miller Williams. CP-WillM

Man in the black twill and gold braid of a pilot, A. Running on Silk. Galway Kinnell. SP-KinnGN

Man in the Chair, The. Galway Kinnell. SP-KinnGN

Man in the Dead Machine, The. Donald Hall. CP-HallD

Man in the Dining Car, The. Tennessee Williams. CP-WillT

Man in / the eye clinic. Postcards. Rae Armantrout. SP-ArmaA

Man in the Landscape. Sam Hamill. SP-HamiS

Man in the Moon, The. Billy Collins. SP-CollB

Man in the Moon, The. James Whitcomb Riley. CP-RileJ

Man in the Street, The. D. H. Lawrence. CP-LawrD

Man in the West. Two Priests, The. Archibald MacLeish. CP-MacLA

Man in the Wind, The. Thomas Merton. CP-MertT

Man in whom Tao, The. Man of Tao, The. Chuang Tzu. CP-MertT

Man inside the Chipmunk Suit, The. Thomas Lux. SP-LuxT

Man inside the mandolin, The. Refrain. Rita Dove. SP-DoveR

Man into Men. Langston Hughes. CP-HughL; CP-HughL2

Man, introverted man, having crossed. Science. Robinson Jeffers. CP-JefR1

Man invented the machine. Man and Machine. D. H. Lawrence. CP-LawrD

Man is A. Two-legged. Heather McHugh. SP-McHuH

Man is a glutton. Quick, Hammacher, My Stomacher! Ogden Nash. CP-NashO

Man is a lump[e], where all beasts kneaded be[e]. To Sir Edward Herbert, at Juliers [or Julyers]. John Donne. CP-DonnJ; MW-DonnJ

Man Is a Spirit. Stevie Smith. CP-SmitS

Man is a Watch, wound up at first, but never. Watch, The. Robert Herrick. CP-HerrR

Man is an animal who thinks himself important. Moment of Truth, The. Thomas Merton. CP-MertT

Man Is Born in Tao. Chuang Tzu. CP-MertT, *tr. by* Thomas Merton

Man is coming out of the mountains. Touch and Go. Stevie Smith. CP-SmitS

Man is compos'd here of a two-fold part. Upon Man. Robert Herrick. CP-HerrR

Man is immoral because he has got a mind. Immoral Man. D. H. Lawrence. CP-LawrD

Man is killing time—there's nothing else, The. Drinker, The. Robert Lowell. SP-LoweR

Man is leaning on a cold iron rail, A. Man Who Loved Islands, The. Derek Walcott. CP-WalcD

Man Is More than *Homo Sapiens*. D. H. Lawrence. CP-LawrD

Man is my darling, my love and my pain. God and Man. Stevie Smith. CP-SmitS

Man is not quite a man. Man Is More than *Homo Sapiens*. D. H. Lawrence. CP-LawrD

Man is old and—, The. Seated Man. George Oppen. CP-OppGN

Man is said to want but little here below. Jangle Bells. Ogden Nash. CP-NashO

Man is singing on the bus, A. Ordinary Morning, An. Philip Levine. SP-LeviP

Man is the world, and death the ocean. Elegy on the Lady Markham. John Donne. CP-DonnJ; MW-DonnJ

Man is the writing instrument. Man and Nature. Richard Eberhart. CP-EberR

Man Is to Man a Beast. Kenneth Patchen. CP-PatcK

Man is watching down the sun. All day, A. Machiavelli in Exile. Charles Tomlinson. CP-TomlC

Man knocked three times, A. Madam and the Wrong Visitor. Langston Hughes. CP-HughL; CP-HughL2

Man knows his day, it has. Seven Songs, The. Charles Olson. CP-OlsoC

Man knows nothing. Know-All. D. H. Lawrence. CP-LawrD

Man know[e]s where first he ships himsel[f]e], but he. Man's Dying-Place Uncertain. Robert Herrick. CP-HerrR

Man like That on a Bald Mountain in Jerusalem, A. Yehuda Amichai. SP-AmicY, *tr. by* Chana Bloch

Man Listening to Disc. Billy Collins. SP-CollB

Man Lives Here, A. Kenneth Patchen. CP-PatcK

Man lives less than a hundred years, A. Han-shan. CP-ColdM, *tr. by* Red Pine

Man Locked inside the Oak, The. Robert Bly. SP-BlyR

Man looking into the sea. Grave, A. Marianne Craig Moore. CP-MoorM

Man looks at his watch to see, A. Mind. Heather McHugh. SP-McHuH

Man-Made World, A. Stephen Spender. CP-SpenS

Man Man is the Devil. Henry David Thoreau. CP-ThorH

Man may at first transgress, but next do well. Bad May Be Better. Robert Herrick. CP-HerrR

Man may make a Remark, A. Emily Dickinson. CP-DickE

Man may want land to live in; but for all. Buriall. Robert Herrick. CP-HerrR

Man Meets a Woman in the Street, A. Randall Jarrell. CP-JarrR

Man-Moth, The. Elizabeth Bishop. CP-BishE

Man must do well out of a good intent. Feare. Robert Herrick. CP-HerrR

Man must not be engaged if he is to float to the moon, A. Matinée. Andrei Codrescu. SP-CodrA

Man my age, A. Faces. Grace Paley. CP-PalGC

Man, my friend, whose conscious heart, The. Ode 1.22: Translations of Horace ("Integer vitae"). Horace. CP-JohnS *Fr.* Odes.

Man named Finchley once, A. Missouri Fable, A. John Ciardi. CP-CiarJ

Man named Philander S. Goo, A. Philander. Theodore Roethke. CP-RoetT

Man needs ammunition, A. Jack Ruby on Ice. Ai. SP-Ai

Man of Evil. Robert Graves. CP-GravR

Man of Feeling, The. James Vincent Cunningham. CP-CunnJ

Man of firm and noble soul, The. Translation from Horace. Lord Byron. CP-Byron

Man of La Mancha. W. H. Auden.
  Golden Age, The. CP-AudeW
  Recitative by Death. CP-AudeW
  ("Ladies and gentlemen, you have made most remarkable.") CP-AudeW

Man of law, The. Lorine Niedecker. CP-NiedL

Man of letters is of letters wary, A. A. Heather McHugh. SP-McHuH

Man of Life Upright, The. Thomas Campion. CP-CampT

Man of low degree was sore oppressed, A. Crisis, The. Paul Laurence Dunbar. CP-DunbP

Man of Many Parts, A. James Whitcomb Riley. CP-RileJ

Man of massive meditation, A. Analogue of Unity in Multeity. Richard Eberhart. CP-EberR

Man of Science, The. Jones Very. CP-VeryJ

Man of Sung did business, A. Hat Salesman and a Capable Ruler, A. Chuang Tzu. CP-MertT

Man of Tao, The. Chuang Tzu. CP-MertT

Man of the Middle Class, A. Gwendolyn Brooks. SP-BrooG

Man of Tyre, The. D. H. Lawrence. CP-LawrD

Man of words and not of deeds, A. Voyage Autour de Mes Cartes Postales. James Schuyler. CP-SchuJ

Man on his deathbed left instructions, A. Night Air, The. Jelaluddin Rumi. SP-Rumi, *tr.* by Coleman Barks

Man, on the dubious waves of error toss'd. Truth. William Cowper. CP-CowpW

Man on the Dump, The. Wallace Stevens. CP-StevW; CP-StevWP

Man on the foreshore cooking a fish breakfast, The. Sea of Tiberias. Donald Davie. CP-DaviDC

Man on the radio mourns, The. Frontier, The. James Wright. CP-WrigJ

Man on this four-drachma piece, The. Orophernis. Constantine P. Cavafy. CP-CavaC, *tr.* by Theoharis Constantine Theoharis

Man out of the fire rises, A. To the Tune of an Ancient Song. Kenneth Patchen. CP-PatcK

Man out walking alone in the snow, A. Winter Exercise. Howard Nemerov. CP-NemeH

Man Outside, The. Raymond Carver. CP-CarvR

Man owes me two hundred and fifty dollars, A. To a Friendly Dun. James Wright. CP-WrigJ

Man peeing / by the woodpile. South Window. Grace Paley. CP-PalGC

Man prepar'd against all ills to come, A. Christian Militant. Robert Herrick. CP-HerrR

Man Reaches a Point. D. H. Lawrence. CP-LawrD

Man remembers from the tales the rocket, The. Romance of Science, The. Randall Jarrell. CP-JarrR

Man riding on the meaning of rivers, A. Are You Born? / I. Muriel Rukeyser. CP-RukeM

Man risked his life to write the words, A. I Love You Sweetheart. Thomas Lux. SP-LuxT

Man said to the universe, A. Stephen Crane. CP-CranS

Man sat in the felon's tank, alone, A. In the Tank. Thom Gunn. CP-GunnT

Man Saul, The. Stevie Smith. CP-SmitS

Man saw a ball of gold in the sky, A. Stephen Crane. CP-CranS

Man saw the whole world as a grinning skull and cross-bones, The, A. Bath. Carl Sandburg. CP-SandC

Man Seeking Experience Enquires His Way of a Drop of Water, The. Ted Hughes. SP-HughTN

Man, sen thy lyf is ay in weir. William Dunbar. CP-DunbW

Man shot through back while. Simplicity of Everything in Viet Nam, The. Charles Bukowski. SP-BukC2

Man should never earn his living, A. Living, A. D. H. Lawrence. CP-LawrD

Man should not love the moon, A. Should, Should Not. Czeslaw Milosz. CP-MiloC; CP-MiloCN

Man sick with whirling, A. 1789–1939. Randall Jarrell. CP-JarrR

Man sits in a timelessness, The. Rescue, The. Robert Creeley. CP-CreeR

Man sits in the rocking bedroom, claws, The. Muriel Rukeyser. CP-RukeM

Man / slapped her bottom, The. Covers. Rae Armantrout. SP-ArmaA

Man Speaks: / Though you move with a quiet grace, like a cloud, The. Drama,

A. D. H. Lawrence. CP-LawrD

Man standing there, who is he?, The. Three Stanzas from Goethe. James Wright. CP-WrigJ

Man staring into the fire, A. Miracle, The. Philip Levine. SP-LeviP

Man steps in out of the blizzard with his Klootch, The. Sweet, The. Ai. SP-Ai

Man still light of foot, but ageing, took, A. Thinking of Mr D. Thomas Kinsella. CP-KinsT

Man stomping over my bed in boots. Neighbor, The. Marge Piercy. SP-PierM

Man stoops low on the overcast plain, A. He is earthing. Landscape and Figure. Thomas Kinsella. CP-KinsT

Man Takes His Daughter, Age Five, to a Public Execution by Guillotine, Paris, 1857, A. Thomas Lux. SP-LuxT

Man, tamed by wine, by dress, by talk. Wild Life and Tamed Life. Richard Eberhart. CP-EberR

Man that had six mortal wounds, a man, A. Cuchulain Comforted. William Butler Yeats. CP-YeatW

Man that is man is more than a man. Third Song of Huitzilopochtli. D. H. Lawrence. CP-LawrD

Man that is open of heart to his neighbor, The. Neighbours. Rudyard Kipling. CP-KiplR

Man that rooms next door to me, The. Quiet Lodger, The. James Whitcomb Riley. CP-RileJ

Man the hare has met, The. Names of the Hare, The. *Unknown.* SP-HeanSO, *tr.* by Seamus Heaney

Man, the illogical animal. The others go wrong by anachronistic. To the Story-Tellers. Robinson Jeffers. CP-JefR3

Man, the Man-Hunter. Carl Sandburg. CP-SandC

Man the Master. Thomas Merton. CP-MertT

Man the Moon Shooter. Carl Sandburg. CP-SandC

Man, tied to a tree, thinks he is beginning to feel something, A. Behind His Eyes. David Ignatow. SP-IgnaD

Man to a Woman, A. William Carlos Williams. CP-WilW1

Man toiled on a burning road, A. Stephen Crane. CP-CranS

Man under his fig tree telephoned the man under his vine, The. Sort of an Apocalypse. Yehuda Amichai. SP-AmicY, *tr.* by Stephen Mitchell

Man undergoes pain sitting at a piano, A. Michael Palmer. SP-PalmM

Man wades the deep north, A. Rose for Solitude, A. Sam Hamill. SP-HamiS

Man Walking and Singing, A. Wendell Berry. CP-BerrW

Man walks, I learn, in fear of woman. Lore. Howard Nemerov. CP-NemeH

Man walks on the southern beach, The. Conversation, A. Margaret Atwood. SP-AtwM2

Man was crucified. He came to the city a stranger, was accused, and, The. Silver Nails. Carl Sandburg. CP-SandC

Man Was Drawing Near to Me, A. Thomas Hardy. CP-HardT

Man Was Made to Mourn, a Dirge. Robert Burns. CP-BurnR

Man went before a strange god, A. Stephen Crane. CP-CranS

Man who ate mushrooms, The. Mistaken Identity. Richard Eberhart. CP-EberR

Man Who Believes in Five, The. Miller Williams. CP-WillM

Man Who Carries the Desert Around inside Himself, The: For Wally. Yusef Komunyakaa. CP-KomuY

Man who cloaked his bitterness within, The. Thomas Hood. Edwin Arlington Robinson. CP-RobiE

Man Who Could Write, The. Rudyard Kipling. CP-KiplR
  (Shun—shun the Bowl! That fatal, facile drink.) CP-KiplR

Man who cultivates his garden, as Voltaire wished, A. Just, The. Jorge Luis Borges. SP-BorgJ, *tr.* by Alastair Reid

Man Who Died, A. D. H. Lawrence. CP-LawrD

Man Who Dreamed of Faeryland, The. William Butler Yeats. CP-YeatW

Man who fiercest charged in fight, The. Stonewall Jackson. Herman Melville. SP-MelvH

Man who first saw nothing, The. On Zero. Alan Dugan. CP-DugaA

Man Who Forgot, The. Thomas Hardy. CP-HardT

Man who found the aardvark, The. Bestiary, A. Kenneth Rexroth. CP-RexrK

Man who goes for Christian resignation, The. James Vincent Cunningham. CP-CunnJ

Man who had fallen among thieves, A. E. E. Cummings. CP-CummE; SP-CummE

Man who lives on rose-colored clouds, A. Han-shan. CP-ColdM, *tr.* by Red Pine

Man Who Loved Islands, The. Derek Walcott. CP-WalcD

Man Who Owns Sleep, The. C. K. Williams. CP-WillC

Man who pants for ample Sway, The. Boethius. CP-JohnS *Fr.* Consolation of Philosophy, The ("De Consolacione Philosophie").

Man Who Rode Away, The. Lawrence Ferlinghetti. SP-FerlL

Man who sold his lawn to standard oil, The. War against the Trees, The. Stanley Kunitz. CP-KunSC

Man Who Stays Up Late, The. Miller Williams. CP-WillM

Man who stood beside me, The. Sweet Will. Philip Levine. SP-LeviP

Man who tells you which is the whiter wash, The. Love and How It Becomes

Important in Our Day to Day Lives. Miller Williams. CP-WillM

Man who took 38 steelhead out, The. Its Course. Raymond Carver. CP-CarvR

Man who was about to hang himself, A. Circumstance. *Unknown*. CP-ShelP

Man Who Was Blown Down by the Wind, A. Richard Eberhart. CP-EberR

Man Who Was Pregnant with Envy, The. Robert Stock. SP-StocR

Man Who Was, The. Rudyard Kipling. *Fr.* Life's Handicap.

Man Who Writes Ants, The. W. S. Merwin. SP-MerwW

Man, whom Science had made wise, A. Man of Science, The. Jones Very. CP-VeryJ

Man who's happy many a year, one hour, A. Michelangelo Buonarroti. CP-Miche, *tr. by* John Frederick Nims

Man who's married an attractive, somewhat younger woman conceives a painful jealousy of her, A. Cautionary, The. C. K. Williams. SP-WillC

Man Whose Pharynx Was Bad, The. Wallace Stevens. CP-StevW; CP-StevWP

Man will surely fail who dares delay, The. Ovid. CP-JohnS *Fr.* Remediae Amoris.

Man with a box walked up to a woman with a boy, A. Poem: "Man with a box walked up to a woman with a boy, A." Alan Dugan. CP-DugaA

Man with a good head and belly, A. Han-shan. CP-ColdM, *tr. by* Red Pine

Man with a leaf in his head, A. Mulch, The. Stanley Kunitz. CP-KunSC

Man with a Past, The. Thomas Hardy. CP-HardT

Man with a scythe: the torrent of his swing. Gardens No Emblems. Donald Davie. CP-DaviDC

Man with a tail heads eastward for the Fair. World-Telegram. John Berryman. CP-BerrJ

Man with his lion under the shed of wars, The. Song of the Borderguard, The. Robert Duncan. SP-DuncR

Man with knapsack in the marketplace, Brother. Yehuda Amichai. SP-AmicYL, *tr. by* Benjamin Harshav *and* Barbara Harshav

Man with Night Sweats, The. Thom Gunn. CP-GunnT

Man with One Foot and the Marsh Pheasant, The. Chuang Tzu. CP-MertT

Man with One Leaf in October Night. W. S. Merwin. SP-MerwW

Man with the axe stands profound and termless, The. Randall Jarrell. CP-JarrR

Man with the Blue Guitar, The. Wallace Stevens. CP-StevW; CP-StevWP

Man with the Broken Fingers, The. Carl Sandburg. CP-SandC

Man with the Broken Fingers throws a shadow, The. Man with the Broken Fingers, The. Carl Sandburg. CP-SandC

Man with the Golden Adam's Apple, The. Kenneth Patchen. CP-PatcK

Man with the Hot Nose, The. Charles Bukowski. SP-BukC2

Man with the red hat, The. Glazunoviana. John Ashbery. SP-AshbJ

Man with Two New Suits, The. Ogden Nash. CP-NashO

Man with wooden leg escapes prison. He's caught. James Tate. SP-TateJ

Man within a woman—no, I'd say, A. Michelangelo Buonarroti. CP-Miche, *tr. by* John Frederick Nims

Man without Sense of Direction. John Crowe Ransom. SP-RansJ

Man worn down by time, A. Someone. Jorge Luis Borges. SP-BorgJ, *tr. by* W. S. Merwin

Man Writes to a Part of Himself, A. Robert Bly. SP-BlyR

Man wrote to me: We missed it, you and I, A. Correspondence in After Years. D. H. Lawrence. CP-LawrD

Man, you too, aren't you, one of these rough followers of the criminal? In the Servants' Quarters. Thomas Hardy. CP-HardT

Man Young and Old, A. William Butler Yeats. CP-YeatW

Mana of the Sea. D. H. Lawrence. CP-LawrD

Management Area of Cherokee, The. Trout Map, The. Allen Tate. CP-TateA

Managers, The. W. H. Auden. CP-AudeW

Manciple there was, one of a Temple, A. Manciple's Tale—A Modernization, The. Geoffrey Chaucer. CP-WorW1 *Fr.* Canterbury Tales, The.

Manciple's Tale—A Modernization, The. Geoffrey Chaucer. CP-WorW1 *Fr.* Canterbury Tales, The.

Mandalay. Rudyard Kipling. CP-KiplR

Mandarin ducks roost for the night. Han-shan. CP-ColdM, *tr. by* Red Pine

Mandarins. T. S. Eliot. SP-ElioT

Mandelstam in the Crimea. Donald Davie. CP-DaviDC

Mandelstam, on Dante. Donald Davie. CP-DaviDC

Mandelstam's Hope for the Best. Donald Davie. CP-DaviDC

Mandolin and Liqueurs. Wallace Stevens. CP-StevWP

Mandorla. Paul Celan. SP-CelaP, *tr. by* John Felstiner

Mandrakes. Thom Gunn. CP-GunnT

Maner of Passyng to Confessioun, The. William Dunbar. CP-DunbW

Maneuver [*or* Manoeuvre], The. William Carlos Williams. CP-WilW2

Manfred. Lord Byron. CP-Byron

Manfred. George Meredith. CP-MerG1

Mangel-Bury, The. Ivor Gurney. SP-GurnI

Mangham. James Dickey. CP-DickJ

Mango Tree, The. Hart Crane. CP-CranH

Manhattan. Amy Clampitt. CP-ClamA

Manhattan Island Poem. Gregory Orr. SP-OrrG

Manhattan May Day Midnight. Allen Ginsberg. CP-GinsA; SP-GinsA

Manhattan Movements. John Logan. CP-LogaJ

Manhattan Thirties Flash. Allen Ginsberg. CP-GinsA

Manhattan's streets I saunter'd pondering. Song of Prudence. Walt Whitman. CP-WhitW

Manhole Covers. Karl Shapiro. SP-ShapK

Manhood. Henry David Thoreau. CP-ThorH

Manichaeans, The. Gary Snyder. CP-SnydG

Manifest reason glared at you and me. What Will Be, Is. Robert Graves. CP-GravR

Manifestation, The. Theodore Roethke. CP-RoetT

Manifesto. Andrei Codrescu. SP-CodrA

Manifesto. Allen Ginsberg. CP-GinsA

Manifesto. D. H. Lawrence. CP-LawrD

Manifesto. Nicanor Parra.
  I Move that We Adjourn the Meeting. CP-MertT, *tr. by* Thomas Merton

Manifesto: the Mad Farmer Liberation Front. Wendell Berry. CP-BerrW

Manifold Fusions, The. Kenneth Patchen. CP-PatcK

Manifold Usefulness of an Education, The. Miller Williams. CP-WillM

Manila. Robert Creeley. SP-CreeR

Manita's the Queen, Love and Love. Innocence. Olga Broumas. SP-BrouO

Manitoba Childe Roland. Carl Sandburg. CP-SandC

Mankind and Ocean. Robert Graves. CP-GravR

Mankind, you dismay me. Thoughts at Midnight. Thomas Hardy. CP-HardT

Manliness. John Donne. CP-DonnJ
  (Juggler, The.) MW-DonnJ

Manna. Robert Herrick. CP-HerrR

Manna. James Tate. SP-TateJ

Mannahatta. Walt Whitman. CP-WhitW

Manner of its Death, The. Emily Dickinson. CP-DickE

Manners. Elizabeth Bishop. CP-BishE

Manners. Ralph Waldo Emerson. CP-EmerR

Mannikins, we command you. Caligari. Carl Sandburg. CP-SandC

Manocalzata (Gloved Hand). John Ciardi. CP-CiarJ

Manor Garden, The. Sylvia Plath. CP-PlatS

Manos Karastefanís. James Merrill. SP-MerrJ

Man's Accountability. Jones Very. CP-VeryJ

Man's and woman's bodies lay without souls. Childish Prank, A. Ted Hughes. SP-HughTN

Man's destination is his own village, A. To the Indians Who Died in Africa. T. S. Eliot. CP-ElioT

Man's Devotion. James Whitcomb Riley. CP-RileJ

Mans disposition is for to requite. Revenge. Robert Herrick. CP-HerrR

Man's Divine Equality. G. K. Chesterton. CP-ChesG

Man's Dying-Place Uncertain. Robert Herrick. CP-HerrR

Man's earliest pastime, I suppose. And How Keen Was the Vision of Sir Launfal? Ogden Nash. CP-NashO

Man's First Experience of Winter. Jones Very. CP-VeryJ

Man's full console of cries, his howls and whines. One of the Old Ones. Robert Stock. SP-StocR

Man's Glory. Allen Ginsberg. CP-GinsA

Man's Greed and Envy Are So Great. Richard Eberhart. CP-EberR

Man's harvest is past, his summer is ended. For All. Christina Georgina Rossetti. CP-RosC2

Man's Heart Prophesieth of Peace. Jones Very. CP-VeryJ

Man's Household, A. Wisława Szymborska. SP-SzymWM, *tr. by* Joanna Trzeciak

Man's Image. D. H. Lawrence. CP-LawrD
  (Morality.) CP-LawrD

Man's life is but a working day / Whose tasks are set aright. Christina Georgina Rossetti. CP-RosC2

Man's life is death. Yet Christ endured to live. Wednesday in Holy Week. Christina Georgina Rossetti. CP-RosC2

Man's life is threescore years and ten. Imminent Seventies, The. Robert Graves. CP-GravR

Man's Medley. George Herbert. CP-HerbG

Man's Need of a Spiritual Birth. Jones Very. CP-VeryJ

Man's paradise is his good nature, A. Canto 93: "Man's paradise is his good nature, A." Ezra Pound. SP-PounE *Fr.* Cantos.

Man's Requirements, A. Elizabeth Barrett Browning. CP-BroEB

Man's soul is like, A. Yehuda Amichai. SP-AmicYL, *tr. by* Benjamin Harshav *and* Barbara Harshav

Man's struggle against man. Cold Comfort. Hans Magnus Enzensberger. SP-EnzeH

Mans transgressions God do's then remit, A. Penitencie. Robert Herrick. CP-HerrR

Man's Type. Richard Eberhart. CP-EberR

Man's Wisdom Is in What He Writes. Shmuel HaNagid. SP-HaNaS, *tr.* by Peter Cole

Man's Work, A. Archibald MacLeish. CP-MacLA

Mansion. A. R. Ammons. CP-AmmoA

Mansion burned. Maids, The. Hayden Carruth. CP-CarHS *Fr.* Clay Hill Anthology, The.

Mansion, string of cottages, a farm, A. Inherited Estate, The. Thom Gunn. CP-GunnT

Manso. John Milton. CP-MiltJ

  (To Manso.) CP-CowpW

Mantegna on all the walls. Mantova. Charles Wright. SP-WrigC

"Mantis." Louis Zukofsky. CP-ZukLS

"Mantis," an Interpretation. Louis Zukofsky. CP-ZukLS

Mantis! praying mantis! since your wings' leaves. "Mantis." Louis Zukofsky. CP-ZukLS

Mantle of St. John de Matha, The. John Greenleaf Whittier. CP-WhitJ

Mantled in grey, the dusk steals slowly in. Winter Nocturne. Philip Larkin. CP-LarkP

Mantova. Charles Wright. SP-WrigC

Manual, A. Vincent Bourne. CP-CowpW

Manual System. Carl Sandburg. CP-SandC

Manuel Flores is doomed to die. Milonga of Manuel Flores. Jorge Luis Borges. SP-BorgJ, *tr.* by Alastair Reid

Manuel Komninos. Constantine P. Cavafy. CP-CavaC, *tr.* by Theoharis Constantine Theoharis

Manuelzinho. Elizabeth Bishop. CP-BishE

Manufactured Gods. Carl Sandburg. CP-SandC

Manufacturing. Rae Armantrout. SP-ArmaA

Manuscript Found in a Book of Joseph Conrad. Jorge Luis Borges. SP-BorgJ, *tr.* by Alastair Reid

Many a flower hath perfume for its dower. Exultate Deo. Christina Georgina Rossetti. CP-RosC2

Many a green isle needs must be. Lines Written among the Euganean Hills. Percy Bysshe Shelley. CP-ShelP

Many a phrase has the English language. Emily Dickinson. CP-DickE

Many a time driving over the Coast Range. Looking for Someone. William Stafford. SP-StafWW

Many a year is in its grave. Passage, The. Paul Laurence Dunbar. CP-DunbP

Many an angel, with its needle. Emily Dickinson. SP-DickE

Many an infant that screams like a calliope. Pediatric Reflection. Ogden Nash. CP-NashO

Many and many a time I thought. Dead Bastard, The. Thomas Hardy. CP-HardT

Many animals that our fathers killed in America. Fear Is What Quickens Me. James Wright. CP-WrigJ

Many Are Called. Edwin Arlington Robinson. CP-RobiE

Many are the deceivers. Red-Riding Hood. Anne Sexton. CP-SextA

Many are the thoughts that come to me. My Thoughts. Ralph Waldo Emerson. CP-EmerR

Many arrivals make us live: the tree becoming. Manifestation, The. Theodore Roethke. CP-RoetT

Many birds and the beating of wings. Margaret. Carl Sandburg. CP-SandC

Many by valour have deserved renown. Ode 4.9: "Many by valour have deserved renown." Horace. CP-RaleW *Fr.* Odes.

Many can boast a hollyhock. Emily Dickinson. SP-DickE

Many centures ago in China. Autumn Air. Charles Simic. SP-SimiCE

Many claimed him, squabbled over him. After Death. Yannis Ritsos. SP-RitsY, *tr.* by Kimon Friar

Many clocks in many towers. Bells Toll Kindly, The. Langston Hughes. CP-HughL; CP-HughL3

Many Colored Squares. Philip Whalen. SP-WhalP

Many compacted summers. Sounds of a Devon Village. Donald Davie. CP-DaviDC

Many cross the Rhine. Emily Dickinson. CP-DickE

Many desire, but few or none deserve. Advice, The. Sir Walter Ralegh. CP-RaleW

Many Famous Feet Have Trod. Philip Larkin. CP-LarkP

Many gathered many friends maybe everyone. Dream Called "The House of Jews," A. Michael Palmer. SP-PalmM

Many gentlemen there are born not babes. Laura Riding Jackson. CP-RidiL

Many Handles. Carl Sandburg. CP-SandC

Many Happy Returns. W. H. Auden. CP-AudeW

Many Happy Returns. Ted Berrigan. SP-BerrT

Many Hats. Carl Sandburg. CP-SandC

Many have Earth's lovers been. Human Tree, The. G. K. Chesterton. CP-ChesG

Many have sung of love a root of bane. At Last. Christina Georgina Rossetti. CP-RosC2

Many ingenius lovely things are gone. Nineteen Hundred and Nineteen. William

Butler Yeats. CP-YeatW

Many Loves. Allen Ginsberg. CP-GinsA; SP-GinsA

Many-maned scud-thumper, tub. Winter Ocean. John Updike. CP-UpdiJ

Many Mansions. D. H. Lawrence. CP-LawrD

Many Mansions, The. Denise Levertov. SP-LeveDL

Many of Our Waters: Variations on a Poem by a Black Child. James Wright. CP-WrigJ

Many of the English. English, The. Stevie Smith. CP-SmitS

Many of the three hundred and sixty-five days of the year are followed. Good-by, Old Year, You Oaf or Why Don't They Pay the Bonus. Ogden Nash. CP-NashO

Many of us too often now have granted. For a Self-Possessed Friend. Robert Penn Warren. CP-WarrR

Many our needs, yet we spare prayers. Hafiz. CP-EmerR *Fr.* Odes.

Many Pages Must Be Thrown Away. Philip Whalen. SP-WhalP

Many paths in the woods have chos- / en me, many a time. Lost. Hayden Carruth. CP-CarHS

Many people have asked me what was the most beautiful sight I. Pipe Dreams. Ogden Nash. CP-NashO

Many pleasures of Youth have been buoyantly sung. As I Sit in the Silence. James Whitcomb Riley. CP-RileJ

Many poems may be composed upon the same theme. Praising the Poets of That Country. Howard Nemerov. CP-NemeH

Many prophets have failed, their voices silent. Ode to Failure. Allen Ginsberg. CP-GinsA

Many red devils ran from my heart. Stephen Crane. CP-CranS

Many roses in the wind. Love Storm. D. H. Lawrence. CP-LawrD

Many seek and never see. Eye Altering Alters All, The. Allen Ginsberg. CP-GinsA

Many sow, but only the chosen reap, The. Lines to My Father. Countee Cullen. CP-CullC

Many talents, oh hers was greatest, The. Her Talents . . . Of. Kenneth Patchen. CP-PatcK

Many tedious hours. M. Philip Whalen. SP-WhalP

Many the wonders I this day have seen. To My Brother George. John Keats. CP-KeatJ

Many Things Are Hidden by the Light. William Stafford. SP-StafWW

Many things I might have said today. Aprons of Silence. Carl Sandburg. CP-SandC

Many things in the world have. In the White Sky. William Stafford. SP-StafW

Many things to absorb I teach to help you become eleve of mine. To a Western Boy. Walt Whitman. CP-WhitW

Many times a last time I will look. Harmless Streets. Tess Gallagher. SP-GallT

Many times loneliness. Dogs. W. S. Merwin. SP-MerwW

Many trees can stand unshaded. Trees and Cattle. James Dickey. CP-DickJ

Many-volumned authoresses. Agatha Christie and Beatrix Potter. John Updike. CP-UpdiJ

Many Wagons Ago. John Ashbery. SP-AshbJ

Many waters cannot quench love. Old Saying, An. Algernon Charles Swinburne. SP-SwinA

Many ways to spell good night. Good Night. Carl Sandburg. CP-SandC

Many we are, and yet but few possesse. Few Fortunate. Robert Herrick. CP-HerrR

Many Wines, The. Jelaluddin Rumi. SP-Rumi, *tr.* by Coleman Barks

Many workmen / Built a huge ball of masonry. Stephen Crane. CP-CranS

Many years ago in China. Autumn Air. Charles Simic. SP-SimiC

Many years, and one still harder. Eugenio Montale. CP-MontE, *tr.* by Jonathan Galassi

Many years have I still to burn, detained. At a Loose End. D. H. Lawrence. CP-LawrD

Manyone Flying. May Swenson. SP-SwenM

Manzanita. Gary Snyder. CP-SnydG

Map, The. Elizabeth Bishop. CP-BishE

Map of Europe, A. Derek Walcott. CP-WalcD

Map of places passes, The. Laura Riding Jackson. CP-RidiL

Map of the City, A. Thom Gunn. CP-GunnT

Map of the New World. Derek Walcott. CP-WalcD

Map of the Western Part of the County of Essex in England, A. Denise Levertov. SP-LeveDP; SP-LeveDS

Maple. Robert Frost. CP-FrosR

"Maple leaf forever" / "in 1867—," The. Canada. Robert Creeley. CP-CreeR

Maple leaves are brilliant, The. Red Maple Leaves. Kenneth Rexroth. CP-RexrK

Maple on the Hill. Charles Wright. SP-WrigCN

Maple strews the embers of its leaves, The. Lullaby: "Maple strews the embers of its leaves, The." James Whitcomb Riley. CP-RileJ

Maple Syrup. Donald Hall. CP-HallD

Maples in a Spruce Forest. John Updike. CP-UpdiJ

Mapmaker on His Art, The. Howard Nemerov. CP-NemeH

Mara. Robinson Jeffers. CP-JefR3

Marat Dead. Charles Tomlinson. CP-TomlC

Marathon. Louise Glück. SP-GlucL
   Song of Invisible Boundaries. SP-GlucL

"Marat's Death." Donald Hall. CP-HallD

Marble-Streeted Town, The. Thomas Hardy. CP-HardT

Marble stumps, the plundered archeology of games, The. Olympia. Amy
   Clampitt. CP-ClamA

Marble Tablet, The. Thomas Hardy. CP-HardT

Marble, weep[e], for thou dost cover. On Margaret Ratcliffe [or Radcliffe]. Ben
   Jonson. CP-JonsB; SP-JonsB

Marble-white close-up of the past-cum-future hybrid, A. Centaurs 3. Joseph
   Brodsky. CP-BrodJ

March. Jane Cooper. CP-CoopJ

March. Hart Crane. CP-CranH

March. Donald Davie. CP-DaviDC

March. Ivor Gurney. SP-GurnI

March. A. E. Housman. CP-HousA

March. Archibald MacLeish. CP-MacLA

March. Lorine Niedecker. CP-NiedL

March. Wyatt Prunty. SP-PrunW

March. Edmund Spenser. CP-Spens Fr. Shepheardes [or Shepeards or
   Shepherd's] Calender, The.

March. Richard Wilbur. CP WilbR

March. William Carlos Williams. CP-WilW1

March. James Wright. CP-WrigJ

March, A. Denise Levertov. SP-LeveDP

March, The. Li Po. CP-WilW2, tr. by David Rafael Wang and William Carlos
   Williams

March 1, The. Robert Lowell. SP-LoweR

March 2, The. Robert Lowell. SP-LoweR

March: A Birthday Poem. John Updike. CP-UpdiJ

March Calf, A. Ted Hughes. SP-HughTN

March 4th. Anne Sexton. CP-SextA

March / goes flying by. Proverb: "March / goes flying by." Federico García
   Lorca. CP-GarcF, tr. by Alan S. Trueblood Fr. Theories.

March has come to the bridge head. Poem by the Bridge at Ten-shin. Li Po. SP-
   PounE, tr. by Ezra Pound

March Here. James Schuyler. CP-SchuJ

March in the Ranks Hard-Prest, and the Road Unknown, A. Walt Whitman. CP-
   WhitW

March interrupted the light afternoon, The. March Past, The. Philip Larkin. CP-
   LarkP

March into Russia, The. Raymond Carver. CP-CarvR

March into Virginia, The. Herman Melville. SP-MelvH

March Is a Light. William Carlos Williams. CP-WilW1

March is the Month of Expectation. Emily Dickinson. CP-DickE

March is the month of slow fire. Easter 1989. Charles Wright. SP-WrigCN

March Journal. Charles Wright. SP-WrigC

March-Mad. May Sarton. SP-SartM

March Moon. Langston Hughes. CP-HughL; CP-HughL1

March Morning. John Ciardi. CP-CiarJ

March, 1937. Laura Riding Jackson. CP-RidiL

March of the Hungry Mountains. Carl Sandburg. CP-SandC

March Past, The. Philip Larkin. CP-LarkP

March 7th. Anne Sexton. CP-SextA

March Snow. Wendell Berry. CP-BerrW

March . . . Someone has walked across the snow. Vacancy in the Park. Wallace
   Stevens. CP-StevW; CP-StevWP

March Song. A. R. Ammons. CP-AmmoA

March, the fierce! like a wind of garters. Poem in January. Frank O'Hara. SP-
   OharF

March! The mud is cakin' good about our trousies. "Birds of Prey" March.
   Rudyard Kipling. CP-KiplR

March. The Museum. Buffalo. De Chirico. John Logan. CP-LogaJ

March to the Sea, The. Herman Melville. SP-MelvH

March 22, 1968. Wendell Berry. CP-BerrW

March Twilight. Louise Bogan. CP-BogaL

March wind on the ocean turns everything solemn. Heavy Surf, A. Pablo
   Neruda. SP-NeruP

Marché aux Oiseaux. Richard Wilbur. CP-WilbR

Märchen, The. Randall Jarrell. CP-JarrR

Märchenbilder. John Ashbery. SP-AshbJ

Marching. Charles Simic. SP-SimiC; SP-SimiCE

Marching, a dream of wind in our chests. Curse of the Earth Magician on a
   Metal Land. Marge Piercy. SP-PierM

Marching through a Novel. John Updike. CP-UpdiJ

Marching through Georgia to bed, he stopped, listened. Child's Christmas in
   Georgia, A. Wyatt Prunty. SP-PrunW

Marchioness of Brinvilliers, The. Herman Melville. SP-MelvH

Marcus Cato 95–42 B.C. Robert Lowell. SP-LoweR

Marcus Cato 234–149 B.C. Robert Lowell. SP-LoweR

Mare Alix breaks the world's trotting record in one day. I see her heels, The.
   Alix. Carl Sandburg. CP-SandC

Mare Rubrum. Paul Laurence Dunbar. CP-DunbP

Marenghi. Percy Bysshe Shelley. CP-ShelP

Marengo. Mary Oliver. SP-OlivM

Mare's Nest, The. Rudyard Kipling. CP-KiplR

Mares of the Camargue, The. Frédéric Mistral. CP-MerG1, tr. by George
   Meredith Fr. Mirèio.

Mare's skeleton in the clearing: another sign of life, The. Adrienne Rich. SP-
   RicA2 Fr. Shooting Script.

Marfa. James Tate. SP-TateJ

Marga Barr. William Corbett. SP-CorbW

Margaret. Carl Sandburg. CP-SandC

Márgarét, áre you gríeving. Spring and Fall. Gerard Manley Hopkins. CP-
   HopkG

Margaret Clitheroe. Gerard Manley Hopkins. CP-HopkG

Margaret Fuller. Lorine Niedecker. CP-NiedL

Margaret Fuller Drowned. Robert Lowell. SP-LoweR

Margaret Fuller, 1847. Amy Clampitt. CP-ClamA

Margaret has a milking-pail, / And she rises early. Christina Georgina Rossetti.
   CP-RosC2

Margaret's Bridal-Eve. George Meredith. CP-MerG1

Margaret's Speech. Norman Dubie. CP-DubiN

Margate. Amy Clampitt. CP-ClamA

Marge. Hayden Carruth. CP-CarHS

Margery. Christina Georgina Rossetti. CP-RosC3

Marginal Employment. Amy Clampitt. CP-ClamA

Marginalia. W. H. Auden. CP AudeW

Marginalia. Billy Collins. SP-CollB

Marginalia. Richard Wilbur. CP-WilbR

Margins of Choice. Josephine Jacobsen. CP-JacoJ

Margo. Raymond Carver. CP-CarvR

Margrave. Robinson Jeffers. CP-JefR2

Margrave's Birthnight, The. Herman Melville. SP-MelvH

Marguerite. John Greenleaf Whittier. CP-WhitJ

Marguerite-chain all color not royal-or-blue. Chrysanthemum. Louis Zukofsky.
   CP-ZukLS

Mari Magno. Arthur Hugh Clough.
   Clergyman's Second Tale, The. SP-ClouA
   Currente Calamo. SP-ClouA

Mari Magno I. Arthur Hugh Clough. SP-ClouA

Mari Magno II. Arthur Hugh Clough. See Songs in Absence

Maria, could Horace have guess'd. To Mrs. Throckmorton. William Cowper.
   CP-CowpW

María del Reposo, / again I encounter. Encounter ("María del Reposo, / again I
   encounter"). Federico García Lorca. CP-GarcF, tr. by Jerome Rothenberg
   Fr. Garden in Umber; or The Garden of the Brownhaired Girls.

Maria Holt / Was not the dolt. Bereavement. Stevie Smith. CP-SmitS

Maria! I have ev'ry good. Poet's New-Year's Gift, The. William Cowper. CP-
   CowpW

Maria Speaks. Robert Creeley. SP-CreeR

Maria Wentworth. Thomas Carew. CP-CareT

Marian: "Clouds fly fast across the moon, The." George Meredith. CP-MerG2

Marian: "She can be as wise as we." George Meredith. CP-MerG1

Mariana. Christina Georgina Rossetti. CP-RosC2

Mariana. Alfred Tennyson. CP-TennA

Mariana in the South. Alfred Tennyson. CP-TennA

Marianne Moore. E. E. Cummings. CP-CummE

Marianne Moore. William Carlos Williams. CP-WilW1

Marianne, My Mother, and Me. Maxine W. Kumin. SP-KumiM

Marianne's Dream. Percy Bysshe Shelley. CP-ShelP

Maria's Gift. Michael Palmer. SP-PalmM

Marica Lart. W. S. Merwin. SP-MerwW

Marie's irises / what with the furnace. William Corbett. SP-CorbW

Marigold. Louis Zukofsky. CP-ZukLS

Marijuana Notation. Allen Ginsberg. CP-GinsA; SP-GinsA

Marilyn Marilyn. Dorothy Parker. CP-ParkD

Marin-An. Gary Snyder. CP-SnydG

Marin! je te connais, rentier du cinquième. Tristan Corbière. T. S. Eliot. SP-
   ElioT

Marina. T. S. Eliot. CP-ElioT

Marina: here are shells and pebbles. To Marina Zwetajewa-Efron. Rainer Maria

Rilke. CP-RilkFr, *tr. by* A. Poulin, Jr.

Marine. Yannis Ritsos. SP-RitsY, *tr. by* Kostas Myrsiades

Marine. Charles Tomlinson. CP-TomlC

Marine Surface, Low Overcast. Amy Clampitt. CP-ClamA

Mariner, The. G. K. Chesterton. CP-ChesG

Mariner unpracticed. Unsounded. Adrienne Rich. CP-RicAE

Marino Faliero, Doge of Venice. Lord Byron. CP-Byron

Marion, why that pensive brow? To Marion. Lord Byron. CP-Byron

Marionettes, The. Walter De la Mare. CP-DeLaW

Mariposa. Edna St. Vincent Millay. CP-MillE

Maritime Ode. Fernando Pessoa. SP-PessF, *tr. by* Susan M. Brown *and* Edwin Honig

Mark. James Schuyler. CP-SchuJ

Mark, The. A. R. Ammons. CP-AmmoA

Mark, The. Louise Bogan. CP-BogaL

Mark 4; Why Are Yee Afraid, O Yee of Little Faith? Bible, *N.T.* CP-CrasR *Fr.* St. Mark.

Mark 7; The Dumbe Healed, and the People Enjoyned Silence. Bible, *N.T.* CP-CrasR *Fr.* St. Mark.

Mark 10; The Blind Cured by the Word of Our Saviour. Bible, *N.T.* CP-CrasR *Fr.* St. Mark.

Mark 12; (Give to Cæsar———) (And to God———). Bible, *N.T.* CP-CrasR *Fr.* St. Mark.

Mark by what wretched steps Great [Marlborough] grows. Character of Marlborough, A. Alexander Pope. CP-PopeA *Fr.* Essay on Man, An.

Mark. Hair, one strand of it, can curl. Judas. James Dickey. CP-DickJ

Mark how the bashful morn in vain. Boldness[e] in Love. Thomas Carew. CP-CareT

Mark how the feathered tenants of the flood. Water Fowl. William Wordsworth. CP-WorW1

Mark how this polished [*or* polish'd] Eastern sheet. Fancy, A. Thomas Carew. CP-CareT

Mark, how yond eddy steals away. To My Mistress Sitting by a River's Side; an Eddy. Thomas Carew. CP-CareT

Mark mar ha forest 1 a boundary manic a land a. Secret History of the Dividing Line. Susan Howe. SP-HoweSE

Mark the concentrated hazels that enclose. William Wordsworth. CP-WorW1

Mark the man I am with. Contact, The. Raymond Carver. CP-CarvR

Mark them with signs. Remember the clothes. Yehuda Amichai. SP-AmicYL, *tr. by* Benjamin Harshav *and* Barbara Harshav

Mark this holy chapel well! Tell's Birth-Place. Samuel Taylor Coleridge. CP-ColeS

Mark Twain Centenary. Gertrude Stein. CP-SteiG

Mark Twain's opinion was, he was entitled. Authors' Residences. John Updike. CP-UpdiJ

Mark Van Doren and the Brook. Archibald MacLeish. CP-MacLA

Mark yonder pomp of costly fashion. Song: "Mark yonder pomp of costly fashion." Robert Burns. CP-BurnR

Mark you how the peacock's eye. Peacock's Eye, The. Gerard Manley Hopkins. CP-HopkG

Mark you the floor[e]? that square and speckled stone. Church-Floor[e], The. George Herbert. CP-HerbG

Mark[e] but this flea, and mark[e] in this. Flea, The. John Donne. CP-DonnJ; MW-DonnJ

Markes that did limit *Lands* in former times. Of This Ensuing Discourse. Thomas Campion. CP-CampT

Market, The. Shmuel HaNagid. SP-HaNaS, *tr. by* Peter Cole

Market at Turk. Thom Gunn. CP-GunnT

Market Discounts Love. James Laughlin. CP-LaugJ

Market Economy, The. Marge Piercy. SP-PierM

Market-Place, The. Walter De la Mare. CP-DeLaW

Market-Place, The. Howard Nemerov. CP-NemeH

Markings. Seamus Heaney. SP-HeanSO

Marks and numbers / Cut in skin. Thomas Merton. CP-MertT

Mark's Sheep. Archibald MacLeish. CP-MacLA

Mark's sheep, I said, but they were only. Mark's Sheep. Archibald MacLeish. CP-MacLA

Marl Pits, The. Charles Tomlinson. CP-TomlC; SP-TomlC

Marl white road, the Dorée rushing cool, The. Tales of the Islands. Derek Walcott. CP-WalcD

Marlene Dietrich is singing a lament. Blue Angel, The. Allen Ginsberg. CP-GinsA

Marlowe. Robert Lowell. SP-LoweR

Marmion. Sir Walter Scott.

  Battle, The ("Not far advanc'd was morning day"). SP-ScotW

  (Douglas and Marmion.) SP-ScotW

  Death of Marmion, The. SP-ScotW

  Edinburgh from the Pentland Hills. SP-ScotW

  (Edinburgh From Blackford Hill.) SP-ScotW

  English Advance at Flodden, The. SP-ScotW

  Fitz-Eustace's Song. SP-ScotW

  Lochinvar. SP-ScotW

  Lords Strand of Northumberland, The. SP-ScotW

  Norham Castle. SP-ScotW

  Saint of Holy Island, The. SP-ScotW

Marni, do you remember. Homefires. William Corbett. SP-CorbW

Marni's Birthday. William Corbett. SP-CorbW

Maroon with Silver Frost. Carl Sandburg. CP-SandC

Marooned by night in a canvas cathedral under bare bulbs. Flower Show. Louis MacNeice. CP-MacNL

Marostica, Val di Ser. Bassano del Grappa. Self-Portrait. Charles Wright. SP-WrigC

Marpessa's Selection. Yannis Ritsos. SP-RitsY, *tr. by* N. C. Germanacos

Marquis de Sade / Wasn't always mad, The. Literary Scene, The. Ogden Nash. CP-NashO

Marquita had blossom fists. Portrait of a Child Settling Down for an Afternoon Nap. Carl Sandburg. CP-SandC

Marrakech. Richard Eberhart. CP-EberR

Marrèd Drives of Windsor, The. Rudyard Kipling. CP-KiplR *Fr.* Muse among the Motors, The.

Marriage. Wendell Berry. CP-BerrW

Marriage. William Blake. CP-BlakW

Marriage. Raymond Carver. CP-CarvR

Marriage. Marianne Craig Moore. CP-MoorM

Marriage. William Carlos Williams. CP-WilW1

Marriage, A. Robert Creeley. CP-CreeR

Marriage, The. Denise Levertov. SP-LeveDS

Marriage 2, The. Denise Levertov. SP-LeveDS

Marriage aged one, A. Anniversary, The. Ogden Nash. CP-NashO

Marriage, an Elegy, A. Wendell Berry. CP-BerrW

Marriage Counsel. John Updike. CP-UpdiJ

Marriage in the 'Sixties, A. Adrienne Rich. CP-RicAE; SP-RicA1; SP-RicA2

Marriage is not / a house or even a tent. Habitation. Margaret Atwood. SP-AtwM1

Marriage of Heaven and Earth, The. Howard Nemerov. CP-NemeH (Firelight in Sunlight.) CP-NemeH

Marriage of Heaven and Hell, The. William Blake. CP-BlakW

Marriage of Insult to Injury, The. Andrei Codrescu. SP-CodrA

Marriage of Psyche, The. Kathleen Jessie Raine. SP-RainK

Marriage of Psyche and Cupid. Elizabeth Barrett Browning. CP-BroEB

Marriage of St Katharine, by the same, A; in the Hospital of St John at Bruges. Dante Gabriel Rossetti. CW-RossD

Marriage of Souls, The. William Carlos Williams. CP-WilW2

Marriage of Strongbow and Aoife, The. Paul Muldoon. CP-MuldP

Marriage Portion, The. Adrienne Rich. CP-RicAE

Marriage Ritual, A. William Carlos Williams. CP-WilW1

Marriage Song: "We begin with the osprey who cries, 'Clang, clang!'" Carolyn Kizer. CP-KizeC

Marriage Song, A. G. K. Chesterton. CP-ChesG

Marriage Song for Florence and Harry, A. Louis Zukofsky. CP-ZukLS

Marriage Vow. Federico García Lorca. CP-GarcF, *tr. by* Alan S. Trueblood *Fr.* Back of the World.

Marriage, with Beasts. Mona Van Duyn. SP-VanDM

Marriages. Philip Larkin. CP-LarkP

Married in June. D. H. Lawrence. CP-LawrD

Married Man, The. Rudyard Kipling. CP-KiplR

Married Walk in a Hot Place, A. Marge Piercy. SP-PierM

Married Woman, A. Thomas Carew. CP-CareT

Marrow, The. Theodore Roethke. CP-RoetT

Marrow unvisited, / And then, visited. Marry the Marrow. Charles Olson. CP-OlsoC

Marrucinus Asinius, that sinister. Catullus. *See* While everyone else is laughing & drinking

Marry, and love thy Flavia, for, she. Anagram, The. John Donne. MW-DonnJ *Fr.* Elegies.

Marry Nettie. Gertrude Stein. CP-SteiG

Marry. Sweets, tarts and sweets. General Prothalamion for Wartimes. Alan Dugan. CP-DugaA

Marry the Marrow. Charles Olson. CP-OlsoC

Marrying left your maiden name disused. Maiden Name. Philip Larkin. CP-LarkP

Marrying the Hangman. Margaret Atwood. SP-AtwM2

Mars. Howard Nemerov. CP-NemeH

Mars is braw in crammasy. Bonnie Broukit Bairn, The. Hugh MacDiarmid. SP-MacDH

Marsh flat where they graze, The. Buffalo in Compound: Alberta. Margaret Atwood. SP-AtwM1

Marsh, Hawk. Margaret Atwood. SP-AtwM2

Marsh hummocks that were a sabbath hill. Sea Marshes in Winter. John Ciardi. CP-CiarJ

Marshal the quaint barren fogbeats in harbors. Prayer Not to Go to Paradise with the Asses. Kenneth Patchen. CP-PatcK

Marshall Washer. Hayden Carruth. CP-CarHS

Marshalling of the Achaians. Homer. CP-MerG1 *Fr.* Iliad, The.

Marston. Stephen Spender. CP-SpenS

Marsyas. James Merrill. SP-MerrJ

Marta (Brazil, 1928). Denise Levertov. SP-LeveDL

Marten. John Clare. SP-ClarJ

Marten cat, long-shagged, of courage good, The. Marten. John Clare. SP-ClarJ

Martha. Walter De la Mare. CP-DeLaW

Martha. Audre Lorde. SP-LordA

Martha as the Angel Gabriel. Marge Piercy. SP-PierM

Martha Graham. James Laughlin. CP-LaugJ

Martha, Martha. Robert Herrick. CP-HerrR

Martha this is a catalog of days. Martha. Audre Lorde. SP-LordA

Martha's Vineyard. Ogden Nash. CP-NashO

Marthy Ellen. James Whitcomb Riley. CP-RileJ

Martial Cadenza. Wallace Stevens. CP-StevW; CP-StevWP

Martial Choreograph. Maya Angelou. SP-AngeM

Martial courage of a day is vain, The. William Wordsworth. CP-WorW1

Martial. Epigram XLVII, Book X. Ben Jonson. CP JonsB

Martial Law Carol, A. Joseph Brodsky. CP-BrodJ

Martial, Lib. I. Epig. I. Lord Byron. CP-Byron

Martial, thou gav'st far[re] nobler epigrams [*or* epigrammes]. To the Ghost of Martial. Ben Jonson. CP-JonsB; SP-JonsB

Martial—12, 52. Kenneth Rexroth. CP-RexrK

Martin and Katherine. William Carlos Williams. CP-WilW1

Martin Luther King, Malcolm X. Muriel Rukeyser. CP-RukeM

Martin Relph. Robert Browning. CP-BroR2

Martin said "every sane man" would hesitate to believe what we were now about to see. Martin's Predicament or Atlas Watches Every Evening. Thomas Merton. CP-MertT

Martin sat young upon his bed. St. Martin and the Beggar. Thom Gunn. CP-GunnT

Martini-time: time to draw the curtains and. Garrison, The. W. H. Auden. CP-AudeW

Martin's Predicament or Atlas Watches Every Evening. Thomas Merton. CP-MertT

Martin's Puzzle. George Meredith. CP-MerG1

Martins: September. Walter De la Mare. CP-DeLaW

Martyr, A. Charles Baudelaire. CP-BaudC, *tr. by* Walter Martin

Martyr, A. Christina Georgina Rossetti. CP-RosC2

Martyr, A. Christina Georgina Rossetti. CP-RosC3

Martyr à la Mode. D. H. Lawrence. CP-LawrD

Martyr, The. Herman Melville. SP-MelvH

Martyr, The. Christina Georgina Rossetti. CP-RosC3

Martyr Poets—did not tell, The. Emily Dickinson. CP-DickE

Martyrdom of Bishop Farrar, The. Ted Hughes. SP-HughTN

Martyrdom of St. Eulalia. Federico García Lorca. CP-GarcF, *tr. by* Will Kirkland

Martyrdom of Saint Eulalia, The. Federico García Lorca. SP-GarcF, *tr. by* A. L. Lloyd

Martyrs' Song. Christina Georgina Rossetti. CP-RosC1

Marvel No More. Sir Thomas Wyatt. CP-WyatT

Marvel of Marvels. Christina Georgina Rossetti. CP-RosC2

Marvel of our age, the Telephone!, The. Telephone, The. Jones Very. CP-VeryJ

Marvel [*or* Marvaill] no more although [*or* all tho]. Marvel No More. Sir Thomas Wyatt. CP-WyatT

Marvelous children, The. In Jack-o'-Lantern's Weather. Tennessee Williams. CP-WillT

Marvin McCabe. Hayden Carruth. CP-CarHS

Marvoil. Ezra Pound. CP-PoEar

Marxist Analysis of the Fifth Labor of Hercules. Alan Dugan. CP-DugaA

Mary. William Blake. CP-BlakW

Mary. George Oppen. CP-OppGN

Mary and I were having an emotion. Donne Ch'avete Intellètto d'Amore. John Ciardi. CP-CiarJ

Mary and the Seasons. Kenneth Rexroth. CP-RexrK

Mary Bly. James Wright. CP-WrigJ

Mary Coldwell. Jane Cooper. CP-CoopJ

Mary Desti's Ass. Frank O'Hara. SP-OharF

Mary Farl Powers: *Pink Spotted Torso.* Paul Muldoon. CP-MuldP

Mary Garvin. John Greenleaf Whittier. CP-WhitJ

Mary Gloster, The. Rudyard Kipling. CP-KiplR

Mary green / cheerful & generous. E. E. Cummings. CP-CummE

Mary Gulliver to Capt. Lemuel Gulliver. John Gay *and* Alexander Pope. CP-PopeA

Mary has a thingamajig clamped on her ears. Manual System. Carl Sandburg. CP-SandC

Mary, I call them pigs, not Picts, those Scots. Twenty Sonnets to Mary Queen of Scots. Joseph Brodsky. CP-BrodJ, *tr. by* Peter France

Mary! I want a lyre with other strings. To Mary Unwin. William Cowper. CP-CowpW

Mary in the noisy seascape. Inlet. George Oppen. CP-OppGN

Mary is an old woman without shoes. My Dream about the Second Coming. Lucille Clifton. SP-ClifL

Mary Jane, she's after me. Black Hoyden. Donald Davie. CP-DaviDC

Mary June's brother Willard always had. Style. William Stafford. SP-StafWW

Mary Magdalen and I. Czeslaw Milosz. CP-MiloC; CP-MiloCN, *tr. by* Robert Hass

Mary Magdalene and the Other Mary. Christina Georgina Rossetti. CP-RosC2

Mary Magdalene at the Door of Simon the Pharisee. Dante Gabriel Rossetti. CW-RossD

Mary Magdalene lives over the grocery store. Gospel Hour. Charles Simic. SP-SimiCE

Mary McDonald. Allen Tate. CP-TateA

Mary mine that art Mary's Rose. Rose Mary. Dante Gabriel Rossetti. CW-RossD

Mary Morison. Robert Burns. CP-BurnR

Mary of Holyrood may smile indeed. Namesake. G. K. Chesterton. CP-ChesG

Mary on the Death of Joachim. Robert Stock. SP-StocR

Mary [*or* Marie] Magdalene. George Herbert. CP-HerbG

Mary, Pity Women! Rudyard Kipling. CP-KiplR

Mary sat musing on the lamp-flame at the table. Death of the Hired Man, The. Robert Frost. CP-FrosR

Mary Sheffield. James Dickey. CP-DickJ

Mary Sleeth. Muriel Rukeyser. CP-RukeM

Mary Stuart. Robert Lowell. SP-LoweR

Mary the Cook-Maid's Letter to Dr. Sheridan. Jonathan Swift. CP-SwifJ

Mary Winslow. Robert Lowell. SP-LoweR

Mary Wollstonecraft and Fuseli. Robert Browning. CP-BroR2

Mary, your great. Jesus Suckles. Anne Sexton. CP-SextA; SP-SextA

Maryam. Ingeborg Bachmann. CP-KizeC, *tr. by* Carolyn Kizer

Maryland, Virginia, Caroline. Emblems. Allen Tate. CP-TateA

Mary's Fancy. Robert Creeley. CP-CreeR

Mary's Girlhood. Dante Gabriel Rossetti. CW-RossD

Mary's heart's so unprotected. To a Friend. Rainer Maria Rilke. CP-RilkFr, *tr. by* A. Poulin, Jr. *Fr.* Affectionate Taxes to France.

Mary's Son. Rudyard Kipling. CP-KiplR

Mary's Song. Sylvia Plath. CP-PlatS

Mary's Song. Anne Sexton. CP-SextA

Mas-Soñer / Restaurat—Any. House, The ("Mas-Soñer / Restaurat—Any"). Robert Creeley. SP-CreeR

Mascots. Carl Sandburg. CP-SandC

Mask. Carl Sandburg. CP-SandC

Mask. Philip Whalen. SP-WhalP

Mask, A. John Milton. *See* Comus; a Masque Presented at Ludlow Castle

Mask, The. Charles Baudelaire. CP-BaudC, *tr. by* Walter Martin

Mask, The. Elizabeth Barrett Browning. CP-BroEB

Mask, The. Laura Riding Jackson. CP-RidiL

Mask, The. Rainer Maria Rilke. CP-RilkFr, *tr. by* A. Poulin, Jr.

Mask, The. William Butler Yeats. CP-YeatW

Mask, a perpetual natural disguiser of herself, A. Visor'd. Walt Whitman. CP-WhitW

Mask [*or* Masque] of Anarchy, The. Percy Bysshe Shelley. CP-ShelP

Mask of Love. Thomas Kinsella. CP-KinsT

Mask, The. Look how the mask. Dance of Death. Federico García Lorca. CP-GarcF, *tr. by* Greg Simon *and* Steven F. White

Mask thy wisdom with delight. Ralph Waldo Emerson. CP-EmerR

Masked Face, The. Thomas Hardy. CP-HardT

Masks. Ezra Pound. CP-PoEar

Masks offer themselves to us. Rainer Maria Rilke. CP-RilkFr, *tr. by* A. Poulin, Jr.

Mason is dead the gentle drunk, The. Dry Stone Mason, The. W. S. Merwin. SP-MerwW

Masque of Augurs, The. Ben Jonson.
    Ballad: "Though it may seem rude." CP-JonsB
    "Which way and whence the lightning flew." CP-JonsB

Masque of Beauty, The. Ben Jonson.
    "Had those that dwell in error foul." CP-JonsB
    "If all these Cupids now were blind." CP-JonsB

"So beauty on the waters stood." CP-JonsB

"Still turn, and imitate the heaven." CP-JonsB

"When Love at first did move." CP-JonsB

Masque of Blackness, The. Ben Jonson.

"Daughters of the subtle flood." CP-JonsB

"Now Dian, with her burning face." CP-JonsB

"Sound, sound aloud / The welcome of the orient flood." CP-JonsB

Masque of Hymen. Ben Jonson.

"Bid all profane away." CP-JonsB

Epithalamion: "Glad time is at his point arrived." CP-JonsB

"Now, now begin to set." CP-JonsB

"O know to end, as to begin." CP-JonsB

"These, these are they." CP-JonsB

"Think yet how night doth waste." CP-JonsB

Masque of Mercy, A. Robert Frost. CP-FrosR

Masque of Plenty, The. Rudyard Kipling. CP-KiplR

Masque of Queen Bersabe, The. Algernon Charles Swinburne. SP-SwinA

Masque of Queens, The. Ben Jonson.

"Help, help all tongues to celebrate this wonder." CP-JonsB

"Who, Virtue, can thy power forget." CP-JonsB

Witches' Charms, The.

Charm[e]. CP-JonsB

Masque of Reason, A. Robert Frost. CP-FrosR

Masque of the Seasons, A. James Whitcomb Riley. CP-RileJ

Mass creates, The. The systematic mind or Form misunderstands. On Translation. Andrei Codrescu. SP-CodrA

Mass for the Day of St. Thomas Didymus. Denise Levertov. SP-LeveDL; SP-LeveDS

Mass hysteria, wave after breaking wave. Willowware Cup. James Merrill. SP-MerrJ

Mass Man. Derek Walcott. CP-WalcD

Massachusetts. Robert Creeley. CP-CreeR

Massachusetts. John Greenleaf Whittier. CP-WhitJ

Massachusetts to Virginia. John Greenleaf Whittier. CP-WhitJ

Massacre, The. Olga Broumas. SP-BrouO

Massacre, The. Walter De la Mare. CP-DeLaW

Massacre of Perugia, The. Christina Georgina Rossetti. CP-RosC3

Massed in her creaseless black. Fat Woman, The. Walter De la Mare. CP-DeLaW

Masses. Carl Sandburg. CP-SandC

Masses and Classes. D. H. Lawrence. CP-LawrD

Masseuse, The. Olga Broumas. SP-BrouO

Massive engines lift beautifully from the deck. Teeth Mother Naked at Last, The. Robert Bly. SP-BlyR

Massive Retaliation. John Ciardi. CP-CiarJ

Massive with gems, he bends aside. Mithridates 5. Robert Stock. SP-StocR

Massy Ways Carried across These Heights, The. William Wordsworth. CP-WorW2

Mast, The. Charles Olson. CP-OlsoC

Mast / Inaudibly soars; bole-like, tapering, The. George Oppen. CP-OppGN

Mastah drink his ol' Made'a. Preference, A. Paul Laurence Dunbar. CP-DunbP

Master, The. "H. D." CP-DoolH

Master, The. Seamus Heaney. SP-HeanSO Fr. Sweeney Redivivus.

Master, The. Czeslaw Milosz. CP-MiloC; CP-MiloCN

Master, The. Edwin Arlington Robinson. CP-RobiE

Master & Man. Donald Davie. CP-DaviDC

Master and Mistress. Stanley Kunitz. CP-KunSC

Master and the Leaves, The. Thomas Hardy. CP-HardT

Master and the slave go hand in hand, The. Sonnet: "Master and the slave go hand in hand, The." Edwin Arlington Robinson. CP-RobiE

Master at a Mediterranean Port, The. Howard Nemerov. CP-NemeH

Master-Cook, The. Rudyard Kipling. CP-KiplR Fr. Land and Sea Tales.

Master, Grieved with Age, The. Hayden Carruth. CP-CarHS

Master-hand whose pencils trace, The. Summer Sunrise, A. James Whitcomb Riley. CP-RileJ

Master hasn't been among us long, The. Interview with a Child. Wisława Szymborska. SP-SzymWM, tr. by Joanna Trzeciak

Master Hugues of Saxe-Gotha. Robert Browning. CP-BroR1

Master Is Come, and Calleth for Thee, The. Christina Georgina Rossetti. CP-RosC1

Master Keng Sang Chu, a disciple of Lao Tzu. Keng Sang Chu. Chuang Tzu. CP-MertT

Master Ki had eight sons. Good Fortune. Chuang Tzu. CP-MertT

'Master Love,' my grim instructor assured me. Old Harry. Thomas Kinsella. CP-KinsT

Master Meng said: There was once a fine forest on the Ox Mountain. Ox Mountain Parable, The. Mencius. CP-MertT

Master, my dear master! Fernando Pessoa. SP-PessF, tr. by Susan M. Brown and Edwin Honig

Master of a house (as I have read), A. Good Husband, A. Robert Herrick. CP-HerrR

Master of All. Robert Creeley. CP-CreeR

Master of eloquence and Rome's potent line. Catullus. See Silver-tongued among the sons of Rome

Master of masters in the days of yore. Lord Bacon. James Whitcomb Riley. CP-RileJ

Master of Rime told me, You must learn to lose heart, The. Robert Duncan. SP-DuncR Fr. Structure of Rime, The.

Master of the brush and the sword, A. Han-shan. CP-ColdM, tr. by Red Pine

Master of the Dance, The. Nicholas Vachel Lindsay. CP-LindV

Master of the Golden Glow, The. James Schuyler. CP-SchuJ

Master of the GREEK and ROMAN page, The. Epitaph on Henry Fielding, Esq. Christopher Smart. SP-SmarC

Master of the murmuring courts. Love's Nocturn. Dante Gabriel Rossetti. CW-RossD

Master played the bishop's pawn, The. Atherton's Gambit. Edwin Arlington Robinson. CP-RobiE

Master-Player, The. Paul Laurence Dunbar. CP-DunbP

Master Speed, The. Robert Frost. CP-FrosR

Master Surveyor, you that first began. Expostulation with Inigo Jones, An. Ben Jonson. CP-JonsB; SP-JonsB

Master, this is Thy Servant. He is rising eight / weeks old. His Apologies. Rudyard Kipling. CP-KiplR

Master Tung Kwo asked Chuang. Where Is Tao? Chuang Tzu. CP-MertT

Master Will, so cussed human. Piazza San Marco. Ezra Pound. CP-PoEar

Masterman and Chesterton. G. K. Chesterton. CP-ChesG

Masters, The. Hart Crane. CP-CranH

Masters, The. Paul Laurence Dunbar. CP-DunbP

Masters, the mock orange is blooming in Syracuse without scent, having been bred. Of Distress Being Humiliated by the Classical Chinese Poets. Hayden Carruth. CP-CarHS

Matachines, The. Charles Tomlinson. CP-TomlC

Matador. Richard Eberhart. CP-EberR

Matadors, The. Josephine Jacobsen. CP-JacoJ

Match. Donald Hall. CP-HallD

Match, A. Ted Hughes. SP-HughTN

Match, The. Andrew Marvell. CP-MarvA

Match with the Moon, A. Dante Gabriel Rossetti. CW-RossD

Matches. Adam Zagajewski. SP-ZagaA, tr. by Renata Gorczynski, Benjamin Ivry and C. K. Williams

Matches among other things that were not allowed. Burnt Child, The. W. S. Merwin. SP-MerwWF

Matchstick-Viewed-without-Regard-to-Its-Outer-Surface, A. Kenneth Patchen. CP-PatcK

Mater Jesu mei. Ad Matrem Virginem. Gerard Manley Hopkins. CP-HopkG

Material. Donald Hall. CP-HallD

Maternal Grief. William Wordsworth. CP-WorW1

Math. James Dickey. CP-DickJ

Mathematical Problem, A. Samuel Taylor Coleridge. CP-ColeS

Mathematical Secret, and the Apron, The. Charles Olson. CP-OlsoC

Mathematicians and physics men, The. Robinson Jeffers. CP-JefR3

Mathematics of Chaos, The. James Laughlin. CP-LaugJ

Mather, mother, let me go. Queen and the Young Princess, The. Stevie Smith. CP-SmitS

Mathilde in Normandy. Adrienne Rich. CP-RicAE

Matière de Bretagne. Paul Celan. SP-CelaP, tr. by John Felstiner

Matilda Gathering Flowers. Dante Alighieri. CP-ShelP Fr. Divina Commedia.

Matilda! I have heard a sweet tune played. To Matilda Betham from a Stranger. Samuel Taylor Coleridge. CP-ColeS

Matilde, sleeping / that feverish sleep, a day or a year. Final. Pablo Neruda. SP-NeruP, tr. by Ben Belitt

Matinée. Andrei Codrescu. SP-CodrA

Matinee. John Logan. CP-LogaJ

Matinee that Saturday, A. Adultery. Raymond Carver. CP-CarvR

Matinees. James Merrill. SP-MerrJ

Matins. John Berryman. CP-BerrJ

Matins. John Ciardi. CP-CiarJ

Matins. George Herbert. See Mattens

Matins. Denise Levertov. SP-LeveDP

Matins. James McMichael. SP-McMiJ

Matins [or Mattens], or Morning Prayer. Robert Herrick. CP-HerrR

Matisse at the Modern, Magritte at the Met. Lawrence Ferlinghetti. SP-FerlL

Matoaka. Amy Clampitt. CP-ClamA

Matris pennigerum alites Amorum. De obitu Phil. Sydnaei equitis aurati generosissimi. Thomas Campion. CP-CampT

Matrix of your legs. Sleep. Robert Creeley. CP-CreeR

Matrix (Villa Serbelloni, Lake Como). Amy Clampitt. CP-ClamA

Matron of Jedborough and Her Husband, The. William Wordsworth. CP-WorW1; MW-WorW

Mattens. George Herbert. CP-HerbG

(Matins.) CP-HerbG

Matter for Gratitude. Ambrose Bierce. SP-BierA

Matter for mirth, Cato, & a smile, A. Carmen 56. Catullus. CP-ZukLS *Fr.* Carmina.

Matter is palsy: the land heaving, water. From Heraclitus. Alan Dugan. CP-DugaA

Matter of Locality, A. Paul Laurence Dunbar. CP-DunbP

Matter Over, The. Heather McHugh.

Matter, The. C. K. Williams. CP-WillC

Matthew. Clarence Major. SP-MajoC

Matthew. William Wordsworth. CP-WorW1; MW-WorW

Matthew 8; I Am Not Worthy that Thou Should'st Come Under my Roofe. Bible, *N.T.* CP-CrasR *Fr.* St. Matthew.

Matthew 16:25; Whosoever Shall Loose His Life. Bible, *N.T.* CP-CrasR *Fr.* St. Matthew.

Matthew 22; Neither Durst Any Man from that Day Aske Him Any More Questions. Bible, *N.T.* CP-CrasR *Fr.* St. Matthew.

Matthew 23; Yee Build the Sepulchres of the Prophets. Bible, *N.T.* CP-CrasR *Fr.* St. Matthew.

Matthew 25:30. Jorge Luis Borges. SP-BorgJ, *tr. by* Alastair Reid

Matthew 27; And He Answered Them Nothing. Bible, *N.T.* CP-CrasR *Fr.* St. Matthew.

Matthew 28; Come See the Place where the Lord Lay. Bible, *N.T.* CP-CrasR *Fr.* St. Matthew.

Matthew and Mark and Luke and holy John. Epi-strauss-ium. Arthur Hugh Clough. SP-ClouA

Matthew VIII, 28 ff. Richard Wilbur. CP-WilbR

Matutinal. Mother-of-Pearl. Pillowed Head, A. Seamus Heaney. SP-HeanSO

Maturity. Allen Ginsberg. SP-GinsA

Maturity. Philip Larkin. CP-LarkP

Maturity. Yannis Ritsos. SP-RitsY, *tr. by* Gwendolyn MacEwen *and* Nikos Tsingos

Maturity only enhances mystery. Emily Dickinson. SP-DickE

Mauchline Wedding, The. Robert Burns. CP-BurnR

Maud [A Monodrama]. Alfred Tennyson. CP-TennA

Maud Miller worked at making hay. That Other Maud Miller. James Whitcomb Riley. CP-RileJ

Maud Muller. John Greenleaf Whittier. CP-WhitJ

Maude Clare. Christina Georgina Rossetti. CP-RosC1

Maude, the brightest of the sex. Moral Tales for the Young ("Maude, the brightest of the sex"). Dorothy Parker. CP-ParkD

Maudgalyâyana Saw Hell. Gary Snyder. CP-SnydG *Fr.* Myths and Texts.

Maudit. George Oppen. CP-OppGN

Maudlin. Sylvia Plath. CP-PlatS

Maundy Thursday. Wilfred Owen. CP-OwenW

Maundy Thursday. Christina Georgina Rossetti. CP-RosC2

Maundy Thursday's Candles. Donald Hall. CP-HallD

Maureen in England, Joseph in Guelph. Wishbone, The. Paul Muldoon. CP-MuldP

Mausoleum, The. Charles Tomlinson. CP-TomlC

Mauve into purple, bent on foam-green stems. For Jean Migrenne. Marilyn Hacker. SP-HackM

Max an' Jim. Max and Jim. James Whitcomb Riley. CP-RileJ

Max and Jim. James Whitcomb Riley. CP-RileJ

Max Schling, Max Schling, Lend Me Your Green Thumb. Ogden Nash. CP-NashO

Maxima Dona Ferens. James Laughlin. CP-LaugJ

Maximian, Elegy 5. Kenneth Rexroth. CP-RexrK

Maximilian Esterhazy. Stevie Smith. CP-SmitS

Maximum surge would place you. Seine Split. Clarence Major. SP-MajoC

Maximus. D. H. Lawrence. CP-LawrD

Maximus, at the Harbor. Charles Olson. SP-OlsoC *Fr.* Maximus Poems, The.

Maximus, from Dogtown-1. Charles Olson. SP-OlsoC *Fr.* Maximus Poems, The.

Maximus, in Gloucester Sunday, LXV. Charles Olson. SP-OlsoC *Fr.* Maximus Poems, The.

Maximus Letter # Whatever. Charles Olson. SP-OlsoC *Fr.* Maximus Poems, The.

Maximus of Gloucester. Charles Olson. SP-OlsoC *Fr.* Maximus Poems, The.

Maximus Poems, The. Charles Olson.

   "Added to / making a Republic." SP-OlsoC

   "And now let all the ships come in." SP-OlsoC

   April Today Main Street. SP-OlsoC

   "At the boundary of the mighty world" H. (T) 620 foll." SP-OlsoC

   "Blow is Creation, / & the Twist the Nasturtium, The." SP-OlsoC

   "Boats' lights in the dawn going so swiftly the, The." SP-OlsoC

   "Bottled up for days, mostly." SP-OlsoC

   Celestial Evening, October 1967. SP-OlsoC

   Chronicles. SP-OlsoC

   Cole's Island. SP-OlsoC

   Got Me Home, the Light Snow Gives the Air, Falling. SP-OlsoC

   Gulf of Maine, The. SP-OlsoC

   "Having descried the nation." SP-OlsoC

   Hotel Steinplatz, Berlin, December 25 (1966). SP-OlsoC

   "Hour of evening—supper hour, for my neighbors—quietness, The." SP-OlsoC

   "I have been an ability—a machine—up to." SP-OlsoC

   "I live underneath / the light of day." SP-OlsoC

   "I looked up and saw." SP-OlsoC

   "Imbued / with the light." SP-OlsoC

   John Burke. SP-OlsoC

   Later Note on Letter #15, A. SP-OlsoC

   "Main Street / is deserted, the hills." SP-OlsoC

   Maximus, at the Harbor. SP-OlsoC

   Maximus, from Dogtown-1. SP-OlsoC

   Maximus, in Gloucester Sunday, LXV. SP-OlsoC

   Maximus Letter # Whatever. SP-OlsoC

   Maximus of Gloucester. SP-OlsoC

   Maximus, to Gloucester. SP-OlsoC

   Maximus, to Gloucester, Letter 27. SP-OlsoC

     (Maximus to Gloucester, Letter 27 [withheld].) SP-OlsoC

   Maximus, to Himself. SP-OlsoC

   Maximus to Himself June 1964. SP-OlsoC

   "Out of the light of Heaven the flower." SP-OlsoC

   Plantation a Beginning, A. SP-OlsoC

   Some Good News. SP-OlsoC

   Stevens Song. SP-OlsoC

   "Swimming through the air, in schools upon the highways." SP-OlsoC

   Telesphere, The. SP-OlsoC

   Twist, The. SP-OlsoC

   West Gloucester. SP-OlsoC

   "When do poppies bloom I ask myself, stopping again." SP-OlsoC

   "Wholly absorbed / into my own conduits to." SP-OlsoC

Maximus, to Gloucester. Charles Olson. SP-OlsoC *Fr.* Maximus Poems, The.

Maximus, to Gloucester, Letter 27. Charles Olson. SP-OlsoC *Fr.* Maximus Poems, The.

Maximus to Gloucester, Letter 27 [withheld]. Charles Olson. *See* Maximus Poems, The

Maximus, to Himself. Charles Olson. SP-OlsoC *Fr.* Maximus Poems, The.

Maximus to Himself June 1964. Charles Olson. SP-OlsoC *Fr.* Maximus Poems, The.

Maxwell, if merit here you crave. To Dr Maxwell, on Miss Jessy Staig's Recovery. Robert Burns. CP-BurnR

May. Edmund Spenser. CP-Spens *Fr.* Shepheardes [*or* Shepeards *or* Shepherd's] Calender, The.

May. W. H. Auden. CP-AudeW

May. Ralph Waldo Emerson. CP-EmerR

May. Christina Georgina Rossetti. CP-RosC1

May. Christina Georgina Rossetti. CP-RosC3

May 1st Tomorrow. William Carlos Williams. CP-WilW2

May and Death. Robert Browning. CP-BroR1

May be swimming, not drowning. People Who See Bubbles Rise. James Schuyler. CP-SchuJ

May be true what I had heard. Berrying. Ralph Waldo Emerson. CP-EmerR

May circling years with Joy unmix'd return. Lines Impromptu on Miss Morgans Birth Day. Annis Boudinot Stockton. CP-StocA

May come up with bird-din. Nuts in May. Louis MacNeice. CP-MacNL

May-Day. Ralph Waldo Emerson. CP-EmerR

May Day Dancing, The. Howard Nemerov. CP-NemeH

May Day Sermon to the Women of Gilmer County, Georgia, by a Woman Preacher Leaving the Baptist Church. James Dickey. CP-DickJ

May days as white as snow descend. Bridal Wish Adressed to Mr S. Stockton and His Lady the Morning after Their Maraige, The. Annis Boudinot Stockton. CP-StocA

May Days 1988. Allen Ginsberg. SP-GinsA

May drew in its breath and smelled June's roses. Looking Forward to See Jane Real Soon. James Schuyler. CP-SchuJ

May Evening. Richard Eberhart. CP-EberR

May Flower, The. Jones Very. CP-VeryJ

May flowers are opening. Emily Jane Brontë. CP-BronE

May flowers of dirt and. For Lisa. Alan Dugan. CP-DugaA

May God be praised for woman. On Woman. William Butler Yeats. CP-YeatW

May has come, but flowers are rare. First of May, The. Jones Very. CP-VeryJ

May heaven's anger blaze down on your head! Petrarch. CP-Petra, *tr.* by J. G. Nichols

May his eyes go on unblinking. Attempt to Spell, Incantate and Annoy. Andrei Codrescu. SP-CodrA

May his pretty Duke-ship grow. Poets Good Wishes for the Most Hopefull and Handsome Prince, the Duke of Yorke, The. Robert Herrick. CP-HerrR

May I Ask You a Question, Mr. Youngstown Sheet & Tube? Kenneth Patchen. CP-PatcK

May i be gay. E. E. Cummings. CP-CummE

May i feel said he. E. E. Cummings. CP-CummE; SP-CummE

May I for my own self song's truth reckon. Seafarer, The. *Unknown.* CP-PoEar; SP-PounE, *tr.* by Ezra Pound

May I forever a Muse. Vow. John Updike. CP-UpdiJ

May I join you in the doghouse, Rover? Children's Party. Ogden Nash. CP-NashO

May I print, Shelley, how it came to pass. Cenciaja. Robert Browning. CP-BroR2

May I tell you the news of my eyes. Guido Cavalcanti. CP-CavaG, *tr.* by Marc Cirigliano

May I upon thy beauty gaze. Moon & Sun. James Laughlin. CP-LaugJ

May is come again:—how sweet, The. William Wordsworth. *See* Beneath these fruit-tree boughs that shed

May is Mary's month, and I. May Magnificat, The. Gerard Manley Hopkins. CP-HopkG

May it please my lord the king,—there's a Jew at the door. William Rufus and the Jew. Ralph Waldo Emerson. CP-EmerR

May Janet. Algernon Charles Swinburne. SP-SwinA

May Journal. Charles Wright. SP-WrigC

May-June, 1940. Robinson Jeffers. CP-JefR3 (Battle.) CP-JefR3

May Lines. Gerard Manley Hopkins. CP-HopkG

May Magnificat, The. Gerard Manley Hopkins. CP-HopkG

May Morning. Henry David Thoreau. CP-ThorH

May Morning Admonition. Robert Stock. SP-StocR

May Morning: Hudson Pastoral. Marya Alexandrovna Zaturenska. SP-ZatuM

May Mornings, The. Denise Levertov. SP-LeveDL

May mornings wear. May Mornings, The. Denise Levertov. SP-LeveDL

May my heart always be open to little. E. E. Cummings. CP-CummE; SP-CummE

May 1943. "H. D." CP-DoolH

May, 1972. James Schuyler. CP-SchuJ

May none, whose scattered names honour my book. To All, to Whom I Write. Ben Jonson. CP-JonsB; SP-JonsB

May not whole nations, as the single man. Do Nations Ever Become Insane? Jones Very. CP-VeryJ

May others fear, fly, and traduce thy name. To the Learnèd Critic. Ben Jonson. CP-JonsB; SP-JonsB

May Our Right Hands Lose Their Cunning. Denise Levertov. SP-LeveDL

May-Pole, The. Robert Herrick. CP-HerrR

May 16, 1973. Wisława Szymborska. SP-SzymW, *tr.* by Stanislaw Barańczak *and* Clare Cavanagh

May Song. Wendell Berry. CP-BerrW

May Song. George Meredith. CP-MerG2

May sun—whom, The. Tulip Bed, The. William Carlos Williams. CP-WilW1

May 10th. Maxine W. Kumin. SP-KumiM *Fr.* Joppa Diary.

May the smell of thyme and lavender accompany us on our journey. On Pilgrimage. Czesław Miłosz. CP-MiloC; CP-MiloCN, *tr.* by Robert Hass

May the tide / that is entering even now. Blessing the Boats. Lucille Clifton. SP-ClifL

May the weather next week be good to us. Broken Sonnet. Carl Sandburg. CP-SandC

May 30th. Anne Sexton. CP-SextA

May 31, 1961. Charles Olson. CP-OlsoC; SP-OlsoC

May-Time. Christina Georgina Rossetti. CP-RosC2

May Time. Sir Thomas Wyatt. CP-WyatT

May 24, 1980. Joseph Brodsky. CP-BrodJ, *tr.* by Joseph Brodsky

May 24th or So. James Schuyler. CP-SchuJ

May 20, 1959. Charles Olson. CP-OlsoC

May we be able to begin with ourselves. For a Time and Place. James Dickey. CP-DickJ

May we live, my Lesbia, love while we may. Catullus. *See* Lesbia / live with me

May Weather. Philip Larkin. CP-LarkP

May with its light behaving. May. W. H. Auden. CP-AudeW

May you not drop your little jewel. Guido Cavalcanti. CP-CavaG, *tr.* by Marc Cirigliano

Maya. Eleanor Wilner. SP-WilnE

Maya Against Itzas. Charles Olson. CP-OlsoC

Maya-Quechua Indians plodding to market on feet as flat and tough as toads were semi-starving, The. Guatemala: 1964. C. K. Williams. SP-WillC

Mayakovsky. Frank O'Hara. SP-OharF

Mayakovsky / has it! Over Brooklyn Bridge. Charles Tomlinson. CP-TomlC; SP-TomlC

Mayan Ground, The. George Oppen. CP-OppGN

Maybe. Robert Creeley. SP-CreeR

Maybe. Langston Hughes. CP-HughL; CP-HughL3

Maybe. D. H. Lawrence. CP-LawrD

Maybe. Mary Oliver. SP-OlivM

Maybe. Carl Sandburg. CP-SandC

Maybe. William Stafford. SP-StafWW

Maybe All This. Wisława Szymborska. SP-SzymW, *tr.* by Stanislaw Barańczak *and* Clare Cavanagh

Maybe god / is a child. E. E. Cummings. CP-CummE

Maybe he believes me, maybe not. Maybe. Carl Sandburg. CP-SandC

Maybe he does not even have to exist. First Darkness, The. W. S. Merwin. SP-MerwW

Maybe He looked indeed. Salvator Mundi: Via Crucis. Denise Levertov. SP-LeveDS

Maybe I'll win the Irish Sweepstakes. Eaten by Butterflies. Charles Bukowski. SP-BukC2

Maybe I'm seven in the open field—. Sudden Journey. Tess Gallagher. SP-GallT

Maybe it ain't right. Live and Let Live. Langston Hughes. CP-HughL; CP-HughL3

Maybe it is true we have to return. Obsessions. Denise Levertov. SP-LeveDS

Maybe (it's a fear), maybe. Maybe. William Stafford. SP-StafWW

Maybe it's his wife. Exercise. William Carlos Williams. CP-WilW2

Maybe it's not as bad as we like to think: no melodramatic rendings, sackcloths, nothing so acute. Failure. C. K. Williams. SP-WillC

Maybe it's our nature to be naming. When the Future Is Black. Heather McHugh. SP-McHuH

Maybe Love. Allen Ginsberg. CP-GinsA

Maybe love will come. Maybe Love. Allen Ginsberg. CP-GinsA

Maybe my father. What I Think When I Ride the Train. Lucille Clifton. SP-ClifL

Maybe once more I will be driven mad. Hundred Times Nothing, A. Jaroslav Seifert. SP-SeifJ, *tr.* by Ewald Osers

Maybe one morning, walking in dry, glassy air. Eugenio Montale. CP-MontE, *tr.* by Jonathan Galassi

Maybe, so I'd look kindly on souls in need. Michelangelo Buonarroti. CP-Miche, *tr.* by John Frederick Nims

Maybe, Someday. Yannis Ritsos. SP-RitsY, *tr.* by Edmund Keeley

Maybe someone comes to the door and says. Easter Morning. William Stafford. SP-StafWW

Maybe someone stumbles across that child. Over the Mountains. William Stafford. SP-StafWW

Maybe the martyrology until today. Elegy for a Trappist. Thomas Merton. CP-MertT

Maybe this summer I shall revisit Palermo. Vucceria. James Fenton. SP-FentJ

Maybe / this way again. Maybe. Robert Creeley. SP-CreeR

Maybe we knew each other better. Coda: "Maybe we knew each other better." Louis MacNeice. CP-MacNL

Maybe You Can't Take It with You, but Look What Happens When You Leave It Behind. Ogden Nash. CP-NashO

Maybe you ranted in the grove. Ezry. Archibald MacLeish. CP-MacLA

Maybe you spoke to someone. City. Gerrit Achterberg. CP-RicAE

Maybe you thought it was a bird. Hand, The: "Brightness Falls from the Air" Gregory Orr. SP-OrrG

Mayday on Holderness. Ted Hughes. SP-HughTN

Mayday: two came to field in such wise. Bucolics. Sylvia Plath. CP-PlatS

Maydes are simple, some men say. Thomas Campion. CP-CampT

Mayflower. Sylvia Plath. CP-PlatS

Mayflowers, The. John Greenleaf Whittier. CP-WhitJ

Mayfly. Louis MacNeice. CP-MacNL

Maymie's Story of Red Riding-Hood. James Whitcomb Riley. CP-RileJ *Fr.* Child-World, A.

Mayo Tao, The. Derek Mahon. CP-MahoD

Mayor. Yehuda Amichai. SP-AmicY, *tr.* by Stephen Mitchell

Mayor of Gary, The. Carl Sandburg. CP-SandC

Mayor, The. Yehuda Amichai. SP-AmicYL, *tr.* by Benjamin Harshav *and* Barbara Harshav

Mays Landing. A. R. Ammons. CP-AmmoA

May's Love. Elizabeth Barrett Browning. CP-BroEB

May's, whose mouth was. Death in the West, A. Donald Davie. CP-DaviDC

Mayten, The. Gabriela Mistral. SP-MistG, *tr.* by Maria Giachetti [*or* Jacketti]

Mazdaism / has overcome. Charles Olson. CP-OlsoC

Maze. Richard Eberhart. CP-EberR

Maze, The. W. H. Auden. CP-AudeW

Maze, The. Vincent Bourne. CP-CowpW

Maze, The. James Laughlin. CP-LaugJ

Maze under the loess, The. Dead, The. Randall Jarrell. CP-JarrR

Mazeppa. Lord Byron. CP-Byron

McAllister, of talents rich and rare. Ambrose Bierce. SP-BierA

McAndrew's Hymn. Rudyard Kipling. CP-KiplR

McFeeters' Fourth. James Whitcomb Riley. CP-RileJ

McKane's Falls. James Merrill. SP-MerrJ

McLean Asylum, Somerville. Jones Very. CP-VeryJ

McPherson's Farewell. Robert Burns. *See* Macpherson's Farewell

Me. Charles Bukowski. SP-BukC1

Me. Kenneth Rexroth. CP-RexrK

Me Again. Kenneth Rexroth. CP-RexrK

Me an' Bert an' Minnie-Belle. Fool-Youngens. James Whitcomb Riley. CP-RileJ

Me an' ma baby's. Negro Dancers. Langston Hughes. CP-HughL; CP-HughL1

Me and Mary. James Whitcomb Riley. CP-RileJ

Me and my gift: kind Lord, behold. Christina Georgina Rossetti. CP-RosC2

Me and My Song. Langston Hughes. CP-HughL; CP-HughL2

Me and the Mule. Langston Hughes. CP-HughL; CP-HughL2

Me, change! Me, alter! Emily Dickinson. CP-DickE

Me—come! My dazzled face. Emily Dickinson. CP-DickE

Me from Myself—to banish. Emily Dickinson. CP-DickE

Me, go to Florida! This Is Pioneer Weather. William Carlos Williams. CP-WilW2

Me! he says, hand on his chest. Myself I Sing. George Oppen. CP-OppGN

Me Heart. G. K. Chesterton. CP-ChesG

Me, I'm Chinese. One More Loss to Count. Yusef Komunyakaa. CP-KomuY

Me Imperturbe. Walt Whitman. CP-WhitW

Me list no more to sing. Sir Thomas Wyatt. CP-WyatT

Me n' Asræ perferre jubes oblivia? et Asræ. Ad Vilmum Axiologum. Samuel Taylor Coleridge. CP-ColeS

Me prove it now—Whoever doubt. Emily Dickinson. CP-DickE

Me that 'ave been what I've been. Chant-Pagan. Rudyard Kipling. CP-KiplR

Me thought, (last night) love in an anger came. Dream, The. Robert Herrick. CP-HerrR

Me Time has Crook'd. no good Workman. From Cratetos. William Blake. CP-BlakW

Me to whatever state the Gods assign. To Delia. William Cowper. CP-CowpW

Me too, perchance, in future days. Stanzas on Milton's Remains. William Cowper. CP-CowpW

Me up at does. E. E. Cummings. CP-CummE

Me you often meet / In London's crowded street. Christina Georgina Rossetti. CP-RosC3

Meadow, A. Czeslaw Milosz. CP-MiloCN, *tr.* by Robert Hass

Meadow Bridge. James Dickey. CP-DickJ

Meadow House. Hayden Carruth. CP-CarHS

Meadow in Summer. Carl Sandburg. CP-SandC

Meadow Lark, The. Paul Laurence Dunbar. CP-DunbP

Meadow Mouse, The. Theodore Roethke. CP-RoetT

Meadow of wild grass, heather, and sage, A. Point Lobos, 1950. Helen Pinkerton. CP-PinkH

Meadow, The. Wendell Berry. CP-BerrW

Meadow, The. Raymond Carver. CP-CarvR

Meadowlark Country. Amy Clampitt. CP-ClamA

Meadows are empty, The. There are two villages. Hours, The. Norman Dubie. CP-DubiN

Meadows of golden dust. The silver. In Midas' Country. Sylvia Plath. CP-PlatS

Meadowsounds. Jelaluddin Rumi. SP-Rumi, *tr.* by Coleman Barks

Meadowsweet centuries friends allowably carol. Spirea. Louis Zukofsky. CP-ZukLS

Meager earth, very meager, burnt bushes, stones. Evening Procession. Yannis Ritsos. SP-RitsY, *tr.* by N. C. Germanacos

Mealy-bugs, shootflies in squadrons, mites. Pismire Rising. Thomas Lux. SP-LuxT

Mean. A. R. Ammons. CP-AmmoA

Mean fate surrounds our life with fear, A. World Is a Round Earthenware Plate, The. Pablo Antonio Cuadra. CP-MertT

Mean grimy houses, shades drawn. May I Ask You a Question, Mr. Youngstown Sheet & Tube? Kenneth Patchen. CP-PatcK

,Mean- / hum / a)now / (nit. E. E. Cummings. CP-CummE

Mean Old Yesterday. Langston Hughes. CP-HughL; CP-HughL3

Meandering River Poems, The. Tu Fu. CP-KizeC, *tr.* by Carolyn Kizer

Meane in Our Meanes, A. Robert Herrick. CP-HerrR

Meane, The. Robert Herrick. CP-HerrR

Meane, The. Robert Herrick. CP-HerrR

Meane Things Overcome Mighty. Robert Herrick. CP-HerrR

Meanest man I ever saw, The. Equity—? James Whitcomb Riley. CP-RileJ

Meaning. Czeslaw Milosz. CP-MiloCN, *tr.* by Robert Hass

Meaning Business. Heather McHugh. SP-McHuH

Meaning of Art, The. Yannis Ritsos. SP-RitsY, *tr.* by Kimon Friar *and* Kostas Myrsiades

Meaning of Death, The. Allen Tate. CP-TateA

Meaning of Life, The. Kenneth Patchen. CP-PatcK

Meaning of Life, The. Allen Tate. CP-TateA

Meaning of Simplicity, The. Yannis Ritsos. SP-RitsY, *tr.* by Kimon Friar

Meaning of the Look, The. Elizabeth Barrett Browning. CP-BroEB

Meaningless Institution, A. Allen Ginsberg. CP-GinsA

Meaningless Poem. Richard Eberhart. CP-EberR

Means there is something to hold. Fact of a Doorframe, The. Adrienne Rich. SP-RicA1

Meantime. Heather McHugh. SP-McHuH

Meantool amuck with her. Muck with her mean tool ah? Geared I. Catullus. *See* Stuffing, O'Toole naturally stuffs with his tool

Meantool inhabits in style three times ten hewed acres, forty. Catullus. *See* O'Toole is the proud master of

Meantool reconnoiters Pipléa scanning Their mountain. Catullus. *See* O'Toole / attempting an entry of the *mons Parnassus*

Meanwhile. Laura Riding Jackson. CP-RidiL

Meanwhile, the last of the human faculties. Happy on Heimaey. Hugh MacDiarmid. SP-MacDH

Mearl Blankenship. Muriel Rukeyser. CP-RukeM

Mease brags of Pullets which he eats; but Mease. Upon Mease. Robert Herrick. CP-HerrR

Measure. Clarence Major. SP-MajoC

Measure. Charles Olson. CP-OlsoC

Measure by your footsteps, sd the voice, the days. Kin. Charles Olson. CP-OlsoC

Measure everything well, calculate with precision. Other Precision, The. Yannis Ritsos. SP-RitsY, *tr.* by Kimon Friar

Measure of Casualness, A. Robert Graves. CP-GravR

Measure of Poetry, The. Howard Nemerov. CP-NemeH

Measure, The. Elizabeth Barrett Browning. CP-BroEB

Measure, The. Robert Creeley. CP-CreeR

Measured blood beats out the year's delay, The. Simple Autumnal. Louise Bogan. CP-BogaL

Measured Tread, A. Donald Davie. CP-DaviDC

Measurements. John Ciardi. CP-CiarJ

Meat. Thom Gunn. CP-GunnT

Meat I ate M E A T I ate meat. Raging Desire & c. Philip Whalen. SP-WhalP

Meat without Mirth. Robert Herrick. CP-HerrR

Meben. Kenneth Patchen. CP-PatcK

Mecanic on Duty at All Times. Miller Williams. CP-WillM

Mechanic, The. Robert Creeley. CP-CreeR

Mechanical Heart, The. Kenneth Patchen. CP-PatcK

Mechanically, the academic file. Ode for School Convocation. John Ciardi. CP-CiarJ

Mechanics. A. R. Ammons. CP-AmmoA

Mechanism. A. R. Ammons. CP-AmmoA

Mechanist, The. Richard Wilbur. CP-WilbR

Medal [*or* Medall], The. John Dryden.

   "Almighty crowd, thou shorten'st all dispute." SP-DrydJ

Medal, The. John Dryden. CP-DryJ2

Medallion. Robert Creeley. CP-CreeR

Medallion. Sylvia Plath. CP-PlatS

Medallion. Carl Sandburg. CP-SandC

Meddow Verse; or, Aniversary to Mistris Bridget Lowman, The. Robert Herrick. CP-HerrR

Medea. Euripides.

   "This is the chief felicity of life." CP-JohnS

   Translations from the *Medea* of Euripedes. CP-JohnS

Medea. Euripides. CP-JefR3, *tr.* by Robinson Jeffers

Medea. Kathleen Jessie Raine. SP-RainK

Mediaevalism. G. K. Chesterton. CP-ChesG

Mediation. A. R. Ammons. CP-AmmoA

Mediator, The. Elizabeth Barrett Browning. CP-BroEB

Mediators, reconcilers, compromisers, appeasers, The. UN Headquarters in the High Commissioner's Residence in Jerusalem. Yehuda Amichai. SP-AmicYL, *tr.* by Benjamin Harshav *and* Barbara Harshav

Mediators, the peacemakers, the compromise-shapers, the comforters, The. U.N. Headquarters in the High Commissioner's House in Jerusalem, The. Yehuda Amichai. SP-AmicY, *tr.* by Stephen Mitchell

Medicine. Raymond Carver. CP-CarvR

Medicine. Alice Walker. CP-WalkA

Medicine Bow. John Logan. CP-LogaJ

Medicine for Tight Spots. A. R. Ammons. CP-AmmoA

Medicine ("Practice of medicine, The"). Carolyn Kizer. CP-KizeC

Medicine ("When the nurses, interns, doctors came running full tilt down the hall"). Carolyn Kizer. CP-KizeC

Medieval Miniature, A. Wisława Szymborska. SP-SzymW, *tr. by* Stanislaw Barańczak *and* Clare Cavanagh

Medieval town, with frieze, The. What Is Poetry. John Ashbery. SP-AshbJ

Mediocrity in Love Rejected. Thomas Carew. CP-CareT

Meditatio. Ezra Pound. SP-PounE

Meditation. Charles Baudelaire. CP-BaudC, *tr. by* Walter Martin

Meditation. John Berryman. CP-BerrJ

Meditation. Hart Crane. CP-CranH

Meditation. Czeslaw Milosz. CP-MiloCN, *tr. by* Robert Hass

Meditation. William Stafford. SP-StafW; SP-StafWW

Meditation. Wallace Stevens. CP-StevWP

Meditation. Wallace Stevens. CP-StevWP

Meditation, A. Richard Eberhart. CP-EberR

Meditation, A. A. K. Ramanujan. CP-RamaA

Meditation before an Ancient Poem. Pablo Antonio Cuadra. CP-MertT

Meditation Celestial & Terrestrial. Wallace Stevens. CP-StevW; CP-StevWP

Meditation for His Mistress[e], A. Robert Herrick. CP-HerrR

Meditation in Hydrotherapy. Theodore Roethke. CP-RoetT

Meditation in the Presence of "Ostrich Walk" Hayden Carruth. CP-CarHS

Meditation in the Spring Rain. Wendell Berry. CP-BerrW

Meditation in the Waiting Room. William Stafford. SP-StafWW

Meditation in Time of War, A. William Butler Yeats. CP-YeatW

Meditation of Leaves, A. Peter Blue Cloud. SP-BlueP

Meditation of My Lady of Sorrows. Kenneth Patchen. CP-PatcK

Meditation of the Old Fisherman, The. William Butler Yeats. CP-YeatW

Meditation on a Holiday. Thomas Hardy. CP-HardT

Meditation on a Memoir. James Vincent Cunningham. CP-CunnJ

Meditation on a News Item. John Updike. CP-UpdiJ

Meditation on Form and Measure. Charles Wright. SP-WrigCN

Meditation on John Constable, A. Charles Tomlinson. CP-TomlC; SP-TomlC

Meditation on Philosophy, A. Robert Bly. SP-BlyR

Meditation on Saviors. Robinson Jeffers. CP-JefR1

Meditation on Song and Structure. Charles Wright. SP-WrigCN

Meditation on Statistical Method. James Vincent Cunningham. CP-CunnJ

Meditation on Summer and Shapelessness. Charles Wright. SP-WrigCN

Meditation on the 3d Verse of the 28th Chapter of Mathew. Annis Boudinot Stockton. CP-StocA

Meditation on the *Wen-Fu*. Eleanor Wilner. SP-WilnE

Meditation Two. Richard Eberhart. CP-EberR

Meditation under Stars. George Meredith. CP-MerG1

Meditations for a Savage Child. Adrienne Rich. SP-RicA2

Meditations in an Emergency. Frank O'Hara. SP-OharF

Meditations in Time of Civil War. William Butler Yeats. CP-YeatW

    Ancestral Houses. CP-YeatW

    I See Phantoms of Hatred and of the Heart's Fullness and of the Coming Emptiness. CP-YeatW

    My Descendants. CP-YeatW

    My House. CP-YeatW

    My Table. CP-YeatW

    Road at My Door, The. CP-YeatW

    Stare's Nest by My Window, The. CP-YeatW

Meditations of an Old Woman. Theodore Roethke. CP-RoetT

Meditations of Marcus Aurelius, The. Carpenter, The. G. K. Chesterton. CP-ChesG

Meditations on a Dingo. Yusef Komunyakaa. CP-KomuY

Meditations on Death. Giuseppe Ungaretti. CP-KunSC, *tr. by* Stanley Kunitz

Mediterranean. Eugenio Montale. CP-MontE, *tr. by* Jonathan Galassi

Mediterranean. Federico García Lorca. CP-GarcF, *tr. by* Jerome Rothenberg *Fr.* Palm Tree, The.

Mediterranean. Thomas McGrath. SP-McGrT

Mediterranean. Muriel Rukeyser. CP-RukeM

Mediterranean. May Sarton. SP-SartM

Mediterranean Basin. Robert Penn Warren. CP-WarrR

Mediterranean in January. D. H. Lawrence. CP-LawrD

Mediterranean Song. Richard Eberhart. CP-EberR

Mediterranean, The. Allen Tate. CP-TateA

Mediterranean, The. Charles Tomlinson. CP-TomlC; SP-TomlC

Medium. A. R. Ammons. CP-AmmoA

Medium, The. Theodore Weiss. SP-WeisT

Mediums. Walt Whitman. CP-WhitW

Medlars and Sorb-Apples. D. H. Lawrence. CP-LawrD

Medley. Carl Sandburg. CP-SandC

Medusa. Louise Bogan. CP-BogaL

Medusa. Amy Clampitt. CP-ClamA

Medusa. Hart Crane. CP-CranH

Medusa. Countee Cullen. CP-CullC

Medusa. Sylvia Plath. CP-PlatS

Medusa. C. K. Williams. SP-WillC

Medusa at Broadstairs. Amy Clampitt. CP-ClamA

Meek Have Inherited, The. Charles Bukowski. SP-BukC1

Meek, The. Jones Very. CP-VeryJ

Meekly the sea. Even Sea, The. May Swenson. SP-SwenM

Meet me again as at that time. To Louisa in the Lane. Thomas Hardy. CP-HardT

Meet me where sky and air. Voyage. Marya Alexandrovna Zaturenska. SP-ZatuM

Meet mr universe(who clean). E. E. Cummings. CP-CummE

Meeting. Matthew Arnold. *See* Switzerland

Meeting. John Berryman. CP-BerrJ

Meeting. Ted Hughes. SP-HughTN

Meeting. David Ignatow. SP-IgnaD

Meeting. George Meredith. CP-MerG2

Meeting. W. S. Merwin. SP-MerwW

Meeting. Christina Georgina Rossetti. CP-RosC3

Meeting. William Butler Yeats. CP-YeatW

Meeting, A. Wendell Berry. CP-BerrW

Meeting, A. Mary Oliver. SP-OlivM

Meeting, The. Louise Bogan. CP-BogaL

Meeting, The. Tess Gallagher. SP-GallT

Meeting, The. Robert Graves. CP-GravR

Meeting, The. George Meredith. CP-MerG1

Meeting, The. Muriel Rukeyser. CP-RukeM

Meeting, The. John Greenleaf Whittier. CP-WhitJ

Meeting among the Mountains. D. H. Lawrence. CP-LawrD

Meeting and Passing. Robert Frost. CP-FrosR

Meeting at Night. Robert Browning. CP-BroR1; SP-BroR

Meeting by Accident. Emily Dickinson. CP-DickE

Meeting ended, and the delegates. Social Work. Thomas Kinsella. CP-KinsT

Meeting Her in Chapultepec. Jay Wright. SP-WrigJ

Meeting his mother makes him lose ten years. Between the Porch and the Altar. Robert Lowell. SP-LoweR

Meeting is well worth parting. Emily Dickinson. SP-DickE

Meeting of Cultures, A. Donald Davie. CP-DaviDC

Meeting on the way to the same there. Talking World, The. Laura Riding Jackson. CP-RidiL

Meeting-Place. Dorothy Parker. CP-ParkD

Meeting Point. Louis MacNeice. CP-MacNL

Meeting the British. Paul Muldoon. CP-MuldP

Meeting the Mountains. Gary Snyder. CP-SnydG

'Meeting' was what / I had intended. Misprint. Charles Tomlinson. CP-TomlC

Meeting when all the world was in the bud. Loves of the Puppets. Richard Wilbur. CP-WilbR

Meeting with Despair, A. Thomas Hardy. CP-HardT

Meeting with Time, slack thing, said I. Time. George Herbert. CP-HerbG

Meetings Like Hungry Beaks. Marge Piercy. SP-PierM

Meg Merrilies [*or* Merrilees]. John Keats. CP-KeatJ

    (Old Meg She Was a Gipsy.) CP-KeatJ

Megaceph, chosen to serve the State. Egotist. Ambrose Bierce. SP-BierA *Fr.* Devil's Dictionary, The.

Megg yesterday was troubled with a Pose. Upon Megg. Robert Herrick. CP-HerrR

Mei Axis Mundi. James Laughlin. CP-LaugJ

Mei-mei, here is the table. Michael Palmer. SP-PalmM

Mein Kampf. William Stafford. SP-StafWW

Meiosis. W. H. Auden. CP-AudeW

Meister Eckhart. Norman Dubie. CP-DubiN

Melampus. George Meredith. CP-MerG1

Melancholia. Charles Bukowski. SP-BukC1

Melancholia. Paul Laurence Dunbar. CP-DunbP

Melancholy. Samuel Taylor Coleridge. CP-ColeS

Melancholy. William Corbett. SP-CorbW

Melancholy face Charles Carville had, A. Charles Carville's Eyes. Edwin Arlington Robinson. CP-RobiE

Melancholy Hours. Constantine P. Cavafy. CP-CavaC, *tr. by* Theoharis Constantine Theoharis

Melancholy Moon, The. Charles Baudelaire. CP-BaudC, *tr. by* Walter Martin

Melancholy of Jason Kleander; Poet in Kommagini; 595 A.D.. Constantine P. Cavafy. CP-CavaC, *tr. by* Theoharis Constantine Theoharis

Melancholy of Storm Windows, The. John Updike. CP-UpdiJ

Mélange Adultère de Tout. T. S. Eliot. CP-ElioT

Melchior Vulpius. Marianne Craig Moore. CP-MoorM

Meleager, one of Jason's heroes, died. Carving the Turkey. John Ciardi. CP-CiarJ

Mélisande. Charles Tomlinson. CP-TomlC

Mellea mi si abeam promittit basia septem. In Melleam. Thomas Campion. CP-CampT

Mellow. Langston Hughes. CP-HughL; CP-HughL3

Mellow hazes, lowly trailing. Dream of Autumn, A. James Whitcomb Riley. CP-RileJ

Mellow, mellow, at thrush-hour. Smile, The. Robert Penn Warren. CP-WarrR

Mellow touch of musick most doth wound, The. Soft Musick. Robert Herrick. CP-HerrR

Mellowed *those*, I call *those* eyes, Juventius. Catullus. *See* Iuventius, / were I allowed

Melodious Arethusa, o'er my verse. Virgil. CP-ShelP *Fr.* Eclogues.

Melodious skeletons, for all of last night's music. Fish-Scale Sunrise, A. Wallace Stevens. CP-StevW; CP-StevWP

Melody. Charles Tomlinson. CP-TomlC

Melody Grundy. Denise Levertov. SP-LeveDP

Melody / moving / downstream. Music, A. Denise Levertov. SP-LeveDP

Melon. Rainer Maria Rilke. CP-RilkFr

Melon-Seller, The. Robert Browning. CP-BroR2

Melongène. Richard Wilbur. CP-WilbR

Melpomene among her livid people. Two Masks, The. George Meredith. CP-MerG1

Melpomene in Manhattan. David Ignatow. SP-IgnaD

Melrose by Moonlight. Sir Walter Scott. SP-ScotW *Fr.* Lay of the Last Minstrel, The.

Melt earth to sea, sea flow to air. Ben Jonson. CP-JonsB *Fr.* Oberon, the Fairy Prince.

Melted iron, noon, stone shadows. Summer Noon at Karlovasi. Yannis Ritsos. SP-RitsY, *tr. by* Kimon Friar

Melted Money. Heather McHugh. SP-McHuH

Melted snow the verdure now restores, The. Horace. *See* Snow dissolv'd no more is seen, The

Melting. John Updike. CP-UpdiJ

Melville's Letter to William Clark Russell. Helen Pinkerton. CP-PinkH

Melvilliana. Helen Pinkerton. CP-PinkH

Memento, homo, quod cinis es. William Dunbar. CP-DunbW

Memento ("I have laid out the singer"). Federico García Lorca. CP-GarcF, *tr. by* Jerome Rothenberg *Fr.* Epitaph for a Bird.

Memento ("Moon is dead already, The"). Federico García Lorca. CP-GarcF, *tr. by* Jerome Rothenberg *Fr.* Six Songs at Nightfall.

Memento Mori. Christina Georgina Rossetti. CP-RosC2

Memento ("When we die / we'll take with us"). Federico García Lorca. CP-GarcF, *tr. by* Jerome Rothenberg *Fr.* Shadow.

Memo from the Cave. Louise Glück. SP-GlucL

Memo: Preliminary Draft of a Prayer to God the Father. John Ciardi. CP-CiarJ

Memo to Non-White Peoples. Langston Hughes. CP-HughL; CP-HughL3

Memo to the Dark Angel. James Tate. SP-TateJ

Memoir. James Vincent Cunningham. CP-CunnJ

Memoir. Robinson Jeffers. CP-JefR2

Memoir. Robert Pinsky. CP-PinsR

Memoir. Carl Sandburg. CP-SandC

Memoir of a One-Armed Harp Teacher. John Ciardi. CP-CiarJ

Memoir of a Proud Boy. Carl Sandburg. CP-SandC

Memoirs. William Meredith. SP-MereW

Memoirs of a Spinach-Picker. Sylvia Plath. CP-PlatS

Memoirs of Glückel of Hameln, The. Randall Jarrell. CP-JarrR

Memorabilia. Robert Browning. CP-BroR1; SP-BroR

Memorabilia. E. E. Cummings. CP-CummE; SP-CummE

Memoranda. William Dickey. SP-DickW

Memoranda. Carl Sandburg. CP-SandC

Memoranda to Horace. Louis MacNeice. CP-MacNL

Memorandum. Kenneth Rexroth. CP-RexrK

Memorandum. Wallace Stevens. CP-StevWP

Memorandum Book. Primo Levi. CP-LeviP, *tr. by* Ruth Feldman

Memoria Voraciae Simplex. Andrei Codrescu. SP-CodrA

Memorial. Thomas McGrath. SP-McGrT

Memorial. Robert Pinsky. CP-PinsR

Memorial, A. John Greenleaf Whittier. CP-WhitJ

Memorial Brass, The: 186–. Thomas Hardy. CP-HardT

Memorial Day. John Ciardi. CP-CiarJ

Memorial Day. Paul Laurence Dunbar. CP-DunbP

Memorial Day. Lorine Niedecker. CP-NiedL

Memorial Day. Charles Olson. CP-OlsoC

Memorial Day. Gregory Orr. SP-OrrG

Memorial Day. Wyatt Prunty. SP-PrunW

Memorial Day 1950. Frank O'Hara. SP-OharF

Memorial Evening. Dan Pagis. SP-PagiD, *tr. by* Stephen Mitchell

Memorial for My Mother, A. William Stafford. SP-StafWW

Memorial for the City. W. H. Auden. CP-AudeW

Memorial I. Audre Lorde. SP-LordA

Memorial Rain. Archibald MacLeish. CP-MacLA

Memorial Service at Poros. Yannis Ritsos. SP-RitsY, *tr. by* N. C. Germanacos

Memorial Service for the Invasion Beach Where the Vacation in the Flesh Is Over. Alan Dugan. CP-DugaA

Memorial Services. Yannis Ritsos. SP-RitsY, *tr. by* N. C. Germanacos

Memorial: Son Bret, A. William Stafford. SP-StafW; SP-StafWW

Memorial III—from a Phone Booth on Broadway. Audre Lorde. SP-LordA

Memorial Thresholds. Dante Gabriel Rossetti. CW-RossD *Fr.* House of Life, The.

Memorial to D. C. Edna St. Vincent Millay. CP-MillE

Epitaph: "Heap not on this mound." CP-MillE

MemorialII. Audre Lorde. SP-LordA

Memorial Verses. Matthew Arnold. SP-ArnoM

Memorials of a Tour in Italy, 1837. William Wordsworth. CP-WorW2

Memorials of a Tour of the Continent; 1820. William Wordsworth. CP-WorW2

Bruges ("Bruges I saw attired with golden light"). MW-WorW

Bruges ("Spirit of Antiquity—enshrined, The"). MW-WorW

Incident at Bruges. MW WorW

Memories. Rudyard Kipling. CP-KiplR

Memories. Dorothy Parker. CP-ParkD

Memories. Walt Whitman. CP-WhitW

Memories. John Greenleaf Whittier. CP-WhitJ

Meditations & Allegories of Water. Federico García Lorca. CP-GarcF, *tr. by* Jerome Rothenberg

Memories of a Boss in an Ad Agency. Alan Dugan. CP-DugaA

Memories of John Keats. Denise Levertov. SP-LeveDS

Memories of Mortalities. Laura Riding Jackson. CP-RidiL

Memories of Muzot. Rainer Maria Rilke. CP-RilkFr, *tr. by* A. Poulin, Jr.

Memories of 1936–7. Alan Dugan. CP-DugaA

Memories of President Lincoln. Walt Whitman. CP-WhitW

Memories of the Ancient World. Carlos Drummond de Andrade. CP-MertT

Memories of the Bowery. Alan Dugan. CP-DugaA

Memories of Verdun. Alan Dugan. CP-DugaA

Memories of West Street and Lepke. Robert Lowell. SP-LoweR

Memory. Federico García Lorca. CP-GarcF, *tr. by* Jerome Rothenberg *Fr.* Night (Suite for Piano and Poet's Voice).

Memory. Louise Bogan. CP-BogaL

Memory. Constantine P. Cavafy. CP-CavaC, *tr. by* Theoharis Constantine Theoharis

Memory. G. K. Chesterton. CP-ChesG

Memory. Lucille Clifton. SP-ClifL

Memory. Richard Eberhart. CP-EberR

Memory. Ivor Gurney. SP-GurnI

Memory. Ted Hughes. SP-HughTN

Memory. Walter De la Mare. CP-DeLaW

Memory. Arthur Rimbaud. CP-RimbA, *tr. by* Martin Sorrell

Memory. Theodore Roethke. CP-RoetT

Memory. Christina Georgina Rossetti. CP-RosC1

Memory. Dante Gabriel Rossetti. CW-RossD

Memory ("Soon the silver chord is broken"). Jones Very. CP-VeryJ

Memory ("Soon the waves, so lightly bounding"). Jones Very. CP-VeryJ

Memory. Miller Williams. CP-WillM

Memory. William Wordsworth. CP-WorW2

Memory. William Butler Yeats. CP-YeatW

Memory 1. Raymond Carver. CP-CarvR

Memory 2. Raymond Carver. CP-CarvR

Memory, A. Ted Hughes. SP-HughTN

Memory, A. John Greenleaf Whittier. CP-WhitJ

Memory, The. Maya Angelou. SP-AngeM

Memory, The. Robert Creeley. CP-CreeR

Memory and Hope. Elizabeth Barrett Browning. CP-BroEB

Memory and I. Thomas Hardy. CP-HardT

Memory as a building or a city. Seamus Heaney. SP-HeanSO *Fr.* Squarings.

Memory at 'The Modern'. George Oppen. CP-OppGN

Memory believes / fragrance of a town(whose). E. E. Cummings. CP-CummE

Memory / carved on stelae of, A. Two Egyptian Portrait Masks. Robert Earl Hayden. CP-HaydR

Memory Cave. Yusef Komunyakaa. CP-KomuY

Memory Forgotten. Robert Penn Warren. CP-WarrR

Memory ("Fresh, A"). Robert Creeley. SP-CreeR

Memory Gardens. Allen Ginsberg. CP-GinsA; SP-GinsA

Memory Green. Archibald MacLeish. CP-MacLA

Memory, hither come. Song: "Memory, hither come." William Blake. CP-BlakW

Memory: I can take my head and strike it on a wall on Cumberland /Island Island. Shark's Parlor, The. James Dickey. CP-DickJ

Memory is a highway. Rapture. Ai. SP-Ai

Memory is a strange Bell. Emily Dickinson. SP-DickE

Memory is a watery flower, when watered. In the Garden. Richard Eberhart. CP-EberR

Memory is not good. There is something loose, The. Amnesty. Howard Nemerov. CP-NemeH

Memory is the Sherry Flower. Emily Dickinson. SP-DickE

Memory is when you look back. Scroll. Carl Sandburg. CP-SandC

Memory, Mind, and Will. Charles Olson. CP-OlsoC

Memory ("Nancy finally"). Robert Creeley. SP-CreeR

Memory, 1930. Robert Creeley. SP-CreeR

Memory of April. William Carlos Williams. CP-WilW1

Memory of Burns, The. John Greenleaf Whittier. CP-WhitJ

Memory of Cape Cod. Edna St. Vincent Millay. CP-MillE

Memory of Cassis. Edna St. Vincent Millay. CP-MillE

Memory of Edwin Muir is green, The. Edwin Muir. Archibald MacLeish. CP-MacLA

Memory of England. Edna St. Vincent Millay. CP-MillE

Memory of Love—Image. Yehuda Amichai. SP-AmicYL, tr. by Benjamin Harshav and Barbara Harshav

Memory of Love—Opening the Will. Yehuda Amichai. SP-AmicYL, tr. by Benjamin Harshav and Barbara Harshav

Memory of Love—Terms and Conditions. Yehuda Amichai. SP-AmicYL, tr. by Benjamin Harshav and Barbara Harshav

Memory of Martha, The. Paul Laurence Dunbar. CP-DunbP

Memory of My Friend, A. Howard Nemerov. CP-NemeH

Memory of Oars. George Oppen. CP-OppGN

Memory of Old Forms under Hell's Angels. Alan Dugan. CP-DugaA

Memory of rain falling slowly, The. Philip Levine. SP-LeviP Fr. Poem with No Ending, A.

Memory of snow, The. Das Kleine Weinjahr. Rainer Maria Rilke. CP-RilkFr, tr. by A. Poulin, Jr.

Memory of Spring. W. S. Merwin. SP-MerwW

Memory of Summer Facing West. W. S. Merwin. SP-MerwWF

Memory of Swans. May Sarton. SP-SartM

Memory of the Loss of Wings. W. S. Merwin. SP-MerwW

Memory of the Sad Chair, A. John Ciardi. CP-CiarJ

Memory of the War, A. Howard Nemerov. CP-NemeH

Memory of time is here imprisoned, The. In a Strange House. Stanley Kunitz. CP-KunSC

Memory of time, The. Gunnar Thorgilsson (1816-1979). Jorge Luis Borges. SP-BorgJ, tr. by Hoyt Rogers

Memory of W.H. Auden. Thomas Kinsella. CP-KinsT

Memory of you is . . . a blue spear of flower. Two. Carl Sandburg. CP-SandC

Memory of Youth, A. William Butler Yeats. CP-YeatW

Memory Piece / for Baby Jane. Olga Broumas. SP-BrouO

Memory says: Want to do right? Don't count on me. Adrienne Rich. SP-RicA1 Fr. Eastern War Time.

Memory Unsettled. Thom Gunn. CP-GunnT

Memory worsening — let it go as rain. Sorrel. Geoffrey Hill. CP-HillG

Memphis. Lucille Clifton. SP-ClifL

Memphis, 2 P.M [or 2:00 P.M.]. Miller Williams. CP-WillM

Men. Maya Angelou. SP-AngeM

Men. Robert Creeley. SP-CreeR

Men. Archibald MacLeish. CP-MacLA

Men. Dorothy Parker. CP-ParkD

Men. William Stafford. SP-StafWW

Men. Gertrude Stein. CP-SteiG

Men. C. K. Williams. SP-WillC

Men, The. William Carlos Williams. CP-WilW1

Men; A Hate Song. Dorothy Parker. CP-ParkD

Men all, and birds, and creeping beasts. Sleep. Walter De la Mare. CP-DeLaW

Men always praise an honest whore, keen. Carmen 110. Catullus. CP-ZukLS Fr. Carmina.

Men and Man. George Meredith. CP-MerG1

Men and Women. D. H. Lawrence. CP-LawrD

Men are not alike in the sight of God. Sight of God, The. D. H. Lawrence. CP-LawrD

Men Are Not Bad. D. H. Lawrence. CP-LawrD

Men are not born Kings, but are men renown'd. Kings. Robert Herrick. CP-HerrR

Men are suspicious; prone to discontent. Present Government Grievous. Robert Herrick. CP-HerrR

Men are what they do, women are what they are. In Nature There Is Neither Right nor Left nor Wrong. Randall Jarrell. CP-JarrR

Men ask the way to Cold Mountain. Gary Snyder. CP-SnydG

Men asleep in their underwear. Tōji. Gary Snyder. CP-SnydG

Men, brother men, that after us yet live. Epitaph in Form of a Ballad, The. François Villon. SP-SwinA, tr. by Algernon Charles Swinburne

Men delight to praise men; and to edge. Lock Keeper, The. Ivor Gurney. SP-GurnI

Men (XVIII), The. Pablo Neruda. SP-NeruP Fr. Separate Rose, The.

Men fear the hollow man at the top of the tree. Leader, The. Stevie Smith. CP-SmitS

Men fight for liberty, and win it with hard knocks. Liberty's Old Old Story. D. H. Lawrence. CP-LawrD

Men, fires, feasts. Demeter. "H. D." CP-DoolH

Men (IV), The. Pablo Neruda. SP-NeruP Fr. Separate Rose, The.

Men give their hearts away. Beacon, The. James Vincent Cunningham. CP-CunnJ

Men have worked all week, The. If they have talked. Bronx Zoo. George Oppen. CP-OppGN

Men hiked on a loop trail, The. Tsankawi. Arthur Sze. SP-SzeA

Men! if manhood still ye claim. To Faneuil Hall. John Greenleaf Whittier. CP-WhitJ

Men, if you love us, play no more. In the Person of Womankind [A Song Apologetic]. Ben Jonson. CP-JonsB

Men I'm Not Married To. Dorothy Parker. CP-ParkD

Men Improve with the Years. William Butler Yeats. CP-YeatW

Men in Arab robes. Two. James Schuyler. CP-SchuJ

Men in my life were, The. Robert Creeley. SP-CreeR

Men in New Mexico. D. H. Lawrence. CP-LawrD

Men in the kitchens, The. Louis Zukofsky. CP-ZukLS

Men kept to themselves, The. Landscape of a Pissing Multitude. Federico García Lorca. CP-GarcF, tr. by Greg Simon and Steven F. White

Men know but little more than we. Caged Thrush Freed and Home Again, The. Thomas Hardy. CP-HardT

Men laughed and baaed like sheep, The. Memories of Verdun. Alan Dugan. CP-DugaA

Men leave the car, The. Lorine Niedecker. CP-NiedL

Men Like Gods. G. K. Chesterton. CP-ChesG

Men Like Gods. D. H. Lawrence. CP-LawrD

Men Like Gods. D. H. Lawrence. CP-LawrD

Men live and die in secret; none can see. Death. Jones Very. CP-VeryJ

Men live and die in secret; none can see. Life and Death. Jones Very. CP-VeryJ

Men Loved Wholly Beyond Wisdom. Louise Bogan. CP-BogaL

Men Made out of Words. Wallace Stevens. CP-StevW; CP-StevWP

Men make them fires on the hearth. Fires, The. Rudyard Kipling. CP-KiplR

Men marry what they need. I marry you. John Ciardi. CP-CiarJ

Men may sing of their Havanas, elevating to the stars. My Corn-Cob Pipe. Paul Laurence Dunbar. CP-DunbP

Men Mind No State in Sicknesse. Robert Herrick. CP-HerrR

Men must have Bounds how far[re] to walk[e]; for we. Rules for Our Reach. Robert Herrick. CP-HerrR

Men (IX), The. Pablo Neruda. SP-NeruP Fr. Separate Rose, The.

Men (XIX), The. Pablo Neruda. SP-NeruP Fr. Separate Rose, The.

Men of business, of pleasure. Felicity's Fourth Order. Donald Davie. CP-DaviDC

Men of Eleusis, ye that with long staves. At Eleusis. Algernon Charles Swinburne. SP-SwinA

Men of England, wherefore plough. Song to the Men of England. Percy Bysshe Shelley. CP-ShelP

Men of My Century Loved Mozart. Archibald MacLeish. CP-MacLA

Men of Old, The. John Greenleaf Whittier. CP-WhitJ

Men of our race, we send you one. Voyage of the "Ophir," The. George Meredith. CP-MerG2

Men of Sheepshead, The. George Oppen. CP-OppGN

Men of the North-land! where's the manly spirit. Summons, A. John Greenleaf Whittier. CP-WhitJ

Men of the Western World! In Fate's Dark Book. William Wordsworth. CP-WorW2

Men phone and ask me that, The. How Come You're Not Unlisted? Charles Bukowski. SP-BukC1

Men, ropes, horses, strain. Wheel King, The. Howard Nemerov. CP-NemeH

Men said at vespers: "All is well!" Chicago. John Greenleaf Whittier. CP-WhitJ

Men say they know many things. Henry David Thoreau. CP-ThorH

Men say y'are faire; and faire ye are, 'tis true. Upon a Painted Gentlewoman. Robert Herrick. CP-HerrR

Men seldom make passes. News Item. Dorothy Parker. CP-ParkD

Men should group themselves into a new order. Sun-Men. D. H. Lawrence. CP-LawrD

Men start digging in the ground. Missing in Action. Yusef Komunyakaa. CP-KomuY

Men talking, The. Eclogue: "Men talking, The." George Oppen. CP-OppGN

Men tell how many blossoms will appear. Swift, The. Jones Very. CP-VeryJ

Men That Are Falling, The. Wallace Stevens. CP-StevW; CP-StevWP

Men that are safe, and sure, in all they do[e]. Epistle Answering to One That Asked to Be Sealed of the Tribe of Ben, An. Ben Jonson. CP-JonsB; SP-JonsB

Men that cut their graves in the grey rocks, The. Widow of Naim, The. Thomas Merton. CP-MertT

Men That Fought at Minden, The. Rudyard Kipling. CP-KiplR

Men that worked for England, The. Elegy in a Country Churchyard. G. K. Chesterton. CP-ChesG

Men the Angels eyed. Men and Man. George Meredith. CP-MerG1

Men think that men have more sense than women and women. Just Wrap It Up, and I'll Throw It Away Later. Ogden Nash. CP-NashO

Men (II), The. Pablo Neruda. SP-NeruP *Fr.* Separate Rose, The.

Men wanted to be like gods. Men Like Gods. D. H. Lawrence. CP-LawrD

Men who are out hate those in play. Rivals, The. *Unknown.* CP-SherT

Men who could drink the wolf's hot blood. Goths, The. Tennessee Williams. CP-WillT

Men who find happiness in whores. Laments of an Icarus, The. Charles Baudelaire. CP-BaudC, *tr. by* Walter Martin

Men who here in harness died, The. On the Home Guards. Herman Melville. SP-MelvH

Men who imagine themselves covered with fur and sprouting. Werewolf Movies. Margaret Atwood. SP-AtwM2

Men Who March Away. Thomas Hardy. CP-HardT

Men who ride strange wild horses. Tapestry. Langston Hughes. CP-HughL; CP-HughL1

Men with picked voices chant the names. Overture to a Dance of Locomotives. William Carlos Williams. CP-WilW1

Men With Small Heads. Thomas Lux. SP-LuxT

Men Working. Edna St. Vincent Millay. CP-MillE

Men working on the building going up here have got these great, The. Sanctity, The. C. K. Williams. CP-WillC; SP-WillC

Men you strike. Euripides. CP-DoolH *Fr.* Hippolytus.

Men you've loved are one man, The. David Ignatow. SP-IgnaD

Menace. Rainer Maria Rilke. CP-RilkFr

Menace, The. Thom Gunn. CP-GunnT

Menagerie at Versailles in 1775, The. John Updike. CP-UpdiJ

Mendicant Order, A. Tennessee Williams. CP-WillT

Mending Wall. Robert Frost. CP-FrosR

Mendings. Muriel Rukeyser. CP-RukeM

Menenius' wife, / a red-headed cat from Bologna. Carmen 59. Catullus. CP-ZukLS *Fr.* Carmina.

Men's can at Café Society Uptown, The. Let's All Hear It for Mildred Bailey! James Schuyler. CP-SchuJ

Mens Sana in Corpore Sano. Donald Davie. CP-DaviDC

Menses. Edna St. Vincent Millay. CP-MillE

Menstruation at Forty. Anne Sexton. CP-SextA; SP-SextA

Mental Cases. Wilfred Owen. CP-OwenW

Mental Hospital Garden, The. William Carlos Williams. CP-WilW2

Mental picture which the, The. Lady in Black. Robert Creeley. CP-CreeR

Mental Traveller, The. William Blake. CP-BlakW

Mention any cousin's death. Any Cow's Horn Can Do It. A. K. Ramanujan. CP-RamaA

Mentor. Audre Lorde. SP-LordA

Mentor and Pupils. George Meredith. CP-MerG2

Mentors. Gwendolyn Brooks. SP-BrooG

Menu, The. Robert Creeley. CP-CreeR

Merax & Mullin. W. H. Auden. CP-AudeW

Mercator, vigiles oculos ut fallere possit. Translation of Prior's Chloe and Euphelia. Matthew Prior. CP-CowpW

Merce of Egypt. Charles Olson. CP-OlsoC; SP-OlsoC

Mercedes is a jungle-lily in a death house. To the Dark Mercedes of "El Palacio de Amor." Langston Hughes. CP-HughL; CP-HughL1

Mercenary Muse, The. Charles Baudelaire. CP-BaudC, *tr. by* Walter Martin

Merchant, as crafty a man is he, The. Do You Plan to Speak Bantu? or Abbreviation is the Thief of Sanity. Ogden Nash. CP-NashO

Merchant is, A. Home Federal. Rae Armantrout. SP-ArmaA

Merchant man, whom many seas have taught, The. Sir Philip Sidney. SP-SidnP *Fr.* Arcadia.

Merchant of the Picturesque, The. Emily Dickinson. CP-DickE

Merchantmen, The. Rudyard Kipling. CP-KiplR

Merchants have multiplied more than the stars of heaven. Executive's Death, The. Robert Bly. SP-BlyR

Merchants. of the sea and of finance. Move Over. Charles Olson. CP-OlsoC; SP-OlsoC

Merci Beaucoup. William Stafford. SP-StafWW

Mercian Hymns. Geoffrey Hill. CP-HillG

Merciful Hand, The. Nicholas Vachel Lindsay. CP-LindV

Mercifully. Marianne Craig Moore. CP-MoorM

Merciles[s] Beaute [*or* Beautée *or* Beauty]. Geoffrey Chaucer. CP-ChauG

Merciless, callous and sinister god! Clock, The. Charles Baudelaire. CP-BaudC, *tr. by* Walter Martin

Merciless Madrigal. Charles Baudelaire. CP-BaudC, *tr. by* Walter Martin

Mercurius Gallo-Belgicus. John Donne. CP-DonnJ; MW-DonnJ

Mercury Carries Psyche to Olympus. Elizabeth Barrett Browning. CP-BroEB

Mercury, god of larceny. Accomplice, The. Robert Graves. CP-GravR

Mercury shew'd Apollo, Bartas Book. Nathaniel Ward. CP-BradA

Mercury showed Apollo Bartas' book. Nathaniel Ward. *See* Mercury shew'd Apollo, Bartas Book

Mercury Vindicated. Ben Jonson.
   "How young and fresh I am tonight." CP-JonsB
   "Soft, subtle fire, thou soul of art." SP-JonsB

Mercutio. Walter De la Mare. CP-DeLaW

Mercy. Olga Broumas. SP-BrouO

Mercy. James Dickey. CP-DickJ

Mercy. Robert Herrick. CP-HerrR

Mercy and Love. Robert Herrick. CP-HerrR

Mercy, O Eternal One!, The. Hymns of the Brahmo Somaj. John Greenleaf Whittier. CP-WhitJ

Mercy on Maryanne who through a hole beneath her collarbone drinks. Infusion Room, The. Jane Cooper. CP-CoopJ

Mercy on us for our many birthdays. Sestina for Warm Seasons. Mona Van Duyn. SP-VanDM

Mercy Seat, The. Norman Dubie. CP-DubiN

Mercy, the wise Athenians held to be. Mercy. Robert Herrick. CP-HerrR

Mercy there is to ask: but not of these. Verdict, A. G. K. Chesterton. CP-ChesG

Mercy, Wherever You Are, Come Running in to Me and Grab Me in Your Good Arms—. Charles Bukowski. SP-BukC2

Mere intruder in the lavish gardens, A. To Johannes Brahms. Jorge Luis Borges. SP-BorgJ, *tr. by* Stephen Kessler

Mere mortal once. Divine, though, born to be. Michelangelo Buonarroti. CP-Miche, *tr. by* John Frederick Nims

Mere trees cast no coolness where you go, The. Girl Walking into a Shadow, A. James Wright. CP-WrigJ

Meredith Nicholson. James Whitcomb Riley. CP-RileJ

Merely the landscape of a vanished whim. Versailles. Adrienne Rich. CP-RicAE

Merely to Know. Adrienne Rich. CP-RicAE; SP-RicA2

Merely to look upon your sacred City. Petrarch. CP-Petra, *tr. by* J. G. Nichols

Merely to name them is the prose. Islands. Derek Walcott. CP-WalcD

Merest nub of a notion, nothing more, The. Playing the Inventions. Howard Nemerov. CP-NemeH

Merger, The. G. K. Chesterton. CP-ChesG

Merging into place against a slope of trees. Song. A. R. Ammons. CP-AmmoA

Meridian. Amy Clampitt. CP-ClamA

Meridian. Louise Glück. SP-GlucL

Meridians are a net. Objects. Richard Wilbur. CP-WilbR

Merits Make the Man. Robert Herrick. CP-HerrR

Merle Bascom's .22. Donald Hall. CP-HallD

Merlin. Ralph Waldo Emerson. CP-EmerR

Merlin. Geoffrey Hill. CP-HillG

Merlin. Edwin Arlington Robinson. CP-RobiE

Merlin and the Deer. Thomas Merton. CP-MertT

Merlin Enthralled. Richard Wilbur. CP-WilbR

Merlin in the Cave: He Speculates without a Book. Thom Gunn. CP-GunnT

Merlins Prophecy. William Blake. CP-BlakW

Merlin's Song. Ralph Waldo Emerson. CP-EmerR

Mermaid. Robert Lowell. SP-LoweR

Mermaid Emerging. Robert Lowell. SP-LoweR

Mermaid, The. Ogden Nash. CP-NashO

Mermaids, The. Walter De la Mare. CP-DeLaW

Merman, The. Paul Muldoon. CP-MuldP

Merman, The. James Whitcomb Riley. CP-RileJ

Mermen, The. Hart Crane. CP-CranH

Merops. Ralph Waldo Emerson. CP-EmerR

Merrily, merrily goes the bark. Voyage to Arran, The. Sir Walter Scott. SP-ScotW *Fr.* Lord of the Isles, The.

Merrily 'mid the faded leaves. To Robin Redbreast. George Meredith. CP-MerG1

Merrimac, The. John Greenleaf Whittier. CP-WhitJ

Merriment that followed was subdued, The. Bewildering Emotions. James Whitcomb Riley. CP-RileJ *Fr.* Child-World, A.

Merritt Parkway. Denise Levertov. SP-LeveDS

Merrow Down. Rudyard Kipling. CP-KiplR *Fr.* Just-So Stories.

Merry Autumn. Paul Laurence Dunbar. CP-DunbP

Merry Christmas, China. Langston Hughes. CP-HughL; CP-HughL1

Merry clerks of Oxenford they stretch themselves at ease, The. Clerks and the Bells, The. Rudyard Kipling. CP-KiplR

Merry-go-round. Federico García Lorca. CP-GarcF, *tr.* by Alan S. Trueblood *Fr.* Theories.

Merry-Go-Round. Langston Hughes. CP-HughL; CP-HughL2; CP-HughL3

Merry-Go-Round with White Swan. Jaroslav Seifert. SP-SeifJ, *tr.* by Ewald Osers

Merry Guide, The. A. E. Housman. CP-HousA

Merry Hae I Been Teethin a Heckle. Robert Burns. CP-BurnR

Merry heart is a continual feast, A. Then I Commended Mirth. Christina Georgina Rossetti. CP-RosC2

Merry, La Belle / *antichi*, tilling. 4 Other Countries. Louis Zukofsky. CP-ZukLS

Merry Madness Hall. James Laughlin. CP-LaugJ

Merry Maid. John Clare. SP-ClarJ

Merry Maid, The. Edna St. Vincent Millay. CP-MillE

Merry [*or* Merrie] world did on a day, The. Quip, The. George Herbert. CP-HerbG

Merrymaking in Question, A. Thomas Hardy. CP-HardT

Meru. William Butler Yeats. CP-YeatW

Mescaline. Allen Ginsberg. CP-GinsA

Meseemeth I heard cry and groan. Complaint of the Fair Armoress [*or* Armouress], The. François Villon. SP-SwinA, *tr.* by Algernon Charles Swinburne

Mesmerism. Robert Browning. CP-BroR1; SP-BroR

Mesmerism. Ezra Pound. CP-PoEar

Mesmerized eyes on one's. Seeing through Me. Donald Davie. CP-DaviDC

Mesopotamia. Raymond Carver. CP-CarvR

Mesopotamia. Rudyard Kipling. CP-KiplR

Mess of Love, The. D. H. Lawrence. CP-LawrD

Mess-room by Night. Arthur Rimbaud. CP-RimbA, *tr.* by Martin Sorrell

Messae from the Wanderer, A. William Stafford. SP-StafWW

Message. Fernando Pessoa. SP-PessF, *tr.* by Susan M. Brown *and* Edwin Honig

Message. John Berryman. CP-BerrJ

Message. Allen Ginsberg. CP-GinsA; SP-GinsA

Message. Denise Levertov. SP-LeveDP

Message. Kathleen Jessie Raine. SP-RainK

Message. Yannis Ritsos. SP-RitsY, *tr.* by Edmund Keeley

Message. Philip Whalen. SP-WhalP

Message, The. Robert Creeley. CP-CreeR

Message, The. John Donne. CP-DonnJ; MW-DonnJ

Message, The. Denise Levertov. SP-LeveDP

Message, The ("On the bare alder bough"). Jones Very. CP-VeryJ

Message, The ("There is no voice but it is born of Me"). Jones Very. CP-VeryJ

Message II. Allen Ginsberg. CP-GinsA

Message at Sunset for Bishop Berkeley. Heather McHugh. SP-McHuH

Message for the Sinecurist. Tess Gallagher. SP-GallT

Message from a secretary tells me first, A. Elegy for Frank Stanford. Thomas Lux. SP-LuxT

Message from Abroad. Allen Tate. CP-TateA

Message from Home. Kathleen Jessie Raine. SP-RainK

Message from Outside. Gary Snyder. CP-SnydG

Message from Space, A. William Stafford. SP-StafWW

Message from the Assistant Chief of the Fly People, A. Kenneth Patchen. CP-PatcK

Message Hidden in an Empty Wine Bottle that I Threw into a Gully of Maple Trees One Night at an Indecent Hour, A. James Wright. CP-WrigJ

Message of Thelma Sayles, The. Lucille Clifton. SP-ClifL

Message to Be Inscribed on Mark Van Doren's Hamilton Medal. Thomas Merton. CP-MertT

Message to the President. Langston Hughes. CP-HughL; CP-HughL3

Message you brought back again and again, The. Remembering Robert Lowell. William Meredith. SP-MereW

Messages. Jane Cooper. CP-CoopJ

Messages. James Dickey. CP-DickJ

Messages. Yusef Komunyakaa. CP-KomuY

Messenger. Yannis Ritsos. SP-RitsY, *tr.* by Kimon Friar

Messenger, The. Thomas Kinsella. CP-KinsT

Messenger, The. Thom Gunn. CP-GunnT

Messenger, The. Thomas Merton. CP-MertT

Messenger, The. Eleanor Wilner. SP-WilnE

Messenger descending. Garden, The. Eugenio Montale. CP-MontE, *tr.* by Jonathan Galassi

Messenger from the Horizon, A. Thomas Merton. CP-MertT

Messenger runs, not carrying the news, The. Messenger, The. Eleanor Wilner. SP-WilnE

Messengers. Louise Glück. SP-GlucL

Messengers much like ourselves? Explain it. By Disposition of Angels. Marianne Craig Moore. CP-MoorM

Messengers, The. Robert Creeley. CP-CreeR

Messiah [a Sacred Eclogue, in Imitation of Virgil's Pollio]. Alexander Pope. CP-PopeA

Messiah, The. Louis MacNeice. CP-MacNL

Messias. Thomas Merton. CP-MertT

Messias. Karl Shapiro. SP-ShapK

Metacom. John Greenleaf Whittier. CP-WhitJ

Metal door groans, The. Re-creating the Scene. Yusef Komunyakaa. CP-KomuY

Metal for Resistance. D. H. Lawrence. CP-LawrD

Metal harps of the high gates, The. Leaving the Asylum. Gregory Orr. SP-OrrG

Metal smokestack, The. Exercise No. 2. William Carlos Williams. CP-WilW2

Metals. Donald Davie. CP-DaviDC

Metamorphic Journal. Denise Levertov. SP-LeveDL
    Part 2—February. SP-LeveDL

Metamorphoses. Ovid.
    "All the more reason, then, that men and women." CP-MuldP
    "Bura and Helice on Achaian ground." CP-RaleW
    "East winde with Aurora hath abiding, The." CP-RaleW
    Fable of Dryope, The. CP-PopeA
    "From thence our kinde hard-hearted is, enduring paine and care." CP-RaleW
    Galatea. CP-MahoD
    "Joyfull Spring did ever last, The." CP-RaleW
    "More holy than the rest, and understanding more." CP-RaleW
    "No man was better, nor more just than hee." CP-RaleW
    "Nought from my birth or ancestors I claim." CP-JohnS
    "Various ills ordain'd to man by fate, The." CP-JohnS
    Vertumnus and Pomona. CP-PopeA
    "World discernes it selfe, while I the world behold, The." CP-RaleW

Metamorphoses. Geoffrey Hill. CP-HillG

Metamorphoses. Howard Nemerov. CP-NemeH

Metamorphoses at a College for Women. Eleanor Wilner. SP-WilnE

Metamorphoses of the Moon. Sylvia Plath. CP-PlatS

Metamorphoses of the Vampire. Charles Baudelaire. CP-BaudC, *tr.* by Walter Martin

Metamorphoses, The. Randall Jarrell. CP-JarrR

Metamorphosis. Louise Glück. SP-GlucL

Metamorphosis. E. E. Cummings. CP-CummE

Metamorphosis. Robinson Jeffers. CP-JefR3

Metamorphosis. Carl Sandburg. CP-SandC

Metamorphosis. May Sarton. SP-SartM

Metamorphosis. Wallace Stevens. CP-StevW; CP-StevWP

Metamorphosis. Robert Stock. SP-StocR

Metamorphosis. Chuang Tzu. CP-MertT

Metamorphosis, The. David Ignatow. SP-IgnaD

Metamorphosis, The. Sir John Suckling. CP-SuckJ

Metamorphosis, The. Charles Tomlinson. CP-TomlC; SP-TomlC

Metaphor as Degeneration. Wallace Stevens. CP-StevW; CP-StevWP

Metaphor, The. Robert Graves. CP-GravR

Metaphor to Action. Muriel Rukeyser. CP-RukeM

Metaphors. Sylvia Plath. CP-PlatS

Metaphors of a Magnifico. Wallace Stevens. CP-StevW; CP-StevWP

Metaphysical Amorist, The. James Vincent Cunningham. CP-CunnJ

Metaphysical Automobile, The. Howard Nemerov. CP-NemeH

Metaphysical Garden, The. May Sarton. SP-SartM

Metaphysical Insomnia Jazz. Mumonkan XXIX. Philip Whalen. SP-WhalP

Metaphysical Sonnet, A. William Meredith. SP-MereW

Metaphysical Town Hall and Bookshop, The. Philip Whalen. SP-WhalP

Metaphysics. Allen Ginsberg. CP-GinsA; SP-GinsA

Metaphysics of the Night. Marya Alexandrovna Zaturenska. SP-ZatuM

Metastasis. Arthur Sze. SP-SzeA

Metempsychosis. Margaret Atwood. SP-AtwM2

Metempsychosis. "Rubén Dario." SP-DariR, *tr.* by Alberto Acereda *and* Will Derusha

Metempsychosis. Kenneth Rexroth. CP-RexrK

Meteor flying and the planets' chime. Poet as Mute. Josephine Jacobsen. CP-JacoJ

Meteorite, The. Randall Jarrell. CP-JarrR

Meteorologist, September. Donald Davie. CP-DaviDC

Meteorologists, The. Jones Very. CP-VeryJ

Meteorology. A. R. Ammons. CP-AmmoA

Meteors. Jane Cooper. CP-CoopJ

Meteor's arc of quiet; a voiceless rain, The. Faint Music. Walter De la Mare. CP-DeLaW

Methedrine Vision in Hollywood, A. Allen Ginsberg. CP-GinsA

Methinks all things have travelled since you shined. On the Sun Coming Out in the Afternoon. Henry David Thoreau. CP-ThorH

Methinks that by a strict behavior. Henry David Thoreau. CP-ThorH

Methinks the ills of life I fain would shun. Christina Georgina Rossetti. CP-RosC3

Methinks this heart should rest awhile. Emily Jane Brontë. CP-BronE

Methinks 'twere no unprecedented feat. William Wordsworth. CP-WorW2 *Fr.* River Duddon [A Series of Sonnets], The.

Methinks we do as fretful children do. Prospect, The. Elizabeth Barrett Browning. CP-BroEB

Methinnks I see thee decently array'd. William Cowper. CP-CowpW

Method, A. Robert Creeley. CP-CreeR

Method, The. George Herbert. CP-HerbG

Method for Optimism. Yannis Ritsos. SP-RitsY, *tr. by* Kimon Friar

Method. For Ronald Gaskell. Donald Davie. CP-DaviDC

Method must be purest meat, The. On Burroughs, Work. Allen Ginsberg. CP-GinsA

Method of Actuality, The. Robert Creeley. CP-CreeR

Method of Salvation. Yannis Ritsos. SP-RitsY, *tr. by* Kostas Myrsiades

Methodus Amandi. Thomas Cary. CP-CareT

Methought an angel from the air. After Rochester (or somebody). James Laughlin. CP-LaugJ

Methought I saw a dark and lonely tower. Doubt. G. K. Chesterton. CP-ChesG

Methought I saw (as I did dream[e] in bed). Vision, The. Robert Herrick. CP-HerrR

Methought I saw the footsteps of a throne. William Wordsworth. CP-WorW1; MW-WorW

Methought I saw the grave where Laura lay. Vision upon This Concei[p]t of the Faerie [*or* Faery] Queen[e], A. Sir Walter Ralegh. CP-RaleW *Fr.* Commendatory Verses to Edmund Spenser's Fairy Queen.

Methought I was a billow in the crowd. Fragment: "Methought I was a billow in the crowd." Percy Bysshe Shelley. CP-ShelP

Methought [*or* Mee thought] I saw my late espoused saint. On His Deceased Wife. John Milton. CP-MiltJ

Methusaleh Saw Many Repeaters. Carl Sandburg. CP-SandC

Methusaleh was a witness to many cabbages and kings. Methusaleh Saw Many Repeaters. Carl Sandburg. CP-SandC

Methusaleh was a witness to many cabbages and kings. Three Fragments for Fishers of Destiny. Carl Sandburg. CP-SandC

Métier of Blossoming, The. Denise Levertov. SP-LeveDS

Metric Figure. William Carlos Williams. CP-WilW1

Metric Figure. William Carlos Williams. CP-WilW2

Metrical Feet. Samuel Taylor Coleridge. CP-ColeS; MW-ColeS

Metropolis of Bruges, which long ago, The. Vulnerant Omnes, Ultima Necat. Constantine P. Cavafy. CP-CavaC, *tr. by* Theoharis Constantine Theoharis

Metropolitan. Arthur Rimbaud. CP-RimbA, *tr. by* Martin Sorrell

Metropolitan Bard. James Laughlin. CP-LaugJ

Metropolitan Christmas, A. Eugenio Montale. CP-MontE, *tr. by* Jonathan Galassi

Metropolitan Melancholy. Wallace Stevens. CP-StevWP

Metropolitan Museum. Langston Hughes. CP-HughL; CP-HughL3

Metropolitan Sunday. Howard Nemerov. CP-NemeH

Mettle and Metal. Robert Browning. CP-BroR2

Mexcity drugstore table, giant. Violence. Allen Ginsberg. CP-GinsA

Mexican dancer shook her fans at, The. Yellow Cab. Charles Bukowski. SP-BukC1

Mexican Divertimento. Joseph Brodsky. CP-BrodJ, *tr. by* Alan Myers

Mexican Girls, The. Charles Bukowski. SP-BukC2

Mexican Guitar, A. Frank O'Hara. SP-OharF

Mexican Market Woman. Langston Hughes. CP-HughL; CP-HughL1

Mexican Peacock, The. Josephine Jacobsen. CP-JacoJ

Mexican Valley. James Dickey. CP-DickJ

Mexico. Robert Lowell.
   "As if we chewed dry twigs and salt grasses." SP-LoweR
   "Difficulties, the impossibilities, The." SP-LoweR
   "Lizard rusty as a leaf rubbed rough." SP-LoweR
   "Midwinter in Cuernavaca, tall red flowers." SP-LoweR
   "No artist perhaps, you go beyond their phrases;" SP-LoweR
   "Poor child, you were kissed so much you thought you were walked on;" SP-LoweR
   "South of Boston, south of Washington." SP-LoweR
   "Three pillows, end on end, rolled on a daybed." SP-LoweR

Mexico. Jorge Luis Borges. SP-BorgJ, *tr. by* Stephen Kessler

(Mexico) could not. This. Charles Olson. CP-OlsoC

Mexico is a Foreign Country: Five Studies in Naturalism. Robert Penn Warren. CP-WarrR

Meyer is a bum. He eats his pie. What They Call Red Cherry Pie. Wallace Stevens. CP-StevWP

Mezentius and Lausus. Virgil. CP-DryJ2, *tr. by* John Dryden *Fr.* Aeneid (Dryden translation).

Mezzo Cammin. Henry Wadsworth Longfellow. SP-LongH

Mezzo Forte. William Carlos Williams. CP-WilW1

Miami. John Updike. CP-UpdiJ

Michael [A Pastoral Poem]. William Wordsworth. CP-WorW1; MW-WorW

Michael and Christine. Arthur Rimbaud. CP-RimbA, *tr. by* Martin Sorrell

Michael Angelo. D. H. Lawrence. CP-LawrD
  (God shook thy roundness in His finger's cup.) CP-LawrD

Michael F. M. Rossetti. Christina Georgina Rossetti. CP-RosC3

Michael Flynn and the Baby. James Whitcomb Riley. CP-RileJ

Michael, Michael: Michael of the Morning. To St. Michael, in Time of Peace. G. K. Chesterton. CP-ChesG

Michael Robartes and the Dancer. William Butler Yeats. CP-YeatW

Michael Robartes Bids His Beloved Be at Peace. William Butler Yeats. CP-YeatW
  (He Bids His Beloved Be at Peace.) CP-YeatW

Michaelmas. Ivor Gurney. SP-GurnI

Michelangelo's Kiss. Dante Gabriel Rossetti. CW-RossD *Fr.* House of Life, The.

Michigan Water, a Few Riffs before Dawn. Hayden Carruth. CP-CarHL

Miching Mallecho. Robinson Jeffers. CP-JefR3

Michtam. Louis Zukofsky. CP-ZukLS

Microscopic monster. Euglena. Miller Williams. CP-WillM

Mictlantecuhtli. Charles Tomlinson. CP-TomlC

Mid-August. A. R. Ammons. CP-AmmoA

Mid-August at Sourdough Mountain Lookout. Gary Snyder. CP-SnydG

Mid-August meltdown, Assurbanipal in the west. Opus Posthumous 3. Charles Wright. SP-WrigCN

Mid-Country Blow. Theodore Roethke. CP-RoetT

'Mid crowded obelisks and urns. To the Sons of Burns, after Visiting the Grave of Their Father. William Wordsworth. CP-WorW1

Mid-day. "H. D." CP-DoolH

Mid-Day Verse, The. D. H. Lawrence. CP-LawrD

Mid-December but still the ground's unfrozen, taking. Mild Winter. Hayden Carruth. CP-CarHS

Mid-leap in her escape, the nymph. Some Kind of Pine. Heather McHugh. SP-McHuH

Mid-Lent. Christina Georgina Rossetti. CP-RosC2

Mid-May—after May frosts that killed the Camellias. Two Tortoiseshell Butterflies. Ted Hughes. SP-HughTN

Mid-morning / the light, what light. This Soft October. James Schuyler. CP-SchuJ

Mid-noon is past;—upon the sultry mead. Resting-Place, The. William Wordsworth. CP-WorW2 *Fr.* River Duddon [A Series of Sonnets], The.

Mid-Rapture. Dante Gabriel Rossetti. CW-RossD *Fr.* House of Life, The.

Mid-September, and I miss my daughter. Towards Autumn. Marilyn Hacker. SP-HackM

Mid-Term Break. Seamus Heaney. SP-HeanSO

Mid the trunks and roots gigantic. G. K. Chesterton. CP-ChesG *Fr.* Vision of Edens, A.

Mid-Twentieth-Century Portrait. Czeslaw Milosz. CP-MiloC; CP-MiloCN, *tr. by* Jan Darowski

Mid-winter Snowfall in the Piazza Dante. Charles Wright. SP-WrigCN

Mid-Winter Waking. Robert Graves. CP-GravR

Midafternoon / I come. April. A. R. Ammons. CP-AmmoA

Midas. Jones Very. CP-VeryJ

Midas and Wife. Mona Van Duyn. SP-VanDM

Midas eyes the seasonable glints. Legend. Charles Tomlinson. CP-TomlC

Midas watched the golden crust. Ungrateful Garden, The. Carolyn Kizer. CP-KizeC

Midas, we are in story told. Fable of Midas, The. Jonathan Swift. CP-SwifJ

Midbay, the Nikonos. Before the Elegy. Olga Broumas. SP-BrouO

Midday Construction. Pablo Neruda. SP-NeruP

Middle. William Carlos Williams. CP-WilW1

Middle, The. Ogden Nash. CP-NashO

Middle Age. Robert Lowell. SP-LoweR

Middle Age. A. K. Ramanujan. CP-RamaA

Middle-Age Enthusiasms. Thomas Hardy. CP-HardT

Middle-Age Poem. Grace Paley. CP-PalGC

Middle age you wouldn't wait, The. Progress Report. Maxine W. Kumin. SP-KumiM

Middle-aged life is merry, and I love to lead it. Peekaboo, I Almost See You. Ogden Nash. CP-NashO

Middle-aged man is approaching an all-night lavatory, A. Christopher Logue.

SP-LoguC

Middle-Aged Midwesterner at Waikiki Again. John Logan. CP-LogaJ

Middle-Aged, The. Adrienne Rich. CP-RicAE; SP-RicA2

Middle Class Blues. Hans Magnus Enzensberger. SP-EnzeH, *tr. by* Hans Magnus Enzensberger *and* Michael Hamburger

Middle-Class Children. D. H. Lawrence. CP-LawrD

Middle-Class Vantage. Eleanor Wilner. SP-WilnE

Middle Classes, The. D. H. Lawrence. CP-LawrD

Middle-northern March, now as always, A. Celebration, A. William Carlos Williams. CP-WilW1

Middle of May, when the iris blows. Iris. Muriel Rukeyser. CP-RukeM

Middle of the Month, The. Ogden Nash. CP-NashO

Middle of the night, she's wide awake, carefully lying as far away as she can from him, The. Question, The. C. K. Williams. SP-WillC

Middle of the Summer, The. W. S. Merwin. SP-MerwWF

Middle of the Way. Galway Kinnell. SP-KinnGN

Middle of the World. D. H. Lawrence. CP-LawrD

Middle Passage. Robert Earl Hayden. CP-HaydR

Middleness of the Road, The. Robert Frost. CP-FrosR

Middlesex. Donald Davie. CP-DaviDC

Midget, The. Philip Levine. SP-LeviP

Midlands. Charles Tomlinson. CP-TomlC

Midlands' *a* is mostly an *i*, The. Stratford-on-Avon. Louis Zukofsky. CP-ZukLS

Midnight. John Ciardi. CP-CiarJ

Midnight. Robert Creeley. CP-CreeR

Midnight. Ivor Gurney. SP-GurnI

Midnight. David Ignatow. SP-IgnaD

Midnight. Dorothy Parker. CP-ParkD

Midnight. Yannis Ritsos. SP-RitsY, *tr. by* Athan Anagnostopoulos

Midnight. Robert Penn Warren. CP-WarrR

Midnight 2. David Ignatow. SP-IgnaD

Midnight Chippie's Lament. Langston Hughes. CP-HughL; CP-HughL2

Midnight Dancer. Langston Hughes. CP-HughL
  (To a Black Dancer in "The Little Savoy") CP-HughL1

Midnight has come, and the great Christ Church Bell. All Souls' Night. William Butler Yeats. CP-YeatW *Fr.* Vision, A.

Midnight in Early Spring. W. S. Merwin. SP-MerwW

Midnight—in no midsummer tune. Prefatory Poem to My Brother's Sonnets. Alfred Tennyson. CP-TennA

Midnight in the mid-Atlantic. On deck. On Deck. Sylvia Plath. CP-PlatS

Midnight is not more bewildering, The. Serenade, The: "Midnight is not more bewildering, The." James Whitcomb Riley. CP-RileJ

Midnight Moscow Airport / sucks me in from Siberia. Moscow in the Wilderness, Segovia in the Snow. Lawrence Ferlinghetti. SP-FerlL

Midnight Oil. Edna St. Vincent Millay. CP-MillE

Midnight on Beechen, 187–. Thomas Hardy. CP-HardT

Midnight on the Great Western. Thomas Hardy. CP-HardT

Midnight Outcry. Robert Penn Warren. CP-WarrR

Midnight Raffle. Langston Hughes. CP-HughL; CP-HughL2

Midnight shadow has drooped and drooped, The. At Midnight. D. H. Lawrence. CP-LawrD

Midnight shadows have come over what was the green of Spring. Sympathy. D. H. Lawrence. CP-LawrD

Midnight Special. Kenneth Patchen. CP-PatcK

Midnight Stroll. Yannis Ritsos. SP-RitsY, *tr. by* Kimon Friar *and* Kostas Myrsiades

Midnight: the field becomes white stone. Builders, The. Gregory Orr. SP-OrrG

Midnight wooed the Morning-Star, The. Barrier, The. Paul Laurence Dunbar. CP-DunbP

Midpoint. John Updike. CP-UpdiJ

Midpoint. Charles Simic. SP-SimiC; SP-SimiCE

Mi(dreamlike)st / makes / big each dim. E. E. Cummings. CP-CummE

Midst all the darke and knotty Snares. Matthew 22; Neither Durst Any Man from that Day Aske Him Any More Questions. Bible, *N.T.* CP-CrasR *Fr.* St. Matthew.

'Midst the men and things which will. Abram Morrison. John Greenleaf Whittier. CP-WhitJ

'Midst the palace bowers of Hungary, imperial Presburg's pride. Isabella of Austria. John Greenleaf Whittier. CP-WhitJ

Midsummer. Derek Walcott.
  "At the Queen's Park Hotel, with its white, high-ceilinged rooms." CP-WalcD
  "Before that thundercloud breaks from its hawsers." CP-WalcD
  "Camps hold [*or* held] their distance—[of] brown chestnuts and grey smoke, The." CP-WalcD
  "Chicago's avenues, as white as Poland." CP-WalcD
  "Companion in Rome, whom Rome makes as old as Rome." CP-WalcD
  "Grey English road hissed emptily under the tires, The." CP-WalcD

"I can sense it coming from far, too, Maman, the tide." CP-WalcD

"I heard them marching the leaf-wet roads of my head." CP-WalcD

"I once gave my daughters, separately, two conch shells." CP-WalcD

"In the other 'eighties, a hundred midsummers gone." CP-WalcD

"Long, white, summer cloud, like a cleared linen table, A." CP-WalcD

Midsummer. CP-WalcD

"Midsummer sea, the hot pitch road, this grass, these shacks that made me, The." CP-WalcD

"Midsummer stretches beside me with its cat's yawn." CP-WalcD

Midsummer: XXX. CP-WalcD

"Mud. Clods. The sucking heel of the rain-flinger." CP-WalcD

"My double, tired of morning, closes the door." CP-WalcD

"Oak inns creak in their joints as light declines, The." CP-WalcD

"Our houses are one step from the gutter. Plastic curtains." CP-WalcD

"Since all of your work was really an effort to appease." CP-WalcD

"Something primal in our spine makes the child swing." CP-WalcD

"Sun has fired my face to terra-cotta, The." CP-WalcD

"There was one Syrian, with his bicycle, in our town." CP-WalcD

"Those grooves in that forehead of sand-coloured flesh." CP-WalcD

Tropic Zone. CP-WalcD

Watteau. CP-WalcD

"Wind-scraped headland, a sludgy, dishwater sea, A." CP-WalcD

"With the frenzy of an old snake shedding its skin." CP-WalcD

"With the stampeding hiss and scurry of green lemmings." CP-WalcD

Midsummer. Derek Walcott. CP-WalcD *Fr.* Midsummer.

Midsummer. Thomas Kinsella. CP-KinsT

Midsummer Dawn. Archibald MacLeish. CP-MacLA

Midsummer Duet. Robert Graves. CP-RidiL

Midsummer in the Blueberry Barrens. Amy Clampitt. CP-ClamA

Midsummer. Irish overcast. Oatmeal-colored sky. Jesuit Graves. Charles Wright. SP-WrigCN

Midsummer Mobile. Sylvia Plath. CP-PlatS

Midsummer Night, 1940. Philip Larkin. CP-LarkP

Midsummer Night, whose dream we knew. Midsummer Night's Dream, A. G. K. Chesterton. CP-ChesG

Midsummer Night's Dream, A. G. K. Chesterton. CP-ChesG

Midsummer sea, the hot pitch road, this grass, these shacks that made me, The. Derek Walcott. CP-WalcD *Fr.* Midsummer.

Midsummer stretches beside me with its cat's yawn. Derek Walcott. CP-WalcD *Fr.* Midsummer.

Midsummer, Tobago. Derek Walcott. CP-WalcD

Midsummer, was it, when They died. Emily Dickinson. CP-DickE

Midsummer: XXX. Derek Walcott. CP-WalcD *Fr.* Midsummer.

Midsummer's Day. Howard Nemerov. CP-NemeH

Midsummer's Daymare. Ogden Nash. CP-NashO

Midsummer's Eve. Donald Davie. CP-DaviDC

Midway the Journey of This Life. Eleanor Wilner. SP-WilnE

Midwest. William Stafford. SP-StafWW

Midwinter. William Carlos Williams. CP-WilW2

Midwinter Blues. Langston Hughes. CP-HughL; CP-HughL1

Midwinter in Cuernavaca, tall red flowers. Robert Lowell. SP-LoweR *Fr.* Mexico.

Midwinter night. Open Window on Chicago, An. Allen Ginsberg. CP-GinsA

Midwinter, Presolstice. Margaret Atwood. SP-AtwM1

Midwinter Waking. Philip Larkin. CP-LarkP

Midwives, The. Hans Magnus Enzensberger. SP-EnzeH, *tr. by* Michael Hamburger

Mien to move a Queen, A. Emily Dickinson. CP-DickE

Might have been. Certainly these ashes might have been pleasures. This Place Rumord to Have Been Sodom. Robert Duncan. SP-DuncR

Might / have gone with them. Might. To be. Caliban Remembers. Theodore Weiss. SP-WeisT

Might he [Cro-Magnon] have drawn bi- / son to induct a mys-. Cave Painting. Hayden Carruth. CP-CarHS

Might I as well within my song belay. Sir Thomas Wyatt. CP-WyatT

Might I, if you can find it, be given. Saint Nicholas. Marianne Craig Moore. CP-MoorM

Might I lie where leans her lute. Song: "Might I lie where leans her lute." George Meredith. CP-MerG2

Might these be thrushes climbing through almost(do they). E. E. Cummings. CP-CummE

Mightiest moments pass uncalendared, The. V.R. 1819–1901. Thomas Hardy. CP-HardT

Mighty Britain, tremble! Gandhi Is Fasting. Langston Hughes. CP-HughL; CP-HughL3

Mighty creature is the germ, A. Germ, The. Ogden Nash. CP-NashO

Mighty dog with three colossal necks, A. Psyche and Cerberus. Elizabeth Barrett

Browning. CP-BroEB

Mighty dome is rear'd in solemn state, A. Congress of Nations, The. George Meredith. CP-MerG2

Mighty dying of my Father, The. Emily Dickinson. SP-DickE

Mighty Eagle. Percy Bysshe Shelley. CP-ShelP

Mighty Fountain, A. Samuel Taylor Coleridge. CP-ColeS

Mighty guest of merely me. E. E. Cummings. CP-CummE

Mighty man and the mother-egg, The. From the Inca. Charles Olson. CP-OlsoC

Mighty Neptune, may it please. Another to Neptune. Robert Herrick. CP-HerrR

Mighty Soviet armies marching on the West. Salute to Soviet Armies. Langston Hughes. CP-HughL; CP-HughL2

Mighty struggle in the world goes on, A. Struggle, The. Jones Very. CP-VeryJ

Mighty wind was blowing, A. The deep, dark cypress. Generalization of Distrust. Yannis Ritsos. SP-RitsY, *tr. by* N. C. Germanacos

Mignon he was or *mignonette*. Little Horse. Tennessee Williams. CP-WillT

Mignon's Song. Johann Wolfgang von Goethe. CP-ColeS

Migrant. Langston Hughes. CP-HughL; CP-HughL2

Migrant Camps, The. Gregory Orr. SP-OrrG

Migrant tribe of spiders, A. Encampment at Morning, An. W. S. Merwin. SP-MerwWF

Migration. Raymond Carver. CP-CarvR

Migration. Langston Hughes. CP-HughL; CP-HughL2

Migration. W. S. Merwin. SP-MerwWF

Migration: C.P.R. Margaret Atwood. SP-AtwM1

Migration of Birds. Gary Snyder. CP-SnydG

Migration of Cities, The. Thomas McGrath. SP-McGrT

Migration of Powers, The. Rainer Maria Rilke. CP-RilkFr, *tr. by* A. Poulin, Jr.

Mihrab Shah. Robert Browning. CP-BroR2

Mike. James Schuyler. CP-SchuJ

Milady has picked up a whisper of lilac chiffon. Lady with No One at All, The. Tennessee Williams. CP-WillT

Milady Reflects. John Updike. CP-UpdiJ

Milan Cathedral. Herman Melville. SP-MelvH

Milarepa Taste. Allen Ginsberg. CP-GinsA; SP-GinsA

Mild dose of prussic acid, A. To the Revolutionary Cadres of Balboa, Malibu & Santa Barbara. Philip Whalen. SP-WhalP

Mild noon air of Spring again, The. Riddle, A. Walter De la Mare. CP-DeLaW

Mild parochial talk was ours, A. In the Garden. Walter De la Mare. CP-DeLaW

Mild-Spoken Citizen Finally Writes to the White House, A. William Meredith. SP-MereW

Mild the mist upon the hill. Emily Jane Brontë. CP-BronE

Mild Winter. Hayden Carruth. CP-CarHS

Mildred. G. K. Chesterton. CP-ChesG

Mile out in the marshes, under a sky, A. Town Dump, The. Howard Nemerov. CP-NemeH

Miles above them, miles below. Desert Parable. Eleanor Wilner. SP-WilnE

Miles back. There ("Miles back"). Robert Creeley. SP-CreeR

Miles. Birdland 1959. At first he. Hero. William Corbett. SP-CorbW

Miles Davis and Elizabeth Bishop Fake the Break. Charles Wright. SP-WrigCN

Miles go sliding by, The. Walking Song. Ivor Gurney. SP-GurnI

Milesian Encounter on the Sligachan. Ted Hughes. SP-HughTN

Milestone by the Rabbit-Burrow, The. Thomas Hardy. CP-HardT

Militant. Langston Hughes. CP-HughL; CP-HughL3 (Pride.) CP-HughL1

Military Appointment, A. Thomas Hardy. CP-HardT

Military surprises and the capture of capitals, are the events of a by-gone age. D'Israeli. Jones Very. CP-VeryJ

Milk. James Schuyler. CP-SchuJ

Milk-drops on your chin, Helga, The. Winter Milk. Carl Sandburg. CP-SandC

Milk Factory, The. Seamus Heaney. SP-HeanSO

Milk-glass bowl hanging by three chains, A. Corpse-Plant, The. Adrienne Rich. CP-RicAE; SP-RicA2

Milk of Millennia, The. Jelaluddin Rumi. SP-Rumi, *tr. by* Coleman Barks

Milk stil your Fountains, and your Springs, for why? Draw, and Drinke. Robert Herrick. CP-HerrR

Milk to be boiled. Visit, A. Denise Levertov. SP-LeveDL

Milk used to come in tall glass, heavy and uncrystalline as frozen melted. Milk. James Schuyler. CP-SchuJ

Milk-White Moon, Put the Cows to Sleep. Carl Sandburg. CP-SandC

Milk-Wort and Bog Cotton. Hugh MacDiarmid. SP-MacDH

Milkers Broken Up. Donald Hall. CP-HallD

Milking-Maid, The. Christina Georgina Rossetti. CP-RosC1 (Farm Walk, A.) CP-RosC1

Milkmaid, The. Thomas Hardy. CP-HardT

Milkman and His Son, The. Thomas Lux. SP-LuxT

Milkman came in the moonlight and the moonlight, The. Les Plus Belles Pages. Wallace Stevens. CP-StevW; CP-StevWP

Milkweed. Peter Blue Cloud. SP-BlueP

Milkweed. Philip Levine. SP-LeviP

Milkweed. James Wright. CP-WrigJ

Milkweed and Monarch. Paul Muldoon. CP-MuldP

Milkweed flower, The. In Deepest Summer. Grace Paley. CP-PalGC

Milky love of this bland child, The. Governess, The. Stevie Smith. CP-SmitS

Milky Way Is a Cowpath, The. Robert Frost. CP-FrosR

Mill-Doors. Carl Sandburg. CP-SandC

Mill-stream, now that noises cease, The. A. E. Housman. CP-HousA

Mill, The. Edwin Arlington Robinson. CP-RobiE

Mill, The. Richard Wilbur. CP-WilbR

Millais Loquacious. Robert Stock. SP-StocR

"Millennium," yes; "pandemonium"! Hometown Piece for Messrs. Alston and Reese. Marianne Craig Moore. CP-MoorM

Miller, The. Randall Jarrell. CP-JarrR

Miller's Man, The. Robert Graves. CP-GravR

Miller's wife had waited long, The. Mill, The. Edwin Arlington Robinson. CP-RobiE

Million buds are born that never blow, A. Buds and Babies. Christina Georgina Rossetti. CP-RosC2

Million whirling spinning-wheels of flowing gossamer, A. Genesis. Louis MacNeice. CP-MacNL

Million Young Workmen, 1915, A. Carl Sandburg. CP-SandC

Millionaire, The. Charles Bukowski. SP-BukC2

Millions of babies watching the skies. September on Jessore Road. Allen Ginsberg. CP-GinsA; SP-GinsA

Millions of miles away at evening the sun. By the Deschutes Shore. William Stafford. SP-StafWW

Millions of people cheering and waving flags for joy in Manhattan. After the Big Parade. Allen Ginsberg. SP-GinsA

Millipede, The. John Updike. CP-UpdiJ

Millpond Lost. Robert Penn Warren. CP-WarrR

Millpond, The. Yusef Komunyakaa. CP-KomuY

Mills of God, The. D. H. Lawrence. CP-LawrD

Mills of the Kavanaughs, The. Robert Lowell. SP-LoweR

Mills / That grind and grind, The. Steel Mills. Langston Hughes. CP-HughL; CP-HughL1

Milonga of Albornoz. Jorge Luis Borges. SP-BorgJ, *tr. by* Alastair Reid

Milonga of Don Nicanor Paredes. Jorge Luis Borges. SP-BorgJ, *tr. by* Eric McHenry

Milonga of Manuel Flores. Jorge Luis Borges. SP-BorgJ, *tr. by* Alastair Reid

Miltiades! thy valour best. On Miltiades. *Unknown*. CP-CowpW

Milton. William Blake. CP-BlakW

Milton. John Dryden. CP-HopkG

Milton. George Meredith. CP-MerG2

Milton. John Greenleaf Whittier. CP-WhitJ

Milton: A Sonnet. Robert Penn Warren. CP-WarrR

Milton Avery Altmar. Anthem: "Milton Avery Altmar." William Corbett. SP-CorbW

Milton by Firelight. Gary Snyder. CP-SnydG

Milton! I think thy spirit hath passed away. To Milton. Oscar Wilde. CP-WildO

Milton paints purple trees. Avery. Thinking of Winter at the Beginning of Summer. Charles Wright. SP-WrigCN

Milton! thou shouldst be living at this hour. London 1802. William Wordsworth. CP-WorW1; MW-WorW

Milton Über Alles. Robert Creeley. SP-CreeR

Milton unlocked hell for us. Our Hells. Carl Sandburg. CP-SandC

Miltonic Sonnet for Mr. Johnson on His Refusal of Peter Hurd's Official Portrait, A. Richard Wilbur. CP-WilbR

Mime. John Updike. CP-UpdiJ

Mime the loud wind in pain. To the Loud Wind. Donald Hall. CP-HallD

Mimiambi of Herodas, The. Constantine P. Cavafy. CP-CavaC, *tr. by* Theoharis Constantine Theoharis

Min Schleppner. William Carlos Williams. CP-WilW1

Mince-pies grant Wishes: let each name his Prize. Some Wishes at Xmas. G. K. Chesterton. CP-ChesG

Mind. Heather McHugh. SP-McHuH

Mind. Richard Wilbur. CP-WilbR

Mind and Nature. Richard Eberhart. CP-EberR

Mind Breaths. Allen Ginsberg. CP-GinsA; SP-GinsA

Mind can't sleep, can only lie awake and, The. Winter Insomnia. Raymond Carver. CP-CarvR

Mind does not forget; that which is limned, The. Two Metaphysical Sonnets. Tennessee Williams. CP-WillT

Mind has shown itself at times, The. For the Marriage of Faustus and Helen. Hart Crane. CP-CranH

Mind Hesitant, The. William Carlos Williams. CP-WilW2

Mind in its [*or* the] purest play is like some bat. Mind. Richard Wilbur. CP-

WilbR

Mind, Intractable Thing, The. Marianne Craig Moore. CP-MoorM

Mind is a most delicate evidence. On the Fragility of Mind. Richard Eberhart. CP-EberR

Mind Is an Enchanting Thing, The. Marianne Craig Moore. CP-MoorM

Mind is its own beautiful prisoner, The. E. E. Cummings. CP-CummE

Mind is so near itself, The. Emily Dickinson. SP-DickE

Mind is the great poem of winter, the man, The. Man and Bottle. Wallace Stevens. CP-StevW; CP-StevWP

Mind is the terriblest force in the world, father, The. Saint John and the Back-Ache. Wallace Stevens. CP-StevW; CP-StevWP

Mind lives on the Heart, The. Emily Dickinson. CP-DickE

Mind of mortals, in perverseness strong, The. Juvenal. CP-JohnS *Fr.* Satires.

Mind of Professor Primrose, The. Ogden Nash. CP-NashO

Mind of the Frontispiece to a Book, The. Ben Jonson. CP-JonsB

Mind-Reader, The. Richard Wilbur. CP-WilbR

Mind reels, The. End of the Line, The. Eleanor Wilner. SP-WilnE

Mind the Greatest Mystery, The. Jones Very. CP-VeryJ

Mind (the soul) is not, The. Attar of Roses. Donald Davie. CP-DaviDC

Mind was six feet deep in a, The. Introspection. T. S. Eliot. SP-ElioT

Mind went forth with naked eye, The. Druidic Rimes. Howard Nemerov. CP-NemeH

Mindes of men are ever so affected, The. Homer. CP-RaleW *Fr.* Odyssey.

Mindful of the shambles of the day. Nightwalker. Thomas Kinsella. CP-KinsT

Mindful of you the sodden earth in spring. Edna St. Vincent Millay. CP-MillE

Mindless, meaning no harm. Amoeba. John Updike. CP-UpdiJ

Mind's a queer sponge, The. May 1st Tomorrow. William Carlos Williams. CP-WilW2

Mind's anchored to a stone, The. They Say in Yellow Jacket. Yusef Komunyakaa. CP-KomuY

Mind's eye sees as the heart mirrors:, The. To Sleep. Robert Graves. CP-GravR

Mind's Games, The. William Carlos Williams. CP-WilW2

Mind's Heart. Robert Creeley. CP-CreeR

Mind's heart, it must / be that some. Mind's Heart. Robert Creeley. CP-CreeR

Mind's(/ I never you never), The. E. E. Cummings. CP-CummE

Mind's Notice, The. Charles Olson. CP-OlsoC

Mine are the night and morning. Song of Nature. Ralph Waldo Emerson. CP-EmerR

Mine—by the Right of the White Election! Emily Dickinson. CP-DickE

Mine Enemy is growing old. Emily Dickinson. CP-DickE

Mine eyes, like clouds, were drizzling rain. Rainbow; or Curious Covenant, The. Robert Herrick. CP-HerrR

Mine eyes were dim with tears unshed. To Mary Wollstonecraft Godwin. Percy Bysshe Shelley. CP-ShelP

Mine is a body that should die at sea! Burial. Edna St. Vincent Millay. CP-MillE

Mine is a dauntless spirit, meaning a spirit that is hard to daunt. I'm a Pleasure to Shop for. Ogden Nash. CP-NashO

Mine is a hollow tree upside-down in the ground, A. On an Architect. Alan Dugan. CP-DugaA

Mine old dear enemy [*or* en'my], my froward master. Translation from Petrarch. Petrarch. CP-WyatT

Mine [*or* Myne] own[e] John Poyntz, since [*or* sins] ye delight to know. Of the Courtier's Life. Sir Thomas Wyatt. CP-WyatT *Fr.* Satires.

Mine Sweepers. Rudyard Kipling. CP-KiplR

Mine there is no Man would own, A. Emily Dickinson. CP-DickE

Mine to watch the sun at work. Thermometer. Ralph Waldo Emerson. CP-EmerR

Mine was a midwest home—you can keep your world. One Home. William Stafford. SP-StafW; SP-StafWW

Mine was the life planned to go wrong. Prologue. David Ignatow. SP-IgnaD

Mine was the woman to me, darkling I found her. First Chantey, The. Rudyard Kipling. CP-KiplR

Mine will last though others fall to dust. Enigma, The. Richard Eberhart. CP-EberR

Mined Country. Richard Wilbur. CP-WilbR

Minefield Revisited. Joseph Brodsky. CP-BrodJ

Miners. Wilfred Owen. CP-OwenW

Miners. James Wright. CP-WrigJ

Minerva has vowed since the bishops do slight her. On Wisdom's Defeat in a Learned Debate. Jonathan Swift. CP-SwifJ

Mingle with the genial bowl. Translation from Anacreon. Lord Byron. CP-Byron

Mingled / breath and smell. Subway Rush Hour. Langston Hughes. CP-HughL; CP-HughL3

Mingled the moonlight with daylight—the last in the narrowing west. Thomas Hardy. Walter De la Mare. CP-DeLaW

Mingling scent of flowers is in the air, The. Spring and Summer Flowers. Jones Very. CP-VeryJ

Miniature. William Meredith. SP-MereW

Miniature. Yannis Ritsos. SP-RitsY, *tr. by* Kimon Friar

Miniature Greek gods support the Roman hour. On a Baroque Clock. Alan Dugan. CP-DugaA

Minimal, The. Theodore Roethke. CP-RoetT

Minister to my friends, Saint Peregrine. Fanny Howe. SP-HoweF *Fr.* O'Clock.

Minister wet to lee, pour the Falernian. Catullus. *See* Falernian, / old Falernian!

Minister's Daughter, The. John Greenleaf Whittier. CP-WhitJ

Ministers / Don't like bar sinisters. Birth Comes to the Archbishop. Ogden Nash. CP-NashO

Miniver Cheevy. Edwin Arlington Robinson. CP-RobiE

Miniver Cheevy, child of scorn, Miniver Cheevy. Edwin Arlington Robinson. CP-RobiE

Mink. Paul Muldoon. CP-MuldP

Mink escaped from a mink-farm, A. Mink. Paul Muldoon. CP-MuldP

Minneapolis Poem, The. James Wright. CP-WrigJ

Minneapolis Story. Robert Penn Warren. CP-WarrR

Minnelied. W. H. Auden. CP-AudeW *Fr.* Three Posthumous Poems.

Minnesota Recollection. Robert Penn Warren. CP-WarrR

Minnesota Thanksgiving. John Berryman. CP-BerrJ

(For that free Grace bringing us past great risks.) CP-BerrJ

Minnie and Mattie. Christina Georgina Rossetti. CP-RosC2

Minnie bakes oaten cakes, / Minnie brews ale. Christina Georgina Rossetti. CP-RosC2

Minnie Sings Her Blues. Langston Hughes. CP-HughL; CP-HughL1

Minnow, go to sleep and dream. Lullaby for the Cat. Elizabeth Bishop. CP-BishE

Minoan Snake Goddess is flanked by a Chardin still-life, somber, The. Postcards: A Triptych, The. Denise Levertov. SP-LeveDP

Minor Bird, A. Robert Frost. CP-FrosR

Minor Epic. Eleanor Wilner. SP-WilnE

Minor Impulse to Complain, A. Charles Bukowski. SP-BukC2

Minor Poet, The. Josephine Jacobsen. CP-JacoJ

Minor poet sits at meat, The. Minor Poet, The. Josephine Jacobsen. CP-JacoJ

Minor Sacrifice, A. A. K. Ramanujan. CP-RamaA

Minor Song. Federico García Lorca. CP-GarcF, *tr. by* Catherine Brown

Minor stupidities, The. Education a Failure. William Carlos Williams. CP-WilW2

Minor Toys of the Year are alike, The. Emily Dickinson. SP-DickE

Minor Tremor, A. Amy Clampitt. CP-ClamA

Minorities in Danger. D. H. Lawrence. CP-LawrD

Minority Report. John Updike. CP-UpdiJ

Minotaur, The. Muriel Rukeyser. CP-RukeM

Minott, Lee, Willard, Hosmer, Meriam, Flint. Hamatreya. Ralph Waldo Emerson. CP-EmerR

Minstrel came singing in the way, A. Unheard Melodies. Walter De la Mare. CP-DeLaW

Minstrel Man. Langston Hughes. CP-HughL; CP-HughL1

Minstrel, what have you to do. To a Poet that Died Young. Edna St. Vincent Millay. CP-MillE

Minstrels. Eugenio Montale. CP-MontE, *tr. by* Jonathan Galassi

Minstrel's mystic wand, The. Ole Bull. James Whitcomb Riley. CP-RileJ

Mint. Seamus Heaney. SP-HeanSO

Mint a spiked attar hot. Spearmint. Louis Zukofsky. CP-ZukLS

Mint bed is in / bloom: lavender haze, the. Sunday. James Schuyler. CP-SchuJ

Minuet, The. Raymond Carver. CP-CarvR

Minuet has long ceased to be danced, The. Moscow. Jaroslav Seifert. SP-SeifJ, *tr. by* Ewald Osers

Minus One. John Ciardi. CP-CiarJ

Minute before Meeting, The. Thomas Hardy. CP-HardT

Minute garden / you must not enter, A. In Verdi Square. Charles Tomlinson. CP-TomlC

Minute I heard my first love story, The. Jelaluddin Rumi. SP-Rumi, *tr. by* Coleman Barks

Minute I'm out of town, The. 20:vii:58, On Which I Renounce the Notion of Social Responsiblity. Philip Whalen. SP-WhalP

Minute my brother gets out of jail I want, The. Autobiographical. Thomas Lux. SP-LuxT

Minutely Hurt. Countee Cullen. CP-CullC

Minutes are flying swiftly, and as yet. On Receiving a Laurel Crown from Leigh Hunt. John Keats. CP-KeatJ

Minutes have their trusts as they go by, The. Hours, The. Jones Very. CP-VeryJ

Mirabeau Bridge. Guillaume Apollinaire. CP-WilbR, *tr. by* Richard Wilbur

Miracle. Raymond Carver. CP-CarvR

Miracle, The. Donald Davie. CP-DaviDC

Miracle, The. Ralph Waldo Emerson. CP-EmerR

Miracle, The. Thom Gunn. CP-GunnT

Miracle, The. Philip Levine. SP-LeviP

Miracle, The. Walter De la Mare. CP-DeLaW

Miracle, The. George Meredith. CP-MerG2

Miracle, The. Sir John Suckling. CP-SuckJ

Miracle at Sea, The. Shmuel HaNagid. SP-HaNaS, *tr. by* Peter Cole

Miracle Fair. Wisława Szymborska. SP-SzymW, *tr. by* Stanisław Barańczak *and* Clare Cavanagh

Miracle Fair. Wisława Szymborska. SP-SzymWM, *tr. by* Joanna Trzeciak

Miracle for Breakfast, A. Elizabeth Bishop. CP-BishE

Miracle in Manila. Ai. SP-Ai

Miracle is the Shortest Time, The. Charles Bukowski. SP-BukC3

Miracle of our land's speech—so known, The. Birthright, The. Rudyard Kipling. CP-KiplR *Fr.* Debits and Credits.

Miracle of Purun Bhagat, The. Rudyard Kipling. *Fr.* Second Jungle Book, The.

Miracle of the Bottle and the Fishes, The. Charles Tomlinson. SP-TomlC

Miracle of the children the brilliant. Exodus. George Oppen. CP-OppGN

Miracle of the Roses, The. Robert Stock. SP-StocR

Miracles. Arthur Sze. SP-SzeA

Miracles. Walt Whitman. CP-WhitW

Miracles, The. Rudyard Kipling. CP-KiplR

Mirage. Walter De la Mare. CP-DeLaW

Mirage. Christina Georgina Rossetti. CP-RosC1

Mirages. Walt Whitman. CP-WhitW

Mirages, The. Robert Earl Hayden. CP-HaydR

Mired in it! Stuck in the various. Zion. Donald Davie. CP-DaviDC

Mirèio. Frédéric Mistral.
     Mares of the Camargue, The. CP-MerG1, *tr. by* George Meredith

Miriam. John Greenleaf Whittier. CP-WhitJ

Miriam and Horlick spend a great deal of time putting off going to bed. Goodnight. Stevie Smith. CP-SmitS

Miriam Tazewell. John Crowe Ransom. SP-RansJ

Miriam's Lucky Day. Ogden Nash. CP-NashO

Miriam's Song. Eleanor Wilner. SP-WilnE

Miror surgentem per puram Oriona noctem. Gerard Manley Hopkins. CP-HopkG

Mirror. Federico García Lorca. CP-GarcF, *tr. by* Jerome Rothenberg *Fr.* Secrets.

Mirror. James Merrill. SP-MerrJ

Mirror. Sylvia Plath. CP-PlatS

Mirror. Kenneth Rexroth. CP-RexrK

Mirror, The. Jorge Luis Borges. SP-BorgJ, *tr. by* Hoyt Rogers

Mirror, The. Robert Creeley. CP-CreeR

Mirror, The. Michael Davitt. CP-MuldP, *tr. by* Paul Muldoon

Mirror, The. Robert Duncan. SP-DuncR

Mirror, The. Louise Glück. SP-GlucL

Mirror, The. Howard Nemerov. CP-NemeH

Mirror, The. James Tate. SP-TateJ

Mirror, The. Robert Penn Warren. CP-WarrR

Mirror, The. C. K. Williams. SP-WillC

Mirror above my fireplace reflects the reflected, The. Reflections. Louis MacNeice. CP-MacNL

Mirror cared less and less at the last, The. At the Grave of My Brother. William Stafford. SP-StafWW

Mirror does not lie to me, the sight is true, The. Dünya Güzeli. Constantine P. Cavafy. CP-CavaC, *tr. by* Theoharis Constantine Theoharis

Mirror for Poets, A. Thom Gunn. CP-GunnT

Mirror from the twenties. What the Owl Sees. Marge Piercy. SP-PierM

Mirror Girl, The. James Laughlin. CP-LaugJ

Mirror hangs on the wall of the draughty cupola, A. Cupola, The. Louise Bogan. CP-BogaL

Mirror hung on the broken, A. Mirror in the Woods, The. Kenneth Rexroth. CP-RexrK

Mirror in February. Thomas Kinsella. CP-KinsT

Mirror in the Roadway, The. Charles Tomlinson. CP-TomlC

Mirror in the Vestibule, The. Constantine P. Cavafy. CP-CavaC, *tr. by* Theoharis Constantine Theoharis

Mirror in the Woods, The. Kenneth Rexroth. CP-RexrK

Mirror in Which Two Are Seen as One, The. Adrienne Rich. SP-RicA2

Mirror Lake, The. Summer Song. Li Po. CP-WilW2

Mirror, let us through the glass. Flight into Egypt, The. W. H. Auden. CP-AudeW *Fr.* For the Time Being; a Christmas Oratorio.

Mirror, mirror on the wall. Conduct and Work. Donald Hall. CP-HallD

Mirror of Madmen, The. G. K. Chesterton. CP-ChesG

Mirror Perilous, The. Alan Dugan. CP-DugaA

Mirror Suite. Federico García Lorca.
     Air ("Air / pregnant with rainbows, The"). CP-GarcF, *tr. by* Jerome Rothenberg
     Berceuse for a Sleeping Mirror. CP-GarcF, *tr. by* Jerome Rothenberg
     Capriccio ("Behind each mirror"). CP-GarcF, *tr. by* Jerome Rothenberg
     Confusion ("Is my heart / your heart?"). CP-GarcF, *tr. by* Jerome Rothenberg
     Earth ("We walk on / an unsilvered"). CP-GarcF, *tr. by* Jerome Rothenberg

     Eyes. CP-GarcF, *tr. by* Jerome Rothenberg
     Giant Mirror, The. CP-GarcF, *tr. by* Jerome Rothenberg
     Initium. CP-GarcF, *tr. by* Jerome Rothenberg
     Pool, The. CP-GarcF, *tr. by* Jerome Rothenberg
     Rays. CP-GarcF, *tr. by* Jerome Rothenberg
     Reflection. CP-GarcF, *tr. by* Jerome Rothenberg
     Replica. CP-GarcF, *tr. by* Jerome Rothenberg
     Shinto. CP-GarcF, *tr. by* Jerome Rothenberg
     Symbol. CP-GarcF, *tr. by* Jerome Rothenberg

Mirrored in the waters lie. South River at Sunset, The. Jones Very. CP-VeryJ

Mirrored Room, The. Marya Alexandrovna Zaturenska. SP-ZatuM

Mirrored / the rear window. Carscape. Charles Tomlinson. CP-TomlC

Mirrorment. A. R. Ammons. CP-AmmoA

Mirrors. Jorge Luis Borges. SP-BorgJ, *tr. by* Alastair Reid

Mirrors are not more wrapt in silences. To a Cat. Jorge Luis Borges. SP-BorgJ, *tr. by* Alastair Reid

Mirrors in the hall were a strange backwater, The. Northwind Escarpment. Norman Dubie. CP-DubiN

Mirror's Mission, The. Jorge Carrera Andrade. CP-MertT

Mirrors of Life and Death. Christina Georgina Rossetti. CP-RosC2

Mirrors, reflecting each other. Georgy Vladimirovich Ivanov. SP-WeisT, *tr. by* Theodore Weiss

Mirrors, The. William Carlos Williams. CP-WilW2

Mirra. Kenneth Patchen. CP-PatcK

Mirth. G. K. Chesterton. CP-ChesG

Mirth. Robert Herrick. CP-HerrR

Misael, civil servant in the Ministry of Labor, 63 years old. Brazilian Tragedy. Manuel Bandeira. CP-BishE

Misanthropos. Thom Gunn. CP-GunnT

Misapprehension. Paul Laurence Dunbar. CP-DunbP

Miscellaneous weed / strands, stems, debris—. Cod Head, The. William Carlos Williams. CP-WilW1

Misconception. Thomas Hardy. CP-HardT

Misconceptions. Robert Browning. CP-BroR1

Misconstructions. Yannis Ritsos. SP-RitsY, *tr. by* Kimon Friar

Mise-en-Scène. Miller Williams. CP-WillM

Miser, The. Mona Van Duyn. SP-VanDM

Miser, The. Jones Very. CP-VeryJ

Miser and the Mouse, The. Lucilius. SP-SmarC
     (To a Mouse says a Miser my dear Mr Mouse.) SP-SmarC

Miser, traversing his house, A. Another. *Unknown.* CP-CowpW

Miser with an eager face, A. World's Miser, The. G. K. Chesterton. CP-ChesG

Miserable Catullus, stop being foolish. Catullus viii. Louis Zukofsky. CP-ZukLS

Miserable day, his dog had leapt, A. Riven Doggeries. James Tate. SP-TateJ

Miserable little woman. Divertimiento. William Carlos Williams. CP-WilW1

Misericordia. William Carlos Williams. CP-WilW1

Miseries. Robert Herrick. CP-HerrR

Miserly, is the best description of that poor fool. Con Brio. William Carlos Williams. CP-WilW1

"Miserrimus!" and neither name nor date. Gravestone upon the Floor in the Cloisters of Worcester Cathedral, A. William Wordsworth. CP-WorW2

Misery. Langston Hughes. CP-HughL; CP-HughL1

Misery. D. H. Lawrence. CP-LawrD

Misery [*or* Miserie]. George Herbert. CP-HerbG

Misery weighed by drachms and scruples. Drachms and Scruples. Ivor Gurney. SP-GurnI

Misfit, The. A. R. Ammons. CP-AmmoA

Misfortune Is on the Way. Charles Simic. SP-SimiCE

Misgiving. Robert Frost. CP-FrosR

Misgivings. Herman Melville. SP-MelvH

Mismatched Shoes. Yusef Komunyakaa. CP-KomuY

Mismet. Thomas Hardy. CP-HardT

Misprint. Charles Tomlinson. CP-TomlC

Misremembered Edwin Denby Line. William Corbett. SP-CorbW

Miss. A. R. Ammons. CP-AmmoA

Miss Blues'es Child. Langston Hughes. CP-HughL; CP-HughL3

Miss Brown, my woman, died. Matthew. Clarence Major. SP-MajoC

Miss Carney handed us out blank paper and marla. Settings. Thomas Kinsella. CP-KinsT

Miss Drake Proceeds to Supper. Sylvia Plath. CP-PlatS

Miss Gardner's in her garden. Southern Mammy Sings. Langston Hughes. CP-HughL; CP-HughL2

Miss Gee. W. H. Auden. CP-AudeW

Miss Green's Reply. Mrs. Austen. CP-AustJ

Miss Helen Slingsby was my maiden aunt. Aunt Helen. T. S. Eliot. CP-ElioT

Miss her, Catullus? don't be so inept to rail. Catullus. *See* Break off / fallen Catullus

Miss Isadora Quigley pays. Our Own Home Talent. Dorothy Parker. CP-ParkD

Miss Lloyd has now sent to Miss Green. Lines *Supposed* to Have Been Sent to an Uncivil Dress Maker. Jane Austen. CP-AustJ

Miss Loo. Walter De la Mare. CP-DeLaW

Miss Lorence, until I get to be somebody else—big me. Another Day. In a Field of Peace the Child, Playing. The Child Preparing for Daytime Sleep. Muriel Rukeyser. CP-RukeM

Miss Lorence, we are new to each other. Another Day (Miss Lorence). Muriel Rukeyser. CP-RukeM

Miss Lorence, you are a tree with leaves on. Muriel Rukeyser. CP-RukeM

Miss Lucy. Wyatt Prunty. SP-PrunW

Miss Marfy sco'n young Issac so. Suitor, The. Paul Laurence Dunbar. CP-DunbP

Miss Millicent Maxse was fond of her Ma. George Meredith. CP-MerG2

Miss Moore at Assembly. John Updike. CP-UpdiJ

Miss Murphy in first grade. Halley's Comet. Stanley Kunitz. CP-KunSC

Miss Nancy Ellicott. Cousin Nancy. T. S. Eliot. CP-ElioT

Miss Olivia Branton. John Ciardi. CP-CiarJ

Miss Pauncefort sang at the top of her voice. Songster, The. Stevie Smith. CP-SmitS

Miss Puma, Miss Who? Tennessee Williams. CP-WillT

Miss Puma was popular barely. Miss Puma, Miss Who? Tennessee Williams. CP-WillT

Miss Rafferty wore taffeta. Private Dining Room, The. Ogden Nash. CP-NashO

Miss Scarlet, Mr. Rhett and other Latter-Day Saints. Maya Angelou. SP-AngeM

Miss Story's character! too much you ask. Gerard Manley Hopkins. CP-HopkG

Missed Train, The. Thomas Hardy. CP-HardT

Missile to launch a missile, The. Venus and the Ark. Anne Sexton. CP-SextA

Missing. W. H. Auden. CP-AudeW

Missing, The. Thom Gunn. CP-GunnT

Missing All—prevented Me, The. Emily Dickinson. CP-DickE

Missing in Action. Yusef Komunyakaa. CP-KomuY

Missing is a pain. Never-Never. Marge Piercy. SP-PierM

Missing Persons. Miller Williams. CP-WillM

Missing the Bo in the Henhouse. Hayden Carruth. CP-CarHS

Missing the Point. Adrienne Rich. CP-RicAE

Missing the Sea. Derek Walcott. CP-WalcD

Missing You. "Shu Ting." CP-KizeC, *tr. by* Carolyn Kizer *and* Y. H. Zhao

Mission. Yehuda Amichai. SP-AmicYL, *tr. by* Benjamin Harshav *and* Barbara Harshav

Mission. A. R. Ammons. CP-AmmoA

Mission, The. Robert Penn Warren. CP-WarrR

Mission of the Friends to the Emperor Nicholas, The. Jones Very. CP-VeryJ

Mission with the Night, A. Jane Cooper. CP-CoopJ

Missionary from the Mau Mau told me, A. Magus, A. John Ciardi. CP-CiarJ

Missionary, The. John Greenleaf Whittier. CP-WhitJ

Mississippi. Langston Hughes. CP-HughL; CP-HughL3

Mississippi Anatomy. Josephine Jacobsen. CP-JacoJ

Mississippi at Midnight, The. Walt Whitman. CP-WhitW

Mississippi John Hurt. Yusef Komunyakaa. CP-KomuY

Mississippi Levee. Langston Hughes. CP-HughL; CP-HughL2

Mississippi River. Kenneth Rexroth. CP-RexrK

Mississippi Winter I. Alice Walker. CP-WalkA

Mississippi Winter II. Alice Walker. CP-WalkA

Mississippi Winter III. Alice Walker. CP-WalkA

Mississippi Winter IV. Alice Walker. CP-WalkA

Missive Missile, A. Robert Frost. CP-FrosR

Missouri Fable, A. John Ciardi. CP-CiarJ

Missus Dora. Lorine Niedecker. CP-NiedL

Mist. E. E. Cummings. CP-CummE

Mist. Robert Graves. CP-GravR

Mist. Walter De la Mare. CP-DeLaW

Mist. W. S. Merwin. SP-MerwW

Mist, The. Carl Sandburg. CP-SandC

Mist after frost. The woodlands. Last of Night, The. Charles Tomlinson. CP-TomlC

Mist and Rain. Charles Baudelaire. CP-BaudC, *tr. by* Walter Martin

Mist came up as a man's hand. New Weather. Carl Sandburg. CP-SandC

Mist clears and the cavities, The. Derry Morning. Derek Mahon. CP-MahoD

Mist Forms. Carl Sandburg. CP-SandC

Mist has left the greening plain, The. Morning. Paul Laurence Dunbar. CP-DunbP

Mist hung on the slope, growing whiter, The. Tara. Thomas Kinsella. CP-KinsT

Mist in St. James Street. Earrings of Madame de, The. William Corbett. SP-CorbW

Mist in the trees, and soiled water and grass cuttings splotch. Yard Journal. Charles Wright. SP-WrigC

Mist in the Valley. Edna St. Vincent Millay. CP-MillE

Mist keeps pushing between the peaks, A. Down From Colonnata. Charles Tomlinson. SP-TomlC

Mist Marches Across the Valley. Carl Sandburg. CP-SandC

Mist-Net, The. Paul Muldoon. CP-MuldP

Mist rain this morning made glass, The. Early Morning in Early April. A. R. Ammons. CP-AmmoA

Mist, the weather changing. Instructions to Painters by Wang Wei, Eighth Century. Eleanor Wilner. SP-WilnE

Mistake, A. Czeslaw Milosz. CP-MiloC; CP-MiloCN, *tr. by* Renata Gorczynski *and* Robert Hass

Mistake, The. Thomas Carew. CP-CareT

Mistaken Identity. Richard Eberhart. CP-EberR

Mistaking him for a leaf, I cut a toad. Territory. Maxine W. Kumin. SP-KumiM

Mistaking Water Hemlock for Parsley. Arthur Sze. SP-SzeA

Mr. & Mrs. John Ciardi. CP-CiarJ

Mr. and Mrs. Billings. Donald Hall. CP-HallD

Mr. and Mrs. F.X. Pleasants. Lines To Be Mumbled At Ovington's. Ogden Nash. CP-NashO

Mr. and Mrs. Scott, and I. Christina Georgina Rossetti. CP-RosC3

Mr. Apollinax. T. S. Eliot. CP-ElioT

Mr. Artesian's Conscientiousness. Ogden Nash. CP-NashO

Mr. Attila. Carl Sandburg. CP-SandC

Mister Backlash, Mister Backlash. Backlash Blues, The. Langston Hughes. CP-HughL; CP-HughL3

Mr. Barcalow's Breakdown. Ogden Nash. CP-NashO

Mister Beringer, whose son. Yehuda Amichai. SP-AmicYL *Fr.* Elegies on the War Dead.

Mr. Berryman's songs and sonnets say. Thank-You Note. Elizabeth Bishop. CP-BishE

Mr. Betts's Mind a Kingdom Is. Ogden Nash. CP-NashO

Mr. Brodsky. Charles Tomlinson. CP-TomlC; SP-TomlC

Mr. Burgess, Meet Mr. Barmecide. Ogden Nash. CP-NashO

Mr. Carew to His Friend. Thomas Carew. CP-CareT

Mr Chernobyl is. Chernobyl. A Disaster. Donald Davie. CP-DaviDC

Mr Cromek to Mr Stothard. William Blake. CP-BlakW

Mr. Edwards and the Spider. Robert Lowell. SP-LoweR

Mr. Eliot's Sunday Morning Service. T. S. Eliot. CP-ElioT; SP-ElioT

Mr Flood's Party. Edwin Arlington Robinson. CP-RobiE

Mr. Foley's Christmas. James Whitcomb Riley. CP-RileJ

Mr. Hammond's Parable. James Whitcomb Riley. CP-RileJ *Fr.* Child-World, A.

Mister Hanusevich. Czeslaw Milosz. CP-MiloCN, *tr. by* Robert Hass

Mr. Hericke his Daughter's Dowrye. Robert Herrick. CP-HerrR

[Mr. Herrys,] His Epitaph. Richard Crashaw. CP-CrasR

Mr. High-Mind. John Updike. CP-UpdiJ

Mister Hop-Toad. James Whitcomb Riley. CP-RileJ

Mister Humbug. Nothing to Do with Janice Drake. Yusef Komunyakaa. CP-KomuY

Mr J who had been poor for years. To the Memory Of. Philip Whalen. SP-WhalP

Mr. Jason Hassard, a Woolen Draper in Dublin. Jonathan Swift. CP-SwifJ

Mr. Lizard is crying. Federico García Lorca. CP-GarcF, *tr. by* Alan S. Trueblood *Fr.* Songs for Children.

Mr. Longfellow and His Boy. Carl Sandburg. CP-SandC

Mr. Longfellow, Henry Wadsworth Longfellow. Mr. Longfellow and His Boy. Carl Sandburg. CP-SandC

Mr. Mandragon, the Millionaire, he wouldn't have wine or wife. Good Rich Man, The. G. K. Chesterton. CP-ChesG

Mr. Mine. Anne Sexton. CP-SextA; SP-SextA

Mister Minister, I found. Why I Turned Vegetarian. Rita Dove. SP-DoveR

Mr. or Mrs. Nobody. William Stafford. SP-StafW

Mr. Osmosis / Is all right in small doses. Mistress Osmosis. Stevie Smith. CP-SmitS

Mr. Peachey's Predicament or No Mot Parades. Ogden Nash. CP-NashO

Mr. Pope. Allen Tate. CP-TateA

Mr. President, kindly please. Message to the President. Langston Hughes. CP-HughL; CP-HughL3

Mr. Robert Hericke His Farwell unto Poetrie. Robert Herrick. CP-HerrR

Mister Sandman. Langston Hughes. CP-HughL

Mr Sharp in Florence. Donald Davie. CP-DaviDC

Mr. Sheridan's Prologue to the Greek Play of Phaedra and Hippolytus; Designed to Have Been Spoke by a Boy of Six Years Old. Thomas Sheridan. CP-SherT

Mister Shih had two sons. Han-shan. CP-ColdM, *tr. by* Red Pine

Mr Sludge, "The Medium" Robert Browning. CP-BroR1; SP-BroR

Mr. smith / is reading / his letter. E. E. Cummings. CP-CummE

Mr Stothard to Mr Cromek. William Blake. CP-BlakW

Mr T. / bareheaded. Artist, The. William Carlos Williams. CP-WilW2

Mr u will not be missed. E. E. Cummings. CP-CummE

Mr. Van Ess bought 14 washcloths? Lorine Niedecker. CP-NiedL

Mr. Wakeville on Interstate 90. Donald Hall. CP-HallD

Mister Wang the Graduate. Han-shan.

Mr. What's-His-Name. James Whitcomb Riley. CP-RileJ

Mr. White Man, White Man. Do You Reckon? Langston Hughes. CP-HughL; CP-HughL3

Mr youse needn't be so spry. E. E. Cummings. CP-CummE; SP-CummE

Mistlines. Charles Tomlinson. CP-TomlC

Mistral Over the Graves. Archibald MacLeish. CP-MacLA

Mistress, The. Abraham Cowley.
Against Hope. CP-CrasR
(On Hope.) CP-CrasR

Mistress Adrienne, I have been given a bed with a pink dresser. Her Monologue of Dark Crepe with Edges of Light. Norman Dubie. CP-DubiN

Mrs. Alfred Uruguay. Wallace Stevens. CP-StevW; CP-StevWP

Mrs / and mr across the way are kind of. E. E. Cummings. CP-CummE

Mrs. Arbuthnot. Stevie Smith. CP-SmitS

Mrs. Blow and her Animals. Stevie Smith. CP-SmitS

Mrs. Choate's House-Warming. John Greenleaf Whittier. CP-WhitJ

Mistress Dampgress, the Mother Joel—Don't, oh don't go barefoot. Down in Ol' Dontcaradama. Kenneth Patchen. CP-PatcK

Mrs. Eliz. Wheeler, Under the Name of the Lost Shepardesse. Robert Herrick. CP-HerrR

Mistress Fell. Walter De la Mare. CP-DeLaW

Mrs. Gabrielle Giovanitti comes along Peoria Street every morning. Onion Days. Carl Sandburg. CP-SandC

Mrs. Grundy. Walter De la Mare. CP-DeLaW

Mrs. Harris's Petition. Jonathan Swift. CP-SwifJ

Mrs. Hattie Boomer Spink. Lines to a Three-Name Lady. Ogden Nash. CP-NashO

Mrs. Leamington stood on a cloud. Roots. William Meredith. SP-MereW

Mrs. Mandrill. Howard Nemerov. CP-NemeH

Mrs. Marmaduke Moore, at the age of ten. Seven Spiritual Ages of Mrs. Marmaduke Moore, The. Ogden Nash. CP-NashO

Mrs Masters's fuchsias hung. Lodging-House Fuchsias, The. Thomas Hardy. CP-HardT

Mrs. Mouse / Come out of your house. Cat Asks Mouse Out. Stevie Smith. CP-SmitS

Mistress of Poets, The. Jaroslav Seifert. SP-SeifJ, tr. by Ewald Osers

Mistress of scenes, good-by. Your maidenhead. James Vincent Cunningham. CP-CunnJ

Mistress [or Mistris], since you so much desire. Mistris [or Mistress] Since You So Much Desire. Thomas Campion. CP-CampT

Mistress Osmosis. Stevie Smith. CP-SmitS

Mrs. Pondicherry was / fat and mean. Pondicherry Blues. Josephine Jacobsen. CP-JacoJ

Mrs. Purvis Dreads Room Service. Ogden Nash. CP-NashO

Mrs. Sexton went out looking for the gods. Gods. Anne Sexton. CP-SextA

Mrs. Shepherd of Danbury, Conn., A. Malice Domestic. Ogden Nash. CP-NashO

Mrs. Someone's been to Asia. Importer, An. Robert Frost. CP-FrosR

Mrs Throckmorton's bull-finch sang a song. Homage to William Cowper. Donald Davie. CP-DaviDC

Mistress Tsou of Tiyen. Han-shan. CP-ColdM, tr. by Red Pine

Mrs. Wilmot sate scribbling a play. Another Simple Ballat. Lord Byron. CP-Byron

Mistris [or Mistress] Since You So Much Desire. Thomas Campion. CP-CampT

Mistrust of the Beloved. William Carlos Williams. CP-WilW2

Mistrustful minds be moved. Sir Thomas Wyatt. CP-WyatT

Mists of fortune, The. Fortune's Mist. Richard Eberhart. CP-EberR

Mists Over the River. William Carlos Williams. CP-WilW2

Misty and cool. Morning. Who are you, with one hand. Waking Dream about a Lost Child. William Meredith. SP-MereW

Misty Day, A. Paul Laurence Dunbar. CP-DunbP

Misty heat, now that the spring has gone, A. Midsummer's Day. Howard Nemerov. CP-NemeH

Misty memory—faint, far away, A. Enduring, The. James Whitcomb Riley. CP-RileJ

Misunderstanding, A. W. H. Auden. CP-AudeW

Misunderstandings. Yannis Ritsos. SP-RitsY, tr. by Kimon Friar

Misuse of the word hope- / fully spread through the lin-, The. I Have Heard. James Laughlin. CP-LaugJ

Mitchell Case, The. Langston Hughes. CP-HughL; CP-HughL3

Mites. John Updike. CP-UpdiJ

Mithras, God of the morning, our trumpets waken the Wall! Song to Mithras, A. Rudyard Kipling. CP-KiplR Fr. Puck of Pook's Hill.

Mithridates. Ralph Waldo Emerson. CP-EmerR

Mithridates 5. Robert Stock. SP-StocR

Mithridates at Chios. John Greenleaf Whittier. CP-WhitJ

Mithridates, glorious and powerful. On the March to Sinopi. Constantine P. Cavafy. CP-CavaC, tr. by Theoharis Constantine Theoharis

Mitosis. Olga Broumas. SP-BrouO

Mitre, The. G. K. Chesterton. CP-ChesG

Mittelbergheim. Czeslaw Milosz. CP-MiloC; CP-MiloCN, tr. by Richard Lourie

Mix a Pancake. Christina Georgina Rossetti. CP-RosC2

Mix the Ingredients. Hayden Carruth. CP-CarHS

Mix your red mouth with mine. Summer Madrigal. Federico García Lorca. CP-GarcF, tr. by Catherine Brown

Mixed crop. I dig a clump, A. Parsnips. Charles Tomlinson. CP-TomlC

Mixed Feelings. John Ashbery. SP-AshbJ

Mixed Marriage, The. Paul Muldoon. CP-MuldP

Mixer, The. Louis MacNeice. CP-MacNL

Mixup of kinkhead and high yaller. Prelude in Boricua. Luis Palés Matos. CP-WilW2

M'Liss and Louie. Carl Sandburg. CP-SandC

Mmm, yes, narcissus, mmm. Volupté. Denise Levertov. SP-LeveDL

Mneme begin. Inspire, ye sacred nine. On Recollection. Phillis Wheatley. CP-WheaP

Mnemogasoline. Andrei Codrescu. SP-CodrA

Mnemosyne. Dante Gabriel Rossetti. CW-RossD

Moan. Langston Hughes. CP-HughL; CP-HughL1

Moan / (ls) / ing / the she of the. E. E. Cummings. CP-CummE

Moan the loss, another. Scream to the Editor, A. Charles Olson. CP-OlsoC

Moaning and Groaning. Charles Bukowski. SP-BukC1

Mob within the heart, The. Emily Dickinson. CP-DickE

Mobile Homes. Robert Creeley. CP-CreeR

Mobile, immaculate and austere. Pastoral, A: "Mobile, immaculate and austere." Geoffrey Hill. CP-HillG

Mobile of Birds. John Updike. CP-UpdiJ

Mobiles: / that the wind can catch at. Still Life Or. Robert Creeley. CP-CreeR

Mobs are like the Gulf Stream. Would-Be Merman, The. Nicholas Vachel Lindsay. CP-LindV

Moccasin Flowers. Mary Oliver. SP-OlivM

Mock Confessional. Lawrence Ferlinghetti. SP-FerlL

Mock On, Mock On, Voltaire, Rousseau. William Blake. CP-BlakW

Mock Orange. Louise Glück. SP-GlucL

Mock Translation from the Greek. Alan Dugan. CP-DugaA

Mock Wife, The. Thomas Hardy. CP-HardT

Mockers Go to Kansas in Spring. Carl Sandburg. CP-SandC

Mockery Against the Irish Censorship. Alan Dugan. CP-DugaA

Mockingbird, The. Randall Jarrell. CP-JarrR

Mocking-bird on a branch, A. Wyncote, Pennsylvania: A Gloss. Thomas Kinsella. CP KinsT

Mocking Birds. Kenneth Rexroth. CP-RexrK

Mockingbirds, that pair, arrive, The. Of Pairs. Josephine Jacobsen. CP-JacoJ

Mode of the person becomes the mode of the world, The. Conversation with Three Women of New England. Wallace Stevens. CP-StevWP

Model, The. W. H. Auden. CP-AudeW

Model, The. Jaroslav Seifert. SP-SeifJ, tr. by Ewald Osers

Model for an Object in X Space. Robert Stock. SP-StocR

Model for an Object in Y Space. Robert Stock. SP-StocR

Model for an Object in Z Space. Robert Stock. SP-StocR

Model for the Laureate, A. William Butler Yeats. CP-YeatW

Model Towards a Theory of Cognition. Hans Magnus Enzensberger. SP-EnzeH

Model Work. Andrei Codrescu. SP-CodrA

Models, The. Yannis Ritsos. SP-RitsY, tr. by Kimon Friar

Moderate, The. John Updike. CP-UpdiJ

Moderation. Robert Herrick. CP-HerrR

Moderation. Yannis Ritsos. SP-RitsY, tr. by Andonis Decavalles

Modern, The. C. K. Williams. SP-WillC

Modern Athens, The. William Wordsworth. CP-WorW2

Modern Craft. Hart Crane. CP-CranH

Modern Declaration. Edna St. Vincent Millay. CP-MillE

Modern Elfland. G. K. Chesterton. CP-ChesG

Modern Fable, A. David Ignatow. SP-IgnaD

Modern Girl, A. Yehuda Amichai. SP-AmicYL, tr. by Benjamin Harshav and Barbara Harshav

Modern Incident, A. George Oppen. CP-OppGN

Modern life is a tale told by an idiot. Tale Told by an Idiot, A. D. H. Lawrence. CP-LawrD

Modern Love. George Meredith. CP-MerG1

Modern Love. James Vincent Cunningham. CP-CunnJ

Modern Magic, The. G. K. Chesterton. CP-ChesG

Modern Manichee, The. G. K. Chesterton. CP-ChesG

Modern Patriot, The. William Cowper. CP-CowpW

Modern Poet, A. Howard Nemerov. CP-NemeH

Modern Prayer. D. H. Lawrence. CP-LawrD

Modern Problems. D. H. Lawrence. CP-LawrD

Modern society is a mill. Give Us the Thebaïd. D. H. Lawrence. CP-LawrD

Modern Superstition. Laura Riding Jackson. CP-RidiL

Modernities. Edwin Arlington Robinson. CP-RobiE

Modes of Being. Denise Levertov. SP-LeveDL

Modes of Pleasure. Thom Gunn. CP-GunnT

Modest Achievement, The. William Carlos Williams. CP-WilW2

Modest, and fair, for fair and good are near. Ben Jonson. CP-JonsB *Fr.* Epicoene; or, The Silent Woman.

Modest bard, like many a bard unknown, The. Lines Written in the Travellers' Book at Orchomenus. Lord Byron. CP-Byron

Modest front of this small floore, The. Epitaph upon Mr. Ashton, a Conformable Citizen, An. Richard Crashaw. CP-CrasR

Modest little country by the sea, A. Lithuanian Divertissement. Joseph Brodsky. CP-BrodJ, *tr.* by Alan Myers

Modest Mound of Bones, A. John Updike. CP-UpdiJ

Modest Proposal, A. James Laughlin. CP-LaugJ

Modest rose puts forth a thorn, The. Lily, The. William Blake. CP-BlakW *Fr.* Songs of Experience.

Modest singer, with meek soul and heart, A. Humble Singer, A. James Whitcomb Riley. CP-RileJ

Modest Sum, A. Dan Pagis. SP-PagiD, *tr.* by Stephen Mitchell

Modesties. Philip Larkin. CP-LarkP

Modigliani's Death Mask. John Updike. CP-UpdiJ

Modulation is that footfalling, A. Footfalling. Laura Riding Jackson. CP-RidiL

Modulations for Solo Voice. Denise Levertov. SP-LeveDL

Modus Vivendi. Tennessee Williams. CP-WillT

Moebius Strip, The. Charles Olson. CP-OlsoC

Moenkopi. Arthur Sze. SP-SzeA

Mogg Megone. John Greenleaf Whittier. CP-WhitJ

Mohammed. Kenneth Patchen. CP-PatcK

Mohammed Bek Hadjetlache. Carl Sandburg. CP-SandC

Mohammedans say that the sound of bells, The. Bells. D. H. Lawrence. CP-LawrD

Mohini Chatterjee. William Butler Yeats. CP-YeatW

Moiré. Eugenio Montale. CP-MontE, *tr.* by Jonathan Galassi

Moise and the World of Reason. Tennessee Williams. "I have a vast traumatic eye." CP-WillT

Moist Moon People. Carl Sandburg. CP-SandC

Moist[e]ned Osyer [or osier] of the hoarie Willow, The. Coracle, The. Lucan. CP-RaleW *Fr.* Civil War [Bellum Civile] *or* Pharsalia.

Mole, angel-dog of the pit. Star-Nosed Mole. Anne Sexton. CP-SextA; SP-SextA

Mole-Catcher, The. John Clare. SP-ClarJ

Mollis abuti, / Has an acuti. Anglo-Latin Verses. Jonathan Swift. CP-SwifJ

Molly Gone. Thomas Hardy. CP-HardT

Moloch in State Street. John Greenleaf Whittier. CP-WhitJ

Molten gold flows away from the sun, A. Evening Sea Wind. Carl Sandburg. CP-SandC

Moly. Thom Gunn. CP-GunnT

Mom said I didn't have a belt that fit and. Suspenders. Raymond Carver. CP-CarvR

Moment. A. R. Ammons. CP-AmmoA

Moment. Robert Creeley. CP-CreeR

Moment. Howard Nemerov. CP-NemeH

Moment. Yannis Ritsos. SP-RitsY, *tr.* by Kimon Friar

Moment. Adam Zagajewski. SP-ZagaA, *tr.* by Renata Gorczynski

Moment. Adam Zagajewski. SP-ZagaA, *tr.* by Clare Cavanagh

Moment, A. Gregory Orr. SP-OrrG

Moment, The. Walter De la Mare. CP-DeLaW

Moment, The. Kathleen Jessie Raine. SP-RainK

Moment, The. Theodore Roethke. CP-RoetT

Moment, The. Charles Tomlinson. CP-TomlC; SP-TomlC

Moment Again. William Stafford. SP-StafWW

Moment and / over and with, A. Rachmaninoff's Third. James Schuyler. CP-SchuJ

Moment at the Louvre, A. Dan Pagis. SP-PagiD, *tr.* by Stephen Mitchell

Moment Between Masks. Rainer Maria Rilke. CP-RilkFr, *tr.* by A. Poulin, Jr.

Moment comes when my sound senses, The. Time of Waiting, A. Robert Graves. CP-GravR

Moment Fugue. Hart Crane. CP-CranH

Moment in Eternity, A. Hugh MacDiarmid. SP-MacDH

Moment in Troy, A. Wisława Szymborska. SP-SzymW, *tr.* by Stanislaw Barańczak *and* Clare Cavanagh

Moment of Contrition. Yannis Ritsos. SP-RitsY, *tr.* by Kimon Friar

Moment of Creation, The. Arthur Sze. SP-SzeA

Moment of Equilibrium among the Islands. Richard Eberhart. CP-EberR

Moment of quiet covenant, A. Covenant. Adam Zagajewski. SP-ZagaA, *tr.* by Renata Gorczynski, Benjamin Ivry *and* C. K. Williams

Moment of silence, first, then there it is, A. Dial Tone, The. Howard Nemerov. CP-NemeH

Moment of Truth, The. Thomas Merton. CP-MertT

Moment of Vision, The. Richard Eberhart. CP-EberR

Moment on Earth, A. James Laughlin. CP-LaugJ

Moment to / moment the. Time ("Moment to / moment the"). Robert Creeley. CP-CreeR

Moment tries to come in, A. Approaching Prayer. James Dickey. CP-DickJ

Momentary Bafflement with Return Home at Dawn. Andrei Codrescu. SP-CodrA

Momento Mori. Ai. SP-Ai

Moments. Ivor Gurney. SP-GurnI

Moments of Dawn Riders. Carl Sandburg. CP-SandC

Moments of Glory. Robinson Jeffers. CP-JefR3

Moments of Minnie. John Crowe Ransom. SP-RansJ

Moments of Old Age. Dan Pagis. SP-PagiD, *tr.* by Stephen Mitchell

Moments of Song. Federico García Lorca.
    At Songfall. CP-GarcF, *tr.* by Jerome Rothenberg
    Landscape Minus Song. CP-GarcF, *tr.* by Jerome Rothenberg
    Sesame. CP-GarcF, *tr.* by Jerome Rothenberg
    Song under Tears. CP-GarcF, *tr.* by Jerome Rothenberg
    Song with Reflections. CP-GarcF, *tr.* by Jerome Rothenberg
    Unopened Song. CP-GarcF, *tr.* by Jerome Rothenberg

Moments of the Garden. Federico García Lorca. CP-GarcF, *tr.* by Jerome Rothenberg *Fr.* In the Garden of the Lunar Grapefruits.

Moments of Vision. Thomas Hardy. CP-HardT

Moments passed as at a play, The. Memory of Youth, A. William Butler Yeats. CP-YeatW

Moment's patience, gentle Mistris Anne, A. William Shakespeare to Mrs Anne, Regular Servant to the Rev. Mr Precentor of York. Thomas Gray. CP-GrayT

Moment's Peace, A. Thomas Kinsella. CP-KinsT

Moments Return, The. Allen Ginsberg. CP-GinsA

Moments that shared us, The. First Snow. Sam Hamill. SP-HamiS

Moments / when I care about nothing. Apologies. Marge Piercy. SP-PierM

Momma Welfare Roll. Maya Angelou. SP-AngeM

Mommy. Robert Creeley. SP-CreeR

Mommy. / I want to be all silver. Silly Song. Federico García Lorca. CP-GarcF, *tr.* by Alan S. Trueblood *Fr.* Songs for Children.

Mommy, The. On Board. Robert Creeley. SP-CreeR

Mommy mommy come and see. Ballad from Childhood. Audre Lorde. SP-LordA

Momus. Edwin Arlington Robinson. CP-RobiE

Momus. Carl Sandburg. CP-SandC

Mon cher Monsieur le Secretaire. Monsieur le Secretaire. James Whitcomb Riley. CP-RileJ

Monotone of the rain is beautiful, The. Monotone. Carl Sandburg. CP-SandC

Mona, by nature formed a jay. Linnet and the Jay, The. *Unknown, sometimes at. to* Thomas Sheridan. CP-SherT

Mona Machree! och, the sootherin' flow of it. James Whitcomb Riley. CP-RileJ

Monadnoc. Ralph Waldo Emerson. CP-EmerR

Monadnock through the Trees. Edwin Arlington Robinson. CP-RobiE

Monads. Kenneth Rexroth. CP-RexrK

Monarch and fritillary, swallowtail. Practicing for Death. Jane Cooper. CP-CoopJ

Monarch of Gods and Dæmons, and all Spirits. Prometheus Unbound [A Lyrical Drama in Four Acts]. Percy Bysshe Shelley. CP-ShelP

Monarchs, the butterflies, are commanded, The. Untitled Poem. Alan Dugan. CP-DugaA

Monastery at Vršac, The. Charles Wright. SP-WrigC

Monastery's careful austerity, A. Office Party, The. Miller Williams. CP-WillM

Monday. A. R. Ammons. CP-AmmoA

Monday. Primo Levi. CP-LeviP, *tr.* by Ruth Feldman *and* Brian Swann

Monday Beach, Cold Day. Charles Bukowski. SP-BukC2

Monday / Dearest, / It is snowing, grotesquely snowing. Letter Written During a January Northeaster. Anne Sexton. CP-SextA

Monday in Holy Week. Christina Georgina Rossetti. CP-RosC2

Monday is the day that everything starts all over again. Every Day Is Monday. Ogden Nash. CP-NashO

Monday Morning. Billy Collins. SP-CollB

Monday Morning. James Vincent Cunningham. CP-CunnJ

Monday Morning: London. John Ciardi. CP-CiarJ

Monday, Tuesday: thorns. Thursday: iron. Yannis Ritsos. SP-RitsY *Fr.* First Series.

Monday, Wednesday, and Friday. Federico García Lorca. CP-GarcF, *tr.* by Alan S. Trueblood *Fr.* Moon Songs.

Mondays must be lovely where you are, The. Coast Hillside. Helen Pinkerton. CP-PinkH

Mondo Angelico. Charles Wright. SP-WrigCN

Mondo Henbane. Charles Wright. SP-WrigCN

Monessie Gorge. Kathleen Jessie Raine. SP-RainK

Monet's "Waterlilies" Robert Earl Hayden. CP-HaydR

Money. A. R. Ammons. CP-AmmoA

Money. Raymond Carver. CP-CarvR

Money. Robert Creeley. SP-CreeR

Money. Randall Jarrell. CP-JarrR

Money. Philip Larkin. CP-LarkP

Money. D. H. Lawrence. CP-LawrD

Money. Thomas Lux. SP-LuxT

Money. Howard Nemerov. CP-NemeH

Money. Miller Williams. CP-WillM

Money and art. Plaint. Langston Hughes. CP-HughL; CP-HughL3

Money and fame break in the room. Strife between the Poet and Ambition, The. Thomas Merton. CP-MertT

Money and Grass. David Ignatow. SP-IgnaD

Money cannot fill our needs. Song for the First of the Month. Dorothy Parker. CP-ParkD

Money Gets the Mastery [or Masterie]. Robert Herrick. CP-HerrR

Money is cheap / in the fall, The. In the Fall. Robert Creeley. CP-CreeR

Money is flesh and bone. Honestly got. Money. Miller Williams. CP-WillM

Money is nothing now, even if I had it. Half Moon In a High Wind. Carl Sandburg. CP-SandC

Money Is the Roost of All Eagles. Philip Whalen. SP-WhalP

Money-Madness. D. H. Lawrence. CP-LawrD

Money Makes the Mirth. Robert Herrick. CP-HerrR

Money Musk. James Schuyler. CP-SchuJ

Money, Politics, Love, and Glory. Carl Sandburg. CP-SandC

Money Swing, The. Anne Sexton. CP-SextA; SP-SextA

Money, thou bane of bliss and source of woe. Avarice. George Herbert. CP-HerbG

Money thou ow'st me; prithee fix a day. Upon Bunce: Epigram. Robert Herrick. CP-HerrR

Mongan Laments the Change That Has Come upon Him and His Beloved. William Butler Yeats. CP-YeatW

(He Mourns for the Change That Has Come upon Him and His Beloved, and Longs for the End of the World.) CP-YeatW

Mongolian Idiot. Karl Shapiro. SP-ShapK

Mongrel, The. Thomas Hardy. CP-HardT

Mongrel image for all summer, our scene for breakfast:, A. WIldrose. Robert Lowell. SP-LoweR

'Mongst the Hills o' Somerset. James Whitcomb Riley. CP-RileJ

'Mongst those long rowes of crownes that guild your racc. To the Queen's Majesty. Richard Crashaw. CP-CrasR

Monk, The. William Blake. CP-BlakW Fr. Jerusalem.

Monk, The. Andrei Codrescu. SP-CodrA

Monk, The. Thomas Kinsella. CP-KinsT

Monk is American, he is wheat treated Bethlehem steel, The. Dear Editors. Andrei Codrescu. SP-CodrA

Monk locks himself up so that his god, The. Rainer Maria Rilke. CP-RilkFr, tr. by A. Poulin, Jr. Fr. Fragments.

Monk sat in his den, The. Weak Monk, The. Stevie Smith. CP-SmitS

Monkey House, The. Yusef Komunyakaa. CP-KomuY

Monkey of Stars. Carl Sandburg. CP-SandC

Monkey Puzzle, The. Marianne Craig Moore. CP-MoorM

Monkeyman. Audre Lorde. SP-LordA

Monkey's Address to Others of His Kind, A. Robert Stock. SP-StocR

Monkeys, The. Marianne Craig Moore. CP-MoorM

Monkhood. John Berryman. CP-BerrJ

Monks are dying out at Hosios Loukas, The. Reservoirs of Mount Helicon, The. Amy Clampitt. CP-ClamA

Monk's Walk, The. Paul Laurence Dunbar. CP-DunbP

Monmouth. George Meredith. CP-MerG2

Monmouthshire. Donald Davie. CP-DaviDC

Monna Innominata. Christina Georgina Rossetti. CP-RosC2

Monochord, The. Dante Gabriel Rossetti. CW-RossD Fr. House of Life, The.

Monody. Herman Melville. SP-MelvH

Monody. Dorothy Parker. CP-ParkD

Monody on Maria. Robert Burns. CP-BurnR

Monody on the Death of Chatterton. Samuel Taylor Coleridge. CP-ColeS

("O what a wonder seems the fear of death.") MW-ColeS

Monody on the Death of the Right Hon. R. B. Sheridan. Lord Byron. CP-Byron

Monolith of a double flight, The. Informative Object, An. William Carlos Williams. CP-WilW2

Monologue at Midnight. Robert Penn Warren. CP-WarrR

Monologue at 3 A.M. Sylvia Plath. CP-PlatS

Monologue for a Sixth Avenue Screamer. Alan Dugan. CP-DugaA

Monologue for the Good Friday Christ. John Logan. CP-LogaJ

Monologue of a Commercial Fisherman. Alan Dugan. CP-DugaA

Monologue of a Mother. D. H. Lawrence. CP-LawrD

Monologue of Two Moons, Nudes with Crests. 1938. Norman Dubie. CP-DubiN

Monologue, The. Walter De la Mare. CP-DeLaW

Monologues of the Son of Saul. John Logan. CP-LogaJ

"Ah, so our first load of honey heavy Christmas trees." CP-LogaJ

"Far off the road on the left on a slight rolling hill." CP-LogaJ

"I did but taste a little of the honey with the." CP-LogaJ

"If the half moon stamp of a sacred hoof showed Cadmus." CP-LogaJ

"In my dream I know I see my father Saul a king." CP-LogaJ

Monoon Season. Yusef Komunyakaa. CP-KomuY

Monosyllabic. Carl Sandburg. CP-SandC

Monosyllabic European called Sax, A. Ginza Samba. Robert Pinsky. CP-PinsR

Monosyllable, The. Josephine Jacobsen. CP-JacoJ

Monotone. Carl Sandburg. CP-SandC

Monotony. Constantine P. Cavafy. CP-CavaC, tr. by Theoharis Constantine Theoharis

Monotony. Langston Hughes. CP-HughL; CP-HughL1

Monotony Song, The. Theodore Roethke. CP-RoetT

Monovasia. Yannis Ritsos.

Coins. SP-RitsY

Dead, The. SP-RitsY

Deceptive Discoveries. SP-RitsY

Finishing Touch. SP-RitsY

Geographic Origins. SP-RitsY

Inside the Rust. SP-RitsY

Items of Identification. SP-RitsY

Leaving Monovasia. SP-RitsY

Monovasia. SP-RitsY

Remembrances. SP-RitsY

Time. SP-RitsY

White. SP-RitsY

Monovasia. Yannis Ritsos. SP-RitsY Fr. Monovasia.

Monroe's Blues. Langston Hughes. CP-HughL; CP-HughL2

Monroe's fell on evil days. Monroe's Blues. Langston Hughes. CP-HughL; CP-HughL2

Monsieur Étienne de Silhouette. Some Frenchmen. John Updike. CP-UpdiJ

Monsieur le Secretaire. James Whitcomb Riley. CP-RileJ

M. Mallarmé has put a curse on me. Tuesday at 87 Rue de Rome. James Laughlin. CP-LaugJ

Monsieur Pussy-Cat, Blackmailer. Stevic Smith. CP-SmitS

Monster, The. G. K. Chesterton. CP-ChesG

Monster, The. Thom Gunn. CP-GunnT

Monster owl, A. Lorine Niedecker. CP-NiedL

Monstering horror swallows, A. Thanksgiving (1956). E. E. Cummings. CP-CummE

Monstrous and three-headed cur, The. Dream Recalled on Waking. Robert Graves. CP-GravR

Monstrous Marriage, The. William Carlos Williams. CP-WilW2

Mont Blanc. Percy Bysshe Shelley. CP-ShelP

Montage. Charles Tomlinson. CP-TomlC

Montaigne. W. H. Auden. CP-AudeW

Montaigne and His Kitten. Herman Melville. SP-MelvH

Montalban: Near the Ancient Fort. Clarence Major. SP-MajoC

Montana Fifty Years Ago. James Vincent Cunningham. CP-CunnJ

Montana Pastoral. James Vincent Cunningham. CP-CunnJ

Montefiore. Ambrose Bierce. SP-BierA

Montes Scripturarum, the Mounts of the Scriptures. Robert Herrick. CP-HerrR

Montgomery! true, the common lot. Answer to a Beautiful Poem, Entitled "The Common Lot" Lord Byron. CP-Byron

Month—a year—of idle work, A. Song: "Month—a year—of idle work, A." Wallace Stevens. CP-StevWP

Month after month the gathered rains descend. To the Nile. Percy Bysshe Shelley. CP-ShelP

Month after month, year after year. Emily Jane Brontë. CP-BronE

Month ago in fields, A. May Weather. Philip Larkin. CP-LarkP

Month before Easter, A. Lamb, The. John Ciardi. CP-CiarJ

Month in Summer, A. Carolyn Kizer. CP-KizeC

Month of Cleansing. Yannis Ritsos. SP-RitsY, tr. by Kimon Friar

Month of flowering's finished, The. The fruit's in. Poem for a Birthday. Sylvia Plath. CP-PlatS

Month of roses. My rhymes go. In Spring. "Rubén Dario." SP-DariR, tr. by Alberto Acereda and Will Derusha

Month of Saints, A. John Logan. CP-LogaJ

Month of the drowned dog, The. After long rain the land. November. Ted Hughes. SP-HughTN

Month of vigilance draws to its close, A. Nothing Now Astonishes. Robert Graves. CP-GravR

Month or twain to live on honeycomb, A. Before Parting. Algernon Charles Swinburne. SP-SwinA

Month to the hour, A. Next Moon, The. W. S. Merwin. SP-MerwWF

Month when farmers escape the heat, The. Han-shan. CP-ColdM, tr. by Red Pine

Months: A Pageant, The. Christina Georgina Rossetti. CP-RosC2

Months, The. Christina Georgina Rossetti. CP-RosC2

Months after the Muse. Illustration [—a Footnote], The. Denise Levertov. SP-LeveDP

Month's Calendar, The. Thomas Hardy. CP-HardT

Month's eye blurs, The. After a Sentence in "Malte Laurids Brigge" Adrienne Rich. CP-RicAE

Months have ends—the Years—a knot, The. Emily Dickinson. CP-DickE

Months of it, and the inarticulate mist so thick. Long Summers. Robert Lowell. SP-LoweR

Months on, you hold me still. Two Songs [for Doreen]. Derek Mahon. CP-MahoD

Monticello. May Sarton. SP-SartM

Montmartre. Langston Hughes. CP-HughL; CP-HughL2

Montrachet-le-Jardin. Wallace Stevens. CP-StevW; CP-StevWP

Monument. Robinson Jeffers. CP-JefR3

Monument. George Oppen. CP-OppGN

Monument and the Shrine, The. John Logan. CP-LogaJ

Monument for the Soldiers, A. James Whitcomb Riley. CP-RileJ

Monument-Maker, The. Thomas Hardy. CP-HardT

Monument Rescue Dim. Philip Whalen. SP-WhalP

Monument, The. Elizabeth Bishop. CP-BishE

Monument, The. Wyatt Prunty. SP-PrunW

Monuments to events that never took place: to bloody. Postcard from Lisbon. Joseph Brodsky. CP-BrodJ

Mood. Countee Cullen. CP-CullC

Mood. Dorothy Parker. CP-ParkD

Mood Apart, A. Robert Frost. CP-FrosR

Mood Indigo. James Schuyler. CP-SchuJ

Moods, The. William Butler Yeats. CP-YeatW

Moody. Alice Walker. CP-WalkA

Moody child and wildly wise, A. Motto to "The Poet" Ralph Waldo Emerson. CP-EmerR

Mool 'tis homos,' Naso 'n' queer take 'im mool 'tis ho most he. Catullus. See Naso! an elevated personage

Moon. James Schuyler. CP-SchuJ

Moon. James Wright. CP-WrigJ

Moon, The. Jorge Luis Borges. SP-BorgJ, tr. by Alan S. Trueblood

Moon, The. Jorge Luis Borges. SP-BorgJ, tr. by Willis Barnstone

Moon, The. Robert Creeley. CP-CreeR

Moon, The. Donald Hall. CP-HallD

Moon, The. Henry David Thoreau. CP-ThorH

Moon, The. William Carlos Williams. CP-WilW1

Moon / and clouds, will. Eye, The. Robert Creeley. CP-CreeR

Moon and Five Planets. Robinson Jeffers. CP-JefR3

Moon and mandrake. Air. Christopher Logue. CP-LoguC

Moon and Panorama of the Insects. Federico García Lorca. CP-GarcF, tr. by Greg Simon and Steven F. White

Moon and Stars. William Carlos Williams. CP-WilW2

Moon & Sun. James Laughlin. CP-LaugJ

Moon and the Night and the Men, The. John Berryman. CP-BerrJ

Moon and the Waves, The. Samuel Taylor Coleridge. CP-ColeS

Moon and the Yew Tree, The. Sylvia Plath. CP-PlatS

Moon-Annoyed, Cognac's Ashen Thrill. Thomas Lux. SP-LuxT

Moon Appears, The. Federico García Lorca. CP-GarcF, tr. by Alan S. Trueblood Fr. Moon Songs.

Moon at the Fair, A. Federico García Lorca. CP-GarcF, tr. by Jerome Rothenberg Fr. Fairs.

Moon begins her stately ride, The. Evening. Paul Laurence Dunbar. CP-DunbP

Moon came out full, you could see the white breathing of the. Kenneth Patchen. CP-PatcK

Moon came to the forge, The. Ballad of the Moon Moon. Federico García Lorca. CP-GarcF, tr. by Christopher Maurer

Moon came up late, because the sandstone bluff across the river, The. Journal Entry (With the Udalls, June 1968). William Meredith. SP-MereW

Moon circles the sky, The. Thamar and Amnon. Federico García Lorca. CP-GarcF, tr. by Will Kirkland

Moon Clock. Donald Hall. CP-HallD

Moon, cloud, tower, a patch of the battistero all of a whiteness. Canto 79:

"Moon, cloud, tower, a patch of the battistero all of a whiteness." Ezra Pound. SP-PounE Fr. Cantos.

Moon Compasses. Robert Frost. CP-FrosR

Moon Conjunct Ace of Cups. Olga Broumas. SP-BrouO

Moon "Continued" Kenneth Patchen. CP-PatcK

Moon could rest in the end along the pure white curve of the horses, The. Crucifixion. Federico García Lorca. CP-GarcF, tr. by Greg Simon and Steven F. White

Moon cuts through, The. Somewhere Near Phu Bai. Yusef Komunyakaa. CP-KomuY

Moon drops one or two feathers into the field, The. Beginning. James Wright. CP-WrigJ

Moon-drowned. James Whitcomb Riley. CP-RileJ

Moon falls through the autumn Behind prisons she grins, The. E. E. Cummings. CP-CummE

Moon fastens on the sea, The. Second Anniversary ("Moon fastens on the sea, The"). Federico García Lorca. CP-GarcF, tr. by Alan S. Trueblood Fr. Moon Songs.

Moon Flock. James Dickey. CP-DickJ

Moon glued to the windowpane like a canceled postage stamp, A. Earth's Attraction, The. Yannis Ritsos. SP-RitsY, tr. by Kimon Friar and Kostas Myrsiades

Moon goes over the water, The. Half Moon. Federico García Lorca. SP-GarcF, tr. by W. S. Merwin

Moon goes through the water. Half Moon. Federico García Lorca. CP-GarcF, tr. by Jerome Rothenberg Fr. Backwaters.

Moon golden towards the full. Kathleen Jessie Raine. SP-RainK

Moon Hammock. Carl Sandburg. CP-SandC

Moon has a swollen cheek, The. Ezra Pound. See Moon, cloud, tower, a patch of the battistero all of a whiteness

Moon has left the sky, love, The. Night of Love. Paul Laurence Dunbar. CP-DunbP

Moon has passed to the panes of the south-aisle wall, The. In Sherborne Abbey. Thomas Hardy. CP-HardT

Moon has set now, and, The. Deduke Men A Selanna. Sappho. CP-CunnJ, tr. by James Vincent Cunningham

Moon has set: while yet the dawn, The. Moloch in State Street. John Greenleaf Whittier. CP-WhitJ

Moon—how definite its orb!, The. Lunar Entrancement. Samuel Taylor Coleridge. CP-ColeS

Moon hung low o'er Provence vales, The. Godfrey of Boulogne. Henry David Thoreau. CP-ThorH

Moon impoverished amid stars curtailed, A. Greatest of These Is Charity, The. Christina Georgina Rossetti. CP-RosC2

Moon in the bureau mirror, The. Insomnia. Elizabeth Bishop. CP-BishE

Moon in the river, mother, is a red, red moon tonight, The. River Moon. Carl Sandburg. CP-SandC

Moon in the sky is a custard-pie, The. Bub Says. James Whitcomb Riley. CP-RileJ

Moon-in-the-Trees, / The old canoe awaits you. E. E. Cummings. CP-CummE

Moon ink is too bright to read. Fanny Howe. SP-HoweF Fr. O'Clock.

Moon Is a Diamond, The. Arthur Sze. SP-SzeA

Moon Is a Painter, The. Nicholas Vachel Lindsay. CP-LindV

Moon is a sow, The. Song for Ishtar. Denise Levertov. SP-LeveDP; SP-LeveDS

Moon is able to command the valley tonight, The. Moist Moon People. Carl Sandburg. CP-SandC

Moon is alone in the sky, The. Song. George Meredith. CP-MerG1

Moon is black, The. Noah's / Dove. Arthur Sze. SP-SzeA

Moon is broken in twain, and half a moon, The. Troth with the Dead. D. H. Lawrence. CP-LawrD

Moon is but a candle-glow, The. What the Forester Said. Nicholas Vachel Lindsay. CP-LindV

Moon is but a censer swung, The. Censer-Moon, The. Nicholas Vachel Lindsay. CP-LindV

Moon is but a golden skull, The. What the Hyena Said. Nicholas Vachel Lindsay. CP-LindV

Moon is dark, The. We have our drinks on a terrace. Aesthetic Distance. Miller Williams. CP-WillM

Moon is dead already, The. Memento. Federico García Lorca. CP-GarcF, tr. by Jerome Rothenberg Fr. Six Songs at Nightfall.

Moon is dead, is dead, The. Two Evening Moons. Federico García Lorca. CP-GarcF, tr. by Alan S. Trueblood Fr. Moon Songs.

Moon is dead, you lovers!, The. Selene Afterwards. Archibald MacLeish. CP-MacLA

Moon is distant from the Sea, The. Emily Dickinson. CP-DickE

Moon is fat and old tonight, The. Change. Langston Hughes. CP-HughL; CP-HughL1

Moon is full this winter night, The. M. Douglas to E.R. Gleneden. Emily Jane Brontë. CP-BronE

Moon Is Full Tonight, The. Philip Larkin. CP-LarkP

Moon is hiding in, The. E. E. Cummings. CP-CummE

Moon is in sight, The. Owl, The. János Hegedüs. CP-LogaJ, *tr.* by John Logan

Moon is moving away, The. Fanny Howe. SP-HoweF *Fr.* Robeson Street.

Moon is naked, The. March Moon. Langston Hughes. CP-HughL; CP-HughL1

Moon is now an opening flower, The. Rose of Midnight, The. Nicholas Vachel Lindsay. CP-LindV

Moon is round. Game of Moons, A. Federico García Lorca. CP-GarcF, *tr.* by Jerome Rothenberg *Fr.* Barrage of Firework Poems on the Occasion of the Poet's Birthday.

Moon is Salome's, The. Salome & the Moon. Federico García Lorca. CP-GarcF, *tr.* by Jerome Rothenberg *Fr.* Sublunar Cantos.

Moon is the mother of pathos and pity, The. Lunar Paraphrase. Wallace Stevens. CP-StevW; CP-StevWP

Moon Is the Number 18, The. Charles Olson. CP-OlsoC; SP-OlsoC

Moon? It is a griffin's egg, The. Yet Gentle Will the Griffin Be. Nicholas Vachel Lindsay. CP-LindV *Fr.* Poems about the Moon.

Moon Landing. W. H. Auden. CP-AudeW

Moon-lit snow is falling like strange candy into the big eyes of the, The. E. E. Cummings. CP-CummE

Moon looked into my window, The. E. E. Cummings. CP-CummE

Moon Looks In, The. Thomas Hardy. CP-HardT

Moon Memory. D. H. Lawrence. CP-LawrD

Moon-minded the sun goes. Gemini. Audre Lorde. SP-LordA

Moon moves up her smooth and sheeny path, The. Henry David Thoreau. CP-ThorH

Moon must be in Perigee the sea, The. May 20, 1959. Charles Olson. CP-OlsoC

Moon never makes use of the Sun's palette, The. Colours of Night, The. Robert Graves. CP-GravR

Moon New-Risen. D. H. Lawrence. CP-LawrD

Moon now rises to her absolute rule, The. Henry David Thoreau. CP-ThorH

Moon of Mind Against the Wooden Louver, The. Olga Broumas. SP-BrouO

Moon of Other Days, The. Rudyard Kipling. CP-KiplR

Moon, old fossil. After the Flight of Ranger 7. May Swenson. SP-SwenM

Moon, one tree, one star, The. Old Martinmas Eve. Ivor Gurney. SP-GurnI

Moon over gai. E. E. Cummings. CP-CummE

MOOn Over tOwns mOOn. E. E. Cummings. CP-CummE

Moon / ovoid, The. View. William Carlos Williams. CP-WilW1

Moon Path. Carl Sandburg. CP-SandC

Moon revolves around outside; possibly, black air, The. Study in a Late Subway. Muriel Rukeyser. CP-RukeM

Moon revolves in the sky, The. Thamar and Amnon. Federico García Lorca. SP-GarcF, *tr.* by J. L. Gili *and* Stephen Spender

Moon Riders. Carl Sandburg. CP-SandC

Moon rises. The red cubs rolling, The. Breath of Night, The. Randall Jarrell. CP-JarrR

Moon Rising, The. Federico García Lorca. SP GarcF, *tr.* by Lysander Kemp

Moon Rondeau. Carl Sandburg. CP-SandC

Moon / round / goes around while going around a. Of Rounds. May Swenson. SP-SwenM

Moon: royal crown of an enormous head. Divine Falling of Leaves, A. César Vallejo. CP-WrigJ

Moon smiles like a queen, The. Thomas Merton. CP-MertT

Moon Song, Woman Song. Anne Sexton. CP-SextA

Moon Songs. Federico García Lorca.

    Dead at Daybreak. CP-GarcF, *tr.* by Alan S. Trueblood

    First Anniversary. CP-GarcF, *tr.* by Alan S. Trueblood

    Flower. CP-GarcF, *tr.* by Alan S. Trueblood

    Monday, Wednesday, and Friday. CP-GarcF, *tr.* by Alan S. Trueblood

    Moon Appears, The. CP-GarcF, *tr.* by Alan S. Trueblood

    Second Anniversary ("Moon fastens on the sea, The"). CP-GarcF, *tr.* by Alan S. Trueblood

    Two Evening Moons. CP-GarcF, *tr.* by Alan S. Trueblood

Moon stepped like a dead thing, The. Twilight Land. John Logan. CP-LogaJ

Moon still sends its mellow light, The. To a Dead Friend. Langston Hughes. CP-HughL; CP-HughL1

Moon, svelte person. To the Moon. Rainer Maria Rilke. CP-RilkFr, *tr.* by A. Poulin, Jr.

Moon, that against the lintel of the west. Edna St. Vincent Millay. CP-MillE

Moon, the landscape, the train, The. Moon, the Train, The. Raymond Carver. CP-CarvR

Moon, the Train, The. Raymond Carver. CP-CarvR

Moon upon her fluent Route, The. Emily Dickinson. CP-DickE

Moon was but a Chin of Gold, The. Emily Dickinson. CP-DickE

Moon was grieving, the. Seraphim in tears. Apparition. Stéphane Mallarmé. CP-MallS, *tr.* by Henry Weinfield

Moon was like a full cup tonight, The. Cows at Night, The. Hayden Carruth. CP-CarHS

Moon was shining on the deck, The. Jones Very. CP-VeryJ

Moon-white dunes and the water like violets. Beach, The. Robinson Jeffers. CP-JefR1

Moon Will Restore the Virginity of My Sister, The. Josephine Jacobsen. CP-JacoJ

Moon will run all consciences to cover, The. Ditty. Allen Tate. CP-TateA

Moon with Roman numerals, there, A. Clock With No Hands, A. Howard Nemerov. CP-NemeH

Moon with Venus in her sickle blade, The. Captain Nicholas Strong. John Ciardi. CP-CiarJ

Moonbeam, leave the shadowy vale. To the Moonbeam. Percy Bysshe Shelley. CP-ShelP

Moonbow. Federico García Lorca. CP-GarcF, *tr.* by Jerome Rothenberg *Fr.* In the Garden of the Lunar Grapefruits.

Moonchild. Lucille Clifton. SP-ClifL

Moonless darkness stands between. Gerard Manley Hopkins. CP-HopkG

Moonlight. Walter De la Mare. CP-DeLaW

Moonlight and Maggots. Carl Sandburg. CP-SandC

Moonlight behind the tall branches, The. Fernando Pessoa. SP-PessF *Fr.* Keeper of Sheep, The.

Moonlight fills the laurels. Confusion of the Senses. Kenneth Rexroth. CP-RexrK

Moonlight filters on the prairie, The. Moonlight and Maggots. Carl Sandburg. CP-SandC

Moonlight in Valencia: Civil War. Langston Hughes. CP-HughL; CP-HughL2

Moonlight is failin', The. Serenade—To Nora. James Whitcomb Riley. CP-RileJ

Moonlight landscape, sheep. Thoughts on Looking at a Samuel Palmer Etching at the Tate. Gary Snyder. CP-SnydG

Moonlight Night. Joseph, Freiherr von Eichendorff. CP-MerG2

Moonlight Night: Carmel. Langston Hughes. CP-HughL; CP-HughL2

Moonlight now on Malibu. Air and Angels. Kenneth Rexroth. CP-RexrK

Moonlight on antebellum skin. Too Pretty for Serious Business. Yusef Komunyakaa. CP-KomuY

Moonlight on my bed keeps me awake, The. Night Sounds. Carolyn Kizer. CP-KizeC

Moonlight Sonata. Yannis Ritsos. SP-RitsY, *tr.* by Kimon Friar

Moonlight stumbles with bright heel. Dream of a Dream. Robert Penn Warren. CP-WarrR

Moonlight through my gauze curtains. Skein, The. Emperor Wu of Han. CP-KizeC, *tr.* by Carolyn Kizer

Moonlight washes the west side of the house. Winter Verse for His Sister. William Meredith. SP-MereW

Moonlight's Dream, The. Robert Penn Warren. CP-WarrR

Moonmouth and grasshopper that flee our page. Name for All, A. Hart Crane. CP-CranH

Moonrise. "H. D." CP-DoolH

Moonrise. Gerard Manley Hopkins. CP-HopkG

    (Moonrise June 19 1876.) CP-HopkG

Moonrise. D. H. Lawrence. CP-LawrD

Moonrise. Sylvia Plath. CP-PlatS

Moonrise gleams above the mountain, sunset glimmers through the wood. Simon de Montfort. G. K. Chesterton. CP-ChesG

Moonrise June 19 1876. Gerard Manley Hopkins. *See* Moonrise

Moon's a brass-hooped water-keg, The. What the Miner in the Desert Said. Nicholas Vachel Lindsay. CP-LindV

Moon's a cottage with a door, The. Drying Their Wings. Nicholas Vachel Lindsay. CP-LindV

Moon's a gong, hung in the wild, The. What the Gray-Winged Fairy Said. Nicholas Vachel Lindsay. CP-LindV

Moon's a holy owl-queen, The. What Grandpa Mouse Said. Nicholas Vachel Lindsay. CP-LindV

Moon's a little prairie-dog, The. What the Rattlesnake Said. Nicholas Vachel Lindsay. CP-LindV

Moon's a monk, unmated, The. Strength of the Lonely, The. Nicholas Vachel Lindsay. CP-LindV

Moon's a paper jumping hoop, The. What the Clown Said. Nicholas Vachel Lindsay. CP-LindV

Moon's a peck of corn. It lies, The. Old Horse in the City, The. Nicholas Vachel Lindsay. CP-LindV

Moon's a snowball. See the drifts, The. What the Snow Man Said. Nicholas Vachel Lindsay. CP-LindV

Moon's a steaming chalice, The. What Semiramis Said. Nicholas Vachel Lindsay. CP-LindV

Moon's an open furnace door, The. What the Coal-Heaver Said. Nicholas Vachel Lindsay. CP-LindV

Moon's Last Quarter, The. Robert Graves. CP-GravR

Moon's man stands in his shell, The. Everlasting Monday, The. Sylvia Plath. CP-PlatS

Moons of Jupiter, The. John Updike. CP-UpdiJ

Moon's Tear, The. Robert Graves. CP-GravR

Moon's the North Wind's Cooky, The. Nicholas Vachel Lindsay. CP-LindV

Moonset. Hayden Carruth. CP-CarHS

Moonset. Carl Sandburg. CP-SandC

Moonset, Gloucester, December 1, 1957, 1:58 A.M. Charles Olson. CP-OlsoC; SP-OlsoC

Moonshine. Yusef Komunyakaa. CP-KomuY

Moonshine. Howard Nemerov. CP-NemeH

Moonshine. Christina Georgina Rossetti. CP-RosC3

Moonshiner's Serenade. James Whitcomb Riley. CP-RileJ

Moonsnails. Eleanor Wilner. SP-WilnE

Moonsong at Morning. Sylvia Plath. CP-PlatS

Moonstar, The. Dante Gabriel Rossetti. CW-RossD *Fr.* House of Life, The.

Moony breadth of virgin face, A. Lines on the Portrait of a Celebrated Publisher. John Greenleaf Whittier. CP-WhitJ

Moored to the same ring. Ships Are Made Ready in Silence, The. W. S. Merwin. SP-MerwW

Moorish King rides up and down, The. Very Mournful Ballad, A. Lord Byron. CP-Byron

Moors. Ted Hughes. SP-HughTN

Moose. Anne Sexton. CP-SextA

Moose in the Morning, Northern Maine. Mona Van Duyn. SP-VanDM

Moose, The. Elizabeth Bishop. CP-BishE

Moose Wallow, The. Robert Earl Hayden. CP-HaydR

Mop-eyed I am, as some have said. Upon Himself. Robert Herrick. CP-HerrR

Mora Sponsi, the Stay of the Bridegroome. Robert Herrick. CP-HerrR

Moral, The. Rudyard Kipling. CP-KiplR *Fr.* Muse among the Motors, The.

Moral, The. William Carlos Williams. CP-WilW2

Moral Clothing. D. H. Lawrence. CP-LawrD

Moral Dream. Alan Dugan. CP-DugaA

Moral Poem, A. James Vincent Cunningham. CP-CunnJ

Moral Poem Freely Accepted from Sappho, A. James Wright. CP-WrigJ

Moral Tale, A. David Ignatow. SP-IgnaD

Moral Tales for the Young ("Little Gormley stole a purse"). Dorothy Parker. CP-ParkD

Moral Tales for the Young ("Maude, the brightest of the sex"). Dorothy Parker. CP-ParkD

Moral Warfare, The. John Greenleaf Whittier. CP-WhitJ

Moralists tell us that Loving is Sinning, The. Queries to Casuists. Lord Byron. CP-Byron

Moralities. Thomas Kinsella. CP-KinsT

Morality. D. H. Lawrence. *See* Man's Image

Morality. D. H. Lawrence. CP-LawrD

Morality, A. Howard Nemerov. CP-NemeH

Morality of Poetry, The. James Wright. CP-WrigJ

Moralizer Corrected, The. William Cowper. CP-CowpW

Morandi. Adam Zagajewski. SP-ZagaA, *tr. by* Renata Gorczynski, Benjamin Ivry *and* C. K. Williams

Morass is bulging and aborting, The. Memory. Ted Hughes. SP-HughTN

Mordanto fills the trump of fame. To the Earl of Peterborough. Jonathan Swift. CP-SwifJ

More. Ai. SP-Ai

More a Man Has the More a Man Wants, The. Paul Muldoon. CP-MuldP

More About People. Ogden Nash. CP-NashO

More about Poems. Andrei Codrescu. SP-CodrA

More and More. Margaret Atwood. SP-AtwM1

More and more empty chairs. Chairs. Charles Simic. SP-SimiCE

More and more lately, as, not even minding the slippages yet, the aches / and sad softenings. Repression. C. K. Williams. SP-WillC

More beautiful and soft than any moth. Landscape near an Aerodrome, The. Stephen Spender. CP-SpenS

More circumspect good friend, if by "deceive" Marilyn Hacker. SP-HackM *Fr.* Separations.

More Clues. Muriel Rukeyser. CP-RukeM

More concert than the quick have, have the dead. Metaphysical Sonnet, A. William Meredith. SP-MereW

More Country People. Carl Sandburg. CP-SandC

More discontents I never had. Discontents in Devon. Robert Herrick. CP-HerrR

More do I love cold. Old. Louis Zukofsky. CP-ZukLS

More experiences and sights, stranger, than you'd think for. Mirages. Walt Whitman. CP-WhitW

More food! The food of anxiety! The vivacious. Jingling the Cookery. Andrei Codrescu. SP-CodrA

More Foreign Cities. Charles Tomlinson. CP-TomlC; SP-TomlC

More gaily, dance. Quick-Step. Robert Creeley. CP-CreeR

More Girl than Boy. Yusef Komunyakaa. CP-KomuY

More Grammar for a Sentence. Gertrude Stein. CP-SteiG

More happily than I no ship has ever. Petrarch. CP-Petra, *tr. by* J. G. Nichols

More holy than the rest, and understanding more. Ovid. CP-RaleW *Fr.* Metamorphoses.

More I leaf through the dictionary in my physician's waiting, The. What the Well-Read Patient Is Talking About, or, Look, Ma, What I Got! Ogden Nash. CP-NashO

More I spread wings of desire to fly, The. Petrarch. CP-Petra, *tr. by* J. G. Nichols

More it seems I agonize, the more, The. Michelangelo Buonarroti. CP-Miche, *tr. by* John Frederick Nims

More Life—went out—when He went. Emily Dickinson. CP-DickE

More like a man it is, The. Apparition. W. S. Merwin. SP-MerwW

More like a vault—you pull the handle out. Refrigerator, 1957. Thomas Lux. SP-LuxT

More Love to His Life. Alice Walker. CP-WalkA

More lovely than all others. What Is It Makes One Girl. James Laughlin. CP-LaugJ

More Loving One, The. W. H. Auden. CP-AudeW

More May not Be by Human Art Exprest. William Wordsworth. CP-WorW2

More Mighty, the More Merciful, The. Robert Herrick. CP-HerrR

More Modest, More Manly. Robert Herrick. CP-HerrR

More money's lost, old gamblers understand. Two Pair. Howard Nemerov. CP-NemeH

More of a Corpse Than a Woman. Muriel Rukeyser. CP-RukeM

More often than not he stops at the headrig to light. Cauliflowers. Paul Muldoon. CP-MuldP

More Pleasant Adventures. John Ashbery. SP-AshbJ

More pleasurable to look than feed upon. Walgh-Vogel, The. Richard Wilbur. CP-WilbR

More Potent, Lesse Peccant. Robert Herrick. CP-HerrR

More real than ever, as I move. Way It Is, The. Denise Levertov. SP-LeveDL

More safely truth to urge her claim presumes. Juvenal. CP-JohnS *Fr.* Satires.

More shower than shine. Valentines to My Mother, 1880. Christina Georgina Rossetti. CP-RosC3

More Sonnets at Christmas. Allen Tate. CP-TateA

More strange than wonders of the earth, or skies. Inward Phenomena. Jones Very. CP-VeryJ

More Sufficient, The. Yannis Ritsos. SP-RitsY, *tr. by* Edmund Keeley

More sweet than my refrain. Ralph Waldo Emerson. CP-EmerR

More than a common tower. Belltower's Song. Rainer Maria Rilke. CP-RilkFr, *tr. by* A. Poulin, Jr. *Fr.* Valaisian Quatrains, The.

More Than a Fool's Song. Countee Cullen. CP-CullC

More than half my life long. Obliterate Tomb, The. Thomas Hardy. CP-HardT

More than halfway up the pass. Times Table, The. Robert Frost. CP-FrosR

More than once taking both roads one night. Mother, 1972. Robert Lowell. SP-LoweR

More than one cuckoo? Boys Then and Now. Thomas Hardy. CP-HardT

More than other song. Humming a Tune for an Old Lady in West Virginia. James Wright. CP-WrigJ

More than the ash stays you from nothingness! Phoenix, The. James Vincent Cunningham. CP-CunnJ

More than the dove, more than the mulberry. Lonely One, The. Paul Celan. SP-CelaP, *tr. by* John Felstiner

More than the Grave is closed to me. Emily Dickinson. CP-DickE

More than the sennet of the solstice pipe. Song, The: "More than the sennet of the solstice pipe." Charles Olson. CP-OlsoC; SP-OlsoC

More than this flecked thing . . . ? Under a Tree. Kenneth Patchen. CP-PatcK

More that— / who? the world. 1959 Valentine. Louis Zukofsky. CP-ZukLS

More Under Saturn. William Dickey. SP-DickW

More voice was in her cough tonight: its first harsh, stripping sound would weaken abruptly. Helen. C. K. Williams. SP-WillC

More white then whitest lilies far. To Electra. Robert Herrick. CP-HerrR

More you tackle the property dragon, The. St George and the Dragon. D. H. Lawrence. CP-LawrD

Morgan the lonely. Elegy for the Poet Morgan Blum, An. James Wright. CP-WrigJ

Morgante Maggiore, The. Luigi Pulci. CP-Byron

Morgenlied. Tennessee Williams. CP-WillT

Morituri Salutamus. Henry Wadsworth Longfellow. SP-LongH

Moriturus. Edna St. Vincent Millay. CP-MillE

Morlaix: Into the Future with Neil Young. Lawrence Ferlinghetti. SP-FerlL

Mormon Question, The. Ambrose Bierce. SP-BierA

Morn is breaking see the rising sun, The. Flee to the Mountains. Jones Very. CP-VeryJ

Morn may lend its golden smile, The. Jones Very. CP-VeryJ

Morn when first it thunders in March, The. Old Pictures in Florence. Robert Browning. CP-BroR1

Morning. William Blake. CP-BlakW

Morning. Louise Bogan. CP-BogaL

Morning. John Ciardi. CP-CiarJ

Morning. Billy Collins. SP-CollB

Morning ("Light's bright glimmer"). Robert Creeley. SP-CreeR

Morning ("Shadows, on the far wall"). Robert Creeley. SP-CreeR

Morning. Donald Davie. CP-DaviDC

Morning. Emily Dickinson. CP-DickE
(Will there really be a "Morning"?) CP-DickE

Morning. Paul Laurence Dunbar. CP-DunbP

Morning. Allen Ginsberg. CP-GinsA

Morning. Louise Glück. SP-GlucL

Morning. Federico García Lorca. CP-GarcF, tr. by Catherine Brown

Morning. Gabriela Mistral. SP-MistG, tr. by Maria Giachetti [or Jacketti]

Morning. Mary Oliver. SP-OlivM

Morning. John Crowe Ransom. SP-RansJ

Morning. James Whitcomb Riley. CP-RileJ

Morning. Arthur Rimbaud. CP-RimbA, tr. by Martin Sorrell

Morning. Yannis Ritsos. SP-RitsY, tr. by Kimon Friar

Morning. Henry David Thoreau. CP-ThorH

Morning. Jones Very. CP-VeryJ

Morning. William Carlos Williams. CP-WilW1

Morning, A. Margaret Atwood. SP-AtwM1

Morning, A. James Dickey. CP-DickJ

Morning, The. W. S. Merwin. SP-MerwWF

Morning, The. James Schuyler. CP-SchuJ

Morning, a glass door, flashes. Arrival. Philip Larkin. CP-LarkP

Morning After. Langston Hughes. CP-HughL; CP-HughL2

Morning after moonsnow, the bone dunes, The. Storm. John Ciardi. CP-CiarJ

Morning after Woe, The. Emily Dickinson. CP-DickE

Morning and evening. Goblin Market. Christina Georgina Rossetti. CP-RosC1

Morning at Great Pond. Mary Oliver. SP-OlivM

Morning at Last: There in the Snow. Philip Larkin. CP-LarkP

Morning at Speed Products. Alan Dugan. CP-DugaA

Morning at the Window. T. S. Eliot. CP-ElioT; SP-ElioT

Morning at the Zagorsk Monastery Outside Moscow. Miller Williams. CP-WillM

Morning Athletes. Marge Piercy. SP-PierM

Morning breaks like a pomegranate, The. Wedding Morn. D. H. Lawrence. CP-LawrD

Morning by a tree of blood was dewed, The. Adam. Federico García Lorca. SP-GarcF, tr. by Roy Campbell

Morning by tree of blood is moistened. Adam. Stephen Spender. CP-SpenS

Morning changes in the sun, The. Dogdays. James Vincent Cunningham. CP-CunnJ

Morning, clear morning. Love Song to a Morning. Jorge Guillén. CP-WrigJ

Morning Coffee. Thomas Kinsella. CP-KinsT

Morning comes, and thickening clouds prevail, The. Clouded Morning, The ("Morning comes, and thickening clouds prevail, The"). Jones Very. CP-VeryJ

Morning comes; and thickening fogs prevail, The. Clouded Morning, The ("Morning comes; and thickening fogs prevail, The"). Jones Very. CP-VeryJ

Morning comes. The old woman, a spot, The. Grief. Wendell Berry. CP-BerrW

Morning cried by the bed. Thousands of Days. Muriel Rukeyser. CP-RukeM

Morning ("Dam's broke"). Robert Creeley. SP-CreeR

Morning Dream, The. William Cowper. CP-CowpW

Morning (8:10 AM). Robert Creeley. SP-CreeR

Morning, evening, noon and night. Boy and the Angel, The. Robert Browning. CP-BroR1

Morning Exercise, A. William Wordsworth. CP-WorW2

Morning fair: A noontide dubious, A. New Year's Day, 1848. Walt Whitman. CP-WhitW

Morning: from sleep to confusion. On Being Easy in the Ritual of Separation. Alan Dugan. CP-DugaA

Morning glories, pale as a mist drying. Bees and Morning Glories. John Ciardi. CP-CiarJ

Morning Glory Blue. Carl Sandburg. CP-SandC

Morning glory vine. Next Day, The. A. R. Ammons. CP-AmmoA

Morning Half-Life Blues, The. Marge Piercy. SP-PierM

Morning Has Spread Again. Philip Larkin. CP-LarkP

Morning haunted by black dragonfly. Ginkakuji Michi. Philip Whalen. SP-WhalP

Morning Hymn for a Little Child. Jones Very. CP-VeryJ

Morning Hymn to a Dark Girl. James Wright. CP-WrigJ

Morning: I Know Perfectly How in a Minute You Will Stretch and Smile. John Ciardi. CP-CiarJ

Morning in a New Land. Mary Oliver. SP-OlivM

Morning in Salerno 4. Yannis Ritsos. SP-RitsY, tr. by Kostas Myrsiades

Morning in the Hospital Solarium. Sylvia Plath. CP-PlatS

Morning in the Park. John Ciardi. CP-CiarJ

Morning in Vicenza, A. Adam Zagajewski. SP-ZagaA, tr. by Clare Cavanagh

Morning is due to all. Emily Dickinson. CP-DickE

Morning is so gray that the grass is gray and the side of the white horse grazing, The. On Learning of a Friend's Illness. C. K. Williams. CP-WillC; SP-WillC

Morning—is the place for Dew. Emily Dickinson. CP-DickE

Morning / island light begins, The. Dawn and a Woman. John Logan. CP-LogaJ

Morning: Leaving Calle Gigantes. Jay Wright. SP-WrigJ

Morning lights / whiteness that has touched the world, The. March Snow. Wendell Berry. CP-BerrW

Morning man came in to report, The. People Who Went By in Winter. William Stafford. SP-StafWW

"Morning"—means "Milking"—to the Farmer. Emily Dickinson. CP-DickE

Morning Melancholy. Rainer Maria Rilke. CP-RilkFr, tr. by A. Poulin, Jr.

Morning, Midday, and Evening Sacrifice. Gerard Manley Hopkins. CP-HopkG

Morning Moon, The. Derek Walcott. CP-WalcD

Morning, My Prince—the Eye That Walks. Kenneth Patchen. CP-PatcK

Morning News, The. Charles Olson. CP-OlsoC

Morning newspaper is useful, The. Press is Peculiar, The. Carl Sandburg. CP-SandC

Morning of Drunkenness. Arthur Rimbaud. CP-RimbA, tr. by Martin Sorrell

Morning of 1649, A. Jorge Luis Borges. SP-BorgJ, tr. by Alastair Reid

Morning of the Dying Gigolo, The. Alan Dugan. CP-DugaA

Morning of the life there is, A. Morning. John Ciardi. CP-CiarJ

Morning of the Poem, The. James Schuyler. CP-SchuJ

Morning of the world, the western afternoon, The. May Morning: Hudson Pastoral. Marya Alexandrovna Zaturenska. SP-ZatuM

Morning on the St. John's. Jane Cooper. CP-CoopJ

Morning, or heartache. In / the night it rained. Good Morning. James Schuyler. CP-SchuJ

Morning Poem. Mary Oliver. SP-OlivM

Morning quivers in the thorns; above the budded snowdrops. To Autumn. Louise Glück. SP-GlucL

Morning Radio. Derek Mahon. CP-MahoD

Morning rattles the tall spike fence. Half Past Home. Marge Piercy. SP-PierM

Morning Sea. Constantine P. Cavafy. CP-CavaC

Morning Shutters. Arthur Sze. SP-SzeA

Morning Song. Alan Dugan. CP-DugaA

Morning Song. Gregory Orr. SP-OrrG

Morning Song. Sylvia Plath. CP-PlatS

Morning Song. Wallace Stevens. CP-StevWP

Morning Song in the Jungle. Rudyard Kipling. CP-KiplR Fr. Second Jungle Book, The.

Morning Song of Love. Paul Laurence Dunbar. CP-DunbP

Morning Star, The. Emily Jane Brontë. CP-BronE

Morning star is not a star, The. Gary Snyder. CP-SnydG Fr. Myths and Texts.

Morning Sun. Louis MacNeice. CP-MacNL

Morning Sun. Howard Nemerov. CP-NemeH

Morning sun seemed fair as though, The. Mute Singer, The. James Whitcomb Riley. CP-RileJ

Morning sunlight—a patch of clear memory. Irwin Street. Thomas Kinsella. CP-KinsT

Morning Swim. Maxine W. Kumin. SP-KumiM

Morning that comes but once. Emily Dickinson. CP-DickE

Morning that I first loved you, The. New Clouds, The. William Carlos Williams. CP-WilW2

Morning: the phone jangles me from words: you. Marilyn Hacker. SP-HackM Fr. Taking Notice.

Morning, Thinking of Empire. Raymond Carver. CP-CarvR

Morning up the eastern stair. God's Acre. A. E. Housman. CP-HousA

Morning Walk, A. Philip Whalen. SP-WhalP

Morning Watch, The. Jones Very. CP-VeryJ

Morning watch was come; the vessel lay, The. Island, The. Lord Byron. CP-Byron

Morning. / Who never sang before is singing. Lying In. Olga Broumas. SP-BrouO

Morning wind, making the lanterns flare, A. First Light. Charles Baudelaire. CP-BaudC, tr. by Walter Martin

Morning wind spreads its fresh smell, The. Jelaluddin Rumi. SP-Rumi, tr. by Coleman Barks

Morning without you is a dwindled Dawn. Emily Dickinson. SP-DickE

Morning Work. D. H. Lawrence. CP-LawrD

Mornings, after leg lifts and knee bends. Body and Soul: A Meditation. Maxine W. Kumin. SP-KumiM

Mornings are blind as newborn cars. Ode to Softness. Adam Zagajewski. SP-ZagaA, tr. by Renata Gorczynski

Morning's brightness cannot make thee glad, The. True Light, The. Jones Very. CP-VeryJ

Mornings: Catherine. C. K. Williams. SP-WillC

Mornings, curled asleep in our soft beds. Creation of the World, The. Adam Zagajewski. SP-ZagaA, *tr.* by Renata Gorczynski, Benjamin Ivry *and* C. K. Williams

Mornings in a New House. James Merrill. SP-MerrJ

Mornings in bed / Are energetic mornings. In Bed. Kenneth Koch. SP-KochK

Mornings Innocent. May Swenson. SP-SwenM

Morning's News, The. Wendell Berry. CP-BerrW

Mornings / of an impossible love. Alice Walker. CP-WalkA

Mornings on Bourbon Street. Tennessee Williams. CP-WillT

Mornings Remembering Last Nights. Olga Broumas. SP-BrouO

Morning's the woman time of day. Off. A. R. Ammons. CP-AmmoA

Morns are meeker than they were, The. Emily Dickinson. CP-DickE

Morns are meeker than they were, The. Morns are meeker than they were, The. Emily Dickinson. CP-DickE

Morns like these—we parted. Emily Dickinson. CP-DickE

Morro Bay. Robinson Jeffers. CP-JefR3

Morrow's Message, The. Dante Gabriel Rossetti. CW-RossD *Fr.* House of Life, The.

Mors nox perpetua est; mori proinde. In Morachum. Thomas Campion. CP-CampT

Morsel miraculous and meaningless. E. E. Cummings. CP-CummE

Mort de A.D. Samuel Beckett. CP-BeckS

Mortal. Laura Riding Jackson. CP-RidiL

Mortal Answers, The. G. K. Chesterton. CP-ChesG

Mortal body quickly dies, The. This Mortal Shall put on Immortality. Jones Very. CP-VeryJ

Mortal Combat. Charles Baudelaire. CP-BaudC, *tr.* by Walter Martin

Mortal Enemy. Dorothy Parker. CP-ParkD

Mortal field of moons. Song of a Little Death. Federico García Lorca. CP-GarcF, *tr.* by Greg Simon *and* Steven F. White

Mortal Flesh, Is Not Your Place in the Ground? Edna St. Vincent Millay. CP-MillE

Mortal Girl. Muriel Rukeyser. CP-RukeM

Mortal in things I want to pray with you. Insomniac of a Zen-Garden Fruit. Olga Broumas. SP-BrouO

Mortal Limit. Robert Penn Warren. CP-WarrR

Mortal mixed of middle clay. Guy. Ralph Waldo Emerson. CP-EmerR

Mortal my mate, bearing my rock-a-heart. To His Watch. Gerard Manley Hopkins. CP-HopkG

Mortal Prudence, handmaid of divine Providence. Testament of Perpetual Change, The. William Carlos Williams. CP-WilW2

Mortales decem tela inter Gallica caesos. In Barnum. Thomas Campion. CP-CampT

Mortales tua forma quod misellos. Ad Chloen. Thomas Campion. CP-CampT

Mortality. Paul Laurence Dunbar. CP-DunbP

Mortals around your destin'd heads. William Cowper. CP-CowpW

Mortals) / climbi / ng i / nto eachness begi. E. E. Cummings. CP-CummE

Mortals know present events. Wise Sense Imminent Events, The. Constantine P. Cavafy. CP-CavaC, *tr.* by Theoharis Constantine Theoharis

Morte d'Arthur. Alfred Tennyson. CP-TennA

Morte parmi. Samuel Beckett. CP-BeckS

Mortesto. George Meredith. CP-MerG2

Mortification. George Herbert. CP-HerbG

Mortmain. Robert Penn Warren. CP-WarrR

Mortmain Reappears. Herman Melville. SP-MelvH *Fr.* Clarel: A Poem and Pilgrimage in the Holy Land.

Morton. James Whitcomb Riley. CP-RileJ

Mortul Prayer, A. James Whitcomb Riley. CP-RileJ

Morwenna's Cliff. Charles Tomlinson. CP-TomlC

Mosaic. Olga Broumas. SP-BrouO

Mosaic: St. Praxed's. Raissa Maritain. CP-MertT

Mosaicist of minute, A. On Eleventh Street. Charles Tomlinson. CP-TomlC

Moscow. Langston Hughes. CP-HughL; CP-HughL1

Moscow. Jaroslav Seifert. SP-SeifJ, *tr.* by Ewald Osers

Moscow in the Wilderness, Segovia in the Snow. Lawrence Ferlinghetti. SP-FerlL

Moses. Howard Nemerov. CP-NemeH

Moses. Adam Zagajewski. SP-ZagaA, *tr.* by Renata Gorczynski, Benjamin Ivry *and* C. K. Williams

Moses and the Shepherd. Jelaluddin Rumi. SP-Rumi, *tr.* by Coleman Barks

Moses as Leader of Israel. Jones Very. CP-VeryJ

Moses at the Bush. Jones Very. CP-VeryJ

Moses heard a shepherd on the road praying. Moses and the Shepherd. Jelaluddin Rumi. SP-Rumi, *tr.* by Coleman Barks

Moses in Infancy. Jones Very. CP-VeryJ

"Moses" of Michael Angelo, The. Robert Browning. CP-BroR2

Moses on Pisgah. Robert Stock. SP-StocR

Moslems' Angel of Death, The. Thomas Merton. CP-MertT

Mosque in Jaffa, The. Raymond Carver. CP-CarvR

Mosquito. John Updike. CP-UpdiJ

Mosquito & / moth. Scream. Federico García Lorca. CP-GarcF, *tr.* by Jerome Rothenberg *Fr.* Fairs.

Mosquito Knows, The. D. H. Lawrence. CP-LawrD

Mosquito, The. D. H. Lawrence. CP-LawrD

Moss. Andrei Codrescu. SP-CodrA

Moss and Its Teachings. The. Jones Very. CP-VeryJ

Moss-Gathering. Theodore Roethke. CP-RoetT

Moss of His Skin, The. Anne Sexton. CP-SextA; SP-SextA

Mossbawn. Seamus Heaney. SP-HeanSO

Most, The. Charles Bukowski. SP-BukC1

Most, The. Heather McHugh. SP-McHuH

Most Alluring Clouds That Mount the Sky, The. William Wordsworth. CP-WorW2

Most ancient Metaphysics, (poor Metaphysics!). Madonnas Touched Up with Goatees [*or* a goatee]. Charles Simic. SP-SimiC; SP-SimiCE

Most astonishing thing, A. Imitated from the Japanese. William Butler Yeats. CP-YeatW

Most beautiful, haunting, The. Celestial. A. R. Ammons. CP-AmmoA

Most beautiful, most dear. Timor Dei. James Vincent Cunningham. CP-CunnJ

Most beautiful! the red-flowering eucalyptus. Torso, The. Robert Duncan. SP-DuncR *Fr.* Passages.

Most binding labor / is, The. 86'd. Charles Bukowski. SP-BukC2

Most brainy woman, the sexuality of your thought. Sonnet: "Most brainy woman, the sexuality of your thought." Hayden Carruth. CP-CarHS *Fr.* Sonnets.

Most candid critic, what if I. To a Critic. Samuel Taylor Coleridge. CP-ColeS

Most dear, and dearest at this moment most. Dakar Doldrums. Allen Ginsberg. CP-GinsA

Most delectable mess. O, July 1992. William Corbett. SP-CorbW

Most excruciating / thing, The. C. K. Williams. CP-WillC

Most Expensive Picture in the World, The. Howard Nemerov. CP-NemeH

Most glorious Virgin, you are clothed in glory. Petrarch. CP-Petra, *tr.* by J. G. Nichols

Most highly respected Professor Nietzsche. Talk with Friedrich Nietzsche, A. Adam Zagajewski. SP-ZagaA, *tr.* by Renata Gorczynski, Benjamin Ivry *and* C. K. Williams

Most holy Satyr. Holy Satyr. "H. D." CP-DoolH

Most important population, The. Emily Dickinson. CP-DickE

Most intimate, most far, most ethereally near. Lost, The. Richard Eberhart. CP-EberR

Most marvelous is not, The. Hard Core of Beauty, The. William Carlos Williams. CP-WilW2

Most mornings I get away, slip out. Run before Dawn. William Stafford. SP-StafW; SP-StafWW

Most mornings we go running side by side. Morning Athletes. Marge Piercy. SP-PierM

Most of his friends, as expected. As Expected. Thom Gunn. CP-GunnT

Most of It, The. Robert Frost. CP-FrosR

Most of our Moments. Emily Dickinson. SP-DickE

Most of the continent. Fanny Howe. SP-HoweF *Fr.* O'Clock.

Most of the world's poetry. Codicil. Kenneth Rexroth. CP-RexrK

Most ontimely old man yit! Pen-Pictur' of a Cert'in Frivvolus Old Man, A. James Whitcomb Riley. CP-RileJ

Most pathetic thing I do, The. Emily Dickinson. CP-DickE

Most patients believe. Art of Healing, The. W. H. Auden. CP-AudeW

Most people don't do very well and I get discouraged with. 60 Yard Pass. Charles Bukowski. SP-BukC3

Most people from Idaho are crazed rednecks. Running Away from Home. Carolyn Kizer. CP-KizeC

Most people know more as they get older. Winter Palace, The. Philip Larkin. CP-LarkP

Most people, today, are chimaera. Chimaera. D. H. Lawrence. CP-LawrD

Most people's downy couches have a footboard and a headboard. Have You Tried Staying Awake? or, They'll Find a Way to Stop That, Too. Ogden Nash. CP-NashO

Most poems are of emerald seas. Demon Smoke. Tennessee Williams. CP-WillT

Most quaintly touching, in her German tongue. Christine. James Whitcomb Riley. CP-RileJ

Most recent in the long race that descends. Doodler, The. James Merrill. SP-MerrJ

Most Saturday afternoons. Weepies, The. Paul Muldoon. CP-MuldP

Most she touched me by her muteness. Emily Dickinson. CP-DickE

Most sweet and pleasing are thy wayes, O God. Thomas Campion. CP-CampT

Most tangible of all the gods that be. To Santa Claus. James Whitcomb Riley. CP-RileJ

Most travelers eavesdrop / As unintentionally as autumn leaves drop. Everybody Wants to Get into the Baedeker. Ogden Nash. CP-NashO

Most triumphant Bird I ever knew or met, The. Emily Dickinson. CP-DickE

Most truly hono[u]red, and as truly dear. To Her Father, with Some Verses. Anne Bradstreet. CP-BradA

Most truth of what is most usual, The. It Is the Same Place Always Once Again. John Ciardi. CP-CiarJ

Most wandering thing is a heart that stopped wandering, The. Yehuda Amichai. SP-AmicYL *Fr.* At Right Angles.

Most were married teenagers. Glory. Yusef Komunyakaa. CP-KomuY

Most what I know of war is what I learned. Memory of the War, A. Howard Nemerov. CP-NemeH

Most wicked words!-forbear to speak them out. Edna St. Vincent Millay. CP-MillE

Most Words, Lesse Workes. Robert Herrick. CP-HerrR

Most wounds can Time repair. At Ease. Walter De la Mare. CP-DeLaW

Most wretched heart, most miserable. Sir Thomas Wyatt. CP-WyatT

Mostly, folks is law-abidin'. Down on Wriggle Crick. James Whitcomb Riley. CP-RileJ

Mostly the animals dream. Dreams of the Animals. Margaret Atwood. SP-AtwM1

Mostly you don't see the ocean. Road Behind the Last Dune, The. Marge Piercy. SP-PierM *Fr.* Sand Roads.

Mostly you look back and say, Well, Ok. Things might have. Afterwards. William Stafford. SP-StafWW

Most(people / simply / can't). E. E. Cummings. CP-CummE

Motel in Troy, New York, A. Josephine Jacobsen. CP-JacoJ

Motel was made for love, The. Up Here. James Tate. SP-TateJ

Motes that still disturbed her lidded calm, The. Night. Adrienne Rich. CP-RicAE; SP-RicA2

Motet. Louis Zukofsky. CP-ZukLS

Moth, The. Walter De la Mare. CP-DeLaW

Moth and Rust. D. H. Lawrence. CP-LawrD

Moth-browed girl in town, A. Han-shan. CP-ColdM, *tr.* by Red Pine

Moth-force a small town always has. Strength of Fields, The. James Dickey. CP-DickJ

Moth Hour. Adrienne Rich. CP-RicAE; SP-RicA2

Moth in the Schoolroom. May Sarton. SP-SartM

Moth-Signal, The. Thomas Hardy. CP-HardT

Moth That Made God Blind, The. Hart Crane. CP-CranH

Moth the hue of this, A. Emily Dickinson. CP-DickE

Moth under the eaves, The. Prelude to Winter. William Carlos Williams. CP-WilW2

Mother. Hayden Carruth. CP-CarHL

Mother. Raymond Carver. CP-CarvR

Mother. Donald Davie. CP-DaviDC

Mother. Marilyn Hacker. SP-HackM

Mother. James Whitcomb Riley. CP-RileJ

Mother. Stevie Smith. CP-SmitS

Mother, The. George Crabbe. SP-CrabG *Fr.* Tales.

Mother, among the Dustbins. Stevie Smith. CP-SmitS

Mother and Babe. Walt Whitman. CP-WhitW

Mother and Child. George Oppen. CP-OppGN

Mother and Child. Christina Georgina Rossetti. CP-RosC3

Mother and Daughter. Anne Sexton. CP-SextA; SP-SextA

Mother and Father 1. Robert Lowell. SP-LoweR

Mother and Father 2. Robert Lowell. SP-LoweR

Mother and Father have fulfilled their promise. Chill, The. Denise Levertov. SP-LeveDL

Mother and father knew God and were glad to explain. Echoes. John Ciardi. CP-CiarJ

Mother and Jack and the Rain. Anne Sexton. CP-SextA

Mother and listener she is, but she does not listen. Question, The. Muriel Rukeyser. CP-RukeM

Mother and Poet. Elizabeth Barrett Browning. CP-BroEB

Mother and Son. Charles Bukowski. SP-BukC2

Mother and Son. Allen Tate. CP-TateA

Mother, because you never spoke to me. More Clues. Muriel Rukeyser. CP-RukeM

Mother carried her child in the white moonlight, The. Sebastian in the Dream. John Logan. CP-LogaJ

Mother Country. Christina Georgina Rossetti. CP-RosC1

Mother, / each time I talk to God. Praying on a 707. Anne Sexton. CP-SextA

Mother Earth: Her Whales. Gary Snyder. CP-SnydG

Mother, Father. Money Swing, The. Anne Sexton. CP-SextA; SP-SextA

Mother Garden's Round. Muriel Rukeyser. CP-RukeM

Mother Goose. Kenneth Rexroth. CP-RexrK

Mother Goose. James Whitcomb Riley. CP-RileJ

Mother Goose's Garland. Archibald MacLeish. CP-MacLA

Mother-hands no further toil may know, The. To the Mother. James Whitcomb

Riley. CP-RileJ

Mother, help me. I feel as if I'm falling. Knock, Knock. Ai. SP-Ai

Mother!, I am sick. For an Obligate Parasite. Alan Dugan. CP-DugaA

Mother, I love you so. Human Affection. Stevie Smith. CP-SmitS

Mother, I'm heavy on my bed, and everything I wear. Cursed Child. Rainer Maria Rilke. CP-RilkFr, *tr.* by A. Poulin, Jr.

Mother-in-Law. Adrienne Rich. SP-RicA2

Mother, in my unwanted suffering. Bread Itself, The. David Ignatow. SP-IgnaD

Mother in Wartime. Langston Hughes. CP-HughL; CP-HughL3

Mother Is Dead. Lorine Niedecker. *See* Element Mother, The

Mother is often lop-. Fanny Howe. SP-HoweF *Fr.* Sea-Garden, The.

Mother, is this the darkness of the end. For "Our Lady of the Rocks" by Leonardo da Vinci. Dante Gabriel Rossetti. CW-RossD

Mother Junkie. Clarence Major. SP-MajoC

Mother-Lodge, The. Rudyard Kipling. CP-KiplR

Mother Marie Therese. Robert Lowell. SP-LoweR

Mother mine / Whom every year. 1879. Christina Georgina Rossetti. CP-RosC3

Mother (mother) unbent to give to / anyone, The. Method of Actuality, The. Robert Creeley. CP-CreeR

Mother, mother, what illbred aunt. Disquieting Muses, The. Sylvia Plath. CP-PlatS

Mother Mourns, The. Thomas Hardy. CP-HardT

Mother my good girl. Life's Work. Maxine W. Kumin. SP-KumiM

Mother, my Mary Gray. Division of Parts, The. Anne Sexton. CP-SextA; SP-SextA

Mother, 1972. Robert Lowell. SP-LoweR

Mother o' Mine. Rudyard Kipling. CP-KiplR *Fr.* Light That Failed, The.

Mother, O mother! forever I cry for you. Mother-Song, A. James Whitcomb Riley. CP-RileJ

Mother of All. G. K. Chesterton. CP-ChesG

Mother of Darkness, Our Lady. Winter-Worship. Charles Wright. SP-WrigCN

Mother of flames. Crude Lament. William Carlos Williams. CP-WilW1

Mother of God! Our Lady! For Eleanor and Bill Monahan. William Carlos Williams. CP-WilW2

Mother of God, The. William Butler Yeats. CP-YeatW

Mother of heaven, regina of the clouds. Le Monocle de Mon Oncle. Wallace Stevens. CP-StevW; CP-StevWP

Mother of Hermes! and still youthful Maia! Fragment of an Ode to Maia Written on May Day, 1818. John Keats. CP-KeatJ

Mother of Latin games and Grecian rites. Lesbos. Charles Baudelaire. CP-BaudC, *tr.* by Walter Martin

Mother of memories, mistress divine. Balcony, The. Charles Baudelaire. CP-BaudC, *tr.* by Walter Martin

Mother of my birth, for how long were we together. Kaddish. David Ignatow. SP-IgnaD

Mother of Riddles, dark desperate vivid. Present Time, The. G. K. Chesterton. CP-ChesG

Mother of roots, you have not seeded. Goodbye to the Poetry of Calcium. James Wright. CP-WrigJ

Mother of the Buddhas, Queen of Heaven, Mother of the Sun; Marici, Goddess of the Dawn. Gary Snyder. CP-SnydG

Mother of the Fair Delight. Ave. Dante Gabriel Rossetti. CW-RossD

Mother of the Groom. Seamus Heaney. SP-HeanSO

Mother of the little boy that sleeps, The. Little David. James Whitcomb Riley. CP-RileJ

Mother, picked for jury duty, managed to get through. Long Line of Doctors, A. Carolyn Kizer. CP-KizeC

Mother Pomegranate. Gabriela Mistral. SP-MistG, *tr.* by Maria Giachetti [or Jacketti]

Mother procure for me a golden crown. Crown of Gold, The. Stevie Smith. CP-SmitS

Mother-Right. Adrienne Rich. SP-RicA2

Mother said if I wore this hat. My Hat. Stevie Smith. CP-SmitS

Mother, Said the Child. Randall Jarrell. CP-JarrR

Mother Sainted, The. James Whitcomb Riley. CP-RileJ

Mother shake the cherry-tree. Let's Be Merry. Christina Georgina Rossetti. CP-RosC2

Mother slew her unborn babe, A. But Murderous. Stevie Smith. CP-SmitS

Mother-Song, A. James Whitcomb Riley. CP-RileJ

Mother, / strange goddess face. Dreaming the Breasts. Anne Sexton. CP-SextA; SP-SextA

Mother, Summer, I. Philip Larkin. CP-LarkP

Mother, the pleasure. To return is, The. La Chute III. Charles Olson. CP-OlsoC

Mother, the sweet peas have gushed out of. 108 East 19th. William Stafford. SP-StafW; SP-StafWW

Mother ties the hair-ribbons of the child, The. Extraordinary References. Wallace Stevens. CP-StevW; CP-StevWP

Mother to Babe. George Meredith. CP-MerG1

"Mother," to me, is so sacred a Name. Emily Dickinson. SP-DickE

Mother to Son. Langston Hughes. CP-HughL; CP-HughL1

Mother II. Marilyn Hacker. SP-HackM

Mother was a crack of light. Three Floors. Stanley Kunitz. CP-KunSC

Mother was going through, The. Cheesecake. Paul Muldoon. CP-MuldP

Mother when does the. When Does the Play Begin? James Laughlin. CP-LaugJ

Mother, when I open a book of yours. Soul-Cake, A. Denise Levertov. SP-LeveDL; SP-LeveDS

Mother will not turn, who thinks she hears, The. Broken Music. Dante Gabriel Rossetti. CW-RossD *Fr.* House of Life, The.

Motherhood. Rita Dove. SP-DoveR

Motherhood. Rainer Maria Rilke. CP-RilkFr, *tr. by* A. Poulin, Jr.

Motherhood. May Swenson. SP-SwenM

Mothering Blackness, The. Maya Angelou. SP-AngeM

Motherland. Langston Hughes. CP-HughL; CP-HughL2

Motherless baby and babyless mother. Christina Georgina Rossetti. CP-RosC2

Motherless soft lambkin / Alone upon a hill. Christina Georgina Rossetti. CP-RosC2

Mothers. Margaret Atwood. SP-AtwM2

Mothers. Anne Sexton. CP-SextA

Mothers are doubtless happier for their babes. Gerard Manley Hopkins. CP-HopkG

Mother's Day. William Stafford. SP-StafW; SP-StafWW

Mother's Day is a very fine day. Please Leave Father Alone. Ogden Nash. CP-NashO

Mother's dying almost stunned my spirit. Emily Dickinson. SP-DickE

Mother's gone a-visitin' to spend a month er two. Lonesome. Paul Laurence Dunbar. CP-DunbP

Mother's Hearse, A. Stevie Smith. CP-SmitS

Mother's Lament for the Death of Her Son, A. Robert Burns. CP-BurnR (Mother's Lament for the Loss of Her Only Son, A.) CP-BurnR

Mother's Lament for the Loss of Her Only Son, A. Robert Burns. *See* Mother's Lament for the Death of Her Son, A

Mothers! Mothers! It was visions of mothers that had been relentlessly haunting me. Epilogue to Mother's Day, Which Is To Be Published on Any Day But Mother's Day. Ogden Nash. CP-NashO

Mothers of America / let your kids go to the movies! Ave Maria. Frank O'Hara. SP-OharF

Mothers pass, / Sweet watermelon in a baby carriage. Summer Evening (Calumet Avenue). Langston Hughes. CP-HughL; CP-HughL2

Mothers smear bitter neem. Images. A. K. Ramanujan. CP-RamaA

Mother's Son, The. Rudyard Kipling. CP-KiplR

Mother's Tale, The. Ai. SP-Ai

Mothers you have met before still need you. Thomas Merton. CP-MertT

Moths. Adam Zagajewski. SP-ZagaA, *tr. by* Renata Gorczynski, Renata Gorczynski, Benjamin Ivry *and* C. K. Williams

Moths, The. Norman Dubie. CP-DubiN

Moths, The. James Laughlin. CP-LaugJ

Moths, The. W. S. Merwin. SP-MerwW

Moths, The. Mary Oliver. SP-OlivM

Moths watched us through. Moths. Adam Zagajewski. SP-ZagaA, *tr. by* Renata Gorczynski, Renata Gorczynski, Benjamin Ivry *and* C. K. Williams

Motif. Ezra Pound. CP-PoEar

Motion. A. R. Ammons. CP-AmmoA

Motion for Motion. A. R. Ammons. CP-AmmoA

Motion: not things / moving where the harp's. Music's Trinity. Charles Tomlinson. CP-TomlC

Motion, The. Charles Olson. CP-OlsoC

Motion, The. Theodore Roethke. CP-RoetT

Motionless—His sons. Death Bed. Thomas Kinsella. CP-KinsT

Motions and means, on land and sea at war. Steamboats, Viaducts, and Railways. William Wordsworth. CP-WorW2

Motions of waking trouble winter air. Fare Well. John Berryman. CP-BerrJ

Motion's the dead give away. Viable. A. R. Ammons. CP-AmmoA

Motive. Jones Very. CP-VeryJ

Motive for Metaphor, The. Wallace Stevens. CP-StevW; CP-StevWP

Motive of All of It, The. Muriel Rukeyser. CP-RukeM

Motives of a Two-Headed Turtle. Robert Stock. SP-StocR

Motley. Walter De la Mare. CP-DeLaW

Motley. George Meredith. CP-MerG2

Motor-Barge, The. William Carlos Williams. CP-WilW2

Motor cars / like china. Lorine Niedecker. CP-NiedL

Motorbike, A. Ted Hughes. SP-HughTN

Motorcycle, count my sins. Thirteenth and Pennsylvania. William Stafford. SP-StafWW

Motorcycle strums the empty streets. Bed in the Sky, The. Gary Snyder. CP-SnydG

Motorcyclists, The. James Tate. SP-TateJ

Mots survivants. Samuel Beckett. CP-BeckS

Mottled afternoon shall shade, The. Afternoon of a Doll. Marya Alexandrovna Zaturenska. SP-ZatuM

Motto. Langston Hughes. CP-HughL; CP-HughL3

Motto, A. James Whitcomb Riley. CP-RileJ

Motto Intended for Poems on the Naming of Places. William Wordsworth. CP-WorW1

Motto on the King's Clock. William Cowper. CP-CowpW

Motto on the Sundial, The. Kenneth Rexroth. CP-RexrK

Motto to "Circles" Ralph Waldo Emerson. *See* Circles

Motto to "Considerations by the Way" Ralph Waldo Emerson. CP-EmerR

Motto to "Fate" Ralph Waldo Emerson. CP-EmerR

Motto to "Gifts" Ralph Waldo Emerson. CP-EmerR

Motto to "Illusions" Ralph Waldo Emerson. *See* Illusions

Motto to "Intellect" Ralph Waldo Emerson. *See* Intellect

Motto to "Nature" Ralph Waldo Emerson. *See* Nature [1836]

Motto to "Nature" Ralph Waldo Emerson. *See* Nature [1844]

Motto to "New England Reformers" Ralph Waldo Emerson. CP-EmerR

Motto to "Nominalist and Realist" Ralph Waldo Emerson. *See* Nominalist and Realist

Motto to "Power" Ralph Waldo Emerson. CP-EmerR

Motto to "Prudence" Ralph Waldo Emerson. *See* Theme no poet gladly sung

Motto to "The Poet" Ralph Waldo Emerson. CP-EmerR

Motto to the Songs of Innocence & of Experience. William Blake. CP-BlakW

Mottoes to "History" Ralph Waldo Emerson. CP-EmerR *Fr.* History.

Mould-green is the house of oblivion. Sand from the Urns, The. Paul Celan. SP-CelaP, *tr. by* John Felstiner

Mould's not alone in this, A. Michelangelo Buonarroti. CP-Miche, *tr. by* John Frederick Nims

Moulting. A. K. Ramanujan. CP-RamaA

Moulting has first to find a thorn at a suitable height to pin and fix the growing numbness in the tail. Moulting. A. K. Ramanujan. CP-RamaA

Mound, The. Thomas Hardy. CP-HardT

Mound Builders, The. Stanley Kunitz. CP-KunSC

Mound Builders, The. Jones Very. CP-VeryJ

Mount Agiochook. John Greenleaf Whittier. CP-WhitJ

Mount Aso uplands. Volcano in Kyushu, A. Gary Snyder. CP-SnydG

Mount Caribou at Night. Charles Wright. SP-WrigC

Mt. Fuji and the Martial Arts. Eleanor Wilner. SP-WilnE

Mt. Gabriel. Derek Mahon. CP-MahoD

Mount Kearsarge. Donald Hall. CP-HallD

Mount, not wearisome and bare and steep, A. To a Young Friend. Samuel Taylor Coleridge. CP-ColeS

Mount of the Muses, The. Robert Herrick. CP-HerrR

Mount Zion. Ted Hughes. SP-HughTN

Mountain, The. Elizabeth Bishop. CP-BishE

Mountain, The. Hayden Carruth. CP-CarHS

Mountain, The. Robert Frost. CP-FrosR

Mountain, The. Louise Glück. SP-GlucL

Mountain, The. James Laughlin. CP-LaugJ

Mountain, The. Jones Very. CP-VeryJ

Mountain Afterglow, The. James Laughlin. CP-LaugJ

Mountain air from the mountain up behind. Seamus Heaney. SP-HeanSO *Fr.* Squarings.

Mountain Cabin, The. Hayden Carruth. CP-CarHS

Mountain comes and goes, The. Elusive. Denise Levertov. SP-LeveDS

Mountain Days. W. S. Merwin. SP-MerwWF

Mountain gorses, ever-golden. Lessons from the Gorse. Elizabeth Barrett Browning. CP-BroEB

Mountain I live on, The. Han-shan. CP-ColdM, *tr. by* Red Pine

Mountain Impasse. John Updike. CP-UpdiJ

Mountain is red, The. The sea is green. Accented Colors. Yannis Ritsos. SP-RitsY, *tr. by* Athan Anagnostopoulos

Mountain Laurel. Louis Zukofsky. CP-ZukLS

Mountain Liar. A. R. Ammons. CP-AmmoA

Mountain Lion. D. H. Lawrence. CP-LawrD

Mountain Lovers. Robert Graves. CP-GravR

Mountain man lives under thatch, A. Han-shan. CP-ColdM, *tr. by* Red Pine

Mountain / Mesquite. Flint and Steel. Thomas McGrath. SP-McGrT

Mountain, mountain, mountain. Into the Interior. Denise Levertov. SP-LeveDP

Mountain Mystery. Robert Penn Warren. CP-WarrR

Mountain: One from Bryant. Muriel Rukeyser. CP-RukeM

Mountain Pictures. John Greenleaf Whittier. CP-WhitJ

Mountain Plateau. Robert Penn Warren. CP-WarrR

Mountain risen, A. High & Low. A. R. Ammons. CP-AmmoA

Mountain road ends here, The. Lyell's Hypothesis Again. Kenneth Rexroth. CP-

RexrK

Mountain sat upon the Plain, The. Emily Dickinson. CP-DickE

Mountain skies, The. Chess under Trees. A. K. Ramanujan. CP-RamaA

Mountain Talk. A. R. Ammons. CP-AmmoA

Mountain Tomb, The. William Butler Yeats. CP-YeatW

Mountain Town. W. S. Merwin. SP-MerwW

Mountaineer and Poet. Elizabeth Barrett Browning. CP-BroEB

Mountains, The. Walter De la Mare. CP-DeLaW

Mountains, The. W. S. Merwin. SP-MerwW

Mountains, a moment's earth-waves rising and hollowing; the earth too's an ephemerid; the stars. Treasure, The. Robinson Jeffers. CP-JefR1

Mountains and mountains and mountains. Autumn Leaves. James Schuyler. CP-SchuJ

Mountains and Rivers without End. Sam Hamill. SP-HamiS

Mountains and the shadows move away, The. Silence of Volcanoes. Muriel Rukeyser. CP-RukeM

Mountains are so cold, The. Han-shan. CP-ColdM, tr. by Red Pine

Mountains between our lands and the sea, The. In the Clear Season of Grapes. Wallace Stevens. CP-StevW; CP-StevWP

Mountains blanket-wrapped. Men in New Mexico. D. H. Lawrence. CP-LawrD

Mountains bloom in spring they shine in summer. Summits. W. S. Merwin. SP-MerwW

Mountains blue now, The. Mountains in the Desert, The. Robert Creeley. CP-CreeR

Mountains, cities, all so. Nanao Knows. Gary Snyder. CP-SnydG

Mountains cover me like rain. For an Atheist. Countee Cullen. CP-CullC

Mountains Covered with Cats. Wallace Stevens. CP-StevW; CP-StevWP

Mountain's Daily Speech is Silence, The. Denise Levertov. SP-LeveDS

Mountains, from this downward turn in the road, The. At a Glance. Charles Tomlinson. CP-TomlC

Mountains grow—unnoticed, The. Emily Dickinson. CP-DickE

Mountains in the Desert, The. Robert Creeley. CP-CreeR

Mountains in the Horizon, The. Henry David Thoreau. CP-ThorH

Mountains, monuments, all forms. Elegiac Stanzas: On a Visit to Dove Cottage. Geoffrey Hill. CP-HillG

Mountains of twine and. Ted Berrigan. SP-BerrT Fr. Sonnets, The.

Mountains said they were, The. Mountain Liar. A. R. Ammons. CP-AmmoA

Mountains stand up around the main street in Harper's Ferry. Landscape Including Three States of the Union. Carl Sandburg. CP-SandC

Mountains stood in Haze, The. Emily Dickinson. CP-DickE

Mountains stood on their bottom ends, The. Smoke Blue. Carl Sandburg. CP-SandC

Mountains vanish, / cattle wander. Night. Gabriela Mistral. SP-MistG, tr. by Maria Giachetti [or Jacketti] and Maria Jacketti

Mountaintop. Federico García Lorca. CP-GarcF, tr. by Jerome Rothenberg Fr. Shadow.

Mountaintop stands in silence a minute after the murder, The. Orpheus. Muriel Rukeyser. CP-RukeM

Mountebanks. Guillaume Apollinaire. SP-MereW, tr. by William Meredith

Mountebanks appear like smoke, The. Mountebanks. Guillaume Apollinaire. SP-MereW, tr. by William Meredith

Mounted as an Amazon. William Carlos Williams. CP-WilW2

Mourn, Israel! Sons of Israel, mourn! Israel's Lament. Samuel Taylor Coleridge. CP-ColeS

Mourner Betrayed. Josephine Jacobsen. CP-JacoJ

Mourner, The. W. S. Merwin. SP-MerwW

Mourner, The. Jones Very. CP-VeryJ

Mournful Young Man. D. H. Lawrence. CP-LawrD

Mournfully to and fro, to and fro the trees are waving. Passing-Bell, A. D. H. Lawrence. CP-LawrD

Mourning. Andrew Marvell. CP-MarvA

Mourning Dove. Lorine Niedecker. CP-NiedL

Mourning Grace. Maya Angelou. SP-AngeM

Mourning Mother, The. Elizabeth Barrett Browning. CP-BroEB

Mourning my heart doth sore oppress. Sir Thomas Wyatt. CP-WyatT

Mourning Picture. Jane Cooper. CP-CoopJ

Mourning Picture. Adrienne Rich. CP-RicAE; SP-RicA2

Mourning Poem for the Queen of Sunday. Robert Earl Hayden. CP-HaydR

Mourn'st Thou Now? Walter De la Mare. CP-DeLaW

Mouse, The. Hayden Carruth. CP-CarHS

Mouse, The. Inference. Miller Williams. CP-WillM

Mouse and a frog meet every morning on the riverbank, A. Jelaluddin Rumi. SP-Rumi, tr. by Coleman Barks

Mouse and the Camel, The. Jelaluddin Rumi. SP-Rumi, tr. by Coleman Barks

Mouse asks the beloved frog, The. Long String, The. Jelaluddin Rumi. SP-Rumi, tr. by Coleman Barks

Mouse caught hold of a camel's lead rope, A. Mouse and the Camel, The. Jelaluddin Rumi. SP-Rumi, tr. by Coleman Barks

Mouse fell from a screech-owl's beak, A—a thing that I can not pretend. Mouse Metamorphosed Into a Maid, The. Marianne Craig Moore. CP-MoorM Fr. Fables of La Fontaine.

Mouse got in, from some hole or other, A. Primo Levi. CP-LeviP, tr. by Ruth Feldman

Mouse in the cupboard repeats himself, The. Fables about Error. William Meredith. SP-MereW

Mouse Metamorphosed Into a Maid, The. Marianne Craig Moore. CP-MoorM Fr. Fables of La Fontaine.

Mouse Sex. John Updike. CP-UpdiJ

Mouse sharpens his teeth, The. Mouse, The. Hayden Carruth. CP-CarHS

Mouse That Gnawed the Oak-Tree Down, The. Nicholas Vachel Lindsay. CP-LindV

Mouse was startled by its own unimpearled shadow, The. On the South-West Coast of Erehwemos Stands a Romantic Little Village. Kenneth Patchen. CP-PatcK

Mousemeal. Howard Nemerov. CP-NemeH

Mouse)Won / derfully is. E. E. Cummings. CP-CummE

Mousia, the clock is still. Memo to the Dark Angel. James Tate. SP-TateJ

Mouth of the Hudson, The. Robert Lowell. SP-LoweR

Mouth of this man is a gaunt strong mouth, The. Tall Man, A. Carl Sandburg. CP-SandC

Mouth of truth, The. Lawrence Ferlinghetti. SP-FerlL

Mouthings of water at the end of a world. Rubh An' Dunain. Charles Tomlinson. CP-TomlC

Mouths Nuzz. Robert Creeley. CP-CreeR

Move, The. James Tate. SP-TateJ

Move / deeply,rain / (dream hugely)wish. E. E. Cummings. CP-CummE

Move Eastward, Happy Earth, and Leave. Alfred Tennyson. CP-TennA

Move him into the sun. Futility. Wilfred Owen. CP-OwenW

Move Over. Charles Olson. CP-OlsoC; SP-OlsoC

Move to California, The. William Stafford. SP-StafWW
  Written on the Stub of the First Paycheck. SP-StafW

Movement. Raymond Carver. CP-CarvR

Movement. Denise Levertov. SP-LeveDL

Movement. Arthur Rimbaud. CP-RimbA, tr. by Martin Sorrell

Movement of Fish, The. James Dickey. CP-DickJ

Movement Song. Audre Lorde. SP-LordA

Movement? Weighed down by hails of trumpets and days, what is it? In Transformation of an Imago. Robert Stock. SP-StocR

Movements. Charles Tomlinson. CP-TomlC

Movie. Muriel Rukeyser. CP-RukeM

Movie House. John Updike. CP-UpdiJ

Movie of Robert, A. Bresson's Movies. Robert Creeley. SP-CreeR

Movie Run Backward, The. Robert Creeley. SP-CreeR

Movies. Langston Hughes. CP-HughL; CP-HughL3

Movies; A Hymn of Hate. Dorothy Parker. CP-ParkD

Movies, The. Billy Collins. SP-CollB

Movies are badder. Saturday Afternoon at the Movies. John Logan. CP-LogaJ

Movies, the Old Law. TV is the New. Late Late Show. Howard Nemerov. CP-NemeH

Moving. Randall Jarrell. CP-JarrR

Moving from Cheer to Joy, from Joy to All. Next Day. Randall Jarrell. CP-JarrR

Moving from left to left, the light. View of the Capitol from the Library of Congress. Elizabeth Bishop. CP-BishE

Moving in her radiant care. Carmen 34. Catullus. CP-ZukLS Fr. Carmina.

Moving in Winter. Adrienne Rich. CP-RicAE; SP-RicA2

Moving must be in our nature. Premises. Karl Shapiro. SP-ShapK

Moving of stones, that sly jockeying thrust, The. Stones. Maxine W. Kumin. SP-KumiM

Moving on or going back to where you came from. Procession at Candlemas, A. Amy Clampitt. CP-ClamA

Moving Out Or the End of Cooperative Living. Audre Lorde. SP-LordA

Moving over the hills, crossing the irrigation. Some San Francisco Poems. George Oppen. CP-OppGN

Moving Picture. David Ignatow. SP-IgnaD

Moving slowly sweating a lot. Post the Lake Poets Ballad. Frank O'Hara. SP-OharF

Moving sun-shapes on the spray, The. Going and Staying. Thomas Hardy. CP-HardT

Moving through the silent crowd. Unemployed. Stephen Spender. CP-SpenS

Mow the grass in the cemetery, darkies. Two at Norfolk. Wallace Stevens. CP-StevW; CP-StevWP

Mower, The. Philip Larkin. CP-LarkP

Mower Against Gardens, The. Andrew Marvell. CP-MarvA

Mower stalled, twice, The; kneeling, I found. Mower, The. Philip Larkin. CP-LarkP

Mower to the Glowworms [or Glow-Worms or Glo-Worms], The. Andrew

Marvell. CP-MarvA

Mowers begin, The. Watchers. W. S. Merwin. SP-MerwW

Mower's Song, The. Andrew Marvell. CP-MarvA

Mowers, The. D. H. Lawrence. CP-LawrD

Mowgli's Brothers. Rudyard Kipling. *Fr.* Jungle Book, The.

Mowgli's Song Against People. Rudyard Kipling. CP-KiplR *Fr.* Second Jungle Book, The.

Mowing. Robert Frost. CP-FrosR

Mowing the lawn, having done with a tangle. Politics. Miller Williams. CP-WillM

Mox Note. Heather McHugh. SP-McHuH

Mozart Chemisier. Frank O'Hara. SP-OharF

Mozart, Goethe, and the Duke of Wellington. Augsburg Adoration, The. Randall Jarrell. CP-JarrR

Mozart, 1935. Wallace Stevens. CP-StevW; CP-StevWP

Mr. Beringer, whose son. Seven Laments for the War-Dead. Yehuda Amichai. SP-AmicY, *tr.* by Chana Bloch

Mr Bleaney. Philip Larkin. CP-LarkP

Mr. Cromek [*or* On Cromek]. William Blake. CP-BlakW

Mr. Dodd's Son. Robert Penn Warren. CP-WarrR

Mr. Ford. G. K. Chesterton. CP-ChesG

Mr Gladstone was a very good man. Daddy-Do-Nothing. D. H. Lawrence. CP-LawrD

"Mr John Keats Five Feet Tall" Sails Away. Thomas Lux. SP-LuxT

Mr Krösing's Top Hat. Jaroslav Seifert. SP-SeifJ, *tr.* by Ewald Osers

Mr Leonard Magnus. G. K. Chesterton. CP-ChesG

Mr Leonard Magnus, being endowed for research with several large state bounties. Mr Leonard Magnus. G. K. Chesterton. CP-ChesG

Mr. Mahoney. Josephine Jacobsen. CP-JacoJ

Mr. Over. Stevie Smith. CP-SmitS

Mr. Pope. Thomas Lux. SP-LuxT

Mr. Silberberg. James Whitcomb Riley. CP-RileJ

Mr Smith, Mr Smith. Great Newspaper Editor to His Subordinate, The. D. H. Lawrence. CP-LawrD

Mr Squire. D. H. Lawrence. CP-LawrD

Mr. Tantripp's Day. Josephine Jacobsen. CP-JacoJ

see also Mister, etc.

Mrs. Baines. G. K. Chesterton. CP-ChesG

Mrs. Benjamin Harrison. James Whitcomb Riley. CP-RileJ

Mrs Simpkins. Stevie Smith. CP-SmitS

Mrs. Small. Gwendolyn Brooks. SP-BrooG

Mrs. Walpurga. Muriel Rukeyser. CP-RukeM

see also Mistress, etc.

Ms. Found in a Quagmire. Ogden Nash. CP-NashO

Ms. Found under a Serviette in a Lovely Home. Ogden Nash. CP-NashO

Ms. Lot. Muriel Rukeyser. CP-RukeM

see also Miss, etc.

Mt in my head surpasses you, The. Reversal. A. R. Ammons. CP-AmmoA

Mt. Shasta: A Painting, by H. O. Young. Jones Very. CP-VeryJ

Much ado about trees lichen. Gamut. Louis Zukofsky. CP-ZukLS

Much as I own I owe. Closed for Good. Robert Frost. CP-FrosR

Much-beaten-upon-looking, bedraggled blackbird, not a starling, with a mangled or tumourous claw, A. Greed. C. K. Williams. SP-WillC

Much comes out of the body and, by and large. Self-Control. Miller Williams. CP-WillM

Much did I rage when young. Youth and Age. William Butler Yeats. CP-YeatW

Much—discerning Public hold, A. Rudyard Kipling. *See* I had seen, as dawn was breaking

Much have I travell'd [*or* travelled *or* traveled] in the realms of gold. On First Looking into Chapman's Homer. John Keats. CP-KeatJ

Much having traveled in the funkier realms of Ac. Homer, A.D. 1982. Amy Clampitt. CP-ClamA

Much i cannot) / tear up the world:& toss. E. E. Cummings. CP-CummE

Much I owe to the Lands that grew. Two-Sided Man, The. Rudyard Kipling. CP-KiplR *Fr.* Kim.

Much-loved Pastor! thou hast gone. To the Memory of the Rev. James Flint, D. D. Jones Very. CP-VeryJ

Much Madness is divinest Sense. Emily Dickinson. CP-DickE

Much-more, provides, and hoords up like an Ant. Upon Much-More. Robert Herrick. CP-HerrR

Much of transfiguration that we hear. Interlude, The. Karl Shapiro. SP-ShapK

Much of what I had thought mine. Wind is the Wall of the Year. Marge Piercy. SP-PierM

Much of what is said here. Blues, The. Billy Collins. SP-CollB

Much on my early youth I love to dwell. To a Young Lady. Samuel Taylor Coleridge. CP-ColeS

Much they admire the wild flowers scattered wide. Same, The. Jones Very. CP-VeryJ

Much time and trouble this poor play has cost. Epilogue: "Much time and trouble this poor play has cost." Nathaniel Lee. CP-DryJ2 *Fr.* Duke of Guise, The.

Much wonder I—here long low-laid. Bedridden Peasant, The. Thomas Hardy. CP-HardT

Muckers. Carl Sandburg. CP-SandC

Muckle-Mouth Meg. Robert Browning. CP-BroR2

Mud. Maxine W. Kumin. SP-KumiM

Mud. Clods. The sucking heel of the rain-flinger. Derek Walcott. CP-WalcD *Fr.* Midsummer.

Mud is very deep, The. Emily Dickinson. SP-DickE

Mud Master. Wallace Stevens. CP-StevW; CP-StevWP

Mud-mattressed under the sign of the hag. Maudlin. Sylvia Plath. CP-PlatS

Mud put / upon mud. House, The ("Mud put / upon mud"). Robert Creeley. CP-CreeR

Mud Season. May Sarton. SP-SartM

Mud Soup. Carolyn Kizer. CP-KizeC

Mud Turtle, The. Howard Nemerov. CP-NemeH

Mud Vision, The. Seamus Heaney. SP-HeanSO

Muddy rivers of spring, The. Mud Master. Wallace Stevens. CP-StevW; CP-StevWP

Mudge every morning to the Postern comes. Upon Mudge. Robert Herrick. CP-HerrR

Mudroom, The. Paul Muldoon. CP-MuldP

Muffled by a Belt across the Mouth. Andrei Codrescu. SP-CodrA

Mugging. Allen Ginsberg. CP-GinsA

"Tonite I walked out of my red apartment door on East tenth street's dusk." SP-GinsA

Muhammad and the Huge Eater. Jelaluddin Rumi. SP-Rumi, *tr.* by Coleman Barks

Muhammad could mediate. Witness, the Darling, The. Jelaluddin Rumi. SP-Rumi, *tr.* by Coleman Barks

Muhammad, in the presence of Gabriel. Private Banquet, The. Jelaluddin Rumi. SP-Rumi, *tr.* by Coleman Barks

Muhammad says, / "I come before dawn." I Come Before Dawn. Jelaluddin Rumi. SP-Rumi, *tr.* by Coleman Barks

Muiopotmos: or The Fate of the Butterflie. Edmund Spenser. CP-Spens

Muirland Meg. Robert Burns. CP-BurnR

Mujer. William Carlos Williams. CP-WilW1

Mulatto. Langston Hughes. CP-HughL; CP-HughL1

Mulberry is a double tree, The. Banjo Boomer. Wallace Stevens. CP-StevWP

Mulberry Street. Grace Paley.

Mulberry Tree, The. James Whitcomb Riley. CP-RileJ

Mulch, The. Stanley Kunitz. CP-KunSC

Mulch, The. Eleanor Wilner. SP-WilnE

Mulciber at West Egg. Amy Clampitt. CP-ClamA

Mule. John Ciardi. CP-CiarJ

Mule kicked out in the trees, A. An Early. Poem. Norman Dubie. CP-DubiN

Mule of water, The. Kenneth Patchen. CP-PatcK

Mule Song. A. R. Ammons. CP-AmmoA

Mules. Paul Muldoon. CP-MuldP

Mules, The. Ogden Nash. CP-NashO

Mules, I think, will not be here this hour, The. Empedocles on Etna. Matthew Arnold. SP-ArnoM

Muléykeh. Robert Browning. CP-BroR2

Mulford. John Greenleaf Whittier. CP-WhitJ

Mulholland's Contract. Rudyard Kipling. CP-KiplR

Mulish, unregenerate. In the North. Adrienne Rich. CP-RicAE

Mulled hosts their countries yet mulled there by a core of wake tossed. Catullus. *See* Journeying over many seas and through many countries

Multas per gentes et multa per aequora vectus. Deconstructed Man, The. James Laughlin. CP-LaugJ

Multi-colored chart without a boundary, A. Missing You. "Shu Ting." CP-KizeC, *tr.* by Carolyn Kizer and Y. H. Zhao

Multidimensional. Yannis Ritsos. SP-RitsY, *tr.* by Kostas Myrsiades

Multiple song that carries to our ears. Rainer Maria Rilke. CP-RilkFr, *tr.* by A. Poulin, Jr. *Fr.* Fragments.

Multiple Troubles of Man, The. Shmuel HaNagid. SP-HaNaS, *tr.* by Peter Cole

Multiples. Michael Palmer. SP-PalmM

Multitude. Robert Herrick. CP-HerrR

Multitude of stars is the late night's light, The. Han-shan. CP-ColdM, *tr.* by Red Pine

Multitudes. D. H. Lawrence. CP-LawrD

Mumbe-jumble drones on, the hangman waits; the shabby surviving, The. War-Guilt Trials. Robinson Jeffers. CP-JefR3

Mumble Peg. Yusef Komunyakaa. CP-KomuY

Mumbo jumbo, what have we here? Midsummer's Daymare. Ogden Nash. CP-NashO

Mummer's Rhyme. Tennessee Williams. CP-WillT

Mummies. Nicanor Parra. CP-MertT, *tr. by* Thomas Merton

Mummies, The. Maxine W. Kumin. SP-KumiM

Mummified spider hung in its own web in the rafters striped legs coiled tightly, The. Spider Psyche. C. K. Williams. SP-WillC

Mummy. Carl Sandburg. CP-SandC

Munching a plum on. To a Poor Old Woman. William Carlos Williams. CP-WilW1

Mundus et Infans. W. H. Auden. CP-AudeW

Munich. John Updike. CP-UpdiJ

Munich Courier, The. James Laughlin. CP-LaugJ

Munich Mannequins, The. Sylvia Plath. CP-PlatS

Municipal. Rudyard Kipling. CP-KiplR

   ("Why is my District death-rate low?") CP-KiplR

Municipal Gallery Revisited, The. William Butler Yeats. CP-YeatW

Munificence and Modesty. Christopher Smart. SP-SmarC

Murals Not Yet Dreamed. Philip Whalen. SP-WhalP

Murder. D. H. Lawrence. CP-LawrD

Murder. Federico García Lorca. CP-GarcF, *tr by* Greg Simon *and* Steven F. White

Murder. Stevie Smith. CP-SmitS

Murder of Two Men by a Young Kid Wearing Lemon-colored Gloves, The. Kenneth Patchen. CP-PatcK

Murder of William Remington, The. Howard Nemerov. CP-NemeH

Murdered, I went, risen. Life, The. James Wright. CP-WrigJ

Murdered Lover, The. Paul Laurence Dunbar. CP-DunbP

Murderer, The. David Ignatow. SP-IgnaD

Murderer, The. Stevie Smith. CP-SmitS

Murderer's House, The. Mary Oliver. SP-OlivM

Murderer's little daughter, The. Sympathetic Portrait of a Child. William Carlos Williams. CP-WilW1

Murderer's Wine. Charles Baudelaire. CP-BaudC, *tr. by* Walter Martin

Murderess, The. Louise Glück. SP-GlucL

Murderfully in midmost o.c.an. E. E. Cummings. CP-CummE

Murdering Beauty. Thomas Carew. CP-CareT

  (Song: Murdering Beauty.) CP-CareT

Murderous Weapons. D. H. Lawrence. CP-LawrD

Murelandis man of vplandis mak, Ane. William Dunbar. CP-DunbW

Muriel, Muriel, marry me Muriel. Sorrowful Girl, The. Stevie Smith. CP-SmitS

Murine and Kleenex were lovers. M & K. James Laughlin. CP-LaugJ

Murkiness of the local garage is not so dense, The. Pinup. Billy Collins. SP-CollB

Murmur, The. Arthur Sze. SP-SzeA

Murmur; and your house gets blurred, A. In the Rain. Eugenio Montale. CP-MontE, *tr. by* Jonathan Galassi

Murmur in the Trees—to note, A. Emily Dickinson. CP-DickE

Murmur of a Bee, The. Emily Dickinson. CP-DickE

Murmur of clear water on stones, The. By a Stream. Czeslaw Milosz. CP-MiloCN, *tr. by* Tony Milosz

Murmuring of Bees, has ceased, The. Emily Dickinson. CP-DickE

Murmurings in a Field Hospital. Carl Sandburg. CP-SandC

Murmurs in the Gloom. Thomas Hardy. CP-HardT

Murrays have moved to a house, The. You Have More Freedom in a House. Ogden Nash. CP-NashO

Murry, on finding *le Bon Dieu.* On Reading "God" G. K. Chesterton. CP-ChesG

Muscles which move the eyeballs, The. Poem: "Muscles which move the eyeballs, The." Charles Tomlinson. CP-TomlC

Muse. A. R. Ammons. CP-AmmoA

Muse, A. Carolyn Kizer. CP-KizeC

Muse, The. Miller Williams. CP-WillM

Muse, The. Eleanor Wilner. SP-WilnE

Muse affrighted at the clash of arms, The. Addressed to General Washington, in the Year 1777, after the Battles of Trenton and Princeton. Annis Boudinot Stockton. CP-StocA

Muse among the Motors, The. Rudyard Kipling.

  Advertisement, The. CP-KiplR

  Arterial. CP-KiplR

  Ballad of the Cars, The. CP-KiplR

  Beginner, The. CP-KiplR

  Bother, The. CP-KiplR

  Braggart, The. CP-KiplR

  Carmen Circulare. CP-KiplR

  Child's Garden, A. CP-KiplR

  Consolations of Memory, The. CP-KiplR

  Contradictions. CP-KiplR

  Dying Chauffer, The. CP-KiplR

  Fastness. CP-KiplR

  Four Points, The. CP-KiplR

  Idiot Boy, The. CP-KiplR

  Inventor, The. CP-KiplR

  Justice's Tale, The. CP-KiplR

  Lady Geraldine's Hardship. CP-KiplR

  Landau, The. CP-KiplR

  Marrèd Drives of Windsor, The. CP-KiplR

  Moral, The. CP-KiplR

  Progress of the Spark, The. CP-KiplR

  Sepulchral. CP-KiplR

  To a Lady, Peruading Her to a Car. CP-KiplR

  To Motorists. CP-KiplR

  Tour, The. CP-KiplR

  When the Journey Was Intended to the City. CP-KiplR

Muse as Medusa, The. May Sarton. SP-SartM

Muse / Can at pleasure use, The. Ralph Waldo Emerson. CP-EmerR

Muse Considered As a Demon Lover, The. Frank O'Hara. SP-OharF

Muse—Hide his name of whom I sing. Cock-Fighters Garland. William Cowper. CP-CowpW

Muse / in her dark habit, The. Well, The. Denise Levertov. SP-LeveDP

Muse / is the "fate" of the poem, The. Charles Olson. CP-OlsoC

Muse not that by thy mind thy body is led. To Mr R. W ("Muse not that by thy mind thy body is led"). John Donne. CP-DonnJ; MW-DonnJ

Muse of Midnight. Gregory Orr. SP-OrrG

Muse of the Evening. Miller Williams. CP-WillM

Muse of the many-twinkling feet! whose charms. Waltz, The. Lord Byron. CP-Byron

Muse of Water, A. Carolyn Kizer. CP-KizeC

Muse salutes thee as the females pride, The. On Seeing Mrs Macauly Graham. Annis Boudinot Stockton. CP-StocA

Muse, sing the deeds of golden Aphrodite. Homer's Hymn to Venus. *Unknown.* CP-ShelP, *tr. by* Percy Bysshe Shelley *Fr.* Homeric Hymns.

Muse, / tell me of this man of wit. Homer. CP-DoolH *Fr.* Odyssey.

Muse that makes pretensions to discourse, The. Owl Minerva, The. Donald Davie. CP-DaviDC

Muse that stirs my blood, The. Bird and the Muse. Marya Alexandrovna Zaturenska. SP-ZatuM

Muse this one Verse to learn'd Pigot addresses, The. Presentation Verses to Nathaniel Pigott. Alexander Pope. CP-PopeA

Muse, 'tis enough: at length thy labour ends. Occasioned by Some Verses of his Grace the Duke of Buckingham. Alexander Pope. CP-PopeA

Muse! where shall I begin the spacious feild. Address to the Atheist, by P. Wheatley at the Age of 14 Years—1767, An. Phillis Wheatley. CP-WheaP

Muse, you have bitten through my fool's-finger. Hercules at Nemea. Robert Graves. CP-GravR

Musée des Beaux Arts. W. H. Auden. CP-AudeW

Musers Afar Will Say. Ivor Gurney. SP-GurnI

Museum. Jorge Luis Borges. SP-BorgJ, *tr. by* Ken Krabbenhoft

Museum. Thomas Kinsella. CP-KinsT

Museum. A. K. Ramanujan. CP-RamaA

Museum. Wisława Szymborska. SP-SzymW, *tr. by* Stanislaw Barańczak *and* Clare Cavanagh

Museum at Akhziv. Yehuda Amichai. SP-AmicYL, *tr. by* Benjamin Harshav *and* Barbara Harshav

Museum man!, The. Lorine Niedecker. CP-NiedL

Museum Piece. Hayden Carruth. CP-CarHS

Museum Piece. Richard Wilbur. CP-WilbR

Museums. Louis MacNeice. CP-MacNL

Museums in Chapultepec, The. Jay Wright. SP-WrigJ

Museums offer us, running from among the buses. Museums. Louis MacNeice. CP-MacNL

Mushroom Gatherers, The. Adam Mickiewicz. CP-DaviDC, *tr. by* Donald Davie

Mushroom Hunting in the Jemez Mountains. Arthur Sze. SP-SzeA

Mushroom is the Elf of Plants, The. Emily Dickinson. CP-DickE

Mushroom, Soft Ear, Old Memory. Bring the North. William Stafford. SP-StafWW

Mushrooms. Margaret Atwood. SP-AtwM2

Mushrooms. Mary Oliver. SP-OlivM

Mushrooms. Sylvia Plath. CP-PlatS

Mushrooms. Charles Tomlinson. CP-TomlC; SP-TomlC

Mushrooms feel like stiff pricks made of rot, The. Rising in Fall. Alan Dugan. CP-DugaA

Music. Charles Baudelaire. CP-BaudC, *tr. by* Walter Martin

Music. Raymond Carver. CP-CarvR

Music. G. K. Chesterton. CP-ChesG

Music. Andrei Codrescu. SP-CodrA

Music. E. E. Cummings. CP-CummE

Music. Ralph Waldo Emerson. CP-EmerR

Music. Walter De la Mare. CP-DeLaW

Music. William Meredith. SP-MereW

Music. Frank O'Hara. SP-OharF

Music. Wilfred Owen. CP-OwenW

Music. Rainer Maria Rilke. CP-RilkFr, *tr.* by A. Poulin, Jr.

Music. Percy Bysshe Shelley. CP-ShelP

Music. Henry David Thoreau. CP-ThorH

Music, A. Wendell Berry. CP-BerrW

Music, A. Denise Levertov. SP-LeveDP

Music, The. Jelaluddin Rumi. SP-Rumi, *tr.* by Coleman Barks

Music and Drum. Archibald MacLeish. CP-MacLA

Music and painting and all that. All the Fancy Things. William Carlos Williams. CP-WilW1

Music Box. Jorge Luis Borges. SP-BorgJ, *tr.* by Willis Barnstone

"Music" by David Hume. Michael Palmer. SP-PalmM

Music comes and goes on the wind, The. Listening to Jefferson Airplane. Thom Gunn. CP-GunnT

Music composed during a war. Family. Olga Broumas. SP-BrouO

Music divides the evening. Tu Do Street. Yusef Komunyakaa. CP-KomuY

Music does not happen in a place. Palace, The. W. S. Merwin. SP-MerwW

Music in a Snowy Street. Thomas Hardy. CP-HardT

Music is a dance, The. Los Guitaristas. Robert Creeley. CP-CreeR

Music is clear about such freshness and colour. Song of Autumn. Ivor Gurney. SP-GurnI

Music Is International. W. H. Auden. CP-AudeW

Music is sweet from the thrush's throat! Music. E. E. Cummings. CP-CummE

Music, lady, The. Lorine Niedecker. CP-NiedL

Music Master. Jelaluddin Rumi. SP-Rumi, *tr.* by Coleman Barks

Music of Japan. Drops of slow honey. Music Box. Jorge Luis Borges. SP-BorgJ, *tr.* by Willis Barnstone

Music of music is stillness, you birds, The. D. H. Lawrence. *See* Trees rise taller and taller, lifted, The

Music of October, The. All Things. Hayden Carruth. CP-CarHS

Music of the spheres, The—that ends in Silence. Funny Death. Allen Ginsberg. CP-GinsA

Music of words, The. Pieces. Adrienne Rich. CP-RicAE; SP-RicA2

Music of your feeling has its form, The. Man of Feeling, The. James Vincent Cunningham. CP-CunnJ

Music Rewritten. Michael Palmer. SP-PalmM

Music Swims Back to Me. Anne Sexton. SP-SextA; SP-SextA

Music That Hurts, The. Yusef Komunyakaa. CP-KomuY

Music Unheard. Walter De la Mare. CP-DeLaW

Music was going on, The. At the Fillmore. Philip Levine. SP-LeviP

Music, when soft voices die. To ———: "Music, when soft voices die." Percy Bysshe Shelley. CP-ShelP

Music!—Yea, and the airs you play. On Reading Dr. Henry van Dyke's Volume of Poems—Music. James Whitcomb Riley. CP-RileJ

Musica Ficta. Michael Palmer. SP-PalmM

Musical, A. Paul Laurence Dunbar. CP-DunbP

Musical Box, The. Thomas Hardy. CP-HardT

Musical Comedy Thought, A. Dorothy Parker. CP-ParkD

Musical Incident, A. Thomas Hardy. CP-HardT

Musical Instrument, A. Elizabeth Barrett Browning. CP-BroEB

Musical instrument tuned. Born Pretty in a Poor Country. Yusef Komunyakaa. CP-KomuY

Musical Strife, The; in a Pastoral Dialogue. Ben Jonson. CP-JonsB; SP-JonsB

Musical Toys. Lorine Niedecker. CP-NiedL

Musician. Louise Bogan. CP-BogaL

Musician late at night in his little house, The. Æolian. Hayden Carruth. CP-CarHS

Musicians wrestle everywhere. Emily Dickinson. CP-DickE

Musick strides through these poems. Ted Berrigan. SP-BerrT *Fr.* Sonnets, The.

Music[k], thou queen of heaven, care-charming spell. To Music: A Song. Robert Herrick. CP-HerrR

Music[k]'s Duel[l]. Richard Crashaw. CP-CrasR

Musicks maister, and the offspring. To the Worthy Author. Thomas Campion. CP-CampT

Music's Empire. Andrew Marvell. CP-MarvA

Music's Trinity. Charles Tomlinson. CP-TomlC

Musing allone this hinder nicht. William Dunbar. CP-DunbW

Musing and marvelling on the miserie. Prologe, The: "Musing and marvelling on the miserie." Sir David Lyndsay. SP-LyndD *Fr.* Dialog betwix Experience and ane Courteour, Ane.

Musing Maiden, The. Thomas Hardy. CP-HardT

Musing on the fate of Daphne. Daphne. George Meredith. CP-MerG1

Musing on the roaring ocean. Robert Burns. CP-BurnR

Musingly she mouths the end of her ballpoint pen as she stares down at the sheet of paper. Fast Food. C. K. Williams. SP-WillC

Musique de l'indifférence. Samuel Beckett. CP-BeckS

Musk-ox smells, The. Long River, The. Donald Hall. CP-HallD

Musketaquid. Ralph Waldo Emerson. CP-EmerR

Muskets triggered a white smoke. Execution of Maximilian, The. Arthur Sze. SP-SzeA

Muskingum Valley!—How longin' the gaze, The. James Whitcomb Riley. CP-RileJ

Mussel Hunter at Rock Harbor. Sylvia Plath. CP-PlatS

Mussels. Mary Oliver. SP-OlivM

Must be a Woe. Emily Dickinson. CP-DickE

Must be almost four. Night in NYC. Robert Creeley. CP-CreeR

Must be the Black Maria. Black Maria. Langston Hughes. CP-HughL; CP-HughL2

Must be thousands of sweet gourmets rustling through. Voznesensky's "Silent Tingling." Allen Ginsberg. CP-GinsA

Must being shall. E. E. Cummings. CP-CummE

Must Ethiopians be employ'd for you? Address to the Deist—1767, An. Phillis Wheatley. CP-WheaP

Must Ethiopians be imploy'd for you. Deism. Phillis Wheatley. CP-WheaP

Must fall occasionally a new. Into Each Life. James Laughlin. CP-LaugJ

Must genius always struggle, always exaggerate. Sonnet: "Must genius always struggle, always exaggerate." Hayden Carruth. CP-CarHS *Fr.* Sonnets.

Must I lose the Friend that saved my Life. Emily Dickinson. SP-DickE

Must I tell again. Daemon, The. Louise Bogan. CP-BogaL

Must represent the governess. Xenophobia. Rae Armantrout. SP-ArmaA

Must she then languish, and we sorrow thus. Upon the Sickness of E.S. Thomas Carew. CP-CareT

Must thou go, my glorious Chief. From the French. Lord Byron. CP-Byron

Must we believe that what ascends aspires? Pencil Stub Journals. John Ciardi. CP-CiarJ

Must we for ever eye through space? and make. Separation, The. Thom Gunn. CP-GunnT

Must you leave, John Holmes, with the prayers and psalms. Somewhere in Africa. Anne Sexton. CP-SextA; SP-SextA

Mustard Seed, The. Jones Very. CP-VeryJ

Muster, The. Herman Melville. SP-MelvH

Mustered into the Avant-Garde. Donald Davie. CP-DaviDC

Mutability. William Wordsworth. MW-WorW *Fr.* Ecclesiastical Sonnets.

Mutability. Percy Bysshe Shelley. CP-ShelP

Mutations. Louis MacNeil. CP-MacNL

Mutchmore and Not-So. Stevie Smith. CP-SmitS

Mute autumn smells. The. Paul Celan. SP-CelaP, *tr.* by John Felstiner

Mute Opinion. Thomas Hardy. CP-HardT

Mute Phenomena, The. Gérard de Nerval. CP-MahoD, *tr.* by Derek Mahon

Mute Singer, The. James Whitcomb Riley. CP-RileJ

Mute thy Coronation. Emily Dickinson. CP-DickE

Muted Music. Robert Penn Warren. CP-WarrR

Mutely the mole toils on. Quiet. Walter De la Mare. CP-DeLaW

Muteness, afresh, roomy, a house. Into the Distance. Paul Celan. SP-CelaP, *tr.* by John Felstiner

Mutes, The. Denise Levertov. SP-LeveDP; SP-LeveDS

Mutilation. D. H. Lawrence. CP-LawrD

Mutinous & free I drifted off. Form, The. John Berryman. CP-BerrJ

Muttering "fine upland staple," "prime Sea Island finer" What State Street Said to South Carolina, and What South Carolina Said to State Street. John Greenleaf Whittier. CP-WhitJ

Mutterings. John Ciardi. CP-CiarJ

Mutterings Over the Crib of a Deaf Child. James Wright. CP-WrigJ

Mutual Concessions. Yannis Ritsos. SP-RitsY, *tr.* by Andonis Decavalles

Mutual Forbearance. William Cowper. CP-CowpW

Mutual forgiveness of each vice. Gates of Paradise, The. William Blake. CP-BlakW

Mutual Lullaby, A. Yehuda Amichai. SP-AmicY, *tr.* by Chana Bloch

My adult unemployed son and I. Back Bay. John Updike. CP-UpdiJ

My age fallen away like white swaddling. Age. Philip Larkin. CP-LarkP

My Alba. Allen Ginsberg. CP-GinsA

My aloneness with no rest! Ballad of the Marked Man. Federico García Lorca. CP-GarcF, *tr.* by Will Kirkland

My Ambition. James Laughlin. CP-LaugJ

My answers are inadequate. Daylight Savings. Dorothy Parker. CP-ParkD

My apologies to chance for calling it necessity. Under One Small Star. Wisława Szymborska. SP-SzymW, *tr.* by Stanisław Barańczak *and* Clare Cavanagh

My apologies to chance for calling it necessity. Under a Certain Little Star. Wisława Szymborska. SP-SzymWM, *tr.* by Joanna Trzeciak

My apple branch dressed. Charles Olson. CP-OlsoC

My apple tree. Orchard, March. Federico García Lorca. CP-GarcF, *tr.* by Alan S.

Trueblood *Fr.* Songs to End With.

My architects, forsaking me. This Day This World. Stanley Kunitz. CP-KunSC

My ardours for emprize nigh lost. On an Invitation to the United States. Thomas Hardy. CP-HardT

My Arkansas. Maya Angelou. SP-AngeM

My aspens dear, whose airy cages quelled. Binsey Poplars (Felled 1879). Gerard Manley Hopkins. CP-HopkG

My Associates. Rae Armantrout. SP-ArmaA

My astonishment almost felicity. Giovanni Diodati. Charles Tomlinson. CP-TomlC

My attention has been recently focussed. Locust-Lovers, Attention! Ogden Nash. CP-NashO

My aunt kept turnips in a flock. Randall Jarrell. CP-JarrR

My aunt was an herb doctor, one-eyed with crooked yellow teeth. To-ta Ti-om. Peter Blue Cloud. SP-BlueP

My Aunts. Adam Zagajewski. SP-ZagaA, *tr.* by Clare Cavanagh

My baby has a father and a mother. Christina Georgina Rossetti. CP-RosC1

My baby has a mottled fist. Christina Georgina Rossetti. CP-RosC2

My Bachelor Chum. James Whitcomb Riley. CP-RileJ

My Baptismal Birthday [*or* Birth-Day]. Samuel Taylor Coleridge. CP-ColeS

My bean-pod boat you see here. Carmen 4. Catullus. CP-ZukLS *Fr.* Carmina.

My beard is thick, my eyelids half cover. Greek Portrait. Czeslaw Milosz. CP-MiloC; CP-MiloCN, *tr.* by Peter Dale Scott

My beard rough as the beginning. In the Woods. David Ignatow, SP-IgnaD

My Beatrice. Charles Baudelaire. CP-BaudC, *tr.* by Walter Martin

My beautiful wooden leader. Margaret Atwood. SP-AtwM1

My bed grows narrower as I grow old. Bed, The. Archibald MacLeish. CP-MacLA

My bedclothes were stuffed with ashes. Fanny Howe. SP-HoweF *Fr.* Quietist, The.

My belly / sounds like an owl. Charles Olson. CP-OlsoC

My Beloved. Langston Hughes. CP-HughL; CP-HughL1

My Beloved. Charles Simic. SP-SimiCE

My beloved land. Minority Report. John Updike. CP-UpdiJ

My beloved little billiard balls. Poem to Some of my Recent Poems. James Tate. SP-TateJ

My best Acquaintances are those. Emily Dickinson. CP-DickE

My Best Girl. Paul Laurence Dunbar. CP-DunbP

My biography / in the absence of facts. Biographical Notes. Andrei Codrescu. SP-CodrA

My Birthday. John Greenleaf Whittier. CP-WhitJ

My black face fades. Facing It. Yusef Komunyakaa. CP-KomuY

My black sun, my. Song for a Dark Voice. Denise Levertov. SP-LeveDP

My blessed mother dozing in her chair. Valentine to My Mother, A. Christina Georgina Rossetti. CP-RosC3

My blessings on ye, honest wife. At Roslin Inn. Robert Burns. CP-BurnR

My blinds drawn down against siesta heat. Roseapples and Nudes. Robert Stock. SP-StocR

My boat is being made to order. Right now it's about to leave. Raymond Carver. CP-CarvR

My boat is on the shore. To Thomas Moore. Lord Byron. CP-Byron

My Boat Is on the Shore. Lord Byron. *See* To Thomas Moore

My boat moves and I with her delighting. March. Ivor Gurney. SP-GurnI

My body a rounded stone. Living Tenderly. May Swenson. SP-SwenM

My Body in the Walls Captived. Sir Walter Ralegh. CP-RaleW

My body opens over San Francisco like the day. Splittings. Adrienne Rich. SP-RicA1; SP-RicA2

My body, spill-proof but not quite. Tête-à-Tête. Andrei Codrescu. SP-CodrA

My body trots semblably. L'Epreuve. Thom Gunn. CP-GunnT

My body was never married. Gregory Orr. SP-OrrG

My Bohemia (Fantasy). Arthur Rimbaud. CP-RimbA, *tr.* by Martin Sorrell

My Bones Flew Apart. Richard Eberhart. CP-EberR

My bones start singing through my skin. Fast, The. Gregory Orr. SP-OrrG

My Bonie Laddie's Young but He's Growin Yet. Robert Burns. CP-BurnR

My Bonnie [*or* Bony] Mary. Robert Burns. *See* Silver Tassie, The

My Book, My Book. C. K. Williams. SP-WillC

My Boots. Henry David Thoreau. CP-ThorH

My Boy. James Whitcomb Riley. CP-RileJ

My Boy Jack. Rudyard Kipling. CP-KiplR

My Brains Are Slipping in the Fields of Eros. Richard Eberhart. CP-EberR

My breast waited. Wedlock, The. Anne Sexton. CP-SextA

'My brethren . . .' And a bland, elastic smile. Evangelist, The. Donald Davie. CP-DaviDC

My Bride That Is to Be. James Whitcomb Riley. CP-RileJ

My Brother. Hendrik de Vries. CP-RicAE

My brother being the eldest had / for his bike the most elaborate. Our Bicycles. James Laughlin. CP-LaugJ

My brother comes home from work. You Can Have It. Philip Levine. SP-LeviP

My brother died in France—but I came back. Colored Soldier, The. Langston Hughes. CP-HughL; CP-HughL1

My brother, / He never left the old fireside. Ballad of the Black Sheep. Langston Hughes. CP-HughL; CP-HughL3

My brother, I am hungry, give me food. Ye Gave Me No Meat. Jones Very. CP-VeryJ

My brother is crouched at the edge. Heaven. Lucille Clifton. SP-ClifL

My brother Jack was wild. Tuesday's Child. Tennessee Williams. CP-WillT

My brother kneels, so saith Kabir. Prayer, The: "My brother kneels, so saith Kabir." Rudyard Kipling. CP-KiplR *Fr.* Kim.

My Brother Luis. Stephen Spender. CP-SpenS

My brother saw a pig root in a field. Meat. Thom Gunn. CP-GunnT

My Brothers the Silent. W. S. Merwin. SP-MerwW

My Brown self. Beast. May Swenson. SP-SwenM

My Burial Place. Robinson Jeffers. CP-JefR3

My business is words. Words are like labels. Said the Poet to the Analyst. Anne Sexton. CP-SextA; SP-SextA

My Butterfly. Robert Frost. CP-FrosR

My Canary Bird. Walt Whitman. CP-WhitW

My candle burned alone in an immense valley. Valley Candle. Wallace Stevens. CP-StevW; CP-StevWP

My candle burns at both ends. First Fig. Edna St. Vincent Millay. CP-MillE

My cane, my pocket change, this ring of keys. Things. Jorge Luis Borges. SP-BorgJ, *tr.* by Stephen Kessler

My carrier pigeon is a "fancy" pigeon. 4th May Morning. Christina Georgina Rossetti. CP-RosC3

My Cat Major. Stevie Smith. CP-SmitS

My Cats. Stevie Smith. CP-SmitS

My chair rock-rocks by the door all day. Lonesome Man. Tennessee Williams. CP-WillT

My cheap toy lamp. Child's Song. Robert Lowell. SP-LoweR

My cheek was hit and hit. Hailstones. Seamus Heaney. SP-HeanSO

My chest gapes open sometimes. Bereavement. D. H. Lawrence. CP-LawrD

My child and I hold hands on the way to school. September, the First Day of School. Howard Nemerov. CP-NemeH

My child as yet unborn, the doctors nod. March: A Birthday Poem. John Updike. CP-UpdiJ

My child is like a bird's wing, a bird's wing, a bird's wing. How Dulcenia del Toboso Is Like the Left Wing of a Bird. Nicholas Vachel Lindsay. CP-LindV

"My Child Is Phlegmatic . . . "—Anxious Parent. Ogden Nash. CP-NashO

My child is so sad. I Was the Moon. Yehuda Amichai. SP-AmicYL, *tr.* by Benjamin Harshav *and* Barbara Harshav

My child, my child, watch how he goes. Hast Du Dich Verirrt? Stevie Smith. CP-SmitS

My child, my sister. L'Invitation au Voyage. Charles Baudelaire. CP-WilbR, *tr.* by Richard Wilbur

My Child Wafts Peace. Yehuda Amichai. SP-AmicYL, *tr.* by Benjamin Harshav *and* Barbara Harshav

My child wants dolls, a tutu, that girls' world made. Marilyn Hacker. SP-HackM *Fr.* Taking Notice.

My Childhood's Home. Abraham Lincoln. CP-LincA

My childhood's home I see again. My Childhood's Home. Abraham Lincoln. CP-LincA

My Children. Yehuda Amichai. SP-AmicYL, *tr.* by Benjamin Harshav *and* Barbara Harshav

My children are, to me, / what is uncommon: they are dumb. Charm, The. Robert Creeley. CP-CreeR

My Children at the Dump. John Updike. CP-UpdiJ

My Chinese uncle, gouty, deaf, half-blinded. Grotesques. Robert Graves. CP-GravR

My chosen bride shall bless the plough. Song: "My chosen bride shall bless the plough." George Meredith. CP-MerG2

My Church. Jones Very. CP-VeryJ

My Cicely. Thomas Hardy. CP-HardT

My City, my beloved, my white! Ah, slender. N. Y. Ezra Pound. CP-PoEar

My city's fit and noble name resumed. Mannahatta. Walt Whitman. CP-WhitW

My client is a scoundrel and a thief. In Extremis *in Hardy, Arkansas.* Miller Williams. CP-WillM

My clock jumped on cement. Clock, The. Josephine Jacobsen. CP-JacoJ

My clothes grow dull in the closet. Casting. Andrei Codrescu. SP-CodrA

My clothes leaped up when I came in. Courtesy Call. John Updike. CP-UpdiJ

My Coat Is Dirty. Kenneth Patchen. CP-PatcK

My coat threadbare. Lorine Niedecker. CP-NiedL

My Cocoon tightens—Colors tease. Emily Dickinson. CP-DickE

My Collier Laddie. Robert Burns. CP-BurnR

My Comforter. Emily Jane Brontë. CP-BronE

My comforts drop and melt away like snow. Answer, The. George Herbert. CP-HerbG

My companion kept exclaiming. Cypress Avenue, The. Donald Davie. CP-DaviDC

My Comrades. Charles Bukowski. SP-BukC1

My Conscience. James Whitcomb Riley. CP-RileJ

My Corn-Cob Pipe. Paul Laurence Dunbar. CP-DunbP

My cot was down by a cypress grove. Lesson, The. Paul Laurence Dunbar. CP-DunbP

My country need not change her gown. Union. Emily Dickinson. CP-DickE

My country, O my land, my friends. Purgatorio. Hart Crane. CP-CranH

My country, 'tis of thee. Rational Anthem, A. Ambrose Bierce. SP-BierA

My Country, 'tis of thee. Emily Dickinson. SP-DickE

My Cousin in April. Louise Glück. SP-GlucL

My cousin knows buildings. Real Estate. A. K. Ramanujan. CP-RamaA

My Cousin Muriel. Amy Clampitt. CP-ClamA

My cross! / Your cross? Stephen Crane. CP-CranS

My Crow. Raymond Carver. CP-CarvR

My curse be on the day when first I saw. Sonnet: To the Lady Pietra degli Scrovigni. Dante Alighieri. CW-RossD, tr. by Dante Gabriel Rossetti

My curse on your envenom'd stang. Address to the Tooth-Ache. Robert Burns. CP-BurnR

My cuticles are a mess. Oh honey, by the way. Motorcyclists, The. James Tate. SP-TateJ

My dad is at the stove in front of a pan with brains. Balsa Wood. Raymond Carver. CP-CarvR

My Daddy. Ogden Nash. CP-NashO

My daddy played the market. January 1st. Anne Sexton. CP-SextA

My daddy rides me piggy-back. Piggy-back. Langston Hughes. CP-HughL

My Dad's Wallet. Raymond Carver. CP-CarvR

My Dancin'-Days Is Over. James Whitcomb Riley. CP-RileJ

My darling read my heart, for she left on. Jewels. Charles Baudelaire. CP-BaudC, tr. by Walter Martin

My darling since / you and. E. E. Cummings. CP-CummE

My darling's love shall close me up. Song: "My darling's love shall close me up." George Meredith. CP-MerG2

My Daughter and Apple Pie. Raymond Carver. CP-CarvR

My daughter, at eleven. Little Girl, My String Bean, My Lovely Woman. Anne Sexton. CP-SextA; SP-SextA

My Daughter Is Coming! Alice Walker. CP-WalkA

My daughter is most. Sitting in a Sandwich Joint. Charles Bukowski. SP-BukC1

My daughter marks the day that spring begins. Equinox. Audre Lorde. SP-LordA

My daughter, the old woman says, the weaver. Soothsayer, The. Denise Levertov. SP-LeveDL

My daughters left home. Depression Years. Lorine Niedecker. CP-NiedL

My Daughter's Wedding. John Logan. CP-LoganJ

My Day of Life. Ambrose Bierce. SP-BierA

My dayes delight, my spring tyme joyes foredun. Conjectural First Draft of the Petition to Queen Anne. Sir Walter Ralegh. CP-RaleW

My days are burning. Counter, The. William Carlos Williams. CP-WilW2

My day's delights, my spring[e]time joy[e]s for[e]done. End of the Boo[c]k[e]s, of the Ocean's Love to Cynthia [or Scinthia], and the Beginning[e] of the 12 [or 22] Boo[c]k, Entreating of Sorrow, The. Sir Walter Ralegh. CP-RaleW Fr. Ocean's Love to Cynthia, The.

My days have gone by swifter than a deer. Petrarch. CP-Petra, tr. by J. G. Nichols

My day's plan to write. Kathleen Jessie Raine. SP-RainK

My days roll by me like a train of dreams. Ralph Waldo Emerson. CP-EmerR

My dead are shining like washed gold. Arrivals, The. Josephine Jacobsen. CP-JacoJ

My dead-in-battle, my turned-to-ashes, my earth. Dream, A. Wisława Szymborska. SP-SzymWM, tr. by Joanna Trzeciak

My dead, to whom I pray so they may pray. Shore of Versilia. Eugenio Montale. CP-MontE, tr. by Jonathan Galassi

My Dear Brother Washington. Jones Very. CP-VeryJ

My dear, darkened in sleep, turned from the moon. To Judith Asleep. John Ciardi. CP-CiarJ

My Dear, How Ever Did You Think Up This Delicious Salad? Ogden Nash. CP-NashO

My dear —: / I do thank you, that we hear from you, but the. Letter for Melville 1951. Charles Olson. CP-OlsoC

My dear, I wonder if before the end. To D———, Dead by Her Own Hand. Howard Nemerov. CP-NemeH

My dear, it was a moment. Expatriates, The. Anne Sexton. CP-SextA

My dear Kafka. Literary World, The. Philip Larkin. CP-LarkP

My Dear Love. Robinson Jeffers. CP-JefR3

My dear love died last night. Paul Laurence Dunbar. CP-DunbP

My dear Mrs. Bloomer. Part of a True Story. Marilyn Hacker. SP-HackM

My Dear Mr. Murray. Lord Byron. CP-Byron

My dear, my dear, I know. To a Young Girl. William Butler Yeats. CP-YeatW

My dear old friends—It jes' beats all. Writin' Back to the Home Folks. James Whitcomb Riley. CP-RileJ

My dear Papa / Though superstitious Folks may say. Lines Addressed to his Father on Making Him a Present of a Knife. James Edward Austen-Leigh. CP-AustJ

My dear Telemachus, / The Trojan War. Odysseus to Telemachus. Joseph Brodsky. CP-BrodJ, tr. by George L. Kline

My dear wife asked me this morn- / ing at breakfast nothing I said. What Are You Smiling About. James Laughlin. CP-LaugJ

My dear, you moved so rapidly through my life. Halation. Carolyn Kizer. CP-KizeC

My dearest Frank, I wish you joy. Jane Austen. CP-AustJ

My dearest Love, since thou wilt go. Dialogue Betwixt Himselfe and Mistresse Eliza: Wheeler, Under the Name of Amarillis, A. Robert Herrick. CP-HerrR

My dearest Mary, wherefore hast thou gone. To Mary Shelley. Percy Bysshe Shelley. CP-ShelP

My Dearest Mistress. William Corkine. CP-CampT
(My deerest mistrisse, let us live and love.) CP-CampT

My dearest mistress, let us live and love. My Dearest Mistress. William Corkine. CP-CampT

My dearest rival, lest [or least] our love. Sir John Suckling. CP-SuckJ

My dears, do you know, one short. Christmas-Time Jingle, A. James Whitcomb Riley. CP-RileJ

My dears, don't I know? I esteem you more than you think. To Certain English Poets. Donald Davie. CP-DaviDC

My dears, don't look at me, I am merely terrified of you. Don't Look at Me. D. H. Lawrence. CP-LawrD

My Death. Raymond Carver. CP-CarvR

My death is what I live on; seems to me. Michelangelo Buonarroti. CP-Miche, tr. by John Frederick Nims

My death was arranged by special plans in Heaven. New England Bachelor, A. Richard Eberhart. CP-EberR

My deathly body's deadly lady. E. E. Cummings. CP-CummE

My deep-dyed husband trusts me. On Martock Moor. Thomas Hardy. CP-HardT

My deerest mistrisse, let us live and love. William Corkine. See My dearest mistress, let us live and love

My Departure. Walt Whitman. CP-WhitW

My Descendants. William Butler Yeats. CP-YeatW Fr. Meditations in Time of Civil War.

My destiny is in the Spanish language. To the German Language. Jorge Luis Borges. SP-BorgJ, tr. by Alastair Reid

My dice are crystal inlaid with gold. A. R. Ammons. CP-AmmoA

My Dim-Wit Cousin. Theodore Roethke. CP-RoetT

My disappointments, large as capsized tugs. Return of Odysseus, The. Richard Eberhart. CP-EberR

My dissent is cheer. Definition. Grace Paley. CP-PalGC

My doctor has just come into his office. Stethoscope Case, A. Charles Bukowski. SP-BukC1

My doctor, the comedian. Cripples and Other Stories. Anne Sexton. CP-SextA; SP-SextA

My dog lay dead five days without a grave. Pardon, The. Richard Wilbur. CP-WilbR

My dog's dead. / I buried him in the garden near the wreck. Dead Dog. Pablo Neruda. SP-NeruP

My Dolphin, you only guide me by surprise. Dolphin. Robert Lowell. SP-LoweR

My double, tired of morning, closes the door. Derek Walcott. CP-WalcD Fr. Midsummer.

My dove, my doe. Aubade: "My dove, my doe." Stevie Smith. CP-SmitS

My Doves. Elizabeth Barrett Browning. CP-BroEB

My dread, my ignorance, my. Finally. W. S. Merwin. SP-MerwW

My Dream. Christina Georgina Rossetti. CP-RosC1

My Dream. John Greenleaf Whittier. CP-WhitJ

My dream a drink with Lonnie Johnson we discuss the code. Sonnet: "My dream a drink with Lonnie Johnson we discuss the code." Ted Berrigan. SP-BerrT Fr. Sonnets, The.

My Dream About Being White. Lucille Clifton. SP-ClifL

My Dream About Falling. Lucille Clifton. SP-ClifL

My Dream About God. Lucille Clifton. SP-ClifL

My Dream About the Cows. Lucille Clifton. SP-ClifL

My Dream About the Poet. Lucille Clifton. SP-ClifL

My Dream About the Second Coming. Lucille Clifton. SP-ClifL

My Dream About Time. Lucille Clifton. SP-ClifL

My dream is of an island-place. Island, An. Elizabeth Barrett Browning. CP-BroEB

My dreams are of a field afar. A. E. Housman. CP-HousA

My Dreams, My Works Must Wait Till after Hell. Gwendolyn Brooks. SP-BrooG

My driver's license is lapsing and so I appear. Vision Test, The. Mona Van Duyn. SP-VanDM

My drum, hollowed out thru the thin slit. La Chute. Charles Olson. CP-OlsoC; SP-OlsoC

My ear is full of summer sounds. Summons, The. John Greenleaf Whittier. CP-WhitJ

My ear is listening for the sound. Heralds of the Spring, The. Jones Very. CP-VeryJ

My earliest love, that stabbed and lacerated. Growing Pains. Robert Graves. CP-GravR

My earnestness, which might at first offend. Edna St. Vincent Millay. CP-MillE

My ears catch less and less of conversations, and my eyes have weakened, though they are still insatiable. Honest Description of Myself with a Glass of Whiskey at an Airport, Let Us Say, in Minneapolis, An. Czeslaw Milosz. CP-MiloCN, tr. by Robert Hass

My elder, / Born into death like a message into a bottle. To My Brother Hanson. W. S. Merwin. SP-MerwW

My eldest sister arrived home that morning. Cuba. Paul Muldoon. CP-MuldP

My Elusive Guest. Maxine W. Kumin. SP-KumiM

My embarrassment at his nakedness. Pool, The. Robert Creeley. CP-CreeR

My end came while I was happy. Kimon, Son of Learchos, Age 22, Student of Greek Literature (in Kyrini). Constantine P. Cavafy. CP-CavaC, tr. by Theoharis Constantine Theoharis

My Enemies. David Ignatow. SP-IgnaD

My enemies came to get me. Form of Adaptation, A. Robert Creeley. CP-CreeR

My Enemy. D. H. Lawrence. CP-LawrD

My enemy, who often lets you gaze. Petrarch. CP-Petra, tr. by J. G. Nichols

My Eppie. Robert Burns. CP-BurnR

My Erotic Double. John Ashbery. SP-AshbJ

My Eye is fuller than my vase. Emily Dickinson. CP-DickE

My eyes are closing, my eyes are opening. Anemone. Muriel Rukeyser. CP-RukeM

My eyes are feverish and dull. Mad Lover, The. James Whitcomb Riley. CP-RileJ

My eyes are fond of the east side. E. E. Cummings. CP-CummE

My eyes are saddened by so much they see. Michelangelo Buonarroti. CP-Miche, tr. by John Frederick Nims

My eyes being downcast. Assuming the Burden. D. H. Lawrence. CP-LawrD

My eyes catch and stick. Consumer, The. Marge Piercy. SP-PierM

My eyes fondle carved metal and stone. Look Look Look. Philip Whalen. SP-WhalP

My eyes in your pledge, Quintius. Carmen 82. Catullus. CP-ZukLS Fr. Carmina.

My eyes make pictures, when they are shut. Day-Dream, A. Samuel Taylor Coleridge. CP-ColeS

My eyes, my eyes are tired. Lost Nights. Rainer Maria Rilke. CP-RilkFr, tr. by A. Poulin, Jr.

My eyes, that sun of ours is shut away. Petrarch. CP-Petra, tr. by J. G. Nichols

My face and hair are changing; I grow old. Petrarch. CP-Petra, tr. by J. G. Nichols

My face ends inside you. Portions of Manslayer. C. K. Williams. CP-WillC

My faint spirit was sitting in the light. From the Arabic: An Imitation. Percy Bysshe Shelley. CP-ShelP

My faith / is a great weight. Small Wire. Anne Sexton. CP-SextA; SP-SextA

My faith is in my native land. Britain. George Meredith. CP-MerG2

My Faith is larger than the Hills. Emily Dickinson. CP-DickE

My faithful friend, if you can see. Impossibilities to His Friend. Robert Herrick. CP-HerrR

My faithful glass has very often told. Petrarch. CP-Petra, tr. by J. G. Nichols

My Faithful Mother Tongue. Czeslaw Milosz. CP-MiloC; CP-MiloCN, tr. by Robert Pinsky

My falcon to my wrist. On Thought in Harness. Edna St. Vincent Millay. CP-MillE

My family of Apparitions. Emily Dickinson. SP-DickE

My family slept those level miles. Across Kansas. William Stafford. SP-StafWW

My Farm. May Swenson. SP-SwenM

My Father and I and Billy Two Rivers. Paul Muldoon. CP-MuldP

My father and I are catching spricklies. Waking Father, The. Paul Muldoon. CP-MuldP

My father and mother both. Mississippi Winter IV. Alice Walker. CP-WalkA

My father and mother, my brother and sister. Sightseers, The. Paul Muldoon. CP-MuldP

My Father at 85. Grace Paley. CP-PalGC

My Father at 89. Grace Paley. CP-PalGC

My father / (back blistered). Democratic Order, The: Such Things in Twenty Years I Understood. Alice Walker. CP-WalkA

My father brought out his donkey-jacket. Early Warning. Paul Muldoon. CP-MuldP

My father brought the emigrant bundle. Europe and America. David Ignatow. SP-IgnaD

My father built a great worry around me like a dock. Autobiography in the Year 1952. Yehuda Amichai. SP-AmicYL, tr. by Benjamin Harshav and Barbara Harshav

My father built over me a worry big as a shipyard. Autobiography, 1952. Yehuda Amichai. SP-AmicY, tr. by Stephen Mitchell

My father could hear a little animal step. Listening. William Stafford. SP-StafW; SP-StafWW

My father didn't really belong in history. Parentage. William Stafford. SP-StafW; SP-StafWW

My father died again in dreams, a twin. For Elektra. Marilyn Hacker. SP-HackM

My Father Died Imperfect as a Man. John Ciardi. CP-CiarJ

My father, Eating Small Boat. Autobiographical Note. Kenneth Patchen. CP-PatcK

My father entered the kingdom of roots. 1933. Philip Levine. SP-LeviP

My father fell asleep in his new life. Disappearee's Song. Heather McHugh. SP-McHuH

My father fished here summers, scaled and cleaned. Elegy at Beaverhead County, Montana. Helen Pinkerton. CP-PinkH

My father, for example. Visitor, A. Mary Oliver. SP-OlivM

My father got on his horse and went to the field. Infancy. Carlos Drummond de Andrade. CP-BishE, tr. by Elizabeth Bishop

My father groaned; my mother wept. Rite. Muriel Rukeyser. CP-RukeM

My father in a dream he lay. Host. Olga Broumas. SP-BrouO

My Father in a White Space Suit. Yehuda Amichai. SP-AmicY, tr. by Chana Bloch

My Father-in-Law's Coat. William Corbett. SP-CorbW

My father is a quiet man. Fruit of the Flower. Countee Cullen. CP-CullC

My father is standing on a railroad platform. Departure. Louise Glück. SP-GlucL

My father kept a vaulted conch. On the Decline of Oracles. Sylvia Plath. CP-PlatS

My father knew. How to Be Uncle Sam. John Updike. CP-UpdiJ

My father laughing over the morning paper. Reading Before We Read, Horoscope and Weather. Wyatt Prunty. SP-PrunW

My father lay fifty years in St. Michael's bed. Epithalamium at St. Michael's Cemetary. John Ciardi. CP-CiarJ

My father liked Edgar Allan. Dear Pa and Ma. Charles Bukowski. SP-BukC3

My father, listening to music, that's me. Requiem, A: "My father, listening to music, that's me." David Ignatow. SP-IgnaD

My Father Moved Through Dooms Of Love. E. E. Cummings. CP-CummE; SP-CummE

My father never finished. Rafters, The. James Dickey. CP-DickJ

My Father: October 1942. William Stafford. SP-StafW; SP-StafWW

My Father on Passover Eve. Yehuda Amichai. SP-AmicYL, tr. by Benjamin Harshav and Barbara Harshav

My Father Paints the Summer. Richard Wilbur. CP-WilbR

My Father Said. Grace Paley. CP-PalGC

My father said / how will they get out of it. My Father at 85. Grace Paley. CP-PalGC

My father said "I remember" Lorine Niedecker. CP-NiedL

My father sat in his chair recovering. Out. Ted Hughes. SP-HughTN

My father sent me on an errand to the house of his friend Averroës. Song for the Death of Averroës. Thomas Merton. CP-MertT

My father spent four years inside their war. Yehuda Amichai. SP-AmicY, tr. by Stephen Mitchell Fr. We Loved Here.

My father spent his last winter. Ice. Mary Oliver. SP-OlivM

My father stands in the warm evening. Starlight. Philip Levine. SP-LeviP

My father, suddenly, left all the places. My Father's Death. Yehuda Amichai. SP-AmicYL, tr. by Benjamin Harshav and Barbara Harshav

My father used to say. Silence. Marianne Craig Moore. CP-MoorM

My father was a farmer upon the Carrick border O. Song: "My father was a farmer upon the Carrick border O." Robert Burns. CP-BurnR

My Father was a scholar and knew Greek. Development. Robert Browning. CP-BroR2

My father was a servant-boy. Mixed Marriage, The. Paul Muldoon. CP-MuldP

My father was a warrior, he wore the white. Easter. Olga Broumas. SP-BrouO

My father was a working man. Red-Herring. D. H. Lawrence. CP-LawrD

My father was born in a house by a river. Oars, The. W. S. Merwin. SP-MerwWF

My father was born in Horton. Lancashire. Donald Davie. CP-DaviDC

My father was born with a spade in his hand and traded it. Elegy: "My father was born with a spade in his hand and traded it." John Ciardi. CP-CiarJ

My father was brilliant embarrassed funny handsome. Family. Grace Paley. CP-PalGC

My father was ribald / about religion: when. Mark. James Schuyler. CP-SchuJ

My father was the whipper-in. Whipper-In, The. Thomas Hardy. CP-HardT

My father who found the English landscape tame. Woods. Louis MacNeice. CP-MacNL

My father, who since his death. Our Family. Leo Vroman. CP-RicAE

My father worked with a horse-plough. Follower. Seamus Heaney. SP-HeanSO

My father writes all day, all night. Poem: "My father writes all day, all night." Charles Simic. SP-SimiC; SP-SimiCE

My Father's Birthday. Kathleen Jessie Raine. SP-RainK

My Father's Chair. Rudyard Kipling. CP-KiplR

My Father's Close. Unknown. CW-RossD, tr. by Dante Gabriel Rossetti

My Father's Death. Yehuda Amichai. SP-AmicYL, tr. by Benjamin Harshav and Barbara Harshav

My Father's Death. May Sarton. SP-SartM

My Father's Face. Hayden Carruth. CP-CarHL

My father's father came. Legend. Louise Glück. SP-GlucL

My father's father saw it not. British-Roman Song, A. Rudyard Kipling. CP-KiplR Fr. Puck of Pook's Hill.

My father's gravestone said, "I knew it was time" Why I Am a Poet. William Stafford. SP-StafWW

My father's halls, so rich and rare. James Whitcomb Riley. CP-RileJ

My Father's Honour. Donald Davie. CP-DaviDC

My Father's House. Jones Very. CP-VeryJ

My Father's house, I find no entrance there. My Father's House. Jones Very. CP-VeryJ

My Father's Love Letters [or Loveletters]. Yusef Komunyakaa. CP-KomuY

My father's madness is to own himself. Complex, The. David Ignatow. SP-IgnaD

My father's Memory Book. Coat of Arms. Alan Dugan. CP-DugaA

My Father's Neckties. Maxine W. Kumin. SP-KumiM

My father's ripped pants. Heir Apparent, The. Theodore Weiss. SP-WeisT

My Fathers sit on benches. Song for the Old Ones. Maya Angelou. SP-AngeM

My Father's Telescope. Rita Dove. SP-DoveR

My Father's Voice. Gregory Orr. SP-OrrG

My Father's Watch. John Ciardi. CP-CiarJ

My Father's Wedding. Robert Bly. SP-BlyR

My favorite time to write is in the late afternoon. Purity. Billy Collins. SP-CollB

My feet in the ever-moving sea. Kathleen Jessie Raine. SP-RainK

My feet took a walk in heavenly grass. Heavenly Grass. Tennessee Williams. CP-WillT

My feet wait there listening, and when. Freedom of Expression. William Stafford. SP-StafWW

My fellow man I do not care for. Bas Ben Adhem, A. Ogden Nash. CP-NashO

My fervent prayer, if any pity me. Michelangelo Buonarroti. CP-Miche, tr. by John Frederick Nims

My Fifth Trip to Washington Ended in Northeast Delaware. Audre Lorde. SP-LordA

My fingers have crept. Pablo Neruda. SP-LoguC, tr. by Christopher Logue Fr. Red Bird.

My first and only wife. About Pain. Charles Bukowski. SP-BukC3

My First Days in New York. Yehuda Amichai. SP-AmicYL, tr. by Benjamin Harshav and Barbara Harshav

My first displays the wealth and pomp of kings. Charade. Jane Austen. CP-AustJ Fr. Emma.

My first is no proof of my second. Charades. Christina Georgina Rossetti. CP-RosC3

My first love, whom all beauties did adorn. Guiltless Inconstant, The. Sir John Suckling. CP-CareT; CP-SuckJ

My first may be the firstborn. Charade. Christina Georgina Rossetti. CP-RosC3

My first shuts out Thieves from your house or your Room. Charade on Dr Thomas Barnard. Samuel Johnson. CP-JohnS

My First Spectacles. James Whitcomb Riley. CP-RileJ

My first thought was, he lied in every word. Childe Roland to the Dark Tower Came. Robert Browning. CP-BroR1; SP-BroR

My first well Day—since many ill. Emily Dickinson. CP-DickE

My First Womern. James Whitcomb Riley. CP-RileJ

My five-word poems number five hundred. Han-shan. CP-ColdM, tr. by Red Pine

My flesh is at a distance from me. Virgin, The. Laura Riding Jackson. CP-RidiL

My flesh turned earth, my bones turned naked shame. Michelangelo Buonarroti. CP-Miche, tr. by John Frederick Nims

My flocks hadst thou e'er seen them, where they feed. Shepherd's Life, The. Jones Very. CP-VeryJ

My flowers are near and foreign. Emily Dickinson. SP-DickE

My flowers are reflected. Florists Wears Knee-Breeches, The. Wallace Stevens. CP-StevWP

My Fly. C. K. Williams. SP-WillC

My Foe? You name yourself, then,—I refuse. James Whitcomb Riley. CP-RileJ

My fool walks on wobbling roads. Spirit of Noplace, The. Kenneth Patchen. CP-PatcK

My foolish eyes, that first looked. Guido Cavalcanti. CP-CavaG, tr. by Marc Cirigliano

My foot is blue with blood although. Prayer for One Leg. Alan Dugan. CP-DugaA

My former hopes are fled. William Cowper. CP-CowpW Fr. Olney Hymns.

My former student is in the traffic police. Yehuda Amichai. SP-AmicYL, tr. by Benjamin Harshav and Barbara Harshav

My forty-year-old father learned to fly. Hang-Glider's Daughter, The. Marilyn Hacker. SP-HackM

My four-year-old daughter. Katie at the Pool. Derek Mahon. CP-MahoD

My frame hath often trembled with delight. Tributary Stream. William Wordsworth. CP-WorW2 Fr. River Duddon [A Series of Sonnets], The.

My Friend. Charles Bukowski. SP-BukC3

My Friend. Jane Cooper. CP-CoopJ

My Friend. James Whitcomb Riley. CP-RileJ

My Friend. Christina Georgina Rossetti. CP-RosC1

My friend, are you sleeping? Two Eclipses. Shmuel HaNagid. SP-HaNaS, tr. by Peter Cole

My friend attacks my friend! Emily Dickinson. CP-DickE

My friend Daniels met us in her Subaru. Manhattan Movements. John Logan. CP-LogaJ

My friend Dave knew a famous writer who used to have screwdrivers for breakfast. Friends. C. K. Williams. CP-WillC

My Friend Felix. Donald Hall. CP-HallD

My friend from Asia has powers and magic, he plucks a blue leaf from the young blue-gum. Credo. Robinson Jeffers. CP-JefR1

My friend hands me a coin of ancient stamp. Cleopatra. George Meredith. CP-MerG2

My friend, I have to go. Departure. Rainer Maria Rilke. CP-RilkFr, tr. by A. Poulin, Jr.

My friend, I must leave you. Four Poems after Rilke. Heather McHugh. SP-McHuH

My friend is worried about dying. Doom and Siesta Time. Charles Bukowski. SP-BukC1

My friend keeps kissing me goodbye, the kisses. Devotion: That It Flow; That There Be Concentration. Tess Gallagher. SP-GallT

My friend Klaus a German goes. Hard to Translate. James Laughlin. CP-LaugJ

My friend must be a Bird. Emily Dickinson. CP-DickE

My Friend, My Friend. Anne Sexton. SP-SextA

My friend says I was not a good son. Yesterday. W. S. Merwin. SP-MerwWF

My friend tells me. This Life. Grace Paley. CP-PalGC

My friend the black and white collie. Lorine Niedecker. CP-NiedL

My friend the ecologist tells. End of It All, The. James Laughlin. CP-LaugJ

My Friend the Philosopher and Hanukah. Yehuda Amichai. SP-AmicYL, tr. by Benjamin Harshav and Barbara Harshav

My friend, this body is made of bone. Origin of the Praise of God, The. Robert Bly. SP-BlyR

My friend, this body is made of energy compacted and whirling. We Love This Body. Robert Bly. SP-BlyR

My friend, this body offers to carry us for nothing. Finding the Father. Robert Bly. SP-BlyR

My friend tree. Lorine Niedecker. CP-NiedL

My friend uses a blackboard and chalk and rustling. My Friend the Philosopher and Hanukah. Yehuda Amichai. SP-AmicYL, tr. by Benjamin Harshav and Barbara Harshav

My friend, what you're doing now. Yehuda Amichai. SP-AmicYL, tr. by Benjamin Harshav and Barbara Harshav

My friend writes of rejection and editors. Letter from the North. Charles Bukowski. SP-BukC2

My friends all know that I am shy. Chipmunk, The. Ogden Nash. CP-NashO

My friends are those who find agreement with me. Joan and Darby. Robert Graves. CP-GravR

My friends, I hope you will not swim here. Snake Lake. Thomas Lux. SP-LuxT

My friends: If thirty people gather in a room. Open Letter, Personal. Mona Van Duyn. SP-VanDM

My friends, my noble friends, know ye. Henry David Thoreau. CP-ThorH

My friends, why should we live? Henry David Thoreau. CP-ThorH

My friend's wife has a lover; I come to this conclusion—not suspicion, mind, conclusion. Signs. C. K. Williams. SP-WillC

My friends without shields walk on the target. W. S. Merwin. SP-MerwW

My future will not copy fair my past. Past and Future. Elizabeth Barrett Browning. CP-BroEB

My galley [or galy] charged with forgetfulness. Galley, The. Petrarch. CP-WyatT, tr. by Sir Thomas Wyatt Fr. Sonnets to Laura.

My Garden. Ralph Waldo Emerson. CP-EmerR

My Garden. Jones Very. CP-VeryJ

My garden blazes brightly with the rose-bush and the peach. In Springtime. Rudyard Kipling. CP-KiplR

My garden blossoms pink and white. Story of Mrs. W———. Dorothy Parker. CP-ParkD

My Garden—like the Beach. Emily Dickinson. CP-DickE

My garden roses long ago. Winter Roses. John Greenleaf Whittier. CP-WhitJ

My gaze saw no mere mortal on the day. Michelangelo Buonarroti. CP-Miche, *tr. by* John Frederick Nims

My Generation Reading the Newspapers. Kenneth Patchen. CP-PatcK

My gentle Anne, whom heretofore. To Anne Bodham. William Cowper. CP-CowpW

My gentle hill, I rest. Song (2). Wendell Berry. CP-BerrW

My gesture that destroys. Fernando Pessoa. SP-PessF, *tr. by* Susan M. Brown *and* Edwin Honig

My Ghost. Robert Graves. CP-GravR

My Girl. James Tate. SP-TateJ

My girl, another summer's gone dark. Both Together and Each Apart. Yehuda Amichai. SP-AmicYL, *tr. by* Benjamin Harshav *and* Barbara Harshav

My girl coming by. Wind Gust. Federico García Lorca. CP-GarcF, *tr. by* Jerome Rothenberg *Fr.* Return, The.

My girl she give me the go onest. Private Ortheris's Song. Rudyard Kipling. CP-KiplR *Fr.* Life's Handicap.

My girl she's airy, she's buxom and gay. Song: "My girl she's airy, she's buxom and gay." Robert Burns. CP-BurnR

My girl went down to the sea. Federico García Lorca. CP-GarcF, *tr. by* Alan S. Trueblood *Fr.* Andalusian Songs.

My girl's tall with hard long eyes. E. E. Cummings. CP-CummE

My glance is clear like a sunflower. Fernando Pessoa. SP-PessF *Fr.* Keeper of Sheep, The.

My glass is filled with a wine that trembles like flame. Rhenish Night. Guillaume Apollinaire. SP-MereW, *tr. by* William Meredith

My glasses are. This Morning. May Swenson. SP-SwenM

My God, a verse is not a crown. Quidditie [*or* Quiddity], The. George Herbert. CP-HerbG

My God, Bill, what have you done? Fragment: "My God, Bill, what have you done?" William Carlos Williams. CP-WilW2

My God—He sees thee. Emily Dickinson. CP-DickE

My God, I am weeping for the life that I live. Eternal Dice, The. César Vallejo. CP-WrigJ

My God, I have come with. Abandoned. Federico García Lorca. CP-GarcF, *tr. by* Christopher Maurer

My God, I heard this day. Man. George Herbert. CP-HerbG

My God, I read this day. Afflction (5). George Herbert. CP-HerbG

My God, if writings may. Obedience. George Herbert. CP-HerbG

My God, I'm wounded by my sin. To God: an Anthem, Sung in the Chapel at White-Hall, Before the King. Robert Herrick. CP-HerrR

My God! looke on me with thine eye. His Ejaculation to God. Robert Herrick. CP-HerrR

My God, my God, have mercy on my sin. Ash Wednesday. Christina Georgina Rossetti. CP-RosC2

My God, my God, what queer corner am I in? In the Deep Museum. Anne Sexton. CP-SextA; SP-SextA

My God, my God, why hast thou forsaken me? Psalm 22: "My God, my God, why hast thou forsaken me?" Bible, *O.T.* SP-SidnP *Fr.* Psalms.

My God, the poor expressions of my Love. Perseverance. George Herbert. CP-HerbG

My God, the soul you gave me. Yehuda Amichai. SP-AmicYL, *tr. by* Benjamin Harshav *and* Barbara Harshav

My God, the wind is rising! on those edges. Hell's Prayer. Ivor Gurney. SP-GurnI

My God, Thyself being Love Thy Heart is love. Trinity Sunday. Christina Georgina Rossetti. CP-RosC2

My God, to live: how didst Thou bear to live. None With Him. Christina Georgina Rossetti. CP-RosC3

My God, where is that ancient heat towards Thee. Sonnet: "My God, where is that ancient heat towards Thee." George Herbert. CP-HerbG

My God, wilt Thou accept, and will not we / Give aught to Thee? Christina Georgina Rossetti. CP-RosC2

My godlike Friend—nay do not stare. To Alexander Cunnignham. Robert Burns. CP-BurnR

My Golden and My Fierce Assays. Richard Eberhart. CP-EberR

My golden ring. Mirror. Federico García Lorca. CP-GarcF, *tr. by* Jerome Rothenberg *Fr.* Secrets.

My goldfish stares with watery eyes. Goldfish. Charles Bukowski. SP-BukC2

My good blade carves the casques of men. Sir Galahad [*or* The Purple Heart]. Alfred Tennyson. CP-TennA

My Good Father. Carolyn Kizer. CP-KizeC

My good father grown old. Priest at the Serapeion. Constantine P. Cavafy. CP-CavaC, *tr. by* Theoharis Constantine Theoharis

My good friend gave me a sheepskin coat. Sheepskin Coat. Yehuda Amichai. SP-AmicYL, *tr. by* Benjamin Harshav *and* Barbara Harshav

My Grampa he's a-allus sayin'. Song o' Cheer, A. James Whitcomb Riley. CP-RileJ

My grampa was short and thick and German. Letter to Robert Hedin. Sam Hamill. SP-HamiS

My grandaddy told me a man is nothing but appetite. Blood in the Water. Ai. SP-Ai

My Granddaughter. James Laughlin. CP-LaugJ

My Grandfather found / his grandchild's fogbound solitudes. Dunbarton. Robert Lowell. SP-LoweR

My grandfather Remmers was a German immigrant. Piano Scholar, The. John Logan. CP-LogaJ

My grandfather said to me. Manners. Elizabeth Bishop. CP-BishE

My grandfather says he remembers he saw, when a youngster long ago. Martin Relph. Robert Browning. CP-BroR2

My Grandfather Sigismund Kunat. Czeslaw Milosz. CP-MiloCN, *tr. by* Robert Hass

"My grandfather Squeers," said The Raggedy Man. Grandfather Squeers. James Whitcomb Riley. CP-RileJ

My grandfather was a tall German. Gold Pocket Watch, A. Charles Bukowski. SP-BukC1

My grandfather, who blessed me as a child. Age Gap. Robert Graves. CP-GravR

My grandfather's name was Augusto. Carlotta's Confession. Donald Hall. CP-HallD

My Grandfather's Wake. Paul Muldoon. CP-MuldP

My Grandmother. Karl Shapiro. SP-ShapK

My grandmother moves to my mind in context of sorrow. My Grandmother. Karl Shapiro. SP-ShapK

My grandmother said I was an atheist. God and Man. Richard Eberhart. CP-EberR

My grandmother used it. Dutch Cleanser. Dutch Cleanser. John Updike. CP-UpdiJ

My Grandmother's Ghost. James Wright. CP-WrigJ

My Grandmother's Love Letters. Hart Crane. CP-CranH

My grandpa wasn't salty. I Must Tell You about My Novel. Ogden Nash. CP-NashO

My great-aunt Elizabeth Fortune. Strawberry Moon. Mary Oliver. SP-OlivM

My great brother. Psalm Praising the Hair of Man's Body, A. Denise Levertov. SP-LeveDP

My great-grandfather spoke to Edmund Burke. Seven Sages, The. William Butler Yeats. CP-YeatW

My Great-Grandfather's Slaves. Wendell Berry. CP-BerrW

My Great Great Etc. Uncle Patrick Henry. James Tate. SP-TateJ

My great wars close. Treaties. A. R. Ammons. CP-AmmoA

My greetings to you, sir, whose memory. Apparition, The. William Carlos Williams. CP-WilW2

My ground is high. Henry David Thoreau. CP-ThorH

My Groupie. Charles Bukowski. SP-BukC1

My grown-ups told me when I started out. To the Bleeding Hearts Association of American Novelists. Howard Nemerov. CP-NemeH

My gudewife—she that is tae be. Gudewife, The. James Whitcomb Riley. CP-RileJ

My Guilt. Maya Angelou. SP-AngeM

My halting Muse, that dragg'st by choice along. John Milton. *See* O Muse who willingly drags along with a limping step

My hand, a little raised, might press a star. Sonnet On An Alpine Night. Dorothy Parker. CP-ParkD

My hand by chance. Web, The. Robert Earl Hayden. CP-HaydR

My hand clicked on. Dead Man's Room, The. John Logan. CP-LogaJ

My Hands. William Stafford. SP-StafW

My hands are no longer mine. Three Carriers, The. Rainer Maria Rilke. CP-RilkFr, *tr. by* A. Poulin, Jr.

My hands have long been busy cutting from each. Book of Life, The. Jones Very. CP-VeryJ

My hands have not touched pleasure since your hands. Hart Crane. *See* My hands have not touched water since your hands,—

My hands have not touched water since your hands,—. Carrier Letter. Hart Crane. CP-CranH

My hands that were not born completely. From Time. James Dickey. CP-DickJ

My Harry was a gallant gay. Highland Harry Back Again. Robert Burns. CP-BurnR

My hartis tresure and swete assured fo. William Dunbar. CP-DunbW

My harvest is done, its promise is ended. For Each. Christina Georgina Rossetti. CP-RosC2

My Hat. Stevie Smith. CP-SmitS

My hawk is tir'd of perch and hood. Lay of the Imprisoned Huntsman. Sir Walter Scott. SP-ScotW *Fr.* Lady of the Lake, The.

My head and shoulders, and my book. Signature of All Things, The. Kenneth Rexroth. CP-RexrK

My head can lend no succour. In Hac Spe Vivo. James Laughlin. CP-LaugJ

My head didn't grow anymore. Last Word Is Captain, The. Yehuda Amichai. SP-AmicYL, *tr. by* Benjamin Harshav *and* Barbara Harshav

My head doth ake. Head-Ake, The. Robert Herrick. CP-HerrR

My head hangs. Annabelle. Yusef Komunyakaa. CP-KomuY

My head hurts like hell! Comfort. William Carlos Williams. CP-WilW2

My head is heavy, my limbs are weary. Fragment: Death in Life. Percy Bysshe Shelley. CP-ShelP

My head is wild with weeping for a grief. Fragment: "My head is wild with weeping for a grief." Percy Bysshe Shelley. CP-ShelP

My head knocks against the stars. Who Am I? Carl Sandburg. CP-SandC

My head made wilderness, crowned of weed. Cuckoo King, The. Howard Nemerov. CP-NemeH

My head, my heart, mine Eyes, my life, nay more. Letter to Her Husband, Absent upon Public[k] Employment, A. Anne Bradstreet. CP-BradA

My Heart. Billy Collins. SP-CollB

My Heart. Heinrich Heine. CP-MerG2

My Heart. Frank O'Hara. SP-OharF

My heart aches and a drowsy numbness pains. Ode to a Nightingale. John Keats. CP-KeatJ

My Heart and I. Elizabeth Barrett Browning. CP-BroEB

My Heart, Being Hungry. Edna St. Vincent Millay. CP-MillE

My heart did heave, and there came forth, O God! Affliction (3). George Herbert. CP-HerbG

My heart faints in me for the distant sea. Sea-Magic. Walter De la Mare. CP-DeLaW

My heart felt need to die. Scourge, The. Stanley Kunitz. CP-KunSC

My heart flashed like a gull above the spars. Voyage to Cythera, A. Charles Baudelaire. CP-BaudC, *tr.* by Walter Martin

My Heart Goes Out. Stevie Smith. CP-SmitS

My Heart Has Reopened to You. Alice Walker. CP-WalkA

My heart has thanked [*or* thank'd] thee, Bowles! for those soft strains. To the Rev. [*or* Reverend] W. L. Bowles. Samuel Taylor Coleridge. MW-ColeS *Fr.* Effusions.

My heart hath uttered. Word—a Responsory, The. Thomas Merton. CP-MertT

My heart I gave thee not to do it pain. Sir Thomas Wyatt. CP-WyatT

My heart is a-breaking, dear Tittie. Tam Glen. Robert Burns. CP-BurnR

My heart is a walled. Friends, The. Shmuel HaNagid. SP-HaNaS

My heart is aching. Relief. Langston Hughes. CP-HughL; CP-HughL3

My heart is easy, and my burthen light. Happy Solitude—Unhappy Men. Jeanne Marie Bouvier de la Motte- Guyon. CP-CowpW

My heart is fairly melting at the thought of Julian Eltinge. Musical Comedy Thought, A. Dorothy Parker. CP-ParkD

My heart is fallen in despair. Broken Friendship, The. Stevie Smith. CP-SmitS

My heart is heavy. For I saw Fionnuala. White Shoulders. Paul Muldoon. CP-MuldP

My heart is like a singing bird. Birthday, A. Christina Georgina Rossetti. CP-RosC1

My heart is resting by the cool spring's banks. Dream. Federico García Lorca. CP-GarcF, *tr.* by Catherine Brown

My heart is sair—I dare na tell. Somebody. Robert Burns. CP-BurnR

My heart is wae and unco wae. Scots Ballad. Robert Burns. CP-BurnR

My heart is what it was before. Alms. Edna St. Vincent Millay. CP-MillE

My heart is yearnig: / Behold my yearning heart. Like As the Hart Desireth the Water Brooks. Christina Georgina Rossetti. CP-RosC2

My heart leaps up when I behold. Song to Be Sung by the Father of Infant Female Children. Ogden Nash. CP-NashO

My heart leaps up when I behold. William Wordsworth. CP-WorW1; MW-WorW

My heart leaps up with streams of joy. Word, The. Stevie Smith. CP-SmitS

My heart lies wrapped in red under your pillow. Arrears of Moonlight. Robert Graves. CP-GravR

My Heart ran so to thee. Emily Dickinson. CP-DickE

My heart sank with our Claret-flask. Nationality in Drinks. Robert Browning. CP-BroR1

My heart says, puzzled, "Why do men kill each other?" And He Had Wilder Moments. Kenneth Patchen. CP-PatcK

My heart, so rarely rent. Dream Journey of the Head and Heart. Richard Eberhart. CP-EberR

My heart to thy heart. Song: "My heart to thy heart." Paul Laurence Dunbar. CP-DunbP

My heart upon a little Plate. Emily Dickinson. CP-DickE

My heart was ance as blythe and free. To the Weaver's Gin Ye Go. Robert Burns. CP-BurnR

My Heart Was Full. Stevie Smith. CP-SmitS

My heart was heavy, for its trust had been. Forgiveness. John Greenleaf Whittier. CP-WhitJ

My heart, we must abdicate this waiting. Rainer Maria Rilke. CP-RilkFr, *tr.* by A. Poulin, Jr. *Fr.* Fragments.

My heart went fluttering with fear. Surprise. Dorothy Parker. CP-ParkD

My heart would take the shape of a shoe. Moon and Panorama of the Insects. Federico García Lorca. CP-GarcF, *tr.* by Greg Simon *and* Steven F. White

My heartbeat always beats me again. My Sleep. Yehuda Amichai. SP-AmicYL, *tr.* by Benjamin Harshav *and* Barbara Harshav

My heart's aflutter! Mayakovsky. Frank O'Hara. SP-OharF

My Heart's as Gay as a Young Sunflower. Kenneth Rexroth. CP-RexrK

My heart's in the Highlands, my heart is not here. My Heart's in the Highlands. Robert Burns. CP-BurnR

My Heat. Frank O'Hara. SP-OharF

My Heavenly Shiner (Elizabeth). Robert Lowell. SP-LoweR

My heavy life is hanging on a thread. Petrarch. CP-Petra, *tr.* by J. G. Nichols

My heavy step is treacherous in the shallows. Lost Fish. Robert Lowell. SP-LoweR

My heid did yak yester nicht. Magryme, The. William Dunbar. CP-DunbW

My Henry. James Whitcomb Riley. CP-RileJ

My Hens Are Hatching. Thomas Sheridan. CP-SherT

My Hero Bares His Nerves. Dylan Thomas. CP-ThomD

My hips are a desk. Secretary Chant, The. Marge Piercy. SP-PierM

My history extends / Where moved my tourist hands. Abroad Thoughts from Home. Donald Hall. CP-HallD

My home is below green cliffs. Han-shan. CP-ColdM, *tr.* by Red Pine

My Home Town. Tu Fu. CP-KizeC, *tr.* by Carolyn Kizer

My home was at Cold Mountain from the start. Gary Snyder. CP-SnydG

My honored colonel, deep I feel. Poem on Life. Robert Burns. CP-BurnR

My hope, alas, hath me abused. Sir Thomas Wyatt. CP-WyatT

My horsemen wheel in a great circle shutting out the sun. Old Lean Over the Tombstones, The. Kenneth Patchen. CP-PatcK

My horse's feet beside the lake. Farewell, A: "My horse's feet beside the lake." Matthew Arnold. SP-ArnoM *Fr.* Switzerland.

My House. William Butler Yeats. CP-YeatW *Fr.* Meditations in Time of Civil War.

My house, my fairy / palace. Jerónimo's House. Elizabeth Bishop. CP-BishE

My human love, my She-human. Her Vision. Denise Levertov. SP-LeveDL

My humorous ghost precisely will. E. E. Cummings. CP-CummE

My hungry eyes, through greedy covetize. Sonnet 35. Edmund Spenser. CP-Spens *Fr.* Amoretti.

My Husband Says. Alice Walker. CP-WalkA

My husband walks in the frosted field. Wereman, The. Margaret Atwood. SP-AtwM1

My husband was hanging wet sheets, almost in disbelief. New Age at Airport Mesa. Norman Dubie. CP-DubiN

My Hut. Hayden Carruth. CP-CarHS

My ideas are a curse. February 3rd. Anne Sexton. CP-SextA; SP-SextA

My ills oppress me, and I fear the worst. Petrarch. CP-Petra, *tr.* by J. G. Nichols

My infinite thoughts, so many gone awry. Michelangelo Buonarroti. CP-Miche, *tr.* by John Frederick Nims

My Instructions. James Laughlin. CP-LaugJ

My intense friend was tall & strongly made. Freshman Blues. John Berryman. CP-BerrJ

My jolly friar, / Now lift thy cowl. George Meredith. CP-MerG2

My Jolly Friend's Secret. James Whitcomb Riley. CP-RileJ

My Kate. Elizabeth Barrett Browning. CP-BroEB

My kingdom is within you haste to find. Snare, The. Jones Very. CP-VeryJ

My kingdom is within you seek it there. Kingdom of God Is Within You, The. Jones Very. CP-VeryJ

My kiss was a pomegranate. Madrigal: "My kiss was a pomegranate." Federico García Lorca. CP-GarcF, *tr.* by Catherine Brown

My knees recall the pockets. Far Memory. Lucille Clifton. SP-ClifL

My Knight is over the sea, cried Kate. Squireless Kate. George Meredith. CP-MerG2

My Laddie wi' the Bashfu' Grace. James Whitcomb Riley. CP-RileJ

My lady / fair with / soft. Token, A. Robert Creeley. CP-CreeR

My Lady has Diana's brows. George Meredith. CP-MerG2

My lady, how comes it about—what all can see. Michelangelo Buonarroti. CP-Miche, *tr.* by John Frederick Nims

My lady, if it's true. Michelangelo Buonarroti. CP-Miche, *tr.* by John Frederick Nims

My Lady in Her White Silk Shawl. Nicholas Vachel Lindsay. CP-LindV

My lady is an ivory garden. E. E. Cummings. CP-CummE

My Lady Is Compared to a Young Tree. Nicholas Vachel Lindsay. CP-LindV

My lady is so impetuous, devil-may-care. Michelangelo Buonarroti. CP-Miche, *tr.* by John Frederick Nims

My lady love lives far away. Lyric, A: "My lady love lives far away." Paul Laurence Dunbar. CP-DunbP

My Lady of Castle Grand. Paul Laurence Dunbar. CP-DunbP

My lady, these eyes see vividly—far, near. Michelangelo Buonarroti. CP-Miche, *tr.* by John Frederick Nims

My lady walks her morning round. Henchman, The. John Greenleaf Whittier. CP-WhitJ

My lady, you raise me so. Michelangelo Buonarroti. CP-Miche, *tr.* by John Frederick Nims

My Lady's Gown There's Gairs upon't. Robert Burns. CP-BurnR

My Lady's Lamentation and Complaint against the Dean. Jonathan Swift. CP-SwifJ

My Lady's Law. Rudyard Kipling. CP-KiplR *Fr.* Naulahka, The.

My Lalalards I cucomplain. Joshua Battus's Spepeech to the Paparliament. Thomas Sheridan. CP-SherT

My land is bare of chattering folk. Sanctuary. Dorothy Parker. CP-ParkD

My landlord has a little pad. Upon Mr. Sheridan's Turning Author, 1716. *Unknown*. CP-SherT

My large back tooth, without a mate for years. Back Tooth. Muriel Rukeyser. CP-RukeM

My Last Afternoon with Uncle Devereux Winslow. Robert Lowell. SP-LoweR

My last—Cornificius—your Catullus'. Catullus. *See* Angst, / ennui & angst

My last defense. Old Mary. Gwendolyn Brooks. SP-BrooG

My Last Duchess. Robert Browning. CP-BroR1; SP-BroR

My last fringed gentians. Language of Flowers, Etc, The. Hayden Carruth. CP-CarHS

My Last Poem. Manuel Bandeira. CP-BishE

My Last Tiger. Jorge Luis Borges. SP-BorgJ, *tr.* by Ken Krabbenhoft

My latest cruel misfortune. Guido Cavalcanti. CP-CavaG, *tr.* by Marc Cirigliano

My latest tribute here I send. Verses on I Know Not What. Jonathan Swift. CP-SwifJ

My left hind-foot. Coyote. William Stafford. SP-StafWW

My Legacy. Walt Whitman. CP-WhitW

My legs hinge on my foreshortened bathtub. 1930's. Robert Lowell. SP-LoweR

My Lesbia let us love and live. Catullus. *See* Lesbia / live with me

My lids with grief were tumid yet. John Milton. *See* As yet my cheeks were not dry with flowing tears

My life. My Life by Water. Lorine Niedecker. CP-NiedL

My Life. William Stafford. SP-StafWW

My life ain't nothin'. Love Again Blues. Langston Hughes. CP-HughL; CP-HughL2

My life as yet is but an infant's walk. Eternal Life. Jones Very. CP-VeryJ

My Life Before Dawn. Louise Glück. SP-GlucL

My Life by Water. Lorine Niedecker. CP-NiedL

My life closed twice before its close. Emily Dickinson. CP-DickE

My life / has appeared unclothed in court. Talking to Sheep. Anne Sexton. CP-SextA

My life has been the poem I would have writ. Henry David Thoreau. CP-ThorH

My life has been too simple and stern. Emily Dickinson. SP-DickE

My Life Has Turned to Blue. Maya Angelou. SP-AngeM

My life, I ask of you no stable. Eugenio Montale. CP-MontE, *tr.* by Jonathan Galassi

My life is all made into lit. Volcanic Dirge & Co. Andrei Codrescu. SP-CodrA

My life is bitter with thy love; thine eyes. Anactoria. Algernon Charles Swinburne. SP-SwinA

My life is hung up. Lorine Niedecker. CP-NiedL

My life is like a stately warrior horse. Life. Henry David Thoreau. CP-ThorH

My life is vile. Reason, The. Stevie Smith. CP-SmitS

My life more civil are and free. Independence. Henry David Thoreau. CP-ThorH

My life was never so precious. Inscription for the Tank. James Wright. CP-WrigJ

My life, your light green eyes. Last Words. James Merrill. SP-MerrJ

My Life's Delight. Thomas Campion. CP-CampT

My life's on an even keel. Jean's TV. Raymond Carver. CP-CarvR

My limbs are wasted with a flame. La Bella Donna della Mia Mente. Oscar Wilde. CP-WildO

My limbs thicken with. His Brother's Illness. Shmuel HaNagid. SP-HaNaS

My limits crowd around me. Green Limits. Muriel Rukeyser. CP-RukeM

My little Balm might be o'erlooked. Emily Dickinson. SP-DickE

My Little 'Bout-Town Gal Has Gone. Gwendolyn Brooks. SP-BrooG

My little box. Little Box from Olinalá, The. Gabriela Mistral. SP-MistG, *tr.* by Maria Giachetti [*or* Jacketti] *and* Maria Jacketti

My Little Critics. D. H. Lawrence. CP-LawrD

My little dark baby. Lullaby (For a Black Mother). Langston Hughes. CP-HughL; CP-HughL1

My little dog ten years ago. For a Good Dog. Ogden Nash. CP-NashO

My little doves have left a nest. My Doves. Elizabeth Barrett Browning. CP-BroEB

My little finger's stuck in a. Constant Defender. James Tate. SP-TateJ

My little girl keeps talking to me. Conversation. John Updike. CP-UpdiJ

My little happiness. Self-Glamourer, A. Thomas Hardy. CP-HardT

My little heart is so wonderfully sorry. E. E. Cummings. CP-CummE

My little love, my darling. Virgin Mother, The. D. H. Lawrence. CP-LawrD

My Little Lovebirds. Arthur Rimbaud. CP-RimbA, *tr.* by Martin Sorrell

My Little March Girl. Paul Laurence Dunbar. CP-DunbP

My little one whose tongue is dumb. Tennessee Williams. CP-WillT

My little son comes running with open arms! Poem: "My little son comes running with open arms!" Thomas McGrath. SP-McGrT

My little son, laughing, singing . . . . Poem: "My little son, laughing, singing . . . " Thomas McGrath. SP-McGrT

My little son, my Florentine. Tale of Villafranca, A. Elizabeth Barrett Browning. CP-BroEB

My little soul, my vagrant charmer. Emperor Hadrian. CP-CunnJ, *tr.* by James Vincent Cunningham

My little story, Cousin Rufus said. Cousin Rufus' Story. James Whitcomb Riley. CP-RileJ *Fr.* Child-World, A.

My little woman, of you I sing. Little Woman, The. James Whitcomb Riley. CP-RileJ

My live telephone swings crippled to solitude. Marcus Cato 234–149 B.C. Robert Lowell. SP-LoweR

My lizard, my lively writher. Wish for a Young Wife. Theodore Roethke. CP-RoetT

My lonely chamber next the sea. Flower in a Letter, A. Elizabeth Barrett Browning. CP-BroEB

My long two-pointed ladder's sticking through a tree. After Apple-Picking. Robert Frost. CP-FrosR

My Lord, a diamond to me you sent. To the Right Hon. the Lord Chancellor (Bacon). George Herbert. CP-HerbG

My Lord a hunting he is gane. My Lady's Gown There's Gairs upon't. Robert Burns. CP-BurnR

My Lord and Lady Darlington. Written in the Strangers' Book at "The Station," Opposite Bowness. William Wordsworth. CP-WorW2

My Lord complains, that Pope, stark mad with gardens. Epigram: "My Lord complains, that Pope, stark mad with gardens." Alexander Pope. CP-PopeA

My lord, how beautifully you write! Tu Fu to Li Po. Tu Fu. CP-KizeC, *tr.* by Carolyn Kizer

My Lord, I know not what you mean. Letter of Advice to the Right Hon. John Earl of Orrery, A. Thomas Sheridan. CP-SherT

My Lord, I know, your noble ear. Humble Petition of Bruar Water to the Noble Duke of Athole, The. Robert Burns. CP-BurnR

My Lord, I loved strawberry jam. Confession, A. Czeslaw Milosz. CP-MiloC; CP-MiloCN, *tr.* by Robert Hass

My Lord, in every trivial work, 'tis known. To My Much Honoured Friend, Henry, Lord Carey of Leppington, Upon His Translation of Malvezzi. Thomas Carew. CP-CareT

My Lord, My Lord. Just Like Job. Maya Angelou. SP-AngeM

My Lord, my Love! in pleasant pain. Imitated From the Arpa Evangelica: Page 121. Christina Georgina Rossetti. CP-RosC3

My lord; / Poor wretched states, pressed by extremities. To the Right Honourable, the Lord High Treasurer of England. An Epistle Mendicant. 1631. Ben Jonson. CP-JonsB; SP-JonsB

My Lord to find out who must deal. Ballad on the Game of Traffic, A. Jonathan Swift. CP-SwifJ

My lordis of chalker, pleis yow to heir. William Dunbar. CP-DunbW

My lost William, thou in whom. To William Shelley. Percy Bysshe Shelley. CP-ShelP

My Lost Youth. Henry Wadsworth Longfellow. SP-LongH

My loud machine for making hay. Old Field Mowed for Appearances' Sake, An. William Meredith. SP-MereW

My lov'd [*or* loved], my honor'd [*or* honored], much respected friend. Cotter's Saturday Night [nscribed to Robert Aiken [*or* R. A****], Esq.], The. Robert Burns. CP-BurnR

My Love. Robert Creeley. CP-CreeR

My love, and not I, is the egoist. Fernando Pessoa. SP-PessF *Fr.* 35 Sonnets.

My love, be calmer! Werner; or, The Inheritance. Lord Byron. CP-Byron

My Love bound me with a kiss[e]. Kisses. Thomas Campion. CP-CampT

My love, do you recall that thing we saw. Carrion. Charles Baudelaire. CP-BaudC, *tr.* by Walter Martin

My love for you has never wearied me. Petrarch. CP-Petra, *tr.* by J. G. Nichols

My love for you is a dark hall. David Ignatow. SP-IgnaD

My love for you, though true, wears the. Compact. Robert Graves. CP-GravR

My love had gone; tho my soul. Complaint, The. John Logan. CP-LogaJ *Fr.* Epilogue, Songs of the Spouses, Complaint of Love.

My love has a long white dress. Instead of Words. Yehuda Amichai. SP-AmicYL, *tr.* by Benjamin Harshav *and* Barbara Harshav

My love has a very long white gown. Instead of Words. Yehuda Amichai. SP-AmicY, *tr.* by Chana Bloch

My love has come to ride me home. Do We Understand Each Other? Allen Ginsberg. CP-GinsA

My Love Hath Vowd. Thomas Campion. *See* Maid's Complaint, A

My love hath vow[e]d he he[e] will forsake me[e]. Maid's Complaint, A. Thomas Campion. CP-CampT

My love & I are yours to command. Carmen 15. Catullus. CP-ZukLS *Fr.* Carmina.

My Love Irene. Paul Laurence Dunbar. CP-DunbP

My love is a boat. Oh Love ("My love is a boat"). Robert Creeley. SP-CreeR

My love is a deep flame / that hides beneath the waters. Aria. Ezra Pound. CP-PoEar

My mother was a romantic girl. Papa Love Baby. Stevie Smith. CP-SmitS

My mother was a snake, but warm. Memories of Mortalities. Laura Riding Jackson. CP-RidiL

My Mother Was a Soldier. William Stafford. SP-StafWW

My Mother Was a Soldier. William Stafford. SP-StafWW

My mother was afraid. In Fear and Valor. William Stafford. SP-StafWW

My mother was Dutch. Portrait (II). Stevie Smith. CP-SmitS

My mother was very small. Gabriela Mistral. SP-MistG, tr. by Maria Giachetti [or Jacketti]

My mother white on her bed in the world. My Mother's Death and the Lost Battles for the Future of Her Children. Yehuda Amichai. SP-AmicYL, tr. by Benjamin Harshav and Barbara Harshav

My mother, who hates thunderstorms. Mother, Summer, I. Philip Larkin. CP-LarkP

My mother, who opened my eyes, who. Ruby Was Her Name. William Stafford. SP-StafWW

My mother works here. Toy Factory. Charles Simic. SP-SimiC; SP-SimiCF

My Mother Would Be a Falconress. Robert Duncan. SP-DuncR

My Mother's Birthday. Kathleen Jessie Raine. SP-RainK

My Mother's Death and the Lost Battles for the Future of Her Children. Yehuda Amichai. SP-AmicYL, tr. by Benjamin Harshav and Barbara Harshav

My mother's friend cooked for the drunk-and-disorderlies. In the Hospital for Tests. Mona Van Duyn. SP-VanDM

My mother's gold serpent bit its tail. Things, The. Josephine Jacobsen. CP-JacoJ

My mother's insomnia over at last. Chain, The. Maxine W. Kumin. SP-KumiM

My mother's lamp once out. Scenes of Childhood. James Merrill. SP-MerrJ

My Mother's Life. William Meredith. SP-MereW

My Mother's Lips. C. K. Williams. CP-WillC; SP-WillC

My mother's maids [or maydes] when they did sew [or sowe] and spin [or spynne]. Sir Thomas Wyatt. CP-WyatT Fr. Satires.

My Mother's Pears. Stanley Kunitz. CP-KunSC

My Mother's Portrait. Eleanor Wilner. SP-WilnE

My Mother's R & R. Galway Kinnell. SP-KinnGN

My Mother's Voice. Jones Very. CP-VeryJ

My mother's voice! I hear it now. My Mother's Voice. Jones Very. CP-VeryJ

My mountain belly and incontinent girth. Toby to Aguecheek. Donald Davie. CP-DaviDC

My Mouse. Christina Georgina Rossetti. CP-RosC3

My mouth blooms like a cut. Kiss, The. Anne Sexton. CP-SextA

My mouth holds round. Toome. Seamus Heaney. SP-HeanSO

My mouth hovers across your breasts. Adrienne Rich. SP-RicA1 Fr. Contradictions: Tracking Poems.

My muscles unravel. Why I Will Not Get Out of Bed. James Tate. SP-TateJ

My Muse. James Laughlin. CP-LaugJ

My Muse. Stevie Smith. CP-SmitS

My muse in meads has spent her many hours. To Mistress Katherine Bradshaw, the Lovely, That Crowned Him with Laurel. Robert Herrick. CP-HerrR

My muse keeps irregular hours. My Muse. James Laughlin. CP-LaugJ

My Muse what ails this ardour. Sir Philip Sidney. SP-SidnP Fr. Arcadia.

My muvver's ist the nicest one. Appreciation. Paul Laurence Dunbar. CP-DunbP

My My. Ogden Nash. CP-NashO

My Naked Aunt. Archibald MacLeish. CP-MacLA

My naked lady framed. E. E. Cummings. CP-CummE

'My name? Alex Zink.' 'Where were you born?'. On Trial. Primo Levi. CP-LeviP, tr. by Ruth Feldman

My Name and I. Robert Graves. CP-GravR

My name, as the title shows. Laura and Francisca. Laura Riding Jackson. CP-RidiL

My name engraved herein. Valediction, A: of My Name in the Window. John Donne. CP-DonnJ; MW-DonnJ

My name is / Black Golden Amber / Changing. To a Man. Maya Angelou. SP-AngeM

My name is Ebenezer Brown. James Vincent Cunningham. CP-CunnJ

My name is Edgar Poe and I was born. On the Edge. Philip Levine. SP-LeviP

My name is James A. Wright, and I was born. At the Executed Murderer's Grave. James Wright. CP-WrigJ

My Name Is Jesus. D. H. Lawrence. CP-LawrD

My name is Jesus, I am Mary's son. My Name Is Jesus. D. H. Lawrence. CP-LawrD

My name is John Majuba-Jink. Evolution. G. K. Chesterton. CP-ChesG

My name is Johnson. Madam's Past History. Langston Hughes. CP-HughL; CP-HughL2

My name is Lord Piggly-Wiggly Wogglesfoot Brown. Envoy to Africa. Langston Hughes. CP-HughL; CP-HughL3

My name is not my own. Meeting, The. Tess Gallagher. SP-GallT

My name is O'Kelly, I've heard the Revelly. Shillin' a Day. Rudyard Kipling. CP-KiplR

My name is Oriane, / the lurcher. Oriane. James Schuyler. CP-SchuJ

My name is Severino. João Cabral de Melo Neto. CP-BishE Fr. Death and Life of a Severino, The.

My name is Solomon Levi. Old Cracked Tune, An. Stanley Kunitz. CP-KunSC

My name is Timmy Torin. Muriel Rukeyser. CP-RukeM

My Name Is William Tell. William Stafford. SP-StafWW

My name meant "Arms." But little help to me. Michelangelo Buonarroti. CP-Miche, tr. by John Frederick Nims

My Namesake. John Greenleaf Whittier. CP-WhitJ

My Nannie's Awa'. Robert Burns. CP-BurnR

My Naughty Book. D. H. Lawrence. CP-LawrD

My neighbor, a scientist and art-collector, telephones me in a. Burning of Paper instead of Children, The. Adrienne Rich. SP-RicA1; SP-RicA2

My neighbor and his children are shoveling snow. January 2, 1978. John Ciardi. CP-CiarJ

My neighbor in the country, Henry Manley. Hello, Hello Henry. Maxine W. Kumin. SP-KumiM

My Neighbor in the Mirror. Louise Glück. SP-GlucL

My neighbor is a nice guy but he utterly. Puzzle, The. Charles Bukowski. SP-BukC3

My neighbor lives on the hill. Differences. Paul Laurence Dunbar. CP-DunbP

My neighbor used to come to our hut. Rwanda. Ai. SP-Ai

My neighbour moves less and less, attempts less. Green Wolf, The. Ted Hughes. SP-HughTN

My nephew / And my new. Louis Zukofsky. CP-ZukLS

My-ness. Czeslaw Milosz. CP-MiloC; CP-MiloCN, tr. by Robert Hass

My New-Cut Ashlar. Rudyard Kipling. CP-KiplR Fr. Life's Handicap.

My new friend, Maisie, who works where I work. Valley of the Fallen, The. Carolyn Kizer. CP-KizeC

My New Year's drink is mulled to-night. Ancestors. Robert Graves. CP-GravR

My next book will have a poem for each. Andrei Codrescu. SP-CodrA

My next-door neighbor is robust. Wooden Heart. Primo Levi. CP-LeviP, tr. by Ruth Feldman

My Night. James Whitcomb Riley. CP-RileJ

My night sweats grease his breakfast plate. Jailer, The. Sylvia Plath. CP-PlatS

My noble lord, all that I have in mind. Petrarch. CP-Petra, tr. by J. G. Nichols

My nonarrival in the city of N. Railroad Station, The. Wisława Szymborska. SP-SzymW, tr. by Stanislaw Barańczak and Clare Cavanagh

My northern pines are good enough for me. Boston. Edwin Arlington Robinson. CP-RobiE

My nosegays are for Captives. Emily Dickinson. CP-DickE

My November Guest. Robert Frost. CP-FrosR

My Number. Billy Collins. SP-CollB

My offended contempt for the mental & stylistic workings of. Crisis. John Berryman. CP-BerrJ

My old admiration before I was twenty. Christina Georgina Rossetti. CP-RosC3

My old body. Those Who Wait. Federico García Lorca. CP-GarcF, tr. by Jerome Rothenberg Fr. Suite.

My old books closed upon Paphos's name. Stéphane Mallarmé. CP-MallS, tr. by Henry Weinfield

My old flame, my wife! Old Flame, The. Robert Lowell. SP-LoweR

My Old Friend. James Whitcomb Riley. CP-RileJ

My old friend has departed, he is making the inevitable journey. Leave-taking, A. James Laughlin. CP-LaugJ

My old friend, the owner. Plan, The. Wendell Berry. CP-BerrW

My Old Friends. Christina Georgina Rossetti. CP-RosC3

My Old Gray Sweater. James Laughlin. CP-LaugJ

My old lady died of a common cold. Kitchen Door Blues. Tennessee Williams. CP-WillT

My Old Man. Charles Bukowski. SP-BukC1

My old man's a white old man. Cross. Langston Hughes. CP-HughL; CP-HughL1

My old mule. Me and the Mule. Langston Hughes. CP-HughL; CP-HughL2

My old time daddy. Lover's Return. Langston Hughes. CP-HughL; CP-HughL1; CP-HughL2

My old Uncle Sidney he says it's a sign. Goldie Goodwin. James Whitcomb Riley. CP-RileJ

My old Welsh neighbor over the way. Robin, The. John Greenleaf Whittier. CP-WhitJ

My oldest son comes to visit me. Having Been Asked "What is a Man?" I Answer. Philip Levine. SP-LeviP

My ole man named Silas: he. Gladness. James Whitcomb Riley. CP-RileJ

My only Love, be merciful to me! Out of the Depths I Called to Thee. Charles Baudelaire. CP-BaudC, tr. by Walter Martin

My only son, more God's than mine. Jesus and His Mother. Thom Gunn. CP-GunnT

My other favorite cat seemed to be dying and. Terminology. Charles Bukowski. SP-BukC3

My Own. Dorothy Parker. CP-ParkD

My own country my countrymen the exchanges. Island in the Harbor, An. W. S. Merwin. SP-MerwW

My own dear love, he is strong and bold. Love Song: "My own dear love, he is strong and bold." Dorothy Parker. CP-ParkD

My Own Heart. Gerard Manley Hopkins. *See* My Own Heart Let Me More Have Pity On

My Own Heart Let Me More Have Pity On. Gerard Manley Hopkins. CP-HopkG

  (My Own Heart.) CP-HopkG

My Own House. David Ignatow. SP-IgnaD

My Paistin Finn is my sole desire. Two Songs Rewritten for the Tune's Sake. William Butler Yeats. CP-YeatW

My Papa's Waltz. Theodore Roethke. CP-RoetT

My Parents. Stephen Spender. SP-SpenS

My parents, my husband, my brother, my sister. My-ness. Czeslaw Milosz. CP-MiloC; CP-MiloCN, *tr.* by Robert Hass

My parents stayed busy enough. Han-shan. CP-ColdM, *tr.* by Red Pine

My parrot is emerald green. Parrot, A. May Sarton. SP-SartM

My past is a stupid butterfly's overseas voyage. Frivolous Conversation, A. Czeslaw Milosz. CP-MiloC; CP-MiloCN, *tr.* by Lillian Vallee

My path led through an old cemetery. Han-shan. CP-ColdM, *tr.* by Red Pine

My Pedagogue Dear, I Read with Surprise. Thomas Sheridan. CP-SherT

My Peggy's Face. Robert Burns. CP-BurnR

My Pen. Sir Thomas Wyatt. CP-WyatT

My pen moves along the page. Budapest. Billy Collins. SP-CollB

My pen, take pain a little space. My Pen. Sir Thomas Wyatt. CP-WyatT

My pens are all spilt, and my ink-glass is dry. William Cowper. CP-CowpW

My pensive Sara! thy soft cheek reclined [*or* reclin'd]. Eolian Harp, The. Samuel Taylor Coleridge. MW-ColeS *Fr.* Effusions.

My peonies have lovely leaves. What Ails My Fern? James Schuyler. CP-SchuJ

My People. Langston Hughes. CP-HughL

  (Poem.) CP-HughL1

My People. Carl Sandburg. CP-SandC

My People are destroyed for lack of Knowledge.—Hosea 4:6. Jones Very. CP-VeryJ

My people are gray. My People. Carl Sandburg. CP-SandC

My people come to me and make their moan. Saith the Czar. Ambrose Bierce. SP-BierA

My period had come for Prayer. Emily Dickinson. CP-DickE

My Philosofy. James Whitcomb Riley. CP-RileJ

My phoenix long ago secured. Phoenix, The. Hafiz. CP-EmerR *Fr.* Odes.

My Picture-Gallery. Walt Whitman. CP-WhitW

My Picture Left in Scotland. Ben Jonson. CP-JonsB; SP-JonsB

My piglets cling to me. Her Task. Denise Levertov. SP-LeveDL

My pillow won't tell me. Apparition, The. Theodore Roethke. CP-RoetT

My Place. David Ignatow. SP-IgnaD

My 'place of clear water.' Anahorish. Seamus Heaney. SP-HeanSO

My Playmate. John Greenleaf Whittier. CP-WhitJ

My poems are poems alright. Shih-te. CP-ColdM, *tr.* by Red Pine

My poems no longer are "Beautiful" Reply, A. David Ignatow. SP-IgnaD

My Poetry Is for the Night. David Ignatow. SP-IgnaD

My Poets. Philip Levine. SP-LeviP

My pooped heart oozes. Tortured Heart. Arthur Rimbaud. CP-RimbA, *tr.* by Martin Sorrell

My poor dumb body. Charles Olson. CP-OlsoC

My Portion is Defeat—today. Emily Dickinson. CP-DickE

My post-war father was so silent. Dust As We Are. Ted Hughes. SP-HughTN

My Prayer. E. E. Cummings. CP-CummE

My prayers must meet a brazen heaven. Gerard Manley Hopkins. CP-HopkG

My present life is a Sunday-morning cartoon. Syncopated Cakewalk, The. Clarence Major. SP-MajoC

My Pretty Animals. Kenneth Patchen. CP-PatcK

My pretty cousin, ten years old. Sexual Conduct. Clarence Major. SP-MajoC

My Pretty Rose-Tree. William Blake. CP-BlakW *Fr.* Songs of Experience.

My prince in God, gif the guid grace. William Dunbar. CP-DunbW

My Problem. Rae Armantrout. SP-ArmaA

My proper prudence toward his proper probe. Riders to the Blood-Red Wrath. Gwendolyn Brooks. SP-BrooG

My Psalm. John Greenleaf Whittier. CP-WhitJ

My quality is such as common things. Having Been Near. Kenneth Patchen. CP-PatcK

My quietness has a man in it, he is transparent. In Memory of My Feelings. Frank O'Hara. SP-OharF

My race began as the sea began. Names. Derek Walcott. CP-WalcD

My real trouble is. True Confessions. Philip Whalen. SP-WhalP

My reason, out of sorts with me, deplores. Michelangelo Buonarroti. CP-Miche, *tr.* by John Frederick Nims

My Rebel Grandmother. John Logan. CP-LogaJ

My Reward for Being, was This. Emily Dickinson. CP-DickE

My right hand has suffered an amputation. Good Resolution, The. Mona Van Duyn. SP-VanDM

My Rival. Rudyard Kipling. CP-KiplR

My rival, obscurely effeminate. Man-Giraffe. Robert Stock. SP-StocR

My River runs to thee. Emily Dickinson. CP-DickE

My room in Florence was the color of air. Above the Arno. May Swenson. SP-SwenM

My room is whitewashed. Silence, The. Anne Sexton. CP-SextA; SP-SextA

My Rose, Gravina, blooms anew. To Gravina. William Cowper. CP-CowpW

My Ruthers. James Whitcomb Riley. CP-RileJ

My Sad Captains. Thom Gunn. CP-GunnT

My Sad Self. Allen Ginsberg. CP-GinsA; SP-GinsA

My sadness, don't desert me. Encounter. Eugenio Montale. CP-MontE, *tr.* by Jonathan Galassi

My Sandy gied to me a ring. I Love My Love in Secret. Robert Burns. CP-BurnR

My science-friend, my noblest woman-friend. Going Somewhere. Walt Whitman. CP-WhitW

My scrolls are filled with the poems of immortals. Han-shan. CP-ColdM, *tr.* by Red Pine

My Seasonal Body. Clarence Major. SP-MajoC

My Season's furthest Flower. Emily Dickinson. CP-DickE

My Secret. James Laughlin. CP-LaugJ

My Secrets. Czeslaw Milosz. CP-MiloCN, *tr.* by Robert Hass

My secrets cry aloud. Open House. Theodore Roethke. CP-RoetT

My 71st Year. Walt Whitman. CP-WhitW

My shadow and I. Some Notes on Shadows. Gregory Orr. SP-OrrG

My shadow glides in silence. Debussy. Federico García Lorca. CP-GarcF, *tr.* by Alan S. Trueblood *Fr.* Three Portraits with Shading.

My shared bedroom's window. Elegies for Paradise Valley. Robert Earl Hayden. CP-HaydR

My Sheep. Jones Very. CP-VeryJ

My Sheep Are Thoughts. Sir Philip Sidney. SP-SidnP *Fr.* Arcadia.

My sheep are thoughts, which I both guide and serve. My Sheep Are Thoughts. Sir Philip Sidney. SP-SidnP *Fr.* Arcadia.

My Shepherd. Heather McHugh. SP-McHuH

My Shepherd, I'm still where I lie. Earthquake, The. Shmuel HaNagid. SP-HaNaS, *tr.* by Peter Cole

My ship passes over-slowly through the foreign lands. First Prelude. Dream in Ohio: The Father. John Logan. CP-LogaJ *Fr.* Poem in Progress.

My ship passes overslowly through the foreign lands. Poem in Progress. John Logan. CP-LogaJ

My shirt is a token and symbol. Shirt. Carl Sandburg. CP-SandC

My Shoes. Charles Simic. SP-SimiC; SP-SimiCE

My shoes are almost dead. Caesar. W. S. Merwin. SP-MerwW

My shoes as I lean. Nightingales, The. William Carlos Williams. CP-WilW1

My Shy Hand. Wilfred Owen. CP-OwenW

My sight with the clouds'. Kathleen Jessie Raine. SP-RainK

My silks and fine array. Song: "My silks and fine array." William Blake. CP-BlakW

My silver stag is fallen—on the grass. Silver Stag, The. Kathleen Jessie Raine. SP-RainK

My sincerity doth surpass. To the Comet. Henry David Thoreau. CP-ThorH

My sister and I are sewing. Red Shirt, A. Margaret Atwood. SP-AtwM2

My sister, by the chiming kinks. Silverpoint. Louise Glück. SP-GlucL

My sister doesn't write poems. In Praise of My Sister. Wisława Szymborska. SP-SzymW, *tr.* by Stanisław Barańczak *and* Clare Cavanagh

My sister got me the script. I couldn't. Sanctuary. Norman Dubie. CP-DubiN

My sister has my hair my mouth my eyes. Family Resemblance, A. Audre Lorde. SP-LordA

My sister! my sweet sister! if a name. Epistle to Augusta. Lord Byron. CP-Byron

My sister rubs the doll's face in mud. Kid, The. Ai. SP-Ai

My Sisters. Stanley Kunitz. CP-KunSC

My sisters, / do you remember the fiddlers. Wonderful Musician, The. Anne Sexton. CP-SextA

My Sister's Letter. Bogomil Gjuzel. CP-KizeC, *tr.* by Carolyn Kizer

My Sisters, O My Sisters. May Sarton. SP-SartM

My Sister's Sleep. Dante Gabriel Rossetti. CW-RossD

My Sleep. Yehuda Amichai. SP-AmicYL, *tr.* by Benjamin Harshav *and* Barbara Harshav

My Small Aunt. Josephine Jacobsen. CP-JacoJ

My smallheaded pearshaped. E. E. Cummings. CP-CummE

My Son. Yehuda Amichai. SP-AmicYL, *tr.* by Benjamin Harshav *and* Barbara Harshav

My Son and I. Philip Levine. SP-LeviP

My son and I gao walking in the garden. New Season. Philip Levine. SP-LeviP

My son as a child saying. Little Stone in the Middle of the Road, in Florida, A. Muriel Rukeyser. CP-RukeM

My son enters the classroom. For Danny. Grace Paley. CP-PalGC

My son invites me to witness with him. Mousemeal. Howard Nemerov. CP-NemeH

My Son, My Executioner. Donald Hall. CP-HallD

My Son, My Son, My Head, My Head. Yehuda Amichai. SP-AmicYL, *tr. by* Benjamin Harshav *and* Barbara Harshav

"My son," said the Norman Baron, "I am dying, and you will be heir" Norman and Saxon. Rudyard Kipling. CP-KiplR

My son squats in the snow in his blue snowsuit. Illuminations. Louise Glück. SP-GlucL

My son, the softness of your face already shows. Yehuda Amichai. SP-AmicYL, *tr. by* Benjamin Harshav *and* Barbara Harshav

My son was born in Asuta hopital and since then. Yehuda Amichai. SP-AmicYL, *tr. by* Benjamin Harshav *and* Barbara Harshav

My son who is stranger. Variation, A. Robert Creeley. CP-CreeR

My son, you were conceived in love, that's all I will ever know about you. Yokimura. Czeslaw Milosz. CP-MiloCN, *tr. by* Robert Hass

My Song, I fear that thou wilt find but few. Epipsychidion. Percy Bysshe Shelley. CP-ShelP

My song! It is time! Rendezvous. William Carlos Williams. CP-WilW1

My Songs Are Kandym in the Waste Land. Hugh MacDiarmid. SP-MacDH

My songs remade that I send greet the world. To Ysolt. For Pardon. Ezra Pound. CP-PoEar

My sonnet is A light goes on in. E. E. Cummings. CP-CummE

My sorrow, when she's here with me. My November Guest. Robert Frost. CP-FrosR

My sorrows he said. Convergence. A. R. Ammons. CP-AmmoA

My Sort o' Man. Paul Laurence Dunbar. CP-DunbP

My Soul. Stevie Smith. CP-SmitS

My Soul—accused me—And I quailed. Emily Dickinson. CP-DickE

My Soul and I. John Greenleaf Whittier. CP-WhitJ

My soul and I last night. Night Thought. Kathleen Jessie Raine. SP-RainK

My soul, calm sister, ascends toward your brow. Sigh. Stéphane Mallarmé. CP-MallS, *tr. by* Henry Weinfield

My soul came apart like an empty jar. Note. Fernando Pessoa. SP-PessF, *tr. by* Susan M. Brown *and* Edwin Honig

My soul goes there crying when. To Crickley. Ivor Gurney. SP-GurnI

My soul has had a long, hard day. Fatigue. D. H. Lawrence. CP-LawrD

My Soul Is Dark. Lord Byron. CP-Byron

My soul is, in the middle of the night. Confusion. Constantine P. Cavafy. CP-CavaC, *tr. by* Theoharis Constantine Theoharis

My soul is in the streets. Streets, The. Jorge Luis Borges. SP-BorgJ, *tr. by* Stephen Kessler

My soul is out back eating your soul. For Gail, When I Was Five. C. K. Williams. CP-WillC; SP-WillC

My soul is wildly terrified. Guido Cavalcanti. CP-CavaG, *tr. by* Marc Cirigliano

My soul looked down from a vague height, with Death. Show, The. Wilfred Owen. CP-OwenW

My soul, lost in the music's mist. Song, The: "My soul, lost in the music's mist." Paul Laurence Dunbar. CP-DunbP

My soul, prophetic of your coming loss. Petrarch. CP-Petra, *tr. by* J. G. Nichols

My soul, rejoice thou in thy God. Anne Bradstreet. CP-BradA

My soul, who see, hear, read, think, speak, and write. Petrarch. CP-Petra, *tr. by* J. G. Nichols

My soul within the shades of night. Recluse, The. Stevie Smith. CP-SmitS

My soul without a friend, without a guide. Michelangelo Buonarroti. SP-ZatuM, *tr. by* Marya Alexandrovna Zaturenska

My soule would one day goe and seeke. How His Soule Came Ensnared. Robert Herrick. CP-HerrR

My Soul's Shadow. Federico García Lorca. CP-GarcF, *tr. by* Catherine Brown

My Special Fate. John Berryman. CP-BerrJ

My specialty is living said. E. E. Cummings. CP-CummE; SP-CummE

My Spectre around Me Night and Day. William Blake. CP-BlakW

My spirit is too weak—mortality. On Seeing the Elgin Marbles. John Keats. CP-KeatJ

My spirit like a charmèd bark doth swim. Fragment: To One Singing. Percy Bysshe Shelley. CP-ShelP

My spirit on which, after God, I lean. Shmuel HaNagid. SP-HaNaS, *tr. by* Peter Cole

My Spirit, Sore from Marching. Edna St. Vincent Millay. CP-MillE

My spirit to yours dear brother. To Him That Was Crucified. Walt Whitman. CP-WhitW

My Spirit Will Not Haunt the Mound. Thomas Hardy. CP-HardT

My Spouse! in whose presence I live. Aspirations of the Soul after God. Jeanne Marie Bouvier de la Motte- Guyon. CP-CowpW

My Star. Robert Browning. CP-BroR1

My stick fingers click with a snicker. Player Piano. John Updike. CP-UpdiJ

My stock has gone down and my tailor has sent. Companion's Progress, A. Paul Laurence Dunbar. CP-DunbP

My stock lies dead, and no increase. Grace. George Herbert. CP-HerbG

My story begins in the town of Cambridge, Mass. Mind of Professor Primrose, The. Ogden Nash. CP-NashO

My story is. Blues Chant Hoodoo Rival. Yusef Komunyakaa. CP-KomuY

My strength becoming wistful in a glib. E. E. Cummings. CP-CummE

My students look at me expectantly. Mountain, The. Louise Glück. SP-GlucL

My stutter, my cough, my unfinished sentences. Second-Fated, The. Robert Graves. CP-GravR

My subject's / still the wind still. Project. A. R. Ammons. CP-AmmoA

My sun has set, I dwell. Despised and Rejected. Christina Georgina Rossetti. CP-RosC1

My Sweeney, Mr. Eliot. Sweeney. Anne Sexton. CP-SextA

My sweet ache / is gone. Ache's End. Marge Piercy. SP-PierM

My sweet, alas, forget me not. Sir Thomas Wyatt. CP-WyatT

My Sweet Brown Gal. Paul Laurence Dunbar. CP-DunbP

My sweet European homeland. Earth. Czeslaw Milosz. CP-MiloC; CP-MiloCN, *tr. by* Robert Hass

My sweet-faced, tattle-tale brother was born blind. Twins, The. Mona Van Duyn. SP-VanDM

My sweet old etcetera. E. E. Cummings. CP-CummE; SP-CummE

"My sweet," you sang, and, "Sweet," I sang. Spring Reminiscence. Countee Cullen. CP-CullC

My sweetest Lesbia, let us live and love. Catullus. *See* Lesbia / live with me

My Sweetest Lesbia [Let Us Live and Love]. Catullus. *See* Carmina

My Sweetheart is the TRUTH BEYOND THE MOON. Beyond the Moon. Nicholas Vachel Lindsay. CP-LindV

My swirling wants. Your frozen lips. Valediction Forbidding Mourning, A. Adrienne Rich. CP-RicAE; SP-RicA1; SP-RicA2

My Table. William Butler Yeats. CP-YeatW *Fr.* Meditations in Time of Civil War.

My teacher lies on the floor with a bad back. Piano Lessons. Billy Collins. SP-CollB

My thankful heart with glorying tongue. Anne Bradstreet. CP-BradA

My Thanks. John Greenleaf Whittier. CP-WhitJ

My Theme. George Meredith. CP-MerG1

My Theme: Continued. George Meredith. CP-MerG1

My theory withstood the light of the Hyades. *Principia Mathematica:* Einstein's Exile in an Old Dutch Winter. Norman Dubie. CP-DubiN

My Thoughts. Ralph Waldo Emerson. CP-EmerR

My thoughts are all in yonder town. Friend's Burial, The. John Greenleaf Whittier. CP-WhitJ

My thoughts are crabbed and sallow. Jilted. Sylvia Plath. CP-PlatS

My thoughts are crowded with death. In Time of Plague. Thom Gunn. CP-GunnT

My thoughts arise and fade in solitude. Fragment: Thoughts Come and Go in Solitude. Percy Bysshe Shelley. CP-ShelP

My thoughts talked with each other pleasantly. Petrarch. CP-Petra, *tr. by* J. G. Nichols

My thoughts through yours refracted into speech. Sonnet: "My thoughts through yours refracted into speech." Muriel Rukeyser. CP-RukeM

My thoughts turn south. White City, A. James Schuyler. CP-SchuJ

My thousand-thousand-leaved. Elm. John Updike. CP-UpdiJ

My three sisters are sitting. Women. Adrienne Rich. CP-RicAE; SP-RicA2

My tie is made of terylene. In Praise of $(C_{10}H_9O_5)x$. John Updike. CP-UpdiJ

My time / moves on in a spiral. Spiral. Federico García Lorca. CP-GarcF, *tr. by* Jerome Rothenberg *Fr.* Caracols / Snails.

My time, O ye Grattans, was happily spent. Song, The: "My time, O ye Grattans, was happily spent." Thomas Sheridan. CP-SherT

My titillations have no foot-notes. Jasmine's Beautiful Thoughts Underneath the Willow. Wallace Stevens. CP-StevW; CP-StevWP

My title as an Genius thus is provd. William Blake. CP-BlakW

My Tocher's the Jewel. Robert Burns. CP-BurnR

My toes feel like nothing they are so cold. Muriel Rukeyser. CP-RukeM

My tongue is prone to lose the way. Letters. Ralph Waldo Emerson. CP-EmerR

My touch has little force. Girl on a Swing. Thomas Kinsella. CP-KinsT

My townspeople, beyond in the great world. Gulls. William Carlos Williams. CP-WilW1

My track the first. Thickening Mat, The. May Swenson. SP-SwenM

My Tribe. John Ciardi. CP-CiarJ

My Trip Daorba. Ogden Nash. CP-NashO

My Triumph. John Greenleaf Whittier. CP-WhitJ

My Triumph lasted till the Drums. Emily Dickinson. CP-DickE

My true friend's poems about aging and death held my mind as in a sea-surge. No Supervening Thought of Grace. Hayden Carruth. CP-CarHS

My true home is on Cold Mountain. Han-shan.

My true love breathed her latest breath. Murderer, The. Stevie Smith. CP-SmitS

My true love hath my heart [*or* hart], and I have his. Sir Philip Sidney. SP-SidnP *Fr.* Arcadia.

My turn. The history of one of my madnesses. Second Delirium. Alchemy of the Word. Arthur Rimbaud. CP-RimbA, *tr. by* Martin Sorrell

My two-fold book! single in show. John Milton. *See* Two-part book rejoicing in single garb

My uncle, a child in the terrible second coming. Josephine Jacobsen. CP-JacoJ

My uncle, a craftsman of hammers and wood. Willy Lyons. James Wright. CP-WrigJ

My Uncle Alec's friend, Dominic Cataldo. Feasts. John Ciardi. CP-CiarJ

My uncle believed he had. Parity. Kenneth Rexroth. CP-RexrK

My uncle / Daniel fought in the civil. E. E. Cummings. CP-CummE

My Uncle from the realms of Death. Le Revenant. Stevie Smith. CP-SmitS

My uncle is buried at Sheikh Badr, my other uncle. Luxury, A. Yehuda Amichai. SP-AmicY, *tr. by* Stephen Mitchell

My uncle is buried in Sheikh Badr, my other uncle. Luxury. Yehuda Amichai. SP-AmicYL, *tr. by* Benjamin Harshav *and* Barbara Harshav

My unexpected knocking at the door. Literate Farmer and the Planet Venus, The. Robert Frost. CP-FrosR

My valiant helper, a small-sized tiger. To Mrs. Professor in Defense of My Cat's Honor and Not Only. Czeslaw Milosz. CP-MiloCN, *tr. by* Robert Hass

My very good lord, 'tis a very hard task. Verses Left in a Window of Dublin Castle. Jonathan Swift. CP-SwifJ

My very soul smiles as I listen to. Laughter of the Rain, The. James Whitcomb Riley. CP-RileJ

My vessel laden with oblivion. Petrarch. CP-Petra, *tr. by* J. G. Nichols

My vineyard that is mine I have to keep. Yea, I Have a Goodly Heritage. Christina Georgina Rossetti. CP-RosC3

My vixen, I myself was once the *poète*. From a Swiss Lake. Eugenio Montale. CP-MontE, *tr. by* Jonathan Galassi

My Voice. Oscar Wilde. CP-WildO

My voice is a minor one, but I must raise it. I Spy, or, The Depravity of Privacy. Ogden Nash. CP-NashO

My Voice Not Being Proud. Louise Bogan. CP-BogaL

My Walk It Is Finished. Thomas Sheridan. CP-SherT

My wandered brother wind wild bloweth now. Fratello Mio, Zephyrus. Ezra Pound. CP-PoEar

My Wars are laid away in Books. Emily Dickinson. CP-DickE

My way is in the sand flowing. Samuel Beckett. CP-BeckS

My Way Is Not Thy Way. D. H. Lawrence. CP-LawrD

My wearied bark, O let it now be crowned! To Crown[e] It. Robert Herrick. CP-HerrR

My Weariness of Epic Proportions. Charles Simic. SP-SimiC; SP-SimiCE

My wedding-ring lies in a basket. Wedding-Ring. Denise Levertov. SP-LeveDL; SP-LeveDS

My wheel is in the dark! Emily Dickinson. CP-DickE

My whining lover, what needs all. Against Absence. Sir John Suckling. CP-SuckJ

My whiskey is / a tough way of life. Drink. William Carlos Williams. CP-WilW1

My White Bread. James Whitcomb Riley. CP-RileJ

My whole dream shuts down tight. Dreams. Federico García Lorca. CP-GarcF, *tr. by* Jerome Rothenberg *Fr.* Blue River.

My whole eye was sunset red. Eye and Tooth. Robert Lowell. SP-LoweR

My Whole Life. Jorge Luis Borges. SP-BorgJ, *tr. by* W. S. Merwin

My whole life has led me here. Woolworth's. Donald Hall. CP-HallD

My whole life is mine, but whoever says so. Water Lily. Rainer Maria Rilke. CP-RilkFr, *tr. by* A. Poulin, Jr.

My wife a-rattling. Addenda Quaedam. Jonathan Swift. CP-SwifJ

My wife and I lived all alone. Ballad of the Despairing Husband. Robert Creeley. CP-CreeR

My wife, because she daydreams catalogues. Obsolescence. John Ciardi. CP-CiarJ

My wife deserved to be shot. Penis Envy. Ai. SP-Ai

My wife has disappeared along with her clothes. Raymond Carver. CP-CarvR

My wife, I dread to come and tell you. Consolation. David Ignatow. SP-IgnaD

My wife is dead. I'm free to get. Murderer's Wine. Charles Baudelaire. CP-BaudC, *tr. by* Walter Martin

My wife is ill! Thomas Jefferson. Lorine Niedecker. CP-NiedL

My wife is in the other half of this mobile home. Other Life, The. Raymond Carver. CP-CarvR

My Wife Reads the Paper at Breakfast on the Birthday of the Scottish Poet. Miller Williams. CP-WillM

My wife said, "There's an angel at the door!" Glory, The. John Ciardi. CP-CiarJ

My Wife's a Wanton Wee Thing. Robert Burns. CP-BurnR

My Wife's a Winsome Wee Thing. Robert Burns. CP-BurnR

My wife's new pink slippers. Thinker, The. William Carlos Williams. CP-WilW1

My wind is turned to bitter north. Arthur Hugh Clough. SP-ClouA

My window shews the travelling clouds. Alchemist in the City, The. Gerard Manley Hopkins. CP-HopkG

My wish has always been to live alone. Petrarch. CP-Petra, *tr. by* J. G. Nichols

My woods belong to woodcock and to deer. Guest, A. May Sarton. SP-SartM

My wooing's ended: now my wedding's neere. To Rosemary and Baies. Robert Herrick. CP-HerrR

My word will teach obedience thou wilt learn. Obedience. Jones Very. CP-VeryJ

My words and thoughts do both express this notion. Our Life Is Hid with Christ in God. George Herbert. CP-HerbG

My words, in hope to blaze my steadfast mind. Sir Philip Sidney. SP-SidnP *Fr.* Arcadia.

My words that once were virtuous and expressed. Edna St. Vincent Millay. CP-MillE

My Work. Raymond Carver. CP-CarvR

My World Is Pyramid. Dylan Thomas. CP-ThomD

My world would not fit into yours. Animus Mundi. Sam Hamill. SP-HamiS

My worship from this hour the Sparrow-Drawn. Edna St. Vincent Millay. CP-MillE

My worst habit is I get so tired of winter. Jelaluddin Rumi. SP-Rumi, *tr. by* Coleman Barks

My Worthiness is all my Doubt. Emily Dickinson. CP-DickE

My wrath, where's the edge. Song: "My wrath, where's the edge." Theodore Roethke. CP-RoetT

My writing and judgment aren't that bad. Han-shan. CP-ColdM, *tr. by* Red Pine

My writing hand moves washed in the same light now. Conspiracy, The. Charles Tomlinson. CP-TomlC

My yard with its pines is almost spherical in winter. Widow Speaks to the Auroras of a December Night, A. Norman Dubie. CP-DubiN

My yoke is easy and my burthen light. Yoke, The. Jones Very. CP-VeryJ

My young blossom. Guido Cavalcanti. CP-CavaG, *tr. by* Marc Cirigliano

My young lord's the lover. Youth and Lordship. *Unknown.* CW-RossD, *tr. by* Dante Gabriel Rossetti

My young mother, her face narrow. Jane Cooper. CP-CoopJ

My younger days, my sensual life. Understanding. Constantine P. Cavafy. CP-CavaC, *tr. by* Theoharis Constantine Theoharis

My youth is. Yacht for Sale. Archibald MacLeish. CP-MacLA

My youthful lady will have other lovers. E. E. Cummings. CP-CummE

Mycelium, the delicate white threads. Dream Inscape. Denise Levertov. SP-LeveDL

Mycenae. Donald Hall. CP-HallD

Mycenae Lookout. Seamus Heaney. SP-HeanSO

Mycilla dyes her locks, 'tis said. On an Old Woman. Lucilius. CP-CowpW, *tr. by* William Cowper

My(his from daughter's mother's zero mind). E. E. Cummings. CP-CummE

Mylo Jones's wife was all. James Whitcomb Riley. CP-RileJ

Myopia: a Night. Robert Lowell. SP-LoweR

Myopic Child, A. Yannis Ritsos. SP-RitsY, *tr. by* Gwendolyn MacEwen *and* Nikos Tsingos

Myris: Alexandria, 340 A.D.. Constantine P. Cavafy. CP-CavaC, *tr. by* Theoharis Constantine Theoharis

Myrrhina. Robert Graves. CP-GravR

Myrtilla's tripping down the street. To Myrtilla, On Easter Day. Dorothy Parker. CP-ParkD

Myrtle. Theodore Roethke. CP-RoetT

Myrtle Bough. "H. D." CP-DoolH

Myrtle-leaf that, ill besped. To an Unfortunate Woman Whom the Author Had Known in the Days of Her Innocence. Samuel Taylor Coleridge. CP-ColeS

Myrtle's Cousin. Theodore Roethke. CP-RoetT

Myself. Robert Creeley. SP-CreeR

Myself. Walter De la Mare. CP-DeLaW

Myself and Mine. Walt Whitman. CP-WhitW

Myself and Pangur. *Unknown.* CP-MuldP, *tr. by* Paul Muldoon

Myself and Pangur, my white cat. Myself and Pangur. *Unknown.* CP-MuldP, *tr. by* Paul Muldoon

Myself can read the Telegrams. Emily Dickinson. CP-DickE

Myself, I rather like the bat. Bat, The. Ogden Nash. CP-NashO

Myself I Sing. George Oppen. CP-OppGN

Myself, Rousseau, a Few Others. William Meredith. SP-MereW

Myself to Me. May Sarton. SP-SartM

Myself unholy, from myself unholy. Gerard Manley Hopkins. CP-HopkG

Myself,walking in Dragon st. E. E. Cummings. CP-CummE

Myself was formed—a Carpenter. Emily Dickinson. CP-DickE

Myselves / The grievers. Ceremony after a Fire Raid. Dylan Thomas. CP-ThomD

Mysteries. Alice Walker. CP-WalkA

Mysteries, The. John Berryman. CP-BerrJ

Mysteries, The. "H. D." CP-DoolH

Mysteries of human nature, The. Emily Dickinson. SP-DickE

Mysterious Biography. Carl Sandburg. CP-SandC

Mysterious Cat, The. Nicholas Vachel Lindsay. CP-LindV

Mysterious didactic urgency informs the compelling bedtime stories he is obsessively recounted, A. Herakles. C. K. Williams. SP-WillC

Mysterious Disappearance, The. James Laughlin. CP-LaugJ

Mysterious Song in the Spring of the Year, A. Thomas Merton. CP-MertT

Mystery. Langston Hughes. CP-HughL; CP-HughL3

Mystery. D. H. Lawrence. CP-LawrD

Mystery, A. Ambrose Bierce. SP-BierA

Mystery, A. John Greenleaf Whittier. CP-WhitJ

Mystery, The. G. K. Chesterton. CP-ChesG

Mystery, The. Paul Laurence Dunbar. CP-DunbP

'Mystery Boy' Looks for Kin in Nashville. Robert Earl Hayden. CP-HaydR

Mystery does not get clearer by repeating the question, The. Jelaluddin Rumi. SP-Rumi, *tr. by* Coleman Barks

Mystery: God, Man's Life, born into man. Virgin and Child, by Hans Memmeling, A; in the Academy of Bruges. Dante Gabriel Rossetti. CW-RossD

Mystery: Katharine, the bride of Christ. Marriage of St Katharine, by the same, A; in the Hospital of St John at Bruges. Dante Gabriel Rossetti. CW-RossD

Mystery! lo! betwixt the sun and moon. Astarte Syriaca. Dante Gabriel Rossetti. CW-RossD

Mystery (Oaxaca, Mexico), A. Denise Levertov. SP-LeveDL

Mystery of creation is the divine urge of creation, The. Work of Creation, The. D. H. Lawrence. CP-LawrD

Mystery of Deep Candor, The. Denise Levertov. SP-LeveDS

Mystery of Life, the Mystery, The. Mirrors of Life and Death. Christina Georgina Rossetti. CP-RosC2

Mystery of mysteries, the crude and hurried ceaseless flame, spontaneous, bearing on itself, The. Thought of Columbus, A. Walt Whitman. CP-WhitW

Mystery of the Abstract. Richard Eberhart. CP-EberR

Mystery of the Charity of Charles Péguy, The. Geoffrey Hill. CP-HillG

Mystery. Seed of every motion. Living Alone. Hayden Carruth. CP-CarHS

Mystery Story. Howard Nemerov. CP-NemeH

Mystic. D. H. Lawrence. CP-LawrD

Mystic. Sylvia Plath. CP-PlatS

Mystic finishes in time, The. Insomniacs, The. Adrienne Rich. CP-RicAE

Mystic Moment. James Tate. SP-TateJ

Mystic River. John Ciardi. CP-CiarJ

Mystic Sea, The. Paul Laurence Dunbar. CP-DunbP

Mystic shadow, bending near me. Stephen Crane. CP-CranS

Mystic Trumpeter, The. Walt Whitman. CP-WhitW

Mystical. Arthur Rimbaud. CP-RimbA, *tr. by* Martin Sorrell

Mystical Beast in the Shadows, The. Richard Eberhart. CP-EberR

Mystically I live on two planes at once. Programme for the Double Barrel Life When It Hits, A. Andrei Codrescu. SP-CodrA

Mysticism for Beginners. Adam Zagajewski. SP-ZagaA, *tr. by* Clare Cavanagh

Mysticism Has Not the Patience To Wait for God's Revelation. Richard Eberhart. CP-EberR

Mystic's Christmas, The. John Greenleaf Whittier. CP-WhitJ

Mystique. David Ignatow. SP-IgnaD

Myth. Muriel Rukeyser. CP-RukeM

Myth. May Sarton. SP-SartM

Myth of Arthur, The. G. K. Chesterton. CP-ChesG

Myth of Mountain Sunrise. Robert Penn Warren. CP-WarrR

Myth of the Blaze. George Oppen. CP-OppGN

Myth & Ritual. Howard Nemerov. CP-NemeH

Mythic Fragment. Louise Glück. SP-GlucL

Mythical Founding of Buenos Aires, The. Jorge Luis Borges. SP-BorgJ, *tr. by* Alastair Reid

Mythological Introduction. Philip Larkin. CP-LarkP

Mythologies 1. A. K. Ramanujan. CP-RamaA

Mythologies 2. A. K. Ramanujan. CP-RamaA

Mythologies 3. A. K. Ramanujan. CP-RamaA

Mythology in an Age of Reason. Johann Christoph Friedrich von Schiller. CP-ColeS *Fr.* Piccolomini, The.

Mythology of Dark and Light, The. Hayden Carruth. CP-CarHL

Mythology reflects its region, A. Here. Wallace Stevens. CP-StevWP

Myths and Texts. Gary Snyder.
    ("But ye shall destroy their altars.") CP-SnydG

Myxomatosis. Philip Larkin. CP-LarkP

N

N is for NANNYGOAT—the silly. John Ciardi. CP-CiarJ

N / ot eth / eold almos. E. E. Cummings. CP-CummE

N / OthI / n / g can / s / urPas / s. E. E. Cummings. CP-CummE

N. Truro Light—1946. Robert Creeley. SP-CreeR

N / Umb a / stree / t's wintr. E. E. Cummings. CP-CummE

N. Y. Ezra Pound. CP-PoEar

Na Audiart. Ezra Pound. CP-PoEar; SP-PounE

NAACP. Langston Hughes. CP-HughL; CP-HughL2

Naaman's Song. Rudyard Kipling. CP-KiplR

Naches River. Just below the falls. Woman Bathing. Raymond Carver. CP-CarvR

Nachtwache. Primo Levi. CP-LeviP, *tr. by* Ruth Feldman

Nadya, pink-cheeked, happy, her eyes shining with tears. Don't Run. Raymond Carver. CP-CarvR

Nae gentle dames tho' ne'er sae fair. Highland Lassie O. Robert Burns. CP-BurnR

Nae Heathen Name shall I prefix. To Miss Ferrier. Robert Burns. CP-BurnR

Nagasaki Days. Allen Ginsberg. CP-GinsA; SP-GinsA
    Everybody's Fantasy, SP-GinsA

Nagging questions, taunting remarks, objections. Frogs of Bikini, The. Hans Magnus Enzensberger. SP-EnzeH

Nahant. Ralph Waldo Emerson. CP-EmerR

Nahoa Urn, for a Woman. Pablo Antonio Cuadra. CP-MertT

Nail his neck to the cross nail it with a nail. William Blake. CP-BlakW

Nailing up chicken wire on the frame house. Opal, The. Arthur Sze. SP-SzeA

Nails, The. W. S. Merwin. SP-MerwW

Nails, The. Yannis Ritsos. SP-RitsY, *tr. by* Kostas Myrsiades

Nails dropped off a roof onto flagstone. Ice Floe. Arthur Sze. SP-SzeA

Naked. Alvaro Figueredo. CP-WilW2

Naked. William Carlos Williams. CP-WilW1

Naked and grey the Cotswolds stand. Edgehill Fight. Rudyard Kipling. CP-KiplR

Naked and the Nude, The. Robert Graves. CP-GravR

Naked Ape, The. John Updike. CP-UpdiJ

Naked, astride an elephant. Yannis Ritsos. SP-RitsY *Fr.* Second Series.

Naked at 92 Degrees. Charles Bukowski. SP-BukC3

Naked before the glass she said. Young Woman. Howard Nemerov. CP-NemeH

Naked, but with my boots on / my son. Incunabula, 1958. Charles Olson. CP-OlsoC

Naked cornucopia of autumn fields, The. Cornucopia. Carl Sandburg. CP-SandC

Naked Eye of the Aunt, The. Wallace Stevens. CP-StevWP

Naked Face. Yannis Ritsos. SP-RitsY, *tr. by* Kimon Friar *and* Kostas Myrsiades

Naked foot steps out onto bare baked mud, A. Check. Thomas Kinsella. CP-KinsT

Naked, he climbed to the wolf's lair. Holy Thursday. Geoffrey Hill. CP-HillG

Naked he found her? Two Women Talking. Archibald MacLeish. CP-MacLA

Naked, he lies in the blinded room. Soledad, Robert Earl Hayden. CP-HaydR

Naked I came, naked I leave the scene. Epitaph for Someone or Other. James Vincent Cunningham. CP-CunnJ *Fr.* Five Epigrams.

Naked in Borneo. May Swenson. SP-SwenM

Naked Jaina monk, A. Pleasure. A. K. Ramanujan. CP-RamaA

Naked Land, The. Kenneth Patchen. CP-PatcK

Naked man jumps in the river, hornets swarming, A. Zikr. Jelaluddin Rumi. SP-Rumi, *tr. by* Coleman Barks

Naked, marble, invisible statues lined up. Shelters. Yannis Ritsos. SP-RitsY, *tr. by* N. C. Germanacos

Naked on the ground. After Piero di Cosimo's *Venus, Mars, and Amor*. Gregory Orr. SP-OrrG

Naked—she took her red handkerchief. Beauty. Yannis Ritsos. SP-RitsY, *tr. by* Minas Savvas

Naked solitude with neither gesture nor word. Transparent in the orchard. Sketch for an Ode. Federico García Lorca. CP-GarcF, *tr. by* Christopher Maurer

Naked spike chocolaty men white. Pachysandra. Louis Zukofsky. CP-ZukLS

Naked traveller, The. Ash Wednesday. Thomas Merton. CP-MertT

Naked / unarmored / before the open window. 6 A.M. Charles Bukowski. SP-BukC2

Naked woman and a dead dwarf, A. Stephen Crane. CP-CranS

Nakedly muscular, the beech no longer regrets. Beech, The. Charles Tomlinson. CP-TomlC

Namaste. Olga Broumas. SP-BrouO

Name. Robert Graves. CP-GravR

Name, A. John Greenleaf Whittier. CP-WhitJ

Name, The. Robert Creeley. CP-CreeR

Name, The. Wyatt Prunty. SP-PrunW

Name, The. Tomas Transtromer. CP-CarvR, *tr. by* Robert Bly

Name any gentleman you spy. New Enigmas. Christina Georgina Rossetti. CP-RosC3

Name Day. Robert Graves. CP-GravR

Name Day, A. James Schuyler. CP-SchuJ

Name-Day Night. Charles Olson. CP-OlsoC

Name Edmund, The. Adam Zagajewski. SP-ZagaA, *tr. by* Clare Cavanagh

Name for a curtain at night. Encounter. W. S. Merwin. SP-MerwW

Name for All, A. Hart Crane. CP-CranH

Name in a footnote. Faceless name. Crispus Attucks. Robert Earl Hayden. CP-HaydR

Name is spelled without letters how can this be, The. First Figure. Michael Palmer. SP-PalmM

Name Is Too Familiar, The. Ogden Nash. CP-NashO

Name names, Paul Goodman. Black Mt. College Has a Few Words for a Visitor. Charles Olson. CP-OlsoC

Name not his deed: in shuddering and in haste. Earth's Shame, The. G. K. Chesterton. CP-ChesG

Name of a fact: at home in that leafy world, The. Thoughts on Looking into a Thicket. John Ciardi. CP-CiarJ

Name—of it—is "Autumn," The. Name—of it—is "Autumn," The. Emily Dickinson. CP-DickE

Name of Jesus, The. Christina Georgina Rossetti. CP-RosC2

Name of Old Glory, The. James Whitcomb Riley. CP-RileJ

Name of the author is the first to go, The. Forgetfulness. Billy Collins. SP-CollB

Name of the Place "Trieste," The. Yehuda Amichai. SP-AmicYL, *tr. by* Benjamin Harshav *and* Barbara Harshav

Name? Rank? Regiment? Number? Reveille. Tennessee Williams. CP-WillT

Name the Gallic exile bore, The. Name, A. John Greenleaf Whittier. CP-WhitJ

Name the Gods! D. H. Lawrence. CP-LawrD

Name the thing knowledge—name it liberty. Free Love: A Sonnet. G. K. Chesterton. CP-ChesG

Name Us a King. Carl Sandburg. CP-SandC

Name Us No Names No More. James Whitcomb Riley. CP-RileJ

Named them / and they danced. Orpheus. Donald Davie. CP-DaviDC

Nameless. James Dickey. CP-DickJ

Nameless and gay my days have been. Apology, An. G. K. Chesterton. CP-ChesG

Nameless lavender, a lavender of April, A. April. Dan Pagis. SP-PagiD, *tr. by* Stephen Mitchell

Nameless Thing. Robert Penn Warren. CP-WarrR

Nameless Voyage, The. James Laughlin. CP-LaugJ

Nameless / white poppy. White Summer Flower. W. S. Merwin. SP-MerwWF

Names. Hayden Carruth. CP-CarHS

Names. Samuel Taylor Coleridge. CP-ColeS

Names. Robert Creeley. CP-CreeR

Names. Robert Earl Hayden. CP-HaydR

Names. Derek Walcott. CP-WalcD

Names, The. Robert Browning. CP-BroR2; SP-BroR

Names, The. Robert Creeley. CP-CreeR

Names, The. Allen Ginsberg. CP-GinsA; SP-GinsA

Names and things named don't match. Essex. Donald Davie. CP-DaviDC

Name's another thing, A. My Shepherd. Heather McHugh. SP-McHuH

Names of Horses. Donald Hall. CP-HallD

Names of the Hare, The. *Unknown*. SP-HeanSO, *tr. by* Seamus Heaney

Namesake. G. K. Chesterton. CP-ChesG

Namesake, The. Wyatt Prunty. SP-PrunW

Naming for Love. Hayden Carruth. CP-CarHS

Naming the Beast. Sam Hamill. SP-HamiS

Nanao and myself at the pond. Hobo Bird. Peter Blue Cloud. SP-BlueP

Nanao Knows. Gary Snyder. CP-SnydG

Nancy finally. Memory ("Nancy finally"). Robert Creeley. SP-CreeR

Nancy Hanks dreams by the fire. Fire-Logs. Carl Sandburg. CP-SandC

Nancy, Jimmy, Larry, Frank, & Berdie. Lady. Ted Berrigan. SP-BerrT

Nancy where art thou? Ezra Pound. *See* Ain' committed no federal crime

Nandin's Tail. Eleanor Wilner. SP-WilnE

Nanine. Ambrose Bierce. SP-BierA

Nanny was Irish, I told my mother, *born* in Scotland. Children's Ward, The. Jane Cooper. CP-CoopJ

Nansen. Gary Snyder. CP-SnydG

Nantucket. William Carlos Williams. CP-WilW1

Nantucket Morning / This World. Gregory Orr. SP-OrrG

Nap. Mona Van Duyn. SP-VanDM

Naphtha. Frank O'Hara. SP-OharF

Naples. John Greenleaf Whittier. CP-WhitJ

Naples, too credulous, ah! boast no more. John Milton. *See* Why, credulous Naples, do you vaunt your clear-voiced Siren

Napoléon. George Meredith. CP-MerG1

Napoleon. Robert Lowell. SP-LoweR

Napoleon. Walter De la Mare. CP-DeLaW

Napoleon on St. Helena. Bonapartisme. Kenneth Rexroth. CP-RexrK

Napoleon shifted / Restless in the old sarcophagus. Statistics. Carl Sandburg.

CP-SandC

Napoleon III in Italy. Elizabeth Barrett Browning. CP-BroEB

Napoleon!—years ago, and that great word. Crowned and Buried. Elizabeth Barrett Browning. CP-BroEB

Napoleon's Farewell. Lord Byron. CP-Byron

Napoleon's hat is an obvious choice I guess to list as a famous hat. List of Famous Hats, The. James Tate. SP-TateJ

Napoleon's Snuff-Box. Lord Byron. CP-Byron

Narcisses: Vision and Retrospect. John Logan. CP-LogaJ

Narcissus. Federico García Lorca.
Door. CP-GarcF, *tr. by* Jerome Rothenberg
I. CP-GarcF, *tr. by* Jerome Rothenberg

Narcissus. Federico García Lorca. CP-GarcF, *tr. by* Alan S. Trueblood *Fr.* Three Portraits with Shading.

Narcissus. D. H. Lawrence. CP-LawrD

Narcissus. Federico García Lorca. SP-GarcF, *tr. by* William Jay Smith

Narcissus. Rainer Maria Rilke. CP-RilkFr, *tr. by* A. Poulin, Jr.

Narcissus. May Sarton. SP-SartM

Narcissus. Louis Zukofsky. CP-ZukLS

Narcissus in the Desert. Nicolas Calas. CP-WilW1

Narcissus Moving. John Berryman. CP-BerrJ

Narcissus. / The smell of you. Federico García Lorca. CP-GarcF, *tr. by* Alan S. Trueblood *Fr.* Love.

Narcissus 2. Alan Dugan. CP-DugaA

Narcissus Unbound. William Dickey. SP-DickW

Narcissus. / Your fragrance. Narcissus. Federico García Lorca. SP-GarcF, *tr. by* William Jay Smith

Narcotic Alcohol. Ezra Pound. CP-PoEar

Narrative. George Oppen. CP-OppGN

Narrative, A. George Oppen. CP-OppGN

Narrow backyard garden, The. Hermes and Mr Shaw. Donald Davie. CP-DaviDC

Narrow-bodied, iron head like the flat side. Sturgeon, The. Raymond Carver. CP-CarvR

Narrow Escape, A. James Merrill. SP-MerrJ

Narrow girdle of rough stones and crags, A. William Wordsworth. CP-WorW1; MW-WorW

Narrow Hemisphere, The. Marya Alexandrovna Zaturenska. SP-ZatuM

Narrow Road to the Deep North, The. Paul Muldoon. CP-MuldP

Narrow Sea, The. Robert Graves. CP-GravR

Narrow street rears up from memory, The. From Memory. Adam Zagajewski. SP-ZagaA, *tr. by* Clare Cavanagh

Narrow Way, The. Jones Very. CP-VeryJ

Narrowing line. / Walking on the burning ground, The. What Is the Beautiful? Kenneth Patchen. CP-PatcK

Nashe's old queens who bartered young and fair. Lament: "Nashe's old queens who bartered young and fair." Richard Wilbur. CP-WilbR

Nashville Mornings. Donald Davie. CP-DaviDC

Naso! an elevated personage. Carmen 112. Catullus. CP-ZukLS *Fr.* Carmina.

Nasturtium. Thom Gunn. CP-GunnT

Nasty surprise in a sandwich, A. God, A Poem. James Fenton. SP-FentJ

Nasuh. Jelaluddin Rumi. SP-Rumi, *tr. by* Coleman Barks

Nat Bacon's Bones. Archibald MacLeish. CP-MacLA

Natcha, offering love. Langston Hughes. CP-HughL; CP-HughL1

Nathaniel Hawthorne. Robert Creeley. CP-CreeR

Nation. George Oppen. CP-OppGN

Nation, A. Czeslaw Milosz. CP-MiloC; CP-MiloCN, *tr. by* Robert Hass

Nation spoke to a Nation, A. Our Lady of the Snows. Rudyard Kipling. CP-KiplR

National Anthem; Imitation of Carlos Drummond de Andrade's "*Hino Nacional*" Robert Stock. SP-StocR

National Gallery, The. Louis MacNeice. CP-MacNL

National Security. Archibald MacLeish. CP-MacLA

National Thanksgiving, The. Jones Very. CP-VeryJ

National Thoughts. Yehuda Amichai. SP-AmicY, *tr. by* Stephen Mitchell

National Thoughts. Yehuda Amichai. SP-AmicYL, *tr. by* Benjamin Harshav *and* Barbara Harshav

National Unity ("Nobler unity, than that which came, A"). Jones Very. CP-VeryJ

National Unity ("Unity complete, assured, and high, A"). Jones Very. CP-VeryJ

Nationality in Drinks. Robert Browning. CP-BroR1

Nations and kings conspire against the Lord. Conspiracy, The. Jones Very. CP-VeryJ

Nations have used up their desire, The. Madder. C. K. Williams. CP-WillC

Nation's Life of Slow Growth, A. Jones Very. CP-VeryJ

Nations ten thousand years before these States, and many times ten thousand years before these States. Unnamed Lands. Walt Whitman. CP-WhitW

Native. Rae Armantrout. SP-ArmaA

Native. Olga Broumas. SP-BrouO

Native-Born, The. Rudyard Kipling. CP-KiplR

Native Moments. Walt Whitman. CP-WhitW

Native Speech. Philip Whalen. SP-WhalP

Native Wisdom. Thomas Kinsella. CP-KinsT

Natives here have given up their backyards, The. Champagne. Rita Dove. SP-DoveR

Native's myth, as lavish as the night, The. Improvisation for a Southern Night. John Ciardi. CP-CiarJ

Nativity. Joseph Brodsky. CP-BrodJ

Nativity. May Sarton. SP-SartM

Nativity, A. Rudyard Kipling. CP-KiplR

Nativity, A. William Butler Yeats. CP-YeatW

Nativity, The. G. K. Chesterton. CP-ChesG

Nativity, The. Jeanne Marie Bouvier de la Motte- Guyon. CP-CowpW

Nativity by Botticelli, The. G. K. Chesterton. CP-ChesG

Nativity Poem. Louise Glück. SP-GlucL

Natura Naturans. Arthur Hugh Clough. SP-ClouA

Natura Naturans. Kathleen Jessie Raine. SP-RainK

Natural Complexion. D. H. Lawrence. CP-LawrD

Natural Enemies of the Conch, The. Alan Dugan. CP-DugaA

Natural History. Rae Armantrout. SP-ArmaA

Natural History. Sam Hamill. SP-HamiS

Natural History. Thomas Merton. CP-MertT

Natural History. Sylvia Plath. CP-PlatS

Natural History. Robert Penn Warren. CP-WarrR

Natural History. Eleanor Wilner. SP-WilnE

Natural Linguistics. W. H. Auden. CP-AudeW

Natural Magic. Robert Browning. CP-BroR2

Natural Music. Robinson Jeffers. CP-JefR1

Natural Perversities. James Whitcomb Riley. CP-RileJ

Natural Question. John Updike. CP-UpdiJ

Natural Resources. Adrienne Rich. SP-RicA2

Natural Star. Alice Walker. CP-WalkA

Natural strange beatitudes. Cycle. Geoffrey Hill. CP-HillG

Natural, The. George Oppen. CP-OppGN

Natural Theology. Rudyard Kipling. CP-KiplR

Naturalist, The. James Whitcomb Riley. CP-RileJ

Naturally it is night. Air: "Naturally it is night." W. S. Merwin. SP-MerwW

Naturally tender, flesh and such. Under the Skin of It. Gary Snyder. CP-SnydG

Naturally the Foundation Will Bear Your Expenses. Philip Larkin. CP-LarkP

Nature. Robert Creeley. SP-CreeR

Nature. Ralph Waldo Emerson. CP-EmerR

Nature. George Herbert. CP-HerbG

Nature. Henry Wadsworth Longfellow. SP-LongH

Nature. Mary Oliver. SP-OlivM

Nature. May Swenson. SP-SwenM

Nature. Henry David Thoreau. CP-ThorH

Nature. John Updike. CP-UpdiJ

Nature ("Bubbling brook doth leap when I come by, The"). Jones Very. CP-VeryJ

Nature ("I love to sit on the green hill's side"). Jones Very. CP-VeryJ

Nature ("Nature, my love for thee is deeper far"). Jones Very. CP-VeryJ

Nature ("Nature would speak through her first master man"). Jones Very. CP-VeryJ

Nature 1. Ralph Waldo Emerson. CP-EmerR

Nature 2. Ralph Waldo Emerson. CP-EmerR

Nature [1836]. Ralph Waldo Emerson. CP-EmerR
(Motto to "Nature") CP-EmerR

Nature [1844]. Ralph Waldo Emerson. CP-EmerR
(Motto to "Nature") CP-EmerR

Nature a Living Teacher. Jones Very. CP-VeryJ

Nature affects to be sedate. Emily Dickinson. CP-DickE

Nature Alive. Jorge Guillén. CP-WrigJ

Nature and Art. Paul Laurence Dunbar. CP-DunbP

Nature and Free Animals. Stevie Smith. CP-SmitS

Nature and God—I neither knew. Emily Dickinson. CP-DickE

Nature and Life. George Meredith. CP-MerG1

Nature and Man. George Meredith. CP-MerG2

Nature and Nature's Laws lay hid in Night. Intended for Sir Isaac Newton. Alexander Pope. CP-PopeA

Nature & Art in this together Suit. Pretty Epigram for [Those] the Entertainment of Those Who [Pay] Have Paid Great Sums in the Venetian & Flemish Ooze, A. William Blake. CP-BlakW

Nature Assigns the Sun. Emily Dickinson. CP-DickE

Nature assigns the Sun. Nature Assigns the Sun. Emily Dickinson. CP-DickE

Nature, by nature, has no answers. Saturday Morning Journal. Charles Wright. SP-WrigC

Nature can do no more. Emily Dickinson. CP-DickE

Nature centres into balls. Circles. Ralph Waldo Emerson. CP-EmerR

Nature Does Not Suffer Decay. John Milton. CP-MiltJ
(Nature Unimpaired by Time.) CP-CowpW

Nature doth have her dawn each day. Stanzas. Henry David Thoreau. CP-ThorH

Nature from life by piece and piece. Of Experience. Howard Nemerov. CP-NemeH

Nature gives her love. Emily Dickinson. SP-DickE

Nature had long a treasure made. Match, The. Andrew Marvell. CP-MarvA

Nature had made them hide in crevices. New Hampshire, February. Richard Eberhart. CP-EberR

Nature has her sickly years. Potato Blight, The. Jones Very. CP-VeryJ

Nature here / is the multiplicity of luck. Mirror in the Roadway, The. Charles Tomlinson. CP-TomlC

Nature Intelligible. Jones Very. CP-VeryJ

Nature invades: old rooks in each college garden. Oxford. W. H. Auden. CP-AudeW

Nature is a Haunted House. Emily Dickinson. SP-DickE

Nature is full of teeth. Wall, The. Anne Sexton. CP-SextA

Nature is our eldest mother. Emily Dickinson. SP-DickE

"Nature" is what we see. Emily Dickinson. CP-DickE

Nature Knows Best. Ogden Nash. CP-NashO

Nature knows what it's doing: one cruel as you. Michelangelo Buonarroti. CP-Miche, tr. by John Frederick Nims

Nature Morte. Joseph Brodsky. CP-BrodJ, tr. by George L. Kline

Nature Morte. Louis MacNeice. CP-MacNL

Nature Morte. Howard Nemerov. CP-NemeH

Nature must be too young to feel. Emily Dickinson. SP-DickE

Nature, my love for thee is deeper far. Nature. Jones Very. CP-VeryJ

Nature? No, not Nature. Robinson Jeffers at Point Sur. Donald Davie. CP-DaviDC

Nature Note, A. Robert Frost. CP-FrosR

Nature Note: The California Poison Oak. Helen Pinkerton. CP-PinkH

Nature Notes. Louis MacNeice. CP-MacNL

Nature of a Mirror, The. Robert Penn Warren. CP-WarrR

Nature of an Action, The. Thom Gunn. CP-GunnT

Nature of This City, The. Grace Paley. CP-PalGC

Nature of This Flower Is to Bloom, The. Alice Walker. CP-WalkA

Nature Poem. Charles Tomlinson. CP-TomlC

Nature Poem: Demanding Stiff Sentences. James Tate. SP-TateJ

Nature rarer uses Yellow. Emily Dickinson. CP-DickE

Nature repeats her lessons; day and night. Nature Repeats Her Lessons. Jones Very. CP-VeryJ

Nature responds so beautifully. Roses. D. H. Lawrence. CP-LawrD

Nature saith / I am not infinite. Ralph Waldo Emerson. CP-EmerR

Nature says, / These craggy hills that front the dawn. Ralph Waldo Emerson. CP-EmerR

Nature seemed monstrous to his thirteen years. Orient and Immortal Wheat. Derek Walcott. CP-WalcD

Nature, seems it to myself. Emily Dickinson. SP-DickE

Nature, so far as in her lies. On a Mourner. Alfred Tennyson. CP-TennA

Nature—sometimes sears a Sapling. Emily Dickinson. CP-DickE

Nature Teaches Only Love. Jones Very. CP-VeryJ

Nature Teaches Us of Time and Its Duration. Jones Very. CP-VeryJ

Nature that gave the bee so feat a grace. Sir Thomas Wyatt. CP-WyatT

Nature that washt her hands in milke. Poem of Sir Walter Rawleighs, A. Sir Walter Ralegh. CP-RaleW

Nature—the Gentlest Mother is. Emily Dickinson. CP-DickE

Nature, through these generations. Genitrix Laesa. Thomas Hardy. CP-HardT

Nature Unimpaired by Time. John Milton. See Nature Does Not Suffer Decay

Nature-Walks, or, Not to Mention a Dopping of Sheldrakes. Ogden Nash. CP-NashO

Nature will not lose. Ralph Waldo Emerson. CP-EmerR

Nature within her inmost self divides. From Iron. Robert Frost. CP-FrosR

Nature would speak through her first master man. Nature ("Nature would speak through her first master man"). Jones Very. CP-VeryJ

Nature's faithful Blossoms. Emily Dickinson. SP-DickE

Nature's first green is gold. Nothing Gold Can Stay. Robert Frost. CP-FrosR

Nature's Help for the Soul. Jones Very. CP-VeryJ

Nature's Invitation. Jones Very. CP-VeryJ

Nature's Law. Robert Burns. CP-BurnR

Nature's lay idiot [or ideot], I taught thee to love. John Donne. MW-DonnJ Fr. Elegies.

Nature's Lineaments. Robert Graves. CP-GravR

Nature's Questioning. Thomas Hardy. CP-HardT

Nature's Remorses. Elizabeth Barrett Browning. CP-BroEB

Nature's Thanksgiving. Tennessee Williams. CP-WillT

Natures web star broidered. Ralph Waldo Emerson. CP-EmerR

Naught are all Women: I say no. Defence for Women, A. Robert Herrick. CP-HerrR

Naughty Boy. Robert Creeley. CP-CreeR

Naughty Child, The. Langston Hughes. CP-HughL; CP-HughL1

Naughty Claude. James Whitcomb Riley. CP-RileJ

Nauhaught, the Deacon. John Greenleaf Whittier. CP-WhitJ

Naulahka, The. Rudyard Kipling.

  "Beat off in our last fight were we?" CP-KiplR

  "Because I sought it far from men." CP-KiplR

  "Beware the man who's crossed in love." CP-KiplR

  Kingdom, The. CP-KiplR

  Lie, The. CP-KiplR

  My Lady's Law. CP-KiplR

  "Now it is not good for the Christian's health to hustle the Aryan brown." CP-KiplR

  Nursing Sister, The. CP-KiplR

  Sack of the Gods, The. CP-KiplR

  "There was a strife 'twixt man and maid." CP-KiplR

  "This I saw when the rites were done." CP-KiplR

  "We be the Gods of the East." CP-KiplR

  "We meet in an evil land." CP-KiplR

  "When a lover hies abroad." CP-KiplR

  "Will they gape for the husks that ye proffer." CP-KiplR

  "Your patience, Sirs. The Devil took me up." CP-KiplR

Naumkeck River. Jones Very. CP-VeryJ

Nausea. William Meredith. SP-MereW

Nausea, Coincidence. James Tate. SP-TateJ

Nauset Billerica — to get the fid in. Encounter, The. Charles Olson. CP-OlsoC

Nautilus Island's hermit. Skunk Hour. Robert Lowell. SP-LoweR

Navajo. William Carlos Williams. CP-WilW2

Navajo Blanket, The. Maurice Sendak. SP-SwenM

Navajo Setting the Record Straight. John Berryman. CP-BerrJ

Naval Battle, The. Constantine P. Cavafy. CP-CavaC, *tr.* by Theoharis Constantine Theoharis

Navigator. Charles Simic. SP-SimiCE

Navigator. Charles Simic. SP-SimiC

Navigator of the day, The. Helmsmen, The. W. S. Merwin. SP-MerwWF

Navigators. Thomas Kinsella. CP-KinsT

Navigators, The. Marilyn Hacker.

  "Across the mud flats and the wide roads, over rivers and borders." SP-HackM

  "Between us on our wide bed we cuddle an incubus." SP-HackM

  His Wife at Bellevue. SP-HackM

  "Orpheus and animus, / drawing back to journeys now." SP-HackM

  "When you told me that he was in jail." SP-HackM

  "You made algebra: his tastes in food." SP-HackM

Navy Field. William Meredith. SP-MereW

Nay but you, who do not love her. Song: "Nay but you, who do not love her." Robert Browning. CP-BroR1

Nay Cousin, Dearest. Elixir. D. H. Lawrence. CP-LawrD

Nay, dearest Anna! why so grave? To a Lady. Samuel Taylor Coleridge. CP-ColeS

Nay, Death, thou mightiest of all. General Lew Wallace. James Whitcomb Riley. CP-RileJ

Nay, do not dream, designer dark. Death's Valley. Walt Whitman. CP-WhitW

Nay draw not yet the cork, my friend. Arthur Hugh Clough. SP-ClouA

Nay, if I had come back so. Where's Agnes? Elizabeth Barrett Browning. CP-BroEB

Nay, learnèd doctor, these fine leeches fresh. Edna St. Vincent Millay. CP-MillE

Nay, let us walk from fire unto fire. Panthea. Oscar Wilde. CP-WildO

Nay, Lord, not thus! white lilies in the spring. Sonnet on Hearing the *Dies Iræ* Sung in the Sistine Chapel. Oscar Wilde. CP-WildO

Nay, nay, / You must not stay. Ben Jonson. CP-JonsB *Fr.* Oberon, the Fairy Prince.

Nay, read & spare not, Passenger. Epitaph on a Man who Had a Scold to His Wife. Robert Herrick. CP-HerrR

Nay, Tell Me Not To-day the Publish'd Shame. Walt Whitman. CP-WhitW

Nay, that, Furini, never I at least. With Francis Furini. Robert Browning. CP-BroR2

Nay, Traveller. Lines: "Nay, Traveller." William Wordsworth. CP-WorW1; MW-WorW

Nazi at the Puppet Show, The. Thomas Lux. SP-LuxT

Nazi Doll, The. Yusef Komunyakaa. CP-KomuY

Ndebele. Alice Walker. CP-WalkA

Ne manquez pas à Stuttgart. Samuel Beckett. CP-BeckS

Ne manquez pas à Tanger. Samuel Beckett. CP-BeckS

Ne Plus Ultra. Samuel Taylor Coleridge. CP-ColeS; MW-ColeS

Ne' sogni ti veggo. Christina Georgina Rossetti. CP-RosC3

Ne tu me crudelis ames, nec basia labris. Ad Caspiam. Thomas Campion. CP-CampT

Neaera when I'm there is adamant. George Buchanan. CP-CunnJ, *tr.* by James Vincent Cunningham

Neal Cassady was my animal: he brought me to my knees. Many Loves. Allen Ginsberg. CP-GinsA; SP-GinsA

Near. William Stafford. SP-StafW; SP-StafWW

Near a bright-lit tobacco shop window. Tobacco Shop Window, The. Constantine P. Cavafy. CP-CavaC, *tr.* by Theoharis Constantine Theoharis

Near Alexandria. Joseph Brodsky. CP-BrodJ

Near and the Far, The. Charles Tomlinson. CP-TomlC

Near are we, Lord. Tenebrae. Paul Celan. SP-CelaP, *tr.* by John Felstiner

Near Brussels—A Half-way Pause. Dante Gabriel Rossetti. CW-RossD

Near Capua. Eugenio Montale. CP-MontE, *tr.* by Jonathan Galassi

Near Ceibwr. Charles Tomlinson. CP-TomlC

Near Corinium. Charles Tomlinson. CP-TomlC

Near Darien. James Dickey. CP-DickJ

Near Dover, September 1802. William Wordsworth. CP-WorW1; MW-WorW (September, 1802. Near Dover.) CP-WorW1

Near Eclipse, The. Robert Graves. CP-GravR

Near, far, unearthly, break the birds. Dawn. Walter De la Mare. CP-DeLaW

Near Finistère. Eugenio Montale. CP-MontE, *tr.* by Jonathan Galassi

Near Hartland. Charles Tomlinson. CP-TomlC

Near, in the aorta's arch. Paul Celan. SP-CelaP, *tr.* by John Felstiner

Near Keokuk. Carl Sandburg. CP-SandC

Near Klamath. Raymond Carver. CP-CarvR

Near Lanivet, 1872. Thomas Hardy. CP-HardT

Near Mexico, near April, in the morning. Target Practice. Muriel Rukeyser. CP-RukeM

Near on Salem's rocky shore. Baker's Island Light, The. Jones Very. CP-VeryJ

Near Pah-Gotzin-Kay. Thomas McGrath. SP-McGrT

Near Perigord. Ezra Pound. SP-PounE

Near Rhyme. Rae Armantrout. SP-ArmaA

Near Siena. Eugenio Montale. CP-MontE, *tr.* by Jonathan Galassi

Near Sonnet. Andrei Codrescu. SP-CodrA

Near Spring. Ivor Gurney. SP-GurnI

Near the beginning was the horse. George Oppen. CP-OppGN

Near the big spruce, on the path that goes. Squire Hazard Walks. William Meredith. SP-MereW

Near the Bridge of Saint-Cloud. Norman Dubie. CP-DubiN

Near the dry river's water-mark we found. Note Left in Jimmy Leonard's Shack, A. James Wright. CP-WrigJ

Near the eighth tee, sixty yards off into the words from the green links. Chanterelles, The. Josephine Jacobsen. CP-JacoJ

Near the Giant's House. Robert Bly. SP-BlyR

Near the Haunted Castle. C. K. Williams. CP-WillC; SP-WillC

Near the lone pile with ivy overspread. Elegy Imitated from One of Akenside's Blank-Verse Inscriptions. Samuel Taylor Coleridge. CP-ColeS

Near the Ocean. Robert Lowell. SP-LoweR

Near the Old People's Home. Howard Nemerov. CP-NemeH

Near the peak. A clear morning. Pilgrimage. Robert Pinsky. CP-PinsR

Near the top a bad turn some dare. Well. Whether There Is Sorrow in the Demons. John Berryman. CP-BerrJ

Near the train, we saw layers of rock in a row. I Told You It Would Be So—And You Didn't Believe. Yehuda Amichai. SP-AmicYL, *tr.* by Benjamin Harshav *and* Barbara Harshav

Near the wall of a house painted. Yehuda Amichai. SP-AmicY, *tr.* by Chana Bloch

Near the waterfront / Mouth of a wide shed open. Burnishing, Oakland. Muriel Rukeyser. CP-RukeM

Near Vienna. Eugenio Montale. CP-MontE, *tr.* by Jonathan Galassi

Near York. Charles Tomlinson. CP-TomlC

Near your eyes. George Oppen. CP-OppGN

Near Zermatt: The Drahtseilbahn. James Laughlin. CP-LaugJ

Nearer:breath of my breath:take not thy tingling. E. E. Cummings. CP-CummE

Nearest Dream recedes—unrealized, The. Emily Dickinson. CP-DickE

Nearing Forty. Derek Walcott. CP-WalcD

Nearly. Raymond Carver. CP-CarvR

Nearly. Laura Riding Jackson. CP-RidiL

Nearly a landscape. The full figure count. At Carol Willink's Exhibition. Joseph Brodsky. CP-BrodJ, *tr.* by Jamey Gambrell

Nearly expressed obscurity. Nearly. Laura Riding Jackson. CP-RidiL

Nearly landless and on the way to water. Lorine Niedecker. CP-NiedL

Nearly right, The. To the Tune of The Coventry Carol. Stevie Smith. CP-SmitS

Nearness of Graves. Paul Celan. SP-CelaP, *tr.* by John Felstiner

Nearness of remoteness like a lion's eye, The. Revenant, The. Louis MacNeice. CP-MacNL

Nearness to Tremendousness, A. Emily Dickinson. CP-DickE

Nearsighted child has taken off her glasses, The. Country Stars. William Meredith. SP-MereW

Neat person. Shang Dynasty Oracle Bone 2 Say. Charles Olson. CP-OlsoC

Neat sky was tall, full of sliding birds, The. Study for a Geographical Trail. Clarence Major. SP-MajoC

'Neath a shed-roof that shouldered the tempest. Song of the Cradle, The. G. K. Chesterton. CP-ChesG

'Neath my moon what doest thou. Night and the Merry Man. Elizabeth Barrett Browning. CP-BroEB

'Neath skies that winter never knew. "I Was a Stranger and Ye Took Me in" John Greenleaf Whittier. CP-WhitJ

Neatness Is All. Kenneth Rexroth. CP-RexrK

Nebraska. Karl Shapiro. SP-ShapK

Nebuchadnezzar, Solus. Howard Nemerov. CP-NemeH

Nebuchadnezzar the King of the Jews. Pioneers, O Pioneers. G. K. Chesterton. CP-ChesG

Nebuchadnezzar's Dream. John Keats. CP-KeatJ

Nebulous, freezingly moist. Winter's Talents. Donald Davie. CP-DaviDC

Necessarily, we must think of the. Interjection #2: Caveat. Robert Penn Warren. CP-WarrR

Necessary Dirge, A. Ogden Nash. CP-NashO

Necessary Explanation. Yannis Ritsos. SP-RitsY, *tr.* by Kimon Friar

Necessitarian, The. Rudyard Kipling. CP-KiplR

Necessitarian's Epitaph, A. Thomas Hardy. CP-HardT

Necessities of Life. Adrienne Rich. CP-RicAE; SP-RicA1; SP-RicA2

Necessity. Richard Eberhart. CP-EberR

Necessity. Langston Hughes. CP-HughL; CP-HughL3

Necessity, The. Denise Levertov. SP-LeveDP

Necessity of Faith, The. Wendell Berry. CP-BerrW

Necessity of Self-Abasement. Jeanne Marie Bouvier de la Motte- Guyon. CP-CowpW

Necessity, the impact of whose sidelong course. Old Actor Addresses Julius Caesar, An. Decimus Laberius. CP-CunnJ, *tr.* by James Vincent Cunningham

Neck of, The. Real, The. Charles Olson. CP-OlsoC

Necklace, The. Robert Graves. CP-GravR

Necrological. John Crowe Ransom. SP-RansJ

Necromance. Rae Armantrout. SP-ArmaA

Necropolis. Karl Shapiro. SP-ShapK

Ned Bratts. Robert Browning. CP-BroR2; SP-BroR

Ned Skinner. Paul Muldoon. CP-MuldP

Need. Robert Herrick. CP-HerrR

Need, The. David Ignatow. SP-IgnaD

Need: A Chorale for Black Woman Voices. Audre Lorde. SP-LordA

Need for Dictionaries II, The. Thomas McGrath. SP-McGrT

Need For Hell, A. Laura Riding Jackson. CP-RidiL

Need for Stoicism in the Stoa of Attalus, The. Thomas McGrath. SP-McGrT

Need gotta be, The. Blue Light Lounge Sutra for the Performance Poets at Harold Park Hotel. Yusef Komunyakaa. CP-KomuY

Need is no vice at all; though here it be. Want. Robert Herrick. CP-HerrR

Need of Being Versed in Country Things, The. Robert Frost. CP-FrosR

Need of Proof. Yannis Ritsos. SP-RitsY, *tr.* by Kimon Friar

Need of this man was her ignoble secret:. Lamia in Love. Robert Graves. CP-GravR

Need to Confide, The. Laura Riding Jackson. CP-RidiL

Need to Express. Yannis Ritsos. SP-RitsY, *tr.* by Andonis Decavalles

Need to Win, The. Chuang Tzu. CP-MertT, *tr.* by Thomas Merton

Needing one, I invented her. Aunt Leaf. Mary Oliver. SP-OlivM

Needle. Charles Simic. SP-SimiCE

Needle, The. Ezra Pound. CP-PoEar

Needle, needle, dip and dart. Satin Dress, The. Dorothy Parker. CP-ParkD

Needle-point's swaying reminder, The. Way In, The. Charles Tomlinson. CP-TomlC; SP-TomlC

Needle small, as small can be, A. Ænigma, An. Vincent Bourne. CP-CowpW

Needled by death for change, for simple change. Vegetable Garden, The. Wyatt Prunty. SP-PrunW

Needle's Eye, A. William Butler Yeats. CP-YeatW

Needles of the pine, The. Henry David Thoreau. CP-ThorH

Needless Alarm, The. William Cowper. CP-CowpW

Needs. A. R. Ammons. CP-AmmoA

Needs most / happily mutual. Night ("Needs most / happily mutual"). Robert Creeley. CP-CreeR

Ne'er felt I parting from a woman loved. Partenza di Venezia. Ezra Pound. CP-PoEar

"NEFAS" / the Roman said. Philip Whalen. SP-WhalP

Negation. Wallace Stevens. CP-StevW; CP-StevWP

Negative. Wisława Szymborska. SP-SzymWM, *tr.* by Joanna Trzeciak

Negative Hands. Pablo Neruda. SP-NeruP

Negative Indicative. Philip Larkin. CP-LarkP

Negative Love. John Donne. CP-DonnJ; MW-DonnJ

Negative, The. Arthur Sze. SP-SzeA

Negatives. Derek Walcott. CP-WalcD

Negatives 2. Charles Wright. SP-WrigCN

Neglect. Robert Herrick. CP-HerrR

Neglect. C. K. Williams. SP-WillC

Neglected Child, The. G. K. Chesterton. CP-ChesG

Neglected now is the old guitar. Old Guitar, The. James Whitcomb Riley. CP-RileJ

Negress, A. Stéphane Mallarmé. CP-MallS, *tr.* by Henry Weinfield

Negress roused by demons is on fire, A. Negress, A. Stéphane Mallarmé. CP-MallS, *tr.* by Henry Weinfield

Negress serene though underground. Eurydice. John Updike. CP-UpdiJ

Negro. Langston Hughes. CP-HughL

(Proem.) CP-HughL1

Negro Cemetery Next to a White One, A. Howard Nemerov. CP-NemeH

Negro Dancers. Langston Hughes. CP-HughL; CP-HughL1

Negro Ghetto. Langston Hughes. CP-HughL; CP-HughL1

"Negro" Hero. Gwendolyn Brooks. SP-BrooG

Negro Love Song, A. Paul Laurence Dunbar. CP-DunbP

Negro Mother, The. Langston Hughes. CP-HughL1

Negro Mother's Lullaby, A. Countee Cullen. CP-CullC

Negro Servant. Langston Hughes. CP-HughL; CP-HughL2

Negro Speaks of Rivers, The. Langston Hughes. CP-HughL; CP-HughL1

Negro, / With the trumpet at his lips, The. Trumpet Player. Langston Hughes. CP-HughL; CP-HughL2

Negro Woman, A. William Carlos Williams. CP-WilW2

Negroes, / Sweet and docile. Roland Hayes Beaten (Georgia: 1942). Langston Hughes. CP-HughL2

Negro's Complaint, The. William Cowper. CP-CowpW

Neighbor. Langston Hughes. CP-HughL; CP-HughL3

Neighbor, The. Marge Piercy. SP-PierM

Neighbor, The. Miller Williams. CP-WillM

Neighbor of mine in the village, A. Girl's Garden, A. Robert Frost. CP-FrosR

Neighbor / rejects chemotherapy and the hospital, A. Cloud Chamber, The. Arthur Sze. SP-SzeA

Neighborhood. William Corbett. SP-CorbW

Neighborhood of Make-Believe, The. Thomas Lux. SP-LuxT

Neighbors. Robert Creeley. SP-CreeR

Neighbors. David Ignatow. SP-IgnaD

Neighbors. Audre Lorde. SP-LordA

Neighbors. George Oppen. CP-OppGN

Neighbors. Gregory Orr. SP-OrrG

Neighbors. Edwin Arlington Robinson. CP-RobiE

Neighbors. Carl Sandburg. CP-SandC

Neighbors. James Tate. SP-TateJ

Neighbors' dog will not stop barking, The. Another Reason Why I Don't Keep a Gun in the House. Billy Collins. SP-CollB

Neighbors have a teenaged girl, The. Below the hill. Music. William Meredith. SP-MereW

Neighbors, please don't. Ogoni. Yusef Komunyakaa. CP-KomuY

Neighbours. Rudyard Kipling. CP-KiplR

Neither all nor any angels arrive in the mind where. Popham of the New Song. Norman Dubie. CP-DubiN

Neither awake / (there's your general). E. E. Cummings. CP-CummE

Neither Blood Nor Bowed. Dorothy Parker. CP-ParkD

Neither childhood / nor future. Confession. George Oppen. CP-OppGN

Neither could say / (it comes so slow). E. E. Cummings. CP-CummE

Neither daylight, starlight, moonlight. Twilight Stories. James Whitcomb Riley. CP-RileJ

Neither dead nor alive, neither asleep nor awake. Revenge for Love. Donald Davie. CP-DaviDC

Neither fearing Extinction. Emily Dickinson. SP-DickE

Neither her voice, her name. Night Dream, The. Archibald MacLeish. CP-MacLA

Neither in Heaven nor Earth. Emily Dickinson. SP-DickE

Neither of them was better than the other. From Plane to Plane. Robert Frost. CP-FrosR

Neither our vices nor our virtues. Poetry, a Natural Thing. Robert Duncan. SP-DuncR

Neither Out Far Nor In Deep. Robert Frost. CP-FrosR

Neither rose leaves were gathered in a jar—respectably in Boston—these—nor. Whirls. Carl Sandburg. CP-SandC

Neither sadness nor desire. Robert Creeley. CP-CreeR

Neither sinners nor saints, their visions maintain. Prophets, The. Robert Stock. SP-StocR

Neither the harps nor the crowns amused, nor the cherubs' dove-winged races. Return of the Children, The. Rudyard Kipling. CP-KiplR

Neither the intimacy of your look, your brow fair as a feast day. Anticipation of Love. Jorge Luis Borges. SP-BorgJ, tr. by Robert Fitzgerald

Neither the symbolic detail. Year's End. Jorge Luis Borges. SP-BorgJ, tr. by W. S. Merwin

Neither useful nor beautiful. Agave. Primo Levi. CP-LeviP, tr. by Ruth Feldman

Nel Biancheggiar. Ezra Pound. CP-PoEar

Nel mezzo del camino I found myself / in the middle class. Circle Jerk. Andrei Codrescu. SP-CodrA

Nel Mezzo del Cammin di Nostra Vita. Robert Duncan. SP-DuncR

Nel verno accanto al fuoco. Christina Georgina Rossetti. CP-RosC3

Nell and the other maids danced their best. Harvest-Supper, The. Thomas Hardy. CP-HardT

Nell Gwyn, / It says in the dictionary. King!, The. William Carlos Williams. CP-WilW2

Nell scolded in so loud a din. Quiet Life and a Good Name, A. Jonathan Swift. CP-SwifJ

Nell's Circular Poem. Christopher Logue. SP-LoguC

Nelly Myers. A. R. Ammons. CP-AmmoA

Nemesis. Ralph Waldo Emerson. CP-EmerR

Nemesis. D. H. Lawrence. CP-LawrD

Nempe ea formosa est: adeo omne quod aut facit aut fit. Incomplete Latin Version of "In all things beautiful" by Robert Bridges. Robert Bridges. CP-HopkG

Nempe sic innumero succrescunt agmine libri. Dignissimo Suo Amico Doctori Witty. Andrew Marvell. CP-MarvA

Neo-Classical Urn, The. Robert Lowell. SP-LoweR

Neo-neolithic urban nomad school of poetry, The. Fanny Howe. SP-HoweF Fr. Q.

Neoclassicist, A. Kenneth Rexroth. CP-RexrK

Neon Signs. Langston Hughes. CP-HughL; CP-HughL3

Neotony. John Updike. CP-UpdiJ

Neptune's Triumph. Ben Jonson. "Come, noble nymphs, and do not hide." CP-JonsB

Nereid, The. James Laughlin. CP-LaugJ

Nereids have departed. A century, The. Seriphos Unvisited. Amy Clampitt. CP-ClamA

Nereids of Seriphos, The. Amy Clampitt. CP-ClamA

Nero commanded; but withdrew his eyes. Cruelties. Robert Herrick. CP-HerrR

Nero did not worry when he heard. Nero's Term. Constantine P. Cavafy. CP-CavaC, tr. by Theoharis Constantine Theoharis

Nero sleeps in his royal palace. Footsteps of the Eumenides, The. Constantine P. Cavafy. CP-CavaC, tr. by Theoharis Constantine Theoharis

Nero's Term. Constantine P. Cavafy. CP-CavaC, tr. by Theoharis Constantine Theoharis

Nerthus. Seamus Heaney. SP-HeanSO

Neruda, the Wine. Muriel Rukeyser. CP-RukeM

Neruda's "Que dispierte el leñador" Allen Ginsberg. CP-GinsA

Nerve, The. Clarence Major. SP-MajoC

Nerve to make a high toss and the sense, The. Tennis. Robert Pinsky. CP-PinsR

Nerve us with patience, Lord, to toil or rest. Where Neither Rust Nor Moth Doth Corrupt. Christina Georgina Rossetti. CP-RosC2

Nerves. Robinson Jeffers. CP-JefR3

Nerves Are Staves, and When the Tears Come There Is Voice, The. Charles Olson. CP-OlsoC

Nervous face of my dear wife, The. Devil-My-Wife, The. Stevie Smith. CP-SmitS

Nervous smile as gaze meets, A. Face to Face. Denise Levertov. SP-LeveDP

Nervousness of Memory, The. Kenneth Patchen. CP-PatcK

Nervy with neons, the main drag. At Barstow. Charles Tomlinson. CP-TomlC

Nescit Vox Missa Reverti. J. V. Cunningham. CP-CunnJ

Nessmuk. James Whitcomb Riley. CP-RileJ

N'est-ce pas assez de ne me point haïr? Stevie Smith. CP-SmitS

Nest of Vampires. James Fenton. CP-FentJ

Nesting-Ground. Seamus Heaney. SP-HeanSO

Nestor's Bathtub. Rita Dove. SP-DoveR

Nests in the caves stir in the dawn. Open the Blind. Kenneth Rexroth. CP-RexrK

Nestus Gurley. Randall Jarrell. CP-JarrR

Net, The. Raymond Carver. CP-CarvR

Net-Menders, The. Sylvia Plath. CP-PlatS

Net to Snare the Moonlight, A. Nicholas Vachel Lindsay. CP-LindV

Netherlands, The. Samuel Taylor Coleridge. CP-ColeS

Nets newly tarred, The. Reapers of the Water. James Tate. SP-TateJ

Nettles, The. Thomas Hardy. CP-HardT

Nettles and poppy mar each rock-hewn seat. Theatre at Argos, The. Oscar Wilde. CP-WildO

Network. William Stafford. SP-StafWW

Network, The. Arthur Sze. SP-SzeA

Network that emerges. At the ocean, A. Muriel Rukeyser. CP-RukeM

Neurotics. Philip Larkin. CP-LarkP

Neutral island facing the Atlantic, The. Neutrality. Louis MacNeice. CP-MacNL

Neutral Tones. Thomas Hardy. CP-HardT

Neutrality. Louis MacNeice. CP-MacNL

Neutrality Loathsome. Robert Herrick. CP-HerrR

Neutrals, The. Robinson Jeffers. CP-JefR3

Neutrinos, they are very small. Cosmic Gall. John Updike. CP-UpdiJ

Never a careworn wife but shows. Wives in the Sere. Thomas Hardy. CP-HardT

Never afraid of those huge creatures. Horseback. Carolyn Kizer. CP-KizeC

Never Again. Stevie Smith. CP-SmitS

Never again remind me of it. Bank Account. Robert Graves. CP-GravR

Never again / When the heat overwhelms us. Long Hot Summer. Archibald MacLeish. CP-MacLA

Never Again Would Birds' Song Be The Same. Robert Frost. CP-FrosR

Never alone / While over unending sky. Cloud. Kathleen Jessie Raine. SP-RainK

Never and never, my girl riding far and near. In Country Sleep. Dylan Thomas. CP-ThomD

Never any more. In a Year. Robert Browning. CP-BroR1; SP-BroR

Never Apologize for Poetry. Eleanor Wilner. SP-WilnE

Never be disenchanted of. Through Nightmare. Robert Graves. CP-GravR

Never be happy until the golden hour. Formative Mastership. Richard Eberhart. CP-EberR

Never Being. Stephen Spender. CP-SpenS

Never believe I leave you. Hiding Our Love. Emperor Wu of Han. CP-KizeC, tr. by Carolyn Kizer

Never, believe me, / Appear the Immortals. Visit of the Gods, The. Samuel Taylor Coleridge. CP-ColeS

Never believe me, if I love. Careless Lover, The. Sir John Suckling. CP-SuckJ

Never Born. Carl Sandburg. CP-SandC

Never Call a Babysitter in a Thunderstorm. Thomas Merton. CP-MertT

Never can spring be known so well. Time Exposure. Josephine Jacobsen. CP-JacoJ

Never comes now the through-and-through clear. Not-Returning, The. Ivor Gurney. SP-GurnI

Never could anyone / who simply lives to die. E. E. Cummings. CP-CummE

Never did sculptor's dream unfold. Sonnet of Michel Angelo Buonaroti. Michelangelo Buonarroti. CP-EmerR

Never do sea birds sing. Lost Speakers, The. Archibald MacLeish. CP-MacLA

Never enlivened with the liveliest ray. Companion to the Foregoing [Love Lies Bleeding]. William Wordsworth. CP-WorW2

Never finding itself. Ruin. Federico García Lorca. CP-GarcF, tr. by Greg Simon and Steven F. White

Never for ever, for ever never, oh. Intimation of Immortality. Stevie Smith. CP-SmitS

Never for Society. Emily Dickinson. CP-DickE

Never forget who brings the rain. Turn of the Moon. Robert Graves. CP-GravR

Never Give All the Heart. William Butler Yeats. CP-YeatW

Never happy any more! Lady's Lament, The. Dante Gabriel Rossetti. CW-RossD

Never has she known. Leader of Fashion, A. Thomas Hardy. CP-HardT

Never have I been sad or glad. Quandary. Robert Frost. CP-FrosR

Never in all my life have I seen. Rat, O Rat. Christopher Logue. SP-LoguC

Never in any circumstances think you can tell the men from the boys. (Or the sheep from the goats). Incorrigible Dirigible, The. Hayden Carruth. CP-CarHS

Never Land. Yusef Komunyakaa. CP-KomuY

Never let it be said. "H. D." CP-DoolH Fr. Electra-Orestes.

Never let me lose the marvel. Sonnet of the Sweet Complaint. Federico García Lorca. CP-GarcF, tr. by Angela Jaffray

Never love a simple lad. For a Favorite Grand-Daughter. Dorothy Parker. CP-ParkD

Never love unless you can. Advice to a Girl. Thomas Campion. CP-CampT

Never love with all your heart. Song in Spite of Myself. Countee Cullen. CP-CullC

Never mind the day we left, or the day the women clung to us. Klondike, The. Edwin Arlington Robinson. CP-RobiE

Never Mind the Overcoat, Button Up That Lip. Ogden Nash. CP-NashO

Never More, Sailor. Walter De la Mare. CP-DeLaW

Never my Book's perfection did appeare. To the High and Noble Prince, George, Duke, Marquesse, and Earle of Buckingham. Robert Herrick. CP-HerrR

Never, my young men. No Joy in Life. D. H. Lawrence. CP-LawrD

Never Naught Song, A. Robert Frost. CP-FrosR

Never-Never. Marge Piercy. SP-PierM

Never, never again? To See Him Again. Gabriela Mistral. SP-MistG, *tr. by* Maria Giachetti [*or* Jacketti]

Never, never again / This moment, never. Moment, The. Kathleen Jessie Raine. SP-RainK

Never, never may the fruit be plucked from the bough. Edna St. Vincent Millay. CP-MillE

Never, no never, listen too long. Fool's Song, The. Walter De la Mare. CP-DeLaW

Never, O never, / Since dewy sweet Flora. Rape of Aurora, The. George Meredith. CP-MerG1

Never offer your heart. Never Offer Your Heart to Someone Who Eats Hearts. Alice Walker. CP-WalkA

Never on one single pore Eternity. Being Alone. C. K. Williams. CP-WillC; SP-WillC

Never on this side of the grave again. Life's Parallels, A. Christina Georgina Rossetti. CP-RosC2

Never Pharaoh's Night. In the Desert. Herman Melville. SP-MelvH

Never seek [*or* pain] to tell thy love. Love's Secret. William Blake. CP-BlakW

Never shall a young man. For Anne Gregory. William Butler Yeats. CP-YeatW

Never Stronger. W. H. Auden. CP-AudeW

Never Such Love. Robert Graves. CP-GravR

Never take her away. Song: "Never take her away." Vinícius de Moraes. CP-WilbR, *tr. by* Richard Wilbur

Never talk back! sich things is repperhensible. James Whitcomb Riley. CP-RileJ

Never tell me that not one star of all. Star in a Stoneboat, A. Robert Frost. CP-FrosR

Never / the chess game. Poem, The ("Never / the chess game"). George Oppen. CP-OppGN

Never the Time and the Place. Robert Browning. CP-BroR2; SP-BroR

Never the tramp of foot or horse. Farewell to Anactoria. Sappho. CP-TateA, *tr. by* Allen Tate

Never-To-Be. Walter De la Mare. CP-DeLaW

Never to be lonely like that. Face to Face. Adrienne Rich. CP-RicAE; SP-RicA1; SP-RicA2

Never to fight unless from a pure motive. Bottleneck. Louis MacNeice. CP-MacNL

Never to hear, I know in myself complete. Certain Music, A. Muriel Rukeyser. CP-RukeM

Never to say no to the algae suddenly. To the Algae. Charles Olson. CP-OlsoC

Never to walk from the station's lamps and laurels. Negative Indicative. Philip Larkin. CP-LarkP

Never Too Late to Dye. Robert Herrick. CP-HerrR

Never Try to Trick Me with a Kiss. Sylvia Plath. CP-PlatS

Never Two Songs the Same. Carl Sandburg. CP-SandC

Never until the mankind making. Refusal to Mourn the Death, by Fire, of a Child in London, A. Dylan Thomas. CP-ThomD

Never until this night have I been stirred. Image from a Past Life, An. William Butler Yeats. CP-YeatW

Never was Day so over-sick with showres. Upon the Bishop of Lincolne's Imprisonment. Robert Herrick. CP-HerrR

Never was so profound a shadow thrown. Birth of Angels. Robert Graves. CP-GravR

Never was there a man much uglier. Vain Gratuities. Edwin Arlington Robinson. CP-RobiE

Never weather-beaten sail[e] more willing bent to shore. O Come Quickly! Thomas Campion. CP-CampT

Never will you depart. Strange Captivity. Marya Alexandrovna Zaturenska. SP-ZatuM

Never—yes, never—before these months just passed. Acquaintance with Time in Early Autumn. Robert Penn Warren. CP-WarrR

Neverland. Galway Kinnell. SP-KinnGN

Nevertheless. Marianne Craig Moore. CP-MoorM

Nevertheless. Ogden Nash. CP-NashO

Nevertheless, sleep / And as your eyes close. William Dickey. SP-DickW *Fr.* At Your Old House.

Nevertheless the Moon. Muriel Rukeyser. CP-RukeM

New. Gertrude Stein. CP-SteiG

New Age, The. Stevie Smith. CP-SmitS

New Age at Airport Mesa. Norman Dubie. CP-DubiN

New and more commendable delight, A. Michelangelo Buonarroti. CP-Miche, *tr. by* John Frederick Nims

New Animals. Donald Hall. CP-HallD

New Aqueduct, The. Jones Very. CP-VeryJ

New Being, The. Kenneth Patchen. CP-PatcK

New Birth, The. Jones Very. CP-VeryJ

New Body, The. Jones Very. CP-VeryJ

New bomb, big one, drops, A. On the 32nd Anniversary of the Bombing of

Hiroshima and Nagasaki. Denise Levertov. SP-LeveDL

New books of poetry will be written. Coronal, A. William Carlos Williams. CP-WilW1

New Boots, The. Thomas Hardy. CP-HardT

New Brooms. D. H. Lawrence. CP-LawrD

New Cabaret Girl, The. Langston Hughes. CP-HughL; CP-HughL1

New Car. C. K. Williams. SP-WillC

New Cathedral Overlooking the Park, The. William Carlos Williams. CP-WilW1

New Charon, The. Robert Herrick. CP-HerrR

New Clouds, The. William Carlos Williams. CP-WilW2

New coated / a winter white. White Van, The. Charles Tomlinson. CP-TomlC

New creatures; the Creator still the Same. Christina Georgina Rossetti. CP-RosC2

New Cry, The. Ben Jonson. CP-JonsB; SP-JonsB

New Dance, The. Yannis Ritsos. SP-RitsY, *tr. by* Kimon Friar *and* Karelisa Hartigan

New-dated from the terms that reappear. To Oxford. Gerard Manley Hopkins. CP-HopkG

New Dawn. Robert Penn Warren. CP-WarrR

New Dawn's Business, The. Thomas Hardy. CP-HardT

New Day, A. Philip Levine. SP-LeviP

New Decalogue, The. Ambrose Bierce. SP-BierA

New depths of truth within God's holy Word. Puritan Church and State 2., The. Jones Very. CP-VeryJ

New desire to understand, A. R. G. E. Richard Eberhart. CP-EberR

New England. William Carlos Williams. CP-WilW1

New England and the morning. Cambridge. Jorge Luis Borges. SP-BorgJ, *tr. by* Hoyt Rogers

New England, Autumn. Norman Dubie. CP-DubiN

New England Bachelor, A. Richard Eberhart. CP-EberR

New England Capitalist. Ralph Waldo Emerson. CP-EmerR

New England doesn't kid around. Granite. John Updike. CP-UpdiJ

New England first a wilderness was found. America. Phillis Wheatley. CP-WheaP

New England March. Charles Olson. CP-OlsoC

New England, 1967. Jorge Luis Borges. SP-BorgJ, *tr. by* Stephen Kessler

New England Spring, 1942. Edna St. Vincent Millay. CP-MillE

New England, Springtime. Norman Dubie. CP-DubiN

New England Verses. Wallace Stevens. CP-StevW; SP-StevWP

New England Weather. Archibald MacLeish. CP-MacLA

New Enigmas. Christina Georgina Rossetti. CP-RosC3

New Entrepreneurial Plan. Nelle Richmond Eberhart. CP-EberR

New Era the Army of the Future the Egg of an Army, The. George Meredith. CP-MerG2

New Eternity, The. Robert Graves. CP-GravR

New Every Day. William Stafford. SP-StafWW

New every morning is the love. Horae Canonicae. Donald Davie. CP-DaviDC

New Exodus, The. John Greenleaf Whittier. CP-WhitJ

New Eyes Each Year. Philip Larkin. CP-LarkP

New Face. Alice Walker. CP-WalkA

New face, strange face, for my unrest. Modes of Pleasure. Thom Gunn. CP-GunnT

New Faces, The. William Butler Yeats. CP-YeatW

New Farm Tractor. Carl Sandburg. CP-SandC

New Feet. Carl Sandburg. CP-SandC

New feet within my garden go. Emily Dickinson. CP-DickE

New Fiction, The. G. K. Chesterton. CP-ChesG

New Flowers. Langston Hughes. CP-HughL

New Foal. Ted Hughes. SP-HughTN

New Freethinker, The. G. K. Chesterton. CP-ChesG

New Gazette, The. Andrei Codrescu. SP-CodrA

New Georgia. Randall Jarrell. CP-JarrR

New ghost is that what you are. Is That What You Are. W. S. Merwin. SP-MerwW

New Gold Mountain. Yusef Komunyakaa. CP-KomuY

New Hampshire. Robert Frost. CP-FrosR

New Hampshire. Donald Hall. CP-HallD

New Hampshire. John Greenleaf Whittier. CP-WhitJ

New Hampshire Again. Carl Sandburg. CP-SandC

New Hampshire, February. Richard Eberhart. CP-EberR

New Hartford. Hayden Carruth. CP-CarHS

New Heart. Federico García Lorca. CP-GarcF, *tr. by* Catherine Brown

New Heaven and Earth. D. H. Lawrence. CP-LawrD

New Helen, The. Oscar Wilde. CP-WildO

New homeland was built, The. Yehuda Amichai. SP-AmicYL *Fr.* Poems of the Land of Zion and Jerusalem.

New Houses, New Clothes. D. H. Lawrence. CP-LawrD

New Inn, The. Ben Jonson.
   "It was a beauty that I saw." CP-JonsB; SP-JonsB
New Jerusalem. Louis MacNeice. CP-MacNL
New Jerusalem, The ("I saw the city, 'twas not built by hands"). Jones Very. CP-VeryJ
New Jerusalem, The ("There are towers; where they are"). Jones Very. CP-VeryJ
New Jingle on Tom Dingle, A. *Unknown*. CP-SherT
New Jules Verne, The. Joseph Brodsky. CP-BrodJ
New Knighthood, The. Rudyard Kipling. CP-KiplR
New Land. Mona Van Duyn. SP-VanDM
New Legends. Robert Graves. CP-GravR
New Letters from Thomas Jefferson. William Stafford. SP-StafWW
New Life. Joseph Brodsky. CP-BrodJ, *tr.* by David MacFadyen
New Life. Wallace Stevens. CP-StevWP
New Life, A. Amy Clampitt. CP-ClamA
New love, new love, where are you to lead me? Last Question, The. Dorothy Parker. CP-ParkD
New Love, The. Dorothy Parker. CP-ParkD
New Lover, A. Dan Pagis. SP-PagiD, *tr.* by Stephen Mitchell
New Man, The. Jones Very. CP-VeryJ
New Mexican Mountain. Robinson Jeffers. CP-JefR2
New Mexico. William Carlos Williams. CP-WilW2
New Mexico peels off. Loneliness. Yusef Komunyakaa. CP-KomuY
New ministers when first they get in place. Epilogue to the King and Queen. John Dryden. CP-DryJ2
New Mistress, The. A. E. Housman. CP-HousA
New Moon. Robert Creeley. SP-CreeR
New Moon. Langston Hughes. CP-HughL; CP-HughL2
New Moon. D. H. Lawrence. CP-LawrD
New moon, The. Yannis Ritsos. SP-RitsY *Fr.* Second Series.
New Moon, Hilal. Jelaluddin Rumi. SP-Rumi, *tr.* by Coleman Barks
New Moon in January. Ted Hughes. SP-HughTN
New Moon in November. W. S. Merwin. SP-MerwW
New moon looks down on our sick sweet planet, A. Death on All Fronts. Allen Ginsberg. CP-GinsA
New-mown hay smell and wind of the plain made her a woman whose. Population Drifts. Carl Sandburg. CP-SandC
New National Anthem, A. Percy Bysshe Shelley. CP-ShelP
New neighbors came to the corner house at Congress and Green Streets. Clean Curtains. Carl Sandburg. CP-SandC
New Numbers. Christopher Logue. SP-LoguC
New Objectives, New Cadres. Kenneth Rexroth. CP-RexrK
New Omar, The. G. K. Chesterton. CP-ChesG
New Orleans. Hayden Carruth. CP-CarHS
New Pair, A. May Swenson. SP-SwenM
New People, The. George Oppen. CP-OppGN
New Personal Poem. Ted Berrigan. SP-BerrT
New Place, The. Charles Bukowski. SP-BukC2
New Place, The. William Dickey. SP-DickW
New Poem. John Logan. CP-LogaJ
New Poem. Charles Olson. CP-OlsoC
New Poet, The. Tennessee Williams. CP-WillT
New Pretexts. Yannis Ritsos. SP-RitsY, *tr.* by Minas Savvas
New Prologue Spoken at the Representation of *Comus*, A. Samuel Johnson. CP-JohnS
New Province, A. Czeslaw Milosz. CP-MiloCN, *tr.* by Robert Hass
New Psalm for the Chapel of Kilmarnock, on the Thanksgiving-Day for His Majesty's Recovery, A. Robert Burns. CP-BurnR
New Readings. Gerard Manley Hopkins. CP-HopkG
New Realism, The. John Ashbery.
   "There was calm rapture in the way she spoke." SP-AshbJ
New! / Reason explodes. Atomic split. Lorine Niedecker. CP-NiedL
New red houses spring like plants, The. Flat Suburbs, S.W., in the Morning. D. H. Lawrence. CP-LawrD
New Religion is the True, The. True Religion, The. James Vincent Cunningham. CP-CunnJ
New Remorse, The. Oscar Wilde. CP-WildO
New Ribbon. Thomas Merton. CP-MertT
New ring oppresses the finger, The. New Ring, The. Karl Shapiro. SP-ShapK
New Ring, The. Karl Shapiro. SP-ShapK
New Roof, The. Wendell Berry. CP-BerrW
New Rule, The. Jelaluddin Rumi. SP-Rumi, *tr.* by Coleman Barks *and* Robert Bly
New Saddhus, The. Robert Pinsky. CP-PinsR
New-sawed. Lorine Niedecker. CP-NiedL
New Sea, The. Jones Very. CP-VeryJ
New Season. Philip Levine. SP-LeviP

New Season, The. W. S. Merwin. SP-MerwWF
New silence. Plumbing, The. W. S. Merwin. SP-MerwW
New Simile for the Ladies, A. Thomas Sheridan. CP-SherT
New snow onto old ice last night. Now. Cadillacs and Poetry. Raymond Carver. CP-CarvR
New Song, A. Seamus Heaney. SP-HeanSO
New Song, A. Langston Hughes. CP-HughL; CP-HughL1
New Song, A: "Sylvia the fair, in the bloom of fifteen." John Dryden. CP-DryJ2
New Song, The. Clement of Alexandria. CP-MertT
New Song for Indiana Ophelias. Carl Sandburg. CP-SandC
New Song to the Tune of "Whare Hae Ye Been a' Day, My Boy Tammy O? Courting O' a Young Thing, Just Come Frae Her Mammie O?" Lord Byron. CP-Byron
New Songs. Federico García Lorca. CP-GarcF, *tr.* by Catherine Brown
New Stanzas. Eugenio Montale. CP-MontE, *tr.* by Jonathan Galassi
New Stanzas for *Amazing Grace*. Allen Ginsberg. SP-GinsA
New star has been discovered, A. Surplus. Wisława Szymborska. SP-SzymWM, *tr.* by Joanna Trzeciak
New surprises? No. No new surprises. Berryman. Donald Davie. CP-DaviDC
New Tenants, The. Edwin Arlington Robinson. CP-RobiE
New Territory. Wyatt Prunty. SP-PrunW
New to the blood. Children. Ted Hughes. SP-HughTN
New Toy, The. Thomas Hardy. CP-HardT
New-vamped Abbey shaped apace, The. Abbey Mason, The. Thomas Hardy. CP-HardT
New Vicar of Bray, The. Lord Byron. CP-Byron
New Victory. Yannis Ritsos. SP-RitsY, *tr.* by Kimon Friar
New volcano has erupted, A. Crusoe in England. Elizabeth Bishop. CP-BishE
New Wave. Arthur Sze. SP-SzeA
New Weapons in the Old War. Howard Nemerov. CP-NemeH
New Weather. Carl Sandburg. CP-SandC
New Wife and the Old, The. John Greenleaf Whittier. CP-WhitJ
New wood as old as carpentry. The. Carpenter's Boat. George Oppen. CP-OppGN
New Word, The. D. H. Lawrence. CP-LawrD
New World. Derek Walcott. CP-WalcD
New World. Adam Zagajewski. SP-ZagaA, *tr.* by Clare Cavanagh
New World, The. Jones Very. CP-VeryJ
New world honors him whose lofty plea, The. Milton. John Greenleaf Whittier. CP-WhitJ
New Year. Langston Hughes. CP-HughL; CP-HughL1
New Year. Philip Larkin. CP-LarkP
New Year, The. Kenneth Rexroth. CP-RexrK
New Year, The. Jones Very. CP-VeryJ
New Year, The. John Greenleaf Whittier. CP-WhitJ
New year ends a year of sorrow, The. Han-shan. CP-ColdM, *tr.* by Red Pine
New Year Greeting, A. W. H. Auden. CP-AudeW
New Year Letter. W. H. Auden. CP-AudeW
New Year Morning. Adrienne Rich. CP-RicAE
New Year! New Year! come over the snow. New Year's Eve. George Meredith. CP-MerG2
New Year on Dartmoor. Sylvia Plath. CP-PlatS
New Year Wishes for the English. Donald Davie. CP-DaviDC
New Year's. Robert Creeley. CP-CreeR
New Year's Burden, A. Dante Gabriel Rossetti. CW-RossD
New Year's Dawn, 1947. Robinson Jeffers. CP-JefR3
New Year's Day. Audre Lorde. SP-LordA
New Year's Day, 1848. Walt Whitman. CP-WhitW
New Year's Eve. John Berryman. CP-BerrJ
New Year's Eve. John Ciardi. CP-CiarJ
New Year's Eve. Ivor Gurney. SP-GurnI
New Year's Eve. Thomas Hardy. CP-HardT
New Year's Eve. A. E. Housman. CP-HousA
New Year's Eve. Robinson Jeffers. CP-JefR2
New Year's Eve. D. H. Lawrence. CP-LawrD
New Year's Eve. George Meredith. CP-MerG2
New Year's Eve in War Time, A. Thomas Hardy. CP-HardT
New Year's Eve, 1979. Charles Wright. SP-WrigC
New Year's Gift for Bec, A. Jonathan Swift. CP-SwifJ
New Year's Gift for the Dean of St. Patrick's Given Him at Quilca, 1723/24, A. Thomas Sheridan. CP-SherT
New Year's Gift Sung to King Charles. 1635, A. Ben Jonson. CP-JonsB
New Year's Gift. To the King, A. Thomas Carew. CP-CareT
New Years Gift. To the Queen, A. Thomas Carew. CP-CareT
New Year's Night. D. H. Lawrence. CP-LawrD
New Year's Nursery Jingle. James Whitcomb Riley. CP-RileJ
New-Year's [*or* New-Yeares] Gift Sent to Sir Simeon Steward, A. Robert

Herrick. CP-HerrR

New years [or yeares], expect new gifts: sister, your harp[e]. Ben Jonson. CP-JonsB

New Year's Plaint, A. James Whitcomb Riley. CP-RileJ

New Year's Sacrifice: To Lucinda, A. Thomas Carew. CP-CareT

New Year's Time at Willards's, A. James Whitcomb Riley. CP-RileJ

New-Yeeres Gift, or Circumcisions Song, Sung to the King in the Presence at White Hall, The. Robert Herrick. CP-HerrR

New-Yeeres Gift, The. Robert Herrick. CP-HerrR

New York. Andrei Codrescu. SP-CodrA

New York. Thom Gunn. CP-GunnT

New York. Federico García Lorca. CP-GarcF, tr. by Greg Simon and Steven F. White

New York. Marianne Craig Moore. CP-MoorM

New York—Albany. Lawrence Ferlinghetti. SP-FerlL

New York Blues. Allen Ginsberg. SP-GinsA

New York City. Audre Lorde. See New York City 1970

New York City 1970. Audre Lorde. SP-LordA

  (New York City.) SP-LordA

New York dawn has, The. Dawn, The. Federico García Lorca. SP-GarcF, tr. by J. L. Gili and Stephen Spender

New York: 5 March 1957. James Vincent Cunningham. CP-CunnJ

New York in August. Boris Leonidovich Pasternak. CP-DaviDC, tr. by Donald Davie

New York is a city of many cats. Three Slants at New York. Carl Sandburg. CP-SandC

New York Lullaby. Joseph Brodsky. CP-BrodJ Fr. Shorts.

New York 1962: Fragment. Robert Lowell. SP-LoweR

New York Scene: May 1958. John Logan. CP-LogaJ

New Yorker, A. James Schuyler. CP-SchuJ

New Yorkers. Langston Hughes. CP-HughL; CP-HughL3

New York's lovely weather / hurts my forehead. Bean Spasms. Ted Berrigan. SP-BerrT

New York's lovely weather hurts my forehead. For You. Ted Berrigan. SP-BerrT

Newborn Death ("And thou, O Life, the lady of all bliss"). Dante Gabriel Rossetti. CW-RossD Fr. House of Life, The.

Newborn Death ("To-day Death seems to me an infant child"). Dante Gabriel Rossetti. CW-RossD Fr. House of Life, The.

Newcomer's Wife, The. Thomas Hardy. CP-HardT

Newer garden of creation, no primal solitude, A. Prairie States, The. Walt Whitman. CP-WhitW

Newly / cued / motif smites truly to beautifully. E. E. Cummings. CP-CummE

Newly / cued / motif smites truly to beautifully, The. E. E. Cummings. See Surely / Cued / motif smites truly to Beautifully, The

Newly Discovered "Homeric" Hymn, A. Charles Olson. CP-OlsoC; SP-OlsoC

Newly say dickered my love air my own would marry me all. Catullus. See Lesbia says she'ld rather marry me

Newlys of silence. E. E. Cummings. CP-CummE

Newlywed's Cuisine, The. Wang Chien. CP-WilW2

Newlyweds, The. John Updike. CP-UpdiJ

Newport Beach, 1979. Yusef Komunyakaa. CP-KomuY

News. Richard Eberhart. CP-EberR

News. Randall Jarrell. CP-JarrR

News. Walter De la Mare. CP-DeLaW

News. Lorine Niedecker. CP-NiedL

News about the outcome of the sea-battle, at Actium, The. In a Township of Asia Minor. Constantine P. Cavafy. CP-CavaC, tr. by Theoharis Constantine Theoharis

News and the Weather, The. Thomas McGrath. SP-McGrT

News and the Weather, The. Wallace Stevens. CP-StevW; CP-StevWP

News Bulletin. Allen Ginsberg. CP-GinsA

News Carried to Macedonia, The. Raymond Carver. CP-CarvR

News clip; the invasion of Biafra, A. Negatives. Derek Walcott. CP-WalcD

News comes that a friend far away. James. W. S. Merwin. SP-MerwWF

News for Her Mother. Thomas Hardy. CP-HardT

News for the Delphic Oracle. William Butler Yeats. CP-YeatW

News from Mount Amiata. Eugenio Montale. CP-MontE, tr. by Jonathan Galassi

News from the Cabin. May Swenson. SP-SwenM

News from the New World. Ben Jonson.

  "Howe'er the brightness may amaze." CP-JonsB

  "Now look and see in yonder throne." CP-JonsB

News from the School at Chartres. Thomas Merton. CP-MertT

News from the Underworld. John Updike. CP-UpdiJ

News gave me a scare, The. I tried to look. Lifelike. Heather McHugh. SP-McHuH

News Item. Dorothy Parker. CP-ParkD

News Items. Denise Levertov. SP-LeveDL

NEWS (o the latest). A B Cs (3—for Rimbaud). Charles Olson. CP-OlsoC

News of the Assassin. W. S. Merwin. SP-MerwW

News of the World. Robert Creeley. SP-CreeR

News Photo. Robert Penn Warren. CP-WarrR

News-Reel, The. Louis MacNeice. CP-MacNL

News Report. David Ignatow. SP-IgnaD

News Report. Yannis Ritsos. SP-RitsY, tr. by Gwendolyn MacEwen and Nikos Tsingos

News, The. Robert Creeley. CP-CreeR

News, The. Paul Laurence Dunbar. CP-DunbP

News! / What is the word that they tell now—now—now! Runners, The. Rudyard Kipling. CP-KiplR

Newsboy knocks. Madam and the Newsboy. Langston Hughes. CP-HughL; CP-HughL2

Newspaper comes. It, The. Sky Eats Up the Trees, The. James Schuyler. CP-SchuJ

Newspaper is a collection of half-injustices, A. Stephen Crane. CP-CranS

Newspaper Picture of Spectators at a Hotel Fire, A. Miller Williams. CP-WillM

Newspaper, The. Jones Very. CP-VeryJ

Newspaper, the coffee cup, the dog's, The. Coffee Cup, The. Donald Hall. CP-HallD

Newspaper Vendor, The. Stéphane Mallarmé. CP-MallS Fr. Street Songs.

Newspaper Vendor, The. Stéphane Mallarmé. CP-MallS, tr. by Henry Weinfield

Newspapermen say that of all work, newspaper work is the infernalist. I Am Full of Previous Experience. Ogden Nash. CP-NashO

Newspapers cover the floor. Metropolitan Sunday. Howard Nemerov. CP-NemeH

Newspapers rise high in the air over Maryland. At a March against the Vietnam War. Robert Bly. SP-BlyR

Newsreel. Adrienne Rich. SP-RicA2 Fr. Shooting Script.

Newsreel: Man and Firing Squad. Margaret Atwood. SP-AtwM1

Newstead Abbey. Lord Byron. CP-Byron

Newstead! fast-falling, once-resplendent dome! Elegy on Newstead Abbey. Lord Byron. CP-Byron

Newton. Federico García Lorca.

  Harmony. CP-GarcF, tr. by Jerome Rothenberg

  In the Woods. CP-GarcF, tr. by Jerome Rothenberg

  "Onto the nose of Newton." CP-GarcF, tr. by Jerome Rothenberg

  Philosopher's Last Walk, The. CP-GarcF, tr. by Jerome Rothenberg

  Question. CP-GarcF, tr. by Jerome Rothenberg

  Reply. CP-GarcF, tr. by Jerome Rothenberg

Newton / was taking a walk. Philosopher's Last Walk, The. Federico García Lorca. CP-GarcF, tr. by Jerome Rothenberg Fr. Newton.

Next! Ogden Nash. CP-NashO

Next Day. Randall Jarrell. CP-JarrR

Next Day, The. A. R. Ammons. CP-AmmoA

Next Door. Raymond Carver. CP-CarvR

Next Door. Richard Wilbur. CP-WilbR

Next door the windows are yellow. Factory, The. Aleksandr Aleksandrovich Blok. SP-BlokA, tr. by Peter France and Jon Stallworthy

Next door they've finally brought home the new baby. For Every Last Batch When the Next One Comes Along. William Dickey. SP-DickW

Next is your lot, fair, to be numbered one. To His Kinswoman, Mrs. Penelope Wheeler. Robert Herrick. CP-HerrR

Next Moon, The. W. S. Merwin. SP-MerwWF

Next Morning. D. H. Lawrence. CP-LawrD

Next morning Troilus began to clear. Troilus and Cresida. William Wordsworth. CP-WorW1

Next of Kin. Christina Georgina Rossetti. CP-RosC3

Next, Please. Philip Larkin. CP-LarkP

Next poem I write will have firewood, The. Pipe, The. Raymond Carver. CP-CarvR

Next Summer. Josephine Jacobsen. CP-JacoJ

Next Table, The. Constantine P. Cavafy. CP-CavaC, tr. by Theoharis Constantine Theoharis

Next, The. W. S. Merwin. SP-MerwW

Next Time. William Stafford. SP-StafWW

Next time I'll travel by dream. Fanny Howe. SP-HoweF Fr. O'Clock.

Next Time, The. Robert Graves. CP-GravR

Next time what I'd do is look at. Next Time. William Stafford. SP-StafWW

Next to of course god america i. E. E. Cummings. CP-CummE; SP-CummE

Next to the Café Chaos. Olga Broumas. SP-BrouO

Next to the Last Poem about God, The. C. K. Williams. CP-WillC

Next to the tiny bladeless windmill. Small Tin Parrot Pin, A. Thomas Lux. SP-LuxT

Next to these ladies, but in nought allied. Contented Peasant, The. George Crabbe. SP-CrabG Fr. Parish Register, The.

Next War, The. Wilfred Owen. CP-OwenW

Next week, alas, BOULANGERIE. Farewell to the Shopping District of Antibes.

John Updike. CP-UpdiJ

Next woman that comes through here that I, The. "Horrible Incredible Lies" : Keith Lampe Spontaneously. Philip Whalen. SP-WhalP

Next Year. Raymond Carver. CP-CarvR

Next Year or I Fly My Rounds Tempestuous. Lorine Niedecker. CP-NiedL

Next year the grave grass will cover us. Street Corner College. Kenneth Patchen. CP-PatcK

Next year we are to bring the soldiers home. Homage to a Government. Philip Larkin. CP-LarkP

Nexus. Rita Dove. SP-DoveR

Nexus. Richard Eberhart. CP-EberR

Ni las noches de amor que no. El camino de amor. James Laughlin. CP-LaugJ

Niagara. Nicholas Vachel Lindsay. CP-LindV

Nice Day for a Lynching. Kenneth Patchen. CP-PatcK

Nice Place, A. Charles Bukowski. SP-BukC2

Nice Try. Charles Bukowski. SP-BukC3

Niceties of symbolism & identification. In & Out. John Berryman. CP-BerrJ

Nicholas Oberting. James Whitcomb Riley. CP-RileJ

Nichori. Constantine P. Cavafy. CP-CavaC, *tr.* by Theoharis Constantine Theoharis

Nick and the Candlestick. Sylvia Plath. CP-PlatS

Nick said, radiant, being helped upstairs. Nothing I Meant to Keep. Jane Cooper. CP-CoopJ

Nicked a gin-ace seeing hour. Four-o'clock. Louis Zukofsky. CP-ZukLS

Nickel nickel dime. Penny for the Old Guy, A. Philip Whalen. SP-WhalP

Nickname of Hell, The. C. K. Williams. CP-WillC; SP-WillC

Nicodemus. Howard Nemerov. CP-NemeH

Nicóla—he would shout—drive a bit more slowly. I want to see. Immobilizing the Boundless. Yannis Ritsos. SP-RitsY, *tr.* by Kostas Myrsiades

Nicotine. Ezra Pound. CP-PoEar

Nid, am i Ti fy ngwared i. Ochenaid Sant Francis Xavier, Apostol Yr Indiaid. Gerard Manley Hopkins. CP-HopkG

Niece. George Oppen. CP-OppGN

Nieh Ch'ueh, who had no teeth. Importance of Being Toothless, The. Chuang Tzu. CP-MertT

Niether the wild tulip, poignant. Palm Sunday. Amy Clampitt. CP-ClamA

Nieves / Is a girl. To the Muse. George Oppen. CP-OppGN

Nigger. Carl Sandburg. SP-SandC

Nigger. Karl Shapiro. SP-ShapK

Nigger: as if it were not. Internal Injuries. Robert Penn Warren. CP-WarrR

Nigger comes home from work, A. Man into Men. Langston Hughes. CP-HughL; CP-HughL2

Nigger Song: An Odyssey. Rita Dove. SP-DoveR

Nigh on twice a thousand springs. Man's Divine Equality. G. K. Chesterton. CP-ChesG

Night. Sir Philip Sidney. SP-SidnP *Fr.* Arcadia.

Night. Federico García Lorca. SP-GarcF *Fr.* Poem of the Saeta.

Night. Robert Bly. SP-BlyR

Night. Louise Bogan. CP-BogaL

Night. E. E. Cummings. CP-CummE

Night ("Born and bred / in Wellington"). Robert Creeley. SP-CreeR

Night ("Needs most / happily mutual"). Robert Creeley. CP-CreeR

Night. "H. D." CP-DoolH

Night. Paul Laurence Dunbar. CP-DunbP

Night. David Ignatow. SP-IgnaD

Night. Robinson Jeffers. CP-JefR1

Night. D. H. Lawrence. CP-LawrD

Night. Walter De la Mare. CP-DeLaW

Night. Walter De la Mare. CP-DeLaW

Night. Gabriela Mistral. SP-MistG, *tr.* by Maria Giachetti [*or* Jacketti] *and* Maria Jacketti

Night. Adrienne Rich. CP-RicAE; SP-RicA2

Night. Gary Snyder. CP-SnydG

Night. Jones Very. CP-VeryJ

Night. William Carlos Williams. CP-WilW1

Night. Adam Zagajewski. SP-ZagaA, *tr.* by Renata Gorczynski, Benjamin Ivry *and* C. K. Williams

Night. Adam Zagajewski. SP-ZagaA, *tr.* by Clare Cavanagh

Night. A dream so drowned my mind. Scream, The. Charles Tomlinson. CP-TomlC; SP-TomlC

Night. A major storm. The lonely woman hears. Method of Salvation. Yannis Ritsos. SP-RitsY, *tr.* by Kostas Myrsiades

Night (Suite for Piano and Poet's Voice). Federico García Lorca.

  At the Poorhouse. CP-GarcF, *tr.* by Jerome Rothenberg

  Below. CP-GarcF, *tr.* by Jerome Rothenberg

  Comet. CP-GarcF, *tr.* by Jerome Rothenberg

  Great Sadness, The. CP-GarcF, *tr.* by Jerome Rothenberg

  In a Corner of the Sky. CP-GarcF, *tr.* by Jerome Rothenberg

  Memory. CP-GarcF, *tr.* by Jerome Rothenberg

  One. CP-GarcF, *tr.* by Jerome Rothenberg

  Prelude: "Bullock / slowly, The." CP-GarcF, *tr.* by Jerome Rothenberg

  Sketches. CP-GarcF, *tr.* by Jerome Rothenberg

  Star, A. CP-GarcF, *tr.* by Jerome Rothenberg

  Swath. CP-GarcF, *tr.* by Jerome Rothenberg

  Ursa Major ("Bear mother / gives suck to the stars"). CP-GarcF, *tr.* by Jerome Rothenberg

  Venus ("Open sesame / by day"). CP-GarcF, *tr.* by Jerome Rothenberg

  Whole Works, The. CP-GarcF, *tr.* by Jerome Rothenberg

Night, The. Charles Olson. CP-OlsoC

Night, The. James Schuyler. CP-SchuJ

Night acrobats laid down in a dark carriage. In the morning. Acrobat, An. Yannis Ritsos. SP-RitsY, *tr.* by Kostas Myrsiades

Night after night. James Dean. Ai. SP-Ai

Night after night forever the dolls lay stiff. Dolls, The. John Ciardi. CP-CiarJ

Night after night, it was very nearly enough. Whippoorwill in the Woods, A. Amy Clampitt. CP-ClamA

Night after night of muffled. Anniversary, The. Amy Clampitt. CP-ClamA

Night after night the dead moon lit. Difficult Resolution, The. Randall Jarrell. CP-JarrR

Night Air, The. Jelaluddin Rumi. SP-Rumi, *tr.* by Coleman Barks

Night always still. Balance. Federico García Lorca. CP-GarcF, *tr.* by Alan S. Trueblood *Fr.* Theories.

Night and Day. Ludovico Ariosto. CP-MahoD, *tr.* by Derek Mahon

Night and day arrive, and day after day goes by. For My Son Noah, Ten Years Old. Robert Bly. SP-BlyR

Night and Death. Christina Georgina Rossetti. CP-RosC3

Night and full moon. Dreams of Wild Horses, The. Thomas McGrath. SP-McGrT

Night, and my wristwatch is slow. It's the wrist's fault. Toward Home. Dan Pagis. SP-PagiD, *tr.* by Stephen Mitchell

Night and the City. John Berryman. CP-BerrJ

Night and the Merry Man. Elizabeth Barrett Browning. CP-BroEB

Night and the Merry Man. Elizabeth Barrett Browning. CP-BroEB

NIght-Apple, The. Allen Ginsberg. CP-GinsA

Night Arrival of Sea-Trout. Ted Hughes. SP-HughTN

Night arrives. 30 January 1949. Yannis Ritsos. SP-RitsY *Fr.* Exile's Journals 2.

Night at the Opera, A. James Laughlin. CP-LaugJ

Night at the Opera, A. Charles Tomlinson. CP-TomlC

Night attendant, a B.U. sophomore, The. Waking in the Blue. Robert Lowell. SP-LoweR

Night before Christmas, The. Howard Nemerov. CP-NemeH

Night before he was to be ordained, The. Bishop, The. Paul Muldoon. CP-MuldP

Night before Thanksgiving, The. Norman Dubie. CP-DubiN

Night before the Night before Christmas, The. Randall Jarrell. CP-JarrR

Night Bells. Carl Sandburg. CP-SandC

Night below Zero. Kenneth Rexroth. CP-RexrK

Night Bird. James Dickey. CP-DickJ

Night-Blooming Cereus, The. Robert Earl Hayden. CP-HaydR

Night Blooming Cereus, The. Jones Very. CP-VeryJ

Night-bound fire, A. Black Nude. Charles Tomlinson. CP-TomlC

Night, by the light of whatever would burn. Without Regret. Eleanor Wilner. SP-WilnE

Night café 4 A.M., The. Havana 1953. Allen Ginsberg. CP-GinsA

Night calls many witnesses. Tall Timber. Carl Sandburg. CP-SandC

Night came on the Waters—all was rest, The. Julian [A Fragment]. Lord Byron. CP-Byron

Night City. Elizabeth Bishop. CP-BishE

Night closed my windows and. Plough of Time, The. Lawrence Ferlinghetti. SP-FerlL

Night comes, an angel stands. Nocturn: "Night comes, an angel stands." Kathleen Jessie Raine. SP-RainK

Night Conference, Wood Quay: 6 June 1979. Thomas Kinsella. CP-KinsT

Night covers the pond with its wing. Pond, The. Louise Glück. SP-GlucL

Night Crawlers. Robert Stock. SP-StocR

Night creep down erlong de lan, De. Tryst, The. Paul Laurence Dunbar. CP-DunbP

Night Crow. Theodore Roethke. CP-RoetT

Night Dampness. Raymond Carver. CP-CarvR

Night Dances, The. Sylvia Plath. CP-PlatS

Night, Death, Mississippi. Robert Earl Hayden. CP-HaydR

Night, Dim Night. Paul Laurence Dunbar. CP-DunbP

Night does not want to come. Ghazal of Desperate Love. Federico García Lorca. CP-GarcF, *tr.* by Catherine Brown *Fr.* Ghazals.

Night does not wish to come, The. Gacela of Desperate Love. Federico García Lorca. SP-GarcF, *tr.* by W. S. Merwin

Night Dream, The. Archibald MacLeish. CP-MacLA

Night Drive. Seamus Heaney. SP-HeanSO

Night Drive. Rainer Maria Rilke. CP-MahoD, *tr.* by Derek Mahon

Night falls in the borough. We can't sleep. We Are Waiting. Yannis Ritsos. SP-RitsY, *tr.* by Thanasis Maskaleris

Night Feeding. Muriel Rukeyser. CP-RukeM

Night Fishers. Charles Tomlinson. CP-TomlC; SP-TomlC

Night Fishing in the Sound. Eleanor Wilner. SP-WilnE

Night Flight. Mary Oliver. SP-OlivM

Night Flight. Marge Piercy. SP-PierM

Night Flight : New York. Muriel Rukeyser *and* Leif Sjoberg. CP-RukeM

Night Flight, over Ocean. John Updike. CP-UpdiJ

Night-Flowering Cactus. Thomas Merton. CP-MertT

Night: Four Songs. Langston Hughes. CP-HughL; CP-HughL2

Night Freight, Michigan. John Ciardi. CP-CiarJ

Night Frogs. Robert Bly. SP-BlyR

Night from a railroad car window. Window. Carl Sandburg. CP-SandC

Night frost glitter glazes. Energies. Donald Davie. CP-DaviDC

Night full of talking that hurts, A. Jelaluddin Rumi. SP-Rumi, *tr.* by Coleman Barks *and* John Moyne *Fr.* Three Quatrains.

Night Funeral in Harlem. Langston Hughes. CP-HughL; CP-HughL3

Night Game, The. Robert Pinsky. CP-PinsR

Night Gleam. Allen Ginsberg. CP GinsA; SP GinsA

Night has a sea which quenches the machine. Nocturne: "Night has a sea which quenches the machine." Thomas Merton. CP-MertT

Night Has Been as Beautiful as Virginia. Kenneth Patchen. CP-PatcK

Night Has Come. Rainer Maria Rilke. CP-RilkFr, *tr.* by A. Poulin, Jr.

Night has come like something crawling. 22,000 Dollars in 3 Months. Charles Bukowski. SP-BukC2

Night has cut, The. Night. "H. D." CP-DoolH

Night hath no wings, to him that cannot sleep. To His Sweet Saviour. Robert Herrick. CP-HerrR

Night here already. Song: "Night here already." Federico García Lorca. CP-GarcF, *tr.* by Jerome Rothenberg *Fr.* Backwaters.

Night Herons. Gary Snyder. CP-SnydG

Night herons nest in the cypress. Night Herons. Gary Snyder. CP-SnydG

Night hides our thefts; all faults then pardoned be. In the Dark None Dainty. Robert Herrick. CP-HerrR

Night House, The. Billy Collins. SP-CollB

Night! how I love thy silent shades. *see also* Watching unto God in the Night-Season. Jeanne Marie Bouvier de la Motte- Guyon. CP-CowpW

Night huddled our town. In Dear Detail, by Ideal Light. William Stafford. SP-StafWW

Night I Fucked My Alarm Clock, The. Charles Bukowski. SP-BukC1

Night I wrote your name in biro on my wrist, The. Asra. Paul Muldoon. CP-MuldP

Night in a World, A. Heather McHugh. SP-McHuH

Night in Hell. Arthur Rimbaud. CP-RimbA, *tr.* by Martin Sorrell

Night in June, A. William Wordsworth. CP-WorW1; MW-WorW

Night in Martindale. Kathleen Jessie Raine. SP-RainK

Night in May!, A. Ode: "Night in May!, A." Wallace Stevens. CP-StevWP

Night in NYC. Robert Creeley. CP-CreeR

Night in November, A. Thomas Hardy. CP-HardT

Night in the Kitchen. Adrienne Rich. CP-RicAE

Night in the Old Home. Thomas Hardy. CP-HardT

Night is / a black diamond, The. Listening to a Broken Radio. Arthur Sze. SP-SzeA

Night is beautiful, The. My People. Langston Hughes. CP-HughL

Night is covered with signs. The body and face of man, The. Akiba. Muriel Rukeyser. CP-RukeM

Night is darkening round me, The. Spellbound. Emily Jane Brontë. CP-BronE

Night is dewy as a maiden's mouth, The. Summer's Night, A. Paul Laurence Dunbar. CP-DunbP

Night is far spent, the day is at hand, The. Awake, Thou That Sleepest. Christina Georgina Rossetti. CP-RosC2

Night is filled with indecisions, The. Night, The. James Schuyler. CP-SchuJ

Night is for sorrow and dawn is for joy. With the Lark. Paul Laurence Dunbar. CP-DunbP

Night is my favorite Day. Emily Dickinson. SP-DickE

Night is my sister, and how deep in love. Edna St. Vincent Millay. CP-MillE

Night is o'er England, and the winds are still. Peace. Walter De la Mare. CP-DeLaW

Night is on these hills, and some can sleep, The. Letter to His Brother. John Berryman. CP-BerrJ

Night is quiet, The. Letter Poem #3. James Schuyler. CP-SchuJ

Night is still, The. The unfailing surf. J. V. Cunningham. CP-CunnJ

Night is uneasy, armed between streetlamps, The. Evening Stroll in the Suburbs. Mona Van Duyn. SP-VanDM

Night it was a holy [*or* haly] night, The. Godly Girzie. Robert Burns. CP-BurnR

Night Journal. Charles Wright. SP-WrigC

Night Journal II. Charles Wright. SP-WrigC

Night Journey. Theodore Roethke. CP-RoetT

Night knows nothing of the chants of night, The. Re-statement of Romance. Wallace Stevens. CP-StevW; CP-StevWP

Night Launch. Maxine W. Kumin. SP-KumiM

Night Letter. Stanley Kunitz. CP-KunSC

Night Letter. Marge Piercy. SP-PierM

Night lies down. In Summer. Denise Levertov. SP-LeveDL

Night light, my calm confidante. Rainer Maria Rilke. CP-RilkFr, *tr.* by A. Poulin, Jr. *Fr.* Orchards.

Night, like a dying mother. By Morning Twilight. George Meredith. CP-MerG1

Night Litany. Ezra Pound. CP-PoEar

Night Mail, The. W. H. Auden. CP-AudeW

Night makes no difference 'twixt the Priest and Clerk. No Difference in the Dark [*or* i'th'dark]. Robert Herrick. CP-HerrR

Night-March, The. Herman Melville. SP-MelvH

Night-Mare Death in Life, The. Samuel Taylor Coleridge. CP-ColeS

Night Movement—New York. Carl Sandburg. CP-SandC

Night Muse & Mortar Round. Yusef Komunyakaa. CP-KomuY

Night-Music. Muriel Rukeyser. CP-RukeM

Night-Music. Philip Larkin. CP-LarkP

Night-Music. Muriel Rukeyser. CP-RukeM

Night my father died the moon shone on the snow, The. Circle of Breath. William Stafford. SP-StafWW

Night my father got me, The. Culprit, The. A. E. Housman. CP-HousA

Night odors: wet grass, wet trees. Love Against Death. Clarence Major. SP-MajoC

Night of a Faun. Andrei Codrescu. SP-CodrA

Night of Destiny, The. Thomas Merton. CP-MertT

Night of First Snow. Robert Bly. SP-BlyR

Night of four moons. Dead at Daybreak. Federico García Lorca. CP-GarcF, *tr.* by Alan S. Trueblood *Fr.* Moon Songs.

Night of four moons. He Died at Dawn. Federico García Lorca. SP-GarcF, *tr.* by Greville Texidor

Night of Frost in May. George Meredith. CP-MerG1

Night of Love. Paul Laurence Dunbar. CP-DunbP

Night of my cousin's wedding, The. How We Danced. Anne Sexton. SP-SextA *Fr.* Death of the Fathers, The.

Night of Questionings, A. Thomas Hardy. CP-HardT

Night of Sleepless Love. Federico García Lorca. CP-GarcF, *tr.* by Angela Jaffray

Night of storms has passed, The. Emily Jane Brontë. CP-BronE

Night of the comet, The. Recompense, The. Charles Tomlinson. CP-TomlC

Night of the Dance, The. Thomas Hardy. CP-HardT

Night of the Iguana, The. Tennessee Williams.
    Drunken Fiddler, The. CP-WillT
    "How calmly does the orange branch." CP-WillT
    "Youth must be wanton, youth must be quick." CP-WillT

Night of the Shirts, The. W. S. Merwin. SP-MerwW

Night of the two moons. Night: Four Songs. Langston Hughes. CP-HughL; CP-HughL2

Night of Trafalgar, The. Thomas Hardy. CP-HardT *Fr.* Dynasts, The.

Night of wonder! piled afar, A. Evening in Burmah. John Greenleaf Whittier. CP-WhitJ

Night on a Visa Card. Charles Bukowski. SP-BukC3

Night on Hatchet Cove. Denise Levertov. SP-LeveDP

Night on the Chesapeake. Paul Laurence Dunbar. CP-DunbP

Night on the city of the Moor! Derne. John Greenleaf Whittier. CP-WhitJ

Night on the Prairies. Walt Whitman. CP-WhitW

Night. Only one look. A noiseless bullet. Unjust, The. Yannis Ritsos. SP-RitsY, *tr.* by Minas Savvas

Night open wide. Fair by Starlight. Federico García Lorca. CP-GarcF, *tr.* by Jerome Rothenberg *Fr.* Fairs.

Night, our [*or* the] black summer, simplifies her smells. Nights in the Gardens of Port of Spain. Derek Walcott. SP-WalcD

Night over England's interrupted pastoral. Foxes' Moon. Charles Tomlinson. CP-TomlC

Night Patrol. Josephine Jacobsen. CP-JacoJ

Night-piece. James Vincent Cunningham. CP-CunnJ

Night Piece. Louise Glück. SP-GlucL

Night-Piece. Stanley Kunitz. CP-KunSC

Night-Piece, A. William Wordsworth. CP-WorW1
    (Sky is overspread, The.) MW-WorW

Night Piece for My Twenty-seventh Birthday. John Ciardi. CP-CiarJ

Night Piece, The. Thom Gunn. CP-GunnT

Night-Piece: The Near and the Far. Charles Tomlinson. CP-TomlC

Night-Piece, to Julia, The. Robert Herrick. CP-HerrR

Night-Pieces: For a Child. Adrienne Rich. CP-RicAE; SP-RicA2

Night Poem. Margaret Atwood. SP-AtwM2

Night Pool, The. James Dickey. CP-DickJ

Night prevails where Phoebus—that's our sun, The. Michelangelo Buonarroti. CP-Miche, tr. by John Frederick Nims

Night Rain. Countee Cullen. CP-CullC

Night rain, dripping unseen, The. Embankment at Night, before the War: Outcasts. D. H. Lawrence. CP-LawrD

Night Ride. Charles Tomlinson. CP-TomlC

Night Ride. Jay Wright. SP-WrigJ

Night Rider, The. William Carlos Williams. CP-WilW2

Night Ritual. Yannis Ritsos. SP-RitsY, tr. by Kostas Myrsiades

Night Room Composition. Peter Blue Cloud. SP-BlueP

Night Scene. George Oppen. CP-OppGN

Night Scene before Combat. Alan Dugan. CP-DugaA

Night-Scene, The. Samuel Taylor Coleridge. CP-ColeS

Night sends this white eye. Full Moonlight in Spring. W. S. Merwin. SP-MerwW

Night shall eat these girls and boys. E. E. Cummings. CP-CummE

Night Shift. Sylvia Plath. CP-PlatS

Night Sky. Kathleen Jessie Raine. SP-RainK

Night Sky, A. Robert Creeley. CP-CreeR

Night—sky bird's world. Myth of the Blaze. George Oppen. CP-OppGN

Night sky is only a sort of carbon paper, The. Insomniac. Sylvia Plath. CP-PlatS

Night Sky, The. Michael Palmer. SP-PalmM

Night slowly stretches o'er the changing skies. Original—"Apropos" Ralph Waldo Emerson. CP-EmerR

Night So Bright A Squirrel Reads, The. Thomas Lux. SP-LuxT

Night so bright a squirrel reads, The. Night So Bright A Squirrel Reads, The. Thomas Lux. SP-LuxT

Night Sober Goddess nurse of tender thought. Ode, to Amanda, An. Annis Boudinot Stockton. CP-StocA

Night Song. Langston Hughes. CP-HughL; CP-HughL2

Night-Song. Wallace Stevens. CP-StevWP

Night Song for a Boy. Alan Dugan. CP-DugaA

Night Song of the Andalusian Sailors. Federico García Lorca. CP-GarcF, tr. by Christopher Maurer

Night Songs. D. H. Lawrence. CP-LawrD

Night Songs. Thomas Kinsella. CP-KinsT

Night Sounds. Carolyn Kizer. CP-KizeC

Night. Street. Lamp. Drugstore. Scene, The. Aleksandr Aleksandrovich Blok. CP-KunSC Fr. Dances of Death.

Night Stuff. Carl Sandburg. CP-SandC

Night Surf, The. W. S. Merwin. SP-MerwWF

Night Sweat. Robert Lowell. SP-LoweR

Night Taxi. Thom Gunn. CP-GunnT

Night that has no star lit up by God, The. New World, The. Jones Very. CP-VeryJ

Night, that old woman, jabs the sun. 29 (A Dream in Two Parts). Ai. SP-Ai

Night the cold the solitude, The. From the Outside. Paul Éluard. CP-WilW2

Night the flowers were butchered, The. Provider, The. Josephine Jacobsen. CP-JacoJ

Night the half-moon was like a dancing-girl, A. Tamar. Robinson Jeffers. CP-JefR1

Night. The little bell of the mess hall. 6 November 1948. Yannis Ritsos. SP-RitsY Fr. Exile's Journals 1.

Night—there lay the Days between, A. Emily Dickinson. CP-DickE

Night They Took Whitey, The. Charles Bukowski. SP-BukC2

Night Thought. Kathleen Jessie Raine. SP-RainK

Night Thought, A. William Wordsworth. CP-WorW2

Night Thoughts. Stevie Smith. CP-SmitS

Night tightens its noose. Two Brothers. Ai. SP-Ai

Night Time. Robert Creeley. SP-CreeR

Night-Time in Mid-Fall. Thomas Hardy. CP-HardT

Night-Time in the Cemetery. Stevie Smith. CP-SmitS

Night Train. The. Thomas Merton. CP-MertT

Night-Train, The. Charles Tomlinson. CP-TomlC

Night Transfigured. Charles Tomlinson. CP-TomlC

Night Traveler, The. Mary Oliver. SP-OlivM

Night turns slowly round, The. Going Back. D. H. Lawrence. CP-LawrD

Night undresses you. Her hands tremble. Nocturnal. Yannis Ritsos. SP-RitsY, tr. by Edmund Keeley

Night up we two with the full moon. Night of Sleepless Love. Federico García Lorca. CP-GarcF, tr. by Angela Jaffray

Night Visit. Tennessee Williams. CP-WillT

Night-Walk, The. George Meredith. CP-MerG1

Night Walking. Robert Penn Warren. CP-WarrR

Night walks the earth with silver feet. George Meredith. CP-MerG2

Night was a failure, The. First Morning. D. H. Lawrence. CP-LawrD

Night was almost too long to bear, The. Conclusively. Fanny Howe. SP-HoweF

Night was cloyed with flowers, The. Outskirts, The. Walter De la Mare. CP-DeLaW

Night was dark and I alone, The. Thieves, The. Jones Very. CP-VeryJ

Night was dark, yet winter breathed, The. Emily Jane Brontë. CP-BronE

Night was down among the mountains. Judith at the Tent of Holofernes. John Greenleaf Whittier. CP-WhitJ

Night was near, a day was near, A. Hope Carol, A. Christina Georgina Rossetti. CP-RosC2

Night was still, and o'er the hill, The. Robert Burns. CP-BurnR

Night was wide, and furnished scant, The. Emily Dickinson. CP-DickE

Night Watch. Rita Dove. SP-DoveR

Night Watch. Adrienne Rich. CP-RicAE; SP-RicA2

Night Watch. May Sarton. SP-SartM

Night Watch in the City of Boston. Archibald MacLeish. CP-MacLA

Night Watch of the Trojans before Troy. Homer. CP-MerG2 Fr. Iliad, The.

Night Watchman, The. Josephine Jacobsen. CP-JacoJ

Night we bailed out Jolene from Riker's Island, The. Amaranth and Moly. Amy Clampitt. CP-ClamA

Night we felt the earth would move, The. Rudyard Kipling. CP-KiplR Fr. Second Jungle Book, The.

Night when wastes of uplands wan were grey with silvering snow, A. Even unto the End of the World. G. K. Chesterton. CP-ChesG

Night Wind. W. S. Merwin. SP-MerwW

Night Wind, The. Emily Jane Brontë. CP-BronE

Night-wind of August, The. Wallace Stevens. CP-StevWP

Night! with all thine eyes look down! Another Version of the Same. Percy Bysshe Shelley. CP-ShelP

Night, with all thine eyes look down! Epithalamium: "Night, with all thine eyes look down!" Percy Bysshe Shelley. CP-ShelP

Night without Sleep. Robinson Jeffers. CP-JefR2

Night Work. Thomas McGrath. SP-McGrT

Night you got away, I dreamed you rose, The. To a Fugitive. James Wright. CP-WrigJ

Nightbird. Yusef Komunyakaa. CP-KomuY

Nightbreak. Adrienne Rich. CP-RicAE; SP-RicA1; SP-RicA2

Nightclub. Billy Collins. SP-CollB

Nightfall, cold eye—neither disheartens. Beggars, The. Sylvia Plath. CP-PlatS

Nightfall, that saw the morning-glories float. On the Skeleton of a Hound. James Wright. CP-WrigJ

Nightgown. James Merrill. SP-MerrJ

Nighthawks: after Hopper's Painting. John Logan. CP-LogaJ

Nightingale, The. Samuel Taylor Coleridge. CP-ColeS; MW-ColeS

Nightingale, The. Gerard Manley Hopkins. CP-HopkG

Nightingale and Glow-Worm, The. William Cowper. CP-CowpW

Nightingale Road. Denise Levertov. SP-LeveDL

Nightingale, that all day long, A. Nightingale and Glow-Worm, The. William Cowper. CP-CowpW

Nightingale, that so harmoniously, The. Petrarch. CP-Petra, tr. by J. G. Nichols

Nightingale . . . , whose heart. Small Notebook. Rainer Maria Rilke. CP-RilkFr, tr. by A. Poulin, Jr.

Nightingales. Paul Muldoon. CP-MuldP

Nightingales, The. William Carlos Williams. CP-WilW1

Nightingales warbled without. In the Garden at Swainston. Alfred Tennyson. CP-TennA

Nightly I await you. Why Do You Never Enter My Dreams. James Laughlin. CP-LaugJ

Nightly I chose to keep this covenant. Sleeping with Animals. Maxine W. Kumin. SP-KumiM

Nightly, in some old suburban square. Ragpickers' Wine. Charles Baudelaire. CP-BaudC, tr. by Walter Martin

Nightmare. Jorge Luis Borges. SP-BorgJ, tr. by Willis Barnstone

Nightmare. G. K. Chesterton. CP-ChesG

Nightmare. Rita Dove. SP-DoveR

Nightmare. Howard Nemerov. CP-NemeH

Nightmare, The. Laura Riding Jackson. CP-RidiL

Nightmare, and the Next Thing, A. Thomas Hardy. CP-HardT

Nightmare Boogie. Langston Hughes. CP-HughL; CP-HughL3

Nightmare Factory, The. Maxine W. Kumin. SP-KumiM

Nightmare of beasthood, snorting, how to wake. Moly. Thom Gunn. CP-GunnT

Nightmare of Senility. Robert Graves. CP-GravR

Nightmare of the Suburbs, A. Jane Cooper. CP-CoopJ

Nightmare shower room. My tormentor leers, The. Days of 1941 and '44. James Merrill. SP-MerrJ

Nightmare Song. Robert Stock. SP-StocR

Nightpiece. Robinson Jeffers. CP-JefR3

Nights are very unclear here, The. Romanticism. Raymond Carver. CP-CarvR

Nights belong to / What hurts. Rafael Alberti. CP-MertT *Fr.* Roman Nocturnes.

Night's black mirror is broken. Upon Reflection. Lawrence Ferlinghetti. SP-FerlL

Night's blind-black, an' I 'low the stars's, The. Moonshiner's Serenade. James Whitcomb Riley. CP-RileJ

Night's blood / flows through the arteries. Aside. Federico García Lorca. CP-GarcF, *tr. by* Jerome Rothenberg *Fr.* Water Jets.

Night's capacity varies. Emily Dickinson. SP-DickE

Night's eye / he could say / blandly, The. So Big. Robert Creeley. CP-CreeR

Nights in the Gardens of Port of Spain. Derek Walcott. CP-WalcD

Night's Nothings Again. Carl Sandburg. CP-SandC

Nights of 1965: the Old Reliable. Marilyn Hacker. SP-HackM

(Nights of 1964–1966: The Old Reliable.) SP-HackM

Nights of 1964–1966: The Old Reliable. Marilyn Hacker. *See* Nights of 1965: the Old Reliable

Nights of 1962: The River Merchant's Wife. Marilyn Hacker. SP-HackM

Nights, streets, faces, lights. Unhidden. The. Yannis Ritsos. SP-RitsY, *tr. by* N. C. Germanacos

Nights, the railway-arches, the bad sky, The. Rimbaud. W. H. Auden. CP-AudeW

Night's wanderers! why hang ye there. Stars, The. Jones Very. CP-VeryJ

Nights with guns firing and walls. Afterwards, quiet. 1972. Yannis Ritsos. SP-RitsY, *tr. by* Kimon Friar *and* Kostas Myrsiades

Nightshade on the Way to School. Margaret Atwood. SP-AtwM2

Nightsong. Carl Sandburg. CP-SandC

Nightwalker. Thomas Kinsella. CP-KinsT

Nihil Obstat. Sam Hamill. SP-HamiS

Nihilist as Hero, The. Robert Lowell. SP-LoweR

Nike. James Merrill. SP-MerrJ

Nil, not my aim to study you, Caesar, to be—well, a placater. Catullus. *See* Utter indifference to your welfare, Caesar

Nil Ptolomaeus agit, caelique volumina nescit. De Regis reditu e Scotia. Thomas Campion. CP-CampT

Nils Lykke. Ezra Pound. CP-PoEar

The / nimble / heat / had. E. E. Cummings. CP-CummE

Nimmo. Edwin Arlington Robinson. CP-RobiE

Nina Answers Back. Arthur Rimbaud. CP-RimbA, *tr. by* Martin Sorrell

Nine are the enabling elements. Coda: "Nine are the enabling elements." Thomas Kinsella. CP-KinsT

Nine birds(rising / through a gold moment)climb. E. E. Cummings. CP-CummE

Nine Black Poppies for Chac. Norman Dubie. CP-DubiN

Nine completely naked girls. New Numbers. Christopher Logue. SP-LoguC

Nine drops of water bead the jessamine. Wet August, A. Thomas Hardy. CP-HardT

9:45 AM. Robert Creeley. SP-CreeR

Nine furlongs strecht lies Tityus, who for his wicked deedes. Sir Walter Ralegh. CP-RaleW

Nine harvests & nine winters since its inception. Carmen 95. Catullus. CP-ZukLS *Fr.* Carmina.

Nine Inch Will Please a Lady. Robert Burns. CP-BurnR

Nine leaves a minute. Best She Could, The. Thomas Hardy. CP-HardT

Nine Little Goblins, The. James Whitcomb Riley. CP-RileJ

Nine Lives. William Corbett. SP-CorbW

Nine Miles to the Railroad. Ogden Nash. CP-NashO

Nine months I waited in the dark beneath. Pro Sua Vita. Robert Penn Warren. CP-WarrR

Nine Nectarines. Marianne Craig Moore. CP-MoorM

Nine o'Clock Bell, The. Jones Very. CP-VeryJ

9:00 p.m. Federico García Lorca. CP-GarcF, *tr. by* Jerome Rothenberg *Fr.* Summer Hours.

Nine Poems for the Unborn Child. Muriel Rukeyser. CP-RukeM

Nine posts, five doors, up the Clivus. Carmen 37. Catullus. CP-ZukLS *Fr.* Carmina.

9 Rings. Charles Bukowski. SP-BukC2

Nine stories high Second Avenue. 44th Birthday Evening, at Harris's. Ted Berrigan. SP-BerrT

Nine times Latona's son had turned his gaze. Petrarch. CP-Petra, *tr. by* J. G. Nichols

Nine truckloads of jewels. Figueras Castle. William Carlos Williams. CP-WilW2

Nine Variations in a Chinese Winter Setting. Charles Tomlinson. CP-TomlC; SP-TomlC

Nine Variations on Themes from Petrarch. Petrarch. SP-ZatuM, *tr. by* Marya Alexandrovna Zaturenska

Nine white chickens come. Black November Turkey, A. Richard Wilbur. CP-WilbR

Nine years old! The first of any. Hector in the Garden. Elizabeth Barrett Browning. CP-BroEB

Ninefold table of Heaven, The. Hafiz. CP-EmerR *Fr.* Odes.

1984. Yusef Komunyakaa. CP-KomuY

1959 Valentine. Louis Zukofsky. CP-ZukLS

1951. Frank O'Hara. SP-OharF

Nineteen Forty. Norman Dubie. CP-DubiN

1940. William Stafford. SP-StafW; SP-StafWW

1945. Donald Davie. CP-DaviDC

1945. Czeslaw Milosz. CP-MiloC; CP-MiloCN, *tr. by* Robert Hass

1945—1985: Poem for the Anniversary. Mary Oliver. SP-OlivM

1945: The Death of the Gods. Randall Jarrell. CP-JarrR

1914. Randall Jarrell. CP-JarrR

MCMXIV. Philip Larkin. CP-LarkP

1914. Wilfred Owen. CP-OwenW

1905. David Ignatow. SP-IgnaD

Nineteen Hundred and Nineteen. William Butler Yeats. CP-YeatW

1935. Kenneth Patchen. CP-PatcK

19 May 1950. Yannis Ritsos. SP-RitsY *Fr.* Exile's Journals 3.

MCMXCV. Joseph Brodsky. CP-BrodJ

MCMXCIV. Joseph Brodsky. CP-BrodJ

1994. Lucille Clifton. SP-ClifL

1991. William Corbett. SP-CorbW

Nineteen-Seventeen. Donald Davie. CP-DaviDC

1917–18–19. Portrait of the Author as a Young Anarchist. Kenneth Rexroth. CP-RexrK

1978 Reunion of Palmach Veterans at Ma-ayan Harod. Yehuda Amichai. SP-AmicY, *tr. by* Chana Bloch

1975. Thom Gunn. CP-GunnT

1971. Jorge Luis Borges. SP-BorgJ, *tr. by* Alastair Reid

1971. Robert Creeley. CP-CreeR

1971. Alice Walker. CP-WalkA

1976. Marilyn Hacker. SP-HackM

1973. Marilyn Hacker. SP-HackM

1972. Jorge Luis Borges. SP-BorgJ, *tr. by* Alastair Reid

1972. Joseph Brodsky. CP-BrodJ, *tr. by* Alan Myers

1972. Yannis Ritsos. SP-RitsY, *tr. by* Kimon Friar *and* Kostas Myrsiades

1964. Jorge Luis Borges. SP-BorgJ, *tr. by* Alastair Reid

1969. Adam Zagajewski. SP-ZagaA, *tr. by* Clare Cavanagh

1967. Thomas Hardy. CP-HardT

1910. Federico García Lorca. CP-GarcF, *tr. by* Greg Simon *and* Steven F. White

1913. Czeslaw Milosz. CP-MiloC; CP-MiloCN, *tr. by* Robert Hass

1930's. Robert Lowell. SP-LoweR

Nineteen Thirty-Eight. John Berryman. CP-BerrJ

1938. Yusef Komunyakaa. CP-KomuY

1938: at 5 in the morning I vomited on the grass in front of my house. Diaries of Death. Charles Olson. CP-OlsoC

1938: Tales from the Vienna Woods. Randall Jarrell. CP-JarrR

1938: The Spring Dances. Randall Jarrell. CP-JarrR

1934. Richard Eberhart. CP-EberR

1934. Donald Hall. CP-HallD

1931. Yusef Komunyakaa. CP-KomuY

Nineteen-thirty, our window had for view. Etruria Vale. Charles Tomlinson. CP-TomlC

1937. Lorine Niedecker. CP-NiedL

1933. Philip Levine. SP-LeviP

1932. William Stafford. SP-StafWW

1924. Yehuda Amichai. SP-AmicY, *tr. by* Chana Bloch

1924. Yehuda Amichai. SP-AmicYL, *tr. by* Benjamin Harshav *and* Barbara Harshav

1929. W. H. Auden. CP-AudeW

Nineteen years this city was divided. Yehuda Amichai. SP-AmicY, *tr. by* Chana Bloch *Fr.* Songs of Zion the Beautiful.

XIX, The. Pablo Neruda. SP-NeruP

Nineteenth Century and After, The. William Butler Yeats. CP-YeatW

Nineteenth Hole, The. Wyatt Prunty. SP-PrunW

90th Year, The. Denise Levertov. SP-LeveDL; SP-LeveDS

95°. Jane Cooper. CP-CoopJ

99 to One. Charles Bukowski. SP-BukC1

90 North. Randall Jarrell. CP-JarrR

Ninety percent of the mass of the Universe. Certainty before Lunch. John Berryman. CP-BerrJ

Ninna nanna, ninna nanna! Christina Georgina Rossetti. CP-RosC3

Ninon De L'Enclos, on Her Last Birthday. Dorothy Parker. CP-ParkD

Ninth-circle concrete. North Jersey. A. R. Ammons. CP-AmmoA

Ninth Elegy. The Antagonists. Muriel Rukeyser. CP-RukeM

Ninth Symphony of Beethoven Understood at Last as a Sexual Message, The. Adrienne Rich. SP-RicA2

Niobe. John Donne. CP-DonnJ; MW-DonnJ

Niobe. Kenneth Patchen. CP-PatcK

Niobe. Yannis Ritsos. SP-RitsY, *tr.* by Kimon Friar *and* Karelisa Hartigan

Niobe in Distress for Her Children Slain by Apollo, from *Ovid's Metamorphoses*, Book 6. And from a View of the Painting of Mr. *Richard Wilson*. Phillis Wheatley. CP-WheaP

Niobe Now. Muriel Rukeyser. CP-RukeM

Niobe, your tears. Hayden Carruth. CP-CarHS *Fr.* Clay Hill Anthology, The.

Nipping Pussy's Feet in Fun. Stevie Smith. CP-SmitS

Nis, he makes Verses; but the Lines he writes. Upon Nis. Robert Herrick. CP-HerrR

Nisus and Euryalus ("From thence his way the Trojan hero bent"). Virgil. CP-DryJ2, *tr.* by John Dryden *Fr.* Aeneid (Dryden translation).

Nisus and Euryalus ("Trojan camp the common danger shared, The"). Virgil. CP-DryJ2, *tr.* by John Dryden *Fr.* Aeneid (Dryden translation).

Nisus, the guardian of the portal, stood. Episode of Nisus and Euryalus, The. Lord Byron. CP-Byron

Nite) / thatthis / crou / ched. E. E. Cummings. CP-CummE

Nithsdale's Welcome Hame. Robert Burns. CP-BurnR

Nitrate. Philip Levine. SP-LeviP

Nixon's the One. William Meredith. SP-MereW

NJ Transit. Yusef Komunyakaa. CP-KomuY

No. John Berryman. CP-BerrJ

No. Robert Creeley. CP-CreeR

No! Kenneth Rexroth. CP-RexrK

No access to the Duke! You have not said. Scene from "Tasso." Percy Bysshe Shelley. CP-ShelP

No ache, love, 's the way to start the New Year. Celia's Birthday Poem. Louis Zukofsky. CP-ZukLS

No Action Hard to Affection. Robert Herrick. CP-HerrR

No age was less assured a heaven waits. On Seeing Projected Figures for War Dead in the Twentieth Century. Miller Williams. CP-WillM

No aimless wanderers, by the fiend Unrest. Christian Tourists, The. John Greenleaf Whittier. CP-WhitJ

No Amnesiac King. A. K. Ramanujan. CP-RamaA

No artist perhaps, you go beyond their phrases. Robert Lowell. SP-LoweR *Fr.* Mexico.

No Autumn's intercepting Chill. Emily Dickinson. CP-DickE

No barometer but yellow. One, The. James Dickey. CP-DickJ

No Bashfulnesse in Begging. Robert Herrick. CP-HerrR

No begging forgiveness. Sex, Magnolias, & Speed. Yusef Komunyakaa. CP-KomuY

No Bell-Ringing. Thomas Hardy. CP-HardT

No Berserk thirst of blood had they. Lexington. John Greenleaf Whittier. CP-WhitJ

No better day to come. Old Woman's Vision, An. Norman Dubie. CP-DubiN

No better lost than any other woman. Marilyn Hacker. SP-HackM *Fr.* Taking Notice.

No better love than love with no object. Jelaluddin Rumi. SP-Rumi, *tr.* by Coleman Barks

No Better than a "Withered Daffodil." Marianne Craig Moore. CP-MoorM

No Bird. Theodore Roethke. CP-RoetT

No Bird Does Call. Robert Penn Warren. CP-WarrR

No bird-song floated down the hill. River Path, The. John Greenleaf Whittier. CP-WhitJ

No bitterness: our ancestors did it. Ave Caesar. Robinson Jeffers. CP-JefR2

No blanch witloof handboud dry. Dandelion. Louis Zukofsky. CP-ZukLS

No boats oar slow, no barges pass. George Meredith. CP-MerG2

No Bobolink—reverse His Singing. Emily Dickinson. CP-DickE

No books, no songs. Old Man at Valdez. Charles Tomlinson. CP-TomlC

No Boy Knows. James Whitcomb Riley. CP-RileJ

No, boy, we must not—so began. Filippo Baldinucci on the Privilege of Burial. Robert Browning. CP-BroR2

No breath of air to break the wave. Giaour, The. Lord Byron. CP-Byron

No Brigadier throughout the Year. Emily Dickinson. CP-DickE

No Buyers [or No Buyers: A Street Scene]. Thomas Hardy. CP-HardT

No calculation holds the miles endured. Old Declaratives. Wyatt Prunty. SP-PrunW

No cars go by. Dry Places. Thomas Merton. CP-MertT

No Categories! Stevie Smith. CP-SmitS

No cause, nor client fat, will Cheveril [or Cheverel] leese. On Cheveril [or Cheverel] the Lawyer. Ben Jonson. CP-JonsB; SP-JonsB

No Change of Place. W. H. Auden. *See* Who Will Endure

No changes of support—only. Last Month. John Ashbery. SP-AshbJ

No Cherub's heart or hand for us might ache. Good Friday Evening. Christina Georgina Rossetti. CP-RosC2

No Churchman am I for to rail and to write. Song: "No Churchman am I for to rail and to write." Robert Burns. CP-BurnR

No cloud, no relique of the sunken day. Nightingale, The. Samuel Taylor Coleridge. CP-ColeS; MW-ColeS

No clouds out the window. Robert Creeley. CP-CreeR

No Color Man. Donald Hall. CP-HallD

No Coming to God without Christ. Robert Herrick. CP-HerrR

No Comparison. James Laughlin. CP-LaugJ

No Coward Soul is Mine. Emily Jane Brontë. CP-BronE

No Crowd that has occurred. Emily Dickinson. CP-DickE

No Danger to Men Desperate. Robert Herrick. CP-HerrR

No, darling, the world is not ruled by sense, not sense. Alligators and Paris and North America. William Dickey. SP-DickW

No day for work; a day to strut and ramp. Epistle to Suzanne Joslyn Fosberg. Robert Stock. SP-StocR

No day has an age of its own. By the Cloud Path. W. S. Merwin. SP-MerwW

No Deposit. Donald Hall. CP-HallD

No Despight to the Dead. Robert Herrick. CP-HerrR

No Difference in the Dark [or i'th'dark]. Robert Herrick. CP-HerrR

No differently the guilty wretch hangs back. Michelangelo Buonarroti. CP-Miche, *tr.* by John Frederick Nims

No dignity without chromium. Ballad of Faith. William Carlos Williams. CP-WilW2

No Doctors Today, Thank You. Ogden Nash. CP-NashO

No, don't ask me to give you. Moon Flock. James Dickey. CP-DickJ

No, don't say a word! Fernando Pessoa. SP-PessF, *tr.* by Susan M. Brown *and* Edwin Honig

No doubt but ye are the People—your throne is above the King's. Islanders, The. Rudyard Kipling. CP-KiplR

No doubt he could remember how in the past. Milton: A Sonnet. Robert Penn Warren. CP-WarrR

No doubt he'd once had eyes to see. Archibald MacLeish. CP-MacLA *Fr.* Happy Marriage, The.

No doubt I will end my life as poor as you. Talking to My Grandmother Who Died Poor. Alice Walker. CP-WalkA

No doubt much peril lies. Michelangelo Buonarroti. CP-Miche, *tr.* by John Frederick Nims

No doubt she was a singer. Girl Who Died #2, The. Alice Walker. CP-WalkA

No doubt to-morrow I will hide. At Mass. Nicholas Vachel Lindsay. CP-LindV

No doubt we are intelligent. But far. Dept. of Philosophy. Hans Magnus Enzensberger. SP-EnzeH

No Druid can control a woman's longing. Druid Love. Robert Graves. CP-GravR

No duties. I don't have to be profound. Good Night. Czeslaw Milosz. CP-MiloCN, *tr.* by Robert Hass

No Earthly Enterprise. Edna St. Vincent Millay. CP-MillE

No empty bed blues. 29 Songs. Louis Zukofsky. CP-ZukLS

No End of Fun. Wisława Szymborska. SP-SzymW, *tr.* by Stanislaw Barańczak *and* Clare Cavanagh

No Epitaph. Donald Davie. CP-DaviDC

No Escaping the Scourging. Robert Herrick. CP-HerrR

No event of Wind or Bird. Emily Dickinson. SP-DickE

No faculty not ill at ease. After a Long Illness. Robert Duncan. SP-DuncR

No faith of partnership dominion owns. Lucan. CP-JohnS *Fr.* Civil War [Bellum Civile] *or* Pharsalia.

No farther out / than in—. No. Robert Creeley. CP-CreeR

No fate, save by the victim's fault, is low. Ralph Waldo Emerson. CP-EmerR

No Fault in Women. Robert Herrick. CP-HerrR

No fiction was it of the antique age. Faery Chasm, The. William Wordsworth. CP-WorW2 *Fr.* River Duddon [A Series of Sonnets], The.

No Fifth Man. A. K. Ramanujan. CP-RamaA

No Fixed Place. Alice Walker. CP-WalkA

No Flag. Jelaluddin Rumi. SP-Rumi, *tr.* by Coleman Barks

No flag touched our this year. Old Glory. William Stafford. SP-StafWW

No flame, no sleepless nights, no heat. Senza Flash. Adam Zagajewski. SP-ZagaA, *tr.* by Clare Cavanagh

No flower grew where I was bred. Slum Child, The. Walter De la Mare. CP-DeLaW

No foot could endure it. Night City. Elizabeth Bishop. CP-BishE

No, for I'll save it! Seven years since. Apparent Failure. Robert Browning. CP-BroR1; SP-BroR

No Frog Prince ever had a pond. To a Waterbed. John Updike. CP-UpdiJ

No front yard to speak of. House on Bishop Street, The. Rita Dove. SP-DoveR

No further from me than my hand. Edna St. Vincent Millay. CP-MillE

No generous action can delay. Delay. Henry David Thoreau. CP-ThorH

No gloom o'er Nature's face is spread. William Cullen Bryant. Jones Very. CP-VeryJ

No-Good Blues. Yusef Komunyakaa. CP-KomuY

No Good Too. William Carlos Williams. CP-WilW2

No grave for woe, yet earth my watrie teares devoures. Thomas Campion *and* Philip Rosseter. CP-CampT

No grief is grown so desperate, but the ill. Will Makes the Work, or Consent Makes the Cure, The. Robert Herrick. CP-HerrR

No Harm Shall Come. Olga Broumas. SP-BrouO

No hawk at wrist, but blessed by sudden sun. Portrait of Mrs. Spaxton. Charles Tomlinson. CP-TomlC

No hawk hangs over in this air. Snow Storm, The. Edna St. Vincent Millay. CP-MillE

No, he doesn't want to let go; the rope shakes; he shuts his eyes. Tightrope Walker, The. Yannis Ritsos. SP-RitsY, *tr. by* Christian McEwen *and* Nikos Tsingos

No Hearing. Robert Lowell. SP-LoweR

No heart that broke but further went. Emily Dickinson. SP-DickE

No Heroics, Please. Raymond Carver. CP-CarvR

No Holy Wars for Them. Robert Frost. CP-FrosR

No hope in life; yet is there hope. What Good Shall My Life Do Me? Christina Georgina Rossetti. CP-RosC3

No hope, no change! The clouds have shut us in. Two Months. Rudyard Kipling. CP-KiplR

No house accepted us. Bedouin in Love. Yehuda Amichai. SP-AmicYL, *tr. by* Benjamin Harshav *and* Barbara Harshav

No hyacinthine imagination can express this clock of meat bleakly pining. Hymn: "No hyacinthine imagination can express this clock of meat bleakly pining." Allen Ginsberg. CP-GinsA

No, I can't touch these mountains. George Seferis in Sonora. Sam Hamill. SP-HamiS

No, I don't want anything. Lisbon Revisited (1923). Fernando Pessoa. SP-PessF, *tr. by* Susan M. Brown *and* Edwin Honig

No, I had set no prohibiting sign. Trespass. Robert Frost. CP-FrosR

No, I have never found. Places, Loved Ones. Philip Larkin. CP-LarkP

No, I want no more: no. Rainer Maria Rilke. CP-RilkFr, *tr. by* A. Poulin, Jr. *Fr.* Fragments.

No, I was wrecked here. Hayden Carruth. CP-CarHS *Fr.* Clay Hill Anthology, The.

No, I will go alone. Concert, The. Edna St. Vincent Millay. CP-MillE

No, I will never forget you and your great eyes. Song: "No, I will never forget you and your great eyes." May Sarton. SP-SartM

No idea, Gelli, spurred me to mirror you faithful. Catullus. *See* In this hopeless & wasting love of mine

No, I'll not do it. I'll not! Conscript. Imitation of Horace; Carmina 1.6. Robert Stock. SP-StocR

No, I'm not ashamed. By Proxy. Yusef Komunyakaa. CP-KomuY

No I'm not in Sing Sing. Prisoner's Song, The. James Laughlin. CP-LaugJ

No, I'm not tired, the tide. Thetis. Olga Broumas. SP-BrouO

No! Indeed. Sir Thomas Wyatt. CP-WyatT

No Infant Sotheby, Whose Dauntless Head. Lord Byron. CP-Byron

No interval of manner. George Oppen. CP-OppGN

No introspective chaos . . . I accept. Lettres d'un Soldat. Wallace Stevens. CP-StevWP

No, it does not happen. Snakes. A. K. Ramanujan. CP-RamaA

No, it won't do, my sweet theologians. Theodicy. Czeslaw Milosz. CP-MiloC; CP-MiloCN, *tr. by* Robert Hass

No it would not mean a damn (quick whim referred to pure). Catullus. *See* As God is my witness where is the difference between

No, it's not that Apollo took back his pledge. Actual Cause, The. Yannis Ritsos. SP-RitsY, *tr. by* Kostas Myrsiades

No Joy in Life. D. H. Lawrence. CP-LawrD

No Labor-Saving Machine. Walt Whitman. CP-WhitW

No lack of counsel from the shrewd and wise. Edna St. Vincent Millay. CP-MillE

No ladder needs the bird but skies. Emily Dickinson. CP-DickE

No lame excuses can gloss over. Green Rock, Winthrop Bay. Sylvia Plath. CP-PlatS

No Lamp Has Ever Shown Us Where to Look. Archibald MacLeish. CP-MacLA

No Letter. Robert Graves. CP-GravR

No Life can pompless pass away. Emily Dickinson. CP-DickE

No lift odd mere horror, harrowed (why boy?) that no woman will. Catullus. *See* Do not wonder when the wench declines

No limbo this week. Or next. Now it turns out. Limbo Dancer, The. Josephine Jacobsen. CP-JacoJ

No Loathsomnesse in Love. Robert Herrick. CP-HerrR

No Lock against Lechery. Robert Herrick. CP-HerrR

No longer burn the hands that seized. Stanza: "No longer burn the hands that seized." Louise Bogan. CP-BogaL

No longer I follow a sound. Song on Peace. William Cowper. CP-CowpW

No longer throne of a goddess to whom we pray. Full Moon. Robert Earl Hayden. CP-HaydR

No longer torn by what she knows. Poor Relation, The. Edwin Arlington Robinson. CP-RobiE

No Loser, No Weeper. Maya Angelou. SP-AngeM

No Love. Grace Paley. CP-PalGC

No love by test, my love, 'll air then, time, say the care of all my time. Catullus. *See* No woman loved, in truth, Lesbia

No love cried the last fling. No Love. Grace Paley. CP-PalGC

No Love in This House. Yusef Komunyakaa. CP-KomuY

No love is so dear (quivered Cupid, fly!). Elegy 2.5: "No love is so dear (quivered Cupid, fly!)." Ovid. CP-MarlC *Fr.* Elegies.

No lovelier hills than thine have laid. England. Walter De la Mare. CP-DeLaW

No lover ever found a cure for love. Cure, The. Robert Graves. CP-GravR

No lover saith, I love, nor any other. Paradox, The. John Donne. CP-DonnJ; MW-DonnJ

No loving mother doting on her son. Petrarch. CP-Petra, *tr. by* J. G. Nichols

No Luck in Love. Robert Herrick. CP-HerrR

No Man can compass a Despair. Emily Dickinson. CP-DickE

No man comes late unto that place from whence. Never Too Late to Dye. Robert Herrick. CP-HerrR

No man has seen the third hand. Mystique. David Ignatow. SP-IgnaD

No man hath dared to write this thing as yet. Histrion. Ezra Pound. CP-PoEar

No man, if men are gods;but if gods must. E. E. Cummings. CP-CummE; SP-CummE

No Man Is an Island. A. K. Ramanujan. CP-RamaA

No man is tempted so, but may o'recome. Temptations. Robert Herrick. CP-HerrR

No man may him hyde. Sun. Marianne Craig Moore. CP-MoorM

No man saw awe, nor to his house. Emily Dickinson. CP-DickE

No man should stand before the moon. Sense of Humor, A. Nicholas Vachel Lindsay. CP-LindV

No man so well a Kingdom Rules, as He. Another on the Same. Robert Herrick. CP-HerrR

No man such rare paths hath, that he can swim. No Man without Money. Robert Herrick. CP-HerrR

No man, unless he has died, and learned to be alone. Initiation Degrees. D. H. Lawrence. CP-LawrD

No man was better, nor more just than hee. Ovid. CP-RaleW *Fr.* Metamorphoses.

No Man without Money. Robert Herrick. CP-HerrR

No manner of address will do. Metamorphoses. Geoffrey Hill. CP-HillG

No map traces the street. Sleepers, The. Sylvia Plath. CP-PlatS

No, Mary, there was nothing—not a word. Lazarus. Edwin Arlington Robinson. CP-RobiE

No matter how dull your soul, you cannot help. Playing Skittles. Howard Nemerov. CP-NemeH

No matter how lofty your spirit. Han-shan. CP-ColdM, *tr. by* Red Pine

No matter how much he called them "harmless," there was always a danger. Displacement. Yannis Ritsos. SP-RitsY, *tr. by* Kimon Friar

No matter how she tilts her head to hear. Going Deaf. Miller Williams. CP-WillM

No Matter, Never Mind. Gary Snyder. CP-SnydG

No matter—now—Sweet. Emily Dickinson. CP-DickE

No Matter What, after All, and That Beautiful Word So. Hayden Carruth. CP-CarHS

No matter what color my pants are. Swinging Down Central. Robert Creeley. CP-CreeR

No matter what I am. Poet Answers the Accuser, The. Kathleen Jessie Raine. SP-RainK

No matter what I say. Eel-Grass. Edna St. Vincent Millay. CP-MillE

No matter what life you lead. Snow White and the Seven Dwarfs. Anne Sexton. CP-SextA; SP-SextA

No matter what went on around them; no matter. Nativity. Joseph Brodsky. CP-BrodJ

No matter what you call it. James Whitcomb Riley. Paul Laurence Dunbar. CP-DunbP

No matter what you do. Irreconcilabilia. Thomas Lux. SP-LuxT

No matter where my route may lie. Men I'm Not Married To. Dorothy Parker. CP-ParkD

No matter where the Saints abide. Emily Dickinson. CP-DickE

No matter where they lived the same dream came. Castaways, The. Marya Alexandrovna Zaturenska. SP-ZatuM

No matter where you are. Lorine Niedecker. CP-NiedL

No matter why, nor whence, nor when she came. Story of the Ashes and the Flame, The. Edwin Arlington Robinson. CP-RobiE

No McTavish. Genealogical Reflection. Ogden Nash. CP-NashO

No Messiah. Robert Lowell. SP-LoweR

No mischief worthier of our fear. On Flatterers. *Unknown.* CP-CowpW

No! Mr Lawrence! D. H. Lawrence. CP-LawrD

No, Mr. Lawrence, it's not like that! No! Mr Lawrence! D. H. Lawrence. CP-

LawrD

No money to bury him. Ballad of the Man Who's Gone. Langston Hughes. CP-HughL; CP-HughL2

No moral doctor could more nicely pose. Motives of a Two-Headed Turtle. Robert Stock. SP-StocR

No More. Czeslaw Milosz. CP-MiloC; CP-MiloCN, tr. by Tony Milosz

No More Are Lovely Palaces. Laura Riding Jackson. CP-RidiL

No more around the social board. Song: "No more around the social board." Jones Very. CP-VeryJ

No more, blind god! for see, my heart. Truce in Love Intreated. Thomas Carew. CP-CareT

No more cinders, the cellar water is iced over. Fanny Howe. SP-HoweF Fr. Lines Out to Silence.

No more football. On Wearing Glasses. Alan Dugan. CP-DugaA

No more for us the sighing. Threnos. Ezra Pound. CP-PoEar

No More Ghosts. Robert Graves. CP-GravR

No more let Greece her bolder fables tell. On the Famous Voyage. Ben Jonson. CP-JonsB; SP-JonsB

No more loud Fall / October is suddenly over / Sunk in snow. Early Blizzard. Thomas Merton. CP-MertT

No more muffled drums! In Baghdad, Dreaming of Cairo: In Cairo, Dreaming of Baghdad. Jelaluddin Rumi. SP-Rumi, tr. by Coleman Barks

No more my little song comes back. Small Hours, The. Dorothy Parker. CP-ParkD

No more my Silvia, do I mean to pray. To Silvia. Robert Herrick. CP-HerrR

No more my visionary soul shall dwell. Pantisocracy. Samuel Taylor Coleridge. CP-ColeS

No more, no more, no more! On Being Forbidden to Feed the Dog. G. K. Chesterton. CP-ChesG

No more, O my spirit. Euripides. CP-DoolH Fr. Hippolytus.

No more of your titled acquaintances boast. Toadeater, The. Robert Burns. CP-BurnR

No more our mother meets our sight. Our Dear Mother. Jones Very. CP-VeryJ

No More People. Stevie Smith. CP-SmitS

No more phrases, Swenson: I was once. Lions in Sweden. Wallace Stevens. CP-StevW; CP-StevWP

No more sand art, no sand book, no masters. Paul Celan. SP-CelaP, tr. by John Felstiner

No More Sea. Louis MacNeice. CP-MacNL

No more shall hapless Celia's ears. Song: "No more shall hapless Celia's ears." William Cowper. CP-CowpW

No more shall I, since I am driven hence. To Larr [or Lar]. Robert Herrick. CP-HerrR

No more shall meads be deckt [or deck'd] with flowers. Protestation [A Sonnet], The. Thomas Carew. CP-CareT

No more stalling. Saying Goodbye to Love. Charles Bukowski. SP-BukC2

No more summer for Molly and me. Molly Gone. Thomas Hardy. CP-HardT

No More than Is. Laura Riding Jackson. CP-RidiL

No more: the end is sudden and abrupt. Apology. William Wordsworth. CP-WorW2

No more the flow'ry scenes of pleasure rise. On the Death of J. C. an Infant. Phillis Wheatley. CP-WheaP

No more the thunderous trumpets tell. Crooner, The. G. K. Chesterton. CP-ChesG

No more the white refulgent streets. Elegy: "No more the white refulgent streets." Allen Tate. CP-TateA

No more the white refulgent streets. Euthanasia. Allen Tate. CP-TateA

No more these simple flowers belong. Burns. John Greenleaf Whittier. CP-WhitJ

No more thus brooding o'er yon heap. Vanity of Wealth, The. Samuel Johnson. CP-JohnS

No more 'twixt conscience staggering and the Pope. Lines Suggested by the Last Words of Berengarius. Samuel Taylor Coleridge. CP-ColeS; MW-ColeS

No more violets. Pastorale. Hart Crane. CP-CranH

No more, / where the tidal river rushes. Maximus to Himself June 1964. Charles Olson. SP-OlsoC Fr. Maximus Poems, The.

No more! while sun and planets fly. I See that All Things Come to an End. Christina Georgina Rossetti. CP-RosC2

No more wine for me! Center of the Fire, The. Jelaluddin Rumi. SP-Rumi, tr. by Coleman Barks

No more wine? then we'll push back chairs and talk. Bishop Blougram's Apology. Robert Browning. CP-BroR1

No more with overflowing light. For a Dead Lady. Edwin Arlington Robinson. CP-RobiE

No more, ye warblers of the wood, no more. Sonnet on the Death of Robert Riddel, Esq. of Glen Riddel, April 1794. Robert Burns. CP-BurnR

No mortal man beneath the sky. Epitaph for George Moore. Thomas Hardy. CP-HardT

No mortal object did these eyes behold. Michelangelo Buonarroti. CP-WorW1

No moss nor mottle stains. No Epitaph. Donald Davie. CP-DaviDC

No, Music, thou art not the "food of Love." Another Fragment to Music. Percy Bysshe Shelley. CP-ShelP

No My Dear. James Laughlin. CP-LaugJ

No Name. Margaret Atwood. SP-AtwM2

No Need. Raymond Carver. CP-CarvR

No need at all for your angel loveliness. Michelangelo Buonarroti. CP-Miche, tr. by John Frederick Nims

No need for spurs, for bits or reins. Lover's Wine. Charles Baudelaire. CP-BaudC, tr. by Walter Martin

No need to attack the faults of others. Han-shan. CP-ColdM, tr. by Red Pine

No need to break the mirror. Economy. W. S. Merwin. SP-MerwW

No need to get home early. Father's Voice. William Stafford. SP-StafW; SP-StafWW

No News. D. H. Lawrence. CP-LawrD

No news of navies burnt at seas. New-Year's [or New-Yeares] Gift Sent to Sir Simeon Steward, A. Robert Herrick. CP-HerrR

No nightingale: water, dense, still. Rococo Birdbath with Figurine of Daphne as Warning to Virgins. Robert Stock. SP-StocR

No, no,—forget your Cricket and your Ant. Leffingwell. Edwin Arlington Robinson. CP-RobiE

No, no! Go from me. I have left her lately. Virginal, A. Ezra Pound. CP-PoEar; SP-PounE

No, no, go not to Lethe, neither twist. Ode on Melancholy. John Keats. CP-KeatJ

No, no. Guard thee. Get thee gone. Not that way. Walter De la Mare. CP-DeLaW

No; no; / It must not be so. Paths of Former Time. Thomas Hardy. CP-HardT

No No No No. Maya Angelou. SP-AngeM

No no the dead have no brothers. Hydra, The. W. S. Merwin. SP-MerwW

No, no, the falling blossom is no sign. Song: "No, no, the falling blossom is no sign." George Meredith. CP-MerG1

No. No. The woman is cheerful, she smiles at her stomach. Eighth Psalm. Anne Sexton. SP-SextA Fr. O Ye Tongues.

No no: they definitely were. Testimony. Dan Pagis. SP-PagiD, tr. by Stephen Mitchell

No, no, you're no spring chicken, dear. Rara Avis. Charles Baudelaire. CP-BaudC, tr. by Walter Martin

No. Not really red. Song for a Red Nightgown. Anne Sexton. CP-SextA

No, not Sprung Rhythm. Blue Tonality. Yusef Komunyakaa. CP-KomuY

No, not that door—never! But. I Am Dreaming of a White Christmas: The Natural History of a Vision. Robert Penn Warren. CP-WarrR

No, not the downfall. Rumba! Rumba! William Carlos Williams. CP-WilW2

No—not where I shall make my own. Her Late Husband. Thomas Hardy. CP-HardT

No Notice gave She, but a Change. Emily Dickinson. CP-DickE

No novice / In those elaborate rituals. Miss Drake Proceeds to Supper. Sylvia Plath. CP-PlatS

No, now I wish the sunshine would stop. And Oh—That the Man I Am Might Cease to Be. D. H. Lawrence. CP-LawrD

No, of course we were never. Song: Of Course. Robert Graves. CP-GravR

No one believes in the calm. Belief. Philip Levine. SP-LeviP

No one can die twice of the same fever? Twice of the Same Fever. Robert Graves. CP-GravR

No one can hear the loud voice of the city. Ohio River—Louisville, The. Thomas Merton. CP-MertT

No one can help him anymore. Company. Rita Dove. SP-DoveR

No one can truly write a book. To be. Ariosto and the Arabs. Jorge Luis Borges. SP-BorgJ, tr. by Eric McHenry

No One Can Watch the Wasichu. Alice Walker. CP-WalkA

No one can wish nothing. Emeritus Addresses the School, An. John Ciardi. CP-CiarJ

No one did anything at first. Technical Supplement, A. Thomas Kinsella. CP-KinsT

No one / else in the room. Here ("No one / else in the room"). Robert Creeley. CP-CreeR

No one escapes the perjury of time. Old Photograph, An. Howard Nemerov. CP-NemeH

No one ever saw it. Home-made Riddles. James Whitcomb Riley. CP-RileJ

No one ever walking this our only earth, various, very clouded. He Had a Quality of Growth. Muriel Rukeyser. CP-RukeM

No one ever works alone. Kenneth Patchen. CP-PatcK

No one explains me because. Song for Muriel, A. Carolyn Kizer. CP-KizeC

No one gives you a thought, as day by day. Neurotics. Philip Larkin. CP-LarkP

No one had taken care of the garden for years. And yet. Renaissance. Yannis Ritsos. SP-RitsY, tr. by Kimon Friar

No one in his family has ever died of love. Family Album. Wisława Szymborska. SP-SzymW, tr. by Stanislaw Barańczak and Clare Cavanagh

No one, in the vast and virgin jungle. Fernando Pessoa. SP-PessF, tr. by Susan M. Brown and Edwin Honig

No one is left to eat by my fire. Signs. Audre Lorde. SP-LordA

No one is lovely. To a Woman Seen Once. William Carlos Williams. CP-WilW2

No one is missed in the garden. Nobody's there. Egoist. Pablo Neruda. SP-NeruP

No one is perfection, yet. Absence. Stephen Spender. CP-SpenS

No one is the homeland. Not even the rider. Ode Written in 1966. Jorge Luis Borges. SP-BorgJ, *tr. by* W. S. Merwin

No one is to open or close a single door. Bust of Janus Speaks, A. Jorge Luis Borges. SP-BorgJ, *tr. by* Alan S. Trueblood

No one is "Woman" to another. Mother II. Marilyn Hacker. SP-HackM

No one kneads us again out of earth and clay. Psalm: "No one kneads us again out of earth and clay." Paul Celan. SP-CelaP, *tr. by* John Felstiner

No one knows how mastered we are. Rainer Maria Rilke. CP-RilkFr, *tr. by* A. Poulin, Jr. *Fr.* Orchards.

No one knows how this naked statue came to be found on the mezzanine floor. Statue in the Cafe, The. Yannis Ritsos. SP-RitsY, *tr. by* Kimon Friar *and* Kostas Myrsiades

No one knows, / the heart of a child "H. D." CP DoolH *Fr.* Electra-Orestes.

No one knows what the banging is all about. Neighbor, The. Miller Williams. CP-WillM

No one knows yet. Violence. Adrienne Rich. CP-RicAE

No one, not even Cambridge, was to blame. A. E. Housman. W. H. Auden. CP-AudeW

No one, not even God, can put back a leaf on to a tree. Fatality. D. H. Lawrence. CP-LawrD

No one now imagines you answer idle questions. Short Ode to the Cuckoo. W. H. Auden. CP-AudeW

No one prays for me . . . Giovanna or the others. Dante 3. Buonconte. Robert Lowell. SP-LoweR

No One Remembers. Philip Levine. SP-LeviP

No one should read self-pity or reproach. Poem of the Gifts. Jorge Luis Borges. SP-BorgJ, *tr. by* Alastair Reid

No one speaks of them, and yet. Rainer Maria Rilke. CP-RilkFr

No / one / thing. Loop, A. Robert Creeley. CP-CreeR

No one understood the perfume. Gacela of Unforeseen Love. Federico García Lorca. SP-GarcF, *tr. by* W. S. Merwin

No one understood the perfume, ever. Ghazal of Love Unforeseen. Federico García Lorca. CP-GarcF, *tr. by* Catherine Brown *Fr.* Ghazals.

No one was in the fields. Tom's Angel. Walter De la Mare. CP-DeLaW

No one was looking at his lonely case. Any Size We Please. Robert Frost. CP-FrosR

No one was with me there. Estranged. Walter De la Mare. CP-DeLaW

No one will come with water and white rags. No one. Indian Summer. Norman Dubie. CP-DubiN

No one will ever understand that evening. Evening Plaza, San Miguel. Muriel Rukeyser. CP-RukeM

No one's going to. Seventeenth Floor: Echoes of Singapore. Robert Creeley. SP-CrecR

No one's serious when they're seventeen. Romance. Arthur Rimbaud. CP-RimbA, *tr. by* Martin Sorrell

No Other can reduce. Emily Dickinson. CP-DickE

No other handsome face such power possessed. Michelangelo Buonarroti. CP-Miche, *tr. by* John Frederick Nims

No other such luxuriance: the. Gentle Negress, The. William Carlos Williams. CP-WilW2

No other word will do. For that's what it was. Gravy. Gravy. Raymond Carver. CP-CarvR

No outward service doth the Lord require. True Worshipers, The. Jones Very. CP-VeryJ

No Page (Unturned). Michael Palmer. SP-PalmM

No Paines, No Gaines. Robert Herrick. CP-HerrR

No paraphrase does. English A. John Ciardi. CP-CiarJ

No Passenger was known to flee. Emily Dickinson. CP-DickE

No physician has a balsam for my wo. Hafiz. CP-EmerR *Fr.* Odes.

No Pindar I, but a poor gentleman. Torch and Crown, 1968. Robert Graves. CP-GravR

No place for a lady, this. Sisterhood. Marilyn Hacker. SP-HackM

No, Plato, No. W. H. Auden. CP-AudeW

No, please! Then night. Report from the Lucky Country. Yusef Komunyakaa. CP-KomuY

No Pleasure, without Some Payne. Sir Walter Ralegh. CP-RaleW

No poet should admit to limitation. Great High Feasts on the Birthdays of Little Men. Robert Stock. SP-StocR

No point in looking. The. Sunday Morning. Donald Davie. CP-DaviDC

No Possum, No Sop, No Taters. Wallace Stevens. CP-StevW; CP-StevWP

No Praise, No Blame. William Stafford. SP-StafWW

No pretense no more than the. Cézanne. William Carlos Williams. CP-WilW2

No Prisoner be. Emily Dickinson. CP-DickE

No protesting, dearest! Saint Martin's Summer. Robert Browning. CP-BroR2;

SP-BroR

No question but Dols cheecks wo'd soon rost dry. Upon Dol. Robert Herrick. CP-HerrR

No question but, when my desire's aflame. Michelangelo Buonarroti. CP-Miche, *tr. by* John Frederick Nims

No Rack can torture me. Emily Dickinson. CP-DickE

No rage. No hate. A single blow. Self-Tormentor, The. Charles Baudelaire. CP-BaudC, *tr. by* Walter Martin

No real Style of Colouring ever appears. William Blake. CP-BlakW

No record tells of lance opposed to lance. William Wordsworth. CP-WorW2 *Fr.* River Duddon [A Series of Sonnets], The.

No Regrets. Langston Hughes. CP-HughL; CP-HughL3

No resolution. Visit, The. Robert Creeley. SP-CreeR

No Respect. Stevie Smith. CP-SmitS

No Rest for the Gambler. James Tate. SP-TateJ

No Rest for the Wicked. Derek Mahon. CP-MahoD

No rest here for the wicked, as folk say. Michelangelo Buonarroti. CP-Miche, *tr. by* John Frederick Nims

No Resurrection. Robinson Jeffers. CP-JefR2

No retiring summer stroke. Lorine Niedecker. CP-NiedL

No ripening curve can be allowed to sag. Cherry Ripe. Donald Davie. CP-DaviDC

No Road. Philip Larkin. CP-LarkP

No Romance sold unto. Emily Dickinson. CP-DickE

No roofes of golf o're riotous tables shining. Description of a Religious House and Condition of Life. Richard Crashaw. CP-CrasR

No Room for Form. Jelaluddin Rumi. SP-Rumi, *tr. by* Coleman Barks

No rose that in a garden ever grew. Edna St. Vincent Millay. CP-MillE

No Rose, yet felt myself a'bloom. Emily Dickinson. SP-DickE

No sadness. Here Again ("No sadness"). Robert Creeley. SP-CreeR

No salt here, old sea father, holy giant. Far-removed Mountain Men, The. Hayden Carruth. CP-CarHS

No sculptur'd marble here, nor pompous lay. Epitaph. Here Lies Robert Fergusson, Poet. Robert Burns. CP-BurnR

No Second Troy. William Butler Yeats. CP-YeatW

No shaken seas confuse me now. Tennessee Williams. CP-WillT

No sheltered ear can miss. February Midnight. Josephine Jacobsen. CP-JacoJ

No shields now / Cross the knoll. Iceland. Louis MacNeice. CP-MacNL

No ship of all that under sail or steam. Immigrants. Robert Frost. CP-FrosR

No Shipwrack of Vertue. To a Friend. Robert Herrick. CP-HerrR

No Shoes No Shirt No Service. Gary Snyder. CP-SnydG

No Single Thing by Itself. Clarence Major. SP-MajoC

No skilled hands. In Abeyance. Denise Levertov. SP-LeveDP

No sleep, not tonight. The window blazes. Lullaby. Adam Zagajewski. SP-ZagaA, *tr. by* Renata Gorczynski, Benjamin Ivry *and* C. K. Williams

No sleep. Somewhere near here in the woods, fear. Conspirators. Raymond Carver. CP-CarvR

No sleep. The sultriness pervades the air. House-Top, The. Herman Melville. SP-MelvH

No slightest chance on earth her heavenly eyes. Michelangelo Buonarroti. CP-Miche, *tr. by* John Frederick Nims

No smile so innocent or angelic. Against Witchcraft. Robert Graves. CP-GravR

No smoke says law light-/ Ning arrest alarm for. Comedy Card for a Serious Case. Thomas Merton. CP-MertT

No smoke spreads out of this chimney-pot. Starlings on the Roof. Thomas Hardy. CP-HardT

No So. Not So. Anne Sexton. CP-SextA

No soldiers in the scenery. Clear Day and No Memories, A. Wallace Stevens. CP-StevWP

No song is mine of Arab steed. Iron Horse, The. James Whitcomb Riley. CP-RileJ

No song nor dance I bring from yon great city. Prologue: "No song nor dance I bring from yon great city." Robert Burns. CP-BurnR

No song so tuneful, quoth the fox. Ralph Waldo Emerson. CP-EmerR

No sooner come [*or* came] but gone, and fallen [*or* fall'n] asleep. On My Dear Grandchild Simon Bradstreet, [Who Died on 16th November, 1669, Being but a Month and One Day Old]. Anne Bradstreet. CP-BradA

No sooner had I left A. Midpoint. Charles Simic. SP-SimiC; SP-SimiCE

No Sorrow Peculiar to the Sufferer. Vincent Bourne. CP-CowpW

No sort of learning ever hurts his head. Lout, The: "No sort of learning ever hurts his head." John Clare. SP-ClarJ

No sound—a spell—on, on out. Father and Son. William Stafford. SP-StafWW

No sound falls. After. Maya Angelou. SP-AngeM

No sound of any storm that shakes. Hillcrest. Edwin Arlington Robinson. CP-RobiE

No spade for leagues had won a rood of earth. William Wordsworth. CP-WorW1

No Spartan tube, no Attic shell. Ode [for General Washington's Birthday]. Robert Burns. CP-BurnR

No specious splendour of this stone. Cornelian, The. Lord Byron. CP-Byron

No Speech from the Scaffold. Thom Gunn. CP-GunnT

No speed of wind or water rushing by. Master Speed, The. Robert Frost. CP-FrosR

No spot of earth where men have so fiercely for ages of time. Antrim. Robinson Jeffers. CP-JefR2

No Spouse but a Sister. Robert Herrick. CP-HerrR

No spring, nor summer beauty hath such grace. Autumnal[l], The. John Donne. MW-DonnJ *Fr.* Elegies.

No sprouted wheat and soya shoots. Health-Food Diner, The. Maya Angelou. SP-AngeM

No sun these months. Ice-dark and cold. Robert Earl Hayden. CP-HaydR *Fr.* Snow Lamp, The.

No sunlight ever. Bleak trees whisper ironies. Sunday in the Park. Louis MacNeice. CP-MacNL

No sunset, but a grey, great, struggling sky. Sonnet: "No sunset, but a grey, great, struggling sky." E. E. Cummings. CP-CummE

No Supervening Thought of Grace. Hayden Carruth. CP-CarHS

No Swan So Fine. Marianne Craig Moore. CP-MoorM

No, Thank You, John. Christina Georgina Rossetti. CP-RosC1

No, that carved angel whose still smile. Chartres Annunciation, The. Kathleen Jessie Raine. SP-RainK

No that is not it. To Have Done Nothing. William Carlos Williams. CP-WilW1

No, the night has gone. William Dickey. SP-DickW *Fr.* At Your Old House.

No, the serpent did not. Theology. Ted Hughes. SP-HughTN

No / the two legg'd beasts. No No No No. Maya Angelou. SP-AngeM

No theory will stand up to a chicken's guts. David Ignatow. SP-IgnaD

No, there will be no explanations then. On the Final Day. Donald Davie. CP-DaviDC

No, they are come; their horn is lifted up. Gerard Manley Hopkins. CP-HopkG

No thing is great on this side of the grave. Heaviness May Endure for a Night, but Joy Cometh in the Morning. Christina Georgina Rossetti. CP-RosC2

No thing less than one thing. Flowers. Robert Creeley. CP-CreeR

No: this, my love, is neither you nor I. This Beast, This Angel. Adrienne Rich. CP-RicAE

No! those days are gone away. Robin Hood. John Keats. CP-KeatJ

No time ago / or else a life. E. E. Cummings. CP-CummE; SP-CummE

No Time for Self-Pity. Clarence Major. SP-MajoC

No Time in Eternity. Robert Herrick. CP-HerrR

No Title Required. Wisława Szymborska. SP-SzymW, *tr. by* Stanisław Barańczak *and* Clare Cavanagh

No Title Required. Wisława Szymborska. SP-SzymWM, *tr. by* Joanna Trzeciak

No trail / can't be followed. Target Practice. Gary Snyder. CP-SnydG

No trellises, no vines. Iron Landscapes (and the Statue of Liberty). Thom Gunn. CP-GunnT

No trump tells thy virtues—the grave where they rest. On Robert Emmet's Grave. Percy Bysshe Shelley. CP-ShelP

No trust to Metals nor to Marbles, when. Epitaph on the Tomb of Sir Edward Giles and His Wife in the South Aisle of Dean Prior Church. Robert Herrick. CP-HerrR

No unfit place is this wherein to vote. Voting in the Old North Church. Jones Very. CP-VeryJ

No use hoping, or feeling vext. He Wonders about Himself. Thomas Hardy. CP-HardT

No use in my going. Blue Monday. Langston Hughes. CP-HughL; CP-HughL3

No use invoking Apollo in a case like theirs. Epigoni, The. W. H. Auden. CP-AudeW

No use, no use, now, begging Recognize! Amnesiac. Sylvia Plath. CP-PlatS

No use to look for signs of old affection. To One Who Went Too Far. Miller Williams. CP-WillM

No use whistling for Lyonnesse! Lyonnesse. Sylvia Plath. CP-PlatS

No, Virgil, no. Secondary Epic. W. H. Auden. CP-AudeW

No vow once sworn may ever be annulled. Vow, The. Robert Graves. CP-GravR

No Voyage. Mary Oliver. SP-OlivM

No vulture is here, hardly a hawk. Low Sky, The. Robinson Jeffers. CP-JefR2

No Want Where There's Little. Robert Herrick. CP-HerrR

No waste is trackless: all terrain the lost. Sestina 2: "No waste is trackless: all terrain the lost." Howard Nemerov. CP-NemeH

No water is still, on top. Movement of Fish, The. James Dickey. CP-DickJ

No water so still as the / dead fountains of Versailles. No swan. No Swan So Fine. Marianne Craig Moore. CP-MoorM

No waxing or waning essentially still. Shih-te. CP-ColdM, *tr. by* Red Pine

No way he who undid me can restore. Michelangelo Buonarroti. CP-Miche, *tr. by* John Frederick Nims

No weary weather-beaten mariner. Petrarch. CP-Petra, *tr. by* J. G. Nichols

No whimsy of the purse is here. Inscription for the Moss-Hut at Dove Cottage. William Wordsworth. CP-WorW1

No White Birds Sings. John Ciardi. CP-CiarJ

No wind-wakeness here. A cricket's creed. Sunday in the Country. May Swenson. SP-SwenM

No wit (and none needed) but. Atlantic City Convention, The. William Carlos Williams. CP-WilW1

No Woe Is Gossamer to Mr. Bessemer. Ogden Nash. CP-NashO

No woman loved, in truth, Lesbia. Carmen 87. Catullus. CP-ZukLS *Fr.* Carmina.

No Wonder Our Fathers Died. Ogden Nash. CP-NashO

No wonder, shaggy saint, breast-deep in Jordan's. Salome. James Merrill. SP-MerrJ

No wonder / The river Humber. River Humber, The. Stevie Smith. CP-SmitS

No wonder we exclaim: How like a child! Paul Klee. Robert Stock. SP-StocR

No Word. Kenneth Rexroth. CP-RexrK

No words can express, my dear Aunt, my surprise. To Miss J. Austen. James Edward Austen-Leigh. CP-AustJ

NO WORK is master of the mine today. Tunnel, The. Muriel Rukeyser. CP-RukeM

No, worldling, no, 'tis not thy gold. Second Rapture, The. Thomas Carew. CP-CareT

No Worst, There Is None. Pitched Past Pitch of Grief. Gerard Manley Hopkins. CP-HopkG

No wrath of Men, or rage of Seas. Purposes. Robert Herrick. CP-HerrR

No writing-desk crammed full of music, twine. Black Bile ("No writing-desk crammed full of music, twine"). Charles Baudelaire. CP-BaudC, *tr. by* Walter Martin

Noah drunken, taking. Dancing Measures. Donald Davie. CP-DaviDC

Noah retrieves the dove again. After the Flood. Robert Graves. CP-GravR

Noah the first was (as Tradition sayes). Fast, or Lent, The. Robert Herrick. CP-HerrR

Noah's / Dove. Arthur Sze. SP-SzeA

Noah's Raven. W. S. Merwin. SP-MerwW

Nobil rosa ancor non crebbe. L'Incognita. Christina Georgina Rossetti. CP-RosC3

Noble. D. H. Lawrence. CP-LawrD

Noble and Ethereal. Stevie Smith. CP-SmitS

Noble beyond degree. Anabasis, The. Allen Tate. CP-TateA

Noble company, that early band, A. East India Marine Museum, The. Jones Very. CP-VeryJ

Noble Englishman, The. D. H. Lawrence. CP-LawrD

(I Know a Noble Englishman.) CP-LawrD

Noble hall our fathers planned, The. Hymn: Sung at the Dedication of the Peabody Academy of Science, Aug. 18, 1869. Jones Very. CP-VeryJ

Noble in Nature, great in arms. Ode to General Draper. Christopher Smart. SP-SmarC

Noble Lady of the Italian shore, A. Sonnet on the Nuptials of the Marquis Antonio Cavalli with the Countess Clelia Rasponi of Ravenna. Lord Byron. CP-Byron

Noble Lady's Tale, The. Thomas Hardy. CP-HardT

Noble life, well spent in learning's cause, A. To the Memory of Alpheus Crosby. Jones Very. CP-VeryJ

Noble lineage with calm humility. Petrarch. CP-Petra, *tr. by* J. G. Nichols

Noble Man, The. Richard Eberhart. CP-EberR

Noble Maxwels and their powers, The. Nithsdale's Welcome Hame. Robert Burns. CP-BurnR

Noble Old Elm, The. James Whitcomb Riley. CP-RileJ

Noble sire fallen on evil days, The. Virginia—the West. Walt Whitman. CP-WhitW

Noble Sisters. Christina Georgina Rossetti. CP-RosC1

Noble spirit, the ruler of that body. Petrarch. CP-Petra, *tr. by* J. G. Nichols

Noble theme demands a noble verse, A. To Mrs. Newton. William Cowper. CP-CowpW

Noble tree, which I loved well and long, The. Petrarch. CP-Petra, *tr. by* J. G. Nichols

Nobler king had never breath, A. Guinevere at Her Fireside. Dorothy Parker. CP-ParkD

Nobler unity, than that which came, A. National Unity ("Nobler unity, than that which came, A"). Jones Very. CP-VeryJ

Noblest Service, The. James Whitcomb Riley. CP-RileJ

Nobly, nobly Cape Saint Vincent to the North-west died away. Home-Thoughts, from the Sea. Robert Browning. CP-BroR1

Nobody. Robert Graves. CP-GravR

Nobody, ancient mischief, nobody. Nobody. Robert Graves. CP-GravR

Nobody Comes. Thomas Hardy. CP-HardT

Nobody comes here to stay: that's. Ship. A. R. Ammons. CP-AmmoA

Nobody could come because ours was the house. 1932. William Stafford. SP-StafWW

Nobody could / in superhuman flights. E. E. Cummings. CP-CummE

Nobody heard him, the dead man. Not Waving but Drowning. Stevie Smith. CP-SmitS

Nobody hears me, nobody sees me. Widowhood or the Home-Coming of Lady

Ross. Stevie Smith. CP-SmitS

Nobody here likes a wet dog. To a Stranger Born in Some Distant Country Hundreds of Years from Now. Billy Collins. SP-CollB

Nobody home. Long threads of sunlight slant. Pierce Street. Thom Gunn. CP-GunnT

Nobody in the lane, and nothing, nothing but blackberries. Blackberrying. Sylvia Plath. CP-PlatS

Nobody in the widow's household. Passing Through. Stanley Kunitz. CP-KunSC

Nobody knows if the water will dry up. Doomsday Books, The. Howard Nemerov. CP-NemeH

Nobody knows the beginning of the city. Legend, A. Czeslaw Milosz. CP-MiloC; CP-MiloCN, tr. by Robert Hass

Nobody knows this little Rose. Emily Dickinson. CP-DickE

Nobody knows what I feel about Freddy. Freddy. Stevie Smith. CP-SmitS

Nobody knows what love is anymore. Cartographer's Wedding, The. Sam Hamill. SP-HamiS

Nobody knows who she was, the Immortal. Late Beethoven. Adam Zagajewski. SP-ZagaA, tr. by Renata Gorczynski

Nobody lies in this earth. Cemetery in Pernambuco: Our Lady of Light. João Cabral de Melo Neto. CP-CoopJ, tr. by Jane Cooper

Nobody loses all the time. E. E. Cummings. CP-CummE; SP-CummE

Nobody loved this. E. E. Cummings. CP-CummE

Nobody noogers the shaff of a sloo. On a Flimmering Floom You Shall Ride. Carl Sandburg. CP-SandC

Nobody on the old farm here but Mother, me and John. How John Quit the Farm. James Whitcomb Riley. CP-RileJ

Nobody picks a red rose when the winter wind. Red and White. Carl Sandburg. CP-SandC

Nobody planted roses, he recalls. Summertime and the Living. Robert Earl Hayden. CP-HaydR

Nobody says: Ah, that is the place. Places. Thomas Hardy. CP-HardT

Nobody speaks of it but destiny is currency today. Stock Report. Andrei Codrescu. SP-CodrA

Nobody steps into the same river twice. Heraclitus on Rivers. Derek Mahon. CP-MahoD

Nobody there: / no body. On the Mountain. Charles Tomlinson. CP-TomlC

Nobody told me anything much. I was born. Bedlam Revisited. John Ciardi. CP-CiarJ

Nobody understood Juan. Juan's Twilight Dance. Marge Piercy. SP-PierM

Nobody wears a yellow. E. E. Cummings. CP-CummE

Nobody's Business. James Tate. SP-TateJ

Nobody's hero, George Vancouver, ever. Vancouver. Donald Davie. CP-DaviDC

Nobody's interested / (and how!). Every Tie. Andrei Codrescu. SP-CodrA

Nobody's (not Rilke's even, whose). White Mind and Roses. Heather McHugh. SP-McHuH

Nocht lang ago, efter the hour of pryme. Tragedie of the Cardinall, The. Sir David Lyndsay. SP-LyndD

Noctivagi terror, ganeonis triste flagellum. Acc. by English translation. Christopher Marlowe. CP-MarlC

Nocturn: "Night comes, an angel stands." Kathleen Jessie Raine. SP-RainK

Nocturn 4: "Claims of the sea, of the tide, move out, The." Carl Sandburg. CP-SandC

Nocturn Cabbage. Carl Sandburg. CP-SandC

Nocturnal. Yannis Ritsos. SP-RitsY, tr. by Edmund Keeley

Nocturnal Darkness. Jaroslav Seifert. SP-SeifJ, tr. by Ewald Osers

Nocturnal Divertimento. Jaroslav Seifert. SP-SeifJ, tr. by Ewald Osers

Nocturnal Episode. Yannis Ritsos. SP-RitsY, tr. by Kimon Friar

Nocturnal[l] upon Saint Lucy's [or S. Lucy's or S. Lucies] Day, Being the Shortest Day, A. John Donne. CP-DonnJ; MW-DonnJ

Nocturnally Pursed. Paul Celan. SP-CelaP, tr. by John Felstiner

Nocturne: "Always I knew that it could not last." Dorothy Parker. CP-ParkD

Nocturne: "Appearing unannounced, the moon." W. H. Auden. CP-AudeW

Nocturne: "As he was walking alone in the deserted street." Yannis Ritsos. SP-RitsY, tr. by Kimon Friar

Nocturne: "Dark blood of night-time, The." Louis MacNeice. CP-MacNL

Nocturne: "Do squamous and squiggling fish." W. H. Auden. CP-AudeW

Nocturne: "Earth, still heavy and warm with afternoon, The." Archibald MacLeish. CP-MacLA

Nocturne: "High-beam light swung, The." Yusef Komunyakaa. CP-KomuY

Nocturne: "I am afraid / of dead leaves." Federico García Lorca. CP-GarcF, tr. by Catherine Brown

Nocturne: "I stare at the stars." Federico García Lorca. CP-GarcF, tr. by Jerome Rothenberg Fr. Seaside Prints.

Nocturne: "I want to express my anguish in verses that tell." "Rubén Dario." SP-DariR, tr. by Alberto Acereda and Will Derusha

Nocturne: "Leopard no more secret, A." Stanley Kunitz. CP-KunSC

Nocturne: "Night has a sea which quenches the machine." Thomas Merton. CP-MertT

Nocturne: "Silence of the night, a sorrowful silence." "Rubén Dario." SP-DariR, tr. by Alberto Acereda and Will Derusha

Nocturne: "Sleep not. Be on your guard." Paul Celan. SP-CelaP, tr. by John Felstiner

Nocturne: "Their six-weeks-old daughter lies." Stephen Spender. CP-SpenS

Nocturne: "Those of you who auscultated the heart of the night." "Rubén Dario." SP-DariR, tr. by Alberto Acereda and Will Derusha

Nocturne: "'Tis not my voice now speaks; but as a bird." Walter De la Mare. CP-DeLaW

Nocturne: "When the lithe moonlight silently." E. E. Cummings. CP-CummE

Nocturne: "Where now has our young Adam." John Crowe Ransom. SP-RansJ

Nocturne for the Drums. Langston Hughes. CP-HughL; CP-HughL1

Nocturne for the Heirs of Light. Kenneth Patchen. CP-PatcK

Nocturne in a Deserted Brickyard. Carl Sandburg. CP-SandC

Nocturne in Outline. Federico García Lorca. CP-GarcF, tr. by Alan S. Trueblood Fr. Theories.

Nocturne Militaire. Thomas McGrath. SP-McGrT

Nocturne of Emptied Space. Federico García Lorca. CP-GarcF, tr. by Greg Simon and Steven F. White

Nocturne of the Drowned Youth. Federico García Lorca. CP-GarcF, tr. by Catherine Brown

Nocturne: Traveling Salesman in Hotel Bedroom. Robert Penn Warren. CP-WarrR

Nocturnes from the Window. Federico García Lorca. CP-GarcF, tr. by Alan S. Trueblood

Nod. Walter De la Mare. CP-DeLaW

Noddin' by de Fire. Paul Laurence Dunbar. CP-DunbP

Nodding. Stevie Smith. CP-SmitS

Nodding, its great head rattling like a gourd. Original Sin[: A Short Story]. Robert Penn Warren. CP-WarrR

Nodding Meadow Lily, The. Jones Very. CP-VeryJ

Noey Bixler ketched him, an' fetched him in to me. Pet Coon, The. James Whitcomb Riley. CP-RileJ

Noey's Night-Piece. James Whitcomb Riley. CP-RileJ Fr. Child-World, A.

Noguchi. Muriel Rukeyser. CP-RukeM

Noir for example, negro, as in any case. Maria's Gift. Michael Palmer. SP-PalmM

Noire soeur. Samuel Beckett. CP-BeckS

Noise. E. E. Cummings. CP-CummE

Noise of Battle. D. H. Lawrence. CP-LawrD

Noise of falls I am possessèd by, A. Gerard Manley Hopkins. CP-HopkG

Noise of the square is behind me, The. For Leopoldo Lugones. Jorge Luis Borges. SP-BorgJ, tr. by Ken Krabbenhoft

Noise of the vans woke us before we would. Narcissus Moving. John Berryman. CP-BerrJ

Noise of water teased his literal ear[s], The. Persistent Explorer. John Crowe Ransom. SP-RansJ

Noise will startle the dolphins, The. Insufficiency. Yannis Ritsos. SP-RitsY Fr. Wavering Scales, The.

Noises new to sea and land. Big Tent under the Roof, The. Ogden Nash. CP-NashO

Noli Me Tangere. D. H. Lawrence. CP-LawrD

Nollekens. Randall Jarrell. CP-JarrR

Nomad Exquisite. Wallace Stevens. CP-StevW; CP-StevWP

Nomad Songs. W. S. Merwin. SP-MerwW

Nomads gather in autumn. Assembly. W. S. Merwin. SP-MerwWF

Nombril Walketh on the Loam. Thomas Merton. CP-MertT

Nomenclature. Alan Dugan. CP-DugaA

Nominalist and Realist. Ralph Waldo Emerson. CP-EmerR
(Motto to "Nominalist and Realist.") CP-EmerR

Nomine Dracus erat signatus ut incolat undas. De Fran. Draco. Thomas Campion. CP-CampT

Non-action of the wise man is not inaction, The. Action and Non-Action. Chuang Tzu. CP-MertT

Non-Birthday Poem for My Father, A. Jay Wright. SP-WrigJ

Non Cogunt Astra. Robert Graves. CP-GravR

Non-Entity, The. William Carlos Williams. CP-WilW2

Non Est Mortale Quod Opto. Sir John Suckling. CP-SuckJ

Non-Existence. D. H. Lawrence. CP-LawrD

Non Nobis Domine! Rudyard Kipling. CP-KiplR

Non Omnis Moriar. Allen Tate. CP-TateA

Non Sum Dignus. Josephine Jacobsen. CP-JacoJ

Non Ti Fidar. Louis Zukofsky. CP-ZukLS

Non-World, The. James Laughlin. CP-LaugJ

Nona Domenica Garnaro sits in the sun. Fragments [or Poems] from Italy. John Ciardi. CP-CiarJ

Nona poured oil on the water and saw the eye. Evil Eye, The. John Ciardi. CP-CiarJ

Nonconformist, The. Donald Davie. CP-DaviDC

Nondescript. Amy Clampitt. CP-ClamA

Nondescript express in from the South, A. Gare du Midi. W. H. Auden. CP-AudeW

Nondum. Gerard Manley Hopkins. CP-HopkG

None. Hayden Carruth. CP-CarHS

None but a lioness moaned this, Libya's mountains. Catullus. *See* Hard. Hard. As she-cat whelped in desert mountains

None but one beheld him dying. Emily Jane Brontë. CP-BronE

None can experience stint. Emily Dickinson. CP-DickE

None dares with impious steel the grove to rend. Lucan. CP-JohnS *Fr.* Civil War [Bellum Civile] *or* Pharsalia.

None ever loved as Molly loved me then. Strangling in Merrion Square, The. Robert Graves. CP-GravR

None ever shar'd the social feast. Sparrows Self-Domesticated. Vincent Bourne. CP-CowpW

None Free from Fault. Robert Herrick. CP-HerrR

None goes to warfare, but with this intent. Hope Heartens. Robert Herrick. CP-HerrR

None, none can tell where I shall be. Where Is Thy Victory? Walter De la Mare. CP-DeLaW

None of It Was. Clarence Major. SP-MajoC

None of my kindred now can tell. Emily Jane Brontë. CP-BronE

None of the Books Have Time. Philip Larkin. CP-LarkP

None of us are as young. Shorts [1972–1973]. W. H. Auden. CP-AudeW

None of us have felt good this year. Immortals, The. James Tate. SP-TateJ

None spares another yet it pleases me. Ralph Waldo Emerson. CP-EmerR

None still had their entire wings. "Victories," The. Rainer Maria Rilke. CP-RilkFr, *tr. by* A. Poulin, Jr.

None the Wiser. Robert Graves. CP-GravR

None Truly Happy Here. Robert Herrick. CP-HerrR

None who saw it ever told it. Emily Dickinson. CP-DickE

"None whole or clean," we cry, "or free from stain." Last Department, The. Rudyard Kipling. CP-KiplR

None with Him. Christina Georgina Rossetti. CP-RosC3

None yet have been good jocund days. Spring 1974. Robert Graves. CP-GravR

Nonentity. D. H. Lawrence. CP-LawrD

Nones. John Berryman. CP-BerrJ

Nones. James McMichael. SP-McMiJ

Nonette. Langston Hughes. CP-HughL; CP-HughL1

Nonsense Rhyme, A. James Whitcomb Riley. CP-RileJ

Nonsun blob a / cold to. E. E. Cummings. CP-CummE

Nooksack Valley. Gary Snyder. CP-SnydG

Noon. James Vincent Cunningham. CP-CunnJ

Noon. Paul Laurence Dunbar. CP-DunbP

Noon. Josephine Jacobsen. CP-JacoJ

Noon. Robinson Jeffers. CP-JefR1

Noon. Philip Levine. SP-LeviP

Noon. Adrienne Rich. CP-RicAE

Noon. Yannis Ritsos. SP-RitsY, *tr. by* Minas Savvas

Noon. Henry David Thoreau. CP-ThorH

Noon, and a wind on the hill. New Life. Wallace Stevens. CP-StevWP

Noon and Night Flower. Walter De la Mare. CP-DeLaW

Noon at St. Michael's. Derek Mahon. CP-MahoD

Noon breaks to thunder and the iron hawk. Letter Homeward. John Ciardi. CP-CiarJ

Noon casts no shadow. Any other time. Advice from the Holy Tomb. Howard Nemerov. CP-NemeH

Noon-Clearing. Wallace Stevens. CP-StevWP

Noon heat in the yard, The. Hen Woman, The. Thomas Kinsella. CP-KinsT

Noon Hour. Carl Sandburg. CP-SandC

Noon Interval, A. James Whitcomb Riley. CP-RileJ

Noon—is the Hinge of Day. Emily Dickinson. CP-DickE

Noon light on the jacaranda fans. Bicoastal Journal. Charles Wright. SP-WrigC

Noon Lull, A. James Whitcomb Riley. CP-RileJ

Noon of the Sunbather. Marge Piercy. SP-PierM

Noon Office. James Schuyler. CP-SchuJ

Noon, streams of the melting crowd. Van Gogh's Face. Adam Zagajewski. SP-ZagaA, *tr. by* Renata Gorczynski

Noon summer solstice light shines on a creation spiral petroglyph. Metastasis. Arthur Sze. SP-SzeA

Noon sun big as a knuckle, / tight over Ponte S. Polo. Passing the Morning under the Serenissima. Charles Wright. SP-WrigCN

Noon. The luminous tide. Ballydavid Pier. Thomas Kinsella. CP-KinsT

Noon. The tall trees uphold the sky. Dragon-Fly, The. Charles Olson. CP-OlsoC

Noon-time and June-time, down around the river! Down around the River. James Whitcomb Riley. CP-RileJ

Noon Walk on the Asylum Lawn. Anne Sexton. CP-SextA

Noon was approaching and the quiet. Chaplet of Sage, A. Jaroslav Seifert. SP-SeifJ, *tr. by* Ewald Osers

Noon was shady, and soft airs, The. Dog and the Water-Lily, The. William Cowper. CP-CowpW

Noone and a star stand,am to am. E. E. Cummings. CP-CummE

Noone" autumnal this great lady's gaze. E. E. Cummings. CP-CummE

Noone-day and Midnight shall at once be seene. His Protestation to Perilla. Robert Herrick. CP-HerrR

Noon's World. Alan Dugan. CP-DugaA

Nor art thou lesse esteem'd, that I have plac'd. To Doctor Alabaster. Robert Herrick. CP-HerrR

Nor Buying or Selling. Robert Herrick. CP-HerrR

Nor can ambition make this garden theirs. Hidden Garden, The. Robert Graves. CP-GravR

Nor cold, nor stern, my soul! yet I detest. Lines Composed in a Concert-Room. Samuel Taylor Coleridge. CP-ColeS

Nor did Saint Cuthbert's daughters fail. Saint of Holy Island, The. Sir Walter Scott. SP-ScotW *Fr.* Marmion.

Nor do you think that their legs is all. Ben Jonson. CP-JonsB *Fr.* Christmas His Masque.

Nor dread nor hope attend. Death. William Butler Yeats. CP-YeatW

Nor from the compass-quarter of the rising sun. Solis Ortus Cardine, A. Sedulius. CP-MertT

Nor happiness, nor majesty, nor fame. Sonnet: Political Greatness. Percy Bysshe Shelley. CP-ShelP

Nor is my Number full, till I inscribe. To His Worthy Kinsmen, Mr. Stephen Soame. Robert Herrick. CP-HerrR

Nor is this the setting for extravagance. Trees. Northern Spring. Charles Tomlinson. CP-TomlC; SP-TomlC

Nor Mountain hinder Me. Emily Dickinson. CP-DickE

Nor oils of balmy scent produce. On Pallas Bathing, from a Hymn of Callimachus. Callimachus. CP-CowpW *Fr.* Hymns.

Nor skin nor hide nor fleece. Lethe. "H. D." CP-DoolH

Nor slightly pass those early planters by. Old Planters, The. Jones Very. CP-VeryJ

Nor Southerne heat nor Northerne snow. Ode 3.24: "Nor Southerne heat nor Northerne snow." Horace. CP-RaleW *Fr.* Odes.

Nor thinke that Thou in this my Booke art worst. To the Most Accomplisht Gentleman Master Michael Oulsworth. Robert Herrick. CP-HerrR

Nor travels my meandering eye. Lines Written at Shurton Bars, near Bridgewater, September 1795, in Answer to a Letter from Bristol. Samuel Taylor Coleridge. MW-ColeS *Fr.* Poetical Epistles.

Nor was meant to be let. Two Fragments from Pausanias. James Laughlin. CP-LaugJ

Nor We of Her to Him. Stevie Smith. CP-SmitS

Nor woman / (just as it be). E. E. Cummings. CP-CummE

Nor yet, nor yet, O you in this night blessed. Ben Jonson. CP-JonsB *Fr.* Oberon, the Fairy Prince.

Nora: A Serenade. Paul Laurence Dunbar. CP-DunbP

Norembega. John Greenleaf Whittier. CP-WhitJ

Noretorp-Noretsyh. Kenneth Rexroth. CP-RexrK

Norfolk. Donald Davie. CP-DaviDC

Norham Castle. Sir Walter Scott. SP-ScotW *Fr.* Marmion.

Normal Occurence. Yannis Ritsos. SP-RitsY, *tr. by* N. C. Germanacos

Norman and Saxon. Rudyard Kipling. CP-KiplR

Norman Boy, The. William Wordsworth. CP-WorW2

Normandy Beach. Miller Williams. CP-WillM

Norman's Rocks. Jones Very. CP-VeryJ

Norsemen, The. John Greenleaf Whittier. CP-WhitJ

North. Federico García Lorca. CP-GarcF, *tr. by* Jerome Rothenberg *Fr.* Cross.

North. Seamus Heaney. SP-HeanSO

North American Bear. Charles Wright. SP-WrigCN

North American Sequence. Theodore Roethke. CP-RoetT

North American Time. Adrienne Rich. SP-RicA1; SP-RicA2

North & South. Donald Davie. CP-DaviDC

North and South. Robert Herrick. CP-HerrR

North and South. James Whitcomb Riley. CP-RileJ

North and South. Derek Walcott. CP-WalcD

North and the South, The. Elizabeth Barrett Browning. CP-BroEB

North Atlantic. Carl Sandburg. CP-SandC

North Baltic. Joseph Brodsky. CP-BrodJ

North Beach Alba. Gary Snyder. CP-SnydG

North Coast, The. Gary Snyder. CP-SnydG

North Country, The. D. H. Lawrence. CP-LawrD

North Dublin. Donald Davie. CP-DaviDC

North Haven. Elizabeth Bishop. CP-BishE

North Island Songs. Heather McHugh. SP-McHuH

North Jersey. A. R. Ammons. CP-AmmoA

North Labrador. Hart Crane. CP-CranH

North of Beer Sheba. Yehuda Amichai. SP-AmicYL, *tr. by* Benjamin Harshav *and* Barbara Harshav

North of Beersheba. Yehuda Amichai. SP-AmicY, *tr. by* Chana Bloch

North of Delphi. Joseph Brodsky. CP-BrodJ

North of San Francisco. Yehuda Amichai. SP-AmicY, *tr. by* Chana Bloch

North of San Francisco. Yehuda Amichai. SP-AmicYL, *tr. by* Benjamin Harshav *and* Barbara Harshav

North Palisade, the End of September, 1939. Kenneth Rexroth. CP-RexrK

North people known for silence. Long. They Accuse Me of Not Talking. Hayden Carruth. CP-CarHS

North Rim, The. May Swenson. SP-SwenM

North River. Jones Very. CP-VeryJ

North Sea, The. Donald Davie. CP-DaviDC

North Sea, The. Louis MacNeice. CP-MacNL

North Sea, in a Snowstorm, The. Donald Davie. CP-DaviDC

North Sea Patrol, The. Rudyard Kipling. CP-KiplR

North Sea, Protestant sea. North Sea, The. Donald Davie. CP-DaviDC

North Ship, The. Philip Larkin. CP-LarkP

North Star Whispers to the Blacksmith's Son, The. Nicholas Vachel Lindsay. CP-LindV

North summer wind swept the hay, The. Meadow in Summer. Carl Sandburg. CP-SandC

North to Taos. Arthur Sze. SP-SzeA

North Wind. W. S. Merwin. SP-MerwWF

North wind doth blow, The. Ma, What's a Banker? or, Hush, My Child. Ogden Nash. CP-NashO

North wind like a fine drill. China Journal. Charles Wright. SP-WrigC

North Wind: Portrush. Derek Mahon. CP-MahoD

North Winter. Hayden Carruth. CP-CarHL

Northampton, 1922–San Francisco, 1939. Kenneth Rexroth. CP-RexrK

Northamptonshire. Donald Davie. CP-DaviDC

Northeast wind was the wind off the lake, The. Cook County. Archibald MacLeish. CP-MacLA

Norther—Key West, A. Elizabeth Bishop. CP-BishE

Northern April. Edna St. Vincent Millay. CP-MillE

Northern countryside of China, The. Spring in the Snow-Drenched Garden. Mao Tse-tung. CP-WilW2

Northern Exposure. Charles Simic. SP-SimiC; SP-SimiCE

Northern Farmer: New Style. Alfred Tennyson. CP-TennA

Northern Heather. Robinson Jeffers. CP-JefR2

Northern Lass, The. Robert Burns. CP-BurnR

Northern Liberal. Langston Hughes. CP-HughL; CP-HughL3

Northern lights. I wouldn't have noticed them, The. I Know, I Remember, but How Can I Help You. Hayden Carruth. CP-CarHS

Northern Metres. Donald Davie. CP DaviDC

Northern Pike. James Wright. CP-WrigJ

Northern Snows, The. Randall Jarrell. CP-JarrR

Northern Spring. Charles Tomlinson. CP-TomlC; SP-TomlC

Northern Star. Derek Mahon. CP-MahoD

Northern Statement for St. Cecilia. Alan Dugan. CP-DugaA

Northern Suburb. Jorge Luis Borges. SP-BorgJ, *tr. by* Charles Tomlinson

Northumberland. Donald Davie. CP-DaviDC

Northumberland House. Stevie Smith. CP-SmitS

Northward I came, and knocked in the coated wall. Rodez. Donald Davie. CP-DaviDC

Northwest Montana, high country, and downward. First Time, The. Robert Penn Warren. CP-WarrR

Northwest Passage. Allen Ginsberg. CP-GinsA

Northwind blows glitter. Marni's Birthday. William Corbett. SP-CorbW

Northwind Escarpment. Norman Dubie. CP-DubiN

Northwood Path. Louise Glück. SP-GlucL

Norumbega Hall. John Greenleaf Whittier. CP-WhitJ

Nose. Donald Hall. CP-HallD

Nose, The. Samuel Taylor Coleridge. CP-ColeS

Nose and chin would shame a knocker. On Sam Rogers. Lord Byron. CP-Byron

Nose and palate never doubt, The. Smelt and Tasted. W. H. Auden. CP-AudeW

Nose-end that twitches, the old imperfections, The. Companionable Ills, The. Sylvia Plath. CP-PlatS

Nosegay, The. Donald Davie. CP-DaviDC

Nossis. "H. D." CP-DoolH

Nostalgia. Billy Collins. SP-CollB

Nostalgia. D. H. Lawrence. CP-LawrD

Nostalgia. Louis MacNeice. CP-MacNL

Nostalgia. Rainer Maria Rilke. CP-RilkFr, *tr. by* A. Poulin, Jr.

Nostalgia. C. K. Williams. SP-WillC

Nostalgia for a Language. Alan Dugan. CP-DugaA

Nostalgia for Edith Sitwell. Richard Eberhart. CP-EberR

Nostalgia for India. May Sarton. SP-SartM

Nostalgia for the Present. Jorge Luis Borges. SP-BorgJ, *tr. by* Alan S. Trueblood

Nostalgia, incantation, escape. Sports Page. Louis MacNeice. CP-MacNL

Nostalgia of old men. In Praise of Necessity. Thomas McGrath. SP-McGrT

Nostalgias. Derek Mahon. CP-MahoD

Noster was a ship of swank, The. E. E. Cummings. CP-CummE

Nostrarum quoties prendit me nausea rerum. Ad Ed. Mychelburnum. Thomas Campion. CP-CampT

Not a breath of air. Airey-Force Valley. William Wordsworth. CP-WorW2; MW-WorW

Not a Day on Any Calendar. Jelaluddin Rumi. SP-Rumi, *tr. by* Coleman Barks

Not a derangement of the senses but yes there is an occult other. Poetry Disarranged. Robert Duncan. SP-DuncR

Not a flake assaults my birds. Emily Dickinson. SP-DickE

Not a flow'r can be found in the fields. Innocent Thief, The. Vincent Bourne. CP-CowpW

Not a friend hated time. Wild Geranium. Louis Zukofsky. CP-ZukLS

Not a line of her writing have I. Thoughts of Phena. Thomas Hardy. CP-HardT

Not a Movie. Langston Hughes. CP-HughL; CP-HughL3

Not a Pot to Piss In. Andrei Codrescu. SP-CodrA

Not a rat-hole, a cat-hole: the knife of time; on the ledge, overlooking. Charles Olson. CP-OlsoC

Not a sigh was heard, not a tear was shed. Death and Burial of McDonald Clarke, a Parody, The. Walt Whitman. CP-WhitW

Not a Sin. Heather McHugh. SP-McHuH

Not a single star will be left in the night. Suicide, The. Jorge Luis Borges. SP-BorgJ, *tr. by* Alastair Reid

Not a Soul; Blanket Roll Blues. Tennessee Williams. CP-WillT *Fr.* Fugitive Kind, The.

Not a tree but the tree. There Is Only One of Everything. Margaret Atwood. SP-AtwM1

Not a vapour had stained the breezeless blue. Emily Jane Brontë. CP-BronE

Not able to be honest in person. Truth Is Forced, The. May Swenson. SP-SwenM

Not Again. Robert Creeley. CP-CreeR

Not Aladdin magian. On Visiting Staffa. John Keats. CP-KeatJ

Not all die early, dying young. Emily Dickinson. CP-DickE

Not all harsh sounds displease. Lorine Niedecker. CP-NiedL

Not all of life to live, is it. Emily Dickinson. SP-DickE

Not all of my eyes see, wándering on the world. Ashboughs. Gerard Manley Hopkins. CP-HopkG

Not all of them were human. Village Tudda, The. Kenneth Patchen. CP-PatcK

Not All That Bad. Charles Bukowski. SP-BukC3

Not all that's heard is music. We leave. Lorine Niedecker. CP-NiedL

Not all thy flushing suns are set. Ode to Master Endymion Porter, upon His Brother's Death, An. Robert Herrick. CP-HerrR

Not alone those camps of white, old comrades of the wars. Camps of Green. Walt Whitman. CP-WhitW

Not always as the whirlwind's rush. Call of the Christian, The. John Greenleaf Whittier. CP-WhitJ

Not always should the tear's ambrosial dew. Pitt. Samuel Taylor Coleridge. MW-ColeS *Fr.* Effusions.

Not always so prized and cherished by us all. Michelangelo Buonarroti. CP-Miche, *tr. by* John Frederick Nims

Not an epic, being not loosely architectured. King John's Castle. Thomas Kinsella. CP-KinsT

Not any flower that blows. Noon and Night Flower. Walter De la Mare. CP-DeLaW

Not any higher stands the Grave. Emily Dickinson. CP-DickE

Not any more to be lacked. Emily Dickinson. CP-DickE

Not any sunny tone. Emily Dickinson. CP-DickE

Not architecture, not. Gloucestershire. Donald Davie. CP-DaviDC

Not as a poor requital of the joy. To J. P. John Greenleaf Whittier. CP-WhitJ

Not as beholding with our mortal sight. For We Walk by Faith, Not by Sight. Jones Very. CP-VeryJ

Not, as it used to be, round. Poison, The. Hans Magnus Enzensberger. SP-EnzeH, *tr. by* Hans Magnus Enzensberger *and* Michael Hamburger

Not as that dream Napoleon, rumour's dread and centre. Like a Vocation. W. H. Auden. CP-AudeW

Not as the World giveth. Jones Very. CP-VeryJ

Not as two errant spheres together grin. To Maude. Ambrose Bierce. SP-BierA

Not as with Sundering of the Earth. Algernon Charles Swinburne. SP-SwinA *Fr.* Atalanta in Calydon.

Not at Home. Samuel Taylor Coleridge. CP-ColeS

Not at Home. Robert Graves. CP-GravR

Not at Home to Callers. Tree in Winter. Emily Dickinson. CP-DickE

Not aware of it much of the time, but of course we are. Une Présence Absolue.

Hayden Carruth. CP-CarHS

Not bad mouth / in bad mouth. Bad Mouth. C. K. Williams. CP-WillC

Not because of his eyes. Turtle, The. William Carlos Williams. CP-WilW2

Not because they are far, but because so near. Dead, The. Kathleen Jessie Raine. SP-RainK

Not blue—she says—the sky is red. Untamed. Yannis Ritsos. SP-RitsY, *tr. by* Kimon Friar

Not boskiest bow'r. Epigraph to "The Woodlanders." Thomas Hardy. CP-HardT

Not Both. William Meredith. SP-MereW

Not bound by slavish bondage to the Past. Puritan Church and State 3, The. Jones Very. CP-VeryJ

Not branchless as the fear tree. Anxiety. A. K. Ramanujan. CP-RamaA

Not by growth / But the. Drawing. George Oppen. CP-OppGN

Not by one measure mayst thou mete our love. Equal Troth. Dante Gabriel Rossetti. CW-RossD *Fr.* House of Life, The.

Not by the railing tongues of angry men. Slavery. Jones Very. CP-VeryJ

Not by water, fire or flesh. Signs of Knowledge, The. Laura Riding Jackson. CP-RidiL

Not Caesar's birth made Caesar to survive. Vertue the Best Monument. *Unknown, sometimes at. to* Sir Walter Ralegh. CP-RaleW

Not Caesar's deeds, nor all his honours won. To Clement Edmonds, on His *Caesar's Commentaries* Observed, and Translated. Ben Jonson. CP-JonsB; SP-JonsB

Not Cecrops kept my bees. My olives bore. Fernando Pessoa. SP-PessF *Fr.* Inscriptions.

Not, Celia, that I look for rest. After Charles Sedley. Louis Zukofsky. CP-ZukLS

Not Christian or Jew or Muslim, not Hindu. Only Breath. Jelaluddin Rumi. SP-Rumi, *tr. by* Coleman Barks

Not Compostela where these pilgrims journey. On Watteau's *Pilgrimage to Cythera* (1717) in the Louvre. Helen Pinkerton. CP-PinkH

Not deaf to ghosts yet not expecting them. Thomas and Emma. Donald Davie. CP-DaviDC

Not death so much, but its terror rescues me. Michelangelo Buonarroti. CP-Miche, *tr. by* John Frederick Nims

Not deerpark, royal chase. Sylvae. Donald Davie. CP-DaviDC

Not drawn but flown by glistening mares. Night Drive. Rainer Maria Rilke. CP-MahoD, *tr. by* Derek Mahon

Not easy to state the change you made. Love Letter. Sylvia Plath. CP-PlatS

Not Else—But. Langston Hughes. CP-HughL; CP-HughL3

Not enough. The question: what is. Love ("Not enough. The question: what is"). Robert Creeley. CP-CreeR

Not envying Latian shades—if yet they throw. William Wordsworth. CP-WorW2 *Fr.* River Duddon [A Series of Sonnets], The.

Not ere the bitter herb we taste. Lesson of Grief, The. George Meredith. CP-MerG1

Not even dried-up leaves. Thesis, Antithesis and Nostalgia. Alan Dugan. CP-DugaA

Not even for a moment. He knew, for one thing, what he was. Leda. Mona Van Duyn. SP-VanDM

Not Even for Brunch. Ogden Nash. CP-NashO

Not even if with a wizard force I might. Caput Mortuum. Edwin Arlington Robinson. CP-RobiE

Not even in darkest August. Old Woman. Robert Pinsky. CP-PinsR

Not even, in dreams sent soaring, can I imagine. Michelangelo Buonarroti. CP-Miche, *tr. by* John Frederick Nims

Not even poetry, then, not even poetry. Yannis Ritsos. SP-RitsY, *tr. by* Andonis Decavalles

Not ever, now, any more, upon this mildewed planet. If, in the Foggy Aleutians. Edna St. Vincent Millay. CP-MillE

Not Every Day Fit for Verse. Robert Herrick. CP-HerrR

Not every man has gentians in his house. Bavarian Gentians. D. H. Lawrence. CP-LawrD

Not every morning that you awaken. What's Next on the Agenda, Mr. Williams? Tennessee Williams. CP-WillT

Not everyone can see the truth, but he can be it. Charles Wright. SP-WrigCN

Not exactly disembodied, but speaking from no mouth. Quiet Afternoon at Home, A. Mona Van Duyn. SP-VanDM

Not far advanc'd was morning day. Battle, The ("Not far advanc'd was morning day"). Sir Walter Scott. SP-ScotW *Fr.* Marmion.

Not far from hence. From yonder pointed hill. Orpheus. Percy Bysshe Shelley. CP-ShelP

Not far from here someone. Raymond Carver. CP-CarvR

Not far from Mellstock—so tradition saith. By the Barrows. Thomas Hardy. CP-HardT

Not far from the railroad tracks, near the fickle post office. "Rustle of History's Wings," as They Used to Say Then, The. Yehuda Amichai. SP-AmicY, *tr. by* Chana Bloch

Not far from the railroad tracks, near the painful Post Office. "History's Wings Beating," They Used to Say. Yehuda Amichai. SP-AmicYL, *tr. by* Benjamin Harshav *and* Barbara Harshav

Not faster in the summer's ray. Seneca. CP-JohnS *Fr.* Hippolytus.

Not feeling well, my wood uncut. Lorine Niedecker. CP-NiedL

Not finding where the flowers were. Automobile Accident. Lorine Niedecker. CP-NiedL

Not first the things, which we behold. Hymn: The Word before All Things. Jones Very. CP-VeryJ

Not for a Nation. Edna St. Vincent Millay. CP-MillE

Not for Charity. James Vincent Cunningham. CP-CunnJ

Not for me marring or making. Mariana. Christina Georgina Rossetti. CP-RosC2

Not for myself I make this prayer. Pagan Prayer. Countee Cullen. CP-CullC

Not for the naked make I this my prayer. Ballade of Soul. E. E. Cummings. CP-CummE

Not for these lovely blooms that prank your chambers did I come. Indeed. Rendezvous. Edna St. Vincent Millay. CP-MillE

Not forgetting Ko-jen, that. More Foreign Cities. Charles Tomlinson. CP-TomlC; SP-TomlC

Not from successful love alone. Halcyon Days. Walt Whitman. CP-WhitW

Not from that / could you get it. City, The. Robert Creeley. CP-CreeR

Not from the earth, or skies. Health of Body Dependent on the Soul. Jones Very. CP-VeryJ

Not from This Anger. Dylan Thomas. CP-ThomD

Not George Washington's, Not Abraham Lincoln's, but Mine. Ogden Nash. CP-NashO

Not glad, like those that have new hopes, or suits. To the Same [Robert, Earl of Salisbury] [Upon the Accension of the Treasurership to Him]. Ben Jonson. CP-JonsB; SP-JonsB

Not God, / not God. Orestes Theme. "H. D." CP-DoolH

Not good any more, not beautiful. Face, The. Randall Jarrell. CP-JarrR

Not great, not / among the acerbic. Homage to John Lyly and Frankie Newton. Hayden Carruth. CP-CarHS

Not gusts of wind that hold the streets. Note to Whistler. Stéphane Mallarmé. CP-MallS, *tr. by* Henry Weinfield

Not he that flies the court for want of clothes. To Sir Ra[l]ph Shelton. Ben Jonson. CP-JonsB; SP-JonsB

Not heart not soul—some spirit. Recipe. Raissa Maritain. CP-MertT

Not Heat Flames Up and Consumes. Walt Whitman. CP-WhitW

Not Heaving from My Ribb'd Breast Only. Walt Whitman. CP-WhitW

Not him I prize who poorly gains. Martial. CP-JohnS *Fr.* Epigrams.

Not honey, / not the plunder of the bee. Fragment 113: "Not honey, / not the plunder of the bee." "H. D." CP-DoolH

Not hour after hour, / but grief after grief the day passes. Initial. Pablo Neruda. SP-NeruP

Not house-proud: garden-proud are the people here. Carmel. Robinson Jeffers. CP-JefR3

Not hurled precipitous from steep to steep. William Wordsworth. CP-WorW2 *Fr.* River Duddon [A Series of Sonnets], The.

Not hurrying, my quiet friend. Autumn Day. Aleksandr Aleksandrovich Blok. SP-BlokA, *tr. by* Peter France *and* Jon Stallworthy

Not, I keep being told, the Time. Six Epistles to Eva Hesse. Donald Davie. CP-DaviDC

Not I myself know all my love for thee. Dark Glass, The. Dante Gabriel Rossetti. CW-RossD *Fr.* House of Life, The.

Not I, not I, but the wind that blows through me! Song of a Man Who Has Come Through. D. H. Lawrence. CP-LawrD

Not Ideas about the Thing but the Thing Itself. Wallace Stevens. CP-StevW; CP-StevWP

Not If He Has Any Sense, He Won't Be Back. Kenneth Patchen. CP-PatcK

Not, I'll not, carrion comfort, Despair, not feast on thee. Carrion Comfort. Gerard Manley Hopkins. CP-HopkG

Not in a gorgeous hall of pride / Mid tears of grief and friendship's sigh. My Departure. Walt Whitman. CP-WhitW

Not in a gorgeous hall of pride / Where tears fall thick, and loved ones sigh. Death of the Nature-Lover, The. Walt Whitman. CP-WhitW

Not in a silver casket cool with pearls. Edna St. Vincent Millay. CP-MillE

Not in Baedeker. W. H. Auden. CP-AudeW

Not in believing, but in pretending. Not in knowing, but in pretending. Imagining in Writing. Robert Duncan. SP-DuncR

Not in Marble Palaces. Pedro Salinas. CP-WrigJ

Not in rich furniture, or fine array. H[oly] Communion, The. George Herbert. CP-HerbG

Not in shyness but in disgust. This Morning Again It Was in the Dusty Pines. Mary Oliver. SP-OlivM

Not in the camp his victory lies. Reformers, The. Rudyard Kipling. CP-KiplR

Not in the days of Adam and Eve, but when Adam. In the Days of Prismatic Color. Marianne Craig Moore. CP-MoorM

Not in the Headlines. William Stafford. SP-StafWW

Not in the Lucid Intervals of Life. William Wordsworth. CP-WorW2

Not in the rustle of water, the air's noise. Night in Martindale. Kathleen Jessie Raine. SP-RainK

Not in the streets, not in the white streets. Theory of Prayer. Thomas Merton. CP-MertT

Not in the thick of the fight. Verdicts, The. Rudyard Kipling. CP-KiplR

Not in their houses stand the stars. To the Shah, from Enweri. "Anvari." CP-EmerR

Not in this chamber only at my birth. Edna St. Vincent Millay. CP-MillE

Not in this grave. Defiance to Cupid. William Carlos Williams. CP-WilW2

Not in this World to see his face. Emily Dickinson. CP-DickE

Not in thy body is thy life at all. Life-in-Love. Dante Gabriel Rossetti. CW-RossD *Fr.* House of Life, The.

Not it was no dream of coming death. Louis Zukofsky. CP-ZukLS

Not jealousy but pale disgust complains. Bedside Rune, A. Jane Cooper. CP-CoopJ

Not just those who hate and those who envy us. Fernando Pessoa. SP-PessF, *tr. by* Susan M. Brown *and* Edwin Honig

Not Kenesaw high-arching. March to the Sea, The. Herman Melville. SP-MelvH

Not kind! to freeze me with forecast. Gerard Manley Hopkins. CP-HopkG

Not knowing he rose from earth, not having seen him rise. On First Having Heard the Skylark. Edna St. Vincent Millay. CP-MillE

Not knowing them in very heart. Sketch, A. Herman Melville. SP-MelvH *Fr.* Clarel: A Poem and Pilgrimage in the Holy Land.

Not knowing what to say to her. A. K. Ramanujan. CP-RamaA

Not knowing when the Dawn will come. Emily Dickinson. CP-DickE

Not Known. Thomas Hardy. CP-HardT

Not leaves, not lightning, not the greatness of rivers. Muriel Rukeyser. CP-RukeM

Not leaves, not lightning, not the greatness of rivers. Muriel Rukeyser. CP-RukeM

Not Leaving the House. Gary Snyder. CP-SnydG

Not less a Queen, because I wear. Queen Zuleima. George Meredith. CP-MerG2

Not less because in purple I descended. Tea at the Palaz of Hoon. Wallace Stevens. CP-StevW; CP-StevWP

Not like a beast borne on the flood of passion, boat without oars, but mindful of all his dignity. Humanist's Tragedy, The. Robinson Jeffers. CP-JefR1

Not like a Cypress. Yehuda Amichai. SP-AmicYL, *tr. by* Benjamin Harshav *and* Barbara Harshav

Not like a Cypress. Yehuda Amichai. SP-AmicY, *tr. by* Stephen Mitchell

Not like That. Adrienne Rich. CP-RicAE

Not living for each other's sake. Knowledge. Howard Nemerov. CP-NemeH

Not long ago. Song of the Imperial Carrion, The. Christopher Logue. SP-LoguC

Not long ago, the writer of these lines. To ————: "Not long ago, the writer of these lines." Edgar Allan Poe. CP-PoeEd

Not Love, Not War, nor the Tumultuous Swell. William Wordsworth. CP-WorW2

Not magnitude, not lavishness. Greek Architecture. Herman Melville. SP-MelvH

Not many enchant you (put to it) popular is he, Juventi. Catullus. *See* Surely, Iuventius, one of this throng in Rome

Not Many Kingdoms Left. Kenneth Patchen. CP-PatcK

Not many moonlit nights. Reading Seferis. Sam Hamill. SP-HamiS

Not many years but long enough to see. Emily Jane Brontë. CP-BronE

Not Marble nor the Gilded Monuments. Archibald MacLeish. CP-MacLA

Not Martha nor Diana—only a woman. On Vermeer's *Young Woman with a Water Jug* (1658) in the Metropolitan Museum. Helen Pinkerton. CP-PinkH

Not me alone. Union. Langston Hughes. CP-HughL; CP-HughL1

Not Meagre, Latent Boughs Alone. Walt Whitman. CP-WhitW

Not 'mid the World's vain objects that enslave. Composed while the Author Was Engaged in Writing a Tract, Occasioned by the Convention of Cintra. William Wordsworth. CP-WorW1

Not much but something. Before the morning glories. Quirks. John Ciardi. CP-CiarJ

Not My Enemies Ever Invade Me. Walt Whitman. CP-WhitW

Not 'neath the altar only,—yet, in sooth. Vox Ecclesiae, Vox Christi. Dante Gabriel Rossetti. CW-RossD

Not Now. Robert Creeley. CP-CreeR

Not o'er thy dust let there be spent. Whittier. Paul Laurence Dunbar. CP-DunbP

Not of father nor of mother. Song of Blodeuwedd, The. *Unknown.* CP-GravR, *tr. by* Robert Graves

Not of one sect thy kingdom is. Kingdom of the Truth, The. Jones Very. CP-VeryJ

Not of School Age. Robert Frost. CP-FrosR

Not of self-will are States and Nations born. Set Times, and the Boundaries of Nations, Appointed by God, The. Jones Very. CP-VeryJ

Not of the dead: of the face on face. God of the Living, The. G. K. Chesterton. CP-ChesG

Not of the dust, but of the wave. For Joseph Conrad. Countee Cullen. CP-CullC

Not of the earth, nor sense are we. Teachings of the Spirit, The. Jones Very. CP-VeryJ

Not Often. Langston Hughes. CP-HughL

Not on Penobscot's wooded bank the spires. Norumbega Hall. John Greenleaf Whittier. CP-WhitJ

Not One by Heaven defrauded stay. Emily Dickinson. CP-DickE

Not one corner of a foreign field. Fragment: "Not one corner of a foreign field." Wilfred Owen. CP-OwenW

Not one leaf stirs, though a high few. Platonic Lassitude. Robert Penn Warren. CP-WarrR

Not one not dandled a man high up in the air. White Pines, Felled 1984. Richard Eberhart. CP-EberR

Not one to lose. Skeffington's Daughter. Paul Muldoon. CP-MuldP

Not Only. Walter De la Mare. CP-DeLaW

Not only can I not remember anecdotes that are racy. What's in a Name? Some Letter I Always Forget. Ogden Nash. CP-NashO

Not only doesn't the Ohio. Elegy: "Not only doesn't the Ohio." Gregory Orr. SP-OrrG

Not Only I. Thomas Hardy. CP-HardT

Not only love plus awful grief. Edna St. Vincent Millay. CP-MillE

Not only master of his art was he. At His Wintry Tent. James Whitcomb Riley. CP-RileJ

Not only pretences, but actual motives and great results. New Dance, The. Yannis Ritsos. SP-RitsY, *tr. by* Kimon Friar *and* Karelisa Hartigan

Not only sands and gravels. One Step Taken Backward. Robert Frost. CP-FrosR

Not only that one hand when it is bare. Petrarch. CP-Petra, *tr. by* J. G. Nichols

Not only the gaze of those. Rainer Maria Rilke. CP-RilkFr, *tr. by* A. Poulin, Jr *Fr.* Valaisian Quatrains, The.

Not only through the dense bush cleared by fires. Rescuers, The. Robert Stock. SP-StocR

Not Oral Roberts' city of heavenly glitz. Tulsa. John Updike. CP-UpdiJ

Not Our Good Luck. Robinson Jeffers. CP-JefR1

Not out of mercy / Did I launch this transaction. Epitaph for a Public Servant. Thomas Merton. CP-MertT

Not Pan / & not Leda. Second Page. Federico García Lorca. CP-GarcF, *tr. by* Jerome Rothenberg *Fr.* White Album.

Not picnics or pageants or the improbable. Terror. Robert Penn Warren. CP-WarrR

Not probable—The barest Chance. Emily Dickinson. CP-DickE

Not quite diaphanous, not Spanish. Savannah. Amy Clampitt. CP-ClamA

Not Quite like a Top. Robert Penn Warren. CP-WarrR

Not Quite So Soon. Charles Bukowski. SP-BukC2

Not Quite Social. Robert Frost. CP-FrosR

Not quite yet. First, / around the corner for a visit. Dining Out with Doug and Frank. James Schuyler. CP-SchuJ

Not resting but / moving her lovely butt. Visit of the Queen of Sheba, The. Yehuda Amichai. SP-AmicY, *tr. by* Stephen Mitchell

Not-Returning, The. Ivor Gurney. SP-GurnI

Not "Revelation" 'tis, that waits. Emily Dickinson. CP-DickE

Not Sacco and Vanzetti. Countee Cullen. CP-CullC

Not Sato's sword, not Sato's "consecrated blade." Point, The. Paul Muldoon. CP-MuldP

Not seeing, still we know. Emily Dickinson. CP-DickE

Not seldom, when her semblance has been kind. Petrarch. CP-Petra, *tr. by* J. G. Nichols

Not Sickness stains the Brave. Emily Dickinson. CP-DickE

Not slowly wrought, nor treasured for their form. Snowflakes. Howard Nemerov. CP-NemeH

Not So Far as the Forest. Edna St. Vincent Millay. CP-MillE

Not so he felt, who with her was to pay. Condemned Felon, The. George Crabbe. SP-CrabG *Fr.* Borough, The.

Not so that Pair whose youthful spirits dance. Same Subject, The. William Wordsworth. CP-WorW2 *Fr.* River Duddon [A Series of Sonnets], The.

Not so the infinite Relations—Below. Emily Dickinson. CP-DickE

Not solitarily in fields we find. Earth's Secret. George Meredith. CP-MerG1

Not soon, as late as the approach of my ninetieth year. Late Ripeness. Czeslaw Milosz. CP-MiloCN, *tr. by* Robert Hass

Not stars that wander through the open sky. Petrarch. CP-Petra, *tr. by* J. G. Nichols

Not suffering for their sins in former state. Jones Very. CP-VeryJ *Fr.* Origin of Man, The.

Not tears alone for natural grief. Hymn: "Not tears alone for natural grief." Jones Very. CP-VeryJ

Not that he goes—we love him more. Emily Dickinson. CP-DickE

Not that he holds with church, but Henry goes. Rejoicing with Henry. Maxine W. Kumin. SP-KumiM

Not that I care who's sleeping with whom. Paul Muldoon. CP-MuldP *Fr.* Last Poems.

Not that I look to my eyes more than your love. Catullus. *See* If, my irrepressible Calvus, I didn't

Not that I love thy children, whose dull eyes. Sonnet to Liberty. Oscar Wilde. CP-WildO

Not that in colour it was like thy hair. Bracelet, The. John Donne. MW-DonnJ

Fr. Elegies.

Not that it matters, not that my heart's cry. Edna St. Vincent Millay. CP-MillE

Not that it matters, or not much, and not. Incident. John Ciardi. CP-CiarJ

Not that it was beautiful. For John, Who Begs Me Not to Enquire Further. Anne Sexton. CP-SextA; SP-SextA

Not that, of course, you couldn't stick it out. To a Friend. Howard Nemerov. CP-NemeH

Not that she didn't recognize him in the fireside light; nor was it. Penelope's Despair. Yannis Ritsos. SP-RitsY, *tr.* by Kostas Myrsiades

Not that she had no equal, not that she was. Fallgrief's Girlfriends. Ted Hughes. SP-HughTN

Not that the earth is changing, O my God! On Refusal of Aid between Nations. Dante Gabriel Rossetti. CW-RossD

Not that the widespread wings of wrong brood o'er a moaning earth. Adveniat Regnum Tuum. G. K. Chesterton. CP-ChesG

Not that way. Walter De la Mare. CP-DeLaW

Not that we are not all. To a Man Dying on His Feet. William Carlos Williams. CP-WilW2

Not the action of rowing. Christian Hero, A. Donald Davie. CP-DaviDC

Not the branches. All of December toward New Year's. Louis Zukofsky. CP-ZukLS

Not the city lights. We want. View. Rae Armantrout. SP-ArmaA

Not the cricket but the cat. To Liuba, Leaving. Eugenio Montale. CP-MontE, *tr.* by Jonathan Galassi

Not the Cuckold's Dream. Norman Dubie. CP-DubiN

Not the expression of collective emotion. Note on War Poetry, A. T. S. Eliot. CP-ElioT

Not the least enviable of your many gifts. At the Cradle of Genius. Donald Davie. CP-DaviDC

Not the Moon. Margaret Atwood. SP-AtwM2

Not the more. Fragment: Redundance. William Wordsworth. CP-WorW1

Not the one of an armistice. Wild Peace. Yehuda Amichai. SP-AmicYL, *tr.* by Benjamin Harshav *and* Barbara Harshav

Not the peace of a cease-fire. Wildpeace. Yehuda Amichai. SP-AmicY, *tr.* by Chana Bloch

Not the Pilot. Walt Whitman. CP-WhitW

Not the sea-wave so bellows abroad when it bursts upon shingle. Clash in Arms of the Achaians and Trojans. Homer. CP-MerG1, *tr.* by George Meredith *Fr.* Iliad, The.

Not the soft sighs of vernal gales. Song, A: "Not the soft sighs of vernal gales." Samuel Johnson. CP-JohnS

Not the Ticino, Arno, Varo, Tiber. Petrarch. CP-Petra, *tr.* by J. G. Nichols

Not the whole warbling grove in concert heard. To the Cuckoo. William Wordsworth. CP-WorW2

Not the wild Walkyr maid alone. Gentlemen Prefer Blondes. G. K. Chesterton. CP-ChesG

Not There. Tess Gallagher. SP-GallT

Not These Hills. W. S. Merwin. SP-MerwW

Not They Who Soar! Paul Laurence Dunbar. CP-DunbP

Not thinking other than how the hand works. Ice-Fishing. William Stafford. SP-StafWW

Not This Way. Czeslaw Milosz. CP-MiloC; CP-MiloCN, *tr.* by Lillian Vallee

Not this week nor this month dare I lie down. Training. Wilfred Owen. CP-OwenW

Not though you die to-night, O Sweet, and wail. Rudyard Kipling. CP-KiplR *Fr.* Plain Tales from the Hills.

Not through the rational mind. Recapitulation, The. Richard Eberhart. CP-EberR

Not till old age did I learn. Canal Gardens. Jaroslav Seifert. SP-SeifJ, *tr.* by Ewald Osers

Not time's how(anchored in what mountaining roots). E. E. Cummings. CP-CummE

Not to admire, is all the Art I know. Sixth Epistle of the First Book of Horace Imitated, The. Alexander Pope. CP-PopeA

Not to ask, not to be answered. Unthronged Oracle, The. Laura Riding Jackson. CP-RidiL

Not to avoid him but. 1. Business Jacob, the Angel Wrestler. Alan Dugan. CP-DugaA

Not to Be Printed, Not to Be Said, Not to Be Thought. Muriel Rukeyser. CP-RukeM

Not to be shattered. Paxdominisit Sem Pervobiscum Etcumspiri Tutuo. Kenneth Patchen. CP-PatcK

Not to Choose. Alan Dugan. CP-DugaA

Not to Covet Much Where Little is the Charge. Robert Herrick. CP-HerrR

Not to discover weakness is. Emily Dickinson. CP-DickE

Not to encroach on Abel's herds. First Row, The. Robert Stock. SP-StocR

Not to exclude or demarcate, or pick out evils from their formidable masses (even to expose them). L. of G.'s Purport. Walt Whitman. CP-WhitW

Not to glance at anyone else, looking full in the face. Six Moral Virtues, The: Grace, Style, Class, Kindness, and Wisdom. Miller Williams. CP-WillM

Not to have guessed is better: what is, ends. Sphinx's Riddle to Oedipus, The. Randall Jarrell. CP-JarrR

Not to Keep. Robert Frost. CP-FrosR

Not to know vice at all, and keep[e] true state. Epode: "Not to know vice at all, and keep[e] true state." Ben Jonson. CP-JonsB; SP-JonsB

Not to let ourselves know. Even Now You Are Leaving. Tess Gallagher. SP-GallT

Not to Live. John Berryman. CP-BerrJ

Not to Love. Robert Herrick. CP-HerrR

Not, to me, less lavish—though my dreams have been splendid. Edna St. Vincent Millay. CP-MillE

Not to permit himself to be. Charles Olson. CP-OlsoC

Not to Sleep. Robert Graves. CP-GravR

Not to sleep all the night long, for pure joy. Not to Sleep. Robert Graves. CP-GravR

Not to the midnight of the gloomy past. On the Dedication of Dorothy Hall. Paul Laurence Dunbar. CP-DunbP

Not to Worry. Charles Bukowski. SP-BukC3

Not to You. Stephen Spender. CP-SpenS

Not to you / Unborn generations. Sentiments for a Dedication. Archibald MacLeish. CP-MacLA

Not today, not tomorrow. Song: Yesterday Only. Robert Graves. CP-GravR

Not tornado I sing, not wind for wind's unruly sake. Wind in the Mirror. Robert Stock. SP-StocR

Not Touching. Billy Collins. SP-CollB

Not Transhistorical Death, or at Least Not Quite. Hayden Carruth. CP-CarHS

Not true that it's always grim with mortal sin. Michelangelo Buonarroti. CP-Miche, *tr.* by John Frederick Nims

Not twice a twelvemonth [*or* twelve-month] you appear in Print. Epilogue to the Satires, in Two Dialogues. Alexander Pope. CP-PopeA

Not unconcerned Wachusett rears his head. Henry David Thoreau. CP-ThorH

Not unto men alone has come. Original Hymn ("Not unto men alone has come"). Jones Very. CP-VeryJ

Not unto us who did but seek. Hymn for the Celebration of Emancipation at Newburyport. John Greenleaf Whittier. CP-WhitJ

Not vainly did old poets tell. Channing. John Greenleaf Whittier. CP-WhitJ

Not vainly doth the earnest voice of man. To Alex. Smith, the "Glasgow Poet," on His Sonnet to "Fame." George Meredith. CP-MerG2

Not vainly we waited and counted the hours. Quakers Are Out, The. John Greenleaf Whittier. CP-WhitJ

Not very affectionate; she likes to kiss. Dog under False Pretences. William Dickey. SP-DickW

Not Very Loud. William Stafford. SP-StafWW

Not want / jesus, The. Sting, The. C. K. Williams. CP-WillC

Not Waving but Drowning. Stevie Smith. CP-SmitS

Not what I think / or see (I can't). Labor Day. James Schuyler. CP-SchuJ

Not what the stars have done. Emily Dickinson. SP-DickE

Not What Was. Langston Hughes. CP-HughL3

Not what We did, shall be the test. Emily Dickinson. CP-DickE

Not what's done, but what. Ecclesiastical Polity. Donald Davie. CP-DaviDC

Not while, but long after he had told me. Each Bird Walking. Tess Gallagher. SP-GallT

Not with a Club, the Heart is broken. Emily Dickinson. CP-DickE

Not with an iron will, no. More like a whip. Steps for a Dancer. Howard Nemerov. CP-NemeH

Not with an order but a question. Light. Rae Armantrout. SP-ArmaA

Not with an outcry to Allah nor any complaining. Captive, The. Rudyard Kipling. CP-KiplR

Not with bright forms alone, that please the eye. Guido's Aurora. Jones Very. CP-VeryJ

Not with libations, but with shouts and laughter. Edna St. Vincent Millay. CP-MillE

Not with the splendors of the days of old. Pennsylvania Hall. John Greenleaf Whittier. CP-WhitJ

Not without envy Wealth at times must look. Problem, The. John Greenleaf Whittier. CP-WhitJ

Not without heavy grief of heart did He. Gabriello Chiabrera. CP-WorW1

Not without Knowledge. Tennessee Williams. CP-WillT

Not without thee, our God, the skies. Hymn in Drought. Jones Very. CP-VeryJ

Not writ in water[,] nor in mist. For John Keats, Apostle of Beauty. Countee Cullen. CP-CullC *Fr.* Four Epitaphs.

Not Writing Poems about Children. Carolyn Kizer. CP-KizeC

Not Yet. Muriel Rukeyser. CP-RukeM

Not yet did I know your laws, enticing Amathusia. Elegy 7: "Not yet did I know your laws, enticing Amathusia." John Milton. CP-CowpW; CP-MiltJ

Not yet had History's Ætna smoked the skies. Revolution, The. George Meredith. CP-MerG1

Not yet old enough, still only a kid. Honeysuckle. William Stafford. SP-StafWW

Not yet the thirtieth year, the thirtieth. Fragment of a Meditation. Allen Tate.

CP-TateA

Not you but your beauty. Luxury in August. Philip Whalen. SP-WhalP

Not you, lean quarterlies and swarthy periodicals. To the Film Industry in Crisis. Frank O'Hara. SP-OharF

Not your dark poisons again. Sleep. Georg Trakl. CP-WrigJ

Not your defeats, no. Inscription for a Burned Bridge. W. S. Merwin. SP-MerwW

Not your eyes, but what they disguise. Speech out of Shadow. Ted Hughes. SP-HughTN

Not Yours but You. Christina Georgina Rossetti. CP-RosC3

Not Youth Pertains to Me. Walt Whitman. CP-WhitW

Nota: man is the intelligence of his soil. Comedian as the Letter C, The. Wallace Stevens. CP-StevW; CP-StevWP

Notations from a Muddled Indolence. Charles Bukowski. SP-BukC2

Note. Andrei Codrescu. SP-CodrA

Note. Alan Dugan. CP-DugaA

Note. Fernando Pessoa. SP-PessF, tr. by Susan M. Brown and Edwin Honig

Note. Charles Simic. SP-SimiC; SP-SimiCE

Note. William Stafford. SP-StafWW

Note, A. Wisława Szymborska. SP-SzymWM, tr. by Joanna Trzeciak

Note, A. William Carlos Williams. CP-WilW2

Note / as it gets darker. Elegy: "Note / as it gets darker." Charles Simic. SP-SimiC; SP-SimiCE

Note for a Diary. Kenneth Patchen. CP-PatcK

Note for a Fantastic Story. Jorge Luis Borges. SP-BorgJ, tr. by Stephen Kessler

Note from Leyden, A. Amy Clampitt. CP-ClamA

Note how the bear. Hispaniola. Amy Clampitt. CP-ClamA

Note in Honor of Machiavelli, A. Thomas Merton. CP-MertT

Note in Music. Langston Hughes. CP-HughL; CP-HughL1

Note Left in Jimmy Leonard's Shack, A. James Wright. CP-WrigJ

Note of Quits. Alan Dugan. CP-DugaA

Note of Thanks, A. Wyatt Prunty. SP-PrunW

Note on Commercial Theatre. Langston Hughes. CP-HughL; CP-HughL2

Note on Moonlight. Wallace Stevens. CP-StevW; CP-StevWP

Note on the Late Elections, A. Thomas McGrath. SP-McGrT

Note on War Poetry, A. T. S. Eliot. CP-ElioT

Note, Passed to Superman. Lucille Clifton. SP-ClifL

Note read re / letter of Lawrence's. Robert Creeley. CP-CreeR

Note Slipped under a Door. Charles Simic. SP-SimiC; SP-SimiCE

Note: The Sea Grinds Things Up. Alan Dugan. CP-DugaA

Note to All Nazis Fascists and Klansmen. Langston Hughes. CP-HughL; CP-HughL2

Note to God Concerning a Point from an Earlier Communication, A. Miller Williams. CP-WillM

Note to Grandparents. Grace Paley. CP-PalGC

Note to Music: Brahms 1st Piano Concerto. William Carlos Williams. CP-WilW2

Note to Olga (1966), A. Denise Levertov. SP-LeveDP

Note to the Boys in the Back Room, A. Charles Bukowski. SP-BukC3

Note to the Previous Tenants. John Updike. CP-UpdiJ

Note to Wang Wei. John Berryman. CP-BerrJ

Note to Whistler. Stéphane Mallarmé. CP-MallS, tr. by Henry Weinfield

Note upon the Love Letters of Beethoven. Charles Bukowski. SP-BukC3

Noteless stream, the Birchbrook runs, A. Birchbrook Mill. John Greenleaf Whittier. CP-WhitJ

Notes. Thomas Kinsella. CP-KinsT

Notes. John Ciardi. CP-CiarJ

Notes. Czeslaw Milosz. CP-MiloC; CP-MiloCN, tr. by Lillian Vallee

Notes for a Biography. Louis MacNeice. CP-MacNL

Notes for a Lecture. David Ignatow. SP-IgnaD

Notes for a Little Play. Ted Hughes. SP-HughTN

Notes for a Poem. Muriel Rukeyser. CP-RukeM

Notes for an Elegy. William Meredith. SP-MereW

Notes for Canto 111. Ezra Pound. See Cantos

Notes for Echo Lake 1. Michael Palmer. SP-PalmM

Notes for Echo Lake 2. Michael Palmer. SP-PalmM

Notes for Echo Lake 3. Michael Palmer. SP-PalmM

Notes for Echo Lake 4. Michael Palmer. SP-PalmM

Notes for Echo Lake 5. Michael Palmer. SP-PalmM

Notes for Echo Lake 6. Michael Palmer. SP-PalmM

Notes for Echo Lake 7. Michael Palmer. SP-PalmM

Notes for Echo Lake 8. Michael Palmer. SP-PalmM

Notes for Echo Lake 9. Michael Palmer. SP-PalmM

Notes for Echo Lake 10. Michael Palmer. SP-PalmM

Notes for Echo Lake 11. Michael Palmer. SP-PalmM

Notes for Echo Lake 12. Michael Palmer. SP-PalmM

Notes for Nobody. Donald Hall. CP-HallD

Notes for the Program. William Stafford. SP-StafWW

Notes from a Lenten Bar. Josephine Jacobsen. CP-JacoJ

Notes from a Nonexistent Himalayan Expedition. Wisława Szymborska. SP-SzymW, tr. by Stanislaw Barańczak and Clare Cavanagh

Notes from a Suburban Heart. Mona Van Duyn. SP-VanDM

Notes from a Tunisian Journal. Rita Dove. SP-DoveR

Notes from India. May Sarton. SP-SartM

Notes from Robin Hill Cottage. Hayden Carruth. CP-CarHS

Notes from the Agent on Earth: How to be Human. Miller Williams. CP-WillM

Notes from the Childhood and the Girlhood. Gwendolyn Brooks. SP-BrooG

Notes from the provinces always start. May Journal. Charles Wright. SP-WrigC

Notes I fall for fall from the lip of the sky, The. Spring Abstract. Charles Wright. SP-WrigC

Notes of a Parachute Jumper. Jorge Carrera Andrade. CP-MertT

Notes on the State of Virginia. Amy Clampitt. CP-ClamA

Notes on the tuned frame of strings. Sub Contra. Louise Bogan. CP-BogaL

Notes to a Neophyte. Sylvia Plath. SP-PlatS

Notes toward a Spring Offensive. Alan Dugan. CP-DugaA

Notes toward a Supreme Fiction. Wallace Stevens. CP-StevW; CP-StevWP

Notes toward Time. Josephine Jacobsen. CP-JacoJ

Notes towards a Poem That Can Never Be Written. Margaret Atwood. SP-AtwM2

Nothin' to say, my daughter! Nothin' at all to say! James Whitcomb Riley. CP-RileJ

Nothing. Margaret Atwood. SP-AtwM2

Nothing. James Fenton. SP-FentJ

Nothing. Robert Graves. CP-GravR

Nothing and the Incident in the Streets. Gregory Orr. SP-OrrG

Nothing better for singing of life. Ballad in Honor of the Muses of Flesh and Blood. "Rubén Darío." SP-DariR, tr. by Alberto Acereda and Will Derusha

Nothing Big. Yusef Komunyakaa. CP-KomuY

Nothing but Change. Richard Eberhart. CP-EberR

Nothing but Color. Ai. SP-Ai

Nothing but me is moving. Bridges, The. W. S. Merwin. SP-MerwW

Nothing but Nature. Ogden Nash. CP-NashO

Nothing but one life: all stands. Springhouse, Menses, Held Apple, House and Beyond. James Dickey. CP-DickJ

Nothing can be more loathsome, then to see. Cruelty Base in Commanders. Robert Herrick. CP-HerrR

Nothing can ever happen twice. Nothing Twice. Wisława Szymborska. SP-SzymW, tr. by Stanislaw Barańczak and Clare Cavanagh

Nothing Can Heal the Severed Nerves of a Hand? Arthur Sze. SP-SzeA

Nothing certain of this world. Land of Loss, The. Thomas Kinsella. CP-KinsT

Nothing comes Free-cost here; Jove will not let. Nothing Free-Cost. Robert Herrick. CP-HerrR

Nothing comes of nothing. We are nothing. Fernando Pessoa. SP-PessF, tr. by Susan M. Brown and Edwin Honig

Nothing day full of, A. Closed Gentian Distances. James Schuyler. CP-SchuJ

Nothing Down. Rita Dove. SP-DoveR

Nothing else in this song—only your face. Paula. Carl Sandburg. CP-SandC

Nothing endures, / Not even love. Countee Cullen. CP-CullC

Nothing exists that is not married; therefore. Therefore. William Dickey. SP-DickW

Nothing false and possible is love. E. E. Cummings. CP-CummE; SP-CummE

Nothing for a dirty man. All That Is Lovely in Men. Robert Creeley. CP-CreeR

Nothing forced those kids. Nothing and the Incident in the Streets. Gregory Orr. SP-OrrG

Nothing Free-Cost. Robert Herrick. CP-HerrR

Nothing Gold Can Stay. Robert Frost. CP-FrosR

Nothing hard, or harsh can prove. No Action Hard to Affection. Robert Herrick. CP-HerrR

Nothing has changed. Torture. Wisława Szymborska. SP-SzymWM, tr. by Joanna Trzeciak

Nothing has changed. Tortures. Wisława Szymborska. SP-SzymW, tr. by Stanislaw Barańczak and Clare Cavanagh

Nothing holds me to anything. Lisbon Revisited (1926). Fernando Pessoa. SP-PessF, tr. by Susan M. Brown and Edwin Honig

Nothing I Meant to Keep. Jane Cooper. CP-CoopJ

Nothing in her Life became her. Emily Dickinson. SP-DickE

Nothing in life has been made by man for man's using. Untimely. Rudyard Kipling. CP-KiplR Fr. Debits and Credits.

Nothing in life is so exciting. Fanny Howe. SP-HoweF Fr. Joy Had I Known.

Nothing in this bright region melts or shifts. From the Highest Camp. Thom Gunn. CP-GunnT

Nothing inclusive of a human Heart. Emily Dickinson. SP-DickE

Nothing is better, I well think. Leper, The. Algernon Charles Swinburne. SP-SwinA

NOTHING is circular. Nothing. Robert Graves. CP-GravR

Nothing is entirely as one. In Some Doubt but Willingly. John Ciardi. CP-CiarJ

Nothing is ever really lost, or can be lost. Continuities. Walt Whitman. CP-WhitW

Nothing is flat-lit and tabula rasaed in Charlottesville. Umbrian Dreams. Charles Wright. SP-WrigCN

Nothing is glummer. Fahrenheit *Gesundheit*. Ogden Nash. CP-NashO

Nothing is happening / Nothing. Event. Charles Tomlinson. CP-TomlC; SP-TomlC

Nothing is more certain than the flower. Two Aspects of April. William Carlos Williams. CP-WilW1

Nothing is more exactly terrible than. E. E. Cummings. CP-CummE

Nothing is new: we walk where others went. Nothing New. Robert Herrick. CP-HerrR

Nothing is plumb, level or square. Love Song: I and Thou. Alan Dugan. CP-DugaA

Nothing is quite as secretive as the way the stars. Star Turn. Charles Wright. SP-WrigCN

Nothing is re-enacted. Nothing. Holy Writ. Robert Penn Warren. CP-WarrR

Nothing is really any fun, to-day. Always This Paying. D. H. Lawrence. CP-LawrD

Nothing Is Really Hard but to Be Real. John Ciardi. CP-CiarJ

Nothing Is Right. Alice Walker. CP-WalkA

Nothing is simple, / not even simplification. Throwing away the Mail. Wendell Berry. CP-BerrW

Nothing is so beautiful as Spring—. Spring. Gerard Manley Hopkins. CP-HopkG

Nothing is so magnificent. Opulence. Richard Eberhart. CP-EberR

Nothing is so sure that it. Looking Glass, The. Walter De la Mare. CP-DeLaW

Nothing like love to put blood. Nothing. Margaret Atwood. SP-AtwM2

Nothing like the freedom of vision. Life as Visionary Spirit. Richard Eberhart. CP-EberR

Nothing Matters Much. Thomas Hardy. CP-HardT

Nothing moves. In its cage, the broken. Returning a Lost Child. Louise Glück. SP-GlucL

Nothing New. Robert Herrick. CP-HerrR

Nothing nothinged itself for me as well. Wisława Szymborska. SP-SzymWM, *tr. by* Joanna Trzeciak

Nothing nourishing. Lorine Niedecker. CP-NiedL

Nothing Now Astonishes. Robert Graves. CP-GravR

Nothing odd. Lion Grotto, The. Norman Dubie. CP-DubiN

Nothing, of course, comes entirely by itself. Encounter. Yannis Ritsos. SP-RitsY, *tr. by* Kimon Friar

Nothing on the walls. Cave, The. Wisława Szymborska. SP-SzymWM, *tr. by* Joanna Trzeciak

Nothing only / what it was. Hut. Robert Pinsky. CP-PinsR

Nothing particular. Yannis Ritsos. SP-RitsY *Fr.* Paper Poems 2.

Nothing prolongs. Neither the bronze plaque. Memorial. Thomas McGrath. SP-McGrT

Nothing remained: Nothing, the wanton name. Annihilation of Nothing, The. Thom Gunn. CP-GunnT

Nothing says that you must. Dozens, The. Audre Lorde. SP-LordA

Nothing seemed so incongruous. Santa Claus in Oaxaca. Richard Eberhart. CP-EberR

Nothing Significant Was Really Said. Philip Larkin. CP-LarkP

Nothing so far but moonlight. Laura Riding Jackson. CP-RidiL

Nothing so true as what you once let fall. Epistle [II,] to a Lady[: Of the Characters of Women]. Alexander Pope. CP-PopeA

Nothing Stays Put. Amy Clampitt. CP-ClamA

Nothing Subtle. Charles Bukowski. SP-BukC2

Nothing That's Lovely Can My Love Escape. James Laughlin. CP-LaugJ

Nothing the best of artists can conceive. Michelangelo Buonarroti. CP-Miche, *tr. by* John Frederick Nims

Nothing, the cross-haired sky tells lenses. Letter from a Pander. John Ciardi. CP-CiarJ

"Nothing" the unjust man complained. E. E. Cummings. CP-CummE

Nothing, this foam, virgin verse. Salutation. Stéphane Mallarmé. CP-MallS, *tr. by* Henry Weinfield

Nothing to Be Said. Philip Larkin. CP-LarkP

Nothing to be said about it, and everything. Dying. Robert Pinsky. CP-PinsR

Nothing to do I climbed Flower Peak. Han-shan. CP-ColdM, *tr. by* Red Pine

Nothing to Do with Janice Drake. Yusef Komunyakaa. CP-KomuY

Nothing to Save. D. H. Lawrence. CP-LawrD

Nothing to say to all those marriages! Place for a Third. Robert Frost. CP-FrosR

Nothing to speak of. Lorine Niedecker. CP-NiedL

Nothing Twice. Wisława Szymborska. SP-SzymW, *tr. by* Stanisław Barańczak *and* Clare Cavanagh

Nothing was left of me. Dream of Burial, A. James Wright. CP-WrigJ

Nothing was less than its seemed, my darling. Long Past Moncada. Muriel Rukeyser. CP-RukeM

Nothing we add, A. Scale. Rainer Maria Rilke. CP-RilkFr, *tr. by* A. Poulin, Jr.

Nothing whichful about / thick big this. E. E. Cummings. CP-CummE

Nothing Will Cure the Sick Lion but to Eat an Ape. Marianne Craig Moore. CP-MoorM

Nothing will do but. Standards. W. S. Merwin. SP-MerwW

Nothing will hold him much longer—let him go. Sunken Crown, The. Edwin Arlington Robinson. CP-RobiE

Nothing Will Yield. Howard Nemerov. CP-NemeH

Nothing worth noting. Linnaeus in Lapland. Lorine Niedecker. CP-NiedL

Nothing would sleep in that cellar, dank as a ditch. Root Cellar. Theodore Roethke. CP-RoetT

Nothing you have when you awake. Rondel: "Nothing you have when you awake." Stéphane Mallarmé. CP-MallS, *tr. by* Henry Weinfield

Nothingness, for our / names' sake. Paul Celan. SP-CelaP, *tr. by* John Felstiner

Nothing's a gift, it's all on loan. Wisława Szymborska. SP-SzymW, *tr. by* Stanisław Barańczak *and* Clare Cavanagh

Nothing's certain. Crossing, on this longest day. Hermit Thrush, A. Amy Clampitt. CP-ClamA

Nothing's final, not even. Matches. Adam Zagajewski. SP-ZagaA, *tr. by* Renata Gorczynski, Benjamin Ivry *and* C. K. Williams

Nothing's going to become of anyone. Play. A. R. Ammons. CP-AmmoA

Nothing's Left. Rainer Maria Rilke. CP-RilkFr, *tr. by* A. Poulin, Jr.

Nothing's / today and. Poor. Robert Creeley. SP-CreeR

Notice each windowpane has a different. Frost. Arthur Sze. SP-SzeA

Notice how each particle moves. Special Plates. Jelaluddin Rumi. SP-Rumi, *tr. by* Coleman Barks

Notice how he has numbered the blue veins. Mr. Mine. Anne Sexton. CP-SextA; SP-SextA

Notice of Loss. Hans Magnus Enzensberger. SP-EnzeH

Notice that is called the Spring, The. Emily Dickinson. CP-DickE

Notice the convulsed orange inch of moon. E. E. Cummings. CP-CummE

Notice What This Poem Is Not Doing. William Stafford. SP-StafWW

Notre Dame. Rainer Maria Rilke. CP-RilkFr, *tr. by* A. Poulin, Jr.

Notre Dame de Chartres. William Meredith. SP-MereW

Nottingham's New University. D. H. Lawrence. CP-LawrD

Nottinghamshire. Donald Davie. CP-DaviDC

Nought from my birth or ancestors I claim. Ovid. CP-JohnS *Fr.* Metamorphoses.

Nought is more honorable to a knight. Book 5, Canto 2. Edmund Spenser. CP-Spens *Fr.* Faerie Queene, The.

Nought loves another as itself. Little Boy Lost, A. William Blake. CP-BlakW *Fr.* Songs of Experience.

Noun Verse. Caroline Mary Craven Austen. CP-AustJ

Nouns to nouns / wan / wan. E. E. Cummings. CP-CummE

Nourish Me on an Egg. Stevie Smith. CP-SmitS

Nourished by figs be the heart. Remembrance. Paul Celan. SP-CelaP, *tr. by* John Felstiner

Nourishment before Battle. Homer. CP-MerG2 *Fr.* Iliad, The.

Nous N'osons Plus Chanter les Roses. Constantine P. Cavafy. CP-CavaC, *tr. by* Theoharis Constantine Theoharis

Nova. Robinson Jeffers. CP-JefR2

Novel, The. Denise Levertov. SP-LeveDP

Novel, The. Wallace Stevens. CP-StevW; CP-StevWP

Novelettes. Louis MacNeice. CP-MacNL

Novelist, The. W. H. Auden. CP-AudeW

Novelists. Howard Nemerov. CP-NemeH

Novella. Adrienne Rich. CP-RicAE; SP-RicA2

Novelty, A. G. K. Chesterton. CP-ChesG

November. Margaret Atwood. SP-AtwM1

November. Billy Collins. SP-CollB

November. Robert Frost. CP-FrosR

November. Ted Hughes. SP-HughTN

November. Federico García Lorca. CP-GarcF, *tr. by* Catherine Brown

November. Archibald MacLeish. CP-MacLA

November. W. S. Merwin. SP-MerwWF

November. Gregory Orr. SP-OrrG

November. James Schuyler. CP-SchuJ

November. Stevie Smith. CP-SmitS

November. William Stafford. SP-StafWW

November. John Updike. CP-UpdiJ

November always seemed to me. Emily Dickinson. SP-DickE

November and trees blown bare and leaves stippling. Winter Music. John Ciardi. CP-CiarJ

November brings no rain. Brown stubble blackens. Autumn Drought. Helen Pinkerton. CP-PinkH

November by the Sea. D. H. Lawrence. CP-LawrD

November Day at McClure's Beach. Robert Bly. SP-BlyR

November 8, a cold rain. Hazard discovered. Nixon's the One. William

Meredith. SP-MereW

November, 1806. William Wordsworth. CP-WorW1; MW-WorW

November, 1813. William Wordsworth. CP-WorW1

November, 1836. William Wordsworth. CP-WorW2; MW-WorW

November for Beginners. Rita Dove. SP-DoveR

November Ghosts, The. Randall Jarrell. CP-JarrR

November Graveyard. Sylvia Plath. CP-PlatS

November has hung the locust. Kenneth Rexroth. CP-RexrK

November in afterpiece. Local Journal. Charles Wright. SP-WrigC

November in Ohio. Kenneth Patchen. CP-PatcK

November: Indian Summer. Hayden Carruth. CP-CarHS

November Jeans Song. Hayden Carruth. CP-CarHS

November Late. Theodore Weiss. SP-WeisT

November Night. May Swenson. SP-SwenM

November night. Waning moon. Xmas Coming. Kenneth Rexroth. CP-RexrK

November 1918. Jaroslav Seifert. SP-SeifJ, tr. by Ewald Osers

November 1968. Adrienne Rich. CP-RicAE; SP-RicA2

November 1 [1815]. William Wordsworth. CP-WorW2

November Rain. Jaroslav Seifert. SP-SeifJ, tr. by Ewald Osers

November 6, 1984. Andrei Codrescu. SP-CodrA

November sun invites me, The. Nutting Song. Paul Laurence Dunbar. CP-DunbP

November Surf. Robinson Jeffers. CP-JefR2

November Talks. Michael Palmer. SP-PalmM

November. The sun, having risen on an empty stomach. Thames at Chelsea, The. Joseph Brodsky. CP-BrodJ, tr. by David Rigsbee

11/22/63. George Oppen. CP OppGN

November 23, 1989. Norman Dubie. CP-DubiN

Nov. 23, 1963: Alone. Allen Ginsberg. CP-GinsA

Novice, The. Christina Georgina Rossetti. CP-RosC3

Novice, hear me what I say. Hafiz. CP-EmerR Fr. Odes.

Novice was sitting on a cornice, A. Illustration. John Ashbery. SP-AshbJ

Novices. Marianne Craig Moore. CP-MoorM

Novices, The. Denise Levertov. SP-LeveDP

Novitiates sing Ave. Miss Scarlet, Mr. Rhett and other Latter-Day Saints. Maya Angelou. SP-AngeM

Novum Organum. Ambrose Bierce. SP-BierA

Now. Robert Browning. SP-BroR

Now. Charles Bukowski. SP-BukC3

Now. Robert Creeley. SP-CreeR

Now. David Ignatow. SP-IgnaD

NOW. Audre Lorde. SP-LordA

NOW. Grace Paley. CP-PalGC

Now. Anne Sexton. CP ScxtA

Now. Dylan Thomas. CP-ThomD

Now a daring blue heron. Fanny Howe. SP-HoweF Fr. Vineyard, The.

Now above all is the time for the minorities of men. Minorities in Danger. D, H Lawrence. CP-LawrD

Now, after all, let no man. Phoenix Analysed, The. Ben Jonson. CP-JonsB

Now again and now for ever breaks the great illusion. Gulf, The. D. H. Lawrence. CP-LawrD

Now air is air and thing is thing:no bliss. E. E. Cummings. CP-CummE

Now all day long the man who is not dead. Mother and Son. Allen Tate. CP-TateA

Now all is done, learned spectators, tell. Epilogue, The: "Now all is done, learned spectators, tell." Thomas Sheridan. CP-SherT

Now all my teachers are dead except silence. Scale in May, A. W. S. Merwin. SP-MerwW

Now all of change. Sir Thomas Wyatt. CP-WyatT

Now all our saws sing holy sonnets in this world of timber. Trappists, Working. Thomas Merton. CP-MertT

Now all the balls your daddy hit. Nineteenth Hole, The. Wyatt Prunty. SP-PrunW

Now all the fingers of this tree(darling)have. E. E. Cummings. CP-CummE; SP-CummE

Now all the hosts are marching to the grave. Resurrection. D. H. Lawrence. CP-LawrD

Now all the truth is out. To a Friend Whose Work Has Come to Nothing. William Butler Yeats. CP-YeatW

Now and again. Virgin Youth. D. H. Lawrence. CP-LawrD

Now and Again. W. S. Merwin. SP-MerwW

Now and perpetually, over. Grievances. William Meredith. SP-MereW

Now and Then. James Schuyler. CP-SchuJ

Now and then he assures himself he didn't see, he doesn't know. Normal Occurence. Yannis Ritsos. SP-RitsY, tr. by N. C. Germanacos

Now and then some animals stops you. Rainer Maria Rilke. CP-RilkFr, tr. by A. Poulin, Jr. Fr. Fragments.

Now and then the intolerable crooks. King of Ice, The. A. R. Ammons. CP-

AmmoA

Now and then the smell of apples. Homeland. Amy Clampitt. CP-ClamA

Now Are We Remembered. Robert Stock. SP-StocR

Now armed with biting ice, now tongues of fire. Michelangelo Buonarroti. CP-Miche, tr. by John Frederick Nims

Now Art has lost its mental Charms. William Blake. CP-BlakW

Now as at all times I can see in the mind's eye. Magi, The. William Butler Yeats. CP-YeatW

Now as from maple to elm the flittermice skitter and twirl. Idyll: "Now as from maple to elm the flittermice skitter and twirl." Theodore Roethke. CP-RoetT

Now as he rolled these matters within him in heart & in spirit. Odysseus Encircled. Homer. CP-MerG2 Fr. Iliad, The.

Now as Heaven is my Lot, they're the Pests of the Nation! Soliloquy on the Full Moon, She Being in a Mad Passion, A. Samuel Taylor Coleridge. CP-ColeS

Now, as I sink in sleep. Night Songs. Thomas Kinsella. CP-KinsT

Now as I was young and easy under the apple boughs. Fern Hill. Dylan Thomas. CP-ThomD

Now as I watch the progress of the plague. Missing, The. Thom Gunn. CP-GunnT

Now as I watch you, strong of arm and endurance, battling and struggling. To the Swimmer. Countee Cullen. CP-CullC

Now as the train bears west. Night Journey. Theodore Roethke. CP-RoetT

Now as the year turns toward its darkness. Going Away. Howard Nemerov. CP-NemeH

Now ashen gray tinges the balding brow. Fernando Pessoa. SP-PessF, tr. by Susan M. Brown and Edwin Honig

Now at Liberty. Dorothy Parker. CP-ParkD

Now at ninety this frail and lightsome woman. Examination of Psyche: Thoughts of Home. Richard Eberhart. CP-EberR

Now at our island's shining rim. Aubade: Bermuda. Thomas Merton. CP-MertT

Now, at the rising of Venus—the steady star. North and South. Derek Walcott. CP-WalcD

Now autumn has finished scolding. Winter: He Shapes Up. William Meredith. SP-MereW

Now autumn nibbles its leaf from my hand: we are friends. Love Crown. Paul Celan. CP-PinsR, tr. by Robert Pinsky

Now, being invisible, I walk without mantilla. Souls of Women at Night, The. Wallace Stevens. CP-StevWP

Now blessed be the day, the month, the year. Petrarch. CP-Petra, tr. by J. G. Nichols

Now but she's the same sweet. Persephone Wears Bluejeans. James Laughlin. CP-LaugJ

Now hy a sudden shift of eye. Olive-Yard, The. Robert Graves. CP-GravR

Now by the path I climbed, I journey back. Edna St. Vincent Millay. CP-MillE

Now, by the verdure on thy thousand hills. Adequacy. Elizabeth Barrett Browning. CP-BroEB

Now by this moon, before this moon shall wane. Edna St. Vincent Millay. CP-MillE

Now can you see the monument? It is of wood. Monument, The. Elizabeth Bishop. CP-BishE

Now Chil the Kite brings home the night. Rudyard Kipling. CP-KiplR Fr. Jungle Book, The.

Now Close the Windows. Robert Frost. CP-FrosR

Now come to me all men. Experience Evoked. Richard Eberhart. CP-EberR

Now comes the good rain farmers pray for(and). E. E. Cummings. CP-CummE

Now constantly there is the sound. October 10. Wendell Berry. CP-BerrW

Now could I but describe with what sweet breath. Petrarch. CP-Petra, tr. by J. G. Nichols

Now cumis aige quhair yewth hes bene. William Dunbar. CP-DunbW

Now Dædalus, behold, by fate assign'd. Ovid. CP-JohnS Fr. Art of Love, The.

Now dawns all waxen to your seal of life. George Meredith. CP-MerG2

Now dearest comrade, lift me to your face. To the Reader at Parting. Walt Whitman. CP-WhitW

Now deeply drunk, always where you have found him. G.F. Died 1954, Aged 27. William Dickey. SP-DickW

Now Dian, with her burning face. Ben Jonson. CP-JonsB Fr. Masque of Blackness, The.

Now did you mark a falcon. Noble Sisters. Christina Georgina Rossetti. CP-RosC1

Now dis "daughter" uv eve(who aint precisely slim)sim. E. E. Cummings. CP-CummE

Now do our eyes behold. Lament for the Two Brothers Slain by Each Other's Hand. Aeschylus. CP-HousA Fr. Seven against Thebes, The.

Now do you know of Avalon. Jingo and the Minstrel, The. Nicholas Vachel Lindsay. CP-LindV

Now does our world descend. E. E. Cummings. CP-CummE

Now does Spain's fleet her spacious wings unfold. On the Victory Obtained by Blake over the Spaniards, in the Bay of Santa [or Sancta] Cruz, in the Island of Tenerife, 1657. Andrew Marvell. CP-MarvA

Now, don't sir! Don't expose me! Just this once! Mr Sludge, "The Medium." Robert Browning. CP-BroR1; SP-BroR

Now dreams / Are not available. Oppression. Langston Hughes. CP-HughL; CP-HughL2; CP-HughL3

Now dreary dawns the eastern light. A. E. Housman. CP-HousA

Now dumb is he who waked the world to speak. On Hearing the News from Venice. George Meredith. CP-MerG1

Now earth and sky are still, winds blow no more. Petrarch. CP-Petra, tr. by J. G. Nichols

Now Europe's balanc'd neither Side prevails. Balance of Europe, The. Alexander Pope. CP-PopeA

Now farewell to you! you are. Lines to a Friend Visiting America. George Meredith. CP-MerG1

Now fear, the engine of all turnaround. Lullaby for Now. Robert Stock. SP-StocR

Now Finalè to the Shore. Walt Whitman. CP-WhitW

Now first of all he means the night. Song for the Middle of the Night, A. James Wright. CP-WrigJ

Now flesh and bones burn inside my mouth. Dying Tooth Song. Philip Whalen. SP-WhalP

Now flower the oldest seeds. Doom in Bloom. Laura Riding Jackson. CP-RidiL

Now for the first time on the night of your death your name is mentioned in convents, *ne cadas in obscurum*. Elegy for Ernest Hemingway, An. Thomas Merton. CP-MertT

Now for the hour when swaying on its stem. Evening Harmony. Charles Baudelaire. CP-BaudC, tr. by Walter Martin

Now from my window-sill I watch the night. Watchers, The. W. H. Auden. CP-AudeW

Now frost has broken summer like a glass. Der Abschied. May Sarton. SP-SartM

Now ginnes this goodly frame of temperaunce. Book 2, Canto 12. Edmund Spenser. CP-Spens *Fr.* Faerie Queene, The.

Now give us lands where the olives grow. North and the South, The. Elizabeth Barrett Browning. CP-BroEB

Now go to the party. Lorine Niedecker. CP-NiedL

Now God wants even. Celestial Desolations. Gregory Orr. SP-OrrG

Now goes under, and I watch it go under, the sun. To a Friend Estranged from Me. Edna St. Vincent Millay. CP-MillE

Now grapes are plush upon the vines. Contrary Theses (I). Wallace Stevens. CP-StevV; CP-StevWP

Now green, now burning, I make a way for peace. Tenth Elegy. Elegy in Joy. Muriel Rukeyser. CP-RukeM

Now grey-ey'd hazy Eve's begun. Evening. John Clare. SP-ClarJ

Now had the loophole of that dungeon, still. Ugolino. Dante Alighieri. CP-ShelP *Fr.* Divina Commedia.

Now hardly here and there a hackney-coach. Description of the Morning, A. Jonathan Swift. CP-SwifJ

Now has come, an easy time. I let it. Why I Am Happy. William Stafford. SP-StafWW

Now has the brittle incandescent day. Autumn Twilight Piece. Robert Penn Warren. CP-WarrR

Now has the rapier of iron wrought. Odyssey, Book Twenty-three. Jorge Luis Borges. SP-BorgJ, tr. by Robert Fitzgerald

Now having seen so many smiles sink. Second Letter to Junk Jeannee of NYC. Andrei Codrescu. SP-CodrA

Now he has become one who upon that coast. His Head is Full of Faces. Muriel Rukeyser. CP-RukeM

Now he plays with the other children. Muriel Rukeyser. CP-RukeM

Now health forsakes that angel face. Fragment: "Now health forsakes that angel face." Robert Burns. CP-BurnR

Now here is peace for one who knew. No Bird. Theodore Roethke. CP-RoetT

Now his nose's bridge is broken, one eye. On Hurricane Jackson. Alan Dugan. CP-DugaA

Now hollow fires burn out to black. A. E. Housman. CP-HousA

Now homing tradesmen scatter through the streets. Place Pigalle. Richard Wilbur. CP-WilbR

Now honest William's gaen to Heaven. Elegy on Mister William Cruikshank A. M. Robert Burns. CP-BurnR

Now I am afraid for a child. Midsummer's Eve. Donald Davie. CP-DaviDC

Now I am all. Mystery. D. H. Lawrence. CP-LawrD

Now I am come again, to you who have so desired. Return. D. H. Lawrence. CP-LawrD

Now I am dead you sing to me. Upbraiding, An. Thomas Hardy. CP-HardT

Now I am going. Thing Itself, The. Alice Walker. CP-WalkA

Now I am minded to take a pipe in hand. Gerard Manley Hopkins. CP-HopkG

Now I am old and free from time. Winter Paradise. Kathleen Jessie Raine. SP-RainK

Now I am out of element. Against Disaster. Theodore Roethke. CP-RoetT

Now I am surer where they were going. For W. H. Auden. Richard Wilbur. CP-WilbR

Now I am tired of being Japanese. Two Japanese Poems. William Meredith. SP-MereW

Now I am young and credulous. Wisdom Cometh with the Years. Countee Cullen. CP-CullC

Now I Become Myself. May Sarton. SP-SartM

Now I believe tradition, which doth call. Upon the Author. By a Known Friend. Benjamin Woodbridge. CP-BradA

Now I can be sure of my sleep. On the Hill below the Lighthouse. James Dickey. CP-DickJ

Now I Can Go On and On. Eleanor Wilner. SP-WilnE

Now I commend this body to this earth. It Is for Us the Living. Kenneth Patchen. CP-PatcK

Now I feast not just my eyes. On the Greve. Eugenio Montale. CP-MontE, tr. by Jonathan Galassi

Now I go down here and bring up a moon. Auctioneer. Carl Sandburg. CP-SandC

Now I have become a man. Ode: My 24th Year. Allen Ginsberg. CP-GinsA

Now I have lain awake imagining murder. Poem at Christmas, 1972, during the Terror-Bombing of North Vietnam, A. Denise Levertov. SP-LeveDL

Now I have no notion whether I will be able. Letter to My Son. John Logan. CP-LogaJ

Now I hear two unsynchronized steel hammers pounding on steel. David Ignatow. SP-IgnaD

Now I knew I lost her. Emily Dickinson. CP-DickE

Now I know. Delphi. "H. D." CP-DoolH

Now I know I never shall. Ted Hughes. SP-HughTN *Fr.* Prometheus on His Crag.

Now I know where they live, like the night owls. Yehuda Amichai. SP-AmicYL *Fr.* At Right Angles.

Now I lay thee down to Sleep. Emily Dickinson. CP-DickE

Now i lay(with everywhere around). E. E. Cummings. CP-CummE

Now I long for the Pierian fountains. To My Father. John Milton. CP-MiltJ

Now I must sit naked. Sweat, The. Gary Snyder. CP-SnydG

Now I must tell you of our grandeur. Rydal Mount. Amy Clampitt. CP-ClamA

Now I out walking. Away! Robert Frost. CP-FrosR

Now I put on the thimble of dream. Red Bird Tapestry, The. May Swenson. SP-SwenM

Now I remember: in our town the druggist. Serving with Gideon. William Stafford. SP-StafW; SP-StafWW

Now I remember, letting the dark. Many Things are Hidden by the Light. William Stafford. SP-StafWW

Now I remember songs you might have sung. Apologia for Grief. Robert Penn Warren. CP-WarrR

Now I see something in my listeners. After the Meditation. Jelaluddin Rumi. SP-Rumi, tr. by Coleman Barks

Now I understand myself running back. Where Nothing Is Hidden. David Ignatow. SP-IgnaD

Now I Went Down to the Ringside and Little Henry Armstrong Was There. Kenneth Patchen. CP-PatcK

Now I will abandon the route of my life. Mr. Wakeville on Interstate 90. Donald Hall. CP-HallD

Now I will enter the house of affliction. Love's Dozen. Jay Wright. SP-WrigJ

Now I will shut you in a box. La Prisonnière. Thom Gunn. CP-GunnT

Now I will tell Meader's story; I have a moral in view. Story, A. Czeslaw Milosz. CP-MiloC; CP-MiloCN, tr. by Renata Gorczynski *and* Robert Pinsky

Now if not love, what is it that I feel? Petrarch. CP-Petra, tr. by J. G. Nichols

Now if You. Kenneth Patchen. CP-PatcK

Now, if you love me, tell me. Nor Buying or Selling. Robert Herrick. CP-HerrR

Now, if You Were Teaching Creative Writing, He Asked, What Would You Tell Them? Charles Bukowski. SP-BukC1

Now I'll also tell what food. Gary Snyder. CP-SnydG *Fr.* Myths and Texts.

Now I'll record my secret vision, impossible sight of the face of God. Psalm 4. Allen Ginsberg. CP-GinsA; SP-GinsA

Now in a thought, now in a shadowed word. L'Envoi. Edwin Arlington Robinson. CP-RobiE

Now in her green mantle blythe nature arrays. My Nannie's Awa'. Robert Burns. CP-BurnR

Now, / In June. After Many Springs. Langston Hughes. CP-HughL; CP-HughL1

Now in midsummer come and all fools slaughtered. Credences of Summer. Wallace Stevens. CP-StevV; CP-StevWP

Now in November nearer comes the sun. November by the Sea. D. H. Lawrence. CP-LawrD

Now in one year. Lorine Niedecker. CP-NiedL

Now in the din before the silence. Yehuda Amichai. SP-AmicYL, tr. by Benjamin Harshav *and* Barbara Harshav

Now, in the middle of the limpid evening. Evening. Thomas Merton. CP-MertT

Now, in the night, all music haunts us here. Johnny Appleseed Speaks of the Appleblossom Amaranth That Will Come to This City. Nicholas Vachel

Lindsay. CP-LindV

Now in the storm before the calm. Yehuda Amichai. SP-AmicY, *tr. by* Stephen Mitchell

Now in the suburbs and the falling light. Father and Son. Stanley Kunitz. CP-KunSC, *tr. by* Jack Bevan

Now in this evening land of fire and shadow. From Yellow Lake: An Interval. Mona Van Duyn. SP-VanDM

Now in This Thankless World the Givers. *Unknown, sometimes at. to* Thomas Sheridan. CP-SherT

Now incense fills the air. After Yeats. Allen Ginsberg. CP-GinsA

Now, innocent, within the deep. M., Singing. Louise Bogan. CP-BogaL

Now is a ship / which captain am. E. E. Cummings. CP-CummE

Now Is the Air Made of Chiming Balls. Richard Eberhart. CP-EberR

Now is the day of our farewell in fear, lean pages. Poet, to His Book, The. Thomas Merton. CP-MertT

Now is the globe shrunk tight. Snowdrop. Ted Hughes. SP-HughTN

Now is the hour to rhyme a song for death. Admonition to Those Who Mourn. Robert Penn Warren. CP-WarrR

Now is the season for dry smell of powder. September Shooting. Howard Nemerov. CP-NemeH

Now is the season / of hungry mice, / cold rabbits. Wolf Moon. Mary Oliver. SP-OlivM

Now is the time for mirth. To Live Merrily, and to Trust to Good Verses. Robert Herrick. CP-HerrR

Now is the time of the moths that come. Not Very Loud. William Stafford. SP-StafWW

Now is the time, when all the lights wax dim. To Anthea. Robert Herrick. CP-HerrR

Now is the time when weakness comes,—& strength goes. Salve Senescentem. Sadi. CP-EmerR

Now is the world withdrawn all. Carol: "Now is the world withdrawn all." Howard Nemerov. CP-NemeH

Now is your turne (my Dearest) to be set. To his deare Valentine, Mistresse Margaret Falconbrige. Robert Herrick. CP-HerrR

Now it begins: / sprays of forsythia against wet brick. Breaking Camp. Marge Piercy. SP-PierM

Now it happens in these years at unguarded intervals. Apparitions. W. S. Merwin. SP-MerwWF

Now it is almost night, from the bronzey soft sky. Storm in the Black Forest. D. H. Lawrence. CP-LawrD

Now it is autumn and the falling fruit. Ship of Death, The. D. H. Lawrence. CP-LawrD

Now it is clear to me that no leaves are mine. W. S. Merwin. SP-MerwW

Now it is fifteen years you have lain in the meadow. Lines for an Interment. Archibald MacLeish. CP-MacLA

Now it is gone, all of it. Stones. Donald Hall. CP-HallD

Now it is late winter. Two Spring Charms. *Unknown.* CP-WrigJ, *tr. by* James Wright

Now, it is night and time. I Got the Fat Poet into a Corner. Kenneth Patchen. CP-PatcK

Now it is night, now in the brilliant room. De Anima. Howard Nemerov. CP-NemeH

Now it is no longer the war, but a war. 1914. Randall Jarrell. CP-JarrR

Now it is not good for the Christian's health to hustle the Aryan brown. Rudyard Kipling. CP-KiplR *Fr.* Naulahka, The.

Now it is September and the web is woven. Dwarf, The. Wallace Stevens. CP-StevW; CP-StevWP

Now it is the 27th. Poem: "Now it is the 27th." Frank O'Hara. SP-OharF

Now it is time. Labor Storm. Langston Hughes. CP-HughL; CP-HughL2

Now it seems to me that since the Word Himself has come down from heaven to us, we no longer have any need for the schooling of men. Logos Our Teacher, The. Clement of Alexandria. CP-MertT

Now it's autumn. All glasses broken at weddings, didn't bounce. Yehuda Amichai. SP-AmicYL *Fr.* At Right Angles.

Now it's Borodin . . . 4:18 A.M. Fleg. Charles Bukowski. SP-BukC2

Now It's Happened. D. H. Lawrence. CP-LawrD

Now it's over, and now it's done. Finis. Dorothy Parker. CP-ParkD

Now it's windy and the waves are running crisscross. Letters to a Roman Friend. Joseph Brodsky. CP-BrodJ, *tr. by* George L. Kline

Now I've said all I would, mother. Life out of Death. Christina Georgina Rossetti. CP-RosC3

Now Johnson would go up to join the [great] simulacra of men. Up Rising. Robert Duncan. SP-DuncR *Fr.* Passages.

Now Jones had left his new-wed bride to keep his house in order. Code of Morals, A. Rudyard Kipling. CP-KiplR

Now, joy and thanks forevermore! Pæan. John Greenleaf Whittier. CP-WhitJ

Now Kennedy if foot or horse. To Mr. John Kennedy. Robert Burns. CP-BurnR

Now let all lovely things embark. Lament: "Now let all lovely things embark." Countee Cullen. CP-CullC

Now let forever the phlox and the rose be tended. Hardy Garden, The. Edna St. Vincent Millay. CP-MillE

Now let her change and spare not. Thomas Campion. CP-CampT

Now let me tell you why I said that. Nothing Is Really Hard but to Be Real. John Ciardi. CP-CiarJ

Now let no man abide. Bombarded City, The. Thomas Merton. CP-MertT

Now let the legless boy show the great lady. In the Children's Hospital. Hugh MacDiarmid. SP-MacDH

Now let the mouth of wailing for a time. Edna St. Vincent Millay. CP-MillE

Now let this present act. Recollection on the Day of a First Book. John Logan. CP-LogaJ

Now let us honor with violin and flute. Song: "Now let us honor with violin and flute." May Sarton. SP-SartM

Now Lift Me Close. Walt Whitman. CP-WhitW

Now light dies from the pleasance. Pleasance Window, The. Ivor Gurney. SP-GurnI

Now light is less; noon skies are wide and deep. Slow Season. Theodore Roethke. CP-RoetT

Now list to my morning's romanza, I tell the signs of the Answerer. Song of the Answerer. Walt Whitman. CP-WhitW

Now littlely wandering . . . littlely dressed in rainment suitable to. Deathsong for a Maiden. Kenneth Patchen. CP-PatcK

Now loneliness enters the marrow. Distance. Josephine Jacobsen. CP-JacoJ

Now Long Ago. Maya Angelou. SP-AngeM

Now look and see in yonder throne. Ben Jonson. CP-JonsB *Fr.* News from the New World.

Now look here. Altercation. D. H. Lawrence. CP-LawrD

Now lookahere, gal. Argument ("Now lookahere, gal"). Langston Hughes. CP-HughL; CP-HughL1

Now Lord, or never, they'l[l] believe [*or* beleeve] on Thee. On the Miracle of Loaves. Richard Crashaw. CP-CrasR

Now lost, things a child heard. Loss of Sounds. Josephine Jacobsen. CP-JacoJ

Now Love Speaks. James Laughlin. CP-LaugJ

Now luck for us and a kind hearty pit. Prologue to *The Spanish Friar*. John Dryden. SP-DrydJ *Fr.* Spanish Friar [*or* Fryar], The.

Now lythis off ane gentill knycht. William Dunbar. CP-DunbW

Now mind is clear. Desolation, A. Allen Ginsberg. CP-GinsA

Now mist takes the hemlocks and nothing. Selectivity. John Ciardi. CP-CiarJ

Now more and more on my concern with the lifted waves of genius gaining. On the Ocean Floor. Hugh MacDiarmid. SP-MacDH

Now Morning from her orient chamber came. Imitation of Spenser. John Keats. CP-KeatJ

Now muse divine, thy heav'nly aid impart. Ocean. Phillis Wheatley. CP-WheaP

Now must all satisfaction. Certain Mercies. Robert Graves. CP-GravR

Now must I learn to feign. Sir Thomas Wyatt. CP-WyatT

Now must I le[a]rn[e] to live [*or* lyve] at rest. Sir Thomas Wyatt. CP-WyatT

Now must I these three praise. Friends. William Butler Yeats. CP-YeatW

Now my body flat. Exchange, The. May Swenson. SP-SwenM

Now, my cunning lady moon. Ben Jonson. CP-JonsB *Fr.* Oberon, the Fairy Prince.

Now my love explains me as the commentators in their prime. Yehuda Amichai. SP-AmicYL *Fr.* At Right Angles.

Now nature cleeds the flowery lea. Lassie wi' the Lintwhite Locks. Robert Burns. CP-BurnR

Now Nature hangs her mantle green. Lament of Mary Queen of Scots on the Approach of Spring. Robert Burns. CP-BurnR

Now night perfumes lie upon the air. Summer Nocturne. Philip Larkin. CP-LarkP

Now night with sable wings the world o'erspread. Speech of Venus to Vulcan, The. Virgil. CP-DryJ2, *tr. by* John Dryden *Fr.* Aeneid (Dryden translation).

Now, not a tear begun. Woman Mourned by Daughters, A. Adrienne Rich. CP-RicAE; SP-RicA2

Now not every man has the makings of a barber. Ohio River Blues. Kenneth Patchen. CP-PatcK

Now! / Not now! In a Balcony. Robert Browning. CP-BroR1

Now not to smile again. After Smiling. Laura Riding Jackson. CP-RidiL

Now, Now. Paul Muldoon. CP-MuldP

Now—now, as low I stooped, thought I. Snowdrop, The. Walter De la Mare. CP-DeLaW

Now, now begin to set. Ben Jonson. CP-JonsB *Fr.* Masque of Hymen.

Now, now the mirth comes. Twelfe Night, or King and Queene. Robert Herrick. CP-HerrR

Now, now's the time so oft by Truth. Epithalamy to Sir Thomas Southwell and His Lady, An. Robert Herrick. CP-HerrR

Now o'er the sea from her old love comes she. Elegy 1.13: "Now o'er the sea from her old love comes she." Ovid. CP-MarlC *Fr.* Elegies.

Now of wemen this I say, for me. In Prais[e] of Women [*or* Wemen]. William Dunbar. CP-DunbW

Now on the great stage a silence falls. Proletarian in Abstract Light. Thomas

McGrath. SP-McGrT

Now on the left foot shuffling, now the right. Michelangelo Buonarroti. CP-Miche, *tr. by* John Frederick Nims

Now, on this day of the first hundred flowers. We Come Back. Kenneth Rexroth. CP-RexrK

Now on you is the hungry equinox. Kentucky Mountain Farm. Robert Penn Warren. CP-WarrR

Now once more gray mottled buckeye branches. Andrée Rexroth ("Now once more gray mottled buckeye branches"). Kenneth Rexroth. CP-RexrK

Now one of you turn this way. Instructions to Four Walls. W. S. Merwin. SP-MerwW

Now only when the skies are washed, rain-cleared. Quiet Countries: The World of Hans Christian Andersen. Marya Alexandrovna Zaturenska. SP-ZatuM

Now, parting from the festive board. Parting Hymn. Jones Very. CP-VeryJ

Now Patrick with his footmanship has done. Upon Patrick a Footman. Robert Herrick. CP-HerrR

Now Pine-Needles. Stevie Smith. CP-SmitS

Now praise the Gods of Time and Chance. Song of French Roads, A. Rudyard Kipling. CP-KiplR

Now Precedent Songs, Farewell. Walt Whitman. CP-WhitW

Now prose. How to Tell a Story (My Method) (Most of the Time). Grace Paley. CP-PalGC

Now ravel up the roots of workman oak trees. Dirge for the World Joyce Died In. Thomas Merton. CP-MertT

Now Returned Home. Robinson Jeffers. CP-JefR2

Now Robin lies in his last lair. Elegy on the Death of Robert Ruisseaux. Robert Burns. CP-BurnR

Now rosy May comes in wi' flowers. Dainty Davie. Robert Burns. CP-BurnR

Now secretness dies of the open. For the Nightly Ascent of the Hunter Orion over a Forest Clearing. James Dickey. CP-DickJ

Now seed their Magus (of Gelli's mother wrestling confounded). Catullus. *See* Let there stem (Gellius)

Now seven days from land the gulls still wheel. Transport. William Meredith. SP-MereW

Now shall I sing. Prophetess, The. Thomas Hardy. CP-HardT

Now she burn[e]s as well as I. Song: To Her Again[e], She Burning in a Fe[a]ver. Thomas Carew. CP-CareT

Now she is still not beautiful but more. Eve. Jane Cooper. CP-CoopJ

Now she will lean away to fold. Girl in a Window, A. James Wright. CP-WrigJ

Now she's breathing quietly, I said. No, she's. Yehuda Amichai. SP-AmicY, *tr. by* Chana Bloch

Now should great men die. On the Death of Winston Churchill. David Ignatow. SP-IgnaD

Now should my life endure to this extent. Petrarch. CP-Petra, *tr. by* J. G. Nichols

Now shut your eyes. Old Orchard, The. D. H. Lawrence. CP-LawrD

Now simmer blinks on flowery braes. Robert Burns. *See* Bonnie lassie, will ye go, will ye go, will ye go

Now sing, O slight girls. Euripides. CP-DoolH *Fr.* Iphigenia [*or* Iphigeneia] in Aulis.

Now sits the autumn cricket in the grass. Autumn. Edna St. Vincent Millay. CP-MillE

Now small boys come to stare across the garden. Murderer's House, The. Mary Oliver. SP-OlivM

Now some men must get up and depart. Departure. D. H. Lawrence. CP-LawrD

Now spring bursts. Carmen 46. Catullus. CP-ZukLS *Fr.* Carmina.

Now Spring has clad the grove in green. Scotch Song. Robert Burns. CP-BurnR

Now, starflake frozen on the windowpane. Moment. Howard Nemerov. CP-NemeH

Now Strike the Golden Lyre Again. James Laughlin. CP-LaugJ

Now strike up a concert of action in the electric nest. Tune for Festive Dances in the Nineteen Sixties, A. Thomas Merton. CP-MertT

Now Tell Me about Yourself. Ogden Nash. CP-NashO

Now tells the flower. Hafiz. CP-EmerR *Fr.* Odes.

Now thanked be the great god *Pan*. Sir Philip Sidney. SP-SidnP *Fr.* Arcadia.

Now that a crimson rambler. Crimson Rambler. Carl Sandburg. CP-SandC

Now that a letter gives me ground at last. Beach Head, The. Thom Gunn. CP-GunnT

Now that a Parthenon acends to crown. Modern Athens, The. William Wordsworth. CP-WorW2

Now that a revolution really is needed, those who once were fervent are quite cool. Sarajevo. Czeslaw Milosz. CP-MiloCN, *tr. by* Robert Hass

Now that all hearts are glad, all faces bright. November, 1813. William Wordsworth. CP-WorW1

Now that autumn is over and all. Northern Statement for St. Cecilia. Alan Dugan. CP-DugaA

Now that fierce few. E. E. Cummings. CP-CummE

Now that he's famous fame will not elude me. Memoir. James Vincent Cunningham. CP-CunnJ

Now that he's free, relatively, often he shuffles. Holiday, The. Hans Magnus

Enzensberger. SP-EnzeH, *tr. by* Hans Magnus Enzensberger *and* Michael Hamburger

Now that I am all but blind. Tribute to Neruda the Poet Collector of Seashells. William Carlos Williams. CP-WilW2

Now that I am fifty-six. Rondel: "Now that I am fifty-six." Muriel Rukeyser. CP-RukeM

Now that I Am Forever with Child. Audre Lorde. SP-LordA

Now that I Am in Madrid and Can Think. Frank O'Hara. SP-OharF

Now that I am in Paris. Postcard from France, A. Joseph Brodsky. CP-BrodJ *Fr.* Shorts.

Now that I have cooled to you. Postlude. William Carlos Williams. CP-WilW1

Now that I have your face by heart, I look. Song for the Last Act. Louise Bogan. CP-BogaL

Now that I know. Knowledge. Louise Bogan. CP-BogaL

Now that I know you are gone. Creation, The. Mona Van Duyn. SP-VanDM

Now that I, tying thy glass mask tightly. Laboratory, The (Ancien Régime). Robert Browning. CP-BroR1

Now that I'm banned and routed from the fire. Michelangelo Buonarroti. CP-Miche, *tr. by* John Frederick Nims

Now that in the distance a mirage. Correspondences. Eugenio Montale. CP-MontE, *tr. by* Jonathan Galassi

Now that I've wasted. My Alba. Allen Ginsberg. CP-GinsA

Now that,more nearest even than your fate. E. E. Cummings. CP-CummE

Now that my page is exiled,—doomed, maybe. To a Lady. Thomas Hardy. CP-HardT

Now that our hero has come back to us. On Seeing Larry Rivers' *Washington Crossing the Delaware* at the Museum of Modern Art. Frank O'Hara. SP-OharF

Now that Samurai bow & arrow, Sumi brush, teacup. Homage Vajracarya. Allen Ginsberg. SP-GinsA

Now that summer is lying with a stone for a lantern. Now and Again. W. S. Merwin. SP-MerwW

Now that the bird of life. Voix Glauque. Lawrence Ferlinghetti. SP-FerlL

Now that the Book Is Finished. Alice Walker. CP-WalkA

Now that the cameras zero in from space. Weather of the World, The. Howard Nemerov. CP-NemeH

Now that the choir of rock partridges. To My Mother. Eugenio Montale. CP-MontE, *tr. by* Jonathan Galassi

Now that the clouds have come like cattle. Aubade—the City. Thomas Merton. CP-MertT

Now that the day is done. Centaur Song. "H. D." CP-DoolH

Now that the hearth [*or* harth] is crowned [*or* crown'd] with smiling fire. Ode. To Sir William Sydney, on His Birthday. Ben Jonson. CP-JonsB; SP-JonsB

Now that the hillside woods are dense with summer. Witnesses, The. Charles Tomlinson. CP-TomlC

Now that the night is here. Night. D. H. Lawrence. CP-LawrD

Now that the number of steps you were given. Epilogue: "Now that the number of steps you were given." Jorge Luis Borges. SP-BorgJ, *tr. by* Stephen Kessler

Now that the river has changed, my dear. Muriel Rukeyser. CP-RukeM

Now that the Shapes of Mist. Louis MacNeice. SP-MacNL

Now that the Water Presses Hard. Yehuda Amichai. SP-AmicYL, *tr. by* Benjamin Harshav *and* Barbara Harshav

Now that the west is washed of clouds and clear. Edna St. Vincent Millay. CP-MillE

Now that the Winter's gone, the earth hath lost. Spring, The. Thomas Carew. CP-CareT

Now that they've abolished chrome work. Ask Daddy, He Won't Know. Ogden Nash. CP-NashO

Now that thy servants all may sing. Ut Queant. Paul the Deacon. CP-MertT

Now that we're almost settled in our house. In Memory of Major Robert Gregory. William Butler Yeats. CP-YeatW

Now that we've come to the end. Avenue, The. Paul Muldoon. CP-MuldP

Now that with a flourish you've stubbed out. New Stanzas. Eugenio Montale. CP-MontE, *tr. by* Jonathan Galassi

Now that you have gone. Except. Wendell Berry. CP-BerrW

Now that you have read of. Courtesies of Authorship, The. Laura Riding Jackson. CP-RidiL

Now that your hopes are shamed, you stand. Afterward. Adrienne Rich. CP-RicAE; SP-RicA1; SP-RicA2

Now that your soul is loosened from that knot. Petrarch. CP-Petra, *tr. by* J. G. Nichols

Now that you've gone away for five days. Still Looking Out for Number One. Raymond Carver. CP-CarvR

Now that you've written it. To a Romantic Novelist. Allen Tate. CP-TateA

Now the active young attorneys. Helter Skelter. Jonathan Swift. CP-SwifJ

Now the autumn shudders. Autumn Chant. Edna St. Vincent Millay. CP-MillE

Now the bright morning Star, Dayes [*or* day's] harbinger. Song: on [*or* of] May Morning. John Milton. CP-MiltJ

Now the Cats with Jewelled Claws. Tennessee Williams. "They that come late to the dance." CP-WillT

Now the children are asleep. Listening Landscape, The. Marya Alexandrovna Zaturenska. SP-ZatuM

Now the devout James coming from the remote north. On the Fifth of November. John Milton. CP-MiltJ

Now the disorder of your words. Mississippi John Hurt. Yusef Komunyakaa. CP-KomuY

Now the Four-way Lodge is opened, now the Hunting Winds are loose. Feet of the Young Men, The. Rudyard Kipling. CP-KiplR

Now the frog, all lean and weak. Sweet o' the Year, The. George Meredith. CP-MerG1

Now the frost is on the pane. Word about Winter, A. Ogden Nash. CP-NashO

Now the golden morn aloft. Ode on the Pleasure Arising from Vicissitude. Thomas Gray. CP-GrayT

Now the Grass is Glass. Emily Dickinson. SP-DickE

Now the hours of my life grow small. Obsolete Models. Philip Whalen. SP-WhalP

N(o)w / the / how / dis(appeared cleverly)world. E. E. Cummings. CP-CummE

Now the keen rigour of the winter's o'er. Town Eclogue, A. Jonathan Swift. CP-SwifJ

Now the last day of many days. To Jane: The Recollection. Percy Bysshe Shelley. CP-ShelP

Now the lean children of the God of armies. Rahab's House. Thomas Merton. CP-MertT

Now the lifeguards have all gone home. The bay. Yehuda Amichai. SP-AmicY, tr. by Chana Bloch

Now, the locust, tall and green. Noon-Clearing. Wallace Stevens. CP-StevWP

Now the lone world is streaky as a wall of marble. Evening: Zero Weather. Thomas Merton. CP-MertT

Now the midwinter grind. Middle Age. Robert Lowell. SP-LoweR

Now the New Year, reviving last Year's Debt. Rupaiyat of Omar Kal'vin, The. Rudyard Kipling. CP-KiplR

Now the New Year reviving old desires. Exiles' Line, The. Rudyard Kipling. CP-KiplR

Now the North wind ceases. Tardy Spring. George Meredith. CP-MerG1

Now the official nerve is analyzed. Thomas Merton. CP-MertT

Now the official nerve is cauterized. And So Goodbye to Cities. Thomas Merton. CP-MertT

Now the old ways that have brought us. At a Country Funeral. Wendell Berry. CP-BerrW

Now the pain beginneth and the word is spoken. Zara. Christina Georgina Rossetti. CP-RosC3

Now the preacher told Willie when he said his last prayer. Willie Francis and the Electric Chair. Charles Olson. CP-OlsoC

Now the reviving sea. Young Dancers, The. Marya Alexandrovna Zaturenska. SP-ZatuM

Now the ridge. Mid-August. A. R. Ammons. CP-AmmoA

Now the river is rich, but her voice is low. River in March, The. Ted Hughes. SP-HughTN

Now the singers leave the darkened garden. Lament for the Makers of Songs. Kenneth Patchen. CP-PatcK

Now the snow / lies on the ground. Winter. William Carlos Williams. CP-WilW1

Now the sordid tragedy crashes to a close. Neutrals, The. Robinson Jeffers. CP-JeffR3

Now the stone house on the lake front is finished and the workmen are beginning the fence. Fence, A. Carl Sandburg. CP-SandC

Now the storm begins to lower. Fatal Sisters, The. Thomas Gray. CP-GrayT

Now the strong horse goes loose at last. Near Spring. Ivor Gurney. SP-GurnI

Now the sun-lit hours are o'er. Night and Death. Christina Georgina Rossetti. CP-RosC3

Now the trumpet sounds with a mighty voice calling the soldiers of the world to arms, announcing war. Soldiers of Peace. Clement of Alexandria. CP-MertT

Now the violets are all gone, the rhinoceroses, the cymbals. Poem: "Now the violets are all gone, the rhinoceroses, the cymbals." Frank O'Hara. SP-OharF

Now the winter nights begin. Postcript to Iceland. Louis MacNeice. CP-MacNL

Now, the wry Rosenbloom is dead. Cortège for Rosenbloom. Wallace Stevens. CP-StevW; CP-StevWP

Now Then. Robert Creeley. CP-CreeR

Now there is. Robert Creeley. CP-CreeR

Now there is nothing wrong with me. Child's Garden, A. Rudyard Kipling. CP-KiplR Fr. Muse among the Motors, The.

Now there will be nobody, you say. Thorn, The. Langston Hughes. CP-HughL; CP-HughL3

Now they are all moving. Reading Translated Poets, Feb. 1. Thomas Merton. CP-MertT

Now they are resting. Fine Work with Pitch and Copper. William Carlos Williams. CP-WilW1

Now They Bury Her Again. Carl Sandburg. CP-SandC

Now They Desire. Christina Georgina Rossetti. CP-RosC3

Now They Desire a Better Country. Christina Georgina Rossetti. CP-RosC2

Now they've come before Jerusalem. Constantine P. Cavafy. See Now they've gotten to Jerusalem

Now they've gotten to Jerusalem. To Jerusalem. Constantine P. Cavafy. CP-CavaC, tr. by Theoharis Constantine Theoharis

Now, this is the cup the White Men drink. Song of the White Men, A. Rudyard Kipling. CP-KiplR

Now this is the price of a stirrup-cup. Ballad of the Cars, The. Rudyard Kipling. CP-KiplR Fr. Muse among the Motors, The.

Now this is the story of Lucy Brown. Biographies. Dorothy Parker. CP-ParkD

Now this is the tale of the Council the German Kaiser decreed. Imperial Rescript, An. Rudyard Kipling. CP-KiplR

Now this must be the sweetest place. Landscape. Dorothy Parker. CP-ParkD

Now this particular girl. Spinster. Sylvia Plath. CP-PlatS

Now this remains: the thunder stopped. Country Excursion. Kenneth Patchen. CP-PatcK

Now this the Law of the Jungle—as old and as true as the sky. Law of the Jungle, The. Rudyard Kipling. CP-KiplR Fr. Second Jungle Book, The.

Now, this, to my notion, is pleasant cheer. Beggar's Soliloquy, The. George Meredith. CP-MerG1

Now thou art dead, no eye shall ever see. Upon His Spaniel[l] Tracie [or Tracy]. Robert Herrick. CP-HerrR

Now thou hast lov'd me one whole day. Woman's Constancy. John Donne. CP-DonnJ; MW-DonnJ

Now thread my voice / with lies. How I Can Lie to You. Maya Angelou. SP-AngeM

Now tidy your house. Chicago Zen. A. K. Ramanujan. CP-RamaA

Now Time's Andromeda on this rock rude. Andromeda. Gerard Manley Hopkins. CP-HopkG

Now 'tis Spring on wood and wold. Invitation to the Country. George Meredith. CP-MerG1

Now to Break. Yehuda Amichai. SP-AmicYL, tr. by Benjamin Harshav and Barbara Harshav

Now to her lap the incestuous earth. A. E. Housman. CP-HousA

Now to Lampoon Myself for My Presumption. Thomas Sheridan. CP-SherT

Now to my Lady I would speak. To My Lady in a Distant Land that She Forget Me Not. James Laughlin. CP-LaugJ

Now to the come of the poem, let me be worthy. Fragment 1956. Allen Ginsberg. CP-GinsA

Now to the dry hillside. Education. Kenneth Rexroth. CP-RexrK

Now Tomlinson gave up the ghost at his house in Berkeley Square. Tomlinson. Rudyard Kipling. CP-KiplR

Now trust a heart that trusts in you. Emily Jane Brontë. CP-BronE

Now, Tudens, you sit on this knee—and 'scuse. Session with Uncle Sidney, A. James Whitcomb Riley. CP-RileJ

Now twenty-four or maybe twenty-five. Inside and Outside. Allen Tate. CP-TateA

Now two old ladies sit peacefully knitting. E. E. Cummings. CP-CummE

Now utter calm and rest. Mrs. Benjamin Harrison. James Whitcomb Riley. CP-RileJ

Now Vole art dead. To a Dead Vole. Stevie Smith. CP-SmitS

Now Walter White / Is mighty light. Ballad of Walter White. Langston Hughes. CP-HughL; CP-HughL3

Now was our heav'nly vault deprived of the light. Sir Philip Sidney. SP-SidnP Fr. Arcadia.

Now we are come to our Kingdom. Kingdom, The. Rudyard Kipling. CP-KiplR Fr. Naulahka, The.

Now we are partners in such legal trade. Friendship. Henry David Thoreau. CP-ThorH

Now we are thirty-five we no longer enjoy red neon. Literary Life in the Golden West. Philip Whalen. SP-WhalP

Now we are tired of boisterous joy. Blind Highland Boy, The; A Tale Told by the Fire-side, after Returning to the Vale of Grasmere. William Wordsworth. CP-WorW1

Now / We do not even know. Marica Lart. W. S. Merwin. SP-MerwW

Now we have buried the face we never knew. Easter, 1968. May Sarton. SP-SartM

Now we have taught our love to know. To His Rival. Sir John Suckling. CP-SuckJ

Now we must get up quickly. Two Lines from the Brothers Grimm. Gregory Orr. SP-OrrG

Now we remember all: the wild pear-tree. Pictures by Vuillard. Adrienne Rich. CP-RicAE

Now we, returning from the vaulted domes. Doom of Exiles. Sylvia Plath. CP-PlatS

Now we shall open boxes and look. Keepsake Boxes. Carl Sandburg. CP-SandC

Now westlin winds, and slaught'ring guns. Song, Composed in August. Robert Burns. CP-BurnR

Now westward Sol had spent the richest beam[e]s. Music[k]'s Duel[l]. Richard Crashaw. CP-CrasR

Now we've made a child. And What about the Children. Audre Lorde. SP-LordA

Now what is Love, I praie thee tell. Description of Love, A. Sir Walter Ralegh. CP-RaleW

Now what were motionless move(exists no). E. E. Cummings. CP-CummE

Now, when he and I meet, after all these years. Bitch. Carolyn Kizer. CP-KizeC

Now when I lay me down to sleep. Insomnia the Gem of the Ocean. John Updike. CP-UpdiJ

Now when I walk around at lunchtime. Personal Poem. Frank O'Hara. SP-OharF

Now when the frogs. Associate Professor Delivers an Exhortation to His Failing Students, The. Miller Williams. CP-WillM

Now when the Gods had crushed the Asian State. Virgil. CP-WorW2 *Fr.* Aeneid [*or* Eneados *or* Aeneis], The.

Now when the primrose makes a splendid show. Poor Robin. William Wordsworth. CP-WorW2

Now when those girls, all thirty-six, go. Rockettes, The. John Updike. CP-UpdiJ

Now when we depart. Hunt, Its Chant, A. Peter Blue Cloud. SP-BlueP

Now where the hills of Languedoc are blue with vineyards. St. John's Night. Thomas Merton. CP-MertT

Now, while that tree just past bud, the leaves. Tree in Spring, A. May Swenson. SP-SwenM

Now? Why— / whirlpools of. Virtue. William Carlos Williams. CP-WilW1

Now will you stand for me, in this cool light. Love in the Museum. Adrienne Rich. CP-RicAE

Now William pulled the lever down. William Blake. Allen Tate. CP-TateA

Now winging selves sing sweetly, while ghosts(there). E. E. Cummings. CP-CummE

Now winter downs the dying of the year. Year's End. Richard Wilbur. CP-WilbR

Now Winter Nights Enlarge. Thomas Campion. CP-CampT

Now, with all my knowledge, honorable newts. In a Jar. Czeslaw Milosz. CP-MiloC; CP-MiloCN, *tr. by* Robert Hass

Now with no weak unballast wing. Ode 2.20: Translation of Horace: *Odes* 2.20. Horace. CP-JohnS *Fr.* Odes.

Now, with your palms on the blades of my shoulders. Dead Still. Andrey Andreievich Voznesensky. CP-WilbR, *tr. by* Richard Wilbur

Now would I weave her portrait out of all dim splendour. Portrait. Ezra Pound. CP-PoEar

Now you are a priest. Priest. "H. D." CP-DoolH

Now you are gone, and with your unreturning goes. Therefore, Adieu. Countee Cullen. CP-CullC

Now you are holding my skull in your hand. Meditation, A. Richard Eberhart. CP-EberR

Now you are mine, to-night at last I say it. New Year's Night. D. H. Lawrence. CP-LawrD

Now you are ready to build your human brain. Cybernetics. Howard Nemerov. CP-NemeH

Now, you great stanza, you heroic mould. Single Sonnet. Louise Bogan. CP-BogaL

Now you have come. Foot-Washing, The. A. R. Ammons. CP-AmmoA

Now you have freely given me leave to love. To a Lady That Desired I Would Love Her. Thomas Carew. CP-CareT

Now you have read them all; or if not all. Rahel to Varnhagen. Edwin Arlington Robinson. CP-RobiE

Now you have stabbed her good. Kreutzer Sonata. Ted Hughes. SP-HughTN

Now you, John Henry, 'tain't no use. Charity. Paul Laurence Dunbar. CP-DunbP

Now you must bear with your poor soul. In Salem. Czeslaw Milosz. CP-MiloC; CP-MiloCN, *tr. by* Robert Hass

Now You See It, Now I Don't. Ogden Nash. CP-NashO

Now you take. Judge William Hastie. Langston Hughes. CP-HughL; CP-HughL3

Now you're caressing. Yannis Ritsos. SP-RitsY *Fr.* Paper Poems 2.

Now Zephirus brings back the better weather. Petrarch. CP-Petra, *tr. by* J. G. Nichols

Nowadays. James Laughlin. CP-LaugJ

Nowadays everybody wants to be young. Old People. D. H. Lawrence. CP-LawrD

Nowadays, to talk of humility is a sin against the Holy Ghost. Humility. D. H. Lawrence. CP-LawrD

Nowhere. John Berryman. CP-BerrJ

(Traitoring *words*, tearing my thought across.) CP-BerrJ

Nowhere before you. Backwards. Robert Creeley. CP-CreeR

Now(more near ourselves than we). E. E. Cummings. CP-CummE

Nowness and nowness sings the crow. Michael Palmer. SP-PalmM

Nu. Federico García Lorca. CP-GarcF, *tr. by* Alan S. Trueblood *Fr.* Eros with a Cane.

Nuances of a Theme by Williams. Wallace Stevens. CP-StevW; CP-StevWP

Nuclear Winter. Thomas McGrath. SP-McGrT

Nucleus. A. R. Ammons. CP-AmmoA

Nuda Natens. John Updike. CP-UpdiJ

Nude bodies like peeled logs. Sonnet in Search of an Author. William Carlos Williams. CP-WilW2

Nude Interrogation. Yusef Komunyakaa. CP-KomuY

Nude Kneeling in Sand. John Logan. CP-LogaJ

Nude Pictures. Yusef Komunyakaa. CP-KomuY

Nude Swim, The. Anne Sexton. CP-SextA

Nude Tango. Yusef Komunyakaa. CP-KomuY

Nude Young Dancer. Langston Hughes. CP-HughL; CP-HughL1

Nudity at the Capital. Wallace Stevens. CP-StevW; CP-StevWP

Nudity in the Colonies. Wallace Stevens. CP-StevW; CP-StevWP

Nuisance, The. Marge Piercy. SP-PierM

Nuit Blanche. Edna St. Vincent Millay. CP-MillE

Nuit qui fais tant. Samuel Beckett. CP-BeckS

Nullus. D. H. Lawrence. CP-LawrD

Numb Your Ass and Your Brain and Your Heart—. Charles Bukowski. SP-BukC1

Numb(and / that was). E. E. Cummings. CP-CummE

Number. Langston Hughes. CP-HughL; CP-HughL3

Number, A. W. S. Merwin. SP-MerwW

Number, The. Laura Riding Jackson. CP-RidiL

Number is a secret, The. Number, The. Laura Riding Jackson. CP-RidiL

Number Man. Carl Sandburg. CP-SandC

Number of Britons killed, The. Lorine Niedecker. CP-NiedL

Number of Two, The. Robert Herrick. CP-HerrR

Number runner / Come to my door. Madam and the Number Writer. Langston Hughes. CP-HughL; CP-HughL2

Number, said the skull Pythagoras. Under the Bell Jar. Howard Nemerov. CP-NemeH

No. 13 Hymn Written in Concord Sept. 1814. Ralph Waldo Emerson. CP-EmerR

Numbered. Langston Hughes. CP-HughL; CP-HughL3

Numbered Apartment. W. S. Merwin. SP-MerwWF

Numberless. Heather McHugh. SP-McHuH

Numbers. Robert Creeley. CP-CreeR

Numbers. Langston Hughes. CP-HughL; CP-HughL3

Numbers. Stevie Smith. CP-SmitS

Numbers and Faces. W. H. Auden. CP-AudeW

Numbers in heaven grow. Tree-Sense. Laura Riding Jackson. CP-RidiL

Numbers, in league, The. Paul Celan. SP-CelaP, *tr. by* John Felstiner

Numbers who can't even hear me. Math. James Dickey. CP-DickJ

Numpholeptos. Robert Browning. CP-BroR2

Nunc Dimittis. Joseph Brodsky. CP-BrodJ, *tr. by* George L. Kline

Nunc Est Bibendum, Cleopatra's Death. Robert Lowell. SP-LoweR

Nuns are allowed full liberty of conscience. Gooseflesh Abbey. Robert Graves. CP-GravR

Nuns are the brides of Christ. Life Story. Ai. SP-Ai

Nun's Aspiration. Ralph Waldo Emerson. CP-EmerR

Nuns fret not at their convent's narrow room. Sonnet: "Nuns fret not at their convent's narrow room." William Wordsworth. CP-WorW1; MW-WorW

Nuns in the Wind. Muriel Rukeyser. CP-RukeM

Nuns, monks and swamis. Fanny Howe. SP-HoweF *Fr.* O'Clock.

Nuns Painting Water-Lilies. Wallace Stevens. CP-StevWP

Nun's Song. William Carlos Williams. CP-WilW2

Nun's Well, Brigham. William Wordsworth. CP-WorW2

Nuptial Sleep. Dante Gabriel Rossetti. CW-RossD *Fr.* House of Life, The.

Nuptiall Song, or Epithalamie, on Sir Clipseby Crew and His Lady, A. Robert Herrick. CP-HerrR

Nuptiall Verse to Mistresse Elizabeth Lee, Now Lady Tracie. Robert Herrick. CP-HerrR

Nuptials. Allen Tate. CP-TateA

Nuptials of Attila, The. George Meredith. CP-MerG1

Nurse. David Ignatow. SP-IgnaD

Nurse carried him up the stair, The. At Thomas Hardy's Birthplace, 1953. James Wright. CP-WrigJ

Nurse is at the tree, and if I'm thirsty no one minds, The. Christmas Roses, The. Randall Jarrell. CP-JarrR

Nurse on the battlefield, A. Dien Bien Phu. Adrienne Rich. SP-RicA2

Nursery, The. Fanny Howe. SP-HoweF

Nursery Rhyme. W. H. Auden. CP-AudeW

Nursery Rhyme. Lorine Niedecker. CP-NiedL

Nursery Rhyme. May Sarton. SP-SartM

Nursery Rhyme. Charles Simic. SP-SimiC; SP-SimiCE

Nursery Rhyme, A. G. K. Chesterton. CP-ChesG

Nursery Rhyme, A. Randall Jarrell. CP-JarrR

Nursery Rhymes. Robert Penn Warren. CP-WarrR

Nursery Rhymes No. 1: Property. G. K. Chesterton. CP-ChesG

Nursery Rhymes No. 2: Education. G. K. Chesterton. CP-ChesG

Nursery Rhymes No. 3. G. K. Chesterton. CP-ChesG

Nursery Tale. Philip Larkin. CP-LarkP

Nurses, The. Rudyard Kipling. CP-KiplR *Fr.* Land and Sea Tales.

Nurses and nuns. Noon at St. Michael's. Derek Mahon. CP-MahoD

Nurse's Song. William Blake. CP-BlakW *Fr.* Songs of Experience.

Nurse's Song. Louise Glück. SP-GlucL

Nurse's Song, The. G. K. Chesterton. CP-ChesG

Nursing Sister, The. Rudyard Kipling. CP-KiplR *Fr.* Naulahka, The.

Nursing your nerves / to rest, I've roused my own; well. Afterwake, The. Adrienne Rich. CP-RicAE; SP-RicA2

Nurture. Maxine W. Kumin. SP-KumiM

Nut, The. C. K. Williams. CP-WillC

Nuts in May. Louis MacNeice. CP-MacNL

Nutting. William Wordsworth. CP-WorW1; MW-WorW

Nutting Song. Paul Laurence Dunbar. CP-DunbP

Nw / O / h / S / LoW. E. E. Cummings. CP-CummE

NY Youth Call Annunciation. Allen Ginsberg. SP-GinsA

Nyanu was appointed. Early Losses: a Requiem. Alice Walker. CP-WalkA

NYC—. Robert Creeley. CP-CreeR

Nylon is a wonderful thing in a city with trees. Leaves of Nerves. Andrei Codrescu. SP-CodrA

Nymph and shepherd raise electric tridents. Chances "R." Allen Ginsberg. CP-GinsA

Nymph and swain, Sheelah and Dermot hight. A Pastoral Dialogue, A. Jonathan Swift. CP-SwifJ

Nymph and the Shepherd, or She Went That-a-Way, The. Ogden Nash. CP-NashO

Nymph Complaining for the Death of Her Faun [*or* Fawn], The. Andrew Marvell. CP-MarvA

Nymph, forever dressing. Small Fountain. Rainer Maria Rilke. CP-RilkFr, *tr. by* A. Poulin, Jr. *Fr.* Valaisian Quatrains, The.

Nymph her graces here express'd may find, The. Of Her Picture. Alexander Pope. CP-PopeA

Nymph must lose her female friend, The. Lily and the Rose, The. William Cowper. CP-CowpW

Nymph of the downward smile, and sidelong glance. To Georgiana Augusta Wylie. John Keats. CP-KeatJ

Nymph of the forest, only in whose honour, The. Ambience. Robert Graves. CP-GravR

Nymph to Narcissus, The. Heather McHugh. SP-McHuH

Nymph who wrote this in an amorous fit, The. Answer to Vanessa's Rebus, The. Jonathan Swift. CP-SwifJ

Nymph, would you learn the only art. Lines from Cadenus to Vanessa. Jonathan Swift. CP-SwifJ

Nympha potens Thamesis soli cessura Dianae. Ad Thamesin. Thomas Campion. CP-CampT

Nymphs bewail'd poor Daphnis hapless death, The. Translation of Virgil: Pastoral V. Virgil. CP-JohnS *Fr.* Pastorals.

Nymphs of Himera—for you remember Daphnis and Hylas. Damon's Epitaph. John Milton. CP-MiltJ

Nymph's [*or* Nimphs] Reply to the Shepherd [*or* Sheepheard], The. Sir Walter Ralegh. CP-MarlC; CP-RaleW

Nymph's Passion, A. Ben Jonson. CP-JonsB

NyQuil. Raymond Carver. CP-CarvR

NYU. Yehuda Amichai. SP-AmicYL, *tr. by* Benjamin Harshav *and* Barbara Harshav

O

Ö. Rita Dove. SP-DoveR

O. Robert Graves. CP-GravR

O! ("O happiness! To see an iris"). Czeslaw Milosz. CP-MiloCN, *tr. by* Robert Hass

O! ("O lips half opened, eyes half closed, the rosy nipple of your unveiled nakedness, Judith!"). Czeslaw Milosz. CP-MiloCN, *tr. by* Robert Hass

O! ("O the quiet of water under the rocks, and the yellow silence of the afternoon"). Czeslaw Milosz. CP-MiloCN, *tr. by* Robert Hass

O! ("O what sadness unaware that it's sadness!"). Czeslaw Milosz. CP-MiloCN, *tr. by* Robert Hass

O a little lonely in Cambridge [all] that first Fall. Transit. John Berryman. CP-BerrJ

O a new song, a free song. Song of the Banner at Daybreak. Walt Whitman. CP-WhitW

O a' ye pious, godly flocks. Holy Tulzie, The. Robert Burns. CP-BurnR

O Adolescence, O Adolescence. Tarkington, Thou Should'st Be Living in This Hour. Ogden Nash. CP-NashO

O ailing Love, compose your struggling wing! Edna St. Vincent Millay. CP-MillE

O All down within the Pretty Meadow. Kenneth Patchen. CP-PatcK

O all ye exorcizers come and exorcize now, and ye clergymen draw. So Does Everybody Else, only Not So Much. Ogden Nash. CP-NashO

O all ye fair ladies with your colours and your graces. Revenant, The. Walter De la Mare. CP-DeLaW

O! Americans. D. H. Lawrence. CP-LawrD

O an Ye Were Dead Gudeman. Robert Burns. CP-BurnR

O and we sang then whose voices. Poem for Bob Leed. Robert Creeley. CP-CreeR

O apple-seed I planted in a silly shallow place. Fairy from the Apple-Seed, The. Nicholas Vachel Lindsay. CP-LindV

O are you tangled up in yourself. Self-Conscious People. D. H. Lawrence. CP-LawrD

O Ary Scheffer! when beneath thine eye. On a Prayer-Book. John Greenleaf Whittier. CP-WhitJ

O Atthis. Ezra Pound. SP-PounE

(Imerro.) SP-PounE

O Autumn, laden with fruit, and stained. To Autumn. William Blake. CP-BlakW

O Ay My Wife She Dang Me. Robert Burns. CP-BurnR

O Bacchus, what a world of toil, both now. Cyclops, The. Euripides. CP-ShelP, *tr. by* Percy Bysshe Shelley

O be swift. Helmsman, The. "H. D." CP-DoolH

O beauteous daughter, the bright pitcher of death. All That Night Lights Were Seen Moving in Every Direction. Kenneth Patchen. CP-PatcK

O, beauteous is the earth! and fair. Love That Is Hereafter, The. Walt Whitman. CP-WhitW

O beautiful Forever! I Saw Eternity. Louise Bogan. CP-BogaL

O beautiful star with the crimson mouth! Under the Balcony. Oscar Wilde. CP-WildO

O Beauty, in a beauteous Body dight! Veil of Spirit, The. Samuel Taylor Coleridge. CP-ColeS

O bella mia patria in Verona. Cultural Note. James Laughlin. CP-LaugJ

O Best of All Nights, Return and Return Again. James Laughlin. CP-LaugJ

O between distress and pleasure. Song: "O between distress and pleasure." Emily Jane Brontë. CP-BronE

O Big Old Tree, so tall an' fine. Noble Old Elm, The. James Whitcomb Riley. CP-RileJ

O blessed body [*or* bodie]! Whither art thou thrown? Sepulchre. George Herbert. CP-HerbG

O, blessed of the gods. Ode 4.6: "O, blessed of the gods." Horace. CP-CummE *Fr.* Odes.

O blessed Paul elect to grace, / Arise and wash away thy sin. Conversion of St. Paul. Christina Georgina Rossetti. CP-RosC2

O blessed souls, who high in heaven delight. Michelangelo Buonarroti. CP-Miche, *tr. by* John Frederick Nims

O blithe New-comer! I have heard. To the Cuckoo. William Wordsworth. CP-WorW1; MW-WorW

O blow of the building. Midday Construction. Pablo Neruda. SP-NeruP

O Blush Not So! O Blush Not So! John Keats. CP-KeatJ

O bonie was yon rosy brier. Scotish Song. Robert Burns. CP-BurnR

O Book! infinite sweetness! let my heart. Holy Scriptures (1), The. George Herbert. CP-HerbG

O Boston city lecture-hearing. Ralph Waldo Emerson. CP-EmerR

O briar-scents, on yon wet wing. Breath of the Briar. George Meredith. CP-MerG1

O bright, O swift and bright. Birds of Vietnam, The. Hayden Carruth. CP-CarHS

O [*or* Oh], Brignal[l] banks are wild and fair. Edmund's Songs. Sir Walter Scott. SP-ScotW *Fr.* Rokeby.

O, but the racked clear tired strained frames we had! Billet. Ivor Gurney. SP-GurnI

O but there is wisdom. Consolation. William Butler Yeats. CP-YeatW

O but we talked at large before. Sixteen Dead Men. William Butler Yeats. CP-YeatW

O by the by / has anybody seen. E. E. Cummings. CP-CummE; SP-CummE

O Caesar, we who are about to die. Morituri Salutamus. Henry Wadsworth Longfellow. SP-LongH

O Caledonia! stern and wild. Sir Walter Scott. SP-ScotW *Fr.* Lay of the Last Minstrel, The.

O cam ye here the fight to shun. Battle of Sherra-Moor, The. Robert Burns. CP-BurnR

O Carib Isle! Hart Crane. CP-CranH

O Chatterton, how very sad thy fate! To Chatterton. John Keats. CP-KeatJ

O Cheese. Donald Hall. CP-HallD

O Childish Mind! Walter De la Mare. CP-DeLaW

O Christ my God Who seest the unseen. Christina Georgina Rossetti. CP-RosC2

O Christ of God! whose life and death. Vesta. John Greenleaf Whittier. CP-WhitJ

O Christ our All in each, our All in all! Christina Georgina Rossetti. CP-RosC2

O Christ our Light, Whom even in darkness we. Light of Light. Christina

Georgina Rossetti. CP-RosC2

O Christ the Life, look on me where I lie / Ready to die. Half Dead. Christina Georgina Rossetti. CP-RosC2

O Christ the Vine with living Fruit. I Know You Not. Christina Georgina Rossetti. CP-RosC3

O! Christmas Day, Oh! happy day! Homeless. Samuel Taylor Coleridge. CP-ColeS

O ciliegia infiorita. Christina Georgina Rossetti. CP-RosC3

O city ladies. George Oppen. CP-OppGN

O, cleave not to the things of earth. Jones Very. CP-VeryJ

O cloud-pale eyelids, dream-dimmed eyes. He Tells of the Perfect Beauty. William Butler Yeats. CP-YeatW

O Colonia, whose wishes build a long bridge to dance on. Catullus. *See* Cologna Veneta - / where the good folk

O come again; what chains withhold. Emily Jane Brontë. CP-BronE

O come all ye faithful. Christopher Logue. SP-LoguC

O come, dearest Emma! the rose is full blown. To Emma. John Keats. CP-KeatJ

O come here! a sunflower! Day of Rabblement. Kenneth Patchen. CP-PatcK

O Come Quickly! Thomas Campion. CP-CampT

O come with me, thus ran the song. Emily Jane Brontë. CP-BronE

O composite, / O unconscious. Ode to a Bird. Czeslaw Milosz. CP-MiloC; CP-MiloCN, *tr.* by Robert Pinsky

O cool unto the sense of pain. During Music. Dante Gabriel Rossetti. CW-RossD

O could I give thee India's wealth. To Mr. McMurdo, with a Pound of Lundiefoot Snuff. Robert Burns. CP-BurnR

O crimson salamander. Ordeal, The. William Carlos Williams. CP-WilW1

O cross, more splendid than all the stars. Thomas Merton. CP-MertT

O cruel cloudless space. Nativity. May Sarton. SP-SartM

O cruel Death, give three things back. Three Things. William Butler Yeats. CP-YeatW

O, cruel heart, where is thy faith? Sir Thomas Wyatt. CP-WyatT

O cruel star, or say instead, cruel will. Michelangelo Buonarroti. CP-Miche, *tr.* by John Frederick Nims

O cruell Deith! To greit is thy puissance! Deploratioun of the Deith of Quene Magdalene, The. Sir David Lyndsay. SP-LyndD

O Cupid, that dost never cease my smart. Elegy 2.9: "O Cupid, that dost never cease my smart." Ovid. CP-MarlC *Fr.* Elegies.

O curlew, cry no more in the air. He Reproves the Curlew. William Butler Yeats. CP-YeatW

O Daedalus, Fly Away Home. Robert Earl Hayden. CP-HaydR

O dandelion, rich and haughty. Dandelion, The. Nicholas Vachel Lindsay. CP-LindV

O Day! he cannot die. Death Scene, A. Emily Jane Brontë. CP-BronE

O Day most calm, most bright. Sunday. George Herbert. CP-HerbG

O day, O hour, O instant at the last. Petrarch. CP-Petra, *tr.* by J. G. Nichols

O dear cool you couldn't be virile—you couldn't a parent he. Catullus. *See* Sweet entrance to a husband's pleasure

O Dear Minny What Shall I Do? Robert Burns. CP-BurnR

O dear Mother outline of knowledge most sage. William Blake. CP-BlakW

O dear sweet rosy. Asphodel, An. Allen Ginsberg. CP-GinsA

O deare, that I with thee might live. Thomas Campion. CP-CampT

O dearer far than light and life are dear. To ———: "O dearer far than light and life are dear." William Wordsworth. CP-WorW2; MW-WorW

O dearest bloom the seasons know. Easter Flower Gift, An. John Greenleaf Whittier. CP-WhitJ

O dearest glances, O persuasive breath. Petrarch. CP-Petra, *tr.* by J. G. Nichols

O dearly loved! / And worthy of our love! No more. Daniel Wheeler. John Greenleaf Whittier. CP-WhitJ

O, Death! a black and pierceless pall. Time to Come. Walt Whitman. CP-WhitW

O Death, Death, He is come. Gerard Manley Hopkins. CP-HopkG

O death, hadst thou but spar'd his life. Epigram on Said Occasion. Robert Burns. CP-BurnR

O death, so dear to me. Poem: "O death, so dear to me." James Dickey. CP-DickJ

O death! thou tyrant fell and bloody! Elegy on Captain Matthew Henderson [*or* Capt. M——— H———] [A *Gentleman* Who Held the Patent for His Honours Immediately from Almighty God!]. Robert Burns. CP-BurnR

O Death Where Is Thy Sting? Christina Georgina Rossetti. CP-RosC3

O Death! whose sceptre, trembling realms obey. To Mr. and Mrs.—, on the Death of Their Infant Son. Phillis Wheatley. CP-WheaP

O deep unknown, guttering candle. Mass for the Day of St. Thomas Didymus. Denise Levertov. SP-LeveDL; SP-LeveDS

O destiny, destiny. Destiny. D. H. Lawrence. CP-LawrD

O Deus, Ego Amo Te. Gerard Manley Hopkins. CP-HopkG

O Dieu, Purifiez nos coeurs! Night Litany. Ezra Pound. CP-PoeEar

O distant, distant; deep unapproachable; receive always. Distant, The. Yannis Ritsos. SP-RitsY, *tr.* by Edmund Keeley

O distant song, supreme lyre. Distant Song. Rainer Maria Rilke. CP-RilkFr, *tr.* by A. Poulin, Jr.

O Distinct / Lady of my unkempt adoration. E. E. Cummings. CP-CummE

O Do Not Love Too Long. William Butler Yeats. CP-YeatW

O do not praise my beauty more. Beauty, The. Thomas Hardy. CP-HardT

O do not use me / After my sin[ne]s! look not on my desert. Sighs and Groans [*or* Grones]. George Herbert. CP-HerbG

O does some blind fool now stand on my hill. Above Ashleworth. Ivor Gurney. SP-GurnI

O dreadful Justice, what a fright and terror. Justice (2). George Herbert. CP-HerbG

O Dream, where art thou now? Emily Jane Brontë. CP-BronE

O dreamer, that I might. Another Fan; of Mademoiselle Mallarmé. Stéphane Mallarmé. CP-MallS, *tr.* by Henry Weinfield

"O Dreary life," we cry, "O dreary life!" Patience Taught by Nature. Elizabeth Barrett Browning. CP-BroEB

O Duty, / Why hast thou not the visage of a sweetie or a cutie? Kind of an Ode to Duty. Ogden Nash. CP-NashO

O dwellers in the stately towns. June on the Merrimac. John Greenleaf Whittier. CP-WhitJ

O early one morning I walked out like Agag. Streets of Laredo, The. Louis MacNeice. CP-MacNL

O Earth! Earth! Earth heare thou my voice, and be. To His Paternall Countrey. Robert Herrick. CP-HerrR

O Earth, lie heavily upon her eyes. Rest. Christina Georgina Rossetti. CP-RosC1

O Ease My Spirit. Hugh MacDiarmid. SP-MacDH

O—eh—lee! La—La! Sicilian Emigrant's Song. William Carlos Williams. CP-WilW1

O elegant whore! Carmen 43. Catullus. CP-ZukLS *Fr.* Carmina.

O embittered joy. Fiend's Weather. Louise Bogan. CP-BogaL

O England, may God punish thee! England to Germany in 1914. Thomas Hardy. CP-HardT

O Envy, enemy to all that's good. Petrarch. CP-Petra, *tr.* by J. G. Nichols

O epic-famed, god-haunted Central Sea. Genoa and the Mediterranean. Thomas Hardy. CP-HardT

O Eros, silently smiling one, hear me. Hymn to Eros. Denise Levertov. SP-LeveDP

O evening, why is thy light so sad? Emily Jane Brontë. CP-BronE

O ever gracious Airs from Arcady! Written in Bunner's "Airs from Arcady." James Whitcomb Riley. CP-RileJ

O Everliving Queen! Kenneth Patchen. CP-PatcK

O exquisite. On Foscombe Hill. Ivor Gurney. SP-GurnI

O face within the sky. Cruelkind Swans, The. Kenneth Patchen. CP-PatcK

O fahter, fahter. Epigraph to *Call Me Ishmael*. Charles Olson. CP-OlsoC

O faint sad noises. Glassy Harbor, The. James Tate. SP-TateJ

O fair and stately maid, whose eyes. To Eva. Ralph Waldo Emerson. CP-EmerR

O fair is Love's first hope to gentle mind! First Advent of Love. Samuel Taylor Coleridge. CP-ColeS

O, fair the golden Hills of Hell. Golden Hills of Hell, The. Robert Penn Warren. CP-WarrR

O fair wind blowing from the sea! Euripides. CP-WildO *Fr.* Hecuba.

O Fairest flower no sooner blown but blasted. On the Death of a Fair Infant Dying of a Cough. John Milton. CP-MiltJ

O fairest Pattern to a failing Age! Epitaph on John Knight, Who Died Oct. 2, 1733. Alexander Pope. CP-PopeA

O farm, dear nest, or say Sabine, ah say Tibur's. Catullus. *See* It depends who's talking if you're a 'Sabine'

O fatal emblem, thou, of all our happiness! Funereal Toast. Stéphane Mallarmé. CP-MallS, *tr.* by Henry Weinfield

O father, answer me. Dialogue. Howard Nemerov. CP-NemeH

O fields of the sun! Age of Pericles, The. Kenneth Patchen. CP-PatcK

O fiery river / Flow out over the land. Kenneth Patchen. CP-PatcK

O fiery tiger walking down through the air. I Have No Place to Take Thee. Kenneth Patchen. CP-PatcK

O fill pull willand lean of that gleam. At the Entrance to the Other World. Kenneth Patchen. CP-PatcK

O Fill Your Sack with Tiger Cubs. Kenneth Patchen. CP-PatcK

O Firstfruits of our grain, / Infant and Lamb appointed to be slain. Feast of the Presentation. Christina Georgina Rossetti. CP-RosC2

O flag of the nation! O Red, White and Blue! Our Flag. E. E. Cummings. CP-CummE

"O Flodden Field." Donald Hall. CP-HallD

O Florida, Venereal Soil. Wallace Stevens. CP-StevW; CP-StevWP

O flower of all that springs from gentle blood. Gabriello Chiabrera. CP-WorW1

O follow the sonnet's flight. Hafiz. CP-EmerR *Fr.* Odes.

O foolish Soul! to make thy count / For languid falls and much forgiven. Christina Georgina Rossetti. CP-RosC2

O for a dirge! But why complain? Elegiac Stanzas (Addressed to Sir G.H.B. upon the Death of His Sister-in-Law). William Wordsworth. CP-WorW2

O, for a kindling touch from that pure flame. Siege of Vienna Raised by John Sobieski February, 1816. William Wordsworth. CP-WorW2

O for a pair like turtles wear. Ecquis Binas. Gerard Manley Hopkins. CP-HopkG

O For a voice like thunder, and a tongue. Prologue, Intended for a Dramatic Piece of King Edward the Fourth. William Blake. CP-BlakW

O, for Ane-and-Twenty Tam. Robert Burns. CP-BurnR

O for God's sake / they are connected. Islands. Muriel Rukeyser. CP-RukeM

O for my ain king, quo gude Wallace. Gude Wallace. Robert Burns. CP-BurnR

O for wings. Chorus sing of escape, The. Euripides. CP-DoolH *Fr.* Hippolytus.

O form'd t' illume a sunless world forlorn. To William Godwin. Samuel Taylor Coleridge. CP-ColeS

O fram'd at once to charm the ear and sight. To Mrs. Dacosta. Christopher Smart. SP-SmarC

O Frame the strains anew. Bible, *O.T. See* O sing unto the Lord a new song; for he hath done marvellous [*or* marvelous] things

O Frères Humains. James Laughlin. CP-LaugJ

O friend blame not Hafiz. Hafiz. CP-EmerR *Fr.* Odes.

O Friend! I know not which way I must look. Written in London, September, 1802. William Wordsworth. CP-WorW1; MW-WorW

O Friend! O Teacher! God's great Gift to me! To W. Wordsworth. Samuel Taylor Coleridge. CP-ColeS

O Friend! There is no way. Charles H. Philips. James Whitcomb Riley. CP-RileJ

O friend, who hast attained thyself in her. S.T.E.E. Cummings. CP-CummE

O Friends of mine, whose kindly words come to me. Unknown Friends. James Whitcomb Riley. CP-RileJ

O friends! with whom my feet have trod. Eternal Goodness, The. John Greenleaf Whittier. CP-WhitJ

O "fruitful and purified"—an identity in the Invisible! Nothing. Time to Believe!, A. Kenneth Patchen. CP-PatcK

O Future bards. Prophecy, A. Allen Ginsberg. CP-GinsA

O Galloway Tam cam here to woo. Galloway Tam. Robert Burns. CP-BurnR

O generation of the thoroughly smug / and thoroughly uncomfortable. Salutation. Ezra Pound. SP-PounE

O Gentle death, bow down and sip. Dream of Death, The. James Whitcomb Riley. CP-RileJ *Fr.* Adjustable Lunatic, An.

O gentle Sleep! do they belong to thee. To Sleep. William Wordsworth. CP-WorW1

O Gentlest kinsman of Humanity! Longfellow. James Whitcomb Riley. CP-RileJ

O ghost in the bluehearing grove. Each Is Alone, Each Is Everything. Kenneth Patchen. CP-PatcK

O gie the lass her fairin' lad. Gie the Lass her Fairin'. Robert Burns. CP-BurnR

O Gloriosa Domina. Richard Crashaw. CP-CrasR

O glorious sea that in each climbing wave. Christina Georgina Rossetti. CP-RosC3

O Goat-foot God of Arcady! Pan: Double Villanelle. Oscar Wilde. CP-WildO

O God, have mercy on Levallois. Ballad of Levallois. Czeslaw Milosz. CP-MiloC; CP-MiloCN, *tr. by* Robert Hass

O God, I love thee, I love thee—. O Deus, Ego Amo Te. Gerard Manley Hopkins. CP-HopkG

O God, in the dream the terrible horse began. Dream, The. Louise Bogan. CP-BogaL

O God! My God! have mercy now. Supposed Confessions of a Second-rate Sensitive Mind. Alfred Tennyson. CP-TennA

O God, O God, O God, how can I be. Michelangelo Buonarroti. CP-Miche, *tr. by* John Frederick Nims

O God, O Venus, O Mercury, patron of thieves. Lake Isle, The. Ezra Pound. SP-PounE

O, God of Columbia! O, Shield of the Free! Ode: "O, God of Columbia! O, Shield of the Free!" Walt Whitman. CP-WhitW

O God of earth and altar. Hymn, A. G. K. Chesterton. CP-ChesG

O God of heaven! the dream of horror. Emily Jane Brontë. CP-BronE

O God of my salvation. Psalm 88: "O God of my salvation." Bible, *O.T.* CP-MiltJ *Fr.* Psalms.

O God! who dost the nations lead. Hymn: Sung at the Eulogy on Abraham Lincoln June 1st 1865. Jones Very. CP-VeryJ

O goddess excellently bright. She-Bear, The. Charles Olson. CP-OlsoC

O Goddess! hear these tuneless numbers, wrung. Ode to Psyche. John Keats. CP-KeatJ

O golden-tongued Romance with serene lute! On Sitting Down to Read "King Lear" Once Again. John Keats. CP-KeatJ

O goodly hand. Sir Thomas Wyatt. CP-WyatT

O Gowdie, terror o' the whigs. Epistle to John Goldie in Kilmarnock, Author of, the Gospel Recovered. Robert Burns. CP-BurnR

O gracious Lord, how shall I know. Holy Communion, The. George Herbert. CP-HerbG

O gracious princes guid and fair. William Dunbar. CP-DunbW

O grande Amor possente. Amore E Dispetto. Christina Georgina Rossetti. CP-RosC3

O, Great God of Cold and Winter. Prayer for a Winter Night. Langston Hughes. CP-HughL; CP-HughL1

O great heart of God. Heart of God. Nicholas Vachel Lindsay. CP-LindV

O Great Priestess. Address to the Boobus. Philip Whalen. SP-WhalP

O Griefe, how divers are they shapes wherein men languish! To the Most Sacred King James. Thomas Campion. CP-CampT

O griefe, O spight, to see poore Vertue scorn'd. Thomas Campion. CP-CampT

O gude ale comes and gude ale goes. Guid Ale Keeps the Heart Aboon. Robert Burns..CP-BurnR

O had truth power the guiltless could not fall. Sir Walter Ralegh's [*or* S.W. Raghlies] Petition to the Queene 1618. Sir Walter Ralegh. CP-RaleW

O Hafiz, give me thought. Hafiz. CP-EmerR *Fr.* Odes.

O Hafiz! speak not of thy need. Hafiz. CP-EmerR *Fr.* Odes.

O half moon. Thalidomide. Sylvia Plath. CP-PlatS

O hand that smooths the air's flesh. Morning, My Prince—the Eye That Walks. Kenneth Patchen. CP-PatcK

O happiness! To see an iris. O! ("O happiness! To see an iris"). Czeslaw Milosz. CP-MiloCN, *tr. by* Robert Hass

O happy are they that have forgiveness got. Bible, *O.T. See* Blessed is he whose transgression is forgiven, whose sin is covered

O Happy Dogs of England. Stevie Smith. CP-SmitS

O happy rose-bud blooming. Gone for Ever. Christina Georgina Rossetti. CP-RosC1

O happy Rose, red Rose, that bloomest lonely. Solitary Rose, The. Christina Georgina Rossetti. CP-RosC3

O happy spirit that so charmingly. Petrarch. CP-Petra, *tr. by* J. G. Nichols

O happy they whose hearts receive. Arthur Hugh Clough. SP-ClouA

O happy time of youthful lovers (thus). Vaudracour and Julia. William Wordsworth. CP-WorW1

O have you seen my Tuck? my bonny bonny Tuck! George Meredith. CP-MerG2

O have you seen the Stratton flood. Stratton Water. Dante Gabriel Rossetti. CW-RossD

O he can hold her hand, and full and fair. Unspoken. James Whitcomb Riley. CP-RileJ

O heart, be at peace, because. Against Unworthy Praise. William Butler Yeats. CP-YeatW

O heart, hold thee secure. Courage. Walter De la Mare. CP-DeLaW

O heart o' me / Heart o' all that is true in me. Rune, The. Ezra Pound. CP-PoEar

O heart of mine, we shouldn't. Kissing the Rod. James Whitcomb Riley. CP-RileJ

O Heart: this is a dream I had, or not a dream. Poem: "O Heart: this is a dream I had, or not a dream." Stanley Kunitz. CP-KunSC

O Heaven, and thou most loving family. Arthur Hugh Clough. SP-ClouA

O heaven born muse! inspire my humble lay. Jones Very. CP-VeryJ

O helpless few in my country. Rest, The. Ezra Pound. SP-PounE *Fr.* Lustra.

O Henriette / I remember yet. Henriette. D. H. Lawrence. CP-LawrD

O. Henry, Afrite-chef of all delight! James Whitcomb Riley. CP-RileJ

O her beautiful eyes! they are as blue as the dew. Her Beautiful Eyes. James Whitcomb Riley. CP-RileJ

O her eyes are amber-fine. Judith. James Whitcomb Riley. CP-RileJ

O Hermes Trismegistus. James Laughlin. CP-LaugJ

O he's suffering—maybe dying—and I not there to aid. Telegram, The. Thomas Hardy. CP-HardT

O hide your eyes. Archibald MacLeish. CP-MacLA *Fr.* Happy Marriage, The.

O hideous little bat, the size of snot. Fly, The. Karl Shapiro. SP-ShapK

O high hilarity. Bones of Coleridge, The. Richard Eberhart. CP-EberR

O hinder me by no delay. Emily Jane Brontë. CP-BronE

O ho for the bus that rolls down the dirt road. Bus Ride Ballad Road to Suva. Allen Ginsberg. SP-GinsA

O-ho! ye sunny, sonnet-singin' vagrant. To James Newton Matthews. James Whitcomb Riley. CP-RileJ

O holy, blessèd, glorious Trinity. Sinner's Sacrifice, The. Ben Jonson. CP-JonsB

O Holy Father! just and true. Hymn: "O Holy Father! just and true." John Greenleaf Whittier. CP-WhitJ

O holy virgin! clad in purest white. To Morning. William Blake. CP-BlakW

O homesick, brood no more! Homesick. Walter De la Mare. CP-DeLaW

O how came Love, that is himself a fire. Ben Jonson. CP-JonsB *Fr.* Love Restored.

O how can I be blythe and glad. Bonie Lad That's Far Awa, The. Robert Burns. CP-BurnR

O! How I Love, on a Fair Summer's Eve. John Keats. CP-KeatJ

O how shall I, unskilfu', try. Lovely Davies. Robert Burns. CP-BurnR

O, how sick and weary I. In a Myrtle [*or* Mirtle] Shade. William Blake. CP-BlakW

O Howling Cells. Kenneth Patchen. CP-PatcK

O hurry where by water among the trees. Ragged Wood, The. William Butler Yeats. CP-YeatW

O hushed October morning mild. October. Robert Frost. CP-FrosR

O Hymen! O Hymenee! Walt Whitman. CP-WhitW

O I admire and sorrow! The heart's eye grieves. On the Portrait of Two Beautiful Young People. Gerard Manley Hopkins. CP-HopkG

O I am happy! O Swami Shivananda—a smile! Today. Allen Ginsberg. CP-GinsA; SP-GinsA

"O I am weary!" she sighed, as her billowy. Bride, A. James Whitcomb Riley. CP-RileJ

O I forbid you, maidens a' [or all]. Tam Lin. *Unknown*. CP-BurnR

O! I had my gyp *prepare* that tea. Tea. John Berryman. CP-BerrJ

O I say you Joe. William Blake. CP-BlakW *Fr.* Island in the Moon, An.

O I will walk with you, my lad, whichever way you fare. Song of the Road, A. James Whitcomb Riley. CP-RileJ

O, I wish that yesterday. Yesterday and Today. Langston Hughes. CP-HughL; CP-HughL2

O I Won't Lead a Homely Life. Thomas Hardy. CP-HardT

O I would I had a lover! Song: "O I would I had a lover!" James Whitcomb Riley. CP-RileJ

O, if a flame is in you, be it so! Be It So. D. H. Lawrence. CP-LawrD

O if the birds sang while the clouds felt bored by singing. Flourish. Joseph Brodsky. CP-BrodJ

O ill-fated mother of the best of offspring, Five, O. Pros Karolon ton Basilea [To King Charles]. Andrew Marvell. CP-MarvA

O in her bower let me lie. Flavius to Postumia. James Laughlin. CP-LaugJ

O in the depths of midnight. In the Dark. James Whitcomb Riley. CP-RileJ

O is for ox, by which word we. John Ciardi. CP-CiarJ

O Isis my goddess. Her Prayer. Denise Levertov. SP-LeveDL

O! it is pleasant, with a heart at ease. Fancy in Nubibus. Samuel Taylor Coleridge. CP-ColeS; MW-ColeS

O it was but a dream I had. While the Musician Played. James Whitcomb Riley. CP-RileJ

O it was Puck! I saw him yesternight. Puck. James Whitcomb Riley. CP-RileJ

O it was sad enough, weak enough, mad enough. Going of the Battery, The. Thomas Hardy. CP-HardT

O Italy, my land, words cannot heal. Petrarch. CP-Petra, *tr.* by J. G. Nichols

O it's good to ketch a relative 'at's richer and don't run. Our Old Friend Neverfail. James Whitcomb Riley. CP-RileJ

O, it's many's the scenes which is dear to my mind. Mulberry Tree, The. James Whitcomb Riley. CP-RileJ

O It's Nice To Get Up In,the slipshod mucous kiss. E. E. Cummings. CP-CummE

O ivory, delicate hands! Epigrams: "O ivory, delicate hands!" Ezra Pound. CP-PoEar

O Jealousie, that art. To Jealousie. Robert Herrick. CP-HerrR

O Jehovah our Lord, how wondrous great. Bible, *O.T. See* O Lord our Lord, how excellent is thy name in all the earth!

O Jesu, better than Thy gifts / Art Thou Thine only Self to us! Chiefest among Ten Thousand, The. Christina Georgina Rossetti. CP-RosC2

O Jesu, gone so far apart / Only my heart can follow Thee. Vigil of St. Peter. Christina Georgina Rossetti. CP-RosC2

"O Jesus Christ! I'm hit," he said; and died. Last Laugh, The. Wilfred Owen. CP-OwenW

O Jesus, thou who sittest up there on the right. Sonnet: "O Jesus, thou who sittest up there on the right." Hayden Carruth. CP-CarHS *Fr.* Sonnets.

O, July 1992. William Corbett. SP-CorbW

O Jupiter, sho'd I speake ill. In Praise of Women. Robert Herrick. CP-HerrR

O Kangaroo, O Kangaroo. Kangaroo, The. Ogden Nash. CP-NashO

O ken ye what Meg o' the mill has gotten. Ken Ye What Meg o' the Mill Has Gotten. Robert Burns. CP-BurnR

O Kenmure's on and awa, Willie. Robert Burns. CP-BurnR

O kind watchers came. Kenneth Patchen. CP-PatcK

O Kindness, Kindness. These virtues are. Thank You. Robert Creeley. CP-CreeR

O king, if you make an end of me, a lawful person. Philosopher on His Way to His Death Suddenly Sent This Message to a Certain King Who Had Unawares Condemned Him, Unrecognized and Innocent, when He Was Seized by Chance among Criminals, A. John Milton. CP-MiltJ

O know to end, as to begin. Ben Jonson. CP-JonsB *Fr.* Masque of Hymen.

O know you what I have done. Brother, The. Thomas Hardy. CP-HardT

O Lady fair, these silks of mine are beautiful and rare. Vaudois Teacher, The. John Greenleaf Whittier. CP-WhitJ

O Lady Mary Ann looks o'er the castle-wa'. My Bonie Laddie's Young but He's Growin Yet. Robert Burns. CP-BurnR

O Lady Moon. Christina Georgina Rossetti. CP-RosC2

O Lady Moon, your horns point toward the east. O Lady Moon. Christina Georgina Rossetti. CP-RosC2

O Lady, my city, and new flower of the prairie. After Reading the Sad Story of the Fall of Babylon. Nicholas Vachel Lindsay. CP-LindV

O lady of the lucent hair. To a Lady Passing Time Better Left Unpassed. Ogden Nash. CP-NashO

O lady, when the tipped cup of the moon blessed you. Song: "O lady, when the tipped cup of the moon blessed you." Ted Hughes. SP-HughTN

O land alive with miracles! Song: Contemplation. Thomas Merton. CP-MertT

O land of Empire, art and love. Resignation—to Faustus. Arthur Hugh Clough.

SP-ClouA

O land of mine, O land I love. Apostrophe to the Land. Countee Cullen. CP-CullC

O Lapwing! William Blake. CP-BlakW

O lapwing, thou fliest around the heath. O Lapwing! William Blake. CP-BlakW

O lassie art thou sleeping yet. Let Me in This Ae Night. Robert Burns. CP-BurnR

O late fall. Lorine Niedecker. CP-NiedL

O Lay Thy Loof in Mine Lass. Robert Burns. CP-BurnR

O learned man who never learned to learn. Myth of Arthur, The. G. K. Chesterton. CP-ChesG

O leave novels, ye Mauchline belles. Robert Burns. CP-BurnR

O leave your hand where it lies cool. Song and Music. Dante Gabriel Rossetti. CW-RossD

O leeze me on my spinning-wheel. Bess[y] and Her Spinning-Wheel. Robert Burns. CP-BurnR

O Lelius, beauteous flower of gentleness. Gabriello Chiabrera. CP-WorW1

O let the seeds be planted. Rogation Sunday. William Carlos Williams. CP-WilW2

O let's glee glow as we go. Lorine Niedecker. CP-NiedL

O Liberty, God-gifted. To the Bartholdi Statue. Ambrose Bierce. SP-BierA

O Life! O Beyond! James Whitcomb Riley. CP-RileJ

O life with the sad seared face. To Life. Thomas Hardy. CP-HardT

O like a young tree rooted near the water. Marya Alexandrovna Zaturenska. SP-ZatuM

O li'l lamb out in de col'. Hymn: "O li'l lamb out in de col'." Paul Laurence Dunbar. CP-DunbP

O lips half opened, eyes half closed, the rosy nipple of your unveiled nakedness, Judith! O! ("O lips half opened, eyes half closed, the rosy nipple of your unveiled nakedness, Judith!"). Czeslaw Milosz. CP-MiloCN, *tr.* by Robert Hass

O lithest Shirley! & the other worlds. Shirley & Auden. John Berryman. CP-BerrJ

O little forests, meekly. Love Winter when the Plant Says Nothing. Thomas Merton. CP-MertT

O littleblood, hiding from the mountains in the mountains. Littleblood. Ted Hughes. SP-HughTN *Fr.* Crow.

O Living Always, Always Dying. Walt Whitman. CP-WhitW

O, Logan, sweetly didst thou glide. Song: "O, Logan, sweetly didst thou glide." Robert Burns. CP-BurnR

O lonely bay of Trinity. Cable Hymn, The. John Greenleaf Whittier. CP-WhitJ

O lonely man. Speech from the Stairs. Tennessee Williams. CP-WillT

O long expected up in Heaven, O blest. Petrarch. CP-Petra, *tr.* by J. G. Nichols

O longing for the places that weren't loved. Rainer Maria Rilke. CP-RilkFr, *tr.* by A. Poulin, Jr. *Fr.* Orchards.

O Lord Almighty, Who hast formed us weak. Ascension Eve. Christina Georgina Rossetti. CP-RosC2

O Lord, as I thee have both prayed and pray. Bible, *O.T. See* O Lord, rebuke me not in thy wrath

O Lord, fulfil Thy Will / Be the days few or many, good or ill. Will of the Lord Be Done, The. Christina Georgina Rossetti. CP-RosC2

O Lord God, hear the silence of each soul, / Its cry unutterable of ruth and shame. I Will Come and Heal Him. Christina Georgina Rossetti. CP-RosC2

O lord, have patience. T. S. Eliot. SP-ElioT

O lord, he said, Japanese women. Japanese Wife, The. Charles Bukowski. SP-BukC2

O Lord, how canst Thou say Thou lovest me? When My Heart Is Vexed, I Will Complain. Christina Georgina Rossetti. CP-RosC1

"O Lord, How Long?" Jones Very. CP-VeryJ

O Lord, I am ashamed to seek Thy Face / As tho' I loved Thee as Thy saints love Thee. Christina Georgina Rossetti. CP-RosC2

O Lord, I cannot plead my love of Thee. Christina Georgina Rossetti. CP-RosC3

O Lord, it was all night. Sun. James Dickey. CP-DickJ

O Lord Jesus Christ, son of the living God. Prayer, A. Richard Crashaw. CP-CrasR

O Lord, my best desire fulfil. William Cowper. CP-CowpW *Fr.* Olney Hymns.

O Lord my God, in thee do I put my trust. Psalm 7: "O Lord my God, in thee do I put my trust." Bible, *O.T.* CP-MiltJ *Fr.* Psalms.

O Lord of all compassionate control. Portrait, The. Dante Gabriel Rossetti. CW-RossD *Fr.* House of Life, The.

O Lord, on Whom we gaze and dare not gaze, / Increase our faith that gazing we may see. Christina Georgina Rossetti. CP-RosC2

O Lord our Lord, how excellent is thy name in all the earth! Psalm 8: "O Lord our Lord, how excellent is thy name in all the earth!" Bible, *O.T.* CP-MiltJ *Fr.* Psalms.

O Lord, rebuke me not in thine anger. Psalm 6: "O Lord, rebuke me not in thine anger." Bible, *O.T.* CP-MiltJ; CP-WyatT *Fr.* Psalms.

O Lord, rebuke me not in thy wrath. Psalm 38: "O Lord, rebuke me not in thy wrath." Bible, *O.T.* CP-WyatT *Fr.* Psalms.

O Lord, seek us, O Lord, find us / In Thy patient care. Lord, Save Us, We Perish. Christina Georgina Rossetti. CP-RosC2

O Lord, since in my mouth thy mighty name. Bible, *O.T. See* O Lord, rebuke me not in thine anger

O Lord, the hard-won miles. Prayer, A: "O Lord, the hard-won miles." Paul Laurence Dunbar. CP-DunbP

O Lord, thou hearest my daily moan. In My Solitary Hours in My Dear Husband His Absence. Anne Bradstreet. CP-BradA

O Lord, thy land has favour found. Bible, *O.T. See* Lord, thou hast been favourable unto thy land

O Lord, when Thou didst call me, didst Thou know. Christina Georgina Rossetti. CP-RosC2

O Lord, why grievest Thou? By the Earth's Corpse. Thomas Hardy. CP-HardT

O love, be fed with apples while you may. Sick Love. Robert Graves. CP-GravR

O love is a deep thing. Deeper than Love. D. H. Lawrence. CP-LawrD

O love is like an untamed steed! Bedouin. James Whitcomb Riley. CP-RileJ

O love, love, hold me fast. Hour and the Ghost, The. Christina Georgina Rossetti. CP-RosC1

O Love, Love, Love! O withering might! Fatima. Alfred Tennyson. CP-TennA

O Love, O thou that, for my fealty. Sonnet: To Love, in great Bitterness. Cino da Pistoia. CW-RossD, *tr. by* Dante Gabriel Rossetti

O Love, of pure and heav'nly birth! Truth and Divine Love Rejected by the World. Jeanne Marie Bouvier de la Motte- Guyon. CP-CowpW

O love sweet love. Francesca in Winter. Stevie Smith. CP-SmitS

O love, what hours were thine and mine. Daisy, The. Alfred Tennyson. CP-TennA

O Love, where are thy Shafts, thy Quiver, and thy Bow? Thomas Campion. CP-CampT

O love, you airtight bird. Memo from the Cave. Louise Glück. SP-GlucL

O lovely apple! Perfection. William Carlos Williams. CP-WilW2

O lovely hand, clutched tightly round my heart. Petrarch. CP-Petra, *tr. by* J. G. Nichols

O lovely hand, that thy sweet self dost lave. La Bella Mano. Dante Gabriel Rossetti. CW-RossD

O lovely horn, from where are you. Cornucopia. Rainer Maria Rilke. CP-RilkFr, *tr. by* A. Poulin, Jr. *Fr.* Orchards.

O lovely lovely so lovely. Song: "O lovely lovely so lovely." James Laughlin. CP-LaugJ

O Lucifer, Son of the Morning! Christina Georgina Rossetti. CP-RosC2

O lucky me, to look upon me dead! Michelangelo Buonarroti. CP-Miche, *tr. by* John Frederick Nims

O Lull Me, Lull Me. Theodore Roethke. CP-RoetT

O luve will venture in where it daur na weel be seen. Posie, The. Robert Burns. CP-BurnR

O Lyric March. Marya Alexandrovna Zaturenska. SP-ZatuM

O Magnet-South. Walt Whitman. CP-WhitW

O maiden aunt, you have come to call. Tour, The. Sylvia Plath. CP-PlatS

O Maiden! heir of kings! Victoria's Tears. Elizabeth Barrett Browning. CP-BroEB

O Make Me a Mask. Dylan Thomas. CP-ThomD

O Mally's Meek, Mally's Sweet. Robert Burns. CP-BurnR

O, many a panting, noble heart. Fame's Vanity. Walt Whitman. CP-WhitW

O marinaro che mi apporti tu? Christina Georgina Rossetti. CP-RosC3

O Mary Barrie, Mary Barrie. George Meredith. CP-MerG2

O Mary dear, that you were here. To Mary———. Percy Bysshe Shelley. CP-ShelP

O Mary, fragile mother. For the Year of the Insane. Anne Sexton. CP-SextA; SP-SextA

O mater! O fils! Apostroph. Walt Whitman. CP-WhitW

O matutini rores, auræque salubres. Votum. William Cowper. CP-CowpW

O Maximilian stern and wild. Maximilian Esterhazy. Stevie Smith. CP-SmitS

O may I see thy face for without thee. Simmons Mobile Alabama. Jones Very. CP-VeryJ

O May, thy morn was ne'er sae sweet. Robert Burns. CP-BurnR

O me, man of slack faith so long. All Is Truth. Walt Whitman. CP-WhitW

O me, my pleasant rambles by the lake. Edwin Morris. Alfred Tennyson. CP-TennA

O Me! O Life! Walt Whitman. CP-WhitW

O meek attendant of Sol's setting blaze. To the Evening Star. Samuel Taylor Coleridge. CP-ColeS

O meikle thinks my luve o' my beauty. My Tocher's the Jewel. Robert Burns. CP-BurnR

"O 'Melia, my dear, this does everything crown!" Ruined Maid, The. Thomas Hardy. CP-HardT

O mellow month and merry month. August. James Whitcomb Riley. CP-RileJ

O melody of sap rising. Spring. Rainer Maria Rilke. CP-RilkFr, *tr. by* A. Poulin, Jr. *Fr.* Orchards.

O memory, where is now my youth. Memory and I. Thomas Hardy. CP-HardT

O mercy, O me miserable man! Bitter Reflection, A. Samuel Taylor Coleridge.

CP-ColeS

O merry hae I been teethin a heckle. Merry Hae I Been Teethin a Heckle. Robert Burns. CP-BurnR

O might I load my arms with thee. Crown of Love, The. George Meredith. CP-MerG1

O mighty mind, in whose deep stream this age. Fragment: To Byron. Percy Bysshe Shelley. CP-ShelP

O Mighty *Nothing!* unto thee. Matthew 27; And He Answered Them Nothing. Bible, *N.T.* CP-CrasR *Fr.* St. Matthew.

O Miller Knox, whom we knew well. At the Mill. Thomas Hardy. CP-HardT

O mind, beset by music never for a moment quiet. Northern April. Edna St. Vincent Millay. CP-MillE

O mine enemy / Rejoice not over me! Christina Georgina Rossetti. CP-RosC2

O miserable sorrow withouten cure! Sir Thomas Wyatt. CP-WyatT

O mister Eckhart! calling. Morning News, The. Charles Olson. CP-OlsoC

O months of blossoming, months of transfigurations. Lilacs and the Roses, The. Louis Aragon. CP-MacNL, *tr. by* Louis MacNeice

O Moon, discreetly worshipped in the past. Affronted Moon, The. Charles Baudelaire. CP-BaudC, *tr. by* Walter Martin

O Moon! / Gradually. To the Moon. Philip Whalen. SP-WhalP

O Moon! if e'er I joyed when thy soft light. Written in a Grotto. William Wordsworth. CP-WorW1

O moon of illusion. Moonsong at Morning. Sylvia Plath. CP-PlatS

O Moon, Thou Cool, Hart Crane. CP-CranH

O Most High, you willed to create me a poet and now it is time for me to present a report. Report. Czeslaw Milosz. CP-MiloCN, *tr. by* Robert Hass

O most just Vizier, send away. Sick King in Bokhara, The. Matthew Arnold. SP-ArnoM

O Mother Earth! Upon thy lap. Randolph of Roanoke. John Greenleaf Whittier. CP-WhitJ

O Mother Gaia. Gary Snyder. CP-SnydG

O mother, I am not regretting. Emily Jane Brontë. CP-BronE

O Mother Race! to thee I bring. Ode to Ethiopia. Paul Laurence Dunbar. CP-DunbP

O Mother State! the winds of March. Sumner. John Greenleaf Whittier. CP-WhitJ

O mount and go. Captain's Lady, The. Robert Burns. CP-BurnR

O mountain Stream! the Shepherd and his Cot. William Wordsworth. CP-WorW2; MW-WorW *Fr.* River Duddon [A Series of Sonnets], The.

O mud, mud, how fluid! Words Heard, by Accident, over the Phone. Sylvia Plath. CP-PlatS

O Muse, get me high out of my mind. Life and Death and a Letter to My Mother beyond Them Both. Philip Whalen. SP-WhalP

O Muse! / I don't dare summon you. Plums, Metaphysics, an Investigation, a Visit, and a Short Funeral Ode. Philip Whalen. SP-WhalP

O Muse! O Music! Voice and Lyre. On Gratitude. Christopher Smart. SP-SmarC

O Muse who willingly drags along with a limping step. To Salzilli, a Roman Poet, Being Ill. John Milton. CP-CowpW; CP-MiltJ

O my chief good. Good Friday. George Herbert. CP-HerbG

O my darling troubles heaven. Kenneth Patchen. CP-PatcK

O my daughter, supple bird on my branch. For Sharon, as Soon as She Wants It. Robert Stock. SP-StocR

O my dearest [*or* deerest], I shall grieve thee. Complement, The. Thomas Carew. CP-CareT

O my dearest / While the sun still spends its fabulous money. For Miriam. Kenneth Patchen. CP-PatcK

O my first Love! You are in my life forever. Of My First Love. Hugh MacDiarmid. SP-MacDH

O my friends, all of you, I renounce. Rainer Maria Rilke. CP-RilkFr, *tr. by* A. Poulin, Jr. *Fr.* Orchards.

O my grey hairs! Spring. William Carlos Williams. CP-WilW1

O my Lady, didn't you see him. Guido Cavalcanti. CP-CavaG, *tr. by* Marc Cirigliano

O my life, how I'd want to be him who responds. Nostalgia. Rainer Maria Rilke. CP-RilkFr, *tr. by* A. Poulin, Jr.

O my Lord, I am not eloquent. Somber Prayer. John Berryman. CP-BerrJ

O my love / The pretty towns. Kenneth Patchen. CP-PatcK

O my lover! the night like a broad smooth wave. Shemselnihar. George Meredith. CP-MerG1

O[h] my Luve's [*or* love's *or* love is *or* luve is] like a red, red rose. Red, Red Rose, A. Robert Burns. CP-BurnR

O My Name It Is Sam Hall. Randall Jarrell. CP-JarrR

O my pretty pink frock. Pink Frock, The. Thomas Hardy. CP-HardT

O my sister remember the stars the tears the trains. To My Sister. Theodore Roethke. CP-RoetT

O My songs. Coda: "O My songs." Ezra Pound. SP-PounE

O my soul, keep the rest unknown! He Resolves to Say No More. Thomas Hardy. CP-HardT

O my thirteen pictures are in prison! 13 Pictures. D. H. Lawrence. CP-LawrD

O my trade it is the rarest one. Stranger's Song, The. Thomas Hardy. CP-HardT

O my wholly unwise and definite. E. E. Cummings. CP-CummE

O nature I do not aspire. Nature. Henry David Thoreau. CP-ThorH

O never girl beneath the skies of Italy. Feminine Charm. Stevie Smith. CP-SmitS

O never harm the dreaming world. Vegetation. Kathleen Jessie Raine. SP-RainK

O never rudely will I blame his faith. Mythology in an Age of Reason. Johann Christoph Friedrich von Schiller. CP-ColeS *Fr.* Piccolomini, The.

O never to be moved. Thomas Campion. CP-CampT

O new-born State, what lovely flowers are thine! On Some Blue and Golden Columbines from Pike's Peak, Colorado. Jones Very. CP-VeryJ

O night, comforting night, dark though you are. Michelangelo Buonarroti. CP-Miche, *tr. by* John Frederick Nims

O night of admiration, full of choirs. Dark Encounter, The. Thomas Merton. CP-MertT

O night, the ease of care, the pledge of pleasure. Night. Sir Philip Sidney. SP-SidnP *Fr.* Arcadia.

O nightingale! how hast thou learnt. To a Nightingale. George Meredith. CP-MerG1

O Nightingale, that on yon bloomy Spray. Sonnet 1: "O Nightingale, that on yon bloomy Spray." John Milton. CP-MiltJ

O Nightingale! thou surely art. William Wordsworth. CP-WorW1; MW-WorW

O nimis semper mea vere amata. Ad Melleam. Thomas Campion. CP-CampT

O / nly this / darkness(in). E. E. Cummings. CP-CummE

O, no, except for newsreels, books. Theodore Weiss. SP-WeisT *Fr.* Polish Question, The.

O noble heart, and brave impetuous hand! T. C. Philips. James Whitcomb Riley. CP-RileJ

O noble soul, glowing with worthiness. Petrarch. CP-Petra, *tr. by* J. G. Nichols

O noble soul, in whom, as mirrored, show. Michelangelo Buonarroti. CP-Miche, *tr. by* John Frederick Nims

O noble, true and pure and lovable. To Elizabeth. James Whitcomb Riley. CP-RileJ

O Norah, lay your basket down. Kathleen. John Greenleaf Whittier. CP-WhitJ

O! nothing earthly save the ray. Al Aaraaf. Edgar Allan Poe. CP-PoeEd

O now that the genius of Bewick were mine. Two Thieves, The; or, the Last Stage of Avarice. William Wordsworth. CP-WorW1; MW-WorW

'O Now the Drenched Land Wakes.' Kenneth Patchen. CP-PatcK

O now the drenched land wakes. 'O Now the Drenched Land Wakes.' Kenneth Patchen. CP-PatcK

O now you've got a very different look. Lost Poem, A. Kenneth Patchen. CP-PatcK

O ocean sea, for all your being vast. Does No One at All Ever Feel This Way in the Least? Robert Frost. CP-FrosR

O once I loved [*or* lov'd] a bonnie lass. Song: "O once I loved [*or* lov'd] a bonnie lass." Robert Burns. CP-BurnR

O only Source of all our light and life. Qui Laborat, Orat. Arthur Hugh Clough. SP-ClouA

O, open the door, some pity to show. Palmer, The. Sir Walter Scott. SP-ScotW

O [*or A or* Oh] ye wha are sae guid yoursel. Address to the Unco Guid, or the Rigidly Righteous. Robert Burns. CP-BurnR

O [*or* Oh] listen, listen, ladies gay! Rosabelle. Sir Walter Scott. SP-ScotW *Fr.* Lay of the Last Minstrel, The.

O [*or* Oh] Mary, at the window be. Mary Morison. Robert Burns. CP-BurnR

O [*or* Oh] Wert Thou in the Cauld Blast. Robert Burns. CP-BurnR

O / out of a bed of love. Holy Spring. Dylan Thomas. CP-ThomD

O Outrider! / when you come to the threshold of the stars. Robert Duncan. SP-DuncR *Fr.* Structure of Rime, The.

O Painter of the fruits and flowers. Garden. John Greenleaf Whittier. CP-WhitJ

O Pan is the goodliest god, I wist. Great God Pan, The. James Whitcomb Riley. CP-RileJ

O parakeets & avocets, O immortelles. Old Man Goes South Again Alone. John Berryman. CP-BerrJ

O Passenger, pray list and catch. Levelled Churchyard, The. Thomas Hardy. CP-HardT

O Peace! and dost thou with thy presence bless. On Peace. John Keats. CP-KeatJ

O people-chosen! are ye not. To the Thirty-Ninth Congress. John Greenleaf Whittier. CP-WhitJ

O per se O, O per se O! O. Robert Graves. CP-GravR

O Philly, happy be that day. Song: "O Philly, happy be that day." Robert Burns. CP-BurnR

O pillow cold and wet with tears! Cancelled Passage. Percy Bysshe Shelley. CP-ShelP

O Pino / What a bean-o! To Pino. D. H. Lawrence. CP-LawrD

O playmate of the far-away. George A. Carr. James Whitcomb Riley. CP-RileJ

O poet, come you haunting here. At a House in Hampstead. Thomas Hardy. CP-HardT

O poet rare and old! Astræa. John Greenleaf Whittier. CP-WhitJ

O poore distracted world, partly a slave. To the World. Thomas Campion. CP-CampT

O poortith cauld, and restless love. Song: "O poortith cauld, and restless love." Robert Burns. CP-BurnR

O poverty, by thee the soul is wrapp'd. Canzone: A Song against Poverty. Guido Cavalcanti. CW-RossD, *tr. by* Dante Gabriel Rossetti

O Power! that waits not on man's feeble will. Reconciling Power, The. Jones Very. CP-VeryJ

O pr / gress verily thou art m. E. E. Cummings. CP-CummE

O praedestinata bis. May Lines. Gerard Manley Hopkins. CP-HopkG

O Praise the Lord, and bless his name. Bible, *O.T. See* Praise ye the Lord. Praise ye the name of the Lord; praise him, O ye servants of the Lord

O precious liberty, how you reveal. Petrarch. CP-Petra, *tr. by* J. G. Nichols

O pretty village . . . aye, mine own home. To Say if You Love Someone. Kenneth Patchen. CP-PatcK

O princely poet!—kingly heir. Your Height Is Ours. James Whitcomb Riley. CP-RileJ

O printerman of sallow face. Ancient Printerman, The. James Whitcomb Riley. CP-RileJ

O prophets with your backs turned to the sea. Research Council. Hans Magnus Enzensberger. SP-EnzeH

O Pug! Stevie Smith. CP-SmitS

O purple finch / please tell me why. E. E. Cummings. CP-CummE

O Queen of Heaven. La Gretchen de Nos Jours (II). Stevie Smith. CP-SmitS

O queenly month of indolent repose! June. James Whitcomb Riley. CP-RileJ

O Qui Me—! Arthur Hugh Clough. SP-ClouA

O qui sonora coelites altos cheli. Ad Io. Dolundum. Thomas Campion. CP-CampT

O quick floss silk of the Juventii, form. Catullus. *See* Best sprig of the clan

O rabid sirocco. Agave on the Reef, The. Eugenio Montale. CP-MontE, *tr. by* Jonathan Galassi

O raging Fortune's withering blast. Robert Burns. CP-BurnR

O ram ridicule home, Cato, the jokes some. Catullus. *See* Matter for mirth, Cato, & a smile, A

O rattlin, roarin Willie. Rattlin, Roarin Willie. Robert Burns. CP-BurnR

O Reader behold the Philosophers Grave. William Blake. CP-BlakW

O restless fingers—not that music make! Music. Walter De la Mare. CP-DeLaW

O river winding to the sea! Haverhill. John Greenleaf Whittier. CP-WhitJ

O rock my baby on the tree tops. Coming out of Sleep. Lorine Niedecker. CP-NiedL

O Rome thou art, at coffee break, O Rome. Thomas Kinsella. CP-KinsT

O Roneo, Roneo, wherefore art thou Roneo? To Rhoda. G. K. Chesterton. CP-ChesG

O room of silences, alien land. Mirror, The. Howard Nemerov. CP-NemeH

O[h] Rose, thou art sick. Sick Rose, The. William Blake. CP-BlakW *Fr.* Songs of Experience.

O Rose, thou flower of flowers, thou fragrant wonder. Rose, The. Christina Georgina Rossetti. CP-RosC3

O rose, who dares to name thee? Dead Rose, A. Elizabeth Barrett Browning. CP-BroEB

O rosy fair and rosy sweet. Ballad of the Lady Eglantine, The. George Meredith. CP-MerG2

O rough, rude, ready-witted R******. Epistle to J. R******, Enclosing Some Poems. Robert Burns. CP-BurnR

! / o(rounD)moon,how. E. E. Cummings. CP-CummE

O Rourk's noble fare. Description of an Irish Feast, The. Hugh MacGowran. CP-SwifJ, *tr. by* Jonathan Swift

O ruff-embastioned vast Elizabeth. On Certain Elizabethan Revivals. Dante Gabriel Rossetti. CW-RossD

O sacred Providence, who from end to end. Providence. George Herbert. CP-HerbG

O sad and heavy should I part. Sae Far Awa. Robert Burns. CP-BurnR

O sad little horses. Wooden Horses. Federico García Lorca. CP-GarcF, *tr. by* Jerome Rothenberg *Fr.* Fairs.

O sad man, now a long dead man. Pair He Saw Pass, The. Thomas Hardy. CP-HardT

O Sailor, Come Ashore. Christina Georgina Rossetti. CP-RosC2

O St. James Road. Swath. Federico García Lorca. CP-GarcF, *tr. by* Jerome Rothenberg *Fr.* Night (Suite for Piano and Poet's Voice).

O! save ye Gods, omnipotent and kind. Seneca. CP-JohnS *Fr.* Hercules Furens.

O saw ye bonny Lesley. Bonnie Lesley. Robert Burns. CP-BurnR

O saw ye my dearie, my Eppie Mcnab? Eppie McNab. Robert Burns. CP-BurnR

O saw ye my dearie, my Phely. Saw Ye My Phely (Quasi Dicat, Phillis). Robert Burns. CP-BurnR

O Saw Ye My Maggie. Robert Burns. CP-BurnR

O say not he is dead. Lee O. Harris. James Whitcomb Riley. CP-RileJ

O seal the shining! this stillness binds the stars. Firing, The. Kenneth Patchen. CP-PatcK

O seasons, o châteaux. Arthur Rimbaud. CP-RimbA, *tr. by* Martin Sorrell

O see what I have made! Homunculus. Louise Bogan. CP-BogaL

O Seraph, pause no more! Seraphim, The. Elizabeth Barrett Browning. CP-

BroEB

O shallow ground. Words to be Spoken. Archibald MacLeish. CP-MacLA

O She Is as Lovely-Often as Every Day. Kenneth Patchen. CP-PatcK

O she that made the brave appeal. George Meredith. CP-MerG1 *Fr.* France.

O she was full of loving fuss. One of the Principal Causes of War. Hugh MacDiarmid. SP-MacDH

O she whom I cannot abide. One Night in Oz. Ogden Nash. CP-NashO

O Shepherd with the bleeding Feet. Good Shepherd, The. Christina Georgina Rossetti. CP-RosC2

O Sheridan, the muses' pet, sweet friend. Ad Amicum Eruditum Thomam Sheridan [To My Learned Friend, Thomas Sheridan]. Jonathan Swift. CP-SherT, *tr. by* Robert Hogan

O ship in a bottle. Ships in Bottles. D. H. Lawrence. CP-LawrD

O shrive me Friar, my ghostly Friar! George Meredith. CP-MerG2

O sight of pity, shame and dole! Singer in the Prison, The. Walt Whitman. CP-WhitW

O simple as the rhymes that tell. Lincoln—The Boy. James Whitcomb Riley. CP-RileJ

O, sing a new Song to the L——! New Psalm for the Chapel of Kilmarnock, on the Thanksgiving-Day for His Majesty's Recovery, A. Robert Burns. CP-BurnR

O sing unto the Lord a new song; for he hath done marvellous [*or* marvelous] things. Psalm 98: "O sing unto the Lord a new song; for he hath done marvellous [*or* marvelous] things." Bible, *O.T.* SP-SmarC *Fr.* Psalms.

O Singer of Persephone! Theocritus: A Villanelle. Oscar Wilde. CP-WildO

O Sister! couldst thou know as thou wilt know. Antigone. George Meredith. CP-MerG1

O sister of the shadow. Meditations on Death. Giuseppe Ungaretti. CP-KunSC, *tr. by* Stanley Kunitz

O sixteen hundred and ninety-one. Two Witches, The. Robert Graves. CP-GravR

O skylark! I see thee and call thee joy! To a Skylark. George Meredith. CP-MerG1

O Slain for love of me, canst Thou be cold. Zion Said. Christina Georgina Rossetti. CP-RosC3

O sleeping falls the maiden snow. Kenneth Patchen. CP-PatcK

O Sleepless Night. James Schuyler. CP-SchuJ

O sleepy city of reeling wheelchairs. Wheelchair Butterfly, The. James Tate. SP-TateJ

O sluggish, hard, ingrate, what doest thou? Canzone: A Dispute with Death. Guido Cavalcanti. CW-RossD, *tr. by* Dante Gabriel Rossetti

O small St. Agnes, dressed in gold. Prelude: For the Feast of St. Agnes, A. Thomas Merton. CP-MertT

O smooth flatterers, go over sea. Pax Saturni. Ezra Pound. CP-PoEar

O snake, you are an argument / for poetry. Psalm to Snake. Margaret Atwood. SP-AtwM2

O soft embalmer of the still midnight! To Sleep. John Keats. CP-KeatJ

O Solitude! If I Must with Thee Dwell. John Keats. CP-KeatJ

O solo mio, hot diggety, nix 'I wather think I can.' Poem: "O solo mio, hot diggety, nix 'I wather think I can.'" Frank O'Hara. SP-OharF

O some will court and compliment. John Come Kiss Me Now. Robert Burns. CP-BurnR

O soul of mine, look out and see. My Bride That Is to Be. James Whitcomb Riley. CP-RileJ

O sov'reign of an isle renown'd. On His Majesty's Sea Bathing. William Cowper. CP-CowpW

O Spirit blest! / Whether th' eternal Throne around. Samuel Taylor Coleridge. CP-ColeS *Fr.* Monody on the Death of Chatterton.

O Spirit, / spark by spark. Euripides. CP-DoolH *Fr.* Hippolytus.

O spiteful bitter thought. Assurance. George Herbert. CP-HerbG

O splendid to reach a craft and creed. Magic Car, The. Kenneth Patchen. CP-PatcK

O Spring without end, without limit. Aleksandr Aleksandrovich Blok. SP-BlokA, *tr. by* Peter France *and* Jon Stallworthy

O spring, you who aren't human, speak. Spring. Rainer Maria Rilke. CP-RilkFr, *tr. by* A. Poulin, Jr.

O stagnant east-wind, palsied mare. Room on a Garden, A. Wallace Stevens. CP-StevWP

O Star of France (1870–71). Walt Whitman. CP-WhitW

O Star (the fairest one in sight). Choose Something like a Star. Robert Frost. CP-FrosR

O staring eyes, searchlight disks. Van der Lubbe. Stephen Spender. CP-SpenS

O! Start a Revolution. D. H. Lawrence. CP-LawrD

O State prayer-founded! never hung. To Pennsylvania. John Greenleaf Whittier. CP-WhitJ

O Statue of Liberty Spouse of Europa Destroyer of Past Present Future. Stotras to Kali Destroyer of Illusions. Allen Ginsberg. CP-GinsA

O stay, sweet warbling woodlark stay. Address to the Woodlark. Robert Burns. CP-BurnR

O stealing time, the subject of delay. Sir Philip Sidney. SP-SidnP *Fr.* Arcadia.

O steer her up and had her gaun. Robert Burns. CP-BurnR

O stiffly shapen houses that change not. Suburbs on a Hazy Day. D. H. Lawrence. CP-LawrD

O storied vale of Merrimac. One of the Signers. John Greenleaf Whittier. CP-WhitJ

O stormy, stormy world. Happiness Makes Up in Height for What It Lacks in Length. Robert Frost. CP-FrosR

O strange devices that alone divide. Eyes. Walter De la Mare. CP-DeLaW

O strange face there in the glass! On His Own Face in a Glass. Ezra Pound. CP-PoEar

O strange old shadow among us, O sweet-voiced mystery. Mother of All. G. K. Chesterton. CP-ChesG

O stream, descending to the sea. Arthur Hugh Clough. SP-ClouA

O strong, upwelling prayers of faith. Hermit of the Thebaid, The. John Greenleaf Whittier. CP-WhitJ

O sun, and moonlight shining in the woods. Carmen Saeculare. Charles Hubert Sisson. SP-SmarC, *tr. by* Christopher Smart

O Sun! Instigator of cocks! Salute. Archibald MacLeish. CP-MacLA

O Sun of Real Peace. Walt Whitman. CP-WhitW

O sun! take off thy hood of clouds. Ralph Waldo Emerson. CP-EmerR

O Sun! With your eye of a great bird. Maya against Itzas. Charles Olson. CP-OlsoC

O sundown, sundown / Like blood on Sion! Sundown. Thomas Merton. CP-MertT

O! Superstition is the Giant Shadow. Superstition. Samuel Taylor Coleridge. CP-ColeS

O / sure)but / nobody unders(no). E. E. Cummings. CP-CummE

O, sweep of stars over Harlem streets. Stars. Langston Hughes. CP-HughL; CP-HughL2

O sweet delight, O more than human[e] bliss[e]. Song: "O sweet delight, O more than human[e] bliss[e]." Thomas Campion. CP-CampT

O sweet escape! O smiling flight! Communion, The. Thomas Merton. CP-MertT

O sweet everlasting Voices be still. Everlasting Voices, The. William Butler Yeats. CP-YeatW

O Sweet Irrational Worship. Thomas Merton. CP-MertT

O sweet pleasure lifting us toward. Bitter Pleasure. Rainer Maria Rilke. CP-RilkFr, *tr. by* A. Poulin, Jr.

O sweet sincerity!— / Where modern methods be. To Sincerity. Thomas Hardy. CP-HardT

O Sweet Spontaneous. E. E. Cummings. CP-CummE; SP-CummE

O sweet spontaneous. O Sweet Spontaneous. E. E. Cummings. CP-CummE; SP-CummE

O sweet To-morrow! Song of Hope. Thomas Hardy. CP-HardT

O sweet woods, the delight of solitariness! Delight of Solitariness, The. Sir Philip Sidney. SP-SidnP *Fr.* Arcadia.

O Sylvia, Sylvia. Sylvia's Death. Anne Sexton. CP-SextA

O synfull man, thir ar the fourty dayis. Maner of Passyng to Confessioun, The. William Dunbar. CP-DunbW

O take my gift. At Croton. "H. D." CP-DoolH

O take my hand Walt Whitman! Salut au Monde! Walt Whitman. CP-WhitW

O Tan-Faced Prairie-Boy. Walt Whitman. CP-WhitW

O Tannenbaum. Lorine Niedecker. CP-NiedL

O Taste and See. Denise Levertov. SP-LeveDP; SP-LeveDS

O te te nimis, & nimis beatum! Psalmus 1. Richard Crashaw. CP-CrasR

O tell me, friends, while yet we part. Sectantem levia nervi deficiunt. Arthur Hugh Clough. SP-ClouA

O tell me, Harper, wherefore flow. On the Massacre of Glencoe, 1692. Sir Walter Scott. SP-ScotW

O tell me of the Russians, Communist, my son! Communist, John Berryman. CP-BerrJ

O tell me where, in lands or seas. Ballade of the Ladies of Time Past. François Villon. CP-WilbR, *tr. by* Richard Wilbur

O tender-heartedness right bitter grown. Fragmenti. Ezra Pound. CP-PoEar

O tenderly the haughty day. Ode Sung in the Town Hall. Ralph Waldo Emerson. CP-EmerR

O terrible is the highest thing. Kenneth Patchen. CP-PatcK

O th' oppressive, irksome weight. Uncertainty in Love. Samuel Taylor Coleridge. CP-ColeS

O that a chariot of cloud were mine! Percy Bysshe Shelley. CP-ShelP

O that a week could be an age, and we. To James Rice. John Keats. CP-KeatJ

O that I could a sin once see! Sin (2): "O that I could a sin once see!" George Herbert. CP-HerbG

O that I Had Ne'er Been Married. Robert Burns. CP-BurnR

O that I knew how all thy lights combine. Holy Scriptures (2), The. George Herbert. CP-HerbG

O that I Now. Algernon Charles Swinburne. SP-SwinA *Fr.* Atalanta in Calydon.

O that I were where Helen lies. Where Helen Lies. Robert Burns. CP-BurnR

O, that joy so soon should waste! Ben Jonson. CP-JonsB *Fr.* Cynthia's Revels.

O that the rain would come—the rain in big battalions. Precursors. Louis

MacNeice. CP-MacNL

O that warm February morning! The inopportune South wind came to rekindle the memories. Workers. Arthur Rimbaud. CP-RimbA, *tr. by* Martin Sorrell

O that's the lassie o' my heart. Robert Burns. *See* O wat ye wha that lo'es me

O the ashen face, the horsehair escutcheon. Arthur Rimbaud. CP-RimbA, *tr. by* Martin Sorrell

O the beautiful garment. Flowering of the Rod, The. "H. D." CP-DoolH

O the bitter shame and sorrow. Hymn: "O the bitter shame and sorrow." Christina Georgina Rossetti. CP-RosC3

O the clammy cold November. Apathy and Enthusiasm. Herman Melville. SP-MelvH

O the clear moment, when from the mouth. Fragment of a Lost Poem. Robert Graves. CP-GravR

O the days gone by! O the days gone by! Days Gone By, The. James Whitcomb Riley. CP-RileJ

O the drum! Drum, The. James Whitcomb Riley. CP-RileJ

O the dummies in the windows! Dummies. Randall Jarrell. CP-JarrR

O the enormous avenues of the holy land, the temple terraces! Lives. Arthur Rimbaud. CP-RimbA, *tr. by* Martin Sorrell

O the gentle fool / He fell in love. Antipoem 1. Thomas Merton. CP-MertT

O the green glimmer of apples in the orchard. Ballad of Another Ophelia. D. H. Lawrence. CP-LawrD

O the jungle is beautiful the jungle is wild. Recollection of Childhood. Richard Eberhart. CP-EberR

O the lands of Where-Away! Where-Away. James Whitcomb Riley. CP-RileJ

O the Little Lady's dainty. Little Lady, The. James Whitcomb Riley. CP-RileJ

O the little tiny kickshaw that Mither sent tae me. Little Tiny Kickshaw, The. James Whitcomb Riley. CP-RileJ

O the Lockerbie Fair!—Have you heard of its fame. Lockerbie Fair. James Whitcomb Riley. CP-RileJ

O the Lord is good. Lord Is Good, The. Thomas Merton. CP-MertT

O the night was dark and the night was late. Treasure of the Wise Man, The. James Whitcomb Riley. CP-RileJ

O the old trundle-bed where I slept when a boy! Old Trundle-Bed, The. James Whitcomb Riley. CP-RileJ

O the old wall here! How I could pass. Prologue: "O the old wall here! How I could pass." Robert Browning. CP-BroR2

O the opal and the sapphire of that wandering western sea. Beeny Cliff. Thomas Hardy. CP-HardT

O the Poet of the Future! He will come to us as comes. Poet of the Future, The. James Whitcomb Riley. CP-RileJ

O the precipice Titanic. Canticle, A. Herman Melville. SP-MelvH

O the quiet of water under the rocks, and the yellow silence of the afternoon. O! ("O the quiet of water under the rocks, and the yellow silence of the afternoon"). Czeslaw Milosz. CP-MiloCN, *tr. by* Robert Hass

O the Raggedy Man! He works fer Pa. Raggedy Man, The. James Whitcomb Riley. CP-RileJ

O / the round / little man we. E. E. Cummings. CP-CummE

O the sledbirds rides over the willow. Kenneth Patchen. CP-PatcK

O the slums of Dublin fermenting with children. Slum Song. Louis MacNeice. CP-MacNL

O the snows last so long. Despair. Richard Eberhart. CP-EberR

O the stale old dogs who pretend to guard. Young and Their Moral Guardians, The. D. H. Lawrence. CP-LawrD

O the Summer-time to-day. Summer-Time, The. James Whitcomb Riley. CP-RileJ

O the sun and the rain, and the rain and the sun! Song of the Cruise, A. James Whitcomb Riley. CP-RileJ

O the sun comes up-up-up in the opening. E. E. Cummings. CP-CummE

O / the sweet & aged people. oDE: "O / the sweet & aged people." E. E. Cummings. CP-CummE

O the waiting in the watches of the night! Watches of the Night, The. James Whitcomb Riley. CP-RileJ

O the way that Billy could ride! Billy Could Ride. James Whitcomb Riley. CP-RileJ

O the wind, the wind, the wind doth blow. Song: "O the wind, the wind, the wind doth blow." George Meredith. CP-MerG2

O Theos Meta Sou. Arthur Hugh Clough. SP-ClouA

O Theotropia, my empress consort. Byzantine Mosaic, A. Wisława Szymborska. SP-SzymW, *tr. by* Stanislaw Barańczak *and* Clare Cavanagh

O there were three jolly hunters. Three Jolly Hunters, The. James Whitcomb Riley. CP-RileJ

O these wakeful[l] wounds of thine! On the Wounds of Our Crucified Lord. Richard Crashaw. CP-CrasR

O they canna' do without it. Song: "O they canna' do without it." George Meredith. CP-MerG2

O th'hate I move love. Quarry it fact I am, for that's so re queries. Catullus. *See* I hate and I love. And if you ask me how

O think what joy that now. Midsummer Duet. Robert Graves. CP-RidiL

O this is no my ain lassie. Song: "O this is no my ain lassie." Robert Burns. CP-BurnR

O this is the way the baby came. Way the Baby Came, The. James Whitcomb Riley. CP-RileJ

O Thoth O wise one. O Hermes Trismegistus. James Laughlin. CP-LaugJ

O Thou bright jewel in my aim I strive. On Virtue. Phillis Wheatley. CP-WheaP

O thou bright Sun! beneath the dark blue line. Evening: To Harriet. Percy Bysshe Shelley. CP-ShelP

O thou dread Pow'r, who reign'st above! Lying at a Reverend Friend's House One Night, the Author Left the Following *Verses* in the Room Where He Slept. Robert Burns. CP-BurnR

O Thou, far off and here, whole and broken. To the Holy Spirit. Wendell Berry. CP-BerrW

O Thou Father of splendor, Giver of light. Prayer of Thanksgiving Written for Victor Hammer, A. Thomas Merton. CP-MertT

O Thou, fierce God of armies, Mars the red. Queen Annelida and False Arcite. Geoffrey Chaucer. CP-BroEB

O Thou great Being! what Thou art. Prayer, under the Pressure of Violent Anguish, A. Robert Burns. CP-BurnR

O thou immortal deity. Fragment: "O thou immortal deity." Percy Bysshe Shelley. CP-ShelP

O thou, in whom we live and move. Grace after Meat. Robert Burns. CP-BurnR

O Thou mocked heart that cowerest by the door. Sonnet in Tenzone. Ezra Pound. CP-PoEar

O thou Most High, who rulest all. Upon My Dear and Loving Husband His Going into England. Anne Bradstreet. CP-BradA

O thou Mother Oberoi / Crosseyed goddess of death. Songs of Experience; India, One. Thomas Merton. CP-MertT

O Thou my monster, Thou my guide. Prayer in Mid-Passage. Louis MacNeice. CP-MacNL

O thou new comer [*or* newcomer] who seek'st Rome in Rome. Rome. Joachim Du Bellay. CP-PoEar, *tr. by* Ezra Pound

O Thou, of British Orators the chief. Catullus. *See* Silver-tongued among the sons of Rome

O, Thou Opening, O. Theodore Roethke. CP-RoetT

O thou pale Orb, that silent shines. Lament. Occasioned by the Unfortunate Issue of a Friend's Amour, The. Robert Burns. CP-BurnR

O, Thou that doth all things devise. Hymb of Faith, A. James Whitcomb Riley. CP-RileJ

O thou that from thy mansion. For My Funeral. A. E. Housman. CP-HousA

O thou that hearest the prayers of thine. In Thankful Acknowledgement for the Letters I Received from My Husband out of England. Anne Bradstreet. CP-BradA

O Thou that in the heavens does dwell! Holy Willie's Prayer. Robert Burns. CP-BurnR

O Thou, that sit'st upon a throne. Song to David, A. Christopher Smart. SP-SmarC

O Thou, the first, the greatest friend. *First Six Verses* of the Ninetieth Psalm, The. Robert Burns. CP-BurnR

O thou the span of whose Omnipotence. Out of *Grotius* His Tragedy of *Christes* Sufferings. Richard Crashaw. CP-CrasR

O thou, the wonder of all day[e]s! Dirge of Jephthah's Daughter, The. Robert Herrick. CP-HerrR

O Thou to whom the musical white spring. E. E. Cummings. CP-CummE

O thou, to whose fury the nations are. King Edward the Third. William Blake. CP-BlakW

O Thou unknown, Almighty Cause. Prayer, in the Prospect of Death, A. Robert Burns. CP-BurnR

O Thou! What e'er may thy attention draw. Michael Tracey. CP-SherT *Fr.* Critical Minute, The.

O thou! whatever title suit thee. Address to the Deil. Robert Burns. CP-BurnR

O thou which to search out the secret parts. To Mr S. B. John Donne. CP-DonnJ; MW-DonnJ

O thou who at Love's hour ecstatically. Love's Testament. Dante Gabriel Rossetti. CW-RossD *Fr.* House of Life, The.

O thou who giving helm and sword. Dreamer, The. Walter De la Mare. CP-DeLaW

O Thou, who kindly dost [*or* doth] provide. Grace before Dinner, Extempore, A. Robert Burns. CP-BurnR

O Thou who movest onward with a mind. Gabriello Chiabrera. CP-WorW1

O thou, who passest through [*or* thro'] our valleys [*or* vallies] in. To Summer. William Blake. CP-BlakW

O thou who pausest here. Thorn, The. Walter De la Mare. CP-DeLaW

O thou, who plumed with strong desire. Two Spirits[: An Allegory], The. Percy Bysshe Shelley. CP-ShelP

O thou! who rollest in yon azure field. Version of Ossian's Address to the Sun, A. Lord Byron. CP-Byron

O thou who tell'st me that all hope is over. Christina Georgina Rossetti. CP-RosC3

O thou whom Poetry [*or* Poesy] abhors. On Elphinston's Translation of Martial.

Robert Burns. CP-BurnR

O thou, whose all-creating hands sustain. Boethius. CP-PopeA *Fr.* Consolation of Philosophy, The ("De Consolacione Philosophie").

O Thou whose exit wraps in boundless woe. Elegy Sacred to the Memory of the Rev'd Samuel Cooper, D.D., An. Phillis Wheatley. CP-WheaP

O Thou whose exit wraps in boundless woe. Elegy, Sacred to the Memory of that Great Divine, the Reverend and Learned Dr. Samuel Cooper, An. Phillis Wheatley. CP-WheaP

O Thou Whose Face Hath Felt the Winter's Wind. John Keats. CP-KeatJ

O thou! whose fancies from afar are brought. To H. C., Six Years Old. William Wordsworth. CP-WorW1; MW-WorW

O thou whose image in the shrine. Hymnos Aymnos. Arthur Hugh Clough. SP-ClouA

O thou whose name, being alone, aloud. Dante Gabriel Rossetti. CW-RossD

O thou whose pow'r o'er moving worlds presides. Boethius. CP-JohnS *Fr.* Consolation of Philosophy, The ("De Consolacione Philosophie").

O Thou, whose presence went before. Hymn: "O Thou, whose presence went before." John Greenleaf Whittier. CP-WhitJ

O thou, with dewy locks, who lookest down. To Spring. William Blake. CP-BlakW

O thou yclep'd by vulgar sons of Men. Farewell Petition to J.C.H., Esq. Lord Byron. CP-Byron

O thought, fly to her when the end of day. Old Memory. William Butler Yeats. CP-YeatW

O thrilling voice of Zeus. Sophocles. CP-SpenS *Fr.* Oedipus Rex [*or* Oedipus the King, *or* Oedipus Tyrannus].

O throw it away, throw it all away on the wind. Song for a Revolutionary Love. Sylvia Plath. CP-PlatS

O thy flamed cheek, / Those locks with weeping wet. Forgiveness. Walter De la Mare. CP-DeLaW

O time, O turning sky, speeding away. Petrarch. CP-Petra, *tr. by* J. G. Nichols

O Time—the heedless child you are! Moment, The. Walter De la Mare. CP-DeLaW

O Time, whence comes the Mother's moody look amid her labours. Lacking Sense, The. Thomas Hardy. CP-HardT

O Times most bad. Upon the Troublesome Times. Robert Herrick. CP-HerrR

O 'tis my delight / In the dead of the night. George Meredith. CP-MerG2

O to Be A Dragon. Marianne Craig Moore. CP-MoorM

O to be born ardent and sad. L'Indifférent. Rainer Maria Rilke. CP-RilkFr, *tr. by* A. Poulin, Jr. *Fr.* Affectionate Taxes to France.

O[h], to be in England. Home-Thoughts, from Abroad. Robert Browning. CP-BroR1; SP-BroR

O to be in finland. E. E. Cummings. CP-CummE, SP-CummE

O to break loose, like the chinook. Waking Early Sunday Morning. Robert Lowell. SP-LoweR

O to make the most jubilant song! Song of Joys, A. Walt Whitman. CP-WhitW

O tongue / licking. To an Old Jaundiced Woman. William Carlos Williams. CP-WilW1

O too dull brain, O unpiercing nerves. Revenant, The. Archibald MacLeish. CP-MacLA

O touch me with your hands. Passing of a Heart, The. James Whitcomb Riley. CP-RileJ

O transient voyager of heaven! To a Wreath of Snow. Emily Jane Brontë. CP-BronE

O Tree of Pride. Ivor Gurney. SP-GurnI

O trip and skip, Elvire! Link arm in arm with me! Fifine at the Fair. Robert Browning. CP-BroR2

O truly, Lily was a lulu. Pop Smash, out of Echo Chamber. John Updike. CP-UpdiJ

O Tu Pater splendoris Dator luminis. Prayer of Thanksgiving Written for Victor Hammer, A. Thomas Merton. CP-MertT

O two-tongued angel, on my grief a hundred. Breakup, The. Boris Leonidovich Pasternak. SP-WeisT, *tr. by* Theodore Weiss

O unknown city, cool cradle. City Unknown. Adam Zagajewski. SP-ZagaA, *tr. by* Renata Gorczynski

O uommibatto / Agil, giocondo. Christina Georgina Rossetti. CP-RosC3

O venerable plank burning. One Time. W. S. Merwin. SP-MerwW

O Vocables of Love. Laura Riding Jackson. CP-RidiL

O Voice of Approbation, bless. Munificence and Modesty. Christopher Smart. SP-SmarC

O. W. Holmes on His Eightieth Birthday. John Greenleaf Whittier. CP-WhitJ

O wander not so far away! Emily Jane Brontë. CP-BronE

O wasted steps, O wanderings in the mind. Petrarch. CP-Petra, *tr. by* J. G. Nichols

O wastfull Riot, never well content. Lucan. CP-RaleW *Fr.* Civil War [Bellum Civile] *or* Pharsalia.

O wat ye wha that lo'es me. Song: "O wat ye wha that lo'es me." Robert Burns. CP-BurnR

O wat ye wha's in yon town. Song: "O wat ye wha's in yon town." Robert Burns. CP-BurnR

O Wave God who broke through me today. Burning Island. Gary Snyder. CP-SnydG

O, We Are the Outcasts. Charles Bukowski. SP-BukC2

O weary Champion of the Cross, lie still. Cardinal Newman. Christina Georgina Rossetti. CP-RosC3

O weary mariners, here shaded, fed. Randall Jarrell. CP-JarrR

O well for him who lives at ease. Aeschylus. CP-WildO *Fr.* Agamemnon.

O well for him whose will is strong! Will. Alfred Tennyson. CP-TennA

O were I on Parnassus hill. Robert Burns. CP-BurnR

O! were I one of the Olympian twelve. Extracts from an Opera. John Keats. CP-KeatJ

O Were My Love Yon Lilac[k] Fair. Robert Burns. CP-BurnR

O were there anything by half. Song: "O were there anything by half." Ivor Gurney. SP-GurnI

O wert thou, Love, but near me. Robert Burns. *See* Forlorn, my love, no comfort near

O Western Wind. George Oppen. CP-OppGN

O wha my babie-clouts will buy? Rantin' Dog, the Daddie o't, The. Robert Burns. CP-BurnR

O wha will to Saint Stephen's house. Fête Champetre, The. Robert Burns. CP-BurnR

O wha'll m-w me now, my jo. Wha'll M-w Me Now. Robert Burns. CP-BurnR

O whar did ye get that hauver-meal bannock? Bonic Dundee. Robert Burns. CP-BurnR

O what a physical effect it has on me. In Love with You. Kenneth Koch. SP-KochK

O What a Revolution! Kenneth Patchen. CP-PatcK

O what a silence is this wilderness! Gerard Manley Hopkins. CP-HopkG

O, what a thing is man! how far from power. Giddiness. George Herbert. CP-HerbG

O what a weary while it is to stand. Eternity. James Whitcomb Riley. CP-RileJ

O what a wonder seems the fear of death. Samuel Taylor Coleridge. *See* When faint and sad o'er Sorrow's desart wild

O what an endelesse worke have I in hand. Book 4, Canto 12. Edmund Spenser. CP-Spens *Fr.* Faerie Queene, The.

O what are heroes prophets men. Ralph Waldo Emerson. CP-EmerR

O what astonishment if you. Spite of Mirrors. Robert Graves. CP-GravR

O[h] what can ail thee, knight-at-arms [*or* wretched wight]. La Belle Dame sans Merci [A Ballad]. John Keats. CP-KeatJ

O what could be more nice. Light Listened. Theodore Roethke. CP-RoetT

O what daybreak in the windows! Cannons salute. Amazement. Czeslaw Milosz. CP-MiloC; CP-MiloCN, *tr. by* Lillian Vallee

O what did the little boy do? Youthful Patriot, The. James Whitcomb Riley. CP-RileJ

O what has made that sudden noise? Ghost of Roger Casement, The. William Butler Yeats. CP-YeatW

O What have I to do. Ralph Waldo Emerson. CP-EmerR

O what is Heaven but the fellowship. Ralph Waldo Emerson. CP-EmerR

"O, what is Life at last," says you. Lines to an Onsettled Young Man. James Whitcomb Riley. CP-RileJ

O What Is That Sound [Which So Thrills the Ear]. W. H. Auden. CP-AudeW

O What Is the Setting Sun's Radiance to Me. Aleksandr Aleksandrovich Blok. SP-BlokA, *tr. by* Peter France *and* Jon Stallworthy

O what sadness unaware that it's sadness! O! ("O what sadness unaware that it's sadness!"). Czeslaw Milosz. CP-MiloCN, *tr. by* Robert Hass

O what to me the little room. Heart of the Woman, The. William Butler Yeats. CP-YeatW

O, what undeserved cruelty. Sir Thomas Wyatt. CP-WyatT

O what unhop't for sweet supply! Thomas Campion. CP-CampT

O what will you turn out, book, to be. First Poem. Ivor Gurney. SP-GurnI

O what's the gain, my worthy Sir. Forbidden Banns, The. Thomas Hardy. CP-HardT

O what's the weather in a Beard? Dinky. Theodore Roethke. CP-RoetT

O when I grunted, over lines and her. Images of Elspeth. John Berryman. CP-BerrJ

O when I take my love out walking. Kenneth Patchen. CP-PatcK

O when in San Fransisco do. Scenic. John Updike. CP-UpdiJ

O when she cam ben she bobbed fu' law. When She Cam Ben She Bobbed. Robert Burns. CP-BurnR

O when the world's at peace. Mad Farmer's Love Song, The. Wendell Berry. CP-BerrW

O when you were little, you were really big. Duet. Theodore Roethke. CP-RoetT

O whence do you come. Sailor's Mother, The. Thomas Hardy. CP-HardT

O where hae ye been, Lord Ronald, my son? Lord Ronald My Son. Robert Burns. CP-BurnR

O where is it, the wilderness. Gerard Manley Hopkins. CP-HopkG

O whistle, and I'll come to you [*or* ye], my lad. Whistle, and I'll Come to You, My Lad. Robert Burns. CP-BurnR

O white-faced mimes. For Dead Mimes. Langston Hughes. CP-HughL; CP-

HughL2

O white, white, white. White city where women carry bread and vegetables. Whiteness. Czeslaw Milosz. CP-MiloC; CP-MiloCN, *tr.* by Richard Lourie

O who can ever gaze his fill. Death's Echo. W. H. Auden. CP-AudeW

O[h], who shall from this dungeon raise. Dialogue between the Soul and [the] Body, A. Andrew Marvell. CP-MarvA

O who will give me tears? Come all ye springs. Grief. George Herbert. CP-HerbG

O who will show me those delights on high? Heaven. George Herbert. CP-HerbG

O who'll get me a healthy child. Practical Woman, A. Thomas Hardy. CP-HardT

O why did we uncover to view. Clasped Skeleton, The. Thomas Hardy. CP-HardT

O, why judge Myrrhina. Myrrhina. Robert Graves. CP-GravR

O why the deuce should I repine. Extempore. Robert Burns. CP-BurnR

O Why Was I Born with a Different Face? William Blake. CP-BlakW (To Thomas Butts, 16 August 1803.) CP-BlakW

O Wild Chaos! Richard Eberhart. CP-EberR

O[h] wild West Wind, thou breath of Autumn's being. Ode to the West Wind. Percy Bysshe Shelley. CP-ShelP

O "William," in thy blithe companionship. To Edgar Wilson Nye. James Whitcomb Riley. CP-RileJ

O Willie brew'd a peck o' maut. Willie Brew'd [or Brewed] a Peck o' Maut. Robert Burns. CP-BurnR

O wilt thou go wi' me, sweet Tibbie Dunbar. Tibbie Dunbar. Robert Burns. CP-BurnR

O wind, where have you been. Christina Georgina Rossetti. CP-RosC2

O wind, why do you never rest. Christina Georgina Rossetti. CP-RosC2

O Winter! bar thine adamantine doors. To Winter. William Blake. CP-BlakW

O winter, what a deadly foe. Impromptu on Winter. John Clare. SP-ClarJ

O woe is me for the merry life. Lament of the Border Cattle Thief, The. Rudyard Kipling. CP-KiplR

O woe, woe, / People are born and die. Song in the Manner of Housman. Ezra Pound. CP-PoEar

O women, kneeling by your altar-rails long hence. Lover Speaks to the Hearers of His Songs in Coming Days, The. William Butler Yeats. CP-YeatW

O wonderful nonsense of lotions of Lucky Tiger. Haircut. Karl Shapiro. SP-ShapK

"O words are lightly spoken." Rose Tree, The. William Butler Yeats. CP-YeatW

O Words Which Fall. Sir Philip Sidney. SP-SidnP *Fr.* Arcadia.

O words, which fall like summer dew on me! O Words Which Fall. Sir Philip Sidney. SP-SidnP *Fr.* Arcadia.

O world, I cannot hold thee close enough! God's World. Edna St. Vincent Millay. CP-MillE

O world! O life! O time! Lament, A: "O world! O life! O time!" Percy Bysshe Shelley. CP-ShelP

O World of Many Worlds. Wilfred Owen. CP-OwenW

O worthy of belief I hold it was. Pan and Luna. Robert Browning. CP-BroR2

O Would that Enemy I Dread, My Fate. Thomas Sheridan. CP-SherT

O wreche [or wretch], be war [or beware], this warld [or world] will wend the[e] fro. William Dunbar. CP-DunbW

O wrestler, the sun on the sand as you sleep. Summer Sadness. Stéphane Mallarmé. CP-MallS, *tr.* by Henry Weinfield

O ye, all ye that walk in Willowwood. Willowwood ("O ye, all ye that walk in Willowwood"). Dante Gabriel Rossetti. CW-RossD *Fr.* House of Life, The.

O ye red-blushing summer roses, ye. Floral Teaching. Christina Georgina Rossetti. CP-RosC3

O Ye Tongues. Anne Sexton. CP-SextA

    Eighth Psalm. SP-SextA

    First Psalm. SP-SextA

    Fourth Psalm. SP-SextA

    Tenth Psalm. SP-SextA

O ye, who are not dead and fit. Christina Georgina Rossetti. CP-RosC2

O ye who love today, / Turn away / From Patience with her silver ray. Christina Georgina Rossetti. CP-RosC2

O ye who tread the Narrow Way. Buddha at Kamakura. Rudyard Kipling. CP-KiplR

O ye whose cheek the tear of pity stains. For the Author's Father. Robert Burns. CP-BurnR

O ye young and thoughtless youth. Poem for Children with Thoughts on Death, A. Jupiter Hammon. CP-WheaP

O years [or yeares]! and age! farewell. Eternity [or Eternitie]. Robert Herrick. CP-HerrR

O yet how early, and before her time. Ben Jonson. CP-JonsB *Fr.* Oberon, the Fairy Prince.

O you are sad on Twelfth Night. Burning the Holly. Thomas Hardy. CP-HardT

O, you can't find a buddy. Death of Do Dirty: A Rounder's Song. Langston Hughes. CP-HughL; CP-HughL1

O you, center of the game. Eros. Rainer Maria Rilke. CP-RilkFr, *tr.* by A.

Poulin, Jr. *Fr.* Orchards.

O you chorus of indolent reviewers. Hendecasyllabics. Alfred Tennyson. CP-TennA

O you Dr. Ycas you! Bitter Life, A. John Updike. CP-UpdiJ

O you hard-boiled conservatives, and you soft-boiled liberals. Hard-Boiled Conservatives. D. H. Lawrence. CP-LawrD

O you, my one inestimable gem. Petrarch. CP-Petra, *tr.* by J. G. Nichols

O you so long dead. To My Brother: Killed: Hammont Wood: October, 1918. Louise Bogan. CP-BogaL

O! You the Virgins nine! Hymne to the Muses, A. Robert Herrick. CP-HerrR

O You Whom I Often and Silently Come. Walt Whitman. CP-WhitW

O your hands—they are strangely fair! Her Beautiful Hands. James Whitcomb Riley. CP-RileJ

O youth whose heart is right. Sage to the Young Man, The. A. E. Housman. CP-HousA

O yr facing reality now—. Broken Back Blues. Robert Creeley. CP-CreeR

Oafishness Sells Good, like an Advertisement Should. Ogden Nash. CP-NashO

Oak, The. Richard Eberhart. CP-EberR

Oak and the Broom, The; A Pastoral. William Wordsworth. CP-WorW1; MW-WorW

Oak and the Poplar, The. Jones Very. CP-VeryJ

Oak Arms. Carl Sandburg. CP-SandC

Oak burns steady and hot and long. Shadows of the Burning. Marge Piercy. SP-PierM

Oak inns creak in their joints as light declines, The. Derek Walcott. CP-WalcD *Fr.* Midsummer.

Oak-Leaves, The. Edna St. Vincent Millay. CP-MillE

Oak Leaves Are Hands. Wallace Stevens. CP-StevW; CP-StevWP

Oak of Guernica! Tree of holier power. William Wordsworth. CP-WorW1

Oak Openings. Donald Davie. CP-DaviDC

Oak twig drops, An. Acorns. Donald Hall. CP-HallD

Oaken, broken elbow-chair, An. True and Faithful Inventory of the Goods Belonging to Dr. Swift, Vicar of Laracor; upon Lending His House to the Bishop of Meath, until His Own Was Built [or till His Palace Was Rebuilt], A. Jonathan Swift. CP-SherT

Oaks, how subtle and marine, The. Bearded Oaks. Robert Penn Warren. CP-WarrR

Oaks shone / gaunt gold, The. Lightning. Mary Oliver. SP-OlivM

Oars, The. W. S. Merwin. SP-MerwWF

Oasis. Alan Dugan. CP-DugaA

Oath, The. Robert Graves. CP-GravR

Oath, The. Allen Tate. CP-TateA

Oatmeal. Galway Kinnell. SP-KinnGN

Oaxaca. Audre Lorde. SP-LordA

Oaxaca Bus, The. Charles Tomlinson. CP-TomlC; SP-TomlC

Oaxaca 1925. Kenneth Rexroth. CP-RexrK

Obedience. Rita Dove. SP-DoveR

Obedience. George Herbert. CP-HerbG

Obedience. Robert Herrick. CP-HerrR

Obedience. Jones Very. CP-VeryJ

Obedience in Subjects. Robert Herrick. CP-HerrR

Obedient daily dress. Skin. Philip Larkin. CP-LarkP

Oberon, the Fairy Prince. Ben Jonson.

    Catch, A. CP-JonsB

    "Gentle knights, / Know some measure of your nights." CP-JonsB

    "Melt earth to sea, sea flow to air." CP-JonsB

    "Nay, nay, / You must not stay." CP-JonsB

    "Nor yet, nor yet, O you in this night blessed." CP-JonsB

    "Now, my cunning lady moon." CP-JonsB

    "O yet how early, and before her time." CP-JonsB

    "Solemn rites are well begun, The." CP-JonsB

Oberon's Feast. Robert Herrick. CP-HerrR

Oberon's Palace. Robert Herrick. CP-HerrR

Obit. John Ciardi. CP-CiarJ

Obit. Robert Lowell. SP-LoweR

Obit. Charles Olson. CP-OlsoC

Obiter Dicta. Donald Davie. CP-DaviDC

Obituary. A. K. Ramanujan. CP-RamaA

Object. A. R. Ammons. CP-AmmoA

Object, An. Ezra Pound. CP-PoEar; SP-PounE

Object among dreams, you sit here with your shoes off, An. Girl in a Library, A. Randall Jarrell. CP-JarrR

Object in a Setting. Charles Tomlinson. CP-TomlC

Object Lesson. Charles Bukowski. SP-BukC2

Objection to Being Stepped On, The. Robert Frost. CP-FrosR

Objector. William Stafford. SP-StafW; SP-StafWW

Objects. W. H. Auden. CP-AudeW

Objects. Richard Wilbur. CP-WilbR

Objects, The. Charles Olson. CP-OlsoC

Objects & Apparitions. Octavio Paz. CP-BishE, *tr. by* Elizabeth Bishop

Obligations. Jane Cooper. CP-CoopJ

Obliged by frequent visits of this man. Flecknoe, an English Priest at Rome. Andrew Marvell. CP-MarvA

Oblique cloud of purple smoke, An. Woman Walking. William Carlos Williams. CP-WilW1

Oblique light on the trite, on brick and tile. Courtyards in Delft. Derek Mahon. CP-MahoD

Oblique Rain. Fernando Pessoa.
    "Inside, the church lights up today's rain." SP-PessF

Obliterate / mythology as you unwind. Cavern, The. Charles Tomlinson. CP-TomlC; SP-TomlC

Obliterate Tomb, The. Thomas Hardy. CP-HardT

Obliteration, The. Lorine Niedecker. CP-NiedL

Oblivion. Stevie Smith. CP-SmitS

Oblivious window of Quiet. Tuning the Sky. Susan Howe. SP-HoweS

O'Brien, most disconsolate of Men. Arthur Hugh Clough. SP-ClouA

Obscene Poem, An. Robert Creeley. CP-CreeR

Obscenity. D. H. Lawrence. CP-LawrD

Obscure, The. Norman Dubie. CP-DubiN

Obscure, unpriz'd, and dark, the magnet lies. Claudian. CP-JohnS

Obscure Writer, An. John Donne. CP-DonnJ; MW-DonnJ

Obscurely yet most surely called to praise. Praise in Summer. Richard Wilbur. CP-WilbR

Obscurest night involved [*or* involv'd] the sky. Castaway, The. William Cowper. CP-CowpW

Obscurity has its tale to tell. Focus. Adrienne Rich. CP-RicAE; SP-RicA1; SP-RicA2

Obsequial Ode. D. H. Lawrence. CP-LawrD

Obsequies for a Poetess. James Vincent Cunningham. CP-CunnJ

Obsequies to the Lady Anne Hay. Thomas Carew. CP-CareT

Obsequies to the Lord Harrington, Brother to the Lady Lucy, Countess of Bedford. John Donne. CP-DonnJ; MW-DonnJ

Observance. Wendell Berry. CP-BerrW

Observant of the way she told. Tact. Edwin Arlington Robinson. CP-RobiE

Observation. Robert Herrick. CP-HerrR

Observation. Philip Larkin. CP-LarkP

Observation. Dorothy Parker. CP-ParkD

Observation of Facts. Charles Tomlinson. CP-TomlC

Observation of October. Howard Nemerov. CP-NemeH

Observations in a Cornish Teashop. Kenneth Rexroth. CP-RexrK

Observations in the Art of English Poesie. Thomas Campion. CP-CampT
    Rose-cheeked Laura, Come. CP-CampT
    ("Rose-cheekt *Lawra* come.") CP-CampT

Observations of P. Ovidus Naso on the Incidence of Sex in the Contemporary Novel. Archibald MacLeish. CP-MacLA

Observatory. Yusef Komunyakaa. CP-KomuY

Observe Details. Christopher Logue. SP-LoguC

Observe how it will be at last. Summing Up in Italy. Elizabeth Barrett Browning. CP-BroEB

Observe. Ridged, raised, tactile, the horror. "Scream, The." Donald Hall. CP-HallD

Observe the Convalescent Child. Happy Xmas, A ("Observe the Convalescent Child"). G. K. Chesterton. CP-ChesG

Observe the dying father speak. Faggot, The. Jonathan Swift. CP-SwifJ

Observe the wisdom of the Florentine. Lesson, The. Stanley Kunitz. CP-KunSC

Observed from down the beach, the seal. Seal in Nature. John Updike. CP-UpdiJ

Observer, The. Adrienne Rich. CP-RicAE; SP-RicA2

Observer, The. William Carlos Williams. CP-WilW2

Obsession. Charles Baudelaire. CP-BaudC, *tr. by* Walter Martin

Obsession. James Laughlin. CP-LaugJ

Obsession, The. Frédéric Mistral. SP-MistG, *tr. by* Maria Giachetti [*or* Jacketti]

Obsessions. Denise Levertov. SP-LeveDS

Obsessive Combination of Ontological Inscape, Trickery and Love, An. Anne Sexton. SP-SextA

Obsolescence. John Ciardi. CP-CiarJ

Obsolete as books in leather bindings. Relics. Louis MacNeice. CP-MacNL

Obsolete Models. Philip Whalen. SP-WhalP

Obstructions. James Dickey. CP-DickJ

Obtaining but our own Extent. Emily Dickinson. CP-DickE

Obtrusive and absurd, the guilty mind. Pelican. Donald Davie. CP-DaviDC

Obviously. Czeslaw Milosz. CP-MiloCN, *tr. by* Brian Glazer *and* Martin Sabiniewicz

Obviously, in a plutocracy. Childe Harold to the Round Tower Came. William Carlos Williams. CP-WilW2

Occasional Address, Spoken by Miss Fontenell, on Her Benefit-Night, Decr. 4th. 1793.—Written by Mr Burns. Robert Burns. CP-BurnR

Occasional Dilemmas. Philip Whalen. SP-WhalP

Occasional Meditations: "By night, when others soundly slept." Anne Bradstreet. CP-BradA

Occasional Prologue Delivered previous to the Performance of "The Wheel of Fortune" at a Private Theatre, An. Lord Byron. CP-Byron

Occasional Yarrow, The. Stevie Smith. CP-SmitS

Occasioned by Sir William Temple's Late Illness and Recovery. Jonathan Swift. CP-SwifJ

Occasioned by Some Verses of His Grace the Duke of Buckingham. Alexander Pope. CP-PopeA

Occasioned by the Battle of Waterloo February, 1816. William Wordsworth. CP-WorW2

Occasioned by the Battle of Waterloo (the Last Six Lines Intended for an Inscription) February, 1816. William Wordsworth. CP-WorW2

Occidit. Ezra Pound. CP-PoEar

Occidit brevis lux. James Laughlin. CP-LaugJ

Occludes wild dawn. Up thro' green ragged clouds. Prime. John Berryman. CP-BerrJ

Occultation of Orion, The. Henry Wadsworth Longfellow. SP-LongH

Occultation, The. Thomas Hardy. CP-HardT

Occurrences, The ("Limited air drafts"). George Oppen. CP-OppGN

Occurrences, The ("Simplest / Words say the grass blade, The"). George Oppen. CP-OppGN

Ocean. Federico García Lorca. CP-GarcF, *tr. by* Catherine Brown

Ocean. Robinson Jeffers. CP-JefR3

Ocean. Robinson Jeffers. CP-JefR1

Ocean. Czeslaw Milosz. CP-MiloC; CP-MiloCN, *tr. by* Peter Dale Scott

Ocean. Phillis Wheatley. CP-WheaP

Ocean. John Greenleaf Whittier. CP-WhitJ

Ocean, The. Moschus. CP-ShelP, *tr. by* Percy Bysshe Shelley

Ocean City. A. R. Ammons. CP-AmmoA

Ocean glittered quietly in the moonlight, The. Rock Music. Derek Mahon. CP-MahoD

Ocean has not been so quiet for a long while, The. Evening Ebb. Robinson Jeffers. CP-JefR2

Ocean is / the Lucifer of blue, The. Ocean. Federico García Lorca. CP-GarcF, *tr. by* Catherine Brown

Ocean said to me once, The. Stephen Crane. CP-CranS

Ocean twanging away there, The. Parting: I, The. Adrienne Rich. CP-RicAE; SP-RicA2

Ocean, whale-shaped, rocking between the dunes. May Swenson. SP-SwenM

Oceans beyond the nearest war we fought. Chelsea Naval Hospital. John Ciardi. CP-CiarJ

Ocean's Love to Cynthia, The. Sir Walter Ralegh.
    11th: and Last Booke of the Ocean to Scinthia, The. CP-RaleW
    End of the Boo[c]k[e]s, of the Ocean's Love to Cynthia [*or* Scinthia], and the Beginning[e] of the 12 [*or* 22] Boo[c]k, Entreating of Sorrow, The. CP-RaleW

Ocean's Treasures. Jones Very. CP-VeryJ

Ocean's Tribute, The. Robinson Jeffers. CP-JefR3

Ochenaid Sant Francis Xavier, Apostol Yr Indiaid. Gerard Manley Hopkins. CP-HopkG

O'Clock. Fanny Howe.
    "After this girl was grown." SP-HoweF
    "Bracken by the tracks." SP-HoweF
    "Clotted cream and heather, Bronte way to heavenshire." SP-HoweF
    "Converse airwaves." SP-HoweF
    "Dirt feels sweet, The." SP-HoweF
    "Edge of the dome is slipping, The." SP-HoweF
    "Every glance works its way to infinity." SP-HoweF
    "From the bray of gray donkeys." SP-HoweF
    "Full Irish breakfast, A." SP-HoweF
    "Go on out but come back in." SP-HoweF
    "He was a cold-hearted Saxon." SP-HoweF
    "Hello eternal life in the light." SP-HoweF
    "Herds of the deer wander—their heads like wands." SP-HoweF
    "Hive-sized creams are on the chestnut tree." SP-HoweF
    "I feel like the end." SP-HoweF
    "I have backed up / into my silence." SP-HoweF
    "I often believe that nothing can be lost." SP-HoweF
    "I suffer from ire, it's electric." SP-HoweF
    "I won't be able to write from the grave." SP-HoweF
    "Iced stones in a nice hotel." SP-HoweF
    "If you mess up, run to the west." SP-HoweF
    "In envy's carriage there's a witness." SP-HoweF
    "Inked-in / nerve endings." SP-HoweF

"Into the forest I went walking—to get lost." SP-HoweF
"Late afternoon—the shadows lengthen." SP-HoweF
"Like a sheep sweating inside." SP-HoweF
"Limits have wintered me, The." SP-HoweF
"Minister to my friends, Saint Peregrine." SP-HoweF
"Moon ink is too bright to read." SP-HoweF
"Most of the continent." SP-HoweF
"Next time I'll travel by dream." SP-HoweF
"Nuns, monks and swamis." SP-HoweF
"On azure seats." SP-HoweF
"Parent above, look down and see." SP-HoweF
"Pass the small churchyard hamlet." SP-HoweF
"Production continues into the alienated night." SP-HoweF
"Prosaic poetry—an animal." SP-HoweF
"Rain—red rhododendron tree." SP-HoweF
"Rambling snowmounds and still sheep along." SP-HoweF
"Red shirt for anarchy, A." SP-HoweF
"Sallying off to the pub." SP-HoweF
"Slit should be blue, The." SP-HoweF
"So leave the field." SP-HoweF
"Soft fist of feathers." SP-HoweF
"Sometimes a goodbye." SP-HoweF
"Sometimes it seems." SP-HoweF
"Spring wind blows trumpet." SP-HoweF
"Stains of blackberries near Marx's grave, The." SP-HoweF
"Three is a city of terror where." SP-HoweF
"Under sky that is water." SP-HoweF
"Unmanned ship—a bed." SP-HoweF
"War occurred in the vicinity, A." SP-HoweF
"Welcome television to this rug-ruined room." SP-HoweF
"When one more means on less, you are a drudge." SP-HoweF
"When was when." SP-HoweF
"Where twigs are breaking stones." SP-HoweF
"Wild garlic flowers." SP-HoweF
"You float inside your water." SP-HoweF
"You travel a path on paper." SP-HoweF
Octave. Ezra Pound. CP-PoEar
Octaves. Edwin Arlington Robinson. CP-RobiE
Octets. Osip Emilevich Mandelstam. CP-DaviDC, tr. by Donald Davie
October. Paul Laurence Dunbar. CP-DunbP
October. Robert Frost. CP-FrosR
October. Robert Earl Hayden. CP-HaydR
October. Denise Levertov. SP-LeveDP
October. Audre Lorde. SP-LordA
October. W. S. Merwin. SP-MerwW
October. Mary Oliver. SP-OlivM
October. Gregory Orr. SP-OrrG
October. James Schuyler. CP-SchuJ
October. May Swenson. SP-SwenM
October. Charles Tomlinson. CP-TomlC
October ("All day, amidst the forests' splendor bright"). Jones Very. CP-VeryJ
October ("How beautiful the sight of woods still fair"). Jones Very. CP-VeryJ
October. Charles Wright. SP-WrigC
October 2. Charles Wright. SP-WrigCN
October 1950. Paul Muldoon. CP-MuldP
October again. Faint pheasant tail. Maple on the Hill. Charles Wright. SP-WrigCN
October—An Etching. Edna St. Vincent Millay. CP-MillE
October Dawn. Ted Hughes. SP-HughTN
October days / Red admirals. Late Butterflies. Howard Nemerov. CP-NemeH
October, 1803 ("One might believe that natural miseries"). William Wordsworth. CP-WorW1; MW-WorW
October, 1803: ("These times strike monied worldlings with dismay.") William Wordsworth. CP-WorW1
("These times touch moneyed Worldlings with dismay.") MW-WorW
October, 1803 ("When, looking on the present face of things"). William Wordsworth. CP-WorW1; MW-WorW
October Evening. Robinson Jeffers. CP-JefR1
October First. Philip Whalen. SP-WhalP
October 5, 1981. James Schuyler. CP-SchuJ
October Frost. Sam Hamill. SP-HamiS
October Garden, An. Christina Georgina Rossetti. CP-RosC2
October hangs in grape. Evening Wind. James Schuyler. CP-SchuJ
October. Here in this dank, unfamiliar kitchen. Photograph of My Father in His Twenty-second Year. Raymond Carver. CP-CarvR
October in Bloomsbury. Louis MacNeice. CP-MacNL

October in Hyde Park. Derek Mahon. CP-MahoD
October in mission creep, / autumnal reprise and stand down. October 2. Charles Wright. SP-WrigCN
October is marigold, and yet. October Dawn. Ted Hughes. SP-HughTN
October is the treasurer of the year. October. Paul Laurence Dunbar. CP-DunbP
October Maples, Portland. Richard Wilbur. CP-WilbR
October 19. Andrei Codrescu. SP-CodrA
October 1973. Carolyn Kizer. CP-KizeC
October-November. Hart Crane. CP-CranH
October Paint. Carl Sandburg. CP-SandC
October Picnic Long Ago. Robert Penn Warren. CP-WarrR
October Salmon[, An]. Ted Hughes. SP-HughTN
October 17. Andrei Codrescu. SP-CodrA
October 16: The Raid. Langston Hughes. CP-HughL; CP-HughL2; CP-HughL3
(Perhaps today.) CP-HughL2
October Song. Tennessee Williams. CP-WillT
October sun warms our faces, The. Yehuda Amichai. SP-AmicY, tr. by Chana Bloch *Fr.* Songs of Zion the Beautiful.
October 10. Wendell Berry. CP-BerrW
October Textures. May Swenson. SP-SwenM
October: the falling leaves resume the earth. Autumnal. Howard Nemerov. CP-NemeH
October Tune. Joseph Brodsky. CP-BrodJ, tr. by Joseph Brodsky
October 21, 1905. George Meredith. CP-MerG2
October. Twilight / flutters like cloth of silver. Hayden Carruth. CP-CarHS *Fr.* Clay Hill Anthology, The.
October Week-End. Robinson Jeffers. CP-JefR2
October woods, wherein. Ralph Waldo Emerson. CP-EmerR
Octopus, An. Marianne Craig Moore. CP-MoorM
Octopus, The. James Merrill. SP-MerrJ
Octopus, The. Ogden Nash. CP-NashO
Octopus is a solitary creature, and for it, The. Art of the Octopus: Variations on a Found Theme, The. Denise Levertov. SP-LeveDL
Octopus would be my model—, The. If I Could Be like Wallace Stevens. William Stafford. SP-StafW; SP-StafWW
Odd planet, and those on it are odd, too, An. People on the Bridge, The. Wisława Szymborska. SP-SzymW, tr. by Stanislaw Barańczak *and* Clare Cavanagh
Odd stillness of your body, The. Clutter-up People. Alice Walker. CP-WalkA
Odd, that Mozart, the frock-coated. XIX, The. Pablo Neruda. SP-NeruP
Odd—the Gnostic. Asphodels. Hans Magnus Enzensberger. SP-EnzeH, tr. by Rita Dove *and* Fred Viebahn
Odd, the inward turned, the isolated, The. They Never Were Found. Josephine Jacobsen. CP-JacoJ
Odd we've never met there. Dream Habitués, The. Josephine Jacobsen. CP-JacoJ
Oddjob, a Bull Terrier. Derek Walcott. CP-WalcD
Oddly Lovely Day Alone, An. John Updike. CP-UpdiJ
Odds can be terribly tempting, The. All the same. Caution. Miller Williams. CP-WillM
Ode: "Ask me no more." Olga Broumas. SP-BrouO
Ode: "Bards of passion and of mirth." John Keats. CP-KeatJ
Ode. Fernando Pessoa.
"Come, selfsame and ageless Night." SP-PessF
Ode: "Idea of justice may be precious, An." Frank O'Hara. SP-OharF
Ode: "If men, and times were now." Ben Jonson. CP-JonsB; SP-JonsB
Ode: "Night in May!, A." Wallace Stevens. CP-StevWP
Ode: "O, God of Columbia! O, Shield of the Free!" Walt Whitman. CP-WhitW
oDE: "O / the sweet & aged people." E. E. Cummings. CP-CummE
Ode: "So long as memory, valour, and faith endure." Rudyard Kipling. CP-KiplR
Ode: "Though aware of our rank and alert to obey orders." W. H. Auden. CP-AudeW
Ode: "To-night is so coarse with chocolate." Louis MacNeice. CP-MacNL
Ode: "Who rises on the banks of Seine." William Wordsworth. CP-WorW2
Ode, An: "At length revolving fates th' expected year." Francis Williams. CP-WheaP
Ode, An: "Early Queen of Light arise." Thomas Sheridan. CP-SherT
Ode, An: "Helen, did Homer never see." Ben Jonson. CP-JonsB; SP-JonsB
Ode, An: "High-spirited friend." Ben Jonson. CP-JonsB; SP-JonsB
Ode, An: "I'm going to write a novel, hey." John Updike. CP-UpdiJ
Ode, An: "Stern winter now, by spring repress'd." Samuel Johnson. CP-JohnS
Ode, An. *Unknown, sometimes at. to* Thomas Sheridan.
"See! the sacred scion springs." CP-SherT
Ode, An: "Yes tis an easy thing to view." Annis Boudinot Stockton. CP-StocA
Ode Allegoric. Ben Jonson. CP-JonsB
Ode and Elegy of the Roads. Constantine P. Cavafy. CP-CavaC, tr. by Theoharis Constantine Theoharis

Ode Composed on May Morning. William Wordsworth. CP-WorW2

Ode, De Skia Insula. Samuel Johnson. CP-JohnS

Ode: 1815. William Wordsworth. CP-WorW2

Ode: 1814. William Wordsworth. CP-WorW2

Ode Enthusiastic. Ben Jonson. CP-JonsB

Ode for Christmas Day, An. Annis Boudinot Stockton. CP-StocA

Ode [for General Washington's Birthday]. Robert Burns. CP-BurnR

Ode for Him [or Ben Jonson], An. Robert Herrick. CP-HerrR

Ode for Memorial Day. Paul Laurence Dunbar. CP-DunbP

Ode for Music. Thomas Gray. CP-GrayT

Ode for Music on St. Cecilia's Day. Alexander Pope. CP-PopeA

Ode for School Convocation. John Ciardi. CP-CiarJ

Ode for Ted. Sylvia Plath. CP-PlatS

Ode for the American Dead in Asia. Thomas McGrath. *See* Ode for the American Dead in Korea

Ode for the American Dead in Korea. Thomas McGrath. SP-McGrT
    (Ode for the American Dead in Asia.) SP-McGrT

Ode for the Eightieth Birthday of Pope John Paul II. Czeslaw Milosz. CP-MiloCN, *tr. by* Robert Hass

Ode for You. Philip Whalen. SP-WhalP

Ode from the French. Lord Byron. CP-Byron

Ode in the Manner of Anacreon, An. Samuel Taylor Coleridge. CP-ColeS

Ode, Inscribed to W.H. Channing. Ralph Waldo Emerson. CP-EmerR

Ode. Intimations of Immortality from Recollections of Early Childhood. William Wordsworth. CP-WorW1; MW-WorW

Ode: My 24th Year. Allen Ginsberg. CP-GinsA

Ode of Verses on the Much-lamented Death of the Rev. Mr. George Whitefield, Late Chaplain to the Countess of Huntingdon, An. Phillis Wheatley. *See* On the Death of the Rev. Mr. George Whitefield [1770]

Ode on a Distant Prospect of Eton College. Thomas Gray. CP-GrayT

Ode on a Grecian Urn. John Keats. CP-KeatJ

Ode on a Lady Leaving Her Place of Abode; Almost Impromptu, An. Samuel Johnson. CP-JohnS

Ode on a Prayer-Book. Richard Crashaw. CP-CrasR

Ode on Causality. Frank O'Hara. SP-OharF

Ode on Friendship, An. Samuel Johnson. CP-JohnS

Ode on Independence Day, July 4th 1918. T. S. Eliot. SP-ElioT

Ode on Indolence. John Keats. CP-KeatJ

Ode on Melancholy. John Keats. CP-KeatJ

Ode on Nativity, An. Charles Olson. CP-OlsoC; SP-OlsoC

Ode on Necrophilia. Frank O'Hara. SP-OharF

Ode on *Sir Charles Grandison*. William Cowper. CP-CowpW

Ode on Solitude. Alexander Pope. CP-PopeA

Ode on the Birth Day of the Illustrious George Washington President of the United States, An. Annis Boudinot Stockton. CP-StocA

Ode on the Birth of Our Saviour, An. Robert Herrick. CP-HerrR

Ode on the Death of a Favo[u]rite Cat, Drowned in a Tub [or Bowl] of Gold Fishes. Thomas Gray. CP-GrayT

Ode on the Death of a Lady. Vincent Bourne. CP-CowpW

Ode on the Death of the Duke of Wellington. Alfred Tennyson. CP-TennA

Ode on the Departing Year. Samuel Taylor Coleridge. CP-ColeS
    (Ode to the Departing Year.) MW-ColeS

Ode on the Installation of His Royal Highness Prince Albert as Chancellor of the University of Cambridge, July, 1847. William Wordsworth. CP-WorW2

Ode on the Marriage of a Friend. William Cowper. CP-CowpW

Ode on the Ottery and Tiverton Church Music. Samuel Taylor Coleridge. CP-ColeS

Ode on the Pleasure Arising from Vicissitude. Thomas Gray. CP-GrayT

Ode on the Spring. Thomas Gray. CP-GrayT

Ode on Venice. Lord Byron. CP-Byron

Ode, or Psalme, to God, An. Robert Herrick. CP-HerrR

Ode, or Song, by All the Muses, An. Ben Jonson. CP-JonsB

Ode, Sacred to the Memory of Mrs. ———— of ————. Robert Burns. CP-BurnR

Ode: Salute to the French Negro Poets. Frank O'Hara. SP-OharF

Ode: Secundum Artem, An. William Cowper. CP-CowpW

Ode Sung in the Town Hall. Ralph Waldo Emerson. CP-EmerR

Ode: The Dying Christian to His Soul. Alexander Pope. CP-PopeA

Ode: The Morning of the Day Appointed for a General Thanksgiving. January 18, 1816. William Wordsworth. CP-WorW2

Ode to a Bird. Czeslaw Milosz. CP-MiloC; CP-MiloCN, *tr. by* Robert Pinsky

Ode to a Drum. Yusef Komunyakaa. CP-KomuY

Ode to a Lady Whose Lover Was Killed by a Ball, Which at the Same Time Shivered a Portrait next His Heart. Lord Byron. CP-Byron

Ode to a Nightingale. John Keats. CP-KeatJ

Ode to Admiral Sir George Pocock. Christopher Smart. SP-SmarC

Ode to All Rebels. Hugh MacDiarmid.

"I mind when ny first wife died." SP-MacDH

"Think not that I forget a single pang." SP-MacDH

Ode, to Amanda, An. Annis Boudinot Stockton. CP-StocA

Ode to Apollo. William Cowper. CP-CowpW

Ode to Apollo. John Keats. CP-KeatJ

Ode to Apollo. William Wordsworth. CP-WorW1

Ode to Arnold Schoenberg. Charles Tomlinson. CP-TomlC; SP-TomlC

Ode to Beauty. Ralph Waldo Emerson. CP-EmerR

Ode to Concrete. Joseph Brodsky. CP-BrodJ

Ode to Constantius. Annis Boudinot Stockton. CP-StocA

Ode to Curiosity. Andrei Codrescu. SP-CodrA

Ode to Dinah. Langston Hughes. CP-HughL; CP-HughL3

Ode to Doctor Smith on His Birth Day March the 16th, 1791, An. Annis Boudinot Stockton. CP-StocA

Ode to Dr. William Sancroft. Jonathan Swift. CP-SwifJ

Ode to Duty. William Wordsworth. CP-WorW1; MW-WorW

Ode to Ethiopia. Paul Laurence Dunbar. CP-DunbP

Ode to Failure. Allen Ginsberg. CP-GinsA

Ode to Fear. Allen Tate. CP-TateA

Ode to Freedom. Jones Very. CP-VeryJ

Ode to Gaea. W. H. Auden. CP-AudeW

Ode to Garlic. William Stafford. SP-StafWW

Ode to General Draper. Christopher Smart. SP-SmarC

Ode to Georgiana, Duchess of Devonshire. Samuel Taylor Coleridge. CP-ColeS

Ode to Heaven. Percy Bysshe Shelley. CP-ShelP

Ode to Hengist and Horsa. Robinson Jeffers. CP-JefR3

Ode to H.I.M. Napoleon 3d. George Meredith. CP-MerG2

Ode to Himself, An. Ben Jonson. CP-JonsB; SP-JonsB

Ode to Himself[e]. Ben Jonson. CP-JonsB
    (On *The New Inn*: Ode. To Himself.) SP-JonsB

Ode to Innocence. Eleanor Wilner. SP-WilnE

Ode to James, Earl of Desmond, An. Ben Jonson. CP-JonsB

Ode (to Joseph Lesueur) on the Arrow That Flieth by Day. Frank O'Hara. SP-OharF

Ode to Lady Harriot. Christopher Smart. SP-SmarC

Ode to Laryngitis. Andrei Codrescu. SP-CodrA

Ode to Laziness. Pablo Neruda. CP-WilW2, *tr. by* William Carlos Williams

Ode to Liberty. Percy Bysshe Shelley. CP-ShelP

Ode to Liberty. Rudyard Kipling. CP-KiplR
    (Greek National Anthem, The.) CP-KiplR

Ode to Liberty. Percy Bysshe Shelley. CP-ShelP

Ode to Lycoris. William Wordsworth. CP-WorW2

Ode to Lycoris; May, 1817. William Wordsworth. CP-WorW2

Ode to Master Endymion Porter, upon His Brother's Death, An. Robert Herrick. CP-HerrR

Ode to May. Fragment. John Keats. *See* Fragment of an Ode to Maia Written on May Day, 1818

Ode to Michael Goldberg ('s Birth and Other Births). Frank O'Hara. SP-OharF

Ode to Music, The. Philip Whalen. SP-WhalP

Ode to Naples. Percy Bysshe Shelley. CP-ShelP

Ode to Napoleon Buonaparte. Lord Byron. CP-Byron

Ode to Neptune. Phillis Wheatley. CP-WheaP

Ode to Our Young Pro-consuls of the Air. Allen Tate. CP-TateA

Ode to Peace. William Cowper. CP-CowpW

Ode to Pity. Jane Austen. CP-AustJ

Ode to Pleasure. Richard Wilbur. CP-WilbR

Ode to Plurality. Adam Zagajewski. SP-ZagaA, *tr. by* Renata Gorczynski

Ode to Psyche. John Keats. CP-KeatJ

Ode to Rouse. John Milton. *See* To John Rouse

Ode to Salvador Dalí. Federico García Lorca. CP-GarcF, *tr. by* William Bryant Logan

Ode to Silence. Richard Eberhart. CP-EberR

Ode to Silence. Edna St. Vincent Millay. CP-MillE

Ode to Sir Clipsebie Crew, An. Robert Herrick. CP-HerrR

Ode. To Sir William Sydney, on His Birthday. Ben Jonson. CP-JonsB; SP-JonsB

Ode (to Sleep. Samuel Taylor Coleridge. CP-ColeS

Ode to Softness. Adam Zagajewski. SP-ZagaA, *tr. by* Renata Gorczynski

Ode to Solitude Inscribed to Mrs Boudinot, An. Annis Boudinot Stockton. CP-StocA

Ode to Spring. Robert Burns. CP-BurnR

Ode to Tanaquil Leclercq: "Smiling through my own memories of painful excitement your wide eyes." Frank O'Hara. SP-OharF

Ode to Terminus. W. H. Auden. CP-AudeW

Ode to the Athenian Society. Jonathan Swift. CP-SwifJ

Ode to the Chinese Paper Snake. Richard Eberhart. CP-EberR

Ode to the Confederate Dead. Allen Tate. CP-TateA

Ode to the Departed Regency-Bill—1789. Robert Burns. CP-BurnR

Ode to the Departing Year. Samuel Taylor Coleridge. *See* Ode on the Departing Year

Ode to the Diencephalon. W. H. Auden. CP-AudeW

Ode to the Framers of the Frame Bill, An. Lord Byron. CP-Byron

Ode to the Honourable Sir William Temple. Jonathan Swift. CP-SwifJ

Ode to the King. Jonathan Swift. CP-SwifJ

Ode to the Medieval Poets. W. H. Auden. CP-AudeW

Ode to the Most Holy Sacrament of the Altar. Federico García Lorca. CP-GarcF, *tr. by* Greg Simon *and* Steven F. White

Ode to the Present Century. Thomas Merton. CP-MertT

Ode to the Rain, An. Samuel Taylor Coleridge. CP-ColeS

Ode to the Setting Sun. Allen Ginsberg. CP-GinsA

Ode to the Spectral Thief, Alpha. Norman Dubie. CP-DubiN

Ode to the Spirit of Earth in Autumn. George Meredith. CP-MerG1

Ode to the Swallow. Elizabeth Barrett Browning. CP-BroEB

Ode to the West Wind. Percy Bysshe Shelley. CP-ShelP

Ode to Tranquillity. Samuel Taylor Coleridge. CP-ColeS

Ode to Walt Whitman. Federico García Lorca. SP-GarcF, *tr. by* J. L. Gili *and* Stephen Spender

Ode to Walt Whitman. Federico García Lorca. CP-GarcF, *tr. by* Greg Simon *and* Steven F. White

Ode Written in 1966. Jorge Luis Borges. SP-BorgJ, *tr. by* W. S. Merwin

Ode Written October, 1819, An. Percy Bysshe Shelley. CP-ShelP

Ode—Written 1756, An. Annis Boudinot Stockton. CP-StocA

Odes. Hafiz.

  "Ah, could I hide me in my song." CP-EmerR

  "Alas! till now I had not known." CP-EmerR

  "All day the rain." CP-EmerR

  "And had Hafiz." CP-EmerR

  "And since round lines are drawn." CP-EmerR

  "Art thou wise, four things resign." CP-EmerR

  "Blame me not thou hoarse preacher." CP-EmerR

  "Boy bring the bowl full of wine." CP-EmerR

  "Bring wine release me." CP-EmerR

  "Builder of heaven, The." CP-EmerR

  "By breath of beds of roses drawn." CP-EmerR

  "Chemist of love, The." CP-EmerR

  "Come let us strew roses." CP-EmerR

  "Come!—the palace of heaven rests on aëry pillars." CP-EmerR

  "Desire no bread, forsake the guest hall of the earth." CP-EmerR

  "Drink, hear my counsel, my son, that the world fret thee not." CP-EmerR

  "Drink till the turbans are all unbound." CP-EmerR

  "Drink wine, and the heaven." CP-EmerR

  "Early after the night long revel." CP-EmerR

  "Fair fall thy soft heart!" CP-EmerR

  "Fit for the Pleiads' azure chord." CP-EmerR

  "For his constant dwelling place has Hafiz." CP-EmerR

  "Free thyself from wo." CP-EmerR

  "Good is what goes on the road of Nature." CP-EmerR

  "Hafiz since on the world." CP-EmerR

  "Hafiz thou art from Eternity." CP-EmerR

  "Has thine enemy slandered thy house." CP-EmerR

  "Hear what the glass will tell thee." CP-EmerR

  "High heart, O Hafiz! though not thine." CP-EmerR

  "His learning truly lifted Hafiz to Heaven." CP-EmerR

  "I am: what I am." CP-EmerR

  "I batter the wheel of heaven." CP-EmerR

  "I have no hoarded treasure." CP-EmerR

  "I know this perilous love-lane." CP-EmerR

  "I never went out of my country." CP-EmerR

I said to heaven that glowed above.

  From Hafiz. CP-EmerR

  "If my darling should depart." CP-EmerR

  "I said to the East wind." CP-EmerR

  "I shall go from my sickbed to heaven." CP-EmerR

  "I will be drunk and down with wine." CP-EmerR

  "If thy darling favor thee." CP-EmerR

  "In bounding youth the night & train." CP-EmerR

  "In the kingdom of Poesy Hafiz waves like a banner." CP-EmerR

  "In thy holiday of life." CP-EmerR

  "It is certain that who his mind." CP-EmerR

  "Knowst thou the luck the friends face to see." CP-EmerR

  "Lament not, o Hafiz, the distribution." CP-EmerR

  "Lo! where from Heaven's high roof." CP-EmerR

  "Loose the knots of the heart; never think on thy fate." CP-EmerR

  "Many our needs, yet we spare prayers." CP-EmerR

  "Ninefold table of Heaven, The." CP-EmerR

  "No physician has a balsam for my wo." CP-EmerR

  "Novice, hear me what I say." CP-EmerR

  "Now tells the flower." CP-EmerR

  "O follow the sonnet's flight." CP-EmerR

  "O friend blame not Hafiz." CP-EmerR

  "O Hafiz, give me thought." CP-EmerR

  "O Hafiz! speak not of thy need." CP-EmerR

  "Oft have I said, I say it once more." CP-EmerR

  "Our Shah's counsel is the efflux." CP-EmerR

  "Out of the East, and out of the West, no man understands me." CP-EmerR

Phoenix, The. CP-EmerR

  "Plunge in yon angry waves." CP-EmerR

  "Prince the ball of heaven should." CP-EmerR

  "Reach me wine No counsel weakens the conclusion of the lot." CP-EmerR

  "Red rose blooms, The." CP-EmerR

  "Roguish wind and I, The." CP-EmerR

  "Ruler after word & thought." CP-EmerR

  "Secretly to love & to drink, what is it? tis a dissolute day's work." CP-EmerR

  "See & hear the fraud, the malice of the change of fortune." CP-EmerR

  "See how the roses burn!" CP-EmerR

  "Should I shed my tears." CP-EmerR

  "Since you set no worth on the heart." CP-EmerR

  "So long as there's a trace." CP-EmerR

  "Spare thou neither time nor blood for thy friend." CP-EmerR

  "Stand up, that we may sacrifice the soul." CP-EmerR

  "Stately bride is the shining world, A." CP-EmerR

  "Take my heart in thy hand, O beautiful boy of Schiraz!" CP-EmerR

  "There resides in the grieving." CP-EmerR

  "They strew in the path of kings and czars." CP-EmerR

  "This effervescing gentleman who despises a secret." CP-EmerR

  "Thou who with thy long hair." CP-EmerR

  "Thousand dangers of ruin has the street of love." CP-EmerR

  "Thy poems Hafiz shame the rose leaves." CP-EmerR

  "Thy songs O Hafiz." CP-EmerR

  "'Tis write on Paradise's gate." CP-EmerR

  "To be wise the dull brain so earnestly throbs." CP-EmerR

  "To whom a glass full of red wine." CP-EmerR

  "Treacherous wind pipes a lewd song, The." CP-EmerR

  "Understanding's copper coin, The." CP-EmerR

  "Untruth is become the mode." CP-EmerR

  "Way of love is unlimited, The." CP-EmerR

  "We wish like the glass." CP-EmerR

  "We would do nought but good." CP-EmerR

  "What lovelier forms things wear." CP-EmerR

  "When in eternity the light." CP-EmerR

  "Where o where is the message which today." CP-EmerR

  "Who compares a poem." CP-EmerR

  "Who dedicates himself to the glass." CP-EmerR

  "Who ever suffered as I from separation?" CP-EmerR

  "Who gave thy cheek the mixed tint." CP-EmerR

  "Who royally bedded." CP-EmerR

  "Wine resembles the Lord Jesus." CP-EmerR

  "World is a bride superbly dressed, The." CP-EmerR

  "Yet all comes out of this, that one door." CP-EmerR

Odes. Horace.

  "Brasen tower [*or* Tower] with doors [*or* dores] close barred [*or* bar'd], The." CP-RaleW

Ode 1.1: To Maecenas: "Maecenas, of a race renown'd." SP-SmarC

Ode 1.2: How to Live. CP-MahoD

Ode 1.3: To the Ship in Which Virgil Sailed to Athens: "So may the [*or* th'] auspicious Queen of love." CP-DryJ2, *tr. by* John Dryden

Ode 1.4: "Fetters of winter are shattered,shatter, The." CP-CummE

Ode 1.4: "Grateful change! Favonius, and the spring, A." SP-SmarC

Ode 1.5: "What slender youth bedewed [*or* bedew'd] with liquid odours." CP-MiltJ, *tr. by* John Milton

  (Fifth Ode of Horace, The.) CP-MiltJ

Ode 1.9: "See how resplendent in deep snow." CP-CunnJ

Ode 1.9: "See'st thou yon mountains laden with deep snow." CP-CowpW

Ode 1.9: To Thaliarchus. CP-DryJ2

Ode 1.22: Translations of Horace ("Integer vitae"). CP-JohnS

  (To Aristius Fuscus.) CP-JohnS

Ode 1.24: "I mist my end, and lost my way." CP-JohnS

Ode 1.24: "Who chides the tears that weep so dear a head?." CP-CummE

Ode 1.38: Simplicity. CP-CowpW; CP-HopkG

("Ah child, no Persian—perfect art.") CP-HopkG, *tr. by* Gerard Manley Hopkins

(Another Translation of the Same Ode.) CP-CowpW, *tr. by* William Cowper

("Boy! I detest all Persian fopperies.") CP-CowpW, *tr. by* William Cowper

(Horace: Persicos Odi, Puer, Apparatus.) CP-HopkG, *tr. by* Gerard Manley Hopkins

("Persian pomps, boy, ever I renounce them.") SP-SmarC, *tr. by* Christopher Smart

(To His Servant.) SP-SmarC, *tr. by* Christopher Smart

Ode 2.1: "With heedless feet on fires you go." CP-JohnS

Ode 2.5: "Maid whom now you court in vain, The." CP-JohnS

Ode 2.9: Translation of Horace: *Odes* 2.9. CP-JohnS

Ode 2.10: "Receive, dear friend, the truths I teach." CP-CowpW

Ode 2.14: "Ah, Postumus, fleet-footed are the years!." CP-CummE

("Ah! Posthumus, the years, the years.") SP-SmarC

(To Posthumus.) SP-SmarC

Ode 2.14: Translation of Horace *Odes* 2.14 ("Eheu Fugaces"). CP-JohnS

Ode 2.15: Upon the Luxury of the Age He Lived In. SP-SmarC

Ode 2.16: To Grosphus. SP-SmarC

("Ease is the weary merchant's pray'r.") CP-CowpW

Ode 2.18: "Gold or iv'ry's not intended." SP-SmarC, *tr. by* Christopher Smart

Ode 2.20: Translation of Horace: *Odes* 2.20. CP-JohnS

Ode 3.1: "Tread back—and back, the lewd and lay."

(Horace: Odi Profanum Volgus Et Arceo.) CP-HopkG

Ode 3.2: "Seldome the villaine, though much hast he make." CP-RaleW

Ode 3.2: "Stranger to folly and to fear." CP-JohnS

Ode 3.4: "Who rules the duller earth, the wind-swolne streames." CP-RaleW

Ode 3.7: "To taint th'attentive mind she tries." CP-JohnS

Ode 3.9: Dialogue between Horace and Lydia, A ("Donec gratus eram"). CP-HerrR, *tr. by* Robert Herrick

Ode 3.9: To Lydia. Dialogue of Horace and Lydia. CP-JonsB

Ode 3.12: To Neobule. SP-SmarC

Ode 3.13: Translation of Horace's Ode 3.13. CP-WorW1

Ode 3.16: "By gifts the Macedon clave Gates a-sunder." CP-RaleW

Ode 3.16: To Maecenas. SP-SmarC

Ode 3.22: Pine Tree for Diana, The ("Montium custos nemorumque"). SP-SmarC

("Queen of the mountains far and near.") SP-SmarC

Ode 3.23: "If rustic Phidyle her prayer renews." CP-JohnS

Ode 3.24: "He whom the dread of want ensnares." CP-JohnS

Ode 3.24: "Nor Southerne heat nor Northerne snow." CP-RaleW

Ode 3.29: To Maecenas. CP-DryJ2, *tr. by* John Dryden

Ode 4.1: To Venus. CP-JonsB

Ode 4.2: Praise of Pindar, The ("Pindarum quisquis studet aemulari"). SP-SmarC

(To Antonius Julus, the Son of Mark Antony, to the Triumvirate.) SP-SmarC

("Whoever vies with Pindar's strain.") SP-SmarC

Ode 4.2: "Such as like heavenly wights doe come." CP-RaleW

Ode 4.3: To Melpomene. SP-SmarC

Ode 4.6: "O, blessed of the gods." CP-CummE

Ode 4.7: "Farewell,runaway snows! For the meadow is green,and the tree stands." CP-CummE

Ode 4.7: "Snow dissolv'd no more is seen, The." CP-JohnS, *tr. by* Samuel Johnson

("Melted snow the verdure now restores, The.") SP-SmarC

(To L. Manlius Torquatus.) SP-SmarC

(Translation of Horace *Odes* IV vii ("Diffugere nives").) CP-JohnS

Ode 4.9: "Many by valour have deserved renown." CP-RaleW

Ode 4.11: To Phyllis. SP-SmarC

Out of Horace. CP-CrasR

Odessa Steps, The. Amy Clampitt. CP-ClamA

Odor from a star, An. Carnet de Voyage. Wallace Stevens. CP-StevWP

Odor of charred embers penetrates, The. Crossing the Pedregal. Helen Pinkerton. CP-PinkH

Odor of death everywhere. Downwind. Clarence Major. SP-MajoC

Odorous bush I seek, An. Wallace Stevens. CP-StevWP

Odour, The. (2 Corinthians 2). George Herbert. CP-HerbG

Odour from the flower is gone, The. On a Faded Violet. Percy Bysshe Shelley. CP-ShelP

O'Driscoll drove with a song. Host of the Air, The. William Butler Yeats. CP-YeatW

Odysseus Encircled. Homer. CP-MerG2 *Fr.* Iliad, The.

Odysseus on Hermes. Thom Gunn. CP-GunnT

Odysseus, Penelope. World Is Not a Meditation, The. Eleanor Wilner. SP-WilnE

Odysseus to Telemachus. Joseph Brodsky. CP-BrodJ, *tr. by* George L. Kline

Odyssey. Homer.

Daughters of Pandarus, The. CP-BroEB, *tr. by* Elizabeth Barrett Browning

("So the storms bore the daughters of Pandarus out into thrall.") CP-BroEB, *tr. by* Elizabeth Barrett Browning

Gardens of Alcinous, The. CP-PopeA, *tr. by* Alexander Pope

"Mindes of men are ever so affected, The." CP-RaleW, *tr. by* Sir Walter Ralegh

"Muse, / tell me of this man of wit." CP-DoolH, *tr. by* "H.D."

"Sun descending, the *Phæacian* train, The." CP-PopeA, *tr. by* Alexander Pope

Odyssey. Tennessee Williams. CP-WillT

Odyssey, Book Twenty-three. Jorge Luis Borges. SP-BorgJ, *tr. by* Robert Fitzgerald

Oeconomia Divina. Czeslaw Milosz. CP-MiloC; CP-MiloCN

Oedipean Mom and Dad, An. James Vincent Cunningham. CP-CunnJ

Oedipus. Constantine P. Cavafy. CP-CavaC, *tr. by* Theoharis Constantine Theoharis

Oedipus. Richard Eberhart. CP-EherR

Oedipus and the Enigma. Jorge Luis Borges. SP-BorgJ, *tr. by* Alan S. Trueblood

Oedipus at Colonus. Sophocles.

Chorus: "What man is he that yearneth." CP-HousA

Colonus' Praise. CP-YeatW

"Stranger, this is shining Colonos." CP-SpenS

Oedipus Reformed. David Ignatow. SP-IgnaD

Oedipus Rex [*or* Oedipus the King, *or* Oedipus Tyrannus]. Sophocles. "O thrilling voice of Zeus." CP-SpenS

Oedipus slew his father near this muddy field. On the Way to Delphi. John Updike. CP-UpdiJ

Oedipus Tyrannus. John Ciardi. CP-CiarJ

Oedipus Tyrannus; or, Swellfoot the Tyrant. Percy Bysshe Shelley. CP-ShelP

Œnone. Alfred Tennyson. CP-TennA

O'er all the city comes a glow. Sunset after a Clouded Day in April. Jones Very. CP-VeryJ

O'er Ice the rapid Skaiter flies. Translations of Roy's Verses on Skaters. Samuel Johnson. CP-JohnS

O'er the bare woods, whose outstretched hands. Last Walk in Autumn, The. John Greenleaf Whittier. CP-WhitJ

O'er the garden water goes the wind alone. "Anvari." CP-EmerR

O'er the glad waters of the dark blue sea. Corsair, The. Lord Byron. CP-Byron

O'er the night-black city gazing, broken by the blaze and spark. Humanity ("O'er the night-black city gazing, broken by the blaze and spark.") G. K. Chesterton. CP-ChesG

O'er the raised earth the gales of evening sigh. Fragment: "O'er the raised earth the gales of evening sigh." Samuel Taylor Coleridge. CP-ColeS

O'er the Water to Charlie. Robert Burns. CP-BurnR

O'er the wide earth, on mountain and on plain. William Wordsworth. CP-WorW1

O'er wayward childhood would'st thou hold firm rule. Love, Hope, and Patience in Education. Samuel Taylor Coleridge. CP-ColeS

O'erhung with yew, midway the Muses mount. Mighty Fountain, A. Samuel Taylor Coleridge. CP-ColeS

O'erweening Statesmen have full long relied. 1810. William Wordsworth. CP-WorW1

O'Erwhelming sorrow now demands my song. To a Lady and Her Children, on the Death of Her Son and Their Brother. Phillis Wheatley. CP-WheaP

Of a few years. Of Years. Robert Creeley. CP-CreeR

Of a green color, standing in a shed alongside rakes and spades. Watering Can. Czeslaw Milosz. CP-MiloCN, *tr. by* Robert Hass

Of a Lady Singing to Her Lute. Alexander Pope. CP-PopeA

Of a Ministry pitiful, angry, mean. On Sir Home Popham's Sentence—April 1807. Jane Austen. CP-AustJ

Of a Son. Walter De la Mare. CP-DeLaW

Of a steady winking beat between. Paraphrase. Hart Crane. CP-CranH

Of a Sun She Can Remember. Eleanor Wilner. SP-WilnE

Of A' the Airts [the Wind Can Blaw]. Robert Burns. CP-BurnR

(I Love My Jean.) CP-BurnR

Of a Vanished Kingdom. Yehuda Amichai. SP-AmicYL, *tr. by* Benjamin Harshav *and* Barbara Harshav

Of a Woman, Dead Young. Dorothy Parker. CP-ParkD

Of a worthy Dublin drapier. Drapier's Ballad, The. Thomas Sheridan. CP-SherT

Of Adam's first wife, Lilith, it is told. Body's Beauty. Dante Gabriel Rossetti. CW-RossD *Fr.* House of Life, The.

Of all among the fallen from on high. Doctor of Billiards. Edwin Arlington Robinson. CP-RobiE

Of all disquiets sorrow is most serene. Reflexive. Hayden Carruth. CP-CarHS

Of all God's creatures give me man. Song for a Temperature of a Hundred and One. Ogden Nash. CP-NashO

Of all good gifts that the Lord lets fall. Best of All. James Whitcomb Riley. CP-RileJ

Of all grandeur that was Solomon's. At the Wailing Wall in Jerusalem. Countee Cullen. CP-CullC

Of all green trees, I love a nevergreen. Blue Spruce. Muriel Rukeyser. CP-RukeM

Of all her appalling virtues, none. Damn Her. John Ciardi. CP-CiarJ

Of all implements, the pitchfork was the one. Pitchfork, The. Seamus Heaney. SP-HeanSO

Of all our antic sights and pageantry. Medal, The. John Dryden. CP-DryJ2

Of all our parts, the eyes expresse. Bashfulnesse. Robert Herrick. CP-HerrR

Of all returns in man's device. Lines with a Pocket Book. Christopher Smart. SP-SmarC

Of all that ever in extreme disease. Edna St. Vincent Millay. CP-MillE

Of all that Orient lands can vaunt. Haschish, The. John Greenleaf Whittier. CP-WhitJ

Of all the birds that rove and sing. Jenny Wren. Walter De la Mare. CP-DeLaW

Of all the blessings which to man. E. E. Cummings. CP-CummE; SP-CummE

Of all the cities in Romanian lands. Theodore and Honoria, from [Fables Ancient and Modern from] Boccace. John Dryden. SP-DrydJ

Of all the disgraceful and abominable things. This Is Disgraceful and Abominable. Stevie Smith. CP-SmitS

Of all the doctors I could cite you to in this-'ere town. Doc Sifers. James Whitcomb Riley. CP-RileJ

Of all the downfalls in the world, / The flutter of an Autumn leaf. Vanity of Vanities. Christina Georgina Rossetti. CP-RosC2

Of all the gods that were. They. James Vincent Cunningham. CP-CunnJ

Of all the good things whatsoe're we do. Robert Herrick. CP-HerrR

Of all the heroes whom the poets sing. Perfection. G. K. Chesterton. CP-ChesG

Of all the numerous ills that hurt our peace. Remorse. Robert Burns. CP-BurnR

Of all the off'rings thanks can find. Epistle to John Sherratt, Esq, An. Christopher Smart. SP-SmarC

Of all the questions you might want to ask. Questions about Angels. Billy Collins. SP-CollB

Of all the rhymes of all the climes. New Year's Nursery Jingle. James Whitcomb Riley. CP-RileJ

Of all the rides since the birth of time. Skipper Ireson's Ride. John Greenleaf Whittier. CP-WhitJ

Of all the sights in Yosemite. Homage to John Muir. John Logan. CP-LogaJ

Of all the Souls that stand create—. Choice. Emily Dickinson. CP-DickE

Of all the Sounds despatched abroad. Wind, The. Emily Dickinson. CP-DickE

Of all the things that I would rather. In Which the Poet Is Ashamed but Pleased. Ogden Nash. CP-NashO

Of all the thoughts of God that are. Sleep, The. Elizabeth Barrett Browning. CP-BroEB

Of all the trees that grow so fair. Tree Song, A. Rudyard Kipling. CP-KiplR Fr. Puck of Pook's Hill.

Of all the twice ten thousand bards. Ballad: "Of all the twice ten thousand bards." Lord Byron. CP-Byron

Of all the ways in which this country. American Cancer Society or There Is More than One Way to Skin a Coon. Audre Lorde. SP-LordA

Of All the World. Laura Riding Jackson. CP-RidiL

Of all things, lady, be not proud. Advice to a Beauty. Countee Cullen. CP-CullC

Of all things under our. E. E. Cummings. CP-CummE

Of all those streets that blur into the sunset [or wander to the west]. Limits. Jorge Luis Borges. SP-BorgJ, tr. by Alastair Reid

Of all those three-brave-brothers, faln i'th'Warre. To the Right Gratious Prince, Lodwick, Duke of Richmond and Lenox. Robert Herrick. CP-HerrR

Of all who hail thy presence as the morning. To M. L. S——. Edgar Allan Poe. CP-PoeEd

Of an Evening Pulling Off a Little Experience (with the english language). Hart Crane. CP-CranH

Of an it ignoblest he, The. E. E. Cummings. CP-CummE

Of appearance / speak in the unchosen. Tongues, The. George Oppen. CP-OppGN

Of asphodel, that greeny flower. Asphodel, That Greeny Flower. William Carlos Williams. CP-WilW2

Of asphodel, that greeny flower, the least. Paterson, Book 5: The River of Heaven. William Carlos Williams. CP-WilW2 Fr. Asphodel, That Greeny Flower.

Of Beginning Light. Charles Tomlinson. CP-TomlC; SP-TomlC

Of Being. Denise Levertov. SP-LeveDS

Of Being is a Bird. Emily Dickinson. CP-DickE

Of Being Numerous. George Oppen. CP-OppGN

Of Being Woven. Jelaluddin Rumi. SP-Rumi, tr. by Coleman Barks

Of both our Fortunes good and bad we find. Felicitie Knowes No Fence. Robert Herrick. CP-HerrR

Of bricks . . . Who built it? Like some crazy balloon. Our Youth. John Ashbery. SP-AshbJ

Of Bright & Blue Birds & the Gala Sun. Wallace Stevens. CP-StevW; CP-StevWP

Of Bronze—and Blaze. Aurora. Emily Dickinson. CP-DickE

Of Brook and Stone. Hayden Carruth. CP-CarHS

Of Brussels—it was not. Emily Dickinson. CP-DickE

Of buildings, this building, / frame a stream of windows. Arches. James Schuyler. CP-SchuJ

Of Carthage he, that worthy warrior. Sir Thomas Wyatt. CP-WyatT

Of Chloe all the town has rung. Strephon and Chloe. Jonathan Swift. CP-SwifJ

Of Colored Glass. Constantine P. Cavafy. CP-CavaC, tr. by Theoharis Constantine Theoharis

Of Coming-into-Being and Passing-Away. Geoffrey Hill. CP-HillG

Of Commerce and Society: Variations on a Theme. Geoffrey Hill. CP-HillG

Of Consciousness, her awful Mate. Emily Dickinson. CP-DickE

Of course across the winter wood. Winter Song. William Meredith. SP-MereW

Of / Course I could go to sleep right here. Metaphysical Insomnia Jazz. Mumonkan XXIX. Philip Whalen. SP-WhalP

Of course I don't say what I really think. Obviously. Czeslaw Milosz. CP-MiloCN, tr. by Brian Glazer and Martin Sabiniewicz

Of course I may be remembering it all wrong. Santarém. Elizabeth Bishop. CP-BishE

Of Course—I prayed. Emily Dickinson. CP-DickE

Of course, if you make naughtiness nasty. Our Moral Age. D. H. Lawrence. CP-LawrD

Of course it sounds cold. More Under Saturn. William Dickey. SP-DickW

Of course, Lou noticed the angels. Rilke and Lou. Thomas Lux. SP-LuxT

Of course make love not. Hayden Carruth. CP-CarHS Fr. Clay Hill Anthology, The.

Of course, mankind—and the brain of it, brawn of it. On Canann Mountain Meadow. Hayden Carruth. CP-CarHS

Of course not all the watchers of the dawn. Longford Dawns. Ivor Gurney. SP-GurnI

"Of course, of course, of course," I heard you intone. Hug, The. Paul Muldoon. CP-MuldP

Of course, of course! Who else would die. Germans Are Lunatics, The. Randall Jarrell. CP-JarrR

Of course the dead outnumber us. Death's Door. Thom Gunn. CP-GunnT

Of course, the entire effort is to put my [or one] self. Thoughts during an Air Raid. Stephen Spender. CP-SpenS

Of course the plane is late. Poet Dreams of a Nice Warm Motel, The. Marge Piercy. SP-PierM

Of course there were. How High the Moon. Adam Zagajewski. SP-ZagaA, tr. by Clare Cavanagh

Of course, we were all fucked-up, I was suicidal but hitting the. Old Gang, The. Charles Bukowski. SP-BukC3

Of course you're dreaming. That's how I got here. Ghost of His Wife Comes to Tell Him How It Is, The. Miller Williams. CP-WillM

Of Cruelty. Ivor Gurney. SP-GurnI

Of Death. Ben Jonson. CP-JonsB; SP-JonsB

Of Death I try to think like this. Emily Dickinson. CP-DickE

Of death / the barber. Death the Barber. William Carlos Williams. CP-WilW1

Of Dimitrios Sotir (162–150 B.C.). Constantine P. Cavafy. CP-CavaC, tr. by Theoharis Constantine Theoharis

Of Distress Being Humiliated by the Classical Chinese Poets. Hayden Carruth. CP-CarHS

Of draftsmanship zero. Strange Are the Products. George Oppen. CP-OppGN

Of dying fall, dead winter, dirty spring. Mist and Rain. Charles Baudelaire. CP-BaudC, tr. by Walter Martin

Of each sad word which is more sorrowful. Christina Georgina Rossetti. CP-RosC2

Of earthly civilization, what shall we say? Tidings. Czeslaw Milosz. CP-MiloC; CP-MiloCN, tr. by Lillian Vallee

Of Eastbourn, Mr. Gell. On the Marriage of Mr. Gell of East Bourn to Miss Gill. Jane Austen. CP-AustJ

Of English blood, of Tuscan birth. Child's Grave at Florence, A. Elizabeth Barrett Browning. CP-BroEB

Of Epigram. Thomas Sheridan. CP-SherT

Of Equality—as if it harm'd me, giving others the same chances and rights as myself—as if it were not indispensible to my own rights that others possess the same. Thought. Walt Whitman. CP-WhitW

Of Ever-Ever Land i speak. E. E. Cummings. CP-CummE; SP-CummE

Of evident invisibles / exquisite the hovering. E. E. Cummings. CP-CummE

Of Experience. Howard Nemerov. CP-NemeH

Of falling leaves and melting. Artful Pose. Maya Angelou. SP-AngeM

Of Fields with dead bestrew'd around. Upon the Feast of St Simon and St Jude. Samuel Johnson. CP-JohnS

Of Figures Peculiar to Prosody. Thomas Sheridan. CP-SherT

Of Fish and Fishermen. John Ciardi. CP-CiarJ

Of Flanks and Chines of Beefe doth Gorrell boast. Great Boast, Small Rost. Robert Herrick. CP-HerrR

Of Flora did his luster spring. Testa Dell' Effebo. Tennessee Williams. CP-WillT

Of Florence and of Beatrice. Dante at Verona. Dante Gabriel Rossetti. CW-RossD

Of foul matters I must speak. Guido Cavalcanti. CP-CavaG, *tr.* by Marc Cirigliano

Of foure teeth onely Bridget was possest. Upon Bridget. Robert Herrick. CP-HerrR

Of gentle Philips will I ever sing. Three Gentle Shepherds, The. Alexander Pope. CP-PopeA

Of Glory not a Beam is left. Emily Dickinson. CP-DickE

Of God we ask one favor. Emily Dickinson. CP-DickE

Of gold the bread on which he banqueted. Caligula's Dream. John Updike. CP-UpdiJ

Of Grandcourt. Ivor Gurney. SP-GurnI

Of green and hexagonal glass. Bottle, The. Walter De la Mare. CP-DeLaW

Of Grief. May Sarton. SP-SartM

Of Hartford in a Purple Light. Wallace Stevens. CP-StevW; CP-StevWP

Of H[ayley]s birth this was the happy lot. William Blake. CP-BlakW

Of Heaven and Hell. Jorge Luis Borges. SP-BorgJ, *tr.* by Alastair Reid

Of Heaven Considered as a Tomb. Wallace Stevens. CP-StevW; CP-StevWP

Of her arms, this was her sin. Hutch. Anne Sexton. CP-SextA

Of Her Picture. Alexander Pope. CP-PopeA

Of Her Sickness. Alexander Pope. CP-PopeA

Of Her Sighing. Alexander Pope. CP-PopeA

Of Her Walking in a Garden after a Shower. Alexander Pope. CP-PopeA

Of heroes, history, grand events, premises, myths, poems. Few Drops Known, The. Walt Whitman. CP-WhitW

Of Him I Love Day and Night. Walt Whitman. CP-WhitW

Of Him That Was Ready to Perish. Christina Georgina Rossetti. CP-RosC2

Of Himself. William Cowper. CP-CowpW

Of History and Hope. Miller Williams. CP-WillM

Of Hours. George Oppen. CP-OppGN

Of how that current ran in, and turned. Silhouette. John Ashbery. SP-AshbJ

Of ice. Deceptively reserved and flat. Octopus, An. Marianne Craig Moore. CP-MoorM

Of interest to John Calvin and Thomas Aquinas. Why God Permits Evil: For Answers to This Question of Interest to Many Write Bible Answers, Dept. E-7. Miller Williams. CP-WillM

Of it, the trees have the wind willing one thing—pretty feet. On My Side. Kenneth Patchen. CP-PatcK

Of Jacopo del Sellaio. Ezra Pound. CP-PoEar; SP-PounE

Of John Davidson. Hugh MacDiarmid. SP-MacDH

Of Justice—as if Justice could be any thing but the same ample law, expounded by natural judges and saviors. Thought. Walt Whitman. CP-WhitW

Of keeping; the competition of brutal law. O Fill Your Sack with Tiger Cubs. Kenneth Patchen. CP-PatcK

Of Kindness. William Meredith. SP-MereW

Of Knowing the Gender of Nouns by Termination. Thomas Sheridan. Declension 1. CP-SherT

Of Lady Grange. Charles Tomlinson. CP-TomlC; SP-TomlC

Of Lady, of Beauty, of Stream. Charles Olson. CP-OlsoC

Of late, in one of those most weary hours. Garden of Boccaccio, The. Samuel Taylor Coleridge. CP-ColeS

Of late they leave the light on in my entry. Words for Muffin, a Guinea Pig. Robert Lowell. SP-LoweR

Of Late Two Dainties Were before Me Placed. John Keats. CP-KeatJ

Of lead and emerald. Note to Olga (1966), A. Denise Levertov. SP-LeveDP

Of Life and Death. Ben Jonson. CP-JonsB; SP-JonsB

Of life and knowledge. Biblical Tree, The. George Oppen. CP-OppGN

Of Life to own. Emily Dickinson. CP-DickE

Of Love. Robert Herrick. CP-HerrR

Of Love. A Sonnet. Robert Herrick. CP-HerrR

Of love, perhaps, or perhaps of women. Lunar Ironmongery. Jaroslav Seifert. SP-SeifJ, *tr.* by Ewald Osers

Of lovers sad calamities of old. Book 4, Canto 1. Edmund Spenser. CP-Spens *Fr.* Faerie Queene, The.

Of Manners gentle, of Affections mild. On Mr. Gay, in Westminster Abbey, 1732. Alexander Pope. CP-PopeA

Of Many a Smutch'd Deed Reminiscent. Walt Whitman. CP-WhitW

Of Mathilde. Charles Olson. CP-OlsoC

Of me and of my theme think what thou wilt. My Theme. George Meredith. CP-MerG1

Of medium nature, this farouche extreme. Bouquet, The. Wallace Stevens. CP-StevW; CP-StevWP

Of men he would have raised to light he fell. Gordon of Khartoum. George Meredith. CP-MerG1

Of Mere Being. Wallace Stevens. CP-StevWP

Of Merlin wise I learned a song. Merlin's Song. Ralph Waldo Emerson. CP-EmerR

Of moderate height. Magician's Retreat, The. Marianne Craig Moore. CP-MoorM

Of Modern Poetry. Wallace Stevens. CP-StevW; CP-StevWP

Of Money. And the Past. Muriel Rukeyser. CP-RukeM

Of morning, Iowa City, blue. Poem: "Of morning, Iowa City, blue." Ted Berrigan. SP-BerrT

Of mortal Justice if thou scorn the rod. Virgil. CP-JohnS *Fr.* Aeneid [*or* Eneados *or* Aeneis], The.

Of mortal parents is the Hero born. Hofer. William Wordsworth. CP-WorW1

Of mother of sex. When the Glass of My Body Broke. Anne Sexton. CP-SextA

Of Mothers. A. K. Ramanujan. CP-RamaA

Of music, in a cavernous house. Note to Music: Brahms 1st Piano Concerto. William Carlos Williams. CP-WilW2

Of my city the worst that men will ever say is this. They Will Say. Carl Sandburg. SP-SandC

Of:/ my crow / Pluto. To Victor Hugo of My Crow Pluto. Marianne Craig Moore. CP-MoorM

Of My First Love. Hugh MacDiarmid. SP-MacDH

Of my grandmother / who at over eighty. Teachings, The. Robert Creeley. CP-CreeR

Of my heart que les loups se. This Is the Morte Saison. James Laughlin. CP-LaugJ

Of My Life. Christina Georgina Rossetti. CP-RosC3

Of my / soul a street is. E. E. Cummings. CP-CummE

Of my three certainly most impassioned students. Memoir of a One-Armed Harp Teacher. John Ciardi. CP-CiarJ

Of Nature I shall have enough. Emily Dickinson. CP-DickE

Of nearness to her sundered Things. Emily Dickinson. CP-DickE

Of Neptune's empire [*or* Empyre] let us sing. Hymn in Praise of Neptune, A. Thomas Campion. CP-CampT

Of Nicolette. E. E. Cummings. CP-CummE

Of noble minds and noble hearts. John Boyle O'Reilly. Paul Laurence Dunbar. CP-DunbP

Of obedience, faith, adhesiveness. Thought. Walt Whitman. CP-WhitW

Of old sat Freda on the heights. Lines by the Late Lord Tennyson (On Miss Spencer Being Transferred with Her Typewriter from the Study to the Dining Room). G. K. Chesterton. CP-ChesG

Of old, when mummers mummed on Christmas Day. Prologue to the Old Vic Pantomime. G. K. Chesterton. CP-ChesG

Of old with a divided heart. Blessed Are the Peacemakers. G. K. Chesterton. CP-ChesG

Of olden time, when it came to pass. Blood-Money. Walt Whitman. CP-WhitW

Of one scrap of science I've evidence ocular. Verses Trivocular. Samuel Taylor Coleridge. CP-ColeS

Of our religious beliefs. You Didn't Understand. Constantine P. Cavafy. CP-CavaC, *tr.* by Theoharis Constantine Theoharis

Of ownership—as if one fit to own things could not at pleasure enter upon all, and incorporate them into himself or herself. Thoughts. Walt Whitman. CP-WhitW

Of Pacchiarotto, and How He Worked in Distemper. Robert Browning. CP-BroR2

Of Pairs. Josephine Jacobsen. CP-JacoJ

Of Paradise' existence. Emily Dickinson. CP-DickE

Of Paradise, O hermit wise. Ghaselle. Hafiz. CP-EmerR

Of Paul and Silas it is said. Emily Dickinson. CP-DickE

Of people running down the street. Picture, A. Howard Nemerov. CP-NemeH

Of persons arrived at high positions, ceremonies, wealth, scholarships, and the like. Thought. Walt Whitman. CP-WhitW

Of Politics, & Art. Norman Dubie. CP-DubiN

Of Possessions, in Winter. William Meredith. SP-MereW

Of Prosody. Thomas Sheridan.
  "Words from their root their quantity." CP-SherT

Of public opinion. Thoughts. Walt Whitman. CP-WhitW

Of purpose Love chose first for to be blind. Sir Thomas Wyatt. CP-WyatT

Of Pushes Spalt has such a knottie race. Upon Spalt. Robert Herrick. CP-HerrR

Of Quantity Which Depends upon the Authority of the Poets. Thomas Sheridan. CP-SherT

Of rhymes I printed seven volumes. E Nihilo Nihil. Lord Byron. CP-Byron

Of rights and of wrongs. Mrs. Choate's House-Warming. John Greenleaf Whittier. CP-WhitJ

Of Robert Frost. Gwendolyn Brooks. SP-BrooG

Of Robin Redbreast's babes I told. George Meredith. CP-MerG2

Of Roses. Tennessee Williams. CP-WillT

Of Rounds. May Swenson. SP-SwenM

Of sailors—those two Corsicans at Marseille. Traveller Born, A. Hart Crane. CP-CranH

Of seven sparrows on a country wire. Minus One. John Ciardi. CP-CiarJ

Of Silken Speech and Specious Shoe. Emily Dickinson. CP-DickE

Of simple choice they are the villagers; their clothes come. Adrienne Rich. SP-RicA2 *Fr.* Shooting Script.

Of Small Delights in Idleness. William Corbett. SP-CorbW

Of so divine a Loss. Emily Dickinson. CP-DickE

Of such deadly ancestry. Volkswagen. George Oppen. CP-OppGN

Of Suicide. John Berryman. CP-BerrJ

Of That Blithe Throat of Thine. Walt Whitman. CP-WhitW

Of That Fire. David Ignatow. SP-IgnaD

Of that gentleman with the sallow, dry complexion. Readers. Jorge Luis Borges. SP-BorgJ, *tr.* by Alastair Reid

Of that short Roll of friends writ in my heart. To Mr I. L. ("Of that short Roll of friends writ in my heart"). John Donne. CP-DonnJ; MW-DonnJ

Of the barn's shadow we declared our field. Grown Men at Touch. Wyatt Prunty. SP-PrunW

Of the beast . . . an angel. Everlasting Contenders, The. Kenneth Patchen. CP-PatcK

Of the birds which in wing-voice raise speech. Of All the World. Laura Riding Jackson. CP-RidiL

Of the Courtier's Life. Sir Thomas Wyatt. CP-WyatT *Fr.* Satires.

Of the electric guitar as a percussion instrument. Prayer to the Mountain, A. John Ciardi. CP-CiarJ

Of the Four Ages of Man. Anne Bradstreet. CP-BradA

Of the Four Humors in Man's Constitution. Anne Bradstreet. CP-BradA

Of the four louts who threw him off the dock. Finished Man, A. Richard Wilbur. CP-WilbR

Of the Genders of Nouns. Thomas Sheridan. CP-SherT

Of the goddess there is only the marble shoulder and one. Interrupted, The. Josephine Jacobsen. CP-JacoJ

Of the Great World he knew not much. Epitaph: "Of the Great World he knew not much." Howard Nemerov. CP-NemeH

Of the handsome bluey-brown bodies, they might just as well be gutta-percha. Sea-Bathers. D. H. Lawrence. CP-LawrD

Of the Heart that goes in, and closes the Door. Emily Dickinson. CP-DickE

Of the incertain game. Deposition, The. Howard Nemerov. CP-NemeH

Of the Lady Lu there were stories told. Caricature, The. Thomas Hardy. CP-HardT

Of the Lady Who Could Not Sleep in a Stormy Night. Alexander Pope. CP-PopeA

Of the main-road canal bridge. Long Tunnel Ceiling, The. Ted Hughes. SP-HughTN

Of the many histories, Earth tells only one. Things in the Wild Need Salt. William Stafford. SP-StafWW

Of the million or two, more or less. Instans Tyrannus. Robert Browning. CP-BroR1

Of the North I wove a dream. North and South. James Whitcomb Riley. CP-RileJ

Of the old heroes when the warlike shades. Loyal Scot, The. Andrew Marvell. CP-MarvA

Of the primeval Priests assum'd power. Book of Urizen [*or* First Book of Urizen], The. William Blake. CP-BlakW

Of the Progress of the Soul: The Second Anniversary. John Donne. CP-DonnJ; MW-DonnJ

Of the right way. As to How Much. Louis Zukofsky. CP-ZukLS

Of the same beauty were stars made. Kenneth Patchen. CP-PatcK

Of the Seasons. May Sarton. SP-SartM

Of the Stones of the Place. Robert Frost. CP-FrosR

Of the Surface of Things. Wallace Stevens. CP-StevW; CP-StevWP

Of the Terrible Doubt of Appearances. Walt Whitman. CP-WhitW

Of the three voices, it is hers that stays. Die Älte Frau, Die Älte Marschallin. William Dickey. SP-DickW

Of the three Wise Men. Carol of the Brown King. Langston Hughes. CP-HughL; CP-HughL3

Of the two cardinals the female is both bolder and more "beautiful." She comes. Meditation in the Presence of "Ostrich Walk." Hayden Carruth. CP-CarHS

Of the two flowers growing. Nightmare, The. Laura Riding Jackson. CP-RidiL

Of the two, one / faces one. In. One Way. Robert Creeley. CP-CreeR

Of the United States. Charles Olson. CP-OlsoC

Of the visages of things—And of piercing through to the accepted hells beneath. Thoughts—I: Visages. Walt Whitman. CP-WhitW

Of the wealth of facts and fancies. Friday Afternoon. James Whitcomb Riley. CP-RileJ

Of the Winter Ball Game. Charles Tomlinson. CP-TomlC

Of the world of that passion. To Make Much. George Oppen. CP-OppGN

Of thee, kind boy, I ask no red and white. Sonnet: "Of thee, kind boy, I ask no red and white." Sir John Suckling. CP-SuckJ

Of their peculiar light. Emily Dickinson. CP-DickE

Of the Jews (50 A.D.). Constantine P. Cavafy. CP-CavaC, *tr.* by Theoharis Constantine Theoharis

Of them, undefined / repetitions / inactual, The. It Is at Times. Robert Creeley.

CP-CreeR

Of these two thousand "I" and "We" people. Saladin's Begging Bowl. Jelaluddin Rumi. SP-Rumi, *tr.* by Coleman Barks

Of these years I sing. Thoughts. Walt Whitman. CP-WhitW

Of This All Things. George Oppen. CP-OppGN

Of this / all things. Little Pin, The: Fragment. George Oppen. CP-OppGN

Of this aspiring burgher who disdained. Lasalle. Donald Davie. CP-DaviDC

Of This Cloth Doll Which. Michael Palmer. SP-PalmM

Of this cloth doll which. Of This Cloth Doll Which. Michael Palmer. SP-PalmM

Of this Ensuing Discourse. Thomas Campion. CP-CampT

Of this is Day composed. Emily Dickinson. CP-DickE

Of this profusion. Middle. William Carlos Williams. CP-WilW1

Of this sunset(which is so). E. E. Cummings. CP-CummE

Of this wilting wall the colour drub. E. E. Cummings. CP-CummE

Of those ideas in his head. Little Passion, The ("Of those ideas in his head"). T. S. Eliot. SP-ElioT *Fr.* Agony in the Garret, An.

Of thousands grown climb head-on-head. "X." Louis Zukofsky. CP-ZukLS

Of Three or Four in a Room. Yehuda Amichai. SP-AmicY, *tr.* by Stephen Mitchell

Of tides that toss the souls of men. Turnip-Hoer, The. Thomas Hardy. CP-HardT

Of Tolling Bell I ask the cause? Emily Dickinson. CP-DickE

Of tomorrow I have nothing to say. Night Surf, The. W. S. Merwin. SP-MerwWF

Of Tribulation, these are They. Emily Dickinson. CP-DickE

Of turning a girl into an ikon. Is There a Danger. James Laughlin. CP-LaugJ

Of venture capitalists are. Small Group, A. James Laughlin. CP-LaugJ

Of very funny affairs. Han-shan. CP-ColdM, *tr.* by Red Pine

Of wars o western / wind and storm. Disasters. George Oppen. CP-OppGN

Of waste and again of waste, and of the waste of wasting, o void, o desolation. I Tell You for Several Years of My Madness I Heard the Voice of Lilith Singing in the Trees of Chicago. Hayden Carruth. CP-CarHS

Of western New York state. As You Came from the Holy Land. John Ashbery. SP-AshbJ

Of what an easy quick access. Prayer (2). George Herbert. CP-HerbG

Of what anticipation. Rainer Maria Rilke. CP-RilkFr, *tr.* by A. Poulin, Jr. *Fr.* Affectionate Taxes to France.

Of what I write from myself—As if that were not the resumé. Thoughts—6: "Of What I Write." Walt Whitman. CP-WhitW

Of what importance, O my lovely girls, my dancers, O my lovely boys. Edna St. Vincent Millay. CP-MillE

Of What Is Past. C. K. Williams. CP-WillC; SP-WillC

Of what mould did Nature frame me[?]. Tinder, The. Thomas Carew. CP-CareT

Of which I am the sand—. This Florida: 1924. William Carlos Williams. CP-WilW1

Of white and tawny, black as ink. Variation on a Sentence. Louise Bogan. CP-BogaL

Of who we and all they are. Grapevine, The. John Ashbery. SP-AshbJ

Of whom so dear. Emily Dickinson. CP-DickE

Of whom two will make love. What happens. Here There Are Three of Us Driving South in This Expensive Car. William Dickey. SP-DickW

Of Wickedness the Word. Herman Melville. SP-MelvH *Fr.* Clarel: A Poem and Pilgrimage in the Holy Land.

Of writing many books there is no end. Aurora Leigh. Elizabeth Barrett Browning. CP-BroEB

Of Years. Robert Creeley. CP-CreeR

Of Yellow was the outer Sky. Emily Dickinson. CP-DickE

Off. A. R. Ammons. CP-AmmoA

Off a pane)the. E. E. Cummings. CP-CummE

Off benefice, sir, at everie feist. William Dunbar. CP-DunbW

Off Cape Colona. Herman Melville. SP-MelvH

Off every asking followis nocht. William Dunbar. CP-DunbW

Off Februar the fyiftene nycht. William Dunbar. CP-DunbW

Off garbage outside the diner. Outside the Diner. Thom Gunn. CP-GunnT

Off Highway 106. Cherrylog Road. James Dickey. CP-DickJ

Of[f] Lentren in the first mornyng [*or* morning]. William Dunbar. CP-DunbW

Off Spectacle Island. Richard Eberhart. CP-EberR

Off that landspit of stony mouth-plugs. Medusa. Sylvia Plath. CP-PlatS

Off the bluff, huge white sails wind. At Rexroth's Grave. Sam Hamill. SP-HamiS

Off the coast of Ireland. Seascape. Langston Hughes. CP-HughL; CP-HughL1

Off the Hook. Eleanor Wilner. SP-WilnE

Off the Peg. Louis MacNeice. CP-MacNL

Off the Trail. Gary Snyder. CP-SnydG

Off to Patagonia. Theodore Weiss. SP-WeisT

Off to the Cemetery. David Ignatow. SP-IgnaD

Offending Eel, The. Raymond Carver. CP-CarvR

Offense, The. James Wright. CP-WrigJ

Offer, The. Henry David Thoreau. CP-ThorH

Offer 'em up to me—bullneck crook of the baths. Catullus. *See* Vibennius & son, renowned

Offer it up plank it down. Ooftish. Samuel Beckett. CP-BeckS

Offer no borrowed proof or energy; the dust. That We Here Highly Resolve. Kenneth Patchen. CP-PatcK

Offer thy gift; but first the Law commands. To Julia. Robert Herrick. CP-HerrR

Offering. Thomas McGrath. SP-McGrT

Offering. William Carlos Williams. CP-WilW1

Offering, An. George Herbert. CP-HerbG

Offering and Rebuff. Carl Sandburg. CP-SandC

Offering for Mr. Bluehart, An. James Wright. CP-WrigJ

Offering of the New Law, the One Oblation Once Offered, The. Christina Georgina Rossetti. CP-RosC3

Offerings. Walt Whitman. CP-WhitW

Offertory. Olga Broumas. SP-BrouO

Office Building: Evening. Langston Hughes. CP-HughL; CP-HughL3

Office Love. Karl Shapiro. SP-ShapK

Office of the Dead. Thomas Kinsella. CP-KinsT

Office Party, The. Miller Williams. CP-WillM

Officers' Prison Camp Seen from a Troop-Train, An. Randall Jarrell. CP-JarrR

Official acropolis surpasses the most colossal conceptions of modern barbarity, The. Cities ("Official acropolis surpasses the most colossal conceptions of modern barbarity, The"). Arthur Rimbaud. CP-RimbA, *tr.* by Martin Sorrell

Official Notice. Langston Hughes. CP-HughL; CP-HughL3

Official Piety. John Greenleaf Whittier. CP-WhitJ

Offscape, the in-folds, secreted, The. At the Edge. Charles Tomlinson. CP-TomlC

Offset. A. R. Ammons. CP-AmmoA

Offspring of Jove, Calliope, once more. Homer's Hymn to the Sun. *Unknown.* CP-ShelP, *tr.* by Percy Bysshe Shelley *Fr.* Homeric Hymns.

Oft as I paced the deck. At Sea, September 1833. Ralph Waldo Emerson. CP-EmerR

Oft bend the Bow, and thou with ease shalt do. By Use Comes Easinesse. Robert Herrick. CP-HerrR

Oft had I heard of Lucy Gray. William Wordsworth. *See* Oft I had heard of Lucy Gray

Oft has our Poet wisht [*or* wished], this happy Seat. Epilogue Spoken by Mrs. Boutell. John Dryden. SP-DrydJ

Oft have I heard both Youths and Virgins say. To His Valentine, on S. Valentines Day. Robert Herrick. CP-HerrR

Oft have I looked on France with envy vain. To P.A. Labouchère Esq. George Meredith. CP-MerG2

Oft Have I Mused. Sir Philip Sidney. SP-SidnP

Oft have I mused, but now at length I find. Oft Have I Mused. Sir Philip Sidney. SP-SidnP

Oft have I said, I say it once more. Hafiz. CP-EmerR *Fr.* Odes.

Oft have I seen, ere Time had ploughed my cheek. Decay of Piety. William Wordsworth. CP WorW2

Oft have I sigh'd for him that heares me not. Thomas Campion. CP-CampT

Oft have we trod the vales of Castaly. Amor Intellectualis. Oscar Wilde. CP-WildO

Oft have you seen a swan superbly frowning. To Charles Cowden Clarke. John Keats. CP-KeatJ

Oft I had heard of Lucy Gray. Lucy Gray; or, Solitude. William Wordsworth. CP-WorW1

Oft in Danger yet alive. To Mrs Thrale [on Her Thirty-fifth Birthday]. Samuel Johnson. CP-JohnS

Oft in the stilly night. Who Did Which? or Who Indeed? Ogden Nash. CP-NashO

Oft is the medal faithful to its trust. *see also* Inscription in the Grounds of Coleorton, the Seat of Sir George Beaumont, BART., Leicestershire *and* Written at the Request of Sir George Beaumont, BART., and in His Name, for an Urn, Placed by Him at the T. William Wordsworth. CP-WorW1

Oft o'er my brain does that strange fancy roll. Sonnet Composed on a Journey Homeward; the Author Having Received Intelligence of the Birth of a Son, 20 September 1796. Samuel Taylor Coleridge. CP-ColeS

Oft, oft methinks, the while with thee. Happy Husband, The. Samuel Taylor Coleridge. CP-ColeS

Oft times, when rapture swells the heart. To the President of the United States. Annis Boudinot Stockton. CP-StocA

Oft we enhance our ills by discontent. By Philemon. Philemon. CP-CowpW

Oft when I look I may descry. Dart, The. Thomas Carew. CP-CareT

Oft when I'm sitting without anything to read. Lines to a World-famous Poet Who Failed to Complete a World-famous Poem; or, Come Clean, Mr. Guest! Ogden Nash. CP-NashO

Often a mask empties itself before believers. Migration of Powers, The. Rainer Maria Rilke. CP-RilkFr, *tr.* by A. Poulin, Jr.

Often an easterly churns. Letter from our Man in Blossomtime. Louise Glück.

SP-GlucL

Often beneath the wave, wide from this ledge. At Melville's Tomb. Hart Crane. CP-CranH

Often, half-way to sleep. In Procession. Robert Graves. CP-GravR

Often hands are like faces. Hands. Yannis Ritsos. SP-RitsY, *tr.* by Edmund Keeley

Often I Am Permitted to Return to a Meadow. Robert Duncan. SP-DuncR

Often I leave my television set to listen to my wireless. This Is My Own, My Native Tongue. Ogden Nash. CP-NashO

Often I looked at you—stood at the window I had started. Great Night, The. Randall Jarrell. CP-JarrR

Often I meet, on walking from a door. Signals, The. Theodore Roethke. CP-RoetT

Often I saw, as on my balcony. Christ Church Meadows, [Oxford]. Donald Hall. CP-HallD

Often I squinted my courage to see the spot. Vanishing Point, The. Miller Williams. CP-WillM

Often I think of the beautiful town. My Lost Youth. Henry Wadsworth Longfellow. SP-LongH

Often, in these blue meadows. Pursuit from Under. James Dickey. CP-DickJ

Often I've encountered evil. Eugenio Montale. CP-MontE, *tr.* by Jonathan Galassi

Often rebuked, yet always back returning. Stanzas: "Often rebuked, yet always back returning." Emily Jane Brontë. CP-BronE

Often the mockingbird is only a mocker. Kansas Lessons. Carl Sandburg. CP-SandC

Often Was It. Kenneth Patchen. CP-PatcK

Often when I go out I. What the Pencil Writes. James Laughlin. CP-LaugJ

Often when Warring. Thomas Hardy. CP-HardT

Ogham stone stands foursquare as the fridge, An. Fridge, The. Paul Muldoon. CP-MuldP

Ogoni. Yusef Komunyakaa. CP-KomuY

Ogre, The. William Carlos Williams. CP-WilW1

Ogre does what ogres can, The. August 1968. W. H. Auden. CP-AudeW

Ogres and Pygmies. Robert Graves. CP-GravR

Oh. Robert Creeley. SP-CreeR

Oh. Seal Lullaby. Rudyard Kipling. CP-KiplR *Fr.* Jungle Book, The.

Oh. Grace Paley.

Oh. Anne Sexton. CP-SextA

Oh a lovely husband he was known. Lovely Husband, The. James Whitcomb Riley. CP-RileJ

Oh, a rare old wine ye brewed for me. Stephen Crane. CP-CranS

Oh a thin ribbon with streaming ends. To Madame Jeanne-Renée Dubost. Rainer Maria Rilke. CP-RilkFr, *tr.* by A. Poulin, Jr.

O[h] *all ye*, who pass[e] by, whose eyes and mind[e]. Sacrifice, The. George Herbert. CP-HerbG

Oh, America / The sun sets in you. Evening Land, The. D. H. Lawrence. CP-LawrD

Oh, Ammons rolled the octaves slow. Expatiation on the Combining of Weathers at Thirty-Seventh and Indiana where the Southern More or Less Crosses the Dog, An. Hayden Carruth. CP-CarHS

Oh, Anne! your offences to me have been grievous. To Anne. Lord Byron. CP-Byron

Oh, ask not what is love, she said. Arthur Hugh Clough. SP-ClouA

Oh, Auntie, isn't he a beauty! And is he a gentleman or a lady? Puss-Puss! D. H. Lawrence. CP-LawrD

"Oh! banish care"—such ever be. Epistle to a Friend. Lord Byron. CP-Byron

Oh be a demon. Be a Demon! D. H. Lawrence. CP-LawrD

Oh be thou blest with all that Heav'n can send. To Mrs. M. B. on Her Birth-Day. Alexander Pope. CP-PopeA

Oh, bid the desert blossom as the rose. Desert, The. Jones Very. CP-VeryJ

Oh, black Persian cat! Mujer. William Carlos Williams. CP-WilW1

Oh, both my shoes are shiny new. Autobiography. Dorothy Parker. CP-ParkD

Oh Brittannia's got a baby, a baby, a baby. Brittannia's Baby. D. H. Lawrence. CP-LawrD

Oh but is it not hard, Dear? Mary Wollstonecraft and Fuseli. Robert Browning. CP-BroR2

Oh, but it is dirty! Filling Station. Elizabeth Bishop. CP-BishE

Oh, cabaret dancer, I know a dancer. How a Little Girl Danced. Nicholas Vachel Lindsay. CP-LindV

Oh, Castlereagh! thou art a patriot now. Epigrams: "Oh, Castlereagh! thou art a patriot now." Lord Byron. CP-Byron

Oh Christianity, Christianity. Stevie Smith. CP-SmitS

Oh cold and ferocious are the children of the cross. Children of the Cross, The. Stevie Smith. CP-SmitS

Oh, come again to Astolat! Elaine. Edna St. Vincent Millay. CP-MillE

Oh Come Lavinia dear lov'd maid. Invitation Ode to a Young Lady in New York from Her Friend in the Country—New Brunswick May the 22d 1753, An. Annis Boudinot Stockton. CP-StocA

Oh, come, my lad, or go, my lad. Betrothal, The. Edna St. Vincent Millay. CP-MillE

Oh come, my love, and join with me. Passionate Screen Writer to His Love, The. Dorothy Parker. CP-ParkD

Oh, comrade, comrade, I have missed you so! Comrade. Paul Laurence Dunbar. CP-DunbP

Oh, Congo brother. We, Too. Langston Hughes. CP-HughL; CP-HughL3

Oh! could Le Sage's demon's gift. Granta—A Medley. Lord Byron. CP-Byron

Oh curse them not nor rail. Bureaucrats: Diggers. Thomas Merton. CP-MertT

Oh Daddy, look at that man, excuse my pointing, but just look at him! Machinery Doesn't Answer, Either, but You Aren't Married to It. Ogden Nash. CP-NashO

Oh days given over to a fruitless. That Man. Jorge Luis Borges. SP-BorgI, tr. by Alan S. Trueblood

Oh, de clouds is mighty heavy. Keep a Song Up on de Way. Paul Laurence Dunbar. CP-DunbP

Oh, de grubbin'-hoe's a-rustin' in de co'nah. Deserted Plantation, The. Paul Laurence Dunbar. CP-DunbP

Oh, de weathah it is balmy an' de breeze is sighin' low. Li'l' Gal. Paul Laurence Dunbar. CP-DunbP

Oh dead punk lady with the knack. Victim, The. Thom Gunn. CP-GunnT

Oh dear, / the plane is so small the baggage. East Hampton—Boston by Air. John Updike. CP-UpdiJ

Oh death / about you I know nothing, nothing. Gladness of Death. D. H. Lawrence. CP-LawrD

Oh, dere's lots o' keer an' trouble. Banjo Song, A. Paul Laurence Dunbar. CP-DunbP

Oh destiny of Borges. Elegy: "Oh destiny of Borges." Jorge Luis Borges. SP-BorgI, tr. by Alastair Reid

Oh! did those eyes, instead of fire. To M——. Lord Byron. CP-Byron

Oh! did you ne'er hear of a jolly young Carpenter. Jolly Young Carpenter, The. George Meredith. CP-MerG2

Oh do not die, for I shall hate. Fever, A. John Donne. CP-DonnJ; MW-DonnJ

Oh, do not tell me the heavens as well are a wheel. Wandering Cosmos, The. D. H. Lawrence. CP-LawrD

Oh do[e] not wanton with those eyes. Ben Jonson. CP-JonsB

Oh down at the tavern. Portrait of an Old Woman on the College Tavern Wall. Anne Sexton. CP-SextA

Oh, dwarfed and wronged, and stained with ill. Woman, A. John Greenleaf Whittier. CP-WhitJ

Oh, early every afternoon. Cat Naps Are Too Good for Cats. Ogden Nash. CP-NashO

Oh, East is East, and West is West, and never the twain shall meet. Ballad of East and West, The. Rudyard Kipling. CP-KiplR

Oh effervescent palisades of ferns in drippage. From Rome, for More Public Fountains in New York City. Alan Dugan. CP-DugaA

Oh factious viper! whose envenom'd tooth. Lord Byron. CP-Byron

Oh fair enough are sky and plain. A. E. Housman. CP-HousA

Oh fair Milly Brandon, a young maid, a fair maid! Brandons Both. Christina Georgina Rossetti. CP-RosC2

Oh, Fair to See. Christina Georgina Rossetti. CP-RosC2 Fr. Sing-Song.

Oh fair to see / Bloom-laden cherry tree. Christina Georgina Rossetti. CP-RosC2

Oh fallen star! a darkened light, / A glory hurtled form its car. O Lucifer, Son of the Morning! Christina Georgina Rossetti. CP-RosC2

Oh, fields of wonder. Birth. Langston Hughes. CP-HughL; CP-HughL2

Oh flame falling, as shaken, as the stories. Fire, The. Robert Creeley. CP-CreeR

Oh, fond attempt to give a deathless lot. On Observing Some Names of Little Note Recorded in the "Biographia Britannica." William Cowper. CP-CowpW

Oh for a knight like Bayard. Hero, The. John Greenleaf Whittier. CP-WhitJ

Oh for a poet—for a beacon bright. Sonnet: "Oh for a poet—for a beacon bright." Edwin Arlington Robinson. CP-RobiE

Oh for my love, my only love. Dream, A. Christina Georgina Rossetti. CP-RosC3

O[h]! for some honest lover's ghost. Sonnet: "O[h]! for some honest lover's ghost." Sir John Suckling. CP-SuckJ

Oh for the breath of the briny deep. Sailor's Song, A. Paul Laurence Dunbar. CP-DunbP

Oh for the time gone by when thought of Christ. Come unto Me. Christina Georgina Rossetti. CP-RosC3

Oh fountain of pale turquoise! Prison Sentence, The. Gabriela Mistral. SP-MistG, tr. by Maria Giachetti [or Jacketti]

Oh, Friend, for ever loved, for ever dear! Epitaph on a Friend. Lord Byron. CP-Byron

Oh Future! thou secreted peace. Emily Dickinson. CP-DickE

Oh, gallant was our galley from her carven steering-wheel. Galley-Slave, The. Rudyard Kipling. CP-KiplR

Oh, gallant was the first love, and glittering and fine. Pictures in the Smoke. Dorothy Parker. CP-ParkD

Oh, Galuppi, Baldassaro, this is very sad to find! Toccata of Galuppi's, A.

Robert Browning. CP-BroR1; SP-BroR

Oh General, Oh Spy, Oh Bureaucrat! Wyatt Prunty. SP-PrunW

O[h,] gentle Love, do not forsake the guide. Upon Some Alterations in My Mistress, after My Departure into France. Thomas Carew. CP-CareT

Oh, gipsies, proud and stiff-necked and perverse. I Know All This when Gipsy Fiddles Cry. Nicholas Vachel Lindsay. CP-LindV

Oh give it Motion—deck it sweet. Emily Dickinson. CP-DickE

Oh give me of thy waters pure and clear. Relief. Jones Very. CP-VeryJ

Oh, give us pleasure in the flowers today. Prayer in Spring, A. Robert Frost. CP-FrosR

Oh, glorious are the guarded heights. Wage-Slaves, The. Rudyard Kipling. CP-KiplR

O[h] glorious spirits, who after all your bands. To All Angels and Saints. George Herbert. CP-HerbG

Oh God help me now to cry out and bear witness. Restless Night, The. Thomas McGrath. SP-McGrT

Oh, god, let's go. / This is a poem for Kenneth Patchen. Please. Robert Creeley. CP-CreeR

Oh, God of dust and rainbows, help us see. Two Somewhat Different Epigrams. Langston Hughes. CP-HughL; CP-HughL3

Oh God supreme, on whom my soul depends. On Exodus 30.18. Annis Boudinot Stockton. CP-StocA

Oh Grateful Colours, Bright Looks! Stevie Smith. CP-SmitS

Oh, greenly and fair in the lands of the sun. Pumpkin, The. John Greenleaf Whittier. CP-WhitJ

Oh! had each SCOT of ancient times. On Miss J. Scott, of Ayr. Robert Burns. CP-BurnR

Oh! had my fate been join'd with thine. To a Lady. Lord Byron. CP-Byron

Oh had we known it turns out so. Boris Leonidovich Pasternak. CP-DaviDC, tr. by Donald Davie

Oh Hale green song. Fragment to W. C. W.'s Romance. William Carlos Williams. CP-PoEar, tr. by Ezra Pound

Oh half as fearful for the yawning day. Terce. John Berryman. CP-BerrJ

Oh hand me down my old cigar with its Havana wrapper. What to Do until the Doctor Goes or It's Tomorrow than You Think. Ogden Nash. CP-NashO

Oh happy happy land! Christian and Jew. A Dialogue. Christina Georgina Rossetti. CP-RosC1

Oh happy shades—to me unblest! Shrubbery, The. William Cowper. CP-CowpW

Oh hard is the bed they have made him. Illic Jacet. A. E. Housman. CP-HousA

Oh, he is sweet. I do love him sometimes. Muriel Rukeyser. CP-RukeM

Oh, heavenly gift of Love Divine. Hymn: Prayer for the Gift of the Holy Spirit. Jones Very. CP-VeryJ

Oh hell, there once again hunger. One Way. W. S. Merwin. SP-MerwW

Oh hell, what do mine eyes. Milton by Firelight. Gary Snyder. CP-SnydG

Oh, her beauty was such that it dazzled my eyes. James Whitcomb Riley. CP-RileJ

Oh, here the air is sweet and still. Little Hill, The. Edna St. Vincent Millay. CP-MillE

Oh, here we are at the mammoth banquet. Banquet, The. Ogden Nash. CP-NashO

Oh, his death sure was a neat trick; he played dead. Ready Man, The. Yannis Ritsos. SP-RitsY, tr. by Christian McEwen and Nikos Tsingos

Oh ho uncircumcised Sadducee I see. Jew Is Angry with His Friend Who Does Not Believe in Circumcision, A. Stevie Smith. CP-SmitS

Oh, honey of an hour. Emily Dickinson. CP-DickE

Oh! House of Refuge; for those weary souls. McLean Asylum, Somerville. Jones Very. CP-VeryJ

Oh, how I love Humanity. World State, The. G. K. Chesterton. CP-ChesG

Oh How I Wish that an Embargo. Lord Byron. CP-Byron

Oh how the women. Little Peasant, The. Anne Sexton. CP-SextA

Oh how there in the glittering. Times at Bellosguardo. Eugenio Montale. CP-MontE, tr. by Jonathan Galassi

Oh, how worried they are about my. Soul. Charles Bukowski. SP-BukC1

Oh how you used to walk. Just for a Time. Maya Angelou. SP-AngeM

Oh, Hubshee, carry your shoes in your hand and bow your head on your breast! Kitchener's School. Rudyard Kipling. CP-KiplR

Oh humble me! I cannot bide the joy. Humility. Jones Very. CP-VeryJ

Oh I am a cat that likes to. Galloping Cat, The. Stevie Smith. CP-SmitS

Oh, I am come to the low Countrie. Highland Widow's Lament, The. Robert Burns. CP-BurnR

Oh, I am grown so free from care. Merry Maid, The. Edna St. Vincent Millay. CP-MillE

Oh, I am hurt to death, my Love. One Life. Paul Laurence Dunbar. CP-DunbP

Oh I am of the people! Amo Sacrum Vulgus. D. H. Lawrence. CP-LawrD

Oh I approached and bowed. Courting Song: Attack! Attack! Attack! Alan Dugan. CP-DugaA

Oh I believe that all of us real poets string pickers. Us. Andrei Codrescu. SP-CodrA

Oh I came up from anywhere. To Paris: Fear of the Heights Reached. Alan

Dugan. CP-DugaA

Oh I can praise a cloistered virtue, such. Three Moral Discoveries. Donald Davie. CP-DaviDC

Oh, I can smile for you, and tilt my head. Certain Lady, A. Dorothy Parker. CP-ParkD

Oh, I des received a letter f'om de sweetest little gal. Love Letter, A. Paul Laurence Dunbar. CP-DunbP

Oh, I do like a little bit of gossip. This Was Told Me in Confidence. Ogden Nash. CP-NashO

Oh I got jammed among the bodies as. I Dreamed I Got a Letter from Ezra Pound. Alan Dugan. CP-DugaA

Oh I got up and went to work. On a Seven-Day Diary. Alan Dugan. CP-DugaA

Oh, I have done those things that my Soul fears. Arthur Hugh Clough. SP-ClouA

Oh I have felt these same. Lament in Spring. John Logan. CP-LogaJ

Oh I have loved my fellow-men. But I Say unto You: Love One Another. D. H. Lawrence. CP-LawrD

Oh, I have n't got long to live, for we all. Border Ballad, A. Paul Laurence Dunbar. CP-DunbP

Oh, I have walked in Kansas. Kansas. Nicholas Vachel Lindsay. CP-LindV

Oh I know / if I'd practised the piano. Gradus ad Parnassum. Muriel Rukeyser. CP-RukeM

Oh, I must have it I feed on it. Like Him I Need the Past. James Laughlin. CP-LaugJ

Oh, I shall be, till Gabriel's trump. Accursed, The. Dorothy Parker. CP-ParkD

Oh, I should like to ride the seas. Song of Perfect Propriety. Dorothy Parker. CP-ParkD

Oh I suppose I should. Le Médecin Malgré Lui. William Carlos Williams. CP-WilW1

Oh I wish that there were some wing, some wing. I Wish. Stevie Smith. CP-SmitS

Oh, I'd been better dying. Trusting Heart, The. Dorothy Parker. CP-ParkD

Oh, If Only. Stevie Smith. CP-SmitS

Oh, if we had a rich boss. "Blue-Monday" at the Shoe Shop. James Whitcomb Riley. CP-RileJ

Oh I'm not upset that a chariot wheel. Favor of Alexander Valas, The. Constantine P. Cavafy. CP-CavaC, tr. by Theoharis Constantine Theoharis

Oh, in a harsh suspicious time. Émigrés, The. Marya Alexandrovna Zaturenska. SP-ZatuM

Oh, in the pen, oh, in the pen. Penological Study: Southern Exposure. Robert Penn Warren. CP-WarrR

Oh, in the world of the flesh of man. What Then Is Evil? D. H. Lawrence. CP-LawrD

Oh is it the jar of nations. Jar of Nations, The. A. E. Housman. CP-HousA

Oh, is it, then, Utopian. De Profundis. Dorothy Parker. CP-ParkD

Oh ivy green. Lorine Niedecker. CP-NiedL

Oh just hanging around. What You Up To? Allen Ginsberg. SP-GinsA

Oh! kangaroos, sequins, chocolate sodas! Today. Frank O'Hara. SP-OharF

Oh kindle up thine altar! see the brands. Altar, The. Jones Very. CP-VeryJ

O[h] King of grief! (a title strange, yet true). Thanksgiving, The. George Herbert. CP-HerbG

Oh kiss me once before I go. Husband and Wife. Christina Georgina Rossetti. CP-RosC3

Oh knell of a passing time, / Will it never cease to chime? Christina Georgina Rossetti. CP-RosC2

Oh Lady! when I left the shore. To Florence. Lord Byron. CP-Byron

Oh, late withdrawn from human-kind. Portent, The. Rudyard Kipling. CP-KiplR Fr. Debits and Credits.

Oh, lay my ashes on the wind. Curse, The. Edna St. Vincent Millay. CP-MillE

Oh, le petit rondelay! Chanson. Robert Creeley. CP-CreeR

Oh, lead me to a quiet cell. Portrait of the Artist. Dorothy Parker. CP-ParkD

Oh, let it be a night of lyric rain. Testament. Dorothy Parker. CP-ParkD

Oh, let me not serve so, as those men serve. John Donne. MW-DonnJ Fr. Elegies.

Oh let me see You everywhere I go! Michelangelo Buonarroti. CP-Miche, tr. by John Frederick Nims

Oh, let's go up the hill and scare ourselves. Bonfire, The. Robert Frost. CP-FrosR

Oh, life is a glorious cycle of song. Comment. Dorothy Parker. CP-ParkD

Oh life lived since who knows when! Rainer Maria Rilke. CP-RilkFr, tr. by A. Poulin, Jr. Fr. Fragments.

Oh, Light was the world that he weighed in his hands! Song of Kabir, A. Rudyard Kipling. CP-KiplR Fr. Second Jungle Book, The.

Oh like a bird. Oh. Robert Creeley. SP-CreeR

Oh lion in a peculiar guise. Roman Road, The. Stevie Smith. CP-SmitS

Oh listen, listen; for the Earth. World's Harmonies, The. Christina Georgina Rossetti. CP-RosC3

Oh, little did the Wolf-Child care. Romulus and Remus. Rudyard Kipling. CP-KiplR

Oh little fledgling out of the nest. Paul Laurence Dunbar. CP-DunbP

Oh, little rose tree, bloom! Three Songs from "The Lamp and the Bell." Edna St. Vincent Millay. CP-MillE

Oh little voices of the throats of men. T. S. Eliot. SP-EliotT

Oh, long had we paltered. Hymn of the Triumphant Airman. Rudyard Kipling. CP-KiplR

Oh Look—I Can Do It Too. Dorothy Parker. CP-ParkD

Oh Lord have mercy on my soul. Suicide's Epitaph. Stevie Smith. CP-SmitS

"Oh Lord, our Lord! how wondrously," (quoth she). Prioress' Tale—A Modernization, The. Geoffrey Chaucer. CP-WorW1 Fr. Canterbury Tales, The.

Oh lost garden Paradise. Afterthought, An. Christina Georgina Rossetti. CP-RosC3

Oh lov'd! but not enough—though dearer far. Glory to God Alone. Jeanne Marie Bouvier de la Motte Guyon. CP-CowpW, tr. by William Cowper

Oh Love ("My love is a boat"). Robert Creeley. SP-CreeR

Oh, Love ("Oh love, falling"). Robert Creeley. CP-CreeR

Oh Love, Love, thou that from the eyes diffusest. Robert Browning. CP-BroR2

Oh, Love—no, Love! All the noise below, Love. Epilogue: "Oh, Love—no, Love! All the noise below, Love." Robert Browning. CP-BroR2

Oh, love, why do we argue like this? Curse against Elegies, A. Anne Sexton. CP-SextA

Oh, Lovely Rock. Robinson Jeffers. CP-JefR2

Oh Lucy of Granada! Madrigal: "Oh Lucy of Granada!" Federico García Lorca. CP-GarcF, tr. by Jerome Rothenberg Fr. Palimpsests.

Oh Mabel. Robert Creeley. CP-CreeR

Oh, Mariamne! now for thee. Herod's Lament for Mariamne. Lord Byron. CP-Byron

Oh Matchless Earth—We underrate. Emily Dickinson. SP-DickE

Oh Max. Robert Creeley. SP-CreeR

Oh! May sits crowned with hawthorn-flower. Fin di Maggio. Dante Gabriel Rossetti. CW-RossD

Oh men, living men, vivid men, ocean and fire. Hold Back! D. H. Lawrence. CP-LawrD

Oh, mercifullest one of all. After a Spanish Proverb. Dorothy Parker. CP-ParkD

Oh! might I kiss those eyes of fire. Catullus. See Iuventius, / were I allowed

Oh mirk, mirk is this midnight hour. Lord Gregory. Robert Burns. CP-BurnR

Oh! Mr. Best, you're very bad. Jane Austen. CP-AustJ

Oh Mr. Pussy-Cat. Nipping Pussy's Feet in Fun. Stevie Smith. CP-SmitS

Oh moment, inconceivable to all. Rainer Maria Rilke. CP-RilkFr, tr. by A. Poulin, Jr. Fr. Fragments.

Oh, morning fresh and clear as heavenly light. Cold Morning Sky. Marya Alexandrovna Zaturenska. SP-ZatuM

Oh most delightful hour by man. On a Similar Occasion for the Year 1789. William Cowper. CP-CowpW

Oh mother. Mothers. Anne Sexton. CP-SextA

Oh, Mother, / Virgin Mother. Jesus, the Actor, Plays the Holy Ghost. Anne Sexton. CP-SextA; SP-SextA

Oh muse, not to be a boxer is not to be at all. Poetry Reading. Wisława Szymborska. SP-SzymWM, tr. by Joanna Trzeciak

Oh my bald head. Apostrophe to a Buddhist Monk. D. H. Lawrence. CP-LawrD

Oh, my belovèd, have you thought of this. Sonnet: "Oh, my belovèd, have you thought of this." Edna St. Vincent Millay. CP-MillE

Oh my darling Goosey-Gander. True Tyrant or the Spirit of Duty Rebuked, The. Stevie Smith. CP-SmitS

Oh my God what a bitter shame. And Jude the Obscure and His Beloved. D. H. Lawrence. CP-LawrD

Oh my Good, my Beauty! Atrocious fanfare in which I do not waver! Morning of Drunkenness. Arthur Rimbaud. CP-RimbA, tr. by Martin Sorrell

Oh my Gracious Preserver! Prayer: "Oh my Gracious Preserver!" Phillis Wheatley. CP-WheaP

Oh! my heart, although it sounds better. Poem in Envy of Cavalcanti, A. Frank O'Hara. SP-OharF

Oh!—my lonely—lonely—lonely Pillow! Stanzas: "Oh!—my lonely—lonely—lonely Pillow!" Lord Byron. CP-Byron

"Oh My Love." Robert Creeley. CP-CreeR

Oh my love and my own deary! What to Do? Christina Georgina Rossetti. CP-RosC3

Oh my mute city, honey-gold. To See. Adam Zagajewski. SP-ZagaA, tr. by Clare Cavanagh

Oh, my old, venerable teacher, life. Yehuda Amichai. SP-AmicYL, tr. by Benjamin Harshav and Barbara Harshav

Oh never talk again to me. Girl of Cadiz, The. Lord Byron. CP-Byron

Oh never try to knock on rotten wood. Admonitions. Sylvia Plath. CP-PlatS

Oh No. Robert Creeley. CP-CreeR

Oh, no one can deny. Self's the Man. Philip Larkin. CP-LarkP

"Oh no," said It: "her lifedoings." Absolute Explains, The. Thomas Hardy. CP-HardT

Oh noble, rich, glowing color of blood. That Noble Flower. Robinson Jeffers.

CP-JefR3

Oh nobody's a long time. Lonesome Boy Blues. Kenneth Patchen. CP-PatcK

Oh, none in all the world before. Hymn Sung at Christmas by the Scholars of St. Helena's Island, S.C. John Greenleaf Whittier. CP-WhitJ

Oh, not inexplicable. Death explains. Hemingway. Archibald MacLeish. CP-MacLA

Oh, not the loss of the accomplished thing! Two Poems from the War. Archibald MacLeish. CP-MacLA

Oh, Oh, you will be sorry for that word! Edna St. Vincent Millay. CP-MillE

Oh old dry rose of God. Imaginary Rose in a Book, An. Allen Ginsberg. CP-GinsA

Oh, on an early morning I think I shall live forever! Poem in Three Parts. Robert Bly. SP-BlyR

Oh on my breast in days hereafter. A. E. Housman. CP-HousA

Oh, once I walked a garden. On the Garden Wall. Nicholas Vachel Lindsay. CP-LindV

Oh, once I walked in Heaven, all alone. How Johnny Appleseed Walked Alone in the Jungles of Heaven. Nicholas Vachel Lindsay. CP-LindV

Oh, once there lived in Kankakee. Tune for an Ill-Tempered Clavichord. Ogden Nash. CP-NashO

Oh, open the door, some pity to shew. Open the Door to Me, Oh! Robert Burns. CP-BurnR

Oh [or O] that those lips had language! Life has passed [or pass'd]. On the Receipt of My Mother's Picture out of Norfolk [the Gift of My Cousin Ann Bodham]. William Cowper. CP-CowpW

Oh [or O], young Lochinvar is come out of the west. Lochinvar. Sir Walter Scott. SP-ScotW Fr. Marmion.

Oh, over the factory cities there seems to hover a doom. Factory Cities, The. D. H. Lawrence. CP-LawrD

Oh Patsey dear and did you hear. To Patricia Gilgert Who Acted. G. K. Chesterton. CP-ChesG

Oh peacock, Argus-eyed and blind. From the Greek Anthology. Alan Dugan. CP-DugaA

Oh pile of white shirts who is coming. Night of the Shirts, The. W. S. Merwin. SP-MerwW

Oh pity the dead that are dead, but cannot take. Houseless Dead, The. D. H. Lawrence. CP-LawrD

Oh pleasant eventide! Twilight Calm. Christina Georgina Rossetti. CP-RosC1

Oh! pleasant exercise of hope and joy! French Revolution as It Appeared to Enthusiasts at Its Commencement. Reprinted from "The Friend." William Wordsworth. CP-WorW1

Oh, Please Don't Get Up! Ogden Nash. CP-NashO

Oh, ponder, friend, the porcupine. Parable for a Certain Virgin. Dorothy Parker. CP-ParkD

Oh practical end of my poetry! Reality. Pier Paolo Pasolini. SP-PasoP, tr. by Norman MacAfee and Luciano Martinengo

Oh praise the Lord! let every heart be glad! Praise. Jones Very. CP-VeryJ

Oh, Prue she has a patient man. She Is Overheard Singing. Edna St. Vincent Millay. CP-MillE

"Oh! Raining! Look!" she whispered. Episodes. Walter De la Mare. CP-DeLaW

Oh read the verses of the loaded scourges. Biography, The. Thomas Merton. CP-MertT

Oh, "rorty" was a mid-Victorian word. You Can Be a Republican, I'm a Genocrat. Ogden Nash. CP-NashO

Oh roses for the flush of youth. Song: "Oh roses for the flush of youth." Christina Georgina Rossetti. CP-RosC1

Oh sad thy lot before I came. Light Love. Christina Georgina Rossetti. CP-RosC1

Oh Sad vicissitude of human woe. Elegy on the Death of Mrs Wilson, April the 19, 1786, An. Annis Boudinot Stockton. CP-StocA

Oh, saw I there. Daisy, The. Walter De la Mare. CP-DeLaW

Oh say not, sweet Anne, that the Fates have decreed. To the Same. Lord Byron. CP-Byron

Oh secret voice of dark love! Federico García Lorca. CP-GarcF, tr. by Angela Jaffray

Oh see how thick the goldcup flowers. A. E. Housman. CP-HousA

Oh, seek, my love, your newer way. Godspeed. Dorothy Parker. CP-ParkD

Oh seekers, when you leave off seeking. Seekers. D. H. Lawrence. CP-LawrD

Oh sensitive mimosa, you have. On Naming a Baby Mimosa. Alan Dugan. CP-DugaA

Oh Shadow on the Grass. Emily Dickinson. CP-DickE

Oh sharp diamond, my mother! Christmas Eve. Anne Sexton. CP-SextA

Oh, show me how a rose can shut and be a bud again! Scholars, The. Rudyard Kipling. CP-KiplR

Oh, Shucks, Ma'am, I Mean Excuse Me. Ogden Nash. CP-NashO

Oh, sick I am to see you, will you never let me be? New Mistress, The. A. E. Housman. CP-HousA

Oh, silver tree! Jazzonia. Langston Hughes. CP-HughL; CP-HughL1

Oh slavery! thou bane of human kind. Lines, Written on Reading Stuart's Account of the Treatment of Slaves in Charleston. Jones Very. CP-VeryJ

"Oh, sleep forever in the Latmian cave." Edna St. Vincent Millay. CP-MillE

Oh! Snatch'd Away in Beauty's Bloom. Lord Byron. CP-Byron'

Oh, soap bubbles! Soap Bubbles. Rainer Maria Rilke. CP-RilkFr, tr. by A. Poulin, Jr.

Oh sock, sock, sock! Brilliance, The. William Carlos Williams. CP-WilW2

Oh, some people grieve for New Year's Eve. Middle of the Month, The. Ogden Nash. CP-NashO

Oh, sometimes I sit around and think, what would you do if you. How Now, Sirrah? Oh, Anyhow. Ogden Nash. CP-NashO

Oh, sometimes I wish I had the wings of an angel because then I. It's Snug to Be Smug. Ogden Nash. CP-NashO

Oh soul, fear things grandiose. Ides of March, The. Constantine P. Cavafy. CP-CavaC, tr. by Theoharis Constantine Theoharis

Oh, soul, sometimes—often—still say when I'm trying to convince my inner self of something. Thinking Thought. C. K. Williams. SP-WillC

Oh stay at home, my lad, and plough. A. E. Housman. CP-HousA

Oh stay locked and free. Incantation. Eugenio Montale. CP-MontE, tr. by Jonathan Galassi

Oh, Stop Being Thankful All over the Place. Ogden Nash. CP-NashO

Oh strong-ridged and deeply hollowed. Smell. William Carlos Williams. CP-WilW1

Oh Stubborn Race of Cadmus' Seed. Stevie Smith. CP-SmitS

Oh, summer has clothed the earth. In Summer. Paul Laurence Dunbar. CP-DunbP

Oh summer's happiness: the carillon chimes. Rainer Maria Rilke. CP-RilkFr, tr. by A. Poulin, Jr. Fr. Valaisian Quatrains, The.

Oh Sumptuous moment. Emily Dickinson. CP-DickE

Oh swell my bosom deeper with thy love. River, The. Jones Very. CP-VeryJ

Oh! take the pure gem to where southerly breezes. On an Icicle That Clung to the Grass of a Grave. Percy Bysshe Shelley. CP-ShelP

Oh, talk not to me of a name great in story. Stanzas Written on the Road between Florence and Pisa. Lord Byron. CP-Byron

Oh! tell me a tale of the airly days. Tale of the Airly Days, A. James Whitcomb Riley. CP-RileJ

Oh tell me once and tell me twice. One Foot on Sea, and One on Shore. Christina Georgina Rossetti. CP-RosC2

Oh thank you for giving me the chance. Thank You. Kenneth Koch. SP-KochK

Oh that horse I see so high. Gift of Great Value, A. Robert Creeley. CP-CreeR

Oh, that last long ride is a. Widow Woman. Langston Hughes. CP-HughL; CP-HughL2

Oh That my young life were a lasting dream! Dreams. Edgar Allan Poe. CP-PoeEd

Oh that Pieria's spring would thro' my breast. John Milton. See Now I long for the Pierian fountains

Oh, that this lashing wind was something more. Chaos in Motion and Not in Motion. Wallace Stevens. CP-StevW

Oh that was not a scrap of flying Daily News. Poem: "Oh that was not a scrap of flying Daily News." Alan Dugan. CP-DugaA

Oh, the beautiful girl, too white. Gold Hair: A Story of Pornic. Robert Browning. CP-BroR1; SP-BroR

Oh the breeze is blowin' balmy. Till the Wind Gets Right. Paul Laurence Dunbar. CP-DunbP

Oh the cheerful budding-time. Seasons. Christina Georgina Rossetti. CP-RosC3

Oh! the Circus-Day Parade! How the bugles played and played! Circus-Day Parade, The. James Whitcomb Riley. CP-RileJ

Oh, the day has set me dreaming. Little Lucy Landman. Paul Laurence Dunbar. CP-DunbP

Oh the destroyed or never finished temple! How. To Natalie Clifford Barney. Rainer Maria Rilke. CP-RilkFr, tr. by A. Poulin, Jr.

"Oh," the doctor mumbled, "she's doing as well." I Can Only Stay for Fifteen Minutes. Miller Williams. CP-WillM

Oh, the golden afternoon! Some Imitations. James Whitcomb Riley. CP-RileJ

Oh the green glimmer of apples in the orchard. Another Ophelia. D. H. Lawrence. CP-LawrD

Oh the happy ending, the happy ending. Sphere, The. Kathleen Jessie Raine. SP-RainK

Oh, the hobo's life is a roving life. Hobo Voluntary, A. James Whitcomb Riley. CP-RileJ

Oh the innocent girl. Jeune Fille, The. D. H. Lawrence. CP-LawrD

Oh, the leaky boundaries of man-made states! Psalm: "Oh, the leaky boundaries of man-made states!" Wisława Szymborska. SP-SzymW, tr. by Stanisław Barańczak and Clare Cavanagh

Oh, the little bird is rocking in the cradle of the wind. Farm Child's Lullaby, The. Paul Laurence Dunbar. CP-DunbP

Oh the maple! Two Trees, The. Archibald MacLeish. CP-MacLA

Oh! the old swimmin'-hole! whare the crick so still and deep. Old Swimmin'-Hole, The. James Whitcomb Riley. CP-RileJ

Oh, the poets may sing of their Lady Irenes. To Louise. Paul Laurence Dunbar. CP-DunbP

Oh the rose of England is a single rose. Rose of England, The. D. H. Lawrence.

CP-LawrD

Oh the rose of keenest thorn! Iniquity of the Fathers upon the Children, The. Christina Georgina Rossetti. CP-RosC1

Oh, the ruins of the human heart. Dresden Cattle. Sam Hamill. SP-HamiS

Oh the slave trade. Is There a Difference between Men and Women. Grace Paley. CP-PalGC

Oh / the sumac died. Some Simple Measures in the American Idiom and the Variable Foot. William Carlos Williams. CP-WilW2

Oh the sun stood still above the Passport Office. Jericho. Louis MacNeice. CP-MacNL

Oh, the Virgin, / the pilgrimage to see. Ballad of Our Lady of the Boat. Federico García Lorca. CP-GarcF, tr. by Catherine Brown

Oh the year before I was born. Song Stanzas of Private Luck; To Be Added Sometimes and Sometimes to Be Subtracted from as Events Prove One More Wrong than Right. Grace Paley. CP-PalGC

Oh then be nameless and be never seen! Resurrection of the Flesh. D. H. Lawrence. CP-LawrD

Oh! there are spirits of the air. To ———: "Oh! there are spirits of the air." Percy Bysshe Shelley. CP-ShelP

Oh there hasn't been much change. Grange, The. Stevie Smith. CP-SmitS

Oh, there is evil, there is an evil world-soul. Evil World-Soul, The. D. H. Lawrence. CP-LawrD

Oh there is much to speak of. Emily Dickinson. SP-DickE

Oh, there once was a lady, and so I've been told. Fable: "Oh, there once was a lady, and so I've been told." Dorothy Parker. CP-ParkD

Oh they were doing custom. On a Hymn, Misprinted. Alan Dugan. CP-DugaA

Oh, thicker, deeper, darker growing. Memorial, A. John Greenleaf Whittier. CP-WhitJ

Oh, think not I am faithful to a vow! Edna St. Vincent Millay. CP-MillE

Oh, this is the tale the grandmas tell. Ballad of the Brown Girl, The. Countee Cullen. CP-CullC

Oh those altars where fruit was placed. Rainer Maria Rilke. CP-RilkFr, tr. by A. Poulin, Jr. Fr. Valaisian Quatrains, The.

Oh thou, by long experience tried. Soul That Loves God Finds Him Every Where, The. Jeanne Marie Bouvier de la Motte Guyon. CP-CowpW, tr. by William Cowper

Oh thou that liftest up thy hands in prayer. Belgium. E. E. Cummings. CP-CummE

Oh! thou that roll'st above thy glorious Fire. Ossian's Address to the Sun in "Carthon." Lord Byron. CP-Byron

Oh! Thou that veileth from all eyes. Mortul Prayer, A. James Whitcomb Riley. CP-RileJ

Oh thou, whose fixed bewildered eye. Septimi Gades. William Wordsworth. CP-WorW1

Oh, thy bright eyes must answer now. Emily Jane Brontë. See God of Visions

Oh, time of our lyrical laughter. Song of a Hopeful Heart. Dorothy Parker. CP-ParkD

Oh to be at Crowdieknowe. Crowdieknowe. Hugh MacDiarmid. SP-MacDH

Oh to Be Odd! Ogden Nash. CP-NashO

Oh, to be Orville Prescott. Tome-Thoughts, from the *Times*. John Updike. CP-UpdiJ

Oh to cast the mind. Subconscious Sea. May Swenson. SP-SwenM

Oh, to fall easily, easily, easily in Love. Love Song: "Oh, to fall easily, easily, easily in Love." Carolyn Kizer. CP-KizeC

Oh to have you in May. In May. Paul Laurence Dunbar. CP-DunbP

Oh / Together. As by Water. W. S. Merwin. SP-MerwW

Oh, tree outside my window, we are kin. To a Tree. Elizabeth Bishop. CP-BishE

Oh turn not in from marching. A. E. Housman. CP-HousA

Oh unforgotten! / How long ago? one spirit saith. Unforgotten. Christina Georgina Rossetti. CP-RosC3

Oh unfortunate generation! Poetry of the Tradition, The. Pier Paolo Pasolini. SP-PasoP, tr. by Norman MacAfee and Luciano Martinengo

Oh Venice! Venice! when thy marble walls. Ode on Venice. Lord Byron. CP-Byron

Oh virgin queen of mountain-side and woodland. Ode 3.22: Pine Tree for Diana, The ("Montium custos nemorumque"). Horace. SP-SmarC Fr. Odes.

Oh, wash-woman, / Arms elbow-deep in white suds. Song to a Negro Wash-woman, A. Langston Hughes. CP-HughL; CP-HughL1

Oh, we are the bold expatriate band! Song of Americans Resident in France. Dorothy Parker. CP-ParkD

Oh we have moved forward in pain. Looking Back. W. S. Merwin. SP-MerwW

Oh, weep for Mr. and Mrs. Bryan! Lion, The. Ogden Nash. CP-NashO

Oh weep for the glory departed. Counsel, A. Christina Georgina Rossetti. CP-RosC3

Oh! Weep for Those. Lord Byron. CP-Byron

Oh well done Lord E———n! and better done R———r! Ode to the Framers of the Frame Bill, An. Lord Byron. CP-Byron

Oh! well I know your subtle Sex. To ———: "Oh! well I know your subtle Sex." Lord Byron. CP-Byron

Oh, well may Essex sit forlorn. William Francis Bartlett. John Greenleaf Whittier. CP-WhitJ

Oh well, they had such a big garden. Mona Van Duyn. SP-VanDM

Oh, Wellington! (or "Villainton") for fame. Canto the Ninth. Lord Byron. CP-Byron Fr. Don Juan.

Oh were he and I together. A. E. Housman. CP-HousA

Oh we've got to trust. Trust. D. H. Lawrence. CP-LawrD

Oh what a crush of people. Floating Bridges. Federico García Lorca. CP-GarcF, tr. by Jerome Rothenberg Fr. In the Garden of the Lunar Grapefruits.

O[h] what a cunning guest. Confession. George Herbert. CP-HerbG

Oh, what a dawn of day! Lovers' Quarrel, A. Robert Browning. CP-BroR1; SP-BroR

Oh what a Grace is this. Emily Dickinson. CP-DickE

Oh what a hard time I have. It's True. Federico García Lorca. CP-GarcF, tr. by Alan S. Trueblood Fr. Andalusian Songs.

Oh what a pity, Oh! don't you agree. Innocent England. D. H. Lawrence. CP-LawrD

Oh, what a shining town were Death. Valentine. Edna St. Vincent Millay. CP-MillE

Oh what a shuddering! Last Nocturne. Federico García Lorca. CP-GarcF, tr. by Jerome Rothenberg Fr. Cúckoo-Cuckoo-Cuckóo.

Oh What a Wreck! How Changed in Mien and Speech! William Wordsworth. CP-WorW2

Oh, what an effort it is. It Is True. Federico García Lorca. SP-GarcF, tr. by Harriet de Onís

Oh what can be happening pray what are they at? Friskers, or, Gods and Men. Stevie Smith. CP-SmitS

Oh what cold perfumes / what hyacinths! White Smell. Federico García Lorca. CP-GarcF, tr. by Jerome Rothenberg Fr. In the Garden of the Lunar Grapefruits.

Oh what comes over the sea. Song: "Oh what comes over the sea." Christina Georgina Rossetti. CP-RosC1

Oh! what ef little childerns all. Her Poet-Brother. James Whitcomb Riley. CP-RileJ

Oh what fools! what shattered fools we are. Our (American) Ragcademicians. William Carlos Williams. CP-WilW1

Oh, what in the world could be more fun. September Morn. Ogden Nash. CP-NashO

Oh what is earth, that we should build / Our houses here, and seek concealed. Then Whose Shall Those Things Be? Christina Georgina Rossetti. CP-RosC2

Oh what is that country. Mother Country. Christina Georgina Rossetti. CP-RosC1

Oh what is the terrible thing he has done. Oh What Is the Thing He Done? Stevie Smith. CP-SmitS

Oh What Is the Thing He Done? Stevie Smith. CP-SmitS

Oh, what shall I do? I am wholly upset. Disturber, The. Paul Laurence Dunbar. CP-DunbP

Oh, what soft wings shall rise above this place. In a Garden. Wallace Stevens. CP-StevWP

Oh, what sorrow! Mississippi. Langston Hughes. CP-HughL; CP-HughL3

Oh, what sorrow to have. Crossroad. Federico García Lorca. CP-GarcF, tr. by Catherine Brown

Oh, what we want on earth. Temples. D. H. Lawrence. CP-LawrD

Oh what wealth of stucco flowers. Dirge for the City of Miami. Thomas Merton. CP-MertT

Oh what's the matter? What's the matter? Goody Blake and Harry Gill. William Wordsworth. CP-WorW1; MW-WorW

Oh, when I flung my heart away. Healed. Dorothy Parker. CP-ParkD

Oh, when I think of the industrial millions, when I see some of them. We Die Together. D. H. Lawrence. CP-LawrD

Oh, When I Was In Love. A. E. Housman. CP-HousA

Oh, when I was in love with you. Oh, When I Was In Love. A. E. Housman. CP-HousA

Oh when Mercury came to London. London Mercury. D. H. Lawrence. CP-LawrD

Oh when shall the grave hide for ever my sorrow? To Caroline. Lord Byron. CP-Byron

Oh, when the grass flowers, the grass. Magnificent Democracy. D. H. Lawrence. CP-LawrD

Oh, when the world is hopeless. What Is a Man to Do? D. H. Lawrence. CP-LawrD

Oh when you gonna / lie down by my side. 4 AM Blues. Allen Ginsberg. SP-GinsA

Oh when you're young. They Come No More, Those Words, Those Finches. Archibald MacLeish. CP-MacLA

Oh whence do you come, my dear friend, to me. Poor Ghost, The. Christina Georgina Rossetti. CP-RosC1

Oh where are ye going ye human faces. Where Are You Going? Stevie Smith. CP-SmitS

Oh where are you going to, all you Big Steamers. Big Steamers. Rudyard Kipling. CP-KiplR

Oh where are you going with your lovelocks flowing. Amor Mundi. Christina Georgina Rossetti. CP-RosC1

Oh where have you fallen to. Lucille Clifton. SP-ClifL

Oh, whither is my fair sun fled. Lady, Rescued from Death by a Knight, Who in the Instant Leaves Her, Complains Thus, A. Thomas Carew. CP-CareT

Oh who is / so cosy with. End of the Day, The. Robert Creeley. CP-CreeR

Oh who is that young sinner with the handcuffs on his wrists? A. E. Housman. CP-HousA

Oh, who is the Lord of the land of life. Masters, The. Paul Laurence Dunbar. CP-DunbP

Oh, who will shoe your pretty little foot. My Heart's as Gay as a Young Sunflower. Kenneth Rexroth. CP-RexrK

Oh, who would be sad tho' the sky be a-graying. Winter-Song. Paul Laurence Dunbar. CP-DunbP

Oh, who would live in a silent house. Little Feet. Ogden Nash. CP-NashO

Oh who would not want such a wonderful thing. Eskimo Song. G. K. Chesterton. CP-ChesG

Oh, Why? Walter De la Mare. CP-DeLaW

Oh, why does man pursue the smelt? Smelt, The. Ogden Nash. CP-NashO

Oh why is heaven built so far. De Profundis. Christina Georgina Rossetti. CP-RosC2

Oh, why should a *hen*. Trouvée. Elizabeth Bishop. CP-BishE

Oh wind I hear you faltering. From the Lookout Rock. Richard Wilbur. CP-WilbR

Oh, wind of the spring-time, oh, free wind of May. Roses. Paul Laurence Dunbar. CP-DunbP

Oh wine-sweet ghost how are we borne apart. In Morte De. Ezra Pound. CP-PoEar

Oh Wonderful Machine! D. H. Lawrence. CP-LawrD

Oh would I were a politician. Yes and No. Ogden Nash. CP-NashO

Oh would that I were a reliable spirit careering around. Longing for Death because of Feebleness. Stevie Smith. CP-SmitS

Oh! would that I were very far away. Wishes: Sonnet. Christina Georgina Rossetti. CP-RosC3

Oh, ye who hold the written clue. Things and the Man. Rudyard Kipling. CP-KiplR

Oh, Yes. Charles Bukowski. SP-BukC3

Oh yes, I love you, book of my confessions. Chinese Tomb Guardians. Robert Bly. SP-BlyR

Oh yes, I, too, am one of those. Residual Light. Hans Magnus Enzensberger. SP-EnzeH

Oh yes, I will own we were dear to each other. To George, Earl Delawarr. Lord Byron. CP-Byron

Oh, yes, I'd love to go to the play. Wednesday Matinee. Ogden Nash. CP-NashO

Oh you are never tame. Twilight. W. S. Merwin. SP-MerwWF

Oh you brown bacon machine. Hog. Anne Sexton. CP-SextA

Oh you, passing by this hill—one. Epitaph: "Oh you, passing by this hill—one." Primo Levi. CP-LeviP, *tr. by* Ruth Feldman *and* Brian Swann

Oh you stiff shapes, swift transformation seethes. Transformations. D. H. Lawrence. CP-LawrD

Oh you, the sprightliest & most puggish, the brightest star. After Peire Vidal, & Myself. Ted Berrigan. SP-BerrT

Oh You, Who in All Names Can Tickle the Town. Lord Byron. CP-Byron

Oh you, whose eyes carry. Guido Cavalcanti. CP-CavaG, *tr. by* Marc Cirigliano

Oh you'd think the British Public. Lucky Little Britisher. D. H. Lawrence. CP-LawrD

Oh young men oh young comrades. Us. Stephen Spender. CP-SpenS

Oh za ki tan ke parlay lot. Za Ki Tan Ke Parlay Lot. Audre Lorde. SP-LordA

Ohio. John Updike. CP-UpdiJ

Ohio River Blues. Kenneth Patchen. CP-PatcK

Ohio River—Louisville, The. Thomas Merton. CP-MertT

Ohld song / you Know. E. E. Cummings. CP-CummE

Oi! oi! *noli me tangere*, no argument. Millipede, The. John Updike. CP-UpdiJ

Oibò, piccina / Tutto atterrita. Christina Georgina Rossetti. CP-RosC3

Oil. Gary Snyder. CP-SnydG

Oil and Blood. William Butler Yeats. CP-YeatW

Oil & Wine, / Sparkling gems, & rich attire. Ralph Waldo Emerson. CP-EmerR

Oil brown smog over Denver. Who Runs America? Allen Ginsberg. CP-GinsA

Oil for extreme unction must be blessed, The. Rule, The. Richard Wilbur. CP-WilbR

Oil in wild Aladdin's lamp, The. Rose in Candlelight, A. Walter De la Mare. CP-DeLaW

Oil is spilling down the little stream. Breaking of Rainbows, The. Howard Nemerov. CP-NemeH

Oil Painting of the Artist as the Artist. Archibald MacLeish. CP-MacLA

Oil tel duh woil doi sez. E. E. Cummings. CP-CummE

Ointment, The. Thomas Merton. CP-MertT

OK, lift this mask. Happy-Go-Lucky's Wolf Skull Dream Mask. Yusef Komunyakaa. CP-KomuY

OK Neal / aethereal Spirit. Elegy for Neal Cassady. Allen Ginsberg. CP-GinsA; SP-GinsA

Okay, today I'm the teacher. Measure. Clarence Major. SP-MajoC

Ōkeanos and the Golden Sickle. Kenneth Rexroth. CP-RexrK

Okeanos rages, tears rocks back in his path. Maximus, at the Harbor. Charles Olson. SP-OlsoC *Fr.* Maximus Poems, The.

Oklahoma Ligno and Lithograph Co, The. Corporate Entity. Archibald MacLeish. CP-MacLA

Ol' Bunk's Band. William Carlos Williams. CP-WilW2

Ol' time's gone, de new time's hyeah, De. Long Ago. Paul Laurence Dunbar. CP-DunbP

Ol' Tunes, The. Paul Laurence Dunbar. CP-DunbP

Olbers' Paradox. Lawrence Ferlinghetti. SP-FerlL

Old. Paul Laurence Dunbar. CP-DunbP

Old. David Ignatow. SP-IgnaD

Old. Thomas Merton. CP-MertT

Old. Anne Sexton. CP-SextA; SP-SextA

Old. Louis Zukofsky. CP-ZukLS

Old Actor Addresses Julius Caesar, An. Decimus Laberius. CP-CunnJ, *tr. by* James Vincent Cunningham

Old Adam, The. Denise Levertov. SP-LeveDP

Old Age. Sir Philip Sidney. SP-SidnP *Fr.* Arcadia.

Old Age. Ralph Waldo Emerson. CP-EmerR

Old Age. Langston Hughes. CP-HughL; CP-HughL3

Old Age. Jones Very. CP-VeryJ

Old Age Compensation. James Wright. CP-WrigJ

Old Age Echoes. Philip Whalen. SP-WhalP

Old age hath clawed me with his scaly clutch. Robinson Jeffers. CP-JefR3

Old age is. To Waken an Old Lady. William Carlos Williams. CP-WilW1

Old Age of Queen Maeve, The. William Butler Yeats. CP-YeatW

Old age sticks / up Keep. E. E. Cummings. CP-CummE

Old age (the name that others give it). In Praise of Darkness. Jorge Luis Borges. SP-BorgJ, *tr. by* Hoyt Rogers

Old Age's Lambent Peaks. Walt Whitman. CP-WhitW

Old Age's Ship & Crafty Death's. Walt Whitman. CP-WhitW

Old Amusement Park. Marianne Craig Moore. CP-MoorM

Old, and abandon'd by each venal friend. Impromptu. Thomas Gray. CP-GrayT

Old and New Art (Not as These). Dante Gabriel Rossetti. CW-RossD *Fr.* House of Life, The.

Old and New Art (St Luke the Painter). Dante Gabriel Rossetti. CW-RossD *Fr.* House of Life, The.

Old and New Art (The Husbandmen). Dante Gabriel Rossetti. CW-RossD *Fr.* House of Life, The.

Old and New Year Ditties. Christina Georgina Rossetti. CP-RosC1

Old and sick final years over a hundred. Han-shan. CP-ColdM, *tr. by* Red Pine

Old and the New Masters, The. Randall Jarrell. CP-JarrR

Old Angler, The. Walter De la Mare. CP-DeLaW

Old Apple-Tree, The. Paul Laurence Dunbar. CP-DunbP

Old Archangels. D. H. Lawrence. CP-LawrD

Old Archibald, in his eternal chair. Archibald's Example. Edwin Arlington Robinson. CP-RobiE

Old Band, The. James Whitcomb Riley. CP-RileJ

Old Barn at the Bottom of the Fogs, The. Robert Frost. CP-FrosR

Old Barque's picture we took from the wall, The. Barque Aurelia of Boston, The. Jones Very. CP-VeryJ

Old beast ended in this place, An. Burnt-out Spa, The. Sylvia Plath. CP-PlatS

Old Becker crawling in the night. Coronation Murder, The. Robert Graves. CP-GravR

Old Ben. Walter De la Mare. CP-DeLaW

Old black-man showed me, The. Canthara. William Carlos Williams. CP-WilW1

Old, black, rutting tomcat, An. Old Tom. Richard Eberhart. CP-EberR

Old blanket, The. The crumbs of rubbed wool turning up. Adrienne Rich. SP-RicA2 *Fr.* Shooting Script.

Old blind woman was sitting on her doorstep by the street, An. Scrutiny. Yannis Ritsos. SP-RitsY, *tr. by* Kimon Friar

Old Blue. William Stafford. SP-StafWW

Old Boards. Robert Bly. SP-BlyR

Old Boast, The. W. S. Merwin. SP-MerwW

Old Bob-white and Chipbird, The. Few of the Bird-Family, A. James Whitcomb Riley. CP-RileJ

Old Bob White's a funny bird! James Whitcomb Riley. CP-RileJ

Old Bones. Sam Hamill. SP-HamiS

Old boys, the cracked boards spread before. Bread. James Dickey. CP-DickJ

Old brown hen and the old blue sky, The. Continual Conversation with a Silent Man. Wallace Stevens. CP-StevW; CP-StevWP

Old brown thorn-trees break in two high over Cummen Strand, The. Red

Hanrahan's Song about Ireland. William Butler Yeats. CP-YeatW

Old buccaneers are leaving, The. Move, The. James Tate. SP-TateJ

Old buddha road is deserted, The. Shih-te. CP-ColdM, *tr.* by Red Pine

Old Buddy, An. Charles Bukowski. SP-BukC3

Old Burying-Ground, The. John Greenleaf Whittier. CP-WhitJ

Old Cabin, The. Paul Laurence Dunbar. CP-DunbP

Old Cadets, The. Wyatt Prunty. SP-PrunW

Old Care with Industry and Art. Care and Generosity. Christopher Smart. SP-SmarC

Old Chants. Walt Whitman. CP-WhitW

Old Chartist, The. George Meredith. CP-MerG1

Old Chums. James Whitcomb Riley. CP-RileJ

Old Chung north of town. Han-shan. CP-ColdM, *tr.* by Red Pine

Old church tower and garden wall, The. Emily Jane Brontë. CP-BronE

Old Cities. Andrei Codrescu. SP-CodrA

Old Clothes Man, The. Stanley Kunitz. CP-KunSC

Old-Clothes Woman, The. Stéphane Mallarmé. CP-MallS *Fr.* Street Songs.

Old cloud passes mourning her daughter. Sunset after Rain. W. S. Merwin. SP-MerwW

Old clown hands out flyers at the station, An. How Clowns Go. Adam Zagajewski. SP-ZagaA, *tr.* by Clare Cavanagh

Old coach-road through a common of furze, The. Meeting, The. George Meredith. CP-MerG1

Old colleague, / Puritan New England's famous scholar. Night Watch in the City of Boston. Archibald MacLeish. CP-MacLA

Old Colonial Imperialist, An. Howard Nemerov. CP-NemeH

Old Comedian, The. James Laughlin. CP-LaugJ

Old Country, The. Howard Nemerov. CP-NemeH

Old Countryside. Louise Bogan. CP-BogaL

Old Couple. Charles Simic. SP-SimiC; SP-SimiCE

Old Couples. Hans Magnus Enzensberger. SP-EnzeH

Old courtesans, installed in threadbare chairs. Games of Chance. Charles Baudelaire. CP-BaudC, *tr.* by Walter Martin

Old Cracked Tune, An. Stanley Kunitz. CP-KunSC

Old creation Thou hast formed is dead, The. Old Things Are Passed Away. Jones Very. CP-VeryJ

Old Cuckoo's Song, The. Federico García Lorca. CP-GarcF, *tr.* by Jerome Rothenberg *Fr.* Cúckoo-Cuckoo-Cuckóo.

Old Cumberland Beggar, The. William Wordsworth. CP-WorW1; MW-WorW

Old Danvers Burying-Ground, The. Jones Very. *See* Lines on the Old Danvers Burying Ground

Old Darned Man, The. Stanley Kunitz. CP-KunSC

Old daughter, small traveler. Making the Jam without You. Maxine W. Kumin. SP-KumiM

Old Davis owned a solid mica mountain. Fountain, a Bottle, a Donkey's Ears and Some Books, A. Robert Frost. CP-FrosR

Old Day the gardener seemed. Figure of Time, A. Denise Levertov. SP-LeveDP

Old Days, The. Raymond Carver. CP-CarvR

Old Days, The. Howard Nemerov. CP-NemeH

Old days—the far days, The. James Whitcomb Riley. CP-RileJ

Old Declaratives. Wyatt Prunty. SP-PrunW

Old Deep Sing-Song. Carl Sandburg. CP-SandC

Old desperation of the flesh, An. Observation of October. Howard Nemerov. CP-NemeH

Old Detective Begins His Last Interrogation Looking for the Truth as Always, The. Miller Williams. CP-WillM

Old Dichotomy: Choosing Sides. Richard Eberhart. CP-EberR

Old dissembler who lived out his lie, An. Epigrams: "Old dissembler who lived out his lie, An." James Vincent Cunningham. CP-CunnJ

Old Dog Dead. Robert Penn Warren. CP-WarrR

Old Dog Queenie. Langston Hughes. CP-HughL

Old Dog's Song, The. Grace Paley. CP-PalGC

Old Dr God. James Laughlin. CP-LaugJ

Old Dreams. Ivor Gurney. SP-GurnI

Old Dutch Woman, The. Gary Snyder. CP-SnydG

Old Dwarf Heart. Anne Sexton. CP-SextA; SP-SextA

Old Earth keepeth her watch the same, The. Earth's Vigil, The. G. K. Chesterton. CP-ChesG

Old Eben Flood, climbing alone one night. Mr Flood's Party. Edwin Arlington Robinson. CP-RobiE

Old Ebenezer Bryce the. Cincinnatus in Utah. James Laughlin. CP-LaugJ

Old Eddie's face, wrinkled with river lights. Glory Trumpeter, The. Derek Walcott. CP-WalcD

Old Ella Mason keeps cats, eleven at last count. Ella Mason and Her Eleven Cats. Sylvia Plath. CP-PlatS

Old Elm Tree by the River, The. Wendell Berry. CP-BerrW

Old Euclid drew a circle. Euclid. Nicholas Vachel Lindsay. CP-LindV *Fr.* Poems about the Moon.

Old Excursions. Thomas Hardy. CP-HardT

Old fabulous rendering up. Flame of a Candle, The. Howard Nemerov. CP-NemeH

Old farm-house is Mother's yet and mine, The. Where the Children Used to Play. James Whitcomb Riley. CP-RileJ

Old farmers, travelers, workmen (no matter how crippled or bent). True Conquerors. Walt Whitman. CP-WhitW

Old-Fashioned Air. Ted Berrigan. SP-BerrT

Old Fashioned American Business Man, An. Richard Eberhart. CP-EberR

Old-fashioned Bible, The. James Whitcomb Riley. CP-RileJ

Old-Fashioned German Christmas Card, An. William Carlos Williams. CP-WilW2

Old-Fashioned Lightning Rod. John Updike. CP-UpdiJ

Old-Fashioned Requited Love. Carl Sandburg. CP-SandC

Old-Fashioned Roses. James Whitcomb Riley. CP-RileJ

Old-fashioned shadows hanging down, that difficulty in love too soon. 37 Haiku. John Ashbery. SP-AshbJ

Old fat fish of everlasting life. Lines on a Carp. Gary Snyder. CP-SnydG

Old father Ocean calls my tide. Song: "Old father Ocean calls my tide." John Dryden. CP-DryJ2; SP-DrydJ *Fr.* Albion and Albanius.

Old fathers, great-grandfathers. Love's Loneliness. William Butler Yeats. CP-YeatW

Old Field Mowed for Appearances' Sake, An. William Meredith. SP-MereW

Old fir young fir. Roadside. Olga Broumas. SP-BrouO

Old Fitz, who from your suburb grange. To E. Fitzgerald. Alfred Tennyson. CP-TennA

Old Flag. W. S. Merwin. SP-MerwW

Old Flagman, The. Carl Sandburg. CP-SandC

Old flagman has great-grandchildren, The. Old Flagman, The. Carl Sandburg. CP-SandC

Old Flame. Robert Penn Warren. CP-WarrR

Old Flame, The. Robert Lowell. SP-LoweR

Old Florist. Theodore Roethke. CP-RoetT

Old folks play a game, The. Traffic Signals. Charles Bukowski. SP-BukC1

Old Fools, The. Philip Larkin. CP-LarkP

Old frescoes on great abbey walls portray. Bad Monk, The. Charles Baudelaire. CP-BaudC, *tr.* by Walter Martin

Old Friend, An. James Whitcomb Riley. CP-RileJ

Old friend, I dressed in my very best. Final Meeting. Carolyn Kizer. SP-KizeC

Old friend, it's easy. However you behave. Anent Socrates, or Somebody. Hayden Carruth. CP-CarHS

Old friend, kind friend! lightly down. To My Old Schoolmaster. John Greenleaf Whittier. CP-WhitJ

Old friend of mine, whose chiming name. Dan Paine. James Whitcomb Riley. CP-RileJ

Old Friends. Peter Blue Cloud. SP-BlueP

Old friends allus is the best. Back from Town. James Whitcomb Riley. CP-RileJ

Old Front Gate, The. Paul Laurence Dunbar. CP-DunbP

Old fun is too true for the truth. Old. Thomas Merton. CP-MertT

Old Furniture. Thomas Hardy. CP-HardT

Old Gang, The. Charles Bukowski. SP-BukC3

Old Garden. W. S. Merwin. SP-MerwWF

Old garden of grayish and ochre lichen. To the Rock That Will Be a Cornerstone of the House. Robinson Jeffers. CP-JefR1

Old Gentleman in the Park, The. G. K. Chesterton. CP-ChesG

Old Ghosts. Stevie Smith. CP-SmitS

Old Glory. William Stafford. SP-StafWW

Old Glory at halfmast. From the New World. Donald Davie. CP-DaviDC

Old Glory! say, who. Name of Old Glory, The. James Whitcomb Riley. CP-RileJ

Old goatherds swear how all night long they hear. Goatsucker. Sylvia Plath. CP-PlatS

Old Gods, The. Carolyn Kizer. SP-KizeC *Fr.* Heine Journal, A.

Old Gown, The. Thomas Hardy. CP-HardT

Old Granny Dusk, when the sun goes down. James Whitcomb Riley. CP-RileJ

Old Gray Couple (1), The. Archibald MacLeish. CP-MacLA

Old Gray Couple (2), The. Archibald MacLeish. CP-MacLA

Old grey Alp has caught the cold, The. By the Rosanna. George Meredith. CP-MerG1

Old grey mother she thrummed on her knee, The. Margaret's Bridal-Eve. George Meredith. CP-MerG1

Old Guitar, The. James Whitcomb Riley. CP-RileJ

Old guy / next door, The. Patriot of Life, A. Charles Bukowski. SP-BukC3

Old guy put down his beer, The. Do the Dead Know What Time It Is? Kenneth Patchen. CP-PatcK

Old half blinded hawk—but how can he hunt with only one eye?—, The. Robinson Jeffers. CP-JefR3

Old Hall of Elbë, ruined, lonely now. Emily Jane Brontë. CP-BronE

Old Hamer Place. William Stafford. SP-StafWW

Old Hamilton hailed the man from the grocery store. Lorine Niedecker. CP-NiedL

Old Hand-Organ, The. James Whitcomb Riley. CP-RileJ

Old Harry. Thomas Kinsella. CP-KinsT

Old have a secret, The. Trying to Tell It. William Stafford. SP-StafWW

Old Haymow, The. James Whitcomb Riley. CP-RileJ

Old Haymow's the place to play, The. Old Haymow, The. James Whitcomb Riley. CP-RileJ

Old he was but not yet wax. My Father's Face. Hayden Carruth. CP-CarHL

Old heavens, you used to tweak above us. John Ashbery. SP-AshbJ *Fr.* Skaters, The.

Old Hec's Idolatry. James Whitcomb Riley. CP-RileJ

Old High School and the New, The. Paul Laurence Dunbar. CP-DunbP

Old hill town in northern Pennsylvania, a missed connection for a bus, an hour to kill, An. Neglect. C. K. Williams. SP-WillC

Old Hokusai Print. Carl Sandburg. CP-SandC

Old Home by the Mill, The. James Whitcomb Riley. CP-RileJ

Old Home-Folks, The. James Whitcomb Riley. CP-RileJ *Fr.* Child-World, A.

Old Home Week. Donald Hall. CP-HallD

Old Homestead, The. Paul Laurence Dunbar. CP-DunbP

Old Horn to All Atlantic said. Frankie's Trade. Rudyard Kipling. CP-KiplR

Old horse dies slow, The. When Structure Fails Rhyme Attempts to Come to the Rescue. William Carlos Williams. CP-WilW2

Old Horse in the City, The. Nicholas Vachel Lindsay. CP-LindV

Old hound wags his shaggy tail, The. Over the Hills. George Meredith. CP-MerG2

Old House, The. Yannis Ritsos. SP-RitsY, *tr. by* Kostas Myrsiades

Old House, The. William Carlos Williams. CP-WilW2

Old House, The. Marya Alexandrovna Zaturenska. SP-ZatuM

Old house grows, adding rooms of silence, The. House Growing, The. John Updike. CP-UpdiJ

Old Houses. Donald Hall. CP-HallD

Old houses, and new-fangled violence. Ransom. Robert Penn Warren. CP-WarrR

Old Houses of Salem: Illustrated by George M. White. Jones Very. CP-VeryJ

Old Icons, The. Seamus Heaney. SP-HeanSO *Fr.* Sweeney Redivivus.

Old Idea of Sacrifice, The. D. H. Lawrence. CP-LawrD

Old Indian Belief. A. K. Ramanujan. CP-RamaA

Old Indiany, 'course we know. James Whitcomb Riley. CP-RileJ

Old inventive Poets, had they seen, The. Plain of Donnerdale, The. William Wordsworth. CP-WorW2 *Fr.* River Duddon [A Series of Sonnets], The.

Old Ireland. Walt Whitman. CP-WhitW

Old is the song that I sing. Rudyard Kipling. *See* Ahasuerus Jenkins of the "Operatic Own"

Old Issue, The. Rudyard Kipling. CP-KiplR

Old Italians Dying, The. Lawrence Ferlinghetti. SP-FerlL

Old Jewish Cemetery, The. Lost Paradise. Jaroslav Seifert. SP-SeifJ, *tr. by* Ewald Osers

Old John Clevenger lets on. Old John Clevenger on Buckeyes. James Whitcomb Riley. CP-RileJ

Old John Clevenger on Buckeyes. James Whitcomb Riley. CP-RileJ

Old John Henry. James Whitcomb Riley. CP-RileJ

Old John's jes' made o' the commonest stuff. Old John Henry. James Whitcomb Riley. CP-RileJ

Old joints of the house, The. Winter Gale. Alan Dugan. CP-DugaA

Old King, The. Denise Levertov. SP-LeveDS

Old King Cole. Edwin Arlington Robinson. CP-RobiE

Old King's New Jester, The. Edwin Arlington Robinson. CP-RobiE

Old Ladies' Home. Sylvia Plath. CP-PlatS

Old ladies' skulls. Shadow Boxes. Tennessee Williams. CP-WillT

Old lady walking, wears gloves. It is a shady, The. Linkwood Road. Josephine Jacobsen. CP-JacoJ

Old lady who lives to the east, An. Han-shan. CP-ColdM, *tr. by* Red Pine

Old lady with the pince-nez whirling. Odessa Steps, The. Amy Clampitt. CP-ClamA

Old lady writes me in a spidery style, An. Letter from Brooklyn, A. Derek Walcott. CP-WalcD

Old Lady's Old Men! Arthur Rimbaud. CP-RimbA, *tr. by* Martin Sorrell

Old Latimer preaching did fairly describe. On the Irish Bishops. Jonathan Swift. CP-SwifJ

Old Lean over the Tombstones, The. Kenneth Patchen. CP-PatcK

Old lean over the tombstones, the, The. Kenneth Patchen. CP-PatcK

Old Lewis thus the terms of peace to burnish. Jonathan Swift. CP-SwifJ *Fr.* Dunkirk to be Let.

Old liar, death, do you think I don't see you? Challenger, The. Mona Van Duyn. SP-VanDM

Old *Life* photograph, An. Sister by the Pond, A. Donald Hall. CP-HallD

Old Likeness, An. Thomas Hardy. CP-HardT

Old Lines. Eugenio Montale. CP-MontE, *tr. by* Jonathan Galassi

Old lion hunter and I, The. Sense of Proportion. Kenneth Rexroth. CP-RexrK

Old Lizard, The. Federico García Lorca. CP-GarcF, *tr. by* Catherine Brown

Old Lizard, The. Federico García Lorca. SP-GarcF, *tr. by* Lysander Kemp

Old Love. Robert Penn Warren. CP-WarrR

Old love is old resentment, novelty. James Vincent Cunningham. CP-CunnJ

Old Lutheran Bells at Home, The. Wallace Stevens. CP-StevW; CP-StevWP

Old, mad, blind, despised, and dying king, An. England in 1819. Percy Bysshe Shelley. CP-ShelP

Old maid early eer I knew, An. William Blake. CP-BlakW

Old Man. John Ciardi. CP-CiarJ

Old Man. Kenneth Patchen. CP-PatcK

Old Man, An. Constantine P. Cavafy. CP-CavaC, *tr. by* Theoharis Constantine Theoharis

Old Man, An. Robert Pinsky. CP-PinsR

Old man alone in a house, An. Prognosis. James Laughlin. CP-LaugJ

Old Man, The. John Clare. SP-ClarJ

Old Man, The. George Oppen. CP-OppGN

Old Man, The. James Whitcomb Riley. CP-RileJ

Old Man and Jim, The. James Whitcomb Riley. CP-RileJ

Old Man and the Child, The. "Ping Hsin." CP-WilW2

Old man asked me: What is Love? I turned, An. Grown Cold. Christina Georgina Rossetti. CP-RosC3

Old Man Asleep, An. Wallace Stevens. CP-StevW; CP-StevWP

Old Man at Valdez. Charles Tomlinson. CP-TomlC

Old man bending I come among new faces, An. Wound-Dresser, The. Walt Whitman. CP-WhitW

Old man bundled into a long ulster, An. Mulciber at West Egg. Amy Clampitt. CP-ClamA

Old man cocked his ear upon a bridge, An. Phases of the Moon, The. William Butler Yeats. CP-YeatW

Old man, come out in the sun. Bermuda. Jane Cooper. CP-CoopJ

Old Man Confesses, An. John Ciardi. CP-CiarJ

Old man, contemptuous, black-hearted, An. Separate Notebooks, The. Czeslaw Milosz. CP-MiloCN

Old Man, Dead in a Room. Charles Bukowski. SP-BukC2

Old Man Drunk. James Wright. CP-WrigJ

Old Man Goes South Again Alone. John Berryman. CP-BerrJ

Old man had his box and wheel, The. Scissors-Grinder, The. Nicholas Vachel Lindsay. CP-LindV

Old man, it's four flights up and for what? Doors, Doors, Doors. Anne Sexton. CP-SextA

Old Man Leaves His Church for the Last Time, An. Miller Williams. CP-WillM

Old man never had much to say. Old Man and Jim, The. James Whitcomb Riley. CP-RileJ

Old Man of the Alps, The. Samuel Taylor Coleridge. CP-ColeS

Old Man of the Sea, The. James Whitcomb Riley. CP-RileJ

Old man planted and dug and tended, An. Disappointed. Paul Laurence Dunbar. CP-DunbP

Old Man Playing with Children. John Crowe Ransom. SP-RansJ

Old man realizes that he is seeing signs of a bodily reversion to his youth, An. Scenario. David Ignatow. SP-IgnaD

Old man remembers to old man. Old Home Week. Donald Hall. CP-HallD

Old man riding his slow bike, An. Crash. Gary Snyder. CP-SnydG

Old Man Shoveling Snow. Thomas Lux. SP-LuxT

Old man sits, An. Six Significant Landscapes. Wallace Stevens. CP-StevW; CP-StevWP

Old man sits on the doorsill, The. Evening. Alone. Black Boat, The. Yannis Ritsos. SP-RitsY, *tr. by* Kostas Myrsiades

Old man sleeping in the evening train, An. Evening Train. Denise Levertov. SP-LeveDS

Old man, tapping with his cane, aware of his silence, An. Retired. Czeslaw Milosz. CP-MiloCN, *tr. by* Robert Hass

Old man to the child, The. Old Man and the Child, The. "Ping Hsin." CP-WilW2

Old Man to the Lizard, The. Archibald MacLeish. CP-MacLA

Old Man Travelling [Animal Tranquillity and Decay, a Sketch]. William Wordsworth. MW-WorW

Old Man Whiskery-Whee-Kum-Wheeze. James Whitcomb Riley. CP-RileJ

Old man who can undress before you, The. Nurse. David Ignatow. SP-IgnaD

Old man who goes about, The. Pastoral 1: "Old man who goes about, The." William Carlos Williams. CP-WilW1

Old man who had dug the small pit, The. Burial. May Sarton. SP-SartM

Old man who seined. Lorine Niedecker. CP-NiedL

Old man whose black face, An. Rainwalkers, The. Denise Levertov. SP-LeveDP

Old man, with hair made of newspaper cutting. Public Son of a Public Man, The. Stephen Spender. CP-SpenS

Old man Woolworth put up a building. Again? Carl Sandburg. CP-SandC

Old man, you surface seldom. Full Fathom Five. Sylvia Plath. CP-PlatS

Old Man's Beard. Charles Tomlinson. CP-TomlC

Old man's blood had spoken the word: 'Enough,' The. Small Events. Ted Hughes. SP-HughTN

Old man's heart sleeping in its morgue, An. Dead, The. Rainer Maria Rilke. CP-RilkFr, tr. by A. Poulin, Jr.

Old Man's Journey. Archibald MacLeish. CP-MacLA

Old man's lazy, The. Peter Blue Cloud. SP-BlueP

Old Man's Memory, An. James Whitcomb Riley. CP-RileJ

Old Man's Nursery Rhyme. James Whitcomb Riley. CP-RileJ

Old Man's Road, The. W. H. Auden. CP-AudeW

Old Man's Thought of School, An. Walt Whitman. CP-WhitW

Old man's wasting brain, An; a ruined city. Life and Letters. Adrienne Rich. CP-RicAE

Old Man's Winter Night, An. Robert Frost. CP-FrosR

Old Mansion. John Crowe Ransom. SP-RansJ

Old maple hairytrunks root asphalt grass marge, November branches rare leaved. Have You Seen This Movie? Allen Ginsberg. CP-GinsA

Old Marlborough Road, The. Henry David Thoreau. CP-ThorH

Old Martinmas Eve. Ivor Gurney. SP-GurnI

Old marvel of will, me, famished for vanity. Poem to Me. William Meredith. SP-MereW

Old Mary. Gwendolyn Brooks. SP-BrooG

Old master yourself now, Auden, An. As You Like It. Theodore Weiss. SP-WeisT

Old Masters Abroad. Louis MacNeice. CP-MacNL

Old meeting-house bell. Henry David Thoreau. CP-ThorH

Old Meg. Thom Gunn. CP-GunnT

Old Meg She Was a Gipsy. John Keats. See Meg Merrilies [or Merrilees]

Old Meg she was a gipsy [or gypsy]. Meg Merrilies [or Merrilees]. John Keats. CP-KeatJ

Old Melancholy. Federico García Lorca. CP-GarcF, tr. by Jerome Rothenberg

Old Memory. William Butler Yeats. CP-YeatW

Old Memory, An. Paul Laurence Dunbar. CP-DunbP

Old Men. D. H. Lawrence. CP-LawrD

Old Men. Ogden Nash. CP-NashO

Old Men, The. Walter De la Mare. CP-DeLaW

Old Men, The. Rudyard Kipling. CP-KiplR

Old Men, The. William Carlos Williams. CP-WilW1

Old Men Admiring Themselves in the Water, The. William Butler Yeats. CP-YeatW

Old men and women walk by my window. Winter Afternoon. Grace Paley. CP-PalGC

Old Men Are Fond. Tennessee Williams. CP-WillT

Old men are talking about sex, The. On the Deck. Grace Paley. CP-PalGC

Old Men at Pevensey. Rudyard Kipling. Fr. Puck of Pook's Hill.

Old Men Go Mad at Night. Tennessee Williams. CP-WillT

Old Men in the Leaf Smoke, The. Archibald MacLeish. CP-MacLA

Old men live a life. Hebrides. Archibald MacLeish. CP-MacLA

Old men rake the yards for winter, The. Old Men in the Leaf Smoke, The. Archibald MacLeish. CP-MacLA

Old men say, The. Why the Telephone Wires Dip and the Poles Are Cracked and Crooked. John Updike. CP-UpdiJ

Old men, son, drink whisky, for they know, The. Moonshine. Howard Nemerov. CP-NemeH

Old men walking abroad. Old Men with Sticks. Tennessee Williams. CP-WillT

Old men wept when the Old Man in blue, The. Ancestor. John Berryman. CP-BerrJ

Old Men with Sticks. Tennessee Williams. CP-WillT

Old Men's Souls, The. Constantine P. Cavafy. CP-CavaC, tr. by Theoharis Constantine Theoharis

Old mr ly / fresh from a fu. E. E. Cummings. CP-CummE

Old Mole. Primo Levi. CP-LeviP, tr. by Ruth Feldman

Old monk is turned loose / And can travel!, The. Thomas Merton. CP-MertT

Old moon my eyes are now moon with human footprint. Poem Rocket. Allen Ginsberg. CP-GinsA

Old Mother Act and her child Fact-of-Act. That Ancient Line. Laura Riding Jackson. CP-RidiL

Old Mother Laidinwool. Rudyard Kipling. CP-KiplR

Old Mother turns blue and from us. Lorine Niedecker. CP-NiedL

Old motorbike she was, The. Greta. Derek Mahon. CP-MahoD

Old Mountain Road. Charles Simic. SP-SimiC; SP-SimiCE

Old Mrs. Kawabata. Yase: September. Gary Snyder. CP-SnydG

Old Music for Quiet Hearts. Carl Sandburg. CP-SandC

Old nails, their large flat heads. Two Artists. Denise Levertov. SP-LeveDL

Old Neighbour and the New, The. Thomas Hardy. CP-HardT

Old New England. Derek Walcott. CP-WalcD

Old newspapers. 1 December 1948. Yannis Ritsos. SP-RitsY Fr. Exile's Journals 2.

Old Nigger on One-Mule Cart Encountered Late at Night when Driving Home from Party in the Back Country. Robert Penn Warren. CP-WarrR

Old Night and Sleep. Norman Dubie. CP-DubiN

Old Noah he had an ostrich farm and fowls on the largest scale. Wine and Water. G. K. Chesterton. CP-ChesG

Old Nollekens? No, Little Nollekens. Nollekens. Randall Jarrell. CP-JarrR

Old Norbert with the flat blue cap. Leipzig. Thomas Hardy. CP-HardT

Old now, / your eyes nearly blank. Benjamin Banneker Sends His Almanac to Thomas Jefferson. Jay Wright. SP-WrigJ

Old No. 1. May Swenson. SP-SwenM

Old oak, old timber, sunk and rooted. G. M. B. Donald Davie. CP-DaviDC

Old Oats. Ted Hughes. SP-HughTN

Old oblivion-book, that I lay open. Accountability. Gerrit Achterberg. CP-RicAE

Old October's purt' nigh gone. James Whitcomb Riley. CP-RileJ

Old, old widow Greedy needs wo'd wed, An. Upon Greedy. Robert Herrick. CP-HerrR

Old, Old Wish, The. James Whitcomb Riley. CP-RileJ

Old ones to the side. Psalm: "Old ones to the side." Charles Simic. SP-SimiC; SP-SimiCE

Old ones want to be young, and they aren't young, The. Grudge of the Old, The. D. H. Lawrence. CP-LawrD

Old Orchard, The. D. H. Lawrence. CP-LawrD

Old orchard in the middle of the forest, The. Randall Jarrell. CP-JarrR

Old Organ of the East Society Salem, The. Jones Very. CP-VeryJ

Old Osawatomie. Carl Sandburg. CP-SandC

Old pagan burials, uninscribed rock, The. Delusion of Saints. Robinson Jeffers. CP-JefR2

Old Paintings on Italian Walls. Kathleen Jessie Raine. SP-RainK

Old Pair of Shoes, An. Kenneth Patchen. CP-PatcK

Old Parson Beanes hunts six days [or dayes] of the week. Upon Parson Beanes. Robert Herrick. CP-HerrR

Old Penobscot Indian, The. Flux. Richard Eberhart. CP-EberR

Old People. D. H. Lawrence. CP-LawrD

Old People Dozing. Denise Levertov. SP-LeveDL

Old People's Home. W. H. Auden. CP-AudeW

Old person of Troy, An. First Limick. Ogden Nash. CP-NashO

Old Photo. Andrei Codrescu. SP-CodrA

Old Photograph, An. Howard Nemerov. CP-NemeH

Old Photograph of Strangers, An. William Meredith. SP-MereW

Old Photograph of the Future. Robert Penn Warren. CP-WarrR

Old photographs would have her bookish, sitting. Ma. Paul Muldoon. CP-MuldP

Old Picture, An. Howard Nemerov. CP-NemeH

Old Pictures in Florence. Robert Browning. CP-BroR1

Old Pilot, The. Donald Hall. CP-HallD

Old Planters, The. Jones Very. CP-VeryJ

Old Played-out Song, A. James Whitcomb Riley. CP-RileJ

Old Poems. Randall Jarrell. CP-JarrR

Old poems from long ago. Sorting Old Papers. Donald Davie. CP-DaviDC

Old Poet Moves to a New Aprtment 14 Times, The. Louis Zukofsky. CP-ZukLS

Old Poet, Poetry's final subject glimmers months ahead. Don't Grow Old. Allen Ginsberg. CP-GinsA Fr. Don't Grow Old.

Old Pond. Allen Ginsberg. CP-GinsA; SP-GinsA

Old pond—a frog jumps in, kerplunk!, The. Old Pond. Allen Ginsberg. CP-GinsA; SP-GinsA

Old powers rise and do return to me. San Vio. June. Ezra Pound. CP-PoEar

Old priest Peter Gilligan, The. Ballad of Father Gilligan, The. William Butler Yeats. CP-YeatW

Old Prof. William Stafford. SP-StafWW

Old Question. Richard Eberhart. CP-EberR

Old radio, its dial showing all the names of the cities, glows again, The. Sominex. Dan Pagis. SP-PagiD, tr. by Stephen Mitchell

Old Retired Sea-Captain, The. James Whitcomb Riley. CP-RileJ

Old Revolution. Hans Magnus Enzensberger. SP-EnzeH

Old Riddle, An. G. K. Chesterton. CP-ChesG

Old Road, The. Jones Very. CP-VeryJ

Old road followed, The. Memory of Old Forms under Hell's Angels. Alan Dugan. CP-DugaA

Old Roman sow / Bears a new litter now, The. Fable for a War. Thomas Merton. CP-MertT

Old Room, The. W. S. Merwin. SP-MerwW

Old Roscoff. Tristan Corbière. CP-MahoD, tr. by Derek Mahon

Old Roses. Donald Hall. CP-HallD

Old Rotting Tree Trunk Down. Gary Snyder. CP-SnydG

Old rusty-belly thing will soon be gone. Sappa Creek, The. Gary Snyder. CP-SnydG

Old Sailor. Langston Hughes. CP-HughL; CP-HughL2

Old Sailors, The. Lawrence Ferlinghetti. SP-FerlL

Old Salt Kossabone. Walt Whitman. CP-WhitW

Old sandpiper contemplates his age, The. Summer's Early End at Hudson's Bay. Hayden Carruth. CP-CarHS

Old Saying. Robert Creeley. SP-CreeR

Old Saying, An. Algernon Charles Swinburne. SP-SwinA

Old School-Chum, The. James Whitcomb Riley. CP-RileJ

Old sea-captain has sailed the seas, The. Old Retired Sea-Captain, The. James Whitcomb Riley. CP-RileJ

Old shoe, an old pot, an old skin, An. Autumn Sequence. Adrienne Rich. CP-RicAE

Old sick green parrot, The. Parrot. Stevie Smith. CP-SmitS

Old sir, I think of you in this tardy spring. To Lu Chi. Howard Nemerov. CP-NemeH

Old sisters at our Maris Stella House. Mother Marie Therese. Robert Lowell. SP-LoweR

Old Snaps, The. Derek Mahon. CP-MahoD

Old snapshot from Venice 1952. Robert Lowell. SP-LoweR

Old snow gets up and moves taking its, The. December among the Vanished. W. S. Merwin. SP-MerwW

Old Soldiers' Home, The. Howard Nemerov. CP-NemeH

Old Song. Hart Crane. CP-CranH

Old Song. Robert Creeley. CP-CreeR

Old Song. D. H. Lawrence. CP-LawrD

Old Song, An. Randall Jarrell. CP-JarrR

Old Song, An. Rudyard Kipling. CP-KiplR

Old Song, The. G. K. Chesterton. CP-ChesG

Old Song and Dance, The. Kenneth Rexroth. CP-RexrK

Old Song Ended, An. Dante Gabriel Rossetti. CW-RossD

Old souse, how often, before head clears. To My Inebriety. Robert Stock. SP-StocR

Old South Boston Aquarium stands, The. For the Union Dead. Robert Lowell. SP-LoweR

Old sow in the mud. Mother of the Buddhas, Queen of Heaven, Mother of the Sun; Marici, Goddess of the Dawn. Gary Snyder. CP-SnydG

Old spoon, An. Spoon. Charles Simic. SP-SimiC; SP-SimiCE

Old Squire said, as he stood by his gate, The. Valuation. John Greenleaf Whittier. CP-WhitJ

Old / star / shuts her bleary eyes, The. In a Corner of the Sky. Federico García Lorca. CP-GarcF, *tr. by* Jerome Rothenberg *Fr.* Night (Suite for Piano and Poet's Voice).

Old Stoic, The. Emily Jane Brontë. CP-BronE

Old Stone Cross, The. William Butler Yeats. CP-YeatW

Old Stone-Mason, The. Robinson Jeffers. CP-JefR3

Old Story, An. Edwin Arlington Robinson. CP-RobiE

Old Story, The. Paul Laurence Dunbar. CP-DunbP

Old Street. Kenneth Rexroth. CP-RexrK

Old Summerhouse, The. Walter De la Mare. CP-DeLaW

Old Susan. Walter De la Mare. CP-DeLaW

Old Sweet Dove of Wiveton, The. Stevie Smith. CP-SmitS

Old sweetheart of mine!—Is this her presence here with me, An. James Whitcomb Riley. CP-RileJ

Old Swimmin'-Hole, The. James Whitcomb Riley. CP-RileJ

Old Tale, An. Marya Alexandrovna Zaturenska. SP-ZatuM

Old, the cautious, the over-wise, The. Elderly Leaders. Langston Hughes. CP-HughL; CP-HughL3

Old, the young—they sit, The. Sitting on Farm Lawn on Sunday Afternoon. Robert Penn Warren. CP-WarrR

Old Things. Tennessee Williams. CP-WillT

Old Things Are Passed Away. Jones Very. CP-VeryJ

Old things, like the button drawer. Mean. What's in My Journal. William Stafford. SP-StafWW

Old things need not be therefore true. Arthur Hugh Clough. SP-ClouA

Old Thought. Ivor Gurney. SP-GurnI

Old-time blues. Blues. Robert Creeley. SP-CreeR

Old-Time Childhood in Kentucky. Robert Penn Warren. CP-WarrR

Old-Timer, An. James Whitcomb Riley. CP-RileJ

Old Timers. Carl Sandburg. CP-SandC

Old Timer's Day. Donald Hall. *See Couplet*

Old Times. Ivor Gurney. SP-GurnI

Old Times Were the Best, The. James Whitcomb Riley. CP-RileJ

Old Tom. Richard Eberhart. CP-EberR

Old Tom Again. William Butler Yeats. CP-YeatW

Old Tom would tell us. Peter Blue Cloud. SP-BlueP

Old Trails. Edwin Arlington Robinson. CP-RobiE

Old Tramp, The. James Whitcomb Riley. CP-RileJ

Old Tramp slep' in our stable wunst, A'. Old Tramp, The. James Whitcomb Riley. CP-RileJ

Old Tree by the Penobscot. Richard Eberhart. CP-EberR

Old trees are witnesses. Kind of Ethics, A. Thom Gunn. CP-GunnT

Old Trundle-Bed, The. James Whitcomb Riley. CP-RileJ

Old Village before I Die, The. Allen Ginsberg. CP-GinsA

Old voice of the ocean, the bird-chatter of little rivers, The. Natural Music. Robinson Jeffers. CP-JefR1

Old Walt Whitman / Went finding and seeking. Langston Hughes. CP-HughL; CP-HughL3

Old War-Dreams. Walt Whitman. CP-WhitW

Old Warplane, An. Howard Nemerov. CP-NemeH

Old Warrior Terror, The. Alice Walker. CP-WalkA

Old watch: their, The. Vapor Trail Reflected in the Frog Pond. Galway Kinnell. SP-KinnGN

Old widow lady, and went out to do her chore, An. Mona Van Duyn. SP-VanDM

Old widow Prouse to do her neighbours evill. Upon an Old Woman. Robert Herrick. CP-HerrR

Old Widow Shopter, when so ere she cryes. Upon Shopter. Robert Herrick. CP-HerrR

Old Wife in High Spirits. Hugh MacDiarmid. SP-MacDH

Old willow with hollow branches, An. Epitaph: "Old willow with hollow branches." William Carlos Williams. CP-WilW1

Old winds have replaced us on the bare plains. Postponed Decision. Yannis Ritsos. SP-RitsY, *tr. by* Athan Anagnostopoulos

Old Winter, with his frosty beard. Impromptu, on Mrs. W. Riddell's Birthday, 4th Novr. 1793. Robert Burns. CP-BurnR

Old Winters on the Farm. James Whitcomb Riley. CP-RileJ

Old wives have often told, how they. Upon Cupid. Robert Herrick. CP-HerrR

Old Wives Prayer, The. Robert Herrick. CP-HerrR

Old Wolf My Father, The. Robinson Jeffers. CP-JefR3

Old Woman. Robert Pinsky. CP-PinsR

Old Woman. Carl Sandburg. CP-SandC

Old Woman, The. Thom Gunn. CP-GunnT

Old woman across the way, The. Whipping, The. Robert Earl Hayden. CP-HaydR

Old woman, An. Rembrandt's Old Woman Cutting Her Nails. George Oppen. CP-OppGN

Old woman comes, The. Clarence Major. SP-MajoC

Old woman from the country, An. Fountain, The. W. S. Merwin. SP-MerwWF

Old Woman Nature. Gary Snyder. CP-SnydG

Old woman sits on a bench before the door and quarrels, The. Fawn's Foster-Mother. Robinson Jeffers. CP-JefR1 ·

Old Woman's Vision, An. Norman Dubie. CP-DubiN

Old Women. Czeslaw Milosz. CP-MiloC; CP-MiloCN, *tr. by* Robert Hass

Old women came from their caves to close the too many doors, The. Robert Duncan. SP-DuncR *Fr.* Structure of Rime, The.

Old women come here to die. Nurses. In the Ward. Charles Tomlinson. CP-TomlC

Old wood stands uncut, of long years' space, An. Elegy 3.1: "Old wood stands uncut, of long years' space, An." Ovid. CP-MarlC *Fr.* Elegies.

Old wooden steps to the front door, The. Time Past, A. Denise Levertov. SP-LeveDL

Old words: *trust fidelity.* For Memory. Adrienne Rich. SP-RicA1; SP-RicA2

Old Workman, The. Thomas Hardy. CP-HardT

Old-World Thicket, An. Christina Georgina Rossetti. CP-RosC2

Old, worn harp that had been played, An. Master-Player, The. Paul Laurence Dunbar. CP-DunbP

Old Worshipper, The. William Carlos Williams. CP-WilW1

Old wortermelon time is a-comin' round ag'in. Wortermelon Time. James Whitcomb Riley. CP-RileJ

Old wound in my ass, The. Fabrication of Ancestors. Alan Dugan. CP-DugaA

Old Year and the New, The. James Whitcomb Riley. CP-RileJ

Old Year's Address, An. James Whitcomb Riley. CP-RileJ

Old Youth. Langston Hughes. CP-HughL; CP-HughL1

Older children pedal past, The. Learning the Bicycle. Wyatt Prunty. SP-PrunW

Oldest Conversation, The. Kenneth Patchen. CP-PatcK

Oldest Desire, The. Eleanor Wilner. SP-WilnE

Oldest joke / in the world, The. My Father's Telescope. Rita Dove. SP-DoveR

Oldest Killed Lake in North America, The. Hayden Carruth. CP-CarHS

Oldest Soldier, The. Robert Graves. CP-GravR

Oldest Song, The. Rudyard Kipling. CP-KiplR

Oldest wheel, the setting sun, The. (E)Motion. Yusef Komunyakaa. CP-KomuY

Ole Bull. James Whitcomb Riley. CP-RileJ

Ole 'Sephus (Monologue to a Coon Dog). Tennessee Williams. CP-WillT

Oleander. Yehuda Amichai. SP-AmicYL, *tr. by* Benjamin Harshav *and* Barbara Harshav

Oleander: coral. Garden, The. Rae Armantrout. SP-ArmaA

Oleander on the wall, The. By the Arno. Oscar Wilde. CP-WildO

O'Leary was a poet—for a while. Shadrach O'Leary. Edwin Arlington Robinson. CP-RobiE

Oleaster, The. Robert Graves. CP-GravR

Oleum Misericordiae. John Ashbery. SP-AshbJ

Olga Poems. Denise Levertov. SP-LeveDP; SP-LeveDS

Olim fungus ego, silex verebar. In se. Thomas Campion. CP-CampT

Olim te duro cernebam tempore Martis. Ad Rob. Caraeum Equitem Auratum Nobilissimum. Thomas Campion. CP-CampT

Olive, The. A. E. Housman. CP-HousA

Olive Branch, The. Robert Herrick. CP-HerrR

Olive Branch, The. George Meredith. CP-MerG1

Olive Garden, The. Randall Jarrell. CP-JarrR

Olive-green, sky-blue, gravel-brown. September Landscape. Robert Graves. CP-GravR

Olive Grove. James Merrill. SP-MerrJ

Olive Grove, The. May Sarton. SP-SartM

Olive Grove, The. Arthur Sze. SP-SzcA

Olive grove's his only country, An. Cops Call Him Charlie, The. Yusef Komunyakaa. CP-KomuY

Olive Groves of Thasos, The. Amy Clampitt. CP-ClamA

Olive Night. Arthur Sze. SP-SzeA

Olive Tree, The. Karl Shapiro. SP-ShapK

Olive trees were rising, The. Song of Despair. Federico García Lorca. CP-GarcF, tr. by Christopher Maurer

Olive Wood Fire, The. Galway Kinnell. SP-KinnGN

Olive Yard, The. Robert Graves. CP-GravR

Oliver C. Felton, Esq., of Brookfield. Jones Very. CP-VeryJ

Oliver wanted to write about reality. Make Big Money at Home! Write Poems in Spare Time! Howard Nemerov. CP-NemeH

Oliverio Girondo. Pablo Neruda. SP-NeruP

Olivet, Olivet! Where heaven robbed us. Whitsun Canticle, A. Thomas Merton. CP-MertT

Olney Hymns. William Cowper. CP-CowpW

    Lively Hope, and Gracious Fear. CP-CowpW

    Lord Will Happiness Divine, The. CP-CowpW

        (Contrite Heart, The.) CP-CowpW

    True Pleasures. CP-CowpW

        (Shining Light, The.) CP-CowpW

        (Submission.) CP-CowpW

Olor Iscanus queries: "Why should we." To Samuel E. Sewall and Harriet W. Sewall. John Greenleaf Whittier. CP-WhitJ

Oltre la Torre: Rolando. Ezra Pound. CP-PoEar

Olympia. Amy Clampitt. CP-ClamA

Olympia. Yusef Komunyakaa. CP-KomuY

Olympian, The. James Dickey. CP-DickJ

Olympian before the Olympics, that inhuman backdrop, An. Noble Man, The. Richard Eberhart. CP-EberR

Olympian gods, mark now my bedside lamp. Edna St. Vincent Millay. CP-MillE

Olympic Rain Forest. Jane Cooper. CP-CoopJ

Olympics have descended into, The. Big Beat. Allen Ginsberg. CP-GinsA

Olympus. John Berryman. CP-BerrJ

Om. "Rubén Dario." SP-DariR

Om! is the luminous sun. Om. "Rubén Dario." SP-DariR

OM MANI PADME HUM / LET US ERECT A COLUMN, an epicene column. Our Respectful Homages to M. Laurent Tailhade. Ezra Pound. CP-PoEar

OM—the pride of perfumed money, food music from China, a place to sit. Thoughts Sitting Breathing. Allen Ginsberg. CP-GinsA

Omaha. Carl Sandburg. CP-SandC

Omar and the Old Poet. Jelaluddin Rumi. SP-Rumi, tr. by Coleman Barks

Omega. Federico García Lorca. CP-GarcF, tr. by Greg Simon and Steven F. White

Omega. John Updike. CP-UpdiJ

Omelet of sunset vibrates in the great flat pan, The. Winter Wheat: Oklahoma. Robert Penn Warren. CP-WarrR

Omen. Yusef Komunyakaa. CP-KomuY

Omen, An. David Ignatow. SP-IgnaD

Omen, The. Walter De la Mare. CP-DeLaW

Ominous bird sang from its branch, An. Beware! Walter De la Mare. CP-DeLaW

Omnibus across the bridge, An. Symphony in Yellow. Oscar Wilde. CP-WildO

Omnipresence of the sound of water: rain, The. Rain at Bellagio. Amy Clampitt. CP-ClamA

On a bank, beside a willow. Tears of Amynta for the Death of Damon, The. John Dryden. CP-DryJ2

On a Bank of Flowers. Robert Burns. CP-BurnR

On a bare tree in a hollow place. Epigram on a Painting of Golgotha. Allen Ginsberg. CP-GinsA

On a Baroque Clock. Alan Dugan. CP-DugaA

On a Bath. Plato. CP-CowpW

On a Battered Beauty. Unknown. CP-CowpW, tr. by William Cowper

On a Beach. Czeslaw Milosz. CP-MiloCN, tr. by Robert Hass

On a Beautiful Bar Butterfly in the Black Cat. Kenneth Rexroth. CP-RexrK

On a bed of gravel moving. Folk Singer of the Thirties, A. James Dickey. CP-DickJ

On a Bed of Guernsey Lilies. Christopher Smart. SP-SmarC

On a Benign Bureaucratization of Death. Alan Dugan. CP-DugaA

On a Bird Singing in its Sleep. Robert Frost. CP-FrosR

On a Bright Day, Next Week. Maya Angelou. SP-AngeM

On a brilliant morning in May. Riding Song for a Semi-Feudal Army, for Glubb Pasha, for Tortured Colonels. Alan Dugan. CP-DugaA

On a Cataract. Samuel Taylor Coleridge. CP-ColeS

On a Celebrated Ruling Elder. Robert Burns. CP-BurnR

On a Certain Engagement South of Seoul. Hayden Carruth. CP-CarHS

On a Certain Lady at Court. Alexander Pope. CP-PopeA

On a Change of Masters at a Great Public School. Lord Byron. CP-Byron

On a Christmas Night. Langston Hughes. CP-HughL; CP-HughL3

On a Church Lawn. William Stafford. SP-StafWW

On a Clean Book. Paul Laurence Dunbar. CP-DunbP

On a clear day how thin the horizon. Horizon. Robert Graves. CP-GravR

On a clear day, the jealous. Danger of Loss, The. Robert Bly. SP-BlyR

On a clear spring windless sky. Feathered Robe, The. Gary Snyder. CP-SnydG

On a cold evening, summer almost gone. Loon's Cry, The. Howard Nemerov. CP-NemeH

On a cold late. Day. A. R. Ammons. CP-AmmoA

On a cold night I came through the cold rain. James Vincent Cunningham. CP-CunnJ

On a Columnar Self. Emily Dickinson. CP-DickE

On a Cornelian Heart Which Was Broken. Lord Byron. CP-Byron

On a Daffodil, the First Flower the Author Had Seen That Year. Samuel Johnson. CP-JohnS

On a Damask[e] Rose, Sticking upon a Lady's Breast. Thomas Carew. CP-CareT

On a day I long since started. Call It a Day. John Ciardi. CP-CiarJ

On a Day in August. Thomas Merton. CP-MertT

On a day in fall, when high winds trouble the country. Hymn for the Feast of Duns Scotus. Thomas Merton. CP-MertT

On a day like this the rain comes. Fauré's Second Piano Quartet. James Schuyler. CP-SchuJ

On a day of dry wind. Danger in the Air, The. Archibald MacLeish. CP-MacLA

On a day when the trees are exchanging the cured gold of the sun. In Early Autumn. Thomas McGrath. SP-McGrT

On a Delhi Sundial. A. K. Ramanujan. CP-RamaA

On a Desolation of the Animals at Night. Alan Dugan. CP-DugaA

On a Discovered Curl of Hair. Thomas Hardy. CP-HardT

On a Dispossess Precept. 1. Alan Dugan. CP-DugaA

On a Dispossess Precept. 2. Alan Dugan. CP-DugaA

On a Distant View of the Village and School of Harrow on the Hill. Lord Byron. CP-Byron

On a Dog of Lord Eglinton's. Robert Burns. CP-BurnR

On a Drawing by Flavio. Philip Levine. SP-LeviP

On a Dream. John Keats. CP-KeatJ

    (Dream, after Reading Dante's Episode of Paolo and Francesca, A.) CP-KeatJ

On a Drop of Dew. Andrew Marvell. CP-MarvA

On a Faded Violet. Percy Bysshe Shelley. CP-ShelP

On a Fallen Statue Forbidden to the Women at Pompeii. Alan Dugan. CP-DugaA

On a Fan of the Author's Design, in Which Was Painted the Story of CEPHALUS and PROCRIS, with the Motto, AURA VENI. Alexander Pope. CP-PopeA

On a Ferry across Chesapeake Bay. Robert Bly. SP-BlyR

On a Fête at Carlton House: Fragment. Percy Bysshe Shelley. CP-ShelP

On a Fine Day. Franco Sacchetti. CW-RossD, tr. by Dante Gabriel Rossetti

On a Fine Morning. Thomas Hardy. CP-HardT

On a flat road runs the well-train'd runner. Runner, The. Walt Whitman. CP-WhitW

On a Flimmering Floom You Shall Ride. Carl Sandburg. CP-SandC

On a flower of dark sobs / & waters you left me. Little Song of the Unborn Child. Federico García Lorca. CP-GarcF, tr. by Jerome Rothenberg Fr. In the Garden of the Lunar Grapefruits.

On a Fly-Leaf. James Whitcomb Riley. CP-RileJ

On a Fly-Leaf of Longfellow's Poems. John Greenleaf Whittier. CP-WhitJ

On a Flyleaf of Rime—Gaspara Stampa. Kenneth Rexroth. CP-RexrK

On a Foule Morning, Being Then to Take a Journey. Richard Crashaw. CP-CrasR

On a Fowler. Isidorus. CP-CowpW, tr. by William Cowper

On a frozen pond a mole north of Liberal. One Evening. William Stafford. SP-

StafWW

On a Gift of Leaves From Dove Cottage Close, Grasmere. Robert Stock. SP-StocR

On a Goldfinch Starved to Death in His Cage. William Cowper. CP-CowpW

On a Good Man. *Unknown.* CP-CowpW, *tr.* by William Cowper

On a gray day in March in his first year. We Stood There Singing. Maxine W. Kumin. SP-KumiM

On a gray evening. History. Charles Simic. SP-SimiC; SP-SimiCE

On a ground beaten gold by running and. Game of Ball, A. Muriel Rukeyser. CP-RukeM

On a Heath. Thomas Hardy. CP-HardT

On a High Part of the Coast in Cumberland. William Wordsworth. CP-WorW2

On a Highway East of Selma, Alabama. Gregory Orr. SP-OrrG

On a Horse Carved in Wood. Donald Hall. CP-HallD

On a hot summer Sunday. Cemetery at Academy, California, The. Philip Levine. SP-LeviP

On a Hyacinth from Georgia. Jones Very. CP-VeryJ

On a Hymn, Misprinted. Alan Dugan. CP-DugaA

On a Journey. Paul Celan. SP-CelaP, *tr.* by John Felstiner

On a kind of Christmas day. Reminiscent of a Wave at the Curl. Marianne Craig Moore. CP-MoorM

On a Lady Who P-ssed [*or* P———st] at the Tragedy of Cato. Alexander Pope. CP-PopeA

On a Lady's Presenting a Sprig of Myrtle to a Gentleman. Samuel Johnson. CP-JohnS

On a Landscape by Li Ch'eng. Charles Tomlinson. CP-TomlC

On a Late Connubial Rupture in High Life. Samuel Taylor Coleridge. CP-ColeS

On a Leander Gem which Miss Reynolds, My Kind Friend, Gave Me. John Keats. CP-KeatJ

On a Letter. James Cunningham. CP-CunnJ

On a Letter of Miss Fanshawe. William Cowper. CP-CowpW

On a Lichen from North Cape: Gathered by Mr. J. M. Richards, July 3d, 1874. Jones Very. CP-VeryJ

On a Line from Bodenham's "Belvedere." James Vincent Cunningham. CP-CunnJ

On a Line from Julian. Carolyn Kizer. CP-KizeC

On a Line from Sophocles. Carolyn Kizer. CP-KizeC

On a Line from Valéry. Carolyn Kizer. CP-KizeC

On a Little Boy Going to Play on a Place from Whence He Had Just Fallen. Annis Boudinot Stockton. CP-StocA

On a long block. Drawn to Perspective. Charles Simic. SP-SimiC; SP-SimiCE

On a low cedar-bush. Eagle in New Mexico. D. H. Lawrence. CP-LawrD

On a low couch reclining. Spanish Lady, The. Walt Whitman. CP-WhitW

On a May Night. Charles Tomlinson. CP-TomlC

On a Mexican Straw Christ. Charles Tomlinson. CP-TomlC

On a mid-December day. Since. W. H. Auden. CP-AudeW

On a Midsummer Eve. Thomas Hardy. CP-HardT

On a Military Graveyard. Simonides. CP-RexrK, *tr.* by Kenneth Rexroth

On a Mischievous Bull. William Cowper. CP-CowpW

On a Miser. Lucilius.

On a Mistake in His Translation of Homer. William Cowper. CP-CowpW

On a morning sick as the day of doom. In a Waiting-Room. Thomas Hardy. CP-HardT

On a mound an Arab lay. Hermione. Ralph Waldo Emerson. CP-EmerR

On a mountain-side the real estate agents. Landscape. Carl Sandburg. CP-SandC

On a Mourner. Alfred Tennyson. CP-TennA

On a Myth. On a Conventional Wisdom. Alan Dugan. CP-DugaA

On a naked slope of a poor province. Crucified, The. G. K. Chesterton. CP-ChesG

On a New Generation. Laura Riding Jackson. CP-RidiL

On a Night of the Full Moon. Audre Lorde. SP-LordA

On a Night You Don't Sleep. Charles Bukowski. SP-BukC2

On a Noisy Polemic. Robert Burns. CP-BurnR

On a Painting by Todd Price of the 16th Michigan Infantry on Little Round Top, July 2, 1863. Helen Pinkerton. CP-PinkH

On a Pallet of Straw. Langston Hughes. CP-HughL; CP-HughL3

On a Party. Alan Dugan. CP-DugaA

On a Perfum'd Lady. Robert Herrick. CP-HerrR

On a Photo of Sgt. Ciardi a Year Later. John Ciardi. CP-CiarJ

On a Photograph by Aaron Siskind. John Logan. CP-LogaJ

On a Photograph of My Mother at Seventeen. Miller Williams. CP-WillM

On a Picture of a Black Centaur by Edmund Dulac. William Butler Yeats. CP-YeatW

On a Pig's Head. Charles Tomlinson. CP-TomlC

On a Plant of Virgin's Bower. William Cowper. CP-CowpW

On a Pocketknife. On Carrying. Alan Dugan. CP-DugaA

On a Political Prisoner. William Butler Yeats. CP-YeatW

On a Portrait of Honoré Daumier. Charles Baudelaire. CP-BaudC, *tr.* by Walter Martin

On a Portrait of the Duke of Wellington upon the Field of Waterloo, by Haydon. William Wordsworth. CP-WorW2

On a Portrait of Wordsworth by B. R. Haydon. Elizabeth Barrett Browning. CP-BroEB

On a Prayer-Book. John Greenleaf Whittier. CP-WhitJ

On a Printer's Being Sent to Newgate. Jonathan Swift. CP-SwifJ

On a Prize Crucifix by a Student Sculptor. John Logan. CP-LogaJ

On a Professional Couple in a Side-Show. Alan Dugan. CP-DugaA

On a Prohibitionist Poem. G. K. Chesterton. CP-ChesG

On a Proposed Celebration of Ezra Pound. Donald Davie. CP-DaviDC

On a Proposed Trip South. William Carlos Williams. CP-WilW1

On a Railroad Right of Way. Carl Sandburg. CP-SandC

On a rainy night / On a rainy night in April. April 4th 1968. Thomas Merton. CP-MertT

On a Raised Beach. Hugh MacDiarmid. SP-MacDH

On a raisin stone. Ralph Waldo Emerson. CP-EmerR

On a relief map. Sioux Haiku. William Stafford. SP-StafW

On a Review Condemning Thelyphthora. William Cowper. CP-CowpW

On a Robbery. Ben Jonson. CP-JonsB; SP-JonsB

On a roof in the Old City. Jerusalem. Yehuda Amichai. SP-AmicY, *tr.* by Stephen Mitchell

On a Row of Cabins / Next My Home. Lorine Niedecker. CP-NiedL

On a Royal Visit to the Vaults. Lord Byron. CP-Byron

On a Sabbath eve, at dusk on a summer day. Song of Lies on Sabbath Eve, A. Yehuda Amichai. SP-AmicY, *tr.* by Chana Bloch

On a Schoolmaster in Cleish Parish, Fifeshire. Robert Burns. *See* Epitaph on a Schoolmaster

On a Scotch Bard Gone to the West Indies. Robert Burns. CP-BurnR

On a Seven-Day Diary. Alan Dugan. CP-DugaA

On a Shell-strewn Beach. Kathleen Jessie Raine. SP-RainK

On a shrub in the heart of the garden. Leaf-eater. Thomas Kinsella. CP-KinsT

On a Similar Character. Lucianus.

On a Similar Occasion for the Year 1788. William Cowper. CP-CowpW

On a Similar Occasion for the Year 1789. William Cowper. CP-CowpW

On a Similar Occasion for the Year 1790. William Cowper. CP-CowpW

On a Similar Occasion for the Year 1792. William Cowper. CP-CowpW

On a Similar Occasion for the Year 1793. William Cowper. CP-CowpW

On a Skunked Fox. Alan Dugan. CP-DugaA

On a Snake. Alan Dugan. CP-DugaA

On a snug evening I shall watch her fingers. Piano after War. Gwendolyn Brooks. SP-BrooG

On a Spaniel Called Beau Killing a Young Bird. William Cowper. CP-CowpW

On a Splendud Match. James Whitcomb Riley. CP-RileJ

On a Squirrel Crossing the Road in Autumn, in New England. Richard Eberhart. CP-EberR

On a staircase as cheerless. Esprit d'Escalier. Adam Zagajewski. SP-ZagaA, *tr.* by Renata Gorczynski

On a stale morning. Hotel Breakfast. Archibald MacLeish. CP-MacLA

On a starred [*or* starr'd] night Prince Lucifer uprose. Lucifer in Starlight. George Meredith. CP-MerG1

On a still, silent night, scarce could I number. His Dream. Sir John Suckling. CP-SuckJ

On a street without people. 5:00 p.m. Federico García Lorca. CP-GarcF, *tr.* by Jerome Rothenberg *Fr.* Summer Hours.

On a sultry morning, Mother. Family, A. Czeslaw Milosz. CP-MiloC; CP-MiloCN, *tr.* by Robert Hass

On a Summer Goddess Who Should Be Nameless. Alan Dugan. CP-DugaA

On a summer's back road. Road 37C. Peter Blue Cloud. SP-BlueP

On a summer's day as I sat by a stream. Song, A: "On a summer's day as I sat by a stream." Paul Laurence Dunbar. CP-DunbP

On a sunny brae alone I lay. Day Dream, A. Emily Jane Brontë. CP-BronE

On a terribly clear day. Fernando Pessoa. SP-PessF *Fr.* Keeper of Sheep, The.

On a Text: Jonah IV, xi. Howard Nemerov. CP-NemeH

On a thawed-out patch of green. Little Priest of the Fen, The. Aleksandr Aleksandrovich Blok. SP-BlokA, *tr.* by Peter France *and* Jon Stallworthy

On a Theme by Lawrence, Hearing Purcell. Robert Creeley. SP-CreeR

On a theme fantastic, a light / *aria*, by some altogether monstrous woman in. Trap, The. Robert Creeley. CP-CreeR

On a Theme from Julian's Chapter 20. Denise Levertov. SP-LeveDS

On a Thief. *Unknown.* CP-CowpW, *tr.* by William Cowper

On a Trailways Bus a Man Who Holds His Head Strangely Speaks to the Seat Behind Him. Miller Williams. CP-WillM

On a Travel Story from Wormwood Valley. Alan Dugan. CP-DugaA

On a Tree Fallen across the Road. Robert Frost. CP-FrosR

On a tributary of the Amazon. Lass of Aughrim, The. Paul Muldoon. CP-MuldP

On a True Friend. *Unknown.* CP-CowpW, *tr.* by William Cowper

On a Very Old Glass. Jonathan Swift. CP-SwifJ

On a Volunteer Singer. Samuel Taylor Coleridge. CP-ColeS

On a Wedding Anniversary. Dylan Thomas. CP-ThomD

On a Wet Day. Franco Sacchetti. CW-RossD, *tr.* by Dante Gabriel Rossetti

On a wet pavement the white sky recedes. Bitter World of Spring, The. William Carlos Williams. CP-WilW2

On a white chariot which four mules. Before the Statue of Endymion. Constantine P. Cavafy. CP-CavaC, *tr.* by Theoharis Constantine Theoharis

On a Winter Night. May Sarton. SP-SartM

On a Youthful Portrait of Stevenson. James Whitcomb Riley. CP-RileJ

On Acid. Robert Creeley. CP-CreeR

On Acquiring an Encyclopedia. Jorge Luis Borges. SP-BorgJ, *tr.* by Alan S. Trueblood

On Addy Road. May Swenson. SP-SwenM

On afternoons of drowsy calm. Afternoon Service at Mellstock. Thomas Hardy. CP-HardT

On Aging. Maya Angelou. SP-AngeM

On Albina. Christina Georgina Rossetti. CP-RosC3

On Alexander and Aristotle, on a Black-on-Red Greek Plate. Alan Dugan. CP-DugaA

On all fours around the roof. And I, Too, Am Something of a Stranger Here, My Friend. Kenneth Patchen. CP-PatcK

On All Sides. Charles Olson. CP-OlsoC

On all that strand. Roundelay: "On all that strand." Samuel Beckett. CP-BeckS

On all the streetcorners the children are standing. Flying Red Horse, The. Muriel Rukeyser. CP-RukeM

On almost the incendiary eve. Deaths and Entrances. Dylan Thomas. CP-ThomD

On alternating levels the world pounds in. Overworld, The. Kenneth Patchen. CP-PatcK

On an Accident: On a Newspaper Story. Alan Dugan. CP-DugaA

On an Ancient Isle. Kathleen Jessie Raine. SP-RainK

On an Anthology of Chinese Poems. Robinson Jeffers. CP-JefR3

On an Architect. Alan Dugan. CP-DugaA

On an Eagle Confined in a College-Court. Christopher Smart. SP-SmarC

On an Ear of Wheat Brought, by My Brother, from the Field of Waterloo. Jones Very. CP-VeryJ

On an Early Cycladic Harpist (2500 B.C.) in the Archaeological Museum in Athens. Helen Pinkerton. CP-PinkH

On an Early Cycladic Harpist (2600-2500 B.C.) in the J. Paul Getty Museum. Helen Pinkerton. CP-PinkH

On an East Wind from the Wars. Alan Dugan. CP-DugaA

On an empty morning a small clerk. Lake in the Park, The. Louis MacNeice. CP-MacNL

On an empty stomach I send you a wish for health. Elegy 6: To Charles Deodati. John Milton. CP-CowpW; CP-MiltJ

On an Enclosure of Roses in Which Is the Grave of Miss Mary Morgan a Young Lady of 13 Years of Age Daughter of Col Morgan. Annis Boudinot Stockton. CP-StocA

On an Icicle That Clung to the Grass of a Grave. Percy Bysshe Shelley. CP-ShelP

On an Industrial Ruin. Andrei Codrescu. SP-CodrA

On an Infant. Lucianus. CP-CowpW

On an Infant Which Died before Baptism. Samuel Taylor Coleridge. CP-ColeS

On an Innkeeper in Tarbolton. Robert Burns. CP-BurnR

On an Insignificant. Samuel Taylor Coleridge. CP-ColeS

On an Invitation to the United States. Thomas Hardy. CP-HardT

On an Island. John Updike. CP-UpdiJ

On an Italian Shore. Constantine P. Cavafy. CP-CavaC, *tr.* by Theoharis Constantine Theoharis

On an oak in autumn. Survivor. Archibald MacLeish. CP-MacLA

On an Old Advertisement and after a Photograph by Alfred Stieglitz. Alan Dugan. CP-DugaA

On an Old Horn. Wallace Stevens. CP-StevW; CP-StevWP

On an Old Photograph of My Son. Raymond Carver. CP-CarvR

On an old shore, the vulgar ocean rolls. Somnambulisma. Wallace Stevens. CP-StevW; CP-StevWP

On an Old Woman. Lucilius. CP-CowpW, *tr.* by William Cowper

On an olive beach, beneath a turquoise sky. Sunglasses. John Updike. CP-UpdiJ

On an Ugly Fellow. *Unknown.* CP-CowpW, *tr.* by William Cowper

On an undiscovered island. Economics. G. K. Chesterton. CP-ChesG

On an Unwritten Letter. Eugenio Montale. CP-MontE, *tr.* by Jonathan Galassi

On ancient rocks are ancient tracks. Han-shan. CP-ColdM, *tr.* by Red Pine

On and off the Road. Charles Bukowski. CP-BukC3

On and On and On. D. H. Lawrence. CP-LawrD

On and on like so, in the azure black. What the Poet Is Told on the Subject of Flowers. Arthur Rimbaud. CP-RimbA, *tr.* by Martin Sorrell

On Andrew Turner. Robert Burns. CP-BurnR

On Angels. Czeslaw Milosz. CP-MiloC; CP-MiloCN

On Anne Spencer's table. Anne Spencer's Table. Langston Hughes. CP-HughL; CP-HughL1

On Any Ordenary Man in a High State of Laughture and Delight. James Whitcomb Riley. CP-RileJ

On April twenty-seventh, 1932, Hart Crane. Voyages. Amy Clampitt. CP-ClamA

On, as thou hast begunne, brave youth, and get. To His Nephew, to Be Prosperous in His Art of Painting. Robert Herrick. CP-HerrR

On ashes of old volcanoes. Lost Loves. Galway Kinnell. SP-KinnGN

On azure seats. Fanny Howe. SP-HoweF *Fr.* O'Clock.

On back roads you can find people. Fixers. William Stafford. SP-StafWW

On bank and brake the moonshine quakes. Miller, The. Randall Jarrell. CP-JarrR

On Bank the Usurer. Ben Jonson. CP-JonsB; SP-JonsB

On Bawds and Usurers. Ben Jonson. CP-JonsB; SP-JonsB

On Beauty. Kenneth Koch. SP-KochK

On Beechen Cliff self-commune I. Midnight on Beechen, 187–. Thomas Hardy. CP-HardT

On Being a Householder. Alan Dugan. CP-DugaA

On Being a Member of the Jury for a Poetry Prize. Howard Nemerov. CP-NemeH

On Being a Woman. Dorothy Parker. CP-ParkD

On Being Asked for a Peace Poem. Howard Nemerov. CP-NemeH

On Being Asked for a War Poem. William Butler Yeats. CP-YeatW

On Being Asked How Do You Feel after an Operation for Inadequate Anesthesia. This Is How I Feel. Alan Dugan. CP-DugaA

On Being Asked to Leave a Place of Honor for One of Comfort, Preferably in the Northern Suburbs. Alice Walker. CP-WalkA

On Being Asked to Write a Poem against the War in Vietnam. Hayden Carruth. CP-CarHS

On Being Asked to Write a Poem for the Centenary of the Civil War. Maxine W. Kumin. SP-KumiM

On Being Asked to Write a Poem in Memory of Anne Sexton. Maxine W. Kumin. SP-KumiM

On Being Asked What Was the "Origin of Love." Lord Byron. CP-Byron

On Being Asked Why God Had Made Miss D——— So Little and Mrs A——— So Big. Robert Burns. CP-BurnR

On Being Brought from Africa to America. Phillis Wheatley. CP-WheaP

On Being Chosen Poet of Vermont. Robert Frost. CP-FrosR

On Being Easy in the Ritual of Separation. Alan Dugan. CP-DugaA

On Being Forbidden to Feed the Dog. G. K. Chesterton. CP-ChesG

On Being Given Time. May Sarton. SP-SartM

On Being Idolized. Robert Frost. CP-FrosR

On Being Out-Classed by Class. Alan Dugan. CP-DugaA

On Being Recognized. Charles Bukowski. SP-BukC3

On Being Sure and of What. John Ciardi. CP-CiarJ

On Being Thanked for a Favor. G. K. Chesterton. CP-ChesG

On Being 20. Charles Bukowski. SP-BukC3

On Being Twenty-Six. Philip Larkin. CP-LarkP

On Being Unhappily in Love with Reason. Alan Dugan. CP-DugaA

On Benjamin Disraeli. Robert Browning. CP-BroR2

On Bertrand Russell's 'Portraits from Memory.' Donald Davie. CP-DaviDC

On black gallows, one-armed friend. Hanged Men Dance. Arthur Rimbaud. CP-RimbA, *tr.* by Martin Sorrell

On Blakelock's *Moonlit Landscape* in the de Young Museum. Helen Pinkerton. CP-PinkH

On blue evenings in summer, down paths. Sensation. Arthur Rimbaud. CP-RimbA, *tr.* by Martin Sorrell

On Board. Robert Creeley. SP-CreeR

On Boston Common a red star. Winter's Tale, A. Sylvia Plath. CP-PlatS

On bravely through the sunshine & the showers. Ralph Waldo Emerson. CP-EmerR

On Breeding, from Plutarch. Alan Dugan. CP-DugaA

On Breughel the Elder's *The Harvesters* (1565) in the Metropolitan Museum. Helen Pinkerton. CP-PinkH

On Britain Europe's safety lies. To Mr. Harley's Surgeon. Jonathan Swift. CP-SwifJ

On Building with Stone. Robinson Jeffers. CP-JefR1

On Burning a Dull Poem. Jonathan Swift. CP-SwifJ

On Burns. Dante Gabriel Rossetti. CW-RossD

On Burroughs, Work. Allen Ginsberg. CP-GinsA

On Cabin Fever, on Boredom in the Countryside. Alan Dugan. CP-DugaA

On Canann Mountain Meadow. Hayden Carruth. CP-CarHS

On Capt. Foote's Marriage with Miss Patton. James Leigh Perrot. CP-AustJ

On Captain Hazard the Cheater. Ben Jonson. CP-JonsB; SP-JonsB

On Captn. L———lles. Robert Burns. CP-BurnR

On Capt. W——— R-dd-ck of C-rb—ton. Robert Burns. CP-BurnR

On Caravaggio's *Conversion of St. Paul* (1600) in Santa Maria del Popolo, Rome. Helen Pinkerton. CP-PinkH

On Cashiered Capt[ain] Surly. Ben Jonson. CP-JonsB; SP-JonsB

On Castle Hill. Marge Piercy. SP-PierM

On Censure. Jonathan Swift. CP-SwifJ

On Certain Elizabethan Revivals. Dante Gabriel Rossetti. CW-RossD

On Certain Wits. Howard Nemerov. CP-NemeH

On Cessnock banks a lassie dwells. Song: "On Cessnock banks a lassie dwells." Robert Burns. CP-BurnR

On Cheating the Fiddler. Dorothy Parker. CP-ParkD

On Cheveril [or Cheverel]. Ben Jonson. CP-JonsB; SP-JonsB

On Cheveril [or Cheverel] the Lawyer. Ben Jonson. CP-JonsB; SP-JonsB

On Chloris Requesting Me to Give Her a Spray of a Sloe-Thorn in Full Blossom. Robert Burns. CP-BurnR

On Chuff, Banks the Usurer's Kinsman. Ben Jonson. CP-JonsB

On city bridges steep as hills I change countries. Beginning of the Plains. W. S. Merwin. SP-MerwW

On clear days it's fast black dead west sixty miles. What I See when I Drive to Work. Thomas Lux. SP-LuxT

On Climbing the Sierra Matterhorn Again after Thirty-One Years. Gary Snyder. CP-SnydG

On Cold Mountain Road. Han-shan. CP-ColdM, tr. by Red Pine

On Cold Mountain there's a naked bug. Han-shan. CP-ColdM, tr. by Red Pine

On Columbus Day he set out for the north. Lorine Niedecker. CP-NiedL

On Combe Bottom: Surrey. George Meredith. CP-MerG2

On coming up on deck Palm Sunday morning, oh. Sailing to Jerusalem. Alan Dugan. CP-DugaA

On Commissary Goldie's Brains. Robert Burns. CP-BurnR

On Como. George Meredith. CP-MerG2

On Correggio. Robert Browning. CP-BroR2

On Correggio's Leda. James Vincent Cunningham. CP-CunnJ

On Court-Parrot. Ben Jonson. CP-JonsB; SP-JonsB

On Court-Worm[e]. Ben Jonson. CP-JonsB; SP-JonsB

On Cruachan's plain slept he. Tom at Cruachan. William Butler Yeats. CP-YeatW

On Cutting Down the Old Thorn at Market Hill. Jonathan Swift. CP-SwifJ

On Dan Jackson's Picture. Jonathan Swift. CP-SwifJ

On days like these. Washing. Randall Jarrell. CP-JarrR

On Death. Percy Bysshe Shelley. CP-ShelP

On Death, without Exaggeration. Wisława Szymborska. SP-SzymW, tr. by Stanislaw Barańczak and Clare Cavanagh

On Death, without Exaggeration. Wisława Szymborska. SP-SzymWM, tr. by Joanna Trzeciak

On Death's domain intent I fix my eyes. To a Gentleman and Lady on the Death of the Lady's Brother and Sister, and a Child of the Name Avis, Aged One Year. Phillis Wheatley. CP-WheaP

On Death's face all religion dances. Eros. Olga Broumas. SP-BrouO

On Deck. Sylvia Plath. CP-PlatS

On Dieric Bouts's Virgin and Child (1460) in the California Palace of the Legion of Honor. Helen Pinkerton. CP-PinkH

On distant sides of the bed. In the Child's Night. James Dickey. CP-DickJ

On Diverse Deviations. Maya Angelou. SP-AngeM

On Doctor Drink. James Vincent Cunningham. CP-CunnJ

On Dr. Rundle. Jonathan Swift. CP-SwifJ

On Doctor Rushes Birth Day the 5th of January—after Ten Days Thick Fog. Annis Boudinot Stockton. CP-StocA

On Don Surly. Ben Jonson. CP-JonsB; SP-JonsB

On Donne's First Poem. Samuel Taylor Coleridge. CP-ColeS

On Donne's Poetry. Samuel Taylor Coleridge. CP-ColeS; MW-ColeS

On downward slope gigantic wheels. On into the Night. Robert Penn Warren. CP-WarrR

On Dreams. Jonathan Swift. CP-SwifJ

On dreams, on mathematics, and on death. Du rêve, de la mathématique, et de la mort. Howard Nemerov. CP-NemeH

On Dürer's Etching of Pilate Washing His Hands (1512). Helen Pinkerton. CP-PinkH

On Dwelling. Robert Graves. CP-GravR

On Each Journey. W. S. Merwin. SP-MerwW

On each receding bush. Second Song. Charles Tomlinson. SP-TomlC

On ear and ear two noises too old to end. Sea and the Skylark, The. Gerard Manley Hopkins. CP-HopkG

On Earth. Olga Broumas. SP-BrouO

On earth are many sights of woe. We All Shall Rest at Last. Walt Whitman. CP-WhitW

On earth, it's no unworthy soul that nurses. Michelangelo Buonarroti. CP-Miche, tr. by John Frederick Nims

On earth's wide thoroughfares below. Omar Khayyám. CP-EmerR

On Easter morning two egrets. Two Egrets. John Ciardi. CP-CiarJ

On Edges. Adrienne Rich. CP-RicAE; SP-RicA1; SP-RicA2

On Edmund Spenser's House in Ireland. Donald Davie. CP-DaviDC

On either side of the white line. James Vincent Cunningham. CP-CunnJ

On either side the river lie. Lady of Shalott, The. Alfred Tennyson. CP-TennA

On elbows propped Europa lies. Message. Fernando Pessoa. SP-PessF, tr. by Susan M. Brown and Edwin Honig

On Eleventh Street. Charles Tomlinson. CP-TomlC

On Elphinston's Translation of Martial. Robert Burns. CP-BurnR

(To Mr. E——— on His Translation of and Commentaries on Martial.) CP-BurnR

On Emily Dickinson. Helen Pinkerton. CP-PinkH

On English Monsieur. Ben Jonson. CP-JonsB; SP-JonsB

On Envy. Unknown. CP-CowpW, tr. by William Cowper

On Erastus Salisbury Field's The Israelites Crossing the Red Sea (1863?). Helen Pinkerton. CP-PinkH

On Ethnic Definitions. Eleanor Wilner. SP-WilnE

On evenings like this. Tango. Louise Glück. SP-GlucL

On every thought I have the countless shadows fall. Light and Shadow. Hugh MacDiarmid. SP-MacDH

On Evidence, on Deeds, on Bills. Unexpounded. Ambrose Bierce. SP-BierA

On Exodus 30.18. Annis Boudinot Stockton. CP-StocA

On eyes embarked for sleep the only light. For Ellen. Richard Wilbur. CP-WilbR

On Fabricius. Unknown, sometimes at. to Thomas Sheridan. CP-SherT

On Falling Asleep by Firelight. William Meredith. SP-MereW

On Falling Asleep to Birdsong. William Meredith. SP-MereW

On Fame ("Fame, like a wayward girl"). John Keats. CP-KeatJ Fr. Two Sonnets on Fame.

On Fame ("How fever'd is the man who cannot look"). John Keats. CP-KeatJ Fr. Two Sonnets on Fame.

On Fanny Godwin. Percy Bysshe Shelley. CP-ShelP

On Female Inconstancy. Unknown. CP-CowpW, tr. by William Cowper

On Fergusson. Robert Burns. CP-BurnR

On fields oer which the reaper's hand has passed. Henry David Thoreau. CP-ThorH

On Finding a Fan. Lord Byron. CP-Byron

On Finding the Meaning of "Radiance." Alan Dugan. CP-DugaA

On Finding the Tree of Life. Alan Dugan. CP-DugaA

On Finding the Truth. Jones Very. CP-VeryJ

On Fingernails in Bloody Times. Alan Dugan. CP-DugaA

On First Having Heard the Skylark. Edna St. Vincent Millay. CP-MillE

On First Looking into Chapman's Homer. John Keats. CP-KeatJ

On First Opening the Lyric Year. William Carlos Williams. CP-WilW1

On Fishing Being a Chancy Life. Alan Dugan. CP-DugaA

On Fitz Hugh Lane's Approaching Storm, Owl's Head, 1860. Helen Pinkerton. CP-PinkH

On Flatterers. Unknown. CP-CowpW, tr. by William Cowper

On Flaxman and Stothard. William Blake. CP-BlakW

On Flaxman's Penelope. William Cowper. CP-CowpW

On Fleeing His City. Shmuel HaNagid. SP-HaNaS, tr. by Peter Cole

On Flower Wreath Hill. Kenneth Rexroth. CP-RexrK

On Flowers. On Negative Evolution. Alan Dugan. CP-DugaA

On Flunking a Nice Boy out of School. John Ciardi. CP-CiarJ

On forelands high in heaven. A. E. Housman. CP-HousA

On Form. Yannis Ritsos. SP-RitsY, tr. by Kimon Friar

On Fortune. Robert Herrick. CP-HerrR

On Forty-first Street. Neighbors. Carl Sandburg. CP-SandC

On Foscombe Hill. Ivor Gurney. SP-GurnI

On four lions' paws. Tub, A. Charles Simic. SP-SimiCE

On Freedom. David Ignatow. SP-IgnaD

On Freedom's Ground. Richard Wilbur. CP-WilbR

On Fridays he'd open a can of Jax. My Father's Love Letters [or Loveletters]. Yusef Komunyakaa. CP-KomuY

On Friendship. Phillis Wheatley. CP-WheaP

On G.B. Tiepolo's Etching Adoration of the Magi (1753) in the Stanford Museum. Helen Pinkerton. CP-PinkH

On Gabriel Richardson. Robert Burns. CP-BurnR

On Gaining a Soul. Alan Dugan. CP-DugaA

On Gari Melchers's Writing (1905) in the Los Angeles County Museum of Art. Helen Pinkerton. CP-PinkH

On Gay Wallpaper. William Carlos Williams. CP-WilW1

On Gelli-Flowers Begotten. Robert Herrick. CP-HerrR

On Generous Lines. Donald Davie. CP-DaviDC

On getting a card. Poem: "On getting a card." William Carlos Williams. CP-WilW2

On Getting out of Vietnam. Howard Nemerov. CP-NemeH

On Giles and Joan. Ben Jonson. CP-JonsB; SP-JonsB

On Giving. Robert Graves. CP-GravR

On Going Back to the Street after Viewing an Art Show. Charles Bukowski. SP-BukC2

On Going Latent. Alan Dugan. CP-DugaA

On Going Unnoticed. Robert Frost. CP-FrosR

On Going up to Surgery in the Morning and in Favor of Pain-Killing Drugs. Alan Dugan. CP-DugaA

On golden seas of drink, so the Greek poet said. Alcohol. Louis MacNeice. CP-MacNL

On Goya's *Duel with Cudgels* (ca. 1820), a "Black Painting" in the Prado. Helen Pinkerton. CP-PinkH

On Gratitude. Christopher Smart. SP-SmarC

On Groin. Ben Jonson. CP-JonsB; SP-JonsB

On Gut. Ben Jonson. CP-JonsB; SP-JonsB

On gypsum slabs of preternatural whiteness. Animal, Vegetable and Mineral. Louise Bogan. CP-BogaL

On Gypsy. Ben Jonson. CP-JonsB; SP-JonsB

On Halloween. Alan Dugan. CP-DugaA

On Handling Some Small Shells from the Windward Islands. May Swenson.

On Hat: On Vertical Mobility as a Concept. Alan Dugan. CP-DugaA

On Having Mis-identified a Wild Flower. Richard Wilbur. CP-WilbR

On Hayley. William Blake. CP-BlakW

On H[ayley] the Pick Thank. William Blake. CP-BlakW

On H[ayle]ys Friendship. William Blake. CP-BlakW

On Hayley's Portrait. William Cowper. CP-CowpW

On he goes, the little one. Tortoise Family Connections. D. H. Lawrence. CP-LawrD

On Hearing a Symphony of Beethoven. Edna St. Vincent Millay. CP-MillE

On Hearing about the Death of Mitzi Mayfair. Miller Williams. CP-WillM

On Hearing Miss Thrale Deliberate about Her Hat. Samuel Johnson. CP-JohnS

On Hearing of Love. Constantine P. Cavafy. CP-CavaC, *tr.* by Theoharis Constantine Theoharis

On hearing of powerful love, tremble, and feel it. On Hearing of Love. Constantine P. Cavafy. CP-CavaC, *tr.* by Theoharis Constantine Theoharis

On Hearing of the News of the Capture of Lord Cornwallis and the British Army, by Gen. Washington. Annis Boudinot Stockton. CP-StocA

On Hearing of the Out Powering of the Divine Spirit in Nassau Hall, Feb 24 1757. Annis Boudinot Stockton. CP-StocA

On Hearing that General Warren Was Killed on Bunker-Hill, on the 17th of June 1775. Annis Boudinot Stockton. CP-StocA

On Hearing the Clock Strike, in Harmony Grove. Jones Very. CP-VeryJ

On Hearing the Cooing of a Dove, a Song. Annis Boudinot Stockton. CP-StocA

On Hearing the News from Venice. George Meredith. CP-MerG1

On Hearing / the Wood Pewee. Lorine Niedecker. CP-NiedL

On Heaven. Robert Herrick. CP-HerrR

On Hell's high gates to thunder. Lawrence [Solomon]. G. K. Chesterton. CP-ChesG

On Her Endeavoring to Conceal Her Grief at Parting. William Cowper. CP-CowpW

On her great venture, Man. Earth and Man. George Meredith. CP-MerG1

On her shut lids the lightning flickers. Rhea. Robert Graves. CP-GravR

On her side, reclining on her elbow. So-and-So Reclining on Her Couch. Wallace Stevens. CP-StevW; CP-StevWP

On her 36th birthday, Thomas had shown her. Wingfoot Lake. Rita Dove. SP-DoveR

On Hermocratia. *Unknown.* CP-CowpW

On Herodotus. Alan Dugan. CP-DugaA

On Hibernation in the Country. Alan Dugan. CP-DugaA

On High Feast-Days they were given a public airing. Rois Fainéants. W. H. Auden. CP-AudeW

On Himself. G. K. Chesterton. CP-ChesG

On Himself. Robert Herrick. CP-HerrR

On Himselfe. Robert Herrick. CP-HerrR

On His Approaching Visit to Hayley. William Cowper. CP-CowpW

On His Booke. Robert Herrick. CP-HerrR

On His Deceased Wife. John Milton. CP-MiltJ
   (Sonnet 23.) CP-MiltJ

On His Grotto at Twickenham. Alexander Pope. CP-PopeA

On his knees with that pickaxe. Gold on Mule. Thomas Lux. SP-LuxT

On His Majesty's Sea Bathing. William Cowper. CP-CowpW

On His Mistress [*or* Mistris]. John Donne. MW-DonnJ *Fr.* Elegies.

On His Mistress[e] Going to Sea. Thomas Cary. CP-CareT

On his morning rounds the Master. Incident Characteristic of a Favourite Dog. William Wordsworth. CP-WorW1

On His Own Deafness. Jonathan Swift. CP-SwifJ

On His Own Face in a Glass. Ezra Pound. CP-PoEar

On His Portrait. William Cowper. CP-CowpW

On Hope. Abraham Cowley. *See* Mistress, The

On horseback, and. There He Was. Alan Dugan. CP-DugaA

On Hurricane Jackson. Alan Dugan. CP-DugaA

On Ignaz Moscheles. Robert Browning. CP-BroR2

On Illness. Allen Ginsberg. CP-GinsA

On Imagination. Phillis Wheatley. CP-WheaP

On Inter-Relatedness in the Universe. Alan Dugan. CP-DugaA

On Into the Night. Robert Penn Warren. CP-WarrR

On Invalids. *Unknown.* CP-CowpW, *tr.* by William Cowper

On Its Way. May Swenson. SP-SwenM

On its way I see. Kathleen Jessie Raine. SP-RainK

On Jas. Grieve, Laird of Boghead, Tarbolton. Robert Burns. *See* Epitaph on James Grieve, Laird of Boghead

On Jan van Huysum's *Vase of Flowers* (1722) in the J. Paul Getty Museum. Helen Pinkerton. CP-PinkH

On Jane Street in October. Arboreal Mystery, An. Grace Paley. CP-PalGC

On Jenkins' Hill. William Meredith. SP-MereW

On Jessy Lewars. Robert Burns. CP-BurnR

On J-hn M-r-ne, Laird of L-gg-n. Robert Burns. CP-BurnR

On John McMurdo. Robert Burns. CP-BurnR

On Johnson's Opinion of Hampden. Robert Burns. CP-BurnR

On Jone. Robert Herrick. CP-HerrR

On Jordan's Banks. Lord Byron. CP-Byron

On Journeys through the States. Walt Whitman. CP-WhitW

On Julia's Breath. Robert Herrick. CP-HerrR

On Julias Lips. Robert Herrick. CP-HerrR

On Julia's Picture. Robert Herrick. CP-HerrR

On June 5th, '90: / closed shops. Six Something. James Schuyler. CP-SchuJ

On Keats, 18 January, 1948 (Eve of St Agnes). Christina Georgina Rossetti. CP-RosC3

On Lady Mary Wortley Montagu's Portrait. Alexander Pope. CP-PopeA

On Late-acquired Wealth *or* Riches. *Unknown.* CP-CowpW, *tr.* by William Cowper

On Learning of a Friend's Illness. C. K. Williams. CP-WillC; SP-WillC

On learning that he was about. James Laughlin. CP-LaugJ

On Leaving London for Wales. Percy Bysshe Shelley. CP-ShelP

On Leaving Newstead Abbey. Lord Byron. CP-Byron

On Leaving Some Friends at an Early Hour. John Keats. CP-KeatJ

On Leaving Town. Alan Dugan. CP-DugaA

On Leaving Ullswater. Kathleen Jessie Raine. SP-RainK

On Leonard Baskin's Etching *Benevolent Angel*. Helen Pinkerton. CP-PinkH

On Lieutenant Shift. Ben Jonson. CP-JonsB; SP-JonsB

On life, on morals, be thy thoughts employ'd. Automedon. CP-JohnS

On Lifting the Siege. Shmuel HaNagid. SP-HaNaS, *tr.* by Peter Cole

On Lines 69–70, Book 4, of Virgil's *Aeneid*. Alan Dugan. CP-DugaA

On Lip[pe] the Teacher. Ben Jonson. CP-JonsB

On littlest this / the of twig three. E. E. Cummings. CP-CummE

On, loitering Muse—the swift stream chides us—on! Hints for the Fancy. William Wordsworth. CP-WorW2 *Fr.* River Duddon [A Series of Sonnets], The.

On longer evenings. Coming. Philip Larkin. CP-LarkP

On Looking at *La Grande Jatte*, the Czar Wept Anew. Frank O'Hara. SP-OharF

On Looking East to the Sea with a Sunset behind Me. John Ciardi. CP-CiarJ

On Looking for Models. Alan Dugan. CP-DugaA

On Looking into the Eyes of a Demon Lover. Sylvia Plath. CP-PlatS

On Looking Up by Chance at the Constellations. Robert Frost. CP-FrosR

On Lookout Mountain. Robert Earl Hayden. CP-HaydR

On Lord Carteret's Arms. Jonathan Swift. CP-SwifJ

On Lord Galloway. Robert Burns. *Fr.* Epigrams on Lord Galloway.

On Losing the Power of Speech. Samuel Johnson. CP-JohnS

On Love. Joseph Brodsky. CP-BrodJ, *tr.* by Daniel Weissbort

On Love. Robert Herrick. CP-HerrR

On Loyalty. William Cowper. CP-CowpW

On Lucian Oldershaw, Who Introduced Him to Frances. G. K. Chesterton. CP-ChesG

On Lucy, Countess[e] of Bedford. Ben Jonson. CP-JonsB; SP-JonsB

On Madan's Answer to Newton. William Cowper. CP-CowpW

On Madison. Charles Tomlinson. CP-TomlC

On Main one night when they sounded the chimes. In Medias Res. William Stafford. SP-StafWW

On Man, on Nature, and on Human Life. Prospectus to *The Recluse*. William Wordsworth. CP-WorW2 *Fr.* Recluse, The.

On Margaret Ratcliffe [*or* Radcliffe]. Ben Jonson. CP-JonsB; SP-JonsB

On Marriage. Robert Burns. CP-BurnR

On Marriage. Richard Crashaw. CP-CrasR

On Martock Moor. Thomas Hardy. CP-HardT

[On] Maxwell of Cardoness. Robert Burns. CP-BurnR

On Meeting Miss B. John Ciardi. CP-CiarJ

On Memory. A. K. Ramanujan. CP-RamaA

On Messrs Hussey and Coffin. Phillis Wheatley. CP-WheaP

On Mill, My Lady's Woman. Ben Jonson. CP-JonsB; SP-JonsB

On Receiving a Curious Shell, and a Copy of Verses, from the Same Ladies. John Keats. CP-KeatJ

On Receiving a Flower from the Rev. C. H. A. Dall, in India. Jones Very. CP-VeryJ

On Receiving a Laurel Crown from Leigh Hunt. John Keats. CP-KeatJ

On Receiving an Account that His Only Sister's Death Was Inevitable. Samuel Taylor Coleridge. CP-ColeS

On Receiving an Eagle's Quill from Lake Superior. John Greenleaf Whittier. CP-WhitJ

On Receiving from a Lady a Present of a Ring. George Crabbe. SP-CrabG

On Receiving from the Right Hon. the Lady Frances Shirley a Standish and Two Pens. Alexander Pope. CP-PopeA

On Receiving Hayley's Picture. William Cowper. CP-CowpW

On Receiving Heyne's Virgil. William Cowper. CP-CowpW

On Recollection. Phillis Wheatley. CP-WheaP

  (Recollection. To Miss A—M—, humbly inscribed by the Authoress.) CP-WheaP

On Reformed Gamester. Ben Jonson. CP-JonsB; SP-JonsB

On Refusal of Aid between Nations. Dante Gabriel Rossetti. CW-RossD

On Religion's holy hill. Fragment of an Intended Poem on Milton, Written in the Copy of *Paradise Lost* Which Belonged to Wordsworth at Cambridge. William Wordsworth. CP-WorW1

On Rembrandt's Etching of Joseph Telling His Dream (1636). Helen Pinkerton. CP-PinkH

On Rembrandt's Self-Portrait (1658) in the Frick Museum. Helen Pinkerton. CP-PinkH

On Resurrection Day your body testifies agains you. Jelaluddin Rumi. SP-Rumi, *tr. by* Coleman Barks

On Returning to a Lake in Spring. Richard Eberhart. CP-EberR

On Revisiting Harrow. Lord Byron. CP-Byron

On Revisiting the Sea-Shore, after Long Absence. Samuel Taylor Coleridge. CP-ColeS

On Righteous Indignation. G. K. Chesterton. CP-ChesG

On Rising Early. Robert Graves. CP-GravR

On Rising from the Dead. Carolyn Kizer. CP-KizeC

On roadsides, / in fall fields, / in rumpy bunches. Goldenrod. Mary Oliver. SP-OlivM

On Robert Emmet's Grave. Percy Bysshe Shelley. CP-ShelP

On Robert Riddel. Robert Burns. CP-BurnR

On St Brigid's Day the new life could be entered. Seamus Heaney. SP-HeanSO *Fr.* Squarings.

On St. *Peter* Casting Away His Nets at Our Saviours Call. Richard Crashaw. CP-CrasR

On Saint Peter Cutting of Malchus His Eare. Richard Crashaw. CP-CrasR

On St. Winefred. Gerard Manley Hopkins. CP-HopkG

On Sam Rogers. Lord Byron. CP-Byron

On Saturday, the power-mowers' whine. Suburban Prophecy. Howard Nemerov. CP-NemeH

On Scaring Some Waterfowl in Loch Turit, a Wild Scene among the Hills of Oughtertyre. Robert Burns. CP-BurnR

On scattered battlefields they lie. Unsepulchred, 1914–1918, The. Marya Alexandrovna Zaturenska. SP-ZatuM

On 'Scursion-days—an' Shows—an' Fairs. Little Lame Boy's Views, A. James Whitcomb Riley. CP-RileJ

On Seeing a Lock of Milton's Hair. John Keats. CP-KeatJ

On Seeing a Needlecase in the Form of a Harp; the Work of E.M.S. William Wordsworth. CP-WorW2

On Seeing a Photograph by Mathew Brady. Miller Williams. CP-WillM

On Seeing a Portrait of Mrs Montagu. Samuel Johnson. CP-JohnS

On Seeing a Wounded Hare Limp by Me, Which a Fellow Had Just Shot At. Robert Burns. CP-BurnR

On Seeing a Youth Affectionately Welcomed by a Sister. Samuel Taylor Coleridge. CP-ColeS

On Seeing an Egyptian Mummy in Berlin, 1932. Richard Eberhart. CP-EberR

On Seeing an Old Civil War Painting with My Love. Charles Bukowski. SP-BukC2

On Seeing Larry Rivers' *Washington Crossing the Delaware* at the Museum of Modern Art. Frank O'Hara. SP-OharF

On Seeing Miss Fontenelle in a Favourite Character. Robert Burns. CP-BurnR

On Seeing Mrs. Kemble in Yarico. Robert Burns. CP-BurnR

On Seeing Mrs Macauly Graham. Annis Boudinot Stockton. CP-StocA

On seeing my own play. 15 Years Later. William Carlos Williams. CP-WilW2

On Seeing Projected Figures for War Dead in the Twentieth Century. Miller Williams. CP-WillM

On Seeing Some Tourists of the Lakes Pass by Reading; a Practice Very Common. William Wordsworth. CP-WorW1

On Seeing the Elgin Marbles. John Keats. CP-KeatJ

On Seeing the Portrait of Helen Ruthven Waterston. Jones Very. CP-VeryJ

On Seeing the Victoria Regia in Bloom, at the Garden of J. Fisk Allen Esq. July

22d, 1853. Jones Very. CP-VeryJ

On Seeing the White Mountains from Cook's Hill, in West Peabody. Jones Very. CP-VeryJ

On Seeing Verses Written upon Windows in Inns. Jonathan Swift. CP-SwifJ

On Sending Home My Civilian Clothes. John Ciardi. CP-CiarJ

On September 2, 1945. Formalities, The. John Ciardi. CP-CiarJ

On Shakespear[e]. John Milton. CP-MiltJ

On shallow slates the pigeons shift together. Pigeons. Philip Larkin. CP-LarkP

On shallow straw, in shadeless glass. Take One Home for the Kiddies. Philip Larkin. CP-LarkP

On Sherman's Men. Herman Melville. SP-MelvH

On Shields. Against World War 3. Alan Dugan. CP-DugaA

On Shooting Particles beyond the World. Richard Eberhart. CP-EberR

On short, still days. Gathering Wood. Philip Larkin. CP-LarkP

On shoulders whirled in some eccentric orbit. Henry David Thoreau. CP-ThorH

On Sight. Alice Walker. CP-WalkA

On Sight of a Gentlewoman's Face in the Water. Thomas Carew. CP-CareT

On Silence. Alexander Pope. CP-PopeA

On Singers. Robert Browning. CP-BroR2

On Sir Cod the Perfumed. Ben Jonson. CP-JonsB; SP-JonsB

On Sir Home Popham's Sentence—April 1807. Jane Austen. CP-AustJ

On Sir John Roe ("In place of scutcheons, that should deck thy hearse"). Ben Jonson. CP-JonsB; SP-JonsB

On Sir John Roe ("What two brave perils of the private sword"). Ben Jonson. CP-JonsB; SP-JonsB

On Sir Joshua Reynolds. William Blake. CP-BlakW

On Sir Voluptuous Beast. Ben Jonson. CP-JonsB; SP-JonsB

On Sitting Down to Read "King Lear" Once Again. John Keats. CP-KeatJ

On 69th Street. 11/22/63. George Oppen. CP-OppGN

On Sleep. Publius Papinius Statius. CP-CunnJ *Fr.* Sylvae [*or* Silvae].

On Some Beautiful Crocuses: In Front of the House of B. H. Silsbee, Esq. Jones Very. CP-VeryJ

On Some Blue and Golden Columbines from Pike's Peak, Colorado. Jones Very. CP-VeryJ

On Some Eternals from a Friend's Garden. Jones Very. CP-VeryJ

On some evening, shall we say, when the innocent tourist, away from our economic horrors. Historic Evening. Arthur Rimbaud. CP-RimbA, *tr. by* Martin Sorrell

On Some Other Planet You May Be Right. Yehuda Amichai. SP-AmicY, *tr. by* Chana Bloch

On Something, that Walk[e]s Somewhere. Ben Jonson. CP-JonsB; SP-JonsB

On Somme. Ivor Gurney. SP-GurnI

On souls robbed of their birth-right's better part. E. E. Cummings. CP-CummE

On Spies. Ben Jonson. CP-JonsB; SP-JonsB

On St. Valentine's Day. William Carlos Williams. CP-WilW2

On starry heights. Conflict of Convictions, The. Herman Melville. SP-MelvH

On Stella's Birthday, 1718/1719. Jonathan Swift. *See* Stella's Birthday; Written in the Year 1718[/9]

On Stephen Duck, the Thresher, and Favourite Poet. Jonathan Swift. CP-SwifJ

On stern Blencartha's perilous height. Thought, A. Samuel Taylor Coleridge. CP-ColeS

On still days when country telephone. Troubleshooting. William Stafford. SP-StafW; SP-StafWW

On Stinsford Hill at Midnight. Thomas Hardy. CP-HardT

On Stone. Ambrose Bierce. SP-BierA

On storm-struck deck, wind sirens caterwaul. Channel Crossing. Sylvia Plath. CP-PlatS

On Stothard. William Blake. CP-BlakW

On Stripping Bark from Myself. Alice Walker. CP-WalkA

On Stuffing a Goose. Theodore Weiss. SP-WeisT

On Sturminster Foot-Bridge. Thomas Hardy. CP-HardT

On such a night, or such a night. Emily Dickinson. CP-DickE

On such Subjects no Wonder that she shou'd write well. To Miss Jane Austen the Reputed Author of Sense and Sensibility a Novel Lately Publish'd. James Austen. CP-AustJ

On summer nights I sleep naked. Letter of Recommendation, A. Yehuda Amichai. SP-AmicY, *tr. by* Chana Bloch

On summer nights, under the shopfront's piercing eyes. Arthur Rimbaud. CP-RimbA, *tr. by* Martin Sorrell

On Sunday, day of rest, I stroll the park. Statement for the Times. David Ignatow. SP-IgnaD

On Sunday I go to church and pray with all the others. Helene's Religion. Czeslaw Milosz. CP-MiloCN, *tr. by* Robert Hass

On Sunday Walks. W. H. Auden. CP-AudeW

On sunny summer Sunday afternoons in Harlem. Passing. Langston Hughes. CP-HughL; CP-HughL3

On Sutton Strand. Donald Davie. CP-DaviDC

On sweet young earth where the myrtle presses. Willow, The. Dorothy Parker.

CP-ParkD

On Swimming. Adam Zagajewski. SP-ZagaA, *tr. by* Clare Cavanagh

On Taking a Batchelor's Degree. Christopher Smart. SP-SmarC

On Taking from the Top to Broaden the Base. Robert Frost. CP-FrosR

On Taking Physicke. Richard Crashaw. *See* Temperance or the Cheap Physitian upon the Translation of Lessius

On Tam the Chapman. Robert Burns. *See* Tam the Chapman

On That Day. D. H. Lawrence. CP-LawrD

On that day the Yellow Emperor showed the poet his palace. Parable of the Palace. Jorge Luis Borges. SP-BorgJ, *tr. by* Ken Krabbenhoft

On that dear Frame the Years had worn. Emily Dickinson. CP-DickE

On that gray night of mournful drone. Man Was Drawing Near to Me, A. Thomas Hardy. CP-HardT

On that great night of her success. Aimée. George Meredith. CP-MerG2

On that night the poet went. Ralph Waldo Emerson. CP-EmerR

On that specific Pillow. Emily Dickinson. CP-DickE

On the Adequacy of Landscape. Wallace Stevens. CP-StevW; CP-StevWP

On the Anniversary of My Baptism. Thomas Merton. CP-MertT

On the anvil of love my flesh has been hammered out. How Long Is the Night? Stanley Kunitz. CP-KunSC

On the Archbishop of Cashel and Bettesworth. Jonathan Swift. CP-SwifJ

On the Astrologers. *Unknown.* CP-CowpW, *tr. by* William Cowper

An an Attic Red-Figured Amphora (490 B.C.) by the "Berlin Painter" in the Metropolitan Museum. Helen Pinkerton. CP-PinkH

On the Author of Letters on Literature. William Cowper. CP-CowpW

On the Author, Work, and Translator. Ben Jonson. CP-JonsB

On the Balcony. D. H. Lawrence. CP-LawrD

On the Bank Street Pier. Grace Paley. CP-PalGC

On the Banks o' Deer Crick. James Whitcomb Riley. CP-RileJ

On the Banks of a Rocky Stream. William Wordsworth. CP-WorW2

On the banks of the. News Carried to Macedonia, The. Raymond Carver. CP-CarvR

On the Banks of the Niemen was published in 1888. Undressing Justine. Czeslaw Milosz. CP-MiloCN, *tr. by* Robert Hass

On the Banks of the Styx. Wisława Szymborska. SP-SzymW, *tr. by* Stanislaw Barańczak *and* Clare Cavanagh

On the Baptized Ethiopian. Richard Crashaw. CP-CrasR, *tr. by* Richard Crashaw (Acts 8; On the Baptized Æthiopian.) CP-CrasR, *tr. by* Richard Crashaw

On the bare alder bough. Message, The ("On the bare alder bough"). Jones Very. CP-VeryJ

On the Beach at Night. Walt Whitman. CP-WhitW

On the Beach at Night Alone. Walt Whitman. CP-WhitW

On the beach where we had been idly. Gracious Goodness. Marge Piercy. SP-PierM

On the Beautiful Roses, in front of the Mansion of John Hodges, Esq. Jones Very. CP-VeryJ

On the Belgian Expatriation. Thomas Hardy. CP-HardT

On the Big Horn. John Greenleaf Whittier. CP-WhitJ

On the big staircase in this picture. Old Photograph of Strangers, An. William Meredith. SP-MereW

On the Biographia Britannica. William Cowper. *See* On Observing Some Names of Little Note Recorded in the "Biographia Britannica"

On the Birth Day of the Revd Doctor Witherspoon, 1788. Annis Boudinot Stockton. CP-StocA

On the Birth of a Posthumous Child, Born in Peculiar Circumstances of Family Distress. Robert Burns. CP-BurnR

On the Birth of Good & Evil during the Long Winter of '28. Philip Levine. SP-LeviP

On the Birth of John William Rizzo Hoppner. Lord Byron. CP-Byron

On the black stage he. Mime. John Updike. CP-UpdiJ

On the blackboard in his study, time. Visit to a Physicist. Dan Pagis. SP-PagiD, *tr. by* Stephen Mitchell

On the blackboard map your country. Comic Books vs. History. Margaret Atwood. SP-AtwM1

On the Bleeding Wounds of Our Crucified Lord. Richard Crashaw. CP-CrasR

On the Blessed Virgins Bashfulnesse. Richard Crashaw. CP-CrasR

On the bottom of this ocean of air which aeons ago. Outside an Air Base, California. Dan Pagis. SP-PagiD, *tr. by* Stephen Mitchell

On the Breakwater. Carl Sandburg. SP-SandC

On the brink of sleep, stretched in a wide bed. Friday Night. Robert Graves. CP-GravR

On the broad sidewalk across from the university gate. NYU. Yehuda Amichai. SP-AmicYL, *tr. by* Benjamin Harshav *and* Barbara Harshav

On the brown trail. Stephen Crane. CP-CranS

On the Bunyan Tableau. Jones Very. CP-VeryJ

On the Burning of Lord Mansfield's Library. William Cowper. CP-CowpW

On the Burning of Whitehall in 1698. Jonathan Swift. CP-SwifJ

On the Bust of Helen by Canova. Lord Byron. CP-Byron

(In This Beloved Marble View.) CP-Byron

On the Capture of General Lee. Phillis Wheatley. CP-WheaP

On the Card[e]s, and Dice. Sir Walter Ralegh. CP-RaleW

On the cedars and yews. Shore Fog. A. R. Ammons. CP-AmmoA

On the Celebration of the Birth of the Dauphin of France. Annis Boudinot Stockton. CP-StocA

On the chamber, on the stairs. Ralph Waldo Emerson. CP-EmerR

On the Chinese Abduction of Tibet's Child Panchen Lama. Norman Dubie. CP-DubiN

On the Christening of a Friend's Child. Samuel Taylor Coleridge. CP-ColeS

On the Christmaswhite plains of the floured and flowering kitchen table. Bread of this World; Praises III, The. Thomas McGrath. SP-McGrT

On the Circuit. W. H. Auden. CP-AudeW

On the Civil War on the East Coast of the United States of North America 1860–64. Alan Dugan. CP-DugaA

On the coast of ARMORICA. A monastery. Le Poète Contumace. Randall Jarrell. CP-JarrR

On the coast of Chile where Neruda lived. General Song of Humanity, The. Lawrence Ferlinghetti. SP-FerlL

On the Collar of Mrs. Dingley's Lap-Dog. Jonathan Swift. CP-SwifJ

On the Columbia River near Vantage. Bobber. Raymond Carver. CP-CarvR

On the Completion of the Pacific Telegraph. Jones Very. CP-VeryJ

On the Continent. Charles Bukowski. SP-BukC1

On the Coosawattee. James Dickey. CP-DickJ

On the Corner. Philip Levine. SP-LeviP

On the counter among many. Writings of the Mystics, The. Charles Simic. SP-SimiC; SP-SimiCE

On the Countess of Burlington Cutting Paper. Alexander Pope. CP-PopeA

On the cover of an ancient box, a parting man and woman are drawn. Yehuda Amichai. SP-AmicYL *Fr.* At Right Angles.

On the curving, dusty roads. Indonesia. Mary Oliver. SP-OlivM

On the Danger of War. George Meredith. CP-MerG1

On the dark lake below, the fishermen's bells. Recollection of Bellagio. William Meredith. SP-MereW

On the day I left, spring broke out. Yehuda Amichai. SP-AmicY, *tr. by* Chana Bloch

On the day it was delivered. Box, The. James Laughlin. CP-LaugJ

On the Day My Daughter Was Born No One Died. Yehuda Amichai. SP-AmicY, *tr. by* Chana Bloch

On the day my daughter was born not a single person. On the Day My Daughter Was Born No One Died. Yehuda Amichai. SP-AmicY, *tr. by* Chana Bloch

On the Day My Daughter Was Born Not a Single Person Died. Yehuda Amichai. SP-AmicYL, *tr. by* Benjamin Harshav *and* Barbara Harshav

On the day of breasts and small hips. Song for a Lady. Anne Sexton. CP-SextA; SP-SextA

On the Day of Judgement. Jonathan Swift. *See* Day of Judgement, The

On the Day of the Destruction of Jerusalem by Titus. Lord Byron. CP-Byron

On the day of the explosion. Explosion, The. Philip Larkin. CP-LarkP

On the day of their excursion up the Thames. Royal Prospect, A. Seamus Heaney. SP-HeanSO

On the day the sienna-skinned man. Killing Floor. Ai. SP-Ai

On the day when the flies were made. Flies. W. S. Merwin. SP-MerwW

On the day when the Savoy. Projection. Langston Hughes. CP-HughL; CP-HughL3

On the day when youth is no more upon me. To Wish Myself Courage. William Carlos Williams. CP-WilW1

On the Death of a Cat. Christina Georgina Rossetti. CP-RosC3

On the Death of a Fair Infant Dying of a Cough. John Milton. CP-MiltJ

On the Death of a German Philosopher. Stevie Smith. CP-SmitS

On the Death of a Middle-Aged Man. Miller Williams. CP-WillM

On the Death of a Poem. A. K. Ramanujan. CP-RamaA

On the Death of a Poet. Czeslaw Milosz. CP-MiloCN, *tr. by* Robert Hass

On the Death of a Young Gentleman. Phillis Wheatley. CP-WheaP

On the Death of a Young Lady. Lord Byron. CP-Byron

On the Death of a Young Lady of Five Years of Age. Phillis Wheatley. CP-WheaP

On the Death of an Unfortunate Lady. William Wordsworth. CP-WorW1

On the Death of Damon. John Milton. *See* Damon's Epitaph

On the Death of Dr [*or* Mr] Robert Levet [a Practiser in Physic]. Samuel Johnson. CP-JohnS

On the Death of Dr. Samuel Marshall. 1771. Phillis Wheatley. CP-WheaP
(On the Death of Doctor Samuel Marshall [variant 2].) CP-WheaP

On the Death of Dr. Samuel Marshall [variant 1]. Phillis Wheatley. *See* On the Death of Dr. Samuel Marshall. 1771

On the Death of Doctor Samuel Marshall [variant 2]. Phillis Wheatley. *See* On the Death of Dr. Samuel Marshall. 1771

On the Death of Echo, a Lap-Dog. Robert Burns. CP-BurnR

On the Death of General Montgomery. Annis Boudinot Stockton. CP-StocA

On the Death of General Wooster. Phillis Wheatley. CP-WheaP

On the Death of Her Mother. Muriel Rukeyser. CP-RukeM

On the Death of His Majesty (George the Third). William Wordsworth. CP-WorW2

On the Death of Isaac, His Brother. Shmuel HaNagid. SP-HaNaS

On the Death of J. C. an Infant. Phillis Wheatley. CP-WheaP

On the Death of José de Ciria y Escalante. Federico García Lorca. CP-GarcF, tr. by Christopher Maurer

On the Death of Keats; Lines for Those Who Drown Twice. John Logan. CP-LogaJ

On the Death of Little Mahala Ashcraft. James Whitcomb Riley. CP-RileJ

On the Death of Mr. Snider Murder'd by Richardson. Phillis Wheatley. CP-WheaP

On the Death of Mr. John Haskins. Ralph Waldo Emerson. CP-EmerR

On the Death of Norman Dukes. Alan Dugan. CP-DugaA

On the Death of Russell. William Cowper. CP-CowpW

On the Death of Sir J. Hunter Blair. Robert Burns. CP BurnR

On the Death of the Bishop of Ely. John Milton. CP-CowpW; CP-MiltJ
   (My lids with grief were tumid yet.) CP-CowpW

On the Death of the Late Lord President Dundas. Robert Burns. CP-BurnR

On the Death of the Poet's Mother Thirty-Three Years Later. John Logan. CP-LogaJ

On the Death of the Rev'd Dr. Sewall. 1769. [variant 3]. Phillis Wheatley. See On the Death of the Rev. Dr. Sewall. 1769

On the Death of the Rev. Dr. Sewell. 1769. Phillis Wheatley. CP-WheaP
   (On the Death of the Rev'd Dr. Sewall. 1769. [variant 3].) CP-WheaP

On the Death of the Rev. Mr. George Whitefield [1770]. Phillis Wheatley. CP-WheaP
   (Ode of Verses on the Much-lamented Death of the Rev. Mr. George Whitefield, Late Chaplain to the Countess of Huntingdon, An.) CP-WheaP

On the Death of the Vice-Chancellor, a Physician. John Milton. CP-CowpW; CP-MiltJ
   (Learn, ye nations of the earth.) CP-CowpW

On the Death of W. C. Paul Laurence Dunbar. CP-DunbP

On the Death of Winston Churchill. David Ignatow. SP-IgnaD

On the Death of Zhukov. Joseph Brodsky. CP-BrodJ, tr. by George L. Kline

On the Decease of the Rev'd Doctr. Sewall [variant 1]. Phillis Wheatley. See On the Death of the Rev. Dr. Sewell. 1769

On the Decease of the Rev'd Dr. Sewell [variant 2]. Phillis Wheatley. See On the Death of the Rev. Dr. Sewell. 1769

On the Deck. Grace Paley. CP-PalGC

On the Decline of Oracles. Sylvia Plath. CP-PlatS

On the Dedication of Dorothy Hall. Paul Laurence Dunbar. CP-DunbP

On the deep snowy field. Tenth Grade. Grace Paley. CP-PalGC

On the Departure of Sir Walter Scott from Abbotsford, for Naples. William Wordsworth. CP-WorW2; MW-WorW

On the Departure Platform. Thomas Hardy. CP-HardT

On the desert. Stephen Crane. CP-CranS

On the Detraction Which Followed the Publication of a Certain Poem. William Wordsworth. CP-WorW2

On the Detraction Which Followed upon My Writing Certain Treatises. John Milton. CP-MiltJ
   (Sonnet 12.) CP-MiltJ

On the Difficulty of Conjuring Up a Dryad. Sylvia Plath. CP-PlatS

On the difficulty of writing. Difficulty. A. K. Ramanujan. CP-RamaA

On the Disadvantages of Central Heating. Amy Clampitt. CP-ClamA

On the door you will not enter. Catarina to Camoens. Elizabeth Barrett Browning. CP-BroEB

On the Doorstep. Thomas Hardy. CP-HardT

On the Downs. G. K. Chesterton. CP-ChesG

On the Downs, in the Weald, on the Marshes. Very Many People. Rudyard Kipling. CP-KiplR

On the Dresser. James Schuyler. CP-SchuJ

On the Drum. D. H. Lawrence. CP-LawrD

On the Duchess of Gordon's Reel Dancing. Robert Burns. CP-BurnR

On the Duke of Buckingham. Thomas Carew. CP-CareT

On the Edge. Philip Levine. SP-LeviP

On the Edge. May Swenson. SP-SwenM

On the edge of woods. Igor Stravinsky. Charles Olson. CP-OlsoC

On the Elk, Unwitnessed. Alan Dugan. CP-DugaA

On the Engraver of His Likeness. John Milton. CP-MiltJ

On the Engraver of His Pourtrait. William Cowper. CP-CowpW

On the equator east of my son I Orion bequeath to him my riches. Charles Olson. CP-OlsoC

On the Esplanade. Walter De la Mare. CP-DeLaW

On the Esplanade. Thomas Hardy. CP-HardT

On the Eternity of the Supreme Being. Christopher Smart. SP-SmarC
   "Hail wonrous being who in power supreme." CP-StocA

On the eve of All-Souls' Day. Night of Questionings, A. Thomas Hardy. CP-HardT

On the evening in memory fo Whatsisname, the veteran poet. Memorial Evening. Dan Pagis. SP-PagiD, tr. by Stephen Mitchell

On the evening of July 25, 1936. Mediterranean. Muriel Rukeyser. CP-RukeM

On the Extinction of the Venetian Republic. William Wordsworth. CP-WorW1; MW-WorW

On the Eyes of an SS Officer. Richard Wilbur. CP-WilbR

On the Eyes of Miss A——— H———. Lord Byron. CP-Byron

On the Failure of a Poet. Charles Bukowski. SP-BukC2

On the fair green hills of Rio. Burglar of Babylon, The. Elizabeth Bishop. CP-BishE

On the Fall of Zalona. Emily Jane Brontë. CP-BronE

On the Famous Voyage. Ben Jonson. CP-JonsB; SP-JonsB

On the far side of the water, high on a sand bar. Arkansas Traveller. Charles Wright. SP-WrigC

On the Ferry. Wallace Stevens. CP StevWP

On the Field of Kulikovo. Aleksandr Aleksandrovich Blok. SP-BlokA, tr. by Peter France and Jon Stallworthy

On the 15th day of November in the year of the motorcar. Ted Berrigan. SP-BerrT Fr. Sonnets, The.

On the Fifth of November. John Milton. CP-MiltJ

On the Final Day. Donald Davie. CP-DaviDC

On the Final Submission of the Tyrolese. William Wordsworth. CP WorW1

On the fine wire of his whine he walked. Mosquito. John Updike. CP-UpdiJ

On the First Church Built by the Puritans in 1634. Jones Very. CP-VeryJ

On the first day. How God Was Made. Kenneth Patchen. CP-PatcK

On the first day of Ruin. Chase, The. W. S. Merwin. SP-MerwW

On the first day when light came through the curtain. Widow. William Stafford. SP-StafWW

On the first few nights of the new year, a week. Sex. Hayden Carruth. CP-CarHS

On the first of the Feast of Feasts. Epilogue: "On the first of the Feast of Feasts." Robert Browning. CP-BroR1; SP-BroR

On the first page of my dreambook. Empire of Dreams. Charles Simic. SP-SimiC; SP-SimiCE

On the Five Ladies at Sot's Hole, with the Doctor at Their Head. Jonathan Swift. CP-SwifJ

On the flat road a man at last appears. Light Snow-Fall after Frost, A. Thomas Hardy. CP-HardT

On the Forcers of Conscience. John Milton.

On the Fourth Floor. Grace Paley. CP-PalGC

On the Fourth of July at the beach. At the Beach. James Schuyler. CP-SchuJ

On the Fragility of Mind. Richard Eberhart. CP-EberR

On the frigid face of the heath-hemmed pond. At Rushy-Pond. Thomas Hardy. CP-HardT

On the Frontispiece of Isaacsons Chronologie Explained. Richard Crashaw. CP-CrasR

On the Garden Wall. Nicholas Vachel Lindsay. CP-LindV

On the Gift of a Sapphire to My Wife Ann. James Laughlin. CP-LaugJ

On the Goodness of the Supreme Being. Christopher Smart. SP-SmarC

On the Grasshopper. Unknown. CP-CowpW, tr. by William Cowper

On the Grasshopper and [the] Cricket. John Keats. CP-KeatJ

On the grassy banks / Lambkins at their pranks. Lambs at Play. Christina Georgina Rossetti. CP-RosC2

On the Grave. Herman Melville. SP-MelvH

On the Great Atlantic Rainway. Kenneth Koch. SP-KochK

On the Great Divisions of the Christian Church, the Catholic, the Protestant, and the Greek. Jones Very. CP-VeryJ

On the Great Earthquake in New Grenada. Jones Very. CP-VeryJ

On the Great Encouragement Given by English Nobility & Gentry to Correggio Rubens Rembrandt Reynolds Gainsborough Catalani Ducrowe & Dilbury Doodle. William Blake. CP-BlakW

On the Great Wall. Rudyard Kipling. Fr. Puck of Pook's Hill.

On the green a white boy goes / And he walks. Three ciphers and a faint fakir. Penn Station. Ted Berrigan. SP-BerrT Fr. Sonnets, The.

On the green a white boy goes / We may read about all those radio waves. Ted Berrigan. SP-BerrT Fr. Sonnets, The.

On the green margin of the brook. Song, A: "On the green margin of the brook." William Cowper. CP-CowpW

On the green riverbank. Old Sailors, The. Lawrence Ferlinghetti. SP-FerlL

On the green / with lignum vitae balls and ivory markers. Bowls. Marianne Craig Moore. CP-MoorM

On the greensward there was a milk-white deer. Petrarch. CP-Petra, tr. by J. G. Nichols

On the Greve. Eugenio Montale. CP-MontE, tr. by Jonathan Galassi

On the grey rock of Cashel the mind's eye. Double Vision of Michael Robartes, The. William Butler Yeats. CP-YeatW

On the grey sand beside the shallow stream. Ego Dominus Tuus. William Butler Yeats. CP-YeatW

On the grim and crowded tumbrils high he reared his giant frame. Danton. G. K. Chesterton. CP-ChesG

On the Gunpowder Plot. John Milton. CP-MiltJ

On the Gunpowder-Treason. Richard Crashaw. CP-CrasR

On the Hall at Stowey. Charles Tomlinson. CP-TomlC; SP-TomlC

On the Heart's Beginning to Cloud the Mind. Robert Frost. CP-FrosR

On the hedges grew the low melon moons. Epitaph on a Street Dog. A. K. Ramanujan. CP-RamaA

On the High Price of Fish. William Cowper. CP-CowpW

On the high rocks you have turned. For Mercedes in Her Flight. Federico García Lorca. CP-GarcF, *tr.* by Christopher Maurer

On the Highest Column. Eugenio Montale. CP-MontE, *tr.* by Jonathan Galassi

On the Hill below the Lighthouse. James Dickey. CP-DickJ

On the hill is cool! Even the dead. Morning. William Carlos Williams. CP-WilW1

On the Hill Late at Night. Wendell Berry. CP-BerrW

On the Home Guards. Herman Melville. SP-MelvH

On the Honoured Poems of His Honoured Friend, Sir John Beaumont, Baronet. Ben Jonson. CP-JonsB

On the horizon the peaks assembled. Stephen Crane. CP-CranS

On the horizon, through the steam of exhausted blast furnaces fog yes. Ax God: Sea Pursuit, The. James Dickey. CP-DickJ

On the hour he shuts the door and walks out of town. Face of the Dam: Vivian Jones. Muriel Rukeyser. CP-SpenS

On the House of a Friend. John Logan. CP-LogaJ

On the housetop, the floor of the boundless. New Roof, The. Wendell Berry. CP-BerrW

On the Ice Islands Seen Floating in the German Ocean. William Cowper. CP-CowpW

On the idle hill of summer. A. E. Housman. CP-HousA

On the Immensity of the Supreme Being. Christopher Smart. SP-SmarC

On the Inclusion of Miniature Dinosaurs in Breakfast Cereal Boxes. John Updike. CP-UpdiJ

On the Increase in Crime Since the Late Civil War. Jones Very. CP-VeryJ

On the Inequality of Men. Czeslaw Milosz. CP-MiloCN, *tr.* by Robert Hass

On the Inventor of Gunpowder. John Milton. CP-MiltJ
    (On the Inventor of Guns.) CP-CowpW

On the Inventor of Guns. John Milton. *See* On the Inventor of Gunpowder

On the Irish Bishops. Jonathan Swift. CP-SwifJ

On the Irish Club. Jonathan Swift. CP-SwifJ

On the island where the Argonaut of immortal Fantasy. Colloquy of the Centaurs. "Rubén Dario." SP-DariR, *tr.* by Alberto Acereda *and* Will Derusha

On the isle of Penikese. Prayer of Agassiz, The. John Greenleaf Whittier. CP-WhitJ

On the Jamb-Statues of the Portail Royal (1150) on Chartres Cathedral. Helen Pinkerton. CP-PinkH

On the King's Birthday. Ben Jonson. CP-JonsB

On the kitchen wall a flash. World Outside, The. Denise Levertov. SP-LeveDP

On the Lamented Death of Mrs. Throckmorton's Bullfinch. William Cowper. CP-CowpW
    (On Mrs. Throckmorton's Bulfinch.) CP-CowpW

On the land and on the sea. For H.P. Christina Georgina Rossetti. CP-RosC3

On the lap of the mountain meadow. Youth Stares at Minoan Sunset. Robert Penn Warren. CP-WarrR

On the last day of a rough but fortunate voyage, near the farthest end of the known world. Atlas and the Fatman. Thomas Merton. CP-MertT

On the last words of Trumpeldor. Yehuda Amichai. SP-AmicY, *tr.* by Chana Bloch *Fr.* Songs of Zion the Beautiful.

On the Late Captain Grose's Peregrinations thro' Scotland, Collecting the Antiquities of That King. Robert Burns. CP-BurnR

On the late Disgraceful Scene in Congress. Jones Very. CP-VeryJ

On the Late Mild Winter. Jones Very. CP-VeryJ

On the Late Tornado, at Wallingford, Conn. Jones Very. CP-VeryJ

On the Lawn at Ira's. Gregory Orr. SP-OrrG

On the lawn, beside the red house. Weeds, The. Gregory Orr. SP-OrrG

On the left shore of the Tyrrhenian Sea. Petrarch. CP-Petra, *tr.* by J. G. Nichols

On the Life of Man. Sir Walter Ralegh. *See* What Is Our Life?

On the lips of the child Janet float changing dreams. Sixteen Months. Carl Sandburg. CP-SandC

On the Liquidation of Zoology. Alan Dugan. CP-DugaA

On the little bank, below the orchard. At the Cearne. D. H. Lawrence. CP-LawrD

On the Little House by the Churchyard of Castleknock. Jonathan Swift. CP-SwifJ

On the Llobregat. Eugenio Montale. CP-MontE, *tr.* by Jonathan Galassi

On the London Train. John Berryman. CP-BerrJ

On the Long Island Railroad System. Alan Dugan. CP-DugaA

On the long shore, lit by the moon. Goose Fish, The. Howard Nemerov. CP-NemeH

On the Loss of the *Royal George*. William Cowper. CP-CowpW

On the lot that was a short-cut for lovers. Yehuda Amichai. SP-AmicYL *Fr.* Poems of the Land of Zion and Jerusalem.

On the Madam's best april the. E. E. Cummings. CP-CummE

On the Magnetic Lady. Ben Jonson. CP-JonsB

On [*or* Of] the Manner of Addressing Clouds. Wallace Stevens. CP-StevW; CP-StevWP

On the March. D. H. Lawrence. CP-LawrD

On the March to Sinopi. Constantine P. Cavafy. CP-CavaC, *tr.* by Theoharis Constantine Theoharis

On the Marginal Way. Richard Wilbur. CP-WilbR

On the *Maria Crowther*. "Mr John Keats Five Feet Tall" Sails Away. Thomas Lux. SP-LuxT

On the Marriage of a Virgin. Dylan Thomas. CP-ThomD

On the Marriage of Miss Camilla Wallop & the Revd. [Henry] Wake. Jane Austen. CP-AustJ

On the Marriage of Mr. Gell of East Bourn to Miss Gill. Jane Austen. CP-AustJ

On the Marriage of T. K. and C. C.: The Morning Stormy. Thomas Carew. CP-CareT

On the Massacre of Glencoe, 1692. Sir Walter Scott. SP-ScotW

On the Medusa of Leonardo da Vinci in the Florentine Gallery. Percy Bysshe Shelley. CP-ShelP

On the Miracle of Loaves. Richard Crashaw. CP-CrasR

On the Miracle of Multiplied [*or* Multiplyed] Loaves. Richard Crashaw. CP-CrasR

On the Morning of Christ's Nativity. John Milton. CP-MiltJ

On the morning of May. Faith on Trial, A. George Meredith. CP-MerG1

On the morning you woke beside me—already thinking of going away. Mornings / of an impossible love. Alice Walker. CP-WalkA

On the most westerly Blasket. Given Note, The. Seamus Heaney. SP-HeanSO

On the Mountain. W. S. Merwin. SP-MerwWF

On the Mountain. Charles Tomlinson. CP-TomlC

On the mountain after Vesuvius. Back. John Ciardi. CP-CiarJ

On the Mountain Ash Tree: In front of the house of the late Capt. Robert W. Gould. Jones Very. CP-VeryJ

On the mountain trail, all afternoon. Mountain Mystery. Robert Penn Warren. CP-WarrR

On the Move. Thom Gunn. CP-GunnT

On the Murder of Lieutenant José Del Castillo by the Falangist Bravo Martinez, July 12, 1936. Philip Levine. SP-LeviP

On the Nature of Perspective. Clarence Major. SP-MajoC

On the Nebraska Bill. Jones Very. CP-VeryJ

ON THE NEED TO DRAW BOUNDARIES. Notes. Czeslaw Milosz. CP-MiloCN; CP-MiloCN, *tr.* by Lillian Vallee

On the Neglect of Public Worship. Jones Very. CP-VeryJ

On the Neglect of the Study of History. Jones Very. CP-VeryJ

On the New Hot-House. Ben Jonson. CP-JonsB; SP-JonsB

On *The New Inn*: Ode. To Himself. Ben Jonson. *See* Ode to Himself[e]

On the New Motion. Ben Jonson. CP-JonsB; SP-JonsB

On the Night of a Friend's Wedding. Edwin Arlington Robinson. CP-RobiE

On the night of the Belgian surrender the moon rose. Moon and the Night and the Men, The. John Berryman. CP-BerrJ

On the night that Mrs. Mandrill entered Nature. Mrs. Mandrill. Howard Nemerov. CP-NemeH

On the night there are shown dim few stars timorous. Ivor Gurney. SP-GurnI

On the night when you cross the street. No Room for Form. Jelaluddin Rumi. SP-Rumi, *tr.* by Coleman Barks

On the north side of the telephone pole wet snow stuck. Anniversary. Charles Olson. CP-OlsoC

On the note you do not send me. Christina Georgina Rossetti. CP-RosC3

On the Ocean Floor. Hugh MacDiarmid. SP-MacDH

On the old bridge, the bridge. Advertising in Paris. Alan Dugan. CP-DugaA

On the Old Roman Road. Clarence Major. SP-MajoC

On the Omniscience of the Supreme Being. Christopher Smart. SP-SmarC

On the one hand the steel works. Joliet. Carl Sandburg. CP-SandC

On the one, the / only. Havdalah. Paul Celan. SP-CelaP, *tr.* by John Felstiner

On the orchard of the sea far out are whitecaps. On a Ferry across Chesapeake Bay. Robert Bly. SP-BlyR

On the Orthodoxy and Creed of My Power Mower. John Ciardi. CP-CiarJ

On the Other Hand. C. K. Williams. SP-WillC

On the other phone, Persephone: "He crushed me,—he creased my britches." Allegory of Wealth, The. Charles Olson. CP-OlsoC

On the other shore, in the grey morning. Shore. Hans Magnus Enzensberger. SP-EnzeH, *tr.* by Michael Hamburger

On the Other Side. Czeslaw Milosz. CP-MiloC; CP-MiloCN, *tr.* by Jan Darowski

On the other side of the world's narrow lane. Fact of the Act. Robert Graves.

CP-GravR

On the pampas tonight a gaucho. Raymond Carver. CP-CarvR

On the path. Erotica. Robert Creeley. SP-CreeR

On the path, / by this wet site. Under the Maud Moon. Galway Kinnell. SP-KinnGN

On the Patio. John Ciardi. CP-CiarJ

On the paved parapet. Thetis. "H. D." CP-DoolH

On the Photograph of Corps Commander. Herman Melville. SP-MelvH

On the Picture of a Sleeping Child. Vincent Bourne. CP-CowpW

On the plains of Thessaly. Having Eaten of the Tree of Knowledge. Eleanor Wilner. SP-WilnE

On the Platform. Howard Nemerov. CP-NemeH

On the Platonic Idea as Aristotle Understood It. John Milton. CP-CowpW; CP-MiltJ

   (Ye sister pow'rs, who o'er the sacred groves.) CP-CowpW

On the Plethora of Dryads. Sylvia Plath. CP-PlatS

On the Poet as a Damned Poor Thing. John Ciardi. CP-CiarJ

On the Portrait of a Woman about to Be Hanged. Thomas Hardy. CP-HardT

On the Portrait of Two Beautiful Young People. Gerard Manley Hopkins. CP-HopkG

On the Post Office. Kenneth Rexroth. CP-RexrK

On the Power of Sound. William Wordsworth. CP-WorW2; MW-WorW

On the Power of the Supreme Being. Christopher Smart. SP-SmarC

On the precious verge of danger. Jewels and After. Laura Riding Jackson. CP-RidiL

On the Principle of Blowclocks. Charles Tomlinson. CP-TomlC; SP-TomlC

On the Projected Kendal and Windermere Railway. William Wordsworth. CP-WorW2

On the Promotion of Thurlow. William Cowper. CP-CowpW

On the Prospect of Establishing a Pantisocracy in America. Samuel Taylor Coleridge. CP-ColeS

On the proud banks of great Euphrates' flood. Bible, *O.T. See* By the rivers of Babylon, there we sat down, yea, we wept, when [*or* then] we remembered Zion

On the Quay. Theodore Roethke. CP-RoetT

On the Queens's Visit to London. William Cowper. CP-CowpW

On the Quotation "And My True Faith Can Alter Never, though Thou Art Gone Perhaps Forever." Lord Byron. CP-Byron

On the radio a canary bewailed her luck. Lightnin' Blues. Rita Dove. SP-DoveR

On the Railway Platform. Randall Jarrell. CP-JarrR

On the Ramblas a Tree a Girl. Grace Paley. CP-PalGC

On the Receipt of My Mother's Picture out of Norfolk [the Gift of My Cousin Ann Bodham]. William Cowper. CP-CowpW

On the Recently Minted Hundred-Cent Piece. John Updike. CP-UpdiJ

On the red-on-black amphora. I Saw Her First. James Laughlin. CP-LaugJ

On the Reed. *Unknown.* CP-CowpW, *tr. by* William Cowper

On the Reservations. Ted Hughes. SP-HughTN

On the Return of Col Laurens from His Confinement in the Tower of London. Annis Boudinot Stockton. CP-StocA

On the Revd. Dr. Swift, D. S. P. D. Leaving His Fortune to Build an Hospital for Idiots and Lunatics. *Unknown, sometimes at. to* Thomas Sheridan. CP-SherT

On the Right Honourable and Virtuous Lord Weston, L[ord] High Treasurer of England, upon the Day He Was Made Earl of Portland, 17. Febr. 1632. To the Envious. Ben Jonson. CP-JonsB

On the River. Paul Laurence Dunbar. CP-DunbP

On the Road. Seamus Heaney. SP-HeanSO *Fr.* Sweeney Redivivus.

On the Road. Paul Laurence Dunbar. CP-DunbP

On the Road. D. H. Lawrence. CP-LawrD

On the Road. Czeslaw Milosz. CP-MiloC; CP-MiloCN, *tr. by* Renata Gorczynski *and* Robert Hass

On the road Home. Wallace Stevens. CP-StevW; CP-StevWP

On the road to Bangor, we spotted a domed stone. Bringing a Turtle Home. Robert Lowell. SP-LoweR

On the Road to Larry Robin's Bookstore. Eleanor Wilner. SP-WilnE

On the Road to Nowhere. Nicholas Vachel Lindsay. CP-LindV

On the Road to Wockensutter. John Crowe Ransom. SP-RansJ

On the Road to Woodlawn. Theodore Roethke. CP-RoetT

On the roads at night I saw the glitter of eyes. Eyes of Night-Time. Muriel Rukeyser. CP-RukeM

On the Roof. C. K. Williams. CP-WillC

On the Sacrifice of a Siamese Twin at Birth. Miller Williams. CP-WillM

On the Same. William Cowper. CP-CowpW

On the Same. Thomas Sheridan. CP-SherT

On the Same. *Unknown, sometimes at. to* Thomas Sheridan. CP-SherT

On the Same ["James derided the Purgatorial fire of the soul"]. John Milton. CP-MiltJ

On the Same ["Thus did you strive to vouchsafe James to Heaven"]. John

Milton. CP-MiltJ

On the Same ["Whom impious Rome had just marked out for her curses"]. John Milton. CP-MiltJ

On the Same Beast. Ben Jonson. CP-JonsB; SP-JonsB

On the Same Nobleman. Robert Burns. *See* Epigrams on Lord Galloway

On the Same Occasion. William Wordsworth. CP-WorW2

On the Same Occasion [on Seeing the Foundation Preparing for the Erection of Rydal Chapel]. William Wordsworth. CP-WorW2

On the Same Picture. Walt Whitman. CP-WhitW

On the Sea. John Keats. CP-KeatJ

On the sea and at the Hogue, sixteen hundred ninety-two. Hervé Riel. Robert Browning. CP-BroR2

On the Sea Wall. Paul Laurence Dunbar. CP-DunbP

On the Seas and Far Away. Robert Burns. CP-BurnR

On the secret map the assassins. Rivers and Mountains. John Ashbery. SP-AshbJ

On the seventeenth. Hotel Merlin. Robert Creeley. SP-CreeR

On the sheep-cropped summit, under hot sun. Cat and Mouse. Ted Hughes. SP-HughTN

On the shoals of Nowhere. Flotsam. Langston Hughes. CP-HughL; CP-HughL3

On the Shore. Charles Olson. CP-OlsoC

On the Shortness of Life. William Cowper. CP-CowpW

On the sidewalk. Construction. William Carlos Williams. CP-WilW2

On the Sight of a Manse in the South of Scotland. William Wordsworth. CP-WorW2

On the Silent Anniversary of a Reunion. W. S. Merwin. SP-MerwW

On the Site of a Mulberry-Tree; Planted by Wm. Shakespeare; felled by the Rev. F. Gastrell. Dante Gabriel Rossetti. CW-RossD

On the Skeleton of a Hound. James Wright. CP-WrigJ

On the Slain Collegians. Herman Melville. SP-MelvH

On the slope of the bank angels turn their robes of wool in pastures of steel and emerald. Mystical. Arthur Rimbaud. CP-RimbA, *tr. by* Martin Sorrell

On the small marble-paved platform. Margrave. Robinson Jeffers. CP-JefR2

On the Snuff of a Candle. Sir Walter Ralegh. CP-RaleW

   (Sir W. Ralegh, on the Snuff of a Candle the Night before He Died.) CP-RaleW

On the south terraces of the glass palace. Mourner, The. W. S. Merwin. SP-MerwW

On the South-West Coast of Erehwemos Stands a Romantic Little Village. Kenneth Patchen. CP-PatcK

On the southwest side of Capri. Nude Swim, The. Anne Sexton. CP-SextA

On the Southworth and Hawes Daguerreotype of Massachusetts Supreme Court Chief Justice Lemuel Shaw (1851). Helen Pinkerton. CP-PinkH

On the square, tailored into meagre lawns. To Music. Arthur Rimbaud. CP-RimbA, *tr. by* Martin Sorrell

On the Stairs. Constantine P. Cavafy. CP-CavaC, *tr. by* Theoharis Constantine Theoharis

On the Star of "The Legion of Honour." Lord Byron. CP-Byron

On the Statue of *Cleopatra*, Made into a Fountain by *Leo* the Tenth. Baldassare, Count of Novilara Castiglione. CP-PopeA

On the steep slope by the drive he. Three Gardens. James Schuyler. CP-SchuJ

On the stiff twig up there. Black Rook in Rainy Weather. Sylvia Plath. CP-PlatS

On the Still Surviving Markes of Our Saviours Wounds. Richard Crashaw. CP-CrasR

On "The Story of Rimini." John Keats. CP-KeatJ

On the street I am met with constant hostility. Fragment, A: "On the street I am met with constant hostility." Robert Creeley. CP-CreeR

On the street / Slung on his shoulder is a handle half way across. Shovel Man, The. Carl Sandburg. CP-SandC

On the Subject of Doctors. James Tate. SP-TateJ

On the Subtle Man. Richard Eberhart. CP-EberR

On the Sudden Snow. Jones Very. CP-VeryJ

On the summit: it stands on a fair summit. Grace's House. Thomas Merton. CP-MertT

On the Sun Coming Out in the Afternoon. Henry David Thoreau. CP-ThorH

On the Sunny Side. James Whitcomb Riley. CP-RileJ

On the Suns Setting Clear after a Three Days Storm. Annis Boudinot Stockton. CP-StocA

On the Supposed Immorality of Orchids. Alan Dugan. CP-DugaA

On the Swing. Federico García Lorca. CP-GarcF, *tr. by* Jerome Rothenberg *Fr.* Fairs.

On the Symbolic Consideration of Hands and the Significance of Death. Miller Williams. CP-WillM

On the tallest day in time, the dead came back. V-J Day. John Ciardi. CP-CiarJ

On the Tennis Court at Night. Galway Kinnell. SP-KinnGN

On the Terrace. Charles Tomlinson. SP-TomlC *Fr.* For A Granddaughter.

On the third day i contemplate. Lazarus ("On the third day i contemplate"). Lucille Clifton. SP-ClifL

On the third day, when we unlocked the room, we found nothing. Subject for an

Oil Painting. Yannis Ritsos. SP-RitsY, *tr.* by Kostas Myrsiades

On the third finger of my left hand. Ceremony. William Stafford. SP-StafW; SP-StafWW

On the third night of autumn. New Season, The. W. S. Merwin. SP-MerwWF

On the 32nd Anniversary of the Bombing of Hiroshima and Nagasaki. Denise Levertov. SP-LeveDL

On the Three Hundredth Anniversary of Shakespeare's Birthday. Jones Very. CP-VeryJ

On the Threshhold. Eugenio Montale. CP-MontE, *tr.* by Jonathan Galassi

On the threshold of heaven, the figures in the street. To an Old Philosopher in Rome. Wallace Stevens. CP-StevW; CP-StevWP

On the Threshold of His Greatness, the Poet Comes Down with a Sore Throat. Howard Nemerov. CP-NemeH

On the tidal mud, just before sunset. Daybreak. Galway Kinnell. SP-KinnGN

On the Tlacolula Bus. Charles Tomlinson. CP-TomlC

On the top of my red banner. Song for Elizabeth, A. Nicholas Vachel Lindsay. CP-LindV

On the Town's Honest Man. Ben Jonson. CP-JonsB; SP-JonsB

On the Towpath. John Ashbery. SP-AshbJ

On the Trans-Siberian Railway I traveled to Krasnoyarsk. La Belle Époque. Czeslaw Milosz. CP-MiloC; CP-MiloCN, *tr.* by Robert Hass

On the Tune Called the Old-Hundred-and-Fourth. Thomas Hardy. CP-HardT

On the turf's edge—grass flashing like a knife. Conscript, The. Stephen Spender. CP-SpenS

On the Two Marys in a Fresco of the Crucifixion. Helen Pinkerton. CP-PinkH

On the unbreathing sides of hills. Squatter's Children. Elizabeth Bishop. CP-BishE

On the Union. Ben Jonson. CP-JonsB; SP-JonsB

On the University Carrier Who Sick'n'd [*or* Sickened] in the Time of His Vacancy [Being Forbid to go to London, by Reason of the Plague]. John Milton. CP-MiltJ

On the upper slope. Who It Is. W. S. Merwin. SP-MerwW

On the Venetian Painter. William Blake. CP-BlakW

On the Very Possible Jaundice of an Unborn Daughter. A. K. Ramanujan. CP-RamaA

On the Victory Obtained by Blake over the Spaniards, in the Bay of Santa [*or* Sancta] Cruz, in the Island of Tenerife, 1657. Andrew Marvell. CP-MarvA

On the Virgin and Child Carved in Oak (Auvergne, 1150-1200) in the Metropolitan Museum. Helen Pinkerton. CP-PinkH

On the Virginity of the Virgin Mary & Johanna Southcott. William Blake. CP-BlakW

On the 'Vita Nuova' of Dante. Dante Gabriel Rossetti. CW-RossD

On the Water of Our Lord's Baptism[e]. Richard Crashaw. CP-CrasR

On the water, solid. George Oppen. CP-OppGN

On the water the first wind. Spring. W. S. Merwin. SP-MerwW

On the Way. Thomas Hardy. CP-HardT

On the Way. Denise Levertov. SP-LeveDL

On the Way. Edwin Arlington Robinson. CP-RobiE

On the Way. Carl Sandburg. CP-SandC

On the Way Back. Bogomil Gjuzel. CP-KizeC, *tr.* by Carolyn Kizer

On the Way Home from Nowhere, New Year's Eve. Miller Williams. CP-WillM

On the way to a woman, I give. Into the Stone. James Dickey. CP-DickJ

On the Way to Delphi. John Updike. CP-UpdiJ

On the Way to the Bus. Wallace Stevens. CP-StevWP

On the way to the / valley of transformation. On the Way. Denise Levertov. SP-LeveDL

On the Wide Heath. Edna St. Vincent Millay. CP-MillE

On the wide lawn the snow lay deep. Red Riding-Hood. John Greenleaf Whittier. CP-WhitJ

On the wide level of a mountain's head. Time, Real and Imaginary. Samuel Taylor Coleridge. MW-ColeS

On the wide stairs going down to the Western Wall. On the Wide Stairs—Lurking for Happiness. Yehuda Amichai. SP-AmicYL, *tr.* by Benjamin Harshav *and* Barbara Harshav

On the Wide Stairs—Lurking for Happiness. Yehuda Amichai. SP-AmicYL, *tr.* by Benjamin Harshav *and* Barbara Harshav

On the wide Texan and New Mexican ranches. Oysters. Robinson Jeffers. CP-JefR3

On the wide veranda white. Corn-Song, A. Paul Laurence Dunbar. CP-DunbP

On the Wild Flowers of the Art Exhibition. Jones Very. CP-VeryJ

On the wind of January. Year's Windfalls, A. Christina Georgina Rossetti. CP-RosC1

On the Wing. Christina Georgina Rossetti. CP-RosC1

On the Words "Brother Protestants and Fellow Christians." Jonathan Swift. CP-SwifJ

On the World you colored. Emily Dickinson. CP-DickE

On the World's Birthday. James Tate. SP-TateJ

On the Wounds of Our Crucified Lord. Richard Crashaw. CP-CrasR

On thee has God conferred. Ralph Waldo Emerson. CP-EmerR

On Their Couches Stretched Out at the Treasury. Shmuel HaNagid. SP-HaNaS, *tr.* by Peter Cole

On these cold days. Cemetary Angels. Galway Kinnell. SP-KinnGN

On these green banks, where falls too soon. Outdoor Reception, An. John Greenleaf Whittier. CP-WhitJ

On these low hills, a life meant to go on a long time. Kibbutz Gvar-'Am. Yehuda Amichai. SP-AmicYL, *tr.* by Benjamin Harshav *and* Barbara Harshav

On this bald hill the new year hones its edge. Parliament Hill Fields. Sylvia Plath. CP-PlatS

On This Day I Complete My Thirty-sixth Year. Lord Byron. CP-Byron

On this day man's disgust is known. On Shooting Particles beyond the World. Richard Eberhart. CP-EberR

On this day of errors. June 15th. Maxine W. Kumin. SP-KumiM *Fr.* Joppa Diary.

On this day tradition allots. New Year Greeting, A. W. H. Auden. CP-AudeW

On this decline of Christmas Day. Nightmare, and the Next Thing, A. Thomas Hardy. CP-HardT

On this evening, I think again. Yehuda Amichai. SP-AmicYL, *tr.* by Benjamin Harshav *and* Barbara Harshav

On this exquisite sky. Sundown ("On this exquisite sky"). Federico García Lorca. CP-GarcF, *tr.* by Jerome Rothenberg *Fr.* Shadow.

On this flashing afternoon of Ascension Thursday let me sit. Ceremony for Edward Dahlberg. Thomas Merton. CP-MertT

On This Island. W. H. Auden. CP-AudeW

On this kindly yellow day of mild low-travelling winter sun. Spellbound Palace, A. Thomas Hardy. CP-HardT

On this long storm the Rainbow rose. Emily Dickinson. CP-DickE

On this side of the tapestry. Tapestry, The. Howard Nemerov. CP-NemeH

On this sweet bank your head thrice sweet and dear. Youth's Spring-Tribute. Dante Gabriel Rossetti. CW-RossD *Fr.* House of Life, The.

On this tree thrown up. Spindrift. Galway Kinnell. SP-KinnGN

On this winebowl of pure silver. Craftsman of Winebowls. Constantine P. Cavafy. CP-CavaC, *tr.* by Theoharis Constantine Theoharis

On this wondrous sea. Eternity. Emily Dickinson. CP-DickE

On those islands / The west wind drops its message of indolence. Hebrides, The. Louis MacNeice. CP-MacNL

On Those That Hated "The Playboy of the Western World" 1907. William Butler Yeats. CP-YeatW

On Thought in Harness. Edna St. Vincent Millay. CP-MillE

On thrones from China to Peru. Model for the Laureate, A. William Butler Yeats. CP-YeatW

On Thurlow. William Cowper. CP-CowpW

On Time. John Milton. CP-MiltJ

On to the old haunts. Return to St. Paul's School, A. G. K. Chesterton. CP-ChesG

On Tomasin Parsons. Robert Herrick. CP-HerrR

On top of that if you know me I pronounce you an ignu. Ignu. Allen Ginsberg. CP-GinsA; SP-GinsA

On Trading Time for Life by Work. Alan Dugan. CP-DugaA

On Translation. Andrei Codrescu. SP-CodrA

On Trees. Alan Dugan. CP-DugaA

On Trial. Primo Levi. CP-LeviP, *tr.* by Ruth Feldman

On Tuesday's bus I heard the man from State. Two Women on the Potomac Parkway. Norman Dubie. CP-DubiN

On Turning Ten. Billy Collins. SP-CollB

On two days it steads not to run from thy grave. Omar Khayyám. CP-EmerR

On up the sea slant. Sea Slant. Carl Sandburg. CP-SandC

On uplands bleak and bare to wind. Companions, The. Ivor Gurney. SP-GurnI

On Vacation. Robert Creeley. CP-CreeR

On vacation. Well / earned, twice and. You're. James Schuyler. CP-SchuJ

On Valentine's Day to Friends. Louis Zukofsky. CP-ZukLS

On vent'rous wing in quest of praise I go. Virgil. CP-JohnS *Fr.* Georgics.

On Vermeer's *Young Woman with a Water Jug* (1658) in the Metropolitan Museum. Helen Pinkerton. CP-PinkH

On Viewing the Falls of Niagara, as Photographed by George Barker. Jones Very. CP-VeryJ

On Virtue. Phillis Wheatley. CP-WheaP

On Visiting a Veterans Hospital. Alan Dugan. CP-DugaA

On Visiting Central Park Zoo. Alan Dugan. CP-DugaA

On Visiting Staffa. John Keats. CP-KeatJ

On visiting the beautiful estate of H. H. Hunnewell, Esq., at Wellesley. Jones Very. CP-VeryJ

On Visiting the Tomb of Burns. John Keats. CP-KeatJ

On Voyage. Alan Dugan. CP-DugaA

On Vulture Peak. Gary Snyder. CP-SnydG

On W. R———, Esq. Robert Burns. CP-BurnR

On Waking to the Third Rainy Morning of a Long Week End. Ogden Nash. CP-

NashO

On Walking Slowly after an Accident. Stevie Smith. CP-SmitS

On Water. Charles Tomlinson. CP-TomlC; SP-TomlC

On Watteau's *Pilgrimage to Cythera* (1717) in the Louvre. Helen Pinkerton. CP-PinkH

On Wearing Glasses. Alan Dugan. CP-DugaA

On Wednesday night. Wednesday Night Prayer Meeting. Jay Wright. SP-WrigJ

On Wee Johnie. Robert Burns. CP-BurnR

On Wenlock Edge. A. E. Housman. CP-HousA

On Wenlock Edge the wood's in trouble. On Wenlock Edge. A. E. Housman. CP-HousA

On What Planet. Kenneth Rexroth. CP-RexrK

On When McCarthy Was a Wolf among a Nation of Queer-Queers. Alan Dugan. CP-DugaA

On which to shoot pool (that). Table of Green Fields, A. James Schuyler. CP-SchuJ

On white linen the silk. Ripple, The. Denise Levertov. SP-LeveDP

On whom I sat went by the. Kenners' Cat, The. James Laughlin. CP-LaugJ

On William Graham [*or* W———— Gr-h-m], Esq., of Mossknowe [*or* M-sskn-w]. Robert Burns. CP-BurnR

On Willie Chalmers. Robert Burns. CP-BurnR

On wings too stiff to flap. Milky Way Is a Cowpath, The. Robert Frost. CP-FrosR

On Winslow Homer's *Moonlight on Water* (1895) in the Los Angeles County Museum of Art. Helen Pinkerton. CP-PinkH

On Winter's Margin. Mary Oliver. SP-OlivM

On Wisdom's Defeat in a Learned Debate. Jonathan Swift. CP-SwifJ

On with thy work[e], though thou beest hardly priest. Rest. Robert Herrick. CP-HerrR

On Woman. William Butler Yeats. CP-YeatW

On Wood the Ironmonger. Jonathan Swift. CP-SwifJ

On Word that the Old Children's Stories Have Been Brought Up to Date. Miller Williams. CP-WillM

On Work. Alan Dugan. CP-DugaA

On Working White Liberals. Maya Angelou. SP-AngeM

On yonder hills soft twilight dwells. Longest Day, The. George Meredith. CP-MerG1

On you go now! Run, son, like the devil. Errand, The. Seamus Heaney. SP-HeanSO

On you th' affections of your Fathers Friends. To My Worthy Friend, Mr. John Mounson, Sonne and Heyre to Sir Thomas Mounson, Knight and Baronet. Thomas Campion. CP-CampT

On your feet like paws and if a board might squeak. Part of the Series on the Paths, A. Charles Olson. CP-OlsoC

On your midnight pallet lying. A. E. Housman. CP-HousA

On Your Own. Tess Gallagher. SP-GallT

On your piano a plaster Beethoven stands. Picture Postcard from Our Youth. Dan Pagis. SP-PagiD, *tr. by* Stephen Mitchell

On Zero. Alan Dugan. CP-DugaA

Once. Alice Walker. CP-WalkA

Once. Christina Georgina Rossetti. CP-RosC3

Once, a man, clambering to the house-tops. Stephen Crane. CP-CranS

Once a man was traveling through the woods, and. Maximus Letter # Whatever. Charles Olson. SP-OlsoC *Fr.* Maximus Poems, The.

Once a pair of savages found a stranded tree. Junk and the Dhow, The. Rudyard Kipling. CP-KiplR *Fr.* Land and Sea Tales.

Once a ripple came to land. Ripple Song, A. Rudyard Kipling. CP-KiplR *Fr.* Second Jungle Book, The.

Once a volcano here belched with zest. Ischia in October. Joseph Brodsky. CP-BrodJ

Once a woman went into the woods. Sound of the Axe. Denise Levertov. SP-LeveDL

Once a year in some self-secreting Lent. Corpus Christi. John Ciardi. CP-CiarJ

Once, after long-drawn revel at The Mermaid. Craftsman, The. Rudyard Kipling. CP-KiplR

Once, after storm, I stood at the cliff-head. Cross, The. Robert Penn Warren. CP-WarrR

Once, Again. Alice Walker. CP-WalkA

Once again the hour's turning silver. Rainer Maria Rilke. CP-RilkFr, *tr. by* A. Poulin, Jr. *Fr.* Valaisian Quatrains, The.

Once again the Steamer at Calais— the tackles. Song of Seventy Horses. Rudyard Kipling. CP-KiplR

Once again they were dismayed. Exploits of a Machine Age. Thomas Merton. CP-MertT

Once again to wake, nor wish to sleep. But Thy Commandment Is Exceeding Broad. Christina Georgina Rossetti. CP-RosC2

Once. / Always excited to say twice. Brim Beauvais. Gertrude Stein. CP-SteiG

Once and Again. Hayden Carruth. CP-CarHS

Once, and but once found in thy company. Perfume, The. John Donne. MW-DonnJ *Fr.* Elegies.

Once and for all, have done with it. Have Done with It. D. H. Lawrence. CP-LawrD

Once, animals spewed sperm as they charged. Arthur Rimbaud. CP-RimbA, *tr. by* Martin Sorrell

Once around a daisy counting. Counting on Flowers. John Ciardi. CP-CiarJ

Once as a child, out in a field of sheep. Seamus Heaney. SP-HeanSO *Fr.* Squarings.

Once as I was travelling. Highway Stripper. A. K. Ramanujan. CP-RamaA

Once as my carriage wearily dragg'd. Three Gipsies, The. Nikolaus Lenau. CP-MerG2

Once at Cold Mountain, troubles cease. Gary Snyder. CP-SnydG

Once at mid-day in late spring. Fernando Pessoa. SP-PessF *Fr.* Keeper of Sheep, The.

Once at midnight in the fall. Muse Considered as a Demon Lover, The. Frank O'Hara. SP-OharF

Once at Swanage. Thomas Hardy. CP-HardT

Once, at the Agricultural Show. Pat of Butter, The. Thomas Hardy. CP-HardT

Once at the Plaza, looking out into the park. Three Bills. Randall Jarrell. CP-JarrR

Once below a Time. Dylan Thomas. CP-ThomD

Once born, death's our destination. Michelangelo Buonarroti. CP-Miche, *tr. by* John Frederick Nims

Once branching light startles the hair of the coconuts. Hurucan. Derek Walcott. CP-WalcD

Once by a bitter candle. Later in Belleville: Career. Margaret Atwood. SP-AtwM1

Once by the Pacific. Robert Frost. CP-FrosR

Once, camping on a high bluff. Singing Voice, A. Kenneth Rexroth. CP-RexrK

Once did She hold the gorgeous east in fee. On the Extinction of the Venetian Republic. William Wordsworth. CP-WorW1; MW-WorW

Once down on my knees to growing plants. Mood Apart, A. Robert Frost. CP-FrosR

Once Duffy's Circus had shaken out its tent. Duffy's Circus. Paul Muldoon. CP-MuldP

Once, early in the morning. Devil's Walk, The. Percy Bysshe Shelley. CP-ShelP

Once every man wore a hat. Death of the Hat, The. Billy Collins. SP-CollB

Once Fairly Set Out on His Party of Pleasure. Lord Byron. CP-Byron

Once flamingoes reminded me of long-legged aunts in white cottons. Zoo Gardens Revisited. A. K. Ramanujan. CP-RamaA

Once fondly lov'd, and still rememb'red dear. Wrote on the Blank Leaf of a Copy of My First Edition, Which I Sent to an Old Sweetheart, Then Married. Robert Burns. CP-BurnR

Once for All. (Margaret). Christina Georgina Rossetti. CP-RosC1

Once from a big, big building. Visit to the Asylum, A. Edna St. Vincent Millay. CP-MillE

Once from thy awful quiver ruthless death. Elegy in the Extreme Illness of a Friend Whose Disorder Was the Bursting of a Blood Vesel in His Breast, An. Annis Boudinot Stockton. CP-StocA

Once he was seduced by the soft luxurious hill. Puritan, The. May Sarton. SP-SartM

Once he went inside a pool hall. Well-Ordered Life, The. Miller Williams. CP-WillM

Once hid in a fiery twist. Scratch, The. James Dickey. CP-DickJ

Once hooked ever after lives in lack, The. Nescit Vox Missa Reverti. J. V. Cunningham. CP-CunnJ

Once I ached for thy dear sake: / Wilt thou cause Me now to ache? Monday in Holy Week. Christina Georgina Rossetti. CP-RosC2

Once I adopted. Madam and the Charity Child. Langston Hughes. CP-HughL; CP-HughL2

Once I am sure there's nothing going on. Church Going. Philip Larkin. CP-LarkP

Once I began to write. Irregular Ode, An. Philip Whalen. SP-WhalP

Once I believed in you. Spirit Wooed, The. Philip Larkin. CP-LarkP

Once I could hail (howe'er serene the sky). William Wordsworth. CP-WorW2; MW-WorW

Once I demanded annihilation and frenzy. Confession of Heresy. Alan Dugan. CP-DugaA

Once I fell in the ocean when. This Time. Michael Palmer. SP-PalmM

Once I followed a drunken young gypsy. Tourist Poem. Alan Dugan. CP-DugaA

Once I gave birth to living metaphors. Not Writing Poems about Children. Carolyn Kizer. CP-KizeC

Once I got so skinny. Elegy for a Magician. Alan Dugan. CP-DugaA

Once I had a Comrade. Good Comrade, The. Ludwig Uhland. CP-MerG2

Once I had a son named John. Abandoned Church. Federico García Lorca. CP-GarcF, *tr. by* Greg Simon *and* Steven F. White

Once I had dreamed of return to a sunlit land. Old Dreams. Ivor Gurney. SP-GurnI

Once I had hopes (so fervent was my rhyme). Petrarch. CP-Petra, *tr. by* J. G.

Nichols

Once I had 1000 roses. Abundance. John Ciardi. CP-CiarJ

Once, / I heard him. Paul Celan. SP-CelaP, *tr. by* John Felstiner

Once I heard your voice. Kathleen Jessie Raine. SP-RainK

Once, I knew a fine song. Stephen Crane. CP-CranS

Once I knew answers. "Sit down!" said God. And didn't blink. Yehuda Amichai. SP-AmicYL *Fr.* At Right Angles.

Once I lived at a Riverside. By the Riverside. Carolyn Kizer. CP-KizeC

Once I looked down at my bootlaces. Bootlaces. G. K. Chesterton. CP-ChesG

Once I looked inside / the darkness. Hermit Crab, The. Mary Oliver. SP-OlivM

Once I loved a fairy. Queen Mab in the Village. Nicholas Vachel Lindsay. CP-LindV

Once I loved a spider. Spider and the Ghost of the Fly, The. Nicholas Vachel Lindsay. CP-LindV

Once I musing was in spirit. Hymn on the Logos: The Light Still Shining in the Darkness. Jones Very. CP-VeryJ

Once I Pass'd through a Populous City. Walt Whitman. CP-WhitW

Once I rambled in a wood. Dead City, The. Christina Georgina Rossetti. CP-RosC3

Once I reached Cold Mountain. Han-shan. CP-ColdM, *tr. by* Red Pine

Once I read a story. Story, The. Dan Pagis. SP-PagiD, *tr. by* Stephen Mitchell

Once I said lightly. Ted Hughes. SP-HughTN

Once I saw a grown man fall from a tree. Death and the Maiden. Howard Nemerov. CP-NemeH

Once I saw mountains angry. Stephen Crane. CP-CranS

Once I saw thee idly rocking. Stephen Crane. CP-CranS

Once I thought to sit so high. Offering of the New Law, the One Oblation Once Offered, The. Christina Georgina Rossetti. CP-RosC3

Once I was a small grain. Last Step, The. Philip Levine. SP-LeviP

Once, / I was afraid of dying. I Was Afraid of Dying. James Wright. CP-WrigJ

Once I was immortal. Maiden, The. Audre Lorde. SP-LordA

Once I was part of the music I heard. Youth in Age. George Meredith. CP-MerG2

Once I was water, full of scaly fish. Two Riddles from Aldhelm. Richard Wilbur. CP-WilbR

Once I wished I might rehearse. Freedom. Ralph Waldo Emerson. CP-EmerR

Once, I'd only heard. Image for Politics, An. A. K. Ramanujan. CP-RamaA

Once, if I remember well, my life was a banquet where all hearts opened. Arthur Rimbaud. CP-RimbA, *tr. by* Martin Sorrell

Once in a California Sierra. Auspex. Robert Frost. CP-FrosR

Once in a dark restaurant I caught the eyes of another. Behind the Mirror. Thom Gunn. CP-GunnT

Once in a dream (for once I dreamed of you). On the Wing. Christina Georgina Rossetti. CP-RosC1

Once, in a dream, I saw a man. Fame. James Whitcomb Riley. CP-RileJ

Once in a dream I saw the flowers. Paradise. Christina Georgina Rossetti. CP-RosC1

Once in a lonely hamlet I sojourned. Emigrant Mother, The. William Wordsworth. CP-WorW1

Once, in a night as black as ink. How Samson Bore Away the Gates of Gaza. Nicholas Vachel Lindsay. CP-LindV

Once in a while / we'd find a patch. Children, The. William Carlos Williams. CP-WilW2

Once in an Ancient Book. Marya Alexandrovna Zaturenska. SP-ZatuM

Once, / in August. Keeping the City. Anne Sexton. CP-SextA

Once in Canandaigua, hitchhiking from Ann Arbor. Faces. John Ciardi. CP-CiarJ

Once, in dream. To Rilke. Denise Levertov. SP-LeveDS

Once in late summer. Certain Village, A. Theodore Weiss. SP-WeisT

Once in life I watched a Star. Penalty, The. Rudyard Kipling. CP-KiplR

Once, in Rotterdam, a whore once, in a bar, a sailors' bar, a hooker bar, opened up her legs. Medusa. C. K. Williams. SP-WillC

Once in September, having crossed the desert. Return, The. Helen Pinkerton. CP-PinkH

Once in snowed-in winter I was caught. Twice, Away from Jack, I Thought of Him. John Ciardi. CP-CiarJ

"Once in so often," King Solomon said. Banquet Night. Rudyard Kipling. CP-KiplR *Fr.* Debits and Credits.

Once, in summer, / in the blueberries. Picking Blueberries, Austerlitz, New York, 1957. Mary Oliver. SP-OlivM

Once, in the city of Kalamazoo. Kalamazoo. Nicholas Vachel Lindsay. CP-LindV

Once in the 40s. William Stafford. SP-StafWW

Once in the wind of morning. Merry Guide, The. A. E. Housman. CP-HousA

Once in winter I, too, sailed in. Homage to Girolamo Marcello. Joseph Brodsky. CP-BrodJ

Once in your grace I know I was. Sir Thomas Wyatt. CP-WyatT

Once it had gorged itself. On a Pig's Head. Charles Tomlinson. CP-TomlC

Once it made music, tiny, frail, yet sweet. Sallie's Musical Box. Walter De la Mare. CP-DeLaW

Once it smiled a silent dell. Valley of Unrest, The. Edgar Allan Poe. CP-PoeEd

Once it was my brother on. Figure on the Far Side, The. Jane Cooper. CP-CoopJ

Once It Was the Colour of Saying. Dylan Thomas. CP-ThomD

Once Law was sitting on the bench. Law. Ambrose Bierce. SP-BierA

Once like a broken bow Mark sprang aside. St. Mark. Christina Georgina Rossetti. CP-RosC2

Once like a lady / In a silken dress. To the Three for Whom the Book. Countee Cullen. CP-CullC

Once like a spark. E. E. Cummings. CP-CummE

Once, Lily and I fell from a ladder. Monologue of Two Moons, Nudes with Crests. 1938. Norman Dubie. CP-DubiN

Once Love grew bold and arrogant of air. Love's Chastening. Paul Laurence Dunbar. CP-DunbP

Once made a fairy rooster from. For My Sister Molly Who in the Fifties. Alice Walker. CP-WalkA

Once men touch one another, then the modern industrial. Future States. D. H. Lawrence. CP-LawrD

Once More. Hayden Carruth. CP-CarHS

Once more again my mentor fate is kind. Dream, an Ode, 1756, The. Annis Boudinot Stockton. CP-StocA

Once more bright Sol has traveld round the Sky. Birth Day Ode, A. Annis Boudinot Stockton. CP-StocA

Once More by the Potomac. Joseph Brodsky. CP-BrodJ

Once more, dear friends, you meet beneath. Anniversary Poem. John Greenleaf Whittier. CP-WhitJ

Once more he sees his companions' faces. Survivor, The. Primo Levi. CP-LeviP, *tr. by* Ruth Feldman *and* Brian Swann

Once more he turned to that which could not be fixed. Two Versions of the Same Poem. Wallace Stevens. CP-StevW; CP-StevWP

Once more I dare to rouse the sounding string. On the Immensity of the Supreme Being. Christopher Smart. SP-SmarC

Once more I go over your earthly body. Rediscovery. Thomas McGrath. SP-McGrT

Once more I welcome Thee, and Thou, fair Plant. Tuft of Primroses, The. William Wordsworth. CP-WorW1

Once more into my arid days like dew. Edna St. Vincent Millay. CP-MillE

Once more it is early summer. Venice. Kenneth Rexroth. CP-RexrK

Once more Love sends to me that pleasing thought. Petrarch. CP-Petra, *tr. by* J. G. Nichols

Once more, my now bewildered Dove. Emily Dickinson. CP-DickE

Once more, O all-adjusting Death! Samuel J. Tilden. John Greenleaf Whittier. CP-WhitJ

Once more, O Mountains of the North, unveil. Mountain Pictures. John Greenleaf Whittier. CP-WhitJ

Once More, O Ye. Richard Eberhart. CP-EberR

Once more on yonder laurelled height. Our River. John Greenleaf Whittier. CP-WhitJ

Once more our awful poet arms, t' engage. Upon the Author of the following Poem. Nahum Tate. CP-DryJ2

Once more, sweet Stream! with slow foot wand'ring near. Lines to a Beautiful Spring in a Village. Samuel Taylor Coleridge. CP-ColeS

Once more the cauldron of the sun. Sun on the Bookcase, The. Thomas Hardy. CP-HardT

Once more the changed year's turning wheel returns. Barren Spring. Dante Gabriel Rossetti. CW-RossD *Fr.* House of Life, The.

Once more the country calls. Ode to Our Young Pro-consuls of the Air. Allen Tate. CP-TateA

Once more the earth is sending up its juices. Spanish Vineyards. Jaroslav Seifert. SP-SeifJ, *tr. by* Ewald Osers

Once more / The guns roar. Some Day. Langston Hughes. CP-HughL; CP-HughL2

Once more the hills. Purgatory. A. W. S. Merwin. SP-MerwW

Once more the irises are blooming. Zdziechowski. Czeslaw Milosz. CP-MiloCN, *tr. by* Robert Hass

Once more the long twilight. In April. Wallace Stevens. CP-StevWP

Once more the man stood, saying "A cottage-door." Fragment: "Once more the man stood, saying 'A cottage-door.'" G. K. Chesterton. CP-ChesG

Once more the predawn throbs on engine sound. Poem for My Twenty-ninth Birthday. John Ciardi. CP-CiarJ

Once More, the Round. Theodore Roethke. CP-RoetT

Once more the storm is howling, and half hid. Prayer for My Daughter, A. William Butler Yeats. CP-YeatW

Once more / the sun roaming on the carpenter's back. Is It True? Anne Sexton. CP-SextA

Once more / The yellow iris on the wrack-strewn shore. Kore. Kathleen Jessie Raine. SP-RainK

Once more we step. Word for Spring, A. Sam Hamill. SP-HamiS

Once my salary wasn't transferred from the place where I work to my bank.

Box, The. Yehuda Amichai. SP-AmicY, *tr. by* Chana Bloch

Once my wife and I were invited out trap-fishing because. On Fishing Being a Chancy Life. Alan Dugan. CP-DugaA

Once, on a glittering ice-field, ages and ages ago. Story of Ung, The. Rudyard Kipling. CP-KiplR

Once on a Lord-Mayors day, in Cheapside, when. Way in a Crowd. Robert Herrick. CP-HerrR

Once on a night in spring. Hayden Carruth. CP-CarHS *Fr.* Bloomingdale Papers, The.

Once on a time, as old stories rehearse. Ballad to the Tune of the Cutpurse [*or* "The Cut-Purse"], A. Jonathan Swift. CP-SwifJ

Once on a time in merry mood. Original of Punning, The. Thomas Sheridan. CP-SherT

Once on a time, the ancient legends tell. Legend of Truth, A. Rudyard Kipling. CP-KiplR *Fr.* Debits and Credits.

Once on a time was a King anxious to understand. King's Job, The. Rudyard Kipling. CP-KiplR

Once on a time when thought began. Drinking Song. Thomas Hardy. CP-HardT

Once on his star-gemmed, dazzling throne. Punishment of Pride, The. Walt Whitman. CP-WhitW

Once on returning home, purse-proud and hale. Auction, The. Theodore Roethke. CP-RoetT

Once on Saipan at the end of the rains. Island Galaxy, An. John Ciardi. CP-CiarJ

Once on the beach at night I heard the waves. Untitled Poem: "Once on the beach at night I heard the waves." Alan Dugan. CP-DugaA

Once on the brow of yonder Hill I stopped. Home at Grasmere. William Wordsworth. MW-WorW

Once on the kind of day called "weather breeder." Encounter, An. Robert Frost. CP-FrosR

Once, once, in Washington. Patriotic Tour and Postulate of Joy. Robert Penn Warren. CP-WarrR

Once once only in the deluge. Eagles and Alone. George Oppen. CP-OppGN

Once . . . once upon a time. Martha. Walter De la Mare. CP-DeLaW

Once, one of my students read a book we had. Untitled Poem: "Once, one of my students read a book we had." Alan Dugan. CP-DugaA

Once Only. Denise Levertov. SP-LeveDS

Once Only. Gary Snyder. SP-SnydG

Once only did I see / the sun so blood-red. Jaroslav Seifert. SP-SeifJ, *tr. by* Ewald Osers

Once [*or* Ons], as methought, Fortune me kissed [*or* kist *or* kyst]. Promise, A. Sir Thomas Wyatt. CP-WyatT

Once over water, to you borne brightly. True Nature of Time, The. Robert Penn Warren. CP-WarrR

Once Poore, Still Penurious. Robert Herrick. CP-HerrR

Once riding in Old Baltimore. Incident. Countee Cullen. CP-CullC

Once (says an Author, where, I need not say). Verbatim from Boileau. Alexander Pope. CP-PopeA

Once Seen, and No More. Robert Herrick. CP-HerrR

Once slain for Him Who first was slain for them. All Saints: Martyrs. Christina Georgina Rossetti. CP-RosC2

Once started nothing stops. Death. Robert Creeley. SP-CreeR

Once / starving in Philadelphia. Night I Fucked My Alarm Clock, The. Charles Bukowski. SP-BukC1

Once swept elm leaves. Found in a Notebook. William Corbett. SP-CorbW

Once the broom has started. Sorting the Personae. Donald Davie. CP-DaviDC

Once the Dream Begins. Yusef Komunyakaa. CP-KomuY

Once the fair Romance of story. George Meredith. CP-MerG2

Once the priest / Lived in an age. Ralph Waldo Emerson. CP-EmerR

Once the two of us. Gregory Orr. SP-OrrG

Once there came a man. Stephen Crane. CP-CranS

Once there was a cabin here, and once there was a man. Stafford's Cabin. Edwin Arlington Robinson. CP-RobiE

Once there was a couple named Mr. and Mrs. Pepperloaf. Frailty, Thy Name Is a Misnomer. Ogden Nash. CP-NashO

Once there was a fair young damsel and she early went. Rapunzel, Rapunzel, Let's Let Down Our Hair. Ogden Nash. CP-NashO

Once there was a girl named Miriam. Miriam's Lucky Day. Ogden Nash. CP-NashO

Once there was a handsome man named Mr. Beamington and. Love Me but Leave My Dog Alone. Ogden Nash. CP-NashO

Once there was a lonely man named Mr. Powers. Solitude of Mr. Powers, The. Ogden Nash. CP-NashO

Once there was a lyric writer named Mr. Amazon. Strange Case of the Renegade Lyric Writer, The. Ogden Nash. CP-NashO

Once there was a man. Stephen Crane. CP-CranS

Once there was a man, and he was named Mr. Barcalow, to be exact. Mr. Barcalow's Breakdown. Ogden Nash. CP-NashO

Once there was a man named Jarvis Gravel who was just a man. Individualist, The. Ogden Nash. CP-NashO

Once there was a man named Mr. Arents. Father, Dear Father, Go Jump in the Lake, or, You're Costlier than You Think. Ogden Nash. CP-NashO

Once there was a man named Mr. Culpepper Wood. Strange Case of Mr. Wood's Frustration, or, A Team That Won't Be Beaten Better Stay off the Field, The. Ogden Nash. CP-NashO

Once there was a man named Mr. O'Banion. Strange Case of Mr. O'Banion's Come-Uppance, The. Ogden Nash. CP-NashO

Once there was a man named Mr. Palliser and he asked his wife. Strange Case of Mr. Palliser's Palate, The. Ogden Nash. CP-NashO

Once there was a man named Mr. Pauncefoot to whom Fate could. Strange Case of Mr. Pauncefoot's Broad Mind, The. Ogden Nash. CP-NashO

Once there was a man named Mr. Peachey and he lived on Park. Mr. Peachey's Predicament or No Mot Parades. Ogden Nash. CP-NashO

Once there was a man named Mr. Train who wasn't called Choo-choo. Happy Ending of Mr. Train, The. Ogden Nash. CP-NashO

Once there was a man named Mr. Artesian and his activity was tremendous. Mr. Artesian's Conscientiousness. Ogden Nash. CP-NashO

Once there was a man who lived by the ocean named Mr. Strawbridge. Poor Mr. Strawbridge. Ogden Nash. CP-NashO

Once / there was a plumb-line. Beginnings. Raymond Carver. CP-CarvR

Once there was a poem, and it was serious and not in jest. Birdies, Don't Make Me Laugh. Ogden Nash. CP-NashO

Once there was a time in England, for a random space alone. Before a Statue of Cromwell. G. K. Chesterton. CP-ChesG

Once There Was a Woman Smiled at Me. David Ignatow. SP-IgnaD

Once there was an Archer. Version. Robert Frost. CP-FrosR

Once there was blood One-Legged Man, The. Anne Sexton. CP-SextA

Once There Were Glaciers. May Swenson. SP-SwenM

Once there were some children and they were uninterested in chores. Child Is Father to the Man, but with More Authority, The. Ogden Nash. CP-NashO

Once there were two men named Mr. Webster and Mr. Merriam. To Ee Is Human. Ogden Nash. CP-NashO

Once they were sticks and stones. Names. Robert Earl Hayden. CP-HaydR

Once to the verge of yon steep barrier came. Home at Grasmere. William Wordsworth. CP-WorW1 *Fr.* Recluse, The.

Once upon a little planet. Professor Tucholsky's Facts. Christopher Logue. SP-LoguC

Once upon a Massachusetts midnight. Go. Ai. SP-Ai

Once upon a midnight dreary, while I pondered [*or* ponder'd], weak and weary. Raven, The. Edgar Allan Poe. CP-PoeEd

Once upon a sandy beach. Gift of Stone. Peter Blue Cloud. SP-BlueP

Once upon a time. Boy and the Man, The. E. E. Cummings. CP-CummE

Once upon a time. Crow's Elephant Totem Song. Ted Hughes. SP-HughTN

Once upon a time a certain phantom. Good Fight, The. Thomas Kinsella. CP-KinsT

Once upon a time a man stole a wolf from among its pack. Modern Fable, A. David Ignatow. SP-IgnaD

Once, upon a time, invented zero. Poem in Honor Of, A. Wisława Szymborska. SP-SzymWM, *tr. by* Joanna Trzeciak

Once upon a time—the old storytellers. Prospect of Prague, A. Jaroslav Seifert. SP-SeifJ, *tr. by* Ewald Osers

Once upon a time there was a beautiful woman named Mrs. Geraldine. Strange Case of the Dead Divorcee, The. Ogden Nash. CP-NashO

Once upon a time there was a boy named Robin Bideawee. Strange Case of the Ambitious Caddy, The. Ogden Nash. CP-NashO

Once upon a time there was a flock of doves. Strange Case of the Blackmailing Dove, The. Ogden Nash. CP-NashO

Once upon a time there was a man named Mr. Lionel Fortague. Strange Case of Mr. Fortague's Disappointment, The. Ogden Nash. CP-NashO

Once upon a time there was a man named Mr. Sponsoon who was. Strange Case of the Girl o' Mr. Sponsoon's Dreams, The. Ogden Nash. CP-NashO

Once upon a time there was a man named Mr. Donnybrook. Strange Case of Mr. Donnybrooks's Boredom, The. Ogden Nash. CP-NashO

Once upon a time there was a man named Orlando Tregennis and he was in love with his wife. Unselfish Husband, The. Ogden Nash. CP-NashO

Once upon a time there was a taxi-driver named Llewellyn Abdullah. Strange Case of the Pleasing Taxi-Driver, The. Ogden Nash. CP-NashO

Once upon a time there was a young man named Harold Scrutiny. Strange Case of the Irksome Prude, The. Ogden Nash. CP-NashO

Once upon a time there was an attorney named Mr. Ballantine. Strange Case of Mr. Ballantine's Valentine, The. Ogden Nash. CP-NashO

Once upon a time there was an Italian. Columbus. Ogden Nash. CP-NashO

Once upon a time when I. Parable, A. James Laughlin. CP-LaugJ

Once upon a time, when the clocks were slow. Since the Noon Mail Stopped. Wyatt Prunty. SP-PrunW

Once upon earth they stood. Dreams. Kathleen Jessie Raine. SP-RainK

Once was every woman the witch. Witches. Ted Hughes. SP-HughTN

Once water lilies floated on this pool. Water Lilies: A Nocturne. Marya Alexandrovna Zaturenska. SP-ZatuM

Once we feared The Beast—when he followed us we ran. Song of the Men's

Side. Rudyard Kipling. CP-KiplR

Once we have driven past Mundo Nuevo trace. Crusoe's Journal. Derek Walcott. CP-WalcD

Once We Meant It. Thomas McGrath. SP-McGrT

Once we painted our house and went into it. How the Real Bible Is Written. William Stafford. SP-StafWW

Once we presumed to found ourselves for good. Disappearing Island, The. Seamus Heaney. SP-HeanSO

Once we're born we're confused. Han-shan. CP-ColdM, *tr. by* Red Pine

Once when an honest weaver slept. Apology of Bottom the Weaver, The. G. K. Chesterton. CP-ChesG

Once, when he had saved the human race again. Apollo. Alan Dugan. CP-DugaA

Once, when I liked a German girl. Nostalgia for a Language. Alan Dugan. CP-DugaA

Once when I saw a cripple. Cripple. Carl Sandburg. CP-SandC

Once, when I wandered in the woods alone. Amaryllis. Edwin Arlington Robinson. CP-RobiE

Once, when I was young and true. Very Short Song, A. Dorothy Parker. CP-ParkD

Once when I was young, Juanito. Mother's Tale, The. Ai. SP-Ai

Once when, like birds, we feared the hunter's gun. Snare, The. Thomas Merton. CP-MertT

Once, when midnight smote the air. On Those That Hated "The Playboy of the Western World" 1907. William Butler Yeats. CP-YeatW

Once when my soul was newly shriven. Light, The. Paul Laurence Dunbar. CP-DunbP

Once when our eyes were clean as noon, our rooms. Cana. Thomas Merton. CP-MertT

Once, when the grand nudes, golden as fields of grain—. Trinc: Praises II. Thomas McGrath. SP-McGrT

Once when the snow of the year was beginning to fall. Runaway, The. Robert Frost. CP-FrosR

Once when the white clouds praised you, Yorkshire. Rievaulx: St. Ailred. Thomas Merton. CP-MertT

Once when Theology was in her prime. Punishment of Pride. Charles Baudelaire. CP-BaudC, *tr. by* Walter Martin

Once White & Gold / daisy in the dust. E. E. Cummings. CP-CummE

Once within, within for evermore: / There the long beatitudes begin. He Shall Go No More Out. Christina Georgina Rossetti. CP-RosC2

Once you have let the first blade. Salt Marsh, The. James Dickey. CP-DickJ

Once you said joking slyly, *If I'm killed*. Faithful, The. Jane Cooper. CP-CoopJ

Once, you say, we felt love's blisses. Memories. Dorothy Parker. CP-ParkD

Once you were young. Parisian Beggar Woman. Langston Hughes. CP-HughL; CP-HughL1

"Ondumonde" / (first than caref. E. E. Cummings. CP-CummE

One. Robert Creeley. SP-CreeR

One. Federico García Lorca. CP-GarcF, *tr. by* Jerome Rothenberg *Fr.* Night (Suite for Piano and Poet's Voice).

One. Langston Hughes. CP-HughL; CP-HughL2

One. Carolyn Kizer. CP-KizeC *Fr.* Pro Femina.

One. Thomas Kinsella. CP-KinsT

1. Thomas Kinsella. CP-KinsT

One. Stephen Spender. CP-SpenS

One, The. James Dickey. CP-DickJ

One after another, hard-pressed waves. Fernando Pessoa. SP-PessF, *tr. by* Susan M. Brown *and* Edwin Honig

One after one do they leave thee. Salve O Pontifex! Ezra Pound. CP-PoEar

One Afternoon. James Whitcomb Riley. CP-RileJ

One afternoon Cabbage visited Carrot. Cabbage and Carrot. Joseph Brodsky. CP-BrodJ

One afternoon I was seraph on gold leaf. Seamus Heaney. SP-HeanSO *Fr.* Squarings.

One afternoon the last week in April. Axe Handles. Gary Snyder. CP-SnydG

One afternoon you step outside. Saying It Back. Wyatt Prunty. SP-PrunW

One among friends who stood above your grave. Auden's Funeral. Stephen Spender. CP-SpenS

One and. Piece, A. Robert Creeley. CP-CreeR

One and Many. Czeslaw Milosz. CP-MiloCN, *tr. by* Martin Sabiniewicz *and* Jennifer Scappettone

One and One—are One. Emily Dickinson. CP-DickE

1 and 1 are 2— / That's for me and you. Christina Georgina Rossetti. CP-RosC2

One and Two. Tennessee Williams. CP-WillT

One Angel. James Whitcomb Riley. CP-RileJ

One Anguish—in a Crowd. Emily Dickinson. CP-DickE

One ant turns backward. Hayden Carruth. CP-CarHS *Fr.* Clay Hill Anthology, The.

One April dusk the. E. E. Cummings. CP-CummE

One arch of the sky. Love in Labrador. Carl Sandburg. CP-SandC

One-armed explorer, The. Gardens of Zuñi, The. W. S. Merwin. SP-MerwW

One-Armed Man, The. Yannis Ritsos. SP-RitsY, *tr. by* Kostas Myrsiades

One-armed, one-legged, and one-headed. Terms. Randall Jarrell. CP-JarrR

One around me and, The. I Live in Three Worlds. James Laughlin. CP-LaugJ

One Art. Elizabeth Bishop. CP-BishE

One ask'd me where the roses grew? Rosarie, The. Robert Herrick. CP-HerrR

One beautiful morning, in a country of very gentle people. Royalty. Arthur Rimbaud. CP-RimbA, *tr. by* Martin Sorrell

One Birth our Saviour had; the like none yet. Christs Birth. Robert Herrick. CP-HerrR

One black thing was blowing down the road. Fanny Howe. SP-HoweF *Fr.* Q.

One Blessing had I than the rest. Emily Dickinson. CP-DickE

One bliss for which / There is no match. Taboo to Boot. Ogden Nash. CP-NashO

One book able to give me stable advice, The. Millais Loquacious. Robert Stock. SP-StocR

One bottle is cast in gold. Han-shan. CP-ColdM, *tr. by* Red Pine

One breath opens operatic breaches in the walls. Vulgar Nocturne. Arthur Rimbaud. CP-RimbA, *tr. by* Martin Sorrell

One-Breath Song. Yusef Komunyakaa. CP-KomuY

One by one I proclaim your songs. Three Nahuatl Poems. William Carlos Williams. CP-WilW2

One by one lights of a skyscraper fling their checkering cross work on the. Skyscraper Loves Night, The. Carl Sandburg. CP-SandC

One by one the bells have broken their music. Cathedral. John Ciardi. CP-CiarJ

One by one, the words. Reading Hölderlin on the Patio with the Aid of a Dictionary. Rita Dove. SP-DoveR

One by one they appear in. My Sad Captains. Thom Gunn. CP-GunnT

One by one / they fall away. Passing Bell, The. Denise Levertov. SP-LeveDL

One came from the skies. Stephen Crane. CP-CranS

One can be tolerant with a bore. Tolerance. D. H. Lawrence. CP-LawrD

One can do one begins to one can only. Reincarnation (II). James Dickey. CP-DickJ

One can say more of sunlight. Light Is Speech. Marianne Craig Moore. CP-MoorM

One candle will do. Such light, so faint. That They Might Appear. Constantine P. Cavafy. CP-CavaC, *tr. by* Theoharis Constantine Theoharis

One cannot now help thinking. Now It's Happened. D. H. Lawrence. CP-LawrD

One cantaloupe is ripe and lush. Cantaloupe, The. Ogden Nash. CP-NashO

One Certainty, The. Christina Georgina Rossetti. CP-RosC1

One chemical afternoon in mid-autumn. Contrary Theses (II). Wallace Stevens. CP-StevW; CP-StevWP

One Christmas in the early din. What "Old Santa" Overheard. James Whitcomb Riley. CP-RileJ

One Christmastime Fats Waller in a fur coat. History of My Heart. Robert Pinsky. CP-PinsR

One Circumlocution. W. H. Auden. CP-AudeW

One clear glass slipper; a slender blue single-rose vase. Cranston near the City Line. Ted Berrigan. SP-BerrT

One cloud in the sky comes from Greece. Paestum. James Dickey. CP-DickJ

One comes across the strangest things in walks. Cotswold Ways. Ivor Gurney. SP-GurnI

One Comes Back. Pablo Neruda. SP-NeruP

One composing seminal works sat oblivious. A. R. Ammons. CP-AmmoA

1 Corinthians 13: Commentary. James Vincent Cunningham. CP-CunnJ

One could not see or think, the heat overcame one. Cloud, The. Ivor Gurney. SP-GurnI

One could pass valuable months. Allen Ginsberg. SP-GinsA *Fr.* Siesta in Xbalba.

One creature, not the mollusk. Sleeping with You. John Updike. CP-UpdiJ

One crown that no one seeks. Emily Dickinson. CP-DickE

One Crucifixion is recorded—only. Emily Dickinson. CP-DickE

One damn time (7th inning). The. Ball Game, The. Robert Creeley. CP-CreeR

One Day. Robert Creeley. CP-CreeR

One Day. Grace Paley. CP-PalGC

One Day. Christina Georgina Rossetti. CP-RosC1

One day a nigger. E. E. Cummings. CP-CummE

One day a sufi sees an empty food sack hanging on a nail. Food Sack, The. Jelaluddin Rumi. SP-Rumi, *tr. by* Coleman Barks

One day a woman picking peaches in Georgia. Miller Williams. CP-WillM

One day across the lake where echoes come now. Animal That Drank up Sound, The. William Stafford. SP-StafWW

One day, along the electric wire. Rantoul. John Greenleaf Whittier. CP-WhitJ

One day, an obscure youth, a wanderer. Ambition. Walt Whitman. CP-WhitW

One day apes made their grab for power. Apes. Adam Zagajewski. SP-ZagaA, *tr. by* Renata Gorczynski, Benjamin Ivry *and* C. K. Williams

One day, he finished the pitchers, the flower pots, the cooking pots. Some clay. Potter, The. Yannis Ritsos. SP-RitsY, *tr. by* Kostas Myrsiades

One day, his mother took him on the tram. Portrait of the Artist I. Charles Tomlinson. CP-TomlC

One day I complained about the periphery. Periphery. A. R. Ammons. CP-AmmoA

One Day I Decided. Grace Paley. CP-PalGC

One day I decided to not grow any older. One Day I Decided. Grace Paley. CP-PalGC

One day I forgot Jerusalem and my right arm is withered. Warning, A. Grace Paley. CP-PalGC

One day I left the mountains. Han-shan. CP-ColdM, *tr. by* Red Pine

One day I sought with her hart-thrilling eies. Sonnet 12. Edmund Spenser. CP-Spens *Fr.* Amoretti.

One day in early Spring. Song: Fig Tree in Leaf. Robert Graves. CP-GravR

One day in my family's life. Immigrant Story, The. Grace Paley. CP-PalGC

One day in Paradise. Quietness. William Carlos Williams. CP-WilW1

One day in the Library. Further Advantages of Learning. Kenneth Rexroth. CP-RexrK

One Day is there of the Series. Emily Dickinson. CP-DickE

One day it thundered and lightened. Adam, Lilith, and Eve. Robert Browning. CP-BroR2

One day lying on my stomach in the afternoon trying to sleep. One Day. Grace Paley. CP-PalGC

One day / Marilyn marched. Chic Freedom's Reflection. Alice Walker. CP-WalkA

One day more. Wallace Stevens. CP-StevWP

One Day of Autumn. Charles Tomlinson. CP-TomlC

One day our noses will be in heaven. Crossed Hands. Andrei Codrescu. SP-CodrA

One day / she fell. Monosyllable, The. Josephine Jacobsen. CP-JacoJ

One day Sun found a new canyon. People of the South Wind. William Stafford. SP-StafW; SP-StafWW

One day the elephant gets up and lumbers. Short History of Philosophy, A. Eleanor Wilner. SP-WilnE

One day the king assembled his courtiers. Ayaz and the King's Pearl. Jelaluddin Rumi. SP-Rumi, *tr. by* Coleman Barks

One day the men pulled a house off float logs. Edna Bay. Arthur Sze. SP-SzeA

One day the Nouns were clustered in the street. Permanently. Kenneth Koch. SP-KochK

One day 3 poets & 60 ears sat under a green-striped Chautauqua tent in Aurora. Nagasaki Days. Allen Ginsberg. CP-GinsA; SP-GinsA

One day we lay beneath an apple tree. One Day We Played a Game. Countee Cullen. CP-CullC

One Day We Played a Game. Countee Cullen. CP-CullC

One day when I am written off as dead. Half-Finished Letter, The. Robert Graves. CP-GravR

One day when I was a child long ago. Grace Paley. CP-PalGC

One day when I was feeling absolutely healthy. Peaks. John Ciardi. CP-CiarJ

One day when I was looking from my window. Petrarch. CP-Petra, *tr. by* J. G. Nichols

One day you finally knew. Journey, The. Mary Oliver. SP-OlivM

One day you look at the mirror and it's open. Glass. W. S. Merwin. SP-MerwW

One debarred from enrollment at Harvard. In Lieu of the Lyre. Marianne Craig Moore. CP-MoorM

1 December 1948. Yannis Ritsos. SP-RitsY *Fr.* Exile's Journals 2.

One dervish to another, *What was your vision of God's presence?* Question, The. Jelaluddin Rumi. SP-Rumi, *tr. by* Coleman Barks

One Desire, The. Paul Muldoon. CP-MuldP

One died, and the soul was wrenched out. Street Musicians. John Ashbery. SP-AshbJ

One dignity delays for all. Emily Dickinson. CP-DickE

One does not expect to see them, out there. Sails on All Saints' Day. John Updike. CP-UpdiJ

One dot / Grainily shifting we at roadside and. Bee, The. James Dickey. CP-DickJ

One Dull Thing You Did Was to Die, Fletcher, The. John Ciardi. CP-CiarJ

One Eare tingles; some there be. On Himselfe. Robert Herrick. CP-HerrR

One earring's smile. Summery Weather. Kenneth Koch. SP-KochK

One Easter Not on the Calendar I Woke. John Ciardi. CP-CiarJ

One erases only in order to write again. Negatives 2. Charles Wright. SP-WrigCN

One Evening. William Stafford. SP-StafWW

One evening Eros took me by the hand. To the Bitter Sweet-heart: a Dream. Wilfred Owen. CP-OwenW

One evening i return. Coming of Fox, The. Lucille Clifton. SP-ClifL

One evening the Fork said to the Knife. At the Helmet and Sword. Joseph Brodsky. CP-BrodJ

One ever hangs where shelled roads part. At a Calvary near the Ancre. Wilfred Owen. CP-OwenW

One Eye? a thousand rather, and a Thousand more. It Is Better to Go into

Heaven with One Eye. Richard Crashaw. CP-CrasR

One-Eye, Two-Eyes, Three-Eyes. Anne Sexton. CP-SextA; SP-SextA

One face looks out from all his canvas[s]es. In An Artist's Studio. Christina Georgina Rossetti. CP-RosC3

One face, two face, three. True Numbers. Charles Olson. CP-OlsoC

One fairest of the ripe unwedded left. Sage Enamoured and the Honest Lady, The. George Meredith. CP-MerG1

One faith is bondage. Two. Homecoming, A. Wendell Berry. CP-BerrW

One feather is a bird. Voice, The. Theodore Roethke. CP-RoetT

One feeds on Lard, and yet is leane. Littlenesse No Cause of Leanesse. Robert Herrick. CP-HerrR

One Fine Day. E. E. Cummings. CP-CummE

(One fine day) / let's take the train. One Fine Day. E. E. Cummings. CP-CummE

One fire than other burnes more forcibly. Sir Walter Ralegh. CP-RaleW

One flame-winged brought a white-winged harp-player. Passion and Worship. Dante Gabriel Rossetti. CW-RossD *Fr.* House of Life, The.

One Fond Embrace. Thomas Kinsella. CP-KinsT

One foot down, then hop! It's hot. Harlem Hopscotch. Maya Angelou. SP-AngeM

One Foot on Sea, and One on Shore. Christina Georgina Rossetti. CP-RosC2

One for Old Snaggle-Tooth. Charles Bukowski. SP-BukC1

One for the Old Boy. Charles Bukowski. SP-BukC3

One for the Rose. Philip Levine. SP-LeviP

One for the Shoeshine Man. Charles Bukowski. SP-BukC1

One Forever Alien. Howard Nemerov. CP-NemeH

One friend. Louis Zukofsky. CP-ZukLS

1 from 9 is 8. Alice Faye at Ruby Foo's. James Schuyler. CP-SchuJ

One from the ends of the earth—gifts at an open door. Song of the Sons, The. Rudyard Kipling. CP-KiplR

One garland. Divorcing. Denise Levertov. SP-LeveDL; SP-LeveDS

One generation passeth away, and another generation cometh: but the earth abideth for ever. Ecclesiastes 1:4. Jones Very. CP-VeryJ

1. Get smart with general biggle in the quadrangle of math and fun. Twenty Three Point Prospectus for Small College in the Badlands. Thomas Merton. CP-MertT

One Girl. Sappho. CW-RossD, *tr. by* Dante Gabriel Rossetti

One-gloved beasts in cleats, they come clattering. Golfers. John Updike. CP-UpdiJ

One God is born. Others die. Truth. Christmas. Fernando Pessoa. SP-PessF, *tr. by* Susan M. Brown *and* Edwin Honig

One good poet gives an age its voice. Guide to Poetry, A. John Ciardi. CP-CiarJ

One got peace of heart at last, the dark march over. After War. Ivor Gurney. SP-GurnI

One granite ridge. Piute Creek. Gary Snyder. CP-SnydG

One great plain and five great chieftains. G. K. Chesterton. CP-ChesG *Fr.* Vision of Edens, A.

One grief on me is laid. Burden, The. Rudyard Kipling. CP-KiplR *Fr.* Debits and Credits.

One had a lovely face. Memory. William Butler Yeats. CP-YeatW

One Hand in Space. Tennessee Williams. CP-WillT

One hand washes the other. Ralph Waldo Emerson. CP-EmerR

One Hard Look. Robert Graves. CP-GravR

One has flippers. This one is like a seal. Ones that Are Thrown Out, The. Miller Williams. CP-WillM

One Home. William Stafford. SP-StafW; SP-StafWW

One Hope, The. Dante Gabriel Rossetti. CW-RossD *Fr.* House of Life, The.

One Hour to Madness and Joy. Walt Whitman. CP-WhitW

One hellgrammite that I think we could all dispense with. King Leer. Ogden Nash. CP-NashO

One humid night a clanking in the plumbing. Reverse Metamorphosis. Robert Stock. SP-StocR

One Hundred and Ninety-Nine Pounds of Clay Leaning Forward. Charles Bukowski. SP-BukC2

136 Syllables at Rocky Mountain Dharma Center. Allen Ginsberg. SP-GinsA

125th Street. Langston Hughes. CP-HughL; CP-HughL3

One hundred black sailors. Moments of the Garden. Federico García Lorca. CP-GarcF, *tr. by* Jerome Rothenberg *Fr.* In the Garden of the Lunar Grapefruits.

108 East 19th. William Stafford. SP-StafW; SP-StafWW

One hundred feet overhead the fog from the Pacific. Another Early Morning Exercise. Kenneth Rexroth. CP-RexrK

151st Psalm, The. Robert Stock. SP-StocR

140 Syllables. Kenneth Rexroth. CP-RexrK

103 Degrees. Charles Bukowski. SP-BukC1

One hundred years with their events have fled. To the Salem Gazette, on the Completion of Its First Century. Jones Very. CP-VeryJ

One hymn more, O my lyre! Hymns from the French of Lamartine. John Greenleaf Whittier. CP-WhitJ

One I kept. Three. Tennessee Williams. CP-WillT

1. I will tell you what you can do ask me if you do not understand what I just said. Proverbs. Thomas Merton. CP-MertT

One idle afternoon, today. Bill of Fare. Hans Magnus Enzensberger. SP-EnzeH, *tr.* by Michael Hamburger

One imagines a surgeon to be. Surgeons. Robert Creeley. CP-CreeR

One imagines himself / addressing his peers. To C. T. George Oppen. CP-OppGN

One in the musical throng. Unheard, The. James Whitcomb Riley. CP-RileJ

One in the Public Gallery. Walter De la Mare. CP-DeLaW

One in the upper left-hand corner, The. Victoria's Secret. Billy Collins. SP-CollB

One in thy thousand statues we salute thee. Black Virgin, The. G. K. Chesterton. CP-ChesG

One Incident of Many. William Dickey. SP-DickW

One innocent spring. Now Long Ago. Maya Angelou. SP-AngeM

One instant of morning. Greeting, The. Charles Tomlinson. CP-TomlC

One is large and lazy. Furies, The. May Sarton. SP-SartM

One Jay at a Time. John Ciardi. CP-CiarJ

One Joy of so much anguish. Emily Dickinson. CP-DickE

One kind of person when catching a train always wants to allow. We Don't Need to Leave Yet, Do We? Or, Yes We Do. Ogden Nash. CP-NashO

One knows by now one is no amnesiac. No Amnesiac King. A. K. Ramanujan. CP-RamaA

One-l lama, / He's a priest, The. Lama, The. Ogden Nash. CP-NashO

One laughs / is worried. Other, The. Hans Magnus Enzensberger. SP-EnzeH, *tr.* by Michael Hamburger

One Law for the Lion and Ox is Oppression. Standings. Donald Davie. CP-DaviDC

One leaf fell, / a second. Waltz in the Branches. Federico García Lorca. CP-GarcF, *tr.* by Greg Simon *and* Steven F. White

One leaf left on a branch. David Ignatow. SP-IgnaD

One leaves his leaves at home. Great Mullen. William Carlos Williams. CP-WilW1

One-Legged Man, The. Anne Sexton. CP-SextA

One-legged Stool, The. Yusef Komunyakaa. CP-KomuY

One lesson, Nature, let me learn of [*or* from] thee. Quiet Work. Matthew Arnold. SP-ArnoM

One Life. Paul Laurence Dunbar. CP-DunbP

One Life of so much Consequence! Emily Dickinson. CP-DickE

One likes to see a laggard rook's high. Combat Cultural. Marianne Craig Moore. CP-MoorM

One lives by commerce, said the guide. Guide to the Ruins. Howard Nemerov. CP-NemeH

One long table supported by three sets of winged lions. What? Writing in the Dining Room? Philip Whalen. SP-WhalP

One looks from the train. Orient Express, The. Randall Jarrell. CP-JarrR

One loud whistle, then another. Star Vehicle (My Senior Year in High School). Ai. SP-Ai

One loves the temporal, some unique manifestation. Hugh MacDiarmid. SP-MacDH *Fr.* Battle Continues, The.

One lucky hour in middle of my tiredness. Brimscombe. Ivor Gurney. SP-GurnI

One luncheon party in Andy's rooms in Magdalene. Meeting. John Berryman. CP-BerrJ

One lutenist played *look*; your through was *drink*. Louis Zukofsky. CP-ZukLS

One Man. William Stafford. SP-StafWW

One Man Down. Ai. SP-Ai

One man in a house. To Landrum Guy, Beginning to Write at Sixty. James Dickey. CP-DickJ

One man in a thousand, Solomon says. Thousandth Man, The. Rudyard Kipling. CP-KiplR

One man in me is locked inside an oakwomb. Man Locked inside the Oak, The. Robert Bly. SP-BlyR

One man killed another. The saying between them had been "I'd give you." Hate. Carl Sandburg. CP-SandC

One man repentant is of more esteem. Position in the Hebrew Divinity, A. Robert Herrick. CP-HerrR

One man shall smile one day and say goodbye. Cambodia. James Fenton. SP-FentJ

One Man Walking a Deserted Platform. Philip Larkin. CP-LarkP

One / man who will, The. Curse. Robert Creeley. CP-CreeR

One Man's Meed Is Another Man's Overemphasis. Ogden Nash. CP-NashO

One:Many. A. R. Ammons. CP-AmmoA

1 May 1950. Yannis Ritsos. SP-RitsY *Fr.* Exile's Journals 3.

One may say courage. Kind of Garden, A: A Poem for My Sister. George Oppen. CP-OppGN

One midnight, after a day when lilies. Digging. Donald Hall. CP-HallD

One might believe that natural miseries. October, 1803 ("One might believe that natural miseries"). William Wordsworth. CP-WorW1; MW-WorW

One might talk of the sanity of the atom. Sane Universe, The. D. H. Lawrence. CP-LawrD

One mile more is. News for Her Mother. Thomas Hardy. CP-HardT

One minute I had the windows open. Forge, and a Scythe, A. Raymond Carver. CP-CarvR

One misty evening, one another's guide. Iris by Night. Robert Frost. CP-FrosR

One Modern Poet. Carl Sandburg. CP-SandC

One moment bid the horses wait. Ballade of Jakko Hill, A. Rudyard Kipling. CP-KiplR

One Moment in Eternity. Howard Nemerov. CP-NemeH

One moment past our bodies cast. Morning Song in the Jungle. Rudyard Kipling. CP-KiplR *Fr.* Second Jungle Book, The.

One monotonous day follows. Monotony. Constantine P. Cavafy. CP-CavaC, *tr.* by Theoharis Constantine Theoharis

One Month. Muriel Rukeyser. CP-RukeM

One moonlight, in the simple-colored night, The. Note on Moonlight. Wallace Stevens. CP-StevW; CP-StevWP

One More. Raymond Carver. CP-CarvR

One More after Reading Homer. A. K. Ramanujan. CP-RamaA

One More Brevity. Robert Frost. CP-FrosR

One more by Thee, Love, and Desert have sent. To Mistresse Mary Willand. Robert Herrick. CP-HerrR

One more casualty. To Clio, Muse of History. Howard Nemerov. CP-NemeH

One more Christmas ends. Martial Law Carol, A. Joseph Brodsky. CP-BrodJ

One More Contradiction. Czeslaw Milosz. CP-MiloC

One More Day. Czeslaw Milosz. CP-MiloCN; CP-MiloCN, *tr.* by Robert Hass

One more day gone, / done, found in / the form of days. Again. Robert Creeley. CP-CreeR

One more is gone. Funeral Bell, The. Henry David Thoreau. CP-ThorH

One More Loss to Count. Yusef Komunyakaa. CP-KomuY

One More New Botched Beginning. Stephen Spender. CP-SpenS

One More on a Deathless Theme. A. K. Ramanujan. CP-RamaA

One More Round. Maya Angelou. SP-AngeM

One More "S" in the U.S.A. Langston Hughes. CP-HughL; CP-HughL1

One More Time. A. R. Ammons. CP-AmmoA

One morn before me were three figures seen. Ode on Indolence. John Keats. CP-KeatJ

One Morning. Ambrose Bierce. SP-BierA

One Morning. John Ciardi. CP-CiarJ

One morning Beebe. Jungle Knot. A. R. Ammons. CP-AmmoA

One morning early I met armoured cars. Toome Road, The. Seamus Heaney. SP-HeanSO

One morning I put in the pocket of my shirt. Believing in Symbols. Miller Williams. CP-WillM

One morning I shall find. Maisie. James Merrill. SP-MerrJ

One Morning in New Hampshire. May Swenson. SP-SwenM

One morning in summer. Cart, The. W. S. Merwin. SP-MerwWF

One morning in the month of June. Blackbird, The. Derek Mahon. CP-MahoD

One morning of the first sad Fall. Lay of Old Time, A. John Greenleaf Whittier. CP-WhitJ

One morning (raw it was and wet). Sailor's Mother, The. William Wordsworth. CP-WorW1

One morning the days have grown shorter. Fireweed. W. S. Merwin. SP-MerwWF

One morning the Grand Seigneur. Great Horned Owl, The. Charles Simic. SP-SimiC; SP-SimiCE

One morning / the wind scouring. Death of See, The. William Carlos Williams. CP-WilW1

One morning you step out, still in pajamas. Saturday, March 6. John Ciardi. CP-CiarJ

One mummy walks on snow. Mummies. Nicanor Parra. CP-MertT, *tr.* by Thomas Merton

One musician is sure. Harp, The. Ralph Waldo Emerson. CP-EmerR

One must be happy to find God. To Madame the Baronness Renée De Brimont. Rainer Maria Rilke. CP-RilkFr, *tr.* by A. Poulin, Jr.

One must be sitting in one's chair. Instruction. Olga Broumas. SP-BrouO

One must have a mind of winter. Snow Man, The. Wallace Stevens. CP-StevW; CP-StevWP

One need not be a Chamber—to be Haunted. Emily Dickinson. CP-DickE

One Night. Constantine P. Cavafy. CP-CavaC, *tr.* by Theoharis Constantine Theoharis

One Night. W. S. Merwin. SP-MerwWF

One Night. William Stafford. SP-StafWW

One night a man was crying. Love Dogs. Jelaluddin Rumi. SP-Rumi, *tr.* by Coleman Barks

One night as I did wander. Fragment, A: "One night as I did wander." Robert Burns. CP-BurnR

One night he dreamed of a palace fair. Ralph Waldo Emerson. CP-EmerR

One night I dreamed I was locked in my Father's watch. My Father's Watch. John Ciardi. CP-CiarJ

One night I reached a cave: I slept, my head. Incident on a Journey. Thom Gunn. CP-GunnT

One night I read philosophy. Colossus in Quicksand, The. John Ciardi. CP-CiarJ

One night i' th' yeare [or in the year], my dearest Beauties, come. To His Lovely Mistresses. Robert Herrick. CP-HerrR

One night I thirsted like a prince. Diabetes. James Dickey. CP-DickJ

One night in Albany. Drunks. John Berryman. CP-BerrJ

One night in my room, still and beamless. Phantom Kiss, The. Paul Laurence Dunbar. CP-DunbP

One Night in Oz. Ogden Nash. CP-NashO

One night in the desert. Man and a Woman Arguing, A. Jelaluddin Rumi. SP-Rumi, tr. by Coleman Barks

One Night Ma / Lay with Pa. Charles Olson. CP-OlsoC

One Night Stand. Charles Bukowski. SP-BukC2

One night the water lay so deathly still. Oldest Killed Lake in North America, The. Hayden Carruth. CP-CarHS

One night we find ourselves near the giant's house. Near the Giant's House. Robert Bly. SP-BlyR

One night when he seemed a little drunk he said in a funny tone of voice. Contradictions. Yannis Ritsos. SP-RitsY, tr. by Gwendolyn MacEwen and Nikos Tsingos

One nonsufficiently inunderstood. E. E. Cummings. CP-CummE

One noonday, at my window in the town. Ball's Bluff. Herman Melville. SP-MelvH

1. Now you are all here you might as well know this is America we do what we like. Thomas Merton. CP-MertT

"One oak fool box";—the pun. Louis Zukofsky. CP-ZukL3

One o'clock in the letter-box. Meeting, The. Muriel Rukeyser. CP-RukeM

One of God's creatures, just as much as you. Snake. Robert Lowell. SP-LoweR

One of her hands on one of her cheeks lay under. Supplement of an Imperfect Copy of Verses of Mr. William Shakespeare's, by the Author, A. Sir John Suckling. CP-SuckJ

One of Many. Stevie Smith. CP-SmitS

One of my favorite dreams. Skiing without Skis. James Laughlin. CP-LaughJ

One of My Favorite Songs Is Stormy Weather. Philip Whalen. SP-WhalP

One of my frequent little. Bad Night on Third Avenue, A. James Laughlin. CP-LaughJ

One of my marionettes is dead. Humouresque. T. S. Eliot. SP-ElioT

One of my neighbors began digging himself. Fable of Survival, A. John Ciardi. CP-CiarJ

One of my wings beat faster. Growing Up. William Stafford. SP-StafWW

One of my wishes is that those dark trees. Into My Own. Robert Frost. CP-FrosR

One of our new aristocrats. Stuttgart: In a Nightclub (Illegal). James Laughlin. CP-LaughJ

One of the Bracci, I. Now, as you see. Michelangelo Buonarroti. CP-Miche, tr. by John Frederick Nims

One of the Crowd on the Shore Tells How It Was. Miller Williams. CP-WillM

One of the Dead. Christina Georgina Rossetti. CP-RosC3

One of the dead woman's days, the ghost of a day. Constantine P. Cavafy. CP-CavaC, tr. by Theoharis Constantine Theoharis

One of the five straight branches of my hand. Upon the Losse of His Finger. Robert Herrick. CP-HerrR

One of the foremost organs of beauty. Back, The. Karl Shapiro. SP-ShapK

One of the gentlest, as it looks from here. Miniature. William Meredith. SP-MereW

One of the hardest explanations to be found. I'm Sure She Said Six-Thirty. Ogden Nash. CP-NashO

One of the Hottest. Charles Bukowski. SP-BukC1

One of the Inhabitants of the West. Wallace Stevens. CP-StevW; CP-StevWP

One of the Many Epilogs. Pier Paolo Pasolini. SP-PasoP, tr. by Norman MacAfee and Luciano Martinengo

One of the Muses. C. K. Williams. CP-WillC

One of the Old Ones. Robert Stock. SP-StocR

One of the ones that Midas touched. Emily Dickinson. CP-DickE

One of the Principal Causes of War. Hugh MacDiarmid. SP-MacDH

One of the Signers. John Greenleaf Whittier. CP-WhitJ

One of the Softer Sorrows of Age. Grace Paley. CP-PalGC

One of the Soldiers with a Spear Pierced His Side. Christina Georgina Rossetti. CP-RosC2

One of the Strangest. May Swenson. SP-SwenM

One of the surprises of nature. Tree Swallows. Richard Eberhart. CP-EberR

One of the / things I found out by being. 1837 War in Retrospect. Margaret Atwood. SP-AtwM1

"One of the wits of the school" your chum would say. Your Birthday in Wisconsin You Are 140. John Berryman. CP-BerrJ

One of Their Gods. Constantine P. Cavafy. CP-CavaC, tr. by Theoharis Constantine Theoharis

One of These Days. Lawrence Ferlinghetti. SP-FerlL

One of these days I'm gonna leave you, baby. Spinejacking. A. R. Ammons. CP-AmmoA

One of These Nights. Derek Mahon. CP-MahoD

One of those great, garishly emerald flies that always look freshly generated from fresh excrement. My Fly. C. K. Williams. SP-WillC

One of Those Hibiscuses of Damozels. Wallace Stevens. CP-StevWP

One of those many dates. May 16, 1973. Wisława Szymborska. SP-SzymW, tr. by Stanisław Barańczak and Clare Cavanagh

One of Those Rare Occurrences on a City Bus. Miller Williams. CP-WillM

One of us had to make the official identification of Dylan's body at the Medical Examiner's Morgue. Dylan. James Laughlin. CP-LaughJ

One of you is a major made of cord and catskin. Lent in a Year of War. Thomas Merton. CP-MertT

One, one / Lives all alone. Perpetual Motion. Thomas McGrath. SP-McGrT

One onely fire has Hell; but yet it shall. Hell Fire. Robert Herrick. CP-HerrR

One or Two. I've Finished. Gertrude Stein. CP-SteiG

One or Two Things. Mary Oliver. SP-OlivM

One ought not to have to care. Hill Wife, The. Robert Frost. CP-FrosR

One parson, one poet, one belman, one crier. William Cowper. CP-CowpW

One part Indian, one part Tennessee. Ritual for Singing Bat. John Ciardi. CP-CiarJ

One Parting. Carl Sandburg. CP-SandC

One passed me like a flash of lightning by. For One Sake. Christina Georgina Rossetti. CP-RosC3

One Perfect Rose. Dorothy Parker. CP-ParkD

One person present steps on his pedal of speech. Talker, The. Mona Van Duyn. SP-VanDM

One poet tells us. Before the Night. Theodore Weiss. SP-WeisT

One poet used to take. Beauti-ful. Charles Bukowski. SP-BukC3

One prosecutor (bald, speaks in a low voice). Trial, The. Adam Zagajewski. SP-ZagaA, tr. by Renata Gorczynski

One puts on one's white socks. Score, The. Heather McHugh. SP-McHuH

One Queen Artemisa, as old stories tell. Another [Epigram on Said Occasion]. Robert Burns. CP-BurnR

One Ralph Blossom Soliloquizes. Thomas Hardy. CP-HardT

One Reads. A. K. Ramanujan. CP-RamaA

One Remains, The. Wilfred Owen. CP-OwenW

One resting now on a plant stem, The. Butterfly Effect, The. Billy Collins. SP-CollB

One rope one single twist one sole man. Uncertain of the Crime. Paul Éluard. CP-WilW2

One royal afternoon. Birdcage Walk. Thomas Merton. CP-MertT

One said: Here is my hand to lean upon. False and True. James Whitcomb Riley. CP-RileJ

One saint to another I heard say, "How long?" "O Lord, How Long?" Jones Very. CP-VeryJ

One Saturday morning he went to the river to play. From the Childhood of Jesus. Robert Pinsky. CP-PinsR

One scene as I bow to pour her coffee. Vacation. William Stafford. SP-StafWW

One Sea-Side Grave. Christina Georgina Rossetti. CP-RosC2

One Self. Laura Riding Jackson. CP-RidiL

1 September 1939. John Berryman. CP-BerrJ

One should have known, I suppose, that you can't even trust. Annual and Perennial Problem, An. Mona Van Duyn. SP-VanDM

"One Should Not Talk to a Skilled Hunter about What Is Forbidden by the Buddha." Gary Snyder. CP-SnydG

One-sided relationship is developing quite well, A. Silence of Plants, The. Wisława Szymborska. SP-SzymWM, tr. by Joanna Trzeciak

One sigh stretches heaven. O Lull Me, Lull Me. Theodore Roethke. CP-RoetT

One silent night of late. Cheat of Cupid; or, The Ungentle Guest, The. Robert Herrick. CP-HerrR

One silver spoon shines in the house of Croot. Upon Croot. Robert Herrick. CP-HerrR

One simple and effective rhyme. Woodpigeons at Raheny. Donald Davie. CP-DaviDC

One Sister have I in our house. Emily Dickinson. CP-DickE

One sleep, one stirring. Enough. Laura Riding Jackson. CP-RidiL

One slipslouch twi / tterstamp. E. E. Cummings. CP-CummE

One small joy still left. Notes from Robin Hill Cottage. Hayden Carruth. CP-CarHS

One Soldier. Muriel Rukeyser. CP-RukeM

One Song, America, Before I Go. Walt Whitman. CP-WhitW

One sorrow more? I thought the tale complete. Whom the Lord Loveth He Chasteneth. Christina Georgina Rossetti. CP-RosC2

One sound. Then the hiss and whir. Garden, The. Louise Glück. SP-GlucL

One speculates—or doesn't one? Song of Social Life in Hollywood. Dorothy Parker. CP-ParkD

One spring the circus gave. Hill of Beans, A. Rita Dove. SP-DoveR

One star in the dark pass of the houses. Evening Star, The. Randall Jarrell. CP-JarrR

One stays or leaves. The one who returns is not. Phoenix Park. Thomas Kinsella. CP-KinsT

One step more, and the race is ended; / One word more, and the lesson's done. Septuagesima. Christina Georgina Rossetti. CP-RosC2

One Step Taken Backward. Robert Frost. CP-FrosR

One stood still, looking stupid. The other. Willets, The. May Swenson. SP-SwenM

One-story is disheartening, A. Pyromaniac, The. Wyatt Prunty. SP-PrunW

One Struggle More, and I Am Free. Lord Byron. CP-Byron

One sudden week (the roads still salty,). Styles of Bloom. John Updike. CP-UpdiJ

One summer, like a stone. What of the Night? Stanley Kunitz. CP-KunSC

One sung of thee who left the tale untold. Fragment: A Tale Untold. Percy Bysshe Shelley. CP-ShelP

One Swallow Does Not Make a Summer. Christina Georgina Rossetti. CP-RosC3

One / t / hi / s / snowflake. E. E. Cummings. CP-CummE

One tenth of the population. America's Young Black Joe! Langston Hughes. CP-HughL; CP-HughL3

One that is ever kind said yesterday. Folly of Being Comforted, The. William Butler Yeats. CP-YeatW

1. The shield. Three Functions of Irony. Thomas McGrath. SP-McGrT

One, the summer fire. Two Fires, The. Margaret Atwood. SP-AtwM1

One / the Sun / Moon / one. Robert Creeley. CP-CreeR

(One!) / the wisti-twisti barber. E. E. Cummings. CP-CummE

One thing about the past. Ho, Varlet! My Two Cents' Worth of Penny Postcard! Ogden Nash. CP-NashO

On thing alone does not exist—oblivion. Everness. Jorge Luis Borges. SP-BorgJ, tr. by Alastair Reid

One thing does not exist: Oblivion. Everness. Jorge Luis Borges. CP-WilbR, tr. by Richard Wilbur

One thing / done, the. Robert Creeley. CP-CreeR

One thing has a shelving bank. Drumlin Woodchuck, A. Robert Frost. CP-FrosR

One thing is certain, we've got to take hands off love. Love. D. H. Lawrence. CP-LawrD

One thing of it we borrow. Emily Dickinson. CP-DickE

One thing, strikes in. Talk ("One thing, strikes in"). Robert Creeley. SP-CreeR

One thing that sustained, The. Grace. James Tate. SP-TateJ

One thing the old will never understand, The. Stop It. D. H. Lawrence. CP-LawrD

One Third of a Calendar. Ogden Nash. CP-NashO

One Thought Ever at the Fore. Walt Whitman. CP-WhitW

One Time. W. S. Merwin. SP-MerwW

One Time. William Stafford. SP-StafWW

One time a mighty plague did pester. Fable of the Lion and Other Beasts, A. Unknown, sometimes at. to Thomas Sheridan. CP-SherT

One time an honest wine poured out its soul. Spirit of the Wine, The. Charles Baudelaire. CP-BaudC, tr. by Walter Martin

One time I thought that sunset's flaming air. Fair Cuirass Shattered. Allen Tate. CP-TateA

One time I was invited to see Croce. Love among the Ruins. Richard Eberhart. CP-EberR

One time, sweet creature, and one time only. Confession. Charles Baudelaire. CP-BaudC, tr. by Walter Martin

One time / there was Rene who. Ass but No Class. Charles Bukowski. SP-BukC3

One time, when we'z at Aunty's house. At Aunty's House. James Whitcomb Riley. CP-RileJ

One time Wind World. Wind World. William Stafford. SP-StafW

One to Nothing. Carolyn Kizer. CP-KizeC

One to one / walking talk, The. Walking the Dog. Robert Creeley. CP-CreeR

One to the Breastplate. Charles Bukowski. SP-BukC1

One touch of your finger on the drum sets off every sound and starts the new harmony. To a Reason. Arthur Rimbaud. CP-RimbA, tr. by Martin Sorrell

One travels. Traveling. W. S. Merwin. SP-MerwW

One tries to be sober and respectable. Untitled Poem: "One tries to be sober and respectable." Alan Dugan. CP-DugaA

One trouble with a cough. Can I Get You a Glass of Water? or, Please Close the Glottis after You. Ogden Nash. CP-NashO

One, Two, Maybe Three, Arguments against Suicide. A. K. Ramanujan. CP-RamaA

One . . . two . . . three. Federico García Lorca. CP-GarcF, tr. by Jerome Rothenberg Fr. In the Forest of Clocks.

One two three four five. Opposable Thumb, The. A. K. Ramanujan. CP-RamaA

One understands your sort of sun, Piero. Ballade to be Read in the Medici Gardens. Robert Stock. SP-StocR

One used to be able to say. Untitled Poem: "One used to be able to say." Alan Dugan. CP-DugaA

One Version of Events. Wisława Szymborska. SP-SzymW, tr. by Stanislaw Barańczak and Clare Cavanagh

One Version of Events. Wisława Szymborska. SP-SzymWM, tr. by Joanna Trzeciak

One vessel leaves, another comes. 6 May 1950. Yannis Ritsos. SP-RitsY Fr. Exile's Journals 3.

One Viceroy Resigns. Rudyard Kipling. CP-KiplR

One Volume Missing. Rita Dove. SP-DoveR

One wading a Fall meadow finds on all sides. Beautiful Changes, The. Richard Wilbur. CP-WilbR

One Waking in a Northern Fall. Alan Dugan. CP-DugaA

One wants to say to them: even Florida, if they'd have just left even Florida alone. Every Man His Own Matador; or for That Matter Any Member of the Family. Charles Olson. CP-OlsoC

One was put in the lockup. My Poets. Philip Levine. SP-LeviP

One Way. Robert Creeley. CP-CreeR

One Way. W. S. Merwin. SP-MerwW

One Way. Howard Nemerov. CP-NemeH

One way I need you, the way I come to need. Time of Year, the Time of Day, The. Robert Pinsky. CP-PinsR

One Way of Love. Robert Browning. CP-BroR1

One way or another. Fernando Pessoa. SP-PessF Fr. Keeper of Sheep, The.

One way remains to loose me yet, dear Lord. Michelangelo Buonarroti. CP-Miche, tr. by John Frederick Nims

One-Way Ticket. Langston Hughes. CP-HughL; CP-HughL2

One way to be honest. Igni Natura Renovatur Integra (Nature Is Completely Renewed by Fire). Andrei Codrescu. SP-CodrA

One way to be very happy is to be very rich. Lines Indited with All the Depravity of Poverty. Ogden Nash. CP-NashO

One We Knew. Thomas Hardy. CP-HardT

One Wet Iota. John Ciardi. CP-CiarJ

One whistle, a short husky breath. Not There. Tess Gallagher. SP-GallT

One who could repeat the Summer day, The. Emily Dickinson. CP-DickE

One who has loved the hills and died, a man. Pony Rock. Archibald MacLeish. CP-MacLA

One who lights the wood stove, The. February. Charles Simic. SP-SimiC; SP-SimiCE

One Who made, and from utter nothing too, The..Michelangelo Buonarroti. CP-Miche, tr. by John Frederick Nims

One Who Married above Him. Thomas Hardy. CP-HardT

One who sees giant Orion, the torches of winter midnight. Flight of Swans. Robinson Jeffers. CP-JefR2

One who sings "chansons vulgaires." Young Singer. Langston Hughes. CP-HughL; CP-HughL1

One Who Was Different, The. Randall Jarrell. CP-JarrR

One who was suffering tumult in his soul. Composed during a Storm. William Wordsworth. CP-WorW2

One who works. One Who Works and Buys Himself Books. Shmuel HaNagid. SP-HaNaS, tr. by Peter Cole

One Who Works and Buys Himself Books. Shmuel HaNagid. SP-HaNaS, tr. by Peter Cole

One Who Wraps Himself. Jelaluddin Rumi. SP-Rumi, tr. by Coleman Barks

One winds through firs—their weeds are ferns. Leave. Randall Jarrell. CP-JarrR

One winter afternoon / (at the magical hour). E. E. Cummings. CP-CummE

One winter morning as a child. Vision of the Garden, A. James Merrill. SP-MerrJ

One with a Song. James Whitcomb Riley. CP-RileJ

One with the golden eagle of the morning. Monster, The. G. K. Chesterton. CP-ChesG

One with the stone cups, The. Aphrodite. Olga Broumas. SP-BrouO

One without looks in to-night [or tonight]. Fallow Deer at the Lonely House, The. Thomas Hardy. CP-HardT

One woe is past. Come what come will. Christina Georgina Rossetti. CP-RosC2

One Woman to All Women. D. H. Lawrence. CP-LawrD

One Word. Yannis Ritsos. SP-RitsY, tr. by Kostas Myrsiades

One Word as the Complete Poem. Charles Olson. CP-OlsoC

One word is too often profaned. To———: "One word is too often profaned." Percy Bysshe Shelley. CP-ShelP

One Word More. Robert Browning. CP-BroR1

One word—'tis all I ask of thee. Dying Man to His Betrothed, The. Christina Georgina Rossetti. CP-RosC3

One World. Robert Creeley. SP-CreeR

One World. Charles Tomlinson. CP-TomlC

One world you say. One World. Charles Tomlinson. CP-TomlC

One would assume a difference in tempermentts. Edgar Allan Poe Meets Sarah Hale (Author of "Mary Had a Little Lamb"). Thomas Lux. SP-LuxT

One would be in less danger. Family Court. Ogden Nash. CP-NashO

One would know nothing. Io. Olga Broumas. SP-BrouO

One would remember still. Laventie. Ivor Gurney. SP-GurnI

One X. E. E. Cummings. CP-CummE

One Year. Gary Snyder. CP-SnydG

One Year ago—jots what? Emily Dickinson. CP-DickE

One year floods rose. Canto 9: "One year floods rose." Ezra Pound. SP-PounE *Fr.* Cantos.

One year I seem to have started north many times. Old Garden. W. S. Merwin. SP-MerwWF

One Year Later. Lucille Clifton. SP-ClifL

One-Year-Old, The. John Updike. CP-UpdiJ

One year, you gave us. Classmate. Adrienne Rich. CP-RicAE

One young life lost, two happy young lives blighted. Death of a First-Born, A. Christina Georgina Rossetti. CP-RosC3

One young singer, clay-red on sheer black, The. On an Attic Red-Figured Amphora (490 B.C.) by the "Berlin Painter" in the Metropolitan Museum. Helen Pinkerton. CP-PinkH

One(Floatingly)arrive / (silent)one by(alive). E. E. Cummings. CP-CummE

Oneiromancy. Ambrose Bierce. SP-BierA

One's grand flights, one's Sunday baths. Sense of the Sleight-of-Hand Man, The. Wallace Stevens. CP-StevW; CP-StevWP

One's not half two. It's two are halves of one. E. E. Cummings. CP-CummE; SP-CummE

One's-Self I Sing. Walt Whitman. CP-WhitW

Ones that Are Thrown Out, The. Miller Williams. CP-WillM

Ones that disappeared are back, The. Emily Dickinson. CP-DickE

One's the pictur' of his Pa. Twins, The. James Whitcomb Riley. CP-RileJ

Ones who camped on the slopes, below the bare summit, The. 7/13/68. Adrienne Rich. CP-RicAE *Fr.* Ghazals: Homage to Ghalib.

Ones who left were ours, The. We felt their loss. Alterations. Yannis Ritsos. SP-RitsY, *tr. by* Kostas Myrsiades

Ongoing. Rae Armantrout. SP-ArmaA

Ongoing Story, The. John Ashbery. SP-AshbJ

Onion, The. Wisława Szymborska. SP-SzymW, *tr. by* Stanislaw Barańczak *and* Clare Cavanagh

Onion Days. Carl Sandburg. CP-SandC

Onion, now that's something else, The. Onion, The. Wisława Szymborska. SP-SzymW, *tr. by* Stanislaw Barańczak *and* Clare Cavanagh

Onion tears fall from the eyes of saints. The Debts. Andrei Codrescu. SP-CodrA

Onions. Jonathan Swift. *See* Verses Made for the Women Who Cry Apples, etc

Only. Yannis Ritsos. SP-RitsY, *tr. by* N. C. Germanacos

Only a Curl. Elizabeth Barrett Browning. SP-BroEB

Only a dish of blueberries could pull me. It's Not the Heat So Much as the Humidity. James Tate. SP-TateJ

Only a Dream. James Whitcomb Riley. CP-RileJ

Only a dream unfinished; only a form at rest. Dream Unfinished, A. James Whitcomb Riley. CP-RileJ

Only a few faint elements of order hint. Yellow of the Mask, The. Charles Olson. CP-OlsoC

Only a few weeks ago, the sonogram of Jean's womb. Sonogram, The. Paul Muldoon. CP-MuldP

Only a madman could mistake. Arrow Shots. Robert Graves. CP-GravR

Only a man harrowing clods. In Time of "The Breaking of Nations." Thomas Hardy. CP-HardT

Only a Shrine, but Mine. Emily Dickinson. CP-DickE

Only a single bird / is singing. Replica. Federico García Lorca. CP-GarcF, *tr. by* Jerome Rothenberg *Fr.* Mirror Suite.

Only a small wrought-iron gate that's always open. Birds' Voices in the Tree Tops. Jaroslav Seifert. SP-SeifJ, *tr. by* Ewald Osers

Only accidents preserve. Athena in the Front Lines. Marge Piercy. SP-PierM

Only acquaintances / Seem do we. In the Street. Thomas Hardy. CP-HardT

Only Alice. Josephine Jacobsen. CP-JacoJ

Only an ear in the spring / Sunlight in Central Park it could. *Spring* by Robert Lowell / (Photograph by Trudi Fuller). May Swenson. SP-SwenM

Only as what(out of a flophouse)floats. E. E. Cummings. CP-CummE

Only Balmless Wound, The. Emily Dickinson. SP-DickE

Only Believe. Christina Georgina Rossetti. CP-RosC3

Only Breath. Jelaluddin Rumi. SP-Rumi, *tr. by* Coleman Barks

Only brooms / Know the devil. Brooms. Charles Simic. SP-SimiC; SP-SimiCE

Only close up could you make out the wings on their horses. Evidence? What Evidence . . . ? Kenneth Patchen. SP-PatcK

Only comfort of my life, The. His Comfort. Robert Herrick. CP-HerrR

Only death remains. John Ledyard. Richard Eberhart. CP-EberR

Only dumb guys fight. Prize Fighter. Langston Hughes. CP-HughL; CP-HughL1

Only from the back / could I be seen clearly. What's for Dinner. Robert Creeley. CP-CreeR

Only Ghost I ever saw, The. Emily Dickinson. CP-DickE

Only God—detect the Sorrow. Emily Dickinson. CP-DickE

Only hope is to catch the moment as it flies, The. Truth, The. Richard Eberhart. CP-EberR

Only hungers left, The. Sacrifice. Audre Lorde. SP-LordA

Only in boks the flat and final happens. Observation. Philip Larkin. CP-LarkP

Only in books I knew you. A la Mystérieuse. Gregory Orr. SP-OrrG

Only in flight could you gather at a glance. Carrara Revisited. Charles Tomlinson. SP-TomlC

Only in music are there similar surprises. Soloist. Rainer Maria Rilke. CP-RilkFr, *tr. by* A. Poulin, Jr.

Only in the beauty created. In the Beauty Created by Others. Adam Zagajewski. SP-ZagaA, *tr. by* Renata Gorczynski

Only in the Dream. Richard Eberhart. CP-EberR

Only let it form within his hands once more—. Brandy Glass, The. Louis MacNeice. CP-MacNL

Only Love can wound. Emily Dickinson. SP-DickE

Only loving, only knowing. Tears of the Excavator, The. Pier Paolo Pasolini. SP-PasoP, *tr. by* Norman MacAfee *and* Luciano Martinengo

Only Man. D. H. Lawrence. CP-LawrD

Only man that eer I knew, The. William Cowper Esqre. William Blake. CP-BlakW

Only my enemy for all time. Chess. Primo Levi. CP-LeviP, *tr. by* Ruth Feldman

Only my written word / I've sacrificed every thing, including sex and woman. Maximus of Gloucester. Charles Olson. SP-OlsoC *Fr.* Maximus Poems, The.

Only name the day, and we'll fly away. Passionate Freudian to His Love, The. Dorothy Parker. CP-ParkD

Only Nature is divine, and she's not divine. Fernando Pessoa. SP-PessF *Fr.* Keeper of Sheep, The.

Only News I know, The. Emily Dickinson. CP-DickE

Only now, at this late hour of my life. Nocturnal Darkness. Jaroslav Seifert. SP-SeifJ, *tr. by* Ewald Osers

Only [*or* Onely] a little more. His Poetry His Pillar. Robert Herrick. CP-HerrR

Only people I ever heard talk about My Lady Poverty, The. Poverty. D. H. Lawrence. CP-LawrD

Only people who should really sin, The. Inter-Office Memorandum. Ogden Nash. CP-NashO

Only poem to write I now have in mind, The. Robert Penn Warren. CP-WarrR

Only question to ask today, about man or woman, The. Egoists, The. D. H. Lawrence. CP-LawrD

Only reason for living is being fully alive, The. Being Alive. D. H. Lawrence. CP-LawrD

Only right then it was! Federico García Lorca. CP-GarcF, *tr. by* Jerome Rothenberg *Fr.* Water Jets

Only salvation is to realise that we know nothing about it, The. Salvation. D. H. Lawrence. CP-LawrD

Only some spires of bright green grass. Emily Jane Brontë. CP-BronE

Only Son, The. Rudyard Kipling. CP-KiplR

Only stand high a long enough time your lightning will come; that is what blunts the peaks of redwoods. Summit Redwood, The. Robinson Jeffers. CP-JefR1

Only tangible thing of his that remained was his coat, The. Under Oblivion. Yannis Ritsos. SP-RitsY, *tr. by* Kimon Friar

Only teaching on Tuesdays, book-worming. Memories of West Street and Lepke. Robert Lowell. SP-LoweR

Only the Best Matters. D. H. Lawrence. CP-LawrD

Only the dead can be born again, and then not much. Stray Paragraphs in April, Year of the Rat. Charles Wright. SP-WrigCN

Only the dead have an enduring city. Situation Does Not Change, The. Howard Nemerov. CP-NemeH

Only the Dreamer Can Change the Dream. John Logan. CP-LogaJ

Only the gods may act with perfect impudence—. Purana, Meaning Once upon a Time. Hayden Carruth. CP-CarHS

Only the Polished Skeleton. Countee Cullen. CP-CullC

Only the Pope partook, the cardinals, priests, monks. Sex in History. Thomas Lux. SP-LuxT

Only the priest. Charioteer. "H. D." CP-DoolH

Only the prism's obstruction shows aright. Deaf and Dumb. Robert Browning. CP-BroR1

Only the Red Fox, Only the Crow. Charles Olson. CP-OlsoC

Only the rich remember the past. Arcades of Philadelphia the Past. Wallace Stevens. CP-StevW; CP-StevWP

Only the slave knows of the slave. Henry David Thoreau. CP-ThorH

Only the wanderer. Song: "Only the wanderer." Ivor Gurney. SP-GurnI

Only the wide-awake can tell their dreams. Somnium Narrare, Vigilantis Est. James Vincent Cunningham. CP-CunnJ

Only their hands are living, to the wheel attracted. Casino. W. H. Auden. CP-AudeW

Only themselves understand themselves and the like of themselves. Perfections. Walt Whitman. CP-WhitW

Only thing for a man to do now, or a woman, The. What's to Be Done. D. H.

Lawrence. CP-LawrD

Only thing I have of Jane MacNaughton, The. Leap, The. James Dickey. CP-DickJ

Only thing to be done, now, The. Be Still! D. H. Lawrence. CP-LawrD

Only this evening I saw again low in the sky. Martial Cadenza. Wallace Stevens. CP-StevW; CP-StevWP

Only this much light was left from our life. They've Blocked Every Window. Tibor Tollas. CP-LogaJ, *tr.* by John Logan

Only this table is certain. Heavy. Of massive wood. Table 1. Czeslaw Milosz. CP-MiloC; CP-MiloCN, *tr.* by Robert Hass

Only thou livest. Centuries wheel and pass. Helen. E. E. Cummings. CP-CummE

Only three things lengthen life. *Unknown.* CP-EmerR, *tr.* by Ralph Waldo Emerson

Only time, I swear, I ever fell more than abstractly in love with someone else's wife, The. Ethics. C. K. Williams. SP-WillC

Only to have a grief. Peeling Onions. Adrienne Rich. CP-RicAE; SP-RicA2

Only to name again. Wallace Stevens. CP-StevWP

Only Truth is as deep as the ocean. Remark for Historians. Robert Penn Warren. CP-WarrR

Only two African kopjes. Two Kopjes. Rudyard Kipling. CP-KiplR

Only until this cigarette is ended. Edna St. Vincent Millay. CP-MillE

Only way it makes sense, The. Undead, The. C. K. Williams. SP-WillC

Only way to be quiet, The. Poetry. Frank O'Hara. SP-OharF

Only way to settle the property question, The. Way Out, The. D. H. Lawrence. CP-LawrD

Only, when I am sudden loss. Promise Me. Stanley Kunitz. CP-KunSC

Only with fire can men at forge and flue. Michelangelo Buonarroti. CP-Miche, *tr.* by John Frederick Nims

Only Woman Blues. Langston Hughes. CP-HughL; CP-HughL2

Only Years. Kenneth Rexroth. CP-RexrK

Only your hot heart, / nothing more. Desire. Federico García Lorca. CP-GarcF, *tr.* by Catherine Brown

Onomatopoeia. Thomas Lux. SP-LuxT

"Onora, Onora,"—her mother is calling. Lay of the Brown Rosary, The. Elizabeth Barrett Browning. CP-BroEB

Onrushing spring, Oh secret will. Rainer Maria Rilke. CP-RilkFr, *tr.* by A. Poulin, Jr. *Fr.* Fragments.

Onset, The. Robert Frost. CP-FrosR

Ontario. Paul Muldoon. CP-MuldP

Onto the nose of Newton. Federico García Lorca. CP-GarcF, *tr.* by Jerome Rothenberg *Fr.* Newton.

Ontological Episode of the Asylum. Hayden Carruth. CP-CarHS

Ontology, An. David Ignatow. SP-IgnaD

Onward led the road again. Hell Gate. A. E. Housman. CP-HousA

Onward Trail, The. James Whitcomb Riley. CP-RileJ

Onyons. Jonathan Swift. CP-SwifJ *Fr.* Verses Made for the Women Who Cry Apples, etc.

Ooftish. Samuel Beckett. CP-BeckS

Oolong. Arthur Sze. SP-SzeA

Oomba. Carl Sandburg. CP-SandC

Oomba went along years. Oomba. Carl Sandburg. CP-SandC

Oonts. Rudyard Kipling. CP-KiplR

Oozing, then / weedy stillness on the banks. Paul Celan. SP-CelaP, *tr.* by John Felstiner

Opal, The. Arthur Sze. SP-SzeA

Opals hiding in your lids, The. Jane Awake. Frank O'Hara. SP-OharF

Open. A. R. Ammons. CP-AmmoA

Open-Air Museum. Adrienne Rich. CP-RicAE; SP-RicA2

Open city / uncluttered as a map. Night Taxi. Thom Gunn. CP-GunnT

Open Closets Are Sad. Yehuda Amichai. SP-AmicYL, *tr.* by Benjamin Harshav *and* Barbara Harshav

Open Court. Thomas Kinsella. CP-KinsT

Open Door, The. Rudyard Kipling. CP-KiplR

Open Door. Federico García Lorca. CP-GarcF, *tr.* by Jerome Rothenberg *Fr.* Secrets.

Open door says, "Come in," An. Doors. Carl Sandburg. CP-SandC

Open doors / all give on a chasm. Open Door. Federico García Lorca. CP-GarcF, *tr.* by Jerome Rothenberg *Fr.* Secrets.

Open-field / blue-wheeled. Chicory Flower / on Campus. Lorine Niedecker. CP-NiedL

Open Fire near a Shed. Tess Gallagher. SP-GallT

Open green those / (dear). E. E. Cummings. CP-CummE

Open Happens in the Midst of Beings, The. Norman Dubie. CP-DubiN

Open his head,baby. E. E. Cummings. CP-CummE

Open horizons round. George Meredith. CP-MerG2

Open House. Theodore Roethke. CP-RoetT

Open Internalized. Yehuda Amichai. SP-AmicYL, *tr.* by Benjamin Harshav *and* Barbara Harshav

Open Letter from a Constant Reader. Mona Van Duyn. SP-VanDM

Open Letter, Personal. Mona Van Duyn. SP-VanDM

Open Letter to the Poet Archibald MacLeish Who Has Forsaken His Massachusetts Farm to Make Propaganda for Freedom. Carl Sandburg. CP-SandC

Open Letter to the South. Langston Hughes. CP-HughL; CP-HughL1

Open Letter to Voyager II, An. John Updike. CP-UpdiJ

Open, love, open. Unclench Yourself. Marge Piercy. SP-PierM

Open-mouthed, the baby god. I Want, I Want. Sylvia Plath. CP-PlatS

Open my eyes on the welcome. Advent. James Schuyler. CP-SchuJ

Open. Open bubbling pools and. T / O. Philip Whalen. SP-WhalP

Open our eyes that we the world may see. Spirit Land, The ("Open our eyes that we the world may see"). Jones Very. CP-VeryJ

Open Prospect. William Wordsworth. CP-WorW2 *Fr.* River Duddon [A Series of Sonnets], The.

Open rosette flowering continually cyme. African Violet. Louis Zukofsky. CP-ZukLS

Open Sea, The. William Meredith. SP-MereW

Open Secret. Denise Levertov. SP-LeveDS

Open secret, the elementary chemistry of Greek fire. What is Worthless? Robinson Jeffers. CP-JefR3

Open sesame / by day. Venus ("Open sesame / by day"). Federico García Lorca. CP-GarcF, *tr.* by Jerome Rothenberg *Fr.* Night (Suite for Piano and Poet's Voice).

Open the barn door, farm woman. She Opens the Barn Door Every Morning. Carl Sandburg. CP-SandC

Open the Blind. Kenneth Rexroth. CP-RexrK

Open the book of tales you knew by heart. Living Memory. Adrienne Rich. SP-RicA1

Open the door now. Pearl Fog. Carl Sandburg. CP-SandC

Open the Door, open the Door. Emily Dickinson. SP-DickE

Open the Door to Me, Oh! Robert Burns. CP-BurnR

Open the Gates. Stanley Kunitz. CP-KunSC

Open the old cigar-box, get me a Cuba stout. Betrothed, The. Rudyard Kipling. CP-KiplR

Open the soft string that clasps in series. Ritual of Departure ("Open the soft string that clasps in series"). Thomas Kinsella. CP-KinsT

Open thy gates. To Heaven. Robert Herrick. CP-HerrR

Open water facing Bradbury snags fog in its spruce. Penobscot. James Schuyler. CP-SchuJ

Open Window on Chicago, An. Allen Ginsberg. CP-GinsA

Open window. On the television screen colors. Open Internalized. Yehuda Amichai. SP-AmicYL, *tr.* by Benjamin Harshav *and* Barbara Harshav

Open with care the journal of those years. For Memory. Muriel Rukeyser. CP-RukeM

Open your heart: / i'll give you a treasure. E. E. Cummings. CP-CummE

Open yourself up: today. Domestic Life. Gregory Orr. SP-OrrG

Opening a bus window in N.Y. You Might Get in Trouble. Allen Ginsberg. CP-GinsA

Opening and the Close, The. Emily Dickinson. CP-DickE

Opening is read by the tongue, The. Michael Palmer. SP-PalmM

Opening like a marigold. I Will Not Be Your Sickness. Marge Piercy. SP-PierM

Opening of Eyes. Laura Riding Jackson. CP-RidiL

Opening of the chambers close. E. E. Cummings. CP-CummE

Opening of the doors. Dark, The. Sun-Artist, The. Muriel Rukeyser. CP-RukeM

Opening out and out, The. Broken Ground, The. Wendell Berry. CP-BerrW

Opening Paths. David Ignatow. SP-IgnaD

Opening Poem. Jaroslav Seifert. SP-SeifJ, *tr.* by Ewald Osers

Opening scene, The. The yellow, coal-fed fog. Poem with Refrains. Robert Pinsky. CP-PinsR

Opening the book at a bright window. Sun and Rain. W. S. Merwin. SP-MerwWF

Opening the Door of a Barn I Thought Was Empty on New Year's Eve. Robert Bly. SP-BlyR

Opening the Window. Kenneth Patchen. CP-PatcK

Opening to Satan, An. Dan Pagis. SP-PagiD, *tr.* by Stephen Mitchell

Openings. Winandermere and Derwentwater. Elgin Marbles, The. Amy Clampitt. CP-ClamA

Openness. Wisława Szymborska. SP-SzymWM, *tr.* by Joanna Trzeciak

Opera. T. S. Eliot. SP-ElioT

Operation, The. Robert Creeley. CP-CreeR

Operation, The. Anne Sexton. CP-SextA; SP-SextA

Operation, The. Charles Tomlinson. SP-TomlC

Operations: Desert Shield, Desert Storm. Eleanor Wilner. SP-WilnE

Operations of Desire, The. Andrei Codrescu. SP-CodrA

Operators stood around the cold shop, The. Morning at Speed Products. Alan Dugan. CP-DugaA

Ophelia. Walter De la Mare. CP-DeLaW

Ophelia. Ted Hughes. SP-HughTN

Ophelia. Arthur Rimbaud. CP-RimbA, *tr. by* Martin Sorrell

Opinion is a flitting thing. Emily Dickinson. CP-DickE

Opinion is not worth a rush. Michael Robartes and the Dancer. William Butler Yeats. CP-YeatW

Opinion on the Question of Pornography, An. Wisława Szymborska. SP-SzymW, *tr. by* Stanislaw Barańczak *and* Clare Cavanagh

Opium Eater. Fernando Pessoa. SP-PessF, *tr. by* Susan M. Brown *and* Edwin Honig

Opium for Archie Anderson. Andrei Codrescu. SP-CodrA

Opium for Britt Wilkie. Andrei Codrescu. SP-CodrA

Opium, horse, nothing. Sappers. Yusef Komunyakaa. CP-KomuY

Opportunity. Paul Laurence Dunbar. CP-DunbP

Opportunity, The. Thomas Hardy. CP-HardT

Opposable Thumb, The. A. K. Ramanujan. CP-RamaA

Opposed to Each Other. Czeslaw Milosz. CP-MiloCN, *tr. by* Robert Hass

Opposite House, The. Robert Lowell. SP-LoweR

Opposition. Richard Eberhart. CP-EberR

Opposition lurks, An. Menace, The. Thom Gunn. CP-GunnT

Oppositions. Charles Tomlinson. CP-TomlC

Oppress'd with grief, oppress'd with care. Despondency, an Ode. Robert Burns. CP-BurnR

Oppression. Langston Hughes. CP-HughL; CP-HughL2; CP-HughL3

Optimist, The. D. H. Lawrence. CP-LawrD

Opulence. Richard Eberhart. CP-EberR

Opulent house had in its vestibule, The. Mirror in the Vestibule, The. Constantine P. Cavafy. CP-CavaC, *tr by* Theoharis Constantine Theoharis

Opulent park: serene, we chose the heights, An. Lo Yu Park. Tu Fu. CP-KizeC, *tr. by* Carolyn Kizer

Opus Dei. John Berryman. CP-BerrJ

Opus 131 in C Sharp Minor. Ted Hughes. SP-HughTN

Opus Posthumous. Charles Wright. SP-WrigCN

Opus Posthumous. Adam Zagajewski. SP-ZagaA, *tr. by* Clare Cavanagh

Opus Posthumous 2. Charles Wright. SP-WrigCN

Opus Posthumous 3. Charles Wright. SP-WrigCN

Opusculum paedagogum. Study of Two Pears. Wallace Stevens. CP-StevW; CP-StevWP

Opusthirteen. Hayden Carruth. CP-CarHS

Or. C. K. Williams. CP-WillC

Or a crippled sloop falters, about to go under. Volume, The. Robert Pinsky. CP-PinsR

Or a Valentine. Louis Zukofsky. CP-ZukLS

Or as the embryo, whose vital band. So Make Them Melt as the Dishoused Snail. Donald Davie. CP-DaviDC

Or, as we said. Fodder. Seamus Heaney. SP-HeanSO

Or Captain Philip Sheridan. Civil War, The. Charles Olson. CP-OlsoC

Or Consider Prometheus. Amy Clampitt. CP-ClamA

Or, conversely, hungers. Beethoven, Opus 111. Amy Clampitt. CP-ClamA

Or Else. Heather McHugh. SP-McHuH

Or else their cooings came from bays of trees. Gerard Manley Hopkins. CP-HopkG

Or ever the battered liners sank. Changelings, The. Rudyard Kipling. CP-KiplR *Fr.* Debits and Credits.

Or, from That Sea of Time. Walt Whitman. CP-WhitW

Or: I work at the language as a spring of water works at the rock. Source. Robert Duncan. SP-DuncR

Or if I will not rape. Pedigree, The. Robert Creeley. CP-CreeR

Or in My Throat. John Ashbery. CP-AshbJ

Or listen to the clocktowers. Time and Time Again. A. K. Ramanujan. CP-RamaA

Or looked [*or* lookt] I back unto the times hence flown. To M. Denham, on His Prospective Poem. Robert Herrick. CP-HerrR

Or me wanting another man's / wife, etc. Europeans, The. Robert Creeley. CP-CreeR

Or must I say, Vain Word, false thought! Alteram Partem. Arthur Hugh Clough. SP-ClouA

Or scorn[e], or pity [*or* pittie] on me take. Dream[e], The. Ben Jonson. CP-JonsB

Or shall we run with Artemis. Vital Choice, The. George Meredith. CP-MerG1

Or she would turn up *The Songs of Leonard Cohen.* Kissing and Telling. Paul Muldoon. CP-MuldP

Or, Solitude. Donald Davie. CP-DaviDC

Or the single path— / Which the cool moon sheds. George Meredith. CP-MerG2

Or: *They are come near me that.* Thou Art Near at Hand, O Lord. Donald Davie. CP-DaviDC

Or to Perish before Day. Robert Graves. CP-GravR

Or Traveller's Joy. Charles Tomlinson. CP-TomlC

Or was it Princess Fall Winter Spring Summer? Princess Summer Fall Winter

Spring. Thomas Lux. SP-LuxT

Or were he a Jew or a. To My Friend Ezra Pound. William Carlos Williams. CP-WilW2

Or what is closer to the truth. When I Buy Pictures. Marianne Craig Moore. CP-MoorM

Or who and who. E. E. Cummings. CP-CummE

Or with a rush. Sluggishly. William Carlos Williams. CP-WilW1

Oracle. Seamus Heaney. SP-HeanSO

Oracle, The. Thomas Merton. CP-MertT

Oracle of the market! thence you drew. Camelus Saltat: Continued. George Meredith. CP-MerG1

Oracles. Kathleen Jessie Raine. SP-RainK

Oracles, The. A. E. Housman. CP-HousA

O'Rahilly, The. William Butler Yeats. CP-YeatW

Oral Messages. Lawrence Ferlinghetti.

   "I am waiting for my case to come up." SP-FerlL

Orananaoig, or, the Song of Death. Robert Burns. CP-BurnR

Orange and lemon. Federico García Lorca. CP-GarcF, *tr. by* Alan S. Trueblood *Fr.* Games.

Orange Bears, The. Kenneth Patchen. CP-PatcK

Orange blossoms have dropped their threads. Landscape with Seated Figure and Olive Trees. Charles Wright. SP-WrigC

Orange Buds by Mail from Florida. Walt Whitman. CP-WhitW

Orange Clock, An. Ted Berrigan. SP-BerrT

Orange devours, An. In Earliest Morning. James Schuyler. CP-SchuJ

Orange flower on the other side of that pane, The. Close Up. Fanny Howe. SP-HoweF

Orange hawkeye stronger than thought winking above a thousand thin grassblades. Independence Day. Allen Ginsberg. CP-GinsA

Orange in the middle of a table. Against Still Life. Margaret Atwood. SP-AtwdM1

Orange on its way. On Its Way. May Swenson. SP-SwenM

Orange translucent butterflies are cruising. Above. Howard Nemerov. CP-NemeH

Orange tree, in various light, The. In a Green Night. Derek Walcott. CP-WalcD

Oranges fell to the ground, The. Yannis Ritsos. SP-RitsY *Fr.* First Series.

Oratio Patris Condren: O Jesu Vivens in Maria. Gerard Manley Hopkins. CP-HopkG

Oration, The. Carolyn Kizer. CP-KizeC

Oration: Half-Moon in Vermont. Norman Dubie. CP-DubiN

Orator dismal of Nottinghamshire, An. Excellent New Song, An. Jonathan Swift. CP-SwifJ

Orator of the Opposition, The. G. K. Chesterton. CP-ChesG

Orator Prigg. William Blake. CP-BlakW

Orb-weaver shivering. Waterfall, The. Amy Clampitt. CP-ClamA

Orbit. Heather McHugh. SP-McHuH

Orbital Complexion. Andrei Codrescu. SP-CodrA

Orbiter 5 Shows How Earth Looks from the Moon. May Swenson. SP-SwenM

Orca. Robinson Jeffers. CP-JefR3

Orchard. Yehuda Amichai. SP-AmicY, *tr. by* Chana Bloch

Orchard. "H. D." CP-DoolH

Orchard. Richard Eberhart. CP-EberR

Orchard. Rainer Maria Rilke. CP-RilkFr, *tr. by* A. Poulin, Jr.

Orchard, The. Rainer Maria Rilke. CP-RilkFr, *tr. by* A. Poulin, Jr. *Fr.* Orchards.

Orchard, The. William Carlos Williams. CP-WilW2

Orchard and the Heath, The. George Meredith. CP-MerG1

Orchard Keeper, The. Robert Bly. SP-BlyR

Orchard Lands of Long Ago, The. James Whitcomb Riley. CP-RileJ

Orchard, March. Federico García Lorca. CP-GarcF, *tr. by* Alan S. Trueblood *Fr.* Songs to End With.

Orchard Pathway, The. William Wordsworth. CP-WorW1

Orchard-Pit, The. Dante Gabriel Rossetti. CW-RossD

Orchard Trees, January. Richard Wilbur. CP-WilbR

Orchards. Rainer Maria Rilke.

   "All my goodbyes are said. Many separations." CP-RilkFr, *tr. by* A. Poulin, Jr.

   "All of our ancestors' pleasures." CP-RilkFr, *tr. by* A. Poulin, Jr.

   "And yet how many ports, and in those ports." CP-RilkFr, *tr. by* A. Poulin, Jr.

   "Angels' view: perhaps the tips of trees, The." CP-RilkFr, *tr. by* A. Poulin, Jr.

   "As Venetian glass." CP-RilkFr, *tr. by* A. Poulin, Jr.

   "Between the masques of mist and green." CP-RilkFr, *tr. by* A. Poulin, Jr.

   "Can such light offer." CP-RilkFr, *tr. by* A. Poulin, Jr.

   "Centaur has good reason, The." CP-RilkFr, *tr. by* A. Poulin, Jr.

   Cornucopia. CP-RilkFr, *tr. by* A. Poulin, Jr.

   "Do our humble things." CP-RilkFr, *tr. by* A. Poulin, Jr.

   Doe, The. CP-RilkFr, *tr. by* A. Poulin, Jr.

   Eros. CP-RilkFr, *tr. by* A. Poulin, Jr.

   "Everything happens a little." CP-RilkFr, *tr. by* A. Poulin, Jr.

Flag, The. CP-RilkFr, *tr. by* A. Poulin, Jr.
Fountain, The. CP-RilkFr, *tr. by* A. Poulin, Jr.
Goddess, The. CP-RilkFr, *tr. by* A. Poulin, Jr.
"Have the angels turned discreet!" CP-RilkFr, *tr. by* A. Poulin, Jr.
"How can I recognize again." CP-RilkFr, *tr. by* A. Poulin, Jr.
"How many strange secrets." CP-RilkFr, *tr. by* A. Poulin, Jr.
"Hurried, running water—forgetful water." CP-RilkFr, *tr. by* A. Poulin, Jr.
"If we sing a god, that god." CP-RilkFr, *tr. by* A. Poulin, Jr.
"In the animal eye I saw." CP-RilkFr, *tr. by* A. Poulin, Jr.
"In the multiple encounter." CP-RilkFr, *tr. by* A. Poulin, Jr.
Interior Portrait. CP-RilkFr, *tr. by* A. Poulin, Jr.
"Isn't it sad that our eyes close?" CP-RilkFr, *tr. by* A. Poulin, Jr.
"It's that we must consent." CP-RilkFr, *tr. by* A. Poulin, Jr.
"It's the endless landscape, it's a bell." CP-RilkFr, *tr. by* A. Poulin, Jr.
Ivory Fragment. CP-RilkFr, *tr. by* A. Poulin, Jr.
"Let the god content himself with us." CP-RilkFr, *tr. by* A. Poulin, Jr.
"Let's stop a while, let's talk." CP-RilkFr, *tr. by* A. Poulin, Jr.
"Little porcelain angel." CP-RilkFr, *tr. by* A. Poulin, Jr.
"Night light, my calm confidante." CP-RilkFr, *tr. by* A. Poulin, Jr.
"No one knows how mastered we are." CP-RilkFr, *tr. by* A. Poulin, Jr.
"O longing for the places that weren't loved." CP-RilkFr, *tr. by* A. Poulin, Jr.
"O my friends, all of you, I rencounce." CP-RilkFr, *tr. by* A. Poulin, Jr.
Orchard, The. CP-RilkFr, *tr. by* A. Poulin, Jr.
"Our next-to-last word will be one." CP-RilkFr, *tr. by* A. Poulin, Jr.
Palm. CP-RilkFr, *tr. by* A. Poulin, Jr.
"Since everything must pass." CP-RilkFr, *tr. by* A. Poulin, Jr.
Sleeping Woman. CP-RilkFr, *tr. by* A. Poulin, Jr.
"Sometimes it's good to be." CP-RilkFr, *tr. by* A. Poulin, Jr.
"Soul-bird often, The." CP-RilkFr, *tr. by* A. Poulin, Jr.
Spring. CP-RilkFr, *tr. by* A. Poulin, Jr.
"Stay still, if the Angel." CP-RilkFr, *tr. by* A. Poulin, Jr.
"Sublime is a departure, The." CP-RilkFr, *tr. by* A. Poulin, Jr.
Summer Passer-By. CP-RilkFr, *tr. by* A. Poulin, Jr.
"Swan swims on the water, A." CP-RilkFr, *tr. by* A. Poulin, Jr.
"This horse drinking at the fountain." CP-RilkFr, *tr. by* A. Poulin, Jr.
"Tonight my heart makes." CP-RilkFr, *tr. by* A. Poulin, Jr.
"Tonight there was something in the air." CP-RilkFr, *tr. by* A. Poulin, Jr.
"Two wagons full of bricks." CP-RilkFr, *tr. by* A. Poulin, Jr.
"We arrange and we compose." CP-RilkFr, *tr. by* A. Poulin, Jr.
"We've forgotten so well." CP-RilkFr, *tr. by* A. Poulin, Jr.
"When the candle has burned out." CP-RilkFr, *tr. by* A. Poulin, Jr.
"Whole night rests, The." CP-RilkFr, *tr. by* A. Poulin, Jr.
"Who's coming to finish Love's temple?" CP-RilkFr, *tr. by* A. Poulin, Jr.
Window, The. CP-RilkFr, *tr. by* A. Poulin, Jr.
"Winter's total silence." CP-RilkFr, *tr. by* A. Poulin, Jr.
"Without being less venerable." CP-RilkFr, *tr. by* A. Poulin, Jr.
Orchards half the way, The. First of May, The. A. E. Housman. CP-HousA
Orchestra, The. William Carlos Williams. CP-WilW2
Orchestras have so long been speaking. Music Is International. W. H. Auden. CP-AudeW
Orchestration of events, An. Composing. A. R. Ammons. CP-AmmoA
Orchid, The. C. K. Williams. SP-WillC
Orchids. Theodore Roethke. CP-RoetT
Orchids are poisonous blooms, though. On the Supposed Immorality of Orchids. Alan Dugan. CP-DugaA
Ordeal, The. William Carlos Williams. CP-WilW1
Order for A Song, An. James Whitcomb Riley. CP-RileJ
Order of Diet. May Swenson. SP-SwenM
Order of Saying, The. Charles Tomlinson. CP-TomlC
Order of Service, An. Geoffrey Hill. CP-HillG
Order of the small town on the riverbank, The. 8/1/68. Adrienne Rich. CP-RicAE *Fr.* Ghazals: Homage to Ghalib.
Order on the kitchen's wooden door, An. 27 November 1948. Yannis Ritsos. SP-RitsY *Fr.* Exile's Journals 2.
Order. Order. The bottle contains. Divisions. Robert Creeley. CP-CreeR
Order to View. Louis MacNeice. CP-MacNL
Ordered cruly and plain cabbages, The. Garden, The. Ivor Gurney. SP-GurnI
Orderly hand of man, hollowing, The. Switzerland. John Updike. CP-UpdiJ
Orders. John Ciardi. CP-CiarJ
Orders for the Day. Theodore Roethke. CP-RoetT
Ordinary Afternoon in Charlottesville, An. Charles Wright. SP-WrigCN
Ordinary Detail. Jane Cooper. CP-CoopJ
Ordinary Evening in New Haven, An. Wallace Stevens. CP-StevW; CP-StevWP
Ordinary evening in Wisconsin, An. Witness. Amy Clampitt. CP-ClamA
Ordinary God. Donald Davie. CP-DaviDC
Ordinary milkman brought that dawn, The. Trial of Man, The. Sylvia Plath. CP-PlatS
Ordinary Morning, An. Philip Levine. SP-LeviP
Ordinary Newscaster, An. Robinson Jeffers. CP-JefR3
Ordinary people are peculiar too. Conversation. Louis MacNeice. CP-MacNL
Ordinary people ordinarily do not care. Force of Habit, The. Hans Magnus Enzensberger. SP-EnzeH, *tr. by* Michael Hamburger
Ordinary Women, The. Wallace Stevens. CP-StevW; CP-StevWP
Ordination, The. Robert Burns. CP-BurnR
Ordonnance. Thomas McGrath. SP-McGrT
Oread. "H. D." CP-DoolH
Oregon Landscape with Lost Lover. Olga Broumas. SP-BrouO
Oregon Message, An. William Stafford. SP-StafW; SP-StafWW
Orestes. Yannis Ritsos. SP-RitsY, *tr. by* Philip Pastras *and* George Pilitsis
Orestes at Tauris. Randall Jarrell. CP-JarrR
Orestes Theme. "H. D." CP-DoolH
Orfeo. James Merrill. SP-MerrJ
Orford. Boris Leonidovich Pasternak. CP-DaviDC, *tr. by* Donald Davie
Organ. Alfonso Cortes. CP-MertT
Organ is moaning, The. Emily Dickinson. SP-DickE
Organ smites the ear with solemn notes, The. Evening Choir, The. Jones Very. CP-VeryJ
Organ swells, the trumpets sound, The. Emily Jane Brontë. CP-BronE
Organic Bloom. Stanley Kunitz. CP-KunSC
Organic Form. Sam Hamill. SP-HamiS
Organization Men in Affluent Society. Kenneth Rexroth. CP-RexrK
Organization of clear purposes, An. Stations. John Ciardi. CP-CiarJ
Organized crime, The. Kissing Seat, The. Paul Muldoon. CP-MuldP
Organized knowledge in story and picture. From Morning-Glory to Petersburg. Adrienne Rich. CP-RicAE; SP-RicA2
Organon. Kenneth Rexroth. CP-RexrK
Organs and War News / Radio static from Saigon. These States: into L.A. Allen Ginsberg. CP-GinsA
Orgasm. David Ignatow. SP-IgnaD
Orgy. Muriel Rukeyser. CP-RukeM
Oriane. James Schuyler. CP-SchuJ
Orient and Immortal Wheat. Derek Walcott. CP-WalcD
Orient Express, The. Randall Jarrell. CP-JarrR
Orient Wheat. Adrienne Rich. CP-RicAE
Oriental Ballerina, The. Rita Dove. SP-DoveR
Oriental histories tell a tale, The. John I:14. Jorge Luis Borges. SP-BorgJ, *tr. by* Willis Barnstone
Oriental Maxims. John Greenleaf Whittier. CP-WhitJ
Oriental Visitor, An. Donald Davie. CP-DaviDC
Orientale. A. R. Ammons. CP-AmmoA
Origami. Miller Williams. CP-WillM
Origen. Thomas Merton. CP-MertT
Origin. Howard Nemerov. CP-NemeH
Origin of Baseball, The. Kenneth Patchen. CP-PatcK
Origin of Electricity, The. Andrei Codrescu. SP-CodrA
Origin of Laughter, The. John Updike. CP-UpdiJ
"Origin of Love!"—Ah! why, The. On Being Asked What Was the "Origin of Love." Lord Byron. CP-Byron
Origin of Man, The. Jones Very. CP-VeryJ
  "Man has forgot his Origin; in vain." CP-VeryJ
  "Not suffering for their sins in former state." CP-VeryJ
Origin of the Marble Forest. Gregory Orr. SP-OrrG
Origin of the Praise of God, The. Robert Bly. SP-BlyR
Original—"Apropos." Ralph Waldo Emerson. CP-EmerR
Original artist, you have become. Decorated Skull in a University Museum. Howard Nemerov. CP-NemeH
Original Aversions. William Meredith. SP-MereW
Original Child Bomb. Thomas Merton. CP-MertT
Original Hymn ("Not unto men alone has come"). Jones Very. CP-VeryJ
Original Hymn ("We welcome, with the opening year"). Jones Very. CP-VeryJ
Original Memory. Arthur Sze. SP-SzeA
Original of Punning, The. Thomas Sheridan. CP-SherT
Original Poetry by Victor and Cazire. Percy Bysshe Shelley. CP-ShelP
Original Sin. James Vincent Cunningham. CP-CunnJ
Original Sin. Robinson Jeffers. CP-JefR3
Original Sin. Helen Pinkerton. CP-PinkH
Original Sin. Miller Williams. CP-WillM
Original Sin [: A Short Story]. Robert Penn Warren. CP-WarrR
Originally. Laura Riding Jackson. CP-RidiL
Originally being meant. Originally. Laura Riding Jackson. CP-RidiL
Originators, The. Thomas Merton. CP-MertT
Origins. Derek Walcott. CP-WalcD

Origins. Jay Wright. SP-WrigJ

Oriole, a charred and singing coal, The. Amherst. Amy Clampitt. CP-ClamA

Oriole on a flowering branch, An. Han-shan. CP-ColdM, *tr. by* Red Pine

Oriole sings in the greening grove, The. Summer in the South. Paul Laurence Dunbar. CP-DunbP

Orioles live in the elms, and in classical verse. Summer Solstice. Osip Emilevich Mandelstam. CP-KunSC, *tr. by* Stanley Kunitz

Orion. Adrienne Rich. CP-RicAE; SP-RicA1; SP-RicA2

Orion Dead. "H. D." CP-DoolH

Orion over Farne. Charles Tomlinson. SP-TomlC

Orion plunges like a drunken hunter. Adrienne Rich. SP-RicA1 *Fr.* Spirit of Place, The.

Orion swung southward aslant. Before Marching and After. Thomas Hardy. CP-HardT

Orlando Furioso. Ludovico Ariosto.
   "Orlando who great length of time had been." CP-WorW1

Orlando who great length of time had been. Ludovico Ariosto. CP-WorW1 *Fr.* Orlando Furioso.

Orlie Wilde. James Whitcomb Riley. CP-RileJ

Ormerod was deeply troubled. Distractions and the Human Crowd. Stevie Smith. CP-SmitS

Ornamental clouds. Evening Love Song. Rainer Maria Rilke. CP-RilkFr, *tr. by* A. Poulin, Jr.

Ornithology for Beginners. Dorothy Parker. CP-ParkD

Oropheriris. Constantine P. Cavaty. CP-CavaC, *tr. by* Theoharis Constantine Theoharis

O'Rourk's noble fare. Description of an Irish Feast, The. Jonathan Swift. CP-SwifJ

Orphan, The. Thomas McGrath. SP-McGrT

Orphan, The. Rainer Maria Rilke. CP-RilkFr, *tr. by* A. Poulin, Jr.

Orphan arrived in outlandish hat, The. Arrival (North Wales, 1897), An. Denise Levertov. SP-LeveDL

Orphan at the Door, An. Nuala Ni Dhomhnaill. CP-MahoD, *tr. by* Derek Mahon

Orphan Hours, the Year is dead. Dirge for the Year. Percy Bysshe Shelley. CP-ShelP

Orphan, I was wandering in black and with an eye vacant of family. Reminiscence. Stéphane Mallarmé. CP-MallS, *tr. by* Henry Weinfield

Orphan is looking for parents, The. Orphan Reformed, The. Stevie Smith. CP-SmitS

Orphan Reformed, The. Stevie Smith. CP-SmitS

Orphan Song. Rainer Maria Rilke. CP-RilkFr

Orphan Wind. Rainer Maria Rilke. CP-RilkFr, *tr. by* A. Poulin, Jr.

Orphanage Boy. Robert Penn Warren. CP-WarrR

Orphanage of possibility, The. Sea Mouse. Amy Clampitt. CP-ClamA

Orphaned, I cry to thee. Sleep. James Whitcomb Riley. CP-RileJ

Orphaned Old Maid, The. Thomas Hardy. CP-HardT

Orphans' New Year Gifts. Arthur Rimbaud. CP-RimbA, *tr. by* Martin Sorrell

Orpheus. W. H. Auden. CP-AudeW

Orpheus. Donald Davie. CP-DaviDC

Orpheus. Alan Dugan. CP-DugaA

Orpheus. Robert Herrick. CP-HerrR

Orpheus. James Laughlin. CP-LaugJ

Orpheus. William Meredith. SP-MereW

Orpheus. George Oppen. CP-OppGN

Orpheus. Muriel Rukeyser. CP-RukeM

Orpheus. Percy Bysshe Shelley. CP-ShelP

Orpheus! an Orpheus! yes, Faith may grow bold, An. Power of Music. William Wordsworth. CP-WorW1; MW-WorW

Orpheus and animus, / drawing back to journeys now. Marilyn Hacker. SP-HackM *Fr.* Navigators, The.

Orpheus and Eurydice. Geoffrey Hill. CP-HillG

Orpheus and Eurydice. Virgil. CP-WorW1 *Fr.* Georgics.

Orpheus and Pluto. Robert Herrick. CP-HerrR

Orpheus Descending. Tennessee Williams. CP-WillT

Orpheus, for so the Gentiles call'd thy name. On the Goodness of the Supreme Being. Christopher Smart. SP-SmarC

Orpheus he went (as poets tell). Orpheus. Robert Herrick. CP-HerrR

Orpheus liked the glad personal quality. Syringa. John Ashbery. SP-AshbJ

Orpheus (1). Margaret Atwood. SP-AtwM2

Orpheus (2). Margaret Atwood. SP-AtwM2

Orphic Scenario. Howard Nemerov. CP-NemeH

Orphic Soul, The. Kenneth Rexroth. CP-RexrK

Orsha is a bad station. In Orsha a train risks stopping for days. Fear-Dream (1918). Czeslaw Milosz. CP-MiloC; CP-MiloCN, *tr. by* Robert Hass

Orso, there never was a lake or river. Petrarch. CP-Petra, *tr. by* J. G. Nichols

Orso, upon your charger you may put. Petrarch. CP-Petra, *tr. by* J. G. Nichols

Orson of the Muse, An. George Meredith. CP-MerG1

Orthodontia. John Updike. CP-UpdiJ

Orthodox, Orthodox, wha [*or* who] believe in John Knox. Kirk's Alarm, The. Robert Burns. CP-BurnR

Orthography. Ambrose Bierce. SP-BierA *Fr.* Devil's Dictionary, The.

Orvieto. The King of Clubs. Donald Davie. CP-DaviDC

O'Ryan. Charles Olson. CP-OlsoC

O'Ryan 11-15. Charles Olson. CP-OlsoC

Osawatomie. Carl Sandburg. CP-SandC

Oscar. Paul Muldoon. CP-MuldP

Oscar C. McCulloch. James Whitcomb Riley. CP-RileJ

Oscar of Alva. Lord Byron. CP-Byron

Osceola. Walt Whitman. CP-WhitW

Osiris pales; the palace walls. Dilemma in the Delta. John Updike. CP-UpdiJ

Osmund Dutch, and John Gallop, mariners, their wages. Maximus, in Gloucester Sunday, LXV. Charles Olson. SP-OlsoC *Fr.* Maximus Poems, The.

Ospreys in Cry. Richard Eberhart. CP-EberR

Ossian's Address to the Sun in "Carthon." Lord Byron. CP-Byron

Ossian's Grave. Robinson Jeffers. CP-JefR2

Osso Buco. Billy Collins. SP-CollB

Ossuary. Rainer Maria Rilke. CP-RilkFr, *tr. by* A. Poulin, Jr.

Ostinato and Drone. Charles Wright. SP-WrigCN

Ostjuden. Primo Levi. CP-LeviP, *tr. by* Ruth Feldman *and* Brian Swann

Oswald Incognito & Astral Travels. Ai. SP-Ai

Other, The. James Dickey. CP-DickJ

Other, The. Hans Magnus Enzensberger. SP-EnzeH, *tr. by* Michael Hamburger

Other, The. Ted Hughes. CP-HughTN

Other, The. Gabriela Mistral. SP-MistG, *tr. by* Maria Giachetti [*or* Jacketti]

Other, The. Sylvia Plath. CP-PlatS

Other, The. Theodore Roethke. CP-RoetT

Other, The. Anne Sexton. CP-SextA

Other acquainted years. On Reaching Forty. Maya Angelou. SP-AngeM

Other animals see her pass by and ask each other what heavenly thing is worthy of that high neck. Giraffe, The. Gabriela Mistral. SP-MistG, *tr. by* Maria Giachetti [*or* Jacketti]

Other Cambridge, The. John Berryman. CP-BerrJ

Other Cindy, The. John Ashbery. SP-AshbJ

Other day, The. Day the Epileptic Spoke, The. Charles Bukowski. SP-BukC3

Other day a witch came to call, The. Intruder, An. May Sarton. SP-SartM

Other day I heard in the movies, The. Folk Singer, The. David Ignatow. SP-IgnaD

Other day we spent, The. Carmen 50. Catullus. CP-ZukLS *Fr.* Carmina.

Other days still to come. Let's Wait. Pablo Neruda. SP-NeruP

Other guineahen, The. E. E. Cummings. CP-CummE

Other kids romped around the playground; their voices, The. Myopic Child, A. Yannis Ritsos. SP-RitsY, *tr. by* Gwendolyn MacEwen *and* Nikos Tsingos

Other lads, their ways are daring. Folk Tune. Dorothy Parker. CP-ParkD

Other Life, The. Raymond Carver. CP-CarvR

Other Lines. Eugenio Montale. CP-MontE, *tr. by* Jonathan Galassi

Other loves may sink and settle, other loves may loose and slack. Strange Music, The. G. K. Chesterton. CP-ChesG

Other Man, The. Rudyard Kipling. *Fr.* Plain Tales from the Hills.

Other Man, The. Yannis Ritsos. SP-RitsY, *tr. by* Kimon Friar *and* Kostas Myrsiades

Other mens sins wee ever beare in mind. Our Owne Sinnes Unseen. Robert Herrick. CP-HerrR

Other night I saw . . . / Who did I see?, The. Rafael Alberti. CP-MertT *Fr.* Roman Nocturnes.

Other one, Borges, is the one things happen to, The. Borges and I. Jorge Luis Borges. SP-BorgJ, *tr. by* Ken Krabbenhoft

Other Precision, The. Yannis Ritsos. SP-RitsY, *tr. by* Kimon Friar

Other props are gone, The. Je T'adore. Thomas Kinsella. CP-KinsT

Other Sea-Cities. "H. D." CP-DoolH

Other Side, The. Seamus Heaney. SP-HeanSO

Other Side, The. C. K. Williams. CP-WillC

Other Side of the River, The. Charles Wright. SP-WrigC

Other Side of the Wall, The. Clarence Major. SP-MajoC

Other Side: The Green Home, The. Kenneth Patchen. CP-PatcK

Other stones the æra tell. Inscription for a Stone. William Cowper. CP-CowpW

Other Than. Charles Olson. CP-OlsoC

Other Tiger, The. Jorge Luis Borges. SP-BorgJ, *tr. by* Alastair Reid

Other Tradition, The. John Ashbery. SP-AshbJ

Other Travelers to the River. W. S. Merwin. SP-MerwW

Other Two, The. Sylvia Plath. CP-PlatS

Other Wing, The. Louis MacNeice. CP-MacNL

Other Women Have Reared in Me. D. H. Lawrence. CP-LawrD

Other world's not for me, The. Song, A: "Other world's not for me, The." Gregory Orr. SP-OrrG

Others abide our question. Thou art free. Shakespeare. Matthew Arnold. SP-

ArnoM

Others beat timbrels with uplifted hands. History of a Malady. Charles Tomlinson. CP-TomlC

Others because you did not keep. Deep-sworn Vow, A. William Butler Yeats. CP-YeatW

Others have sought publicity. Lives of the Saints. Paul Muldoon. CP-MuldP

Others, I am not the first. A. E. Housman. CP-HousA

Others in museums pass them by. Roman Portrait Busts. John Updike. CP-UpdiJ

Others may need new life in Heaven. Speculative. Robert Browning. CP-BroR2

Others May Praise What They Like. Walt Whitman. CP-WhitW

Others see a rush, a carnival, a million. Some People. A. K. Ramanujan. CP-RamaA

Others taunt me with having knelt at well-curbs. For Once, Then, Something. Robert Frost. CP-FrosR

Others were the tempest, The. To M. Rainer Maria Rilke. CP-RilkFr, *tr.* by A. Poulin, Jr.

Otherwise. John Ashbery. SP-AshbJ

Otherwise. Lorine Niedecker. CP-NiedL

Otherworld. Muriel Rukeyser. CP-RukeM

Otho. Percy Bysshe Shelley. CP-ShelP

Otho the Great. John Keats. CP-KeatJ

Otho's scooped nut its pusillanimity. Catullus. *See* If not by all that his friends boast

O'Toole / attempting an entry of the *mons Parnassus*. Carmen 105. Catullus. CP-ZukLS *Fr.* Carmina.

O'Toole is generally accounted. Carmen 114. Catullus. CP-ZukLS *Fr.* Carmina.

O'Toole is the proud master of. Carmen 115. Catullus. CP-ZukLS *Fr.* Carmina.

Ot's a leedle Gristmas story. Dot Leedle Boy. James Whitcomb Riley. CP-RileJ

Otter, An. Ted Hughes. SP-HughTN

Otter, The. Seamus Heaney. SP-HeanSO

Ottffssente. Kenneth Rexroth. CP-RexrK

Otto. Theodore Roethke. CP-RoetT

Otto ore suonano: / Picchia il postino! Christina Georgina Rossetti. CP-RosC3

Ouija. Sylvia Plath. CP-PlatS

Our (American) Ragcademicians. William Carlos Williams. CP-WilW1

Our Ancestors' Short Lives. Wisława Szymborska. SP-SzymW, *tr.* by Stanislaw Barańczak *and* Clare Cavanagh

Our angels, sir, surely recognized each other. To Odilon-Jean Périer. Rainer Maria Rilke. CP-RilkFr, *tr.* by A. Poulin, Jr.

Our April must replenish the delightful wells. April Manifesto, An. Louis MacNeice. CP-MacNL

Our argute voices vied among the bracken. Hampshire. Donald Davie. CP-DaviDC

Our Autocrat. John Greenleaf Whittier. CP-WhitJ

Our baby was weaned during the first days. Yehuda Amichai. SP-AmicY, *tr.* by Chana Bloch *Fr.* Songs of Zion the Beautiful.

Our bane and physic the same earth bestows. Ovid. CP-JohnS *Fr.* Remediae Amoris.

Our bark's on the water; come down, come down. Love and Death. Christina Georgina Rossetti. CP-RosC3

Our Bastard-children are but like to Plate. Bastards. Robert Herrick. CP-HerrR

Our Bias. W. H. Auden. CP-AudeW

Our Bicycles. James Laughlin. CP-LaugJ

Our boat is asleep on Serchio's stream. Boat on the Serchio, The. Percy Bysshe Shelley. CP-ShelP

Our Bodies. Denise Levertov. SP-LeveDP

Our Bog Is Dood. Stevie Smith. CP-SmitS

Our bones are scattered at the grave's mouth. Metaphysics of the Night. Marya Alexandrovna Zaturenska. SP-ZatuM

Our Boyhood Haunts. James Whitcomb Riley. CP-RileJ

Our brains ache, in the merciless iced east winds that knive us . . . . Exposure. Wilfred Owen. CP-OwenW

Our breed of trinket-burying avatars. Death and the Professor. Thomas Kinsella. CP-KinsT

Our brethren of England, who love us so dear. Excellent New Ballad, An. Jonathan Swift. CP-SwifJ

Our brows are wreathed with spindrift and the weed is on our knees. Coastwise Lights, The. Rudyard Kipling. CP-KiplR

Our building floated heavily through the cold. Window. Robert Pinsky. CP-PinsR

Our buttocks aren't like theirs. Many times I've seen. Arthur Rimbaud. CP-RimbA, *tr.* by Martin Sorrell

Our canoe idles in the idling current. Floating. Kenneth Rexroth. CP-RexrK

Our car was fierce enough. Trip, The. William Stafford. SP-StafWW

Our Castle is East of the Sun. Ubi Ecclesia. G. K. Chesterton. CP-ChesG

Our Cave. William Stafford. SP-StafWW

Our chief amusement was to lie naked. Written after Reading an Item in the Paper about a Young Lady Who Went Mad upon Forsaking Her Lover. He Is Here Assumed to Speak. Kenneth Patchen. CP-PatcK

Our Child Doesn't Know Anything. Ogden Nash. CP-NashO

Our Children, Coming of Age. Wendell Berry. CP-BerrW

Our Church Palms are Budding Willow Twigs. Christina Georgina Rossetti. CP-RosC2

Our City Is Guarded by Automatic Rockets. William Stafford. SP-StafWW

Our clothes are still wet from wading. Huts at Esquimaux, The. Norman Dubie. CP-DubiN

Our cookbook is bound like Whitman's *Leaves of Grass*-. Beethoven. Robert Lowell. SP-LoweR

Our Country. Henry David Thoreau. CP-ThorH

Our Country. John Greenleaf Whittier. CP-WhitJ

Our Cousins. Dorothy Parker. CP-ParkD

Our Crosses are no other then the rods. Crosses. Robert Herrick. CP-HerrR

Our Curious Position. Charles Bukowski. SP-BukC3

Our Daily Bread. César Vallejo. CP-WrigJ, *tr.* by James Wright

Our darkness stays, the self-made dark we know. Degrees of Shade. Helen Pinkerton. CP-PinkH

Our daughter dreamt of magnolias. New England, Autumn. Norman Dubie. CP-DubiN

Our Day Is Over. D. H. Lawrence. CP-LawrD

Our days as in ancient times, in ancient times. You Will Speak. Yehuda Amichai. SP-AmicYL, *tr.* by Benjamin Harshav *and* Barbara Harshav

Our dead fathers came down to us in the river. Desert Deportation of 1915, The. Norman Dubie. CP-DubiN

Our Dear Mother. Jones Very. CP-VeryJ

Our dearest, our white youth. La Jeunesse Blanche. Constantine P. Cavafy. CP-CavaC, *tr.* by Theoharis Constantine Theoharis

Our divinations, / Mechanisms of angelic thought. One of the Inhabitants of the West. Wallace Stevens. CP-StevW; CP-StevWP

Our Doom to Bloom. Robert Frost. CP-FrosR

Our dreams of a land with vines. Fanny Howe. SP-HoweF *Fr.* Vineyard, The.

Our earth in 1969. Doggerel by a Senior Citizen. W. H. Auden. CP-AudeW

Our efforts are those of men caught in calamity. Trojans. Constantine P. Cavafy. CP-CavaC, *tr.* by Theoharis Constantine Theoharis

Our England is a garden that is full of stately views. Glory of the Garden, The. Rudyard Kipling. CP-KiplR

Our epoch takes a voluptuous satisfaction. Hypocrite Auteur. Archibald MacLeish. CP-MacLA

Our era is dying. Death of Our Era, The. D. H. Lawrence. CP-LawrD

Our Eunuch Dreams. Dylan Thomas. CP-ThomD

Our Euripedes, the human / With his droppings of warm tears. Balaustion's Adventure. Robert Browning. CP-BroR1

Our eyeless bark sails free. Earth, The. Ralph Waldo Emerson. CP-EmerR

Our eyes by day are good enough: only the birds. Robinson Jeffers. CP-JefR3

Our eyes have viewed the burnished vineyards where. Letter to a Friend. Robert Penn Warren. CP-WarrR

Our eyes meet: kookaburra. Delicate Conspiracy, A. Yusef Komunyakaa. CP-KomuY

Our eyes on the hill. Red Pagoda. Yusef Komunyakaa. CP-KomuY

Our Family. Leo Vroman. CP-RicAE

Our Father. Donald Davie. CP-DaviDC

Our Father. James Schuyler. CP-SchuJ

Our father is three months dead. Woodcutting on Lost Mountain. Tess Gallagher. SP-GallT

Our father sleeps. It is the hour when they. Heaven and Earth. Lord Byron. CP-Byron

Our Fathers Also. Rudyard Kipling. CP-KiplR

Our fathers' God! from out whose hand. Centennial Hymn. John Greenleaf Whittier. CP-WhitJ

Our Fathers in a wondrous age. Heritage, The. Rudyard Kipling. CP-KiplR

Our fathers in their books and speech. Orient Wheat. Adrienne Rich. CP-RicAE

Our fathers liked to carry persian beards. Jean Sans Terre Reviews the Fathers. Iwan Goll. CP-WilW2

Our Fathers of Old. Rudyard Kipling. CP-KiplR

Our fathers of this earth. Ostjuden. Primo Levi. CP-LeviP, *tr.* by Ruth Feldman *and* Brian Swann

Our fathers to creed and tradition were tied. Commercial Candour. G. K. Chesterton. CP-ChesG

Our fathers, whose art was Heaven. Statement. John Ciardi. CP-CiarJ

Our favoured wrestler, the Mohawk Indian. My Father and I and Billy Two Rivers. Paul Muldoon. CP-MuldP

Our feet shall tread upon the stars. Eye Hath Not Seen. Christina Georgina Rossetti. CP-RosC3

Our fellow-countrymen in chains! Expostulation. John Greenleaf Whittier. CP-WhitJ

Our fingers played each other like a blue guitar. Breasts. Yusef Komunyakaa. CP-KomuY

Our First House in Sacramento. Raymond Carver. CP-CarvR

Our Flag. E. E. Cummings. CP-CummE

Our flesh that was a battle-ground. Litany of the Dark People, The. Countee Cullen. CP-CullC

Our flowers are numbered. Last People. W. S. Merwin. SP-MerwW

Our forefathers the tortoise and the sea lizard tramped. Modest Sum, A. Dan Pagis. SP-PagiD, *tr. by* Stephen Mitchell

Our Future Lot. Walt Whitman. CP-WhitW

Our gaieties, our luxuries / Our pleasures and our glee. In Stratis Viarum II. Arthur Hugh Clough. SP-ClouA

Our German teacher used to say. Untitled Poem: "Our German teacher used to say." Alan Dugan. CP-DugaA

Our Gloves are stiff with the frozen blood. Angutivaun Taina. Rudyard Kipling. CP-KiplR *Fr.* Second Jungle Book, The.

Our God was to be a breath, and not a postcard. View from Pisgah, The. Howard Nemerov. CP-NemeH

Our God who made two lovers in a garden. Wedding in War-Time, A. G. K. Chesterton. CP-ChesG

Our good knight, Ted, girds his broadsword on. Knight, The. Paul Laurence Dunbar. CP-DunbP

Our good old friend is gone, gone to his rest. Translation of Verses to Lloyd. William Cowper. CP-CowpW

Our grandfathers were strangers and their absurd notions. Seekers, The. Thomas McGrath. SP-McGrT

Our Ground Time Here Will Be Brief. Maxine W. Kumin. SP-KumiM

Our Guardian Angels and Their Children. Nicholas Vachel Lindsay. CP-LindV

Our half-thought thoughts divide in sifted wisps. Train to Dublin. Louis MacNeice. CP-MacNL

Our hammock swung between Americas. Elegy: "Our hammock swung between Americas." Derek Walcott. CP-WalcD

Our Hearts. Kenneth Koch. SP-KochK

Our heaven must be within ourselves / Our home and heaven the work of faith. Christina Georgina Rossetti. CP-RosC2

Our Hells. Carl Sandburg. CP-SandC

Our hero's happy in the play's conclusion. Epilogue: "Our hero's happy in the play's conclusion." Nathaniel Lee. CP-DryJ2 *Fr.* Constantine the Great.

Our hill has made its submission and the green. Homage to Clio. W. H. Auden. CP-AudeW

Our hired girl, she's 'Lizabuth Ann. James Whitcomb Riley. CP-RileJ

Our Hired Girl, when it's bakin'-day. 'Lizabuth-Ann on Bakin'-Day. James Whitcomb Riley. CP-RileJ

Our history is grave noble and tragic. Men. Archibald MacLeish. CP-MacLA

Our Hold on the Planet. Robert Frost. CP-FrosR

Our Home Is in the Rocks. Kenneth Rexroth. CP-RexrK

Our honeymoon. Bridal Piece. Louise Glück. SP-GlucL

Our Honours, and our Commendations be, Merits Make the Man. Robert Herrick. CP-HerrR

Our houses are built on other, straightlined houses, made of marble. Perspective. Yannis Ritsos. SP-RitsY, *tr. by* Kimon Friar

Our houses are one step from the gutter. Plastic curtains. Derek Walcott. CP-WalcD *Fr.* Midsummer.

Our Houshold-gods our Parents be. Primitiæ to Parents, The. Robert Herrick. CP-HerrR

Our Hunting Fathers. W. H. Auden. CP-AudeW

Our iron drum of timbers blazed and sparked. Night Conference, Wood Quay: 6 June 1979. Thomas Kinsella. CP-KinsT

Our Islet out of Helgoland, dismissed. Islet the Dachs. George Meredith. CP-MerG1

Our Jatti, palace wrestler of Mysore. At Forty. A. K. Ramanujan. CP-RamaA

Our journey had advanced. Emily Dickinson. CP-DickE

Our Kind. William Stafford. SP-StafW; SP-StafWW

Our Kind of a Man. James Whitcomb Riley. CP-RileJ

Our King went forth on pilgrimage. King's Pilgrimage, The. Rudyard Kipling. CP-KiplR

Our Lady. Donald Davie. CP-DaviDC

Our Lady Moon still hidden. Memory. Federico García Lorca. CP-GarcF, *tr. by* Jerome Rothenberg *Fr.* Night (Suite for Piano and Poet's Voice).

Our Lady of Ardboe. Paul Muldoon. CP-MuldP

Our Lady of the Sackcloth. Rudyard Kipling. CP-KiplR

Our Lady of the Snows. Rudyard Kipling. CP-KiplR

Our Lady of Wain. G. K. Chesterton. CP-ChesG

Our Lady of Žižkov. Jaroslav Seifert. SP-SeifJ, *tr. by* Ewald Osers

Our Lady went into a strange country. Regina Angelorum. G. K. Chesterton. CP-ChesG

Our Lady's Winter Words. Theodore Roethke. CP-RoetT

Our Land. Langston Hughes. CP-HughL; CP-HughL1

Our Land. Yannis Ritsos. SP-RitsY, *tr. by* Andonis Decavalles

Our Land—our Home!—the common home indeed. Indiana. James Whitcomb Riley. CP-RileJ

Our large hands. Greeting to the Vietnamese Delegates to the U.N. Denise Levertov. SP-LeveDL

Our last connection with the mythic. Planting Trees. John Updike. CP-UpdiJ

Our last free summer we mooned about at odd hours. Chrysalides. Thomas Kinsella. CP-KinsT

Our last morning in that long room. In the Last Few Moments Came the Old German Cleaning Woman. Jane Cooper. CP-CoopJ

Our letters cross by nosing silver. Letter from India. Louis MacNeice. CP-MacNL

Our Life Is Hid with Christ in God. George Herbert. CP-HerbG (Colossians 3:3.) CP-HerbG

Our life is long. Not so, wise Angels say. Christina Georgina Rossetti. CP-RosC2

Our life is two fold: Sleep hath its own world. Dream, The. Lord Byron. CP-Byron

Our Lighthouses. Jones Very. CP-VeryJ

Our little baby fell asleep. Christina Georgina Rossetti. CP-RosC2

Our Little Girl. James Whitcomb Riley. CP-RileJ

Our little Kinsmen—after Rain. Emily Dickinson. CP-DickE

Our little secrets slink away. Emily Dickinson. CP-DickE

Our lives are circumscribed by dust. Han-shan. CP-ColdM, *tr. by* Red Pine

Our lives are Swiss. Emily Dickinson. CP-DickE

Our Lombard country-girls along the coast. Last Confession, A. Dante Gabriel Rossetti. CW-RossD

Our Lord in His Circumcision to His Father. Richard Crashaw. CP-CrasR

Our Lord is set in his great oak throne, Ballad Rosalind. Ezra Pound. CP-PoEar

Our Lord Who did the Ox command. Carol, A: "Our Lord Who did the Ox command." Rudyard Kipling. CP-KiplR

Our lords are to the mountains gane. Hughie Graham. Robert Burns. CP-BurnR

Our love will not come back on fortune's wheel. Obit. Robert Lowell. SP-LoweR

Our man has mown today. Emily Dickinson. SP-DickE

Our marriage book, it. Drill, The. Charles Bukowski. SP-BukC1

Our Martyred Soldiers. Paul Laurence Dunbar. CP-DunbP

Our Master. John Greenleaf Whittier. CP-WhitJ

Our Master lies asleep and is at rest. Mary Magdalene and the Other Mary. Christina Georgina Rossetti. CP-RosC2

Our Meetings. James Laughlin. CP-LaugJ

Our Moral Age. D. H. Lawrence. CP-LawrD

Our mortall parts may wrapt in Seare-cloths lye. Great Spirits Supervive. Robert Herrick. CP-HerrR

Our Mother. Thomas Kinsella. CP-KinsT

Our mother knew our worth. Our Kind. William Stafford. SP-StafW; SP-StafWW

Our Mother Pocahontas. Nicholas Vachel Lindsay. CP-LindV

Our Mothers, lovely women pitiful; / Our sisters, gracious in their life and death. Christina Georgina Rossetti. CP-RosC2

Our mound of earth dug up. Epithalamion: "Our mound of earth dug up." Olga Broumas. SP-BrouO

Our muffled phone & the through. Love Lines. Olga Broumas. SP-BrouO

Our names had to each other been two rumours. Friendship on Visit. Laura Riding Jackson. CP-RidiL

Our Native Sparrows. Jones Very. CP-VeryJ

Our Nature. Rae Armantrout. SP-ArmaA

Our neighbor Laura Foley used to love. Take Care. Heather McHugh. SP-McHuH

Our neighbors at the / beach have got their. Full Life, The. James Laughlin. CP-LaugJ

Our next-to-last word will be one. Rainer Maria Rilke. CP-RilkFr, *tr. by* A. Poulin, Jr. *Fr.* Orchards.

Our Office; An Intimate Glimpse of Vanity Fair—en Famille a Hate Song. Dorothy Parker. CP-ParkD

Our Office Cat. Stevie Smith. CP-SmitS

Our Old Feuillage. Walt Whitman. CP-WhitW

Our Old Friend Dualism. Thomas Hardy. CP-HardT

Our Old Friend Neverfail. James Whitcomb Riley. CP-RileJ

Our Old Men. Yannis Ritsos. SP-RitsY, *tr. by* Martin McKinsey

Our one foreboding was: we might forget. Brief Reunion. Robert Graves. CP-GravR

Our orchestra / is the cat's nuts. Shoot It Jimmy! William Carlos Williams. CP-WilW1

Our Own. James Whitcomb Riley. CP-RileJ

Our Own Home Talent. Dorothy Parker. CP-ParkD

Our own possessions—though our own. Emily Dickinson. CP-DickE

Our Owne Sinnes Unseen. Robert Herrick. CP-HerrR

Our pallid Egypt. Sam el Nesim. Constantine P. Cavafy. CP-CavaC, *tr. by* Theoharis Constantine Theoharis

Our passions are most like to floods and stream[e]s. Sir Walter Ralegh to the Queen. Sir Walter Ralegh. CP-RaleW

Our People. William Stafford. SP-StafWW

Our play's a parallel: the Holy League. Prologue: "Our play's a parallel: the Holy League." Nathaniel Lee. CP-DryJ2 *Fr.* Duke of Guise, The.

Our poor angel how sick. Hounding Mercy. C. K. Williams. CP-WillC

Our portion of fire. Manichaeans, The. Gary Snyder. CP-SnydG

Our Prayer of Thanks. Carl Sandburg. CP-SandC

Our present Teares here (not our present laughter). Teares. Robert Herrick. CP-HerrR

Our Princess married. Forlorn Sea, The. Stevie Smith. CP-SmitS

Our Queer Old World. James Whitcomb Riley. CP-RileJ

Our Respectful Homages to M. Laurent Tailhade. Ezra Pound. CP-PoEar

Our River. John Greenleaf Whittier. CP-WhitJ

Our River Is Dry. Thomas Sheridan. CP-SherT

Our road is no wider than yours. We often fall. Saltimbanques. Rainer Maria Rilke. CP-RilkFr, *tr. by* A. Poulin, Jr.

Our ropes are the roots. Sand Flesh and Sky. Clarence Major. SP-MajoC

Our royal king and queen, God bless. Ben Jonson's Grace before King James. Ben Jonson. CP-JonsB

Our sad coats assemble at the counter. In the M5 Restaurant. Ted Hughes. SP-HughTN

Our sainted great-great. Gallows Etiquette. Charles Simic. SP-SimiC; SP-SimiCE

Our sardine fishermen work at night in the dark of the moon; daylight or moonlight. Purse-Seine, The. Robinson Jeffers. CP-JefR2

Our Self. Robert Graves. CP-GravR

Our set of strollers, wandering up and down. Billet to the Company of Players. Jonathan Swift. CP-SwifJ

Our Shah's counsel is the efflux. Hafiz. CP-EmerR *Fr.* Odes.

Our share of night to bear. Emily Dickinson. CP-DickE

Our shells clacked on the plates. Oysters. Seamus Heaney. SP-HeanSO

Our Ship Comes Home! G. K. Chesterton. CP-ChesG

Our ship (in this easy metaphor I employ). Læstrygonians, The. William Dickey. SP-DickW

Our Singing Strength. Robert Frost. CP-FrosR

Our single purpose was to walk through snow. Polar Exploration. Stephen Spender. CP-SpenS

Our sister sayeth such and such. Nursing Sister, The. Rudyard Kipling. CP-KiplR *Fr.* Naulahka, The.

Our Sister Water. Louis MacNeice. CP-MacNL

Our Soldiers' Graves. Jones Very. CP-VeryJ

Our songs went up and out the chimney. At the Entering of the New Year. Thomas Hardy. CP-HardT

Our souls shall be Leviathans. Red Sea, The. G. K. Chesterton. CP-ChesG

Our Stars Come from Ireland. Wallace Stevens. CP-StevW; CP-StevWP

Our State. John Greenleaf Whittier. CP-WhitJ

Our storm[e] is past, and that storm[e]'s tyrannous rage. Calm[e], The. John Donne. CP-DonnJ; MW-DonnJ

Our Story. William Stafford. SP-StafWW

Our summer's gone. My Life Has Turned to Blue. Maya Angelou. SP-AngeM

Our talk, our books. Club 26. Lorine Niedecker. CP-NiedL

Our talk was of Too Much, of. Zurich, at the Stork. Paul Celan. SP-CelaP, *tr. by* John Felstiner

Our Tears. Rainer Maria Rilke. CP-RilkFr, *tr. by* A. Poulin, Jr.

Our three cats is Maltese cats. Find the Favorite. James Whitcomb Riley. CP-RileJ

Our Times, Virginia, of which you are a doctor. Letter to Virginia Johnson. John Ciardi. CP-CiarJ

Our touching hearts slenderly comprehend. E. E. Cummings. CP-CummE

Our Tree of Opposites. Wyatt Prunty. SP-PrunW

Our trouble. Knowing the Unknown. Denise Levertov. SP-LeveDL

Our twentieth century was going to improve on the others. Century's Decline, The. Wisława Szymborska. SP-SzymW, *tr. by* Stanisław Barańczak *and* Clare Cavanagh

Our Twentieth Wedding Anniversary (Elizabeth). Robert Lowell. SP-LoweR

Our Two Worthies. John Crowe Ransom. SP-RansJ

Our uncrowned kings have no such regal rind. Melongène. Richard Wilbur. CP-WilbR

Our valentine the heart proposed by three. Record, The. Louis Zukofsky. CP-ZukLS

Our vales are sweet with fern and rose. Old Burying-Ground, The. John Greenleaf Whittier. CP-WhitJ

Our voices / are like. Voices. Federico García Lorca. CP-GarcF, *tr. by* Christopher Maurer

Our voices with our hearts we lift. Hymn: "Our voices with our hearts we lift." Jones Very. CP-VeryJ

Our Walk in Yorkshire. Donald Hall. CP-HallD

Our walk was far among the ancient trees. To M. H. William Wordsworth. CP-WorW1; MW-WorW

Our Way Those Days before These Days. William Stafford. SP-StafWW

Our wealth has wasted all away. I Look for the Lord. Christina Georgina Rossetti. CP-RosC3

Our whistling son called his canary Hector. Boy, Cat, Canary. Stephen Spender. CP-SpenS

Our Whole Life. Adrienne Rich. CP-RicAE; SP-RicA1; SP-RicA2

Our Widowed Queen. Christina Georgina Rossetti. CP-RosC3

Our young lady's a huntin gane. Rowin 't in Her Apron, The. Robert Burns. CP-BurnR

Our / YOUR FRIEND CHARLIE pawnshop. Riot: 60's. Maya Angelou. SP-AngeM

Our Youth. John Ashbery. SP-AshbJ

Ours. James Whitcomb Riley. CP-RileJ

Ours are the streets where Bess first met her. Bess. William Stafford. SP-StafWW

Ours is a low, curst, under-swamp land. Connections. William Stafford. SP-StafWW

Ours Is No Wedlock. Robert Graves. CP-GravR

Ours is the ancient story. For Daughters of Magdalen. Countee Cullen. CP-CullC

Ours is the country of Jack Armstrong. Looking at Images Reflected in the Showcase Plate Glass. Clarence Major. SP-MajoC

Ours would be a worldly wisdom, heaven-sent. Paul Muldoon. CP-MuldP *Fr.* Last Poems.

Ourselves we do inter with sweet derision. Emily Dickinson. CP-DickE

Ourselves were wed one summer—dear. Emily Dickinson. CP-DickE

Out. Margaret Atwood. SP-AtwM2

Out. Raymond Carver. CP-CarvR

Out. Robert Creeley. CP-CreeR

Out. Ted Hughes. SP-HughTN

Out, all the way, without. Applause. Charles Olson. CP-OlsoC

Out alone in the winter rain. Thatch, The. Robert Frost. CP-FrosR

Out and in the river is winding. Red River Voyageur, The. John Greenleaf Whittier. CP-WhitJ

Out at Woodruff Place—afar. June at Woodruff. James Whitcomb Riley. CP-RileJ

Out beyond ideas of wrongdoing and rightdoing. Jelaluddin Rumi. SP-Rumi, *tr. by* Coleman Barks

Out door here. Nature. Robert Creeley. SP-CreeR

Out for a walk, after a week in bed. Urban Convalescence, An. James Merrill. SP-MerrJ

Out for stars he. Body Politic. A. R. Ammons. CP-AmmoA

Out from Behind This Mask. Walt Whitman. CP-WhitW

Out from Jerusalem / The king rode with his great. King Solomon and the Ants. John Greenleaf Whittier. CP-WhitJ

Out Here. Robert Creeley. SP-CreeR

Out here on Cottage Grove it matters. The galloping. Pyrography. John Ashbery. SP-AshbJ

Out here there are no hearthstones. Sleep in the Mojave Desert. Sylvia Plath. CP-PlatS

Out, hunchback! / I was born so, mother! Deformed Transformed, The. Lord Byron. CP-Byron

Out in de night a sad bird moans. Memory of Martha, The. Paul Laurence Dunbar. CP-DunbP

Out in It. Maxine W. Kumin. SP-KumiM

Out in the elegy country, summer evenings. Blue Suburban. Howard Nemerov. CP-NemeH

Out in the green sun-dancing cane a mad half-Spaniard. Fugitive. Thomas Merton. CP-MertT

Out in the harbor breaths of smoke. Mercy. Olga Broumas. SP-BrouO

Out in the Lane I Pause. Philip Larkin. CP-LarkP

Out in the late amber afternoon. In Shadow. Hart Crane. CP-CranH

Out in the morning. Old Times. Ivor Gurney. SP-GurnI

Out in the Pasture. James Laughlin. CP-LaugJ

Out in the rain a world is growing green. Easter Monday. Christina Georgina Rossetti. CP-RosC2

Out in the sky, no one sleeps. No one, no one. Sleepless City. Federico García Lorca. CP-GarcF, *tr. by* Greg Simon *and* Steven F. White

Out in the sky the great dark clouds are massing. Ships That Pass in the Night. Paul Laurence Dunbar. CP-DunbP

Out in the soundless / World that the window. Anxious View of a Tree. Hayden Carruth. CP-CarHS

Out in this desert we are testing bombs. Trying to Talk with a Man. Adrienne Rich. SP-RicA1; SP-RicA2

Out Is Out. Ogden Nash. CP-NashO

Out mountainward, I explained I've already. Schooling. A. R. Ammons. CP-AmmoA

Out o' the wilderness, dusty an' dry. Columns. Rudyard Kipling. CP-KiplR

Out of a bellicose fore-time, thundering. River Profile. W. H. Auden. CP-AudeW

Out of a bow-windowed, mingy, doleful. Dejection: A Footnote. Amy Clampitt. CP-ClamA

Out of a Clear Sky. Miller Williams. CP-WillM

Out of a crowd he steps. In a Dream 1. David Ignatow. SP-IgnaD

Out of a dark into the dark she leaped. All the Beautiful Are Blameless. James Wright. CP-WrigJ

Out of a distant past this tableau sticks. Scene from Life. Robert Stock. SP-StocR

Out of a fired ship, which, by no way. Burnt Ship, A. John Donne. CP-DonnJ; MW-DonnJ

Out of a gothic North, the pallid children. Good-Bye to the Mezzogiorno. W. H. Auden. CP-AudeW

Out of a government grant to poets, I paid. Economics. Mona Van Duyn. SP-VanDM

Out of a sealed window. In Another Town. Miller Williams. CP-WillM

Out of a supermetamathical subpreincestures. E. E. Cummings. CP-CummE

Out of a thousand ladies I saw one. Petrarch. CP-Petra, tr. by J. G. Nichols

Out of beaten gold, just. In Front of a Candle. Paul Celan. SP-CelaP, tr. by John Felstiner

Out of Bounds. Walter De la Mare. CP-DeLaW

Out of burlap sacks, out of bearing butter. They Feed They Lion. Philip Levine. SP-LeviP

Out of Catullus. Ausonius. CP-CrasR

Out of doors the season dies, a fountain. Museum. Thomas Kinsella. CP-KinsT

Out of East Anglia. Donald Davie. CP-DaviDC

Out of Egypt. Mary's Song. Anne Sexton. CP-SextA

Out of Euphormio. Richard Crashaw. CP-CrasR

Out of every hundred people. Word on Statistics, A. Wisława Szymborska. SP-SzymWM, tr. by Joanna Trzeciak

Out of Grotius his Tragedy of Christes Sufferinges. Richard Crashaw. CP-CrasR

Out of her womb of pain my mother spat me. Story Books on a Kitchen Table. Audre Lorde. SP-LordA Fr. Story Books on a Kitchen Table.

Out of him that I loved. Our Stars Come from Ireland. Wallace Stevens. CP-StevW; CP-StevWP

Out of Honolulu. Heading for Nandi. John Updike. CP-UpdiJ

Out of Horace. Horace. CP-CrasR Fr. Odes.

Out of Line. Dan Pagis. SP-PagiD, tr. by Stephen Mitchell

Out of love, / No regrets. No Regrets. Langston Hughes. CP-HughL; CP-HughL3

Out of Martiall. Martial. CP-CrasR

Out of May's Shows Selected. Walt Whitman. CP-WhitW

Out of midsummer's blazing most not night. E. E. Cummings. CP-CummE

Out of Mind. Olga Broumas. SP-BrouO

Out of mist, God's. Interjection #6: What You Sometimes Feel on Your Face at Night. Robert Penn Warren. CP-WarrR

Out of Mobile I saw a rusty [or '60] Ford. Plain. Miller Williams. CP-WillM

Out of more find than seeks. E. E. Cummings. CP-CummE

Out of my flesh that hungers. On a Night of the Full Moon. Audre Lorde. SP-LordA

Out of my heart, one day, I wrote a song. Misapprehension. Paul Laurence Dunbar. CP-DunbP

Out of my heart, one treach'rous winter's day. Love and Grief. Paul Laurence Dunbar. CP-DunbP

Out of my own great woe. Last Translation, The. Elizabeth Barrett Browning. CP-BroEB

Out of my poverty. Conversation by the Body's Light. Jane Cooper. CP-CoopJ

Out of My Soul's Depth. Thomas Campion. CP-CampT

Out of Nazareth. James Whitcomb Riley. CP-RileJ

Out of night's almosT Floats a colour(in). E. E. Cummings. CP-CummE

Out of one's birth. Horoscope. James Vincent Cunningham. CP-CunnJ

Out of our own mouths we are sentenced. Last Journal. Charles Wright. SP-WrigC

Out of Petronius. Petronius Arbiter. CP-CrasR, tr. by Richard Crashaw

Out of poverty. White. Charles Simic. SP-SimiC

Out of poverty / to begin. Song, the Winds of Downhill. George Oppen. CP-OppGN

Out of Ptolemy's principle. Neatness Is All. Kenneth Rexroth. CP-RexrK

Out of Reach. James Whitcomb Riley. CP-RileJ

Out of shape, / my legs ache. Walk, The. James Schuyler. CP-SchuJ

Out of Sight. Robert Creeley. CP-CreeR

Out of Sight in the Direction of My Body. Paul Éluard. CP-BeckS

Out of sight? What of that? Emily Dickinson. CP-DickE

Out of silence walks delight. Delight. Robert Penn Warren. CP-WarrR

Out of Sleep Awakened. Archibald MacLeish. CP-MacLA

Out of the bigg / est the knownun. E. E. Cummings. CP-CummE

Out of the black mouth of the big king. Out. Raymond Carver. CP-CarvR

Out of the Blue. Charles Baudelaire. CP-BaudC, tr. by Walter Martin

Out of the Blue. Charles Bukowski. SP-BukC

Out of the blue, in plaster from wrist to bicep. Strato in Plaster. James Merrill. SP-MerrJ

Out of the bone landscape. Figure. Josephine Jacobsen. CP-JacoJ

Out of the bosom of the Air. Snow-Flakes. Henry Wadsworth Longfellow. SP-LongH

Out of the church she followed [or follow'd] them. Maude Clare. Christina Georgina Rossetti. CP-RosC1

Out of the churned aureoles. Marine Surface, Low Overcast. Amy Clampitt. CP-ClamA

Out of the Cradle Endlessly Rocking. Walt Whitman. CP-WhitW

Out of the Dark and the Dearth. James Whitcomb Riley. CP-RileJ

Out of the darkness, fretted sometimes in its sleeping. Blueness. D. H. Lawrence. CP-LawrD

Out of the Deep. Christina Georgina Rossetti. CP-RosC3

Out of the Depths I Called to Thee. Charles Baudelaire. CP-BaudC, tr. by Walter Martin

Out of the dust of dreams. Fairies. Langston Hughes. CP-HughL

Out of the earth beneath the water. Mud Turtle, The. Howard Nemerov. CP-NemeH

Out of the East, and out of the West, no man understands me. Hafiz. CP-EmerR Fr. Odes.

Out of the east window a storm. Wednesday of Holy Week, 1940. Kenneth Rexroth. CP-RexrK

Out of the filing cabinet of true steel. Crucifix in the Filing Cabinet, The. Karl Shapiro. SP-ShapK

Out of the fire. Pool. Carl Sandburg. CP-SandC

Out of the fire out of the mouth. Stevens Song. Charles Olson. SP-OlsoC Fr. Maximus Poems, The.

Out of the first warmth of spring. Celle Qui Fût Héaulmiette. Wallace Stevens. CP-StevW; CP-StevWP

Out of the garden. Hayden Carruth. CP-CarHS Fr. Clay Hill Anthology, The.

Out of the Greeke Cupid's Cryer. Moschus. CP-CrasR, tr. by Richard Crashaw

Out of the hitherwhere into the YON. James Whitcomb Riley. CP-RileJ

Out of the imprecise, the murk. Bayou Afternoon. Amy Clampitt. CP-ClamA

Out of the incorruptible green of the camphor tree. On the Llobregat. Eugenio Montale. CP-MontE, tr. by Jonathan Galassi

Out of the Italian. Giovanni Giambattista. CP-CrasR, tr. by Richard Crashaw

Out of the Italian. Ammianus Marcellinus. CP-CrasR

Out of the Italian; a Song. Richard Crashaw. CP-CrasR

Out of the lie of no. E. E. Cummings. CP-CummE

Out of the light of Heaven the flower. Charles Olson. SP-OlsoC Fr. Maximus Poems, The.

Out of the little chapel I burst. Christmas-Eve. Robert Browning. CP-BroR1

Out of the living word. Book of Kells, The. Howard Nemerov. CP-NemeH

Out of the mid-wood's twilight. In the Forest. Oscar Wilde. CP-WildO

Out of the mountain of his soul comes. E. E. Cummings. CP-CummE

Out of the mud two strangers came. Two Tramps in Mud Time. Robert Frost. CP-FrosR

Out of the murk of heaviest clouds. Spain, 1873–74. Walt Whitman. CP-WhitW

Out of the overhanging gray mist. Xenia ("Out of the overhanging gray mist"). Ezra Pound. CP-PoEar

Out of the pants which cover me. E. E. Cummings. CP-CummE

Out of the past there rises a week. Change, The. Thomas Hardy. CP-HardT

Out of the Picture. Louis MacNeice. CP-MacNL

Out of the Rainbow End. Carl Sandburg. CP-SandC

Out of the Rolling Ocean the Crowd. Walt Whitman. CP-WhitW

"Out of the Rolling Ocean, the Crowd . . ." Robert Bly. SP-BlyR

Out of the Sea, Early. May Swenson. SP-SwenM

Out of the seagull cries and wind. To Liberty. Hart Crane. CP-CranH

Out of the shut cell of that solitude there is. Something: a Direction. Charles Tomlinson. SP-TomlC Fr. Antecedents.

Out of the Sighs. Dylan Thomas. CP-ThomD

Out of the small domestic jungle. Junction, on a Warm Afternoon, The. Howard Nemerov. CP-NemeH

Out of the sump rise the marigolds. Marengo. Mary Oliver. SP-OlivM

Out of the sun and the dispersing stars. Concert, The. Robert Duncan. SP-DuncR Fr. Passages.

Out of the sunshine and out of the heat. Dove, The. Paul Laurence Dunbar. CP-DunbP

Out of the table endlessly rocking. Just Friends. Robert Creeley. CP-CreeR

Out of the testimony of such relcutant lips, out of the oaths and mouths. Hogh Conspiratorial Persons. Carl Sandburg. CP-SandC

Out of the tomb, we bring Badroulbadour. Worms at Heaven's Gate, The. Wallace Stevens. CP-StevW; CP-StevWP

Out of the water call. Logbook of Judgments. Jay Wright. SP-WrigJ

Out of the world he must, who once comes in. None Free from Fault. Robert Herrick. CP-HerrR

Out of the world of blood and snatters. Salmon of Knowledge, The. Paul Muldoon. CP-MuldP

Out of their loneliness for each other. Spirit of Place: Great Blue Heron. William Stafford. SP-StafWW

Out of this oubliette between the mountains. Misery. D. H. Lawrence. CP-

LawrD

Out of those hallways. March, A. Denise Levertov. SP-LeveDP

Out of Three or Four People in a Room. Yehuda Amichai. SP-AmicYL, *tr.* by Benjamin Harshav *and* Barbara Harshav

Out of Time. Stevie Smith. CP-SmitS

Out of Time, Out of Tune. Robert Herrick. CP-HerrR

Out of Virgil, in the Praise of the Spring. Virgil. CP-CrasR *Fr.* Georgics.

Out of what secret English summer evening. To the Nightingale. Jorge Luis Borges. SP-BorgJ, *tr.* by Alastair Reid

Out of White Lips. Carl Sandburg. CP-SandC

Out of Work. Langston Hughes. CP-HughL; CP-HughL2

Out of your whole life give but a moment! Now. Robert Browning. SP-BroR

Out on the high "bird islands," Ciboux and Hertford. Cape Breton. Elizabeth Bishop. CP-BishE

Out on the lawn I lie in bed. Summer Night, A. W. H. Auden. CP-AudeW

Out on the prairie my heart. Song with Reflections. Federico García Lorca. CP-GarcF, *tr.* by Jerome Rothenberg *Fr.* Moments of Song.

Out on the Strait the water is whitecapping. For Tess. Raymond Carver. CP-CarvR

Out on the town having. I Like to Think of You. James Laughlin. CP-LaugJ

"Out, Out—." Robert Frost. CP-FrosR

Out, out, away! my blood boils up! Hungarian Horse-Herd, The. Karl Beck. CP-MerG2

Out, out, / push some more, lady. He'll Come Out for Sure. Dan Pagis. SP-PagiD, *tr.* by Stephen Mitchell

Out over the Forth, I look to the North. I Look to the North. Robert Burns. CP-BurnR

Out picking cowslips on the meadows of the sea. Calentures. Robert Stock. SP-StocR

Out Picking up Corn. Robert Bly. SP-BlyR

Out shines again the glorious round sun. Near Eclipse, The. Robert Graves. CP-GravR

Out—so this means you render them, ten sestertia, Silo. Catullus. *See* Either give me my hundred pounds back, Silo

Out somewhere in the middle of the crickets. School of Summer, The. Randall Jarrell. CP-JarrR

Out the same picture window the pine bow. Clouds, The. Charles Olson. CP-OlsoC

Out the window. Arroyo. Robert Creeley. SP-CreeR

Out the window, the cow out the window. Simplicity of the Unknown Past, The. Kenneth Koch. SP-KochK

Out there in the fighting. What the Old Women Say. Archibald MacLeish. CP-MacLA

Out there, out there beyond the air. Spy, The. Howard Nemerov. CP-NemeH

Out there. The mind of the river. Study of History. Adrienne Rich. CP-RicAE; SP-RicA2

Out there, / the scene that won't compare. Made by Hand. Eleanor Wilner. SP-WilnE

Out There There Be Dragons. Yusef Komunyakaa. CP-KomuY

Out there, we've walked quite friendly up to Death. Next War, The. Wilfred Owen. CP-OwenW

Out through the fields and the woods. Reluctance. Robert Frost. CP-FrosR

Out through the frosty archipelago. Voyage from Stockholm to Take Advantage of Lower Prices on the Finnish Island of Åland. James Tate. SP-TateJ

Out through the neighborhood with nothing more. Downtown Bus, The. Wyatt Prunty. SP-PrunW

Out to Old Aunt Mary's. James Whitcomb Riley. CP-RileJ

Out Walking. Adam Zagajewski. SP-ZagaA, *tr.* by Clare Cavanagh

Out walking along the river. Groom Falconer. Norman Dubie. CP-DubiN

Out walking in the frozen swamp one gray [*or* grey] day. Wood-Pile, The. Robert Frost. CP-FrosR

Out window roof's slope. Time ("Out window roof's slope"). Robert Creeley. SP-CreeR

Out Window: Taylor's Mistake. Robert Creeley. SP-CreeR

Out-worn heart, in a time out-worn. Into the Twilight. William Butler Yeats. CP-YeatW

Out-worn Sappho, An. James Whitcomb Riley. CP-RileJ

Outbound, your bark awaits you. Were I one. Godspeed. John Greenleaf Whittier. CP-WhitJ

Outcome of Mr. Buck's Superstition, The. Ogden Nash. CP-NashO

Outcrop stone is miserly. Still Life. Ted Hughes. SP-HughTN

Outcry. Heather McHugh.

Outdoor Concert, The. Thom Gunn. CP-GunnT

Outdoor Gallery, An. Thomas Kinsella. CP-KinsT

Outdoor Reception, An. John Greenleaf Whittier. CP-WhitJ

Outer and Inner. George Meredith. CP-MerG1

Outer Banks, The. Muriel Rukeyser. CP-RukeM

Outer Bar, The. Amy Clampitt. CP-ClamA

Outer—from the Inner, The. Emily Dickinson. CP-DickE

Outing with a Woman. Yehuda Amichai. SP-AmicYL, *tr.* by Benjamin Harshav *and* Barbara Harshav

Outlandish Agon. Mona Van Duyn. SP-VanDM

Outlandish as a circus, the ravaged face. Ravaged Face, The. Sylvia Plath. CP-PlatS

Outlaw, The. G. K. Chesterton. CP-ChesG

Outlaw, The. Seamus Heaney. SP-HeanSO

Outlaw, The. David Ignatow. SP-IgnaD

Outlaw of the Lowest Planet, The. Kenneth Patchen. CP-PatcK

Outlaws. Robert Graves. CP-GravR

Outlaws, The. Rudyard Kipling. CP-KiplR

Outline of History. G. K. Chesterton. CP-ChesG

Outlines for a Tomb. Walt Whitman. CP-WhitW

Outlivers (Harriet and Elizabeth). Robert Lowell. SP-LoweR

Outlook gives an interview, The. Ballade pour la Grosse Lulu. T. S. Eliot. SP-ElioT

Outpost. Muriel Rukeyser. CP-RukeM

Outside. Robert Creeley. SP-CreeR

Outside. William Stafford. SP-StafWW

Outside an Air Base, California. Dan Pagis. SP-PagiD, *tr.* by Stephen Mitchell

Outside comes in, The. Xerox the Spirit and Be Well. Andrei Codrescu. SP-CodrA

Outside Fargo, North Dakota. James Wright. CP-WrigJ

Outside his library window he could see. Montaigne. W. H. Auden. CP-AudeW

Outside in the street I hear. Family Reunion. Sylvia Plath. CP-PlatS

Outside it is cold. Inside. Winter for an Untenable Situation. Alan Dugan. CP-DugaA

Outside memory worship never dies. Sappho's Gymnasium. Olga Broumas. SP-BrouO

Outside my mother's town in Avellino. Manocalzata (Gloved Hand). John Ciardi. CP-CiarJ

Outside of the movies. Revolt. Kenneth Rexroth. CP-RexrK

Outside of Wedlock. Wallace Stevens. CP-StevWP

Outside snow decays the country. Fanny Howe. SP-HoweF *Fr.* Joy Had I Known.

Outside the Casement. Thomas Hardy. CP-HardT

Outside the Crowd. George Meredith. CP-MerG2

Outside the Diner. Thom Gunn. CP-GunnT

Outside, the freezing desert night. Tent, The. Jelaluddin Rumi. SP-Rumi, *tr.* by Coleman Barks

Outside the great clanging cathedrals of rust and smoke. Poem Written under an Archway in a Discontinued Railroad Station, Fargo, North Dakota, A. James Wright. CP-WrigJ

Outside, the heirs of purity pick by. Violet and Jasper. Richard Wilbur. CP-WilbR

Outside the Hospital. Wallace Stevens. CP-StevWP

Outside the hotel window, unenlightened pigeons. Jain Bird Hospital in Delhi, The. William Meredith. SP-MereW

Outside the House. Le Singe qui swing. Stevie Smith. CP-SmitS

Outside the house an ash-tree hung its terrible whips. Discord in Childhood. D. H. Lawrence. CP-LawrD

Outside, the night is glowing. Second Language. Tess Gallagher. SP-GallT

Outside the porthole life, or what is. Flight. George Oppen. CP-OppGN

Outside, the rain, pinafore of gray water, dresses the town. Child Beater. Ai. SP-Ai

Outside the rain upon the street. Musical. A. Paul Laurence Dunbar. CP-DunbP

Outside the river entrance, between the Potomac. Dahlia Gardens, The. Amy Clampitt. CP-ClamA

Outside the vineyard is a caravan. Graffiti from the Gare Saint-Manqué. Marilyn Hacker. SP-HackM

Outside the window past the two hills there is the city. City of the Olesha Fruit, The. Norman Dubie. CP-DubiN

Outside, to corpse and fish, means atmosphere. Inside-Outside Game, The. Thom Gunn. CP-GunnT

Outside, upon warm air. Death of the Infanta, The. Charles Tomlinson. CP-TomlC

Outskirts, The. Walter De la Mare. CP-DeLaW

Outsong in the Jungle. Rudyard Kipling. CP-KiplR *Fr.* Second Jungle Book, The.

Outward Conquests Not Enough. Jones Very. CP-VeryJ

Ouzo for Robin. James Merrill. SP-MerrJ

Ouzo Unclouded. Robert Graves. CP-GravR

Oval Portrait: Jessie Wilkie, The. Kathleen Jessie Raine. SP-RainK

Oval the golden moon. Kathleen Jessie Raine. SP-RainK

Oval the sweep, the motion horizontal. On an Early Cycladic Harpist (2600–2500 B.C.) in the J. Paul Getty Museum. Helen Pinkerton. CP-PinkH

Oven Bird, The. Robert Frost. CP-FrosR

Over. Rae Armantrout. SP-ArmaA

Over all this / grief of yours: no. Sluice, The. Paul Celan. SP-CelaP, *tr. by* John Felstiner

Over America. Adam Zagajewski. SP-ZagaA, *tr. by* Renata Gorczynski

Over an ash-fawn beach fronting a sea which keeps. Fiascherino. Charles Tomlinson. CP-TomlC; SP-TomlC

Over and around grass banked and packed short and holding back. Messages. James Dickey. CP-DickJ

Over and back. At Ithaca. "H. D." CP-DoolH

Over and over. Hayden Carruth. CP-CarHS *Fr.* Clay Hill Anthology, The.

Over and over I have heard. Portrait. Edna St. Vincent Millay. CP-MillE

Over and over, like a Tune. Emily Dickinson. CP-DickE

Over and over something would remain. For Proust. James Merrill. SP-MerrJ

Over and over thru the dull material world the call is made. Night Gleam. Allen Ginsberg. CP-GinsA; SP-GinsA

Over and through the burial chant. Interpolation Sounds. Walt Whitman. CP-WhitW

Over back where they speak of life as staying. Investment, The. Robert Frost. CP-FrosR

Over Brooklyn Bridge. Charles Tomlinson. CP-TomlC; SP-TomlC

Over Denver Again. Allen Ginsberg. CP-GinsA

Over-dew / Became a dread name for Cynthia. House of Over-Dew, The. Stevie Smith. CP-SmitS

Over-elaboration of scaffolding. Resolution of Hesitancies. Alan Dugan. CP-DugaA

Over Elizabeth Bridge: a Circumvention. Charles Tomlinson. CP-TomlC

Over forty years, and I haven't left your weather. First Flight. Mona Van Duyn. SP-VanDM

Over-Heart, The. John Greenleaf Whittier. CP-WhitJ

Over her flesh the skin. Dance of the Skin, The. James Laughlin. CP-LaugJ

Over in Montana. William Stafford. SP-StafWW

Over its cliffs. Little Rapids, The. May Swenson. SP-SwenM

Over Kansas. Allen Ginsberg. CP-GinsA

Over knowledge of death. I Have Increased Power. Allen Ginsberg. CP-GinsA

Over Laramie. Allen Ginsberg. CP-GinsA

Over low, rolling hills patch-worked by live oak. Destination Zero. Sam Hamill. SP-HamiS

Over meadows of Brittany, the lark. Another Dimension. Robert Penn Warren. CP-WarrR

Over men's graves we lightly tread! Christ's Final Victory. Jones Very. CP-VeryJ

Over my bed / My father stood. Fathers and Sons. Donald Hall. CP-HallD

Over my desk Georgia O'Keeffe says. Calling, A. Maxine W. Kumin. SP-KumiM

Over my head, I see the bronze butterfly. Lying in a Hammock at William Duffy's Farm in Pine Island, Minnesota. James Wright. CP-WrigJ

Over my paws. Moon Will Restore the Virginity of My Sister, The. Josephine Jacobsen. CP-JacoJ

Over night it had emerged. Moth in the Schoolroom. May Sarton. SP-SartM

Over our heads, if we but knew. At a Party. Louise Bogan. CP-BogaL

Over our scattered tents by night. Psalm: People Power at the Die-in. Denise Levertov. SP-LeveDL

Over Paris the moon's. Colors. Federico García Lorca. CP-GarcF, *tr. by* Jerome Rothenberg *Fr.* Sublunar Cantos.

Over Peoria we lost the sun. Homage to Emerson, on Night Flight to New York. Robert Penn Warren. CP-WarrR

Over silent waters / day descending. Finis. E. E. Cummings. CP-CummE

Over Sir John's Hill. Dylan Thomas. CP-ThomD

Over stone walls and barns. Going Gone. Anne Sexton. CP-SextA

Over sunny earth, meadow. Steps, The. Josephine Jacobsen. CP-JacoJ

Over the ankles in snow and numb past pain. Secret Sharer, The. Thom Gunn. CP-GunnT

Over the Arafura sea, the China sea. For John Chappell. Gary Snyder. CP-SnydG

Over the ball of it. Pisgah-Sights. I. Robert Browning. CP-BroR2

Over the Carnage Rose Prophetic a Voice. Walt Whitman. CP-WhitW

Over the chessboard now. Artificial Intelligence. Adrienne Rich. CP-RicAE; SP-RicA2

Over the course of time I think your smile. Petrarch. CP-Petra, *tr. by* J. G. Nichols

Over the dead line we have called to you. To a Dead Man. Carl Sandburg. CP-SandC

Over the Door at the Entrance into the Apollo. Ben Jonson. CP-JonsB

Over the dumb Campagna-sea. View across the Roman Campagna. Elizabeth Barrett Browning. CP-BroEB

Over the edge of the purple down. City of Sleep, The. Rudyard Kipling. CP-KiplR

Over the Eyes of Gladness. James Whitcomb Riley. CP-RileJ

Over the fence. Emily Dickinson. CP-DickE

Over the ferry, and over the ferry. Song: "Over the ferry, and over the ferry." George Meredith. CP-MerG2

Over the flat slope of St. Eloi. Poem: Abbreviated from the Conversation of Mr. T. E. H. Ezra Pound. CP-PoEar

Over the florid capitals. Randall Jarrell. CP-JarrR

Over the flowery, sharp pasture's edge. Flowers by the Sea. William Carlos Williams. CP-WilW1

Over the grasses Love had spread his net. Petrarch. CP-Petra, *tr. by* J. G. Nichols

Over the gray, massed blunder of her face. Woman Waiting. Mona Van Duyn. SP-VanDM

Over the great inland. White. Amy Clampitt. CP-ClamA

Over the ground of slate and light gravel. Sanctuary, The. Howard Nemerov. CP-NemeH

Over the half-finished houses. Roofwalker, The. Adrienne Rich. CP-RicAE; SP-RicA1; SP-RicA2

Over the heady wine. Symposium, The. James Vincent Cunningham. CP-CunnJ

Over the heart of the west, the Taos desert, Red Wolf, The. D. H. Lawrence. CP-LawrD

Over the hill and over the dale. Dawlish Fair. John Keats. CP-KeatJ

Over the hill came horsemen, horsemen whistling. Stared Story, A. William Stafford. SP-StafWW

Over the Hills. Paul Laurence Dunbar. CP-DunbP

Over the Hills. George Meredith. CP-MerG2

Over the Hills. James Schuyler. CP-SchuJ

Over the houses and into the sky. Street Songs. Wallace Stevens. CP-StevWP

Over the landscape walk the mailboxes disguised as whores. Russia or The Weakness of Photography. Andrei Codrescu. SP-CodrA

Over the local stations, one by one. Beyond the Snow Belt. Mary Oliver. SP-OlivM

Over the Medes and light Sabaeans reigns [*or* raignes]. Claudian. CP-RaleW *Fr.* Against Eutropius.

Over the Mountains. William Stafford. SP-StafWW

Over the North Jetty. William Stafford. SP-StafWW

Over the phone a good friend asks. Theodore Weiss. SP-WeisT *Fr.* Polish Question, The.

Over the pianissimo / of gold. Solitaire. Federico García Lorca. CP-GarcF, *tr. by* Jerome Rothenberg *Fr.* Six Songs at Nightfall.

Over the river / mosquitoes. Unopened Song. Federico García Lorca. CP-GarcF, *tr. by* Jerome Rothenberg *Fr.* Moments of Song.

Over the rounded sides of the Rockies, the aspens of autumn. Autumn at Taos. D. H. Lawrence. CP-LawrD

Over the snow at night. Winter Lightning, The. Howard Nemerov. CP-NemeH

Over the stone wall her hand comes. Some with Wings, Some with Manes. Tess Gallagher. SP-GallT

Over the threshold of his pleasant home. Banished from Massachusetts. John Greenleaf Whittier. CP-WhitJ

Over the water. Thistledown Night. Federico García Lorca. CP-GarcF, *tr. by* Jerome Rothenberg *Fr.* Summer Hours.

Over the water, where I lie alive. Song, from "Mr. Amazeen on the River." Muriel Rukeyser. CP-RukeM

Over the Western sea hither from Niphon come. Broadway Pageant, A. Walt Whitman. CP-WhitW

Over there the old shoe-shine boy. Sightseeing Tour. Hans Magnus Enzensberger. SP-EnzeH

Over These Brooks. Sir Philip Sidney. SP-SidnP *Fr.* Arcadia.

Over these brooks trusting to ease mine eyes. Over These Brooks. Sir Philip Sidney. SP-SidnP *Fr.* Arcadia.

Over Timberline. Josephine Jacobsen. CP-JacoJ

Over 2000 Illustrations and a Complete Concordance. Elizabeth Bishop. CP-BishE

Over us if(as what dusk becomes). E. E. Cummings. CP-CummE

Over Vinegar Hill somehow the sky. Tryst on Vinegar Hill. Robert Penn Warren. CP-WarrR

Over wide awake houses. Confusion ("Over wide awake houses"). Federico García Lorca. CP-GarcF, *tr. by* Jerome Rothenberg *Fr.* Fairs.

Over your body the clouds go. Gulliver. Sylvia Plath. CP-PlatS

Over your mother's grave. Semblance, A. David Ignatow. SP-IgnaD

Overall, mover of the unnumbered. O'Ryan. Charles Olson. CP-OlsoC

Overboard. May Swenson. SP-SwenM

Overcast, Hot. James Schuyler. CP-SchuJ

Overcast morning in July, An. A Taste of ashes wafts throught the air. Phrases ("Overcast morning in July, An. A Taste of ashes wafts throught the air"). Arthur Rimbaud. CP-RimbA, *tr. by* Martin Sorrell

Overcoat, The. Charles Simic. SP-SimiCE

Overcome—O bitter sweetness. From the 'Antigone.' Sophocles. CP-YeatW *Fr.* Antigone.

Overcome with frustration I sing a few songs. Song to Begin *Rohatsu*. Philip Whalen. SP-WhalP

Overfaithful sword returns the user, The. Pro-Consuls, The. Rudyard Kipling. CP-KiplR

Overflowing with your dream. Rainer Maria Rilke. CP-RilkFr, *tr.* by A. Poulin, Jr. *Fr.* Roses, The.

Overhang of grass and seedling birch. Seamus Heaney. SP-HeanSO *Fr.* Squarings.

Overhead Mirrors. Charles Bukowski. SP-BukC3

Overheard. Denise Levertov. SP-LeveDP

(Overheard at the) Maykovsky Station. Michael Palmer. SP-PalmM

Overhearing. Rae Armantrout. SP-ArmaA

Overland Mail, The. Rudyard Kipling. CP-KiplR

Overland to the Islands. Denise Levertov. SP-LeveDS

Overlooking the River Stour. Thomas Hardy. CP-HardT

Overnight, very. Mushrooms. Sylvia Plath. CP-PlatS

Overnights. Alice Walker. CP-WalkA

Overpopulation. Lawrence Ferlinghetti. SP-FerlL

Overpopulation, overpopulation / Give me 3 acres of land. Allen Ginsberg. SP-GinsA *Fr.* These States: into L.A.

Overruled. John Greenleaf Whittier. CP-WhitJ

Overseas Prayer. John Berryman. CP-BerrJ

Oversifted fine white flour / with little crust. Boer War Bread Strike. James Schuyler. CP-SchuJ

Overtakelessness of those, The. Emily Dickinson. CP-DickE

Overtaken by Fog while Climbing. Gregory Orr. SP-OrrG

Overthrow, An. John Ciardi. CP-CiarJ

Overthrow of One o'Clock at Night, The. Muriel Rukeyser. CP-RukeM

Overture. Thomas Kinsella. CP-KinsT

Overture. A shutter opens. Down. Trees Listening to Bach. James Merrill. SP-MerrJ

Overture: The Hostages. Randall Jarrell. CP-JarrR

Overture to a Dance of Locomotives. William Carlos Williams. CP-WilW1

Overview. Federico García Lorca. CP-GarcF, *tr.* by Jerome Rothenberg *Fr.* In the Forest of Clocks.

Overworld, The. Kenneth Patchen. CP-PatcK

Ovid in Love. Ovid. CP-MahoD *Fr.* Amores.

Ovid in the Third Reich. Geoffrey Hill. CP-HillG

Ovid in Tomis. Derek Mahon. CP-MahoD

Ovid, Old Buddy, I Would Discourse with You a While. Hayden Carruth. CP-CarHS

Ovidian Elegiac Metre, The. Samuel Taylor Coleridge. CP-ColeS

Owen Aherne and His Dancers. William Butler Yeats. CP-YeatW

Owen's praise demands my song. Triumphs of Owen, The. Thomas Gray. CP-GrayT

Owl. Sylvia Plath. CP-PlatS

Owl, An. Gabriela Mistral. SP-MistG, *tr.* by Maria Giachetti [*or* Jacketti]

Owl, The. János Hegedüs. CP-LogaJ, *tr.* by John Logan

Owl, The. Walter De la Mare. CP-DeLaW

Owl, The. W. S. Merwin. SP-MerwW

Owl, The. Arthur Sze. SP-SzeA

Owl, The. Robert Penn Warren. CP-WarrR

Owl and Phoenix. Chuang Tzu. CP-MertT

Owl, and wagtail / and huo-hu, the fire-fox. Canto 112, From: "Owl, and wagtail / and huo-hu, the fire-fox." Ezra Pound. CP-PoCan *Fr.* Cantos.

Owl-car clatters along, dogged by the echo, The. Old Woman. Carl Sandburg. CP-SandC

Owl hoots my dead friend's name, An. Cenotaph. Yusef Komunyakaa. CP-KomuY

Owl in the Sarcophagus, The. Wallace Stevens. CP-StevW; CP-StevWP

Owl King, The. James Dickey. CP-DickJ

Owl of Minerva, The. Donald Davie. CP-DaviDC

Owl of Minerva, The. James Laughlin. CP-LaugJ

Owl sound wandered along the road with me, An. Malheur before Dawn. William Stafford. SP-StafWW

Owl winks in the shadows, An. Mother Earth: Her Whales. Gary Snyder. CP-SnydG

Owl[e] is abroad, the bat, and the toad, The. Charm[e]. Ben Jonson. CP-JonsB *Fr.* Masque of Queens, The.

Owls. Charles Baudelaire. CP-BaudC, *tr.* by Walter Martin

Owl's Bedtime Story, The. Randall Jarrell. CP-JarrR

Owl's Clover. Wallace Stevens. CP-StevWP

Owls sit perched in rows to wait, The. Owls. Charles Baudelaire. CP-BaudC, *tr.* by Walter Martin

Owl's Song. Ted Hughes. SP-HughTN

Owls that cry in the night. Hoot Owls. Richard Eberhart. CP-EberR

Owls–they whinny down the night. Outlaws. Robert Graves. CP-GravR

Owl's torches gutter. Chaos clouds the globe, The. Goats and Monkeys. Derek Walcott. CP-WalcD

Own mother dear, / We all rejoicing here. Valentine, 1877, A. Christina Georgina Rossetti. CP-RosC3

Owned a pair o' skates onc't. Hoodoo, The. James Whitcomb Riley. CP-RileJ

Owners over the ocean sailed, The. Fanny Howe. SP-HoweF *Fr.* Vineyard, The.

Ox-bow. Donald Davie. CP-DaviDC

Ox Cart Man. Donald Hall. CP-HallD

Ox, long fed with musty hay, An. Recantation. Samuel Taylor Coleridge. CP-ColeS; MW-ColeS

Ox Mountain Parable, The. Mencius. CP-MertT

Ox-Tamer, The. Walt Whitman. CP-WhitW

Oxalis. Louis Zukofsky. CP-ZukLS

Oxbow. Federico García Lorca. CP-GarcF, *tr.* by Jerome Rothenberg *Fr.* Return, The.

Oxen, The. Thomas Hardy. CP-HardT

Oxen gone, the house is fallen where, The. Trial, The. John Berryman. CP-BerrJ

Oxen: Ploughing at Fiesole. Charles Tomlinson. CP-TomlC; SP-TomlC

Oxford. W. H. Auden. CP-AudeW

Oxford Bells. Gerard Manley Hopkins. CP-HopkG
   (Like Shuttles Fleet the Clouds.) CP-HopkG

Oxford, May 30, 1820. William Wordsworth. CP-WorW2

Oxford, May Thirtieth, Eighteen Twenty. William Wordsworth. CP-WorW2

Oxford, Thirty Years After. John Updike. CP-UpdiJ

Oxford Voice, The. D. H. Lawrence. CP-LawrD

Oxfordshire. Donald Davie. CP-DaviDC

Oxymoron sisters, Snowflake and Acetylene, The. Thomas Lux. SP-LuxT

Oxymoronic Hospital Blues. Alan Dugan. CP-DugaA

Oya. Audre Lorde. SP-LordA

Oyntment to Alure Fish to the Bait. Raymond Carver. CP-CarvR

Oyster, The. Ogden Nash. CP-NashO

Oyster, cast upon the shore, An. Poet, the Oyster, and Sensitive Plant, The. William Cowper. CP-CowpW

Oyster that went to bed x-million years ago, An. Goodnight. John Ciardi. CP-CiarJ

Oysters. Anne Sexton. SP-SextA *Fr.* Death of the Fathers, The.

Oysters. Joseph Brodsky. CP-BrodJ *Fr.* Shorts.

Oysters. Seamus Heaney. SP-HeanSO

Oysters. Robinson Jeffers. CP-JefR3

Oysters and Hermits. Donald Hall. CP-HallD

Oysters, like girls, like pearls. Oysters. Joseph Brodsky. CP-BrodJ *Fr.* Shorts.

Oysters we ate. Death of the Fathers, The. Anne Sexton. SP-SextA

Oysters we ate. Oysters. Anne Sexton. SP-SextA *Fr.* Death of the Fathers, The.

Ozell, at Sanger's call, invok'd his muse. Translator, The. Alexander Pope. CP-PopeA

Ozone. Heather McHugh. SP-McHuH

Ozymandias. George Oppen. CP-OppGN

Ozymandias. Percy Bysshe Shelley. CP-ShelP

Ozymandias II. Howard Nemerov. CP-NemeH

P

P—. Robert Creeley. SP-CreeR

P.O.W. Jane Cooper. CP-CoopJ

P.R.B, The. Christina Georgina Rossetti. CP-RosC3

P.S. Olga Broumas. SP-BrouO

£ S. D. Robert Graves. CP-GravR

Pa he bringed me here to stay. Christmas Memory, A. James Whitcomb Riley. CP-RileJ

Pa McCabe. Hayden Carruth. CP-CarHS

Pa wunst he scold' an' says to me. Uncle Sidney's Logic. James Whitcomb Riley. CP-RileJ

Pablo and Pedro, and black Serafin. Bacardi Spreads the Eagle's Wing. Hart Crane. CP-CranH

Pablo Casals. Archibald MacLeish. CP-MacLA

Pace Is the Essence. Charles Bukowski. SP-BukC3

Pace like That, A. Yehuda Amichai. SP-AmicY, *tr.* by Chana Bloch

Pacer in the Fresco, The. John the Baptist. Donald Davie. CP-DaviDC

Pacha sank at last upon his knee, The. Giaour and the Pacha, The. Richard Wilbur. CP-WilbR

Pachysandra. Louis Zukofsky. CP-ZukLS

Pacific Gazer. Robert Penn Warren. CP-WarrR

Pacific: in Russian as. Out of East Anglia. Donald Davie. CP-DaviDC

Pacific Lament. Charles Olson. CP-OlsoC

Pacific Telephone. Charles Bukowski. SP-BukC1

Pacifist's Song, The. John Berryman. CP-BerrJ

Pacing as with some consequent. Robert Creeley. CP-CreeR

Pack your heavy suitcase. Putting the Sonnet to Work. William Stafford. SP-StafWW

Packed in my mind lie all the clothes. Inward Morning, The. Henry David Thoreau. CP-ThorH

Packet of Letters. Louise Bogan. CP-BogaL

Pact, A. Ezra Pound. SP-PounE

Pact, The. Robert Graves. CP-GravR

Pact that we made was the ordinary pact, The. From a Survivor. Adrienne Rich. SP-RicA1; SP-RicA2

Pad, Pad. Stevie Smith. CP-SmitS

Padding down the street, the. No Shoes No Shirt No Service. Gary Snyder. CP-SnydG

Paddy's Choice. *Unknown, sometimes at. to* Thomas Sheridan. CP-SherT

Pads in a quilted bathrobe to the door. Callers, The. Marilyn Hacker. SP-HackM

Paean. Dorothy Parker. CP-ParkD

Pæan. John Greenleaf Whittier. CP-WhitJ

Paean to Place. Lorine Niedecker. CP-NiedL

Paesaggio Notturno. Charles Wright. SP-WrigCN

Paestum. James Dickey. CP-DickJ

Paestum of the twice blooming. Golden Section. Kenneth Rexroth. CP-RexrK

Pagan. Alice Walker. CP-WalkA

Pagan Prayer. Countee Cullen. CP-CullC

Pagan Saturday. John Logan. CP-LogaJ

Pagani's, November 8. Ezra Pound. SP-PounE

Pagans, The. G. K. Chesterton. CP-ChesG

Pagan's myths through marble lips are spoken, The. Worship. John Greenleaf Whittier. CP-WhitJ

Pagan's Prayer, The. Charles Baudelaire. CP-BaudC, *tr. by* Walter Martin

Page from a Tale. Wallace Stevens. CP-StevW; CP-StevWP

Page from the Koran. James Merrill. SP-MerrJ

Page my acre; A, B, C, are buildings, The. My Farm. May Swenson. SP-SwenM

Page to Commemorate Colonel Suárez, Victor at Junín, A. Jorge Luis Borges. SP-BorgJ, *tr. by* Alastair Reid

Pageant, The. John Greenleaf Whittier. CP-WhitJ

Pageant of Elizabeth, A. Rudyard Kipling. CP-KiplR

Pages in an Album. Dan Pagis. SP-PagiD, *tr. by* Stephen Mitchell

Pagett, M. P. Rudyard Kipling. CP-KiplR

Pagget, a schoolboy, got a sword, and then. Upon Pagget. Robert Herrick. CP-HerrR

Paging Saint Patrick. Dorothy Parker. CP-ParkD

Paid on Both Sides. W. H. Auden. CP-AudeW

Pail droops on chain, rotten, The. Tree House, The. Louise Glück. SP-GlucL

Pain. Ivor Gurney. SP-GurnI

Pain. A. K. Ramanujan. CP-RamaA

Pain. John Updike. CP-UpdiJ

Pain, The. Shmuel HaNagid. SP-HaNaS, *tr. by* Peter Cole

Pain and weariness, aching eyes and head. Sick Child's Meditation, A. Christina Georgina Rossetti. CP-RosC3

Pain can make a whole winter bright. Humpty Dumpty. May Sarton. SP-SartM

Pain—expands the Time. Emily Dickinson. CP-DickE

Pain flattens the world—its bubbles. Pain. John Updike. CP-UpdiJ

Pain for a Daughter. Anne Sexton. CP-SextA; SP-SextA

Pain Has an Element of Blank. Emily Dickinson. CP-DickE

Pain has but one Acquaintance. Emily Dickinson. CP-DickE

Pain in Ilium and wailing. Priam's Speeding Forth at Night. Constantine P. Cavafy. CP-CavaC, *tr. by* Theoharis Constantine Theoharis

Pain in Pleasure. Elizabeth Barrett Browning. CP-BroEB

Pain Is an Eagle Clinging to Your Name. Pablo Antonio Cuadra. CP-MertT

Pain is impossible to describe. Beyond. Laura Riding Jackson. CP-RidiL

Pain is in this dark room like many speakers. Teachers. W. S. Merwin. SP-MerwW

Pain is seen to have been transitory. On Seeing an Egyptian Mummy in Berlin, 1932. Richard Eberhart. CP-EberR

Pain of all pain, the most grievous pain. Sir Thomas Wyatt. CP-WyatT

Pain of love's a better fate, The. Sadi. CP-EmerR

Pain of loving you, The. Young Wife, A. D. H. Lawrence. CP-LawrD

Pain, pain continual; pain unending. Pain. Ivor Gurney. SP-GurnI

Pain-people think that God is the god of joy, The. At the Seashore. Yehuda Amichai. SP-AmicY, *tr. by* Chana Bloch

PAIN: Trying to Find a Metaphor. A. K. Ramanujan. CP-RamaA

Pain was pulled down over his eyes like a fool's hat. God, A. Ted Hughes. SP-HughTN

Paine and Pleasure. Robert Herrick. CP-HerrR

Pain[e] Ends in Pleasure. Robert Herrick. CP-HerrR

Paines without Profit. Robert Herrick. CP-HerrR

Painfully Banal. Thomas Lux. SP-LuxT

Painfully grinning faces like dogs' or. Old Masters Abroad. Louis MacNeice. CP-MacNL

Painkillers. Thom Gunn. CP-GunnT

Pains enough thou hast given me. Tanck's Song about His Birthday. Hayden Carruth. CP-CarHS *Fr.* Songs about What Comes Down: The Complete

Works of Mr. Septic Tanck.

Pains in my ankle flicker, nerve ends. Pain. A. K. Ramanujan. CP-RamaA

Pains of Sleep, The. Samuel Taylor Coleridge. CP-ColeS; MW-ColeS

Paint a Wall. David Ignatow. SP-IgnaD

Paint me a cavernous waste shore. Sweeney Erect. T. S. Eliot. CP-ElioT; SP-ElioT

Paint 'til You Faint. James Tate. SP-TateJ

Paintbrush and lute-string or new modeling clay. Izhab-O-Rasai (Expression and Reach). N. M. Rashid. CP-KizeC, *tr. by* Carolyn Kizer

Painted. Constantine P. Cavafy. CP-CavaC, *tr. by* Theoharis Constantine Theoharis

Painted beams aren't for me. Han-shan. CP-ColdM, *tr. by* Red Pine

Painted Columbine, The. Jones Very. CP-VeryJ

Painted Cup, The. Michael Palmer. SP-PalmM

Painted Head. John Crowe Ransom. SP-RansJ

Painted Lace. Gertrude Stein. CP-SteiG

Painted wind has sprung, A. E. E. Cummings. CP-CummE

Painted Wives. John Updike. CP-UpdiJ

Painter, The. John Ashbery. SP-AshbJ

Painter and poet, runner and discus-thrower. Of the Jews (50 A.D.). Constantine P. Cavafy. CP-CavaC, *tr. by* Theoharis Constantine Theoharis

Painter & the Fish, The. Raymond Carver. CP-CarvR

Painter at Xyochtl. Josephine Jacobsen. CP-JacoJ

Painter Dreaming in the Scholar's House, The. Howard Nemerov. CP-NemeH

Painter in China once painted a hall, A. Body and Soul. "Anvari." CP-EmerR

Painter indicates the time of day, A. Moment of Creation, The. Arthur Sze. SP-SzeA

Painter one afternoon drew a train, A. Abstracted Painter. Yannis Ritsos. SP-RitsY, *tr. by* Kimon Friar

Painter, this likeness is too strong. Another ["Painter, this likeness is too strong"]. *Unknown.* CP-CowpW, *tr. by* William Cowper

Painters. Muriel Rukeyser. CP-RukeM

Painters, The. William Corbett. SP-CorbW

Painter's Dream, The. Lawrence Ferlinghetti. SP-FerlL

Painter's eye follows relation out, The. Painter Dreaming in the Scholar's House, The. Howard Nemerov. CP-NemeH

Painters of Spain, The. Spanish School. Stevie Smith. CP-SmitS

Painter's Wife, The. D. H. Lawrence. CP-LawrD

Painting, The. William Carlos Williams. CP-WilW2

Painting a Mountain Stream. Howard Nemerov. CP-NemeH

Painting and Sculpture. Ralph Waldo Emerson. CP-EmerR

Painting by Winifred Nicholson, A. Kathleen Jessie Raine. SP-RainK

Painting, finished, A. Theodore Weiss. SP-WeisT *Fr.* Polish Question, The.

Painting Sometimes Permitted. Robert Herrick. CP-HerrR

Painting the North San Juan School. Gary Snyder. CP-SnydG

Paintings in the Museums of Munich and Vienna. James Laughlin. CP-LaugJ

Pair, A. May Swenson. SP-SwenM

Pair He Saw Pass, The. Thomas Hardy. CP-HardT

Pair in One. Langston Hughes. CP-HughL; CP-HughL3

Pair of crystal eyes will lead me, A. Ralph Waldo Emerson. CP-EmerR

Pair of great blue herons should, A. Searching for Eagles. Peter Blue Cloud. SP-BlueP

Pair of newlyweds, A. Imperfect Lover, The. Nicanor Parra. CP-MertT

Pair of Shoes, A. Theodore Weiss. SP-WeisT

Pair of Stays to Mend the Shape, A. William Blake. CP-BlakW

Pairing Time Anticipated. William Cowper. CP-CowpW

Paisant Chronicle. Wallace Stevens. CP-StevW; CP-StevWP

Pal was her friend, her lover, and, dismissed. Love's Progress. James Vincent Cunningham. CP-CunnJ

Palace, The. Rudyard Kipling. CP-KiplR

Palace, The. W. S. Merwin. SP-MerwW

Palace in smoky light. Canto 4: "Palace in smoky light." Ezra Pound. SP-PounE *Fr.* Cantos.

Palace is not infinite, The. Jorge Luis Borges. SP-BorgJ, *tr. by* Alastair Reid

Palace of Art, The. Alfred Tennyson. CP-TennA

Palace of the Babies. Wallace Stevens. CP-StevW; CP-StevWP

Palace of unreality, where the place. Airport. John Updike. CP-UpdiJ

Palace-roof of cloudless night! Ode to Heaven. Percy Bysshe Shelley. CP-ShelP

Palace weeps, the king weeps, The. Aristovoulos. Constantine P. Cavafy. CP-CavaC, *tr. by* Theoharis Constantine Theoharis

Palaeolithic Fertility Fetish, A. Wisława Szymborska. SP-SzymW, *tr. by* Stanislaw Barańczak *and* Clare Cavanagh

Palais de justice of chambermaids, The. Surprises of the Superhuman, The. Wallace Stevens. CP-StevW; CP-StevWP

Palais des Arts. Louise Glück. SP-GlucL

Palatine, The. John Greenleaf Whittier. CP-WhitJ

Palaver's No Prayer. John Ciardi. CP-CiarJ

Pale at first and cold. Finding of Love, The. Robert Graves. CP-GravR

Pale beech and pine so blue. Thomas Hardy. *See* Pale beech and pine-tree blue

Pale beech and pine-tree blue. In a Wood. Thomas Hardy. CP-HardT

Pale Bliss. John Updike. CP-UpdiJ

Pale blossoms, each balanced on a single jointed stem. Carnations. Theodore Roethke. CP-RoetT

Pale brows, still hands and dim hair. Lover Mourns for the Loss of Love, The. William Butler Yeats. CP-YeatW

Pale bubbles, The. She Looks Back. D. H. Lawrence. CP-LawrD

Pale, delightful lady. Pale Lady. Langston Hughes. CP-HughL; CP-HughL1

Pale Dream came to a Lady fair, A. Marianne's Dream. Percy Bysshe Shelley. CP-ShelP

Pale face pathetically lit with laughter. Mildred. G. K. Chesterton. CP-ChesG

Pale Genius roves alone. Ralph Waldo Emerson. CP-EmerR

Pale gold of the walls, gold. Gold. Donald Hall. CP-HallD

Pale inner left arm pierced and withdrawn, The. Visiting Hour. Thomas Kinsella. CP-KinsT

Pale Lady. Langston Hughes. CP-HughL; CP-HughL1

Pale man walks on flower-dotted lawns, The. Caesars' Rage. Arthur Rimbaud. CP-RimbA, *tr. by* Martin Sorrell

Pale orange, green and crimson, and. Colors. Wallace Stevens. CP-StevWP

Pale Panther, The. Louis MacNeice. CP-MacNL

Pale sad face of her I wronged, The. Zara. Christina Georgina Rossetti. CP-RosC3

Pale sand edges England's Old. Virginia Britannia. Marianne Craig Moore. CP-MoorM

Pale sky, hovering over a world that is dying, A. Phenomenon of the Future, A. Stéphane Mallarmé. CP-MallS, *tr. by* Henry Weinfield

Pale sunlight. Jelaluddin Rumi. SP-Rumi, *tr. by* Coleman Barks

Pale, the cold, and the moony smile, The. On Death. Percy Bysshe Shelley. CP-ShelP

Pale woman is cradling a large red fish, A. Fish, The. Norman Dubie. CP-DubiN

Paled in by many a lofty hill. Magic Castle, The. Sir Walter Scott. SP-ScotW *Fr.* Bridal of Trierman, The.

Palely intent, he urged his keel. At the Cannon's Mouth. Herman Melville. SP-MelvH

Paler, not quite so fair as in her life. One of the Dead. Christina Georgina Rossetti. CP-RosC3

Palestine. John Greenleaf Whittier. CP-WhitJ

Palette, The. What You Need for Painting. Raymond Carver. CP-CarvR

Palimpsest. Yusef Komunyakaa. CP-KomuY

Palimpsest. Philip Whalen. SP-WhalP

Palimpsest: "Written in an old Aeolian dialect." "Rubén Dario." SP-DariR, *tr. by* Alberto Acereda *and* Will Derusha

Palimpsests. Federico García Lorca.

    Air ("Full of scars / & fast asleep"). CP-GarcF, *tr. by* Jerome Rothenberg

    City. CP-GarcF, *tr. by* Jerome Rothenberg

    Corridor. CP-GarcF, *tr. by* Jerome Rothenberg

    Front Page. CP-GarcF, *tr. by* Jerome Rothenberg

    Madrigal: "Oh Lucy of Granada!" CP-GarcF, *tr. by* Jerome Rothenberg

Palinodia. Thomas Sheridan. CP-SherT

Palio. Eugenio Montale. CP-MontE, *tr. by* Jonathan Galassi

Palladiums. Carl Sandburg. CP-SandC

Pallas, a goddess chaste and wise. Storm, The. Jonathan Swift. CP-SwifJ

Pallas grew vap'rish once and odd. On the Countess of Burlington Cutting Paper. Alexander Pope. CP-PopeA

Pallas, observing Stella's wit. To Stella, Visiting Me in My Sickness. Jonathan Swift. CP-SwifJ

Pallas saw *Venus* arm'd, and streight she cry'd. Upon the Same. Ausonius. CP-CrasR

Pallid, mis-shapen he stands. The World's grimed thumb. In the Dock. Walter De la Mare. CP-DeLaW

Pallid white theories / with blinded eyes. Avenue. Federico García Lorca. CP-GarcF, *tr. by* Jerome Rothenberg *Fr.* In the Garden of the Lunar Grapefruits.

Pallid Wreath, The. Walt Whitman. CP-WhitW

Palm. W. S. Merwin. SP-MerwWF

Palm. Rainer Maria Rilke. CP-RilkFr, *tr. by* A. Poulin, Jr. *Fr.* Orchards.

Palm, The. Federico García Lorca. CP-GarcF, *tr. by* Jerome Rothenberg *Fr.* Palm Tree, The.

Palm at the end of the mind, The. Of Mere Being. Wallace Stevens. CP-StevWP

Palm-house in Belfast's Botanic Gardens, The. One Desire, The. Paul Muldoon. CP-MuldP

Palm is air, The. Palm, The. Federico García Lorca. CP-GarcF, *tr. by* Jerome Rothenberg *Fr.* Palm Tree, The.

Palm is in no hurry, The. Palm. W. S. Merwin. SP-MerwWF

Palm of the Hand. Charles Tomlinson. CP-TomlC

Palm print confirms the stars, but what confirms the hand?, A. Meditation on

Form and Measure. Charles Wright. SP-WrigCN

Palm, soft unmade bed. Palm. Rainer Maria Rilke. CP-RilkFr, *tr. by* A. Poulin, Jr. *Fr.* Orchards.

Palm Sunday. Amy Clampitt. CP-ClamA

Palm Sunday. Paul Muldoon. CP-MuldP

Palm Sunday. Christina Georgina Rossetti. CP-RosC2

Palm Sunday. Adam Zagajewski. SP-ZagaA, *tr. by* Renata Gorczynski

Palm Tree. Federico García Lorca. CP-GarcF, *tr. by* Jerome Rothenberg *Fr.* Palm Tree, The.

Palm Tree, The. Federico García Lorca.

    Limits. CP-GarcF, *tr. by* Jerome Rothenberg

    Mediterranean. CP-GarcF, *tr. by* Jerome Rothenberg

    Palm, The. CP-GarcF, *tr. by* Jerome Rothenberg

    Palm Tree. CP-GarcF, *tr. by* Jerome Rothenberg

Palm-Tree, The. John Greenleaf Whittier. CP-WhitJ

Palm-tree, single and apart. Song: The Palm Tree. Robert Graves. CP-GravR

Palmer, The. Sir Walter Scott. SP-ScotW

Palms for a Catholic Child. Kenneth Patchen. CP-PatcK

Palms grow in the garden where. Tarbes. Adam Zagajewski. SP-ZagaA, *tr. by* Clare Cavanagh

Palms of Mammon have disowned, The. Revealer, The. Edwin Arlington Robinson. CP-RobiE

Palos Verdes Cliffs. Muriel Rukeyser. CP-RukeM

Pals. Carl Sandburg. CP-SandC

Paltry-Looking People. D. H. Lawrence. CP-LawrD

Paltry Nude Starts on a Spring Voyage, The. Wallace Stevens. CP-StevW; CP-StevWP

Pambo. Robert Browning. CP-BroR2

Pamela. Rita Dove. SP-DoveR

Pamela was too gentle to deceive. Tree in Pamela's Garden, The. Edwin Arlington Robinson. CP-RobiE

Pamphilia to Amphilanthus. Mary Sidney, Countess of Montgomery Wroth. CP-WrotM

Pamphylian. Louis Zukofsky. CP-ZukLS

Pan. Federico García Lorca. CP-GarcF, *tr. by* Jerome Rothenberg *Fr.* Secrets.

Pan. James Whitcomb Riley. CP-RileJ

Pan and Luna. Robert Browning. CP-BroR2

Pan came out of the woods one day. Pan with Us. Robert Frost. CP-FrosR

Pan: Double Villanelle. Oscar Wilde. CP-WildO

Pan, Echo, and the Satyr. Moschus. CP-ShelP, *tr. by* Percy Bysshe Shelley

Pan in Vermont. Rudyard Kipling. CP-KiplR

Pan is dead. Great Pan is dead. Ezra Pound. CP-PoEar

Pan loved his neighbour Echo—but that child. Pan, Echo, and the Satyr. Moschus. CP-ShelP, *tr. by* Percy Bysshe Shelley

Pan with Us. Robert Frost. CP-FrosR

Panacea. Muriel Rukeyser. CP-RukeM

Pandora. Robert Graves. CP-GravR

Pandora. Dante Gabriel Rossetti. CW-RossD

Pandora's Box, an Ode. Ted Berrigan. SP-BerrT

Panegyre, on the Happy Entrance of James, Our Sovereign, to His First High Session of Parliament in This Kingdom, the 19 of March, 1603, A. Ben Jonson. CP-JonsB

Panegyric on the Dean, A. Jonathan Swift. CP-SwifJ

Panegyric on the Reverend Dean Swift, A. Jonathan Swift. CP-SwifJ

Panegyric to Sir Lewis Pemberton, A. Robert Herrick. CP-HerrR

Panel board of the table, The. Nature Alive. Jorge Guillén. CP-WrigJ

Panels. Carl Sandburg. CP-SandC

Pang is more conspicuous in Spring, A. Emily Dickinson. CP-DickE

Pang More Sharp than All, The. Samuel Taylor Coleridge. CP-ColeS; MW-ColeS

Pang of Reminiscence, A. D. H. Lawrence. CP-LawrD

Pangloss's Song: A Comic-Opera Lyric. Richard Wilbur. CP-WilbR

Pangolin, The. Marianne Craig Moore. CP-MoorM

Panoply of Paradise is mine. Ralph Waldo Emerson. CP-EmerR

Panorama. Jaroslav Seifert. SP-SeifJ, *tr. by* Ewald Osers

Panorama, The. John Greenleaf Whittier. CP-WhitJ

Panorama of ruined houses, walls, A. Trial and Death, a Double Feature. Howard Nemerov. CP-NemeH

Panoramas are not what they used to be. Botanist on Alp (No. 1). Wallace Stevens. CP-StevW; CP-StevWP

Pansies. Charles Bukowski. SP-BukC2

Pansies, lilies, kingcups, daisies. To the Small Celandine. William Wordsworth. CP-WorW1; MW-WorW

Pansies! Pansies! How I love you, pansies! James Whitcomb Riley. CP-RileJ

Panthea. Oscar Wilde. CP-WildO

Panther, The. Paul Muldoon. CP-MuldP

Panther, The. Ogden Nash. CP-NashO

Panthera. Thomas Hardy. CP-HardT

Pantisocracy. Samuel Taylor Coleridge. CP-ColeS

Pantoum. Marilyn Hacker. SP-HackM

Pantoum on Some Lines from Camões. Robert Stock. SP-StocR

Pap had one old-fashioned sayin'. Pap's Old Sayin'. James Whitcomb Riley. CP-RileJ

Pap he allus ust to say. Them Old Cheery Words. James Whitcomb Riley. CP-RileJ

Papa above! Emily Dickinson. CP-DickE

Papa and Mama Dance, The. Anne Sexton. CP-SextA; SP-SextA

Papa called her Pearl when he came home. Taking in Wash. Rita Dove. SP-DoveR

Papa died in the gas chamber. Uses. Anne Sexton. CP-SextA

Papa, don't you see my shoes? Barefoot Blues. Langston Hughes. CP-HughL; CP-HughL2

Papa eats bread. Sut Lovingood. Charles Olson. CP-OlsoC

Papa Joffre, the shoulders of him wide as the land of France. Memoir. Carl Sandburg. CP-SandC

Papa Love Baby. Stevie Smith. CP-SmitS

Papal nuncio, John Burchard, writes calmly, The. For the Record. Raymond Carver. CP-CarvR

Paparazzi, The. Ai. SP-Ai

Papas Blondine / Grew tall & wise. Ralph Waldo Emerson. CP-EmerR

Papa's House, Son's Room. John Logan. CP-LogaJ

Paper Anniversary. Muriel Rukeyser. CP-RukeM

Paper Bag, A. Margaret Atwood. SP-AtwM2

Paper book is sent by Boyle, A. Jonathan Swift. CP-SwifJ

Paper by Maillol, no kiddin' End of the Rope, The. William Carlos Williams. CP-WilW2

Paper Cranes. Thomas Merton. CP-MertT

Paper Flute. Olga Broumas. SP-BrouO

Paper is two kinds, to write on, to wrap with. Paper I. Carl Sandburg. CP-SandC

Paper Nautilus, The. Marianne Craig Moore. CP-MoorM

Paper on Humor. Andrei Codrescu. SP-CodrA

Paper I. Carl Sandburg. CP-SandC

Paper Palace, The. E. E. Cummings. CP-CummE

Paper Poems 1. Yannis Ritsos.

  "Better this way." SP-RitsY

  "Glory / is the second child." SP-RitsY

  "He whitewashed the house." SP-RitsY

  "Put the flower pots." SP-RitsY

  "Wall is yellow, The." SP-RitsY

  "White on white." SP-RitsY

  "Words have another shell." SP-RitsY

  "You can't count." SP-RitsY

Paper Poems 2. Yannis Ritsos.

  "Ah cock, cock of treachery." SP-RitsY

  "Body / thin as a matchstick." SP-RitsY

  "Hammering of the nails, The." SP-RitsY

  "Look at it from this side." SP-RitsY

  "Nothing particular." SP-RitsY

  "Now you're caressing." SP-RitsY

  "This severed / marble hand." SP-RitsY

  "Wicked old women with candles and sheets." SP-RitsY

  "Word had me, The." SP-RitsY

  "You who seek the truth." SP-RitsY

Paper Poems 3. Yannis Ritsos.

  "How to prove." SP-RitsY

  "I saw the water flow." SP-RitsY

  "That same night." SP-RitsY

Paper product, A. We say it's green. Money. Thomas Lux. SP-LuxT

Paper Roses. Federico García Lorca. CP-GarcF, tr. by Jerome Rothenberg Fr. Fairs.

Paper II. Carl Sandburg. CP-SandC

Paper universe of primes. Michael Palmer. SP-PalmM

Paperboy shakes me awake, The. "I have been dreaming you'd come." Iowa Summer. Raymond Carver. CP-CarvR

Paperboys, The. John Logan. CP-LogaJ

Papers to sign and documents to read. Sa Majestá Très Chrétienne. Arthur Hugh Clough. SP-ClouA

Paphian Ball, The. Thomas Hardy. CP-HardT

Papilio et Limax. John Gay. CP-CowpW

Pappy Wants a Poppy. Ogden Nash. CP-NashO

Pap's got his pattent-right, and rich as all creation. Griggsby's Station. James Whitcomb Riley. CP-RileJ

Pap's Old Sayin'. James Whitcomb Riley. CP-RileJ

Parable. Thomas McGrath. SP-McGrT

Parable. Richard Wilbur. CP-WilbR

Parable, A. Louise Glück. SP-GlucL

Parable, A. James Laughlin. CP-LaugJ

Parable, A. Gregory Orr. SP-OrrG

Parable for a Certain Virgin. Dorothy Parker. CP-ParkD

Parable for Sports Writers, Society Columnists, Bond Salesmen, and Poets or Go Get a Reputation, A. Ogden Nash. CP-NashO

Parable of Cervantes and Don Quixote. Jorge Luis Borges. SP-BorgJ

Parable of the Blind, The. William Carlos Williams. CP-WilW2 Fr. Pictures from Brueghel.

Parable of the Old Men and the Young, The. Wilfred Owen. CP-OwenW

Parable of the Palace. Jorge Luis Borges. SP-BorgJ, tr. by Ken Krabbenhoft

Parables ("Raven flapped o'er the rich man's roof, A"). G. K. Chesterton. CP-ChesG

Parables ("There was a man who dwelt in the east centuries ago"). G. K. Chesterton. CP-ChesG

Paracelsus. Robert Browning. CP-BroR1

Paracelsus in Excelsis. Ezra Pound. CP-PoEar

Parade. Langston Hughes. CP-HughL; CP-HughL3

Parade. Arthur Rimbaud. CP-RimbA, tr. by Martin Sorrell

Parade-Song of the Camp Animals. Rudyard Kipling. CP-KiplR Fr. Jungle Book, The.

Paradelle for Susan. Billy Collins. SP-CollB

Parades, heroes, wreathes. Yannis Ritsos. SP-RitsY Fr. First Series.

Parades of 1949, The. Eugenio Montale. CP-MontE, tr. by Jonathan Galassi

Parades. Rattle of palm trees. The silver planes. Muriel Rukeyser. CP-RukeM

Paradigm, The. Allen Tate. CP-TateA

Paradigm of Seasons. Robert Penn Warren. CP-WarrR

Paradise. George Herbert. CP-HerbG

Paradise. Robert Herrick. CP-HerrR

Paradise. Gabriela Mistral. SP-MistG, tr. by Maria Giachetti [or Jacketti]

Paradise. Gregory Orr. SP-OrrG

Paradise. Christina Georgina Rossetti. CP-RosC1

Paradise. Jones Very. CP-VeryJ

Paradise / endless movie. You, An. Kingdoms of Heaven. Denise Levertov. SP-LeveDP

Paradise: in a Symbol. Christina Georgina Rossetti. CP-RosC3

Paradise is (as from the Learn'd I gather). Paradise. Robert Herrick. CP-HerrR

Paradise is of the option. Emily Dickinson. CP-DickE

Paradise is that old mansion. Emily Dickinson. CP-DickE

Paradise lasts for a day. Crowns of the palms lift. Day Like Rousseau's Dream, A. May Swenson. SP-SwenM

Paradise Lightning Dazzle. Gregory Orr. SP-OrrG

Paradise Lost. John Milton. CP-MiltJ

Paradise might have appeared here. Aristocracy, The. Wendell Berry. CP-BerrW

Paradise of Squares. Nicanor Parra. CP-MertT

Paradise Re-entered. D. H. Lawrence. CP-LawrD

Paradise Regained [or Regain'd]. John Milton. CP-MiltJ

Paradise too is a schizophrenic slum. Poem for Kyra. Andrei Codrescu. SP-CodrA

Paradiso 31, 108. Jorge Luis Borges. SP-BorgJ, tr. by Ken Krabbenhoft

Paradox. Thomas Hardy. CP-HardT

Paradox. Robert Penn Warren. CP-WarrR

Paradox, The. G. K. Chesterton. CP-ChesG

Paradox, The. Robert Creeley. CP-CreeR

Paradox, The. John Donne. CP-DonnJ; MW-DonnJ

Paradox, The. Paul Laurence Dunbar. CP-DunbP

Paradox of Time. Robert Penn Warren. CP-WarrR

Paradoxes and Oxymorons. John Ashbery. SP-AshbJ

Paragraphs. Hayden Carruth. CP-CarHS

Paraguay. G. K. Chesterton. CP-ChesG

Parallax. Arthur Sze. SP-SzeA

Parallax Monograph for Rodin, The. Norman Dubie. CP-DubiN

Parallel coherent worlds tectonic plates. Cohere Britannia. Andrei Codrescu. SP-CodrA

Parallel Invention. Muriel Rukeyser. CP-RukeM

Parallelism therefore is in fact Black Stone to Footstool of. For Mac Hammond. Charles Olson. CP-OlsoC

Paralytic. Sylvia Plath. CP-PlatS

Paranæticall, or Advisive Verse, to His Friend, M. John Wicks. Robert Herrick. CP-HerrR

Parang. Derek Walcott. CP-WalcD

Paraphrase. Hart Crane. CP-CranH

Paraphrase. Samuel Johnson. CP-JohnS

  (Ant, The.) CP-JohnS

Paraphrase from Notebooks. Howard Nemerov. CP-NemeH

Paraphrase on Psalm 114, A. John Milton. CP-MiltJ

Paraphrase on Thomas à Kempis, A. Alexander Pope. CP-PopeA

Parasceve, or Preparation, The. Robert Herrick. CP-HerrR

Parasol is the umbrella's daughter, The. Emily Dickinson. CP-DickE

Paratrooper. Mona Van Duyn. SP-VanDM

Parcæ, The; or, Three Dainty Destinies: The Armilet. Robert Herrick. CP-HerrR

Parcell-gil't-Poetry. Robert Herrick. CP-HerrR

Pardon. Robert Herrick. CP-HerrR

Pardon, The. Robert Graves. CP-GravR

Pardon, The. Richard Wilbur. CP-WilbR

Pardon, a few towns over. William Corbett. SP-CorbW

Pardon a stranger hand that gives. Album Verses. John Greenleaf Whittier. CP-WhitJ

Pardon, dear Lady, if this Christmas time. Stilton and Milton; or Literature in the 17th and 20th Centuries. G. K. Chesterton. CP-ChesG

Pardon Me. Pablo Neruda. SP-NeruP

Pardon me God, (once more I Thee intreat). To God. Robert Herrick. CP-HerrR

Pardon me if, to my eyes. Pardon Me. Pablo Neruda. SP-NeruP

Pardon my injuries. Eve. William Carlos Williams. CP-WilW1

Pardon my trespasse (Silvia) I confesse. To Silvia. Robert Herrick. CP-HerrR

Pardon of Christmas, The. G. K. Chesterton. CP-ChesG

Pardon, old fathers, if you still remain. Prologue to Responsibilities. William Butler Yeats. CP-YeatW

Pardon the faults in me. Wife to Husband. Christina Georgina Rossetti. CP-RosC1

Pardons. Robert Herrick. CP-HerrR

Parent, The. Ogden Nash. CP-NashO

Parent above, look down and see. Fanny Howe. SP-HoweF *Fr.* O'Clock.

Parent of golden dreams, Romance! To Romance. Lord Byron. CP-Byron

Parent Reprimanded, A. James Whitcomb Riley. CP-RileJ

Parentage. William Stafford. SP-StafW; SP-StafWW

Parenthesis. Federico García Lorca. CP-GarcF, *tr.* by Jerome Rothenberg *Fr.* In the Garden of the Lunar Grapefruits.

Parenthetical Address. Lord Byron. CP-Byron

Parents. William Meredith. SP-MereW

Parents. Stevie Smith. CP-SmitS

Parents left the child with his grandparents, The. Yehuda Amichai. SP-AmicY, *tr.* by Chana Bloch

Parents of Beauty, The. Emily Dickinson. SP-DickE

Parents' Pantoum. Carolyn Kizer. CP-KizeC

Parergon. John Ashbery. SP-AshbJ

Paring the Apple. Charles Tomlinson. CP-TomlC; SP-TomlC

Paris. Paul Muldoon. CP-MuldP

Paris and Diomedes. Homer. CP-MerG1 *Fr.* Iliad, The.

Paris came to Ida. Euripides. CP-DoolH *Fr.* Iphigenia [*or* Iphigeneia] in Aulis.

Paris, 1856. Jorge Luis Borges. SP-BorgJ, *tr.* by Willis Barnstone

Paris in Sixty-Nine. Charles Tomlinson. SP-TomlC

Paris, 7 A.M. Elizabeth Bishop. CP-BishE

Paris,*₊*is April sunset completely utters. E. E. Cummings. CP-CummE

Paris,thou art not. E. E. Cummings. CP-CummE

Paris Transformations. Lawrence Ferlinghetti. SP-FerlL

Paris War-Cry. Arthur Rimbaud. CP-RimbA, *tr.* by Martin Sorrell

Parish. Norman Dubie. CP-DubiN

Parish Register, The. George Crabbe.
   Contented Peasant, The. SP-CrabG
   Phoebe Dawson. SP-CrabG

Parisian Beggar Woman. Langston Hughes. CP-HughL; CP-HughL1

Parisian Dream. Charles Baudelaire. CP-BaudC, *tr.* by Walter Martin

Parisian Orgy, or Paris Filling Up Again. Arthur Rimbaud. CP-RimbA, *tr.* by Martin Sorrell

Parisina. Lord Byron. CP-Byron

Parity. Olga Broumas. SP-BrouO

Parity. Kenneth Rexroth. CP-RexrK

Park ("Like in the Brownie Books"). Robert Creeley. SP-CreeR

Park ("Why did that man"). Robert Creeley. SP-CreeR

Park, The. Andrei Codrescu. SP-CodrA

Park, The. Ralph Waldo Emerson. CP-EmerR

Park, The. Louis MacNeice. CP-MacNL

Park, The. C. K. Williams. SP-WillC

Park / "a Darling Walk / for the Mind," The. Lorine Niedecker. CP-NiedL

Park Bench. Langston Hughes. CP-HughL; CP-HughL1

Park Benching. Langston Hughes. CP-HughL; CP-HughL1

Park in the Public's or in the Public, Parks. Kenneth Rexroth. CP-RexrK

Parked among oak pews, in church corners. Poor People in Church. Arthur Rimbaud. CP-RimbA, *tr.* by Martin Sorrell

Parked in the fields. Forms of Love, The. George Oppen. CP-OppGN

Parker River, The. Richard Eberhart. CP-EberR

Parking lot was, The. Being and Becoming. Clarence Major. SP-MajoC

Parkinson's Disease. Galway Kinnell. SP-KinnGN

Parkinsons Shade to the House of Mr. Pallauicine Taking His Death Ill. Robert Herrick. CP-HerrR

Parklands, The. Stevie Smith. CP-SmitS

Parks & ponds are good by day. Ralph Waldo Emerson. CP-EmerR

Parkway. George Oppen. CP-OppGN

Parlement of Foules, The. Geoffrey Chaucer. CP-ChauG

Parliament Hill Fields. Sylvia Plath. CP-PlatS

Parliament Hill in the Evening. D. H. Lawrence. CP-LawrD

Parliament of Roses to Julia, The. Robert Herrick. CP-HerrR

Parliamentary Oscillators. Samuel Taylor Coleridge. CP-ColeS

Parnassus. Alfred Tennyson. CP-TennA

Parnell. William Butler Yeats. CP-YeatW

Parnell came down the road, he said to a cheering man. Parnell. William Butler Yeats. CP-YeatW

Parnell's Funeral. William Butler Yeats. CP-YeatW

Parochial Theme. Wallace Stevens. CP-StevW; CP-StevWP

Parodies of Bishop Percy's *Hermit of Warkworth*. Samuel Johnson. *See* Ballad: "I put my hat upon my head"

Parodies of Bishop Percy's *Hermit of Warkworth*. Samuel Johnson. *See* Ballad: "I therefore pray thee, Renny dear"

Parodies of Bishop Percy's *Hermit of Warkworth*. Samuel Johnson. *See* Ballad: "Tender infant, meek and mild, The"

Parody [*or* Parodie], A. George Herbert. CP-HerbG

Parody of Alfred Austin. George Meredith. CP-MerG2

Paros, far-shining star of dark-blue earth. Banished Gods, The. Derek Mahon. CP-MahoD

Parquet barely gleams, a lake, The. In the Hall of Mirrors. James Merrill. SP-MerrJ

Parrat protests 'tis he, and only he. Upon Parrat. Robert Herrick. CP-HerrR

Parrot. Stevie Smith. CP-SmitS

Parrot, A. May Sarton. SP-SartM

Parrot, The. Vincent Bourne. CP-CowpW

Parrot, The. Gabriela Mistral. SP-MistG, *tr.* by Maria Giachetti [*or* Jacketti]

Parrot / a talking parrot, A. No Comparison. James Laughlin. CP-LaugJ

Parrot Asylum, The. Yusef Komunyakaa. CP-KomuY

Parrot Fish, The. James Merrill. SP-MerrJ

Parrot, from east India to me sent, The. Elegy 2.6: "Parrot, from east India to me sent, The." Ovid. CP-MarlC *Fr.* Elegies.

Parrot in its palmy boughs, The. Communications of Meaning. Wallace Stevens. CP-StevWP

Parrot / Is eating a carrot, The. Who Killed Lawless Lean? Stevie Smith. CP-SmitS

Parrots live in western lands. Han-shan. CP-ColdM, *tr.* by Red Pine

Parsi Woman, The. Edna St. Vincent Millay. CP-MillE

Parsley. Rita Dove. SP-DoveR

Parsley. Further Reflection on Parsley. Ogden Nash. CP-NashO

Parsley for Vice-President! Ogden Nash. CP-NashO

Parsnip, The. Ogden Nash. CP-NashO

Parsnips. Charles Tomlinson. CP-TomlC

Parsnips, those rabbis, The. In the Root Cellar. Maxine W. Kumin. SP-KumiM

Parson, these things in thy possessing. Happy Life of a Country Parson, The. Alexander Pope. CP-PopeA

Parson to his pallid spouse, The. Questions in a Wood. Robert Graves. CP-GravR

Parsonage in Oxfordshire, A. William Wordsworth. CP-WorW2

Parson's Case, The. Jonathan Swift. CP-SwifJ

Parson's Looks, The. Robert Burns. CP-BurnR
   (In Answer to One Who Affirmed of a Well Known Character Here, Dr B——, that There Was Falsehood in His Very Looks.) CP-BurnR

Part, The. Denise Levertov. SP-LeveDP

Part 2—February. Denise Levertov. SP-LeveDL *Fr.* Metamorphic Journal.

Part fenced by man, part by a rugged steep. Place of Burial in the South of Scotland, A. William Wordsworth. CP-WorW2

Part of a Hero. Tennessee Williams. CP-WillT

Part of a Letter. Richard Wilbur. CP-WilbR

Part of a Novel, Part of a Poem, Part of a Play. Marianne Craig Moore.
   Hero, The. CP-MoorM
   Steeple-Jack, The. CP-MoorM

Part of a Summer, The. Jonathan Swift. CP-SwifJ

Part of a Tarot Fortune. Robert Stock. SP-StocR

Part of a True Story. Marilyn Hacker. SP-HackM

Part of Speech, A. Joseph Brodsky. CP-BrodJ, *tr.* by Daniel Weissbort

Part of the Forest. George Oppen. CP-OppGN

Part of the Ninth Ode of Horace Imitated. Alexander Pope. CP-PopeA

Part of the Ninth Ode of the Fourth Book of Horace. Jonathan Swift. CP-SwifJ

Part of the Series on the Paths, A. Charles Olson. CP-OlsoC

Part of the time when I move it's for. Crossing Our Campground. William Stafford. SP-StafWW

Part of the work[e] remains [or remaines]; one part is past. End of His Work, The. Robert Herrick. CP-HerrR

Part of What Might Have Been a Short Story, Almost Forgotten. Robert Penn Warren. CP-WarrR

Part otter, part snake, part bird the bird Anhinga. Waterbird. May Swenson. SP-SwenM

Part ravishing beauty, part sofa, in the vernacular—Sophie. Centaurs 2. Joseph Brodsky. CP-BrodJ

Part Song, with Concert of Recorders. William Dickey. SP-DickW

  "And he lies dead." SP-DickW

  "And I, who lay so warm and quiet there—." SP-DickW

  "Come, Doctor, we must fly someotherwhere." SP-DickW

  "Doctor, I did not see that you were there." SP-DickW

  "For we have gone a curious way from there." SP-DickW

  "I did not know you when you came in there." SP-DickW

  "Who made you come and find the door to there?" SP-DickW

Parta Quies. A. E. Housman. CP-HousA

Partake as doth the Bee. Emily Dickinson. CP-DickE

Partaking of the miraculous. Apparition of Splendor. Marianne Craig Moore. CP-MoorM

Parted. Paul Laurence Dunbar. CP-DunbP

Parted Love. Dante Gabriel Rossetti. CW-RossD Fr, House of Life, The.

Parted Presence. Dante Gabriel Rossetti. CW-RossD

Partenza di Venezia. Ezra Pound. CP-PoEar

Parthenia. Allen Tate. CP-TateA

Parthenon, The. Herman Melville. SP-MelvH

Partial Analysis. Marilyn Hacker. SP-HackM

Partial Comfort. Dorothy Parker. CP-ParkD

Partial Explanation, The. Charles Simic. CP-SimiC; SP-SimiCE

Partial Resemblance. Denise Levertov. SP-LeveDP

Partial to pine cliffs and lonely trails. Shih-te. CP-ColdM, tr. by Red Pine

Particular Lullaby. Stanley Kunitz. CP-KunSC

Particularly near sundown. Left. A. R. Ammons. CP-AmmoA

Particulars they want. Envoi: "Particulars they want." Robert Creeley. CP-CreeR

Parties; A Hymn of Hate. Dorothy Parker. CP-ParkD

Parting. Jorge Luis Borges. SP-BorgJ, tr. by W. S. Merwin

Parting. Jaroslav Seifert. SP-SeifJ, tr. by Ewald Osers

Parting. William Butler Yeats. CP-YeatW

Parting: I, The. Adrienne Rich. CP-RicAE; SP-RicA2

Parting: II, The. Adrienne Rich. CP-RicAE; SP-RicA2

Parting after parting, / Sore loss and gnawing pain. Christina Georgina Rossetti. CP-RosC2

Parting as Descent. John Berryman. CP-BerrJ

Parting at Dawn. John Crowe Ransom. SP-RansJ

Parting at Morning. Robert Browning. CP-BroR1; SP-BroR

Parting, Celia Weeps. Thomas Carew. CP-CareT

Parting Guest, A. James Whitcomb Riley. CP-RileJ

Parting Hymn. Jones Very. CP-VeryJ

Parting, I take with me completed June. Stanley Kunitz. CP-KunSC

Parting is one of the exactions. Emily Dickinson. SP-DickE

Parting Lovers. Elizabeth Barrett Browning. CP-BroEB

Parting of the Columns, The. Rudyard Kipling. CP-KiplR

Parting-Scene, A. Thomas Hardy. CP-HardT

Parting up/down from / one on the shore, two egrets—. Hayden Carruth. CP-CarHS Fr. Clay Hill Anthology, The.

Parting Verse, or Charge to His Supposed Wife when He Travelled, The. Robert Herrick. CP-HerrR

Parting Verse, the Feast There Ended, The. Robert Herrick. CP-HerrR

Parting with a View. Wisława Szymborska. SP-SzymW, tr. by Stanislaw Barańczak and Clare Cavanagh

Parting with a View. Wisława Szymborska. SP-SzymWM, tr. by Joanna Trzeciak

Parting with Thee reluctantly. Emily Dickinson. CP-DickE

Parting, without a Sequel. John Crowe Ransom. SP-RansJ

Partisan. Primo Levi. CP-LeviP, tr. by Ruth Feldman

Partisan, she condemns. Resistance, The. George Oppen. CP-OppGN

Partiti Vestimenta Mea Miserunt Sortem Contra Me ad Incarte Cla a Filii a Eniol Liebee Braya Braguesca et Belzebuth. Andrei Codrescu. SP-CodrA

Partition. W. H. Auden. CP-AudeW

Partly to think, more to be left alone. Book of Annandale, The. Edwin Arlington Robinson. CP-RobiE

Partly work[e] and partly play. Saint Distaffs Day, or the Morrow after Twelfth Day. Robert Herrick. CP-HerrR

Partnership. Edwin Arlington Robinson. CP-RobiE

Partnership dissolved. Sale. Miller Williams. CP-WillM

Parts of an Opera, Parts of a Guitar, Part of Nowhere. Charles Bukowski. SP-BukC2

Party, The. Raymond Carver. CP-CarvR

Party, The. Paul Laurence Dunbar. CP-DunbP

Party, The. Ogden Nash. CP-NashO

Party is going strong, The. Tribute to Kafka for Someone Taken. Alan Dugan. CP-DugaA

Party Knee. John Updike. CP-UpdiJ

Party Next Door, The. Ogden Nash. CP-NashO

Party on Olympus, The. James Laughlin. CP-LaugJ

Party on Shipboard. George Oppen. CP-OppGN

Party Piece. Paul Muldoon. CP-MuldP

Party Politics. Philip Larkin. CP-LarkP

Party Question, A. G. K. Chesterton. CP-ChesG

Parunts knows lots more than us. Intellectual Limitations. James Whitcomb Riley. CP-RileJ

Parva qudem regio, sed relligione primorum. Samuel Johnson. CP-JohnS

Parvenu. Nicholas Vachel Lindsay. CP-LindV

(Parvenue) delinquent, who will now. Late Comer, The. Robert Creeley. CP-CreeR

Pas à pas. Samuel Beckett. CP-BeckS

Pas davantage. Samuel Beckett. CP-BeckS

Pasa Thalassa Thalassa. Edwin Arlington Robinson. CP-RobiE

Pascal's own shadow seemed a wild abyss. Abyss, The. Charles Baudelaire. CP-BaudC, tr. by Walter Martin

Paschal smoke, floating, with. Paul Celan. SP-CelaP, tr. by John Felstiner

Paske, though his debt be due upon the day. Upon Paske a Draper. Robert Herrick. CP-HerrR

Paso. Federico García Lorca. SP-GarcF Fr. Poem of the Saeta.

Paso por Aquí. William Stafford. SP-StafWW

Pass, The. John Logan. CP-LogaJ

Pass by! Stand from between me and my tree! Miracle of the Roses, The. Robert Stock. SP-StocR

Pass forth, my wonted cries. Sir Thomas Wyatt. CP-WyatT

Pass, Friend. Carl Sandburg. CP-SandC

Pass me through, Beloved, as light through glass. Sixth Station, The. Robert Stock. SP-StocR

Pass now in metaphor beyond birds. Dancing Flame. Robert Graves. CP-GravR

Pass of Kirkstone, The. William Wordsworth. CP-WorW2; MW-WorW

Pass of Sand. Shmuel HaNagid. SP-HaNaS, tr. by Peter Cole

Pass of the Sierra, The. John Greenleaf Whittier. CP-WhitJ

Pass the small churchyard hamlet. Fanny Howe. SP-HoweF Fr. O'Clock.

Pass to thy Rendezvous of Light. Emily Dickinson. CP-DickE

Pass we to another land. Song: "Pass we to another land." George Meredith. CP-MerG2

Passage. A. R. Ammons. CP-AmmoA

Passage. Hart Crane. CP-CranH

Passage. W. S. Merwin. SP-MerwWF

Passage, The. Robert Creeley. CP-CreeR

Passage, The. Paul Laurence Dunbar. CP-DunbP

Passage, The. Richard Eberhart. CP-EberR

Passage Bird, The. Jones Very. CP-VeryJ

Passage from John Wilson's The Angler's Tent. William Wordsworth. CP-WorW1

Passage from Mary Barker's Lines Addressed to a Noble Lord (His Lordship Will Know Why). William Wordsworth. CP-WorW2

Passage of lights without hands. She Who Was Gone. W. S. Merwin. SP-MerwW

Passage of the Apennines. Percy Bysshe Shelley. CP-ShelP

Passage over Water. Robert Duncan. SP-DuncR

Passage Steamer. Louis MacNeice. CP-MacNL

Passage to godhead, fitfully glared upon. Lynchings of Jesus, The. Muriel Rukeyser. CP-RukeM

Passage to India. Walt Whitman. CP-WhitW

Passage to Worship. Donald Hall. CP-HallD

Passages. Robert Duncan.

  Architecture, The. SP-DuncR

  Before the Judgment. SP-DuncR

  Concert, The. SP-DuncR

  Fire, The. SP-DuncR

  In Blood's Domaine. SP-DuncR

  Stage Directions. SP-DuncR

  Torso, The. SP-DuncR

  Tribal Memories. SP-DuncR

  Up Rising. SP-DuncR

Passages. Thomas McGrath. SP-McGrT

Passaic, N.J. William Carlos Williams. CP-WilW2

Passed and repassed on the way to Vespers. Antiphonal. Amy Clampitt. CP-ClamA

Passed from you, mother, to the custody. Our Father. Donald Davie. CP-DaviDC

Passed On. William Corbett. SP-CorbW

Passed through the dark wall. Long Hunter, The. Wendell Berry. CP-BerrW

Passel o' the boys last night, A. Tom Johnson's Quit. James Whitcomb Riley. CP-RileJ

Passenger Pigeons. Robinson Jeffers. CP-JefR3

Passenger who e're thou art. [Mr. Herrys,] His Epitaph. Richard Crashaw. CP-CrasR

Passengers. Billy Collins. SP-CollB

Passer-By, The. Thomas Hardy. CP-HardT

Passer Domesticus. William Carlos Williams. CP-WilW2

Passer Mortuus Est. Edna St. Vincent Millay. CP-MillE

Passers-by. Carl Sandburg. CP-SandC

Passers-by on Snowy Night. Robert Penn Warren. CP-WarrR

Passing. Langston Hughes. CP-HughL; CP-HughL3

Passing a Flemish village and a burning city. Brueghel: The Triumph of Time. Howard Nemerov. CP-NemeH

Passing and Glassing. Christina Georgina Rossetti. CP-RosC2

Passing at my pleasure's pace. No More People. Stevie Smith. CP-SmitS

Passing away the bliss, / The anguish passing away. Christina Georgina Rossetti. CP-RosC3

Passing-Bell, A. D. H. Lawrence. CP-LawrD

Passing Bell, The. Denise Levertov. SP-LeveDL

Passing by, he could be anybody. Night Traveler, The. Mary Oliver. SP-OlivM

Passing Cloud, The. Stevie Smith. CP-SmitS

Passing cyclist winks; well, let her, let her!, A. Sears Roebuck. Randall Jarrell. CP-JarrR

Passing Glance, A. Charles Baudelaire. CP-BaudC, tr. by Walter Martin

Passing Glimpse, A. Robert Frost. CP-FrosR

Passing Hail, A. James Whitcomb Riley. CP-RileJ

Passing her in the day he had but dared. Archibald MacLeish. CP-MacLA Fr. Happy Marriage, The.

Passing into the wilderness of twisted trees. Souvenir, The. Robert Creeley. CP-CreeR

Passing Love. Langston Hughes. CP-HughL; CP-HughL1

Passing men in the street who are dead. Conclusion. Audre Lorde. SP-LordA

Passing my house in the suburbs. To a Chinese Woman. William Carlos Williams. CP-WilW2

Passing of a Heart, The. James Whitcomb Riley. CP-RileJ

Passing of the Year, The. E. E. Cummings. CP-CummE

Passing On. Adrienne Rich. CP-RicAE

Passing Remark. William Stafford. SP-StafW; SP-StafWW

Passing Show, The. Ambrose Bierce. SP-BierA

Passing stranger! you do not know how longingly I look upon you. To a Stranger. Walt Whitman. CP-WhitW

Passing the Morning under the Serenissima. Charles Wright. SP-WrigCN

Passing the Strait. Wendell Berry. CP-BerrW

Passing Through. Ai. SP-Ai

Passing Through. Constantine P. Cavafy. CP-CavaC, tr. by Theoharis Constantine Theoharis

Passing Through. Stanley Kunitz. CP-KunSC

Passing through huddled and ugly walls. Harbor, The. Carl Sandburg. CP-WilbR

Passing through the Banford Tolls. Alan Dugan. CP-DugaA

Passing Time. Maya Angelou. SP-AngeM

Passing Visit to Helen. D. H. Lawrence. CP-LawrD

Passion. Robert Herrick. CP-HerrR

Passion, The. John Milton. CP-MiltJ

Passion and Love. Paul Laurence Dunbar. CP-DunbP

Passion and Worship. Dante Gabriel Rossetti. CW-RossD Fr. House of Life, The.

Passion Flower hath sprung up tall, The. Christina Georgina Rossetti. CP-RosC2

Passion for Roman order seized the plains, A. Indianapolis. John Updike. CP-UpdiJ

Passion is never fact. Passion. James Vincent Cunningham. CP-CunnJ

Passion may call for a partner. Evening Sunsets Witness and Pass On, The. Carl Sandburg. CP-SandC

Passion of the Mad Rabbit, The. Anne Sexton. CP-SextA

Passion, too intemperate. Somewhere Else. Richard Eberhart. CP-EberR

Passionate Freudian to His Love, The. Dorothy Parker. CP-ParkD

Passionate love is temporary. Landscape with Leaves and Figure. Olga Broumas. SP-BrouO

Passionate Man[']s Pilgrimage, The. Sir Walter Ralegh. CP-RaleW

Passionate Pagan and the Dispassionate Public, The. Ogden Nash. CP-NashO

Passionate peace is in the sky. Truce of Christmas, The. G. K. Chesterton. CP-ChesG

Passionate Screen Writer to His Love, The. Dorothy Parker. CP-ParkD

Passionate Shepherd to His Love, The. Christopher Marlowe. CP-MarlC

Passions. Yusef Komunyakaa. CP-KomuY

Passion's Cry. Robert Burns. CP-BurnR

Passiontide. Christina Georgina Rossetti. CP-RosC2

Passive and dark, dead river. Dead River. Howard Nemerov. CP-NemeH

Passive I lie, looking up through leaves. Seventh Day. Kathleen Jessie Raine. SP-RainK

Passover. Primo Levi. CP-LeviP, tr. by Ruth Feldman

Passover in the Holy Family, The. Dante Gabriel Rossetti. CW-RossD

Passport. Sam Hamill. SP-HamiS

Password. Adam Zagajewski. SP-ZagaA, tr. by Renata Gorczynski, Benjamin Ivry and C. K. Williams

Past, The. Jane Cooper. CP-CoopJ

Past, The. Ralph Waldo Emerson. CP-EmerR

Past, The. Percy Bysshe Shelley. CP-ShelP

Past, The. Stevie Smith. CP-SmitS

Past, The. Jones Very. CP-VeryJ

Past, The. C. K. Williams. SP-WillC

Past a swim-by of deep-sea fish. At the Natural History Museum. William Meredith. SP-MereW

Past ancient dust Antigua bright blue water above Port Royal. Past Ruin'd Ilion. Philip Whalen. SP-WhalP

Past and Coming Year, The. John Greenleaf Whittier. CP-WhitJ

Past and Future. Elizabeth Barrett Browning. CP-BroEB

Past and Future Turn About. Kenneth Rexroth. CP-RexrK

Past and Present. G. K. Chesterton. CP-ChesG

Past crag and scarp. History. Robert Penn Warren. CP-WarrR

Past Days of Gales. Philip Larkin. CP-LarkP

Past death / past rainy days. Deep Religious Faith. William Carlos Williams. CP-WilW2

Past has been a mint, The. History. Langston Hughes. CP-HughL; CP-HughL1; CP-HughL3

Past is like a story, The. Letter to a Friend, A. James Whitcomb Riley. CP-RileJ

Past is not a package, The. Emily Dickinson. SP-DickE

Past is past, and if one. Salute. James Schuyler. CP-SchuJ

Past is such a curious Creature, The. Emily Dickinson. CP-DickE

Past Is the Present, The. Marianne Craig Moore. CP-MoorM

Past Madonna dell'Orto. Visit to Fadin. Eugenio Montale. CP-MontE, tr. by Jonathan Galassi

Past mesas in yellow ruin. Drive to Los Alamos, A. Thom Gunn. CP-GunnT

Past midnight and I. Ever So. James Laughlin. CP-LaugJ

Past midnight / rain driven hard. Dead Letter. Sam Hamill. SP-HamiS

Past Mobile Home Estates. Prison. Miller Williams. CP-WillM

Past my window dawn and down. Song: "Past my window dawn and down." Ivor Gurney. SP-GurnI

Past parentage or gender. Silence, A. Amy Clampitt. CP-ClamA

Past Ruin'd Ilion. Philip Whalen. SP-WhalP

Past ruined cities down the grass. Wandering Scholar's Prayer to St. Catherine of Egypt, The. James Vincent Cunningham. CP-CunnJ

Past Silver Durango Over Mexic Sierra-Wrinkles. Allen Ginsberg. CP-GinsA

Past the angular maguey fields, a ride on the optic nerve. Into Mexico. Mona Van Duyn. SP-VanDM

Past the hills that peep. Epeisodia. Thomas Hardy. CP-HardT

Past the turpentine camps. Jo Jo's Fireworks—Next Exit. James Tate. SP-TateJ

Past thousands of layers of mountains and clouds. Shih-te. CP-ColdM, tr. by Red Pine

Past time—those. Here ("Past time—those"). Robert Creeley. CP-CreeR

Past towns, states, deserts, hills, and rivers borne. Catullus. See Journeying over many seas and through many countries

Pastels by Degas. Czeslaw Milosz. CP-MiloCN, tr. by Robert Hass

Pastime. Christina Georgina Rossetti. CP-RosC2

Pastime. James Schuyler. CP-SchuJ

Pastor Caballero, The. Wallace Stevens. CP-StevW; CP-StevWP

Pastor Errante. Donald Davie. CP-DaviDC

Pastor / of grief and dreams, The. Cure of Souls, A. Denise Levertov. SP-LeveDP

Pastoral: "Autumn blows a withered hand on." Andrei Codrescu. SP-CodrA

Pastoral: "Between the little clouds of heaven." Langston Hughes. CP-HughL; CP-HughL3

Pastoral: "Can you still stand out on that balcony." Sam Hamill. SP-HamiS

Pastoral: "Dove walks with sticky feet, The." Kenneth Patchen. CP-PatcK

Pastoral: "Enquiring fields, courtesies, The." Allen Tate. CP-TateA

Pastoral: "Girl lies down on the hill, The." William Meredith. SP-MereW

Pastoral: "I came to a meadow." Charles Simic. SP-SimiCE

Pastoral: "I came to a meadow." Charles Simic. SP-SimiC

Pastoral: "If I say I have heard voices." William Carlos Williams. CP-WilW1

Pastoral: "If it were only still!" Edna St. Vincent Millay. CP-MillE

Pastoral: "It happened so fast. Fenya was in the straight." Norman Dubie. CP-DubiN

Pastoral: "Little sparrows, The." William Carlos Williams. CP-WilW1

Pastoral: "When I was younger." William Carlos Williams. CP-WilW1

Pastoral: "Young lady opposite, The." Ezra Pound. CP-PoEar

Pastoral 1: "Old man who goes about, The." William Carlos Williams. CP-WilW1

Pastoral 2: "If I talk to things." William Carlos Williams. CP-WilW1

Pastoral, A: "Mobile, immaculate and austere." Geoffrey Hill. CP-HillG

Pastoral Dialogue, A. Frank O'Hara. SP-OharF

Pastoral Dialogue, A. Jonathan Swift. CP-SwifJ

Pastoral Dialogue between Richmond Lodge and Marble Hill, A. Jonathan Swift. CP-SwifJ

Pastoral Jazz. Olga Broumas. SP-BrouO

Pastoral Letter, The. John Greenleaf Whittier. CP-WhitJ

Pastoral Nun, A. Wallace Stevens. CP-StevW; CP-StevWP

Pastorale. Hart Crane. CP-CranH

Pastoral[l] Dialogue, A. Thomas Carew. CP-CareT

Pastorall Sung to the King; Montano, Silvio, and Mirtillo, Shepards, A. Robert Herrick. CP-HerrR

Pastorall upon the Birth of Prince Charles, A. Robert Herrick. CP-HerrR

Pastorals. George Meredith. CP-MerG1

Pastorals. Alexander Pope. CP-PopeA

Pastorals. Virgil.
  Translation of Virgil; Pastoral V. CP-JohnS
  Translation of Virgil; Pastoral I. CP-JohnS

Pastry-cook once moulded up a t——, A. Tale of the T——d, The. Thomas Sheridan. CP-SherT

Pasture Alp is webbed with shade, The. George Meredith. CP-MerG2

Pasture, stone wall, and steeple. Question in a Field. Louise Bogan. CP-BogaL

Pasture, The. Robert Frost. CP-FrosR

Pat Dugan . . . my grandfather . . . throat cancer . . . 1947. People Who Died. Ted Berrigan. SP-BerrT

Pat of Butter, The. Thomas Hardy. CP-HardT

Patch of meadow & upland, A. Ralph Waldo Emerson. CP-EmerR

Patch of Old Snow, A. Robert Frost. CP-FrosR

Patch Work. Thom Gunn. CP-GunnT

Patent of a lord, The. Stephen Crane. CP-CranS

Patent Pending. James Laughlin. CP-LaugJ

Paternity suit was brought at ten o'clock, A. Synapse, The. Robert Stock. SP-StocR

Paterson. Allen Ginsberg. CP-GinsA; SP-GinsA

Paterson. William Carlos Williams
  "Better than flowers." CP-WilW1
  Episode 17. CP-WilW1
  "I bought a new." CP-WilW1
  Paterson. CP-WilW1
  "When I saw." CP-WilW1

Paterson, Book 5: The River of Heaven. William Carlos Williams. CP-WilW2 Fr. Asphodel, That Greeny Flower.

Paterson: The Falls. William Carlos Williams. CP-WilW2

Path. A. R. Ammons. CP-AmmoA

Path, The. Paul Laurence Dunbar. CP-DunbP

Path, The. Kathleen Jessie Raine. SP-RainK

Path at my feet disappears, The. Overtaken by Fog while Climbing. Gregory Orr. SP-OrrG

Path climbs up to the left, toward the Plantation, The. Liffey Hill, The. Thomas Kinsella. CP-KinsT

Path crowded with thistle fern blue daisy. Bixby Canyon. Allen Ginsberg. CP-GinsA

Path in the Sky, The. Nicholas Vachel Lindsay. CP-LindV

Path of Peace, The. Jones Very. CP-VeryJ

Path to Han-shan's place is laughable, The. Gary Snyder. CP-SnydG

Path was purple in the dusk, The. Owl, The. Arthur Sze. SP-SzeA

Pathological Case in Pliny, A. John Logan. CP-LogaJ

Pathological Puzzle. Langston Hughes. CP-HughL; CP-HughL3

Pathos of Applause, The. James Whitcomb Riley. CP-RileJ Fr. Child-World, A.

Paths. Dorothy Parker. CP-ParkD

Paths and Thingscape. Margaret Atwood. SP-AtwM1

Paths are dutiful, The. Queen Anne Cottage, The. James McMichael. SP-McMiJ

Paths of Former Time. Thomas Hardy. CP-HardT

Paths of Peace, The. James Whitcomb Riley. CP-RileJ

Pathway, The. Kenneth Patchen. CP-PatcK

Patience. Robert Graves. CP-GravR

Patience. Sir Thomas Wyatt. CP-WyatT

Patience, Dudley, we are two dried paltries. To Dudley Fitts. John Ciardi. CP-CiarJ

Patience, for I have wrong. Sir Thomas Wyatt. CP-WyatT

Patience for my device. Sir Thomas Wyatt. CP-WyatT

Patience, Hard Thing! Gerard Manley Hopkins. See Sonnet: "Patience, hard thing! the hard thing but to pray"

Patience, hard thing! the hard thing but to pray. Sonnet: "Patience, hard thing! the hard thing but to pray." Gerard Manley Hopkins. CP-HopkG

Patience—has a quiet Outer. Emily Dickinson. CP-DickE

Patience! I'll weave myself another web. Arachne. Primo Levi. CP-LeviP, tr. by Ruth Feldman

Patience in Princes. Robert Herrick. CP-HerrR

Patience: In the Mill. James Dickey. CP-DickJ

Patience Is when You Stop Waiting. C. K. Williams. CP-WillC

Patience, little Heart! Forecast. D. H. Lawrence. CP-LawrD

Patience must dwell with Love, for Love and Sorrow. Christina Georgina Rossetti. CP-RosC2

Patience of all my smart. Sir Thomas Wyatt. CP-WyatT

Patience of an Angel. Max Jacob. CP-BishE

Patience of Hope. Christina Georgina Rossetti. CP-RosC2

Patience, or Comforts in Crosses. Robert Herrick. CP-HerrR

Patience Taught by Nature. Elizabeth Barrett Browning. CP-BroEB

Patience though I have not. Patience. Sir Thomas Wyatt. CP-WyatT

Patient brute was Balaam's Ass, A. Ass of Balaam, The. George Meredith. CP-MerG2

Patient Chief, who lab'ring long, arriv'd, The. Fragment of Brutus, an Epic. Alexander Pope. CP-PopeA

Patient children stand in line, The. Nazi at the Puppet Show, The. Thomas Lux. SP-LuxT

Patient, in the fire of noon. Ariadne at the Labyrinth. Thomas Merton. CP-MertT

Patient Lovers, The. Carolyn Kizer. CP-KizeC

Patient Pan / Drunken with nectar, The. Ralph Waldo Emerson. CP-EmerR

Patients in the waiting room, The. Untitled Poem: "Patients in the waiting room, The." Alan Dugan. CP-DugaA

Patio. Jorge Luis Borges. SP-BorgJ, tr. by Robert Fitzgerald

Patio. Robert Stock. SP-StocR

Patna-Benares Express. Allen Ginsberg. CP-GinsA; SP-GinsA

Patriarch, The. Robert Burns. CP-BurnR

Patriarch wrestled with the angel long, The. Jacob Wrestling with the Angel. Jones Very. CP-VeryJ

Patriarchal bed with four posts, The. No More Ghosts. Robert Graves. CP-GravR

Patriarchal Poetry. Gertrude Stein. CP-SteiG

Patriot, The [An Old Story]. Robert Browning. CP-BroR1; SP-BroR

Patriot Engineer, The. George Meredith. CP-MerG1

Patriot of Life, A. Charles Bukowski. SP-BukC3

Patriotic Song, A. G. K. Chesterton. CP-ChesG

Patriotic Tour and Postulate of Joy. Robert Penn Warren. CP-WarrR

Patrolling Barnegat. Walt Whitman. CP-WhitW

Patron of all those luckless brains. Ode to Apollo. William Cowper. CP-CowpW

Patronage. Heather McHugh. SP-McHuH

Patronymic. Robinson Jeffers. CP-JefR3

Patsy's / brother / Bill—. Home. Robert Creeley. CP-CreeR

Pattern. Dorothy Parker. CP-ParkD

Pattern, The. Robert Creeley. CP-CreeR

Pattern of the sun, The. Emily Dickinson. CP-DickE

Patterns / of sounds, endless. Method, A. Robert Creeley. CP-CreeR

Patting good-bye, doubtless they told the lad. S.I.W. Wilfred Owen. CP-OwenW

Paudeen. William Butler Yeats. CP-YeatW

Paul. William Carlos Williams. CP-WilW2

Paul. James Wright. CP-WrigJ

Paul Blackburn. Ted Berrigan. SP-BerrT

Paul, did you mention chicory? Chicory. Hayden Carruth. CP-CarHS

Paul, he began ill, but he ended well. Beginnings and Endings. Robert Herrick. CP-HerrR

Paul, hello / what do you know. Lorine Niedecker. CP-NiedL

Paul Klee. Robert Stock. SP-StocR

Paul Klee: They're Biting. Paul Muldoon. CP-MuldP

Paul Laurence Dunbar. Robert Earl Hayden. CP-HaydR

Paul / now six years old. Lorine Niedecker. CP-NiedL

Paul Revere's Ride [The Landlord's Tale]. Henry Wadsworth Longfellow. SP-LongH Fr. Tales of a Wayside Inn.

Paul, that friend and heir to Christ. Ballad of the Four Saints. Josephine Jacobsen. CP-JacoJ

Paul / when the leaves. Lorine Niedecker. CP-NiedL

Paula. Carl Sandburg. CP-SandC

Paula Becker to Clara Westhoff. Adrienne Rich. SP-RicA2

Paula is digging and shaping the loam of a salvia. June. Carl Sandburg. CP-SandC

Pauline [*or* Pauline; A Fragment of a Confession]. Robert Browning. CP-BroR1

Pauline, mine own, bend o'er me—thy soft breast. Pauline [*or* Pauline; A Fragment of a Confession]. Robert Browning. CP-BroR1

Pauls hands do give, what give they bread or meat. Upon Paul. Robert Herrick. CP-HerrR

Paul's Wife. Robert Frost. CP-FrosR

Paumanok. Amy Clampitt. CP-ClamA

Paumanok. Walt Whitman. CP-WhitW

Paumanok Picture, A. Walt Whitman. CP-WhitW

Paunch. Paul Muldoon. CP-MuldP

Pauper, A. Allen Tate. CP-TateA

Pause, A. Christina Georgina Rossetti. CP-RosC3

Pause, The. William Carlos Williams. CP-WilW2

Pause by the Water. W. S. Merwin. SP-MerwWF

Pause, courteous Spirit!—Baldi supplicates. Gabriello Chiabrera. CP-WorW1

Pause en Route. Thomas Kinsella. CP-KinsT

Pause here, and think: a monitory rhime. Inscription for the Tomb of Hamilton. William Cowper. CP-CowpW

Pause of the Clock. Federico García Lorca. SP-GarcF, *tr.* by Stanley Read

Pause of Thought, A. Christina Georgina Rossetti. CP-RosC1 *Fr.* Three Stages.

Paused at the more than Brocken summit. At the Trade Center. Charles Tomlinson. CP-TomlC

Pavement, The. Charles Olson. CP-OlsoC

Pavements are quiet under press of their feet, The. Heine, Too, Lived in Germany. Kenneth Patchen. CP-PatcK

Pavilion. Billy Collins. SP-CollB

Pavilion pierces the green sky, The. Solo. Li Po. CP-WilW2

Paw, The. W. S. Merwin. SP-MerwW

Pawn, The. Constantine P. Cavafy. CP-CavaC, *tr.* by Theoharis Constantine Theoharis

Pawnbroker, The. Maxine W. Kumin. SP-KumiM

Pawn-shop man knows hunger, The. Street Window. Carl Sandburg. CP-SandC

Paws there. Snout there as well. Mustiness. Mould. Midwinter Waking. Philip Larkin. CP-LarkP

Pax. D. H. Lawrence. CP-LawrD

Pax Saturni. Ezra Pound. CP-PoEar

Pax Vobis. Dante Gabriel Rossetti. CW-RossD

Paxdominisit Sem Pervobiscum Etcumspiri Tutuo. Kenneth Patchen. CP-PatcK

Pay. Robert Creeley. CP-CreeR

Pay close attention: the world that appears now. Lesson in Observation, A. Dan Pagis. SP-PagiD, *tr.* by Stephen Mitchell

Pay me my price, Potters! and I will sing. Epigram of Homer, An. Homer. CP-CowpW

Paying Calls. Thomas Hardy. CP-HardT

Paying Some Slight Attention to His Birthday the Associate Professor Goes about His Business Considering What He Sees and a Kind of Praise. Miller Williams. CP-WillM

Paynefull smith with force of fervent heat, The. Sonnet 32. Edmund Spenser. CP-Spens *Fr.* Amoretti.

Paysage Moralisé. W. H. Auden. CP-AudeW

Paysage Triste. T. S. Eliot. SP-ElioT

Pcheek pcheek pcheek pcheek pcheek. Avenue Bearing the Initial of Christ into the New World, The. Galway Kinnell. SP-KinnGN

Pea Brush. Robert Frost. CP-FrosR

Pea pods cling to stems. Pods. Carl Sandburg. CP-SandC

Peace. Ted Berrigan. SP-BerrT

Peace ("Waiting for a bus"). Robert Creeley. CP-CreeR

Peace ("You're looking at a chopper"). Robert Creeley. SP-CreeR

Peace. Walter De la Mare. CP-DeLaW

Peace. George Herbert. CP-HerbG

Peace. Gerard Manley Hopkins. CP-HopkG

Peace. Langston Hughes. CP-HughL; CP-HughL3

Peace. David Ignatow. SP-IgnaD

Peace. D. H. Lawrence. CP-LawrD

Peace. Lorine Niedecker. CP-NiedL

Peace. Adrienne Rich. CP-RicAE

Peace. Yannis Ritsos. SP-RitsY, *tr.* by Kimon Friar

Peace. C. K. Williams. SP-WillC

Peace. William Carlos Williams. CP-WilW1

Peace. William Butler Yeats. CP-YeatW

Peace, a Pastoral Dialogue.—Part the Second. Annis Boudinot Stockton. CP-StocA

Peace and Dunkirk. Jonathan Swift. CP-SwifJ

Peace and War. D. H. Lawrence. CP-LawrD

Peace Autumn, The. John Greenleaf Whittier. CP-WhitJ

Peace belongs with the birds. Peace. David Ignatow. SP-IgnaD

Peace between Wars. Carl Sandburg. CP-SandC

Peace Conference in an American Town. Langston Hughes. CP-HughL; CP-HughL2

Peace Congress the Promise of a Higher Civilization, The. Jones Very. CP-VeryJ

Peace Convention at Brussels, The. John Greenleaf Whittier. CP-WhitJ

Peace for Awhile. David Ignatow. SP-IgnaD

Peace has unveil'd her smiling face. Entire Surrender, The. Jeanne Marie Bouvier de la Motte- Guyon. CP-CowpW

Peace-Hymn of the Republic, A. James Whitcomb Riley. CP-RileJ

Peace I have from the core of the atom, from the core of space. Wealth. D. H. Lawrence. CP-LawrD

Peace I Leave with You. Christina Georgina Rossetti. CP-RosC2

Peace in her chamber, wheresoe'er. First Love Remembered. Dante Gabriel Rossetti. CW-RossD

Peace in Our Time. Howard Nemerov. CP-NemeH

Peace in this green field. Kenneth Patchen. CP-PatcK

Peace in thy hands / Peace in thine eyes. Ghost, The. Walter De la Mare. CP-DeLaW

Peace is a fiction of our Faith. Emily Dickinson. CP-DickE

Peace is at last confirmed for us. Solomon's Seal. Robert Graves. CP-GravR

Peace is declared, an' I return. Return, The. Rudyard Kipling. CP-KiplR

Peace is something most often to be preferred. War and Peace. Miller Williams. CP-WillM

Peace is written on the doorstep. Peace. D. H. Lawrence. CP-LawrD

Peace, life—he found them in my open eyes. Michelangelo Buonarroti. CP-Miche, *tr.* by John Frederick Nims

Peace mutt'ring thoughts, and do not grudge to keep. Content. George Herbert. CP-HerbG

Peace, Night, Sleep. Carl Sandburg. CP-SandC

Peace Not Permanent. Robert Herrick. CP-HerrR

Peace of Cities, The. Richard Wilbur. CP-WilbR

Peace of Dives, The. Rudyard Kipling. CP-KiplR

Peace of Europe, The. John Greenleaf Whittier. CP-WhitJ

Peace of great doors be for you, The. For You. Carl Sandburg. CP-SandC

Peace of green summer lay over this meadow so deeply once, The. Once and Again. Hayden Carruth. CP-CarHS

Peace of Mind. Kathleen Jessie Raine. SP-RainK

"Peace of mind," my parents said, "a person must." Peace of Mind, Peace of Mind. Yehuda Amichai. SP-AmicYL, *tr.* by Benjamin Harshav *and* Barbara Harshav

Peace of Mind, Peace of Mind. Yehuda Amichai. SP-AmicYL, *tr.* by Benjamin Harshav *and* Barbara Harshav

Peace of Petrol, The. G. K. Chesterton. CP-ChesG

Peace of Wild Things, The. Wendell Berry. CP-BerrW

Peace-Offering, The. Thomas Hardy. CP-HardT

Peace on Earth. Edwin Arlington Robinson. CP-RobiE

Peace on Earth. William Carlos Williams. CP-WilW1

Peace on New England, on the shingled white houses, on golden. Jehu. Louis MacNeice. CP-MacNL

Peace, peace, peace, do you say? First News from Villafranca. Elizabeth Barrett Browning. CP-BroEB

Peace Peal, The. Thomas Hardy. CP-HardT

Peace prat[t]ler, do not lour [*or* lowre]. Conscience. George Herbert. CP-HerbG

Peace the day says, and *peace*. Noon. Josephine Jacobsen. CP-JacoJ

Peace the great meaning has not been defined. Muriel Rukeyser. CP-RukeM

Peace, the Wasp. César Vallejo. CP-MertT

Peace, the wild valley streaked with torrents. Straw, The. Robert Graves. CP-GravR

"Peace upon earth!" was said. We sing it. Christmas: 1924. Thomas Hardy. CP-HardT

Peace Walk. William Stafford. SP-StafW; SP-StafWW

Peace, war, religion. This Tokyo. Gary Snyder. CP-SnydG

Peace which others seek they find, The. Forsaken, The. William Wordsworth. CP-WorW1

Peaceable Kingdom, The. Marge Piercy. SP-PierM

Peaceful and slow, peaceful and slow. Truck-Garden Market-Day. Edna St. Vincent Millay. CP-MillE

Peaceful Kingdom. Charles Simic. SP-SimiC; SP-SimiCE

Peaceful life—just toil and rest, A. Lincoln. James Whitcomb Riley. CP-RileJ

Peaceful Shepherd, The. Robert Frost. CP-FrosR

Peaceful Trees. Charles Simic. SP-SimiC; SP-SimiCE

Peaceful Western Wind, The. Thomas Campion. CP-CampT (Peacefull westerne winde, The.) CP-CampT

Peaceful yard, silent, A. The sickly trees, saḍ. Yard, The. Yannis Ritsos. SP-RitsY, *tr.* by Andonis Decavalles

Peacefull westerne winde, The. Thomas Campion. *See* Peaceful Western Wind, The

Peacefull westerne winde the wintrye stormes hath calmde, The. Thomas Campion. CP-CampT

Peach. D. H. Lawrence. CP-LawrD

Peach Blossoms. Carl Sandburg. CP-SandC

Peach tree on the southern wall, The. Christina Georgina Rossetti. CP-RosC2

Peach would bloom through summer, The. Han-shan. CP-ColdM, *tr. by* Red Pine

Peacock. D. H. Lawrence. CP-LawrD

Peacock, The. James Merrill. SP-MerrJ

Peacock, The. Gabriela Mistral. SP-MistG, *tr. by* Maria Giachetti [*or* Jacketti]

Peacock, The. William Butler Yeats. CP-YeatW

Peacock has a score of eyes, The. Christina Georgina Rossetti. CP-RosC2

Peacock nobly born and bred, A. To the Right Honorable the Lord Viscount Mont-Cassel. Thomas Sheridan. CP-SherT

Peacock Room, The. Robert Earl Hayden. CP-HaydR

Peacock's Eye, The. Gerard Manley Hopkins. CP-HopkG

Peacocks of Perilampes, The. Yannis Ritsos. SP-RitsY, *tr. by* Kimon Friar

Peak. A. R. Ammons. CP-AmmoA

Peaked in an immortal flame. World; The Lovers; Falling Stars, The. Thomas McGrath. SP-McGrT

Peaks. John Ciardi. CP-CiarJ

Peal of Bells, A. Christina Georgina Rossetti. CP-RosC1

Peal of the Bells, The. Henry David Thoreau. CP-ThorH

Pealing, The. Olga Broumas. SP-BrouO

Peapes he do's strut, and pick his Teeth, as if. Upon Adam Peapes. Robert Herrick. CP-HerrR

Pear-Blossom. D. H. Lawrence. CP-LawrD

Pear like a Potato, A. John Updike. CP-UpdiJ

Pear Tree. "H. D." CP-DoolH

Pear Tree, The. Edna St. Vincent Millay. CP-MillE

Pear tree that last year, The. Shimmer. James Schuyler. CP-SchuJ

Pear tree, why blossom? Query. John Updike. CP-UpdiJ

Pearl. Carolyn Kizer. CP-KizeC

Pearl. Stevie Smith. CP-SmitS

Pearl, The. Robert Graves. CP-GravR

Pearl, a Girl, A. Robert Browning. CP-BroR2

Pearl Avenue runs past the high-school lot. Ex-Basketball Player. John Updike. CP-UpdiJ

Pearl better, The. Without the Season of Structure, Modes Lie like Gods Thrown Down, Helpless before the Newness Upsets Genesis when the Young Men Pour In. Charles Olson. CP-OlsoC

Pearl Fog. Carl Sandburg. CP-SandC

Pearl Harbor. Susan Howe. SP-HoweS

Pearl Harbor. Robinson Jeffers. CP-JefR3

Pearl Horizons. Carl Sandburg. CP-SandC

Pearl. It's baroque. Regular-irregular. A bad dialectic, The. What's Wrong with Pindar. Charles Olson. CP-OlsoC

Pearl of Biloxi, The. Nicholas Vachel Lindsay. CP-LindV

Pearl Oyster. Primo Levi. CP-LeviP, *tr. by* Ruth Feldman

Pearl, The. Matth. 13;45. George Herbert. CP-HerbG

Pearls. Rita Dove. SP-DoveR

Pears hang on the tree by stems. Sunday. James Schuyler. CP-SchuJ

Peasant. W. S. Merwin. SP-MerwW

Peasant to his lord pay'd yearly court, A. John Milton. *See* Every year a peasant gathered from an appletree the most savory fruit

Peasant's Confession, The. Thomas Hardy. CP-HardT

Pebble spoke and down, The. Orientale. A. R. Ammons. CP-AmmoA

Pebbles. Herman Melville. CP-MelvH

Pebbles are beneath, but we stand softly. Sea-Marge. Ivor Gurney. SP-GurnI

Peccatology. Charles Wright. SP-WrigCN

Peck of Gold, A. Robert Frost. CP-FrosR

Pecked to Death by Swans. Thomas Lux. SP-LuxT

Pedagogue's Answer, The. Thomas Sheridan. CP-SherT

Pedantic Literalist. Marianne Craig Moore. CP-MoorM

Pedants all / They would be original. Ralph Waldo Emerson. CP-EmerR

Pedants of deconstruction, The. Maledictus In Plebe Sit. James Laughlin. CP-LaugJ

Pedestrian. Thomas Lux. SP-LuxT

Pedestrian. George Oppen. CP-OppGN

Pedestrian, The. Thomas Hardy. CP-HardT

Pediatric Reflection. Ogden Nash. CP-NashO

Pedicabo et irrumabo. Carmen 16. Catullus. CP-ZukLS *Fr.* Carmina.

Pedigree, The. Robert Creeley. CP-CreeR

Pedigree, The. Thomas Hardy. CP-HardT

Pedigree of Honey, The. Emily Dickinson. CP-DickE

Pediment of Appearance, The. Wallace Stevens. CP-StevW; CP-StevWP

Pedlar I am, that take great care, A. Pedlar of Small-Wares, A. Sir John Suckling. CP-SuckJ

Pedlar of Small-Wares, A. Sir John Suckling. CP-SuckJ

Pedro is the when and the how. Pedro Is When. Pablo Neruda. SP-NeruP

Pedro Is When. Pablo Neruda. SP-NeruP

Peekaboo, I Almost See You. Ogden Nash. CP-NashO

Peeling a hard boiled egg. Shower in June, A. William Corbett. SP-CorbW

Peeling Onions. Adrienne Rich. CP-RicAE; SP-RicA2

Peepers in Our Meadow, The. Archibald MacLeish. CP-MacLA

Peeping Tom. Lucille Clifton. SP-ClifL

Peeping Tom. Walter De la Mare. CP-DeLaW

Peer re foot own his. Grecian Windflower. Louis Zukofsky. CP-ZukLS

Peering, stung. Poem: Tears, Spray, and Steam. John Logan. CP-LogaJ

Peerless and solitary. For the Prince in Exile. Tu Fu. CP-KizeC, *tr. by* Carolyn Kizer

Peg Nicholson was a good bay mare. Elegy on Peg Nicholson. Robert Burns. CP-BurnR

Peg Ratcliff the Hostess's Invitation to Dean Swift. *Unknown, sometimes at. to* Thomas Sheridan. CP-SherT

Peg said, "This one," and we bought it. Mother's Day. William Stafford. SP-StafW; SP-StafWW

Pegasus. Rainer Maria Rilke. CP-RilkFr, *tr. by* A. Poulin, Jr. *Fr.* Affectionate Taxes to France.

Pelasgian Image. Constantine P. Cavafy. CP-CavaC, *tr. by* Theoharis Constantine Theoharis

Pelayo. William Wordsworth. CP-WorW1

Peleg Lookout. William Stafford. SP-StafWW

Pelican. Donald Davie. CP-DaviDC

Pelican, The. Richard Wilbur. CP-WilbR

Pelicans. Robinson Jeffers. CP-JefR1

Pelicans. Czeslaw Milosz. CP-MiloCN, *tr. by* Robert Hass

Pelion and Ossa flourish side by side. William Wordsworth. CP-WorW1

Pelion could one time prong its top worthy keel in pines. Catullus. *See* In old days / driving through soft waters

PELLICANUS is the word / For a certain breed of bird. Pelican, The. Richard Wilbur. CP-WilbR

Pen-Pictur' of a Cert'in Frivvolus Old Man, A. James Whitcomb Riley. CP-RileJ

Pen that told the truth, The. Raymond Carver. CP-CarvR

Pen—to register; a key, A. Memory. William Wordsworth. CP-WorW2

Penal Cavalry, The. Andrei Codrescu. SP-CodrA

Penalty, The. Rudyard Kipling. CP-KiplR

Penalty of Genius, The. James Whitcomb Riley. CP-RileJ

Penance. Thomas Hardy. CP-HardT

Penance. C. K. Williams. CP-WillC

Penates. Tennessee Williams. CP-WillT

Pencil Sketch. Clarence Major. SP-MajoC

Pencil Sketch of Self & Other. Jane Cooper. CP-CoopJ

Pencil Stub Journals. John Ciardi. CP-CiarJ

Pencils. Carl Sandburg. CP-SandC

Pencils / telling where the wind comes from. Pencils. Carl Sandburg. CP-SandC

Penelope. Donald Davie. CP-DaviDC

Penelope. Norman Dubie. CP-DubiN

Penelope. Dorothy Parker. CP-ParkD

Penelope, for her Ulisses sake. Sonnet 23. Edmund Spenser. CP-Spens *Fr.* Amoretti.

Penelope's Despair. Yannis Ritsos. SP-RitsY, *tr. by* Kostas Myrsiades

Penetration and Trust. George Meredith. CP-MerG1

P'eng That Was a K'un, The. Chuang Tzu. CP-GravR

Peninsula, The. Seamus Heaney. SP-HeanSO

Peninsula seen from the hills near Bath, The. Moths, The. Norman Dubie. CP-DubiN

Peninsular arm, Sirmio, insular arm, well. Carmen 31. Catullus. *Fr.* Carmina.

Peninsulas are held by an ancient people, The. Land's End. Archibald MacLeish. CP-MacLA

Penis Envy. Ai. SP-Ai

Penitence. Robert Herrick. CP-HerrR

Penitencie. Robert Herrick. CP-HerrR

Penitent, The. Robert Creeley. CP-CreeR

Penitent, The. Edna St. Vincent Millay. CP-MillE

Penitent Considers Another Coming of Mary, A. Gwendolyn Brooks. SP-BrooG

Penitential Psalms. Sir Thomas Wyatt.

 Prologue: "Love, to give law unto his subject hearts." CP-WyatT

Penitential Thought, in the Hour of Remorse—Intended for a Tragedy, A. Robert Burns. CP-BurnR

Penmaen Pool. Gerard Manley Hopkins. CP-HopkG

Penn Station. Ted Berrigan. SP-BerrT *Fr.* Sonnets, The.

Pennacesse Leper Colony for Women, Cape Cod, The: 1922. Norman Dubie. CP-DubiN

Pennies of sun's fire jazzing like silver foil. Poreč. Donald Davie. CP-DaviDC

Penniless to our surprise. For Fred Carpenter Who Died in His Sleep. Miller Williams. CP-WillM

Pennsylvania. Carl Sandburg. CP-SandC

Pennsylvania Hall. John Greenleaf Whittier. CP-WhitJ

Pennsylvania Pilgrim, The. John Greenleaf Whittier. CP-WhitJ

Pennsylvania Station in New York, The. Langston Hughes. CP-HughL; CP-HughL1

Penny for the Old Guy, A. Philip Whalen. SP-WhalP

Pennycandystore beyond the El, The. Lawrence Ferlinghetti. SP-FerlL

Penobscot. George Oppen. CP-OppGN

Penobscot. James Schuyler. CP-SchuJ

Penological Study: Southern Exposure. Robert Penn Warren. CP-WarrR

Pens, The. W. S. Merwin. SP-MerwW

Pens to mend, and hands to guide. Henry David Thoreau. CP-ThorH

Penshurst Place. Derek Mahon. CP-MahoD

Pensive and Faltering. Walt Whitman. CP-WhitW

Pensive Flower. Rainer Maria Rilke. CP-RilkFr, *tr. by* A. Poulin, Jr.

Pensive gnu, the staid aardvark, The. For an Amorous Lady. Theodore Roethke. CP-RoetT

Pensive golden girl's come-hither stare, The. Wine of the Solitary Man, The. Charles Baudelaire. CP-BaudC, *tr. by* Walter Martin

Pensive on Her Dead Gazing. Walt Whitman. CP-WhitW

Pensive They Sit, and Roll Their Languid Eyes. John Keats. CP-KeatJ

Pensive we sat the silent hours. Bible, *O.T. See* By the rivers of Babylon, there we sat down, yea, we wept, when [*or* then] we remembered Zion

Pentagon code / for end of the world. Smart and Final Iris. James Tate. SP-TateJ

Pentagon Exorcism. Allen Ginsberg. CP-GinsA

Pente cõst under the body of the gull flying directly over. Charles Olson. CP-OlsoC

Pentecost. Ai. SP-Ai

Pentecost Castle, The. Félix Lope de Vega Carpio. CP-HillG, *tr. by* Geoffrey Hill

Penthesileia. Robert Graves. CP-GravR

Pentimento. Denise Levertov. SP-LeveDS

Pentimento. Arthur Sze. SP-SzeA

Pentucket. John Greenleaf Whittier. CP-WhitJ

Penumbra. Dante Gabriel Rossetti. CW-RossD

Penumbrae. John Updike. CP-UpdiJ

Peograms. Charles Olson. CP-OlsoC

Poem Written under an Archway in a Discontinued Railroad Station, Fargo, North Dakota, A. James Wright. CP-WrigJ

Peonies. Mary Oliver. SP-OlivM

Peony Stalks. Mona Van Duyn. SP-VanDM

People. Robert Creeley. CP-CreeR

People. D. H. Lawrence. CP-LawrD

People. Ogden Nash. CP-NashO

People. Miller Williams. CP-WillM

People, The. Robert Creeley. CP-CreeR

People, The. D. H. Lawrence. CP-LawrD

People, The. William Butler Yeats. CP-YeatW

People along the sand, The. Neither out Far nor in Deep. Robert Frost. CP-FrosR

People always make war when they say they love peace. Peace and War. D. H. Lawrence. CP-LawrD

People and a Heron. Robinson Jeffers. CP-JefR1

People and things crowd in. Nature Morte. Joseph Brodsky. CP-BrodJ, *tr. by* George L. Kline

People are divided. Division. W. S. Merwin. SP-MerwW

People are like leaves, fluttering and gay on the bush of the globe. Difference, The. D. H. Lawrence. CP-LawrD

People are putting up storm windows now. Storm Windows. Howard Nemerov. CP-NemeH

People Are So Busy: Or: That's Life! Thomas McGrath. SP-McGrT

People are the plot. Plaza, The. Charles Tomlinson. SP-TomlC

People around me, The. Wovoka's Witness. William Stafford. SP-StafWW

People Boxes, The. James Laughlin. CP-LaugJ

People came to watch him. Apocrypha. David Ignatow. SP-IgnaD

People can't explain. Han-shan. CP-ColdM, *tr. by* Red Pine

People crowd by in the dust. Shih-te. CP-ColdM, *tr. by* Red Pine

People don't act / like they act. Changes, The. Robert Creeley. CP-CreeR

People expect old men to die. Old Men. Ogden Nash. CP-NashO

People filling the street, The. In a Gradually Moving Car Somewhere in Calcutta. Miller Williams. CP-WillM

People Getting Divorced. Lawrence Ferlinghetti. SP-FerlL

People go on singing when they have no song in them. Keep It Up. D. H. Lawrence. CP-LawrD

People had celebrated him as a god. In the Dark House. Stanley Kunitz. CP-KunSC

People have dangled like fish on hooks that were baited. Buying and Selling. Miller Williams. CP-WillM

People have eaten fried fish. In Answer to Your Silly Question. Alice Walker. CP-WalkA

People having a good time. Out Here. Robert Creeley. SP-CreeR

People I live among, unforgivingly, The. First Neighbours. Margaret Atwood. SP-AtwM1

People I love the best, The. To Be of Use. Marge Piercy. SP-PierM

People I see in the village. The. Han-shan. CP-ColdM, *tr. by* Red Pine

People, if you have any prayers. Verses Made Up in a Dream. G. K. Chesterton. CP-ChesG

People in My Family. Grace Paley. CP-PalGC

People in the dark always see people. Yehuda Amichai. SP-AmicYL, *tr. by* Benjamin Harshav *and* Barbara Harshav

People in the elevator all, The. Fiction. Howard Nemerov. CP-NemeH

People in the hall lighted so it hurts. Great Calm: Questions and Answers. Yehuda Amichai. SP-AmicYL, *tr. by* Benjamin Harshav *and* Barbara Harshav

People in the painfull bright auditorium, The. Great Tranquillity: Questions and Answers, A. Yehuda Amichai. SP-AmicY, *tr. by* Chana Bloch

People in the village. Macarius and the Pony. Thomas Merton. CP-MertT

People laugh about my poems. Han-shan. CP-ColdM, *tr. by* Red Pine

People like me can't feel. Wanderer's Daysong. Denise Levertov. SP-LeveDL

People live forever in Jacksonville and St. Petersburg and Tampa. Come On in, the Senility Is Fine. Ogden Nash. CP-NashO

People made a ring, The. Hemorrhage, The. Stanley Kunitz. CP-KunSC

People moves as one spirit unfettered, The. De Jure Belli ac Pacis. Geoffrey Hill. CP-HillG

People of England, ye who toil and groan. Fragment: To the People of England. Percy Bysshe Shelley. CP-ShelP

People of the Eastern Ice, they are melting like the snow, The. Rudyard Kipling. CP-KiplR *Fr.* Second Jungle Book, The.

People of the Eaves, I Wish You Good Morning. Carl Sandburg. CP-SandC

People of the Other Village, The. Thomas Lux. SP-LuxT

People of the South Wind. William Stafford. SP-StafW; SP-StafWW

People on the avenue at noon, The. Near the Old People's Home. Howard Nemerov. CP-NemeH

People on the Bridge. Wisława Szymborska. SP-SzymWM, *tr. by* Joanna Trzeciak

People on the Bridge, The. Wisława Szymborska. SP-SzymW, *tr. by* Stanislaw Barańczak *and* Clare Cavanagh

People on wheels hate people on feet. Hi-Ho the Ambulance-O. Ogden Nash. CP-NashO

People on whom I do not bother to dote. Election Day Is a Holiday. Ogden Nash. CP-NashO

People pass under my windows deeply absorbed in garter belts. Fascination. Andrei Codrescu. SP-CodrA

People, people. Lorine Niedecker. CP-NiedL

People—people of my kind, my own, The. To the Lacedemonians. Allen Tate. CP-TateA

People say cares never depart. Han-shan. CP-ColdM, *tr. by* Red Pine

People say that spiritism is a joke and a swizz, The. From the County Lunatic Asylum. Stevie Smith. CP-SmitS

People scratched their names. Beit Guvrin. Yehuda Amichai. SP-AmicYL, *tr. by* Benjamin Harshav *and* Barbara Harshav

People search for cloud roads. Han-shan. CP-ColdM, *tr. by* Red Pine

People sit on the porch. Ramatayim. Yehuda Amichai. SP-AmicYL, *tr. by* Benjamin Harshav *and* Barbara Harshav

People spruce themselves for a party. Magdalene. Donald Davie. CP-DaviDC

People that build their houses inland. Inland. Edna St. Vincent Millay. CP-MillE

People that live in the biggest houses. Hieroglyphica. Wallace Stevens. CP-StevWP

People, the People, The. George Oppen. CP-OppGN

People think the body's their root. Han-shan. CP-ColdM, *tr. by* Red Pine

People travel a long distance to be able to say: this reminds me. Yehuda Amichai. SP-AmicY, *tr. by* Chana Bloch *Fr.* Songs of Zion the Beautiful.

People travel all day long. Travel by Train. Yehuda Amichai. SP-AmicYL, *tr. by* Benjamin Harshav *and* Barbara Harshav

People upstairs, The. Ogden Nash. CP-NashO

People use each other. Love Poem: "People use each other." Yehuda Amichai. SP-AmicYL, *tr. by* Benjamin Harshav *and* Barbara Harshav

People wait for their mail, dogs wait for their can. Don't Wait for Me. Andrei Codrescu. SP-CodrA

People Welcome the Rich. Shmuel HaNagid. SP-HaNaS, *tr. by* Peter Cole

People were bathing and posturing themselves on the beach. Gods! The Gods!, The. D. H. Lawrence. CP-LawrD

People were leaving. Federico García Lorca. CP-GarcF, *tr. by* Alan S. Trueblood *Fr.* Games.

People who are always praising the past. Past, The. Stevie Smith. CP-SmitS

People Who Care. D. H. Lawrence. CP-LawrD

People who complain of loneliness must have lost something. Uprooted, The. D.

H. Lawrence. CP-LawrD

People Who Died. Ted Berrigan. SP-BerrT

People who have what they want are very fond of telling people. Terrible People, The. Ogden Nash. CP-NashO

People who leave home want to be free. Shih-te. CP-ColdM, *tr. by* Red Pine

People who meet Cold Mountain. Han-shan. CP-ColdM, *tr. by* Red Pine

People Who Must. Carl Sandburg. CP-SandC

People Who See Bubbles Rise. James Schuyler. CP-SchuJ

People who, The. E. E. Cummings. CP-CummE

People who wander among clouds. Han-shan. CP-ColdM, *tr. by* Red Pine

People Who Went By in Winter. William Stafford. SP-StafWW

People who were better than us were *comfortable*, The. Shiftless. Raymond Carver. CP-CarvR

People who work for me don't smoke. Night Crawlers. Robert Stock. SP-StocR

People with no future love people. Yehuda Amichai. SP-AmicYL, *tr. by* Benjamin Harshav *and* Barbara Harshav

People with Proud Chins. Carl Sandburg. CP-SandC

People without their own scene. Robert Creeley. CP-CreeR

People, Yes, The. Carl Sandburg. CP-SandC

   "Aster, a farewell-summer flower, stays long in the last fall weeks, An." CP-SandC

   "Have you seen men handed refusals." CP-SandC

   "Hold down the skylines now with your themes." CP-SandC

   "In paper sacks the customers carry away millions of tons of goods daily." CP-SandC

   "In the days of the cockade and the brass pistol." CP-SandC

   "Let the nickels and dimes explain." CP-SandC

People! your chains are severing link by link. Composed after Reading a Newspaper of the Day. William Wordsworth. CP-WorW2

People's Surroundings. Marianne Craig Moore. CP-MoorM

Peopleshaped toomany-ness far too, A. E. E. Cummings. CP-CummE

Pepper. Yusef Komunyakaa. CP-KomuY

Peracute Lucidity. A. R. Ammons. CP-AmmoA

Perceiving that in the masked ball. Nothing Will Cure the Sick Lion but to Eat an Ape. Marianne Craig Moore. CP-MoorM

Perception as a Guided Missile. Richard Eberhart. CP-EberR

Perception can force you to crawl. Looking a Mad Dog Dead in the Eyes. Yusef Komunyakaa. CP-KomuY

Perception of an object costs. Emily Dickinson. CP-DickE

Perch, The. Galway Kinnell. SP-KinnGN

Perch Less. Louis Zukofsky. CP-ZukLS

Perch less, bird. Perch Less. Louis Zukofsky. CP-ZukLS

Perched for the nonce among such verticals. Matrix (Villa Serbelloni, Lake Como). Amy Clampitt. CP-ClamA

Percy Bysshe Shelley. Dante Gabriel Rossetti. CW-RossD *Fr.* Five English Poets.

Perdita. Louis MacNeice. CP-MacNL

Perdona al primo eccesso. Lisetta all' Amante. Christina Georgina Rossetti. CP-RosC3

Perdy [*or* Perdie *or* Perdye], I said[e] it [*or* yt] not. Sir Thomas Wyatt. CP-WyatT

Pere Bouhours' Fountain Made Muddy by the Translator. *Unknown.* CP-SherT, *tr. by* Thomas Sheridan

Perennial. Olga Broumas. SP-BrouO

Perennial Answer, The. Adrienne Rich. CP-RicAE; SP-RicA2

Perfect. Hugh MacDiarmid. SP-MacDH

Perfect beneath an eight-rayed sun you lie. La Mejicana. Robert Graves. CP-GravR

Perfect god puts forth no dogma, cant, The. Thomas Lux. SP-LuxT

Perfect half-moon glistens, A. True Illumination Is Habitude. Sam Hamill. SP-HamiS

Perfect Husband, The. Ogden Nash. CP-NashO

Perfect is the word I can never hear. Rhymes. Charles Tomlinson. CP-TomlC

Perfect Joy. Chuang Tzu. CP-MertT

Perfect line of horizon, A. Without a blot. A swanky. New Jules Verne, The. Joseph Brodsky. CP-BrodJ

Perfect Love Casteth Out Everything. Randall Jarrell. CP-JarrR

Perfect Love Casteth Out Fear. Christina Georgina Rossetti. CP-RosC2

Perfect Love that Casts Out Fear, The. Jones Very. CP-VeryJ

Perfect Marriage, The. Nicholas Vachel Lindsay. CP-LindV

Perfect Match, The. Clarence Major. SP-MajoC

Perfect rainbow! a wide, A. Storm, The. William Carlos Williams. CP-WilW2

Perfect reliance on the impossible. To Put It Simply. Robert Graves. CP-GravR

Perfect Sacrifice, The. Jeanne Marie Bouvier de la Motte Guyon. CP-CowpW, *tr. by* William Cowper

Perfect skin of things is stretched across them, The. From the Lives of Things. Adam Zagajewski. SP-ZagaA, *tr. by* Renata Gorczynski, Benjamin Ivry *and* C. K. Williams

Perfect swan upon the perfect lake, The. Proverbs of the Middle World. Thomas McGrath. SP-McGrT

Perfection. G. K. Chesterton. CP-ChesG

Perfection. Alice Walker. CP-WalkA

Perfection. William Carlos Williams. CP-WilW2

Perfection, The. Charles Tomlinson. CP-TomlC

Perfection is terrible, it cannot have children. Munich Mannequins, The. Sylvia Plath. CP-PlatS

Perfection now is tended and observed. At Hertford House. Adrienne Rich. CP-RicAE

Perfection, of a kind, was what he was after. Epitaph on a Tyrant. W. H. Auden. CP-AudeW

Perfection Wasted. John Updike. CP-UpdiJ

Perfectionists. Robert Graves. CP-GravR

Perfections. Walt Whitman. CP-WhitW

Perfectly a year, we watched Together les enfants jumping and. E. E. Cummings. CP-CummE

Perfectly Free Association, A. Randall Jarrell. CP-JarrR

Perforation. Yannis Ritsos. SP-RitsY, *tr. by* N. C. Germanacos

Performance. Ted Hughes. SP-HughTN

Performance, The. James Dickey. CP-DickJ

Performances. William Dickey. SP-DickW

Performers, The. Robert Earl Hayden. CP-HaydR

Perfume, The. John Donne. MW-DonnJ *Fr.* Elegies.

Perfume, The. Robert Herrick. CP-HerrR

Perfume!, The. Charles Olson. CP-OlsoC

Perfume-flask, The. Charles Baudelaire. CP-BaudC, *tr. by* Walter Martin

Perfume / of flowers! A haw, The. Charles Olson. CP-OlsoC

Perfume / of Flowers!, The. Charles Olson. CP-OlsoC

Perfume of the iris, sweet citron, The. Words, the Words, the Words, The. William Carlos Williams. CP-WilW2

Pergola. Federico García Lorca. CP-GarcF, *tr. by* Jerome Rothenberg *Fr.* In the Garden of the Lunar Grapefruits.

Perhaps. James Schuyler. CP-SchuJ

Perhaps. Stephen Spender. SP-SpenS

Perhaps . . . "Shu Ting." CP-KizeC, *tr. by* Carolyn Kizer *and* Y. H. Zhao

Perhaps I always knew what they were saying. Prophets, The. W. H. Auden. CP-AudeW

Perhaps I asked too large. Emily Dickinson. CP-DickE

Perhaps I have had enough of summer's. Cycle. Robert Penn Warren. CP-WarrR

Perhaps I was born kneeling. Cigarettes and Whiskey and Wild, Wild Women. Anne Sexton. CP-SextA

Perhaps I'll find my lover. Rainer Maria Rilke. CP-RilkFr, *tr. by* A. Poulin, Jr. *Fr.* Fragments.

Perhaps it is to avoid some great sadness. Sleeping on the Wing. Frank O'Hara. SP-OharF

Perhaps it is to feel strike. E. E. Cummings. CP-CummE

Perhaps it isn't as we like to think, the last resort, the end of something, thwarted choice or attempt. Suicide: Anne. C. K. Williams. SP-WillC

Perhaps it was Myself sits down in this chair. There were two chairs, in fact. E. E. Cummings. CP-CummE

Perhaps it's not more than the fire's reflection. Fire's Reflection. Rainer Maria Rilke. CP-RilkFr, *tr. by* A. Poulin, Jr.

Perhaps Mr. Bessemer is not a pessimist but, last and first. No Woe Is Gossamer to Mr. Bessemer. Ogden Nash. CP-NashO

Perhaps one day I shall let myself. Open Secret. Denise Levertov. SP-LeveDS

Perhaps some needful service of the State. Gabriello Chiabrera. CP-WorW1

Perhaps the Best Time. William Meredith. SP-MereW

Perhaps the cello meant. Confessing My Ignorance. Yusef Komunyakaa. CP-KomuY

Perhaps the dear, grieved Heart. Emily Dickinson. SP-DickE

Perhaps the earth is floating. Poet of Ignorance, The. Anne Sexton. CP-SextA

Perhaps the epithalamic sea beckons. Catalonian Woman. Gabriela Mistral. SP-MistG, *tr. by* Maria Giachetti [*or* Jacketti]

Perhaps there has been some mistake. Man Born on the Earth, A. G. K. Chesterton. CP-ChesG

Perhaps there's time to write a poem. Perhaps. James Schuyler. CP-SchuJ

Perhaps these thoughts of ours. Perhaps . . . "Shu Ting." CP-KizeC, *tr. by* Carolyn Kizer *and* Y. H. Zhao

Perhaps they do not go so far. Emily Dickinson. CP-DickE

Perhaps they have some value. Yannis Ritsos. SP-RitsY, *tr. by* Kostas Myrsiades

Perhaps thy lot in life is higher. Ralph Waldo Emerson. CP-EmerR

Perhaps today. Langston Hughes. *See* Perhaps / You will remember

Perhaps we desire death: or why is poison so sweet? Sirens, The. Robinson Jeffers. CP-JefR3

Perhaps we humans. Freedom. Denise Levertov. SP-LeveDL

Perhaps we ought to feel with more imagination. Recent Past, The. John Ashbery. SP-AshbJ

Perhaps what's wrong is simply lack of vitality. What's Wrong. D. H. Lawrence. CP-LawrD

Perhaps you never thought of it. Crescenzago. Primo Levi. CP-LeviP, *tr. by* Ruth Feldman *and* Brian Swann

Perhaps you smile at me. Emily Dickinson. SP-DickE

Perhaps you think me stooping. Emily Dickinson. CP-DickE

Perhaps / You will remember. October 16: The Raid. Langston Hughes. CP-HughL; CP-HughL2; CP-HughL3

Perhaps you'd like a marching song for the embattled prolet-. Ars Poetica: Or: Who Lives in the Ivory Tower? Thomas McGrath. SP-McGrT

Perhaps you'd like to buy a flower. Emily Dickinson. CP-DickE

Peri Poietikes. Louis Zukofsky. CP-ZukLS

Periander. George Meredith. CP-MerG1

Peril. W. S. Merwin. SP-MerwW

Peril, The. Thomas Merton. CP-MertT

Peril as a Possession. Emily Dickinson. CP-DickE

Peril of Hope. Robert Frost. CP-FrosR

Peril upon the paths of this desire. Edna St. Vincent Millay. CP-MillE

Perilous yellow sun follows with its slant eyes, The. Tsushima Screen. Joseph Brodsky. CP-BrodJ

Perils of the ocean safely o'er, The. Winter ("Perils of the ocean safely o'er, The"). Jones Very. CP-VeryJ

Perimeters. Allen Tate. CP-TateA

Period Period. Ogden Nash. CP-NashO

Period Piece: 1834. William Carlos Williams. CP-WilW2

Peripherally the ocean. Expressions of Sea Level. A. R. Ammons. CP-AmmoA

Periphery. A. R. Ammons. CP-AmmoA

Perirrhanterium. George Herbert. CP-HerbG

Perishable devours the perishable in broad daylight, The. At the City Dump in Nantucket. Joseph Brodsky. CP-BrodJ

Perished have safe small. E. E. Cummings. CP-CummE

Périsprit. Olga Broumas. SP-BrouO

Perjury Excused. Sir John Suckling. CP-SuckJ

Perlegi Versus Versos, Jonathan Bone, Tersos. Thomas Sheridan. CP-SherT, *tr. by* Robert Hogan

Permanence. G. K. Chesterton. CP-ChesG

Permanence. David Ignatow. SP-IgnaD

Permanent Migrations, The. Kenneth Patchen. CP-PatcK

Permanent Way, A. W. H. Auden. CP-AudeW

Permanently. Kenneth Koch. SP-KochK

Permeo terras, ubi nuda rupes. Ode, De Skia Insula. Samuel Johnson. CP-JohnS

Permit a sister muse to soar. To Laura—a Card. Annis Boudinot Stockton. CP-StocA

Permit me, Julia, now to goe away. To Julia. Robert Herrick. CP-HerrR

Permit mine eyes to see. On Heaven. Robert Herrick. CP-HerrR

Permit them one more day with their small words. Like a Prayer. Yannis Ritsos. SP-RitsY, *tr. by* Kimon Friar *and* Kostas Myrsiades

Permitted to assist you, let me see. St. Valentine. Marianne Craig Moore. CP-MoorM

Perpetual angle / of earth & sky. Worlds. Federico García Lorca. CP-GarcF, *tr. by* Jerome Rothenberg *Fr.* Countries.

Perpetual Migration, The. Marge Piercy. SP-PierM

Perpetual Motion. Thomas McGrath. SP-McGrT

Perpetuum Mobile: The City. William Carlos Williams. CP-WilW1

Perplexed Music. Elizabeth Barrett Browning. CP-BroEB

Persecutions Profitable. Robert Herrick. CP-HerrR

Persecutions Purifie. Robert Herrick. CP-HerrR

Persephone. Stevie Smith. CP-SmitS

Persephone. Adam Zagajewski. SP-ZagaA, *tr. by* Clare Cavanagh

Persephone awaits him in the dim boudoir. Adonis in Winter. Kenneth Rexroth. CP-RexrK

Persephone goes underground again. Persephone. Adam Zagajewski. SP-ZagaA, *tr. by* Clare Cavanagh

Persephone Pauses. Carolyn Kizer. CP-KizeC

Persephone Wears Bluejeans. James Laughlin. CP-LaugJ

Perseus. Amy Clampitt. CP-ClamA

Perseus. Robert Earl Hayden. CP-HaydR

Perseus. Louis MacNeice. CP-MacNL

Perseus. Sylvia Plath. CP-PlatS

Perseus Airborne. Amy Clampitt. CP-ClamA

Perseverance. George Herbert. CP-HerbG

Perseverance. Robert Herrick. CP-HerrR

Persian, The. Stevie Smith. CP-SmitS

Persian Arrow. Joseph Brodsky. CP-BrodJ

Persian Lesson, A. Walt Whitman. CP-WhitW

Persian pomps, boy, ever I renounce them. Horace. *See* Boy, I hate their empty shows

Persian Version, The. Robert Graves. CP-GravR

Persian's flowery gifts, the shrine, The. For an Autumn Festival. John Greenleaf Whittier. CP-WhitJ

Persimmons, The. Gary Snyder. CP-SnydG

Persistence of 1937. Donald Hall. CP-HallD

Persistent Explorer. John Crowe Ransom. SP-RansJ

Persistent is the thought for me of that. Sonnet: "Persistent is the thought for me of that." Hayden Carruth. CP-CarHS *Fr.* Sonnets.

Person. Robert Creeley. CP-CreeR

Person, The. James Laughlin. CP-LaugJ

Person crowns the Place; your lot doth fall, The. To His Sister in Law, M. Susanna Herrick. Robert Herrick. CP-HerrR

Person is very self-conscious about his head, A. Thoughts on One's Head (In Plaster, with a Bronze Wash). William Meredith. SP-MereW

Person of this plant with heart-shaped leaves, The. Philodendron. Alan Dugan. CP-DugaA

Person who can do, The. Poem: "Person who can do, The." Alan Dugan. CP-DugaA

Personable shadow, you follow me into this. Corona. Tess Gallagher. SP-GallT

Personae seek provisional assent. Mamertinus on Rhetoric, A.D. 291. Donald Davie. CP-DaviDC

Personae Separatae. Eugenio Montale. CP-MontE, *tr. by* Jonathan Galassi

Personage is seen, A. Landscape. Thomas Merton. CP-MertT

Personal. Langston Hughes. CP-HughL; CP-HughL2

Personal Devil, The. Robert Pinsky. CP-PinsR

Personal Helicon. Seamus Heaney. SP-HeanSO

Personal idiom of a corn shock staisfies me, The. Personalia. Carl Sandburg. CP-SandC

Personal Packaging, Inc. Robert Graves. CP-GravR

Personal Places. Thomas Kinsella. CP-KinsT

Personal Poem. Frank O'Hara. SP-OharF

Personal Poem #9. Ted Berrigan. SP-BerrT *Fr.* Sonnets, The.

Personal Talk. William Wordsworth. CP-WorW1; MW-WorW

Personalia. Carl Sandburg. CP-SandC

Personality. Carl Sandburg. CP-SandC

Personality—amour / brings me to death. For a Play. Ezra Pound. CP-PoEar

Personality and dourness of winter, The. Charles Olson. CP-OlsoC

Personally I don't care whether a detective-story writer was. Don't Guess, Let Me Tell You. Ogden Nash. CP-NashO

Personals. Miller Williams. CP-WillM

Personals Ad. Allen Ginsberg. SP-GinsA

Personas propriis recte virtutibus ornas. Eiusdem ad Authorem. Thomas Campion. CP-CampT

Persons. Robert Creeley. CP-CreeR

Persons. Czeslaw Milosz. CP-MiloCN, *tr. by* Robert Hass

Persons wane and fade, they fade out of meaning. Personal greatness, The. Teheran. Robinson Jeffers. CP-JefR3

Persons who have something to say like to talk about the arts and politics and economics. Never Mind the Overcoat, Button Up That Lip. Ogden Nash. CP-NashO

Perspective. Federico García Lorca. CP-GarcF, *tr. by* Jerome Rothenberg *Fr.* In the Garden of the Lunar Grapefruits.

Perspective. Yannis Ritsos. SP-RitsY, *tr. by* Kimon Friar

Perspective betrays with its dichotomy. Love Is a Parallax. Sylvia Plath. CP-PlatS

Perspectives. Denise Levertov. SP-LeveDP

Perspectives. Louis MacNeice. CP-MacNL

Perspicuity like a sanctuary: against, A. Peracute Lucidity. A. R. Ammons. CP-AmmoA

Perspiration: A Travelling Eclogue. Samuel Taylor Coleridge. CP-ColeS

Persuasion, A. Hart Crane. CP-CranH

Persuasions to Enjoy. Thomas Carew. CP-CareT

Pertussin. Allen Ginsberg. CP-GinsA

Peruse my leaves through every part. Verses Wrote in a Lady's Ivory Table-Book. Jonathan Swift. CP-SwifJ

Perverse Explanation for Mutilated Statuary. Alan Dugan. CP-DugaA

Perverse habit of cat-goddesses—, A. Cat-Goddesses. Robert Graves. CP-GravR

Perversity. James Whitcomb Riley. CP-RileJ

Perverted Village, The. Ambrose Bierce. SP-BierA

Pervigilium Veneris. *Unknown. See* Vigil of Venus, The

Pesano rena e pena. Christina Georgina Rossetti. CP-RosC3

Peschiera. Arthur Hugh Clough. SP-ClouA

Pessimist, The. G. K. Chesterton. CP-ChesG

Pet Coon, The. James Whitcomb Riley. CP-RileJ

Pet Deer, The. James Tate. SP-TateJ

Pet Lamb, The; A Pastoral. William Wordsworth. CP-WorW1

Pet-Name, The. Elizabeth Barrett Browning. CP-BroEB

Pet Shop. Louis MacNeice. CP-MacNL

Pet shops were advertising non-rabid bats, The. Week That Was, The. John Ciardi. CP-CiarJ

Pet was never mourned as you. Last Words to a Dumb Friend. Thomas Hardy. CP-HardT

Petal, colorless and without form, A. Flower, The. William Carlos Williams. CP-WilW1

Petal of white rose. Kathleen Jessie Raine. SP-RainK

Petals and leaves look much alike, in shape. Look Closer. May Swenson. SP-SwenM

Petals of the cosmos, The. After a Visit. Tennessee Williams. CP-WillT

Peter. James Merrill. SP-MerrJ

Peter. Marianne Craig Moore. CP-MoorM

Peter. Richard Wilbur. CP-WilbR

Peter Bell; a Tale. William Wordsworth. CP-WorW1; MW-WorW

Peter Bell the Third. Percy Bysshe Shelley. CP-ShelP

Peter Bells, one, two and three. Peter Bell the Third. Percy Bysshe Shelley. CP-ShelP

Peter complains, that God has given. Epigram: "*Peter* complains, that God has given." Alexander Pope. CP-PopeA

Peter Grump. Christina Georgina Rossetti. CP-RosC3

Peter Jackson was a-preaching. When Peter Jackson Preached in the Old Church. Nicholas Vachel Lindsay. CP-LindV

Peter Parasol. Wallace Stevens. CP-StevWP

Peter-penny, The. Robert Herrick. CP-HerrR

Peter Quince at the Clavier. Wallace Stevens. CP-StevW; CP-StevWP

Peter Warshall says that the slow lorls moves approximately. Public Opinions. Philip Whalen. SP-WhalP

Peterborough. Marilyn Hacker. SP-HackM

Peter's Diary in Goodentown. Kenneth Patchen. CP-PatcK

Pethox the Great. Jonathan Swift. CP-SwifJ

Petit Epître. T. S. Eliot. SP-ElioT

Petit Poème en Prose. Frank O'Hara. SP-OharF

Petite Histoire of Red Fascism, A. Andrei Codrescu. SP-CodrA

Petite Madeleine. Andrei Codrescu. SP-CodrA

Petition of the Gray Horse, Auld Dunbar, [The]. William Dunbar. CP-DunbW

Petrels, The. Jones Very. CP-VeryJ

Petrolio, vaunting his Mercedes' power. Braggart, The. Rudyard Kipling. CP-KiplR *Fr.* Muse among the Motors, The.

Petrou his name was sorrow. Lorine Niedecker. CP-NiedL

Petrus Aponensis—there was a magician! Pietro of Abano. Robert Browning. CP-BroR2

Pettiness really gets petty. Han-shan. CP-ColdM, *tr. by* Red Pine

Pettius no more I verses write. Translation of Horace: Epode xi. Horace. CP-JohnS *Fr.* Epodes.

Petty fury, The. Drunk and the Sailor, The. William Carlos Williams. CP-WilW2

Petty sneaking Knave I knew, A. Mr. Cromek [*or* On Cromek]. William Blake. CP-BlakW

Petunia. Louis Zukofsky. CP-ZukLS

Petunia, The. William Carlos Williams. CP-WilW2

Pewter bowls heavy and swelling with metal. Dutch Painters. Adam Zagajewski. SP-ZagaA, *tr. by* Clare Cavanagh

Ph.D. Langston Hughes. CP-HughL; CP-HughL1

Phaedo. Kenneth Rexroth. CP-RexrK

Phaedra. "H. D." CP-DoolH

Phaedra. Algernon Charles Swinburne. SP-SwinA

Phaedra in the Farm House. Thom Gunn. CP-GunnT

Phaéthôn. George Meredith. CP-MerG1

Phaneron. Muriel Rukeyser. CP-RukeM

Phantasia for Elvira Shatayev. Adrienne Rich. SP-RicA1; SP-RicA2

Phantasmagoria. Yusef Komunyakaa. CP-KomuY

Phantasmal fears, / And the flap of the flame. New Year's Eve in War Time, A. Thomas Hardy. CP-HardT

Phantasy. George Meredith. CP-MerG1

Phantom. Samuel Taylor Coleridge. CP-ColeS

Phantom, A. Charles Baudelaire. CP-BaudC, *tr. by* Walter Martin
    Black Brightness. CP-BaudC, *tr. by* Walter Martin
    Frame, The. CP-BaudC, *tr. by* Walter Martin
    Portrait, The. CP-BaudC, *tr. by* Walter Martin
    Scent, The. CP-BaudC, *tr. by* Walter Martin

Phantom, A. James Whitcomb Riley. CP-RileJ

Phantom, The. Walter De la Mare. CP-DeLaW

Phantom Bark, The. Hart Crane. CP-CranH
    (So Dream Thy Sails . . .) CP-CranH

Phantom Horsewoman, The. Thomas Hardy. CP-HardT

Phantom Kiss, The. Paul Laurence Dunbar. CP-DunbP

Phantom laboratory smoked in the hills, A. Filina. Czeslaw Milosz. CP-MiloC; CP-MiloCN, *tr. by* Robert Hass

Phantom Limbs. Yusef Komunyakaa. CP-KomuY

Phantom or Fact? Samuel Taylor Coleridge. CP-ColeS

Pharaoh and the Sergeant. Rudyard Kipling. CP-KiplR

Pharaoh, I just have a hunch. Lively Watering Hole, A. Charles Baudelaire. CP-BaudC, *tr. by* Walter Martin

Pharaohs were sealed up in their own dust, The. Crocodile at the Ancient Tombs. Howard Nemerov. CP-NemeH

Phase. A. R. Ammons. CP-AmmoA

Phasellus Ille. Ezra Pound. CP-PoEar

Phases. Wallace Stevens. CP-StevWP

Phases of the Moon, The. William Butler Yeats. CP-YeatW

Pheasant. Sylvia Plath. CP-PlatS

Phebe drest like beauties Queen. William Blake. CP-BlakW *Fr.* Island in the Moon, An.

Phèdre. Stevie Smith. CP-SmitS

Phèdre. Oscar Wilde. CP-WildO

Pheidippides. Robert Browning. CP BroR2

Phenomena. Robinson Jeffers. CP-JefR1

Phenomena. John Updike. CP-UpdiJ

Phenomenal Survivals of Death in Nantucket. Louise Glück. SP-GlucL

Phenomenal Woman. Maya Angelou. SP-AngeM

Phenomenology of Anger, The. Adrienne Rich. SP-RicA1; SP-RicA2

Phenomenon, The. Raymond Carver. CP-CarvR

Phenomenon of the Future, A. Stéphane Mallarmé. CP-MallS, *tr. by* Henry Weinfield

Philadelphia. Rudyard Kipling. CP-KiplR

Philadelphia city lights boiling under the. These States: to Miami Presidential Convention. Allen Ginsberg. CP-GinsA

Philadelphia: 1978. C. K. Williams. SP-WillC

Philai Te Kou Philai. George Oppen. CP-OppGN

Philander. Theodore Roethke. CP-RoetT

Philanthropist, The. G. K. Chesterton. CP-ChesG

Philanthropy before Nationality. Jones Very. CP-VeryJ

Philemon and Baucis. Thom Gunn. CP-GunnT

Philhellene. Constantine P. Cavafy. CP-CavaC, *tr. by* Theoharis Constantine Theoharis

Philip, has the white man's charm. King Philip. Jones Very. CP-VeryJ

Philiper Flash. James Whitcomb Riley. CP-RileJ

Philis's Reply to the Answer in Our Last by the Gentleman in the Navy. Phillis Wheatley. CP-WheaP

P[hillips] loved me, not as he loved his Friends. William Blake. CP-BlakW

Phillips! the suff'rer less by law than pow'r. Sonnet Addressed to Mr. Phillips, A. William Cowper. CP-CowpW

Phillips, whose touch harmonious could remove. Epitaph upon the Celebrated Claudy Phillips, Musician, Who Died Very Poor, An. Samuel Johnson. CP-JohnS

Phillis the Fair. Robert Burns. CP-BurnR

Philo Vance. Literary Reflection. Ogden Nash. CP-NashO

Philo, with twelve years' study, hath been grieved. Obscure Writer, An. John Donne. CP-DonnJ; MW-DonnJ

Philoctetes. Sophocles.
    Choral Song: "Soft sleep, thou stranger to all pain." CP-SherT
    Chorus: "I heard of those eternal pains." CP-SherT
    Voices from Lemnos. SP-HeanSO

Philoctetes. / Hercules. / Odysseus. Voices from Lemnos. Sophocles. SP-HeanSO *Fr.* Philoctetes.

Philoctetes; The Ultimate Mask. Yannis Ritsos. SP-RitsY, *tr. by* Peter Bien

Philodendron. Alan Dugan. CP-DugaA

Philological. John Updike. CP-UpdiJ

Philology. Czeslaw Milosz. CP-MiloCN, *tr. by* Robert Hass

Philomel. Yannis Ritsos. SP-RitsY, *tr. by* N. C. Germanacos

Philomela. John Crowe Ransom. SP-RansJ

Philomena Andronico. William Carlos Williams. CP-WilW2

Philosopher, The. Emily Jane Brontë. CP-BronE

Philosopher, The. Robert Graves. CP-GravR

Philosopher, The. Edna St. Vincent Millay. CP-MillE

Philosopher and the King, The. William Cowper. CP-CowpW

Philosopher Nietzsche, The. There They Stand Unaware of Their Wretchedness. Charles Simic. SP-SimiCE

Philosopher on His Way to His Death Suddenly Sent This Message to a Certain King Who Had Unawares Condemned Him, Unrecognized and Innocent, when He Was Seized by Chance among Criminals, A. John Milton. CP-MiltJ

Philosopher! 'tis said you wail. George Meredith. CP-MerG2

Philosophers. Adam Zagajewski. SP-ZagaA, *tr. by* Clare Cavanagh

Philosophers, The. Thomas Merton. CP-MertT

Philosophers are lined with eyes within. Ralph Waldo Emerson. CP-EmerR

Philosophers have measured [*or* measur'd] mountains. Agony [*or* Agonie], The. George Herbert. CP-HerbG

Philosopher's Home, A. Czeslaw Milosz. CP-MiloCN, *tr.* by Robert Hass

Philosopher's Last Walk, The. Federico García Lorca. CP-GarcF, *tr.* by Jerome Rothenberg *Fr.* Newton.

Philosophic prince of ancient days, The. To Aspasio. Annis Boudinot Stockton. CP-StocA

Philosophical Fantasy, A. Thomas Hardy. CP-HardT

Philosophical Poem. John Ciardi. CP-CiarJ

Philosophical Trinity, The. Samuel Taylor Coleridge. CP-ColeS

Philosophus et Phasiani. John Gay. CP-CowpW

Philosophy. Paul Laurence Dunbar. CP-DunbP

Philosophy. Howard Nemerov. CP-NemeH

Philosophy. Dorothy Parker. CP-ParkD

Philosophy. Jaroslav Seifert. SP-SeifJ, *tr.* by Ewald Osers

Philosophy and Religion. Jones Very. CP-VeryJ

Phizzog. Carl Sandburg. CP-SandC

Phlox. Louis Zukofsky. CP-ZukLS

Phocas the peasant, my son, who has had. To Phocas the Peasant. "Rubén Dario." SP-DariR, *tr.* by Alberto Acereda *and* Will Derusha

Phoebe Dawson. George Crabbe. SP-CrabG *Fr.* Parish Register, The.

Phoebus and Dian, queen of bow'rs. Charles Hubert Sisson. *See* O sun, and moonlight shining in the woods

Phoebus Farewell. Sir Philip Sidney. SP-SidnP *Fr.* Arcadia.

Phoebus farewell, a sweeter saint I serve. Phoebus Farewell. Sir Philip Sidney. SP-SidnP *Fr.* Arcadia.

Phoebus, make haste, the day's too long, be gone. Another. Anne Bradstreet. CP-BradA

Phoebus now shortening every shade. Apollo Outwitted. Jonathan Swift. CP-SwifJ

PHOEBUS, Phoebus, ere thou slay. Sophocles. SP-PounE, *tr.* by Ezra Pound *Fr.* Women of Trachis.

Phoebus shineth ere his splendour flieth. Alba Belingalis. Ezra Pound. CP-PoEar

Phœbus! when that I a Verse. To Apollo. Robert Herrick. CP-HerrR

Phoebus with Admetus. George Meredith. CP-MerG1

Phoenician galley and the sweating slave. Empire. Robert Penn Warren. CP-WarrR

Pheonician Women, The [*or* Phœnissae]. Euripides. "Exiles, the proverb says, subsist on hope." CP-JohnS

Phoenicians first (if Fame may credit have). Lucan. CP-RaleW *Fr.* Civil War [Bellum Civile] *or* Pharsalia.

Phoenicians guarded a recipe that required, The. Ten Thousand to One. Arthur Sze. SP-SzeA

Phoenix. D. H. Lawrence. CP-LawrD

Phoenix, The. James Vincent Cunningham. CP-CunnJ

Phoenix, The. Hafiz. CP-EmerR *Fr.* Odes.

Phœnix, The. Ogden Nash. CP-NashO

Phoenix, The. Howard Nemerov. CP-NemeH

Phoenix, The. May Sarton. SP-SartM

Phoenix Analysed, The. Ben Jonson. CP-JonsB

Phoenix and the Tortoise, The. Kenneth Rexroth. CP-RexrK

Phoenix and the Tortoise, The. William Carlos Williams. CP-WilW2

Phoenix Park. Thomas Kinsella. CP-KinsT

Phoenix Undying, *sel.* Kuo Mo-jo. CP-WilW2

Phone. Hayden Carruth. CP-CarHS

Phone. Robert Creeley. CP-CreeR

Phone Booth. Andrey Andreievich Voznesensky. CP-WilbR

Phone Booth, The. Raymond Carver. CP-CarvR

Phone rings, The. Macho Man. Charles Bukowski. SP-BukC3

Phonemes, The. George Oppen. CP-OppGN

Phonograph may(if it likes)be prophe, The. E. E. Cummings. CP-CummE

Phonograph's voice like a keen spider skipping, The. E. E. Cummings. CP-CummE

Phony now has good fortune and a wife. Epigrams: "*Phony* now has good fortune and a wife." Helen Pinkerton. CP-PinkH

Phosphor Reading by His Own Light. Wallace Stevens. CP-StevW; CP-StevWP

Photo. Robert Creeley. CP-CreeR

Photo Genic. Olga Broumas. SP-BrouO

Photo is taken of the family, A. And That Night. David Ignatow. SP-IgnaD

Photo of Emily, The. Lawrence Ferlinghetti. SP-FerlL

Photo of someone else's childhood, A. Old Adam, The. Denise Levertov. SP-LeveDP

Photo on the mantel, A. Neighbors. Gregory Orr. SP-OrrG

Photo Torn from The Times. Denise Levertov. SP-LeveDL

Photograph. Lucille Clifton. SP-ClifL

Photograph. W. S. Merwin. SP-MerwWF

Photograph, A. Joseph Brodsky. CP-BrodJ

Photograph, A. Czeslaw Milosz. CP-MiloCN, *tr.* by Robert Hass

Photograph, A. James Schuyler. CP-SchuJ

Photograph, The. Paul Laurence Dunbar. CP-DunbP

Photograph, The. Thomas Hardy. CP-HardT

Photograph, The. Stevie Smith. CP-SmitS

Photograph, The. Stephen Spender. CP-SpenS

Photograph, The: A Lynching. Lucille Clifton. SP-ClifL

Photograph and Pearls. Tennessee Williams. CP-WillT

Photograph of a Girl, The. Howard Nemerov. CP-NemeH

Photograph of a Lighthouse Through Fog. Tess Gallagher. SP-GallT

Photograph of Kavafis, A. Sam Hamill. SP-HamiS

Photograph of My Father in His Twenty-second Year. Raymond Carver. CP-CarvR

Photograph of the Unmade Bed, The. Adrienne Rich. CP-RicAE; SP-RicA2

Photograph, U.S. Army Flying School, College Park, Maryland, 1909. Maxine W. Kumin. SP-KumiM

Photograph where we smile, The. February 21st. Anne Sexton. CP-SextA; SP-SextA

Photographer's Annual, The. Norman Dubie. CP-DubiN

Photographic chamber of the eye, The. Tale of a Tub. Sylvia Plath. CP-PlatS

Photographs. Charles Bukowski. SP-BukC1

Photographs. Mona Van Duyn. SP-VanDM

Photographs of China. Donald Hall. CP-HallD

Photograph, Maryland Agricultural College Livestock Show, 1924. Maxine W. Kumin. SP-KumiM

Photosynthesis. A. R. Ammons. CP-AmmoA

Photovoltaic. Olga Broumas. SP-BrouO

Phrases ("Overcast morning in July, An. A Taste of ashes wafts throught the air"). Arthur Rimbaud. CP-RimbA, *tr.* by Martin Sorrell

Phrases ("When the world has been reduced to a single dark wood for our four astonished eyes"). Arthur Rimbaud. CP-RimbA, *tr.* by Martin Sorrell

Phrasing Must Change, The. Jelaluddin Rumi. SP-Rumi, *tr.* by Coleman Barks

Phronesis. Kenneth Rexroth. CP-RexrK

Phryne. John Donne. CP-DonnJ; MW-DonnJ

Phryne. Alexander Pope. CP-PopeA

Phyllis. Paul Laurence Dunbar. CP-DunbP

Phyllis, ah, Phyllis, my life is a gray day. Phyllis. Paul Laurence Dunbar. CP-DunbP

Phyllis Corydon clutched to him. Carmen 45. Catullus. CP-ZukLS *Fr.* Carmina.

Phyllis [*or* Phillis] [*or* Progress of Love, The]. Jonathan Swift. CP-SwifJ

Phyllis Wounded. Marge Piercy. SP-PierM

Physical Moon beyond Paterson, A. Norman Dubie. CP-DubiN

Physical world is meaningless tonight, The. Jouga. Wallace Stevens. CP-StevW; CP-StevWP

Physician, The. Jones Very. CP-VeryJ

Physician Nature! let my spirit blood! To Fanny. John Keats. CP-KeatJ

Physics. Pablo Neruda. SP-NeruP

Physitians. Robert Herrick. CP-HerrR

Physitians say Repletion springs. Repletion. Robert Herrick. CP-HerrR

Pi. Wisława Szymborska. SP-SzymW, *tr.* by Stanislaw Barańczak *and* Clare Cavanagh

Pi. Wisława Szymborska. SP-SzymWM, *tr.* by Joanna Trzeciak

Piano. D. H. Lawrence. CP-LawrD

Piano, The. D. H. Lawrence. CP-LawrD

Piano after War. Gwendolyn Brooks. SP-BrooG

Piano & Everything Nice. Andrei Codrescu. SP-CodrA

Piano Lessons. Billy Collins. SP-CollB

Piano Practice. Derek Walcott. CP-WalcD

Piano Practice at the Academy of the Holy Angels. Wallace Stevens. CP-StevWP

Piano Scholar, The. John Logan. CP-LogaJ

Piano, so long untuned, A. Arroyo Seco. Charles Tomlinson. CP-TomlC

Piano Solo. Nicanor Parra. CP-WilW2, *tr.* by William Carlos Williams

Piano Tuner, Untune Me That Tune. Ogden Nash. CP-NashO

Piazza di Spagna, Early Morning. Richard Wilbur. CP-WilbR

Piazza Piece. John Crowe Ransom. SP-RansJ

Piazza San Marco. Ezra Pound. CP-PoEar

Pibroch. Ted Hughes. SP-HughTN

Pibroch of Donuil Dhu. Sir Walter Scott. SP-ScotW

Pibroch's note, discountenanced or mute. William Wordsworth. CP-WorW2

Picasso: "Dream." Oil 1932. May Swenson. SP-SwenM

Picasso made me tough and quick, and the world. Memorial Day 1950. Frank O'Hara. SP-OharF

Picasso / you give us Things. E. E. Cummings. CP-CummE

Piccadilly. Ezra Pound. CP-PoEar

Piccadilly Circus at Night. D. H. Lawrence. CP-LawrD

Piccola Commedia. Richard Wilbur. CP-WilbR

Piccolo, The. Yusef Komunyakaa. CP-KomuY

Piccolo played, then a drum, A. Learning. William Stafford. SP-StafWW

Piccolomini, The. Johann Christoph Friedrich von Schiller. Mythology in an Age of Reason. CP-ColeS

Pick-Offs. Carl Sandburg. CP-SandC

Pick Up the Evening Paper. Kenneth Patchen. CP-PatcK

Pickaxe, The. Jelaluddin Rumi. SP-Rumi, *tr. by* Coleman Barks

Pickaxes of the roosters. Ballad of Black Pain. Federico García Lorca. CP-GarcF, *tr. by* Christopher Maurer

Picked up, a hermit crab who seems. Life Comparison. Alan Dugan. CP-DugaA

Picker. Miller Williams. CP-WillM

Pickin Em Up and Layin Em Down. Maya Angelou. SP-AngeM

Picking and Choosing. Marianne Craig Moore. CP-MoorM

Picking Blueberries, Austerlitz, New York, 1957. Mary Oliver. SP-OlivM

Picking Mushrooms by Moonlight. Charles Tomlinson. SP-TomlC

Pickle Belt. Theodore Roethke. CP-RoetT

Picnic. Adrienne Rich. CP-RicAE; SP-RicA2

Picnic, The. Robert Creeley. CP-CreeR

Picnic, The. John Logan. CP-LogaJ

Picnic Boat. Carl Sandburg. CP-SandC

Picnic Cantata, A. James Schuyler. CP-SchuJ

Picnic, Lightning. Billy Collins. SP-CollB

Picnic Remembered. Robert Penn Warren. CP-WarrR

Picnics is fun 'at's purty hard to beat. In Fervent Praise of Picnics. James Whitcomb Riley. CP-RileJ

Pico Farnese Elegy. Eugenio Montale. CP-MontE, *tr. by* Jonathan Galassi

Pict Song, A. Rudyard Kipling. CP-KiplR *Fr.* Puck of Pook's Hill.

Pictor Ignotus. Robert Browning. CP-BroR1

Picture. Robert Pinsky. CP-PinsR

Picture, A. Robert Creeley. CP-CreeR

Picture, A. Howard Nemerov. CP-NemeH

Picture, The. Samuel Taylor Coleridge. CP-ColeS

Picture, The. Charles Olson. CP-OlsoC

Picture, The. Ezra Pound. CP-PoEar

Picture a stony desert, baked and still. Dream. Thomas Kinsella. CP-KinsT

Picture and book remain. Acre of Grass, An. William Butler Yeats. CP-YeatW

Picture in the Paper, A. Randall Jarrell. CP-JarrR

Picture of a Black Child with a White Doll. Thomas Merton. CP-MertT

Picture of a Nativity. Geoffrey Hill. CP-HillG

Picture of a Nude in a Machine Shop. William Carlos Williams. CP-WilW2

Picture of a Young Man, Twenty-three, Done by His Friend of the Same Age, an Amateur. Constantine P. Cavafy. CP-CavaC, *tr. by* Theoharis Constantine Theoharis

Picture of Daniel in the Lions' Den, at Hamilton Palace. William Wordsworth. CP-WorW2

Picture of J. T. in a Prospect of Stone, The. Charles Tomlinson. CP-TomlC; SP-TomlC

Picture of Lee Ying, A. Thomas Merton. CP-MertT

Picture of Little J. A. in a Prospect of Flowers, The. John Ashbery. SP-AshbJ

Picture of Little T. C. in a Prospect of Flowers, The. Andrew Marvell. CP-MarvA

Picture of the pretty Home, The. Emily Dickinson. SP-DickE

Picture Postcard from Our Youth. Dan Pagis. SP-PagiD, *tr. by* Stephen Mitchell

Picture Showing. William Carlos Williams. CP-WilW1

Picture some Isle smiling green 'mid the white-foaming ocean. Poetry of Shakespeare, The. George Meredith. CP-MerG1

Pictures. John Greenleaf Whittier. CP-WhitJ

Pictures at an Exhibition. Norman Dubie. CP-DubiN

Pictures by Vuillard. Adrienne Rich. CP-RicAE

Pictures from Brueghel. William Carlos Williams. CP-WilW2 Parable of the Blind, The. CP-WilW2

Pictures in the air have few visitors, The. Self-Portait. Charles Wright. SP-WrigC

Pictures in the Smoke. Dorothy Parker. CP-ParkD

Pictures of Philippa. Donald Hall. CP-HallD

Pictures of the People in the War. Louise Glück. SP-GlucL

Pictures of the Rhine. George Meredith. CP-MerG1

Pictures on the television, The. Grandpa's Stories. Langston Hughes. CP-HughL

Pictures to the Wall. Langston Hughes. CP-HughL; CP-HughL1

Pie-wedge petals / deeply pinked and. Yellow Flowers. James Schuyler. CP-SchuJ

Piece, A. Robert Creeley. CP-CreeR

Piece by piece I SEEM. Necessities of Life. Adrienne Rich. CP-RicAE; SP-RicA1; SP-RicA2

Piece of flesh gives off, A. Dead Shall Be Raised Incorruptible, The. Galway Kinnell. SP-KinnGN

Piece of me, curiously. Billfold. Robert Creeley. CP-CreeR

Piece of thread ripped-out from a fierce design, A. 8/8/68: ii. Adrienne Rich.

CP-RicAE *Fr.* Ghazals: Homage to Ghalib.

Piecemeal. Rae Armantrout. SP-ArmaA

Piecemeal the summer dies. Exeunt. Richard Wilbur. CP-WilbR

Pieces. Robert Creeley. CP-CreeR

Pieces. Adrienne Rich. CP-RicAE; SP-RicA2

Pieces. Wallace Stevens. CP-StevW; CP-StevWP

Pieces for Other Lives. W. S. Merwin. SP-MerwW

Pieces(in darker / than small is dirtiest). E. E. Cummings. CP-CummE

Pieces of animals, pieces of all my friends. Ninth Elegy. The Antagonists. Muriel Rukeyser. CP-RukeM

Pieces of cake crumbling. Robert Creeley. CP-CreeR

Pieces of my voice have been thrown, The. Rack. A. R. Ammons. CP-AmmoA

Pied Beauty. Gerard Manley Hopkins. CP-HopkG

Pied Piper, The. John Ashbery. SP-AshbJ

Pied Piper of Hamelin, The. Robert Browning. CP-BroR1; SP-BroR

Pier-Glass, The. Robert Graves. CP-GravR

Pier: Under Pisces, The. James Merrill. SP-MerrJ

Pierce Street. Thom Gunn. CP-GunnT

Piercing eye with which you see, The. Old-Clothes Woman, The. Stéphane Mallarmé. CP-MallS *Fr.* Street Songs.

Piere Vidal Old. Ezra Pound. CP-PoEar

Piero in wraps, the True Cross *sotto restauro*. With Eddie and Nancy in Arezzo at the Caffè Grande. Charles Wright. SP-WrigCN

Piero Luca, known of all the town. Brother of Mercy, The. John Greenleaf Whittier. CP-WhitJ

Pierrot. Langston Hughes. CP-HughL; CP-HughL1

Pierrot. Wallace Stevens. CP-StevWP

Pierrot Le Fou. Adrienne Rich. CP-RicAE; SP-RicA2

Pierrot / Took his heart. Heart. Langston Hughes. CP-HughL; CP-HughL2

Piers are pummelled by the waves, The. Fall of Rome, The. W. H. Auden. CP-AudeW

Pierson College. Czeslaw Milosz. CP-MiloCN, *tr. by* Robert Hass

Piet. Rudyard Kipling. CP-KiplR

Pietà. Donald Davie. CP-DaviDC

Pietà. Louise Glück. SP-GlucL

Pietà. Robert Stock. CP-StocR

Pietà. Wisława Szymborska. SP-SzymW, *tr. by* Stanisław Barańczak *and* Clare Cavanagh

Pietà, Rhenish, 14th C., the Cloisters, The. Mona Van Duyn. SP-VanDM

Pietro has twenty red and blue balloons on a string. Five Cent Balloons. Carl Sandburg. CP-SandC

Pietro of Abano. Robert Browning. CP-BroR2

Piety. Charles Simic. SP-SimiC; SP-SimiCE

Pievish doth boast, that he's the very first. Upon Pievish. Robert Herrick. CP-HerrR

Pig. Rudyard Kipling. *Fr.* Plain Tales from the Hills.

Pig, The. Ogden Nash. CP-NashO

Pig, if I am not mistaken, The. Pig, The. Ogden Nash. CP-NashO

Pig lay on a barrow dead, The. View of a Pig. Ted Hughes. SP-HughTN

Pig-song. Denise Levertov. SP-LeveDL

Pigalle: / A neon rose. Montmartre. Langston Hughes. CP-HughL; CP-HughL2

Pigalone. Sylvia. Dogbrothers. Denise Levertov. SP-LeveDL

Pigeon. Carl Sandburg. CP-SandC

Pigeon, who are to me. Reckoning, The. Stanley Kunitz. CP-KunSC

Pigeon Woman. May Swenson. SP-SwenM

Pigeons. Philip Larkin. CP-LarkP

Pigeons, The. Edna St. Vincent Millay. CP-MillE

Pigeons, The. Karl Shapiro. SP-ShapK

Pigeons fly from the dark bough, The. George Oppen. CP-OppGN

Pigeons shake their wings on the copper church roof. Fourth Floor, Dawn, Up All Night Writing Letters. Allen Ginsberg. CP-GinsA; SP-GinsA

Piggy-back. Langston Hughes. CP-HughL

Piggy to Joey. Stevie Smith. CP-SmitS

Pigheaded Poet. William Carlos Williams. CP-WilW2

Pigment of wax apples bleeds into. Visit to Aunt Francesca, A. John Ciardi. CP-CiarJ

Pigmy seraphs—gone astray. Emily Dickinson. CP-DickE

Pignus Amoris. Lord Byron. CP-Byron

Pigs devour dead human flesh. Han-shan. CP-ColdM, *tr. by* Red Pine

Pig's-Eye View of Literature, A. Dorothy Parker. CP-ParkD

Pike. Ted Hughes. SP-HughTN

Pike, The. Theodore Roethke. CP-RoetT

Pike, three inches long, perfect. Pike. Ted Hughes. SP-HughTN

Pilas volare qui iubebat impius. In obitum Gual. Devoreux fratris clariss. Comitus Essexiae. Thomas Campion. CP-CampT

Pilate. Donald Davie. CP-DaviDC

Pilate. Gerard Manley Hopkins. CP-HopkG

Pilate. W. S. Merwin. SP-MerwW

Pile high the hickory and the light. Winter Night. Edna St. Vincent Millay. CP-MillE

Pile of Years is not so high, The. Emily Dickinson. CP-DickE

Pile the bodies high at Austerlitz and Waterloo. Grass. Carl Sandburg. CP-SandC

Piled deep below the screening apple-branch. Orchard-Pit, The. Dante Gabriel Rossetti. CW-RossD

Pilgrim, The. Jones Very. CP-VeryJ

Pilgrim, The. William Butler Yeats. CP-YeatW

Pilgrim Dreaming, A. Denise Levertov. SP-LeveDL

Pilgrim Fish Heads. Robert Bly. SP-BlyR

Pilgrim passes swiftly, The. Three Postcards from the Monastery. Thomas Merton. CP-MertT

Pilgrim, when the summer day, A. Pilgrim's Dream; or, The Star and the Glow-Worm, The. William Wordsworth. CP-WorW2

Pilgrimage. Robert Pinsky. CP-PinsR

Pilgrimage. Marya Alexandrovna Zaturenska. SP-ZatuM

Pilgrims, The. Ralph Waldo Emerson. CP-EmerR

Pilgrim's Dream; or, The Star and the Glow-Worm, The. William Wordsworth. CP-WorW2

Pilgrims' Song. Thomas Merton. CP-MertT

Pilgrims stopping over who have kept, The. Pico Farnese Elegy. Eugenio Montale. CP-MontE, tr. by Jonathan Galassi

Pilgrim's Way, A. Rudyard Kipling. CP-KiplR

Pili's Wall. Philip Levine. SP-LeviP

Pillar, The. Eleanor Wilner. SP-WilnE

Pillar and the Post, The. Hart Crane. CP-CranH

Pillar at Sebzevar, A. Robert Browning. CP-BroR2

Pillar Box, The. G. K. Chesterton. CP-ChesG

Pillar of Fame, The. Robert Herrick. CP-HerrR

Pillar [or Piller] perished [or pearisht] is whe[a]rto I le[a]nt, The. Sir Thomas Wyatt. CP-WyatT

Pillars. Raissa Maritain. CP-MertT

Pillow. John Updike. CP-UpdiJ

Pillow, The. Charles Simic. SP-SimiC; SP-SimiCE

Pillowed Head, A. Seamus Heaney. SP-HeanSO

Pillows are going insane, The. Flat. C. K. Williams. CP-WillC; SP-WillC

Pilot, The. Edwin Arlington Robinson. CP-RobiE

Pilot from the Carrier, A. Randall Jarrell. CP-JarrR

Pilot in the Jungle, The. John Ciardi. CP-CiarJ

Pilot, returned, sees the village, The. In the Sleep of Reason. Thomas McGrath. SP-McGrT

Pilots, The. Denise Levertov. SP-LeveDL

Pilots, Man Your Planes. Randall Jarrell. CP-JarrR

Primitiæ to Parents, The. Robert Herrick. CP-HerrR

Pimps wear their summer hats, The. Langston Hughes. See Some pimps wear summer hats

Pin Has a Head, A. Christina Georgina Rossetti. CP-RosC2

Pin-swin or spine-swine, The. His Shield. Marianne Craig Moore. CP-MoorM

Pinch, The. Robert Stock. SP-StocR

Pinch lies in the shoe of state, The. Pinch, The. Robert Stock. SP-StocR

Pinch-penny light, rifted, pitied light. On the Failure of a Poet. Charles Bukowski. SP-BukC2

Pin'd I am, and like to die. Thomas Campion. CP-CampT

Pindar is imitable by none. Ode 4.2: Praise of Pindar, The ("Pindarum quisquis studet aemulari"). Horace. SP-SmarC Fr. Odes.

Píndaro no soy, sino caballero. Antorcha Y Corona, 1968. Robert Graves. CP-GravR

Pine. James Dickey. CP-DickJ

Pine-Apple and the Bee, The. William Cowper. CP-CowpW

Pine-apples, in triple row, The. Pine-Apple and the Bee, The. William Cowper. CP-CowpW

Pine Forest. Gabriela Mistral. SP-MistG, tr. by Maria Giachetti [or Jacketti]

Pine Forest of the Cascine Near Pisa, The. Percy Bysshe Shelley. CP-ShelP

Pine moon looks so cold, The. Shih-te. CP-ColdM, tr. by Red Pine

Pine not, my child, to distant lands to go. Nature's Invitation. Jones Very. CP-VeryJ

Pine Planters, The. Thomas Hardy. CP-HardT

Pine River. Gary Snyder. CP-SnydG

Pine-Tree, The. John Greenleaf Whittier. CP-WhitJ

Pine Tree Tops. Gary Snyder. CP-SnydG

Pine-trees bend to listen to the autumn wind as it mutters, The. At the Window. D. H. Lawrence. CP-LawrD

Pine trees will not converse with foreigners. Their aim. Zipangu. Charles Tomlinson. SP-TomlC

Pine with gray tips is moist still, The. Summer Landscape. Richard Eberhart. CP-EberR

Pineapple knows nothing, The. Song of Wild Fruit, A. G. K. Chesterton. CP-ChesG

Pinecones on the Tree Above. Yehuda Amichai. SP-AmicYL, tr. by Benjamin Harshav and Barbara Harshav

Pines, aggressive as erect tails of cats. Forest. May Swenson. SP-SwenM

Pines are darkly swaying, The. Schubert's "Farewell." George Meredith. CP-MerG2

Pines. The white, ochre-pocked houses. Sky unflawed. Upon so. Another August. James Merrill. SP-MerrJ

Pines, under pines. Gary Snyder. CP-SnydG Fr. Myths and Texts.

Pines were dark on Ramoth hill, The. My Playmate. John Greenleaf Whittier. CP-WhitJ

Pink and purple. Shower. Wallace Stevens. CP-StevWP

Pink as a dawn in Galilee. Choral: The Pink Church. William Carlos Williams. CP-WilW2

Pink-cheeked Jesus, The. Cold Blue Tinge. Charles Simic. SP-SimiC; SP-SimiCE

Pink confused with white. Pot of Flowers, The. William Carlos Williams. CP-WilW1

Pink Dog. Elizabeth Bishop. CP-BishE

Pink Dominoes. Rudyard Kipling. CP-KiplR

  ("They are fools who kiss and tell") CP-KiplR

Pink Frock, The. Thomas Hardy. CP-HardT

Pink Locust, The. William Carlos Williams. CP-WilW2

Pink primrose from the plant he knows, A. Unplanted Primrose, The. Thomas Hardy. CP-HardT

Pink—small—and punctual. Emily Dickinson. CP-DickE

Pink tits, or grace of white thighs. Long Distance. Charles Olson. CP-OlsoC

Pinned to Mrs R———'s Carriage. Robert Burns. See Extempore Pinned to a Lady's Coach

Pinup. Billy Collins. SP-CollB

Pioneers. Lorine Niedecker. CP-NiedL

Pioneers, O Pioneers. G. K. Chesterton. CP-ChesG

Pioneers! O Pioneers! Walt Whitman. CP-WhitW

Pious magistrate! sound his praise throughout, A. Official Piety. John Greenleaf Whittier. CP-WhitJ

Pipe. Charles Baudelaire. CP-BaudC, tr. by Walter Martin

Pipe, The. Raymond Carver. CP-CarvR

Pipe, The. Stéphane Mallarmé. CP-MallS, tr. by Henry Weinfield

Pipe Dreams. Ogden Nash. CP-NashO

Piper, The. W. S. Merwin. SP-MerwW

Piper coming from far away is you, The. Keeping Going. Seamus Heaney. SP-HeanSO

Piper's Son, The. James Whitcomb Riley. CP-RileJ

Pipes at Lucknow, The. John Greenleaf Whittier. CP-WhitJ

Pipes of Pan, The. James Whitcomb Riley. CP-RileJ

Pipes of Pan! Not idler now are they, The. Pipes of Pan, The. James Whitcomb Riley. CP-RileJ

Pipes of the misty moorlands. Pipes at Lucknow, The. John Greenleaf Whittier. CP-WhitJ

Piping, beaus, I'll go whoosh and I'll rumble you. Catullus. See Pedicabo et irrumabo

Pipit sate upright in her chair. Cooking Egg, A. T. S. Eliot. CP-EliotT; SP-EliotT

Pippa Passes. Robert Browning. CP-BroR1

  Pippa's Song.

    (Song.) SP-BroR

  "There goes a swallow to Venice—the stout seafarer!" SP-BroR

Pippa's Song. Robert Browning. Fr. Pippa Passes.

Piranhas / in a wine-dark river. Arthur Sze. SP-SzeA

Pirates in England, The. Rudyard Kipling. CP-KiplR

Pirouette. Federico García Lorca. CP-GarcF, tr. by Jerome Rothenberg Fr. Capriccios.

Pirouette. Audre Lorde. SP-LordA

  (I saw your hands.) SP-LordA

Pisa's Leaning Tower. Herman Melville. SP-MelvH

Pisgah-Sights. I. Robert Browning. CP-BroR2

Pisgah-Sights. II. Robert Browning. CP-BroR2

Pismire Rising. Thomas Lux. SP-LuxT

Piso's own comates, his, corps an inane as. Catullus. See In Piso's suite / are empty pockets

Pit—but Heaven over it, A. Emily Dickinson. CP-DickE

Pit where the buffalo cooled his hide. Rudyard Kipling. CP-KiplR Fr. Plain Tales from the Hills.

Pitch here the tent, while the old horse grazes. Juggling Jerry. George Meredith. CP-MerG1

Pitch Lake. Josephine Jacobsen. CP-JacoJ

Pitcher, how / exactly is. Charles Olson. CP-OlsoC

Pitcher that went to the well too often, The. Need for Stoicism in the Stoa of Attalus, The. Thomas McGrath. SP-McGrT

Pitchfork, The. Seamus Heaney. SP-HeanSO

Pite, that I have sought so yore agoo. Complaint unto Pity, The. Geoffrey Chaucer. CP-ChauG

Piteous my rhyme is / What while I muse of love and pain. Christina Georgina Rossetti. CP-RosC2

Piteous Sight, A. James Laughlin. CP-LaugJ

Piteous sobs that choke the Virgin's breath, The. Sonnet [to Charles Lloyd]. Samuel Taylor Coleridge. CP-ColeS

Pithos. Rita Dove. SP-DoveR

Pitia a Damone. Christina Georgina Rossetti. CP-RosC3

Pitie to the Prostrate. Robert Herrick. CP-HerrR

Pitiful brother! What atrocious nights of wakefulness I owed him! Tramps. Arthur Rimbaud. CP-RimbA, tr. by Martin Sorrell

Pitiful Case, A. William Blake. CP-BlakW

Pitiful dupes of old illusion, lost. Sparrows in a Hillside Drift. James Wright. CP-WrigJ

Pitiful hundred-year house, A. Han shan. CP-ColdM, tr. by Red Pine

Pitiful lovers broken by your loves. Twelve Line Poem. William Carlos Williams. CP-WilW2

Pitiless, pitiless spoilers. Fierce Horsemen, The. Robert Penn Warren. CP-WarrR

Pitmirk the nicht: God's waukrife yet. Dying Earth, The. Hugh MacDiarmid. SP-MacDH

Pitt. Samuel Taylor Coleridge. MW-ColeS Fr. Effusions.

Pittie, and Punishment. Robert Herrick. CP-HerrR

Pity. Robert Graves. CP-GravR

Pity. Richard Wilbur. CP-WilbR

Pity, A. We Were Such a Good Invention. Yehuda Amichai. SP-AmicY, tr. by Stephen Mitchell

Pity all the frightened ones. Good Bluffers. Langston Hughes. CP-HughL; CP-HughL3

Pity and Fear. Miller Williams. CP-WillM

Pity Ascending with the Fog. James Tate. SP-TateJ

Pity beyond all telling, A. Pity of Love, The. William Butler Yeats. CP-YeatW

Pity came to lonely me. Guido Cavalcanti. CP-CavaG, tr. by Marc Cirigliano

Pity could be no more. Human Image, The. William Blake. CP-BlakW

Pity for him who suffers from his waste. Suffer the Children. Audre Lorde. SP-LordA

Pity for Poor Africans. William Cowper. CP-CowpW

Pity his how illimitable plight. E. E. Cummings. CP-CummE

Pity, if true. Hearts-Of-Gold. Herman Melville. SP-MelvH

Pity lifts from me. I touch my cheek while everyone sleeps. Ithaca: Little Summer in Winter. Olga Broumas. SP-BrouO

Pity me not because the light of day. Edna St. Vincent Millay. CP-MillE

Pity mourns in plaintive tone. Catullus. See Who loves beauty / veil her statues

Pity of It, The. Thomas Hardy. CP-HardT

Pity of Love, The. William Butler Yeats. CP-YeatW

Pity of the Leaves, The. Edwin Arlington Robinson. CP-RobiE

Pity, says the Theban Bard. On Envy. Unknown. CP-CowpW

Pity the deep in love. Countee Cullen. CP-CullC

Pity the nightly tiger: fierce and wise. Fear of Beasts, The. William Meredith. SP-MereW

Pity the sorrows of a poor old Dog. Word for the Dumb, A. Christina Georgina Rossetti. CP-RosC3

Pity this busy monster,manunkind. E. E. Cummings. CP-CummE; SP-CummE

Pity, We Were a Good Invention. Yehuda Amichai. SP-AmicYL, tr. by Benjamin Harshav and Barbara Harshav

Pity would be no more. Human Abstract, The. William Blake. CP-BlakW Fr. Songs of Experience.

Pity's Sake. Archibald MacLeish. CP-MacLA

Piute Creek. Gary Snyder. CP-SnydG

Pivot, The. Stanley Kunitz. CP-KunSC

Pixy People, The. James Whitcomb Riley. CP-RileJ

Placard for a Poll Bearing an Old Shirt. William Wordsworth. CP-WorW2

Placation of Reality. Richard Eberhart. CP-EberR

Placatory pumice ledged. Kavyria. Donald Davie. CP-DaviDC

Place ("Faded mind, / fading colors"). Robert Creeley. CP-CreeR

Place ("Let's take / any"). Robert Creeley. SP-CreeR

Place ("Long gone time"). Robert Creeley. SP-CreeR

Place ("There was a path"). Robert Creeley. CP-CreeR

Place ("Thinking of you asleep on a"). Robert Creeley. CP-CreeR

Place ("This is an empty landscape"). Robert Creeley. SP-CreeR

Place, A. Robert Creeley. CP-CreeR

Place, The ("Swoop of hawk"). Robert Creeley. SP-CreeR

Place, The ("What is the form is the gro- / tesquerie—the accident"). Robert Creeley. CP-CreeR

Place, The. Richard Eberhart. CP-EberR

Place, The. Kenneth Rexroth. CP-RexrK

Place, The. Charles Simic. SP-SimiC; SP-SimiCE

Place, The. Robert Penn Warren. CP-WarrR

Place (Any Place) to Transcend All Places, A. William Carlos Williams. CP-WilW2

Place at Albert Bay, The. Muriel Rukeyser. CP-RukeM

Place-bound and time-bound in evening rain. Human Arrangement. Wallace Stevens. CP-StevW; CP-StevWP

Place de la Bastille, Paris. Dante Gabriel Rossetti. CW-RossD

Place Didn't Look Bad, The. Charles Bukowski. SP-BukC1

Place for a Third. Robert Frost. CP-FrosR

Place for No Story, The. Robinson Jeffers. CP-JefR2

Place, for the Marshal of the Masque! Charles the First. Percy Bysshe Shelley. CP-ShelP

Place: Fragments, A. Margaret Atwood. SP-AtwM1

Place in mind. Up Here. Robert Creeley. SP-CreeR

Place in which he lived, / Is called Scete, The. Macarius the Younger. Thomas Merton. CP-MertT

Place is forgotten now; when I was a child, The. Quarry, The. Howard Nemerov. CP-NemeH

Place is growing difficult, The. Flails of bramble. Secret Garden, The. Thomas Kinsella. CP-KinsT

Place is so landlocked that it's getting mountainous, The. Swiss Blue. Joseph Brodsky. CP-BrodJ

Place is the focus. What is the language. In Defence of Metaphysics. Charles Tomlinson. CP-TomlC

Place it, / make the space. Edge, The ("Place it, / make the space"). Robert Creeley. CP-CreeR

Place me where flowers and grass scorch in the sun. Petrarch. CP-Petra, tr. by J. G. Nichols

Place names, the names of streams. Matoaka. Amy Clampitt. CP-ClamA

Place of a Skull. Louis MacNeice. CP-MacNL

Place of Backs, The. W. S. Merwin. SP-MerwW

Place of Burial in the South of Scotland, A. William Wordsworth. CP-WorW2

Place of clear concepts is taken by images, anima telluris, The. Writ, The. Charles Olson. CP-OlsoC

Place of Death, The. Randall Jarrell. CP-JarrR

Place of Kindness, A. Denise Levertov. SP-LeveDL

Place of Laughter, The. Theodore Weiss. SP-WeisT

Place of Pilgrimage. Jaroslav Seifert. SP-SeifJ, tr. by Ewald Osers

Place of the Damned [or Damn'd], The. Jonathan Swift. CP-SwifJ

Place of the Skull, The. James Dickey. CP-DickJ

Place of the Solitaires, The. Wallace Stevens. CP-StevW; CP-StevWP

Place of Value, The. Howard Nemerov. CP-NemeH

Place on the Map, The. Thomas Hardy. CP-HardT

Place Pigalle. Richard Wilbur. CP-WilbR

Place-Rituals. Muriel Rukeyser. CP-RukeM

Place so, A. There ("Place so, A"). Robert Creeley. CP-CreeR

Place that Solomon made to worship in, The. Far Mosque, The. Jelaluddin Rumi. SP-Rumi, tr. by Coleman Barks

Place this bunch of mignonette. Dirge: "Place this bunch of mignonette." Paul Laurence Dunbar. CP-DunbP

Place Where I Never Was, The. Yehuda Amichai. SP-AmicYL, tr. by Benjamin Harshav and Barbara Harshav

Place where I've retired, The. Han-shan. CP-ColdM, tr. by Red Pine

Place where pain and beauty, A. Square d'Orléans. Adam Zagajewski. SP-ZagaA, tr. by Clare Cavanagh

Place Where the Rainbow Ends, The. Paul Laurence Dunbar. CP-DunbP

Place Where Things Got. Heather McHugh. SP-McHuH

Place Where We Are Right, The. Yehuda Amichai. SP-AmicY, tr. by Stephen Mitchell

Place without associations, A. End of the World, The. Louise Glück. SP-GlucL

Placenta of love: Letters, A. Yehuda Amichai. SP-AmicYL, tr. by Benjamin Harshav and Barbara Harshav

Places ("All but / for me and Paul"). Robert Creeley. SP-CreeR

Places ("When I wake next"). Robert Creeley. CP-CreeR

Places. Thomas Hardy. CP-HardT

Places. Carl Sandburg. CP-SandC

Places. Marya Alexandrovna Zaturenska. SP-ZatuM

Places among the stars. Stephen Crane. CP-CranS

Places, Loved Ones. Philip Larkin. CP-LarkP

Places of Refuge. Yannis Ritsos. SP-RitsY, tr. by Kimon Friar

Places with Meaning. William Stafford. SP-StafWW

Placet Experiri. Mona Van Duyn. SP-VanDM

Placid lake that rested far below, The. Passage from John Wilson's The Angler's Tent. William Wordsworth. CP-WorW1

Placid Man's Epitaph, A. Thomas Hardy. CP-HardT

Plague, The. Christina Georgina Rossetti. CP-RosC3

Plague Column, The. Jaroslav Seifert. SP-SeifJ, tr. by Ewald Osers

Plague has stricken the moths, the moths are dying, A. Lament for the Moths. Tennessee Williams. CP-WillT

Plague of Dead Sharks. Alan Dugan. CP-DugaA

Plague of Starlings, A. Robert Earl Hayden. CP-HaydR

Plague on your languages, German and Norse!, A. Written in Germany on One of the Coldest Days of the Century. William Wordsworth. CP-WorW1

Plagued Journey, A. Maya Angelou. SP-AngeM

Plagues of Egypt, The. Jones Very. CP-VeryJ

Plaid Dress, The. Edna St. Vincent Millay. CP-MillE

Plain. Miller Williams. CP-WillM

Plain be the phrase, yet apt the verse. Utilitarian View of the Monitor's Fight, A. Herman Melville. SP-MelvH

Plain black cotton dress, A. Piety. Charles Simic. SP-SimiC; SP-SimiCE

Plain hoss-sense in poetry-writin'. Wholly Unscholastic Opinion, A. James Whitcomb Riley. CP-RileJ

Plain in front of me, A. Weary Walker, The. Thomas Hardy. CP-HardT

Plain of Donnerdale, The. William Wordsworth. CP-WorW2 *Fr.* River Duddon [A Series of Sonnets], The.

Plain Sense of Things, The. Wallace Stevens. CP-StevW; CP-StevWP

Plain Sermons. James Whitcomb Riley. CP-RileJ

Plain Song for Comadre, A. Richard Wilbur. CP-WilbR

Plain Speaking. Louis MacNeice. CP-MacNL

Plain Tales from the Hills. Rudyard Kipling.

  Bank Fraud, A.

    "He drank strong waters and his speech was coarse." CP-KiplR

  Beyond the Pale.

    Love Song of Har Dyal, The. CP-KiplR

  Bisara of Pooree, The.

    "Little Blind Fish, thou art marvellous wise!" CP-KiplR

  Broken-Link Handicap, The.

    "While the snaffle holds or the long-neck stings." CP-KiplR

  Bronkhorst Divorce Case, The.

    "In the daytime, when she moved about me." CP-KiplR

  By Word of Mouth.

    "Not though you die to-night, O Sweet, and wail." CP-KiplR

  Consequences.

    "Rosicrucian subtleties / In the Orient had rise." CP-KiplR

  Conversion of Aurelian McGoggin, The.

    "Ride with an idle whip, ride with an unused heel." CP-KiplR

  Cupid's Arrows.

    "Pit where the buffalo cooled his hide." CP-KiplR

  False Dawn.

    "To-night, God knows what thing shall tide." CP-KiplR

  Germ-Destroyer, A.

    "Pleasant it is for the Little Tin Gods." CP-KiplR

  Hadramauti. CP-KiplR

  His Chance in Life.

    "Then a pile of heads he laid." CP-KiplR

  His Wedded Wife.

    "Cry "Murder" in the market-place, and each." CP-KiplR

  In Error.

    "They burnt a corpse upon the sand." CP-KiplR

  In the House of Suddhoo.

    "Stone's throw out on either hand, A." CP-KiplR

  In the Pride of His Youth.

    "'Stopped in the straight when the race was his own." CP-KiplR

  Kidnapped.

    There Is a Tide. CP-KiplR

  Lispeth.

    Look, You Have Cast Out Love! CP-KiplR

  Other Man, The.

    "When the earth was sick and the skies were grey." CP-KiplR

  Pig.

    "Go, stalk the red dear o'er the heather." CP-KiplR

  Rescue of Pluffles, The.

    "Thus, for a season, they fought it fair." CP-KiplR

  Rout of the White Hussars, The.

    "It was not in the open fight." CP-KiplR

  Taking of Lungtungpen, The.

    "So we loosed a bloomin' volley." CP-KiplR

  Thrown Away.

    "And some are sulky, while some will plunge." CP-KiplR

  To Be Filed for Reference.

    By the Hoof of the Wild Goat. CP-KiplR

  Tod's Amendment.

    "World hath set its heavy yoke, The." CP-KiplR

Wressley of the Foreign Office.

  Tarrant Moss. CP-KiplR

Plain tilt-bonnet on her head, A. In the Days of Crinoline. Thomas Hardy. CP-HardT

Plain was grassy, wild and bare, The. Dying Swan, The. Alfred Tennyson. CP-TennA

Plain ye, mine eyes. Accompany my heart. Sir Thomas Wyatt. CP-WyatT

Plain youth, Lady, and a simple lover, A. Sonnet Translated from the Italian of Milton. William Wordsworth. CP-WorW1

Plainness in Diversity. John Ashbery. SP-AshbJ

Plaint. Langston Hughes. CP-HughL; CP-HughL3

Plaint. Theodore Roethke. CP-RoetT

Plaint Human, The. James Whitcomb Riley. CP-RileJ

Plaint of the Poet in an Ignorant Age. Carolyn Kizer. CP-KizeC

Plaint to Man, A. Thomas Hardy. CP-HardT

Plaited Like the Generations of Men. Hugh MacDiarmid.

  "All life's million conflicting interests and relationships." SP-MacDH

  "Come, follow me into the realms of music. Here is the gate." SP-MacDH

  "Everlasting layers / Of ideas, images, feelings." SP-MacDH

Plakkopytrixophylisperambulantiobatrix. G. K. Chesterton. CP-ChesG

Plan, The. Rae Armantrout. SP-ArmaA

Plan, The. Wendell Berry. CP-BerrW

Plan, The. Robert Creeley. CP-CreeR

Plan du Centre de Paris à Vol d'Oiseau. Lawrence Ferlinghetti. SP-FerlL

Plan Is the Body, The. Robert Creeley. CP-CreeR

Plan of Future Works. Pier Paolo Pasolini. SP-PasoP, *tr. by* Norman MacAfee *and* Luciano Martinengo

Plan of Self-Subjection, A. Thom Gunn. CP-GunnT

Plane. W. S. Merwin. SP-MerwW

Plane. Howard Nemerov. CP-NemeH

Plane goes by, A. Sky Writing. Charles Tomlinson. CP-TomlC; SP-TomlC

Plane leaves, The. Autumn Rain. D. H. Lawrence. CP-LawrD

Plane Ticket. Robert Lowell. SP-LoweR

Plane tilts in to Nashville, The. Homecoming Singer, The. Jay Wright. SP-WrigJ

Planes arc like arrows through the highest sky. Plotted. Robert Lowell. SP-LoweR

Plane's flight your helix, transcontinental blood. Birth's Obituary. Charles Olson. CP-OlsoC

Planes, trains, lorries simmer through the garden. In the Mail. Robert Lowell. SP-LoweR

Planet, The. Josephine Jacobsen. CP-JacoJ

Planet on the Table, The. Wallace Stevens. CP-StevW; CP-StevWP

Planet once got married to a star, A. Through Two Points Only One Straight Line Can Pass. Yehuda Amichai. SP-AmicY, *tr. by* Stephen Mitchell

Planetarium. Adrienne Rich. CP-RicAE; SP-RicA1; SP-RicA2

Planetarium. Adam Zagajewski. SP-ZagaA, *tr. by* Clare Cavanagh

Planh. Ezra Pound. CP-PoEar

Planh for the Young English King. Bertrans de Born. CP-PoEar; SP-PounE, *tr. by* Ezra Pound

Planing in, on the autumn gusts. Geese Going South. Charles Tomlinson. SP-TomlC

Planners, The. Robert Frost. CP-FrosR

Plant, The. Jones Very. CP-VeryJ

Plant and Phantom. Louis MacNeice. CP-MacNL

Plant Called Yarrow, The. Robert Stock. SP-StocR

Plant it springs it rears its drooping head, The. Harvest, The ("Plant it springs it rears its drooping head, The"). Jones Very. CP-VeryJ

Plant Magic dust / expect hope doubt. E. E. Cummings. CP-CummE

Plant of noble stemme, forward and faire, A. Upon the Death of Mister Herrys. Richard Crashaw. CP-CrasR

Plant the small seed, the mustard grain within. Mustard Seed, The. Jones Very. CP-VeryJ

Plant the tea-plant on my grave. Testamentum. Wallace Stevens. CP-StevWP

Plant your toes in the cool swamp mud. Flight. Langston Hughes. CP-HughL; CP-HughL1; CP-HughL2 *Fr.* Three Songs about Lynching.

Plantation, The. Seamus Heaney. SP-HeanSO

Plantation a Beginning, A. Charles Olson. SP-OlsoC *Fr.* Maximus Poems, The.

Plantation Child's Lullaby, The. Paul Laurence Dunbar. CP-DunbP

Plantation Hymn. James Whitcomb Riley. CP-RileJ

Plantation Melody, A. Paul Laurence Dunbar. CP-DunbP

Plantation Portrait, A. Paul Laurence Dunbar. CP-DunbP

Planted deeper than roots. Stone Church Damaged by a Bomb, A. Philip Larkin. CP-LarkP

Planters, The. Margaret Atwood. SP-AtwM1

Planting. Philip Levine. SP-LeviP

Planting a Mailbox. John Updike. CP-UpdiJ

Planting Crocuses. Wendell Berry. CP-BerrW

Planting Trees. Wendell Berry. CP-BerrW

Planting Trees. John Updike. CP-UpdiJ

Planting trees early in spring. For the Future. Wendell Berry. CP-BerrW

Plants against the light, The. Dec. 28, 1974. James Schuyler. CP-SchuJ

Plants and trees made poore and old, The. Albinovanus Pedo. CP-RaleW

Plants that careless grow shall flower and bud, The. Ramble, The. Jones Very. CP-VeryJ

Plants went into camp last night, The. Emily Dickinson. SP-DickE

Plaster. Carl Sandburg. CP-SandC

Plaster, The. W. S. Merwin. SP-MerwW

Plaster Model. Yannis Ritsos. SP-RitsY, tr. by Kimon Friar

Plastic surgeon who has, The. Poem: "Plastic surgeon who has, The." William Carlos Williams. CP-WilW2

Plate Glass Window, A. Charles Bukowski. SP-BukC1

Plate in light upon a table is not a plate of hunger, A. Salvages: An Evening Place. Robert Duncan. SP-DuncR

Plate of Steaming Fish, A. Kenneth Patchen. CP-PatcK

Plated Life—diversified, A. Emily Dickinson. CP-DickE

Platform, The. Adrienne Rich. CP-RicAE

Platitudinous Reflection. Ogden Nash. CP-NashO

Plato, despair! Meditation on Statistical Method. James Vincent Cunningham. CP-CunnJ

Plato Elaborated. Joseph Brodsky. CP-BrodJ, tr. by George L. Kline

Plato Told. E. E. Cummings. CP-CummE; SP-CummE

Plato told / him:he couldn't. Plato Told. E. E. Cummings. CP-CummE; SP-CummE

Platonic Drowse. Robert Penn Warren. CP-WarrR

Platonic Passitude. Robert Penn Warren. CP-WarrR

Plato's Dialogues. Czeslaw Milosz. CP-MiloCN, tr. by Robert Hass

Plaudite, or End of Life, The. Robert Herrick. CP-HerrR

Play. A. R. Ammons. CP-AmmoA

Play. William Carlos Williams. CP-WilW1

Play, The. Richard Eberhart. CP-EberR

Play, The. Anne Sexton. CP-SextA

Play Again. David Ignatow. SP-IgnaD

Play children's games one. Two Children. James Laughlin. CP-LaugJ

Play full smiles around the dimpled mouth, The. On Lady Mary Wortley Montagu's Portrait. Alexander Pope. CP-PopeA

Play-Ground, The. Walt Whitman. CP-WhitW

Play I could once; but, gentle friend, you see. To His Friend, on the Untunable Times. Robert Herrick. CP-HerrR

Play it across the table. Cahoots. Carl Sandburg. CP-SandC

Play it once. Saturday Night. Langston Hughes. CP-HughL; CP-HughL1

Play me a game like Blind Man's dance. Bump d'Bump. Maya Angelou. SP-AngeM

Play, Phoebus, on thy lute. Canticle to Apollo, A. Robert Herrick. CP-HerrR

Play seems out for an almost infinite run, The. It Bids Pretty Fair. Robert Frost. CP-FrosR

Play that thing, / Jazz band! Jazz Band in a Parisian Cabaret. Langston Hughes. CP-HughL, CP-HughL1

Play the [or de] blues for me. Misery. Langston Hughes. CP-HughL; CP-HughL1

Play the St. Louis Blues. Request for Requiems. Langston Hughes. CP-HughL; CP-HughL2

Play their offensive and defensive parts. Good Christians. Robert Herrick. CP-HerrR

Play your guitar, boy. Blues on a Box. Langston Hughes. CP-HughL; CP-HughL2

Playboy. Richard Wilbur. CP-WilbR

Playboy of the dawn. Gone Boy. Langston Hughes. CP-HughL; CP-HughL3

Played-Out Game, A. D. H. Lawrence. CP-LawrD

Player Piano. John Updike. CP-UpdiJ

Player Piano, The. Randall Jarrell. CP-JarrR

Player Piano, The. Wyatt Prunty. SP-PrunW

Players Ask for a Blessing on the Psalteries and on Themselves, The. William Butler Yeats. CP-YeatW

Player's Club, The. G. K. Chesterton. CP-ChesG

Players pause, The. After Music. Wallace Stevens. CP-StevWP

Playful birches in the / Where the mind goes off in austerity. Four Exposures. Richard Eberhart. CP-EberR

Playhouse, The. May Swenson. SP-SwenM

Playing a phonograph record of a windy morning. From the Duck-Pond to the Carousel. Muriel Rukeyser. CP-RukeM

Playing alone, I found the wall. And I'd Love You to Be in It. John Ashbery. SP-AshbJ

Playing at bob cherry / Tom and Nell and Hugh. Christina Georgina Rossetti. CP-RosC2

Playing by Ear. Wyatt Prunty. SP-PrunW

Playing chess on the oil tablecloth at Sparky's. Exeter Revisited. Joseph Brodsky. CP-BrodJ

Playing her parchment moon. Preciosa and the Wind. Federico García Lorca. CP-GarcF, tr. by Christopher Maurer

Playing It Out. Charles Bukowski. SP-BukC3

Playing Skittles. Howard Nemerov. CP-NemeH

Playing the Inventions. Howard Nemerov. CP-NemeH

Playing the quarter slots. Gambling at Reno. William Dickey. SP-DickW

Playmate, The. Rudyard Kipling. CP-KiplR

Playthings. Yusef Komunyakaa. CP-KomuY

Playwright, by chance, hearing some toys I had writ. On Playwright ("Playwright, by chance, hearing some toys I had writ"). Ben Jonson. CP-JonsB; SP-JonsB

Playwright convict of public wrongs to men. On Playwright ("Playwright convict of public wrongs to men"). Ben Jonson. CP-JonsB; SP-JonsB

Playwright me reads, and still my verses damns. To Playwright. Ben Jonson. CP-JonsB; SP-JonsB

Plaza, The. Charles Tomlinson. SP-TomlC

Plea. Dorothy Parker. CP-ParkD

Plea, A. John Ciardi. CP-CiarJ

Plea, A. Paul Laurence Dunbar. CP-DunbP

Plea, The. Yusef Komunyakaa. CP-KomuY

Plea for a League of Sleep, A. Ogden Nash. CP-NashO

Plea for Authors, May, 1838, A. William Wordsworth. CP-WorW2

Plea for Mercy, A. William Carlos Williams. CP-WilW2

Plea of the Simla Dancers, The. Rudyard Kipling. CP-KiplR (Too late, alas! the song.) CP-KiplR

Plea to Boys and Girls, A. Robert Graves. CP-GravR

Plead for Me. Emily Jane Brontë. See God of Visions

Plead my cause, O Lord, with them that strive with me. Psalm 35: "Plead my cause, O Lord, with them that strive with me." Bible, O.T. SP-SidnP Fr. Psalms.

Pleas stuck in the cracks of the Wailing Wall. Jerusalem 1985. Yehuda Amichai. SP-AmicYL, tr. by Benjamin Harshav and Barbara Harshav

Pleasance Window, The. Ivor Gurney. SP-GurnI

Pleasant isle of Rügen looks the Baltic water o'er, The. Brown Dwarf of Rügen, The. John Greenleaf Whittier. CP-WhitJ

Pleasant it is for the Little Tin Gods. Rudyard Kipling. CP-KiplR Fr. Plain Tales from the Hills.

Pleasant obduracy, and calm rejection. Petrarch. CP-Petra, tr. by J. G. Nichols

Pleasant smell of frying sausages, A. Mixed Feelings. John Ashbery. SP-AshbJ

Pleasant Thought from Whitehead, A. Frank O'Hara. SP-OharF

Pleas'd in these lines, Belinda, you may view. To Belinda on the Rape of the Lock. Alexander Pope. CP-PopeA

Please. Robert Creeley. CP-CreeR

Please. Yusef Komunyakaa. CP-KomuY

Please do not tell me there is no voodoo. Exposure. John Updike. CP-UpdiJ

Please do not think of me as a surly guest. Traffic Victim Sends a Sonnet of Confused Thanks to God as the Sovereign Host, A. John Ciardi. CP-CiarJ

Please don't anybody ask me to decide anything. Suppose He Threw It in Your Face. Ogden Nash. CP-NashO

Please forgive me, sir. When in Rome—Apologia. Yusef Komunyakaa. CP-KomuY

Please Keep on Forwarding. Ogden Nash. CP-NashO

Please keep your icecream hands. Poem to a Most Affectionate Lady. Charles Bukowski. SP-BukC2

Please Leave Father Alone. Ogden Nash. CP-NashO

Please let me sleep again . . . During long. Sleeper, The. Rainer Maria Rilke. CP-RilkFr, tr. by A. Poulin, Jr. Fr. Affectionate Taxes to France.

Please Master. Allen Ginsberg. CP-GinsA; SP-GinsA

Please master can I touch your cheek. Please Master. Allen Ginsberg. CP-GinsA; SP-GinsA

Please, my daimonion, ease off just a bit. To My Daimonion. Czeslaw Milosz. CP-MiloCN, tr. by Robert Hass

Please Open the Window and Let Me In. Allen Ginsberg. CP-GinsA

Please Pass the Biscuit. Ogden Nash. CP-NashO

Please read this letter when you are alone. Mild-Spoken Citizen Finally Writes to the White House, A. William Meredith. SP-MereW

Please rest the Life so many own. Emily Dickinson. SP-DickE

Please tell me, Love, if that lady had a soul. Michelangelo Buonarroti. CP-Miche, tr. by John Frederick Nims

Please your Grace, from out your store. Beggar to Mab, the Fairy [or Fairie] Queen, The. Robert Herrick. CP-HerrR

Please yourself how you have it. Loggerheads. D. H. Lawrence. CP-LawrD

Pleasing form, a firm, yet cautious mind, A. Epitaph on Sir William Trumbal. Alexander Pope. CP-PopeA

Pleasing is the water's voice. Alhambra. Jorge Luis Borges. SP-BorgJ, tr. by Hoyt Rogers

Pleasure. A. K. Ramanujan. CP-RamaA

Pleasure ("Goddess of pleasure, where thy golden car?"). Jones Very. CP-VeryJ

Pleasure ("With business haste, or with a worldly mind"). Jones Very. CP-VeryJ

Pleasure in the Flesh. Constantine P. Cavafy. CP-CavaC, *tr. by* Theoharis Constantine Theoharis

Pleasure Island. W. H. Auden. CP-AudeW

Pleasure of the wit sustains, The. For W.C.W. Robert Creeley. CP-CreeR

Pleasure Pier. Robert Pinsky. CP-PinsR

Pleasure, Pleasure. Theodore Weiss. SP-WeisT

Pleasure Reconciled to Virtue. Ben Jonson.
  "Come on, come on! And where you go." CP-JonsB
  "Eye of looking back were well, An." CP-JonsB
  Hymn: "Room, room, make room for the bouncing belly." CP-JonsB
  "It follows now you are to prove." CP-JonsB

Pleasure Seas. Elizabeth Bishop. CP-BishE

Pleasure space crammed. Paradise Lightning Dazzle. Gregory Orr. SP-OrrG

Pleasure, whom had we lacked from earliest hour. Ode to Pleasure. Richard Wilbur. CP-WilbR

Pleasures. Robinson Jeffers. CP-JefR3

Pleasures. Denise Levertov. SP-LeveDS

Pleasures newly found are sweet. To the Same Flower [The Small Celandine]. William Wordsworth. CP-WorW1; MW-WorW

Pleasures of Friendship, The. Stevie Smith. CP-SmitS

Pleasures of Merely Circulating, The. Wallace Stevens. CP-StevW; CP-StevWP

Pleasures of pain. Robert Creeley. CP-CreeR

Pleasures of Peace, The. Kenneth Koch. SP-KochK

Pleasures of This Gentle Day. Kenneth Patchen. CP-PatcK

Pleasures Pernicious. Robert Herrick. CP-HerrR

Plena Timoris. Thomas Hardy. CP-HardT

Plentiful sacrifice and believers in redemption. When the Saints Come Marching In. Audre Lorde. SP-LordA

Plessy vs Ferguson: Theme and Variations. Thomas Merton. CP-MertT

Plexus. A. R. Ammons. CP-AmmoA

Plight of a pawn tells the king what it's all about, The. North of Delphi. Joseph Brodsky. CP-BrodJ

Plight of the Troubadour. Billy Collins. SP-CollB

Plighted Promise. Dante Gabriel Rossetti. CW-RossD

Plighted to Shame. Laura Riding Jackson. CP-RidiL

Pliny. Primo Levi. CP-LeviP, *tr. by* Ruth Feldman

Pliny—9, 36—Lampridius—29. Kenneth Rexroth. CP-RexrK

Plod! Plod! Elephants Plodding. D. H. Lawrence. CP-LawrD

Plot, The. Rae Armantrout. SP-ArmaA

Plot, The. Paul Muldoon. CP-MuldP

Plot against the Giant, The. Wallace Stevens. CP-StevW; CP-StevWP

Plot-Culture. Robert Browning. CP-BroR2

Plotinus. Ezra Pound. CP-PoEar

Plotless tale: the passing hours, A. Rower. Charles Tomlinson. CP-TomlC

Plots Not Still Prosperous. Robert Herrick. CP-HerrR

Plotted. Robert Lowell. SP-LoweR

Plotting with the Dead. Wisława Szymborska. SP-SzymW, *tr. by* Stanislaw Barańczak *and* Clare Cavanagh

Plough of Time, The. Lawrence Ferlinghetti. SP-FerlL

Plough, The / the only constellation we are. Look at the Night (Temple, Early '60's), A. Denise Levertov. SP-LeveDL

Ploughed field and the fallow field, The. Generations. Ivor Gurney. SP-GurnI

Ploughing on Sunday. Wallace Stevens. CP-StevW; CP-StevWP

Ploughman, The. Robert Burns. CP-BurnR

Ploughman he's a bony lad, The. Ploughman, The. Robert Burns. CP-BurnR

Plovers. Paul Muldoon. CP-MuldP

Plovers come down hard, then clear again, The. Plovers. Paul Muldoon. CP-MuldP

Plow Cemetery. John Updike. CP-UpdiJ

Plow Horses. Kenneth Patchen. CP-PatcK

Plow: one of the three-mile inns that nicked, The. Plow Cemetery. John Updike. CP-UpdiJ

Plow over bars of sea plowing. Fins. Carl Sandburg. CP-SandC

Plow, they say, to plow the snow, A. Plowmen. Robert Frost. CP-FrosR

Plow thrust into the earth, A. A large smoke-blackened pot. Gradually Stripped Bare. Yannis Ritsos. SP-RitsY, *tr. by* Kimon Friar *and* Kostas Myrsiades

Plowboy. Carl Sandburg. CP-SandC

Plowdens, Finns. Beginnings. Robert Earl Hayden. CP-HaydR

Plowmen. Robert Frost. CP-FrosR

Pluck the florets from. Song: "Pluck the florets from." William Carlos Williams. CP-WilW2

Plucked from their sockets like eyes that gave offense. Assent to Wildflowers, An. William Meredith. SP-MereW

Plum Gatherer, The. Edna St. Vincent Millay. CP-MillE

Plumber in his blue overalls on the ladder, The. Message. Yannis Ritsos. SP-RitsY, *tr. by* Edmund Keeley

Plumbing, The. W. S. Merwin. SP-MerwW

Plumet Basilisk, The. Marianne Craig Moore. CP-MoorM

Plump cherubs ride the star-rays down to see. On G.B. Tiepolo's Etching *Adoration of the Magi* (1753) in the Stanford Museum. Helen Pinkerton. CP-PinkH

Plump, green-gold, Worcester's pride. My Mother's Pears. Stanley Kunitz. CP-KunSC

Plump mate to my head, you alone absorb. Pillow. John Updike. CP-UpdiJ

Plump Mr. Pl'f is washing his hands of America, The. Oil Painting of the Artist as the Artist. Archibald MacLeish. CP-MacLA

Plums, Metaphysics, an Investigation, a Visit, and a Short Funeral Ode. Philip Whalen. CP-WhalP

Plunder. A. R. Ammons. CP-AmmoA

Plunder, The. Robert Herrick. CP-HerrR

Plunge. Ezra Pound. CP-PoEar

Plunge, The. Thom Gunn. CP-GunnT

Plunge beneath the ledge of coral. Reef Fisher, The. Archibald MacLeish. CP-MacLA

Plunge in yon angry waves. Hafiz. CP-EmerR *Fr.* Odes.

Plunger. Carl Sandburg. CP-SandC

Plunging and labouring on in a tide of visions. In Front of the Landscape. Thomas Hardy. CP-HardT

Plunging donkey puberty devi. Go Round. Gary Snyder. CP-SnydG

Plunging into the Improbable. Olga Broumas. SP-BrouO

Plunging towards Phrygia over violent water. Carmen 63. Catullus. CP-ZukLS *Fr.* Carmina.

Plunking the keys until sent out. Playing by Ear. Wyatt Prunty. SP-PrunW

Plural of "Jack-in-the-Box," The. John Ashbery. SP-AshbJ

Plural the verdicts we cast on the creatures we have to shake hands with. Talking to Mice. W. H. Auden. CP-AudeW

Pluralist. A. R. Ammons. CP-AmmoA

Plurality. Louis MacNeice. CP-MacNL

Plurality in death. How We Learn. Josephine Jacobsen. CP-JacoJ

Plus. Raymond Carver. CP-CarvR

Plus Ça Change. Philip Whalen. SP-WhalP

Plus loin un autre commémore. Samuel Beckett. CP-BeckS

Plutonian Ode. Allen Ginsberg. CP-GinsA; SP-GinsA

Pluvius, venting spleen on all enclaves. Black Bile ("Pluvius, venting spleen on all enclaves"). Charles Baudelaire. CP-BaudC, *tr. by* Walter Martin

Plymouth. Philip Larkin. CP-LarkP

Po' Boy Blues. Langston Hughes. CP-HughL; CP-HughL1

Po Chu-i, balding old politician. As I Step over a Puddle at the End of Winter, I Think of an Ancient Chinese Governor. James Wright. CP-WrigJ

Po-sy, a Po-sy, A. Charles Olson. CP-OlsoC

Po, you are quick to take my outer shell. Petrarch. CP-Petra, *tr. by* J. G. Nichols

Pock-marked player of the accordion, The. Wedding Party. Donald Hall. CP-HallD

Pocket handkerchief to hem, A. Christina Georgina Rossetti. CP-RosC2

Pocket watch, I tick well. Gigolo. Sylvia Plath. CP-PlatS

Pockets. Howard Nemerov. CP-NemeH

Pockets of our greatcoats full of barley, The. Requiem for the Croppies. Seamus Heaney. SP-HeanSO

Pocomania. Derek Walcott. CP-WalcD

Pod of the Milkweed. Robert Frost. *See* From a Milkweed Pod

Pods. Carl Sandburg. CP-SandC

Pods of summer crowd around the door. Fall Wind. William Stafford. SP-StafWW

Poem. Langston Hughes. *See* Garden

Poem. Langston Hughes. *See* My People

Poem. Langston Hughes. *See* Youth

Poem: "About the size of an old-style dollar bill." Elizabeth Bishop. CP-BishE

Poem: "After your first poetry reading." Alan Dugan. CP-DugaA

Poem: "Ah, / My black one." Langston Hughes. CP-HughL; CP-HughL1

Poem: "All the tom-toms of the jungles beat in my blood." Langston Hughes. CP-HughL; CP-HughL1

Poem: "Always prudent but unprepared." Alan Dugan. CP-DugaA

Poem: "And tomorrow morning at 8 o'clock in Springfield, Massachusetts." Frank O'Hara. SP-OharF

Poem: "As at the beginning of birth." Yehuda Amichai. SP-AmicYL, *tr. by* Benjamin Harshav *and* Barbara Harshav

Poem: "As the cat." William Carlos Williams. CP-WilW1

Poem: "At night Chinamen jump." Frank O'Hara. SP-OharF

Poem: "Chalky swallow shit." William Corbett. SP-CorbW

Poem: "Daniel Boone, the father of Kentucky." William Carlos Williams. CP-WilW1

Poem: "Down the small and crooked road." Thomas McGrath. SP-McGrT

Poem: "Eager note on my door said 'Call me,' The." Frank O'Hara. SP-OharF

Poem: "Every morning I forget how it is." Charles Simic. SP-SimiC; SP-SimiCE

Poem: "Feeling chilled in that cold country." Kenneth Patchen. CP-PatcK

Poem: "Flowering balls!" Alan Dugan. CP-DugaA

Poem: "For having left the birds that left me." James Dickey. CP-DickJ

Poem: "French blue morning." William Corbett. SP-CorbW

Poem: "Friend o' the Poet, tired and leal." Robert Burns. CP-BurnR

Poem: "Green going through the jungle of those years." Muriel Rukeyser. CP-RukeM

Poem: "Hate is only one of many responses." Frank O'Hara. SP-OharF

Poem: "Here is the man of the islands." Thomas Merton. CP-MertT

Poem: "High in Hollywood Hills a door opens." James Tate. SP-TateJ

Poem: "How about an oak leaf." James Schuyler. CP-SchuJ

Poem: "How could I have come so far?" Thomas McGrath. SP-McGrT

Poem: "I am tired of you." David Ignatow. SP-IgnaD

Poem: "I do not always understand what you say." James Schuyler. CP-SchuJ

Poem: "I don't know as I get what D.H. Lawrence is driving at." Frank O'Hara. SP-OharF

Poem: "I got my hair cut." James Schuyler. CP-SchuJ

Poem: "I lived in the first century of world wars." Muriel Rukeyser. CP-RukeM

Poem: "I loved my friend." Langston Hughes. CP-HughL; CP-HughL1

Poem: "I ran through the snow like a young Czarevitch!" Frank O'Hara. SP-OharF

Poem: "I watched an armory combing its bronze bricks." Frank O'Hara. SP-OharF

Poem: "I would like my love to die." Samuel Beckett. CP-BeckS

Poem: "In the early evening, as now, a man is bending." Louise Glück. SP-GlucL

Poem: "In the list of one thousand false addresses." Thomas McGrath. SP-McGrT

Poem: "In the old days either the plaintiff or the defendant won or lost." Alan Dugan. CP-DugaA

Poem: "Instant coffee with slightly sour cream." Frank O'Hara. SP-OharF

Poem: "It falls onto my page like rain." Charles Tomlinson. CP-TomlC

Poem: "It is no wonder that new lovers run." Alan Dugan. CP-DugaA

Poem: "Ivy is trembling in the hammock, The." Frank O'Hara. SP-OharF

Poem: "Khrushchev is coming on the right day!" Frank O'Hara. SP-OharF

Poem: "Language was almost impossible in those days." James Tate. SP-TateJ

Poem: "Let's take a walk, you." Frank O'Hara. SP-OharF

Poem: "Light clarity avocado salad in the morning." Frank O'Hara. SP-OharF

Poem: "Light flares from the tombstones . . . ." Thomas McGrath. SP-McGrT

Poem: "Light plays like a radio in the iron tree." Thomas Merton. CP-MertT

Poem: "Long wound of the summer—, The." Thomas McGrath. SP-McGrT

Poem: "Looking up, of a sudden." William Carlos Williams. CP-WilW2

Poem: "Love, I shall perfect for you the child." Seamus Heaney. SP-HeanSO

Poem: "Man applying gold leaf, A." Alan Dugan. CP-DugaA

Poem: "Man with a box walked up to a woman with a boy, A." Alan Dugan. CP-DugaA

Poem: "Mule kicked out in the trees, A. An Early." Norman Dubie. CP-DubiN

Poem: "Muscles which move the eyeballs, The." Charles Tomlinson. CP-TomlC

Poem: "My father writes all day, all night." Charles Simic. SP-SimiC; SP-SimiCE

Poem: "My little son comes running with open arms!" Thomas McGrath. SP-McGrT

Poem: "My little son, laughing, singing . . . ." Thomas McGrath. SP-McGrT

Poem: "Now it is the 27th." Frank O'Hara. SP-OharF

Poem: "Now the violets are all gone, the rhinoceroses, the cymbals." Frank O'Hara. SP-OharF

Poem: "O death, so dear to me." James Dickey. CP-DickJ

Poem: "O Heart: this is a dream I had, or not a dream." Stanley Kunitz. CP-KunSC

Poem: "O solo mio, hot diggety, nix 'I wather think I can.'" Frank O'Hara. SP-OharF

Poem: "Of morning, Iowa City, blue." Ted Berrigan. SP-BerrT

Poem: "Oh that was not a scrap of flying Daily News." Alan Dugan. CP-DugaA

Poem: "On getting a card." William Carlos Williams. CP-WilW2

Poem: "Person who can do, The." Alan Dugan. CP-DugaA

Poem: "Plastic surgeon who has, The." William Carlos Williams. CP-WilW2

Poem: "Pythagorean Silences, The." Alan Dugan. CP-DugaA

Poem: "Rose fades, The." William Carlos Williams. CP-WilW2

Poem: "Silence that tunnels forever, A." James Tate. SP-TateJ

Poem: "Sky, the blueness of quiet light." Fernando Pessoa. SP-PessF, tr. by Susan M. Brown and Edwin Honig

Poem: "So many echoes in my head." Frank O'Hara. SP-OharF

Poem: "Some are too much at home in the role of wanderer." Denise Levertov. SP-LeveDS

Poem: "Space / window / that looks into itself." Charles Tomlinson. CP-TomlC

Poem: "Supreme test of one's poem, The." Andrei Codrescu. SP-CodrA

Poem: "Swans on the river, a great, The." William Meredith. SP-MereW

Poem: "That's not a cross look it's a sign of life." Frank O'Hara. SP-OharF

Poem: "There I could never be a boy." Frank O'Hara. SP-OharF

Poem: "Thing / To do / Is organize / The sea, The." Kenneth Koch. SP-KochK

Poem: "This beauty that I see." James Schuyler. CP-SchuJ

Poem: "This life like no other." Gregory Orr. SP-OrrG

Poem: "Through the fog / The gulls." Thomas McGrath. SP-McGrT

Poem: "To be idiomatic in a vacuum." Frank O'Hara. SP-OharF

Poem: "Tree was wet with the moon's, The." Alan Dugan. CP-DugaA

Poem: "Truth's in myth not fact, The." Gregory Orr. SP-OrrG

Poem: "Twin spheres full of fur and noise." Frank O'Hara. SP-OharF

Poem: "Upended, it crouches on broken limbs." Charles Tomlinson. CP-TomlC

Poem: "Wakening with the window over fields." Charles Tomlinson. CP-TomlC

Poem: "Watching, among the rifled branches, for the sun, our hero." Thomas Merton. CP-MertT

Poem: "We will not go out or hear the 'mysterious and private'." Michael Palmer. SP-PalmM

Poem: "What was once an island with birds." Alan Dugan. CP-DugaA

Poem: "Whatever was living is dead." Alan Dugan. CP-DugaA

Poem: "What's the balm." Alan Dugan. CP-DugaA

Poem: "When I am feeling depressed and anxious sullen." Frank O'Hara. SP-OharF

Poem: "When I carry my little son in the cold." Thomas McGrath. SP-McGrT

Poem: "When young spring comes." Langston Hughes. CP-HughL; CP-HughL1

Poem: "Willing to die, / you give up." Wendell Berry. CP-BerrW

Poem: "Wind tears up the sun, The." James Schuyler. CP-SchuJ

Poem: "You out there, so secret." Thomas McGrath. SP-McGrT

Poem: "You were asleep. I wake you." Jorge Luis Borges. SP-BorgJ, tr. by Alastair Reid

Poem: "Your enchantment / enchains me, stretched." James Schuyler. CP-SchuJ

Poem, A: "If the water forms." Robert Creeley. CP-CreeR

Poem, A: "Tags of songs, like salvaged buttons." James Schuyler. CP-SchuJ

Poem, A: "Ye Sons of Levi, Church Divines." Samuel Owens. CP-SherT

Poem, The: "Coming late, as always." W. S. Merwin. SP-MerwW

Poem, The: "Gnarled avenues the years have mapped." Wyatt Prunty. SP-PrunW

Poem, The: "How shall I light." George Oppen. CP-OppGN

Poem, The: "It discovers by night." Donald Hall. CP-HallD

Poem, The: "It's all in / the sound. A song." William Carlos Williams. CP-WilW2

Poem, The: "Never / the chess game." George Oppen. CP-OppGN

Poem, The: "Poetry of the meaning of words, A." George Oppen. CP-OppGN

Poem: A Reminder. Robert Graves. CP-GravR

Poem: Abbreviated from the Conversation of Mr. T. E. H. Ezra Pound. CP-PoEar

Poem about Breasts, A. James Wright. CP-WrigJ

Poem about George Doty in the Death House, A. James Wright. CP-WrigJ

Poem about Morning. William Meredith. SP-MereW

Poem about Oxford. Philip Larkin. CP-LarkP

Poem about People. Robert Pinsky. CP-PinsR

Poem about Repairs to My House. Yehuda Amichai. SP-AmicYL, tr. by Benjamin Harshav and Barbara Harshav

Poem about Storytelling, A. Grace Paley. CP-PalGC

Poem about the Future. Hans Magnus Enzensberger. SP-EnzeH, tr. by Michael Hamburger

Poem about the Garden, A. George Oppen. CP-OppGN

Poem about tradition could easily be, A. Tradition. Wallace Stevens. CP-StevWP

Poem Almost Wholly in My Own Manner. Charles Wright. SP-WrigCN

Poem and Prayer for an Invading Army. Edna St. Vincent Millay. CP-MillE

Poem as Abstract. Donald Davie. CP-DaviDC

Poem as Mask, The. Muriel Rukeyser. CP-RukeM

Poem as Trajectory, The. Richard Eberhart. CP-EberR

Poem at Christmas, 1972, during the Terror-Bombing of North Vietnam, A. Denise Levertov. SP-LeveDL

Poem at the Fairground. Federico García Lorca. CP-GarcF, tr. by Jerome Rothenberg Fr. Fairs.

Poem at Thirty-nine. Alice Walker. CP-WalkA

Poem Beginning "The." Louis Zukofsky. CP-ZukLS

Poem Beginning with a Line by Pindar, A. Robert Duncan. SP-DuncR

Poem by Garnie Braxton, A. James Wright. CP-WrigJ

Poem by the Bridge at Ten-shin. Li Po. SP-PounE, tr. by Ezra Pound

Poem Circling Hamtramck, Michigan, All Night in Search of You, The. Philip Levine. SP-LeviP

Poem-closed, poem-open. Paul Celan. SP-CelaP, tr. by John Felstiner

Poem Delivered to the Reverend Doctor Swift, Dean of St. Patrick's, Dublin, by a Young Nobleman, November 30, 1725, Being the Dean's Birthday, A. Thomas Sheridan. CP-SherT

Poem Factory, The. James Laughlin. CP-LaugJ

Poem for a Birthday. Sylvia Plath. CP-PlatS

Poem for a Far Land. John Updike. CP-UpdiJ

Poem for a Poet. Audre Lorde. *See* Poem for a Poet, A

Poem for a Poet, A. Audre Lorde. SP-LordA
    (Poem for a Poet.) SP-LordA

Poem for a Soldier's Girl. John Ciardi. CP-CiarJ

Poem for an Intellectual on the Way Up to Submit to His Lady. Langston Hughes. CP-HughL; CP-HughL2

Poem for Arbor Day. Yehuda Amichai. SP-AmicY, *tr.* by Stephen Mitchell

Poem for Beginners. Robert Creeley. CP-CreeR

Poem for Benn's Graduation from High School, A. John Ciardi. CP-CiarJ

Poem for Bhain, A. John Berryman. CP-BerrJ

Poem for Bob Leed. Robert Creeley. CP-CreeR

Poem for Children with Thoughts on Death, A. Jupiter Hammon. CP-WheaP

Poem for D. H. Lawrence. Robert Creeley. CP-CreeR

Poem for Dr Pratt, a Lady Pathologist. Raymond Carver. CP-CarvR

Poem for Elliot Carter on His 90th Birthday. Alan Dugan. CP-DugaA

Poem for Emily, A. Miller Williams. CP-WillM

Poem for Hemingway & W. C. Williams. Raymond Carver. CP-CarvR

Poem for J. Wendell Berry. CP-BerrW

Poem for Karl Wallenda, Aerialist Supreme. Raymond Carver. CP-CarvR

Poem for Kathleen Ferrier. James Wright. CP-WrigJ

Poem for Kyra. Andrei Codrescu. SP-CodrA

Poem for Liz. Charles Bukowski. SP-BukC2

Poem for Me Mother. William Corbett. SP-CorbW

Poem for My Brother. John Logan. CP-LogaJ

Poem for My Father. Charles Tomlinson. CP-TomlC; SP-TomlC

Poem for My 43rd Birthday. Charles Bukowski. SP-BukC2

Poem for My Friend, Clare. Or, With White Stupas We Remember Buddha. Norman Dubie. CP-DubiN

Poem for My Friend Peter at Pihana. John Logan. CP-LogaJ

Poem for My Son. John Logan. CP-LogaJ

Poem for My Thirty-ninth Birthday. John Ciardi. CP-CiarJ

Poem for My Twenty-ninth Birthday. John Ciardi. CP-CiarJ

Poem for Norman Macleod, A. William Carlos Williams. CP-WilW1

Poem for Old Walt. Lawrence Ferlinghetti. SP-FerlL

Poem for Someone Killed in Spain, A. Randall Jarrell. CP-JarrR

Poem for the End of the Century, A. Czeslaw Milosz. CP-MiloCN *Fr.* Two Poems.

Poem for the Governments, A. C. K. Williams. CP-WillC

Poem for the Sandman. James Tate. SP-TateJ

Poem for the Time of Change. Archibald MacLeish. CP-MacLA

Poem for Women in Rage, A. Audre Lorde. SP-LordA

Poem for Your Birthday. Carolyn Kizer. CP-KizeC

Poem for Youth. Langston Hughes. CP-HughL; CP-HughL1

Poem from a Single Pallet. Fanny Howe.
    "But I, too, want to be a poet." SP-HoweF
    "Three bags of gold, a fairytale." SP-HoweF
    "Wildness of the flower is all in the tone, The." SP-HoweF

Poem Half in the Manner of Li Ho. Charles Wright. SP-WrigCN

Poem her belly marched through me as, The. E. E. Cummings. CP-CummE

Poem (I Can't Speak for the Wind). James Tate. SP-TateJ

Poem I Didn't Write, The. Raymond Carver. CP-CarvR

Poem in a Straight Line. Fernando Pessoa. SP-PessF, *tr.* by Susan M. Brown *and* Edwin Honig

Poem in Envy of Cavalcanti, A. Frank O'Hara. SP-OharF

Poem in Honor Of, A. Wisława Szymborska. SP-SzymWM, *tr.* by Joanna Trzeciak

Poem in January. Frank O'Hara. SP-OharF

Poem in New York. Gregory Orr. SP-OrrG

Poem in October. Dylan Thomas. CP-ThomD

Poem in Praise of Menstruation. Lucille Clifton. SP-ClifL

Poem in Progress. John Logan. CP-LogaJ
    First Prelude. Dream in Ohio: The Father. CP-LogaJ

Poem in Prose. Louise Bogan. CP-BogaL

Poem in Prose. Archibald MacLeish. CP-MacLA

Poem in Stretching, A. Robert Duncan. SP-DuncR

Poem in Thanks. Thomas Lux. SP-LuxT

Poem in the American Manner. Dorothy Parker. CP-ParkD

Poem in the ancient mode for you. When I Wrote a Little. Hayden Carruth. CP-CarHS

Poem in the Form of a Letter: to Lauro de Bosis. Kenneth Patchen. CP-PatcK

Poem in the Modern Manner. Ted Berrigan. SP-BerrT *Fr.* Sonnets, The.

Poem in the Rain and the Sun. Thomas Merton. CP-MertT

Poem in the Traditional Manner. Ted Berrigan. SP-BerrT *Fr.* Sonnets, The.

Poem in Three Parts. Robert Bly. SP-BlyR

Poem in Translation, A. Tess Gallagher. SP-GallT

Poem in Two Parts. Michael Palmer. SP-PalmM

Poem / is a discipline, The. Self, The. William Carlos Williams. CP-WilW2

Poem is just beyond the corner of the eye, The. Corner of the Eye, The. Robert Penn Warren. CP-WarrR

Poem is less an orange than a grid, A. Poem as Abstract. Donald Davie. CP-DaviDC

Poem is the cry of its occasion, The. Another Duffer. Sam Hamill. SP-HamiS

Poem is this, The. Poet and His Poems, The. William Carlos Williams. CP-WilW2

Poem Left in Sourdough Mountain Lookout. Gary Snyder. CP-SnydG

Poem must not charm us like a play [*or* film], The. Against the False Magicians. Thomas McGrath. SP-McGrT

Poem must resist the intelligence, The. Man Carrying Thing. Wallace Stevens. CP-StevW; CP-StevWP

Poem: 1939. Thomas Merton. CP-MertT

Poem Not against Songbirds, A. Raymond Carver. CP-CarvR

Poem of Exile, A. Eleanor Wilner. SP-WilnE

Poem of Flight, The. Philip Levine. SP-LeviP

Poem of Margery Kempe, A. Howard Nemerov. CP-NemeH

Poem of Night. Galway Kinnell. SP-KinnGN

Poem of Quantity. Jorge Luis Borges. SP-BorgJ, *tr.* by Alastair Reid

Poem of Remembrances for a Girl or a Boy of These States. Walt Whitman. CP-WhitW

Poem of Sir Walter Rawleighs, A. Sir Walter Ralegh. CP-RaleW

Poem of Spring. Yehuda Amichai. SP-AmicYL, *tr.* by Benjamin Harshav *and* Barbara Harshav

Poem of Thanks, A. Wendell Berry. CP-BerrW

Poem of the Fourth Element. Jorge Luis Borges. SP-BorgJ, *tr.* by Alastair Reid

Poem of the Gifts. Jorge Luis Borges. SP-BorgJ, *tr.* by Alastair Reid

Poem of the Gypsy *Siguiriya*. Federico García Lorca. CP-GarcF, *tr.* by Cola Franzen

Poem of the mind in the act of finding, The. Of Modern Poetry. Wallace Stevens. CP-StevW; CP-StevWP

Poem of the Saeta. Federico García Lorca. CP-GarcF, *tr.* by Cola Franzen *and* Robert Nasatir
    Archers. SP-GarcF
    Arrow. SP-GarcF
    Balcony. SP-GarcF
    Early Morning. SP-GarcF
    Night. SP-GarcF
    Paso. SP-GarcF
    Procession. SP-GarcF
    Seville. SP-GarcF

Poem of the *Soleá*. Federico García Lorca. CP-GarcF, *tr.* by Cola Franzen, Christopher Maurer *and* Robert Nasatir

Poem of Women. Kadya Molodovsky.

Poem on America, A. Allen Ginsberg. CP-GinsA

Poem on Eloquence by R. W. Emerson. Ralph Waldo Emerson. CP-EmerR

Poem on His Birthday. Dylan Thomas. CP-ThomD

Poem on Holy Saturday. Robert Stock. SP-StocR

Poem on Life. Robert Burns. CP-BurnR

Poem on My Birthday, July 2. Raymond Carver. CP-CarvR

Poem on Particulars, A. A. K. Ramanujan. CP-RamaA

Poem on the Death of Charles Eliot, Aged 12 Months, A [variant 1]. Phillis Wheatley. *See* Funeral Poem on the Death of C. E. an Infant of Twelve Months, A

Poem on the Death of Charles Eliot Aged 12 Months, A [variant 2]. Phillis Wheatley. *See* Funeral Poem on the Death of C. E. an Infant of Twelve Months, A

Poem on the Death of Mrs. Smith, A. Mary Field Stockton Harrison. CP-StocA

Poem on the Death of Richard Stockton, A. Elizabeth Graeme Fergusson. CP-StocA

Poem on Tom Pun——bi on Occasion of His Late Death, and in Vindication of Some Verses Written, Entitled "Sheridan's Resurrection," A. *Unknown.* CP-SherT

Poem Only. Laura Riding Jackson. CP-RidiL

Poem, or Beauty Hurts Mr. Vinal. E. E. Cummings. CP-CummE; SP-CummE

Poem out of Childhood. Muriel Rukeyser. CP-RukeM

Poem perfect through its parts and in its whole, The. Ultimate Poem, The. Robert Stock. SP-StocR

Poem Put into My Lady Laiton's Pocket, A. Sir Walter Ralegh. CP-RaleW
    (Poem Put into My Lady Laiton's Pocket by Sr W. Rawleigh, A.) CP-RaleW

Poem Put into My Lady Laiton's Pocket by Sr W. Rawleigh, A. Sir Walter Ralegh. *See* Poem Put into My Lady Laiton's Pocket, A

Poem Read at Joan Mitchell's. Frank O'Hara. SP-OharF

Poem Recalled, A. Theodore Weiss. SP-WeisT

Poem Rising by Its Own Weight, The. Denise Levertov. SP-LeveDL

Poem Rocket. Allen Ginsberg. CP-GinsA

Poem Seen as a Shell Game, The. James Laughlin. CP-LaugJ

Poem Sent Me by Sir William Burlase, A. Ben Jonson. CP-JonsB

Poem should be palpable and mute, A. Ars Poetica. Archibald MacLeish. CP-MacLA

Poem, Slow to Come, on the Death of Cummings (1894-1962). John Logan. CP-LogaJ

Poem, Small and Delible. Carolyn Kizer. CP-KizeC

Poem so hard it has no heart, A. Why. Richard Eberhart. CP-EberR

Poem, Spoken before the ΦBK Society, August, 1834. Ralph Waldo Emerson. CP-EmerR

Poem taken by the New Yorker, A. Snowy Owl. Richard Eberhart. CP-EberR

Poem talking silence not dead death. Poem Only. Laura Riding Jackson. CP-RidiL

Poem: Tears, Spray, and Steam. John Logan. CP-LogaJ

Poem That Took the Place of a Mountain, The. Wallace Stevens. CP-StevW, CP-StevWP

Poem to a Dead Soldier. Langston Hughes. CP-HughL; CP-HughL1

Poem to a Most Affectionate Lady. Charles Bukowski. SP-BukC2

Poem to Be Printed on a Very White Page. Robert Stock. SP-StocR

Poem to Me. William Meredith. SP-MereW

Poem to My Uterus. Lucille Clifton. SP ClifL

Poem to Some of my Recent Poems. James Tate. SP-TateJ

Poem to the Mother. Gregory Orr. SP-OrrG

Poem to Uncle Sam. Langston Hughes. CP-HughL; CP-HughL3

Poem—Unfinished Poem. Thomas McGrath. SP-McGrT

Poem upon the Death of His Late Highness the Lord Protector, A. Andrew Marvell. *See* Poem upon the Death of Oliver Cromwell, A

Poem upon the Death of Oliver Cromwell, A. Andrew Marvell. CP-MarvA
    (Poem upon the Death of His Late Highness the Lord Protector, A.) CP-MarvA

Poem upon the page is as massive as, The. Ted Berrigan. SP-BerrT *Fr.* Sonnets, The.

Poem V (F) W. Frank O'Hara. SP-OharF

Poem White Page White Page Poem. Muriel Rukeyser. CP-RukeM

Poem with Capital Letters, A. Jane Cooper. CP-CoopJ

Poem with No Ending, A. Philip Levine.
    "Across the world / in the high mountains of the West." SP-LeviP
    "How many lives were torn apart." SP-LeviP
    "I reenter a day in a late summer." SP LeviP
    "Memory of rain falling slowly, The." SP-LeviP
    "To get west you go east." SP-LeviP
    "We sat by the shore." SP-LeviP

Poem with One Fact. Donald Hall. CP-HallD

Poem with Refrains. Robert Pinsky. CP-PinsR

Poem with Rhythms. Wallace Stevens. CP-StevW; CP-StevWP

Poem with the Answer, A. Sir John Suckling. CP-SuckJ

Poem without a Title. Charles Simic. SP-SimiC; SP-SimiCE

Poem without an End. Yehuda Amichai. SP-AmicY, *tr.* by Chana Bloch

Poem Written after Reading Certain Poets Sired by the English School and Bitched by the C.P. Kenneth Patchen. CP-PatcK

Poem Written at Morning. Wallace Stevens. CP-StevW; CP-StevWP

Poem Written in a Copy of *Beowulf*. Jorge Luis Borges. SP-BorgJ, *tr.* by Alastair Reid

Poem Written on the Typewriter. Robert Stock. SP-StocR

Poème d'Automne. Langston Hughes. CP-HughL; CP-HughL1

Poemless Rhymes for the Times. Charles Olson. CP-OlsoC

POEM(or "the divine right of majorities, that illegitimate offspring of the divine right of kings" Homer Lea). E. E. Cummings. CP-CummE

Poems. Raymond Carver. CP-CarvR

Poems about the Moon. Nicholas Vachel Lindsay.
    Euclid. CP-LindV
    Yet Gentle Will the Griffin Be. CP-LindV

Poems along the Hudson River. Yehuda Amichai. SP-AmicYL, *tr.* by Benjamin Harshav *and* Barbara Harshav

Poems are be not intended. Intention. Andrei Codrescu. SP-CodrA

Poems are hard to read. Major Work, A. William Meredith. SP-MereW

Poems are talking to them- / selves again they're bored, The. Poem Factory, The. James Laughlin. CP-LaugJ

Poems at the Porthole. Lorine Niedecker. CP-NiedL

Poems Composed or Suggested during a Tour, in the Summer of 1833. William Wordsworth. CP-WorW2

Poems Done on a Late Night Car. Carl Sandburg. CP-SandC

Poems for a Woman. Yehuda Amichai. SP-AmicY, *tr.* by Stephen Mitchell

Poems for Camillo Sbarbaro. Eugenio Montale. CP-MontE, *tr.* by Jonathan Galassi

Poems for My Cousin. Josephine Jacobsen. CP-JacoJ

Poems from Buenos Aires. Yehuda Amichai. SP-AmicYL, *tr.* by Benjamin Harshav *and* Barbara Harshav

Poems from poems, songs. River, A. Adam Zagajewski. SP-ZagaA

Poems from St. Irvyne, or, The Rosicrucian. Percy Bysshe Shelley. CP-ShelP

Poems have too much point, The. Phonemes, The. George Oppen. CP-OppGN

Poems here at home!—Who'll write 'em down, The. James Whitcomb Riley. CP-RileJ

Poems, like lives, are doing what we can. Esthetic Theories: Art as Expression. Randall Jarrell. CP-JarrR

Poems of Akhziv. Yehuda Amichai. SP-AmicYL, *tr.* by Benjamin Harshav *and* Barbara Harshav

Poems of continuity, mines and graves. Yehuda Amichai. SP-AmicYL, *tr.* by Benjamin Harshav *and* Barbara Harshav

Poems of Lies and Beauty. Yehuda Amichai. SP-AmicYL, *tr.* by Benjamin Harshav *and* Barbara Harshav

Poems of others he clipped and saved in those distant summers, The. Uses of the Lost Poets. Thomas McGrath. SP-McGrT

Poems of Our Climate, The. Wallace Stevens. CP-StevW; CP-StevWP

Poems of Resigning. Yehuda Amichai. SP-AmicYL, *tr.* by Benjamin Harshav *and* Barbara Harshav

Poems of Spring in the Appalachian Mountains. Yehuda Amichai. SP-AmicYL, *tr.* by Benjamin Harshav *and* Barbara Harshav

Poems of the Hot Wind. Yehuda Amichai. SP-AmicYL, *tr.* by Benjamin Harshav *and* Barbara Harshav

Poems of the Land of Zion and Jerusalem. Yehuda Amichai.
    "And in spite of all that, I must." SP-AmicYL
    "Blood that stands the member erect, The." SP-AmicYL
    "City where I was born was destroyed by cannons, The." SP-AmicYL
    "Even my loves are measured by the wars." SP-AmicYL
    "I have nothing to say about the war." SP-AmicYL
    "I left the Evening Land by the will of the night." SP-AmicYL
    "In the summer, nations come to one another." SP-AmicYL
    "Let Memory Mountain remember instead of me." SP-AmicYL
    "New homeland was built, The." SP-AmicYL
    "On the lot that was a short-cut for lovers." SP-AmicYL
    "Sometimes I think of my fathers." SP-AmicYL
    "War broke out in autumn, in the no-man's land." SP-AmicYL
    "What was the message of the burned man?" SP-AmicYL
    "Where was he wounded?" "You don't know." SP-AmicYL

Poems on Poland. Adam Zagajewski. SP ZagaA, *tr.* by Renata Gorczynski

Poems on the Shore of Caesarea. Yehuda Amichai.
    "And so we live here. Like the sea." SP-AmicYL
    "Come again next winter." SP-AmicYL
    "I swam alone far away." SP-AmicYL
    "Sea preserves in salt, The." SP-AmicYL
    "Weary salt said: Here, The." SP-AmicYL
    "Woman that disappeared beyond, The." SP-AmicYL

Poems, Potatoes. Sylvia Plath. CP-PlatS

Poems rise in my brain. Reading French Poetry. Allen Ginsberg. CP-GinsA

"Poems," says the title. George Meredith. CP-MerG2

Poems Speaking of Buddha, Prince Siddartha. Nicholas Vachel Lindsay. CP-LindV

Poems to a Brown Cricket. James Wright. CP-WrigJ

Poems to a Girl on the Seashore. Yehuda Amichai. SP-AmicYL, *tr.* by Benjamin Harshav *and* Barbara Harshav

Poems which are written by the soul. Kenneth Patchen. CP-PatcK

Poesie Abrutie. Wallace Stevens. CP-StevW; CP-StevWP

Poesie to Prove Affection is Not Love, A. Sir Walter Ralegh. CP-RaleW

Poet. Archibald MacLeish. CP-MacLA

Poet. Karl Shapiro. SP-ShapK

Poet! Stevie Smith. CP-SmitS

Poet, A. Thomas Hardy. CP-HardT

Poet, The. Elizabeth Barrett Browning. CP-BroEB

Poet, The. Hayden Carruth. CP-CarHS

Poet, The. Countee Cullen. CP-CullC

Poet, The. "H. D." CP-DoolH

Poet, The. Paul Laurence Dunbar. CP-DunbP

Poet, The. Richard Eberhart. CP-EberR

Poet, The. Ivor Gurney. SP-GurnI

Poet, The. John Keats. CP-KeatJ

Poet, The. Rainer Maria Rilke. CP-RilkFr, *tr.* by A. Poulin, Jr.

Poet, The. Jones Very. CP-VeryJ

Poet: A Lying Word. Laura Riding Jackson. CP-RidiL

Poet and friend of poets, if thy glass. To E. C. S. John Greenleaf Whittier. CP-WhitJ

Poet and His Book, The. Edna St. Vincent Millay. CP-MillE

Poet and His Poems, The. William Carlos Williams. CP-WilW2

Poet and His Song, The. Paul Laurence Dunbar. CP-DunbP

Poet and Person. Denise Levertov. SP-LeveDL; SP-LeveDS

Poet and the Baby, The. Paul Laurence Dunbar. CP-DunbP

Poet and the Bird, The. Elizabeth Barrett Browning. CP-BroEB

Poet and the Caged Turtledove, The. William Wordsworth. CP-WorW2

Poet and the Children, The. John Greenleaf Whittier. CP-WhitJ

Poet and the Muse, The. Constantine P. Cavafy. CP-CavaC, *tr. by* Theoharis Constantine Theoharis

Poet Answers the Accuser, The. Kathleen Jessie Raine. SP-RainK

Poet as Eagle Scout, The. Howard Nemerov. CP-NemeH

Poet as Fisherman. Lawrence Ferlinghetti. SP-FerlL

Poet as Mute. Josephine Jacobsen. CP-JacoJ

Poet asks, and *Phillis* can't refuse, The. Answer to the *Rebus*, by the Author of These Poems, An. Phillis Wheatley. CP-WheaP

Poet Asks His Love about the "Enchanted City" of Cuenca, The. Federico García Lorca. CP-GarcF, *tr. by* Angela Jaffray

Poet Asks His Love to Write Him, The. Federico García Lorca. CP-GarcF, *tr. by* Angela Jaffray

Poet at Forty, The. Howard Nemerov. CP-NemeH

Poet at Seventy. Czeslaw Milosz. CP-MiloC; CP-MiloCN

Poet, be seated at the piano. Mozart, 1935. Wallace Stevens. CP-StevW; CP-StevWP

Poet bred in Saadi's school. Proteus. Ralph Waldo Emerson. CP-EmerR

Poet Burns to Be Honored, the headline read. My Wife Reads the Paper at Breakfast on the Birthday of the Scottish Poet. Miller Williams. CP-WillM

Poet comes with his white pain to save mankind, The. Broken Wing Theory. Richard Eberhart. CP-EberR

Poet could not sleep aright, A. Vision of Poets, A. Elizabeth Barrett Browning. CP-BroEB

· Poet Dreams of a Nice Warm Motel, The. Marge Piercy. SP-PierM

Poet Egan O'Rahilly, Homesick in Old Age, The. Egan O'Rahilly. CP-KinsT, *tr. by* Thomas Kinsella

Poet, exquisite and pale, The. After Reading a Book of Modern Verse. G. K. Chesterton. CP-ChesG

Poet Hath Lost His Pipe, The. Robert Herrick. CP-HerrR

Poet hath the child's sight in his breast, The. Poet, The. Elizabeth Barrett Browning. CP-BroEB

Poet!—He Hath Put His Heart to School, A. William Wordsworth. CP-WorW2

Poet Hin, The. Stevie Smith. CP-SmitS

Poet I'm too near your and my sod daily. Catullus. *See* Fetch, papyrus / our soft-measured poet

Poet in his lone yet genial hour, The. Apologia pro Vita Sua. Samuel Taylor Coleridge. CP-ColeS

Poet in Residence. Karl Shapiro. SP-ShapK

Poet is a faker, The. He. Autopsychography. Fernando Pessoa. SP-PessF, *tr. by* Susan M. Brown *and* Edwin Honig

Poet is at home, A. Ralph Waldo Emerson. CP-EmerR

Poet is born, A. Elegy on the Death of Kenneth Patchen, An. Lawrence Ferlinghetti. SP-FerlL

Poet is of those, The. Kathleen Jessie Raine. SP-RainK

Poet is Priest. Death to Van Gogh's Ear! Allen Ginsberg. CP-GinsA; SP-GinsA

Poet Li Po Admiring a Waterfall, The. Denise Levertov. SP-LeveDL

Poet Loves a Mistress, but Not to Marry, The. Robert Herrick. CP-HerrR

Poet Mário Faustino Descends into Hades and Rises to the Empyrean. Robert Stock. SP-StocR

Poet must rescue etymology from among the footnotes, The. Oppositions. Charles Tomlinson. CP-TomlC

Poet named Robert Browning eloped with a poetess named Elizabeth Barrett, A. Old Is for Books. Dorothy Nash. CP-NashO

· Poet of Ignorance, The. Anne Sexton. CP-SextA

Poet of Nature, thou hast wept to know. To Wordsworth. Percy Bysshe Shelley. CP-ShelP

Poet of nouns has left my attic, The. Message for the Sinecurist. Tess Gallagher. SP-GallT

Poet of poets / Is Time, the distiller. Ralph Waldo Emerson. CP-EmerR

Poet of the Future, The. James Whitcomb Riley. CP-RileJ

Poet of the Prison Isle: Ritsos against the Colonels, The. Thomas McGrath. SP-McGrT

Poet of the Thirteenth Century, A. Jorge Luis Borges. SP-BorgJ, *tr. by* Alan S. Trueblood

Poet often strives, on eagle's wings, The. Sonnet, To the Rev. James Flint, D. D., On reading his Collection of Poems. Jones Very. CP-VeryJ

Poet, pallid and perverse, A. Humanity ("Poet, pallid and perverse, A"). G. K. Chesterton. CP-ChesG

Poet Percival said: I struck a lode. Lorine Niedecker. CP-NiedL

Poet Phernazis is shaping, The. Dareios. Constantine P. Cavafy. CP-CavaC, *tr. by* Theoharis Constantine Theoharis

Poet Pleads with the Elemental Powers, The. William Butler Yeats. CP-YeatW

Poet, poet, what is your task. Poet, The. Countee Cullen. CP-CullC

Poet Prays to the Virgin for Help, The. Federico García Lorca. CP-GarcF, *tr. by* Greg Simon *and* Steven F. White

Poet professor in autumn years. Personals Ad. Allen Ginsberg. SP-GinsA

Poet put in his verses, The. "Rubén Dario." SP-DariR, *tr. by* Alberto Acereda *and* Will Derusha

Poet Redeemed & Dead. Donald Davie. CP-DaviDC

Poet-Scholar, The. Donald Davie. CP-DaviDC

Poet Scratches His Head, The. John Logan. CP-LogaJ

Poet scrawled upon a page of verse, A. In the Balance. G. K. Chesterton. CP-ChesG

Poet Speaks with His Beloved on the Telephone, The. Federico García Lorca. CP-GarcF, *tr. by* Angela Jaffray

Poet Tells the Truth, The. Federico García Lorca. CP-GarcF, *tr. by* Angela Jaffray

Poet, the Oyster, and Sensitive Plant, The. William Cowper. CP-CowpW

Poet, thou art dead and damned. Poet! Stevie Smith. CP-SmitS

Poet to Bigot. Langston Hughes. CP-HughL; CP-HughL3

Poet to His Beloved, A. William Butler Yeats. CP-YeatW

Poet, to His Book, The. Thomas Merton. CP-MertT

Poet to His Grandchild; Sequel to "A Plea for Authors." William Wordsworth. CP-WorW2

Poet to Patron. Langston Hughes. CP-HughL; CP-HughL1

Poet Whose Photo Never Grows Old, A. Yusef Komunyakaa. CP-KomuY

Poet with a painted face, A. Inscription in "Poems and Ballads." G. K. Chesterton. CP-ChesG

Poet would a-wishing go, A. A-Wishing Well. Robert Frost. CP-FrosR

Poet wrote a long story with the first name, A. Claims. Louis Zukofsky. CP-ZukLS

Poetaster. Theodore Roethke. CP-RoetT

Poetaster, The. Ben Jonson.

  "Blush, folly, blush: here's none that fears." CP-JonsB

  "Love is blind, and a wanton." CP-JonsB

  Song: "If I freely may discover." CP-JonsB

  "Swell me a bowl with lusty wine." CP-JonsB

  "Wake! Our mirth begins to die." CP-JonsB

Poetic State, A. Czeslaw Milosz. CP-MiloC; CP-MiloCN, *tr. by* Robert Hass

Poetical Abstracts. Hayden Carruth. CP-CarHS

Poetical Correspondence between Palemon and Æmilia, A. Annis Boudinot Stockton. CP-StocA

Poetical Epistle, Addressed by a Lady of New-Jersey, to Her Niece, upon Her Marriage, in This City, A. Annis Boudinot Stockton. CP-StocA

Poetical Epistle to Dr. Sheridan, A. Jonathan Swift. CP-SwifJ

Poetical Epistles. Samuel Taylor Coleridge. CP-ColeS

  Lines Written at Shurton Bars, near Bridgewater, September 1795, in Answer to a Letter from Bristol. MW-ColeS

Poetical Inscription, for an Altar to Independence at Kerrouchtry, the Seat of Mr. Heron, Written in Summer 1795. Robert Burns. CP-BurnR

Poetical lady whom I find, A. Fisherwoman, The. James Laughlin. CP-LaugJ

Poetical Remains. Archibald MacLeish. CP-MacLA

Poetics. A. R. Ammons. CP-AmmoA

Poetics. Robert Browning. CP-BroR2

Poetics. Yusef Komunyakaa. CP-KomuY

Poetics of Paperwood. Yusef Komunyakaa. CP-KomuY

Poetry. John Ciardi. CP-CiarJ

Poetry. Andrei Codrescu. SP-CodrA

Poetry. Frank O'Hara. SP-OharF

Poetry. William Stafford. SP-StafWW

Poetry, a Natural Thing. Robert Duncan. SP-DuncR

Poetry and Games. Richard Eberhart. CP-EberR

Poetry and Our City. A. K. Ramanujan. CP-RamaA

Poetry and Science. Hugh MacDiarmid. SP-MacDH

Poetry as Continuity. Jane Cooper. CP-CoopJ

Poetry as salutation; taste. History as Poetry. Geoffrey Hill. CP-HillG

Poetry Disarranged. Robert Duncan. SP-DuncR

Poetry Ends with Me. Nicanor Parra. CP-MertT

Poetry full of *cynghanedd*, and hair-trigger relationships, A. Hugh MacDiarmid. SP-MacDH *Fr.* Kind of Poetry I Want, The.

Poetry: "I, too, dislike it: there are things that are important beyond all this fiddle." Marianne Craig Moore. CP-MoorM

  (I, too, dislike it. / Reading it, however, with a perfect contempt for it, one discovers in.) CP-MoorM

Poetry in which all connections will constantly render such services, A. Hugh MacDiarmid. SP-MacDH *Fr.* Kind of Poetry I Want, The.

Poetry Is a Destructive Force. Wallace Stevens. CP-StevW; CP-StevWP

Poetry is a discourse. Poetry. Andrei Codrescu. SP-CodrA

Poetry is a projection across silence of cadences arranged to break that silence. Tentative (First Model) Definitions of Poetry. Carl Sandburg. CP-SandC

Poetry is dead? So they say. Now They Bury Her Again. Carl Sandburg. CP-SandC

Poetry is like fishing. Deep Fishing. Richard Eberhart. CP-EberR

Poetry is not instruments. To Gottfried Benn. Frank O'Hara. SP-OharF

Poetry is the supreme fiction, madame. High-Toned Old Christian Woman, A. Wallace Stevens. CP-StevW; CP-StevWP

"Poetry," John Wieners. William Corbett. SP-CorbW

Poetry like a lance at rest, A. Hugh MacDiarmid. SP-MacDH *Fr. Further Passages from* The Kind of Poetry I Want.

Poetry like the barrel of a gun, A. Hugh MacDiarmid. SP-MacDH *Fr. Further Passages from* The Kind of Poetry I Want.

Poetry like the character of Indian culture, A. Hugh MacDiarmid. SP-MacDH *Fr.* Kind of Poetry I Want, The.

Poetry like the hope of achieving ere very long. Hugh MacDiarmid. SP-MacDH *Fr.* Kind of Poetry I Want, The.

Poetry, music, I have loved, and yet. Spirit Medium, The. William Butler Yeats. CP-YeatW

Poetry of Chaucer, The. George Meredith. CP-MerG1

Poetry of Coleridge, The. George Meredith. CP-MerG1

Poetry of Departures. Philip Larkin. CP-LarkP

Poetry of earth is never dead, The. On the Grasshopper and [the] Cricket. John Keats. CP-KeatJ

Poetry of Keats, The. George Meredith. CP-MerG1

Poetry of Milton, The. George Meredith. CP-MerG1

Poetry of Shakespeare, The. George Meredith. CP-MerG1

Poetry of Shelley, The. George Meredith. CP-MerG1

Poetry of Southey, The. George Meredith. CP-MerG1

Poetry of Spenser, The. George Meredith. CP-MerG1

Poetry of such an integration as cannot be effected. Hugh MacDiarmid. SP-MacDH *Fr.* Kind of Poetry I Want, The.

Poetry of the meaning of words, A. Poem, The ("Poetry of the meaning of words, A"). George Oppen. CP-OppGN

Poetry of the Tradition, The. Pier Paolo Pasolini. SP-PasoP, *tr. by* Norman MacAfee *and* Luciano Martinengo

Poetry of tragedy is never dead, The. Am I My Neighbor's Keeper. Richard Eberhart. CP-EberR

Poetry of Wordsworth, The. George Meredith. CP-MerG1

Poetry: I. Adrienne Rich. SP-RicA1

Poetry Paper. Andrei Codrescu. SP-CodrA

Poetry Perpetuates the Poet. Robert Herrick. CP-HerrR

Poetry Reading. Wisława Szymborska. SP-SzymW, *tr. by* Stanisław Barańczak *and* Clare Cavanagh

Poetry Reading. Wisława Szymborska. SP-SzymWM, *tr. by* Joanna Trzeciak

Poetry should treat. Formula. Langston Hughes. CP-HughL; CP-HughL1

Poetry that goes all the way, A. Hugh MacDiarmid. SP-MacDH *Fr.* Kind of Poetry I Want, The.

Poetry that never for a moment forgets, A. Hugh MacDiarmid. SP-MacDH *Fr.* Kind of Poetry I Want, The.

Poetry the quality of which, A. Hugh MacDiarmid. SP-MacDH *Fr.* Kind of Poetry I Want, The.

Poetry: III. Adrienne Rich. SP-RicA1

Poets. Robert Herrick. CP-HerrR

Poets. Ted Hughes. SP-HughTN

Poets. James Laughlin. CP-LaugJ

Poet's age is sad: for why?, The. Prologue: "Poet's age is sad: for why?, The." Robert Browning. CP-BroR2

Poets and writers. Stage Fright. Wisława Szymborska. SP-SzymWM, *tr. by* Joanna Trzeciak

"Poets are born"—and so are whores—the trade is. John Clare. SP-ClarJ *Fr.* Don Juan.

Poets are colorpots. Ralph Waldo Emerson. CP-EmerR

Poets are going home now, The. Ingathering. Carolyn Kizer. CP-KizeC

Poets are guardians. Title of Poet, The. Robert Graves. CP-GravR

Poets are invited to submit poems appropriate to the above title. Inner Life of the Septic Tank, The. James Laughlin. CP-LaugJ

Poets Are Silent, The. Stevie Smith. CP-SmitS

Poets aren't very useful. Everybody Makes Poets. Ogden Nash. CP-NashO

Poets attempt the noblest task they can. In Memory of John Thornton. William Cowper. CP-CowpW

Poet's Bestiary. Robert Stock. SP-StocR

Poet's cat, sedate and grave, A. Retired Cat, The. William Cowper. CP-CowpW

Poet's Chair. Seamus Heaney. SP-HeanSO

Poets, come out of your closets. Populist Manifesto. Lawrence Ferlinghetti. SP-FerlL

Poets' Corner, The. Laura Riding Jackson. CP-RidiL

Poet's Curse, The. Robert Graves. CP-GravR

Poet's Delay, The. Henry David Thoreau. CP-ThorH

Poet's Dream, The. William Wordsworth. CP-WorW2

Poet's Epitaph, A. William Wordsworth. CP-WorW1
(Art thou a Statesman, in the van.) MW-WorW

Poet's eye obscenely seeing, The. Lawrence Ferlinghetti. SP-FerlL

Poet's Final Instructions, The. John Berryman. CP-BerrJ

Poets, from paupers to well-heeled. Letter to John Fuller. James Fenton. SP-FentJ

Poets Good Wishes for the Most Hopefull and Handsome Prince, the Duke of Yorke, The. Robert Herrick. CP-HerrR

Poet's hand has placed thee there. Withered Leaf—seen on a Poet's Table, A. Jones Very. CP-VeryJ

Poet's hope: to be, A. Shorts II [1958–1971]. W. H. Auden. CP-AudeW

Poet's Household, A. Carolyn Kizer. CP-KizeC

Poet's Laughter. Archibald MacLeish. CP-MacLA

Poet's lie!, A. Wild Boar Clough. Donald Davie. CP-DaviDC

Poets light but Lamps, The. Emily Dickinson. CP-DickE

Poets like lawful monarchs ruled the stage. Prologue, A: "Poets like lawful monarchs ruled the stage." Thomas Southerne. CP-DryJ2 *Fr.* Loyal Brother, The.

Poets, my dear, are much the same as you. To Be Read Later On. Charles Tomlinson. SP-TomlC *Fr.* For A Granddaughter.

Poet's New-Year's Gift, The. William Cowper. CP-CowpW

Poet's Occasional Alternative, The. Grace Paley. CP-PalGC

Poets of the Land of Indra write, The. Godhulivela. Hayden Carruth. CP-CarHS

Poet's Plea, The. Jones Very. CP-VeryJ

Poets pour us wine, The. Epilogue: "Poets pour us wine, The." Robert Browning. CP-BroR2

Poet's Prescription of Shamelessness, The. Robert Stock. SP-StocR

Poet's Space, The. Yannis Ritsos. SP-RitsY, *tr. by* Kimon Friar

Poets survive in fame. Lector Aere Perennior. James Vincent Cunningham. CP-CunnJ

Poet's Tale: The Birds of Killingworth, The. Henry Wadsworth Longfellow. *See* Tales of a Wayside Inn

Poets tell us of an age of unalloyed felicity, The. Golden Age, The. W. H. Auden. CP-AudeW *Fr.* Man of La Mancha.

Poet's Thoughts, A. Thomas Hardy. CP-HardT

Poet's to Come. Walt Whitman. CP-WhitW

Poet's Vow, The. Elizabeth Barrett Browning. CP-BroEB

Poets, we must lift again our warning cry. Challenge to Poets, A. Tennessee Williams. CP-WillT

Poet's Welcome to His Love-Begotten Daughter [the First Instance that Entitled Him to the Venerable Appellation of Father], A. Robert Burns. CP-BurnR

Poets with whom I'd learned my trade. Grey Rock, The. William Butler Yeats. CP-YeatW

Poet's Wooing, A. James Whitcomb Riley. CP-RileJ

Poet's Words, The. John Ciardi. CP-CiarJ

Poet's Work. Lorine Niedecker. CP-NiedL

Poets yeggs and thirsties. E. E. Cummings. CP-CummE

Poets, your subjects, have their parts assigned. Prologue to the University of Oxford, 1674. John Dryden. SP-DrydJ

Point, A. Andrei Codrescu. SP-CodrA

Point, The. Hayden Carruth. CP-CarHS

Point, The. Robert Earl Hayden. CP-HaydR

Point, The. Paul Muldoon. CP-MuldP

Point, The. Charles Simic. SP-SimiC; SP-SimiCE

Point Joe. Robinson Jeffers. CP-JefR1

Point Lobos, 1950. Helen Pinkerton. CP-PinkH

Point of Age, A. John Berryman. CP-BerrJ

Point of Departure. Dan Pagis. SP-PagiD, *tr. by* Stephen Mitchell

Point of No Return. Robert Graves. CP-GravR

Point of No Return, The. Charles Baudelaire. CP-BaudC, *tr. by* Walter Martin

Point of Origin. Heather McHugh. SP-McHuH

Point of Taste, The. George Meredith. CP-MerG1

Point Pinos and Point Lobos. Robinson Jeffers. CP-JefR1

Point Reyes. Gary Snyder. CP-SnydG

Point Shirley. Sylvia Plath. CP-PlatS

Poised beneath a twig-wigged tree. Coloratura. Wisława Szymborska. SP-SzymW, *tr. by* Stanisław Barańczak *and* Clare Cavanagh

Poised for the leap she. 3 Stances. William Carlos Williams. CP-WilW2

Poised impossibly on the high tight-rope. Acrobats. Robert Graves. CP-GravR

Poised upside down on its duncecap. In the Cold Kingdom. Mona Van Duyn. SP-VanDM

Poison. Charles Baudelaire. CP-BaudC, *tr. by* Walter Martin

Poison. D. H. Lawrence. CP-LawrD

Poison, The. Hans Magnus Enzensberger. SP-EnzeH, *tr. by* Hans Magnus Enzensberger *and* Michael Hamburger

Poison of Asps. Rudyard Kipling. CP-KiplR

Poison Tree, A. William Blake. CP-BlakW *Fr.* Songs of Experience.

Poisoned Day. Robert Graves. CP-GravR

Poisoned in Nassau. John Updike. CP-UpdiJ

Poisoned Man, The. James Dickey. CP-DickJ

Poland. G. K. Chesterton. CP-ChesG

Poland, France, Judea ran in her veins. Electric Sign Goes Dark, An. Carl Sandburg. CP-SandC

Poland like a dry fever on. Fever. Adam Zagajewski. SP-ZagaA, *tr. by* Renata Gorczynski

Polar Bear, The. William Carlos Williams. CP-WilW2

Polar Exploration. Stephen Spender. CP-SpenS

Polar Explorer, A. Joseph Brodsky. CP-BrodJ

Polar ice-caps are melting, the mountain glaciers, The. Robinson Jeffers. CP-JefR3

Pole Star. Archibald MacLeish. *See* Pole Star for This Year

Pole Star for This Year. Archibald MacLeish. CP-MacLA
   (Pole Star.) CP-MacLA

Poles / are within us, The. Paul Celan. SP-CelaP, *tr. by* John Felstiner

Pole's shadow qualifies. Qualia. Rae Armantrout. SP-ArmaA

Polestar and northern capital: equal as scepter and orb. Visit in Winter to the Temple of His Mystical Majesty, A. Tu Fu. CP-KizeC, *tr. by* Carolyn Kizer

Police, The. Andrei Codrescu. SP-CodrA

Police are probing tonight for the bodies, The. Miners. James Wright. CP-WrigJ

Police dog eating grass, A. Variant, The. Charles Simic. SP-SimiC; SP-SimiCE

Police Spies. D. H. Lawrence. CP-LawrD

Policeman buys shoes slow and careful, The. Psalm of Those Who Go Forth before Daylight. Carl Sandburg. CP-SandC

Policeman in front of a bank 3 A.M. . . . lonely. Stripes. Carl Sandburg. CP-SandC

Polish Biographical Dictionary in a Library in Houston, The. Adam Zagajewski. SP-ZagaA, *tr. by* Clare Cavanagh

Polish Question, The. Theodore Weiss. SP-WeisT

   "But suppose / you could, like a painter, nail down." SP-WeisT

   "By this eye, north of its frowning." SP-WeisT

   Envoy: "So, to complete the spectrum." SP-WeisT

   "O, no, except for newsreels, books." SP-WeisT

   "Over the phone a good friend asks." SP-WeisT

   "Painting, finished, A." SP-WeisT

   "Stacks of illustrations." SP-WeisT

   "Suppose your powers such." SP-WeisT

   Theory of Repetition, The. SP-WeisT

   "Thick smoke coils up, the shriveled." SP-WeisT

   "We talked the last of the mild." SP-WeisT

   "Words, words, such deeds words, come." SP-WeisT

Polish Rider, The. Derek Walcott. CP-WalcD

Polish'd with endless toil, my lays. Publius Papinius Statius. CP-JohnS *Fr.* Sylvae [*or* Silvae].

Polishing the Mirror. Jelaluddin Rumi. SP-Rumi, *tr. by* Coleman Barks

Political Ambition. Jones Very. CP-VeryJ

Political Economy. Ambrose Bierce. SP-BierA

Political Poem, A. Yehuda Amichai. SP-AmicYL, *tr. by* Benjamin Harshav *and* Barbara Harshav

Political Poem, A. George Oppen. CP-OppGN

Political Reflection. Ogden Nash. CP-NashO

Political Song for the Year's End. Thomas McGrath. SP-McGrT

Politician is an arse upon, A. E. E. Cummings. CP-CummE; SP-CummE

Politics. Andrei Codrescu. SP-CodrA

Politics. Ralph Waldo Emerson. CP-EmerR

Politics. Heather McHugh. SP-McHuH

Politics. William Meredith. SP-MereW

Politics. Miller Williams. CP-WillM

Politics. C. K. Williams. SP-WillC

Politics. William Butler Yeats. CP-YeatW

Polka-dot Dress, A. Czeslaw Milosz. CP-MiloCN, *tr. by* Robert Hass

Pollicie in Princes. Robert Herrick. CP-HerrR

Pollie. Walter De la Mare. CP-DeLaW

Polluted tide, / Desecrated earth destroyed. Kathleen Jessie Raine. SP-RainK

Polly—An Almost-True Story. Kenneth Patchen. CP-PatcK

Polly had a kind of electric beauty—it flashed out of her eye and. Polly—An Almost-True Story. Kenneth Patchen. CP-PatcK

Polly Red Top Thermos is with us. With Frank and George at Lexington. James Schuyler. CP-SchuJ

Polly's Tree. Sylvia Plath. CP-PlatS

Polo Ponies Practicing. Wallace Stevens. CP-StevWP

Polonaise: A Variation. Joseph Brodsky. CP-BrodJ

Polonius. Walter De la Mare. CP-DeLaW

Polonius Passing through a Stage. Howard Nemerov. CP-NemeH

Polterguest, My Polterguest. Ogden Nash. CP-NashO

Polyphiloprogenitive / The sapient sutlers of the Lord. Mr. Eliot's Sunday

Morning Service. T. S. Eliot. CP-ElioT; SP-ElioT

Pomade. Rita Dove. SP-DoveR

Pomander Bracelet, The. Robert Herrick. CP-HerrR

Pomegranate. Louise Glück. SP-GlucL

Pomegranate. D. H. Lawrence. CP-LawrD

Pomo Basketmaker. Peter Blue Cloud. SP-BlueP

Pompeii. John Updike. CP-UpdiJ

Pompeii. Jones Very. CP-VeryJ

Ponchus Pilut *ust* to be. James Whitcomb Riley. CP-RileJ

Pond, The. Louise Glück. SP-GlucL

Pond, The. Edna St. Vincent Millay. CP-MillE

Pond, The. Howard Nemerov. CP-NemeH

Pond, The. Gregory Orr. SP-OrrG

Pond lilies are like little executions, The. Friary at Blossom, Prologue & Instructions, The. Norman Dubie. CP-DubiN

Ponder, darling, these busted statues. Verses in the Night. Dorothy Parker. CP-ParkD

Ponder, darling, these busted statues. E. E. Cummings. CP-CummE

Ponder my words, if so that any be. Request to the Graces, An. Robert Herrick. CP-HerrR

Pondering over the testimony of his predecessors he knew that he was entering the age of the mind. Philosopher's Home, A. Czeslaw Milosz. CP-MiloCN, *tr. by* Robert Hass

Pondicherry Blues. Josephine Jacobsen. CP-JacoJ

Ponds, The. Mary Oliver. SP-OlivM

Pondy Woods. Robert Penn Warren. CP-WarrR

Pont-Y-Wern. Arthur Hugh Clough. SP-ClouA

Ponte de Lima. Charles Tomlinson. SP-TomlC *Fr.* Portuguese Pieces.

Ponte dell' Angelo, Venice. Robert Browning. CP-BroR2

Ponte Veneziano. Charles Tomlinson. CP-TomlC

Ponti profundis clausa recessibus. Skia, an Ode on the Isle of Skye. Samuel Johnson. CP-JohnS

Pontiac fires Detroit! Donald Davie. CP-DaviDC

Pontoosuce. Herman Melville. SP-MelvH

Pony Rock. Archibald MacLeish. CP-MacLA

Pooem. John Updike. CP-UpdiJ

Pool. Eugenio Montale. CP-MontE, *tr. by* Jonathan Galassi

Pool. Carl Sandburg. CP-SandC

Pool, The. Robert Creeley. CP-CreeR

Pool, The. "H. D." CP-DoolH

Pool, The. Paul Laurence Dunbar. CP-DunbP

Pool, The. Federico García Lorca. CP-GarcF, *tr. by* Jerome Rothenberg *Fr.* Mirror Suite.

Pool, The. Helen Pinkerton. CP-PinkH

Pool of Bethesda. Carl Sandburg. CP-SandC

Poolville, N.Y. Charles Tomlinson. CP-TomlC

Poona Train Window. A. K. Ramanujan. CP-RamaA

Poor. Robert Creeley. SP-CreeR

Poor, The. Jones Very. CP-VeryJ

Poor, The. William Carlos Williams. CP-WilW1

Poor and desperate men. Revisionist Poem: Machado. Thomas McGrath. SP-McGrT

Poor and inadequate the shadow-play. At Eventide. John Greenleaf Whittier. CP-WhitJ

Poor and Their Dwellings, The. George Crabbe. SP-CrabG *Fr.* Borough, The.

Poor bird! destined to lead thy life. To a Stray Fowl. Henry David Thoreau. CP-ThorH

Poor Bit of a Wench! D. H. Lawrence. CP-LawrD

Poor But TerFLY / went(flesh is grass). E. E. Cummings. CP-CummE

Poor Child with the Hooked Hands, The. Kenneth Patchen. CP-PatcK

Poor child, you were kissed so much you thought you were walked on. Robert Lowell. SP-LoweR *Fr.* Mexico.

Poor church / but an obstinate devotion, A. In Michoacán. Charles Tomlinson. CP-TomlC

Poor Clergyman, The. Jones Very. CP-VeryJ

Poor clerk I, "Arnaut the less" they call me, A. Marvoil. Ezra Pound. CP-PoEar

Poor conductor, in his tin shelter, The. State of Siege? Arthur Rimbaud. CP-RimbA, *tr. by* Martin Sorrell

Poor cricket longs for a song, and I, The. October Frost. Sam Hamill. SP-HamiS

Poor donkey is short by a bushel, A. Han-shan. CP-ColdM, *tr. by* Red Pine

Poor dying thing; it was my dog, not I. To a Snake. Edna St. Vincent Millay. CP-MillE

Poor floating isle, tossed on ill fortune's waves. Horace, Book I, Ode XIV. Jonathan Swift. CP-SwifJ

Poor Ghost, The. Christina Georgina Rossetti. CP-RosC1

Poor Girl. Maya Angelou. SP-AngeM

Poor Girl's Ruination. Langston Hughes. CP-HughL

Poor God was always there. Tabernacle, The. James Tate. SP-TateJ

Poor Gorrel. Kenneth Patchen. CP-PatcK

Poor heart, lament. Method, The. George Herbert. CP-HerbG

Poor, honest George, Swift's works to print. To the Editor of *The Dublin Journal. Unknown, sometimes at. to* Thomas Sheridan. CP-SherT

Poor Honest Men. Rudyard Kipling. CP-KiplR

Poor Hope. C. K. Williams. CP-WillC

Poor human race that must. So to Fatness Come. Stevie Smith. CP-SmitS

Poor in my youth, and in life's later scenes. On Late-acquired Wealth *or* Riches. *Unknown.* CP-CowpW, *tr. by* William Cowper

Poor john, who joined in make of wrong. Welcome the Wrath. Stanley Kunitz. CP-KunSC

Poor kids are active in the penny arcades, The. Scene (1946–7). Alan Dugan. CP-DugaA

Poor ladies! Though their business be to play. Hardship Put upon Ladies, The. Jonathan Swift. CP-SwifJ

Poor little bird, singing as you flit by. Petrarch. CP-Petra, *tr. by* J. G. Nichols

Poor little book, *The Sleeping Beauty* died. Sonnet: "Poor little book, *The Sleeping Beauty* died." Hayden Carruth. CP-CarHS *Fr. Sonnets.*

Poor little Heart! Emily Dickinson. CP-DickE

Poor loves his music, The. Dollar Dance. Andrei Codrescu. SP-CodrA

Poor Mailie's Elegy. Robert Burns. CP-BurnR

Poor Man and a Lady, A. Thomas Hardy. CP-HardT

Poor man weeps—here G————N sleeps, The. For G. H. Esq. Robert Burns. CP-BurnR

Poor man went to the rich man's doors, The. Precedent. Paul Laurence Dunbar. CP-DunbP

Poor man? Yes, I must confess, A, Poor Man's Wealth, A. James Whitcomb Riley. CP-RileJ

Poor man's history will brown the gold, A. If Eyes Can See. A. K. Ramanujan. CP-RamaA

Poor Man's Riches 1, A. A. K. Ramanujan. CP-RamaA

Poor Man's Riches 2, A. A. K. Ramanujan. CP-RamaA

Poor Man's Wealth, A. James Whitcomb Riley. CP-RileJ

Poor Mr. Strawbridge. Ogden Nash. CP-NashO

Poor Myrtle would sigh, "Sweet my Coz." Goo Girl. Theodore Roethke. CP-RoetT

Poor nation, whose sweet sap and juice. Jews, The. George Herbert. CP-HerbG

Poor noble Ghost that comes from place of pain. King Hamlet's Ghost. Stevie Smith. CP-SmitS

Poor old Abner, poor old white-haired nigger! Time the Hangman. William Carlos Williams. CP-WilW1

Poor. Old. China. Man. William Corbett. SP-CorbW

Poor Others. Robert Graves. CP-GravR

Poor pale child, why do you bawl out your sharp, cheeky songs. Stéphane Mallarmé. CP-MallS, *tr. by* Henry Weinfield

Poor parched man, we had to squeeze. Words for Some Ash. Thom Gunn. CP-GunnT

Poor People in Church. Arthur Rimbaud. CP-RimbA, *tr. by* Martin Sorrell

Poor Poet-Ape, that would be thought our chief. On Poet-Ape. Ben Jonson. CP-JonsB; SP-JonsB

Poor, poor fool! Ballad of the Fool. Langston Hughes. CP-HughL; CP-HughL3

Poor procurator, why do you ask someone else. Reply to Papini. Wallace Stevens. CP-StevW; CP-StevWP

Poor Relation, The. Edwin Arlington Robinson. CP-RobiE

Poor Relations. G. K. Chesterton. CP-ChesG

Poor Robin. William Wordsworth. CP-WorW2

Poor Rover. Langston Hughes. CP-HughL

Poor savages / Of ghost and glitter. Merely rolling now. Mayan Ground, The. George Oppen. CP-OppGN

Poor sheepish plaything. For Sale. Robert Lowell. SP-LoweR

Poor Sherry, inglorious. Sheridan's Submission. Jonathan Swift. CP-SwifJ

Poor silly soul, whose hope and head lies low. Vanity (2). George Herbert. CP-HerbG

Poor Soul, Poor Girl! Stevie Smith. CP-SmitS

Poor Stella hourly is perplexed. Humble Petition of Stella's Friends, The. Thomas Sheridan. CP-SherT

Poor Student, The. James Whitcomb Riley. CP-RileJ

Poor talker mouthperson. In France. Grace Paley. CP-PalGC

Poor the pleasure / Doled out by measure. Memento Mori. Christina Georgina Rossetti. CP-RosC2

Poor, thick, white. Three Poems on Morris Graves' Paintings. John Logan. CP-LogaJ

Poor Tom, wilt thou never accept a defiance. Swift to Sheridan. Jonathan Swift. CP-SwifJ

Poor torn heart, a tattered heart, A. Emily Dickinson. CP-DickE

Poor Vestris, griev'd beyond all measure. Card, A. William Cowper. CP-CowpW

Poor victim of that vulture curse. Luther Benson. James Whitcomb Riley. CP-RileJ

Poor Voter on Election Day, The. John Greenleaf Whittier. CP-WhitJ

"Poor wanderer," said the leaden sky. Subalterns, The. Thomas Hardy. CP-HardT

Poor Washed Up by Chicago Winter, The. James Wright. CP-WrigJ

Poor wearied singer at the gates of death. To E. B. B. Ezra Pound. CP-PoEar

Poor Withered Rose. Paul Laurence Dunbar. CP-DunbP

Poor Young Things. D. H. Lawrence. CP-LawrD

Poore Mans Part, The. Robert Herrick. CP-HerrR

Poores Portion, The. Robert Herrick. CP-HerrR

Pop Smash, out of Echo Chamber. John Updike. CP-UpdiJ

Popcorn-can cover. Lorine Niedecker. CP-NiedL

Popcorn peanuts clams and gum. Bar-Room Matins. Louis MacNeice. CP-MacNL

Pope and the Net, The. Robert Browning. CP-BroR2

Pope from penance purgatorial, The. George Buchanan. CP-CunnJ, *tr. by* James Vincent Cunningham

Pope has the talent well to speak. Dr. Swift to Mr. Pope. Jonathan Swift. CP-SwifJ

Pope he was saying the high, high mass. Gray Brother, The. Sir Walter Scott. SP-ScotW

Pope on Christmas Day, The. Christmas Gifts. Elizabeth Barrett Browning. CP-BroEB

Pope was riding a bicycle around inside, The. In Memoriam. Donald Mark Fall. Alan Dugan. CP-DugaA

Popham of the New Song. Norman Dubie. CP-DubiN

Poplar, absolute danseuse. Poplar, Sycamore. Richard Wilbur. CP-WilbR

Poplar and Elm. Carl Sandburg. CP-SandC

Poplar and oak awake. Life around Us, The. Denise Levertov. SP-LeveDS

Poplar and tower. / Living shade. Federico García Lorca. CP-GarcF, *tr. by* Christopher Maurer

Poplar Field, The. William Cowper. CP-CowpW

Poplar lanes move on, The. Prelude: "Poplar lanes move on, The." Federico García Lorca. CP-GarcF, *tr. by* Alan S. Trueblood *Fr. Love.*

Poplar, Sycamore. Richard Wilbur. CP-WilbR

Poplar tree under the stars, A. Stems. Denise Levertov. SP-LeveDP

Poplar Trees, The. Gabriela Mistral. SP-MistG, *tr. by* Maria Giachetti [*or* Jacketti]

Poplar trees follow us, The. Poplar Trees, The. Gabriela Mistral. SP-MistG, *tr. by* Maria Giachetti [*or* Jacketti]

Poplars, The. Yusef Komunyakaa. CP-KomuY

Poplars are fading away, The. Daydreams of a River. Federico García Lorca. CP-GarcF, *tr. by* Jerome Rothenberg

Poplars are felled [*or* fell'd], farewell to the shade, The. Poplar Field, The. William Cowper. CP-CowpW

Poplars gray as a ghost by the creek, The. High Noon. Amy Clampitt. CP-ClamA

Poplar's Shadow, The. May Swenson. SP-SwenM

Poppies. Mary Oliver. SP-OlivM

Poppies. Carl Sandburg. CP-SandC

Poppies in July. Sylvia Plath. CP-PlatS

Poppies in October. Sylvia Plath. CP-PlatS

Poppy Anemone. Louis Zukofsky. CP-ZukLS

Poppy Flower. Langston Hughes. CP-HughL; CP-HughL2

Poppy under a young. Necromance. Rae Armantrout. SP-ArmaA

Popular Heart is a Cannon first, The. Emily Dickinson. CP-DickE

Popular Personage at Home, A. Thomas Hardy. CP-HardT

Popular Revivals 1956. John Updike. CP-UpdiJ

Popular Songs. John Ashbery. SP-AshbJ

Popularity. Robert Browning. CP-BroR1

Population. George Oppen. CP-OppGN

Population Drifts. Carl Sandburg. CP-SandC

Population Explosion. Archibald MacLeish. CP-MacLA

Populist. George Oppen. CP-OppGN

Populist Manifesto. Lawrence Ferlinghetti. SP-FerlL

Porcelain Bowl. Louise Glück. SP-GlucL

Porch over the River, The. Wendell Berry. CP-BerrW

Porco la zucca / Fitta in parrucca! Christina Georgina Rossetti. CP-RosC3

Porcupine. Anne Sexton. CP-SextA

Porcupine, The. Galway Kinnell. SP-KinnGN

Porcupine, The. Ogden Nash. CP-NashO

Porcupine Meditation. Margaret Atwood. SP-AtwM2

Porcupine Tree. Margaret Atwood. SP-AtwM2

Pore afflicted Evagene! Evagene Baker. James Whitcomb Riley. CP-RileJ

Pore-folks lives at Lonesomeville. Folks at Lonesomeville. James Whitcomb Riley. CP-RileJ

Poreč. Donald Davie. CP-DaviDC

Poring over calendars is apt to give people round shoulders. There Are More Ways to Roast a Pig than Burning the House Down or You Can Always Stick Your Head in a Volcano. Ogden Nash. CP-NashO

Porky and Socration, two-eye sins as try. Catullus. *See* Lucius Calpurnius Piso Caesoninus

Porky & porkie. E. E. Cummings. CP-CummE

Pornographic Poem. Marilyn Hacker. SP-HackM

Porous. William Carlos Williams. CP-WilW1

Porphyria's Lover. Robert Browning. CP-BroR1; SP-BroR

Porphyro in Akron. Hart Crane. CP-CranH

Porpoise, The. Ogden Nash. CP-NashO

Port, The. W. S. Merwin. SP-MerwW

Port Bou. Stephen Spender. CP-SpenS

Port of Aerial Embarkation. John Ciardi. CP-CiarJ

Port of Call. Andrei Codrescu. SP-CodrA

Port of Embarkation. Randall Jarrell. CP-JarrR

Port of London Authority, The. G. K. Chesterton. CP-ChesG

Port of Peace has many Coves, The. Emily Dickinson. SP-DickE

Port Town. Langston Hughes. CP-HughL; CP-HughL1

Porta San Pancrazio. Joseph Brodsky. CP-BrodJ

Portable garden, Bill's shed in Point Richmond, moth. Lemon Trees. Philip Whalen. SP-WhalP

Portal, A. Czeslaw Milosz. CP-MiloC; CP-MiloCN, *tr.* by Robert Hass

Portal as of shadowy adamant, A. Allegory, An. Percy Bysshe Shelley. CP-ShelP

Portals. Walt Whitman. CP-WhitW

Portent. William Carlos Williams. CP-WilW1

Portent, The. Rudyard Kipling. CP-KiplR *Fr.* Debits and Credits.

Portent, The. Herman Melville. SP-MelvH

Portentous change when History can appear. In Allusion to Various Recent Histories and Notices of the French Revolution. William Wordsworth. CP-WorW2

Portentous sound! mysteriously vast. Lines: "Portentous sound! mysteriously vast." James Whitcomb Riley. CP-RileJ

Portents. Thomas McGrath. SP-McGrT

Porter. Langston Hughes. CP-HughL; CP-HughL1

Portia. Oscar Wilde. CP-WildO

Portico ("Clang clang / The air, having been killed"). Federico García Lorca. CP-GarcF, *tr.* by Jerome Rothenberg *Fr.* In the Garden of the Lunar Grapefruits.

Portico ("Water / taps its silver"). Federico García Lorca. CP-GarcF, *tr.* by Jerome Rothenberg *Fr.* Garden in Umber; or The Garden of the Brownhaired Girls.

Portion of this yew. Transformations. Thomas Hardy. CP-HardT

Portions of Manslayer. C. K. Williams. CP-WillC

Portland Coliseum. Allen Ginsberg. CP-GinsA

Portland, 1968. Louise Glück. CP-GlucL

Portland, the Isle of Portland—how I love. Boris Leonidovich Pasternak. CP-DaviDC, *tr.* by Donald Davie

Portobello Carnival 1973. Charles Tomlinson. CP-TomlC

Portola Valley. Amy Clampitt. CP-ClamA

Portrait. Louise Bogan. CP-BogaL

Portrait. E. E. Cummings. CP-CummE; SP-CummE

Portrait. James Vincent Cunningham. CP-CunnJ

Portrait. Alan Dugan. CP-DugaA

Portrait. Louise Glück. SP-GlucL

Portrait. Philip Larkin. CP-LarkP

Portrait. Edna St. Vincent Millay. CP-MillE

Portrait. Ezra Pound. CP-PoEar

Portrait. Carl Sandburg. CP-SandC

Portrait (I). Stevie Smith. CP-SmitS

Portrait (II). Stevie Smith. CP-SmitS

Portrait, A. Elizabeth Barrett Browning. CP-BroEB

Portrait, A ("Fair faces crowd on Christmas night"). G. K. Chesterton. CP-ChesG

Portrait, A ("Her hair is as a floating fire"). G. K. Chesterton. CP-ChesG

Portrait, A. Walter De la Mare. CP-DeLaW

Portrait, A. John Keats. CP-KeatJ

(Character of Charles Brown.) CP-KeatJ

Portrait, A. Dorothy Parker. CP-ParkD

Portrait, A. Christina Georgina Rossetti. CP-RosC1

Portrait, The. Charles Baudelaire. CP-BaudC, *tr.* by Walter Martin *Fr.* Phantom, A.

Portrait, The. Robert Graves. CP-GravR

Portrait, The. Stanley Kunitz. CP-KunSC

Portrait, The. Dan Pagis. SP-PagiD, *tr.* by Stephen Mitchell

Portrait, The. Dante Gabriel Rossetti. CW-RossD

Portrait, The. Dante Gabriel Rossetti. CW-RossD *Fr.* House of Life, The.

Portrait, The. Jones Very. CP-VeryJ

Portrait by a Neighbour. Edna St. Vincent Millay. CP-MillE

Portrait by Holbein. May Sarton. SP-SartM

Portrait d'une Femme. Ezra Pound. CP-PoEar; SP-PounE

Portrait from the Infantry. Alan Dugan. CP-DugaA

Portrait from the Life, A. Jonathan Swift. CP-SherT; CP-SwifJ

Portrait in Greys, A. William Carlos Williams. CP-WilW1

Portrait in Stone. Charles Tomlinson. CP-TomlC

Portrait in the Form of an Extended Conceit. Alan Dugan. CP-DugaA

Portrait Now before Then. Michael Palmer. SP-PalmM

Portrait of a Child Settling Down for an Afternoon Nap. Carl Sandburg. CP-SandC

Portrait of a House Detective. Hans Magnus Enzensberger. SP-EnzeH, *tr.* by Michael Hamburger

Portrait of a Lady. Alan Dugan. CP-DugaA

Portrait of a Lady. T. S. Eliot. CP-ElioT; SP-ElioT

Portrait of a Lady. Kenneth Rexroth. CP-RexrK

Portrait of a Lady. William Carlos Williams. CP-WilW1

Portrait of a Local Politician. Alan Dugan. CP-DugaA

Portrait of a Man, with a Background of Holdings. Muriel Rukeyser. CP-RukeM

Portrait of a Motorcar. Carl Sandburg. CP-SandC

Portrait of a Woman at Her Bath. William Carlos Williams. CP-WilW2

Portrait of a Woman in Bed. William Carlos Williams. CP-WilW1

Portrait of a Young Man with a Bad Heart. William Carlos Williams. CP-WilW1

Portrait of an Old Woman on the College Tavern Wall. Anne Sexton. CP-SextA

Portrait of Gertrude Stein. Robert Stock. SP-StocR

Portrait of Her Lover. Gaspara Stampa. SP-ZatuM, *tr.* by Marya Alexandrovna Zaturenska

Portrait of Mrs. Spaxton. Charles Tomlinson. CP-TomlC

Portrait of my mother, The. Virtuoso, The. Stevie Smith. CP-SmitS

Portrait of Rilke. Richard Eberhart. CP-EberR

Portrait of the Artist. Dorothy Parker. CP-ParkD

Portrait of the Artist I. Charles Tomlinson. CP-TomlC

Portrait of the Artist II. Charles Tomlinson. CP-TomlC

Portrait of the Artist, A. Thomas Kinsella. CP-KinsT

Portrait of the Artist, A. Derek Mahon. CP-MahoD

Portrait of the Artist as a Prematurely Old Man. Ogden Nash. CP-NashO

Portrait of the Artist as an Interior Decorator. Kenneth Patchen. CP-PatcK

Portrait of the Artist with Hart Crane. Charles Wright. SP-WrigC

Portrait of the Artist with Li Po. Charles Wright. SP-WrigC

Portrait of the Author. William Carlos Williams. CP-WilW1

Portrait of the Author as a Young Anarchist. Kenneth Rexroth. CP-RexrK

Portrait of the Engineer, A. Thomas Kinsella. CP-KinsT

Portrait of the Man Who Drowned Wearing His Best Suit and Shoes. Thomas Lux. SP-LuxT

Portrait of the Queen in Tears. Louise Glück. SP-GlucL

Portrait of the Times, A. William Carlos Williams. CP-WilW2

Portrait of Three Conspirators. Howard Nemerov. CP-NemeH

Portrait of Tragedy. Joseph Brodsky. CP-BrodJ

Portrait on an American Theme. Kenneth Patchen. CP-PatcK

Portrait with a Cat, A. Czeslaw Milosz. CP-MiloC; CP-MiloCN, *tr.* by Robert Hass

Portraits. Ivor Gurney. SP-GurnI

Portraits. D. H. Lawrence. CP-LawrD

Portraits. Christina Georgina Rossetti. CP-RosC3

Portraits are to daily faces. Emily Dickinson. CP-DickE

Portraits of Three Ladies. Robert Penn Warren. CP-WarrR

Ports of death are sins; of life, good deeds, The. Of Life and Death. Ben Jonson. CP-JonsB; SP-JonsB

Portugeuse Pieces. Charles Tomlinson.

Alto Minho. SP-TomlC

In Lisbon. SP-TomlC

Ponte De Lima. SP-TomlC

Soajo. SP-TomlC

Swallows. SP-TomlC

Poseidonians. Constantine P. Cavafy. CP-CavaC, *tr.* by Theoharis Constantine Theoharis

Poseidonians forgot the Greek language, The. Poseidonians. Constantine P. Cavafy. CP-CavaC, *tr.* by Theoharis Constantine Theoharis

Poseidon's Law. Rudyard Kipling. CP-KiplR

Posie, The. Robert Burns. CP-BurnR

Posies from a Second Childhood, or, Hark How Gaffer Do Chaffer. Ogden Nash. CP-NashO

Posing. Clarence Major. SP-MajoC

Position in the Hebrew Divinity, A. Robert Herrick. CP-HerrR

Position is where you. Window, The. Robert Creeley. CP-CreeR

Position without a Magnitude. Charles Simic. SP-SimiC; SP-SimiCE

Positions. A. R. Ammons. CP-AmmoA

Possesions. Robert Herrick. CP-HerrR

Possessed. Charles Baudelaire. CP-BaudC, *tr. by* Walter Martin

Possessed. Robert Graves. CP-GravR

Possessed, The. John Berryman. CP-BerrJ

Possession. Paul Laurence Dunbar. CP-DunbP

Possession. Dante Gabriel Rossetti. CW-RossD

Possessions. Hart Crane. CP-CranH

Possessions. Ivor Gurney. SP-GurnI

Possessions. Diana Gurney. SP-GurnI

Possessions. Pablo Neruda. SP-NeruP

Possessions Are Nine Points of Conversation. Ogden Nash. CP-NashO

Possessor. Things. W. S. Merwin. SP-MerwW

Possibilities. John Ciardi. CP-CiarJ

Possibilities. Rudyard Kipling. CP-KiplR

Possibility, A. Ambrose Bierce. SP-BierA

Possibility along a Line of Difference. A. R. Ammons. CP-AmmoA

Possible, The. Raymond Carver. CP-CarvR

Possible by now, one would suppose. Having Lunch at Brasenose. Amy Clampitt. CP-ClamA

Possibles we dare!, The. Love's Progress. Theodore Roethke. CP-RoetT

Possibly. Robert Graves. CP-GravR

Possibly because she's already so striking—tall, well dressed, very clear, pure skin. Hooks. C. K. Williams. SP-WillC

Possibly is not a monosyllable. Possibly. Robert Graves. CP-GravR

Possibly thrice we glimpsed. E. E. Cummings. CP-CummE

Possum. Paul Laurence Dunbar. CP-DunbP

'Possum in de 'tater-patch. Noon Lull, A. James Whitcomb Riley. CP-RileJ

Possum Trot. Paul Laurence Dunbar. CP-DunbP

Possum work, world's windowlust, lens of the Byzantine. Opus Posthumous. Charles Wright. SP-WrigCN

Possum's a greasy critter, The. Roast Possum. Rita Dove. SP-DoveR

Post-boy drove with fierce career, The. Alice Fell; or, Poverty. William Wordsworth. CP-WorW1; MW-WorW

Post Cards. Robert Creeley. CP-CreeR

Post-Graduate. Dorothy Parker. CP-ParkD

Post-historic herbivore, A. On the Inclusion of Miniature Dinosaurs in Breakfast Cereal Boxes. John Updike. CP-UpdiJ

Post-Impressionist Susurration for the First of November, 1983, A. Hayden Carruth. CP-CarHS

Post Mortem. Robinson Jeffers. CP-JefR1

Post-Recessional. G. K. Chesterton. CP-ChesG

Post That Fitted, The. Rudyard Kipling. CP-KiplR

(Though tangled and twisted the course of true love.) CP-KiplR

Post the Lake Poets Ballad. Frank O'Hara. SP-OharF

Post-Therapy Room. William Dickey. SP-DickW

Post Virginal, The. Charles Olson. CP-OlsoC

Postal authorities of the United States of America, The. Legal Reflection. Ogden Nash. CP-NashO

Postcard. Margaret Atwood. SP-AtwM2

Postcard. Denise Levertov. SP-LeveDL

Postcard. Adrienne Rich. CP-RicAE

Postcard, A. Joseph Brodsky. CP-BrodJ

Postcard from France, A. Joseph Brodsky. CP-BrodJ *Fr.* Shorts.

Postcard from John Ashbery, A. Frank O'Hara. SP-OharF

Postcard from Lisbon. Joseph Brodsky. CP-BrodJ

Postcard from Provincetown. Heather McHugh. SP-McHuH

Postcard from Spain. Langston Hughes. CP-HughL; CP-HughL1

Postcard from the Garden. Marge Piercy. SP-PierM

Postcard from the Volcano, A. Wallace Stevens. CP-StevW; CP-StevWP

Postcard held, A. Trestle, The. W. S. Merwin. SP-MerwWF

Postcard to Baudelaire. Thomas Lux. SP-LuxT

Postcards. Rae Armantrout. SP-ArmaA

Postcards. Adam Zagajewski. SP-ZagaA, *tr. by* Clare Cavanagh

Postcards: A Triptych, The. Denise Levertov. SP-LeveDP

Postcards from Cape Split. Mona Van Duyn. SP-VanDM

Postcards from Rotterdam. Carolyn Kizer. CP-KizeC

Postcards from Soviet Cities. John Updike. CP-UpdiJ

Postcript to Iceland. Louis MacNeice. CP-MacNL

Posterity. Philip Larkin. CP-LarkP

Posthumous Fragments of Margaret Nicholson. Percy Bysshe Shelley. CP-ShelP

Posthumous Letter to Gilbert White. W. H. Auden. CP-AudeW

Posthumous Remorse. Charles Baudelaire. CP-BaudC, *tr. by* Walter Martin

Posthumous Tales. George Crabbe.

Ancient Mansion, The. SP-CrabG

Posthumous Work. Charles Baudelaire. CP-BaudC, *tr. by* Walter Martin

Postillion, The. Nikolaus Lenau. CP-MerG2

Posting to Printing. Robert Herrick. CP-HerrR

Postlude. William Carlos Williams. CP-WilW1

Postman, The. Christina Georgina Rossetti. CP-RosC2

Postman comes when I am still in bed, The. Sick Child, A. Randall Jarrell. CP-JarrR

Postponed Decision. Yannis Ritsos. SP-RitsY, *tr. by* Athan Anagnostopoulos

Postponement. Thomas Hardy. CP-HardT

Postponement of Self. Laura Riding Jackson. CP-RidiL

Postscript. Hart Crane. CP-CranH

Postscript. Seamus Heaney. SP-HeanSO

Postscript. Eleanor Wilner. SP-WilnE

Postscript, A. Hart Crane. CP-CranH

Postscript [To W. S*****n, Ochiltree]. Robert Burns. CP-BurnR

Posture of an innocence presumes. Form of Pity, A. Robert Stock. SP-StocR

Posture of the tree, The. Lovers in Winter. Robert Graves. CP-GravR

Posy [*or* Posie], The. George Herbert. CP-HerbG

Pot-au-feu. Mona Van Duyn. SP-VanDM

Pot of Earth, The. Archibald MacLeish. CP-MacLA

Pot of Flowers, The. William Carlos Williams. CP-WilW1

Pot of gold at the rainbow end, The. Gold Mud. Carl Sandburg. CP-SandC

Pot of Musk, A. Walter De la Mare. CP-DeLaW

Pot was empty, The. Ballad of Roosevelt. Langston Hughes. CP-HughL; CP-HughL1

Potato. Richard Wilbur. CP-WilbR

Potato Blight, The. Jones Very. CP-VeryJ

Potato Blossom Songs and Jigs. Carl Sandburg. CP-SandC

Potato smell came out from the kitchen door, A. Dura Mater. Thomas Kinsella. CP-KinsT

Potatoes' Dance, The. Nicholas Vachel Lindsay. CP-LindV

Potent tiller reck to copper. Cinquefoil. Louis Zukofsky. CP-ZukLS

Potentates. Robert Herrick. CP-HerrR

Potflower on the windowsill says to me, The. Power of Suicide, The. Muriel Rukeyser. CP-RukeM

Potiphar Gubbins, C. E. Study of an Elevation, in Indian Ink. Rudyard Kipling. CP-KiplR

Potomac River Mist. Carl Sandburg. CP-SandC

Potomac Town in February. Carl Sandburg. CP-SandC

Potter, The. Yannis Ritsos. SP-RitsY, *tr. by* Kostas Myrsiades

Potter nor iron-founder. 'Sculpture' of Rhyme, The. Donald Davie. CP-DaviDC

Potter, Vidalia. Miller Williams. CP-WillM

Pouilly-Fuissé. Arthur Sze. SP-SzeA

Pound at Spoleto. Lawrence Ferlinghetti. SP-FerlL

Pound pound pound / on thy cold grey corona oh P. E. E. Cummings. CP-CummE

Pounding VW motor. Riding with Sal. Robert Creeley. SP-CreeR

Pour Away That Youth. Philip Larkin. CP-LarkP

Pour Prendre Congé. Dorothy Parker. CP-ParkD

Pour the unhappiness out. Another Weeping Woman. Wallace Stevens. CP-StevW; CP-StevWP

Pour the wasteland into your eye-sacks. Paul Celan. SP-CelaP, *tr. by* John Felstiner

Pour the wine! pour the wine! Ralph Waldo Emerson. CP-EmerR

Pour wine and dance if manhood still have pride. Mountain Tomb, The. William Butler Yeats. CP-YeatW

Pouring Milk Away. Muriel Rukeyser. CP-RukeM

Poussin. Louis MacNeice. CP-MacNL

Poverty. D. H. Lawrence. CP-LawrD

Poverty. A. K. Ramanujan. CP-RamaA

Poverty. Henry David Thoreau. CP-ThorH

Poverty and Riches. Robert Herrick. CP-HerrR

Poverty is a stranger now. Poverty. A. K. Ramanujan. CP-RamaA

Poverty Programs, The. Howard Nemerov. CP-NemeH

Poverty the Greatest Pack. Robert Herrick. CP-HerrR

Powder, chunks of road, twisted. Bringing to Light. Thom Gunn. CP-GunnT

Powder-Monkey. Raymond Carver. CP-CarvR

Power. Andrei Codrescu. SP-CodrA

Power. Adrienne Rich. SP-RicA1; SP-RicA2

Power. Muriel Rukeyser. CP-RukeM

Power and Light. James Dickey. CP-DickJ

Power and Peace. Robert Herrick. CP-HerrR

Power death has of touching The hard, The. Drizzle off the Ocean. Andrei Codrescu. SP-CodrA

Power-house, A. Classic Scene. William Carlos Williams. CP-WilW1

Power in the People, The. Robert Herrick. CP-HerrR

Power is a familiar growth. Emily Dickinson. CP-DickE

Power is an inferiority complex wound up like a clock by an inability to relax.

Power. Andrei Codrescu. SP-CodrA

Power is mute (the trees tell me). This Is Simple. Pablo Neruda. SP-NeruP

Power is my aphrodisiac. Aphrodisiac, The. Arthur Sze. SP-SzeA

Power-mown morning of this spang, The. Saturday. John Ciardi. CP-CiarJ

Power never dominion. / Some other power. Muriel Rukeyser. CP-RukeM

Power of a beautiful face lifts me to heaven, The. Michelangelo Buonarroti. CP-EmerR

Power of a lovely face impels me where? Michelangelo Buonarroti. CP-Miche, tr. by John Frederick Nims

Power of Armies is a visible thing, The. 1811. William Wordsworth. CP-WorW1

Power of Music. William Wordsworth. CP-WorW1; MW-WorW

Power of Poesy, The. James Laughlin. CP-LaugJ

Power of Princes rests in the Consent, The. Obedience. Robert Herrick. CP-HerrR

Power of Suicide, The. Muriel Rukeyser. CP-RukeM

Power of the Dog, The. Rudyard Kipling. CP-KiplR

Power of Time, The. Jonathan Swift. CP-SwifJ

Power of war leads to a plan of lives, The. Muriel Rukeyser. CP-RukeM

Power rigs drift like lights out past the breakwater. Journal of True Confessions, A. Charles Wright. SP-WrigC

Power, the Enchanted World. George Oppen. CP-OppGN

Power! / The power alone, The. Appian Way, The. Kenneth Patchen. CP-PatcK

Power, this / coil thumping around. & Power. Andrei Codrescu. SP-CodrA

Power to be true to You, The. Emily Dickinson. CP-DickE

Power to fly is sweet, The. Emily Dickinson. SP-DickE

Power to the People. Howard Nemerov. CP-NemeH

Powerful and armed, neutral in the midst of madness, we might have held. Shine, Empire. Robinson Jeffers. CP-JefR3

Powerful aroma of hot olive oil, The. Cooking. Sam Hamill. SP-HamiS

Powerless emperor, The. Hard Listener, The. William Carlos Williams. CP-WilW1; CP-WilW2

Powers. Czeslaw Milosz. CP-MiloC; CP-MiloCN, tr. by Robert Hass

Powers, The. George Oppen. CP-OppGN

Powers Unconfessed. Robert Graves. CP-GravR

Powers whose name and shape no living creature knows, The. Poet Pleads with the Elemental Powers, The. William Butler Yeats. CP-YeatW

Practical People. Robinson Jeffers. CP-JefR1

Practical Program for Monks, A. Thomas Merton. CP-MertT

Practical Woman, A. Thomas Hardy. CP-HardT

"Practically all you newspaper people." Clown, The. Donald Hall. CP-HallD

Practically speaking / the great words of great men. Trick to Dull Our Bleeding, A. Charles Bukowski. SP-BukC2

Practice. Charles Bukowski. SP-BukC2

Practice. Charles Bukowski. SP-BukC3

Practice makes perfect, the old folks said. Magic. Rita Dove. SP-DoveR

Practice of medicine, The. Medicine ("Practice of medicine, The"). Carolyn Kizer. CP-KizeC

Practice of Oratory. Gertrude Stein. CP-SteiG

Practice of piety, The. The practice of music. The practice of calligraphy. Failing. Philip Whalen. SP-WhalP

Practicing for Death. Jane Cooper. CP-CoopJ

Pragmatical old Capulet, the head. Bride of Reason, The. Donald Davie. CP-DaviDC

Prague. Jaroslav Seifert. SP-SeifJ, tr. by Ewald Osers

Prague! / Who has seen her but once. Verses from an Old Tapestry. Jaroslav Seifert. SP-SeifJ, tr. by Ewald Osers

Prairie. Carl Sandburg. CP-SandC

Prairie, The. Amy Clampitt. CP-ClamA

Prairie, The. Rudyard Kipling. CP-KiplR

Prairie Battlements, The. Nicholas Vachel Lindsay. CP-LindV

Prairie-Grass Dividing, The. Walt Whitman. CP-WhitW

Prairie Harvest. Robert Penn Warren. CP-WarrR

Prairie States, The. Walt Whitman. CP-WhitW

Prairie Sunset, A. Walt Whitman. CP-WhitW

Prairie Town. William Stafford. SP-StafW; SP-StafWW

Prairie Waters by Night. Carl Sandburg. CP-SandC

Prairie Woodland. Carl Sandburg. CP-SandC

Praise. Wendell Berry. CP-BerrW

Praise. G. K. Chesterton. CP-ChesG

Praise. Jane Cooper. CP-CoopJ

Praise. Jones Very. CP-VeryJ

Praise. Robert Penn Warren. CP-WarrR

Praise (1). George Herbert. CP-HerbG

Praise (2). George Herbert. CP-HerbG

Praise (3). George Herbert. CP-HerbG

Praise, A. Wendell Berry. CP-BerrW

Praise for All Dancers. Robert Bly. SP-BlyR

Praise for an Urn. Hart Crane. CP-CranH

Praise for Death. Donald Hall. CP-HallD

Praise in old times the sage Prometheus won. John Milton. See Antiquity in blindness praised the son of Iapetus

Praise in Summer. Richard Wilbur. CP-WilbR

Praise it—'tis dead. Emily Dickinson. CP-DickE

Praise Life. Robinson Jeffers. CP-JefR2

Praise of Distance. Paul Celan. SP-CelaP, tr. by John Felstiner

Praise of Dust, The. G. K. Chesterton. CP-ChesG

Praise of Good Poets in a Bad Age, A. John Ciardi. CP-CiarJ

Praise of Love. Christina Georgina Rossetti. CP-RosC3

Praise of the Committee. Muriel Rukeyser. CP-RukeM

Praise of Ysolt. Ezra Pound. CP-PoEar

Praise [or prayse] of meaner wits this work[e] like profit brings, The. Another of the Same. Sir Walter Ralegh. CP-RaleW Fr. Commendatory Verses to Edmund Spenser's Fairy Queen.

Praise praise as fast is lasting. Lark. Olga Broumas. SP-BrouO

Praise Song. Lucille Clifton. SP-ClifL

Praise the spells and bless the charms. Always Marry an April Girl. Ogden Nash. CP-NashO

Praise they that will Times past, I joy to see. Present Time but Pleaseth, The. Robert Herrick. CP-HerrR

Praise to the emptiness that blanks out existence. Existence. This World Which Is Made of Our Love for Emptiness. Jelaluddin Rumi. SP-Rumi, tr. by Coleman Barks

Praise to the End! Theodore Roethke. CP-RoetT

Praise to the lonely ones! Purveyors General. Ezra Pound. CP-PoEar

"Praise Woman still!" his Lordship says. To Maria. Robert Burns. CP-BurnR

Praise ye the Lord. Praise God in his sanctuary. Psalm 150: "Praise ye the Lord. Praise God in his sanctuary." Bible, O.T. SP-SmarC Fr. Psalms.

Praise ye the Lord. Praise ye the Lord from the heavens. Psalm 148: "Praise ye the Lord. Praise ye the Lord from the heavens." Bible, O.T. SP-SmarC Fr. Psalms.

Praise ye the Lord. Praise ye the name of the Lord; praise him, O ye servants of the Lord. Psalm 135: "Praise ye the Lord. Praise ye the name of the Lord; praise him, O ye servants of the Lord." Bible, O.T. SP-SmarC Fr. Psalms.

Praise ye the Lord. Sing unto the Lord a new song. Psalm 149: "Praise ye the Lord. Sing unto the Lord a new song." Bible, O.T. SP-SmarC Fr. Psalms.

Praise youth's hot blood if you will, I think that happiness. Age in Prospect. Robinson Jeffers. CP-JefR1

Prais[e]d be Diana[']s fair[e] and harmles[s] light. Homage to Diana. Sir Walter Ralegh. CP-RaleW

Praised be the climate. Anthem: "Praised be the climate." Joseph Brodsky. CP-BrodJ

Praised be the God of love. Antiphon (2): "Praised be the God of love." George Herbert. CP-HerbG

Praised by the Art whose subtle power could stay. Upon the Sight of a Beautiful Picture. William Wordsworth. CP-WorW1

Praisers of women in their proud and beautiful poems, The. Not Marble nor the Gilded Monuments. Archibald MacLeish. CP-MacLA

Praises. Thomas McGrath. SP-McGrT

Praises, The. Charles Olson. CP-OlsoC

Praises for Mrs. Dodd. Robert Penn Warren. CP-WarrR

Praises IV. Thomas McGrath. SP-McGrT

Praises of a Country Life, The. Horace. CP-JonsB; SP-JonsB, tr. by Ben Jonson Fr. Epodes.

Praising Dark Places. Yusef Komunyakaa. CP-KomuY

Praising the Poets of That Country. Howard Nemerov. CP-NemeH

Prank of the Heart at play on the Heart, The. Emily Dickinson. SP-DickE

Prat he writes Satyres; but herein's the fault. On Poet Prat. Robert Herrick. CP-HerrR

Pray and Prosper. Robert Herrick. CP-HerrR

Pray Billy Pitt explain thy rigs. On Mr. Pitt's [or Pit's] Hair-Powder Tax. Robert Burns. CP-BurnR

Pray, butcher, spare yon tender calf. Calf, The. Ogden Nash. CP-NashO

"Pray for me and die rotten," the men's. Memories of the Bowery. Alan Dugan. CP-DugaA

Pray give the "Atlantic." To Lucy Larcom. John Greenleaf Whittier. CP-WhitJ

Pray, mother, for thy prayer may keep. Hymn: The Efficacy of a Mother's Prayer. Jones Very. CP-VeryJ

Pray / pay / no attention to my greatness. Brief Lief. William Carlos Williams. CP-WilW2

Pray, pray for rain; thou may'st not know. Prayer for Rain. Jones Very. CP-VeryJ

Pray, Reader, have you eaten ortolans. Prologue: "Pray, Reader, have you eaten ortolans." Robert Browning. CP-BroR2

Pray steal me not, I'm Mrs. Dingley's. On the Collar of Mrs. Dingley's Lap-Dog. Jonathan Swift. CP-SwifJ

Pray tell me, Love, if what my eyes can see. Michelangelo Buonarroti. CP-Miche, tr. by John Frederick Nims

Pray thee, take care, that tak'st my book[e] in hand. To the Reader ("Pray thee, take care, that tak'st my book[e] in hand"). Ben Jonson. CP-JonsB; SP-JonsB

Pray to what earth does this sweet cold belong. Henry David Thoreau. CP-ThorH

Pray, what can dreams avail. Dream Song II. Paul Laurence Dunbar. CP-DunbP

Pray, what is this Bank of which the town rings? Bank Thrown Down, The. Jonathan Swift. CP-SwifJ

Pray why are you so bare, so bare. Haunted Oak, The. Paul Laurence Dunbar. CP-DunbP

Pray You Young Woman. Hayden Carruth. CP-CarHS

Prayer: "Approaching ninety, and still with a hope." Czeslaw Milosz. CP-MiloCN, tr. by Robert Hass

Prayer: "Gather up / In the arms of your pity." Langston Hughes. CP-HughL; CP-HughL2

Prayer: "Give me the moon at my feet." D. H. Lawrence. CP-LawrD

Prayer: "God, I need a job because I need money." Alan Dugan. CP-DugaA

Prayer : "I ask you this: / Which way to go?" Langston Hughes. CP-HughL; CP-HughL1

Prayer: "If I must of my Senses lose." Theodore Roethke. CP-RoetT

Prayer: "Oh my Gracious Preserver!" Phillis Wheatley. CP-WheaP

Prayer: "Prayer, that is said alone." Robert Herrick. CP-HerrR

Prayer: "Summe Deus, cui cæca patent penetralia cordis." Samuel Johnson. CP-JohnS

Prayer: "To her depths the sea has taken a sailor." Constantine P. Cavafy. CP-CavaC, tr. by Theoharis Constantine Theoharis

Prayer: "Whatever happens. Whatever." Galway Kinnell. SP-KinnGN

Prayer: "When white haired." William Corbett. SP-CorbW

Prayer: "White, O white face." "H. D." CP-DoolH

Prayer (1): "Prayer the Church's banquet, Angels' age." George Herbert. CP-HerbG

Prayer (2). George Herbert. CP-HerbG

Prayer, A. Richard Crashaw. CP-CrasR

Prayer, A. Robert Creeley. CP-CreeR

Prayer, A. Walter De la Mare. CP-DeLaW

Prayer, A: "O Lord, the hard-won miles." Paul Laurence Dunbar. CP-DunbP

Prayer, The. Denise Levertov. SP-LeveDP; SP-LeveDS

Prayer, The: "Father! help them who walk in their own light." Jones Very. CP-VeryJ

Prayer, The: "My brother kneels, so saith Kabir." Rudyard Kipling. CP-KiplR Fr. Kim.

Prayer, The: "Wilt Thou not visit me?" Jones Very. CP-VeryJ

Prayer after All, A. John Berryman. CP-BerrJ

Prayer after Eating. Wendell Berry. CP-BerrW

Prayer after World War. Carl Sandburg. CP-SandC

Prayer at Morning, A. Randall Jarrell. CP JarrR

Prayer at the End of a Rope. Ogden Nash. CP-NashO

Prayer before Birth. Louis MacNeice. CP-MacNL

Prayer before Study. Theodore Roethke. CP-RoetT

Prayer before Work. May Sarton. SP-SartM

Prayer Blues. Allen Ginsberg. SP-GinsA

Prayer for a New Mother. Dorothy Parker. CP-ParkD

Prayer for a Prayer. Dorothy Parker. CP-ParkD

Prayer for a Winter Night. Langston Hughes. CP-HughL; CP-HughL1

Prayer for His Lady's Life. Propertius. CP-PoEar, tr. by Ezra Pound

Prayer for My Daughter. Marilyn Hacker. SP-HackM

Prayer for My Daughter, A. William Butler Yeats. CP-YeatW

Prayer for My Son, A. William Butler Yeats. CP-YeatW

Prayer for Old Age, A. William Butler Yeats. CP-YeatW

Prayer for One Leg. Alan Dugan. CP-DugaA

Prayer for Rain. Jones Very. CP-VeryJ

Prayer for Revolutionary Love. Denise Levertov. SP-LeveDL; SP-LeveDS

Prayer for the Dead (To Verlaine). "Rubén Dario." SP-DariR, tr. by Alberto Acereda and Will Derusha

Prayer for the Great Family. Gary Snyder. CP-SnydG

Prayer in Bad Weather. Charles Bukowski. SP-BukC1

Prayer in Mid-Passage. Louis MacNeice. CP-MacNL

Prayer in My Sickness, A. James Wright. CP-WrigJ

Prayer in Spring, A. Robert Frost. CP-FrosR

Prayer, in the Prospect of Death, A. Robert Burns. CP-BurnR

Prayer is the little implement. Emily Dickinson. CP-DickE

Prayer Meeting. Langston Hughes. CP-HughL; CP-HughL1

Prayer Not to Go to Paradise with the Asses. Kenneth Patchen. CP-PatcK

Prayer of Agassiz, The. John Greenleaf Whittier. CP-WhitJ

Prayer of Columbus. Walt Whitman. CP-WhitW

Prayer of Jabez, The. Jones Very. CP-VeryJ

Prayer of Jabez, too, should be our prayer, The. Prayer of Jabez, The. Jones

Very. CP-VeryJ

Prayer of Miriam Cohen, The. Rudyard Kipling. CP-KiplR

Prayer of Nature, The. Lord Byron. CP-Byron

Prayer of One Not Indifferent Enough. Rainer Maria Rilke. CP-RilkFr, tr. by A. Poulin, Jr. Fr. Affectionate Taxes to France.

Prayer of Thanksgiving Written for Victor Hammer, A. Thomas Merton. CP-MertT

Prayer of the Eyes, A. W. S. Merwin. SP-MerwW

Prayer of the Middle-Aged Man, The. John Berryman. CP-BerrJ

Prayer on Going into My House. William Butler Yeats. CP-YeatW

Prayer Perfect, The. James Whitcomb Riley. CP-RileJ

Prayer-Seeker, The. John Greenleaf Whittier. CP-WhitJ

Prayer the Church's banquet, Angels' age. Prayer (1): "Prayer the Church's banquet, Angels' age." George Herbert. CP-HerbG

Prayer to All the Dead among Mine Own People, A. Nicholas Vachel Lindsay. CP-LindV

Prayer to Escape from the Market Place, A. James Wright. CP-WrigJ

Prayer to Go to Paradise with the Donkeys, A. Francis Jammes. CP-WilbR, tr. by Richard Wilbur

Prayer to Hermes. Robert Creeley. SP-CreeR

Prayer to My Mother. Pier Paolo Pasolini. SP-PasoP, tr. by Norman MacAfee and Luciano Martinengo

Prayer to the Lord Ramakrishna, A. James Wright. CP-WrigJ

Prayer to the Mountain, A. John Ciardi. CP-CiarJ

Prayer to the Wind, A. Thomas Carew. CP-CareT

Prayer, under the Pressure of Violent Anguish, A. Robert Burns. CP-BurnR

Prayer with Martial Stance. Olga Broumas. SP-BrouO

Prayers and Praises are those spotless two. Gods Prt. Robert Herrick. CP-HerrR

Prayers and Sayings of the Mad Farmer. Wendell Berry. CP-BerrW

Prayers Must Have Poise. Robert Herrick. CP-HerrR

Prayers of many summers come. Migration. W. S. Merwin. SP-MerwWF

Prayers of Steel. Carl Sandburg. CP-SandC

Prayers to Lord Murugan. A. K. Ramanujan. CP-RamaA

Praying Always. Christina Georgina Rossetti. CP-RosC2

Praying on a 707. Anne Sexton. CP-SextA

Praying to Big Jack. Anne Sexton. CP-SextA

Pre-Amphibian. Margaret Atwood. SP-AtwM1

Pre-Petrarchan Sonnet. Michael Palmer. SP-PalmM

Pre-Raphaelite Notebook, A. Geoffrey Hill. CP-HillG

Preacher, The. Jones Very. CP-VeryJ

Preacher, The. John Greenleaf Whittier. CP-WhitJ

Preacher's Boy, The. James Whitcomb Riley. CP-RileJ

Preaching from a Spanish Ballad, A. George Meredith. CP-MerG1

Preamble. Muriel Rukeyser. CP-RukeM

Preceded by mounted police. George Oppen. CP-OppGN

Precedence. Rae Armantrout. SP-ArmaA

Precedent. Paul Laurence Dunbar. CP-DunbP

Precepts. Robert Herrick. CP-HerrR

Precession of the Equinoxes. Kenneth Rexroth. CP-RexrK

Preciosa and the Wind. Federico García Lorca. CP-GarcF, tr. by Christopher Maurer

Precious Five. W. H. Auden. CP-AudeW

Precious in the light of the early sun the Housatonic. From a Train Window. Edna St. Vincent Millay. CP-MillE

Precious—moldering pleasure—'tis, A. Emily Dickinson. CP-DickE

Precious Moments. Carl Sandburg. CP-SandC

Precious to Me—She still shall be. Emily Dickinson. CP-DickE

Precipitous is the shape and stance of the spruce. Kodiak Poem, A. William Meredith. SP-MereW

Precipitous rock—all day long drinking the scorching sun. Geographic Origins. Yannis Ritsos. SP-RitsY Fr. Monovasia.

Precise counterpart, The. Orchestra, The. William Carlos Williams. CP-WilW2

Precise woman with a short haircut brings order, A. Yehuda Amichai. SP-AmicY, tr. by Chana Bloch

Precise woman with a short haircut makes order, A. Yehuda Amichai. SP-AmicYL, tr. by Benjamin Harshav and Barbara Harshav

Precise yet furtive etiquette of dogs, The. Dogs in the Park. Louis MacNeice. CP-MacNL

Precisely as unbig a why as i'm. E. E. Cummings. CP-CummE

Precognition. Margaret Atwood. SP-AtwM2

Precursors. A. R. Ammons. CP-AmmoA

Precursors. Hans Magnus Enzensberger. SP-EnzeH, tr. by Michael Hamburger

Precursors. Louis MacNeice. CP-MacNL

Predecessor of Perseus, A. Howard Nemerov. CP-NemeH

Predestination. Robert Herrick. CP-HerrR

Predestined Space, The. James Vincent Cunningham. CP-CunnJ

Predestined to the catacomb. Phantom, A. Charles Baudelaire. CP-BaudC, tr. by

Walter Martin

Predestined to the catacomb. Black Brightness. Charles Baudelaire. CP-BaudC, *tr.* by Walter Martin *Fr.* Phantom, A.

Predicter of Famine, The. William Carlos Williams. CP-WilW2

Preface. Theodore Weiss. SP-WeisT

Preface, A: "If he goes rowing in the park tho he may row so well that." George Oppen. CP-OppGN

Preface, A: "To all to whom this little book may come." Rudyard Kipling. CP-KiplR *Fr.* Land and Sea Tales.

Preface: "First, plain speech in the mother tongue." Czeslaw Milosz. CP-MiloC, *tr.* by Robert Hass *Fr.* Treatise on Poetry, A.

Preface, The: "Continous fabric (nerve movie?) exactly as wide as these lines, A." Philip Whalen. SP-WhalP

Preface first: the two of them, the brittle, A. Yehuda Amichai. SP-AmicY, *tr.* by Stephen Mitchell *Fr.* We Loved Here.

Preface to "Bob Taylor's Birthday" Nicholas Vachel Lindsay. CP-LindV

Preface to the Past. Ogden Nash. CP-NashO

Prefatory Poem to My Brother's Sonnets. Alfred Tennyson. CP-TennA

Preference. Langston Hughes. CP-HughL; CP-HughL3

Preference, A. Paul Laurence Dunbar. CP-DunbP

Preferences. Heather McHugh. SP-McHuH

Preferred: / tired little poems, taut. How to Get in the Best Magazines. Eleanor Wilner. SP-WilnE

Preferring laxatives to wine. America's Plutonic Ecstasies. Hart Crane. CP-CranH

Pregnant again with th' old twins hope, and fear. To Mr T. W ("Pregnant again with th' old twins hope, and fear"). John Donne. CP-DonnJ; MW-DonnJ

Pregnant moon of August, A. One of These Nights. Derek Mahon. CP-MahoD

Pregnant women are jealously guarded by their Angels, The. Souls Looking for Bodies. Andrei Codrescu. SP-CodrA

Preguntas sin respuestas for Nicanor Parra. James Laughlin. CP-LaugJ

Prejudice, The. Robert Creeley. CP-CreeR

Prejudice against the Past, The. Wallace Stevens. CP-StevW; CP-StevWP

Prelude, A. Charles Tomlinson. CP-TomlC

Prelude, A: "I know only the bare rocks of today." William Carlos Williams. CP-WilW1

Prelude: "Bullock / slowly, The." Federico García Lorca. CP-GarcF, *tr.* by Jerome Rothenberg *Fr.* Night (Suite for Piano and Poet's Voice).

Prelude: For the Feast of St. Agnes, A. Thomas Merton. CP-MertT

Prelude: "I drew solitude over me, on the lone shore." Robinson Jeffers. CP-JefR1

Prelude: "I, with legs crossed along the daylight, watch." Derek Walcott. CP-WalcD

Prelude in Boricua. Luis Palés Matos. CP-WilW2

Prelude: "Limit of the song is this, The." Michael Palmer. SP-PalmM

Prelude: Over the Ognisanti. Ezra Pound. CP-PoEar

Prelude: "Poplar lanes move on, The." Federico García Lorca. CP-GarcF, *tr.* by Alan S. Trueblood *Fr.* Love.

Prelude, Prefixed to the Volume Entitled "Poems Chiefly of Early and Late Years" William Wordsworth. CP-WorW2

Prelude, The; Growth of a Poet's Mind [1805 vers.]. William Wordsworth. CP-WorW3; MW-WorW

Prelude, The; Growth of a Poet's Mind [1850 vers.]. William Wordsworth. CP-WorW3

   Books.

   "There was a boy;—ye knew him well, ye cliffs." CP-WorW1

   Introduction—Childhood and School-Time.

   Influence of Natural Objects [in Calling Forth and Strengthening the Imagination in Boyhood and Early Youth]. CP-WorW1

Prelude to a Parting. Maya Angelou. SP-AngeM

Prelude to "Departmental Ditties." Rudyard Kipling. CP-KiplR

Prelude to Objects. Wallace Stevens. CP-StevW

Prelude to Our Age. Langston Hughes. CP-HughL; CP-HughL3

Prelude to Winter. William Carlos Williams. CP-WilW2

Preludes. T. S. Eliot. CP-ElioT; SP-ElioT

Prelusive. Herman Melville. SP-MelvH *Fr.* Clarel: A Poem and Pilgrimage in the Holy Land.

Premises. Karl Shapiro. SP-ShapK

Premonition. Paul Laurence Dunbar. CP-DunbP

Premonition, The. Theodore Roethke. CP-RoetT

Premonitions. Thomas Hardy. CP-HardT

Premonitions. David Ignatow. SP-IgnaD

Premula's Problem. James Laughlin. CP-LaugJ

Preoccupation's Gift. Donald Davie. CP-DaviDC

Preparation. Paul Laurence Dunbar. CP-DunbP

Preparation. Czeslaw Milosz. CP-MiloC; CP-MiloCN, *tr.* by Robert Hass

Preparation for Life's Voyage. Jones Very. CP-VeryJ

Preparation for the Highest Being. Kenneth Patchen. CP-PatcK

Prepare for death. But how can you prepare. Speculation. Howard Nemerov. CP-NemeH

Prepare for Songs; He's come, He's come. New-Yeeres Gift, or Circumcisions Song, Sung to the King in the Presence at White Hall, The. Robert Herrick. CP-HerrR

Prepare, prepare, the iron helm of war. War Song [to Englishmen], A. William Blake. CP-BlakW

Prepare the ground when maple buds have burst. Planting a Mailbox. John Updike. CP-UpdiJ

Prepared for death and unprepared. Two Poems of the Military. James Dickey. CP-DickJ

Prepared Statement, The. Robert Graves. CP-GravR

Prepared, the sailor o'er the ocean sails. Preparation for Life's Voyage. Jones Very. CP-VeryJ

Preparing for Exile. Derek Walcott. CP-WalcD

Preparing to Leave Home. Jay Wright. SP-WrigJ

Preponderance, The. William Meredith. SP-MereW

Preposterous is that Government, (and rude). Ill Government. Robert Herrick. CP-HerrR

Prepost'rous is that order, when we run. First Work, and Then Wages. Robert Herrick. CP-HerrR

Presage and caveat not only seem. Window Sill, The. Robert Graves. CP-GravR

Prescience. Maya Angelou. SP-AngeM

Prescience. Robert Herrick. CP-HerrR

Prescient, my hands soothing. Walt Whitman in the Civil War Hospitals. David Ignatow. SP-IgnaD

Prescription. Czeslaw Milosz. CP-MiloCN, *tr.* by Robert Hass

Prescription of Painful Ends. Robinson Jeffers. CP-JefR3

Presence. Denise Levertov. SP-LeveDS

Presence. Yannis Ritsos. SP-RitsY, *tr.* by N. C. Germanacos

Presence. Adam Zagajewski. SP-ZagaA, *tr.* by Renata Gorczynski, Benjamin Ivry *and* C. K. Williams

Presence, The. Robert Graves. CP-GravR

Presence, The. Maxine W. Kumin. SP-KumiM

Presence, The. Denise Levertov. SP-LeveDP

Presence, The. Jones Very. CP-VeryJ

Presence and Absence. Robert Herrick. CP-HerrR

Presence of an External Master of Knowledge. Wallace Stevens. CP-StevWP

Presence of Love, The. Samuel Taylor Coleridge. CP-ColeS

Presences. Josephine Jacobsen. CP-JacoJ

Presences. William Butler Yeats. CP-YeatW

Presences are always said to brood. Tuscan Morning. Donald Davie. CP-DaviDC

Present. Tess Gallagher. SP-GallT

Present. Langston Hughes. CP-HughL; CP-HughL2

Present, The. John Logan. CP-LogaJ

Present, The. W. S. Merwin. SP-MerwW

Present again / present present. "Follow the Drinking Gourd." Robert Creeley. CP-CreeR

Present and Future. Christina Georgina Rossetti. CP-RosC3

Present for Tu Fu from Li Po, A. Li Po. CP-KizeC, *tr.* by Carolyn Kizer

Present Government Grievous. Robert Herrick. CP-HerrR

Present: or, The Bag of the Bee, The. Robert Herrick. CP-HerrR

Present Time, The. G. K. Chesterton. CP-ChesG

Present Time But Pleaseth, The. Robert Herrick. CP-HerrR

Presentation of Two Birds to My Son, A. James Wright. CP-WrigJ

Presentation Piece. Marilyn Hacker. SP-HackM

Presentation Verses to Nathaniel Pigott. Alexander Pope. CP-PopeA

Presentiment. Ambrose Bierce. SP-BierA

Presentiment—is that long Shadow—on the lawn. Emily Dickinson. CP-DickE

Presentiments. William Wordsworth. CP-WorW2

Presenting a *Lark*. Alexander Pope. CP-PopeA

Presently at our touch the teacup stirred. Voices from the Other World. James Merrill. SP-MerrJ

President and Poet. Donald Hall. CP-HallD

President of my country his face flushed, The. Nickname of Hell, The. C. K. Williams. CP-WillC; SP-WillC

President of shame has his own flag, The. Presidents. W. S. Merwin. SP-MerwW

President of the Holding Company, The. Lorine Niedecker. CP-NiedL

President of the, The. Confidential Report. James Laughlin. CP-LaugJ

President Roosevelt, you. Dear Mr. President. Langston Hughes. CP-HughL; CP-HughL2

President Slumming, The. James Tate. SP-TateJ

Presidentiad, The. Donald Hall. CP-HallD

Presidential Address to a Party of Exiles. Howard Nemerov. CP-NemeH

Presidents. W. S. Merwin. SP-MerwW

President's Four Freedoms, The. How About It, Dixie. Langston Hughes. CP-HughL; CP-HughL2

President's Speech, The. Hayden Carruth. CP-CarHS

Press, The. Rudyard Kipling. CP-KiplR

Press is Peculiar, The. Carl Sandburg. CP-SandC

Press reports the enemy in power: the solo, The. Fields of Earth. Kenneth Patchen. CP-PatcK

Press[e] me not to take more pleasure. Rose, The. George Herbert. CP-HerbG

Pressed Gentian, The. John Greenleaf Whittier. CP-WhitJ

Pressed with conflicting thoughts of love and fear. St Paul's. William Wordsworth. CP-WorW1; MW-WorW

Presses were busy enough. George Oppen. CP-OppGN

Pressing down I remember. In Your Own Words Without Lying Tell Something of Your Background With Particular Attention to Anything Relating to the Position For Which You Are Applying. Press Down. Miller Williams. CP-WillM

Pressure as it crushes gags the moan, The. Iceberg, The. Randall Jarrell. CP-JarrR

Pressure of sun on the rockslide. Water. Gary Snyder. CP-SnydG

Prest by the load of life, the weary mind. Prologue to Goldsmith's *The Good Natur'd Man*. Samuel Johnson. CP-JohnS

Prester John on his lands looked down. Modern Magic, The. G. K. Chesterton. CP-ChesG

Prestige. George Meredith. CP-MerG2

Prestige. D. H. Lawrence. CP-LawrD

Presumption has it's Affliction. Emily Dickinson. SP-DickE

Presumptuous bard! How could you dare. Answer to a Scandalous Poem, An. Jonathan Swift. CP-SwifJ

Presumptuous Poet, could you dare. Jonathan Swift. *See* Presumptuous bard! How could you dare

Pretension has it / you can't. For the Graduation. Robert Creeley. CP-CreeR

Pretension's. Robert Creeley. CP-CreeR

Preternaturally Early Snowfall in Mating Season. Robert Penn Warren. CP-WarrR

Pretrial Hearing. Alan Dugan. CP-DugaA

Pretty. Stevie Smith. CP-SmitS

Pretty. Louis Zukofsky. CP-ZukLS

Pretty a day, A. E. E. Cummings. CP-CummE; SP-CummE

Pretty Blue Apron. James McMichael. SP-McMiJ

Pretty boarders are leaving the trees, The. Emily Dickinson. SP-DickE

Pretty Epigram for [Those] the Entertainment of Those Who [Pay] Have Paid Great Sums in the Venetian & Flemish Ooze, A. William Blake. CP-BlakW

Pretty glow on the water. Kenneth Patchen. CP-PatcK

Pretty Halcyon Days. Ogden Nash. CP-NashO

Pretty Love, I Must Outlive You. Edna St. Vincent Millay. CP-MillE

Pretty party for people, A. And. Robert Creeley. CP-CreeR

Pretty, pretty girl, A. Profile of a Lady. Tu Fu. CP-WilW2

Pretty Rain from those sweet Eaves, The. Emily Dickinson. CP-DickE

Pretty Redhead, The. Guillaume Apollinaire. CP-WrigJ

Pretty Woman, A. Robert Browning. CP-BroR1

Pretty women wonder where my secret lies. Phenomenal Woman. Maya Angelou. SP-AngeM

Prevalent At One Time. Marianne Craig Moore. CP-MoorM

Previous Existence. Charles Baudelaire. CP-BaudC, *tr.* by Walter Martin

Previous night is now, A. Laura Riding Jackson. CP-RidiL

Prevision, or Provision. Robert Herrick. CP-HerrR

Prey swooped up, the iron love seat shudders. Up and Down. James Merrill. SP-MerrJ

Priam's Speeding Forth at Night. Constantine P. Cavafy. CP-CavaC, *tr.* by Theoharis Constantine Theoharis

Price, The. W. H. Auden. CP-AudeW

Price, The. Charles Bukowski. SP-BukC1

Pricing. David Ignatow. SP-IgnaD

Prickle a lamb. Conjuring Roethke. James Tate. SP-TateJ

Prickles is waspish, and puts forth his sting. Upon Prickles. Robert Herrick. CP-HerrR

Pride. Langston Hughes. *See* Militant

Pride Allowable in Poets. Robert Herrick. CP-HerrR

Pride Goeth Before a Raise or Ah, There, Mrs. Cadwallader-Smith. Ogden Nash. CP-NashO

Pride of Head. Laura Riding Jackson. CP-RidiL

Pride of Love. Robert Graves. CP-GravR

Pride of Progeny. Robert Graves. CP-GravR

Pride of the Dead, The. Thomas Merton. CP-MertT

Pride of Youth. Dante Gabriel Rossetti. CW-RossD *Fr.* House of Life, The.

Pride's Crossing. James Tate. SP-TateJ

Priest. "H. D." CP-DoolH

Priest, The. Jones Very. CP-VeryJ

Priest at the Serapeion. Constantine P. Cavafy. CP-CavaC, *tr.* by Theoharis Constantine Theoharis

Priest from a different land, A. Tree. Ted Hughes. SP-HughTN

Priest, is any song-bird stricken. Outlaw, The. G. K. Chesterton. CP-ChesG

Priesthood, The. George Herbert. CP-HerbG

Priestley. Samuel Taylor Coleridge. CP-ColeS; MW-ColeS *Fr.* Effusions.

Priest's Confession, The. Ai. SP-Ai

Priest's Curse on Dancing, The. Howard Nemerov. CP-NemeH

Priests of the Old Gods, The. Clement of Alexandria. CP-MertT *Fr.* Diatribe Against the Old Gods.

Prig now drinks Water, who before drank Beere. Upon Prig. Robert Herrick. CP-HerrR

Prigg, when he comes to houses, oft doth use. Upon Prigg. Robert Herrick. CP-HerrR

Primal Passions, The. D. H. Lawrence. CP-LawrD

Primary Wonder. Denise Levertov. SP-LeveDS

Prime. John Berryman. CP-BerrJ

Prime. Langston Hughes. CP-HughL; CP-HughL3

Prime. James McMichael. SP-McMiJ

Primer. Charles Simic. SP-SimiC; SP-SimiCE

Primer, The. Josephine Jacobsen. CP-JacoJ

Primer for the Nuclear Age. Rita Dove. SP-DoveR

Primer Lesson. Carl Sandburg. CP-SandC

Primer of the Daily Round, A. Howard Nemerov. CP-NemeH

Primeval fish was like a squid, all mouth, The. Criticism of Bergson and Darwin. Alan Dugan. CP-DugaA

Primeval Landscape with Politician and Dodo Bird. Robert Stock. SP-StocR

Primitive. George Oppen. CP-OppGN

Primitive head, That. Bad Island, The—Easter. Robert Frost. CP-FrosR

Primitive Journal. Charles Wright. SP-WrigC

Primitive Journal II. Charles Wright. SP-WrigC

Primitive like an Orb, A. Wallace Stevens. CP-StevW; CP-StevWP

Primitive Worship. Jones Very. CP-VeryJ

Primordia. Wallace Stevens. CP-StevWP

Primordial locutions and ventures. Seven Archaic Images. Thomas Merton. CP-MertT

Primrose. William Carlos Williams. CP-WilW1

Primrose, The. Robert Burns. CP-BurnR

Primrose, The. Robert Herrick. CP-HerrR

Primrose Bed, The. Robert Graves. CP-GravR

Primrose of the Rock, The. William Wordsworth. CP-WorW2

Primrose petal's edge, A. Ted Hughes. SP-HughTN

Primrose, The; Being at Montgomery Castle, upon the hill, on which it is situate. John Donne. CP-DonnJ; MW-DonnJ

Primroses; salutations; the miry skull. Pre-Raphaelite Notebook, A. Geoffrey Hill. CP-HillG

Prince, The. Randall Jarrell. CP-JarrR

Prince Athanase; a Fragment. Percy Bysshe Shelley. CP-ShelP

Prince from Western Libya, A. Constantine P. Cavafy. CP-CavaC, *tr.* by Theoharis Constantine Theoharis

Prince Harry turns from Percy's pouring sides. Up, Jack. Richard Wilbur. CP-WilbR

Prince Hohenstiel-Schwangau, Saviour of Society. Robert Browning. CP-BroR1

Prince leans to the girl in scarlet heels, The. Cinderella. Sylvia Plath. CP-PlatS

Prince of Bards was old Aneurin. Aneurin's Harp. George Meredith. CP-MerG1

Prince of calm, treasure of fascinating cuts on my arm. Spirit Ink, The. Frank O'Hara. SP-OharF

Prince of the church whose lofty mind. Acknowledgement. Archibald MacLeish. CP-MacLA

Prince of This World governs number, The. One and Many. Czeslaw Milosz. CP-MiloCN, *tr.* by Martin Sabiniewicz *and* Jennifer Scappettone

Prince Roman Sanguszko treks across Siberia. Polish Biographical Dictionary in a Library in Houston, The. Adam Zagajewski. SP-ZagaA, *tr.* by Clare Cavanagh

Prince Rupert's drop, paper muslin ghost. Pedantic Literalist. Marianne Craig Moore. CP-MoorM

Prince the ball of heaven should. Hafiz. CP-EmerR *Fr.* Odes.

Prince was vexed that he had only ever spent his time perfecting acts of banal generosity, A. Tale. Arthur Rimbaud. CP-RimbA, *tr.* by Martin Sorrell

Prince Wen Hui's cook. Cutting up an Ox. Chuang Tzu. CP-MertT, *tr.* by Thomas Merton

Prince, Yorkshire holds me now. Invitation Declined, An. G. K. Chesterton. CP-ChesG

Princely cockroach, inheritor. Kneeling at the Pipes. Marge Piercy. SP-PierM

Princes and Favourites. Robert Herrick. CP-HerrR

Prince's Progress, The. Christina Georgina Rossetti. CP-RosC1

Princess, The. Alfred Tennyson. CP-TennA

Princess and the Goblins, The. Sylvia Plath. CP-PlatS

Princess and the Pea, The. Paul Muldoon. CP-MuldP

Princess Di. James Schuyler. CP-SchuJ

Princess! in envy of the fate of a Hebe. Futile Petition. Stéphane Mallarmé. CP-MallS, *tr.* by Henry Weinfield

Princess in the eastern tale, A. Sleeping City, The. George Meredith. CP-MerG1

Princess is sad . . . What is wrong with the princess?, The. Sonatina. "Rubén Darío." SP-DariR, *tr.* by Alberto Acereda *and* Will Derusha

Princess of Cleves, The. Nathaniel Lee.
Epilogue: "Qualm of conscience brings me back again, A." CP-DryJ2
Prologue: "Ladies! (I hope there's none behind to hear)." CP-DryJ2

Princess Recalls Her One Adventure, The. Edna St. Vincent Millay. CP-MillE

Princess Summer Fall Winter Spring. Thomas Lux. SP-LuxT

Princess Wakes in the Wood, The. Randall Jarrell. CP-JarrR

Principia Mathematica: Einstein's Exile in an Old Dutch Winter. Norman Dubie. CP-DubiN

Principle, The. David Ignatow. SP-IgnaD

Principle of all things; entrails made, The. Lucretius. CP-EmerR *Fr.* De Rerum Natura (On the Nature of Things).

Print is too small, distressing me, The. Last Decision, The. Maya Angelou. SP-AngeM

Prints, The. W. S. Merwin. SP-MerwW

Prior to Miss Belle's Appearance. James Whitcomb Riley. CP-RileJ

Prioress' Tale—A Modernization, The. Geoffrey Chaucer. CP-WorW1 *Fr.* Canterbury Tales, The.

Priory of St Saviour, Glendalough, The. Donald Davie. CP-DaviDC

Prism. James Merrill. SP-MerrJ

Prism. Howard Nemerov. CP-NemeH

Prisms. Laura Riding Jackson. CP-RidiL

Prison. Charles Simic. SP-SimiCE

Prison. Jones Very. CP-VeryJ

Prison. Miller Williams. CP-WillM

Prison gets to be a friend, A. Emily Dickinson. CP-DickE

Prison house is full, there is no cell, The. Prison. Jones Very. CP-VeryJ

Prison Island. James Fenton. SP-FentJ

Prison Poem. Tibor Tollas. CP-LogaJ, *tr.* by John Logan

Prison Sentence, The. Gabriela Mistral. SP-MistG, *tr.* by Maria Giachetti [*or* Jacketti]

Prison Song. Alan Dugan. CP-DugaA

Prison Tree and the Women, The. Yannis Ritsos. SP-RitsY, *tr.* by Kimon Friar

Prison Walls. Robert Graves. CP-GravR

Prisoner. Maya Angelou. SP-AngeM

Prisoner. Dorothy Parker. CP-ParkD

Prisoner, The. Emily Jane Brontë. CP-BronE

Prisoner, The. Ai. SP-Ai

Prisoner, The. Elizabeth Barrett Browning. CP-BroEB

Prisoner, The. Raissa Maritain. CP-MertT

Prisoner, The. Charles Simic. SP-SimiC; SP-SimiCE

Prisoner, The. Jones Very. CP-VeryJ

Prisoner at a Desk. May Sarton. SP-SartM

Prisoner for Debt, The. John Greenleaf Whittier. CP-WhitJ

Prisoner in this space perpetually narrow, A. When. James Dickey. CP-DickJ

Prisoner of Childhood, The. James Laughlin. CP-LaugJ

Prisoner of Chillon, The. Lord Byron. CP-Byron

Prisoner of Zenda, The. Richard Wilbur. CP-WilbR

Prisoner ran forward, The. First his head. Essay on Death. Hayden Carruth. CP-CarHS

Prisoners. "H. D." CP-DoolH

Prisoners. Randall Jarrell. CP-JarrR

Prisoners. Yusef Komunyakaa. CP-KomuY

Prisoners. Rainer Maria Rilke. CP-RilkFr, *tr.* by A. Poulin, Jr.

Prisoners, The. Robert Earl Hayden. CP-HaydR

Prisoners, The. Adrienne Rich. CP-RicAE; SP-RicA2

Prisoners, The. Stephen Spender. CP-SpenS

Prisoner's Dream, The. Eugenio Montale. CP-MontE, *tr.* by Jonathan Galassi

Prisoners of infinite choice, The. Leaves. Derek Mahon. CP-MahoD

Prisoners of Naples, The. John Greenleaf Whittier. CP-WhitJ

Prisoner's Song, The. James Laughlin. CP-LaugJ

Prithee, Gentle Lady, List. William Wordsworth. CP-WorW2

Privacy. Kenneth Rexroth. CP-RexrK

Private Banquet, The. Jelaluddin Rumi. SP-Rumi, *tr.* by Coleman Barks

Private Dining Room, The. Ogden Nash. CP-NashO

Private Eye, The. Howard Nemerov. CP-NemeH

Private First Class. Charles Bukowski. SP-BukC1

Private Ground. Sylvia Plath. CP-PlatS

Private Intrigue of Melancholy, The. James Tate. SP-TateJ

Private Life of the Sphinx. Muriel Rukeyser. CP-RukeM

Private Man on Public Men, A. Thomas Hardy. CP-HardT

Private Means Is Dead. Stevie Smith. CP-SmitS

Private Ortheris's Song. Rudyard Kipling. CP-KiplR *Fr.* Life's Handicap.

Private Place. Yannis Ritsos. SP-RitsY, *tr.* by Kimon Friar

Private Space, A. Eleanor Wilner. SP-WilnE

Private Theatricals. James Whitcomb Riley. CP-RileJ

Privato commune bonum, Lea, cum melius fit. Ad Leam. Thomas Campion. CP-CampT

Privet. Louis Zukofsky. CP-ZukLS

Prize Fighter. Langston Hughes. CP-HughL; CP-HughL1

Prize, The. Raymond Carver. CP-CarvR

Prized memorial this slight work may prove, A. With a Small Present. William Wordsworth. CP-WorW2

Pro-Consuls, The. Rudyard Kipling. CP-KiplR

Pro Femina. Carolyn Kizer.
Erotic Philosophers, The. CP-KizeC
Fanny. CP-KizeC
One. CP-KizeC
Three. CP-KizeC
Two. CP-KizeC

Pro Nobis. George Oppen. CP-OppGN

Pro Sua Vita. Robert Penn Warren. CP-WarrR

Probabilities. Yannis Ritsos. SP-RitsY, *tr.* by Athan Anagnostopoulos

Probable Truth. Robert Creeley. SP-CreeR

Probably death fits all right in the world. This Day. C. K. Williams. CP-WillC

Probably I am an ordinary middle-class. Fire. Adam Zagajewski. SP-ZagaA, *tr.* by Renata Gorczynski

Probably in a battered trunk. Somewhere in France. James Laughlin. CP-LaugJ

Probatur Aliter. Jonathan Swift. CP-SwifJ

Probity. George Oppen. CP-OppGN

Problem. Tennessee Williams. CP-WillT

Problem from Milton, A. Richard Wilbur. CP-WilbR

Problem. I cannot come among Your saints. Nones. John Berryman. CP-BerrJ

Problem, The. Ralph Waldo Emerson. CP-EmerR

Problem, The. Robert Creeley. CP-CreeR

Problem, The. Thomas Hardy. CP-HardT

Problem, The. Jonathan Swift. CP-SwifJ

Problem, The. John Greenleaf Whittier. CP-WhitJ

Problem, The. William Carlos Williams. CP-WilW2

Problem in Spatial Composition, A. Robert Penn Warren. CP-WarrR

Problem in the pool is plain, The. Dytiscus. Hugh MacDiarmid. SP-MacDH

Problem is urgent, yes, for this hot light, The. To a Woman. John Berryman. CP-BerrJ

Problem of Autobiography / Vague Recollection or Dream? Robert Penn Warren. CP-WarrR

Problem of Knowledge. Robert Penn Warren. CP-WarrR

Problem Struck Me, The. James Laughlin. CP-LaugJ

Problem, unstated until now, is how, The. Adrienne Rich. SP-RicA1 *Fr.* Contradictions: Tracking Poems.

Problem was to get first things, The. Grace to Be Said before Committee Meetings. Howard Nemerov. CP-NemeH

Problems. Langston Hughes. CP-HughL

Problems About the Other Woman. Charles Bukowski. SP-BukC1

Problems Of Gender. Robert Graves. CP-GravR

Procedures for Underground. Margaret Atwood. SP-AtwM1

Proceeding sidewise by inattention I arrive. Passing through the Banford Tolls. Alan Dugan. CP-DugaA

Process. Yannis Ritsos. SP-RitsY, *tr.* by Kimon Friar

Process, A. Charles Tomlinson. CP-TomlC

Process, The. May Swenson. SP-SwenM

Process in the Weather of the Heart, A. Dylan Thomas. CP-ThomD

Process of time worketh such wonder. Sir Thomas Wyatt. CP-WyatT

Procession. Federico García Lorca. SP-GarcF *Fr.* Poem of the Saeta.

Procession. James Schuyler. CP-SchuJ

Procession. Allen Tate. CP-TateA

Procession at Candlemas, A. Amy Clampitt. CP-ClamA

Procession of Dead Days, A. Thomas Hardy. CP-HardT

Procession of Dionysus. Constantine P. Cavafy. CP-CavaC, *tr.* by Theoharis Constantine Theoharis

Procession that has been crossing, The. For Nikolai, Many Thousand Miles Away. Denise Levertov. SP-LeveDL

Procession winds like a little snake, The. Island Funeral. Hugh MacDiarmid. SP-MacDH

Processions that lack high stilts have nothing that catches the eye. High Talk. William Butler Yeats. CP-YeatW

Proclamation. Allen Ginsberg. SP-GinsA

Proclamation, The. John Greenleaf Whittier. CP-WhitJ

Procne, Philomela, and Itylus. Philomela. John Crowe Ransom. SP-RansJ

Procne your charming servant has. Two Letters on Samos. James Laughlin. CP-

LaugJ

Procrastination Is All of the Time. Ogden Nash. CP-NashO

Prodigal. A. R. Ammons. CP-AmmoA

Prodigal, The. Elizabeth Bishop. CP-BishE

Prodigal, The. Jones Very. CP-VeryJ

Prodigal of loves and barbecues. To the (Supposed) Patron. Geoffrey Hill. CP-HillG

Prodigal Son, A. Christina Georgina Rossetti. CP-RosC2

Prodigal Son, The. Rudyard Kipling. CP-KiplR *Fr.* Kim.

Prodigal Son, The. Robert Bly. SP-BlyR

Prodigal Son is kneeling in the husks, The. Prodigal Son, The. Robert Bly. SP-BlyR

Prodigious goals—Flakes boat starmarsh—Great Highone I care. I Care What Happens. Kenneth Patchen. CP-PatcK

Prodigious Madness of the writing Race! Prologue to Garrick's *Lethe.* Samuel Johnson. CP-JohnS

Prodigious, prodigal, crags steel-ringing. Myth of Mountain Sunrise. Robert Penn Warren. CP-WarrR

Prodigious this! the Frail-one of our Play. Epilogue to Mr. Rowe's *Jane Shore.* Alexander Pope. CP-PopeA

Prodigy. Charles Simic. SP SimiC; SP-SimiCE

Prodigy, The. C. K. Williams. SP-WillC

Product. George Oppen. CP-OppGN

Production continues into the alienated night. Fanny Howe. SP-HoweF *Fr.* O'Clock.

Products of my Farm are these, The. Emily Dickinson. CP-DickE

Proem. Langston Hughes. *See* Negro

Proem: "Child-World—long and long since lost to view, The." James Whitcomb Riley. CP-RileJ *Fr.* Child-World, A.

Proem: "I love the old melodious lays." John Greenleaf Whittier. CP-WhitJ

Proem to "Home-Folks." James Whitcomb Riley. CP-RileJ

Proem: "We found him in that Far-away that yet to us seems near." James Whitcomb Riley. CP-RileJ

Proensa. Charles Olson. CP-OlsoC

Proetus of Argos gives his greeting's breath. Bellerophon and the Portable Universe. Robert Stock. SP-StocR

Profession, A. Primo Levi. CP-LeviP, *tr.* by Ruth Feldman

Professionals of snow. Camel in the Snow. Theodore Weiss. SP-WeisT

Professionals see the signs in the dice, the signs in the cards and clouds, The. Muriel Rukeyser. CP-RukeM

Professor. Miller Williams. CP-WillM

Professor Tucholsky's Facts. Christopher Logue. SP-LoguC

Professor Varder handles Dante. Humanities Course. John Updike. CP-UpdiJ

Professor's Song, A. John Berryman. CP-BerrJ

Professors, The. Charles Bukowski. SP-BukC1

Proffered Love Rejected. Sir John Suckling. CP-SuckJ

Profile. W. H. Auden. CP-AudeW

Profile of a Lady. Tu Fu. CP-WilW2

Profile of a man who waits, The. Shaving at Night. Charles Simic. SP-SimiC; SP-SimiCE

Profit and Batten. Villains. Stevie Smith. CP-SmitS

Profound and thrilling vibration of justice, sense of ultimate justice, The. Vibration of Justice. D. H. Lawrence. CP-LawrD

Profound lover rising from the earth. Rainer Maria Rilke. CP-RilkFr, *tr.* by A. Poulin, Jr. *Fr.* Fragments.

Profound sensual experience of truth: Yea, this *is*! Satisfaction. D. H. Lawrence. CP-LawrD

Profoundest of all our sensualitites, The. Deepest Sensuality, The. D. H. Lawrence. CP-LawrD

Profumo. Paul Muldoon. CP-MuldP

Profuse announcement. Paul Celan. SP-CelaP, *tr.* by John Felstiner

Prognosis. James Laughlin. CP-LaugJ

Prognosis. Louis MacNeice. CP-MacNL

Prognosis. Theodore Roethke. CP-RoetT

Prognosis: A Short Story, the End of Which You Will Know Soon Enough. Robert Penn Warren. CP-WarrR

What the Joree Said, The Joree Being Only a Bird. CP-WarrR

Prognostick, A. Robert Herrick. CP-HerrR

Programme for the Double Barrel Life When It Hits, A. Andrei Codrescu. SP-CodrA

Programme Note. Charles Tomlinson. CP-TomlC

Progress. George Meredith. CP-MerG1

Progress? W. H. Auden. CP-AudeW

Progress, The. Gwendolyn Brooks. SP-BrooG

Progress, The. Robert Graves. CP-GravR

Progress at Building Site With (Fewer) Pigeons. Amy Clampitt. CP-ClamA

Progress, big baby, wore shoes by Humanity. Arthur Rimbaud. CP-RimbA, *tr.* by Martin Sorrell

Progress of Beauty, The. Jonathan Swift. CP-SwifJ

Progress of Error, The. William Cowper. CP-CowpW

Progress of Faust, The. Karl Shapiro. SP-ShapK

Progress of Marriage, The. Jonathan Swift. CP-SwifJ

Progress of Œnia, The. Allen Tate. CP-TateA

Progress of Poesy, The. Thomas Gray. CP-GrayT

Progress of Poetry, The. Jonathan Swift. CP-SwifJ

Progress of the Soul, The. John Donne. CP-DonnJ; MW-DonnJ

Progress of the Soul, The. Thomas McGrath. SP-McGrT

Progress of the Spark, The. Rudyard Kipling. CP-KiplR *Fr.* Muse among the Motors, The.

Progress Report. Maxine W. Kumin. SP-KumiM

Progress Report. Audre Lorde. SP-LordA

Progress to a View of Life. Kenneth Patchen. CP-PatcK

Progress you have made is very remarkable, The. Recitative by Death. W. H. Auden. CP-AudeW *Fr.* Man of La Mancha.

Progression. George Meredith. CP-MerG2

Progression. Lorine Niedecker. CP-NiedL

Progression. Stevie Smith. CP-SmitS

Progressive Insanities of a Pioneer. Margaret Atwood. SP-AtwM1

Prohibition, The. John Donne. CP-DonnJ; MW-DonnJ

Prohibition, The. Robert Graves. CP-GravR

Project. A. R. Ammons. CP-AmmoA

Project, The. Richard Eberhart. CP-EberR

Project of Linear Inquiry, The. Michael Palmer. SP-PalmM

Projected from the bilious Childe. Manfred. George Meredith. CP-MerG1

Projected Slide of an Unknown Soldier. Margaret Atwood. SP-AtwM1

Projectile, The. Raymond Carver. CP-CarvR

Projection. Langston Hughes. CP-HughL; CP-HughL3

Projection. Howard Nemerov. CP-NemeH

Projector. "H. D." CP-DoolH

Projector II. "H. D." CP-DoolH

Prokofiev's sick prince can't laugh. Love for One Orange, The. Randall Jarrell. CP-JarrR

Prolegomenon. Sam Hamill.

Prolegomenon to a Theodicy, A. Kenneth Rexroth. CP-RexrK

Proletarian in Abstract Light. Thomas McGrath. SP-McGrT

Proletarian Portrait. William Carlos Williams. CP-WilW1

Proletarian Speaker, A. Yannis Ritsos. SP-RitsY, *tr.* by Minas Savvas

Proletariat for your Messiah, the poor and many are to seize power, The. Blind Horses. Robinson Jeffers. CP-JefR2

Prolific Spell, The. Donald Davie. CP-DaviDC

Prologe, The: "Musing and marvelling on the miserie." Sir David Lyndsay. SP-LyndD *Fr.* Dialog betwix Experience and ane Courteour, Ane.

Prologo. Thomas Merton. CP-MertT

Prologue, The. Anne Bradstreet. CP-BradA

Prologue, A: "Poets like lawful monarchs ruled the stage." Thomas Southerne. CP-DryJ2 *Fr.* Loyal Brother, The.

Prologue, A: "What light hath passed us in the silent ways?" Ezra Pound. CP-PoEar

Prologue and Questions for St. Augustine On His Sixteenth Centenary. John Logan. CP-LogaJ

Prologue at Sixty. W. H. Auden. CP-AudeW

Prologue Design'd for Mr. Durfy's Last Play. Alexander Pope. CP-PopeA

Prologue Designed for the Play of *Oedipus*, Written in Greek, and Performed by Mr. Sheridan's Scholars, at the King's Inn Hall, on Tuesday the 10th of December, 1723, A. Thomas Sheridan. CP-SherT

Prologue: "Full twenty years and more our labouring stage." John Dryden. CP-DryJ2 *Fr.* Albion and Albanius.

Prologue: "Here, my God, / is my heart." Federico García Lorca. CP-GarcF, *tr.* by Catherine Brown

Prologue: "How comes it, gentlemen, that nowadays." Thomas Southerne. CP-DryJ2 *Fr.* Disappointment, The.

Prologue: "I am going on a long trip." Federico García Lorca. CP-GarcF, *tr.* by Jerome Rothenberg *Fr.* In the Forest of the Lunar Grapefruits.

Prologue: "I have taken leave of the friends I love the most & have set out on a short dramatic journey." Federico García Lorca. CP-GarcF, *tr.* by Jerome Rothenberg *Fr.* In the Garden of the Lunar Grapefruits.

Prologue in Heaven. Johann Wolfgang von Goethe. CP-ShelP *Fr.* Faust.

Prologue: "In these stern times of ours, when crimson strife." Thomas Hardy. CP-HardT *Fr.* Dynasts, The.

Prologue, Intended for a Dramatic Piece of King Edward the Fourth. William Blake. CP-BlakW

Prologue: "Ladies! (I hope there's none behind to hear)." Nathaniel Lee. CP-DryJ2 *Fr.* Princess of Cleves, The.

Prologue: "Love, to give law unto his subject hearts." Sir Thomas Wyatt. CP-WyatT *Fr.* Penitential Psalms.

Prologue: "Mine was the life planned to go wrong." David Ignatow. SP-IgnaD

Prologue: "No song nor dance I bring from yon great city." Robert Burns. CP-BurnR

Prologue: "O the old wall here! How I could pass." Robert Browning. CP-BroR2

Prologue of the Author's to a Masque at Witten, A. Sir John Suckling. CP-SuckJ

Prologue: "Our play's a parallel: the Holy League." Nathaniel Lee. CP-DryJ2 *Fr.* Duke of Guise, The.

Prologue: "Poet's age is sad: for why?, The." Robert Browning. CP-BroR2

Prologue: "Pray, Reader, have you eaten ortolans." Robert Browning. CP-BroR2

Prologue Spoke by Mr. Elrington at the Theatre-Royal on Saturday the First of April, A. Thomas Sheridan. CP-SherT

Prologue Spoken at Mr. Sheridan's School. Thomas Sheridan. CP-SherT

Prologue Spoken before a Greek Play, at the Reverend Dr. Sheridan's School, at the Breaking-Up of His Scholars for Christmas, 1728. Thomas Sheridan. CP-SherT

Prologue Spoken by Mr[.] Garrick at the Opening of the Theatre in Drury Lane, 1747. Samuel Johnson. CP-JohnS

Prologue to a Play for Mr. Dennis's Benefit, in 1733, when He Was Old, Blind, and in Great Distress, a Little before His Death, A. Alexander Pope. CP-PopeA

Prologue to a Play Performed at Mr. Sheridan's School Spoke by One of His Scholars, A. Thomas Sheridan. CP-SherT

Prologue to a Saga. Dorothy Parker. CP-ParkD

Prologue: "To be a poet is no easy task." Jaroslav Seifert. SP-SeifJ, *tr.* by Ewald Osers

Prologue to *Don Sebastian*. John Dryden. SP-DrydJ *Fr.* Don Sebastian.

Prologue to Garrick's *Lethe*. Samuel Johnson. CP-JohnS

Prologue to Goldsmith's *The Good Natur'd Man*. Samuel Johnson. CP-JohnS

Prologue to *Hippolytus*, Spoken by a Boy of Six Years Old. Richard Helsham. CP-SherT

Prologue to His Royal Highness. John Dryden. CP-DryJ2

Prologue to Hugh Kelly's *A Word to the Wise*. Samuel Johnson. CP-JohnS

Prologue to King John. William Blake. CP-BlakW

Prologue to Mr. Addison's *Tragedy of Cato*. Alexander Pope. CP-PopeA

Prologue to Responsibilities. William Butler Yeats. CP-YeatW

Prologue to "Rhymes to be Traded for Bread." Nicholas Vachel Lindsay. CP-LindV

Prologue to Spring. Sylvia Plath. CP-PlatS

Prologue to the Duchess. John Dryden. CP-DryJ2

Prologue to the Farce of *Punch Turned Schoolmaster*. Thomas Sheridan. CP-SherT

Prologue to the King and Queen at the Opening of their Theatre. John Dryden. CP-DryJ2

Prologue to the Old Vic Pantomime. G. K. Chesterton. CP-ChesG

Prologue to *The Spanish Friar*. John Dryden. SP-DrydJ *Fr.* Spanish Friar [*or* Fryar], The.

Prologue to *The Tempest* [or *The Enchanted Island*]. John Dryden. SP-DrydJ

Prologue to the *Three Hours after Marriage*. Alexander Pope. CP-PopeA

Prologue to the University of Oxford, 1673. John Dryden. SP-DrydJ

Prologue to the University of Oxford, 1674. John Dryden. SP-DrydJ

Prologue to Wiley on November 17, 1941. Randall Jarrell. CP-JarrR

Prologue: "When by a generous Public's kind acclaim." Robert Burns. CP-BurnR

Prologues are over. It is a question, now, The. Asides on the Oboe. Wallace Stevens. CP-StevW

Prologues to What Is Possible. Wallace Stevens. CP-StevW; CP-StevWP

Prolonged Sonnet: He finds fault with the Conceits of the foregoing Sonnet. Guido Orlandi. CW-RossD, *tr.* by Dante Gabriel Rossetti

Prolonged Sonnet: When the Troops were Returning from Milan. Niccolò degli Albizzi. CW-RossD, *tr.* by Dante Gabriel Rossetti

Proludium. Ben Jonson. CP-JonsB

Promenade. Charles Bukowski. SP-BukC3

Promenade. David Ignatow. SP-IgnaD

Promenade. Eugenio Montale. CP-MontE, *tr.* by Jonathan Galassi

Promenade. William Carlos Williams. CP-WilW1

Promenading their / skirted galleons of sex. Return to Work, The. William Carlos Williams. CP-WilW1

Prometheus. Lord Byron. CP-Byron

Prometheus. Paul Laurence Dunbar. CP-DunbP

Prometheus. Richard Eberhart. CP-EberR

Prometheus. Robert Graves. CP-GravR

Prometheus. Ezra Pound. CP-PoEar

Prometheus. Jonathan Swift. CP-SwifJ

Prometheus. Charles Tomlinson. CP-TomlC; SP-TomlC

Prometheus Bound. Aeschylus. CP-BroEB, *tr.* by Elizabeth Barrett Browning

Prometheus Bound. Aeschylus.

"But Fortune governed all their works[,] till when." CP-RaleW

Prometheus in Straits. John Crowe Ransom. SP-RansJ

Prometheus on His Crag. Ted Hughes.
  "Now I know I never shall." SP-HughTN
  "Prometheus On His Crag." SP-HughTN

Prometheus On His Crag. Ted Hughes. SP-HughTN *Fr.* Prometheus on His Crag.

Prometheus Passes the Toast. Robert Stock. SP-StocR

Prometheus stole from Heaven the sacred fire. Prometheus. Paul Laurence Dunbar. CP-DunbP

Prometheus Unbound [A Lyrical Drama in Four Acts]. Percy Bysshe Shelley. CP-ShelP

Promise. Paul Laurence Dunbar. CP-DunbP

Promise. Dorothy Parker. CP-ParkD

Promise, A. Charles Olson. CP-OlsoC

Promise, A. Sir Thomas Wyatt. CP-WyatT

Promise, The. Charles Bukowski. SP-BukC1

Promise, The. Charles Tomlinson. CP-TomlC

Promise in a Pair of Eyes, The. Charles Baudelaire. CP-BaudC, *tr.* by Walter Martin

Promise in Disturbance, The. George Meredith. CP-MerG1

Promise is firmer than a Hope, A. Emily Dickinson. SP-DickE

Promise Me. Stanley Kunitz. CP-KunSC

Promise me no promises. Promises like Pie-Crust. Christina Georgina Rossetti. CP-RosC3

Promise, The ("I come the rushing wind that shook the place"). Jones Very. CP-VeryJ

Promise, The ("Words I give thee they are not thine own, The"). Jones Very. CP-VeryJ

Promise This, When You be Dying. Emily Dickinson. CP-DickE

Promise to California, A. Walt Whitman. CP-WhitW

Promised Ballad, The. Robert Graves. CP-GravR

Promised Land, The. Langston Hughes. CP-HughL; CP-HughL3

Promisers, The. Wilfred Owen. CP-OwenW

Promises. Robert Penn Warren. CP-WarrR

Promises. Rita Dove. SP-DoveR

Promises like Pie-Crust. Christina Georgina Rossetti. CP-RosC3

Promises, Promises. Paul Muldoon. CP-MuldP

Promises they give, alas, to fail!, The. Rain Clouds. Jones Very. CP-VeryJ

Promising Author. Carolyn Kizer. CP-KizeC

Promontory. Arthur Rimbaud. CP-RimbA, *tr.* by Martin Sorrell

Promontory Moment, The. May Swenson. SP-SwenM

Promotion, The. Miller Williams. CP-WillM

Prompt—executive Bird is the Jay, A. Emily Dickinson. CP-DickE

Promptress of unnumber'd sighs. To Fortune. Samuel Taylor Coleridge. CP-ColeS

Prone couple still sleeps, A. First Light. Thomas Kinsella. CP-KinsT

Proof. Czeslaw Milosz. CP-MiloC; CP-MiloCN, *tr.* by Lillian Vallee

Proof, The. Richard Wilbur. CP-WilbR

Proof and Disproof. Elizabeth Barrett Browning. CP-BroEB

Proof to No Purpose. Robert Herrick. CP-HerrR

Proper Pride. D. H. Lawrence. CP-LawrD

Proper Soul / in the Proper Body, The. Charles Olson. CP-OlsoC

Proper way to eat a fig, in society, The. Figs. D. H. Lawrence. CP-LawrD

Properate Tempus. James Laughlin. CP-LaugJ

Propertius wrote that it. Ingenium Nobis Ipsa Puella Facit. James Laughlin. CP-LaugJ

Property and No-Property. D. H. Lawrence. CP-LawrD

Property is now Solomon's baby. Solomon's Baby. D. H. Lawrence. CP-LawrD

Property is poverty. Lorine Niedecker. CP-NiedL

Property Question, The. D. H. Lawrence. CP-LawrD

Prophecy. Robert Penn Warren. CP-WarrR

Prophecy, A. Allen Ginsberg. CP-GinsA

Prophecy February, 1807, A. William Wordsworth. CP-WorW1

Prophecy of Dante, The. Lord Byron. CP-Byron

Prophecy of Samuel Sewall, The. John Greenleaf Whittier. CP-WhitJ

Prophecy on Lethe. Stanley Kunitz. CP-KunSC

Prophesying. Reading water or words, signs are cards in their multi-. Poem in Stretching, A. Robert Duncan. SP-DuncR

Prophet. D. H. Lawrence. CP-LawrD

Prophet. Thomas Merton. CP-MertT

Prophet, The. Jones Very. CP-VeryJ

Prophet at Creation's door, The. Creation and the Prophet. George Meredith. CP-MerG2

Prophet beware: there is a tricky urchin in nature. Urchin, The. Robinson Jeffers. CP-JefR3

Prophet in the Rose Garden, The. D. H. Lawrence. CP-LawrD

Prophet Johnson's white beard. Cooling Board, The. Yusef Komunyakaa. CP-

KomuY

Prophet Muhammad said, The. Basket of Fresh Bread, A. Jelaluddin Rumi. SP-Rumi, *tr. by* Coleman Barks

Prophet of disaster ceased to shout, The. Broken Drought, The. Robert Frost. CP-FrosR

Prophet said, "There are some who see me," The. Chinese Art and Greek Art. Jelaluddin Rumi. SP-Rumi, *tr. by* Coleman Barks

Prophet speaks, the world attentive stands!, The. Prophet, The. Jones Very. CP-VeryJ

Prophet stood, The. Deity, The. John Greenleaf Whittier. CP-WhitJ

Prophetess, The. Thomas Hardy. CP-HardT

Prophetic Soul. Dorothy Parker. CP-ParkD

Prophetic thought of Unity, and Peace. There shall be one Flock, one Shepherd. Jones Very. CP-VeryJ

Prophets, The. W. H. Auden. CP-AudeW

Prophets, The. Robert Stock. SP-StocR

Prophets at Home. Rudyard Kipling. CP-KiplR *Fr.* Puck of Pook's Hill.

Prophets have honour all over the Earth. Prophets at Home. Rudyard Kipling. CP-KiplR *Fr.* Puck of Pook's Hill.

Proposal. Raymond Carver. CP-CarvR

Proposal for Recycling Wastes, A. Marge Piercy. SP-PierM

Propriety. Marianne Craig Moore. CP-MoorM

Props. Carl Sandburg. CP-SandC

Props assist the House, The. Emily Dickinson. CP-DickE

Pros Karolon ton Basilea [To King Charles]. Andrew Marvell. CP-MarvA

Prosaic poetry—an animal. Fanny Howe. SP-HoweF *Fr.* O'Clock.

Prose. Stéphane Mallarmé. CP-MallS, *tr. by* Henry Weinfield

Prose for the Children of Aborted Revolution. Robert Stock. SP-StocR

Prose in Advent Time. *Unknown.* CP-MertT

Prose or Verse—or Verse or Prose? James Whitcomb Riley. CP-RileJ

Prose Parables. Robert Stock. SP-StocR

Prose Poem. Alan Dugan. CP-DugaA

Prose Poem. Rainer Maria Rilke. CP-RilkFr, *tr. by* A. Poulin, Jr.

Prose Poem. James Tate. SP-TateJ

Prose Poem. Charles Tomlinson. CP-TomlC; SP-TomlC

Prose Poem in Six Parts. David Ignatow. SP-IgnaD

Prose Take-Out, Portland, 13:ix:58. Philip Whalen. SP-WhalP

Proserpina. Dante Gabriel Rossetti. CW-RossD

Prosopopoia: or Mother Hubberds Tale. Edmund Spenser. CP-Spens

Prospect. Robert Creeley. SP-CreeR

Prospect. Louis MacNeice. CP-MacNL

Prospect. Sylvia Plath. CP-PlatS

Prospect, The. Elizabeth Barrett Browning. CP-BroEB

Prospect, The. Thomas Hardy. CP-HardT

Prospect, The. Adrienne Rich. CP-RicAE

Prospect, The. By a Lady in Princeton. Annis Boudinot Stockton. CP-StocA

Prospect of Prague, A. Jaroslav Seifert. SP-SeifJ, *tr. by* Ewald Osers

Prospecting. A. R. Ammons. CP-AmmoA

Prospective Glimpse, A. James Whitcomb Riley. CP-RileJ

Prospective Immigrants Please Note. Adrienne Rich. CP-RicAE; SP-RicA1; SP-RicA2

Prospective Visit, A. James Whitcomb Riley. CP-RileJ *Fr.* Child-World, A.

Prospectus to *The Recluse.* William Wordsworth. CP-WorW2 *Fr.* Recluse, The.

Prosperity has stolen stupor from me. Sleepless in Scarsdale. John Updike. CP-UpdiJ

Prospero and Sycorax. Ted Hughes. SP-HughTN

Prosperous and beautiful, The. Park, The. Ralph Waldo Emerson. CP-EmerR

Prospice. Robert Browning. CP-BroR1

Prosser. Raymond Carver. CP-CarvR

Prostitution. Bogomil Gjuzel. CP-KizeC, *tr. by* Carolyn Kizer

Protagonists. Richard Eberhart. CP-EberR

Protean Maiden, The. Thomas Hardy. CP-HardT

Protecting each other, right in the center. Burning a Book. William Stafford. SP-StafWW

Protection of Moveable Cultural Heritage. Yusef Komunyakaa. CP-KomuY

Protesilaus and Laodamia. Donald Davie. CP-DaviDC

Protest. Countee Cullen. CP-CullC

Protest. Paul Laurence Dunbar. CP-DunbP

Protest, A. Sir Thomas Wyatt. CP-WyatT

Protest After a Dream. John Logan. CP-LogaJ

Protest against the Ballot. William Wordsworth. CP-WorW2

Protestant Churches, The. D. H. Lawrence. CP-LawrD

Protestant Easter. Anne Sexton. CP-SextA; SP-SextA

Protestation [A Sonnet], The. Thomas Carew. CP-CareT

Protesters in their houses built of placards, The. Washington: Tourist View. John Updike. CP-UpdiJ

Protests multiplied—protests of actors, The. Fate of the Observer, The. Yannis

Ritsos. SP-RitsY, *tr. by* N. C. Germanacos

Proteus. Ralph Waldo Emerson. CP-EmerR

Proteus. Stanley Kunitz. CP-KunSC

Proteus. May Sarton. SP-SartM

Prothalamion. Edmund Spenser. CP-Spens

Prothalamion. Maxine W. Kumin. SP-KumiM

Prothalamion. Heather McHugh. SP-McHuH

Prothalamion. May Sarton. SP-SartM

Prothalamion of Quantum Mechanics and Astrophysics against the Text "Philosophia Biou Kubernetes" (Philosophy the Guide of Life). Alan Dugan. CP-DugaA

Protocols. Randall Jarrell. CP-JarrR

Protus. Robert Browning. CP-BroR1

Proud and Beautiful. Carl Sandburg. CP-SandC

Proud banner of death. Tomorrow's Seed. Langston Hughes. CP-HughL; CP-HughL3

Proud crumbling of these towers. Rainer Maria Rilke. CP-RilkFr, *tr. by* A. Poulin, Jr. *Fr.* Valaisian Quatrains, The.

Proud Death with Swelling Port. Stevie Smith. CP-SmitS

Proud elephant, by accident of bulk. High-Hearts, The. John Updike. CP-UpdiJ

Proud Heart, The. Countee Cullen. CP-CullC

Proud mountains, Kallídromon, Oéta, Óthrys. First Sensual Delight, The. Yannis Ritsos. SP-RitsY, *tr. by* Kimon Friar

Proud Music of the Storm. Walt Whitman. CP-WhitW

Proud of his scientific attitude. E. E. Cummings. CP-CummE; SP CummE

Proud of my broken heart, since thou didst break it. Emily Dickinson. CP-DickE

Proud of Their Rags. Carl Sandburg. CP-SandC

Proud Ship, The. Charles Baudelaire. CP-BaudC, *tr. by* Walter Martin

Proud Songsters. Thomas Hardy. CP-HardT

Proud Torsos. Carl Sandburg. CP-SandC

Proud, very beautiful woman sold me, A. Autumn Rain in Tel Aviv. Yehuda Amichai. SP-AmicY, *tr. by* Chana Bloch

Proud Were Ye, Mountains, When, in Times of Old. William Wordsworth. CP-WorW2

Proudest now is but my peer, The. Poor Voter on Election Day, The. John Greenleaf Whittier. CP-WhitJ

Proudest pearl of the wide world. Pearl of Biloxi, The. Nicholas Vachel Lindsay. CP-LindV

Proudly, the fedoras march on the heads of the somewhat. Sky Pieces. Carl Sandburg. CP-SandC

Proust, doing penance. Les Saints Nouveaux. John Updike. CP-UpdiJ

Proust's Madeleine. Kenneth Rexroth. CP-RexrK

Prove whether I do change, my dear. Sir Thomas Wyatt. CP-WyatT

Proved Etherege prudish, selfish, hypocrite, heartless. Gerard Manley Hopkins. CP-HopkG

Proverb: "March / goes flying by." Federico García Lorca. CP-GarcF, *tr. by* Alan S. Trueblood *Fr.* Theories.

Proverbs. Thomas Merton. CP-MertT

Proverbs of the Middle World. Thomas McGrath. SP-McGrT

Proverbs: "What shul these clothes thus manyfold." Geoffrey Chaucer. CP-ChauG

Provide, Provide. Robert Frost. CP-FrosR

Provide your friend with almanacs. Song: "Provide your friend with almanacs." Howard Nemerov. CP-NemeH

Provided for! Provided for. Reticence. Donald Davie. CP-DaviDC

Providence. George Herbert. CP-HerbG

Providence. Yusef Komunyakaa. CP-KomuY

Providence. Charles Tomlinson. CP-TomlC

Provider, The. Josephine Jacobsen. CP-JacoJ

Province, The. Robert Creeley. CP-CreeR

Province, The. William Carlos Williams. CP-WilW2

Province of the Saved, The. Emily Dickinson. CP-DickE

Provinces are celebrating Christmas, The. Anno Domini. Joseph Brodsky. CP-BrodJ, *tr. by* Daniel Weissbort

Provincetown. Robert Creeley. SP-CreeR

Provincetown *Totentanz.* Alan Dugan. CP-DugaA

Provincial Spring. Yannis Ritsos. SP-RitsY, *tr. by* N. C. Germanacos

Provincial town-boy he,—frail, lame. Boy's Dream, The. Thomas Hardy. CP-HardT

Provision. W. S. Merwin. SP-MerwW

Provocation of the Dream, The. Marge Piercy. SP-PierM

Provocatively, our epoch swings her breasts. Prostitution. Bogomil Gjuzel. CP-KizeC, *tr. by* Carolyn Kizer

Proxy. Primo Levi. CP-LeviP, *tr. by* Ruth Feldman

Prudence. Ralph Waldo Emerson. CP-EmerR
   (Motto to "Prudence"). CP-EmerR

Prudence Caution and Foresight: A Story of Avignon. Gertrude Stein. CP-SteiG

Prudence is a tedious one. Emily Dickinson. SP-DickE

Prudent field mouse, The. Harvests. Dan Pagis. SP-PagiD, *tr. by* Stephen Mitchell

Prudent Hind intent on Gain, The. Boethius. CP-JohnS *Fr.* Consolation of Philosophy, The ("De Consolacione Philosophie").

Prudent Simplicity. Goronwy Owen. CP-CowpW, *tr. by* William Cowper

Prue loved her man: to clean, to mend. James Vincent Cunningham. CP-CunnJ

Prue, my dearest maid, is sick. Upon Prudence Baldwin Her Sickness[e]. Robert Herrick. CP-HerrR

Prufrock in Wonderland. Kenneth Rexroth. CP-RexrK

Prufrock's Pervigilium. T. S. Eliot. SP-ElioT *Fr.* Love Song of J. Alfred Prufrock, The.

Prune us serried teen sear. Chokecherry. Louis Zukofsky. CP-ZukLS

Prune your corn in the gray of the morn. Charms. James Whitcomb Riley. CP-RileJ

Pruned Roses, The. William Dickey. SP-DickW

Psalm: "How leaky are the borders of man-made states!" Wisława Szymborska. SP-SzymWM, *tr. by* Joanna Trzeciak

Psalm: "In the small beauty of the forest." George Oppen. CP-OppGN

Psalm: "No one kneads us again out of earth and clay." Paul Celan. SP-CelaP, *tr. by* John Felstiner

Psalm: "Oh, the leaky boundaries of man-made states!" Wisława Szymborska. SP-SzymW, *tr. by* Stanisław Barańczak *and* Clare Cavanagh

Psalm: "Old ones to the side." Charles Simic. SP-SimiC; SP-SimiCE

Psalm: "Psalm on the day, A." Yehuda Amichai. SP-AmicY, *tr. by* Chana Bloch

Psalm: "Their shoes are stuccoed with sawdust and blood." Grace Paley. CP-PalGC

Psalm: Our Fathers. W. S. Merwin. SP-MerwW

Psalm: People Power at the Die-in. Denise Levertov. SP-LeveDL

Psalm I. Allen Ginsberg. CP-GinsA

Psalm II: "Ah, still Lord, ah sweet Divinity" Allen Ginsberg. CP-GinsA

Psalm III: "To God: to illuminate all men. Beginning with Skid Road." Allen Ginsberg. CP-GinsA

Psalm 4. Allen Ginsberg. CP-GinsA; SP-GinsA

Psalm 23. Norman Dubie. CP-DubiN

Psalm 114. John Milton. CP-MiltJ

Psalm 132: A Modern Monastic Revision. Thomas Merton. CP-MertT

Psalm 136. John Milton. CP-MiltJ

Psalm, A: "When psalms surprise me with their music." Thomas Merton. CP-MertT

Psalm Concerning the Castle. Denise Levertov. SP-LeveDP

Psalm of Life, A. Henry Wadsworth Longfellow. SP-LongH

Psalm of the Bloodbank. Carl Sandburg. CP-SandC

Psalm of Those Who Go Forth before Daylight. Carl Sandburg. CP-SandC

Psalm on the day, A. Psalm: "Psalm on the day, A." Yehuda Amichai. SP-AmicY, *tr. by* Chana Bloch

Psalm Praising the Hair of Man's Body, A. Denise Levertov. SP-LeveDP

Psalm to Snake. Margaret Atwood. SP-AtwM2

Psalme or Hymne to the Graces, A. Robert Herrick. CP-HerrR

Psalms. Bible, *O.T.*

Psalm 1: "Blessed is the man that walketh not in the counsel of the ungodly [or wicked]." CP-MiltJ

("Blest is the man who hath not walk'd astray.") CP-MiltJ

Psalm 2: "Why do the heathen rage."

Psalm 3: "Lord, how are they increased that trouble me!." CP-MiltJ

("Lord how many are my foes.") CP-MiltJ

Psalm 4: "Hear me when I call, O God of my righteousness." CP-MiltJ

("Answer me when I call / God of my righteousness.") CP-MiltJ

Psalm 5: "Give ear to my words, O Lord, consider my meditation." CP-MiltJ

("Jehovah to my words give ear.") CP-MiltJ

Psalm 6: "O Lord, rebuke me not in thine anger." CP-MiltJ; CP-WyatT

("Lord in thine anger do not reprehend me.") CP-MiltJ

("O Lord, since in my mouth thy mighty name.") CP-WyatT

Psalm 7: "O Lord my God, in thee do I put my trust." CP-MiltJ

("Lord my God to thee I flie / Save me and secure me all.") CP-MiltJ

Psalm 8: "O Lord our Lord, how excellent is thy name in all the earth!." CP-MiltJ

("O Jehovah our Lord, how wondrous great.") CP-MiltJ

Psalm 12: "Help, Lord; for the godly man ceaseth." SP-SidnP

("Lord, help, it is high time for me to call.") SP-SidnP

Psalm 18: "I will love thee, O Lord, my strength." SP-SmarC

("Thee will I love, O Lord, my tow'r.") SP-SmarC

Psalm 22: "My God, my God, why hast thou forsaken me?." SP-SidnP

Psalm 23: "Lord is my shepherd; I shall not want, The." CP-CrasR; SP-SidnP

("Happy me! o happy sheepe!") CP-CrasR

("Lord, the Lord my shepherd is, The.") SP-SidnP

Psalm 24: "Earth is the Lord's and the fulness thereof, The." SP-SmarC, *tr. by* Christopher Smart

("Earth is God's, with all she bears, The.") SP-SmarC

Psalm 25: "Unto thee, O Lord, do I lift up my soul." SP-SmarC

("Lord and Master, to thine altar.") SP-SmarC

Psalm 28: "Unto thee will I cry, O Lord my rock." SP-SidnP

("To Thee, Lord, my cry I send.") SP-SidnP

Psalm 32: "Blessed is he whose transgression is forgiven, whose sin is covered." CP-WyatT

("O happy are they that have forgiveness got.") CP-WyatT

Psalm 33: "Rejoice in the Lord, O ye righteous: for praise is comely for the upright." SP-SmarC

("Rejoice in God, ye saints above.") SP-SmarC

Psalm 35: "Plead my cause, O Lord, with them that strive with me." SP-SidnP

("Speak Thou for me against wrong-speaking foes.") SP-SidnP

Psalm 37: "Fret not thyself because of evildoers." CP-WyatT

("Although thou see th'outrageous climb aloft.") CP-WyatT

Psalm 38: "O Lord, rebuke me not in thy wrath." CP-WyatT

("O Lord, as I thee have both prayed and pray.") CP-WyatT

Psalm 51: "Have mercy upon me, O God, according to thy lovingkindness." CP-WyatT

("Rue on me, Lord, for thy goodness and grace.") CP-WyatT

Psalm 68: "Let God arise, let his enemies be scattered." SP-SmarC

("Arouse—and let thy foes disperse.") SP-SmarC

Psalm 80: "Give ear, O Shepherd of Israel, thou that leadest Joseph like a flock." CP-MiltJ

("Thou Shepherd that dost Israel keep.") CP-MiltJ

Psalm 81: "Sing aloud unto God our strength." CP-MiltJ

("To God our strength sing loud, and clear.") CP-MiltJ

Psalm 82: "God standeth in the congregation of the mighty." CP-MiltJ

("God in the great assembly stands.") CP-MiltJ

Psalm 83: "Keep not thou silence, O God." CP-MiltJ

("Be not thou silent now at length.") CP-MiltJ

Psalm 84: "How amiable are thy tabernacles, O Lord of hosts!." CP-MiltJ

("How lovely are thy dwellings fair!") CP-MiltJ

Psalm 84: "How amiable are thy tabernacles, O Lord of hosts!." CP-MiltJ

("*par. by* Milton.") CP-MiltJ

Psalm 85: "Lord, thou hast been favourable unto thy land." CP-MiltJ; SP-SmarC

("O Lord, thy land has favour found.") SP-SmarC

("Thy Land to favour graciously.") CP-MiltJ

Psalm 86: "Bow down thine ear, O Lord, hear me." CP-MiltJ

("Thy gracious ear, O Lord, encline.") CP-MiltJ

Psalm 87: "His foundation is in the holy mountains." CP-MiltJ

("Among the holy Mountains high.") CP-MiltJ

Psalm 88: "O God of my salvation." CP-MiltJ

("Lord God that dost me save and keep.") CP-MiltJ

Psalm 91: "He that dwelleth in the secret place of the most High." CP-PopeA

("He who beneath thy shelt'ring wing resides.") CP-PopeA

Psalm 98: "O sing unto the Lord a new song; for he hath done marvellous [or marvelous] things." SP-SmarC

("O Frame the strains anew.") SP-SmarC

Psalm 102: "Hear my prayer, O Lord, and let my cry come unto thee." CP-WyatT

("Lord hear [or here] my prayer [or prayre] and let my cry[e] pass[e].") CP-WyatT

Psalm 127: "Except the Lord build the house." SP-SmarC

("If the work be not direct.") SP-SmarC

Psalm 130: "Out of the deep [or depths] have I called [or cried unto] thee, O Lord."

Psalm 134: "Behold, bless ye the Lord, all ye servants of the Lord." SP-SmarC

("Attend to the music divine.") SP-SmarC

Psalm 135: "Praise ye the Lord. Praise ye the name of the Lord; praise him, O ye servants of the Lord." SP-SmarC

("O Praise the Lord, and bless his name.") SP-SmarC

Psalm 137: "By the rivers of Babylon, there we sat down, yea, we wept, when [or then] we remembered Zion." CP-CowpW; CP-CrasR; SP-SmarC

("On the proud banks of great Euphrates' flood.") CP-CrasR

("Pensive we sat the silent hours.") SP-SmarC

("To Babylon's proud waters brought.") CP-CowpW

Psalm 143: "Hear my prayer, O Lord, give ear to my supplications." CP-WyatT

("Hear my prayer, O Lord, hear my request.") CP-WyatT

Psalm 148: "Praise ye the Lord. Praise ye the Lord from the heavens." SP-SmarC

("Hallelujah! kneel and sing / Praises to the heav'nly king.") SP-SmarC, *tr. by* Christopher Smart

Psalm 149: "Praise ye the Lord. Sing unto the Lord a new song." SP-SmarC

("Hosanna! God be prais'd.") SP-SmarC

Psalm 150: "Praise ye the Lord. Praise God in his sanctuary." SP-SmarC

("Hosanna! praise the Lord, and bless.") SP-SmarC

Psalms. Bible, *O.T.*

Psalm 130. De profundis clamavi. CP-WyatT, *tr. by* Sir Thomas Wyatt

Psalms are said and three potted lilies nod, The. Easter Morning: Crosby Junction. Robert Penn Warren. CP-WarrR

Psalms of Assize. Geoffrey Hill. CP-HillG

Psalmus 1. Richard Crashaw. CP-CrasR

Pseudo-Questions. W. H. Auden. CP-AudeW

Psyche. Samuel Taylor Coleridge. CP-ColeS

Psyche. "H. D." CP-DoolH

Psyche and Cerberus. Elizabeth Barrett Browning. CP-BroEB

Psyche and Pan. Elizabeth Barrett Browning. CP-BroEB

Psyche and Proserpine. Elizabeth Barrett Browning. CP-BroEB

Psyche and Venus. Elizabeth Barrett Browning. CP-BroEB

Psyche Gazing on Cupid. Elizabeth Barrett Browning. CP-BroEB

Psyche Propitiating Ceres. Elizabeth Barrett Browning. CP-BroEB

Psyche-type (Psychotype). Fernando Pessoa. SP-PessF, *tr. by* Susan M. Brown *and* Edwin Honig

Psyche Wafted by Zephyrus. Elizabeth Barrett Browning. CP-BroEB

Psyche with the Candle. Archibald MacLeish. CP-MacLA

Ptolemy Philopator receives. Hospitality of Lagides, The. Constantine P. Cavafy. CP-CavaC, *tr. by* Theoharis Constantine Theoharis

Puase at the top of a leap, A. Grass Beginning July. W. S. Merwin. SP-MerwWF

Public Affairs. Thomas Merton. CP-MertT

Public Bar TV. Ted Hughes. *See* Boom

Public Bath, The. Gary Snyder. CP-SnydG

Public Garden, The. Robert Lowell. SP-LoweR

Public Letter to Emily Dickinson. Carl Sandburg. CP-SandC

Public Opinions. Philip Whalen. SP-WhalP

Public silence indeed is nothing. Monument. George Oppen. CP-OppGN

Public Son of a Public Man, The. Stephen Spender. CP-SpenS

Public sorrow, the acquired. Autumnal. Louise Glück. SP-GlucL

Public Square, The. Wallace Stevens. CP-StevW; CP-StevWP

Public Waste. Rudyard Kipling. CP-KiplR

    (Walpole talks of "a man and his price") CP-KiplR

Publication—is the Auction. Emily Dickinson. CP-DickE

Publius Vergilius Maro, the Madison Avenue Hick. John Updike. CP-UpdiJ

Puccini in hog-butchering time. Cadenza, A. Amy Clampitt. CP-ClamA

Puccini was Latin, and Wagner Teutonic. Birds, The. Ogden Nash. CP-NashO

Puck. James Whitcomb Riley. CP-RileJ

Puck and the woodland elves shall weep with me. Mrs. Baines. G. K. Chesterton. CP-ChesG

Puck of Pook's Hill. Rudyard Kipling.

    Centurion of the Thirtieth, A.

        British-Roman Song, A. CP-KiplR

        Cities and Thrones and Powers. CP-KiplR

    Dymchurch Flit.

        Bee-Boy's Song, The. CP-KiplR

        Three-Part Song, A. CP-KiplR

    Hal o' the Draft.

        Prophets at Home. CP-KiplR

        Smuggler" Song, A. CP-KiplR

    Knights of the Joyous Venture, The.

        Harp Song of the Dane Women. CP-KiplR

        Thorkild's Song. CP-KiplR

    Land of Our Birth. CP-KiplR

        (Children's Song, The.) CP-KiplR

    Old Men at Pevensey.

        Runes on Weland's Sword, The. CP-KiplR

    On the Great Wall.

        Song to Mithras, A. CP-KiplR

    Puck's Song. CP-KiplR

    Rimini. CP-KiplR

    Treasure and the Law, The.

        Song of the Fifth River. CP-KiplR

    Weland's Sword.

        Tree Song, A. CP-KiplR

    Winged Hats, The.

        Pict Song, A. CP-KiplR

    Young Men at the Manor.

        Sir Richard's Song. CP-KiplR

Puckered and obscure, like a violet's eye. Idol, The. Arsehole Sonnet. Arthur Rimbaud. CP-RimbA, *tr. by* Martin Sorrell

Puck's Song. Rudyard Kipling. CP-KiplR *Fr.* Puck of Pook's Hill.

Puddles / shine with the sky's light, The. Students Gather, The. George Oppen. CP-OppGN

Pueblo. Federico García Lorca. CP-GarcF, *tr. by* Jerome Rothenberg *Fr.* Shadow.

Pueblo Pot. Edna St. Vincent Millay. CP-MillE

Puella Mea. E. E. Cummings. CP-CummE

Puella Parvula. Wallace Stevens. CP-StevW; CP-StevWP

Puff of air or dry or damp, A. Ralph Waldo Emerson. CP-EmerR

Puisque je suis / Imaginaire. Le Secret. Thomas Merton. CP-MertT

Pull at the rope! Lynching Song. Langston Hughes. CP-HughL; CP-HughL1; CP-HughL2 *Fr.* Three Songs about Lynching.

Pull back the curtains, quick now that we've caught the mood of. Hymn to the Virgin. Elizabeth Bishop. CP-BishE

"Pull! crew" 's convenient to reprobate kin hides. Catullus. *See Caesar Mamurraque! /* A peerless pair of brazen buggers

Pull my arm back, Seymour. Seymour and Chantelle or Un Peu de Vice. Stevie Smith. CP-SmitS

Pull My Daisy. Allen Ginsberg. CP-GinsA, SP-GinsA

Pull my daisy. Fie My Fum. Allen Ginsberg. CP-GinsA

Pull out the pissed-on clinkers. Form. James Dickey. CP-DickJ

Pull yourself out of the mire. Homage to Gödel. Hans Magnus Enzensberger. SP-EnzeH

Pulley, The. George Herbert. CP-HerbG

Pulling Back. Miller Williams. CP-WillM

Pulling / into their pots. Crabbing. Lucille Clifton. SP-ClifL

Pulling the garden I always think. After the Harvest. Maxine W. Kumin. SP-KumiM

Pulsating city overrun with dreams. Seven Old Men, The. Charles Baudelaire. CP-BaudC, *tr. by* Walter Martin

Pulse. Tennessee Williams. CP-WillT

Pulse, A. Rae Armantrout. SP-ArmaA

Pulse, The. Denise Levertov. SP-LeveDP

Pulse, The. Arthur Sze. SP-SzeA

Pulse of / Violin, The. Tango. Josephine Jacobsen. CP-JacoJ

Pulsing stops where time has been, The. Bed, The. Thom Gunn. CP-GunnT

Pummeling the winds it came, spoiling for a brawl. Poet Mário Faustino Descends Into Hades and Rises to the Empyrean. Robert Stock. SP-StocR

Pumping away pumping away / now everyone is pumping away. For a Screaming Lady. Robert Creeley. CP-CreeR

Pumpkin, The. John Greenleaf Whittier. CP-WhitJ

Pumpkin's hollow head returns her gaze, The. Widow's Halloween, The. Wyatt Prunty. SP-PrunW

Pun, The. Ambrose Bierce. SP-BierA

Puñal. Denise Levertov. SP-LeveDP

Punch Minus Judy. Charles Simic. SP-SimiCE

Punch . . . Punch . . . as yet you hardly know. To Punch. G. K. Chesterton. CP-ChesG

Punch Rubicundus. Thom Gunn. CP-GunnT

Punchdrunk. Yusef Komunyakaa. CP-KomuY

Punch's Petition to the Ladies. *Unknown, sometimes at. to* Thomas Sheridan. CP-SherT

Punctual to the midnight—lurch, ruck and chime. Night Freight, Michigan. John Ciardi. CP-CiarJ

Punctually now, by all we learned at school. Night Piece for My Twenty-seventh Birthday. John Ciardi. CP-CiarJ

Puncture. John Crowe Ransom. SP RansJ

Punegyric upon Tom Pun-sibi's *Ars Pun-ica,* A. *Unknown.* CP-SherT

Pungent atom in the Air, The. Emily Dickinson. CP-DickE

Pungent smells of a California winter, The. Winter. Czeslaw Milosz. CP-MiloC; CP-MiloCN, *tr. by* Robert Hass

Punisher, The. D. H. Lawrence. CP-LawrD

Punishing the Myth. John Ashbery. SP-AshbJ

Punishment. Seamus Heaney. SP-HeanSO

Punishment of Pride. Charles Baudelaire. CP-BaudC, *tr. by* Walter Martin

Punishment of Pride, The. Walt Whitman. CP-WhitW

Punk Rock Your My Big Crybaby. Allen Ginsberg. CP-GinsA; SP-GinsA

Punta del Mesco. Eugenio Montale. CP-MontE, *tr. by* Jonathan Galassi

Pupa. Clarence Major. SP-MajoC

Pupil. Heather McHugh. SP-McHuH

Pupils of the eye expand, The. Or To Perish Before Day. Robert Graves. CP-GravR

Puppet-Show, The. *Unknown.*

    "Tell Tom he draws a farce in vain." CP-SherT

Purana, Meaning Once Upon a Time. Hayden Carruth. CP-CarHS

Puranic shastras tell us that, The. Mathematics of Chaos, The. James Laughlin. CP-LaugJ

Purdah. Sylvia Plath. CP-PlatS

Pure air trembles, O pitiless God, The. Noon. Robinson Jeffers. CP-JefR1

Pure Death. Robert Graves. CP-GravR

Pure element of waters! wheresoe'er. Suggested by Mr W. Westall's Views of the Caves, etc., in Yorkshire. William Wordsworth. CP-WorW2

Pure fasted faces draw unto this feast. Easter Communion. Gerard Manley Hopkins. CP-HopkG

Pure Fury, The. Theodore Roethke. CP-RoetT

Pure Good of Theory, The. Wallace Stevens. CP-StevW; CP-StevWP

Pure in Heart, The. Jones Very. CP-VeryJ

Pure melody, love without alteration. Testament. Robert Graves. CP-GravR

Pure products of America, The. To Elsie. William Carlos Williams. CP-WilW1

Pure sun—throwing off, The. Glazier, The. Stéphane Mallarmé. CP-MallS *Fr.* Street Songs.

Pure sun—throwing off, The. Glazier, The. Stéphane Mallarmé. CP-MallS, *tr. by* Henry Weinfield

Pure? What does it mean? Fever 103°. Sylvia Plath. CP-PlatS

Purely Local. Adrienne Rich. CP-RicAE

Purer Eve and the impure, The. On the Two Marys in a Fresco of the Crucifixion. Helen Pinkerton. CP-PinkH

Purer than purest pure. E. E. Cummings. CP-CummE

Purest of nations on earth when it's judged by a flash of lightning, The. Nation, A. Czeslaw Milosz. CP-MiloC; CP-MiloCN, *tr. by* Robert Hass

Purest soul that e'er was sent, The. Another [Epitaph on the Lady Mary Villiers]. Thomas Carew. CP-CareT

Purgation. James Dickey. CP-DickJ

Purgation. James Dickey. CP-DickJ

Purgatorio. Dante Alighieri. *Fr.* Divina Commedia.

Purgatorio. Hart Crane. CP-CranH

Purgatorio. Hans Magnus Enzensberger. SP-EnzeH, *tr. by* Michael Hamburger

Purgatory. John Berryman. CP-BerrJ

Purgatory. Robert Herrick. CP-HerrR

Purgatory. Maxine W. Kumin. SP-KumiM

Purgatory, A. W. S. Merwin. SP-MerwW

Purgatory Blind. Charles Olson. CP-OlsoC

Purge soul for the guest awaited. Ballad of Your Puzzlement. Robert Penn Warren. CP-WarrR

Purification. Robert Graves. CP-GravR

Purification, A. Wendell Berry. CP-BerrW

Purification of St. Mary the Virgin, The. Christina Georgina Rossetti. CP-RosC2

Purification of the Temple, The. Jones Very. CP-VeryJ

Purifying the Language of the Tribe. William Stafford. SP-StafW; SP-StafWW

Purist, The. Ogden Nash. CP-NashO

Purists Will Object. John Ashbery. SP-AshbJ

Puritan, The. May Sarton. SP-SartM

Puritan Church and State 1., The. Jones Very. CP-VeryJ

Puritan Church and State 2., The. Jones Very. CP-VeryJ

Puritan Church and State 3., The. Jones Very. CP-VeryJ

Puritan Ethos, The. Robert Creeley. CP-CreeR

Puritan is insane, The. Sane and Insane. D. H. Lawrence. CP-LawrD

Puritans, The. Richard Wilbur. CP-WilbR

Purity. Billy Collins. SP-CollB

Purity. Reflection On a Wicked World. Ogden Nash. CP-NashO

Purity born of a Maid: / Was such a Virgin defiled? Purification of St. Mary the Virgin, The. Christina Georgina Rossetti. CP-RosC2

Purloining while you played in honeyed youth. Carmen 99. Catullus. CP-ZukLS *Fr.* Carmina.

Purple. Wilfred Owen. CP-OwenW

Purple and green, blue and white. Andrée Rexroth ("Purple and green, blue and white"). Kenneth Rexroth. CP-RexrK

Purple Anemones. D. H. Lawrence. CP-LawrD

Purple— / Color of a Queen, is this, The. Emily Dickinson. CP-DickE

Purple! / for months unknown. Petunia, The. William Carlos Williams. CP-WilW2

Purple—is fashionable twice. Emily Dickinson. CP-DickE

Purple Martins. Carl Sandburg. CP-SandC

Purple woman with a lavender tongue, A. Metropolitan Melancholy. Wallace Stevens. CP-StevWP

Purples of Barley. Michael Palmer. SP-PalmM

Purpose. Rae Armantrout. SP-ArmaA

Purposely Ungrammatical Love Song. Dorothy Parker. CP-ParkD

Purposes. Robert Herrick. CP-HerrR

Purpurea rosa / Dolce, odorosa. Christina Georgina Rossetti. CP-RosC3

Purse-Seine, The. Robinson Jeffers. CP-JefR2

Pursuing you in your transitions. Emily Dickinson. CP-DickE

Pursuit. "H. D." CP-DoolH

Pursuit. Sylvia Plath. CP-PlatS

Pursuit. Wisława Szymborska. SP-SzymWM, *tr. by* Joanna Trzeciak

Pursuit. Robert Penn Warren. CP-WarrR

Pursuit from Under. James Dickey. CP-DickJ

Pursuit of Happiness, The. John Ashbery. SP-AshbJ

Purveyors General. Ezra Pound. CP-PoEar

Pus-filled growths, cratered skin, green rings under. Seated. Arthur Rimbaud. CP-RimbA, *tr. by* Martin Sorrell

Push yourself in on others. Boy, the. Robert Creeley. CP-CreeR

Pushed into the corner. Black Panther. Langston Hughes. CP-HughL; CP-HughL3

Pusher, The. Maya Angelou. SP-AngeM

Pushing children in plaid & silver prams. Fanny Howe. SP-HoweF *Fr.* Robeson Street.

Pushing in All the Buttons. Yusef Komunyakaa. CP-KomuY

Pushing it back to. N. Truro Light—1946. Robert Creeley. SP-CreeR

Pushkin. A Didactic Poem. Donald Davie. CP-DaviDC

Puss-Puss! D. H. Lawrence. CP-LawrD

Pusse and her Prentice both at Draw-gloves play. Upon Pusse and her Prentice. Robert Herrick. CP-HerrR

Pussy Blues. Allen Ginsberg. CP-GinsA

Pussy can sit by the fire and sing. Rudyard Kipling. CP-KiplR *Fr.* Just-So Stories.

Pussy has a whiskered face, / Kitty has such pretty ways. Christina Georgina Rossetti. CP-RosC2

Pussy put her paw into the pail of paint. Epithalamion: "Pussy put her paw into the pail of paint." Ted Berrigan. SP-BerrT

Pussy Willow. Louis Zukofsky. CP-ZukLS

Pussycat on Causeway Street is closed, The. In Memoriam Felis Felis. John Updike. CP-UpdiJ

Put a dog in a bottle. It won't bark. Keeping. John Ciardi. CP-CiarJ

Put a sun in Sunday, Sunday. Yet Dish. Gertrude Stein. CP-SteiG

Put away the painted masque. Mummer's Rhyme. Tennessee Williams. CP-WillT

Put away those insipid spoons. Music That Hurts, The. Yusef Komunyakaa. CP-KomuY

Put Back Those Whiskers, I Know You. Ogden Nash. CP-NashO

Put by thy days like withered flowers. Unregarding. Walter De la Mare. CP-DeLaW

Put-Down Come On, The. A. R. Ammons. CP-AmmoA

Put Down Your Cigarette Rag (Dont Smoke). Allen Ginsberg. SP-GinsA

Put 5 and 5 together. Addition ("Put 5 and 5 together"). Langston Hughes. CP-HughL; CP-HughL3

Put forth thy leaf, thou lofty plane. In Stratis Viarum IV. Arthur Hugh Clough. SP-ClouA

Put forth to watch, unschooled, alone. Rudyard Kipling. CP-KiplR

Put high walls around the part of you that dreams yourself. Advice. Fernando Pessoa. SP-PessF, *tr. by* Susan M. Brown *and* Edwin Honig

Put him this way. Charles Olson. CP-OlsoC

Put in, drive home the sightless wedges. Ralph Waldo Emerson. CP-EmerR

Put it down! I say; put it down,—here, give it to me, I know. Tristan. Edna St. Vincent Millay. CP-MillE

Put it there, Mr. Longwell, put it there! Two Songs for a Boss Named Mr. Longwell. Ogden Nash. CP-NashO

Put mommy on the front steps. Creams. C. K. Williams. CP-WillC

Put Not Your Trust in Princes. Donald Davie. CP-DaviDC

"Put off that mask of burning gold." Mask, The. William Butler Yeats. CP-YeatW

Put Off the Wedding Five Times and Nobody Comes to It. Carl Sandburg. CP-SandC

Put off Thy robe of purple, then go on. Good Friday: Rex Tragicus, or, Christ Going to His Cross[e]. Robert Herrick. CP-HerrR

Put off your faces,Death:for day is over. E. E. Cummings. CP-CummE

Put on a clean shirt. Clothes. Anne Sexton. CP-SextA; SP-SextA

Put on thy *Holy Fillitings*, and so. Julia's Churching, or Purification. Robert Herrick. CP-HerrR

Put on yo' red silk stockings. Red Silk Stockings. Langston Hughes. CP-HughL; CP-HughL1

Put on your silks, and piece by piece. To His Mistresses. Robert Herrick. CP-HerrR

Put one more s in the U.S.A. One More "S" in the U.S.A. Langston Hughes. CP-HughL; CP-HughL1

Put out that Light. Light of Life, The. Stevie Smith. CP-SmitS

Put out the lights and stop the clocks. Madrid [—1937]. Langston Hughes. CP-HughL; CP-HughL1

Put the broidery-frame away. Bertha in the Lane. Elizabeth Barrett Browning. CP-BroEB

Put the flower pots. Yannis Ritsos. SP-RitsY *Fr.* Paper Poems 1.

Put the rest away, O put the rest away! Kenneth Patchen. CP-PatcK

Put These in Your Pipe. William Stafford. SP-StafWW

Put things in their place. Sky Is Blue, The. David Ignatow. SP-IgnaD

Put This Design in Your Carpet. Jelaluddin Rumi. SP-Rumi, *tr. by* Coleman Barks

Put up my lute! Emily Dickinson. CP-DickE

"Put up the sword!" The voice of Christ once more. Disarmament. John Greenleaf Whittier. CP-WhitJ

Put your face to the wind. Of a Vanished Kingdom. Yehuda Amichai. SP-AmicYL, *tr. by* Benjamin Harshav *and* Barbara Harshav

Put your / self out. Chasm. A. R. Ammons. CP-AmmoA

Put yourself where you'll be. Then ("Put yourself where you'll be"). Robert Creeley. SP-CreeR

Putrefaction. Robert Herrick. CP-HerrR

Puttin' the Baby Away. Paul Laurence Dunbar. CP-DunbP

Putting in the Seed. Robert Frost. CP-FrosR

Putting out the Lamp. Yannis Ritsos. SP-RitsY, *tr. by* Kimon Friar

Putting out the light. Trees at Night. Charles Simic. SP-SimiC; SP-SimiCE

Putting socks away. William Corbett. SP-CorbW

Putting the Sonnet to Work. William Stafford. SP-StafWW

Putting to Sea. Louise Bogan. CP-BogaL

Puzzle, The. Charles Bukowski. SP-BukC3

Puzzle, The. David Ignatow. SP-IgnaD

Puzzle, The. Howard Nemerov. CP-NemeH

Puzzle assembled, The. Solution. George Oppen. CP-OppGN

Puzzle faces in the dying elms. 'Mystery Boy' Looks for Kin in Nashville. Robert Earl Hayden. CP-HaydR

Puzzled. Langston Hughes. *See* Harlem ("Here on the edge of hell")

Puzzled Game-Birds, The. Thomas Hardy. CP-HardT

Puzzlement. Langston Hughes. CP-HughL; CP-HughL3

Puzzler, The. Rudyard Kipling. CP-KiplR

PX wives who smuggled the dinette, The. After Lunch. Olga Broumas. SP-BrouO

Pyche and the Eagle. Elizabeth Barrett Browning. CP-BroEB

Pygmalion. "H. D." CP-DoolH

Pygmalion lived for years alone. Galatea. Ovid. CP-MahoD *Fr.* Metamorphoses.

Pygmalion lived for years alone. Galatea. Ovid. CP-MahoD, *tr. by* Derek Mahon

Pylons, The. Stephen Spender. CP-SpenS

Pyramids, Arches, Obelisks, were but the irregularity of vainglory. Fauré Ballade, The. James Schuyler. CP-SchuJ

Pyramids of flesh sweated pyramids of stone. Track of the Master Builder, The. Marge Piercy. SP-PierM

Pyramids rooted in a rubble of beggars and bored camels, The. Sonnet to Man-Made Grandeur. John Updike. CP-UpdiJ

Pyramus and Thisbe. John Donne. CP-DonnJ; MW-DonnJ

Pyrography. John Ashbery. SP-AshbJ

Pyromaniac, The. Wyatt Prunty. SP-PrunW

Pyrra, jugo tandem vitulum junges-ne leoni? Jugum Improbum. Robert Graves. CP-GravR

Pythagoras planned it. Why did the people stare? Statues, The. William Butler Yeats. CP-YeatW

Pythagorean Silence. Susan Howe. SP-HoweS

Pythagorean Silences, The. Poem: "Pythagorean Silences, The." Alan Dugan. CP-DugaA

Pythian Odes. Pindar.
   "For not the brave, or wise, or great." CP-JohnS

Q

Q. Fanny Howe.
   "After a good beating on a cold day." SP-HoweF
   "Creation was the end that preceded means." SP-HoweF
   "Heaven has been my nation-state." SP-HoweF
   "I light up the grids." SP-HoweF
   "I was sick of my wits." SP-HoweF
   "Lambs don't fight being itinerant." SP-HoweF
   "Little clover's on autumn lawns, A." SP-HoweF
   "Neo-neolithic urban nomad school of poetry, The." SP-HoweF
   "One black thing was blowing down the road." SP-HoweF
   "Snow rises as it falls." SP-HoweF
   "We moved to be happy." SP-HoweF
   "Wherever I am becomes an end." SP-HoweF

Q may as well be for QUEEN. John Ciardi. CP-CiarJ

Q:dwo / we know of anything which can. E. E. Cummings. CP-CummE

Qasida of One Wounded by Water. Federico García Lorca. CP-GarcF, *tr. by* Catherine Brown *Fr.* Qasidas.

Qasida of the Branches. Federico García Lorca. CP-GarcF, *tr. by* Catherine Brown *Fr.* Qasidas.

Qasida of the Dark Doves. Federico García Lorca. CP-GarcF, *tr. by* Catherine Brown *Fr.* Qasidas.

Qasida of the Dream in Open Air. Federico García Lorca. CP-GarcF, *tr. by* Catherine Brown *Fr.* Qasidas.

Qasida of the Golden Girl. Federico García Lorca. CP-GarcF, *tr. by* Catherine Brown *Fr.* Qasidas.

Qasida of the Impossible Hand. Federico García Lorca. CP-GarcF, *tr. by* Catherine Brown *Fr.* Qasidas.

Qasida of the Rose. Federico García Lorca. CP-GarcF, *tr. by* Catherine Brown *Fr.* Qasidas.

Qasida of the Weeping. Federico García Lorca. CP-GarcF, *tr. by* Catherine Brown *Fr.* Qasidas.

Qasida of the Women Prone. Federico García Lorca. CP-GarcF, *tr. by* Catherine Brown *Fr.* Qasidas.

Qasidas. Federico García Lorca.
   Qasida of One Wounded by Water. CP-GarcF, *tr. by* Catherine Brown
   Qasida of the Branches. CP-GarcF, *tr. by* Catherine Brown
   Qasida of the Dark Doves. CP-GarcF, *tr. by* Catherine Brown
   Qasida of the Dream in Open Air. CP-GarcF, *tr. by* Catherine Brown
   Qasida of the Golden Girl. CP-GarcF, *tr. by* Catherine Brown
   Qasida of the Impossible Hand. CP-GarcF, *tr. by* Catherine Brown
   Qasida of the Rose. CP-GarcF, *tr. by* Catherine Brown
   Qasida of the Weeping. CP-GarcF, *tr. by* Catherine Brown
   Qasida of the Women Prone. CP-GarcF, *tr. by* Catherine Brown

QPP, The. Alice Walker. CP-WalkA

Qua Cursum Ventus. Arthur Hugh Clough. SP-ClouA

Quadroon mermaids, Afro angels, black saints. Ballad of Remembrance, A. Robert Earl Hayden. CP-HaydR

Quæ lenta accedit, quam velox præterit hora! Motto on the King's Clock. William Cowper. CP-CowpW

Quae linquam, aut nihil, aut nihili, aut vix sunt mea. Sordes. Epitaphium Testamentarium. Samuel Taylor Coleridge. CP-ColeS

Quae ratio, aut quis te furor impulit, improbe Sanni. In Sannium. Thomas Campion. CP-CampT

Quaerendo Invenietis. Howard Nemerov. CP-NemeH

Quai d'Orléans. Elizabeth Bishop. CP-BishE

Quail. Charles Olson. CP-OlsoC

Quail, The. James Wright. CP-WrigJ

Quail, and the wild mountain aster, The. Obit. Charles Olson. CP-OlsoC

Quail flutters like a forlorn castle falling, The. Quantity of Mercy, The. Kenneth Patchen. CP-PatcK

Quake last night was nothing personal, The. Earth Tremors Felt in Missouri. Mona Van Duyn. SP-VanDM

Quake, quake, let us turn Quaker all! George Meredith. CP-MerG2

Quaker Alumni, The. John Greenleaf Whittier. CP-WhitJ

Quaker Graveyard in Nantucket, The. Robert Lowell. SP-LoweR

Quaker of the Olden Time, The. John Greenleaf Whittier. CP-WhitJ

Quakers Are Out, The. John Greenleaf Whittier. CP-WhitJ

Quales aërii montis de vertice nubes. Translation of a Simile in Paradise Lost. John Milton. CP-CowpW

Qualia. Rae Armantrout. SP-ArmaA

Qualifications of Survivors. Alan Dugan. CP-DugaA

Quality of Genius, The. Denise Levertov. SP-LeveDL

Quality of Heaven, The. William Carlos Williams. CP-WilW2

Quality of Light, A. Yusef Komunyakaa. CP-KomuY

Quality of Mercy. Allen Tate. CP-TateA

Quality of these trees, green height; of the sky, shining; of water, The. Shine, Republic. Robinson Jeffers. CP-JefR2

Qualm. John Ashbery. SP-AshbJ

Qualm of conscience brings me back again, A. Epilogue: "Qualm of conscience brings me back again, A." Nathaniel Lee. CP-DryJ2 *Fr.* Princess of Cleves, The.

Quand on n'a pas ce que l'on aime, il faut aimer ce que l'on a—. Stevie Smith. CP-SmitS

Quandary. Robert Frost. CP-FrosR

Quanta. Richard Eberhart. CP-EberR

Quantity of Mercy, The. Kenneth Patchen. CP-PatcK

Quanto a Lei grata io sono. Christina Georgina Rossetti. CP-RosC3

Quantum Mutata. Oscar Wilde. CP-WildO

Quantum Theory Made Simple. Miller Williams. CP-WillM

Quarai. Charles Tomlinson. CP-TomlC

Quarrel. Grace Paley.

Quarrel, The. William Meredith. SP-MereW

Quarrel, The. James Whitcomb Riley. CP-RileJ

Quarrel, The. Theodore Weiss. SP-WeisT

Quarrel ("Bob and I / in different rooms"). Grace Paley. CP-PalGC

Quarrel in Old Age. William Butler Yeats. CP-YeatW

Quarrel with a Cloud. Richard Eberhart. CP-EberR

Quarried from snow, the dark walks lead to doors. Windows. Randall Jarrell. CP-JarrR

Quarry, The. Amy Clampitt. CP-ClamA

Quarry, The. Walter De la Mare. CP-DeLaW

Quarry, The. Howard Nemerov. CP-NemeH

Quarry, The. Charles Tomlinson. CP-TomlC

Quarry out the stone. Two Quits and a Drum, and Elegy for Drinkers. Alan Dugan. CP-DugaA

Quarry, Pigeon Cove. Maxine W. Kumin. SP-KumiM

Quart jar of silver dollars, The. Omen. Yusef Komunyakaa. CP-KomuY

Quarter of pleasures where the rich are always waiting. Capital, The. W. H. Auden. CP-AudeW

Quarterly, is it, money reproaches me. Money. Philip Larkin. CP-LarkP

Quartermasters and filibusterers. War on the Mind in a Time of Love. Charles Olson. CP-OlsoC

Quartet. William Corbett. SP-CorbW

Quartet in F Major. William Meredith. SP-MereW

Quartz opens its eyes in the snow. Pablo Neruda. SP-NeruP *Fr.* Skystones.

Quas ad Lucinam tot epistoles. Maxima Dona Ferens. James Laughlin. CP-LaugJ

Quatrain: "Do not, at this high time, desert." Charles Olson. CP-OlsoC

Quatrain: "Go not, young cloud, too boldly through the sky." Wallace Stevens. CP-StevWP

Quatrain: "He sought the music of the distant spheres." Wallace Stevens. CP-StevWP

Quatrain? Is that, A. Sound of Waves, The. William Carlos Williams. CP-WilW2

Quatrains. Ralph Waldo Emerson. CP-EmerR

Quatrains for Ishi. Yusef Komunyakaa. CP-KomuY

Quattrocento. Margaret Atwood. SP-AtwM2

Quavering cry. Screech-owl? A. Night, Death, Mississippi. Robert Earl Hayden. CP-HaydR

Quay recedes, The. Hurrah! Ahead we go! Colonel's Soliloquy, The. Thomas Hardy. CP-HardT

Que ferais-je sans ce monde sans visage sans questions. Samuel Beckett. CP-BeckS

Que J'ay Dit Devant. Louis Zukofsky. CP-ZukLS

Quebec, rattling chains of Separatism. Peter Blue Cloud. SP-BlueP

Quebec Suite. Mona Van Duyn. SP-VanDM

Quechuan Song. Gabriela Mistral. SP-MistG, *tr. by* Maria Giachetti [*or* Jacketti]

Queen and huntress, chaste and fair. Hymn[e] to Cynthia. Ben Jonson. CP-JonsB; SP-JonsB *Fr.* Cynthia's Revels.

Queen and the Young Princess, The. Stevie Smith. CP-SmitS

Queen Anne Cottage, The. James McMichael. SP-McMiJ

Queen Annelida and False Arcite. Geoffrey Chaucer. CP-BroEB

Queen Anne's Lace. Robert Stock. SP-StocR

Queen-Anne's-Lace. William Carlos Williams. CP-WilW1

Queen Anne's Lace. Louis Zukofsky. CP-ZukLS

Queen Bess was Harry's daughter. Stand forward partners all! Looking Glass, The. Rudyard Kipling. CP-KiplR

Queen Caroline to Her Guests. Thomas Hardy. CP-HardT

Queen Djenira. Walter De la Mare. CP-DeLaW

Queen has lately lost a part, The. Verses Said to Be Written on the Union. Jonathan Swift. CP-SwifJ

Queen Henrietta Maria. Oscar Wilde. CP-WildO

Queen Is in the Parlor, The. Ogden Nash. CP-NashO

Queen Mab. Percy Bysshe Shelley. CP-ShelP

Queen Mab in the Village. Nicholas Vachel Lindsay. CP-LindV

Queen of Bubbles, The. Nicholas Vachel Lindsay. CP-LindV

Queen of Hearts, The. Christina Georgina Rossetti. CP-RosC1

Queen of Sharon in the valley. Song: To a Rose. Robert Graves. CP-GravR

Queen of the Crabs, accept this claw. With the Gift of a Lion's Claw. Robert Graves. CP-GravR

Queen of the mountains far and near. Horace. *See* Oh virgin queen of mountain-side and woodland

Queen of the stars!—so gentle, so benign. To the Moon (Rydal). William Wordsworth. CP-WorW2

Queen of wit and beauty, Betty. To Betty the Grisette. Jonathan Swift. CP-SwifJ

Queen rejoices in her peers, A. Ralph Waldo Emerson. CP-EmerR

Queen Rose. Christina Georgina Rossetti. CP-RosC3

Queen she sent to look for me, The. Grenadier. A. E. Housman. CP-HousA

Queen Sheba loads forty mules with gold bricks. Sheba's Gifts to Solomon. Jelaluddin Rumi. SP-Rumi, *tr. by* Coleman Barks

Queen Theodolind has built. Song of Theodolinda, The. George Meredith. CP-MerG1

Queen Venus, come now, be my heroine. Flying House, and the May Queen Eternal, The. Nicholas Vachel Lindsay. CP-LindV

Queen Wasp, A. Walter De la Mare. CP-DeLaW

Queen Zuleima. George Meredith. CP-MerG2

Queene anone commands the waightie bowle, The. Virgil. CP-RaleW *Fr.* Aeneid [*or* Eneados *or* Aeneis], The.

Queens Cemetery, Setting Sun. Lawrence Ferlinghetti. SP-FerlL

Queen's Complaint, The. Sylvia Plath. CP-PlatS

Queen's Crowning, The. Gerard Manley Hopkins. CP-HopkG

Queen's Men, The. Rudyard Kipling. CP-KiplR

Queens of Hell had lissome necks to crane, The. Tall Girl, The. John Crowe Ransom. SP-RansJ

Queer are the ways of a man I know. Phantom Horsewoman, The. Thomas Hardy. CP-HardT

Queer Client and the Forest-Inn, The. Kenneth Patchen. CP-PatcK

Queer thing about those waters: there are no, A. Across the Bay. Donald Davie. CP-DaviDC

Quenching the Red. Kathleen Jessie Raine. SP-RainK

Quentin Durward. Sir Walter Scott.

　Serenade, A: "Ah! County Guy, the hour is nigh." SP-ScotW (County Guy.) SP-ScotW

Queries to Casuists. Lord Byron. CP-Byron

Queries to My Seventieth Year. Walt Whitman. CP-WhitW

Queries, you ask how many times must I kiss. Catullus. *See* Curious to learn / how many kiss- / es of your lips

Query. John Updike. CP-UpdiJ

Query: was ever a quainter. Of Pacchiarotto, and How He Worked in Distemper. Robert Browning. CP-BroR2

Quest, The. W. H. Auden. CP-AudeW

Quest, The. Rudyard Kipling. CP-KiplR

Quest, The. James Whitcomb Riley. CP-RileJ

Quest, The. James Wright. CP-WrigJ

Quest of the Fathers, The. James Whitcomb Riley. CP-RileJ

Quest of the Purple-Fringed, The. Robert Frost. CP-FrosR

Question. Robert Creeley. SP-CreeR

? E. E. Cummings. CP-CummE

Question. Federico García Lorca. CP-GarcF, *tr. by* Jerome Rothenberg *Fr.* Newton.

Question. D. H. Lawrence. CP-LawrD

Question. Grace Paley. CP-PalGC

Question. May Swenson. SP-SwenM

Question, A. Paul Laurence Dunbar. CP-DunbP

Question, A. Robert Frost. CP-FrosR

Question, The. W. H. Auden. CP-AudeW

Question, The: "All of us believe." W. H. Auden. CP-AudeW

Question, The. Robert Creeley. CP-CreeR

Question, The. David Ignatow. SP-IgnaD

Question, The. Rudyard Kipling. CP-KiplR

Question: "Man fades at the distant end of the street, A." Yannis Ritsos. SP-RitsY, *tr. by* Minas Savvas

Question, The. Dante Gabriel Rossetti. CW-RossD

Question, The. Muriel Rukeyser. CP-RukeM

Question, The. Jelaluddin Rumi. SP-Rumi, *tr. by* Coleman Barks

Question, The. Percy Bysshe Shelley. CP-ShelP

Question, The. Charles Tomlinson. CP-TomlC

Question, The. Charles Tomlinson. CP-TomlC

Question, The. C. K. Williams. SP-WillC

Question, The. Marya Alexandrovna Zaturenska. SP-ZatuM

Question and Answer. Elizabeth Barrett Browning. CP-BroEB

Question and Answer. Langston Hughes. CP-HughL; CP-HughL3

Question and Answer. Robert Penn Warren. CP-WarrR

Question and Answer. William Carlos Williams. CP-WilW1

Question at Cliff-Thrust. Robert Penn Warren. CP-WarrR

Question Book. Pablo Neruda.

　"And why is the sun such a poor friend." SP-NeruP

　"Are the salt and the sugar at work." SP-NeruP

　"At whom is the rice grinning." SP-NeruP

　"Can't you think death lives." SP-NeruP

　"Do you hear yellow detonations." SP-NeruP

　"Don't you also feel danger." SP-NeruP

　"How long would a rhinoceros last." SP-NeruP

　"If all rivers are sweet." SP-NeruP

　"If I'm dead and don't know it." SP-NeruP

　"Is all peace a dove's peace?" SP-NeruP

　"Is 4 always 4 for everybody?" SP-NeruP

　"Is it true that amber contains." SP-NeruP

　"Is there anything crazier in this life." SP-NeruP

　"Spelling book, can you love me." SP-NeruP

　"Tell me, is the rose really naked." SP-NeruP

　"That solemn Senator / who claimed I had castles." SP-NeruP

　"To whom does the raggedy condor." SP-NeruP

　"What are you hiding under your hump?" SP-NeruP

　"What can it mean to endure." SP-NeruP

　"What forced labor / for Hitler in Hell?" SP-NeruP

"What will the Poles think of my hat." SP-NeruP

"When does the butterfly read." SP-NeruP

"Where is the child that I was." SP-NeruP

"Who can persuade the sea." SP-NeruP

"Whom can I ask / what I meant to achieve in this world?" SP-NeruP

"Won't our life be a tunnel." SP-NeruP

Question in a Field. Louise Bogan. CP-BogaL

Question is: how does one hold an apple, The. Five Poems about Poetry. George Oppen. CP-OppGN

Question Is, Who Is Afraid of What, The? Kenneth Patchen. CP-PatcK

Question Mark. Richard Eberhart. CP-EberR

Question of Identity, A. Stephen Spender. CP-SpenS

Question of Marriage, A. Thomas Hardy. CP-HardT

Question of Personnel, The. Andrei Codrescu. SP-CodrA

Question of Time, A. Miller Williams. CP-WillM

Question ("Said the lady, *Can you do*"). Langston Hughes. CP-HughL; CP-HughL3

Question: / Tell me, where do fairy queens, The. Cold Sunbeams. Nicholas Vachel Lindsay. CP-LindV

Question, upon Being Told in Jest by Mr Stockton that He Was Not Loved Much, The. Annis Boudinot Stockton. CP-StocA

Question ("When the old junk man Death"). Langston Hughes. CP-HughL; CP-HughL1

Question Whither, The. George Meredith. CP-MerG1

Questioner Who Sits So Sly, The. W. H. Auden. CP-AudeW

Questioning Faces. Robert Frost. CP-FrosR

Questioning Spirit, The. Arthur Hugh Clough. SP-ClouA

Questionnaire. Carl Sandburg. CP-SandC

Questions. Hayden Carruth. CP-CarHS

Questions. Howard Nemerov. CP-NemeH

Questions. A. K. Ramanujan. CP-RamaA

Questions, The. James Laughlin. CP-LaugJ

Questions, The. Robert Pinsky. CP-PinsR

Questions about Angels. Billy Collins. SP-CollB

Questions Are Remarks. Wallace Stevens. CP-StevW; CP-StevWP

Questions in a Wood. Robert Graves. CP-GravR

Questions of Life. John Greenleaf Whittier. CP-WhitJ

Questions of Travel. Elizabeth Bishop. CP-BishE

Questions to Tourists Stopped by a Pineapple Field. W. S. Merwin. SP-MerwWF

Questions You Must Learn to Live Past. Robert Penn Warren. CP-WarrR

Quetzalcoatl Looks Down on Mexico. D. H. Lawrence. CP-LawrD

Quha will behald of vice the chance. William Dunbar. CP-DunbW

Quhat is this lyfe bot ane straucht way to deid. William Dunbar. CP-DunbW

Quhen Merche wes with variand windis past. William Dunbar. CP-DunbW

Quho that antique stories reidis. Squyer Meldrum. Sir David Lyndsay. SP-LyndD

Quho thinkis that he hes sufficence. William Dunbar. CP-DunbW

Quhom to sall I compleine my wo. William Dunbar. CP-DunbW

Quhy will ye, merchantis of renoun. To the Merchant[i]s of Edinburgh. William Dunbar. CP-DunbW

Qui Laborat, Orat. Arthur Hugh Clough. SP-ClouA

Qui Nunquam Amavit. James Laughlin. CP-LaugJ

Qui subito ex imis rerum in fastigia surgit. Papilio et Limax. John Gay. CP-CowpW

Quia Absurdum. Robinson Jeffers. CP-JefR3

Quia Amore Langueo. Ezra Pound. CP-PoEar

Quia Multum Amavi. Oscar Wilde. CP-WildO

Quibbling Elegy on the Worshipful Judge Boat, A. Jonathan Swift. CP-SwiftJ

Quick! a last poem before I go. On Rachmaninoff's Birthday. Frank O'Hara. SP-OharF

Quick as a knife-blade there you were. Vampire, The. Charles Baudelaire. CP-BaudC, *tr. by* Walter Martin

Quick bird sings and pierces me, The. Song: "Quick bird sings and pierces me, The." George Meredith. CP-MerG2

Quick death, Catullus! what more horrors may hurry! Catullus. *See* Drop dead, Catullus, lie right down where you are & die

Quick, Hammacher, My Stomacher! Ogden Nash. CP-NashO

Quick, Henry, the Flit! James Schuyler. CP-SchuJ

Quick i the death of thing. E. E. Cummings. CP-CummE

Quick on my feet in those Novembers of my loneliness. Mad Fight Song for William S. Carpenter, 1966, A. James Wright. CP-WrigJ

Quick, painter, quick the moment seize. Currente Calamo. Arthur Hugh Clough. SP-ClouA *Fr.* Mari Magno.

Quick pink; Soutine meat-streaks in the west. Looking Again at What I Looked at for Seventeen Years. Charles Wright. SP-WrigCN

Quick Poem, A. Adam Zagajewski. SP-ZagaA, *tr. by* Clare Cavanagh

Quick sparks on the gorse bushes are leaping, The. Wild Common, The. D. H. Lawrence. CP-LawrD

Quick-Step. Robert Creeley. CP-CreeR

Quick sun brings, exciting mountains warm, The. Power. Muriel Rukeyser. CP-RukeM

Quick talk / their speech—. Robert Creeley. CP-CreeR

Quick! there's that. Turn of the Head, A. Denise Levertov. SP-LeveDP

Quick-thinking people I meet, The. Han-shan. CP-ColdM, *tr. by* Red Pine

Quickening of St. John the Baptist, The. Thomas Merton. CP-MertT

Quickening Sun, that bough I love alone. Petrarch. CP-Petra, *tr. by* J. G. Nichols

Quicker deceit dies, The. Emily Dickinson. SP-DickE

Quicker / than that, can't. Sight, A. Robert Creeley. CP-CreeR

Quicker than the inquisition's night. Malady. Theodore Weiss. SP-WeisT

Quickly melting snow ran through the street, The. White Dove and the Snow, The. Jones Very. CP-VeryJ

Quickly, my letter, run through the boundless deep. Elegy 4: To Thomas Young. John Milton. CP-CowpW; CP-MiltJ

Quicksand Years. Walt Whitman. CP-WhitW

Quicquid in adversis potuit constantia rebus. Ad Tho. Munsonium, equitem Auratum et Baronetum. Thomas Campion. CP-CampT

Quid, fact it is Gelli? quick'ning mother, at (queer) sis, all three. Catullus. *See* What, Gellius, of the man

Quid Hic Agis? Thomas Hardy. CP-HardT

Quidditie [*or* Quiddity], The. George Herbert. CP-HerbG

Quiddity, Gelli, quarry, rosy as these too lips belie. Catullus. *See* How is it, Gellius

Quids, The. Laura Riding Jackson. CP-RidiL

Quies. Ezra Pound. CP-PoEar

Quiet. Walter De la Mare. CP-DeLaW

Quiet afternoon, A. Compulsory Chapel. Alice Walker. CP-WalkA

Quiet Afternoon at Home, A. Mona Van Duyn. SP-VanDM

Quiet as is proper for such places. Return. Robert Creeley. CP-CreeR

Quiet Clean Girls in Gingham Dresses. Charles Bukowski. SP-BukC1

Quiet Countries: The World of Hans Christian Andersen. Marya Alexandrovna Zaturenska. SP-ZatuM

Quiet deepens, The. You will not persuade. Farewell to Van Gogh. Charles Tomlinson. CP-TomlC; SP-TomlC

Quiet Enemy, The. Walter De la Mare. CP-DeLaW

Quiet fading out of life, The. Magnolia Flowers. Langston Hughes. CP-HughL; CP-HughL1

Quiet Fireshine. Ivor Gurney. SP-GurnI

Quiet Glades of Eden, The. Robert Graves. CP-GravR

Quiet House, The. Marya Alexandrovna Zaturenska. SP-ZatuM

Quiet is fireshine when the light is gone. Quiet Fireshine. Ivor Gurney. SP-GurnI

Quiet Joy, A. Yehuda Amichai. SP-AmicY, *tr. by* Chana Bloch

Quiet Life and a Good Name, A. Jonathan Swift. CP-SwifJ

Quiet little harbor—paintings, ships, colors. Calm. Yannis Ritsos. SP-RitsY, *tr. by* Athan Anagnostopoulos

Quiet Lodger, The. James Whitcomb Riley. CP-RileJ

Quiet man showed me around campus, The. At the University of New Orleans. Yehuda Amichai. SP-AmicYL, *tr. by* Benjamin Harshav *and* Barbara Harshav

Quiet Nights. Raymond Carver. CP-CarvR

Quiet Normal Life, A. Wallace Stevens. CP-StevW; CP-StevWP

Quiet setting the rough hairy roots. At the Core. Marge Piercy. SP-PierM

Quiet Talk. Ivor Gurney. SP-GurnI

Quiet Talk with Oneself, A. Charles Simic. SP-SimiC; SP-SimiCE

Quiet voice, / In the midst of those blazing. Echo for the Promise of Georg Trakl's Life. James Wright. CP-WrigJ

Quiet way the sun hangs dead center, The. Hard Up. Yusef Komunyakaa. CP-KomuY

Quiet Work. Matthew Arnold. SP-ArnoM

Quieter the people are, The. Sign Board, The. Robert Creeley. CP-CreeR

Quietist, The. Fanny Howe.

    "Holy one called, The." SP-HoweF

    "Mad God, mad thought." SP-HoweF

    "My bedclothes were stuffed with ashes." SP-HoweF

    "Sex is made on a bed which is too loose." SP-HoweF

    "Two waters—squared." SP-HoweF

    "What does serpent mean?" SP-HoweF

    "When she was alone in her cell, she didn't exist." SP-HoweF

    "Zero built a nest." SP-HoweF

Quietly at the corner table. Leafy Angel, A. Andrei Codrescu. SP-CodrA

Quietly pacifist peaceful, The. QPP, The. Alice Walker. CP-WalkA

Quietly, quietly, why have I been waiting? To Wang Wei. Meng Hao Jan. CP-WilW2

Quietness. Jelaluddin Rumi. SP-Rumi, *tr. by* Coleman Barks

Quietness. William Carlos Williams. CP-WilW1

Quietness clings to the air. Snow Fall, The. Archibald MacLeish. CP-MacLA

Quietude of a soft wind, The. Creditor, The. Louis MacNeice. CP-MacNL

Quilca House to the Dean. Henry Brooke. CP-SherT

Quilt-Pattern, A. Randall Jarrell. CP-JarrR

Quilting. Lucille Clifton. SP-ClifL

Quilting, The. Paul Laurence Dunbar. CP-DunbP

Quilts the pond and / out from under its plumped-upness. Rain. James Schuyler. CP-SchuJ

Quince. W. S. Merwin. SP-MerwW

Quince Bush, The. A. R. Ammons. CP-AmmoA

Quinine is to cinchona. Wasabi. Arthur Sze. SP-SzeA

Quinquagesima. Christina Georgina Rossetti. CP-RosC2

Quinque. Robert Graves. CP-GravR

Quinque tibi luces vibrant in nomine: quinque. Quinque. Robert Graves. CP-GravR

Quintell, The. Robert Herrick. CP-HerrR

Quinti, see if't be wish of cool eyes day bear your Catullus. Catullus. *See* My eyes in your pledge, Quintius

Quintia's *foremost* to multitudes; my eye can deed her *long, e—*. Catullus. *See* We have heard of Quintia's beauty. To me she is tall, slender

Quintius her mentor tries. Premula's Problem. James Laughlin. CP-LaugJ

Quip, The. George Herbert. CP-HerbG

Quips and players, seeming to vend astringency off-hours. Second Avenue. Frank O'Hara. SP-OharF

Quique haec membra malis vis esse obnoxia multis. Gerard Manley Hopkins. CP-HopkG

Quiquern. Rudyard Kipling. *Fr.* Second Jungle Book, The.

Quirks. John Ciardi. CP-CiarJ

Quisnam adeo, mortale genus, praecordia versat? Hortus. Andrew Marvell. CP-MarvA

Quit 'at, ole 'Sephus. Ole 'Sephus (Monologue to a Coon Dog). Tennessee Williams. CP-WillT

QUIT PLAYING GAMES! Penal Cavalry, The. Andrei Codrescu. SP-CodrA

Quit writing / and in Morocco. Africa. William Carlos Williams. CP-WilW1

Quite convincing axiom, A. Private Theatricals. James Whitcomb Riley. CP-RileJ

Quite empty, quite at rest. Emily Dickinson. CP-DickE

Quite Forsaken. D. H. Lawrence. CP-LawrD

Quite suddenly the evening clears at last. Rain. Jorge Luis Borges. SP-BorgJ, *tr. by* Alastair Reid

Quite unexpectedly as Vasserot. End of the World, The. Archibald MacLeish. CP-MacLA

Quivering wings of the winter ant, The. Winter Poem. Robert Bly. SP-BlyR

Quo Vadis. William Stafford. SP-StafWW

Quòd festas luces juvat instaurare Beatis. Ad Episcopum Salopiensem. Gerard Manley Hopkins. CP-HopkG

Quod nostros, Davisi, laudas recitasque libellos. Ad Io. Davisium. Thomas Campion. CP-CampT

Quoit, The. W. S. Merwin. SP-MerwWF

Quondam was I in my lady's grace. Sir Thomas Wyatt. CP-WyatT

Quoof. Paul Muldoon. CP-MuldP

Quotation, A. G. K. Chesterton. CP-ChesG

Quotations. George Oppen. CP-OppGN

Quotations. Carl Sandburg. CP-SandC

Quotations. Charles Wright. SP-WrigCN

Quoth an inquirer, "Praise the Merciful!" Mihrab Shah. Robert Browning. CP-BroR2

Quoth King Robin, our ribbons I see are too few. Verses on the Revival of the Order of the Bath. Jonathan Swift. CP-SwifJ

Quoth one: "Sir, solve a scruple! No true sage." Two Camels. Robert Browning. CP-BroR2

Quoth Saadi, when I stood before. Ralph Waldo Emerson. CP-EmerR

Quoth the thief to the dog; "let me into your door." Dog and the Thief, The. Jonathan Swift. CP-SwifJ

R

R.A.F. "H. D." CP-DoolH

R. Alcona to J. Brenzaida. Emily Jane Brontë. *See* Remembrance

R. C. Dallas. Lord Byron. CP-Byron

R. G. E. Richard Eberhart. CP-EberR

R is for RAT, the noise in man's wall. John Ciardi. CP-CiarJ

R. L. S. A. E. Housman. CP-HousA

R.M.D. Hayden Carruth. CP-CarHS

R-p-o-p-h-e-s-s-a-g-r. E. E. Cummings. CP-CummE

R R Bums, The. William Carlos Williams. CP-WilW2

R.S.S. William Cowper. CP-CowpW

R. S. S., at Deer Island on the Merrimac. John Greenleaf Whittier. CP-WhitJ

R.S.S. Written in a Fit of Illness. William Cowper. CP-CowpW

R. Says. Adam Zagajewski. SP-ZagaA, *tr. by* Renata Gorczynski, Benjamin Ivry *and* C. K. Williams

R². Charles Olson. CP-OlsoC

Rabbi, The. Robert Earl Hayden. CP-HaydR

Rabbi Ben Ezra. Robert Browning. CP-BroR1

Rabbi Ishmael. John Greenleaf Whittier. CP-WhitJ

Rabbi Nakhman of Bratslav. Yehuda Amichai. SP-AmicYL, *tr. by* Benjamin Harshav *and* Barbara Harshav

Rabbi Nathan twoscore years and ten, The. Two Rabbins, The. John Greenleaf Whittier. CP-WhitJ

Rabbi told me: On the day allowed, A. Doctor———. Robert Browning. CP-BroR2

Rabbi, we Gadarenes. Matthew VIII, 28 ff. Richard Wilbur. CP-WilbR

Rabbi's Song, The. Rudyard Kipling. CP-KiplR

Rabbit. James Whitcomb Riley. CP-RileJ

Rabbit, The. Edna St. Vincent Millay. CP-MillE

Rabbit, The. Mary Oliver. SP-OlivM

Rabbit as King of the Ghosts, A. Wallace Stevens. CP-StevW; CP-StevWP

Rabbit Catcher, The. Sylvia Plath. CP-PlatS

Rabbit crossed and dodged and turned, The. Chase, The. James Vincent Cunningham. CP-CunnJ

Rabbit Fights for His Life the Leopard Eats Lunch, The. C. K. Williams. CP-WillC

Rabbit Hunter, The. Robert Frost. CP-FrosR

Rabbit hurries to the brim of its wood, The. Randall Jarrell. CP-JarrR

Rabbit in his burrow keeps, The. Haunted. Walter De la Mare. CP-DeLaW

Rabbit in the Cross-Ties. James Whitcomb Riley. CP-RileJ

Rabbit leaps, The. Henry David Thoreau. CP-ThorH

Rabbit loves his hoppity and the wallaby loves his hippity, The. Don't Look for the Silver Lining, Just Wait for It. Ogden Nash. CP-NashO

Rabbit Snared in the Night. D. H. Lawrence. CP-LawrD

Rabbit tracks in an inch or so of new snow. Ditto. Thomas Lux. SP-LuxT

Rabbit who used to belong to Matthew, The. Sojourners. Marge Piercy. SP-PierM

Rabbits breed, flies breed, said the virgin lady. Unborn Song. Muriel Rukeyser. CP-RukeM

Rabbit's dreamy eyes grow dreamier, The. Bulletin Has Just Come In, A. Ogden Nash. CP-NashO

Rabbits, The. Ogden Nash. CP-NashO

(..rabid or dog-dull.) Let me tell you how. Professor's Song, A. John Berryman. CP-BerrJ

Raccoon. Anne Sexton. CP-SextA

Raccoon Journal. Stanley Kunitz. CP-KunSC

Raccoons have invaded the crawl space. In the Old Neighborhood. Rita Dove. SP-DoveR

Race, The. Nuala Ní Dhomhnaill. CP-MahoD, *tr. by* Derek Mahon

Race, The. Howard Nemerov. CP-NemeH

Race, The. Charles Tomlinson. CP-TomlC

Race and Battle. D. H. Lawrence. CP-LawrD

Race is not to the swift, The. Race and Battle. D. H. Lawrence. CP-LawrD

Race-Memory. G. K. Chesterton. CP-ChesG

Race of the Flood, The. C. K. Williams. CP-WillC

Race of Veterans. Walt Whitman. CP-WhitW

Race Relations. Carolyn Kizer. CP-KizeC

Race with the sun as he downed, A. Cynic's Epitaph. Thomas Hardy. CP-HardT

Racer's Widow, The. Louise Glück. SP-GlucL

Rachel. Walter De la Mare. CP-DeLaW

Rachel. Jones Very. CP-VeryJ

Rachel and Leah. Robert Stock. SP-StocR

Rachel Had Said. Robert Creeley. CP-CreeR

Rachel sings sweet— / Oh, yes, at night. Rachel. Walter De la Mare. CP-DeLaW

Rachmaninoff's Third. James Schuyler. CP-SchuJ

Racists. C. K. Williams. SP-WillC

Rack. A. R. Ammons. CP-AmmoA

Rack of Paperbacks, A. John Updike. CP-UpdiJ

Racketing catcalls spiral down. Mediterranean. Eugenio Montale. CP-MontE, *tr. by* Jonathan Galassi

Radar and rocket-plane, the applications of chemistry, the tricks of. Staggering Back Toward Life. Robinson Jeffers. CP-JefR3

Raderus. John Donne. CP-DonnJ; MW-DonnJ

Radiance in a Dark Wood, The. Kenneth Patchen. CP-PatcK

Radiation is like oppression. Long Death, The. Marge Piercy. SP-PierM

Radiator cockroach. Come Back Christmas: Blues Stanza. Allen Ginsberg. SP-GinsA

Radiator's last hiss and steam-clang done, he, The. Reading Late at Night, Thermometer Falling. Robert Penn Warren. CP-WarrR

Radical Departure, A. James Tate. SP-TateJ

Radicals. Jorge Carrera Andrade. CP-MertT

Radio. Frank O'Hara. SP-OharF

Radio Again, The. Philip Whalen. SP-WhalP

Radio fades, The. The blues are out, and then. Denomination. Heather McHugh. SP-McHuH

Radio Horse, The. Paul Muldoon. CP-MuldP

Radio silence of aircraft over the dense ocean. Muriel Rukeyser. CP-RukeM

Radio Sky. Norman Dubie. CP-DubiN

Radio Waves. Raymond Carver. CP-CarvR

Radiometer. James Merrill. SP-MerrJ

Radius of the bomb was twelve inches, The. Yehuda Amichai. SP-AmicYL, *tr. by* Benjamin Harshav *and* Barbara Harshav

Radix, Matrix. Paul Celan. SP-CelaP, *tr. by* John Felstiner

Rafael Sublime Majestic Graceful Wise. William Blake. CP-BlakW

Raft. A. R. Ammons. CP-AmmoA

Raft, The. Robert Graves. CP-GravR

Rafters, The. James Dickey. CP-DickJ

Rafts, The. Adrienne Rich. CP-RicAE

Rag Man, The. Robert Earl Hayden. CP-HaydR

Rag of black plastic, shred of a kite. Goodbye, Goldeneye. May Swenson. SP-SwenM

Rag woman, half a child, A. Roman Diary: 1951. John Ciardi. CP-CiarJ

Rage. Mary Oliver. SP-OlivM

Rage. Alice Walker. CP-WalkA

Rage, closest to reason in the mind. On Being Unhappily in Love with Reason. Alan Dugan. CP-DugaA

Rage for Order. Derek Mahon. CP-MahoD

Ragged and thrashing. Messages. Jane Cooper. CP-CoopJ

Ragged Island. Edna St. Vincent Millay. CP-MillE

Ragged poet, languishing in hell, The. 'Tasso in Prison' by Delacroix. Charles Baudelaire. CP-BaudC, *tr. by* Walter Martin

Ragged Wood, The. William Butler Yeats. CP-YeatW

Raggedy Man on Children, The. James Whitcomb Riley. CP-RileJ

Raggedy Man, The. James Whitcomb Riley. CP-RileJ

Raggs. Robert Herrick. CP-HerrR

Raging Desire & c. Philip Whalen. SP-WhalP

Raging from every quarter. Wreath of Women. Muriel Rukeyser. CP-RukeM

Ragnarök. Jorge Luis Borges. SP-BorgJ, *tr. by* Ken Krabbenhoft

Ragpickers' Wine. Charles Baudelaire. CP-BaudC, *tr. by* Walter Martin

Rahab's House. Thomas Merton. CP-MertT

Rahel to Varnhagen. Edwin Arlington Robinson. CP-RobiE

Rahere. Rudyard Kipling. CP-KiplR *Fr.* Debits and Credits.

Rahere, King Henry's Jester, feared by all the Norman Lords. Rahere. Rudyard Kipling. CP-KiplR *Fr.* Debits and Credits.

Raid. Langston Hughes. CP-HughL; CP-HughL2

Raid, A. G. K. Chesterton. CP-ChesG

Rail on, Rail on, ye heartless Crew! To a Knot of Ungenerous Critics. Lord Byron. CP-Byron

Rail Road, The. Jones Very. CP-VeryJ

Railroad Avenue. Langston Hughes. CP-HughL; CP-HughL1

Railroad baron in the West, A. I, Too, Have Been to the Huntington. James Vincent Cunningham. CP-CunnJ

Railroad Station, The. Wisława Szymborska. SP-SzymW, *tr. by* Stanisław Barańczak *and* Clare Cavanagh

Railroad track is miles away, The. Travel. Edna St. Vincent Millay. CP-MillE

Railroad yard in San Jose. In Back of the Real. Allen Ginsberg. CP-GinsA; SP-GinsA

Railway bore him through, The. After a Romantic Day. Thomas Hardy. CP-HardT

Railway Children, The. Seamus Heaney. SP-HeanSO

Railway Junction, The. Walter De la Mare. CP-DeLaW

Railway stationery lay upon, The. Railway Stationery, The. Kenneth Koch. SP-KochK

Railway Stationery, The. Kenneth Koch. SP-KochK

Railway stations of our daily plight. Platform, The. Adrienne Rich. CP-RicAE

Rain. Wendell Berry. CP-BerrW

Rain. Jorge Luis Borges. SP-BorgJ, *tr. by* Alastair Reid

Rain. Raymond Carver. CP-CarvR

Rain. Constantine P. Cavafy. CP-CavaC, *tr. by* Theoharis Constantine Theoharis

Rain. Andrei Codrescu. SP-CodrA

Rain. Robert Creeley. CP-CreeR

Rain. Ted Hughes. SP-HughTN

Rain. Mary Oliver. SP-OlivM

Rain. James Schuyler. CP-SchuJ

Rain. William Carlos Williams. CP-WilW1

Rain. James Wright. CP-WrigJ

Rain, The. G. K. Chesterton. CP-ChesG

Rain, The. Robert Creeley. CP-CreeR

Rain, The. James Whitcomb Riley. CP-RileJ

Rain, The ("Rain descends; each drop some drooping flower, The"). Jones Very. CP-VeryJ

Rain (2). Robert Creeley. CP-CreeR

Rain and rain! and rain and rain! We to Sigh Instead of Sing. James Whitcomb Riley. CP-RileJ

Rain, and then / the cool pursed. Mushrooms. Mary Oliver. SP-OlivM

Rain and thunder beat down and flooded the streets. Cartagena. Gary Snyder. CP-SnydG

Rain at Bellagio. Amy Clampitt. CP-ClamA

Rain at Wildwood. May Swenson. SP-SwenM

Rain baptizes the ravaged counties. Midlands. Charles Tomlinson. CP-TomlC

Rain-beaten stones: great tussocks of dead grass. Wind-bags, The. Hugh MacDiarmid. SP-MacDH

Rain blows my eyelashes upwards toward. October 19. Andrei Codrescu. SP-CodrA

Rain-charm for the Duchy. Ted Hughes. SP-HughTN

Rain Clouds. Jones Very. CP-VeryJ

Rain comes down, it comes without our call, The. Winter Rain, The. Jones Very. CP-VeryJ

Rain comes flapping through the yard, The. Gathering Mushrooms. Paul Muldoon. CP-MuldP

Rain descends; each drop some drooping flower, The. Rain, The ("Rain descends; each drop some drooping flower, The"). Jones Very. CP-VeryJ

Rain Downriver. Philip Levine. SP-LeviP

Rain-drenched, Rhine-drained. Note from Leyden, A. Amy Clampitt. CP-ClamA

Rain / Drips down / O'er fields, The. Early Summer Sketch. E. E. Cummings. CP-CummE

Rain-drop on the eyelids of the earth, A. Sonnet: "Rain-drop on the eyelids of the earth, A." E. E. Cummings. CP-CummE

Rain extravagantly that morning kept us. Story of a Citizen, The. Tess Gallagher. SP-GallT

Rain falls on Santiago. Madrigal for the City of Santiago. Federico García Lorca. CP-GarcF, *tr. by* Catherine Brown

Rain falls on the faces of my friends. Rain on the Battlefield. Yehuda Amichai. SP-AmicYL, *tr. by* Benjamin Harshav *and* Barbara Harshav

Rain fell like grass growing, The. Rain at Wildwood. May Swenson. SP-SwenM

Rain. Floods. Frost. And after frost, rain. Rain. Ted Hughes. SP-HughTN

Rain-god Tlaloc, hungering for blood, The. War Memorial, The. Amy Clampitt. CP-ClamA

Rain greases all false lips. Earth quacks. Some of These Days. Philip Whalen. SP-WhalP

Rain Guitar, The. James Dickey. CP-DickJ

Rain had long since stopped, The. View from Charles Bridge. Jaroslav Seifert. SP-SeifJ, *tr. by* Ewald Osers

Rain has come, and the earth must be very glad, The. Soaking, The. Ivor Gurney. SP-GurnI

Rain has spoiled the farmer's day, The. Suum Cuique. Ralph Waldo Emerson. CP-EmerR

Rain hisses onto stones as old men and women. Sudden Rain. Raymond Carver. CP-CarvR

Rain imprinted the step's wet shine, The. On the Doorstep. Thomas Hardy. CP-HardT

Rain in Ohio. Mary Oliver. SP-OlivM

Rain in the night; now cock-crow and engine-hum. Roman Script. Derek Mahon. CP-MahoD

Rain Is a Handsome Animal, The. E. E. Cummings. CP-CummE

Rain is raining all around, The. Quick, Henry, the Flit! James Schuyler. CP-SchuJ

Rain is speaking quietly, The. Six Poems for Tamar. Yehuda Amichai. SP-AmicY, *tr. by* Stephen Mitchell

Rain it rains without a stay, The. Floods, The. Rudyard Kipling. CP-KiplR

Rain, it streams on stone and hillock, The. A. E. Housman. CP-HousA

Rain, its tiny pressure, The. Romanze, or the Music Students. Frank O'Hara. SP-OharF

Rain, now as all night, is tapping. Seattle Uplift. John Updike. CP-UpdiJ

Rain of Blood, The. Adrienne Rich. CP-RicAE

Rain of bombs, well placed, A. Snow Begins, The. William Carlos Williams. CP-WilW2

Rain of London pimples, The. London Rain. Louis MacNeice. CP-MacNL

Rain of the white valley the clear rain, The. June Rain. W. S. Merwin. SP-MerwWF

Rain on a Grave. Thomas Hardy. CP-HardT

Rain on South-East England. Donald Davie. CP-DaviDC

Rain on the Battlefield. Yehuda Amichai. SP-AmicYL, *tr. by* Benjamin Harshav *and* Barbara Harshav

Rain on the dock, cold, in a place. Off the Hook. Eleanor Wilner. SP-WilnE

Rain on the windows, creaking doors. Division, The. Thomas Hardy. CP-HardT

Rain or hail / sam done. E. E. Cummings. CP-CummE; SP-CummE

Rain or Shine. Charles Bukowski. SP-BukC1

Rain patters on a sea that tilts and sighs. Absences. Philip Larkin. CP-LarkP

Rain pools in the old lumber yard, The. Lumber Yard Pools at Sunset. Carl Sandburg. CP-SandC

Rain—red rhododendron tree. Fanny Howe. SP-HoweF *Fr.* O'Clock.

Rain set early in tonight, The. Porphyria's Lover. Robert Browning. CP-BroR1; SP-BroR

Rain-shafts splintered on me, The. Christmastide. Thomas Hardy. CP-HardT

Rain slants from the clouded light, The. November Ghosts, The. Randall Jarrell. CP-JarrR

Rain smites more and more, The. January Night, A. Thomas Hardy. CP-HardT

Rain-Songs. Paul Laurence Dunbar. CP-DunbP

Rain Spirit Passing. Denise Levertov. SP-LeveDL

Rain squalls on afternoon's tin roof. Costa Rican Pastoral. Robert Stock. SP-StocR

Rain Stick, The. Seamus Heaney. SP-HeanSO

Rain still falls, the wind moves. Sharp Lookout. A. R. Ammons. CP-AmmoA

Rain straight up and down upon the sword ferns. Spring Musick. Philip Whalen. SP-WhalP

Rain streams down like harp-strings from the sky, The. Rain-Songs. Paul Laurence Dunbar. CP-DunbP

Rain that ripens oranges, The. And Now, the Weather. Karl Shapiro. SP-ShapK

Rain, the earliest creature. Jaguar Myth, The. Pablo Antonio Cuadra. CP-MertT

Rain! the rain! the rain!, The. Rain, The. James Whitcomb Riley. CP-RileJ

Rain to the wind said, The. Lodged. Robert Frost. CP-FrosR

Rain unslanting, unceasing. Winter Afternoons in the V & A, Pre-W.W.II. Denise Levertov. SP-LeveDL

Rain upon the window, rain upon the day. Lucubration. Richard Eberhart. CP-EberR

Rain-Wet Asphalt Heat, Garbage Curbed Cans Overflowing. Allen Ginsberg. CP-GinsA; SP-GinsA

Rain Winds Blow Doors Open. Carl Sandburg. CP-SandC

Rainbow. Max Jacob. CP-BishE

Rainbow. D. H. Lawrence. CP-LawrD

Rainbow, The. Robert Herrick. CP-HerrR

Rainbow, The. Gerard Manley Hopkins. CP-HopkG

Rainbow, The. D. H. Lawrence. CP-LawrD

Rainbow, The. Christina Georgina Rossetti. CP-RosC2

Rainbow at Evening. Archibald MacLeish. CP-MacLA

Rainbow, beautiful and clear light, A. Kathleen Jessie Raine. SP-RainK

Rainbow Body. Gary Snyder. CP-SnydG

Rainbow Grocery, The. William Dickey. SP-DickW

Rainbow never tells me, The. Emily Dickinson. CP-DickE

Rainbow; or Curious Covenant, The. Robert Herrick. CP-HerrR

Rainbow over evening, my. Rainbow at Evening. Archibald MacLeish. CP-MacLA

Raindrop fell on my hand, A. Water. Wisława Szymborska. SP-SzymWM, *tr. by* Joanna Trzeciak

Raindrops on a Briar. William Carlos Williams. CP-WilW2

Raindrops / On the crumbling walls. Poem for Youth. Langston Hughes. CP-HughL; CP-HughL1

Raindrops on the tin roof. Falling Asleep. Wendell Berry. CP-BerrW

Rainer, / the man who was about to celebrate his 52nd birthday. Death of Europe, The. Charles Olson. CP-OlsoC; SP-OlsoC

Raining here / in little pieces. Funny. Robert Creeley. CP-CreeR

Raining in Magens Bay. John Updike. CP-UpdiJ

Rainless darkness drew o'er the lake, A. On Como. George Meredith. CP-MerG2

Rainmakers are these second growths, The. Gently Bent to Ease Us. Norman Dubie. CP-DubiN

Rain's all right. The boys who physic. Biography of Southern Rain. Kenneth Patchen. CP-PatcK

Rains at length have ceased, the winds are stilled, The. William Wordsworth. CP-WorW1

Rain's lovely gray daughter has lost her tall lover. Fog. Kenneth Patchen. CP-PatcK

Rains, the rains, The. Louis Zukofsky. CP-ZukLS

Rainstorms that blacken like a headache. Grasmere. Amy Clampitt. CP-ClamA

Rainsweet / s / tillnes / s. E. E. Cummings. CP-CummE

Rainwalkers, The. Denise Levertov. SP-LeveDP

Rainy evening in exhausted gray. Evening ("Rainy evening in exhausted gray"). Federico García Lorca. CP-GarcF, *tr. by* Catherine Brown

Rainy 4th. Marge Piercy. SP-PierM

Rainy Morning, The. James Whitcomb Riley. CP-RileJ

Rainy Night. Dorothy Parker. CP-ParkD

Rainy Night at the Writers' Colony. Josephine Jacobsen. CP-JacoJ

Rainy Pleiads wester, The. A. E. Housman. CP-HousA

Rainy Saturday, Larry dead / almost three weeks now. Thinking about the Poet Larry Levis One Afternoon in Late May. Charles Wright. SP-WrigCN

Rainy Season, The. Clarence Major. SP-MajoC

Rainy Season; Sub-Tropics. Elizabeth Bishop. CP-BishE

Rainy skies, misty mountains. Fifty. Kenneth Rexroth. CP-RexrK

Rainy, smoky Fall, clouds tower. Noretorp-Noretsyh. Kenneth Rexroth. CP-RexrK

Rainy vacations / Try people's patience. Tomorrow, Partly Cloudy. Ogden Nash. CP-NashO

Raise from these rocky cliffs your heads. First Song, The. Thomas Carew. CP-CareT *Fr.* Carew's Masque.

Raise girls but not too many. Han-shan. CP-ColdM, *tr. by* Red Pine

Raise me; undraw the curtain; that is well. Ellen Middleton. Christina Georgina Rossetti. CP-RosC3

Raise the shade. E. E. Cummings. CP-CummE; SP-CummE

Raised are the dripping oars. Youth of Nature, The. Matthew Arnold. SP-ArnoM

Raised high on tripod, flashing bright, the Holy Silver Urn. Tea Poet, The. G. K. Chesterton. CP-ChesG

Raised on high, above the city. Cross, The ("Raised on high, above the city"). Jones Very. CP-VeryJ

Raisin, The. Donald Hall. CP-HallD

Raising our glasses, smilingly. Libation. Denise Levertov. SP-LeveDL; SP-LeveDS

Raja, I wish I knew. To Raja Rao. Czeslaw Milosz. CP-MiloC; CP-MiloCN

Rake-hell Muses. Thomas Hardy. CP-HardT

Rakeoff and the Getaway, The. Carl Sandburg. CP-SandC

Ralegh's Prizes. Robert Pinsky. CP-PinsR

Raleigh Was Right. William Carlos Williams. CP-WilW2

Raleigh's Cell in the Tower. Dante Gabriel Rossetti. CW-RossD

Rallying-Point. D. H. Lawrence. CP-LawrD

Ralph pares his nayles, his warts, his cornes, and Raph. Upon Ralph. Robert Herrick. CP-HerrR

Ralphius. John Donne. CP-DonnJ; MW-DonnJ

Ramatayim. Yehuda Amichai. SP-AmicYL, *tr. by* Benjamin Harshav *and* Barbara Harshav

Ramble, The. Jones Very. CP-VeryJ

Rambler, The. Thomas Hardy. CP-HardT

Rambling I looked for an old abode. Life Laughs Onward. Thomas Hardy. CP-HardT

Rambling snowmounds and still sheep along. Fanny Howe. SP-HoweF *Fr.* O'Clock.

Rambo-Tree, The. James Whitcomb Riley. CP-RileJ

Rampage, The. C. K. Williams. CP-WillC; SP-WillC

Ramshackles, archipelagoes, loose constellations. Unifying Principle, The. A. R. Ammons. CP-AmmoA

Rancorous heart, cruel, pitiless, though showing. Michelangelo Buonarroti. CP-Miche, *tr. by* John Frederick Nims

Rancorous man—he would remember all that was gloomy—this is what he underlined, A. Method for Optimism. Yannis Ritsos. SP-RitsY, *tr. by* Kimon Friar

Randall Jarrell 1. October 1965. Robert Lowell. SP-LoweR

Randall Jarrell 2. Robert Lowell. SP-LoweR

Randall Jarrell 3. Robert Lowell. SP-LoweR

Randall Jarrell, Office Hours 10-11. Randall Jarrell. CP-JarrR

Randolph of Roanoke. John Greenleaf Whittier. CP-WhitJ

Randy old / woman said, The. In Her Burning. Muriel Rukeyser. CP-RukeM

Rang and rang, rang in a small boy's head. Muriel Rukeyser. CP-RukeM

Range after range of mountains. On Climbing the Sierra Matterhorn Again after Thirty-One Years. Gary Snyder. CP-SnydG

Range-finding. Robert Frost. CP-FrosR

Range in the Desert, The. Randall Jarrell. CP-JarrR

Ranger, The. John Greenleaf Whittier. CP-WhitJ

Ranges / of clinker heaps. John Maydew or The Allotment. Charles Tomlinson. CP-TomlC; SP-TomlC

Ransom. Robert Penn Warren. CP-WarrR

Ransom, The. Charles Baudelaire. CP-BaudC, *tr. by* Walter Martin

Ransomed of the Lord, The. Christina Georgina Rossetti. CP-RosC2

Ranstead yellow fringes dragon clusters. Butter-and-Eggs. Louis Zukofsky. CP-ZukLS

Rant, A. Frank O'Hara. SP-OharF

Rantin' Dog, the Daddie o't, The. Robert Burns. CP-BurnR

Rantin Laddie, The. Robert Burns. CP-BurnR

Rantin, Rovin Robin. Robert Burns. CP-BurnR

Rantoul. John Greenleaf Whittier. CP-WhitJ

Rape. Adrienne Rich. SP-RicA2

Rape in the Engineering Building. James Tate. SP-TateJ

Rape of Aurora, The. George Meredith. CP-MerG1

Rape of the bourgeoisie accomplished, the men, The. Life on a Battleship. Wallace Stevens. CP-StevWP

Rape of the Cataract, The. Richard Eberhart. CP-EberR

Rape of the Lock, The; an Heroi-Comical Poem. Alexander Pope. CP-PopeA

Rape of the Swan, The. Archibald MacLeish. CP-MacLA

Rape Poem. Marge Piercy. SP-PierM

Raper from Passenack, The. William Carlos Williams. CP-WilW1

Raphael. John Greenleaf Whittier. CP-WhitJ

Raphael, they've asked you to compose. For Ammonis, Who at Died at 29, in 610. Constantine P. Cavafy. CP-CavaC, tr. by Theoharis Constantine Theoharis

Rapid Transit. William Carlos Williams. CP-WilW1

Rapidly cruising or lying on the air there is a bird. Frigate Pelican, The. Marianne Craig Moore. CP-MoorM

Rapine Brings Ruine. Robert Herrick. CP-HerrR

Rapine has yet tooke nought from me. To God, in Time of Plundering. Robert Herrick. CP-HerrR

Rapture. Ai. SP-Ai

Rapture. Galway Kinnell. SP-KinnGN

Rapture, A. Thomas Carew. CP-CareT

Rapture The. Theodore Weiss. SP-WeisT

Rapture in exile—paradox. Fanny Howe. SP-HoweF Fr. Sea-Garden, The.

Rapunzel. Olga Broumas. SP-BrouO

Rapunzel. Anne Sexton. CP-SextA; SP-SextA

Rapunzel Rapunzel let down your hair. After-Thought, The. Stevie Smith. CP-SmitS

Rapunzel, Rapunzel, Let's Let Down Our Hair. Ogden Nash. CP-NashO

Raquel the Queen of Diamonds and La Hire. Voyage to the Moon. Robert Pinsky. CP-PinsR

Rara Avis. Charles Baudelaire. CP-BaudC, tr. by Walter Martin

Rare are thy cheeks, Susanna, which do show. Upon Mistresse Susanna Southwell, Her Cheeks. Robert Herrick. CP-HerrR

Rare Gist, The. William Carlos Williams. CP-WilW2

Rare is the voice it selfe; but when we sing. Voice and Violl, The. Robert Herrick. CP-HerrR

Rare-sweet the air in that unimagined country. Unfinished Dream, The. Walter De la Mare. CP-DeLaW

Rare temples thou hast seen, I know. Fairy Temple; or, Oberon's Chapel, The. Robert Herrick. CP-HerrR

Rarely, rarely, comest thou. Song: "Rarely, rarely, comest thou." Percy Bysshe Shelley. CP-ShelP

Rarest mood of all the year! With the Current. James Whitcomb Riley. CP-RileJ

Rarity and value of scientific knowledge, The. Poetry and Science. Hugh MacDiarmid. SP-MacDH

'Ras Wilson, I respect you, 'cause. Erasmus Wilson. James Whitcomb Riley. CP-RileJ

Rash author, 'tis a vain presumptuous crime. Art of Poetry, The. Nicolas Boileau-Despéaux. CP-DryJ2, tr. by John Dryden

Rash Bride, The. Thomas Hardy. CP-HardT

Raspberry. Louis Zukofsky. CP-ZukLS

Raspe playes at Ninc-holes; and 'tis known he gets. Upon Raspe. Robert Herrick. CP-HerrR

Rastignac at 45. Thom Gunn. CP-GunnT

Rat, The. Emily Dickinson. CP-DickE

Rat, The. Gabriela Mistral. SP-MistG, tr. by Maria Giachetti [or Jacketti]

Rat, The. Edwin Arlington Robinson. CP-RobiE

Rat, The. William Carlos Williams. CP-WilW1

Rat came on stage, A. Note. Charles Simic. SP-SimiC; SP-SimiCE

Rat is in the trap, it is in the trap, The. Song of a Rat. Ted Hughes. SP-HughTN

Rat is the conciest Tenant, The. Rat, The. Emily Dickinson. CP-DickE

Rat, O Rat. Christopher Logue. SP-LoguC

Rat ran to a deer, A. Rat, The. Gabriela Mistral. SP-MistG, tr. by Maria Giachetti [or Jacketti]

Rat Riddles. Carl Sandburg. CP-SandC

Rat Rises, A. Charles Bukowski. SP-BukC2

Rat sits up and works his, The. Rat, The. William Carlos Williams. CP-WilW2

Rat surrendered here, A. Emily Dickinson. CP-DickE

Rat-tat-tat-tash of shields upon Ida. Other Wing, The. Louis MacNeice. CP-MacNL

Rather arid delight. Emily Dickinson. CP-DickE

"Rather dead than spotted"; and believe it. Then the Ermine. Marianne Craig Moore. CP-MoorM

Rather Foolish Sentiment, A. A. K. Ramanujan. CP-RamaA

Rather Like a Dream. Robert Penn Warren. CP-WarrR

Rather notice, mon cher. To a Solitary Disciple. William Carlos Williams. CP-WilW1

Rather remote, all of it. Vanished Work. Hans Magnus Enzensberger. SP-EnzeH, tr. by Hans Magnus Enzensberger and Michael Hamburger

Rather than evade itself. Rainer Maria Rilke. CP-RilkFr, tr. by A. Poulin, Jr. Fr. Valaisian Quatrains, The.

Rather than permit him. Early Martyr, An. William Carlos Williams. CP-WilW1

Rather than set her to music, keep her in stone's. Red Clay Speech. Robert Stock. SP-StocR

Rather the flight of the bird passing and leaving no trace. Fernando Pessoa. SP-PessF Fr. Keeper of Sheep, The.

Rathlin. Derek Mahon. CP-MahoD

Rational Anthem, A. Ambrose Bierce. SP-BierA

Rationality. George Oppen. CP-OppGN

Rats. John Updike. CP-UpdiJ

Rats, The. Georg Trakl. CP-WrigJ

Rats Live on No Evil Star. Anne Sexton. CP-SextA

Rattle, rattle. There is no question. He Speaks to His Arguing Friends and to Himself. Miller Williams. CP-WillM

Rattlesnake Country. Robert Penn Warren. CP-WarrR

Rattlesnake Glyph. Arthur Sze. SP-SzeA

Rattlesnakes I've had them. Abiquiu. Charles Tomlinson. CP-TomlC

Rattlin, Roarin Willie. Robert Burns. CP-BurnR

Rav / of Northern White Russia declined, The. Illustrious Ancestors. Denise Levertov. SP-LeveDS

Ravaged Face, The. Sylvia Plath. CP-PlatS

Ravaged Villa, The. Herman Melville. SP-MelvH

Raveling of the evenings is ours, too, The. Indian Serenade. Eugenio Montale. CP-MontF, tr. by Jonathan Galassi

Raven, The. Samuel Taylor Coleridge. CP-ColeS

Raven, The. Edgar Allan Poe. CP-PoeEd

Raven, The. Adrienne Rich. CP-RicAE

Raven, Don't Stay Away from My Door—A Chant for April First. Ogden Nash. CP-NashO

Raven flapped o'er the rich man's roof, A. Parables ("Raven flapped o'er the rich man's roof, A"). G. K. Chesterton. CP-ChesG

Raven, while with glossy breast, A. Fable, A: "Raven, while with glossy breast, A." William Cowper. CP-CowpW

Ravening through the persistent bric-à-brac. On the Difficulty of Conjuring Up a Dryad. Sylvia Plath. CP-PlatS

Ravenna. Oscar Wilde. CP-WildO

Ravenna. Aleksandr Aleksandrovich Blok. SP-BlokA, tr. by Peter France and Jon Stallworthy

Ravenna. Louis MacNeice. CP-MacNL

Ravenous the flock. Maine Winter. Charles Tomlinson. CP-TomlC

Ravenousness of fondness, The. Emily Dickinson. SP-DickE

Ravens. Ted Hughes. SP-HughTN

Ravine, The. Ai. SP-Ai

Ravine, The. Hayden Carruth. CP-CarHS

Raving winds around her blowing. Robert Burns. CP-BurnR

Ravings of the Depraved Monk Benno of St. Gall Who Went Mad from Carnal Longing in His Cell and Forgot How to Write Good Latin. James Laughlin. CP-LaugJ

Raw-boned and an ignorant man, A. St. Christopher. Louise Bogan. CP-BogaL

Raw Data for an Unfinished Questionnaire. Yusef Komunyakaa. CP-KomuY

Rawdon Brown. Robert Browning. CP-BroR2

Ray. Hayden Carruth. CP-CarHS

Ray Charles! His voice. Hanoi Hannah. Yusef Komunyakaa. CP-KomuY

Ray Wells, a big Nisqually, and I. Gary Snyder. CP-SnydG Fr. Myths and Texts.

Raymond Hodgkins, his dragger last seen. Handed Down. Amy Clampitt. CP-ClamA

Rays. Federico García Lorca. CP-GarcF, tr. by Jerome Rothenberg Fr. Mirror Suite.

Ray's letterpoem. William Corbett. SP-CorbW

Rays of Dazzling Light. Czeslaw Milosz. CP-MiloCN, tr. by Jessica Fisher and Bozena Gilewska

Raze these long blocks of brick and stone. Truce of Piscataqua, The. John Greenleaf Whittier. CP-WhitJ

Razed House, The. Wyatt Prunty. SP-PrunW

Razors pain you. Résumé. Dorothy Parker. CP-ParkD

Razzle dazzle maggots are summary, The. Easter. Frank O'Hara. SP-OharF

Re-Acquaintance. Hayden Carruth. CP-CarHS

Re-Born. G. K. Chesterton. CP-ChesG

Re C—. Robert Creeley. CP-CreeR

Re-creating the Scene. Yusef Komunyakaa. CP-KomuY

Re-Enactment, The. Thomas Hardy. CP-HardT

Re-entry, without pillow, dear and the pieces. Examples—for Richard Bridgeman. Charles Olson. CP-OlsoC

Re-forming the Crystal. Adrienne Rich. SP-RicA1; SP-RicA2

Re-interment: Recollection of a Grandfather. Robert Penn Warren. CP-WarrR

Re-place me in the firmament. Saturn. "H. D." CP-DoolH Fr. Temple of the Sun.

Re-Rooting. Denise Levertov. SP-LeveDL

Re-statement of Romance. Wallace Stevens. CP-StevW; CP-StevWP

Reach me a blue pencil of the moon. Ur Burial. Richard Eberhart. CP-EberR

Reach me a quill, pluckt from the flaming wing. Upon the Gunpowder Treason. Richard Crashaw. CP-CrasR

Reach me wine No counsel weakens the conclusion of the lot. Hafiz. CP-EmerR *Fr.* Odes.

Reach Over. D. H. Lawrence. CP-LawrD

Reach, with your whiter hands, to me. To the Water Nymphs, Drinking at the Fountain. Robert Herrick. CP-HerrR

Reach your hand to me, my friend. James Whitcomb Riley. CP-RileJ

Reaching. Raymond Carver. CP-CarvR

Reaching down arm-deep into bright water. Shells. Kathleen Jessie Raine. SP-RainK

Reaching my own block. Walking Home at Night. Allen Ginsberg. CP-GinsA

Reaching Out to Turn on a Light. William Stafford. SP-StafWW

Read a thousand books! Linked Verses. Carolyn Kizer. CP-KizeC

Read by Moonlight. Thomas Hardy. CP-HardT

Read here: / This is the story of Evarra-man. Evarra and His Gods. Rudyard Kipling. CP-KiplR

Read history: so learn your place in Time. Edna St. Vincent Millay. CP-MillE

Read history: thus learn how small a space. Edna St. Vincent Millay. CP-MillE

Read in these roses the sad story. Red and White Roses. Thomas Carew. CP-CareT

Read Me a Lesson, Muse, and Speak It Loud. John Keats. CP-KeatJ

Read me, ere age. Bookplate. James Vincent Cunningham. CP-CunnJ

Read me Euripides. Follies of Adam, The. Theodore Roethke. CP-RoetT

Read—Sweet—how others—strove. Emily Dickinson. CP-DickE

Read the Great Poets. James Tate. SP-TateJ

Read the Signs. Clarence Major. SP-MajoC

Read thou my lines, my Swetnaham, if there be. To M. Laurence Swetnaham. Robert Herrick. CP-HerrR

Reade, you that have some teares left yet unspent. Elegie upon the Untimely Death of Prince *Henry,* An. Thomas Campion. CP-CampT

Reader, The. Randall Jarrell. CP-JarrR

Reader, The. Thomas Merton. CP-MertT

Reader, The. Wallace Stevens. CP-StevW; CP-StevWP

Reader! behold a monument. Another. William Cowper. CP-CowpW

Reader (did he buy it, borrow, beg), A. On Doctor Drink. James Vincent Cunningham. CP-CunnJ

Reader, it's time reality was faced. James Vincent Cunningham. CP-CunnJ

Reader my friend, is in the words here, somewhere. Cheer, The. William Meredith. SP-MereW

Reader of the Sentences, The. Norman Dubie. CP-DubiN

Reader over My Shoulder, The. Robert Graves. CP-GravR

Reader, stay, / And if I had no more to say. Epitaph on Master Philip Gray, An. Ben Jonson. CP-JonsB

Reader, when these dumb stones have told. Another [On the Duke of Buckingham]. Thomas Carew. CP-CareT

Reader, you must have noticed how. Scent, The. Charles Baudelaire. CP-BaudC, *tr. by* Walter Martin *Fr.* Phantom, A.

Readers. Jorge Luis Borges. SP-BorgJ, *tr. by* Alastair Reid

Readers, The. Laura Riding Jackson. CP-RidiL

Readers of poetry, the writers of, The. Redwing. Tess Gallagher. SP-GallT

Readers of the *Boston Evening Transcript,* The. *Boston Evening Transcript,* The. T. S. Eliot. CP-ElioT

Readers wee entreat ye pray. Purgatory. Robert Herrick. CP-HerrR

Readie Pome. William Carlos Williams. CP-WilW1

Readier than flags rippling in the sun. Test Case. Thomas Kinsella. CP-KinsT

Readiness, The. Dan Pagis. SP-PagiD, *tr. by* Stephen Mitchell

Readinesse. Robert Herrick. CP-HerrR

Readinesse of doing, doth expresse, The. Readinesse. Robert Herrick. CP-HerrR

Reading. Raymond Carver. CP-CarvR

Reading. William Corbett. SP-CorbW

Reading a Letter. D. H. Lawrence. CP-LawrD

Reading a life of Alexander the Great, Alexander. Wine. Raymond Carver. CP-CarvR

Reading Aloud. Tess Gallagher. SP-GallT

Reading Aloud at Dusk. Josephine Jacobsen. CP-JacoJ

Reading an Anglo-Saxon love poem in its extravagance. Good Silence, The. Robert Bly. SP-BlyR

Reading an Anthology of Chinese Poems of the Sung Dynasty, I Pause to Admire the Length and Clarity of Their Titles. Billy Collins. SP-CollB

Reading and Talking. Louis Zukofsky. CP-ZukLS

Reading Apollinaire by the Rogue River. Lawrence Ferlinghetti. SP-FerlL

Reading at Night. David Ignatow. SP-IgnaD

Reading Bai Juyi. Allen Ginsberg.

   China Bronchitis. SP-GinsA

   "I grew up in Paterson New Jersey and was." SP-GinsA

"I'm a traveller in a strange country." SP-GinsA

"Tho the body's heavy meat's sustained." SP-GinsA

Reading Before We Read, Horoscope and Weather. Wyatt Prunty. SP-PrunW

Reading books, ah, we kept forgetting. Adam Zagajewski. SP-ZagaA, *tr. by* Renata Gorczynski

Reading C. K. Williams's "The Critic." William Corbett. SP-CorbW

Reading: Early Sorrow. C. K. Williams. SP-WillC

Reading Flowers. Rainer Maria Rilke. CP-RilkFr, *tr. by* A. Poulin, Jr.

Reading French Poetry. Allen Ginsberg. CP-GinsA

Reading *Genesis* to a Blind Child. James Dickey. CP-DickJ

Reading her, I realized how rich she was and myself, how poor. Reading the Notebook of Anna Kamienska. Czeslaw Milosz. CP-MiloCN, *tr. by* Robert Hass

Reading his own lines over, he'd been. Margate. Amy Clampitt. CP-ClamA

Reading Hölderlin on the Patio with the Aid of a Dictionary. Rita Dove. SP-DoveR

Reading how even the Swiss had thrown the sponge. Beyond the Alps. Robert Lowell. SP-LoweR

Reading in Fall Rain. Robert Bly. SP-BlyR

Reading in Li Po. After the Last Dynasty. Stanley Kunitz. CP-KunSC

Reading, in the chair. For Pen ("Reading, in the chair"). Robert Creeley. SP-CreeR

Reading in the Evening. D. H. Lawrence. CP-LawrD

Reading Lao Tzu Again in the New Year. Charles Wright. SP-WrigCN

Reading Late at Night, Thermometer Falling. Robert Penn Warren. SP-WarrR

Reading Late in the Cottage. Gregory Orr. SP-OrrG

Reading late, / last-awake in the country. September 22nd. Maxine W. Kumin. SP-KumiM *Fr.* Joppa Diary.

Reading Myself. Robert Lowell. SP-LoweR

Reading of Rex Stout, A. Mona Van Duyn. SP-VanDM

Reading on the Beach. Josephine Jacobsen. CP-JacoJ

Reading Room, The New York Public Library. Richard Eberhart. CP-EberR

Reading Rorty and Paul Celan One Morning in Early June. Charles Wright. SP-WrigCN

Reading Seferis. Sam Hamill. SP-HamiS

Reading Something in the Restaurant. Raymond Carver. CP-CarvR

Reading the Bible Backwards. Eleanor Wilner. SP-WilnE

Reading the Headlines. David Ignatow. SP-IgnaD

Reading the Japanese Poet Issa (1762–1826). Czeslaw Milosz. CP-MiloC; CP-MiloCN, *tr. by* Robert K. Haas

Reading the Names of the Vietnam War Dead. Thomas McGrath. SP-McGrT

Reading the Newspaper at the Village Store. Grace Paley. CP-PalGC

Reading the Newspaper on Microfilm. Miller Williams. CP-WillM

Reading the Notebook of Anna Kamienska. Czeslaw Milosz. CP-MiloCN, *tr. by* Robert Hass

Reading the Obituary Page in *The Times.* James Laughlin. CP-LaugJ

Reading the sentences, November sun. Sentences, The. Robert Pinsky. CP-PinsR

Reading this, you are waiting for the curtain. Programme Note. Charles Tomlinson. CP-TomlC

Reading Time : 1 Minute 26 Seconds. Muriel Rukeyser. CP-RukeM

Reading Translated Poets, Feb. 1. Thomas Merton. CP-MertT

Reading: Winter. C. K. Williams. SP-WillC

Reading with Little Sister: A Recollection. William Stafford. SP-StafWW

Reading Yeats I do not think. 26. Lawrence Ferlinghetti. SP-FerlL

Reading Your Poems in Your House While You Are Away. Carolyn Kizer. CP-KizeC

Reading your words. Bloodroot. Jane Cooper. CP-CoopJ

Readings. Czeslaw Milosz. CP-MiloC; CP-MiloCN, *tr. by* Lillian Vallee

Readings from Ibn Abbad. Thomas Merton. CP-MertT

Readings in French. Thom Gunn. CP-GunnT

Readings in those college towns were hell, The. Hustle, The. Charles Bukowski. SP-BukC3

Readings of History. Adrienne Rich. CP-RicAE

Ready. Yannis Ritsos. SP-RitsY, *tr. by* Martin McKinsey

Ready for parting, as if my back were turned. Dan Pagis. SP-PagiD, *tr. by* Stephen Mitchell

Ready Man, The. Yannis Ritsos. SP-RitsY, *tr. by* Christian McEwen *and* Nikos Tsingos

Ready page, with hurried hand, The. Bale-Fire, The. Sir Walter Scott. SP-ScotW *Fr.* Lay of the Last Minstrel, The.

Ready to Kill. Carl Sandburg. CP-SandC

Ready to Roll. Allen Ginsberg. CP-GinsA

Real, The. Charles Olson. SP-OlsoC

Real and Half Real. Robinson Jeffers. CP-JefR3

Real Anthem, The. G. K. Chesterton. CP-ChesG

Real as a dream. Understand That This Is a Dream. Allen Ginsberg. CP-GinsA

Real Avenue News. Carl Sandburg. CP-SandC

Real Bones. James Laughlin. CP-LaugJ

Real dark alley, A. Shortcut. Charles Simic. SP-SimiCE

Real Democracy. D. H. Lawrence. CP-LawrD

Real emeralds are worth more than synthetics. True or False. John Ciardi. CP-CiarJ

Real Estate. Amy Clampitt. CP-ClamA

Real Estate. A. K. Ramanujan. CP-RamaA

Real Hands. Yannis Ritsos. SP-RitsY, tr. by Kimon Friar and Kostas Myrsiades

Real hero of The Binding of Isaac was the ram, The. Yehuda Amichai. SP-AmicY, tr. by Chana Bloch

Real Hero of the Sacrifice of Isaac, The. Yehuda Amichai. SP-AmicYL, tr. by Benjamin Harshav and Barbara Harshav

Real hero of the sacrifice was the ram, The. Real Hero of the Sacrifice of Isaac, The. Yehuda Amichai. SP-AmicYL, tr. by Benjamin Harshav and Barbara Harshav

Real immorality, as far as I can see it, The. Immorality. D. H. Lawrence. CP-LawrD

Real-Life Story. Dan Pagis. SP-PagiD

Real People. William Stafford. SP-StafWW

Real Question, The. Paul Laurence Dunbar. CP-DunbP

Real sphinx, The. He. Federico García Lorca. CP-GarcF, tr. by Jerome Rothenberg Fr. In the Forest of Clocks.

Real thing is always an imitation, The. Dharmakaya. Philip Whalen. SP-WhalP

Real value comes with madness. Jelaluddin Rumi. SP-Rumi, tr. by Coleman Barks

Real Work, The. Gary Snyder. CP-SnydG

Realism. Czeslaw Milosz. CP-MiloCN, tr. by Robert Hass

Realists, The. William Butler Yeats. CP-YeatW

Realities. Howard Nemerov. CP-NemeH

Reality. Pier Paolo Pasolini. SP-PasoP, tr. by Norman MacAfee and Luciano Martinengo

Reality and Willie Yeats. John Ciardi. CP-CiarJ

Reality and Yeats were two. Reality and Willie Yeats. John Ciardi. CP-CiarJ

Reality being too thorny for my great character,—I found myself nevertheless at my lady's. Bottom. Arthur Rimbaud. CP-RimbA, tr. by Martin Sorrell

Reality Demands. Wisława Szymborska. SP-SzymWM, tr. by Joanna Trzeciak

Reality Demands. Wisława Szymborska. SP-SzymW, tr. by Stanislaw Barańczak and Clare Cavanagh

Reality is a question. Terms in Which I Think of Reality, The. Allen Ginsberg. CP-GinsA

Reality Is an Activity of the Most August Imagination. Wallace Stevens. CP-StevWP

Reality is and is. For Selma Gubin's Umbrellas. Louis Zukofsky. CP-ZukLS

Reality / is like a contemporary string. Dazzled. Arthur Sze. SP-SzeA

Reality is to be sought, not in concrete. Aesthetic. Charles Tomlinson. CP-TomlC; SP-TomlC

Reality of Peace, 1916. D. H. Lawrence. CP-LawrD

Reality! said the stone-minded man. Maia. Howard Nemerov. CP-NemeH

Reality's gossed guzzlings. Meteorology. A. R. Ammons. CP-AmmoA

Really, it is not the. In This Age of Hard Trying, Nonchalance Is Good and. Marianne Craig Moore. CP-MoorM

Really, must you. You. W. H. Auden. CP-AudeW

Really, too stupid, those village churches. First Communions. Arthur Rimbaud. CP-RimbA, tr. by Martin Sorrell

Really what keeps us apart. Love Poem for a Wife, 1. A. K. Ramanujan. CP-RamaA

Reaper, The. Robert Duncan. SP-DuncR

Reaper, The. Jones Very. CP-VeryJ

Reapers Are the Angels, The. Jones Very. CP-VeryJ

Reapers of the Water. James Tate. SP-TateJ

Reape's eyes so rawe are, that (it seemes) the flyes. Upon Reape. Robert Herrick. CP-HerrR

Rearmament. Robinson Jeffers. CP-JefR2

Rearrange a "Wife's" affection! Emily Dickinson. CP-DickE

Reas'ning at every step he treads. Doves, The. William Cowper. CP-CowpW

Reason. Samuel Taylor Coleridge. CP-ColeS

Reason. George Meredith. CP-MerG2

Reason, A. Robert Creeley. CP-CreeR

Reason, The. Stevie Smith. CP-SmitS

Reason and Imagination. Christopher Smart. SP-SmarC

Reason and Nature. James Vincent Cunningham. CP-CunnJ

Reason blinded by sin, Lesbia. Carmen 75. Catullus. CP-ZukLS Fr. Carmina.

Reason Dixie, The. Total War. Langston Hughes. CP-HughL; CP-HughL3

Reason for Love's Blindness. Samuel Taylor Coleridge. CP-ColeS

Reason for Skylarks, The. Kenneth Patchen. CP-PatcK

Reason let others give and realness bring. E. E. Cummings. CP-CummE

Reason of the saint that he is saintly, The. Reasons of Each, The. Laura Riding Jackson. CP-RidiL

Reason, tell me thy mind, if here be reason. Love and Reason. Sir Philip Sidney. SP-SidnP Fr. Arcadia.

Reason will not decide at last; the sword will decide. Contemplation of the Sword. Robinson Jeffers. CP-JefR2

Reasonable Constitution, A. Herman Melville. SP-MelvH

Reasonable, reasonable, reasonable . . . we walked through. Hangman, The. Anne Sexton. CP-SextA

Reasons for Attendance. Philip Larkin. CP-LarkP

Reasons for Music. Archibald MacLeish. CP-MacLA

Reasons of Each, The. Laura Riding Jackson. CP-RidiL

Reasons Why. Langston Hughes. CP-HughL; CP-HughL1

Reassessing. A. R. Ammons. CP-AmmoA

Reassurance. Alice Walker. CP-WalkA

Reassurance, The. Thom Gunn. CP-GunnT

Reawakening, The. Walter De la Mare. CP-DeLaW

Reb Nachman sat in his hovel one day in spring. Rhyme of Reb Nachman, The. Robert Pinsky. CP-PinsR

Rebecca at Play. Miller Williams. CP-WillM

Rebecca's Hymn. Sir Walter Scott. SP-ScotW Fr. Ivanhoe.

Rebeginning and beginnings is what she told me or what she showed me. Idem 2. Michael Palmer. SP-PalmM

Rebel Color-Bearers at Shiloh. Herman Melville. SP-MelvH

Rebel, The. Charles Baudelaire. CP-BaudC, tr. by Walter Martin

Rebellion is my theme all day. Modern Paulot, The. William Cowper. CP-CowpW

Rebellious. Living. Nature of This Flower Is to Bloom, The. Alice Walker. CP-WalkA

Rebels, The. Lawrence Ferlinghetti. SP-FerlL

Rebirth. Rudyard Kipling. CP-KiplR

Rebuke the company of spearmen. Women and War. Donald Davie. CP-DaviDC

Rebuked. D. H. Lawrence. CP-LawrD

Rebus, by I. B., A. James Bowdoin. CP-WheaP

Recalcitrance / of whorl-wheel fossils, The. Near Corinium. Charles Tomlinson. CP-TomlC

Recalcitrants, The. Thomas Hardy. CP-HardT

Recall, The. Rudyard Kipling. CP-KiplR

Recall it you? That Kiss in the Dark. Thomas Hardy. CP-HardT

Recalled. Edwin Arlington Robinson. CP-RobiE

Recalling who I was, I see somebody else. Fernando Pessoa. SP-PessF, tr. by Susan M. Brown and Edwin Honig

Recantation. Samuel Taylor Coleridge. CP-ColeS; MW-ColeS

Recantation. Sylvia Plath. CP-PlatS

Recantation, A. Rudyard Kipling. CP-KiplR

Recapitulation, The. Richard Eberhart. CP-EberR

Receipt for a Pudding, A. Mrs. Austen. CP-AustJ

Receipt to Frighten away the Dean, A. Peter Murray. CP-SherT

Receipt to Restore Stella's Youth, A. Jonathan Swift. CP-SwifJ

Receive a gift which more rewards myself. With a Copy of Stevens' Harmonium. J. V. Cunningham. CP-CunnJ

Receive, dear friend, the truths I teach. Ode 2.10: "Receive, dear friend, the truths I teach." Horace. CP-CowpW Fr. Odes.

Receiving the Stigmata. Rita Dove. SP-DoveR

Recent Past, The. John Ashbery. SP-AshbJ

Recently in the south of England. Ode to Hengist and Horsa. Robinson Jeffers. CP-JefR3

Recently regilded / General Sherman marches bravely. Sherman's March Reglitterized. Lawrence Ferlinghetti. SP-FerlL

Receptionist has shiny fingernails, The. On Trading Time for Life by Work. Alan Dugan. CP-DugaA

Recessional. Rudyard Kipling. CP-KiplR

Réchauffé. Louis MacNeice. CP-MacNL

Recipe. Raissa Maritain. CP-MertT

Recipe for Contemplation. William Corbett. SP-CorbW

Recipe for Sleep. James Tate. SP-TateJ

Reciprocal Kindness the Primary Law of Nature. Vincent Bourne. CP-CowpW

Recital. John Updike. CP-UpdiJ

Recital? "Concert" is the word. Rescue With Yul Brynner. Marianne Craig Moore. CP-MoorM

Recital of Water over Stones. Yusef Komunyakaa. CP-KomuY

Recitative. Hart Crane. CP-CranH

Recitative by Death. W. H. Auden. CP-AudeW Fr. Man of La Mancha.

Reciting Adrienne Rich on Cole and Haight. Differences, The. Thom Gunn. CP-GunnT

Reckless Head. Ted Hughes. SP-HughTN

Recklessly you offered me your all. Hoopoe Tells Us How, The. Robert Graves. CP-GravR

Reckoning, The. Stanley Kunitz. CP-KunSC

Reckoning, The. Theodore Roethke. CP-RoetT

"Reclining Figure." Donald Hall. CP-HallD

Reclining Position, The. James Laughlin. CP-LaugJ

Recluse, The. William Wordsworth.
Home at Grasmere. CP-WorW1
Prospectus to *The Recluse*. CP-WorW2

Recluse, The. Stevie Smith. CP-SmitS

Recluse Hsu Su Kwei had come to see Prince Wu, The. Advising the Prince. Chuang Tzu. CP-MertT

Recognition. Richard Eberhart. CP-EberR

Recognition. Robert Graves. CP-GravR

Recognition. W. S. Merwin. SP-MerwW

Recognition. Dan Pagis. SP-PagiD, *tr. by* Stephen Mitchell

Recognition. Yannis Ritsos. SP-RitsY, *tr. by* Athan Anagnostopoulos

Recognition, A. May Sarton. SP-SartM

Recognition, The. Wendell Berry. CP-BerrW

Recognition, The. Johann N. Vogl. CP-MerG2

Recognition Not Enough. Stevie Smith. CP-SmitS

Recoil. William Stafford. SP-StafWW

Recoleta Cemetary. Jorge Luis Borges. SP-BorgJ, *tr. by* Stephen Kessler

Recollect the Face of me. Emily Dickinson. CP-DickE

Recollection. Arthur Rimbaud. CP-RimbA, *tr. by* Martin Sorrell

Recollection in Upper Ontario, from Long Before. Robert Penn Warren. CP-WarrR

Recollection of Bellagio. William Meredith. SP-MereW

Recollection of Childhood. Richard Eberhart. CP-EberR

Recollection of George Oppen in a Letter to an English Friend. Donald Davie. CP-DaviDC

Recollection of the Portrait of King Henry Eighth, Trinity Lodge, Cambridge. William Wordsworth. CP-WorW2

Recollection on the Day of a First Book. John Logan. CP-LogaJ

Recollection. To Miss A—M—, humbly inscribed by the Authoress. Phillis Wheatley. *See* On Recollection

Recollections of Love. Samuel Taylor Coleridge. CP-ColeS

Recommendation, The. Richard Crashaw. CP-CrasR

Recompence. Robert Herrick. CP-HerrR

Recompence, The. Robert Herrick. CP-HerrR

Recompense, The. Charles Tomlinson. CP-TomlC

Reconciliation. Walter De la Mare. CP-DeLaW

Reconciliation. Czeslaw Milosz. CP-MiloCN, *tr. by* Robert Hass

Reconciliation. Walt Whitman. CP-WhitW

Reconciliation. William Butler Yeats. CP-YeatW

Reconciling Power, The. Jones Very. CP-VeryJ

Reconstructing a Crime. Yusef Komunyakaa. CP-KomuY

Reconstruction. Robert Stock. SP-StocR

Record, The. Louis Zukofsky. CP-ZukLS

Record Stride, A. Robert Frost. CP-FrosR

'Recorded ambience'—this. In the Studio. Charles Tomlinson. CP-TomlC

Recorders Ages Hence. Walt Whitman. CP-WhitW

Recorders in Italy. Adrienne Rich. CP-RicAE

Records. Robert Graves. CP-GravR

Records. Robert Lowell. SP-LoweR

Records. Allen Tate. CP-TateA

Recoveries. Theodore Weiss. SP-WeisT

Recovering. Muriel Rukeyser. CP-RukeM

Recovery. A. R. Ammons. CP-AmmoA

Recovery. Maya Angelou. SP-AngeM

Recovery. John Berryman. CP-BerrJ

Recovery. Rita Dove. SP-DoveR

Recovery. Mona Van Duyn. SP-VanDM

Recovery. Wyatt Prunty. SP-PrunW

Recovery. Eleanor Wilner. SP-WilnE

Recruit, The. A. E. Housman. CP-HousA

Rectitude. A. R. Ammons. CP-AmmoA

Rectitude, and the terrible upstanding member. Washington in Love. John Berryman. CP-BerrJ

Rector's Memory, A. Rudyard Kipling. CP-KiplR

Rector's pallid neighbor at The Firs, The. Villagers and Death, The. Robert Graves. CP-GravR

Recuerdo. Tennessee Williams. CP-WillT

Recuerdo. Edna St. Vincent Millay. CP-MillE

Recurrence. Dorothy Parker. CP-ParkD

Red. D. H. Lawrence. CP-LawrD

Red and White. Carl Sandburg. CP-SandC

Red and White Roses. Thomas Carew. CP-CareT

Red as the banner which enshrouds. Metacom. John Greenleaf Whittier. CP-WhitJ

Red barns and red heifers spot the green. Omaha. Carl Sandburg. CP-SandC

Red Bird. Pablo Neruda.
"Drunk as drunk on turpentine." SP-LoguC, *tr.* by Christopher Logue
"Lithe girl, brown girl." SP-LoguC, *tr.* by Christopher Logue
"My fingers have crept." SP-LoguC, *tr.* by Christopher Logue
"Sometimes it's like you're dead." SP-LoguC, *tr.* by Christopher Logue
"Steep gloom among pine trees." SP-LoguC, *tr.* by Christopher Logue
"That you may hear me, my words." SP-LoguC, *tr.* by Christopher Logue
"Tonight, I write sadly. Write." SP-LoguC, *tr.* by Christopher Logue
"Wings whirr by moon and midnight." SP-LoguC, *tr.* by Christopher Logue

Red Bird Tapestry, The. May Swenson. SP-SwenM

Red—Blaze—is the Morning, The. Emily Dickinson. CP-DickE

Red Branch, The. Donald Hall. CP-HallD

Red Brick and Brown Stone. James Schuyler. CP-SchuJ

Red brick monastery in, The. Semblables, The. William Carlos Williams. CP-WilW2

Red bridge fastening this city to the forest, A. Muriel Rukeyser. CP-RukeM

Red chair, blue chair, white chair, big chair, chair. To a Composer. Arthur Sze. SP-SzeA

Red cheeked boyfriends tenderly kiss me sweet mouthed. Tethnakin D'oligo Pideuis Fainom Alaia. Allen Ginsberg. CP-GinsA; SP-GinsA

Red Clay Blues. Langston Hughes. CP-HughL; CP-HughL1

Red Clay Speech. Robert Stock. SP-StocR

Red Coats & the Blue, The. George Meredith. CP-MerG2

Red Cotton Night-Cap Country. Robert Browning. CP-BroR2

Red cradle of the night. Portent. William Carlos Williams. CP-WilW1

Red Cross. Langston Hughes. CP-HughL; CP-HughL2

Red Cross Warrior, The. G. K. Chesterton. CP-ChesG

Red curtain moving in the still room, The. One Waking in a Northern Fall. Alan Dugan. CP-DugaA

Red Dance, The. Anne Sexton. CP-SextA

Red Dog. Rudyard Kipling. *Fr.* Second Jungle Book, The.

Red Dress, The. Dorothy Parker. CP-ParkD

Red drips from my chin where I have been eating. Fight. Carl Sandburg. CP-SandC

Red Dust. Philip Levine. SP-LeviP

Red Earl, and will ye take for guide. Ballad of the Red Earl, The. Rudyard Kipling. CP-KiplR

Red-eyed as Rikki-Tikki glows. Dishwasher as Absolution. Josephine Jacobsen. CP-JacoJ

Red face / Texas. Good Loser, The. Charles Bukowski. SP-BukC1

Red Fern, The. Wallace Stevens. CP-StevW; CP-StevWP

Red Fish-of-Bones, The. Charles Olson. CP-OlsoC

Red flower falls to its dim reflection, A. Kiss, A. D. H. Lawrence. CP-LawrD

Red fox, the vixen, The. Abnegation. Adrienne Rich. CP-RicAE; SP-RicA2

Red Front, The. Louis Aragon. CP-CummE

Red Geranium and Godly Mignonette. D. H. Lawrence. CP-LawrD

Red glow in the sky, the dead night underground, A. Aleksandr Aleksandrovich Blok. SP-BlokA, *tr.* by Peter France *and* Jon Stallworthy

Red gold of pools. Harvest Sunset. Carl Sandburg. CP-SandC

Red granite and black diorite, with the blue. Skeleton of the Future, The. Hugh MacDiarmid. SP-MacDH

Red grapes shielded from the sun by thick, velvety leaves. Vines with Their. Kenneth Patchen. CP-PatcK

Red Guards battling country workers. Returning North of Vortex. Allen Ginsberg. CP-GinsA

Red hair / real. Red Up and Down. Charles Bukowski. SP-BukC1

Red Hanrahan's Song about Ireland. William Butler Yeats. CP-YeatW

Red-Headed Resstaurant Cashier. Carl Sandburg. CP-SandC

Red-Herring. D. H. Lawrence. CP-LawrD

Red Hook: December. George Oppen. CP-OppGN

Red-Hot Fruit. Jaroslav Seifert. SP-SeifJ, *tr.* by Ewald Osers

Red-hot needle, A. Hornet. Anne Sexton. CP-SextA; SP-SextA

Red House, The. W. S. Merwin. SP-MerwWF

Red Huitzilopochtli / Keeps day and night apart. Huitzilopochtli's Watch. D. H. Lawrence. CP-LawrD

Red is the Alabama road. Ballad of Ozie Powell. Langston Hughes. CP-HughL; CP-HughL1

Red Jacket (from Aloft). Walt Whitman. CP-WhitW

Red Jacket's Grave. James Wright. CP-WrigJ

Red leaf. And beside it, a red leaf alive. Salamander. Muriel Rukeyser. CP-RukeM

Red Leaves take the Green Leaves place, The. Emily Dickinson. SP-DickE

Red Lily, The. William Carlos Williams. CP-WilW1

Red lily, if one day, The. Eugenio Montale. CP-MontE, *tr.* by Jonathan Galassi

Red lips are not so red. Greater Love. Wilfred Owen. CP-OwenW

Red lips, green eyes, black hair. Reconstruction. Robert Stock. SP-StocR

Red Loves Kit. Wallace Stevens. CP-StevWP

Red Mallows. Charles Olson. CP-OlsoC

Red Man told me, "Your father." Dance, of the Grizzly Bear, The. Charles Olson. CP-OlsoC

Red Maple Leaves. Kenneth Rexroth. CP-RexrK

Red mills and farms clumped soothingly here and there. Battlefield, A. Donald Davie. CP-DaviDC

Red moon hung above the pines that night, A. Travelling South. John Berryman. CP-BerrJ

Red Moon-Rise. D. H. Lawrence. CP-LawrD

Red Mountain. Robinson Jeffers. CP-JefR2

Red oak leaves rustle in the wind. Leaves of a Dream Are the Leaves of an Onion, The. Arthur Sze. SP-SzeA

Red Octopus. Arthur Sze. SP-SzeA

Red Pagoda. Yusef Komunyakaa. CP-KomuY

Red paper box, The. Composition. William Carlos Williams. CP-WilW1

Red-rag and pink-flag. E. E. Cummings. CP-CummF; SP-CummE

Red rain spatter under the redhaw, The. Redhaw Rain. Carl Sandburg. CP-SandC

Red, Red Rose, A. Robert Burns. CP-BurnR

Red Riding-Hood. James Whitcomb Riley. CP-RileJ

Red-Riding Hood. Anne Sexton. CP-SextA

Red Riding-Hood. John Greenleaf Whittier. CP-WhitJ

Red River Voyageur, The. John Greenleaf Whittier. CP-WhitJ

Red Rock of Utah. Donald Davie. CP-DaviDC

Red rose blooms, The. Hafiz. CP-EmerR Fr. Odes.

Red Rose, proud Rose, sad Rose of all my days! To the Rose upon the Rood of Time. William Butler Yeats. CP-YeatW

Red Roses. Langston Hughes. CP-HughL; CP-HughL1

Red Roses. Anne Sexton. CP-SextA

Red Roses for Bronze. "H. D." CP-DoolH

Red Scabies on the Skin. Smoke Rolling Down Street. Allen Ginsberg. CP-GinsA

Red Sea, The. G. K. Chesterton. CP-ChesG

"Red Sea," indeed! Talk not to me. Emily Dickinson. CP-DickE

Red Shift. Ted Berrigan. SP-BerrT

Red Shirt. Jelaluddin Rumi.

Red Shirt, A. Margaret Atwood. SP-AtwM2

Red shirt for anarchy, A. Fanny Howe. SP-HoweF Fr. O'Clock.

Red Shoes, The. Anne Sexton. CP-SextA

Red Shower, The. Robert Graves. CP-GravR

Red Silk Stockings. Langston Hughes. CP HughL; CP-HughL1

Red Son, The. Carl Sandburg. CP-SandC

Red Stains. Allen Tate. CP-TateA

Red sunset. Yannis Ritsos. SP-RitsY Fr. So?

Red-Tail Hawk and Pyre of Youth. Robert Penn Warren. CP-WarrR

Red-Tailed Hawk. Helen Pinkerton. CP-PinkH

Red teat of the sun. Harlequin. Federico García Lorca. CP-GarcF, tr. by Alan S. Trueblood Fr. Theories.

Red tulips / living into their death. Tulips, The. Denise Levertov. SP-LeveDP; SP-LeveDS

Red Up and Down. Charles Bukowski. SP-BukC1

Red Wheelbarrow, The. William Carlos Williams. CP-WilW1

Red Wine and Yellow Hair. Kenneth Patchen. CP-PatcK

Red wine / from the / Black Sea. Conversation in Moscow. Denise Levertov. SP-LeveDL

Red-Wing Blackbird, The. William Carlos Williams. CP-WilW2

Red-winged Blackbird. Peter Blue Cloud. SP-BlueP

Red-winged blackbird, The. Bay Bank. A. R. Ammons. CP-AmmoA

Red Wolf, The. D. H. Lawrence. CP-LawrD

Red Wolf came, and Passenger Pigeon. Roll Call. Wendell Phillips Stafford. SP-StafWW

Red woman, / (Keep Christ out). Navajo. William Carlos Williams. CP-WilW2

Red X, correction. Red check, yes. Fanny Howe. SP-HoweF Fr. Vineyard, The.

Redbreast Chasing the Butterfly, The. William Wordsworth. CP-WorW1

Redbreast, early in the morning. Emily Jane Brontë. CP-BronE

Redbreast, The [Suggested in a Westmoreland Cottage]. William Wordsworth. CP-WorW2

Redeem the surrogate goodbyes. Da Tagte Es. Samuel Beckett. CP-BeckS

Redeemed, The. Jones Very. CP-VeryJ

Redeemer, A. Robinson Jeffers. CP-JefR1

Redeeming the Time. Christina Georgina Rossetti. CP-RosC2

Redeeming the Time. Jones Very. CP-VeryJ

Redemption. Richard Eberhart. CP-EberR

Redemption. George Herbert. CP-HerbG

Redeployment. Howard Nemerov. CP-NemeH

Redhaw Rain. Carl Sandburg. CP-SandC

Rediscovery. Thomas McGrath. SP-McGrT

Redivivus. Ezra Pound. CP-PoEar

Redondillas, or Something of That Sort. Ezra Pound. CP-PoEar

Redoubted knights, and honorable Dames. Book 3, Canto 9. Edmund Spenser. CP-Spens Fr. Faerie Queene, The.

Redoutit roy, your ragment I have red. Answer to the Kingis Flyting, The. Sir David Lyndsay. SP-LyndD

Redshifting Web, The. Arthur Sze. SP-SzeA

Reduced Sentence, A. Robert Graves. CP-GravR

Reduced to This. Thomas Merton. CP-MertT

Redwing. Tess Gallagher. SP-GallT

Reed, A. Elizabeth Barrett Browning. CP-BroEB

Reed Boat, A. Yusef Komunyakaa. CP-KomuY

Reed Flute's Song, The. Jelaluddin Rumi. SP-Rumi, tr. by Coleman Barks

Reed in voice and gesture, A. Tree of Song. Federico García Lorca. CP-GarcF, tr. by Alan S. Trueblood Fr. Games.

Reed, / slashed and torn. Sea Lily. "H. D." CP-DoolH

Reed that softly, The. Eugenio Montale. CP-MontE, tr. by Jonathan Galassi

Reedbeds of the Hackensack, The. Amy Clampitt. CP-ClamA

Reeds. Charles Tomlinson. CP-TomlC

Reeds give, The. Small Song. A. R. Ammons. CP-AmmoA

Reeds of Runnymede, The. Rudyard Kipling. CP-KiplR

Reef Fisher, The. Archibald MacLeish. CP-MacLA

Reef Mantra. Allen Ginsberg. SP-GinsA

Reel. John Updike. CP-UpdiJ

Reel o' Stumpie, The. Robert Burns. CP-BurnR

Reference Back. Philip Larkin. See Referred Back

Referendum. Adam Zagajewski. SP-ZagaA, tr. by Clare Cavanagh

Referred Back. Philip Larkin. CP-LarkP

(Reference Back.) CP-LarkP

Refinery, The. Robert Pinsky. CP-PinsR

Refining Mallarmé at last destroyed. Readings in French. Thom Gunn. CP-GunnT

Reflected in rose gleams on "crystal walls." On Erastus Salisbury Field's The Israelites Crossing the Red Sea (1863?). Helen Pinkerton. CP-PinkH

Reflected is / the real, The. Sesame. Federico García Lorca. CP-GarcF, tr. by Jerome Rothenberg Fr. Moments of Song.

Reflecting Trees of Being and Not Being, The. Kenneth Rexroth. CP-RexrK

Reflection. Federico García Lorca. CP-GarcF, tr. by Jerome Rothenberg Fr. Mirror Suite.

Reflection. Ezra Pound. CP-PoEar

Reflection. Christina Georgina Rossetti. CP-RosC3

Reflection by a Mailbox. Stanley Kunitz. CP-KunSC

Reflection of the Fallibility of Nemesis. Ogden Nash. CP-NashO

Reflection On a Wicked World. Ogden Nash. CP-NashO

Reflection on Babies. Ogden Nash. CP-NashO

Reflection on Caution. Ogden Nash. CP-NashO

Reflection on Ingenuity. Ogden Nash. CP-NashO

Reflection on the Foregoing Ode. William Cowper. CP-CowpW

Reflection on the Passage of Time, Its Inevitability and Its Quirks. Ogden Nash. CP-NashO

Reflections. Federico García Lorca. CP-GarcF, tr. by Jerome Rothenberg Fr. In the Forest of the Lunar Grapefruits.

Reflections. Robert Creeley. SP-CreeR

Reflections. Yusef Komunyakaa. CP-KomuY

Reflections. Louis MacNeice. CP-MacNL

Reflections. Walter De la Mare. CP-DeLaW

Reflections. Charles Tomlinson. CP-TomlC

Reflections at Lake Louise. Allen Ginsberg. CP-GinsA

Reflections in a Forest. W. H. Auden. CP-AudeW

Reflections in an Old House. Allen Tate. CP-TateA

Reflections in Sleepy Eye. Allen Ginsberg. CP-GinsA

Reflections in the forest of the dying child, The. 1938: Tales from the Vienna Woods. Randall Jarrell. CP-JarrR

Reflections On a Centaur. Marya Alexandrovna Zaturenska. SP-ZatuM

Reflections on Deafness. Donald Davie. CP-DaviDC

Reflections on Having Left a Place of Retirement. Samuel Taylor Coleridge. CP-ColeS; MW-ColeS

Reflections on Ice-breaking. Ogden Nash. CP-NashO

Reflections on Milkweed. Peter Blue Cloud. SP-BlueP

Reflections on Reading a Life of Dickens. Robert Browning. CP-BroR2

Reflections on the History of Nations. Jones Very. CP-VeryJ

Reflections on the St. Lawrence Seaway. Peter Blue Cloud. SP-BlueP

Reflections on the Vernacular. Ogden Nash. CP-NashO

Reflective. A. R. Ammons. CP-AmmoA

Reflex, A. Robert Frost. CP-FrosR

Reflexion of a Novelist. Howard Nemerov. CP-NemeH

Reflexions on suicide, & on my father, possess me. Of Suicide. John Berryman.

CP-BerrJ

Reflexions on the Seizure of the Suez, and on a Proposal to Line the Banks of That Canal with Billboard Advertisements. Howard Nemerov. CP-NemeH

Reflexive. Hayden Carruth. CP-CarHS

Reformation. Yannis Ritsos. SP-RitsY, *tr. by* Kimon Friar

Reformer, The. John Greenleaf Whittier. CP-WhitJ

Reformers, The. Rudyard Kipling. CP-KiplR

Refrain. Rita Dove. SP-DoveR

Refrain. Allen Ginsberg. CP-GinsA

Refrain, echoing. Minstrels. Eugenio Montale. CP-MontE, *tr. by* Jonathan Galassi

Refrains. Richard Eberhart. CP-EberR

Refreshment. Gabriela Mistral. SP-MistG, *tr. by* Maria Giachetti [*or* Jacketti]

Refrigerator falls silent, The. Night in the Kitchen. Adrienne Rich. CP-RicAE

Refrigerator, 1957. Thomas Lux. SP-LuxT

Refuge, Serpent-Riders. C. K. Williams. CP-WillC

Refugee. Langston Hughes. CP-HughL; CP-HughL2

Refugee in America. Langston Hughes. CP-HughL2
(Words Like Freedom.) CP-HughL; CP-HughL3

Refugee road, refugee road. Song of the Refugee Road. Langston Hughes. CP-HughL; CP-HughL3

Refugees. Louis MacNeice. CP-MacNL

Refugees. Adam Zagajewski. SP-ZagaA, *tr. by* Clare Cavanagh

Refugees, The. Randall Jarrell. CP-JarrR

Refusal. Maya Angelou. SP-AngeM

Refusal, A. Thomas Hardy. CP-HardT

Refusal, The. James Wright. CP-WrigJ

Refusal of a Kindness Offered. Howard Nemerov. CP-NemeH

Refusal to Mourn, A. Derek Mahon. CP-MahoD

Refusal to Mourn the Death, by Fire, of a Child in London, A. Dylan Thomas. CP-ThomD

Refuse Man, The. David Ignatow. SP-IgnaD

Refused Friendship. D. H. Lawrence. CP-LawrD

Refusing Silence. Tess Gallagher. SP-GallT

Refutation. G. K. Chesterton. CP-ChesG

Regard Me. Charles Bukowski. SP-BukC2

Regard that white gallant. Dance of the Moon in Santiago. Federico García Lorca. SP-GarcF, *tr. by* Norman Thomas Di Giovanni

Regard the capture here, O Janus-faced. Recitative. Hart Crane. CP-CranH

Regardin' Terry Hut. James Whitcomb Riley. CP-RileJ

Regarding Chainsaws. Hayden Carruth. CP-CarHS

Regarding Wave. Gary Snyder. CP-SnydG

Regards to Mr. Glover. Lorine Niedecker. CP-NiedL

Regatta, The. Richard Wilbur. CP-WilbR

Regeneration, The. Jay Wright. SP-WrigJ

Regent's Park Sonnets, The. Marilyn Hacker. SP-HackM

Regiment of Pleasure, The. Constantine P. Cavafy. CP-CavaC, *tr. by* Theoharis Constantine Theoharis

Regina Angelorum. G. K. Chesterton. CP-ChesG

Region November, The. Wallace Stevens. CP-StevWP

Regression Spoiles Resolution. Robert Herrick. CP-HerrR

Regret, The. Thomas Merton. CP-MertT

Regret Not Me. Thomas Hardy. CP-HardT

Regret of War Ways. Laura Riding Jackson. CP-RidiL

Regretfully, I proffer my excuses. Lines Declining a Transatlantic Dinner Invitation. Marilyn Hacker. SP-HackM

Regrets After Death. Ivor Gurney. SP-GurnI

Regulars, The. C. K. Williams. CP-WillC; SP-WillC

Rehearsal. Rae Armantrout. SP-ArmaA

Rehearsal, The. Stevie Smith. CP-SmitS

Rehearsal, The. Arthur Sze. SP-SzeA

Rehearsal to Ourselves. Emily Dickinson. CP-DickE

Rehearse to me, ye sacred sisters nine. Teares of the Muses, The. Edmund Spenser. CP-Spens

Reincarnation (I) ["Still, passed through the spokes of an old wheel, on and around"]. James Dickey. CP-DickJ

Reincarnation (II). James Dickey. CP-DickJ

Reincarnation of Captain Cook, The. Margaret Atwood. SP-AtwM1

Reincarnations. "Rubén Dario." SP-DariR, *tr. by* Alberto Acereda *and* Will Derusha

Reindeer and Engine. Josephine Jacobsen. CP-JacoJ

Reiteration, The. Robert Graves. CP-GravR

Reject me not if I should say to you. Love Song, A: "Reject me not if I should say to you." D. H. Lawrence. CP-LawrD

Reject the complicated life. From Father to Son. Rainer Maria Rilke. CP-RilkFr, *tr. by* A. Poulin, Jr.

Rejected Member's Wife, The. Thomas Hardy. CP-HardT

Rejoice a child is born a son is given. Unto you is born a Saviour. Jones Very. CP-VeryJ

Rejoice in God, ye saints above. Bible, *O.T. See* Rejoice in the Lord, O ye righteous: for praise is comely for the upright

Rejoice in the Abyss. Stephen Spender. CP-SpenS

Rejoice in the clefts of Gehenna. Drama of Exile, A. Elizabeth Barrett Browning. CP-BroEB

Rejoice in the Lord, O ye righteous: for praise is comely for the upright. Psalm 33: "Rejoice in the Lord, O ye righteous: for praise is comely for the upright." Bible, *O.T.* SP-SmarC *Fr.* Psalms.

Rejoice, Liars. Laura Riding Jackson. CP-RidiL

Rejoice, mackerel, and whosoever is of the fish in the deep. Verse from Defensio Secunda. John Milton. CP-MiltJ

Rejoice, the witch of truth has perished. Rejoice, Liars. Laura Riding Jackson. CP-RidiL

Rejoice with Me. Christina Georgina Rossetti. CP-RosC2

Rejoice ye weary! ye whose spirits mourn. Soul's Rest, The. Jones Very. CP-VeryJ

Rejoice ye weary! ye whose spirits mourn! Weary and Heavy Laden, The. Jones Very. CP-VeryJ

Rejoicing with Henry. Maxine W. Kumin. SP-KumiM

Rejoinder to a Critic. Donald Davie. CP-DaviDC

Rejoining Time after fifty years. Seth Thomas: A Love Poem. Denise Levertov. SP-LeveDL

Relation of Art and Life, A. Howard Nemerov. CP-NemeH

Relation of the Late Royall Entertainment Given by the Right Honourable the Lord *Knowles*, at *Cawsome*-House neere *Redding*, A. Thomas Campion. CP-CampT

Relation of the Unrelated, The. Yannis Ritsos. SP-RitsY, *tr. by* Kimon Friar

Relations. John Berryman. CP-BerrJ

Relationships. Mona Van Duyn. SP-VanDM

Relative and an Absolute, A. Mona Van Duyn. SP-VanDM

Relative to cost, the high figures / of production. Surf: An Elegy, The. Robert Creeley. CP-CreeR

Relatives. John Updike. CP-UpdiJ

Relatives; A Hate Song. Dorothy Parker. CP-ParkD

Relativity. Yehuda Amichai. SP-AmicY, *tr. by* Chana Bloch

Relativity. D. H. Lawrence. CP-LawrD

Relaxing below Cold Cliff. Han-shan. CP-ColdM, *tr. by* Red Pine

Relay Tower, The. Jaroslav Seifert. SP-SeifJ, *tr. by* Ewald Osers

Relearning the Alphabet. Denise Levertov. SP-LeveDS

Relearning the Language of April. Maxine W. Kumin. SP-KumiM

Release. D. H. Lawrence. CP-LawrD

Release, The. Thom Gunn. CP-GunnT

Release her now. Yehuda Amichai. SP-AmicYL, *tr. by* Benjamin Harshav *and* Barbara Harshav

Release of Demonic Energies in the name of, The. Spel Against Demons. Gary Snyder. CP-SnydG

Release Time. Audre Lorde. SP-LordA

Relentless confetti of dollars!, The. Twilight Sustenance Hiatus. James Tate. SP-TateJ

Relentless man loved France, A. Is There Any Easy Road to Freedom? Carl Sandburg. CP-SandC

Relevant Is Different Points on the Circle. Audre Lorde. SP-LordA

Relic. Ted Hughes. SP-HughTN

Relic, The. John Donne. CP-DonnJ; MW-DonnJ

Relic, The. John Greenleaf Whittier. CP-WhitJ

Relic of Memory. Seamus Heaney. SP-HeanSO

Relics. Louis MacNeice. CP-MacNL

Relief. Langston Hughes. CP-HughL; CP-HughL3

Relief. Jones Very. CP-VeryJ

Relieved, I let the book fall behind a stone. Depressed by a Book of Bad Poetry, I Walk toward an Unused Pasture and Invite the Insects to Join Me. James Wright. CP-WrigJ

Religio Laici. John Dryden. CP-DryJ2; SP-DrydJ

Religion. Paul Laurence Dunbar. CP-DunbP

Religion. D. H. Lawrence. CP-LawrD

Religion. Jones Very. CP-VeryJ

Religion Back Home. William Stafford. SP-StafWW

Religion? Huh! Whenever I hear the word. Two Memories. Hugh MacDiarmid. SP-MacDH

Religion Is That I Love You. Kenneth Patchen. CP-PatcK

Religion of My Time, The. Pier Paolo Pasolini. SP-PasoP, *tr. by* Norman MacAfee *and* Luciano Martinengo

'Religion's never mentioned here,' of course. Seamus Heaney. SP-HeanSO *Fr.* Whatever You Say Say Nothing.

Religious Articles. Donald Hall. CP-HallD

Religious faith is a most filling vapor. Innate Helium. Robert Frost. CP-FrosR

Religious Man, A. Stevie Smith. CP-SmitS

Religious Musings. Samuel Taylor Coleridge. CP-ColeS; MW-ColeS

Religious Question. Alan Dugan. CP-DugaA

Reliquary. Adrienne Rich. CP-RicAE

Reluctance. Paul Laurence Dunbar. CP-DunbP

Reluctance. Robert Frost. CP-FrosR

Reluctant call it was; the rite delayed. Upon the Late General Fast. March, 1832. William Wordsworth. CP-WorW2

Reluctant Confession. Thomas Hardy. CP-HardT

Reluctant whispers of kissed lips. Jaroslav Seifert. SP-SeifJ, *tr.* by Ewald Osers

Reluctantly, my son goes with me. Ask Him. Raymond Carver. CP-CarvR

REM Sleep. William Meredith. SP-MereW

Remark for Historians. Robert Penn Warren. CP-WarrR

Remarked Robinson Jefferson. E. E. Cummings. CP-CummE

Remarks on My Character. William Stafford. SP-StafWW

Rembrandt. Robert Lowell. CP-LoweR

Rembrandt to Rembrandt. Edwin Arlington Robinson. CP-RobiE

Rembrandt's Old Woman Cutting Her Nails. George Oppen. CP-OppGN

Remediae Amoris. Ovid.
   "At busy hearts in vain love's arrows fly." CP-JohnS
   "Man will surely fail who dares delay, The." CP-JohnS
   "Our bane and physic the same earth bestows." CP-JohnS
   "While furie gallops on the way." CP-RaleW

Remedies, Maladies, Reasons. Mona Van Duyn. SP-VanDM

Remember. Robert Creeley. SP-CreeR

Remember? Alice Walker. CP-WalkA

Remember all those renowned generations. Three Marching Songs. William Butler Yeats. CP-YeatW

Remember, and already the lapse in. Croce e Delizia al Cor. Tess Gallagher. SP-GallT

Remember, Body. Constantine P. Cavafy. CP-CavaC, *tr.* by Theoharis Constantine Theoharis

Remember Him Whom Passion's Power. Lord Byron. CP-Byron

Remember how bright it is. Artist, Come Home. William Stafford. SP-StafWW

Remember how close we sat in Sifnos having dinner by the water! Olga Broumas. SP-BrouO *Fr.* Black Holes, Black Stockings.

Remember how Daylight Saving used to end. Old Days, The. Howard Nemerov. CP-NemeH

Remember how / Twenty-five years ago in Cincinnati. Remembering Cincinnati, 1953. Stephen Spender. CP-SpenS

Remember how unimportant. Milkweed. Philip Levine. SP-LeviP

Remember, if I claim too much of you. By Way of Remembrance. Christina Georgina Rossetti. CP-RosC3

Remember kissing, haste of embrace. Eventual Love. Laura Riding Jackson. CP-RidiL

Remember, master, I asked you / to take this child Godfrey, my kinsman. News from the School at Chartres. Thomas Merton. CP-MertT

Remember [Me]. Christina Georgina Rossetti. CP-RosC1

Remember me? Remember? Alice Walker. CP-WalkA

Remember me? I was the one. Hood. C. K. Williams. CP-WillC; SP-WillC

"Remember me" implored the Thief! Emily Dickinson. CP-DickE

Remember me when I am gone away. Remember [Me]. Christina Georgina Rossetti. CP-RosC1

Remember: not making. Walter Armistead. James Dickey. CP-DickJ

Remember now, my Love, what piteous thing. Carrion, A. Charles Baudelaire. CP-TateA, *tr.* by Allen Tate

Remember now there were others before this. From the Paris Commune to the Kronstadt Rebellion. Kenneth Rexroth. CP-RexrK

Remember on our far-flung fronts. Fourth of July Thought. Langston Hughes. CP-HughL; CP-HughL3

Remember that leader with the funny mustache? Explaining the Big One. William Stafford. SP-StafWW

Remember that person you thought you were? That summer. Sure You Do. William Stafford. SP-StafWW

Remember the line in the sand? Entering History. William Stafford. SP-StafWW

Remember the 1340s? We were doing a dance called the Catapult. Nostalgia. Billy Collins. SP-CollB

Remember the way you. Flower, The. Robert Creeley. CP-CreeR

Remember the wise philosophers. Philosophy. Jaroslav Seifert. SP-SeifJ, *tr.* by Ewald Osers

Remember Thee! Remember Thee! Lord Byron. CP-Byron

Remember those awful parties. Brighton Beach. Derek Mahon. CP-MahoD

Remember those wingovers and loops and spins? Dream of Flying Comes of Age, The. Howard Nemerov. CP-NemeH

Remember what a night of storm. George Meredith. CP-MerG2

Remember, when the nurses lose you. Standing Invitation, A. G. K. Chesterton. CP-ChesG

Remember when you were the first one awake, the first. Little Girl Wakes Early.

Robert Penn Warren. CP-WarrR

Rememberance for a great man is this. In a Back Alley. Carl Sandburg. CP-SandC

Remembered. Paul Laurence Dunbar. CP-DunbP

Remembered as octagonal, dark-panelled. Room 28. John Updike. CP-UpdiJ

Remembered Women. Carl Sandburg. CP-SandC

Remembering. Maya Angelou. SP-AngeM

Remembering. Denise Levertov. SP-LeveDP

Remembering. William Stafford. SP-StafW; SP-StafWW

Remembering a Boatman. W. S. Merwin. SP-MerwWF

Remembering an Account Executive. Alan Dugan. CP-DugaA

Remembering Brother Bob. William Stafford. SP-StafW; SP-StafWW

Remembering Cincinnati, 1953. Stephen Spender. CP-SpenS

Remembering glitter on the first river. Shuttles, The. W. S. Merwin. SP-MerwWF

Remembering Greece. Amy Clampitt. CP-ClamA

Remembering how thou didst beguile. Elegy Written in the Same Place upon the Same Occasion. William Wordsworth. CP-WorW1; MW-WorW

Remembering Loves and Deaths. Thomas McGrath. SP-McGrT

Remembering movies love. Song: Remembering Movies. Muriel Rukeyser. CP-RukeM

Remembering Old Wars. Thomas Kinsella. CP-KinsT

Remembering Robert Lowell. William Meredith. SP-MereW

Remembering Spello, Sitting Outside in Prampolini's Garden. Charles Wright. SP-WrigCN

Remembering Teheran. Ted Hughes. SP-HughTN

Remembering the Birth of Lucifer. Lucille Clifton. SP-ClifL

Remembering the Children of Auschwitz. Thomas McGrath. SP-McGrT

Remembering the Man. Miller Williams. CP-WillM

Remembering the past. What the Bones Know. Carolyn Kizer. CP-KizeC

Remembering the Strait of Belle Isle or. Large Bad Picture. Elizabeth Bishop. CP-BishE

Remembering the 'Thirties. Donald Davie. CP-DaviDC

Remembering Walter. Miller Williams. CP-WillM

Remembering Williams. Charles Tomlinson. CP-TomlC

Remember'st thou. Hungarian Air. George Meredith. CP-MerG2

Remembrance. Maya Angelou. SP-AngeM

Remembrance. Emily Jane Brontë. CP-BronE
   (R. Alcona to J. Brenzaida.) CP-BronE

Remembrance. Lord Byron. CP-Byron

Remembrance. Paul Celan. SP-CelaP, *tr.* by John Felstiner

Remembrance. Langston Hughes. CP-HughL; CP-HughL2

Remembrance. James Laughlin. CP-LaugJ

Remembrance. Walter De la Mare. CP-DeLaW

Remembrance. Yannis Ritsos. SP-RitsY, *tr.* by Kimon Friar

Remembrance. Percy Bysshe Shelley. CP-ShelP

Remembrance. John Greenleaf Whittier. CP-WhitJ

Remembrance has a Rear and Front. Emily Dickinson. CP-DickE

Remembrance of Belgian Friends. Stéphane Mallarmé. CP-MallS, *tr.* by Henry Weinfield

Remembrance of Collins, Composed upon the Thames near Richmond. William Wordsworth. CP-WorW1

Remembrance of My Forgotten Skinniness. Andrei Codrescu. SP-CodrA

Remembrances. Yannis Ritsos. SP-RitsY *Fr.* Monovasia.

Remembrances of Senility. Arthur Rimbaud. CP-RimbA

Remind me again—together we. Our Story. William Stafford. SP-StafWW

Remind Me Not, Remind Me Not. Lord Byron. CP-Byron

Reminded. Ambrose Bierce. SP-BierA

Reminded of Bougainville. Donald Davie. CP-DaviDC

Reminder. D. H. Lawrence. CP-LawrD

Reminder, The. Thomas Hardy. CP-HardT

Reminder, The. Theodore Roethke. CP-RoetT

Reminds me of the sense. Your Love. James Laughlin. CP-LaugJ

Reminiscence. Yusef Komunyakaa. CP-KomuY

Reminiscence. Stéphane Mallarmé. CP-MallS, *tr.* by Henry Weinfield

Reminiscences of a Dancing Man. Thomas Hardy. CP-HardT

Reminiscent of a Wave At the Curl. Marianne Craig Moore. CP-MoorM

Reminiscent Reflection. Ogden Nash. CP-NashO

Remnant of some lost orchard. Half-Dead Black Cherry Tree across the Road from My Childhood House, A. Gregory Orr. SP-OrrG

Remnant Water. James Dickey. CP-DickJ

Remnants of hearing, of seeing, in. Paul Celan. SP-CelaP, *tr.* by John Felstiner

Remonstrance, The. Walter De la Mare. CP-DeLaW

Remora. James Merrill. SP-MerrJ

Remorse. Samuel Taylor Coleridge.
   Invocation, An: "Hear, sweet spirit, hear the spell." CP-ColeS

Remorse. Jorge Luis Borges. SP-BorgJ, *tr.* by Willis Barnstone

Remorse. Robert Burns. CP-BurnR

Remorse. Yannis Ritsos. SP-RitsY, *tr. by* Kimon Friar

Remorse. Carl Sandburg. CP-SandC

Remorse for Any Death. Jorge Luis Borges. SP-BorgJ, *tr. by* W. S. Merwin

Remorse for Intemperate Speech. William Butler Yeats. CP-YeatW

Remorse for Time, The. Howard Nemerov. CP-NemeH

Remorse—is Memory—awake. Emily Dickinson. CP-DickE

Remote control factors. For Rene Ricard. Robert Creeley. SP-CreeR

Remote House. Hans Magnus Enzensberger. SP-EnzeH, *tr. by* Michael Hamburger

Remote, it lives now in a tiny glass. Looking Glass. Thom Gunn. CP-GunnT

Remote sky, prolonged to the sea's brim, A. For "Ruggiero and Angelica" by Ingres. Dante Gabriel Rossetti. CW-RossD

Removal, The. W. S. Merwin. SP-MerwW

Removal, The. Jones Very. CP-VeryJ

Remove away that blackning church. Ancient Proverb, An. William Blake. CP-BlakW

Remove—from Accident of Loss. Emily Dickinson. CP-DickE

Remove me from this land of slaves. Ireland. Jonathan Swift. CP-SwifJ

Removing the Plate of the Pump on the Hydraulic System of the Backhoe. Gary Snyder. CP-SnydG

Renaissance. Hayden Carruth. CP-CarHS

Renaissance. D. H. Lawrence. *See* Renascence

Renaissance. Yannis Ritsos. SP-RitsY, *tr. by* Kimon Friar

Renaming the Kings. Philip Levine. SP-LeviP

Renascence. Edna St. Vincent Millay. CP-MillE

Renascence. D. H. Lawrence. CP-LawrD

(Renaissance.) CP-LawrD

Rencontres Funestes. Stevie Smith. CP-SmitS

Rend, rend thine hair, Cassandra: he will go. Cassandra. Dante Gabriel Rossetti. CW-RossD

Rendezvous. Yusef Komunyakaa. CP-KomuY

Rendezvous. Edna St. Vincent Millay. CP-MillE

Rendezvous. William Carlos Williams. CP-WilW1

Rendition, The. John Greenleaf Whittier. CP-WhitJ

Renegade. Eleanor Wilner. SP-WilnE

Renewal. Stéphane Mallarmé. CP-MallS, *tr. by* Henry Weinfield

Renewal, A. James Merrill. SP-MerrJ

Renewal, The. Theodore Roethke. CP-RoetT

Renga: "We hunger for the iridescent shine of an abalone shell." Arthur Sze. SP-SzeA

Renoir, whose painting I don't much like. Quotations. Charles Wright. SP-WrigCN

Renovated Temple, The. Archibald MacLeish. CP-MacLA

Renovating. A. R. Ammons. CP-AmmoA

Renownit, ryall, right reuerend and serene. William Dunbar. CP-DunbW

Rent. Jane Cooper. CP-CoopJ

Rent in the Screen, The. Howard Nemerov. CP-NemeH

Rent man knocked, The. Madam and the Rent Man. Langston Hughes. CP-HughL; CP-HughL2

Rent-Party Shout: For a Lady Dancer. Langston Hughes. CP-HughL; CP-HughL1

Rented Room, The. Tennessee Williams. CP-WillT

Rentrer / À la nuit. Samuel Beckett. CP-BeckS

Renunciation. Emily Dickinson. CP-DickE

Renunciation. Dorothy Parker. CP-ParkD

Renunciation—is a piercing Virtue. Emily Dickinson. CP-DickE

Renunciation of the Desert Primrose, A. Norman Dubie. CP-DubiN

Reparation. G. K. Chesterton. CP-ChesG

Repealer, The: "You're Too Wild." Alan Dugan. CP-DugaA

Repeat and repeat till they say what you. Brainwashing. Carl Sandburg. CP-SandC

Repeat that, repeat. Cuckoo, The. Gerard Manley Hopkins. CP-HopkG

Repeat That, Repeat. Gerard Manley Hopkins. *See* Cuckoo, The

Repeated Journey, The. Thomas McGrath. SP-McGrT

Repeated Shapes, The. Donald Hall. CP-HallD

Repeating fly, blueback, thumbthick—so gross, A. Harriet. Robert Lowell. SP-LoweR

Repent. Maxine W. Kumin. SP-KumiM

Repent for the kingdom of Heaven is at hand. Jones Very. CP-VeryJ

Repent, repent, the day of wrath is near! Repent for the kingdom of Heaven is at hand. Jones Very. CP-VeryJ

Repentance. George Herbert. CP-HerbG

Repentance; A Pastoral Ballad. William Wordsworth. CP-WorW1

Repentance of Lady T, The. Stevie Smith. CP-SmitS

Repetition of the name made known, The. Martha, Martha. Robert Herrick. CP-HerrR

Repetitions. Carl Sandburg. CP-SandC

Repetitions—he says—repetitions without end;—what fatigue, my God. Talos. Yannis Ritsos. SP-RitsY, *tr. by* N. C. Germanacos

Repetitions of a Young Captain. Wallace Stevens. CP-StevW; CP-StevWP

Rephan. Robert Browning. CP-BroR2

Repining. Christina Georgina Rossetti. CP-RosC3

Replacing the lid of air. Thinking of the Goldfish. Paul Muldoon. CP-MuldP

Repletion. Robert Herrick. CP-HerrR

Replica. Federico García Lorca. CP-GarcF, *tr. by* Jerome Rothenberg *Fr.* Mirror Suite.

Replies to Challenges to Rhyme. Robert Browning. CP-BroR2

Reply. Federico García Lorca. CP-GarcF, *tr. by* Jerome Rothenberg *Fr.* Newton.

Reply, A. David Ignatow. SP-IgnaD

Reply, The. Allen Ginsberg. CP-GinsA

Reply, The. Theodore Roethke. CP-RoetT

Reply of the County of Surrey to the Poet's Pathetic Address in Dispraise of Jean. George Meredith. CP-MerG2

Reply to a Lady Editor. Theodore Roethke. CP-RoetT

Reply to Censure. Theodore Roethke. CP-RoetT

Reply to Impromptu Verses by Baretti, A. Samuel Johnson. *See* Verses in Baretti's Commonplace Book

Reply to Mr. Wordsworth. Archibald MacLeish. CP-MacLA

Reply to Papini. Wallace Stevens. CP-StevW; CP-StevWP

Reply to Robert Burns. Robert Burns. CP-BurnR

Reply to S. K. John Ciardi. CP-CiarJ

Reply to Some Verses of J.M.B. Pigot, Esq., on the Cruelty of His Mistress. Lord Byron. CP-Byron

Reply to Wang Wei. Charles Wright. SP-WrigCN

Replying to Reviewers. Donald Davie. CP-DaviDC

Report. Czeslaw Milosz. CP-MiloCN, *tr. by* Robert Hass

Report, A. A. K. Ramanujan. CP-RamaA

Report from a Far Place. William Stafford. SP-StafWW

Report from the angel of eden. Lucille Clifton. SP-ClifL

Report from the Lucky Country. Yusef Komunyakaa. CP-KomuY

Report from the Skull's Diorama. Yusef Komunyakaa. CP-KomuY

Report of an Adjudged Case. William Cowper. CP-CowpW

Report of Health. John Updike. CP-UpdiJ

Report on a Happening in Washington Square San Francisco, A. Lawrence Ferlinghetti. SP-FerlL

Report to Crazy Horse. William Stafford. SP-StafW; SP-StafWW

Report Upon the Consumption of Myself, A. Charles Bukowski. SP-BukC2

Reporting Back. William Stafford. SP-StafWW

Reportless Subjects, to the Quick. Emily Dickinson. CP-DickE

Repose in God. Jeanne Marie Bouvier de la Motte- Guyon. CP-CowpW

Repose of Rivers. Hart Crane. CP-CranH

Representing Far Places. William Stafford. SP-StafWW

Representing the Universe. Alice Walker. CP-WalkA

Repression. C. K. Williams. SP-WillC

Reprieve, The. Hans Magnus Enzensberger. SP-EnzeH, *tr. by* Michael Hamburger

Reprieve and Admixture. Charles Bukowski. SP-BukC2

Reprimand, The. Elizabeth Bishop. CP-BishE

Reprisal[1], The. George Herbert. CP-HerbG

Reprise. Langston Hughes. *See* Heaven

Reproach. Robert Graves. CP-GravR

Reproach, The. Louise Glück. SP-GlucL

Reproach to Dead Poets. Archibald MacLeish. CP-MacLA

Reproach we may the living; not the dead. No Despight to the Dead. Robert Herrick. CP-HerrR

Reproof and Reply, The. Samuel Taylor Coleridge. CP-ColeS

Reprove not love, though fondly thou hast lost. Thomas Campion *and* Philip Rosseter. CP-CampT

Repulse the staring eye. Reply to Censure. Theodore Roethke. CP-RoetT

Repulsed. D. H. Lawrence. CP-LawrD

Request. Maya Angelou. SP-AngeM

Request. Richard Eberhart. CP-EberR

Request. Langston Hughes. CP-HughL; CP-HughL3

Request, The. Charles Tomlinson. CP-TomlC

Request for Blanca, A. Gabriela Mistral. SP-MistG, *tr. by* Maria Giachetti [*or* Jacketti]

Request for Offering. Richard Eberhart. CP-EberR

Request for Requiems. Langston Hughes. CP-HughL; CP-HughL2

Request to the Graces, An. Robert Herrick. CP-HerrR

Requiem. Sam Hamill. SP-HamiS

Requiem: "Strawberries along the roadbank in the hills bloomed, The." A. R. Ammons. CP-AmmoA

Requiem: "There was a young belle of old Natchez." Ogden Nash. CP-NashO

Requiem: "Thousand leaves slant down across the rain, A." Kenneth Rexroth. CP-RexrK

Requiem: "We will see no more." Wendell Berry. CP-BerrW

Requiem: "Where faces are hueless, where eyelids are dewless." George Meredith. CP-MerG1

Requiem, A: "My father, listening to music, that's me." David Ignatow. SP-IgnaD

Requiem for the Croppies. Seamus Heaney. SP-HeanSO

Requiem for the Death of a Boy. Randall Jarrell. CP-JarrR

Requiem for the Plantagenet Kings. Geoffrey Hill. CP-HillG

Requiem for the Spanish Dead. Kenneth Rexroth. CP-RexrK

Requiescam. Countee Cullen. CP-CullC

Requiescat. Matthew Arnold. SP-ArnoM

Requiescat. Dorothy Parker. CP-ParkD

Requiescat. James Whitcomb Riley. CP-RileJ

Requiescat. Oscar Wilde. CP-WildO

Requirement. John Greenleaf Whittier. CP-WhitJ

Requiring something lovely on his arm. Labor Day. Louise Glück. SP-GlucL

Requisitioning. John Ciardi. CP-CiarJ

Requital. John Greenleaf Whittier. CP-WhitJ

Rescue. James Tate. SP-TateJ

Rescue, The. Robert Creeley. CP-CreeR

Rescue, The. John Logan. CP-LogaJ

Rescue of Pluffles, The. Rudyard Kipling. Fr. Plain Tales from the Hills.

Rescue the Dead. David Ignatow. SP-IgnaD

Rescue With Yul Brynner. Marianne Craig Moore. CP-MoorM

Rescued! new-white. Old House, The. William Carlos Williams. CP-WilW2

Rescued Year, The. William Stafford. SP-StafW; SP-StafWW

Rescuers, The. Robert Stock. SP-StocR

Rescuing gate is wide, The. Like a Mourningless Child. Kenneth Patchen. CP-PatcK

Research and Development: Classified. Robert Graves. CP-GravR

Research Council. Hans Magnus Enzensberger. SP-EnzeH

Research Team in the Mountains, The. William Stafford. SP-StafW; SP-StafWW

Resemblance, The. William Carlos Williams. CP-WilW2

Resembles Life what once was deem'd of Light. What Is Life? Samuel Taylor Coleridge. CP-ColeS; MW-ColeS

Resentment. C. K. Williams. SP-WillC

Reservation. Heather McHugh. SP-McHuH

Reserved. Walter De la Mare. CP-DeLaW

Reservoirs of Mount Helicon, The. Amy Clampitt. CP-ClamA

Residence, The. Joseph Brodsky. CP-BrodJ

Residencies. Thomas McGrath. SP-McGrT

Resident Dispenser of Bromides, The. Being Called. John Ciardi. CP-CiarJ

Residual Light. Hans Magnus Enzensberger. SP-EnzeH

Resignation. Matthew Arnold. SP-ArnoM

Resignation. Paul Laurence Dunbar. CP-DunbP

Resignation, an Elegiac Ode, February the 28th, 1788. Annis Boudinot Stockton. CP-StocA

Resignation—to Faustus. Arthur Hugh Clough. SP-ClouA

Resign'd to live, prepar'd to die. To Mr. Thomas Southern, on His Birth-Day, 1742. Alexander Pope. CP-PopeA

Resist anxiety. Mitosis. Olga Broumas. SP-BrouO

Resistance, The. George Oppen. CP-OppGN

Resistless, unresisting, as some swift spear upon the flood. Fortunatus. Ezra Pound. CP-PoEar

Resolute will can't be rolled up, A. Han-shan. CP-ColdM, tr. by Red Pine

Resolution. W. S. Merwin. SP-MerwW

Resolution. Robert Penn Warren. CP-WarrR

Resolution and Independence. William Wordsworth. CP-WorW1; MW-WorW

Resolution of Hesitancies. Alan Dugan. CP-DugaA

Resolutions. Donald Davie. CP-DaviDC

Resolve. Sylvia Plath. CP-PlatS

Resolve, The. Denise Levertov. SP-LeveDP

Resolve, The. George Oppen. CP-OppGN

Resolved my annual verse to pay. Stella's Birthday (1723). Jonathan Swift. CP-SwifJ

Resolved my gratitude to show. Panegyric on the Dean, A. Jonathan Swift. CP-SwifJ

Resort. George Oppen. CP-OppGN

Resound my voice [or voyse], ye woods [or wodes] that hear [or here] me plain. 'Resound my voice, ye woods.' Sir Thomas Wyatt. CP-WyatT

'Resound my voice, ye woods.' Sir Thomas Wyatt. CP-WyatT

Respect and Discretion. Shmuel HaNagid. SP-HaNaS, tr. by Peter Cole

Respect for the Dead. Laura Riding Jackson. CP-RidiL

Respect his obstinacy of undefeat. Traditionalist, The. Robert Graves. CP-GravR

Respect my faith, regard my service past. Thomas Campion. CP-CampT

Respectability. Robert Browning. CP-BroR1

Respectable Burgher, The. Thomas Hardy. CP-HardT

Respectable folks, The. Henry David Thoreau. CP-ThorH

Respondez! Walt Whitman. CP-WhitW

Response. Paul Laurence Dunbar. CP-DunbP

Response. John Greenleaf Whittier. CP-WhitJ

Response to a Translation by Longfellow. Robert Browning. CP-BroR2

Response to Hopkins. Charles Tomlinson. SP-TomlC

Responsibilities roost on our fingers and toes. Under the Grind. Marge Piercy. SP-PierM

Responsibility. Grace Paley. CP-PalGC

Responsible Romance, The. James Tate. SP-TateJ

Responsible sound of the lawnmower, The. Elegy: "Responsible sound of the lawnmower, The." William Stafford. SP-StafWW

Responsory, A. Thomas Merton. CP-MertT

Responsory, 1948, A. Thomas Merton. CP-MertT

Republica. Geoffrey Hill. CP-HillG

Rest. Robert Herrick. CP-HerrR

Rest. Christina Georgina Rossetti. CP-RosC1

Rest. Wallace Stevens. CP-StevWP

Rest, The. Ezra Pound. SP-PounE Fr. Lustra.

Rest, The. Margaret Atwood. SP-AtwM2

Rest, The. Raymond Carver. CP-CarvR

Rest, The. James Whitcomb Riley. CP-RileJ

Rest and Be Thankful! William Wordsworth. CP-WorW2

Rest for the body's residue. Urn-Burial and the Butterfly Migration. Amy Clampitt. CP-ClamA

Rest, heart of the tired world. Kenneth Patchen. CP-PatcK

Rest House, The. Louis MacNeice. CP-MacNL

Rest I Will Tell to Those Below in Hades, The. Constantine P. Cavafy. CP-CavaC, tr. by Theoharis Constantine Theoharis

'Rest is not our business.' Come the end or, The. Reminded of Bougainville. Donald Davie. CP-DaviDC

Rest Master, for we be aweary, weary. Cry of the Eyes, The. Ezra Pound. CP-PoEar

Rest me with Chinese colours. Song of the Degrees, A. Ezra Pound. SP-PounE

Rest of the Flight, The. Flemish, 1521. Hans Magnus Enzensberger. SP-EnzeH

Rest Refreshes. Robert Herrick. CP-HerrR

Rest remains when all is done, / Work and vigil, prayer and fast. There Remaineth Therefore a Rest to the People of God. Christina Georgina Rossetti. CP-RosC2

Rest, rest, perturbèd Earth! Invocation to the Earth; February, 1816. William Wordsworth. CP-WorW2

Rest, rest; the troubled breast. Dream, The. Christina Georgina Rossetti. CP-RosC3

Restaurant Car. Louis MacNeice. CP-MacNL

Restaurant serving Char-Broiled Meats, The. Ice Cream at Blauenberg. Charles Tomlinson. CP-TomlC

Restaurant's expensive and German, but, The. Sugar. Tess Gallagher. SP-GallT

Restful place, reviver of my smart, The. Sir Thomas Wyatt. CP-WyatT

Resting Figure. Denise Levertov. SP-LeveDP

Resting from faring among those ice-flares, halt birth and the unprojectiled never (O peace) to grapple. Wandering Jew and the Heavenly Hosts, The. Robert Stock. SP-StocR

Resting-Place, The. William Wordsworth. CP-WorW2 Fr. River Duddon [A Series of Sonnets], The.

Restless and Sad. Charles Baudelaire. CP-BaudC, tr. by Walter Martin

Restless Ghost, A. Robert Graves. CP-GravR

Restless, I find no other cause. Three Poems from Michelangelo. Helen Pinkerton. CP-PinkH

Restless Night, The. Thomas McGrath. SP-McGrT

Restlessness. D. H. Lawrence. CP-LawrD

Restoration of a Stolen Fan, The. To ———. Annis Boudinot Stockton. CP-StocA

Restoration of the Pictures, The. Raissa Maritain. CP-MertT

Restore my truth, love, or have done for good. Poet's Curse, The. Robert Graves. CP-GravR

Restored, The. Theodore Roethke. CP-RoetT

Restrictive Covenants. Langston Hughes. CP-HughL; CP-HughL2

Rests at Night. Emily Dickinson. CP-DickE

Result. Charles Bukowski. SP-BukC3

Results of Thought, The. William Butler Yeats. CP-YeatW

Résumé. Dorothy Parker. CP-ParkD

Resume unequal days in chilly thrall. Perception as a Guided Missile. Richard Eberhart. CP-EberR

Resumption, Or Possibly a Remission, A. Amy Clampitt. CP-ClamA

Resurgam. Emily Dickinson. CP-DickE

Resurgam. Christina Georgina Rossetti. CP-RosC2

Resurgam. Allen Tate. CP-TateA

Resurgemus. Walt Whitman. CP-WhitW

Resurrected Christ, The. Rainer Maria Rilke. CP-RilkFr, *tr.* by A. Poulin, Jr.

Resurrection. Yehuda Amichai. SP-AmicY, *tr.* by Stephen Mitchell

Resurrection. Margaret Atwood. SP-AtwM1

Resurrection. G. K. Chesterton. CP-ChesG

Resurrection. Robinson Jeffers. CP-JefR2

Resurrection. D. H. Lawrence. CP-LawrD

Resurrection, The. William Butler Yeats.
   Two Songs from a Play. CP-YeatW

Resurrection, The. Robert Herrick. CP-HerrR

Resurrection, The. Jones Very. CP-VeryJ

Resurrection Eve. Christina Georgina Rossetti. CP-RosC3

Resurrection, Imperfect. John Donne. CP-DonnJ; MW-DonnJ

Resurrection of the Flesh. D. H. Lawrence. CP-LawrD

Resurrection of the Right Side. Muriel Rukeyser. CP-RukeM

Resurrection, Possible, and Probable, The. Robert Herrick. CP-HerrR

Retainer of the bridge club win and loss. Effervescent Mrs. G, The. Wyatt
   Prunty. SP-PrunW

Retaliation. William Cowper. CP-CowpW

Reticence. Donald Davie. CP-DaviDC

Reticent volcano keeps, The. Emily Dickinson. CP-DickE

Reticulations creep upon the slack stream's face. On Sturminster Foot-Bridge.
   Thomas Hardy. CP-HardT

Retire abandon world sd Swami Bhaktivedanta my age 47 approaching half-
   century. What I'd Like to Do. Allen Ginsberg. CP-GinsA

Retired. Czeslaw Milosz. CP-MiloCN, *tr.* by Robert Hass

Retired Ballerinas, Central Park West. Lawrence Ferlinghetti. SP-FerlL

Retired Cat, The. William Cowper. CP-CowpW

Retired Colonel, The. Ted Hughes. SP-HughTN

Retired, with purpose your fair worth to praise. To His Lady, Then Mrs Cary.
   Ben Jonson. CP-JonsB; SP-JonsB

Retirement. William Cowper. CP-CowpW

Retirement. Karl Shapiro. SP-ShapK

Retirement. William Stafford. SP-StafWW

Retirement. William Wordsworth. CP-WorW2

Retirement Catalogue, A. Wyatt Prunty. SP-PrunW

Retort. Paul Laurence Dunbar. CP-DunbP

Retort to Jesus. D. H. Lawrence. CP-LawrD

Retort to Whitman. D. H. Lawrence. CP-LawrD

Retourne agayne, my forces late dismayd. Sonnet 14. Edmund Spenser. CP-
   Spens *Fr.* Amoretti.

Retraction. Alan Dugan. CP-DugaA

Retreat, The. Charles Bukowski. SP-BukC1

Retribution. Aleksandr Aleksandrovich Blok.
   "In those far years of inertia." SP-BlokA

Retrieval System, The. Maxine W. Kumin. SP-KumiM

Retro me, Sathana! Dante Gabriel Rossetti. CW-RossD *Fr.* House of Life, The.

Retroduction to American History. Allen Tate. CP-TateA

Retrospect. Robert Creeley. SP-CreeR

Retrospect, A: 1951-91. Charles Tomlinson. SP-TomlC

Retrospect, The: CWM Elan, 1812. Percy Bysshe Shelley. CP-ShelP

Retrospection. Paul Laurence Dunbar. CP-DunbP

Retrospective Forelook. Richard Eberhart. CP-EberR

Retty used to shake her head. Retty's Phases. Thomas Hardy. CP-HardT

Retty's Phases. Thomas Hardy. CP-HardT

Return. William Wordsworth. CP-WorW2 *Fr.* River Duddon [A Series of
   Sonnets], The.

Return. A. R. Ammons. CP-AmmoA

Return. Raymond Carver. CP-CarvR

Return. Constantine P. Cavafy. CP-CavaC, *tr.* by Theoharis Constantine
   Theoharis

Return. Robert Creeley. CP-CreeR

Return. Robert Graves. CP-GravR

Return. Robinson Jeffers. CP-JefR2

Return. D. H. Lawrence. CP-LawrD

Return. Audre Lorde. SP-LordA

Return. Archibald MacLeish. CP-MacLA

Return. Czeslaw Milosz. CP-MiloCN, *tr.* by Robert Hass

Return. George Oppen. CP-OppGN

Return. Yannis Ritsos. SP-RitsY, *tr.* by N. C. Germanacos

Return. May Sarton. SP-SartM

Return, The. Charles Tomlinson. SP-TomlC

Return, The. Federico García Lorca.
   "I'm coming back / for my wings." CP-GarcF, *tr.* by Jerome Rothenberg

   In Motion. CP-GarcF, *tr.* by Jerome Rothenberg

   Oxbow. CP-GarcF, *tr.* by Jerome Rothenberg

   Saying Goodbye. CP-GarcF, *tr.* by Jerome Rothenberg

   Towards. CP-GarcF, *tr.* by Jerome Rothenberg

   Wind Gust. CP-GarcF, *tr.* by Jerome Rothenberg

Return, The. Richard Eberhart. CP-EberR

Return, The. Louise Glück. SP-GlucL

Return, The. Robert Earl Hayden. CP-HaydR

Return, The. Rudyard Kipling. CP-KiplR

Return, The. Louis MacNeice. CP-MacNL

Return, The. Thomas McGrath. SP-McGrT

Return, The. Edna St. Vincent Millay. CP-MillE

Return, The. Eugenio Montale. CP-MontE, *tr.* by Jonathan Galassi

Return, The. Mary Oliver. SP-OlivM

Return, The. Charles Olson. CP-OlsoC

Return, The. Helen Pinkerton. CP-PinkH

Return, The. Ezra Pound. CP-PoEar; SP-PounE

Return, The. Kathleen Jessie Raine. SP-RainK

Return, The. Theodore Roethke. CP-RoetT

Return, The. Muriel Rukeyser. CP-RukeM

Return, Content! for fondly I pursued. William Wordsworth. CP-WorW2 *Fr.*
   River Duddon [A Series of Sonnets], The.

Return from Greece. Constantine P. Cavafy. CP-CavaC, *tr.* by Theoharis
   Constantine Theoharis

Return from Town, The. Edna St. Vincent Millay. CP-MillE

Return of a Deserter. Yannis Ritsos. SP-RitsY, *tr.* by John Stathatos

Return of Aphrodite, The. May Sarton. SP-SartM

Return of Eve, The. G. K. Chesterton. CP-ChesG

Return of Imray, The. Rudyard Kipling. *Fr.* Life's Handicap.

Return of Kral Majales. Allen Ginsberg. SP-GinsA

Return of Love, The. James Laughlin. CP-LaugJ

Return of Morgan and Fingal, The. Edwin Arlington Robinson. CP-RobiE

Return of Odysseus, The. Richard Eberhart. CP-EberR

Return of Returns. D. H. Lawrence. CP-LawrD

Return of the Children, The. Rudyard Kipling. CP-KiplR

Return of the Columbine, The. Jones Very. CP-VeryJ

Return of the Evening Grosbeaks, The. Adrienne Rich. CP-RicAE

Return of the Goddess [Artemis]. Robert Graves. CP-GravR

Return of the Heroes, The. Walt Whitman. CP-WhitW

Return of the Savior, The. Jones Very. CP-VeryJ

Return often and take me. Return. Constantine P. Cavafy. CP-CavaC, *tr.* by
   Theoharis Constantine Theoharis

Return, The: An Elegy. Robert Penn Warren. CP-WarrR

Return / the night women's. Hospital Kitchen. Lorine Niedecker. CP-NiedL

Return to D'Ennery; Rain. Derek Walcott. CP-WalcD

Return to Hinton. Charles Tomlinson. CP-TomlC

Return to Kraków in 1880. Czeslaw Milosz. CP-CarvR; CP-MiloC; CP-MiloCN,
   tr. by Robert Hass

Return to Lahore. Louis MacNeice. CP-MacNL

Return to Love. Hayden Carruth. CP-CarHS

Return to Marsh Street. Thomas McGrath. SP-McGrT

Return to Sea. Langston Hughes. CP-HughL; CP-HughL3

Return to St. Paul's School, A. G. K. Chesterton. CP-ChesG

Return to the Island. John Logan. CP-LogaJ

Return to Work, The. William Carlos Williams. CP-WilW1

Returned to Say. William Stafford. SP-StafW; SP-StafWW

Returned to the Yaak Cabin, I Overhear an Old Greek Song. Charles Wright. SP-
   WrigCN

Returning. Wendell Berry. CP-BerrW

Returning. Robert Lowell. SP-LoweR

Returning a Lost Child. Louise Glück. SP-GlucL

Returning after I left my home in childhood. Ho Ch'e Ch'ang. CP-WilW2

Returning Birds. Wisława Szymborska. SP-SzymW, *tr.* by Stanislaw Barańczak
   and Clare Cavanagh

Returning each morning from a timeless world. Dark Years, The. W. H. Auden.
   CP-AudeW

Returning from Church. Kathleen Jessie Raine. SP-RainK

Returning Home. John Ciardi. CP-CiarJ

Returning Home. John Logan. CP-LogaJ

Returning Home. "Shu Ting." CP-KizeC, *tr.* by Carolyn Kizer *and* Y. H. Zhao

Returning, I find her just the same. Passing Visit to Helen. D. H. Lawrence. CP-
   LawrD

Returning Janus now prepares. New Year's Gift for Bec, A. Jonathan Swift. CP-
   SwifJ

Returning Native. John Updike. CP-UpdiJ

Returning (1975). Yusef Komunyakaa. CP-KomuY

Returning North of Vortex. Allen Ginsberg. CP-GinsA

Returning the Borrowed Road. Yusef Komunyakaa. CP-KomuY

Returning to Europe. Howard Nemerov. CP-NemeH

Returning to Glasgow after long exile. Glasgow, 1960. Hugh MacDiarmid. SP-MacDH

Returning to Paris with Pissarro. Lawrence Ferlinghetti. SP-FerlL

Returning to that house. Birthplace: New Rochelle. George Oppen. CP-OppGN

Returning to the Country for a Brief Visit. Allen Ginsberg. CP-GinsA

Returning to the spent house its emptiness. Stillness. Wyatt Prunty. SP-PrunW

Returning Turtle. Robert Lowell. SP-LoweR

Returns to punishment as we all return, in agonized initiation. Chapman. Muriel Rukeyser. CP-RukeM

Reuben Bright. Edwin Arlington Robinson. CP-RobiE

Reuben's Children. Dorothy Parker. CP-ParkD

Reunion. Charles Bukowski. SP-BukC2

Reunion. W. S. Merwin. SP-MerwW

Reunion, A. James Schuyler. CP-SchuJ

Reunion, The. John Greenleaf Whittier. CP-WhitJ

Reunions with a Ghost. Ai. SP-Ai

Rêve / sans fin. Samuel Beckett. CP-BeckS

Reveal the dragon thro' the human; coursing swift as fire. William Blake. CP-BlakW

Revealer, The. Edwin Arlington Robinson. CP-RobiE

Reveille. Joseph Brodsky. CP-BrodJ

Reveille. A. E. Housman. CP-HousA

Reveille. Primo Levi. CP-LeviP, *tr. by* Ruth Feldman *and* Brian Swann

Reveille. Tennessee Williams. CP-WillT

Reveille rung on telephones awakes. Wafflebutt. John Ciardi. CP-CiarJ

Revelation. Robert Frost. CP-FrosR

Revelation. John Updike. CP-UpdiJ

Revelation. Jones Very. CP-VeryJ

Revelation. Robert Penn Warren. CP-WarrR

Revelation. John Greenleaf Whittier. CP-WhitJ

Revelation, The. Robert Creeley. CP-CreeR

Revelation, The. William Carlos Williams. CP-WilW1

Revelation, The. James Wright. CP-WrigJ

Revelation 20:11–15. Norman Dubie. CP-DubiN

Revelation According to the Beloved. Robert Stock. SP-StocR

Revelation at Cap Ferrat. Clarence Major. SP-MajoC

Revelation came on Jane, A. Jump-to-Glory Jane. George Meredith. CP-MerG1

Revelation of the Spirit Through the Material World, The. Jones Very. CP-VeryJ

Revelations. Norman Dubie. CP-DubiN

Revelations every two hours on the Lounge. I Know. John Berryman. CP-BerrJ

Revenant, The. Walter De la Mare. CP-DeLaW

Revenant, The. Archibald MacLeish. CP-MacLA

Revenant, The. Louis MacNeice. CP-MacNL

Revenant, The. William Meredith. SP-MereW

Revenants, The. James Laughlin. CP-LaugJ

Revenge. Robert Herrick. CP-HerrR

Revenge Fable. Ted Hughes. SP-HughTN

Revenge for Love. Donald Davie. CP-DaviDC

Revered, beloved—O you that hold. To the Queen. Alfred Tennyson. CP-TennA

Revered Defender of beauteous Stuart. Epistle to Mr Tytler of Woodhouselee, Author of a Defence of Mary Queen of Scots. Robert Burns. CP-BurnR

Reverence. Robert Herrick. CP-HerrR

Reverence. Jones Very. CP-VeryJ

Reverence to Riches. Robert Herrick. CP-HerrR

Reverend Butler came by. Madam and the Minister. Langston Hughes. CP-HughL; CP-HughL2

Rev. Dr. Barclay outgrew his profession, The. Women at Point Sur, The. Robinson Jeffers. CP-JefR1

Reverential Comparison. Yannis Ritsos. SP-RitsY, *tr. by* Kimon Friar

Reverie. Sophocles. CP-CummE *Fr.* Electra.

Reverie. Robert Browning. CP-BroR2

Reverie. Walter De la Mare. CP-DeLaW

Reverie. Gregory Orr. SP-OrrG

Reverie and Invocation. William Carlos Williams. CP-WilW2

Reverie during Briefing. John Ciardi. CP-CiarJ

Reverie of Poor Susan, The. William Wordsworth. CP-WorW1

Reverie on the Harlem River. Langston Hughes. CP-HughL; CP-HughL2

Reversal. A. R. Ammons. CP-AmmoA

Reversals. Walt Whitman. CP-WhitW

Reverse. Andrei Codrescu. SP-CodrA

Reverse cannot befall. Emily Dickinson. CP-DickE

Reverse Metamorphosis. Robert Stock. SP-StocR

Reverse on the Back Side, The. Ben Jonson. CP-JonsB

Reverse Side. Yannis Ritsos. SP-RitsY, *tr. by* Kimon Friar

Reverses. Maya Angelou. SP-AngeM

Reversibility. Charles Baudelaire. CP-BaudC, *tr. by* Walter Martin

Reversionary. Stevie Smith. CP-SmitS

Reversions, always. Hayden Carruth. CP-CarHS *Fr.* Clay Hill Anthology, The.

Reviewing the Summer and Winter Calender of the Next Life. Maxine W. Kumin. SP-KumiM

Revision for Clarinda. Robert Burns. CP-BurnR

Revisionist Poem: Machado. Thomas McGrath. SP-McGrT

Revisionist Poem—Octavio Paz. Thomas McGrath. SP-McGrT

Revisit to the Room of a Saint. John Logan. CP-LogaJ

Revisitation, The. Thomas Hardy. CP-HardT

Revisited. John Greenleaf Whittier. CP-WhitJ

Revival. Yannis Ritsos. SP-RitsY, *tr. by* Kimon Friar

Revivalist in Boston, A. Adrienne Rich. CP-RicAE

Revivals. Denise Levertov. SP-LeveDP

Revives in Escudero's constant of the plumbline. Style. Marianne Craig Moore. CP-MoorM

Revolt. Ezra Pound. CP-PoEar

Revolt. Kenneth Rexroth. CP-RexrK

Revolt of Islam, The. Percy Bysshe Shelley. CP-ShelP

Revolution. A. E. Housman. CP-HousA

Revolution. Langston Hughes. CP-HughL; CP-HughL1

Revolution, A. Philip Whalen. SP-WhalP

Revolution, The. George Meredith. CP-MerG1

Revolution, The. Donald Hall. CP-HallD

Revolution at Market Hill, The. Jonathan Swift. CP-SwifJ

Revolution in the Revolution in the Revolution. Gary Snyder. CP-SnydG

Revolution / is accomplished, The. Poem for Norman Macleod, A. William Carlos Williams. CP-WilW1

Revolution Is One Form of Social Change. Audre Lorde. SP-LordA

Revolution is the Pod. Emily Dickinson. CP-DickE

REVOLUTION it says. Revolution Piazza Di Spagna. Charles Tomlinson. SP-TomlC

Revolution of the Children. Archibald MacLeish. CP-MacLA

Revolution Piazza Di Spagna. Charles Tomlinson. SP-TomlC

Revolution shall be a toy of peace to you. Child and Mother. Muriel Rukeyser. CP-RukeM

Revolutionary palingenesis. Bonpland. Lorine Niedecker. CP-NiedL

Revolutionary Petunias. Alice Walker. CP-WalkA

Revolutionary, The. D. H. Lawrence. CP-LawrD

Revolutionist, The: or Lines to a Statesman. G. K. Chesterton. CP-ChesG

Revolutionists Stop for Orangeade, The. Wallace Stevens. CP-StevW; CP-StevWP

Revolutions as Such! D. H. Lawrence. CP-LawrD

Revolving in oval loops of solar speed. Dead, The. Sylvia Plath. CP-PlatS

Revolving Meditation. Stanley Kunitz. CP-KunSC

Revulsion. Donald Davie. CP-DaviDC

Revulsion. Thomas Hardy. CP-HardT

Rewaking, The. William Carlos Williams. CP-WilW2

Reward. A. R. Ammons. CP-AmmoA

Reward, The. David Ignatow. SP-IgnaD

Reward, The. Jones Very. CP-VeryJ

Reward, The. John Greenleaf Whittier. CP-WhitJ

Reward of curiosity, The. Further Details. Laura Riding Jackson. CP-RidiL

Rewarded porters opening their smiles, The. On the Railway Platform. Randall Jarrell. CP-JarrR

Rewards. Robert Herrick. CP-HerrR

Rewards and Punishments. Robert Herrick. CP-HerrR

Rex. Ralph Waldo Emerson. CP-EmerR

Rexroth and Patchen and Fearing—their mothers. Kenneths. John Updike. CP-UpdiJ

Rexroth's face reflecting human. Scribble. Allen Ginsberg. CP-GinsA

Reynolds, come, thy pencil prove. Anacreon. William Wordsworth. CP-WorW1

Rhapsody. Frank O'Hara. SP-OharF

Rhapsody of Life's Progress, A. Elizabeth Barrett Browning. CP-BroEB

Rhapsody on a Windy Night. T. S. Eliot. CP-ElioT; SP-ElioT

Rhapsody on Irish Themes, A. Randall Jarrell. CP-JarrR

Rhea. Robert Graves. CP-GravR

Rhenish Night. Guillaume Apollinaire. SP-MereW, *tr. by* William Meredith

Rhenish Winter. Charles Tomlinson. CP-TomlC

Rhetoric. Marilyn Hacker. SP-HackM

Rhetoric for Danny Keough to Recite at the Bar, A. John Ciardi. CP-CiarJ

Rhine-Land. George Meredith. CP-MerG2

Rhinoceros, The. Ogden Nash. CP-NashO

Rhode Island. William Meredith. SP-MereW

Rhodes. Raymond Carver. CP-CarvR

Rhodes Memorial, Table Mountain. Rudyard Kipling. CP-KiplR

Rhododendrons. Tess Gallagher. SP-GallT

Rhododendrons. Ted Hughes. SP-HughTN

Rhodora, The [On Being Asked Whence Is the Flower]. Ralph Waldo Emerson. CP-EmerR

Rhyme. Louise Bogan. CP-BogaL

Rhyme. James Laughlin. CP-LaugJ

Rhyme. Sylvia Plath. CP-PlatS

Rhyme, The. Robert Creeley. CP-CreeR

Rhyme About an Electrical Advertising Sign, A. Nicholas Vachel Lindsay. CP-LindV

Rhyme Against Living. Dorothy Parker. CP-ParkD

Rhyme for a Child Viewing a Naked Venus in a Painting [of "The Judgement of Paris"]. Robert Browning. CP-BroR2

Rhyme for a Parlour Game. G. K. Chesterton. CP-ChesG

Rhyme for All Zionists, A. Nicholas Vachel Lindsay. CP-LindV

Rhyme is after, The. For W.C.W. Robert Creeley. CP-CreeR

Rhyme o' The Raggedy Man's 'at's best, The. Lugubrious Whing-Whang, The. James Whitcomb Riley. CP-RileJ

Rhyme of an Involuntary Violet. Dorothy Parker. CP-ParkD

Rhyme of Dust, A. G. K. Chesterton. CP-ChesG

Rhyme of Reb Nachman, The. Robert Pinsky. CP-PinsR

Rhyme of the Duchess May. Elizabeth Barrett Browning. CP-BroEB

Rhyme of the Three Captains, The. Rudyard Kipling. CP-KiplR

Rhyme of the Three Sealers, The. Rudyard Kipling. CP-KiplR

Rhyme on Edward Burne-Jones. Robert Browning. CP-BroR2

Rhyme [or Rime], the rack of finest wits. Fit of Rhyme [or Rime] against Rhyme [or Rime], A. Ben Jonson. CP-JonsB; SP-JonsB

Rhymed Address: The Lobster. William Carlos Williams. CP-WilW1

Rhymes. Charles Tomlinson. CP-TomlC

Rhymes mean nothing to me. Only rarely. Fernando Pessoa. SP-PessF *Fr.* Keeper of Sheep, The.

Rhymes of Ironquill, The. James Whitcomb Riley. CP-RileJ

Rhyming Exercises. Robert Browning. CP-BroR2

Rhythm, The. Robert Creeley. CP-CreeR

Rhythm, Charts and Changes. Jay Wright. SP-WrigJ

Rhythm is, The. Four Motions for the Pea Vines. A. R. Ammons. CP-AmmoA

Rhythm Method. Yusef Komunyakaa. CP-KomuY

Rhythm of life, The. Lenox Avenue: Midnight. Langston Hughes. CP-HughL; CP-HughL1

Rhythms of Love. Laura Riding Jackson. CP-RidiL

Rib, The. James Dickey. CP-DickJ

Ribblesdale. Gerard Manley Hopkins. CP-HopkG

Ribbons. C. K. Williams. CP-WillC

Ribbons of the Year. Emily Dickinson. CP-DickE

Ribh at the Tomb of Baile and Aillinn. William Butler Yeats. CP-YeatW

Ribh Considers Christian Love Insufficient. William Butler Yeats. CP-YeatW

Ribh Denounces Patrick. William Butler Yeats. CP-YeatW

Ribh in Ecstasy. William Butler Yeats. CP-YeatW

Rice. Mary Oliver. SP-OlivM

Rich, The. Charles Tomlinson. CP-TomlC

Rich are small in number, The. Shmuel HaNagid. SP-HaNaS, *tr. by* Peter Cole

Rich black blend of musk and nicotine, A. Still Unsatisfied. Charles Baudelaire. CP-BaudC, *tr. by* Walter Martin

Rich have so many cares, The. Han-shan. CP-ColdM, *tr. by* Red Pine

Rich Interior, After Thomas Mann. Philip Whalen. SP-WhalP

Rich labour is the struggle to be wise. Discipline of Wisdom, The. George Meredith. CP-MerG1

Rich *Lazarus!* richer in those gems, thy teares. Upon Lazarus His Teares. Richard Crashaw. CP-CrasR

Rich man's Heir, his father's spirit fled, The. Grief of an Heir, The. William Cowper. CP-CowpW

Rich men met in an elegant hall. Han-shan. CP-ColdM, *tr. by* Red Pine

Rich profusion of familiar flowers, A. Garden of Childhood, The. May Sarton. SP-SartM

Rich, thou hadst many lovers—poor, hast none. On Female Inconstancy. *Unknown.* CP-CowpW

Richard. Gerard Manley Hopkins. CP-HopkG

Richard Coeur-de-Lion. Louis Aragon. CP-MacNL

Richard Cory. Edwin Arlington Robinson. CP-RobiE

Richard Hunt's "Arachne." Robert Earl Hayden. CP-HaydR

Richard Lionheart. George Meredith. CP-MerG2

Richard Nixon / is standing. On Being Asked How Do You Feel after an Operation with Inadequate Anesthesia. This Is How I Feel. Alan Dugan. CP-DugaA

Richard Roe and John Doe. Robert Graves. CP-GravR

Richard Roe wished himself Solomon. Richard Roe and John Doe. Robert Graves. CP-GravR

Richard would wait till George the tale should ask. Ruth. George Crabbe. SP-CrabG *Fr.* Tales of the Hall.

Richard's Youth. George Crabbe. SP-CrabG *Fr.* Tales of the Hall.

Richer than Miser o'er his countless hoards. Lines Written at the King's Arms, Ross, Formerly the House of the "Man of Ross." Samuel Taylor Coleridge. CP-ColeS

Riches. William Blake. CP-BlakW

Riches. D. H. Lawrence. CP-LawrD

Riches. Gabriela Mistral. SP-MistG, *tr. by* Maria Giachetti [*or* Jacketti]

Riches and Poverty. Robert Herrick. CP-HerrR

Richmond. John Updike. CP-UpdiJ

Richness at the center of a rose, The. Rose, The. Gabriela Mistral. SP-MistG, *tr. by* Maria Giachetti [*or* Jacketti]

Richt arely one Ask Wedinsday. William Dunbar. CP-DunbW

Rickshaw-Wallah, The. A. K. Ramanujan. CP-RamaA

Rid of a vexing and a heavy load. Michelangelo Buonarroti. CP-WorW1

Rid of the world's injustice, and his pain. Grave of Keats, The. Oscar Wilde. CP-WildO

Rid of this nagging nattering cadaver. Michelangelo Buonarroti. CP-Miche, *tr. by* John Frederick Nims

Riddle: "I am just two and two, I am warm, I am cold." William Cowper. CP-CowpW

Riddle: "What'd you throw it on the floor for?" Robert Creeley. SP-CreeR

Riddle, A. Walter De la Mare. CP-DeLaW

Riddle, A. Richard Wilbur. CP-WilbR

Riddle, A: "Because I am by nature blind." Thomas Sheridan. CP-SherT

Riddle, A: "There is one that has a head without an eye." Christina Georgina Rossetti. CP-RosC2

Riddle, The. W. H. Auden. CP-AudeW

Riddle, The. Robert Creeley. CP-CreeR

Riddle, The. Thomas Hardy. CP-HardT

Riddle, The. Seamus Heaney. SP-HeanSO

Riddle, The. Louis MacNeice. CP-MacNL

Riddle by T-m Pun——i, Addressed to D——h, A. *Unknown, sometimes at. to* Thomas Sheridan. CP-SherT

Riddle for Men, The. George Meredith. CP-MerG1

Riddle of the Conjurer, The. G. K. Chesterton. CP-ChesG

Riddle Song, A. Walt Whitman. CP-WhitW

Riddle the Sphinx Forgot, A. Howard Nemerov. CP-NemeH

Riddle we can guess, The. Emily Dickinson. CP-DickE

Riddlers, The. Walter De la Mare. CP-DeLaW

Riddles. Jonathan Swift. CP-SwifJ

Riddles: "Two brothers wisely kept apart, together are employ'd." James Leigh Perrot. CP-AustJ

Riddles: "When my 1st is a task to a young girl of spirit." Jane Austen. CP-AustJ

Riddles and Charades. Mrs. Austen. CP-AustJ

Riddles and Whims. Carl Sandburg. CP-SandC

Riddling Letter, A. Jonathan Swift. CP-SwifJ

Ride a black horse with tan feet. Striped Cats, Old Men and Proud Stockings. Carl Sandburg. CP-SandC

Ride, The. Stevie Smith. CP-SmitS

Ride, The. Richard Wilbur. CP-WilbR

Ride 'em, and, by the ride, down all night, all. Adamo Me. Charles Olson. CP-OlsoC

Ride, Red, Ride. Langston Hughes. CP-HughL; CP-HughL3

Ride to Stirling, The. Sir Walter Scott. SP-ScotW *Fr.* Lady of the Lake, The.

Ride with an idle whip, ride with an unused heel. Rudyard Kipling. CP-KiplR *Fr.* Plain Tales from the Hills.

"Ride you this fair cool morning?" said the Squire. Ellen. George Crabbe. SP-CrabG *Fr.* Tales of the Hall.

Rider of the Knee, The. James Whitcomb Riley. CP-RileJ

Rider remained on the plain, half-hidden in the grass, The. Episode. Yannis Ritsos. SP-RitsY, *tr. by* Minas Savvas

Riders. Robert Frost. CP-FrosR

Riders. Clarence Major. SP-MajoC

Riders of the wind, The. Bitter Summer Thoughts. Carl Sandburg. CP-SandC

Rider's Song. Federico García Lorca. CP-GarcF, *tr. by* Alan S. Trueblood *Fr.* Andalusian Songs.

Rider's Song. Federico García Lorca. SP-GarcF, *tr. by* J. L. Gili *and* Stephen Spender

Rider's Song (1860). Federico García Lorca. CP-GarcF, *tr. by* Alan S. Trueblood *Fr.* Andalusian Songs.

Riders to the Blood-Red Wrath. Gwendolyn Brooks. SP-BrooG

Riding against the east. To Beachey, 1912. Carl Sandburg. CP-SandC

Riding all night, the bus half empty, toward the interior. Iola, Kansas. Amy Clampitt. CP-ClamA

Riding along in the beautiful day (there go two). Letter Poem #2. James

Schuyler. CP-SchuJ

Riding from Topeka, Kansas, to Manhattan, Kansas. Mockers Go to Kansas in Spring. Carl Sandburg. CP-SandC

Riding home from credulous blue domes. Terminal. Sylvia Plath. CP-PlatS

Riding on a Railroad Train. Ogden Nash. CP-NashO

Riding on his bike. Only the Dreamer Can Change the Dream. John Logan. CP-LogaJ

Riding slowly along the banks of a canal. Ride, The. Stevie Smith. CP-SmitS

Riding Song for a Semi-Feudal Army, for Glubb Pasha, for Tortured Colonels. Alan Dugan. CP-DugaA

Riding the black express from heaven to hell. Lucifer in the Train. Adrienne Rich. CP-RicAE

Riding the Elevator into the Sky. Anne Sexton. CP-SextA; SP-SextA

Riding the horse as was my wont. Don't Sign Anything. Robert Creeley. CP-CreeR

Riding to Town. Paul Laurence Dunbar. CP-DunbP

Riding with Sal. Robert Creeley. SP-CreeR

Ridway robbed Duncote of three hundred pound. On a Robbery. Ben Jonson. CP-JonsB; SP-JonsB

Rien nul / n'aura été. Samuel Beckett. CP-BeckS

Rievaulx: St. Ailred. Thomas Merton. CP-MertT

Riez Bailleul ("Behind the line there mending reserve posts, looking"). Ivor Gurney. SP-GurnI

Riez Bailleul in blue tea-time. Riez Bailleul ("Riez Bailleul in blue tea-time"). Ivor Gurney. SP-GurnI

Riez Bailleul ("Riez Bailleul in blue tea-time"). Ivor Gurney. SP-GurnI

Rifkin Movement. Richard Eberhart. CP-EberR

Rifle goes up; / Does what a rifle does. Soldier and the Star, The. Kenneth Patchen. CP-PatcK

Rift, The. Thomas Hardy. CP-HardT

Rigamarole. William Carlos Williams. CP-WilW1

Rigged poker-stiff on her back. All the Dead Dears. Sylvia Plath. CP-PlatS

Right. Ambrose Bierce. SP-BierA

Right after the Moon was got rid of, a moon was brought on. The. Moon "Continued." Kenneth Patchen. CP-PatcK

Right Arm, The. Paul Muldoon. CP-MuldP

Right arm: a many-splendored. Peter. James Merrill. SP-MerrJ

Right down the shocked street with a siren-blast. Fire-Truck, A. Richard Wilbur. CP-WilbR

Right from the start he is dressed in his best—his blacks and his whites. March Calf, A. Ted Hughes. SP-HughTN

Right Hand, The. Robert Herrick. CP-HerrR

Right here at home, boys, in old Hoosierdom. James Whitcomb Riley. CP-RileJ

Right here in the street. Amazing Potato Peeler, The. Charles Simic. SP-SimiCE

Right here the other night something. E. E. Cummings. CP-CummE

Right in midtown walking in broad daylight. Happens Every Day. W. S. Merwin. SP-MerwWF

Right in My Eye. Charles Olson. CP-OlsoC

Right in the track where Sherman. Howard at Atlanta. John Greenleaf Whittier. CP-WhitJ

Right in the Trail. Gary Snyder. CP-SnydG

Right Lads, The. Donald Davie. CP-DaviDC

Right Now. Grace Paley.

Right of Way, The. William Carlos Williams. CP-WilW1

Right off we started inflicting history. This Is a Sin. C. K. Williams. CP-WillC

Right On. A. R. Ammons. CP-AmmoA

Right Possessor, The. Thom Gunn. CP-GunnT

Right, Sir! your text I'll prove it true. Calf, The. Robert Burns. CP-BurnR

Right Thing, The. Theodore Roethke. CP-RoetT

Right Thinking Man. Marge Piercy. SP-PierM

Right to Die. William Stafford. SP-StafWW

Right to Die, The. Paul Laurence Dunbar. CP-DunbP

Right to Grief, The. Carl Sandburg. CP-SandC

Right to Life. Marge Piercy. SP-PierM

Right to Life, The: What Can the White Man Say to the Black Woman? Alice Walker. CP-WalkA

Right to perish might be thought, The. Emily Dickinson. CP-DickE

Right to the end, that man, he was so hot. Miracle, The. Thom Gunn. CP-GunnT

Right true it is and said full yore ago. Sir Thomas Wyatt. CP-WyatT

Right trusty, and so forth,—We let you to know. Apollo to the Dean. Jonathan Swift. CP-SwifJ

Right under their noses, the green. Dusk of Horses, The. James Dickey. CP-DickJ

Right up there this side the Five Chimneys Corners. Block. Hayden Carruth. CP-CarHS

Right well I wote, most mighty Soveraine. Book 2. Edmund Spenser. CP-Spens Fr. Faerie Queene, The.

Right Wing Sympathies. Donald Davie. CP-DaviDC

Rightful name that thou art called by, The. Thy Name. Jones Very. CP-VeryJ

Rightful One, The. David Ignatow. SP-IgnaD

Rights of Man, The. Jones Very. CP-VeryJ

Rights of Woman—Spoken by Miss Fontenelle on Her Benefit Night, The. Robert Burns. CP-BurnR

Right's Security. Paul Laurence Dunbar. CP-DunbP

Rigid sleeps the house in darkness, I alone. Late at Night. D. H. Lawrence. CP-LawrD

Rigid, uncompromising throughout his entire life. Life, A. Yannis Ritsos. SP-RitsY, tr. by John Stathatos

Rigorists. Marianne Craig Moore. CP-MoorM

Rigs o' Barley, The. Robert Burns. CP-BurnR (Song.) CP-BurnR

Rijl. Tess Gallagher. SP-GallT

Rikki-Tikki-Tavi. Rudyard Kipling. Fr. Jungle Book, The.

Rilke and Lou. Thomas Lux. SP-LuxT

Rilke thought it was the human part. Infinite Reason, The. Archibald MacLeish. CP-MacLA

Rilke writes of the expectation. Limper, The. James Laughlin. CP-LaugJ

Rilke's Epitaph. Thomas Merton. CP-MertT

Rillons, Rillettes. Richard Wilbur. CP-WilbR

Rillons, Rillettes, they taste the same. Rillons, Rillettes. Richard Wilbur. CP-WilbR

Rimbaud. W. H. Auden. CP-AudeW

Rime of the Ancient Mariner, The. Samuel Taylor Coleridge. CP-ColeS; MW-ColeS

("It is an ancyent Marinere.") CP-ColeS

Rime of the Ancyent Marinere, The. Samuel Taylor Coleridge. See Rime of the Ancient Mariner, The

Rimini. Rudyard Kipling. CP-KiplR Fr. Puck of Pook's Hill.

Rimmon. Rudyard Kipling. CP-KiplR

Rimrock, Where It Is. Hayden Carruth. CP-CarHS

Ring, The. Langston Hughes. CP-HughL; CP-HughL1

Ring of, The. Charles Olson. CP-OlsoC; SP-OlsoC

Ring of a doorbell, The. Being Here. Miller Williams. CP-WillM

Ring of gold and a milk-white dove, A. Chanson. Oscar Wilde. CP-WildO

Ring out the Old, Ring in the New, but Don't Get Caught in Between. Ogden Nash. CP-NashO

Ring out, ye bells! Christmas Carol: "Ring out, ye bells!" Paul Laurence Dunbar. CP-DunbP

Ring Posy, A. Christina Georgina Rossetti. CP-RosC1

Ring Presented to Julia, A. Robert Herrick. CP-HerrR

Ring the big bells. Contemporary Announcement. Maya Angelou. SP-AngeM

Ring to me Cecilia sends, A. On Receiving from a Lady a Present of a Ring. George Crabbe. SP-CrabG

Ring upon her finger, / Walks the bride, A. Christina Georgina Rossetti. CP-RosC2

Ringed / with monstrous / a doomed. E. E. Cummings. CP-CummE

Ringing Doorbells. Amy Clampitt. CP-ClamA

Ringing the Bells. Anne Sexton. CP-SextA; SP-SextA

Ringlety-jing! Nonsense Rhyme, A. James Whitcomb Riley. CP-RileJ

Ringling. Muriel Rukeyser. CP-RukeM

Ringling Brothers, Barnum and Bailey. Mona Van Duyn. SP-VanDM

Rings of birch bark. Love Song: "Rings of birch bark." A. R. Ammons. CP-AmmoA

Rings of iron gray smoke; a woman's steel face . . . looking . . . looking. Fog Portrait. Carl Sandburg. CP-SandC

Ringworm Frank. James Whitcomb Riley. CP-RileJ

Rinsed and flooded, flooded. Summer Thunderstorm, A. Theodore Weiss. SP-WeisT

Rinsing our mouths. Good Man in a Bad Time, A. Archibald MacLeish. CP-MacLA

Rio. Wyatt Prunty. SP-PrunW

Rio de Janeiro. Four Sambas. Unknown. CP-BishE

Rio de Janeiro. John Updike. CP-UpdiJ

Rio Samba. Joseph Brodsky. CP-BrodJ

Riot Act, April 29, 1992. Ai. SP-Ai

Riot: 60's. Maya Angelou. SP-AngeM

RIP. James Wright. CP-WrigJ

Rip, whoosh, wing-whistle: and out of. Sunset Walk in Thaw-Time in Vermont. Robert Penn Warren. CP-WarrR

Riparian origins . . . did you know. Amazonian. Donald Davie. CP-DaviDC

Ripe apples were caught like red fish in the nets. Great Scarf of Birds, The. John Updike. CP-UpdiJ

Ripe Corn. Carl Sandburg. CP-SandC

Ripe grassheads bend in the starlight, The. On the Hill Late at Night. Wendell Berry. CP-BerrW

Ripeness Is All. James Vincent Cunningham. CP-CunnJ

Ripening. Wendell Berry. CP-BerrW

Ripening there / among the entanglement of leaves. Green Quinces. Charles Tomlinson. CP-TomlC

Ripest Peach is highest on the tree, The. James Whitcomb Riley. CP-RileJ

Riposte. Marilyn Hacker. SP-HackM

Riposte. William Carlos Williams. CP-WilW1

Ripple, The. Denise Levertov. SP-LeveDP

Ripple Song, A. Rudyard Kipling. CP-KiplR *Fr.* Second Jungle Book, The.

Rippled nut, The. Hollow Walnut, The. Gabriela Mistral. SP-MistG, *tr.* by Maria Giachetti [*or* Jacketti]

Ripples on the Surface. Gary Snyder. CP-SnydG

Rippling eyelids. Robert Creeley. CP-CreeR

Rippling in the ocean of that darkening room. Woman at the Piano. Marya Alexandrovna Zaturenska. SP-ZatuM

Riprap. Gary Snyder. CP-SnydG

Rise early and look at the sky. Shmuel HaNagid. SP-HaNaS, *tr.* by Peter Cole

Rise from your bed of langour. Company. Stevie Smith. CP-SmitS

Rise heart; thy Lord is risen. Sing his praise. Easter. George Herbert. CP-HerbG

Rise, Heire of fresh Eternity. Easter Day. Richard Crashaw. CP-CrasR

Rise, Household-gods, and let us goe. To His Household Gods. Robert Herrick. CP-HerrR

Rise in the World, A. D. H. Lawrence. CP-LawrD

Rise O Days from Your Fathomless Deeps. Walt Whitman. CP-WhitW

Rise, Royall SION! rise and sing. Lauda Sion Salvatorem. Richard Crashaw. CP-CrasR

Rise then, immortall maid! *Religion* rise! Upon the Ensuing Treatises [of Mr. Shelford]. Richard Crashaw. CP-CrasR

Rise, thou best and brightest morning! Hymn for New Year's Day. Richard Crashaw. CP-CrasR

Rise to the surface, flex and spin and dart. Pool, The. Helen Pinkerton. CP-PinkH

Rise up, poets, phalanx of the just. Killer, The. Richard Eberhart. CP-EberR

Rise with superior light auspicious morn. Impromptu Ode before Day on the 24th of Dec, Christmas Morning, An. Annis Boudinot Stockton. CP-StocA

Risen, The. Ted Hughes. SP-HughTN

Risen Image Shines, The. Muriel Rukeyser. CP-RukeM

Risen in a / welter of waters. Birth of Venus, The. Muriel Rukeyser. CP-RukeM

Risen Lord, The. D. H. Lawrence. CP-LawrD

Rises at five, just when a late moon. Insomniac Sleeps Well for Once and, The. Hayden Carruth. CP-CarHS

Risible nice go when from mud a crony. Catullus. *See* I laughed. Calvus. I laughed today

Rising. Wendell Berry. CP-BerrW

Rising a Little. Kenneth Patchen. CP-PatcK

Rising beyond the sky. Han-shan. CP-ColdM, *tr.* by Red Pine

Rising early and walking in the garden. On Rising Early. Robert Graves. CP-GravR

Rising hills, the slopes, The. For the Children. Gary Snyder. CP-SnydG

Rising in Fall. Alan Dugan. CP-DugaA

Rising of the Storm, The. Paul Laurence Dunbar. CP-DunbP

Rising Over Night-Blackened Detroit Streets. Allen Ginsberg. CP-GinsA

Rising Sun, The. Randall Jarrell. CP-JarrR

Rising Waters. Langston Hughes. CP-HughL; CP-HughL1

Risk, The. Robert Graves. CP-GravR

Risk, The. Anne Sexton. CP-SextA

Risk is the Hair that holds the Tun. Emily Dickinson. CP-DickE

Risks and Possibilities. A. R. Ammons. CP-AmmoA

Risks of Immortality, The. Emily Dickinson. SP-DickE

Rite. Muriel Rukeyser. CP-RukeM

Rite, The. John Ciardi. CP-CiarJ

Rite, The. Czeslaw Milosz. CP-MiloCN, *tr.* by Robert Hass

Rites, The. Robert Creeley. CP-CreeR

Rites deriv'd from ancient days, The. Translations from the *Medea* of Euripedes. Euripides. CP-JohnS *Fr.* Medea.

Rites for the Extrusion of a Leper. Thomas Merton. CP-MertT

Rites of Darkness, The. Kenneth Patchen. CP-PatcK

Rites of Passage. Thom Gunn. CP-GunnT

Rites of Passage. Audre Lorde. SP-LordA

Rites of War. Louis MacNeice. CP-MacNL

Ritner. John Greenleaf Whittier. CP-WhitJ

Ritornelli. Geoffrey Hill. CP-HillG

Ritornello. Charles Tomlinson. CP-TomlC

Ritual for Eating the World. A. R. Ammons. CP-AmmoA

Ritual for Singing Bat. John Ciardi. CP-CiarJ

Ritual of Departure ("Open the soft string that clasps in series"). Thomas Kinsella. CP-KinsT

Ritual of Memories, The. Tess Gallagher. SP-GallT

Ritual One. David Ignatow. SP-IgnaD

Ritual to Read to Each Other, A. William Stafford. SP-StafW; SP-StafWW

Ritualists, The. William Carlos Williams. CP-WilW2

Rituals. Miller Williams. CP-WillM

Rituals of Departure. Thomas Kinsella. CP-KinsT

Rival, A. G. K. Chesterton. CP-ChesG

Rival, The. Thomas Hardy. CP-HardT

Rival, The. Sylvia Plath. CP-PlatS

Rival, The. James Whitcomb Riley. CP-RileJ

Rival Poet, The. Billy Collins. SP-CollB

Rivals. Christina Georgina Rossetti. CP-RosC3

Rivals, The. Paul Laurence Dunbar. CP-DunbP

Rivals, The. *Unknown.* CP-SherT

Rivals, The; or the Showman's Ruse. James Whitcomb Riley. CP-RileJ

Riven Doggeries. James Tate. SP-TateJ

River. A. R. Ammons. CP-AmmoA

River. Ted Hughes. SP-HughTN

River, The. Raymond Carver. CP-CarvR

River, The. Gregory Orr. SP-OrrG

River, The. Alexander Pope. CP-PopeA

River, The. Jones Very. CP-VeryJ

River, A. A. K. Ramanujan. CP-RamaA

River, A. Adam Zagajewski. SP-ZagaA

River Between the Train and the Highway, The. Thomas Lux. SP-LuxT

River blackens in a frame of snow, The. Hometown after a War. John Ciardi. CP-CiarJ

River Blindness (Onchocerciasis). Thomas Lux. SP-LuxT

River Bridged and Forgot, The. Wendell Berry. CP-BerrW

River brought down, The. How We Heard the Name. Alan Dugan. CP-DugaA

River Deben, The. Stevie Smith. CP-SmitS

River Down Home, The. James Wright. CP-WrigJ

River Duddon [A Series of Sonnets], The. William Wordsworth. CP-WorW2

    After-Thought. CP-WorW2

    (River Duddon, The.) MW-WorW

    American Tradition. CP-WorW2

    Change Me, Some God, Into That Breathing Rose! CP-WorW2

    Conclusion: "But here no cannon thunders to the gale." CP-WorW2

    Faery Chasm, The. CP-WorW2

    "From this deep chasm, where quivering sunbeams play." CP-WorW2

    Hints for the Fancy. CP-WorW2

    Journey Renewed. CP-WorW2

    "KIRK OF ULPHA to the pilgrim's eye, The." CP-WorW2

    "Methinks 'twere no unprecedented feat." CP-WorW2

    "No record tells of lance opposed to lance." CP-WorW2

    "Not envying Latian shades—if yet they throw." CP-WorW2

    "Not hurled precipitous from steep to steep." CP-WorW2

    "O mountain Stream! the Shepherd and his Cot." CP-WorW2; MW-WorW

    Open Prospect. CP-WorW2

    Plain of Donnerdale, The. CP-WorW2

    Resting-Place, The. CP-WorW2

    Return. CP-WorW2

    "Return, Content! for fondly I pursued." CP-WorW2

    Same Subject, The. CP-WorW2

    Seathwaite Chapel. CP-WorW2

    Sheep-Washing. CP-WorW2

    Stepping-Stones, The. CP-WorW2

    Tradition. CP-WorW2

    Tributary Stream. CP-WorW2

    "Whence that low voice?—A whisper from the heart." CP-WorW2

    "Who swerves from innocence, who makes divorce." CP-WorW2

River Duddon, The. William Wordsworth. *See* River Duddon [A Series of Sonnets], The

River falls and over the walls the coffins of cold funerals, The. River in Spate. Louis MacNeice. CP-MacNL

River glides out of the grass. A river or a serpent, A. Long Alley, The. Theodore Roethke. CP-RoetT

River God, The. Stevie Smith. CP-SmitS

River gravel. In the beginning, that. Gravel Walks, The. Seamus Heaney. SP-HeanSO

River Guadalquivir, The. Ballad of the Three Rivers. Federico García Lorca. CP-GarcF, *tr.* by Robert Nasatir

River hemmed with leaning trees, The. Mystery, A. John Greenleaf Whittier. CP-WhitJ

River Humber, The. Stevie Smith. CP-SmitS

River in All Lights, from an Upstairs Window, The. Jane Cooper. CP-CoopJ

River in its abundance, The. Eros at Temple Stream. Denise Levertov. SP-LeveDP; SP-LeveDS

River in March, The. Ted Hughes. SP-HughTN

River in Spate. Louis MacNeice. CP-MacNL

River in the Valley. Gary Snyder. CP-SnydG

River Incident. Theodore Roethke. CP-RoetT

River irises, The. Grass. James Merrill. SP-MerrJ

River is full, The. Solstice. William Carlos Williams. CP-WilW1

River is gold under a sunset of Illinois, The. Letter S. Carl Sandburg. CP-SandC

River is rising with the breathless sound of a fever, The. High Water. W. S. Merwin. SP-MerwWF

River is slow, The. Port, The. W. S. Merwin. SP-MerwW

River-marsh-drowse. Lorine Niedecker. CP-NiedL

River-mirror mirrors the cold sky, The. Mists Over the River. William Carlos Williams. CP-WilW2

River Moon. Carl Sandburg. CP-SandC

River Moons. Carl Sandburg. CP-SandC

River of Bees, The. W. S. Merwin. SP-MerwW

River of green stone. Renaming the Kings. Philip Levine. SP-LeviP

River of Mist, The. E. E. Cummings. CP-CummE

River of Rivers in Connecticut, The. Wallace Stevens. CP-StevW; CP-StevWP

River of Ruin, The. Paul Laurence Dunbar. CP-DunbP

River of sweetness that runs through the meadow of lies, The. Hill Dream of Youth, Thirty Years Later. Richard Eberhart. CP-EberR

River opens out, crawls grieving on its way, The. On the Field of Kulikovo. Aleksandr Aleksandrovich Blok. SP-BlokA, tr. by Peter France and Jon Stallworthy

River Path, The. John Greenleaf Whittier. CP-WhitJ

River Poem. James Merrill. SP-MerrJ

River Profile. W. H. Auden. CP-AudeW

River Rhyme. William Carlos Williams. CP-WilW2

River Rhyme II. William Carlos Williams. CP-WilW2

River Road. Stanley Kunitz. CP-KunSC

River Roads. Carl Sandburg. CP-SandC

River Roses. D. H. Lawrence. CP-LawrD

River Rouge, 1932. John Berryman. CP-BerrJ

River shines in the jungle's, A. Monoon Season. Yusef Komunyakaa. CP-KomuY

River sleeps beneath the sky, The. Sunset. Paul Laurence Dunbar. CP-DunbP

River Song, The. Li Po. SP-PounE, tr. by Ezra Pound

River Still To Be Found, A. Lawrence Ferlinghetti. SP-FerlL

River Styx, Ohio, The. Mary Oliver. SP-OlivM

River takes the land, and leaves nothing, The. Slip, The. Wendell Berry. CP-BerrW

River Thames (?). Christina Georgina Rossetti. CP-RosC3

River That Is East, The. Galway Kinnell. SP-KinnGN

River that rollest by the ancient walls. Stanzas to the Po. Lord Byron. CP-Byron

River That Scolds at All the Other Rivers, The. Thomas Lux. SP-LuxT

River turns, The. Pike, The. Theodore Roethke. CP-RoetT

River wandering down. Robert Creeley. SP-CreeR

River Water Music. Richard Eberhart. CP-EberR

River winds through the wilderness, The. Looking Outside the Cabin Window, I Remember a Line by Li Po. Charles Wright. SP-WrigCN

Riverbank, the long rigs. Broagh. Seamus Heaney. SP-HeanSO

Rivergut girlriver damn drowned. I Was Born to Hustle Roses Down the Avenues of the Dead. Charles Bukowski. SP-BukC2

Riverly is a flower. E. E. Cummings. CP-CummE

Riverman, The. Elizabeth Bishop. CP-BishE

Rivermouth Rocks are fair to see. Wreck of Rivermouth, The. John Greenleaf Whittier. CP-WhitJ

Rivers ("'So lasting they are, the rivers!' Only think. Sources somewhere in the mountains"). Czeslaw Milosz. CP-MiloCN, tr. by Robert Hass

Rivers ("Under various names, I have praised only you, rivers!"). Czeslaw Milosz. CP-MiloC; CP-MiloCN, tr. by Renata Gorczynski and Robert Hass

Rivers and Mountains. John Ashbery. SP-AshbJ

River's blue where it reflects the sky, The. Absence of Noise Presence of Sound. Olga Broumas. SP-BrouO

Rivers flow on idly in their light, The. Wallace Stevens. CP-StevWP

Rivers grow small. Cities grow small. And splendid gardens. Czeslaw Milosz. CP-MiloC; CP-MiloCN

River's mirrorings remake a world. Below Tintern. Charles Tomlinson. CP-TomlC

Rivers of this country are sweet, The. On Swimming. Adam Zagajewski. SP-ZagaA, tr. by Clare Cavanagh

Rivers rustling, martins preparing for flight. Moses. Adam Zagajewski. SP-ZagaA, tr. by Renata Gorczynski, Benjamin Ivry and C. K. Williams

River's Story. James Tate. SP-TateJ

River's Tale, The. Rudyard Kipling. CP-KiplR

Rivers were made by the commingling. Theory of Nato-geography as Advanced by the Tiaphidian Man, With a Comment on the Character of His Penal

System, A. Kenneth Patchen. CP-PatcK

Roach, foulest of creatures. Cockroach. Anne Sexton. CP-SextA

Roaches spit out, The. In a Neighborhood of Murder. Charles Bukowski. SP-BukC1

Road. W. S. Merwin. SP-MerwWF

Road, The. Raymond Carver. CP-CarvR

Road, The. Federico García Lorca. CP-GarcF, tr. by Catherine Brown

Road, The. Muriel Rukeyser. CP-RukeM

Road, The. Tennessee Williams. CP-WillT

Road 37C. Peter Blue Cloud. SP-BlueP

Road ahead, The. On the Road. Seamus Heaney. SP-HeanSO Fr. Sweeney Redivivus.

Road and the End, The. Carl Sandburg. CP-SandC

Road at My Door, The. William Butler Yeats. CP-YeatW Fr. Meditations in Time of Civil War.

Road at the top of the rise, The. Middleness of the Road, The. Robert Frost. CP-FrosR

Road Back, The. Anne Sexton. CP-SextA

Road Behind the Last Dune, The. Marge Piercy. SP-PierM Fr. Sand Roads.

Road Between Here and There, The. Galway Kinnell. SP-KinnGN

Road ends here, The. If your way. Far Point. Charles Tomlinson. SP-TomlC

Road extended o'er a heath, The. William Wordsworth. CP-WorW1

Road goes down, The. It stops at the sea. West of Here, William Stafford. SP-StafWW

Road had steepened and the sun sharpened on the high ridges; the stream probably was dry, The. Redeemer, A. Robinson Jeffers. CP-JefR1

Road in Kentucky, A. Robert Earl Hayden. CP-HaydR

Road is a hard road, The. Driving to Passalacqua, 1960. Charles Wright. SP-WrigC

Road is left that once was trod, The. Old Road, The. Jones Very. CP-VeryJ

Road led straight to the temple, The. Hall, A. Czeslaw Milosz. CP-MiloCN, tr. by Robert Hass

Road Map, The. Thom Gunn. CP-GunnT

Road marked closed, The. Blockade. Olga Broumas. SP-BrouO

Road Not Taken, The. Robert Frost. CP-FrosR

Road-Runner, The. Philip Whalen. SP-WhalP

Road-side Dog. Czeslaw Milosz. CP-MiloCN, tr. by Robert Hass

Road-Song of the Bandar-Log. Rudyard Kipling. CP-KiplR Fr. Jungle Book, The.

Road that had wound us 20,000 miles, A. Homecoming. Hayden Carruth. CP-CarHS

Road that turns and plays. Rainer Maria Rilke. CP-RilkFr, tr. by A. Poulin, Jr. Fr. Valaisian Quatrains, The.

Road to Avrillé, The. Edna St. Vincent Millay. CP-MillE

Road to En-dor is easy to tread, The. En-Dor. Rudyard Kipling. CP-KiplR

Road to Paradise is plain, The. Emily Dickinson. CP-DickE

Road to Roundabout, The. G. K. Chesterton. CP-ChesG

Road to the great canyon always feels, The. Turning the Wheel. Adrienne Rich. SP-RicA1; SP-RicA2 Fr. Turning the Wheel.

Road to the Past, The. Edna St. Vincent Millay. CP-MillE

Road Up. Stevie Smith. CP-SmitS

Road was lit with Moon and star, The. Emily Dickinson. CP-DickE

Road winds down through autumn hills, The. Tour 5. Robert Earl Hayden. CP-HaydR

Roadmender, The. Stéphane Mallarmé. CP-MallS Fr. Street Songs.

Roads. Robert Creeley. CP-CreeR

Roads Also, The. Wilfred Owen. CP-OwenW

Roads getting emptier, air in a steadily purer, The. Dudwood. Donald Davie. CP-DaviDC

Roads leading nowhere. Rainer Maria Rilke. CP-RilkFr, tr. by A. Poulin, Jr. Fr. Valaisian Quatrains, The.

Roadside. Olga Broumas. SP-BrouO

Roadside Stand, A. Robert Frost. CP-FrosR

Roadway, A. Paul Laurence Dunbar. CP-DunbP

Roadway, The. Adrienne Rich. CP-RicAE

Roadway's sallow, puddled furrow, The. Alders. Amy Clampitt. CP-ClamA

Roaming in Thought. Walt Whitman. CP-WhitW

Roan Stallion. Robinson Jeffers. CP-JefR1

Roar and clatter, The. Man and Nature. William Carlos Williams. CP-WilW1

Roar, China! / Roar, old lion of the East! Langston Hughes. CP-HughL; CP-HughL1

Roar through the Tall Twin Elm-Trees, A. George Meredith. CP-MerG1

Roaring. Robert Herrick. CP-HerrR

Roaring alongside he takes for granted, The. Sandpiper. Elizabeth Bishop. CP-BishE

Roaring company that festive night, A. Dark and the Fair, The. Stanley Kunitz. CP-KunSC

Roaring Tinker if you like, The. Three Songs to the One Burden. William Butler

Yeats. CP-YeatW

Roast Possum. Rita Dove. SP-DoveR

Roast[ing] Potatoes. Denise Levertov. SP-LeveDS

Roasting alive of rabbis, The. In the Absence of Bliss. Maxine W. Kumin. SP-KumiM

Rob Roy's Grave. William Wordsworth. CP-WorW1; MW-WorW

Robbed by Death—but that was easy. Emily Dickinson. CP-DickE

Robber Bridegroom, The. Margaret Atwood. SP-AtwM2

Robber Bridegroom, The. Allen Tate. CP-TateA

Robber Woman, The. Marilyn Hacker. SP-HackM

Robbers' Den. Robert Graves. CP-GravR

Robe, The. Jones Very. CP-VeryJ

Robecq Again. Ivor Gurney. SP-GurnI

Robecq had straw and a comfortable tavern. Robecq Again. Ivor Gurney. SP-GurnI

Robed in Light. Jaroslav Seifert.
   First Canto. SP-SeifJ

Robert Bruce's March to Bannockburn. Robert Burns. See Scots, wha hae wi' Wallace bled

Robert Burns' Answer [to Epistle from a Taylor]. Robert Burns. CP-BurnR

Robert Burns Wilson. James Whitcomb Riley. CP-RileJ

Robert Frost. Robert Lowell. SP-LoweR

Robert Gould Shaw. Paul Laurence Dunbar. CP-DunbP

Robert Louis Stevenson! To Robert Louis Stevenson. James Whitcomb Riley. CP-RileJ

Robert Rawlin!—Frosts were falling. Ranger, The. John Greenleaf Whittier. CP-WhitJ

Robert Schumann. Mary Oliver. SP-OlivM

Robert Schumann, Or: Musical Genius Begins with Affliction. Rita Dove. SP-DoveR

Robes of the judges are red [or magnificent], The. Summons, The. Charles Simic. SP-SimiC; SP-SimiCE

Robeson Street. Fanny Howe.
   "Away from the park and zoo." SP-HoweF
   "Blight was on the oaks, A." SP-HoweF
   "Flamingo pink on the chimney stacks." SP-HoweF
   "In the sylvan section of the old zoo." SP-HoweF
   "Moon is moving away, The." SP-HoweF
   "Pushing children in plaid & silver prams." SP-HoweF
   "When snow falls on Franklin Park." SP-HoweF

Robespierre and Mozart as Stage. Robert Lowell. SP-LoweR

Robespierre could live with himself: "The Republic." Robespierre and Mozart as Stage. Robert Lowell. SP-LoweR

Robin. Emily Dickinson. CP-DickE

Robin. W. S. Merwin. SP-MerwWF

Robin, A. Walter De la Mare. CP-DeLaW

Robin, The. Thomas Hardy. CP-HardT

Robin, The. Jones Very. CP-VeryJ

Robin, The. John Greenleaf Whittier. CP-WhitJ

Robin and Harry. Jonathan Swift. CP-SwifJ

Robin cam to the wren's nest, The. Wren's Nest, The. Robert Burns. CP-BurnR

Robin cries: rain!, The. Rain in Ohio. Mary Oliver. SP-OlivM

Robin for the Crumb, The. Emily Dickinson. CP-DickE

Robin has begun his early song, The. Robin's Song, The. Jones Very. CP-VeryJ

Robin, he is strong and sure. Folk Song. Dorothy Parker. CP-ParkD

Robin Hood. John Keats. CP-KeatJ

Robin is a Gabriel, The. Robin. Emily Dickinson. CP-DickE

Robin is a lovely lad. Dance, The. Thomas Campion. CP-CampT Fr. Ayres that Were Sung and Played, at Brougham Castle in Westmerland, in the Kings Entertainment, The.

Robin is the One, The. Emily Dickinson. CP-DickE

Robin Redbreast. Stanley Kunitz. CP-KunSC

Robin said: The Spring will never come, A. Wintry Sonnet, A. Christina Georgina Rossetti. CP-RosC2

Robin Shure in Hairst. Robert Burns. CP-BurnR

Robin Song. Ted Hughes. SP-HughTN

Robin stood by my porch, A. Easter. Lorine Niedecker. CP-NiedL

Robin, to beggars, with a curse. Robin and Harry. Jonathan Swift. CP-SwifJ

Robins' green-blue eggs, The. Morning. Louise Bogan. CP-BogaL

Robin's my Criterion for Tune, The. Emily Dickinson. CP-DickE

Robins' Other Name, The. James Whitcomb Riley. CP-RileJ

Robins sang in the orchard, the buds into blossoms grew, The. Marguerite. John Greenleaf Whittier. CP-WhitJ

Robin's Song, The. Jones Very. CP-VeryJ

"Robins?" They are writing now, The. Emily Dickinson. SP-DickE

Robin's whistled stave, The. Speech. Walter De la Mare. CP-DeLaW

Robinson Jeffers at Point Sur. Donald Davie. CP-DaviDC

Robinsonade. Joseph Brodsky. CP-BrodJ, tr. by Jonathan Aaron

Roblinus is our leading lit- / erary pot-shotter (iconoclasm). After Martial. James Laughlin. CP-LaugJ

Robot-Democracy. D. H. Lawrence. CP-LawrD

Robot Feelings. D. H. Lawrence. CP-LawrD

Rock. Kathleen Jessie Raine. SP-RainK

Rock. Miller Williams. CP-WillM

Rock, The. W. S. Merwin. SP-MerwWF

Rock, The. Wallace Stevens. CP-StevW; CP-StevWP

Rock, The. Jones Very. CP-VeryJ

Rock, a leaf, mud, even the grass, A. Concealment, The: Ishi, the Last Wild Indian. William Stafford. SP-StafW; SP-StafWW

Rock and Hawk. Robinson Jeffers. CP-JefR2

Rock and precipice. Landscape. Octavio Paz. CP-TomlC, tr. by Charles Tomlinson

Rock and sand and no water. Flight. Primo Levi. CP-LeviP, tr. by Ruth Feldman

Rock Climbing. Jane Cooper. CP-CoopJ

Rock drops in a bucket, A. Waters. Donald Hall. CP-HallD

Rock Flow, River Mix. Muriel Rukeyser. CP-RukeM

"Rock" in El Ghor, The. John Greenleaf Whittier. CP-WhitJ

Rock insults us, hard and so boldly browed. Giacometti. Richard Wilbur. CP-WilbR

Rock Music. Derek Mahon. CP-MahoD

Rock. Nothing else. The wild fig tree and the ironstone. Monovasia. Yannis Ritsos. SP-RitsY Fr. Monovasia.

Rock of Rubies: and The Quarrie of Pearls, The. Robert Herrick. CP-HerrR

Rock-Old Dogma, The. William Carlos Williams. CP-WilW2

Rock-plant wife is dead, The. Rock-Plant Wife, The. Josephine Jacobsen. CP-JacoJ

Rock-Plant Wife, The. Josephine Jacobsen. CP-JacoJ

Rock reproduces rock / In miniature. Gli Scafari. Charles Tomlinson. CP-TomlC

Rock-Study with Wanderer. John Berryman. CP-BerrJ

Rock the boat to a fare-thee-well. Rites of Passage. Audre Lorde. SP-LordA

Rock there is whose homely front, A. Primrose of the Rock, The. William Wordsworth. CP-WorW2

Rock-Tomb of Bradore, The. John Greenleaf Whittier. CP-WhitJ

Rock where the sword was stuck, The. Minor Epic. Eleanor Wilner. SP-WilnE

Rocker, The. Donald Hall. CP-HallD

Rockets. Federico García Lorca. CP-GarcF, tr. by Jerome Rothenberg Fr. Barrage of Firework Poems on the Occasion of the Poet's Birthday.

Rockets, The. David Ignatow. SP-IgnaD

Rockettes, The. John Updike. CP-UpdiJ

Rocking. Gabriela Mistral. SP-MistG, tr. by Maria Giachetti [or Jacketti]

Rocking across the lapis lazuli sea. Epitaph in Three Parts. Sylvia Plath. CP-PlatS

Rocking-chairs, The. Sunday at Key West. Elizabeth Bishop. CP-BishE

Rocking Woman, The. William Carlos Williams. CP-WilW2

Rocks, The. Robert Creeley. CP-CreeR

Rocks and the firm roots of trees. Spirituals. Langston Hughes. CP-HughL; CP-HughL2

Rocks and trees in silence stood, The. Will Man Ever Face Fact and Not Feel Flat? Stevie Smith. SP-SmitS

Rocks Push. Yusef Komunyakaa. CP-KomuY

Rocky Acres. Robert Graves. CP-GravR

Rocky nook with hill-tops three, The. Boston. Ralph Waldo Emerson. CP-EmerR

Rococo Birdbath with Figurine of Daphne as Warning to Virgins. Robert Stock. SP-StocR

Rococo compositions of decay. Via Portello. Donald Davie. CP-DaviDC

Rod, The. Robert Herrick. CP-HerrR

Rod was but a harmless wand, The. Virtues of Sid Hamet the Magician's Rod, The. Jonathan Swift. CP-SwifJ

Rodent, The. James Laughlin. CP-LaugJ

Rodez. Donald Davie. CP-DaviDC

Rodin: The Cathedral. Miller Williams. CP-WillM

Rodina Feldervatova. Graveside. James Tate. SP-TateJ

Rodin's Orpheus, floodlit, hacked. Postcard. Adrienne Rich. CP-RicAE

Rodric Lesley. 1830. Emily Jane Brontë. CP-BronE

Roe (and my joy to name) th'art now, to go. To William Roe ("Roe (and my joy to name) th'art now, to go"). Ben Jonson. CP-JonsB; SP-JonsB

Roe-Deer. Ted Hughes. SP-HughTN

Roe Deer, The. Charles Tomlinson. CP-TomlC

Rogation Sunday. William Carlos Williams. CP-WilW2

Rogationtide. Christina Georgina Rossetti. CP-RosC2

Roger Casement. William Butler Yeats. CP-YeatW

Roger Clay's Proposal. James Merrill. SP-MerrJ

Rogers Group, A. Robert Frost. CP-FrosR

Rogue River Jet-Boat Trip, Gold Beach, Oregon, July 4, 1977. Raymond Carver.

CP-CarvR

Rogues' and Gonifs' Ditty. A. Paul Celan. SP-CelaP, *tr. by* John Felstiner

Roguish wind and I, The. Hafiz. CP-EmerR *Fr.* Odes.

Rois Fainéants. W. H. Auden. CP-AudeW

Rokeby. Sir Walter Scott.

   Dawn and Sunrise. SP-ScotW

   Edmund's Songs. SP-ScotW

   Evening. SP-ScotW

   Thorsgill. SP-ScotW

Roland Hayes Beaten (Georgia: 1942). Langston Hughes. CP-HughL2
   (Warning.) CP-HughL; CP-HughL3

Role of the Idea in Poetry, The. Wallace Stevens. CP-StevWP

Roll Call. Yusef Komunyakaa. CP-KomuY

Roll Call. Wendell Phillips Stafford. SP-StafWW

Roll of drums and the bugle's wailing, The. Revisited. John Greenleaf Whittier.
   CP-WhitJ

"Roll on," said Gilbert to the earth. To a Holy Roller. G. K. Chesterton. CP-
   ChesG

Roll On, Thou Deep and Dark Blue Copy Writer—Roll! Ogden Nash. CP-
   NashO

Roll open this rug; a minx is. Props. Carl Sandburg. CP-SandC

Roll stones down on our head! On Taking from the Top to Broaden the Base.
   Robert Frost. CP-FrosR

Rolled in the grass. Grandfather-Father Poem, The. Charles Olson. CP-OlsoC

Rolled over on Europe: the sharp dew frozen to stars. Cornet Cornelius Rilke.
   Stephen Spender. CP-SpenS

Rollicking into Bleecker Street. Halloween Parade, The. Amy Clampitt. CP-
   ClamA

Rolling along through Ohio. Ohio. John Updike. CP-UpdiJ

Rolling English Road, The. G. K. Chesterton. CP-ChesG

Rolling Thunder Stones. Allen Ginsberg. CP-GinsA

Rolling wheele, that runneth often round, The. Sonnet 18. Edmund Spenser. CP-
   Spens *Fr.* Amoretti.

Roma I. Charles Wright. SP-WrigC

Roma II. Charles Wright. SP-WrigC

Roman Antiquities. William Wordsworth. CP-WorW2

Roman Antiquities Discovered at Bishopstone, Herefordshire. William
   Wordsworth. CP-WorW2

Roman Centurion's Song, The. Rudyard Kipling. CP-KiplR

Roman Diary: 1951. John Ciardi. CP-CiarJ

Roman Dream. Jane Cooper. CP-CoopJ

Roman Elegies. Joseph Brodsky. CP-BrodJ, *tr. by* Joseph Brodsky

Roman Fountain. Louise Bogan. CP-BogaL

Roman Gravemounds, The. Thomas Hardy. CP-HardT

Roman had an, A / artist, a freedman. Jerboa, The. Marianne Craig Moore. CP-
   MoorM

Roman Master stands on the Grecian ground, A. *see also* Upon the Same Event.
   William Wordsworth. CP-WorW1

Roman Morn. Lawrence Ferlinghetti. SP-FerlL

Roman Nocturnes. Rafael Alberti.

   "From empty windows / Voice of dead eyes." CP-MertT

   "Nights belong to / What hurts." CP-MertT

   "Other night I saw . . . / Who did I see?, The." CP-MertT

   "Take, O take the key of Rome." CP-MertT

   "You did not come to Rome to dream." CP-MertT

Roman Portrait Busts. John Updike. CP-UpdiJ

Roman Road, The. Thomas Hardy. CP-HardT

Roman Road, The. Stevie Smith. CP-SmitS

Roman Script. Derek Mahon. CP-MahoD

Roman slave appeared one day, A. Inauspiciously. Ambrose Bierce. SP-BierA

Roman Virgil [*or* Vergil], thou that singest. To Virgil [*or* Vergil]. Alfred
   Tennyson. CP-TennA

Romance. Denise Levertov. SP-LeveDL

Romance. Edgar Allan Poe. CP-PoeEd

Romance. Arthur Rimbaud. CP-RimbA, *tr. by* Martin Sorrell

Romance. Miller Williams. CP-WillM

Romance for a Demoiselle Lying in the Grass. Wallace Stevens. CP-StevWP

Romance Moderne. William Carlos Williams. CP-WilW1

Romance of a Youngest Daughter. John Crowe Ransom. SP-RansJ

Romance of Science, The. Randall Jarrell. CP-JarrR

Romance of the Escaped Children. Alan Dugan. CP-DugaA

Romance of the Ganges, A. Elizabeth Barrett Browning. CP-BroEB

Romance of the precise is not the elision, The. Adult Epigram. Wallace Stevens.
   CP-StevW; CP-StevWP

Romance of the Swan's Nest, The. Elizabeth Barrett Browning. CP-BroEB

Romance [*or* Romaunt] of the Rose, The. Guillaume de Lorris *and* Jean de
   Meun. CP-ChauG

Romance was always young. To Lady Jane. Nicholas Vachel Lindsay. CP-LindV

Romance, who loves to nod and sing. Romance. Edgar Allan Poe. CP-PoeEd

Romancer's a nightingale, The. Three Several Birds. James Whitcomb Riley.
   CP-RileJ

Romancin'. James Whitcomb Riley. CP-RileJ

Romans Angry about the Inner World. Robert Bly. SP-BlyR

Romantic, The. Louise Bogan. CP-BogaL

Romantic & Beautiful Poem Inspired by the Recollection of William Butler
   Yeats, His Life & Work, A. Philip Whalen. SP-WhalP

Romantic Eros, The. Helen Pinkerton. CP-PinkH

Romanticism. Raymond Carver. CP-CarvR

Romany Girl, The. Ralph Waldo Emerson. CP-EmerR

Romanze, or the Music Students. Frank O'Hara. SP-OharF

Romaunt of King Mordameer, The. James Whitcomb Riley. CP-RileJ

Romaunt of Margret, The. Elizabeth Barrett Browning. CP-BroEB

Romaunt of the Page, The. Elizabeth Barrett Browning. CP-BroEB

Rome. Joachim Du Bellay. CP-PoEar, *tr. by* Ezra Pound

Rome. "Panormitanus." CP-CunnJ, *tr. by* James Vincent Cunningham

Rome: At the Pyramid of Cestius near the Graves of Shelley and Keats. Thomas
   Hardy. CP-HardT

Rome: Building a New Street in the Ancient Quarter. Thomas Hardy. CP-HardT

Rome conquered earth with arms, the sea with ships. George Buchanan. CP-
   CunnJ, *tr. by* James Vincent Cunningham

Rome has fallen, ye see it lying. Fragment: Rome and Nature. Percy Bysshe
   Shelley. CP-ShelP

'Rome I dislike,' you said in French. To Vasko Popa In Rome. Charles
   Tomlinson. SP-TomlC

Rome: In the Café. James Laughlin. CP-LaugJ

Rome never looks where she treads. Pict Song, A. Rudyard Kipling. CP-KiplR
   Fr. Puck of Pook's Hill.

Rome: On the Palatine. Thomas Hardy. CP-HardT

Rome: The Vatican: Sala delle Muse. Thomas Hardy. CP-HardT

Rome Unvisited. Oscar Wilde. CP-WildO

Rome! what a scroll of History thine has been. Urbs Sacra Æterna. Oscar Wilde.
   CP-WildO

Rome Zoo. A. R. Ammons. CP-AmmoA

Romiosini. Yannis Ritsos. SP-RitsY, *tr. by* Kimon Friar

Romney! expert infallibly to trace. To George Romney, Esq. William Cowper.
   CP-CowpW

Romulus and Remus. Rudyard Kipling. CP-KiplR

Ronalds of the Bennals, The. Robert Burns. CP-BurnR

Rondeau: "Give me a rose, cool-petaled, virgin white." Dorothy Parker. CP-
   ParkD

Rondeau: "It isn't fair, to me, when you're away." Dorothy Parker. CP-ParkD

Rondeau: "It's easy to talk." Hans Magnus Enzensberger. SP-EnzeH, *tr. by*
   Michael Hamburger

Rondeau: "Year has cast its cloak away, The." Charles, Duc d'Orléans. CP-
   WilbR

Rondeau of a Conscientious Objector. D. H. Lawrence. CP-LawrD

Rondeau Redoublé. Dorothy Parker. CP-ParkD

Rondel. Algernon Charles Swinburne. *See* Kissing Her Hair

Rondel: "Nothing you have when you awake." Stéphane Mallarmé. CP-MallS,
   tr. by Henry Weinfield

Rondel: "Now that I am fifty-six." Muriel Rukeyser. CP-RukeM

Rondel: "We'll love each other if you choose." Stéphane Mallarmé. CP-MallS,
   tr. by Henry Weinfield

Roof Garden. James Schuyler. CP-SchuJ

Roof overwoven by a soft tussle of leaves. Wellfleet: The House. Richard
   Wilbur. CP-WilbR

Roof pours upward. View, The. Robert Creeley. SP-CreeR

Roofed in with the snows of December. Pardon of Christmas, The. G. K.
   Chesterton. CP-ChesG

Roofless and eyeless, weed-sodden, dank, old, cold. Abandoned Church, An.
   Walter De la Mare. CP-DeLaW

Roofless houses, cartons of chalk. Sahara Bus Trip, The. Rita Dove. SP-DoveR

Roofless, the wreck of a house and byre. Idrigill. Charles Tomlinson. CP-TomlC

Roofs. Philip Levine. SP-LeviP

Roof's peak is eye. Sitting Here. Robert Creeley. CP-CreeR

Rooftop, The. Thom Gunn. CP-GunnT

Roofwalker, The. Adrienne Rich. CP-RicAE; SP-RicA1; SP-RicA2

Rook Grimshaw posed the problem neat. Young Grimshaw. Robert Stock. SP-
   StocR

Rook[e] he sells feathers, yet he still doth cry. Upon Rook: Epigram. Robert
   Herrick. CP-HerrR

Rooks flew across the sky, bright February watched. February Dawn. Ivor
   Gurney. SP-GurnI

Rooks In October. Walter De la Mare. CP-DeLaW

Room. Langston Hughes. CP-HughL; CP-HughL3

Room. Laura Riding Jackson. CP-RidiL

Room. Denise Levertov. SP-LeveDL

Room. C. K. Williams. SP-WillC

Room, The. W. S. Merwin. SP-MerwW

Room, The. Gregory Orr. SP-OrrG

Room above the Square, The. Stephen Spender. CP-SpenS

Room after room. Love in a Life. Robert Browning. CP-BroR1

Room after room without a voice no one to say. Red House, The. W. S. Merwin. SP-MerwWF

Room all the way across america, A. Bringing It Home. C. K. Williams. CP-WillC

Room darkened, darkened until, The. Blessing, The. John Updike. CP-UpdiJ

Room designed by Orrery receives, A. Dublin Georgian. Donald Davie. CP-DaviDC

'Room for manœuvre,' I say. Intervals in a Busy Life. Donald Davie. CP-DaviDC

"Room for the spheres!"—then first they shined. Three Dimensions, The. Ralph Waldo Emerson. CP-EmerR

Room I work in is as foursquare, The. Adam Zagajewski. SP-ZagaA, *tr. by* Clare Cavanagh

Room in Rome, A. Karl Shapiro. SP-ShapK

Room is all a stupid quietness, The. Happy Families. Louis MacNeice. CP-MacNL

Room is already white, The. Trim it in blue. Life in the City: In Memoriam Edward Gibbon. Philip Whalen. SP-WhalP

Room is full of shadow and the sad, The. Orphans' New Year Gifts. Arthur Rimbaud. CP-RimbA, *tr. by* Martin Sorrell

Room is full of you!—As I came in, The. Interim. Edna St. Vincent Millay. CP-MillE

Room is like a cave, the webs of night, The. Clock, The. Thom Gunn. CP-GunnT

Room is sparsely furnished, The. Thrall. Carolyn Kizer. CP-KizeC

Room of My Life, The. Anne Sexton. CP-SextA

Room of the guilty one / Evil place of bad luck. Aegeus in Prison. Alfonso Cortes. CP-MertT

Room on a Garden, A. Wallace Stevens. CP-StevWP

Room opens onto a slate-blue sky, The. Young Couple. Arthur Rimbaud. CP-RimbA, *tr. by* Martin Sorrell

Room, room, make room for the bouncing belly. Hymn: "Room, room, make room for the bouncing belly." Ben Jonson. CP-JonsB *Fr.* Pleasure Reconciled to Virtue.

Room 28. John Updike. CP-UpdiJ

Room was filled with black boxes, The. Blues for Casanova. Andrei Codrescu. SP-CodrA

Room was poor and shabby, The. One Night. Constantine P. Cavafy. CP-CavaC, *tr. by* Theoharis Constantine Theoharis

Room was small but neat and when I visited him, The. Result. Charles Bukowski. SP-BukC3

Room was suddenly rich and the great bay-window was, The. Snow. Louis MacNeice. CP-MacNL

Room where you lived, The. Mysterious Disappearance, The. James Laughlin. CP-LaugJ

Rooming Houses are Old Women. Audre Lorde. SP-LordA

Roominghouse, Winter. Margaret Atwood. SP-AtwM1

Rooms are grotesque with furniture of snow. Return, The. Robert Earl Hayden. CP-HaydR

Rooms gone, hallways and stairwells, The. Vacant Lot with Tumbleweed and Pigeons. Amy Clampitt. CP-ClamA

Rooms in Bloomsbury. Marilyn Hacker. SP-HackM

Rooms Without Walls. Wyatt Prunty. SP-PrunW

Roomy Eternity / Casts her schemes rarely. Ralph Waldo Emerson. CP-EmerR

Roosevelt. Nicholas Vachel Lindsay. CP-LindV

Roosevelt died and met Wilson, who said, "I blundered into it." Wilson in Hell. Robinson Jeffers. CP-JefR3

Roosevelt, Renaissance, Gem, Alhambra, The. Movies. Langston Hughes. CP-HughL; CP-HughL3

Rooster. James Tate. SP-TateJ

Rooster, The. Ogden Nash. CP-NashO

Roosters. Elizabeth Bishop. CP-BishE

Root an acceptable connection, The. What Appears to Be Yours. Frank O'Hara. SP-OharF

Root Canal, The. Marge Piercy. SP-PierM

Root Cellar. Theodore Roethke. CP-RoetT

Root-light, or the Lawyer's Daughter. James Dickey. CP-DickJ

Root of Our Evil, The. D. H. Lawrence. CP-LawrD

Root of our present evil is that we buy and sell, The. Root of Our Evil, The. D. H. Lawrence. CP-LawrD

Rooted in the most unconscionable romance. Law of Poetry, The. George Oppen. CP-OppGN

Roots. William Meredith. SP-MereW

Roots. Adrienne Rich. CP-RicAE; SP-RicA2

Roots. Gary Snyder. CP-SnydG

Roots and Branches. Robert Duncan. SP-DuncR

Roots and Leaves Themselves Alone. Walt Whitman. CP-WhitW

Roots, go deep: wrap your coils; fasten your knots. Wind Horses. Carl Sandburg. CP-SandC

Roots grow from my feet, Apollo, like a tree. Daphne. Marya Alexandrovna Zaturenska. SP-ZatuM

Roots had no money; yet he went o'th score. Upon Roots. Robert Herrick. CP-HerrR

Roots of the World, The. Yannis Ritsos. SP-RitsY, *tr. by* Athan Anagnostopoulos

Roots out of the ground and ongoing. Craters. James Dickey. CP-DickJ

Rope's End, The. Howard Nemerov. CP-NemeH

Ropes, pulleys, shawls. Kudzu Dormant. Amy Clampitt. CP-ClamA

Ropewalk, The. Henry Wadsworth Longfellow. SP-LongH

Rorate, celi, desuper! William Dunbar. CP-DunbW

Ros. Andrew Marvell. CP-MarvÀ

Rosa Mundi. Kenneth Rexroth. CP-RexrK

Rosa Mystica. Gerard Manley Hopkins. CP-HopkG

Rosa Sanguinea, The. Henry David Thoreau. CP-ThorH

Rosa Sempiterna. Ezra Pound. CP-PoEar

Rosabelle. Sir Walter Scott. SP-ScotW *Fr.* Lay of the Last Minstrel, The.

Rosalia. Charles Simic. SP-SimiC

    Dimly Outlined by a Police Artist. SP-SimiC

Rosalie. Ambrose Bierce. SP-BierA

Rosalind. George Meredith. CP-MerG2

Rosalind. Christina Georgina Rossetti. CP-RosC3

Rosalind and Helen; A Modern Eclogue. Percy Bysshe Shelley. CP-ShelP

Rosamond C. Bailey. James Whitcomb Riley. CP-RileJ

Rosarie, The. Robert Herrick. CP-HerrR

Rosary Beads. Herman Melville. SP-MelvH

Rose. Walter De la Mare. CP-DeLaW

Rose. Kathleen Jessie Raine. SP-RainK

Rose. Rainer Maria Rilke. CP-RilkFr, *tr. by* A. Poulin, Jr.

Rose, The. William Cowper. CP-CowpW

Rose, The. Robert Creeley. CP-CreeR

Rose, The. Robert Graves. CP-GravR

Rose, The. George Herbert. CP-HerbG

Rose, The. Robert Herrick. CP-HerrR

Rose, The. Gabriela Mistral. SP-MistG, *tr. by* Maria Giachetti [*or* Jacketti]

Rose, The. John Crowe Ransom. SP-RansJ

Rose, The. James Whitcomb Riley. CP-RileJ

Rose, The. Christina Georgina Rossetti. CP-RosC3

Rose, The. Jones Very. CP-VeryJ

Rose, The. William Carlos Williams. CP-WilW2

Rose, The. William Carlos Williams. CP-WilW1

Rose, a lily, and the Face of Christ, A. Thou Art Fairer Than the Children of Men. Christina Georgina Rossetti. CP-RosC2

Rose, against whom. Rainer Maria Rilke. CP-RilkFr, *tr. by* A. Poulin, Jr. *Fr.* Roses, The.

Rose and Cabbage. D. H. Lawrence. CP-LawrD

Rose and Milton, A. Jorge Luis Borges. SP-BorgJ, *tr. by* Alastair Reid

Rose-Ann. Thomas Hardy. CP-HardT

Rose at the edge of my tax structure, The. On the Patio. John Ciardi. CP-CiarJ

Rose Bawn. Carl Sandburg. CP-SandC

Rose, certainly earthly and our equal. Rainer Maria Rilke. CP-RilkFr, *tr. by* A. Poulin, Jr. *Fr.* Roses, The.

Rose-cheeked Laura, Come. Thomas Campion. CP-CampT *Fr.* Observations in the Art of English Poesie.

Rose-cheekt *Lawra* come. Thomas Campion. *See* Rose-cheeked Laura, Come

Rose-colored cup and saucer. Song on Porcelain. Czeslaw Milosz. CP-MiloC; CP-MiloCN, *tr. by* Robert Pinsky

Rose Colored Glasses. Kenneth Rexroth. CP-RexrK

Rose did caper on her cheek, The. Emily Dickinson. CP-DickE

Rose, did you have to be left. Rainer Maria Rilke. CP-RilkFr, *tr. by* A. Poulin, Jr. *Fr.* Roses, The.

Rose, do you prefer to be the ardent friend. Rainer Maria Rilke. CP-RilkFr, *tr. by* A. Poulin, Jr. *Fr.* Roses, The.

Rose fades, The. Poem: "Rose fades, The." William Carlos Williams. CP-WilW2

Rose Family, The. Robert Frost. CP-FrosR

Rose for Janet, A. Charles Tomlinson. SP-TomlC

Rose for Solitude, A. Sam Hamill. SP-HamiS

Rose had been wash'd, just wash'd in a shower, The. Rose, The. William Cowper. CP-CowpW

Rose, harsh rose. Sea Rose. "H. D." CP-DoolH

Rose has thorns as well as honey, A. Christina Georgina Rossetti. CP-RosC2

Rose-hips. Charles Tomlinson. CP-TomlC

Rose I set within my "Paradise," A. Rosa Sempiterna. Ezra Pound. CP-PoEar

Rose in a mystery, where is it found?, The. Rosa Mystica. Gerard Manley Hopkins. CP-HopkG

Rose in Candlelight, A. Walter De la Mare. CP-DeLaW

Rose in Ice. Robert Stock. SP-StocR

Rose in October, A. James Whitcomb Riley. CP-RileJ

Rose, in tatters on the garden path, A. Answer, The. Rudyard Kipling. CP-KiplR

Rose in the high garden you desire, A. Ode to Salvador Dalí. Federico García Lorca. CP-GarcF, *tr.* by William Bryant Logan

Rose in the park. 10/14. William Carlos Williams. CP-WilW2

Rose in Water, A. Walter De la Mare. CP-DeLaW

Rose is a rose, The. Rose Family, The. Robert Frost. CP-FrosR

Rose / is dying the, The. E. E. Cummings. CP-CummE

Rose is Love's own flower, and Love's no less, The. To My Fior-Di-Lisa. Christina Georgina Rossetti. CP-RosC3

Rose Is Not a Cabbage, A. D. H. Lawrence. CP-LawrD

Rose-Lady, The. James Whitcomb Riley. CP-RileJ

Rose late: the jarring and whining. Morning. Donald Davie. CP-DaviDC

Rose, like dim battlements, the hills and reared. Macbeth. Walter De la Mare. CP-DeLaW

Rose Mary. Dante Gabriel Rossetti. CW-RossD

Rose, O pure / Contradiction / Longing to be nobody's. Rilke's Epitaph. Thomas Merton. CP-MertT

Rose, O you completely perfect thing. Rainer Maria Rilke. CP-RilkFr, *tr.* by A. Poulin, Jr. *Fr.* Roses, The.

Rose of all Roses, Rose of all the World! Rose of Battle, The. William Butler Yeats. CP-YeatW

Rose of All the World. D. H. Lawrence. CP-LawrD

Rose of all the world is not for me, The. Little White Rose, The. Hugh MacDiarmid. SP-MacDH

Rose of Battle, The. William Butler Yeats. CP-YeatW

Rose of England, The. D. H. Lawrence. CP-LawrD

Rose of light, a crumbling wall. Rainer Maria Rilke. CP-RilkFr, *tr.* by A. Poulin, Jr. *Fr.* Valaisian Quatrains, The.

Rose of Marion, The. James Schuyler. CP-SchuJ

Rose of Midnight, The. Nicholas Vachel Lindsay. CP-LindV

Rose of neon darkness. Chippy. Langston Hughes. CP-HughL; CP-HughL2

Rose of Peace, The. William Butler Yeats. CP-YeatW

Rose-of-Sharon. Louis Zukofsky. CP-ZukLS

Rose of spirit, rose of light. On Reading William Blake's "The Sick Rose." Allen Ginsberg. CP-GinsA

Rose of the future and lode withheld. Useless Song. Federico García Lorca. CP-GarcF, *tr.* by Alan S. Trueblood *Fr.* Songs to End With.

Rose of the World, The. William Butler Yeats. CP-YeatW

Rose on Sunday. Rainer Maria Rilke. CP-RilkFr, *tr.* by A. Poulin, Jr.

Rose, on this terrace fifty years ago. Roses on the Terrace, The. Alfred Tennyson. CP-TennA

Rose once grew within, A. Lay of the Early Rose, A. Elizabeth Barrett Browning. CP-BroEB

Rose Plant in Jericho, A. Christina Georgina Rossetti. CP-RosC1

Rose Pogonias. Robert Frost. CP-FrosR

Rose / red sunlight, A. Destroying Beauty. Charles Bukowski. SP-BukC2

Rose, Rose. Charles Bukowski. SP-BukC2

Rose sericea: its red. Of Coming-into-Being and Passing-Away. Geoffrey Hill. CP-HillG

Rose, so cherished by our customs. Rainer Maria Rilke. CP-RilkFr, *tr.* by A. Poulin, Jr. *Fr.* Roses, The.

Rose, so clear and yet so fiery. Rainer Maria Rilke. CP-RilkFr, *tr.* by A. Poulin, Jr. *Fr.* Roses, The.

Rose that blushes rosy red, The. Christina Georgina Rossetti. CP-RosC2

Rose that drinks the fountain dew, The. To Constantia. Percy Bysshe Shelley. CP-ShelP

Rose thou showst me has lost all its hue, The. Rose, The. Jones Very. CP-VeryJ

Rose Tree, The. William Butler Yeats. CP-YeatW

Rose / was not looking for the dawn, The. Qasida of the Rose. Federico García Lorca. CP-GarcF, *tr.* by Catherine Brown *Fr.* Qasidas.

Rose was sick and smiling died [*or* di'd], The. Funeral[l] Rites of the Rose, The. Robert Herrick. CP-HerrR

Rose which spied one swallow, A. One Swallow Does Not Make a Summer. Christina Georgina Rossetti. CP-RosC3

Rose with such a bonny blush, The. Christina Georgina Rossetti. CP-RosC2

Rose / with the deepdown corolla. Roulette. Federico García Lorca. CP-GarcF, *tr.* by Jerome Rothenberg *Fr.* Wheels of Fortune.

Roseapples and Nudes. Robert Stock. SP-StocR

Rosebay willow herb pushing. Nottinghamshire. Donald Davie. CP-DaviDC

Rosebud, The. Robert Burns. CP-BurnR

Rosebud, knot of worms. Words for a Nursery. Sylvia Plath. CP-PlatS

Rosebud Morales, my friend. Pentecost. Ai. SP-Ai

Rosebush hangs over the wall, witness to bliss, A. Yehuda Amichai. SP-AmicYL, *tr.* by Benjamin Harshav *and* Barbara Harshav

Rosebush in an Unlikely Garden, A. William Carlos Williams. CP-WilW2

Rosemarie Branch, The. Robert Herrick. CP-HerrR

Rosemary. Edna St. Vincent Millay. CP-MillE

Rosemary. Marianne Craig Moore. CP-MoorM

Rosemary ("Ah, no, I dare not lose myself in dreams"). Dorothy Parker. CP-ParkD

Rosemary ("I wear your fragrant memory, like a spray of mignonette"). Dorothy Parker. CP-ParkD

Roses. Rita Dove. SP-DoveR

Roses. Paul Laurence Dunbar. CP-DunbP

Roses. D. H. Lawrence. CP-LawrD

Roses. Mary Oliver. SP-OlivM

Roses. Louis Zukofsky. CP-ZukLS

Roses, The. Rainer Maria Rilke.

  "Abandon surrounds abandon." CP-RilkFr, *tr.* by A. Poulin, Jr.

  "All alone, O abundant flower." CP-RilkFr, *tr.* by A. Poulin, Jr.

  "All that spinning on your stem." CP-RilkFr, *tr.* by A. Poulin, Jr.

  "Bright cool rose leaning." CP-RilkFr, *tr.* by A. Poulin, Jr.

  "Do you set yourself up as example?" CP-RilkFr, *tr.* by A. Poulin, Jr.

  "Except from your inner." CP-RilkFr, *tr.* by A. Poulin, Jr.

  "Friend of hours when no on remains." CP-RilkFr, *tr.* by A. Poulin, Jr.

  "I see you, rose, half-open book." CP-RilkFr, *tr.* by A. Poulin, Jr.

  "If we're sometimes so amazed." CP-RilkFr, *tr.* by A. Poulin, Jr.

  "I'm conscious of your being." CP-RilkFr, *tr.* by A. Poulin, Jr.

  "Infinitely at ease." CP-RilkFr, *tr.* by A. Poulin, Jr.

  "It's you who in you is preparing." CP-RilkFr, *tr.* by A. Poulin, Jr.

  "Late-blooming rose that the bitter." CP-RilkFr, *tr.* by A. Poulin, Jr.

  "Let's not speak of you. Ineffable." CP-RilkFr, *tr.* by A. Poulin, Jr.

  "Overflowing with your dream." CP-RilkFr, *tr.* by A. Poulin, Jr.

  "Rose, against whom." CP-RilkFr, *tr.* by A. Poulin, Jr.

  "Rose, certainly earthly and our equal." CP-RilkFr, *tr.* by A. Poulin, Jr.

  "Rose, did you have to be left." CP-RilkFr, *tr.* by A. Poulin, Jr.

  "Rose, do you prefer to be the ardent friend." CP-RilkFr, *tr.* by A. Poulin, Jr.

  "Rose, O you completely perfect thing." CP-RilkFr, *tr.* by A. Poulin, Jr.

  "Rose, so cherished by our customs." CP-RilkFr, *tr.* by A. Poulin, Jr.

  "Rose, so clear and yet so fiery." CP-RilkFr, *tr.* by A. Poulin, Jr.

  "Single rose is every rose, A." CP-RilkFr, *tr.* by A. Poulin, Jr.

  "Summer: for a few days being." CP-RilkFr, *tr.* by A. Poulin, Jr.

  "Surely it was us who encouraged." CP-RilkFr, *tr.* by A. Poulin, Jr.

  "You again, you rising." CP-RilkFr, *tr.* by A. Poulin, Jr.

  "You're touched by all that touches us." CP-RilkFr, *tr.* by A. Poulin, Jr.

Roses and gold. Places. Carl Sandburg. CP-SandC

Roses and lilies grow above the place. Life Hidden. Christina Georgina Rossetti. CP-RosC3

Roses and Pearls. Paul Laurence Dunbar. CP-DunbP

Roses and Rue. Oscar Wilde. CP-WildO

Roses are sweet to smell and see. April Moon. Walter De la Mare. CP-DeLaW

Roses are things which Christmas is not a bed of them. April Yule, Daddy! Ogden Nash. CP-NashO

Roses at first were white. How Roses Came Red. Robert Herrick. CP-HerrR

Roses bloom too late for me. I Do Set My Bow in the Cloud. Christina Georgina Rossetti. CP-RosC3

Roses blushing red and white, / For delight. Christina Georgina Rossetti. CP-RosC2

Roses hardy as clover return. Roses. Louis Zukofsky. CP-ZukLS

Roses, Late Summer. Mary Oliver. SP-OlivM

Roses lift from the strawberry-like leaves, The. Bouquet of Ten Roses, A. Robert Bly. SP-BlyR

Roses lingered in her cheeks, The. On Albina. Christina Georgina Rossetti. CP-RosC3

Roses of irony blossom, The. Nosegay, The. Donald Davie. CP-DaviDC

Roses of Life, The. Kenneth Patchen. CP-PatcK

Roses of love glad the garden of life, The. Love's Last Adieu. Lord Byron. CP-Byron

Roses on a brier, / Pearls from out the bitter sea. Christina Georgina Rossetti. CP-RosC2

Roses on the Breakfast Table. D. H. Lawrence. CP-LawrD

Roses on the Terrace, The. Alfred Tennyson. CP-TennA

Roses red and roses white. Blue Roses. Rudyard Kipling. CP-KiplR *Fr.* Light That Failed, The.

Roses, rooted warm in earth. Lines on Reading Too Many Poets. Dorothy Parker. CP-ParkD

Roses slanted crimson sobs, The. Testimony Regarding a Ghost. Carl Sandburg. CP-SandC

Roses tremble; oh, the sunflower's eye, The. Listening to Distant Guns. Denise Levertov. SP-LeveDS

Roses with the scent bred out. In Lieu. Louis MacNeice. CP-MacNL

Roses, you can never die. To Roses in Julia's Bosome. Robert Herrick. CP-HerrR

Rosetree,rosetree / —you're a song to see:whose. E. E. Cummings. CP-CummE

Rosicrucian subtleties / In the Orient had rise. Rudyard Kipling. CP-KiplR *Fr.* Plain Tales from the Hills.

Rosina. Emily Jane Brontë. CP-BronE

Rosny. Robert Browning. CP-BroR2

Ross-shire Hills, The. Hugh MacDiarmid. SP-MacDH

Rossville Lectur' Course, The. James Whitcomb Riley. CP-RileJ

Rosy. Louise Glück. SP-GlucL

Rosy, It Was. Charles Olson. CP-OlsoC

Rosy maiden Winifred, / With a milkpail on her head. Christina Georgina Rossetti. CP-RosC2

Rotarians. G. K. Chesterton. CP-ChesG

Rotha, my Spiritual Child! this head was grey. To Rotha Q—. William Wordsworth. CP-WorW2

Rothebât. Stevie Smith. CP-SmitS

Roto: How the Bourgeoisie Dream. Andrei Codrescu. SP-CodrA

Rotting Ginsberg, I stared in the mirror naked today. Mescaline. Allen Ginsberg. CP-GinsA

Rou-cou spoke the dove. Song of Fixed Accord. Wallace Stevens. CP-StevW; CP-StevWP

Rouge In Appearance. Shmuel HaNagid. SP-HaNaS, *tr.* by Peter Cole

Rough draft, getting rougher, A. Drafts. A. K. Ramanujan. CP-RamaA

Rough Metaphors. Jelaluddin Rumi. SP-Rumi, *tr.* by Coleman Barks

Rough Outline. Charles Simic. SP-SimiC; SP-SimiCE

Rough Sketch, A. James Whitcomb Riley. CP-RileJ

Rough Song of Animals Dying. Lawrence Ferlinghetti. SP-FerlL

Rough Times. Marge Piercy. SP-PierM

Rough wind, that moanest loud. Dirge, A: "Rough wind, that moanest loud." Percy Bysshe Shelley. CP-ShelP

Roughly figured, this man of moderate habits. Life Cycle of Common Man. Howard Nemerov. CP-NemeH

Roughly Square. Yannis Ritsos. SP-RitsY, *tr.* by N. C. Germanacos

Roulette. Federico García Lorca. CP-GarcF, *tr.* by Jerome Rothenberg *Fr.* Wheels of Fortune.

Round. A. R. Ammons. CP-AmmoA

Round. Robert Pinsky. CP-PinsR

Round, The. Stanley Kunitz. CP-KunSC

Round, The. Walter De la Mare. CP-DeLaW

Round & a Canon, A. Charles Olson. CP-OlsoC

Round a so moon could dream(i sus). E. E. Cummings. CP-CummE

Round about midnight. Plea, The. Yusef Komunyakaa. CP-KomuY

Round and a Hope for Smithgirls, A. Thomas Merton. CP-MertT

Round and Round. Thom Gunn. CP-GunnT

Round and round / again, and. For the Graduation: Bolinas, 1972. Robert Creeley. CP-CreeR

Round and sad-eyed man puffed cigars as if, The. Song of the Round Man. Michael Palmer. SP-PalmM

Round and smooth, my body in the bath, The. Young Woman's Song. John Berryman. CP-BerrJ

Round clouds roll in the arms of the wind. Come Spring, Come Sorrow. D. H. Lawrence. CP-LawrD

Round face near the top of the stairs, A. E. E. Cummings. CP-CummE

Round Fish, The. Eleanor Wilner. SP-WilnE

Round graves, below. In. Sketch of a Landscape. Paul Celan. SP-CelaP, *tr.* by John Felstiner

Round Midnight. Clarence Major. SP-MajoC

Round moon suffocates the neighbouring stars, A. Lure of Murder. Robert Graves. CP-GravR

Round of Argentina, The. Argentine Round. Gabriela Mistral. SP-MistG, *tr.* by Maria Giachetti [*or* Jacketti]

Round of Aromas. Gabriela Mistral. SP-MistG, *tr.* by Maria Giachetti [*or* Jacketti]

Round of Colors. Gabriela Mistral. SP-MistG, *tr.* by Maria Giachetti [*or* Jacketti]

Round of gold, The. Girl's Ring, A. E. E. Cummings. CP-CummE

Round of the Rainbow. Gabriela Mistral. SP-MistG, *tr.* by Maria Giachetti [*or* Jacketti]

Round Robin, A. Robert Browning. CP-BroR2

Round silence of night, The. Hour of Stars. Federico García Lorca. CP-GarcF, *tr.* by Catherine Brown

Round Susan, somewhere Susan. Trajectory of the Traveling Susan. Marge Piercy. SP-PierM

Round the cape of a sudden came the sea. Parting at Morning. Robert Browning. CP-BroR1; SP-BroR

Round the Corner. Louis MacNeice. CP-MacNL

Round the green fountain thick with women. Adult Bookstore. Karl Shapiro. SP-ShapK

Round the house were lilacs and strawberries. Twenty Years Ago. D. H. Lawrence. CP-LawrD

Round the three actors in any blessed event. Blessed Event. W. H. Auden. CP-AudeW

Round the wide earth, from the red field your valour has won. Conquerors, The. Paul Laurence Dunbar. CP-DunbP

Round Thurlow's head in early youth. On the Promotion of Thurlow. William Cowper. CP-CowpW

Round Time. Heather McHugh. SP-McHuH

Round yellow light, A. Egg, the. Sam Hamill. SP-HamiS

Roundabout hours of air, slanting past Massachusetts above the. Lat. 10 Degrees North, Long. 45 Degrees West. Muriel Rukeyser. CP-RukeM

Roundclouds occluding patches of the. Struggle of Wings. William Carlos Williams. CP-WilW1

Rounded Catalogue Divine Complete, The. Walt Whitman. CP-WhitW

Rounded world is fair to see, The. Nature [1844]. Ralph Waldo Emerson. CP-EmerR

Roundel: "I come unto thee thru the hidden ways." Joachim Du Bellay. CP-PoEar, *tr.* by Ezra Pound

Roundel: "She's passing fair; but so demure is she." Dorothy Parker. CP-ParkD

Roundel for Arms. Ezra Pound. CP-PoEar

Roundel seems to fit a round of days, A. Christina Georgina Rossetti. CP-RosC3

Roundelay: "On all that strand." Samuel Beckett. CP-BeckS

Rounding steeps and jostles were one thing, The. Ferris Wheel, The. Wyatt Prunty. SP-PrunW

Rounding the mountain's rim-ledge. Delaware Water Gap. A. R. Ammons. CP-AmmoA

Rouse, A. Ezra Pound. CP-PoEar

Rouse for Stevens, A. Theodore Roethke. CP-RoetT

Rouse now, my dullard, and thy wits awake. Imp Within, The. Walter De la Mare. CP-DeLaW

Rouse up thyself, my gentle muse. On the King's Birthday. Ben Jonson. CP-JonsB

Roused, you ask, "Wasn't that . . . ?" Over. Rae Armantrout. SP-ArmaA

Rouses in its cave. Grosse Fuge. Ted Hughes. SP-HughTN

Rousseau in His Day. Donald Davie. CP-DaviDC

Rousseau, Voltaire, our Gibbon, and De Staël. Sonnet to Lake Leman. Lord Byron. CP-Byron

Rout of the White Hussars, The. Rudyard Kipling. *Fr.* Plain Tales from the Hills.

Route. George Oppen. CP-OppGN

Route Marchin'. Rudyard Kipling. CP-KiplR

Route of Evanescence, A. Hummingbird, A. Emily Dickinson. CP-DickE

Route of the Táin, The. Thomas Kinsella. CP-KinsT

Route Six. Stanley Kunitz. CP-KunSC

Route Two. Howard Nemerov. CP-NemeH

Route with No Number. W. S. Merwin. SP-MerwW

Routine Day Sonnet. A. K. Ramanujan. CP-RamaA

Rover Come Home, The. Thomas Hardy. CP-HardT

Rover was in clover. Poor Rover. Langston Hughes. CP-HughL

Roving boy comes, staff in hand, A. Recognition, The. Johann N. Vogl. CP-MerG2

Roving Gypsies. Charles Baudelaire. CP-BaudC, *tr.* by Walter Martin

Roving, roving, as it seems. Una. Ralph Waldo Emerson. CP-EmerR

Row after row with strict impunity. Ode to the Confederate Dead. Allen Tate. CP-TateA

Row of thick pillars, A. Stephen Crane. CP-CranS

Row us out from Desenzano, to your Sirmione row! Frater Ave Atque Vale. Alfred Tennyson. CP-TennA

Rowan like a lip-sticked girl, A. Song: "Rowan like a lip-sticked girl, A." Seamus Heaney. SP-HeanSO

Rowdy wind pushed out the sky, A. Regatta, The. Richard Wilbur. CP-WilbR

Rower. Charles Tomlinson. CP-TomlC

Rowers, The. Rudyard Kipling. CP-KiplR

Rowin 't in Her Apron, The. Robert Burns. CP-BurnR

Rowing. Anne Sexton. CP-SextA; SP-SextA

Rowing between Pond and Western Islands. Loon Call, A. Richard Eberhart. CP-EberR

Rowing Endeth, The. Anne Sexton. CP-SextA; SP-SextA

Rowle of Parchment Clunn about him beares, A. Upon Clunn. Robert Herrick. CP-HerrR

Roxy. James Schuyler. CP-SchuJ

Royal and Dower-royal, I the Queen. Song of the Cities, The. Rudyard Kipling. CP-KiplR

Royal nature, and a most refined, A. Petrarch. CP-Petra, *tr.* by J. G. Nichols

Royal Palm. Hart Crane. CP-CranH

Royal Pavilion, The. Jaroslav Seifert. SP-SeifJ, *tr. by* Ewald Osers

Royal Princess, A. Christina Georgina Rossetti. CP-RosC1

Royal Prospect, A. Seamus Heaney. SP-HeanSO

Royal roads were cow paths, The. First Kingdom, The. Seamus Heaney. SP-HeanSO *Fr.* Sweeney Redivivus.

Royal Sponsors. Thomas Hardy. CP-HardT

Royals. James Schuyler. CP-SchuJ

Royalty. Arthur Rimbaud. CP-RimbA, *tr. by* Martin Sorrell

Rozewicz. Czeslaw Milosz. CP-MiloCN, *tr. by* Robert Hass

Rub thou thy battered lamp: nor claim nor beg. State of Age, The. George Meredith. CP-MerG1

Rubáiyát. Jorge Luis Borges. SP-BorgJ, *tr. by* Charles Tomlinson

Rubaiyat for Sue Ella Tucker. Miller Williams. CP-WillM

Rubáiyát of Doc Sifers. James Whitcomb Riley. CP-RileJ

Rubber gloves, for the kitchen—brutish, efficient. Devotion. Dan Pagis. SP-PagiD, *tr. by* Stephen Mitchell

Rubbing her mouth along my mouth she lost. Eleutheria. James Wright. CP-WrigJ

Rubbing of the sleeping bag on my ear made me dream, The. Ant Mansion, The. Robert Bly. SP-BlyR

Rubble railroad, The. O Frères Humains. James Laughlin. CP-LaugJ

Rubens, Garden of Indolence. Nepenthe's source. Guiding Lights, The. Charles Baudelaire. CP-BaudC, *tr. by* Walter Martin

Rubens had been a Statesman or a Saint. William Blake. *See* I Rubens am a Statesman & a Saint

Rubens' Women. Wisława Szymborska. SP-SzymW, *tr. by* Stanislaw Barańczak *and* Clare Cavanagh

Rubens' Women. Wisława Szymborska. SP-SzymW, *tr. by* Joanna Trzeciak

Rubh An' Dunain. Charles Tomlinson. CP-TomlC

Rubies. Ralph Waldo Emerson. CP-EmerR

Ruby and Amethyst. Robert Graves. CP-GravR

Ruby Brown. Langston Hughes. CP-HughL; CP-HughL1

Ruby Daggett. Richard Eberhart. CP-EberR

Ruby Disc, The. Federico García Lorca. CP-GarcF, *tr. by* Jerome Rothenberg *Fr.* Barrage of Firework Poems on the Occasion of the Poet's Birthday.

Ruby Tells All. Miller Williams. CP-WillM

Ruby Was Her Name. William Stafford. SP-StafWW

Ruby wine is drunk by knaves. Heroism. Ralph Waldo Emerson. CP-EmerR

Rucksack, The. Paul Muldoon. CP-MuldP

Ruddy drop of manly blood, A. Friendship. Ralph Waldo Emerson. CP-EmerR

Rude is this Edifice, and Thou hast seen. Written with a Pencil upon a Stone in the Wall of the House (an Out-House), on the Island at Grasmere. William Wordsworth. CP-WorW1

Rude man, 'tis vain thy damsel to commend. Elegy 3.4: "Rude man, 'tis vain thy damsel to commend." Ovid. CP-MarlC *Fr.* Elegies.

Rude wind is singing, The. Fragment: "Rude wind is singing, The." Percy Bysshe Shelley. CP-ShelP

Rudel to the Lady of Tripoli. Robert Browning. CP-BroR1

Rudolph Reed was oaken. Ballad of Rudolph Reed, The. Gwendolyn Brooks. SP-BrooG

Rudyerd, as lesser dames, to great ones use. To Benjamin Rudyerd. Ben Jonson. CP-JonsB; SP-JonsB

Rue Carpenter. Archibald MacLeish. CP-MacLA

Rue de Vaugirard. Samuel Beckett. CP-BeckS

Rue on me, Lord, for thy goodness and grace. Bible, *O.T. See* Have mercy upon me, O God, according to thy lovingkindness

Rufey my how frustrate unquickened and craved the tie I'm equal. Catullus. *See* Whom I have trusted to no end (Rufus)

Rufus Woodpecker visited the President. Charles Olson. CP-OlsoC

Rugged Black of Anger, The. Laura Riding Jackson. CP-RidiL

Rugged forhead that with grave foresight, The. Book 4. Edmund Spenser. CP-Spens *Fr.* Faerie Queene, The.

Ruhama. Yehuda Amichai. SP-AmicY, *tr. by* Chana Bloch

Ruhr-Gebiet. Allen Ginsberg. CP-GinsA; SP-GinsA

Ruin. Charles Baudelaire. CP-BaudC, *tr. by* Walter Martin

Ruin. Federico García Lorca. CP-GarcF, *tr. by* Greg Simon *and* Steven F. White

Ruin. Christina Georgina Rossetti. CP-RosC3

Ruin, The. Charles Tomlinson. CP-TomlC

Ruin falls on blackening skies. Lullaby: "Ruin falls on blackening skies." Marya Alexandrovna Zaturenska. SP-ZatuM

Ruin. I lie passionately in the moonlight. Romantic & Beautiful Poem Inspired by the Recollection of William Butler Yeats, His Life & Work, A. Philip Whalen. SP-WhalP

Ruin seize thee, ruthless King! Bard, The [A Pindaric Ode]. Thomas Gray. CP-GrayT

Ruination. D. H. Lawrence. CP-LawrD

Ruined capitals. Uta Mound, The. Sam Hamill. SP-HamiS

Ruined Cottage, The. William Wordsworth. MW-WorW

Ruined Cross, The. Christina Georgina Rossetti. CP-RosC3

Ruined Gal, A. Langston Hughes. CP-HughL; CP-HughL1

Ruined Maid, The. Thomas Hardy. CP-HardT

Ruined, time ruined, all these once good things. Rimrock, Where It Is. Hayden Carruth. CP-CarHS

Ruines of Time, The. Edmund Spenser. CP-Spens

Ruins of a Great House. Derek Walcott. CP-WalcD

Ruins of Rome. Joachim Du Bellay. CP-Spens, *tr. by* Edmund Spenser

Ruins under the Stars. Galway Kinnell. SP-KinnGN

Rule of the majority is / strictly enforced in all matters, The. Hayden Carruth. CP-CarHS *Fr.* Bloomingdale Papers, The.

Rule, The. Richard Wilbur. CP-WilbR

Rule which by obeying grows. Intellect. Ralph Waldo Emerson. CP-EmerR

Ruler, A. A. K. Ramanujan. CP-RamaA

Ruler after word & thought. Hafiz. CP-EmerR *Fr.* Odes.

Rules for Our Reach. Robert Herrick. CP-HerrR

Rules to men made evident, The. Ralph Waldo Emerson. CP-EmerR

Rum asks—see, fortune won't molest you. Catullus. *See* Where / if it's not too much to ask

Rum tiddy um, / tiddy um. Potato Blossom Songs and Jigs. Carl Sandburg. CP-SandC

Rumba! Rumba! William Carlos Williams. CP-WilW2

Rumble-rattle, rumble-rattle. Lifeline Train to Puerto Limón, Robert Stock. SP-StocR

Rumble, tumble, growl and grate! Impromptu on Roller Skates, An. James Whitcomb Riley. CP-RileJ

Rumbling, buzzing, turning, whirling Wheels. Stephen Crane. CP-CranS

Rumbling: it is, A. Paul Celan. SP-CelaP, *tr. by* John Felstiner

Ruminant pillows! Gregarious soft boulders! Black Faced Sheep, The. Donald Hall. CP-HallD

Rumination. Richard Eberhart. CP-EberR

Rummage. Hayden Carruth. CP-CarHS

Rummaging inside yourself. Death of Fathers, The. Theodore Weiss. SP-WeisT

Rumor at twilight of whisper, crepuscular. Robert Penn Warren. CP-WarrR

Rumor. / Though nothing may remain but the rumor. Desire of a Statue. Federico García Lorca. SP-GarcF, *tr. by* W. S. Merwin

Rumor Verified. Robert Penn Warren. CP-WarrR

Rumors from an Aeolian Harp. Henry David Thoreau. CP-ThorH

Rumour. Charles Tomlinson. CP-TomlC

Rump-Trumpet, the Critic. Refusal of a Kindness Offered. Howard Nemerov. CP-NemeH

Rumpe is a Turne-broach, yet he seldome can. Upon Rumpe. Robert Herrick. CP-HerrR

Rumpelstiltskin. Olga Broumas. SP-BrouO

Rumpelstiltskin. Anne Sexton. CP-SextA

Rumpled river, The. River Rhyme. William Carlos Williams. CP-WilW2

Rumpled sheet, A. Term, The. William Carlos Williams. CP-WilW1

Run, A. Czeslaw Milosz. CP-MiloCN, *tr. by* Tony Milosz

Run before Dawn. William Stafford. SP-StafW; SP-StafWW

Run of the Downs, The. Rudyard Kipling. CP-KiplR

Run on, you still dead to the sound of a name. Louis Zukofsky. CP-ZukLS *Fr.* 29 Poems.

Run out the boat, my broken comrades. Thalassa. Louis MacNeice. CP-MacNL

Run-Through, The. A. R. Ammons. CP-AmmoA

Run upon the Bankers, The. Jonathan Swift. CP-SwifJ

Runagate Runagate. Robert Earl Hayden. CP-HaydR

Runaway. Kenneth Rexroth. CP-RexrK

Runaway, The. Robert Frost. CP-FrosR

Runaway, The. Marya Alexandrovna Zaturenska. SP-ZatuM

Runaway Boy, The. James Whitcomb Riley. CP-RileJ

Runaway Colors. Carl Sandburg. CP-SandC

Runaway Pond. William Corbett. SP-CorbW

Runaway Slave at Pilgrim's Point, The. Elizabeth Barrett Browning. CP-BroEB

Runaway Sun. Pablo Neruda. SP-NeruP

Rune. Paul Muldoon. CP-MuldP

Rune. Muriel Rukeyser. CP-RukeM

Rune, The. Ezra Pound. CP-PoEar

Rune of the Finland Woman. Marilyn Hacker. SP-HackM

Runes. Howard Nemerov. CP-NemeH

Runes, The. Denise Levertov. SP-LeveDP

Runes, Blurs, Sap Rising. Amy Clampitt. CP-ClamA

Runes on Weland's Sword, The. Rudyard Kipling. CP-KiplR *Fr.* Puck of Pook's Hill.

Rungs. C. K. Williams. SP-WillC

Runner Artist, The. Dan Pagis. SP-PagiD, *tr. by* Stephen Mitchell

Runner, The. Walt Whitman. CP-WhitW

Runners, The. Rudyard Kipling. CP-KiplR

Running. Richard Wilbur. CP-WilbR

Running ahead beside the sea. Paradox. Robert Penn Warren. CP-WarrR

Running and standing still at once. Painting a Mountain Stream. Howard Nemerov. CP-NemeH

Running Away from Home. Carolyn Kizer. CP-KizeC

Running Footsteps. James Schuyler. CP-SchuJ

Running into Things. Miller Williams. CP-WillM

Running of the Grunion, The. Muriel Rukeyser. CP-RukeM

Running on Silk. Galway Kinnell. SP-KinnGN

Running on the Shore. May Swenson. SP-SwenM

Running peoples on their bloody way, The. Fear. Randall Jarrell. CP-JarrR

Running to Paradise. William Butler Yeats. CP-YeatW

Running Water Music. Gary Snyder. CP-SnydG

Running Water Music II. Gary Snyder. CP-SnydG

Running water never disappointed. Seamus Heaney. SP-HeanSO *Fr.* Squarings.

Runoff. A. R. Ammons. CP-AmmoA

Runs falls rises stumbles on from darkness into darkness. Runagate Runagate. Robert Earl Hayden. CP-HaydR

Rupaiyat of Omar Kal'vin, The. Rudyard Kipling. CP-KiplR

Ruptured underbelly of a black horse flew overhead, The. Apocrypha of Jacques Derrida, The. Norman Dubie. CP-DubiN

Rural Architecture. William Wordsworth. CP-WorW1; MW-WorW

Rural Delivery. Charles Simic. SP-SimiC; SP-SimiCE

Rural Illusions. William Wordsworth. CP-WorW2

Rural Life. George Crabbe. *See* Village, The

Rural Reflections. Adrienne Rich. CP-RicAE; SP-RicA2

Rus in Urbe. William Meredith. SP-MereW

Rush of rain against the glass, The. New England Spring, 1942. Edna St. Vincent Millay. CP-MillE

Rush saves his shooes, in wet and snowie wether. Upon Rush. Robert Herrick. CP-HerrR

Rushes in a watery place, / And reeds in a hollow. Summer. Christina Georgina Rossetti. CP-RosC2

Rushing music, seizing on her dance, A. L'Etoile. Richard Wilbur. CP-WilbR

Rushing river, forcing your rapid way. Petrarch. CP-Petra, *tr. by* J. G. Nichols

Russet Gold. A. R. Ammons. CP-AmmoA

Russia. Aleksandr Aleksandrovich Blok. SP-BlokA, *tr. by* Peter France *and* Jon Stallworthy

Russia. William Carlos Williams. CP-WilW2

Russia and America circle each other. Woman Unconscious, A. Ted Hughes. SP-HughTN

Russia and I, must we suffer one destiny? Aleksandr Aleksandrovich Blok. SP-BlokA, *tr. by* Peter France *and* Jon Stallworthy

Russia Comes Into Poland. Adam Zagajewski. SP-ZagaA, *tr. by* Renata Gorczynski, Benjamin Ivry *and* C. K. Williams

Russia, most feminine of lands. Poem for a Far Land. John Updike. CP-UpdiJ

Russia or The Weakness of Photography. Andrei Codrescu. SP-CodrA

Russia! Russia! you might say. Song: "Russia! Russia! you might say." William Carlos Williams. CP-WilW2

Russia to the Pacifists. Rudyard Kipling. CP-KiplR

Russian Fugitive, The. William Wordsworth. CP-WorW2

Russian Jew, for you. Mandelstam, on Dante. Donald Davie. CP-DaviDC

Russian leaning with all his might, A. In Praise of the New Russian Writers. Andrei Codrescu. SP-CodrA

Russian Lesson. Theodore Weiss. SP-WeisT

Russo, rimless. Youth. William Corbett. SP-CorbW

Rust. Lucille Clifton. SP-ClifL

Rust, a little pile of western color, lies, The. We Continue. W. S. Merwin. SP-MerwW

Rust cat leaps through the gap in the screen, The. Cambridge Revery. John Logan. CP-LogaJ

Rust-hulled freighters in. Saloniki. Amy Clampitt. CP-ClamA

Rustication. Adrienne Rich. CP-RicAE

Rustice, sta, paucis dum te moror, auribus adsis. Ad Rusticum. Thomas Campion. CP-CampT

Rusticity's ungainly form. Robert Burns. CP-BurnR

Rustle of Acacias, The. Joseph Brodsky. CP-BrodJ, *tr. by* Daniel Weissbort

"Rustle of History's Wings," as They Used to Say Then, The. Yehuda Amichai. SP-AmicY, *tr. by* Chana Bloch

Rustum Beg of Kolazai—slightly backward Native State. Legend of the Foreign Office, A. Rudyard Kipling. CP-KiplR

Rusty autumn to your breast again I come Memorial tears. May Swenson. SP-SwenM

Rusty Crimson. Carl Sandburg. CP-SandC

Rusty-gold green trees, The. Non-Entity, The. William Carlos Williams. CP-WilW2

Rusty Man, The. Herman Melville. SP-MelvH

Rusty Romanian tanker, wallowing out in the azure, A. Venice: Lido. Joseph

Brodsky. CP-BrodJ, *tr. by* Alan Myers

Ruth. George Crabbe. SP-CrabG *Fr.* Tales of the Hall.

Ruth had been moved out of her job in an. Honolulu and Back. John Logan. CP-LogaJ

Ruth [or, The Influences of Nature]. William Wordsworth. CP-WorW1

Ruthie? That you? Well, how's it go- / ing back there, good? Yeah. Look. Phone. Hayden Carruth. CP-CarHS

Rutland. Donald Davie. CP-DaviDC

Ruts. Arthur Rimbaud. CP-RimbA, *tr. by* Martin Sorrell

Rwanda. Ai. SP-Ai

RX Creative Writing: Identity. William Stafford. SP-StafWW

Rycht potent prince, of hie imperial blude. Dreme, The. Sir David Lyndsay. SP-LyndD

Rydal Mount. Amy Clampitt. CP-ClamA

Ryder. Muriel Rukeyser. CP-RukeM

Ryght as the stern of day begouth to schyne. Goldyn [*or* Golden] Targe, The. William Dunbar. CP-DunbW

(Ryokan's scroll). Louis Zukofsky. CP-ZukLS

S

S & M. Yusef Komunyakaa. CP-KomuY

S. Dead. Marge Piercy. SP-PierM

S. Eliason 66: *Double Portrait of Emily Dickinson and the Rev. Charles Wadsworth.* Jane Cooper. CP-CoopJ

S.F.D. E. E. Cummings. CP-CummE

S.I.W. Wilfred Owen. CP-OwenW

S M. Alice Walker. CP-WalkA

S.P.Q.R. A Letter from Rome. John Ciardi. CP-CiarJ

S. R. Ralph Waldo Emerson. CP-EmerR

S-sss-ss-sh! Langston Hughes. CP-HughL; CP-HughL2

S.T. E. E. Cummings. CP-CummE

S(/ these out of in). E. E. Cummings. CP-CummE

S. Thomae Aquinatis Rhythmus ad SS. Sacramentum. Gerard Manley Hopkins. CP-HopkG

S.ti:rstuso,nce♂:n. E. E. Cummings. CP-CummE

Sa Majestá Très Chrétienne. Arthur Hugh Clough. SP-ClouA

Saadi. Ralph Waldo Emerson. CP-EmerR

Saadi held the Muse in awe. Ralph Waldo Emerson. CP-EmerR

Saadi loved the new & old. Ralph Waldo Emerson. CP-EmerR

Sabbath, The. W. H. Auden. CP-AudeW

Sabbath, The ("Bright is the morn, and hushed is every sound"). Jones Very. CP-VeryJ

Sabbath, The ("Thy rest has come thy long expected rest"). Jones Very. CP-VeryJ

Sabbath evening privacy at home. Eben Haëzer. Gerrit Achterberg. CP-RicAE

Sabbath Morning at Sea, A. Elizabeth Barrett Browning. CP-BroEB

Sabbath of Mutual Respect, The. Marge Piercy. SP-PierM

Sabbath Scene, A. John Greenleaf Whittier. CP-WhitJ

Sabbaths. Robert Herrick. CP-HerrR

Sabbaths are threefold (as S. Austine sayes:). Sabbaths. Robert Herrick. CP-HerrR

Sabbaths, W.I. Derek Walcott. CP-WalcD

Sabbatia, The. Jones Very. CP-VeryJ

Sabinus, I don't like you. You know why? Martial. CP-CunnJ, *tr. by* James Vincent Cunningham

Sack of the Gods, The. Rudyard Kipling. CP-KiplR *Fr.* Naulahka, The.

Sacks, The. James Laughlin. CP-LaugJ

Sacre de Printemps. Tennessee Williams. CP-WillT

Sacred, blithesome, undenied, / With benisons from East and West. Kiss to the Bride, A. Walt Whitman. CP-WhitW

Sacred Goddess, Mother Earth. Song of Proserpine. Percy Bysshe Shelley. CP-ShelP

Sacred Heart. Thom Gunn. CP-GunnT

Sacred Heart 2. Thomas Merton. CP-MertT

Sacred Hearth Fire, The. Amy Clampitt. CP-ClamA

Sacred is secret: at the confluence. There. Howard Nemerov. CP-NemeH

Sacred Lake. Muriel Rukeyser. CP-RukeM

Sacred? or sacrosanct? Ironist, The. Donald Davie. CP-DaviDC

Sacred Place. Rainer Maria Rilke. CP-RilkFr, *tr. by* A. Poulin, Jr.

Sacred Religion! "mother of form and fear." Seathwaite Chapel. William Wordsworth. CP-WorW2 *Fr.* River Duddon [A Series of Sonnets], The.

Sacred song that on mine ear, The. To the Hon. Mrs. George Lamb. Lord Byron. CP-Byron

Sacred sycamore and the odor of cedar wood (the odor of the buried boat). Boat, The. Charles Olson. CP-OlsoC

Sacred to the Memory. Thomas Hardy. CP-HardT

Sacred to the poet, honor-worthy inkwell. Inkwell, The. Constantine P. Cavafy. CP-CavaC, *tr. by* Theoharis Constantine Theoharis

Sacred watcher, wave thy bells! To the Bluebell. Emily Jane Brontë. CP-BronE

Sacrifice. Ted Hughes. SP-HughTN

Sacrifice. Thomas Kinsella. CP-KinsT

Sacrifice. Audre Lorde. SP-LordA

Sacrifice. Jones Very. CP-VeryJ

Sacrifice, The. Richard Eberhart. CP-EberR

Sacrifice, The. George Herbert. CP-HerbG

Sacrilege, The. Thomas Hardy. CP-HardT

Sacrifice, by Way of Discourse betwixt Himselfe and Julia, The. Robert Herrick. CP-HerrR

Sacrifice of Er-Heb, The. Rudyard Kipling. CP-KiplR

Sad Advice. Robert Creeley. SP-CreeR

Sad and lovely face, with upturned eyes, A. Sonnet to a Picture by Lucca Giordano in the Mureo Borbonico at Naples. William Wordsworth. CP-WorW2

Sad as he sits on the white sea-stone. Tarantella. D. H. Lawrence. CP-LawrD

Sad Boy, The. Laura Riding Jackson. CP-RidiL

Sad Children's Song, The. Grace Paley. CP-PalGC

Sad confession from the heart of man, A. Man's Heart Prophesieth of Peace. Jones Very. CP-VeryJ

Sad creatures of a transient existence. Han-shan. CP-ColdM, *tr. by* Red Pine

Sad Dust Glories. Allen Ginsberg. CP-GinsA
    "Teacher / bring me to heaven." SP-GinsA

Sad-Fyed Mules of Men. Charles Bukowski. SP-BukC2

Sad Friend. Shmuel HaNagid. SP-HaNaS, *tr. by* Peter Cole

Sad Heart, The. Stevie Smith. CP-SmitS

Sad heart, the gymnast of inertia, does not count. Sad Indian, The. Hart Crane. CP-CranH

Sad Indian, The. Hart Crane. CP-CranH

Sad is old Ben Tristlewaite. Old Ben. Walter De la Mare. CP-DeLaW

Sad little lake, your. Exercise, The. Thom Gunn. CP-GunnT

Sad lot, to have no Hope! Though lowly kneeling. Visionary Hope, The. Samuel Taylor Coleridge. CP-ColeS; MW-ColeS

Sad man on a summer day, A. Man and Nature. Elizabeth Barrett Browning. CP-BroEB

Sad Mayflower! watched by winter stars. Mayflowers, The. John Greenleaf Whittier. CP-WhitJ

Sad Mother, The. Gabriela Mistral. SP-MistG, *tr. by* Maria Giachetti [*or* Jacketti]

Sad Mother, The. Stevie Smith. CP-SmitS

Sad music of roads lined with larches, The. Afghanistan. Raymond Carver. CP-CarvR

Sad One, The. Sir John Suckling. CP-SuckJ

Sad Perversity. James Whitcomb Riley. CP-RileJ

Sad Poem, A. Charles Bukowski. SP-BukC3

Sad refrain I heard, from poet sad, A. Forevermore. Jones Very. CP-VeryJ

Sad seamstress, The. House Guest. Elizabeth Bishop. CP-BishE

Sad Shepherd, The. Ben Jonson.
    "Though I am young, and cannot tell." CP-JonsB; SP-JonsB

Sad Shepherd, The. William Butler Yeats. CP-YeatW

Sad Song. Philip Whalen. SP-WhalP

Sad Steps. Philip Larkin. SP-LarkP

Sad Strains of a Gay Waltz. Wallace Stevens. CP-StevW; CP-StevWP

Sad the matter of which I speak. Ballade of a Complete Flop. Dorothy Parker. CP-ParkD

Sad thoughts, avaunt!—partake we their blithe cheer. Sheep-Washing. William Wordsworth. CP-WorW2 *Fr.* River Duddon [A Series of Sonnets], The.

Sad thy tale, thou idle page. On Reading, in a Newspaper, the Death of J———— McL————, Esq. Brother to a Young Lady, a Particular Friend of the Author's. Robert Burns. CP-BurnR

Sad, tired, lonely, and not pretty. Adam Zagajewski. SP-ZagaA, *tr. by* Renata Gorczynski

Sadder aspect wears the spring, A. Hymn: Nature's Sympathy with Freedom. Jones Very. CP-VeryJ

Saddest Day, The. D. H. Lawrence. CP-LawrD

Saddest noise, the sweetest noise, The. Emily Dickinson. CP-DickE

Saddest silence falls when Laughter lays, The. Edgar Wilson Nye. James Whitcomb Riley. CP-RileJ

Saddhu of Couva, The. Derek Walcott. CP-WalcD

Saddle and ride, I heard a man say. Alternative Song for the Severed Head in "The King of the Great Clock Tower." William Butler Yeats. CP-YeatW

S'addormentò la nostra figliolina. Christina Georgina Rossetti. CP-RosC3

Sadly I walk't within the field. Olive Branch, The. Robert Herrick. CP-HerrR

Sadness, The. W. S. Merwin. SP-MerwW

Sadness and Happiness. Robert Pinsky. CP-PinsR

Sadness of Eyes and Descriptions of a Voyage. Yehuda Amichai. SP-AmicYL, *tr. by* Benjamin Harshav *and* Barbara Harshav

Sadness of My Neighbors, The. James Tate. SP-TateJ

Sadness of the Sea, The. William Carlos Williams. CP-WilW1

Sadness of Things for Sappho's Sickness, The. Robert Herrick. CP-HerrR

Sadness Unhinged. Andrei Codrescu. SP-CodrA

Sadness we bring back from sleep, The. Waking. Archibald MacLeish. CP-MacLA

Sae Far Awa. Robert Burns. CP-BurnR

Sae flaxen were her ringlets. She Says She Lo'es Me Best of A'. Robert Burns. CP-BurnR

Saeta. James Laughlin. CP-LaugJ

Safe Conduct. Norman Dubie. CP-DubiN

Safe Despair it is that raves. Emily Dickinson. CP-DickE

Safe from the wild storms off Cape Hatteras. Season of Lovers and Assassins. Carolyn Kizer. CP-KizeC

Safe in Shade. Robert Penn Warren. CP-WarrR

Safe Subjects. Yusef Komunyakaa. CP-KomuY

Safe upon the solid rock the ugly houses stand. Second Fig. Edna St. Vincent Millay. CP-MillE

Safe where I cannot lie yet, / Safe where I hope to lie too. Christina Georgina Rossetti. CP-RosC2

Safety on the Shore. Robert Herrick. CP-HerrR

Safety To Look to Ones Selfe. Robert Herrick. CP-HerrR

Saffron. Stevie Smith. CP-SmitS

Sagacity. Richard Eberhart. CP-EberR

Sage, The. Edwin Arlington Robinson. CP-RobiE

Sage Enamoured and the Honest Lady, The. George Meredith. CP-MerG1

Sage lectured brilliantly, The. Stephen Crane. CP-CranS

Sage of Cold Mountain, The. Han-shan. CP-ColdM, *tr. by* Red Pine

Sage of Darien, The. Ogden Nash. CP-NashO

Sage to the Young Man, The. A. E. Housman. CP-HousA

Sage, who said he should be proud, The. On Seeing Verses Written upon Windows in Inns. Jonathan Swift. CP-SwifJ

Sagging hayricks file into the lanc, The. Haymaking. May Swenson. SP-SwenM

Saggy-bellied cat of Bar Maria, The. Italian Kittens, The. Carolyn Kizer. CP-KizeC

Saginaw Song, The. Theodore Roethke. CP-RoetT

Sagittarius Approaching Thirty-Five. Yusef Komunyakaa. CP-KomuY

Sagittarius, Scorpio Rising. William Dickey. SP-DickW

Sahara Bus Trip, The. Rita Dove. SP-DoveR

Sahara doth not keep her livid hell. On the Road to Wockensutter. John Crowe Ransom. SP-RansJ

Said a people to a poet—"Go out from among us straightway!" Poet and the Bird, The. Elizabeth Barrett Browning. CP-BroEB

Said a wistful daw in Saint Peter's tower. Peace Peal, The. Thomas Hardy. CP-HardT

Said Abner, "At last thou art come! Ere I tell, ere thou speak." Saul. Robert Browning. CP-BroR1

Said Adam. Charles Olson. CP-OlsoC

Said Death to Passion. Emily Dickinson. CP-DickE

Said England unto Pharaoh, "I must make a man of you." Pharaoh and the Sergeant. Rudyard Kipling. CP-KiplR

Said Harvey Swados to Herbert Gold. Vision, A. John Updike. CP-UpdiJ

Said lady once to lover. Three Bushes, The. William Butler Yeats. CP-YeatW

Said Myrtias (a Syrian student). Dangerous Remarks. Constantine P. Cavafy. CP-CavaC, *tr. by* Theoharis Constantine Theoharis

Said Pound (out of Homer). Knowledge. James Laughlin. CP-LaugJ

Said Propertius oculi sunt. Eyes Are the Guides of Love. James Laughlin. CP-LaugJ

Said red-ribboned Evans. Squib on Colonel Evans, A. William Wordsworth. CP-WorW2

Said Rinpoche Chögyam Trungpa Tulku in the marble glittering apartment lobby. What Would You Do If You Lost It. Allen Ginsberg. CP-GinsA

Said Robinson, stone axe at a breadfruit tree. Solo for Four. Robert Stock. SP-StocR

Said Rockefeller, senior, to his boy. Compliance. Ambrose Bierce. SP-BierA

Said Secrecy to Cowardice and Fraud. William Wordsworth. CP-WorW2

Said the Damaged Angel to the Improved Ape. Dialogue in the Shade, A. John Ciardi. CP-CiarJ

Said the Governor of Louisiana. Ipse Dixit. James Laughlin. CP-LaugJ

Said the grave Dean of Westminster. Refusal, A. Thomas Hardy. CP-HardT

Said the lady, *Can you do*. Question ("Said the lady, *Can you do*"). Langston Hughes. CP-HughL; CP-HughL3

Said the Lord God, "Build a house." Kingdom of Heaven, The. G. K. Chesterton. CP-ChesG

Said the owl was dehu- / manization it wasn't. Your Error. James Laughlin. CP-LaugJ

Said the panama hat to the fedora. Quotations. Carl Sandburg. CP-SandC

Said the Poet to the Analyst. Anne Sexton. CP-SextA; SP-SextA

Said the Presidential Skeleton. Ballad of the Skeletons, The. Allen Ginsberg. SP-GinsA

Said The Raggedy Man, on a hot afternoon. Man in the Moon, The. James Whitcomb Riley. CP-RileJ

Said the red-cloaked crone. Signs and Tokens. Thomas Hardy. CP-HardT

Said the Speaker. Michael Palmer. SP-PalmM

Said the Undertaker to the Overtaker. Tweedledee and Tweedledoom. Ogden Nash. CP-NashO

Said the Watcher by the Way. Town Down the River, The. Edwin Arlington Robinson. CP-RobiE

Saigon Bar Girls, 1975. Yusef Komunyakaa. CP-KomuY

Sail and Oar. Robert Graves. CP-GravR

Sail before the morning breeze. Archipelago, The. Herman Melville. SP-MelvH

Sail-bellyer, exciter of boys, come bang. Autumnal Equinox on Mediterranean Beach. Robert Penn Warren. CP-WarrR

Sail, Monarchs, rising and falling. Roots and Branches. Robert Duncan. SP-DuncR

Sail of Claustra, Aelis, Azalais. Alchemist, The. Ezra Pound. CP-PoEar

Sail of Ulysses, The. Wallace Stevens. CP-StevWP

Sail Out for Good, Eidólon Yacht! Walt Whitman. CP-WhitW

Sailing. Clarence Major. SP-MajoC

Sailing after Lunch. Wallace Stevens. CP-StevW; CP-StevWP

Sailing at dawn into the Narrows. Arrival, The. Charles Tomlinson. CP-TomlC

Sailing Date. Langston Hughes. CP-HughL; CP-HughL2

Sailing Home from Rapallo. Robert Lowell. SP-LoweR

Sailing on Cakes of Ice in the North River. Jones Very. CP-VeryJ

Sailing Orders. Louis MacNeice. CP-MacNL

Sailing thru the straits of Demos. Lawrence Ferlinghetti. SP-FerlL

Sailing to Buck's Harbor. Richard Eberhart. CP-EberR

Sailing to Byzantium. William Butler Yeats. CP-YeatW

Sailing to Jerusalem. Alan Dugan. CP-DugaA

Sailing to Tauris: the pitchy cave. Orestes at Tauris. Randall Jarrell. CP-JarrR

Sailor. Langston Hughes. CP-HughL; CP-HughL1

Sailor cannot see the North, The. Emily Dickinson. SP-DickE

Sailor in Africa, the. Rita Dove. SP-DoveR

Sailor's Mother, The. Thomas Hardy. CP-HardT

Sailor's Mother, The. William Wordsworth. CP-WorW1

Sailor's Song, A. Paul Laurence Dunbar. CP-DunbP

Sailors there are of gentlest breed. Commemorative of a Naval Victory. Herman Melville. SP-MelvH

Sailors who come ashore, The. Fleet Visit. W. H. Auden. CP-AudeW

Sails. Adam Zagajewski. SP-ZagaA, tr. by Renata Gorczynski, Benjamin Ivry and C. K. Williams

Sails on All Saints' Day. John Updike. CP-UpdiJ

Saint. Stéphane Mallarmé. CP-MallS, tr. by Henry Weinfield

Saint. Frank O'Hara. SP-OharF

Saint About to Fall, A. Dylan Thomas. CP-ThomD

St. Agnes: A Responsory. Thomas Merton. CP-MertT

St Agnes' Eve—Ah, bitter chill it was! Eve of St Agnes, The. John Keats. CP-KeatJ

St. Alberic. Thomas Merton. CP-MertT

Saint and demon blindly stare. Europe. Howard Nemerov. CP-NemeH

Saint and the Hunchback, The. William Butler Yeats. CP-YeatW

St. Andrew's Church. Christina Georgina Rossetti. CP-RosC3

Saint Anthony and the Rose of Life. Stevie Smith. CP-SmitS

St Antony of Padua. Robert Graves. CP-GravR

St. Armorer's Church from the Outside. Wallace Stevens. CP-StevW; CP-StevWP

St. Armorer's was once an immense success. St. Armorer's Church from the Outside. Wallace Stevens. CP-StevW; CP-StevWP

St. Augustine and the Arctic Bear. Charles Wright. SP-WrigCN

St. Augustine-by-the-Sea. May Swenson. SP-SwenM

St. Barnabas. Christina Georgina Rossetti. CP-RosC2

St. Barnabas, with John his sister's son. St. Barnabas. Christina Georgina Rossetti. CP-RosC2

St. Bartholomew. Christina Georgina Rossetti. CP-RosC2

Saint Catherine. Rainer Maria Rilke. CP-RilkFr, tr. by A. Poulin, Jr.

St Catherine of Ledbury. William Wordsworth. CP-WorW2

St. Catherine's Clock. Thomas Kinsella. CP-KinsT

Saint Cecilia: / between. Nashville Mornings. Donald Davie. CP-DaviDC

St. Christopher. Louise Bogan. CP-BogaL

Saint Distaffs Day, or the Morrow after Twelth Day. Robert Herrick. CP-HerrR

St. Dorothea. Gerard Manley Hopkins. CP-HopkG

St. Elizabeth of Hungary. Christina Georgina Rossetti. CP-RosC3

Saint Francis and the Sow. Galway Kinnell. SP-KinnGN

St. Francis, Buddha, Tolstoi, and St. John. Above the Battle's Front. Nicholas Vachel Lindsay. CP-LindV

St. Gabriel. Federico García Lorca. CP-GarcF, tr. by Will Kirkland

St George's Basilica. Jaroslav Seifert. SP-SeifJ, tr. by Ewald Osers

St George's, Hardwicke Street. North Dublin. Donald Davie. CP-DaviDC

St Godnait's Graveyard, Ballyvourney: That Evening. Thomas Kinsella. CP-KinsT Fr. Selected Life, A.

Saint Gregory's Guest. John Greenleaf Whittier. CP-WhitJ

Saint Harmony, many / years I have stript. Freedom and Discipline. Hayden Carruth. CP-CarHS

St. Helena Lullaby, A. Rudyard Kipling. CP-KiplR

Saint Jason. Thomas Merton. CP-MertT

Saint Jerome and his lion. Leonardo Da Vinci's. Marianne Craig Moore. CP-MoorM

Saint Jerome lived with a community. Elegy for Wright & Hugo. Norman Dubie. CP-DubiN

St John. D. H. Lawrence. CP-LawrD

Saint John. Kenneth Rexroth. CP-RexrK

St. John. John Greenleaf Whittier. CP-WhitJ

Saint John and the Back-Ache. Wallace Stevens. CP-StevW; CP-StevWP

St. John, as Duvet's angel leads him. Woodcut, A. Denise Levertov. SP-LeveDS

St. John Baptist. Thomas Merton. CP-MertT

Saint John of the Cross in Prison. James Tate. SP-TateJ

St. John tells how, at Cana's wedding-feast. Wedding Toast, A. Richard Wilbur. CP-WilbR

St. John, whose love indulg'd my labours past. First Epistle of the First Book of Horace Imitated, The. Alexander Pope. CP-PopeA

St. John's Night. Thomas Merton. CP-MertT

St. Johnswort! [or Saint-John's-wort!]. Grace Paley. CP-PalGC

Saint Judas. James Wright. CP-WrigJ

Saint-Just: his name seems stolen from the Missal. Saint-Just 1767–93. Robert Lowell. SP-LoweR

Saint-Just 1767–93. Robert Lowell. SP-LoweR

St Kevin and the Blackbird. Seamus Heaney. SP-HeanSO

St. Launce's Revisited. Thomas Hardy. CP-HardT

St. Lirriper. James Whitcomb Riley. CP-RileJ Fr. Child-World, A.

Saint-Lô. Samuel Beckett. CP-BeckS

St. Luke. D. H. Lawrence. CP-LawrD

St. Maedoc. Thomas Merton. CP-MertT

St. Malachy. Thomas Merton. CP-MertT

St Mark. D. H. Lawrence. CP-LawrD

St. Mark. Christina Georgina Rossetti. CP-RosC2

St. Martin and the Beggar. Thom Gunn. CP-GunnT

Saint Martin's Summer. Robert Browning. CP-BroR2; SP-BroR

St. Martin's Summer. John Greenleaf Whittier. CP-WhitJ

St Matthew. D. H. Lawrence. CP-LawrD

Saint Matthew and All. William Stafford. SP-StafW; SP-StafWW

St. Michael. Federico García Lorca. CP-GarcF, tr. by Christopher Maurer

St. Michael and all Angels. Christina Georgina Rossetti. CP-RosC2

Saint Monday. Alan Dugan. CP-DugaA

Saint Nicholas. Marianne Craig Moore. CP-MoorM

Saint Nicholas Patron of Nicholls. 'Thank-You' for Coming to Tea, A. G. K. Chesterton. CP-ChesG

Saint of Holy Island, The. Sir Walter Scott. SP-ScotW Fr. Marmion.

Saint of the Uplands, The. W. S. Merwin. SP-MerwW

Saint on the pillar stands, The. Stylite. Louis MacNeice. CP-MacNL

St Patrick bound unto himself. Comforter, The. Donald Davie. CP-DaviDC

Saint Patrick, slave to Milcho of the herds. Proclamation, The. John Greenleaf Whittier. CP-WhitJ

Saint Patrick was a proper man, a man to be admired. It's a Grand Parade It Will Be, Modern Design. Ogden Nash. CP-NashO

St. Paul. Thomas Merton. CP-MertT

St. Paul and All That. Frank O'Hara. SP-OharF

St. Paul never saw a sight like this. United 555. Richard Eberhart. CP-EberR

St Paul's Rocks: 16 February 1832. Thomas Kinsella. CP-KinsT

St. Peter. Christina Georgina Rossetti. CP-RosC2

St. Peter once: "Lord, dost Thou wash my feet?" St. Peter. Christina Georgina Rossetti. CP-RosC2

Saint Peter sat by the celestial gate. Vision of Judgment, The. Lord Byron. CP-Byron

Saint Peter's Denial. Charles Baudelaire. CP-BaudC, tr. by Walter Martin

St. Philip's Church in Antigua. Archibald MacLeish. CP-MacLA

St. Raphael. Federico García Lorca. CP-GarcF, tr. by Will Kirkland

Saint Raphael (Córdoba). Federico García Lorca. SP-GarcF, tr. by Rolfe Humphries

St. Roach. Muriel Rukeyser. CP-RukeM

Saint sat down with the sinner, The. Fusion. George Meredith. CP-MerG2

Saint Sex. C. K. Williams. CP-WillC; SP-WillC

St. Simeon Stylites. Alfred Tennyson. CP-TennA

Saint Sulpice. Rainer Maria Rilke. CP-RilkFr, *tr.* by A. Poulin, Jr.

St. Thérèse. George Meredith. CP-MerG2

St. Thomas Aquinas. Thomas Merton. CP-MertT

St. Thomas Didymus. Denise Levertov. SP-LeveDS

Saint Valentine. Marianne Craig Moore. *See* St. Valentine

Saint Valentine, / although late, would "some interested law." For February 14th. Marianne Craig Moore. CP-MoorM

St. Valentine's Day 1881. Christina Georgina Rossetti. CP-RosC3

St. Valentine's. Winter is in us. Half February. Charles Wright. SP-WrigCN

St. Vincent's. W. S. Merwin. SP-MerwWF

St. Winefred's Well. Gerard Manley Hopkins. CP-HopkG

Sainte Anne De Beaupré. Richard Eberhart. CP-EberR

Sainte Lucie. Derek Walcott. CP-WalcD

Sainte-Nitouche. Edwin Arlington Robinson. CP-RobiE

Saintly yogi Hari-Hara-Baba, The. At Benares. James Laughlin. CP-LaugJ

Saints, The. Robert Creeley. CP-CreeR

Saints and Angels. Christina Georgina Rossetti. CP-RosC1

Saints are gathering at the real, The. Confirmers, The. A. R. Ammons. CP-AmmoA

Saints are like roses when they flush rarest. I Gave a Sweet Smell. Christina Georgina Rossetti. CP-RosC2

Saints-bell calls; and, Julia, I must read, The. To Julia. Robert Herrick. CP-HerrR

Saints Come Marching In, The. Anne Sexton. CP-SextA

Saints of Negativity, The. Norman Dubie. CP-DubiN

Saipan. John Ciardi. CP-CiarJ

Saith the Czar. Ambrose Bierce. SP-BierA

Sakyamuni Coming Out from the Mountain. Allen Ginsberg. CP-GinsA

Salad, The. William Cowper. CP-CowpW

Saladin's Begging Bowl. Jelaluddin Rumi. SP-Rumi, *tr.* by Coleman Barks

Salamander. Muriel Rukeyser. CP-RukeM

Salamanders. A. K. Ramanujan. CP-RamaA

Salami. Philip Levine. SP-LeviP

Sale. Theodore Roethke. CP-RoetT

Sale. Miller Williams. CP-WillM

Sale, The. William Carlos Williams. CP-WilW2

Salem. Richard Eberhart. CP-EberR

Salem ("Boast not, my native spot, thy sons were first"). Jones Very. CP-VeryJ

Salem ("They reach a harbor spacious and secure"). Jones Very. CP-VeryJ

Sales. Arthur Rimbaud. CP-RimbA, *tr.* by Martin Sorrell

Salesman, A. E. E. Cummings. CP-CummE; SP-CummE

Salesman is an it that stinks excuse, A. Salesman, A. E. E. Cummings. CP-CummE; SP-CummE

Saleswomen in Bakery Shops. Mona Van Duyn. SP-VanDM

Saliences. A. R. Ammons. CP-AmmoA

Saliences are humming bee paths. Summer Session. A. R. Ammons. CP-AmmoA

Salisbury Plain. William Wordsworth. MW-WorW

Sallie's Musical Box. Walter De la Mare. CP-DeLaW

Sallow Bird, The. Stevie Smith. CP-SmitS

Sallying off to the pub. Fanny Howe. SP-HoweF *Fr.* O'Clock.

Salmon are very sure. On Being Sure and of What. John Ciardi. CP-CiarJ

Salmon Brook. Henry David Thoreau. CP-ThorH

Salmon Eggs. Ted Hughes. SP-HughTN

Salmon Fishing. Robinson Jeffers. CP-JefR1

Salmon of Knowledge, The. Paul Muldoon. CP-MuldP

Salmon were just down there, The. Salmon Eggs. Ted Hughes. SP-HughTN

Salmoneus, as the Grecian tale is. On Wood the Ironmonger. Jonathan Swift. CP-SwifJ

Salome. Constantine P. Cavafy. CP-CavaC, *tr.* by Theoharis Constantine Theoharis

Salomé. Yusef Komunyakaa. CP-KomuY

Salome. James Merrill. SP-MerrJ

Salome & the Moon. Federico García Lorca. CP-GarcF, *tr.* by Jerome Rothenberg *Fr.* Sublunar Cantos.

Salome's Dancing-Lesson. Dorothy Parker. CP-ParkD

Saloniki. Amy Clampitt. CP-ClamA

Saloon is gone up the creek, The. Hemmed-in Males. William Carlos Williams. CP-WilW1 *Fr.* Folded Skyscraper, A.

Salt. Yusef Komunyakaa. CP-KomuY

Salt. D. H. Lawrence. CP-LawrD

Salt and water. Sea ("Salt and water"). Robert Creeley. CP-CreeR

Salt Garden, The. Howard Nemerov. CP-NemeH

Salt hacks, tavern boys, what skews, can't you burn alleys. Catullus. *See* Nine posts, five doors, up the Clivus

Salt Marsh, The. James Dickey. CP-DickJ

Salt of the Earth. D. H. Lawrence. CP-LawrD

Salt of the soil and liquor of the rock. Order of Diet. May Swenson. SP-SwenM

Salt seas, mountains, deserts. Toward Climax. Gary Snyder. CP-SnydG

Salt shining behind its glass cylinder. Morning. Mary Oliver. SP-OlivM

Salt weather on the East River, A. For the Squadron. Howard Nemerov. CP-NemeH

Salta, ranocchio, e mostrati. Christina Georgina Rossetti. CP-RosC3

Saltimbanques. Rainer Maria Rilke. CP-RilkFr, *tr.* by A. Poulin, Jr.

Salts and Oils. Philip Levine. SP-LeviP

Salubrious air, free of the low fogs that were. Winchester: The Autumn Equinox. Amy Clampitt. CP-ClamA

Saluiour, suppois my sensualite. William Dunbar. CP-DunbW

Salut au Monde! Walt Whitman. CP-WhitW

Salutation. Robert Herrick. CP-HerrR

Salutation. Stéphane Mallarmé. CP-MallS, *tr.* by Henry Weinfield

Salutation. Ezra Pound. SP-PounE

Salutation, A. Federico García Lorca. CP-GarcF, *tr.* by Jerome Rothenberg

Salutation to Walt Whitman. Fernando Pessoa. SP-PessF, *tr.* by Susan M. Brown *and* Edwin Honig

Salute. Archibald MacLeish. CP-MacLA

Salute. James Schuyler. CP-SchuJ

Salute to Donald Davie. Eleanor Wilner. SP-WilnE

Salute to Soviet Armies. Langston Hughes. CP-HughL; CP-HughL2

Salute to the Madrid Barricades. Jaroslav Seifert. SP-SeifJ, *tr.* by Ewald Osers

Salvador Díaz Mirón. "Rubén Darío." SP-DariR, *tr.* by Alberto Acereda *and* Will Derusha

Salvage. Amy Clampitt. CP-ClamA

Salvage. Robinson Jeffers. CP-JefR3

Salvage. Carl Sandburg. CP-SandC

Salvaged Parts. William Stafford. SP-StafW; SP-StafWW

Salvages: An Evening Place. Robert Duncan. SP-DuncR

Salvation. D. H. Lawrence. CP-LawrD

Salvation comes by [Jesus] Christ alone. Evening Thought, An. Salvation by Christ with Penetential Cries. Jupiter Hammon. CP-WheaP

Salvation Is of the Lord: The Book of Jonah 2.9. Jones Very. CP-VeryJ

Salvationists. Ezra Pound. SP-PounE

Salvation's angel in a tree. Christmas Eve. John Ciardi. CP-CiarJ

Salvator Mundi: Via Crucis. Denise Levertov. SP-LeveDS

Salvé, next, minimal, poor little nosey. Catullus. *See* O elegant whore!

Salve O Pontifex! Ezra Pound. CP-PoEar

Salve, quae fingis proprio modulamine carmen. Christopher Smart. *See* Hail heav'nly harp, where Memnon's skill is shewn

Salve Senescentem. Sadi. CP-EmerR

Sam and Poll Go Back to the City. Hayden Carruth. CP-CarHS

Sam el Nesim. Constantine P. Cavafy. CP-CavaC, *tr.* by Theoharis Constantine Theoharis

Sam Solomon said. Ballad of Sam Solomon. Langston Hughes. CP-HughL; CP-HughL2

Sam the whorehouse man. Little Tigers Everywhere. Charles Bukowski. SP-BukC1

Samad says: Give me my daily pita. Concert of Wishes. Hans Magnus Enzensberger. SP-EnzeH, *tr.* by Michael Hamburger

Samaden, the Julier, Tiefenkasten . . . the raw egg. Immoralist, The. Norman Dubie. CP-DubiN

Same. Robert Creeley. CP-CreeR

Same, The. Jones Very. CP-VeryJ

Same and not quite the same, I walked through oak forests, The. Magpiety. Czeslaw Milosz. CP-MiloC; CP-MiloCN, *tr.* by Peter Dale Scott

Same as Always. Yannis Ritsos. SP-RitsY, *tr.* by Kostas Myrsiades

Same can be said of you, Victius, The. Carmen 98. Catullus. CP-ZukLS *Fr.* Carmina.

Same Embroidery, the Same Pattern, The. Yehuda Amichai. SP-AmicYL, *tr.* by Benjamin Harshav *and* Barbara Harshav

Same faces, and then the same scandels, The. Wind in the Street. Thom Gunn. CP-GunnT

Same gold of summer was on the winter hills, The. Winter Gold. Carl Sandburg. CP-SandC

Same in Blues. Langston Hughes. CP-HughL *Fr.* Lenox Avenue Mural.

Same Kiss After Many Years, The. Tess Gallagher. SP-GallT

Same leaves over and over again, The! In Hardwood Groves. Robert Frost. CP-FrosR

Same Meaning, The. Yannis Ritsos. SP-RitsY, *tr.* by N. C. Germanacos

Same old baffling questions! O my friend, The. Trust. John Greenleaf Whittier. CP-WhitJ

Same old story told again, The. James Whitcomb Riley. CP-RileJ

Same Star, The. Yannis Ritsos. SP-RitsY, *tr.* by Edmund Keeley

Same Story. Pablo Neruda. SP-NeruP

Same Subject, The. William Wordsworth. CP-WorW2 *Fr.* River Duddon [A Series of Sonnets], The.

Same Tits. James Tate. SP-TateJ

Same to me are sombre days and gay, The. Rondeau Redoublé. Dorothy Parker. CP-ParkD

Same tunes hang on pegs in the cloakrooms of the mind, The. Off the Peg. Louis MacNeice. CP-MacNL

Same, who crownes the Conquerour, will be, The. Comforts in Contentions. Robert Herrick. CP-HerrR

Same wind that uproots trees, The. Grasses, The. Jelaluddin Rumi. SP-Rumi, tr. by Coleman Barks

Samedi répit. Samuel Beckett. CP-BeckS

Sam'l Johnson in his famous. Temporary Poems. James Laughlin. CP-LaugJ

Sammy Lou of Rue. Revolutionary Petunias. Alice Walker. CP-WalkA

Samson. Primo Levi. CP-LeviP, tr. by Ruth Feldman

Samson Agonistes. John Milton. CP-MiltJ

Samson Agonistes. Ogden Nash. CP-NashO

Samson of Tinnata, the rebel. Delilah. Primo Levi. CP-LeviP, tr. by Ruth Feldman

Samson stark at Dagon's knee. Ralph Waldo Emerson. CP-EmerR

Samson to His Delilah. Richard Crashaw. CP-CrasR

Samuel. Anté Popovski.
   "There was nothing left for man." CP-KizeC, tr. by Carolyn Kizer

Samuel Beckett's Dublin. Donald Davie. CP-DaviDC

Samuel E. Sewall. John Greenleaf Whittier. CP-WhitJ

Samuel J. Tilden. John Greenleaf Whittier. CP-WhitJ

Samuel Pepys. Rudyard Kipling. CP-KiplR

Samuel Taylor Coleridge. Dante Gabriel Rossetti. CW-RossD Fr. Five English Poets.

San Francisco chronicle, A. Head Lines. Louis Zukofsky. CP-ZukLS

San Francisco for Whomever. Andrei Codrescu. SP-CodrA

San Francisco Poem. John Logan. CP-LogaJ

San Francisco Streets. Thom Gunn. CP-GunnT

San Fruttuoso. Charles Tomlinson. CP-TomlC; SP-TomlC

San Jose Symphony Reception. Lawrence Ferlinghetti. SP-FerlL

San Miniato. Oscar Wilde. CP-WildO

San Pietro. Joseph Brodsky. CP-BrodJ, tr. by Barry Rubin

San Sebastian. Thomas Hardy. CP-HardT

San Sebastiano de Sodoma. Tennessee Williams. CP-WillT

San Vio. June. Ezra Pound. CP-PoEar

Sanai. Jelaluddin Rumi. SP-Rumi, tr. by Coleman Barks

Sanct saluatour, send siluer sorrow! William Dunbar. CP-DunbW

Sancta Maria Dolorum. Richard Crashaw. CP-CrasR

Sancti Dominici Pallium. Samuel Taylor Coleridge. CP-ColeS

Sanctity, The. C. K. Williams. CP-WillC; SP-WillC

Sanctuary. John Berryman. CP-BerrJ

Sanctuary. Norman Dubie. CP-DubiN

Sanctuary. Dorothy Parker. CP-ParkD

Sanctuary. Tennessee Williams. CP-WillT

Sanctuary, The. Howard Nemerov. CP-NemeH

Sand-bed, they said. And gravel-bed. Before. Seamus Heaney. SP-HeanSO Fr. Squarings.

Sand Dollar. John Updike. CP-UpdiJ

Sand Dunes. Robert Frost. CP-FrosR

Sand Flesh and Sky. Clarence Major. SP-MajoC

Sand from the Urns, The. Paul Celan. SP-CelaP, tr. by John Felstiner

Sand has the ants, clay ferny weeds for play. Possessions. Ivor Gurney. SP-GurnI

Sand here's like meal. La Conca. Robert Creeley. SP-CreeR

Sand in the Air. Louis MacNeice. CP-MacNL

Sand is swift, overflowing, The. Snake. Dan Pagis. SP-PagiD, tr. by Stephen Mitchell

Sand-Man, The. Paul Laurence Dunbar. CP-DunbP

Sand Man, The. Thom Gunn. CP-GunnT

Sand-man he's a jolly old fellow, The. Johnny Speaks. Paul Laurence Dunbar. CP-DunbP

Sand of the sea runs red. Flux. Carl Sandburg. CP-SandC

Sand-Quarry with Moving Figures. Muriel Rukeyser. CP-RukeM

Sand Roads. Marge Piercy.
   Development, The. SP-PierM
   Road Behind the Last Dune, The. SP-PierM

Sand, sand; hills of sand. Mermaids, The. Walter De la Mare. CP-DeLaW

Sand Scribblings. Carl Sandburg. CP-SandC

Sandalphon. Ezra Pound. CP-PoEar

Sandals. Yehuda Amichai. SP-AmicY, tr. by Chana Bloch

Sandals are the skeleton of a full shoe. Yehuda Amichai. SP-AmicYL, tr. by Benjamin Harshav and Barbara Harshav

Sandals are the skeleton of a whole shoe. Sandals. Yehuda Amichai. SP-AmicY, tr. by Chana Bloch

Sanders Theater. Richard Eberhart. CP-EberR

Sandhill People. Carl Sandburg. CP-SandC

Sandhills That None May Visit. Peter Blue Cloud. SP-BlueP

Sandhog. Yusef Komunyakaa. CP-KomuY

Sandinista Avioncitos. Lawrence Ferlinghetti. SP-FerlL

Sandman walks abroad tonight, The. Mister Sandman. Langston Hughes. CP-HughL

Sandmartins' nests were loopholes of darkness in the riverbank, The. Nesting-Ground. Seamus Heaney. SP-HeanSO

Sandpiper. Elizabeth Bishop. CP-BishE

Sandpipers. Howard Nemerov. CP-NemeH

Sandpipers. Carl Sandburg. CP-SandC

Sandpipers at the margin. Point Reyes. Gary Snyder. CP-SnydG

Sandra. Charles Bukowski. SP-BukC1

Sands of the Well. Denise Levertov. SP-LeveDS

Sand's still blue with the receding water, sky topples, The. Formosa. Muriel Rukeyser. CP-RukeM

Sands, sunset, toilets. Kitville. Frank O'Hara. SP-OharF

Sandstone Keepsake. Seamus Heaney. SP-HeanSO

Sandy and Jockie. Robert Burns. CP-BurnR

Sandy's Sunday Best. Ted Berrigan. SP-BerrT

Sandys's Ghost, or a Proper New Ballad on the New Ovid's Metamorphosis as it Was Intended to Be. Alexander Pope. CP-PopeA

Sane and Insane. D. H. Lawrence. CP-LawrD

Sane, random, negligent hours. Supplement Hours. Walt Whitman. CP-WhitW

Sane Revolution, A. D. H. Lawrence. CP-LawrD

Sane Universe, The. D. H. Lawrence. CP-LawrD

Sang from the Heart, Sire. Emily Dickinson. CP-DickE

Sang off-key so mouthed the words. Sequence. Wyatt Prunty. SP-PrunW

Sang old Tom the lunatic. Tom the Lunatic. William Butler Yeats. CP-YeatW

Sang Solomon to Sheba. Solomon to Sheba. William Butler Yeats. CP-YeatW

Sang the angel in the tree. Tree Angel. Josephine Jacobsen. CP-JacoJ

Sanies I. Samuel Beckett. CP-BeckS

Sanies II. Samuel Beckett. CP-BeckS

Sanine to Leda. Robert Creeley. CP-CreeR

Sanjusangendo. Philip Whalen. SP-WhalP

Sank through easeful. Diver, The. Robert Earl Hayden. CP-HaydR

Sans Name. Charles Olson. CP-OlsoC

Sanskrit root word, The. Hayden Carruth. CP-CarHS Fr. Clay Hill Anthology, The.

Santa. Anne Sexton. SP-SextA Fr. Death of the Fathers, The.

Santa Claus. Howard Nemerov. CP-NemeH

Santa Claus in Oaxaca. Richard Eberhart. CP-EberR

Santa Decca. Oscar Wilde. CP-WildO

Santa Fe Sketches. Carl Sandburg. CP-SandC

Santa-Fé Trail (A Humoresque), The. Nicholas Vachel Lindsay. CP-LindV

Santa Maria Dei Frari. Clarence Major. SP-MajoC

Santa Maria delle Nevi. Charles Tomlinson. CP-TomlC

Santarém. Elizabeth Bishop. CP-BishE

Santayana's. Lorine Niedecker. CP-NiedL

Santo. James Merrill. SP-MerrJ

Santorini: Stopping the Leak. James Merrill. SP-MerrJ

São Paulo. John Updike. CP-UpdiJ

Sap Is Gone Out of the Trees, The. A. R. Ammons. CP-AmmoA

Sap rises from the sodden ditch. For Jane Myers. Louise Glück. SP-GlucL

Sapho, I will chuse to go. To Sapho. Robert Herrick. CP-HerrR

Sapling springs, the milkweed blooms, The: obsolete Nature. Adrienne Rich. CP-RicAE

Sappa Creek, The. Gary Snyder. CP-SnydG

Sappers. Rudyard Kipling. CP-KiplR

Sappers. Yusef Komunyakaa. CP-KomuY

Sapphic Fragment. Sappho. CP-HardT, tr. by Thomas Hardy

Sapphics. Sir Philip Sidney. SP-SidnP Fr. Arcadia.

Sapphics. Sappho. SP-SwinA, tr. by Algernon Charles Swinburne

Sapphics. E. E. Cummings. CP-CummE

Sappho. Christina Georgina Rossetti. CP-RosC3

Sappho. Sappho. CP-WilW2

Sappho. James Wright. CP-WrigJ

Sappho / and the Venus de Milo. In Longfellow's Library. Charles Tomlinson. CP-TomlC

Sappho, Be Comforted. William Carlos Williams. CP-WilW2

Sappho Crosses the Dark River into Hades. Edna St. Vincent Millay. CP-MillE

Sappho, Sappho, Sappho! initiate. To a Lovely Old Bitch. William Carlos Williams. CP-WilW2

Sappho to Phaon. Alexander Pope. CP-PopeA

Sappho to Philaenis. John Donne. MW-DonnJ Fr. Elegies.

Sappho's Gymnasium. Olga Broumas. SP-BrouO

Saprophyte. Sam Hamill. SP-HamiS

Sara in Her Father's Arms. George Oppen. CP-OppGN

Sarabande. Howard Nemerov. CP-NemeH

Saracen's Head, The. G. K. Chesterton. CP-ChesG

"Saraeen's Head" looks down the lane, The. Saracen's Head, The. G. K. Chesterton. CP-ChesG

Sarah Greenleaf, of eighteen years. Home-Coming of the Bride, The. John Greenleaf Whittier. CP-WhitJ

Sarah's Choice. Eleanor Wilner. SP-WilnE

Sarah's Letter to Peter. Carl Sandburg. CP-SandC

Sarajevo. Czeslaw Milosz. CP-MiloCN, *tr.* by Robert Hass

Sarajevo. Howard Nemerov. CP-NemeH

Sarcasm against the Ladies in a Newspaper, A; An Impromptu Answer. Annis Boudinot Stockton. CP-StocA

Sarcastic Science, she would like to know. Why Wait for Science. Robert Frost. CP-FrosR

Sarcophagi. Eugenio Montale. CP-MontE, *tr.* by Jonathan Galassi

Sardanapalus. Lord Byron. CP-Byron

Sardines in Striped Dresses. Charles Bukowski. SP-BukC3

Saris go by me from the embassies, The. Woman at the Washington Zoo, The. Randall Jarrell. CP-JarrR

Sarolla's women in their picture hats. Lawrence Ferlinghetti. SP-FerlL

Saroyan on his deathbed said. Our Curious Position. Charles Bukowski. SP-BukC3

Sarrasin's Wealth Song. Andrei Codrescu. SP-CodrA

Sash the faces of Just Orange Clock, An. Ted Berrigan. SP-BerrT

Sat in the car beside my doctor father. Migrant Camps, The. Gregory Orr. SP-OrrG

Satan. Robert Herrick. CP-HerrR

Satan himself came up the stairs. Total Harmony. Charles Baudelaire. CP-BaudC, *tr.* by Walter Martin

Sather Gate Illumination. Allen Ginsberg. CP-GinsA

Satin-Clad. Stevie Smith. CP-SmitS

Satin Dress, The. Dorothy Parker. CP-ParkD

Satin Shoes, The. Thomas Hardy. CP-HardT

Satire 1 [A London Street]. John Donne. MW-DonnJ *Fr.* Satires.

Satire 1.1: "What doating bigot to his faults so blind." Horace. CP-JohnS *Fr.* Satires.

Satire 1.5: "'Twas a long journey lay before us." Horace. CP-CowpW *Fr.* Satires.

Satire 1.9: "Saunt'ring along the street one day." Horace. CP-CowpW *Fr.* Satires.

Satire 2. John Donne. MW-DonnJ *Fr.* Satires.

Satire 2.1: "In books the various scenes of life he drew." Horace. CP-JohnS *Fr.* Satires.

Satire 2.6. Horace. *Fr.* Satires.

Satire 2.6: "This was the summit of my views." Horace. SP-SmarC *Fr.* Satires.

Satire 2.13: "Thirsting Tantalus doth catch at stream[e]s that from him flee, The." Horace. CP-RaleW *Fr.* Satires.

Satire 3 [Religion]. John Donne. MW-DonnJ *Fr.* Satires.

Satire 4. John Donne. MW-DonnJ *Fr.* Satires.

Satire 5. John Donne. MW-DonnJ *Fr.* Satires.

Satire IV of Dr. John Donne, Versified. Alexander Pope. CP-PopeA

Satire on an Inconstant Lover, A. Jonathan Swift. CP-SwifJ

Satire on the Fashionable Pompoons Worn by the Ladies in the Year 1753. by a Gentleman, A; Answered by a Young Lady of Sixteen. Annis Boudinot Stockton. CP-StocA

Satire, The. Walter De la Mare. CP-DeLaW

Satire II of Dr. John Donne, Versified. Alexander Pope. CP-PopeA

Satires. John Donne. CP-DonnJ

   Satire 1 [A London Street]. MW-DonnJ

   Satire 2. MW-DonnJ

   Satire 3 [Religion]. MW-DonnJ

   Satire 4. MW-DonnJ

   Satire 5. MW-DonnJ

Satires. Juvenal.

   "Beasts of each kind their fellows spare." CP-JohnS

   "Egyptians [or Aegyptians] think[e] it sin[ne] to root[e] up, or to bite." CP-RaleW

   "Fickle crowd with fortune comes and goes, The." CP-JohnS

   "Mind of mortals, in perverseness strong, The." CP-JohnS

   "More safely truth to urge her claim presumes." CP-JohnS

   "See the wild purchase of the bold and vain." CP-JohnS

   "Vain man runs headlong, to caprice resign'd." CP-JohnS

Satires. Sir Thomas Wyatt.

   "My mother's maids [or maydes] when they did sew [or sowe] and spin [or spynne]." CP-WyatT

   Of the Courtier's Life. CP-WyatT

To Sir Francis Brian. CP-WyatT

Satires. Horace.

   Satire 1.1: "What doating bigot to his faults so blind." CP-JohnS

   Satire 1.5: "'Twas a long journey lay before us." CP-CowpW

   Satire 1.9: "Saunt'ring along the street one day." CP-CowpW

   Satire 2.1: "In books the various scenes of life he drew." CP-JohnS

   Satire 2.6.

     "Thus after plain repast each cheerful guest." CP-SherT

   Satire 2.6: "This was the summit of my views." SP-SmarC

     ("Chearful sage, when solemn dictatees fail.") CP-JohnS

   Satire 2.13: "Thirsting Tantalus doth catch at stream[e]s that from him flee, The." CP-RaleW

Satires of Circumstance in Fifteen Glimpses. Thomas Hardy. CP-HardT

Satirical Elegy on the Death of a Late Famous General, A. Jonathan Swift. CP-SwifJ

Satirical Shrub, A. Ben Jonson. CP-JonsB

Satirist, The. Louis MacNeice. CP-MacNL

Satisfaction. D. H. Lawrence. CP-LawrD

Satisfaction Coal Company, The. Rita Dove. SP-DoveR

Satisfaction for Sufferings. Robert Herrick. CP-HerrR

Satisfaction—is the Agent. Emily Dickinson. CP-DickE

Satisfactions of the Mad Farmer, The. Wendell Berry. CP-BerrW

Satisfied loves eat big breakfasts. I. Marilyn Hacker. SP-HackM *Fr.* Separations.

Satrapy, The. Constantine P. Cavafy. CP-CavaC, *tr.* by Theoharis Constantine Theoharis

Saturated meadow, A. Rose Pogonias. Robert Frost. CP-FrosR

Saturday. John Ciardi. CP-CiarJ

Saturday. C. K. Williams. CP-WillC

Saturday, A. Jorge Luis Borges. SP-BorgJ, *tr.* by Eric McHenry

Saturday Afternoon. Robert Creeley. CP-CreeR

Saturday Afternoon at the Movies. John Logan. CP-LogaJ

Saturday. Early afternoon. High. Early Saturday Afternoon, Early Evening. Charles Wright. SP-WrigCN

Saturday. / (Garden gate). Schoolboy's Song. Federico García Lorca. CP-GarcF, *tr.* by Alan S. Trueblood *Fr.* Theories.

Saturday late afternoon. Coming Home. Robert Creeley. SP-CreeR

Saturday, March 6. John Ciardi. CP-CiarJ

Saturday Morning Journal. Charles Wright. SP-WrigC

Saturday Night. Langston Hughes. CP-HughL; CP-HughL1

Saturday Night. James Schuyler. CP-SchuJ

Saturday Night at the Chiropodist's. Wallace Stevens. CP-StevWP

Saturday night in August when, A. Last Meeting. Robert Penn Warren. CP-WarrR

Saturday Night in the Parthenon. Kenneth Patchen. CP-PatcK

Saturday noon: the morning of the mind. On Rising from the Dead. Carolyn Kizer. CP-KizeC

Saturday on Seventh Street. Fields, The. W. S. Merwin. SP-MerwWF

Saturday Sweeping. Philip Levine. SP-LeviP

Saturdays. A. K. Ramanujan. CP-RamaA

Saturday's Child. Countee Cullen. CP-CullC

Saturn. "H. D." CP-DoolH *Fr.* Temple of the Sun.

Saturnalia. Louise Glück. SP-GlucL

Saturnalia. Thom Gunn. CP-GunnT

Saturne descending from the heavens high. Virgil. CP-RaleW *Fr.* Aeneid [or Eneados *or* Aeneis], The.

Saturne to be the fatter is not knowne. Sir Walter Ralegh. CP-RaleW

Saturnian Dilemma. Andrei Codrescu. SP-CodrA

Saturnian Hypotyposes, Ex-Belmontet. Arthur Rimbaud. CP-RimbA, *tr.* by Martin Sorrell

Satyr, A. Jonathan Smedley.

   "Science and Arts are at a stand." CP-SherT

Satyr Formalist. A. R. Ammons. CP-AmmoA

Satyr spied a Goddess in her bath, A. Teaching of the Nude, The. George Meredith. CP-MerG1

Satyricon. Petronius Arbiter.

   "I saw the Sibyl at Cumæ." CW-RossD

Satyrs dance! All the deformities take wing. Tribute to the Painters. William Carlos Williams. CP-WilW2

Sauce for Sorrowes. Robert Herrick. CP-HerrR

Saucer holds a Cup, A. Emily Dickinson. CP-DickE

Sauchs in the Reuch Heuch Hauch, The. Hugh MacDiarmid. SP-MacDH

Saul. Robert Browning. CP-BroR1

Saul. Lord Byron. CP-Byron

Sauntering the pavement or riding the country by-road, lo, such faces! Faces. Walt Whitman. CP-WhitW

Saunt'ring along the street one day. Satire 1.9: "Saunt'ring along the street one day." Horace. CP-CowpW *Fr.* Satires.

Savage Beast, The. William Carlos Williams. CP-WilW2

Savage I was sitting in my house, late, lone. Householder, The. Robert Browning. CP-BroR2

Savage's romance, The. New York. Marianne Craig Moore. CP-MoorM

Savannah. Amy Clampitt. CP-ClamA

Savannah. Donald Davie. CP-DaviDC

Savantism. Walt Whitman. CP-WhitW

Save for a lusterless honing-stone of moon. Olive Tree, The. Karl Shapiro. SP-ShapK

Save me from the idolatry. Emily Dickinson. SP-DickE

Save some room. Epic. Robert Creeley. SP-CreeR

Save ye, Merry gentlemen! Vagabonds and Rovers. Rouse, A. Ezra Pound. CP-PoEar

Saving, The. Robert Pinsky. CP-PinsR

Saving Just the Real. Clarence Major. SP-MajoC

Saving the Appearances. Charles Tomlinson. CP-TomlC

Saving Way, The. Hayden Carruth. CP-CarHS

Savior! I've no one else to tell. Emily Dickinson. CP-DickE

Savior looked on Peter. Ay, no word, The. Look, The. Elizabeth Barrett Browning. CP-BroEB

Savior must have been, The. Emily Dickinson. CP-DickE

Savior's only signature, The. Emily Dickinson. SP-DickE

Savoir Faire. Carl Sandburg. CP-SandC

Savonarola. W. S. Merwin. SP-MerwW

Savoring sleep, the figure. Sleeping Woman. Rainer Maria Rilke. CP-RilkFr, tr. by A. Poulin, Jr. Fr. Orchards.

Savoy. Frank O'Hara. SP-OharF

Saw a girl in a food. Crystal Palace Market. James Laughlin. CP-LaugJ

Saw Carrara's marble mountains. Carrara, Looking Seaward. Lawrence Ferlinghetti. SP-FerlL

Saw I Never the Righteous Forsaken. Donald Davie. CP-DaviDC

Saw ye my Maggie? O Saw Ye My Maggie. Robert Burns. CP-BurnR

Saw Ye My Phely (Quasi Dicat, Phillis). Robert Burns. CP-BurnR

Sawyer's Rage against Trees Noble as Horses, A. Alan Dugan. CP-DugaA

Saxifrage. Robert Stock. SP-StocR

Saxo Cere. James Laughlin. CP-LaugJ

Saxon (A.D. 449), A. Jorge Luis Borges. SP-BorgJ, tr. by Alastair Reid

Saxon peasant girl, A. Marta (Brazil, 1928). Denise Levertov. SP-LeveDL

Saxophone and subway. Rock, The. W. S. Merwin. SP-MerwWF

Saxophone / Has a vulgar tone, The. Conservatory Student Struggles with Higher Instrumentation. Langston Hughes. CP-HughL; CP-HughL2

Say. George Oppen. CP-OppGN

Say a man tells a woman that he was blind. He Shuts His Eyes for the Layman's Long Prayer about Lust and the Mind of the Young Preacher Wanders Again. Miller Williams. CP-WillM

Say a mass for my soul's repose, my brother. Murdered Lover, The. Paul Laurence Dunbar. CP-DunbP

Say a master of the track. When This Clangor in the Brain. Adrienne Rich. CP-RicAE

Say farewell, and let me go. Song of Parting. James Whitcomb Riley. CP-RileJ

Say first he loved the dear homehearts, and then. William Pinkney Fishback. James Whitcomb Riley. CP-RileJ

Say, goddesses, guardians of the sacred groves. On the Platonic Idea as Aristotle Understood It. John Milton. CP-CowpW; CP-MiltJ

Say good-by er howdy-do. Good-by er Howdy-do. James Whitcomb Riley. CP-RileJ

Say Good-bye to Big Daddy. Randall Jarrell. CP-JarrR

Say, heav'nly muse, what king, or mighty God. Isaiah 63. 1–8. Phillis Wheatley. CP-WheaP

Say I Am You. Jelaluddin Rumi. SP-Rumi, tr. by Coleman Barks

Say I was where in dream I seemed to be. Elementals, The. Kathleen Jessie Raine. SP-RainK

Say in what country, where. Dames du Temps Jadis. Robert Lowell. SP-LoweR

Say, is it day, is it dusk in thy bower. Song of the Bower, The. Dante Gabriel Rossetti. CW-RossD

Say it depends on the interpretation. Muriel Rukeyser. CP-RukeM

Say it, / you're afraid. Box. Robert Creeley. SP-CreeR

Say it's a picnic on the Fourth of July. Places with Meaning. William Stafford. SP-StafWW

Say it's an important event like this. Off to Patagonia. Theodore Weiss. SP-WeisT

Say, lad, have you things to do? A. E. Housman. CP-HousA

Say life is the one-way trip, the one-way flight. Watchmaker God. Robert Lowell. SP-LoweR

Say, lovely youth, that dost my heart command. Sappho to Phaon. Alexander Pope. CP-PopeA

Say, muse divine, can hostile scenes delight. To Captain H—D, of the 65th Regiment. Phillis Wheatley. CP-WheaP

Say my love is easy had. Fighting Words. Dorothy Parker. CP-ParkD

Say never the strong heart. Eagle, The. Allen Tate. CP-TateA

Say not Eve needed Adam's pardon. He Digs, He Dug, He Has Dug. Ogden Nash. CP-NashO

Say not, that in old age. Old Age. Jones Very. CP-VeryJ

Say not the mermaid is a myth. Mermaid, The. Ogden Nash. CP-NashO

Say Not the Struggle Nought Availeth. Arthur Hugh Clough. SP-ClouA

Say not the struggle nought [or naught] availeth. Say Not the Struggle Nought Availeth. Arthur Hugh Clough. SP-ClouA

Say nothing: let us sit within arm's reach. Meeting. George Meredith. CP-MerG2

Say of the gulls that they are flying. Variations on a Summer Day. Wallace Stevens. CP-StevW; CP-StevWP

Say pardon to a bum. David Ignatow. SP-IgnaD

Say, Robin, what can Traulus mean. Traulus. Jonathan Swift. CP-SwifJ

Say Something. Robert Creeley. SP-CreeR

Say something, man, say something before the nations and. Class of 1934. Kenneth Patchen. CP-PatcK

Say something to me! I've waited so long. James Whitcomb Riley. CP-RileJ

Say that a ballad. Speeches at the Barriers. Susan Howe. SP-HoweS

Say that it is a crude effect, black reds. Bouquet of Roses in Sunlight. Wallace Stevens. CP-StevW; CP-StevWP

Say that the men of the old black tower. Black Tower, The. William Butler Yeats. CP-YeatW

Say that We Saw Spain Die. Edna St. Vincent Millay. CP-MillE

Say that you're / lonely—and want / something to. Chicago. Robert Creeley. CP-CreeR

Say the face I'm speaking of now, hers I mean. Michelangelo Buonarroti. CP-Miche, tr. by John Frederick Nims

Say to me only. Sotto Voce. Stanley Kunitz. CP-KunSC

Say to the lover when the lane. Laughter. G. K. Chesterton. CP-ChesG

Say, what am I? or what are we? Riddles and Charades. Mrs. Austen. CP-AustJ

Say, what is Honour?—"Tis the finest sense." William Wordsworth. CP-WorW1

Say What Is Love—To Live In Vain. Song: "Say What Is Love—To Live In Vain." John Clare. SP-ClarJ Fr. Child Harold.

Say what we like, our civilisation has learnt a great lesson. Young Are Not Greedy, The. D. H. Lawrence. CP-LawrD

Say what you will, and scratch my heart to find. Edna St. Vincent Millay. CP-MillE

Say: Who is this that cometh royally. Triumph of Man, The ("Say: Who is this that cometh royally"). G. K. Chesterton. CP-ChesG

Say, whose is this fair picture, which the light. Missionary, The. John Greenleaf Whittier. CP-WhitJ

Say, ye apostate and profane. Ode on Sir Charles Grandison. William Cowper. CP-CowpW

Say, ye far-travelled clouds, far-seeing hills. On the Sight of a Manse in the South of Scotland. William Wordsworth. CP-WorW2

Say Yes. Thomas Lux. SP-LuxT

Say Yes to all and be condensed in fact! Yes Log, The. Andrei Codrescu. SP-CodrA

Say! you feller! You. Sutter's Claim. James Whitcomb Riley. CP-RileJ

Saying. A. R. Ammons. CP-AmmoA

Saying Farewell at the Monastery After Hearing the Old Master Lecture on "Return to the Source." Gary Snyder. CP-SnydG

Saying Good-bye. Thomas Hardy. CP-HardT

Saying Goodbye. Federico García Lorca. CP-GarcF, tr. by Jerome Rothenberg Fr. Return, The.

Saying Goodbye to Love. Charles Bukowski. SP-BukC2

Saying it Back. Wyatt Prunty. SP-PrunW

Saying It to Keep It from Happening. John Ashbery. SP-AshbJ

Saying of Farewell, A. James Dickey. CP-DickJ

Saying to the square that is always open good-bye. Going from the Green Window. W. S. Merwin. SP-MerwWF

Sayings. Jones Very. CP-VeryJ

Sayings from the Northern Ice. William Stafford. SP-StafW; SP-StafWW

Sayings of Henry Stephens. Carl Sandburg. CP-SandC

Sayings of the Blind. William Stafford. SP-StafWW

Says. Walt Whitman. CP-WhitW

Says Alcaeus echthairo ton. I Hate Love. James Laughlin. CP-LaugJ

Says Audrey to herself in the mirror, adjusting. Painfully Banal. Thomas Lux. SP-LuxT

Says Death 'I've been trying these three weeks or more.' Dialogue between Death and Mrs A. Mrs. Austen. CP-AustJ

Says England to Germany: "Africa's ours." Strained Relations. Ambrose Bierce. SP-BierA

Says ol man no body. E. E. Cummings. CP-CummE

Says the pipe to the snuff-box, I can't understand. To Mr. Newton. William Cowper. CP-CowpW

Scaffold, A. Amy Clampitt. CP-ClamA

Scala Coeli. Kathleen Jessie Raine. SP-RainK

Scalded cat, / claws, arched back and blistered pride. Night Letter. Marge Piercy. SP-PierM

Scale. Raymond Carver. CP-CarvR

Scale. Rainer Maria Rilke. CP-RilkFr, *tr. by* A. Poulin, Jr.

Scale in May, A. W. S. Merwin. SP-MerwW

Scalene landscape of foam and olive trees, The. Siren and the Carabineer, The. Federico García Lorca. CP-GarcF, *tr. by* Christopher Maurer

Scales of the Eyes, The. Howard Nemerov. CP-NemeH

Scales of the monster, The. Heaven and Earth. Kenneth Patchen. CP-PatcK

Scaling small rocks, exhaling smog. Central Park. Robert Lowell. SP-LoweR

Scaling your words like crags I found. Mentor. Audre Lorde. SP-LordA

Scamp. Paul Laurence Dunbar. CP-DunbP

Scandal. John Clare. SP-ClarJ

Scapegoats and Rabies. Ted Hughes. SP-HughTN

Scapin's not with it. Fête Galante. Arthur Rimbaud. CP-RimbA, *tr. by* Martin Sorrell

Scar. C. K. Williams. SP-WillC

Scar, The. Charles Tomlinson. CP-TomlC

Scar tissue says, The. Initials on Aspens. Yusef Komunyakaa. CP-KomuY

Scarabs. Dan Pagis. SP-PagiD, *tr. by* Stephen Mitchell

Scarce had the solemn Sabbath-bell. Sabbath Scene, A. John Greenleaf Whittier. CP-WhitJ

Scarce tolerable life, which all life long. Christina Georgina Rossetti. CP-RosC2

Scarcely Disfigured. Paul Éluard. CP-BeckS

Scarcely, I think; yet it indeed *may* be. For "An Allegorical Dance of Women" by Andrea Mantegna. Dante Gabriel Rossetti. CW-RossD

Scar[e]-Fire, The. Robert Herrick. CP-HerrR

Scarecrow, The. Walter De la Mare. CP-DeLaW

Scared Child, The. Robert Graves. CP-GravR

Scarf of June, The. Richard Eberhart. CP-EberR

Scarlet. Charles Bukowski. SP-BukC1

Scarlet Tanager. James Schuyler. CP-SchuJ

Scarlet the sunset, crimson the dawn. Psalm of the Bloodbank. Carl Sandburg. CP-SandC

Scarred Girl, The. James Dickey. CP-DickJ

Scars take us back to places we have been, The. Memoranda. William Dickey. SP-DickW

Scars upon the day, The. Await. James Schuyler. CP-SchuJ

Scatter a few cold cinders into the empty grate. Making a fire. Walter De la Mare. CP-DeLaW

Scatter a fragrant flower. Emily Dickinson. SP-DickE

Scattered humming, perverted silence, A. Gong. Rainer Maria Rilke. CP-RilkFr, *tr. by* A. Poulin, Jr.

Scattered in scattered capitals. Invocation to Joyce. Jorge Luis Borges. SP-BorgJ, *tr. by* Charles Tomlinson

Scattered, with every breeze, I see them fly. Elm Seed, The. Jones Very. CP-VeryJ

Scattered Words for Emily Dickinson. Jane Cooper. CP-CoopJ

Scatterghost, / it can't float away. Rabbit, The. Mary Oliver. SP-OlivM

Scavai la neve,—sì che scavai! Christina Georgina Rossetti. CP-RosC3

Scenario. David Ignatow. SP-IgnaD

Scene. Federico García Lorca. CP-GarcF, *tr. by* Alan S. Trueblood *Fr.* Back of the World.

Scene. Paul Éluard. CP-BeckS

Scene, The. Aleksandr Aleksandrovich Blok. CP-KunSC *Fr.* Dances of Death.

Scene From Life. Robert Stock. SP-StocR

Scene from "Tasso." Percy Bysshe Shelley. CP-ShelP

Scene is the fore-court of a noble dwelling on the island of Rhodes, The. At the Fall of an Age. Robinson Jeffers. CP-JefR2

Scene (1946–7). Alan Dugan. CP-DugaA

Scene of the Lieutenant Colonel of the Civil Guard. Federico García Lorca. CP-GarcF, *tr. by* Christopher Maurer

Scene stands stubborn, The: skinflint trees. November Graveyard. Sylvia Plath. CP-PlatS

Scene, which 'wildered fancy viewed, A. Retrospect, The: CWM Elan, 1812. Percy Bysshe Shelley. CP-ShelP

Scenes. Arthur Rimbaud. CP-RimbA, *tr. by* Martin Sorrell

Scenes are new, and everything compact, The. Prologue Spoken at Mr. Sheridan's School. Thomas Sheridan. CP-SherT

Scenes Favourable to Meditation. Jeanne Marie Bouvier de la Motte Guyon. CP-CowpW

Scenes from a Death. Heather McHugh. SP-McHuH

Scenes from Politian. Edgar Allan Poe. CP-PoeEd

Scenes of Childhood. James Merrill. SP-MerrJ

Scenes of Life at the Capital. Philip Whalen.
  "Today I started late and quit early." SP-WhalP

Scenes with Harlequins. Geoffrey Hill. CP-HillG

Scenic. John Updike. CP-UpdiJ

Scenic View. Donald Hall. CP-HallD

Scent, The. Charles Baudelaire. CP-BaudC, *tr. by* Walter Martin *Fr.* Phantom, A.

Scent / from the apple-loft! Farmer's Wife: at Fostons Ash, The. Charles Tomlinson. CP-TomlC

Scent of Irises. D. H. Lawrence. CP-LawrD

Scent of ripeness from over a wall, A. Unharvested. Robert Frost. CP-FrosR

Scent of smoke from the oil of the Flying Dolphin, The. Two Poems of Greece. John Logan. CP-LogaJ

Scented Herbage of My Breast. Walt Whitman. CP-WhitW

Scepticism with Regard to the Gospels. Jones Very. CP-VeryJ

Schad paced the length of his studio. Agosta the Winged Man and Rasha the Black Dove. Rita Dove. SP-DoveR

Schatten Küsse, Schatten Liebe. Kenneth Rexroth. CP-RexrK

Scheduled: / a two part. Sets. Rae Armantrout. SP-ArmaA

Scheherazade. John Ashbery. SP-AshbJ

Schematic Nocturne. Federico García Lorca. SP-GarcF, *tr. by* Stanley Read

Scherzo. Randall Jarrell. CP-JarrR

Schir, at this feist of benefice. William Dunbar. CP-DunbW

Schir, for your grace, bayth nicht and day. William Dunbar. CP-DunbW

Schir, I beseik thyne excellence. Complaynt of Schir David Lindesay, The. Sir David Lyndsay. SP-LyndD

Schir, I complane off iniuris. William Dunbar. CP-DunbW

Schir Iohine the Ros, ane thing thair is compild. Flyting of Dumbar [or Dunbar] and Kennedie [or Kennedy], The. William Dunbar. CP-DunbW

Schir, lat it neuer in tonne be tald. Petition of the Gray Horse, Auld Dunbar, [The]. William Dunbar. CP-DunbW

Schir, ye haue [or have] mony seruitouris [or servitouris]. William Dunbar. CP-DunbW

Schir, yit remember as befoir. William Dunbar. CP-DunbW

Schizophrene. Louis MacNeice. CP-MacNL

Schizophrenic, wrenched by two styles. Codicil. Derek Walcott. CP-WalcD

Scholar Dreaming, The. Jones Very. CP-VeryJ

Scholar Gypsy, The. Matthew Arnold. SP-ArnoM

Scholar is a ball thats spent. Ralph Waldo Emerson. CP-EmerR

Scholars, The. Rudyard Kipling. CP-KiplR

Scholars, The. William Butler Yeats. CP-YeatW

Scholars at the Orchid Pavilion. John Berryman. CP-BerrJ

Scholars call the masculine swan a cob. Swan, The. Ogden Nash. CP-NashO

School-Boy, The. William Blake. CP-BlakW *Fr.* Songs of Experience.

School boy loitered on his way to school, The. May Morning. Henry David Thoreau. CP-ThorH

School children, The. Upon First Reading the Immortal Literature of the World—. Charles Bukowski. SP-BukC3

School Children, The. Louise Glück. SP-GlucL

School Days. William Stafford. SP-StafWW

School Daze. Andrei Codrescu. SP-CodrA

School for Dark Thoughts. Charles Simic. SP-SimiC; SP-SimiCE

School Holidays. Yannis Ritsos. SP-RitsY, *tr. by* Kimon Friar

School-house next they build, a structure small, The. Common School, The. Jones Very. CP-VeryJ

School in August, The. Philip Larkin. CP-LarkP

School is over. It is too hot. Lonely Street, The. William Carlos Williams. CP-WilW1

School of Summer, The. Randall Jarrell. CP-JarrR

School on the Outskirts. D. H. Lawrence. CP-LawrD

School on the Roof, The. W. S. Merwin. SP-MerwWF

School or Perl of Putney, the Mistress of All Singular Manners, Mistresse Portman, The. Robert Herrick. CP-HerrR

School Play. William Stafford. SP-StafWW

School Play, The. James Merrill. SP-MerrJ

School Song, A. Rudyard Kipling. CP-KiplR

Schoolboy's Favorite, The. James Whitcomb Riley. CP-RileJ

Schoolboy's Song. Federico García Lorca. CP-GarcF, *tr. by* Alan S. Trueblood *Fr.* Theories.

Schoolchildren. W. H. Auden. CP-AudeW

Schoolcraft's Diary Written on the Missouri: 1830. Robert Bly. SP-BlyR

Schooldesk, The. Raymond Carver. CP-CarvR

Schoolgirls in pantyhose. Girls in Pantyhose. Charles Bukowski. SP-BukC1

Schooling. A. R. Ammons. CP-AmmoA

Schoolmaster. Philip Larkin. CP-LarkP

Schoolmaster [A], The. D. H. Lawrence. CP-LawrD
  "How can I teach you when your blue." CP-LawrD

Schoolmaster and Songmaster! Memory. Three Singing Friends. James Whitcomb Riley. CP-RileJ

Schoolmaster [B], The. D. H. Lawrence. CP-LawrD

Schoolsville. Billy Collins. SP-CollB

Schooner Flight, The. Derek Walcott. CP-WalcD

Schopenhauer's Crying. Adam Zagajewski. SP-ZagaA, *tr.* by Renata Gorczynski

Schreckhorn, The. Thomas Hardy. CP-HardT

Schubert's "Farewell." George Meredith. CP-MerG2

Schumann Adds Trombones to His Second Symphony After Mendelssohn Conducts the First Performance. Miller Williams. CP-WillM

Science. Ambrose Bierce. SP-BierA

Science. Robinson Jeffers. CP-JefR1

Science and Arts are at a stand. Jonathan Smedley. CP-SherT *Fr.* Satyr, A.

Science in God. Robert Herrick. CP-HerrR (Knowledge.) CP-HerrR

Science of the Night, The. Stanley Kunitz. CP-KunSC

Science outstrips. Exotic. A. R. Ammons. CP-AmmoA

Science puffs up, sayes Gut, when either Pease. Upon Gut. Robert Herrick. CP-HerrR

Science—so the Savants say, A. Emily Dickinson. CP-DickE

Science, that gives man hope to live without lies. Curb Science? Robinson Jeffers. CP-JefR3

Science, that makes wheels turn, cities grow. Triad. Robinson Jeffers. CP-JefR2

Science, that simple saint, cannot be bothered. Dr. Sigmund Freud Discovers the Sea Shell. Archibald MacLeish. CP-MacLA

Science! true daughter of Old Time thou art! Sonnet—To Science. Edgar Allan Poe. CP-PoeEd

Science will not trust us. Emily Dickinson. SP-DickE

Scientific Doctor, The. D. H. Lawrence. CP-LawrD

Scientist of love, The. Under His Microscope. James Laughlin. CP-LaugJ

Scientists are in terror, The. From Canto 115: "Scientists are in terror, The." Ezra Pound. CP-PoCan *Fr.* Cantos.

Scissor-and-slap abruptness of a latch. Seamus Heaney. SP-HeanSO *Fr.* Squarings.

Scissor man. / (3:00 p.m.). Federico García Lorca. CP-GarcF, *tr.* by Jerome Rothenberg *Fr.* Summer Hours.

Scissors. David Ignatow. SP-IgnaD

Scissors cut the long-grown hair, The. Upon Shaving Off One's Beard. John Updike. CP-UpdiJ

Scissors, glue, clumsy. Gift, The. Gregory Orr. SP-OrrG

Scissors-Grinder, The. Nicholas Vachel Lindsay. CP-LindV

Scobble for whoredom[e] whips his wife, and cries [*or* cryes]. Upon Scobble [Epigram]. Robert Herrick. CP-HerrR

Scoffing, amorous maidens and young men. Canzone: "Scoffing, amorous maidens and young men." John Milton. CP-CowpW; CP-MiltJ

Sconset. Charles Tomlinson. CP-TomlC

Scooped by the / great Eye- / less One. Paul Celan. SP-CelaP, *tr.* by John Felstiner

Score, The. Heather McHugh. SP-McHuH

Score of airy miles will smooth, A. Ralph Waldo Emerson. CP-EmerR

Score of years had come and gone, A. John Underhill. John Greenleaf Whittier. CP-WhitJ

Scorn not the Sonnet; Critic, you have frowned. William Wordsworth. CP-WorW2; MW-WorW

Scorn of God, The. G. K. Chesterton. CP-ChesG

Scornful or Fond Infinity. Laura Riding Jackson. CP-RidiL

Scornful Reprieve. Denise Levertov. SP-LeveDL

Scorning the schemes of nature. At the Children's Hospital in Little Rock. Miller Williams. CP-WillM

Scorns have I seen but Lady Babchen's scorn. Das Babenzorn. Ezra Pound. CP-PoEar

Scorpio. Ted Berrigan. SP-BerrT

Scorpion. Stevie Smith. CP-SmitS

Scotch Drink. Robert Burns. CP-BurnR

Scotch Song. Robert Burns. CP-BurnR

Scotish Ballad. Robert Burns. CP-BurnR

Scotish Song. Robert Burns. CP-BurnR

Scotland. Billy Collins. SP-CollB

Scotland. Hugh MacDiarmid. SP-MacDH

Scotland Small? Hugh MacDiarmid. SP-MacDH

Scots Ballad. Robert Burns. CP-BurnR

Scots Poem. John Berryman. SP-BerrJ

Scots Prologue, *For Mrs. Sutherland's Benefit Night*, Spoken at the Theatre Dumfries. Robert Burns. CP-BurnR

Scots steel tempered wi' Irish fire. Weapon, The. Hugh MacDiarmid. SP-MacDH

Scots, wha hae wi' Wallace bled. Robert Burns. CP-BurnR

Scottish Broom on Birdnest brae, The. Help for the Memory of the Grand Independent; A New Song, A. William Wordsworth. CP-WorW2

Scottish hinds, too poor to house, The. Receipt to Restore Stella's Youth, A. Jonathan Swift. CP-SwifJ

Scottsboro. Langston Hughes. CP-HughL; CP-HughL1

Scottsboro, Too, Is Worth Its Song. Countee Cullen. CP-CullC

Scottsboro's just a little place. Town of Scottsboro, The. Langston Hughes. CP-HughL; CP-HughL1

Scotty's dead.—Of course he is! James Whitcomb Riley. CP-RileJ

Scoundrels, Scoundrels. Triptych. Alan Dugan. CP-DugaA

Scoured like a conch. Night Rider, The. William Carlos Williams. CP-WilW2

Scourge, The. Stanley Kunitz. CP-KunSC

Scourge of life, and death's extreme disgrace, The. Sir Philip Sidney. SP-SidnP

Scouring, The. Richard Eberhart. CP-EberR

Scowl on ye dead that hug the dead, and cleave the air with cries. Union, The. G. K. Chesterton. CP-ChesG

Scrabble. Seamus Heaney. SP-HeanSO *Fr.* Glanmore Revisited.

Scraggle and brush broken through, snow-shower jarred loose. Snowshoeing Back to Camp in Gloaming. Robert Penn Warren. CP-WarrR

Scram, Lion! Ogden Nash. CP-NashO

Scraps. Louise Glück. SP-GlucL

Scraps. James Whitcomb Riley. CP-RileJ

Scratch, The. Raymond Carver. CP-CarvR

Scratch, The. James Dickey. CP-DickJ

Scratch on the Scratch Pad. Philip Larkin. CP-LarkP

Scratchy sound of skin, The. Seeing in the Dark. Yusef Komunyakaa. CP-KomuY

Scrawl, A. James Whitcomb Riley. CP-RileJ

Scream. Federico García Lorca. CP-GarcF, *tr.* by Jerome Rothenberg *Fr.* Fairs.

"Scream, The." Donald Hall. CP-HallD

Scream, The. Ted Hughes. SP-HughTN

Scream, The. Charles Tomlinson. CP-TomlC; SP-TomlC

Scream to the Editor, A. Charles Olson. CP-OlsoC

Screamed the far sea-mew. On the mirroring sands. Flotsam. Walter De la Mare. CP-DeLaW

Screaming Out Loud. Gregory Orr. SP-OrrG

Screaming produced by the great fright machines, The. Fire in Luna Park. Galway Kinnell. SP-KinnGN

Screech-Owl. Donald Davie. CP-DaviDC

Screen door slammed, The. Quartet. William Corbett. SP-CorbW

Screen of supreme good fortune curved, The. Young Son, The. John Ashbery. SP-AshbJ

Screen with the Face with the Voice, The. Ogden Nash. CP-NashO

Screendoor whines, clacks, The. Night on Hatchet Cove. Denise Levertov. SP-LeveDP

Screened Porch in the Country, A. James Dickey. CP-DickJ

Screw-Guns. Rudyard Kipling. CP-KiplR

Scribble. Allen Ginsberg. CP-GinsA

Scribbled wishes stuck between the stones. Jerusalem, 1985. Yehuda Amichai. SP-AmicY, *tr.* by Chana Bloch

Scribbler from the Northern Bear, A. Thomas Sheridan. CP-SherT

Scribe. "H. D." CP-DoolH

Scribe, The. James Laughlin. CP-LaugJ

Scribe, The. Walter De la Mare. CP-DeLaW

Scribes, The. Seamus Heaney. SP-HeanSO *Fr.* Sweeney Redivivus.

Scriblerian Verses. Jonathan Swift. CP-SwifJ

Script. A. R. Ammons. CP-AmmoA

Script of trees before the hill, A. Winter Spring. Richard Wilbur. CP-WilbR

Scriptor Ignotus. Ezra Pound. CP-PoEar

Scriptsmith. Carl Sandburg. CP-SandC

Scripture. Carl Sandburg. CP-SandC

Scritch, scratch, saith the frozen spring snow. Upon the Last Day of His Forty-Ninth Year. John Updike. CP-UpdiJ

Scrivener's Roses, The. Norman Dubie. CP-DubiN

Scroggam. Robert Burns. CP-BurnR

Scroll. Carl Sandburg. CP-SandC

Scroll is defaced; the worm, The. Some Shires Revisited. Donald Davie. CP-DaviDC

Scroppo's Dog. May Swenson. SP-SwenM

Scrotum tumescit Pandaro; tremat scortum. In Pandarum. Thomas Campion. CP-CampT

Scrub. Edna St. Vincent Millay. CP-MillE

Scrubwoman for the old bank and jailhouse, The. Lamentations. Norman Dubie. CP-DubiN

Scrutability. Sam Hamill. SP-HamiS

Scrutinize the Scorpion constellation. Almanac. Carl Sandburg. CP-SandC

Scrutiny. Yannis Ritsos. SP-RitsY, *tr.* by Kimon Friar

Sculptor. Sylvia Plath. CP-PlatS

Sculptor?—Nameless, though once dear to fame. Inscription for a Bust of Homer. William Cowper. CP-CowpW

Sculpture in Soil. Peter Blue Cloud. SP-BlueP

'Sculpture' of Rhyme, The. Donald Davie. CP-DaviDC

Sculptures in Hungary. Donald Davie. CP-DaviDC

Scum has come, The. Lament, for Cocoa. John Updike. CP-UpdiJ

Scummed maunderings that nothing loves but reeds. Reedbeds of the Hackensack, The. Amy Clampitt. CP-ClamA

'Scur'ous-like, said the tree-toad. Tree-Toad, The. James Whitcomb Riley. CP-RileJ

Scurvy with things, human brothers, human sisters. Of Possessions, in Winter. William Meredith. SP-MereW

Scuts of froth swirled from the discharge pipe. Milk Factory, The. Seamus Heaney. SP-HeanSO

Scuttle up the workshop. Lorine Niedecker. CP-NiedL

Scylla and Charybdis. Thomas Kinsella. CP-KinsT

Scyros. Karl Shapiro. SP-ShapK

Scythe. Lorine Niedecker. CP-NiedL

Scythe and axe and hedge-clippers, the shriek. Cot, The. Seamus Heaney. SP-HeanSO *Fr.* Glanmore Revisited.

Scythian Charioteers, The. Donald Davie. CP-DaviDC

Scythians, The. Aleksandr Aleksandrovich Blok. SP-BlokA, *tr. by* Peter France *and* Jon Stallworthy

Sea ("Ever / to sleep"). Robert Creeley. SP-CreeR

Sea ("Salt and water"). Robert Creeley. SP-CreeR

Sea, The. Jorge Luis Borges. SP-BorgJ, *tr. by* John Updike

Sea, The. Robert Creeley. CP-CreeR

Sea, The. Donald Hall. CP-HallD

Sea, The. D. H. Lawrence. CP-LawrD

Sea, The. Ballad of the Water of the Sea. Federico García Lorca. SP-GarcF, *tr. by* Lloyd Mallan

Sea, The. Gabriela Mistral. SP-MistG, *tr. by* Maria Giachetti [*or* Jacketti]

Sea, The. Mary Oliver. SP OlivM

Sea, The. Dorothy Parker. CP-ParkD

Sea, The. May Swenson. SP-SwenM

Sea, The. William Carlos Williams. CP-WilW1

Sea, a body of mysterious calls, The. Homecoming. Christian J. Van Geel. CP-RicAE

Sea: A Summer and Winter View, The. George Crabbe. SP-CrabG *Fr.* Borough, The.

Sea always arriving, The. Farmer and the Sea, The. Wendell Berry. CP-BerrW

Sea and Ourselves at Cape Ann, The. Lawrence Ferlinghetti. SP-FerlL

Sea and Star. G. K. Chesterton. CP-ChesG

Sea and the Hills, The. Rudyard Kipling. CP-KiplR

Sea and the Mirror, The. W. H. Auden. CP-AudeW

Sea and the shore are always next to each other, The. Yehuda Amichai. SP-AmicY, *tr. by* Chana Bloch

Sea and the Skylark, The. Gerard Manley Hopkins. CP-HopkG

Sea at its worst drives a white foam up, The. Chasers. Carl Sandburg. CP-SandC

Sea at last lies over this place, The. Fanny Howe. SP-HoweF *Fr.* Introduction to the World.

Sea at sunset can reflect, The. Edna St. Vincent Millay. CP-MillE

Sea-Bathers. D. H. Lawrence. CP-LawrD

Sea-beauty! stretch'd and basking! Paumanok. Walt Whitman. CP-WhitW

Sea-birds on a windy carousel. John Ciardi. CP-CiarJ

Sea-born Goddesse, let me be. Hymne to Venus, and Cupid, A. Robert Herrick. CP-HerrR

Sea breaks on the sands, I listen to its surge and close my eyes, The. On a Beach. Czeslaw Milosz. CP-MiloCN, *tr. by* Robert Hass

Sea Breeze. Stéphane Mallarmé. CP-MallS, *tr. by* Henry Weinfield

Sea Burial. John Ciardi. CP-CiarJ

Sea Burial from the Cruiser *Reve.* Richard Eberhart. CP-EberR

Sea called, The. Loss. "H. D." CP-DoolH

Sea Calm. Langston Hughes. CP-HughL; CP-HughL1

Sea Canes. Derek Walcott. CP-WalcD

Sea Change. Olga Broumas. SP-BrouO

Sea Change. Charles Tomlinson. CP-TomlC; SP-TomlC

Sea-Chantey, A. Derek Walcott. CP-WalcD

Sea charm / The sea's own children. Langston Hughes. CP-HughL; CP-HughL1

Sea Chest. Carl Sandburg. CP-SandC

Sea-Choros. Euripides. CP-DoolH *Fr.* Hecuba.

Sea Cliffs at Kailua in December, The. W. S. Merwin. SP-MerwWF

Sea-coast looks at the sea, and the cities pour, The. After Melville. Muriel Rukeyser. CP-RukeM

Sea comes up and the sun goes over, The. Tide at Long Point, The. May Swenson. SP-SwenM

Sea Coming Indoors, The. Marilyn Hacker. SP-HackM

Sea Corpse, The. Anne Sexton. CP-SextA

Sea cow, a dugong, finds a special pearl, A. Force of Friendship, The. Jelaluddin Rumi. SP-Rumi, *tr. by* Coleman Barks

Sea cries with its meaningless voice, The. Pibroch. Ted Hughes. SP-HughTN

Sea dances its morning, The. Sea Mercy. Muriel Rukeyser. CP-RukeM

Sea Dream, A. John Greenleaf Whittier. CP-WhitJ

Sea-Elephant, The. William Carlos Williams. CP-WilW1

Sea, False Philosophy. Laura Riding Jackson. CP-RidiL

Sea Fight, The. Thomas Hardy. CP-HardT

Sea Fog. The. Josephine Jacobsen. CP-JacoJ

Sea full of fishes in shoals, the woods that let, The. Mountains Covered with Cats. Wallace Stevens. CP-StevW; CP-StevWP

Sea-Garden, The. Fanny Howe.
   "Among brick pots, buckets and rakes." SP-HoweF
   "Bricks are stuck in earth." SP-HoweF
   "Highway cuts through, The." SP-HoweF
   "Human is a thing, The." SP-HoweF
   "Mother is often lop-." SP-HoweF
   "Rapture in exile—paradox." SP-HoweF

Sea Gods. "H. D." CP-DoolH

Sea Grapes. Derek Walcott. CP-WalcD

Sea-Gull, The. Ogden Nash. CP-NashO

Sea has no oranges, The. Adelina Out Walking. Federico García Lorca. CP-GarcF, *tr. by* Alan S. Trueblood *Fr.* Andalusian Songs.

Sea has not such creatures in its waves, The. Petrarch. CP-Petra, *tr. by* J. G. Nichols

Sea has opened, the limit of his dream, The. Muriel Rukeyser. CP-RukeM

Sea Hates the Land, The. Robert Penn Warren. CP-WarrR

Sea-Hawk. Richard Eberhart. CP-EberR

Sea here used to look, The. At Darien Bridge. James Dickey. CP-DickJ

Sea Heroes. "H. D." CP-DoolH

Sea Hold, The. Carl Sandburg. CP-SandC

Sea Horse, The. Robert Graves. CP-GravR

Sea in Winter, The. Derek Mahon. CP-MahoD

Sea Iris. "H. D." CP-DoolH

Sea is a dragon coiled and crowned, The. Ego. G. K. Chesterton. CP-ChesG

Sea is a wilderness of waves, The. Long Trip. Langston Hughes. CP-HughL; CP-HughL1

Sea is all that they say: it wreaks death one way only, The. Our Lady. Donald Davie. CP-DaviDC

Sea / is an archeology, The. Charles Olson. CP-OlsoC

Sea is awash with roses O they blow, The. For Miriam. Kenneth Patchen. CP-PatcK

Sea is calm tonight [*or* to-night], The. Dover Beach. Matthew Arnold. SP-ArnoM

Sea Is Calm Tonight, The. Lawrence Ferlinghetti. SP-FerlL

Sea is deep, The. Exits. Langston Hughes. CP-HughL; CP-HughL2

Sea is flecked with bars of grey, The. Impressions ("Sea is flecked with bars of grey, The"). Oscar Wilde. CP-WildO

Sea is History, The. Derek Walcott. CP-WalcD

Sea is in its listless chime, The. From the Cliffs: Noon. Dante Gabriel Rossetti. CW-RossD

Sea is known to those who sail it, The. Bride. Olga Broumas. SP-BrouO

Sea is large, The. Sea Hold, The. Carl Sandburg. CP-SandC

Sea is never still, The. Young Sea. Carl Sandburg. CP-SandC

Sea is Open to the Light, The. Charles Tomlinson. CP-TomlC

Sea is unfolding scrolls, The. At Truro. May Swenson. SP-SwenM

Sea Knell. John Updike. CP-UpdiJ

Sea laments with appeasable / Hankering wail of loss, The. Was Thy Wrath against the Sea? Christina Georgina Rossetti. CP-RosC2

Sea lets forth a secret voice, The. Voice from the Sea. Constantine P. Cavafy. CP-CavaC, *tr. by* Theoharis Constantine Theoharis

Sea Lily. "H. D." CP-DoolH

Sea-Limits, The. Dante Gabriel Rossetti. CW-RossD

Sea-lions and birds. Real Work, The. Gary Snyder. CP-SnydG

Sea-lions loafed in the swinging tide in the inlet, long fluent creatures. Orca. Robinson Jeffers. CP-JefR3

Sea-Magic. Walter De la Mare. CP-DeLaW

Sea-Marge. Ivor Gurney. SP-GurnI

Sea Marshes in Winter. John Ciardi. CP-CiarJ

Sea Mercy. Muriel Rukeyser. CP-RukeM

Sea-Mew, The. Elizabeth Barrett Browning. CP-BroEB

Sea mist surprises my heavy eyes. Fanny Howe. SP-HoweF *Fr.* Introduction to the World.

Sea Mouse. Amy Clampitt. CP-ClamA

Sea of Tiberias. Donald Davie. CP-DaviDC

Sea opened its lips / blue with cold, The. Amy Lowell Thoughts. James Schuyler. CP-SchuJ

Sea Poem. Charles Tomlinson. CP-TomlC; SP-TomlC

Sea Poppies. "H. D." CP-DoolH

Sea-preserved, heaped with sea-spoils. Picture of a Nativity. Geoffrey Hill. CP-HillG

Sea preserves in salt, The. Yehuda Amichai. SP-AmicYL *Fr.* Poems on the

Shore of Caesarea.

Sea Raised Up, The. Hart Crane. CP-CranH

Sea reflects the rosy sky, The. Ralph Waldo Emerson. CP-EmerR

Sea repeats itself in light flourishes, The. Moment of Equilibrium among the Islands. Richard Eberhart. CP-EberR

Sea roars, the storm whistles, The. Way of the World, The. Carl Sandburg. CP-SandC

Sea rocks have a green moss, The. Home Thoughts. Carl Sandburg. CP-SandC

Sea Rose. "H. D." CP-DoolH

Sea-Ruck. Richard Eberhart. CP-EberR

Sea said "Come" to the Brook, The. Emily Dickinson. CP-DickE

Sea Serpent Chantey, The. Nicholas Vachel Lindsay. CP-LindV

Sea shines, The. Wind-raked, the waters run light. John Ciardi. CP-CiarJ

Sea-Shore. Ralph Waldo Emerson. CP-EmerR

Sea-shouldering Ithaca. Canal. Muriel Rukeyser. CP-RukeM

Sea Sickness. Andrei Codrescu. SP-CodrA

Sea Side. Robert Graves. CP-GravR

Sea-side walk, A. Elizabeth Barrett Browning. CP-BroEB

Sea Slant. Carl Sandburg. CP-SandC

Sea smiles / in the distance, The. Seawater Ballad. Federico García Lorca. CP-GarcF, tr. by Catherine Brown

Sea-Song from the Shore, A. James Whitcomb Riley. CP-RileJ

Sea speaks a language polite people never repeat, The. Two Nocturns. Carl Sandburg. CP-SandC

Sea speaks to me of you, The. Paul Laurence Dunbar. CP-DunbP

Sea-Spell, A. Dante Gabriel Rossetti. CW-RossD

Sea Storm. Richard Eberhart. CP-EberR

Sea sucks at its own, The. Landcrab II. Margaret Atwood. SP-AtwM2

Sea Surface Full of Clouds. Wallace Stevens. CP-StevW; CP-StevWP

Sea that encloses her young body, The. Sea, The. William Carlos Williams. CP-WilW1

Sea that founders on the other shore, The. Dead, The. Eugenio Montale. CP-MontE, tr. by Jonathan Galassi

Sea, That Has No Ending, The. Stanley Kunitz. CP-KunSC

Sea, the Sea, The. D. H. Lawrence. CP-LawrD

Sea, the sun, the tree, The. And again. Center, The. Yannis Ritsos. SP-RitsY, tr. by Kimon Friar

Sea Took Pity, The. Gerard Manley Hopkins. CP-HopkG

Sea-Trout and Butterfish. William Carlos Williams. CP-WilW1

Sea Unicorns and Land Unicorns. Marianne Craig Moore. CP-MoorM

Sea Violet. "H. D." CP-DoolH

Sea / wants to blow, The. Federico García Lorca. CP-GarcF, tr. by Jerome Rothenberg Fr. Seaside Prints.

Sea-ward, white-gleaming thro' [or through] the busy Scud. Looking Seaward. Samuel Taylor Coleridge. CP-ColeS

Sea was always the sea, The. Sea Wisdom. Carl Sandburg. CP-SandC

Sea was born of the earth without sweet union of love Hesiod says, The. Maximus, from Dogtown-1. Charles Olson. SP-OlsoC Fr. Maximus Poems, The.

Sea was breaking at my feet, The. Faith. James Whitcomb Riley. CP-RileJ

Sea was sapphire coloured, and the sky, The. Impression de Voyage. Oscar Wilde. CP-WildO

Sea-Wash. Carl Sandburg. CP-SandC

Sea-wash never ends, The. Sea-Wash. Carl Sandburg. CP-SandC

Sea waves are green and wet. Sand Dunes. Robert Frost. CP-FrosR

Sea-Weed. D. H. Lawrence. CP-LawrD

Sea-Widow, The. Stevie Smith. CP-SmitS

Sea-Wife, The. Rudyard Kipling. CP-KiplR

Sea will wash in, The. Seafarer. William Carlos Williams. CP-WilW2

Sea Wisdom. Carl Sandburg. CP-SandC

Sea with Two Stars, The. Federico García Lorca. CP-GarcF, tr. by Jerome Rothenberg Fr. Seaside Prints.

Seabattle of Salamis Took Place off Perama. Allen Ginsberg. CP-GinsA

Seacoast late at night and a wheel of wind, A. On the Death of Her Mother. Muriel Rukeyser. CP-RukeM

Seacoasts, / a few blades of sword grass are enough. Eugenio Montale. CP-MontE, tr. by Jonathan Galassi

Seacorps hint imbues blues blue. Chicory. Louis Zukofsky. CP-ZukLS

Seafarer. Archibald MacLeish. CP-MacLA

Seafarer. William Carlos Williams. CP-WilW2

Seafarer, The. Unknown. CP-PoEar; SP-PounE, tr. by Ezra Pound

Seagull. The. Norman Dubie. CP-DubiN

Seagull sitting on the town beach must, The. Dying Seagull and the Great Whore of the World, The. Alan Dugan. CP-DugaA

Seagulls. John Updike. CP-UpdiJ

Seahorse. Charles Bukowski. SP-BukC2

Seal. Heather McHugh. SP-McHuH

Seal. Anne Sexton. CP-SextA

Seal in Nature. John Updike. CP-UpdiJ

Seal Lullaby. Rudyard Kipling. CP-KiplR Fr. Jungle Book, The.

Seal swims like a poodle through the sheet, A. Flaw, The. Robert Lowell. SP-LoweR

Sealed inside the anemone. Pulse, The. Denise Levertov. SP-LeveDP

Sealed into the cocoon. At the Café Parnasse. Donald Davie. CP-DaviDC

Sealed Lips. Seen in Rome. Arthur Rimbaud. CP-RimbA, tr. by Martin Sorrell

Sealed up in fright, the wedding party turned. Nereids of Seriphos, The. Amy Clampitt. CP-ClamA

Sealion, salmon, offshore. Gary Snyder. CP-SnydG Fr. Myths and Texts.

Seals. Robert Lowell. SP-LoweR

Seals and porpoises present. Off Spectacle Island. Richard Eberhart. CP-EberR

Seals at play off Western Isle, The. Seals, Terns, Time. Richard Eberhart. CP-EberR

Seals, Terns, Time. Richard Eberhart. CP-EberR

Seaman's Ditty. Gary Snyder. CP-SnydG

Seamless Garment, The. Hugh MacDiarmid. SP-MacDH

Seamus of the Smart Suit, box player. Harmonies. Thomas Kinsella. CP-KinsT

Séance. Wisława Szymborska. SP-SzymW, tr. by Stanislaw Barańczak and Clare Cavanagh

Séance, The. Marya Alexandrovna Zaturenska. SP-ZatuM

Seanchas. Paul Muldoon. CP-MuldP

Search. Langston Hughes. CP-HughL; CP-HughL1

Search. Pablo Neruda. SP-NeruP

Search, The. John Berryman. CP-BerrJ

Search, The. Jorge Luis Borges. SP-BorgJ, tr. by Charles Tomlinson

Search, The. George Herbert. CP-HerbG

Search, The. John Logan. CP-LogaJ

Search, The. W. S. Merwin. SP-MerwW

Search for Love. D. H. Lawrence. CP-LawrD

Search for nothing any more, nothing. Search for Truth. D. H. Lawrence. CP-LawrD

Search for Sound Free from Motion, The. Wallace Stevens. CP-StevW; CP-StevWP

Search for the Truth Not Vain, The. Jones Very. CP-VeryJ

Search for Truth. D. H. Lawrence. CP-LawrD

Search thou my heart. Confessional. Paul Laurence Dunbar. CP-DunbP

Searched Soul, The. Dorothy Parker. CP-ParkD

Searches the ruins of my youth. Eros as Archaeologist. James Laughlin. CP-LaugJ

Searching. Robert Lowell. SP-LoweR

Searching auld wives' barrels. Extemporaneous Effusion on Being Appointed to the Excise, An. Robert Burns. CP-BurnR

Searching for Eagles. Peter Blue Cloud. SP-BlueP

Searching my heart for its true sorrow. Exiled. Edna St. Vincent Millay. CP-MillE

Searching my verse, to read what I'd once said. Backward Glance, A. Charles Tomlinson. SP-TomlC

Searching / Not Searching. Muriel Rukeyser. CP-RukeM

Searching once I found a flower. Indian Pipe. Richard Eberhart. CP-EberR

Sears Roebuck. Randall Jarrell. CP-JarrR

Sears Roebuck pump, it would snuffle, A. Hydraulics. William Meredith. SP-MereW

Seas netted with ambushes, The. Two Christmas-Cards. Robinson Jeffers. CP-JefR3

Seasalt has rusted the ironwork trellis. San Fruttuoso. Charles Tomlinson. CP-TomlC; SP-TomlC

Seascape. Elizabeth Bishop. CP-BishE

Seascape. Langston Hughes. CP-HughL; CP-HughL1

Seascape. Arthur Rimbaud. CP-RimbA, tr. by Martin Sorrell

Seascape. Stephen Spender. CP-SpenS

Seascape shifts, The. Distinctions. Charles Tomlinson. CP-TomlC

Seashell. Federico García Lorca. CP-GarcF, tr. by Alan S. Trueblood Fr. Songs for Children.

Seashell. Dan Pagis. SP-PagiD, tr. by Stephen Mitchell

Seashore. Ralph Waldo Emerson. CP-EmerR

Seashore through Dark Glasses (Atlantic City). Langston Hughes. CP-HughL; CP-HughL2

Seaside place so tranquil, A. Medusa at Broadstairs. Amy Clampitt. CP-ClamA

Seaside Prints. Federico García Lorca.

Contemplation. CP-GarcF, tr. by Jerome Rothenberg

Guardsmen, The. CP-GarcF, tr. by Jerome Rothenberg

Nocturne: "I stare at the stars." CP-GarcF, tr. by Jerome Rothenberg

"Sea / wants to blow, The." CP-GarcF, tr. by Jerome Rothenberg

Sea with Two Stars, The. CP-GarcF, tr. by Jerome Rothenberg

Seaside Serenade. Ogden Nash. CP-NashO

Season, A. Joseph Brodsky. CP-BrodJ

Season late, day late, sun just down, and the sky. Birth of Love. Robert Penn Warren. CP-WarrR

Season of contaminated mists. 'Eighty-Nine. Amy Clampitt. CP-ClamA

Season of Lovers and Assassins. Carolyn Kizer. CP-KizeC

Season of mists and mellow fruitfulness! To Autumn. John Keats. CP-KeatJ

Season of mists and migraines, rich catarrhs. Portrait of the Artist II. Charles Tomlinson. CP-TomlC

Season of my purest pleasure. see also Watching unto God in the Night-Season. Jeanne Marie Bouvier de la Motte Guyon. CP-CowpW

Season of Phantasmal Peace, The. Derek Walcott. CP-WalcD

Season of Recognition. Yehuda Amichai. SP-AmicYL, tr. by Benjamin Harshav and Barbara Harshav

Season of snows, and season of flowers. Plaint Human, The. James Whitcomb Riley. CP-RileJ

Season Opens on Wild Boar in Chianti. Robert Penn Warren. CP-WarrR

Season stalls, unseasonably fair, The. Indian Summer at Land's End. Stanley Kunitz. CP-KunSC

Season 'tis, my lovely lambs, The. E. E. Cummings. CP-CummE

Season was the childhood of sweet June, The. Fiordispina. Percy Bysshe Shelley. CP-ShelP

Seasonal round never stops, The. Han-shan. CP-ColdM, tr. by Red Pine

Seasonless, The. James Wright. CP-WrigJ

Seasons. Czeslaw Milosz. CP-MiloC; CP-MiloCN, tr. by Renata Gorczynski and Robert Hass

Seasons. Wyatt Prunty. SP-PrunW

Seasons. Christina Georgina Rossetti. CP-RosC3

Seasons. Robert Penn Warren. CP-WarrR

Seasons, The. Richard Eberhart. CP-EberR

Seasons, The. David Ignatow. SP-IgnaD

Seasons, The. Jones Very. CP-VeryJ

Seasons between Yes & No. Yusef Komunyakaa. CP-KomuY

Seasons' Difference, The. William Meredith. SP-MereW

Seasons doubt themselves and give way, The. Seasons, The. David Ignatow. SP-IgnaD

Seasons in a Landscape of Woman, The. Robert Stock. SP-StocR

Seasons, in teaching the years to fly, The. On a Gift of Leaves From Dove Cottage Close, Grasmere. Robert Stock. SP-StocR

Seasons of Her Year, The. Thomas Hardy. CP-HardT

Seasons of the Soul. Allen Tate. CP-TateA

Seasons revolve and the years change, The. Another Spring. Kenneth Rexroth. CP-RexrK

Seasons turn like a great wheel, The. Was It One of the Long Hunters of Kentucky who Discovered Boone at Sunset? Robert Penn Warren. CP-WarrR

Seasons turning, The. Memory flaring. Wenas Ridge. Raymond Carver. CP-CarvR

Seated. Arthur Rimbaud. CP-RimbA, tr. by Martin Sorrell

Seated above the dead. Wind of the Village. William Carlos Williams. CP-WilW1

Seated Figure. Louise Glück. SP-GlucL

Seated Figure. Sam Hamill. SP-HamiS

Seated Man. George Oppen. CP-OppGN

Seated motionless among sliding landscapes. Man in the Dining Car, The. Tennessee Williams. CP-WillT

Seated one day at the dictionary I was pretty weary and also pretty. Where There's a Will, There's Velleity. Ogden Nash. CP-NashO

Seathwaite Chapel. William Wordsworth. CP-WorW2 Fr. River Duddon [A Series of Sonnets], The.

Seatide invades. Pacific Gazer. Robert Penn Warren. CP-WarrR

Seattle Uplift. John Updike. CP-UpdiJ

Seaward. Joseph Brodsky. CP-BrodJ

Seawater Ballad. Federico García Lorca. CP-GarcF, tr. by Catherine Brown

Seaweed. Henry Wadsworth Longfellow. SP-LongH

Sebastian in the Dream. John Logan. CP-LogaJ

Sebastian's Mirror. Heather McHugh. SP-McHuH

Second after, / the first boat touched the shore, A. Settlers, The. Margaret Atwood. SP-AtwM1

Second Air Force. Randall Jarrell. CP-JarrR

Second Anniversary ("Dawn brings us the smell"). Federico García Lorca. CP-GarcF, tr. by Christopher Maurer

Second Anniversary ("Moon fastens on the sea, The"). Federico García Lorca. CP-GarcF, tr. by Alan S. Trueblood Fr. Moon Songs.

Second Attempt, A. Thomas Hardy. CP-HardT

Second Avenue. Frank O'Hara. SP-OharF

Second-Best. Robinson Jeffers. CP-JefR2

Second-Best Bed, The. Howard Nemerov. CP-NemeH

Second Caprice in North Cambridge. T. S. Eliot. SP-ElioT

Second Carolina Said-Song. A. R. Ammons. CP-AmmoA

Second Childhood, A. G. K. Chesterton. CP-ChesG

Second Christmas by the shore, A. Joseph Brodsky. CP-BrodJ, tr. by George L. Kline

Second Coming, The. William Butler Yeats. CP-YeatW

Second-Death. Laura Riding Jackson. CP-RidiL

Second Delirium. Alchemy of the Word. Arthur Rimbaud. CP-RimbA, tr. by Martin Sorrell

Second Didactic Poem. Denise Levertov. SP-LeveDP; SP-LeveDS

Second Elegy. Age of Magicians. Muriel Rukeyser. CP-RukeM

Second Epistle of the Second Book of Horace Imitated, The. Alexander Pope. CP-PopeA

Second Epistle to Davie. Robert Burns. CP-BurnR

Second Epistle to John Lapraik. Robert Burns. CP-BurnR

(To the Same [John Lapraik].) CP-BurnR

Second-Fated, The. Robert Graves. CP-GravR

Second Fig. Edna St. Vincent Millay. CP-MillE

Second floor behind. Under Ideal Conditions. William Corbett. SP-CorbW

Second Generation: New York. Langston Hughes. CP-HughL; CP-HughL2

Second Glance at a Jaguar. Ted Hughes. SP-HughTN

Second Hymn to Lenin. Hugh MacDiarmid.

Ah, Lenin, you were richt. But I'm a poet.

"Are my poems spoken in the factories and fields." SP-MacDH

Second Jungle Book, The. Rudyard Kipling.

How the Fear Came.

Law of the Jungle, The. CP-KiplR

King's Ankus, The.

Song of the Little Hunter, The. CP-KiplR

"These are the four that are never content, that have never been filled since the Dews began." CP-KiplR

Letting in the Jungle.

Morning Song in the Jungle. CP-KiplR

Mowgli's Song Against People. CP-KiplR

"Veil them, cover them, wall them round." CP-KiplR

Miracle of Purun Bhagat, The.

"Night we felt the earth would move, The." CP-KiplR

Song of Kabir, A. CP-KiplR

Quiquern.

Angutivaun Taina. CP-KiplR

"People of the Eastern Ice, they are melting like the snow, The." CP-KiplR

Red Dog.

Chil's Song. CP-KiplR

"For our white and our excellent nights—for the nights of swift running." CP-KiplR

Spring Running, The.

"Man goes to Man! Cry the challenge though the Jungle!" CP-KiplR

Outsong in the Jungle. CP-KiplR

Tiger-Tiger.

"What of the hunting, hunter bold?" CP-KiplR

Undertakers, The.

Ripple Song, A. CP-KiplR

"When ye say to Tabaqui, "My Brother!" when ye call the Hyena to meat." CP-KiplR

Second Language. Tess Gallagher. SP-GallT

Second Letter to Junk Jeannee of NYC. Andrei Codrescu. SP-CodrA

Second Limick. Ogden Nash. CP-NashO

Second Love. Dorothy Parker. CP-ParkD

Second Month It's Not Itemized, The. Ogden Nash. CP-NashO

2nd Musical Form, for Dave Young, A. Charles Olson. CP-OlsoC

Second Nature. Paul Éluard. CP-BeckS

Second Night, The. Thomas Hardy. CP-HardT

2nd Novel, The. Charles Bukowski. SP-BukC1

Second Odyssey, long again, A. Constantine P. Cavafy. CP-CavaC, tr. by Theoharis Constantine Theoharis

Second Oldest Story, The. Dorothy Parker. CP-ParkD

Second Page. Federico García Lorca. CP-GarcF, tr. by Jerome Rothenberg Fr. White Album.

Second People, The. Kenneth Patchen. CP-PatcK

Second Psalm: The Signals. W. S. Merwin. SP-MerwW

Second Rapture, The. Thomas Carew. CP-CareT

Second Satire of the First Book of Horace Imitated, The. Alexander Pope. CP-PopeA

Second Satire of the Second Book of Horace Imitated, The. Alexander Pope. CP-PopeA

Second Series. Yannis Ritsos.

"Guatemala, Nicaragua, Salvador." SP-RitsY

"In the white egg." SP-RitsY

"Naked, astride an elephant." SP-RitsY

"New moon, The." SP-RitsY

"Seek not, want not, be not." SP-RitsY

"They tagged you an illiterate, those idle bureaucrats." SP-RitsY

"Where is the time to light a cigarette." SP-RitsY

Second Shaman Song. Gary Snyder. CP-SnydG *Fr.* Myths and Texts.

Second Sight. W. S. Merwin. SP-MerwW

Second Sight. A. K. Ramanujan. CP-RamaA

Second Song. Louise Bogan. CP-BogaL

Second Song. Charles Tomlinson. SP-TomlC

Second Song, The. Thomas Carew. CP-CareT *Fr.* Carew's Masque.

Second Song of Huitzilopochtli. D. H. Lawrence. CP-LawrD

Second Stanza, A. Donald Hall. CP-HallD

Second Time, The. W. S. Merwin. SP-MerwW

Second Time Around. Carolyn Kizer. CP-KizeC

Second Visit, The. Thomas Hardy. CP-HardT

Second Voyage, The. Rudyard Kipling. CP-KiplR

Second year of drought, and no love, The. Bedouin Goes North, A. Yehuda Amichai. SP-AmicYL, *tr.* by Benjamin Harshav *and* Barbara Harshav

Secondary Epic. W. H. Auden. CP-AudeW

Seconds. Louise Glück. SP-GlucL

Secrecy. G. K. Chesterton. CP-ChesG

Secrecy. Robert Graves. CP-GravR

Secrecy [*or* Secresie] Protested. Thomas Carew. CP-CareT

Secret, A. Sylvia Plath. CP-PlatS

Secret, The. Emily Dickinson. CP-DickE
  (I haven't told my garden yet.) CP-DickE

Secret, The. Paul Laurence Dunbar. CP-DunbP

Secret, The. Denise Levertov. SP-LeveDP; SP-LeveDS

Secret, The. Thomas Merton. CP-MertT

Secret Agent, The. W. H. Auden. CP-AudeW

Secret child walks down the street, The. Christmas Eve. Muriel Rukeyser. CP-RukeM

Secret Garden, The. Rita Dove. SP-DoveR

Secret Garden, The. Thomas Kinsella. CP-KinsT

Secret Garden, The. Eleanor Wilner. SP-WilnE

Secret Gratitude, A. James Wright. CP-WrigJ

Secret Heart, The. Richard Eberhart. CP-EberR

Secret History of the Dividing Line. Susan Howe. SP-HoweSE

Secret I take it a commitment hushed to feed amic—. Catullus. *See* If, Cornelius, we entrust our secrets

Secret is, The. Plot, The. Rae Armantrout. SP-ArmaA

Secret Land, The. Robert Graves. CP-GravR

Secret Love; or, The Maiden Queen. John Dryden.
  Song: "I feed a flame within, which so torments me." SP-DrydJ

Secret Love or Two I Must Confess[e], A. Thomas Campion. CP-CampT

Secret Man. Wallace Stevens. CP-StevWP

Secret my heart keeps, The. Hermetic Poem. Stanley Kunitz. CP-KunSC

Secret of the Burning Stars, The. Pablo Antonio Cuadra. CP-MertT

Secret of the Machines, The. Rudyard Kipling. CP-KiplR

Secret of these hills was stone, and cottages, The. Pylons, The. Stephen Spender. CP-SpenS

Secret Pain of the Decor, The. Yannis Ritsos. SP-RitsY, *tr.* by Andonis Decavalles

Secret Parting. Dante Gabriel Rossetti. CW-RossD *Fr.* House of Life, The.

Secret People, The. G. K. Chesterton. CP-ChesG

Secret remains in the book, The. Michael Palmer. SP-PalmM

Secret Rose, The. William Butler Yeats. CP-YeatW

Secret Sharer, The. Thom Gunn. CP-GunnT

Secret Sits, The. Robert Frost. CP-FrosR

Secret that should not be blown, The. Ralph Waldo Emerson. CP-EmerR

Secret Theatre. Robert Graves. CP-GravR

Secret told, A. Emily Dickinson. CP-DickE

Secret Training. Andrei Codrescu. SP-CodrA

Secret turning in us, A. Jelaluddin Rumi. SP-Rumi, *tr.* by Coleman Barks

Secret walls swing open when a dream loses focus & lights click on inside the head. Floor Plans. Yusef Komunyakaa. CP-KomuY

Secret Waters, The. D. H. Lawrence. CP-LawrD

Secret Words, The. James Laughlin. CP-LaugJ

Secret world turns in us, A. Way the Roundness Feels, The. Clarence Major. SP-MajoC

Secretaries. Czeslaw Milosz. CP-MiloC; CP-MiloCN, *tr.* by Robert Hass

Secretary Chant, The. Marge Piercy. SP-PierM

Secretary's Story, The. James Laughlin. CP-LaugJ

Secretly, the verb is changed and covered. Language of Moss. Josephine Jacobsen. CP-JacoJ

Secretly to love & to drink, what is it? tis a dissolute day's work. Hafiz. CP-EmerR *Fr.* Odes.

Secrets. Federico García Lorca.
  Apothecary. CP-GarcF, *tr.* by Jerome Rothenberg
  Fountain. CP-GarcF, *tr.* by Jerome Rothenberg
  Journey. CP-GarcF, *tr.* by Jerome Rothenberg
  Little Doncella, The. CP-GarcF, *tr.* by Jerome Rothenberg
  Mirror. CP-GarcF, *tr.* by Jerome Rothenberg
  Open Door. CP-GarcF, *tr.* by Jerome Rothenberg
  Pan. CP-GarcF, *tr.* by Jerome Rothenberg
  Woodcutter. CP-GarcF, *tr.* by Jerome Rothenberg

Secrets. W. H. Auden. CP-AudeW

Secrets. C. K. Williams. SP-WillC

Secrets are slimber black worms. Hosts. A. R. Ammons. CP-AmmoA

"Secrets" is a daily word. Emily Dickinson. CP-DickE

Secrets of American Civilization. Muriel Rukeyser. CP-RukeM

Secrets of Divine Love Are To Be Kept, The. Jeanne Marie Bouvier de la Motte Guyon. CP-CowpW

Secrets, you said, would hold us two apart. Plea. Dorothy Parker. CP-ParkD

Sectantem levia nervi deficiunt. Arthur Hugh Clough. SP-ClouA

Secular Masque, The. John Dryden. SP-DrydJ

Secular Ode, The. Charles Hubert Sisson. *See* Carmen Saeculare

Secular Signs. Thomas Merton. CP-MertT

Secure. May Swenson. SP-SwenM

Secured by sooted windows. Through the Inner City to the Suburbs. Maya Angelou. SP-AngeM

Securely, after days. *after* Horace, Book 5, Ode 22. Rudyard Kipling. CP-KiplR *Fr.* Debits and Credits.

Securely sunning in a forest glade. Fable, A. Richard Wilbur. CP-WilbR

Securer a bo? no sacred armpits lair hops as that he-goat's. Catullus. *See* If ever anyone / was deservedly plagued by a goat under his armpits

Security. William Stafford. SP-StafWW

Security Considerations. Hans Magnus Enzensberger. SP-EnzeH

Sed de Correr. Amy Clampitt. CP-ClamA

Sedative Reflection. Ogden Nash. CP-NashO

Seder Night. Amy Clampitt. CP-ClamA

Sediment. David Ignatow. SP-IgnaD

Seductive Piece of Business, A. Randall Jarrell. CP-JarrR

See. David Ignatow. SP-IgnaD

See, and not see; and if thou chance t' espy [*or* espie]. To the Generous Reader. Robert Herrick. CP-HerrR

See, Comini, popular arbiter turned on uncanny senescence. Catullus. *See* If, by general consent, it should be decided

See could we quit coveting hope taunting where hope hid and. Catullus. *See* If ever anyone anywhere, Lesbia, is looking

"See," cries the chorus of admiring preachers. Insectivora. Ambrose Bierce. SP-BierA

See dis pictyah in my han'? Photograph, The. Paul Laurence Dunbar. CP-DunbP

See-er of Cities, The. Randall Jarrell. CP-JarrR

See, even our age has its miracles—miracles which future generations will scarcely believe. To That Most Splendid and Learned Gentleman, Sir Richard Bulstrode, on Account of the Sacred Poems Recently Written by Him. *Unknown, sometimes at. to* Thomas Sheridan. CP-SherT, *tr.* by Robert Hogan

See! from yon low-roofed cottage shines a light. Home, The ("See! from yon low-roofed cottage shines a light"). Jones Very. CP-VeryJ

See, gentle as the light, their Influence spread. Influence of Puritanism. Jones Very. CP-VeryJ

See & hear the fraud, the malice of the change of fortune. Hafiz. CP-EmerR *Fr.* Odes.

See her austere beauty bend. Necessity. Richard Eberhart. CP-EberR

See here a Shadow from that setting Sunne. Richard Crashaw. *See* This reverend shadow cast that setting sun

See here an easy [*or* easie] Feast that know[e]s no wound. On the Miracle of Multiplied [*or* Multiplyed] Loaves. Richard Crashaw. CP-CrasR

See here the diving beetle is split. Creatures. Maxine W. Kumin. SP-KumiM

See, here's the workbox, little wife. Workbox, The. Thomas Hardy. CP-HardT

See his black nose snubbed back, pressed over like a whale's blow-holes. He-Goat. D. H. Lawrence. CP-LawrD

See how efficient it still is. Hatred. Wisława Szymborska. SP-SzymW, *tr.* by Stanislaw Barańczak *and* Clare Cavanagh

See how night opens for you its arms of space. Rainer Maria Rilke. CP-RilkFr, *tr.* by A. Poulin, Jr. *Fr.* Fragments.

See how resplendent in deep snow. Ode 1.9: "See how resplendent in deep snow." Horace. CP-CunnJ *Fr.* Odes.

See how Romance adheres. Ralph Waldo Emerson. CP-EmerR

See how she snuggles against my neck. Baby Songs Ten Months Old. D. H. Lawrence. CP-LawrD

See how Spring opens with disabling cold. Gerard Manley Hopkins. CP-HopkG

See how tall and straight I stand. Vase, The. David Ignatow. SP-IgnaD

See how the archèd earth does here. Upon the Hill and Grove at Bilbrough. Andrew Marvell. CP-MarvA

See how the heights of Almscliff. Epigramma in Duos Montes Amosclivium et Bilboreum: Farfacio [Epigram on Two Mountains, Almscliff and Bilbrough: To Fairfax]. Andrew Marvell. CP-MarvA

See how the orient dew. On a Drop of Dew. Andrew Marvell. CP-MarvA

See how the poore do waiting stand. Upon Her Almes. Robert Herrick. CP-HerrR

See how the roses burn! Hafiz. CP-EmerR *Fr.* Odes.

See how the stubborne damzell doth deprave. Sonnet 29. Edmund Spenser. CP-Spens *Fr.* Amoretti.

See how the sun in dusky skies. Of Her Walking in a Garden after a Shower. Alexander Pope. CP-PopeA

See how these masses mill and swarm. Edna St. Vincent Millay. CP-MillE

See / how they trace. Birds in Snow. "H. D." CP-DoolH

See, I have climbed the mountain side. San Miniato. Oscar Wilde. CP-WildO

See / it was like this when. Lawrence Ferlinghetti. SP-FerlL

See, now, this filigree: 'tis snow. Snowflake, The. Walter De la Mare. CP-DeLaW

See on one hand. Rainbow, The. Gerard Manley Hopkins. CP-HopkG

See one more person. Jaws. Robert Creeley. SP-CreeR

See quick calm moot as gratifying the tombed—sepulchres. Catullus. *See* If, Calvus, effects of grief

See-Saw. Eleanor Wilner. SP-WilnE

See Sir, how as the sun's hot masculine flame. To E. of D. with Six Holy Sonnets. John Donne. CP-DonnJ

See that horseman from the distant land. Visitor, The. Li Po. CP-WilW2

See that lady / Dressed so fine? Lady's Boogie. Langston Hughes. CP-HughL; CP-HughL3

See that stern castle? Clarence Major. SP-MajoC

See that the engraving is done skillfully. Philhellene. Constantine P. Cavafy. CP-CavaC, *tr. by* Theoharis Constantine Theoharis

See the blind and the lame at play. Outside the Hospital. Wallace Stevens. CP-StevWP

See the calm exit of the aged Saint. On the Death of Mr. John Haskins. Ralph Waldo Emerson. CP-EmerR

See! the faint green tinge from the western sky has. Arthur Hugh Clough. SP-ClouA

See the fraud flow by like water. Shmuel HaNagid. SP-HaNaS, *tr. by* Peter Cole

See the girls in shorts on their bicycles. Lorine Niedecker. CP-NiedL

See the high birds! Is their's the song. Sowing of Meanings, The. Thomas Merton. CP-MertT

See. The lamp is adjusted. The ash tray. Now. Anne Sexton. CP-SextA

See! the sacred scion springs. *Unknown, sometimes at. to* Thomas Sheridan. CP-SherT *Fr.* Ode, An.

See, the Ship in the Bay Is Riding. John Keats. CP-KeatJ

See the sign; it flares. Eugenio Montale. CP-MontE, *tr. by* Jonathan Galassi

See the star yonder. George Meredith. CP-MerG2

See the stars, love. In a Boat. D. H. Lawrence. CP-LawrD

See, the sun hath risen! Martyr, The. Christina Georgina Rossetti. CP-RosC3

See the sweet women, friend, that lean beneath. Ballad of Fair Ladies in Revolt, A. George Meredith. CP-MerG1

See the trees lean to the wind's way of learning. Landscape. Carl Sandburg. CP-SandC

See the wild purchase of the bold and vain. Juvenal. CP-JohnS *Fr.* Satires.

See the wild Waste of all-devouring years! Epistle V, to Mr. Addison. Alexander Pope. CP-PopeA

See they come, post haste from Thanet. Lines Written by Jane Austen for the Amusement of a Niece. Jane Austen. CP-AustJ

See, they return; ah, see the tentative. Return, The. Ezra Pound. CP-PoEar; SP-PounE

See this house, how dark it is. Empty House, The. Walter De la Mare. CP-DeLaW

See us, strangers from the land of embarrassed death. Treaty. Josephine Jacobsen. SP-JacoJ

See Virgin forms on carrs of snow descend. Impromptu on the Morning of my Sons Weding Day Which Was Ushered in by a Fall of Snow and Soon after Cleared by a Very Bright Sun. Annis Boudinot Stockton. CP-StocA

See what a trick this is: two meeting bloods. Mule. John Ciardi. CP-CiarJ

See what gay wild flowers deck this earth-built Cot. Highland Hut. William Wordsworth. CP-WorW2

See where, gathered, the wharves. By Cure of—Sulfa. Charles Olson. CP-OlsoC

See Where She Flies. Thomas Campion. CP-CampT

See Where the Thames, the Purest Stream. William Cowper. CP-CowpW

See who ne'er was or will be half read! Verses to Be Placed under the Picture of England's Arch-Poet: Containing a Compleat Catalogue of His Works. Alexander Pope. CP-PopeA

See with how little motion, now, the noon wind. Calypso's Island. Thomas Merton. CP-MertT

See with what simplicity. Picture of Little T. C. in a Prospect of Flowers, The. Andrew Marvell. CP-MarvA

See yon opening flower. Song from the Wandering Jew. Percy Bysshe Shelley. CP-ShelP

See yonder leafless trees against the sky. Ralph Waldo Emerson. CP-EmerR

See you the ferny ride that steals. Puck's Song. Rudyard Kipling. CP-KiplR *Fr.* Puck of Pook's Hill.

See you yond' motion? Not the old fading. On the New Motion. Ben Jonson. CP-JonsB; SP-JonsB

Seeal'd up with Night-gum, Loach each morning lyes. Upon Loach. Robert Herrick. CP-HerrR

Seed. Amy Clampitt. CP-ClamA

Seed, The. Jones Very. CP-VeryJ

Seed-at-Zero, The. Dylan Thomas. CP-ThomD

Seed has started, who can stay it? see, The. Acorn, The. Jones Very. CP-VeryJ

Seed is fallen among the clods, A. Lines Written in Oxford. G. K. Chesterton. CP-ChesG

Seed Leaves. Richard Wilbur. CP-WilbR

Seed Market, The. Jelaluddin Rumi. SP-Rumi, *tr. by* Coleman Barks

Seed of an iron flower, The. Importation of Landscapes. Alan Dugan. CP-DugaA

Seed of Charlemagne, his noble head, The. Petrarch. CP-Petra, *tr. by* J. G. Nichols

Seed of David, The. Dante Gabriel Rossetti. CW-RossD

Seed that goes into the ground, The. Cuckoo Corn. Paul Muldoon. CP-MuldP

Seed that met water spoke a little name, The. B.C. William Stafford. SP-StafWW

Seed-Time. George Meredith. CP-MerG1

Seed-Time and Harvest. John Greenleaf Whittier. CP-WhitJ

Seedling, The. Paul Laurence Dunbar. CP-DunbP

Seedlings in the Mail. Marge Piercy. SP-PierM

Seeds. Raymond Carver. CP-CarvR

Seeds, The. Wendell Berry. CP-BerrW

Seeds begin abstract as their species, The. Seeds, The. Wendell Berry. CP-BerrW

Seeds of treason choake up as they spring, The. Treason. Robert Herrick. CP-HerrR

Seedtime. Denise Levertov. SP-LeveDP

See'est thou a Skylark whose glistening winglets ascending. Poetry of Shelley, The. George Meredith. CP-MerG1

Seeing. Archibald MacLeish. CP MacLA

Seeing. Archibald MacLeish. CP-MacLA

Seeing a chipmunk in the yard. August Evening Outside of Nashville, An. Miller Williams. CP-WillM

Seeing dogwood trees in bloom. Dogwood Trees, The. Robert Earl Hayden. CP-HaydR

Seeing Eye to Eye Is Believing. Ogden Nash. CP-NashO

Seeing Her Leave. Donald Davie. CP-DaviDC

Seeing his stale vocabulary build. Limited Achievement. Donald Davie. CP-DaviDC

Seeing how I love you utterly. To Elinor Wylie. Edna St. Vincent Millay. CP-MillE

Seeing I'm yours, I rouse me from afar. Michelangelo Buonarroti. CP-Miche, *tr. by* John Frederick Nims

Seeing in the Dark. Yusef Komunyakaa. CP-KomuY

Seeing into myth is. Crevice. A. R. Ammons. CP-AmmoA

Seeing is Deceiving. Richard Eberhart. CP-EberR

Seeing Jupiter. May Swenson. SP-SwenM

Seeing me stand there green with fear, my guide. Underworld of Dante, The. Dante Alighieri. CP-ClamA *Fr.* Divina Commedia.

Seeing off the beloved ones, I. Marina Ivanovna Tsvetayeva. CP-BrodJ, *tr. by* Joseph Brodsky

Seeing out of the Sub. Andrei Codrescu. SP-CodrA

Seeing that Patroklos was slaughtered. Horses of Achilles, The. Constantine P. Cavafy. CP-CavaC, *tr. by* Theoharis Constantine Theoharis

Seeing the birds in winter. Vampire. Paul Muldoon. CP-MuldP

Seeing the Bones. Maxine W. Kumin. SP-KumiM

Seeing the child again. Child, The. Raymond Carver. CP-CarvR

Seeing the March rain flood a field. March. Wyatt Prunty. SP-PrunW

Seeing the Moon Rise. Thomas Hardy. CP-HardT

Seeing the snowman standing all alone. Boy at the Window. Richard Wilbur. CP-WilbR

Seeing the sun rise will not mend this day. Sunrise with Crows. William Meredith. SP-MereW

Seeing Thee *Soame*, I see a Goodly man. To His Kinsman, Sir Tho. Soame. Robert Herrick. CP-HerrR

Seeing Things. Seamus Heaney. SP-HeanSO

Seeing Things. Howard Nemerov. CP-NemeH

Seeing thou art fair[e], I bar[re] not thy false playing. Elegy 3.13: "Seeing thou art fair[e], I bar[re] not thy false playing." Ovid. CP-MarlC, *tr. by* Christopher Marlowe *Fr.* Elegies.

Seeing through Me. Donald Davie. CP-DaviDC

Seeing we never spied frail Fairyland. To a Comrade in Flanders. Wilfred Owen. CP-OwenW

Seek not in me the big I capital. Iota Subscript. Robert Frost. CP-FrosR

Seek not, in outward things. Hymn: The Forms of Nature, and the Unity of Their Origin. Jones Very. CP-VeryJ

Seek not the spirit, if it hide. Sursum Corda. Ralph Waldo Emerson. CP-EmerR

Seek not, want not, be not. Yannis Ritsos. SP-RitsY *Fr.* Second Series.

Seek not with mortal sight to pierce the gloom. Future State of the Wicked and Its Duration, The. Jones Very. CP-VeryJ

Seek or record then the benefactor—pree or voluptuous. Catullus. *See* If evocations of past kindness shed

Seek the Lord. Thomas Campion. CP-CampT

(Seeke the Lord, and in his wayes persever.) CP-CampT

Seek who will delight in fable. Westmoreland Girl, The. William Wordsworth. CP-WorW2

Seek[e] and Find[e]. Robert Herrick. CP-HerrR

Seek[e] not to know my love, for she. To One That Desired to Know My Mistress [*or* Mistris]. Thomas Carew. CP-CareT

Seeke the Lord, and in his wayes persever. Thomas Campion. *See* Seek the Lord

Seeker of truth / follow no path. E. E. Cummings. CP-CummE

Seekers. D. H. Lawrence. CP-LawrD

Seekers, The. Thomas McGrath. SP-McGrT

Seeking. James Schuyler. CP-SchuJ

Seeking a Christian Commonwealth to found. Christian Commonwealth, A. Jones Very. CP-VeryJ

Seeking of the Waterfall, The. John Greenleaf Whittier. CP-WhitJ

Seeking Rest. Christina Georgina Rossetti. CP-RosC3

Seeking the Chosen. James Dickey. CP-DickJ

Seele im Raum. Randall Jarrell. CP-JarrR

Seemed enough ambition for anyone with sense. To Be Charmed. Kenneth Patchen. CP-PatcK

Seemed, tho' the soft sheen all enchants. Ralph Waldo Emerson. CP-EmerR

Seemed to be making fun of. Antiphilus. James Laughlin. CP-LaugJ

Seemed to me—never maid. Ralph Waldo Emerson. CP-EmerR

Seeming, The. Muriel Rukeyser. CP-RukeM

Seemingly awash. Hong Kong Window. Robert Creeley. SP-CreeR

Seems lak folks is mighty curus. Foolin' wid de Seasons. Paul Laurence Dunbar. CP-DunbP

Seems like a feller'd ort'o jes' to-day. Full Harvest, A. James Whitcomb Riley. CP-RileJ

Seems like a long time. Partial Explanation, The. Charles Simic. SP-SimiC; SP-SimiCE

Seen by the Waits. Thomas Hardy. CP-HardT

Seen from Above. Wisława Szymborska. SP-SzymW, *tr. by* Stanisław Barańczak *and* Clare Cavanagh

Seen from Above. Wisława Szymborska. SP-SzymWM, *tr. by* Joanna Trzeciak

Seen from above / The foam in the curving bay is a goose-quill. Under the Mountain. Louis MacNeice. CP-MacNL

Seen my lady home las' night. Negro Love Song, A. Paul Laurence Dunbar. CP-DunbP

Seen on the sea, no sign; no sign, no sign. Dead Wingman, The. Randall Jarrell. CP-JarrR

Seen, too clear and historic within us, our sins of omission. Main Regret, The. George Meredith. CP-MerG1

Seen you down at chu'ch las' night. Discovered. Paul Laurence Dunbar. CP-DunbP

Seene? and yet hated thee? they did not see. But Now They Have Seen, and Hated. Richard Crashaw. CP-CrasR

Seeress of the misty Norland. To Fredrika Bremer. John Greenleaf Whittier. CP-WhitJ

Seesaw. Thom Gunn. CP-GunnT

See'st thou that Cloud as silver cleare. Her Bed. Robert Herrick. CP-HerrR

Seest thou that Cloud which rides in State. Cloud, The. Robert Herrick. CP-HerrR

Seest thou those diamonds which she wears. Robert Herrick. CP-HerrR

See'st thou yon mountains laden with deep snow. Ode 1.9: "See'st thou yon mountains laden with deep snow." Horace. CP-CowpW *Fr.* Odes.

Segre Song. Muriel Rukeyser. CP-RukeM

Seine Split. Clarence Major. SP-MajoC

Seine / "transcend, be real," The. Grand Duo. James Schuyler. CP-SchuJ

16 heures / l'Etoile. Two X. E. E. Cummings. CP-CummE

Seize structure / Correspond with the real. Six Canons, The. Muriel Rukeyser. CP-RukeM

Seize the bow, old swarthy fiddler! To an Old Gipsy. Johann N. Vogl. CP-MerG2

Seizure of the World. Laura Riding Jackson. CP-RidiL

Seizures of power. Usurper. Richard Eberhart. CP-EberR

Selavie. Andrei Codrescu. SP-CodrA

Seldom Can't. Christina Georgina Rossetti. CP-RosC2

Seldom "can't," / Seldom "don't." Seldom Can't. Christina Georgina Rossetti. CP-RosC2

"Seldom we find," says Solomon Don Dunce. Enigma, An. Edgar Allan Poe. CP-PoeEd

Seldom Yet Now. Robert Graves. CP-GravR

Seldom yet now: the quality. Seldom Yet Now. Robert Graves. CP-GravR

Seldome the villaine, though much hast he make. Ode 3.2: "Seldome the villaine, though much hast he make." Horace. CP-RaleW *Fr.* Odes.

Selected Life, A. Thomas Kinsella. CP-KinsT

Coolea: 6 October 1971. CP-KinsT

Galloping Green: May 1962. CP-KinsT

St Godnait's Graveyard, Ballyvourney: That Evening. CP-KinsT

Selected Poems of Mañuel Bandeira, The. Robert Stock. SP-StocR

Selecting Iwaszkiewicz's Poems for an Evening of His Poetry at the National Theater in Warsaw. Czeslaw Milosz. CP-MiloCN, *tr. by* Robert Hass

Selection of Concrete Poems, A. Thomas Merton. CP-MertT

Selectivity. John Ciardi. CP-CiarJ

Selene Afterwards. Archibald MacLeish. CP-MacLA

Self. Kathleen Jessie Raine. SP-RainK

Self, The. William Carlos Williams. CP-WilW2

Self, The. Adam Zagajewski. SP-ZagaA, *tr. by* Renata Gorczynski

Self-Centered. David Ignatow. SP-IgnaD

Self-Condemnation. George Herbert. CP-HerbG

Self-Conscious People. D. H. Lawrence. CP-LawrD

Self-contemplation is a curse. Lines upon Leaving a Sanitarium. Theodore Roethke. CP-RoetT

Self-Control. Miller Williams. CP-WillM

Self Criticism. Countee Cullen. CP-CullC

Self-Criticism in February. Robinson Jeffers. CP-JefR2

Self crowned the day displays its plumage. Hymn Among the Ruins. Octavio Paz. CP-WilW2, *tr. by* William Carlos Williams

Self-Dependence. Matthew Arnold. SP-ArnoM

Self-Diffidence. Jeanne Marie Bouvier de la Motte- Guyon. CP-CowpW

Self-drivers may curse their luck. Permanent Way, A. W. H. Auden. CP-AudeW

Self-Effacement of Electra Thorne, The. Ogden Nash. CP-NashO

Self-Employed. David Ignatow. SP-IgnaD

Self-Exhortation on Military Themes. Alan Dugan. CP-DugaA

Self-Glamourer, A. Thomas Hardy. CP-HardT

Self in 1958. Anne Sexton. CP-SextA; SP-SextA

Self-Interrogation. Emily Jane Brontë. CP-BronE

Self is a servant only, The. Fanny Howe. SP-HoweF *Fr.* Vineyard, The.

Self-knower, self-aware. To My Daimon. James Vincent Cunningham. CP-CunnJ

Self-Knowledge. Samuel Taylor Coleridge. CP-ColeS; MW-ColeS

Self Love. John Donne. CP-DonnJ

Self-Love and Truth Incompatible. Jeanne Marie Bouvier de la Motte- Guyon. CP-CowpW

Self-Pity. D. H. Lawrence. CP-LawrD

Self-Pity Is a Kind of Lying, Too. James Schuyler. CP-SchuJ

(It's / snowing defective.) CP-SchuJ

Self-Portait. Charles Wright. SP-WrigC

Self-Portrait. A. R. Ammons. CP-AmmoA

Self-Portrait. Robert Creeley. SP-CreeR

Self-Portrait. A. K. Ramanujan. CP-RamaA

Self-Portrait. Charles Wright. SP-WrigC

Self-Portrait. Adam Zagajewski. SP-ZagaA, *tr. by* Clare Cavanagh

Self-Portrait 1. William Carlos Williams. CP-WilW1

Self-Portrait 2. William Carlos Williams. CP-WilW1

Self-Portrait as a Bear. Donald Hall. CP-HallD

Self-Portrait at Twenty. Gregory Orr. SP-OrrG

Self-Portrait: David, A. Charles Tomlinson. CP-TomlC

Self-Portrait in a Convex Mirror. John Ashbery. SP-AshbJ

Self-Portrait Sad, 22:ix:58. Philip Whalen. SP-WhalP

Self Prepares for an Unwilling Journey, The. William Dickey. SP-DickW

Self-Protection. D. H. Lawrence. CP-LawrD

Self-Respect. Wallace Stevens. CP-StevWP

Self-Sacrifice. D. H. Lawrence. CP-LawrD

Self-Seeker, The. Robert Frost. CP-FrosR

Self-Service. John Updike. CP-UpdiJ

Self to self. Walter De la Mare. CP-DeLaW

Self-Tormentor, The. Charles Baudelaire. CP-BaudC, *tr. by* Walter Martin

Self-Unconscious. Thomas Hardy. CP-HardT

Self-Unseeing, The. Thomas Hardy. CP-HardT

Self[e] Accuser, A. John Donne. CP-DonnJ; MW-DonnJ

Self's the Man. Philip Larkin. CP-LarkP

Selfsame Song, The. Thomas Hardy. CP-HardT

Selfsame toothless voice for death or bridal, The. Bell Speech. Richard Wilbur. CP-WilbR

Selina, Countess of Huntingdon. Donald Davie. CP-DaviDC

Sell me a violin, mister, of old mysterious wood. Kreisler. Carl Sandburg. CP-SandC

Seller of Garlic and Onions, The. Stéphane Mallarmé. CP-MallS *Fr.* Street Songs.

Selling of the Slaves, The. Maxine W. Kumin. SP-KumiM

Selva Oscura. Louis MacNeice. CP-MacNL

Selves. Thom Gunn. CP-GunnT

Semantic. George Oppen. CP-OppGN

Semaphoring chorus. George Oppen. CP-OppGN

Semblables, The. William Carlos Williams. CP-WilW2

Semblance, A. David Ignatow. SP-IgnaD

Semele Recycled. Carolyn Kizer. CP-KizeC

Semi-Detached. Robert Graves. CP-GravR

Semi-Revolution, A. Robert Frost. CP-FrosR

Semi-Spring. E. E. Cummings. CP-CummE

Semidarkness. A black POW is seated on a one-legged stool. One-legged Stool, The. Yusef Komunyakaa. CP-KomuY

Semite. George Oppen. CP-OppGN

Sen Artysty; or, The Artist's Dream. Oscar Wilde. CP-WildO

Sen that I am a presoneir. William Dunbar. CP-DunbW

Sénanque. Adam Zagajewski. SP-ZagaA, *tr. by* Clare Cavanagh

Senator Explains a Vote, The. Miller Williams. CP-WillM

Senator Smoot (Republican, Ut.). Invocation: "Senator Smoot (Republican, Ut.)." Ogden Nash. CP-NashO

Sence I tuk holt o' Gibbses' Churn. Regardin' Terry Hut. James Whitcomb Riley. CP-RileJ

Sence little Wesley went, the place seems all so strange and still. Absence of Little Wesley, The. James Whitcomb Riley. CP-RileJ

SEND FOR THE PIED PIPER AND LET HIM PIPE THE RATS AWAY. Final Call. Langston Hughes. CP-HughL; CP-HughL3

Send home my long strayed [*or* long-strayed *or* long-strayd] eyes to me[e]. Message, The. John Donne. CP-DonnJ; MW-DonnJ

Send me some token, that my hope may live. Sonnet. The Token. John Donne. CP-DonnJ

Send No Money. Philip Larkin. CP-LarkP

Send-Off, The. Wilfred Owen. CP-OwenW

Send peace on all the lands and flickering corn. Anashuya and Vijaya. William Butler Yeats. CP-YeatW

Send regards to Ida the bitch. Louis Zukofsky. CP-ZukLS

Send the Chaperones Away. Jelaluddin Rumi. SP Rumi, *tr. by* Coleman Barks

Send the Lord to the People. Shmuel HaNagid. SP-HaNaS, *tr. by* Peter Cole

Send this man to the mine, this to the battle. Argument for Suicide. William Wordsworth. CP-WorW1

Send this pigeon, a messenger. On Lifting the Siege. Shmuel HaNagid. SP-HaNaS, *tr. by* Peter Cole

Seneca. Thomas Merton. CP-MertT

Senescence begins / And middle age ends. Crossing the Border. Ogden Nash. CP-NashO

Senescente Mundo. Thomas Merton. CP-MertT

Senex, an oak. To Return to the Trees. Derek Walcott. CP-WalcD

Seng-yao I hear was a talented man. Han-shan. CP-ColdM, *tr. by* Red Pine

Sennuccio, I'm half here. Oh, were I all. Petrarch. CP-Petra, *tr. by* J. G. Nichols

Sennuccio, though you leave your friend alone. Petrarch. CP-Petra, *tr. by* J. G. Nichols

Señora, it is true the Greeks are dead. Invocation to the Social Muse. Archibald MacLeish. CP-MacLA

Sensation. Arthur Rimbaud. CP-RimbA, *tr. by* Martin Sorrell

Sensationist Poem, A. Fernando Pessoa. SP-PessF

Sense. Rae Armantrout. SP-ArmaA

Sense, A. Park / "a Darling Walk / for the Mind," The. Lorine Niedecker. CP-NiedL

Sense and Spirit. George Meredith. CP-MerG1

Sense of Comedy, The: 1. Jay Wright. SP-WrigJ

Sense of danger must not disappear, The. Leap Before You Look. W. H. Auden. CP-AudeW

Sense of Distance, A. Charles Tomlinson. CP-TomlC; SP-TomlC

Sense of Humor, A. Nicholas Vachel Lindsay. CP-LindV

Sense of Proportion. Kenneth Rexroth. CP-RexrK

Sense of the Sleight-of-Hand Man, The. Wallace Stevens. CP-StevW; CP-StevWP

Sense of the world is short, The. Eros. Ralph Waldo Emerson. CP-EmerR

Sense of Truth. D. H. Lawrence. CP-LawrD

Sense that sits in the thin skins of lips, The. Betrayal, The. Thomas Merton. CP-MertT

Senseless drops can feel no pain, as they, The. Forbearance. Jones Very. CP-VeryJ

Senseless school, where we must give, A. Young Man's Epigram on Existence, A. Thomas Hardy. CP-HardT

Senses loving Earth or well or ill, The. Sense and Spirit. George Meredith. CP-MerG1

Senses of Insecurity. Maya Angelou. SP-AngeM

Senses of one's / life begin, The. Illness, An. Robert Creeley. CP-CreeR

Sensibility, an Ode. Annis Boudinot Stockton. CP-StocA

Sensibility how charming. Song: "Sensibility how charming." Robert Burns. CP-BurnR

Sensibility! O La! Theodore Roethke. CP-RoetT

Sensibility to the Beauty and Fragrance of Flowers. Jones Very. CP-VeryJ

Sensing death, / The buzzards gather. Dying Beast. Langston Hughes. CP-HughL; CP-HughL1

Sensitive Ears. James Tate. SP-TateJ

Sensitive Girl, The. Raymond Carver. CP-CarvR

Sensitive Plant, The. Percy Bysshe Shelley. CP-ShelP

Sensualist, The. John Updike. CP-UpdiJ

Sensualist and intellectual. Cats. Charles Baudelaire. CP-BaudC, *tr. by* Walter Martin

Sensualists, The. Theodore Roethke. CP-RoetT

Sent straight from suns. Lamplight. John Updike. CP UpdiJ

Sentence, The. Robert Creeley. CP-CreeR

Sentence, The. Robert Graves. CP-GravR

Sentence of death, my love, as if we were destined to squint, A. Now, Now. Paul Muldoon. CP-MuldP

Sentence of John L. Brown, The. John Greenleaf Whittier. CP-WhitJ

Sentence starts out like a lone traveler, A. Winter Syntax. Billy Collins. SP-CollB

Sentence undulates, The. End of the Parade, The. William Carlos Williams. CP-WilW2

Sentence uttered makes a world appear, A. Words. W. H. Auden. CP-AudeW

Sentenced to two consecutive. Knife at the Jugular. Arthur Sze. SP-SzeA

Sentences. Czeslaw Milosz. CP-MiloC; CP-MiloCN, *tr. by* Lillian Vallee

Sentences, The. Robert Pinsky. CP-PinsR

Sentencing goes blithely on its way, The. In a Poem. Robert Frost. CP-FrosR

Sententious Man, The. Theodore Roethke. CP-RoetT

Sentiment, Oeconomy, and Greed. Triad of British Evils, A. George Meredith. CP-MerG2

Sentimental curator has placed, A. In the Museum at Teheran. James Laughlin. CP-LaugJ

Sentimental Delusion, A. Mona Van Duyn. SP-VanDM

Sentimentalist sends his mauve balloon, The. Celebration in the Plaza, The. Adrienne Rich. CP-RicAE

Sentiments are nice, "The Lonely Crowd." John Button Birthday. Frank O'Hara. SP-OharF

Sentiments for a Dedication. Archibald MacLeish. CP-MacLA

Sentinel robins two / guard me and you. E. E. Cummings. CP-CummE

Sentinels, The. Robert Duncan. SP-DuncR

Sentry, The. Wilfred Owen. CP-OwenW

Senza Flash. Adam Zagajewski. SP-ZagaA, *tr. by* Clare Cavanagh

Seoul Sounds. Robert Creeley. SP-CreeR

Sepal, petal, and a thorn, A. Emily Dickinson. CP-DickE

Separate Dead, The. David Ignatow. SP-IgnaD

Separate Lives. Marilyn Hacker. SP-HackM

Separate Notebooks, The. Czeslaw Milosz. CP-MiloCN

Separate place between the thought and felt, A. Corridor, The. Thom Gunn. CP-GunnT

Separate Poem, A. Tennessee Williams. CP-WillT

Separate Rooms. David Ignatow. SP-IgnaD

Separate Rose, The. Pablo Neruda.
    Island (VII), The. SP-NeruP
    Island (VIII), The. SP-NeruP
    Island (XII), The. SP-NeruP
    Island (XVII), The. SP-NeruP
    Island (XX), The. SP-NeruP
    Men (II), The. SP-NeruP
    Men (IV), The. SP-NeruP
    Men (IX), The. SP-NeruP
    Men (XVIII), The. SP-NeruP
    Men (XIX), The. SP-NeruP

Separated. D. H. Lawrence. CP-LawrD

Separation. Robert Stock.
    "Yellow, hurt light shivering over New York, A." SP-StocR

Separation. Audre Lorde. SP-LordA

Separation. W. S. Merwin. SP-MerwW

Separation. Yannis Ritsos. SP-RitsY, *tr. by* Kimon Friar

Separation. Adam Zagajewski. SP-ZagaA, *tr. by* Clare Cavanagh

Separation, The. Thom Gunn. CP-GunnT

Separation from Asra. Samuel Taylor Coleridge. CP-ColeS

Separations. Marilyn Hacker.

    "Culled from the brambled ceiling of my wide." SP-HackM

    "February of the merely real, A." SP-HackM

    "Friend (this is an imaginary letter)." SP-HackM

    "I still balk at my preference for rhyme." SP-HackM

    "I'll dabble in specifics in my bath." SP-HackM

    "More circumspect good friend, if by "deceive"" SP-HackM

    "Satisfied loves eat big breakfasts. I." SP-HackM

    "This is a high and sprawling wooden flat." SP-HackM

Sepia Fashion Show. Maya Angelou. SP-AngeM

Sepia the first part. Caring: A Dream. Maxine W. Kumin. SP-KumiM

September. Edmund Spenser. CP-Spens *Fr.* Shepheardes [*or* Shepeards *or* Shepherd's] Calender, The.

September. Raymond Carver. CP-CarvR

September. W. S. Merwin. SP-MerwW

September. Grace Paley.

September. James Schuyler. CP-SchuJ

September. Adam Zagajewski. SP-ZagaA, *tr. by* Clare Cavanagh

September 1, 1802. William Wordsworth. MW-WorW

September Afternoon at Four O'Clock. Marge Piercy. SP-PierM

September Afternoon in the Abandoned Barracks. Adam Zagajewski. SP-ZagaA, *tr. by* Renata Gorczynski, Benjamin Ivry *and* C. K. Williams

September, and somewhere the last. September. Raymond Carver. CP-CarvR

September, and the butterflies are drifting. Crossing, The. Howard Nemerov. CP-NemeH

September Dark. James Whitcomb Riley. CP-RileJ

September Drift. A. R. Ammons. CP-AmmoA

September, 1815. William Wordsworth. CP-WorW2; MW-WorW (September, 1815.) CP-WorW2

September, 1819. William Wordsworth. CP-WorW2

September, 1802. Near Dover. William Wordsworth. *See* Near Dover, September 1802

September in Gt. Yarmouth. Derek Mahon. CP-MahoD

September Is Summer, Too. Ogden Nash. CP-NashO

September Landscape. Robert Graves. CP-GravR

September Mendocino. Clarence Major. SP-MajoC

September Morn. Ogden Nash. CP-NashO

September 1903. Constantine P. Cavafy. CP-CavaC, *tr. by* Theoharis Constantine Theoharis

September 1961. Denise Levertov. SP-LeveDP; SP-LeveDS

September 1913. William Butler Yeats. CP-YeatW

September Ode. Donald Hall. CP-HallD

September on Jessore Road. Allen Ginsberg. CP-GinsA; SP-GinsA

September 1, 1802. William Wordsworth. CP-WorW1

September Plowing. W. S. Merwin. SP-MerwWF

September rain falls on the house. Sestina: "September rain falls on the house." Elizabeth Bishop. CP-BishE

September Shooting. Howard Nemerov. CP-NemeH

September Song. William Corbett. SP-CorbW

September Song. Geoffrey Hill. CP-HillG

September Song. Christopher Logue. SP-LoguC

September Sowing. Sam Hamill. SP-HamiS

September, the First Day of School. Howard Nemerov. CP-NemeH

September, the fugue of dry weather. Primitive Journal II. Charles Wright. SP-WrigC

September 21. Adrienne Rich. CP-RicAE

September 22nd. Maxine W. Kumin. SP-KumiM *Fr.* Joppa Diary.

SEPTEMBER twenty-second, Sir: today. After the Surprising Conversions. Robert Lowell. SP-LoweR

September 2, 1969. Wendell Berry. CP-BerrW

September yellows. Sickness at the Equinox, A. W. S. Merwin. SP-MerwW

September's Baccalaureate. Emily Dickinson. CP-DickE

Septentrion. René Char. CP-MertT

Septic Tanck. Hayden Carruth. CP-CarHS

Septimi Gades. William Wordsworth. CP-WorW1

Septimius and Acme. Catullus. *See* Carmina

Septimius, the forms you know so well. Another One. Kenneth Rexroth. CP-RexrK

Septimius thus his love addressed. Catullus. *See* Phyllis Corydon clutched to him

Septuagenarian, The. Robert Graves. CP-GravR

Septuagesima. Christina Georgina Rossetti. CP-RosC2

Sepulchral. Rudyard Kipling. CP-KiplR *Fr.* Muse among the Motors, The.

Sepulchral Inscription. Jorge Luis Borges. SP-BorgJ, *tr. by* Robert Fitzgerald

Sepulchre. George Herbert. CP-HerbG

Sepulchre of the Books, The. Jones Very. CP-VeryJ

Sequel, The. Theodore Roethke. CP-RoetT

Sequel to *Beggars* Composed Many Years After. William Wordsworth. CP-WorW2; MW-WorW

Sequence. Wyatt Prunty. SP-PrunW

Sequence, A. Denise Levertov. SP-LeveDP

Sequence 1944-6. Louis Zukofsky. CP-ZukLS

Seraph. William Carlos Williams. CP-WilW1

Seraph and Poet, The. Elizabeth Barrett Browning. CP-BroEB

Seraph scanned the murderer in the dock, The. One in the Public Gallery. Walter De la Mare. CP-DeLaW

Seraph sings before the manifest, The. Seraph and Poet, The. Elizabeth Barrett Browning. CP-BroEB

Seraphic shame generosity causes, The. Emily Dickinson. SP-DickE

Seraphim, The. Elizabeth Barrett Browning. CP-BroEB

Seraphs! around th'Eternal's seat who throng. Anthem for the Children of Christ's Hospital. Samuel Taylor Coleridge. CP-ColeS

Sere ring a pipe wood. Lilac. Louis Zukofsky. CP-ZukLS

Serena I. Samuel Beckett. CP-BeckS

Serena II. Samuel Beckett. CP-BeckS

Serena III. Samuel Beckett. CP-BeckS

Serenade. Christina Georgina Rossetti. CP-RosC3

Serenade: "Down on the riverbanks." Federico García Lorca. CP-GarcF, *tr. by* Alan S. Trueblood *Fr.* Eros with a Cane.

Serenade: "Let the other boys from the village." Billy Collins. SP-CollB

Serenade: "Listen, maiden, to my strain." Ambrose Bierce. SP-BierA

Serenade: "Western wind is blowing fair, The." Oscar Wilde. CP-WildO

Serenade, A: "Ah! County Guy, the hour is nigh." Sir Walter Scott. SP-ScotW *Fr.* Quentin Durward.

Serenade, The: "Midnight is not more bewildering, The." James Whitcomb Riley. CP-RileJ

Serenade at the Villa, A. Robert Browning. CP-BroR1; SP-BroR

Serenade in a Drugstore. John Ciardi. CP-CiarJ

Serenade—To Nora. James Whitcomb Riley. CP-RileJ

Serenades. Seamus Heaney. SP-HeanSO

Serene, and fitted to embrace. Dion. William Wordsworth. CP-WorW2

Serene and purple twilight of the South. Procession. James Schuyler. CP-SchuJ

Serene immediate silliest and whose. E. E. Cummings. CP-CummE

Serene in his unconquerable might. Fragment: Pater Omnipotens. Percy Bysshe Shelley. CP-ShelP

Serene irony of the eternal Sky, The. Azure, The. Stéphane Mallarmé. CP-MallS, *tr. by* Henry Weinfield

Serene night cold November. News and the Weather, The. Thomas McGrath. SP-McGrT

Serfs are glad through Lara's wide domain. Lara. Lord Byron. CP-Byron

Sergeant says that eight and twenty wagons, The. Young Soldier with Bloody Spurs, The. D. H. Lawrence. CP-LawrD

Sgt. stands so fluently in leather, The. On a Photo of Sgt. Ciardi a Year Later. John Ciardi. CP-CiarJ

Sergeant's Song, The. Thomas Hardy. CP-HardT

Sergeant's Weddin', The. Rudyard Kipling. CP-KiplR

Serial Murderer Says Something to the Priest, The. Miller Williams. CP-WillM

Serious Case, A. Mona Van Duyn. SP-VanDM

Serious historians care for coins and weapons. Makers of History. W. H. Auden. CP-AudeW

Serious moment for the water is when it boils, A. Boiling Water, The. Kenneth Koch. SP-KochK

Serious Morning, A. Andrei Codrescu. SP-CodrA

Serious Poem upon William Wood, A. Jonathan Swift. CP-SwifJ

Serious Step Taken Lightly, A. Robert Frost. CP-FrosR

Seriphos Unvisited. Amy Clampitt. CP-ClamA

Sermon Notes. John Ciardi. CP-CiarJ

Sermon of the Rose, The. James Whitcomb Riley. CP-RileJ

Sermon of the Twelve Acknowledgements, The. Anne Sexton. CP-SextA

Serpent. Robert Lowell. SP-LoweR

Serpent, The. Robert Lowell. SP-LoweR

Serpent, The. Theodore Roethke. CP-RoetT

Serpent, The. Jones Very. CP-VeryJ

Serpent does not crouch at Athene's feet, The. Helios and Athene. "H. D." CP-DoolH

Serpent is shut out from Paradise, The. To Edward Williams. Percy Bysshe Shelley. CP-ShelP

Serpents of summer, The. Hooves, The. Josephine Jacobsen. CP-JacoJ

Serpent's Tail. Robert Graves. CP-GravR

Serpent's Tooth, The. Charles Baudelaire. CP-BaudC, *tr. by* Walter Martin

Servant, The. Jones Very. CP-VeryJ

Servant Boy. Seamus Heaney. SP-HeanSO

Servant-Girl at Emmaus (A Painting by Velazquez), The. Denise Levertov. SP-LeveDS

Servant Girl's Bed. Hugh MacDiarmid. SP-MacDH

Servant Thou hast called stands ready shod, The. Servant, The. Jones Very. CP-VeryJ

Servant to Servants, A. Robert Frost. CP-FrosR

Servant When He Reigneth, A. Rudyard Kipling. CP-KiplR

Servant Who Loved His Prayers, The. Jelaluddin Rumi. SP-Rumi, *tr. by* Coleman Barks

Service. D. H. Lawrence. CP-LawrD

Service. W. S. Merwin. SP-MerwWF

Service and strength, God's Angels and Archangels. St. Michael and all Angels. Christina Georgina Rossetti. CP RosC2

Service Man, The. Rudyard Kipling. CP-KiplR

Service, or Latin *sorbus*, European. Life of Service, The. Donald Davie. CP-DaviDC

Service without Hope, The. Emily Dickinson. CP-DickE

Serving-Man, The. Jones Very. CP-VeryJ

Serving no haughty Muse, my hands have here. Valedictory Sonnet. William Wordsworth. CP-WorW2

Serving with Gideon. William Stafford. SP-StafW; SP-StafWW

Servitude. Ivor Gurney. SP-GurnI

Sesame. Federico García Lorca. CP-GarcF, *tr. by* Jerome Rothenberg *Fr.* Moments of Song.

Sessile, unseeing. Progress? W. H. Auden. CP-AudeW

Session with Uncle Sidney, A. James Whitcomb Riley. CP-RileJ

Session[s] was held the other day, A. Wits, The; A Session[s] of the Poets. Sir John Suckling. CP-SuckJ

Sestina: "For a week now our bodies have whispered." Marilyn Hacker. SP-HackM

Sestina: "Hang it all, Ezra Pound, there is only the one sestina." Donald Hall. CP-HallD

Sestina: "I die, no matter what I do I die." Richard Eberhart. CP-EberR

Sestina: "I have reached, alas, the long shadow." Dante Alighieri. CP-SchuJ, *tr. by* James Schuyler

Sestina: Of the Lady Pietra degli Scrovigni. Dante Alighieri. CW-RossD, *tr. by* Dante Gabriel Rossetti

Sestina: "September rain falls on the house." Elizabeth Bishop. CP-BishE

Sestina 1: "Thickness of paint or flesh cannot deface." Howard Nemerov. CP-NemeH

Sestina 2: "No waste is trackless: all terrain the lost." Howard Nemerov. CP-NemeH

Sestina: Altaforte. Ezra Pound. CP-PoEar; SP-PounE

Sestina for Warm Seasons. Mona Van Duyn. SP-VanDM

Sestina for Ysolt. Ezra Pound. CP-PoEar

Sestina of the Tramp-Royal. Rudyard Kipling. CP-KiplR

Set fire to the City, burn the City down. What Had to Go. Charles Olson. CP-OlsoC

Set in their studious corners, the players. Chess. Jorge Luis Borges. SP-BorgJ, *tr. by* Alastair Reid

Set in this stormy Northern sea. Ave Imperatrix. Oscar Wilde. CP-WildO

Set loose on the hills to tramp all night. Forest Fire. Wyatt Prunty. SP-PrunW

Set not thy foot on graves. To J. W. Ralph Waldo Emerson. CP-EmerR

Set of phrases learned [*or* learnt] by rote, A. Furniture of a Woman's Mind, The. Jonathan Swift. CP-SwifJ

Set of Seasons, A. Donald Hall. CP-HallD

Set over Orontes. De Los Cantares. Charles Olson. CP-OlsoC

Set the foot down with distrust upon the crust of the world—it is thin. Underground System. Edna St. Vincent Millay. CP-MillE

Set the table and sweep the floor. Myself to Me. May Sarton. SP-SartM

Set the theme. Still Dancers. Robert Creeley. SP-CreeR

Set Times, and the Boundaries of Nations, Appointed by God, The. Jones Very. CP-VeryJ

Seta cangiante. Eyes. James Schuyler. CP-SchuJ

Seth Thomas: A Love Poem. Denise Levertov. SP-LeveDL

Sets. Rae Armantrout. SP-ArmaA

Settin' round the stove, last night. Liz-Town Humorist, A. James Whitcomb Riley. CP-RileJ

Setting a trotline after sundown. In the Deep Channel. William Stafford. SP-StafW; SP-StafWW

Setting his camera to blink a frame. Thanks to a Botanist, A. John Ciardi. CP-CiarJ

Setting in the wine-house. Wine-O. Langston Hughes. CP-HughL; CP-HughL3

Setting Out. Wendell Berry. CP-BerrW

Setting out East on rain bright highways. Auto Poesy: On the Lam from Bloomington. Allen Ginsberg. CP-GinsA

Setting sun is a red lion, The. Absence. Yannis Ritsos. SP-RitsY, *tr. by* Athan Anagnostopoulos

Settings. Thomas Kinsella. CP-KinsT

Settings. Seamus Heaney. SP-HeanSO *Fr.* Squarings.

Settle Bed, The. Seamus Heaney. SP-HeanSO

Settler, The. Rudyard Kipling. CP-KiplR

Settler, The. Jones Very. CP-VeryJ

Settlers, The. Margaret Atwood. SP-AtwM1

Settling. Denise Levertov. SP-LeveDS

Seur, near Blois. Donald Davie. CP-DaviDC

Seurat and Juan Gris combine this season. Ted Berrigan. SP-BerrT *Fr.* Sonnets, The.

Seven. Thomas Kinsella. CP-KinsT

Seven against Thebes, The. Aeschylus.
  Lament for the Two Brothers Slain by Each Other's Hand. CP-HousA

Seven and Ten addyd to nyne. Jonathan Swift. CP-SwifJ *Fr.* Famous Prediction of Merlin, A.

Seven Archaic Images. Thomas Merton. CP-MertT

Seven bulls of a Sunday. Theory of Regress. Charles Tomlinson. CP-TomlC

Seven buxom women abreast, and arm in arm. Ice on the Highway. Thomas Hardy. CP-HardT

Seven Daughters had Lord Archibald. Seven Sisters, or, the Solitude of Binnorie, The. William Wordsworth. CP-WorW1

Seven days all fog, all mist, and the turbines pounding through high seas. Baltic Fog Notes. Carl Sandburg. CP-SandC

7 December 1948. Yannis Ritsos. SP-RitsY *Fr.* Exile's Journals 2.

Seven Dungeon Songs. Ted Hughes.
  "Dead, she became space-earth." SP-HughTN
  "Earth locked out the light, The." SP-HughTN
  "Face was necessary—I found face." SP-HughTN
  "I walk / Unwind with activity of legs." SP-HughTN
  "If mouth could open its cliff." SP-HughTN

Seven Eleven. Carl Sandburg. CP-SandC

Seven Epigrams. Gerard Manley Hopkins. CP-HopkG

Seven Forbidden Words. Michael Palmer. SP-PalmM

7.IV.64. Gary Snyder. CP-SnydG

Seven hearts / are the hearts that I have. Song of the Seven-Hearted Boy. Federico García Lorca. CP-GarcF, *tr. by* Jerome Rothenberg *Fr.* In the Garden of the Lunar Grapefruits.

Seven Knights a shrine about. Old Riddle, An. G. K. Chesterton. CP-ChesG

Seven ladies / and seventeen gentlemen. Parade. Langston Hughes. CP-HughL; CP-HughL3

Seven Laments for the War-Dead. Yehuda Amichai. SP-AmicY, *tr. by* Chana Bloch

Seven letters, / Seven songs. Ballad of the Seven Songs. Langston Hughes. CP-HughL; CP-HughL2

Seven Lines of Equal Length. Michael Palmer. SP-PalmM

Seven Macabre Songs. Howard Nemerov. CP-NemeH

Seven maidens 'neath the midnight. Romance of the Ganges, A. Elizabeth Barrett Browning. CP-BroEB

7 May 1950. Yannis Ritsos. SP-RitsY *Fr.* Exile's Journals 3.

Seven men from all the world back to Docks again. Ballad of the "Bolivar," The. Rudyard Kipling. CP-KiplR

7, Middagh Street. Paul Muldoon. CP-MuldP

Seven millions stand / Emaciate, in that ancient Delta-land. Appeal to America on Behalf of the Belgian Destitute, An. Thomas Hardy. CP-HardT

Seven Moments of Love; An Un-Sonnet Sequence in Blues. Langston Hughes. CP-HughL; CP-HughL2

Seven nations stood with their hands on the jaws of death. Jaws. Carl Sandburg. CP-SandC

Seven New Ways of Looking at the Moon. John Updike. CP-UpdiJ

Seven o'clock. The seventh day of the seventh month of the year. Birth, The. Paul Muldoon. CP-MuldP

Seven o'clock whistle, The. Whistle, The. Yusef Komunyakaa. CP-KomuY

Seven Odes to Seven Natural Processes. John Updike. CP-UpdiJ

Seven Old Men, The. Charles Baudelaire. CP-BaudC, *tr. by* Walter Martin

7:00 p.m. Federico García Lorca. CP-GarcF, *tr. by* Jerome Rothenberg *Fr.* Summer Hours.

Seven Sages, The. William Butler Yeats. CP-YeatW

Seven Seals. D. H. Lawrence. CP-LawrD

7:VII. Gary Snyder. CP-SnydG

Seven-Sided Poem. Carlos Drummond de Andrade. CP-BishE, *tr. by* Elizabeth Bishop

Seven Sides and Seven Syllables. Edouard J. Maunick. CP-KizeC, *tr. by* Carolyn Kizer

Seven Sisters, or, the Solitude of Binnorie, The. William Wordsworth. CP-

WorW1

Seven Songs, The. Charles Olson. CP-OlsoC

Seven Sonnets. Arthur Hugh Clough. SP-ClouA

Seven sons of the dust that are. Maid's Way, A. G. K. Chesterton. CP-ChesG

Seven Spiritual Ages of Mrs. Marmaduke Moore, The. Ogden Nash. CP-NashO

Seven Stanzas at Easter. John Updike. CP-UpdiJ

Seven stars in the still water. Dole of the King's Daughter, The. *Unknown.* CP-WildO, *tr. by* Oscar Wilde *and* Oscar Wilde

Seven Strophes. Joseph Brodsky. CP-BrodJ, *tr. by* Paul Graves

7 x 7 + love =. Addition ("7 x 7 + love ="). Langston Hughes. CP-HughL; CP-HughL2

Seven Times, The. Thomas Hardy. CP-HardT

Seven unclean spirits of Mary Magdalen, The. Mary Magdalen and I. Czeslaw Milosz. CP-MiloC; CP-MiloCN, *tr. by* Robert Hass

Seven vials hold Thy wrath: but what can hold. Christina Georgina Rossetti. CP-RosC2

Seven Watchmen. Rudyard Kipling. CP-KiplR

Seven-year-old Poets. Arthur Rimbaud. CP-RimbA, *tr. by* Martin Sorrell

Seven Years. Robert Graves. CP-GravR

Seven years a charming woman wore. Lorine Niedecker. CP-NiedL

Seven years' curse is ended now, The. Return. Robert Graves. CP-GravR

7 Years from Somewhere. Philip Levine. SP-LeviP

Seven years I had to think it over. Nebuchadnezzar, Solus. Howard Nemerov. CP-NemeH

Seven years I watched the next-door. Late Snow. Louise Glück. SP-GlucL

Seven years' words wasted. Long Live the Spiderweb. Allen Ginsberg. CP-GinsA

Seventeen. Adam Zagajewski. SP-ZagaA, *tr. by* Renata Gorczynski, Benjamin Ivry *and* C. K. Williams

1789–1939. Randall Jarrell. CP-JarrR

Seventeen Months. Carl Sandburg. CP-SandC

17 November 1948. Yannis Ritsos. SP-RitsY *Fr.* Exile's Journals 1.

Seventeen Questions about KING KONG. Jane Cooper. CP-CoopJ

Seventeen seventy one / and two. In those years the fame. July, 1773. Wendell Berry. CP-BerrW

Seventeen Years. Wendell Berry. CP-BerrW

Seventeen years since first I felt the full. Petrarch. CP-Petra, *tr. by* J. G. Nichols

17th century men / who founded this land. Charles Olson. CP-OlsoC

Seventeenth Floor: Echoes of Singapore. Robert Creeley. SP-CreeR

Seventh Avenue. Muriel Rukeyser. CP-RukeM

Seventh Day. Kathleen Jessie Raine. ŠP-RainK

Seventh dragon turned to his wife, The. Where Two O'clock Came From. Kenneth Patchen. CP-PatcK

Seventh Elegy. Dream-Singing Elegy. Muriel Rukeyser. CP-RukeM

Seventh Epistle of the First Book of Horace Imitated, The. Alexander Pope. CP-PopeA

Seventh of November, The. Robert Burns. CP-BurnR

Seventh Sign, The. Audre Lorde. SP-LordA

Seventieth Birthday. Robinson Jeffers. CP-JefR3

Seventy-four and Twenty. Thomas Hardy. CP-HardT

71 South. Miller Williams. CP-WillM

Seventy years ago my mother labored to bear me. Birthday (Autobiography). Robinson Jeffers. CP-JefR3

Several Large Rocks in a Swiftly Rushing Stream. Robert Stock. SP-StocR

Several Love-Stories. Laura Riding Jackson. CP-RidiL

Several Measures for the Little Lost. Norman Dubie. CP-DubiN

Several Questions Answered. William Blake. CP-BlakW

Several Voices Out of a Cloud. Louise Bogan. CP-BogaL

Several years ago, I wrote haiku in this way. Month in Summer, A. Carolyn Kizer. CP-KizeC

Severe dancer poised before her mirror, The. Times Between, The. Wyatt Prunty. SP-PrunW

Severed Selves. Dante Gabriel Rossetti. CW-RossD *Fr.* House of Life, The.

Severer Service of myself. Emily Dickinson. CP-DickE

Severnside. Charles Tomlinson. CP-TomlC

Seville. Federico García Lorca. SP-GarcF *Fr.* Poem of the Saeta.

Seville is a tower. Seville. Federico García Lorca. SP-GarcF *Fr.* Poem of the Saeta.

Sevillian Ditty. Federico García Lorca. CP-GarcF, *tr. by* Alan S. Trueblood *Fr.* Songs for Children.

Sew. Donald Hall. CP-HallD

Sew the Flags Together. Nicholas Vachel Lindsay. CP-LindV

Sewerplant Grows In Harlem Or I'm a Stranger Here Myself. Audre Lorde. SP-LordA

Sewing Machine. Charles Simic. SP-SimiCE

Sewing together the bits of data. Eyes and No-Eyes. Denise Levertov. SP-LeveDL

Sex. Charles Bukowski. SP-BukC1

Sex. Hayden Carruth. CP-CarHS

Sex and/or Love. Charles Bukowski. SP-BukC3

Sex and Trust. D. H. Lawrence. CP-LawrD

Sex, as they harshly call it. Two Songs. Adrienne Rich. CP-RicAE; SP-RicA2

Sex floated like a moon. Circle, a Square, a Triangle and a Ripple of Water, A. Jane Cooper. CP-CoopJ

Sex in History. Thomas Lux. SP-LuxT

Sex is made on a bed which is too loose. Fanny Howe. SP-HoweF *Fr.* Quietist, The.

Sex Isn't Sin. D. H. Lawrence. CP-LawrD

Sex, Magnolias, & Speed. Yusef Komunyakaa. CP-KomuY

Sex Won't Work. D. H. Lawrence. CP-LawrD

Sexagesima. Christina Georgina Rossetti. CP-RosC2

Sexist Lament: Ruin by Monitor. Alan Dugan. CP-DugaA

Sexless, my brother flies. Song. Summer. Rita Dove. SP-DoveR

Sexpot. Charles Bukowski. SP-BukC1

Sext. John Berryman. CP-BerrJ

Sext. James McMichael. SP-McMiJ

Sexton at Longpuddle, The. Thomas Hardy. CP-HardT

Sexton! My Master's sleeping here. Emily Dickinson. CP-DickE

Sexual Conduct. Clarence Major. SP-MajoC

Sexual intercourse began. Annus Mirabilis. Philip Larkin. CP-LarkP

Sexual Urgency, What a Woman's Laughter Can Do, and the Nature of True Virility. Jelaluddin Rumi. SP-Rumi, *tr. by* Coleman Barks

Seyd planted where the deluge ploughed. Ralph Waldo Emerson. CP-EmerR

Seymour and Chantelle or Un Peu de Vice. Stevie Smith. CP-SmitS

Sez the Junior Orderly Sergeant. Shut-Eye Sentry, The. Rudyard Kipling. CP-KiplR

Sh estiffl / ystrut sal. E. E. Cummings. CP-CummE

Shabby little bird. Passer Domesticus. William Carlos Williams. CP-WilW2

Shabby, tweedy, academic, he was old enough to be her father and I thought he was her father. Dirty Talker: D Line, Boston, The. C. K. Williams. SP-WillC

Shack and a few trees, The. After Work. Gary Snyder. CP-SnydG

Shad-Blow Tree, The. Louise Glück. SP-GlucL

Shad-Time. Richard Wilbur. CP-WilbR

Shadder in de valley. Noon. Paul Laurence Dunbar. CP-DunbP

Shade. Rainer Maria Rilke. CP-RilkFr, *tr. by* A. Poulin, Jr.

Shade, The. Walter De la Mare. CP-DeLaW

Shade, The. C. K. Williams. CP-WillC; SP-WillC

Shade for me, but over thee, The. Sisters, The: A Picture by Barry, The. John Greenleaf Whittier. CP-WhitJ

Shade of Caractacus, if spirits love. Eagle and the Dove, The. William Wordsworth. CP-WorW2

Shade of high shame and honourable blindness. True Lovers. G. K. Chesterton. CP-ChesG

Shade-Seller, The. Josephine Jacobsen. CP-JacoJ

Shade upon the mind there passes, A. Emily Dickinson. CP-DickE

Shaded lamp and a waving blind, A. August Midnight, An. Thomas Hardy. CP-HardT

Shades. D. H. Lawrence. CP-LawrD

Shades. Heather McHugh. SP-McHuH

Shades of Callimachus, Coan ghosts of Philetas. Homage to Sextus Propertius. Ezra Pound. SP-PounE

Shades of Pigmeat. Langston Hughes. CP-HughL; CP-HughL3

Shadow. Walter De la Mare. CP-DeLaW

Shadow. Federico García Lorca.

  Bat. CP-GarcF, *tr. by* Jerome Rothenberg

  End. CP-GarcF, *tr. by* Jerome Rothenberg

  Memento ("When we die / we'll take with us"). CP-GarcF, *tr. by* Jerome Rothenberg

  Mountaintop. CP-GarcF, *tr. by* Jerome Rothenberg

  Pueblo. CP-GarcF, *tr. by* Jerome Rothenberg

  Sundown ("On this exquisite sky"). CP-GarcF, *tr. by* Jerome Rothenberg

  Ursa Major ("Makes me feel sad"). CP-GarcF, *tr. by* Jerome Rothenberg

  Willow. CP-GarcF, *tr. by* Jerome Rothenberg

Shadow, The. Charles Tomlinson. CP-TomlC

Shadow, The. William Carlos Williams. CP-WilW1

Shadow and light both strove to be. Bells, The. Walter De la Mare. CP-DeLaW

Shadow and Shade. Allen Tate. CP-TateA

Shadow and Shine. James Whitcomb Riley. CP-RileJ

Shadow and the Light, The. John Greenleaf Whittier. CP-WhitJ

Shadow and the Real, The. James Wright. CP-WrigJ

Shadow Boxes. Tennessee Williams. CP-WillT

Shadow does not move. It is the water moves, The. Well Disciplined Bargeman, The. William Carlos Williams. CP-WilW2

Shadow faces / In the shadow night. Chord. Langston Hughes. CP-HughL; CP-

HughL3

Shadow falls, A. Motel in Troy, New York, A. Josephine Jacobsen. CP-JacoJ

Shadow his father makes with joined hands, A. Alphabets. Seamus Heaney. SP-HeanSO

Shadow, index of the sun. By Day and by Night. W. S. Merwin. SP-MerwW

Shadow is a clue, The. O shadow! Solving the Riddle. Charles Simic. SP-SimiCE

Shadow is floating through the moonlight, A. Bird of Night, The. Randall Jarrell. CP-JarrR

Shadow kisses, shadow love. Schatten Küsse, Schatten Liebe. Kenneth Rexroth. CP-RexrK

Shadow of a bird / upon the yard upon, The. In Wiry Winter. James Schuyler. CP-SchuJ

Shadow of a butterfly, The. Butterfly. Rainer Maria Rilke. CP-RilkFr, tr. by A. Poulin, Jr.

Shadow of a hilltop, The. Wet Nurse. Yusef Komunyakaa. CP-KomuY

Shadow of a pine-branch quivered, The. Words. Thom Gunn. CP-GunnT

Shadow of a poplar tree, The. Massacre, The. Walter De la Mare. CP-DeLaW

Shadow of Death, The. D. H. Lawrence. CP-LawrD

Shadow of her face upon the wall, The. Two Sketches. Elizabeth Barrett Browning. CP-BroEB

Shadow of the Japanese magnolia, The. Magnolia's Shadow, The. Eugenio Montale. CP-MontE, tr. by Jonathan Galassi

Shadow of the little fishing launch, The. Parrot Fish, The. James Merrill. SP-MerrJ

Shadow of the Venetian blind on the painted wall, The. Forties Flick. John Ashbery. SP-AshbJ

Shadow of War. Stephen Spender. CP-SpenS

Shadow on the Stone, The. Thomas Hardy. CP-HardT

Shadow Play For Guilt, A. Marge Piercy. SP-PierM

Shadow / ran before it lengthening, The. Up at La Serra. Charles Tomlinson. CP-TomlC; SP-TomlC

Shadow Realm. Hans Magnus Enzensberger. SP-EnzeH, tr. by Michael Hamburger

Shadow, shadow on the wall. Three Nuns. Christina Georgina Rossetti. CP-RosC3

Shadow sprang out, The. Hayden Carruth. CP-CarHS Fr. Clay Hill Anthology, The.

Shadow streamed into the wall, The. Shadow and Shade. Allen Tate. CP-TateA

Shadow through the room, a rising, A. Lord Myth. Norman Dubie. CP-DubiN

Shadow was so black, The. Conviction (iii). Stevie Smith. CP-SmitS

Shadow Wood. Tennessee Williams. CP-WillT

Shadowboxing. James Tate. SP-TateJ

Shadowes before the shining sunne do vanish. Thomas Campion. CP-CampT

Shadowing the Ground. David Ignatow. SP-IgnaD

Shadows. Langston Hughes. CP-HughL; CP-HughL1

Shadows. D. H. Lawrence. CP-LawrD

Shadows. A. K. Ramanujan. CP-RamaA

Shadows. C. K. Williams. SP-WillC

Shadows. William Carlos Williams. CP-WilW2

Shadows and Spring Flowers. Kenneth Patchen. CP-PatcK

Shadows at Boxford, The. Norman Dubie. CP-DubiN

Shadows cast by the street light. Shadows. William Carlos Williams. CP-WilW2

Shadows fall along the wall, The. Dennis Shand. Dante Gabriel Rossetti. CW-RossD

Shadows fall between people. Shadows. A. K. Ramanujan. CP-RamaA

Shadows Fall Blue on the Mountains. Carl Sandburg. CP-SandC

Shadows gather round me, while you are in the sun, The. Next of Kin. Christina Georgina Rossetti. CP-RosC3

Shadows grow and deepen round me, The. What the Traveller Said at Sunset. John Greenleaf Whittier. CP-WhitJ

Shadows have their seasons, too, The. Penumbrae. John Updike. CP-UpdiJ

Shadows in his eye sockets like shades, The. Richmond. John Updike. CP-UpdiJ

Shadows in the room. Strange objects. The gladiolas on the coffee table, for instance. Survival as Tao, Beginning at 5:00 A.M. Hayden Carruth. CP-CarHS

Shadows of my chimneys stretch afar, The. Evening Shadows. Thomas Hardy. CP-HardT

Shadows of the ash-trees stride across the hay, The. Death of the Baron, The. D. H. Lawrence. CP-LawrD

Shadows of the banisters march march, The. Intimations of Mortality. Louis MacNeice. CP-MacNL

Shadows of the Burning. Marge Piercy. SP-PierM

Shadows of the ships, The. Sketch. Carl Sandburg. CP-SandC

Shadows / Of too many nights of love, The. Soledad. Langston Hughes. CP-HughL; CP-HughL1

Shadows, on the far wall. Morning ("Shadows, on the far wall"). Robert Creeley. SP-CreeR

Shadows on the wall. Life Doesn't Frighten Me. Maya Angelou. SP-AngeM

Shadows round the inland sea, The. Lakeside, The. John Greenleaf Whittier. CP-WhitJ

Shadows Today. Christina Georgina Rossetti. CP-RosC2

Shadows today, while shadows show God's Will. Shadows Today. Christina Georgina Rossetti. CP-RosC2

Shadowy arch calling the clouds of the sun, A. Gold Leaf. Muriel Rukeyser. CP-RukeM

Shadowy daughter of Urthona stood before red Orc, The. America: A Prophecy. William Blake. CP-BlakW

Shadowy Room. James Schuyler. CP-SchuJ

Shadowy Waters, The. William Butler Yeats. CP-YeatW

Shadrach O'Leary. Edwin Arlington Robinson. CP-RobiE

Shadwell Stair. Wilfred Owen. CP-OwenW

Shady Creek. Peter Blue Cloud. SP-BlueP

Shady friend—for Torrid days, A. Emily Dickinson. CP-DickE

Shaft, The. John Ciardi. CP-CiarJ

Shaft, The. Charles Tomlinson. CP-TomlC; SP-TomlC

Shaft of paralyzed sunlight, The. Platonic Drowse. Robert Penn Warren. CP-WarrR

Shag-Bark Hickory. Carl Sandburg. CP-SandC

Shaggy and heavily natural, they stand. Horses, The. Jorge Guillén. CP-WilbR

Shah Abbas. Robert Browning. CP-BroR2

Shah Sandschar, whose lowest slave. "Anvari." CP-EmerR

Shake back your hair, O red-headed girl. Red-Headed Restaurant Cashier. Carl Sandburg. CP-SandC

Shake hands, we shall never be friends, all's over. A. E. Housman. CP-HousA

Shake of the electric fan above our village; 1930's. Robert Lowell. SP-LoweR

Shake out the ruffle, turn and go. To a Hostess Saying Goodnight. James Wright. CP-WrigJ

Shake, Well Before Using. Hayden Carruth. CP-CarHS

Shake your brown feet, honey. Song for a Banjo Dance. Langston Hughes. CP-HughL; CP-HughL1

Shaken, / The blossoms of lilac. Follies. Carl Sandburg. CP-SandC

Shaker. James Schuyler. CP-SchuJ

Shaker, Why Don't You Sing? Maya Angelou. SP-AngeM

Shakespeare. Matthew Arnold. SP-ArnoM

Shakespeare in Harlem. Langston Hughes. CP-HughL; CP-HughL2

Shakespeare in Vietnam. Robert Stock. SP-StocR

Shakespeare knew Lust by day. Tale of Modernity. Laura Riding Jackson. CP-RidiL

Shakespeare Memorial, The. G. K. Chesterton. CP-ChesG

Shakespeare Say. Rita Dove. SP-DoveR

Shakespeare!—to such name's sounding, what succeeds. Names, The. Robert Browning. CP-BroR2; SP-BroR

Shakespeare, whose life once filled an English home. On the Three Hundredth Anniversary of Shakespeare's Birthday. Jones Very. CP-VeryJ

Shakespearean Cycle, A. Marya Alexandrovna Zaturenska. SP-ZatuM

Shakespearean fish swam the sea, far away from land. Three Movements. William Butler Yeats. CP-YeatW

Shakespeare's Grave. Robinson Jeffers. CP-JefR2

Shaking the head from / side to side, arms. Animal, The. Robert Creeley. CP-CreeR

Shakspere-Bacon's Cipher. Walt Whitman. CP-WhitW

Shakspere. Gerard Manley Hopkins. CP-HopkG

Shaky Spectrum. Gregory Orr. SP-OrrG

Shal I come, if I swim? wide are the waves, you see. Thomas Campion. See Shall I come, if I swim? wide are the waves, you see

Shale and water thrown together so-so first of all, The. Jug. Carl Sandburg. CP-SandC

Shalimar Gardens. Carolyn Kizer. CP-KizeC

Shall Christ hang on the Cross, and we not look? Behold the Man! Christina Georgina Rossetti. CP-RosC2

Shall college suppers be forgot. Song Composed by Mr. J. Very, to be Sung at the Class-Supper of the Sophomore Class of 1834, A. Jones Very. CP-VeryJ

Shall Earth no more inspire thee. Emily Jane Brontë. CP-BronE

Shall Gods Be Said to Thump The Clouds. Dylan Thomas. CP-ThomD

Shall hearts that beat no base retreat. Enthusiast, The. Herman Melville. SP-MelvH

Shall I a daily Begger be. Begger, The. Robert Herrick. CP-HerrR

Shall I again have Lilac week? George Meredith. CP-MerG2

Shall I be prisoner till my pulses stop. Edna St. Vincent Millay. CP-MillE

Shall I be punished more severely. Fate of Actaeon, The. James Laughlin. CP-LaugJ

Shall I begin with Ah, or Oh? Ode: Secundum Artem, An. William Cowper. CP-CowpW

Shall I come, if I swim? wide are the waves, you see. Thomas Campion. CP-CampT

Shall I Come, Sweet Love. Thomas Campion. CP-CampT

Shall I counsel the moon in her ascending? Song of Ruark to Bhanavar the Beautiful. George Meredith. CP-MerG2

Shall I despise you that your colourless tears. To a Young Girl. Edna St. Vincent Millay. CP-MillE

Shall I Forget? Christina Georgina Rossetti. CP-RosC1

Shall I go all my bright days singing. Self Criticism. Countee Cullen. CP-CullC

Shall I go to love and tell. To Electra. Robert Herrick. CP-HerrR

Shall I leave you behind me. Tragedian to Tragedienne. Thomas Hardy. CP-HardT

Shall I let myself be caught. Pygmalion. "H. D." CP-DoolH

Shall I, [(]like an hermit[)], dwell. *Unknown, sometimes at.* to Sir Walter Ralegh. CP-RaleW

Shall I, Like an Hermit, Dwell. Sir Walter Ralegh. CP-RaleW

Shall I love God for causing me to be? Proof, The. Richard Wilbur. CP-WilbR

Shall I make a record of your beauty? My Beloved. Langston Hughes. CP-HughL; CP-HughL1

Shall I never make him look at me again? As a World Would Have It. Edwin Arlington Robinson. CP-RobiE

Shall I say how it is in your clothes? How It Is. Maxine W. Kumin. SP-KumiM

Shall I say, I have gone at dusk through narrow streets. Prufrock's Pervigilium. T. S. Eliot. SP-ElioT *Fr.* Love Song of J. Alfred Prufrock, The.

Shall I say the world has narrowed since my youth? Narrow Hemisphere, The. Marya Alexandrovna Zaturenska. SP-ZatuM

Shall I sonnet-sing you about myself? House. Robert Browning. CP-BroR2; SP-BroR

Shall I stroke your thighs. "I Would Not Change For Thine." William Carlos Williams. CP-WilW2

Shall I Subsume. Hart Crane. CP-CranH

Shall I take thee, the Poet said. Emily Dickinson. CP-DickE

Shall I tell you again the new word. New Word, The. D. H. Lawrence. CP-LawrD

Shall I tell you of my old, old dreams. Pictures to the Wall. Langston Hughes. CP-HughL; CP-HughL1

Shall I tell you the signs of a New Age coming? New Age, The. Stevie Smith. CP-SmitS

Shall I tell you, then, how it is? Shades. D. H. Lawrence. CP-LawrD

Shall I then hope when faith is fled? Thomas Campion. CP-CampT

Shall I then silent be, or shall I speake? Sonnet 43. Edmund Spenser. CP-Spens *Fr.* Amoretti.

Shall not the Judge of all the earth do right? Christina Georgina Rossetti. CP-RosC2

Shall she never out of my mind. Sir Thomas Wyatt. CP-WyatT

Shall the Good Go Down? Langston Hughes. CP-HughL; CP-HughL2

Shall the Muse sing for thousands & not sing. Ralph Waldo Emerson. CP-EmerR

Shall then a traiterous kis or a smile. Thomas Campion *and* Philip Rosseter. CP-CampT

Shall we address it. Birthday, A. Robert Creeley. CP-CreeR

Shall we assume that the world. To Poets' Worksheets in the Air-Conditioned Vault of a Library. Mona Van Duyn. SP-VanDM

"Shall we come back?" the gamblers asked. Rakeoff and the Getaway, The. Carl Sandburg. CP-SandC

Shall we conceal the Case, or tell it. Problem, The. Thomas Hardy. CP-HardT

Shall we have peace my soul. Question, The. Marya Alexandrovna Zaturenska. SP-ZatuM

Shall we let go. To Let Go Or to Hold on—? D. H. Lawrence. CP-LawrD

Shall we roam, my love. To the Queen of My Heart. Percy Bysshe Shelley. CP-ShelP

Shall we turn from the mysterious dark with the pagan prayer and spell. Idolatry. G. K. Chesterton. CP-ChesG

Shall we win at love or shall we lose. Hôtel Transylvanie. Frank O'Hara. SP-OharF

Shallot, A. Richard Wilbur. CP-WilbR

Shallow folds of the wood, The. Woods in Spring. Gerard Manley Hopkins. CP-HopkG

Shallow or deep, snows on Soracte won't. To an American Classicist. Donald Davie. CP-DaviDC

Shallow Pool, The. Tennessee Williams. CP-WillT

Shallow stream, from fountains, A. Voyage of the Jettie. John Greenleaf Whittier. CP-WhitJ

Shallows, brighter, The. Pier: Under Pisces, The. James Merrill. SP-MerrJ

Shalom. Denise Levertov. SP-LeveDP

Shalott. Ezra Pound. CP-PoEar

Shame. Arthur Rimbaud. CP-RimbA, *tr. by* Martin Sorrell

Shame. Richard Wilbur. CP-WilbR

Shame. C. K. Williams. SP-WillC

Shame, The. Robert Creeley. CP-CreeR

Shame checks our first attempts, but then 'tis proved. Sins Loathed, and Yet Loved. Robert Herrick. CP-HerrR

Shame in my heart, I stand among the agates. At the Tomb of the Czech Kings. Jaroslav Seifert. SP-SeifJ, *tr. by* Ewald Osers

Shame is the shawl of Pink. Emily Dickinson. CP-DickE

Shame, No Statist. Robert Herrick. CP-HerrR

Shame of mans face is no more, The. Another. Robert Herrick. CP-HerrR

Shame of thy mother soyle! ill-nurtur'd tree! Out of Horace. Horace. CP-CrasR *Fr.* Odes.

Shame on this faithless heart! that could allow. Oxford, May Thirtieth, Eighteen Twenty. William Wordsworth. CP-WorW2

Shame on You. Langston Hughes. CP-HughL; CP-HughL3

Shameful Profession, The. James Laughlin. CP-LaugJ

Shamelessly, Endlessly Sinning. Aleksandr Aleksandrovich Blok. SP-BlokA, *tr. by* Peter France *and* Jon Stallworthy

Shampoo, The. Elizabeth Bishop. CP-BishE

Shane O'Neill's Cairn. Robinson Jeffers. CP-JefR2

Shang Cup. Louis Zukofsky. CP-ZukLS

Shang Dynasty Oracle Bone 2 Say. Charles Olson. CP-OlsoC

Shank of the afternoon, wan weight-light. Deep Measure. Charles Wright. SP-WrigCN

Shan't be winding. Later ("Shan't be winding"). Robert Creeley. SP-CreeR

Shantung[, or The Empire of China is Crumbling Down]. Nicholas Vachel Lindsay. CP-LindV

Shapcot, to thee the Fairy [*or* faery] State. Oberon's Feast. Robert Herrick. CP-HerrR

Shape of My Tongue, The. Jelaluddin Rumi. SP-Rumi, *tr. by* Coleman Barks

Shape of the Coroner, The. Wallace Stevens. CP-StevWP

Shape of the Fire, The. Theodore Roethke. CP-RoetT

Shape of the world is either a box or a bag, The. Atlas, How Have You Been? Carl Sandburg. CP-SandC

Shape the lips to an *o*, say *a*. Ö. Rita Dove. SP-DoveR

Shapely. David Ignatow. SP-IgnaD

Shapes. Kenneth Patchen. CP-PatcK

Shapes and Intensities of This Man, This Confucius, The. Kenneth Patchen. CP-PatcK

Shapes and Shadows. Derek Mahon. CP-MahoD

Shapes of change take their time, The. Man the Moon Shooter. Carl Sandburg. CP-SandC

Shapes of Leaves, The. Arthur Sze. SP-SzeA

Shapeshifter Poems. Lucille Clifton. SP-ClifL

Shard of History, A. James Laughlin. CP-LaugJ

Sharded in black, like beetles. Old Ladies' Home. Sylvia Plath. CP-PlatS

Share-Croppers. Langston Hughes. CP-HughL; CP-HughL2

Sharecropper's wife, The. Birthday Song. Yusef Komunyakaa. CP-KomuY

Sharing his exile that hath borne the flame. Fifine Answers. Ezra Pound. CP-PoEar

Sharing It With Angels. Robert Stock. SP-StocR

Sharing what sharing quickly who. Knock. James Dickey. CP-DickJ

Shark, The. Ogden Nash. CP-NashO

Shark Meat. Gary Snyder. CP-SnydG

Shark, when he goes to any publick feast. Upon Shark. Robert Herrick. CP-HerrR

Shark's Parlor, The. James Dickey. CP-DickJ

Sharm A-Sheikh. Yehuda Amichai. SP-AmicYL, *tr. by* Benjamin Harshav *and* Barbara Harshav

Sharp and silent in the. Heavy Date. W. H. Auden. CP-AudeW

Sharp in My Heart. Kenneth Rexroth. CP-RexrK

Sharp is the night, but stars with frost alive. Winter Heavens. George Meredith. CP-MerG1

Sharp Lookout. A. R. Ammons. CP-AmmoA

Sharp Ridge, The. Robert Graves. CP-GravR

Sharp shot at the zig-, A. In the Style of Filippo De Pisis, on Sending Him This Book. Eugenio Montale. CP-MontE, *tr. by* Jonathan Galassi

Shattered water made a misty din, The. Once by the Pacific. Robert Frost. CP-FrosR

Shave, water, scrub, and sweep the rink. Zamboni's Law. Wyatt Prunty. SP-PrunW

Shaving at Night. Charles Simic. SP-SimiC; SP-SimiCE

Shaving Mirror. John Updike. CP-UpdiJ

Shaving the Graveyard. Thomas Lux. SP-LuxT

Shaving without a mirror. W. S. Merwin. SP-MerwWF

She. Margaret Atwood. SP-AtwM2

She. Ted Berrigan. SP-BerrT

She. James McMichael. SP-McMiJ

She. Charles Olson. CP-OlsoC

She. Theodore Roethke. CP-RoetT

She. Richard Wilbur. CP-WilbR

She, a beautician, came to see her friend. Beautician, The. Thom Gunn. CP-

GunnT

She, a woman of abrupt features. Ruby Daggett. Richard Eberhart. CP-EberR

She alters all our lives for the better, merely. She (Not to be confused with she, a girl). Ted Berrigan. SP-BerrT

She always had to burn a light. Five Nocturnes. Robert Frost. CP-FrosR

She always said "tu" in such a way. Dark Portrait, A. Lawrence Ferlinghetti. SP-FerlL

She and the Muse. Denise Levertov. SP-LeveDL; SP-LeveDS

She answers the bothersome telephone, takes the message, forgets the message, forgets who called. Alzheimer's: The Wife. C. K. Williams. SP-WillC

She appeared in Triad—Youth, Truth, Beauty. Tousled Pillow. Robert Graves. CP-GravR

She arrives at the volcano almost dead. Heroine, The. William Dickey. SP-DickW

She Asks Me. James Laughlin. CP-LaugJ

She at His Funeral. Thomas Hardy. CP-HardT

She bade me follow to her garden, where. Snap-Dragon. D. H. Lawrence. CP-LawrD

She bade the moon stand still. Two Moon Fantasies. Carl Sandburg. CP-SandC

She-Bear, The. Charles Olson. CP-OlsoC

She-Bear (II), The. Charles Olson. CP-OlsoC

She began to think that jealousy was only an excuse, a front, for something even more rapacious. Image, The. C. K. Williams. SP-WillC

She being Brand, E, E, Cummings. CP-CummE; SP-CummE

She believed herself to have gone through tall gateways. Rose Bawn. Carl Sandburg. CP-SandC

She bent over the side of the bed. Promise, The. Charles Bukowski. SP-BukC1

She bent so low. Morning at the Zagorsk Monastery Outside Moscow. Miller Williams. CP-WillM

She Bitches About Boys. Marilyn Hacker. SP-HackM

She blinks above her sunglasses at the man. Everything Is Fine Here. How Are You? Miller Williams. CP-WillM

She bore it till the simple veins. Emily Dickinson. CP-DickE

She bound her green sleeve on my helm. Dante Gabriel Rossetti. CW-RossD

She brings a drink to the table. Waitress, The. Billy Collins. SP-CollB

She by a sycamore. Stephen and Barberie. Gerard Manley Hopkins. CP-HopkG

She by the river sate, and sitting there. Another upon Her Weeping. Robert Herrick. CP-HerrR

She came among us from the South. Enrica, 1865. Christina Georgina Rossetti. CP-RosC1

She came and stood in the Old South Church. In the "Old South." John Greenleaf Whittier. CP-WhitJ

She came crying down to me. Summer Memory in the Crowded City, A. James Wright. CP-WrigJ

She came every morning to draw water. Drink of Water, A. Seamus Heaney. SP-HeanSO

She Came from The Uttermost Part of the Earth. Christina Georgina Rossetti. CP-RosC2

She came home running. Mothering Blackness, The. Maya Angelou. SP-AngeM

She Came in from the Frost. Aleksandr Aleksandrovich Blok. SP-BlokA, tr. by Peter France and Jon Stallworthy

She came in from the snowing air. Ice. Stephen Spender. CP-SpenS

She Came Out of the Bathroom With Her Flaming Red Hair and Said—. Charles Bukowski. SP-BukC1

She came—she is gone—we have met. Catharina. William Cowper. CP-CowpW

She came to me in a dazzling guise. Werewife, The. James Whitcomb Riley. CP-RileJ

She came to me in the middle of winter. Nell's Circular Poem. Christopher Logue. SP-LoguC

She can be as wise as we. Marian: "She can be as wise as we." George Meredith. CP-MerG1

She cannot leave it alone. New Toy, The. Thomas Hardy. CP-HardT

She carefully wrapped an egg in each sock. Life on Film of St. Theresa, The. Andrei Codrescu. SP-CodrA

She carried a heavy load, but. No Single Thing by Itself. Clarence Major. SP-MajoC

She carried books. Margaret Fuller. Lorine Niedecker. CP-NiedL

She carries her handkerchief, her gloves. Faded. Randall Jarrell. CP-JarrR

She Charged Me. Thomas Hardy. CP-HardT

She cleaned house, and then lay down long. Secret Gratitude, A. James Wright. CP-WrigJ

She comes as in a dream with west wind eggs. Poem in the Modern Manner. Ted Berrigan. SP-BerrT Fr. Sonnets, The.

She comes at eleven every morning. Rome: In the Café. James Laughlin. CP-LaugJ

She comes level with him at. Donahue's Sister. Thom Gunn. CP-GunnT

She comes to mind—no, is already there. Petrarch. CP-Petra, tr. by J. G. Nichols

She confessed to me. I Fall into It Without Trying. Charles Bukowski. SP-BukC3

She Considers Evading Him. Margaret Atwood. SP-AtwM1

She Contrasts with Herself Hippolyta. "H. D." CP-DoolH

She could bind the world's winds in a single strand. Rune of the Finland Woman. Marilyn Hacker. SP-HackM

She could hold me with stories, even. Present. Tess Gallagher. SP-GallT

She could not live upon the Past. Emily Dickinson. CP-DickE

She could tell he loved her. He wanted her there. If Ever There Was One. Miller Williams. CP-WillM

She cut my toenails the night before. 103 Degrees. Charles Bukowski. SP-BukC1

She dealt her pretty words like Blades. Emily Dickinson. CP-DickE

She-death, my green mother, you. Roman Dream. Jane Cooper. CP-CoopJ

She did not answer him again. Undine. Christina Georgina Rossetti. CP-RosC3

She did not know that she was dead. Dinah in Heaven. Rudyard Kipling. CP-KiplR

She Did Not Turn. Thomas Hardy. CP-HardT

She Didn't Even Wave. Ai. SP-Ai

She died at play, / Gambolled away. Emily Dickinson. CP-DickE

She died—this was the way she died. Vanished. Emily Dickinson. CP-DickE

She dipped snuff. Flowers for My Date. Clarence Major. SP-MajoC

She "Displains" It. James Whitcomb Riley. CP-RileJ

She does not place, relate, or name. Her Management. May Swenson. SP-SwenM

She does not want me to speak of her. Joy. Hans Magnus Enzensberger. SP-EnzeH

She doesn't come anymore to visit me in my dreams. She Walks No Longer in the Night. James Laughlin. CP-LaugJ

She dreamed long of waters. American Wedding. James Wright. CP-WrigJ

She dreams a landscape. On her chest. Picasso: "Dream." Oil 1932. May Swenson. SP-SwenM

She dreams the baby's so small she keeps. Motherhood. Rita Dove. SP-DoveR

She dreamt of a lady in light green. Conversation Galante. Charles Olson. CP-OlsoC

She drew back; he was calm. Subverted Flower, The. Robert Frost. CP-FrosR

She dried her tears, and they did smile. Emily Jane Brontë. CP-BronE

She drives into the parking lot while. Turnabout. Charles Bukowski. SP-BukC1

She dropped the bar, she shot the bolt, she fed the fire anew. Only Son, The. Rudyard Kipling. CP-KiplR

She dwelleth in the Ground. Emily Dickinson. CP-DickE

She dwelt among the untrodden ways. William Wordsworth. MW-WorW Fr. Lucy.

She even thinks that up in heaven. For a Lady I Know. Countee Cullen. CP-CullC Fr. Four Epitaphs.

She fanned herself with a violet fan. In a Spanish Tram-Car. D. H. Lawrence. CP-LawrD

She fears him, and will always ask. Eros Turannos. Edwin Arlington Robinson. CP-RobiE

She fell asleep among the flowers. Watchers, The. Christina Georgina Rossetti. CP-RosC3

She fell asleep on Christmas Eve: / At length the long-ungranted shade. My Sister's Sleep. Dante Gabriel Rossetti. CW-RossD

She finally found a place they couldn't find. Deadsong for a Neighbor Child Who Ran Away to the Woods. Miller Williams. CP-WillM

She fluted with her mouth as when one sips. Beauty and the Bird. Dante Gabriel Rossetti. CW-RossD

She folds the four corners into the center. Red Octopus. Arthur Sze. SP-SzeA

She foots it forward down the town. Third Kissing-Gate, The. Thomas Hardy. CP-HardT

She gave a rose. She Gave Me a Rose. Paul Laurence Dunbar. CP-DunbP

She gave me a drink and told me she had tried. At Least with Good Whiskey. John Ciardi. CP-CiarJ

She Gave Me a Rose. Paul Laurence Dunbar. CP-DunbP

She gave me childhood's flowers. Heirloom. Kathleen Jessie Raine. SP-RainK

She gave me the car and two. Hope. Raymond Carver. CP-CarvR

She gave me the flowers—. In Maceio. Tess Gallagher. SP-GallT

She gave up beauty in her tender youth. Portrait, A. Christina Georgina Rossetti. CP-RosC1

She gave with joy her virgin breast. Translation of a Passage in Ottfried's Metrical Paraphrase of the Gospel. Samuel Taylor Coleridge. CP-ColeS

She gives him his eyes, she found them. Bride and Groom Lie Hidden for Three Days. Ted Hughes. SP-HughTN

She gives most dangerous sight. For a Marriage. Louise Bogan. CP-BogaL

She-Goat. D. H. Lawrence. CP-LawrD

She got out of the car here one day. Emily, this Place, and You. William Stafford. SP-StafWW

She grew old. Death Psalm: O Lord of Mysteries. Denise Levertov. SP-LeveDL

She grew so big and sad. Season of Recognition. Yehuda Amichai. SP-AmicYL, tr. by Benjamin Harshav and Barbara Harshav

She grew up in bedeviled southern wilderness. Ballad of Sue Ellen Westerfield,

The. Robert Earl Hayden. CP-HaydR

She grew where every spring. Lorine Niedecker. CP-NiedL

She had a box. Love Beyond Keeping. Carl Sandburg. CP-SandC

She had a coarse and common grace. Homo Sum, Nihil Humani—. Arthur Hugh Clough. SP-ClouA

She had a little time to think. Leda Reconsidered. Mona Van Duyn. SP-VanDM

She had a secret—bonny Bess! George Meredith. CP-MerG2

She had a tall man's height or more. Beggars. William Wordsworth. CP-WorW1

She had a trick that she liked. Hand Trick, The. James Laughlin. CP-LaugJ

She had already kissed Antony's dead lips. Cleopatra. Anna Andreyevna Akhmatova. CP-KunSC, tr. by Max Hayward and Stanley Kunitz

She had amid her ringlets bound. Treachery. Walter De la Mare. CP-DeLaW

She had come, like the river. Eternity. William Carlos Williams. CP-WilW2

She Had Concealed Him in a Deep Dark Cave. Kenneth Patchen. CP-PatcK

She had her feet in the trough. Immolatus. Yusef Komunyakaa. CP-KomuY

She had huge thighs. Place Didn't Look Bad, The. Charles Bukowski. SP-BukC1

She had one with a foreskin and. Esthetics of Circumcision, The. Alan Dugan. CP-DugaA

She had quickly learned to show. Tanck's Song About Women. Hayden Carruth. CP-CarHS Fr. Songs About What Comes Down: The Complete Works of Mr. Septic Tanck.

She had slept with greatness, and its shadows troubled. Empress Marie Louise, The. Marya Alexandrovna Zaturenska. SP-ZatuM

She had that softness which is falsity. E. E. Cummings. CP-CummE

She had thought the studio would keep itself. Living in Sin. Adrienne Rich. SP-RicA1

She had too much so with a smile you took some. Other, The. Ted Hughes. SP-HughTN

She had tumult of the brain. Lorine Niedecker. CP-NiedL

She had wealth of mornings in her year. Ralph Waldo Emerson. CP-EmerR

She has a husband, he a wife. Modern Love. James Vincent Cunningham. CP-CunnJ

She has been condemned to death by hanging. Marrying the Hangman. Margaret Atwood. SP-AtwM2

She has dreams of wolves it bewilders. Landscape Without Touch. Olga Broumas. SP-BrouO

She has finished and sealed the letter. Parting, without a Sequel. John Crowe Ransom. SP-RansJ

She has no need to fear the fall. Portrait. Louise Bogan. CP-BogaL

She has returned, she has returned. Morning. Gabriela Mistral. SP-MistG, tr. by Maria Giachetti [or Jacketti]

She has the shakes, thinks she's gonna die. Mother Junkie. Clarence Major. SP-MajoC

She hastens out and scarcely pins her clothes. Scandal. John Clare. SP-ClarJ

She hath the apple in her hand for thee. Venus Verticordia. Dante Gabriel Rossetti. CW-RossD

She hears a hermit laughing. To a Young Woman Dying at Weir. Norman Dubie. CP-DubiN

She hears me strike the board and say. Father and Child. William Butler Yeats. CP-YeatW

She Hears The Storm. Thomas Hardy. CP-HardT

She held it out. "But you can't both have it," she said. Hatband, The. Thomas Hardy. CP-HardT

She Hid in the Trees from the Nurses. James Wright. CP-WrigJ

She hideth Her the last. Emily Dickinson. CP-DickE

She holds a lily in her hand. Within the Veil. Christina Georgina Rossetti. CP-RosC3

She, I, and They. Thomas Hardy. CP-HardT

She, / In the dark. Helen Keller. Langston Hughes. CP-HughL; CP-HughL1

She Is. Robert Creeley. SP-CreeR

She is a thing too frail to know. Ezra Pound. CP-PoEar

She is a winsome wee thing. My Wife's a Winsome Wee Thing. Robert Burns. CP-BurnR

She is all there. For My Lover, Returning to His Wife. Anne Sexton. CP-SextA; SP-SextA

She is always two blue eyes. She. Ted Berrigan. SP-BerrT

She is as in a field a silken tent. Silken Tent, The. Robert Frost. CP-FrosR

She Is Away [or Marthe Away (She Is Away)]. Kenneth Rexroth. CP-RexrK

She is completely white with an ancient headdress and amber talons. Owl, An. Gabriela Mistral. SP-MistG, tr. by Maria Giachetti [or Jacketti]

She is dead. "H. D." CP-DoolH Fr. Electra-Orestes.

She is devout and plump, but not happy. Baroque Gravure, A. Thomas Merton. CP-MertT

She is eighty and writes in her memoir. Example. Czeslaw Milosz. CP-MiloCN, tr. by Robert Hass

She is foremost of those that I would hear praised. Her Praise. William Butler Yeats. CP-YeatW

She is gamesome and good. Nature 2. Ralph Waldo Emerson. CP-EmerR

She is harnessed for a long journey; on her back she carried an entire store of wool. Alpaca, The. Gabriela Mistral. SP-MistG, tr. by Maria Giachetti [or Jacketti]

She is just leaving the room. S. Eliason 66: Double Portrait of Emily Dickinson and the Rev. Charles Wadsworth. Jane Cooper. CP-CoopJ

She is large and matronly. Lui et Elle. D. H. Lawrence. CP-LawrD

She is like that man. Mission with the Night, A. Jane Cooper. CP-CoopJ

She is listening and writing. Scribe, The. James Laughlin. CP-LaugJ

She is lying on my outstretched arm. Harrowed by These Apprehensions He Resolved to Commit Himself to the Mercy of the Storm. Kenneth Patchen. CP-PatcK

She is making stuffing for the turkey. Shuttle. Arthur Sze. SP-SzeA

She is neither pink nor pale. Witch-Wife. Edna St. Vincent Millay. CP-MillE

She Is No Liar. Robert Graves. CP-GravR

She is no longer the argumentative type of campus radical. Portrait of a Lady. Alan Dugan. CP-DugaA

She is not easy to see. She wears. Virginia Woolf Gathers Mushrooms. William Dickey. SP-DickW

She is not Folly—that I know. Playmate, The. Rudyard Kipling. CP-KiplR

She is not Indian, she's ill. To a Lady in a Train. Stevie Smith. CP-SmitS

She is now water and air. Sea Burial from the Cruiser Reve. Richard Eberhart. CP-EberR

She is out for her daily health / walk she is nicely dressed in a. To Smile or Not to Smile. James Laughlin. CP-LaugJ

She Is Overheard Singing. Edna St. Vincent Millay. CP-MillE

She is painting an eye on the side of the hill. We watch her through binoculars. Lady Painter, The. Andrei Codrescu. SP-CodrA

She Is So Practical. James Laughlin. CP-LaugJ

She is standing on my lids. Lady Love. Paul Éluard. CP-BecksS, tr. by Samuel Beckett

She is struggling through grass-mesh—not flying. Cranefly in September, A. Ted Hughes. SP-HughTN

She is sweet and soft-throated. Decision, A. D. H. Lawrence. CP-LawrD

She is the darkness where I wander. Madrigal: "She is the darkness where I wander." Howard Nemerov. CP-NemeH

She is the knife-thrower's lady. On a Professional Couple in a Side-Show. Alan Dugan. CP-DugaA

She is the Lane to the Indes. Emily Dickinson. SP-DickE

She is the one you call sister. Mirror in Which Two Are Seen as One, The. Adrienne Rich. SP-RicA2

She is the prettiest of creatures. Kenneth Patchen. CP-PatcK

She is walking home from the post. God Bless America! James Laughlin. CP-LaugJ

She is weeping for her lost right arm. Weeping Woman. Denise Levertov. SP-LeveDL

She just shot him, in the Daily News. Cop-Shooting: On a Newspaper Photograph. Alan Dugan. CP-DugaA

She keeps her clavichord. Clavichord, The. May Sarton. SP-SartM

She kept her songs, they took so little space. Love Songs in Age. Philip Larkin. CP-LarkP

She kiltit up her kirtle weel. On the Duchess of Gordon's Reel Dancing. Robert Burns. CP-BurnR

She kneels on the floor, snip snip. Sew. Donald Hall. CP-HallD

She knows, like Ophelia. Prospero and Sycorax. Ted Hughes. SP-HughTN

She knows / The end of the evening will come. Lady in Cabaret. Langston Hughes. CP-HughL; CP-HughL1

She laid her docile Crescent down. Emily Dickinson. CP-DickE

She lay as if at play. Emily Dickinson. CP-DickE

She lay late in bed. Maybe she was sick. My Mother's R & R. Galway Kinnell. SP-KinnGN

She lay like a book. Hayden Carruth. CP-CarHS Fr. Clay Hill Anthology, The.

She lay very still in bed with stubborn eyes. Suppressed Complex. T. S. Eliot. SP-ElioT

She lays her hand on his shoulder. Memory 2. Raymond Carver. CP-CarvR

She leans across a golden table. Epitaph: "She leans across a golden table." Countee Cullen. CP-CullC

She left me at the silent time. Lines Written in the Bay of Lerici. Percy Bysshe Shelley. CP-ShelP

She let her golden ball fall down the well. Frog and the Golden Ball, The. Robert Graves. CP-GravR

She lies, her head beneath her knees. La Belle au Bois Dormant. Randall Jarrell. CP-JarrR

She lies, hip high. George Oppen. CP-OppGN

She lies in the grass and spreads her golden hair. Rebecca at Play. Miller Williams. CP-WillM

She lies on her left side her flank golden. Landscape as a Nude. Archibald MacLeish. CP-MacLA

She lies under July, a blue towel. Sunbather. Yusef Komunyakaa. CP-KomuY

She liked mornings the best—Thomas gone. Weathering Out. Rita Dove. SP-

DoveR

She liked the blue drapes. They made a star. Couple in the Next Room, The. John Ashbery. SP-AshbJ

She likes to split an apple down the middle. About Poetry. William Meredith. SP-MereW

She listened like a cushat dove. Listening. Christina Georgina Rossetti. CP-RosC3

She listened to his voice urgently pleading. What Did You Say? Robert Graves. CP-GravR

She listens, listens, holding. Servant-Girl at Emmaus (A Painting by Velazquez), The. Denise Levertov. SP-LeveDS

She lived in Galveston and was into. T.M. Charles Bukowski. SP-BukC1

She lived in sinful happiness. Girl. Langston Hughes. CP-HughL; CP-HughL2

She lived in storm and strife. That the Night Come. William Butler Yeats. CP-YeatW

She lived out a decent span of years. Departure. Langston Hughes. CP-HughL; CP-HughL3

She loitered to heed his heart's pouring-out. Cold Colloquy. Robert Penn Warren. CP-WarrR

She looked like a bird from a cloud. At the Word "Farewell." Thomas Hardy. CP-HardT

She looked over his shoulder. Shield of Achilles, The. W. H. Auden. CP-AudeW

She looks at me you're. Luck. Grace Paley. CP-PalGC

She Looks Back. D. H. Lawrence. CP-LawrD

She looks far west towards Carmel, shading her eyes with her hand. Evening in Galilee, An. Thomas Hardy. CP-HardT

She looks from the window: still it pours down direly. Henley Regatta. Thomas Hardy. CP-HardT

She Loves. Olga Broumas. SP-BrouO

She loves blood-red poppies for a garden to walk in. Poppies. Carl Sandburg. CP-SandC

She loves him; for her infinite soul is Love. True Woman (Her Love). Dante Gabriel Rossetti. CW-RossD Fr. House of Life, The.

She loves me or loves me not. Song: "She loves me or loves me not." Wallace Stevens. CP-StevWP

She made him a roof with her hands. Fourth Psalm: The Cerements. W. S. Merwin. SP-MerwW

She mark'd where I and Fabian met. Continuation of R. Garnett's Nix. Gerard Manley Hopkins. CP-HopkG

She marries the knight she loves. George Meredith. CP-MerG2

She mediates on how rocks rise. Thorn Merchant's Wife, The. Yusef Komunyakaa. CP-KomuY

She might have followed where our neighbours. To L. K. C. from G. K. C. G. K. Chesterton. CP-ChesG

She might, so noble from head. Thought from Propertius, A. William Butler Yeats. CP-YeatW

She, much more beautiful than others are. Petrarch. CP-Petra, tr. by J. G. Nichols

She must have all the flux and plenitude. Model for an Object in Z Space. Robert Stock. SP-StocR

She must have been kicked unseen or brushed by a car. Dog's Death. John Updike. CP-UpdiJ

She never comes to me. Ralph Waldo Emerson. CP-EmerR

She (Not to be confused with she, a girl). Ted Berrigan. SP-BerrT

She of the Dancing Feet Sings. Countee Cullen. CP-CullC

She of the shining eyes. Astonished Heart, The. Lawrence Ferlinghetti. SP-FerlL

She Opened the Door. Thomas Hardy. CP-HardT

She opened the window shutters, spread the bedsheets on the windowsill, saw the day. Morning. Yannis Ritsos. SP-RitsY, tr. by Kimon Friar

She Opens the Barn Door Every Morning. Carl Sandburg. CP-SandC

She packs the flower beds with leaves. For Fran. Philip Levine. SP-LeviP

She paints with white & red the moors. Ralph Waldo Emerson. CP-EmerR

She phoned me from a far away. Out of the Blue. Charles Bukowski. SP-BukC3

She poured herbal tea to soothe. Herbal Tea. Yehuda Amichai. SP-AmicYL, tr. by Benjamin Harshav and Barbara Harshav

She Prays for Her Husband, the Good Pastor, Lying on His Deathbed at Last. Miller Williams. CP-WillM

She pulled her dress off. Fuck. Charles Bukowski. SP-BukC1

She Rebukes Hippolyta. "H. D." CP-DoolH

She Revisits Alone the Church of Her Marriage. Thomas Hardy. CP-HardT

She rides her hips as. Mounted as an Amazon. William Carlos Williams. CP-WilW2

She rides in the park on a prancing bay. George Meredith. CP-MerG2

She rose as high as His Occasion. Emily Dickinson. CP-DickE

She Rose to His Requirement—Dropt. Emily Dickinson. CP-DickE

She rose to His Requirement—dropt. She Rose to His Requirement—Dropt. Emily Dickinson. CP-DickE

She rushed to meet him: the nurse following. Hector and Andromache. Homer. CP-BroEB Fr. Iliad, The.

She Said. Charles Bukowski. SP-BukC3

She Said. Alice Walker. CP-WalkA

She Said. Stevie Smith. CP-SmitS

She said, and for her lost Galanthis sighs. Fable of Dryope, The. Ovid. CP-PopeA Fr. Metamorphoses.

She Said as Well to Me. D. H. Lawrence. CP-LawrD

She said he was a man who cheated. Jack and Jill. James Vincent Cunningham. CP-CunnJ

She said I would see the future. What the Seer Said. Jane Cooper. CP-CoopJ

She said: "I'm god and all." Against a Sickness: To the Female Double Principle God. Alan Dugan. CP-DugaA

She Said in Apology. James Laughlin. CP-LaugJ

She said that underneath the surface. American Variation on How Rilke Loved a Princess and Got to Stay in Her Castle. Alan Dugan. CP-DugaA

She said to me, He lay there sleeping. Watchers, The. Muriel Rukeyser. CP-RukeM

She said: "When I was with him." She Said. Alice Walker. CP-WalkA

She said / you were a wonderful boy this evening. Boy His Mother, The. Grace Paley. CP-PalGC

She sang a song of May for me. Spring Song and a Later, A. James Whitcomb Riley. CP-RileJ

She sang alone, ere womanhood had known. Lydia H. Sigourney. John Greenleaf Whittier. CP-WhitJ

She sang, and I listened the whole song thro'. Remembered. Paul Laurence Dunbar. CP-DunbP

She sang beyond the genius of the sea. Idea of Order at Key West, The. Wallace Stevens. CP-StevW; CP-StevWP

She sat alway thro' the long day. Repining. Christina Georgina Rossetti. CP-RosC3

She sat and sang alway. Song: "She sat and sang alway." Christina Georgina Rossetti. CP-RosC1

She sat and sewed that hath done me the wrong. Sir Thomas Wyatt. CP-WyatT

She sat on a shelf. Motherhood. May Swenson. SP-SwenM

She sat upon a mountain. Rosalind. Christina Georgina Rossetti. CP-RosC3

She sat upon her Seven Hills. Jealousy. G. K. Chesterton. CP-ChesG

She saw herself a lady. Imaginings. Thomas Hardy. CP-HardT

She Saw Him, She Said. Thomas Hardy. CP-HardT

She says Go fuck yourself. Translating Footsteps. Yusef Komunyakaa. CP-KomuY

She says good-bye, she's sorry, she's signing off. E mail. Miller Williams. CP-WillM

She says he was. Story, A. Yusef Komunyakaa. CP-KomuY

She says, Into the dark. Michael Palmer. SP-PalmM

She says: Seek help! Ha-ha Ha-ha & Christ. No. John Berryman. CP-BerrJ

She Says She Lo'es Me Best of A'. Robert Burns. CP-BurnR

She Says That I Put on Gloves. James Laughlin. CP-LaugJ

She says, you are the negative. Michael Palmer. SP-PalmM

She scarce has a word for Papa. George Meredith. CP-MerG2

She Schools the Flighty Pupils of Her Eyes. Gerard Manley Hopkins. CP-HopkG

She Seemed to Know. James Laughlin. CP-LaugJ

She sends me news of bluejays, frost. Letter from Home, A. Mary Oliver. SP-OlivM

She serves me a piece of it a few minutes. My Daughter and Apple Pie. Raymond Carver. CP-CarvR

She Shall Be Brought unto the King. Christina Georgina Rossetti. CP-RosC2

She shall sing me a song. Song Composed for Fanny Burney, A. Samuel Johnson. CP-JohnS

She, she and she and she. Divestment of Beauty. Laura Riding Jackson. CP-RidiL

"She shoots up in the neck," she told. Junkies. Charles Bukowski. SP-BukC1

She should never have looked at me. Cristina. Robert Browning. CP-BroR1

She showed me her hair turning. Tourist. Yehuda Amichai. SP-AmicYL, tr. by Benjamin Harshav and Barbara Harshav

She shows up in every war. Night Muse & Mortar Round. Yusef Komunyakaa. CP-KomuY

She sights a Bird—she chuckles—. Cat. Emily Dickinson. CP-DickE

She sings by her wheel at that low cottage-door. Yankee Girl, The. John Greenleaf Whittier. CP-WhitJ

She sings the music. To a Poet. Philip Whalen. SP-WhalP

She sits dropping on a caret of clenched arms. E. E. Cummings. CP-CummE

She sits in her night-dress without the door. On the Doorstep. Thomas Hardy. CP-HardT

She sits in the dust at the walls. Noon Hour. Carl Sandburg. CP-SandC

She sits in the tawny vapour. Wife in London, A. Thomas Hardy. CP-HardT

She sits naked on a rock. Last Gods. Galway Kinnell. SP-KinnGN

She sits on the recreation ground. Reading a Letter. D. H. Lawrence. CP-LawrD

She sits up there. Gloomy Lady. Charles Bukowski. SP-BukC1

She sits with. Young Woman at a Window. William Carlos Williams. CP-WilW1

She sits with one hand poised against her head, the. Dialogue. Adrienne Rich. SP-RicA2

She skimmed the yellow water like a moth. My Grandmother's Ghost. James Wright. CP-WrigJ

She sleepeth: would ye wake her if ye could? O Death Where Is Thy Sting? Christina Georgina Rossetti. CP-RosC3

She sleeps not where the gladsome Earth. Lines To ———— On the Death of His Friend. Jones Very. CP-VeryJ

She sleeps on soft, last breaths; but no ghost looms. Kind Ghosts, The. Wilfred Owen. CP-OwenW

She slept beneath a tree. Emily Dickinson. CP-DickE

She slept she slept she blanketed. Landscape with Angels. Olga Broumas. SP-BrouO

She slumps in the booth, weeping. Phone Booth, The. Raymond Carver. CP-CarvR

She smiled as. Treatment, The. Charles Olson. CP-OlsoC

She sought the Studios, beckoning to her side. Heiress and Architect. Thomas Hardy. CP-HardT

She speaks always in her own voice. Portrait, The. Robert Graves. CP-GravR

She speaks with abandonment. Foreign Woman, The. Gabriela Mistral. SP-MistG, *tr. by* Maria Giachetti [*or* Jacketti]

She sped as Petals of a Rose. Emily Dickinson. CP-DickE

She sped through the door. Glimpse, The. Thomas Hardy. CP-HardT

She spends anxious hours. Rainer Maria Rilke. CP-RilkFr, *tr. by* A. Poulin, Jr. *Fr.* Windows, The.

She spoke, dwelling upon me from restraint. Now Are We Remembered. Robert Stock. SP-StocR

She springs from the ground-clinging thicket, her face. Veneris Venefica Agrestis. Lucio Piccolo. CP-TomlC, *tr. by* Charles Tomlinson

She staked her Feathers—Gained an Arc. Emily Dickinson. CP-DickE

She stands alone onstage. Where the Breath Is. Adam Zagajewski. SP-ZagaA

She stands as pale as Parian statues stand. Study (A Soul), A. Christina Georgina Rossetti. CP-RosC3

She stands at the foot of my bed and starts to speak. Woman in the Room, The. Miller Williams. CP-WillM

She stands between the trees and holds. She Hid in the Trees from the Nurses. James Wright. CP-WrigJ

She stands / In the quiet darkness. Troubled Woman. Langston Hughes. CP-HughL; CP-HughL1

She stands now, shy among the destinies. Maiden with Orb and Planets. Howard Nemerov. CP-NemeH

She stayed over after. Last Words of My Grandmother. William Carlos Williams. CP-WilW1

She Steals Birds. George Oppen. CP-OppGN

She stepped out of the framing circle of the dark. Coda, Overture. Eleanor Wilner. SP-WilnE

She steps into the dark swamp. Meeting, A. Mary Oliver. SP-OlivM

She still cries over that dead child. Dim House, Bright Face. Tess Gallagher. SP-GallT

She stole my pencil-case, red leather. Thief, The. Josephine Jacobsen. CP-JacoJ

She / stolen from my bone. Adam Thinking. Lucille Clifton. SP-ClifL

She stood against the kitchen sink, and looked. In the Home Stretch. Robert Frost. CP-FrosR

She stood at the window. There was / a sound, a light. Goodbye. Robert Creeley. CP-CreeR

She,straddling my lap. E. E. Cummings. CP-CummE

She sweeps the kitchen floor of the river bed her husband saw fit. Pomade. Rita Dove. SP-DoveR

She sweeps with many-colored Brooms. Evening. Emily Dickinson. CP-DickE

She talked of you before she went. Emily Dickinson. SP-DickE

She Talks to Her Sister, Briefly By on the Way to West Memphis. Miller Williams. CP-WillM

She taught him the gods. Was it teaching? He went on. Embrace, The. Louise Glück. SP-GlucL

She Tells Her Love While Half Asleep. Robert Graves. CP-GravR

She tells me. Mirror, The. James Tate. SP-TateJ

She tells: / Sing I chant I. Ballad Theme, A. Muriel Rukeyser. CP-RukeM

She that begs a little boon. Salome's Dancing-Lesson. Dorothy Parker. CP-ParkD

She that but little patience knew. On a Political Prisoner. William Butler Yeats. CP-YeatW

She that should most, perceiveth least. Sir Thomas Wyatt. CP-WyatT

She that winked her sandal fan. Wallace Stevens. CP-StevWP

She, then, like snow in a dark night. Like Snow. Robert Graves. CP-GravR

She thinks about skeletons. Daughter. Robert Pinsky. CP-PinsR

She thinks she was hurt this summer. Battered Wife, The. Donald Davie. CP-DaviDC

She thought, without the benefit of knowing. First Meeting with a Possible Mother-in-Law. Thom Gunn. CP-GunnT

She, Thus. Charles Olson. CP-OlsoC

She, to Him. Thomas Hardy. CP-HardT

She to Him. Robert Graves. CP-GravR

She Told Her Beads. Paul Laurence Dunbar. CP-DunbP

She told him, "You were in my dream last night." Realities. Howard Nemerov. CP-NemeH

She told how they used to form for the country dances. One We Knew. Thomas Hardy. CP-HardT

She told the story, and the whole world wept. Harriet Beecher Stowe. Paul Laurence Dunbar. CP-DunbP

She took from her basket four fishes. Fisherwoman, The. David Ignatow. SP-IgnaD

She troubles the waters, and they part and close. Carrier. William Meredith. SP-MereW

She turned in the high pew, until her sight. Church Romance, A. Thomas Hardy. CP-HardT

She turned round to me with her steadfast eyes. Last Answer, The. Christina Georgina Rossetti. CP-RosC3

She turns from the sink. Mary Farl Powers: *Pink Spotted Torso*. Paul Muldoon. CP-MuldP

She turns her head. She Who Turns Her Head. William Carlos Williams. CP-WilW1

She twankled a tune on her light guitar. Her Light Guitar. James Whitcomb Riley. CP-RileJ

She twists scraps of her hair in unshelled snails. Marilyn Hacker. SP-HackM *Fr.* Taking Notice.

She used to come and comfort me in sleep. Petrarch. CP-Petra, *tr. by* J. G. Nichols

She wakes having flown. Aubade: "She wakes having flown." Olga Broumas. SP-BrouO

She walked alone, as she did every morning. Spy. Rita Dove. SP-DoveR

She walked in flowers around my field. Ralph Waldo Emerson. CP-EmerR

She walks beside the river. Two Ghosts Together. Kenneth Patchen. CP-PatcK

She walks in beauty like a lake. Bed, The. Robert Creeley. CP-CreeR

She walks in Beauty like the night. Lord Byron. CP-Byron

She walks in while. Writing Is a State of Trance. Charles Bukowski. SP-BukC3

She Walks No Longer in the Night. James Laughlin. CP-LaugJ

She walks. This never has. What the Hell, Rage, Give in to Natural Graces. Alan Dugan. CP-DugaA

She wanted a little room for thinking. Daystar. Rita Dove. SP-DoveR

She wanted to float free. Floating Free. James Laughlin. CP-LaugJ

She wants to hear. Sunday Greens. Rita Dove. SP-DoveR

She was a fair young girl, yet on her brow. Fair Quakeress, The. John Greenleaf Whittier. CP-WhitJ

She Was a Good Little Wife. D. H. Lawrence. CP-LawrD

She was a modern, you know. Big House, The. William Stafford. SP-StafWW

She was a mourner too. Now she's gone. Lorine Niedecker. CP-NiedL

She was a Phantom of delight. William Wordsworth. CP-WorW1

She was a short one. Sleep. Charles Bukowski. SP-BukC2

She was a symphony of silent smokes. Portrait of a Lady. Kenneth Rexroth. CP-RexrK

She was a vagrant in my heart. Vagrant, The. James Laughlin. CP-LaugJ

She was afraid of men. Chicken-Licken. Maya Angelou. SP-AngeM

She was alive in me upon a time. Petrarch. CP-Petra, *tr. by* J. G. Nichols

She was all of her airs and, for all of her airs. One of Those Hibiscuses of Damozels. Wallace Stevens. CP-StevWP

She was an agèd woman; and the years. Tale of Society As It Is, A: From Facts, 1811. Percy Bysshe Shelley. CP-ShelP

She was as sweet as violets in the Spring. Dirge, A. Christina Georgina Rossetti. CP-RosC3

She was brought up manly for a woman. As If It Happened. Tess Gallagher. SP-GallT

She was cleaning—there is always. Black Silk. Tess Gallagher. SP-GallT

She was cut-luggit, painch-lippit. Auld Man's Mare's Dead, The. Robert Burns. CP-BurnR

She was false, and he was true. Life Term, A. James Whitcomb Riley. CP-RileJ

She was fifteen—had great eyes. Robert Browning. CP-BroR2

She was given crystal flesh for a home. Variations on a Theme. Carl Sandburg. CP-SandC

She was, Grandfather said, *a fly-by-night*. Hattie Bloom. Mary Oliver. SP-OlivM

She was grandma to everyone. Grandma Marie Potts. Peter Blue Cloud. SP-BlueP

She was herself, not his, not anything. Archibald MacLeish. CP-MacLA *Fr.* Happy Marriage, The.

She was in a window mood that day. Rainer Maria Rilke. CP-RilkFr, *tr. by* A. Poulin, Jr. *Fr.* Windows, The.

She was in every way a delect- / able bundle an enticement to. Apotropaic Decision, An. James Laughlin. CP-LaugJ

She was in terrible pain the whole day. Wedding, A. James Tate. SP-TateJ

She was into her forties, her daughter slick, sly, and no good. Prognosis: A Short Story, the End of Which You Will Know Soon Enough. Robert Penn Warren. CP-WarrR

She was less than scantily dressed. First Night. Arthur Rimbaud. CP-RimbA, *tr. by* Martin Sorrell

She was most like a rose, when it flushes rarest. Gone Before. Christina Georgina Rossetti. CP-RosC3

"She was," my father said (in an aside). From My Diary. Stephen Spender. CP-SpenS

She was my sister through the hours that fly. It Is Not Well for Man to Be Alone. G. K. Chesterton. CP-ChesG

She was named Eleutheria. Eleutheria. Carolyn Kizer. CP-KizeC

She was not always so unkind I swear. Portrait (I). Stevie Smith. CP-SmitS

She was not as pretty as women I know. My Kate. Elizabeth Barrett Browning. CP-BroEB

She was [or is] all around me. Blue Wing, The. Donald Hall. CP-HallD

She was pale as one. Another Man's Wife. Ezra Pound. CP-PoEar

She was pretty swacked by the time she. Dinner at George & Katie Schneeman's. Ted Berrigan. SP-BerrT

She was quite mad (paranoid / or schizoid or both) but out. Moment on Earth, A. James Laughlin. CP-LaugJ

She was running in the field with the tall nettles. Until Daybreak. Yannis Ritsos. SP-RitsY, *tr. by* Kimon Friar

She was saying mad things. Illusion, An. David Ignatow. SP-IgnaD

She was sitting in the window. Liberty. Charles Bukowski. SP-BukC1

She was sitting with a pint and a small one. Whim. Paul Muldoon. CP-MuldP

She was such a dab hand, my mother. Such a dab hand. They That Wash on Thursday. Paul Muldoon. CP-MuldP

She was tangled up in her own self-conceit, a woman. Painter's Wife, The. D. H. Lawrence. CP-LawrD

She was taught desire in the street. Trap, The. Nicholas Vachel Lindsay. CP-LindV

She was whiter than the ermine. Once. Christina Georgina Rossetti. CP-RosC3

She was young and beautiful. Ruby Brown. Langston Hughes. CP-HughL; CP-HughL1

She watered the flowers and heard the water dripping from the balcony. Afternoon. Yannis Ritsos. SP-RitsY, *tr. by* Kimon Friar

She wears old clothes she holds a borrowed handkerchief and her sorrow shows us the papers have bad news again today. Picture of Lee Ying, A. Thomas Merton. CP-MertT

She welcomes him with pretty impatience. Visit, The. Ogden Nash. CP-NashO

She went as quiet as the Dew. Emily Dickinson. CP-DickE

She went to bed. Siesta. Stevie Smith. CP-SmitS

She went to buy a brand new hat. Colors. Countee Cullen. CP-CullC

She Went to Stay. Robert Creeley. CP-CreeR

She went with morning on her lips. Valediction: "She went with morning on her lips." Tennessee Williams. CP-WillT

She wept.—Life's purple tide began to flow. Sonnet on Seeing Miss Helen Maria Williams Weep at a Tale of Distress. William Wordsworth. CP-WorW1

She wept, she railed, she spurned the meat. Stanley Kunitz. CP-KunSC

She wept upon her cheeks, and weeping so. Upon Her Weeping. Robert Herrick. CP-HerrR

She who did not come, wasn't she determined. Blank Joy. Rainer Maria Rilke. CP-RilkFr, *tr. by* A. Poulin, Jr.

She who has power to call her man. Unsaid Word, An. Adrienne Rich. CP-RicAE; SP-RicA1; SP-RicA2

She Who Hits at Will. Charles Olson. CP-OlsoC

She, who last felt young during the war. Bluebells. Louis MacNeice. CP-MacNL

She, who on the first night had lain with a god without knowing it. Alcméne. Yannis Ritsos. SP-RitsY, *tr. by* N. C. Germanacos

She Who Saw Not. Thomas Hardy. CP-HardT

She / Who searched for lovers. To a Little Lover-Lass, Dead. Langston Hughes. CP-HughL; CP-HughL1

She who to lift her heavy eyes had tried. Virgil. CP-WorW2 *Fr.* Aeneid [*or* Eneados *or* Aeneis], The.

She Who Turns Her Head. William Carlos Williams. CP-WilW1

She who was burned more than half her body skipped out of death. Praises, The. Charles Olson. CP-OlsoC

She Who Was Gone. W. S. Merwin. SP-MerwW

She who with innocent and tender hands. Monstrous Marriage, The. William Carlos Williams. CP-WilW2

"She will change," I cried. Young Man's Song. William Butler Yeats. CP-YeatW

She will never know I cried for her. Country & Western. Marilyn Hacker. SP-HackM

She will not die, they say. Betrayal. Walter De la Mare. CP-DeLaW

She will not smile. Leave-Taking, A. James Whitcomb Riley. CP-RileJ

She wished of him a lover's kiss and. Communication I. Maya Angelou. SP-AngeM

She with her thighs harder than hooves. Changeling, The. Theodore Roethke.
CP-RoetT

She wore a cloche hat. Photo of Emily, The. Lawrence Ferlinghetti. SP-FerlL

She wore a new 'terra-cotta' dress. Thunderstorm in Town, A. Thomas Hardy. CP-HardT

She wore a platinum blond wig. One of the Hottest. Charles Bukowski. SP-BukC1

She wore the skins of animals. East of the Sun, West of the Moon. Eleanor Wilner. SP-WilnE

She would come back, dripping thick water, from the green bog. Her Grave. Mary Oliver. SP-OlivM

She would plunge all poets in the ninth circle. Afterwards, An. Seamus Heaney. SP-HeanSO

She would say with that succulent. In Another Country. James Laughlin. CP-LaugJ

She Would Welcome Old Tribulations. Thomas Hardy. CP-HardT

She wrapped her soul in a lace of lies. Parted. Paul Laurence Dunbar. CP-DunbP

She wreathed bright flower-wreaths in her hair. Ruined Cross, The. Christina Georgina Rossetti. CP-RosC3

She writes: you'll. Moaning and Groaning. Charles Bukowski. SP-BukC1

She Wrote in Darkness. Adam Zagajewski. SP-ZagaA, *tr. by* Clare Cavanagh

She wrote me for years. Artists. Charles Bukowski. SP-BukC1

Shearing Time. Langston Hughes. CP-HughL

Shears, The. Robinson Jeffers. CP-JefR3

Shears, don't cut away that face. Eugenio Montale. CP-MontE, *tr. by* Jonathan Galassi

Sheath of sleep in the black of the bed. True Night. Gary Snyder. CP-SnydG

Sheath pierces the turf / and the flower unfurls: drooping, The. Snowdrop, The. James Schuyler. CP-SchuJ

Sheba's Gifts to Solomon. Jelaluddin Rumi. SP-Rumi, *tr. by* Coleman Barks

Sheba's Hesitation. Jelaluddin Rumi. SP-Rumi, *tr. by* Coleman Barks

Sheba's Throne. Jelaluddin Rumi. SP-Rumi, *tr. by* Coleman Barks

She'd look upon us, if she could. Voice of Age, The. Edwin Arlington Robinson. CP-RobiE

Shed no tear! O, shed no tear! Fairy Song. John Keats. CP-KeatJ

Shed no tears o'er that tomb. Emily Jane Brontë. CP-BronE

She'd thrust the canyon out of her mind; she never thought of the whispering fall, the ferns, the hawk-haunted. Home. Robinson Jeffers. CP-JefR1

Shedding of Blood. D. H. Lawrence. CP-LawrD

Sheds left out in the darkness. Cornpicker Poem. Robert Bly. SP-BlyR

She[e] is dead; and all which die. Dissolution, The. John Donne. CP-DonnJ; MW-DonnJ

Sheelagh na Gig. Seamus Heaney. SP-HeanSO

Sheep. Ted Hughes. SP-HughTN

"What is it this time the dark barn again." SP-HughTN

Sheep. Carl Sandburg. CP-SandC

Sheep. Anne Sexton. CP-SextA

Sheep and rocks drifting together before sunset. Memory of Summer Facing West. W. S. Merwin. SP-MerwWF

Sheep-Boy, The. Thomas Hardy. CP-HardT

Sheep-boy whistled loud, and lo!, The. Elegiac Verses in Memory of My Brother, John Wordsworth. William Wordsworth. CP-WorW1

Sheep Child, The. James Dickey. CP-DickJ

Sheep Clouds. W. S. Merwin. SP-MerwWF

Sheep Fair, A. Thomas Hardy. CP-HardT

Sheep families are out in the meadow, The. Families. Grace Paley. CP-PalGC

Sheep graze where the cemetery was. Town, The. Charles Olson. CP-OlsoC

Sheep has stopped crying, The. Sheep. Ted Hughes. SP-HughTN

Sheep have formed, The. Out in the Pasture. James Laughlin. CP-LaugJ

Sheep in Fog. Sylvia Plath. CP-PlatS

Sheep in the Ruins, The. Archibald MacLeish. CP-MacLA

Sheep is blind; a passing Owl, The. Blind Sheep, The. Randall Jarrell. CP-JarrR

Sheep like soldiers, The. Lower Field—Enniscorthy. Charles Olson. CP-OlsoC

Sheep move on the grass. Kill, The. Donald Hall. CP-HallD

Sheep mutter as we pass. Our Walk in Yorkshire. Donald Hall. CP-HallD

Sheep start galloping in moon-blind wheels. Man and Woman. Robert Lowell. SP-LoweR

Sheep to Slaughter. Sam Hamill. SP-HamiS

Sheep-Washing. William Wordsworth. CP-WorW2 *Fr.* River Duddon [A Series of Sonnets], The.

Sheepskin Coat. Yehuda Amichai. SP-AmicYL, *tr. by* Benjamin Harshav *and* Barbara Harshav

Sheer over to the other side,—for see. Idiot, The. Hart Crane. CP-CranH

Sheets of night mist travel a long valley, The. Mist Forms. Carl Sandburg. CP-SandC

Sheffield Ghazal 4: Driving West. Galway Kinnell. SP-KinnGN

Sheffield Ghazal 5: Passing the Cemetary. Galway Kinnell. SP-KinnGN

Sheikh Ahmad was continually in debt. Debtor Sheikh, The. Jelaluddin Rumi. SP-Rumi, *tr. by* Coleman Barks

Sheikh Kharraqani and His Wretched Wife. Jelaluddin Rumi. SP-Rumi, *tr. by* Coleman Barks

Sheikh Who Played with Children, The. Jelaluddin Rumi. SP-Rumi, *tr. by* Coleman Barks

Shelf Is a Ledge, A. Gregory Orr. SP-OrrG

Shelf Life. Seamus Heaney. SP-HeanSO

Shelf of worn, chipped, exquisite china oddments. Room. Denise Levertov. SP-LeveDL

Shell. Adam Zagajewski. SP-ZagaA, *tr. by* Clare Cavanagh

Shell, The. Charles Tomlinson. CP-TomlC

Shell arched under my toes, A. River Incident. Theodore Roethke. CP-RoetT

Shell of a doll's head, The. Modigliani's Death Mask. John Updike. CP-UpdiJ

Shelley was drowned near here. Arms at his side. Lerici. Thom Gunn. CP-GunnT

Shelley's Skylark. Thomas Hardy. CP-HardT

Shelling Jacobs Cattle Beans. Maxine W. Kumin. SP-KumiM

Shells. Howard Nemerov. CP-NemeH

Shells. Kathleen Jessie Raine. SP-RainK

Shells. C. K. Williams. SP-WillC

Shells. C. K. Williams. CP-WillC

Shells from the Coast mistaking. Emily Dickinson. CP-DickE

Shelter, The. Jones Very. CP-VeryJ

Shelter this candle from the wind. To the Wife of a Sick Friend. Edna St. Vincent Millay. CP-MillE

Sheltered Garden. "H. D." CP-DoolH

Shelters. Yannis Ritsos. SP-RitsY, *tr. by* N. C. Germanacos

Shemà. Primo Levi. CP-LeviP, *tr. by* Ruth Feldman *and* Brian Swann

Shemselnihar. George Meredith. CP-MerG1

Shenandoah. Charles Olson. CP-OlsoC

Shenandoah. Carl Sandburg. CP-SandC

Shenandoah Journey. Carl Sandburg. CP-SandC

Shepheardes [*or* Shepeards *or* Shepherd's] Calender, The. Edmund Spenser. CP-Spens

  December. CP-Spens

  July. CP-Spens

  June. CP-Spens

  "Loe! I have made a Calender for every yeare." CP-Spens

  March. CP-Spens

  May. CP-Spens

  September. CP-Spens

Shepheards boy (best knowen by that name), The. Colin Clouts Come Home Againe. Edmund Spenser. CP-Spens

Shepheards, that wont on pipes of oaten reed. Astrophel. Edmund Spenser. CP-Spens

Shepherd, The. "H. D." CP-DoolH

Shepherd and Goatherd. William Butler Yeats. CP-YeatW

Shepherd begs to be suckled in snow that drifts, A. Birth of Christ, The. Federico García Lorca. CP-GarcF, *tr. by* Greg Simon *and* Steven F. White

Shepherd, looking eastward softly said, The. William Wordsworth. CP-WorW1

Shephe[a]rd Paris bore the Spartan bride, The. Idyll 27: Daphnis. Theocritus. CP-DryJ2 *Fr.* Idylls.

Shepherd Song. Sir Philip Sidney. SP-SidnP *Fr.* Arcadia.

Shepherd stands by a gate in a white smock-frock, A. Unkindly May, An. Thomas Hardy. CP-HardT

Shepherd touch'd his reed; sweet Philomel, The. Strada's Nightingale. Vincent Bourne. CP-CowpW

Shepherd, with his eye on hazy South, The. Earth and a Wedded Woman. George Meredith. CP-MerG1

Shepherds and the nymphs were seen, The. Cadenus and Vanessa. Jonathan Swift. CP-SwifJ

Shepherds armed with staff and sling. Carol of Patience. Robert Graves. CP-GravR

Shepherd's Brow, The. Gerard Manley Hopkins. CP-HopkG

Shepherd's Life, The. Jones Very. CP-VeryJ

Shepherd's [*or* Shepheards] Calendar, The. John Clare.

  August. SP-ClarJ

  February. SP-ClarJ

  (February: A Thaw.) SP-ClarJ

  ("Snow is gone from cottage tops, The.") SP-ClarJ

  January: A Winters Day. SP-ClarJ

Shepherd's Song at Christmas. Langston Hughes. CP-HughL

Shepherds watch their flocks by night, The. Hymn for Christmas Day, A. Christina Georgina Rossetti. CP-RosC3

Shepherds went their hasty way, The. Christmas Carol, A: "Shepherds went their hasty way, The." Samuel Taylor Coleridge. CP-ColeS

Shepherd's wife cries o'er the knowe, The. Shepherd's Wife, The. Robert Burns. CP-BurnR

Shepherd's Wife, The. Robert Burns. CP-BurnR

Sheridan. W. S. Merwin. SP-MerwWF

Sheridan, a Goose. Jonathan Swift. CP-SwifJ

Sheridan at Cedar Creek. Herman Melville. SP-MelvH

Sheridan to Dan Jackson. Thomas Sheridan. CP-SherT

Sheridan's Masterpiece; or, Tom Pun-Sibi's Folly Complete, *Alexander's Overthrow, or The Downfall of Babylon*, as It Was Acted at Mr. Lyddal's in Dame Street, December 11th, 1721. *Unknown, sometimes at. to* Thomas Sheridan. CP-SherT

Sheridan's Submission. Jonathan Swift. CP-SwifJ

Sherman's March Reglitterized. Lawrence Ferlinghetti. SP-FerlL

She's a big country. Her undulations. Godiva County, Montana. William Stafford. SP-StafWW

She's at the mouth of a river. Two Cranial Murals. Yusef Komunyakaa. CP-KomuY

She's Back! Robert Creeley. SP-CreeR

She's changed, my six-foot. Transformation. Alan Dugan. CP-DugaA

She's Dead. Lorine Niedecker. *Fr.* Element Mother, The.

She's dreaming / of salt again. Nightmare. Rita Dove. SP-DoveR

She's fair and fause that causes my smart. Robert Burns. CP-BurnR

She's from Bengal or Kashmir. Trapper's Bride, The. Yusef Komunyakaa. CP-KomuY

She's from Texas and weighs. Texan. Charles Bukowski. SP-BukC1

She's gone. She was my love, my moon or more. Complaint. James Wright. CP-WrigJ

She's happy, with a new Content. Emily Dickinson. CP-DickE

She's here again. There. Sunset Threnody. Yusef Komunyakaa. CP-KomuY

She's in a Gypsy skirt. Perfect Match, The. Clarence Major. SP-MajoC

She's in a room full of letters, dressed in white. Little Robber Girl Gets On in the Wide World, The. Marilyn Hacker. SP-HackM

She's late. He mixes another drink. Husband. Miller Williams. CP-WillM

She's like a model, proud of her good bones. Dancing Death. Charles Baudelaire. CP-BaudC, *tr. by* Walter Martin

She's made her mind up, the. Michelangelo Buonarroti. CP-Miche, *tr. by* John Frederick Nims

She's not for you, man. Longshot. Charles Bukowski. SP-BukC1

She's not sure if it's song or sermon. Survivor's Ballad. Josephine Jacobsen. CP-JacoJ

She's on Main Street. Sorrow. Yusef Komunyakaa. CP-KomuY

She's passing fair; but so demure is she. Roundel: "She's passing fair; but so demure is she." Dorothy Parker. CP-ParkD

She's the girl. No Good Too. William Carlos Williams. CP-WilW2

She's turning away, about to step. Whispering Gallery, The. Yusef Komunyakaa. CP-KomuY

She's up seeing my doctor. Don't Touch the Girls. Charles Bukowski. SP-BukC1

She's wearing a cotton dress. Backdrop With Lovers, 1931. Tess Gallagher. SP-GallT

Sheweth, with greatest respect and most awful submission. To His Excellency Our Lord Carteret, Lord Lieutenant of Ireland: The Humble Petition of Lord Viscount Mont-Cashel, and the Rest of His School-Fellows. Thomas Sheridan. CP-SherT

Shh, the light is whispering, soft, day's end. Bridge Passage: Variations on Two Scales. Eleanor Wilner. SP-WilnE

Shibboleth. Paul Celan. SP-CelaP, *tr. by* John Felstiner

Shibboleth. Ted Hughes. SP-HughTN

Shibboleth. Josephine Jacobsen. CP-JacoJ

Shield Against the Trampling Foe, A. Robert Stock. SP-StocR

Shield of Achilles, The. Homer. CP-MerG2 *Fr.* Iliad, The.

Shield of Achilles, The. W. H. Auden. CP-AudeW

Shield of Faith, The. Nicholas Vachel Lindsay. CP-LindV

Shifra and Batya promised. Yehuda Amichai. SP-AmicYL, *tr. by* Benjamin Harshav *and* Barbara Harshav

Shift here, in town, not meanest among squires. On Lieutenant Shift. Ben Jonson. CP-JonsB; SP-JonsB

Shift now has cast his clothes: got all things new. Upon Shift. Robert Herrick. CP-HerrR

Shift of Scene, A. Robert Graves. CP-GravR

Shifting brilliancies. Then winter light. Lightenings. Seamus Heaney. SP-HeanSO *Fr.* Squarings.

Shiftless. Raymond Carver. CP-CarvR

Shillin' a Day. Rudyard Kipling. CP-KiplR

Shilling life will give you all the facts, A. Who's Who. W. H. Auden. CP-AudeW

Shillington. John Updike. CP-UpdiJ

Shiloh [A Requiem]. Herman Melville. SP-MelvH

Shimmer. James Schuyler. CP-SchuJ

Shimmer at the ear: a sheen, A. Little Night Music, A. Charles Tomlinson. CP-TomlC

Shimmer of Evil, The. Theodore Roethke. CP-RoetT

Shine alone, shine nakedly, shine like bronze. Nuances of a Theme by Williams. Wallace Stevens. CP-StevW; CP-StevWP

Shine, Empire. Robinson Jeffers. CP-JefR3

Shine miraculous / mottled river. River Rhyme II. William Carlos Williams. CP-WilW2

Shine on, majestic soul, abide. *see also* To the Lady Elizabeth Queen of Bohemia. George Herbert. CP-HerbG

Shine on, O moon of summer. Back Yard. Carl Sandburg. CP-SandC

Shine, Perishing Republic. Robinson Jeffers. CP-JefR1

Shine, Republic. Robinson Jeffers. CP-JefR2

Shines / in the mind of heaven God [*or* heaven God]. Canto 51: "Shines / in the mind of heaven God [*or* heaven God]." Ezra Pound. SP-PounE *Fr.* Cantos.

Shines on top of Mountains where Grey Stone monastery sits & blinks at the sky. Man's Glory. Allen Ginsberg. CP-GinsA

Shining Diamonds & Sequins glitter. December 31, 1978. Allen Ginsberg. CP-GinsA

Shining Light, The. William Cowper. *See* Olney Hymns

Shining neutral summer has no voice, The. In Memory of Ernst Toller. W. H. Auden. CP-AudeW

Shining wave, A. Wave, The. Elizabeth Bishop. CP-BishE

Shinking Song. Ogden Nash. CP-NashO

Shinto. Federico García Lorca. CP-GarcF, *tr.* by Jerome Rothenberg *Fr.* Mirror Suite.

Shinto. Jorge Luis Borges. SP-BorgJ, *tr.* by Hoyt Rogers

Ship. A. R. Ammons. CP-AmmoA

Ship. W. S. Merwin. SP-MerwW

Ship, The. David Ignatow. SP-IgnaD

Ship, The. James Laughlin. CP-LaugJ

Ship, a forest of guilty masts, A. Welcome. Thomas Merton. CP-MertT

Ship after ship after ship. Etesian Winds. Yannis Ritsos. SP-RitsY, *tr.* by Kimon Friar

Ship Ahoy! Walt Whitman. CP-WhitW

Ship-Builders, The. John Greenleaf Whittier. CP-WhitJ

Ship Burning and a Comet All in One Day, A. Richard Eberhart. CP-EberR

Ship comes up the harbor, The. Every sail. Arrival, The. Jones Very. CP-VeryJ

Ship in the Tomb. Archibald MacLeish. CP-MacLA

Ship leaves at nightfall, A. The light glows. Summer at Dhiminio. Yannis Ritsos. SP-RitsY, *tr.* by Kimon Friar

Ship moves, The. 4th of July. William Carlos Williams. CP-WilW1

Ship of Death. D. H. Lawrence. CP-LawrD

Ship of Death, The. D. H. Lawrence. CP-LawrD

Ship of Fools. Archibald MacLeish. CP-MacLA

Ship Rock. Jones Very. CP-VeryJ

Ship rounding, the. Orpheus. George Oppen. CP-OppGN

Ship Starting, The. Walt Whitman. CP-WhitW

Ship that saved us—Uncle Joe!, The. Allied Convoy / Reaches Russia. Lorine Niedecker. CP-NiedL

Ship went on with solemn face, The. Sabbath Morning at Sea, A. Elizabeth Barrett Browning. CP-BroEB

Ship-Wrack. Robert Herrick. CP-HerrR

Shipbored. John Updike. CP-UpdiJ

Ships, The. Constantine P. Cavafy. CP-CavaC, *tr.* by Theoharis Constantine Theoharis

Ships Are Made Ready in Silence, The. W. S. Merwin. SP-MerwW

Ships destroy us above, The. Tin Fish. Rudyard Kipling. CP-KiplR

Ships in Bottles. D. H. Lawrence. CP-LawrD

Ship's Log. Archibald MacLeish. CP-MacLA

Ships on the ocean meet, each other hail. True Knowledge Necessary for the Voyage of Life. Jones Very. CP-VeryJ

Ships? / Sure I'll sail them. Call Letters: Mrs. V.B. Maya Angelou. SP-AngeM

Ships that pass in the night. Reflections on the St. Lawrence Seaway. Peter Blue Cloud. SP-BlueP

Ships That Pass in the Night. Paul Laurence Dunbar. CP-DunbP

Ship's Waiters. Charles Tomlinson. CP-TomlC

Shipwreck. Norman Dubie. CP-DubiN

Shipwreck of Idomeneus, The. George Meredith. CP-MerG1

Shirland Road. Marilyn Hacker. SP-HackM

Shirley & Auden. John Berryman. CP-BerrJ

Shirley came to town with a broken leg. Change of Habit, A. Charles Bukowski. SP-BukC1

Shirt. Robert Pinsky. CP-PinsR

Shirt. Carl Sandburg. CP-SandC

Shirt. Charles Simic. SP-SimiC; SP-SimiCE

Shirt, britches, paper. Hayden Carruth. CP-CarHS *Fr.* Clay Hill Anthology, The.

Shit Time. Charles Bukowski. SP-BukC1

Shiv and the Grasshopper. Rudyard Kipling. CP-KiplR *Fr.* Jungle Book, The.

Shiv, who poured the harvest and made the winds to blow. Shiv and the Grasshopper. Rudyard Kipling. CP-KiplR *Fr.* Jungle Book, The.

Shiva. Robinson Jeffers. CP-JefR2

Shiva and Parvati Hiding in the Rain. Robert Pinsky. CP-PinsR

Shiver, The. Thomas Hardy. CP-HardT

Shivering in the darkness. Portrait of the Artist, A. Derek Mahon. CP-MahoD

Shoal rocks with the sea, The. His Foreboding. Theodore Roethke. CP-RoetT

Shoaled on this shingle. Ship of Fools. Archibald MacLeish. CP-MacLA

Shoals Returning, The. Thomas Kinsella. CP-KinsT

Shock, A. W. H. Auden. CP-AudeW

Shock to find you washed up on the beach, A. Old No. 1. May Swenson. SP-SwenM

Sho'd I not put on Blacks, when each one here. Upon M. William Lawes, the Rare Musitian. Robert Herrick. CP-HerrR

Shoddy furbishings I pick and choose among, The. Russet Gold. A. R. Ammons. CP-AmmoA

Shoe, The. William Corbett. SP-CorbW

Shoe Repairs. W. S. Merwin. SP-MerwW

Shoe that I forgot to tie, A. Old Song, An. Randall Jarrell. CP-JarrR

Shoe the steed with silver. Sheridan at Cedar Creek. Herman Melville. SP-MelvH

Shoe was occupied, kind of a picnic, The. Alfonso Lacklustre. James Tate. SP-TateJ

Shoe with legs, A. Lobster. Anne Sexton. CP-SextA

Shoemaker, The. Stéphane Mallarmé. CP-MallS *Fr.* Street Songs.

Shoemaker, The. James Whitcomb Riley. CP-RileJ

Shoemakers, The. John Greenleaf Whittier. CP-WhitJ

Shoes In Rain Jungle. Robert Penn Warren. CP-WarrR

Shoes of Travel. Carl Sandburg. CP-SandC

Shoes, secret face of my inner life. My Shoes. Charles Simic. SP-SimiC; SP-SimiCE

Shofar place, The. Paul Celan. SP-CelaP, *tr.* by John Felstiner

Sholto Peach Harrison you are no son of mine. Correspondence between Mr. Harrison in Newcastle and Mr. Sholto Peach Harrison in Hull. Stevie Smith. CP-SmitS

Sho[o]e Tying, The. Robert Herrick. CP-HerrR

Shook down shook up on these dead trees they have come. Lord in the Air, the. James Dickey. CP-DickJ

Shoot It Jimmy! William Carlos Williams. CP-WilW1

Shooting. Raymond Carver. CP-CarvR

Shooting Gallery. Muriel Rukeyser. CP-RukeM

Shooting Incident, The. Stevie Smith. CP-SmitS

Shooting pleasures / Ok'd by. Confidential. Rae Armantrout. SP-ArmaA

Shooting Script. Adrienne Rich. CP-RicAE

  Ghazal V. SP-RicA2

  "I was looking for a way out of a lifetime's consolations." SP-RicA2

  "In my imagination I was the pivot of a fresh beginning." SP-RicA2

  "Mare's skeleton in the clearing: another sign of life, The." SP-RicA2

  Newsreel. SP-RicA2

  "Of simple choice they are the villagers; their clothes come." SP-RicA2

  "Old blanket, The. The crumbs of rubbed wool turning up." SP-RicA2

  "They come to you with their descriptions of your soul." SP-RicA2

  "We are driven to odd attempts; once it would not have occurred to." SP-RicA1; SP-RicA2

  "We were bound on the wheel of an endless conversation." SP-RicA1; SP-RicA2

  "Whatever it was: the grains of the glacier caked in the boot-cleats." SP-RicA1; SP-RicA2

  "Woman waking behind grimed blinds slatted across a courtyard, A." SP-RicA1

  "You are beside me like a wall; I touch you with my fingers and." SP-RicA2

Shooting Season. Robinson Jeffers. CP-JefR2

Shooting Star. Arthur Sze. SP-SzeA

Shop. Robert Browning. CP-BroR2

Shop. Andrei Codrescu. SP-CodrA

Shopping in Ferney with Voltaire. Maxine W. Kumin. SP-KumiM

Shops take down their awnings. Almanac, An. James Schuyler. CP-SchuJ

Shore. Hans Magnus Enzensberger. SP-EnzeH, *tr.* by Michael Hamburger

Shore. W. S. Merwin. SP-MerwW

Shore, The. W. S. Merwin. SP-MerwWF

Shore, The. George Oppen. CP-OppGN

Shore Fog. A. R. Ammons. CP-AmmoA

Shore is cabbage green and reeks, The. Early Morning on the Tel Aviv-Haifa Freeway. Rita Dove. SP-DoveR

Shore of Ashkelon, The. Yehuda Amichai. SP-AmicY, *tr.* by Chana Bloch

Shore of Versilia. Eugenio Montale. CP-MontE, *tr.* by Jonathan Galassi

Shore Piece. John Ciardi. CP-CiarJ

Shore Scene. John Logan. CP-LoganJ

Shore Woman. Seamus Heaney. SP-HeanSO

Shorebird-Watching. Amy Clampitt. CP-ClamA

Shoreless Tide, The. A. R. Ammons. CP-AmmoA

Shoring up the ocean. A railroad track. Blood-Sister. Adrienne Rich. SP-RicA2

Shorn moon trembling indistinct on her path, The. Brother and Sister. D. H. Lawrence. CP-LawrD

Short afternoon ends, and the year is over, The. New Year. Philip Larkin. CP-LarkP

Short & baldheaded. Between Angels & Monsters. Yusef Komunyakaa. CP-KomuY

Short and Long Both Likes. Robert Herrick. CP-HerrR

Short Days, The. John Updike. CP-UpdiJ

Short Elegy to the Memory of Her Husband, A. Annis Boudinot Stockton. CP-StocA

Short History of Philosophy, A. Eleanor Wilner. SP-WilnE

Short History of the Bourgeoisie. Hans Magnus Enzensberger. SP-EnzeH, tr. by Hans Magnus Enzensberger and Michael Hamburger

Short Hymne to Larr, A. Robert Herrick. CP-HerrR

Short Hymne to Venus, A. Robert Herrick. CP-HerrR

Short is time, and only time is bleak. Christina Georgina Rossetti. CP-RosC2

Short Life of the Hermit, A. John Logan. CP-LogaJ

Short Ode to the Cuckoo. W. H. Auden. CP-AudeW

Short Poem. William Carlos Williams. CP-WilW2

Short Romance. T. S. Eliot. See Conversation Galante

Short Run to Cambörne. Donald Davie. CP-DaviDC

Short Song of Congratulation, A [or To a Young Heir]. Samuel Johnson. CP-JohnS

Short Story. Edna St. Vincent Millay. CP-MillE

Short Story on a Painting of Gustav Klimt. Lawrence Ferlinghetti. SP-FerlL

Short Summary. Louise Bogan. CP-BogaL

Short Thoughts for Long Nights. Robert Penn Warren. CP-WarrR

Short-timer's Calendar. Yusef Komunyakaa. CP-KomuY

Short Views in Africa. Josephine Jacobsen. CP-JacoJ

Shortcut. Charles Simic. SP-SimiCE

Shortening Days at the Homestead. Thomas Hardy. CP-HardT

Shortest light. Paper Flute. Olga Broumas. SP-BrouO

Shortest Way Home, The. Muriel Rukeyser. CP-RukeM

Shortly after three p.m. today a squall. Squall, A. Raymond Carver. CP-CarvR

Short'nin' Bread Song—Pieced Out, A. James Whitcomb Riley. CP-RileJ

Shorts. Joseph Brodsky.

    Abroad. CP-BrodJ

    Epitaph for a Tyrant. CP-BrodJ

    Epitaph to a Tyrant. CP-BrodJ

    Future. CP-BrodJ

    "Hail the vagina." CP-BrodJ

    "I sit at my desk." CP-BrodJ

    "I went to a museum." CP-BrodJ

    "I've seen the Atlantic." CP-BrodJ

    New York Lullaby. CP-BrodJ

    Oysters. CP-BrodJ

    Postcard from France, A. CP-BrodJ

    To a Fellow Poet. CP-BrodJ

    Valentine, A. CP-BrodJ

    Weather. CP-BrodJ

Shorts I. W. H. Auden. CP-AudeW

Shorts II [1958–1971]. W. H. Auden. CP-AudeW

Shorts [1927–1932]. W. H. Auden. CP-AudeW

Shorts [1939–1947]. W. H. Auden. CP-AudeW

Shorts [1948–1957]. W. H. Auden. CP-AudeW

Shorts [1972–1973]. W. H. Auden. CP-AudeW

Shot. Robert Creeley. CP-CreeR

Shot, The. Robert Graves. CP-GravR

Shot, The. Dan Pagis. SP-PagiD, tr. by Stephen Mitchell

Shot: from crag to crag, A. Hunting Season. W. H. Auden. CP-AudeW

Shot gold, maroon and violet, dazzling silver, emerald, fawn. Prairie Sunset, A. Walt Whitman. CP-WhitW

Shot? so quick, so clean an ending? A. E. Housman. CP-HousA

Shots were heard last night / Out by the burial ground. Ernesto Cardenal. CP-MertT Fr. Three Epigrams.

Should auld acquaintance be forgot. Auld Lang Syne. Robert Burns. CP-BurnR

Should Be Sufficient. Kenneth Patchen. CP-PatcK

Should every creature be as I have been. Elegy: "Should every creature be as I have been." Theodore Roethke. CP-RoetT

Should far this from mankind's unmysteries. E. E. Cummings. CP-CummE

Should I bold in a moment intrude. Doxology. A. R. Ammons. CP-AmmoA

Should I Care. Robert Graves. CP-GravR

Should I say that you're dead? Butterfly, The. Joseph Brodsky. CP-BrodJ, tr. by George L. Kline

Should I shed my tears. Hafiz. CP-EmerR Fr. Odes.

Should I treat it as my own. Discarded Love Poem, The. Robert Graves. CP-GravR

Should I wander with no frown, these idle days. Unpenned Poem, The. Robert Graves. CP-GravR

Should Lanterns Shine. Dylan Thomas. CP-ThomD

Should not the white lie and the unkept promise. Pardon, The. Robert Graves. CP-GravR

Should one of us remember, / And one of us forget. He and She. Christina Georgina Rossetti. CP-RosC2

Should, Should Not. Czeslaw Milosz. CP-MiloC; CP-MiloCN

Should the building totter, run for an archway! Fallen Tower of Siloam, The. Robert Graves. CP-GravR

Should the senses' rapturous burning override. Michelangelo Buonarroti. CP-Miche, tr. by John Frederick Nims

Should the wide world roll away. Stephen Crane. CP-CranS

Should they not have the best of both worlds? Mules. Paul Muldoon. CP-MuldP

Should they whisper false of you. Superfluous Advice. Dorothy Parker. CP-ParkD

Should this fool die. E. E. Cummings. CP-CummE

Should thy love die; / O bury it not under ice-blue eyes! Song: "Should thy love die; / O bury it not under ice-blue eyes!" George Meredith. CP-MerG1

Should unknown messengers appear. Song: From Otherwhere or Nowhere. Robert Graves. CP-GravR

Should you but fail at—Sea. Emily Dickinson. CP-DickE

Should you chance to suffer thirst. Charades: "Should you chance to suffer thirst." Cassandra Elizabeth Austen. CP-AustJ

Should you go to Centre Harbor. Legend of the Lake, A. John Greenleaf Whittier. CP-WhitJ

Should you realize so much, daughter of every season. Such as Sorrow. Yehuda Amichai. SP-AmicY, tr. by Stephen Mitchell

Should you want rhymes again for Graecum. To the Author of "Tom Pun-Sibi Metamorphosed" Thomas Sheridan. CP-SherT

Shoulders sag, / The pull of weighted needling. Junkie Monkey Reel. Maya Angelou. SP-AngeM

Shout. Langston Hughes. CP-HughL; CP-HughL1

Shout, The. Anne Sexton. CP-SextA

Shout, The. Charles Tomlinson. CP-TomlC

Shout comes out of my room, A. Bonfire at Midnight. Jelaluddin Rumi. SP-Rumi, tr. by Coleman Barks

Shout, for a mighty Victory is won! Anticipation. October, 1803. William Wordsworth. CP-WorW1; MW-WorW

Shout for those whose course is done. Song: "Shout for those whose course is done." Ralph Waldo Emerson. CP-EmerR

Shout of a King is common among them. One day may I be, The. What Hath God Wrought! Christina Georgina Rossetti. CP-RosC2

Shout to the Sheperds, A. Ralph Waldo Emerson. CP-EmerR

Shouts, lottery vendors, florists, cardplayers, death. There. Yannis Ritsos. SP-RitsY, tr. by Kimon Friar and Kostas Myrsiades

Shove off from the wharf-edge! Steady. Song of the Red War-Boat. Rudyard Kipling. CP-KiplR

Shovel Man, The. Carl Sandburg. CP-SandC

Shovel of his ashes took, A. Fragment of a Ghost Story. Percy Bysshe Shelley. CP-ShelP

Shoveling Snow with Buddha. Billy Collins. SP-CollB

Show, The. Wilfred Owen. CP-OwenW

Show cat: a soul conferring, The. Cat. Rainer Maria Rilke. CP-RilkFr, tr. by A. Poulin, Jr.

Show Fare, Please. Langston Hughes. CP-HughL; CP-HughL3

Show-fringes, sense-fringes. Paul Celan. SP-CelaP, tr. by John Felstiner

Show is not the Show, The. Emily Dickinson. CP-DickE

Show me again the time. Lines to a Movement in Mozart's E-Flat Symphony. Thomas Hardy. CP-HardT

Show me Eternity, and I will show you Memory. Emily Dickinson. SP-DickE

Show me himselfe, himselfe (bright Sir) O show. Matthew 28; Come See the Place where the Lord Lay. Bible, N.T. CP-CrasR Fr. St. Matthew.

Show me the noblest Youth of present time. Triad, The. William Wordsworth. CP-WorW2

Show me the person who doesn't die. Han-shan. CP-ColdM, tr. by Red Pine

Show [or Shew] me thy feet; show [or shew] me thy legs, thy thighs. To Dianeme. Robert Herrick. CP-HerrR

Show Saturday. Philip Larkin. CP-LarkP

Show thee as I thought thee. To Outer Nature. Thomas Hardy. CP-HardT

Shower. Wallace Stevens. CP-StevWP

Shower, The. James Whitcomb Riley. CP-RileJ

Shower in June, A. William Corbett. SP-CorbW

Shower of stones, A. Volcano? There is no color. Mourning Picture. Jane Cooper. CP-CoopJ

Showered, shaved, splashed / (Ajaccio Violets) I. Ajaccio Violets. James

Schuyler. CP-SchuJ

Showing Late Symptoms She First Tries to Fix Herself in the Minds of Her Children. Miller Williams. CP-WillM

Showing that our ways agreed. For an Evolutionist and His Opponent. Countee Cullen. CP-CullC

Showing the girl. Giovanni's *Rape of the Sabine Women* at Wildenstein's. George Oppen. CP-OppGN

Showings, The: the Lady Julian of Norwich, 1342-1416. Denise Levertov. SP-LeveDS

Showre of Blossomes, The. Robert Herrick. CP-HerrR

Showre of Roses, The. Robert Herrick. CP-HerrR

Shows. D. H. Lawrence. CP-LawrD

Shows you in a London / room: books, a painting. Photograph, A. James Schuyler. CP-SchuJ

Shreds of Steam. Jelaluddin Rumi. SP-Rumi, *tr. by* Coleman Barks

Shrike, The. Sylvia Plath. CP-PlatS

Shrike, The. Henry David Thoreau. CP-ThorH

Shrilling locust slowly sheathes, The. Dusk Song—The Beetle. James Whitcomb Riley. CP-RileJ

Shrine, The. "H. D." CP-DoolH

Shrines. Yusef Komunyakaa. CP-KomuY

Shrinking Lonesome Sestina, The. Miller Williams. CP-WillM

Shrivers, The. Josephine Jacobsen. CP-JacoJ

Shropshire. Donald Davie. CP-DaviDC

Shroud, The. Edna St. Vincent Millay. CP-MillE

Shroud is yet unspread, The. Young Queen, The. Elizabeth Barrett Browning. CP-BroEB

Shroud of Color, The. Countee Cullen. CP-CullC

Shrouded maidens sleep on the wave. Fog Over the Sea and the Sun Going Down. Kenneth Patchen. CP-PatcK

Shrouded Stranger, The. Allen Ginsberg. CP-GinsA; SP-GinsA

Shrubbery, The. William Cowper. CP-CowpW

Shrugging in the flight of its leaves. Old Elm Tree by the River, The. Wendell Berry. CP-BerrW

Shrunken world, A. Epistle. To Enrique Caracciolo Trejo. Donald Davie. CP-DaviDC

Shu Swamp, Spring. May Swenson. SP-SwenM

Shudder[, The]. Donald Hall. CP-HallD

Shudder goes through the universe, even, A. Big Bang. William Stafford. SP-StafWW

Shuffle and cut. What was so large and one. Aftermath. Louis MacNeice. CP-MacNL

Shuffle and shudder of Autumn, The. Autumn Imagined. Donald Davie. CP-DaviDC

Shuffle up the stairs betrays our age, The. Academy. John Updike. CP-UpdiJ

Shun passion, fold the hands of thrift. Ralph Waldo Emerson. CP-EmerR

Shun—shun the Bowl! That fatal, facile drink. Rudyard Kipling. *See* Boanerges Blitzen, servant of the Queen

Shut-Eye Sentry, The. Rudyard Kipling. CP-KiplR

Shut in a white cage. Tongue. Adam Zagajewski. SP-ZagaA, *tr. by* Clare Cavanagh

Shut in kept off. Charles Olson. CP-OlsoC

Shut not me alive away. Commuted Sentence, The. Stevie Smith. CP-SmitS

Shut not so soon; the dull-eyed night. To Daisies, Not to Shut So Soon[e]. Robert Herrick. CP-HerrR

Shut Not Your Doors. Walt Whitman. CP-WhitW

Shut Out. Christina Georgina Rossetti. CP-RosC1

Shut Out That Moon. Thomas Hardy. CP-HardT

Shut, shut the door, good John! (fatigu'd [*or* fatigued] I said). Epistle to Dr. Arbuthnot. Alexander Pope. CP-PopeA

Shut up in woods. Lorine Niedecker. CP-NiedL

Shut up the book and get you now to bed. To One Awake. Robert Penn Warren. CP-WarrR

Shut your eyes then. Nursery Rhyme. May Sarton. SP-SartM

Shutter of time darkening ceaselessly, The. August. Louis MacNeice. CP-MacNL

Shuttle. Arthur Sze. SP-SzeA

Shuttle, The. Tennessee Williams. CP-WillT

Shuttle, The. John Updike. CP-UpdiJ

Shuttles of trains going south, drawing threads of blue. Morning Sun. Louis MacNeice. CP-MacNL

Shuttles, The. W. S. Merwin. SP-MerwWF

Shy at first but quick. Return to Love. Hayden Carruth. CP-CarHS

Shy Man, The. Theodore Roethke. CP-RoetT

Shy one, shy one. To an Isle in the Water. William Butler Yeats. CP-YeatW

Shy One, The. James Tate. SP-TateJ

Shyly it sprinkles, every drop a girl. Small Rain, The. Robert Stock. SP-StocR

Sì che il fratello s'ha falconcello. Christina Georgina Rossetti. CP-RosC3

Si dentro impietrai. Io no piangeva. Sam Hamill. SP-HamiS

Si Peu Séduisante. Stevie Smith. CP-SmitS

Si tu le permets, je veux prendre ton *arrière-train* pour rejoindre Henri Miller à Dijon. L'Abécédérien de la lubricité. James Laughlin. CP-LaugJ

Siamese twins: one, maddened by. Twins. Robert Graves. CP-GravR

Sibb when she saw her face how hard it was. Upon Sibb. Robert Herrick. CP-HerrR

Sibyl. W. S. Merwin. SP-MerwW

Sic a Wife as Willie Had. Robert Burns. CP-BurnR

Sic Itur. Arthur Hugh Clough. SP-ClouA

Sic Semper Mr. Sherman's Temper, or Kindly Place Your Order in English. Ogden Nash. CP-NashO

Sic transit gloria mundi. Emily Dickinson. CP-DickE

Sic Vita. Henry David Thoreau. CP-ThorH

Sicilian Cyclamens. D. H. Lawrence. CP-LawrD

Sicilian Emigrant's Song. William Carlos Williams. CP-WilW1

Sicilian Muse, begin a loftier strain! Eclogue 4: The Messiah. Virgil. CP-DryJ2 *Fr.* Eclogues.

Sicilian Vespers, The. John Greenleaf Whittier. CP-WhitJ

Sick. Robert Creeley. CP-CreeR

Sick. D. H. Lawrence. CP-LawrD

Sick. Robert Lowell. SP-LoweR

Sick, The. Jones Very. CP-VeryJ

Sick African. William Carlos Williams. CP-WilW1

Sick are coming the sick are coming!, The. Chosen, The. Josephine Jacobsen. CP-JacoJ

Sick as I am. Exercise, An. William Carlos Williams. CP-WilW2

Sick Battle-God, The. Thomas Hardy. CP-HardT

Sick Child, A. Randall Jarrell. CP-JarrR

Sick Child's Meditation, A. Christina Georgina Rossetti. CP-RosC3

Sick grapes on the chair by the bed lie prone; at the window, The. Malade. D. H. Lawrence. CP-LawrD

Sick is Anthea, sickly is the spring. To Anthea. Robert Herrick. CP-HerrR

Sick King in Bokhara, The. Matthew Arnold. SP-ArnoM

Sick Lion and the Ass, The. Thomas Sheridan. CP-SherT

Sick Love. Robert Graves. CP-GravR

Sick Man, The. Wallace Stevens. CP-StevWP

Sick Man in the Sun. Pablo Neruda. SP-NeruP

Sick Muse, The. Charles Baudelaire. CP-BaudC, *tr. by* Walter Martin

Sick Nought, The. Randall Jarrell. CP-JarrR

Sick of the piercing company of women. Country Walk, A. Thomas Kinsella. CP-KinsT

Sick of your arms. Head-Aim, The. James Dickey. CP-DickJ

Sick Room. Langston Hughes. CP-HughL; CP-HughL1

Sick Rose, The. William Blake. CP-BlakW *Fr.* Songs of Experience.

Sick with the flu. Trench Warfare. Charles Bukowski. SP-BukC1

Sick with the lightning lay my sister-in-law. Lightning, The. John Berryman. CP-BerrJ

Sickness. D. H. Lawrence. CP-LawrD

Sickness. Jones Very. CP-VeryJ

Sickness, The. Charles Bukowski. SP-BukC3

Sickness at the Equinox. A. W. S. Merwin. SP-MerwW

Sickness Blues. Allen Ginsberg. CP-GinsA; SP-GinsA

Sickness brought me this. Friend's Illness, A. William Butler Yeats. CP-YeatW

Sickness may seem a falling out of love. Pity. Robert Graves. CP-GravR

Sickness of this World it most occasions, A. Emily Dickinson. CP-DickE

Sickness poured through the roads, The. Slow Death of the Dragon. Muriel Rukeyser. CP-RukeM

Sickness, the minister of Death, doth lay. Upon the King's Sickness. Thomas Carew. CP-CareT

Sickness unto Death, The. Anne Sexton. CP-SextA

Sicut et acre piper, mordax epigramma palato. De Epigrammate. Thomas Campion. CP-CampT

Side by Side. Thomas Hardy. CP-HardT

Side by Side. Adrienne Rich. CP-RicAE

Side by side, their faces blurred. Arundel Tomb, An. Philip Larkin. CP-LarkP

Side-Step, O Sons of Men! D. H. Lawrence. CP-LawrD

Side view. Three Views of Horse. Clarence Major. SP-MajoC

Sidereus Nuncius. Primo Levi. CP-LeviP, *tr. by* Ruth Feldman

Sidewalk says, The. Teacher's Lament. Alan Dugan. CP-DugaA

Sidling upon the river, the white boat. Puritans, The. Richard Wilbur. CP-WilbR

Siege. Edna St. Vincent Millay. CP-MillE

Siege. Dan Pagis. SP-PagiD, *tr. by* Stephen Mitchell

Siege, The. Sir John Suckling. *See* Love's Siege

Siege, The. Tennessee Williams. CP-WillT

Siege of Corinth, The. Lord Byron. CP-Byron

Siege of Vienna Raised by John Sobieski February, 1816. William Wordsworth.

CP-WorW2

Siege Perilous. Edwin Arlington Robinson. CP-RobiE

Siegfried. Randall Jarrell. CP-JarrR

"SIEMENS" not. Sign ("'SIEMENS' not"). Robert Creeley. SP-CreeR

Siena. Charles Olson. CP-OlsoC

Siena in Sixty-Eight. Charles Tomlinson. SP-TomlC

Sierra Nevada Hike. Helen Pinkerton. CP-PinkH

Siesta. Stevie Smith. CP-SmitS

Siesta in Xbalba. Allen Ginsberg. CP-GinsA
  "One could pass valuable months." SP-GinsA
  "What solitude I've / finally inherited." SP-GinsA

Sigh. Stéphane Mallarmé. CP-MallS, tr. by Henry Weinfield

Sigh, The. Thomas Hardy. CP-HardT

Sigh No More. D. H. Lawrence. CP-LawrD

Sigh not for richer lands, nor milder skies. Discontent. Jones Very. CP-VeryJ

Sigh paid to be studious when I moved went on to (queer) once. Catullus. See Conscientiously bringing my mind to bear on this problem

Sigh, sigh, pure sigh! Rainer Maria Rilke. CP-RilkFr, tr. by A. Poulin, Jr. Fr. Windows, The.

Sigh that heaves the grasses, The. A. E. Housman. CP-HousA

Sigh, you seven seas. Hayden Carruth. CP-CarHS Fr. Clay Hill Anthology, The.

Sighed Rawdon Brown: "Yes, I'm departing, Toni!" Rawdon Brown. Robert Browning. CP-BroR2

Sighed the wind to the wheat. Gold. Walter De la Mare. CP-DeLaW

Sighing, bursting: steam—sulfur—lava. Arktos. Gary Snyder. CP-SnydG

Sighs and Groans [or Grones]. George Herbert. CP-HerbG

Sighs are my food, drink are my tears. Sir Thomas Wyatt. CP-WyatT

Sight. Dorothy Parker. CP-ParkD

Sight, A. Robert Creeley. CP-CreeR

Sight and Flight. Charles Tomlinson. CP-TomlC

Sight in Camp [in the Daybreak Gray and Dim], A. Walt Whitman. CP-WhitW

Sight of God, The. D. H. Lawrence. CP-LawrD

Sight of her, angelic and serene, The. Petrarch. CP-Petra, tr. by J. G. Nichols

Sight of the Ocean, The. Jones Very. CP-VeryJ

Sights we see, the sounds we hear, The. Interpreting Nature. Jones Very. CP-VeryJ

Sightseeing. Rita Dove. SP-DoveR

Sightseeing Tour. Hans Magnus Enzensberger. SP-EnzeH

Sightseers. Howard Nemerov. CP-NemeH

Sightseers, The. Paul Muldoon. CP-MuldP

Sigil. "H. D." CP-DoolH

Sigismundo Malatesta Brings His Favorite Philosopher's Bones to Italy. Robert Stock. SP-StocR

Sign ("'SIEMENS' not"). Robert Creeley. SP-CreeR

Sign ("What you know of me"). Robert Creeley. CP-CreeR

Sign. Michael Palmer. SP-PalmM

Sign. Marge Piercy. SP-PierM

Sign, A. Walter De la Mare. CP-DeLaW

Sign, The. Randall Jarrell. CP-JarrR

Sign, The. Jones Very. CP-VeryJ

Sign Board, The. Robert Creeley. CP-CreeR

Sign Faehre nach Wilm, The. Stephen Spender. CP-SpenS

Sign Language. Clarence Major. SP-MajoC

Sign of Gemini, star of luck, Capricorn, my star again. Yehuda Amichai. SP-AmicYL Fr. At Right Angles.

Sign of Plenty, Peace, and Joy. On an Ear of Wheat Brought, By My Brother, from the Field of Waterloo. Jones Very. CP-VeryJ

Sign-Post. Robinson Jeffers. CP-JefR2

Sign-Seeker, A. Thomas Hardy. CP-HardT

Signal, The. David Ignatow. SP-IgnaD

Signal, The. Archibald MacLeish. CP-MacLA

Signal from the House, The. Stanley Kunitz. CP-KunSC

Signal light of the firefly in the rose, The. Fireflies. Charles Tomlinson. CP-TomlC; SP-TomlC

Signallers. Ivor Gurney. SP-GurnI

Signals. Yannis Ritsos. SP-RitsY, tr. by Gwendolyn MacEwen and Nikos Tsingos

Signals, The. Theodore Roethke. CP-RoetT

Signature, The. Laura Riding Jackson. CP-RidiL

Signature for Tempo. Archibald MacLeish. CP-MacLA

Signature of All Things, The. Kenneth Rexroth. CP-RexrK

Significance of Corn in American History, The. Alan Dugan. CP-DugaA

Signing the Poem. Robert Stock. SP-StocR

Signorina Angeli, veteran of Vogue. South of the Alps. John Updike. CP-UpdiJ

Signs. Lucille Clifton. SP-ClifL

Signs. Audre Lorde. SP-LordA

Signs. W. S. Merwin. SP-MerwW

Signs. Charles Olson. CP-OlsoC

Signs. Grace Paley. CP-PalGC

Signs. C. K. Williams. SP-WillC

Signs and Evidence in the Orchard of Gan-Hayim. Yehuda Amichai. SP-AmicYL, tr. by Benjamin Harshav and Barbara Harshav

Signs and Portents. Stanley Kunitz. CP-KunSC

Signs and Tokens. Thomas Hardy. CP-HardT

Signs have appeared in heaven, that dog is one. The second. Dog in the Sky, The. Robinson Jeffers. CP-JefR3

Signs in the Natural World. Jones Very. CP-VeryJ

Signs of Knowledge, The. Laura Riding Jackson. CP-RidiL

Signs of Spring. Langston Hughes. CP-HughL

Signs of the Times. Paul Laurence Dunbar. CP-DunbP

Signs of the Times. D. H. Lawrence. CP-LawrD

Sila. Robert Penn Warren. CP-WarrR

Silence. Robert Bly. SP-BlyR
  (Uneasiness in Fall.) SP-BlyR

Silence. Hayden Carruth. CP-CarHS

Silence. G. K. Chesterton. CP-ChesG

Silence. Andrei Codrescu. SP-CodrA

Silence. Walter De la Mare. CP-DeLaW

Silence. Paul Laurence Dunbar. CP-DunbP

Silence. T. S. Eliot. SP-ElioT

Silence. Ralph Waldo Emerson. CP-EmerR

Silence. Robert Herrick. CP-HerrR

Silence. Langston Hughes. CP-HughL; CP-HughL2

Silence. D. H. Lawrence. CP-LawrD

Silence. Marianne Craig Moore. CP-MoorM

Silence. James Whitcomb Riley. CP-RileJ

Silence. Yannis Ritsos. SP-RitsY, tr. by N. C. Germanacos

Silence. Theodore Roethke. CP-RoetT

Silence. William Carlos Williams. CP-WilW2

Silence, A. Amy Clampitt. CP-ClamA

Silence, The. Wendell Berry. CP-BerrW

Silence, The. Anne Sexton. CP-SextA; SP-SextA

Silence, The. Arthur Sze. SP-SzeA

Silence, The. C. K. Williams. SP-WillC

Silence already funereal spreads a pall, The. Homage: "Silence already funereal spreads a pall, The." Stéphane Mallarmé. CP-MallS, tr. by Henry Weinfield

Silence and Tears. Stevie Smith. CP-SmitS

Silence and the Wayfarer. Marya Alexandrovna Zaturenska. SP-ZatuM

Silence, and whirling worlds afar. Night. Paul Laurence Dunbar. CP-DunbP

Silence before Harvest, The. W. S. Merwin. SP-MerwW

Silence! calm, venerable majesty. Address to Silence. William Wordsworth. CP-WorW1

Silence! coeval with Eternity. On Silence. Alexander Pope. CP-PopeA

Silence—except below leaves gorge-deep. Aging Man at Noon in Timeless Noon of Summer. Robert Penn Warren. CP-WarrR

Silence Full of Sleighbells. Jaroslav Seifert. SP-SeifJ, tr. by Ewald Osers

Silence / .is / a / looking. E. E. Cummings. CP-CummE

Silence is a shape that has passed. Green Plant, The. Wallace Stevens. CP-StevW; CP-StevWP

Silence is all we dread. Emily Dickinson. CP-DickE

Silence lies over the headland like a death, A. Headland, The. Charles Tomlinson. SP-TomlC

Silence' oblation to the Ear. Emily Dickinson. SP-DickE

Silence o'er sea and earth. Sicilian Vespers, The. John Greenleaf Whittier. CP-WhitJ

Silence of a City—How awful at midnight, The. Silent City, A. Samuel Taylor Coleridge. CP-ColeS

Silence of a place where there were once horses, The. Horses. W. S. Merwin. SP-MerwW

Silence of after-wars, when through the air. Homage to Christina Rossetti. Marya Alexandrovna Zaturenska. SP-ZatuM

Silence of myrtle and lime. Gypsy Nun, The. Federico García Lorca. CP-GarcF, tr. by Will Kirkland

Silence / of nature, the. Without. Gary Snyder. CP-SnydG

Silence of Plants, The. Wisława Szymborska. SP-SzymWM, tr. by Joanna Trzeciak

Silence of preluded song—, The. South-West Wind in the Woodland. George Meredith. CP-MerG1

Silence of the ether, The. Morning Radio. Derek Mahon. CP-MahoD

Silence of the night, a sorrowful silence. Nocturne: "Silence of the night, a sorrowful silence." "Rubén Dario." SP-DariR, tr. by Alberto Acereda and Will Derusha

Silence of the Year, The. This hour the streets. Landscape of the Star. Adrienne Rich. CP-RicAE

Silence of Volcanoes. Muriel Rukeyser. CP-RukeM

Silence! Oh, well are Death and Sleep and Thou. Fragment: Apostrophe to Silence. Percy Bysshe Shelley. CP-ShelP

Silence on the wooded slopes, a silence on the sea, A. Worship. G. K. Chesterton. CP-ChesG

Silence tel que ce qui fut. Samuel Beckett. CP-BeckS

Silence that tunnels forever, A. Poem: "Silence that tunnels forever, A." James Tate. SP-TateJ

Silence. The man defined. Hand at Callow Hill Farm, The. Charles Tomlinson. CP-TomlC; SP-TomlC

Silence, where are you taking. Elegy: To Silence. Federico García Lorca. CP-GarcF, *tr. by* Catherine Brown

Silence, words into foolishness fading. Black Goddess, The. Robert Graves. CP-GravR

Silences. Thomas Hardy. CP-HardT

Silent, The. Jones Very. CP-VeryJ

Silent Agreement. Yannis Ritsos. SP-RitsY, *tr. by* Kimon Friar

Silent and amazed even when a little boy. Child's Amaze, A. Walt Whitman. CP-WhitW

Silent and small in your wet sleep. Winter's Tale, A. Wyatt Prunty. SP-PrunW

Silent and stealthy days that hour by hour. Runaway, The. Marya Alexandrovna Zaturenska. SP-ZatuM

Silent battles of the sunset, Lines That Could Have Been Written and Lost Round About 1922. Jorge Luis Borges. SP-BorgJ, *tr. by* Charles Tomlinson

Silent City. A. Samuel Taylor Coleridge. CP-ColeS

Silent country whose prophets keep quiet. Rainer Maria Rilke. CP-RilkFr, *tr. by* A. Poulin, Jr. *Fr.* Valaisian Quatrains, The.

Silent friendship of the moon, The. Limit, The. Jorge Luis Borges. SP-BorgJ, *tr. by* Alan S. Trueblood

Silent Generation, The. Charles Wright. SP-WrigCN

Silent history of a word, The. Word, A. Jones Very. CP-VeryJ

Silent I sat, dejected, and alone. John Milton. *See* I was full of sadness, and I was sitting silent with no companion

Silent in America. Philip Levine. SP-LeviP

Silent is the house: all are laid asleep. Visionary, The. Emily Jane Brontë. CP-BronE

Silent is the House—all are laid asleep. Julian M. and A.G. Rochelle. Emily Jane Brontë. CP-BronE

Silent Journal. Charles Wright. SP-WrigC

Silent Man, The. Carolyn Kizer. CP-KizeC

Silent moon is rising, The. Lines Suggested by Hearing the Beach, at F. Peabody's Mills, South Salem. December 21. 1833. Jones Very. CP-VeryJ

Silent Movie. Dan Pagis. SP-PagiD, *tr. by* Stephen Mitchell

Silent night. Silent. And you had stopped. Suddenly. Yannis Ritsos. SP-RitsY, *tr. by* Kimon Friar

Silent Noon. Dante Gabriel Rossetti. CW-RossD *Fr.* House of Life, The.

Silent One. Langston Hughes. CP-HughL; CP-HughL3

Silent One, The. Ivor Gurney. SP-GurnI *Fr.* Silent One, The.

Silent rapt surfaces. Worker in Mirror, at his Bench. Thomas Kinsella. CP-KinsT

Silent room, the heavy creeping shade, The. Fabien dei Franchi. Oscar Wilde. CP-WildO

Silent Shepherds, The. Robinson Jeffers. CP-JefR3

Silent Silent Night. William Blake. CP-BlakW

Silent Singer, The. James Whitcomb Riley. CP-RileJ

Silent Slain, The. Archibald MacLeish. *See* Too-Late Born, The

Silent unday by silently not night. E. E. Cummings. CP-CummE

Silent Victors, The. James Whitcomb Riley. CP-RileJ

Silent Visit. Robert Graves. CP-GravR

Silent Whole, The. Rainer Maria Rilke. CP-RilkFr, *tr. by* A. Poulin, Jr.

Silentium Amoris. Oscar Wilde. CP-WildO

Silently I ascend the western pavilion. Li Yü. CP-WilW2

Silently I footed by an uphill road. Last Signal, The. Thomas Hardy. CP-HardT

Silently if,out of not knowable. E. E. Cummings. CP-CummE

Silently little blue elephant shyly(he was terri), The. E. E. Cummings. CP-CummE

Silently / she was quieter than breathing now. Juliet's Garden. Charles Tomlinson. CP-TomlC

Silently without my window. Melancholia. Paul Laurence Dunbar. CP-DunbP

Silenus' Epitaph. Robert Stock. SP-StocR

Silet. Ezra Pound. CP-PoEar

Silhouette. Langston Hughes. CP-HughL *Fr.* Three Songs about Lynching.

Silhouette. John Ashbery. SP-AshbJ

Silk colour and lit-up candlelight the sheets I saw. Traffic in Sheets. Ivor Gurney. SP-GurnI

Silk glove at my window, A. Glove, The. Raissa Maritain. CP-MertT

Silk I said to myself. One of My Favorite Songs Is Stormy Weather. Philip Whalen. SP-WhalP

Silk Road, The. Arthur Sze. SP-SzeA

Silk Worm, The. Vincent Bourne. CP-CowpW

Silken Snake, The. Robert Herrick. CP-HerrR

Silken Tent, The. Robert Frost. CP-FrosR

Silky / Cap. Stupidities. Arthur Rimbaud. CP-RimbA, *tr. by* Martin Sorrell

Silly. All giggles and ringlets and never. Two Poems for Benn. John Ciardi. CP-CiarJ

Silly Animals. Langston Hughes. CP-HughL

Silly boy, 'tis ful[l] moon[e] yet, thy night as day shines clearly [*or* clearly]. First Love. Thomas Campion. CP-CampT

Silly fool, the silly fool, The. Happy Ending. W. H. Auden. CP-AudeW

Silly girls your heads full of boys. Plainness in Diversity. John Ashbery. SP-AshbJ

Silly Song. Federico García Lorca. CP-GarcF, *tr. by* Alan S. Trueblood *Fr.* Songs for Children.

Silly Song. Federico García Lorca. CP-GarcF, *tr. by* M. D. Herter Norton *and* Harriet de Onís

Siloam. Donald Davie. CP-DaviDC

Silvanus long in love, and long in vain. Sir Philip Sidney. SP-SidnP *Fr.* Lady of May, The.

Silver. A. R. Ammons. CP-AmmoA

Silver Age, The. Thom Gunn. CP-GunnT

Silver and violet leopard of the night, The. Nightmare. G. K. Chesterton. CP-ChesG

Silver bark of beech, and sallow. Counting-out Rhyme. Edna St. Vincent Millay. CP-MillE

Silver birch dances at my window, A. Ivor Gurney. SP-GurnI

Silver bird is E backward in cool pond water, The. Thomas Merton. CP-MertT

Silver burbles of the frogs wind and swirl, The. Frog Songs. Carl Sandburg. CP-SandC

Silver chariots, and copper. Seascape. Arthur Rimbaud. CP-RimbA, *tr. by* Martin Sorrell

Silver Creek Falls. William Dickey. SP-DickW

Silver dust. Pear Tree. "H. D." CP-DoolH

Silver jet, A. Sitting Down, Looking Up. A. R. Ammons. CP-AmmoA

Silver Jubilee, The. Gerard Manley Hopkins. CP-HopkG

Silver key of the fountain of tears. Fragment: To Music, A. Percy Bysshe Shelley. CP-ShelP

Silver leaves of the last summer. Poplar and Elm. Carl Sandburg. CP-SandC

Silver, / lifting. Out Window: Taylor's Mistake. Robert Creeley. SP-CreeR

Silver Nails. Carl Sandburg. CP-SandC

Silver of one star, The. Star Silver. Carl Sandburg. CP-SandC

Silver Plough-Boy, The. Wallace Stevens. CP-StevWP

Silver Point. Carl Sandburg. CP-SandC

Silver point of an evening star, The. Silver Point. Carl Sandburg. CP-SandC

Silver quivering cocoon that shakes, A. Emblem (2). Denise Levertov. SP-LeveDL

Silver scarce-call-silver gloss, A. Gerard Manley Hopkins. CP-HopkG

Silver shadow where the line falls grey, The. Upcountry. Adrienne Rich. SP-RicA1; SP-RicA2

Silver Stag, The. Kathleen Jessie Raine. SP-RainK

Silver stars dot the beam. Shih-te. CP-ColdM, *tr. by* Red Pine

Silver Swan, The. Kenneth Rexroth. CP-RexrK

Silver Tassie, The. Robert Burns. CP-BurnR
   (My Bonnie [*or* Bony] Mary.) CP-BurnR

Silver-tongued among the sons of Rome. Carmen 49. Catullus. CP-ZukLS *Fr.* Carmina.

Silver Trade, The. Arthur Sze. SP-SzeA

Silver trumpets rang across the Dome, The. Easter Day. Oscar Wilde. CP-WildO

Silver will lie where she lies. Mule Song. A. R. Ammons. CP-AmmoA

Silver Wind. Carl Sandburg. CP-SandC

Silverpoint. Louise Glück. SP-GlucL

Silvery leaf of innocence lifts off the bay past dusk, The. Evensong. Olga Broumas. SP-BrouO

Simaetha. "H. D." CP-DoolH

Simeon. Constantine P. Cavafy. CP-CavaC, *tr. by* Theoharis Constantine Theoharis

Simile, A. Jonathan Swift. CP-SwifJ

Simile for Her Smile, A. Richard Wilbur. CP-WilbR

Simile Latinised, A. *Unknown.* CP-CowpW

Similes for Two Political Characters of 1819. Percy Bysshe Shelley. CP-ShelP

Simile's the likeness of a thing, A. Figures of Speech. Thomas Sheridan. CP-SherT

Simmer's a Pleasant Time. Robert Burns. CP-BurnR
   (Ay Waukin O.) CP-BurnR

Simmons Mobile Alabama. Jones Very. CP-VeryJ

Simon. Josephine Jacobsen. CP-JacoJ

Simon de Montfort. G. K. Chesterton. CP-ChesG

Simon Lee, the Old Huntsman; with an incident in which he was concerned. William Wordsworth. CP-WorW1; MW-WorW

Simon the Cyrenian Speaks. Countee Cullen. CP-CullC

Simone Signoret. James Schuyler. CP-SchuJ

Simone Weil Watches the Rhône Valley. Adam Zagajewski. SP-ZagaA, tr. by Renata Gorczynski, Benjamin Ivry and C. K. Williams

Simpering sideways under a picture-hat. Lincolnshire. Donald Davie. CP-DaviDC

Simple. Hayden Carruth. CP-CarHS

Simple. Raymond Carver. CP-CarvR

Simple and extraordinary wall. Wall. Gabriela Mistral. SP-MistG, tr. by Maria Giachetti [or Jacketti]

Simple and fresh and fair from winter's close emerging. First Dandelion, The. Walt Whitman. CP-WhitW

Simple Autumnal. Louise Bogan. CP-BogaL

Simple Bard, rough at the rustic plough, The. Brigs of Ayr, a Poem. Inscribed to J. B*********, Esq; Ayr, The. Robert Burns. CP-BurnR

Simple child, A. We Are Seven. William Wordsworth. CP-WorW1; MW-WorW

Simple Experiment, A. Muriel Rukeyser. CP-RukeM

Simple goatherd between Alp and sky, The. Mountaineer and Poet. Elizabeth Barrett Browning. CP-BroEB

Simple Honesty. Yannis Ritsos. SP-RitsY, tr. by Kostas Myrsiades

Simple misery of survival, The. 9 Rings. Charles Bukowski. SP-BukC2

Simple nosegay! was that much to ask?, A. Troll's Nosegay, The. Robert Graves. CP-GravR

Simple people each with basket or tool, The. Ralph Waldo Emerson. CP-EmerR

Simple Philo of Alexandria. Norman Dubie. CP-DubiN

Simple Recipe, A. James Whitcomb Riley. CP-RileJ

Simple ring with a single stone, A. Pearl, a Girl, A. Robert Browning. CP-BroR2

Simple rustic's soul, The. Soul's Questioning of the Universe, and Its Beginning, The. Jones Very. CP-VeryJ

Simple silly terror, The. Doorknobs. Langston Hughes. CP-HughL; CP-HughL3

Simple Social Lifer is a harmless sort of elf, The. Song of Self-Esteem, A. G. K. Chesterton. CP-ChesG

Simple Sonatina. Tess Gallagher. SP-GallT

Simple-Song. Marge Piercy. SP-PierM

Simple, spontaneous, curious, two souls interchanging. For Us Two, Reader Dear. Walt Whitman. CP-WhitW

Simple stocky belfry that with a sower's gesture. Rainer Maria Rilke. CP-RilkFr, tr. by A. Poulin, Jr. Fr. Valaisian Quatrains, The.

Simple things. Speech. Robert Creeley. SP-CreeR

Simple Trust. Jeanne Marie Bouvier de la Motte Guyon. CP-CowpW

Simple was I and was young. After Reading Psalms XXXIX, XL, etc. Thomas Hardy. CP-HardT

Simplest memory is books by ferny windows, The. Reverie during Briefing. John Ciardi. CP-CiarJ

Simplest / Words say the grass blade, The. Occurrences, The ("Simplest / Words say the grass blade, The"). George Oppen. CP-OppGN

Simplex Sigilum Veri: A Catalogue. William Carlos Williams. CP-WilW1

Simplicity. Jorge Luis Borges. SP-BorgJ, tr. by Stephen Kessler

Simplicity assuages. Predestined Space, The. James Vincent Cunningham. CP-CunnJ

Simplicity, if you. Vocations. W. S. Merwin. SP-MerwW

Simplicity of Everything in Viet Nam, The. Charles Bukowski. SP-BukC2

Simplicity of the Unknown Past, The. Kenneth Koch. SP-KochK

Simplicity yea even to write. Confections. Paul Éluard. CP-BeckS

Simplification, A. Richard Wilbur. CP-WilbR

Simplon Pass, The. William Wordsworth. CP-WorW1

Simply because of a question, my life is implicated. Private Life of the Sphinx. Muriel Rukeyser. CP-RukeM

Simply by opening these eyes. Anonymous Secrets. Robert Stock. SP-StocR

Simulacrum. David Ignatow. SP-IgnaD

Simultaneously. David Ignatow. SP-IgnaD

Simultaneously, five thousand miles apart. Simultaneously. David Ignatow. SP-IgnaD

Sin. Robert Herrick. CP-HerrR

Sin (2): "O that I could a sin once see!" George Herbert. CP-HerbG

Sin against the Holy . . . though what, The. Blasphemies, The. Louis MacNeice. CP-MacNL

Sin and Strife. Robert Herrick. CP-HerrR

Sin City, D.C. John Updike. CP-UpdiJ

Sin for my Master's sake. Sounds. John Ciardi. CP-CiarJ

Sin is an act so free, that if we shall. Another. Robert Herrick. CP-HerrR

Sin is impervious / to past transmutations. Sin of Wanting a New Refrigerator, The. Andrei Codrescu. SP-CodrA

Sin is inferiority. The mother's cooperation in the birth of her daughter. Charles Olson. CP-OlsoC

Sin is the cause of death; and sin's alone. Another. Robert Herrick. CP-HerrR

Sin leads the way, but as it goes, it feels. Sin. Robert Herrick. CP-HerrR

Sin no Existence; Nature none it hath. Sin. Robert Herrick. CP-HerrR

Sin of Wanting a New Refrigerator, The. Andrei Codrescu. SP-CodrA

Sin once reacht up to Gods eternall Sphere. Sin. Robert Herrick. CP-HerrR

Sin (1). George Herbert. CP-HerbG

Sin recognized—but that—may keep us humble. Recognition Not Enough. Stevie Smith. CP-SmitS

Sin Seen. Robert Herrick. CP-HerrR

Sin Severely Punisht. Robert Herrick. CP-HerrR

Sin, stinting, senseless acts and sophistries. To the Reader. Charles Baudelaire. CP-BaudC, tr. by Walter Martin

Sin was mine; I did not understand, The. New Remorse, The. Oscar Wilde. CP-WildO

Sinbad. Allen Tate. CP-TateA

Since. W. H. Auden. CP-AudeW

Since all of your work was really an effort to appease. Derek Walcott. CP-WalcD Fr. Midsummer.

Since all that beat about in Nature's range. Constancy to an Ideal Object. Samuel Taylor Coleridge. CP-ColeS; MW-ColeS

Since all the Riches of this World. William Blake. CP-BlakW

Since / And the rain since. De Votre Bonheur Il ne Reste Que Vos Photos. Archibald MacLeish. CP-MacLA

Since as in night's deck-watch ye show. Herman Melville. SP-MelvH Fr. John Marr.

Since, Bacchus, thou art father. Dedication of the King's New Cellar. To Bacchus, The. Ben Jonson. CP-JonsB

Since bailiffs and mayors, to evade all objection. Trip to Temple-Oge, Stephen's Green and the Bason, A: or, An Election of Dublin Beauties. Unknown, sometimes at. to Thomas Sheridan. CP-SherT

Since Christ embraced the Cross itself, dare I. Cross, The. John Donne. CP-DonnJ; MW-DonnJ

Since Christmas they have lived with us. Balloons. Sylvia Plath. CP-PlatS

Since depth of love is never gauged. Depth of Love. Robert Graves. CP-GravR

Since every sound moves memories. Duettist to her Pianoforte, A. Thomas Hardy. CP-HardT

Since every tree begins to blossom now. Letter Written by Sir H. G. and J. D. alternis vicibus, A. John Donne. CP-DonnJ; MW-DonnJ

Since everyone's anguish is our own. Girl-Child of Pompei, The. Primo Levi. CP-LeviP, tr. by Ruth Feldman

Since everything must pass. Rainer Maria Rilke. CP-RilkFr, tr. by A. Poulin, Jr. Fr. Orchards.

Since faction ebbs, and rogues grow out of fashion. Prologue to the King and Queen at the Opening of their Theatre. John Dryden. CP-DryJ2

Since feeling is first. E. E. Cummings. CP-CummE; SP-CummE

Since feeling is first. Since feeling is first. E. E. Cummings. CP-CummE; SP-CummE

Since fire is not extinguished by more fire. Petrarch. CP-Petra, tr. by J. G. Nichols

Since first the White Horse Banner blew free. Departure, A. Rudyard Kipling. CP-KiplR Fr. Land and Sea Tales.

Since, for the charity they knew. Of Wickedness the Word. Herman Melville. SP-MelvH Fr. Clarel: A Poem and Pilgrimage in the Holy Land.

Since for thy full deserts (with all the rest). To His Peculiar Friend Sir Edward Fish, Knight Baronet. Robert Herrick. CP-HerrR

Since Gander did his prettie Youngling wed. Upon Gander. Robert Herrick. CP-HerrR

Since he had few intimate friends, and little. "Women of Color" Have Rarely Had the Opportunity to Write about Their Love Affairs. Alice Walker. CP-WalkA

Since he is older than Hamlet or Stavrogin. Predecessor of Perseus, A. Howard Nemerov. CP-NemeH

Since he's not jewish. Talismanic Ceremony for Lucian, March 9, 1971, Intersection Church, San Francisco. Andrei Codrescu. SP-CodrA

Since I am a queen and I was once a beggar. Vigilant Woman, The. Gabriela Mistral. SP-MistG, tr. by Maria Giachetti [or Jacketti]

Since I am coming [or comming] to that holy room[e]. Hymn[e] to God My God, In My Sickness[e], A. John Donne. CP-DonnJ; MW-DonnJ

Since I am / Somebody's dream. Secret, The. Thomas Merton. CP-MertT

Since I came to Cold Mountain. Han-shan. CP-ColdM, tr. by Red Pine

Since I came to Tientai Temple. Shih-te. CP-ColdM, tr. by Red Pine

Since I cannot persuade you from this mood. Edna St. Vincent Millay. CP-MillE

Since I can't. Here ("Since I can't"). Robert Creeley. SP-CreeR

Since I did leave the presence of my love. Sonnet 86. Edmund Spenser. CP-Spens Fr. Amoretti.

Since I escaped to Cold Mountain. Han-shan. CP-ColdM, tr. by Red Pine

Since I left the city's heat. At Loafing-Holt. Paul Laurence Dunbar. CP-DunbP

Since I left you, Anne. Letter to Anne, A. Langston Hughes. CP-HughL; CP-HughL1

Since I lost you, I am silence-haunted. Silence. D. H. Lawrence. CP-LawrD

Since I lost you, my darling, the sky has come near. Call into Death. D. H. Lawrence. CP-LawrD

Since I must bear a sorrowing heart. Guido Cavalcanti. CP-CavaG, *tr. by* Marc Cirigliano

Since I no longer speak I. Silent in America. Philip Levine. SP-LeviP

Since I returned, the trees have a Japanese look. Letter to Uehata. Charles Tomlinson. SP-TomlC

Since I was minutely hurt. Minutely Hurt. Countee Cullen. CP-CullC

Since I'm too obligated. Michelangelo Buonarroti. CP-Miche, *tr. by* John Frederick Nims

Since *Jack* and *Jill* both wicked be. Jack and Jill. Robert Herrick. CP-HerrR

Since learning all in such a tremble last night. Echoes. Laura Riding Jackson. CP-RidiL

Since life in sorrow must be spent. Love of God the End of Life, The. Jeanne Marie Bouvier de la Motte- Guyon. CP-CowpW

Since, Lord, to thee / A narrow way and little gate. Holy Baptism (2). George Herbert. CP-HerbG

Since louely sweete, much like unto a Dewe. Elegy: "Since louely sweete, much like unto a Dewe." Robert Herrick. CP-HerrR

Since love is an astonished always. Theme of Death, The. Robert Graves. CP GravR

Since love is such that, as ye wot. Sir Thomas Wyatt. CP-WyatT

Since Love was driving me to my old haunts. Petrarch. CP-Petra, *tr. by* J. G. Nichols

Since Love will needs that I shall love. Sir Thomas Wyatt. CP-WyatT

Since man's life is nothing but a bit of action at a distance. Piano Solo. Nicanor Parra. CP-WilW2, *tr. by* William Carlos Williams

Since Maria left me to go to another star. Autumn Lament. Stéphane Mallarmé. CP-MallS, *tr. by* Henry Weinfield

Since men grow diffident at last. Youth Sings a Song of Rosebuds. Countee Cullen. CP-CullC

Since men have left to do praiseworthy things. To Thomas, Earl of Suffolk. Ben Jonson. CP-JonsB; SP-JonsB

Since men like beasts each other's prey were made. Absalom and Achitophel, Part 2. Nahum Tate. CP-DryJ2

Since mistakes are inevitable, I can easily be taken. At a Lecture. Joseph Brodsky. CP-BrodJ

Since monkeys can be taught. Shih-te. CP-ColdM, *tr. by* Red Pine

Since much at home on. *Song*: The Sundial's Lament. Robert Graves. CP-GravR

Since Munich, what? A tangle of black film. News-Reel, The. Louis MacNeice. CP-MacNL

Since my girlhood, in that small boat. Boat Ride. Tess Gallagher. SP-GallT

Since my mother died, the tone. James Whitcomb Riley. CP-RileJ

Since my old friend is grown so great. Dialogue, A. Alexander Pope. CP-PopeA

Since Nature's works be good, and death doth serve. Why Fear to Die? Sir Philip Sidney. SP-SidnP *Fr.* Arcadia.

Since Nine O'Clock. Constantine P. Cavafy. CP-CavaC, *tr. by* Theoharis Constantine Theoharis

Since no one knows the why of the weather. Why of the Weather, The. Robert Graves. CP-GravR

Since none in virtue to perfection rise. Epilogue Designed to Be Spoken by Alonzo, at the Acting of *The Revenge* by Some Schoolboys. *Unknown, sometimes at. to* Thomas Sheridan. CP-SherT

Since now I dare not ask. Sharp Ridge, The. Robert Graves. CP-GravR

Since now in every public place. Sea Horse, The. Robert Graves. CP-GravR

Since now the hour is come at last. To Emma. Lord Byron. CP-Byron

Since now those clouds, that lately over-cast. To My Honourable Friend, Sr. Thomas Mounson, *Knight and Baronet*. Thomas Campion. CP-CampT

Since of no creature living the last breath. Edna St. Vincent Millay. CP-MillE

Since one of our functions is to forget. Gone. Paul Muldoon. CP-MuldP

Since our Country, our God—Oh, my Sire! Jephtha's Daughter. Lord Byron. CP-Byron

Since Persia fell at Marathon. Villanelle of Change. Edwin Arlington Robinson. CP-RobiE

Since pick av them I'm sore denied. Mr. Foley's Christmas. James Whitcomb Riley. CP-RileJ

Since Reason, with itself dissatisfied. Reason. George Meredith. CP-MerG2

Since Reverend Doctors now declare. Respectable Burgher, The. Thomas Hardy. CP-HardT

Since she, ev'n shee, for whom I liv'd. Thomas Campion. CP-CampT

Since shed or Cottage I have none. To His Peculiar Friend M. Jo: Wicks. Robert Herrick. CP-HerrR

Since, shunning pain, I ease can never find. Sir Philip Sidney. SP-SidnP

Since So Mine Eyes. Sir Philip Sidney. SP-SidnP *Fr.* Arcadia.

Since so mine eyes are subject to your sight. Since So Mine Eyes. Sir Philip Sidney. SP-SidnP *Fr.* Arcadia.

Since so ye please to hear me plain. Sir Thomas Wyatt. CP-WyatT

Since tears become stones. Fanny Howe. SP-HoweF *Fr.* Vineyard, The.

Since that first morning when I crawled. Hornworm: Autumn Lamentation. Stanley Kunitz. CP-KunSC

Since that last evening we have fallen indeed. Adam and Eve. Arthur Hugh Clough. SP-ClouA

Since that moment when in a house with low eaves. Lessons. Czeslaw Milosz. CP-MiloC; CP-MiloCN

Since that my language without eloquence. Sir Thomas Wyatt. CP-WyatT

Since That Stormy Rage. Sir Philip Sidney. SP-SidnP *Fr.* Arcadia.

Since the art of poetry calls for words, I, morose. End of a Beautiful Era, The. Joseph Brodsky. CP-BrodJ, *tr. by* David Rigsbee

Since the devil hopping on. Ralph Waldo Emerson. CP-EmerR

Since the first Adam who beheld the night. Alexandria, A.D. 641. Jorge Luis Borges. SP-BorgJ, *tr. by* Stephen Kessler

Since the Majority of Me. Philip Larkin. CP-LarkP

Since the night in which you stole. Watch, The. Robert Graves. CP-GravR

Since the Noon Mail Stopped. Wyatt Prunty. SP-PrunW

Since the refinement of this polish'd age. Occasional Prologue Delivered Previous to the Performance of "The Wheel of Fortune" at a Private Theatre, An. Lord Byron. CP-Byron

Since the road traveled, if I look back, is longer. Voice That Came with the Coots. Eugenio Montale. CP-MontE, *tr. by* Jonathan Galassi

Since the rumor has been verified, you can, at least. Rumor Verified. Robert Penn Warren. CP-WarrR

Since the sky started crying. Flood at the International Writer's Workshop. Bogomil Gjuzel. CP-KizeC, *tr. by* Carolyn Kizer

Since Then. Yehuda Amichai. SP-AmicYL, *tr. by* Benjamin Harshav *and* Barbara Harshav

Since there are people who complain. Dialogue between an Eminent Lawyer and Dr. Swift, Dean of St. Patrick's. Jonathan Swift. CP-SwifJ

Since there's no help, come, let them kiss and part. Limited, The. Robert Penn Warren. CP-WarrR

Since things have grown empty bit by bit. Exultation. Yannis Ritsos. SP-RitsY, *tr. by* Andonis Decavalles

Since this is the last night I keep you home. Seven Seals. D. H. Lawrence. CP-LawrD

Since through my destiny. Petrarch. CP-Petra, *tr. by* J. G. Nichols

Since to th'Country first I came. To Sir Clipsebie Crew. Robert Herrick. CP-HerrR

Since Tuck is faithless found, no more. Madrigal: "Since Tuck is faithless found, no more." George Meredith. CP-MerG2

Since very soon it is required of you. Noguchi. Muriel Rukeyser. CP-RukeM

Since wailing is a bud of causeful sorrow. Sir Philip Sidney. SP-SidnP *Fr.* Arcadia.

Since we agreed to let the road between us. No Road. Philip Larkin. CP-LarkP

Since we can't go back to Tuscany, Dinty. To My Baby Paul. Louis Zukofsky. CP-ZukLS

Since we had changed. Message. Allen Ginsberg. CP-GinsA; SP-GinsA

Since we have become so cerebral. Touch. D. H. Lawrence. CP-LawrD

Since what I hope for's taking far too long. Petrarch. CP-Petra, *tr. by* J. G. Nichols

Since what you want, not what you ought. I Could Let Tom Go—But What about the Children. Stevie Smith. CP-SmitS

Since when must I draw life from death. Guido Cavalcanti. CP-CavaG, *tr. by* Marc Cirigliano

Since Without Thee We Do No Good. Elizabeth Barrett Browning. CP-BroEB

Since ye delight to know. Sir Thomas Wyatt. CP-WyatT

Since ye distemper and defile. To Motorists. Rudyard Kipling. CP-KiplR *Fr.* Muse among the Motors, The.

Since you and I so many times have seen. Petrarch. CP-Petra, *tr. by* J. G. Nichols

Since you are going to begin to-day. Venus Will Now Say a Few Words. W. H. Auden. CP-AudeW

Since You Ask Me. Philip Whalen. SP-WhalP

Since you ask, most days I cannot remember. Wanting to Die. Anne Sexton. CP-SextA; SP-SextA

Since You Asked Me. Mona Van Duyn. SP-VanDM

Since you did depart. Inheritance, The. D. H. Lawrence. CP-LawrD

Since you first drew my irresistible wave. Cliff and Wave. Robert Graves. CP-GravR

Since you must go, and I must bid farewell. Elegy, An: "Since you must go, and I must bid farewell." Ben Jonson. CP-JonsB

Since you packed your rubber bottom boots. Early Hours. Carl Sandburg. CP-SandC

Since you remember Nimmo, and arrive. Nimmo. Edwin Arlington Robinson. CP-RobiE

Since you set no worth on the heart. Hafiz. CP-EmerR *Fr.* Odes.

Since you will needs that I shall sing. Sir Thomas Wyatt. CP-WyatT

Since you would claim the sources of my thought. Sonnet: "Since you would claim the sources of my thought." Louise Bogan. CP-BogaL

Since your poetic prancer is turned into Cancer. To the Dean of St. Patrick's ("Since your poetic prancer is turned into Cancer"). Thomas Sheridan. CP-SherT

Since you're exasperated. Inside Out. Rae Armantrout. SP-ArmaA

Since you've gone I've fasted having made the soup. Fast. Olga Broumas. SP-BrouO

Sincèrement. Robert Graves. CP-GravR

Sincerity. Robert Herrick. CP-HerrR

Sincerity. Thomas Merton. CP-MertT

Sine Prole. Thomas Hardy. CP-HardT

Sinecure for P. Whalen, A. Gary Snyder. CP-SnydG

Sinew. Raymond Carver. CP-CarvR

Sinful City. Jaroslav Seifert. SP-SeifJ, tr. by Ewald Osers

Sinful painter drapes his goddess warm, The. Painting and Sculpture. Ralph Waldo Emerson. CP-EmerR

Sing a song of joy. Thomas Campion. CP-CampT

Sing a song of Ninepence. To J. L. G. K. Chesterton. CP-ChesG

Sing a song of 'sistence. Two Conceits. Allen Tate. CP-TateA

Sing aloud that she is mine. George Meredith. CP-MerG2

Sing aloud unto God our strength. Psalm 81: "Sing aloud unto God our strength." Bible, O.T. CP-MiltJ Fr. Psalms.

Sing, Ballad-singer, raise a hearty tune. At Casterbridge Fair. Thomas Hardy. CP-HardT

Sing! gangling lad, along the brink. Song of Singing, A. James Whitcomb Riley. CP-RileJ

Sing, heav'nly Muse, of that fair mountain sing. Lines on Mount Auburn. Jones Very. CP-VeryJ

Sing; how 'a would sing! Julie-Jane. Thomas Hardy. CP-HardT

Sing me a hero! Quench my thirst. Tray. Robert Browning. CP-BroR2

Sing me a song of the Revolution. Song of the Revolution. Langston Hughes. CP-HughL; CP-HughL1

Sing me a song— / What shall I sing? Christina Georgina Rossetti. CP-RosC2

Sing me a thrush, bone. Fury of Beautiful Bones, The. Anne Sexton. SP-SextA Fr. Furies, The.

Sing me at morn but only with your laugh. Song of Songs. Wilfred Owen. CP-OwenW

Sing me to death; for til thy voice be cleare. Upon a Hoarse Singer. Robert Herrick. CP-HerrR

Sing miserere / For the men who must die. Litany: "Sing miserere / For the men who must die." Thomas Merton. CP-MertT

Sing, Mister, Sing. Charles Olson. CP-OlsoC

Sing, muse, (if such a theme, so dark, so long). Progress of Error, The. William Cowper. CP-CowpW

Sing, Muse, the son of Maia and of Jove. Hymn to Mercury [or Hermes]. Unknown. CP-ShelP, tr. by Percy Bysshe Shelley Fr. Homeric Hymns.

Sing now no hymn nor chant a dirge. To a Prodigal Old Maid. Allen Tate. CP-TateA

Sing! O Voice of Valor, sing! Nicholas Oberting. James Whitcomb Riley. CP-RileJ

Sing of a love lost and forgotten. Two Parted. Christina Georgina Rossetti. CP-RosC3

Sing of the Great Lord Archibald. Great Lord Archibald, The. G. K. Chesterton. CP-ChesG

Sing of the O'Rahilly. O'Rahilly, The. William Butler Yeats. CP-YeatW

Sing, oh, rarest of roundelays! Name Us No Names No More. James Whitcomb Riley. CP-RileJ

Sing on, sweet thrush, upon the leafless bough. Sonnet—On Hearing a Thrush Sing on a Morning Walk in January. Robert Burns. CP-BurnR

Sing praise for statuary. Touch-and-Go. Sylvia Plath. CP-PlatS

Sing-Song. Christina Georgina Rossetti. CP-RosC2

Oh, Fair to See. CP-RosC2

Sing Song. Robert Creeley. CP-CreeR

Sing-Song of Old Man Kangaroo, The. Rudyard Kipling. Fr. Just-So Stories.

Sing the song of death, O sing it! Song of Death. D. H. Lawrence. CP-LawrD

Sing to me / weather about / one bird. So Good. James Schuyler. CP-SchuJ

Sing unto the Lord a New Song. Donald Davie. CP-DaviDC

Sing us something full of laugher. Laughing Song. James Whitcomb Riley. CP-RileJ

Sing we for love and idleness. Immorality, An. Ezra Pound. CP-PoEar

Sing what you want to sing. Theologize. When I Am Dead, My Dearest. Miller Williams. CP-WillM

Sing your new song in the winepress where these bloody pence. Victory, The. Thomas Merton. CP-MertT

Singapore. Mary Oliver. SP-OlivM

Singer. Constantine P. Cavafy. CP-CavaC, tr. by Theoharis Constantine Theoharis

Singer, The. W. S. Merwin. SP-MerwW

Singer, The. James Whitcomb Riley. CP-RileJ

Singer, The. John Greenleaf Whittier. CP-WhitJ

Singer and tailor am I. Darzee's Chaunt. Rudyard Kipling. CP-KiplR Fr. Jungle Book, The.

Singer Asleep, A. Thomas Hardy. CP-HardT

Singer goes all over the world, The. "Rubén Dario." SP-DariR, tr. by Alberto Acereda and Will Derusha

Singer in the Prison, The. Walt Whitman. CP-WhitW

Singer Will Not Sing, The. Maya Angelou. SP-AngeM

Singer with eyes of sand they said, A. Arthur Sze. SP-SzeA

Singer's House, The. Seamus Heaney. SP-HeanSO

SINGERS / SINGERS LIKE O. Horn of Plenty. Langston Hughes. CP-HughL; CP-HughL3

Singers there are of courtly themes. On a Fly-Leaf. James Whitcomb Riley. CP-RileJ

Singing. Primo Levi. CP-LeviP, tr. by Ruth Feldman and Brian Swann

Singing, The. Robert Stock. SP-StocR

Singing across the orchard. To a Wood Thrush. William Carlos Williams. CP-WilW1

Singing Aloud. Carolyn Kizer. CP-KizeC

Singing, always singing, he was something. Orpheus. Alan Dugan. CP-DugaA

Singing black boatmen. Fog. Langston Hughes. CP-HughL; CP-HughL1

Singing Cat, The. Stevie Smith. CP-SmitS

Singing Flower, The. "Shu Ting." CP-KizeC, tr. by Carolyn Kizer and Y. H. Zhao

Singing in the Rain. Countee Cullen. CP-CullC

Singing Is Fire. Charles Bukowski. SP-BukC2

Singing Kettle & the purring Cat, The. Happy Home, The. Samuel Taylor Coleridge. CP-ColeS

Singing Lovers. Thomas Hardy. CP-HardT

Singing my days. Passage to India. Walt Whitman. CP-WhitW

Singing Nigger. Carl Sandburg. CP-SandC

Singing Prayer, A. Christopher Logue. SP-LoguC

Singing robes fly onto your body and cling there silkily, The. Poem Rising by Its Own Weight, The. Denise Levertov. SP-LeveDL

Singing School. Seamus Heaney. SP-HeanSO

Singing the Pain Back into the Wound. Gregory Orr. SP-OrrG

Singing, / the seven maidens. Song of the Seven Maidens. Federico García Lorca. CP-GarcF, tr. by Alan S. Trueblood Fr. Theories.

Singing Voice. A. Kenneth Rexroth. CP-RexrK

Singing Woman, The. Thomas Hardy. CP-HardT

Singing-Woman from the Wood's Edge, The. Edna St. Vincent Millay. CP-MillE

Single clenched fist lifted and ready, The. Choose. Carl Sandburg. CP-SandC

Single clover Plank, A. Emily Dickinson. CP-DickE

Single dog, A. Dog. Charles Bukowski. SP-BukC1

Single Fare. Richard Graves. CP-GravR

Single flow'r he sent me, since we met, A. One Perfect Rose. Dorothy Parker. CP-ParkD

Single form, they sit in majesty, A. On the Virgin and Child Carved in Oak (Auvergne, 1150-1200) in the Metropolitan Museum. Helen Pinkerton. CP-PinkH

Single Life Most Secure. Robert Herrick. CP-HerrR

Single man stands like a bird-watcher, A. Mouth of the Hudson, The. Robert Lowell. SP-LoweR

Single Most. Rae Armantrout. SP-ArmaA

Single rose is every rose, A. Rainer Maria Rilke. CP-RilkFr, tr. by A. Poulin, Jr. Fr. Roses, The.

Single Screw of Flesh, A. Emily Dickinson. CP-DickE

Single seedling, camp-follower, A. Fireweed. Amy Clampitt. CP-ClamA

Single shine broods gloomily, A. Victorian Rehearsal, A. Thomas Hardy. CP-HardT

Single Sonnet. Louise Bogan. CP-BogaL

Single stalk climbed up, A. White Iris, The. Philip Levine. SP-LeviP

Single Vision. Stanley Kunitz. CP-KunSC

Single Witness, The. Thomas Hardy. CP-HardT

Singleness in Love. Robert Graves. CP-GravR

Singles. Christopher Logue. SP-LoguC

Singular Effects of Malediction. G. K. Chesterton. CP-ChesG Fr. Thought and Reflections.

Singular Metamorphosis, A. Howard Nemerov. CP-NemeH

Sink, thou strange heart, unto thy rest. Futility. Walter De la Mare. CP-DeLaW

Sinking down by the gate I discern the thin moon. Difference, The. Thomas Hardy. CP-HardT

Sinking like a rock in the Sea. Feng-kan. CP-ColdM, tr. by Red Pine

Sinking Like Sediment through the Day. Philip Larkin. CP-LarkP

Sinking Stone. James Laughlin. CP-LaugJ

Sinner. Langston Hughes. CP-HughL; CP-HughL1

Sinner, The. George Herbert. CP-HerbG

Sinners. Robert Herrick. CP-HerrR

Sinners. D. H. Lawrence. CP-LawrD

Sinners confounded are a twofold way. Sinners. Robert Herrick. CP-HerrR

Sinner's own fault? So it was, The. Christina Georgina Rossetti. CP-RosC2

Sinner's Rue. A. E. Housman. CP-HousA

Sinner's Sacrifice, The. Ben Jonson. CP-JonsB

Sins Loathed, and Yet Loved. Robert Herrick. CP-HerrR

Sins of Kalamazoo are neither scarlet nor crimson, The. Sins of Kalamazoo, The. Carl Sandburg. CP-SandC

Sins of Kalamazoo, The. Carl Sandburg. CP-SandC

Sin's Round. George Herbert. CP-HerbG

Sinuously winding through the room. Carmen de Boheme. Hart Crane. CP-CranH

Sinverguenza. Robinson Jeffers. CP-JefR2

Sion. George Herbert. CP-HerbG

Sioux Haiku. William Stafford. SP-StafW

Sioux sat around their wigwam fires, The. Crossing the Paces. Carl Sandburg. CP-SandC

Sipping grog one day at sea. Robert Browning. CP-BroR2

Sir. Miller Williams. CP-WillM

Sir, as your mandate did request. Inventory, The. Robert Burns. CP-BurnR

Sir: Cruising for profit. Slave Ship, The. Louise Glück. SP-GlucL

Sir, / Delany reports it, and he has a shrewd tongue. Left-Handed Letter to Dr. Sheridan, A. Jonathan Swift. CP-SwifJ

Sir, / Ere you pass this threshold, stay. To the King, at His Entrance into Saxham: By Master John Crofts. Thomas Carew. CP-CareT

Sir Eustace Grey. George Crabbe. SP-CrabG

Sir Eustace Grey. Christina Georgina Rossetti. CP-RosC3

Sir Galahad [or The Purple Heart]. Alfred Tennyson. CP-TennA

Sir, I admit your general [or gen'ral] Rule. Epigram from the French: "Sir, I admit your general [or gen'ral] Rule." Alexander Pope. CP-PopeA

Sir, I am thankful, first, to heaven, for you. Epistle to a Friend, An ("Sir, I am thankful, first, to heaven, for you"). Ben Jonson. CP-JonsB

Sir, I arrest you at your country's suit. To Master W. Montague. Thomas Carew. CP-CareT

Sir, I thank you for your comedies. Pedagogue's Answer, The. Thomas Sheridan. CP-SherT

Sir Ihon Sinclair begowthe to dance. William Dunbar. CP-DunbW

Sir, / in reading your letter alone in my hackney. Dean Swift's Answer to the Reverend Dr. Sheridan. Jonathan Swift. CP-SwifJ

Sir Inigo doth fear it as I hear. To a Friend, an Epigram of Him. Ben Jonson. CP-JonsB; SP-JonsB

Sir, it is raining tonight in Towson, Maryland. Memo: Preliminary Draft of a Prayer to God the Father. John Ciardi. CP-CiarJ

Sir John Cope trode the north right far. Johnie Cope. Robert Burns. CP-BurnR

Sir John Mandeville and I Sat Up Talking. Robert Stock. SP-StocR

Sir John Suckling's Answer. Sir John Suckling. CP-SuckJ

Sir John was entombed, and the crypt was closed, and she. Inscription, The. Thomas Hardy. CP-HardT

Sir John Wingfield. John Donne. CP-DonnJ; MW-DonnJ

Sir Jo[s]hua praised Rubens with a Smile. William Blake. CP-BlakW

Sir Joshua Praises Michael Angelo. William Blake. CP-BlakW

Sir Joshua Reynolds. William Blake. CP-BlakW

Sir Joshua sent his own Portrait to. Florentine Ingratitude. William Blake. CP-BlakW

Sir Launcelot and Queen Guinevere. Alfred Tennyson. CP-TennA

Sir Luckless, troth, for luck's sake pass by one. To the Same [Sir Luckless Woo-All]. Ben Jonson. CP-JonsB; SP-JonsB

Sir, more than kisses, letters mingle souls. To Sir Henry Wotton ("Sir, more than kisses, letters mingle souls"). John Donne. CP-DonnJ; MW-DonnJ

Sir Nameless, once of Athelhall, declared. Children and Sir Nameless, The. Thomas Hardy. CP-HardT

Sir, o'er a gill I gat your card. Extempore Epistle to Mr. McAdam of Craigengillian, (Wrote in Nanse Tinnock's, Mauchline) in Answer to an Obliging Letter He Sent in the Commencement of My Poetic Career. Robert Burns. CP-BurnR

Sir, / Our times are much degenerate from those. To His Noble Friend, Mr Richard Lovelace, upon His Poems. Andrew Marvell. CP-MarvA

Sir, perhaps you may wonder, I send you so soon. To the Same. Thomas Sheridan. CP-SherT

Sir, / Pray discruciate what follows: / The dullest beast, and gentleman's liquor. Riddling Letter, A. Jonathan Swift. CP-SwifJ

Sir Richard's Song. Rudyard Kipling. CP-KiplR Fr. Puck of Pook's Hill.

Sir Robert wearied by Will Pulteney's teasings. On Mr. Pulteney Being Put Out of the Council. Jonathan Swift. CP-SwifJ

Sir, starting next month. Unfinished Business. Primo Levi. CP-LeviP, tr. by Ruth Feldman

Sir Thomas More. Robert Lowell. SP-LoweR

Sir, though (I thank God for it) I do hate. Satire 2. John Donne. MW-DonnJ Fr. Satires.

Sir W. Ralegh, on the Snuff of a Candle the Night Before He Died. Sir Walter Ralegh. See On the Snuff of a Candle

Sir Walter Ralegh to the Queen. Sir Walter Ralegh. CP-RaleW

Sir Walter Ralegh's [or S.W. Raghlies] Petition to the Queene 1618. Sir Walter Ralegh. CP-RaleW

Sir Walter Ra[u]le[i]gh to His Son[ne]. Sir Walter Ralegh. CP-RaleW

Sir Walter Rawly made this rime upon the name of a gallant one Mr. Noel. Noe L. From the Diary of John Manningham of the Middle Temple. Sir Walter Ralegh. CP-RaleW

Sir! when I flew to seize the bird. Beau's Reply. William Cowper. CP-CowpW

Sir, / When I left you, I found myself of the grape's juice sick. To Dr. Helsham. Jonathan Swift. CP-SwifJ

Sir, / When I saw you today, as I went with Lord Anglesey. Dean to Thomas Sheridan, The. Jonathan Swift. CP-SwifJ

Sir, / Whether these lines do find you out. Summons to Town, A. Sir John Suckling. CP-SuckJ

Sir, will you let me give you a ride? Pedestrian, The. Thomas Hardy. CP-HardT

Sir Winter. Christina Georgina Rossetti. CP-RosC3

Sir, you are tough and I am tough. To a Fellow Poet. Joseph Brodsky. CP-BrodJ Fr. Shorts.

Sir, you were a credit to whatever. To a Teacher of French. Donald Davie. CP-DaviDC

Sir, your Billingsgate Muse methinks does begin. To the Dean of St. Patrick's ("Sir, your Billingsgate Muse methinks does begin"). Thomas Sheridan. CP-SherT

Sire. W. S. Merwin. SP-MerwW

Siren, A. Umberto Saba. CP-MahoD, tr. by Derek Mahon

Siren and the Carabineer, The. Federico García Lorca. CP-GarcF, tr. by Christopher Maurer

Siren Music. Marya Alexandrovna Zaturenska. SP-ZatuM

Sirens, The. Robinson Jeffers. CP-JefR3

Sirens, The. Richard Wilbur. SP-WilbR

Sirmio, thou dearest dear of strands. Carmen 31. Catullus. Fr. Carmina.

Sirocco at Deyá. Robert Graves. CP-GravR

Sirocco brings the minor devils. Cattivo Tempo. W. H. Auden. CP-AudeW

Sirs, in our youth you love the sight of us. Where I've Been All My Life. Carolyn Kizer. CP-KizeC

Sirs! may I shake your hands? Patriot Engineer, The. George Meredith. CP-MerG1

Sirs, when you are in your last extremity. Gone Away Blues. Thomas McGrath. SP-McGrT

Sis Rapalye. James Whitcomb Riley. CP-RileJ

Sisina. Charles Baudelaire. CP-BaudC, tr. by Walter Martin

Siskins, The. Theodore Roethke. CP-RoetT

Sisley / Walked so nicely. Bag-Snatching in Dublin. Stevie Smith. CP-SmitS

Sissy, The. Miller Williams. CP-WillM

Sister. Langston Hughes. CP-HughL; CP-HughL3

Sister and mother and diviner love. To the One of Fictive Music. Wallace Stevens. CP-StevW; CP-StevWP

Sister, arise: We have no more to sing. Church Porch 2, The. Dante Gabriel Rossetti. CW-RossD

Sister by the Pond, A. Donald Hall. CP-HallD

Sister Elizabeth Michael. Young Nun at Bread Loaf. Maxine W. Kumin. SP-KumiM

Sister, first shake we off the dust we have. Church Porch 1, The. Dante Gabriel Rossetti. CW-RossD

Sister hands it to me—the pod, The. Kennedy's Inauguration. Robert Bly. SP-BlyR

Sister Helen. Dante Gabriel Rossetti. CW-RossD

Sister Hours in circles linked, The. Alsace-Lorraine. George Meredith. CP-MerG1

Sister Johnson Marches. Langston Hughes. CP-HughL; CP-HughL1

Sister Jones's Confession. James Whitcomb Riley. CP-RileJ

Sister Maude. Christina Georgina Rossetti. CP-RosC1

Sister, Morning Is a Time for Miracles. Audre Lorde. SP-LordA

Sister of Ophir. Emily Dickinson. CP-DickE

Sister on the Tracks, A. Donald Hall. CP-HallD

Sister on the way, I was farmed, A. Namesake, The. Wyatt Prunty. SP-PrunW

Sister Poverty, welcome to my cloister. Fanny Howe. SP-HoweF Fr. In the Spirit There Are No Accidents.

'Sister,' said busy Amelotte. Bride's Prelude, The. Dante Gabriel Rossetti. CW-RossD

Sister, tha knows while we was on th' planks. Violets. D. H. Lawrence. CP-LawrD

Sister Water. Robert Penn Warren. CP-WarrR

Sister who told fortunes prophesied, The. From the Cupola. James Merrill. SP-MerrJ

Sisterhood. Marilyn Hacker. SP-HackM

Sisters. Wyatt Prunty. SP-PrunW

Sisters. Adrienne Rich. CP-RicAE; SP-RicA2

Sisters, The. Josephine Jacobsen. CP-JacoJ

Sisters, The. John Greenleaf Whittier. CP-WhitJ

Sisters of Charity. Arthur Rimbaud. CP-RimbA, *tr. by* Martin Sorrell

Sisters of Mercy. Charles Baudelaire. CP-BaudC, *tr. by* Walter Martin

Sisters of Mercy. Adam Zagajewski. SP-ZagaA

Sisters! sisters! who sent you here? Fire, Famine, and Slaughter. Samuel Taylor Coleridge. CP-ColeS; MW-ColeS

Sisters, The: A Picture by Barry, The. John Greenleaf Whittier. CP-WhitJ

Sisyphus. Maxine W. Kumin. SP-KumiM

Sit by the Window and Refuse. Charles Olson. CP-OlsoC

Sit Down. Robert Creeley. SP-CreeR

Sit down and bargain. Song of Those Who Died in Vain. Primo Levi. CP-LeviP, *tr. by* Ruth Feldman

Sit Down in the Lowest Room. Christina Georgina Rossetti. CP-RosC2

Sit, friend. We'll be drinking and I'll tell you why. Kostas Tympakianákis. James Merrill. SP-MerrJ

Sit further, and make room for thine own fame. To His Worthy Friend Doctor Witty upon His Translation of the "Popular Errors." Andrew Marvell. CP-MarvA

Sit Mihi Terra Levis. Robert Graves. CP-GravR

Sit on the bed. I'm blind, and three parts shell. A Terre. Wilfred Owen. CP-OwenW

Sit the noon out, pale and lost in thought. Eugenio Montale. CP-MontE, *tr. by* Jonathan Galassi

Sitalkas. "H. D." CP-DoolH

Site echoes, The. At Delphi. May Sarton. SP-SartM

Sith I myself displease thee. Sir Thomas Wyatt. CP-WyatT

Sith it is so that I am thus refused. Sir Thomas Wyatt. CP-WyatT

Sitôt sorti de l'ermitage. Samuel Beckett. CP-BeckS

Sits up in bed in his navy robe. Unknown Sailor, The. Miller Williams. CP-WillM

Sitting airborne on the. Shuttle, The. John Updike. CP-UpdiJ

Sitting alone (as one forsook). Vision, The. Robert Herrick. CP-HerrR

Sitting Alone at Sunrise: Problems in the Space-Time Continuum. Miller Williams. CP-WillM

Sitting alone I keep slipping away. Han-shan. CP-ColdM, *tr. by* Red Pine

Sitting alone of a summer's evening. Brickenden, Hertfordshire. Stevie Smith. CP-SmitS

Sitting as though suspended from something, cool in my deck chair. Opus Posthumous 2. Charles Wright. SP-WrigCN

Sitting at Dusk in the Back Yard after the Mondrian Retrospective. Charles Wright. SP-WrigCN

Sitting at the top of the stadium. Harvard Stadium. Richard Eberhart. CP-EberR

Sitting between the sea and the buildings. Painter, The. John Ashbery. SP-AshbJ

Sitting by a Bush in Broad Sunlight. Robert Frost. CP-FrosR

Sitting by the glimmer. Something. James Whitcomb Riley. CP-RileJ

Sitting Down. Pablo Neruda. SP-NeruP

Sitting Down, Looking Up. A. R. Ammons. CP-AmmoA

Sitting for a Self-Portrait. Robert Stock. SP-StocR

Sitting Here. Robert Creeley. CP-CreeR

Sitting here in limbo, "there are." For Cheryl. Robert Creeley. SP-CreeR

Sitting here in my house. Suburban Madrigal. John Updike. CP-UpdiJ

Sitting in a cantina, gin. Drunkenness. Robert Stock. SP-StocR

Sitting in a Rocking Chair, Going Blind. Yusef Komunyakaa. CP-KomuY

Sitting in a rowboat. Your Sacred Idiot with Me. Olga Broumas. SP-BrouO

Sitting in a Sandwich Joint. Charles Bukowski. SP-BukC1

Sitting in a Small Screenhouse on a Summer Morning. James Wright. CP-WrigJ

Sitting in a tree-. E. E. Cummings. CP-CummE

Sitting in plane still. 9:45 AM. Robert Creeley. SP-CreeR

Sitting in your family apartment, Lewis. Visit (2). George Oppen. CP-OppGN

Sitting next to you. But You. Robert Creeley. CP-CreeR

Sitting on a bench by the Rogue River, Oregon. Two Immortals. Gary Snyder. CP-SnydG

Sitting on a tree stump with half cup of tea. Cabin in the Rockies. Allen Ginsberg. CP-GinsA

Sitting on Farm Lawn on Sunday Afternoon. Robert Penn Warren. CP-WarrR

Sitting on Some Rocks in Shaw Cove. Robert Bly. SP-BlyR

Sitting on the Bridge. Thomas Hardy. CP-HardT

Sitting once more outside the British Museum. Time for a Smoke. Louis MacNeice. CP-MacNL

Sitting Outside at the End of Autumn. Charles Wright. SP-WrigCN

Sitting up to fill pages. Robert Creeley. CP-CreeR

Sitting with the professors. Professors, The. Charles Bukowski. SP-BukC1

Situation. Federico García Lorca. CP-GarcF, *tr. by* Jerome Rothenberg *Fr.* In the Forest of the Lunar Grapefruits.

Situation. Langston Hughes. CP-HughL; CP-HughL3

Situation Does Not Change, The. Howard Nemerov. CP-NemeH

Situation of feeling increasingly. Robert Creeley. CP-CreeR

Sive canis silvas, Spencere, vel horrida belli. Ad Ed. Spencerum. Thomas Campion. CP-CampT

Six, The. James Dickey. CP-DickJ

Six A.M. / Sat down on excavation gravel. Magpie's Song. Gary Snyder. CP-SnydG

6 A.M. Charles Bukowski. SP-BukC2

Six / are in a room's dark around). E. E. Cummings. CP-CummE

Six-Bits Blues. Langston Hughes. CP-HughL; CP-HughL2

Six Boards, The. Thomas Hardy. CP-HardT

Six calices yellow gold. Kathleen Jessie Raine. SP-RainK

Six Canons, The. Muriel Rukeyser. CP-RukeM

Six Capriccios. Federico García Lorca. CP-GarcF, *tr. by* Cola Franzen

Six Commissioned Texts. W. H. Auden. CP-AudeW

Six days out of all the days. Destruction of Carthage, The. Kenneth Patchen. CP-PatcK

Six Epistles to Eva Hesse. Donald Davie. CP-DaviDC

Six fiery spears / zoom up. Rockets. Federico García Lorca. CP-GarcF, *tr. by* Jerome Rothenberg *Fr.* Barrage of Firework Poems on the Occasion of the Poet's Birthday.

6 Foot Goddess, The. Charles Bukowski. SP-BukC1

Six-foot nest of the sea-hawk, The. Sea-Hawk. Richard Eberhart. CP-EberR

Six hours a day I lay me down. Meditation in Hydrotherapy. Theodore Roethke. CP-RoetT

Six hours outstetched in the sun, yes. On a Theme from Julian's Chapter 20. Denise Levertov. SP-LeveDS

Six hundred years ago, more or less. After a Brubeck Concert. Miller Williams. CP-WillM

Six Illustrations. Michael Palmer. SP-PalmM

Six Inch Chapter—in Verse, A. Charles Olson. CP-OlsoC

Six Lectures in Verse. Czeslaw Milosz. CP-MiloC; CP-MiloCN, *tr. by* Leonard Nathan

Six Maidens, The. Alexander Pope. CP-PopeA

6 May 1950. Yannis Ritsos. SP-RitsY *Fr.* Exile's Journals 3.

Six miasmic women in green. Couples. Carl Sandburg. CP-SandC

Six miles between / my stop and this. Destination: Accomplished. Jay Wright. SP-WrigJ

Six month child, The. Slippery. Carl Sandburg. CP-SandC

Six months to six years added he remained. Epitaph: "Six months to six years added he remained." William Wordsworth. CP-WorW1

Six Moral Virtues, The: Grace, Style, Class, Kindness, and Wisdom. Miller Williams. CP-WillM

Six Naps in One Day. Donald Hall. CP-HallD

6 November 1948. Yannis Ritsos. SP-RitsY *Fr.* Exile's Journals 1.

Six o'clock and / the sun rises. Love Poem: "Six o'clock and / the sun rises." Miller Williams. CP-WillM

Six o'clock in Princes Street. Wilfred Owen. CP-OwenW

Six Persimmons. Arthur Sze. SP-SzeA

Six pigs at the breast of their mother, The. More Country People. Carl Sandburg. CP-SandC

6:00 p.m. Federico García Lorca. CP-GarcF, *tr. by* Jerome Rothenberg *Fr.* Summer Hours.

6 p.m. Curling his upper lip. Fossil Unwound. Joseph Brodsky. CP-BrodJ

Six Poems for Tamar. Yehuda Amichai.

   "Always, you lie." SP-AmicYL

   "Your heart plays hide-and-seek." SP-AmicYL

   "Your laughter likes grapes." SP-AmicYL

Six Poems for Tamar. Yehuda Amichai. SP-AmicY, *tr. by* Stephen Mitchell

Six Significant Landscapes. Wallace Stevens. CP-StevW; CP-StevWP

Six Something. James Schuyler. CP-SchuJ

Six Songs at Nightfall. Federico García Lorca.

   Delirium. CP-GarcF, *tr. by* Jerome Rothenberg

   Fishermen. CP-GarcF, *tr. by* Jerome Rothenberg

   Horizon. CP-GarcF, *tr. by* Jerome Rothenberg

   Last Light. CP-GarcF, *tr. by* Jerome Rothenberg

   Memento ("Moon is dead already, The"). CP-GarcF, *tr. by* Jerome Rothenberg

   Solitaire. CP-GarcF, *tr. by* Jerome Rothenberg

Six street ends come together here. Blue Island Intersection. Carl Sandburg. CP-SandC

Six thankful weeks,—& let it be. Written in a Volume of Goethe. Ralph Waldo Emerson. CP-EmerR

Six thousand veterans practised in war's game. Sonnet in the Pass of Killicranky. William Wordsworth. CP-WorW1; MW-WorW

6/21. Adrienne Rich. SP-RicA1

Six Variations. Denise Levertov. SP-LeveDP

Six whittled chickens. Chinese Toy, A. William Carlos Williams. CP-WilW1

Six Winter Privacy Poems. Robert Bly. SP-BlyR

Six Years. Gary Snyder. CP-SnydG

Six years ago in Ohio we argued free will. On the Lawn at Ira's. Gregory Orr.

SP-OrrG

Six Years Later. Joseph Brodsky. CP-WilbR, *tr. by* Richard Wilbur

Six Young Men. Ted Hughes. SP-HughTN

Sixteen Dead Men. William Butler Yeats. CP-YeatW

Sixteen Lines on Marching. Alan Dugan. CP-DugaA

Sixteen Months. Carl Sandburg. CP-SandC

16. ix. 65. James Merrill. SP-MerrJ

Sixteen Poems in Eight Pairings. John Crowe Ransom. SP-RansJ

16 years old. My Old Man. Charles Bukowski. SP-BukC1

Sixteen years. The narrow rough-gullied backroads. Sources. Adrienne Rich. SP-RicA1

Sixth Elegy. River Elegy. Muriel Rukeyser. CP-RukeM

Sixth Epistle of the First Book of Horace Imitated, The. Alexander Pope. CP-PopeA

Sixth-Month Song in the Foothills. Gary Snyder. CP-SnydG

Sixth Night: Waking, The. Muriel Rukeyser. CP-RukeM

Sixth Satire of the Second Book of Horace Imitated, The. Alexander Pope. CP-PopeA

Sixth Station, The. Robert Stock. SP-StocR

Sixty miles from a lake. Boat in the Forest, A. Thomas Lux. SP-LuxT

Sixty, seventy, eighty: I would see you mellow. Randall Jarrell 1. October 1965. Robert Lowell. SP-LoweR

60 Yard Pass. Charles Bukowski. SP-BukC3

Size, The. George Herbert. CP-HerbG

Size circumscribes—it has no room. Emily Dickinson. CP-DickE

Size of a Fist, The. William Stafford. SP-StafWW

Size of a small skull, and like a skull segmented. To a Box Turtle. John Updike. CP-UpdiJ

Size of Song, The. John Ciardi. CP-CiarJ

Size of Spokane, The. Heather McHugh. SP-McHuH

Size, you said, of silver dollars, The. Moonsnails. Eleanor Wilner. SP-WilnE

Sizzle of the Coleman, The. Voyeur, The. Mona Van Duyn. SP-VanDM

Skald's Death. Hugh MacDiarmid. SP-MacDH

Skateboard. Thom Gunn. CP-GunnT

Skaters, The. John Ashbery.

    "Old heavens, you used to tweak above us." SP-AshbJ

    "Wind thrashes the maple seed-pods, The." SP-AshbJ

Skaters, The. Charles Bukowski. SP-BukC3

Skaters, The. Randall Jarrell. CP-JarrR

Skaters, The. James Laughlin. CP-LaugJ

Skating. E. E. Cummings. CP-CummE

Skeffington's Daughter. Paul Muldoon. CP-MuldP

Skein bottoms them together, A. Charlock per Winkle. Louis Zukofsky. CP-ZukLS

Skein, The. Emperor Wu of Han. CP-KizeC, *tr. by* Carolyn Kizer

Skeleton, The. G. K. Chesterton. CP-ChesG

Skeleton, The. Robert Creeley. CP-CreeR

Skeleton for Mr. Paul in Paradise, A. Norman Dubie. CP-DubiN

Skeleton in Armor [*or* Armour], The. Henry Wadsworth Longfellow. SP-LongH

Skeleton of the Future, The. Hugh MacDiarmid. SP-MacDH

Skeleton produces flesh enemy, The. Solipsism While Dying. Margaret Atwood. SP-AtwM1

Skeletons covered with sores—if they can walk, The. Institute of Defectology. Thomas Lux. SP-LuxT

Skelpick. Donald Davie. CP-DaviDC

Skeptic. Robert Frost. CP-FrosR

Skeptic, The. Ralph Waldo Emerson. CP-EmerR

Sketch. Robert Burns. CP-BurnR

Sketch. Rainer Maria Rilke. CP-RilkFr, *tr. by* A. Poulin, Jr.

Sketch. Carl Sandburg. CP-SandC

Sketch, A. Herman Melville. SP-MelvH *Fr.* Clarel: A Poem and Pilgrimage in the Holy Land.

Sketch, A. Lord Byron. *See* Sketch from Private Life, A

Sketch, A. Christina Georgina Rossetti. CP-RosC3

Sketch, A. Richard Wilbur. CP-WilbR

Sketch for a Landscape. May Swenson. SP-SwenM

Sketch for a Portrait of Henry Ford. William Carlos Williams. CP-WilW2

Sketch for a Portrait of Mme. G———M———. Archibald MacLeish. CP-MacLA

Sketch for an Aesthetic Project. Jay Wright. SP-WrigJ

Sketch for an Elegy. Robert Burns. CP-BurnR

Sketch for an Ode. Federico García Lorca. CP-GarcF, *tr. by* Christopher Maurer

Sketch from Private Life, A. Lord Byron. CP-Byron

    (Sketch, A.) CP-Byron

Sketch. Inscribed to the Rt. Hon. Ch. J. Fox Esq. Robert Burns. CP-BurnR

Sketch. New Year's Day. To Mrs. Dunlop. Robert Burns. CP-BurnR

Sketch of a Landscape. Paul Celan. SP-CelaP, *tr. by* John Felstiner

Sketch of a Poet. Carl Sandburg. CP-SandC

Sketch of His Own Character. Thomas Gray. CP-GrayT

Sketch of the Great Dejection, A. Thom Gunn. CP-GunnT

Sketch of the Ultimate Politician. Wallace Stevens. CP-StevW; CP-StevWP

Sketches. Federico García Lorca. CP-GarcF, *tr. by* Jerome Rothenberg *Fr.* Night (Suite for Piano and Poet's Voice).

Sketching a Thatcher. Ted Hughes. SP-HughTN

Skew Lines. Denise Levertov. SP-LeveDP

Ski-rails run down the sugar-loaf. January 1938. Randall Jarrell. CP-JarrR

Skia, An Ode on the Isle of Skye. Samuel Johnson. CP-JohnS

Skier and the Mountain, The. Richard Eberhart. CP-EberR

Skies can't keep their secret!, The. Emily Dickinson. CP-DickE

Skies grey or green. Temple of Earth, The. G. K. Chesterton. CP-ChesG

Skies have grown troubled and dreary, The. His Last Picture. James Whitcomb Riley. CP-RileJ

Skies held angry clouds when I was young, The. Enemy, The. Charles Baudelaire. CP-BaudC, *tr. by* Walter Martin

Skies may be blue,s. E. E. Cummings. CP-CummE

Skies remind one of one of those mounds of custard, The. Lollipops of the Pomeranian Baroque. James Fenton. SP-FentJ

Skies remind you of those mounds of custard, The. James Fenton. *See* Skies remind one of one of those mounds of custard, The

Skies they were ashen and sober, The. Ulalume [*or* Ulalume—a Ballad]. Edgar Allan Poe. CP-PoeEd

Skiing without Skis. James Laughlin. CP-LaugJ

Skillful, proud, handsome, with a sturdy knife. Marine. Yannis Ritsos. SP-RitsY, *tr. by* Kostas Myrsiades

Skimming lightly, wheeling still. Shiloh [A Requiem]. Herman Melville. SP-MelvH

Skimpy Day at the Solstice. Marge Piercy. SP-PierM

Skin. Philip Larkin. CP-LarkP

Skin is broken, The. The hotel breakfast china. Houseboat Days. John Ashbery. SP-AshbJ

Skin mask, The. Exposure. Dan Pagis. SP-PagiD, *tr. by* Stephen Mitchell

Skin ripples over my body like moon-wooed water, The. Prison Song. Alan Dugan. CP-DugaA

Skin seethes in the heat, The. Sunday Drive, A. Margaret Atwood. SP-AtwM2

Skinful of bowls, he bowls them. Second Glance at a Jaguar. Ted Hughes. SP-HughTN

Skink, The. Ogden Nash. CP-NashO

Skinned corpse of a lion, The. Manifold Fusions, The. Kenneth Patchen. CP-PatcK

Skinns he din'd well to day; how do you think? Upon Skinns. Robert Herrick. CP-HerrR

Skinny girl I never loved and lost, ah how, The. For a Lost Girl. Alan Dugan. CP-DugaA

Skinny kids in shorts get cups. In the House of the Rising Sun. Gary Snyder. CP-SnydG

Skinny voice / of the leatherfaced, The. E. E. Cummings. CP-CummE

Skinny waterfalls, footpaths, The. Lastness. Galway Kinnell. SP-KinnGN

Skip, The. James Fenton. SP-FentJ

Skipper Ireson's Ride. John Greenleaf Whittier. CP-WhitJ

Skirl of the kingfisher was never, The. Hiking on the Coast Range. Kenneth Rexroth. CP-RexrK

Skirting the river road, (my forenoon walk, my rest,). Dalliance of the Eagles, The. Walt Whitman. CP-WhitW

Skoles stinks so deadly, that his Breeches loath. Upon Skoles. Robert Herrick. CP-HerrR

Skopus. May Swenson. SP-SwenM

Skreak and skritter of evening gone, The. Autumn Refrain. Wallace Stevens. CP-StevW; CP-StevWP

Skrew lives by shifts; yet sweares by no small oathes. Upon Skrew. Robert Herrick. CP-HerrR

Skull, A. Czeslaw Milosz. CP-MiloC; CP-MiloCN, *tr. by* Robert Hass

Skull, / museum object. Waking Alone. Anne Sexton. CP-SextA

Skull within, the secret, shuttered heart, The. I. Jorge Luis Borges. SP-BorgJ, *tr. by* Alastair Reid

Skulls. Finalities. They emerge. Skullshapes. Charles Tomlinson. CP-TomlC

Skullshapes. Charles Tomlinson. CP-TomlC

Skunk, The. Seamus Heaney. SP-HeanSO

Skunk Cabbage. Mary Oliver. SP-OlivM

Skunk Hour. Robert Lowell. SP-LoweR

Skunks. Robinson Jeffers. CP-JefR3

Skurffe by his Nine-bones sweares, and well he may. Upon Skurffe. Robert Herrick. CP-HerrR

Sky. Federico García Lorca. CP-GarcF, *tr. by* Jerome Rothenberg *Fr.* In the Garden of the Lunar Grapefruits.

Sky. David Ignatow. SP-IgnaD

Sky. William Stafford. SP-StafWW

Sky. Wisława Szymborska. SP-SzymW, *tr. by* Stanislaw Barańczak *and* Clare Cavanagh

Sky. Wisława Szymborska. SP-SzymWM, *tr. by* Joanna Trzeciak

Sky. Robert Penn Warren. CP-WarrR

Sky, A. A field. A hedge flagrant with gorse. Horses. Paul Muldoon. CP-MuldP

Sky a silver, The. E. E. Cummings. CP-CummE

Sky and lake the same blue. Above Bear Lake. May Swenson. SP-SwenM

Sky and sea and sand. Flag of Summer. May Swenson. SP-SwenM

Sky and sea, horizon-hinged. Hermit at Outermost House, The. Sylvia Plath. CP-PlatS

Sky and the sea put on a show, The. Thimble Islands. Carl Sandburg. CP-SandC

Sky begins to lower and thick'ning Clouds, The. Thunder Storm, A. William Cowper. CP-CowpW

Sky behind, The. For Joe Pernice. William Corbett. SP-CorbW

Sky behind the farthest shore, The. Water Night. Muriel Rukeyser. CP-RukeM

Sky black black clouds and black rain falls. That blond wound. Builders, The. Kenneth Patchen. CP-PatcK

Sky-born and royal. Hercules and Antaeus. Seamus Heaney. SP-HeanSO

Sky burned desolately behind the houses, The. Small Dialogue. Yannis Ritsos. SP-RitsY, *tr. by* Kostas Myrsiades

Sky-coloured bird, blue wings with no more spots of spotless white. Edna St. Vincent Millay. CP-MillE

Sky cries down. Elements. Robert Creeley. SP-CreeR

Sky darkened watching you, The. Jack. Randall Jarrell. CP-JarrR

Sky Diving. Charles Wright. SP-WrigCN

Sky Eats Up the Trees, The. James Schuyler. CP-SchuJ

Sky goes on living it goes, The. Homeland. W. S. Merwin. SP-MerwW

Sky has given over, The. Spring Storm. William Carlos Williams. CP-WilW1

Sky has murder in the eye, and I, The. Nature of a Mirror, The. Robert Penn Warren. CP-WarrR

Sky / in my favor. Lorine Niedecker. CP-NiedL

Sky Is Blue, The. David Ignatow. SP-IgnaD

Sky is laced with fitful red, The. Impression: Le Réveillon. Oscar Wilde. CP-WildO

Sky is lead, and our faces are red, The. Rudyard Kipling. CP-KiplR *Fr.* Life's Handicap.

Sky is low—the Clouds are mean, The. Emily Dickinson. CP-DickE

Sky is overcast, The. Night-Piece, A. William Wordsworth. CP-WorW1

Sky is overspread, The. William Wordsworth. *See* Sky is overcast, The

Sky is perfectly clear, The. Maximian, Elegy 5. Kenneth Rexroth. CP-RexrK

Sky is pitiless. I beg, The. Dog Wants His Dinner, The. James Schuyler. CP-SchuJ

Sky is ruddy in the east, The. Ship-Builders, The. John Greenleaf Whittier. CP-WhitJ

Sky is torn across, The. On a Wedding Anniversary. Dylan Thomas. CP-ThomD

Sky is unmistakeable. Not lurid, not low, not black, The. Haying Before Storm. Muriel Rukeyser. CP-RukeM

Sky is where we should have started, The. Sky. Wisława Szymborska. SP-SzymWM, *tr. by* Joanna Trzeciak

Sky makes no sense to me, The. Blue. David Ignatow. SP-IgnaD

Sky-man in a manhole. Astronomer. A. K. Ramanujan. CP-RamaA

Sky of brightest gray seems dark, The. Comparison. Paul Laurence Dunbar. CP-DunbP

Sky of gray is eaten in six places, The. Broken Sky. Carl Sandburg. CP-SandC

Sky, paid to be blue, The. Raining in Magens Bay. John Updike. CP-UpdiJ

Sky Pieces. Carl Sandburg. CP-SandC

Sky scanned the mind and found behind. Sunday. Laura Riding Jackson. CP-RidiL

Sky seemed so small that winter day, The. Two Illustrations That the World Is What You Make of It. Wallace Stevens. CP-StevW; CP-StevWP

Sky Sign. Charles Bukowski. SP-BukC3

Sky stainless, flawed by one gull, The. Landscape Finally with Human Figure. Josephine Jacobsen. CP-JacoJ

Sky Talk. Carl Sandburg. CP-SandC

Sky tears off / the blindfold. 8:00 p.m. Federico García Lorca. CP-GarcF, *tr. by* Jerome Rothenberg *Fr.* Summer Hours.

Sky, the blueness of quiet light. Poem: "Sky, the blueness of quiet light." Fernando Pessoa. SP-PessF, *tr. by* Susan M. Brown *and* Edwin Honig

Sky today yes and no, The. I am writing a play about a man with a pebble. Dear M ("Sky today yes and no, The. I am writing a play about a man with a pebble"). Michael Palmer. SP-PalmM

Sky unrolls like a rug, / unwelcoming, gun-grey, The. As Our Bodies Rise, Our Names Turn into Light. Charles Wright. SP-WrigCN

The / sky / was / can dy lu. E. E. Cummings. CP-CummE

Sky / was can dy / lu mi, The. E. E. Cummings. CP-CummE

Sky was cold December blue with great tumbling clouds, and the, The. Steelhead, Wild Pig, the Fungus. Robinson Jeffers. CP-JefR2

Sky was like a waterdrop, The. Remembrance. Walter De la Mare. CP-DeLaW

Sky, Water. C. K. Williams. CP-WillC

Sky-Woman. Paul Muldoon. CP-MuldP

Sky Writing. Charles Tomlinson. CP-TomlC; SP-TomlC

Sky Z, in disbelief, agrees that this alphabet. After Sky X. Norman Dubie. CP-DubiN

Skyey Developments. John Updike. CP-UpdiJ

Skylarks. Ted Hughes. SP-HughTN

Skylight, The. Seamus Heaney. SP-HeanSO *Fr.* Glanmore Revisited.

Sky's face so old. November Night. May Swenson. SP-SwenM

Sky's sweet basil, The. Round of Aromas. Gabriela Mistral. SP-MistG, *tr. by* Maria Giachetti [*or* Jacketti]

Skyscraper. Carl Sandburg. CP-SandC

Skyscraper Loves Night, The. Carl Sandburg. CP-SandC

Skyscrapers of the Financial District Dance with Gasman, The. Marge Piercy. SP-PierM

Skyscrapers Stand Proud. Carl Sandburg. CP-SandC

Skystones. Pablo Neruda.

　"From the breach to the iron explosion." SP-NeruP

　"I entered the cave of the amethysts." SP-NeruP

　"I want the jailed / light to awaken: I want." SP-NeruP

　"Quartz opens its eyes in the snow." SP-NeruP

　"Stone, toppled by water and mountain, The." SP-NeruP

　"When all turned to altitude." SP-NeruP

Slabs of the Sunburnt West. Carl Sandburg. CP-SandC

Slack Key Guitar. Allen Ginsberg. SP-GinsA

Slackers; A Hate Song. Dorothy Parker. CP-ParkD

Slain as they lay by the secret, slow. Year's "Casualties", A. Ambrose Bierce. SP-BierA

Slain for man, slain for me, O Lamb of God, look down. Slain from the Foundation of the World. Christina Georgina Rossetti. CP-RosC2

Slain from the Foundation of the World. Christina Georgina Rossetti. CP-RosC2

Slain in their high places: fallen on rest. Christina Georgina Rossetti. CP-RosC2

Slam, Dunk, & Hook. Yusef Komunyakaa. CP-KomuY

Slant of sun on dull brown walls, A. Stephen Crane. CP-CranS

Slanting light casts onto a stucco wall. Arthur Sze. SP-SzeA

Slants at Buffalo, New York. Carl Sandburg. CP-SandC

Slapstick. Wisława Szymborska. SP-SzymW, *tr. by* Stanislaw Barańczak *and* Clare Cavanagh

Slash of angular blacks, A. Public Square, The. Wallace Stevens. CP-StevW; CP-StevWP

Slash of Blue, A. Emily Dickinson. CP-DickE

Slash of the wrist, A. Ways. Langston Hughes. CP-HughL; CP-HughL1

Slate, or dirty-marble colored. Pigeon Woman. May Swenson. SP-SwenM

Slaughtering the Cow. Robert Stock. SP-StocR

Slave. Langston Hughes. CP-HughL; CP-HughL3

Slave, The. Jones Very. CP-VeryJ

Slave, be aware that the Lord. Jelaluddin Rumi. SP-Rumi, *tr. by* Coleman Barks

Slave Coffle. Maya Angelou. SP-AngeM

"Slave, come to my service!" "Yes, my master. Yes?" *Unknown, fr. Sumerian cuneiform.* CP-BrodJ, *tr. by* Joseph Brodsky

Slave Quarters. James Dickey. CP-DickJ

Slave Ship, The. Louise Glück. SP-GlucL

Slave-Ships, The. John Greenleaf Whittier. CP-WhitJ

Slave Singing at Midnight, The. Henry Wadsworth Longfellow. SP-LongH

Slave Song. Langston Hughes. CP-HughL; CP-HughL2

Slave to a God whose sole known verb is *Flatter*! He. Howard Nemerov. CP-NemeH

Slave to love's unbounded sway, A. O Lay Thy Loof in Mine Lass. Robert Burns. CP-BurnR

Slave Trade, The: View from the Middle Passage. Clarence Major. SP-MajoC

Slave yet wearing on my head a crown, A. Epitaph: "Slave yet wearing on my head a crown, A." Christina Georgina Rossetti. CP-RosC3

Slavery. Robert Herrick. CP-HerrR

Slavery. Jones Very. CP-VeryJ

Slave's Critique of Practical Reason, The. Rita Dove. SP-DoveR

Slave's Lament, The. Robert Burns. CP-BurnR

Slaves of Martinique, The. John Greenleaf Whittier. CP-WhitJ

Slaveship[s]. Lucille Clifton. SP-ClifL

Slay with your eyes, Greek. Toward the Piraeus. "H. D." CP-DoolH

Sled Burial, Dream Ceremony. James Dickey. CP-DickJ

Sleds of the children, The. Rites of Darkness, The. Kenneth Patchen. CP-PatcK

Sleek as a lizard at round of a stone. Penetration and Trust. George Meredith. CP-MerG1

Sleek black boys in a cabaret. Harlem Night Club. Langston Hughes. CP-HughL; CP-HughL1

Sleep. Wendell Berry. CP-BerrW

Sleep. Charles Bukowski. SP-BukC2

Sleep. Robert Creeley. CP-CreeR

Sleep. Walter De la Mare. CP-DeLaW

Sleep. Langston Hughes. CP-HughL; CP-HughL2

Sleep. D. H. Lawrence. CP-LawrD

Sleep. James Whitcomb Riley. CP-RileJ

Sleep. Rainer Maria Rilke. CP-RilkFr, *tr.* by A. Poulin, Jr.

Sleep. James Schuyler. CP-SchuJ

Sleep. Charles Simic. SP-SimiCE

Sleep. Georg Trakl. CP-WrigJ

Sleep, The. Elizabeth Barrett Browning. CP-BroEB

Sleep and Poetry. John Keats. CP-KeatJ

Sleep and Waking. D. H. Lawrence. CP-LawrD

Sleep, Angry Beauty. Thomas Campion. CP-CampT

Sleep, angry beauty, sleep, and fear[e] not me. Sleep, Angry Beauty. Thomas Campion. CP-CampT

Sleep at last has fled these eyes. Watching unto God in the Night-Season. Jeanne Marie Bouvier de la Motte- Guyon. CP-CowpW

Sleep at noon. Window blind. Hurricane. Archibald MacLeish. CP-MacLA

Sleep at Sea. Christina Georgina Rossetti. CP-RosC1

Sleep, balmy sleep, has clos'd the eyes of all. Sudden Production of Mrs. Stockton's in One of Those Many Anxious Nights in Which She Watched with Mr. Stockton in His Last Illness, A. Annis Boudinot Stockton. CP-StocA

Sleep! balmy Sleep! has clos'd the eyes of all. Extemporal Ode in a Sleepless Night, An. By a Lady, (Mrs. S. of New-Jersey) while Attending on Her Husband in a Long and Painful Illness. Annis Boudinot Stockton. CP-StocA

Sleep brings no joy to me. Emily Jane Brontë. CP-BronE

Sleep (by Rousseau). A. John Ciardi. CP-CiarJ

Sleep Contravened. Laura Riding Jackson. CP-RidiL

Sleep-crumpled cloud unfurls mealy mizzens, A. Venetian Stanzas 2. Joseph Brodsky. CP-BrodJ, *tr.* by Jane Miller

Sleep. / Do not fear the roaming. Berceuse for a Sleeping Mirror. Federico García Lorca. CP-GarcF, *tr.* by Jerome Rothenberg *Fr.* Mirror Suite.

Sleep fell upon my senses and I dreamed. Contentment. Ambrose Bierce. SP-BierA

Sleep-Gummed Eyes. James Schuyler. CP-SchuJ

Sleep half sleep half silence and with reasons. Ted Berrigan. SP-BerrT *Fr.* Sonnets, The.

Sleep: here's your bed . . . You'll not come, any more, to ours. Afterwards. Randall Jarrell. CP-JarrR

Sleep, horns of a snail. Sleepwalking. Christian J. Van Geel. CP-RicAE

Sleep Impression. Carl Sandburg. CP-SandC

Sleep in Jerusalem. Yehuda Amichai. SP-AmicYL, *tr.* by Benjamin Harshav *and* Barbara Harshav

Sleep in the Mojave Desert. Sylvia Plath. CP-PlatS

Sleep is a maker of makers. Birds sleep. Feet cling to a perch. Look at. Sleepyheads. Carl Sandburg. CP-SandC

Sleep is supposed to be. Emily Dickinson. CP-DickE

Sleep is the gift of many spiders. Drowsy. Carl Sandburg. CP-SandC

Sleep, let me sleep, for I am sick of care. Looking Forward. Christina Georgina Rossetti. CP-RosC3

Sleep, little babe, on my knee. Void in Law. Elizabeth Barrett Browning. CP-BroEB

Sleep, little Baby, sleep, / The holy angels love thee. Holy Innocents. Christina Georgina Rossetti. CP-RosC3

Sleep, little one! The Twilight folds her gloom. Slumber-Song. James Whitcomb Riley. CP-RileJ

Sleep, my child. You Had Me. Gabriela Mistral. SP-MistG, *tr.* by Maria Giachetti [*or* Jacketti]

Sleep, my darling, sleep. Cradle Song: "Sleep, my darling, sleep." Louis MacNeice. CP-MacNL

Sleep not. Be on your guard. Nocturne: "Sleep not. Be on your guard." Paul Celan. SP-CelaP, *tr.* by John Felstiner

Sleep not, dream not; this bright day. Emily Jane Brontë. CP-BronE

Sleep of this night deepens, The. Under Stars. Tess Gallagher. SP-GallT

Sleep on, baby, on the floor. Sleeping and Watching. Elizabeth Barrett Browning. CP-BroEB

Sleep, pretty lady, the night is enfolding you. Lullaby: "Sleep, pretty lady, the night is enfolding you." Dorothy Parker. CP-ParkD

Sleep, sleep, beauty bright. Cradle Song, A: "Sleep, sleep, beauty bright." William Blake. CP-BlakW

Sleep, Sleep Happy Child; All Creation Slept and Smiled. Christina Georgina Rossetti. CP-RosC3

Sleep Sleep; in thy sleep. William Blake. *See* Sleep, sleep, beauty bright

Sleep, sleep, mine Holy One! Virgin Mary to the Child Jesus, The. Elizabeth Barrett Browning. CP-BroEB

Sleep, sleep, my beloved. Sad Mother, The. Gabriela Mistral. SP-MistG, *tr.* by Maria Giachetti [*or* Jacketti]

Sleep sleep old sun, thou canst not have repast [*or* repassed]. Resurrection, Imperfect. John Donne. CP-DonnJ; MW-DonnJ

Sleep, sleep on! forget thy pain. Magnetic Lady to Her Patient, The. Percy Bysshe Shelley. CP-ShelP

Sleep softly . . . eagle forgotten . . . under the stone. Eagle That Is Forgotten, The. Nicholas Vachel Lindsay. CP-LindV

Sleep Song. Carl Sandburg. CP-SandC

Sleep, sweet babe! my cares beguiling. Virgin's Cradle-Hymn, The. Samuel Taylor Coleridge. CP-ColeS

Sleep that comes over me, The. Fernando Pessoa. SP-PessF, *tr.* by Susan M. Brown *and* Edwin Honig

Sleep till death. Nicolas-Sébastien Roch Chamfort. CP-BeckS

Sleep, unforgotten sorrow, sleep awhile. Acme. Christina Georgina Rossetti. CP-RosC3

Sleep was what deviled it. The days were easy. Ten Years Ago when I Played at Being Brave. John Ciardi. CP-CiarJ

Sleep-Worker, The. Thomas Hardy. CP-HardT

Sleeper, The. Walter De la Mare. CP-DeLaW

Sleeper, The. Rainer Maria Rilke. CP-RilkFr, *tr.* by A. Poulin, Jr. *Fr.* Affectionate Taxes to France.

Sleeper, The. Edgar Allan Poe. CP-PoeEd

Sleeper, arise and call upon thy God! Salvation Is of the Lord: The Book of Jonah 2.9. Jones Very. CP VeryJ

Sleepers. James Dickey. CP-DickJ

Sleepers, The. Walt Whitman. CP-WhitW

Sleepers, The. Sylvia Plath. CP-PlatS

Sleeping. Raymond Carver. CP-CarvR

Sleeping. Donald Hall. CP-HallD

Sleeping Alone in a Small Room. Gregory Orr. SP-OrrG

Sleeping and waking in the song of songs. Locket, the. Ted Hughes. SP-HughTN

Sleeping and Watching. Elizabeth Barrett Browning. CP-BroEB

Sleeping at Last. Christina Georgina Rossetti. CP-RosC3

Sleeping at last, the trouble and tumult over. Sleeping at Last. Christina Georgina Rossetti. CP-RosC3

Sleeping Beauty. Ai. SP-Ai

Sleeping Beauty. Olga Broumas. SP-BrouO

Sleeping Beauty. Lucille Clifton. SP-ClifL

Sleeping Beauty. Howard Nemerov. CP-NemeH

Sleeping Beauty, A. James Whitcomb Riley. CP-RileJ

Sleeping Beauty, The. Hayden Carruth. CP-CarHL

Sleeping Beauty, The. Wilfred Owen. CP-OwenW

Sleeping Beauty: Variation of the Prince, The. Randall Jarrell. CP-JarrR

Sleeping Brute, The. William Carlos Williams. CP-WilW2

Sleeping City, The. George Meredith. CP-MerG1

Sleeping face folds down over this human country, The. Boxers Hit Harder When Women Are Around. Kenneth Patchen. CP-PatcK

Sleeping Fury, The. Louise Bogan. CP-BogaL

Sleeping Giant, The. Donald Hall. CP-HallD

Sleeping he saw Ophelia in his dream. Georgy Vladimirovich Ivanov. SP-WeisT, *tr.* by Theodore Weiss

Sleeping in fever, I am unfit. For God While Sleeping. Anne Sexton. CP-SextA

Sleeping in the Forest. Mary Oliver. SP-OlivM

Sleeping map lay green, and we who were never much, The. Leasing of September, The. John Ashbery. SP-AshbJ

Sleeping Mountain, The. W. S. Merwin. SP-MerwW

Sleeping on the Ceiling. Elizabeth Bishop. CP-BishE

Sleeping on the Wing. Frank O'Hara. SP-OharF

Sleeping Out at Easter. James Dickey. CP-DickJ

Sleeping Over. C. K. Williams. CP-WillC

Sleeping Overnight on the Shore. May Swenson. SP-SwenM

Sleeping Pill. Hans Magnus Enzensberger. SP-EnzeH

Sleeping Standing Up. Elizabeth Bishop. CP-BishE

Sleeping Winds. Louis MacNeice. CP-MacNL

Sleeping with Animals. Maxine W. Kumin. SP-KumiM

Sleeping With Friends. Miller Williams. CP-WillM

Sleeping with Women. Kenneth Koch. SP-KochK

Sleeping with You. John Updike. CP-UpdiJ

Sleeping Woman. Rainer Maria Rilke. CP-RilkFr, *tr.* by A. Poulin, Jr. *Fr.* Orchards.

Sleepless. Robert Lowell. SP-LoweR

Sleepless. Stephen Spender. CP-SpenS

Sleepless at Crown Point. Richard Wilbur. CP-WilbR

Sleepless City. Federico García Lorca. CP-GarcF, *tr.* by Greg Simon *and* Steven F. White

Sleepless Dreams. Dante Gabriel Rossetti. CW-RossD *Fr.* House of Life, The.

Sleepless, I stare. Broken Dark, The. Robert Earl Hayden. CP-HaydR

Sleepless in Scarsdale. John Updike. CP-UpdiJ

Sleepless Night, A. James Laughlin. CP-LaugJ

Sleepless Night, A. Philip Levine. SP-LeviP

Sleepmonger, / deathmonger. Addict, The. Anne Sexton. CP-SextA; SP-SextA

Sleep's dream / the nerve-flash in the blood. Subliminal. Lorine Niedecker. CP-NiedL

Sleep's huge soft instruments rustle. Ecstasy of the Pure. Kenneth Patchen. CP-PatcK

Sleepscraps, wedges. Paul Celan. SP-CelaP, tr. by John Felstiner

Sleep'st thou, or wauk'st thou, fairest creature. Lover's Morning Salute to His Mistress, The. Robert Burns. CP-BurnR

Sleepwalk, feed. Terrible Naïve, The. Josephine Jacobsen. CP-JacoJ

Sleepwalking. Christian J. Van Geel. CP-RicAE

Sleepwalking Ballad. Federico García Lorca. CP-GarcF, tr. by Christopher Maurer

Sleepy giant, / You've been resting awhile. Africa. Langston Hughes. CP-HughL; CP-HughL3

Sleepy people, without priests or kings, A. Africa. G. K. Chesterton. CP-ChesG

Sleepyheads. Carl Sandburg. CP-SandC

Sleeve Notes. Paul Muldoon. CP-MuldP

Sleeve, picked out with gold and stones of rare design, of interest. Worn on the. Kenneth Patchen. CP-PatcK

Sleigh Ride. Jones Very. CP-VeryJ

Sleight, A. Theodore Weiss. SP-WeisT Fr. Storeroom, The.

SLEPT / folded in girls. Song of the Slip. Gary Snyder. CP-SnydG

Slice of Wedding Cake, A. Robert Graves. CP-GravR

Sliding Away. Arthur Sze. SP-SzeA

Sliding Mountain, The. Stevie Smith. CP-SmitS

Sliding Rock, The. Jones Very. CP-VeryJ

Sliding Rock! that pleasant spot, The. Sliding Rock, The. Jones Very. CP-VeryJ

Slight Ailment. Yannis Ritsos. SP-RitsY, tr. by Minas Savvas

Slight Relax of Air Where Cold Was, A. Philip Larkin. CP-LarkP

Slight wander of innocence. Anywhere. Robert Creeley. CP-CreeR

Slightest touch, The. Lines to Be Put into Latin. James Laughlin. CP-LaugJ

Slightly before the middle of Congressman Pudd. E. E. Cummings. CP-CummE

Slim and singing copper girl, A. Early Copper. Carl Sandburg. CP-SandC

Slim dragonfly / too rapid for the eye. Arthur Mitchell. Marianne Craig Moore. CP-MoorM

Slim flake of gold that I raised to my eyes and viewed against the light of May, The. In Praise of Gold. Gabriela Mistral. SP-MistG, tr. by Maria Giachetti [or Jacketti]

Slim inquirer, while the old fathers sleep. Earthworm. Anne Sexton. CP-SextA

Slime of all my yesterdays, The. April 18. Sylvia Plath. CP-PlatS

Sling Along. Paul Laurence Dunbar. CP-DunbP

Sling me under the sea. Bones. Carl Sandburg. CP-SandC

Slip, The. Wendell Berry. CP-BerrW

Slip back, Time! St. Launce's Revisited. Thomas Hardy. CP-HardT

Slip of a girl-announcer, The. Lorine Niedecker. CP-NiedL

Slippers. Raymond Carver. CP-CarvR

Slipperwort. Louis Zukofsky. CP-ZukLS

Slippery. Carl Sandburg. CP-SandC

Slippery whinnock, clear across the way, The. Urbanal. Christopher Logue. SP-LoguC

Slipping in blood, by his own hand, through pride. To an Artist, to Take Heart. Louise Bogan. CP-BogaL

Slips of the last rose of summer, The. Emily Dickinson. SP-DickE

Slit should be blue, The. Fanny Howe. SP-HoweF Fr. O'Clock.

Sliver. Langston Hughes. CP-HughL; CP-HughL3

Sliver of Sermon. Langston Hughes. CP-HughL; CP-HughL3

Slivers of rain upon the pane. Echoes. Hart Crane. CP-CranH

Sloe Gin. Seamus Heaney. SP-HeanSO

Sloe was lost in flower, The. A. E. Housman. CP-HousA

Sloop of Amber slips away, A. Emily Dickinson. SP-DickE

Sloops in the Bay are talking in a little bottle, The. James Tate. SP-TateJ

Slop Barrel, The. Philip Whalen. SP-WhalP

Slope. Eugenio Montale. CP-MontE, tr. by Jonathan Galassi

Slope of the heavy woods, The. Source, The. William Carlos Williams. CP-WilW1

Slope woods' snows melt. Easter Sunday. Allen Ginsberg. CP-GinsA

Slopeshouldered shape from scurrying burdens, A. &. Richard Wilbur. CP-WilbR

Slot-O-Topia. Andrei Codrescu. SP-CodrA

Sloth, The. Theodore Roethke. CP-RoetT

Slothful Sleep. John Milton. CP-MiltJ

Slouch he packs up. and goes to sev'rall Faires. Upon Slouch. Robert Herrick. CP-HerrR

Slough of unamiable liars, The. Ezra Pound. See Io venni luogo d'ogni muto

Sloughs of its down once fell to the prairie, like snow. Bringing Back the Trumpeter Swan. Maxine W. Kumin. SP-KumiM

Slow Boat Ride. Richard Eberhart. CP-EberR

Slow de night's a-fallin'. Whip-Poor-Will and Katy-Did. Paul Laurence Dunbar. CP-DunbP

Slow Death of the Dragon. Muriel Rukeyser. CP-RukeM

Slow Dialogue between Pain and Roosevelt. Muriel Rukeyser. CP-RukeM

Slow Down, Mr. Ganderdonk, You're Late. Ogden Nash. CP-NashO

Slow dulcimer, gavotte and bow, in autumn. Impossible to Tell. Robert Pinsky. CP-PinsR

Slow Fuse, A. Theodore Weiss. SP-WeisT

Slow in the dawn, a young man, hollow-eyed. Alchemist, The. Jorge Luis Borges. SP-BorgJ, tr. by Alastair Reid

Slow May. Spring in These Hills. Archibald MacLeish. CP-MacLA

Slow Motion. Amy Clampitt. CP-ClamA

Slow Movement. Louis MacNeice. CP-MacNL

Slow Movement. William Carlos Williams. CP-WilW1

Slow moves the pageant of a climbing race. Slow Through the Dark. Paul Laurence Dunbar. CP-DunbP

Slow Nature, The. Thomas Hardy. CP-HardT

Slow News from Our Place. William Stafford. SP-StafWW

Slow perfume, heart without a scale. Federico García Lorca. CP-GarcF, tr. by Christopher Maurer

Slow Potomac, tarnished water. At the Lincoln Memorial. Archibald MacLeish. CP-MacLA

Slow Process, A. Clarence Major.

Slow Program. Carl Sandburg. CP-SandC

Slow Rain, The. Gabriela Mistral. SP-MistG, tr. by Maria Giachetti [or Jacketti]

Slow River. Czeslaw Milosz. CP-MiloC; CP-MiloCN, tr. by Renata Gorczynski

Slow Season. Theodore Roethke. CP-RoetT

Slow sinks, more lovely ere his race be run. Curse of Minerva, The. Lord Byron. CP-Byron

Slow, slow, fresh fount, keep time with my salt tears. Echo's [or Eccho's] Song. Ben Jonson. CP-JonsB; SP-JonsB Fr. Cynthia's Revels.

Slow slowing—. Robert Creeley. CP-CreeR

Slow Starter, The. Louis MacNeice. CP-MacNL

Slow Through the Dark. Paul Laurence Dunbar. CP-DunbP

Slow Waker. Thom Gunn. CP-GunnT

(I look at the nephew.) CP-GunnT

Slowly. Denise Levertov. SP-LeveDL

Slowly a floor rises, almost becomes a wall. Hurricane at Sea, A. May Swenson. SP-SwenM

Slowly a Nation doth unfold its life. Nation's Life of Slow Growth, A. Jones Very. CP-VeryJ

Slowly, and one by one, with few to see or hear. World of the Salamanders, The. Marya Alexandrovna Zaturenska. SP-ZatuM

Slowly I smoke and hug my knee. Ballade by the Fire. Edwin Arlington Robinson. CP-RobiE

Slowly learning again to love. Sweeping the Garden. Olga Broumas. SP-BrouO

Slowly-moving fingers minutes find, The. Clock, The. Jones Very. CP-VeryJ

Slowly, Prometheus. Always the Same. Adrienne Rich. CP-RicAE

Slowly rising, slowly strengthening moon. La Lune, A. William Carlos Williams. CP-WilW1

Slowly stroking your fingers where they lie. Always. Robert Graves. CP-GravR

Slowly / the dried up pond. Vermont Diary, A. James Schuyler. CP-SchuJ

Slowly the moon is rising out of the ruddy haze. Aware. D. H. Lawrence. CP-LawrD

Slowly the passenger pigeons increased, then suddenly their numbers. Passenger Pigeons. Robinson Jeffers. CP-JefR3

Slowly the roses droop and die. Monody. Dorothy Parker. CP-ParkD

Slowly the salt of the earth becomes salt of the sea. Salt of the Earth. D. H. Lawrence. CP-LawrD

Slowly the toiling images will rise. Stage Directions. Robert Duncan. SP-DuncR Fr. Passages.

Slowly the women file to where he stands. Faith Healing. Philip Larkin. CP-LarkP

Slowly with bleeding nose and aching wrists. Hero, The. Robert Graves. CP-GravR

Slowly, with the blossoms of understanding, I begin to grope. Yehuda Amichai. SP-AmicYL Fr. At Right Angles.

Slowness of Belief in a Spiritual World, The. Jones Very. CP-VeryJ

Slug. Theodore Roethke. CP-RoetT

Slug and the rat possess the dead, The. Burial Ground. Charles Olson. CP-OlsoC

Sluggish smoke curls up from some deep dell, The. Henry David Thoreau. CP-ThorH

Sluggishly. Yannis Ritsos. SP-RitsY, tr. by Kostas Myrsiades

Sluggishly. William Carlos Williams. CP-WilW1

Sluice, The. Paul Celan. SP-CelaP, *tr.* by John Felstiner

Slum Child, The. Walter De la Mare. CP-DeLaW

Slum Dreams. Langston Hughes. CP-HughL; CP-HughL3

Slum Song. Louis MacNeice. CP-MacNL

Slumber did my spirit seal, A. William Wordsworth. MW-WorW *Fr.* Lucy.

Slumber-Song. James Whitcomb Riley. CP-RileJ

Slumberer wakes! Are these the walls, The. Young Drummer Boy of Libby Prison: An Incident Related by Capt. James Hussey, The. Jones Very. CP-VeryJ

Slumped under the impressive genitals. Boston Common. John Berryman. CP-BerrJ

Slums, The. Kenneth Patchen. CP-PatcK

Slung from the gantries cranes. Steel. Charles Tomlinson. CP-TomlC

Slurred and drawled and crooning sounds, The. Toast, A. Louis MacNeice. CP-MacNL

Slyly diverted, a breeze passes. Impromptu with a Breeze. Robert Stock. SP-StocR

Small. John Ciardi. CP-CiarJ

Small, The. Theodore Roethke. CP-RoetT

Small Action Poem. Charles Tomlinson. CP-TomlC

Small barking sounds—. Sunday. William Carlos Williams. CP-WilW1

Small birds fly up. Sparrows. Robert Creeley. SP-CreeR

Small birds puff their cheats and feathers. Fanny Howe. SP-HoweF *Fr.* Introduction to the World.

Small birds rejoice in the green leaves returning, The. Song: "Small birds rejoice in the green leaves returning, The." Robert Burns. CP-BurnR

Small birds swirl around, The. Small, The. Theodore Roethke. CP-RoetT

Small Birds, to Agree with the Leaves, Come in the Fall. Charles Olson. CP-OlsoC

Small black blobs on the beach are the heads, The. Class, The. Josephine Jacobsen. CP-JacoJ

Small blind cripple's face was ready, The. Reading Aloud at Dusk. Josephine Jacobsen. CP-JacoJ

Small blind street off East Commercial Road, A. East-End Curate, An. Thomas Hardy. CP-HardT

Small blue flowers like points. Voice, The. Philip Levine. SP-LeviP

Small Blue Heron, The. James Wright. CP-WrigJ

Small boy in a black hat walks among streaky shadows. Cold Spring in Essex. Donald Davie. CP-DaviDC

Small boy in shock with a blue Popsicle, A. Inside the City Walls. Norman Dubie. CP-DubiN

Small brook gushed on stones hard by, A. Interlude, An. Walter De la Mare. CP-DeLaW

Small, busy flames play through the fresh-laid coals. To My Brothers. John Keats. CP-KeatJ

Small but Brilliant Fire Blazed in the Grate, A. Kenneth Patchen. CP-PatcK

Small Cabin, The. Margaret Atwood. SP-AtwM1

Small Celandine, The. William Wordsworth. CP-WorW1; MW-WorW

Small-City People. John Updike. CP-UpdiJ

Small clematis tumbles, The. Rainer Maria Rilke. CP-RilkFr, *tr.* by A. Poulin, Jr. *Fr.* Valaisian Quatrains, The.

Small Confession. Yannis Ritsos. SP-RitsY, *tr.* by Kimon Friar

Small crimes, like pepper, make things. At Home. Andrei Codrescu. SP-CodrA

Small Dialogue. Yannis Ritsos. SP-RitsY, *tr.* by Kostas Myrsiades

Small dog named for a wing. Ali. W. S. Merwin. SP-MerwWF

Small Elegy. John Ciardi. CP-CiarJ

Small Eternity. Robert Penn Warren. CP-WarrR

Small Events. Ted Hughes. SP-HughTN

Small Excursion, A. Mona Van Duyn. SP-VanDM

Small fact and fingers and farthest one from me. Poem for Emily, A. Miller Williams. CP-WillM

Small Fig Tree, A. Donald Hall. CP-HallD

Small flame pointing, shadowing, picking out. Interiors. Howard Nemerov. CP-NemeH

Small Fountain. Rainer Maria Rilke. CP-RilkFr, *tr.* by A. Poulin, Jr. *Fr.* Valaisian Quatrains, The.

Small Frogs Killed on the Highway. James Wright. CP-WrigJ

Small garden, A. Rain. Constantine P. Cavafy. CP-CavaC, *tr.* by Theoharis Constantine Theoharis

Small Garden Near a Field. Tess Gallagher. SP-GallT

Small gnats that fly. One Hard Look. Robert Graves. CP-GravR

Small golden bells. / Dragon pagoda. Shinto. Federico García Lorca. CP-GarcF, *tr.* by Jerome Rothenberg *Fr.* Mirror Suite.

Small Group, A. James Laughlin. CP-LaugJ

Small Hands, Relinquish All. Edna St. Vincent Millay. CP-MillE

Small Homes. Carl Sandburg. CP-SandC

Small horses on windowsill. Neighbors. Robert Creeley. SP-CreeR

Small Hours, The. Dorothy Parker. CP-ParkD

Small householder now comes out warily, The. Spring Voices. Louis MacNeice. CP-MacNL

Small Invitation, A. Yannis Ritsos. SP-RitsY, *tr.* by Kimon Friar

Small, just / a room, / the altar. Chapel, A. James Schuyler. CP-SchuJ

Small knowledge have we that by knowledge met. Modernities. Edwin Arlington Robinson. CP-RobiE

Small Lady, The. Stevie Smith. CP-SmitS

Small light, furtive, peers, A. Night Watchman, The. Josephine Jacobsen. CP-JacoJ

Small Memory. Langston Hughes. CP-HughL; CP-HughL3

Small mirror hanging on the wall nail, The. Small Song for Éri. Yannis Ritsos. SP-RitsY, *tr.* by Kimon Friar

Small Moment. Howard Nemerov. CP-NemeH

Small Moon. Howard Nemerov. CP-NemeH

Small moon, The. Yannis Ritsos. SP-RitsY *Fr.* First Series.

Small Notebook. Rainer Maria Rilke. CP-RilkFr, *tr.* by A. Poulin, Jr.

Small Plane in Kansas. Thom Gunn. CP-GunnT

Small Poetics, A. Dan Pagis. SP-PagiD, *tr.* by Stephen Mitchell

Small porch of imitation, The. Taylor Street. Thom Gunn. CP-GunnT

Small quantity of musk pervades. That Eyes! Those Nose! Philip Whalen. SP-WhalP

Small Rain, The. Robert Stock. SP-StocR

Small room, the varnished floor, A. Theological Definition, A. George Oppen. CP-OppGN

Small-scale Reflections on a Great House. A. K. Ramanujan. CP-RamaA

Small service is true service while it lasts. To a Child [Written in Her Album]. William Wordsworth. CP-WorW2

Small Song. A. R. Ammons. CP-AmmoA

Small Song. James Dickey. CP-DickJ

Small Song for Éri. Yannis Ritsos. SP-RitsY, *tr.* by Kimon Friar

Small-soul-pleasing, loved with condescension. Ivana. Robert Lowell. SP-LoweR

Small the far away, The. Hospitality to Words. Laura Riding Jackson. CP-RidiL

Small the Theme of My Chant. Walt Whitman. CP-WhitW

Small Tin Parrot Pin, A. Thomas Lux. SP-LuxT

Small Town. Rita Dove. SP-DoveR

Small towns possess humility—it is a natural characteristic. In Praise of Small Towns. Gabriela Mistral. SP-MistG, *tr.* by Maria Giachetti [*or* Jacketti]

Small vellum environment, A. Page from the Koran. James Merrill. SP-MerrJ

Small voice is fretting my house in the night, A. Smallish Son, The. Hayden Carruth. CP-CarHS

Small weight is obnoxious, A. Emily Dickinson. SP-DickE

Small wheel, A. Watch Repair. Charles Simic. SP-SimiC; SP-SimiCE

Small White House. Robert Penn Warren. CP-WarrR

Small wind, A. Cat and the Wind, The. Thom Gunn. CP-GunnT

Small Wire. Anne Sexton. CP-SextA; SP-SextA

Small wonder / he's not been sighted all winter. Brock. Paul Muldoon. CP-MuldP

Small Wonders. Charles Simic. SP-SimiCE

Small, yellow grass-onion, The. To Be Hungry Is to Be Great. William Carlos Williams. CP-WilW1

Smaller, no recall. Kid ("Smaller, no recall"). Robert Creeley. SP-CreeR

Smaller, older *Girl at a Sewing Machine*, The. Two Hoppers. John Updike. CP-UpdiJ

Smaller Orchid, The. Amy Clampitt. CP-ClamA

Smallest Blessing, The. James Laughlin. CP-LaugJ

Smallest flower, The. Compleynt Blossoms April to July. Charles Olson. CP-OlsoC

Smalley Bar. Marge Piercy. SP-PierM

Smallish Son, The. Hayden Carruth. CP-CarHS

Smalltown, South India. A. K. Ramanujan. CP-RamaA

Smart. Robert Herrick. CP-HerrR

Smart and Final Iris. James Tate. SP-TateJ

Smart bombs replace. May Our Right Hands Lose Their Cunning. Denise Levertov. SP-LeveDL

Smart sends his compliments and pray'rs. Epistle to Dr. Nares. Christopher Smart. SP-SmarC

Smash down the cities. And They Obey. Carl Sandburg. CP-SandC

Smashed, and brought up against. After an Accident. Donald Davie. CP-DaviDC

Smashed bones. Gristle of ribs. Encounter at Nightfall. Kenneth Patchen. CP-PatcK

Smell. William Carlos Williams. CP-WilW1

Smell in the diamond morning was, The. On Work. Alan Dugan. CP-DugaA

Smell of coffee and the newspapers, The. Camden, 1892. Jorge Luis Borges. SP-BorgJ, *tr.* by Alastair Reid

Smell of further honey, A. Song of the Foolish Bees. Martinus Nijhoff. CP-RicAE

Smell of Gasoline Ascends in My Nose, The. Yehuda Amichai. SP-AmicY, *tr. by* Stephen Mitchell

Smell of Gasoline in My Nose, The. Yehuda Amichai. SP-AmicYL

Smell of geranium, The. Summer or Its End, A. Yehuda Amichai. SP-AmicYL, *tr. by* Benjamin Harshav *and* Barbara Harshav

Smell of gum wrappers as of Saturday afternoon at movies. Robert Creeley. CP-CreeR

Smell of Lebanon, The. Alice Walker. CP-WalkA

Smell of rain in the air. Pencil Sketch. Clarence Major. SP-MajoC

Smell of snow, stinging in nostrils as the wind lifts it from a beach, The. Crystal Lithium, The. James Schuyler. CP-SchuJ

Smell of stale air, The. Robert Creeley. CP-CreeR

Smell of the heat is boxwood, The. To Daphne and Virginia. William Carlos Williams. CP-WilW2

Smell of the Sacrifice, The. Robert Herrick. CP-HerrR

Smell of the sea in my nostrils, The. Mystic Sea, The. Paul Laurence Dunbar. CP-DunbP

Smell of ubiquitous, The. Meditations on a Dingo. Yusef Komunyakaa. CP-KomuY

Smell of wet geraniums, The. On furry. Digging in the Garden of Age I Uncover a Live Root. May Swenson. SP-SwenM

Smelling bad. Little Rock. Clarence Major. SP-MajoC

Smells are surer than sounds or sights. Lichtenberg. Rudyard Kipling. CP-KiplR

Smells of ordinariness, The. Night Drive. Seamus Heaney. SP-HeanSO

Smells, / sounds. Robert Creeley. CP-CreeR

Smelt, The. Ogden Nash. CP-NashO

Smelt and Tasted. W. H. Auden. CP-AudeW

Smelt Fishing. Robert Earl Hayden. CP-HaydR

Smile, The. William Blake. CP-BlakW

Smile, The. Ted Hughes. SP-HughTN

Smile, The. James Merrill. SP-MerrJ

Smile, The. Stevie Smith. CP-SmitS

Smile, The. Robert Penn Warren. CP-WarrR

Smile and a Sigh, A. Christina Georgina Rossetti. CP-RosC1

Smile at us, pay us, pass us; but do not quite forget. Secret People, The. G. K. Chesterton. CP-ChesG

Smile because the nights are short!, A. Smile and a Sigh, A. Christina Georgina Rossetti. CP-RosC1

Smile fell in the grass, A. Night Dances, The. Sylvia Plath. CP-PlatS

Smile of iceboxes annihilates me, The. Appearance, An. Sylvia Plath. CP-PlatS

Smile of the Moon!—for so I name. Lament of Mary Queen of Scots on the Eve of a New Year. William Wordsworth. CP-WorW2

Smile, Smile, Smile. Wilfred Owen. CP-OwenW

Smilers, smirkers, chucklers, grinners. Woman Who Laughed on Calvary. Heather McHugh. SP-McHuH

Smiles. Wisława Szymborska. SP-SzymW, *tr. by* Stanislaw Barańczak *and* Clare Cavanagh

Smiling back from Coronation. Emily Dickinson. CP-DickE

Smiling Dane, A. William Carlos Williams. CP-WilW2

Smiling face of a happy boy, The. To a Boy Whistling. James Whitcomb Riley. CP-RileJ

Smiling Morne had newly wak't the Day, The. Beginning of Heliodorus, The. Heliodorus. CP-CrasR

Smiling through my own memories of painful excitement your wide eyes. Ode to Tanaquil Leclercq: "Smiling through my own memories of painful excitement your wide eyes." Frank O'Hara. SP-OharF

Smilling spring comes in rejoicing, The. Bonie Bell. Robert Burns. CP-BurnR

Smith makes me, A. Runes on Weland's Sword, The. Rudyard Kipling. CP-KiplR *Fr.* Puck of Pook's Hill.

Smitten Purist, The. James Whitcomb Riley. CP-RileJ

Smog trucks mile after mile high wire. Bayonne Entering NYC. Allen Ginsberg. CP-GinsA

Smoke. Robert Creeley. CP-CreeR

Smoke. Carl Sandburg. CP-SandC

Smoke. William Stafford. SP-StafWW

Smoke. Henry David Thoreau.

Smoke. Adam Zagajewski. SP-ZagaA, *tr. by* Clare Cavanagh

Smoke and Deception. Raymond Carver. CP-CarvR

Smoke and Steel. Carl Sandburg. CP-SandC

Smoke Blue. Carl Sandburg. CP-SandC

Smoke from the train-gulf hid by hoardings blunders upward. Birmingham. Louis MacNeice. CP-MacNL

Smoke of autumn is on it all. Three Pieces on the Smoke of Autumn. Carl Sandburg. CP-SandC

Smoke of Marijuana, The. Jaroslav Seifert. SP-SeifJ, *tr. by* Ewald Osers

Smoke of these landscapes has gone God knows where. Runaway Colors. Carl Sandburg. CP-SandC

Smoke Rolling Down Street. Allen Ginsberg. CP-GinsA

Smoke rolls in stinking, suffocating wrack. By a Reactionary. G. K. Chesterton. CP-ChesG

Smoke Rose Gold. Carl Sandburg. CP-SandC

Smoke Shapes. Carl Sandburg. CP-SandC

Smoke that gathers blue and sinks, The. T. S. Eliot. SP-ElioT

Smoke upon your Altar dies, The. L'Envoi; Departmental Ditties. Rudyard Kipling. CP-KiplR

Smokehouse, The. Yusef Komunyakaa. CP-KomuY

Smoke's way's a good way—find. Smoke. William Stafford. SP-StafWW

Smokin' my pipe on the mountings, sniffin' the mornin'-cool. Screw-Guns. Rudyard Kipling. CP-KiplR

Smoking Pot on the Bus. Thom Gunn. CP-GunnT

Smoky rain riddles the ocean plains, A. My Father Paints the Summer. Richard Wilbur. CP-WilbR

Smooth between sea and land. A. E. Housman. CP-HousA

Smooth Gnarled Crape Myrtle. Marianne Craig Moore. CP-MoorM

Smooth light: all bronze. Brilliant Silence. Charles Tomlinson. CP-TomlC

Smooth talker / slides into my dreams. Eve's version. Lucille Clifton. SP-ClifL

Smooth was the Sea, and seem'd to call. Faire Shewes Deceive. Robert Herrick. CP-HerrR

Smoothing soft the nestling head. Two Loves, The. John Greenleaf Whittier. CP-WhitJ

Smooths and burdens. Snow. Robert Earl Hayden. CP-HaydR

Smothered streams of love, which flow, The. Atlantides, The. Henry David Thoreau. CP-ThorH

Smouldering embers blush, The. Emily Dickinson. CP-DickE

Smudge for the horizon, A. October. May Swenson. SP-SwenM

Smudged eyeballs. Breakfast in a Bowling Alley in Utica, New York. Adrienne Rich. CP-RicAE

Smudgy dawn scarfed with military colors. Ivor Gurney. SP-GurnI

Smuggler's Song, A. Rudyard Kipling. CP-KiplR *Fr.* Puck of Pook's Hill.

Smugglers and Poachers. George Crabbe. SP-CrabG *Fr.* Tales of the Hall.

Snail. Federico García Lorca. SP-GarcF *Fr.* Songs of Childhood.

Snail. Langston Hughes. CP-HughL; CP-HughL2

Snail. Anne Sexton. CP-SextA

Snail, The. Vincent Bourne. CP-CowpW, *tr. by* William Cowper

Snail, The. G. K. Chesterton. CP-ChesG

Snail, The. Primo Levi. CP-LeviP, *tr. by* Ruth Feldman

Snail, The. Gregory Orr. SP-OrrG

Snail gives off stillness, The. Evening. Charles Simic. SP-SimiC; SP-SimiCE

Snail moves like a, The. Hedgehog. Paul Muldoon. CP-MuldP

Snail pushes through a green, The. Considering the Snail. Thom Gunn. CP-GunnT

Snail Sail. Andrei Codrescu. SP-CodrA

Snail sat in the blind man's palm, The. Snail, The. Gregory Orr. SP-OrrG

Snake. D. H. Lawrence. CP-LawrD

Snake. Langston Hughes. CP-HughL; CP-HughL2

Snake. Robert Lowell. SP-LoweR

Snake. Dan Pagis. SP-PagiD, *tr. by* Stephen Mitchell

Snake. Theodore Roethke. CP-RoetT

Snake. Anne Sexton. CP-SextA

Snake, A. Emily Dickinson. CP-DickE

Snake, The. Wendell Berry. CP-BerrW

Snake, The. Emily Dickinson. CP-DickE

Snake came to my water-trough, A. Snake. D. H. Lawrence. CP-LawrD

Snake-Catcher and the Frozen Snake, The. Jelaluddin Rumi. SP-Rumi, *tr. by* Coleman Barks

Snake enters your dreams through paintings:, The. Quattrocento. Margaret Atwood. SP-AtwM2

Snake hunts and sinews, The. She. Margaret Atwood. SP-AtwM2

Snake is one name of God, The. After Heraclitus. Margaret Atwood. SP-AtwM2

Snake Lake. Thomas Lux. SP-LuxT

Snake no bigger, A. Gregory Orr. SP-OrrG

Snake on the blue, The. On a Snake. Alan Dugan. CP-DugaA

Snake was damned, The. Falling: 1. Rae Armantrout. SP-ArmaA

Snake who was afraid of the birdgod Garuda, A. Two Parables from "The Ocean of Story." James Laughlin. CP-LaugJ

Snake Woman. Margaret Atwood. SP-AtwM2

Snakebite. James Dickey. CP-DickJ

Snakecharmer. Sylvia Plath. CP-PlatS

Snakes. A. K. Ramanujan. CP-RamaA

Snakes and Ladders. A. K. Ramanujan. CP-RamaA

Snakes are weeping on the rocks. Valley-sleeper, the Children, the Snakes, and the Giant, The. Kenneth Patchen. CP-PatcK

Snakes, Mongooses, Snake-Charmers, and the Like. Marianne Craig Moore. CP-MoorM

Snakes of September, The. Stanley Kunitz. CP-KunSC

Snap-Comb Wilderness, The. Robert Graves. CP-GravR

Snap-Dragon. D. H. Lawrence. CP-LawrD

Snap the blind; I am not blind. Aubade for Infants. Louis MacNeice. CP-MacNL

Snapped Thread, The. Robert Graves. CP-GravR

Snapping kindling for the kitchen stove. Henry Manley Looks Back. Maxine W. Kumin. SP-KumiM

Snapping turtles in the pond eat bass, sunfish. Pond, The. Gregory Orr. SP-OrrG

Snaps its twig-tether—mounts. Dove, A. Ted Hughes. SP-HughTN

Snapshot. Charles Tomlinson. SP-TomlC

Snapshots. John Updike. CP-UpdiJ

Snapshots of a Daughter-in-Law. Adrienne Rich. CP-RicAE; SP-RicA1; SP-RicA2

Snare, The. Thomas Merton. CP-MertT

Snare, The. Jones Very. CP-VeryJ

Snare, ten i'th'hundred calls his wife; and why? Upon Snare, an Usurer. Robert Herrick. CP-HerrR

Snares of Varuna, The. Hugh MacDiarmid. "As I have often told." SP-MacDH

Snark Was a Boojum Was a Prawn, The. Ogden Nash. CP-NashO

Snarleyow. Rudyard Kipling. CP-KiplR

Snatch of Sliphorn Jazz. Carl Sandburg. CP-SandC

Snatched me from the ivy's tangle. Ezekiel Saw the Wheel. Eugenio Montale. CP-MontE, tr. by Jonathan Galassi

Sneape has a face so brittle, that it breaks. Upon Sneape. Robert Herrick. CP-HerrR

Sneeze, The. Wyatt Prunty. SP-PrunW

Sniff of the real, that's, The. Autobiography. Thom Gunn. CP-GunnT

Sniffle, The. Ogden Nash. CP-NashO

Snip, snip goes wind through the autumn trees. Waiting for Tu Fu. Charles Wright. SP-WrigCN

SNO / a white idea(Listen). E. E. Cummings. CP-CummE

Snob. Langston Hughes. CP-HughL; CP-HughL2

Snorting hippopotamus at the lake's bottom, all snoot. Winter's Tale, by a Wife, A. Mona Van Duyn. SP-VanDM

Snow. Billy Collins. SP-CollB

Snow. Walter De la Mare. CP-DeLaW

Snow. Robert Frost. CP-FrosR

Snow. Ivor Gurney. SP-GurnI

Snow. Robert Earl Hayden. CP-HaydR

Snow. Ted Hughes. SP-HughTN

Snow. Philip Levine. SP-LeviP

Snow. Louis MacNeice. CP-MacNL

Snow. Adrienne Rich. CP-RicAE

Snow. Carl Sandburg. CP-SandC

Snow. Anne Sexton. CP-SextA

Snow, The. Hayden Carruth. CP-CarHS

Snow, The. Robert Creeley. CP-CreeR

Snow, The. Emily Dickinson. CP-DickE

Snow, The. Donald Hall. CP-HallD

Snow, The. W. S. Merwin. SP-MerwWF

Snow, The. Charles Olson. CP-OlsoC

Snow, The. James Schuyler. CP-SchuJ

Snow and Stars. Wallace Stevens. CP-StevW; CP-StevWP

Snow, and the silence of snow, heavy on the rousing day. Snowy Day at School, A. D. H. Lawrence. CP-LawrD

Snow be in this time with us as music. Fanny Howe. SP-HoweF Fr. Lines Out to Silence.

Snow began falling late last night. Wet flakes. Gift, The. Raymond Carver. CP-CarvR

Snow / began here / this morning and all day, The. First Snow. Mary Oliver. SP-OlivM

Snow Begins, The. William Carlos Williams. CP-WilW2

Snow beneath whose chilly softness. Emily Dickinson. CP-DickE

Snow Bird, The. Jones Very. CP-VeryJ

Snow, / blessed snow. Snow. Anne Sexton. CP-SextA

Snow-blizzard sowing. Car Crash. Allen Ginsberg. CP-GinsA

Snow-bound in woodland, a mournful word. Postponement. Thomas Hardy. CP-HardT

Snow-Bound [or Snow-Bound; a Winter Idyl]. John Greenleaf Whittier. CP-WhitJ

Snow brings into view the far hills. Appearance. Charles Tomlinson. CP-TomlC

Snow came down last night like moths, The. First Snow in Alsace. Richard Wilbur. CP-WilbR

Snow came to us in the week of Thanksgiving. Essay on Marriage. Hayden Carruth. CP-CarHS

Snow came with dusk, building itself on windows. New Year's Eve. John Ciardi. CP-CiarJ

Snow Cascades. Richard Eberhart. CP-EberR

Snow / coming / to my window, going up. Hotel Steinplatz, Berlin, December 25 (1966). Charles Olson. SP-OlsoC Fr. Maximus Poems, The.

SNOW / cru / is / ingw Hi. E. E. Cummings. CP-CummE

Snow Day. Billy Collins. SP-CollB

Snow dissolv'd no more is seen, The. Ode 4.7: "Snow dissolv'd no more is seen, The." Horace. CP-JohnS, tr. by Samuel Johnson Fr. Odes.

Snow-Drop, The. Samuel Taylor Coleridge. CP-ColeS

Snow Drop, The. Jones Very. CP-VeryJ

Snow Fall, The. Archibald MacLeish. CP-MacLA

Snow falling and night falling fast oh fast. Desert Places. Robert Frost. CP-FrosR

Snow falling. Snowflakes clung and melted. Snow. Ted Hughes. SP-HughTN

Snow falls deep; the forest lies alone, The. Gipsies: "Snow falls deep; the forest lies alone, The." John Clare. SP-ClarJ

Snow falls in the dusk of Connecticut. The stranger. Sound of Snow, The. Hayden Carruth. CP-CarHS

Snow falls. The fields begin again. Whispered in Winter. William Stafford. SP-StafWW

Snow fell forward forever. Ask the Roses. Philip Levine. SP-LeviP

Snow Fences, The. Charles Tomlinson. CP-TomlC; SP-TomlC

Snow-Flakes. Henry Wadsworth Longfellow. SP-LongH

Snow flakes / I counted till they danced so. Emily Dickinson. CP-DickE

Snow Geese. Robert Bly. SP-BlyR

Snow Geese at Jamaica Bay, The. May Swenson. SP-SwenM

Snow-glitter, snow-gleam, all snow-peaks. Language Barrier. Robert Penn Warren. CP-WarrR

Snow Globe, The. Howard Nemerov. CP-NemeH

Snow had buried Stuyvesant, The. Inauguration Day: January 1953. Robert Lowell. SP-LoweR

Snow-happy hicks of a boy's world. Twelfth Night. Louis MacNeice. CP-MacNL

Snow has fallen on snow for two days behind the Keillen farmhouse. Orchard Keeper, The. Robert Bly. SP-BlyR

Snow has fallen, with no light. A month. Black Flakes. Paul Celan. SP-CelaP, tr. by John Felstiner

Snow has left the cottage top, The. February. John Clare. SP-ClarJ Fr. Shepherd's [or Shepheards] Calendar, The.

Snow in May. James Laughlin. CP-LaugJ

Snow in May. Marge Piercy. SP-PierM

Snow in the Air. James Whitcomb Riley. CP-RileJ

Snow in the City. Jane Cooper. CP-CoopJ

Snow in the Suburbs. Thomas Hardy. CP-HardT

Snow is a process of thinking. Down the street. Snow in the City. Jane Cooper. CP-CoopJ

Snow is a white horse. Poet Whose Photo Never Grows Old, A. Yusef Komunyakaa. CP-KomuY

Snow is deep on the ground, The. Kenneth Patchen. CP-PatcK

Snow is gone from cottage tops, The. John Clare. See Snow has left the cottage top, The

Snow is in the air. Snow in the Air. James Whitcomb Riley. CP-RileJ

Snow is in the oak. Snow, The. Donald Hall. CP-HallD

Snow King, The. Rita Dove. SP-DoveR

Snow Lamp, The. Robert Earl Hayden. CP-HaydR "Across lunar wastes of wind and snow." CP-HaydR "It is beginning oh." CP-HaydR "No sun these months. Ice-dark and cold." CP-HaydR

Snow-Leopard, The. Randall Jarrell. CP-JarrR

Snow, less intransigeant than their marble, The. At the Grave of Henry James. W. H. Auden. CP-AudeW

Snow lies deep upon the ground, The. Christmas in the Heart. Paul Laurence Dunbar. CP-DunbP

Snow lifts it. Winter. Robert Creeley. SP-CreeR

Snow Light, The. May Sarton. SP-SartM

Snow Log. A. R. Ammons. CP-AmmoA

Snow Man, The. Louis MacNeice. CP-MacNL

Snow Man, The. Wallace Stevens. CP-StevW; CP-StevWP

Snow means that / life is a black cannonadin. E. E. Cummings. CP-CummE

Snow mountain fields. Teton Village. Allen Ginsberg. CP-GinsA

Snow names a wreath *snowdrop*. Snowdrop. Louis Zukofsky. CP-ZukLS

Snow on a Southern State. James Dickey. CP-DickJ

Snow on the ground. A day in March. River Rouge, 1932. John Berryman. CP-BerrJ

Snow on the mountain—water in. Song in the Manner of Flannery O'Connor, A. William Stafford. SP-StafW; SP-StafWW

Snow: I. C. K. Williams. SP-WillC

Snow, out over the elephant's rump. Landscape Winter. Anne Sexton. CP-SextA

Snow packs the roadside, sends dunes. Bus to Alliston, Ontario, The. Margaret

Atwood. SP-AtwM2

Snow Party, The. Derek Mahon. CP-MahoD

Snow-piles in dark places are gone, The. Just Before April Came. Carl Sandburg. CP-SandC

Snow Queen, The. Adrienne Rich. CP-RicAE; SP-RicA2

Snow rises as it falls. Fanny Howe. SP-HoweF *Fr.* Q.

Snow Signs. Charles Tomlinson. CP-TomlC; SP-TomlC

Snow, Snow. Marge Piercy. SP-PierM

Snow starts at twilight. All night the house. Twelve Seasons. Donald Hall. CP-HallD

Snow-Storm [*or* Snowstorm], The. Ralph Waldo Emerson. CP-EmerR

Snow Storm, The. Edna St. Vincent Millay. CP-MillE

Snow that makes graces on a soldier's sleeve. Imperial Song for Warmth. Alan Dugan. CP-DugaA

Snow that never drifts, The. Emily Dickinson. CP-DickE

Snow thick and wet, porous. Spring. James Schuyler. CP-SchuJ

Snow Thickets. James Dickey. CP-DickJ

Snow through the fronds, fire flowing into the sea. Account of a Visit to Hawaii, An. William Meredith. SP-MereW

Snow took us away from the smoke valleys into white mountains, we saw. Snow. Carl Sandburg. CP-SandC

Snow turning, The. Snow Whirl. A. R. Ammons. CP-AmmoA

Snow: II. C. K. Williams. SP-WillC

Snow visits us, The. Storm. James Tate. SP-TateJ

Snow Whirl. A. R. Ammons. CP-AmmoA

Snow White. Olga Broumas. SP-BrouO

Snow White and the Seven Dwarfs. Anne Sexton. CP-SextA; SP-SextA

Snow-white ray. Pietà. Donald Davie. CP-DaviDC

Snow White was always waiting for The Prince. Charles Olson. CP-OlsoC

Snow Wine. Aleksandr Aleksandrovich Blok. SP-BlokA, *tr. by* Peter France *and* Jon Stallworthy

Snow would be the easy. November for Beginners. Rita Dove. SP-DoveR

Snow-Wreath. Louis Zukofsky. CP-ZukLS

Snow:/ years of anger following. Blizzard. William Carlos Williams. CP-WilW1

Snow, you are disregarding me. For How Long. Dan Pagis. SP-PagiD, *tr. by* Stephen Mitchell

Snowbanks North of the House. Robert Bly. SP-BlyR

Snowdrop. Ted Hughes. SP-HughTN

Snowdrop. Louis Zukofsky. CP-ZukLS

Snowdrop, The. Walter De la Mare. CP-DeLaW

Snowdrop, The. James Schuyler. CP-SchuJ

Snowdrop is the prophet of the flowers, The. Wild Rose and the Snowdrop, The. George Meredith. CP-MerG1

Snowdrops 1987. John Updike. CP-UpdiJ

Snowfall. W. S. Merwin. SP-MerwW

Snowfall. Robert Penn Warren. CP-WarrR

Snowfall, A. Richard Eberhart. CP-EberR

Snowfall in March. for Lew Welch in a Snowfall. Gary Snyder. CP-SnydG

Snowfall in the Afternoon. Robert Bly. SP-BlyR

Snowfall, thicker and thicker. Homecoming. Paul Celan. CP-PinsR, *tr. by* Robert Pinsky

Snowfalls of Northumbria have known, The. To a Saxon Poet. Jorge Luis Borges. SP-BorgJ, *tr. by* Alastair Reid

Snowflake. Louis Zukofsky. CP-ZukLS

Snowflake, The. Walter De la Mare. CP-DeLaW

Snowflake Which Is Now and Hence Forever, The. Archibald MacLeish. CP-MacLA

Snowflakes. Howard Nemerov. CP-NemeH

Snowheart. Tess Gallagher. SP-GallT

Snowin'. Paul Laurence Dunbar. CP-DunbP

Snowing. Walter De la Mare. CP-DeLaW

Snowline. W. S. Merwin. SP-MerwWF

Snowman on the Moor, The. Sylvia Plath. CP-PlatS

Snowplow was a rattling iron box, The. Safe Conduct. Norman Dubie. CP-DubiN

Snows. Federico García Lorca. CP-GarcF, *tr. by* Jerome Rothenberg *Fr.* Countries.

Snows are fled away, leaves on the shaws, The. Diffugere Nives. A. E. Housman. CP-HousA

Snows of February had buried Christmas, The. Christmas Robin, The. Robert Graves. CP-GravR

Snow)says!Says / over un / graves. E. E. Cummings. CP-CummE

Snowshoe Hare, The. Mary Oliver. SP-OlivM

Snowshoeing Back to Camp in Gloaming. Robert Penn Warren. CP-WarrR

Snowstorm in January. Marya Alexandrovna Zaturenska. SP-ZatuM

Snowstorms in the Midwest. James Wright. CP-WrigJ

Snowy, The. May Swenson. SP-SwenM

Snowy curtain / slides up the sky, A. Noon Office. James Schuyler. CP-SchuJ

Snowy Day at School, A. D. H. Lawrence. CP-LawrD

Snowy Day in School, A. D. H. Lawrence. CP-LawrD

Snowy Heron. John Ciardi. CP-CiarJ

Snowy Owl. Richard Eberhart. CP-EberR

Snowy Weather. Yannis Ritsos. SP-RitsY, *tr. by* Kostas Myrsiades

Snowy Woods, The. Marya Alexandrovna Zaturenska. SP-ZatuM

Snub end of a dismal year. Reading Lao Tzu Again in the New Year. Charles Wright. SP-WrigCN

Snub nose, the guts of twenty mules are in your cylinders and transmission. New Farm Tractor. Carl Sandburg. CP-SandC

Snug at hearthside, while heart of the backlog. Heart of the Backlog. Robert Penn Warren. CP-WarrR

So. Constantine P. Cavafy. CP-CavaC, *tr. by* Theoharis Constantine Theoharis

So? Yannis Ritsos.

    "Dog barked, The." SP-RitsY

    "He changes shirts." SP-RitsY

    "He cracked almonds." SP-RitsY

    "He / sits on the bridge." SP-RitsY

    "Illustrious tree." SP-RitsY

    "In the morning." SP-RitsY

    "Red sunset." SP-RitsY

    "Somewhere / there should be an elephant." SP-RitsY

    "Tangled ball of yarn, A." SP-RitsY

So a new similitude is given us. Spoonbait, The. Seamus Heaney. SP-HeanSO

So about twelve at night, the punk. Dean's Answer to "Upon Stealing a Crown," The. Jonathan Swift. CP-SwifJ

So Abram rose, and clave the wood, and went. Parable of the Old Men and the Young, The. Wilfred Owen. CP-OwenW

So abstract is the idea of your being. Analysis. Fernando Pessoa. SP-PessF, *tr. by* Susan M. Brown *and* Edwin Honig

So active they seem passive, little sheep. Grace. Richard Wilbur. CP-WilbR

So-and-So Reclining on Her Couch. Wallace Stevens. CP-StevW; CP-StevWP

So art thou broken in upon me, Apollo. After Song, An. William Carlos Williams. CP-WilW1

So, art thou feathered, art thou flown. Fledgling, The. Edna St. Vincent Millay. CP-MillE

So autumn comes to an end with these few wet sad stains. Christmas East of the Blue Ridge. Charles Wright. SP-WrigCN

So back you have come from the town, Nan, dear! Military Appointment, A. Thomas Hardy. CP-HardT

So Bartas-like thy fine spun poems been. Anagram, An. *Unknown*. CP-BradA

So bashful when I spied her! Emily Dickinson. CP-DickE

So Be It. Kenneth Patchen. CP-PatcK

So be it. Blare of a cornet. Eugenio Montale. CP-MontE, *tr. by* Jonathan Galassi

So beauty on the waters stood. Ben Jonson. CP-JonsB *Fr.* Masque of Beauty, The.

So Big. Robert Creeley. CP-CreeR

So big / the *out there*. For Chuck Hinman. Robert Creeley. CP-CreeR

So breaks the sun earth's rugged chains. Ben Jonson. CP-JonsB *Fr.* Irish Masque, The.

So brief a life, and then an endless life / Or endless death. All Flesh Is Grass. Christina Georgina Rossetti. CP-RosC2

So-called Life. Czeslaw Milosz. CP-MiloCN, *tr. by* Tony Milosz

So-called poet of love, The. Robert Creeley. CP-CreeR

So-Called Wild Horses of the Water, The. Alan Dugan. CP-DugaA

So Can Anger. Stevie Smith. CP-SmitS

So careful / of anything. Worry. Robert Creeley. SP-CreeR

So careful of the Type she seems. To Dorothy—on Her Birthday—with Love. G. K. Chesterton. CP-ChesG

So condolence visits is what they're here for. Tourists. Yehuda Amichai. SP-AmicY, *tr. by* Chana Bloch

So country-alone, and O so very friendly. Careless Night. Robert Lowell. SP-LoweR

So daylight dies. Moon's Last Quarter, The. Robert Graves. CP-GravR

So dear from far and near and white, and so. Sonnet: "So dear from far and near and white, and so." Stéphane Mallarmé. CP-MallS, *tr. by* Henry Weinfield

So delicate a diffidence. Emily Dickinson. SP-DickE

So delicate my hands, and long. Iseult of Brittany. Dorothy Parker. CP-ParkD

So different, this man. Marriage. William Carlos Williams. CP-WilW1

So Doctor Johnson. Now it serves my pleasure. Epistle to Spencer Holst. Robert Stock. SP-StocR

So does a man. Comment on Stoop. Langston Hughes. CP-HughL3

So Does Everybody Else, Only Not So Much. Ogden Nash. CP-NashO

So down the years the song of the Singing Republic. Paraguay. G. K. Chesterton. CP-ChesG

So Dream Thy Sails . . . . Hart Crane. *See* Phantom Bark, The

So dream thy sails, O phantom bark. Phantom Bark, The. Hart Crane. CP-CranH

So early into a big bed stowed out of sight. Bedtime Stories. Mona Van Duyn. SP-VanDM

So early it's still almost dark out. Happiness. Raymond Carver. CP-CarvR

So Fair, So Sweet, Withal So Sensitive. William Wordsworth. CP-WorW2

So fallen! so lost! the light withdrawn. Ichabod[!]. John Greenleaf Whittier. CP-WhitJ

So Far, and So Far, and On toward the End. Walt Whitman. CP-WhitW

So far as our story approaches the end. Light Woman, A. Robert Browning. CP-BroR1

So far from the murders. Free, The. W. S. Merwin. SP-MerwW

So feeble is the thread that doth the burden stay. Petrarch. CP-WyatT

So few particles of bodyhood engine. Survival of a Heart. Tess Gallagher. SP-GallT

So few things to write about. Late Night, San Francisco. Andrei Codrescu. SP-CodrA

So finally there was nothing. Conjuring in Heaven. Ted Hughes. SP-HughTN

So fond is fire of the frigid stone it waits. Michelangelo Buonarroti. CP-Miche, tr. by John Frederick Nims

So foolish are the hearts of many women. Parting. Jaroslav Seifert. SP-SeifJ, tr. by Ewald Osers

So Forth. Joseph Brodsky. CP-BrodJ

So, Fortinbras: Alas is now the keyword here. Rites of War. Louis MacNeice. CP-MacNL

So, friend, your shop was all your house! Shop. Robert Browning. CP-BroR2

So from the mould / Scarlet and Gold. Emily Dickinson. CP-DickE

So from the years their gifts were showered: each. Sonnets from China. W. H. Auden. CP-AudeW

So Frost Astounds. Robert Penn Warren. CP-WarrR

So gay a Flower. Emily Dickinson. CP-DickE

So, gentle critics, you would have me tilt. Substance or Shadow. Ambrose Bierce. SP-BierA

So give me back to Death. Emily Dickinson. CP-DickE

So glad we are—a Stranger'd deem. Emily Dickinson. CP-DickE

So Going Around Cities. Ted Berrigan. SP-BerrT

So going away slowly now. Mary Sleeth. Muriel Rukeyser. CP-RukeM

So Good. James Schuyler. CP-SchuJ

So good luck came, and on my roof[e] did light. Coming of Good Luck, The. Robert Herrick. CP-HerrR

So Great a Cloud of Witnesses. Christina Georgina Rossetti. CP-RosC2

So great our palaces are now. Ode 2.15: Upon the Luxury of the Age He Lived in. Horace. SP-SmarC Fr. Odes.

So grieves th' advent'rous merchant, when he throws. My Mistress Commanding Me to Return Her Letters. Thomas Carew. CP-CareT

So guns and strong explosives. Murderous Weapons. D. H. Lawrence. CP-LawrD

So, Hall McAllister, you'll not be warned. To an Insolent Attorney. Ambrose Bierce. SP-BierA

So has a Daisy vanished. Emily Dickinson. CP-DickE

So hath myn herte caught in rembraunce. Womanly Noblesse. Geoffrey Chaucer. CP-ChauG

So He Said / on Radio. Lorine Niedecker. CP-NiedL

So he sits down. His host will play for him. Concert Scene. John Logan. CP-LoganJ

So he took her as anointed. April Treason. John Crowe Ransom. SP-RansJ

So he, with a clear shout of laughter. Paris and Diomedes. Homer. CP-MerG1 Fr. Iliad, The.

So, he would pay his 'debt to medicine.' Chekhov on Sakhalin. Seamus Heaney. SP-HeanSO

So here's your Empire. No more wine, then? Good. One Viceroy Resigns. Rudyard Kipling. CP-KiplR

So he's got to have happiness. No End of Fun. Wisława Szymborska. SP-SzymW, tr. by Stanisław Barańczak and Clare Cavanagh

So his friends will think him smart. Mise-en-Scène. Miller Williams. CP-WillM

So how's it going, folks? Boys and Girls, Lenny Bruce, or Back from the Dead. Ai. SP-Ai

So, I am safe emergèd from these broils! Otho the Great. John Keats. CP-KeatJ

So I began my walk of life; no stop. Christina Georgina Rossetti. CP-RosC3

So I came to Rapallo, I was eighteen then. Some Memories of E. P. (Drafts & Fragments). James Laughlin. CP-LaugJ

So I can best endure. Michelangelo Buonarroti. CP-Miche, tr. by John Frederick Nims

So I could look for my childhood, my God! Childhood and Death. Federico García Lorca. CP-GarcF, tr. by Greg Simon and Steven F. White

So I go on, tediously on and on. Winter Song. Carolyn Kizer. CP-KizeC

So I grew half delirious and quite sick. Christina Georgina Rossetti. CP-RosC3

So I have seen the maids in vain. Impromptu ["So I have seen the maids in vain"]. William Cowper. CP-CowpW

So I may say. Epitaph: "So I may say." "H. D." CP-DoolH

So I pull my Stockings off. Emily Dickinson. CP-DickE

So I resigned from the Chu Chin Chowder and Marching Club. Ogden Nash. CP-NashO

So I returned here from the big capitals. Return to Kraków in 1880. Czesław Miłosz. CP-CarvR; CP-MiloC; CP-MiloCN, tr. by Robert Hass

So I Said I Am Ezra. A. R. Ammons. CP-AmmoA

So, I shall see her in three days. In Three Days. Robert Browning. CP-BroR1

So I took her to the river. Faithless Wife, The. Federico García Lorca. SP-GarcF, tr. by J. L. Gili and Stephen Spender

So I took her to the river. Unfaithful Wife, The. Federico García Lorca. CP-GarcF, tr. by Will Kirkland

So I went down to the ancient harbor: human actions. Yehuda Amichai. SP-AmicY, tr. by Chana Bloch

So I would hear out those lungs. Buckdancer's Choice. James Dickey. CP-DickJ

So I'm antiquated. I still like to see. Tanck's Song About November. Hayden Carruth. CP-CarHS Fr. Songs About What Comes Down: The Complete Works of Mr. Septic Tank.

So innocent this scene, I feel it. Lake Scene. A. May Swenson. SP-SwenM

So Intricately Is This World Resolved. Stanley Kunitz. CP-KunSC

So is every one who is born of the spirit. Jones Very. CP-VeryJ

So isn't small one littlest why. E. E. Cummings. CP-CummE

So it came time. Mansion. A. R. Ammons. CP-AmmoA

So It Ends. Kenneth Patchen. CP-PatcK

So it has come to this. Ambition Bird, The. Anne Sexton. CP-SextA

So it is here, then, after so long, and after all. Facing Into It. Eleanor Wilner. SP-WilnE

So it is, my dear. Even So. Dante Gabriel Rossetti. CW-RossD

So it wouldn't need to retrieve the total sum. Michelangelo Buonarroti. CP-Miche, tr. by John Frederick Nims

So it's mind. Web, The. W. S. Merwin. SP-MerwW

So Joseph, yet a youth, expounded well. To My Friend Mr J. Northleigh. John Dryden. CP-DryJ2

So justest lord, may all your judgements be. Epigram. To Thomas Lo[rd] Ellsmere, the Last Term He Sat Chancellor, An. Ben Jonson. CP-JonsB

So large a morning[,] so itself[,] to lean. Song, The: "So large a morning[,] so itself[,] to lean." W. H. Auden. CP-AudeW

So large my Will / The little that I may. Emily Dickinson. CP-DickE

"So lasting they are, the rivers!" Only think. Sources somewhere in the mountains. Rivers ("'So lasting they are, the rivers!' Only think. Sources somewhere in the mountains"). Czesław Miłosz. CP-MiloCN, tr. by Robert Hass

So late in the 20th Century. Au Bout du Temps. Andrei Codrescu. SP-CodrA

So leave the field. Fanny Howe. SP-HoweF Fr. O'Clock.

So let me have the rouge again. Ninon De L'Enclos, On Her Last Birthday. Dorothy Parker. CP-ParkD

So Let Me Live. D. H. Lawrence. CP-LawrD

So let us suppose that after everybody. Coping. Miller Williams. CP-WillM

So like a quiet pigeon in a hollowed rock. Mosaic: St. Praxed's. Raissa Maritain. CP-MertT

So, like him, we cry "l'honneur des hommes: Saint Langage." Hugh MacDiarmid. SP-MacDH Fr. In Memoriam James Joyce.

So like, they seem the same. On an Ancient Isle. Kathleen Jessie Raine. SP-RainK

So Little. Czesław Miłosz. CP-MiloC; CP-MiloCN, tr. by Lillian Vallee

So little he is. E. E. Cummings. CP-CummE

So lone I stood, the very trees seemed drawn. Cyclone, The. James Whitcomb Riley. CP-RileJ

So Long. William Stafford. SP-StafW; SP-StafWW

So Long! Walt Whitman. CP-WhitW

So long adrift, so fast aground. Wise Brothers, The. Edwin Arlington Robinson. CP-RobiE

So long ago that was called Jimmy Yancey. For Papa. Hayden Carruth. CP-CarHS

So long as memory, valour, and faith endure. Ode: "So long as memory, valour, and faith endure." Rudyard Kipling. CP-KiplR

So long as 'neath the Kalka hills. Old Song, An. Rudyard Kipling. CP-KiplR

So long as the blade has. Shame. Arthur Rimbaud. CP-RimbA, tr. by Martin Sorrell

So long as there's a trace. Hafiz. CP-EmerR Fr. Odes.

So long as we speak the same language and never understand each other. Useless Words. Carl Sandburg. CP-SandC

So long had life together been that now. Six Years Later. Joseph Brodsky. CP-WilbR, tr. by Richard Wilbur

So long having foreseen these convulsions, forecast the hemorrhagic. Blood-Guilt, The. Robinson Jeffers. CP-JefR3

So long / is in the song. Langston Hughes. CP-HughL; CP-HughL3

So long (it seem'd) as Maries Faith was small. Upon Woman and Mary. Robert Herrick. CP-HerrR

So long, / So far away. Afro-American Fragment. Langston Hughes. CP-HughL; CP-HughL1

So long / So long as the void. Apollo. James Dickey. CP-DickJ

So long you did not sing, or touch your Lute. Upon a Gentlewoman with a Sweet Voice. Robert Herrick. CP-HerrR

So look the mornings when the Sun. Maiden-Blush, The. Robert Herrick. CP-HerrR

So looks Anthea, when in bed she lyes. To Anthea Lying in Bed. Robert Herrick. CP-HerrR

So Love, emergent out of chaos, brought. Euclia's Hymn. Ben Jonson. CP-JonsB Fr. Love's Triumph through Callipolis.

So, Love, it hasn't healed, not even the least. Michelangelo Buonarroti. CP-Miche, tr. by John Frederick Nims

So lovely, now, the day / quiets. What one hoped. For Benny and Sabina. Robert Creeley. CP-CreeR

So Make Them Melt as the Dishoused Snail. Donald Davie. CP-DaviDC

So many are dead or dying. Crowding. David Ignatow. SP-IgnaD

So many battles, so many wounds, so many honorable defeats and victories. New Victory. Yannis Ritsos. SP-RitsY, tr. by Kimon Friar

So Many Blood-Lakes. Robinson Jeffers. CP-JefR3

So many convolutions and not enough simplicity! To Marina. Kenneth Koch. SP-KochK

So many crutches. Now even the daylight. Landscape with Crutches, A. Charles Simic. SP-SimiC; SP-SimiCE

So many echoes in my head. Poem: "So many echoes in my head." Frank O'Hara. SP-OharF

So many fruits come from roses. Grapes. D. H. Lawrence. CP-LawrD

So many fuckless days and nights. Leaving Fox. Lucille Clifton. SP-ClifL

So many impossible things have already. Haircut, A. Raymond Carver. CP-CarvR

So many kinds of people exist. Han-shan. CP-ColdM, tr. by Red Pine

So many languages have fallen. Here Yet Be Dragons. Lucille Clifton. SP-ClifL

So many little flowers. New Flowers. Langston Hughes. CP-HughL

So many loves have I neglected. Thomas Campion. CP-CampT

So many minds in search of bodies. Adrienne Rich. CP-RicAE

So many nights the solitary lamp had burned. Rousseau in His Day. Donald Davie. CP-DaviDC

So many others have lived in me! Residencies. Thomas McGrath. SP-McGrT

So many poems about the deaths of animals. Essay. Hayden Carruth. CP-CarHS

So many roses in the garden. Dream of Roses, A. Kathleen Jessie Raine. SP-RainK

So many selves(so many fiends and gods). E. E. Cummings. CP-CummE

So many storms and so much havoc and. Pantoum on Some Lines From Camões. Robert Stock. SP-StocR

So many things. Storeroom, The. Theodore Weiss. SP-WeisT

So many things happen. Four Ways of Knowledge. Robert Bly. SP-BlyR

So many tortoises. Race, The. Howard Nemerov. CP-NemeH

So may the [or th'] auspicious Queen of love. Ode 1.3: To the Ship in Which Virgil Sailed to Athens: "So may the [or th'] auspicious Queen of love." Horace. CP-DryJ2, tr. by John Dryden Fr. Odes.

So Much Depends. James Laughlin. CP-LaugJ

So much depends. Red Wheelbarrow, The. William Carlos Williams. CP-WilW1

So much guilt behind them and such beauty! Biography of an Artist. Czeslaw Milosz. CP-MiloCN, tr. by Robert Hass

So much he had from fashion and no more. Troublesome Reign, The. Geoffrey Hill. CP-HillG

So much I loved you, though with words alone. To Prague. Jaroslav Seifert. SP-SeifJ, tr. by Ewald Osers

So much is parchment where I gloom. Black Mesa, The. James Merrill. SP-MerrJ

So much of Heaven has gone from Earth. Emily Dickinson. CP-DickE

So much of man. In a Crowd. Wallace Stevens. CP-StevWP

So much rain, so much life like the swollen sky. Dark August. Derek Walcott. CP-WalcD

So much rain / to make the mud again. Wish, A. Robert Creeley. CP-CreeR

So much slipping by. Business, The. Charles Olson. CP-OlsoC

So much solemn black. Rainer Maria Rilke. CP-RilkFr, tr. by A. Poulin, Jr. Fr. Valaisian Quatrains, The.

So much sorrow comes to me out of your singing. To Madame Alda, Singing a Song, in a White Gown. Wallace Stevens. CP-StevWP

So much Summer. Emily Dickinson. CP-DickE

So much sweetness. Lindens. Adam Zagajewski. SP-ZagaA, tr. by Clare Cavanagh

So much world all at once—how it rustles and bustles! Birthday. Wisława Szymborska. SP-SzymW, tr. by Stanisław Barańczak and Clare Cavanagh

So / mucked up with. C. K. Williams. SP-WillC

So music is supposed to charm. Matinee. John Logan. CP-LogaJ

So my son I would have given my right arm. Lines for His Son in Satin. John Logan. CP-LogaJ

So Near—And Yet. Kenneth Patchen. CP-PatcK

So near to air and water merely. Celery. John Updike. CP-UpdiJ

So near to death yourself. For a Very Old Man, on the Death of His Wife. Jane Cooper. CP-CoopJ

So neck to stubborn neck, and obstinate knee to knee. Antaeus: A Fragment. Wilfred Owen. CP-OwenW

So now I keep my caution company. Silenus' Epitaph. Robert Stock. SP-StocR

So now it's over, my day's long voyage, through. Michelangelo Buonarroti. CP-Miche, tr. by John Frederick Nims

So now it's your turn. Instructions to the Double. Tess Gallagher. SP-GallT

So now my summer task is ended, Mary. Revolt of Islam, The. Percy Bysshe Shelley. CP-ShelP

So now the horses of Aiakides, off wide of the war-ground. Horses of Achilles, The. Homer. CP-MerG1 Fr. Iliad, The.

So now to write the journal of this house. These High White Walls. Jane Cooper. CP-CoopJ

So now we know the worst. Immortal Longings. Before Surgery. Donald Davie. CP-DaviDC

So oft as homeward I from her depart. Sonnet 52. Edmund Spenser. CP-Spens Fr. Amoretti.

So oft as I with state of present time. Book 5. Edmund Spenser. CP-Spens Fr. Faerie Queene, The.

So often and with such cruel fascination I have dreamed the implacable void that contains dream. Dream of Mind: The Gap, A. C. K. Williams. SP-WillC

So old, so delicate, so small. Pablo Casals. Archibald MacLeish. CP-MacLA

So on the seventh day. Apple Tragedy. Ted Hughes. SP-HughTN

So on the Stream the Silver Swan. Thomas Sheridan. CP-SherT

So once again, hearing the tired aunts. In the House of the Dying. Jane Cooper. CP-CoopJ

So, overmasterful, to sea! Furious Voyage, The. Robert Graves. CP-GravR

So parted you as if the world for ever. To the Most Princely and Vertuous the Lady Elizabeth. Thomas Campion. CP-CampT

So, passing through the rustic gate. Burnt Bridge, The. Louis MacNeice. CP-MacNL

So pawed, / by this long last Bear-son. To Gerhardt, There, among Europe's Things of Which He Has Written Us in His "Brief an Creely und Olson." Charles Olson. CP-OlsoC; SP-OlsoC

So Penseroso. Ogden Nash. CP-NashO

So Phoebus makes me worthy of his bays. To Sir Thomas Overbury. Ben Jonson. CP-JonsB; SP-JonsB

So, Pound, you have found the gallows tree. Lustrum for You, E.P, A. Charles Olson. CP-OlsoC

So, praise the gods, at last he's away! From a Letter from Lesbia. Dorothy Parker. CP-ParkD

So proud she was to die. Emily Dickinson. CP-DickE

So questioned one of old, as we. "Are there Few that be Saved?" Luke 13:23. Jones Very. CP-VeryJ

So Quicke, So Hot, So Mad is Thy Fond Sute. Thomas Campion. CP-CampT

So quickly, and so slowly . . . In the tiny elevator of the flat you'd borrowed on the Rue de Pondicherry. Le Petit Salvié. C. K. Williams. SP-WillC

So quiet birds. Ambush. Yusef Komunyakaa. CP-KomuY

So Quietly the World. Eleanor Wilner. SP-WilnE

So ran the schoolday, full of time and stress. Childhood. Rainer Maria Rilke. CP-NemeH

So, salt is the boundary mark between Fire that burns, and the Wet. Boundary Stone, The. D. H. Lawrence. CP-LawrD

So sang he: and as meeting rose and rose. Willowwood ("So sang he: and as meeting rose and rose"). Dante Gabriel Rossetti. CW-RossD Fr. House of Life, The.

"So say the foolish!" Say the foolish so, Love? Poetics. Robert Browning. CP-BroR2

So set its Sun in Thee. Emily Dickinson. CP-DickE

So She Said. James Wright. CP-WrigJ

So shy shy shy(and with a). E. E. Cummings. CP-CummE

So silent I when Love was by. Anecdote. Dorothy Parker. CP-ParkD

So Slender. James Laughlin. CP-LaugJ

So Slight. Laura Riding Jackson. CP-RidiL

So smell those odours that do rise. To the Most Fair and Lovely Mistress Anne Soame, Now Lady Abdie. Robert Herrick. CP-HerrR

So smooth, so sweet, so silv'ry is thy voice. Upon Julia's Voice. Robert Herrick. CP-HerrR

So, so, break[e] off this last lamenting kiss[e]. Expiration, The. John Donne. CP-DonnJ; MW-DonnJ

So soft streams meet, so springs with gladder smiles. Welcome to Sack, The. Robert Herrick. CP-HerrR

So soon as ever your mazed spirit descends. Instructions to the Orphic Adept. Robert Graves. CP-GravR

So Sound You Sleep. A. E. Housman. CP-HousA

So sounds grass, and if it is sun or no sun. Louis Zukofsky. CP-ZukLS

So spake Esaias: so, in words of flame. To George B. Cheever. John Greenleaf Whittier. CP-WhitJ

So spake he, supplicating; and him heard Phoibos Apollo. Vengeance of Apollo, The. Homer. CP-MerG2 *Fr.* Iliad, The.

So spake the Voice; and, as with a single life. Alcaics. Arthur Hugh Clough. SP-ClouA

So standing.our eyes filled with the wind,and the. E. E. Cummings. CP-CummE

So stood of old the holy Christ. Healer, The. John Greenleaf Whittier. CP-WhitJ

So strange, / We are completely out of range. Us: Colored. Langston Hughes. CP-HughL; CP-HughL3

So stumble, heart, under the weight. Heart Attack in Bad Air. Alan Dugan. CP-DugaA

So suddenly, who could have seen it coming. Funeral. Wisława Szymborska. SP-SzymW, *tr. by* Stanisław Barańczak *and* Clare Cavanagh

So summer comes in the end to these few stains. Beginning, The. Wallace Stevens. CP-StevW; CP-StevWP

"So surely is she mine," you say, and turn. Second Love. Dorothy Parker. CP-ParkD

So sweet is thy discourse to me. Thomas Campion. CP-CampT

So sweet / the body. Robert Creeley. CP-CreeR

So take my vows and scatter them to sea. Sonnet for the End of a Sequence. Dorothy Parker. CP-ParkD

So tell me, Death, why not possess some face. Michelangelo Buonarroti. CP-Miche, *tr. by* John Frederick Nims

So that a colony will breed here. We Must Make a Kingdom of It. Gregory Orr. SP-OrrG

So That Even a Lover. Louis Zukofsky. CP-ZukLS

So that the vines burst from my fingers. Canto 17: "So that the vines burst from my fingers." Ezra Pound. SP-PounE *Fr.* Cantos.

So that's it? Just that? Shall our pride—he said—depend. Double Condemnation. Yannis Ritsos. SP-RitsY, *tr. by* N. C. Germanacos

So that's what it's like to be a wheel. Ballad of the Wheel, The. Charles Simic. SP-SimiC; SP-SimiCE

So That's Who I Remind Me Of. Ogden Nash. CP-NashO

So the chattering knaves have vanished, by a mercy all are flown. William of Orange. G. K. Chesterton. CP-ChesG

So the Chosunese would imagine the earth to be flat. Chosun. James Fenton. SP-FentJ

So the church Christ was hit and buried. Le Christianisme. Wilfred Owen. CP-OwenW

So the dark figure falls. Michael Palmer. SP-PalmM

So the distances are Galatea. Distances, The. Charles Olson. CP-OlsoC; SP-OlsoC

So the Eyes accost—and sunder. Emily Dickinson. CP-DickE

So the Norse / were neurotic. Charles Olson. CP-OlsoC

So the rain falls. Cornkind. Frank O'Hara. SP-OharF

So the storms bore the daughters of Pandarus out into thrall. Homer. *See* And so these daughters fair of Pandarus

So, the three Court-ladies began. Which? Robert Browning. CP-BroR2

So the wreckd mariner who tos'd on shore. On a Little Boy Going to Play on a Place from Whence He Had Just Fallen. Annis Boudinot Stockton. CP-StocA

So then she will go away. And what's the loss? Young Instructor Talks to Himself Winding Up the Semester, The. Miller Williams. CP-WillM

So then—the Vandals of our isle. On the Burning of Lord Mansfield's Library. William Cowper. CP-CowpW

So There. Robert Creeley. SP-CreeR

So There! D. H. Lawrence. CP-LawrD

So there sat they. Side by Side. Thomas Hardy. CP-HardT

So there we were stuck. Life of, The. Theodore Weiss. SP-WeisT

So there you are. Poet of the Prison Isle: Ritsos Against the Colonels, The. Thomas McGrath. SP-McGrT

So these are the hills of home. Hazy tiers. Double. Rae Armantrout. SP-ArmaA

So these are the Himalayas. Notes from a Nonexistent Himalayan Expedition. Wisława Szymborska. SP-SzymW, *tr. by* Stanisław Barańczak *and* Clare Cavanagh

So they fought — not easy himself. Kitchen Chair Poem #4. Clarence Major. SP-MajoC

So they hurried to the barn. Quarrel, The. Theodore Weiss. SP-WeisT

So they went out. Story Thus Far, The. Lucille Clifton. SP-ClifL

So, this is all,—the utmost reach. Pastoral Letter, The. John Greenleaf Whittier. CP-WhitJ

So this is death that I. Death. William Carlos Williams. CP-WilW2

So this is his mother. Born. Wisława Szymborska. SP-SzymW, *tr. by* Stanisław Barańczak *and* Clare Cavanagh

So this was I. Lorine Niedecker. CP-NiedL

So this was the story is a story gibbous moon 1:10 AM he falls toward the world from a bridge. Notes for Echo Lake 7. Michael Palmer. SP-PalmM

So Thomas Edison. Lines to Be Embroidered on a Bib, or, The Child Is Father of the Man, but Not for Quite a While. Ogden Nash. CP-NashO

So through that unripe day you bore your head. Philip Larkin. CP-LarkP

So, Time. Thomas Hardy. CP-HardT

So Tir'd Are All My Thoughts. Thomas Campion. CP-CampT

So tired. Robert Creeley. CP-CreeR

So Tired Blues. Langston Hughes. CP-HughL; CP-HughL3

So, to complete the spectrum. Envoy: "So, to complete the spectrum." Theodore Weiss. SP-WeisT *Fr.* Polish Question, The.

So to Fatness Come. Stevie Smith. CP-SmitS

So to Speak. Carl Sandburg. CP-SandC

So unwarely was never no man caught [*or* cawght]. Sir Thomas Wyatt. CP-WyatT

So valiant is the intimacy. Emily Dickinson. SP-DickE

So Various. Thomas Hardy. CP-HardT

So Venus does hang and glitter in the prepared sky. Objects, The. Charles Olson. CP-OlsoC

So vile was poor Wat, such a miscreant slave. On W. R———, Esq. Robert Burns. CP-BurnR

So we loosed a bloomin' volley. Rudyard Kipling. CP-KiplR *Fr.* Plain Tales from the Hills.

So we settled it all when the storm was done. Rudyard Kipling. CP-KiplR *Fr.* Light That Failed, The.

So we, who've supped the self-same cup. After the Quarrel. Paul Laurence Dunbar. CP-DunbP

So We'll Go No More A-Roving. Lord Byron. CP-Byron

So well her mind has taught her eyes their part. Some Traits of the Character of Mrs, Powel as a Model for a Young Lady Who Said She Admired Her More than Any Other Woman. Annis Boudinot Stockton. CP-StocA

So well that I can live without. Emily Dickinson. CP-DickE

So, we've almost arrived, Hermippos. Return from Greece. Constantine P. Cavafy. CP-CavaC, *tr. by* Theoharis Constantine Theoharis

So We've Come at Last to Freud. Alice Walker. CP-WalkA

So what did old Diogenes find. Protest After a Dream. John Logan. CP-LogaJ

So what do you do? What. How the Friends Met. James Tate. SP-TateJ

So what if he walks into red. Punchdrunk. Yusef Komunyakaa. CP-KomuY

So what is a body but a man. Face While Shaving. Charles Bukowski. SP-BukC2

So what is the use of poetry these days. Uses of Poetry. Lawrence Ferlinghetti. SP-FerlL

So what said the others and the sun went down. Mrs. Alfred Uruguay. Wallace Stevens. CP-StevW; CP-StevWP

So what the door was guarded. Curfew. Paul Éluard. CP-WilW2

So, what'd you dream of this time, Gorbunov? Gorbunov and Gorchakov. Joseph Brodsky. CP-BrodJ, *tr. by* Harry Thomas

So, what's this somber and opaque mystery? Saturnian Hypotyposes, Ex-Belmontet. Arthur Rimbaud. CP-RimbA, *tr. by* Martin Sorrell

So when she lay beside me. As She Was Thus Alone in the Clear Moonlight. Kenneth Patchen. CP-PatcK

So when the gods wearing their colored cloaks of nearness. Poem for My Friend, Clare. Or, With White Stupas We Remember Buddha. Norman Dubie. CP-DubiN

So when the year had come full round. Hymn 2: "So when the year had come full round." A. R. Ammons. CP-AmmoA

So while the blear-eyed pimp beside me walked. Easter Day II. Arthur Hugh Clough. SP-ClouA

So why does this dead carnation hold. Song: So Why Does This Dead Carnation. Hayden Carruth. CP-CarHS

So Will had finally broken off with Faith! At Martha's Deli. Paul Muldoon. CP-MuldP

So with his daughter Antigone. Michael Palmer. SP-PalmM

So You Agree with What I Say? Well, What Did I Say? Robert Penn Warren. CP-WarrR

So you are lost to me! Bread upon the Waters. D. H. Lawrence. CP-LawrD

So you are turned—a Someone. Paul Celan. SP-CelaP, *tr. by* John Felstiner

So You Have Been, Despite Parental Ban. Philip Larkin. CP-LarkP

So you have gained the golden crowns, so you have piled together. Lost. G. K. Chesterton. CP-ChesG

So you have swept me back. Eurydice. "H. D." CP-DoolH

So You Put the Dog to Sleep. Thomas Lux. SP-LuxT

So you said you'd go home to work on your father's farm. To a Young Poet Who Fled. John Logan. CP-LogaJ

So you turn up like an old. Lansing Bad Penny Come Again Blues, The. Marge Piercy. SP-PierM

So you're hunting for ann well i'm looking for will. E. E. Cummings. CP-CummE

So you're married, young man. Lorine Niedecker. CP-NiedL

So zestfully canst thou sing? Blinded Bird, The. Thomas Hardy. CP-HardT

Soajo. Charles Tomlinson. SP-TomlC *Fr.* Portugeuse Pieces.

Soaking, The. Ivor Gurney. SP-GurnI

Soap Bubbles. Rainer Maria Rilke. CP-RilkFr, *tr. by* A. Poulin, Jr.

Soap cleans itself the way ice does. Mahayana. Philip Whalen. SP-WhalP

Soap-Pig, The. Paul Muldoon. CP-MuldP

Soap Suds. Louis MacNeice. CP-MacNL

Soar, don't settle for earth. Shmuel HaNagid. SP-HaNaS, *tr.* by Peter Cole

Soaring lark is blest as proud, The. Gold and Silver Fishes in a Vase. William Wordsworth. CP-WorW2

Sobbing of the Bells, The. Walt Whitman. CP-WhitW

Sobieski's Shield. Geoffrey Hill. CP-HillG

Sobriety in Search. Robert Herrick. CP-HerrR

Social. Charles Bukowski. SP-BukC1

Social Note. James Laughlin. CP-LaugJ

Social Note. Dorothy Parker. CP-ParkD

Social Work. Thomas Kinsella. CP-KinsT

Socializing with a Creature. John Ciardi. CP-CiarJ

Society. Robert Herrick. CP-HerrR

Society. George Meredith. CP-MerG1

Society for me my misery. Emily Dickinson. CP-DickE

Society of gnats, A. Gnats. Richard Eberhart. CP-EberR

Sociological Triolets. G. K. Chesterton. CP-ChesG

Sociology of Toyotas and Jade Chrysanthemums, The. Hayden Carruth. CP-CarHS

Soda Crackers. Raymond Carver. CP-CarvR

Soda Fountains. Nicanor Parra. CP-MertT

Sodium pentothal landscape, A. Today I Am Falling. James Tate. SP-TateJ

Soe I may gaine thy death, my life I'le give. Matthew 16:25; Whosoever Shall Loose His Life. Bible, *N.T.* CP-CrasR *Fr.* St. Matthew.

Soeur Louise De La Miséricorde. Christina Georgina Rossetti. CP-RosC2

Sofa in the Forties, A. Seamus Heaney. SP-HeanSO

Soft and softlier hold me, friends! Maiden Speech of the Æolian Harp. Ralph Waldo Emerson. CP-EmerR

Soft As a Cloud Is Yon Blue Ridge. William Wordsworth. CP-WorW2

Soft as beetpulp, the cover. On Reading an Old Baedeker in Schloss Leopoldskron. Maxine W. Kumin. SP-KumiM

Soft as the bed in the earth. Shadow, The. William Carlos Williams. CP-WilW1

Soft as the massacre of Suns. Emily Dickinson. CP-DickE

Soft cat and the scratchy cat, The. Concord Cats. Richard Eberhart. CP-EberR

Soft City, The. Tennessee Williams. CP-WillT

Soft earth turns straight up. Uluru Wild Fig Song. Gary Snyder. CP-SnydG

Soft fist of feathers. Fanny Howe. SP-HoweF *Fr.* O'Clock.

Soft grey ghosts crawl up my sleeve. Remembering. Maya Angelou. SP-AngeM

Soft hairs on the back of his neck, The. Yehuda Ha-Levi. Yehuda Amichai. SP-AmicY, *tr.* by Stephen Mitchell

Soft lights, the companionship, the beers, The. J. V. Cunningham. CP-CunnJ

Soft-littered is the new-year's lambing-fold. Spring. Dante Gabriel Rossetti. CW-RossD

Soft May mists are here again. May, 1972. James Schuyler. CP-SchuJ

Soft Musick. Robert Herrick. CP-HerrR

Soft rain beats upon my windows. Ivor Gurney. SP-GurnI

Soft rain on the. Straits of Malacca 24 Oct 1957. Gary Snyder. CP-SnydG

Soft rainsqualls on the swells. Oil. Gary Snyder. CP-SnydG

Soft Sea washed around the House, A. Emily Dickinson. CP-DickE

Soft siren, let me whisper in your ear. Proud Ship, The. Charles Baudelaire. CP-BaudC, *tr.* by Walter Martin

Soft sleep, thou stranger to all pain. Choral Song: "Soft sleep, thou stranger to all pain." Sophocles. CP-SherT *Fr.* Philoctetes.

Soft Snow. William Blake. CP-BlakW

Soft, subtle fire, thou soul of art. Ben Jonson. CP-JonsB *Fr.* Mercury Vindicated.

Soft, to your places, animals. Thomas Kinsella. CP-KinsT

Soft Toy. Thomas Kinsella. CP-KinsT

Soft unclouded blue of air, The. Lines: "Soft unclouded blue of air, The." Emily Jane Brontë. CP-BronE

Soft voluptuous opiate shades, The. Twilight. Walt Whitman. CP-WhitW

Soft, where the shadow glides. Autumnal. James Wright. CP-WrigJ

Soft white lamb in the daisy meadow. Ballad: "Soft white lamb in the daisy meadow." Christina Georgina Rossetti. CP-RosC3

Soft whoosh, the sunset blaze, A. Leavings. Seamus Heaney. SP-HeanSO

Soft wind, A. No One Remembers. Philip Levine. SP-LeviP

Soft wind southwesterly, something like, A. Vermont Thaw. Robert Penn Warren. CP-WarrR

Soft Wood. Robert Lowell. SP-LoweR

Soft you day, be velvet soft. Gamut, The. Maya Angelou. SP-AngeM

Softening the marbles, day. Dream (Escape from the Sculpture Museum) and Waking. James Merrill. SP-MerrJ

Softens the air so cold & rude. Ralph Waldo Emerson. CP-EmerR

Softly. Josephine Jacobsen. CP-JacoJ

Softly along the road of evening. Nod. Walter De la Mare. CP-DeLaW

Softly from its still lair in Plympton Street. E. E. Cummings. CP-CummE

Softly, in the dusk, a woman is singing to me. Piano. D. H. Lawrence. CP-LawrD

Softly, Then, Softly. D. H. Lawrence. CP-LawrD

Softly wrong, we lie and kiss. In Pity as We Kiss and Lie. John Ciardi. CP-CiarJ

Softness of spring in the yard. Synagogue in Firenze, The. Yehuda Amichai. SP-AmicYL, *tr.* by Benjamin Harshav *and* Barbara Harshav

Sohrab and Rustum. Matthew Arnold.
    "But the majestic river floated on." SP-ArnoM

Soil is ploughed up, The. Inside. North of Beersheba. Yehuda Amichai. SP-AmicY, *tr.* by Chana Bloch

Soil now gets a rumpling soft and damp, The. Strong Are Saying Nothing, The. Robert Frost. CP-FrosR

Soil of Flint, if steady tilled. Emily Dickinson. CP-DickE

Soiled city oblongs stand sprawling, The. City Number. Carl Sandburg. CP-SandC

Soiled Dove. Carl Sandburg. CP-SandC

Soirée. Charles Bukowski. SP-BukC2

Sojourn in the Whale. Marianne Craig Moore. CP-MoorM

Sojourners. Marge Piercy. SP-PierM

Sojourning through a southern realm in youth. Sleeping Beauty, The. Wilfred Owen. CP-OwenW

Sojourns in the Parallel World. Denise Levertov. SP-LeveDS

Solace. Richard Eberhart. CP-EberR

Solace. Dorothy Parker. CP-ParkD

Solace of kisses and cookies and cabbage. Last Words. Theodore Roethke. CP-RoetT

Solar. Philip Larkin. CP-LarkP

Solar Corona. May Swenson. SP-SwenM

Solar floes / big as continents. Transducer. A. R. Ammons. CP-AmmoA

Solar insect on the wing. Ralph Waldo Emerson. CP-EmerR

Solderer, The. Arthur Sze. SP-SzeA

Soldier, A. Robert Frost. CP-FrosR

Soldier, A. Sir John Suckling. CP-SuckJ

Soldier, The. Gerard Manley Hopkins. CP-HopkG

Soldier, The. Randall Jarrell. CP-JarrR

Soldier, The. James Whitcomb Riley. CP-RileJ

Soldier an' Sailor Too. Rudyard Kipling. CP-KiplR

Soldier and the Star, The. Kenneth Patchen. CP-PatcK

Soldier and the Statesman, The. Jones Very. CP-VeryJ

Soldier Dear to Us, A. Stevie Smith. CP-SmitS

Soldier from the wars returning. A. E. Housman. CP-HousA

Soldier, in a curious land. War Song. Dorothy Parker. CP-ParkD

Soldier may forget his Sword, The. Press, The. Rudyard Kipling. CP-KiplR

Soldier!—meek the title, yet divine, The. Soldier, The. James Whitcomb Riley. CP-RileJ

Soldier of the Cross, The. Jones Very. CP-VeryJ

Soldier of Urbina, A. Jorge Luis Borges. SP-BorgJ, *tr.* by Alastair Reid

Soldier, past full retreat, is marching out of the grave, The. Go Ask the Dead. Thomas McGrath. SP-McGrT

Soldier Rejects His Times Addressing His Contemporaries, A. Richard Eberhart. CP-EberR

Soldier, rest! thy warfare o'er. Ellen's Song. Sir Walter Scott. SP-ScotW *Fr.* Lady of the Lake, The.

Soldier runs home, A. Planting. Philip Levine. SP-LeviP

Soldier said to the general, The. Battle Ground. Langston Hughes. CP-HughL; CP-HughL3

Soldier, Soldier. Rudyard Kipling. CP-KiplR

Soldier stepped on his cigarette, The. 1 May 1950. Yannis Ritsos. SP-RitsY *Fr.* Exile's Journals 3.

Soldier [T. P.]. Randall Jarrell. CP-JarrR

Soldier to preserve his Country dies, The. Soldier and the Statesman, The. Jones Very. CP-VeryJ

Soldier Walks under the Trees of the University, The. Randall Jarrell. CP-JarrR

Soldier Who Lived Through the War, The. Howard Nemerov. CP-NemeH

Soldier, young in years, young in ambitions, A. Stephen Crane. CP-CranS

Soldierly at last, for the lines. Poets' Corner, The. Laura Riding Jackson. CP-RidiL

Soldiers and saviors of the homes we love. Soldiers Here To-Day. James Whitcomb Riley. CP-RileJ

Soldiers are marching singing down the lane. Scapegoats and Rabies. Ted Hughes. SP-HughTN

Soldier's Dream. Wilfred Owen. CP-OwenW

Soldiers Here To-Day. James Whitcomb Riley. CP-RileJ

Soldiers in the grave say: you, up there, The. Yehuda Amichai. SP-AmicYL, *tr.* by Benjamin Harshav *and* Barbara Harshav

Soldiers of Peace. Clement of Alexandria. CP-MertT

Soldiers, unshaven, The. 30 May 1950. Yannis Ritsos. SP-RitsY *Fr.* Exile's Journals 3.

Sole Maid, associate sole, to me beyond. Her Thoughts. Samuel Taylor

Coleridge. CP-ColeS

Sole Positive of Night! Ne Plus Ultra. Samuel Taylor Coleridge. CP-ColeS; MW-ColeS

Soledad. Robert Earl Hayden. CP-HaydR

Soledad. Langston Hughes. CP-HughL; CP-HughL1

Solemn-breathing air is ended, The. Ad Lyram. Samuel Taylor Coleridge. CP-ColeS

Solemn dreams / Dreams beautiful as the fair hues that lie. Fragments from the Alfoxden Note-Book (II). William Wordsworth. CP-WorW1

Solemn hour must come tis hastning fast, The. Meditation on the 3d Verse of the 28th Chapter of Mathew. Annis Boudinot Stockton. CP-StocA

Solemn landscape of a dream, The. Parisian Dream. Charles Baudelaire. CP-BaudC, tr. by Walter Martin

Solemn League and Covenant, The. Robert Burns. CP-BurnR

Solemn plain-faced child stands gazing there, A. Portrait, A. Walter De la Mare. CP-DeLaW

Solemn rites are well begun, The. Ben Jonson. CP-JonsB Fr. Oberon, the Fairy Prince.

Solemn thing—it was—I said, A. Emily Dickinson. CP-DickE

Solemn thing within the Soul, A. Emily Dickinson. CP-DickE

Solemnity of a bemused tiger, there in his eyes. Green Eyes. William Carlos Williams. CP-WilW2

Solfeggietto. Adrienne Rich. SP-RicA1

Solid, The. C. K. Williams. SP-WillC

Solid citizens, The. Undertow. Langston Hughes. CP-HughL; CP-HughL3

Solid, Ironical, Rolling Orb. Walt Whitman. CP-WhitW

Solid, solid universe, The. Cupido. Ralph Waldo Emerson. CP-EmerR

Solid Sprite Who Stands Alone, The. Edna St. Vincent Millay. CP-MillE

Soliliguy in a Sleepless Night. Annis Boudinot Stockton. CP-StocA

Soliliquies. C. K. Williams. SP-WillC

Soliloquies. Geoffrey Hill. CP-HillG

Soliloquy: "Whenever I am got under my gravestone." Ted Hughes. SP-HughTN

Soliloquy. Robinson Jeffers. CP-JefR1

Soliloquy for Cassandra. Wisława Szymborska. SP-SzymW, tr. by Stanisław Barańczak and Clare Cavanagh

Soliloquy: Ghost Dance for a Cripple. Alan Dugan. CP-DugaA

Soliloquy in Circles. Ogden Nash. CP-NashO

Soliloquy: Man Talking to a Mirror. Yusef Komunyakaa. CP-KomuY

Soliloquy of a Bard in the Country. Lord Byron. CP-Byron

Soliloquy of a Turkey. Paul Laurence Dunbar. CP-DunbP

Soliloquy of One of the Spies Left in the Wilderness, A. Gerard Manley Hopkins. CP-HopkG

Soliloquy of the Solipsist. Sylvia Plath. CP-PlatS

Soliloquy of the Spanish Cloister. Robert Browning. CP-BroR1; SP-BroR

Soliloquy on the Full Moon, She Being in a Mad Passion, A. Samuel Taylor Coleridge. CP-ColeS

Soliloquy Upon Love. Kathleen Jessie Raine. SP-RainK

Solipsism. Karl Shapiro. SP-ShapK

Solipsism & Solecism. Howard Nemerov. CP-NemeH

Solipsism While Dying. Margaret Atwood. SP-AtwM1

Solipsist. Stephen Spender. CP-SpenS

Solipsist, The. James Vincent Cunningham. CP-CunnJ

Solis Ortus Cardine, A. Sedulius. CP-MertT

Solitaire. Federico García Lorca. CP-GarcF, tr. by Jerome Rothenberg Fr. Six Songs at Nightfall.

Solitaire. John Updike. CP-UpdiJ

Solitaire under the Oaks. Wallace Stevens. CP-StevWP

Solitary, The. Percy Bysshe Shelley. CP-ShelP

Solitary Confinement. Gregory Orr. SP-OrrG

Solitary Gentian, The. Jones Very. CP-VeryJ

Solitary Life. Thomas Merton. CP-MertT

Solitary Observation Brought Back from a Sojourn in Hell. Louise Bogan. CP-BogaL

Solitary Pond, The. John Updike. CP-UpdiJ

Solitary Reaper, The. William Wordsworth. CP-WorW1; MW-WorW

Solitary Rose, The. Christina Georgina Rossetti. CP-RosC3

Solitary Travel. Louis MacNeice. CP-MacNL

Solitary Worshipper, The. Jones Very. CP-VeryJ

Solitary's Solace in the Natural Sciences. Heather McHugh. SP-McHuH

Solitude. Walter De la Mare. CP-DeLaW

Solitude. Federico García Lorca. CP-GarcF, tr. by William Bryant Logan

Solitude. Rainer Maria Rilke. CP-RilkFr, tr. by A. Poulin, Jr.

Solitude. Charles Simic. SP-SimiC; SP-SimiCE

Solitude, A. Denise Levertov. SP-LeveDP

Solitude Calls the Man. G. K. Chesterton. CP-ChesG

Solitude closes down around us. Still on Water. Kenneth Rexroth. CP-RexrK

Solitude Late at Night in the Woods. Robert Bly. SP-BlyR

Solitude of Mr. Powers, The. Ogden Nash. CP-NashO

Solitude: you must be very strong. Lines from the Testament. Pier Paolo Pasolini. SP-PasoP, tr. by Norman MacAfee and Luciano Martinengo

Solo. Li Po. CP-WilW2

Solo for Four. Robert Stock. SP-StocR

Solo for Saturday Night Guitar. Carl Sandburg. CP-SandC

Solo Native. Thomas Lux. SP-LuxT

Soloist. Rainer Maria Rilke. CP-RilkFr, tr. by A. Poulin, Jr.

Solomon and Balkis. Robert Browning. CP-BroR2

Solomon and the Witch. William Butler Yeats. CP-YeatW

Solomon King of the Jews and the Queen of Sheba, Balkis. Solomon and Balkis. Robert Browning. CP-BroR2

Solomon most glorious in array / Put not on his glories without care. Consider the Lilies of the Field. Christina Georgina Rossetti. CP-RosC2

Solomon says to the messengers from Sheba. Solomon to Sheba. Jelaluddin Rumi. SP-Rumi, tr. by Coleman Barks

Solomon to Sheba. Jelaluddin Rumi. SP Rumi, tr. by Coleman Barks

Solomon to Sheba. William Butler Yeats. CP-YeatW

Solomon was busy judging others. Solomon's Crooked Crown. Jelaluddin Rumi. SP-Rumi, tr. by Coleman Barks

Solomon's Baby. D. H. Lawrence. CP-LawrD

Solomon's Crooked Crown. Jelaluddin Rumi. SP-Rumi, tr. by Coleman Barks

Solomon's Mines. Geoffrey Hill. CP-HillG

Solomon's Seal. Robert Graves. CP GravR

Solon. George Meredith. CP-MerG1

Solstice. Louise Glück. SP-GlucL

Solstice. Robinson Jeffers. CP-JefR2

Solstice. Louis MacNeice. CP-MacNL

Solstice. William Carlos Williams. CP-WilW1

Solstice Poem. Margaret Atwood. SP-AtwM2

Solution. Ralph Waldo Emerson. CP-EmerR

Solution. George Oppen. CP-OppGN

'Solution,' they said to my friend, The. Long Way Round, The. Denise Levertov. SP-LeveDL

Solve. Paul Celan. SP-CelaP, tr. by John Felstiner

Solving the Riddle. Charles Simic. SP-SimiCE

Somber figures that wander off into the night. You Must Have Some Idea Where They've Gone. Kenneth Patchen. CP-PatcK

Somber Prayer. John Berryman. CP-BerrJ

Somber Spring. Yehuda Amichai. SP-AmicYL, tr. by Benjamin Harshav and Barbara Harshav

Sombra? Shade-Seller, The. Josephine Jacobsen. CP-JacoJ

Some act of Love's bound to rehearse. Why I Write Not of Love. Ben Jonson. CP-JonsB; SP-JonsB

Some Afternoon. Robert Creeley. CP-CreeR

Some ancient authors wisely write. Poetical Epistle to Dr. Sheridan, A. Jonathan Swift. CP-SwifJ

Some angels were standing on the ground. Angels, The. Richard Eberhart. CP-EberR

Some Are Born. Stevie Smith. CP-SmitS

Some are home-sick—some two or three. Delinquent Travellers, The. Samuel Taylor Coleridge. CP-ColeS

Some are in prison; some are dead. Chums, The. Theodore Roethke. CP-RoetT

Some are laughing, some are weeping. Sound Sleep. Christina Georgina Rossetti. CP-RosC1

Some are pure business, land deals, receipts, a contract. You Sort Old Letters. Robert Penn Warren. CP-WarrR

Some are teethed on a silver spoon. Saturday's Child. Countee Cullen. CP-CullC

Some are too much at home in the role of wanderer. Poem: "Some are too much at home in the role of wanderer." Denise Levertov. SP-LeveDS

Some Arrows slay but whom they strike. Emily Dickinson. CP-DickE

Some ask praise of their fellows. E. E. Cummings. CP-CummE

Some asked me where the rubies grew. Rock of Rubies: and The Quarrie of Pearls, The. Robert Herrick. CP-HerrR

Some Aspects of Immortality. Archibald MacLeish. CP-MacLA

Some autumn leaves a painter took. Sumach Leaves, The. Jones Very. CP-VeryJ

Some awful / grating sound. Sounds. Robert Creeley. CP-CreeR

Some Beasts. Pablo Neruda. CP-WrigJ, tr. by James Wright

Some beating in there. Night Bird. James Dickey. CP-DickJ

Some beetle trilling. Continuum. Denise Levertov. SP-LeveDL

Some Bloody Mutiny. Thomas Merton. CP-MertT

Some books are lies frae end to end. Death and Doctor Hornbook [A True Story]. Robert Burns. CP-BurnR

Some breath breathes out Adonais & Canto General. On Neruda's Death. Allen Ginsberg. CP-GinsA

Some call Lloyd George the Prince of Welshmen; some. To L. K. C. G. K. Chesterton. CP-ChesG

Some can flatter, some can faine. Thomas Campion. CP-CampT

Some can gaze and not be sick. A. E. Housman. CP-HousA

Some candle clear burns somewhere I come by. Candle Indoors, The. Gerard Manley Hopkins. CP-HopkG

Some cartoon kids / watch cartoons. Ongoing. Rae Armantrout. SP-ArmaA

Some certain misty yet tenable signs. Albumania. James Whitcomb Riley. CP-RileJ

Some certified nut. John Ashbery. SP-AshbJ *Fr.* Litany.

Some Christmas Youngsters. James Whitcomb Riley. CP-RileJ

Some *Colinæus* praise, some *Bleau*. Verses to be Prefix'd before Bernard Lintot's New Miscellany. Alexander Pope. CP-PopeA

Some Collisions Bring Luck. Marge Piercy. SP-PierM

Some Comfort in Calamity. Robert Herrick. CP-HerrR

Some commentary on *I was a hidden treasure*. Pickaxe, The. Jelaluddin Rumi. SP-Rumi, *tr. by* Coleman Barks

Some Creature. Pablo Neruda. SP-NeruP

Some credulous chroniclers tell us. Very Tall Boy, A. James Whitcomb Riley. CP-RileJ

Some critic tried to put me down. Gary Snyder. CP-SnydG

Some Critical Annotations, on Various Subjects Which Have Been Handled by Several Authors. Laurence Whyte.

"T-m Punsibi gave us his Art." CP-SherT

Some Day. Langston Hughes. CP-HughL; CP-HughL2

Some day I will go to Aarhus. Tollund Man, The. Seamus Heaney. SP-HeanSO

Some day I'll crank up that Corvette, let it. Old Blue. William Stafford. SP-StafWW

Some day it will rain. As Though I Was Waiting for That. W. S. Merwin. SP-MerwW

Some day our town will grow old. Springfield of the Far Future, The. Nicholas Vachel Lindsay. CP-LindV

Some Days. Grace Paley.

Some days after so long even the sun. Western Country. W. S. Merwin. SP-MerwW

Some days ago, to stop the leaping. Into Summer. Theodore Weiss. SP-WeisT

Some days I put the people in their places at the table. Billy Collins. SP-CollB

Some days in May, little stars. Long Branch Song, A. Robert Pinsky. CP-PinsR

Some days instead of breakfast. Andrei Codrescu. SP-CodrA

Some days, like birthdays, are imported. Imported Days. Andrei Codrescu. SP-CodrA

Some Days retired from the rest. Emily Dickinson. CP-DickE

Some days, though. Living Alone (2). Denise Levertov. SP-LeveDL; SP-LeveDS

Some days when you look out, the land. Mr. or Mrs. Nobody. William Stafford. SP-StafW

Some departure from the norm. Saying It to Keep It from Happening. John Ashbery. SP-AshbJ

Some desperation of the sense. Birth of the Spirit, The. Richard Eberhart. CP-EberR

Some dichty folks. Weekend Glory. Maya Angelou. SP-AngeM

Some die too late and some too soon. Lost Occasion, The. John Greenleaf Whittier. CP-WhitJ

Some dogs who sleep at night. Eulogy to a Hell of a Dame—. Charles Bukowski. SP-BukC3

Some Dreams They Forgot. Elizabeth Bishop. CP-BishE

Some drippage and spillage in. Mean. A. R. Ammons. CP-AmmoA

Some Echo. Robert Creeley. SP-CreeR

Some Echoes. Robert Creeley. CP-CreeR

Some evenings, there are ghosts. There are. Ghosts. Ghosts. Miller Williams. CP-WillM

Some fathers may have some consideration. Left out of vacation. Robert Lowell. SP-LoweR

Some Figures for Who Must Speak. John Ciardi. CP-CiarJ

Some Final Words. Billy Collins. SP-CollB

Some fires are heard most truly. Blowgun and Rattlesnake. James Dickey. CP-DickJ

Some float off on chocolate bars. Lorine Niedecker. CP-NiedL

Some flushed-earth-color pueblo. Sacred Lake. Muriel Rukeyser. CP-RukeM

Some folks think / By burning books. Freedom ("Some folks think / By burning books"). Langston Hughes. CP-HughL; CP-HughL2

Some folks think / By burning churches. Freedom ("Some folks think / By burning churches"). Langston Hughes. CP-HughL; CP-HughL3

Some folks t'inks hit's right an' p'opah. Noddin' by de Fire. Paul Laurence Dunbar. CP-DunbP

Some for a little while do love, and some for long. Sonnet: "Some for a little while do love, and some for long." Countee Cullen. CP-CullC

Some for their looks. Rue Carpenter. Archibald MacLeish. CP-MacLA

Some Foreign Letters. Anne Sexton. CP-SextA; SP-SextA

Some forty years ago or maybe more. Broken Neck. Robert Graves. CP-GravR

Some forty years ago there on your. We Met in a Dream. James Laughlin. CP-LaugJ

Some fowls there be that have so perfect sight. How the Lover Perisheth in His Delight, As the Fly in the Fire. Petrarch. CP-WyatT, *tr. by* Sir Thomas Wyatt *Fr.* Sonnets to Laura.

Some Fragments, Mainly from Manuscripts of 1797–8. Samuel Taylor Coleridge. CP-ColeS

Some Frenchmen. John Updike. CP-UpdiJ

Some Friends from Pascagoula. Wallace Stevens. CP-StevW; CP-StevWP

Some future day, when what is now is not. Mari Magno I. Arthur Hugh Clough. SP-ClouA

Some Future Moon. Boris Leonidovich Pasternak. CP-DaviDC, *tr. by* Donald Davie

Some General Instructions. Kenneth Koch. SP-KochK

Some ghosts are women. Ghosts. Anne Sexton. CP-SextA

Some gnats come from the grass to speak with Solomon. Gnats inside the Wind. Jelaluddin Rumi. SP-Rumi, *tr. by* Coleman Barks

Some gone like boys to school wearing their badges. Elegy: "Some gone like boys to school wearing their badges." John Ciardi. CP-CiarJ

Some Good News. Charles Olson. SP-OlsoC *Fr.* Maximus Poems, The.

Some good, some middling, and some bad. Martial. CP-CunnJ, *tr. by* James Vincent Cunningham

Some have chimes. Lorine Niedecker. CP-NiedL

Some have meant only, though curiously. Darling. John Ciardi. CP-CiarJ

Some have [*or* hae] meat and cannot [*or* canna] eat. Grace at Kirkudbright. Robert Burns. CP-BurnR

Some Herons. Mary Oliver. SP-OlivM

Some Hindus have an elephant to show. Elephant in the Dark. Jelaluddin Rumi. SP-Rumi, *tr. by* Coleman Barks

Some I perceive, content. Advent. Donald Davie. CP-DaviDC

Some Imitations. James Whitcomb Riley. CP-RileJ

Some in the Godspeed, the Susan C. Enough. Marianne Craig Moore. CP-MoorM

Some Indian Uses of History on a Rainy Day. A. K. Ramanujan. CP-RamaA

Some insects feed on rosebuds. Bugs. Ogden Nash. CP-NashO

Some keep the Sabbath going to Church. Emily Dickinson. CP-DickE

Some kind of early waking take about bread (should be). America Inside & Outside Bill Brown's House in Bolinas. Philip Whalen. SP-WhalP

Some Kind of Pine. Heather McHugh. SP-McHuH

Some kind of relaxed and beautiful thing. Dogfish. Mary Oliver. SP-OlivM

Some ladies dress in muslin full and white. Christina Georgina Rossetti. CP-RosC3

Some ladies love the jewels in Love's zone. Love's Lovers. Dante Gabriel Rossetti. CW-RossD *Fr.* House of Life, The.

Some ladies smoke too much and some ladies drink too much and some ladies pray too much. Curl Up and Diet. Ogden Nash. CP-NashO

Some Last Questions. W. S. Merwin. SP-MerwW

Some leading thoroughfares of man. Via Crucis. Herman Melville. SP-MelvH *Fr.* Clarel: A Poem and Pilgrimage in the Holy Land.

Some leaves hang late, some fall. Soughing Wind, The. William Carlos Williams. CP-WilW1

Some Like Poetry. Wisława Szymborska. SP-SzymWM, *tr. by* Joanna Trzeciak

Some Lines Finished Just Before Dawn at the Bedside of a Dying Student It has Snowed All Night. Miller Williams. CP-WillM

Some look. to see the sweet Outlines. William Blake. CP-BlakW

Some Love. Allen Ginsberg. CP-GinsA

Some lucky day each November great waves awake and are drawn. November Surf. Robinson Jeffers. CP-JefR2

Some man unworthy to be possessor. Confined Love. John Donne. CP-DonnJ; MW-DonnJ

Some may have blamed us that we cease to speak. Fault of It, The. Ezra Pound. CP-PoEar

Some may have blamed you that you took away. Reconciliation. William Butler Yeats. CP-YeatW

Some melodies are popular as well as classical, which I suppose makes them popsicles. Everybody's Mind to Me a Kingdom Is, or, A Great Big Wonderful World It's. Ogden Nash. CP-NashO

Some Memories of E. P. (Drafts & Fragments). James Laughlin. CP-LaugJ

Some men break your heart in two. Experience. Dorothy Parker. CP-ParkD

Some Men created for destruction come. William Blake. CP-BlakW

Some men of books or friends not speaking right. To My Truly-Beloved Friend, Mr Browne: on His Pastorals. Ben Jonson. CP-JonsB

Some men, some men. Chant for Dark Hours. Dorothy Parker. CP-ParkD

Some minds have room alone for pageant stories. Motto Intended for Poems on the Naming of Places. William Wordsworth. CP-WorW1

Some Monarchs and a Wish. A. K. Ramanujan. CP-RamaA

Some monster bird, the barn. Cows, a Vision. Tess Gallagher. SP-GallT

Some months ago I went out early. A. R. Ammons. CP-AmmoA

Some mornings of maximal. Making Waves. A. R. Ammons. CP-AmmoA

Some must employ the scythe. Dedicated, The. Philip Larkin. CP-LarkP

Some mysterious phantom's sudden hand. Fernando Pessoa. SP-PessF, *tr. by*

Susan M. Brown *and* Edwin Honig

Some network has bought history, all the rights. Being an American. William Stafford. SP-StafWW

Some nights, a fearful. Robert Creeley. CP-CreeR

Some nights along the sidewalks. Blue Footprints, The. James Laughlin. CP-LaugJ

Some nights stay up till dawn. Jelaluddin Rumi. SP-Rumi, *tr.* by Coleman Barks

Some— / not all, that is. Some Like Poetry. Wisława Szymborska. SP-SzymWM, *tr.* by Joanna Trzeciak

Some Notes on Shadows. Gregory Orr. SP-OrrG

Some Nymphs May Boast External Grace. Thomas Sheridan. CP-SherT

Some Objects of Wood and Stone. Margaret Atwood. SP-AtwM1

Some Oddities. Donald Hall. CP-HallD

Some of My Best Friends Are Children. Ogden Nash. CP-NashO

Some of My Readers. Charles Bukowski. SP-BukC3

Some of the Masts. W. S. Merwin. SP-MerwWF

Some of the mayflies. Summer Canyon. W. S. Merwin. SP-MerwWF

Some of the sky is grey and some of it is white. Moving. Randall Jarrell. CP-JarrR

Some of them write too loud. Influential Writers. William Stafford. SP-StafWW

Some of These Days. Philip Whalen. SP-WhalP

Some of us believe. Night Game, The. Robert Pinsky. CP-PinsR

Some of Us Come to Live. James Laughlin. CP-LaugJ

Some of what we do, we do. Love Poem with Toast. Miller Williams. CP-WillM

Some of you may know, others perhaps can guess. Around the Mountain. Robert Graves. CP-GravR

Some of you will be glad I did what I did. Not Quite Social. Robert Frost. CP-FrosR

Some old Auruncans, I remember well. Virgil. CP-RaleW *Fr.* Aeneid [*or* Eneados *or* Aeneis], The.

Some old Egyptian joke is in the air. By Nilus Once I Knew. Hart Crane. CP-CranH

Some Old Tires. John Ashbery. SP-AshbJ

Some one prepared this mighty show. Emily Dickinson. CP-DickE

Some one who hears the bugle neigh will know. Dirge: "Some one who hears the bugle neigh will know." Thomas Merton. CP-MertT

Some Painful Butterflies Pass Through. Tess Gallagher. SP-GallT

Some parched boxwood shrubs in the summer's armpit. Roots of the World, The. Yannis Ritsos. SP RitsY, *tr.* by Athan Anagnostopoulos

Some part of the lyric wants to exclude. Gregory Orr. SP-OrrG

Some partial cloudiness will flow locally, mostly. Charles Olson. CP-OlsoC

Some particular place fleeting. Susan Howe. SP-HoweS

Some parts may perish; dye thou canst not all. On Himselfe. Robert Herrick. CP-HerrR

Some patios won't allow the shadow of a maid. Fanny Howe. SP-HoweF *Fr.* In the Spirit There Are No Accidents.

Some People. A. K. Ramanujan. CP-RamaA

Some people admire the work of a Fool. William Blake. CP-BlakW

Some people, and it doesn't matter whether they are paupers or millionaires. Possessions Are Nine Points of Conversation. Ogden Nash. CP-NashO

Some people are born simply to pay postage due. Please Keep on Forwarding. Ogden Nash. CP-NashO

Some people are do-it-some-other-timers and other people are do-it-nowers. Splash! Ogden Nash. CP-NashO

Some people are in favor of compromising, while other people. Strange Case of the Lucrative Compromise, The. Ogden Nash. CP-NashO

Some people are popular with other people because their wit is. People. Ogden Nash. CP-NashO

Some people don't want to be doctors because they think doctors. Cousin Euphemia Knows Best, or, Physician, Heal Somebody Else. Ogden Nash. CP-NashO

Some people fear a white head. Han-shan. CP-ColdM, *tr.* by Red Pine

Some people flaunt their practice. Han-shan. CP-ColdM, *tr.* by Red Pine

Some people fleeing some other people. Wisława Szymborska. SP-SzymWM, *tr.* by Joanna Trzeciak

Some people get savage and bitter when to backbiters they refer. Hush, Here They Come. Ogden Nash. CP-NashO

Some people hang portraits up. Likeness, A. Robert Browning. CP-BroR1; SP-BroR

Some people just seem. Down We Go. James Laughlin. CP-LaugJ

Some people lead a feverish life. Plea for a League of Sleep, A. Ogden Nash. CP-NashO

Some people like to hitch and hike. Riding on a Railroad Train. Ogden Nash. CP-NashO

Some people look to the future and others look days of yore-wards. Now You See It, Now I Don't. Ogden Nash. CP-NashO

Some people relate anecdotes about Samuel Goldwyn and Gregory Ratoff. Doctor Fell? I Thought So. Ogden Nash. CP-NashO

Some people set themselves tasks. Life. Grace Paley. CP-PalGC

Some people shave before bathing. And Three Hundred and Sixty-Six in Leap Year. Ogden Nash. CP-NashO

Some people, / they just don't hate enough yet. Beyond. C. K. Williams. CP-WillC

Some People Think. James Laughlin. CP-LaugJ

Some people think that they can beat three two's with a pair of aces. How Long Has This Been Going On? Oh, Quite Long. Ogden Nash. CP-NashO

Some people understand all about machinery. Up from the Wheelbarrow. Ogden Nash. CP-NashO

Some people wept, and not for sorrow—joy. Mycenae Lookout. Seamus Heaney. SP-HeanSO

Some peoples thinks they ain't no Fairies *now*. Bud's Fairy Tale. James Whitcomb Riley. CP-RileJ *Fr.* Child-World, A.

Some Perfume. Rainer Maria Rilke. CP-RilkFr, *tr.* by A. Poulin, Jr.

Some Picnic. Charles Bukowski. SP-BukC1

Some pimps wear summer hats. What? Langston Hughes. CP-HughL

Some Place. Robert Creeley. CP CreeR

Some Power Company employee. Unknown One, The. Charles Simic. SP-SimiCE

Some Power Company Employee. Man, The. Charles Simic. SP-SimiC

Some primal termite knocked on wood. Termite, The. Ogden Nash. CP-NashO

Some prisoned moon in steep cloud-fastnesses. Soul's Sphere, The. Dante Gabriel Rossetti. CW-RossD *Fr.* House of Life, The.

Some Prophecies. G. K. Chesterton. CP-ChesG

Some Prose on *Poetry*. Raymond Carver. CP-CarvR

Some Questions You Might Ask. Mary Oliver. SP-OlivM

Some quickly-weathering rock, perhaps. Twilight on the Waste Lands. Donald Davie. CP-DaviDC

Some Quiet, Plain Poems. Robert Penn Warren. CP-WarrR

Some rain falling. Marga Barr. William Corbett. SP-CorbW

Some Rainbow—coming from the Fair! Emily Dickinson. CP-DickE

Some Relations. A. K. Ramanujan. CP-RamaA

Some Remarks When Richard Hugo Came. William Stafford. SP-StafWW

Some Revelations of Journalism. G. K. Chesterton. CP-ChesG

Some Riddles from Symphosius. Richard Wilbur. CP-WilbR

Some rule of birds kills off the song. Size of Song, The. John Ciardi. CP-CiarJ

Some salve to every sore, we may apply. Upon Love. Robert Herrick. CP-HerrR

Some San Francisco Poems. George Oppen. CP-OppGN

Some say goodnight—at night. Emily Dickinson. CP-DickE

Some say sorrow fades. Trio. Carolyn Kizer. CP-KizeC

Some say that Guy of Warwick. Road to Roundabout, The. G. K. Chesterton. CP-ChesG

Some say that love and joy are one: and so. Sonnet: "Some say that love and joy are one: and so." Christina Georgina Rossetti. CP-RosC3

Some say the fastest living creature is the cheetah. Mrs. Purvis Dreads Room Service. Ogden Nash. CP-NashO

Some say the spot is banned: that the pillar Cross-and-Hand. Lost Pyx, The. Thomas Hardy. CP-HardT

Some say the world will end in fire. Fire and Ice. Robert Frost. CP-FrosR

Some Scattering Remarks of Bub's. James Whitcomb Riley. CP-RileJ

Some Science Fiction. Robert Frost. CP-FrosR

Some seek pleasure in love. Han-shan. CP-ColdM, *tr.* by Red Pine

Some selves are generous. Fanny Howe. SP-HoweF *Fr.* Vineyard, The.

Some seventy years later. Slow Fuse, A. Theodore Weiss. SP-WeisT

Some Shadows. William Stafford. SP-StafW; SP-StafWW

Some shapes cannot be seen in a glass. Holding the Mirror Up to Nature. Howard Nemerov. CP-NemeH

Some Shires Revisited. Donald Davie. CP-DaviDC

Some Simple Measures in the American Idiom and the Variable Foot. William Carlos Williams. CP-WilW2

Some simple / virtue of silence. For Joel. Robert Creeley. CP-CreeR

Some singers sing of ladies' eyes. Clean Platter, The. Ogden Nash. CP-NashO

Some sings of the lilly, and daisy, and rose. Clover, The. James Whitcomb Riley. CP-RileJ

Some sit and stare. Common Grave, The. James Dickey. CP-DickJ

Some slowness across the day. Rainer Maria Rilke. CP-RilkFr, *tr.* by A. Poulin, Jr. *Fr.* Fragments.

Some sneer; some snigger; some simper. To Young Pessimists. G. K. Chesterton. CP-ChesG

Some Songs after Master-Singers. James Whitcomb Riley. CP-RileJ

Some Sort of Game. John Ciardi. CP-CiarJ

Some sort of road does go up there. Sacred Hearth Fire, The. Amy Clampitt. CP-ClamA

Some sort of solitude. Little Air 1. Stéphane Mallarmé. CP-MallS, *tr.* by Henry Weinfield

Some souls / have blue stars. Federico García Lorca. CP-GarcF, *tr.* by Catherine Brown

Some such Butterfly be seen. Emily Dickinson. CP-DickE

Some sway for long and then decline. Oak, The. Richard Eberhart. CP-EberR

Some that have deeper digged love's mine [*or* myne] than [*or* then] I. Love's Alchemy [*or* Alchemie]. John Donne. CP-DonnJ; MW-DonnJ

Some Things Are Dark. Edna St. Vincent Millay. CP-MillE

Some things are never clear. Voice Ways. Robert Frost. CP-FrosR

Some things are truly lost. Think of a sun-hat. Mind-Reader, The. Richard Wilbur. CP-WilbR

Some things, by their affinity light's token. Sunlight. Thom Gunn. CP-GunnT

Some things I do not profess. Abduction, The. Stanley Kunitz. CP-KunSC

Some Things I Like about My Triple Bloods. Alice Walker. CP-WalkA

Some things, niño, some things are like this. Of Bright & Blue Birds & the Gala Sun. Wallace Stevens. CP-StevW; CP-StevWP

Some things that fly there be. Emily Dickinson. CP-DickE

Some thirty years too late. Studying French. Theodore Weiss. SP-WeisT

Some time ago there was a man named Nasuh. Nasuh. Jelaluddin Rumi. SP-Rumi, *tr.* by Coleman Barks

Some time has gone. Louis Zukofsky. CP-ZukLS

Some time in the dark hours. Snowfall. W. S. Merwin. SP-MerwW

Some time is longer than the rest. Emily Dickinson. SP-DickE

Some time now past in the autumnal tide. Contemplations. Anne Bradstreet. CP-BradA

Some time when the river is ice ask me. Ask Me. William Stafford. SP-StafW; SP-StafWW

Some to the cars are yellow, that go. Yellow Cars. William Stafford. SP-StafWW

Some, too fragile for winter winds. Emily Dickinson. CP-DickE

Some Traits of the Character of Mrs. Powel as a Model for a Young Lady Who Said She Admired Her More than Any Other Woman. Annis Boudinot Stockton. CP-StocA

Some Trees. John Ashbery. SP-AshbJ

Some trick of light. Intimation. Denise Levertov. SP-LeveDL

Some war, I bomb their towns from five. Some Remarks When Richard Hugo Came. William Stafford. SP-StafWW

Some we see no more, Tenements of Wonder. Emily Dickinson. CP-DickE

Some weep to find the Golden Pear. Colored Blues Singer. Countee Cullen. CP-CullC

Some were as love loved, some as prizes prized. Fernando Pessoa. SP-PessF *Fr.* Inscriptions.

Some will remember / the flash of light. Remembering the Birth of Lucifer. Lucille Clifton. SP-ClifL

Some winters, taking leave. Storm in April, A. Richard Wilbur. CP-WilbR

Some Wishes at Xmas. G. K. Chesterton. CP-ChesG

  "Mince-pies grant Wishes: let each name his Prize." CP-ChesG

Some with Wings, Some with Manes. Tess Gallagher. SP-GallT

Some women live for the idiotic furniture of their houses. Furniture. D. H. Lawrence. CP-LawrD

Some women marry houses. Housewife. Anne Sexton. SP-SextA; SP-SextA

Some Words. John Ashbery. SP-AshbJ

Some—Work for Immortality. Emily Dickinson. CP-DickE

Some would distinguish nothing here but oaks. Wood, A. Richard Wilbur. CP-WilbR

Some would know / Why I so. His Answer to a Question. Robert Herrick. CP-HerrR

Some Wretched creature, savior take. Emily Dickinson. CP-DickE

Somebody. Robert Burns. CP-BurnR

  (For the Sake o' Somebody.) CP-BurnR

Somebody Always Breaking My Dainty Solitude. Charles Bukowski. SP-BukC2

Somebody Died. Robert Creeley. CP-CreeR

Somebody dies every four minutes. Rapid Transit. William Carlos Williams. CP-WilW1

Somebody Else's Problem Bothers Me. Philip Whalen. SP-WhalP

Somebody has endlessly postponed. Last Time, The. Marilyn Hacker. SP-HackM

Somebody has given my. Proust's Madeleine. Kenneth Rexroth. CP-RexrK

Somebody is shooting at something in our town. Swarm, The. Sylvia Plath. CP-PlatS

Somebody keeps track of how many times. Innings. C. K. Williams. CP-WillC

Somebody knew Lincoln somebody Xerxes. E. E. Cummings. CP-CummE

Somebody left the world last night, I felt it. Elegy: "Somebody left the world last night, I felt it." Olga Broumas. SP-BrouO

Somebody long ago. Hedge of Hemlocks, The. Edna St. Vincent Millay. CP-MillE

Somebody loses whenever somebody wins. Crapshooters. Carl Sandburg. CP-SandC

Somebody who knew him. Unknown Forebear. W. S. Merwin. SP-MerwWF

Somebody who should have been born. Abortion, The. Anne Sexton. CP-SextA; SP-SextA

Somebody'll Hav' to Shoot Ya Down. Norman Dubie. CP-DubiN

Somebody's Aunt Out Swabbing Her Birdbath. Thomas Lux. SP-LuxT

Somebody's grandmother glides through the bracken. Metempsychosis. Margaret Atwood. SP-AtwM2

Somebody's knockin' at th' door. Collier's Wife, The. D. H. Lawrence. CP-LawrD

Somebody's little girl—how easy to make a sob story over who she was once. Crabapple Blossoms. Carl Sandburg. CP-SandC

Somebody's sent a funny little valentine to me. Her Valentine. James Whitcomb Riley. CP-RileJ

Somebody's shout displaces the horizon. Shout, The. Charles Tomlinson. CP-TomlC

Somebody's Song. Dorothy Parker. CP-ParkD

Someday:—So many tearful eyes. James Whitcomb Riley. CP-RileJ

Someday they'll find me out, and my lavish hands. Self-Portrait. Charles Wright. SP-WrigC

Somehow. Marge Piercy. SP-PierM

Somehow I cannot let it go yet, funeral though it is. Pallid Wreath, The. Walt Whitman. CP-WhitW

Somehow it has all. Song Sparrow Singing in the Fall, A. Wendell Berry. CP-BerrW

Somehow myself survived the Night. Emily Dickinson. CP-DickE

Somehow, one expects. Sadness of My Neighbors, The. James Tate. SP-TateJ

Someone. Jorge Luis Borges. SP-BorgJ, *tr.* by W. S. Merwin

Someone approaches to say his life is ruined. Dream, The. David Ignatow. SP-IgnaD

Someone asks him what day it is. What day? Moments of Old Age. Dan Pagis. SP-PagiD, *tr.* by Stephen Mitchell

Someone at a table under a brown metal lamp. Poetry: I. Adrienne Rich. SP-RicA1

Someone brought me a seashell. Seashell. Federico García Lorca. CP-GarcF, *tr.* by Alan S. Trueblood *Fr.* Songs for Children.

Someone calls *Duchess,* our fawn Great Dane, back. Amen. Norman Dubie. CP-DubiN

Someone Digging in the Ground. Jelaluddin Rumi. SP-Rumi, *tr.* by Coleman Barks

Someone else's Leica sitting on the table. Essay on Style. Frank O'Hara. SP-OharF

Someone had a great many dead. Hill, The. Yannis Ritsos. SP-RitsY, *tr.* by Kimon Friar

Someone had been walking in and out. Origin of Baseball, The. Kenneth Patchen. CP-PatcK

Someone has counted the hours. Milonga of Albornoz. Jorge Luis Borges. SP-BorgJ, *tr.* by Alastair Reid

Someone has fallen to the earth. Examination into Life and Death, An. Kenneth Patchen. CP-PatcK

Someone has gathered a shell. Triumph of the Shell, The. Archibald MacLeish. CP-MacLA

Someone has set up a gate here. Gate, The. Charles Tomlinson. CP-TomlC

Someone I know is dying at seventeen. Gray Fox, The. Gregory Orr. SP-OrrG

Someone I tell you will remember us. Sappho. CP-CunnJ, *tr.* by James Vincent Cunningham

Someone identical with Dante. Pre-Petrarchan Sonnet. Michael Palmer. SP-PalmM

Someone in ancient Mas d'Avil. Missive Missile, A. Robert Frost. CP-FrosR

Someone in this room. Olympia. Yusef Komunyakaa. CP-KomuY

Someone is actually playing a dulcimer. Backyard in California, A. Hayden Carruth. SP-CarHS

Someone is always trying to feel something. Trying to Feel Something. John Ciardi. CP-CiarJ

Someone is dead. Lament: "Someone is dead." Anne Sexton. CP-SextA; SP-SextA

Someone is loose is Moscow who won't stop. Phone Booth. Andrey Andreievich Voznesensky. CP-WilbR

Someone is present / On the earth are laid the crowns. Watcher, The. Kenneth Patchen. CP-PatcK

Someone is sitting in the red house. Small Town. Rita Dove. SP-DoveR

Someone kicked him so he limped. Defendant. Alan Dugan. CP-DugaA

Someone lives in a mountain gorge. Han-shan.

Someone makes tracks along the paths of Ithaca. Exile (1977), The. Jorge Luis Borges. SP-BorgJ, *tr.* by Alastair Reid

Someone may be a horse. Should Be Sufficient. Kenneth Patchen. CP-PatcK

Someone moves through the jungle. Drowned Man: Death Between Two Rivers, The. Thomas McGrath. SP-McGrT

Someone must make out the cards. What *Was* Her Name. John Ciardi. CP-CiarJ

Someone offhand to the Caliph of Egypt. Sexual Urgency, What a Woman's Laughter Can Do, and the Nature of True Virility. Jelaluddin Rumi. SP-Rumi, *tr.* by Coleman Barks

Someone points to a cedar. Han-shan. CP-ColdM, *tr.* by Red Pine

Someone said, stirring their tea, "I would." With Neighbors One Afternoon. William Stafford. SP-StafWW

Someone said, "there is no dervish, or if there is a dervish, that dervish is not there." Rough Metaphors. Jelaluddin Rumi. SP-Rumi, *tr.* by Coleman Barks

Someone saw her in Ecbatan. I Don't Know Where She Is Wandering Tonight. James Laughlin. CP-LaugJ

Someone says, *Sanai is dead.* Sanai. Jelaluddin Rumi. SP-Rumi, *tr.* by Coleman Barks

Someone sighed *Cold Mountain sir.* Han-shan. CP-ColdM, *tr.* by Red Pine

Someone Talking to Himself. Richard Wilbur. CP-WilbR

Someone who doesn't know the Tigris River exists. Gift of Water, The. Jelaluddin Rumi. SP-Rumi, *tr.* by Coleman Barks

Someone who goes with half a loaf of bread. Jelaluddin Rumi. SP-Rumi, *tr.* by Coleman Barks

Someone Will Enter between the Gates. D. H. Lawrence. CP-LawrD

Someone's about to enter the doorway . . . One feels the air smiling. Fernando Pessoa. SP-PessF *Fr.* Absurd Hour.

Someone's Blood. Rita Dove. SP-DoveR

Someplace. Yehuda Amichai. SP-AmicYL, *tr.* by Benjamin Harshav *and* Barbara Harshav

Someplace in Arizona. Dogs. Charles Bukowski. SP-BukC3

Somep'n 'at's common-like, and good. Somep'n Common-like. James Whitcomb Riley. CP-RileJ

Somep'n Common-like. James Whitcomb Riley. CP-RileJ

Somerset. Donald Davie. CP-DaviDC

Something. Charles Bukowski. SP-BukC1

Something. Robert Creeley. CP-CreeR

Something. James Whitcomb Riley. CP-RileJ

Something: a Direction. Charles Tomlinson. SP-TomlC *Fr.* Antecedents.

Something Amazing Just Happened. Ted Berrigan. SP-BerrT

Something approaches, about. Old Woman, The. Thom Gunn. CP-GunnT

Something breathless hangs in the air. Breathless, The. Richard Eberhart. CP-EberR

Something broken Something / I need By someone. Nightbreak. Adrienne Rich. CP-RicAE; SP-RicA1; SP-RicA2

Something brought them here. It was an outcropping of peace. Haunted Landscape. John Ashbery. SP-AshbJ

Something / by which. Touchstone. Robert Creeley. SP-CreeR

Something Childish, but Very Natural. Samuel Taylor Coleridge. *See* If I Had but Two Little Wings

Something / cold is in the air. Fury of Sunsets, The. Anne Sexton. SP-SextA *Fr.* Furies, The.

Something comes crawling from St. James's Park, Lullaby for a Summer Recess. James Fenton. SP-FentJ

Something continues and I don't know what to call it. Birthday, A. W. S. Merwin. SP-MerwWF

Something do I see. Head above the Fog, The. Thomas Hardy. CP-HardT

Something Else. Paul Muldoon. CP-MuldP

Something far off buried deep and free. Flash, The. James Dickey. CP-DickJ

Something for a long time has gone wrong. Turning Away. James Dickey. CP-DickJ

Something for Easter. Robert Creeley. CP-CreeR

Something for Hope. Robert Frost. CP-FrosR

Something forgotten for twenty years: though my fathers. Map of the Western Part of the County of Essex in England, A. Denise Levertov. SP-LeveDP; SP-LeveDS

Something gets into us at night. Song Calls the Star Little, The. Heather McHugh. SP-McHuH

Something gnaws inside my head. Kirilov on a Skyscraper. Randall Jarrell. CP-JarrR

Something gone, something gone out with Nelson. Suffolk. Donald Davie. CP-DaviDC

Something had cracked in her mouth as she slept. Gap in the White, The. Thomas Hardy. CP-HardT

Something hangs in back of me. Wings, The. Denise Levertov. SP-LeveDP; SP-LeveDS

Something has happened to the air: a fly. Soliloquy: Ghost Dance for a Cripple. Alan Dugan. CP-DugaA

Something has left itself scattered. Rib, The. James Dickey. CP-DickJ

Something I saw or thought I saw. On the Heart's Beginning to Cloud the Mind. Robert Frost. CP-FrosR

Something I should like to know is, which. Visitors Laugh at Locksmiths or, Hospital Doors Haven't Got Locks Anyhow. Ogden Nash. CP-NashO

Something in a summer's Day, A. Emily Dickinson. CP-DickE

Something in the light of this March afternoon. Tenancy, A. James Merrill. SP-MerrJ

Something in the Papers. Ambrose Bierce. SP-BierA

Something in the water. Lorine Niedecker. CP-NiedL

Something in the wild cherry. Days. John Ciardi. CP-CiarJ

Something inspires the only cow of late. Cow in Apple Time, The. Robert Frost. CP-FrosR

Something is dying, but without blood or. Simple Sonatina. Tess Gallagher. SP-GallT

Something Is Dying Here. Thomas McGrath. SP-McGrT

Something is happening to me. Raymond Carver. CP-CarvR

Something is taking place. Rites of Passage. Thom Gunn. CP-GunnT

Something is there. And teacher here at home. Dream of Waking, The. Randall Jarrell. CP-JarrR

Something is very gently. Thread, The. Denise Levertov. SP-LeveDP

Something isn't right with me. Medicine Bow. John Logan. CP-LogaJ

Something I've Not Done. W. S. Merwin. SP-MerwW

Something like a field in Hungary, but without. Ex Voto. Joseph Brodsky. CP-BrodJ

Something must be done right away. Song for Those Who Know. Hans Magnus Enzensberger. SP-EnzeH, *tr.* by Hans Magnus Enzensberger *and* Michael Hamburger

Something Nice About Myself. Philip Whalen. SP-WhalP

Something not the wind shakes along far. Storm Warnings. William Stafford. SP-StafWW

Something occurred after the operation. Surgical Ward: Men. Robert Graves. CP-GravR

Something of a Departure. Paul Muldoon. CP-MuldP

Something of glass about her, of dead water. Circe. Louis MacNeice. CP-MacNL

Something of the trouble of the mind. How Now, O, Brightener. Wallace Stevens. CP-StevWP

Something of yesterday clings to today. Today Isn't Everything. Pablo Neruda. SP-NeruP

Something old and tyrannical burning there. Coal Fire in Winter, A. Thomas McGrath. SP-McGrT

Something opens our wings. Something. Jelaluddin Rumi. SP-Rumi, *tr.* by Coleman Barks

Something outside my window in the dark. Wind from a Wing, A. William Stafford. SP-StafWW

Something primal in our spine makes the child swing. Derek Walcott. CP-WalcD *Fr.* Midsummer.

Something quiet and subdued, A. At Dusk. James Whitcomb Riley. CP-RileJ

Something removed roars in the ears of this house. Missing the Sea. Derek Walcott. CP-WalcD

Something said: You have nothing to fear. Heard by a Girl. Louise Bogan. CP-BogaL

Something Similar. John Ashbery. SP-AshbJ

Something startles me where I thought I was safest. This Compost. Walt Whitman. CP-WhitW

Something strange is creeping across me. Daffy Duck in Hollywood. John Ashbery. SP-AshbJ

Something Tapped. Thomas Hardy. CP-HardT

Something tells him he is off-limits. Retirement. Karl Shapiro. SP-ShapK

Something That Happens Right Now. William Stafford. SP-StafWW

Something that Saved Him, The. Thomas Hardy. CP-HardT

Something There. Samuel Beckett. CP-BeckS

Something there is that doesn't. Real Estate. Amy Clampitt. CP-ClamA

Something there is that doesn't love a wall. Mending Wall. Robert Frost. CP-FrosR

Something they said next to me. At the Entrance to the Café. Constantine P. Cavafy. CP-CavaC, *tr.* by Theoharis Constantine Theoharis

Something to Believe In. Miller Williams. CP-WillM

Something to Declare. William Stafford. SP-StafWW

Something to dip myself into. Acids. C. K. Williams. CP-WillC

Something to kill songs. White Lady. Yusef Komunyakaa. CP-KomuY

Something to Say. Robert Graves. CP-GravR

Something unkempt about it. Grant's Tomb Revisited. Karl Shapiro. SP-ShapK

Something vague waxes or wanes. Lines for a Friend Who Left. John Logan. CP-LogaJ

Something was being done to the road. Danger / Road under Repair. James Laughlin. CP-LaugJ

Something went crabwise. Presence, The. Maxine W. Kumin. SP-KumiM

Something wrong with my desk the desk. Two Romance Poems. George Oppen. CP-OppGN

Something you can hold on to. Thoughts on the Run 2. Hans Magnus Enzensberger. SP-EnzeH, *tr.* by Rita Dove *and* Fred Viebahn

Sometime around dusk moose lifts. Wife Hits Moose. Thomas Lux. SP-LuxT

Sometime During Eternity. Lawrence Ferlinghetti. SP-FerlL

Sometime during eternity / some guys show up. Sometime During Eternity. Lawrence Ferlinghetti. SP-FerlL

Sometime I fled the fire that me brent. Sir Thomas Wyatt. CP-WyatT

Sometime I must try to write the truth. No Messiah. Robert Lowell. SP-LoweR

Sometime I sigh, sometime I sing. Sir Thomas Wyatt. CP-WyatT

Sometime I'll lay down my wrath. Sometime Jailhouse Blues. Allen Ginsberg. CP-GinsA

Sometime Jailhouse Blues. Allen Ginsberg. CP-GinsA

Sometime nothing has happened. We are home. Key of C— an interlude for Marvin. William Stafford. SP-StafWW

Sometime,perhaps in Paris we will. E. E. Cummings. CP-CummE

Sometime Sportsman Greets the Spring, The. John Updike. CP-UpdiJ

Sometime the pride of my assured truth. Argument, Th'. Sir Thomas Wyatt. CP-WyatT

Sometime turns inside out. Memorial III—from a Phone Booth on Broadway. Audre Lorde. SP-LordA

Sometime you'll walk all night. You'll. Glass Face in the Rain, A. William Stafford. SP-StafWW

Sometimes. Thomas McGrath. SP-McGrT

Sometimes. Grace Paley. CP-PalGC

Sometimes. A. K. Ramanujan. CP-RamaA

Sometimes. James Schuyler. CP-SchuJ

Sometimes a crumb falls. Luck ("Sometimes a crumb falls"). Langston Hughes. CP-HughL

Sometimes a few scraps fall. Luck ("Sometimes a few scraps fall"). Langston Hughes. CP-HughL2

Sometimes a goodbye. Fanny Howe. SP-HoweF *Fr.* O'Clock.

Sometimes a lantern moves along the night. Lantern Out of Doors, The. Gerard Manley Hopkins. CP-HopkG

Sometimes a lover of God may faint. Birdsong from Inside the Egg. Jelaluddin Rumi. SP-Rumi, *tr.* by Coleman Barks

Sometimes / A night funeral. Dead in There. Langston Hughes. CP-HughL; CP-HughL3

Sometimes a word will start it, like. Variant. John Ashbery. SP-AshbJ

Sometimes after you get your ass. About Cranes. Charles Bukowski. SP-BukC1

Sometimes another star chooses. Leda 2. Lucille Clifton. SP-ClifL

Sometimes, apart in sleep, by chance. Trance, The. Stephen Spender. CP-SpenS

Sometimes are living those who have been seen. Veer-Voices: Two Sisters under Crows. James Dickey. CP-DickJ

Sometimes, as a Child. Olga Broumas. SP-BrouO

Sometimes as I woke, the branches beside the stars. New Georgia. Randall Jarrell. CP-JarrR

Sometimes at night he dreams back. Peeping Tom. Lucille Clifton. SP-ClifL

Sometimes at night I think of how we did. My Life Before Dawn. Louise Glück. SP-GlucL

Sometimes, becoming pensive, a flower. Pensive Flower. Rainer Maria Rilke. CP-RilkFr, *tr.* by A. Poulin, Jr.

Sometimes before great events a person will try. Things That Happen. William Stafford. SP-StafWW

Sometimes, charting the heroes and animals of night-time. Clarance Mangan. Thomas Kinsella. CP-KinsT

Sometimes deeply immured in white-washed tower. Tingling Back, The. Karl Shapiro. SP-ShapK

Sometimes disturbed people go to the Public Library. In Favor of a Free Public Library System. Alan Dugan. CP-DugaA

Sometimes for cruel sport a crew will take. Albatross, The. Charles Baudelaire. CP-BaudC, *tr.* by Walter Martin

Sometimes he would try to write a poem. Style. Miller Williams. CP-WillM

Sometimes I almost go hours without crying. Villanelle of the Suicide's Mother. C. K. Williams. SP-WillC

Sometimes i am alive because with. E. E. Cummings. CP-CummE

Sometimes I am ashamed that I have never. Petrarch. CP-Petra, *tr.* by J. G. Nichols

Sometimes I am embarrassed. Not Again. Robert Creeley. CP-CreeR

Sometimes I breathe and. Assuming Control. William Stafford. SP-StafWW

Sometimes I choose a cloud and let it. Quo Vadis. William Stafford. SP-StafWW

Sometimes I dip my pen and find the bottle full of fire. Apology for the Bottle Volcanic, An. Nicholas Vachel Lindsay. CP-LindV

Sometimes I envy others, fear them. Cure, The. William Carlos Williams. CP-WilW2

Sometimes I fain would find in thee some fault. Lamp's Shrine, The. Dante Gabriel Rossetti. CW-RossD *Fr.* House of Life, The.

Sometimes I feel so bad. Family Of. Alice Walker. CP-WalkA

Sometimes I feel thy cheek against my face. Comraderie. Ezra Pound. CP-PoEar

Sometimes I Forget Completely. Jelaluddin Rumi. SP-Rumi, *tr.* by Coleman Barks

Sometimes I have supposed seals. Soft Wood. Robert Lowell. SP-LoweR

Sometimes I hear the veery's clarion. Henry David Thoreau. CP-ThorH

Sometimes I keep. Katydids, The. James Whitcomb Riley. CP-RileJ

Sometimes I play a game that is of interest only to me. Mr. Burgess, Meet Mr. Barmecide. Ogden Nash. CP-NashO

Sometimes I play the music of Charlie Byrd. Kinaesthesia. Richard Eberhart. CP-EberR

Sometimes I remember you, little Ruth. Little Ruth. Yehuda Amichai. SP-AmicYL, *tr.* by Benjamin Harshav *and* Barbara Harshav

Sometimes I see a massive wave of blood. Fountain of Blood. Charles Baudelaire. CP-BaudC, *tr.* by Walter Martin

Sometimes I see an. Banking. A. R. Ammons. CP-AmmoA

Sometimes I still hear the world. Throw Pillows. Yehuda Amichai. SP-AmicYL, *tr.* by Benjamin Harshav *and* Barbara Harshav

Sometimes I think 'at Parunts does. Parent Reprimanded, A. James Whitcomb Riley. CP-RileJ

Sometimes I Think I've Lived Too Long. David Ignatow. SP-IgnaD

Sometimes I think of my fathers. Yehuda Amichai. SP-AmicYL *Fr.* Poems of the Land of Zion and Jerusalem.

Sometimes I think that nothing. Small-scale Reflections on a Great House. A. K. Ramanujan. CP-RamaA

Sometimes in moods of gloom—like mist. Mist. Walter De la Mare. CP-DeLaW

Sometimes in the evening a translator walks out. Walking the Borders. William Stafford. SP-StafWW

Sometimes in the open you look up. Atavism. William Stafford. SP-StafWW

Sometimes / in)Spring a someone will lie(glued). E. E. Cummings. CP-CummE

Sometimes it comes, a gloomy flap of lightning. Ted Hughes. SP-HughTN

Sometimes it is inconceivable that I should be the age I am. Child, The. W. S. Merwin. SP-MerwW

Sometimes it is like a beast. Trucker, A. Thom Gunn. CP-GunnT

Sometimes it occurs to me in the moonlit. Gods. Hayden Carruth. CP-CarHS

Sometimes it seems. Fanny Howe. SP-HoweF *Fr.* O'Clock.

Sometimes it seems to be the inmost land. On Being Given Time. May Sarton. SP-SartM

Sometimes It Turns Dry and the Leaves Fall before They Are Beautiful. William Carlos Williams. CP-WilW2

Sometimes it's difficult, isn't it, not to grow grim and rancorous. Necessary Dirge, A. Ogden Nash. CP-NashO

Sometimes it's good to be. Rainer Maria Rilke. CP-RilkFr, *tr.* by A. Poulin, Jr. *Fr.* Orchards.

Sometimes it's like you're dead. Pablo Neruda. SP-LoguC, *tr.* by Christopher Logue *Fr.* Red Bird.

Sometimes lovers or writers. Rainer Maria Rilke. CP-RilkFr, *tr.* by A. Poulin, Jr. *Fr.* Affectionate Taxes to France.

Sometimes men are kissing. Men are sometimes kissing. Men. Gertrude Stein. CP-SteiG

Sometimes my Conscience says, say he. My Conscience. James Whitcomb Riley. CP-RileJ

Sometimes new ships arrive, with their cargo. Our Old Men. Yannis Ritsos. SP-RitsY, *tr.* by Martin McKinsey

Sometimes, not very frequently, hunting hares in the winter. Keeping Cool. Hans Magnus Enzensberger. SP-EnzeH

Sometimes, oh, often, indeed, in the midst of ugly adversity, beautiful. Edna St. Vincent Millay. CP-MillE

Sometimes / on this green hill. In Hanoi 1969. Grace Paley. CP-PalGC

Sometimes out walking, on a country road. Out Walking. Adam Zagajewski. SP-ZagaA, *tr.* by Clare Cavanagh

Sometimes pus. Ibn Gabirol. Yehuda Amichai. SP-AmicYL, *tr.* by Benjamin Harshav *and* Barbara Harshav

Sometimes pus, / sometimes poetry. Ibn Gabirol. Yehuda Amichai. SP-AmicY, *tr.* by Stephen Mitchell

Sometimes, riding in a car, in Wisconsin. Three Kinds of Pleasures. Robert Bly. SP-BlyR

Sometimes she is a child within mine arms. Heart's Haven. Dante Gabriel Rossetti. CW-RossD *Fr.* House of Life, The.

Sometimes, she remembers, a chipped flint. Imago. Amy Clampitt. CP-ClamA

Sometimes she walks through the village in her little red dress. Child in Red. Rainer Maria Rilke. CP-RilkFr, *tr.* by A. Poulin, Jr.

Sometimes she'd begin to sing to herself before she was out of bed, before, I can remember thinking. Mornings: Catherine. C. K. Williams. SP-WillC

Sometimes the foundering fury that directs. John Ciardi. CP-CiarJ

Sometimes the light when evening fails. Level Light. William Stafford. SP-StafWW

Sometimes the Longing for Death. Richard Eberhart. CP-EberR

Sometimes the mountain. Witness. Denise Levertov. SP-LeveDS

Sometimes the notes are ferocious. Marginalia. Billy Collins. SP-CollB

Sometimes the river. Mind Hesitant, The. William Carlos Williams. CP-WilW2

Sometimes the sun beats up the rocks of capes. Crusoe. Thomas Merton. CP-MertT

Sometimes the sun turns hostile to men. Hostile Sun, The. D. H. Lawrence. CP-LawrD

Sometimes there is a point. On the Nature of Perspective. Clarence Major. SP-MajoC

Sometimes there's a wind in the Georgia dusk. Georgia Dusk. Langston Hughes. CP-HughL; CP-HughL3

Sometimes thou seem'st not as thyself alone. Heart's Compass. Dante Gabriel Rossetti. CW-RossD *Fr.* House of Life, The.

Sometimes up out of this land. Bi-Focal. William Stafford. SP-StafW; SP-StafWW

Sometimes waking, sometimes sleeping. Nestus Gurley. Randall Jarrell. CP-

JarrR

Sometimes, walking for hours through the woods. 1945—1985: Poem for the Anniversary. Mary Oliver. SP-OlivM

Sometimes walking late at night. Butcher Shop. Charles Simic. SP-SimiC; SP-SimiCE

Sometimes we are tied down by memories. Jaroslav Seifert. SP-SeifJ, *tr. by* Ewald Osers

Sometimes we don't say anything. Sometimes. Silence. Hayden Carruth. CP-CarHS

Sometimes we rearticulate history. Henry Hudson. Robert Stock. SP-StocR

Sometimes we remember kisses. By the Spring at Sunset. Nicholas Vachel Lindsay. CP-LindV

Sometimes we see astonishingly clearly. One Circumlocution. W. H. Auden. CP-AudeW

Sometimes when I am wearied suddenly. Edna St. Vincent Millay. CP-MillE

Sometimes, when I bin bad. Uncle Sidney. James Whitcomb Riley. CP-RileJ

Sometimes when I'm lonely. Hope ("Sometimes when I'm lonely"). Langston Hughes. CP-HughL; CP-HughL2

Sometimes When Lovers Lie Quietly Together, Unexpectedly One of Them Will Feel the Other's Pulse. Hayden Carruth. CP-CarHS

Sometimes when my eyes are red. My Sad Self. Allen Ginsberg. CP-GinsA; SP-GinsA

Sometimes / when she would talk about herself. Autobiography. Jaroslav Seifert. SP-SeifJ, *tr. by* Ewald Osers

Sometimes when they shut off the faucets. Good Morning. Andrei Codrescu. SP-CodrA

Sometimes with One I Love. Walt Whitman. CP-WhitW

Sometimes with the Heart. Emily Dickinson. CP-DickE

Sometimes you almost get a punch in. Shadowboxing. James Tate. SP-TateJ

Sometimes you are liked for all the wrong. Funny. Charles Bukowski. SP-BukC3

Sometimes you become. Sometimes. Grace Paley. CP-PalGC

Sometimes you have hardly been born. Bashing the Babies. John Ciardi. CP-CiarJ

Sometimes you hear, fifth-hand. Poetry of Departures. Philip Larkin. CP-LarkP

Somewhat Delayed Spring Song. Dorothy Parker. CP-ParkD

Somewhat familiar landscape, currently flooded, A. Currently. View with a Flood. Joseph Brodsky. CP-BrodJ

Somewhat, to hope for. Emily Dickinson. CP-DickE

Somewhere. Robert Creeley. CP-CreeR

Somewhere. Yusef Komunyakaa. CP-KomuY

Somewhere. Howard Nemerov. CP-NemeH

Somewhere. John Updike. CP-UpdiJ

Somewhere. Robert Penn Warren. CP-WarrR

Somewhere / a black bear / has just risen from sleep. Spring. Mary Oliver. SP-OlivM

Somewhere a king walks in his gallery. Captives—a Psalm, The. Thomas Merton. CP-MertT

Somewhere a white wall faces a white wall. Two Walls. Robert Lowell. SP-LoweR

Somewhere afield here something lies. Shelley's Skylark. Thomas Hardy. CP-HardT

Somewhere beneath that piano's superb sleek black. Piano, The. D. H. Lawrence. CP-LawrD

Somewhere between *Amazing Grace*. Death of Chet Baker, The. Miller Williams. CP-WillM

Somewhere between bells the right angles staggered. Mangham. James Dickey. CP-DickJ

Somewhere between Greenfield and Holyoke. In the Bus. Grace Paley. CP-PalGC

Somewhere between Italian. Flamenco Vignettes. Federico García Lorca. CP-GarcF, *tr. by* Cola Franzen *and* Christopher Maurer

Somewhere beyond. Rage for Order. Derek Mahon. CP-MahoD

Somewhere Else. Richard Eberhart. CP-EberR

Somewhere Else. Yusef Komunyakaa. CP-KomuY

Somewhere i have never travelled, gladly beyond. E. E. Cummings. CP-CummE; SP-CummE

Somewhere i have never travelled, gladly beyond. Somewhere i have never travelled, gladly beyond. E. E. Cummings. CP-CummE; SP-CummE

Somewhere, I think in Dakota. Sound from the Earth, A. William Stafford. SP-StafWW

Somewhere in a Turrent. Marilyn Hacker. SP-HackM

Somewhere in Africa. Anne Sexton. CP-SextA; SP-SextA

Somewhere in everyone's head something points toward home. Shrinking Lonesome Sestina, The. Miller Williams. CP-WillM

Somewhere in France. James Laughlin. CP-LaugJ

Somewhere in or around the turn. Unicorn Defends Himself, The. Paul Muldoon. CP-MuldP

Somewhere in Russia I have heard. In Russia. Hayden Carruth. CP-CarHS

Somewhere in the hour. R.M.D. Hayden Carruth. CP-CarHS

Somewhere in the unknown world. Quilting. Lucille Clifton. SP-ClifL

Somewhere, inside the wintry colonnade. House of Caiphas, The. Thomas Merton. CP-MertT

Somewhere Is Such a Kingdom. John Crowe Ransom. SP-RansJ

Somewhere Near Phu Bai. Yusef Komunyakaa. CP-KomuY

Somewhere on his travels the strange Child. Santa Claus. Howard Nemerov. CP-NemeH

Somewhere on these bare rocks in some bare hall. For a College Yearbook. James Vincent Cunningham. CP-CunnJ

Somewhere Or Other. Christina Georgina Rossetti. CP-RosC1

Somewhere someone is traveling furiously toward you. At North Farm. John Ashbery. SP-AshbJ

Somewhere the balance shifts. See-Saw. Eleanor Wilner. SP-WilnE

Somewhere the flags are frozen. It's Not Cold Here. Eleanor Wilner. SP-WilnE

Somewhere the long mellow note of the blackbird. Study. D. H. Lawrence. CP-LawrD

Somewhere there is a dull room. Place of Kindness, A. Denise Levertov. SP-LeveDL

Somewhere / there should be an elephant. Yannis Ritsos. SP-RitsY *Fr.* So?

Somewhere this dusk. Kissing the Toad. Galway Kinnell. SP-KinnGN

Somewhere up there God has poised. Jermiah at Miminagish. William Stafford. SP-StafWW

Somewhere upon the general Earth. Emily Dickinson. CP-DickE

Somewhere, you and I remember we came. Throwbacks. Carl Sandburg. CP-SandC

Sominex. Dan Pagis. SP-PagiD, *tr. by* Stephen Mitchell

Somme toute / tout compte fait. Samuel Beckett. CP-BeckS

Somnambule Ballad. Federico García Lorca. SP-GarcF, *tr. by* J. L. Gili *and* Stephen Spender

Somnambulisma. Wallace Stevens. CP-StevW; SP-StevWP

Somnambulists along the promenade. Yánnina. James Merrill. SP-MerrJ

Somnium Narrare, Vigilantis Est. James Vincent Cunningham. CP-CunnJ

Somno compositam iacere Clytham. In Lycium et Clytham. Thomas Campion. CP-CampT

Somtyme this world was so stedfast and stable. Lak of Stedfastnesse. Geoffrey Chaucer. CP-ChauG

Son. Raymond Carver. CP-CarvR

Son. W. S. Merwin. SP-MerwWF

Son, A. Denise Levertov. SP-LeveDL

Son, The. Rita Dove. SP-DoveR

Son, The. Denise Levertov. SP-LeveDP

Son, The. Jones Very. CP-VeryJ

Son Altesse. Robert Graves. CP-GravR

Son, and my friend, I had not called you so. Epigram. To a Friend and Son. Ben Jonson. CP-JonsB

Son demands a wife, A. Shih-te. CP-ColdM, *tr. by* Red Pine

Son, I know what happened. Old Detective Begins His Last Interrogation Looking for the Truth as Always, The. Miller Williams. CP-WillM

Son of a sterile mother. Samson. Primo Levi. CP-LeviP, *tr. by* Ruth Feldman

Son of Abraham is studying to be a Jew, A. To a Convert. Yehuda Amichai. SP-AmicY, *tr. by* Chana Bloch

Son of Love and Lord of War I sing, The. Conquest, The. Lord Byron. CP-Byron

Son of Man, The. Jones Very. CP-VeryJ

Son of Man, where shall he find repose?, The. Son of Man, The. Jones Very. CP-VeryJ

Son of Mary, Jesus, hurries up a slope, The. What Jesus Runs Away From. Jelaluddin Rumi. SP-Rumi, *tr. by* Coleman Barks

Son of Melancholy, The. Walter De la Mare. CP-DeLaW

Son of my buried Son, while thus thy hand. Poet to His Grandchild; Sequel to "A Plea for Authors." William Wordsworth. CP-WorW2

Son of the dark solstice descends the tree. Christmas Crown, A. Marilyn Hacker. SP-HackM

Son of the Morning Star. D. H. Lawrence. CP-LawrD

Son of the old moon-mountains African! To the Nile. John Keats. CP-KeatJ

Son ombre une nuit. Samuel Beckett. CP-BeckS

Son, Remember. Christina Georgina Rossetti. CP-RosC2

"Son," said my mother. Ballad of the Harp-Weaver, The. Edna St. Vincent Millay. CP-MillE

Son the One who was also called Sun. Fanny Howe. SP-HoweF *Fr.* In the Spirit There Are No Accidents.

Son to Father to Son. A. K. Ramanujan. CP-RamaA

Son: "What I took in my hand." Robert Creeley. CP-CreeR

Sonata Pathétique. Theodore Weiss. SP-WeisT

Sonatina. "Rubén Dario." SP-DariR, *tr. by* Alberto Acereda *and* Will Derusha

Sonatina Followed by Another, A. Gertrude Stein. CP-SteiG

Sonatina to Hans Christian. Wallace Stevens. CP-StevW; SP-StevWP

Song: "Merging into place against a slope of trees." A. R. Ammons. CP-

AmmoA

Song: "Song tells us of our old way of living, The." John Ashbery. SP-AshbJ

Song: "I am going to have my dinner." Jane Austen. CP-AustJ

Song: "I go to Town." Jane Austen. CP-AustJ

Song: "That Damon was in love with me." Jane Austen. CP-AustJ

Song: "Though misfortunes my footsteps may ever attend." Jane Austen. CP-AustJ

Song: "When Corydon went to the fair." Jane Austen. CP-AustJ

Song: "Age is when to a man." Samuel Beckett. CP-BeckS *Fr.* Words and Music.

Song: "I tell my love in rhyme." Wendell Berry. CP-BerrW

Song: "Summer is over upon the sea." Elizabeth Bishop. CP-BishE

Song. William Blake. *See* How Sweet I Roamed [*or* Roam'd] from Field to Field

Song: "Fresh from the dewy hill, the merry year." William Blake. CP-BlakW

Song: "I love the jocund dance." William Blake. CP-BlakW

Song: "Love and harmony combine." William Blake. CP-BlakW

Song: "Memory, hither come." William Blake. CP-BlakW

Song: "My silks and fine array." William Blake. CP-BlakW

Song: "When early morn walks forth in sober grey." William Blake. CP-BlakW

Song: "It is not now I learn." Louise Bogan. CP-BogaL

Song. Emily Jane Brontë. CP-BronE

Song: "King Julius left the south country." Emily Jane Brontë. CP-BronE

Song: "Linnet in the rocky dells, The." Emily Jane Brontë. CP-BronE

Song: "O between distress and pleasure." Emily Jane Brontë. CP-BronE

Song. Robert Browning. *See* Pippa Passes

Song: "Nay but you, who do not love her." Robert Browning. CP-BroR1

Song. Robert Burns. *See* Contented wi' Little

Song. Robert Burns. *See* Rigs o' Barley, The

Song. Robert Burns. *See* Whistle, and I'll Come to You, My Lad

Song: "Adown winding Nith I did wander." Robert Burns. CP-BurnR

Song: "Again rejoicing Nature sees." Robert Burns. CP-BurnR

Song: "Anna, thy charms my bosom fire." Robert Burns. CP-BurnR

Song: "As I cam down by yon castle wa'." Robert Burns. CP-BurnR

Song: "As I stood by yon roofless tower." Robert Burns. CP-BurnR

Song: "Behind yon hills where Lugar flows." Robert Burns. CP-BurnR

Song: "Behold the hour, the boat arrive." Robert Burns. CP-BurnR

Song: "Blythe hae I been on yon hill." Robert Burns. CP-BurnR

Song: "Farewell, thou stream that winding flows." Robert Burns. CP-BurnR

Song: For A' That and A' That. Robert Burns.

Song: "From thee, ELIZA, I must go." Robert Burns. CP-BurnR

Song: "Full well thou knowest I love thee dear." Robert Burns. CP-BurnR (Fairest maid on Devon banks.) CP-BurnR

Song: "Gloomy night is gath'ring fast, The." Robert Burns. CP-BurnR

Song: "Had I a cave on some wild, distant shore." Robert Burns. CP-BurnR

Song: "I'll tell you a tale of a Wife." Robert Burns. CP-BurnR

Song: "In Mauchline there dwells six proper young Belles." Robert Burns. CP-BurnR

Song: "Let not Woman e'er complain." Robert Burns. CP-BurnR

Song: "Mark yonder pomp of costly fashion." Robert Burns. CP-BurnR

Song: "My father was a farmer upon the Carrick border O." Robert Burns. CP-BurnR

Song: "My girl she's airy, she's buxom and gay." Robert Burns. CP-BurnR

Song: "No Churchman am I for to rail and to write." Robert Burns. CP-BurnR

Song: "O once I loved [*or* lov'd] a bonnie lass." Robert Burns. CP-BurnR

Song: "O Philly, happy be that day." Robert Burns. CP-BurnR

Song: "O poortith cauld, and restless love." Robert Burns. CP-BurnR

Song: "O this is no my ain lassie." Robert Burns. CP-BurnR

Song: "O wat ye wha that lo'es me." Robert Burns. CP-BurnR (O that's the lassie o' my heart.) CP-BurnR

Song: "O wat ye wha's in yon town." Robert Burns. CP-BurnR

Song: "O, Logan, sweetly didst thou glide." Robert Burns. CP-BurnR

Song: "On Cessnock banks a lassie dwells." Robert Burns. CP-BurnR

Song: "Sensibility how charming." Robert Burns. CP-BurnR

Song: "Small birds rejoice in the green leaves returning, The." Robert Burns. CP-BurnR

Song: "Their groves o' sweet myrtle let Foreign Lands reckon." Robert Burns. CP-BurnR

Song: "Tho' women's minds, like winter winds." Robert Burns. CP-BurnR

Song: "Tibby I hae seen the day." Robert Burns. CP-BurnR

Song: "Twas na her bonie blue e'e was my ruin." Robert Burns. CP-BurnR

Song: "Will ye go to the Indies, my Mary." Robert Burns. CP-BurnR

Song: "Breeze of the night in gentler sighs." Lord Byron. CP-Byron

Song: "O sweet delight, O more than human[e] bliss[e]." Thomas Campion. CP-CampT

Song: Beautiful Mistress, A. Thomas Carew. *See* Beautiful Mistress, A

Song: Murdering Beauty. Thomas Carew. *See* Murdering Beauty

Song: The Willing Prisoner to His Mistress. Thomas Carew. CP-CareT (Willing Prisoner to His Mistress, The.) CP-CareT

Song: To Her Again[e], She Burning in a Fe[a]ver. Thomas Carew. CP-CareT (To Her Again, She Burning in a Fever.) CP-CareT

Song: Luxury. Hayden Carruth. CP-CarHS

Song: So Often, So Long I Have Thought. Hayden Carruth. CP-CarHS

Song: So Why Does This Dead Carnation. Hayden Carruth. CP-CarHS

Song: The Famous Vision of America. Hayden Carruth. CP-CarHS

Song: The Old, Old Man. Hayden Carruth. CP-CarHS

Song: The Young Man with the Guitar, Testing. Hayden Carruth. CP-CarHS

Song: "Summer burns on the edges of day." Hayden Carruth. CP-CarHS

Song: "Dying gales of sweet even." John Clare. SP-ClarR *Fr.* Child Harold.

Song: "I peeled bits of straw and I got switches too." John Clare. SP-ClarJ (I peeled bits o strews and I got switches too.) SP-ClarJ

Song: "Say What Is Love—To Live In Vain." John Clare. SP-ClarJ *Fr.* Child Harold.

Song: "Sunny shaft did I behold, A." Samuel Taylor Coleridge. CP-ColeS; MW-ColeS *Fr.* Zapolya.

Song: "Though veiled in spires of myrtle wreath." Samuel Taylor Coleridge. CP-ColeS

Song: "Here I am yours, and here, and here." Jane Cooper. CP-CoopJ

Song: "No more shall hapless Celia's ears." William Cowper. CP-CowpW

Song: "When all within is peace." William Cowper. CP-CowpW

Song: "Lord, when the sense of Thy sweet grace." Richard Crashaw. CP-CrasR

Song: "God give you pardon from gratitude." Robert Creeley. CP-CreeR

Song: "Grit / of things, The." Robert Creeley. CP-CreeR

Song: "How simply / for another." Robert Creeley. CP-CreeR

Song: "I woudn't / embarrass you." Robert Creeley. CP-CreeR

Song: "Love has no other friends." Robert Creeley. SP-CreeR

Song: "Those rivers run from that land." Robert Creeley. CP-CreeR

Song: "Were I myself more blithe." Robert Creeley. CP-CreeR

Song: "What do you / want, love. To be." Robert Creeley. CP-CreeR

Song: "You look out and you see people." Robert Creeley. CP-CreeR

Song: "But we've the may / (for you are in love)." E. E. Cummings. CP-CummE

Song: "You are as gold." H. D. CP-DoolH

Song: "Never take her away." Vinícius de Moraes. CP-WilbR, *tr.* by Richard Wilbur

Song: "Go and catch a falling star." John Donne. CP-DonnJ; MW-DonnJ

Song: "Sweetest love, I do not go[e]." John Donne. CP-DonnJ; MW-DonnJ

Song. John Dryden. *See* Indian Emperor, The

Song. John Dryden. *See* King Arthur

Song. John Dryden. *See* Spanish Friar [*or* Fryar], The

Song. John Dryden. *See* Troilus and Cressida

Song: "Albion, hail; the gods present thee." John Dryden. CP-DryJ2 *Fr.* Albion and Albanius.

Song: "Albion, loved of gods and men." John Dryden. CP-DryJ2 *Fr.* Albion and Albanius.

Song: "All hail, ye royal pair!" John Dryden. CP-DryJ2 *Fr.* Albion and Albanius.

Song: "Fair, sweet and young, receive a prize." John Dryden. SP-DrydJ

Song: "Farewell fair Arminda, my joy and my grief." John Dryden. SP-DrydJ

Song: "From the low palace of old father Ocean." John Dryden. CP-DryJ2 *Fr.* Albion and Albanius.

Song: "Go tell Amynta, gentle swain." John Dryden. CP-DryJ2; SP-DrydJ

Song: "High state and honours to others impart." John Dryden. CP-DryJ2

Song: "How happy the lover." John Dryden. SP-DrydJ *Fr.* King Arthur.

Song: "I feed a flame within, which so torments me." John Dryden. SP-DrydJ *Fr.* Secret Love; or, The Maiden Queen.

Song: "Old father Ocean calls my tide." John Dryden. CP-DryJ2; SP-DrydJ *Fr.* Albion and Albanius.

Song: "Then Zeal and Commonwealth infest." John Dryden. CP-DryJ2 *Fr.* Albion and Albanius.

Song: "Wherever I am, and whatever I do." John Dryden. SP-DrydJ *Fr.* Conquest of Granada, The.

Song: "Ye nymphs, the charge is royal." John Dryden. CP-DryJ2 *Fr.* Albion and Albanius.

Song: "You charmed [*or* charm'd] me not with that fair face." John Dryden. SP-DrydJ *Fr.* Evening's Love, An.

Song: "Bee hit sip some honey f'om de matermony vine, De." Paul Laurence Dunbar. CP-DunbP

Song: "My heart to thy heart." Paul Laurence Dunbar. CP-DunbP

Song: "Wintah, summah, snow er shine." Paul Laurence Dunbar. CP-DunbP

Song: "Shout for those whose course is done." Ralph Waldo Emerson. CP-EmerR

Song: "Weight of the world, The." Allen Ginsberg. CP-GinsA; SP-GinsA

Song: "Joyful / And woful." Johann Wolfgang von Goethe. CP-MerG2

Song: A Phoenix Flame. Robert Graves. CP-GravR

Song: Basket of Blossom. Robert Graves. CP-GravR

Song: Beyond Giving. Robert Graves. CP-GravR

Song: Cherries or Lilies. Robert Graves. CP-GravR

Song: Come, Enjoy Your Sunday! Robert Graves. CP-GravR

Song: Crown of Stars. Robert Graves. CP-GravR

Song: Dew-Drop and Diamond. Robert Graves. CP-GravR

Song: Dream Warning. Robert Graves. CP-GravR

Song: Fig Tree in Leaf. Robert Graves. CP-GravR

Song: From Otherwhere or Nowhere. Robert Graves. CP-GravR

Song: How Can I Care? Robert Graves. CP-GravR

Song: Just Friends. Robert Graves. CP-GravR

Song: Lift-Boy. Robert Graves. CP-GravR

Song: Of Course. Robert Graves. CP-GravR

Song: Olive Tree. Robert Graves. CP-GravR

Song: Once More. Robert Graves. CP-GravR

Song: Reconciliation. Robert Graves. CP-GravR

Song: Seven Fresh Years. Robert Graves. CP-GravR

Song: Sullen Moods. Robert Graves. CP-GravR

Song: Sword and Rose. Robert Graves. CP-GravR

Song: The Clocks of Time. Robert Graves. CP-GravR

Song: The Far Side of Your Moon. Robert Graves. CP-GravR

Song: The Palm Tree. Robert Graves. CP-GravR

Song: The Promise. Robert Graves. CP-GravR

Song: The Queen of Time. Robert Graves. CP-GravR

Song: The Sigil. Robert Graves. CP-GravR

Song: The Sundial's Lament. Robert Graves. CP-GravR

Song: Though Once True Lovers. Robert Graves. CP-GravR

Song: Three Rings for Her. Robert Graves. CP-GravR

Song: To a Rose. Robert Graves. CP-GravR

Song: To Become Each Other. Robert Graves. CP-GravR

Song: Twinned Heart. Robert Graves. CP-GravR

Song: Victims of Calumny. Robert Graves. CP-GravR

Song: Wherever We May Be. Robert Graves. CP-GravR

Song: Yesterday Only. Robert Graves. CP-GravR

Song: "Thyrsis, when we parted, swore." Thomas Gray. CP-GrayT

Song: "I had a girl's fancies." Ivor Gurney. SP-GurnI

Song: "O were there anything by half." Ivor Gurney. SP-GurnI

Song: "Only the wanderer." Ivor Gurney. SP-GurnI

Song: "Past my window dawn and down." Ivor Gurney. SP-GurnI

Song: "Rowan like a lip-sticked girl, A." Seamus Heaney. SP-HeanSO

Song: "Burne, or drowne me, choose ye whether." Robert Herrick. CP-HerrR

Song: "Lovely, dark, and lonely one." Langston Hughes. CP-HughL; CP-HughL1

Song: "From what dog's dish or crocodile's rotten." Ted Hughes. SP-HughTN *Fr.* Bawdry Embraced.

Song: "O lady, when the tipped cup of the moon blessed you." Ted Hughes. SP-HughTN

Song: Not There. Randall Jarrell. CP-JarrR

Song: "If I freely may discover." Ben Jonson. CP-JonsB *Fr.* Poetaster, The.

Song: "To the old, long life and treasure." Ben Jonson. CP-JonsB *Fr.* Gypsies Metamorphosed, The.

Song: "Hush, hush! tread softly! hush, hush my dear." John Keats. CP-KeatJ

Song: "I had a dove and the sweet dove died." John Keats. CP-KeatJ

Song: "Spirit here that reignest!" John Keats. CP-KeatJ

Song: "Stay, ruby-breasted warbler, stay." John Keats. CP-KeatJ

Song: "Engine screams and Murphy, isolate, The." Thomas Kinsella. CP-KinsT

Song: "O lovely lovely so lovely." James Laughlin. CP-LaugJ

Song: "Up in the high." D. H. Lawrence. CP-LawrD

Song: "Malicorn, Malicorn, Malicorn, ho!" Nathaniel Lee. CP-DryJ2 *Fr.* Duke of Guise, The.

Song: "Tell me Thirsis, tell your anguish." Nathaniel Lee. CP-DryJ2 *Fr.* Duke of Guise, The.

Song: "Night here already." Federico García Lorca. CP-GarcF, *tr. by* Jerome Rothenberg *Fr.* Backwaters.

Song: "Wild trees have bought me." Audre Lorde. SP-LordA

Song: Autumn. George Meredith. CP-MerG1

Song: Spring. George Meredith. CP-MerG1

Song: The Wren. George Meredith. CP-MerG2

Song: "Buy, buy, buy, / Is the Peace-markt cry." George Meredith. CP-MerG2

Song: "Come to me in any shape!" George Meredith. CP-MerG1

Song: "Daisy now is out upon the green, The." George Meredith. CP-MerG1

Song: "Fair and false! No dawn will greet." George Meredith. CP-MerG1

Song: "Flower unfolds its dawning cup, The." George Meredith. CP-MerG1

Song: "Forever." George Meredith. CP-MerG2

Song: "Full of thy glory am I." George Meredith. CP-MerG2

Song: "God bless the little Island!" George Meredith. CP-MerG2

Song: "I cannot lose thee for a day." George Meredith. CP-MerG1

Song: "I would be the bounding deer." George Meredith. CP-MerG2

Song: "I would I were the drop of rain." George Meredith. CP-MerG1

Song: "Love within the lover's breast." George Meredith. CP-MerG1

Song: "Might I lie where leans her lute." George Meredith. CP-MerG2

Song: "Moon is alone in the sky, The." George Meredith. CP-MerG1

Song: "My chosen bride shall bless the plough." George Meredith. CP-MerG2

Song: "My darling's love shall close me up." George Meredith. CP-MerG2

Song: "No, no, the falling blossom is no sign." George Meredith. CP-MerG1

Song: "O the wind, the wind, the wind doth blow." George Meredith. CP-MerG2

Song: "O they canna' do without it." George Meredith. CP-MerG2

Song: "Over the ferry, and over the ferry." George Meredith. CP-MerG2

Song: "Pass we to another land." George Meredith. CP-MerG2

Song: "Quick bird sings and pierces me, The." George Meredith. CP-MerG1

Song: "Should thy love die; / O bury it not under ice-blue eyes!" George Meredith. CP-MerG1

Song: "Thou steppest from thy splendour." George Meredith. CP-MerG2

Song: "Thou to me art such a spring." George Meredith. CP-MerG1

Song: "Thou tremblest O my love! thy hand in mine." George Meredith. CP-MerG2

Song: "Twelve arrows, and a bow, and spear." George Meredith. CP-MerG2

Song: "Two wedded lovers watched the rising moon." George Meredith. CP-MerG1

Song: "Under boughs of breathing May." George Meredith. CP-MerG1

Song: "When on my faithful charger." George Meredith. CP-MerG2

Song: "Who says, she is in danger." George Meredith. CP-MerG2

Song: "Woo me now & you'll win me." George Meredith. CP-MerG2

Song: Contemplation. Thomas Merton. CP-MertT

Song: If You Seek. Thomas Merton. CP-MertT

Song: In the Shows of the Round Ox. Thomas Merton. CP-MertT

Song: Sensation Time at the Home, A. Thomas Merton. CP-MertT

Song: "Bottom of the sea has come, The." Thomas Merton. CP-MertT

Song: "Come where the grieving rivers of the night." Thomas Merton. CP-MertT

Song: "When rain, (sings light) rain has devoured my house." Thomas Merton. CP-MertT

Song: on [*or* of] May Morning. John Milton. CP-MiltJ

Song: "Provide your friend with almanacs." Howard Nemerov. CP-NemeH

Song: "Is it dirty." Frank O'Hara. SP-OharF

Song: Early Death of the Mother. Gregory Orr. SP-OrrG

Song: "And shall we build a little nest." Dorothy Parker. CP-ParkD

Song: "Clarabelle has golden hair." Dorothy Parker. CP-ParkD

Song: "When all the world was younger." Dorothy Parker. CP-ParkD

Song: "When summer used to linger." Dorothy Parker. CP-ParkD

Song: "Love thou thy dream." Ezra Pound. CP-PoEar

Song: "You're wondering if I'm lonely." Adrienne Rich. SP-RicA2

Song: "O I would I had a lover!" James Whitcomb Riley. CP-RileJ

Song: "Let's pretend we are shepherds." Rainer Maria Rilke. CP-RilkFr, *tr. by* A. Poulin, Jr.

Song: "You, to whom I don't confide." Rainer Maria Rilke. CP-RilkFr, *tr. by* A. Poulin, Jr.

Song: "From whence cometh song?" Theodore Roethke. CP-RoetT

Song: "My wrath, where's the edge." Theodore Roethke. CP-RoetT

Song: "This fair parcel of summer's." Theodore Roethke. CP-RoetT

Song: "I have loved you for long long years Ellen." Christina Georgina Rossetti. CP-RosC3

Song: "I saw her; she was lovely." Christina Georgina Rossetti. CP-RosC3

Song: "It is not for her even brow." Christina Georgina Rossetti. CP-RosC3

Song: "Oh roses for the flush of youth." Christina Georgina Rossetti. CP-RosC1

Song: "Oh what comes over the sea." Christina Georgina Rossetti. CP-RosC1

Song: "She sat and sang alway." Christina Georgina Rossetti. CP-RosC1

Song: "Stream moaneth as it floweth, The." Christina Georgina Rossetti. CP-RosC3

Song: "Two doves upon the selfsame branch." Christina Georgina Rossetti. CP-RosC1

Song: "We buried her among the flowers." Christina Georgina Rossetti. CP-RosC3

Song: "When I am dead, my dearest." Christina Georgina Rossetti. CP-RosC1

Song: Love in Whose Rich Honor. Muriel Rukeyser. CP-RukeM

Song: Lying in Daylight. Muriel Rukeyser. CP-RukeM

Song: Remembering Movies. Muriel Rukeyser. CP-RukeM

Song: The Star in the Nets of Heaven. Muriel Rukeyser. CP-RukeM

Song: "Voice flew out of the river as morning flew, A." Muriel Rukeyser. CP-RukeM

Song: "World is full of loss; bring, wind, my love, The." Muriel Rukeyser. CP-RukeM

Song: "No, I will never forget you and your great eyes." May Sarton. SP-SartM

Song: "Now let us honor with violin and flute." May Sarton. SP-SartM

Song: "I'm about to go shopping." James Schuyler. CP-SchuJ

Song: "Light lies layered in the leaves, The." James Schuyler. CP-SchuJ

Song: "We wave a handkerchief." Jaroslav Seifert. SP-SeifJ, tr. by Ewald Osers

Song: "Rarely, rarely, comest thou." Percy Bysshe Shelley. CP-ShelP

Song: "Stranger, you who hide my love." Stephen Spender. CP-SpenS

Song: "Beautiful Dove, come back to us in April." Edna St. Vincent Millay. CP-MillE

Song: "Gone, gone again is Summer the lovely." Edna St. Vincent Millay. CP-MillE

Song: "Ah yes! beyond these barren walls." Wallace Stevens. CP-StevWP

Song: "Month—a year—of idle work, A." Wallace Stevens. CP-StevWP

Song: "She loves me or loves me not." Wallace Stevens. CP-StevWP

Song: "There are great things doing." Wallace Stevens. CP-StevWP

Song: "This is the house of her." Wallace Stevens. CP-StevWP

Song: "Crafty boy that had full oft assay'd, The." Sir John Suckling. CP-SuckJ

Song: "Honest lover whosoever." Sir John Suckling. CP-SuckJ

Song: "I prithee send me back my heart." Sir John Suckling. CP-SuckJ

Song: "I prithee spare me, gentle boy." Sir John Suckling. CP-SuckJ

Song: "If you refuse me once and think again." Sir John Suckling. CP-SuckJ

Song: "Unjust decrees, that do at once exact." Sir John Suckling. CP-SuckJ

Song: "When, dearest, I but think on [or of] thee." Sir John Suckling and Owen Feltham. CP-SuckJ

Song. Alfred Tennyson. See Spirit haunts the year's last hours, A

Song: "To enter the real." Charles Tomlinson. SP-TomlC

Song: I Love the Light. Jones Very. CP-VeryJ

Song: The Summer Day. Jones Very. CP-VeryJ

Song: We Have No Ship at Sea. Jones Very. CP-VeryJ

Song: Words of Love to a Parent. Jones Very. CP-VeryJ

Song: "I sought the flowers, but o'er them lay." Jones Very. CP-VeryJ

Song: "No more around the social board." Jones Very. CP-VeryJ

Song: "They sing of Zion, city built of old." Jones Very. CP-VeryJ

Song: "World is full of colored, The." Alice Walker. CP-WalkA

Song: "Girls that have loved me." Tennessee Williams. CP-WillT

Song: "Beauty is a shell." William Carlos Williams. CP-WilW2

Song: "Black-winged gull, The." William Carlos Williams. CP-WilW1

Song: "I'd rather read an account." William Carlos Williams. CP-WilW2

Song: "If I / could count the silence." William Carlos Williams. CP-WilW2

Song: "Pluck the florets from." William Carlos Williams. CP-WilW2

Song: "Russia! Russia! you might say." William Carlos Williams. CP-WilW2

Song: "You are forever April." William Carlos Williams. CP-WilW2

Song: "Life with her weary eyes." Marya Alexandrovna Zaturenska. SP-ZatuM

Song (4). Wendell Berry. CP-BerrW

Song, A. Robert Burns. See Thou Ling'ring Star

Song, A: "As at the bottom of a seething well." Richard Wilbur. CP-WilbR

Song[, A]: "Ask[e] me no more where Jove bestow[e]s." Thomas Carew. CP-CareT

Song, A: "Beneath thy skies, November!" John Greenleaf Whittier. CP-WhitJ

Song, A: "Come, let us here enjoy the shade." Ben Jonson. CP-JonsB

Song, A: "I had wanted a quiet testament." Robert Creeley. CP-CreeR

Song, A: "I thought no more was needed." William Butler Yeats. CP-YeatW

Song, A: "I wish you were here, dear." Joseph Brodsky. CP-BrodJ

Song, A: "Loose no time nor youth but be." Robert Herrick. CP-HerrR

Song, A: "Not the soft sighs of vernal gales." Samuel Johnson. CP-JohnS

Song, A: "On a summer's day as I sat by a stream." Paul Laurence Dunbar. CP-DunbP

Song, A: "On the green margin of the brook." William Cowper. CP-CowpW

Song, A: "Other world's not for me, The." Gregory Orr. SP-OrrG

Song, A: "Sparkling eye, the mantling cheek, The." William Cowper. CP-CowpW

Song, A: "Thou art the soul of a summer's day." Paul Laurence Dunbar. CP-DunbP

Song, A: "When it was day, we heard the panes of windows." Thomas Merton. CP-MertT

Song, The: "So large a morning[,] so itself[,] to lean." W. H. Auden. CP-AudeW

Song, The: "It still makes sense." Robert Creeley. CP-CreeR

Song, The: "My soul, lost in the music's mist." Paul Laurence Dunbar. CP-DunbP

Song, The. David Ignatow. SP-IgnaD

Song, The: "More than the sennet of the solstice pipe." Charles Olson. CP-OlsoC; SP-OlsoC

Song, The. George Oppen. CP-OppGN

Song, The: "I met a ragged man." Theodore Roethke. CP-RoetT

Song, The: "My time, O ye Grattans, was happily spent." Thomas Sheridan. CP-SherT

Song, The. Jones Very. CP-VeryJ

Song, a poem of itself—the word itself a dirge, A. Yonnondio. Walt Whitman. CP-WhitW

Song about a Donkey, A. Jelaluddin Rumi. SP-Rumi, tr. by Coleman Barks

Song about Girls, A. Jaroslav Seifert. SP-SeifJ, tr. by Ewald Osers

Song about Myself, A. John Keats. CP-KeatJ

Song about the happy-go-lucky fellow who hasn't time, The. I Burn Money. Ogden Nash. CP-NashO

Song after Lynching. Langston Hughes. CP-HughL; CP-HughL3

Song against Grocers, The. G. K. Chesterton. CP-ChesG

Song against Singing, A. Elizabeth Barrett Browning. CP-BroEB

Song Against Songs, The. G. K. Chesterton. CP-ChesG

Song, Altered from an Old English One. Robert Burns. See Chloe

Song and Music. Dante Gabriel Rossetti. CW-RossD

Song at Cock-Crow, A. Rudyard Kipling. CP-KiplR

Song at Midnight. Lucille Clifton. SP-ClifL

Song at Shannon's, A. Edwin Arlington Robinson. CP-RobiE

Song at Sunset. Walt Whitman. CP-WhitW

Song at the End, A. Jaroslav Seifert. SP-SeifJ, tr. by Ewald Osers

Song at the Feast of Brougham Castle upon the Restoration of Lord Clifford, the Shepherd, to the Estates and Honours of His Ancestors. William Wordsworth. CP-WorW1

Song at the Winepresses, A. Kenneth Rexroth. CP-RexrK

Song Before Breakfast. Ogden Nash. CP-NashO

Song by Comus and Three Peasants, A. John Dryden. See King Arthur

Song By J. Brenzaida To G.S. Emily Jane Brontë. CP-BronE
(Last Words.) CP-BronE

Song by Julius Angora. Emily Jane Brontë. CP-BronE

Song By Julius Brenzaida To G.S. Emily Jane Brontë. CP-BronE

Song Calls the Star Little, The. Heather McHugh. SP-McHuH

Song Composed by Mr. J. Very, to be Sung at the Class-Supper of the Sophomore Class of 1834, A. Jones Very. CP-VeryJ

Song Composed for Fanny Burney, A. Samuel Johnson. CP-JohnS

Song, Composed in August. Robert Burns. CP-BurnR

Song Contest. Geoffrey Hill. CP-HillG

Song Contest: Lalus and Dorus. Sir Philip Sidney. SP-SidnP Fr. Arcadia.

Song-Day in Autumn. D. H. Lawrence. CP-LawrD

Song Discordant. James Whitcomb Riley. CP-RileJ

Song dripping from the eaves, The. Singer, The. W. S. Merwin. SP-MerwW

Song, ex improviso. Samuel Taylor Coleridge. CP-ColeS

Song 1st By a Shepherd. William Blake. CP-BlakW

Song for a Banjo Dance. Langston Hughes. CP-HughL; CP-HughL1

Song for a Dancer. Kenneth Rexroth. CP-RexrK

Song for a Dark Girl. Langston Hughes. CP-HughL; CP-HughL1

Song for a Dark Voice. Denise Levertov. SP-LeveDP

Song for a Lady. Anne Sexton. CP-SextA; SP-SextA

Song for a Lyre. Louise Bogan. CP-BogaL

Song for a Red Nightgown. Anne Sexton. CP-SextA

Song for a Revolutionary Love. Sylvia Plath. CP-PlatS

Song for a Season. Marya Alexandrovna Zaturenska. SP-ZatuM

Song for a Slight Voice. Louise Bogan. CP-BogaL

Song for a Summer's Day. Sylvia Plath. CP-PlatS

Song for a Temperature of a Hundred and One. Ogden Nash. CP-NashO

Song for a Thin Sister. Audre Lorde. SP-LordA

Song for All Seas, All Ships. Walt Whitman. CP-WhitW

Song for an Afternoon. Charles Baudelaire. CP-BaudC, tr. by Walter Martin

Song for an Allegorical Play. John Ciardi. CP-CiarJ

Song for an April Dusk. Dorothy Parker. CP-ParkD

Song for Billie Holiday. Langston Hughes. CP-HughL; CP-HughL2

Song for Certain Congressmen. Walt Whitman. CP-WhitW

Song for Christmas, A. James Whitcomb Riley. CP-RileJ

Song for Dead Children. Muriel Rukeyser. CP-RukeM

Song for Ditherers. Ogden Nash. CP-NashO

Song for Elizabeth, A. Nicholas Vachel Lindsay. CP-LindV

Song for Happy Feast Days, A. Hart Crane. CP-CranH

Song for Ishtar. Denise Levertov. SP-LeveDP; SP-LeveDS

Song for Muriel, A. Carolyn Kizer. CP-KizeC

Song for Nobody. Thomas Merton. CP-MertT

Song—for November. James Whitcomb Riley. CP-RileJ

Song for Occupations, A. Walt Whitman. CP-WhitW

Song for Our Lady of Cobre. Thomas Merton. CP-MertT

Song for Ourselves. Langston Hughes. CP-HughL; CP-HughL1

Song for Pier Something or Other. Ogden Nash. CP-NashO

Song for St Cecilia's Day, 1687, A. John Dryden. SP-DrydJ

Song / for Sanna. Olga Broumas. SP-BrouO

Song for Seven Parts of the Body. Maxine W. Kumin. SP-KumiM

Song for Simeon, A. T. S. Eliot. CP-ElioT

Song for the Blessed Sacrament. Thomas Merton. CP-MertT

Song for the Death of Averroës. Thomas Merton. CP-MertT

Song for the First of the Month. Dorothy Parker. CP-ParkD

Song for the Last Act. Louise Bogan. CP-BogaL

Song for the Least of All Saints, A. Christina Georgina Rossetti. CP-RosC2

Song for the Middle of the Night, A. James Wright. CP-WrigJ

Song for the Moon. Federico García Lorca. CP-GarcF, tr. by Catherine Brown

Song for the Old Ones. Maya Angelou. SP-AngeM

Song for the Ragged Schools of London, A. Elizabeth Barrett Browning. CP-BroEB

Song for the Rainy Season. Elizabeth Bishop. CP-BishE

Song for the Spinning Wheel (Founded upon a Belief Prevalent among the Pastoral Vales of Westmoreland). William Wordsworth. CP-WorW1

Song for the Squeeze-Box. Theodore Roethke. CP-RoetT

Song for the Time, A. John Greenleaf Whittier. CP-WhitJ

Song for the unsung heroes who rose in the country's need, A. Unsung Heroes, The. Paul Laurence Dunbar. CP-DunbP

Song for the Wandering Jew. William Wordsworth. CP-WorW1

Song for the Women, The. Rudyard Kipling. CP-KiplR

Song for the Year's End, A. Louis Zukofsky. CP-ZukLS

Song for These Crusaders, A. Donald Davie. CP-DaviDC

Song for Those Who Know. Hans Magnus Enzensberger. SP-EnzeH, tr. by Hans Magnus Enzensberger and Michael Hamburger

Song for 2 Balalaikas on the Corner of 3rd & Market. Philip Whalen. SP-WhalP

Song for Young Lovers in a City. Edna St. Vincent Millay. CP-MillE

Song from an Intermezzo. Jaroslav Seifert. SP-SeifJ, tr. by Ewald Osers

Song from "Cleopatra." John Berryman. CP-BerrJ

Song from Heine. Thomas Hardy. CP-HardT

Song, from "Mr. Amazeen on the River." Muriel Rukeyser. CP-RukeM

Song from Puck Fair. Muriel Rukeyser. CP-RukeM

Song from "The Player Queen," A. William Butler Yeats. CP-YeatW

Song from the Wandering Jew. Percy Bysshe Shelley. CP-ShelP

Song / I'll never speak, The. Verlaine. Federico García Lorca. CP-GarcF, tr. by Alan S. Trueblood Fr. Three Portraits with Shading.

Song in a cornfield, A. Songs in a Cornfield. Christina Georgina Rossetti. CP-RosC1

Song in a Minor Key. Dorothy Parker. CP-ParkD

Song in a Year of Catastrophe. Wendell Berry. CP-BerrW

Song in Brown. Federico García Lorca. CP-GarcF, tr. by Jerome Rothenberg Fr. Fairs.

Song in July, A. Nicholas Vachel Lindsay. CP-LindV

Song in Spite of Myself. Countee Cullen. CP-CullC

Song in Storm, A. Rudyard Kipling. CP-KiplR

Song.—In the Character of a Ruined Farmer. Robert Burns. CP-BurnR

Song in the Desert, A. Rudyard Kipling. CP-KiplR

Song in the Manner of Flannery O'Connor, A. William Stafford. SP-StafW; SP-StafWW

Song in the Manner of Housman. Ezra Pound. CP-PoEar

Song in the Songless. George Meredith. CP-MerG1

Song in the Wilderness, A. Paul Celan. SP-CelaP, tr. by John Felstiner

Song in the Worst Possible Taste. Dorothy Parker. CP-ParkD

Song is a violence. Spindle. A. R. Ammons. CP-AmmoA

Song is but a little thing, A. Poet and His Song, The. Paul Laurence Dunbar. CP-DunbP

Song is to emptiness, The. Song, The. David Ignatow. SP-IgnaD

Song o' Cheer, A. James Whitcomb Riley. CP-RileJ

Song of a Camera. Thom Gunn. CP-GunnT

Song of a Contented Heart. Dorothy Parker. CP-ParkD

Song of a Hopeful Heart. Dorothy Parker. CP-ParkD

Song of a Little Death. Federico García Lorca. CP-GarcF, tr. by Greg Simon and Steven F. White

Song of a Man Who Has Come Through. D. H. Lawrence. CP-LawrD

Song of a Man Who Is Loved. D. H. Lawrence. CP-LawrD

Song of a Man Who Is Not Loved. D. H. Lawrence. CP-LawrD

Song of a nightingale sent thro' a slumbrous valley, The. Poetry of Keats, The. George Meredith. CP-MerG1

Song of a Rat. Ted Hughes. SP-HughTN

Song of a Second April. Edna St. Vincent Millay. CP-MillE

Song of Adoration. Langston Hughes. SP-HughL; CP-HughL3

Song of Albert Graeme. Sir Walter Scott. SP-ScotW Fr. Lay of the Last Minstrel, The.

Song of Americans Resident in France. Dorothy Parker. CP-ParkD

Song of an Emigré. Adam Zagajewski. SP-ZagaA, tr. by Renata Gorczynski

Song of Another Tribe, A. Muriel Rukeyser. CP-RukeM

Song of Autobiography, The. Christopher Logue. SP-LoguC

Song of Autumn. Charles Baudelaire. CP-BaudC, tr. by Walter Martin

Song of Autumn. Ivor Gurney. SP-GurnI

Song of Autumn in Springtime. "Rubén Dario." SP-DariR, tr. by Alberto Acereda and Will Derusha

Song of Bananas, A. Rudyard Kipling. CP-KiplR

Song of Blodeuwedd, The. Unknown. CP-GravR, tr. by Robert Graves

Song of canaries, The. Canary, The. Ogden Nash. CP-NashO

Song of China in Europe. Federico García Lorca. CP-GarcF, tr. by Alan S. Trueblood Fr. Songs for Children.

Song of Contrariety. Robert Graves. CP-GravR

Song of Cosmopolitan Courage, A. G. K. Chesterton. CP-ChesG

Song of Courtesy, The. George Meredith. CP-MerG1

Song of Death. D. H. Lawrence. CP-LawrD

Song of Defeat, A. G. K. Chesterton. CP-ChesG

Song of Degrees, A. Howard Nemerov. CP-NemeH

Song of Departing Day. Federico García Lorca. CP-GarcF, tr. by Alan S. Trueblood Fr. Songs to End With.

Song of Despair. Federico García Lorca. CP-GarcF, tr. by Christopher Maurer

Song of Diego Valdez, The. Rudyard Kipling. CP-KiplR

Song of Don Ramon, The. D. H. Lawrence. CP-LawrD

Song of Drab, The. George Meredith. CP-MerG2

Song of Fixed Accord. Wallace Stevens. CP-StevW; CP-StevWP

Song of Flight, A. Christina Georgina Rossetti. CP-RosC2

Song of Four Faeries. John Keats. CP-KeatJ

Song of French Roads, A. Rudyard Kipling. CP-KiplR

Song of Harvest, A. John Greenleaf Whittier. CP-WhitJ

Song of Hiawatha, The. Henry Wadsworth Longfellow.
Hiawatha's Childhood. SP-LongH
Hiawatha's Fasting. SP-LongH

Song of Hope. Thomas Hardy. CP-HardT

Song of Invisible Boundaries. Louise Glück. SP-GlucL Fr. Marathon.

Song of Joys, A. Walt Whitman. CP-WhitW

Song of Kabir, A. Rudyard Kipling. CP-KiplR Fr. Second Jungle Book, The.

Song of Labour, The. G. K. Chesterton. CP-ChesG

Song of Lies on Sabbath Eve, A. Yehuda Amichai. SP-AmicY, tr. by Chana Bloch

Song of Los, The. William Blake. CP-BlakW

Song of Man Chipping an Arrowhead. W. S. Merwin. SP-MerwW

Song of Mercy and Judgment, A. William Cowper. CP-CowpW

Song of Myself. Walt Whitman. CP-WhitW

Song of Natural Capital, The. Christopher Logue. SP-LoguC Fr. Lily-White Boys, The.

Song of Nature. Ralph Waldo Emerson. CP-EmerR

Song of November and April. Federico García Lorca. CP-GarcF, tr. by Alan S. Trueblood Fr. Songs to End With.

Song of One of the Girls. Dorothy Parker. CP-ParkD

Song of Parting. James Whitcomb Riley. CP-RileJ

Song of Paternal Care, A. John Updike. CP-UpdiJ

Song of Perfect Propriety. Dorothy Parker. CP-ParkD

Song of Praise. Countee Cullen. CP-CullC

Song of Praise, A. Countee Cullen. CP-CullC

Song of Proserpine. Percy Bysshe Shelley. CP-ShelP

Song of Prudence. Walt Whitman. CP-WhitW

Song of Purification. Carlos Drummond de Andrade. CP-MertT

Song of Reasons. Robert Pinsky. CP-PinsR

Song of Right and Wrong, The. G. K. Chesterton. CP-ChesG

Song of Ruark to Bhanavar the Beautiful. George Meredith. CP-MerG2

Song of Saul before His Last Battle. Lord Byron. CP-Byron

Song of Self-Esteem, A. G. K. Chesterton. CP-ChesG

Song of Seven Cities, The. Rudyard Kipling. CP-KiplR

Song of Seventy Horses. Rudyard Kipling. CP-KiplR

Song of Seyd [or Seid] Nimetollah of Kuhistan. Seid Nimatullah. CP-EmerR, tr. by Ralph Waldo Emerson

Song of Singing, A. James Whitcomb Riley. CP-RileJ

Song of Slaves in the Desert. John Greenleaf Whittier. CP-WhitJ

Song of Social Life in Hollywood. Dorothy Parker. CP-ParkD

Song of Songs. Wilfred Owen. CP-OwenW

Song of Songs, The. G. K. Chesterton. CP-ChesG

Song of Sour Grapes, A. Countee Cullen. CP-CullC

Song of Spain. Langston Hughes. CP-HughL; CP-HughL1

Song of Summer. Paul Laurence Dunbar. CP-DunbP

Song of Swords, A. G. K. Chesterton. CP-ChesG

Song of Taliesin. Taliesin. CP-EmerR

Song of the Aged Mother which shook the heavens with wrath, The. Vala; or The Four Zoas. William Blake. CP-BlakW

Song of the Answerer. Walt Whitman. CP-WhitW

Song of the Banjo, The. Rudyard Kipling. CP-KiplR

Song of the Banner at Daybreak. Walt Whitman. CP-WhitW

Song of the Barren Orange Tree. Federico García Lorca. SP-GarcF, *tr. by* W. S. Merwin

Song of the Borderguard, The. Robert Duncan. SP-DuncR

Song of the Bower, The. Dante Gabriel Rossetti. CW-RossD

Song of the Bowmen of Shu. Ezra Pound. SP-PounE

Song of the Bridegroom, The. John Berryman. CP-BerrJ

Song of the Broad-Axe [*or* Broad-Ax]. Walt Whitman. CP-WhitW

Song of the Bullet. James Whitcomb Riley. CP-RileJ

Song of the Children, The. G. K. Chesterton. CP-ChesG

Song of the Cities, The. Rudyard Kipling. CP-KiplR

Song of the Conspirators. G. K. Chesterton. CP-ChesG

Song of the Conventions. Dorothy Parker. CP-ParkD

Song of the Cradle, The. G. K. Chesterton. CP-ChesG

Song of the Cruise, A. James Whitcomb Riley. CP-RileJ

Song of the Dead. D. H. Lawrence. CP-LawrD

Song of the Dead Girls. Gabriela Mistral. SP-MistG, *tr. by* Maria Giachetti [*or* Jacketti]

Song of the Dead Orange Tree. Federico García Lorca. CP-GarcF, *tr. by* Alan S. Trueblood *Fr.* Songs to End With.

Song of the Dead Soldier, The. Christopher Logue. SP-LoguC

Song of the Dead, The. Rudyard Kipling. CP-KiplR

Song of the degrees, A. Except the Lord Build the House. Donald Davie. CP-DaviDC

Song of the Degrees, A. Ezra Pound. SP-PounE

Song of the Demented Priest, The. John Berryman. CP-BerrJ

Song of the Dog Quoodle, The. G. K. Chesterton. CP-ChesG

Song of the Dynamo. Rudyard Kipling. CP-KiplR

Song of the Early Spring. Jones Very. CP-VeryJ

Song of the English, A. Rudyard Kipling. CP-KiplR

Song of the Exposition. Walt Whitman. CP-WhitW

Song of the Fairy. Federico García Lorca. CP-GarcF, *tr. by* Alan S. Trueblood *Fr.* Games.

Song of the Fifth River. Rudyard Kipling. CP-KiplR *Fr.* Puck of Pook's Hill.

Song of the Foolish Bees. Martinus Nijhoff. CP-RicAE

Song of the Forsaken Lilac Tree. Marya Alexandrovna Zaturenska. SP-ZatuM

Song of the Fucked Duck. Marge Piercy. SP-PierM

Song of the Galley-Slaves. Rudyard Kipling. CP-KiplR

Song of the Garden-Toad, The. Nicholas Vachel Lindsay. CP-LindV

Song of the GIs & the MGs. James Laughlin. CP-LaugJ

Song of the Great Sea Serpent, The. G. K. Chesterton. CP-ChesG

Song of the Grey Dog, The. D. H. Lawrence. CP-LawrD

Song of the Happy Shepherd, The. William Butler Yeats. CP-YeatW

Song of the Imperial Carrion, The. Christopher Logue. SP-LoguC

Song of the Invisible Corpse in the Field. Gregory Orr. SP-OrrG

Song of the Lathes, The. Rudyard Kipling. CP-KiplR

Song of the Little Hunter, The. Rudyard Kipling. CP-KiplR *Fr.* Second Jungle Book, The.

Song of the Man Forsaken and Obsessed. John Berryman. CP-BerrJ

Song of the Men's Side. Rudyard Kipling. CP-KiplR

Song of the Moon, A. Ben Jonson. CP-JonsB

Song of the Motionless Gardener. Federico García Lorca. CP-GarcF, *tr. by* Jerome Rothenberg *Fr.* In the Garden of the Lunar Grapefruits.

Song of the Native Land. Jaroslav Seifert. SP-SeifJ, *tr. by* Ewald Osers

Song of the New Year. James Whitcomb Riley. CP-RileJ

Song of the New Zealander among the Ruins of Old London. George Meredith. CP-MerG2

Song of the Night. Thomas Kinsella. CP-KinsT

Song of the Nightingale, The. Jaroslav Seifert. SP-SeifJ, *tr. by* Ewald Osers

Song of the Oak, The. G. K. Chesterton. CP-ChesG

Song of the Old Guard, The. Rudyard Kipling. CP-KiplR

Song of the Old Mother, The. William Butler Yeats. CP-YeatW

Song of the Open Country. Dorothy Parker. CP-ParkD

Song of the Open Fireplace. John Updike. CP-UpdiJ

Song of the Open Road. Walt Whitman. CP-WhitW

Song of the Open Road. Ogden Nash. CP-NashO

Song of the Outsider, The. Christopher Logue. SP-LoguC

Song of the Red War-Boat. Rudyard Kipling. CP-KiplR

Song of the Redwood-Tree. Walt Whitman. CP-WhitW

Song of the Refugee Road. Langston Hughes. CP-HughL; CP-HughL3

Song of the Revolution. Langston Hughes. CP-HughL; CP-HughL1

Song of the Rider (1860). Federico García Lorca. SP-GarcF, *tr. by* J. L. Gili *and* Stephen Spender

Song of the Road, A. James Whitcomb Riley. CP-RileJ

Song of the Rolling Earth, A. Walt Whitman. CP-WhitW

Song of the Rose. Sappho. CP-BroEB

Song of the Round Man. Michael Palmer. SP-PalmM

Song of the screech owls, when a rainbow, The. In Sleep. Eugenio Montale. CP-

MontE, *tr. by* Jonathan Galassi

Song of the Sea-Wealth, The. G. K. Chesterton. CP-ChesG

Song of the Seven-Hearted Boy. Federico García Lorca. CP-GarcF, *tr. by* Jerome Rothenberg *Fr.* In the Garden of the Lunar Grapefruits.

Song of the Seven Maidens. Federico García Lorca. CP-GarcF, *tr. by* Alan S. Trueblood *Fr.* Theories.

Song of the Shop Boy. Federico García Lorca. CP-GarcF, *tr. by* Catherine Brown

Song of the Slip. Gary Snyder. CP-SnydG

Song of the Soldiers' Wives and Sweethearts. Thomas Hardy. CP-HardT

Song of the Sons, The. Rudyard Kipling. CP-KiplR

Song of the sorrow of Melisande is a weary song and a dreary song, The. Song Against Songs, The. G. K. Chesterton. CP-ChesG

Song of the Star, The. Christina Georgina Rossetti. CP-RosC3

Song of the Strange Ascetic, The. G. K. Chesterton. CP-ChesG

Song of the Sturdy Snails, The. Nicholas Vachel Lindsay. CP-LindV

Song of the Sweepings. Jaroslav Seifert. SP-SeifJ, *tr. by* Ewald Osers

Song of the Tangle. Gary Snyder. CP-SnydG

Song of the Taste. Gary Snyder. CP-SnydG

Song of the Tortured Girl, The. John Berryman. CP-BerrJ

Song of the Traveller, The. Thomas Merton. CP-MertT

Song of the Two Crows. Hayden Carruth. CP-CarHS

Song of the Universal. Walt Whitman. CP-WhitW

Song of the Vermonters, 1779, The. John Greenleaf Whittier. CP-WhitJ

Song of the Virgin Mother, A. Félix Lope de Vega Carpio. CP-PoEar, *tr. by* Ezra Pound

Song of the Wheel, The. G. K. Chesterton. CP-ChesG

Song of the Wheels, The. G. K. Chesterton. CP-ChesG

Song of the White Men, A. Rudyard Kipling. CP-KiplR

Song of the Wildnerness. Dorothy Parker. CP-ParkD

Song of the Wind, The. Aleksandr Aleksandrovich Blok. SP-BlokA, *tr. by* Peter France *and* Jon Stallworthy

Song of the Wise Children. Rudyard Kipling. CP-KiplR

Song of the Young Hawaiian, The. John Berryman. CP-BerrJ

Song of Theodolinda, The. George Meredith. CP-MerG1

Song of Those Who Died in Vain. Primo Levi. CP-LeviP, *tr. by* Ruth Feldman

Song of Travel, A. Rudyard Kipling. CP-KiplR

Song of Venus. John Dryden. SP-DrydJ *Fr.* King Arthur.

Song Of Wandering Aengus, The. William Butler Yeats. CP-YeatW

Song of Welcome. Joseph Brodsky. CP-BrodJ

Song of Welcome to King Charles, A. Ben Jonson. CP-JonsB

Song of Wild Fruit, A. G. K. Chesterton. CP-ChesG

Song of Yesterday, The. James Whitcomb Riley. CP-RileJ

Song—(On Chloris Being Ill). Robert Burns. CP-BurnR

Song. On Miss P—— K——, A. Robert Burns. CP-BurnR

Song. On Miss W. A. Robert Burns. CP-BurnR

Song on Peace. William Cowper. CP-CowpW

Song on Porcelain. Czeslaw Milosz. CP-MiloC; CP-MiloCN, *tr. by* Robert Pinsky

Song on the Dread of a Chill Spring. John Logan. CP-LogaJ

Song (1). Wendell Berry. CP-BerrW

Song 2nd By a Young Shepherd. William Blake. CP-BlakW

Song / sparrow puts all his, The. Glass. A. R. Ammons. CP-AmmoA

Song Sparrow Singing in the Fall, A. Wendell Berry. CP-BerrW

Song sparrow's limited creativity. To the Poets. Howard Nemerov. CP-NemeH

Song Stanzas of Private Luck; To Be Added Sometimes and Sometimes to Be Subtracted from as Events Prove One More Wrong than Right. Grace Paley. CP-PalGC

Song. Summer. Rita Dove. SP-DoveR

Song Sung. Federico García Lorca. CP-GarcF, *tr. by* Alan S. Trueblood *Fr.* Songs for Children.

Song Sung, A. Federico García Lorca. SP-GarcF *Fr.* Songs of Childhood.

Song tells us of our old way of living, The. Song: "Song tells us of our old way of living, The." John Ashbery. SP-AshbJ

Song That Sounds like This, The. James Fenton. SP-FentJ

Song. That Women Are But Men's Shadows. Ben Jonson. CP-JonsB; SP-JonsB

Song, the Brain-Coral. Muriel Rukeyser. CP-RukeM

Song, The: "Earth flows away from the shore where I stand." Czeslaw Milosz. CP-MiloC; CP-MiloCN

Song, the Winds of Downhill. George Oppen. CP-OppGN

Song Thief, The. Yusef Komunyakaa. CP-KomuY

Song 3rd By an Old Shepherd. William Blake. CP-BlakW

Song (3). Wendell Berry. CP-BerrW

Song-Throe, The. Dante Gabriel Rossetti. CW-RossD *Fr.* House of Life, The.

Song to A.A. Emily Jane Brontë. CP-BronE

Song to a Fair Young Lady, Going Out of the Town in the Spring. John Dryden. SP-DrydJ

Song to a Negro Wash-woman, A. Langston Hughes. CP-HughL; CP-HughL1

Song to an Old Burden. Thomas Hardy. CP-HardT

Song to an Old Tune. G. K. Chesterton. CP-ChesG

Song to Aurore. Thomas Hardy. CP-HardT

Song to Be Sung by the Father of Infant Female Children. Ogden Nash. CP-NashO

Song to Begin *Rohatsu*. Philip Whalen. SP-WhalP

Song. To Celia ("Come my Celia, let us prove"). Ben Jonson. CP-JonsB; SP-JonsB, *tr. by* Ben Jonson *Fr.* Volpone.

Song. To Celia ("Drink to me only with thine eyes"). Ben Jonson. CP-JonsB; SP-JonsB

Song to David, A. Christopher Smart. SP-SmarC

Song to Mithras, A. Rudyard Kipling. CP-KiplR *Fr.* Puck of Pook's Hill.

Song to No Music, A. Joseph Brodsky. CP-BrodJ, *tr. by* David Rigsbee

Song to the Maskers, A. Robert Herrick. CP-HerrR

Song to the Men of England. Percy Bysshe Shelley. CP-ShelP

Song to the Suliotes. Lord Byron. CP-Byron

Song to the Tune of *La Cucaracha*. D. H. Lawrence. CP-LawrD

Song (2). Wendell Berry. CP-BerrW

Song under Tears. Federico García Lorca. CP-GarcF, *tr. by* Jerome Rothenberg *Fr.* Moments of Song.

Song upon Silvia, A. Robert Herrick. CP-HerrR

Song with Movement. Federico García Lorca. CP-GarcF, *tr. by* Alan S. Trueblood *Fr.* Theories.

Song with Reflections. Federico García Lorca. CP-GarcF, *tr. by* Jerome Rothenberg *Fr.* Moments of Song.

Song would like to be light. Federico García Lorca. CP-GarcF, *tr. by* Alan S. Trueblood *Fr.* Theories.

Songbird, The. James Laughlin. CP-LaugJ

Songbook of Sebastian Arrurruz, The. Geoffrey Hill. CP-HillG

Songe d'Athalie. Stevie Smith. CP-SmitS

Songe Made by Sir Walter Rawley, A. *Unknown, sometimes at. to* Sir Walter Ralegh. CP-RaleW

Songless. Alice Walker. CP-WalkA

Songs. Paul Laurence Dunbar. CP-DunbP

Songs. Langston Hughes. CP-HughL; CP-HughL2

Songs. Thomas Merton. CP-MertT

Songs About What Comes Down: The Complete Works of Mr. Septic Tanck. Hayden Carruth.

    Tanck's Brag. CP-CarHS

    Tanck's Epilogue. CP-CarHS

    Tanck's Prolegomenon. CP-CarHS

    Tanck's Song About Brains. CP-CarHS

    Tanck's Song About Dying Young. CP-CarHS

    Tanck's Song About Earl Hines. CP-CarHS

    Tanck's Song About Fear of Falling. CP-CarHS

    Tanck's Song About His Birthday. CP-CarHS

    Tanck's Song About His Unicameral Mind. CP-CarHS

    Tanck's Song About November. CP-CarHS

    Tanck's Song About Pride. CP-CarHS

    Tanck's Song About Silence. CP-CarHS

    Tanck's Song About Survival. CP-CarHS

    Tanck's Song About the Jinx. CP-CarHS

    Tanck's Song About the Transportation Business. CP-CarHS

    Tanck's Song About the Younger Generation. CP-CarHS

    Tanck's Song About Women. CP-CarHS

    Tanck's Song About Youth and Age. CP-CarHS

Songs Come to the Mind. Ivor Gurney. SP-GurnI

Songs for a Colored Singer. Elizabeth Bishop. CP-BishE

Songs for Children. Federico García Lorca.

    Landscape ("By mistake the evening"). CP-GarcF, *tr. by* Alan S. Trueblood

    "Mr. Lizard is crying." CP-GarcF, *tr. by* Alan S. Trueblood

    Seashell. CP-GarcF, *tr. by* Alan S. Trueblood

    Sevillian Ditty. CP-GarcF, *tr. by* Alan S. Trueblood

    Silly Song. CP-GarcF, *tr. by* Alan S. Trueblood

    Song of China in Europe. CP-GarcF, *tr. by* Alan S. Trueblood

    Song Sung. CP-GarcF, *tr. by* Alan S. Trueblood

Songs for Eve. Archibald MacLeish. CP-MacLA

Songs for Marie's Lutebook. Kenneth Rexroth. CP-RexrK

Songs for My Father. Yusef Komunyakaa. CP-KomuY

Songs for the City. G. K. Chesterton. CP-ChesG

Songs from Cyprus. "H. D." CP-DoolH

Songs from Shakespeare, in Latin and Greek. Gerard Manley Hopkins. CP-HopkG

Songs I had are withered, The. Ivor Gurney. SP-GurnI

Songs I Learnt at School. D. H. Lawrence. CP-LawrD

Songs in a Cornfield. Christina Georgina Rossetti. CP-RosC1

Songs in Absence. Arthur Hugh Clough.

(Mari Magno II.) SP-ClouA

Songs in the Distance. Raymond Carver. CP-CarvR

Songs of a Life-Time—with the Singer's head. James Whitcomb Riley. CP-RileJ

Songs of Adrian Zieliński. Czeslaw Milosz. CP-MiloC; CP-MiloCN, *tr. by* Renata Gorczynski *and* Robert Hass

Songs of Childhood. Federico García Lorca.

    Snail. SP-GarcF

    Song Sung, A. SP-GarcF

Songs of continuity, land mines and graves. Yehuda Amichai. SP-AmicY, *tr. by* Chana Bloch

Songs of Degrees. Louis Zukofsky. CP-ZukLS

Songs of Experience. William Blake.

    Ah, Sun-Flower [*or* Ah! Sun-Flower]. CP-BlakW

    Angel, The. CP-BlakW

    Chimney Sweeper, The. CP-BlakW

    Clod and the Pebble, The. CP-BlakW

    Earth's Answer. CP-BlakW

    Garden of Love, The. CP-BlakW

    Holy Thursday [2]. CP-BlakW

    Human Abstract, The. CP-BlakW

    Infant Sorrow. CP-BlakW

    Introduction: "Hear the voice of the Bard!." CP-BlakW

    Lily, The. CP-BlakW

    Little Boy Lost, A. CP-BlakW

    Little Fly. CP-BlakW

    (Fly, The.) CP-BlakW

    ("Woe alas my guilty hand.") CP-BlakW

    Little Girl Found, The. CP-BlakW

    Little Girl Lost, A. CP-BlakW

    Little Girl Lost, The. CP-BlakW

    Little Vagabond, The. CP-BlakW

    London. CP-BlakW

    My Pretty Rose-Tree. CP-BlakW

    Nurse's Song. CP-BlakW

    Poison Tree, A. CP-BlakW

    (Christian Forbearance.) CP-BlakW

    School-Boy, The. CP-BlakW

    Sick Rose, The. CP-BlakW

    To Tirzah. CP-BlakW

    Tyger [*or* Tiger], The. CP-BlakW

    Voice of the Ancient Bard, The. CP-BlakW

Songs of Experience; India, One. Thomas Merton. CP-MertT

Songs of Innocence. William Blake. CP-BlakW

    Little Girl Found, The. CP-BlakW

    Little Girl Lost, The. CP-BlakW

Songs of Praise. Derek Mahon. CP-MahoD

Songs of small birds fade away, The. Sorrel Filly, The. Wendell Berry. CP-BerrW

Songs of the Pixies. Samuel Taylor Coleridge. CP-ColeS; MW-ColeS

Songs of the Psyche. Thomas Kinsella. CP-KinsT

Songs of the Riverbank. Federico García Lorca. CP-GarcF, *tr. by* Alan S. Trueblood *Fr.* Games.

Songs of the Transformed. Margaret Atwood. SP-AtwM1

Songs of Zion the Beautiful. Yehuda Amichai.

    "All these stones, all this sorrow, all this." SP-AmicY, *tr. by* Chana Bloch

    "Armenian funeral on Mount Zion: the coffin, An." SP-AmicY, *tr. by* Chana Bloch

    "Because of the will of the night, I left the land." SP-AmicY, *tr. by* Chana Bloch

    "City where I was born was destroyed by gunfire, The." SP-AmicY, *tr. by* Chana Bloch

    "Even my loves are measured by wars." SP-AmicY, *tr. by* Chana Bloch

    "Every evening God takes his glittery merchandise." SP-AmicY, *tr. by* Chana Bloch

    "Four synagogues are entrenched together." SP-AmicY, *tr. by* Chana Bloch

    "Graves in Jerusalem are the openings, The." SP-AmicY, *tr. by* Chana Bloch

    "I have nothing to say about the war, nothing." SP-AmicY, *tr. by* Chana Bloch

    "In the lot through which lovers took a short-cut." SP-AmicY, *tr. by* Chana Bloch

    "In the summer whole peoples visit one another." SP-AmicY, *tr. by* Chana Bloch

    "I've closed myself up, now I'm like." SP-AmicY, *tr. by* Chana Bloch

    "Jerusalem's a place where everyone remembers." SP-AmicY, *tr. by* Chana Bloch

    "Let the memorial hill remember instead of me." SP-AmicY, *tr. by* Chana Bloch

    "Nineteen years this city was divided." SP-AmicY, *tr. by* Chana Bloch

"October sun warms our faces, The." SP-AmicY, *tr. by* Chana Bloch

"On the last words of Trumpeldor." SP-AmicY, *tr. by* Chana Bloch

"Our baby was weaned during the first days." SP-AmicY, *tr. by* Chana Bloch

"People travel a long distance to be able to say: this reminds me." SP-AmicY, *tr. by* Chana Bloch

"This is the end of the landscape. Among blocks." SP-AmicY, *tr. by* Chana Bloch

"Toys of an only God, The." SP-AmicY, *tr. by* Chana Bloch

"War broke out in the fall, at the empty border." SP-AmicY, *tr. by* Chana Bloch

"What did the man who burned to death." SP-AmicY, *tr. by* Chana Bloch

Songs that break. Gypsy Melodies. Langston Hughes. CP-HughL; CP-HughL2

Songs to End With. Federico García Lorca.

    Cheating Mirror, The. CP-GarcF, *tr. by* Alan S. Trueblood

    In Another Manner. CP-GarcF, *tr. by* Alan S. Trueblood

    Orchard, March. CP-GarcF, *tr. by* Alan S. Trueblood

    Song of Departing Day. CP-GarcF, *tr. by* Alan S. Trueblood

    Song of November and April. CP-GarcF, *tr. by* Alan S. Trueblood

    Song of the Dead Orange Tree. CP-GarcF, *tr. by* Alan S. Trueblood

    Straining Toward Statue. CP-GarcF, *tr. by* Alan S. Trueblood

    Two Sailors Ashore. CP-GarcF, *tr. by* Alan S. Trueblood

    Useless Song. CP-GarcF, *tr. by* Alan S. Trueblood

    "Whither bound, water?" CP-GarcF, *tr. by* Alan S. Trueblood

Songs to the Dark Virgin. Langston Hughes. CP-HughL; CP-HughL1

Songs Tuneless. James Whitcomb Riley. CP-RileJ

Songs We Know Best, The. John Ashbery. SP-AshbJ

Songster, The. Stevie Smith. CP-SmitS

Sonic Boom. John Updike. CP-UpdiJ

"Sonja Hernie," the young girl. Preface. Theodore Weiss. SP-WeisT

Son[ne], The. George Herbert. CP-HerbG

Sonnet. Sam Hamill. SP-HamiS

Sonnet: [From the Italian of Dante.] Dante Alighieri to Guido Cavalcanti. Dante Alighieri.

Sonnet: He imagines a pleasant Voyage for Guido, Lapo Gianni, and himself, with their three Ladies. Dante Alighieri. CW-RossD, *tr. by* Dante Gabriel Rossetti

Sonnet: He rebukes Cino for Fickleness. Dante Alighieri. CW-RossD, *tr. by* Dante Gabriel Rossetti

Sonnet: Of Beatrice de' Portinari, on All Saints' Day. Dante Alighieri. CW-RossD, *tr. by* Dante Gabriel Rossetti

Sonnet: Of Beauty and Duty. Dante Alighieri. CW-RossD, *tr. by* Dante Gabriel Rossetti

Sonnet: On the 9th of June 1290. Dante Alighieri. CW-RossD, *tr. by* Dante Gabriel Rossetti

Sonnet: To certain Ladies; when Beatrice was lamenting her Father's Death. Dante Alighieri. CW-RossD, *tr. by* Dante Gabriel Rossetti

Sonnet: To the Lady Pietra degli Scrovigni. Dante Alighieri. CW-RossD, *tr. by* Dante Gabriel Rossetti

Sonnet: To the same Ladies; with their Answer. Dante Alighieri. CW-RossD, *tr. by* Dante Gabriel Rossetti

Sonnet: Written in Exile. Dante Alighieri. CW-RossD, *tr. by* Dante Gabriel Rossetti

Sonnet: "Each servant stamps the reader with a look." John Ashbery. SP-AshbJ

Sonnet: "My dream a drink with Lonnie Johnson we discuss the code." Ted Berrigan. SP-BerrT *Fr.* Sonnets, The.

Sonnet: "Caught—the bubble." Elizabeth Bishop. CP-BishE

Sonnet: "I am in need of music that would flow." Elizabeth Bishop. CP-BishE

Sonnet: "Dark, underground, is furnished with the bone." Louise Bogan. CP-BogaL

Sonnet: "Since you would claim the sources of my thought." Louise Bogan. CP-BogaL

Sonnet: "Eyes, calm beside thee, (Lady couldst thou know!)." Robert Browning. CP-BroR2

Sonnet: Sin. Hayden Carruth. CP-CarHS *Fr.* Sonnets.

Sonnet: The Recollected Actual Voices of Romanticism. Hayden Carruth. CP-CarHS *Fr.* Sonnets.

Sonnet: "All revolutions in modern times have led." Hayden Carruth. CP-CarHS *Fr.* Sonnets.

Sonnet: "At the hospital where I had the echocardiagram." Hayden Carruth. CP-CarHS *Fr.* Sonnets.

Sonnet: "Bo was three when we slugged through Arizona, The." Hayden Carruth. CP-CarHS *Fr.* Sonnets.

Sonnet: "But still, still . . . / In stillness mystery calls." Hayden Carruth. CP-CarHS *Fr.* Sonnets.

Sonnet: "Cindy, I've used my writing all my life." Hayden Carruth. CP-CarHS *Fr.* Sonnets.

Sonnet: "Cindy, the secret's out. Yes, you're addict-." Hayden Carruth. CP-CarHS *Fr.* Sonnets.

Sonnet: "Dearest, I never knew such loving. There." Hayden Carruth. CP-CarHS

Fr. Sonnets.

Sonnet: "Fear of falling is why the old men walk." Hayden Carruth. CP-CarHS *Fr.* Sonnets.

Sonnet: "Freedom in love? It has been questioned. Think." Hayden Carruth. CP-CarHS *Fr.* Sonnets.

Sonnet: "From our very high window at the Sheraton." Hayden Carruth. CP-CarHS *Fr.* Sonnets.

Sonnet: "Honey, darling, baby . . . but no endearments." Hayden Carruth. CP-CarHS *Fr.* Sonnets.

Sonnet: "How is it, tell me, that this new self can be—." Hayden Carruth. CP-CarHS *Fr.* Sonnets.

Sonnet: "Hubbub of the Hall of Languages, our Babel, The." Hayden Carruth. CP-CarHS *Fr.* Sonnets.

Sonnet: "I think continually of the differences." Hayden Carruth. CP-CarHS *Fr.* Sonnets.

Sonnet: "I want to do a complaint now. Which is to say." Hayden Carruth. CP-CarHS *Fr.* Sonnets.

Sonnet: "If I die today, which statistically speaking." Hayden Carruth. CP-CarHS *Fr.* Sonnets.

Sonnet: "If you see a child that shivers when it hears." Hayden Carruth. CP-CarHS *Fr.* Sonnets.

Sonnet: "In the mind of the kiss occurs a thought so rich." Hayden Carruth. CP-CarHS *Fr.* Sonnets.

Sonnet: "It's said by the thoughtful masters that to know death." Hayden Carruth. CP-CarHS *Fr.* Sonnets.

Sonnet: "Key-reist, I am fed and sick unto death with this." Hayden Carruth. CP-CarHS *Fr.* Sonnets.

Sonnet: "Last night, I don't know if from habit or intent." Hayden Carruth. CP-CarHS *Fr.* Sonnets.

Sonnet: "Like the magnificent stationary animal it is." Hayden Carruth. CP-CarHS *Fr.* Sonnets.

Sonnet: "Loving mind in this death-haunted body, The." Hayden Carruth. CP-CarHS *Fr.* Sonnets.

Sonnet: "Most brainy woman, the sexuality of your thought." Hayden Carruth. CP-CarHS *Fr.* Sonnets.

Sonnet: "Must genius always struggle, always exaggerate." Hayden Carruth. CP-CarHS *Fr.* Sonnets.

Sonnet: "O Jesus, thou who sittest up there on the right." Hayden Carruth. CP-CarHS *Fr.* Sonnets.

Sonnet: "Persistent is the thought for me of that." Hayden Carruth. CP-CarHS *Fr.* Sonnets.

Sonnet: "Poor little book, *The Sleeping Beauty* died." Hayden Carruth. CP-CarHS *Fr.* Sonnets.

Sonnet: "This is our perfect silver maple's day." Hayden Carruth. CP-CarHS *Fr.* Sonnets.

Sonnet: "Thy sting sufficeth, Death. If Heidegger first." Hayden Carruth. CP-CarHS *Fr.* Sonnets.

Sonnet: "To have been Diogenes. Why not? Or de Sade." Hayden Carruth. CP-CarHS *Fr.* Sonnets.

Sonnet: "To rebel is suitable philosophical tactics." Hayden Carruth. CP-CarHS *Fr.* Sonnets.

Sonnet: "To rebel. So I have saved my life, not once." Hayden Carruth. CP-CarHS *Fr.* Sonnets.

Sonnet: "To see a woman long oppressed by fear." Hayden Carruth. CP-CarHS *Fr.* Sonnets.

Sonnet: "To the aged, trembling, illiterate woman yesterday." Hayden Carruth. CP-CarHS *Fr.* Sonnets.

Sonnet: "Was Yahweh chosen by the chosen people?" Hayden Carruth. CP-CarHS *Fr.* Sonnets.

Sonnet: "Well, Jim says that the couplet at the end." Hayden Carruth. CP-CarHS *Fr.* Sonnets.

Sonnet: "Well, she told me I had an aura. 'What?' I said." Hayden Carruth. CP-CarHS

Sonnet: "What if the psychologians, those grand old frauds." Hayden Carruth. CP-CarHS *Fr.* Sonnets.

Sonnet: "While you stood talking at the counter, cutting." Hayden Carruth. CP-CarHS *Fr.* Sonnets.

Sonnet: "Why complain, brothers, to you, my writing." Hayden Carruth. CP-CarHS *Fr.* Sonnets.

Sonnet: "Why extremely do we observe more of." Hayden Carruth. CP-CarHS *Fr.* Sonnets.

Sonnet: "Women in anger, it seems, become theatrical." Hayden Carruth. CP-CarHS *Fr.* Sonnets.

Sonnet: "Word for Today is 'panoptic,' which the goddamn, The." Hayden Carruth. CP-CarHS *Fr.* Sonnets.

Sonnet: "Yes. After all my arguments with myself." Hayden Carruth. CP-CarHS *Fr.* Sonnets.

Sonnet: "You in a tallness slenderly, as a lone." Hayden Carruth. CP-CarHS *Fr.* Sonnets.

Sonnet: "You rose from our embrace and the small light spread." Hayden

Carruth. CP-CarHS *Fr.* Sonnets.

Sonnet: "'Whut do you spose thet thing is,' Oi said. "Whut?" Hayden Carruth. CP-CarHS

Sonnet: A Rapture concerning his Lady. Guido Cavalcanti. CW-RossD, *tr.* by Dante Gabriel Rossetti

Sonnet: From the Italian of Guido Cavalcanti. Cavalcanti to Dante Alighieri. Guido Cavalcanti.

Sonnet: Guido answers the foregoing Sonnet, speaking with shame of his changed Love. Guido Cavalcanti. CW-RossD, *tr.* by Dante Gabriel Rossetti

Sonnet: He compares all Things with his Lady, and finds them wanting. Guido Cavalcanti. CW-RossD, *tr.* by Dante Gabriel Rossetti

Sonnet: He interprets Dante's Dream, related in the first Sonnet of the Vita Nuova. Guido Cavalcanti. CW-RossD, *tr.* by Dante Gabriel Rossetti

Sonnet: He mistrusts the Love of Lapo Gianni. Guido Cavalcanti. CW-RossD, *tr.* by Dante Gabriel Rossetti

Sonnet: He rebukes Dante for his way of Life, after the death of Beatrice. Guido Cavalcanti. CW-RossD, *tr.* by Dante Gabriel Rossetti

Sonnet: He reports, in a feigned Vision, the successful Issue of Lapo Gianni's Love. Guido Cavalcanti. CW-RossD, *tr.* by Dante Gabriel Rossetti

Sonnet: Of an ill-favoured Lady. Guido Cavalcanti. CW-RossD, *tr.* by Dante Gabriel Rossetti

Sonnet: Of his Pain from a new Love. Guido Cavalcanti. CW-RossD, *tr.* by Dante Gabriel Rossetti

Sonnet: Of the Eyes of a certain Mandetta, of Thoulouse, which resemble those of his Lady Joan, of Florence. Guido Cavalcanti. CW-RossD, *tr.* by Dante Gabriel Rossetti

Sonnet: On the Detection of a false Friend. Guido Cavalcanti. CW-RossD, *tr.* by Dante Gabriel Rossetti

Sonnet: To a Friend who does not pity his Love. Guido Cavalcanti. CW-RossD, *tr.* by Dante Gabriel Rossetti

Sonnet: To a newly enriched Man; reminding him of the Wants of the Poor. Guido Cavalcanti. CW-RossD, *tr.* by Dante Gabriel Rossetti

Sonnet: To his Lady Joan, of Florence. Guido Cavalcanti. CW-RossD, *tr.* by Dante Gabriel Rossetti

Sonnet: "High on the wall that holds Jerusalem." G. K. Chesterton. CP-ChesG

Sonnet: "If you have picked your lawn of leaves and snails." G. K. Chesterton. CP-ChesG

Sonnet: "I love to see the summer beaming forth." John Clare. SP-ClarJ

Sonnet: "All we need is fourteen lines, well, thirteen now." Billy Collins. SP-CollB

Sonnet: "Ere elfish Night shall sift another day." Hart Crane. CP-CranH

Sonnet: "I have not loved you in the noblest way." Countee Cullen. CP-CullC

Sonnet: "I know now how a man whose blood is hot." Countee Cullen. CP-CullC

Sonnet: "Some for a little while do love, and some for long." Countee Cullen. CP-CullC

Sonnet: "These are no wind-blown rumors, soft say-sos." Countee Cullen. CP-CullC

Sonnet: "What I am saying now was said before." Countee Cullen. CP-CullC

Sonnet: "For that I have forgot the world these days." E. E. Cummings. CP-CummE

Sonnet: "I dreamed I was among the conquerors." E. E. Cummings. CP-CummE

Sonnet: "Long since, the flicker brushed with shameless wing." E. E. Cummings. CP-CummE

Sonnet: "No sunset, but a grey, great, struggling sky." E. E. Cummings. CP-CummE

Sonnet: "Rain-drop on the eyelids of the earth, A." E. E. Cummings. CP-CummE

Sonnet: To the Blessed Virgin Mary. Fra Guittone d'Arezzo. CW-RossD, *tr.* by Dante Gabriel Rossetti

Sonnet: A Trance of Love. Cino da Pistoia. CW-RossD, *tr.* by Dante Gabriel Rossetti

Sonnet: Death is not without but within him. Cino da Pistoia. CW-RossD, *tr.* by Dante Gabriel Rossetti

Sonnet: He answers Dante, confessing his unsteadfast Heart. Cino da Pistoia. CW-RossD, *tr.* by Dante Gabriel Rossetti

Sonnet: He answers the foregoing Sonnet, and prays Dante, in the name of Beatrice, to continue his great Poem. Cino da Pistoia. CW-RossD, *tr.* by Dante Gabriel Rossetti

Sonnet: He conceives of some Compensation in Death. Cino da Pistoia. CW-RossD, *tr.* by Dante Gabriel Rossetti

Sonnet: He impugns the verdicts of Dante's Commedia. Cino da Pistoia. CW-RossD, *tr.* by Dante Gabriel Rossetti

Sonnet: He interprets Dante's Dream, related in the first Sonnet of the Vita Nuova. Cino da Pistoia. CW-RossD, *tr.* by Dante Gabriel Rossetti

Sonnet: He owes nothing to Guido as a Poet. Cino da Pistoia. CW-RossD, *tr.* by Dante Gabriel Rossetti

Sonnet: Of the grave of Selvaggia, on the Monte della Sambuca. Cino da Pistoia. CW-RossD, *tr.* by Dante Gabriel Rossetti

Sonnet: To Love, in great Bitterness. Cino da Pistoia. CW-RossD, *tr.* by Dante Gabriel Rossetti

Sonnet: "As massive and dispensable as sculpture." Donald Davie. CP-DaviDC

Sonnet: "Emblem of blasted hope and lost desire." Paul Laurence Dunbar. CP-DunbP

Sonnet: "My God, where is that ancient heat towards Thee." George Herbert. CP-HerbG

Sonnet: "Sure Lord, there is enough in thee to dry." George Herbert. CP-HerbG

Sonnet: "Patience, hard thing! the hard thing but to pray." Gerard Manley Hopkins. CP-HopkG

(Patience, Hard Thing!) CP-HopkG

Sonnet: "Where didst thou find, young Bard, thy sounding lyre?" John Keats. CP-KeatJ

Sonnet: Of [*or* To] his Lady in Heaven. Jacopo da Lentino. CW-RossD, *tr.* by Dante Gabriel Rossetti

Sonnet: Of his Lady's Face. Jacopo da Lentino. CW-RossD, *tr.* by Dante Gabriel Rossetti

Sonnet: "I know that my profile will be serene." Federico García Lorca. CP-GarcF, *tr.* by Christopher Maurer

Sonnet: "Specter trailing restless silver, A." Federico García Lorca. CP-GarcF, *tr.* by Alan S. Trueblood *Fr.* Love.

Sonnet: "Lady / who burns without being burnt or trying." Stéphane Mallarmé. CP-MallS, *tr.* by Henry Weinfield

Sonnet: "So dear from far and near and white, and so." Stéphane Mallarmé. CP-MallS, *tr.* by Henry Weinfield

Sonnet: "Hateful are those false themes of speculation." George Meredith. CP-MerG2

Sonnet: On the Religious Memorie of Mrs. Catherine Thomason My Christian Freind Deceas'd Decem. 1646. John Milton. CP-MiltJ

(Sonnet 14.) CP-MiltJ

Sonnet: "Form of Christ cut from dark wood, the pale, A." Howard Nemerov. CP-NemeH

Sonnet: "It seems to be the trouble, everyone." Howard Nemerov. CP-NemeH

Sonnet: "Be slowly lifted up, thou long black arm." Wilfred Owen. CP-OwenW

Sonnet: "In seemly burial, love may not rest." Dorothy Parker. CP-ParkD

Sonnet: "Sweeter your laugh than trill of lark at dawn." Dorothy Parker. CP-ParkD

Sonnet: "Could I say what I think, could I express." Fernando Pessoa. SP-PessF

Sonnet: "If grief dismiss me not to them that rest." Petrarch. CP-WorW1

Sonnet: "Afternoon sun on her back." Robert Pinsky. CP-PinsR

Sonnet: To Eva. Sylvia Plath. CP-PlatS

Sonnet: To Time. Sylvia Plath. CP-PlatS

Sonnet: Chi È Questa? Ezra Pound. CP-PoEar

Sonnet: "If on the tally-board of wasted days." Ezra Pound. CP-PoEar

Sonnet: "Time moves in and out of me." A. K. Ramanujan. CP-RamaA

Sonnet: "Master and the slave go hand in hand, The." Edwin Arlington Robinson. CP-RobiE

Sonnet: "Oh for a poet—for a beacon bright." Edwin Arlington Robinson. CP-RobiE

Sonnet: "When we can all so excellently give." Edwin Arlington Robinson. CP-RobiE

Sonnet: "Some say that love and joy are one: and so." Christina Georgina Rossetti. CP-RosC3

Sonnet: "My thoughts through yours refracted into speech." Muriel Rukeyser. CP-RukeM

Sonnet: "August, tasting of ripe grapes and afternoon sleep." James Schuyler. CP-SchuJ

Sonnet: England in 1819. Percy Bysshe Shelley. *See* England in 1819

Sonnet: Lift Not the Painted Veil: "Lift not the painted veil which those who live." Percy Bysshe Shelley. CP-ShelP

Sonnet: On Launching Some Bottles Filled with Knowledge into the Bristol Channel. Percy Bysshe Shelley. CP-ShelP

Sonnet: Political Greatness. Percy Bysshe Shelley. CP-ShelP

Sonnet: To a Balloon Laden with Knowledge. Percy Bysshe Shelley. CP-ShelP

Sonnet: "Ye hasten to the grave! What seek ye there." Percy Bysshe Shelley. CP-ShelP

Sonnet: "In the forgotten woods, when somber winter glowers." Stéphane Mallarmé. CP-MallS, *tr.* by Henry Weinfield

Sonnet: "Oh, my belovèd, have you thought of this." Edna St. Vincent Millay. CP-MillE

Sonnet: "Time, that renews the tissues of this frame." Edna St. Vincent Millay. CP-MillE

Sonnet: "What lips my lips have kissed, and where, and why." Edna St. Vincent Millay. CP-MillE

Sonnet: "Build up the walls about me; close each door." Wallace Stevens. CP-StevWP

Sonnet: "Explain my spirit—adding word to word." Wallace Stevens. CP-StevWP

Sonnet: "Dost see how unregarded now." Sir John Suckling. CP-SuckJ

Sonnet: "Of thee, kind boy, I ask no red and white." Sir John Suckling. CP-

SuckJ

Sonnet: "O[h]! for some honest lover's ghost." Sir John Suckling. CP-SuckJ

Sonnet: "Could I be sure that I shall see the day." Allen Tate. CP-TateA

Sonnet: "I gazed upon the silent burial-ground." Jones Very. CP-VeryJ

Sonnet: "Of two fair virgins, modest, though admired." Jacopo Vittorelli.

Sonnet: "Winter deepening, the hay all in, The." Richard Wilbur. CP-WilbR

Sonnet: Composed While the Author Was Engaged in Writing a Tract Occasioned by the Convention of Cintra. William Wordsworth. CP-WorW1

(Composed at the Same Time and on the Same Occasion.) CP-WorW1

Sonnet: "England! the time is come when thou shouldst wean." William Wordsworth. CP-WorW1; MW-WorW

Sonnet: "Nuns fret not at their convent's narrow room." William Wordsworth. CP-WorW1; MW-WorW

Sonnet: To————. William Wordsworth. CP-WorW2

(To ————). CP-WorW2

Sonnet: "Why should we weep or mourn, Angelic boy." William Wordsworth. CP-WorW2

Sonnet: 'Each man me telleth.' Sir Thomas Wyatt. CP-WyatT

Sonnet I: "His piercing pince-nez. Some dim frieze." Ted Berrigan. SP-BerrT *Fr.* Sonnets, The.

Sonnet 1: "O Nightingale, that on yon bloomy Spray." John Milton. CP-MiltJ

Sonnet [1–86]. Edmund Spenser. CP-Spens *Fr.* Amoretti.

Sonnet 2: "Charming lady, she whose beautiful name honors." John Milton. CP-CowpW; CP-MiltJ

(Fair Lady! whose harmonious name the Rhine.) CP-CowpW

Sonnet 3: "As on a rugged mountain at the darkening of evening." John Milton. CP-CowpW; CP-MiltJ

(As on a hill-top rude, when closing day.) CP-CowpW

Sonnet III: "Stronger than alcohol, more great than song." Ted Berrigan. SP-BerrT *Fr.* Sonnets, The.

Sonnet 4: "Diodati, and I will say it to you with wonder." John Milton. CP-MiltJ

Sonnet 5: "In truth your fair eyes, my lady." John Milton. CP-CowpW; CP-MiltJ

(Lady! It cannot be, but that thine eyes.) CP-CowpW

Sonnet 6: "Young, gentle, and candid lover that I am." John Milton. CP-CowpW; CP-MiltJ

(Enamour'd, artless, young, on foreign ground.) CP-CowpW

Sonnet 7. John Milton. CP-MiltJ

Sonnet 8. John Milton. *See* When the Assault Was Intended to the City

Sonnet 9: "Ladie [*or* Lady], that in the prime of earliest youth." John Milton. CP-MiltJ

Sonnet 10. John Milton. *See* To the Lady Margaret Ley

Sonnet 11. John Milton. CP-MiltJ

Sonnet 12. John Milton. *See* On the Detraction Which Followed upon My Writing Certain Treatises

Sonnet 13. John Milton. *See* To Mr. H. Lawes On His Airs

Sonnet 14. John Milton. *See* Sonnet: On the Religious Memorie of Mrs. Catherine Thomason My Christian Freind Deceas'd Decem. 1646

Sonnet 15 [On the Lord General Fairfax at the Siege of Colchester]. John Milton.

Sonnet 16. John Milton. *See* To the Lord General Cromwell

Sonnet 17. John Milton. *See* To Sir Henry Vane the Younger

Sonnet 18 [On the Late Massacre in Piedmont]. John Milton. CP-MiltJ

Sonnet 19. John Milton. CP-MiltJ

Sonnet 20. John Milton. *See* To Mr. Lawrence

Sonnet 21. John Milton. *See* To Cyriack Skinner

Sonnet 22. John Milton. *See* To Mr. Cyriack Skinner upon His Blindness

Sonnet 23. John Milton. *See* On His Deceased Wife

Sonnet LV: "Grace to be born and live as variously as possible." Ted Berrigan. SP-BerrT *Fr.* Sonnets, The.

Sonnet LXX: "Sweeter than sour apples flesh to boys." Ted Berrigan. SP-BerrT *Fr.* Sonnets, The.

Sonnet LXXVII: "DEAR CHRIS / It is 3:17 a.m. in New York city, yes, it is." Ted Berrigan. SP-BerrT *Fr.* Sonnets, The.

Sonnet, A: "Ile dote noe more, nor shall mine eyes." Robert Herrick. CP-HerrR

Sonnet, A: "Sonnet is a moment's monument, A." Dante Gabriel Rossetti. CW-RossD *Fr.* House of Life, The.

Sonnet, A: "Thy beauty fades and with it too my love." Jones Very. CP-VeryJ

Sonnet Addressed to Mr. Phillips, A. William Cowper. CP-CowpW

Sonnet at Easter. Howard Nemerov. CP-NemeH

Sonnet Autumnal. Wilfred Owen. CP-OwenW

Sonnet Composed at—Castle. William Wordsworth. *See* Composed at Neidpath Castle, the Property of Lord Queensberry,1803

Sonnet Composed on a Journey Homeward; the Author Having Received Intelligence of the Birth of a Son, 20 September 1796. Samuel Taylor Coleridge. CP-ColeS

Sonnet Dialogue. Countee Cullen. CP-CullC

Sonnet entitled how to run the world). E. E. Cummings. CP-CummE; SP-CummE

Sonnet for Jane Freilicher, A. Frank O'Hara. SP-OharF

Sonnet for Pygmalion. Tennessee Williams. CP-WillT

Sonnet for the End of a Sequence. Dorothy Parker. CP-ParkD

Sonnet IV. E. E. Cummings. CP-CummE

Sonnet from the Book of Regrets. Joachim Du Bellay. CP-StevWP, *tr.* by Wallace Stevens

Sonnet from the Psalms. Christina Georgina Rossetti. CP-RosC3

Sonnet from the Voyage. Yehuda Amichai. SP-AmicY, *tr.* by Stephen Mitchell

Sonnet in Homage to Manuel de Falla Offering Him Some Flowers. Federico García Lorca. CP-GarcF, *tr.* by Christopher Maurer

Sonnet in Search of an Author. William Carlos Williams. CP-WilW2

Sonnet in Tenzone. Ezra Pound. CP-PoEar

Sonnet in the Manner of Góngora in Which the Poet Sends His Beloved a Dove. Federico García Lorca. CP-GarcF, *tr.* by Angela Jaffray

Sonnet in the Pass of Killicranky. William Wordsworth. CP-WorW1; MW-WorW

Sonnet is a moment's monument, A. Sonnet, A: "Sonnet is a moment's monument, A." Dante Gabriel Rossetti. CW-RossD *Fr.* House of Life, The.

Sonnet of Intimacy. Vinícius de Moraes. CP-BishE

Sonnet of Michel Angelo Buonaroti. Michelangelo Buonarroti. CP-EmerR

Sonnet of Perilla, A. Robert Herrick. CP-HerrR

Sonnet of the August Calm. Ezra Pound. CP-PoEar

Sonnet of the Garland of Roses. Federico García Lorca. CP-GarcF, *tr.* by Angela Jaffray

Sonnet of the Sweet Complaint. Federico García Lorca. CP-GarcF, *tr.* by Angela Jaffray

Sonnet on a Still Night. J. V. Cunningham. CP-CunnJ

Sonnet On An Alpine Night. Dorothy Parker. CP-ParkD

Sonnet on Approaching Italy. Oscar Wilde. CP-WildO

Sonnet—On Hearing a Thrush Sing on a Morning Walk in January. Robert Burns. CP-BurnR

Sonnet on Hearing the *Dies Iræ* Sung in the Sistine Chapel. Oscar Wilde. CP-WildO

Sonnet on Milton. William Wordsworth. CP-WorW1

Sonnet on Quitting Christ's Hospital. Samuel Taylor Coleridge. CP-ColeS

Sonnet on Rare Animals. William Meredith. SP-MereW

Sonnet on Receiving a Letter Informing Me of the Birth of a Son. Samuel Taylor Coleridge. CP-ColeS

Sonnet on Seeing Miss Helen Maria Williams Weep at a Tale of Distress. William Wordsworth. CP-WorW1

Sonnet [on the Death of Mr. Richard West]. Thomas Gray. CP-GrayT

Sonnet on the Death of Robert Riddel, Esq. *of Glen Riddel, April* 1794. Robert Burns. CP-BurnR

Sonnet on the Massacre of the Christians in Bulgaria. Oscar Wilde. CP-WildO

Sonnet on the Nuptials of the Marquis Antonio Cavalli with the Countess Clelia Rasponi of Ravenna. Lord Byron. CP-Byron

Sonnet on the Sale by Auction of Keats' Love Letters. Oscar Wilde. CP-WildO

Sonnet—September 1922. Ivor Gurney. SP-GurnI

Sonnet—Silence. Edgar Allan Poe. CP-PoeEd

Sonnet. The Token. John Donne. CP-DonnJ

Sonnet, to a Child. Wilfred Owen. CP-OwenW

Sonnet to a Friend Who Asked How I Felt When the Nurse First Presented My Infant to Me. Samuel Taylor Coleridge. CP-ColeS

Sonnet to a Picture by Lucca Giordano in the Mureo Borbonico at Naples. William Wordsworth. CP-WorW2

Sonnet (To an Octogenarian). William Wordsworth. CP-WorW2

Sonnet to Beauty. Allen Tate. CP-TateA

Sonnet to Byron. Percy Bysshe Shelley. CP-ShelP

(I am afraid these verses will not please you, but.) CP-ShelP

Sonnet [to Charles Lloyd]. Samuel Taylor Coleridge. CP-ColeS

Sonnet to Gath. Edna St. Vincent Millay. CP-MillE

Sonnet, to Genevra. Lord Byron. CP-Byron

Sonnet to Henry Cowper. William Cowper. CP-CowpW

Sonnet to J.M. George Meredith. CP-MerG2

Sonnet to Lake Leman. Lord Byron. CP-Byron

Sonnet to Liberty. Oscar Wilde. CP-WildO

Sonnet to Man-Made Grandeur. John Updike. CP-UpdiJ

Sonnet to Mrs. Unwin. William Cowper. *See* To Mary Unwin

Sonnet to Satan. Sylvia Plath. CP-PlatS

Sonnet—To Science. Edgar Allan Poe. CP-PoeEd

Sonnet to the Noble Lady, the Lady Mary Wroth, A. Ben Jonson. CP-JonsB

Sonnet to the Prince Regent. Lord Byron. CP-Byron

Sonnet, To the Rev. James Flint, D. D., On reading his Collection of Poems. Jones Very. CP-VeryJ

Sonnet to the River Otter. Samuel Taylor Coleridge. CP-ColeS; MW-ColeS

Sonnet, to the Same. Lord Byron. CP-Byron

Sonnet to Wilberforce. William Cowper. *See* To William Wilberforce, Esq

Sonnet to William Linley. Samuel Taylor Coleridge. CP-ColeS

Sonnet to Zante. Ugo Foscolo. CP-PoeEd

Sonnet Translated from the Italian of Milton. William Wordsworth. CP-WorW1

Sonnet upon Sonnets, A. Robert Burns. CP-BurnR

Sonnet with the Compliments of the Season. G. K. Chesterton. CP-ChesG

Sonnet Written by Mr — Immediately after the Death of His Wife. William Wordsworth. CP-WorW1

Sonnet Written in Holy Week at Genoa. Oscar Wilde. CP-WildO

Sonnets. Hayden Carruth.

  Sonnet: "All revolutions in modern times have led." CP-CarHS

  Sonnet: "At the hospital where I had the echocardiagram." CP-CarHS

  Sonnet: "Bo was three when we slugged through Arizona, The." CP-CarHS

  Sonnet: "But still, still . . . / In stillness mystery calls." CP-CarHS

  Sonnet: "Cindy, I've used my writing all my life." CP-CarHS

  Sonnet: "Cindy, the secret's out. Yes, you're addict-." CP-CarHS

  Sonnet: "Dearest, I never knew such loving. There." CP-CarHS

  Sonnet: "Fear of falling is why the old men walk." CP-CarHS

  Sonnet: "Freedom in love? It has been questioned. Think." CP-CarHS

  Sonnet: "From our very high window at the Sheraton." CP-CarHS

  Sonnet: "Honey, darling, baby . . . but no endearments." CP-CarHS

  Sonnet: "How is it, tell me, that this new self can be—." CP-CarHS

  Sonnet: "Hubbub of the Hall of Languages, our Babel, The." CP-CarHS

  Sonnet: "I think continually of the differences." CP-CarHS

  Sonnet: "I want to do a complaint now. Which is to say." CP-CarHS

  Sonnet: "If I die today, which statistically speaking." CP-CarHS

  Sonnet: "If you see a child that shivers when it hears." CP-CarHS

  Sonnet: "In the mind of the kiss occurs a thought so rich." CP-CarHS

  Sonnet: "It's said by the thoughtful masters that to know death." CP-CarHS

  Sonnet: "Key-reist, I am fed and sick unto death with this." CP-CarHS

  Sonnet: "Last night, I don't know if from habit or intent." CP-CarHS

  Sonnet: "Like the magnificent stationary animal it is." CP-CarHS

  Sonnet: "Loving mind in this death-haunted body, The." CP-CarHS

  Sonnet: "Most brainy woman, the sexuality of your thought." CP-CarHS

  Sonnet: "Must genius always struggle, always exaggerate." CP-CarHS

  Sonnet: "O Jesus, thou who sittest up there on the right." CP-CarHS

  Sonnet: "Persistent is the thought for me of that." CP-CarHS

  Sonnet: "Poor little book, *The Sleeping Beauty* died." CP-CarHS

  Sonnet: Sin. CP-CarHS

  Sonnet: The Recollected Actual Voices of Romanticism. CP-CarHS

  Sonnet: "This is our perfect silver maple's day." CP-CarHS

  Sonnet: "Thy sting sufficeth, Death. If Heidegger first." CP-CarHS

  Sonnet: "To have been Diogenes. Why not? Or de Sade." CP-CarHS

  Sonnet: "To rebel is suitable philosophical tactics." CP-CarHS

  Sonnet: "To rebel. So I have saved my life, not once." CP-CarHS

  Sonnet: "To see a woman long oppressed by fear." CP-CarHS

  Sonnet: "To the aged, trembling, illiterate woman yesterday." CP-CarHS

  Sonnet: "Was Yahweh chosen by the chosen people?" CP-CarHS

  Sonnet: "Well, Jim says that the couplet at the end." CP-CarHS

  Sonnet: "What if the psychologians, those grand old frauds." CP-CarHS

  Sonnet: "While you stood talking at the counter, cutting." CP-CarHS

  Sonnet: "Why complain, brothers, to you, my writing." CP-CarHS

  Sonnet: "Why extremely do we observe more of." CP-CarHS

  Sonnet: "Women in anger, it seems, become theatrical." CP-CarHS

  Sonnet: "Word for Today is "panoptic," which the goddamn, The." CP-CarHS

  Sonnet: "Yes. After all my arguments with myself." CP-CarHS

  Sonnet: "You in a tallness slenderly, as a lone." CP-CarHS

  Sonnet: "You rose from our embrace and the small light spread." CP-CarHS

Sonnets are full of love, and this my tome. To My First Love, My Mother. Christina Georgina Rossetti. CP-RosC2

Sonnets at Christmas. Allen Tate. CP-TateA

Sonnets Attempted in the Manner of Contemporary Writers. Samuel Taylor Coleridge. CP-ColeS

Sonnets for the Spring (A Sequence). Tennessee Williams. CP-WillT

Sonnets from an Ungrafted Tree. Edna St. Vincent Millay. CP-MillE

Sonnets from China. W. H. Auden. CP-AudeW

Sonnets from the Portuguese. Elizabeth Barrett Browning. CP-BroEB

Sonnets in Summer Heat. G. K. Chesterton. CP-ChesG

Sonnets of Death 5. Gabriela Mistral. SP-MistG, *tr. by* Maria Giachetti [*or* Jacketti]

Sonnets of the Blood. Allen Tate. CP-TateA

Sonnets of Two Summers. Robert Penn Warren. CP-WarrR

Sonnets, The. Ted Berrigan.

  "Academy of the future is opening its doors, The." SP-BerrT

  "Banging around in a cigarette isn't "in love." SP-BerrT

  "Bulbs burn phosphorescent, white, The." SP-BerrT

  "(Clarity! clarity!) a semblance of motion, omniscience." SP-BerrT

  "Dear Margie, hello. It is 5:15 a.m." SP-BerrT

  "Dear Ron: hello. Your name is now a household name." SP-BerrT

  "Dear Ron: Keats was a baiter of bears etc." SP-BerrT

  "Each tree stands alone in stillness." SP-BerrT

  Final Sonnet, A. SP-BerrT

  "Harum-scarum haze on the Pollock streets / Where Snow White sleeps among the silent dwarfs." SP-BerrT

  "How strange to be gone in a minute / Bearden is dead Gallup is dead Margie is dead." SP-BerrT

  "I like to beat people up." SP-BerrT

  "In Joe Brainard's collage its white arrow." SP-BerrT

  "In my paintings for they are present." SP-BerrT

  "Into the closed air of the slow." SP-BerrT

  "It is a human universe: & I." SP-BerrT

  "It is night. You are asleep. And beautiful tears." SP-BerrT

  "It was summer. We were there. And THERE WAS NO." SP-BerrT

  Lines for Lauren Owen. SP-BerrT

  "Lord, it is time. Summer was very great." SP-BerrT

  "Mountains of twine and." SP-BerrT

  "Musick strides through these poems." SP-BerrT

  "On the 15th day of November in the year of the motorcar." SP-BerrT

  "On the green a white boy goes / We may read about all those radio waves." SP-BerrT

  Penn Station. SP-BerrT

  Personal Poem #9. SP-BerrT

  Poem in the Modern Manner. SP-BerrT

  Poem in the Traditional Manner. SP-BerrT

  "Poem upon the page is as massive as, The." SP-BerrT

  "Seurat and Juan Gris combine this season." SP-BerrT

  "Sleep half sleep half silence and with reasons." SP-BerrT

  Sonnet I: "His piercing pince-nez. Some dim frieze." SP-BerrT

  Sonnet III: "Stronger than alcohol, more great than song." SP-BerrT

  Sonnet LV: "Grace to be born and live as variously as possible." SP-BerrT

  Sonnet LXX: "Sweeter than sour apples flesh to boys." SP-BerrT

  Sonnet LXXVII: "DEAR CHRIS / It is 3:17 a.m. in New York city, yes, it is." SP-BerrT

  Sonnet: "My dream a drink with Lonnie Johnson we discuss the code." SP-BerrT

  "Summer so histrionic, marvelous dirty days." SP-BerrT

Sonnets to Chris. John Berryman. CP-BerrJ

Sonnets to Laura. Petrarch.

  Description of the Contrarious Passions in a Lover. CP-WyatT, *tr. by* Sir Thomas Wyatt

  Galley, The. CP-WyatT, *tr. by* Sir Thomas Wyatt

  How the Lover Perisheth in His Delight, As the Fly in the Fire. CP-WyatT, *tr. by* Sir Thomas Wyatt

  LOVER FOR SHAMEFASTNESS HIDETH HIS DESIRE WITHIN HIS FAITHFUL HEART. CP-WyatT, *tr. by* Sir Thomas Wyatt

Sonnets upon the Punishment of Death. William Wordsworth. CP-WorW2

Sonogram, The. Paul Muldoon. CP-MuldP

Sonora Desert-Edge. Allen Ginsberg. CP-GinsA

Sons of *Greece*, The. Samuel Johnson. CP-JohnS *Fr.* Irene.

Sons of Martha, The. Rudyard Kipling. CP-KiplR

Sons of Mary seldom bother, for they have inherited that good part, The. Sons of Martha, The. Rudyard Kipling. CP-KiplR

Sons of men, from the wombs of wistful women. Side-Step, O Sons of Men! D. H. Lawrence. CP-LawrD

Sons of Old Killie, The. Robert Burns. CP-BurnR

Sons of the Greeks, arise! Translation of the Famous Greek War Song *Deute Paides Tov Ellenon*. Lord Byron. CP-Byron

Sons of Whitman sons of Poe. Adieu À Charlot. Lawrence Ferlinghetti. SP-FerlL

Son's Portrait, The. Thomas Hardy. CP-HardT

Sons, seek not me among these polished stones. Charles Cavendish to His Posterity. Ben Jonson. CP-JonsB

Soon. C. K. Williams. CP-WillC

Soon as *Glumdalclitch* miss'd her pleasing Care. Lamentation of Glumdalclitch for the Loss of Grildrig, The. Alexander Pope. CP-PopeA

Soon as *madonna* comes into my heart. Petrarch. CP-Petra, *tr. by* J. G. Nichols

Soon as the sun forsook the eastern main. Hymn to the Evening, An. Phillis Wheatley. CP-WheaP

Soon as / you stop. Cleavage. A. R. Ammons. CP-AmmoA

Soon did the Almighty Giver of all rest. Upon Perusing the "Epistle [To Sir George Howland Beaumont]" Thirty Years after Its Composition. William Wordsworth. CP-WorW2

Soon fades the rose; once past the fragrant hour. Samuel Johnson. CP-JohnS

Soon I will have to begin. All around me. Spaceship. Dan Pagis. SP-PagiD, *tr. by* Stephen Mitchell

Soon it must come, the great charge. Lorca. Richard Eberhart. CP-EberR

Soon It Will. Kenneth Patchen. CP-PatcK

Soon it will be autumn. The last fruits ripen. Autumn is Near and the Memory of My Parents. Yehuda Amichai. SP-AmicY, *tr. by* Chana Bloch

Soon it will be thirteen years since the nightingale. Letters from the Ming Dynasty. Joseph Brodsky. CP-BrodJ, *tr. by* Derek Walcott

Soon Shall the Winter's Foil Be Here. Walt Whitman. CP-WhitW

Soon the silver chord is broken. Memory ("Soon the silver chord is broken"). Jones Very. CP-VeryJ

Soon the waves, so lightly bounding. Memory ("Soon the waves, so lightly bounding"). Jones Very. CP-VeryJ

Soon to his Name they rear a temple rude. Church, The. Jones Very. CP-VeryJ

Soon to reach you where you are. Friend's Song, A. Marya Alexandrovna Zaturenska. SP-ZatuM

Soon we'll be sunk in cold uncertainty. Song of Autumn. Charles Baudelaire. CP-BaudC, *tr. by* Walter Martin

Soon will blow the changed leaves on the Malvern road. Musers Afar Will Say. Ivor Gurney. SP-GurnI

Sooner let nightmares whinny, if we cannot. Dreams in Middle Age. Louis MacNeice. CP-MacNL

Sooner or late—in earnest or in jest. Hour of the Angel, The. Rudyard Kipling. CP-KiplR *Fr.* Land and Sea Tales.

Sooner or later. Rewaking, The. William Carlos Williams. CP-WilW2

Sooner or later / everyone finds out who his Murderer is. Symmetry. Andrei Codrescu. SP-CodrA

Sooner or later: yet at last / The Jordan must be past. Christina Georgina Rossetti. CP-RosC2

Soonest Mended. John Ashbery. SP-AshbJ

Soonest mended, nothing said; / And help my rise from east or west, The. Fisher-Wife, A. Christina Georgina Rossetti. CP-RosC2

Soot drifted from the engines to the marble, The. Carnegie Library, Juvenile Division, The. Randall Jarrell. CP-JarrR

Soot, house-dust, and tar didn't go far. Painted Wives. John Updike. CP-UpdiJ

Soothing sanity and blitheness of completion, The. Ended Day, An. Walt Whitman. CP-WhitW

Soothsay. Dante Gabriel Rossetti. CW-RossD

Soothsayer, The. Denise Levertov. SP-LeveDL

Soothsaying. Olga Broumas. SP-BrouO

Sopa. Robert Creeley. CP-CreeR

Sophist Departing from Syria. Constantine P. Cavafy. CP-CavaC, *tr. by* Theoharis Constantine Theoharis

Sorcerer Bids Farewell to Seem, A. Sylvia Plath. CP-PlatS

Sorcerer's Daughter, The. Louise Bogan. CP-BogaL

Sorceress!, The. Nicholas Vachel Lindsay. CP-LindV

Sorcery. Walter De la Mare. CP-DeLaW

Sordello. Robert Browning. CP-BroR1

Sorrel. Raymond Carver. CP-CarvR

Sorrel. Geoffrey Hill. CP-HillG

Sorrel Filly, The. Wendell Berry. CP-BerrW

Sorrow. Charles Guérin. CP-ChesG, *tr. by* G. K. Chesterton

Sorrow. Yusef Komunyakaa. CP-KomuY

Sorrow. James Laughlin. CP-LaugJ

Sorrow. D. H. Lawrence. CP-LawrD

Sorrow. Edna St. Vincent Millay. CP-MillE

Sorrow, The. C. K. Williams. CP-WillC

Sorrow almost resents love. Emily Dickinson. SP-DickE

Sorrow, benighted with Fathoms. Emily Dickinson. SP-DickE

Sorrow hath a double voice, / Sharp today but sweet tomorrow. Christina Georgina Rossetti. CP-RosC2

Sorrow how high it is. Dark Song. A. R. Ammons. CP-AmmoA

Sorrow is my own yard. Widow's Lament in Springtime, The. William Carlos Williams. CP-WilW1

Sorrow moves in wide waves. Lorine Niedecker. CP-NiedL

Sorrow of Love, The. William Butler Yeats. CP-YeatW

Sorrow of Obedience, The. John Ciardi. CP-CiarJ

Sorrow of saints is sorrow of a day. Thy Servant Will Go and Fight with This Philistine. Christina Georgina Rossetti. CP-RosC2

Sorrow Song. Lucille Clifton. SP-ClifL

Sorrow Song, The. Hayden Carruth. CP-CarHS

Sorrow, who to this hour scarce knew the way. Elegy on the L. C. John Donne. CP-DonnJ; MW-DonnJ

Sorrowes. Robert Herrick. CP-HerrR

Sorrowes divided amongst many, lesse. Griefe. Robert Herrick. CP-HerrR

Sorrowes our portion are: Ere hence we goe. Sorrowes. Robert Herrick. CP-HerrR

Sorrowful dreams remembered after waking. Edna St. Vincent Millay. CP-MillE

Sorrowful Girl, The. Stevie Smith. CP-SmitS

Sorrows and Joys. George Meredith. CP-MerG1

Sorrows have come before and have stood mute. George Sterling's Death.

Robinson Jeffers. CP-JefR1

Sorrows of Lester Buster, The. Wyatt Prunty. SP-PrunW

Sorrows of Smindyrides, The. James Laughlin. CP-LaugJ

Sorrows Succeed. Robert Herrick. CP-HerrR

Sorry but I'm not in the nursing profession, old man. Rented Room, The. Tennessee Williams. CP-WillT

Sorry I am, my God, sorry I am. Sin's Round. George Herbert. CP-HerbG

"Sorry," said the cop who had shot me. Apprehendee Then Exited Vee-hicle. John Ciardi. CP-CiarJ

Sors adversa gerit stimulum, sed tendit et alas. Simile Latinised, A. *Unknown.* CP-CowpW

Sort of a Song, A. William Carlos Williams. CP-WilW2

Sort of an Apocalypse. Yehuda Amichai. SP-AmicY, *tr. by* Stephen Mitchell

Sort of anxiousness crystal in crystal has, A. Song of the Bridegroom, The. John Berryman. CP-BerrJ

Sort of roll develops out of the bay, A. Calm Day at Drake's Bay. Robert Bly. SP-BlyR

Sort of sexual trauma, A. Café Notre Dame. Lawrence Ferlinghetti. SP-FerlL

Sortes Vergilianae. John Ashbery. SP-AshbJ

Sorting. A. R. Ammons. CP-AmmoA

Sorting Old Papers. Donald Davie. CP-DaviDC

Sorting the Personae. Donald Davie. CP-DaviDC

Sorting, Wrapping, Packing, Stuffing. James Schuyler. CP-SchuJ

Sospetto d'Herode. Giovanni Giambattista. CP-CrasR *Fr.* Strage degli innocenti, La.

Soto! Explore thyself! Emily Dickinson. CP-DickE

Sotto Voce. Walter De la Mare. CP-DeLaW

Sotto Voce. Stanley Kunitz. CP-KunSC

Sottoportico San Zaccaria. Kenneth Rexroth. CP-RexrK

Soufflé. Philip Whalen. SP-WhalP

Soughing Wind, The. William Carlos Williams. CP-WilW1

Soul. Charles Bukowski. SP-BukC1

Soul. Richard Eberhart. CP-EberR

Soul, A. Randall Jarrell. CP-JarrR

Soul, The. George Meredith. CP-MerG2

Soul, The. Charles Olson. CP-OlsoC

Soul, The. Jelaluddin Rumi. CP-EmerR

Soul, The. Adam Zagajewski. SP-ZagaA, *tr. by* Clare Cavanagh

Soul and Body of John Brown, The. Muriel Rukeyser. CP-RukeM

Soul as full of Worth, as void of Pride, A. Epistle to James Craggs, Esq., Secretary of State. Alexander Pope. CP-PopeA

Soul-bird often, The. Rainer Maria Rilke. CP-RilkFr, *tr. by* A. Poulin, Jr. *Fr.* Orchards.

Soul-Cake, A. Denise Levertov. SP-LeveDL; SP-LeveDS

Soul, / Caught in the rose-hued mesh. Donzella Beata. Ezra Pound. CP-PoEar

Soul curls back, A. Effects of Music upon a Company of People. Ezra Pound. CP-PoEar

Soul, Geologically, A. Margaret Atwood. SP-AtwM1

Soul has Bandaged moments, The. Emily Dickinson. CP-DickE

Soul has many motions, body one, The. Motion, The. Theodore Roethke. CP-RoetT

Soul, he said, is composed, The. Anecdote of Men by the Thousand. Wallace Stevens. CP-StevW; CP-StevWP

Soul heeds not, though darkest night, The. Soul in Dreams, The. Jones Very. CP-VeryJ

Soul hired a body, A. Body and Soul. Charles Simic. SP-SimiCE

Soul in Dreams, The. Jones Very. CP-VeryJ

Soul is a region without definite boundaries, The. Terrain. A. R. Ammons. CP-AmmoA

Soul Is the Salt, The. Robert Herrick. CP-HerrR

Soul itself its awful witness is, The. Oriental Maxims. John Greenleaf Whittier. CP-WhitJ

Soul-Light. Dante Gabriel Rossetti. CW-RossD *Fr.* House of Life, The.

Soul lives on, I know it, lying here, The. Michelangelo Buonarroti. CP-Miche, *tr. by* John Frederick Nims

Soul lonely comes and goes; for each our theme. Lachesis. Kathleen Jessie Raine. SP-RainK

Soul Longs to Return Whence It Came, The. Richard Eberhart. CP-EberR

Soul must go by Death alone, The. Emily Dickinson. SP-DickE

Soul, O ganders, flies beyond the parks, The. Invective against Swans. Wallace Stevens. CP-StevW; CP-StevWP

Soul of a Butterfly, The. Nicholas Vachel Lindsay. CP-LindV

Soul of a Spider, The. Nicholas Vachel Lindsay. CP-LindV

Soul of each silkworm who gave each thread, The. Say Yes. Thomas Lux. SP-LuxT

Soul of happy youth is never lost, The. Wallace Stevens. CP-StevWP

Soul of the City Receives the Gift of the Holy Spirit, The. Nicholas Vachel Lindsay. CP-LindV

Soul opens inside you on beauty. Shmuel HaNagid. SP-HaNaS, *tr. by* Peter Cole

Soul rudderless, unbraced. Christina Georgina Rossetti. CP-RosC3

Soul selects her own Society, The. Emily Dickinson. CP-DickE

Soul-Sickness. Jones Very. SP-VeryJ

Soul stop and stare . . . How sickening they are! Blind, The. Charles Baudelaire. CP-BaudC, *tr. by* Walter Martin

Soul, take thy risk. Emily Dickinson. CP-DickE

Soul that hath a Guest, The. Emily Dickinson. CP-DickE

Soul That Loves God Finds Him Every Where, The. Jeanne Marie Bouvier de la Motte- Guyon. CP-CowpW

Soul unto itself, The. Emily Dickinson. CP-DickE

Soul, Wilt thou toss again? Emily Dickinson. CP-DickE

Soulages's space is deep and wide. Moderate, The. John Updike. CP-UpdiJ

Soule, The. Robert Herrick. CP-HerrR

Souls. C. K. Williams. SP-WillC

Soul's Beauty. Dante Gabriel Rossetti. CW-RossD *Fr.* House of Life, The.

Soul's dark cottage, batter'd and decay'd, The. Old King, The. Denise Levertov. SP-LeveDS

Soul's Desert, The. Robinson Jeffers. CP-JefR3

Soul's distinct connection, The. Emily Dickinson. CP-DickE

Soul's Expression, The. Elizabeth Barrett Browning. CP-BroEB

Soul's Freedom, The. Jones Very. SP-VeryJ

Soul's Haven. Marya Alexandrovna Zaturenska. SP-ZatuM

Souls in virginity joined together. Virgin Mirror. Robert Graves. CP-GravR

Soul's Invitation, The. Jones Very. CP-VeryJ

Soul's joy, when thou art gone. Parody [*or* Parodie], A. George Herbert. CP-HerbG

Souls Looking for Bodies. Andrei Codrescu. SP-CodrA

Souls of Poets dead and gone. Lines on the Mermaid Tavern. John Keats. CP-KeatJ

Souls of the day's dead fly up like birds, big sister, The. Composition in Grey and Pink. Charles Wright. SP-WrigC

Souls of the Slain, The. Thomas Hardy. CP-HardT

Souls of Women at Night, The. Wallace Stevens. CP-StevWP

Soul's Opportunities, The. Jones Very. SP-VeryJ

Soul's Preparation for Adversity, The. Jones Very. CP-VeryJ

Soul's Questioning of the Universe, and Its Beginning, The. Jones Very. CP-VeryJ

Soul's Rest, The. Jones Very. CP-VeryJ

Souls rise alive from the body's sad last bed. Michelangelo Buonarroti. CP-Miche, *tr. by* John Frederick Nims

Soul's Season, The. Henry David Thoreau. CP-ThorH

Soul's Sphere, The. Dante Gabriel Rossetti. CW-RossD *Fr.* House of Life, The.

Soul's Superior instants, The. Emily Dickinson. CP-DickE

Souls to Save. D. H. Lawrence. CP-LawrD

Soul's Travelling, The. Elizabeth Barrett Browning. CP-BroEB

Sound. Robert Creeley. CP-CreeR

Sound, The. Robert Creeley. SP-CreeR

Sound as if from bells of silver, A. Pageant, The. John Greenleaf Whittier. CP-WhitJ

Sound. / Even if only sound remains. Straining Toward Statue. Federico García Lorca. CP-GarcF, *tr. by* Alan S. Trueblood *Fr.* Songs to End With.

Sound forth, cælestiall Organs, lett heavens quire. Upon the Kings Coronation. Richard Crashaw. CP-CrasR

Sound from the Earth, A. William Stafford. SP-StafWW

Sound in the Night, A. Thomas Hardy. CP-HardT

Sound is dark; you can barely hear, The. Night Fishing in the Sound. Eleanor Wilner. SP-WilnE

Sound Lag. Arthur Sze. SP-SzeA

Sound now the trumpet warningly! Frémont Campaign Song, A. John Greenleaf Whittier. CP-WhitJ

Sound of a mourning dove, The. Mourning Dove. Lorine Niedecker. CP-NiedL

Sound of Fear, A. Denise Levertov. SP-LeveDL

Sound of music in the house. House of Music, A. Kathleen Jessie Raine. SP-RainK

Sound of passing cars, (if a car comes), The. Ernesto Cardenal. CP-MertT *Fr.* Gethsemani, KY.

Sound of Rapids of Laramie River in Late August. W. S. Merwin. SP-MerwWF

Sound of screaming for thirteen centuries, A. Muriel Rukeyser. CP-RukeM

Sound of Snow, The. Hayden Carruth. CP-CarHS

Sound of the Axe. Denise Levertov. SP-LeveDL

Sound of the closing outside door was all, The. Valley's Singing Day, The. Robert Frost. CP-FrosR

Sound of Time, The. Charles Tomlinson. CP-TomlC

Sound of Trees, The. Robert Frost. CP-FrosR

Sound of trumpets comes, A. Slope. Eugenio Montale. CP-MontE, *tr. by* Jonathan Galassi

Sound of tumult troubles all the air, A. What of the Day? John Greenleaf Whittier. CP-WhitJ

Sound of Waves, The. William Carlos Williams. CP-WilW2

Sound over all waters, reach out from all lands. Christmas Carmen, A. John Greenleaf Whittier. CP-WhitJ

Sound Sleep. Christina Georgina Rossetti. CP-RosC1

Sound slender, quasi tinnula. Canto 20: "Sound slender, quasi tinnula." Ezra Pound. SP-PounE *Fr.* Cantos.

Sound, sound aloud / The welcome of the orient flood. Ben Jonson. CP-JonsB *Fr.* Masque of Blackness, The.

Sound Teeth has Lucie, pure as Pearl, and small. Upon Lucie. Robert Herrick. CP-HerrR

Sound the deep waters. Sleep at Sea. Christina Georgina Rossetti. CP-RosC1

Sound the invisible trumps. In circuit vast. Break of Morning. Walter De la Mare. CP-DeLaW

Sounding brass and tinkling cymbal. Music. G. K. Chesterton. CP-ChesG

Soundless the moth-flit, crisp the death-watch tick. Maerchen. Walter De la Mare. CP-DeLaW

Sounds. Elizabeth Barrett Browning. CP-BroEB

Sounds. John Ciardi. CP-CiarJ

Sounds. Robert Creeley. CP-CreeR

Sounds are ringing on my ear. Death Decay and Change. Jones Very. CP-VeryJ

Sounds are the sea, breaking out of sight, The. Birthday Party, The. Josephine Jacobsen. CP-JacoJ

Sounds, crank. Loner. Robert Creeley. SP-CreeR

Sounds like ball. Here ("Sounds like ball"). Robert Creeley. SP-CreeR

Sounds like big. Waking from a Nap on the Beach. May Swenson. SP-SwenM

Sounds Like Pearls. Maya Angelou. SP-AngeM

Sounds of a Devon Village. Donald Davie. CP-DaviDC

Sounds of labor in the street, hammers at work to open pavement, ignore me, The. Thus Truly. David Ignatow. SP-IgnaD

Sounds of night in the country of the opposites. Muriel Rukeyser. CP-RukeM

Sounds of rain on the roof, The. Secret Man. Wallace Stevens. CP-StevWP

Sounds / Of the Harlem night, The. Summer Night. Langston Hughes. CP-HughL; CP-HughL1

Sounds of the Winter. Walt Whitman. CP-WhitW

Soup ("I know what you'd say"). Robert Creeley. SP-CreeR

Soup ("Trembling / with delight"). Robert Creeley. CP-CreeR

Soup. Carl Sandburg. CP-SandC

Soup of Venus, The. James Tate. SP-TateJ

Soup, The. Charles Simic. SP-SimiCE

Soup, The. Charles Simic. SP-SimiC

Sour smell, The. Getting in the Wood. Gary Snyder. CP-SnydG

Source. Robert Duncan. SP-DuncR

Source, The. George Oppen. CP-OppGN

Source, The. William Carlos Williams. CP-WilW1

Source of love, and light of day. Self-Diffidence. Jeanne Marie Bouvier de la Motte- Guyon. CP-CowpW

Source of Love, my brighter Sun. Necessity of Self-Abasement. Jeanne Marie Bouvier de la Motte- Guyon. CP-CowpW

Sources. Philip Levine. SP-LeviP

Sources. Adrienne Rich. SP-RicA1

Sourdough mountain called a fire in. Text, The. Gary Snyder. CP-SnydG *Fr.* Myths and Texts.

Sourdough Mountain Lookout. Philip Whalen. SP-WhalP

Sours of the Hills. Gary Snyder. CP-SnydG

South. Federico García Lorca. CP-GarcF, *tr. by* Jerome Rothenberg *Fr.* Cross.

South. W. S. Merwin. SP-MerwW

South, The. Jorge Luis Borges. SP-BorgJ, *tr. by* W. S. Merwin

South, The. Langston Hughes. CP-HughL; CP-HughL1

South Africa. Rudyard Kipling. CP-KiplR

South and far south below the Line. With Drake in the Tropics. Rudyard Kipling. CP-KiplR

South Carolina Morning. Yusef Komunyakaa. CP-KomuY

South China Sea [drives in], The. Break from the Bush, A. Yusef Komunyakaa. CP-KomuY

South End. James Tate. SP-TateJ

South-land boasts its teeming cane, The. Our State. John Greenleaf Whittier. CP-WhitJ

South light / wakes us. I turn. Alba. Arthur Sze. SP-SzeA

South Lodge is blue. Kensington Notebook, A. Derek Mahon. CP-MahoD

South, / mirage, / reflection. South. Federico García Lorca. CP-GarcF, *tr. by* Jerome Rothenberg *Fr.* Cross.

South of Boston, south of Washington. Robert Lowell. SP-LoweR *Fr.* Mexico.

South of the Alps. John Updike. CP-UpdiJ

South of the Bridge on Seventeenth. Fifteen. William Stafford. SP-StafW; SP-StafWW

South of the Line, inland from far Durban. Christmas Ghost-Story, A. Thomas

Hardy. CP-HardT

South River at Sunset, The. Jones Very. CP-VeryJ

South Sea King was Act-on-Your-Hunch, The. Two Kings and No-Form. Chuang Tzu. CP-MertT

South: The Name of Home. Alice Walker. CP-WalkA

South-West Wind in the Woodland. George Meredith. CP-MerG1

South-Wester, The. George Meredith. CP-MerG1

South Wind. Ralph Waldo Emerson. CP-EmerR

South Wind and the Sun, The. James Whitcomb Riley. CP-RileJ

South-wind brings, The. Threnody: "South-wind brings, The." Ralph Waldo Emerson. CP-EmerR

South wind. / Dark and burning. Weathervane. Federico García Lorca. CP-GarcF, *tr. by* Catherine Brown

South Wind—has a pathos, A. Emily Dickinson. CP-DickE

South Wind Says So, The. Carl Sandburg. CP-SandC

South wind / striking in—torn. Advent of Today. William Carlos Williams. CP-WilW1

South Window. Grace Paley. CP-PalGC

South Winds jostle them. Emily Dickinson. CP-DickE

Southeast Arkanasia. Maya Angelou. SP-AngeM

Southern Cross, The. Charles Wright. SP-WrigC

Southern Dawn. Pier Paolo Pasolini. SP-PasoP, *tr. by* Norman MacAfee *and* Luciano Martinengo

Southern gentle lady. Silhouette. Langston Hughes. CP-HughL *Fr.* Three Songs about Lynching.

Southern Mammy Sings. Langston Hughes. CP-HughL; CP-HughL2

Southern Negro Speaks. Langston Hughes. CP-HughL; CP-HughL2

Southern Night. D. H. Lawrence. CP-LawrD

Southern Pacific. Carl Sandburg. CP-SandC

Southern Singer, A. James Whitcomb Riley. CP-RileJ

Southern Sunrise. Sylvia Plath. CP-PlatS

Southey! Alas, my writings. Two Intercepted Letters. Donald Davie. CP-DaviDC

Southey! thy melodies steal o'er mine ear. To Robert Southey. Samuel Taylor Coleridge. CP-ColeS

Southward floated over. To Florida. Louise Glück. SP-GlucL

Southwest of Buffalo. Donald Hall. CP-HallD

Southwest the moon. Le Motif. Denise Levertov. SP-LeveDS

Souvenir. Edna St. Vincent Millay. CP-MillE

Souvenir. Edwin Arlington Robinson. CP-RobiE

Souvenir, The. Robert Creeley. CP-CreeR

Souvenir, The. Dan Pagis. SP-PagiD, *tr. by* Stephen Mitchell

Souvenir de Monsieur Poop. Stevie Smith. CP-SmitS

Souvenir of Japan, A. Michael Palmer. SP-PalmM

Souvenirs of Democracy. Walt Whitman. CP-WhitW

Sovereign of the wilderness! Kenneth Patchen. CP-PatcK

Soviet Souvenir. Ted Berrigan. SP-BerrT

Sow. Sylvia Plath. CP-PlatS

Sow Piglet's Escapes, The. Galway Kinnell. SP-KinnGN

Sower, The. Jones Very. CP-VeryJ

Sower's face is secret, The. Daisy-Song. G. K. Chesterton. CP-ChesG

Sowing. Wendell Berry. CP-BerrW

Sowing. Audre Lorde. SP-LordA

Sowing of Meanings, The. Thomas Merton. CP-MertT

Sown in dishonor! Emily Dickinson. CP-DickE

Soy Sauce. Gary Snyder. CP-SnydG

Sozzled, Mo-tsu, after a silence, vouchsafed. Scholars at the Orchid Pavilion. John Berryman. CP-BerrJ

Space. D. H. Lawrence. CP-LawrD

Space, The. George Oppen. CP-OppGN

Space & stars / reflected into sound. Below. Federico García Lorca. CP-GarcF, *tr. by* Jerome Rothenberg *Fr.* Night (Suite for Piano and Poet's Voice).

Space being(don't forget to remember)Curved. E. E. Cummings. CP-CummE

Space Between Two Blades of Grass Meets an Intractable Ego, The. Robert Stock. SP-StocR

Space Creatures. Charles Bukowski. SP-BukC3

Space is ample, east and west. Unity. Ralph Waldo Emerson. CP-EmerR

"Space Is Not Merely a Background for Events, But Possesses an Autonomous Structure." —A. Einstein. Alan Dugan. CP-DugaA

Space mildews at our touch. Moth Hour. Adrienne Rich. CP-RicAE; SP-RicA2

Space of the world is immense, before me and around me, The. Song of a Man Who Is Not Loved. D. H. Lawrence. CP-LawrD

Space—shroud and swaddle—you wore. You, Hart Crane. Charles Olson. CP-OlsoC

Space Song. Alfonso Cortes. CP-MertT, *tr. by* Thomas Merton

Space Soufflé. Andrei Codrescu. SP-CodrA

SPACE (spelled large) the central fact. Local Genius, The. Amy Clampitt. CP-ClamA

Space Travel. A. R. Ammons. CP-AmmoA

Space / window / that looks into itself. Poem: "Space / window / that looks into itself." Charles Tomlinson. CP-TomlC

Spaces between / archetypal openings the aperture. Let the Air Circulate. Amy Clampitt. CP-ClamA

Spaceship. A. R. Ammons. CP-AmmoA

Spaceship. Dan Pagis. SP-PagiD, *tr. by* Stephen Mitchell

Spade! with which Wilkinson hath tilled his lands. To the Spade of a Friend (An Agriculturist). William Wordsworth. CP-WorW1

Spades take up leaves. Gathering Leaves. Robert Frost. CP-FrosR

Spain, 1873–74. Walt Whitman. CP-WhitW

Spain frightened you. Spain. You Hated Spain. Ted Hughes. SP-HughTN

Spain Sits Like a Hidden Flower in My Coffeepot. Charles Bukowski. SP-BukC2

Spake the fire-tinged bramble, bossed with gleaming fruit. Thus Her Tale. Walter De la Mare. CP-DeLaW

Span. W. S. Merwin. SP-MerwW

Spaniard. "Rubén Dario." SP-DariR, *tr. by* Alberto Acereda *and* Will Derusha

Spaniel, Beau, that fares like you, A. On a Spaniel Called Beau Killing a Young Bird. William Cowper. CP-CowpW

Spanish. Carl Sandburg. CP-SandC

Spanish Friar [*or* Fryar], The. John Dryden.
Prologue to *The Spanish Friar*. SP-DrydJ
(Song.) SP-DrydJ

Spanish Guerillas 1811. William Wordsworth. CP-WorW1

Spanish Lady, The. Walt Whitman. CP-WhitW

Spanish Lie, The. Archibald MacLeish. CP-MacLA

Spanish Privilege. D. H. Lawrence. CP-LawrD

Spanish School. Stevie Smith. CP-SmitS

Spanish Sonnets. John Updike. CP-UpdiJ

Spanish Vineyards. Jaroslav Seifert. SP-SeifJ, *tr. by* Ewald Osers

Spanish Wife, The. D. H. Lawrence. CP-LawrD

Spare me, dread angel of reproof. Answer, The. John Greenleaf Whittier. CP-WhitJ

Spare me thy vengeance, G———. To the Same, on the Author Being Threatened with His Resentment. Robert Burns. CP-BurnR *Fr.* Epigrams on Lord Galloway.

Spare thou neither time nor blood for thy friend. Hafiz. CP-EmerR *Fr.* Odes.

Spared by a car or airplane crash or. Accidents of Birth. William Meredith. SP-MereW

Spark, The. Walter De la Mare. CP-DeLaW

Spark of Godhead! child. Soul, The. George Meredith. CP-MerG2

Spark of Laurel, A. Stanley Kunitz. CP-KunSC

Sparkle Depends on Flaws in the Diamond, The. William Stafford. SP-StafWW

Sparkles from the Wheel. Walt Whitman. CP-WhitW

Sparkling eye, the mantling cheek, The. Song, A: "Sparkling eye, the mantling cheek, The." William Cowper. CP-CowpW

Sparks. Charles Bukowski. SP-BukC3

Sparks. Denise Levertov. SP-LeveDP

Sparks. James Schuyler. SP-SchuJ

Sparrow. Thom Gunn. CP-GunnT *Fr.* Three Songs.

Sparrow. Wendell Berry. CP-BerrW

Sparrow, The. Paul Laurence Dunbar. CP-DunbP

Sparrow, The. William Carlos Williams. CP-WilW2

Sparrow and the Robin on a toot, The. Tiger on Parade, The. Nicholas Vachel Lindsay. CP-LindV

Sparrow dips in his wheel-rut bath, The. Five Students, The. Thomas Hardy. CP-HardT

Sparrow in the cobbled street. Stranger's Child. George Oppen. CP-OppGN

Sparrow is / his hunger organized, A. Sparrow. Wendell Berry. CP-BerrW

Sparrow is rich in her nest, The. Ralph Waldo Emerson. CP-EmerR

Sparrow lights on wisteria, A. In the Audience. John Ciardi. CP-CiarJ

Sparrow, my girl's pleasure, delight of my girl. Catullus. *See* Lesbia's sparrow! / Lesbia's plaything

Sparrow Nights. Raymond Carver. CP-CarvR

Sparrow on house-top never was alone. Petrarch. CP-Petra, *tr. by* J. G. Nichols

Sparrow-spry, the orgiastic barnyard. Errant Mole and the Loveliest of Hawks, The. Robert Stock. SP-StocR

Sparrow took a Slice of Twig, A. Emily Dickinson. CP-DickE

Sparrowhawk / flies hard to, The. Anxiety. A. R. Ammons. CP-AmmoA

Sparrows. Hayden Carruth. CP-CarHS

Sparrows. Robert Creeley. SP-CreeR

Sparrows among Dry Leaves. William Carlos Williams. CP-WilW2

Sparrows and the Crop of Weeds, The. Jones Very. CP-VeryJ

Sparrows by the iron fence post, The. Sparrows among Dry Leaves. William Carlos Williams. CP-WilW2

Sparrows in a Hillside Drift. James Wright. CP-WrigJ

Sparrow's Nest, The. William Wordsworth. CP-WorW1
  (Look, five blue eggs are gleaming there!) MW-WorW
Sparrows quarreled outside our window. Waking an Angel. Philip Levine. SP-LeviP
Sparrows Self-Domesticated. Vincent Bourne. CP-CowpW
Sparrows still are lingering here, The. Our Native Sparrows. Jones Very. CP-VeryJ
Spartan, his companion slain, A. From Julianus. Emperor Julian. CP-CowpW
Spartan 'scaping from the fight, A. By Palladas. Palladas. CP-CowpW
Spasmodically cold rain flows down the windows. Little Town, The. Tennessee Williams. CP-WillT
Speak. James Wright. CP-WrigJ
Speak and tell us, our Ximena, looking northward far away. Angels of Buena Vista, The. John Greenleaf Whittier. CP-WhitJ
Speak, did the Bloud of Abel cry. Abels Bloud. Robert Herrick. CP-HerrR
Speak earth and bless me with what is richest. Love Poem. Audre Lorde. SP-LordA
Speak gently to your husband, ma'am. Warning to Wives, A. Ogden Nash. CP-NashO
Speak, Gracious Lord, oh speak; thy Servant hears. Paraphrase on Thomas à Kempis, A. Alexander Pope. CP-PopeA
Speak low to me, my Saviour, low and sweet. Comfort. Elizabeth Barrett Browning. CP-BroEB
Speak, Memory! Mona Van Duyn. SP-VanDM
Speak not, let no word break. Kenneth Rexroth. CP-RexrK
Speak not—whisper not. Sunken Garden, The. Walter De la Mare. CP-DeLaW
Speak, sir, and be wise. Basket. Carl Sandburg. CP-SandC
Speak softly; sun going down. Fall of the Evening Star. Kenneth Patchen. CP-PatcK
Speak softly: you're older than the one. Adam Zagajewski. SP-ZagaA, tr. by Clare Cavanagh
Speak! speak! thou fearful guest! Skeleton in Armor [or Armour], The. Henry Wadsworth Longfellow. SP-LongH
Speak thou and speed, where will or power ought [or aught] help'th. Sir Thomas Wyatt. CP-WyatT
Speak Thou for me against wrong-speaking foes. Bible, O.T. See Plead my cause, O Lord, with them that strive with me
Speak to her heart. Ars Amoris. James Vincent Cunningham. CP-CunnJ
Speak to me friend! Or is the world so wide. W.H.W., Jr. E. E. Cummings. CP-CummE
Speak to me. Take my hand. What are you now? Effort at Speech between Two People. Muriel Rukeyser. CP-RukeM
Speak! yellow men who grub for gold. Josepha. George Meredith. CP-McrG2
Speak You Too. Paul Celan. SP-CelaP, tr. by John Felstiner
Speake in Season. Robert Herrick. CP-HerrR
Speaker and Speaker. Grace Paley.
Speaker in this case, The. Gold Key, The. Anne Sexton. CP-SextA
Speakin' at de Cou't-House. Paul Laurence Dunbar. CP-DunbP
Speakin' in general, I 'ave tried 'em all. Sestina of the Tramp-Royal. Rudyard Kipling. CP-KiplR
Speakin' o' Christmas. Paul Laurence Dunbar. CP-DunbP
Speaking at the Rotary is Praise devoid of Proof, The. Rotarians. G. K. Chesterton. CP-ChesG
Speaking Bitterness. Anne Sexton. CP-SextA
Speaking for Them. Hayden Carruth. CP-CarHS
Speaking mouth's a hearse of wasted days, The. Leaflet (One). Kenneth Patchen. CP-PatcK
Speaking of death / and decay. Exercises on Themes from Life. Alice Walker. CP-WalkA
Speaking of Food. Langston Hughes. CP-HughL; CP-HughL3
Speaking of love(of). E. E. Cummings. CP-CummE
Speaking of Luck. Yusef Komunyakaa. CP-KomuY
Speaking of the skylark in a New England classroom. Meadowlark Country. Amy Clampitt. CP-ClamA
Speaking to mountains (& / hearing them speak!) assiduously. He Said. A. R. Ammons. CP-AmmoA
Speaking Tree, The. Muriel Rukeyser. CP-RukeM
Spearmint. Louis Zukofsky. CP-ZukLS
Special Bulletin. Langston Hughes. CP-HughL; CP-HughL3
Special continuations: the Gethsemani racetrack. Thomas Merton. CP-MertT
Special Plates. Jelaluddin Rumi. SP-Rumi, tr. by Coleman Barks
Special Starlight. Carl Sandburg. CP-SandC
Specially for me, she had some breaded. Breaded Fish. A. K. Ramanujan. CP-RamaA
Species of common garden cat, who are. Lady of Shalott, Her Mirror Broken, The. William Dickey. SP-DickW
Species of thistle no one had ever seen before appeared almost overnight in all the meadows, A. Drought. C. K. Williams. SP-WillC

Specific light, / water, ground. Wanting You. Robert Creeley. CP-CreeR
Specimen of an Induction to a Poem. John Keats. CP-KeatJ
Specimens. Czeslaw Milosz. CP-MiloCN, tr. by Robert Hass
Specimens do not know they are specimens. Specimens. Czeslaw Milosz. CP-MiloCN, tr. by Robert Hass
Speciously individual. Untitled Poem: "Speciously individual." Alan Dugan. CP-DugaA
Speck that would have been beneath my sight, A. Considerable Speck, A. Robert Frost. CP-FrosR
Speckled cat and a tame hare, A. Two Songs of a Fool. William Butler Yeats. CP-YeatW
Speckled frogs leap from my mouth. Fantasy and Conversation. Audre Lorde. SP-LordA
Spectacle of the New York Yacht Club, The. Sailing to Buck's Harbor. Richard Eberhart. CP-EberR
Spectacles. Heather McHugh. SP-McHuH
Specter trailing restless silver, A. Sonnet: "Specter trailing restless silver, A." Federico García Lorca. CP-GarcF, tr. by Alan S. Trueblood Fr. Love.
Spectral Lovers. John Crowe Ransom. SP-RansJ
Spectre, The. Walter De la Mare. CP-DeLaW
Spectres That Grieve. Thomas Hardy. CP-HardT
Speculate with all our might. Emily Dickinson. SP-DickE
Speculation. Howard Nemerov. CP-NemeH
Speculative. Robert Browning. CP-BroR2
Speech. Robert Creeley. SP-CreeR
Speech. Walter De la Mare. CP-DeLaW
Speech. Carl Sandburg. CP-SandC
Speech According to Horace, A. Ben Jonson. CP-JonsB; SP-JonsB
Speech after long silence; it is right. After Long Silence. William Butler Yeats. CP-YeatW
Speech at Soli, The. George Oppen. CP-OppGN
Speech at the Lost and Found, A. Wisława Szymborska. SP-SzymWM, tr. by Joanna Trzeciak
Speech for Aeneas. Alan Dugan. CP-DugaA
Speech: For Antidraft Rally, D.C., March 22, 1980, A. Denise Levertov. SP-LeveDL
Speech for Auden. Alan Dugan. CP-DugaA
Speech for Psyche in the Golden Book of Apuleius. Ezra Pound. CP-PoEar
Speech for the Assistant, from Houdini. Muriel Rukeyser. CP-RukeM
Speech for the Repeal of the McCarran Act. Richard Wilbur. CP-WilbR
Speech from the Stairs. Tennessee Williams. CP-WillT
Speech-Grille. Paul Celan. SP-CelaP, tr. by John Felstiner
"Speech"—is a prank of Parliament. Emily Dickinson. CP-DickE
Speech is one symptom of Affection. Emily Dickinson. CP-DickE
Speech of the Mother, from "The Middle of the Air." Muriel Rukeyser. CP-RukeM
Speech of Venus to Vulcan, The. Virgil. CP-DryJ2, tr. by John Dryden Fr. Aeneid.
Speech Out of Shadow. Ted Hughes. SP-HughTN
Speech Presented unto King James at a Tilting in the Behalf of the Two Noble Brothers S[ir] Robert and S[ir] Henry Rich, Now Earls of Warwick and Holland, A. Ben Jonson. CP-JonsB
Speech Reported, A. G. K. Chesterton. CP-ChesG
Speech to a Crowd. Archibald MacLeish. CP-MacLA
Speech to the Detractors. Archibald MacLeish. CP-MacLA
Speech to the Student Clowns at the Circus Clown School at Sarasota, Florida. Alan Dugan. CP-DugaA
Speech to Those Who Say Comrade. Archibald MacLeish. CP-MacLA
Speeches. Donald Hall. CP-HallD
Speeches at the Barriers. Susan Howe. SP-HoweS
Speeches for Dr Frankenstein. Margaret Atwood. SP-AtwM1
Speechless statue of the Virgin stands, The. Adoration of the Virgin, The. Robert Duncan. SP-DuncR
Speed. May Swenson. SP-SwenM
Speed, Malise, speed! the lake is past. Fiery Cross, The. Sir Walter Scott. SP-ScotW Fr. Lady of the Lake, The.
Speed of Darkness, The. Muriel Rukeyser and Leif Sjoberg. CP-RukeM
Speed, We Say. Muriel Rukeyser. CP-RukeM
Speed, we say of our time: racing my writing word. Speed, We Say. Muriel Rukeyser. CP-RukeM
Speeding from city, feeling day. Driveway. Muriel Rukeyser. CP-RukeM
Speeding of the King's Spite, The. James Whitcomb Riley. CP-RileJ
Speleology. Robert Penn Warren. CP-WarrR
Spell. Raymond Carver. CP-CarvR
Spell, The. Robert Herrick. CP-HerrR
Spell Against Demons. Gary Snyder. CP-SnydG
Spell Against Sorrow. Kathleen Jessie Raine. SP-RainK
Spell before Winter, A. Howard Nemerov. CP-NemeH

Spell cannot be tattered, A. Emily Dickinson. SP-DickE

Spell Is Broke, the Charm is Flown, The. Lord Byron. CP-Byron

Spell of Conjunctivitis, A. Mona Van Duyn. SP-VanDM

Spell of Sleep. Kathleen Jessie Raine. SP-RainK

Spell of the Rose, The. Thomas Hardy. CP-HardT

Spell to Bring Lost Creatures Home. Kathleen Jessie Raine. SP-RainK

Spellbound. Emily Jane Brontë. CP-BronE

Spellbound. Marya Alexandrovna Zaturenska. SP-ZatuM

Spellbound Palace, A. Thomas Hardy. CP-HardT

Spellin'-Bee, The. Paul Laurence Dunbar. CP-DunbP

Spelling Lesson, A. G. K. Chesterton. CP-ChesG

Spelling reformer indicted, A. Orthography. Ambrose Bierce. SP-BierA *Fr.* Devil's Dictionary, The.

Spells and Incantation (a Fragment). Wilfred Owen. CP-OwenW

Spelt from Sibyl's Leaves. Gerard Manley Hopkins. CP-HopkG

Spelunker. Robert Pinsky. CP-PinsR

Spend Harmless shade thy nightly Houres. Upon a Virgin. Robert Herrick. CP-HerrR

Spend the years of learning squandering. Gnome. Samuel Beckett. CP-BeckS

Spending beyond their income on gifts for Christmas. Christmas Shopping. Louis MacNeice. CP-MacNL

Spending hand that alway poureth [*or* powreth] out [*or* owte], A. To Sir Francis Brian. Sir Thomas Wyatt. CP-WyatT *Fr.* Satires.

Spenke has a strong breath, yet short Prayers saith. Upon Spenke. Robert Herrick. CP-HerrR

Spenser! A Jealous Honourer of Thine. John Keats. CP-KeatJ

Spenser's Ireland. Marianne Craig Moore. CP-MoorM

Spent purpose of a perfectly marvellous, The. In Favor of One's Time. Frank O'Hara. SP-OharF

Sperm. Maxine W. Kumin. SP-KumiM

Spes. "Rubén Dario." SP-DariR, *tr.* by Alberto Acereda *and* Will Derusha

Spheral Change. Dante Gabriel Rossetti. CW-RossD

Sphere. Federico García Lorca. CP-GarcF, *tr.* by Jerome Rothenberg *Fr.* Suite.

Sphere. A. R. Ammons. CP-AmmoA

Sphere, the. Kathleen Jessie Raine. SP-RainK

Spheres, The. Jones Very. CP-VeryJ

Sphincter. Allen Ginsberg. SP-GinsA

Sphinx. Richard Eberhart. CP-EberR

Sphinx. Robert Earl Hayden. CP-HaydR

Sphinx. D. H. Lawrence. CP-LawrD

Sphinx, A. Carl Sandburg. CP-SandC

Sphinx, The. Ralph Waldo Emerson. CP-EmerR

Sphinx, The. James Whitcomb Riley. CP-RileJ

Sphinx, The. Oscar Wilde. CP-WildO

Sphinx has fallen upon him, The. Oedipus. Constantine P. Cavafy. CP-CavaC, *tr.* by Theoharis Constantine Theoharis

Sphinx Hour, The. Federico García Lorca. CP-GarcF, *tr.* by Jerome Rothenberg *Fr.* In the Forest of Clocks.

Sphinx's Riddle to Oedipus, The. Randall Jarrell. CP-JarrR

Spice-Tree, The. Nicholas Vachel Lindsay. CP-LindV

Spices in the plants that run. Ralph Waldo Emerson. CP-EmerR

Spider. Czeslaw Milosz. CP-MiloCN, *tr.* by Robert Hass

Spider. Sylvia Plath. CP-PlatS

Spider, The. Charles Bukowski. SP-BukC1

Spider, The. Richard Eberhart. CP-EberR

Spider and the Ghost of the Fly, The. Nicholas Vachel Lindsay. CP-LindV

Spider as an Artist, The. Emily Dickinson. CP-DickE

Spider expects the cold of winter, The. Spider, The. Richard Eberhart. CP-EberR

Spider floats from the apple tree, A. Grandmother. Norman Dubie. CP-DubiN

Spider holds a Silver Ball, The. Emily Dickinson. CP-DickE

Spider is sewing the silence, A. Prison Poem. Tibor Tollas. SP-LogaJ, *tr.* by John Logan

Spider Mums, The. Karl Shapiro. SP-ShapK

Spider mums are yellow, The. Spider Mums, The. Karl Shapiro. SP-ShapK

Spider on the cold expanse. Dusk. Rae Armantrout. SP-ArmaA

Spider or Ribbon Plant. Louis Zukofsky. CP-ZukLS

Spider pendulously waits, The. Breaking Webs. Louis MacNeice. CP-MacNL

Spider Psyche. C. K. Williams. SP-WillC

Spider sewed at Night, A. Emily Dickinson. CP-DickE

Spider spreads her webs, whether she be, The. Letter to Maria Gisborne. Percy Bysshe Shelley. CP-ShelP

Spider, you have long silver legs. Sun Dancer. Carl Sandburg. CP-SandC

Spiders Wanting. Thomas Lux. SP-LuxT

Spiel. A. R. Ammons. CP-AmmoA

Spiel of [the] Three Mountebanks. John Crowe Ransom. SP-RansJ

Spies' March, The. Rudyard Kipling. CP-KiplR

Spies, you are lights in state, but of base stuff. On Spies. Ben Jonson. CP-JonsB; SP-JonsB

Spiked heels, fake fingernails and frizzy curls. Ideal, The. Charles Baudelaire. CP-BaudC, *tr.* by Walter Martin

Spiked sun. The Hudson's. Early December in Croton-on-Hudson. Louise Glück. SP-GlucL

Spikes of new smell driven up nostrils. Gary Snyder. CP-SnydG *Fr.* Myths and Texts.

Spilled. Heather McHugh. SP-McHuH

Spilling the Salt. D. H. Lawrence. CP-LawrD

Spilt Milk. William Butler Yeats. CP-YeatW

Spilth. G. K. Chesterton. CP-ChesG

Spin the ball! I reel, I burn. Song of Seyd [*or* Seid] Nimetollah of Kuhistan. Seid Nimatullah. CP-EmerR, *tr.* by Ralph Waldo Emerson

Spindle. A. R. Ammons. CP-AmmoA

Spindle Song, The. Sir Walter Scott. SP-ScotW

Spindrift. Galway Kinnell. SP-KinnGN

Spindrift, crustacean patience. Swim in Co. Wicklow, A. Derek Mahon. CP-MahoD

Spine hog, / how do you grow? Porcupine. Anne Sexton. CP-SextA

Spinejacking. A. R. Ammons. CP-AmmoA

Spinelessly. Yannis Ritsos. SP-RitsY, *tr.* by N. C. Germanacos

Spinners. Marya Alexandrovna Zaturenska. SP-ZatuM

Spinning Heart, The. John Berryman. CP-BerrJ

Spinning on his heel, the traveller. Flashing Cliff, A. Muriel Rukeyser. CP-RukeM

Spinoza. Jorge Luis Borges. SP-BorgJ, *tr.* by Willis Barnstone

Spinoza grinding lenses brings me. Dancers in a Hospital. A. K. Ramanujan. CP-RamaA

Spinster. Sylvia Plath. CP-PlatS

Spinster at Mass, The. Federico García Lorca. SP-GarcF, *tr.* by Edwin Honig

Spiral. Federico García Lorca. CP-GarcF, *tr.* by Jerome Rothenberg *Fr.* Caracols / Snails.

Spiral Death. Comment. Langston Hughes. CP-HughL; CP-HughL2

Spiral Flame. D. H. Lawrence. CP-LawrD

Spiral of green hay on the end of a rake, A. Last before America. Louis MacNeice. CP-MacNL

Spirals. Lorine Niedecker. CP-NiedL

Spirals and Fugues. Muriel Rukeyser. CP-RukeM

Spire Cranes, The. Dylan Thomas. CP-ThomD

Spirea. Louis Zukofsky. CP-ZukLS

Spirit. Boris Christov. CP-PinsR, *tr.* by Robert Pinsky

Spirit, The. Jones Very. CP-VeryJ

Spirit and nature beat in one breast-bone—. Sententious Man, The. Theodore Roethke. CP-RoetT

Spirit colossal / (& daunted by always). E. E. Cummings. CP-CummE

Spirit cried Go up higher, The. Extremity. Richard Eberhart. CP-EberR

Spirit deft wounds my eyes so. Guido Cavalcanti. CP-CavaG, *tr.* by Marc Cirigliano

Spirit doth our weakness aid, The. Hymn: The Spirit Itself Maketh Intercession for Us. Jones Very. CP-VeryJ

Spirit has an impregnable tower, The. Tower of the Spirit, The. Chuang Tzu. CP-MertT

Spirit has been alone. Slowly. Denise Levertov. SP-LeveDL

Spirit has infinite facets, but the body, The. Tossing and Turning. John Updike. CP-UpdiJ

Spirit haunts the year's last hours, A. Alfred Tennyson. CP-TennA

Spirit here that reignest! Song: "Spirit here that reignest!" John Keats. CP-KeatJ

Spirit in the tree top breathes, A. Voice in the Poplars, The. Jones Very. CP-VeryJ

Spirit Ink, The. Frank O'Hara. SP-OharF

Spirit is in bed, it has been sleeping away, The. Body, The. Boris Christov. CP-PinsR, *tr.* by Robert Pinsky

Spirit is the Conscious Ear, The. Emily Dickinson. CP-DickE

Spirit Land, The ("Father! Thy wonders do not singly stand"). Jones Very. CP-VeryJ

Spirit Land, The ("Open our eyes that we the world may see"). Jones Very. CP-VeryJ

Spirit lasts, but in what mode, The. Emily Dickinson. CP-DickE

Spirit Medium, The. William Butler Yeats. CP-YeatW

Spirit moved, John Harvard walked the yard, A. Villanelle for an Anniversary. Seamus Heaney. SP-HeanSO

Spirit moves, The. Light Breather, A. Theodore Roethke. CP-RoetT

Spirit of air, The. Walter De la Mare. CP-DeLaW

Spirit of Antiquity—enshrined, The. Brugès ("Spirit of Antiquity—enshrined, The"). William Wordsworth. MW-WorW *Fr.* Memorials of a Tour of the Continent; 1820.

Spirit of History, The. Czeslaw Milosz. *Fr.* Treatise on Poetry, A.

Spirit of Noplace, The. Kenneth Patchen. CP-PatcK

Spirit of Place: Great Blue Heron. William Stafford. SP-StafWW

Spirit of Place, The. Adrienne Rich. SP-RicA2
   "Orion plunges like a drunken hunter." SP-RicA1

Spirit of Plato. *Unknown.* CP-ShelP

Spirit of quickness reading *slipperwort*. Slipperwort. Louis Zukofsky. CP-ZukLS

Spirit of romance dies not to those, The. Pictures of the Rhine. George Meredith. CP-MerG1

Spirit of Russia, now has come. Crisis, The. George Meredith. CP-MerG2

Spirit of '76. William Carlos Williams. CP-WilW1

Spirit of Shakespeare, The. George Meredith. CP-MerG1

Spirit of Shakespeare: Continued, The. George Meredith. CP-MerG1

Spirit of the Crusades. Lawrence Ferlinghetti. SP-FerlL

Spirit of the Dead Watching: after Gaugin. John Logan. CP-LogaJ

Spirit of the frozen North. Spirit of the North, The. John Greenleaf Whittier. CP-WhitJ

Spirit of the Laws, The. Czeslaw Milosz. CP-MiloC; CP-MiloCN, *tr. by* John Carpenter *and* Bogdana Carpenter

Spirit of the North, The. John Greenleaf Whittier. CP-WhitJ

Spirit of the Wine, The. Charles Baudelaire. CP-BaudC, *tr. by* Walter Martin

Spirit of this room is dead, The. it was a very good spirit. Good Spirit, The. Andrei Codrescu. SP-CodrA

Spirit Pass'd Before Me, A. Lord Byron. CP-Byron

Spirit seems to pass, A. Lausanne: In Gibbon's Old Garden: 11–12 p.m. Thomas Hardy. CP-HardT

Spirit sped, A. Stephen Crane. CP-CranS

Spirit splits in its asking, On Fleeing His City. Shmuel HaNagid. SP-HaNaS, *tr. by* Peter Cole

Spirit that dispenses, The. Eugenio Montale. CP-MontE, *tr. by* Jonathan Galassi

Spirit That Form'd This Scene. Walt Whitman. CP-WhitW

Spirit the Triumph, The. C. K. Williams. CP-WillC; SP-WillC

Spirit who sweepest the wild Harp of Time! Ode on the Departing Year. Samuel Taylor Coleridge. CP-ColeS

Spirit Whose Work Is Done. Walt Whitman. CP-WhitW

Spirit Wooed, The. Philip Larkin. CP-LarkP

Spirited people make a thousand jewels in verse and prose, and the restlessness of talent. Vices. Robinson Jeffers. CP-JefR1

Spirits among us have departed—friends. Watching Sandhill Cranes. William Stafford. SP-StafWW

Spirits and illusions have died. Life from the Lifeless. Robinson Jeffers. CP-JefR2

Spirits Appeased, The. Denise Levertov. SP-LeveDS

Spirits at Home. James Whitcomb Riley. CP-RileJ

Spirits have dispersed, the woods, The. Dream Play, The. Derek Mahon. CP-MahoD

Spirits of the abnormally born. October. Audre Lorde. SP-LordA

Spirits of the Dead. Edgar Allan Poe. CP-PoeEd

Spirits of the wise, sit on the clouds, The. Ralph Waldo Emerson. CP-EmerR

Spirit's Song. Louise Bogan. CP-BogaL

Spirits Summoned West. D. H. Lawrence. CP-LawrD

Spiritual, A. Paul Laurence Dunbar. CP-DunbP

Spiritual Birth, The. Jones Very. CP-VeryJ

Spiritual Darkness. Jones Very. *See* Dark Day, The

Spiritual Dawn. Charles Baudelaire. CP-BaudC, *tr. by* Walter Martin

Spiritual experience is a modest woman. Put This Design in Your Carpet. Jelaluddin Rumi. SP-Rumi, *tr. by* Coleman Barks

Spiritual Explorations. Stephen Spender. CP-SpenS

Spiritual Intercourse. Jones Very. CP-VeryJ

Spiritual Laws. Ralph Waldo Emerson. CP-EmerR

Spiritual Manifestation, A. John Greenleaf Whittier. CP-WhitJ

Spiritual Woman, A. D. H. Lawrence. *See* These Clever Women

Spirituals. Langston Hughes. CP-HughL1; CP-HughL2

Spit. C. K. Williams. CP-WillC; SP-WillC

Spit the pit in the pit. High Surreal. A. R. Ammons. CP-AmmoA

Spite Fence. Richard Eberhart. CP-EberR

Spite hath no power to make me sad. Sir Thomas Wyatt. CP-WyatT

Spite of Dutch friends and English foes. Peace and Dunkirk. Jonathan Swift. CP-SwifJ

Spite of Mirrors. Robert Graves. CP-GravR

Spite of their spite which they in vain. Sir Thomas Wyatt. CP-WyatT

Spite / spit. Scythe. Lorine Niedecker. CP-NiedL

Spiteful like golden speech this night begins. Late and Deep. Paul Celan. SP-CelaP, *tr. by* John Felstiner

Spits of glitter in lowgrade ore. Conserving the Magnitude of Uselessness. A. R. Ammons. CP-AmmoA

Splash! Ogden Nash. CP-NashO

Splash, Flow. Arthur Sze. SP-SzeA

Splayed, swayback, cheap pipe. Backyard Swingset. Thomas Lux. SP-LuxT

Spleen. Frank O'Hara. SP-OharF

Splendor of ended day floating and filling me. Song at Sunset. Walt Whitman. CP-WhitW

Splendor Paternae Gloriae. Saint Ambrose. CP-MertT

Splendour! O more than mortal. Ode Enthusiastic. Ben Jonson. CP-JonsB

Splendour of the kindling day, The. Fluttered Wings. Christina Georgina Rossetti. CP-RosC2

Splendour's fondly-fostered child! Ode to Georgiana, Duchess of Devonshire. Samuel Taylor Coleridge. CP-ColeS

Splinter. Carl Sandburg. CP-SandC

Splinter, flicked, A. New Moon in January. Ted Hughes. SP-HughTN

Split-cedar / smoked salmon, The. Way West, Underground, The. Gary Snyder. CP-SnydG

Split Mind, The. Denise Levertov. SP-LeveDL

Split Second. Denise Levertov. SP-LeveDL

Split the Lark—and you'll find the Music. Emily Dickinson. CP-DickE

Splitting a bottle of white wine. Pale Bliss. John Updike. CP-UpdiJ

Splitting from Jack Delany's, Sheridan Square. God Rest Ye Merry, Gentlemen. Derek Walcott. CP-WalcD

Splitting Wood. Billy Collins. SP-CollB

Splitting Wood at Six Above. Maxine W. Kumin. SP-KumiM

Splittings. Adrienne Rich. SP-RicA1; SP-RicA2

Spoiled Child, The. James Whitcomb Riley. CP-RileJ

Spoiler's Return, The. Derek Walcott. CP-WalcD

Spoiling daylight inched along the bar-top, The. Mill, The. Richard Wilbur. CP-WilbR

Spoils. Robert Graves. CP-GravR

Spoke joe to jack. E. E. Cummings. CP-CummE; SP-CummE

Spokes of light and shadow, the golden scale, The. Winged Victory. Eleanor Wilner. SP-WilnE

Spokes when he sees a rosted Pig, he swears. Upon Spokes. Robert Herrick. CP-HerrR

Sponge Full of Vinegar, The. Thomas Merton. CP-MertT

Spontaneous Me. Walt Whitman. CP-WhitW

Spontaneous overflows of powerful feeling. Barren Leaves. Thom Gunn. CP-GunnT

Spontaneous singing in thirds. Jewel Lotus Harp. Olga Broumas. SP-BrouO

Spook's Sabbath, Five Bowings. Louis Zukofsky. CP-ZukLS

Spoon. Charles Simic. SP-SimiC; SP-SimiCE

Spoon of desire is crusted, The. Still Life. Olga Broumas. SP-BrouO

Spoonbait, The. Seamus Heaney. SP-HeanSO

Spoons with Realistic Dead Flies on Them. Charles Simic. SP-SimiC; SP-SimiCE

Sport. Langston Hughes. CP-HughL; CP-HughL1

Sport, Dan Pagis. SP-PagiD, *tr. by* Stephen Mitchell

Sporting people, The. Free Fantasia: Tiger Flowers. Robert Earl Hayden. CP-HaydR

Sports and gallantries, the stage, the arts, the antics of dancers. Boats in a Fog. Robinson Jeffers. CP-JefR1

Sports Page. Louis MacNeice. CP-MacNL

Sports without Blood—a Letter to Dylan Thomas (1948). Thomas Merton. CP-MertT

Sposa velata, / Innanellata. Christina Georgina Rossetti. CP-RosC3

Spot, A. Thomas Hardy. CP-HardT

Spot in Space and Time. Heather McHugh. SP-McHuH

Spot of my youth! whose hoary branches sigh. Lines Written beneath an Elm in the Churchyard of Harrow. Lord Byron. CP-Byron

Spotlight her face her face has no light in it. Movie. Muriel Rukeyser. CP-RukeM

Spotting the moonlight at my bedside. Li Po. CP-WilW2

Spouts. William Carlos Williams. CP-WilW1

Sprawled in the pigsty. For a Young Artist. Robert Earl Hayden. CP-HaydR

Sprawled / on our faces in the spring. Hen Flower, The. Galway Kinnell. SP-KinnGN

Sprawled, / on the bottom. To the She-Bear: *The 1st Song.* Charles Olson. CP-OlsoC

Spray. D. H. Lawrence. CP-LawrD

Spray. Carl Sandburg. CP-SandC

Spray of sound, The. Walking to Bells. Charles Tomlinson. CP-TomlC

Spray sprang up across the cusps of the moon, The. Once at Swanage. Thomas Hardy. CP-HardT

Spread back across the air, wings wide. Gulls Land and Cease to Be. John Ciardi. CP-CiarJ

Spread beneath me it lies—lean upland. Flying Above California. Thom Gunn. CP-GunnT

Spread carelessly across my massive chair. Cunning. Arthur Rimbaud. CP-RimbA, *tr. by* Martin Sorrell

Spread of Mrs. Mobey's Lawn. Josephine Jacobsen. CP-JacoJ

Spreading herbs, and flowerets bright. Melrose by Moonlight. Sir Walter Scott. SP-ScotW *Fr.* Lay of the Last Minstrel, The.

Sprengeri. Louis Zukofsky. CP-ZukLS

Spring. Rainer Maria Rilke. CP-RilkFr, *tr. by* A. Poulin, Jr. *Fr.* Orchards.

Spring. Robert Creeley. CP-CreeR

Spring. Gerard Manley Hopkins. CP-HopkG

Spring. Kenneth Koch. SP-KochK

Spring. Philip Larkin. CP-LarkP

Spring. W. S. Merwin. SP-MerwW

Spring. Edna St. Vincent Millay. CP-MillE

Spring. Mary Oliver. SP-OlivM

Spring. Rainer Maria Rilke. CP-RilkFr, *tr. by* A. Poulin, Jr.

Spring. Christina Georgina Rossetti. CP-RosC1

Spring. Dante Gabriel Rossetti. CW-RossD

Spring. Jelaluddin Rumi. SP-Rumi, *tr. by* Coleman Barks

Spring. James Schuyler. CP-SchuJ

Spring ("I have not lived the flesh has hedged me in"). Jones Very. CP-VeryJ

Spring ("Look! Winter now in trembling haste"). Jones Very. CP-VeryJ

Spring ("Spring returns, and, with fresh ardor filled, The"). Jones Very. CP-VeryJ

Spring ("Stem that long has borne the wintry blast, The"). Jones Very. CP-VeryJ

Spring. William Carlos Williams. CP-WilW1

Spring, The. Thomas Carew. CP-CareT

Spring, The. Ezra Pound. SP-PounE

Spring, The. Gary Snyder. CP-SnydG

Spring Abstract. Charles Wright. SP-WrigC

Spring again, can I stand it. Margaret Atwood. SP-AtwM1

Spring and All. William Carlos Williams. CP-WilW1

Spring and Death. Gerard Manley Hopkins. CP-HopkG

Spring, and everything outside is growing. Not a Day on Any Calendar. Jelaluddin Rumi. SP-Rumi, *tr. by* Coleman Barks

Spring and Fall. Gerard Manley Hopkins. CP-HopkG

Spring, and not a Blue Bird. Emily Dickinson. SP-DickE

Spring and Summer Flowers. Jones Very. CP-VeryJ

Spring and the Fall, The. Edna St. Vincent Millay. CP-MillE

Spring: another / joke. / This run-down. C. K. Williams. CP-WillC

Spring Azures. Mary Oliver. SP-OlivM

Spring bursts in the houses. Earth, The. Boris Leonidovich Pasternak. CP-MahoD, *tr. by* Derek Mahon

Spring bursts today, / For Christ is risen and all the earth's at play. Easter Carol, An. Christina Georgina Rossetti. CP-RosC2

Spring by Robert Lowell / (Photograph by Trudi Fuller). May Swenson. SP-SwenM

Spring Call, The. Thomas Hardy. CP-HardT

Spring came. Different and quiet, anonymous blood in a spree. Yehuda Amichai. SP-AmicYL *Fr.* At Right Angles.

Spring Carries Surprises. Carl Sandburg. CP-SandC

Spring Cleaning. Louis MacNeice. CP-MacNL

Spring clouds rest on the walls of the Royal Park. Meandering River Poems, The. Tu Fu. CP-KizeC, *tr. by* Carolyn Kizer

Spring comes and autumn goes. Sparrows. Hayden Carruth. CP-CarHS

Spring comes on the World. Emily Dickinson. CP-DickE

Spring Comes to Murray Hill. Ogden Nash. CP-NashO

Spring Coming. A. R. Ammons. CP-AmmoA

Spring Cries. Carl Sandburg. CP-SandC

Spring crosses over into summer. Crisscross. Carl Sandburg. CP-SandC

Spring Day. John Ashbery. SP-AshbJ

Spring day in the weeds, A. Dog Yoga. Charles Wright. SP-WrigC

SPRING DUSK DARK SHORE. Poem for Old Walt. Lawrence Ferlinghetti. SP-FerlL

Spring Equinox Full Moon. W. S. Merwin. SP-MerwWF

Spring fails, in all its bravery of brilliant gold and green. Her Smile of Cheer and Voice of Song. James Whitcomb Riley. CP-RileJ

Spring Fancies. Christina Georgina Rossetti. CP-RosC3
    Spring Quiet. CP-RosC1

Spring Fashions. Allen Ginsberg. CP-GinsA; SP-GinsA

Spring Fever. Paul Laurence Dunbar. CP-DunbP

Spring Floods. Gregory Orr. SP-OrrG

Spring flowers, autumn moon—when will you end? Bella Donna Iu. Li Yü. CP-WilW2

"Spring-flowers!" While you still delay to take. To Mary Boyle. Alfred Tennyson. CP-TennA

Spring for Lovers. Langston Hughes. CP-HughL; CP-HughL1

Spring, 480 BC. Raymond Carver. CP-CarvR

Spring-Gazing Songs. Hsüeh T'ao. CP-KizeC, *tr. by* Carolyn Kizer

Spring Grass. Carl Sandburg. CP-SandC

Spring grass, there is a dance to be danced. Spring Grass. Carl Sandburg. CP-SandC

Spring had been bulldozed under. Killing the Spring. Anne Sexton. CP-SextA

Spring has been exquisite and the, The. E. E. Cummings. CP-CummE

Spring has come; I look up and see. Robert Bly. SP-BlyR *Fr.* Four Seasons in American Woods.

Spring has come with its smell of Nicaragua. Ernesto Cardenal. CP-MertT *Fr.* Gethsemani, KY.

Spring has gone. The brief hour. Two Poems for Tanabata Matsuri. Sam Hamill. SP-HamiS

Spring Images. James Wright. CP-WrigJ

Spring impels the organism to acts which, in another season. Ecclesiastic, The. Stéphane Mallarmé. CP-MallS, *tr. by* Henry Weinfield

Spring in Belfast. Derek Mahon.

Spring in San Feliu. Robert Creeley. SP-CreeR

Spring in Statue Square. John Ciardi. CP-CiarJ

Spring in the Classroom. Mary Oliver. SP-OlivM

Spring in the Garden. Edna St. Vincent Millay. CP-MillE

Spring in the Snow-Drenched Garden. Mao Tse-tung. CP-WilW2

Spring in the Soul. Jones Very. CP-VeryJ

Spring in These Hills. Archibald MacLeish. CP-MacLA

Spring is a happiness so beautiful. Emily Dickinson. SP-DickE

Spring Is Christ. Jelaluddin Rumi. SP-Rumi, *tr. by* Coleman Barks

Spring is come again not as at first. Christina Georgina Rossetti. CP-RosC3

Spring is Here Again, Sir. William Carlos Williams. CP-WilW2

Spring is like a perhaps hand. E. E. Cummings. CP-CummE; SP-CummE

Spring is like a perhaps hand. Spring is like a perhaps hand. E. E. Cummings. CP-CummE; SP-CummE

Spring is not so beautiful there, The. Water-Front Streets. Langston Hughes. CP-HughL; CP-HughL1

Spring is open windows and Molly Picardo. Spring in Statue Square. John Ciardi. CP-CiarJ

Spring is past, and Summer's past. Skating. E. E. Cummings. CP-CummE

Spring is the Period. Emily Dickinson. CP-DickE

Spring is when the grass turns green and glad. Lines Written for Gene Kelly to Dance To. Carl Sandburg. CP-SandC

Spring larch should set the body shaking. Compensations. Ivor Gurney. SP-GurnI

Spring like smoke in the fruit trees. Broken English. Charles Wright. SP-WrigCN

Spring lingers-out its arrival in these woods. Hesitation, The. Charles Tomlinson. CP-TomlC

Spring!may— / everywhere's here. E. E. Cummings. CP-CummE

Spring: Monastery Farm. Thomas Merton. CP-MertT

Spring Morning. A. E. Housman. CP-HousA

Spring Morning. D. H. Lawrence. CP-LawrD

Spring Morning. Marya Alexandrovna Zaturenska. SP-ZatuM

Spring Mountain Climb. Richard Eberhart. CP-EberR

Spring moved to summer—the rude cold rain. Harriet. Robert Lowell. SP-LoweR

Spring Musick. Philip Whalen. SP-WhalP

Spring 1974. Robert Graves. CP-GravR

Spring 1967. Hayden Carruth. CP-CarHS

Spring Notes from Robin Hill. Hayden Carruth. CP-CarHS

Spring of the Thief. John Logan. CP-LogaJ

Spring Offensive. Wilfred Owen. CP-OwenW

Spring Offensive of the Snail, The. Marge Piercy. SP-PierM

Spring omnipotent goddess thou dost. E. E. Cummings. CP-CummE

Spring People. Audre Lorde. SP-LordA

Spring Pools. Robert Frost. CP-FrosR

Spring pricks a little. I get out the maps. Spring Song, A. Donald Davie. CP-DaviDC

Spring Quiet. Christina Georgina Rossetti. CP-RosC1 *Fr.* Spring Fancies.

Spring Reminiscence. Countee Cullen. CP-CullC

Spring returns, and, with fresh ardor filled, The. Spring ("Spring returns, and, with fresh ardor filled, The"). Jones Very. CP-VeryJ

Spring Revelations. John Logan. CP-LogaJ

Spring rides no horses down the hill. Goose-Girl, The. Edna St. Vincent Millay. CP-MillE

Spring Running, The. Rudyard Kipling. *Fr.* Second Jungle Book, The.

Spring, Says the Child. Josephine Jacobsen. CP-JacoJ

Spring-Shock. James Dickey. CP-DickJ

Spring Snow. Arthur Sze. SP-SzeA

Spring snow coincides with plum blossoms, A. Spring Snow. Arthur Sze. SP-SzeA

Spring Song. A. R. Ammons. CP-AmmoA

Spring Song. Robert Browning. SP-BroR

Spring Song ("Do you remember by morning when the sun"). John Ciardi. CP-CiarJ

Spring Song ("Wake early to the early robin"). John Ciardi. CP-CiarJ

Spring Song. Paul Laurence Dunbar. CP-DunbP

Spring Song. Federico García Lorca. CP-GarcF, *tr.* by Catherine Brown

Spring Song. Edna St. Vincent Millay. CP-MillE

Spring Song. Ogden Nash. CP-NashO

Spring Song. Dorothy Parker. CP-ParkD

Spring Song. Li Po. CP-WilW2

Spring Song. John Updike. CP-UpdiJ

Spring Song. William Carlos Williams. CP-WilW1

Spring Song, A. G. K. Chesterton. CP-ChesG

Spring Song, A. Donald Davie. CP-DaviDC

Spring Song and a Later, A. James Whitcomb Riley. CP-RileJ

Spring Song for Cagli, A. Charles Olson. CP-OlsoC

Spring Song for *Symplocarpus Fœtida* and Me. Alan Dugan. CP-DugaA

Spring spreads one green lap of flowers, The. Death-Watches. Christina Georgina Rossetti. CP-RosC2

Spring / stood there. Lorine Niedecker. CP-NiedL

Spring Storm. Thomas Merton. CP-MertT

Spring Storm. William Carlos Williams. CP-WilW1

Spring Storm. Charles Wright. SP-WrigCN

Spring storm has upended, The. Ark, The. Eugenio Montale. CP-MontE, *tr.* by Jonathan Galassi

Spring Strains. William Carlos Williams. CP-WilW1

Spring Sunshine. Louis MacNeice. CP-MacNL

Spring Symphony, The. Charles Tomlinson. CP-TomlC

Spring: the first morning when that one true block of sweet, laminar, complex scent arrives. From My Window. C. K. Williams. CP-WillC; SP WillC

Spring there, A. Grace. Rae Armantrout. SP-ArmaA

Spring this year in Austria started off benign. Talking to Myself. W. H. Auden. CP-AudeW

Spring Thunder. Adrienne Rich. CP-RicAE

Spring-time, Summer and Fall: days to behold a world. In Due Season. W. H. Auden. CP-AudeW

Spring Uncovered. May Swenson. SP-SwenM

Spring Voices. Louis MacNeice. CP-MacNL

Spring Warning. Philip Larkin. CP-LarkP

Spring Was Begging to Be Born. James Tate. SP-TateJ

Spring water in the green creek is clear. Gary Snyder. CP-SnydG

Spring water is pure in an emerald stream. Han-shan. CP-ColdM, *tr.* by Red Pine

Spring water thawed in an empty alley. Illusion. Aleksandr Aleksandrovich Blok. SP-BlokA, *tr.* by Peter France *and* Jon Stallworthy

Spring Wind. Carl Sandburg. CP-SandC

Spring wind blowing, A. Thought of Something Else, The. Wendell Berry. CP-BerrW

Spring wind blows trumpet. Fanny Howe. SP-HoweF *Fr.* O'Clock.

Spring with its thrusting leaves and jargling birds is here again. Unpredictable but Providential. W. H. Auden. CP-AudeW

Spring with the Larke, most comely Bride, and meet. Nuptiall Verse to Mistresse Elizabeth Lee, Now Lady Tracie. Robert Herrick. CP-HerrR

Spring Wooing, A. Paul Laurence Dunbar. CP-DunbP

Springboard, The. Louis MacNeice. CP-MacNL

Springboard, The. Adrienne Rich. CP-RicAE

Springer Mountain. James Dickey. CP-DickJ

Springfield Magical. Nicholas Vachel Lindsay. CP-LindV

Springfield of the Far Future, The. Nicholas Vachel Lindsay. CP-LindV

Springhouse, Menses, Held Apple, House and Beyond. James Dickey. CP-DickJ

Spring's bright paradise has come to this. Farewell without a Guitar. Wallace Stevens. CP-StevWP

Spring's first conviction is a wealth. Emily Dickinson. SP-DickE

Spring's in the air; from deep. Paris War-Cry. Arthur Rimbaud. CP-RimbA, *tr.* by Martin Sorrell

Springs, The. Wendell Berry. CP-BerrW

Spring(side / walks are)is. E. E. Cummings. CP-CummE

Springtime. Rainer Maria Rilke. CP-RilkFr, *tr.* by A. Poulin, Jr.

Springtime, fresh and green, can never guess, The. Michelangelo Buonarroti. CP-Miche, *tr.* by John Frederick Nims

Springtime's wide. Lorine Niedecker. CP-NiedL

Sprinklers calm summer's wrath, The. Summer Rest and Words. Yehuda Amichai. SP-AmicYL, *tr.* by Benjamin Harshav *and* Barbara Harshav

Sprinter at Forty, The. James Dickey. CP-DickJ

Spruce Has No Taproot, The. Amy Clampitt. CP-ClamA

Sprung from the croup and the flight. Stéphane Mallarmé. CP-MallS, *tr.* by Henry Weinfield

Sprung from the hummocks. Blueberrying in August. Amy Clampitt. CP-ClamA

Sprung Narratives. Charles Wright. SP-WrigCN

Sprung of the father blood, the mother brain. Foresight and Patience. George Meredith. CP-MerG1

Spry Arms of the Wind, The. Emily Dickinson. CP-DickE

Spry, wry, and gray as these March sticks. Among the Narcissi. Sylvia Plath. CP-PlatS

Spunge makes his boasts that he's the onely man. Upon Spunge. Robert Herrick. CP-HerrR

Spunta la margherita. Christina Georgina Rossetti. CP-RosC3

Spur, The. William Butler Yeats. CP-YeatW

Spur jingles now, and sweares by no meane oathes. Upon Spur. Robert Herrick. CP-HerrR

Spurn the temerity. Emily Dickinson. CP-DickE

Spurred altering wake toss Attis his craft racing till marled in the. Catullus. *See* Plunging towards Phrygia over violent water

Sputtering near out, before it touches the moors. Match, A. Ted Hughes. SP-HughTN

Spy. Rita Dove. SP-DoveR

Spy, The. Howard Nemerov. CP-NemeH

Spyres Curten, The. Thomas Campion. CP-CampT

Squall. George Oppen CP-OppGN

Squall, A. Raymond Carver. CP-CarvR

Squalor spreads its hideous length. Tribute, The. "H. D." CP-DoolH

Square. A. R. Ammons. CP-AmmoA

Square D'Orléans. Adam Zagajewski. SP-ZagaA, *tr.* by Clare Cavanagh

Square Matthew Hale's young grafted apple tree. Gold Hesperidee, The. Robert Frost. CP-FrosR

Square sheets—they saw the marble only into. Island Quarry. Hart Crane. CP-CranH

Square, The. Charles Tomlinson. CP-TomlC

Squarings. Seamus Heaney.

    "*All gone into the world of light?* Perhaps." SP-HeanSO

    "And lightening? One meaning of that." SP-HeanSO

    "And strike this scene in gold too, in relief." SP-HeanSO

    "And yes, my friend, we too walked through a valley." SP-HeanSO

    "Annals say: when the monks of Clonmacnoise, The." SP-HeanSO

    "Be literal a moment. Recollect." SP-HeanSO

    "Boat that did not rock or wobble once, A." SP-HeanSO

    "Choose one set of tracks and track a hare." SP-HeanSO

    Crossings. SP-HeanSO

    "Deserted harbour stillness. Every stone." SP-HeanSO

    "For certain ones what was written may come true." SP-HeanSO

    "Heather and kesh and turf stacks reappear." SP-HeanSO

    "I misremembered. He went down on all fours." SP-HeanSO

    "I was four but I turned four hundred maybe." SP-HeanSO

    Lightenings. SP-HeanSO

    "Memory as a building or a city." SP-HeanSO

    "Mountain air from the mountain up behind." SP-HeanSO

    "On St Brigid's Day the new life could be entered." SP-HeanSO

    "Once as a child, out in a field of sheep." SP-HeanSO

    "One afternoon I was seraph on gold leaf." SP-HeanSO

    "Overhang of grass and seedling birch." SP-HeanSO

    "Running water never disappointed." SP-HeanSO

    "Sand-bed, they said. And gravel-bed. Before." SP-HeanSO

    "Scissor-and-slap abruptness of a latch." SP-HeanSO

    Settings. SP-HeanSO

    Squarings. SP-HeanSO

    "Squarings? In the game of marbles, squarings." SP-HeanSO

    "Strange how things in the offing, once they're sensed." SP-HeanSO

    "Three marble holes thumbed in the concrete road." SP-HeanSO

    "Visible sea at a distance from the shore, The." SP-HeanSO

    "We climbed the Capitol by moonlight, felt." SP-HeanSO

    "When you sat, far-eyed and cold, in the basalt throne." SP-HeanSO

    "Where does spirit live? Inside or outside." SP-HeanSO

    "Yeats said, *To those who see spirits, human skin.*" SP-HeanSO

Squarings. Seamus Heaney. SP-HeanSO *Fr.* Squarings.

Squarings? In the game of marbles, squarings. Seamus Heaney. SP-HeanSO *Fr.* Squarings.

Squat in swamp shadows. Second Shaman Song. Gary Snyder. CP-SnydG *Fr.* Myths and Texts.

Squatter's Children. Elizabeth Bishop. CP-BishE

Squatting a day in the sun. Fire in the Hole. Gary Snyder. CP-SnydG

Squatting Down. Arthur Rimbaud. CP-RimbA, *tr.* by Martin Sorrell

Squatting, serious, / His small hand locked on my middle finger. Changeling, The. Thomas McGrath. SP-McGrT

Squaw Lilies: Some Notes. Margaret Atwood. SP-AtwM2

Squeal. Allen Ginsberg. CP-GinsA

Squeal of brakes, A. Stopped Dead. Sylvia Plath. CP-PlatS

Squib on Colonel Evans, A. William Wordsworth. CP-WorW2

Squid, frightened or angry, shoots darkness, The. Ink-Sack. Robinson Jeffers. CP-JefR3

Squince. Derek Mahon. CP-MahoD

Squinting after morning, like a sentry. Gunsight. Theodore Weiss. SP-WeisT

Squinting up at leafy sunlight, I stepped back. History Lessons. Yusef Komunyakaa. CP-KomuY

Squints a blond / job at her. E. E. Cummings. CP-CummE

Squire Hawkins's Story. James Whitcomb Riley. CP-RileJ

Squire Hazard Walks. William Meredith. SP-MereW

Squire Hooper. Thomas Hardy. CP-HardT

Squireless Kate. George Meredith. CP-MerG2

Squirrel, The. Ogden Nash. CP-NashO

Squirrels Mating. John Updike. CP-UpdiJ

Squirrel's Stance, The. George Oppen. CP-OppGN

Squirt-Gun Uncle Maked Me, The. James Whitcomb Riley. CP-RileJ

Squyer Meldrum. Sir David Lyndsay. SP-LyndD

St. Anthony, my father's holy man. Temptation. John Ciardi. CP-CiarJ

St. Francis Einstein of the Daffodils. William Carlos Williams. CP-WilW1

St. Francis of Assisi. G. K. Chesterton. CP-ChesG

St. Francis Xavier. G. K. Chesterton. CP-ChesG

St George and the Dragon. D. H. Lawrence. CP-LawrD

St. John. Bible, *N.T.*

> John 3; But Men Loved Darknesse Rather than Light. CP-CrasR, *tr. by* Richard Crashaw
>
> John 15; Upon Our Lords Last Comfortable Discourse with His Disciples. CP-CrasR
>
> John 16; Verily I Say unto You, Yee Shall Weep and Lament. CP-CrasR

St. John, Apostle. Christina Georgina Rossetti. CP-RosC2

St. Louis Out of Time. Audre Lorde. SP-LordA

St. Luke. Bible, *N.T.*

> Blessed be the Paps which Thou hast Sucked.
> (Luke 11; Blessed Be the Paps Which Thou Hast Sucked.) CP-CrasR
>
> Luke 2; Quærit Jesum Suum Maria. CP-CrasR
>
> Luke 7; She Began To Wash His Feet with Teares and Wipe Them with the Haires of Her Head. CP-CrasR, *tr. by* Richard Crashaw
>
> Luke 10; And a Certaine Priest Comming that Way Looked on Him and Passed by. CP-CrasR
>
> Luke 11; Upon the Dumbe Devill Cast Out, and the Slanderous Jewes Put to Silence. CP-CrasR
>
> Luke 15; On the Prodigall. CP-CrasR
>
> Luke 16; Dives *Asking a Drop.* CP-CrasR

St. Mark. Bible, *N.T.*

> Mark 4; Why Are Yee Afraid, O Yee of Little Faith? CP-CrasR
>
> Mark 7; The Dumbe Healed, and the People Enjoyned Silence. CP-CrasR
>
> Mark 10; The Blind Cured by the Word of Our Saviour. CP-CrasR
>
> Mark 12; (Give to Cæsar———) (And to God———). CP-CrasR

St. Matthew. Bible, *N.T.*

> Matthew 8; I Am Not Worthy that Thou Should'st Come Under my Roofe. CP-CrasR
>
> Matthew 16:25; Whosoever Shall Loose His Life. CP-CrasR
>
> Matthew 22; Neither Durst Any Man from that Day Aske Him Any More Questions. CP-CrasR
>
> Matthew 23; Yee Build the Sepulchres of the Prophets. CP-CrasR
>
> Matthew 27; And He Answered Them Nothing. CP-CrasR
>
> Matthew 28; Come See the Place where the Lord Lay. CP-CrasR

St. Nicholas distributed as he list. Merger, The. G. K. Chesterton. CP-ChesG

St. Patrick's Day. Derek Mahon. CP-MahoD

St Paul's. William Wordsworth. CP-WorW1; MW-WorW

St. Peter and the Angel. Denise Levertov. SP-LeveDS

St. Peter's Shadow. Richard Crashaw. CP-CrasR

> (Act 5; Sicke Implore St. Peter's Shadow, The.) CP-CrasR

St. Thecla. Gerard Manley Hopkins. CP-HopkG

St. Valentine. Marianne Craig Moore. CP-MoorM

> (Saint Valentine.) CP-MoorM

St. Valentine. William Carlos Williams. CP-WilW2

Stab your heart with the arrow of study. Shmuel HaNagid. SP-HaNaS, *tr. by* Peter Cole

Stability. David Ignatow. SP-IgnaD

Stability before Departure. Alan Dugan. CP-DugaA

Stable, The. Thomas Kinsella. CP-KinsT

Stable-lamp is lighted, A. Christmas Hymn, A. Richard Wilbur. CP-WilbR

Stacking the Straw. Amy Clampitt. CP-ClamA

Stacks of illustrations. Theodore Weiss. SP-WeisT *Fr.* Polish Question, The.

Staff and Scrip, The. Dante Gabriel Rossetti. CW-RossD

Staff of Aesculapius, The. Marianne Craig Moore. CP-MoorM

Staffe and Rod, The. Robert Herrick. CP-HerrR

Staff[e] is now greased [*or* greas'd], The. Hag, The. Robert Herrick. CP-HerrR

Stafford's Cabin. Edwin Arlington Robinson. CP-RobiE

Staffordshire. Donald Davie. CP-DaviDC

Staffordshire Murderer, A. James Fenton. SP-FentJ

Stag is retreating, the smoke of its antlers is rising, The. Panorama. Jaroslav Seifert. SP-SeifJ, *tr. by* Ewald Osers

Stage Directions. Robert Duncan. SP-DuncR *Fr.* Passages.

Stage Directions. Lorine Niedecker. CP-NiedL

Stage Fright. Wisława Szymborska. SP-SzymWM, *tr. by* Joanna Trzeciak

Stage is about to be swept of corpses, The. Horatian Epode to the Duchess of Malfi. Allen Tate. CP-TateA

Stage-lit streets. Continuation of a Long Poem of These States. Allen Ginsberg. CP-GinsA

Stages of Ignorance. Yannis Ritsos. SP-RitsY, *tr. by* Kimon Friar *and* Kostas Myrsiades

Stages on a Journey Westward. James Wright. CP-WrigJ

Stagger in air, A. Backward Look, The. Seamus Heaney. SP-HeanSO

Staggering Back Toward Life. Robinson Jeffers. CP-JefR3

Staggering homeward between the stream and the trees the unhappy. New Year's Eve. Robinson Jeffers. CP-JefR2

Staggering, you know / they fall. Comfort. Robert Creeley. CP-CreeR

Stagnant pleasure like a Pool, A. Emily Dickinson. CP-DickE

Stagnant this wintry gloom. Afar. Fog. Walter De la Mare. CP-DeLaW

Stains of blackberries near Marx's grave, The. Fanny Howe. SP-HoweF *Fr.* O'Clock.

Stair, The. Charles Tomlinson. SP-TomlC

Staircase, A. Hans Magnus Enzensberger. SP-EnzeH, *tr. by* Michael Hamburger

Staircase of Notre Dame, Paris, The. Dante Gabriel Rossetti. CW-RossD

Stairs, The. Yannis Ritsos. SP-RitsY, *tr. by* N. C. Germanacos

Stairs are winding up, The. Beyond the Second Landing. Eleanor Wilner. SP-WilnE

Stairs arise out of a village. Mornings Remembering Last Nights. Olga Broumas. SP-BrouO

Stairs lead to the room as bleak as glass, The. Iphigenia: Politics. Thomas Merton. CP-MertT

Stairs squeak like mice caught outside, The. East Side West. David Ignatow. SP-IgnaD

Stairway, face, window. Undermining of the Defense Economy, The. James Wright. CP-WrigJ

Stairway is not, The. Jacob's Ladder, The. Denise Levertov. SP-LeveDP; SP-LeveDS

Stairwell. Heather McHugh. SP-McHuH

Staking Claim. A. R. Ammons. CP-AmmoA

Stalag Luft. Randall Jarrell. CP-JarrR

Stale room of religion, The. Church Interior. George Oppen. CP-OppGN

Stalemated their armies stood, with tottering banners. Snowman on the Moor, The. Sylvia Plath. CP-PlatS

Stalin. Robert Lowell. SP-LoweR

Stalingrad: 1942. Langston Hughes. CP-HughL; CP-HughL2

Stalking a deer I wandered deep into the mountains and from there I saw. How It Was. Czeslaw Milosz. CP-MiloC; CP-MiloCN, *tr. by* Lillian Vallee

Stalking Memory. Ai. SP-Ai

Stall. Heather McHugh. SP-McHuH

Stallions go leap, and rimfire knows. Young Girl of the Mississippi Valley, The. Muriel Rukeyser. CP-RukeM

Stalwart country woman, A. Hobby Lobby, The. Jane Cooper. CP-CoopJ

Stanbury Moor. Ted Hughes. SP-HughTN

"Stand, Bayard, stand!"—The steed obey'd. Ride to Stirling, The. Sir Walter Scott. SP-ScotW *Fr.* Lady of the Lake, The.

Stand by the *Magick* of my powerfull Rhymes. To His Honour'd Friend, Sir Thomas Heale. Robert Herrick. CP-HerrR

Stand by the willow. Cruel Song. Rainer Maria Rilke. CP-RilkFr, *tr. by* A. Poulin, Jr.

Stand forth brave man, since Fate has made thee here. To Sir John Berkeley, Governour of Exeter. Robert Herrick. CP-HerrR

Stand forth,John Keats! On earth thou knew'st me not. Fame Speaks. E. E. Cummings. CP-CummE

Stand here, says the professional TV person. Telyric. Andrei Codrescu. SP-CodrA

Stand-Ins, The. Anne Sexton. CP-SextA

Stand of people, A. Autumn. William Carlos Williams. CP-WilW1

Stand off, Mother, let me go! N'est-ce pas assez de ne me point haïr? Stevie Smith. CP-SmitS

Stand on the highest pavement of the stair. La Figlia Che Piange. T. S. Eliot. CP-ElioT

Stand still, and I will read to thee. Lecture upon the Shadow, A. John Donne. CP-DonnJ; MW-DonnJ

Stand still, my soul, in the silent dark. My Soul and I. John Greenleaf Whittier. CP-WhitJ

Stand still, true poet that you are! Popularity. Robert Browning. CP-BroR1

Stand still, you floods! do[e] not deface. On Sight of a Gentlewoman's Face in the Water. Thomas Carew. CP-CareT

Stand there on the rock. Coming Down to the Desert at Lordsburg, N.M. Hayden Carruth. CP-CarHS

Stand Up. Adrienne Rich. CP-RicAE

Stand Up! D. H. Lawrence. CP-LawrD

Stand up against governments, against God. Cosmopolitan Greetings. Allen Ginsberg. SP-GinsA

Stand up and lift your hand and bless. Saint and the Hunchback, The. William Butler Yeats. CP-YeatW

Stand up, heart, and take it. Money. Robert Creeley. SP-CreeR

Stand up, stand up, thou May Janet. May Janet. Algernon Charles Swinburne. SP-SwinA

Stand up, that we may sacrifice the soul. Hafiz. CP-EmerR *Fr.* Odes.

Stand Whoso List. Sir Thomas Wyatt. CP-WyatT

Stand whoso list upon the slipper top. Stand Whoso List. Sir Thomas Wyatt. CP-WyatT

Stand with thy Graces forth, Brave man, and rise. To Worthy Friend, M. Tho. Falconbirge. Robert Herrick. CP-HerrR

Stand with your lover on the ending earth. E. E. Cummings. CP-CummE

Standards. W. S. Merwin. SP-MerwW

Standards, The. Richard Eberhart. CP-EberR

Standards and Paradise of the Blacks. Federico García Lorca. CP-GarcF, *tr. by* Greg Simon *and* Steven F. White

Standin' at de winder. Blue. Paul Laurence Dunbar. CP-DunbP

Standin' by de lonesome riverside. Ruined Gal, A. Langston Hughes. CP-HughL; CP-HughL1

Standing Afar Off for the Fear of Her Torment. Christina Georgina Rossetti. CP-RosC2

Standing against the gorge, he sees the slides of light. Portrait of a Man, with a Background of Holdings. Muriel Rukeyser. CP-RukeM

Standing alone on a fence in a spasm. Cousin, The. Stevie Smith. CP-SmitS

Standing aloof in giant ignorance. To Homer. John Keats. CP-KeatJ

Standing and Watching. James Schuyler. CP-SchuJ

Standing apart yet oddly sequential. Monument, The. Wyatt Prunty. SP-PrunW

Standing between the sun and moon preserves. Einstein. Archibald MacLeish. CP-MacLA

Standing by the Mantlepiece. Thomas Hardy. CP-HardT

Standing by the wires of your enclosure, I stared into your eyes. Snowy, The. May Swenson. SP-SwenM

Standing Close to Greatness. Miller Williams. CP-WillM

Standing Ground, A. Wendell Berry. CP-BerrW

Standing high on the shoulders of all things, all things. Place at Albert Bay, The. Muriel Rukeyser. CP-RukeM

Standing in front of his students. Paying Some Slight Attention to His Birthday the Associate Professor Goes about His Business Considering What He Sees and a Kind of Praise. Miller Williams. CP-WillM

Standing in the kitchen, ready to rip open the tinfoil. Essay on Criticism, An. Mona Van Duyn. SP-VanDM

Standing Invitation, A. G. K. Chesterton. CP-ChesG

Standing Nowhere. W. S. Merwin. SP-MerwWF

Standing on a boulder you cast a line. Boy, A. Czeslaw Milosz. CP-MiloC; CP-MiloCN, *tr. by* Robert Hass

Standing on a stepladder. Soy Sauce. Gary Snyder. CP-SnydG

Standing on an Alder Bridge over a Creek. Arthur Sze. SP-SzeA

Standing on his hands, he takes no walk. Inversion Factor. Robert Stock. SP-StocR

Standing on the corner / until Tatum passed. On the Corner. Philip Levine. SP-LeviP

Standing on top of the hay. Farm, The. Donald Hall. CP-HallD

Standing-stillness, The. All Nothing, Nothing. Laura Riding Jackson. CP-RidiL

Standing stone still on the path, with long pale chin. Last, The. Thomas Kinsella. CP-KinsT

Standing under the fobbed. Send No Money. Philip Larkin. CP-LarkP

Standing up on lifted, folded rock. By Frazier Creek Falls. Gary Snyder. CP-SnydG

Standings. Donald Davie. CP-DaviDC

Standley's Grove. Jones Very. CP-VeryJ

Stands the Spring! heralded by its bright-clothed. Fragment from May. Philip Larkin. CP-LarkP

Stands there, complete. Mandarins. T. S. Eliot. SP-ElioT

Stanger Minstrel, A. Samuel Taylor Coleridge. CP-ColeS

Stanley Kunitz. Mary Oliver. SP-OlivM

Stanza: "If I walk in Autumn's even." Percy Bysshe Shelley. CP-ShelP

Stanza: "No longer burn the hands that seized." Louise Bogan. CP-BogaL

Stanza from a Translation of the Marseillaise Hymn. Percy Bysshe Shelley. CP-ShelP

Stanza, Written at Bracknell. Percy Bysshe Shelley. CP-ShelP

Stanzas—April, 1814. Percy Bysshe Shelley. CP-ShelP

Stanzas: "At length, my soul! thy fruitless hopes give o'er." François de Malherbe. CP-PopeA

Stanzas: "Bind up thy tresses, thou beautiful one." John Greenleaf Whittier. CP-WhitJ

Stanzas: "Chill and mirk is the nightly blast." Lord Byron. CP-Byron

Stanzas: "Could Love for ever." Lord Byron. CP-Byron

Stanzas for a New Song. James Whitcomb Riley. CP-RileJ

Stanzas for Mary Stuart. Derek Mahon. CP-MahoD

Stanzas for Music. Lord Byron. CP-Byron

Stanzas for the Times. John Greenleaf Whittier. CP-WhitJ

Stanzas from the Grande Chartreuse. Matthew Arnold. SP-ArnoM

Stanzas: "How often we forget all time, when lone." Edgar Allan Poe. CP-PoeEd

Stanzas: "I heard thy fate without a tear." Lord Byron. CP-Byron

Stanzas: "I may sing; but minstrel's singing." Elizabeth Barrett Browning. CP-BroEB

Stanzas: "I'll not weep that thou art going to leave me." Emily Jane Brontë. CP-BronE

Stanzas: "I'm searching vainly for the point the blood." Eugenio Montale. CP-MontE, *tr. by* Jonathan Galassi

Stanzas in Meditation. Gertrude Stein. CP-SteiG

Stanzas in Memory of the Author of "Obermann" Matthew Arnold. SP-ArnoM

Stanzas: "Nature doth have her dawn each day." Henry David Thoreau. CP-ThorH

Stanzas: "Often rebuked, yet always back returning." Emily Jane Brontë. CP-BronE

Stanzas: "Oh!—my lonely—lonely—lonely Pillow!" Lord Byron. CP-Byron

Stanzas: Old Age and the Conventions of Retirement Have Driven My Friends from the Work They Love. Grace Paley. CP-PalGC

Stanzas on Milton's Remains. William Cowper. CP-CowpW

Stanzas on Some Skulls in Beauly Abbey, Near Inverness. John Keats. CP-KeatJ

Stanzas on the Same Occasion [in the Prospect of Death]. Robert Burns. CP-BurnR

Stanzas Printed on Bills of Mortality 1787–1790, 1792, 1793. William Cowper. *See* Stanzas Subjoined to the Yearly Bill of Mortality of the Parish of All Saints, Northampton; for the Year 1787

Stanzas Subjoined to the Yearly Bill of Mortality of the Parish of All Saints, Northampton; for the Year 1787. William Cowper. CP-CowpW

(Stanzas Printed on Bills of Mortality 1787–1790, 1792, 1793.) CP-CowpW

Stanzas: "Through cloudless skies, in silvery sheen." Lord Byron. CP-Byron

Stanzas to———. Emily Jane Brontë. CP-BronE

Stanzas to a Lady on Leaving England. Lord Byron. CP-Byron

Stanzas to a Lady, with the Poems of Camoëns. Lord Byron. CP-Byron

Stanzas to Augusta. Lord Byron. CP-Byron

Stanzas to Jessy. Lord Byron. CP-Byron

Stanzas to Mr. Bentley. Thomas Gray. CP-GrayT

(Stanzas to Mr Richard Bentley.) CP-GrayT

Stanzas to Mr Richard Bentley. Thomas Gray. *See* Stanzas to Mr. Bentley

Stanzas to the Po. Lord Byron. CP-Byron

Stanzas: Written at Night in Radio City. Allen Ginsberg. CP-GinsA

Stanzas Written in Dejection, near Naples [*or* —December 1818, near Naples]. Percy Bysshe Shelley. CP-ShelP

Stanzas Written in My Pocket-Copy of Thomson's "Castle of Indolence." William Wordsworth. CP-WorW1; MW-WorW

Stanzas Written on the Road between Florence and Pisa. Lord Byron. CP-Byron

Stanzas: "You say you love; but with a voice." John Keats. CP-KeatJ

Star. Pablo Neruda. SP-NeruP

Star. Derek Walcott. CP-WalcD

Star, A. Federico García Lorca. CP-GarcF, *tr. by* Jerome Rothenberg *Fr.* Night (Suite for Piano and Poet's Voice).

Star, The. Wendell Berry. CP-BerrW

Star, The. Charles Bukowski. SP-BukC3

Star, The. Kathleen Jessie Raine. SP-RainK

Star, The. Jones Very. CP-VeryJ

Star and coronal and bell. Spring Morning. A. E. Housman. CP-HousA

Star and Crescent. Kenneth Rexroth. CP-RexrK

Star-Apple. Robert Stock. SP-StocR

Star-Apple Kingdom, The. Derek Walcott. CP-WalcD

Star Book. Andrei Codrescu. SP-CodrA

Star by world-connivance seems part of the hill, A. Intelligent Prayer. Laura Riding Jackson. CP-RidiL

Star-crowned cliffs seem hinged upon the sky, The. Glencoe. G. K. Chesterton. CP-ChesG

Star dissolved in evening—the one star, The. Ancestral. Archibald MacLeish. CP-MacLA

Star-Fall. Robert Penn Warren. CP-WarrR

Star-filled seas are smooth to-night, The. Isle of Portland, The. A. E. Housman. CP-HousA

Star-Gazer. Louis MacNeice. CP-MacNL

Star-Gazers. William Wordsworth. CP-WorW1; MW-WorW

Star Guides. Keepsakes. William Stafford. SP-StafWW

Star hit in the hills behind our house, A. Star in the Hills, The. William Stafford. SP-StafW; SP-StafWW

Star in a Stoneboat, A. Robert Frost. CP-FrosR

Star in my, The. Wish. W. S. Merwin. SP-MerwW

Star in the Hills, The. William Stafford. SP-StafW; SP-StafWW

Star in the nets of heaven blazed past your breastbone, The. Song: The Star in the Nets of Heaven. Muriel Rukeyser. CP-RukeM

Star in the sky. Limits. Federico García Lorca. CP-GarcF, tr. by Jerome Rothenberg Fr. Palm Tree, The.

Star Light, Star Bright. Dorothy Parker. CP-ParkD

Star looks down at me, A. Waiting Both. Thomas Hardy. CP-HardT

Star-Nosed Mole. Anne Sexton. CP-SextA; SP-SextA

Star of Bethlehem. Kathleen Jessie Raine. SP-RainK

Star of Bethlehem, The. John Greenleaf Whittier. CP-WhitJ

Star of love was blazing in the east, The. Petrarch. CP-Petra, tr. by J. G. Nichols

Star of My Heart. Nicholas Vachel Lindsay. CP-LindV

Star of our absent ones, O listless mirror. Rainer Maria Rilke. CP-RilkFr, tr. by A. Poulin, Jr. Fr. Fragments.

Star of the brave!—whose beam hath shed. On the Star of "The Legion of Honour." Lord Byron. CP-Byron

Star of the Nativity. Joseph Brodsky. CP-BrodJ

Star Seeker. Langston Hughes. CP-HughL; CP-HughL1

Star seer Copernicus / Only could earn a curse. Ralph Waldo Emerson. CP-EmerR

Star Silver. Carl Sandburg. CP-SandC

Star Sirius, The. George Meredith. CP-MerG1

Star-Song; a Carol to the King; Sung at White-Hall, The. Robert Herrick. CP-HerrR

Star-stricken still / we lie under them. Rebels, The. Lawrence Ferlinghetti. SP-FerlL

Star that beams on Anna's breast, The. To a Lady ["Star that beams on Anna's breast, The"]. William Cowper. CP-CowpW

Star, that gives a gracious dole. Star Light, Star Bright. Dorothy Parker. CP-ParkD

Star, that looked so long among the stones. Meteorite, The. Randall Jarrell. CP-JarrR

Star Turn. Charles Wright. SP-WrigCN

Star Turn 2. Charles Wright. SP-WrigCN

Star two ash stow, A. Aster. Louis Zukofsky. CP-ZukLS

Star Vehicle (My Senior Year in High School). Ai. SP-Ai

Star which comes at close of day to shine, The. To I.F. William Wordsworth. CP-WorW2

Starched unbending candles stir, The. Bidden Guest, The. Geoffrey Hill. CP-HillG

Stare at the monster: remark. Famous Poet. Ted Hughes. SP-HughTN

Stare of the Man from the Provinces, The. Howard Nemerov. CP-NemeH

Stared Story, A. William Stafford. SP-StafWW

Stare's Nest by My Window, The. William Butler Yeats. CP-YeatW Fr. Meditations in Time of Civil War.

Starfish. Mary Oliver. SP-OlivM

Starfish, The. Robert Bly. SP-BlyR

Starfish, The. Josephine Jacobsen. CP-JacoJ

Stargazing. Robert Penn Warren.

Starglow. Louis Zukofsky. CP-ZukLS

Staring at the Sea on the Day of the Death of Another. May Swenson. SP-SwenM

Staring she / kindles. Weasel Snout. William Carlos Williams. CP-WilW1

Stark bewölkt. W. H. Auden. CP-AudeW

Stark Major. Hart Crane. CP-CranH

Starlet. John Ciardi. CP-CiarJ

Starlight. Philip Levine. SP-LeviP

Starlight. William Meredith. SP-MereW

Starlight and Non-Being. Chuang Tzu. CP-MertT

Starlight Night, The. Gerard Manley Hopkins. CP-HopkG

Starlight Scope Myopia. Yusef Komunyakaa. CP-KomuY

Starling, The. Stevie Smith. CP-SmitS

Starling drops / from branch to / branch, it's cold, A. Deep Winter. James Schuyler. CP-SchuJ

Starlings on the Roof. Thomas Hardy. CP-HardT

Star[re], The. George Herbert. CP-HerbG

Starred Coverlet, The. Robert Graves. CP-GravR

Starry, Colossal, blinding, bare. Man, A. G. K. Chesterton. CP-ChesG

Starry Heavens, the Moral Law, The. John Ciardi. CP-CiarJ

Starry Night, A. Paul Laurence Dunbar. CP-DunbP

Starry Night, The. Anne Sexton. CP-SextA; SP-SextA

Starry night shall tidings bring, The. Emily Jane Brontë. CP-BronE

Stars. Robert Earl Hayden. CP-HaydR

Stars. Emily Jane Brontë. CP-BronE

Stars. Robert Frost. CP-FrosR

Stars. Langston Hughes. CP-HughL; CP-HughL2

Stars. Carl Sandburg. CP-SandC

Stars, The. Jones Very. CP-VeryJ

Stars and grass. Weeds. James Dickey. CP-DickJ

Stars are all muffled in shrou'ds, The. Ill Penserosa, an Ode. Annis Boudinot Stockton. CP-StocA

Stars are constellations, The. Traces. A. K. Ramanujan. CP-RamaA

Stars are dropping thick as stones into the twiggy. Stars over the Dordogne. Sylvia Plath. CP-PlatS

Stars are failing, and the sky, The. Wandering Jew, The. James Whitcomb Riley. CP-RileJ

Stars Are Mansions Built by Nature's Hand, The. William Wordsworth. CP-WorW2

Stars are old, that stood for me, The. Emily Dickinson. CP-DickE

Stars are sliding wanton through trees, The. Stars Sliding. Ivor Gurney. SP-GurnI

Stars are soft as flowers, and as near, The. Midnight. Dorothy Parker. CP-ParkD

Stars are too many to count, The. Stars. Carl Sandburg. CP-SandC

Stars at Tallapoosa. Wallace Stevens. CP-StevW; CP-StevWP

Stars Dance, The. Thomas Campion. CP-CampT Fr. Lords Mask[e], The.

Stars / don't have a lover, The. Three Prints of the Sky. Federico García Lorca. CP-GarcF, tr. by Jerome Rothenberg

Stars dwindle / they will not reward me. Separation. Audre Lorde. SP-LordA

Stars fell at night. Five Years Old. James Tate. SP-TateJ

Stars flame. Bell, The. G. K. Chesterton. CP-ChesG

Stars Go Over the Lonely Ocean, The. Robinson Jeffers. CP-JefR3

Stars go to sleep so peacefully, The. Kenneth Patchen. CP-PatcK

Stars have died overhead in their great cold, The. Reading with Little Sister: A Recollection. William Stafford. SP-StafWW

Stars Have Not Dealt Me, The. A. E. Housman. CP-HousA

Stars have not dealt me the worst they could do, The. Stars Have Not Dealt Me, The. A. E. Housman. CP-HousA

Stars, I have seen them fall. A. E. Housman. CP-HousA

Stars in Your Name. Olga Broumas. SP-BrouO

Stars of a strange circus, The. Les Etoiles d'un Cirque. Tennessee Williams. CP-WillT

Stars of the Great Bear drift apart, The. Lesson in Geography, A. Kenneth Rexroth. CP-RexrK

Stars over the Dordogne. Sylvia Plath. CP-PlatS

Stars put out their pale opinions, one by one, The. St. Thomas Aquinas. Thomas Merton. CP-MertT

Stars Sliding. Ivor Gurney. SP-GurnI

Stars, Songs, Faces. Carl Sandburg. CP-SandC

Stars / stripping down, The. Fourth Page. Federico García Lorca. CP-GarcF, tr. by Jerome Rothenberg Fr. White Album.

Stars, that are small lights, The. At Night. William Carlos Williams. CP-WilW1

Stars that open and shut, The. Nonentity. D. H. Lawrence. CP-LawrD

Stars, the sky, the elements have put, The. Petrarch. CP-Petra, tr. by J. G. Nichols

Stars tied to breath. Brain to the Heart, The. Yusef Komunyakaa. CP-KomuY

Star's wept pink deep inside your ears, The. Arthur Rimbaud. CP-RimbA, tr. by Martin Sorrell

Stars were packed so close that night, The. Gerard Manley Hopkins. CP-HopkG

Stars whipped at his gaze, The. Dead Man, The. Paul Celan. SP-CelaP, tr. by John Felstiner

Starspangled cowboy / sauntering out of the almost. Backdrop Addresses Cowboy. Margaret Atwood. SP-AtwM1

Start a system of official spying. Police Spies. D. H. Lawrence. CP-LawrD

Start not—nor deem my spirit fled. Lines Inscribed upon a Cup Formed from a Skull. Lord Byron. CP-Byron

Start not! upon the minister wall. Emily Jane Brontë. CP-BronE

Start such a fire in England, Master Ridley. Oxfordshire. Donald Davie. CP-DaviDC

Start up in gray, / in moist green. Birds. James Schuyler. CP-SchuJ

Start with the house: the smell of the person dead. Where to Turn When Sorrow Comes like a Black Bull in Your Dreams. Miller Williams. CP-WillM

Starter! / Her face is pale. Closing Time. Langston Hughes. CP-HughL; CP-HughL1

Starting from black or. Painting, The. William Carlos Williams. CP-WilW2

Starting from fish-shape Paumanok where I was born. Starting from Paumanok. Walt Whitman. CP-WhitW

Starting from Paumanok. Walt Whitman. CP-WhitW

Starting here, what do you want to remember? You Reading This, Be Ready. William Stafford. SP-StafWW

Starting with a Line from Roethke. Jane Cooper. CP-CoopJ

Starting with eyeball kicks. Over Kansas. Allen Ginsberg. CP-GinsA

Starting with Little Things. William Stafford. SP-StafWW

Startling reality of things, The. Fernando Pessoa. SP-PessF, *tr.* by Susan M. Brown *and* Edwin Honig

Starvation. Maya Angelou. SP-AngeM

Starvation Camp at Jasło. Wisława Szymborska. SP-SzymWM, *tr.* by Joanna Trzeciak

Starved eye devours the seascape for the morsel, The. Castaway, The. Derek Walcott. CP-WalcD

Starved Lovers. Archibald MacLeish. CP-MacLA

Stary Sacz. Adam Zagajewski. SP-ZagaA, *tr.* by Clare Cavanagh

Stasis in darkness. Ariel. Sylvia Plath. CP-PlatS

Stat rosa pristina nomine. Among the Roses. James Laughlin. CP-LaugJ

State, The. Randall Jarrell. CP-JarrR

State Funeral: March 31, 1969. Archibald MacLeish. CP-MacLA

State of Affairs. Yehuda Amichai. SP-AmicYL, *tr.* by Benjamin Harshav *and* Barbara Harshav

State of Age, The. George Meredith. CP-MerG1

State of Siege? Arthur Rimbaud. CP-RimbA, *tr.* by Martin Sorrell

State of the Nation, The. Kenneth Patchen. CP-PatcK

State relies on people, A. Han-shan. CP-ColdM, *tr.* by Red Pine

State Rights. Jones Very. CP-VeryJ

State with the prettiest name, The. Florida. Elizabeth Bishop. CP-BishE

Stately bride is the shining world, A. Hafiz. CP-EmerR *Fr.* Odes.

Stately flower in my garden grows, A. To A.M. George Meredith. CP MerG2

Stately Goddesse, do thou please. Hymne to Juno, An. Robert Herrick. CP-HerrR

Stately music rises on my ear, A. Just Made Perfect, The. Henry David Thoreau. CP-ThorH

Statement. Rae Armantrout. SP-ArmaA

Statement. John Ciardi. CP-CiarJ

Statement. Langston Hughes. CP-HughL; CP-HughL2

Statement by Willkie after Returning from England. Muriel Rukeyser. CP-RukeM

Statement for the Times. David Ignatow. SP-IgnaD

Statement of Being. Ezra Pound. CP-PoEar

Statement: Philippa Allen. Muriel Rukeyser. CP-RukeM

States! Walt Whitman. CP-WhitW

States strong enough to do good are but few. No Holy Wars for Them. Robert Frost. CP-FrosR

States when they black out and lie there rolling when they turn, The. Falling. James Dickey. CP-DickJ

Statesman, I thank thee! and, if yet dissent. To William H. Seward. John Greenleaf Whittier. CP-WhitJ

Statesman is an easy man, A. Old Stone Cross, The. William Butler Yeats. CP-YeatW

Statesman, yet Friend to Truth! of Soul sincere. Epitaph on James Craggs, Esq., in Westminster Abbey. Alexander Pope. CP-PopeA

Statesmen, The. Ambrose Bierce. SP-BierA

Static forces / not a ball of silver, The. On the Principle of Blowclocks. Charles Tomlinson. CP-TomlC; SP-TomlC

Static jet of water, A. Pergola. Federico García Lorca. CP-GarcF, *tr.* by Jerome Rothenberg *Fr.* In the Garden of the Lunar Grapefruits.

Station Island. Seamus Heaney. SP-HeanSO

Stationary sense . . . as, I suppose, A. Maturity. Philip Larkin. CP-LarkP

Stations. Ted Hughes. SP-HughTN

Stations. John Ciardi. CP-CiarJ

Stations of the West, The. Seamus Heaney. SP-HeanSO

Statistics. Yehuda Amichai. SP-AmicY, *tr.* by Chana Bloch

Statistics. James Vincent Cunningham. CP-CunnJ

Statistics. Carl Sandburg. CP-SandC

Statistics. William Butler Yeats. CP-YeatW

Statue. Gerrit Achterberg. CP-RicAE

Statue, The. John Berryman. CP-BerrJ

Statue, The. Robert Creeley. CP-CreeR

Statue and Birds. Louise Bogan. CP-BogaL

Statue and the Bust, The. Robert Browning. CP-BroR1; SP-BroR

Statue has no preferences, not even any objections, The. Witnesses Everywhere. Yannis Ritsos. SP-RitsY, *tr.* by Kimon Friar *and* Kostas Myrsiades

Statue in the Cafe, The. Yannis Ritsos. SP-RitsY, *tr.* by Kimon Friar *and* Kostas Myrsiades

Statue of a Couple. Czeslaw Milosz. CP-MiloC; CP-MiloCN

Statue of Flora, on the Grounds of R. Brookhouse Esq, Washington Street, The. Jones Very. CP-VeryJ

Statue of Liberty. Richard Eberhart. CP-EberR

Statue of Liberty. Karl Shapiro. SP-ShapK

Statue of Liberty, The. Thomas Hardy. CP-HardT

Statue of Old Andrew Jackson, The. Nicholas Vachel Lindsay. CP-LindV

Statue of the founder wears a green, The. Generic College. John Updike. CP-UpdiJ

Statue, tolerant through years of weather, The. Statue, The. John Berryman. CP-BerrJ

Statue turned, The. Two St. Petersburgs. Heather McHugh. SP-McHuH

Statues. Kathleen Jessie Raine. SP-RainK

Statues. Richard Wilbur. CP-WilbR

Statues, The. Yannis Ritsos. SP-RitsY, *tr.* by Minas Savvas

Statues, The. William Butler Yeats. CP-YeatW

Statues in the Cemeteries, The. Yannis Ritsos. SP-RitsY, *tr.* by Edmund Keeley

Statues in the Public Gardens, The. Howard Nemerov. CP-NemeH

Statues naked under the trees in the cemeteries, The. Statues in the Cemeteries, The. Yannis Ritsos. SP-RitsY, *tr.* by Edmund Keeley

Statues suffer the darkness of coffins with their eyes. Little Girl Drowned in the Well. Federico García Lorca. CP-GarcF, *tr.* by Greg Simon *and* Steven F. White

Statues with exposed hearts and barbed-wire crowns. Mud Vision, The. Seamus Heaney. SP-HeanSO

Status indeed and protocol I pay. Church of Ireland. Donald Davie. CP-DaviDC

Status of the Monk, The. Andrei Codrescu. SP-CodrA

Stave of Roving Tim, A. George Meredith. CP-MerG1

Stay Away from the White House. Allen Ginsberg. SP-GinsA

Stay, bold Adventurer; rest awhile thy limbs. Written with a Slate Pencil on a Stone, on the Side of the Mountain of Black Comb. William Wordsworth. CP-WorW1

Stay, coward blood, and do not yield. On Mistress N. Thomas Carew. CP-CareT

Stay here, fond youth, and ask no more. Against Fruition. Sir John Suckling. CP-SuckJ

Stay Home. Wendell Berry. CP-BerrW

Stay, if you list, O passer by the way. Epitaph, An: "Stay, if you list, O passer by the way." A. E. Housman. CP-HousA

Stay, my Charmer, can you leave me. Robert Burns. CP-BurnR

Stay near me—do not take thy flight! To a Butterfly ("Stay near me do not take thy flight!"). William Wordsworth. CP-WorW1; MW-WorW

Stay, passenger! this stone demands thy tears! Elegy on the Death of a Young Lady, An. Annis Boudinot Stockton. CP-StocA

Stay, ruby-breasted warbler, stay. Song: "Stay, ruby-breasted warbler, stay." John Keats. CP-KeatJ

Stay, silver-footed Came, strive not to wed. Elegie on the Death of Doctor Porter, An. Richard Crashaw. CP-CrasR

Stay still, if the angel. Rainer Maria Rilke. CP-RilkFr, *tr.* by A. Poulin, Jr. *Fr.* Affectionate Taxes to France.

Stay still, if the Angel. Rainer Maria Rilke. CP-RilkFr, *tr.* by A. Poulin, Jr. *Fr.* Orchards.

Stay together, friends. Waterwheel, The. Jelaluddin Rumi. SP-Rumi, *tr.* by Coleman Barks

Stay, view this stone: and, if thou beest not such. Ben Jonson. CP-JonsB

Stay where thou art, thou need'st not further go. Invitation, The ("Stay where thou art, thou need'st not further go"). Jones Very. CP-VeryJ

Stay while ye will, or goe. To Carnations. Robert Herrick. CP-HerrR

Stay with the cuckoo I heard. Cuckoo Myth. W. S. Merwin. SP-MerwW

Stayed No Longer in the Place Than to Hire a Guide for the Next Stage. Kenneth Patchen. CP-PatcK

Staying Alive. Denise Levertov.

    At the Justice Department November 15, 1969. SP-LeveDS

    Gandhi's Gun (and Brecht's Vow). SP-LeveDS

    Let Us Sing Unto the Lord a New Song. SP-LeveDS

Staying Awake. John Logan. CP-LogaJ

Staying overnight in a friend's house. Overnights. Alice Walker. CP-WalkA

Staying with It. Andrei Codrescu. SP-CodrA

Steadfast, upstanding, magnanimous Joan. Joan. G. K. Chesterton. CP-ChesG

Steadfastly from his childhood's earliest hour. Claude Matthews. James Whitcomb Riley. CP-RileJ

Steadfastness. Sir Thomas Wyatt. CP-WyatT

Steady, the evening fades. Buffalo Evening. Robert Creeley. SP-CreeR

Steal poems is the license. Why Shouldn't I. James Laughlin. CP-LaugJ

Stealer, The. Thom Gunn. CP-GunnT

Stealing from the night. Dancers. Langston Hughes. CP-HughL; CP-HughL2

Stealing Trout on a May Morning. Ted Hughes. SP-HughTN

Stealth and Subtleties of Growth. Richard Eberhart. CP-EberR

Stealth of the flood tide, the moon dark. August Darks, The. Amy Clampitt. CP-ClamA

Steam fills the bath, and frozen figures on the wall. Steambath, The. Jelaluddin Rumi. SP-Rumi, *tr.* by Coleman Barks

Steam hammer pounds with a regularity on steel I should envy, The. Two. David Ignatow. SP-IgnaD

Steam in Sacrifice. Robert Herrick. CP-HerrR

Steam some sand for your dinner. Han-shan. CP-ColdM, *tr.* by Red Pine

Steambath, The. Jelaluddin Rumi. SP-Rumi, *tr. by* Coleman Barks

Steamboat Whistle, The. Archibald MacLeish. CP-MacLA

Steamboats, Viaducts, and Railways. William Wordsworth. CP-WorW2

Steamer at the pier. George Oppen. CP-OppGN

Steamer, steamer, outward bound. Song for Pier Something or Other. Ogden Nash. CP-NashO

Steaming Ties. James Schuyler. CP-SchuJ

Steaming ties, cutting rue. Steaming Ties. James Schuyler. CP-SchuJ

Steatopygous, sow-dugged. Dame Kind. W. H. Auden. CP-AudeW

Steel. Charles Tomlinson. CP-TomlC

Steel doors—guillotine gates. Prisoners, The. Robert Earl Hayden. CP-HaydR

Steel edge of plough. Dusk. Stephen Spender. CP-SpenS

Steel hardly knows what a hint is, but for thistledown. Different Things. William Stafford. SP-StafWW

Steel Mills. Langston Hughes. CP-HughL; CP-HughL1

Steel Plate, The. Yusef Komunyakaa. CP-KomuY

Steel worker on the girder, The. Building of the Skyscraper, The. George Oppen. CP-OppGN

Steelhead, Wild Pig, the Fungus. Robinson Jeffers. CP-JefR2

Steely light shadows the white horizon, A. On Fitz Hugh Lane's *Approaching Storm, Owl's Head, 1860.* Helen Pinkerton. CP-PinkH

Steep and black the mountain to the graying sky; no star but the morning. Dawn. Robinson Jeffers. CP-JefR3

Steep cliff, round which a child I played. King's Arm Chair, The. Jones Very. CP-VeryJ

Steep gloom among pine trees. Pablo Neruda. SP-LoguC, *tr. by* Christopher Logue *Fr.* Red Bird.

Steep roads, a tunnel through chalk downs, are the approaches. Dover. W. H. Auden. CP-AudeW

Steep up in Lubitavish townland stands. Ossian's Grave. Robinson Jeffers. CP-JefR2

Steeple bush, hardhack. Hayden Carruth. CP-CarHS *Fr.* Clay Hill Anthology, The.

Steeple-Jack, The. Marianne Craig Moore. CP-MoorM *Fr.* Part of a Novel, Part of a Poem, Part of a Play.

Steeple on the House, A. Robert Frost. CP-FrosR

Steepletop. Edna St. Vincent Millay. CP-MillE

Steering my little boat towards a misty islet. Meng Hao Jan. CP-WilW2

Stelae, The. Adrienne Rich. CP-RicAE; SP-RicA2

Stella at Woodpark. Jonathan Swift. CP-SwifJ

Stella Dallas. William Dickey. SP-DickW

Stella in Mourning. Samuel Johnson. CP-JohnS

Stella Maris. James Tate. SP-TateJ

Stella stands in the rain, outside the great house. Stella Dallas. William Dickey. SP-DickW

Stella this day is thirty-four. Stella's Birthday; Written in the Year 1718[/9]. Jonathan Swift. CP-SwifJ

Stella's Birthday (1723). Jonathan Swift. CP-SwifJ

Stella's Birthday, 1725. Jonathan Swift. CP-SwifJ

Stella's Birthday ([March 13,] 1727). Jonathan Swift. CP-SwifJ

Stella's Birthday; Written in the Year 1718[/9]. Jonathan Swift. CP-SwifJ (On Stella's Birthday, 1718/1719.) CP-SwifJ

Stellenbosch. Rudyard Kipling. CP-KiplR

Stem of a departed Flower, The. Emily Dickinson. CP-DickE

Stem that long has borne the wintry blast, The. Spring ("Stem that long has borne the wintry blast, The"). Jones Very. CP-VeryJ

Stempclasp becomes two *cross you.* Jade. Louis Zukofsky. CP-ZukLS

Stems. Denise Levertov. SP-LeveDP

Stentor and Mourning. Alan Dugan. CP-DugaA

Steorra, stir / by the bird's whir. X to the Nth. Charles Olson. CP-OlsoC

Step, A. Robert Creeley. CP-CreeR

Step Away from Them, A. Frank O'Hara. SP-OharF

Step-Children of Paradise. Charles Wright. SP-WrigCN

Step forward and a lesser, A. TWO. Thomas Kinsella. CP-KinsT

Step lightly on this narrow spot. Emily Dickinson. CP-DickE

Step me now a bridal measure. To Dan. Paul Laurence Dunbar. CP-DunbP

Step on His Head. James Laughlin. CP-LaugJ

Step softly, under snow or rain. Wise Men, The. G. K. Chesterton. CP-ChesG

Step through the mirror. Echoes ("Step through the mirror"). Robert Creeley. SP-CreeR

Step very softly, sweet Quiet-foot. Mrs. Grundy. Walter De la Mare. CP-DeLaW

Step wid de banjo an' glide wid de fiddle. Christmas. Paul Laurence Dunbar. CP-DunbP

Stepfather: A Girl's Song. Yusef Komunyakaa. CP-KomuY

Stephanos Skilitsis. Constantine P. Cavafy. CP-CavaC, *tr. by* Theoharis Constantine Theoharis

Stephen and Barberie. Gerard Manley Hopkins. CP-HopkG

Stephen Spender, I write about your face. Face, Ocean. Richard Eberhart. CP-EberR

Stepmother: A Boy's Song. Yusef Komunyakaa. CP-KomuY

Stepmother, The. James Whitcomb Riley. CP-RileJ

Stepping Backward. Hayden Carruth. CP-CarHS

Stepping Backward. Adrienne Rich. CP-RicAE; SP-RicA2

Stepping Outside. Tess Gallagher. SP-GallT

Stepping-Stones, The. William Wordsworth. CP-WorW2 *Fr.* River Duddon [A Series of Sonnets], The.

Stepping-stones, once, The. Dance, A. Wendell Berry. CP-BerrW

Stepping Westward. Denise Levertov. SP-LeveDP

Stepping Westward. William Wordsworth. CP-WorW1; MW-WorW

Steps. Frank O'Hara. SP-OharF

Steps, The. Josephine Jacobsen. CP-JacoJ

Steps for a Dancer. Howard Nemerov. CP-NemeH

Stereopticon. William Stafford. SP-StafWW

Sterile faces squeezed out from squalid tubes of. Mercy, Wherever You Are, Come Running in to Me and Grab Me in Your Good Arms—. Charles Bukowski. SP-BukC2

Sterile these stones. Corner Stone, The. Walter De la Mare. CP-DeLaW

Stern creeds and outward forms must pass away. Influence of Channing, The. Jones Very. CP-VeryJ

Stern Daughter of the Voice of God! Ode to Duty. William Wordsworth. CP-WorW1; MW-WorW

Stern philosophy it is, which says, A. Philosophy and Religion. Jones Very. CP-VeryJ

Stern winter now, by spring repress'd. Ode, An: "Stern winter now, by spring repress'd." Samuel Johnson. CP-JohnS

Stethoscope Case, A. Charles Bukowski. SP-BukC1

Stethoscope tells what everyone fears, The. Academic. Theodore Roethke. CP-RoetT

Stevens Song. Charles Olson. SP-OlsoC *Fr.* Maximus Poems, The.

Stewardess told us to extinguish all smoking materials, A. Yehuda Amichai. SP-AmicYL, *tr. by* Benjamin Harshav *and* Barbara Harshav

Stick, The. May Swenson. SP-SwenM

Stick Builder. Wyatt Prunty. SP-PrunW

Stick is subject to the waves, The. The waves are subject to. Stick, The. May Swenson. SP-SwenM

Stick of Incense, A. William Butler Yeats. CP-YeatW

Stick of the blind man, The. Parable. Thomas McGrath. SP-McGrT

Stick the finger inside. Black Mail. Alice Walker. CP-WalkA

Stick to the hollies. Ghouls of Candlemas, The. Andrei Codrescu. SP-CodrA

Sticks-in-a-drowse droop over sugary loam. Cuttings. Theodore Roethke. CP-RoetT

Sticky music flows slowly, A. Ashkelon. Yehuda Amichai. SP-AmicYL, *tr. by* Benjamin Harshav *and* Barbara Harshav

Stiff-dog death, all froth on a bloody chin. Elegy for Jog. John Ciardi. CP-CiarJ

Stiff spokes of this wheel, The. July in Washington. Robert Lowell. SP-LoweR

Still. A. R. Ammons. CP-AmmoA

Still. Robert Creeley. CP-CreeR

Still. Wisława Szymborska. SP-SzymWM, *tr. by* Joanna Trzeciak

Still, A. Andrei Codrescu. SP-CodrA

Still a Day to Live. Jones Very. CP-VeryJ

Still a day to live, still a day to live. Still a Day to Live. Jones Very. CP-VeryJ

Still Afternoon Light. W. S. Merwin. SP-MerwW

Still and blanched and cold and lone. Mountains, The. Walter De la Mare. CP-DeLaW

Still Another for Mother. A. K. Ramanujan. CP-RamaA

Still Another View of Grace. A. K. Ramanujan. CP-RamaA

Still anxious to secure your partial favor. Occasional Address, Spoken by Miss Fontenell, on Her Bnefit-Night, Decr. 4th. 1793.—Written by Mr Burns. Robert Burns. CP-BurnR

Still as a mountain with dark pines and sun. Goliath. Walter De la Mare. CP-DeLaW

Still, as of old, in Beavor's Vale. Revelation. John Greenleaf Whittier. CP-WhitJ

Still as she looked the iron clouds. Emily Jane Brontë. CP-BronE

Still as the Profile of a Tree. Emily Dickinson. CP-DickE

Still beside that dreary water. Emily Jane Brontë. CP-BronE

Still blooming on, when Summer-flowers all fade. Autumn Flowers. Jones Very. CP-VeryJ

Still-Born, The. Jones Very. CP-VeryJ

Still, Citizen Sparrow. Richard Wilbur. CP-WilbR

Still Dancers. Robert Creeley. SP-CreeR

Still dark, the early morning breathes. Five AM. William Stafford. SP-StafWW

Still dark. / The unknown bird sits on his usual branch. Five Flights Up. Elizabeth Bishop. CP-BishE

Still, Dear, it is incredible to me. Her Second Husband Hears Her Story. Thomas Hardy. CP-HardT

Still Do I Keep My Look, My Identity . . . . Gwendolyn Brooks. SP-BrooG

Still do the southernly Bug waters know. Nearness of Graves. Paul Celan. SP-CelaP, *tr. by* John Felstiner

Still explosions on the rocks, The. Shampoo, The. Elizabeth Bishop. CP-BishE

Still gazing on thy wreath of carved flowers. Statue of Flora, on the Grounds of R. Brookhouse Esq, Washington Street, The. Jones Very. CP-VeryJ

Still go funny, in the face of him. Issue, Mood. Charles Olson. CP-OlsoC

Still half drunk, after a night at cards. Day on the Big Branch, A. Howard Nemerov. CP-NemeH

Still haunted by the cycle of the moon. Morning Moon, The. Derek Walcott. CP-WalcD

Still he wooingly. Theodore Weiss. SP-WeisT *Fr.* Storeroom, The.

Still Here. Langston Hughes. CP-HughL; CP-HughL2; CP-HughL3

Still I bring flowers. Ad Infinitum. William Carlos Williams. CP-WilW1

Still I kneel in the colorless. Narcisses: Vision and Retrospect. John Logan. CP-LogaJ

Still I Rise. Maya Angelou. SP-AngeM

Still, / I would leap too. Small Frogs Killed on the Highway. James Wright. CP-WrigJ

Still in the now of then they remain. After Fifty-five Years. Kathleen Jessie Raine. SP-RainK

Still in thy streets, O Paris! doth the stain. Peace Convention at Brussels, The. John Greenleaf Whittier. CP-WhitJ

Still, it is dear defiance now to carry. Flags. Gwendolyn Brooks. SP-BrooG

Still Life. Buddhadeva Bose. CP-OppGN, *tr. by* George Oppen

Still Life. Olga Broumas. SP-BrouO

Still Life. Andrei Codrescu. SP-CodrA

Still Life. Louise Glück. SP-GlucL

Still Life. Thom Gunn. CP-GunnT

Still Life. Ted Hughes. SP-HughTN

Still Life. A. K. Ramanujan. CP-RamaA

Still Life. Carl Sandburg. CP-SandC

Still Life. C. K. Williams. CP-WillC

Still Life. William Carlos Williams. CP-WilW2

Still Life on a Matchbox Lid. Charles Wright. SP-WrigCN

Still Life I. Howard Nemerov. CP-NemeH

Still Life II. Howard Nemerov. CP-NemeH

Still Life III. Howard Nemerov. CP-NemeH

Still Life Or. Robert Creeley. CP-CreeR

Still Life with Spring and Time to Burn. Charles Wright. SP-WrigCN

Still Life with Stick and Word. Charles Wright. SP-WrigCN

Still Lifes. William Carlos Williams. CP-WilW2

Still linger in our noon of time. Child-Songs. John Greenleaf Whittier. CP-WhitJ

Still Looking Out for Number One. Raymond Carver. CP-CarvR

Still marveling at the light. Return, The. Richard Eberhart. CP-EberR

Still may it stand! For Time himself has spared. On the First Church Built by the Puritans in 1634. Jones Very. CP-VeryJ

Still Moment at Dun Laoghaire. Tess Gallagher. SP-GallT

Still morning. Maria Speaks. Robert Creeley. SP-CreeR

Still must I hear?—shall hoarse Fitzgerald bawl. English Bards and Scotch Reviewers. Lord Byron. CP-Byron

Still must the poet as of old. To Kathleen. Edna St. Vincent Millay. CP-MillE

Still night. The old clock Ticks. Last Night in Calcutta. Allen Ginsberg. CP-GinsA

Still on the spot Lord Marmion stay'd. Edinburgh from the Pentland Hills. Sir Walter Scott. SP-ScotW *Fr.* Marmion.

Still on Water. Kenneth Rexroth. CP-RexrK

Still one more year of preparation. Preparation. Czeslaw Milosz. CP-MiloC; CP-MiloCN, *tr. by* Robert Hass

Still other sheep Thou hast, O Shepherd fair. On the Great Divisions of the Christian Church, the Catholic, the Protestant, and the Greek. Jones Very. CP-VeryJ

Still own thee—still thou art. Emily Dickinson. CP-DickE

Still, passed through the spokes of an old wheel, on and around. Reincarnation (I) ["Still, passed through the spokes of an old wheel, on and around"]. James Dickey. CP-DickJ

Still Pond No More Moving. James Laughlin. CP-LaugJ

Still sits the school-house by the road. In School-Days. John Greenleaf Whittier. CP-WhitJ

Still skies, still seas. Kathleen Jessie Raine. SP-RainK

Still small voice spake unto me, A. Two Voices, The. Alfred Tennyson. CP-TennA

Still Small Voice, The. Jones Very. CP-VeryJ

Still sometimes in my secret heart of hearts. Cor Mio. Christina Georgina Rossetti. CP-RosC3

Still, still my eye will gaze long-fixed on thee. Columbine, The. Jones Very. CP-VeryJ

Still, still without ceasing. Simple Trust. Jeanne Marie Bouvier de la Motte-Guyon. CP-CowpW

Still take advice; though counsels when they flye. Advice the Best Actor. Robert Herrick. CP-HerrR

Still the Mind Smiles. Robinson Jeffers. CP-JefR2

Still the same / day? Still. Robert Creeley. CP-CreeR

Still Though the One I Sing. Walt Whitman. CP-WhitW

Still to be neat, still to be dressed [*or* Drest]. Ben Jonson. CP-JonsB; SP-JonsB *Fr.* Epicoene; or, The Silent Woman.

Still to our gains our chief respect is had. Rewards. Robert Herrick. CP-HerrR

Still Too Young. Robert Creeley. SP-CreeR

Still turn, and imitate the heaven. Ben Jonson. CP-JonsB *Fr.* Masque of Beauty, The.

Still Turning. May Swenson. SP-SwenM

Still Unsatisfied. Charles Baudelaire. CP-BaudC, *tr. by* Walter Martin

Still—Volcano—Life, A. Emily Dickinson. CP-DickE

Still waters of the air, The. Variations. Federico García Lorca. SP-GarcF, *tr. by* Lysander Kemp

Still we turn a corner and there it is. WWI. Miller Williams. CP-WillM

Still weeks before the equinox. Lenten. Olga Broumas. SP-BrouO

Still will I harvest beauty where it grows. Edna St. Vincent Millay. CP-MillE

Still you bring us with our hands bound. Underground, The. Langston Hughes. CP-HughL; CP-HughL2

Still you stand, still you listen, still you smile! Numpholeptos. Robert Browning. CP-BroR2

Stillborn. Sylvia Plath. CP-PlatS

Stillborn. William Stafford. SP-StafWW

Stillborn Love. Dante Gabriel Rossetti. CW-RossD *Fr.* House of Life, The.

Stillness. Wyatt Prunty. SP-PrunW

Stillness. William Carlos Williams. CP-WilW1

Stillness and moonlight, with. Loneliness[: An Outburst of Hexasyllables]. Hayden Carruth. CP-CarHS

Stillness and Vertigo. Clarence Major. SP-MajoC

Stillness! Down the dripping ride. Tunstall Forest. Donald Davie. CP-DaviDC

Stillness of the rose, The. Rose, The. William Carlos Williams. CP-WilW2

Stillness, / of the wood, The. Figures, The. Robert Creeley. CP-CreeR

Stills and Rapids of Your Nakedness, The. John Ciardi. CP-CiarJ

Stilton and Milton; Or Literature in the 17th and 20th Centuries. G. K. Chesterton. CP-ChesG

Stimulus, beyond the Grave, The. Emily Dickinson. CP-DickE

Stimulus of Loss, The. Emily Dickinson. SP-DickE

Sting, The. C. K. Williams. CP-WillC

Sting of bees took away my father, The. Lament: "Sting of bees took away my father, The." Sylvia Plath. CP-PlatS

Stinging / gold swarms. Sunset. E. E. Cummings. CP-CummE

Stinging nettles on my wrists woke me, The. Chief Mystery, The. D. H. Lawrence. CP-LawrD

Stings. Sylvia Plath. CP-PlatS

Stir is on the Worc'ter hills, A. Freshet, The. Henry David Thoreau. CP-ThorH

Stirred . . . the fur-toothed graves. Battle of Unameit, The. Kenneth Patchen. CP-PatcK

Stirring suddenly from long hibernation. Mid-Winter Waking. Robert Graves. CP-GravR

Stirrup Cup, The. Paul Laurence Dunbar. CP-DunbP

Stitch Too Late Is My Fate, A. Ogden Nash. CP-NashO

Stoat danced on the lawns here, A. Strawberry Hill. Ted Hughes. SP-HughTN

Stock-Gilly Flowers, The. Jones Very. CP-VeryJ

Stock Report. Andrei Codrescu. SP-CodrA

Stocky woman at the door, The. Last Day and the First, The. Theodore Weiss. SP-WeisT

Stoic. D. H. Lawrence. CP-LawrD

Stokely Malcolm Me. Langston Hughes. CP-HughL; CP-HughL3

Stolen. Charles Bukowski. SP-BukC1

Stolen and Abandoned. Philip Whalen. SP-WhalP

Stolen Child, The. William Butler Yeats. CP-YeatW

Stolen Jewel. Robert Graves. CP-GravR

Stolen lady was coming on board, A. Discovery of the Madeiras, The. Robert Frost. CP-FrosR

Stomach: lonely. Through Walls. Rae Armantrout. SP-ArmaA

Stomach of goat, crushed. Salami. Philip Levine. SP-LeviP

Stomping with Catullus. Robert Creeley. CP-CreeR

Stone. Robert Creeley. SP-CreeR

Stone. Charles Simic. SP-SimiC; SP-SimiCE

Stone, The. Flower. Paul Celan. SP-CelaP, *tr. by* John Felstiner

Stone, The. Ted Hughes. SP-HughTN

Stone, The. Evolution. May Swenson. SP-SwenM

Stone against stone, they are building back. Churchyard Wall, The. Charles Tomlinson. CP-TomlC; SP-TomlC

Stone Age Figure Far Below, A. Derek Mahon. CP-MahoD

Stone and Flower. Kenneth Rexroth. CP-RexrK

Stone and Flower Series. Charles Olson. CP-OlsoC

Stone at dawn, A. Easter Morning. Amy Clampitt. CP-ClamA

Stone Axe, The. Robinson Jeffers. CP-JefR2

Stone Church Damaged by a Bomb, A. Philip Larkin. CP-LarkP

Stone Crock, The. William Carlos Williams. CP-WilW2

Stone-cutters fighting time with marble, you foredefeated. To the Stone-Cutters. Robinson Jeffers. CP-JefR1

Stone face higher than six horses stood five thousand years gazing. Has-Been, The. Carl Sandburg. CP-SandC

Stone-flake and salmon. Gary Snyder. CP-SnydG *Fr.* Myths and Texts.

Stone goes straight, The. Washington Monument by Night. Carl Sandburg. CP-SandC

Stone Gullets. May Swenson. SP-SwenM

Stone in my tread, The. Holding On. A. R. Ammons. CP-AmmoA

Stone Knife, A. James Schuyler. CP-SchuJ

Stone, / like stillness. After Mallarmé. Robert Creeley. CP-CreeR

Stone Speech. Charles Tomlinson. CP-TomlC; SP-TomlC

Stone, steel, dominions pass. A. E. Housman. CP-HousA

Stone steps, a solid. Hard Times. William Carlos Williams. CP-WilW2

Stone strikes the body, because, The. Parable, A. Gregory Orr. SP-OrrG

Stone sun traveled beside us, A. Recognition. Yannis Ritsos. SP-RitsY, *tr. by* Athan Anagnostopoulos

Stone, toppled by water and mountain, The. Pablo Neruda. SP-NeruP *Fr.* Skystones.

Stone turns over slowly, The. Fit against the Country, A. James Wright. CP-WrigJ

Stone Verdict, The. Seamus Heaney. SP-HeanSO

Stone Walls. Donald Hall. CP-HallD

Stone Walls. May Sarton. SP-SartM

Stone Walls: at Chew Magna. Charles Tomlinson. CP-TomlC

Stone walls emerge from leafy ground. Stone Walls. Donald Hall. CP-HallD

Stone without Edges Has Not Been Mined, The. John Ciardi. CP-CiarJ

Stonecarver's Poem, The. Denise Levertov. SP-LeveDP; SP-LeveDS

Stonecutter's angels were seven, The. Tennessee Williams. CP-WillT

Stoned on Xanax. Lockerbie. William Corbett. SP-CorbW

Stoned & / singing Indian scat. River Still To Be Found, A. Lawrence Ferlinghetti. SP-FerlL

Stonehenge, Newgrange. Easter Island. Paul Muldoon. CP-MuldP

Stones. Donald Hall. CP-HallD

Stones. Maxine W. Kumin. SP-KumiM

Stones. Yannis Ritsos. SP-RitsY, *tr. by* Kimon Friar

Stones, The. Wendell Berry. CP-BerrW

Stones Are Thrown. Tennessee Williams. CP-WillT

Stones, brown tufted grass, but no water. Ravine, The. Hayden Carruth. CP-CarHS

Stones huddled together on the ramparts, The. Faction du Muet. René Char. CP-MertT

Stones of kin and friend, The. Lorelei. James Merrill. SP-MerrJ

Stones of spring, The. Under Libra: Weights and Measures. James Merrill. SP-MerrJ

Stones of time's old house with pelting storms, The. Time's House. Jones Very. CP-VeryJ

Stones on the mountain are always, The. Ballad of the Washed Hair. Yehuda Amichai. SP-AmicY, *tr. by* Stephen Mitchell

Stones only, the disjecta membra of this Great House. Ruins of a Great House. Derek Walcott. CP-WalcD

Stones that rolled in the sea for a thousand years. Old Stone-Mason, The. Robinson Jeffers. CP-JefR3

Stone's throw out on either hand, A. Rudyard Kipling. CP-KiplR *Fr.* Plain Tales from the Hills.

Stones you have gathered, of diverse shapes, The. Consortium of Stones. Robert Graves. CP-GravR

Stonewall Jackson. Herman Melville. SP-MelvH

Stoney Wales / with its slate-grey roofs. Spirit of the Crusades. Lawrence Ferlinghetti. SP-FerlL

Stony Desert of Life, The. Jones Very. CP-VeryJ

Stony Limits. Hugh MacDiarmid. SP-MacDH

Stony Lonesome. Langston Hughes. CP-HughL (Death Chant.) CP-HughL2

Stood there then among. Stars. Robert Earl Hayden. CP-HaydR

Stool-Ball. Robert Herrick. CP-HerrR

Stool Pigeon Blues. Allen Ginsberg. CP-GinsA

Stop. Richard Wilbur. CP-WilbR

Stop bleeding said the knife. Bleeding. May Swenson. SP-SwenM

Stop, Christian passer-by!—Stop, child of God. Epitaph: "Stop, Christian passer-by!—Stop, child of God." Samuel Taylor Coleridge. CP-ColeS; MW-ColeS

Stop deceiving us philosophers. Philosophers. Adam Zagajewski. SP-ZagaA, *tr.*

by Clare Cavanagh

Stop It. D. H. Lawrence. CP-LawrD

Stop, let me have the truth of that! Dîs Aliter Visum; or, Le Byron de Nos Jours. Robert Browning. CP-BroR1; SP-BroR

Stop look & / listen Venezia: incline thine. Memorabilia. E. E. Cummings. CP-CummE; SP-CummE

Stop playing, poet! May a brother speak? Transcendentalism: A Poem in Twelve Books. Robert Browning. CP-BroR1

Stop right now I implore you. Han-shan. CP-ColdM, *tr. by* Red Pine

Stop rowing! This one of our bye-canals. Ponte dell' Angelo, Venice. Robert Browning. CP-BroR2

"Stop thief!" dame Nature call'd to Death. On William Graham [*or* W——Gr-h-m], Esq., of Mossknowe [*or* M-sskn-w]. Robert Burns. CP-BurnR

Stop! Wait! Wherever you are. Immanence. Robert Penn Warren. CP-WarrR

Stopped Dead. Sylvia Plath. CP-PlatS

'Stopped in the straight when the race was his own. Rudyard Kipling. CP-KiplR *Fr.* Plain Tales from the Hills.

Stopping a Kaleidoscope. Richard Eberhart. CP-EberR

Stopping by Woods on a Snowy Evening. Robert Frost. CP-FrosR

Stopping on the bus from Novi Pazar in the rain. Defending the Faith. Allen Ginsberg. CP-GinsA; SP-GinsA

Stopping the diary. Forget What Did. Philip Larkin. CP-LarkP

Stopping to Look at a Crèche in a Jewelry Store Window. Miller Williams. CP-WillM

Stopwatch and an Ordnance Map, A. Stephen Spender. CP-SpenS

Store of courage to me grant. Vow to Mars, A. Robert Herrick. CP-HerrR

Storeroom, The. Theodore Weiss. SP-WeisT

   "Adrift, / distracted." SP-WeisT

   "And yet can she." SP-WeisT

   "And yet how speak of her as one distracted?" SP-WeisT

   "Best of all, / his wide, loving the old man for the memories." SP-WeisT

   "But does she not at times." SP-WeisT

   "But there, just outside." SP-WeisT

   "For suffering the bitter weather of his wars." SP-WeisT

   "Iron though / that, fired to the utmost, can be loving." SP-WeisT

   "Like bugs flying, beams flit around her." SP-WeisT

   "Sleight, A." SP-WeisT

   "Still he wooingly." SP-WeisT

   "Time ripening for the bow, she, lingered." SP-WeisT

   "Web, The / daily spreads the fabulous tales she's drunk." SP-WeisT

   "Without him near, completing her, she feels." SP-WeisT

Stores / guarded / by the lynx-eyed, The. Christmas 1950. William Carlos Williams. CP-WilW2

Stores wore Christmas perfectly, The. Christmas Carol, A: "Stores wore Christmas perfectly, The." John Ciardi. CP-CiarJ

Stories. Donald Hall. CP-HallD

Stories from Kansas. William Stafford. SP-StafWW

Stories to Live in the World With. William Stafford. SP-StafW

Storm. A. R. Ammons. CP-AmmoA

Storm. John Ciardi. CP-CiarJ

Storm. "H. D." CP-DoolH

Storm. Emily Dickinson. CP-DickE

Storm. Wilfred Owen. CP-OwenW

Storm. Robert Stock. SP-StocR

Storm. James Tate. SP-TateJ

Storm. Alice Walker. CP-WalkA

Storm, The. George Herbert. CP-HerbG

Storm, The. Eugenio Montale. CP-MontE, *tr. by* Jonathan Galassi

Storm, The. Theodore Roethke. CP-RoetT

Storm, The. Jonathan Swift. CP-SwifJ

Storm, The. C. K. Williams. SP-WillC

Storm, The. William Carlos Williams. CP-WilW2

Storm and disorder and the giant emotions. Two Illuminations, The. Muriel Rukeyser. CP-RukeM

Storm, and our window frames the ocean, A. Great Thoughts and Noble Feelings. Wyatt Prunty. SP-PrunW

Storm and peril overpast, The. Garrison. John Greenleaf Whittier. CP-WhitJ

Storm and strife and stress. Death. Paul Laurence Dunbar. CP-DunbP

Storm and unconscionable winds once cast. Wreck, The. Walter De la Mare. CP-DeLaW

Storm at Night, The. Thomas Merton. CP-MertT

Storm-beaten old watch-tower, A. Symbols. William Butler Yeats. CP-YeatW

Storm blew in last night and knocked out, A. Window, The. Raymond Carver. CP-CarvR

Storm blowing up, rain and dark weather and the roaring wind, The. Robinson Jeffers. CP-JefR3

Storm built till, The. Heat. A. R. Ammons. CP-AmmoA

Storm came Monday night. On Wednesday we, The. Études de Plusiers Paysages de l'Âme. Hayden Carruth. CP-CarHS

Storm Cone, The. Rudyard Kipling. CP-KiplR

Storm-dances of gulls, the barking game of seals, The. Divinely Superfluous Beauty. Robinson Jeffers. CP-JefR1

Storm, darkness, a cracked hurdle of lightning, The. Lightning Storm on Fuji. Howard Nemerov. CP-NemeH

Storm Fear. Robert Frost. CP-FrosR

Storm-Flower, The. Nicholas Vachel Lindsay. CP-LindV

Storm in April, A. Richard Wilbur. CP-WilbR

Storm in the Black Forest. D. H. Lawrence. CP-LawrD

Storm is done, the sun shines out, The. *Song*: Reconciliation. Robert Graves. CP-GravR

Storm is o'er the rain is done, The. On the Suns Setting Clear after a Three Days Storm. Annis Boudinot Stockton. CP-StocA

Storm is over, and the land has forgotten the storm; the trees are still, The. Cap D'Antibes. Edna St. Vincent Millay. CP-MillE

Storm lifts from Wales. Hanged Man, The. Kenneth Rexroth. CP-RexrK

Storm Mountain Face. Peter Blue Cloud. SP-BlueP

Storm of Angels, A. May Sarton. SP-SartM

Storm of love has burst at last, The. Eros. James Whitcomb Riley. CP-RileJ

Storm of white petals, A. Year, The. Carl Sandburg. CP-SandC

Storm on Lake Asquam. John Greenleaf Whittier. CP-WhitJ

Storm outside, the. Reverse. Andrei Codrescu. SP-CodrA

Storm raged among the live oaks, A. Lady speaks, The. William Carlos Williams. CP-WilW2

Storm rehearses through the bewildered fields, The. Winter's Tale, The. Randall Jarrell. CP-JarrR

Storm that drums the hard, The. Storm, The. Eugenio Montale. CP-MontE, *tr. by* Jonathan Galassi

Storm that entered his body, The. For Jan. Grace Paley. CP-PalGC

Storm that needed a mountain, A. Found in a Storm. William Stafford. SP-StafW; SP-StafWW

Storm Warnings. Adrienne Rich. CP-RicAE; SP-RicA1; SP-RicA2

Storm Warnings. William Stafford. SP-StafWW

Storm wind / was tearing at sleep: as it struck, The. Awakening, The. Charles Tomlinson. CP-TomlC

Storm Windows. Howard Nemerov. CP-NemeH

Storm[e], The. John Donne. CP-DonnJ; MW-DonnJ

Storms are on us, the sailing, The. Short Life of the Hermit, A. John Logan. CP-LogaJ

Storms Begin Far Back. Carl Sandburg. CP-SandC

Storms have beaten on this point of land. Cumulatives. Carl Sandburg. CP-SandC

Storms of the winter, and deepening snows. Shadow and Shine. James Whitcomb Riley. CP-RileJ

Stormy. William Carlos Williams. CP-WilW2

Stormy weather's fireworks, The. News from Mount Amiata. Eugenio Montale. CP-MontE, *tr. by* Jonathan Galassi

Story. Philip Larkin. CP-LarkP

Story. George Oppen. CP-OppGN

Story. Dorothy Parker. CP-ParkD

Story, A. Rae Armantrout. SP-ArmaA

Story, A. Randall Jarrell. CP-JarrR

Story, A. Yusef Komunyakaa. CP-KomuY

Story, A. Czeslaw Milosz. CP-MiloC; CP-MiloCN, *tr. by* Renata Gorczynski *and* Robert Pinsky

Story, A. Charles Olson. CP-OlsoC

Story, A. Muriel Rukeyser. CP-RukeM

Story, A. Miller Williams. CP-WillM

Story, The. Robert Creeley. CP-CreeR

Story, The. Dan Pagis. SP-PagiD, *tr. by* Stephen Mitchell

Story, The. Miller Williams. CP-WillM

Story, a story!, A. Rowing. Anne Sexton. CP-SextA; SP-SextA

Story Books on a Kitchen Table. Audre Lorde. SP-LordA *Fr.* Story Books on a Kitchen Table.

Story for Actors. Alan Dugan. CP-DugaA

Story for Rose on the Midnight Flight to Boston, A. Anne Sexton. CP-SextA

Story goes that in those far-off times, The. Moon, The. Jorge Luis Borges. SP-BorgJ, *tr. by* Alan S. Trueblood

Story I Have Told, The. Stevie Smith. CP-SmitS

Story is like water, A. Story Water. Jelaluddin Rumi. SP-Rumi, *tr. by* Coleman Barks

Story of a Citizen, The. Tess Gallagher. SP-GallT

Story of a Cock and a Bull, A. Christopher Smart. SP-SmarC

Story of an Olson, and Bad Thing, The. Charles Olson. CP-OlsoC

Story of Baucis & Philemon, The. Jonathan Swift. *See* Baucis and Philemon

Story of Ida, The. John Greenleaf Whittier. CP-WhitJ

Story of Mrs. W———. Dorothy Parker. CP-ParkD

Story of My Life, The. John Updike. CP-UpdiJ

Story of Salomon Waste, The. Fernando Pessoa. SP-PessF

Story of Sir Arnulph, The. George Meredith. CP-MerG2

Story of the Ashes and the Flame, The. Edwin Arlington Robinson. CP-RobiE

Story of the Gadsbys, The. Rudyard Kipling. Winners, The. CP-KiplR

Story of the Road, The. Christopher Logue. SP-LoguC

Story of Ung, The. Rudyard Kipling. CP-KiplR

Story of Uriah, The. Rudyard Kipling. CP-KiplR

Story one might read and not know, A. Photo Torn from The Times. Denise Levertov. SP-LeveDL

Story Sassetta Paints, A. Gregory Orr. SP-OrrG

Story That Could Be True, A. William Stafford. SP-StafW; SP-StafWW

Story Thus Far, The. Lucille Clifton. SP-ClifL

Story Time. William Stafford. SP-StafWW

Story to be told below is truthful, The. Homage to Yalta. Joseph Brodsky. CP-BrodJ, *tr. by* Barry Rubin

Story told was how, before, The. Covined Bird, The. Wyatt Prunty. SP-PrunW

Story Water. Jelaluddin Rumi. SP-Rumi, *tr. by* Coleman Barks

Storyteller's face, The. One. Thomas Kinsella. CP-KinsT

S[tothard] in Childhood on the Nursery floor. William Blake. CP-BlakW

Stotras to Kali Destroyer of Illusions. Allen Ginsberg. CP-GinsA

Stout and well-knit in fact. Mandelstam's Hope for the Best. Donald Davie. CP-DaviDC

Stout poet tiptoes, The. Poet's Household, A. Carolyn Kizer. CP-KizeC

Stout Sparta shrined the god of Laughter. Ralph Waldo Emerson. CP-EmerR

Stove expands itself to contain, The. Tsier. Peter Blue Cloud. SP-BlueP

Stove was grey, the coal was gone, The. Forgotten Girlhood. Laura Riding Jackson. CP-RidiL

Strada's Nightingale. Vincent Bourne. CP-CowpW

Strage degli innocenti, La. Giovanni Giambattista. Sospetto d'Herode. CP-CrasR

Strahan, Tonson, Lintot of the times. To Mr. Murray. Lord Byron. CP-Byron

Straight and slender. Love Forgiven. Allen Ginsberg. CP-GinsA; SP-GinsA

Straight-Creek—Great Burn. Gary Snyder. CP-SnydG

Straight down from heaven, and in the flesh, he came. Michelangelo Buonarroti. CP-Miche, *tr. by* John Frederick Nims

Straight from prejudice you leaped to me. Yehuda Amichai. SP-AmicYL, *tr. by* Benjamin Harshav *and* Barbara Harshav

Straight, the swift, the debonair, The. Magnets. Countee Cullen. CP-CullC

Straightway let it be done! Aristodemus the Messenian. Thomas Hardy. CP-HardT

Strained Relations. Ambrose Bierce. SP-BierA

Straining its eyes it scans the horizon. Han-shan. CP-ColdM, *tr. by* Red Pine

Straining Toward Statue. Federico García Lorca. CP-GarcF, *tr. by* Alan S. Trueblood *Fr.* Songs to End With.

Strait, The. A. R. Ammons. CP-AmmoA

Strait, The. Wendell Berry. CP-BerrW

Straits of Malacca 24 Oct 1957. Gary Snyder. CP-SnydG

Strand, The. Seamus Heaney. SP-HeanSO

Strand, The. Louis MacNeice. CP-MacNL

Strand at Lough Beg, The. Seamus Heaney. SP-HeanSO

Strands. Yusef Komunyakaa. CP-KomuY

Strange about shadows, but the sun. Solipsism & Solecism. Howard Nemerov. CP-NemeH

Strange amorist, what can you see in me? Autumn Sonnet. Charles Baudelaire. CP-BaudC, *tr. by* Walter Martin

Strange and wonderful are too much with us, The. Nothing Stays Put. Amy Clampitt. CP-ClamA

Strange Are the Products. George Oppen. CP-OppGN

Strange—as I sat brooding here. Lucy. Walter De la Mare. CP-DeLaW

Strange Attractor. Hans Magnus Enzensberger. SP-EnzeH

Strange bed, whose recurrent dream we are, The. Hotel de l'Univers et Portugal. James Merrill. SP-MerrJ

Strange bird, / His song remains secret. Youth. James Wright. CP-WrigJ

Strange Calendar. Stanley Kunitz. CP-KunSC

Strange Captivity. Marya Alexandrovna Zaturenska. SP-ZatuM

Strange Case of Mr. Ballantine's Valentine, The. Ogden Nash. CP-NashO

Strange Case of Mr. Fortague's Disappointment, The. Ogden Nash. CP-NashO

Strange Case of Mr. Niobob's Transmogrification, The. Ogden Nash. CP-NashO

Strange Case of Mr. O'Banion's Come-Uppance, The. Ogden Nash. CP-NashO

Strange Case of Mr. Palliser's Palate, The. Ogden Nash. CP-NashO

Strange Case of Mr. Pauncefoot's Broad Mind, The. Ogden Nash. CP-NashO

Strange Case of Mr. Wood's Frustration, or, A Team that Won't Be Beaten Better Stay off the Field, The. Ogden Nash. CP-NashO

Strange Case of Mr. Donnybrooks's Boredom, The. Ogden Nash. CP-NashO

Strange Case of the Ambitious Caddy, The. Ogden Nash. CP-NashO

Strange Case of the Blackmailing Dove, The. Ogden Nash. CP-NashO

Strange Case of the Cautious Motorist, The. Ogden Nash. CP-NashO

Strange Case of the Dead Divorcee, The. Ogden Nash. CP-NashO

Strange Case of the Entomologist's Heart, The. Ogden Nash. CP-NashO

Strange Case of the Girl o' Mr. Sponsoon's Dreams, The. Ogden Nash. CP-NashO

Strange Case of the Irksome Prude, The. Ogden Nash. CP-NashO

Strange Case of the Lovelorn Letter Writer, The. Ogden Nash. CP-NashO

Strange Case of the Lucrative Compromise, The. Ogden Nash. CP-NashO

Strange Case of the Pleasing Taxi-Driver, The. Ogden Nash. CP-NashO

Strange Case of the Renegade Lyric Writer, The. Ogden Nash. CP-NashO

Strange / Distorted blades of grass. Garden. Langston Hughes. CP-HughL

Strange dreams of what I used to be. Ban, The. James Whitcomb Riley. CP-RileJ

Strange Erratum in all the Editions, A. To the Royal Academy. William Blake. CP-BlakW

Strange fabled face! From sterile shore to shore. Mirage. Walter De la Mare. CP-DeLaW

Strange fits of passion have I known. William Wordsworth. MW-WorW *Fr.* Lucy.

Strange flower, to ope when day is o'er. Night Blooming Cereus, The. Jones Very. CP-VeryJ

Strange Fruit. Seamus Heaney. SP-HeanSO

Strange Hells. Ivor Gurney. SP-GurnI

Strange House, The. Thomas Hardy. CP-HardT

Strange how these tiny moons across the meadows. Picking Mushrooms by Moonlight. Charles Tomlinson. SP-TomlC

Strange how things in the offing, once they're sensed. Seamus Heaney. SP-HeanSO *Fr.* Squarings.

Strange Hurt. Langston Hughes. CP-HughL; CP-HughL2

Strange judgment upon me. Envoi: "Strange judgment upon me." David Ignatow. SP-IgnaD

Strange life—strangely passed!, A. John Walsh. James Whitcomb Riley. CP-RileJ

Strange light, long lingering in the west. Zodiacal Light, The. Jones Very. CP-VeryJ

Strange Meeting. Wilfred Owen. CP-OwenW

Strange metamorphosis! It was but now. Upon the Kings Coronation. Richard Crashaw. CP-CrasR

Strange Metamorphosis of Poets. Howard Nemerov. CP-NemeH

Strange Moment, A. Charles Bukowski. SP-BukC3

Strange, Moving Lights of People Handle Holinesses Unknown, The. Kenneth Patchen. CP-PatcK

Strange Music, The. G. K. Chesterton. CP-ChesG

Strange New Cottage in Berkeley, A. Allen Ginsberg. CP-GinsA; SP-GinsA

Strange new youth is on me: not of song, A. Re-Born. G. K. Chesterton. CP-ChesG

Strange now to think of you, gone without corsets & eyes, while I walk on the sunny pavement of Greenwich Village. Kaddish. Allen Ginsberg. CP-GinsA; SP-GinsA

Strange part is his head, The. Her head. The strangely ripened. Eel, An. Ted Hughes. SP-HughTN

Strange planet and strange people on it. People on the Bridge. Wisława Szymborska. SP-SzymWM, *tr. by* Joanna Trzeciak

Strange record of a people past away. Mound Builders, The. Jones Very. CP-VeryJ

Strange Song. Denise Levertov. SP-LeveDL

Strange Spirit, The. Walter De la Mare. CP-DeLaW

Strange—strange, O mortal Life. O Life! O Beyond! James Whitcomb Riley. CP-RileJ

Strange that I did not know him then. Old Story, An. Edwin Arlington Robinson. CP-RobiE

Strange, / That in this nigger place. Aesthete [*or* Esthete] in Harlem. Langston Hughes. CP-HughL; CP-HughL1

Strange that sexual jealousy should be so much like sex itself: the same engrossing reveries. Soliliquies. C. K. Williams. SP-WillC

Strange that so many fickle gods, as fickle as the weather. Henry David Thoreau. CP-ThorH

Strange that the dark tree, the unblossomed apple. Dark Tree, The. Ivor Gurney. SP-GurnI

Strange that their dog. Complexity, The. William Carlos Williams. CP-WilW2

Strange thing I said to Sam is the way they die, The. Man Is to Man a Beast. Kenneth Patchen. CP-PatcK

Strange thing surely that my Heart, when love had come unsought, A. Owen Aherne and His Dancers. William Butler Yeats. CP-YeatW

Strange thing that I, by nature nothing prone. Edna St. Vincent Millay. CP-MillE

Strange Times. Yannis Ritsos. SP-RitsY, *tr. by* Kimon Friar

Strange to conceive, how the same objects strike. Occasioned by Sir William

Temple's Late Illness and Recovery. Jonathan Swift. CP-SwifJ

Strange to know nothing, never to be sure. Ignorance. Philip Larkin. CP-LarkP

Strange / To reach that age. Louis Zukofsky. CP-ZukLS

Strange to see that usual dark road paven wet. Going Out at Dawn. Ivor Gurney. SP-GurnI

Strange visitant! that burst'st upon our sight. Comet, The. Jones Very. CP-VeryJ

Strange voices sing among the planets which. Christina Georgina Rossetti. CP-RosC3

Strange walkers! See their processional. Mushroom Gatherers, The. Adam Mickiewicz. CP-DaviDC, *tr. by* Donald Davie

Strange wind off the night, A. Face, The. Philip Levine. SP-LeviP

Strange words are these, that little now we know. Scepticism with Regard to the Gospels. Jones Very. CP-VeryJ

Strange Young Man, The. James Whitcomb Riley. CP-RileJ

Strangely radiant skies have come, The. March-Mad. May Sarton. SP-SartM

Strangeness. Robert Graves. CP-GravR

Strangeness, The. Pair in One. Langston Hughes. CP-HughL; CP-HughL3

Stranger. David Ignatow. SP-IgnaD

Stranger. Thomas Merton. CP-MertT

Stranger. Allen Tate. CP-TateA

Stranger, The. Aleksandr Aleksandrovich Blok. SP-BlokA, *tr. by* Peter France *and* Jon Stallworthy

Stranger, The. Jorge Luis Borges. SP-BorgJ, *tr. by* Alastair Reid

Stranger, The. Walter De la Mare. CP-DeLaW

Stranger, The. Thomas Kinsella. CP-KinsT

Stranger, The. Rudyard Kipling. CP-KiplR

Stranger, The. Kenneth Patchen. CP-PatcK

Stranger, The. Adrienne Rich. CP-RicAE

Stranger, The. Adrienne Rich. SP-RicA1

Stranger! behold, interr'd together. Epitaph for Joseph Blacket. Lord Byron. CP-Byron

Stranger, beside the Ganges I lie, a man. Epitaph: "Stranger, beside the Ganges I lie, a man." Constantine P. Cavafy. CP-CavaC, *tr. by* Theoharis Constantine Theoharis

Stranger came to the door at eve, A. Love and a Question. Robert Frost. CP-FrosR

Stranger, don't forget to say goodbye. Rainer Maria Rilke. CP-RilkFr, *tr. by* A. Poulin, Jr. *Fr.* Fragments.

Stranger from the noisy inn, The. Good Company. Walter De la Mare. CP-DeLaW

Stranger garbed outlandishly, A. Pillar Box, The. G. K. Chesterton. CP-ChesG

Stranger has come, A. Love in the Asylum. Dylan Thomas. CP-ThomD

Stranger, I threaded sunken-hearted, A. Woman I Met, The. Thomas Hardy. CP-HardT

Stranger, if you passing meet me and desire to speak to me, why should you not speak to me? To You. Walt Whitman. CP-WhitW

Stranger, ignore yon loud bassoon. That's Funny, Wasn't It? No, It Won't Be. Ogden Nash. CP-NashO

Stranger in my life. Stranger. David Ignatow. SP-IgnaD

Stranger in the House, The. James Laughlin. CP-LaugJ

Stranger in Town. Langston Hughes. CP-HughL; CP-HughL2

Stranger, striding down the paths of spring, The. Old Man, The. John Clare. SP-ClarJ

Stranger, the wages that we earned. For the Madrid Road. Randall Jarrell. CP-JarrR

Stranger, the world expected You for long days. Messias. Thomas Merton. CP-MertT

Stranger! this hillock of mis-shapen stones. Written with a Slate Pencil upon a Stone, the Largest of a Heap Lying near a Deserted Quarry, upon One of the Islands at Rydal. William Wordsworth. CP-WorW1; MW-WorW

Stranger, this is shining Colonos. Sophocles. CP-SpenS *Fr.* Oedipus at Colonus.

Stranger to folly and to fear. Ode 3.2: "Stranger to folly and to fear." Horace. CP-JohnS *Fr.* Odes.

Stranger, uncover; here you have in view. Trencher-Knight, A. Ambrose Bierce. SP-BierA

Stranger, when you come to Washington. On a Military Graveyard. Simonides. CP-RexrK, *tr. by* Kenneth Rexroth

Stranger, when you see a village wherein nature laughs. Nichori. Constantine P. Cavafy. CP-CavaC, *tr. by* Theoharis Constantine Theoharis

Stranger! whose eyes a look of pity shew. Old Man of the Alps, The. Samuel Taylor Coleridge. CP-ColeS

Stranger within my gate, The. Stranger, The. Rudyard Kipling. CP-KiplR

Stranger, you who hide my love. Song: "Stranger, you who hide my love." Stephen Spender. CP-SpenS

Strangers. Ted Hughes. SP-HughTN

Strangers. Philip Larkin. CP-LarkP

Strangers. May Sarton. SP-SartM

Strangers, The. Jones Very. CP-VeryJ

Stranger's Child. George Oppen. CP-OppGN

Strangers drawn from the ends of the earth, jewelled and plumed were we. Sack of the Gods, The. Rudyard Kipling. CP-KiplR *Fr.* Naulahka, The.

Stranger's Gift, The. Jones Very. CP-VeryJ

Strangers pass me on the street. Tennessee Williams. CP-WillT

Stranger's Song, The. Thomas Hardy. CP-HardT

Strangest is their reality. Dream Objects. John Updike. CP-UpdiJ

Strangest Sight You Ever Did See—, The. Charles Bukowski. SP-BukC1

Strangling in Merrion Square, The. Robert Graves. CP-GravR

Strapped at the center of the blazing wheel. Pilot from the Carrier, A. Randall Jarrell. CP-JarrR

Strapped helpless, monarchs and prelates, round they swung. Wheel of Fortune, The. Thom Gunn. CP-GunnT

Stratagem, The. Walter De la Mare. CP-DeLaW

Stratford on Avon. Donald Davie. CP-DaviDC

Stratford-on-Avon. Louis Zukofsky. CP-ZukLS

Strathallan's Lament. Robert Burns. CP-BurnR

Strathnaver. Donald Davie. CP-DaviDC

Strato in Plaster. James Merrill. SP-MerrJ

Stratosphere was once where angels were, The. Christmas 1944. "H. D." CP-DoolH

Stratton Water. Dante Gabriel Rossetti. CW-RossD

Stravinsky looks upon the mountain. Mountain Impasse. John Updike. CP-UpdiJ

Straw, The. Robert Graves. CP-GravR

Straw, feathers, dust. Note. William Stafford. SP-StafWW

Straw Hat. Rita Dove. SP-DoveR

Straw-stuff'd hamper with his ruthless steel, The. Lines after the Manner of Homer. William Cowper. CP CowpW

Strawberries. W. S. Merwin. SP-MerwWF

Strawberries along the roadbank in the hills bloomed, The. Requiem: "Strawberries along the roadbank in the hills bloomed, The." A. R. Ammons. CP-AmmoA

Strawberries in Wooden Bowls. Arthur Sze. SP-SzeA

Strawberries, pears, fingers, the eyes. Another Elegy. Margaret Atwood. SP-AtwM2

Strawberry Hill. Ted Hughes. SP-HughTN

Strawberry Moon. Mary Oliver. SP-OlivM

Strawberry Shrub, The. Edna St. Vincent Millay. CP-MillE

Stray Paragraphs in April, Year of the Rat. Charles Wright. SP-WrigCN

Stray Paragraphs in February, Year of the Rat. Charles Wright. SP-WrigCN

Stray Pleasures. William Wordsworth. CP-WorW1; MW-WorW

Strayed Message, The. Robert Graves. CP-GravR

Strayed Village, The. Adrienne Rich. CP-RicAE

Streak. Paul Celan. SP-CelaP, *tr.* by John Felstiner

Streak in the eye. Streak. Paul Celan. SP-CelaP, *tr.* by John Felstiner

Streak of Blood That Once Was a Tiny Red Spider, A. Thomas Lux. SP-LuxT

Streaked and fretted with effort, the thick. Street, The. Robert Pinsky. CP-PinsR

Streaking (A Phenomenon Following the Sixties). Alice Walker. CP-WalkA

Stream, The. Charles Simic. SP-SimiC; SP-SimiCE

Stream, The. Mona Van Duyn. SP-VanDM

Stream and Sun at Glendalough. William Butler Yeats. CP-YeatW

Stream, go hide yourself. On a Railroad Right of Way. Carl Sandburg. CP-SandC

Stream moaneth as it floweth, The. Song: "Stream moaneth as it floweth, The." Christina Georgina Rossetti. CP-RosC3

Stream of my fathers! sweetly still. Merrimac, The. John Greenleaf Whittier. CP-WhitJ

STREAM, to mingle with your favourite Dee, A. To the Lady E.B. and the Hon. Miss P. William Wordsworth. CP-WorW2

Streamers. Arthur Sze. SP-SzeA

Streaming simile, the plume, The. Protesilaus and Laodamia. Donald Davie. CP-DaviDC

Stream's Secret, The. Dante Gabriel Rossetti. CW-RossD

Streams shed out of mountains in a white rust. If Anything Will Level with You Water Will. A. R. Ammons. CP-AmmoA

Streams that glide in orient plains. Castle Gordon—*Intended to Be Sung to Morag.* Robert Burns. CP-BurnR

Street. George Oppen. CP-OppGN

Street, The. Robert Pinsky. CP-PinsR

Street Called Crooked, The. Countee Cullen. CP-CullC

Street Cool Clara. Yusef Komunyakaa. CP-KomuY

Street Corner College. Kenneth Patchen. CP-PatcK

Street Corner Dialogue. Grace Paley. CP-PalGC

Street corner to corner he will talk all day. Muriel Rukeyser. CP-RukeM

Street flails, The. Street of Furthest Memory, The. Robert Pinsky. CP-PinsR

Street Has Changed, The. Randall Jarrell. CP-JarrR

Street in Bronzeville, A. Gwendolyn Brooks. SP-BrooG

Street Lamps. Philip Larkin. CP-LarkP

Street Lamps. D. H. Lawrence. CP-LawrD

Street light, The. Late Corner. Langston Hughes. CP-HughL; CP-HughL3

Street Musicians. John Ashbery. SP-AshbJ

Street of Furthest Memory, The. Robert Pinsky. CP-PinsR

Street of the Mute, The. Federico García Lorca. CP-GarcF, *tr.* by Alan S. Trueblood *Fr.* Games.

Street of the Mutes, The. Federico García Lorca. SP-GarcF, *tr.* by W. S. Merwin

Street of this strange metropolis, The. New York. Andrei Codrescu. SP-CodrA

Street-piano, garrulous and frail, A. First Caprice in North Cambridge. T. S. Eliot. SP-ElioT

Street Scene. Louis MacNeice. CP-MacNL

Street Song. A. R. Ammons. CP-AmmoA

Street Song. Thom Gunn. CP-GunnT

Street Song. Langston Hughes. CP-HughL; CP-HughL3

Street Song. Sylvia Plath. CP-PlatS

Street Songs. Wallace Stevens. CP-StevWP

Street Songs. Stéphane Mallarmé. CP-MallS
  Glazier, The. CP-MallS
  Newspaper Vendor, The. CP-MallS
  Old-Clothes Woman, The. CP-MallS
  Roadmender, The. CP-MallS
  Seller of Garlic and Onions, The. CP-MallS
  Shoemaker, The. CP-MallS
  Woman Selling Aromatic Herbs, The. CP-MallS
  Workman's Wife, The. CP-MallS

Street sounds to the soldiers' tread, The. A. E. Housman. CP-HousA

Street Window. Carl Sandburg. CP-SandC

Street with a Pink Corner Store. Jorge Luis Borges. SP-BorgJ, *tr.* by Stephen Kessler

Streetlights bent / the sleet streams as I went, The. Two Cities. Marilyn Hacker. SP-HackM

Streetlights wreathed under saffron curls. It's My Town! Kenneth Patchen. CP-PatcK

Streets, The. Jorge Luis Borges. SP-BorgJ, *tr.* by Stephen Kessler

Streets are new, the harbour, The. Visit to Toronto, with Companions. Margaret Atwood. SP-AtwM1

Streets as ever blocky, grey—square sense of rectangular enclosures. NYC—. Robert Creeley. CP-CreeR

Streets, avenues, signs, names, doors. Uncompromising, The. Yannis Ritsos. SP-RitsY, *tr.* by Kimon Friar

Streets have names, pains have names, ships have names on their prow. Yehuda Amichai. SP-AmicYL *Fr.* At Right Angles.

Streets, in a poor district. Power, the Enchanted World. George Oppen. CP-OppGN

Streets of Laredo, The. Louis MacNeice. CP-MacNL

Streets of Pearl and Gold. Carolyn Kizer. CP-KizeC

Streets of San Francisco, The. Niece. George Oppen. CP-OppGN

Streets of Stockholm are churning with guerrillas, The. Wars in Sweden, The. Carolyn Kizer. CP-KizeC

Streets. Of the mind. Whose gangs, The. First Invention on the Theme of the Adam. Robert Duncan. SP-DuncR

Streets that slept all afternoon in sun, The. Camptown. John Ciardi. CP-CiarJ

Streets Too Old. Carl Sandburg. CP-SandC

Strength of Baptisme, that's within, The. Baptisme. Robert Herrick. CP-HerrR

Strength of Fate, The. Euripides. CP-HousA, *tr.* by A. E. Housman *Fr.* Alcestis.

Strength of Fields, The. James Dickey. CP-DickJ

Strength of my country, whilst I bring to view. To True Soldiers. Ben Jonson. CP-JonsB; SP-JonsB

Strength of the Lonely, The. Nicholas Vachel Lindsay. CP-LindV

Strength of twice three thousand horse, The. Destroyers, The. Rudyard Kipling. CP-KiplR

Strength through Joy. Kenneth Rexroth. CP-RexrK

Strength Thy service cannot tire, A. Lines from a Letter to a Young Clerical Friend. John Greenleaf Whittier. CP-WhitJ

Strength to Support Soveraignty. Robert Herrick. CP-HerrR

Strengthened to live, strengthened to die for. In Distrust of Merits. Marianne Craig Moore. CP-MoorM

Strengthening as secret manna. What? Christina Georgina Rossetti. CP-RosC3

Strephon and Chloe. Jonathan Swift. CP-SwifJ

Stress of his anger set me back. Revelation, The. James Wright. CP-WrigJ

Stretch towards the moonless midnight of the trees. To Dorothy Wellesley. William Butler Yeats. CP-YeatW

Stretch'd on a moulder'd Abbey's broadest wall. Melancholy. Samuel Taylor Coleridge. CP-ColeS

Stretched naked in the sunlit garden. Tammuz in the Garden. Sam Hamill. SP-HamiS

Stretched out under the oak, in the wood's new leaves. Forest Murmurs. Eduard Friedrich Mörike. CP-JarrR, *tr.* by Randall Jarrell

Stretching away to westward the great river lies quiet beneath me. River of Mist, The. E. E. Cummings. CP-CummE

Stretching eyes west / Over the sea. Riddle, The. Thomas Hardy. CP-HardT

Stretto. Paul Celan. SP-CelaP, *tr. by* John Felstiner

Strew all their graves with flowers. Our Soldiers' Graves. Jones Very. CP-VeryJ

Strew on her roses, roses. Requiescat. Matthew Arnold. SP-ArnoM

Strictly Bucolic. Charles Simic. SP-SimiC; SP-SimiCE

Strident high / civic trumpeting, The. Respublica. Geoffrey Hill. CP-HillG

Striders, The. A. K. Ramanujan. CP-RamaA

Striding Over. Yannis Ritsos. SP-RitsY, *tr. by* Edmund Keeley

Strife. D. H. Lawrence. CP-LawrD

Strife between the Poet and Ambition, The. Thomas Merton. CP-MertT

Strike, churl; hurl, cheerless wind, then; heltering hail. Hailstorm in May. Gerard Manley Hopkins. CP-HopkG

Strike home, strong-hearted man! To Ronge. John Greenleaf Whittier. CP-WhitJ

Strike not thy dog with a stick! To Children. George Meredith. CP-MerG1

Strike the bells wantonly. Peal of Bells, A. Christina Georgina Rossetti. CP-RosC1

Striking like lightning to the quick of the real world. Duns Scotus. Thomas Merton. CP-MertT

Striking of the Tower Clock, The. Jaroslav Seifert. SP-SeifJ, *tr. by* Ewald Osers

String, The. James Dickey. CP-DickJ

String, The. Clarence Major. SP-MajoC

String Diamond, The. Arthur Sze. SP-SzeA

String of shiny days we had, A. Dramatists, The. Dorothy Parker. CP-ParkD

String of the scarlet rubies of Ceylon, A. 1945. Donald Davie. CP-DaviDC

String Puppets. Thomas Kinsella. CP-KinsT

Strings' excitement, the applauding drum, The. Family Ghosts. W. H. Auden. CP-AudeW

Strip off kindness. Where Dream Begins. May Sarton. SP-SartM

Strip to the waist and have a seat. The doctor. Words. Miller Williams. CP-WillM

Striped blouse in a clearing by Bazille, A. Ceremony. Richard Wilbur. CP-WilbR

Striped Cats, Old Men and Proud Stockings. Carl Sandburg. CP-SandC

Stripes. Carl Sandburg. CP-SandC

Stripes justly given yerk us (with their fall). Smart. Robert Herrick. CP-HerrR

Stripped Naked. Yannis Ritsos. SP-RitsY, *tr. by* Kimon Friar

Stripped / you're beginning to float free. November 1968. Adrienne Rich. CP-RicAE; SP-RicA2

Stripper, The. Miller Williams. CP-WillM

Stripping and Putting On. May Swenson. SP-SwenM

Strive to sate us, Irish tillers. On Potatoes. *Unknown, sometimes at. to* Thomas Sheridan. CP-SherT, *tr. by* Robert Hogan

Stroke. Heather McHugh. SP-McHuH

Stroke, The. Rita Dove. SP-DoveR

Stroke, The. Stevie Smith. CP-SmitS

Stroke a flint, and there is nothing to admire. Christina Georgina Rossetti. CP-RosC2

Stroke by stroke, in the country of the fragile. Blue Flower, The. Muriel Rukeyser. CP-RukeM

Stroke by / stroke my / body remembers that life and cries for. Sea, The. Mary Oliver. SP-OlivM

Stroll in the Beautiful Gardens of the Valley of the Son of Hinnom, A. Yehuda Amichai. SP-AmicYL, *tr. by* Benjamin Harshav *and* Barbara Harshav

Stroller. William Carlos Williams. CP-WilW1

Strolling along / By the teeming docks. Docks. Carl Sandburg. CP-SandC

Strolling at sunset in my native land. Finis Æternitatis. Ambrose Bierce. SP-BierA

Strong and mighty Angel, A. Mantle of St. John de Matha, The. John Greenleaf Whittier. CP-WhitJ

Strong and slippery / built for the midnight grass-party. Peter. Marianne Craig Moore. CP-MoorM

Strong ankled, sun burned, almost naked. Vitamins and Roughage. Kenneth Rexroth. CP-RexrK

Strong are Saying Nothing, The. Robert Frost. CP-FrosR

Strong Draughts of Their Refreshing Minds. Emily Dickinson. CP-DickE

Strong enough to be neutral—as is now proved, now American power. Historical Choice. Robinson Jeffers. CP-JefR3

Strong I stand, though I have borne. Emily Jane Brontë. CP-BronE

Strong Ilion thou shalt see with walls and towers high. Ovid. CP-RaleW *Fr.* Heroides.

Strong man in its iron still lives on, The. To a Sword at York Minster. Jorge Luis Borges. SP-BorgJ, *tr. by* Charles Tomlinson

Strong Man, The. Jones Very. CP-VeryJ

Strong men keep coming on, The. Upstream. Carl Sandburg. CP-SandC

"Strong Men, Riding Horses." Gwendolyn Brooks. SP-BrooG

Strong men, The. Beach Trip. Charles Bukowski. SP-BukC1

Strong music of hard times, The. Outside of Wedlock. Wallace Stevens. CP-StevWP

Strong rocks hold up the riksdag bridge . . . always strong river waters. Two Items. Carl Sandburg. CP-SandC

Strong sun, that bleach. Plaid Dress, The. Edna St. Vincent Millay. CP-MillE

Strong wind blew, A. The heavy shutters creaked. With These Stones. Yannis Ritsos. SP-RitsY, *tr. by* Kimon Friar

Strong woman is a woman who is straining, A. For Strong Women. Marge Piercy. SP-PierM

Stronger Lessons. Walt Whitman. CP-WhitW

Stronger than alcohol, more great than song. Sonnet III: "Stronger than alcohol, more great than song." Ted Berrigan. SP-BerrT *Fr.* Sonnets, The.

Strongly did Luther seize the mighty thought. Justification by Faith. Jones Very. CP-VeryJ

Strongly it bears us along in swelling and limitless billows. Homeric Hexameter, The. Samuel Taylor Coleridge. CP-ColeS

Strophe of green leaves. Linden Branch, The. Archibald MacLeish. CP-MacLA

Strophes: "Like a glass whose imprint." Joseph Brodsky. CP-BrodJ, *tr. by* David McDuff

Struck through such a dome. Baroque Sunburst, A. Amy Clampitt. CP-ClamA

Struck, was I, not yet by Lightning. Emily Dickinson. CP-DickE

Structure is rising. It takes on shape, it takes on meaning, A. Muriel Rukeyser. CP-RukeM

Structure,miraculous challenge,devout am. E. E. Cummings. CP-CummE

Structure of Rime, The. Robert Duncan.

  "Back to the figure." SP-DuncR

  "Best of ways. That there be a law the Earth gives and the Mountain." SP-DuncR

  "Erecting beyond the boundaries of all government." SP-DuncR

  "I ask the unyielding Sentence that shows Itself forth in the language." SP-DuncR

  "Master of Rime told me, You must learn to lose heart, The." SP-DuncR

  "O Outrider! / when you come to the threshold of the stars." SP-DuncR

  "Old women came from their caves to close the too many doors, The." SP-DuncR

  "There are memories everywhere then. Rememberd, we go out, as in." SP-DuncR

  "This potion is love's portion. This herb." SP-DuncR

  "What of the structure of Rime? I said." SP-DuncR

Structure of the Plane, The. Muriel Rukeyser. CP-RukeM

Struggle, The. Jones Very. CP-VeryJ

Struggle of Wings. William Carlos Williams. CP-WilW1

Struggle with the Angel. Jaroslav Seifert. SP-SeifJ, *tr. by* Ewald Osers

Struggling Rill insensibly is grown, The. Stepping-Stones, The. William Wordsworth. CP-WorW2 *Fr.* River Duddon [A Series of Sonnets], The.

Strumpet Song. Sylvia Plath. CP-PlatS

Strut and wiggle. To Midnight Nan at Leroy's. Langston Hughes. CP-HughL; CP-HughL1

Strut, once a Fore-man of a Shop we knew. Upon Strut. Robert Herrick. CP-HerrR

Stub of a red pencil in your hand, A. World Isn't a Wedding of the Artists of Yesterday, The. Norman Dubie. CP-DubiN

Stubbing the cloud-fields—the searchlight, high. Louis Zukofsky. CP-ZukLS *Fr.* 29 Poems.

Stubborn Man. Rainer Maria Rilke. CP-RilkFr, *tr. by* A. Poulin, Jr.

Stubborn man put out to sea, A. Scouring, The. Richard Eberhart. CP-EberR

Stuck in the need to move on. Fog. A. K. Ramanujan. CP-RamaA

Stuck on the fridge, our favorite pin-up girl. Heather McHugh.

Student, A. Lorine Niedecker. CP-NiedL

Student, The. Elizabeth Barrett Browning. CP-BroEB

Student, The. Marianne Craig Moore. CP-MoorM

Student Dies in 100 Yard Dash. Howard Nemerov. CP-NemeH

Student is sketching a nude girl, The. Drawing Lesson, The. James Laughlin. CP-LaugJ

Student of Clouds. Billy Collins. SP-CollB

Student / The dust of ancient pages, The. Communication II. Maya Angelou. SP-AngeM

Students Gather, The. George Oppen. CP-OppGN

Students, lost in raucousness, The. Hook, The. Theodore Weiss. SP-WeisT

Students of Justice, The. W. S. Merwin. SP-MerwW

Students / went out / of their way, The. Streaking (A Phenomenon Following the Sixties). Alice Walker. CP-WalkA

Studies themselves will languish and decay. Studies to Be Supported. Robert Herrick. CP-HerrR

Studies to Be Supported. Robert Herrick. CP-HerrR

Studio, The. Derek Mahon. CP-MahoD

Studiously by lamp-light I appraised. Man Does, Woman Is. Robert Graves. CP-GravR

Study. D. H. Lawrence. CP-LawrD

Study (A Soul). A. Christina Georgina Rossetti. CP-RosC3

Study for a Geographical Trail. Clarence Major. SP-MajoC

Study in a Late Subway. Muriel Rukeyser. CP-RukeM

Study in Gray, A. Ambrose Bierce. SP-BierA

Study Nature. Gertrude Stein. CP-SteiG

Study of a House with Garden Attached. Robert Stock. SP-StocR

Study of an Elevation, in Indian Ink. Rudyard Kipling. CP-KiplR
  (This ditty is a string of lies.) CP-KiplR

Study of History. Adrienne Rich. CP-RicAE; SP-RicA2

Study of Images 1. Wallace Stevens. CP-StevW; CP-StevWP

Study of Images 2. Wallace Stevens. CP-StevW; CP-StevWP

Study of Loneliness. Czeslaw Milosz. CP-MiloC; CP-MiloCN, *tr. by* Lillian Vallee

Study of Reading Habits, A. Philip Larkin. CP-LarkP

Study of Two Pears. Wallace Stevens. CP-StevW; CP-StevWP

Study the Masters. Lucille Clifton. SP-ClifL

Study to Deserve Death. Stevie Smith. CP-SmitS

Studying French. Theodore Weiss. SP-WeisT

Studying the Signs. Allen Ginsberg. CP-GinsA

Stuff of the moon. Nocturne in a Deserted Brickyard. Carl Sandburg. CP-SandC

Stuffed pink stocking, the neck. One of the Strangest. May Swenson. SP-SwenM

Stuffed quail, A. October Tune. Joseph Brodsky. CP-BrodJ, *tr. by* Joseph Brodsky

Stuffing, O'Toole naturally stuffs with his tool. Carmen 94. Catullus. CP-ZukLS *Fr.* Carmina.

Stumbling up an unfamiliar stairway. Song: The Sigil. Robert Graves. CP-GravR

Stump. Donald Hall. CP-HallD

Stun. James Schuyler. CP-SchuJ

Stunt Flier, The. John Updike. CP-UpdiJ

Stupid. Raymond Carver. CP-CarvR

Stupid? Of course that older lot were stupid. In and Come In. Archibald MacLeish. CP-MacLA

Stupid tranquility, to be most sure. Zero. Tess Gallagher. SP-GallT

Stupidities. Arthur Rimbaud. CP-RimbA, *tr. by* Martin Sorrell

Stupidities—Second Series. Arthur Rimbaud. CP-RimbA, *tr. by* Martin Sorrell

Stupor at the End of May. Andrei Codrescu. SP-CodrA

Stupor of knowledge lacking inwardness—. Pure Fury, The. Theodore Roethke. CP-RoetT

Sturdy I stand, books in my hand. Dark Youth of the U.S.A. Langston Hughes. CP-HughL; CP-HughL1

Sturdy Legs, That. Kenneth Patchen. CP-PatcK

Sturgeon, The. Raymond Carver. CP-CarvR

Stutterer. Alan Dugan. CP-DugaA

Stuttgart: In a Nightclub (Illegal). James Laughlin. CP-LaugJ

Stygian Banks, The. Louis MacNeice. CP-MacNL

Style. Marianne Craig Moore. CP-MoorM

Style. Howard Nemerov. CP-NemeH

Style. Carl Sandburg. CP-SandC

Style. William Stafford. SP-StafWW

Style. Miller Williams. CP-WillM

Style—go ahead talking about style. Style. Carl Sandburg. CP-SandC

Style is the perfection of a point of view. Meditation Two. Richard Eberhart. CP-EberR

Style is the water out of Homer. Garden God, The. Richard Eberhart. CP-EberR

Styles. John Ciardi. CP-CiarJ

Styles of Bloom. John Updike. CP-UpdiJ

Styles of drinking, the cool. She's Back! Robert Creeley. SP-CreeR

Stylist, The. William Carlos Williams. CP-WilW2

Stylite. Louis MacNeice. CP-MacNL

Sub Contra. Louise Bogan. CP-BogaL

Sub Mare. Ezra Pound. SP-PoEar

Sub Terra. William Carlos Williams. CP-WilW1

Subalterns, The. Thomas Hardy. CP-HardT

Subcommittee submits, The. Bill, The. Muriel Rukeyser. CP-RukeM

Subconscious Sea. May Swenson. SP-SwenM

Subject-Cases: The Background of a Detective Story. Gertrude Stein. CP-SteiG

Subject for an Oil Painting. Yannis Ritsos. SP-RitsY, *tr. by* Kostas Myrsiades

Subject for Eisenstein. Constitution Day. Charles Tomlinson. CP-TomlC

Subject, Object, Sentence. Stephen Spender. CP-SpenS

Subject of the Waves, A. May Swenson. SP-SwenM

Subject thought: because he had a verb, A. Subject, Object, Sentence. Stephen Spender. CP-SpenS

Subject To Like Passions as We Are. Christina Georgina Rossetti. CP-RosC2

Subjected Earth. Robinson Jeffers. CP-JefR2

Subjectivity. Helen Pinkerton. CP-PinkH

Sublime Generosity. Jelaluddin Rumi. SP-Rumi, *tr. by* Coleman Barks

Sublime is a departure, The. Rainer Maria Rilke. CP-RilkFr, *tr. by* A. Poulin, Jr. *Fr.* Orchards.

Subliminal. Lorine Niedecker. CP-NiedL

Sublunar Cantos. Federico García Lorca.
  Capriccio ("In the net of moon"). CP-GarcF, *tr. by* Jerome Rothenberg
  Colors. CP-GarcF, *tr. by* Jerome Rothenberg
  Full Moon. CP-GarcF, *tr. by* Jerome Rothenberg
  Salome & the Moon. CP-GarcF, *tr. by* Jerome Rothenberg

Submerged. Czeslaw Milosz. CP-MiloCN, *tr. by* Robert Hass

Submerged Dragon. Thomas Merton. CP-MertT

Submergence. D. H. Lawrence. CP-LawrD

Submission. William Cowper. *See* Olney Hymns

Submission. George Herbert. CP-HerbG

Substance or Shadow. Ambrose Bierce. SP-BierA

Substitute for an Epitaph. Lord Byron. CP-Byron

Substitution. Elizabeth Barrett Browning. CP-BroEB

Subtle chain of countless rings, A. Nature [1836]. Ralph Waldo Emerson. CP-EmerR

Subtle, clever brain, wiser than I am. Play. William Carlos Williams. CP-WilW1

Subtle man, meaning the subtle woman too, The. On the Subtle Man. Richard Eberhart. CP-EberR

Subtle power in perfume found, The. Sweet Fern. John Greenleaf Whittier. CP-WhitJ

Subtle tools. Poems from Buenos Aires. Yehuda Amichai. SP-AmicYL, *tr. by* Benjamin Harshav *and* Barbara Harshav

Subtract from that shower. Rome Zoo. A. R. Ammons. CP-AmmoA

Suburb. Stevie Smith. CP-SmitS

Suburban. John Ciardi. CP-CiarJ

Suburban Classes, The. Stevie Smith. CP-SmitS

Suburban Evening. Langston Hughes. CP-HughL; CP-HughL3

Suburban Exorcism. Alan Dugan. CP-DugaA

Suburban Homecoming. John Ciardi. CP-CiarJ

Suburban Madrigal. John Updike. CP-UpdiJ

Suburban Prophecy. Howard Nemerov. CP-NemeH

Suburban Sicilian Sketches. Carl Sandburg. CP-SandC

Suburbans, The. Carolyn Kizer. SP-KizeC

Suburbs of a Secret, The. Emily Dickinson. CP-DickE

Suburbs on a Hazy Day. D. H. Lawrence. CP-LawrD

Subverted Flower, The. Robert Frost. CP-FrosR

Subway. David Ignatow. SP-IgnaD

Subway. Carl Sandburg. CP-SandC

Subway, The. Allen Tate. CP-TateA

Subway Face. Langston Hughes. CP-HughL; CP-HughL1

Subway from New Britain to the Bronx, The. Randall Jarrell. CP-JarrR

Subway Rush Hour. Langston Hughes. CP-HughL; CP-HughL3

Subway Singer, The. Amy Clampitt. CP-ClamA

Subway Station. Grace Paley.

Succeeding years thy early frame destroy. Ovid. CP-JohnS *Fr.* Heroides.

Success. Langston Hughes. CP-HughL; CP-HughL1

Success Comes to Cow Creek. James Tate. SP-TateJ

Success in life is when one has a goal. Freshman Sonnet: Success. John Ciardi. CP-CiarJ

Success is a played-out game, success, success! Played-Out Game, A. D. H. Lawrence. CP-LawrD

Success is counted sweetest. Emily Dickinson. CP-DickE

Success is dust, but an aim. Emily Dickinson. SP-DickE

Success Is Failure. Philip Whalen. SP-WhalP

Success Story. Philip Larkin. CP-LarkP

Successful and fully satisfied. Alexandros Iannaios, and Alexandra. Constantine P. Cavafy. CP-CavaC, *tr. by* Theoharis Constantine Theoharis

Successful man has thrust himself, The. Stephen Crane. CP-CranS

Successful Species, A. John Ciardi. CP-CiarJ

Succession. Howard Nemerov. CP-NemeH

Succession. Yannis Ritsos. SP-RitsY, *tr. by* Kimon Friar

Succession of Kings, The. Christina Georgina Rossetti. CP-RosC3

Succession of the Foure Sweet Months, The. Robert Herrick. *See* Four Sweet Months, The

Succession of the gen-, The. Generations, The. James Laughlin. CP-LaugJ

Successions. Pablo Neruda. SP-NeruP

Succory, The. Jones Very. CP-VeryJ

Succubus, The. Robert Graves. CP-GravR

Such a day such a day when the rain. Tom's a-Cold. Stephen Spender. CP-SpenS

Such a dear little street it is, nestled away. Lockerbie Street. James Whitcomb Riley. CP-RileJ

Such a depth of charm here always. Ely Place. Thomas Kinsella. CP-KinsT

Such a fine pullet ought to go. Blue Ribbon at Amesbury, A. Robert Frost. CP-FrosR

Such a hubbub in the nests, / Such a bustle and squeak! Freaks of Fashion. Christina Georgina Rossetti. CP-RosC2

Such a lot of confusion, so many killings for nothing. The hero. Apples of the Hesperides 2, The. Yannis Ritsos. SP-RitsY, *tr. by* Gwendolyn MacEwen *and* Nikos Tsingos

Such a Parcel of Rogues in a Nation. Robert Burns. CP-BurnR

Such a starved bank of moss. Robert Browning. CP-BroR2

Such age how beautiful! O Lady bright. To —, in Her Seventieth Year. William Wordsworth. CP-WorW2

Such an alarm. Fox, The. Paul Muldoon. CP-MuldP

Such another peerless queen. Ralph Waldo Emerson. CP-EmerR

Such apt names befall great men. In Legationem Domini Oliveri St John ad Provincias Foederatas [On the Embassy of Lord Oliver St John to the United Provinces]. Andrew Marvell. CP-MarvA

Such are the inlets of the mind. Emily Dickinson. CP-DickE

Such As in Ships. Rudyard Kipling. CP-KiplR

Such as like heavenly wights doe come. Ode 4.2: "Such as like heavenly wights doe come." Horace. CP-RaleW *Fr.* Odes.

Such as Sorrow. Yehuda Amichai. SP-AmicY, *tr. by* Stephen Mitchell

Such as the cause was of two husbands' war. Elegy 1.10: "Such as the cause was of two husbands' war." Ovid. CP-MarlC *Fr.* Elegies.

Such be the end of all the red and gold. Admonition to the Dead. Robert Penn Warren. CP-WarrR

Such brightness, under earth now, put to shame. Michelangelo Buonarroti. CP-Miche, *tr. by* John Frederick Nims

Such Counsels You Gave to Me. Robinson Jeffers. CP-JefR2

Such dayes as weare the badge of holy red. To the Right, Noble, and Vertuous, Henry Lord Clifford, Sonne and Heyre to the Right Honourable, Francis, Earle of Cumberland. Thomas Campion. CP-CampT

Such Diamonds. Raymond Carver. CP-CarvR

Such earnestness! such wear and tear. Ungar and Rolfe. Herman Melville. SP-MelvH *Fr.* Clarel: A Poem and Pilgrimage in the Holy Land.

Such evidence I have of indifference. Voice from the Tomb (3). Stevie Smith. CP-SmitS

Such evening calm, such calm. Rainer Maria Rilke. CP-RilkFr, *tr. by* A. Poulin, Jr. *Fr.* Valaisian Quatrains, The.

Such flowers can bloom. Robert Creeley. SP-CreeR

Such fruitless questions may not long beguile. American Tradition. William Wordsworth. CP-WorW2 *Fr.* River Duddon [A Series of Sonnets], The.

Such glorious faith as fills your limpid eyes. Verse for a Certain Dog. Dorothy Parker. CP-ParkD

Such hap as I am happed in. Sir Thomas Wyatt. CP-WyatT

Such hope, as is the sick despair of good. Fragment: "Such hope, as is the sick despair of good." Percy Bysshe Shelley. CP-ShelP

Such icy wounds the city people bear. Summer Belvedere, The. Tennessee Williams. CP-WillT

Such is Love, it comforts in extremity. Charity Never Faileth. Christina Georgina Rossetti. CP-RosC2

Such is the course that nature's kind hath wrought. Sir Thomas Wyatt. CP-WyatT

Such is the fear those eyes strike into me. Petrarch. CP-Petra, *tr. by* J. G. Nichols

Such is the Force of Happiness. Emily Dickinson. CP-DickE

Such is the loneliness here. Winter in Istanbul. Andrei Codrescu. SP-CodrA

Such love as mourning Husbands have. Life in Death. Samuel Taylor Coleridge. CP-ColeS

Such near aspects had we. Henry David Thoreau. CP-ThorH

Such perfection / of dream would. Dream, The. Robert Creeley. CP-CreeR

Such places are too still for history. Deep Woods. Howard Nemerov. CP-NemeH

Such pleasure as the teeming earth. To the Right Hon[oura]ble Hierome, L[ord] Weston. An Ode Gratulatory for His Return from His Embassy. 1632. Ben Jonson. CP-JonsB

Such should this day be, so the sun should hide. On the Marriage of T. K. and C. C.: The Morning Stormy. Thomas Carew. CP-CareT

Such Simple Love. Thomas McGrath. SP-McGrT

Such strains as, mingled with the lyre. Epilogue to Horace's *Carmen Seculare*. Samuel Johnson. CP-JohnS

Such strangeness of mind I know. Robert Creeley. CP-CreeR

Such things there are, we don't know. Mona Van Duyn. SP-VanDM

Such Tophet was; so looked the grinning fiend. Tophet. Thomas Gray. CP-GrayT

Such vain thought as wonted to mislead me. Sir Thomas Wyatt. CP-WyatT

Such Verse as Bowles, heart-honour'd Poet, sang. Lines to Thomas Poole. Samuel Taylor Coleridge. CP-ColeS

Such Was Our Garden. Kenneth Rexroth. CP-RexrK

Such was the Child-World of the long ago. Old Home-Folks, The. James Whitcomb Riley. CP-RileJ *Fr.* Child-World, A.

Such was the circumstance of our first love. Coronet of Moonlight. Robert Graves. CP-GravR

Such was the power of sleep over him, his unfolded heart swaying. Black Panther and the Little Boy, The. Kenneth Patchen. CP-PatcK

Such wast thou, / Who art now. Her Monument, the Image Cut Thereon. Giacomo Leopardi. CP-PoEar, *tr. by* Ezra Pound

Such water do the gods distill. Henry David Thoreau. CP-ThorH

Such wealth of promise lies. Michelangelo Buonarroti. CP-Miche, *tr. by* John Frederick Nims

Such were the notes thy once-lov'd Poet sung. Epistle to Robert Earl of Oxford and Earl Mortimer. Alexander Pope. CP-PopeA

Such were the trophies, that, in earlier days. John Milton. *See* I with foolish mind and heedless zeal formerly

Suchness. Kenneth Rexroth. CP-RexrK

Suck dove meat from the bones. Legacy. Yusef Komunyakaa. CP-KomuY

Sucking the acid. Woman with Child. Olga Broumas. SP-BrouO

Sudd as Metaphor, The. Thomas Lux. SP-LuxT

Sudden around the curve a high-up and huge. Country Drive-In. Josephine Jacobsen. CP-JacoJ

Sudden blow: the great wings beating still, A. Leda and the Swan. William Butler Yeats. CP-YeatW

Sudden chasm of ghastly light, A. Emily Jane Brontë. CP-BronE

Sudden heart, tightrope walker with no rope. Dan Pagis. SP-PagiD, *tr. by* Stephen Mitchell

Sudden, it comes for you. Ode to Garlic. William Stafford. SP-StafWW

Sudden Journey. Tess Gallagher. SP-GallT

Sudden loss can be cruel, but that other, A. Rainer Maria Rilke. CP-RilkFr, *tr. by* A. Poulin, Jr. *Fr.* Fragments.

Sudden / loss of hope, A. Echoes ("Sudden / loss of hope, A"). Robert Creeley. CP-CreeR

Sudden Production of Mrs. Stockton's in One of Those Many Anxious Nights in Which She Watched with Mr. Stockton in His Last Illness, A. Annis Boudinot Stockton. CP-StocA

Sudden Rain. Raymond Carver. CP-CarvR

Sudden Shower, A. James Whitcomb Riley. CP-RileJ

Sudden the desert changes. Bridge-Guard in the Karroo. Rudyard Kipling. CP-KiplR

Suddenly. Yannis Ritsos. SP-RitsY, *tr. by* Kimon Friar

Suddenly. James Schuyler. CP-SchuJ

Suddenly and as in play. Album Leaf. Stéphane Mallarmé. CP-MallS, *tr. by* Henry Weinfield

Suddenly, at last, the bitter wind veers round. Arrow on the Vane. Robert Graves. CP-GravR

Suddenly, at midnight, when an invisible troupe. God Forsakes Antony, The. Constantine P. Cavafy. CP-CavaC, *tr. by* Theoharis Constantine Theoharis

Suddenly discovering in the eyes of the very beautiful Normande cocotte. Pagani's, November 8. Ezra Pound. SP-PounE

Suddenly he awoke and was running—raw. Bayonet Charge. Ted Hughes. SP-HughTN

Suddenly *here*. Inn / Kyoto. Robert Creeley. SP-CreeR

Suddenly his poor body. Stations. Ted Hughes. SP-HughTN

Suddenly his virtues became universal. Death by Radio. William Carlos Williams. CP-WilW2

Suddenly hooligan baby starlings. Where I Sit Writing My Letter. Ted Hughes. SP-HughTN

Suddenly I recall a place. Rainer Maria Rilke. CP-RilkFr, *tr. by* A. Poulin, Jr. *Fr.* Fragments.

Suddenly I saw the cold and rook-delighting heaven. Cold Heaven, The. William Butler Yeats. CP-YeatW

Suddenly in the Midst. G. K. Chesterton. CP-ChesG

Suddenly in the midst of friends. Suddenly in the Midst. G. K. Chesterton. CP-ChesG

Suddenly in the night the sirens. Ernesto Cardenal. CP-MertT *Fr.* Three Epigrams.

Suddenly into the still air burst thudding. On Somme. Ivor Gurney. SP-GurnI

Suddenly it is late night, there are people in the basement. Colour Machine, The. Thom Gunn. CP-GunnT

Suddenly night crushed out the day and hurled. Unreturning, The. Wilfred Owen. CP-OwenW

Suddenly, not long before. Long Last. Philip Larkin. CP-LarkP

Suddenly out of its still and drowsy lair, the lair of slaves. Europe, the 72d and 73d Year of These States. Walt Whitman. CP-WhitW

Suddenly she doesn't comprehend. Simone Weil Watches the Rhône Valley. Adam Zagajewski. SP-ZagaA, *tr. by* Renata Gorczynski, Benjamin Ivry *and* C. K. Williams

Suddenly they came flying, like a long scarf of smoke. Thing, The. Theodore Roethke. CP-RoetT

Suddenly three angels appeared. Three Angels. Adam Zagajewski. SP-ZagaA, *tr. by* Clare Cavanagh

Suddenly toward the end of 1969 everything is. Toward the End of 1969. Andrei Codrescu. SP-CodrA

Sudds launders bands in piss[e]; and starches them. Upon Sudds, a Laundress[e]. Robert Herrick. CP-HerrR

Sue Ella Tucker was barely in her teens. Rubaiyat for Sue Ella Tucker. Miller Williams. CP-WillM

Sueño Real. Lawrence Ferlinghetti. SP-FerlL

Suffenus is, stay Varus,—whom you've proven—is the. Catullus. *See* I must, Varus, tell you

Suffer, do you? I think if wounds were art. Lines while Walking Home from a Party on Charles Street. John Ciardi. CP-CiarJ

Suffer the Children. Audre Lorde. SP-LordA

(He is forever trapped.) SP-LordA

Suffer the world you're trapped in. Shmuel HaNagid. SP-HaNaS, *tr. by* Peter Cole

Suffer Thou that Canst not Shift. Robert Herrick. CP-HerrR

Suffer thy legs, but not thy tongue to walk. Silence. Robert Herrick. CP-HerrR

Sufferance. Robert Herrick. CP-HerrR

Sufferance of her race is shown, The. Formerly a Slave. Herman Melville. SP-MelvH

Suffering. G. K. Chesterton. CP-ChesG

Suffering has settled like a sly disguise. Korean Woman Seated by a Wall, A. William Meredith. SP-MereW

Suffering in sorrow, in hope to attain. Sir Thomas Wyatt. CP-WyatT

Suffering of the Wheel is relentless, The. Han-shan. CP-ColdM, *tr. by* Red Pine

Suffering Ophthalmologist, The. Alan Dugan. CP-DugaA

Suffering sets us apart. We enjoy too strongly. P.O.W. Jane Cooper. CP-CoopJ

Sufferings. Robert Herrick. CP-HerrR

Sufficed not, madame, that you did tear. Sir Thomas Wyatt. CP-WyatT

Sufficeth it to you [*or* yow] my joy[e]s interred. 11th: and Last Booke of the Ocean to Scinthia, The. Sir Walter Ralegh. CP-RaleW *Fr.* Ocean's Love to Cynthia, The.

Sufficient The, Kenneth Rexroth. CP-RexrK

Suffolk. Donald Davie. CP-DaviDC

Sufi Sam Christian. Robert Creeley. SP-CreeR

Sufi was wandering the world, A. Granary Floor, The. Jelaluddin Rumi. SP-RumI, *tr. by* Coleman Barks

Suflah Spring in the Judean Mountains. Yehuda Amichai. SP-AmicYL, *tr. by* Benjamin Harshav *and* Barbara Harshav

Sugar. Olga Broumas. SP-BrouO

Sugar. Tess Gallagher. SP-GallT

Sugar. Yusef Komunyakaa. CP-KomuY

Sugar I am CALLING you. Not. Islander, The. Louise Glück. SP-GlucL

Sugar in the Cane. Tennessee Williams. CP-WillT

Sugarduke. Dan Pagis. SP-PagiD, *tr. by* Stephen Mitchell

Suggested at Tyndrum in a Storm. William Wordsworth. CP-WorW2

Suggested by a Picture of the Bird of Paradise. William Wordsworth. CP-WorW2

Suggested by a View from an Eminence in Inglewood Forest. William Wordsworth. CP-WorW2

Suggested by Mr W. Westall's Views of the Caves, etc., in Yorkshire. William Wordsworth. CP-WorW2

Suggestion, A. James Laughlin. CP-LaugJ

Suggestion for a Telegraphic Birthday Greeting. Robert Browning. CP-BroR2

Suggestion for an Arrangement. Charles Bukowski. SP-BukC3

Suggestion / recognition. Learning. Robert Creeley. SP-CreeR

Suggestions for the Improvement of a Sunset. Charles Tomlinson. CP-TomlC

Suicide. Charles Bukowski. SP-BukC2

Suicide. Federico García Lorca. CP-GarcF, *tr. by* Alan S. Trueblood *Fr.* Back of the World.

Suicide. Federico García Lorca. SP-GarcF, *tr. by* Edwin Honig

Suicide. Langston Hughes. CP-HughL; CP-HughL1

Suicide. Allen Tate. CP-TateA

Suicide. Alice Walker. CP-AudeW

Suicide, The. Jorge Luis Borges. SP-BorgJ, *tr. by* Alastair Reid

Suicide, The. Walter De la Mare. CP-DeLaW

Suicide, The. Louis MacNeice. CP-MacNL

Suicide, The. Edna St. Vincent Millay. CP-MillE

Suicide: Anne. C. K. Williams. SP-WillC

Suicide Blues. Muriel Rukeyser. CP-RukeM

Suicide, far from content, The. Suicide in The Copse, The. Robert Graves. CP-GravR

Suicide in The Copse, The. Robert Graves. CP-GravR

Suicide Note. Jane Cooper. CP-CoopJ

Suicide Note. Richard Eberhart. CP-EberR

Suicide Note. Anne Sexton. CP-SextA

Suicide off Egg Rock. Sylvia Plath. CP-PlatS

Suicide's Argument, The. Samuel Taylor Coleridge. CP-ColeS

Suicide's Epitaph. Stevie Smith. CP-SmitS

Suicide's Note. Langston Hughes. CP-HughL; CP-HughL1

Suicide's Room, The. Wisława Szymborska. SP-SzymW, *tr. by* Stanislaw

Barańczak *and* Clare Cavanagh

Suit, The. Philip Levine. SP-LeviP

Suitable entrance to this village, A. Permanent Migrations, The. Kenneth Patchen. CP-PatcK

Suitcase Strapped with a Rope, A. Charles Simic. SP-SimiC; SP-SimiCE

Suite. Federico García Lorca.

Landscape Seen with the Nose. CP-GarcF, *tr.* by Jerome Rothenberg

Sphere. CP-GarcF, *tr.* by Jerome Rothenberg

Sundown ("Sun / when it's sundown, The"). CP-GarcF, *tr.* by Jerome Rothenberg

Those Who Wait. CP-GarcF, *tr.* by Jerome Rothenberg

"What's coming up?" CP-GarcF, *tr.* by Jerome Rothenberg

Suite Clownesque. T. S. Eliot. SP-ElioT

Suite for All Clown's Day. Josephine Jacobsen. CP-JacoJ

Suite for Augustus, A. Rita Dove. SP-DoveR

Suite for Lord Timothy Dexter. Muriel Rukeyser. CP-RukeM

Suite for Recorders. Louis MacNeice. CP-MacNL

Suite in Prison. Richard Eberhart. CP-EberR

Suite of Six Pieces for Siskind, A. John Logan. CP-LogaJ

Suitor, The. Paul Laurence Dunbar. CP-DunbP

Suitor, / suitor of mine. Federico García Lorca. CP-GarcF, *tr.* by Alan S. Trueblood *Fr.* Andalusian Songs.

Suitors sinn'd, but with a fair excuse, The. On Flaxman's Penelope. William Cowper. CP-CowpW

Sulkily the sticks burn, and though they crackle. Under the Pot. Robert Graves. CP-GravR

Sullen morning, A. St. Augustine-by-the-Sea. May Swenson. SP-SwenM

Sulmo, Peligny's third part, me contains. Elegy 2.16: "Sulmo, Peligny's third part, me contains." Ovid. CP-MarlC *Fr.* Elegies.

Sulpicia to Cerinthus. Tibullus. CP-TateA

Sultry Dawn. Theodore Weiss. SP-WeisT

Sultry summer day is done, The. Evening. Sir Walter Scott. SP-ScotW *Fr.* Rokeby.

Sum. "Rubén Dario." SP-DariR, *tr.* by Alberto Acereda *and* Will Derusha

Sum, The. Paul Laurence Dunbar. CP-DunbP

Sum of all the parts of Such—, The. Synthetic Such. Robert Graves. CP-GravR

Sum of Destructions, A. Theodore Weiss. SP-WeisT

Sumach and Birds. Carl Sandburg. CP-SandC

Sumach Leaves, The. Jones Very. CP-VeryJ

Sumerian. A. R. Ammons. CP-AmmoA

Summa. Gerard Manley Hopkins. CP-HopkG

Summa wancha. Robert Creeley. SP-CreeR

Summah is de lovin' time. Summer Night, A. Paul Laurence Dunbar. CP-DunbP

Summah night an' sighin' breeze. Lover's Lane. Paul Laurence Dunbar. CP-DunbP

Summah's nice, wif sun a-shinin'. Time to Tinker 'Roun'! Paul Laurence Dunbar. CP-DunbP

Summary. Dorothy Parker. CP-ParkD

Summe, and the Satisfaction, The. Robert Herrick. CP-HerrR

Summe Deus, cui cæca patent penetralia cordis. Prayer: "Summe Deus, cui cæca patent penetralia cordis." Samuel Johnson. CP-JohnS

Summe Pater, quodcunque tuum de corpore Numen. On Losing the Power of Speech. Samuel Johnson. CP-JohnS

Summer. John Ashbery. SP-AshbJ

Summer. Robert Creeley. SP-CreeR

Summer. Eugenio Montale. CP-MontE, *tr.* by Jonathan Galassi

Summer. Yannis Ritsos. SP-RitsY, *tr.* by Kimon Friar

Summer. Christina Georgina Rossetti. CP-RosC2

Summer. Christina Georgina Rossetti. CP-RosC1

Summer. Christina Georgina Rossetti. CP-RosC3

Summer. Adam Zagajewski. SP-ZagaA

Summer Afternoon, A. James Whitcomb Riley. CP-RileJ

Summer Afternoon an Old Man Gives Some Thought to the Central Questions, A. Miller Williams. CP-WillM

Summer Afternoon and Hypnosis. Robert Penn Warren. CP-WarrR

Summer and Winter. Percy Bysshe Shelley. CP-ShelP

Summer and winter close commune. In St. Paul's a While Ago. Thomas Hardy. CP-HardT

Summer apples, showy and sugary, mealy and touchy. Jelly Jelly. James Schuyler. CP-SchuJ

Summer at Dhiminio. Yannis Ritsos. SP-RitsY, *tr.* by Kimon Friar

Summer, be seen no more within this wood. Edna St. Vincent Millay. CP-MillE

Summer begins. In the old cemetary. Yehuda Amichai. SP-AmicY, *tr.* by Chana Bloch

Summer begins to have the look. Emily Dickinson. CP-DickE

Summer Belvedere, The. Tennessee Williams. CP-WillT

Summer Breezes. Frank O'Hara. SP-OharF

Summer burns on the edges of day. Song: "Summer burns on the edges of day." Hayden Carruth. CP-CarHS

Summer by the Lakeside. John Greenleaf Whittier. CP-WhitJ

Summer Canyon. W. S. Merwin. SP-MerwWF

Summer cloud in summer blue, The. Cloud and Flame. John Berryman. CP-BerrJ

Summer cold. No rash. No fever. Nothing. But a dozen times during the night I wake, A. Shade, The. C. K. Williams. CP-WillC; SP-WillC

Summer dawn breaks over the city, A. Thursday. James Schuyler. CP-SchuJ

Summer Day. Rainer Maria Rilke. CP-RilkFr, *tr.* by A. Poulin, Jr.

Summer Day, The. Mary Oliver. SP-OlivM

Summer day on which you came, The. Emily Dickinson. SP-DickE

Summer Doorway. W. S. Merwin. SP-MerwWF

Summer ends now; now, barbarous in beauty, the stooks [a]rise. Hurrahing in Harvest. Gerard Manley Hopkins. CP-HopkG

Summer Evening at the Window with Psalms. Yehuda Amichai. SP-AmicYL, *tr.* by Benjamin Harshav *and* Barbara Harshav

Summer Evening (Calumet Avenue). Langston Hughes. CP-HughL; CP-HughL2

Summer Evening Churchyard, A. Percy Bysshe Shelley. CP-ShelP

Summer Evening in the Jerusalem Mountains. Yehuda Amichai. SP-AmicY, *tr.* by Chana Bloch

Summer Evening in the Jerusalem Mountains. Yehuda Amichai. SP-AmicYL, *tr.* by Benjamin Harshav *and* Barbara Harshav

Summer evening: reclining. Moment's Peace, A. Thomas Kinsella. CP-KinsT

Summer fields shone quiet: and I stood, The. By the Sea. G. K. Chesterton. CP-ChesG

Summer Fog. Raymond Carver. CP-CarvR

Summer: for a few days being. Rainer Maria Rilke. CP-RilkFr, *tr.* by A. Poulin, Jr. *Fr.* Roses, The.

Summer for prose and lemons, for nakedness and languor. Bleecker Street, Summer. Derek Walcott. CP-WalcD

Summer for thee, grant I may be. Emily Dickinson. CP-DickE

Summer Gale. Alan Dugan. CP-DugaA

Summer Grass. Carl Sandburg. CP-SandC

Summer grass aches and whispers. Summer Grass. Carl Sandburg. CP-SandC

Summer grows old, cold-blooded mother. Frog Autumn. Sylvia Plath. CP-PlatS

Summer hail flings crystals on the window. Death of Anne Boleyn. Robert Lowell. SP-LoweR

Summer has been wide and deep, The. Emily Dickinson. SP-DickE

Summer has two Beginnings. Emily Dickinson. CP-DickE

Summer Heaven, Angels, Heaven. Alan Dugan. CP-DugaA

Summer Holiday. Robinson Jeffers. CP-JefR1

Summer Home. Seamus Heaney. SP-HeanSO

Summer Hours. Federico García Lorca.

    8:00 p.m. CP-GarcF, *tr.* by Jerome Rothenberg

    5:00 p.m. CP-GarcF, *tr.* by Jerome Rothenberg

    9:00 p.m. CP-GarcF, *tr.* by Jerome Rothenberg

    "Scissor man. / (3:00 p.m.)." CP-GarcF, *tr.* by Jerome Rothenberg

    7:00 p.m. CP-GarcF, *tr.* by Jerome Rothenberg

    6:00 p.m. CP-GarcF, *tr.* by Jerome Rothenberg

    Thistledown Night. CP-GarcF, *tr.* by Jerome Rothenberg

Summer Idyll. James Vincent Cunningham. CP-CunnJ

Summer in Sacramento, A. Raymond Carver. CP-CarvR

Summer in the City. Yannis Ritsos. SP-RitsY, *tr.* by Kimon Friar

Summer in the South. Paul Laurence Dunbar. CP-DunbP

Summer Is Ended. Christina Georgina Rossetti. CP-RosC2

Summer Is Ended, The. Christina Georgina Rossetti. CP-RosC3

Summer is fading. Afternoons. Philip Larkin. CP-LarkP

Summer is gone with all its roses. Bitter for Sweet. Christina Georgina Rossetti. CP-RosC1

Summer is late, my heart. Touch Me. Stanley Kunitz. CP-KunSC

Summer is over / —it's no use demanding. E. E. Cummings. CP-CummE

Summer is over upon the sea. Song: "Summer is over upon the sea." Elizabeth Bishop. CP-BishE

Summer is shorter than any one. Emily Dickinson. CP-DickE

Summer laid her simple Hat. Emily Dickinson. CP-DickE

Summer Landscape. Richard Eberhart. CP-EberR

Summer Lightning. Donald Davie. CP-DaviDC

Summer like a rajah dies, The. Kipling's Vermont. Ogden Nash. CP-NashO

Summer Madrigal. Federico García Lorca. CP-GarcF, *tr.* by Catherine Brown

Summer Malison, The. Gerard Manley Hopkins. CP-HopkG

Summer Memory in the Crowded City, A. James Wright. CP-WrigJ

Summer Morning. Charles Simic. SP-SimiC; SP-SimiCE

Summer Morning, A. Richard Wilbur. CP-WilbR

Summer morning is risen. Ballad: "Summer morning is risen." John Clare. SP-ClarJ *Fr.* Child Harold.

Summer near the River. Carolyn Kizer. CP-KizeC

Summer Night. Langston Hughes. CP-HughL; CP-HughL1

Summer Night. James Tate. SP-TateJ

Summer Night, A. Matthew Arnold. SP-ArnoM

Summer Night, A. W. H. Auden. CP-AudeW

Summer Night, A. Paul Laurence Dunbar. CP-DunbP

Summer Night, A. Randall Jarrell. CP-JarrR

Summer Night in Hanoi, A. Yusef Komunyakaa. CP-KomuY

Summer night in the desert is as welcome, A. Evening of the Pyramids, The. Norman Dubie. CP-DubiN

Summer Night in the King David Hotel. Yehuda Amichai. SP-AmicYL, *tr.* by Benjamin Harshav *and* Barbara Harshav

Summer Night on the Stone Barrens. W. S. Merwin. SP-MerwWF

Summer nights are short, / Where northern days are long, The. Christina Georgina Rossetti. CP-RosC2

Summer Nocturne. Philip Larkin. CP-LarkP

Summer Noon at Karlovasi. Yannis Ritsos. SP-RitsY, *tr.* by Kimon Friar

Summer of nineteen eighteen, The. Bad Old Days, The. Kenneth Rexroth. CP-RexrK

Summer or Its End. Yehuda Amichai.

    "You washed the fruit." SP-AmicY, *tr.* by Stephen Mitchell

Summer or Its End, A. Yehuda Amichai. SP-AmicYL, *tr.* by Benjamin Harshav *and* Barbara Harshav

Summer or Winter or Spring or Fall. Masque of the Seasons, A. James Whitcomb Riley. CP-RileJ

Summer Oracle. Audre Lorde. SP-LordA

Summer Palace burnt, the Winter Palace, wherever it was, The. 10:X:57, 45 Years Since the Fall of the Ch'ing Dynasty. Philip Whalen. SP-WhalP

Summer Passer-By. Rainer Maria Rilke. CP-RilkFr, *tr.* by A. Poulin, Jr. *Fr.* Orchards.

Summer Pastoral, A. Paul Laurence Dunbar. CP-DunbP

Summer People, The. James Merrill. SP-MerrJ

Summer Pilgrimage, A. John Greenleaf Whittier. CP-WhitJ

Summer Poem. Hans Magnus Enzensberger. SP-EnzeH, *tr.* by Michael Hamburger

Summer Rain, The. Henry David Thoreau.

Summer Rain in Mountains. Robert Penn Warren. CP-WarrR

Summer Resorts; A Hymn of Hate. Dorothy Parker. CP-ParkD

Summer Rest and Words. Yehuda Amichai. SP-AmicYL, *tr.* by Benjamin Harshav *and* Barbara Harshav

Summer Sadness. Stéphane Mallarmé. CP-MallS, *tr.* by Henry Weinfield

Summer Schemes. Thomas Hardy. CP-HardT

Summer Serenade. Ogden Nash. CP-NashO

Summer Session. A. R. Ammons. CP-AmmoA

Summer Shirt Sale. Carl Sandburg. CP-SandC

Summer shirt sale of a downtown haberdasher is glorified in a show, The. Summer Shirt Sale. Carl Sandburg. CP-SandC

Summer Silence. E. E. Cummings. CP-CummE

Summer so histrionic, marvelous dirty days. Ted Berrigan. SP-BerrT *Fr.* Sonnets, The.

Summer Solstice. Osip Emilevich Mandelstam. CP-KunSC, *tr.* by Stanley Kunitz

Summer Song. E. E. Cummings. CP-CummE

Summer Song. Li Po. CP-WilW2

Summer Song. William Carlos Williams. CP-WilW1

Summer Sorrow. Yannis Ritsos. SP-RitsY, *tr.* by Kimon Friar

Summer Stars. Carl Sandburg. CP-SandC

Summer Storm. Charles Wright. SP-WrigCN

Summer sun ray, The. Noon Walk on the Asylum Lawn. Anne Sexton. CP-SextA

Summer Sunrise, A. James Whitcomb Riley. CP-RileJ

Summer. Sunset. Someone is playing. Transient Barracks. Randall Jarrell. CP-JarrR

Summer that I was ten, The. Centaur, The. May Swenson. SP-SwenM

Summer that we did not prize, The. Emily Dickinson. CP-DickE

Summer, this is our flesh. Seasons of the Soul. Allen Tate. CP-TateA

Summer thunder darkens, and its climbing. Prometheus. Charles Tomlinson. CP-TomlC; SP-TomlC

Summer Thunderstorm, A. Theodore Weiss. SP-WeisT

Summer-Time. James Whitcomb Riley. CP-RileJ

Summer-Time and Winter-Time. James Whitcomb Riley. CP-RileJ

Summer warmth has left the sky, The. Hazel Blossoms. John Greenleaf Whittier. CP-WhitJ

Summer was another country, where the birds. Holiday. Adrienne Rich. CP-RicAE

Summer was dead and Autumn was expiring. Zucca, The. Percy Bysshe Shelley. CP-ShelP

Summer—we all have seen. Emily Dickinson. CP-DickE

Summer: West Side. John Updike. CP-UpdiJ

Summer wilderness, a blue light. Loon on Forrester's Pond, The. Hayden Carruth. CP-CarHS

Summer will end. September will come. Once more it's okay to shoot. So Forth. Joseph Brodsky. CP-BrodJ

Summer winds is sniffin' round the bloomin' locus' trees, The. Thoughts fer the Discuraged Farmer. James Whitcomb Riley. CP-RileJ

Summer Wish. Louise Bogan. CP-BogaL

Summer Wish, A. Christina Georgina Rossetti. CP-RosC1

Summergreen for President. Ogden Nash. CP-NashO

Summer's away, I traded my chicks for trees. Lorine Niedecker. CP-NiedL

Summer's Bounty. May Swenson. SP-SwenM

Summer's Day, A. James Whitcomb Riley. CP-RileJ

Summer's day has reached its close, The. Fireflies, The. Jones Very. CP-VeryJ

Summer's Dream, A. Elizabeth Bishop. CP-BishE

Summer's Early End at Hudson's Bay. Hayden Carruth. CP-CarHS

Summer's Elegy. Howard Nemerov. CP-NemeH

Summer's Fullness. Adam Zagajewski. SP-ZagaA, *tr. by* Clare Cavanagh

Summer's last half moon waning high. 16. ix. 65. James Merrill. SP-MerrJ

Summer's last sun nigh unto setting shines. Last Eve of Summer, The. John Greenleaf Whittier. CP-WhitJ

Summer's Night, A. Paul Laurence Dunbar. CP-DunbP

Summers of bloom—and months of frost. Emily Dickinson. SP-DickE

Summer's pastoral looks on barn and bin, A. Letter from a Metaphysical Countryside. John Ciardi. CP-CiarJ

Summer's put the idy in, The. Summer's Day, A. James Whitcomb Riley. CP-RileJ

Summertime and the Living. Robert Earl Hayden. CP-HaydR

Summertime dogs. Bravo. Charles Bukowski. SP-BukC3

Summertime / Is warm and bright. Year Round. Langston Hughes. CP-HughL

Summertime, the cities empty. Saturdays, holidays. Rustle of Acacias, The. Joseph Brodsky. CP-BrodJ, *tr. by* Daniel Weissbort

Summery Weather. Kenneth Koch. SP-KochK

Summing Up in Italy. Elizabeth Barrett Browning. CP-BroEB

Summing-up, The. Stanley Kunitz. CP-KunSC

Summit. Gabriela Mistral. SP-MistG, *tr. by* Maria Giachetti [*or* Jacketti]

Summit and blue air. Wind Coming Down From, The. A. R. Ammons. CP-AmmoA

Summit Redwood, The. Robinson Jeffers. CP-JefR1

Summits. W. S. Merwin. SP-MerwW

Summoned from offices and homes, we came. Disciple, The. John Berryman. CP-BerrJ

Summoned to desolation by the dawn. Morning Hymn to a Dark Girl. James Wright. CP-WrigJ

Summoning artists to participate. For John F. Kennedy; His Inauguration. Robert Frost. CP-FrosR

Summons, A. John Greenleaf Whittier. CP-WhitJ

Summons, The. James Dickey. CP-DickJ

Summons, The. James Laughlin. CP-LaugJ

Summons, The. Ezra Pound. CP-PoEar

Summons, The. Charles Simic. SP-SimiC; SP-SimiCE

Summons, The. John Greenleaf Whittier. CP-WhitJ

Summons because the marvelous prey is fleeing, A. Eraser. Charles Simic. SP-SimiC; SP-SimiCE

Summons to Town, A. Sir John Suckling. CP-SuckJ

Summons was urgent: and forth I went, The. Her Death and After. Thomas Hardy. CP-HardT

Summum Bonum. Robert Browning. CP-BroR2

Sumner. John Greenleaf Whittier. CP-WhitJ

Sumptuous Leonarda. In Málaga. Federico García Lorca. CP-GarcF, *tr. by* Alan S. Trueblood *Fr.* Eros with a Cane.

Sumptuous Leonarda. In Malaga. Federico García Lorca. SP-GarcF, *tr. by* Ben Belitt

Sums. Donald Hall. CP-HallD

Sun. Michael Palmer. SP-PalmM

Sun. Federico García Lorca. CP-GarcF, *tr. by* Jerome Rothenberg *Fr.* Capriccios.

Sun. James Dickey. CP-DickJ

Sun. W. S. Merwin. SP-MerwWF

Sun. Marianne Craig Moore. CP-MoorM

Sun. Michael Palmer. SP-PalmM

Sun, The. Charles Baudelaire. CP-BaudC, *tr. by* Walter Martin

Sun, The. Robert Browning. CP-BroR2

Sun, The. Donald Hall. CP-HallD

Sun, The. Mary Oliver. SP-OlivM

Sun, The. Anne Sexton. CP-SextA

Sun, The. Jones Very. CP-VeryJ

Sun, The. William Carlos Williams. CP-WilW1

Sun again unearthed, colours come up fresh, The. After Cumae. Geoffrey Hill.

CP-HillG

Sun always setting behind us, The. Twelve Hours Out of New York After Twenty-Five Days at Sea. Gary Snyder. CP-SnydG

Sun and Air. Richard Wilbur. CP-WilbR

Sun and Fog Contested, The. Emily Dickinson. CP-DickE

Sun and Moon Flowers: Paul Klee, 1879–1940. Norman Dubie. CP-DubiN

Sun and Moon must make their haste, The. Emily Dickinson. CP-DickE

Sun and Rain. W. S. Merwin. SP-MerwWF

Sun and Rain. James Whitcomb Riley. CP-RileJ

Sun and Skin. Arthur Rimbaud. CP-RimbA, *tr. by* Martin Sorrell

Sun and softness. Sun Song. Langston Hughes. CP-HughL; CP-HughL1

Sun arises from the sea, The. Easter Morning. Christina Georgina Rossetti. CP-RosC3

Sun arises in the East, The. Day. William Blake. CP-BlakW

Sun-Artist, The. Muriel Rukeyser. CP-RukeM

Sun at noon to higher air, The. March. A. E. Housman. CP-HousA

Sun athwart the cloud thought it no sin, The. Ralph Waldo Emerson. CP-EmerR

Sun Bathers, The. William Carlos Williams. CP-WilW1

Sun-beams [*or* Sun-beames] in the east are spred [*or* spread], The. Epithalamion Made at Lincoln's Inn [*or* Lincolnes Inne]. John Donne. CP-DonnJ; MW-DonnJ

Sun binds, The. Back Country. A. R. Ammons. CP-AmmoA

Sun Boat. May Sarton. SP-SartM

Sun breaks over the eucalyptus. Marin-An. Gary Snyder. CP-SnydG

Sun Cab, A. James Schuyler. CP-SchuJ

Sun came up, bigger than all my sorrow. West Country Song. Edna St. Vincent Millay. CP-MillE

Sun Dancer. Carl Sandburg. CP-SandC

Sun, dark sun. Tropic. D. H. Lawrence. CP-LawrD

Sun descending, the *Phæacian* train, The. Homer. CP-PopeA *Fr.* Odyssey.

Sun does not consider any of your hesitations, The. Succession. Yannis Ritsos. SP-RitsY, *tr. by* Kimon Friar

Sun dog hurries a lover, A. Double Limbo. Yusef Komunyakaa. CP-KomuY

Sun doth not the hidden place reveal, The. Who Hath Ears to Hear Let Him Hear! Jones Very. CP-VeryJ

Sun drops daily down the sky, The. North Palisade, the End of September, 1939. Kenneth Rexroth. CP-RexrK

Sun-Face and Moon-Face. Robert Graves. CP-GravR

Sun falls behind Wales, The; the towns and hills. Midsummer Night, 1940. Philip Larkin. CP-LarkP

Sun flower. / River flower. Encounter ("Sun flower. / River flower"). Federico García Lorca. CP-GarcF, *tr. by* Jerome Rothenberg *Fr.* In the Garden of the Lunar Grapefruits.

Sun flung out at the foot of the tree, The. Shadow, The. Charles Tomlinson. SP-TomlC

Sun for all his pride dims out and dies, The. April—Dull Afternoon. Ivor Gurney. SP-GurnI

Sun from the west glares back, The. Coming Up Oxford Street: Evening. Thomas Hardy. CP-HardT

Sun gas coughed, A. A million miles of flame. In the Year of Many Conversions and the Private Soul. John Ciardi. CP-CiarJ

Sun, giver of life and tenderness, The. Sun and Skin. Arthur Rimbaud. CP-RimbA, *tr. by* Martin Sorrell

Sun gives not directly, The. Sunshine. Nicholas Vachel Lindsay. CP-LindV

Sun goes down, and with him takes, The. Romany Girl, The. Ralph Waldo Emerson. CP-EmerR

Sun goes down, each minute the air darker, The. Upward Moon and the Downward Moon, The. Robert Bly. SP-BlyR

Sun goes down in the dusty April night, The. Evening When the Full Moon Rose as the Sun Set, An. Robert Bly. SP-BlyR

Sun goes slowly blind, The. Love in the Valley. Derek Walcott. CP-WalcD

Sun had not gone down. The new moon, The. Journey, The. Charles Tomlinson. CP-TomlC

Sun had rais'd above the mead, The. Country Squire and the Mandrake, The. Christopher Smart. SP-SmarC

Sun had wheeled from Grey's to Dammer's Crest, The. Burghers, The. Thomas Hardy. CP-HardT

Sun has climbed the hill, the day is on the downward slope, The. Mid-Day Verse, The. D. H. Lawrence. CP-LawrD

Sun has fired my face to terra-cotta, The. Derek Walcott. CP-WalcD *Fr.* Midsummer.

Sun has long been set, The. Night in June, A. William Wordsworth. CP-WorW1; MW-WorW

Sun has set, and the long grass now, The. Emily Jane Brontë. CP-BronE

Sun has set; but lit the Light, The. Our Lighthouses. Jones Very. CP-VeryJ

Sun Has Set, The. Federico García Lorca. CP-GarcF, *tr. by* Catherine Brown

Sun has slipped his tether, The. Waiting. Paul Laurence Dunbar. CP-DunbP

Sun hath shed its kindly light, The. Thanksgiving Poem, A. Paul Laurence Dunbar. CP-DunbP

Sun he is sunk in the west, The. Song.—In the Character of a Ruined Farmer. Robert Burns. CP-BurnR

Sun hit shine an' de win' hit blow, De. Winter's Approach. Paul Laurence Dunbar. CP-DunbP

Sun immense and rosy, The. Elegy: "Sun immense and rosy, The." D. H. Lawrence. CP-LawrD

Sun, / in her memory, The. Lost in the Desert. Clarence Major. SP-MajoC

Sun in Me. D. H. Lawrence. CP-LawrD

Sun in reining to the West, The. Emily Dickinson. CP-DickE

Sun in the heaven. Self-Respect. Wallace Stevens. CP-StevWP

Sun is a huntress young, The. Indian Summer Day on the Prairie, An. Nicholas Vachel Lindsay. CP-LindV

Sun is about to come up and the regiments lie, The. At Lake Desolation. Kenneth Rexroth. CP-RexrK

Sun is blazing and the sky is blue, The. Pink Dog. Elizabeth Bishop. CP-BishE

Sun is bleeding its fires upon the mist, The. Ruination. D. H. Lawrence. CP-LawrD

Sun is couched, the sea-fowl gone to rest, The. By the Sea-Side. William Wordsworth. CP-WorW2

Sun is Dead—ye heard the curfew toll, The. Sonnet Written by Mr — Immediately after the Death of His Wife. William Wordsworth. CP-WorW1

Sun is down hopeless, The. Hopeless and Felons. Thomas Merton. CP-MertT

Sun is dressed in black, The. Moon of my life. Possessed. Charles Baudelaire. CP-BaudC, tr. by Walter Martin

Sun is gay or stark, The. Goldsworthy Lowes Dickinson. CP-DickE

Sun / Is gonna go down, The. Sunset in Dixie. Langston Hughes. CP-HughL; CP-HughL2

Sun is hot, the ocean cool, The. The waves. Running on the Shore. May Swenson. SP-SwenM

Sun is like an open furnace door, The. Last Look round St. Martin's Fair. Thomas Hardy. CP-HardT

Sun is love, The. The lover. Jelaluddin Rumi. SP-Rumi, tr. by Coleman Barks

Sun is low, The. On the River. Paul Laurence Dunbar. CP-DunbP

Sun is not yet risen, The. Alice Du Clos. Samuel Taylor Coleridge. CP-ColeS; MW-ColeS

Sun is one—and on the Tare, The. Emily Dickinson. CP-DickE

Sun is set; the swallows are asleep, The. Evening: Ponte al Mare, Pisa. Percy Bysshe Shelley. CP-ShelP

Sun is the sole inconsumable fire, The. Ralph Waldo Emerson. CP-EmerR

Sun is warm, the sky is clear, The. Stanzas Written in Dejection, near Naples [or —December 1818, near Naples]. Percy Bysshe Shelley. CP-ShelP

Sun just drops down through the poplars, The. Nineteen Forty. Norman Dubie. CP-DubiN

Sun—just touched the Morning, The. Emily Dickinson. CP-DickE

Sun just / went behind the / ridge and turned, The. Sunset. James Schuyler. CP-SchuJ

Sun kept setting—setting—still, The. Emily Dickinson. CP-DickE

Sun kept stooping—stooping—low!, The. Emily Dickinson. CP-DickE

Sun like an orange mousse through the trees. Dog Day Vespers. Charles Wright. SP-WrigC

Sun, / Like the red yolk of a rotten egg, The. Sunset—Coney Island. Langston Hughes. CP-HughL; CP-HughL1

Sun made a late and lamented, The. Pale Panther, The. Louis MacNeice. CP-MacNL

Sun makes music as of old, The. Prologue in Heaven. Johann Wolfgang von Goethe. CP-ShelP Fr. Faust.

Sun May Set, The. Catullus. CP-RaleW, tr. by Sir Walter Alexander Raleigh Fr. Carmina.

Sun-Men. D. H. Lawrence. CP-LawrD

Sun now angles downward, and southward, The. Fear and Trembling. Robert Penn Warren. CP-WarrR

Sun of Braccio's under earth, The. The sun. Michelangelo Buonarroti. CP-Miche, tr. by John Frederick Nims

Sun of July beats down on the small white house, The. Small White House. Robert Penn Warren. CP-WarrR

Sun of the Sleepless! Lord Byron. CP-Byron

Sun on his face wakes him. Morning Song. Gregory Orr. SP-OrrG

Sun on the Bookcase, The. Thomas Hardy. CP-HardT

Sun on the faces. On the knotted rocks. Muriel Rukeyser. CP-RukeM

Sun on the Letter, The. Thomas Hardy. CP-HardT

Sun on their naked shoulders. Weekend Bathers. Kenneth Patchen. CP-PatcK

Sun out window's. Hotel Lobby. Robert Creeley. SP-CreeR

Sun, perhaps three of them, one black one red, you know, and her dancing, The. Alma. Frank O'Hara. SP-OharF

Sun retired to a cloud, The. Emily Dickinson. CP-DickE

"Sun Rises and Sets in That Child," So My Grandmother Used to Say, The. Philip Whalen. SP-WhalP

Sun rises at midday, The. Unmeasured Tempo. Maya Angelou. SP-AngeM

Sun Rising, The. John Donne. CP-DonnJ; MW-DonnJ

Sun rushed up the sky; the taxi flew, The. Parting as Descent. John Berryman. CP-BerrJ

Sun said, watching my watering-pot, The. Tenant-for-Life, The. Thomas Hardy. CP-HardT

Sun saw that widening shore, The. Sainte Anne De Beaupré. Richard Eberhart. CP-EberR

Sun Says His Prayers, The. Nicholas Vachel Lindsay. CP-LindV

Sun set, but set not his hope, The. Character. Ralph Waldo Emerson. CP-EmerR

Sun sets as the moon, The. City of the Moon, The. Kenneth Rexroth. CP-RexrK

Sun sets in the cold without friends, The. Dusk in Winter. W. S. Merwin. SP-MerwW

Sun sets out the autumn crocuses, The. Autumn Sunshine. D. H. Lawrence. CP-LawrD

Sun sets unevenly and the people / go to bed, The. Chasing the Bird. Robert Creeley. CP-CreeR

Sun sets wide the yellow crocuses, The. Amour. D. H. Lawrence. CP-LawrD

Sun shakes the man while, The. Getting There. Andrei Codrescu. SP-CodrA

Sun shines fair, the sun shines true, The. Paean. Dorothy Parker. CP-ParkD

Sun shines on the fields and on the town, The. Things. Christopher Logue. SP-LoguC

Sun shines, The. Tommies in the Train. D. H. Lawrence. CP-LawrD

Sun shines warm on seven old soldiers, The. Oldest Soldier, The. Robert Graves. CP-GravR

Sun sings out, as of old, The. Archangel's Song, The. Randall Jarrell. CP-JarrR

Sun / Slanting down, The. Light of Day. George Oppen. CP-OppGN

Sun slides down behind brick dust, The. Urban Renewal. Yusef Komunyakaa. CP-KomuY

Sun smudge on the smoky water. Autumn. Archibald MacLeish. CP-MacLA

Sun Song. Langston Hughes. CP-HughL; CP-HughL1

Sun! stay thy course, this moment stay. Secrets of Divine Love Are To Be Kept, The. Jeanne Marie Bouvier de la Motte- Guyon. CP-CowpW

Sun strikes the whale's back, The. Knowing the Enemy. Eleanor Wilner. SP-WilnE

Sun struts over the asphalt world, The. Noon of the Sunbather. Marge Piercy. SP-PierM

Sun Tan at Dusk. James Wright. CP-WrigJ

Sun, that brave man, The. Brave Man, The. Wallace Stevens. CP-StevW; CP-StevWP

Sun that brief December day, The. Snow-Bound [or Snow-Bound; a Winter Idyl]. John Greenleaf Whittier. CP-WhitJ

Sun, that seemed so mildly to retire, The. On a High Part of the Coast in Cumberland. William Wordsworth. CP-WorW2

Sun, the opulent sun of September, The. September Afternoon in the Abandoned Barracks. Adam Zagajewski. SP-ZagaA, tr. by Renata Gorczynski, Benjamin Ivry and C. K. Williams

Sun This March, The. Wallace Stevens. CP-StevW; CP-StevWP

Sun threw down a radiant spot, The. Sun's Last Look on the Country Girl, The. Thomas Hardy. CP-HardT

Sun. Tree. Beginning. God in a thicket. Crown. Two Portraits of Sex. Philip Larkin. CP-LarkP

Sun Underfoot Among the Sundews, The. Amy Clampitt. CP-ClamA

Sun was black with judgment, and the moon, The. Femina Contra Mundum. G. K. Chesterton. CP-ChesG

Sun was so fragile, so young, The. Morning in Vicenza, A. Adam Zagajewski. SP-ZagaA, tr. by Clare Cavanagh

Sun was strong enough today, The. Courtyard Thaw, A. Richard Wilbur. CP-WilbR

Sun went down—no Man looked on, The. Emily Dickinson. CP-DickE

Sun / when it's sundown, The. Sundown ("Sun / when it's sundown, The"). Federico García Lorca. CP-GarcF, tr. by Jerome Rothenberg Fr. Suite.

Sun! / Who was it named you. Sun. Federico García Lorca. CP-GarcF, tr. by Jerome Rothenberg Fr. Capriccios.

Sun Wields Mercy, The. Charles Bukowski. SP-BukC2

Sun will rise in me, A. Sun in Me. D. H. Lawrence. CP-LawrD

Sun with his hundred horns. Wake Up/Ring Out. Federico García Lorca. CP-GarcF, tr. by Jerome Rothenberg Fr. In the Garden of the Lunar Grapefruits.

Sun woke me this morning loud, The. True Account of Talking to the Sun at Fire Island, A. Frank O'Hara. SP-OharF

Sun-Women. D. H. Lawrence. CP-LawrD

Sun works up to a lather, The. March. Donald Davie. CP-DaviDC

Sun, you may send your haze gold. Haze Gold. Carl Sandburg. CP-SandC

Sunbather. Yusef Komunyakaa. CP-KomuY

Sunbather, to Herself, The. Raymond Carver. CP-CarvR

Sunbathing on a Rooftop in Berkeley. Maxine W. Kumin. SP-KumiM

Sunbeam on the well-waxed oak, A. Chink, The. Robert Graves. CP-GravR

Sunburst. Donald Davie. CP-DaviDC

Sunburst / in crystal, unleashed and surprised, The. Possessions. Pablo Neruda. SP-NeruP

Sunday. George Herbert. CP-HerbG

Sunday. Laura Riding Jackson. CP-RidiL
Sunday. Howard Nemerov. CP-NemeH
Sunday ("Mint bed is in"). James Schuyler. CP-SchuJ
Sunday ("Pears hang on the tree by stems"). James Schuyler. CP-SchuJ
Sunday. John Updike. CP-UpdiJ
Sunday. William Carlos Williams. CP-WilW1
Sunday, A. Walter De la Mare. CP-DeLaW
Sunday Afternoon in Italy. D. H. Lawrence. CP-LawrD
Sunday Afternoons. Yusef Komunyakaa. CP-KomuY
Sunday at Key West. Elizabeth Bishop. CP-BishE
Sunday at the End of Summer. Howard Nemerov. CP-NemeH
Sunday at the State Hospital. David Ignatow. SP-IgnaD
Sunday Before Advent. Christina Georgina Rossetti. CP-RosC2
Sunday. Buttons glitter on every coat. Understanding. Yannis Ritsos. SP-RitsY,
    tr. by Kimon Friar
Sunday by the Combination. Langston Hughes. CP-HughL; CP-HughL3
Sunday Drive, A. Margaret Atwood. SP-AtwM2
Sunday Evening. Adrienne Rich. CP-RicAE
Sunday, first day of summer. George Trakl Journal. Charles Wright. SP-WrigC
Sunday, 4 A.M. Elizabeth Bishop. CP-BishE
Sunday Greens. Rita Dove. SP-DoveR
Sunday in Boston. John Updike. CP-UpdiJ
Sunday in Inwood Park, Picnic. Adrienne Rich. CP-RicAE; SP-RicA2
Sunday in October. Richard Eberhart. CP-EberR
Sunday in the Country. May Swenson. SP-SwenM
Sunday in the Park. Louis MacNeice. CP-MacNL
Sunday is a large closet with winter clothing. 21 November 1948. Yannis Ritsos.
    SP-RitsY Fr. Exile's Journals 1.
Sunday. It's always Sunday. Not everyone can see the truth, but he can be it.
    Charles Wright. SP-WrigCN
Sunday lamb cracks in its fat, The. Mary's Song. Sylvia Plath. CP-PlatS
Sunday Lemons. Derek Walcott. CP-WalcD
Sunday moon, A. Yannis Ritsos. SP-RitsY Fr. First Series.
Sunday Morning. Donald Davie. CP-DaviDC
Sunday Morning. Louis MacNeice. CP-MacNL
Sunday Morning. Derek Mahon.
Sunday Morning. Wallace Stevens. CP-StevW; CP-StevWP
Sunday Morning Apples. Hart Crane. CP-CranH
Sunday Morning Prophecy. Langston Hughes. CP-HughL; CP-HughL2
Sunday Morning Tragedy, A. Thomas Hardy. CP-HardT
Sunday Morning with the Sensational Nightingales. Billy Collins. SP-CollB
Sunday Music. Amy Clampitt. CP-ClamA
Sunday Night. Raymond Carver. CP-CarvR
Sunday night and the park policemen tell each other it is dark as a. Picnic Boat.
    Carl Sandburg. CP-SandC
Sunday Night at Grandfather's. Rita Dove. SP-DoveR
Sunday papers are on the streets, The. Truth of the Matter, The. Howard
    Nemerov. CP-NemeH
Sunday Rain. John Updike. CP-UpdiJ
Sunday School Picnic: What Endures. Gregory Orr. SP-OrrG
Sunday, September Sunday . . . Outdoors. Appalachian Book of the Dead, The.
    Charles Wright. SP-WrigCN
Sunday Sermon. Andrei Codrescu. SP-CodrA
Sunday shuts down on this twentieth-century evening. Boy with His Hair Cut
    Short. Muriel Rukeyser. CP-RukeM
Sunday the fighting-cock. Folk Art. W. S. Merwin. SP-MerwW
Sunday the only day we don't work. Walk, A. Gary Snyder. CP-SnydG
Sunday was calm and airy. Stentor and Mourning. Alan Dugan. CP-DugaA
Sundays Kill More Men Than Bombs. Charles Bukowski. SP-BukC2
Sunday's motor-cars. Lorine Niedecker. CP-NiedL
Sundays of Satin-Legs Smith, The. Gwendolyn Brooks. SP-BrooG
Sundays, They Sleep Late. Muriel Rukeyser. CP-RukeM
Sundays too my father got up early. Those Winter Sundays. Robert Earl Hayden.
    CP-HaydR
Sunder me from my bones, O sword of God. Sword of Surprise, The. G. K.
    Chesterton. CP-ChesG
Sunderland. Howard Nemerov. CP-NemeH
Sundew, The. Algernon Charles Swinburne. SP-SwinA
Sundial on a Wet Day, The. Thomas Hardy. CP-HardT
Sundown. Alfonso Cortes. CP-MertT
Sundown ("On this exquisite sky"). Federico García Lorca. CP-GarcF, tr. by
    Jerome Rothenberg Fr. Shadow.
Sundown ("Sun / when it's sundown, The"). Federico García Lorca. CP-GarcF,
    tr. by Jerome Rothenberg Fr. Suite.
Sundown. Thomas Merton. CP-MertT
Sundown, white with ecstasy, hold. Sundown. Alfonso Cortes. CP-MertT
Sundown's mouth bites. Train Ride. Federico García Lorca. CP-GarcF, tr. by
    Jerome Rothenberg
Sunflower. Federico García Lorca. CP-GarcF, tr. by Jerome Rothenberg Fr.
    Barrage of Firework Poems on the Occasion of the Poet's Birthday.
Sunflower. John Updike. CP-UpdiJ
Sunflower Sutra. Allen Ginsberg. CP-GinsA; SP-GinsA
Sunflowers. Yannis Ritsos. SP-RitsY, tr. by Athan Anagnostopoulos
Sunflowers. William Carlos Williams. CP-WilW2
Sunflowers, The. Mary Oliver. SP-OlivM
Sunflowers, Repossessed. Eleanor Wilner. SP-WilnE
Sunglasses. John Updike. CP-UpdiJ
Sunglasses, The. Howard Nemerov. CP-NemeH
Sunk Lyonesse. Walter De la Mare. CP-DeLaW
Sunken Crown, The. Edwin Arlington Robinson. CP-RobiE
Sunken Garden, The. Walter De la Mare. CP-DeLaW
Sunlicht still on me, you row'd in clood, The. At My Father's Grave. Hugh
    MacDiarmid. SP-MacDH
Sunlight. Thom Gunn. CP-GunnT
Sunlight climbs the snowpeak. Late October Camping in the Sawtooths. Gary
    Snyder. CP-SnydG
Sunlight crumbling from rooftops beheads. Monday Morning: London. John
    Ciardi. CP-CiarJ
Sunlight glitters clean and bright, The. Hampton Beach. John Greenleaf Whittier.
    CP-WhitJ
Sunlight in a child's hair. Blessing, A ("Sunlight in a child's hair"). G. K.
    Chesterton. CP-ChesG
Sunlight in a, The. At the Faucet of June. William Carlos Williams. CP-WilW1
Sunlight Is Imagination. Richard Wilbur. CP-WilbR
Sunlight lies along my table. Weather of Six Mornings, The. Jane Cooper. CP-
    CoopJ
Sunlight, like Rouault, draws a line, The. Tourists at Ensenada. Thomas
    McGrath. SP-McGrT
Sunlight on the Garden, The. Louis MacNeice. CP-MacNL
Sunlight passes through the window into the room, The. You. Norman Dubie.
    CP-DubiN
Sunlight, Piercing the Gloom of this House, The. David Ignatow. SP-IgnaD
Sunlight so blurred with clouds we couldn't tell. Two Dedications. Donald
    Davie. CP-DaviDC
Sunlight strikes a glass of grapefruit juice. Morning in the Hospital Solarium.
    Sylvia Plath. CP-PlatS
Sunlight the tall women may never have seen. Children, the Sandbar, That
    Summer. Muriel Rukeyser. CP RukeM
Sunlight to the river. Ariadne To Theseus. Christina Georgina Rossetti. CP-
    RosC3
Sunlight upon Judæa's hills! Crucifixion, The. John Greenleaf Whittier. CP-
    WhitJ
Sunlight was over. E. E. Cummings. CP-CummE
Sunlit green of a late summer hayfield. Painting by Winifred Nicholson, A.
    Kathleen Jessie Raine. SP-RainK
Sunlit in a museum room. Copper Vat, A. A. K. Ramanujan. CP-RamaA
Sunlit, the lashes fringe the half-closed eyes. Window, The. Walter De la Mare.
    CP-DeLaW
Sunlit tree frog at the lake. Dream in an Old Language. A. K. Ramanujan. CP-
    RamaA
Sunne may set and rise, The. Sun May Set, The. Catullus. CP-RaleW, tr. by Sir
    Walter Alexander Raleigh Fr. Carmina.
Sunned in the South, and here to-day. To Flowers from Italy in Winter. Thomas
    Hardy. CP-HardT
Sunny day's complete Poussiniana, A. Poem Written at Morning. Wallace
    Stevens. CP-StevW; CP-StevWP
Sunny Prestatyn. Philip Larkin. CP-LarkP
Sunny shaft did I behold, A. Song: "Sunny shaft did I behold, A." Samuel
    Taylor Coleridge. CP-ColeS; MW-ColeS Fr. Zapolya.
Sunnyside Child. George Oppen. CP-OppGN
Sunrise. Walter De la Mare. CP-DeLaW
Sunrise. Robert Lowell. SP-LoweR
Sunrise. George Meredith. CP-MerG1
Sunrise. Mary Oliver. SP-OlivM
Sunrise Over Cassis. Adam Zagajewski. SP-ZagaA, tr. by Clare Cavanagh
Sunrise Ruby, The. Jelaluddin Rumi. SP-Rumi, tr. by Coleman Barks
Sunrise runs for Both, The. Emily Dickinson. CP-DickE
Sunrise wakes the lark to sing, The. Bird Raptures. Christina Georgina Rossetti.
    CP-RosC1
Sunrise with Crows. William Meredith. SP-MereW
Sun's a risin'. Hey! Hey! Langston Hughes. CP-HughL; CP-HughL1
Sun's a settin'. Hey! Langston Hughes. CP-HughL; CP-HughL1
Sun's gone dim, and, The. Two-Volume Novel. Dorothy Parker. CP-ParkD
Sun's Last Look on the Country Girl, The. Thomas Hardy. CP-HardT
Suns of eighteen centuries have shone, The. Gallows, The. John Greenleaf

Whittier. CP-WhitJ

Sun's setting, and the corner bar bangs its shutters, The. In Front of Casa Marcello. Joseph Brodsky. CP-BrodJ

Sun's Shame, The ("As some true chief of men, bowed down with stress"). Dante Gabriel Rossetti. CW-RossD *Fr.* House of Life, The.

Sun's Shame, The ("Beholding youth and hope in mockery caught"). Dante Gabriel Rossetti. CW-RossD *Fr.* House of Life, The.

Sun's / sky in / form of, The. Water. Robert Creeley. CP-CreeR

Suns that set, and moons that wane. On the Shortness of Life. William Cowper. CP-CowpW

Sun's white in the high fog, The. Heights, The. Louis Zukofsky. CP-ZukLS

Sun's wind, The. Photosynthesis. A. R. Ammons. CP-AmmoA

Sunset. Robert Creeley. CP-CreeR

Sunset ("Great carnal mountains"). E. E. Cummings. CP-CummE

Sunset ("Stinging / Gold swarms"). E. E. Cummings. CP-CummE

Sunset. Paul Laurence Dunbar. CP-DunbP

Sunset. Allen Ginsberg. CP-GinsA

Sunset. D. H. Lawrence. CP-LawrD

Sunset. James Schuyler. CP-SchuJ

Sunset. Robert Penn Warren. CP-WarrR

Sunset, A. Samuel Taylor Coleridge. CP-ColeS

(Upon the mountain's Edge all lightly resting.) CP-ColeS

Sunset, The. Percy Bysshe Shelley. CP-ShelP

Sunset, The. Jones Very. CP-VeryJ

Sunset after a Clouded Day in April. Jones Very. CP-VeryJ

Sunset after Rain. W. S. Merwin. SP-MerwW

Sunset and Dawn. G. K. Chesterton. CP-ChesG

Sunset and evening star. Crossing the Bar. Alfred Tennyson. CP-TennA

Sunset and Sunrise. William Cowper. CP-CowpW

Sunset at Fossoli. Primo Levi. CP-LeviP, *tr. by* Ruth Feldman *and* Brian Swann

Sunset at Night—is natural. Emily Dickinson. CP-DickE

Sunset at the Fair. Federico García Lorca. CP-GarcF, *tr. by* Jerome Rothenberg *Fr.* Fairs.

Sunset clings to the samovar, abandoning the veranda. Homage to Chekhov. Joseph Brodsky. CP-BrodJ, *tr. by* Jonathan Aaron

Sunset—Coney Island. Langston Hughes. CP-HughL; CP-HughL1

Sunset from Omaha Hotel Window. Carl Sandburg. CP-SandC

Sunset. I pull on. Feeding Time. Maxine W. Kumin. SP-KumiM

Sunset in Derby's Woods. Jones Very. CP-VeryJ

Sunset in Dixie. Langston Hughes. CP-HughL; CP-HughL2

Sunset in Haverhill, A. Jones Very. CP-VeryJ

Sunset, now that we're finally in it. Sunset II. Margaret Atwood. SP-AtwM2

Sunset of such aqueous hints, subdued, A. In Question. Denise Levertov. SP-LeveDS

Sunset of the City, A. Gwendolyn Brooks. SP-BrooG

Sunset on the Bearcamp. John Greenleaf Whittier. CP-WhitJ

Sunset over Villa Ortúzar. Jorge Luis Borges. SP-BorgJ, *tr. by* W. S. Merwin

Sunset Piece, The. Archibald MacLeish. CP-MacLA

Sunset S.S. Azemour. Allen Ginsberg. CP-GinsA

Sunset Scrupulously Observed. Robert Penn Warren. CP-WarrR

Sunset stopped on Cottages, The. Emily Dickinson. CP-DickE

Sunset swept / To the valley's west, you remember, The. Valley Song. Carl Sandburg. CP-SandC

Sunset that screens, reveals. Emily Dickinson. CP-DickE

Sunset: The Canary Islands. Miller Williams. CP-WillM

Sunset Threnody. Yusef Komunyakaa. CP-KomuY

Sunset II. Margaret Atwood. SP-AtwM2

Sunset Verse, The. D. H. Lawrence. CP-LawrD

Sunset Walk in Thaw-Time in Vermont. Robert Penn Warren. CP-WarrR

Sunset Water. W. S. Merwin. SP-MerwWF

Sunset Wings. Dante Gabriel Rossetti. CW-RossD

Sunset worn to its last vermilion he. Union in Disseverance. George Meredith. CP-MerG1

Sunset)edges become swiftly. E. E. Cummings. CP-CummE

Sunsets. Carl Sandburg. CP-SandC

Sunsets and the generations, The. Causes, The. Jorge Luis Borges. SP-BorgJ, *tr. by* Willis Barnstone

Sunshade, The. Thomas Hardy. CP-HardT

Sunshine. Nicholas Vachel Lindsay. CP-LindV

Sunshine. Christina Georgina Rossetti. CP-RosC3

Sunshine in morning field. Childhood Memory. Kathleen Jessie Raine. SP-RainK

Sunshine is wild here!, The. Postcard. Denise Levertov. SP-LeveDL

Sunshine / makes shade / acid blue. Buttered Greens. James Schuyler. CP-SextA

Sunshine on der medders. Warm Day in Winter, A. Paul Laurence Dunbar. CP-DunbP

Sunshine on Sandstone. John Updike. CP-UpdiJ

Sunshine was he. Ralph Waldo Emerson. CP-EmerR

Sunstroke. Ted Hughes. SP-HughTN

Sunstruck. Ted Hughes. SP-HughTN

Sunstruck Foxglove. Ted Hughes. SP-HughTN

Sunt Leones. Stevie Smith. CP-SmitS

Superfluities. Jones Very. CP-VeryJ

Superfluous Advice. Dorothy Parker. CP-ParkD

Superfluous were the Sun. Emily Dickinson. CP-DickE

Superior man's mind is terribly sharp, The. Han-shan. CP-ColdM, *tr. by* Red Pine

Superiorities. Richard Wilbur. CP-WilbR

Superiority to Fate. Emily Dickinson. CP-DickE

Superliminare. George Herbert. CP-HerbG

Superman. John Updike. CP-UpdiJ

Supermarket in California, A. Allen Ginsberg. CP-GinsA; SP-GinsA

Superscription, A. Dante Gabriel Rossetti. CW-RossD *Fr.* House of Life, The.

Superseded, The. Thomas Hardy. CP-HardT

Superstition. Samuel Taylor Coleridge. CP-ColeS

Superstition. Robert Graves. CP-GravR

Supinely we lie in the grove's shady greenery. Uninterpreted. James Whitcomb Riley. CP-RileJ

Supper after the Last, The. Galway Kinnell. SP-KinnGN

Supper o'er, with books, or converse sweet, The. Home, The ("Supper o'er, with books, or converse sweet, The"). Jones Very. CP-VeryJ

Supper with Lindsay. Theodore Roethke. CP-RoetT

Suppertime. Grace Paley. CP-PalGC

Supplanter, The. Thomas Hardy. CP-HardT

Supplanting, The. Wendell Berry. CP-BerrW

Supple haft, the helve, The. William Adams Delano. Archibald MacLeish. CP-MacLA

Supplement Hours. Walt Whitman. CP-WhitW

Supplement of an Imperfect Copy of Verses of Mr. William Shakespeare's, By the Author, A. Sir John Suckling. CP-SuckJ

Supplication for Love, A. Elizabeth Barrett Browning. CP-BroEB

Supplication of the Black Aberdeen. Rudyard Kipling. CP-KiplR

Supplication to the Muses on a Trying Day. Hart Crane. CP-CranH

Support for My Breathing. Yehuda Amichai. SP-AmicYL, *tr. by* Benjamin Harshav *and* Barbara Harshav

Supports, The. Rudyard Kipling. CP-KiplR *Fr.* Debits and Credits.

Suppose. Paul Laurence Dunbar. CP-DunbP

Suppose a lady has no other graces. Michelangelo Buonarroti. CP-Miche, *tr. by* John Frederick Nims

Suppose He Threw It in Your Face. Ogden Nash. CP-NashO

Suppose he wishes balloon routes. Wanting the Impossible. Carl Sandburg. CP-SandC

Suppose I Darken Your Door. Ogden Nash. CP-NashO

Suppose I had ingyne angelicall. Testament and Complaynt of our Soverane Lordis Papyngo, The. Sir David Lyndsay. SP-LyndD

Suppose I move a factory. To Market. C. K. Williams. CP-WillC

Suppose I say *summer*. Hummingbird. Raymond Carver. CP-CarvR

Suppose I were to take you blindfolded. Birthday Exercise, A. William Meredith. SP-MereW

Suppose / Life is an old man carrying flowers on his head. E. E. Cummings. CP-CummE; SP-CummE

Suppose some peddler offered. Market Economy, The. Marge Piercy. SP-PierM

Suppose that we part (work done, comes play). Pambo. Robert Browning. CP-BroR2

Suppose the Ceiling went Outside. Ceiling, The. Theodore Roethke. CP-RoetT

Suppose the dead could crown their wit. Responsory, 1948, A. Thomas Merton. CP-MertT

Suppose this was the root of everything. Golden Woman in a Silver Mirror, A. Wallace Stevens. CP-StevW; CP-StevWP

Suppose we could telephone the dead. Hotel de Dream. Jane Cooper. CP-CoopJ

Suppose we two were cast away. Love Song: "Suppose we two were cast away." Dorothy Parker. CP-ParkD

Suppose you have. Hard. Heather McHugh. SP-McHuH

Suppose you stood facing. Pierrot Le Fou. Adrienne Rich. CP-RicAE; SP-RicA2

Suppose your powers such. Polish Question, The. Theodore Weiss. SP-WeisT

Suppose your powers such. Theodore Weiss. SP-WeisT *Fr.* Polish Question, The.

Suppose you're a solo native here. Solo Native. Thomas Lux. SP-LuxT

Supposed Confessions of a Second-rate Sensitive Mind. Alfred Tennyson. CP-TennA

Supposed of Pamphylax the Antiochene. Death in the Desert, A. Robert Browning. CP-BroR1; SP-BroR

Supposing i dreamed this). E. E. Cummings. CP-CummE

Supposing I say: dogs are my neighbours. As Thyself! D. H. Lawrence. CP-LawrD

Supposing that I should have the courage. Stephen Crane. CP-CranS

Supposing the passionate fire your eyes enkindle. Michelangelo Buonarroti. CP-

Miche, *tr. by* John Frederick Nims

Suppressed Complex. T. S. Eliot. SP-ElioT

Suppressing the Evidence. Carolyn Kizer. CP-KizeC

Sup'rabundance of my store, The. Poores Portion, The. Robert Herrick. CP-HerrR

Supremacy. Edwin Arlington Robinson. CP-RobiE

Supreme Authority of the Imagination, The. Richard Eberhart. CP-EberR

Supreme Fortune Falls Soonest. Robert Herrick. CP-HerrR

Supreme in the distance, veiled. Unreturning Hosts, The. Kenneth Patchen. CP-PatcK

Supreme Surrender. Dante Gabriel Rossetti. CW-RossD *Fr.* House of Life, The.

Supreme test of one's poem, The. Poem: "Supreme test of one's poem, The." Andrei Codrescu. SP-CodrA

Sure. All the time I come upon the evil. Nameless. James Dickey. CP-DickJ

Sure as i am / of the seraphim. Lucifer Speaks in His Own Voice. Lucille Clifton. SP-ClifL

Sure, deck your lower limbs in pants. What's the Use. Ogden Nash. CP-NashO

Sure enough, moving, the thunder became men. Thunder by the Musician. Wallace Stevens. CP-StevW; CP-StevWP

Sure everybody laughs at. Old Dr God. James Laughlin. CP-LaugJ

Sure, / Herbert—. Ice Cream. Robert Creeley. CP-CreeR

Sure I fell in love. Yah. Robert Creeley. SP-CreeR

Sure I know you! White Man. Langston Hughes. CP-HughL; CP-HughL1

Sure Lord, there is enough in thee to dry. Sonnet: "Sure Lord, there is enough in thee to dry." George Herbert. CP-HerbG

Sure never did man see. My Lady's Lamentation and Complaint against the Dean. Jonathan Swift. CP-SwifJ

Sure never was heard so berhymed & beriddled! Time. George Meredith. CP-MerG2

"Sure," Said Benny Goodman. Hayden Carruth. CP-CarHS

Sure, there is a hierarchy. In Absence of the Tree. Clarence Major. SP-MajoC

Sure There Is Food. Kenneth Patchen. CP-PatcK

Sure there's some wondrous joy in doing good. Ode to the King. Jonathan Swift. CP-SwifJ

Sure you are Tyger rightly named. Address to Tyger. James Austen. CP-AustJ

Sure You Do. William Stafford. SP-StafWW

Surely among a rich man's flowering lawns. Meditations in Time of Civil War. William Butler Yeats. CP-YeatW

Surely among a rich man's flowering lawns. Ancestral Houses. William Butler Yeats. CP-YeatW *Fr.* Meditations in Time of Civil War.

Surely / Cued / motif smites truly to Beautifully, The. E. E. Cummings. CP-CummE

Surely He Hath Borne Our Griefs. Christina Georgina Rossetti. CP-RosC2

Surely I will be disquieted. August 17th. Anne Sexton. CP-SextA

Surely it has some virtue, having none. Red Rock of Utah. Donald Davie. CP-DaviDC

Surely it was us who encouraged. Rainer Maria Rilke. CP-RilkFr, *tr. by* A. Poulin, Jr. *Fr.* Roses, The.

Surely it wasn't your cultered mind. Guido Cavalcanti. CP-CavaG, *tr. by* Marc Cirigliano

Surely, Iuventius, one of this throng in Rome. Carmen 81. Catullus. CP-ZukLS *Fr.* Carmina.

Surely one of my finest days, I'd just. Extract from Memoirs. Howard Nemerov. CP-NemeH

Surely there, among the great docks, is peace, my mind. In Harbor. William Carlos Williams. CP-WilW1

Surely there is an aching void within. Christina Georgina Rossetti. CP-RosC3

Surely there was, at first, some love of letters. Full Professor, A. Howard Nemerov. CP-NemeH

Surely we knew our darkling shore. Birth of Venus, The. Hayden Carruth. CP-CarHS

Surely you paused at this roadside oasis. Garage in Co. Cork, A. Derek Mahon. CP-MahoD

Surely you stay my certain own, you stay. Love Note I: Surely. Gwendolyn Brooks. SP-BrooG

Surely you've trodden straight. Obsequial Ode. D. H. Lawrence. CP-LawrD

Surest thing there is is we are riders. Riders. Robert Frost. CP-FrosR

Surf: An Elegy. The. Robert Creeley. CP-CreeR

Surf-Casting. W. S. Merwin. SP-MerwW

Surface shine, the inner steel of track, The. Young Men, The. Muriel Rukeyser. CP-RukeM

Surface, The. May Swenson. SP-SwenM

Surfeits. Robert Herrick. CP-HerrR

Surfers beautiful as men, The. Middle-Aged Midwesterner at Waikiki Again. John Logan. CP-LogaJ

Surge of spirit that goes with using an axe, The. Felling a Tree. Ivor Gurney. SP-GurnI

Surgeon, The. Anne Sexton. CP-SextA

Surgeon at 2 A.M., The. Sylvia Plath. CP-PlatS

Surgeons. Robert Creeley. CP-CreeR

Surgeons must be very careful. Emily Dickinson. CP-DickE

Surgery. Yusef Komunyakaa. CP-KomuY

Surgical Ward: Men. Robert Graves. CP-GravR

Surly One, The. Theodore Roethke. CP-RoetT

Surly's old whore in her new silks doth swim. On Cashiered Capt[ain] Surly. Ben Jonson. CP-JonsB; SP-JonsB

Surplus. Wisława Szymborska. CP-SzymWM, *tr. by* Joanna Trzeciak

Surplus of Flowers in the World. Yehuda Amichai. SP-AmicYL, *tr. by* Benjamin Harshav *and* Barbara Harshav

Surprise. Dorothy Parker. CP-ParkD

Surprise is like a thrilling—pungent. Emily Dickinson. CP-DickE

Surprised by Evening. Robert Bly. SP-BlyR

Surprised by joy—impatient as the Wind. William Wordsworth. CP-WorW1

Surprises of the Superhuman, The. Wallace Stevens. CP-StevW; CP-StevWP

Surrender. Emily Dickinson. CP-DickE

Surreptitious you at bay doom loot is, my little Juventi. Catullus. *See* Purloining while you played in honeyed youth

Surrey. Donald Davie. CP-DaviDC

Surrounded by Mountains. William Stafford. SP-StafWW

Surrounded by Wild Turkeys. Gary Snyder. CP-SnydG

Surrounded by your glance. Tout Entouré de Mon Regard. Charles Tomlinson. CP-TomlC

Surrounded, The. Muriel Rukeyser. CP-RukeM

Sursum Corda. Ralph Waldo Emerson. CP-EmerR

Sursum Corda. Christina Georgina Rossetti. CP-RosC2

Survey of Literature. John Crowe Ransom. SP-RansJ

Survey of the Whole. May Swenson. SP-SwenM

Surveyor straightens from his theodolite, The. Guyana. Derek Walcott. CP-WalcD

Surview [*or* Surview: Cogitavi Vias Meas]. Thomas Hardy. CP-HardT

Survival. Rainer Maria Rilke. CP-RilkFr, *tr. by* A. Poulin, Jr.

Survival. William Stafford. SP-StafWW

Survival as Tao, Beginning at 5:00 A.M. Hayden Carruth. CP-CarHS

Survival in Missouri. John Ciardi. CP-CiarJ

Survival: Infantry. George Oppen. CP-OppGN

Survival of a Heart. Tess Gallagher. SP-GallT

Survival of the Fittest. Kenneth Rexroth. CP-RexrK

Survival Poem, The. Maxine W. Kumin. SP-KumiM

Surviving Love. John Berryman. CP-BerrJ

Surviving the Hurricane. Alan Dugan. CP-DugaA

Survivor. Thomas Kinsella. CP-KinsT

Survivor. Archibald MacLeish. CP-MacLA

Survivor, The. Robert Graves. CP-GravR

Survivor, The. Primo Levi. CP-LeviP, *tr. by* Ruth Feldman *and* Brian Swann

Survivor, The. Miller Williams. CP-WillM

Survivor among Graves, The. Randall Jarrell. CP-JarrR

Survivor and unwitting. Subway Singer, The. Amy Clampitt. CP-ClamA

Survivor sole, and hardly such, of all. Yardley Oak. William Cowper. CP-CowpW

Survivor's Ballad. Josephine Jacobsen. CP-JacoJ

Susana Bombal. Jorge Luis Borges. SP-BorgJ, *tr. by* Alastair Reid

Sushi. Paul Muldoon. CP-MuldP

Suspect, The. Yannis Ritsos. SP-RitsY, *tr. by* Kimon Friar

Suspended. Denise Levertov. SP-LeveDS

Suspended in a moving night. Corner Seat. Louis MacNeice. CP-MacNL

Suspended lion face. Solar. Philip Larkin. CP-LarkP

Suspenders. Raymond Carver. CP-CarvR

Suspense. Emily Dickinson. CP-DickE

Suspense. Thomas Hardy. CP-HardT

Suspense. D. H. Lawrence. CP-LawrD

Suspense. James Whitcomb Riley. CP-RileJ

Suspense—is Hostiler than Death. Emily Dickinson. CP-DickE

Suspension. Audre Lorde. SP-LordA

Suspicion. Constantine P. Cavafy. CP-CavaC, *tr. by* Theoharis Constantine Theoharis

Suspicion, Discontent, and Strife. Single Life Most Secure. Robert Herrick. CP-HerrR

Suspicion Makes Secure. Robert Herrick. CP-HerrR

Suspition upon His Over-much Familiarity with a Gentlewoman, The. Robert Herrick. CP-HerrR

Sussex. Donald Davie. CP-DaviDC

Sussex. Rudyard Kipling. CP-KiplR

Sussex Men are Noted Fools, The. William Blake. CP-BlakW

Sustainment. James Dickey. CP-DickJ

Sut Lovingood. Charles Olson. CP-OlsoC

Sutors o' Selkirk. Robert Burns. CP-BurnR

Sutter's Claim. James Whitcomb Riley. CP-RileJ

Suum Cuique. Ralph Waldo Emerson. CP-EmerR

Suzanne. John Logan. CP-LogaJ

Suzanne. William Carlos Williams. CP-WilW2

Suzy. William Carlos Williams. CP-WilW2

Swaddled to his nose against the chill. Vigil of Corpus Christi, The. Thom Gunn. CP-GunnT

Swaggering Gait, The. William Carlos Williams. CP-WilW2

Swallow, The. Jeanne Marie Bouvier de la Motte- Guyon. CP-CowpW

Swallow brings back blades of grass, The. Lindau. Eugenio Montale. CP-MontE, tr. by Jonathan Galassi

Swallow came from over the sea, The. George Meredith. CP-MerG2

Swallow, my sister, O sister swallow. Itylus. Algernon Charles Swinburne. SP-SwinA

Swallow, noiseless as a shadow, A. Patio. Robert Stock. SP-StocR

Swallow, privileged above the rest, The. John Dryden. SP-DrydJ Fr. Hind and the Panther, The.

Swallow—rebuilding, The. Ted Hughes. SP-HughTN

Swallow the Lake. Clarence Major. SP-MajoC

Swallows. Charles Tomlinson. SP-TomlC Fr. Portugeuse Pieces.

Swallows flew in the curves of an eight, The. Overlooking the River Stour. Thomas Hardy. CP-HardT

Swallows Flown. Walter De la Mare. CP-DeLaW

Swallows in the elderberry. L'Essor Saccadé. Wallace Stevens. CP-StevWP

Swallows in their torpid state, The. To the Rev. Mr. Newton. William Cowper. CP-CowpW

Swallows outshout. Swallows. Charles Tomlinson. SP-TomlC Fr. Portugeuse Pieces.

Swallows Return, The. Richard Eberhart. CP-EberR

Swallows' twisting southward-turning flock, The. Zeno. Randall Jarrell. CP-JarrR

Swallowtail, swallowtail. Backcountry Blues. Kenneth Patchen. CP-PatcK

Swamp, The. Derek Walcott. CP-WalcD

Swamp around the tower was alive, The. Dark Tower, The. Alan Dugan. CP-DugaA

Swamp maples' unmasked sugars'. Thinking Red. Amy Clampitt. CP-ClamA

Swamp Songs. Gregory Orr. SP-OrrG

Swan. Donald Hall. CP-HallD

Swan. D. H. Lawrence. CP-LawrD

Swan, The. Charles Baudelaire. CP-BaudC, tr. by Walter Martin

Swan, The. Ogden Nash. CP-NashO

Swan, The. Mary Oliver. SP-OlivM

Swan, The. Theodore Roethke. CP-RoetT

Swan erected in anger, stiffening his neck, A. Departure Platforms. Thomas Kinsella. CP-KinsT

Swan is the signet, heraldic joy, The. Banners, The. Robert Duncan. SP-DuncR

Swan of the heavens, The. Bird-Queen, The. Kenneth Patchen. CP-PatcK

Swan Ritual, The. A. R. Ammons. CP-AmmoA

Swan Song. Dorothy Parker. CP-ParkD

Swan Song of Parson Avery, The. John Greenleaf Whittier. CP-WhitJ

Swan swims on the water, A. Rainer Maria Rilke. CP-RilkFr, tr. by A. Poulin, Jr. Fr. Orchards.

Swank dinner, A. Food truly wonderful. Commerce. Raymond Carver. CP-CarvR

Swann has visited the Duc and Duchesse de Guermantes. Duchesse's Red Shoes, The. Norman Dubie. CP-DubiN

Swans. Louise Glück. SP-GlucL

Swans. I watch them. Canal. Charles Tomlinson. CP-TomlC; SP-TomlC

Swans, The. May Sarton. SP-SartM

Swans on the river, a great, The. Poem: "Swans on the river, a great, The." William Meredith. SP-MereW

Swans on the River Ayr. Mary Oliver. SP-OlivM

Swans sing before they die—'twere no bad thing. On a Volunteer Singer. Samuel Taylor Coleridge. CP-ColeS

Swans Walk My Brain in April It Rains, The. Charles Bukowski. SP-BukC2

Swarm, The. Sylvia Plath. CP-PlatS

Swarming Bees, The. James Laughlin. CP-LaugJ

Swatara, Swatara, black river. Countryman, The. Wallace Stevens. CP-StevW; CP-StevWP

Swath. Federico García Lorca. CP-GarcF, tr. by Jerome Rothenberg Fr. Night (Suite for Piano and Poet's Voice).

Swath of light climbs up the skyscraper, The. Evening Questions. Carl Sandburg. CP-SandC

Swathed round in mist and crown'd with cloud. George Meredith. CP-MerG1

Swatted a custardy small thing. Small. John Ciardi. CP-CiarJ

Swaying movement by the tumbling riverside, The. Movement. Arthur Rimbaud. CP-RimbA, tr. by Martin Sorrell

Swear by what the sages spoke. Under Ben Bulben. William Butler Yeats. CP-

YeatW

Swear to love and cherish her? To a Bridegroom. Thomas Hardy. CP-HardT

Sweat Lodge—The Afterwards. Peter Blue Cloud. SP-BlueP

Sweat, The. Gary Snyder. CP-SnydG

Sweater. Charles Bukowski. SP-BukC3

Sweating grinds, we stoked the boilers. Voyager Takes Pause, A. Robert Stock. SP-StocR

Sweaty Day in August, A. Charles Bukowski. SP-BukC3

Swede-bread honey and tea to breakfast half a canteloupe. Inside Stuff. Philip Whalen. SP-WhalP

Swedenborg. Lorine Niedecker. CP-NiedL

Sweeney. Anne Sexton. CP-SextA

Sweeney Agonistes. T. S. Eliot. CP-ElioT

Sweeney among the Nightingales. T. S. Eliot. CP-ElioT; SP-ElioT

Sweeney Erect. T. S. Eliot. CP-ElioT; SP-ElioT

Sweeney in Flight. Seamus Heaney. SP-HeanSO

Sweeney Redivivus. Seamus Heaney.

   Artist, An. SP-HeanSO

   Cleric, The. SP-HeanSO

   Drifting Off. SP-HeanSO

   First Flight, The. SP-HeanSO

   First Gloss, The. SP-HeanSO

   First Kingdom, The. SP-HeanSO

   Hermit, The. SP-HeanSO

   Holly. SP-HeanSO

   In Illo Tempore. SP-HeanSO

   In the Beech. SP-HeanSO

   Master, The. SP-HeanSO

   Old Icons, The. SP-HeanSO

   On the Road. SP-HeanSO

   Scribes, The. SP-HeanSO

   Sweeney Redivivus. SP-HeanSO

Sweeney Redivivus. Seamus Heaney. SP-HeanSO Fr. Sweeney Redivivus.

Sweep the house. Dead Baby, The. William Carlos Williams. CP-WilW1

Sweep the house clean. Love Song: "Sweep the house clean." William Carlos Williams. CP-WilW1

Sweeper of Ways, The. Howard Nemerov. CP-NemeH

Sweeping past the florist's came the baby and the girl. Girl and Baby Florist Sidewalk Pram Nineteen Seventy Something. Kenneth Koch. SP-KochK

Sweeping the Garden. Olga Broumas. SP-BrouO

Sweeping Wendy: Study in Fugue. Carl Sandburg. CP-SandC

Sweet, The. Ai. SP-Ai

Sweet, a delicate white mouse, A. Waltzer in the House, The. Stanley Kunitz. CP-KunSC

Sweet Acclamation of Death divulges it, The. Emily Dickinson. SP-DickE

Sweet Alice S. Morris, I am pleased, of course. Reply to a Lady Editor. Theodore Roethke. CP-RoetT

Sweet Amarillis, by a spring's. Upon Mistress Elizabeth Wheeler under the Name of Amarillis. Robert Herrick. CP-HerrR

Sweet and soft as summer, Darlings. Emily Dickinson. SP-DickE

Sweet and various the woodlark. Lawrence Ferlinghetti. SP-FerlL

Sweet anger, sweet disdain, sweet times of peace. Petrarch. CP-Petra, tr. by J. G. Nichols

Sweet are my Julia's lips and cleane. On Julias Lips. Robert Herrick. CP-HerrR

Sweet are the pleasures that to verse belong. To George Felton Mathew. John Keats. CP-KeatJ

Sweet as Eden is the air. Woodland Peace. George Meredith. CP-MerG1

Sweet as it is for seamen, who have sailed. Friendship: To J. M. S. Jones Very. CP-VeryJ

Sweet Auburn! liveliest village of the plain. Perverted Village, The. Ambrose Bierce. SP-BierA

Sweet babe, whose image here express'd. On the Picture of a Sleeping Child. Vincent Bourne. CP-CowpW

Sweet, be not proud of those two eyes. To Dianeme. Robert Herrick. CP-HerrR

Sweet bird, whom the winter constrains. Invitation to the Redbreast. Vincent Bourne. CP-CowpW

Sweet Boy, Gimme Yr Ass. Allen Ginsberg. CP-GinsA

Sweet Breakdowns of Abigail, The. Yehuda Amichai. SP-AmicY, tr. by Chana Bloch

Sweet briar rose has not a form more fair, The. Sabbatia, The. Jones Very. CP-VeryJ

Sweet Briars of the Stairways. Nicholas Vachel Lindsay. CP-LindV

Sweet Bridget blusht, & therewithall. Upon His Kinswoman Mistresse Bridget Herrick. Robert Herrick. CP-HerrR

Sweet brother, if I do not sleep. For My Brother: Reported Missing In Action, 1943. Thomas Merton. CP-MertT

Sweet child, / little girl with well-shaped legs. Ogre, The. William Carlos Williams. CP-WilW1

Sweet closes the evening on Craigieburn-wood. Craigieburn-Wood—A Song. Robert Burns. CP-BurnR

Sweet Corn. Peter Blue Cloud. SP-BlueP

Sweet country life, to such unknown. Country Life, to the Honored Mr. Endymion Porter[, Groome of the Bed-Chamber to His Maj.], The. Robert Herrick. CP-HerrR

Sweet cyder is a great thing. Great Things. Thomas Hardy. CP-HardT

Sweet Dancer. William Butler Yeats. CP-YeatW

Sweet day, so cool, so calm, so bright. Virtue [or Vertue]. George Herbert. CP-HerbG

Sweet Death. Christina Georgina Rossetti. CP-RosC1

Sweet Delia blest with every pleasing art. To a Friend Going to Sea. Annis Boudinot Stockton. CP-StocA

Sweet dimness of her loosened hair's downfall. Love-Sweetness. Dante Gabriel Rossetti. CW-RossD *Fr.* House of Life, The.

Sweet disorder in the dress[e], A. Delight in Disorder. Robert Herrick. CP-HerrR

Sweet earth, he ran and changed his shoes to go. Arrangements with Earth for Three Dead Friends. James Wright. CP-WrigJ

Sweet entrance to a husband's pleasure. Carmen 67. Catullus. CP-ZukLS *Fr.* Carmina.

Sweet, exclude me[e] not, nor be divided. Thomas Campion. CP-CampT

Sweet fa's the eve on Craigieburn. Robert Burns. CP-BurnR

Sweet Fern. John Greenleaf Whittier. CP-WhitJ

Sweet fish tinned in the innocence of sleep. Night Flight, over Ocean. John Updike. CP-UpdiJ

Sweet Flower! belike one day to have. To the Daisy ("Sweet Flower! belike one day to have"). William Wordsworth. CP-WorW1; MW-WorW

Sweet flower! that peeping from thy russet stem. On Observing a Blossom on the First of February 1796. Samuel Taylor Coleridge. CP-ColeS

Sweet floweret, pledge o' meikle love. On the Birth of a Posthumous Child, Born in Peculiar Circumstances of Family Distress. Robert Burns. CP-BurnR

Sweet girl! though only once we met. To a Beautiful Quaker. Lord Byron. CP-Byron

Sweet girls, sweet girls. Listen Here Blues. Langston Hughes. CP-HughL; CP-HughL1

Sweet glove, the witness of my secret bliss. Sir Philip Sidney. SP-SidnP *Fr.* Arcadia.

Sweet Highland Girl, a very shower. To the Highland Girl of Inversneyde. William Wordsworth. CP-WorW1

Sweet hours have perished here. Emily Dickinson. CP-DickE

Sweet Hussy, The. Thomas Hardy. CP-HardT

Sweet I blame you not for mine the fault was, had I not been made of common clay. Oscar Wilde. CP-WildO

Sweet inferno, gusting, funneled, A. Buffalo. Eugenio Montale. CP-MontE, *tr.* by Jonathan Galassi

Sweet is it as Life. Emily Dickinson. SP-DickE

Sweet is the light of infancy, and sweet. Infancy and Age. George Meredith. CP-MerG2

Sweet is the rest the righteous gain! Hymn: The Rest of the Righteous. Jones Very. CP-VeryJ

Sweet is the swamp with its secrets. Snake, A. Emily Dickinson. CP-DickE

Sweet is your antique body, not yet young. Sonnet, to a Child. Wilfred Owen. CP-OwenW

Sweet jesus, superman. Note, Passed to Superman. Lucille Clifton. SP-ClifL

Sweet Jesus, talking / his melancholy madness. Maybe. Mary Oliver. SP-OlivM

Sweet Justice of Norbiton, neighbour of Jones. George Meredith. CP-MerG2

Sweet Kiss, A. James Laughlin. CP-LaugJ

Sweet Lady Sleep, befriend me. Threat to a Fickle Lady. Dorothy Parker. CP-ParkD

"Sweet land" / at last! St. Francis Einstein of the Daffodils. William Carlos Williams. CP-WilW1

Sweet Land of Liberty. Emily Dickinson. SP-DickE

Sweet Levinsky. Allen Ginsberg. CP-GinsA

Sweet Life is dead.— / Not so. May. Christina Georgina Rossetti. CP-RosC3

Sweet Light. Raymond Carver. CP-CarvR

Sweet lips, there are songs about kisses now. Counting. Carl Sandburg. CP-SandC

Sweet little face, so full of slumber now. Mabel. James Whitcomb Riley. CP-RileJ

Sweet little myth of the nursery story. Red Riding-Hood. James Whitcomb Riley. CP-RileJ

Sweet Love,—but oh! most dread Desire of Love. Love's Fatality. Dante Gabriel Rossetti. CW-RossD *Fr.* House of Life, The.

Sweet love, sweet thorn, when lightly to my heart. Edna St. Vincent Millay. CP-MillE

Sweet Mariana gentle maid adieu. Annis Boudinot Stockton. CP-StocA

Sweet Mary the first time she ever was there. Mary. William Blake. CP-BlakW

Sweet Meat Has Sour Sauce. William Cowper. CP-CowpW

Sweet mildness of the late December day. Rent in the Screen, The. Howard Nemerov. CP-NemeH

Sweet mother, sweet muscle. Invocation: "Sweet mother, sweet muscle." Thomas Kinsella. CP-KinsT

Sweet Mountains—Ye tell Me no lie. Emily Dickinson. CP-DickE

Sweet Music. Charles Bukowski. SP-BukC1

Sweet naïveté of feature. On Seeing Miss Fontenelle in a Favourite Character. Robert Burns. CP-BurnR

Sweet night nursing a neighbor—. Night Watch. May Sarton. SP-SartM

Sweet nymph, who art, it seems, accused. To a Young Lady Who Stole a Pen. William Cowper. CP-CowpW

Sweet o' the Year, The. George Meredith. CP-MerG1

Sweet Oahu / Got petroleum. Slack Key Guitar. Allen Ginsberg. SP-GinsA

Sweet Oenone, doe but say. To Oenone. Robert Herrick. CP-HerrR

Sweet peace, where dost thou dwell? I humbly crave. Peace. George Herbert. CP-HerbG

Sweet Pirate of the heart. Emily Dickinson. CP-DickE

Sweet Poet, thou of whom these years that roll. To Philip Bourke Marston, inciting me to Poetic Work. Dante Gabriel Rossetti. CW-RossD

Sweet poplar, / sweet poplar. In Memoriam. Federico García Lorca. CP-GarcF, *tr.* by Catherine Brown

Sweet rains of summer. Sweetgrass. Peter Blue Cloud. SP-BlueP

Sweet recollection, Could the illusive scene. Elegy Inscribed to Richard J Stockton Esqr [Feb. 28, 1787]. Annis Boudinot Stockton. CP-StocA

Sweet, sad / nostalgia— . Robert Creeley. CP-CreeR

Sweet—safe—Houses. Emily Dickinson. CP-DickE

Sweet Sensibility Celestial power. Sensibility, an Ode. Annis Boudinot Stockton. CP-StocA

Sweet shepherd tenderly. Ivory Fragment. Rainer Maria Rilke. CP-RilkFr, *tr.* by A. Poulin, Jr. *Fr.* Orchards.

Sweet-Shop Round The Corner, The. Robert Graves. CP-GravR

Sweet Singer that I loe the maist. To Robert Burns. James Whitcomb Riley. CP-RileJ

Sweet Skepticism of the Heart. Emily Dickinson. CP-DickE

Sweet Sleep, with mellow palms trailed listlessly. Invocation, An. James Whitcomb Riley. CP-RileJ

Sweet smile, the daughter of the Queene of Love. Sonnet 39. Edmund Spenser. CP-Spens *Fr.* Amoretti.

Sweet sounds, begone— / Whose music on my ear. Music Unheard. Walter De la Mare. CP-DeLaW

Sweet sounds, oh, beautiful music, do not cease! On Hearing a Symphony of Beethoven. Edna St. Vincent Millay. CP-MillE

Sweet spot of nature deckd with every charm. Lines to My Brother from a Pavillion in His Garden. Annis Boudinot Stockton. CP-StocA

Sweet spot of nature hallowed by the tomb. On an Enclosure of Roses in Which Is the Grave of Miss Mary Morgan a Young Lady of 13 Years of Age Daughter of Col Morgan. Annis Boudinot Stockton. CP-StocA

Sweet spring day is glad with music, The. To Lydia Maria Child. John Greenleaf Whittier. CP-WhitJ

Sweet spring is your. E. E. Cummings. CP-CummE; SP-CummE

Sweet star, which gleaming o'er the darksome scene. To a Star. Percy Bysshe Shelley. CP-ShelP

Sweet stream-fed glen, why say 'farewell' to thee. Farewell to the Glen. Dante Gabriel Rossetti. CW-RossD *Fr.* House of Life, The.

Sweet stream, that winds through [or thro'] yonder glade. To a Young Lady. William Cowper. CP-CowpW

Sweet streamlet bason! at thy side. Arthur Hugh Clough. SP-ClouA

Sweet summer days had past & gone. Wandering Willie. George Meredith. CP-MerG2

Sweet, sweet, is sleep,—Ah! sweeter, to be stone. Michelangelo Buonarroti. CP-EmerR

Sweet, Sweet Is the Greeting of Eyes. John Keats. CP-KeatJ

Sweet sweet sound of distant waters falling. For Advent. Christina Georgina Rossetti. CP-RosC3

Sweet tenants of this grove! Joy in Martyrdom. Jeanne Marie Bouvier de la Motte- Guyon. CP-CowpW

Sweet Things. Thom Gunn. CP-GunnT

Sweet, thou art pale. Three Enemies, The. Christina Georgina Rossetti. CP-RosC1

Sweet, thou hast trod on a heart. False Step, A. Elizabeth Barrett Browning. CP-BroEB

Sweet, to have had them lost. Emily Dickinson. CP-DickE

Sweet toil for smitten hands. Emily Dickinson. SP-DickE

Sweet tooth taught us to admire, A. Bestiaries Are Out. W. H. Auden. CP-AudeW

Sweet twining hedgeflowers wind-stirred in no wise. Lovers' Walk, The. Dante Gabriel Rossetti. CW-RossD *Fr.* House of Life, The.

Sweet Violets. Dorothy Parker. CP-ParkD

Sweet virgin, that I do not set. Upon His Kinswoman Mistris Elizabeth Herrick.

Robert Herrick. CP-HerrR

Sweet Voice from the Kibbutz, The. Yehuda Amichai. SP-AmicYL, *tr. by* Benjamin Harshav *and* Barbara Harshav

Sweet Voices. Constantine P. Cavafy. CP-CavaC, *tr. by* Theoharis Constantine Theoharis

Sweet warrio[u]r, when shall I have peace with you? Sonnet 57. Edmund Spenser. CP-Spens *Fr.* Amoretti.

Sweet was the walk along the narrow lane. William Wordsworth. CP-WorW1

Sweet were the day[e]s, when thou didst lodge with Lot. Decay. George Herbert. CP-HerbG

Sweet [*or* Swete] were the sauce would please e[a]ch kind of tast[e]. In Commendation of George Gascoigne's Steel Glass. Sir Walter Ralegh. CP-RaleW

Sweet western wind, whose luck it is. To the Western Wind. Robert Herrick. CP-HerrR

Sweet Will. Philip Levine. SP-LeviP

Sweet Words on Race. Langston Hughes. CP-HughL; CP-HughL3

Sweet words that take. Sweet Words on Race. Langston Hughes. CP-HughL; CP-HughL3

Sweet—You forgot—but I remembered. Emily Dickinson. CP-DickE

Sweete, come againe. Thomas Campion *and* Philip Rosseter. CP-CampT

Sweet[e] were the joy[e]s that both might like and last. No Pleasure, Without Some Payne. Sir Walter Ralegh. CP-RaleW

Sweeten these bitter wild crabapples, Illinois. Crabapples. Carl Sandburg. CP-SandC

Sweeter than sour apples flesh to boys. Sonnet LXX: "Sweeter than sour apples flesh to boys." Ted Berrigan. SP-BerrT *Fr.* Sonnets, The.

Sweeter your face than grapes are, stewed to mush. Michelangelo Buonarroti. CP-Miche, *tr. by* John Frederick Nims

Sweeter your laugh than trill of lark at dawn. Sonnet: "Sweeter your laugh than trill of lark at dawn." Dorothy Parker. CP-ParkD

Sweetest blossoms die, The. Sweet Death. Christina Georgina Rossetti. CP-RosC1

Sweetest Elizabeth, accept I pray. To My Friend Elizabeth. Christina Georgina Rossetti. CP-RosC3

Sweetest Heresy received, The. Emily Dickinson. CP-DickE

Sweetest Loue since wee must part. Farewell, The: "Sweetest Loue since wee must part." Robert Herrick. CP-HerrR

Sweetest love, I do not go[e]. Song: "Sweetest love, I do not go[e]." John Donne. CP-DonnJ; MW-DonnJ

Sweetest May. Robert Burns. CP-BurnR

Sweetest of all childlike dreams. Vanishers, The. John Greenleaf Whittier. CP-WhitJ

Sweetest of sweets, I thank you: when displeasure. Church-Music[k]. George Herbert. CP-HerbG

Sweetest of the flowers a-blooming. Lily of the Valley, The. Paul Laurence Dunbar. CP-DunbP

Sweetest Saviour, if my soul. Dialogue, A. George Herbert. CP-HerbG

Sweetest way I think of you, The. Emily Dickinson. SP-DickE

Sweetgrass. Peter Blue Cloud. SP-BlueP

Sweetheart, do not love too long. O Do Not Love Too Long. William Butler Yeats. CP-YeatW

Sweetheart, I beg you to renew and seal. For Ever. Robert Graves. CP-GravR

Sweetheart, losing your looks, go to live in a village. Elegy: "Sweetheart, losing your looks, go to live in a village." Joseph Brodsky. CP-BrodJ

Sweetheart of the Csikos, The. Johann N. Vogl. CP-MerG2

Sweetheart, please send me the notebook I left. Letter. Raymond Carver. CP-CarvR

Sweethearts of the Year. Nicholas Vachel Lindsay. CP-LindV

Sweetness in a man, the very one about to set out to kill a stranger, The. From the Beginning. David Ignatow. SP-IgnaD

Sweetness of rest when Thou sheddest rest. Christina Georgina Rossetti. CP-RosC2

Sweetness of temper unsurpassed and unforgettable, A. Watering-Place Lady Inventoried, A. Thomas Hardy. CP-HardT

Sweetness of the Angelus, divine in the morning, The. "Rubén Dario." SP-DariR, *tr. by* Alberto Acereda *and* Will Derusha

Sweetnesse in Sacrifice. Robert Herrick. CP-HerrR

Sweets of Evening, The. Christopher Smart. SP-SmarC

Sweets of Pillage, can be known, The. Emily Dickinson. CP-DickE

Sweit rois [*or* Sweet rose] of vertew [*or* virtue] and of gentilnes [*or* gentleness]. To a Lady[e]. William Dunbar. CP-DunbW

Swell me a bowl with lusty wine. Ben Jonson. CP-JonsB *Fr.* Poetaster, The.

Swell People. Carl Sandburg. CP-SandC

Swelld limbs with no outline that you can descry. William Blake. CP-BlakW

Sweltering, close. Remember. Robert Creeley. CP-CreeR

Swept by every passing breeze. Whiteweed, The. Jones Very. CP-VeryJ

Swept from his fleet upon that fatal night. Shipwreck of Idomeneus, The. George Meredith. CP-MerG1

Swept snow, Li Po. Lorine Niedecker. CP-NiedL

Swerve, The. William Stafford. SP-StafWW

Swerving east, from rich industrial shadows. Here. Philip Larkin. CP-LarkP

Swi(/ across!gold's / rouNdly. E. E. Cummings. CP-CummE

Swift, The. Jones Very. CP-VeryJ

Swift and Slow. Ivor Gurney. SP-GurnI

Swift and sure the swallow. Christina Georgina Rossetti. CP-RosC2

Swift as a spirit hastening to his task. Triumph of Life, The. Percy Bysshe Shelley. CP-ShelP

Swift boomerang, come get! December 18th. Anne Sexton. SP-SextA *Fr.* Eighteen Days without You.

Swift cloud / across still cloud. Into Distance. Charles Tomlinson. CP-TomlC

Swift Completion of Their Appointed Rounds, The. Robert Stock. SP-StocR

Swift curve of the lip, nose, forehead. Head against White. Margaret Atwood. SP-AtwM1

Swift fall the blows, and men upbraid. George Meredith. CP-MerG1 *Fr.* France.

Swift fly the years! Men call thee mean and old. Hacker School House, The. Jones Very. CP-VeryJ

Swift has sailed into his rest. Swift's Epitaph. William Butler Yeats. CP-YeatW

Swift speeds the time, the time long since foretold. Fulness of the Gentiles, The. Jones Very. CP-VeryJ

Swift to Sheridan. Jonathan Swift. CP-SwifJ

Swift to the western bounds of this wide land. On the Completion of the Pacific Telegraph. Jones Very. CP-VeryJ

Swifter far than summer's flight—. Remembrance. Percy Bysshe Shelley. CP-ShelP

Swifter than aught 'neath the sun the car of Simonides moved him. Sepulchral. Rudyard Kipling. CP-KiplR *Fr.* Muse among the Motors, The.

Swiftly turn the murmuring wheel! Song for the Spinning Wheel (Founded upon a Belief Prevalent among the Pastoral Vales of Westmoreland). William Wordsworth. CP-WorW1

Swiftly walk o'er the western wave. To Night. Percy Bysshe Shelley. CP-ShelP

Swifts. Ted Hughes. SP-HughTN

Swift's Epitaph. William Butler Yeats. CP-YeatW

Swim in Co. Wicklow, A. Derek Mahon. CP-MahoD

Swim / on her. P—. Robert Creeley. SP-CreeR

Swim so now million many worlds in each. E. E. Cummings. CP-CummE

Swimmer, The. Louise Glück. SP-GlucL

Swimmer and Fish Group. Tennessee Williams. CP-WillT

Swimmer in the desert. Away from Water. Olga Broumas. SP-BrouO

Swimmers. May Swenson. SP-SwenM

Swimmers, The. Allen Tate. CP-TateA

Swimming By Night. James Merrill. SP-MerrJ

Swimming Chenango Lake. Charles Tomlinson. CP-TomlC; SP-TomlC

Swimming in the memorial. September. James Schuyler. CP-SchuJ

Swimming in the Pacific. Robert Penn Warren. CP-WarrR

Swimming Lesson, The. Mary Oliver. SP-OlivM

Swimming Pool, The. Thomas Lux. SP-LuxT

Swimming through dark, slow. Love Poem. Denise Levertov. SP-LeveDS

Swimming through the air, in schools upon the highways. Charles Olson. SP-OlsoC *Fr.* Maximus Poems, The.

Swinburne: A Critique. Ezra Pound. CP-PoEar

Swine Who's Eclipsed Me, The. Clarence Major. SP-MajoC

Swing by starwhite bones and. How to Enter a Big City. Thomas Merton. CP-MertT

Swing has its bold rhythm, The. Young Sibyl, The. Robert Graves. CP-GravR

Swing low so I. Gospel. Rita Dove. SP-DoveR

Swing Shift Blues. Alan Dugan. CP-DugaA

Swing-Song. Louis MacNeice. CP-MacNL

Swing, The. Seamus Heaney. SP-HeanSO

Swing yo' lady roun' an' roun'. Frolic, A. Paul Laurence Dunbar. CP-DunbP

Swinging Bridge, The. Richard Eberhart. CP-EberR

Swinging Down Central. Robert Creeley. CP-CreeR

Swinging mill bell changed its rate, The. Lone Striker, A. Robert Frost. CP-FrosR

Swinging / the colored afghan. Just Inside the Vigil of Christmas. Charles Olson. CP-OlsoC

Swirl. Carl Sandburg. CP-SandC

Swirl in the air where your head was once, A. Swirl. Carl Sandburg. CP-SandC

Swirls of Black Dust on Avenue D. Allen Ginsberg. CP-GinsA

Swiss Blue. Joseph Brodsky. CP-BrodJ

Switch on lights yellow as the sun. City Midnight Junk Strains. Allen Ginsberg. CP-GinsA; SP-GinsA

Switzerland. Matthew Arnold.

    Farewell, A: "My horse's feet beside the lake." SP-ArnoM

    Isolation: To Marguerite. SP-ArnoM

    Lake, The. SP-ArnoM

      (Meeting.) SP-ArnoM

    To Marguerite—Continued. SP-ArnoM

Switzerland. John Updike. CP-UpdiJ

Swivelled lantern flares, sheares, The. Navigators. Thomas Kinsella. CP-KinsT

Swollen infant under a tree, rose petals, A. Near the Bridge of Saint-Cloud. Norman Dubie. CP-DubiN

Swoon of noon, a trance of tide, A. In a Bye-Canal. Herman Melville. SP-MelvH

(Swooning)a pillar of youngly. E. E. Cummings. CP-CummE

Swooning swim to less and less. Buddha. Herman Melville. SP-MelvH

Swoop of hawk. Place, The ("Swoop of hawk"). Robert Creeley. SP-CreeR

Sword. Marilyn Hacker. SP-HackM

Sword, The. Charles Bukowski. SP-BukC3

Sword bites for peace, The. Another Voice. Richard Wilbur. CP-WilbR

Sword in his right hand, a stone in his left hand, A. Bronze David of Donatello, The. Randall Jarrell. CP-JarrR

Sword in length a reaping-hook amain. King Harald's Trance. George Meredith. CP-MerG1

Sword of Castruccio Castracani, The. Elizabeth Barrett Browning. CP-BroEB

Sword of Common Sense!—. To the Comic Spirit. George Meredith. CP-MerG1

Sword of sorrow, whetted sharp for me, The. Complaint of Annelida to False Arcite, The. Geoffrey Chaucer. CP-BroEB

Sword of Surprise, The. G. K. Chesterton. CP-ChesG

Sword was sheathed: in April's sun, The. Vow of Washington, The. John Greenleaf Whittier. CP-WhitJ

Sword will die just like the ripening cluster, The. Adam Is Your Ashes. Jorge Luis Borges. SP-BorgJ, tr. by Eric McHenry

Swordfish, I know you are tired: tiredout with the sharpness of your face. Undersea Fragment in Colons. James Dickey. CP-DickJ

Sycamore. Robert Frost. CP-FrosR

Sycamore, The. Wendell Berry. CP-BerrW

Sycamore, The. Marianne Craig Moore. CP-MoorM

Sycamore, by the heap of dead, The. Foreboding. Walter De la Mare. CP-DeLaW

Sycamores, The. John Greenleaf Whittier. CP-WhitJ

Syllable Pain, The. Paul Celan. SP-CelaP, tr. by John Felstiner

Syllables. Heather McHugh. SP-McHuH

Syllogism makes one from many, A. Guido Cavalcanti. CP-CavaG, tr. by Marc Cirigliano

Sylph was it? or a Bird more bright. Rural Illusions. William Wordsworth. CP-WorW2

Sylvae [or Silvae]. Publius Papinius Statius.
   On Sleep. CP-CunnJ
   "Polish'd with endless toil, my lays." CP-JohnS

Sylvae. Donald Davie. CP-DaviDC

Sylvan slopes with corn clad fields, The. September, 1819. William Wordsworth. CP-WorW2

Sylvester's Dying Bed. Langston Hughes. CP-HughL; CP-HughL2

Sylvia, my faithful. Isis Speaks. Denise Levertov. SP-LeveDL

Sylvia said: When I was younger. My Friend. Jane Cooper. CP-CoopJ

Sylvia the fair, in the bloom of fifteen. New Song, A: "Sylvia the fair, in the bloom of fifteen." John Dryden. CP-DryJ2

Sylvia's Death. Anne Sexton. CP-SextA

Symbol. Federico García Lorca. CP-GarcF, tr. by Jerome Rothenberg Fr. Mirror Suite.

Symbol from the first, of mastery, A. Staff of Aesculapius, The. Marianne Craig Moore. CP-MoorM

Symbol inside this poem is my father's feet, The. Pawnbroker, The. Maxine W. Kumin. SP-KumiM

Symbol of war, a war, The. All That is Perfect in Woman. William Carlos Williams. CP-WilW2

Symbols. Christina Georgina Rossetti. CP-RosC1

Symbols. William Butler Yeats. CP-YeatW

Symbols. Everything's symbols. Psyche-type (Psychotype). Fernando Pessoa. SP-PessF, tr. by Susan M. Brown and Edwin Honig

Symmetrical Poem. Michael Palmer. SP-PalmM

Symmetrical Poem: They were afraid of death. Michael Palmer. SP-PalmM

Symmetries & Asymmetries. W. H. Auden. CP-AudeW

Symmetries, harmonies. Mandelstam in the Crimea. Donald Davie. CP-DaviDC

Symmetry. Andrei Codrescu. SP-CodrA

Symmetry of Thought, A. A. R. Ammons. CP-AmmoA

Sympathetic Horror. Charles Baudelaire. CP-BaudC, tr. by Walter Martin

Sympathetic Portrait of a Child. William Carlos Williams. CP-WilW1

Sympathy. Emily Jane Brontë. CP-BronE

Sympathy ("I know what the caged bird feels, alas!"). Paul Laurence Dunbar. CP-DunbP

Sympathy ("Tear another's tears bring forth, The"). Paul Laurence Dunbar. CP-DunbP

Sympathy. D. H. Lawrence. CP-LawrD

Sympathy. Henry David Thoreau. CP-ThorH

Sympathy, A Welcome, A. John Berryman. CP-BerrJ

Sympathy co incidence: that the. George Oppen. CP-OppGN

Sympathy in White Major. Philip Larkin. CP-LarkP

Symphony for a Sea Bird. Chuang Tzu. CP-MertT

Symphony in Yellow. Oscar Wilde. CP-WildO

Symposium. Paul Muldoon. CP-MuldP

Symposium, The. James Vincent Cunningham. CP-CunnJ

Symptom of the Gale, The. Emily Dickinson. CP-DickE

Symptom Recital. Dorothy Parker. CP-ParkD

Symptoms. Robert Lowell. SP-LoweR

Symptoms. James Whitcomb Riley. CP-RileJ

Symptoms Of Love. Robert Graves. CP-GravR

Symptoms of Love, The. William Cowper. CP-CowpW

Synagogue dispirits the deep street, The. Synagogue, The. Karl Shapiro. SP-ShapK

Synagogue in Firenze, The. Yehuda Amichai. SP-AmicYI., tr. by Benjamin Harshav and Barbara Harshav

Synagogue, The. Karl Shapiro. SP-ShapK

Synamism. Lorine Niedecker. CP-NiedL

Synapse, The. Robert Stock. SP-StocR

Syncopated Cakewalk, The. Clarence Major. SP-MajoC

Synonyms. Robert Penn Warren. CP-WarrR

Synthetic Such. Robert Graves. CP-GravR

Syphilitic selling violets calmly, The. Moment Fugue. Hart Crane. CP-CranH

Syria. Eugenio Montale. CP-MontE, tr. by Jonathan Galassi

Syringa. John Ashbery. SP-AshbJ

Syrinx. Amy Clampitt. CP-ClamA

Syrinx. James Merrill. SP-MerrJ

System, The. John Ashbery. SP-AshbJ

System, The. Stanley Kunitz. CP-KunSC

System was breaking down, The. The one who had wandered alone past so. System, The. John Ashbery. SP-AshbJ

Systemic. Rae Armantrout. SP-ArmaA

Syzygy. Yusef Komunyakaa. CP-KomuY

T

T. A. H. Ambrose Bierce. SP-BierA

T.A.M. E. E. Cummings. CP-CummE

T. C. Philips. James Whitcomb Riley. CP-RileJ

T. E. Lawrence. Lorine Niedecker. CP-NiedL

T,h;r:u:h;e:s / are / silent / now. E. E. Cummings. CP-CummE

'T is better to sit here beside the sea. Silence. Paul Laurence Dunbar. CP-DunbP

'T is done—and shivering in the gale. Stanzas to a Lady on Leaving England. Lord Byron. CP-Byron

'T is done—but yesterday a King! Ode to Napoleon Buonaparte. Lord Byron. CP-Byron

'T is done!—I saw it in my dreams. Remembrance. Lord Byron. CP-Byron

'T is fifty years, and yet their fray. Duel, The. Lord Byron. CP-Byron

'T is midnight—but it is not dark. Venice. Lord Byron. CP-Byron

'T is over, Moses! All is lost! Letter, A. John Greenleaf Whittier. CP-WhitJ

'T is said that in the Holy Land. My Thanks. John Greenleaf Whittier. CP-WhitJ

'T is the noon of the spring-time, yet never a bird. April. John Greenleaf Whittier. CP-WhitJ

T.M. Charles Bukowski. SP-BukC1

T / O. Philip Whalen. SP-WhalP

T. S. Eliot (1928). Donald Davie. CP-DaviDC

T' snow is witherin' off'n th' gress—. Drained Cup, The. D. H. Lawrence. CP-LawrD

T the Great. W. H. Auden. CP-AudeW

T, the TURTLE, has been a long time coming. John Ciardi. CP-CiarJ

'T was night. The tranquil moonlight smile. Toussaint L'Ouverture. John Greenleaf Whittier. CP-WhitJ

'T was now the noon of night, and all was still. Soliloquy of a Bard in the Country. Lord Byron. CP-Byron

'T were extreme folly should I dare attempt. Upon the Author. Unknown. CP-BradA

'T will soon appear if we but look. Henry David Thoreau. CP-ThorH

Ta / ppin / g / toe / hip. E. E. Cummings. CP-CummE

Tabernacle. D. H. Lawrence. CP-LawrD

Tabernacle, The. James Tate. SP-TateJ

Tabernacle Window. Paul Celan. SP-CelaP, tr. by John Felstiner

Tabill of Confessioun, The. William Dunbar. CP-DunbW

Tabitha dressed for her wedding. Wedding Morning, The. Thomas Hardy. CP-HardT

Table, The. Carlos Drummond de Andrade. CP-BishE

Table, The. Robert Creeley. SP-CreeR

Table, The. Donald Hall. CP-HallD

Table describes, The. Dish of Fruit, The. William Carlos Williams. CP-WilW2

Table for two will scarcely seat, A. Paris. Paul Muldoon. CP-MuldP

Table hurled itself, to our surprise, The. Lingard and the Stars. Edwin Arlington Robinson. CP-RobiE

Table is cleared of my place, The. Hold Me. Philip Levine. SP-LeviP

Table is laid, The. From Later to Earlier. Laura Riding Jackson. CP-RidiL

Table of Green Fields, A. James Schuyler. CP-SchuJ

Table 1. Czeslaw Milosz. CP-MiloC; CP-MiloCN, tr. by Robert Hass

Table Talk. William Cowper. CP-CowpW

Table Talk. Ogden Nash. CP-NashO

Table Talk. Wallace Stevens. CP-StevWP

Table 2. Czeslaw Milosz. CP-MiloC; CP-MiloCN, tr. by Robert Hass

Tableau. Countee Cullen. CP-CullC

Tableau at Twilight. Ogden Nash. CP-NashO

Tableau de l'Inconstance des Mauvais Anges. Stevie Smith. CP-SmitS

Tableau Vivant. Tess Gallagher. SP-GallT

Tableau Vivant. Gregory Orr. SP-OrrG

Tables Turned, The. William Wordsworth. CP-WorW1
　(Up! up! my friend, and clear your looks.) MW-WorW

Taboo to Boot. Ogden Nash. CP-NashO

Tabula Rasa. Hayden Carruth. CP-CarHS

Taciturn, The. Walter De la Mare. CP-DeLaW

Tact. Ralph Waldo Emerson. CP-EmerR

Tact. Edwin Arlington Robinson. CP-RobiE

Tadpole, it's not time yet to nag you. Upon Seeing An Ultrasound Photo of an Unborn Child. Thomas Lux. SP-LuxT

Tædium Vitæ. Oscar Wilde. CP-WildO

Tag. Langston Hughes. CP-HughL; CP-HughL3

Tags of songs, like salvaged buttons. Poem, A: "Tags of songs, like salvaged buttons." James Schuyler. CP-SchuJ

Tagus farewell, that westward with thy streams. In Spayn. Sir Thomas Wyatt. CP-WyatT

Tail-spinning from the shelves of sky. Jubilo. Allen Tate. CP-TateA

Tail turned to red sunset on a juniper crown a lone magpie cawks. 136 Syllables at Rocky Mountain Dharma Center. Allen Ginsberg. SP-GinsA

Tailor, The. Walter De la Mare. CP-DeLaW

Tailpiece. Samuel Beckett. CP-BeckS

Tailpiece. William Carlos Williams. CP-WilW2

Tails. C. K. Williams. CP-WillC

Take a feller 'at's sick and laid up on the shelf. Them Flowers. James Whitcomb Riley. CP-RileJ

Take a hold now. Pals. Carl Sandburg. CP-SandC

Take a lunatic. Iron Hans. Anne Sexton. CP-SextA

Take a model of the world so big. Rescued Year, The. William Stafford. SP-StafW; SP-StafWW

Take a red book called Telephone. Telephone. Anne Sexton. CP-SextA

Take a trip with me. Small Excursion, A. Mona Van Duyn. SP-VanDM

Take all away. Emily Dickinson. CP-DickE

Take all away from me, but leave me Ecstasy. Emily Dickinson. CP-DickE

Take away all this crystal and silver. Bowls. D. H. Lawrence. CP-LawrD

Take away your knowledge, Doktor. Doctor of the Heart, The. Anne Sexton. CP-SextA

Take Care. Heather McHugh. SP-McHuH

Take Care. A. K. Ramanujan. CP-RamaA

Take Care Of Him. Christina Georgina Rossetti. CP-RosC2

Take care when you speak to me. When You Speak to Me. Tess Gallagher. SP-GallT

Take down its ears first. Dismantling the Silence. Charles Simic. SP-SimiC; SP-SimiCE

Take for example this. E. E. Cummings. CP-CummE

Take from me something. Chance Meeting. "H. D." CP-DoolH

Take Hands. Laura Riding Jackson. CP-RidiL

Take heart! Your zebra will make. Lock, The. Robert Stock. SP-StocR

Take heed betime, lest ye be spied. Sir Thomas Wyatt. CP-WyatT

Take heed of loving me[e]. Prohibition, The. John Donne. CP-DonnJ; MW-DonnJ

Take hold of the shaft of the pen. First Gloss, The. Seamus Heaney. SP-HeanSO Fr. Sweeney Redivivus.

Take in a lyric information. Essay on Poetics. A. R. Ammons. CP-AmmoA

Take It. Charles Bukowski. SP-BukC3

Take it away, and swallow it yourself. Island, An. Edwin Arlington Robinson. CP-RobiE

Take it bright day first hour. Took. Kenneth Rexroth. CP-RexrK

Take it from me kiddo. Poem, or Beauty Hurts Mr. Vinal. E. E. Cummings. CP-CummE; SP-CummE

Take it out in vile whiskey, take it out. Impromptu: The Suckers. William Carlos Williams. CP-WilW1

Take Mans Fat and Cats Fat, of each half an Ounce. Oyntment to Alure Fish to the Bait. Raymond Carver. CP-CarvR

Take me by the hand. Music. Rainer Maria Rilke. CP-RilkFr, tr. by A. Poulin, Jr.

Take me or leave me, cries. Melody Grundy. Denise Levertov. SP-LeveDP

Take mine advise, and go not neere. To his Booke. Robert Herrick. CP-HerrR

Take my heart in thy hand, O beautiful boy of Schiraz! Hafiz. CP-EmerR Fr. Odes.

Take my love, it is not true. Complaint of the Skeleton to Time. Allen Ginsberg. CP-GinsA

Take No Thought for The Morrow. Christina Georgina Rossetti. CP-RosC2

Take, O take the key of Rome. Rafael Alberti. CP-MertT Fr. Roman Nocturnes.

Take of English earth as much. Charm, A. Rudyard Kipling. CP-KiplR

Take-off over Kansas. John Ciardi. CP-CiarJ

Take off your cloak and your hat. December Night. D. H. Lawrence. CP-LawrD

Take off your clothes, love. Old Song. Robert Creeley. CP-CreeR

Take Off Your Socks!! James Laughlin. CP-LaugJ

Take One Home for the Kiddies. Philip Larkin. CP-LarkP

Take one Pompeii-eyed old man. In Walked Bud with a Palette. Clarence Major. SP-MajoC

Take our hands, James Russell Lowell. Welcome to Lowell, A. John Greenleaf Whittier. CP-WhitJ

Take out of time that moment when you stood. Acceptances. Jane Cooper. CP-CoopJ

Take some one in England with brains enough. Genesis. William Carlos Williams. CP-WilW1

Take Something Like a Star. Robert Frost. See Choose Something like a Star

Take telegraph wires, a lonely moor. Telegraph Wires. Ted Hughes. SP-HughTN

Take that, damn you; and that! Mezzo Forte. William Carlos Williams. CP-WilW1

Take the cloak from his face, and at first. After. Robert Browning. CP-BroR1

Take the crystal cup from the fawn. Shmuel HaNagid. SP-HaNaS, tr. by Peter Cole

Take the general mumble. Notes to a Neophyte. Sylvia Plath. CP-PlatS

Take the hands / off of. Hands, The. Robert Creeley. CP-CreeR

Take the lump in your throat. Soup, The. Charles Simic. SP-SimiC

Take the steep stairs up to where the rafters meet. Razed House, The. Wyatt Prunty. SP-PrunW

Take the useful events. Instructions for Angels. Kenneth Patchen. CP-PatcK

Take, then, my answer. K, The. Charles Olson. CP-OlsoC

Take these mortal incarnations. Shih-te. CP-ColdM, tr. by Red Pine

Take these, times tardy truants, sent by me. Upon Two Greene Apricockes Sent to Cowley by Sir Crashaw. Richard Crashaw. CP-CrasR

Take this from one who, though his worth. Mirth. G. K. Chesterton. CP-ChesG

Take this kiss upon the brow! Dream within a Dream, A. Edgar Allan Poe. CP-PoeEd

Take this purse, Beggar! you only whine. Alms. Stéphane Mallarmé. CP-MallS, tr. by Henry Weinfield

Take this, the nexus. Love Charm, The. William Carlos Williams. CP-WilW2

Take thy lute and sing. Flower of the Ruins, The. George Meredith. CP-MerG1

Take Time Out. Maya Angelou. SP-AngeM

Take to thy bosom, gentle earth, a swain. Another ["Take to thy bosom, gentle earth, a swain"]. Unknown. CP-CowpW

Take, 25:iii:59. Philip Whalen. SP-WhalP

Take up the White Man's burden. White Man's Burden, The. Rudyard Kipling. CP-KiplR

Take what you want, we'll throw the rest away. Photographs. Mona Van Duyn. SP-VanDM

Take ye heed, watch and pray: for ye know not when the time is. Mark 13:33. Jones Very. CP-VeryJ

Take your fill of intimate remorse, perfumed sorrow. Right to Grief, The. Carl Sandburg. CP-SandC

Take Your Heaven further on. Emily Dickinson. CP-DickE

Taken. Constantine P. Cavafy. CP-CavaC, tr. by Theoharis Constantine Theoharis

Taken for Granted. Louis MacNeice. CP-MacNL

Taken from men—this morning. Emily Dickinson. CP-DickE

Taken off into / the terrain. Stretto. Paul Celan. SP-CelaP, tr. by John Felstiner

Takeoff on Armageddon —For Ronald Reagan. Alan Dugan. CP-DugaA

Takeover / of America, The. Ethnic Jammies. Andrei Codrescu. SP-CodrA

Taker, The. Anne Sexton. CP-SextA

Takes time where wild the. Thyme. Louis Zukofsky. CP-ZukLS

Taking a husband's duties to heart. Fred. Miller Williams. CP-WillM

Taking a walk on her first retirement day. New Territory. Wyatt Prunty. SP-PrunW

Taking a Walk with You. Kenneth Koch. SP-KochK

Taking Down, The. Wyatt Prunty. SP-PrunW

Taking, giving back their lives. Field Hospital, The. Paul Muldoon. CP-MuldP

Taking in Wash. Rita Dove. SP-DoveR

Taking infection from the vulgar air. Words of the Preacher, The. Stanley Kunitz. CP-KunSC

Taking into consideration all your loveliness. Papa and Mama Dance, The. Anne Sexton. CP-SextA; SP-SextA

Taking Leave of a Friend. Li Po. SP-PounE, *tr.* by Ezra Pound

Taking Notice. Marilyn Hacker.

"And I shout at Iva, whine at you. Easily." SP-HackM

"Angry, I speak, and pass the hurt to you." SP-HackM

"As yoked to her by absence as by prescence." SP-HackM

"Grizzled doorman lets the doctors' wives, The." SP-HackM

"I will never be only a Lesbian." SP-HackM

"If we talk, we're too tired to make love; if we." SP-HackM

"I'll tell you what I don't want: an affair." SP-HackM

"Morning: the phone jangles me from words: you." SP-HackM

"My child wants dolls, a tutu, that girls' world made." SP-HackM

"No better lost than any other woman." SP-HackM

"She twists scraps of her hair in unshelled snails," SP-HackM

"When I read poems to the art students." SP-HackM

"When that jackbooted choreography." SP-HackM

Taking of Little Tony Camborio on the Seville Highway, The. Federico García Lorca. CP-GarcF, *tr.* by Will Kirkland

Taking of Lungtungpen, The. Rudyard Kipling. *Fr.* Plain Tales from the Hills.

Taking off at dawn. If I Take the Wings of the Morning. Donald Davie. CP-DaviDC

Taking off at sunset over the city. Address to the Angels. Maxine W. Kumin. SP-KumiM

Taking Off Emily Dickinson's Clothes. Billy Collins. SP-CollB

Taking off from Kennedy. Grave The Well, The. Donald Hall. CP-HallD

Taking off glasses. LOVE 2: What He Said, Groping. A. K. Ramanujan. CP-RamaA

Taking root in windy sand. Dunes. A. R. Ammons. CP-AmmoA

Taking Stock of Lot. Robert Stock. SP-StocR

Taking up the fair Ideal. Emily Dickinson. CP-DickE

Taking what is, and seeing it as it is. Vermeer. Howard Nemerov. CP-NemeH

Takis Sinopolus, Greek Poet. Yehuda Amichai. SP-AmicYL, *tr.* by Benjamin Harshav and Barbara Harshav

Takis Sinopolus has eyes the color of the sea. Takis Sinopolus, Greek Poet. Yehuda Amichai. SP-AmicYL, *tr.* by Benjamin Harshav and Barbara Harshav

Talbot Road. Thom Gunn. CP-GunnT

Talcahuano. Gabriela Mistral. SP-MistG, *tr.* by Maria Giachetti [*or* Jacketti]

Tale. W. S. Merwin. SP-MerwW

Tale. Howard Nemerov. CP-NemeH

Tale. Arthur Rimbaud. CP-RimbA, *tr.* by Martin Sorrell

Tale, A. Louise Bogan. CP-BogaL

Tale, A. Joseph Brodsky. CP-BrodJ

Tale, A. Robert Burns. CP-BurnR

Tale, A: "In Scotland's realm, where trees are few." William Cowper. CP-CowpW

Tale Begun, A. Wisława Szymborska. SP-SzymW, *tr.* by Stanislaw Barańczak and Clare Cavanagh

Tale for Roman guides to tell, A. Saint Gregory's Guest. John Greenleaf Whittier. CP-WhitJ

Tale, Founded on a Fact, A. William Cowper. CP-CowpW

Tale of a Later Leander. John Logan. CP-LoganJ

Tale of a Tub. Sylvia Plath. CP-PlatS

Tale of Courtship. John Logan. CP-LoganJ *Fr.* Epilogue, Songs of the Spouses, Complaint of Love.

Tale of Custard the Dragon, The. Ogden Nash. CP-NashO

Tale of Modernity. Laura Riding Jackson. CP-RidiL

Tale of Society As It Is, A: From Facts, 1811. Percy Bysshe Shelley. CP-ShelP

Tale of the Airly Days, A. James Whitcomb Riley. CP-RileJ

Tale of the Tiger Tree, The. Nicholas Vachel Lindsay. CP-LindV

Tale of the T——d, The. Thomas Sheridan. CP-SherT

Tale of Time. Robert Penn Warren. CP-WarrR

Tale of Two Cities, A. Rudyard Kipling. CP-KiplR

Tale of Villafranca, A. Elizabeth Barrett Browning. CP-BroEB

Tale Told by an Idiot, A. D. H. Lawrence. CP-LawrD

Taleb, with eyes that saw the gold of Kuwait. Poem about Repairs to My House. Yehuda Amichai. SP-AmicYL, *tr.* by Benjamin Harshav and Barbara Harshav

Talent is what they say. For the Young Who Want To. Marge Piercy. SP-PierM

Talented creatures, on the defensive because. Insignificant Elephants. W. H. Auden. CP-AudeW

Talented old gentleman painting a hedge, A. When Walking. Stevie Smith. CP-SmitS

Tales. George Crabbe.

Edward Shore. SP-CrabG

Frank Courtship, The. SP-CrabG

Mother, The. SP-CrabG

Wager, The. SP-CrabG

Tales of a Wayside Inn. Henry Wadsworth Longfellow.

Birds of Killingworth, The (The Poet's Tale). SP-LongH

(Poet's Tale: The Birds of Killingworth, The.) SP-LongH

Paul Revere's Ride [The Landlord's Tale]. SP-LongH

(Landlord's Tale: Paul Revere's Ride, The.) SP-LongH

Theologian's Tale: Torquemada, The. SP-LongH

Tales of the Hall. George Crabbe.

Ellen. SP-CrabG

Lady Barbara; or, The Ghost. SP-CrabG

Richard's Youth. SP-CrabG

Ruth. SP-CrabG

Smugglers and Poachers. SP-CrabG

Tales of the Islands. Derek Walcott. CP-WalcD

Talismanic Ceremony for Lucian, March 9, 1971, Intersection Church, San Francisco. Andrei Codrescu. SP-CodrA

Talismans. Jorge Luis Borges. SP-BorgJ, *tr.* by Alastair Reid

Talk ("One thing, strikes in"). Robert Creeley. SP-CreeR

Talk ("Talking Ginsbergian"). Robert Creeley. SP-CreeR

Talk. D. H. Lawrence. CP-LawrD

Talk, The. Gregory Orr. SP-OrrG

Talk in the Dark. Denise Levertov. SP-LeveDL

Talk like a jellyfish can ruin a party. At the Chairman's Housewarming. William Stafford. SP-StafWW

Talk not of sad November, when a day. Day, A. John Greenleaf Whittier. CP-WhitJ

Talk not to me of Summer Trees. Emily Dickinson. CP-DickE

Talk of Faith. D. H. Lawrence. CP-LawrD

Talk of Fortune. W. S. Merwin. SP-MerwWF

Talk of Loyalty. D. H. Lawrence. CP-LawrD

Talk with Friedrich Nietzsche, A. Adam Zagajewski. SP-ZagaA, *tr.* by Renata Gorczynski, Benjamin Ivry and C. K. Williams

Talk with prudence to a Beggar. Emily Dickinson. CP-DickE

Talker, The. Mona Van Duyn. SP-VanDM

"Talkin' 'bout yer bees," says Ike. Fessler's Bees. James Whitcomb Riley. CP-RileJ

Talkin' o' poetry,—There's few men yit. Ginoine Ar-tickle, The. James Whitcomb Riley. CP-RileJ

Talking. Robert Creeley. SP-CreeR

Talking. W. S. Merwin. SP-MerwWF

Talking about food won't make you full. Han-shan. CP-ColdM, *tr.* by Red Pine

Talking about her brother, Morris, Tess said. His Bathrobe Pockets Stuffed with Notes. Raymond Carver. CP-CarvR

Talking about myself all day. Interview. Raymond Carver. CP-CarvR

Talking Back (To W. H. Auden). William Meredith. SP-MereW

Talking Ginsbergian. Talk ("Talking Ginsbergian"). Robert Creeley. SP-CreeR

Talking In Bed. Philip Larkin. CP-LarkP

Talking in the Night. Jelaluddin Rumi. SP-Rumi, *tr.* by Coleman Barks

Talking Late with the Governor about the Budget. Gary Snyder. CP-SnydG

Talking Myself to Sleep at One More Hilton. John Ciardi. CP-CiarJ

Talking of death / is like talking of. Eat. Charles Bukowski. SP-BukC2

Talking Picture, The. Philip Whalen. SP-WhalP

Talking through the Door. Jelaluddin Rumi. SP-Rumi, *tr.* by Coleman Barks

Talking to Dogs. W. H. Auden. CP-AudeW

Talking to Grief. Denise Levertov. SP-LeveDL; SP-LeveDS

Talking to Himself He Gets a Few Things Settled in His Mind. Miller Williams. CP-WillM

Talking to His Reflection in a Shallow Pond. Ai. SP-Ai

Talking to Mice. W. H. Auden. CP-AudeW

Talking to My Grandmother Who Died Poor. Alice Walker. CP-WalkA

Talking to My Mailbox. Charles Bukowski. SP-BukC3

Talking to Myself. W. H. Auden. CP-AudeW

Talking to Myself. David Ignatow. SP-IgnaD

Talking to Oneself. Denise Levertov. SP-LeveDL; SP-LeveDS

Talking to Sheep. Anne Sexton. CP-SextA

Talking together, we advance from loneliness. For All Friends. David Ignatow. SP-IgnaD

Talking World, The. Laura Riding Jackson. CP-RidiL

Tall Ambrosia. Henry David Thoreau. CP-ThorH

Tall Atlas, Jupiter, Hercules, Thor. Deities and Beasts. John Updike. CP-UpdiJ

Tall building, A. The walls crept upward in the dark. Dawns. Czeslaw Milosz. CP-MiloC; CP-MiloCN, *tr.* by Robert Hass

Tall buildings swayed / in downtown San Francisco. Shadowy Room. James Schuyler. CP-SchuJ

Tall camels of the spirit, The. "World Without Objects Is a Sensible Emptiness, A" Richard Wilbur. CP-WilbR

Tall / dark. Eyes. Robert Creeley. SP-CreeR

Tall Girl, The. John Crowe Ransom. SP-RansJ

Tall in the evening, arrogant, aloof. Susana Bombal. Jorge Luis Borges. SP-BorgJ, tr. by Alastair Reid

Tall Man, A. Carl Sandburg. CP-SandC

Tall man / Without clothes, A. Karamojongs. Alice Walker. CP-WalkA

Tall marigolds darken, The. Fear of Darkness, The. Wendell Berry. CP-BerrW

Tall mountains, taller clouds, meeting. Presence. Yannis Ritsos. SP-RitsY, tr. by N. C. Germanacos

Tall Order, A. Raymond Carver. CP-CarvR

Tall pine grove! Hunter. Federico García Lorca. CP-GarcF, tr. by Alan S. Trueblood Fr. Theories.

Tall plane trees, muscular torsos of coolness. Harvest of the Void. Yannis Ritsos. SP-RitsY, tr. by Minas Savvas

Tall, sallow guardsmen their horsetails have spread, The. From Perugia. John Greenleaf Whittier. CP-WhitJ

Tall Timber. Carl Sandburg. CP-SandC

Tall timber stood here once. Improved Farm Land. Carl Sandburg. CP-SandC

Tall towers. / Long rivers. Scene. Federico García Lorca. CP-GarcF, tr. by Alan S. Trueblood Fr. Back of the World.

Tall white cliffs of England fade away, The. Departure, The. Jones Very. CP-VeryJ

Tall windows full of sea light. Our Mother. Thomas Kinsella. CP-KinsT

Tall woman wants the tall story, The. Story, The. Robert Creeley. CP-CreeR

Talla spales, The. Servant Girl's Bed. Hugh MacDiarmid. SP-MacDH

Taller To-day. W. H. Auden. CP-AudeW

Taller to-day, we remember similar evenings. Taller To-day. W. H. Auden. CP-AudeW

Tallow worked into a knot, A. Memory Cave. Yusef Komunyakaa. CP-KomuY

Tally, A. Robert Creeley. CP-CreeR

Tally-Ho. Ezra Pound. CP-PoEar

Tally of forces, consequent, A. Tally, A. Robert Creeley. CP-CreeR

Tally, The. Yusef Komunyakaa. CP-KomuY

Talos. Yannis Ritsos. SP-RitsY, tr. by N. C. Germanacos

Tam Cari Capitis. Louis MacNeice. CP-MacNL

Tam Glen. Robert Burns. CP-BurnR

Tam Lin. Unknown. CP-BurnR

Tam o' Shanter; A Tale. Robert Burns. CP-BurnR

Tam Samson's Elegy. Robert Burns. CP-BurnR

Tam the Chapman. Robert Burns. CP-BurnR
  (On Tam the Chapman.) CP-BurnR

Tamales, they like tamales. What Montezuma Fed Cortés and His Men. Thomas Lux. SP-LuxT

Tamar. Robinson Jeffers. CP-JefR1

Tamar and Royce are in love. Assateague. John Logan. CP-LogaJ

Tamarack can cut rain down to size, mist-little, The. Right On. A. R. Ammons. CP-AmmoA

Tambourine Life. Ted Berrigan. SP-BerrT

Tambourines. Langston Hughes. CP-HughL; CP-HughL3

Tame Cat. Ezra Pound. SP-PounE

Tamed by Miltown we lie on Mother's bed; Man And Wife. Robert Lowell. SP-LoweR

Tamely frail body abstain today; today. Upon the Annunciation and Passion Falling upon One Day. 1608. John Donne. CP-DonnJ; MW-DonnJ

Tamer and Hawk. Thom Gunn. CP-GunnT

Tamerlane. Edgar Allan Poe. CP-PoeEd

Tammuz in the Garden. Sam Hamill. SP-HamiS

Tampa Stomp. John Berryman. CP-BerrJ

Tanck's Brag. Hayden Carruth. CP-CarHS Fr. Songs About What Comes Down: The Complete Works of Mr. Septic Tank.

Tanck's Epilogue. Hayden Carruth. CP-CarHS Fr. Songs About What Comes Down: The Complete Works of Mr. Septic Tank.

Tanck's Prolegomenon. Hayden Carruth. CP-CarHS Fr. Songs About What Comes Down: The Complete Works of Mr. Septic Tank.

Tanck's Song About Brains. Hayden Carruth. CP-CarHS Fr. Songs About What Comes Down: The Complete Works of Mr. Septic Tank.

Tanck's Song About Dying Young. Hayden Carruth. CP-CarHS Fr. Songs About What Comes Down: The Complete Works of Mr. Septic Tank.

Tanck's Song About Earl Hines. Hayden Carruth. CP-CarHS Fr. Songs About What Comes Down: The Complete Works of Mr. Septic Tank.

Tanck's Song About Fear of Falling. Hayden Carruth. CP-CarHS Fr. Songs About What Comes Down: The Complete Works of Mr. Septic Tank.

Tanck's Song About His Birthday. Hayden Carruth. CP-CarHS Fr. Songs About What Comes Down: The Complete Works of Mr. Septic Tank.

Tanck's Song About His Unicameral Mind. Hayden Carruth. CP-CarHS Fr. Songs About What Comes Down: The Complete Works of Mr. Septic Tank.

Tanck's Song About November. Hayden Carruth. CP-CarHS Fr. Songs About What Comes Down: The Complete Works of Mr. Septic Tank.

Tanck's Song About Pride. Hayden Carruth. CP-CarHS Fr. Songs About What Comes Down: The Complete Works of Mr. Septic Tank.

Tanck's Song About Silence. Hayden Carruth. CP-CarHS Fr. Songs About What Comes Down: The Complete Works of Mr. Septic Tank.

Tanck's Song About Survival. Hayden Carruth. CP-CarHS Fr. Songs About What Comes Down: The Complete Works of Mr. Septic Tank.

Tanck's Song About the Jinx. Hayden Carruth. CP-CarHS Fr. Songs About What Comes Down: The Complete Works of Mr. Septic Tank.

Tanck's Song About the Transportation Business. Hayden Carruth. CP-CarHS Fr. Songs About What Comes Down: The Complete Works of Mr. Septic Tank.

Tanck's Song About the Younger Generation. Hayden Carruth. CP-CarHS Fr. Songs About What Comes Down: The Complete Works of Mr. Septic Tank.

Tanck's Song About Women. Hayden Carruth. CP-CarHS Fr. Songs About What Comes Down: The Complete Works of Mr. Septic Tank.

Tanck's Song About Youth and Age. Hayden Carruth. CP-CarHS Fr. Songs About What Comes Down: The Complete Works of Mr. Septic Tank.

T'ang Notebook. Charles Wright. SP-WrigC

Tangibles. Carl Sandburg. CP-SandC

Tangier: The Speechless Summer. Tennessee Williams. CP-WillT

Tangle of concerns, A. Memory of W.H. Auden. Thomas Kinsella. CP-KinsT

Tangled ball of yarn, A. Yannis Ritsos. SP-RitsY Fr. So?

Tangled [or Tanglid] I was [or was I] in [or yn] Love's snare. Liberty. Sir Thomas Wyatt. CP-WyatT

Tango. Louise Glück. SP-GlucL

Tango. Josephine Jacobsen. CP-JacoJ

Tanka: "Winter has come." James Laughlin. CP-LaugJ

Tankards, The. Paul Celan. SP-CelaP, tr. by John Felstiner

Tankas. Jorge Luis Borges. SP-BorgJ, tr. by Alastair Reid

Tanker slips behind a distant ridge, The. Being Born. Thom Gunn. CP-GunnT

Tanneries, wine factories, cotton mills—what celebrated silks. Time. Yannis Ritsos. SP-RitsY Fr. Monovasia. tr. by Kimon Friar and Kostas Myrsiades

Tantalized by wind, this flag that flies. At the Grave of My Brother: Bomber Pilot. William Stafford. SP-StafWW

Tanti Vi Sed I Tanti Vi. Thomas Sheridan. CP-SherT

Tanto e Amara. Charles Olson. CP-OlsoC

Tao. Chuang Tzu. CP-MertT

Tao and Unfitness at Inistiogue on the River Nore. Thomas Kinsella. CP-KinsT

Tao in the Yankee Stadium Bleachers. John Updike. CP-UpdiJ

Taoist Painter, The. Arthur Sze. SP-SzeA

Tap (better known then trusted) as we heare. Upon Tap. Robert Herrick. CP-HerrR

Tapers. Robert Herrick. CP-HerrR

Tapestry. John Ashbery. SP-AshbJ

Tapestry. Langston Hughes. CP-HughL; CP-HughL1

Tapestry. Charles Simic. SP-SimiC; SP-SimiCE

Tapestry, The. Howard Nemerov. CP-NemeH

Tapestry and Sail. James Dickey. CP-DickJ

Tapiola. William Carlos Williams. CP-WilW2

Taps. Joseph Brodsky. CP-BrodJ

Tar. C. K. Williams. CP-WillC; SP-WillC

Tara. Thomas Kinsella. CP-KinsT

Tarantella. D. H. Lawrence. CP-LawrD

Tarantians Divert Themselves, The. Constantine P. Cavafy. CP-CavaC, tr. by Theoharis Constantine Theoharis

Tarantula rattling at the lily's foot, The. O Carib Isle! Hart Crane. CP-CranH

Tarantulas on the Lifebuoy. Thomas Lux. SP-LuxT

Tarbes. Adam Zagajewski. SP-ZagaA, tr. by Clare Cavanagh

Tarbolton Lasses, The. Robert Burns. CP-BurnR

Tardy Spring. George Meredith. CP-MerG1

Tares make the corn to grow. By the Road to Upper Midhope. Donald Davie. CP-DaviDC

Target Practice. Muriel Rukeyser. CP-RukeM

Target Practice. Gary Snyder. CP-SnydG

Tarkington, Thou Should'st Be Living in This Hour. Ogden Nash. CP-NashO

Tarnished we! Tarnished! Wastrels all! Decadence, The. Ezra Pound. CP-PoEar

Tarpaper shack and the red rose bush, The. Muriel Rukeyser. CP-RukeM

Tarpon. Derek Walcott. CP-WalcD

Tarquin. Frank O'Hara. SP-OharF

Tarquinia. Charles Tomlinson. CP-TomlC

Tarrant Moss. Rudyard Kipling. CP-KiplR Fr. Plain Tales from the Hills.

Tarry, delight, so seldom met. A. E. Housman. CP-HousA

Tarry sweete love. Thomas Campion. CP-CampT

Tarrying Bridegroom, The. Thomas Hardy. CP-HardT

Tarsier. Wisława Szymborska. SP-SzymW, *tr. by* Stanislaw Barańczak *and* Clare Cavanagh

Tart sun, The. Morning: Leaving Calle Gigantes. Jay Wright. SP-WrigJ

Tarts. D. H. Lawrence. CP-LawrD

Tartufe's Punishment. Arthur Rimbaud. CP-RimbA, *tr. by* Martin Sorrell

Tartuffe. Molière. CP-WilbR

Task, A. Czeslaw Milosz. CP-MiloC; CP-MiloCN, *tr. by* Czeslaw Milosz

Task, The. William Cowper. CP-CowpW

Task, The. John Ashbery. SP-AshbJ

Task, The. Jones Very. CP-VeryJ

Tasker Norcross. Edwin Arlington Robinson. CP-RobiE

Tassajara. Philip Whalen. SP-WhalP

Tasso and Leonora. Christina Georgina Rossetti. CP-RosC3

'Tasso in Prison' by Delacroix. Charles Baudelaire. CP-BaudC, *tr. by* Walter Martin

Taste. John Updike. CP-UpdiJ

Taste, The. David Ignatow. SP-IgnaD

Tasted (and spat out). Waving to the Devil. Denise Levertov. SP-LevcDL

Tata, Baba, Great Spirit—. Sorrow Song, The. Hayden Carruth. CP-CarHS

Tattered and ragg'd, with greatcoat tied in strings. Mole-Catcher, The. John Clare. SP-ClarJ

Tattered Kaddish. Adrienne Rich. SP-RicA1

Tattoo. Wallace Stevens. CP-StevW; CP-StevWP

Tattooed Man, The. Robert Earl Hayden. CP-HaydR

Tattooing in Qazwin. Jelaluddin Rumi. SP-Rumi, *tr. by* Coleman Barks

Tauler James Fenton. SP-FentJ

Tauler. John Greenleaf Whittier. CP-WhitJ

Taurean reaper of the wild apple field. Tattered Kaddish. Adrienne Rich. SP-RicA1

Tavern. Edna St. Vincent Millay. CP-MillE

Tavern, The. Edwin Arlington Robinson. CP-RobiE

Tawdery!—faddery! Feathers and fuss! Jargon-Jingle. James Whitcomb Riley. CP-RileJ

Tawny. Carl Sandburg. CP-SandC

Tawny and lead-gray current of swift river, A. America. Czeslaw Milosz. CP-MiloCN, *tr. by* Robert Hass

Tawny are the leaves turned but they still hold. Antique Harvesters. John Crowe Ransom. SP-RansJ

Tawny in a pasture by the true sea. Forgotten Rock, The. Richard Eberhart. CP-EberR

Tax-Free Encounter. John Updike. CP-UpdiJ

Tax Inspector, The. Charles Tomlinson. SP-TomlC

Taxi driver, A. Eighteen-Dollar Taxi Trip to Tizapan and Back to Chapala. Clarence Major. SP-MajoC

Taxis, The. Louis MacNeice. CP-MacNL

Taxis toot whirl people moving perhaps laugh into the slowly. E. E. Cummings. CP-CummE

Taxis were beyond us. Mother. Donald Davie. CP-DaviDC

Taylor fell thro' the bed, thimble an' a', The. Robert Burns. CP-BurnR

Taylor he cam here to sew, The. Taylor, The. Robert Burns. CP-BurnR

Taylor Street. Thom Gunn. CP-GunnT

Taylor, The. Robert Burns. CP-BurnR

Te escribo cartas, Che / En la sazón de lluvias. Letters to Che: Canto Bilingue. Thomas Merton. CP-MertT

Tea. John Berryman. CP-BerrJ

Tea. Paul Muldoon. CP-MuldP

Tea. Lorine Niedecker. CP-NiedL

Tea. Wallace Stevens. CP-StevW; CP-StevWP

Tea at the Palaz of Hoon. Wallace Stevens. CP-StevW; CP-StevWP

Tea garden shows you how, A. Bridge. A. R. Ammons. CP-AmmoA

Tea is made; the red fogs shut round the house but the gas burns. Idyll, An: "Tea is made; the red fogs shut round the house but the gas burns." G. K. Chesterton. CP-ChesG

Tea leaves I've given up. Recantation. Sylvia Plath. CP-PlatS

Tea leaves wilted in sunlight are shaken. Oolong. Arthur Sze. SP-SzeA

Tea Poet, The. G. K. Chesterton. CP-ChesG

Tea Shop, The. Ezra Pound. SP-PounE

Teach Him—When He makes the names. Emily Dickinson. CP-DickE

Teach me I am forgotten by the dead. Ralph Waldo Emerson. CP-EmerR

Teach me, my God and King. Elixir [*or* Elixer], The. George Herbert. CP-HerbG

Teach me your mood, O patient stars! Ralph Waldo Emerson. CP-EmerR

Teach Us to Number Our Days. Rita Dove. SP-DoveR

Teach your child to earn his meal. *Unknown.* CP-EmerR

Teacher. Langston Hughes. CP-HughL; CP-HughL1

Teacher. Audre Lorde. SP-LordA

Teacher and friend, what you restored to me. Instead of an Essay. Charles Tomlinson. CP-TomlC

Teacher / bring me to heaven. Allen Ginsberg. SP-GinsA *Fr.* Sad Dust Glories.

Teacher let some big boys out at two, The. Transgression, A. Seamus Heaney. SP-HeanSO

Teacher, the preacher, my mother, a mouse, The. Overture: The Hostages. Randall Jarrell. CP-JarrR

Teachers. W. S. Merwin. SP-MerwW

Teachers, The. Gregory Orr. SP-OrrG

Teachers in the Temple, The. Neglected Child, The. G. K. Chesterton. CP-ChesG

Teacher's Lament. Alan Dugan. CP-DugaA

Teacher's Vacation Lament in the Country. Alan Dugan. CP-DugaA

Teaching of History Confirmed, The. Jones Very. CP-VeryJ

Teaching of the Blows of Fortune, The. George Meredith. CP-MerG2

Teaching of the Nude, The. George Meredith. CP-MerG1

Teaching the Ape to Write Poems. James Tate. SP-TateJ

Teachings, The. Robert Creeley. CP-CreeR

Teachings of the Spirit, The. Jones Very. CP-VeryJ

Teage has told lyes so long, that when Teage tells. Upon Teage. Robert Herrick. CP-HerrR

Teamster's Farewell, A. Carl Sandburg. CP-SandC

Tear. Thomas Kinsella. CP-KinsT

Tear. Arthur Rimbaud. CP-RimbA, *tr. by* Martin Sorrell

Tear, The. Lord Byron. CP-Byron

Tear another's tears bring forth, The. Sympathy. Paul Laurence Dunbar. CP-DunbP

Tear Gas. Adrienne Rich. CP-RicAE; SP-RicA2

Tear off the calendar. Month's Calendar, The. Thomas Hardy. CP-HardT

Tear which mourn'd a brother's fate scarce dry, The. On Receiving an Account That His Only Sister's Death Was Inevitable. Samuel Taylor Coleridge. CP-ColeS

Teare Sent to Her from Stanes, The. Robert Herrick. CP-HerrR

Tear[e], The. Richard Crashaw. CP-CrasR

Teares. Robert Herrick. CP-HerrR

Teares, and Laughter. Robert Herrick. CP-HerrR

Teares are Tongues. Robert Herrick. CP-HerrR

Teares most prevaile; with teares too thou mayst move. Teares. Robert Herrick. CP-HerrR

Teares of Saints more sweet by farre, The. Teares. Robert Herrick. CP-HerrR

Teares of the Muses, The. Edmund Spenser. CP-Spens

Teares quickly drie: griefes will in time decay. Faire after Foule. Robert Herrick. CP-HerrR

Teares, though th'are here below the sinners brinc. Upon Teares. Robert Herrick. CP-HerrR

Tearing and tearing / ripped-up bits of paper. Blizzard. James Schuyler. CP-SchuJ

Tearing Down the Hotel. Miller Williams. CP-WillM

Tearing through the lovely landscape. As Far as It Goes, and Back. Eleanor Wilner. SP-WilnE

Tears. Maya Angelou. SP-AngeM

Tears. Elizabeth Barrett Browning. CP-BroEB

Tears. Allen Ginsberg. CP-GinsA

Tears. Josephine Jacobsen. CP-JacoJ

Tears. Walt Whitman. CP-WhitW

Tears and Recriminations. Philip Whalen. SP-WhalP

Tears flow, and cease not, where the good man lies. Epitaph on Mr. Chester. William Cowper. CP-CowpW

Tears from our eyes. Three Words Only. Robert Graves. CP-GravR

Tears here do not soften, The. Jerusalem's Suicide Attempts. Yehuda Amichai. SP-AmicYL, *tr. by* Benjamin Harshav *and* Barbara Harshav

Tears in Sleep. Louise Bogan. CP-BogaL

Tears leave no mark on the soil. Tears. Josephine Jacobsen. CP-JacoJ

Tears of a Painter, The. Vincent Bourne. CP-CowpW

Tears of Amynta for the Death of Damon, The. John Dryden. CP-DryJ2

Tears of delight that on my name-day. Name Day. Robert Graves. CP-GravR

Tears of Friendship. Elegy the Third.—To a Friend Just Married, and Who Had Promised to Write, on Parting, but Had Neglected It. Annis Boudinot Stockton. CP-StocA

Tears of Friendship, The. Elegy the 4th. Annis Boudinot Stockton. CP-StocA

Tears of the Excavator, The. Pier Paolo Pasolini. SP-PasoP, *tr. by* Norman MacAfee *and* Luciano Martinengo

Tears of the Sisters of Phaeton, The. Constantine P. Cavafy. CP-CavaC, *tr. by* Theoharis Constantine Theoharis

Tears of the widow of the military man, The. Silence and Tears. Stevie Smith. CP-SmitS

Tears! tears! tears! / In the night, in solitude, tears. Tears. Walt Whitman. CP-WhitW

Tears that pass, becoming, The. Pulse. Tennessee Williams. CP-WillT

Tease. D. H. Lawrence. CP-LawrD

Technical Notes. James Laughlin. CP-LaugJ

Technical scandal in its day, A. Battle Scene. Robert Stock. SP-StocR

Technical Supplement, A. Thomas Kinsella. CP-KinsT

Technologies. George Oppen. CP-OppGN

Technology of soul restoration, The. Orbital Complexion. Andrei Codrescu. SP-CodrA

Tecumseh. Mary Oliver. SP-OlivM

Ted Roethke was a tearing man. Was a Man. John Ciardi. CP-CiarJ

Tedded hay, the first fruits of the soil, The. Keepsake, The. Samuel Taylor Coleridge. CP-ColeS

Tedium of déjà–vu of home. Christmas. Robert Lowell. SP-LoweR

Teen-age boy in training pants, A. Kai, Today. Gary Snyder. CP-SnydG

Teenyboppers crowd No Exit. Different Story, A. Yusef Komunyakaa. CP-KomuY

Teeth are washed, The. Confession and Penance. Philip Whalen. SP-WhalP

Teeth Mother Naked at Last, The. Robert Bly. SP-BlyR

Teevo cheevo cheevio chee. Woodlark, The. Gerard Manley Hopkins. CP-HopkG

Teheran. Robinson Jeffers. CP-JefR3

Teignmouth. Amy Clampitt. CP-ClamA

Tek a cool night, good an' cleah. Hunting Song. Paul Laurence Dunbar. CP-DunbP

Tel Aviv and *Life on the Mississippi*. Raymond Carver. CP-CarvR

Telegram. Andrei Codrescu. SP-CodrA

Telegram. Carl Sandburg. CP-SandC

Telegram arrived, The. Nobody's Business. James Tate. SP-TateJ

Telegram, The. Thomas Hardy. CP-HardT

Telegram says you have gone away, The. Denouement. Sylvia Plath. CP-PlatS

Telegraph Wires. Ted Hughes. SP-HughTN

Telephone. Anne Sexton. CP-SextA

Telephone, The. Maya Angelou. SP-AngeM

Telephone, The. Robert Frost. CP-FrosR

Telephone, The. Jones Very. CP-VeryJ

Telephone line goes cold, A. Farm on the Great Plains, The. William Stafford. SP-StafW; SP-StafWW

Telephone Poles. John Updike. CP-UpdiJ

Telephone rang in the grocery store, The. Introduction to the Telephone. Alan Dugan. CP-DugaA

Telephus Sedum. Louis Zukofsky. CP-ZukLS

Telescope picks off star dust, The. Pick-Offs. Carl Sandburg. CP-SandC

Telescope's a microscope, The. Stairwell. Heather McHugh. SP-McHuH

Telesila. "H. D." CP-DoolH

Telesphere, The. Charles Olson. SP-OlsoC *Fr.* Maximus Poems, The.

TV Off. Ted Hughes. SP-HughTN

Television set hung, The. Terminal Bar, The. Derek Mahon. CP-MahoD

Television Was a Baby Crawling toward That Deathchamber. Allen Ginsberg. CP-GinsA

"Either we blow ourselves up now and die, like the old tribe of man, arguing among neutrons." SP-GinsA

Tell, acquaint me. French Hill. Hayden Carruth. CP-CarHS

Tell all my mourners. Wake. Langston Hughes. CP-HughL; CP-HughL2

Tell as a Marksman—were forgotten. Emily Dickinson. CP-DickE

Tell brave deeds of war. Stephen Crane. CP-CranS

Tell em to take my bare walls down. Foreclosure. Lorine Niedecker. CP-NiedL

Tell, if thou canst, (and truly) whence doth come. Upon Julia's Unlacing Her Self. Robert Herrick. CP-HerrR

Tell It to the Eskimos or Tell it to the Esquimaux. Ogden Nash. CP-NashO

Tell it to the locked-up trees. Cuckoo Song. Rudyard Kipling. CP-KiplR

Tell Me. Langston Hughes. CP-HughL; CP-HughL3

Tell me a story about the war. Lorine Niedecker. CP-NiedL

Tell me a word. Conundrums. D. H. Lawrence. CP-LawrD

Tell me about yourself they. Word in Edgeways, A. Charles Tomlinson. CP-TomlC

Tell me again the Christmas story. Christmas Story, The. Langston Hughes. CP-HughL; CP-HughL3

Tell me before you hurt me I'm. If You Are Only Flirting. James Laughlin. CP-LaugJ

Tell me bright Boy, tell me my golden Lad. Luke 15; On the Prodigall. Bible, *N.T.* CP-CrasR *Fr.* St. Luke.

Tell me: doth it not grieve thee to lie here. Death Is Swallowed Up in Victory. Christina Georgina Rossetti. CP-RosC3

Tell me, Eutresia, since my fate. Methodus Amandi. Thomas Cary. CP-CareT

Tell me: how is this night different. Passover. Primo Levi. CP-LeviP, *tr. by* Ruth Feldman

Tell me if it is too far for you. Elegy for N. N. Czeslaw Milosz. CP-MiloC; CP-MiloCN, *tr. by* Lawrence Davis

Tell me implacable girl. Visitor, The. James Laughlin. CP-LaugJ

Tell me, is the rose really naked. Pablo Neruda. SP-NeruP *Fr.* Question Book.

Tell me, / Is there peace. Convent. Langston Hughes. CP-HughL; CP-HughL2

Tell me maiden dost thou use. Ralph Waldo Emerson. CP-EmerR

TELL ME, MAMA, CAN I GET MY SHOW. Show Fare, Please. Langston Hughes. CP-HughL; CP-HughL3

Tell me more of the eagle, Cotton. Some Friends from Pascagoula. Wallace Stevens. CP-StevW; CP-StevWP

Tell me, my dear, what wasteful sense. Poet's Prescription of Shamelessness, The. Robert Stock. SP-StocR

Tell me, my girl, does your heart ever soar. Restless and Sad. Charles Baudelaire. CP-BaudC, *tr. by* Walter Martin

Tell me, my love, since Hymen tied [*or* ty'ed]. Hymeneal[l] Dialogue, An. Thomas Carew. CP-CareT

Tell me, my patient friends, awaiters of messages. Speech to a Crowd. Archibald MacLeish. CP-MacLA

Tell me not here, it needs not saying. A. E. Housman. CP-HousA

Tell me not how electricity or. E. E. Cummings. CP-CummE

Tell me not in joyous numbers. Stephen Crane. CP-CranS

Tell me not, in mournful numbers. Psalm of Life, A. Henry Wadsworth Longfellow. SP-LongH

Tell me not that death of grief. Hope in Grief. Christina Georgina Rossetti. CP-RosC3

Tell me now in what hidden way is. Ballad[e] of Dead Ladies, The. François Villon. CW-RossD, *tr. by* Dante Gabriel Rossetti

Tell me, O Octopus, I begs. Octopus, The. Ogden Nash. CP-NashO

Tell me rich man, for what intent. Poore Mans Part, The. Robert Herrick. CP-HerrR

Tell me something / you say. Mother-in-Law. Adrienne Rich. SP-RicA2

Tell me tales of a lilied pool. Song for an April Dusk. Dorothy Parker. CP-ParkD

Tell Me, Tell Me. Marianne Craig Moore. CP-MoorM

Tell me, tell me, smiling child. Emily Jane Brontë. CP-BronE

Tell me, tell me, / Unknown stranger. Galliass, The. Walter De la Mare. CP-DeLaW

Tell me Thirsis, tell your anguish. Song: "Tell me Thirsis, tell your anguish." Nathaniel Lee. CP-DryJ2 *Fr.* Duke of Guise, The.

Tell me, thou Star, whose wings of light. World's Wanderers, The. Percy Bysshe Shelley. CP-ShelP

"Tell me to touch your breast," I wanted to say: "Please, please, please touch me breast" Orchid, The. C. K. Williams. SP-WillC

Tell me, watcher, is it winter? Gleneden's Dream. Emily Jane Brontë. CP-BronE

Tell me, what needs those rich deceits. Upon Julia's Haire, Bundled up in a Golden Net. Robert Herrick. CP-HerrR

Tell me what you see in it. Black Pine Tree in an Orange Light. Sylvia Plath. CP-PlatS

Tell me what you're doing over here, John Gorham. John Gorham. Edwin Arlington Robinson. CP-RobiE

Tell me, when shall these wearie woes have end. Sonnet 36. Edmund Spenser. CP-Spens *Fr.* Amoretti.

Tell me, where do ghosts in love. Ghosts in Love. Nicholas Vachel Lindsay. CP-LindV

Tell me why, behind thee. Stephen Crane. CP-CranS

Tell me, ye juster deities. Expostulation, The. Sir John Suckling. CP-SuckJ

Tell me ye wise ones if ye can. Henry David Thoreau. CP-ThorH

Tell me, ye Zephyrs! that unfold. Flower Garden at Coleorton Hall, Leicestershire, A. William Wordsworth. CP-WorW2

Tell me, you years I had for my life. Remembering Brother Bob. William Stafford. SP-StafW; SP-StafWW

Tell me young man, or did the Muses bring. To his Worthy Friend M. John Hall, Student of Grayes-Inne. Robert Herrick. CP-HerrR

Tell men what they knew before. Ralph Waldo Emerson. CP-EmerR

Tell my friends / that I'm dead. From Out Here. Federico García Lorca. CP-GarcF, *tr. by* Jerome Rothenberg

Tell of us sedum comic. Telephus Sedum. Louis Zukofsky. CP-ZukLS

Tell Story. Robert Creeley. SP-CreeR

Tell that Brave Man, fain thou wo'dst have access. To His Muse, Another to the Same. Robert Herrick. CP-HerrR

Tell that one about Catherine. Story Time. William Stafford. SP-StafWW

Tell the beads of the chromosomes like a rosary. Route. George Oppen. CP-OppGN

Tell the jury your name. Doctors, The. Muriel Rukeyser. CP-RukeM

Tell the story. Think. Robert Creeley. CP-CreeR

Tell them it's not just me. Mission. Yehuda Amichai. SP-AmicYL, *tr. by* Benjamin Harshav and Barbara Harshav

Tell them, though 'tis an awful thing to die. Concluding Lines of Epitaph on Mrs Mason. Thomas Gray. CP-GrayT

Tell them to be quiet, I beg you. Why are they still shouting? Agamemnon. Yannis Ritsos. SP-RitsY, *tr. by* Philip Pastras and George Pilitsis

Tell Them Was Here. James Tate. SP-TateJ

Tell this to ladies: how a hero man. Man without Sense of Direction. John Crowe Ransom. SP-RansJ

Tell Tom he draws a farce in vain. *Unknown.* CP-SherT *Fr.* Puppet-Show, The.

Tell us / how we'll be together in that time. When/Then. Adrienne Rich. SP-RicA2

Tell us, O pilgrim, what strange She. Decoy, The. Walter De la Mare. CP-DeLaW

Tell us, thou clear [or cleere] and heavenly tongue. Star-Song; a Carol to the King; Sung at White-Hall, The. Robert Herrick. CP-HerrR

Tell you a story—an' it's a fac'. Jack the Giant-Killer. James Whitcomb Riley. CP-RileJ

Tell you what I like the best. Knee-deep in June. James Whitcomb Riley. CP-RileJ

Tell your love where the roses blow. Diplomacy. Paul Laurence Dunbar. CP-DunbP

Telling. Alice Walker. CP-WalkA

Telling Our Stories. Lucille Clifton. SP-ClifL

Telling the Bees. John Greenleaf Whittier. CP-WhitJ

Telling you all would take too long. Rainer Maria Rilke. CP-RilkFr, tr. by A. Poulin, Jr.

Tell's Birth-Place. Samuel Taylor Coleridge. CP-ColeS

Telyric, Andrei Codrescu. SP-CodrA

Temeraire, The. Herman Melville. SP-MelvH

Temethos, Antiochian; 400 A.D.. Constantine P. Cavafy. CP-CavaC, tr. by Theoharis Constantine Theoharis

Tempe in the Rain. Amy Clampitt. CP-ClamA

Temper, The. Robert Creeley. CP-CreeR

Temper of Time. Sylvia Plath. CP-PlatS

Temper (1), The. George Herbert. CP-HerbG

Temper (2), The. George Herbert. CP-HerbG

Temperance or the Cheap Physitian upon the Translation of Lessius. Richard Crashaw. CP-CrasR

   (On Taking Physicke.) CP-CrasR

Temperat aestiva fessis sua balnea membris. In S. Winefridam. Gerard Manley Hopkins. CP-HopkG

Tempest and terror below; but Christ the Almighty above. God Is Our Hope and Strength. Christina Georgina Rossetti. CP-RosC2

Tempest cracked on the theatre, A. Quickly. Repetitions of a Young Captain. Wallace Stevens. CP-StevW; CP-StevWP

Tempest over and gone, the calm begun, The. Easter Even. Christina Georgina Rossetti. CP-RosC2

Temple, A. Kenneth Patchen. CP-PatcK

Temple, The. Robert Herrick. CP-HerrR

Temple, The. Jones Very. CP-VeryJ

Temple of Earth, The. G. K. Chesterton. CP-ChesG

Temple of Fame, The. Alexander Pope. CP-PopeA

Temple of the body crumbles, The. Refrains. Richard Eberhart. CP-EberR

Temple of the Sun. "H. D."

   Saturn. CP-DoolH

   Zeus-Provider. CP-DoolH

Temple-pincers / eyed by your cheekbone. Paul Celan. SP-CelaP, tr. by John Felstiner

Temple shall be built, the Holy One, The. Temple, The. Jones Very. CP-VeryJ

Temple stood, holy and perfect, The. Myth. May Sarton. SP-SartM

Temples. D. H. Lawrence. CP-LawrD

Temples he built and palaces of air. Dreamer, The. Paul Laurence Dunbar. CP-DunbP

Temples of Smoke. Yusef Komunyakaa. CP-KomuY

Tempora Mutantur. Ambrose Bierce. SP-BierA

Temporall Goods. Robert Herrick. CP-HerrR

Temporary Poem of My Time. Yehuda Amichai. SP-AmicYL, tr. by Benjamin Harshav and Barbara Harshav

Temporary Poems. James Laughlin. CP-LaugJ

Temporary the All, The. Thomas Hardy. CP-HardT

Temporis interpres, parvum congestus in orbem. De horologio portabili. Thomas Campion. CP-CampT

Temps Perdu. Dorothy Parker. CP-ParkD

Tempt not with cheap words chivalrously given. On Being Thanked for a Favor. G. K. Chesterton. CP-ChesG

Temptation. John Ciardi. CP-CiarJ

Temptation. Paul Laurence Dunbar. CP-DunbP

Temptation. Czeslaw Milosz. CP-MiloC; CP-MiloCN, tr. by Lillian Vallee

Temptation, The. Jones Very. CP-VeryJ

Temptations ("No man is tempted so."). Robert Herrick. CP-HerrR

Temptations ("Temptations hurt not"). Robert Herrick. CP-HerrR

Temptations (&Those Saints, which God loves best"). Robert Herrick. CP-HerrR

Temptations still nest in it like basilisks. Dead Hand. W. S. Merwin. SP-MerwW

Temptress, The. Dorothy Parker. CP-ParkD

Tempus Fugit. Christina Georgina Rossetti. CP-RosC2

10 August '77 . . . Raft trip today. Hilarious God. Lawrence Ferlinghetti. SP-FerlL

Ten Below. C. K. Williams. CP-WillC; SP-WillC

   (It is bad enough crying for children.) CP-WillC

Ten-Day Leave. William Meredith. SP-MereW

Ten Dollars Reward. James Laughlin. CP-LaugJ

10/14. William Carlos Williams. CP-WilW2

Ten hours' light is abating, The. At Day-Close in November. Thomas Hardy. CP-HardT

10 Lions and the End of the World. Charles Bukowski. SP-BukC2

Ten Little Rembrandts. Theodore Weiss. SP-WeisT

Ten men, nine alive. State Funeral: March 31, 1969. Archibald MacLeish. CP-MacLA

Ten miles of flat land along the sea. Sandpipers. Carl Sandburg. CP-SandC

Ten Mills. Robert Frost. CP-FrosR

Ten minutes now I have been looking at this. Ready to Kill. Carl Sandburg. CP-SandC

Ten more miles, it is South Dakota. Sitting in a Small Screenhouse on a Summer Morning. James Wright. CP-WrigJ

Ten o'clock. Lorine Niedecker. CP-NiedL

10:X:57, 45 Years Since the Fall of the Ch'ing Dynasty. Philip Whalen. SP-WhalP

Ten Short Poems. Juan Ramón Jiménez. CP-WrigJ

Ten Songs. W. H. Auden. CP-AudeW

Ten Speeds. Yusef Komunyakaa. CP-KomuY

10:30 AM: Ralph Hotere's. Robert Creeley. SP-CreeR

Ten thousand miles from home. Han-shan. CP-ColdM, tr. by Red Pine

Ten Thousand Sutras. Sam Hamill. SP-HamiS

Ten Thousand to One. Arthur Sze. SP-SzeA

Ten thousand women. Watching Dan- / cers on Skates. Lorine Niedecker. CP-NiedL

10,000-Year-Old Tree Discovered Shades Two and Half Acres. Miller Williams. CP-WillM

Ten years ago it seemed impossible. In Progress. Christina Georgina Rossetti. CP-RosC3

Ten years ago this minute, he possibly sat. Days, The. Donald Hall. CP-HallD

Ten Years Ago when I Played at Being Brave. John Ciardi. CP-CiarJ

Ten years, and it's still on the. Rose Colored Glasses. Kenneth Rexroth. CP-RexrK

Ten years / and will you be. Return to Hinton. Charles Tomlinson. CP-TomlC

Ten Years Since. Thomas Hardy. CP-HardT

Ten years since we were married, since we stood. Long Finish. Paul Muldoon. CP-MuldP

Ten years together without yet a cloud. Firelight. Edwin Arlington Robinson. CP-RobiE

Tenancy, A. James Merrill. SP-MerrJ

Tenant, The. Jones Very. CP-VeryJ

Tenant Farmer, The. Ai. SP Ai

Tenant-for-Life, The. Thomas Hardy. CP-HardT

Tended by Faustina. Faustina, or Rock Roses. Elizabeth Bishop. CP-BishE

Tendencies. Heather McHugh. SP-McHuH

Tender and faithful animals, secretive, very quiet. Gates of the Arsenal, The. Czeslaw Milosz. CP-MiloC; CP-MiloCN, tr. by Robert Hass

Tender as the sweets of Spring. Lines on a Portrait of a Lady. Samuel Taylor Coleridge. CP-ColeS

Tender child of summers three, A. Light That Is Felt, The. John Greenleaf Whittier. CP-WhitJ

Tender floss of my flesh. Close to Me. Gabriela Mistral. SP-MistG, tr. by Maria Giachetti [or Jacketti]

Tender infant, meek and mild, The. Ballad: "Tender infant, meek and mild, The." Samuel Johnson. CP-JohnS

Tender Love's mother, a new poet get. Elegy 3.14: "Tender Love's mother, a new poet get." Ovid. CP-MarlC Fr. Elegies.

Tender nature, happy nature, where so many. Doubt. Rainer Maria Rilke. CP-RilkFr, tr. by A. Poulin, Jr.

Tender Only to One. Stevie Smith. CP-SmitS

Tender Place, The. Ted Hughes. SP-HughTN

Tender Reverence. D. H. Lawrence. CP-LawrD

Tender, semi- / articulate flickers. For My Mother: Genevieve Jules Creeley. Robert Creeley. CP-CreeR

Tender spotted. Lady in the Leopard Coat. Lorine Niedecker. CP-NiedL

Tenderloin. Thom Gunn. CP-GunnT

Tenderness and Resolution. Hart Crane. CP-CranH

Tenderness has not a Date. Emily Dickinson. SP-DickE

Tending Two Shops. Jelaluddin Rumi. SP-RumiJ, tr. by Coleman Barks

Tenebrae. Geoffrey Hill. CP-HillG

Tenebrae. Paul Celan. SP-CelaP, tr. by John Felstiner

Tenebrae. Yusef Komunyakaa. CP-KomuY

Tenebrae. Denise Levertov. SP-LeveDS

Tenementy twilightish landscape. Charles Olson. CP-OlsoC

Tennesee. James Laughlin. CP-LaugJ

Tennessee Line. Charles Wright. SP-WrigCN

Tennis. Robert Pinsky. CP-PinsR

Tennyson. James Whitcomb Riley. CP-RileJ

Tenor Sax Taking the Breaks. Tennessee Williams. CP-WillT

Tent, The. Wyatt Prunty. SP-PrunW

Tent, The. Jelaluddin Rumi. SP-Rumi, *tr. by* Coleman Barks

Tent, The. Jones Very. CP-VeryJ

Tent-lights glimmer on the land, The. At Port Royal. John Greenleaf Whittier. CP-WhitJ

Tent on the Beach, The. John Greenleaf Whittier. CP-WhitJ

Tentacles, the brazen phiz whose glare, The. Medusa. Amy Clampitt. CP-ClamA

Tentative (First Model) Definitions of Poetry. Carl Sandburg. CP-SandC

Tentatively, you. After Basho. Carolyn Kizer. CP-KizeC

Tenth Anniversary Photograph, 1952, A. Miller Williams. CP-WillM

Tenth Elegy. Elegy in Joy. Muriel Rukeyser. CP-RukeM

Tenth Grade. Grace Paley. CP-PalGC

Tenth Muse. Robert Lowell. SP-LoweR

Tenth Muse, Oh my heart-felt Sloth. Tenth Muse. Robert Lowell. SP-LoweR

Tenth Psalm. Anne Sexton. SP-SextA *Fr.* O Ye Tongues.

Tenth year we came upon immense sunlight, a relief, The. Archipelago. Louise Glück. SP-GlucL

Tents climb the hillside one step at a time. Ready. Yannis Ritsos. SP-RitsY, *tr. by* Martin McKinsey

Tenuous and Precarious. Stevie Smith. CP-SmitS

Tenzone. Ezra Pound. SP-PounE *Fr.* Contemporania.

Tenzone. John Ciardi. CP-CiarJ

Teotihuacán. Charles Tomlinson. CP-TomlC

Tepoztlán. Amy Clampitt. CP-ClamA

Tequila & chicken. In a Motel on Lake Erie. James Tate. SP-TateJ

Terce. John Berryman. CP-BerrJ

Terce. James McMichael. SP-McMiJ

Tercets of the Triad. Allen Tate. CP-TateA

Terence, This Is Stupid Stuff. A. E. Housman. CP-HousA

Teresa. Richard Wilbur. CP-WilbR

Teresa, ah, Teresita! King's Gift, The. Elizabeth Barrett Browning. CP-BroEB

Term, The. William Carlos Williams. CP-WilW1

Terminal. Thom Gunn. CP-GunnT

Terminal. Sylvia Plath. CP-PlatS

Terminal Bar, The. Derek Mahon. CP-MahoD

Terminal Days at Beverly Farms. Robert Lowell. SP-LoweR

Terminal Tramps. Charles Tomlinson. CP-TomlC

Terminology. Charles Bukowski. SP-BukC3

Terminus. A. R. Ammons. CP-AmmoA

Terminus ("For thought & not praise"). Ralph Waldo Emerson. CP-EmerR

Terminus ("It is time to be old"). Ralph Waldo Emerson. CP-EmerR

Terminus. Seamus Heaney. SP-HeanSO

Termite is taking her siesta, the house is no more, The. Tetrachlorine. Andrei Codrescu. SP-CodrA

Termite, The. Ogden Nash. CP-NashO

Terms. Randall Jarrell. CP-JarrR

Terms, The. Charles Simic. SP-SimiC; SP-SimiCE

Terms in Which I Think of Reality, The. Allen Ginsberg. CP-GinsA

Tern. Ted Hughes. SP-HughTN

Ternarie of Littles, upon a Pipkin of Jellie [*or* Jelly] Sent to a Lady, A. Robert Herrick. CP-HerrR

Terra Incognita. D. H. Lawrence. CP-LawrD

Terrace, The. Richard Wilbur. CP-WilbR

Terraced Valley, The. Robert Graves. CP-GravR

Terraces of Light. Marya Alexandrovna Zaturenska. SP-ZatuM

Terrain. A. R. Ammons. CP-AmmoA

Terrain that from above, aboard the hurled. Dallas–Fort Worth: Redbud and Mistletoe. Amy Clampitt. CP-ClamA

Terrestrial. Josephine Jacobsen. CP-JacoJ

Terrestrial Cuckoo, A. Frank O'Hara. SP-OharF

Terribilis Est Locus Iste; *Gaugin and the Pont-Aven School.* Geoffrey Hill. CP-HillG

Terrible Naïve, The. Josephine Jacobsen. CP-JacoJ

Terrible People, The. Ogden Nash. CP-NashO

Terrible streets, the manichee hell of twilight. Peace of Cities, The. Richard Wilbur. CP-WilbR

Terrible temper of the day gone dim, The. Sunglasses, The. Howard Nemerov. CP-NemeH

Terrible things coming up. Lorine Niedecker. CP-NiedL

Terrible trains crawl seaward thro' the South, The. Have a Genuine American Horror-&-Mist on the Rocks. John Berryman. CP-BerrJ

Terrible wrath I say, The. Achilles and the King: A Verse Re-telling. John Logan. CP-LogaJ

Terrifying are the attent sleek thrushes on the lawn. Thrushes. Ted Hughes. SP-HughTN

Territory. Maxine W. Kumin. SP-KumiM

Terror. Constantine P. Cavafy. CP-CavaC, *tr. by* Theoharis Constantine Theoharis

Terror. James Laughlin. CP-LaugJ

Terror. Denise Levertov. SP-LeveDS

Terror. Jones Very. CP-VeryJ

Terror. Robert Penn Warren. CP-WarrR

Terror finally becomes almost. There Once Was a Woman Who Put Her Head into an Oven. Charles Bukowski. SP-BukC1

Terror in the house does roar. William Blake. CP-BlakW

Terror of the country, The. Winter in the Country. Mary Oliver. SP-OlivM

Terrorist, He's Watching, The. Wisława Szymborska. SP-SzymW, *tr. by* Stanisław Barańczak *and* Clare Cavanagh

Terrors are to come. The earth. To My Children, Fearing for Them. Wendell Berry. CP-BerrW

Terrors of the scenery, The. Sliding Mountain, The. Stevie Smith. CP-SmitS

Terse old maxim of the poet's pen, The. Child's Home—Long Ago, A. James Whitcomb Riley. CP-RileJ

Terse Verse. Robert Browning. CP-BroR2

Tess's Lament. Thomas Hardy. CP-HardT

Test, A. James Whitcomb Riley. CP-RileJ

Test Case. Thomas Kinsella. CP-KinsT

Test of Love, A. James Whitcomb Riley. CP-RileJ

Test of Love—is Death, The. Emily Dickinson. CP-DickE

Test of Manhood, The. George Meredith. CP-MerG1

Test, The. Ralph Waldo Emerson. CP-EmerR

Testa Dell' Effebo. Tennessee Williams. CP-WillT

Testament. Wendell Berry. CP-BerrW

Testament. Tu Fu. CP-KizeC, *tr. by* Carolyn Kizer

Testament. Robert Graves. CP-GravR

Testament. Langston Hughes. CP-HughL; CP-HughL3

Testament. Dorothy Parker. CP-ParkD

Testament. Carl Sandburg. CP-SandC

Testament, A. G. K. Chesterton. CP-ChesG

Testament, A. Robert Creeley. CP-CreeR

Testament, A. Richard Eberhart. CP-EberR

Testament and Complaynt of our Soverane Lordis Papyngo, The. Sir David Lyndsay. SP-LyndD

Testament of [Mr.] Andro Kennedy, The. William Dunbar. CP-DunbW

Testament of Perpetual Change, The. William Carlos Williams. CP-WilW2

Testament of Squyer Meldrum, The. Sir David Lyndsay. SP-LyndD

Testamentum. Wallace Stevens. CP-StevWP

Testimonial. Langston Hughes. CP-HughL; CP-HughL3

Testimony. Kathleen Jessie Raine. SP-RainK

Testimony. Richard Eberhart. CP-EberR

Testimony. Yusef Komunyakaa. CP-KomuY

Testimony. Dan Pagis. SP-PagiD, *tr. by* Stephen Mitchell

Testimony. César Vallejo. CP-MuldP, *tr. by* Paul Muldoon

Testimony, A. Christina Georgina Rossetti. CP-RosC1

Testimony of Divine Adoption, The. Jeanne Marie Bouvier de la Motte- Guyon. CP-CowpW

Testimony of J. Robert Oppenheimer, The. Ai. SP-Ai

Testimony Regarding a Ghost. Carl Sandburg. CP-SandC

Testing. Testing. Andrei Codrescu. SP-CodrA

Testing-Tree, The. Stanley Kunitz. CP-KunSC

Tests. Walt Whitman. CP-WhitW

Tests are good, The. You need a million of them. Wooden Buildings. John Ashbery. SP-AshbJ

Tête-à-Tête. Andrei Codrescu. SP-CodrA

Tête à Tête. Thomas Kinsella. CP-KinsT

Tethnakin D'oligo Pideuis Fainom Alaia. Allen Ginsberg. CP-GinsA; SP-GinsA

Teton Village. Allen Ginsberg. CP-GinsA

Tetrachlorine. Andrei Codrescu. SP-CodrA

Tewa Victories. Clarence Major. SP-MajoC

Texan. Charles Bukowski. SP-BukC1

Texas. Jorge Luis Borges. SP-BorgJ, *tr. by* Mark Strand

Texas. Czeslaw Milosz. CP-MiloCN, *tr. by* Robert Hass

Texas. John Greenleaf Whittier. CP-WhitJ

Text, The. Gary Snyder. CP-SnydG *Fr.* Myths and Texts.

Text, The. James Whitcomb Riley. CP-RileJ

Text: Love thou thy fellow man!, The. Text, The. James Whitcomb Riley. CP-RileJ

Textures of Space, The. Clarence Major. SP-MajoC

Th' ast dar'd too farre; but Furie now forbeare. To the Fever, Not To Trouble Julia. Robert Herrick. CP-HerrR

Th' Astrologers did all alike presage. On the Astrologers. *Unknown.* CP-CowpW

Th' have left thee naked Lord, O that they had. On Our Crucified Lord Naked, and Bloody. Richard Crashaw. CP-CrasR

Th' old man, our amiable old is gone. Another Version. William Cowper. CP-CowpW

Thalassa. Louis MacNeice. CP-MacNL

Thalia, tell in sober lays. Part of a Summer, The. Jonathan Swift. CP-SwifJ

Thalidomide. Sylvia Plath. CP-PlatS

Thamar and Amnon. Federico García Lorca. SP-GarcF, *tr. by* J. L. Gili *and* Stephen Spender

Thamar and Amnon. Federico García Lorca. CP-GarcF, *tr. by* Will Kirkland

Thames. William Blake. *See* Why Should I Care for the Men of Thames?

Thames at Chelsea, The. Joseph Brodsky. CP-BrodJ, *tr. by* David Rigsbee

Thames flows proudly to the sea, The. Banks of Nith, The. Robert Burns. CP-BurnR

Thames nocturne of blue and gold, The. Impression du Matin. Oscar Wilde. CP-WildO

Than a choice of subject. Château de Muzot. Charles Tomlinson. CP-TomlC

Than Heaven more remote. Emily Dickinson. CP-DickE

Than his chaste wife, though Beast now know no more. On the Same Beast. Ben Jonson. CP-JonsB; SP-JonsB

Than I. Robert Creeley. CP-CreeR

Thanatopsis. Miller Williams. CP-WillM

Than(by you sunset's wintry glow). E. E. Cummings. CP-CummE

Thank God. G. K. Chesterton. CP-ChesG

Thank God, bless God, all ye who suffer not. Tears. Elizabeth Barrett Browning. CP-BroEB

Thank God for Alleys. Charles Bukowski. SP-BukC2

Thank God for rest, where none molest. Peace Autumn, The. John Greenleaf Whittier. CP-WhitJ

Thank God for the old Jewish ladies. Street Corner Dialogue. Grace Paley. CP-PalGC

Thank God for the token! one lip is still free. Ritner. John Greenleaf Whittier. CP-WhitJ

Thank God, I don't have to write a poem. Birthday Poem. Philip Whalen. SP-WhalP

Thank God Life Came For Me, Nerthus Gathered Me Up For Her Annual. This Year. Charles Olson. CP-OlsoC

Thank God, thank God, we do believe. Christmas Carol, A: "Thank God, thank God, we do believe." Christina Georgina Rossetti. CP-RosC3

Thank God there is a world. Emily Dickinson. SP-DickE

Thank god there is no Tsar. Georgy Vladimirovich Ivanov. SP-WeisT, *tr. by* Theodore Weiss

Thank God who seasons thus the year. Soul's Season, The. Henry David Thoreau. CP-ThorH

Thank God Who spared me what I feared! For a Mercy Received. Christina Georgina Rossetti. CP-RosC3

Thank Heaven! the crisis. For Annie. Edgar Allan Poe. CP-PoeEd

Thank her dear power for having come. Emily Dickinson. SP-DickE

Thank the gods thy governors. Ralph Waldo Emerson. CP-EmerR

Thank thee dear distant. Thanksgiving. Federico García Lorca. CP-GarcF, *tr. by* Jerome Rothenberg *Fr.* Epitaph for a Bird.

Thank-You. G. K. Chesterton. CP-ChesG

Thank You. Robert Creeley. CP-CreeR

Thank You. Kenneth Koch. SP-KochK

Thank You. Stevie Smith. CP-SmitS

Thank you, dear Clarinda. To Clarinda. D. H. Lawrence. CP-LawrD

"Thank you" ebbs between us. Emily Dickinson. SP-DickE

Thank You, Fog. W. H. Auden. CP-AudeW

'Thank-You' for Coming to Tea, A. G. K. Chesterton. CP-ChesG

Thank you for leaving the bar of soap. Note to the Previous Tenants. John Updike. CP-UpdiJ

Thank You for Not Cooperating. John Ashbery. SP-AshbJ

Thank you for your letter. Ilford Rose Book. James Schuyler. CP-SchuJ

Thank you in my heart obstructs, The. Emily Dickinson. SP-DickE

Thank You, Lord. Maya Angelou. SP-AngeM

Thank-You Note. Elizabeth Bishop. CP-BishE

Thank-You Note. Wisława Szymborska. SP-SzymW, *tr. by* Stanisław Barańczak *and* Clare Cavanagh

Thank-You Note, A. Wisława Szymborska. SP-SzymWM, *tr. by* Joanna Trzeciak

Thank you. Thank you very much. I'm pleased. Untoward Occurance at Embassy Poetry Reading. Marilyn Hacker. SP-HackM

Thank you very much, how often I have thanked you, how. Sonatina Followed by Another, A. Gertrude Stein. CP-SteiG

"Thank you, whatever comes." And then she turned. Erat Hora. Ezra Pound. CP-PoeEar; SP-PounE

Thankfulness. Czeslaw Milosz. CP-MiloC; CP-MiloCN, *tr. by* Robert Hass

Thankless for favours from on high. On a Similar Occasion for the Year 1792.

William Cowper. CP-CowpW

Thanks. Robert Creeley. SP-CreeR

Thanks. Yusef Komunyakaa. CP-KomuY

Thanks for a Gift of Pheasants. William Cowper. CP-CowpW

Thanks for the omen, that War's rule is spent. Peace Congress the Promise of a Higher Civilization, The. Jones Very. CP-VeryJ

Thanks for the tree / between me & a sniper's bullet. Thanks. Yusef Komunyakaa. CP-KomuY

Thanks for thy gift. To Avis Keene. John Greenleaf Whittier. CP-WhitJ

Thanks for / what will be. Retrospect. Robert Creeley. SP-CreeR

Thanks in Old Age. Walt Whitman. CP-WhitW

Thanks to a Botanist, A. John Ciardi. CP-CiarJ

Thanks to Industrial Essex. Donald Davie. CP-DaviDC

Thanks to the morning light. World-Soul, The. Ralph Waldo Emerson. CP-EmerR

Thanks to those who go & come. Ralph Waldo Emerson. CP-EmerR

Thanksgiving. Federico García Lorca. CP-GarcF, *tr. by* Jerome Rothenberg *Fr.* Epitaph for a Bird.

Thanksgiving. Louise Glück. SP-GlucL

Thanksgiving. Louise Glück. SP-GlucL

Thanksgiving. Robert Herrick. CP-HerrR

Thanksgiving. Kenneth Koch. SP-KochK

Thanksgiving. James Whitcomb Riley. CP-RileJ

Thanksgiving. Yannis Ritsos. SP-RitsY, *tr. by* Kostas Myrsiades

Thanksgiving. A. W. H. Auden. CP-AudeW

Thanksgiving, The. George Herbert. CP-HerbG

Thanksgiving Day at Hunchley's. James Whitcomb Riley. CP-RileJ

Thanksgiving: Detroit. John Berryman. CP-BerrJ

Thanksgiving Dinner. Edna St. Vincent Millay. CP-MillE

Thanksgiving Flowers. Jones Very. CP-VeryJ

Thanksgiving for a former, doth invite. Thanksgiving. Robert Herrick. CP-HerrR

Thanksgiving for a Habitat. W. H. Auden. CP-AudeW

Thanksgiving for My Father, A. William Stafford. SP-StafW

Thanksgiving night: Third Avenue was dead. Thanksgiving's Over. Robert Lowell. SP-LoweR

Thanksgiving (1956). E. E. Cummings. CP-CummE

Thanksgiving Poem, A. Paul Laurence Dunbar. CP-DunbP

Thanksgiving Time. Langston Hughes. CP-HughL

Thanksgiving to God for His House, A. Robert Herrick. CP-HerrR

Thanksgiving's Over. Robert Lowell. SP-LoweR

Th'art hence removing, (like a Shepherds tent). Upon Himself. Robert Herrick. CP-HerrR

That a pansy is transitive. Emily Dickinson. SP-DickE

That a toss of wheat-ears lapping. Seur, near Blois. Donald Davie. CP-DaviDC

That a woman not ask a man to leave meaningful work to follow her. Prayer for Revolutionary Love. Denise Levertov. SP-LeveDL; SP-LeveDS

That Adam would was from the first implied. Metamorphosis. Robert Stock. SP-StocR

That affable, vital, inspired even, and well-paid. Tenzone. John Ciardi. CP-CiarJ

That after Horror—that 'twas us. That after horror that was us. Emily Dickinson. CP-DickE

That after horror that was us. Emily Dickinson. CP-DickE

That afternoon I had been fishing alone. Dream of Retarded Children, A. Robert Bly. SP-BlyR

That afternoon when Monsoor Mouse. Primeval Landscape with Politician and Dodo Bird. Robert Stock. SP-StocR

That aged woman with the bass voice. Great-Grandmother, The. Robert Graves. CP-GravR

That-air young-un ust to set. James Whitcomb Riley. CP-RileJ

That all I learned in books. Write on My Tomb. James Laughlin. CP-LaugJ

That always bitter, always honoured day. Petrarch. CP-Petra, *tr. by* J. G. Nichols

That Ancient Line. Laura Riding Jackson. CP-RidiL

That any just to long for. Root-light, or the Lawyer's Daughter. James Dickey. CP-DickJ

That art is evil (stale). Tolstoy. William Carlos Williams. CP-WilW2

That auto horn sounds familiar. Ernesto Cardenal. CP-MertT *Fr.* Gethsemani, KY.

That Bareheaded life under the grass. Emily Dickinson. SP-DickE

That bleeding beginning that every mourner knows. Emily Dickinson. SP-DickE

That bony potbellied arrow, wing-pumping along. Cormorant in Its Element, The. Amy Clampitt. CP-ClamA

That bravery, which came to flower in you. Petrarch. CP-Petra, *tr. by* J. G. Nichols

That bright chimeric beast. Countee Cullen. CP-CullC

That castle stands the highest in the land. Li Bel Chasteus. Ezra Pound. CP-PoeEar

That center of attention—an infantile face. Old Photograph of the Future. Robert Penn Warren. CP-WarrR

That Centre of Old. Ivor Gurney. SP-GurnI

That cheek of yours that has been tired with weeping. Petrarch. CP-Petra, *tr. by* J. G. Nichols

That chill is in the air. Not So Far as the Forest. Edna St. Vincent Millay. CP-MillE

That Chinese restaurant was a joke. Will to Change, The. Adrienne Rich. CP-RicAE

That Christ did die, the Pagan saith. Resurrection, The. Robert Herrick. CP-HerrR

That Christmas alone in no difference really. Christmas Alone in Key West. John Ciardi. CP-CiarJ

That Christmas quite the animal. Christmas Week, 1948. Donald Davie. CP-DaviDC

That Church they founded on the Word of God. Bible, The. Jones Very. CP-VeryJ

That city was happy and much beloved. In a City. Czeslaw Milosz. CP-MiloCN, *tr. by* Robert Hass

That civilisation may not sink. Long-Legged Fly. William Butler Yeats. CP-YeatW

That cloud—ambiguous, not. Descent of Mr. Aldez, The. John Updike. CP-UpdiJ

That Cod can get no widow, yet a knight. On Sir Cod the Perfumed. Ben Jonson. CP-JonsB; SP-JonsB

That Country. Grace Paley.

That country spire—Samuel Palmer knew. Returning from Church. Kathleen Jessie Raine. SP-RainK

That coursing on, whate'er men's speculations. Calming Thought of All, The. Walt Whitman. CP-WhitW

That crazed girl improvising her music. Crazed Girl, A. William Butler Yeats. CP-YeatW

That crude little old logcabin. Vanishing Institution, A. Kenneth Patchen. CP-PatcK

That cry's from the first cuckoo of the year. Shepherd and Goatherd. William Butler Yeats. CP-YeatW

That Damon was in love with me. Song: "That Damon was in love with me." Jane Austen. CP-AustJ

That darling baby! Alleyway. Philip Whalen. SP-WhalP

That Day. Elizabeth Barrett Browning. CP-BroEB

That Day. Rudyard Kipling. CP-KiplR

That Day. Anne Sexton. CP-SextA

That day / in an oak tree—. Robert Creeley. CP-CreeR

That day of wrath, that dreadful day. Hymn for the Dead. Sir Walter Scott. SP-ScotW *Fr.* Lay of the Last Minstrel, The.

That day, so innocent appeared. Picnic Remembered. Robert Penn Warren. CP-WarrR

That day the eggshell of appearance split. Transfigured Bird. James Merrill. SP-MerrJ

That day, the house was so much a ship. Faring, The. Charles Tomlinson. CP-TomlC; SP-TomlC

That day when oats were reaped, and wheat was ripe, and barley ripening. When Oats Were Reaped. Thomas Hardy. CP-HardT

That day would skin a fairy. Dying Art, A. Derek Mahon. CP-MahoD

That dim shattering character of nerves. Going to Bed. Robert Creeley. CP-CreeR

That Distance was between Us. Emily Dickinson. CP-DickE

That don't peel like an onion. Layers. James Laughlin. CP-LaugJ

That dragonfly, bloated, pinned. Definition in the Face of Unnamed Fury. Rita Dove. SP-DoveR

That dreary lake, that midnight sky. Emily Jane Brontë. CP-BronE

That Dresden clock, which runs slow and strikes. Winter Shiver. Stéphane Mallarmé. CP-MallS, *tr. by* Henry Weinfield

That each should in his house abide. Ralph Waldo Emerson. CP-EmerR

That Eden of earth's sunrise cannot vie. Christina Georgina Rossetti. CP-RosC2

That elbow with its pinpoint bruise. Recovery. Wyatt Prunty. SP-PrunW

That elephantine bray in the upper register, that sagacious rumbling down below. What a Wonder Among the Instruments Is the Walloping Tramboone! Hayden Carruth. CP-CarHS

That Elf. Hare, The. Ted Hughes. SP-HughTN

That evening Sinda thought she heard the drums. Dream, The. Robert Earl Hayden. CP-HaydR

That evening, when night was already at the door. Striking of the Tower Clock, The. Jaroslav Seifert. SP-SeifJ, *tr. by* Ewald Osers

That Eyes! Those Nose! Philip Whalen. SP-WhalP

That famous fatheads find that each. E. E. Cummings. CP-CummE

That far-off day the leaves in flight. Wind and the Rain, The. Robert Frost. CP-FrosR

That fawn-skin-dappled hair of hers. Pretty Woman, A. Robert Browning. CP-BroR1

That fell and iced / the walks and streets. Snow, The. James Schuyler. CP-SchuJ

That fellow on the boattrain who insisted. Lawrence Ferlinghetti. SP-FerlL

That fire I liked to think had been extinguished. Petrarch. CP-Petra, *tr. by* J. G. Nichols

That first Day, when you praised Me, Sweet. Emily Dickinson. CP-DickE

That first green night of their dreaming, asleep beneath the. Sixth Night: Waking, The. Muriel Rukeyser. CP-RukeM

That first summer, what little. Beach Pea, The. Amy Clampitt. CP-ClamA

That first week in Santa Barbara wasn't the worst thing. Next Year. Raymond Carver. CP-CarvR

That flattering glass, whose smooth face wears. Looking-Glass, A. Thomas Carew. CP-CareT

That flow of Gallants which approach. Men Mind No State in Sicknesse. Robert Herrick. CP-HerrR

That flower unseen, that gem of purest ray. In a Churchyard. Richard Wilbur. CP-WilbR

That for seven lustres [*or* lusters] I did never come. To the Reverend Shade of His Religious Father. Robert Herrick. CP-HerrR

That Force. Adam Zagajewski. SP-ZagaA, *tr. by* Renata Gorczynski

That friends we loved, in dying did not die. Faith in the Resurrection Confirmed. Jones Very. CP-VeryJ

That gaiety oh. Lear Is Gay. Robert Earl Hayden. CP-HaydR

That Garden of sedate Philosophy. Garden of Epicurus, The. George Meredith. CP-MerG1

That garland! Hurry! For I'm dying! Sonnet of the Garland of Roses. Federico García Lorca. CP-GarcF, *tr. by* Angela Jaffray

That gloomy cave, that gothic niche. Written in Mrs Field's Album opposite a Pen-and-Ink Sketch in the Manner of a Rembrandt Etching Done by Edmund Field. William Wordsworth. CP-WorW2

That God is colouring Newton does shew. To Venetian Artists. William Blake. CP-BlakW

That God of ours, the Great Geometer. Grace to Be Said at the Supermarket. Howard Nemerov. CP-NemeH

That grandiose colossus who. Letter to a Purist. Sylvia Plath. CP-PlatS

That gray sponge! Christmas on the Hudson. Federico García Lorca. CP-GarcF, *tr. by* Greg Simon *and* Steven F. White

That great feather the mind's wind drives. At Drumcliffe Churchyard, County Sligo. John Logan. CP-LogaJ

That guy three lots down on the oth- / er side? Name of Crawford. Shake, Well Before Using. Hayden Carruth. CP-CarHS

That hackney'd judge of human life. On Marriage. Robert Burns. CP-BurnR

That had a swivel / mirror, a swivel. On the Dresser. James Schuyler. CP-SchuJ

That Happines do's still the longest thrive. Happinesse. Robert Herrick. CP-HerrR

That happy gleam of vernal eyes. Gleaner (Suggested By a Picture), The. William Wordsworth. CP-WorW2

That he is human . . . and living. Emperor Haile Selassie. Langston Hughes. CP-HughL; CP-HughL3

That he knows more of love than you, by far. Gentleman, The. Robert Graves. CP-GravR

That heat! / That terrible heat. Marriage of Souls, The. William Carlos Williams. CP-WilW2

That her serene influence should spread. Two Loves. Richard Eberhart. CP-EberR

That hero my allegiance earns. Everything's Haggis in Hoboken, or, Scots Wha Hae Hae. Ogden Nash. CP-NashO

That his fast-flowing hours with sandy silt. St. Thecla. Gerard Manley Hopkins. CP-HopkG

That holy Hymnes with Lovers cares are knit. To the Reader. Thomas Campion. CP-CampT

That honoured name! Lady Cochrane. Donald Davie. CP-DaviDC

That hump of a man bunching chrysanthemums. Old Florist. Theodore Roethke. CP-RoetT

That I am a bit odd but. I Am Aware. James Laughlin. CP-LaugJ

That I did always love. Emily Dickinson. CP-DickE

That I don't talk to her frankly. She Says That I Put on Gloves. James Laughlin. CP-LaugJ

That I Had Had Courage When Young. Hayden Carruth. CP-CarHS

That I have been looking. Subway Face. Langston Hughes. CP-HughL; CP-HughL1

That I, hereafter, do not think the bar. Epigram to the Coucillor That Pleaded and Carried the Cause, An. Ben Jonson. CP-JonsB

That I now call you by your name. Martial. CP-CunnJ, *tr. by* James Vincent Cunningham

That I once more thy dulcet voice. Now Strike the Golden Lyre Again. James Laughlin. CP-LaugJ

That insect, without antennae, over its. Crane, The. Charles Tomlinson. CP-TomlC; SP-TomlC

That is a quiet place. House of Silence, The. Thomas Hardy. CP-HardT

That is A, that is Anna speaking. That is A, that is no one speaking and it's winter. Portrait Now Before Then. Michael Palmer. SP-PalmM

That is all, merely. Such Was Our Garden. Kenneth Rexroth. CP-RexrK

That is his jacket. These are. Joe's Corner. William Stafford. SP-StafWW

That is no country for old men. The young. Sailing to Byzantium. William Butler Yeats. CP-YeatW

That is not your mother but her body. Dogs Are Eating Your Mother, The. Ted Hughes. SP-HughTN

That is solemn we have ended. Emily Dickinson. CP-DickE

That is, their authors, leave out. History Books. Thomas Lux. SP-LuxT

That is work of waste and ruin. Foresight. William Wordsworth. CP-WorW1

That it doesn't stop there. Thoughts on the Run 3. Hans Magnus Enzensberger. SP-EnzeH, tr. by Rita Dove and Fred Viebahn

That it is true, Master. Emily Dickinson. SP-DickE

That it will never come again. Emily Dickinson. CP-DickE

That Jealousy may rule a mind. Not at Home. Samuel Taylor Coleridge. CP-ColeS

That Justice is a blind goddess. Justice. Langston Hughes. CP-HughL; CP-HughL1; CP-HughL3

That kid's my buddy. Buddy. Langston Hughes. CP-HughL; CP-HughL3

That Kind of Thing. Tess Gallagher. SP-GallT

That Kiss in the Dark. Thomas Hardy. CP-HardT

That kiss meant to sear my heart forever. Time Lapse with Tulips. Tess Gallagher. SP-GallT

That lady whom I always have in mind. Petrarch. CP-Petra, tr. by J. G. Nichols

That lamp thou fill'st in Eros' name to night. Hero's Lamp. Dante Gabriel Rossetti. CW-RossD Fr. House of Life, The.

That lavished sunlight, where. Two Songs in a Stanza of Beddoes'. Richard Wilbur. CP-WilbR

That lime-tree—no, what is it? mulberry? Recollection of George Oppen in a Letter to an English Friend. Donald Davie. CP-DaviDC

That line is the horizon line. Shipbored. John Updike. CP-UpdiJ

That little Negro's married and got a kid. Sister. Langston Hughes. CP-HughL; CP-HughL3

That little pretty [or prettie] bleeding part. To His Savior [or Saviour]. The New Years [or yeers] Gift. Robert Herrick. CP-HerrR

That little yaller gal. New Cabaret Girl, The. Langston Hughes. CP-HughL; CP-HughL1

That lively organ, palpitant and red. Proud Heart, The. Countee Cullen. CP-CullC

That lofty monarch, Monarch Mind. Natural History. Sylvia Plath. CP-PlatS

That Love at length should find me out and bring. Edna St. Vincent Millay. CP-MillE

That Love is all there is. Emily Dickinson. CP-DickE

That Love last long; let it thy first care be. Caution, A. Robert Herrick. CP-HerrR

That love 'twixt men do's ever longest last. On Love. Robert Herrick. CP-HerrR

That lovely climbing vine, so fresh. Conversation with a Japanese Student. Eleanor Wilner. SP-WilnE

That lovely lady who possessed your heart. Petrarch. CP-Petra, tr. by J. G. Nichols

That lovely spot which thou dost see. Upon a Mole in Celia's Bosom. Thomas Carew. CP-CareT

That lover of a night. Crazy Jane on God. William Butler Yeats. CP-YeatW

That love's a bitter sweet, I ne'er conceive. Elegy, An: "That love's a bitter sweet, I ne'er conceive." Ben Jonson. CP-JonsB

That love's dull smart distressed my heart. Her Secret. Thomas Hardy. CP-HardT

That makes me worship. What Is the Need. James Laughlin. CP-LaugJ

That Man. Jorge Luis Borges. SP-BorgJ, tr. by Alan S. Trueblood

That man, / an immense constellation. Paper Roses. Federico García Lorca. CP-GarcF, tr. by Jerome Rothenberg Fr. Fairs.

That man is peer of the gods, who. Sappho. Sappho. CP-WilW2

That Manna, which God on His people cast. Manna. Robert Herrick. CP-HerrR

That march of the funereal Past behold. Il y a Cent Ans. George Meredith. CP-MerG2

That mare stood in the field. All through the Rains. Gary Snyder. CP-SnydG

That matter of the murder is hushed up. Cenci, The. Percy Bysshe Shelley. CP-ShelP

That mean old yesterday. Mean Old Yesterday. Langston Hughes. CP-HughL; CP-HughL3

That melancholy / fellow'll play / his handorgan. E. E. Cummings. CP-CummE

That miracle—which in these days of ours. Petrarch. CP-Petra, tr. by J. G. Nichols

That mirror / Which makes of men a transparency. Moments of Vision. Thomas Hardy. CP-HardT

That Moment. Ted Hughes. SP-HughTN Fr. Crow.

That Moment. Thomas Hardy. CP-HardT

That moment when the high-wire walker suddenly begins to falter, wobble, sway, arms flailing. Vehicle: Conscience. C. K. Williams. SP-WillC

That morn[e] which saw me made a Bride. Upon a Maid That Died [or Dyed]

the Day She Was Married [or Marryed]. Meleager. CP-HerrR, tr. by Robert Herrick

That Morning. Ted Hughes. SP-HughTN

That morning Lars fell. Rucksack, The. Paul Muldoon. CP-MuldP

That morning when I trod the town. Chimes, The. Thomas Hardy. CP-HardT

That Music Always Round Me. Walt Whitman. CP-WhitW

That must be a silver bell. Emily Dickinson. SP-DickE

That nameless son of a bitch of a critic who. February Twelfth Birthday Statement. Alan Dugan. CP-DugaA

That Nature Is a Heraclitean Fire and of the Comfort of the Resurrection. Gerard Manley Hopkins. CP-HopkG

That neither fame nor love might wanting be. To Sir Henry Cary. Ben Jonson. CP-JonsB; SP-JonsB

That Night. James Whitcomb Riley. CP-RileJ

That night came on in Egypt with a step. First-Born of Egypt, The. Robert Browning. CP-BroR2

That night for Gene. Ringing Doorbells. Amy Clampitt. CP-ClamA

That night, that night, / That song, that song! Bygone Occasion, A. Thomas Hardy. CP-HardT

That Night the. Moon came out full, you could see the white breathing of the. Kenneth Patchen. CP-PatcK

That night, the great tree split. Scar, The. Charles Tomlinson. CP-TomlC

That night, when through the mooring-chains. Rudyard Kipling. See 'Twas Fultah Fisher's boarding-house

That night, / winter, / rain. C. K. Williams. CP-WillC; SP-WillC

That night your great guns, unawares. Channel Firing. Thomas Hardy. CP-HardT

That no man schemed it is my hope. Blow, The. Thomas Hardy. CP-HardT

That No Man Take Thy Crown. Christina Georgina Rossetti. CP-RosC2

That Noble Flower. Robinson Jeffers. CP-JefR3

That none beguiled be by time's quick flowing. Love's Clock. Sir John Suckling. CP-SuckJ

That noon we banged like tubs in a blast from Hell's mouth. Launcelot in Hell. John Ciardi. CP-CiarJ

That, not a pair of friends each other see. To Mime. Ben Jonson. CP-JonsB; SP-JonsB

That note you hold, narrowing and rising, shakes. For Sidney Bechet. Philip Larkin. CP-LarkP

That Nova was a moderate star like our good sun; it stored no doubt a. Nova. Robinson Jeffers. CP-JefR2

That nude kneeling so sad-seeming. Touching the River. Thomas Kinsella. CP-KinsT

That oblong book's the Album; hand it here! Inn Album, The. Robert Browning. CP-BroR2

That ocean you of late surveyed. To Mr. Newton [on His Return from Ramsgate]. William Cowper. CP-CowpW

That odd old man is dead a year. Emily Dickinson. CP-DickE

That of the eyes / Opening in the morning. Prison. Charles Simic. SP-SimiCE

That often we were interested, dear Conneau! Exiles. Arthur Rimbaud. CP-RimbA, tr. by Martin Sorrell

That old black goober that I ate. Sopa. Robert Creeley. CP-CreeR

That on her lap she casts her humble Eye. On the Blessed Virgins Bashfulnesse. Richard Crashaw. CP-CrasR

That once which pained to think of. Forgiven Past, The. Laura Riding Jackson. CP-RidiL

That One. Philip Whalen. SP-WhalP

That one who is the dreamer lies mostly in her left arm. Angina. James Dickey. CP-DickJ

That Other Maud Miller. James Whitcomb Riley. CP-RileJ

That other sun by whom the path was shown. Petrarch. CP-Petra, tr. by J. G. Nichols

That Other World. Robert Graves. CP-GravR

That Other World. James Laughlin. CP-LaugJ

That our senses lie and our minds trick us is true, but in general. Advice to Pilgrims. Robinson Jeffers. CP-JefR3

That out of sight is out of mind. Arthur Hugh Clough. SP-ClouA

That pack of scoundrels. System, The. Stanley Kunitz. CP-KunSC

That painting next to the brocaded drapery. Alcohol. Raymond Carver. CP-CarvR

That pale face stretches across the centuries. Yes, I Know. Stevie Smith. CP-SmitS

That 'part / Of consciousness'. Debt. George Oppen. CP-OppGN

That Pass between the False Dawn and the True. Ezra Pound. CP-PoeEar

That Passeth All Understanding. Denise Levertov. SP-LeveDS

That Phaeton of our day. Henry David Thoreau. CP-ThorH

That phrase in the head—that snatch repeated. Melody. Charles Tomlinson. CP-TomlC

That plastic Buddha jars out a Karate screech. Do Not Pick Up the Telephone. Ted Hughes. SP-HughTN

That poetry should be adorn- / ed or complicated I'm. Some People Think.

James Laughlin. CP-LaugJ

That poets are far rarer births than kings. To Elizabeth, Countess of Rutland. Ben Jonson. CP-JonsB; SP-JonsB

That pointless happiness, was it worth it? Georgy Vladimirovich Ivanov. SP-WeisT, *tr.* by Theodore Weiss

That Possession fairest lies. Emily Dickinson. SP-DickE

That powerful lord from whom we cannot hide. Petrarch. CP-Petra, *tr.* by J. G. Nichols

That Prince must govern with a gentle hand. Gentlenesse. Robert Herrick. CP-HerrR

That Prince takes some enough the Victors roome. Prevision, or Provision. Robert Herrick. CP-HerrR

That Prince, who may doe nothing but what's just. King and No King, A. Robert Herrick. CP-HerrR

That Princes may possesse a surer seat. Pollicie in Princes. Robert Herrick. CP-HerrR

That profound cleft. June 9. William Carlos Williams. CP-WilW2

That proper ghoul, the scholar, may exhume. Poet-Scholar, The. Donald Davie. CP-DaviDC

That Providence which had so long the care. Poem upon the Death of Oliver Cromwell, A. Andrew Marvell. CP-MarvA

That public men publish falsehoods. Be Angry at the Sun. Robinson Jeffers. CP-JefR3

That quiet point of light. Letters. Jane Cooper. CP-CoopJ

That reason is a gift of God and that we should believe in its ability to comprehend the world. What I Learned from Jeanne Hersch. Czeslaw Milosz. CP-MiloCN, *tr.* by Robert Hass

That Reminds Me. Ogden Nash. CP-NashO

That rising, of the first, you cause. Of Lady, of Beauty, of Stream. Charles Olson. CP-OlsoC

That road / got no people. Sketches. Federico García Lorca. CP-GarcF, *tr.* by Jerome Rothenberg *Fr.* Night (Suite for Piano and Poet's Voice).

That romantic star. One. Federico García Lorca. CP-GarcF, *tr.* by Jerome Rothenberg *Fr.* Night (Suite for Piano and Poet's Voice).

That round faced woman, she owns the street with her three big dogs. Lower East Side. Allen Ginsberg. SP-GinsA *Fr.* After Whitman & Reznikoff.

That row of icicles along the gutter. Beyond Words. Robert Frost. CP-FrosR

That sacred Closet when you sweep. Emily Dickinson. CP-DickE

That "Sacred to the Memory." Sacred to the Memory. Thomas Hardy. CP-HardT

That sail which leans on light. Sea Grapes. Derek Walcott. CP-WalcD

That same first fiddler who leads the orchéstra to-night. At Madame Tussaud's in Victorian Years. Thomas Hardy. CP-HardT

That same night. Yannis Ritsos. SP-RitsY, *tr.* by Gwendolyn MacEwan *and* Nikos Tsingos *Fr.* Paper Poems 3.

That schoolmen are subtle the world have agreed. Epigram Addressed to Two Clergymen Who Had Been Trying in Jest to Put Some Constructions on the Conversation That Was Not Meant, An. Annis Boudinot Stockton. CP-StocA

That sculptor we knew, the passionate-eyed son of a quarryman. Artist, An. Robinson Jeffers. CP-JefR1

That second time they hunted me. Italian in England, The. Robert Browning. CP-BroR1

That Shadow My Likeness. Walt Whitman. CP-WhitW

That she forgot me was the least. Emily Dickinson. CP-DickE

That she'd been designed for. She Seemed to Know. James Laughlin. CP-LaugJ

That shining moon—watched by that one faint star. Night. Walter De la Mare. CP-DeLaW

That shining, yes, the one that. Paul Celan. SP-CelaP, *tr.* by John Felstiner

That short—potential stir. Emily Dickinson. CP-DickE

That short-sleeved man, our. Modest Mound of Bones, A. John Updike. CP-UpdiJ

That should be obvious. Slums, The. Kenneth Patchen. CP-PatcK

That shoulder. An erotic thing submerged in duration. Pastels by Degas. Czeslaw Milosz. CP-MiloCN, *tr.* by Robert Hass

That shrewd character Will Percy in. University of the South, The. Donald Davie. CP-DaviDC

That shy angle of his daughter's head. Variation on Gaining a Son. Rita Dove. SP-DoveR

That Silent Evening. Galway Kinnell. SP-KinnGN

That simplest gesture which can touch. Goodbye. Robert Penn Warren. CP-WarrR

That second gesture which can touch. If It All Went Up in Smoke. George Oppen. CP-OppGN

That smoke / would remain. If It All Went Up in Smoke. George Oppen. CP-OppGN

That smokestack, for instance. Obedience. Rita Dove. SP-DoveR

That sneaky Thomas Cranmer! Widower. Donald Davie. CP-DaviDC

That snowless, warmthless January sucked. Frost. John Updike. CP-UpdiJ

That solemn Senator / who claimed I had castles. Pablo Neruda. SP-NeruP *Fr.* Question Book.

That Song of Songs which is Solomon's. In the Day of His Espousals. Christina

Georgina Rossetti. CP-RosC2

That Sorrow dare to touch the Loved. Emily Dickinson. SP-DickE

That sound, everywhere about us, of the sea. Ce bruit da la mer. Denise Levertov. SP-LeveDP

That Star. Ted Hughes. SP-HughTN

That star. That Star. Ted Hughes. SP-HughTN

That strange flower, the sun. Gubbinal. Wallace Stevens. CP-StevW; CP-StevWP

That Such have died enable Us. Emily Dickinson. CP-DickE

That summer midnight under her aurora. Transgress, The. Muriel Rukeyser. CP-RukeM

That summer was so hot and muggy. Summer. Adam Zagajewski. SP-ZagaA

That summer when I worked in the frozen foods plant. Life Moving More Rapidly Than Hands Can Manage. William Dickey. SP-DickW

That Sunday morning we had travelled far. Tollund. Seamus Heaney. SP-HeanSO

That sweet Physician, an approaching spring. Emily Dickinson. SP-DickE

That sweet sinewy green nymph. Laocoön is the Name of the Figure. Marge Piercy. SP-PierM

That telephone keeps screaming its little black heart out. Little Black Heart of the Telephone. Robert Penn Warren. CP-WarrR

That the death of a child. Alison's Letter Used as a Bookmark for Ungaretti's Poems. William Corbett. SP-CorbW

That the dialogue of pebbles and brooks. Triadic Node for Tim Reynold's Digestion. Robert Stock. SP-StocR

That the Divine has been human. Emily Dickinson. SP-DickE

That the girls of Cimmeria. Herodotus Reports. James Laughlin. CP-LaugJ

That the glass would melt in heat. Glass of Water, The. Wallace Stevens. CP-StevW; CP-StevWP

That the Night Come. William Butler Yeats. CP-YeatW

That the Sestina is What it is Despite What it is Not. Robert Stock. SP-StocR

That the stream should tremble. Several Large Rocks in a Swiftly Rushing Stream. Robert Stock. SP-StocR

That the world / is going. C. K. Williams. CP-WillC; SP-WillC

That the world will never be quite—what a cliché—the same again. Tam Cari Capitis. Louis MacNeice. CP-MacNL

That then becomes you Have. Assuming the Soul Is a Bitch. Charles Olson. CP-OlsoC

That there are powers above us I admit. Arthur Hugh Clough. SP-ClouA

That there is falsehood in his looks. Parson's Looks, The. Robert Burns. CP-BurnR

That there shall not be violence. Resolve, The. George Oppen. CP-OppGN

That there were men. Downward. May Swenson. SP-SwenM

That there's a God, we all do know. Another. Robert Herrick. CP-HerrR

That they have no earthly measure. Sadness and Happiness. Robert Pinsky. CP-PinsR

That They Might Appear. Constantine P. Cavafy. CP-CavaC, *tr.* by Theoharis Constantine Theoharis

That they that have not been. Blazed. Ezra Pound. CP-PoEar

That things aren't what they should be in the Colony. In a Large Greek Colony, 200 B.C.. Constantine P. Cavafy. CP-CavaC, *tr.* by Theoharis Constantine Theoharis

That this is I, / Not mine, which wakes. Hills, The. George Oppen. CP-OppGN

That this is the gift. Gift, The. Charles Bukowski. SP-BukC2

That this should feel the need of Death. Emily Dickinson. CP-DickE

That this wondering two-footed / notion of abeyance should. Persons. Robert Creeley. CP-CreeR

That thou art loved of God, this work is done. To My L[ord] the King, on the Christening His Second Son James. Ben Jonson. CP-JonsB

That thou hast kept thy love, increased thy will. To the Same [Sir Thomas Roe]. Ben Jonson. CP-JonsB; SP-JonsB

That thou mayst injure no man, dove-like be. Prudent Simplicity. Goronwy Owen. CP-CowpW, *tr.* by William Cowper

That tie, knitted, with a thick knot. Aleksander Wat's Tie. Czeslaw Milosz. CP-MiloCN, *tr.* by Robert Hass

That time I made the winter journey. Authority of Krajova, The. Kenneth Patchen. CP-PatcK

That time I tagged along with my dad to the dry cleaners. Another Mystery. Raymond Carver. CP-CarvR

That time is dead for ever, child! Lines: "That time is dead for ever, child!" Percy Bysshe Shelley. CP-ShelP

That time of day the rapid sky inclines. Petrarch. CP-Petra, *tr.* by J. G. Nichols

That time of the early year. Back of Affluence. Donald Davie. CP-DaviDC

That time that mirth did steer my ship. Sir Thomas Wyatt. CP-WyatT

That Tree. A. K. Ramanujan. CP-RamaA

That tree said. Those Two. Allen Ginsberg. SP-GinsA

That, true to the contours which round it. Derbyshire Turf. Donald Davie. CP-DaviDC

That unripe side of earth, that heavy clime. To the Countess of Huntingdon ("That unripe side of earth, that heavy clime"). John Donne. CP-DonnJ;

MW-DonnJ

That wandering fire to me appears. Ralph Waldo Emerson. CP-EmerR

That was a place, when I was young. Offering for Mr. Bluehart, An. James Wright. CP-WrigJ

That was a pretty one, I heard you call. Referred Back. Philip Larkin. CP-LarkP

That was a strange game of chess. Chicago Cabaret. Kenneth Rexroth. CP-RexrK

That was an imprinted effigy of a river. Wall of a Museum, The. Czeslaw Milosz. CP-MiloCN, *tr.* by Robert Hass

That was by the door. Broken Promise. Archibald MacLeish. CP-MacLA

That was childhood, which won't come back. Sisters of Mercy. Adam Zagajewski. SP-ZagaA

That was I, you heard last night. Serenade at the Villa, A. Robert Browning. CP-BroR1; SP-BroR

That was in a big city, no matter what country, what language. Lastingness. Czeslaw Milosz. CP-MiloCN, *tr.* by Robert Hass

That was in 1875, and we come through. Mona Van Duyn. SP VanDM

That was in 1875, then we moved here. Mona Van Duyn. SP-VanDM

That was my grandfather, nearly went to prison. Mona Van Duyn. SP-VanDM

That was not the genesis. In the Beginning. Laura Riding Jackson. CP-RidiL

That was once her casement. In the Mind's Eye. Thomas Hardy. CP-HardT

That was the chirp of Ariel. Wind on the Lyre. George Meredith. CP-MerG1

That was the day they invited. Beethoven Attends the C Minor Seminar. Charles Tomlinson. CP TomlC

That was the moment when, without. Short History of the Bourgeoisie. Hans Magnus Enzensberger. SP-EnzeH, *tr.* by Hans Magnus Enzensberger *and* Michael Hamburger

That Was the Night. Robert Graves. CP-GravR

That was the proverb. Let my mistress[e] be. Long and Lazy [*or* Lazie]. Robert Herrick. CP-HerrR

That was the year of the bad war. The others—. Interjection #4: Bad Year, Bad War: A New Year's Card, 1969. Robert Penn Warren. CP-WarrR

That was the year / of the black nights and clear. Craigvara House. Derek Mahon. CP-MahoD

That way look, my Infant, lo! Kitten and [the] Falling Leaves, The. William Wordsworth. CP-WorW1

That we are always glad. Secrets. W. H. Auden. CP-AudeW

That we are permanent. Emily Dickinson. SP-DickE

That We Here Highly Resolve. Kenneth Patchen. CP-PatcK

That we the [*or* thy] loss might know, and thou our love. To King James ("That we the [*or* thy] loss might know, and thou our love"). Ben Jonson. CP-JonsB; SP-JonsB

That we've smashed their statues. Ionian. Constantine P. Cavafy. CP-CavaC, *tr.* by Theoharis Constantine Theoharis

That when the good man lowly bent. On Fabricius. *Unknown, sometimes at. to* Thomas Sheridan. CP-SherT

That Where I Am, There Ye May Be Also. Christina Georgina Rossetti. CP-RosC2

That which brings it. Description. Charles Simic. SP-SimiC; SP-SimiCE

That which eludes this verse and any verse. Riddle Song, A. Walt Whitman. CP-WhitW

That which gives me to see. Virtuous Agent, The. William Carlos Williams. CP-WilW2

That Which Hath Been Is Named Already, and It Is Known That It Is Man. Christina Georgina Rossetti. CP-RosC2

That which in colour and in scent outdid. Petrarch. CP-Petra, *tr.* by J. G. Nichols

That which is inside me. Bloodbirth. Audre Lorde. SP-LordA

That which is marred at birth Time shall not mend. Gertrude's Prayer. Rudyard Kipling. CP-KiplR

That which once overbent the turn of chance. Decline of Prophecy. Laura Riding Jackson. CP-RidiL

That which pushes upward. Consulting I Ching Smoking Pot Listening to the Fugs Sing Blake. Allen Ginsberg. CP-GinsA

That which we waited for as a justification of our lives. Fulfillment. Yannis Ritsos. SP-RitsY, *tr.* by Thanasis Maskaleris

That which we who're alive in spite of mirrors. E. E. Cummings. CP-CummE

That which you make you become—he used to say. And the unalterable—said the other. Eyes of the Statue, The. Yannis Ritsos. SP-RitsY, *tr.* by Kimon Friar *and* Kostas Myrsiades

That whiskey will cook the egg. Bar. Langston Hughes. CP-HughL; CP-HughL3

That whisper takes the voice. In a Whispering Gallery. Thomas Hardy. CP-HardT

That white coconut, the sun. Cloud Shadows. John Updike. CP-UpdiJ

That Whitsun, I was late getting away. Whitsun Weddings, The. Philip Larkin. CP-LarkP

That whole way up to your brilliant diadem. Michelangelo Buonarroti. CP-Miche, *tr.* by John Frederick Nims

That wind, I used to hear it swelling. Emily Jane Brontë. CP-BronE

That window has my everlasting hate. Petrarch. CP-Petra, *tr.* by J. G. Nichols

That window where one sun is visible. Petrarch. CP-Petra, *tr.* by J. G. Nichols

That wind's still there that I remember afire. Agrigentum Road, The. Salvatore Quasimodo. CP-WilbR

That winter I stopped loving the President. Suite for Augustus, A. Rita Dove. SP-DoveR

That winter of my third-form year. How to Play Championship Tennis. Paul Muldoon. CP-MuldP

That winter of the war, every day. In Camp. William Stafford. SP-StafW; SP-StafWW

That winter when this thought came—how the river. Living on the Plains. William Stafford. SP-StafW; SP-StafWW

That with this bright believing band. Impercipient, The. Thomas Hardy. CP-HardT

That woman!—eyeing houses. Lorine Niedecker. CP-NiedL

That wood pole's. Greeting. Rae Armantrout. SP-ArmaA

That would be waving and that would be crying. Waving Adieu, Adieu, Adieu. Wallace Stevens. CP-StevW; CP-StevWP

That Year. William Stafford. SP-StafWW

That year he found himself without a job. Days of 1908. Constantine P. Cavafy. CP-CavaC, *tr.* by Theoharis Constantine Theoharis

That year, March began in April. Discrepancies. Charles Tomlinson. CP-TomlC

That year of the cloud, when my marriage failed. River Road. Stanley Kunitz. CP-KunSC

That year the end of winter stood under a sign. Comet, The. Michael Palmer. SP-PalmM

That year the news. Time Capsule. William Stafford. SP-StafW

That you are fair or wise is vain. Fate. Ralph Waldo Emerson. CP-EmerR

That you, friend Marcus, like a Stoic. Parson's Case, The. Jonathan Swift. CP-SwifJ

That you have seen the pride, beheld the sport. Epigram, An: "That you have seen the pride, beheld the sport." Ben Jonson. CP-JonsB

That you may hear me, my words. Pablo Neruda. SP-LoguC, *tr.* by Christopher Logue *Fr.* Red Bird.

That you return to us alive. Emily Dickinson. SP-DickE

That you should still send / yourself to me, that you should. Valentine. Hayden Carruth. CP-CarHS

That you will take the meaning of this verse. To R.H.H. with Daphne. George Meredith. CP-MerG2

That your loved Confederate and yourself. Emily Dickinson. SP-DickE

Thatch of the roof was as golden, The. Nativity, The. G. K. Chesterton. CP-ChesG

Thatch, The. Robert Frost. CP-FrosR

Thatcher. Seamus Heaney. SP-HeanSO

That's Funny, Wasn't It? No, It Won't Be. Ogden Nash. CP-NashO

That's my last Duchess painted on the wall. My Last Duchess. Robert Browning. CP-BroR1; SP-BroR

That's my younger brother with his Navy wings. Family Group. Archibald MacLeish. CP-MacLA

That's never going to fit inside the box. Closing the House. Miller Williams. CP-WillM

That's not a cross look it's a sign of life. Poem: "That's not a cross look it's a sign of life." Frank O'Hara. SP-OharF

That's Sicily. Adam Zagajewski. SP-ZagaA, *tr.* by Clare Cavanagh

That's the condition o't or near. Hugh MacDiarmid. SP-MacDH *Fr.* Frae Anither Window in Thrums.

That's the down-town frieze. Common Life, The. Wallace Stevens. CP-StevW; CP-StevWP

That's the kind of books. Drugstore Library. William Carlos Williams. CP-WilW2

That's the Man. Constantine P. Cavafy. CP-CavaC, *tr.* by Theoharis Constantine Theoharis

That's the Naples packet slipping out of the harbour. Prison Island. James Fenton. SP-FentJ

That's the only image. Wall, A. Charles Simic. SP-SimiC; SP-SimiCE

That's the Sum of It. David Ignatow. SP-IgnaD

That's the way. Robert Creeley. SP-CreeR

That's what love is like. The whole river. Crossing Over. William Meredith. SP-MereW

That's what misery is. Poetry Is a Destructive Force. Wallace Stevens. CP-StevW; CP-StevWP

That's when I saw the old maple. Walking in the Woods. Grace Paley. CP-PalGC

Thaumatrope. Wyatt Prunty. SP-PrunW

Thaw. A. R. Ammons. CP-AmmoA

Thaw. Hayden Carruth. CP-CarHS

Thaw. Philip Larkin. CP-LarkP

Thaw, The. Primo Levi. CP-LeviP, *tr.* by Ruth Feldman

Thaw, The. Henry David Thoreau. CP-ThorH

The. Louis Zukofsky. CP-ZukLS

Theater of Sidon (400 A.D.). Constantine P. Cavafy. CP-CavaC, *tr. by* Theoharis Constantine Theoharis

Theaters crammed, everywhere music. Tarantians Divert Themselves, The. Constantine P. Cavafy. CP-CavaC, *tr. by* Theoharis Constantine Theoharis

Theatre at Argos, The. Oscar Wilde. CP-WildO

Theatre Impressions. Wisława Szymborska. SP-SzymW, *tr. by* Stanislaw Barańczak *and* Clare Cavanagh

Theatrical Reflection. Ogden Nash. CP-NashO

Thebaid. Robinson Jeffers. CP-JefR2

Thebais [*or* Thebaid]. Publius Papinius Statius.
"Fraternal Rage, the guilty Thebes alarms." CP-PopeA

Thee, dear friend, a brother soothes. To Rhea. Ralph Waldo Emerson. CP-EmerR

Thee for my recitative. To a Locomotive in Winter. Walt Whitman. CP-WhitW

Thee, God, I come from, to Thee go. Gerard Manley Hopkins. CP-HopkG

Thee sacrosanct, Thee sweet, Thee crystalline. Firstly Inclined to Take What It Is Told. Gwendolyn Brooks. SP-BrooG

Thee thou on looking out. Michael Palmer. SP-PalmM

Thee, whose refulgent staff, and summons clear. John Milton. *See* You who, conspicuous with your shining mace, were accustomed

Thee will I love, O Lord, my tow'r. Bible, *O.T. See* I will love thee, O Lord, my strength

Thee will i praise between those rivers whose. E. E. Cummings. CP-CummE

Their air binds in sockets. Sext. James McMichael. SP-McMiJ

Their apples fall down. Lorine Niedecker. CP-NiedL

Their Attitudes Differ. Margaret Atwood. SP-AtwM1

Their Barricade against the Sky. Emily Dickinson. CP-DickE

Their Beauty Has More Meaning. Robinson Jeffers. CP-JefR3

THEIR / Book of Stella. Susan Howe. SP-HoweS

Their brains are smooth machines that colonize. Masters, The. Hart Crane. CP-CranH

Their cheeks were fresh and tender. Civil Song. Pier Paolo Pasolini. SP-PasoP, *tr. by* Norman MacAfee *and* Luciano Martinengo

Their dappled importunity. Emily Dickinson. CP-DickE

Their Day. John Ashbery. SP-AshbJ

Their eggs named for his eyes I suppose. Man Who Writes Ants, The. W. S. Merwin. SP-MerwW

Their faces, safe as an interior. Middle-Aged, The. Adrienne Rich. CP-RicAE; SP-RicA2

Their feet on London, their heads in the grey clouds. Whit Monday. Louis MacNeice. CP-MacNL

Their garden has a silent tall stone-wall. Caserta Garden. Richard Wilbur. CP-WilbR

Their groves o' sweet myrtle let Foreign Lands reckon. Song: "Their groves o' sweet myrtle let Foreign Lands reckon." Robert Burns. CP-BurnR

Their hair, pomaded, faces jaded. Sepia Fashion Show. Maya Angelou. SP-AngeM

Their Heads Bent Toward Each Other Like Flowers. Tess Gallagher. SP-GallT

Their Height in Heaven comforts not. Emily Dickinson. CP-DickE

Their high pitched baying. Life of Others, The. Denise Levertov. SP-LeveDL; SP-LeveDS

Their learned kings bent down to chat with frogs. Nursery Rhyme. W. H. Auden. CP-AudeW

Their life, collapsed like unplayed cards. Moving in Winter. Adrienne Rich. CP-RicAE; SP-RicA2

Their Lonely Betters. W. H. Auden. CP-AudeW

Their love for Mickey Mouse. Corners of Night. Yusef Komunyakaa. CP-KomuY

Their marriage is a good one. In our eyes. Common Wisdom, The. Howard Nemerov. CP-NemeH

Their most prized possession. R R Bums, The. William Carlos Williams. CP-WilW2

Their Mouths Full. David Ignatow. SP-IgnaD

Their Origin. Constantine P. Cavafy. CP-CavaC, *tr. by* Theoharis Constantine Theoharis

Their prayers still swarm on me like lost bees. Saint of the Uplands, The. W. S. Merwin. SP-MerwW

Their Rectitude Their Beauty. Donald Davie. CP-DaviDC

Their relationship consisted. Jamesian. Thom Gunn. CP-GunnT

Their sex life was their own business. Cities of the Plain, The. Mona Van Duyn. SP-VanDM

Their shoes are stuccoed with sawdust and blood. Psalm: "Their shoes are stuccoed with sawdust and blood." Grace Paley. CP-PalGC

Their six-weeks-old daughter lies. Nocturne: "Their six-weeks-old daughter lies." Stephen Spender. CP-SpenS

Their supply-lines cut, / The leaves go down to defeat. Alatus. Richard Wilbur. CP-WilbR

Their Sweet Sorrow. James Whitcomb Riley. CP-RileJ

Their thoughts are night gulls. Old People Dozing. Denise Levertov. SP-LeveDL

Their time past, pulled down. Burning the Christmas Greens. William Carlos Williams. CP-WilW2

Their verdure dare not show . . . their verdure dare not show. Valediction: "Their verdure dare not show . . . their verdure dare not show." Louis MacNeice. CP-MacNL

Their voices heard, I stumble suddenly, remembering. One More New Botched Beginning. Stephen Spender. CP-SpenS

Their Voices Rang. Charles Tomlinson. CP-TomlC; SP-TomlC

Their war-boots said big shots to the plank floor. Behold, One of Several Little Christs. Kenneth Patchen. CP-PatcK

Their Week. W. S. Merwin. SP-MerwW

Theirs is a trade for egomaniacs. Novelists. Howard Nemerov. CP-NemeH

Theirs is the bond. Mother and Child. George Oppen. CP-OppGN

Thelonious Sphere Monk. William Corbett. SP-CorbW

Them, Crying. James Dickey. CP-DickJ

Them Flowers. James Whitcomb Riley. CP-RileJ

Them Old Cheery Words. James Whitcomb Riley. CP-RileJ

Them which despair. E. E. Cummings. CP-CummE

Theme and Variation. Robert Earl Hayden. CP-HaydR

Theme and Variations. Edna St. Vincent Millay. CP-MillE

Theme for English B. Langston Hughes. CP-HughL; CP-HughL3

Theme from Louise Labé, A. Marya Alexandrovna Zaturenska. SP-ZatuM

Theme in Yellow. Carl Sandburg. CP-SandC

Theme no poet gladly sung. Prudence. Ralph Waldo Emerson. CP-EmerR

Theme of Carnevale is a secret, The. Clarence Major. SP-MajoC

Theme of Death, The. Robert Graves. CP-GravR

Themes in Contrast. Carl Sandburg. CP-SandC

Themself are all I have. Emily Dickinson. CP-DickE

Then. Grace Paley. CP-PalGC

Then. Muriel Rukeyser. CP-RukeM

Then. Richard Wilbur. CP-WilbR

Then a pile of heads he laid. Rudyard Kipling. CP-KiplR *Fr.* Plain Tales from the Hills.

Then after Eden. New World. Derek Walcott. CP-WalcD

Then all of a sudden there appears to me. At Banagher. Seamus Heaney. SP-HeanSO

Then all the nations of birds lifted together. Season of Phantasmal Peace, The. Derek Walcott. CP-WalcD

Then and Now. Paul Laurence Dunbar. CP-DunbP

Then and Now. Thomas Hardy. CP-HardT

Then and Now. James Laughlin. CP-LaugJ

Then at the very end. Three Songs. Hayden Carruth. CP-CarHS

Then Bacchus' subtle speech her sorrow crossed. How Bacchus Comforts Ariadne. Nonnus. CP-BroEB *Fr.* Dionysiaca.

Then Bernard smiled at me, that I should gaze. Fragment from Dante. G. K. Chesterton. CP-ChesG

Then call me traitor if you must. To Certain Critics. Countee Cullen. CP-CullC

Then Came Flowers. Rita Dove. SP-DoveR

Then came, Oscar, the time of the guns. Long Guns. Carl Sandburg. CP-SandC

Then cried the American poet where she lay supine. Pearl. Stevie Smith. CP-SmitS

Then did I live when I did see. Sonnet of Perilla, A. Robert Herrick. CP-HerrR

Then ("Don't go / to the mountains"). Robert Creeley. SP-CreeR

Then fled, O brethren, the wicked juba. Ballad of Nat Turner, The. Robert Earl Hayden. CP-HaydR

Then follows a description. Laura Riding Jackson. CP-RidiL

Then from their poverty they rose. Ordinary Women, The. Wallace Stevens. CP-StevW; CP-StevWP

Then from tomorrow. Thomas Merton. CP-MertT

Then Guidwife Count the Lawin. Robert Burns. CP-BurnR

Then he laid down the bow of his violin. Red. D. H. Lawrence. CP-LawrD

Then hey, for a lass wi' a tocher, then hey, for a lass wi' a tocher. Robert Burns. *See* Awa wi' your witchcraft o' beauty's alarms

Then I came to Harriet Monroe. To Harriet Monroe. Richard Eberhart. CP-EberR

Then I Commended Mirth. Christina Georgina Rossetti. CP-RosC2

Then I do not know what. Trash Book, The. James Schuyler. CP-SchuJ

Then I forget / The star in the nets of heaven. Campaign. Muriel Rukeyser. CP-RukeM

Then I raised my head. Winter Sunset. William Carlos Williams. CP-WilW1

Then I Saw What the Calling Was. Muriel Rukeyser. CP-RukeM

Then I think of you in bed. December 11th. Anne Sexton. SP-SextA *Fr.* Eighteen Days without You.

Then I was young and had the strength of ten. Autopsy Room, The. Raymond Carver. CP-CarvR

Then I went down to the ancient port: human actions. Yehuda Amichai. SP-AmicYL, *tr. by* Benjamin Harshav *and* Barbara Harshav

Then if this clay thing calls. Executions in Moscow, The. Kenneth Patchen. CP-PatcK

Then it snowed. I / saw it when I let. Afterward. James Schuyler. CP-SchuJ

Then it was dusk in Illinois, the small boy. First Song. Galway Kinnell. SP-KinnGN

Then Jove commanded the god Mercury. Mercury Carries Psyche to Olympus. Elizabeth Barrett Browning. CP-BroEB

Then leave old regret. Moral Poem, A. James Vincent Cunningham. CP-CunnJ

Then let them point my every tear. My Own. Dorothy Parker. CP-ParkD

Then marking this my sacred speech, but truly lend. Saint Justin Martyr. CP-RaleW *Fr.* Hortatory Address to the Greeks.

Then mother Ceres from afar beheld her. Psyche Propitiating Ceres. Elizabeth Barrett Browning. CP-BroEB

Then must I punish you with trustfulness. Nightmare of Senility. Robert Graves. CP-GravR

Then mute days came sprawled on the sidewalks. Belfry. Yannis Ritsos. SP-RitsY, *tr. by* Kimon Friar *and* Kostas Myrsiades

Then One. A. R. Ammons. CP-AmmoA

Then one woman spoke About my son. In San Salvador (II). Grace Paley. CP-PalGC

Then Pancho Villa came to town. Baker, The. Raymond Carver. CP-CarvR

Then Psyche entered in to Proserpine. Psyche and Proserpine. Elizabeth Barrett Browning. CP-BroEB

Then Psyche, weak in body and soul, put on. Psyche Gazing on Cupid. Elizabeth Barrett Browning. CP-BroEB

Then ("Put yourself where you'll be"). Robert Creeley. SP-CreeR

Then Reynolds said O woman most sage. William Blake. *See* O dear Mother outline of knowledge most sage

Then see it! in distressing. Last Turn, The. William Carlos Williams. CP-WilW2

Then shall all the tribes of the earth mourn. Jones Very. CP-VeryJ

Then Shall Perceive. Walt Whitman. CP-WhitW

Then Shall Ye Shout. Christina Georgina Rossetti. CP-RosC2

Then spend an age in whetting thy desire. Henry David Thoreau. CP-ThorH

Then the Brother of the Wind. C. K. Williams. CP-WillC

Then the Cynic sung. William Blake. CP-BlakW *Fr.* Island in the Moon, An.

Then the eighty-year old lady with a sparkle. How It Is. Richard Eberhart. CP-EberR

Then the Ermine. Marianne Craig Moore. CP-MoorM

Then the knee of the wave. "Reclining Figure" Donald Hall. CP-HallD

Then the long sunlight lying on the sea. Insusceptibles, The. Adrienne Rich. CP-RicAE

Then the old man flamed and prayed. Christina. Thomas Merton. CP-MertT

Then the strong trumpets like the guns of God. Music. G. K. Chesterton. CP-ChesG

Then the wise hours, suddenly discovered. 3 A. M. in a War Year. Mona Van Duyn. SP-VanDM

Then there is the story. No Fifth Man. A. K. Ramanujan. CP-RamaA

Then there was Johann. Little Tear Gland That Says, The. Charles Simic. SP-SimiC; SP-SimiCE

Then there was the time in. Spider, The. Charles Bukowski. SP-BukC1

Then there's this giant—tall! So tall he can't. Michelangelo Buonarroti. CP-Miche, *tr. by* John Frederick Nims

Then They That Feared the Lord Spake Often One to Another. Christina Georgina Rossetti. CP-RosC3

Then unto him responding answered fleet-foot Achilles. Nourishment before Battle. Homer. CP-MerG2 *Fr.* Iliad, The.

Then Was My Neophyte. Dylan Thomas. CP-ThomD

Then we brought the lances down—then the trumpets blew. Rudyard Kipling. CP-KiplR *Fr.* Light That Failed, The.

"Then we will have to-night!" we said. On Cheating the Fiddler. Dorothy Parker. CP-ParkD

Then we'll get us some wine and spare ribs. Lewis and Clark Overheard in Conversation. James Tate. SP-TateJ

Then, what do you say to the poem of Mizpah? Dialogue between Father and Daughter. Robert Browning. CP-BroR2

Then what is the answer?—Not to be deluded by dreams. Answer, The. Robinson Jeffers. CP-JefR2

Then when the ample season. Then. Richard Wilbur. CP-WilbR

Then, when the child was gone. Empty House. Stephen Spender. CP-SpenS

Then when the flame forked like a sudden path. Log. James Merrill. SP-MerrJ

Then, when the full moonlight. 52 Oswald Street. Galway Kinnell. SP-KinnGN

Then Wherefore Death. Laura Riding Jackson. CP-RidiL

Then Whose Shall Those Things Be? Christina Georgina Rossetti. CP-RosC2

Then will I not repine. Emily Dickinson. SP-DickE

"Then write," she said. "By all means, if that's" Assignment. Hayden Carruth. CP-CarHS

Then Zeal and Commonwealth infest. Song: "Then Zeal and Commonwealth infest." John Dryden. CP-DryJ2 *Fr.* Albion and Albanius.

Theniel Menzies' Bony Mary. Robert Burns. CP-BurnR

Theocritus: A Villanelle. Oscar Wilde. CP-WildO

Theodicy. Czeslaw Milosz. CP-MiloC; CP-MiloCN, *tr. by* Robert Hass

Theodore and Honoria, From [Fables Ancient and Modern from] Boccace. John Dryden. SP-DrydJ

Theodore Dreiser. After Dawn. Dorothy Parker. CP-ParkD

Theodotos. Constantine P. Cavafy. CP-CavaC, *tr. by* Theoharis Constantine Theoharis

Theogony. Hesiod.
  Bacchus and Ariadne. CP-BroEB

Theologian's Tale: Torquemada, The. Henry Wadsworth Longfellow. SP-LongH *Fr.* Tales of a Wayside Inn.

Theological Definition, A. George Oppen. CP-OppGN

Theological Question, The. George Oppen. CP-OppGN

Theology. Paul Laurence Dunbar. CP-DunbP

Theology. Ted Hughes. SP-HughTN

The(oo)is / lOOk / (aliv / e)e / yes. E. E. Cummings. CP-CummE

Theophilos Palaiologos. Constantine P. Cavafy. CP-CavaC, *tr. by* Theoharis Constantine Theoharis

Theophilus. Edwin Arlington Robinson. CP-RobiE

Theorem. Carl Sandburg. CP-SandC

Theoretikos. Oscar Wilde. CP-WildO

Theories. Federico García Lorca.
  "August. / Facing the sunset." CP-GarcF, *tr. by* Alan S. Trueblood
  Balance. CP-GarcF, *tr. by* Alan S. Trueblood
  Fable: "Unicorns and cyclops." CP-GarcF, *tr. by* Alan S. Trueblood
  Frieze. CP-GarcF, *tr. by* Alan S. Trueblood
  Harlequin. CP-GarcF, *tr. by* Alan S. Trueblood
  Hunter. CP-GarcF, *tr. by* Alan S. Trueblood
  Merry-go-round. CP-GarcF, *tr. by* Alan S. Trueblood
  Nocturne in Outline. CP-GarcF, *tr. by* Alan S. Trueblood
  Proverb: "March / goes flying by." CP-GarcF, *tr. by* Alan S. Trueblood
  Schoolboy's Song. CP-GarcF, *tr. by* Alan S. Trueblood
  Song of the Seven Maidens. CP-GarcF, *tr. by* Alan S. Trueblood
  Song with Movement. CP-GarcF, *tr. by* Alan S. Trueblood
  "Song would like to be light." CP-GarcF, *tr. by* Alan S. Trueblood
  Three Trees Were Cut Down. CP-GarcF, *tr. by* Alan S. Trueblood

Theories. Rae Armantrout. SP-ArmaA

Theory. G. K. Chesterton. CP-ChesG

Theory. Dorothy Parker. CP-ParkD

Theory. Wallace Stevens. CP-StevW; CP-StevWP

Theory, A. Thomas McGrath. SP-McGrT

Theory if you hold it hard enough, A. Etherealizing. Robert Frost. CP-FrosR

Theory of Evil. Robert Earl Hayden. CP-HaydR

Theory of Flight. Muriel Rukeyser. CP-RukeM

Theory of Nato-geography as Advanced by the Tiaphidian Man, With a Comment on the Character of His Penal System, A. Kenneth Patchen. CP-PatcK

Theory of Numbers. Kenneth Rexroth. CP-RexrK

Theory of Poetry. Archibald MacLeish. CP-MacLA

Theory of Prayer. Thomas Merton. CP-MertT

Theory of Prosody, A. Philip Levine. SP-LeviP

Theory of Regress. Charles Tomlinson. CP-TomlC

Theory of Repetition, The. Theodore Weiss. SP-WeisT *Fr.* Polish Question, The.

Theory of the Flower, The. Michael Palmer. SP-PalmM

Theory of Truth. Robinson Jeffers. CP-JefR2

Ther' ain't no use in all this strife. Easy-Goin' Feller, An. Paul Laurence Dunbar. CP-DunbP

Ther nys so high comfort to my pleasaunce. Complaint of Venus, The. Geoffrey Chaucer. CP-ChauG

Therapy. Yannis Ritsos. SP-RitsY, *tr. by* Kimon Friar

There. Langston Hughes. CP-HughL; CP-HughL2

There. Howard Nemerov. CP-NemeH

There. Gregory Orr. SP-OrrG

There. Yannis Ritsos. SP-RitsY, *tr. by* Kimon Friar *and* Kostas Myrsiades

There. William Butler Yeats. CP-YeatW

"There." Robert Creeley. CP-CreeR

There, a rocket in the Wain. Wallace Stevens. CP-StevWP

There ain't no pay beneath the sun. One More Round. Maya Angelou. SP-AngeM

There all the barrel-hoops are knit. There. William Butler Yeats. CP-YeatW

There all the golden codgers lay. News for the Delphic Oracle. William Butler Yeats. CP-YeatW

There, an evening star, there again. Above. Tabula Rasa. Hayden Carruth. CP-CarHS

There are a dozen. Basil 1977-1993. William Corbett. SP-CorbW

There are always, in each of us. Emigration. Eleanor Wilner. SP-WilnE

There are astronomers, mathematicians, men of science, who believe. Explosion. Robinson Jeffers. CP-JefR3

There are beggars in Iran and Araby. Ralph Waldo Emerson. CP-EmerR

There are birds larger than us, I know that. Eagle Exterminating Company, The. James Tate. SP-TateJ

There are bones inside. Crucifixion in the Desert. James Laughlin. CP-LaugJ

There are brilliant heights of sorrow. Paul Laurence Dunbar. CP-DunbP

There are candles that remember for a full twenty-four hours. Yehuda Amichai. SP-AmicY, *tr. by* Chana Bloch

There are candles that remember for twenty-four hours. Yehuda Amichai. SP-AmicYL, *tr. by* Benjamin Harshav *and* Barbara Harshav

There are cannas now on the guarded lawns. Unpeopled, Conventional Rose-Garden, The. Kenneth Rexroth. CP-RexrK

There are certain profitable things to know, and I. Few Axioms for a Young Man, A. Robert Penn Warren. CP-WarrR

There are certain stanzas—sometimes entire poems. Necessary Explanation. Yannis Ritsos. SP-RitsY, *tr. by* Kimon Friar

There are continuities in memory, but. Memory, 1930. Robert Creeley. SP-CreeR

There are dawns when the window. Sleeping Alone in a Small Room. Gregory Orr. SP-OrrG

There are days like this, when the dry air. Pillar, The. Eleanor Wilner. SP-WilnE

There are days when I think the future sets. Mountains, The. W. S. Merwin. SP-MerwW

There are dewdrops. Minor Song. Federico García Lorca. CP-GarcF, *tr. by* Catherine Brown

There Are Different Gardens. Carl Sandburg. CP-SandC

There are different ways of dying without. After the Revolution. Marilyn Hacker. SP-HackM

There are established personal places. Personal Places. Thomas Kinsella. CP-KinsT

There are few of us now, soon. For Eli Jacobson. Kenneth Rexroth. CP-RexrK

There are few songs for domesticity. Hidden Ice. Louis MacNeice. CP-MacNL

There are fields beyond. The world there obeys. Survivor among Graves, The. Randall Jarrell. CP-JarrR

There are five of us in the tent, not counting. Eve of Battle, The. Raymond Carver. CP-CarvR

There are five people in this room. Representing the Universe. Alice Walker. CP-WalkA

There are forked branches of trees. Little Sketch. Carl Sandburg. CP-SandC

There are four caballeros. Garden. Federico García Lorca. CP-GarcF, *tr. by* Jerome Rothenberg *Fr.* Water Jets.

There are four good legs to my Father's Chair. My Father's Chair. Rudyard Kipling. CP-KiplR

There are four men mowing down by the Isar. Youth Mowing, A. D. H. Lawrence. CP-LawrD

There are four vibrators, the world's exactest clocks. Four Quartz Crystal Clocks. Marianne Craig Moore. CP-MoorM

There are great things doing. Song: "There are great things doing." Wallace Stevens. CP-StevWP

There are (I scarce can think it, but [I] am told). First Satire of the Second Book of Horace [Imitated], The. Alexander Pope. CP-PopeA

There are leaves. We Are Leaves. James Schuyler. CP-SchuJ

There are lilies for her sisters. To the End. Christina Georgina Rossetti. CP-RosC3

There are lips as strange and soft. Child Face. Carl Sandburg. CP-SandC

There are longings to kill that cannot be seen. As the Asian War Begins. Robert Bly. SP-BlyR

There are lovers who recall that. Part of the Forest. George Oppen. CP-OppGN

There are many books about the zodiac. Star Book. Andrei Codrescu. SP-CodrA

There are many monsters that a glassen surface. Octopus, The. James Merrill. SP-MerrJ

There are many more Good Fridays. Unkept Good Fridays. Thomas Hardy. CP-HardT

There are many of us. Valentine. George Oppen. CP-OppGN

There are many single women in the world. Imagination and Reality. Charles Bukowski. SP-BukC1

There are many sounds which are neither music nor voice. Ear, The. Louis MacNeice. CP-MacNL

There are many that I miss. Best Cigarette, The. Billy Collins. SP-CollB

There are many things in the world and you. Love Recognized. Robert Penn Warren. CP-WarrR

There are many things that boys may know. No Boy Knows. James Whitcomb Riley. CP-RileJ

There are many wonders on earch. Chorus from *Antigone*, A. Sophocles. SP-LoguC *Fr.* Antigone.

There are masses, and there are classes. Masses and Classes. D. H. Lawrence. CP-LawrD

There are memories everywhere then. Rememberd, we go out, as in. Robert Duncan. SP-DuncR *Fr.* Structure of Rime, The.

There are men and. Hey Red! William Carlos Williams. CP-WilW2

There are moments a man turns from us. Drowning with Others. James Dickey. CP-DickJ

There Are More Ways to Roast a Pig than Burning the House Down or You Can Always Stick Your Head in a Volcano. Ogden Nash. CP-NashO

There are mountains. Third Page. Federico García Lorca. CP-GarcF, *tr. by* Jerome Rothenberg *Fr.* White Album.

There are nights as soft as fur on a foal. Watching Shoah in a Hotel Room in America. Adam Zagajewski. SP-ZagaA, *tr. by* Renata Gorczynski, Benjamin Ivry *and* C. K. Williams

There are no accidents, or so. What Could Hold Us. Heather McHugh. SP-McHuH

There are no angels yet. Gabriel. Adrienne Rich. CP-RicAE

There are no bears among the roses. Virgin Carrying a Lantern, The. Wallace Stevens. CP-StevW; CP-StevWP

There are no beaten paths to Glory's height. Path, The. Paul Laurence Dunbar. CP-DunbP

There are no birds and no flowers. The juncos have gone. September Sowing. Sam Hamill. SP-HamiS

There are / No clocks on the wall. End. Langston Hughes. CP-HughL; CP-HughL2

There are no crosses / on the Hopi graves. They lie. Death in the Desert, A. Charles Tomlinson. CP-TomlC; SP-TomlC

There Are No Gods. D. H. Lawrence. CP-LawrD

There are no handles upon a language. Languages. Carl Sandburg. CP-SandC

There are no imperfect answers from perfect data. Requisitioning. John Ciardi. CP-CiarJ

There are no leaders to lead us to honour, and yet without leaders we sally. Spies' March, The. Rudyard Kipling. CP-KiplR

There are no leaf-eating snakes. Bad Mouth. Margaret Atwood. SP-AtwM2

There are no losses. Kenneth Patchen. CP-PatcK

There are no more shopping days to Christmas. Eve. Howard Nemerov. CP-NemeH

There are no nouns of verse, the earth itself. Memory of Oars. George Oppen. CP-OppGN

There are no reapers in the whitening fields. Reaper, The. Jones Very. CP-VeryJ

There are no roads but the frost. Old Age Compensation. James Wright. CP-WrigJ

There are no rooms here. So Be It. Kenneth Patchen. CP-PatcK

There are no stars tonight. My Grandmother's Love Letters. Hart Crane. CP-CranH

There are no things rain is like. Words into Words Won't Go. Clarence Major. SP-MajoC

There are no tigers. Alice Walker. CP-WalkA

There are no words I know. One. Robert Creeley. SP-CreeR

There are not leaves enough to cover the face. United Dames of America. Wallace Stevens. CP-StevW; CP-StevWP

There are not many meteors over the flat country. Farmers. James Dickey. CP-DickJ

There are only a few games played by a pair. Essay on Chess. Karl Shapiro. SP-ShapK

There are only two men I can really. Playing It Out. Charles Bukowski. SP-BukC3

There are only two things now. New Year's Eve. D. H. Lawrence. CP-LawrD

There are people so near nothing. Anywhere and Everywhere People. Carl Sandburg. CP-SandC

There are people there, beyond the Rockies. Beyond the Rockies. D. H. Lawrence. CP-LawrD

There are people whose sex. Saint Sex. C. K. Williams. CP-WillC; SP-WillC

There are, perhaps, whom passion gives a grace. Aged Lover Discourses in the Flat Style, The. James Vincent Cunningham. CP-CunnJ

There are pieces of the lake. Michael Palmer. SP-PalmM

There are places. My Mother: 33 Years Later. Grace Paley. CP-PalGC

There are places I go when I am strong. Haunts. Carl Sandburg. CP-SandC

There are portraits and still-lifes. Paring the Apple. Charles Tomlinson. CP-TomlC; SP-TomlC

There are possibly 2 1/2 or impossibly 3. E. E. Cummings. CP-CummE

There are rats disguised. On a Dispossess Precept. 2. Alan Dugan. CP-DugaA

There are rivers lapsing down. River Thames (?). Christina Georgina Rossetti. CP-RosC3

There Are Roughly Zones. Robert Frost. CP-FrosR

There are several attitudes towards Christmas. Cultivation of Christmas Trees, The. T. S. Eliot. CP-ElioT

There are several differences between me and Samuel Taylor Coleridge. I Can Hardly Wait for the Sandman. Ogden Nash. CP-NashO

There are several generally recognized grounds for divorce. Boop-Boop-Adieup, Little Group! Ogden Nash. CP-NashO

There are several people who I can claim I am glad I am not. How Do You Say Ha-Ha in French. Ogden Nash. CP-NashO

There are several things in life that keep me guessing. Unanswered by Request. Ogden Nash. CP-NashO

There are shadow figures for a new world. Souvenir of Japan, A. Michael

Palmer. SP-PalmM

There are sicknesses worse than sicknesses. Fernando Pessoa. SP-PessF, *tr. by* Susan M. Brown *and* Edwin Honig

There are similarities / I notice: that the hills. Journey to the Interior. Margaret Atwood. SP-AtwM1

There are 6 doors. E. E. Cummings. CP-CummE

There are 64 panes in each window of the Harrisville church. Green Notebook, The. Jane Cooper. CP-CoopJ

There are sleeping dreams and waking dreams. Ballad of Boding, A. Christina Georgina Rossetti. CP-RosC2

There are so many diseases. Pathological Puzzle. Langston Hughes. CP-HughL; CP-HughL3

There are so many roots to the tree of anger. Who Said It Was Simple. Audre Lorde. SP-LordA

There are so many tictoc. E. E. Cummings. CP-CummE

There are some birds in these valleys. Decoys, The. W. H. Auden. CP-AudeW

There are some creatures in the world with eyes. Petrarch. CP-Petra, *tr.* by J. G. Nichols

There are some days the happy ocean lies. Seascape. Stephen Spender. CP-SpenS

There are some, do you know them? Women Talking. Eleanor Wilner. SP-WilnE

There are some fiestas that the moment you arrive at them you. There's Always an Ubblebub. Ogden Nash. CP-NashO

There are some heights in Wessex, shaped as if by a kindly hand. Wessex Heights. Thomas Hardy. CP-HardT

There are some nights when. Insomniac. Maya Angelou. SP-AngeM

There are some people of whom I would certainly like to be one. Stitch Too Late Is My Fate, A. Ogden Nash. CP-NashO

There are some people who are very resourceful. Hearts of Gold. Ogden Nash. CP-NashO

There are some qualities—some incorporate things. Sonnet—Silence. Edgar Allan Poe. CP-PoeEd

There are some to whom a place means nothing. Lover's Quarrel, A. Sam Hamill. SP-HamiS

There are some words carry a curse with them:. Forbidden Words. Robert Graves. CP-GravR

There Are Sounds. Charles Olson. CP-OlsoC

There are sparkles of rain on the bright. Runaway. Kenneth Rexroth. CP-RexrK

There are spirit presences. In the Night. Carolyn Kizer. CP-KizeC

There are statues moving into a war. War, The. W. S. Merwin. SP-MerwW

There are still bits of night like closed eyes in the walls. In One of the Retreats of Morning. W. S. Merwin. SP-MerwW

There are stonebreakers in straw hats. About Infinity. Norman Dubie. CP-DubiN

There are stones here. Prayer of the Eyes, A. W. S. Merwin. SP-MerwW

There are strange hells within the minds war made. Strange Hells. Ivor Gurney. SP-GurnI

There are streams which are famous in history's story. Vale of the Merrimac, The. John Greenleaf Whittier. CP-WhitJ

There Are Such Springlike Nights. Kadya Molodovsky. CP-RicAE

There are sunsets who whisper a good-by. Sunsets. Carl Sandburg. CP-SandC

There are Sweets of Pathos. Emily Dickinson. SP-DickE

There are teeth marks. Thorn Merchant, The. Yusef Komunyakaa. CP-KomuY

There are terrible nights with thunder, lightning, rain, and. Sparrow Nights. Raymond Carver. CP-CarvR

There are the feminine aspects. Of This All Things. George Oppen. CP-OppGN

There are the few we hear of. Linoleum. Tess Gallagher. SP-GallT

There are the inactive ones who. Stalingrad: 1942. Langston Hughes. CP-HughL; CP-HughL2

There Are the Local. Hart Crane. CP-CranH

There are things. Of Being Numerous. George Oppen. CP-OppGN

There are thirty-six folds to nothing. After Spring Snow, What They Saw. Norman Dubie. CP-DubiN

There are those to whom value is a weapon. Value in Mountains. Kenneth Rexroth. CP-RexrK

There are those who speak of confusion today. Under the Capitol Dome. Carl Sandburg. CP-SandC

There are those who teach only the sweet lessons of peace and safety. Lessons. Walt Whitman. CP-WhitW

There are three degrees of bliss. Jester, The. Rudyard Kipling. CP-KiplR

There are three folk driving in a quaint old chaise. Interloper, The. Thomas Hardy. CP-HardT

There are three names. National Security. Archibald MacLeish. CP-MacLA

There are three things that make me think. Three Things. G. K. Chesterton. CP-ChesG

There are times. Time to Stop. A. K. Ramanujan. CP-RamaA

There are times / no one seems to notice. Improbable Truth. Denise Levertov. SP-LeveDL

There are times of archaic splendor that you saw. Van Black, an Old Farmer in His Dell. Richard Eberhart. CP-EberR

There are too many of you. Presidential Address to a Party of Exiles. Howard Nemerov. CP-NemeH

There Are Too Many People. D. H. Lawrence. CP-LawrD

There are too many waterfalls here; the crowded streams. Questions of Travel. Elizabeth Bishop. CP-BishE

There are towers; where they are. New Jerusalem, The ("There are towers; where they are"). Jones Very. CP-VeryJ

There are toy ships with waves painted on them. Relativity. Yehuda Amichai. SP-AmicY, *tr.* by Chana Bloch

There are tracks which belong to wheels. In the Lupanar at Pompeii. James Dickey. CP-DickJ

There are trucks going down our street tonight. Night Scene before Combat. Alan Dugan. CP-DugaA

There Are Two. Kenneth Patchen. CP-PatcK

There are two classes of men. Classes. D. H. Lawrence. CP-LawrD

There are two facing peacocks. Chenille. James Dickey. CP-DickJ

There are two kinds of intelligence: one acquired. Two Kinds of Intelligence. Jelaluddin Rumi. SP-Rumi, *tr.* by Coleman Barks

There are two kinds of people who blow through life like a breeze. I Have It on Good Authority. Ogden Nash. CP-NashO

There are two Mays. Emily Dickinson. CP-DickE

There are two Ripenings—one—of sight. Emily Dickinson. CP-DickE

There are two things you have. On a Summer Goddess Who Should Be Nameless. Alan Dugan. CP-DugaA

There are two trees in a lonely field. Emily Jane Brontë. CP-BronE

There are two white captains. Sailor in Africa, The. Rita Dove. SP-DoveR

There are vast realms of consciousness still undreamed of. Terra Incognita. D. H. Lawrence. CP-LawrD

There are weeds that flower forth in fall. Seedtime. Denise Levertov. SP-LeveDP

There are who wish to build their houses strong. Builders, The. Jones Very. CP-VeryJ

There are whose study is of smells. *after* Horace, *Book* 5, *Ode* 3. Rudyard Kipling. CP-KiplR

There are wolves in the next room waiting. Wolves, The. Allen Tate. CP-TateA

There are wonder. Langston Hughes. *See* Wonder / And pain

There are words like *Freedom*. Refugee in America. Langston Hughes. CP-HughL2

There are words too ancient to be said by the lips of a child. Spring, Says the Child. Josephine Jacobsen. CP-JacoJ

There are words voluptuous. Love: "There are words voluptuous." Robert Creeley. SP-CreeR

There are worse things than. Oh, Yes. Charles Bukowski. SP-BukC3

There aren't that many pages left. Reading Late in the Cottage. Gregory Orr. SP-OrrG

There as I bent above the broken pot from the mesa pueblo. Pueblo Pot. Edna St. Vincent Millay. CP-MillE

There at Dusk I Found You. Edna St. Vincent Millay. CP-MillE

There at the center. Angels of Fructification, The. Tennessee Williams. CP-WillT

There at the story's close. Peter. Richard Wilbur. CP-WilbR

There be none of Beauty's daughters. Stanzas for Music. Lord Byron. CP-Byron

There be two men of all mankind. Two Men. Edwin Arlington Robinson. CP-RobiE

There Blooms No Bud in May. Walter De la Mare. CP-DeLaW

There by some wrinkled stones round a leafless tree. Twelve, The. Allen Tate. CP-TateA

There came a boy. Last Arrow, The. Walter De la Mare. CP-DeLaW

There came a Day at Summer's full. Renunciation. Emily Dickinson. CP-DickE

There came a Wind like a Bugle. Emily Dickinson. CP-DickE

There came an image in Life's retinue. Death-in-Love. Dante Gabriel Rossetti. CW-RossD *Fr.* House of Life, The.

There came, for lack of sleep. New York in August. Boris Leonidovich Pasternak. CP-DaviDC, *tr.* by Donald Davie

There came one day soon. Oldest Conversation, The. Kenneth Patchen. CP-PatcK

There came such clear opening of the night sky. Night Sky. Kathleen Jessie Raine. SP-RainK

There came to Rhoda's Christmas feast. Happy Xmas, A ("There came to Rhoda's Christmas feast"). G. K. Chesterton. CP-ChesG

There came whisperings in the winds. Stephen Crane. CP-CranS

There can be certain potions. Big Boots of Pain, The. Anne Sexton. CP-SextA

There can be no anniversary. To a Poet Who Read in Gloucester Before the Cape Ann Historical Literary and Scientific Society. Charles Olson. CP-OlsoC

There cannot be a single thing which is. Clouds ("There cannot be a single thing which is"). Jorge Luis Borges. SP-BorgJ, *tr.* by Willis Barnstone

There comes a time of great lassitude. A dazzling morning. Putting out the Lamp. Yannis Ritsos. SP-RitsY, *tr. by* Kimon Friar

There comes a time when everything is laced. Imagination of Necessity, The. Andrei Codrescu. SP-CodrA

There comes a warning like a spy. Emily Dickinson. CP-DickE

There comes an hour when begging stops. Emily Dickinson. CP-DickE

There comes, in certain latitudes, a season. Nondescript. Amy Clampitt. CP-ClamA

There comes upon me will to speak in praise. Sestina for Ysolt. Ezra Pound. CP-PoEar

There could be a book without nations in its chapters. Book of Resemblances, A. Robert Duncan. SP-DuncR

There dwells a mighty pair. Doom and She. Thomas Hardy. CP-HardT

There dwells a wife by the Northern Gate. Sea-Wife, The. Rudyard Kipling. CP-KiplR

There dwelt a lady in a tower high. Oltre la Torre: Rolando. Ezra Pound. CP-PoEar

There dwelt a widow learned and devout. Hearth Eternal, The. Nicholas Vachel Lindsay. CP-LindV

There exists one kind of fool. Han-shan. CP-ColdM, *tr. by* Red Pine

There exists one kind of person. Han-shan. CP-ColdM, *tr. by* Red Pine

There exists one type of person. Han-shan. CP-ColdM, *tr. by* Red Pine

There exists one type of person. Shih-te. CP-ColdM, *tr. by* Red Pine

There exists the eternal fact of conflict. Stephen Crane. CP-CranS

There faded from her features what was her. ICU: Space/Time in the Waiting Room. Miller Williams. CP-WillM

There fared a mother driven forth. House of Christmas, The. G. K. Chesterton. CP-ChesG

There fell a sudden rain. George Meredith. CP-MerG2

There floated the sounds of church-chiming. At the Wicket-Gate. Thomas Hardy. CP-HardT

There goes a swallow to Venice—the stout seafarer! Robert Browning. SP-BroR *Fr.* Pippa Passes.

There goes the Lady Vi. How well. Lady Vi. Thomas Hardy. CP-HardT

There goes the Wapiti. Wapiti, The. Ogden Nash. CP-NashO

There grew upon a sandy hill. Oak and the Poplar, The. Jones Very. CP-VeryJ

There grew, within a favour'd vale. Glastonbury Thorn, The. George Meredith. CP-MerG2

There grows a bonie brier-bush in our kail-yard. Robert Burns. CP-BurnR

There had been boat-sailing on Severn river. Dream, The. Ivor Gurney. SP-GurnI

There had been no such music here until. Girl with 'Cello. May Sarton. SP-SartM

There had been quiet all that afternoon. In Emanuel's Nightmare: Another Coming of Christ. Gwendolyn Brooks. SP-BrooG

There had been years of Passion—scorching, cold. And There Was a Great Calm. Thomas Hardy. CP-HardT

There has been so much noise. Erinnyes. D. H. Lawrence. CP-LawrD

There has fallen on earth for a token. Gloria in Profundis. G. K. Chesterton. CP-ChesG

There has not been for a long time a spring. Slow River. Czeslaw Milosz. CP-MiloC; CP-MiloCN, *tr. by* Renata Gorczynski

There has to be a hero who is not. Homage to John L. Stephens. Donald Davie. CP-DaviDC

There Has to Be a Jail for Ladies. Thomas Merton. CP-MertT

There hasn't been any rain. Sleeping Over. C. K. Williams. CP-WillC

There haunts in Time's bare house an active ghost. Polonius. Walter De la Mare. CP-DeLaW

There have always been tigers in my life. My Last Tiger. Jorge Luis Borges. SP-BorgJ, *tr. by* Ken Krabbenhoft

There Have Been Anguishes. Ivor Gurney. SP-GurnI

There have been so many gods. Spiral Flame. D. H. Lawrence. CP-LawrD

There have been two strangers. Strangers. May Sarton. SP-SartM

There He Was. Alan Dugan. CP-DugaA

There he was, a boy, looking over. Clarence Major. SP-MajoC

There he was—having spent. "Yes, But . . ." Theodore Weiss. SP-WeisT

There Hugo Wolf is buried: fully formed. In a Viennese Cemetery. James Wright. CP-WrigJ

There I could never be a boy. Poem: "There I could never be a boy." Frank O'Hara. SP-OharF

There I was, here I am: a foot in air. Picture in the Paper, A. Randall Jarrell. CP-JarrR

There in New Guinea, by the grounded metal. Baggage King, The. James Dickey. CP-DickJ

There, in the order of traffic. Liberator Explodes, The. James Dickey. CP-DickJ

There Is. Robert Creeley. CP-CreeR

There is a band of dull gold in the west, and say what you like. Sunset. D. H. Lawrence. CP-LawrD

There is a band playing in the early night. Listen to the Band! D. H. Lawrence. CP-LawrD

There is a bird in the poplars. Metric Figure. William Carlos Williams. CP-WilW1

There is a bird who, by his coat. Jackdaw, The. Vincent Bourne. CP-CowpW

There is a bitter river. Bitter River, The. Langston Hughes. CP-HughL; CP-

HughL2

There is a bitter root. Ghazal of the Bitter Root. Federico García Lorca. CP-GarcF, *tr. by* Catherine Brown *Fr.* Ghazals.

There is a bitter root. Gacela of the Bitter Root. Federico García Lorca. SP-GarcF, *tr. by* Edwin Honig

There is a blessing on the wide road. Blessing, The. W. S. Merwin. SP-MerwW

There is a blue star, Janet. Baby Toes. Carl Sandburg. CP-SandC

There is a body, every joint and limb. Physician, The. Jones Very. CP-VeryJ

There is a bondage which is worse to bear. William Wordsworth. *See* There is a bondage worse, far worse, to bear

There is a bondage worse, far worse, to bear. William Wordsworth. CP-WorW1

There is a book, which we may call. Manual, A. Vincent Bourne. CP-CowpW

There is a boy who walks with a fish. Spring Song for Cagli, A. Charles Olson. CP-OlsoC

There is a Bread which You and I propose. Early Mass. Thomas Merton. CP-MertT

There is a budding morrow in midnight. Found. Dante Gabriel Rossetti. CW-RossD

There Is a Budding Morrow in Midnight. Christina Georgina Rossetti. CP-RosC2

There is a change—and I am poor. Complaint, A. William Wordsworth. CP-WorW1; MW-WorW

There is a child. He comes from far. Story, A. Muriel Rukeyser. CP-RukeM

There is a city whose fair houses wizen. Amsterdam. James Merrill. SP-MerrJ

There is a cloud above the sunset hill. Possession. Dante Gabriel Rossetti. CW-RossD

"There is a cloud," / Fairfield used to say. Gray Day. James Schuyler. CP-SchuJ

There is a community of the spirit. Community of the Spirit, A. Jelaluddin Rumi. SP-Rumi, *tr. by* Coleman Barks

There is a cop who is both prowler and father. Rape. Adrienne Rich. SP-RicA2

There is a coppice on Cotswold's edge the winds love. Coppice, The. Ivor Gurney. SP-GurnI

There is a country to cross you will. For My Young Friends Who Are Afraid. William Stafford. SP-StafW; SP-StafWW

There is a cup of sweet or bitter drink. Heart, The. Jones Very. CP-VeryJ

There is a dark memory, the noise of children playing. Sadness of Eyes and Descriptions of a Voyage. Yehuda Amichai. SP-AmicYL, *tr. by* Benjamin Harshav *and* Barbara Harshav

There is a dead pigeon hung. Good Fortune of Pigeons, The. Josephine Jacobsen. CP-JacoJ

There is a deep brooding. My Arkansas. Maya Angelou. SP-AngeM

There is a despair one comes to. Prejudice, The. Robert Creeley. CP-CreeR

There is a desperate lovliness to be seen. Bright Conversation with Saint-Ex. Carl Sandburg. CP-SandC

There is a difference between acting and action. Homo Ludens: On an Argument with an Actor. Alan Dugan. CP-DugaA

There is a dream in the land. Dream of Freedom. Langston Hughes. CP-HughL; CP-HughL3

There is a drear and lonely tract of hell. Supremacy. Edwin Arlington Robinson. CP-RobiE

There is a face I know too well. Face, The. Stevie Smith. CP-SmitS

There is a fault in the universe. Stability. David Ignatow. SP-IgnaD

There is a fearful solitude. Forgot! Stevie Smith. CP-SmitS

There is a fenceless garden overgrown. Garden, The. Edwin Arlington Robinson. CP-RobiE

There is a field through which I often pass. Needless Alarm, The. William Cowper. CP-CowpW

There is a finished feeling. Emily Dickinson. CP-DickE

There is a fish that quivers in the pool. In the Beck. Kathleen Jessie Raine. SP-RainK

There is a flower that Bees prefer. Emily Dickinson. CP-DickE

There is a flower, the Lesser Celandine. Small Celandine, The. William Wordsworth. CP-WorW1; MW-WorW

There is a fork in a branch. Perch, The. Galway Kinnell. SP-KinnGN

There is a garden, far from our idea of it. What Was Going On. Eleanor Wilner. SP-WilnE

There is a garden grey. Myself. Walter De la Mare. CP-DeLaW

There is a ghost town of abandoned love. James Vincent Cunningham. CP-CunnJ

There is a gin mill on the avenue. Juice Joint: Northern City. Langston Hughes. CP-HughL; CP-HughL2

There is a giving beyond giving. Song: Beyond Giving. Robert Graves. CP-GravR

There is a god in whom I do not believe. God the Eater. Stevie Smith. CP-SmitS

There is a great amount of poetry in unconscious. Critics and Connoisseurs. Marianne Craig Moore. CP-MoorM

There is a great river this side of Stygia. River of Rivers in Connecticut, The. Wallace Stevens. CP-StevW; CP-StevWP

There is a great snow / mountain that I know. Mountain, The. James Laughlin.

There is a tranquil star. Star, A. Federico García Lorca. CP-GarcF, *tr.* by Jerome Rothenberg *Fr.* Night (Suite for Piano and Poet's Voice).

There is a travelling fury in his feet. Progress, The. Robert Graves. CP-GravR

There is a truth that travel brings. Familiar Things. George Meredith. CP-MerG2

There is a two-headed goat, a four-winged chicken. Believe It. John Logan. CP-LogaJ

There is a vale which none hath seen. Rumors from an Aeolian Harp. Henry David Thoreau. CP-ThorH

There is a valley which only I know. Valley, A. Primo Levi. CP-LeviP, *tr.* by Ruth Feldman

There is a Void, outside of Existence, which if entered into. Jerusalem. William Blake. CP-BlakW

There is a warm and gentle atmosphere. Fragment: Love's Tender Atmosphere. Percy Bysshe Shelley. CP-ShelP

There Is a Way. Thomas Merton. CP-MertT

There is a way between voice and presence. Jelaluddin Rumi. SP-Rumi, *tr.* by Coleman Barks

There is a way the moon looks into the timber at night. Timber Moon. Carl Sandburg. CP-SandC

There is a way to enter a field. Receiving the Stigmata. Rita Dove. SP-DoveR

There is / A welcome at the door to which no one comes? Angel Surrounded by Paysans. Wallace Stevens. CP-StevW; CP-StevWP

There is a well into whose bottomless eye. Edna St. Vincent Millay. CP-MillE

There is a winter in the godless heart. Winter ("There is a winter in the godless heart"). Jones Very. CP-VeryJ

There is a wolf in me . . . fangs pointed for tearing gashes. Wilderness. Carl Sandburg. CP-SandC

There is a woman on Michigan Boulevard keeps a parrot and goldfish. White Ash. Carl Sandburg. CP-SandC

There is a word / Which bears a sword. Emily Dickinson. CP-DickE

There is a word you often see, pronounce it as you may. Ubique. Rudyard Kipling. CP-KiplR

There is a world. "There." Robert Creeley. CP-CreeR

There is a world outside the one you know. Wilful-Missing. Rudyard Kipling. CP-KiplR

There is a world somewhere else that is unendurable. Dimensions. C. K. Williams. CP-WillC; SP-WillC

There is a Yew-tree, pride of Lorton Vale. Yew-Trees. William Wordsworth. CP-WorW1; MW-WorW

There is a Zone whose even Years. Emily Dickinson. CP-DickE

There is, all around us, / this country. Humpbacks. Mary Oliver. SP-OlivM

There is almost no sound . . . only the redundant stir. Easter Season. Louise Glück. SP-GlucL

There is almost no such fish as this which is. Aquarium. John Ciardi. CP-CiarJ

There is always enough daylight in hell to blind; Sunrise. Robert Lowell. SP-LoweR

There is always something to be made of pain. Love Poem. Louise Glück. SP-GlucL

There is always the cough. In the afternoon. Trees of Madame Blavatsky, The. Norman Dubie. CP-DubiN

There is an amazon in us. Female. Lucille Clifton. SP-ClifL

There is an Amazon tribe that kills its children. Green Mansions. Miller Williams. CP-WillM

There is an arid Pleasure. Emily Dickinson. CP-DickE

There is an Eminence,—of these our hills. William Wordsworth. CP-WorW1

There is an emotion to which we are most of us adduced. Clean Conscience Never Relaxes, A. Ogden Nash. CP-NashO

There is an evening coming in. Going. Philip Larkin. CP-LarkP

There Is an Evil in the Air. Richard Eberhart. CP-EberR

There is an excited nonserious species of snowstorm. Flurry. John Updike. CP-UpdiJ

There is an old. Dawn at Saint Patrick's. Derek Mahon. CP-MahoD

There is an old man in the. Ship, The. James Laughlin. CP-LaugJ

There is an old pine tree facing Penobscot bay. Old Tree by the Penobscot. Richard Eberhart. CP-EberR

There is an orange rotting on the table. Andrei Codrescu. SP-CodrA

There is an order in our daily life. God's Host. Jones Very. CP-VeryJ

There is another Loneliness. Emily Dickinson. CP-DickE

There is another sky. Emily Dickinson. CP-DickE

There is another world above this one; or outside of this one. Through the Smoke Hole. Gary Snyder. CP-SnydG

There is at least one thing I would less rather have in the. What's the Matter, Haven't You Got Any Sense of Humor? Ogden Nash. CP-NashO

There is but one May in the year. May-Time. Christina Georgina Rossetti. CP-RosC2

There is eating one's self. Sure There Is Food. Kenneth Patchen. CP-PatcK

"There is enchantment here!" I mused. Beguiled. October Song. Tennessee Williams. CP-WillT

There is enough treachery, hatred. Genius of the Crowd, The. Charles Bukowski. SP-BukC2

There is far too much of the suburban classes. Suburban Classes, The. Stevie Smith. CP-SmitS

There is for me no sweeter holiday. George Meredith. CP-MerG2

There Is Good News. Josephine Jacobsen. CP-JacoJ

There is grey in your hair. Broken Dreams. William Butler Yeats. CP-YeatW

There is health in thy gray wing. To a Marsh Hawk in Spring. Henry David Thoreau. CP-ThorH

There is her mother's letter on the table. These Words Also. Howard Nemerov. CP-NemeH

There is in age. Guest Room. George Oppen. CP-OppGN

There is in all the sons of men. Ralph Waldo Emerson. CP-EmerR

There is in space a small black hole. Cosmic Comics. Howard Nemerov. CP-NemeH

There is, in the Sistine, Rome. Sealed Lips. Seen in Rome. Arthur Rimbaud. CP-RimbA, *tr.* by Martin Sorrell

There is in your secret refrain. To the Muse. Aleksandr Aleksandrovich Blok. SP-BlokA, *tr.* by Peter France *and* Jon Stallworthy

There is interest in being able to feel what you see. Symmetrical Poem. Michael Palmer. SP-PalmM

There is joy. Welcome Morning. Anne Sexton. CP-SextA

There is lore of more devices. With a Child-Book. James Whitcomb Riley. CP-RileJ

There is love, and it is a deep thing. Deeper Than Love. D. H. Lawrence. CP-LawrD

There is love only. Variations. Robert Creeley. CP-CreeR

There is moonrise under your fingernail—. Guiffre's Nightmusic. Thomas McGrath. SP-McGrT

There is more to Fury. Crash. Allen Ginsberg. CP-GinsA

There is much at work to make the world. Laura Riding Jackson. CP-RidiL

There is much that is precise. Michael Palmer. SP-PalmM

There is much unsaid, though the edges of the said. Untitled. Heather McHugh. SP-McHuH

There is my country under glass. At the Tourist Centre in Boston. Margaret Atwood. SP-AtwM1

There is my spectre. Wallace Stevens. CP-StevWP

There is no. Old Saying. Robert Creeley. SP-CreeR

There is no architect. House, The. Ralph Waldo Emerson. CP-EmerR

There is no beauty in New England like the boats. Product. George Oppen. CP-OppGN

There is no cause for love in such a script. Blue Movie. John Ciardi. CP-CiarJ

There is no change of time and place with Thee. Ark, The. Jones Very. CP-VeryJ

There is no 'cure'. Rationality. George Oppen. CP-OppGN

There is no death with Thee! each plant and tree. Living God, The. Jones Very. CP-VeryJ

There is no deceiving the bird-fancier. He sees and. At the Bird Market. Raymond Carver. CP-CarvR

There is no difference between being raped. Rape Poem. Marge Piercy. SP-PierM

There is no distinction in the encounter, Sweet. Translation. William Carlos Williams. CP-WilW2

There is no drug can shock you into pain. To the Memory of John Wheelwright. Howard Nemerov. CP-NemeH

There is no dusk to be. Eternity, An. Archibald MacLeish. CP-MacLA

There is no end to the / Deception of quiet things. Chinese Banyan, The. William Meredith. SP-MereW

There is no evil but can speak. Ralph Waldo Emerson. CP-EmerR

There is no evil that we do commit. Sin. Robert Herrick. CP-HerrR

There is no faith; the mountain stands within. Faith ("There is no faith; the mountain stands within"). Jones Very. CP-VeryJ

There is no first, or last, in Forever. Emily Dickinson. CP-DickE

There is no fool like an old fool. Fools. Robert Graves. CP-GravR

There is no Frigate like a Book. Emily Dickinson. CP-DickE

There Is No God. Arthur Hugh Clough. SP-ClouA *Fr.* Dipsychus [and the Spirit].

There is no God but God; he is all that exists. Robinson Jeffers. CP-JefR3

"There is no God," the wicked saith. There Is No God. Arthur Hugh Clough. SP-ClouA *Fr.* Dipsychus [and the Spirit].

There is no joy like that in finding Thee. Shelter, The. Jones Very. CP-VeryJ

There Is No Land Yet. Laura Riding Jackson. CP-RidiL

There Is No Language of Destruction. Philip Larkin. CP-LarkP

There is no limit to changes. Han-shan. CP-ColdM, *tr.* by Red Pine

There is no longer any reason to confuse. Heads. James Dickey. CP-DickJ

There is no man can take. Magician [Master]. "H. D." CP-DoolH

There is no moment but whose flight doth bring. Time. Jones Very. CP-VeryJ

There is no money in breathing. Business. David Ignatow. SP-IgnaD

There is no moral treason. Solipsist, The. James Vincent Cunningham. CP-CunnJ

There is no more for me to hope. La Revanche. Lord Byron. CP-Byron

There is no name for brother. Hail to the Sons of Roosevelt. Nicholas Vachel Lindsay. CP-LindV

There Is No Natural Religion. William Blake. CP-BlakW

There is no night I cannot sleep again. Strong Man, The. Jones Very. CP-VeryJ

There is no now for us but always. Envoi: "There is no now for us but always." Robert Graves. CP-GravR

There is no one between you and me. Hymn: "There is no one between you and me." Czeslaw Milosz. CP-MiloC; CP-MiloCN

There is no passion in my life. Worm Turns, The. D. H. Lawrence. CP-LawrD

There is no pause, the day rolls swiftly on. Foe, The. Jones Very. CP-VeryJ

There is no peace beneath the noon. Lotus Leaves. Oscar Wilde. CP-WildO

'There is no place to turn,' she said. Sensualists, The. Theodore Roethke. CP-RoetT

There is no point in work. Work. D. H. Lawrence. CP-LawrD

There is no R in the month of May. What, No Oysters? Ogden Nash. CP-NashO

There is no reason for the surcharge to bother you. Unctuous Platitudes. John Ashbery. SP-AshbJ

There Is No River Which Is Called Lethe. Charles Olson. CP-OlsoC

There is no safety; fear has seized the proud. Terror. Jones Very. CP-VeryJ

There Is No Shelter. Charles Wright. SP-WrigCN

There is no Silence in the Earth—so silent. Emily Dickinson. CP-DickE

There is no sinning against God, what does God care about sin! God and the Holy Ghost. D. H. Lawrence. CP-LawrD

There is no sorrow / Time heals never. Away. Walter De la Mare. CP-DeLaW

There is no sound but thou dost hear my voice. Invitation, The ("There is no sound but thou dost hear my voice"). Jones Very. CP-VeryJ

There is no sound within the cottage now. Midnight. Ivor Gurney. SP-GurnI

There is no spot so lonely, rough, and wild. Bitter-Sweet Rocks. Jones Very. CP-VeryJ

There is no stillness in this wood. This Tower of Sun. James Vincent Cunningham. CP-CunnJ

There / Is no sweetness. For Salome. Langston Hughes. CP-HughL; CP-HughL1

There is no voice but it is born of Me. Message, The ("There is no voice but it is born of Me"). Jones Very. CP-VeryJ

There is no warning rattle at the door. Plagued Journey, A. Maya Angelou. SP-AngeM

There is no way here, shepherds, read the wooden sign. Eclogue by a Five-Barred Gate. Louis MacNeice. CP-MacNL

There Is No Way Out. D. H. Lawrence. CP-LawrD

There is no where in you a paradise that is no place and there. Fall, The. Thomas Merton. CP-MertT

There is no widening distance at the shore. Port of Aerial Embarkation. John Ciardi. CP-CiarJ

There is no worship now—the idol stands. Worship ("There is no worship now—the idol stands"). Jones Very. CP-VeryJ

There is nobody on the road. Wanderer, The. Thomas Hardy. CP-HardT

There Is None, O None but You. Thomas Campion. CP-CampT

There is not much that I can do. At the Railway Station, Upway. Thomas Hardy. CP-HardT

There is not so much Life as talk of Life. Emily Dickinson. SP-DickE

There Is Nothing False in Thee. Kenneth Patchen. CP-PatcK

There is nothing false in thee. There Is Nothing False in Thee. Kenneth Patchen. CP-PatcK

There is nothing for me, Poetry, who was the child of joy. Last of the Book, The. Ivor Gurney. SP-GurnI

There is nothing I hear as well as my name. Fanny Howe. SP-HoweF Fr. Introduction to the World.

There is nothing luminous. Leda 1. Lucille Clifton. SP-ClifL

There is nothing more perky. Turkey, The. Ogden Nash. CP-NashO

There is nothing more that they can do. Easter Even. Christina Georgina Rossetti. CP-RosC3

There is nothing now. To learn. Fortress, The. Louise Glück. SP-GlucL

There is nothing sweeter than Honor, but Love. Emily Dickinson. SP-DickE

There is nothing to be afraid of. Night Poem. Margaret Atwood. SP-AtwM2

There is nothing to be said for you. Guard. To Statecraft Embalmed. Marianne Craig Moore. CP-MoorM

There is nothing to look at anymore. Tourists. D. H. Lawrence. CP-LawrD

There is nothing to save, now all is lost. Nothing to Save. D. H. Lawrence. CP-LawrD

There is nothing / to turn from. Going. Robert Creeley. CP-CreeR

There is nought for thee by thy haste to gain. Jones Very.

There is now not a single. Winter Scene. A. R. Ammons. CP-AmmoA

There is one devil in the lexicon. Merax & Mullin. W. H. Auden. CP-AudeW

There is one fault that I must find with the twentieth century. Put Back Those Whiskers, I Know You. Ogden Nash. CP-NashO

There is one form of life to which I unconditionally surrender. Oh, Please Don't Get Up! Ogden Nash. CP-NashO

There is one phase of life that I have never heard discussed in any seminar. Who Understands Who Anyhow? Ogden Nash. CP-NashO

There is one sin: to call a green leaf grey. Ecclesiastes. G. K. Chesterton. CP-ChesG

There is one story and one story only. To Juan at the Winter Solstice. Robert Graves. CP-GravR

There is one that has a head without an eye. Riddle, A: "There is one that has a head without an eye." Christina Georgina Rossetti. CP-RosC2

There is one thing I do not understand. Do Sphinxes Think? Dorothy Nash. CP-NashO

There is one thing that ought to be taught in all the colleges. Just Keep Quiet and Nobody Will Notice. Ogden Nash. CP-NashO

There is one who all day wishes to die. Appeal for Death, An. Ivor Gurney. SP-GurnI

There Is One Who Watches. Kenneth Patchen. CP-PatcK

There is only content. Space Soufflé. Andrei Codrescu. SP-CodrA

There is only one love. Sappho, Be Comforted. William Carlos Williams. CP-WilW2

There Is Only One of Everything. Margaret Atwood. SP-AtwM1

There is only time to say the first word. Meetings Like Hungry Beaks. Marge Piercy. SP-PierM

There is our herd of cars stopped. Bison Crossing Near Mt. Rushmore. May Swenson. SP-SwenM

There is pleasure in the wet, wet clay. Lie, The. Rudyard Kipling. CP-KiplR Fr. Naulahka, The.

There Is Rain in Me. D. H. Lawrence. CP-LawrD

There is rain on the glass but it all disappears. 20–200 on 747. Heather McHugh. SP-McHuH

There is rust in my mouth. Lost Lie, The. Anne Sexton. CP-SextA

There is St Ignatius Church. Labor Day. Philip Whalen. SP-WhalP

There is silence that saith, "Ah, me!" Golden Silences. Christina Georgina Rossetti. CP-RosC2

There is smoke over the river at the end of the street. Hope against Pollution, A. Alan Dugan. CP-DugaA

There is so little I can do any more. Clearing, The. Thomas Kinsella. CP-KinsT

There is so little that is close and warm. Debris of Life and Mind. Wallace Stevens. CP-StevW; CP-StevWP

There is so much misery in the world. How Thin a Blanket. Langston Hughes. CP-HughL; CP-HughL1

There is so much to write about. Ballad of Negro History, A. Langston Hughes. CP-HughL; CP-HughL3

There is some logic here to trace, and I. Three Darknesses. Robert Penn Warren. CP-WarrR

There is some sentry at the rim of winter. Messenger, The. Thomas Merton. CP-MertT

There / is someone I can bear. W. S. Landor. Marianne Craig Moore. CP-MoorM

There is something. Antique Father. Carolyn Kizer. CP-KizeC

There is something. Mobile of Birds. John Updike. CP-UpdiJ

There is something about a hornet. Hornets by the Sill. Richard Eberhart. CP-EberR

There is something about a Martini. Drink with Something in It, A. Ogden Nash. CP-NashO

There is something terrible. Eleventh Avenue Racket. Carl Sandburg. CP-SandC

There is something there. Hoarder, The. Anne Sexton. CP-SextA

There is something to be said for the Victorians. Don't Look Now. Ogden Nash. CP-NashO

There is sorrow enough in the natural way. Power of the Dog, The. Rudyard Kipling. CP-KiplR

There is stone in me that knows stone. Rock. Kathleen Jessie Raine. SP-RainK

There is such loneliness in that gold. Moon, The. Jorge Luis Borges. SP-BorgJ, tr. by Willis Barnstone

There is that in love. Sentence, The. Robert Creeley. CP-CreeR

There is that moment when. Perfection, The. Charles Tomlinson. CP-TomlC

There is that one word. Semantic. George Oppen. CP-OppGN

There is that sound like the wind. Summer. John Ashbery. SP-AshbJ

There is the grass to play. 1. Enigma: Calm: Addressed to the Air. Alan Dugan. CP-DugaA

There is the hand that has nothing attached to it, no arm no chest. Kenneth Patchen. CP-PatcK

There is the long dream in the afternoon. Ibis. Norman Dubie. CP-DubiN

There is the organic connection, like leaves that belong to a tree. Fallen Leaves. D. H. Lawrence. CP-LawrD

There is the other universe, of the heart of man. Heart of Man, The. D. H. Lawrence. CP-LawrD

There is the sense of neurotic coherence. Ode on Causality. Frank O'Hara. SP-OharF

There is the sign of / the flower—. Rhyme, The. Robert Creeley. CP-CreeR

There is the silence of a copse or croft. Silences. Thomas Hardy. CP-HardT

There is the world, the dream, and the one law. Unscientific Postscript. Howard

Nemerov. CP-NemeH

There is this cave. Jewel, The. James Wright. CP-WrigJ

There is this infinite energy, the power of God forever working. Robinson Jeffers. CP-JefR3

There is this long still knife somehow like a. Literary Life, The. Charles Bukowski. SP-BukC2

There is this other element that shines. Night Pool, The. James Dickey. CP-DickJ

There is this white wall, above which the sky creates itself. Apprehensions. Sylvia Plath. CP-PlatS

There is unknown dust that is near us. Surprised by Evening. Robert Bly. SP-BlyR

There Is Water. Robert Creeley. SP-CreeR

There is—whoe'er will know a bawd aright. Elegy 1.8: "There is—whoe'er will know a bawd aright." Ovid. CP-MarlC *Fr.* Elegies.

There is wind where the rose was. Autumn. Walter De la Mare. CP-DeLaW

There isn't a shabbier street in this whole city. Via Cigna. Primo Levi. CP-LeviP, *tr. by* Brian Swann

There it is, a block of leaping marble. Cousin Florence. Richard Eberhart. CP-EberR

There it stands, though alas, what a little of her. Marble Tablet, The. Thomas Hardy. CP-HardT

There it was, all along. Missing the Point. Adrienne Rich. CP-RicAE

There it was I saw what I shall never forget. Fawn, The. Edna St. Vincent Millay. CP-MillE

There it was, word for word. Poem That Took the Place of a Mountain, The. Wallace Stevens. CP-StevW; CP-StevWP

There journeyed from the south a man. Good Samaritan, The. Jones Very. CP-VeryJ

There late was One whose subtle being. Sunset, The. Percy Bysshe Shelley. CP-ShelP

There let thy bleeding branch atone. Emily Jane Brontë. CP-BronE

There lies a vale in Ida, lovelier. Œnone. Alfred Tennyson. CP-TennA

There! little girl; don't cry! Life-Lesson, A. James Whitcomb Riley. CP-RileJ

There liv'd a man in yonder glen. Johnie Blunt. Robert Burns. CP-BurnR

There liv'd in Lombardy, as authors write. January and May, or the Merchant's Tale. Geoffrey Chaucer. CP-PopeA *Fr.* Canterbury Tales, The.

There lived a carl in Kellyburnbraes. Kellyburnbraes. Robert Burns. CP-BurnR

There lurked a dread that you had gone. Emily Dickinson. SP-DickE

There may be punctilious people. Han-shan. CP-ColdM, *tr. by* Red Pine

There might be working some kind of throwaway. Meadow Bridge. James Dickey. CP-DickJ

There might have been higher music but. From the Theater Lobby. Alan Dugan. CP-DugaA

There ("Miles back"). Robert Creeley. SP-CreeR

There mounts in squalls a sort of rusty mire. Exile's Return, The. Robert Lowell. SP-LoweR

There must be a place. Alone and Not Alone. Carl Sandburg. CP-SandC

There must be / Moments when we see right through. Poet. Archibald MacLeish. CP-MacLA

There must be time when you, too, dream. Memory. Richard Eberhart. CP-EberR

There never breathed a man who, when his life. Gabriello Chiabrera. CP-WorW1

There never yet was honest man. Loving and Beloved. Sir John Suckling. CP-SuckJ

There never yet was woman made. Woman's Constancy. Sir John Suckling. CP-SuckJ

There now, it's finished: there's no more to be done. Work, The. Primo Levi. CP-LeviP, *tr. by* Ruth Feldman

There now, she's passed—that slight. Two Romantic Pieces. Hayden Carruth. CP-CarHS

There now, where the first crumb. Solitude. Charles Simic. SP-SimiC; SP-SimiCE

There on Sirius. Comet. Federico García Lorca. CP-GarcF, *tr. by* Jerome Rothenberg *Fr.* Night (Suite for Piano and Poet's Voice).

There on the top of the down. June Bracken and Heather. Alfred Tennyson. CP-TennA

There Once was a Cow with a Double Udder. Cow, The. Theodore Roethke. CP-RoetT

There once was a girl named Myrtle. Myrtle. Theodore Roethke. CP-RoetT

There once was a sneering wife. Cat and the Meat, The. Jelaluddin Rumi. SP-Rumi, *tr. by* Coleman Barks

There Once Was a Woman Who Put Her Head into an Oven. Charles Bukowski. SP-BukC1

There ought to be a wedding. Jingle. William Carlos Williams. CP-WilW2

There overtook me and drew me in. Gum-Gatherer, The. Robert Frost. CP-FrosR

There pass the careless people. A. E. Housman. CP-HousA

There passes by at dead of night. Ghost, The. Jones Very. CP-VeryJ

There pipes the woodlark, and the song[-]thrush there. Fragment: "There pipes

the woodlark, and the song[-]thrush there." Thomas Gray. CP-GrayT

There ("Place so, A"). Robert Creeley. CP-CreeR

There, quick, a crowd was on me. Jugglers, giants. Her Dream, Half Remembered. Charles Olson. CP-OlsoC

There Remaineth Therefore a Rest. Christina Georgina Rossetti. CP-RosC3

There Remaineth Therefore a Rest for the People of God ("Come blessed sleep"). Christina Georgina Rossetti. CP-RosC3

There Remaineth Therefore a Rest to the People of God ("Rest remains when all is done"). Christina Georgina Rossetti. CP-RosC2

There resides in the grieving. Hafiz. CP-EmerR *Fr.* Odes.

There runs a crisscross pattern of small leaves. Ophelia. Walter De la Mare. CP-DeLaW

There runs a road by Merrow Down. Merrow Down. Rudyard Kipling. CP-KiplR *Fr.* Just-So Stories.

There sandy seems the golden sky. Cliff Dwelling, A. Robert Frost. CP-FrosR

There Seemed a Strangeness. Thomas Hardy. CP-HardT

There seems a spectral power. Emily Dickinson. SP-DickE

There set out, slowly, for a Different World. War, A. Randall Jarrell. CP-JarrR

There Shall Be No More Sea. Kathleen Jessie Raine. SP-RainK

There shall be one Flock, one Shepherd. Jones Very. CP-VeryJ

There shall come faint light. Kenneth Rexroth. CP-RexrK

There she goes up the street with her book in her hand. Martin's Puzzle. George Meredith. CP-MerG1

There she lay so still and pale. Dead Bride, The. Christina Georgina Rossetti. CP-RosC3

There she was, for centuries, the big. Muse, The. Eleanor Wilner. SP-WilnE

There she was. While the flare. Anima. Hayden Carruth. CP-CarHS

There shines the moon, at noon of night. Emily Jane Brontë. CP-BronE

There shines the morning star! Through the forlorn. Wallace Stevens. CP-StevWP

There should be no despair for you. Sympathy. Emily Jane Brontë. CP-BronE

There slouched the drunk, head fallen. Subway. David Ignatow. SP-IgnaD

There, spring lambs jam the sheepfold. In air. Watercolor of Grantchester Meadows. Sylvia Plath. CP-PlatS

There stands a singer in the street. London by Lamplight. George Meredith. CP-MerG1

There stands death, a bluish liquid. Death. Randall Jarrell. CP-JarrR

There still are kindly things for me to know. Homebody, The. Dorothy Parker. CP-ParkD

There still exists one blessed joy. What Cannot Be. Constantine P. Cavafy. CP-CavaC, *tr. by* Theoharis Constantine Theoharis

There stood / a splinter of fig on your lip. Paul Celan. SP-CelaP, *tr. by* John Felstiner

There stood in her street a poor exile of Queen Je'n. George Meredith. CP-MerG2

There stood the citadel—nothing left. Ants of Argos, The. Rita Dove. SP-DoveR

There sunken in deep woods they sang their song. Interlude ("There sunken in deep woods they sang their song"). G. K. Chesterton. CP-ChesG

There swept adown that dreary glen. Emily Jane Brontë. CP-BronE

There, the moon, just appearing. Joy and Agony of Improvisation, The. Hayden Carruth. CP-CarHS

There the Tritone surges. Eugenio Montale. CP-MontE, *tr. by* Jonathan Galassi

There, there where those black spruces crowd. Ragged Island. Edna St. Vincent Millay. CP-MillE

There they are. Fury of Cocks, The. Anne Sexton. SP-SextA *Fr.* Furies, The.

There they are, my fifty men and women. One Word More. Robert Browning. CP-BroR1

There they are now. Three Sentences for a Dead Swan. James Wright. CP-WrigJ

There they are, the gardens, the temples, the justification of the temples. Guardian of the Books, The. Jorge Luis Borges. SP-BorgJ, *tr. by* Charles Tomlinson

There they slept. They left the train. Muriel Rukeyser. CP-RukeM

There They Stand Unaware of Their Wretchedness. Charles Simic. SP-SimiCE

There they were. Charles Olson. CP-OlsoC

There they were. April is the Saddest Month. William Carlos Williams. CP-WilW2

There they were, as if our memory hatched them. Triptych. Seamus Heaney. SP-HeanSO

There trudges one to a merry-making. Autumn Rain-Scene, An. Thomas Hardy. CP-HardT

There uprose a golden giant. Arena, The. G. K. Chesterton. CP-ChesG

There used to be boring afternoons. On Not Working and Then Working on Working and Then Not Working. Alan Dugan. CP-DugaA

There used to be gods in everything, and now they've gone. Companions, The. Howard Nemerov. CP-NemeH

There was a battle in the north. Geordie [An Old Ballad]. *Unknown.* CP-BurnR

There Was a Bonie Lass. Robert Burns. CP-BurnR

There was a boy named river. River's Story. James Tate. SP-TateJ

There was a boy;—ye knew him well, ye cliffs. William Wordsworth. CP-

WorW1 *Fr.* Prelude, The; Growth of a Poet's Mind [1850 vers.].

There was a bridge once that said I'm going. Lorine Niedecker. CP-NiedL

There was a Child. Courage, a Tale. Thom Gunn. CP-GunnT

There Was a Child Went Forth. Walt Whitman. CP-WhitW

There was a curious quiet for a space. Heat-Lightning. James Whitcomb Riley. CP-RileJ *Fr.* Child-World, A.

There was a day. White Snake, The. Anne Sexton. CP-SextA

There was a dog called Clanworthy. Mrs. Blow and her Animals. Stevie Smith. CP-SmitS

There was a fair footman of Torrington Square. George Meredith. CP-MerG2

There was a Fairy—flake of winter. Fairy in Winter, The. Walter De la Mare. CP-DeLaW

There was a feast. The king. Breadmaking. Jelaluddin Rumi. SP-Rumi, *tr. by* Coleman Barks

There was a frost. Frozen Greenhouse, The. Thomas Hardy. CP-HardT

There Was a Gay Bird Named Christine. D. H. Lawrence. CP-LawrD

There was a girl / who danced in the city that night. Red Dance, The. Anne Sexton. CP-SextA

There was a glorious time. He Fears His Good Fortune. Thomas Hardy. CP-HardT

There was a graveyard once—or cemetery. Evening Hour. Robert Penn Warren. CP-WarrR

There was a gray rat looked at me. Rat Riddles. Carl Sandburg. CP-SandC

There was a great Captain with Mary in his sails. Christopher Columbus. Thomas Merton. CP-MertT

There was a great cathedral. Stephen Crane. CP-CranS

There was a great frost those years. Those Years. Yannis Ritsos. SP-RitsY, *tr. by* Kostas Myrsiades

There was a great reckoning. Little Room, The. Raymond Carver. CP-CarvR

There was a green branch hung with many a bell. Dedication to a Book of Stories Selected from the Irish Novelists. William Butler Yeats. CP-YeatW

There was a happy land. Sanies II. Samuel Beckett. CP-BeckS

There was a hardness of stone. Harsh Country, The. Theodore Roethke. CP-RoetT

There was a high majestic fooling. Laughing Corn. Carl Sandburg. CP-SandC

There was a hill once wanted. Height. A. R. Ammons. CP-AmmoA

There was a joke. Joke, The. Robert Creeley. CP-CreeR

There was a jolly gauger, a gauging he did ride. Jolly Gauger, The. Robert Burns. CP-BurnR

There was a jolly tinker came across the sea. Fragments: "There was a jolly tinker came across the sea." T. S. Eliot. SP-ElioT

There was a king who had three. Three Brothers and the Chinese Princess, The. Jelaluddin Rumi. SP-Rumi, *tr. by* Coleman Barks

There was a lad was born in Kyle. Rantin, Rovin Robin. Robert Burns. CP-BurnR

There was a landau deep and wide. Landau, The. Rudyard Kipling. CP-KiplR *Fr.* Muse among the Motors, The.

There was a landscape in my childhood. Autobiography. Archibald MacLeish. CP-MacLA

There was a lass and she was fair. Ballad, A: "There was a lass and she was fair." Robert Burns. CP-BurnR

There was a lass, they ca'd her Meg. Duncan Davison. Robert Burns. CP-BurnR

There was a late autumn cricket. Buckwheat. Carl Sandburg. CP-SandC

There was a lion in Judah. St Mark. D. H. Lawrence. CP-LawrD

There was a little black. James Laughlin. CP-LaugJ *Fr.* America I Love You.

There was a little fliv of a woman loved one man and lost out. And she. Ambassadors of Grief. Carl Sandburg. CP-SandC

There was a little lawny islet. Isle, The. Percy Bysshe Shelley. CP-ShelP

There was a little turtle. Little Turtle, The. Nicholas Vachel Lindsay. CP-LindV

There was a long drought. Crops dried up. Green Ears. Jelaluddin Rumi. SP-Rumi, *tr. by* Coleman Barks

There was a mad old man. Mirror Girl, The. James Laughlin. CP-LaugJ

There was a maidservant. Importance of Gourdcrafting, The. Jelaluddin Rumi. SP-Rumi, *tr. by* Coleman Barks

There was a man. Bedtime Anecdote. Ted Hughes. SP-HughTN

There was a man and a woman. Stephen Crane. CP-CranS

There was a man, born like. Anatomy of Melancholy, The. Thomas Merton. CP-MertT

There was a man walked out. Chillicothe. Carl Sandburg. CP-SandC

There was a man who dwelt in the east centuries ago. Parables ("There was a man who dwelt in the east centuries ago"). G. K. Chesterton. CP-ChesG

There was a man who lived a life of fire. Stephen Crane. CP-CranS

There was a man who was blown down by the wind. Man Who Was Blown Down by the Wind, A. Richard Eberhart. CP-EberR

There was a man whom Sorrow named his friend. Sad Shepherd, The. William Butler Yeats. CP-YeatW

There was a man with tongue of wood. Stephen Crane. CP-CranS

There was a most Monstrous Whale. Whale, The. Theodore Roethke. CP-RoetT

There was a most odious Yak. Yak, The. Theodore Roethke. CP-RoetT

There was a mutter of rain on the leaves and we went back in the. Waiting Can Be Pretty Lousy. Kenneth Patchen. CP-PatcK

There was a naughty boy. Song about Myself, A. John Keats. CP-KeatJ

There was a nothingness, an impulse, a quark. Waking from a Dream. Miller Williams. CP-WillM

There was a path. Place ("There was a path"). Robert Creeley. CP-CreeR

There was a person. Revenge Fable. Ted Hughes. SP-HughTN

There was a priest at Philæ. Our Lady of the Sackcloth. Rudyard Kipling. CP-KiplR

There was a river overhung with trees. In a Notebook. James Fenton. SP-FentJ

There was a river under First and Main. Prairie Town. William Stafford. SP-StafW; SP-StafWW

There was a road ran past our house. Unexplorer, The. Edna St. Vincent Millay. CP-MillE

There was a roaring in the wind all night. Resolution and Independence. William Wordsworth. CP-WorW1; MW-WorW

There was a rose that faded young. Solace. Dorothy Parker. CP-ParkD

There was a row in Silver Street that's near to Dublin Quay. Belts. Rudyard Kipling. CP-KiplR

There Was a Saviour. Dylan Thomas. CP-ThomD

There was a Serpent who had to sing. Serpent, The. Theodore Roethke. CP-RoetT

There was a singing woman. Singing Woman, The. Thomas Hardy. CP-HardT

There was a sky-painter at Folkestone. Folkestone Limerick. Robert Browning. CP-BroR2

There was a spot. William Wordsworth. CP-WorW1

There was a stranger in the. Stranger in the House, The. James Laughlin. CP-LaugJ

There was a strife 'twixt man and maid. Rudyard Kipling. CP-KiplR *Fr.* Naulahka, The.

There was a stunted handpost just on the crest. Near Lanivet, 1872. Thomas Hardy. CP-HardT

There was a sunlit absence. Mossbawn. Seamus Heaney. SP-HeanSO

There was a tall slough grass. Man and Dog on an Early Winter Morning. Carl Sandburg. CP-SandC

There was a time for discoveries. Voyage West. Archibald MacLeish. CP-MacLA

There Was a Time, I Need Not Name. Lord Byron. CP-Byron

There was a time in Europe long ago. Quantum Mutata. Oscar Wilde. CP-WildO

There was a time in former years. She Hears The Storm. Thomas Hardy. CP-HardT

There was a time, Lesbia, when. Carmen 72. Catullus. CP-ZukLS *Fr.* Carmina.

There was a time when Ætna's silent fire. Heroism. William Cowper. CP-CowpW

There was a time when meadow, grove, and stream. Ode: Intimations of Immortality from Recollections of Early Childhood. William Wordsworth. CP-WorW1; MW-WorW

There was a time when my cheek burned. Emily Jane Brontë. CP-BronE

There was a time when Prague. Mr Krösing's Top Hat. Jaroslav Seifert. SP-SeifJ, *tr. by* Ewald Osers

There was a time when the young girls. From the Second Chapter of a Verse History of the World. Thomas Merton. CP-MertT

There was a tower that went before a fall. Babel. Louis MacNeice. CP-MacNL

There was a tree of stars sprang up on a vertical panel of the south. Monkey of Stars. Carl Sandburg. CP-SandC

There was a tree whose leaves were flowers. Tree, The. John Ciardi. CP-CiarJ

There was a whispering in my hearth. Miners. Wilfred Owen. CP-OwenW

There was a wicked woman called Malady Festing. Angel Boley. Stevie Smith. CP-SmitS

There was a Widow in the village known. Smugglers and Poachers. George Crabbe. SP-CrabG *Fr.* Tales of the Hall.

There was a wife wonn'd in Cockpen. Scroggam. Robert Burns. CP-BurnR

There was a wild pigeon came often to Hinkley's timber. Timber Wings. Carl Sandburg. CP-SandC

There was a woman loved a man. Sea Chest. Carl Sandburg. CP-SandC

There was a woman tore off a red velvet gown. Woman with a Past. Carl Sandburg. CP-SandC

There was a worthy, but a simple Pair. Mother, The. George Crabbe. SP-CrabG *Fr.* Tales.

There was a young belle of old Natchez. Requiem: "There was a young belle of old Natchez." Ogden Nash. CP-NashO

There was a young poet of Chelsea. George Meredith. CP-MerG2

There was a youth, who, as with toil and travel. Prince Athanase; a Fragment. Percy Bysshe Shelley. CP-ShelP

There Was a Youth Whose Name Was Thomas Granger. Charles Olson. CP-OlsoC

There was absolutely no reason after the centaur had pawed her and tried to mount her. Hercules, Deianira, Nessus. C. K. Williams. SP-WillC

There was always the inside and. Man Outside, The. Raymond Carver. CP-

CarvR

There was an ease of mind that was like being alone in a boat at sea. Prologues to What Is Possible. Wallace Stevens. CP-StevW; CP-StevWP

There was an infidel who. Water Walker. Richard Wilbur. CP-WilbR

There was an old Crow by the name of Jim. Jim Crow's Last Stand. Langston Hughes. CP-HughL; CP-HughL2

There was an old Dutch lady. For Example. Gary Snyder. CP-SnydG

There was an old man of Calcutta. Arthur. Ogden Nash. CP-NashO

There was an old man of Scoharie. Drusilla. Ogden Nash. CP-NashO

There was an old miser named Clarence. Fragonard. Ogden Nash. CP-NashO

There was an old person of Lapland. Limerick, A: "There was an old person of Lapland." G. K. Chesterton. CP-ChesG

There was an unwanted child. End, Middle, Beginning. Anne Sexton. CP-SextA

There was another, too. Graph. William Carlos Williams. CP-WilW2

There was, before me. Stephen Crane. CP-CranS

There was calm rapture in the way she spoke. John Ashbery. SP-AshbJ *Fr.* New Realism, The.

There was crimson clash of war. Stephen Crane. CP-CranS

There was darkness under Heaven. Helen All Alone. Rudyard Kipling. CP-KiplR

There was debtor's prison before inmates. Empty Pitchforks. Thomas Lux. SP-LuxT

There was earth inside them, and. Paul Celan. SP-CelaP, *tr. by* John Felstiner

There was Father, and Mother, and Emmy, and Jane. Spirits at Home. James Whitcomb Riley. CP-RileJ

There was five Carlins in the South. Five Carlins—A Ballad—Tune, Chevy Chase, The. Robert Burns. CP-BurnR

There Was Glass and There Are Stars. Randall Jarrell. CP-JarrR

There was heaven. Phases. Wallace Stevens. CP-StevWP

There was merry-making. Man with a Past, The. Thomas Hardy. CP-HardT

There was never a Queen like Balkis. Butterfly that Stamped, The. Rudyard Kipling. CP-KiplR *Fr.* Just-So Stories.

There was never a sound beside the wood but one. Mowing. Robert Frost. CP-FrosR

There was never file half so well filed. Sir Thomas Wyatt. CP-WyatT

There was never naught. Never Naught Song, A. Robert Frost. CP-FrosR

There was never nothing more me pained [*or* payned]. Sir Thomas Wyatt. CP-WyatT

There was no more than shadow where. Shadow and the Real, The. James Wright. CP-WrigJ

There was no one inside him, nothing but a trace of chill, a dream dreamt by no one else behind the face. Everything and Nothing. Jorge Luis Borges. SP-BorgJ, *tr. by* Ken Krabbenhoft

There was no one like 'im, 'Orse or Foot. Follow Me 'Ome. Rudyard Kipling. CP-KiplR

There was no place on that plain for a city. Shortest Way Home, The. Muriel Rukeyser. CP-RukeM

There was nothing left for man. Anté Popovski. CP-KizeC, *tr. by* Carolyn Kizer *Fr.* Samuel.

There was nothing to do on the island. Stella Maris. James Tate. SP-TateJ

There was nought in the Valley. Time Passes. Walter De la Mare. CP-DeLaW

There was on a time, but old Time was then young. Caledonia. Robert Burns. CP-BurnR

There was once upon a time a little owl. Owl's Bedtime Story, The. Randall Jarrell. CP-JarrR

There was once was a time when I loved. Faithless Shepherdess, The. Christina Georgina Rossetti. CP-RosC3

There was one a-riding grand. Dorothy Parker. CP-ParkD

There was one hour in the which the Middle Ages. Louis XI. Robert Stock. SP-StocR

There was One I met upon the road. Stephen Crane. CP-CranS

There was one Syrian, with his bicycle, in our town. Derek Walcott. CP-WalcD *Fr.* Midsummer.

There was rain early in November but afterwards. Seventieth Birthday. Robinson Jeffers. CP-JefR3

There was rebellion, Father, and the door was slammed. Father. Robert Lowell. SP-LoweR

There was Rundle, Station Master. Mother-Lodge, The. Rudyard Kipling. CP-KiplR

There was set before me a mighty hill. Stephen Crane. CP-CranS

There was simply / nothing to look at. Shaker. James Schuyler. CP-SchuJ

There was so much talk of the dead. Untenable Situation, An. Pablo Neruda. SP-NeruP

There was something obscene about wrestling that baby-faced boy. Outlandish Agon. Mona Van Duyn. SP-VanDM

There was such speed in her little body. Bells for John Whiteside's Daughter. John Crowe Ransom. SP-RansJ

There was the butcher's hand. Weak Mind in the Mountains, A. Wallace Stevens. CP-StevW; CP-StevWP

There was the mechanicalism. Spook's Sabbath, Five Bowings. Louis Zukofsky. CP-ZukLS

There was the slow girl in art class. Gesture toward an Unfound Renaissance, A. William Stafford. SP-StafWW

There was the sun on the wall—my childhood's. Scream, The. Ted Hughes. SP-HughTN

There was this character come in. How Come He Got Canned at the Ribbon Factory. Allen Ginsberg. CP-GinsA

There was this lady once she used to grow. Tails. C. K. Williams. CP-WillC

There was this man and he was the strongest. Contender, The. Ted Hughes. SP-HughTN

There was this road. Legs, The. Robert Graves. CP-GravR

There was this terrific battle. Crow's Account of the Battle. Ted Hughes. SP-HughTN

There was this time in Boston. Wedding Night, The. Anne Sexton. CP-SextA

There was three kings into the east. John Barleycorn [a Ballad]. Robert Burns. CP-BurnR

There was twa wives, and twa witty wives. Robert Burns. CP-BurnR

There was / what we call "words," Speech. Carl Sandburg. CP-SandC

There wasn't two purtier farms in the state. What Smith Knew about Farming. James Whitcomb Riley. CP-RileJ

There we were in the vaulted tunnel running. Underground, The. Seamus Heaney. SP-HeanSO

There were a few dozen who occupied the field. Afternoon with Irish Cows. Billy Collins. SP-CollB

There were a hundred armed men. Primo Levi. CP-LeviP, *tr. by* Ruth Feldman *and* Brian Swann

There were always little tragedies. Transformation and Disfiguration. Charles Bukowski. SP-BukC3

There were bees about. From the start I thought. Shore Scene. John Logan. CP-LogaJ

There were distinctive. Language of Love. Rae Armantrout. SP-ArmaA

There were evenings, as scarlet as Phoenician sails. Sails. Adam Zagajewski. SP-ZagaA, *tr. by* Renata Gorczynski, Benjamin Ivry *and* C. K. Williams

There were faces to remember in the Valley of the Shadow. Valley of the Shadow, The. Edwin Arlington Robinson. CP-RobiE

There were feet upon the waters in the morning. Meditation. Wallace Stevens. CP-StevWP

There were five howling virgins / Who came. Five Virgins, The. Thomas Merton. CP-MertT

There were four apples on the bough. August. Algernon Charles Swinburne. SP-SwinA

There were four crates of chickens. Man with the Golden Adam's Apple, The. Kenneth Patchen. CP-PatcK

There were ghosts that returned to earth to hear his phrases. Large Red Man Reading. Wallace Stevens. CP-StevW; CP-StevWP

There Were Giants in Those Days or Maybe There Weren't. Ogden Nash. CP-NashO

There were lead-mines here before the Romans. Not in Baedeker. W. H. Auden. CP-AudeW

There were majesties. / Rain tilted his shining spears. I Sent a Mental to My Love. Kenneth Patchen. CP-PatcK

There were many houses like that in Canlin. Investigation of Certain Interesting Questions. Kenneth Patchen. CP-PatcK

There were many who went in huddled procession. Stephen Crane. CP-CranS

There were no antelope on the balcony. Midnight Special. Kenneth Patchen. CP-PatcK

There were no bums in my pores. Music. Andrei Codrescu. SP-CodrA

There were no hidden motives to his life. Epitaph: "There were no hidden motives to his life." David Ignatow. SP-IgnaD

There were no undesirables or girls in my set. Commander Lowell. Robert Lowell. SP-LoweR

There were none of my blood in this battle. Wildwest. Archibald MacLeish. CP-MacLA

There were only two things anyone would want. Cleveland, Oh? Kenneth Patchen. CP-PatcK

There were others; their bodies. Epithalamium: "There were others; their bodies." Louise Glück. SP-GlucL

There were over me three hawks. Poem for the Time of Change. Archibald MacLeish. CP-MacLA

There were palm trees. Alice Walker. CP-WalkA

There were poems all over Broadway that morning. Before Danger. Muriel Rukeyser. CP-RukeM

There were sea-horses and mer-men. Poet, The. "H. D." CP-DoolH

There were several hundred fools. I Cannot Stand Tears. Charles Bukowski. SP-BukC2

There were some dirty plates. Last Words of My English Grandmother, The. William Carlos Williams. CP-WilW1

There Were Some Summers. Thomas Lux. SP-LuxT

There were still shards of an ancient pastoral. Star-Apple Kingdom, The. Derek

Walcott. CP-WalcD

There were the cautionary crows. Crows, The. Wyatt Prunty. SP-PrunW

There were the roses, in the rain. Act, The. William Carlos Williams. CP-WilW2

There were thirty million English who talked of England's might. Last of the Light Brigade, The. Rudyard Kipling. CP-KiplR

There were thoughts that came to Phil. Night Thoughts. Stevie Smith. CP-SmitS

There were three. Three Trees Were Cut Down. Federico García Lorca. CP-GarcF, *tr.* by Alan S. Trueblood *Fr.* Theories.

There were three cherry trees once. Three Cherry Trees, The. Walter De la Mare. CP-DeLaW

There were three eagles percht on a rock. Three Eagles and the Sleepy Lion, The. George Meredith. CP-MerG2

There were three friends / Discussing life. Three Friends. Chuang Tzu. CP-MertT

There were three friends that buried the fourth. Rudyard Kipling. CP-KiplR *Fr.* Light That Failed, The.

There were three in the meadow by the brook. Code, The. Robert Frost. CP-FrosR

There were three maidens met on the highway. Three Maidens, The. George Meredith. CP-MerG1

There were three of them that night. Orgy. Muriel Rukeyser. CP-RukeM

There were twelve ragged children. November in Ohio. Kenneth Patchen. CP-PatcK

There were two who imagined. In Egypt's Land. James Laughlin. CP-LaugJ

There were two youths of equal age. Two Men, The. Thomas Hardy. CP-HardT

There were years vague of measure. Her Apotheosis. Thomas Hardy. CP-HardT

There were years when I knew. Falcons, The. W. S. Merwin. SP-MerwWF

There where the course is. At Galway Races. William Butler Yeats. CP-YeatW

There where the woodcock his long bill among the alders. October—An Etching. Edna St. Vincent Millay. CP-MillE

There where you see a green valley. World, The. Czeslaw Milosz. CP-MiloC; CP-MiloCN

There! Whitman's skull—. Hayden Carruth. CP-CarHS *Fr.* Clay Hill Anthology, The.

There / Why / There / Why. One or Two. I've Finished. Gertrude Stein. CP-SteiG

There will always be a father of all things, in some shape, in our minds. Gods. D. H. Lawrence. CP-LawrD

There will always be an issue: doctrine, dogma, differences of conscience, politics, or creed. Interrogation II. C. K. Williams. SP-WillC

There will always be monkeys and peacocks. Swell People. Carl Sandburg. CP-SandC

There Will Be a Future. Adam Zagajewski. SP-ZagaA, *tr.* by Renata Gorczynski

There will be a rusty gun on the wall, sweetheart. A. E. F. Carl Sandburg. CP-SandC

There will be little enough to forget. 1892—19—. Archibald MacLeish. CP-MacLA

There will be mud on the carpet tonight. Wifebeater, The. Anne Sexton. CP-SextA

There will be no evil. Where Every Prospect. Kenneth Patchen. CP-PatcK

There will be no examination in Long Term Suffering. Long Term Suffering. Richard Eberhart. CP-EberR

There Will Be No Peace. W. H. Auden. CP-AudeW

There will be no simple. Window, The. Robert Creeley. CP-CreeR

There will be no speech from. No Speech from the Scaffold. Thom Gunn. CP-GunnT

There will be one more eye. Confidence. Paul Celan. SP-CelaP, *tr.* by John Felstiner

There will be people left over. Call the Next Witness. Carl Sandburg. CP-SandC

There will be rain. there will be feasts, there. There Will Be a Future. Adam Zagajewski. SP-ZagaA, *tr.* by Renata Gorczynski

There will be rose and rhododendron. Elegy before Death. Edna St. Vincent Millay. CP-MillE

There will be something, later. Paul Celan. SP-CelaP, *tr.* by John Felstiner

There will be surprises: mothers mean harm. When It Happens. A. K. Ramanujan. CP-RamaA

There ("With all I know"). Robert Creeley. SP-CreeR

There, with ten Rembrandts. Ten Little Rembrandts. Theodore Weiss. SP-WeisT

There would be far less masculine gaming and boozing. Thoughts Thought on an Avenue. Ogden Nash. CP-NashO

There would have been the obligatory tour. Chichester. Amy Clampitt. CP-ClamA

There would he stand. Fragments from the Alfoxden Notebook (I). William Wordsworth. CP-WorW1

There you are in the dark. Forgotten Miniature, A. Thomas Hardy. CP-HardT

There! You shed a ray. He Wrote the History Book. Marianne Craig Moore. CP-MoorM

There You Were. Anne Sexton. CP-SextA

Therefore. William Dickey. SP-DickW

Therefore. Grace Paley. CP-PalGC

Therefore, Adieu. Countee Cullen. CP-CullC

Therefore the constant powers do not lessen. Climate of War, The. Kenneth Patchen. CP-PatcK

Therefore the hand of God. Delivery to the Secular Arm, The: A Scene During the Existence of the Spanish Inquisition at Antwerp, 1570. Robert Browning. CP-BroR2

Therefore to us, time's / final lesson: be content. Hayden Carruth. CP-CarHS *Fr.* Clay Hill Anthology, The.

There'll Always Be a War between the Sexes, or, A Woman Can Be Sometimes Pleased, but Never Satisfied. Ogden Nash. CP-NashO

There'll Never Be Peace Till Jamie Comes Hame. Robert Burns. CP-BurnR

There's a bear in the Truro woods. Truro Bear, The. Mary Oliver. SP-OlivM

There's a better shine. Lorine Niedecker. CP-NiedL

There's a bird the color of mustard. The bird. Elegy Asking that It Be the Last. Norman Dubie. CP-DubiN

There's a breathless hush on the freeway tonight. Wild Dreams of a New Beginning. Lawrence Ferlinghetti. SP-FerlL

There's a brilliant man somewhere. Han-shan. CP-ColdM, *tr.* by Red Pine

There's a certain Slant of light. Emily Dickinson. CP-DickE

There's a convict more in the Central Jail. Rudyard Kipling. CP-KiplR *Fr.* Life's Handicap.

There's a curve in the road, and a slow curve in the land. Lonesome Pine Special. Charles Wright. SP-WrigC

There's a deer no gun. Imagination. Yusef Komunyakaa. CP-KomuY

There's a fabulous story. Place Where the Rainbow Ends, The. Paul Laurence Dunbar. CP-DunbP

There's a fly / holding its course, manfully. Book, The. Rae Armantrout. SP-ArmaA

There's a footstep coming; look out and see. Ghost's Petition, The. Christina Georgina Rossetti. CP-RosC1

There's a fortune to be made in just about everything. My Great Great Etc. Uncle Patrick Henry. James Tate. SP-TateJ

There's a grandfather's clock in the hall, watch it closely. The. Robert Penn Warren. CP-WarrR

There's a habit I have nurtured. Scraps. James Whitcomb Riley. CP-RileJ

There's a hole in the bottom of the sea. Do You Want Affidavits? Carl Sandburg. CP-SandC

There's a hole in the earth I'm afraid of. Going Down. David Ignatow. SP-IgnaD

There's a kind of white moth, I don't know. Moths, The. Mary Oliver. SP-OlivM

There's a Legion that never was 'listed. Lost Legion, The. Rudyard Kipling. CP-KiplR

There's a little red-faced man. Bobs. Rudyard Kipling. CP-KiplR

There's a little sunshine in my heart. Sunshine. Christina Georgina Rossetti. CP-RosC3

There's a long-legged girl. Pickin Em Up and Layin Em Down. Maya Angelou. SP-AngeM

There's a lot of the West. Fanny Howe. SP-HoweF *Fr.* Joy Had I Known.

There's a memory keeps a-runnin'. Old Apple-Tree, The. Paul Laurence Dunbar. CP-DunbP

There's a mighty sound a-comin'. For Theodore Roosevelt. Paul Laurence Dunbar. CP-DunbP

There's a naked bug at Cold Mountain. Han-shan. CP-SnydG, *tr.* by Gary Snyder

There's a new skyline in Harlem. Hope for Harlem. Langston Hughes. CP-HughL; CP-HughL3

There's a new young moon. New Moon. Langston Hughes. CP-HughL; CP-HughL2

There's a palace in Florence, the world knows well. Statue and the Bust, The. Robert Browning. CP-BroR1; SP-BroR

There's a pasture in a valley where the hanging woods divide. Alnaschar and the Oxen. Rudyard Kipling. CP-KiplR *Fr.* Debits and Credits.

There's a patch of old snow in a corner. Patch of Old Snow, A. Robert Frost. CP-FrosR

There's a place called Faraway Meadow. Last Mowing, The. Robert Frost. CP-FrosR

There's a place I know where the birds swing low. Song in a Minor Key. Dorothy Parker. CP-ParkD

There's a pulse in Richard. Let Us Sing Unto the Lord a New Song. Denise Levertov. SP-LeveDS *Fr.* Staying Alive.

There's a ripple of fountains. Land o' Used to Be, The. Paul Laurence Dunbar. CP-DunbP

There's a seat, I see, still empty? Carrier, The. Thomas Hardy. CP-HardT

There's a secret boundary hidden in the waving grasses. Two Poems. Adrienne Rich. CP-RicAE

Theres a sort of. Sunflowers. William Carlos Williams. CP-WilW2

There's a space for good to bloom in. As Created. James Whitcomb Riley. CP-RileJ

There's [*or* There is] a special privacy on stage. Gig at Big Al's. Heather McHugh. SP-McHuH

There's a story that a traveling Greek actor. Story for Actors. Alan Dugan. CP-DugaA

There's a strange frenzy in my head. Jelaluddin Rumi. SP-Rumi, *tr. by* Coleman Barks

There's a thing in the East, that inhabits the South. Riddle by T-m Pun——i, Addressed to D——h, A. *Unknown, sometimes at. to* Thomas Sheridan. CP-SherT

There's a thread you follow. It goes among. Way It Is, The. William Stafford. SP-StafWW

There's a Train Leaving Soon. Kenneth Patchen. CP-PatcK

There's a Voice across the Nation like a mighty ocean-hail. Peace-Hymn of the Republic, A. James Whitcomb Riley. CP-RileJ

There's a volcano snow-capped in the air some twenty miles. Resort. George Oppen. CP-OppGN

There's a whisper down the field where the year has shot her yield. Envoi: "There's a whisper down the field where the year has shot her yield." Rudyard Kipling. CP-KiplR

There's a widow in sleepy Chester. Grave of the Hundred Dead, The. Rudyard Kipling. CP-KiplR

There's a woman in the earth, sitting on. Orbiter 5 Shows How Earth Looks from the Moon. May Swenson. SP-SwenM

There's a woman (you tell the gender by the noise of her heels). Sound of Fear, A. Denise Levertov. SP-LeveDL

There's a young man in the next. Hitchhiker, The. James Laughlin. CP-LaugJ

There's a youth in this city, it were a great pity. Robert Burns. CP-BurnR

There's all sorts of gods, all sorts and every sort. All Sorts of Gods. D. H. Lawrence. CP-LawrD

There's Always an Ubblebub. Ogden Nash. CP-NashO

There's always the quiet, stupid grief. Grief. Robert Stock. SP-StocR

There's always weather, weather. Langston Hughes. CP-HughL

There's an angel. In the Labor Camp of Good Intentions. Yusef Komunyakaa. CP-KomuY

There's an old drunk. What Matters. James Laughlin. CP-LaugJ

There's auld Rob Morris that wons in yon glen. Auld Rob Morris. Robert Burns. CP-BurnR

There's Ayisha. Piccolo, The. Yusef Komunyakaa. CP-KomuY

There's been a Death, in the Opposite House. Emily Dickinson. CP-DickE

There's been an eagle on a nickel. Fact. Langston Hughes. CP-HughL; CP-HughL3

There's blood between us, love, my love. Convent Threshold, The. Christina Georgina Rossetti. CP-RosC1

There's Chamfort. He's a sample. Chamfort. Carl Sandburg. CP-SandC

There's death in the cup—sae beware! Inscription on a Goblet. Robert Burns. CP-BurnR

There's four men mowing down by the river. Mowers, The. D. H. Lawrence. CP-LawrD

There's George Fisher, Charles Fleming, and Reginald Shore. Rural Architecture. William Wordsworth. CP-WorW1; MW-WorW

There's hanging moss. Carolina Cabin. Langston Hughes. CP-HughL; CP-HughL2

There's heaven above, and night by night. Johannes Agricola in Meditation. Robert Browning. CP-BroR1; SP-BroR

There's hidden sweetness in the stomach's emptiness. Fasting. Jelaluddin Rumi. SP-Rumi, *tr. by* Coleman Barks

There's in my mind a woman. In Mind. Denise Levertov. SP-LeveDP; SP-LeveDS

There's little in taking or giving. Coda: "There's little in taking or giving." Dorothy Parker. CP-ParkD

There's little to have but the things I had. Ballade of a Great Weariness. Dorothy Parker. CP-ParkD

There's many a strong farmer. Happy Townland, The. William Butler Yeats. CP-YeatW

There's many and many, and not so far. Purposely Ungrammatical Love Song. Dorothy Parker. CP-ParkD

There's my things. Portrait of a Woman in Bed. William Carlos Williams. CP-WilW1

There's nane sall ken, there's nane sall guess. I'll Ay[e] Ca' in by Yon Town. Robert Burns. CP-BurnR

There's News Lasses News. Robert Burns. CP-BurnR

There's no color like the color of an orange. It's Nothing to Laugh About. Charles Bukowski. SP-BukC2

There's no constraint to do amisse. Sin. Robert Herrick. CP-HerrR

There's no more to be done, or feared, or hoped. After the Last Breath. Thomas Hardy. CP-HardT

There's no new spirit abroad. Poets Are Silent, The. Stevie Smith. CP-SmitS

There's no no like money's. Matter, The. C. K. Williams. CP-WillC

There's no replying / To the Wind's sighing. Hollow-Sounding and Mysterious. Christina Georgina Rossetti. CP-RosC2

There's no sense of going further—it's the edge of cultivation. Explorer, The. Rudyard Kipling. CP-KiplR

There's no such thing as death everybody. Then the Brother of the Wind. C. K. Williams. CP-WillC

There's no wind among these seas. Thorkild's Song. Rudyard Kipling. CP-KiplR *Fr.* Puck of Pook's Hill.

There's no winsome woman so winsome as she. Winsome Woman, A. Thomas Hardy. CP-HardT

There's not a joy the world can give like that it takes away. Stanzas for Music. Lord Byron. CP-Byron

There's not a nook within this solemn Pass. Trosachs, The. William Wordsworth. CP-WorW2

There's not a sound tonight. Snow. Ivor Gurney. SP-GurnI

There's not an Echo round me. Child of God Longing To See Him Beloved, A. Jeanne Marie Bouvier de la Motte- Guyon. CP-CowpW

There's not much hill left up from here and after. Sorting. A. R. Ammons. CP-AmmoA

There's not one fact that's certain in. Lines to Catherine. John Logan. CP-LogaJ

There's Nothing Ahead. Jelaluddin Rumi. SP-Rumi, *tr. by* Coleman Barks *and* John Moyne

There's Nothing Like Instinct, Fortunately. Ogden Nash. CP-NashO

There's nothing lower on earth, of less account. Michelangelo Buonarroti. CP-Miche, *tr. by* John Frederick Nims

There's nothing May-like in this toxic air. Pier Paolo Pasolini. CP-MahoD *Fr.* Gramsci's Ashes.

There's nothing more debauched than thinking. Opinion on the Question of Pornography, An. Wisława Szymborska. SP-SzymW, *tr. by* Stanisław Barańczak *and* Clare Cavanagh

There's nothing new the Preacher cries. Behold, I Make All Things New. Jones Very. CP-VeryJ

There's old man Willards; an' his wife. New Year's Time at Willards's, A. James Whitcomb Riley. CP-RileJ

There's pleasure in great favors done, but hidden. Michelangelo Buonarroti. CP-Miche, *tr. by* John Frederick Nims

There's punning Tom Sh-r-d-n, Phoebus's darling. *Unknown.* CP-SherT *Fr.* Epistle in Behalf of Our Irish Poets to the Right Hon. Lady C——t, An.

There's reason good, that you good laws should make. To the Parliament. Ben Jonson. CP-JonsB; SP-JonsB

There's sax eggs in the pan, gudeman. O An Ye Were Dead Gudeman. Robert Burns. CP-BurnR

There's Snow on the Fields. Christina Georgina Rossetti. CP-RosC2

There's so much good in a face, such hope! On the World's Birthday. James Tate. SP-TateJ

There's somebody who's dying. They Warned Him Then They Threw Him Away. C. K. Williams. CP-WillC

There's something disturbing. Worriation. Langston Hughes. CP-HughL; CP-HughL3

There's something holy about. Enlacement, The. James Laughlin. CP-LaugJ

There's something in a flying horse. Peter Bell; a Tale. William Wordsworth. CP-WorW1; MW-WorW

There's something in a stupid ass. Epilogue: "There's something in a stupid ass." Lord Byron. CP-Byron

There's something quieter than sleep. Emily Dickinson. CP-DickE

There's something, sir, that somebody's going to tell you. Man in the Bar Says He Has Something to Say, A. Miller Williams. CP-WillM

There's talk, says Illinois. Colloquy for the States. Archibald MacLeish. CP-MacLA

There's teuch sauchs growin' i' the Reuch Heuch Hauch. Sauchs in the Reuch Heuch Hauch, The. Hugh MacDiarmid. SP-MacDH

There's the Battle of Burgoyne. Emily Dickinson. CP-DickE

There's the story of me sitting in the grass in the dark. In the Dead of the Night. Norman Dubie. CP-DubiN

There's this bird I saw in the paper, they said. Folding His *USA Today* He Makes His Point in the Blue Star Café. Miller Williams. CP-WillM

There's this shape, black as the entrance to a cave. October. Mary Oliver. SP-OlivM

There's this to a good day's sweat. Tree Trimming. John Ciardi. CP-CiarJ

There's *this* to Remember about the Gnu. Gnu, The. Theodore Roethke. CP-RoetT

There's three true gude fellows. Three Gude Fellows Ayont Yon Glen. Robert Burns. CP-BurnR

There's waking and dressing and what a fine day. Dilemmist, The. Laura Riding Jackson. CP-RidiL

Theresa's Friends. Robert Creeley. SP-CreeR

Thermometer. Charles Bukowski. SP-BukC2

Thermometer. Ralph Waldo Emerson. CP-EmerR

Thermopylae. Raymond Carver. CP-CarvR

Thermopylae. Constantine P. Cavafy. CP-CavaC, *tr. by* Theoharis Constantine Theoharis

Thermopylae. Amy Clampitt. CP-ClamA

Thermopylae is a well. Empire of Persia, The. Kenneth Patchen. CP-PatcK

Thersites: On the Surviving Zeus. Ezra Pound. CP-PoEar

These. William Carlos Williams. CP-WilW1

These acres, always again lost. Lost Acres. Robert Graves. CP-GravR

These / admonitory images. Maillol. Charles Tomlinson. CP-TomlC

These All Wait upon Thee. Christina Georgina Rossetti. *See* All Things Wait upon Thee

These alternate nights and days, these seasons. Lines for a Prologue. Archibald MacLeish. CP-MacLA

These ambiguities of his, intolerable; they try us. Misunderstandings. Yannis Ritsos. SP-RitsY, *tr. by* Kimon Friar

These americans just looking. Three Seasons and a Gorilla. C. K. Williams. CP-WillC

These are amazing: each. Some Trees. John Ashbery. SP-AshbJ

These are cities! This is a people for whom these dream Alleghenies and these Lebanons have risen into being! Cities ("These are cities! This is a people for whom these dream Alleghenies and these Lebanons have risen into being!"). Arthur Rimbaud. CP-RimbA, *tr. by* Martin Sorrell

These are diagrams on stilts all wired together. High Tension Lines across a Landscape. John Ciardi. CP-CiarJ

These are fragrant acres where. Clover. Tennessee Williams. CP-WillT

These are men! the gaunt, unforesold, the vocal. Ol' Bunk's Band. William Carlos Williams. CP-WilW2

These are my great ones. Kenneth Patchen. CP-PatcK

These are my legs. I don't have to tell them, legs. Walter Jenks' Bath. William Meredith. SP-MereW

These are no wind-blown rumors, soft say-sos. Sonnet: "These are no wind-blown rumors, soft say-sos." Countee Cullen. CP-CullC

These are not dewdrops, these are tears. Epitaph on a Free but Tame Redbreast. William Cowper. CP-CowpW

These are not the lines that came to me. Lines Lost among Trees. Billy Collins. SP-CollB

These are our brave, these with their hands in on the work. Citation for Horace Gregory. Muriel Rukeyser. CP-RukeM

These are *our* regulations. Boy Scouts' Patrol Song, A. Rudyard Kipling. CP-KiplR

These are prices and costs. Theorem. Carl Sandburg. CP-SandC

These are savannas bluer than your dreams. Deep South. Thomas McGrath. SP-McGrT

These are some canyons. Indian Caves in the Dry Country. William Stafford. SP-StafW; SP-StafWW

These are stone jetties. Facing Africa. James Dickey. CP-DickJ

These Are the Clouds. William Butler Yeats. CP-YeatW

These Are the Days. Rainer Maria Rilke. CP-RilkFr

These are the days I want to. Gentle Rejoinder, The. William Carlos Williams. CP-WilW2

These are the days of elfs and fays. Discovery, The. Paul Laurence Dunbar. CP-DunbP

These are the days of yellow and red. Vermont Idyll. Richard Eberhart. CP-EberR

These are the days that Reindeer love. Emily Dickinson. CP-DickE

These are the days when empty fountains. These Are the Days. Rainer Maria Rilke. CP-RilkFr

These are the dream machines. Nightmare Factory, The. Maxine W. Kumin. SP-KumiM

These are the fields I called for. You Shall Have Homes. Carl Sandburg. CP-SandC

These are the four that are never content, that have never been filled since the Dews began. Rudyard Kipling. CP-KiplR Fr. Second Jungle Book, The.

These are the Idiots chiefest arts. William Blake. CP-BlakW

These are the letters which Endymion wrote. Sonnet on the Sale by Auction of Keats' Love Letters. Oscar Wilde. CP-WildO

These are the lines on which a committee is formed. Praise of the Committee. Muriel Rukeyser. CP-RukeM

These are the names of the companies that have made money from this war. War Profit Litany. Allen Ginsberg. CP-GinsA

These are the Nights that Beetles love. Emily Dickinson. CP-DickE

These are the original monies of the earth. Cabinet of Seeds Displayed, A. Howard Nemerov. CP-NemeH

These are the places. Spring. Robert Creeley. CP-CreeR

These are the proper names. Naming for Love. Hayden Carruth. CP-CarHS

These are the roads to take when you think of your country. Road, The. Muriel Rukeyser. CP-RukeM

These are the Signs to Nature's Inns. Emily Dickinson. CP-DickE

These are the sins for which they cast out angels. Annotation for an Epitaph. Adrienne Rich. CP-RicAE

These are the small resorts. *City of Keansburg*, The. George Oppen. CP-OppGN

These are the tawny days: your face comes back. Tawny. Carl Sandburg. CP-SandC

These are the times when all our feminine notables are beautified. Anybody Else Hate Nickynames? Ogden Nash. CP-NashO

These are the voices of the pastors calling. Old Lutheran Bells at Home, The. Wallace Stevens. CP-StevW; CP-StevWP

These are two friends whose lives were undivided. Epitaph: "These are two friends whose lives were undivided." Percy Bysshe Shelley. CP-ShelP

These as they clack in the wind. In the Pea Patch. Maxine W. Kumin. SP-KumiM

These beds of bracken, climax of the summer's growth. Bracken Hills in Autumn. Hugh MacDiarmid. SP-MacDH

These books you find three weeks behind. To My Sister. James Whitcomb Riley. CP-RileJ

These brief imperfect meetings. Emily Dickinson. SP-DickE

These brittle pages spread before me. Living Room, A. Theodore Weiss. SP-WeisT

These bulbs forgotten in a cellar. Christmas Letter to a Psychiatrist. May Sarton. SP-SartM

These Carols. Walt Whitman. CP-WhitW

These Chairs they have no words to utter. William Wordsworth. CP-WorW1; MW-WorW

These children playing at statues fill. Statues. Richard Wilbur. CP-WilbR

These children singing in stone a. E. E. Cummings. CP-CummE; SP-CummE

These Clever Women. D. H. Lawrence. CP-LawrD
    (Spiritual Woman, A.) CP-LawrD

These coastal bogs, before they settle. Green. Amy Clampitt. CP-ClamA

These coins and calendars stood for the moon, young boys. Of Money. And the Past. Muriel Rukeyser. CP-RukeM

These critics, who to faith no quarter grant. Lines Written in the Monthly Review. William Cowper. CP-CowpW

These Days. Charles Olson. CP-OlsoC

These Days. Alice Walker. CP-WalkA

These days are best when one goes nowhere. Against Travel. Charles Tomlinson. SP-TomlC

These days are long before I die. Yet a Little While. Christina Georgina Rossetti. CP-RosC3

These days, God leaves the earth. Hymn to Summer. Yehuda Amichai. SP-AmicYL, *tr. by* Benjamin Harshav *and* Barbara Harshav

These days I think of Belvie. These Days. Alice Walker. CP-WalkA

These days I think of the wind in your hair. To Hurl Haunting Memories. Yehuda Amichai. SP-AmicYL, *tr. by* Benjamin Harshav *and* Barbara Harshav

These days I've been reading folk songs. Taken. Constantine P. Cavafy. CP-CavaC, *tr. by* Theoharis Constantine Theoharis

These days of disinheritance, we feast. Cuisine Bourgeoise. Wallace Stevens. CP-StevW; CP-StevWP

These days / only the telephone men are spurred. Gloss, A. Charles Olson. CP-OlsoC

These Deathy Leaves. Allen Tate. CP-TateA

These dry, bright winter days. In March. Charles Tomlinson. CP-TomlC

These evenings over the restaurants. Stranger, The. Aleksandr Aleksandrovich Blok. SP-BlokA, *tr. by* Peter France *and* Jon Stallworthy

These faces make a chapel where worship comes easy. English Train Compartment. John Updike. CP-UpdiJ

These farmers dressed in gold and blue. For Milarepa, In Ruse, on Rice Paper. Norman Dubie. CP-DubiN

These Fevered Days—to take them to the Forest. Emily Dickinson. CP-DickE

These fields of thistles are the old. Age. W. S. Merwin. SP-MerwW

These fish have no eyes. Current, The. Raymond Carver. CP-CarvR

These flowers are I, poor Fanny Hurd. Voices from Things Growing in a Churchyard. Thomas Hardy. CP-HardT

These fresh beauties (we can prove). Why Flowers Change Color. Robert Herrick. CP-HerrR

These from my mother's greatgrandmother's rosebush white. E. E. Cummings. CP-CummE

These gardens circle up. Walking Chapultepec. Jay Wright. SP-WrigJ

These gifts from the Friend, a robe. Jelaluddin Rumi. SP-Rumi, *tr. by* Coleman Barks

These golden heads, these common suns. Dandelions. Howard Nemerov. CP-NemeH

These Gothic windows, how they wear me out. Young Glass-Stainer, The. Thomas Hardy. CP-HardT

These grand and fatal movements toward death. Rearmament. Robinson Jeffers. CP-JefR2

These grasses of light. Stanbury Moor. Ted Hughes. SP-HughTN

These hands so well articulated. Ceci est digne de gens sans dieu. Stevie Smith. CP-SmitS

These Have Gone with Silent Hands, Seeking. Kenneth Patchen. CP-PatcK

These have I set up. Dream Forest. Donald Davie. CP-DaviDC

These have no Christ to spit and stoop. Black Magdalens. Countee Cullen. CP-CullC

These heaped-up, half-paved streets. Letter to John Logan from La Push. Sam

Hamill. SP-HamiS

These held their Wick above the West. Emily Dickinson. CP-DickE

These here are words of radical advice for a young man looking for a job. Will Consider Situation. Ogden Nash. CP-NashO

These High White Walls. Jane Cooper. CP-CoopJ

These hills, to hurt me more. Mist in the Valley. Edna St. Vincent Millay. CP-MillE

These Houres, and that which hover's o're my END. Recommendation, The. Richard Crashaw. CP-CrasR

These humble dwellings, old, and quaint. Old Houses of Salem: Illustrated by George M. White. Jones Very. CP-VeryJ

These I assume were words so deeply meant. Ingenuities of Debt, The. Robert Frost. CP-FrosR

These I Singing in Spring. Walt Whitman. CP-WhitW

These Images Remain. May Sarton. SP-SartM

These images will parade until the morning. Shooting Gallery. Muriel Rukeyser. CP-RukeM

These, in the day when heaven was falling. Epitaph on an Army of Mercenaries. A. E. Housman. CP-HousA

These Indian-Summer Days. Emily Dickinson. SP-DickE

These infinite green motions. Tides. Wallace Stevens. CP-StevWP

These keys that draw their silent music out. Imperfect, The. Marya Alexandrovna Zaturenska. SP-ZatuM

These kindly rhymes by which you have made known. Petrarch. CP-Petra, tr. by J. G. Nichols

These laborers of rain, these heavy clouds. Clouds. Rainer Maria Rilke. CP-RilkFr, tr. by A. Poulin, Jr.

These legs need to run. I Kneel. Charles Bukowski. SP-BukC2

These line I give to you in hopes my name. Charles Baudelaire. CP-BaudC, tr. by Walter Martin

These little firs to-day are things. Young Fir-Wood, A. Dante Gabriel Rossetti. CW-RossD

These locks on doors have brought me happiness. Locks. Kenneth Koch. SP-KochK

These locks, which fondly thus entwine. To a Lady Who Presented to the Author a Lock of Hair Braided with His Own, and Appointed a Night in December to Meet Him in the Garden. Lord Byron. CP-Byron

These locusts by day, these crickets by night. Things of August. Wallace Stevens. CP-StevW; CP-StevWP

These loves are the helpless or wanted bliss. 1938: The Spring Dances. Randall Jarrell. CP-JarrR

These magnificent words that I read today. Magnificent Words. Stevie Smith. CP-SmitS

These men look askance, always suspicious. They. Yannis Ritsos. SP-RitsY, tr. by Kostas Myrsiades

These men, the last workers on the world's. Old Photo. Andrei Codrescu. SP-CodrA

These men were kings, albeit they were black. Black Majesty. Countee Cullen. CP-CullC

These men who do not die, but send to death. Not Sacco and Vanzetti. Countee Cullen. CP-CullC

These Mornings of Rain. Alice Walker. CP-WalkA

These mountains have heard God. Tillamook Burn, The. William Stafford. SP-StafWW

These mysteries do point to three more great. Reverse on the Back Side, The. Ben Jonson. CP-JonsB

These nymphs that I would perpetuate. Afternoon of a Faun, The. Stéphane Mallarmé. CP-MallS, tr. by Henry Weinfield

These nymphs, whom I itch to perpetuate—. Afternoon of a Faun. Stéphane Mallarmé. CP-CarHS

These of living emanate a formidable light. Cloth of the Tempest, The. Kenneth Patchen. CP-PatcK

These ornaments as we pass. Facades for Norma Cole. Michael Palmer. SP-PalmM

These people have not heard your name. In a Cathedral City. Thomas Hardy. CP-HardT

These people socalled were not given hearts. E. E. Cummings. CP-CummE

These people, with their illegible diplomas. Metamorphoses. Howard Nemerov. CP-NemeH

These pines, these fall oaks, these rocks. After Drinking All Night with a Friend, We Go Out in a Boat at Dawn to See Who Can Write the Best Poem. Robert Bly. SP-BlyR

These pink-white acres of overcast. From Above. John Updike. CP-UpdiJ

These pods are part of the growth of life within life. Nuns Painting Water-Lilies. Wallace Stevens. CP-StevWP

These poems do not live: it's a sad diagnosis. Stillborn. Sylvia Plath. CP-PlatS

These pods don't seem to light our way. Notes for Echo Lake 12. Michael Palmer. SP-PalmM

These pools that, though in forests, still reflect. Spring Pools. Robert Frost. CP-FrosR

These poor nineteenth-century poets. Immortality. Adam Zagajewski. SP-ZagaA, tr. by Clare Cavanagh

These poplars dream. Consolation Sonata. Carl Sandburg. CP-SandC

These psalms are the workings of the vision haunted mind. Psalm I. Allen Ginsberg. CP-GinsA

These Pure Arches. May Sarton. SP-SartM

These Purists. William Carlos Williams. CP-WilW2

These quiet months of watching for. Song: Once More. Robert Graves. CP-GravR

These retroactive small. First Rain. Robert Creeley. SP-CreeR

These roads will take you into your own country. Book of the Dead, The. Muriel Rukeyser. CP-RukeM

These rolling flowing plunging breaking everlasting weaving waters. There Shall Be No More Sea. Kathleen Jessie Raine. SP-RainK

These rooms are public as a place. Last Wine, The. Tennessee Williams. CP-WillT

These sacks of flesh piled in a pile. Women on a Bus. Randall Jarrell. CP-JarrR

These—saw Visions. Emily Dickinson. CP-DickE

These secretly are going to some place. Grand Central, with Soldiers, in Early Morning. Howard Nemerov. CP-NemeH

These sky-rocket etchings are my life. Prufrock in Wonderland. Kenneth Rexroth. CP-RexrK

These spasms and chrysanthemums of light. Fireworks. John Updike. CP-UpdiJ

These spectres resting on plastic stools. Café in Warsaw. Allen Ginsberg. CP-GinsA

These Springs were Maidens once that lov'd. How Springs Came First. Robert Herrick. CP-HerrR

These States: into L.A. Allen Ginsberg. CP-GinsA
   "Overpopulation, overpopulation / Give me 3 acres of land." SP-GinsA

These States: to Miami Presidential Convention. Allen Ginsberg. CP-GinsA

These still days after frost have let down. Phase. A. R. Ammons. CP-AmmoA

These Strangers, In a Foreign World. Emily Dickinson. CP-DickE

These Strangers, in a foreign World. These Strangers, In a Foreign World. Emily Dickinson. CP-DickE

These Streets. Philip Levine. SP-LeviP

These suggestions by Asians are not taken seriously. Asian Peace Offers Rejected without Publication. Robert Bly. SP-BlyR

These summer-birds did with thy master stay. To His Maid Prew. Robert Herrick. CP-HerrR

These summer landscapes—clump, and croft, and copse. At the Royal Academy. Thomas Hardy. CP-HardT

These tales of old disguisings, are they not. Masks. Ezra Pound. CP-PoEar

These tears flooding my eyes, are they of pain. Wand, The. Robert Graves. CP-GravR

These temp'rall goods God (the most Wise) commends. Temporall Goods. Robert Herrick. CP-HerrR

These tested Our Horizon. Emily Dickinson. CP-DickE

These, the unequalled, vicious. Penitent, The. Robert Creeley. CP-CreeR

These, then, he left, and away where ranks were now clashing the thickest. Agamemnon in the Fight. Homer. CP-MerG1 Fr. Iliad, The.

These, these are they. Ben Jonson. CP-JonsB Fr. Masque of Hymen.

These times strike monied worldlings with dismay. October, 1803. William Wordsworth. CP-WorW1

These times touch moneyed Worldlings with dismay. William Wordsworth. See These times strike monied worldlings with dismay

These Tourists, heaven preserve us! needs must live. Brothers, The. William Wordsworth. CP-WorW1; MW-WorW

These trees are not at ease with lesser air. Romiosini. Yannis Ritsos. SP-RitsY, tr. by Kimon Friar

These trees have the many circles of self-love. Ozone. Heather McHugh. SP-McHuH

These trees like tho'ts that to visions congeal. Ralph Waldo Emerson. CP-EmerR

These two by the stone wall. Burghers of Petty Death. Wallace Stevens. CP-StevW; CP-StevWP

These umbered cliffs and gnarls of masonry. Rome: Building a New Street in the Ancient Quarter. Thomas Hardy. CP-HardT

These Unreturning Destinies. Kenneth Patchen. CP-PatcK

These Untitled Little Verses in Which, at Dawn, Two Obscure Dutch Peasants Struggled with an Auburn Horse. Norman Dubie. CP-DubiN

These vales were saddened with no common gloom. Epitaph in Grasmere Church. William Wordsworth. CP-WorW2

These verses also, Manso, the Pierides are meditating. Manso. John Milton. CP-MiltJ

These verses also to thy praise the Nine. John Milton. See These verses also, Manso, the Pierides are meditating

These vibrant spheres of light were not made. Blue Eyes. Constantine P. Cavafy. CP-CavaC, tr. by Theoharis Constantine Theoharis

These vulgar ways that round me be. Arthur Hugh Clough. SP-ClouA

These walls they knew those shadows. Wall Shadows. Carl Sandburg. CP-SandC

These waters run secretively until. Race, The. Charles Tomlinson. CP-TomlC

These watery diamond spheres. Kathleen Jessie Raine. SP-RainK

These, we are told (in an hour of legends). Expectant Shelters, The. Kenneth Patchen. CP-PatcK

These wells that shine and seem as shallow as pools. Paradox, The. G. K. Chesterton. CP-ChesG

These Were Her Nightly Journeys. May Sarton. SP-SartM

These were my companions going forth by night. Chil's Song. Rudyard Kipling. CP-KiplR *Fr.* Second Jungle Book, The.

These were never your true love's eyes. Oldest Song, The. Rudyard Kipling. CP-KiplR

These were our children who died for our lands: they were dear in our sight. Children, The. Rudyard Kipling. CP-KiplR

These wet rocks where the tide has been. Low-Tide. Edna St. Vincent Millay. CP-MillE

These Winds. Robert Lowell. SP-LoweR

These women are supposed to come. Blue Cheese and Chili Peppers. Charles Bukowski. SP-BukC1

These wonderful things. Last World, A. John Ashbery. SP-AshbJ

These woods are one of my great lies. Owl, The. W. S. Merwin. SP-MerwW

These woods are too impersonal. On a Day in August. Thomas Merton. CP-MertT

These Words Also. Howard Nemerov. CP-NemeH

These words, like heaps of feathers. Yehuda Amichai. SP-AmicYL, *tr. by* Benjamin Harshav *and* Barbara Harshav

These writings are those of a young man, a very young *man.* Deserts of Love, The. Arthur Rimbaud. CP-RimbA, *tr. by* Martin Sorrell

These Years a Winter. Thomas Merton. CP-MertT

Theseus and Ariadne. Robert Graves. CP-GravR

Theseus, if he did destroy the Minotaur. On Getting Out Of Vietnam. Howard Nemerov. CP-NemeH

These(whom;pretends / blue nothing). E. E. Cummings. CP-CummE

Thesis and Antithesis. Arthur Hugh Clough. SP-ClouA

Thesis and Counter-Thesis. Czeslaw Milosz. CP-MiloC; CP-MiloCN

Thesis, Antithesis and Nostalgia. Alan Dugan. CP-DugaA

Thethe / the pink / Tartskids with. E. E. Cummings. CP-CummE

Thetis. Olga Broumas. SP-BrouO

Thetis. "H. D." CP-DoolH

Thetis. "H. D." CP-DoolH

Th'expense in odours is a most vain sin. To the Same Sir Cod. Ben Jonson. CP-JonsB; SP-JonsB

They. W. H. Auden. CP-AudeW

They. Robert Creeley. CP-CreeR

They. Robert Creeley. CP-CreeR

They. James Vincent Cunningham. CP-CunnJ

They. Yannis Ritsos. SP-RitsY, *tr. by* Kostas Myrsiades

They abuse no maiden universe. O Everliving Queen! Kenneth Patchen. CP-PatcK

They Accuse Me of Not Talking. Hayden Carruth. CP-CarHS

They act like drunks all day. Han-shan. CP-ColdM, *tr. by* Red Pine

They, after the slow building of the house. Asmodai. Geoffrey Hill. CP-HillG

"They ain't much 'tale' about it!" Noey said. Noey's Night-Piece. James Whitcomb Riley. CP-RileJ *Fr.* Child-World, A.

They ain't no style about 'em. Old-Fashioned Roses. James Whitcomb Riley. CP-RileJ

They all came, some wore sentiments. Other Tradition, The. John Ashbery. SP-AshbJ

They all climbed up on a high board-fence. Nine Little Goblins, The. James Whitcomb Riley. CP-RileJ

They All Want to Play Hamlet. Carl Sandburg. CP-SandC

They always seem to come up. First Day of the Future. Galway Kinnell. SP-KinnGN

They amputated / your thighs from my hips. Pity, A. We Were Such a Good Invention. Yehuda Amichai. SP-AmicY, *tr. by* Stephen Mitchell

They amputated / Your thighs from my waist. Pity, We Were a Good Invention. Yehuda Amichai. SP-AmicYL, *tr. by* Benjamin Harshav *and* Barbara Harshav

They answer one's questions. People's Surroundings. Marianne Craig Moore. CP-MoorM

They are above us all the time. Angels, The. John Updike. CP-UpdiJ

They are afraid of climbing down from this idiotic tin-pot heaven of ours. Climbing Down. D. H. Lawrence. CP-LawrD

They Are All Dice. Yehuda Amichai. SP-AmicY, *tr. by* Chana Bloch

They are all gone away. House on the Hill, The. Edwin Arlington Robinson. CP-RobiE

They are allowed to inherit. Immigrants, The. Margaret Atwood. SP-AtwM1

They are always there. Virgin, the Doe, and the Leper, The. Marya Alexandrovna Zaturenska. SP-ZatuM

They are always with us, the thin people. Thin People, The. Sylvia Plath. CP-PlatS

They are at the track every. Space Creatures. Charles Bukowski. SP-BukC3

They are born naked. Gods | Children. May Swenson. SP-SwenM

They are chanting now the service of All the Dead. All Souls. D. H. Lawrence. CP-LawrD

They are closing the auto plants. Fall Out. Charles Bukowski. SP-BukC3

They are cowshit farmers, these New Englanders. Marshall Washer. Hayden Carruth. CP-CarHS

They are crying salt tears. Repetitions. Carl Sandburg. CP-SandC

They are dancing the rain dance in Bali. To My Students. John Ciardi. CP-CiarJ

They are fencing the upland against. Snow Fences, The. Charles Tomlinson. CP-TomlC; SP-TomlC

They are flocking from the East / And the West. All Saints. Christina Georgina Rossetti. CP-RosC2

"They are fools who kiss and tell" Rudyard Kipling. *See* Jenny and Me were engaged, you see

They are gathering hay. The truck rolls slowly. Haying. Wyatt Prunty. SP-PrunW

They Are Great Trees. Thomas Hardy. CP-HardT

They are here again. Seventeen Years. Wendell Berry. CP-BerrW

"They are his new boots," she pursued. New Boots, The. Thomas Hardy. CP-HardT

They Are Hostile Nations. Margaret Atwood. SP-AtwM1

They are hunting the boar in the vineyards. Season Opens on Wild Boar in Chianti. Robert Penn Warren. CP-WarrR

They are kneeling upright on a flowered bed. Short Story on a Painting of Gustav Klimt. Lawrence Ferlinghetti. SP-FerlL

They are light as flakes of dandruff with scrawny legs. Crabs. Marge Piercy. SP-PierM

They are massing at the bank. Waking Dream, A. Thom Gunn. CP-GunnT

They are moving the trees in Princeton. In April, in Princeton. Maxine W. Kumin. SP-KumiM

They are murdering all the young men. Thou Shalt Not Kill. Kenneth Rexroth. CP-RexrK

They are not all beasts. St Matthew. D. H. Lawrence. CP-LawrD

They are not dead, but gone before! Early Companions. Jones Very. CP-VeryJ

They are not dead! The sun like a golden lion. Fragment in Correction of D. H. Lawrence. G. K. Chesterton. CP-ChesG

They are not dead, they are not dead! Argonauts, The. D. H. Lawrence. CP-LawrD

They are not, sir, worst owers, that do pay. Epistle to a Friend. Ben Jonson. CP-JonsB

They are not those, are present with their face. To the Most Noble, and above His Titles, Robert, Earl of Somerset. Ben Jonson. CP-JonsB

They are not those who used to feed us. Puzzled Game-Birds, The. Thomas Hardy. CP-HardT

They are old over there, older than we are. Turn of the Wheel. Carl Sandburg. CP-SandC

They are out bathing in the sea at night. Through a Glass Darkly. Norman Dubie. CP-DubiN

They are pounded into the earth. It Is This Way with Men. C. K. Williams. CP-WillC; SP-WillC

They are preparing to begin again. Task, The. John Ashbery. SP-AshbJ

They are rattling breakfast plates in basement kitchens. Morning at the Window. T. S. Eliot. CP-ElioT; SP-ElioT

They are stalking humming birds. It Is a German Honeymoon. Kenneth Rexroth. CP-RexrK

They are stripping the fur of the police. Police, The. Andrei Codrescu. SP-CodrA

They are sure / that a sudden feeling united them. Love at First Sight. Wisława Szymborska. SP-SzymWM, *tr. by* Joanna Trzeciak

They are taking all my letters, and they. Dishonest Mailmen, The. Robert Creeley. CP-CreeR

They are tearing down the oldest hotel. Tearing Down the Hotel. Miller Williams. CP-WillM

They are the last romantics, these candles. Candles. Sylvia Plath. CP-PlatS

They / are the light-hearted races. Laughing Ones, The. Charles Olson. CP-OlsoC

They are the oldest living captive race. Ginkgoes in Fall. Howard Nemerov. CP-NemeH

They are, the surfaces, gorgeous: a master, The. Gorgeous Surfaces. Thomas Lux. SP-LuxT

They are there just the same. Wheels of the Trains, The. W. S. Merwin. SP-MerwW

They are tranquil now. They can sit on the pier to smoke. Finishing Touch. Yannis Ritsos. SP-RitsY *Fr.* Monovasia

They are walking home in tight bunches. Sisters. Wyatt Prunty. SP-PrunW

They are warming up the old horrors; and all that they say is echoes of. Soul's Desert, The. Robinson Jeffers. CP-JefR3

They are watching me die. Six years old. Third Street. William Stafford. SP-

StafWW

They are weighing the babies again on color television. Video Cuisine. Maxine W. Kumin. SP-KumiM

They are with her now, and in her ears, and known. George Meredith. CP-MerG1 *Fr.* France.

They are with us always, but they have the wit. Distances They Keep, The. Howard Nemerov. CP-NemeH

They aren't for everything. What Poems Are For. Heather McHugh. SP-McHuH

They aren't very big are. She Said in Apology. James Laughlin. CP-LaugJ

They arrive inside. Explorers. Charles Simic. SP-SimiC; SP-SimiCE

They ask but our Delight. Emily Dickinson. CP-DickE

They Ask Each Other Where They Came From. Carl Sandburg. CP-SandC

They ask for a knife. Help Wanted. Charles Simic. SP-SimiC; SP-SimiCE

They Ask: Is God, Too, Lonely? Carl Sandburg. CP-SandC

They ask me to handle bronzes. Bronzes. Carl Sandburg. CP-SandC

They ask me to remember. Why some people be mad at me sometimes. Lucille Clifton. SP-ClifL

They bear him to his resting-place. She at His Funeral. Thomas Hardy. CP-HardT

They bear, in place of classic names. Trade, The. Rudyard Kipling. CP-KiplR

They became you, that pair of kid gloves. Toe-Tag, The. Paul Muldoon. CP-MuldP

They bid me sing to thee. Song against Singing, A. Elizabeth Barrett Browning. CP-BroEB

They bob above us all afternoon. Demonstration, The. Gregory Orr. SP-OrrG

They both collected for the March of Dimes. Statistics. James Vincent Cunningham. CP-CunnJ

"They both wanted it," his mother told me. "Both of them" Two Lovers Murdered by a Partridge. Federico García Lorca. CP-GarcF, *tr. by* Greg Simon *and* Steven F. White

They brand themselves with hearts. Messages. Yusef Komunyakaa. CP-KomuY

They briskly bounce out of the future and having cried "Futile!" Centaurs 1. Joseph Brodsky. CP-BrodJ

They brought him in on a stretcher from the world. Grandfather. Derek Mahon. CP-MahoD

They brought me rubies from the mine. Rubies. Ralph Waldo Emerson. CP-EmerR

They built a new temple where the old had fallen. Legend, The. Tennessee Williams. CP-WillT

They burned lime on the hill and dropped it down here in an iron car. Bixby's Landing. Robinson Jeffers. CP-JefR1

They burnt a corpse upon the sand. Rudyard Kipling. CP-KiplR *Fr.* Plain Tales from the Hills.

They butchered the cock, the dove, the goat. With the blood. Night Ritual. Yannis Ritsos. SP-RitsY, *tr. by* Kostas Myrsiades

They Buy with an Eye to Looks. Carl Sandburg. CP-SandC

They call all experience of the senses *mystic,* when the experience / is considered. Mystic. D. H. Lawrence. CP-LawrD

They Call It "Grumus Merdae" Alan Dugan. CP-DugaA

They call it regional, this relevance. Lake Chelan. William Stafford. SP-StafWW

They call me and I go. Complaint. William Carlos Williams. CP-WilW1

They call thee lecherous. Narcotic Alcohol. Ezra Pound. CP-PoEar

They called across to ask me to get some beer and come up and. Opening the Window. Kenneth Patchen. CP-PatcK

They called him Mr. What's-his-name. Mr. What's-His-Name. James Whitcomb Riley. CP-RileJ

They called it Annandale—and I was there. How Annandale Went Out. Edwin Arlington Robinson. CP-RobiE

They called it Neosho, meaning. By a River in the Osage Country. William Stafford. SP-StafW; SP-StafWW

They called me to the Window, for. Emily Dickinson. CP-DickE

They called the place Lookout Farm. Memoirs of a Spinach-Picker. Sylvia Plath. CP-PlatS

They called us. Charm, The. Rita Dove. SP-DoveR

They came at a pace. Lorine Niedecker. CP-NiedL

They came not from afar from lust of gain. Motive. Jones Very. CP-VeryJ

They came on ponies, barefoot. Bolsheviks. Aba Shtoltsenberg. CP-KunSC, *tr. by* Stanley Kunitz

They came that morning, in gowns of pale green and white. Abstraction. Eleanor Wilner. SP-WilnE

They came, the brothers, and took two chairs. Announcement, The. Thomas Hardy. CP-HardT

They came to hear what they have the right to hear. Beside an Open Grave the Mind of the Young Preacher Comes Almost to Terms. Miller Williams. CP-WillM

They can be fists punching the water. Sky, Water. C. K. Williams. CP-WillC

They cannot come to us though we. Spiritual Intercourse. Jones Very. CP-VeryJ

They capped their heads with feathers, masked. Charivari. Margaret Atwood. SP-AtwM1

They Carved an Animal. William Stafford. SP-StafWW

They certainly do move. Dressed to Kill. Clarence Major. SP-MajoC

They cheered when he started out and kept it up. Jonathan Losing. Miller Williams. CP-WillM

They christened my brother of old. Bell Buoy, The. Rudyard Kipling. CP-KiplR

They clamor for a sign with eyeless zeal. Sign, The. Jones Very. CP-VeryJ

They closed the Jaffa port. Closing the Jaffa Port. Yehuda Amichai. SP-AmicYL, *tr. by* Benjamin Harshav *and* Barbara Harshav

They come. Samuel Beckett. CP-BeckS

They come at night, like wisps of fog. Thieves. Primo Levi. CP-LeviP, *tr. by* Ruth Feldman

They come closer together, vines. Who Walks There? Kenneth Patchen. CP-PatcK

They come down from the mountains, proud of their rags. Proud of Their Rags. Carl Sandburg. CP-SandC

They come forth with all four legs folded in. Vealers, The. Maxine W. Kumin. SP-KumiM

They come from the white barrier of noon. Diatribe of the Kite, The. Norman Dubie. CP-DubiN

They come here to visit mourners. Tourists. Yehuda Amichai. SP-AmicYL, *tr. by* Benjamin Harshav *and* Barbara Harshav

They come in in tiny boats . . . . Passages. Thomas McGrath. SP-McGrT

They come in low, wings like dark bandages. Autumn Is the Crows' Time. Kenneth Patchen. CP-PatcK

They Come No More, Those Words, Those Finches. Archibald MacLeish. CP-MacLA

They come on to my clean. Fallen Angels, The. Anne Sexton. CP-SextA

They come to us but once in life. Holidays. George Meredith. CP-MerG2

They come to you with their descriptions of your soul. Adrienne Rich. SP-RicA2 *Fr.* Shooting Script.

They could bend low. Light and Moonbells. Carl Sandburg. CP-SandC

They could not carry much, as soldiers. Gigantomachia. Wallace Stevens. CP-StevW; CP-StevWP

They cover the tree and twitch their coloured capes. Butterflies, The. Charles Tomlinson. SP-TomlC

They crowd near. If you look at them. Last Class, The. William Stafford. SP-StafWW

They crucify me. I have to be the cross, the nails. Accomplice, The. Jorge Luis Borges. SP-BorgJ, *tr. by* Hoyt Rogers

They crush together—a rustling heap of flesh. Ballet, The. Thomas Hardy. CP-HardT

They cut down the last tree. Clarence Major. SP-MajoC

They Desire a Better Country. Christina Georgina Rossetti. CP-RosC1

They did not hear my children. God Said "They Did Not Hear." Thomas Merton. CP-MertT

They did not travel in an airplane. On a Pallet of Straw. Langston Hughes. CP-HughL; CP-HughL3

They did or did not exist. Atlantis. Wisława Szymborska. SP-SzymWM, *tr. by* Joanna Trzeciak

They didn't have much trouble. Teaching the Ape to Write Poems. James Tate. SP-TateJ

They die—the dead return not—Misery. Death. Percy Bysshe Shelley. CP-ShelP

They dither softly at her bedroom door. Cover Her Face. Thomas Kinsella. CP-KinsT

They do not come separately. So Can Anger. Stevie Smith. CP-SmitS

They do not know through the blood of what witchlike women. Harp of Wales, The. Tennessee Williams. CP-WillT

They do not swim alone. Waking. Josephine Jacobsen. CP-JacoJ

They do not toil in heaven; they live and love. Heavenly Rest, The. Jones Very. CP-VeryJ

They Do Not Trade, Sleep, or Remember. Aleksandr Aleksandrovich Blok. SP-BlokA, *tr. by* Peter France *and* Jon Stallworthy

They do say said. Instance, The. Charles Tomlinson. CP-TomlC

They done took Cordelia. Stony Lonesome. Langston Hughes. CP-HughL

They don't come back, he said. Nitrate. Philip Levine. SP-LeviP

They don't get anywhere. Couple Overhead, The. William Meredith. SP-MereW

They don't say gully, cove, cut, gulch. Crow's Mark. Hayden Carruth. CP-CarHS

They don't walk the Noble Path. Han-shan. CP-ColdM, *tr. by* Red Pine

They drift to her. Speaking of Luck. Yusef Komunyakaa. CP-KomuY

They drift unobtrusively into the dream, they linger, then they depart, but they emanate, always. Shadows. C. K. Williams. SP-WillC

They drop the book when it grows clear to them. Inferno 5, 129. Jorge Luis Borges. SP-BorgJ, *tr. by* Alan S. Trueblood

They dropped like Flakes. Emily Dickinson. CP-DickE

They drove to the far side of the island. Olga Broumas. SP-BrouO *Fr.* Black Holes, Black Stockings.

They dug a trench, and threw him in a grave. Young Greek, Killed In The Wars, A. Richard Eberhart. CP-EberR

They dug up the grave, while a banjo and two guitars. Muriel Rukeyser. CP-RukeM

They dunked me in the creek. Baptism. Alice Walker. CP-WalkA

They eat beans mostly, this old yellow pair. Bean Eaters, The. Gwendolyn Brooks. SP-BrooG

They Eat Out. Margaret Atwood. SP-AtwM1

They enter as animals from the outer. Years. Sylvia Plath. CP-PlatS

They enter the bare wood, drawn. Novices, The. Denise Levertov. SP-LeveDP

They envied not the vast Cathedral's pile. Puritan Church and State 1., The. Jones Very. CP-VeryJ

They escape before, but their shadows walk behind. Surrounded, The. Muriel Rukeyser. CP-RukeM

They face us in sea-noon sun, just as he saw them waiting. Suite for Lord Timothy Dexter. Muriel Rukeyser. CP-RukeM

They faced each other: Topaz-brown. Quarrel, The. James Whitcomb Riley. CP-RileJ

They fall through my life and surround me. Twin Falls, The. James Dickey. CP-DickJ

They feed me and feed me and feed me. Point of Origin. Heather McHugh. SP-McHuH

They Feed They Lion. Philip Levine. SP-LeviP

They fill their mouths with alcohol. Young Fire Eaters of Mexico City, The. Raymond Carver. CP-CarvR

They fle[e] from me that sometime [or sometyme] did me se[e]k[e]. Lover Showeth How He Is Forsaken of Such as He Sometime Enjoyed, The. Sir Thomas Wyatt. CP-WyatT

They fought in heavy armor. Gladiators, The. Stanley Kunitz. CP-KunSC

They found him in the fields and called him back to music. Bunk Johnson Blowing. Muriel Rukeyser. CP-RukeM

They fuck you up, your mum and dad. This Be The Verse. Philip Larkin. CP-LarkP

They gave him a crown of bays and dressed him up. Crown of Bays, The. Stevie Smith. CP-SmitS

They gave me in trust. Hayden Carruth. CP-CarHS *Fr.* Clay Hill Anthology, The.

They get drunk, these Great-Sledmakers. Their copper mugs. Great-Sledmakers, The. Kenneth Patchen. CP-PatcK

They get up on their garage roof. 2 Outside, As Bones Break in My Kitchen. Charles Bukowski. SP-BukC2

They give me a bad. Crows. Marge Piercy. SP-PierM

They give to beauty here. Beauty. Langston Hughes. CP-HughL; CP-HughL1

They go on writing. Unkind Poem, An. Charles Bukowski. SP-BukC1

They got me because if a forest has no end I'll go naked. I Take Back All My Kisses. James Tate. CP-TateJ

They got so hungry they all. What the Animals Did. James Laughlin. CP-LaugJ

They had built it up—but not for this the lean. Débâcle. Louis MacNeice. CP-MacNL

They had come in a carriage (which. Epic Expands, The. Robert Creeley. CP-CreeR

They had got used to him. But when they brought. Washing the Corpse. Randall Jarrell. CP-JarrR

They had it wrong. Final Note to Clark. Lucille Clifton. SP-ClifL

They had long met o' Zundays—her true love and she. Bride-Night Fire, The. Thomas Hardy. CP-HardT

They had me laid out in a white. April Fools' Day. Yusef Komunyakaa. CP-KomuY

They had never had one in the house before. Bronzeville Woman in a Red Hat. Gwendolyn Brooks. SP-BrooG

They had not seen, for centuries, such fine gifts at Delphi. Envoys from Alexandria. Constantine P. Cavafy. CP-CavaC, *tr. by* Theoharis Constantine Theoharis

They had supposed their formula was fixed. White Troops Had Their Orders but the Negroes Looked Like Men. Gwendolyn Brooks. SP-BrooG

They had taken off their sandals. My Coat Is Dirty. Kenneth Patchen. CP-PatcK

They had the Boston Bull before I was born. Growing Up Askew. Mona Van Duyn. SP-VanDM

They had this cloud they kept like a zeppelin. Incident. William Stafford. SP-StafWW

They hail me as one living. Dead Man Walking, The. Thomas Hardy. CP-HardT

They hail you as their morning star. Men. Dorothy Parker. CP-ParkD

They happened in us . . . . Remembering Loves and Deaths. Thomas McGrath. SP-McGrT

They harvest the wine of their eyes. Vintagers, The. Paul Celan. SP-CelaP, *tr. by* John Felstiner

They hate the bird's shadow. Standards and Paradise of the Blacks. Federico García Lorca. CP-GarcF, *tr. by* Greg Simon *and* Steven F. White

They Have. John Berryman. CP-BerrJ

They have a little Odor—that to me. Emily Dickinson. CP-DickE

They have a way of looking at us. Animals and Birds. Charles Simic. SP-SimiCE

They have all died and their souls are extinguished; three remnant images. Dear Judas. Robinson Jeffers. CP-JefR2

They have been with us a long time. Telephone Poles. John Updike. CP-UpdiJ

They have brought gold and spices to my King. All Saints. Christina Georgina Rossetti. CP-RosC3

They have brought me a snail. Snail. Federico García Lorca. SP-GarcF *Fr.* Songs of Childhood.

They have carried the mahogany chair and the cane rocker. Mourning Picture. Adrienne Rich. CP-RicAE; SP-RicA2

They have come again to graze the orchard. Thanksgiving. Louise Glück. SP-GlucL

They have connived at those jewelled fascinations. Auspice of Jewels. Laura Riding Jackson. CP-RidiL

They have drunk and always re-drunk. Toys. Rainer Maria Rilke. CP-RilkFr, *tr. by* A. Poulin, Jr.

They have fenced in the dirt road. Burial. Alice Walker. CP-WalkA

They have gone into the gray hills quilled with birches. Mined Country. Richard Wilbur. CP-WilbR

They have gone / into the green hill, by doors without hinges. Apples. Donald Hall. CP-HallD

They have green tram in Florence now. À La Maniere De D. H. Lawrence. D. H. Lawrence. CP-LawrD

They have hung the sky with arrows. E. E. Cummings. CP-CummE

They have lain a long time, these two. Turning the Garden in Middle Age. Maxine W. Kumin. SP-KumiM

They have left me little indeed, how shall I best keep. Memory. Ivor Gurney. SP-GurnI

They have made for Leonora this low dwelling in the ground. Leonora. Edwin Arlington Robinson. CP-RobiE

They have never had a war big enough. Something to Declare. William Stafford. SP-StafWW

They have no song, the sedges dry. Song in the Songless. George Meredith. CP-MerG1

"They have not chosen me," he said. Emily Dickinson. CP-DickE

They have only to look at each other to laugh. Old Gray Couple (1), The. Archibald MacLeish. CP-MacLA

They have painted and sung. Women Washing Their Hair. Carl Sandburg. CP-SandC

They have removed a building to make. United Front, The. William Carlos Williams. CP-WilW2

They have space enough, however cramped their quarters. Dreaming Children. Robert Graves. CP-GravR

They have taken Sun from Woman. Robbers' Den. Robert Graves. CP-GravR

They have taken the ball of earth. Leather Leggings. Carl Sandburg. CP-SandC

They have their moments, and if one loved them they ought to die in. Moments of Glory. Robinson Jeffers. CP-JefR3

They haven't found the *W.* News from the Underworld. John Updike. CP-UpdiJ

They haven't got no noses. Song of the Dog Quoodle, The. G. K. Chesterton. CP-ChesG

They hear Thee not, O God! nor see. Ezekiel. John Greenleaf Whittier. CP-WhitJ

They hold their public meetings where. Three Monuments, The. William Butler Yeats. CP-YeatW

They hunch their heads against the fable of the night. Dolls Play at Hansel and Gretel, The. William Dickey. SP-DickW

They hurried here, as soon as you had died. Condolence. Dorothy Parker. CP-ParkD

They hurt no one. They rove the North. In Fur. William Stafford. SP-StafW

They in their cruel traps, and we in ours. Thoughts in a Zoo. Countee Cullen. CP-CullC

They intimately know just how our fortune lies. Business Acquaintances. John Updike. CP-UpdiJ

They kill mongooses. Always, before they club. On My Island. Josephine Jacobsen. CP-JacoJ

They killed a Child to please the Gods. Rudyard Kipling. CP-KiplR

They killed him on the gallows tree. Galán. Archibald MacLeish. CP-MacLA

They knew it, the fervant pupils of Pythagoras. Cyclical Night, The. Jorge Luis Borges. SP-BorgJ, *tr. by* Alastair Reid

They knew that they were naked, and ashamed. Serpent, The. Jones Very. CP-VeryJ

They know the wilings of the world. Not Known. Thomas Hardy. CP-HardT

They laid their hands upon my head. False Friends, The. Dorothy Parker. CP-ParkD

They laugh at me hey farm boy. Han-shan. CP-ColdM, *tr. by* Red Pine

They lean against the cooling car, backs pressed. Discovery of the Pacific, The. Thom Gunn. CP-GunnT

They lean over the path. Orchids. Theodore Roethke. CP-RoetT

They leave one by one. The rooms empty, grow. Departures 1. Yannis Ritsos. SP-RitsY, *tr. by* N. C. Germanacos

They leave us so to the way we took. In Neglect. Robert Frost. CP-FrosR

They leave us with the Infinite. Emily Dickinson. CP-DickE

They left last night, a tribe of fiery-eyed. Roving Gypsies. Charles Baudelaire. CP-BaudC, *tr.* by Walter Martin

They left my hands like a printer's. Blackberries. Yusef Komunyakaa. CP-KomuY

They left their home of summer ease. Seeking of the Waterfall, The. John Greenleaf Whittier. CP-WhitJ

They let me go. Debtor's Prison Road. Heather McHugh. SP-McHuH

They lie at rest asleep and dead. My Old Friends. Christina Georgina Rossetti. CP-RosC3

They lie at rest, our blessed dead. Christina Georgina Rossetti. CP-RosC2

They lie by the roadside, where they lived. Ancient Burial Places in Peabody, The. Jones Very. CP-VeryJ

They Lied to Us. Yehuda Amichai. SP-AmicYL, *tr.* by Benjamin Harshav *and* Barbara Harshav

They lift / Out of the maternal watery blue lines. Curlews [Lift]. Ted Hughes. SP-HughTN

They live a cool distance. Lorine Niedecker. CP-NiedL

They live by attenuation. Maples in a Spruce Forest. John Updike. CP-UpdiJ

They live down by the sea . . . these men. Gypsies Near Del Mar, The. Charles Bukowski. SP-BukC2

They live promiscuously in the woods. Raccoon Journal. Stanley Kunitz. CP-KunSC

They live to God, they live to God. Hymn: Our Country's Dead. Jones Very. CP-VeryJ

They lived long, and were faithful. Marriage, an Elegy, A. Wendell Berry. CP-BerrW

They lived, Pompeiians. Pompeii. John Updike. CP-UpdiJ

They locked him up in a circle. He still insisted. Invention of the Center. Yannis Ritsos. SP-RitsY, *tr.* by Andonis Decavalles

They look like big dogs badly drawn, drawn wrong. Wolves in the Zoo. Howard Nemerov. CP-NemeH

They look like fact, the bath, the wall, the knife. Marat Dead. Charles Tomlinson. CP-TomlC

They look shabby and crazy but not. Small-City People. John Updike. CP-UpdiJ

They look surreal. Cronkhite Beach. Charles Tomlinson. CP-TomlC

They looked like wood ibis. Millpond, The. Yusef Komunyakaa. CP-KomuY

They love me not, who at my table eat. Harvest, The ("They love me not, who at my table eat"). Jones Very. CP-VeryJ

They made a myth of you, professor. Mr. Attila. Carl Sandburg. CP-SandC

They made for the priest a mitre of many feathers. Mitre, The. G. K. Chesterton. CP-ChesG

They made love among hazel shrubs. Commemoration. Wisława Szymborska. SP-SzymWM, *tr.* by Joanna Trzeciak

They made the chamber sweet with flowers and leaves. Pause, A. Christina Georgina Rossetti. CP-RosC3

They made themselves so tiny. Suitcase Strapped with a Rope, A. Charles Simic. SP-SimiC; SP-SimiCE

They made very little of such events—*Horses rising out of the*. It Takes Few Kinds. Kenneth Patchen. CP-PatcK

They made you complicated. Coats, The. Tess Gallagher. SP-GallT

They make me wince, such vivid dreams rise up. Stone Walls. May Sarton. SP-SartM

They march at God's. Canaan. Geoffrey Hill. CP-HillG

They meet to say farewell: Their way. Their Sweet Sorrow. James Whitcomb Riley. CP-RileJ

They met, and overwhelming her distrust. Job the Rejected. Edwin Arlington Robinson. CP-RobiE

They Met Young. Carl Sandburg. CP-SandC

They Might Have Bothered. Constantine P. Cavafy. CP-CavaC, *tr.* by Theoharis Constantine Theoharis

They might not need me—yet they might. Emily Dickinson. CP-DickE

They mock my toil—the nymphs and am'rous swains. John Milton. *See* Scoffing, amorous maidens and young men

They more than we are what we are. Statues. Kathleen Jessie Raine. SP-RainK

They move at maximum velocity. Hide & Seek. Howard Nemerov. CP-NemeH

They move between the jagged edge. Planters, The. Margaret Atwood. SP-AtwoM1

They must not go alone. Poem and Prayer for an Invading Army. Edna St. Vincent Millay. CP-MillE

They must to keep their certainty accuse. Leaders of the Crowd, The. William Butler Yeats. CP-YeatW

They near the coast; the land-birds hover round. Land. Jones Very. CP-VeryJ

They Never Were Found. Josephine Jacobsen. CP-JacoJ

They nickname Lesbia's brother 'pulcher' Carmen 79. Catullus. CP-ZukLS *Fr.* Carmina.

They offer you many things. Choices. Carl Sandburg. CP-SandC

They operate from elsewhere. Juncos. William Stafford. SP-StafWW

They operated on my brain. First she cut a round slice off the top. Dream (1).

Andrei Codrescu. SP-CodrA

They paid my way here. For John Chamberlain. Robert Creeley. SP-CreeR

They Part. Dorothy Parker. CP-ParkD

They parted—a pallid, trembling pair. Cross-Currents. Thomas Hardy. CP-HardT

They Pass. Marya Alexandrovna Zaturenska. SP-ZatuM

They pass before me one by one riding on animals. Vision of the Bodhisattvas, A. Philip Whalen. SP-WhalP

They photograph you on your porch. Photographs. Charles Bukowski. SP-BukC1

They photographed me young upon a tiger skin. Photograph, The. Stevie Smith. CP-SmitS

They played in the beautiful garden. Warden, The. Stevie Smith. CP-SmitS

They please me not—these solemn songs. Choice, A. Paul Laurence Dunbar. CP-DunbP

They pointed me out on the highway, and they said. Traveller, The. John Berryman. CP-BerrJ

They pray. Security against oldness. Muriel Rukeyser. CP-RukeM

They prefer to sleep on tiny colored stones. Tribes of Rakala, The. Kenneth Patchen. CP-PatcK

They pretend that there's nothing to believe in anymore! Yellow Stones—Sea of Majestic Doves. Kenneth Patchen. CP-PatcK

They promised an unforgettable trip. Rogue River Jet-Boat Trip, Gold Beach, Oregon, July 4, 1977. Raymond Carver. CP-CarvR

They put ma body in the [*or* de] ground. Judgment Day. Langston Hughes. CP-HughL; CP-HughL1

They put me in a small, clean room. Sweet Voice from the Kibbutz, The. Yehuda Amichai. SP-AmicYL, *tr.* by Benjamin Harshav *and* Barbara Harshav

They put my boy-friend. Madam and the Army. Langston Hughes. CP-HughL; CP-HughL2

They put their finger on their lips. Silence. Ralph Waldo Emerson. CP-EmerR

They Put Their Trust in Thee, and Were Not Confounded. Christina Georgina Rossetti. CP-RosC2

They put up big wooden gods. Manufactured Gods. Carl Sandburg. CP-SandC

They put Us far apart. Emily Dickinson. CP-DickE

They ran for their lives up the nightslope, gained the car. Mary Stuart. Robert Lowell. SP-LoweR

They reach a harbor spacious and secure. Salem ("They reach a harbor spacious and secure"). Jones Very. CP-VeryJ

They recall the promises in the books and the. German Girls! The German Girls!, The. Archibald MacLeish. CP-MacLA

They rise into mind. For an Exchange of Rings. Donald Hall. CP-HallD

They rocked on iron benches on the sand. Turner. Kenneth Patchen. CP-PatcK

They rode around in auto-mobiles. Lesson on the Twentieth Century, A. Miller Williams. CP-WillM

They rode right out of the morning sun. King, The. James Whitcomb Riley. CP-RileJ

They rule out of our justice and our despair. Muriel Rukeyser. CP-RukeM

They said he lived in both houses. Fleshing-out the Season. Yusef Komunyakaa. CP-KomuY

They said I got away in a boat. After the Titanic. Derek Mahon. CP-MahoD

They said Mister Dan. Steel Plate, The. Yusef Komunyakaa. CP-KomuY

They said no one would ever care. Gentlemen, I Address You Publicly. Kenneth Rexroth. CP-RexrK

They said, "Po Chü-I, go home" Success Is Failure. Philip Whalen. SP-WhalP

They said that Fame her clarion dropped. On Sherman's Men. Herman Melville. SP-MelvH

They said the Muses were but nine, and then. Plato. CP-CunnJ, *tr.* by J. V. Cunningham

They said their vows in the Church of the Pentecost. Ballad of a Little Delta Town. Miller Williams. CP-WillM

They said to us, or tried to say, and failed. Innocents, The. Adrienne Rich. CP-RicAE

They said we was nowhere. Chanson d'Outre Tombe. Philip Whalen. SP-WhalP

They said (when they had dined at Ciro's). Refutation. G. K. Chesterton. CP-ChesG

They sank the sea. Ballad of Basil, The. Lorine Niedecker. CP-NiedL

They sat in silent watchfulness. Cypress-Tree of Ceylon, The. John Greenleaf Whittier. CP-WhitJ

They saw it take the water—the finished Ark. Trial Run. Josephine Jacobsen. CP-JacoJ

They saw rivers flow west and hoped again. West Virginia. Muriel Rukeyser. CP-RukeM

They Say. Robert Creeley. CP-CreeR

They say a / woman passes at. Photo. Robert Creeley. CP-CreeR

They say eyes clear with age. Long Sight in Age. Philip Larkin. CP-LarkP

They say, George Perry, you're a lawyer. Well. To a Bully. Ambrose Bierce. SP-BierA

They say He was a serious child. Gentlest Lady, The. Dorothy Parker. CP-ParkD

They say I do not realize. Me Again. Kenneth Rexroth. CP-RexrK

They say I fake or lie. This. Fernando Pessoa. SP-PessF, *tr. by* Susan M. Brown *and* Edwin Honig

They say I looked back out of curiosity. Lot's Wife. Wisława Szymborska. SP-SzymW, *tr. by* Stanisław Barańczak *and* Clare Cavanagh

They say I wrote a naughty book. My Naughty Book. D. H. Lawrence. CP-LawrD

They say Ideal beauty cannot enter. Hiram Powers' "Greek Slave." Elizabeth Barrett Browning. CP-BroEB

They Say in Yellow Jacket. Yusef Komunyakaa. CP-KomuY

They say it is very difficult. Fresh Water. D. H. Lawrence. CP-LawrD

They say it is waiting for more, the snow. Snow Signs. Charles Tomlinson. CP-TomlC; SP-TomlC

They say last night radiation. Involved. A. R. Ammons. CP-AmmoA

They say my verse is sad: no wonder. A. E. Housman. CP-HousA

They say of me, and so they should. Neither Blood Nor Bowed. Dorothy Parker. CP-ParkD

They say one king is mad. Perhaps. Who knows? Who Knows? Nicholas Vachel Lindsay. CP-LindV

They say she cried her agony for a long time. For a Dog-killed Doe. Peter Blue Cloud. SP-BlueP

They say she died. Young Bride. Langston Hughes. CP-HughL; CP-HughL1

They say that absence conquers. Emily Dickinson. SP-DickE

They say that God lives very high. Child's Thought of God, A. Elizabeth Barrett Browning. CP-BroEB

They say that Hope is happiness. Stanzas for Music. Lord Byron. CP-Byron

They say that my music is angelic. Master, The. Czeslaw Milosz. CP-MiloC; CP-MiloCN

They say that reality exists only in the spirit. Demiurge. D. H. Lawrence. CP-LawrD

They say that the gold of the under kingdom weighs so. Orpheus Descending. Tennessee Williams. CP-WillT

They say that the power of erasure in our lives. Eraser, The. James Laughlin. CP-LaugJ

They Say That Time Assuages. Emily Dickinson. CP-DickE

They say that "Time assuages." They Say That Time Assuages. Emily Dickinson. CP-DickE

They say that trees scream. High Frequency. Marge Piercy. SP-PierM

They say the ground precisely swept. For the Felling of an Elm in the Harvard Yard. Adrienne Rich. CP-RicAE

They Say the Sea Is Loveless. D. H. Lawrence. CP-LawrD

They say the war is over. But water still. Redeployment. Howard Nemerov. CP-NemeH

They say there is a sweeter air. Carriage from Sweden, A. Marianne Craig Moore. CP-MoorM

They say there is no hope. Sea Gods. "II. D." CP-DoolH

They say they are one flesh. Archibald MacLeish. CP-MacLA *Fr.* Happy Marriage, The.

They Say This Isn't a Poem. Kenneth Rexroth. CP-RexrK

They say, through patience, chalk. Hafiz. CP-EmerR

They say to me, "There is." Idyl: "They say to me, 'There is'." William Carlos Williams. CP-WilW1

They say when Shakyamuni. Han-shan. CP-ColdM, *tr. by* Red Pine

They say you are not for me. Forbidden Things. Alice Walker. CP-WalkA

They say you can jinx a poem. Madmen. Billy Collins. SP-CollB

They say your face. Songs of the Riverbank. Federico García Lorca. CP-GarcF, *tr. by* Alan S. Trueblood *Fr.* Games.

They scarcely waked before they slept. Holy Innocents. Christina Georgina Rossetti. CP-RosC2

They scatter me from church to gutter. Avarice and Ambition Only Were the First Builders of Towns and Founders of Empire. Kenneth Patchen. CP-PatcK

They scrutinize worldly affairs. Han-shan. CP-ColdM, *tr. by* Red Pine

They see his face! Departed, The. Donald Davie. CP-DaviDC

They seek, are sought; to daily battle led. Spanish Guerillas 1811. William Wordsworth. CP-WorW1

They sell meat flowers in that. Shop. Andrei Codrescu. SP-CodrA

They sent him back to her. The letter came. Not to Keep. Robert Frost. CP-FrosR

They sent me away to be bred. Bride, The. Denise Levertov. SP-LeveDL

They servant lord. Lucifer Understanding at Last. Lucille Clifton. SP-ClifL

They set up stones to show where time has ended. Conway Burying Ground. Archibald MacLeish. CP-MacLA

They shall arise in the States. Mediums. Walt Whitman. CP-WhitW

They Shall Be as White as Snow. Christina Georgina Rossetti. CP-RosC2

They shall have breath that never were. A. E. Housman. CP-HousA

They shall not return to us, the resolute, the young. Mesopotamia. Rudyard Kipling. CP-KiplR

They should have called the thistle. Thistle. William Carlos Williams. CP-WilW1

They shut me up in Prose. Emily Dickinson. CP-DickE

They shut the road through the woods. Way Through The Woods, The. Rudyard Kipling. CP-KiplR

They sieved the beach sand and loaded the wagons. Moment of Contrition. Yannis Ritsos. SP-RitsY, *tr. by* Kimon Friar

They sing of Zion, city built of old. Song: "They sing of Zion, city built of old." Jones Very. CP-VeryJ

They sing their dearest songs. During Wind and Rain. Thomas Hardy. CP-HardT

They sit in a room. Outside the world revolves. Portrait of Three Conspirators. Howard Nemerov. CP-NemeH

They slew him, the women. Leader, The. Charles Olson. CP-OlsoC

They smile and bring the food. Windy Night. Charles Bukowski. SP-BukC3

They snarl Over Spain like cur-dogs over a bone, then look at each other. Sinverguenza. Robinson Jeffers. CP-JefR2

They spoke of the horse alive. Horse, The. Philip Levine. SP-LeviP

They spread their legs as a toad. Waking into Sleep. Kenneth Patchen. CP-PatcK

They stack bright pyramids of goods and gather. Avenue. Robert Pinsky. CP-PinsR

They stand contentedly, chewing. Plow Horses. Kenneth Patchen. CP-PatcK

They stand in a corner, on a shadowy shelf. Beginner's Guide. Howard Nemerov. CP-NemeH

They stand there weeping in the stained daylight. Fresco: Departure for an Imperialist War. Thomas McGrath. SP-McGrT

They stole my sleep—now I'll steal theirs. Shmuel HaNagid. SP-HaNaS, *tr. by* Peter Cole

They stood at the foot of the figure. At a Pause in a Country Dance. Thomas Hardy. CP-HardT

They stood on either side the gate. Apart. James Whitcomb Riley. CP-RileJ

They strew in the path of kings and czars. Hafiz. CP-EmerR *Fr.* Odes.

They struggled their legs and blindly loved, those puppies. How It Began. William Stafford. SP-StafWW

They sweep up, crying, riding the wind. Rooks In October. Walter De la Mare. CP-DeLaW

They tagged you an illiterate, those idle bureaucrats. Yannis Ritsos. SP-RitsY *Fr.* Second Series.

They take no shame for dark defeat. Fortitude of the North, The. Herman Melville. SP-MelvH

They talk as slow as Legends grow. Emily Dickinson. CP-DickE

They talk down through / the centuries to us. On Going Back to the Street after Viewing an Art Show. Charles Bukowski. SP-BukC2

They talk of fencing, and the use of arms. Epigram. To William, Earl of Newcastle, An. Ben Jonson. CP-JonsB

They talk of the triumph of the machine. Triumph of the Machine, The. D. H. Lawrence. CP-LawrD

They talk to each other, and he holds her hand. Muriel Rukeyser. CP-RukeM

They tango half the night. Sandhog. Yusef Komunyakaa. CP-KomuY

They tell me how they bought. Wood, The. Paul Muldoon. CP-MuldP

They tell me, Lucy, thou art dead. Lucy Hooper. John Greenleaf Whittier. CP-WhitJ

They tell me on the morrow I must leave. On a Proposed Trip South. William Carlos Williams. CP-WilW1

They tell me that euphoria is the feeling of feeling wonderful, well. No Doctors Today, Thank You. Ogden Nash. CP-NashO

They tell me that these British moral birds. British Sincerity. D. H. Lawrence. CP-LawrD

"They tell me, your carpenters," quoth I to my friend the Russ. Ivàn Ivànovitch. Robert Browning. CP-BroR2

They that come late to the dance. Tennessee Williams. CP-WillT *Fr.* Now the Cats with Jewelled Claws.

They that in course of heavenly spheares are skild. Sonnet 60. Edmund Spenser. CP-Spens *Fr.* Amoretti.

They, that in the Savior sleep. Hymn: So also will God, through Jesus, bring with him them who sleep. Jones Very. CP-VeryJ

They That Wash on Thursday. Paul Muldoon. CP-MuldP

They then to fountain-abundant Ida, mother of wild beasts. Hypnos on Ida. Homer. CP-MerG1 *Fr.* Iliad, The.

They think it's easy to be dead, those. Tableau Vivant. Tess Gallagher. SP-GallT

They think we're simple children. This Puzzles Me. Langston Hughes. CP-HughL; CP-HughL2

They throng from the east and the west, / The north and the south, with a song. As the Doves to Their Windows. Christina Georgina Rossetti. CP-RosC2

They throw in Drummer Hodge, to rest. Drummer Hodge. Thomas Hardy. CP-HardT

They, to Me. Donald Davie. CP-DaviDC

They Toil Not, Neither Do They Spin. Christina Georgina Rossetti. CP-RosC2

They Told Me. Walter De la Mare. CP-DeLaW

They told me I might hold the fairest one. Easy Rider. Kenneth Patchen. CP-PatcK

They told me in an old book. Two Women. Carl Sandburg. CP-SandC

They told me this story a long time ago. Sleeping Beauty. Howard Nemerov. CP-NemeH

They told me—when my heart was glad. Voice of God, The. Jones Very. CP-VeryJ

They told me, "You don't have." Credo. Alan Dugan. CP-DugaA

They took me out. Ku Klux. Langston Hughes. CP-HughL; CP-HughL2; CP-HughL3

They took my man off the street. Private First Class. Charles Bukowski. SP-BukC1

They took out the candelabra into the open air under the trees. Common Miracles. Yannis Ritsos. SP-RitsY, tr. by Kimon Friar and Kostas Myrsiades

They took the plough to the field. Interchanges. Yannis Ritsos. SP-RitsY, tr. by Kimon Friar

They took their time to die, this dynasty. Last of the Princes, The. A. K. Ramanujan. CP-RamaA

They tried to hand it to us on a platter. Two Humpties. Carl Sandburg. CP-SandC

They try to say what you are, spiritual or sexual? Jelaluddin Rumi. SP-Rumi, tr. by Coleman Barks

They turn every heart to stone O for the love. All the Roses of the World. Kenneth Patchen. CP-PatcK

They turned together with a shocked surprise—. Joseph and Mary. Robert Graves. CP-GravR

They (2). Robert Creeley. CP-CreeR

They used to say "deeper" and now we say "higher" Staying with It. Andrei Codrescu. SP-CodrA

They waited all day for the sun to appear. Then. Vigil. Raymond Carver. CP-CarvR

They walk foward now into this death. Those Upon Whom God Has Labored. Kenneth Patchen. CP-PatcK

They walk here with us, hand in hand. Our Own. James Whitcomb Riley. CP-RileJ

They walk in and fall into. Time, The. Robert Creeley. CP-CreeR

They wander, straggling sheep without a fold. Lost, The ("They wander, straggling sheep without a fold"). Jones Very. CP-VeryJ

They want a wilderness with a map. Course in Creative Writing, A. William Stafford. SP-StafWW

They wanted from us. Ars Poetica. Eleanor Wilner. SP-WilnE

They Warned Him Then They Threw Him Away. C. K. Williams. CP-WillC

They wash you / when. C. K. Williams. CP-WillC

They watch me, those informers to the Fates. Fates, The. Wilfred Owen. CP-OwenW

They water-ski over whitecaps. Lake House, The. Wyatt Prunty. SP-PrunW

They wear air. Naked in Borneo. May Swenson. SP-SwenM

They went after him with a long stick. Outlaw, The. David Ignatow. SP-IgnaD

They Went Home. Maya Angelou. SP-AngeM

They went outside then, in the mild night. Quarrel, The. William Meredith. SP-MereW

They were all inaccurate. Margaret Atwood. SP-AtwM1

They were all spared to tell their stories. Morality, A. Howard Nemerov. CP-NemeH

They were always arguing that we. Crimes of Bernard, The. Alan Dugan. CP-DugaA

They were both still. Lamentations. Louise Glück. SP-GlucL

They were calling certain styles of whiskers by the name of "lilacs." Alley Rats. Carl Sandburg. CP-SandC

They were confused at first, being well warned. Reduced Sentence, A. Robert Graves. CP-GravR

They were each other's. Lost Secrets, The. James Laughlin. CP-LaugJ

They were in a big circle. Knights of the White Camellia & Deacons of Defense. Yusef Komunyakaa. CP-KomuY

They were in the living room. Saying their. Late Night with Fog and Horses. Raymond Carver. CP-CarvR

They were intense people, given to migraine. Proteus. May Sarton. SP-SartM

They were into the lambing, up late. Birth (Near Port William), The. Wendell Berry. CP-BerrW

They were introduced in a grave glade. Introduction, The. Louis MacNeice. CP-MacNL

They were outdoors in some sort of fake. Human Honesty. Jelaluddin Rumi. SP-Rumi, tr. by Coleman Barks

They were putting up the statue. Lawrence Ferlinghetti. SP-FerlL

They were so amply beautiful, the maps. Projection. Howard Nemerov. CP-NemeH

They were taking back. Vespers. James McMichael. SP-McMiJ

They were talking about the war. Place, The. Charles Simic. SP-SimiC; SP-SimiCE

They were the strong nudes of a forgotten. Anagram Born of Madness at Czernowitz, 23 November 1920. Norman Dubie. CP-DubiN

They Were There. Hart Crane. CP-CranH

They were trying to catch up. They (2). Robert Creeley. CP-CreeR

They were wedded at midnight. Queen's Crowning, The. Gerard Manley Hopkins. CP-HopkG

They were weeding out the dead at the funeral home. Invasion of Sleep Walkers, The. John Ciardi. CP-CiarJ

They Were Welcome to Their Belief. Robert Frost. CP-FrosR

They Who Feel Death. Alice Walker. CP-WalkA

They who have best succeeded on the stage. Epilogue to the Second Part of The Conquest of Granada. John Dryden. SP-DrydJ Fr. Conquest of Granada, The.

They Who Hunger. Jones Very. CP-VeryJ

They who love me stand in my way. Reward, The. David Ignatow. SP-IgnaD

They will be all fingers and thumbs. Blewits. Paul Muldoon. CP-MuldP

They will be without arms like God. Hummingbirds. Norman Dubie. CP-DubiN

They will forever refuse you the license to carry a gun. License to Carry a Gun, The. Andrei Codrescu. SP-CodrA

They will give you a paperweight. Toward the End. William Stafford. SP-StafWW

They will let you have dope. Memo to Non-White Peoples. Langston Hughes. CP-HughL; CP-HughL3

They will place telescreens there and our life. They Will Place There Telescreens. Czeslaw Milosz. CP-MiloC; CP-MiloCN

They Will Place There Telescreens. Czeslaw Milosz. CP-MiloC; CP-MiloCN

They Will Say. Carl Sandburg. CP-SandC

They will soon be down. For the Last Wolverine. James Dickey. CP-DickJ

They will walk there, the sons of our great-grandsons, and. Time to Come. Ivor Gurney. SP-GurnI

They withheld judgment, looking down at us. Windows of the Summer Vacation Houses, The. Raymond Carver. CP-CarvR

They wonder as they ripen. Four Inscriptions for the Sundial of a Lost Race of Polyphemus. Robert Stock. SP-StocR

They Won't Believe, on New Year's Eve, that New Year's Day Will Come What May. Ogden Nash. CP-NashO

They won't frown always—some sweet Day. Emily Dickinson. CP-DickE

They won't let you in there for no seven cents. It's Because Your Heart Is Pure, Honey. Kenneth Patchen. CP-PatcK

They work with herbs. Doctors. Anne Sexton. CP-SextA

They worshipped Joe. Joe Louis ("They worshipped Joe"). Langston Hughes. CP-HughL; CP-HughL3

They would be none the wiser, even could they overhear. None the Wiser. Robert Graves. CP-GravR

They Would Not Come. Thomas Hardy. CP-HardT

They wuz a Big Day wunst in town. Toy-Balloon, The. James Whitcomb Riley. CP-RileJ

They'd come around and. 2nd Novel, The. Charles Bukowski. SP-BukC1

They'd latch the screendoors [or screen doors]. Sunday Afternoons. Yusef Komunyakaa. CP-KomuY

They'd make you believe that your problem is one of sex. New Being, The. Kenneth Patchen. CP-PatcK

They're afraid of me. For Medgar Evers. David Ignatow. SP-IgnaD

They're alone at the kitchen table in her friend's. Ashtray, The. Raymond Carver. CP-CarvR

They're altogether otherworldly now. Grandparents. Robert Lowell. SP-LoweR

They're at that stage where so much desire streams between them, so much frank need and want. Love: Beginnnings. C. K. Williams. SP-WillC

They're both convinced. Love at First Sight. Wisława Szymborska. SP-SzymW, tr. by Stanislaw Barańczak and Clare Cavanagh

They're counting nails. Tally, The. Yusef Komunyakaa. CP-KomuY

They're discussing the political situation they've been watching evolve in a faraway country. Politics. C. K. Williams. SP-WillC

They're kindly here, to let us linger so late. Holy Thursday. Paul Muldoon. CP-MuldP

They're nice—one would never dream of going over. Healthy Spot, A. W. H. Auden. CP-AudeW

They're nothing, really, all the girls I've known. De Secretis Mulierum. Paul Muldoon. CP-MuldP

They're on a one-way flight, bound from LAX. Miracle. Raymond Carver. CP-CarvR

They're out of the dark's ragbag, these two. Blue Moles. Sylvia Plath. CP-PlatS

They're taking down a tree at the front door. Learning by Doing. Howard Nemerov. CP-NemeH

They're waiting to be murdered. Old Couple. Charles Simic. SP-SimiC; SP-SimiCE

They's a kind o' feel in the air, to me. Feel in the Chris'mas-Air, A. James Whitcomb Riley. CP-RileJ

They's a predjudice allus 'twixt country and town. Town and Country. James Whitcomb Riley. CP-RileJ

They's nothin' in the name to strike. Marthy Ellen. James Whitcomb Riley. CP-RileJ

Theys sO alive. E. E. Cummings. CP-CummE

They've / been here / for thousands of years. You Are in Bear Country. Maxine W. Kumin. SP-KumiM

They've Blocked Every Window. Tibor Tollas. CP-LogaJ, *tr.* by John Logan

They've come every day this month. Poems. Raymond Carver. CP-CarvR

They've covered his face, & he's lost to us. C B M. George Meredith. CP-MerG2

They've forced me to pose. Posing. Clarence Major. SP-MajoC

They've got some pretty horses up in the long dark mountains. Now I Went Down to the Ringside and Little Henry Armstrong Was There. Kenneth Patchen. CP-PatcK

They've lost their leaves. Lorine Niedecker. CP-NiedL

Thick and heavy, with only the finest hairline space be-. Behind the Door. Philip Whalen. SP-WhalP

Thick crust, coarse-grained as limestone rough-cast, A. Churning Day. Seamus Heaney. SP-HeanSO

Thick dew. Passed on. William Corbett. SP-CorbW

Thick ice breaks, it floats away, The. Sailing on Cakes of Ice in the North River. Jones Very. CP-VeryJ

Thick lids of night closed upon me, The Souls of the Slain, The. Thomas Hardy. CP-HardT

Thick lie in Gloucester orchards now. Ypres—Minsterworth. Ivor Gurney. SP-GurnI

Thick man with his back to us squats at the counter, A. Nighthawks: after Hopper's Painting. John Logan. CP-LogaJ

Thick mist-sheet lies over the broken wheat, A. Mutilation. D. H. Lawrence. CP-LawrD

Thick night fell, the folding table unfolded, The. Rest House, The. Louis MacNeice. CP-MacNL

Thick smoke coils up, the shriveled. Theodore Weiss. SP-WeisT *Fr.* Polish Question, The.

Thick-Sprinkled Bunting. Walt Whitman. CP-WhitW

Thick white cloud of mad moths whirls, The. Hitler Spring, The. Eugenio Montale. CP-MontE, *tr.* by Jonathan Galassi

Thickening Mat, The. May Swenson. SP-SwenM

Thickest night, surround my dwelling! Strathallan's Lament. Robert Burns. CP-BurnR

Thickness of paint or flesh cannot deface. Sestina 1: "Thickness of paint or flesh cannot deface." Howard Nemerov. CP-NemeH

Thief. Robert Graves. CP-GravR

Thief. Alice Walker. CP-WalkA

Thief, The. Wendell Berry. CP-BerrW

Thief, The. Josephine Jacobsen. CP-JacoJ

Thief, The. Stanley Kunitz. CP-KunSC

Thief, The. Yannis Ritsos. SP-RitsY, *tr.* by Kimon Friar

Thief, and a murderer! stop her who can!, A. Hue and Cry of John Lewars, The. Robert Burns. CP-BurnR

Thief in the Night. D. H. Lawrence. CP-LawrD

Thief—truly a thief, insignificant, a marked man; he ambushes, A. Thief, The. Yannis Ritsos SP RitsY, *tr.* by Kimon Friar

Thief's Journal, The. Charles Tomlinson. CP-TomlC

Thiers. John Greenleaf Whittier. CP-WhitJ

Thieves. Primo Levi. CP-LeviP, *tr.* by Ruth Feldman

Thieves, The. Robert Graves. CP-GravR

Thieves, The. Jones Very. CP-VeryJ

Thieves, Seasons. Andrei Codrescu. SP-CodrA

Thigh-deep in sedge and marigolds. Other Side, The. Seamus Heaney. SP-HeanSO

Thighs, *trees*— / you want / a place to stand. Trees. Robert Creeley. CP-CreeR

Thimble Islands. Carl Sandburg. CP-SandC

Thimbleberry redcap odor art whose. Raspberry. Louis Zukofsky. CP-ZukLS

Thin Air. John Updike. CP-UpdiJ

Thin are the night-skirts left behind. Insomnia. Dante Gabriel Rossetti. CW-RossD

Thin blue smoke of our campfire, The. For the Boy Who Was Dodger Point Lookout Fifteen Years Ago. Gary Snyder. CP-SnydG

Thin brown orphan in his washed-out blue, A. Dublin Georgian ("Thin brown orphan in his washed-out blue, A"). Donald Davie. CP-DaviDC

Thin brown stain, A. Running Footsteps. James Schuyler. CP-SchuJ

Thin covering of sickly grass, A. Earthworks. James Tate. SP-TateJ

Thin Edge, The. Dorothy Parker. CP-ParkD

Thin Edge of Your Pride, The. Kenneth Rexroth. CP-RexrK

Thin, foul scattering of grim, grey snow, A. Semi-Spring. E. E. Cummings. CP-CummE

Thin green salient aimed at the heart of London, A. Buckinghamshire. Donald Davie. CP-DaviDC

Thin Ice. Gary Snyder. CP-SnydG

Thin long bird. Road-Runner, The. Philip Whalen. SP-WhalP

Thin moonlight with trickling ray, The. Tired Cupid, The. Walter De la Mare. CP-DeLaW

Thin People, The. Sylvia Plath. CP-PlatS

Thin Rain, whom are you haunting. Wraith. Edna St. Vincent Millay. CP-MillE

Thin river woman with a concrete star. Manhattan Island Poem. Gregory Orr. SP-OrrG

Thin sheets of blue smoke among white slabs . . . near the shingle mill. Hemlock and Cedar. Carl Sandburg. CP-SandC

Thin shoulders of the old stones. Trinity Churchyard, Spring 1961. May Swenson. SP-SwenM

Thin snow, and the first small pools of dusk. Faeryland. Robert Pinsky. CP-PinsR

Thin Strips. Carl Sandburg. CP-SandC

Thin wind winds off the water. Touch of Spring. John Updike. CP-UpdiJ

Thine am I, my Chloris fair. Robert Burns. CP-BurnR

Thine are all the gifts, O God! Hymn of the Children. John Greenleaf Whittier. CP-WhitJ

Thine be the volumes, Jessy fair. To a Young Lady, *Miss Jessy L———, Dumfries; with Books which the Bard Presented Her*. Robert Burns. CP-BurnR

Thine emulous fond flowers are dead, too. My Butterfly. Robert Frost. CP-FrosR

Thine eyes' blue tenderness, thy long fair hair. Sonnet, to Genevra. Lord Byron. CP-Byron

Thine Eyes Still Shined. Ralph Waldo Emerson. CP-EmerR

Thine is a grief, the depth of which another. To My Friend on the Death of His Sister. John Greenleaf Whittier. CP-WhitJ

Thine is my all, how little when 'tis told. To My Mother. Walter De la Mare. CP-DeLaW

Thing, A. Andrei Codrescu. SP-CodrA

Thing, The. Theodore Roethke. CP-RoetT

Thing, The. William Carlos Williams. CP-WilW2

Thing about Crows, The. Josephine Jacobsen. CP-JacoJ

Thing about which I know the least, The. So I resigned from the Chu Chin Chowder and Marching Club. Ogden Nash. CP-NashO

Thing 'at's 'bout as tryin' as a healthy man kin meet, A. When the Hearse Comes Back. James Whitcomb Riley. CP-RileJ

Thing comes, The. Love ("Thing comes, The"). Robert Creeley. CP-CreeR

Thing gets made, gets built, and you're the slave, The. Horatian Notion, An. Thomas Lux. SP-LuxT

Thing I loved was Halloween, The. Wallace Stevens Remembers Halloween. Wyatt Prunty. SP-PrunW

Thing is, when Agnieszka and I lay like bride and groom, The. Blissom. Paul Muldoon. CP-MuldP

Thing Itself, The. Alice Walker. CP-WalkA

Thing most new complete fragile intense, A. E. E. Cummings. CP-CummE

Thing no is(of). E. E. Cummings. CP-CummE

Thing O say a sixteenth of an inch, A. They Have. John Berryman. CP-BerrJ

Thing of beauty is joy for ever, A. Endymion: A Poetic Romance. John Keats. CP-KeatJ

Thing that arrests me is, The. Waking in the Dark. Adrienne Rich. SP-RicA1; SP-RicA2

Thing that breaks Hell's prison bars, The. Soul of a Butterfly, The. Nicholas Vachel Lindsay. CP-LindV

Thing that eats the heart comes wild with years, The. Stanley Kunitz. CP-KunSC

Thing that eats the rotting stars, The. Soul of a Spider, The. Nicholas Vachel Lindsay. CP-LindV

Thing to be thought with abated breath, A. Mystery, A. Ambrose Bierce. SP-BierA

Thing / To do / Is organize / The sea, The. Poem: "Thing / To do / Is organize / The sea, the." Kenneth Koch. SP-KochK

Thing Unplanned, The. Thomas Hardy. CP-HardT

Thing Was Moving, The. Charles Olson. CP-OlsoC; SP-OlsoC

Things. Jorge Luis Borges. SP-BorgJ, *tr.* by Stephen Kessler

Things. Christopher Logue. SP-LoguC

Things. W. S. Merwin. SP-MerwW

Things. Gabriela Mistral. SP-MistG, *tr.* by Maria Giachetti [*or* Jacketti]

Things. Miller Williams. CP-WillM

Things, The. Josephine Jacobsen. CP-JacoJ

Things all have their uses. Han-shan. CP-ColdM, *tr.* by Red Pine

Things and people goodbye / It is not that I prefer. Thomas Merton. CP-MertT

Things and the Man. Rudyard Kipling. CP-KiplR

Things are a bit different in. Bit Different, A. James Laughlin. CP-LaugJ

Things are / changing; things are starting to. Last Days. Mary Oliver. SP-OlivM

Things are so changed since last we met. Year Afterwards, A. Christina Georgina Rossetti. CP-RosC3

Things are uncertain, and the more we get. Things Mortal Still Mutable. Robert Herrick. CP-HerrR

Things Before, The. Jones Very. CP-VeryJ

Things / come and go. Step, A. Robert Creeley. CP-CreeR

Things concentrate at the edges; the pond-surface. Marginalia. Richard Wilbur. CP-WilbR

Things do not explode. Endings. Derek Walcott. CP-WalcD

Things ("Fallen volume, hidden by the others, The"). Jorge Luis Borges. SP-BorgJ, *tr.* by Alastair Reid

Things far off the mark and full of high risk. Julian in Nicomedia. Constantine P. Cavafy. CP-CavaC, *tr.* by Theoharis Constantine Theoharis

Things going quiet. Blue Rabbit. Robert Creeley. SP-CreeR

Things have their own lives here. The hall chairs. Dispossessions. Jane Cooper. CP-CoopJ

Things he had loved because he knew them lost. Archibald MacLeish. CP-MacLA *Fr.* Happy Marriage, The.

Things I Learned Last Week. William Stafford. SP-StafW; SP-StafWW

Things in the Wild Need Salt. William Stafford. SP-StafWW

Things Kept. William Dickey. SP-DickW

Things Made by Iron. D. H. Lawrence. CP-LawrD

Things Men Have Made. D. H. Lawrence. CP-LawrD

Things Mortal Still Mutable. Robert Herrick. CP-HerrR

Things of August. Wallace Stevens. CP-StevW; CP-StevWP

Things of Choice, Long a Comming. Robert Herrick. CP-HerrR

Things of the Past. Theodore Weiss. SP-WeisT

Things of this world. Illusion of Eternity, The. Richard Eberhart. CP-EberR

Things of which we want the proof, The. Emily Dickinson. SP-DickE

Things oft miscalling, as the hen-. Ralph Waldo Emerson. CP-EmerR

Things one sees through / a blurred sheet of glass. Rain. Robert Creeley. CP-CreeR

Things out of perfection sail. Old Tom Again. William Butler Yeats. CP-YeatW

Things placed there. Obstructions. James Dickey. CP-DickJ

Things Run Out. Constantine P. Cavafy. CP-CavaC, *tr.* by Theoharis Constantine Theoharis

Things seem empty. On Vacation. Robert Creeley. CP-CreeR

Things she knew, let her forget again, The. Prayer for a New Mother. Dorothy Parker. CP-ParkD

Things that are down should be up, The. Life at Bolinas. The Last of California. Philip Whalen. SP-WhalP

Things that divine us we never touch. Southern Cross, The. Charles Wright. SP-WrigC

Things that give such pleasure to the eye, a clothesline, The. Buenos Días. Olga Broumas. SP-BrouO

Things That Happen. William Stafford. SP-StafWW

Things That Hurt Me. William Stafford. SP-StafWW

Things that make the happier life, are these, The. Martial. Epigram XLVII, Book X. Ben Jonson. CP-JonsB

Things That Might Have Been. Jorge Luis Borges. SP-BorgJ, *tr.* by Hoyt Rogers

Things that never can come back, are several, The. Emily Dickinson. CP-DickE

Things thus agreed: Titan made Saturne sweare. Sir Walter Ralegh. CP-RaleW

Things to Do. James Schuyler. CP-SchuJ

Things To Do in Anne's Room. Ted Berrigan. SP-BerrT

Things To Do in New York (City). Ted Berrigan. SP-BerrT

Things To Do in Providence. Ted Berrigan. SP-BerrT

Things to Do in Tokyo. Robert Creeley. SP-CreeR

Things Unseen. Jones Very. CP-VeryJ

Things we thought that we should do, The. Emily Dickinson. CP-DickE

Things would not have gone on long in any case. In the Evening. Constantine P. Cavafy. CP-CavaC, *tr.* by Theoharis Constantine Theoharis

Think. Robert Creeley. CP-CreeR

Think. James Vincent Cunningham. CP-CunnJ

Think—! D. H. Lawrence. CP-LawrD

Think about Gypsies. Distractions. William Stafford. SP-StafWW

Think about it at will: there is that. Meaning of Life, The. Allen Tate. CP-TateA

Think Also of Horseshoes. Miller Williams. CP-WillM

"Think as I think," said a man. Stephen Crane. CP-CranS

Think, as we lie in this sweet bed. Theory of Numbers. Kenneth Rexroth. CP-RexrK

Think, Delia, with what cruel haste. Written in a Quarrel. William Cowper. CP-CowpW

Think how a peacock in a forest of high trees. Peacock. D. H. Lawrence. CP-LawrD

Think how we predators to every creature. How It's Born in Us to Understand That There Are Two Sides to Every Question. Miller Williams. CP-WillM

Think however you like about this island, its ocean whiteness, grottoes overgrown with vines, under violets, springs. Island. Czeslaw Milosz. CP-MiloC; CP-MiloCN, *tr.* by Lillian Vallee

Think: if Ludwig were alive today. Note Upon the Love Letters of Beethoven. Charles Bukowski. SP-BukC3

Think me not unkind and rude. Apology, The. Ralph Waldo Emerson. CP-EmerR

Think no more, lad; laugh, be jolly. A. E. Housman. CP-HousA

Think no more of me. Soldier Rejects His Times Addressing His Contemporaries, A. Richard Eberhart. CP-EberR

Think not, because I wonder where you fled. Another Dark Lady. Edwin Arlington Robinson. CP-RobiE

Think not 'cause men flattering [*or* flatt'ring] say. To A. L.; Persuasions [*or* Perswasions] to Love. Thomas Carew. CP-CareT

Think not I have not heard. Menses. Edna St. Vincent Millay. CP-MillE

Think not my Phebe [*or* Phœbe], cause a cloud. To His Mistress [*or* Mistris] Confined. James Shirley. CP-CareT

Think not, nor for a moment let your mind. Edna St. Vincent Millay. CP-MillE

Think Not of It, Sweet One, So. John Keats. CP-KeatJ

Think not, should your husband swear. George Meredith. CP-MerG2

Think not that I forget a single pang. Hugh MacDiarmid. SP-MacDH *Fr.* Ode to All Rebels.

Think not that incense-smoke has had its day. Incense. Nicholas Vachel Lindsay. CP-LindV

Think not the gods receive thy prayer. Ralph Waldo Emerson. CP-EmerR

Think not yon tall, rank growth of weeds. Sparrows and the Crop of Weeds, The. Jones Very. CP-VeryJ

Think, O my soul. Phaedra. "H. D." CP-DoolH

Think of a grand metaphor. Fact, The. Robert Creeley. SP-CreeR

Think of an opening page illuminèd. Gerard Manley Hopkins. CP-HopkG

Think of how in a hurricane the winds. Form and Theory of Poetry. Miller Williams. CP-WillM

Think of it:not so long ago. E. E. Cummings. CP-CummE

Think of Judas That He Did Love Jesus. Miller Williams. CP-WillM

Think of man praying. He raises his hands to God. Death in the Mines. Richard Eberhart. CP-EberR

Think of only now, and how this pencil. Promontory Moment, The. May Swenson. SP-SwenM

Think of sweet and chocolate. Anniad, The. Gwendolyn Brooks. SP-BrooG

Think of that great courageous place. Emily Dickinson. SP-DickE

Think of the beds. Beds, Toilets, You and Me—. Charles Bukowski. SP-BukC1

Think of the good times. Spring in San Feliu. Robert Creeley. SP-CreeR

Think of the Serengeti lions looking up. Good Friday. Amy Clampitt. CP-ClamA

Think of the Soul. Walt Whitman. CP-WhitW

Think of the storm roaming the sky uneasily. Little Exercise. Elizabeth Bishop. CP-BishE

Think of the things that can never come true. Idyl. Dorothy Parker. CP-ParkD

Think of those generals at the wax museum. History Display. William Stafford. SP-StafWW

Think Tank. James Merrill. SP-MerrJ

Think that this world against the wind of time. Signature for Tempo. Archibald MacLeish. CP-MacLA

Think that you're gliding out from the face of a cliff. Jelaluddin Rumi. SP-Rumi, *tr.* by Coleman Barks

Think! Think hard. Try to remember. Loss, of Perhaps Love, in Our World of Contingency. Robert Penn Warren. CP-WarrR

Think thou and act; to-morrow thou shalt die. Choice, The ("Think thou and act; to-morrow thou shalt die"). Dante Gabriel Rossetti. CW-RossD *Fr.* House of Life, The.

Think yet how night doth waste. Ben Jonson. CP-JonsB *Fr.* Masque of Hymen.

Thinker, The. William Carlos Williams. CP-WilW1

"THINKER" / in the classic peristyle. Homage to Rodin. Philip Whalen. SP-WhalP

Thinkin' Back. James Whitcomb Riley. CP-RileJ

Thinking ("Had not / thought / of it . . ."). Robert Creeley. CP-CreeR

Thinking ("I've thought of myself"). Robert Creeley. CP-CreeR

Thinking. David Ignatow. SP-IgnaD

Thinking about Being Called Simple by a Critic. William Stafford. SP-StafWW

Thinking about Bill, Dead of AIDS. Miller Williams. CP-WillM

Thinking about Girls. John Ciardi. CP-CiarJ

Thinking About the Night Sky, I Remember a Poem by Tu Fu. Charles Wright. SP-WrigCN

Thinking about the Poet Larry Levis One Afternoon in Late May. Charles Wright. SP-WrigCN

Thinking again of a weekend trip to Ferrara. Italian Days. Charles Wright. SP-WrigC

Thinking Back Toward Christmas: A Statement for the Virgin. William Carlos Williams. CP-WilW2

Thinking for Berky. William Stafford. SP-StafW; SP-StafWW

Thinking Friday Night with a Gothic Storm Going About Final Causes and Logos and Mitzi Mayfair. Miller Williams. CP-WillM

Thinking how it is. Bent, The. Donald Davie. CP-DaviDC

Thinking in terms of one. Counting. Philip Larkin. CP-LarkP

Thinking more and more. Practice. Charles Bukowski. SP-BukC3

Thinking of a Relation between the Images of Metaphors. Wallace Stevens. CP-

StevW; CP-StevWP

Thinking of David Summers at the Beginning of Winter. Charles Wright. SP-WrigCN

Thinking of Death and Dogfood. Maxine W. Kumin. SP-KumiM

Thinking of Inis Oírr in Cambridge, Mass. Derek Mahon. CP-MahoD

Thinking of me / think of what was. William Dickey. SP-DickW *Fr.* In The Dreaming.

Thinking of Mr D. Thomas Kinsella. CP-KinsT

Thinking of rain clouds that rose over the city. St. Vincent's. W. S. Merwin. SP-MerwWF

Thinking of the Goldfish. Paul Muldoon. CP-MuldP

Thinking of the Lost World. Randall Jarrell. CP-JarrR

Thinking of Walter Benjamin. Robert Creeley. SP-CreeR

Thinking of what today adorns the sky. Petrarch. CP-Petra, *tr. by* J. G. Nichols

Thinking of Winter at the Beginning of Summer. Charles Wright. SP-WrigCN

Thinking of Yeats. Robert Creeley. SP-CreeR

Thinking of you asleep on a. Place ("Thinking of you asleep on a"). Robert Creeley. CP-CreeR

Thinking of you I lean over silent water. Sadness, The. W. S. Merwin. SP-MerwW

Thinking out / of the heart. For Pen ("Thinking out / of the heart"). Robert Creeley. SP-CreeR

Thinking Red. Amy Clampitt. CP-ClamA

Thinking Rock. Kenneth Patchen. CP-PatcK

Thinking that I would find you. Flight. Anne Sexton. CP-SextA

Thinking Thought. C. K. Williams. SP-WillC

Thinking too much of death by curves of chance. Expendability. John Ciardi. CP-CiarJ

Think'st thou I saw thy beauteous eyes. To Caroline. Lord Byron. CP-Byron

Think'st thou that this love can stand. Ametas and Thestylis Making Hay-Ropes. Andrew Marvell. CP-MarvA

Think'st thou to seduce me then. Thomas Campion. CP-CampT

Think'st thou to seduce me then with words that have no meaning? Think'st thou to seduce me then. Thomas Campion. CP-CampT

Thinness. James Schuyler. CP-SchuJ

Thir ladeis fair that maks repair. William Dunbar. CP-DunbW

Third Degree. Langston Hughes. CP-HughL; CP-HughL2; CP-HughL3

Third Elegy. The Fear of Form. Muriel Rukeyser. CP-RukeM

Third Epistle to J. Lapraik. Robert Burns. CP-BurnR

Third Kissing-Gate, The. Thomas Hardy. CP-HardT

Third Limick. Ogden Nash. CP-NashO

Third night after wedding, The. Newlywed's Cuisine, The. Wang Chien. CP-WilW2

Third Page. Federico García Lorca. CP-GarcF, *tr. by* Jerome Rothenberg *Fr.* White Album.

Third Psalm: The September Vision. W. S. Merwin. SP-MerwW

Third Series. Yannis Ritsos.
  "Corpses below wooden crosses. At night." SP-RitsY

Third Snowfall. Marilyn Hacker. SP-HackM

Third Song of Huitzilopochtli. D. H. Lawrence. CP-LawrD

Third Song, The. Thomas Carew. CP-CareT *Fr.* Carew's Masque.

Third Street. William Stafford. SP-StafWW

Third Thing, The. D. H. Lawrence. CP-LawrD

Third-week moon reaches its light over my father's farm, The. Late Moon. Robert Bly. SP-BlyR

Third with silence in a tent. Caravan of Silence. Richard Eberhart. CP-EberR

Third World Calling. Lawrence Ferlinghetti. SP-FerlL

Thirst. Emily Dickinson. CP-DickE

Thirst. C. K. Williams. SP-WillC

Thirst for meeting, A. Meeting. W. S. Merwin. SP-MerwW

Thirst of Turtles, The. Thomas Lux. SP-LuxT

Thirst Song. Denise Levertov. SP-LeveDP

Thirsting Tantalus doth catch at stream[e]s that from him flee, The. Satire 2.13: "Thirsting Tantalus doth catch at stream[e]s that from him flee, The." Horace. CP-RaleW *Fr.* Satires.

Thirsty and languorous after their long black sleep. Refinery, The. Robert Pinsky. CP-PinsR

Thirsty Fish, A. Jelaluddin Rumi. SP-Rumi, *tr. by* Coleman Barks

Thirteen as twelve my Murray always took. Tour, The. Rudyard Kipling. CP-KiplR *Fr.* Muse among the Motors, The.

13 Pictures. D. H. Lawrence. CP-LawrD

Thirteen Preludes for Pioneer Square. John Logan. CP-LogaJ

Thirteen Ways of Looking at a Blackbird. Wallace Stevens. CP-StevW; CP-StevWP

Thirteens (Black), The. Maya Angelou. SP-AngeM

Thirteens (White), The. Maya Angelou. SP-AngeM

Thirteenth and Pennsylvania. William Stafford. SP-StafWW

Thirteenth February. In the heart's mouth. In One. Paul Celan. SP-CelaP, *tr. by*

John Felstiner

Thirties, The. Adam Zagajewski. SP-ZagaA, *tr. by* Clare Cavanagh

Thirties / I don't exist yet, The. Thirties, The. Adam Zagajewski. SP-ZagaA, *tr. by* Clare Cavanagh

Thirties Revisited, The. Maxine W. Kumin. SP-KumiM

Thirtieth Anniversary Report of the Class of '41. Howard Nemerov. CP-NemeH

.38. William Stafford. SP-StafWW

35 Seconds. Charles Bukowski. SP-BukC2

35 Sonnets. Fernando Pessoa.
  "As a bad orator, badly o'er-book-skilled." SP-PessF
  "As the lone, frighted user of a night-road." SP-PessF
  "Edge of the green wave whitely doth hiss, The." SP-PessF
  "I could not think of thee as pieced rot." SP-PessF
  "Like a bad suitor desperate and trembling." SP-PessF
  "My love, and not I, is the egoist." SP-PessF
  "We are born at sunset and we die ere morn." SP-PessF
  "When in the widening circle of rebirth." SP-PessF
  "World is woven all of dream and error, The." SP-PessF

34th Street Song. Grace Paley. CP-PalGC

30 January 1949. Yannis Ritsos. SP-RitsY *Fr.* Exile's Journals 2.

30 May 1950. Yannis Ritsos. SP-RitsY *Fr.* Exile's Journals 3.

Thirty-ninth Psalm, Adapted, The. Donald Davie. CP-DaviDC

30 November 1948. Yannis Ritsos. SP-RitsY *Fr.* Exile's Journals 2.

31 B.C. in Alexandria. Constantine P. Cavafy. CP-CavaC, *tr. by* Theoharis Constantine Theoharis

37 Haiku. John Ashbery. SP-AshbJ

Thirty striped rumps in a circle with tails dangling. Ringling Brothers, Barnum and Bailey. Mona Van Duyn. SP-VanDM

Thirty-Three Ring Circus, The. John Logan. CP-LogaJ

Thirty today? Cheer up, my lad! Lines to Be Scribbled on Somebody Else's Thirtieth Milestone. Ogden Nash. CP-NashO

32 Adults. Heather McHugh. SP-McHuH

Thirty-two Greeks are dipping their feet in the creek. Near Keokuk. Carl Sandburg. CP-SandC

Thirty-two times I went out into my life. For My Birthday. Yehuda Amichai. SP-AmicY, *tr. by* Stephen Mitchell

Thirty-two times I went out of my life. On My Birthday. Yehuda Amichai. SP-AmicYL, *tr. by* Benjamin Harshav *and* Barbara Harshav

Thirty-two years since, up against the sun. Zermatt: To the Matterhorn. Thomas Hardy. CP-HardT

Thirty-two years to go. Century Dying, A. Pablo Neruda. SP-NeruP

Thirty yards apart, they face. Too Tenuous. Hayden Carruth. CP-CarHS

Thirty years after. Second Attempt, A. Thomas Hardy. CP-HardT

Thirty years ago: gulls keen in the blue. Woman, A. Robert Pinsky. CP-PinsR

Thirty years since I walked. Man in the Landscape. Sam Hamill. SP-HamiS

Thirty years unremembered. Abbeyforde. Donald Davie. CP-DaviDC

This. Charles Bukowski. SP-BukC2

This. Czeslaw Milosz. CP-MiloCN, *tr. by* Robert Hass

This. Charles Olson. CP-OlsoC

This. Fernando Pessoa. SP-PessF, *tr. by* Susan M. Brown *and* Edwin Honig

This. Wyatt Prunty. SP-PrunW

This. Adam Zagajewski. SP-ZagaA, *tr. by* Renata Gorczynski

This fitting scene would prove. Sunset in Derby's Woods. Jones Very. CP-VeryJ

This admirable gadget, when it is. Gyroscope. Howard Nemerov. CP-NemeH

This Advent moon shines cold and clear. Advent. Christina Georgina Rossetti. CP-RosC1

This after-sunset is a sight for seeing. He Prefers Her Earthly. Thomas Hardy. CP-HardT

This afternoon, darling, when you were here. Letter from a Death Bed. John Ciardi. CP-CiarJ

This afternoon, discomfortable dread. Possessed, The. John Berryman. CP-BerrJ

This afternoon it rains as never before; and I. Down to the Dregs. César Vallejo. CP-WrigJ, *tr. by* James Wright

This afternoon, let me. Whether There Is Enjoyment in Bitterness. Thomas Merton. CP-MertT

This afternoon the Mississippi. Tel Aviv and *Life on the Mississippi*. Raymond Carver. CP-CarvR

This afternoon the thunderstorms were separate and tall. Translating. A. R. Ammons. CP-AmmoA

This air & life of Italy. Italy. George Meredith. CP-MerG2

This all begins on a November day. Hayden Carruth. CP-CarHS *Fr.* Bloomingdale Papers, The.

This ancient hag. Mexican Market Woman. Langston Hughes. CP-HughL; CP-HughL1

This ancient house so notable. Country Mansion, A. Robert Graves. CP-GravR

This, and the Next World. Robert Herrick. CP-HerrR

This anthropologist had learned. In Memoriam. Unfinished. For Robert Barlow.

1950. Alan Dugan. CP-DugaA

This 'appened in a battle to a batt'ry of the corps. Snarleyow. Rudyard Kipling. CP-KiplR

This artist's sculptured, open box of mahogany. Grace. John Logan. CP-LogaJ

This as Including That. Wallace Stevens. CP-StevWP

This augurs well; both in their soft beds. Promised Ballad, The. Robert Graves. CP-GravR

This August evening I've been driving. Transcendental Etude. Adrienne Rich. SP-RicA1; SP-RicA2

This August heat, this momentary breeze. Nature Poem. Charles Tomlinson. CP-TomlC

This Axiom I have often heard. Love. Robert Herrick. CP-HerrR

This babbling gypsy. Jason Visits His Gypsy. Jay Wright. SP-WrigJ

This Band, which bound thy yellow hair. To a Lady. Lord Byron. CP-Byron

This Bauble was preferred of Bees. Emily Dickinson. CP-DickE

This be the meed, that thy Song creates a thousandfold Echo! Tribute to Wordsworth. Samuel Taylor Coleridge. CP-ColeS

This Be The Verse. Philip Larkin. CP-LarkP

This beast that rends me in the sight of all. Edna St. Vincent Millay. CP-MillE

This Beast, This Angel. Adrienne Rich. CP-RicAE

This beautiful ditty / is, for a change, about the city. City, The. Ogden Nash. CP-NashO

This beauty that I see. Poem: "This beauty that I see." James Schuyler. CP-SchuJ

This being human is a guest house. Guest House, The. Jelaluddin Rumi. SP-Rumi, tr. by Coleman Barks

This Black Rich Country. A. R. Ammons. CP-AmmoA

This blue-washed, old, thatched summerhouse. Old Summerhouse, The. Walter De la Mare. CP-DeLaW

This boat is of satō-wood, and its gunwhales are cut magnolia. River Song, The. Li Po. SP-PounE, tr. by Ezra Pound

This body I sometimes call me. One More on a Deathless Theme. A. K. Ramanujan. CP-RamaA

This body, tapped of every drop of breath. Ambergris. Stanley Kunitz. CP-KunSC

This Book is for Harriette. Robert Stock. SP-StocR

This book of Dante's, very sooth to say. Sonnet: He impugns the verdicts of Dante's Commedia. Cino da Pistoia. CW-RossD, tr. by Dante Gabriel Rossetti

This book, when I am dead, will be. Journal. Edna St. Vincent Millay. CP-MillE

This book will live; it hath a genius: this. On the Honoured Poems of His Honoured Friend, Sir John Beaumont, Baronet. Ben Jonson. CP-JonsB

This bossy river, its rate of descent a degree or two greater. River That Scolds at All the Other Rivers, The. Thomas Lux. SP-LuxT

This brand of soap has the same smell as once in the big. Soap Suds. Louis MacNeice. CP-MacNL

This Bread I Break. Dylan Thomas. CP-ThomD

This breast which now alternate burns. Our Future Lot. Walt Whitman. CP-WhitW

This breeze, stirring green laurel and my lady's. Petrarch. CP-Petra, tr. by J. G. Nichols

This Bright Day. A. R. Ammons. CP-AmmoA

This Broken Bell. Pablo Neruda. SP-NeruP

This bronze statue had its place in the midst of winter. Conformity. Yannis Ritsos. SP-RitsY, tr. by Kimon Friar

This bug carries spots on his back. Bug Spots. Carl Sandburg. CP-SandC

This building, graced with Plummer's name. Hymn: Sung at the Dedication of Plummer Hall, Salem, Oct. 6, 1857. Jones Very. CP-VeryJ

This burning behind my eyes as I open a door. Defeated. Robert Bly. SP-BlyR

This cabin, Mary, in my sight appears. Inscription for an Hermitage. William Cowper. CP-CowpW

This can be seen as placing a mirror against the page. Book of the Yellow Castle. Michael Palmer. SP-PalmM

This can happen. They can bring the leaves back. Stereopticon. William Stafford. SP-StafWW

This candle-wax is shaping to a shroud. Standing by the Mantlepiece. Thomas Hardy. CP-HardT

This cap, that so stately appears. Gratitude. William Cowper. CP-CowpW

This carpentered, unpainted, aging house. Letter to Marek about a Photograph, A. Denise Levertov. SP-LeveDL

This celestial seascape, with white herons got up as angels. Seascape. Elizabeth Bishop. CP-BishE

This century, an iron bell of joy, has scarcely rung. Years as Catches, The. Robert Duncan. SP-DuncR

This charm of vacant lots! Second Caprice in North Cambridge. T. S. Eliot. SP-ElioT

This Chasm, Sweet, upon my life. Emily Dickinson. CP-DickE

This child, shovelling away. Tree, The. Charles Tomlinson. CP-TomlC

This cigarette is extremely long. E. E. Cummings. CP-CummE

This circled cosmos whereof man is god. King's Cross Station. G. K. Chesterton. CP-ChesG

This city and its citizens are green. Song of the Outsider, The. Christopher Logue. SP-LoguC

This clonic earth. Serena II. Samuel Beckett. CP-BeckS

This cold puts us in a quandary. 26 November 1948. Yannis Ritsos. SP-RitsY Fr. Exile's Journals 2.

This Compost. Walt Whitman. CP-WhitW

This Configuration. John Ashbery. SP-AshbJ

This Consciousness that is aware. Emily Dickinson. CP-DickE

This coral's shape echoes the hand. Coral. Derek Walcott. CP-WalcD

This country least, but every inhabited country. Praise Life. Robinson Jeffers. CP-JefR2

This covers me, that erst had the blue sky. Fernando Pessoa. SP-PessF, tr. by Susan M. Brown and Edwin Honig Fr. Inscriptions.

This creature fills its mouth with venum. Cobra, The. Ogden Nash. CP-NashO

This creature kneeling / dusted with snow, its teeth. November. Margaret Atwood. SP-AtwM1

This creature with a bear's or tiger's heart. Petrarch. CP-Petra, tr. by J. G. Nichols

This cross-tree here. Cross-tree, The. Robert Herrick. CP-HerrR

This Cryptic Bone. Tennessee Williams. CP-WillT

This crystal sphere. Sometimes It Turns Dry and the Leaves Fall before They Are Beautiful. William Carlos Williams. CP-WilW2

This Dark Apartment. James Schuyler. CP-SchuJ

This darksome burn, horseback brown. Inversnaid. Gerard Manley Hopkins. CP-HopkG

This Day. C. K. Williams. CP-WillC

This day after. Robert Creeley. SP-CreeR

This day among the faithful plac'd. On the Christening of a Friend's Child. Samuel Taylor Coleridge. CP-ColeS

This day, dear Bec, is thy nativity. Bec's Birthday. Jonathan Swift. CP-SwifJ

This day feels put together hastily. New Year's Day. Audre Lorde. SP-LordA

This day is Yours Great Charles! and in this War. To the King, upon His Taking of Leicester. Robert Herrick. CP-HerrR

This day lies under glass. Burning Dawn. Hayden Carruth. CP-CarHS

This day my Julia thou must make. Bride-Cake, The. Robert Herrick. CP-HerrR

This Day, O Soul. Walt Whitman. CP-WhitW

This Day of This Month of This Year of This. W. S. Merwin. SP-MerwW

This day that would tell us what we are. Sunday. John Updike. CP-UpdiJ

This day, the fav'rite of the year. Birthday Poem on the Anniversary of the Birth of the Rev. Dr. Swift, D. S. P. D. Nov. 30, 1737, A. Thomas Sheridan. CP-SherT

This day (the year I dare not tell). Corinna. Jonathan Swift. CP-SwifJ

This day, this night, should be familiar to you. For Wilfred Owen. Josephine Jacobsen. CP-JacoJ

This Day This World. Stanley Kunitz. CP-KunSC

This day throw open all your houses, and forever. Ointment, The. Thomas Merton. CP-MertT

This day, Time winds th' exhausted chain. Sketch. New Year's Day. To Mrs. Dunlop. Robert Burns. CP-BurnR

This day, two hundred years ago. Song of Harvest, A. John Greenleaf Whittier. CP-WhitJ

This day unites a good and virtuous pair. Wish on a Wedding Day Morning, The. Annis Boudinot Stockton. CP-StocA

This day was made of dust. Terrestrial. Josephine Jacobsen. CP-JacoJ

This day, whate'er the fates decree. Stella's Birthday ([March 13,] 1727). Jonathan Swift. CP-SwifJ

This day winding down now. Author's Prologue. Dylan Thomas. CP-ThomD

This day writhes with what? The lecturer. Ultimate Poem Is Abstract, The. Wallace Stevens. CP-StevW; CP-StevWP

This Dear Child-Hearted Woman That Is Dead. James Whitcomb Riley. CP-RileJ

This declaration is that of a secret. Northern Suburb. Jorge Luis Borges. SP-BorgJ, tr. by Charles Tomlinson

This Decoration. Hayden Carruth. CP-CarHS

This devils me: uneasy ease at my window. Flowering Quince. John Ciardi. CP-CiarJ

This dinner is too rich for you, Paul. Another Day. The Children Are All Eating. Muriel Rukeyser. CP-RukeM

This dirty—little—Heart. Emily Dickinson. CP-DickE

This disc, stelliferous. Sand Dollar. John Updike. CP-UpdiJ

This ditty is a string of lies. Rudyard Kipling. See Potiphar Gubbins, C. E

This docile one inter. Emily Dickinson. CP-DickE

This door you might not open, and you did. Bluebeard. Edna St. Vincent Millay. CP-MillE

This down by which we go runs like. Rio. Wyatt Prunty. SP-PrunW

This dream budded bright with leaves round the edges. Dream with Clam-Diggers. Sylvia Plath. CP-PlatS

This dream prorogued. Equation for Marie, An. Kenneth Rexroth. CP-RexrK

This dream the world is having about itself. Vocation. William Stafford. SP-StafW; SP-StafWW

This dry and lusty wind has stirred all night. All Choice Is Error. James Vincent Cunningham. CP-CunnJ

This Dusky Faith. Edna St. Vincent Millay. CP-MillE

This Dust, and its Feature. Emily Dickinson. CP-DickE

This Early Day. Kenneth Patchen. CP-PatcK

This Earth the king said. Return. George Oppen. CP-OppGN

This Easter, Arthur Winslow, less than dead. Death from Cancer. Robert Lowell. SP-LoweR *Fr.* In Memory of Arthur Winslow.

This effervescing gentleman who despises a secret. Hafiz. CP-EmerR *Fr.* Odes.

This eightieth year of thine sits crowned in light. To Carlyle. George Meredith. CP-MerG2

This elderly poet, unpublished for five decades. Ashes, The. Carolyn Kizer. CP-KizeC

This elemental force. Genesis. Theodore Roethke. CP-RoetT

This empty street, this sky to blandness scoured. Triple Time. Philip Larkin. CP-LarkP

This ends: entering the show of silence. Night Has Been as Beautiful as Virginia. Kenneth Patchen. CP-PatcK

This engine started years ago—many. Size of a Fist, The. William Stafford. SP-StafWW

This English Thames is holier far than Rome. Burden of Itys, The. Oscar Wilde. CP-WildO

This Englishwoman. Stevie Smith. CP-SmitS

This escaping mildness. Cemetary in Ragaz. Rainer Maria Rilke. CP-RilkFr, *tr. by* A. Poulin, Jr.

This evangelist / buttons with his big gollywog voice. E. E. Cummings. CP-CummE

This evening, each hour, it grows earlier. Same Story. Pablo Neruda. SP-NeruP

This evening, motherly summer moves in the pond. Mayday on Holderness. Ted Hughes. SP-HughTN

This evening / The river is a beautiful idle woman. Low Water. Ted Hughes. SP-HughTN

This ev'ning, Delia, you and I. William Cowper. CP-CowpW

This face, says art, alone. Michelangelo Buonarroti. CP-Miche, *tr. by* John Frederick Nims.

This face you got. Phizzog. Carl Sandburg. CP-SandC

This faint resemblance of thy charms. To Mary on Receiving Her Picture. Lord Byron. CP-Byron

This fainthearted and gloomy rain. Slow Rain, The. Gabriela Mistral. SP-MistG, *tr. by* Maria Giachetti [*or* Jacketti]

This fair parcel of summer's. Song: "This fair parcel of summer's." Theodore Roethke. CP-RoetT

This fairest lady, who, as well I wot. Sonnet: Death is not without but within him. Cino da Pistoia. CW-RossD, *tr. by* Dante Gabriel Rossetti

This fall you will taste carrots. Digging In. Marge Piercy. SP-PierM

This far south such crippling. Aurora Borealis. Rita Dove. SP-DoveR

This fear is no longer dear. You are not going to America and. E. E. Cummings. CP-CummE

This feast-day of the sun, his altar there. Hill Summit, The. Dante Gabriel Rossetti. CW-RossD *Fr.* House of Life, The.

This fell when dinner-time was done. Fall of Jock Gillespie, The. Rudyard Kipling. CP-KiplR

This fever doubtless comes in punishment. Blanket Charge. Robert Graves. CP-GravR

This Fevers Me. Richard Eberhart. CP-EberR

This field-grass brushed our legs. In the Field. Richard Wilbur. CP-WilbR

This figure, that thou here seest put. To the Reader ("This figure, that thou here seest put"). Ben Jonson. CP-JonsB; SP-JonsB

This fireglow is a red womb. Birth Night. D. H. Lawrence. CP-LawrD

This first book that I ever knew. To Almon Keefer. James Whitcomb Riley. CP-RileJ

This fleur-de-lis. Formal Design, A. William Carlos Williams. CP-WilW2

This Florida: 1924. William Carlos Williams. CP-WilW1

This flower is repeated. Windflower Leaf. Carl Sandburg. CP-SandC

This foot's giving me nothing. Toes, The. Raymond Carver. CP-CarvR

This—For the Moon—Yes? Carl Sandburg. CP-SandC

This / forest pool / A so. E. E. Cummings. CP-CummE

This Form of Life Needs Sex. Allen Ginsberg. CP-GinsA; SP-GinsA

This gentleman the charming duck. Trueblue Gentleman, A. Kenneth Patchen. CP-PatcK

This girl borrowed no dim light of a star. Eager Youths to a Dead Girl. Allen Tate. CP-TateA

This girl child speaks five words. Seventeen Months. Carl Sandburg. CP-SandC

This girlchild was born as usual. Barbie Doll. Marge Piercy. SP-PierM

This glorious oversleeping half through Sunday. Mother and Father 2. Robert Lowell. SP-LoweR

This gold watch and chain. Ballad of the Pawnbroker. Langston Hughes. CP-HughL; CP-HughL2

This golden vengeance is one of those red. Sword. Marilyn Hacker. SP-HackM

This graveyard with its umbrella pines. Island Cemetery, An. W. H. Auden. CP-AudeW

This Gray Age. Theodore Weiss. SP-WeisT

This great purple butterfly. Another Song of a Fool. William Butler Yeats. CP-YeatW

This gun emplacement where we live aims. At Fort Worden: Calling Names. William Stafford. SP-StafWW

This guy / he's got a crazy eye. Hawley's Leaving Town. Charles Bukowski. SP-BukC1

This handful of grass, brown, says little. This quarter-mile field of it. Memoranda. Carl Sandburg. CP-SandC

This handless clock stares blindly from its tower. Clock in the Square, A. Adrienne Rich. CP-RicAE

This harpie with dry red curls. Red Dust. Philip Levine. SP-LeviP

This has nothing / to do with. Conjugation of the Paramecium, The. Muriel Rukeyser. CP-RukeM

This has to be for my school-chum Billy Greaves. Shropshire. Donald Davie. CP-DaviDC

This head meant to be massive and therefore. At the Synod in St Patrick's. Donald Davie. CP-DaviDC

This heap of ashes was a learned girl. La Speakerine de Putney. Stevie Smith. CP-SmitS

This heart that broke so long. Emily Dickinson. CP-DickE

This Height a ministering Angel might select. View from the Top of Black Comb. William Wordsworth. CP-WorW1

This high summer we love will pour its light. Adrienne Rich. SP-RicA1 *Fr.* Contradictions: Tracking Poems.

This hinder nycht, halff sleiping as I lay. William Dunbar. CP-DunbW

This hindir nycht in Dumfermeling. William Dunbar. CP-DunbW

This holy House of God. Letter to My Friends, A. Thomas Merton. CP-MertT

This Holy Month. Robert Graves. CP-GravR

This honest wife, challenged at dusk. With Her Lips Only. Robert Graves. CP-GravR

This horrible but superb painting. Parable of the Blind, The. William Carlos Williams. CP-WilW2 *Fr.* Pictures from Brueghel.

This horse drinking at the fountain. Rainer Maria Rilke. CP-RilkFr, *tr. by* A. Poulin, Jr. *Fr.* Orchards.

This hour is for the lakes. Matins. James McMichael. SP-McMiJ

This house has been far out at sea all night. Wind. Ted Hughes. SP-HughTN

This house is a wreck said the children. Sad Children's Song, The. Grace Paley. CP-PalGC

This House, This Country. Muriel Rukeyser. CP-RukeM

This house where Love a little while abode. Variations on a Theme. Countee Cullen. CP-CullC

This I do, being mad. Siege. Edna St. Vincent Millay. CP-MillE

This I don't believe: rather than take a header. Footling. Paul Muldoon. CP-MuldP

This I saw when the rites were done. Rudyard Kipling. CP-KiplR *Fr.* Naulahka, The.

This I say, and this I know. Wisdom. Dorothy Parker. CP-ParkD

This I will never tell. I slept under a thing. It was a feather. Musica Ficta. Michael Palmer. SP-PalmM

This idol, dark eyes, yellow mane, no family or court, nobler than fables. Childhood. Arthur Rimbaud. CP-RimbA, *tr. by* Martin Sorrell

This, if Japanese, / Would represent grey boulders. Thyme Flowering among Rocks. Richard Wilbur. CP-WilbR

This Ile tell ye by the way. Charmes. Robert Herrick. CP-HerrR

This image was drawn by an untaught hand. On the Engraver of His Likeness. John Milton. CP-MiltJ

This Infant used to howl and yell. Happy Xmas, A ("This Infant used to howl and yell"). G. K. Chesterton. CP-ChesG

This institution / perhaps one should say enterprise. Marriage. Marianne Craig Moore. CP-MoorM

This is a baffling and forbidding world of disreputable international shakedowns. Down the Mousehole, and What Science Missed There. Ogden Nash. CP-NashO

This is a Blossom of the Brain. Emily Dickinson. CP-DickE

This is a book I do not like. To Father O'Connor. G. K. Chesterton. CP-ChesG

This is a brightsome blaze you've lit, good friend, to-night! Wood Fire, The. Thomas Hardy. CP-HardT

This is a Christmas carol. Christmas Season. James Whitcomb Riley. CP-RileJ

This is a circling of itself and you. First Love. Derek Mahon. CP-MahoD

This is a country where there are no mountains. Morning on the St. John's. Jane Cooper. CP-CoopJ

This is a dark woman at a telephone. Judith. Muriel Rukeyser. CP-RukeM

This is a day to celebrate can-openers. Cast Off, The. Marge Piercy. SP-PierM

This is a day when good men die from windows. Death of a Public Servant, The. Carolyn Kizer. CP-KizeC

This is a glove. Village of Reason, The. Michael Palmer. SP-PalmM

This is a good book? Yes? This—For the Moon—Yes? Carl Sandburg. CP-SandC

This is a high and sprawling wooden flat. Marilyn Hacker. SP-HackM Fr. Separations.

This is a land in which you never were. To One Not There. Countee Cullen. CP-CullC

This is a lung disease. Silicate dust makes it. Disease, The. Muriel Rukeyser. CP-RukeM

This is a meditation. First Lesson. James Tate. SP-TateJ

This is a mistake, / these arms and legs. Margaret Atwood. SP-AtwM1

This Is a Photograph of Me. Margaret Atwood. SP-AtwM1

This is a place where a door might be. Door, A ("This is a place where a door might be"). W. S. Merwin. SP-MerwW

This is a poem for you, Ann. Impromptu. Meadow House. Hayden Carruth. CP-CarHS

This is a rope of stars tied to my wrist. Childhood's Body. Charles Wright. SP-WrigC

This is a rubbish of human rind. E. E. Cummings. CP-CummE

This Is a Sin. C. K. Williams. CP-WillC

This is a song for the genius child. Genius Child. Langston Hughes. CP-HughL; CP-HughL2

This is a song to celebrate banks. Bankers Are Just like Anybody Else, except Richer. Ogden Nash. CP-NashO

This is a song to the white-armed one. Fairy Bridal Hymn, The. Nicholas Vachel Lindsay. CP-LindV

This is a spray the Bird clung to. Misconceptions. Robert Browning. CP-BroR1

This is a stern Winter. Emily Dickinson. SP-DickE

This is a story handed down. Creation Myth. Wendell Berry. CP-BerrW

This is a story. You don't have to think about it, it's make-believe. Near the Haunted Castle. C. K. Williams. CP-WillC; SP-WillC

This is a time of lightning without thunder. Waiting. Primo Levi. CP-LeviP, tr. by Ruth Feldman and Brian Swann

This is a very sad ballad. My Dear, How Ever Did You Think Up This Delicious Salad? Ogden Nash. CP-NashO

This is a wild land, country of my choice. Rocky Acres. Robert Graves. CP-GravR

This Is about Death. Allen Ginsberg. CP-GinsA

This Is After All Vacation. Louis Zukofsky. CP-ZukLS

This is after all vacation. All that. This Is After All Vacation. Louis Zukofsky. CP-ZukLS

This is all the story of Salomon Waste. Story of Salomon Waste, The. Fernando Pessoa. SP-PessF

This is all you go with. Out. Margaret Atwood. SP-AtwM2

This is an empty landscape. Place ("This is an empty landscape"). Robert Creeley. SP-CreeR

This is an hour of calm, a quiet hour. Mateja Matevski. CP-KizeC, tr. by Carolyn Kizer Fr. Equinox.

This is an image which put enemies to flight. In Effigiem Oliveri Cromwell [On a Portrait of Oliver Cromwell]. Andrew Marvell. CP-MarvA

This is another of our ancient loves. Quies. Ezra Pound. CP-PoEar

This is at once her pride and her disgrace. Changeling. Tennessee Williams. CP-WillT

This is before electricity. Game after Supper. Margaret Atwood. SP-AtwM1

This is before I'd read Nietzsche. Before Kant or Kierkegaard, even before Whitman and Yeats. Gas Station, The. C. K. Williams. CP-WillC; SP-WillC

This is but a fragment. Emily Dickinson. SP-DickE

This Is Disgraceful and Abominable. Stevie Smith. CP-SmitS

This is earthquake / Weather! Today. Langston Hughes. CP-HughL; CP-HughL2

This is enlightened repose, neither fever nor languor, on the bed or in the meadow. Vigils. Arthur Rimbaud. CP-RimbA, tr. by Martin Sorrell

This is for the kids who die. Kids Who Die. Langston Hughes. CP-HughL; CP-HughL1

This is for the left-handed mothers. Letter from Persephone. Margaret Atwood. SP-AtwM2

This is for you for whom bloom certainly roses. Liturgy of Roses, A. Tennessee Williams. CP-WillT

This is for your body hidden in words. Forage Sestina. Marilyn Hacker. SP-HackM

This is fresh meat right mr nixon? In the Heart of the Beast. C. K. Williams. CP-WillC

This is going to be about smoke. Muriel Rukeyser. CP-RukeM

This is harder than counting stones. Dead at Quang Tri, The. Yusef Komunyakaa. CP-KomuY

This is he, who, felled by foes. Worship. Ralph Waldo Emerson. CP-EmerR

This is her picture as she was. Portrait, The. Dante Gabriel Rossetti. CW-RossD

This is his gift. Projector II. "H. D." CP-DoolH

This is how a human being can change. Worm's Waking, The. Jelaluddin Rumi. SP-Rumi, tr. by Coleman Barks

This is how come I am drowned. Drowning (II). Grace Paley. CP-PalGC

This is how I bend over backward. Life of Poetry, The. James Tate. SP-TateJ

This is how I came to be loved. Cables to Rage Or I've Been Talking On This Street Corner. Audre Lorde. SP-LordA

This is how it feels to do something you are afraid of. Tear Gas. Adrienne Rich. CP-RicAE; SP-RicA2

This is how it is when your animal energies. Dog in the Doorway, The. Jelaluddin Rumi. SP-Rumi, tr. by Coleman Barks

This is how it started: suddenly it felt. Love Song: "This is how it started: suddenly it felt." Yehuda Amichai. SP-AmicY, tr. by Chana Bloch

This is how the wind shifts. Wind Shifts, The. Wallace Stevens. CP-StevW; CP-StevWP

This is, indeed, neither the time nor the place. Toast to Death, A. Robert Graves. CP-GravR

This is just one more. Eclogue at Nash's Grove. James Wright. CP-WrigJ

This Is Just to Say. William Carlos Williams. CP-WilW1

This is King Charles his day. Speak it, thou tower. To the King. On His Birthday. An Epigram Anniversary. Novem[ber] 19, 1632. Ben Jonson. CP-JonsB

This / Is mine, and I can hold it. Edna St. Vincent Millay. CP-MillE

This is Mr. Woolley, Mrs. Dixon. Introduction, The. Ogden Nash. CP-NashO

This is Mortal. David Ignatow. SP-IgnaD

This is my comfort, when she's most unkind. On Fortune. Robert Herrick. CP-HerrR

This is my dream. And always again. Hand. Robert Stock. SP-StocR

This is my father's gray blanket. Inheritance. Charles Simic. SP-SimiC; SP-SimiCE

This is my island. Thirty years ago. Epitaph for John McCutcheon. Archibald MacLeish. CP-MacLA

This is my last. Summer Gale. Alan Dugan. CP-DugaA

This Is My Letter to the World. Emily Dickinson. CP-DickE

This is my letter to the world. This Is My Letter to the World. Emily Dickinson. CP-DickE

This is my mew. On Hearing / the Wood Pewee. Lorine Niedecker. CP-NiedL

This Is My Own, My Native Tongue. Ogden Nash. CP-NashO

This is my piano. Chopin Bukowski. Charles Bukowski. SP-BukC1

This is my Testament of all my gear. Testament, A. G. K. Chesterton. CP-ChesG

This is my wolf. He sits. Appointment, The. Maxine W. Kumin. SP-KumiM

This is newness: every little tawdry. New Year on Dartmoor. Sylvia Plath. CP-PlatS

This is no cell, Holy Woman. To the Virgin as She Now Stands to the Monk after a Beatles Movie. Andrei Codrescu. SP-CodrA

This is no dream. Princess and the Pea, The. Paul Muldoon. CP-MuldP

This is not a pipe. Ceci n'est pas une Pipe. Charles Tomlinson. CP-TomlC

This is not bad. Man Listening to Disc. Billy Collins. SP-CollB

This is not Dante. Identity Check. Hans Magnus Enzensberger. SP-EnzeH

This is not exactly what I mean. World and I, The. Laura Riding Jackson. CP-RidiL

This / is / not / more / snow / to / fall. Valentine, A. Louis Zukofsky. CP-ZukLS

This is not the event. This. On a Mexican Straw Christ. Charles Tomlinson. CP-TomlC

This is not the nest. Blowing Eggs. Paul Muldoon. CP-MuldP

This is not the truth. Blessing. Eleanor Wilner. SP-WilnE

This is not what I meant. Whitsun. Sylvia Plath. CP-PlatS

This is on earth the happiest bit of land. Petrarch. CP-Petra, tr. by J. G. Nichols

This is our lot if we live so long and labour unto the end. Old Men, The. Rudyard Kipling. CP-KiplR

This is our perfect silver maple's day. Sonnet: "This is our perfect silver maple's day." Hayden Carruth. CP-CarHS Fr. Sonnets.

This is our utmost task. To Miss Sophy Giauque. Rainer Maria Rilke. CP-RilkFr, tr. by A. Poulin, Jr.

This is our world, high privet hedge on two sides. Bad Memory Makes You a Metaphysician, a Good One Makes You a Saint, A. Charles Wright. SP-WrigCN

This is ours by natural, not by civil, right. Uncut Diamond, The. Robert Graves. CP-GravR

This is Paul whose habits are. In Paul's Room. John Ciardi. CP-CiarJ

This Is Pioneer Weather. William Carlos Williams. CP-WilW2

This is plum season, the nights. Late August. Margaret Atwood. SP-AtwM1

This Is Simple. Pablo Neruda. SP-NeruP

This is that blessed Mary, pre-elect. Mary's Girlhood. Dante Gabriel Rossetti. CW-RossD

This is that Raphael the Great Source of All. On Raphael. Pietro Bembo. CP-CunnJ, tr. by James Vincent Cunningham

This is the animal that never existed. Unicorn, The. Randall Jarrell. CP-JarrR

This is the arsenal. From floor to ceiling. Arsenal at Springfield, The. Henry Wadsworth Longfellow. SP-LongH

This is the ballad of Boh Da Thone. Rudyard Kipling. *See* Boh Da Thone was a warrior bold

This is the beginning. Aristotle. Billy Collins. SP-CollB

This is the birthday of your death. Birthday Poem for a Childless Man. Carolyn Kizer. CP-KizeC

This is the black day when. Dark Morning, The. Thomas Merton. CP-MertT

This is the blur of dimension, the past arriving. Clock in the Mirror, The. John Ciardi. CP-CiarJ

This is the body of my good gray practical dead. Elegy: "This is the body of my good gray practical dead." John Ciardi. CP-CiarJ

This is the castle where they lived. Chapultepec Castle. Jay Wright. SP-WrigJ

This is the chief felicity of life. Euripides. CP-JohnS *Fr.* Medea.

This is the creature I am! Iron Horse. Allen Ginsberg. CP-GinsA

This is the cripples' hour on Seventh Avenue. Seventh Avenue. Muriel Rukeyser. CP-RukeM

This is the Cross! First Crusades, The! Kenneth Patchen. CP-PatcK

This is the day, this is the day! Judgment Day. Ogden Nash. CP-NashO

This is the debt I pay. Debt, The. Paul Laurence Dunbar. CP-DunbP

This is the desk I sit at. That Day. Anne Sexton. CP-SextA

This is the dream grown young. Lincoln University: 1954. Langston Hughes. CP-HughL; CP-HughL3

This is the dream-journal, knowing the earth slips under. Otherworld. Muriel Rukeyser. CP-RukeM

This is the easy time, there is nothing doing. Wintering. Sylvia Plath. CP-PlatS

This is the end of the landscape. Among blocks. Yehuda Amichai. SP-AmicY, *tr.* by Chana Bloch *Fr.* Songs of Zion the Beautiful.

This is the end whereto men toiled. Fastness. Rudyard Kipling. CP-KiplR *Fr.* Muse among the Motors, The.

This is the face behind my face. You see. Self-Portrait: David, A. Charles Tomlinson. CP-TomlC

This is the field where the battle did not happen. At the Un-National Monument along the Canadian Border. William Stafford. SP-StafW; SP-StafWW

This is the final statement we shall make. Caption for a Photograph of Four Organized Criminals. François Villon. SP-LoguC, *tr.* by Christopher Logue

This is the first rain of spring. First Rain of Spring, The. Maxine W. Kumin. SP-KumiM

This is the first soft snow. First Snow. May Sarton. SP-SartM

This Is the First Thing. Philip Larkin. CP-LarkP

This is the fourth day I've been here. Sensitive Girl, The. Raymond Carver. CP-CarvR

This is the garden:clours come and go. Sonnet IV. E. E. Cummings. CP-CummE

This is the good child. As Soft and as Pink as a Nursery. Eleanor Wilner. SP-WilnE

This is the grass your feet are planted on. Rural Reflections. Adrienne Rich. CP-RicAE; SP-RicA2

This is the hand I dipped in the Missouri. Witness. William Stafford. SP-StafWW

This is the height of Justice, that to doe. Like Pattern, Like People. Robert Herrick. CP-HerrR

This is the house destroyed by Jack. Berlin Wall Tune, The. Joseph Brodsky. CP-BrodJ, *tr.* by Joseph Brodsky

This is the house of Bedlam. Visits to St. Elizabeths. Elizabeth Bishop. CP-BishE

This is the house of her. Song: "This is the house of her." Wallace Stevens. CP-StevWP

This is the image: an old woman in a blue hat. Other Side of the Wall, The. Clarence Major. SP-MajoC

This is the inner sanctum. Here. World Away, A. Charles Baudelaire. CP-BaudC, *tr.* by Walter Martin

This is the key to it. Breast, The. Anne Sexton. CP-SextA; SP-SextA

This is the lair of the landlady. Landlady, The. Margaret Atwood. SP-AtwM1

This—is the land—the Sunset washes. Emily Dickinson. CP-DickE

This is the last day of the last week. Last Day. Margaret Atwood. SP-AtwM2

This is the last day of the world. On the river docks. Downwards. C. K. Williams. CP-WillC; SP-WillC

This is the last of all, then, this is the last! Monologue of a Mother. D. H. Lawrence. CP-LawrD

This is the last; the very, very last! Last Love-Word. Thomas Hardy. CP-HardT

This is the last year. He is the last. Theophilos Palaiologos. Constantine P. Cavafy. CP-CavaC, *tr.* by Theoharis Constantine Theoharis

This Is the Life. Louis MacNeice. CP-MacNL

This is the life of a Congressman. Disease: After-Effects, The. Muriel Rukeyser. CP-RukeM

This is the life of promises. The Greek priest. Yehuda Amichai. SP-AmicYL, *tr.* by Benjamin Harshav *and* Barbara Harshav

This is the light of the mind, cold and planetary. Moon and the Yew Tree, The. Sylvia Plath. CP-PlatS

This is the lilac-bush. Wallace Stevens. CP-StevWP

This is *The Making of America in Five Panels*. Empire Builders. Archibald

MacLeish. CP-MacLA

This is the man who classified the bits. Intellectual Detachment. Allen Tate. CP-TateA

This is the maneater's skull. Ted Hughes. SP-HughTN

This is the midnight—let no star. Storm Cone, The. Rudyard Kipling. CP-KiplR

This is the Month, and this the happy morn. On the Morning of Christ's Nativity. John Milton. CP-MiltJ

This Is the Morte Saison. James Laughlin. CP-LaugJ

This is the most audacious landscape. The gangster's. Alloy. Muriel Rukeyser. CP-RukeM

This is the mouth-filling song of the race that was run by a Boomer. Rudyard Kipling. CP-KiplR *Fr.* Just-So Stories.

This is the night mail crossing the border. Night Mail, The. W. H. Auden. CP-AudeW

This is the night my ship comes in. Johnny Appleseed's Ship Comes In. Nicholas Vachel Lindsay. CP-LindV

This is the night the false Saint Jason. Saint Jason. Thomas Merton. CP-MertT

This is the nightmare you now have frequently. No Name. Margaret Atwood. SP-AtwM2

This is "The Old Home by the Mill"—fer we still call it so. Old Home by the Mill, The. James Whitcomb Riley. CP-RileJ

This is the one and only. Metaphysics. Allen Ginsberg. CP-GinsA; SP-GinsA

This is the other story. There are three. Shirland Road. Marilyn Hacker. SP-HackM

This is the outstretched, tentative toe. Hand Me Down My Old School Sliding Pads, or, There's a Hint of Strawberry Leaves in the Air. Ogden Nash. CP-NashO

This is the place. Notes towards a Poem That Can Never Be Written. Margaret Atwood. SP-AtwM2

This is the place, Craven, the end of our way. Eclogue from Iceland. Louis MacNeice. CP-MacNL

This is the place. Even here the dauntless soul. William Blake. Dante Gabriel Rossetti. CW-RossD *Fr.* Five English Poets.

This is the place they hoped before. Emily Dickinson. CP-DickE

This is the pledge the charter and the seal. Fragment, Janu'ry 1786. Annis Boudinot Stockton. CP-StocA

This is the poem of a month within a year. March, 1937. Laura Riding Jackson. CP-RidiL

This is the reason why Rustum Beg. Rudyard Kipling. *See* Rustum Beg of Kolazai—slightly backward Native State

This is the rock where I my church will build. My Church. Jones Very. CP-VeryJ

This is the sadness of the sea. Sadness of the Sea, The. William Carlos Williams. CP-WilW1

This is the sea then, once. Anchorage. Margaret Atwood. SP-AtwM2

This is the sea, then, this great abeyance. Berck-Plage. Sylvia Plath. CP-PlatS

This is the season when cards are exchanged, or. Departure. Robert Penn Warren. CP-WarrR

This is the sin against the Holy Ghost. Unpardonable Sin, The. Nicholas Vachel Lindsay. CP-LindV

This is the solution: to be happy with slaughter. David Ignatow. SP-IgnaD

This is the song I rested with. Mammy Hums. Carl Sandburg. CP-SandC

This is the song / The spice-tree sings. Spice-Tree, The. Nicholas Vachel Lindsay. CP-LindV

This is the sonnet I wanted to write yesterday. Sonnet: Sin. Hayden Carruth. CP-CarHS *Fr.* Sonnets.

This is the sorrowful story. Legends of Evil, The. Rudyard Kipling. CP-KiplR

This is the sort of book we like. Lines Written in a Picture Book. G. K. Chesterton. CP-ChesG

This is the space where. Private Space, A. Eleanor Wilner. SP-WilnE

This is the spot:—how mildly does the sun. Travelling. William Wordsworth. CP-WorW1; MW-WorW

This is the Spring Symphony. Schumann. Spring Symphony, The. Charles Tomlinson. CP-TomlC

This is the State above the Law. Death-Bed, A. Rudyard Kipling. CP-KiplR

This is the story. Point, The. Charles Simic. SP-SimiC; SP-SimiCE

This is the story a man told me. Wife Comes Back, A. Thomas Hardy. CP-HardT

This is the story of the lake and the three big fish. Three Fish, The. Jelaluddin Rumi. SP-Rumi, *tr.* by Coleman Barks

This is the time. Orchard, The. William Carlos Williams. CP-WilW2

This is the time of night at the delicatessen. Closing Time at the Second Avenue Deli. Alan Dugan. CP-DugaA

This is the time of year. Armadillo, The. Elizabeth Bishop. CP-BishE

This is the time of year. Horned Purple. William Carlos Williams. CP-WilW1

This is the time, when most divine to hear. Religious Musings. Samuel Taylor Coleridge. CP-ColeS; MW-ColeS

This is the Track. Wilfred Owen. CP-OwenW

This is the twentieth century. First on TV, A. David Ignatow. SP-IgnaD

This is the vase, Here. E. E. Cummings. CP-CummE

This is the village where the funeral. Stranger. Allen Tate. CP-TateA

This is the way it goes, the tide. In the Estuary. Charles Tomlinson. CP-TomlC

This is the weather the cuckoo likes. Weathers [*or* Weather]. Thomas Hardy. CP-HardT

This is the white king's palace: snowflakes flounce. Snow, The. Hayden Carruth. CP-CarHS

This is the wind, the wind in a field of corn. Wind. James Fenton. SP-FentJ

This is the witching hour of noon. Dance Unmacabre. Ogden Nash. CP-NashO

This is the word our lips caress, our teeth bite. Place-Rituals. Muriel Rukeyser. CP-RukeM

This is the world. Celestial Globe. Howard Nemerov. CP-NemeH

This is the World that opens and shuts. Emily Dickinson. *See* Is this the Hope that opens and shuts

This is the world we wanted. Gretel in Darkness. Louise Glück. SP-GlucL

This is the year the old ones. September 1961. Denise Levertov. SP-LeveDP; SP-LeveDS

This is their triumph, ripe and rounded. Election Echo, An. G. K. Chesterton. CP-ChesG

This is, this is. Dismal Moment Passing. Clarence Major. SP-MajoC

This is this morning: all. This Morning Here. Alan Dugan. CP-DugaA

This is thy hour O Soul, thy free flight into the wordless. Clear Midnight, A. Walt Whitman. CP-WhitW

This is to-day, a golden summer's day. To an Ingrate. Paul Laurence Dunbar. CP-DunbP

This is to give notice, I Tom the great scribbler. Tom Punsibi's Farewell to the Muses. *Unknown*. CP-SherT

This is to say we remember. Not that remembering saves us. For Victor Jara. Miller Williams. CP-WillM

This is vengeance. Indecent Assumption, the Slaughter Songs, The. Andrei Codrescu. SP-CodrA

This is what, / at last, it is. C. K. Williams. CP-WillC; SP-WillC

This / is what happens when the. Dear Friend. Charles Bukowski. SP-BukC2

This is what I see in my dreams about final exams. Brueghel's Two Monkeys. Wisława Szymborska. SP-SzymW, *tr. by* Stanislaw Barańczak *and* Clare Cavanagh

This is what I vow. Somebody's Song. Dorothy Parker. CP-ParkD

This is what lit the hunters of smoke and the paths of the forest. Muriel Rukeyser. CP-RukeM

This is what was exceptional in him. Days of 1901. Constantine P. Cavafy. CP-CavaC, *tr. by* Theoharis Constantine Theoharis

This is what your cat did to your mouse. Another Cat Poem. To a Cat Person. Alan Dugan. CP-DugaA

This is what your cat does. Note. Alan Dugan. CP-DugaA

This is where I once saw a deaf girl playing in a field. Deaf Girl Playing. James Tate. SP-TateJ

This is where Jack Johnson. Boxing Day. Yusef Komunyakaa. CP-KomuY

This is where the serpent lives, the bodiless. Auroras of Autumn, The. Wallace Stevens. CP-StevW; CP-StevWP

This is winter, this is night, small love. By Candlelight. Sylvia Plath. CP-PlatS

This is your brother the bird. Address to a Bird on a Visit Home. Alan Dugan. CP-DugaA

This is your own lover, Kenneth, Marie. Martial—12, 52. Kenneth Rexroth. CP-RexrK

This isn't Miss Duncan, the noted danseuse? Frozen Motion. Wisława Szymborska. SP-SzymW, *tr. by* Stanislaw Barańczak *and* Clare Cavanagh

This Italian square. Dancers at the Moy. Paul Muldoon. CP-MuldP

This itch to sit at paper and to say. Advertisement for a Reader. John Ciardi. CP-CiarJ

This kid got so dirty. Primer. Charles Simic. SP-SimiC; SP-SimiCE

This knowledge so innocently it goes this sin. From Now On. C. K. Williams. CP-WillC

This lad, when but a child of six. Ariel. Walter De la Mare. CP-DeLaW

This lady was danger, this. H. D. Donald Davie. CP-DaviDC

This Lady's short, that Mistresse she is tall. Short and Long Both Likes. Robert Herrick. CP-HerrR

This land is red, its body is colored of blood. Mississippi Anatomy. Josephine Jacobsen. CP-JacoJ

This Land of Rainbows spanning glens whose walls. Composed in the Glen of Loch Etive. William Wordsworth. CP-WorW2

This land: / The hills, round under straw. George Oppen. CP-OppGN

This land will not always be foreign. Winds of Orisha, The. Audre Lorde. SP-LordA

This late afternoon of April 1964 the despotic old eagle. Celebrating Giacometti. René Char. CP-MertT

This latent mine—these unlaunch'd voices—passionate powers. Font of Type, A. Walt Whitman. CP-WhitW

This Lawn, a Carpet All Alive. William Wordsworth. CP-WorW2

This left hand. Limit, The. A. R. Ammons. CP-AmmoA

This legendary house, this dear enchanted tomb. Monticello. May Sarton. SP-SartM

This level reach of blue is not my sea. Fair Weather. Dorothy Parker. CP-ParkD

This Life. Rita Dove. SP-DoveR

This Life. Grace Paley. CP-PalGC

This life is deep and dense. Remora. James Merrill. SP-MerrJ

This life like no other. Poem: "This life like no other." Gregory Orr. SP-OrrG

This lifeless construction. Doll Believers, The. Clarence Major. SP-MajoC

This light is loss backward; delight by hurt and by bias gained. March Twilight. Louise Bogan. CP-BogaL

This light is the cold light of Brittany. The field holds. Yellow Christ, The; after Gaugin. John Logan. CP-LogaJ

This light, this fire that devours. Wounds of Love. Federico García Lorca. CP-GarcF, *tr. by* Angela Jaffray

This Lime-Tree Bower My Prison. Samuel Taylor Coleridge. CP-ColeS; MW-ColeS

This little bag I hope will prove. Jane Austen. CP-AustJ

This little bride & groom are. E. E. Cummings. CP-CummE; SP-CummE

This little house is sugar. Winter Sweetness. Langston Hughes. CP-HughL

This little house / No smaller than the world. Kathleen Jessie Raine. SP-RainK

This little huge / -eyed per-. E. E. Cummings. CP-CummE

This little lightweight manacle whereby. Omega. John Updike. CP-UpdiJ

This little / pair had a little scare. E. E. Cummings. CP-CummE

This little silent one. Silent One. Langston Hughes. CP-HughL; CP-HughL3

This little vault, this narrow room. Epitaph on the Lady Mary Villiers, An. Thomas Carew. CP-CareT

This Living Hand, Now Warm and Capable. John Keats. CP-KeatJ

This lonely following in the old town. Lines for a Young Wanderer in Mexico. John Logan. CP-LogaJ

This longing to be healed in you. Longing. David Ignatow. SP-IgnaD

This, Lord, was an anxious brother and. Funeral Oration for a Mouse. Alan Dugan. CP-DugaA

This loud morning / sensed a small cry in. Third World Calling. Lawrence Ferlinghetti. SP-FerlL

This love of nature, that allures to take. George Meredith. CP-MerG2

This love of ours, you of my heart, is no light thing. Reverie. Sophocles. CP-CummE *Fr.* Electra.

This Loved One. W. H. Auden. CP-AudeW

This lovely flower fell to seed. For My Grandmother. Countee Cullen. CP-CullC *Fr.* Four Epitaphs.

This loving attention to the details. At a Private Showing in 1982. Maxine W. Kumin. SP-KumiM

This Lunar Beauty. W. H. Auden. CP-AudeW

This maid is from Hantan. Han-shan. CP-ColdM, *tr. by* Red Pine

This makes of you your statue. Cyril Connolly. Stephen Spender. CP-SpenS

This man brings me stones. Debate, The. David Ignatow. SP-IgnaD

This man escaped the dirty fates. Flyer's Fall. Wallace Stevens. CP-StevW; CP-StevWP

This man is o so. Item. E. E. Cummings. CP-CummE

This man is occupied by a problem. Stubborn Man. Rainer Maria Rilke. CP-RilkFr, *tr. by* A. Poulin, Jr.

This man Jones was what you'd call. James Whitcomb Riley. CP-RileJ

This man knew out the secret ways of love. Of Jacopo del Sellaio. Ezra Pound. CP-PoEar; SP-PounE

This man makes a pseudonym. Fearful, The. Sylvia Plath. CP-PlatS

This man, this poet, said. Spark of Laurel, A. Stanley Kunitz. CP-KunSC

This man was generous not because he wanted to see himself as generous. Convergence of the Many. René Char. CP-MertT

This Man Was Your Brother. Kenneth Patchen. CP-PatcK

This man's heart / is true to his. E. E. Cummings. CP-CummE

This Man's Weakness Is Straw. Charles Olson. CP-OlsoC

This Me—that walks and works—must die. Emily Dickinson. CP-DickE

This meal-white snow. Snow. Walter De la Mare. CP-DeLaW

This melodious / prison: crowds. Eastern European Eclogues. Rita Dove. SP-DoveR

This Merit hath the worst. Emily Dickinson. CP-DickE

This metal has come to look at. .38. William Stafford. SP-StafWW

This might be nature—twenty stories high. New York 1962: Fragment. Robert Lowell. SP-LoweR

This mighty empire hath but feet of clay. Theoretikos. Oscar Wilde. CP-WildO

This milky sky of a dragging afternoon. Hokusai on the Trent. Charles Tomlinson. CP-TomlC

This mind made war. E. E. Cummings. CP-CummE; SP-CummE

This mirror inside me shows. Shape of My Tongue, The. Jelaluddin Rumi. SP-Rumi, *tr. by* Coleman Barks

This modest Stone, what few vain Marbles can. Epitaph on Mr. Elijah Fenton, at Easthamstead in Berks, 1730. Alexander Pope. CP-PopeA

This Mohammedan colonel from the Caucasus yells with his voice and. Mohammed Bek Hadjetlache. Carl Sandburg. CP-SandC

This moment this love comes to rest in me. Jelaluddin Rumi. SP-Rumi, *tr.* by Coleman Barks

This moment when the sun is ebbing slowly. Death Is the Serpent. Marya Alexandrovna Zaturenska. SP-ZatuM

This Moment Yearning and Thoughtful. Walt Whitman. CP-WhitW

This month you carried me late and heavy. Crescent Moon like a Canoe. Marge Piercy. SP-PierM

This monument is for the unknown. For the Unknown Enemy. William Stafford. SP-StafWW

This monumental sculpture a / compound of many parts has been. Afternoon Evening and Night in the Courtyard of the Museum of Modern Art. William Dickey. SP-DickW

This Morn, Jones Very. CP-VeryJ

This morn the god of wit and joke. First of April, The. Jonathan Swift. CP-SwifJ

This Morning. Muriel Rukeyser. CP-RukeM
  (Waking this Morning.) CP-RukeM

This Morning. May Swenson. SP-SwenM

This Morning After. William Corbett. SP-CorbW

This Morning Again It Was in the Dusty Pines. Mary Oliver. SP-OlivM

This morning Amanda. Amanda Dreams She Has Died and Gone to the Elysian Fields. Maxine W. Kumin. SP-KumiM

This morning, between two branches of a tree. Dependencies, The. Howard Nemerov. CP-NemeH

This morning blue vast clarity of March sky. Birth of Rainbow. Ted Hughes. SP-HughTN

This morning, flew up the lane. John Crowe Ransom. *See* This morning, there flew up the lane

This morning from a dewy motorway. Seamus Heaney. SP-HeanSO *Fr.* Whatever You Say Say Nothing.

This morning he was almost sick. Slight Ailment. Yannis Ritsos. SP-RitsY, *tr.* by Minas Savvas

This Morning Here. Alan Dugan. CP-DugaA

This morning Hitler spoke in Danzig, we heard his voice. Day is a Poem, The. Robinson Jeffers. CP-JefR3

This morning holds intact the skeletal. Fifth Month, The. Gregory Orr. SP-OrrG

This morning I began a poem on Hamid Ramouz. Hamid Ramouz (1818–1906). Raymond Carver. CP-CarvR

This morning I remembered the young man. Reading Something in the Restaurant. Raymond Carver. CP-CarvR

This morning I 'woke from a quiet repose. Verses to Rhyme with 'Rose'. Elizabeth Austen. CP-AustJ

This morning I woke up to rain. Company. Raymond Carver. CP-CarvR

This morning I'm torn. Debate, The. Raymond Carver. CP-CarvR

This morning in installment property. John Ciardi. CP-CiarJ

This morning is the morning when Mrs. Murphy's treasure chest opens. Excursion: Or: O Columbus!, The. Thomas McGrath. SP-McGrT

This morning my first roadrunner. Reading Your Poems in Your House While You Are Away. Carolyn Kizer. CP-KizeC

This morning reluctance—you gaze on the street below. Uncertain Obligations. Yannis Ritsos. SP-RitsY, *tr.* by Kimon Friar *and* Kostas Myrsiades

This morning the green fists of the peonies are getting ready. Peonies. Mary Oliver. SP-OlivM

This morning / the hawk / rose up. Hawk. Mary Oliver. SP-OlivM

This morning / the hills rolled over. Reading the Newspaper at the Village Store. Grace Paley. CP-PalGC

This morning the wind came, shaking the quince tree. Languedocienne. Marilyn Hacker. SP-HackM

This morning, there flew up the lane. Lady Lost. John Crowe Ransom. SP-RansJ

This morning there was one McGrath in Aitken County. Afternoon of a McGrath. Thomas McGrath. SP-McGrT

This morning tigress Snookums creeps on the porch. May Morning Admonition. Robert Stock. SP-StocR

This morning, timely rapt [*or* wrapt] with holy fire. On Lucy, Countess[e] of Bedford. Ben Jonson. CP-JonsB; SP-JonsB

This morning view / is very plain: thou art. Our Father. James Schuyler. CP-SchuJ

This morning, waking. Campanula. Kathleen Jessie Raine. SP-RainK

This morning was something. A little snow. Raymond Carver. CP-CarvR

This morning we shall spend a few minutes. Money. Howard Nemerov. CP-NemeH

This Mortal Body of a Thousand Days. John Keats. CP-KeatJ

This Mortal Shall put on Immortality. Jones Very. CP-VeryJ

This mossy [*or* mossie] bank they pressed [*or* press'd *or* prest]. Pastoral[l] Dialogue, A. Thomas Carew. CP-CareT

This motion was of love begot. Ben Jonson. CP-JonsB *Fr.* Love Restored.

This movie deals with the epidemic of the way we live now. This Configuration. John Ashbery. SP-AshbJ

This Moving Meaninglessness. John Ciardi. CP-CiarJ

This much I know. Just as I'm about to make that right turn. Hay. Paul Muldoon. CP-MuldP

This much is clear to me now—even then. Our First House in Sacramento. Raymond Carver. CP-CarvR

This much is known. Investigation. Gregory Orr. SP-OrrG

This must be a bad dream. We will wake up. On Leaving Town. Alan Dugan. CP-DugaA

This near-at-hand land breeds pain by measure. Christina Georgina Rossetti. CP-RosC2

This night has been so strange that it seemed. Presences. William Butler Yeats. CP-YeatW

This night presents a play, which publick rage. Prologue to Hugh Kelly's *A Word to the Wise*. Samuel Johnson. CP-JohnS

This night shall thy soul be required of thee. Scorpion. Stevie Smith. CP-SmitS

This nightmare, wearing nothing but a crown. Fantastic Engraving, A. Charles Baudelaire. CP-BaudC, *tr.* by Walter Martin

This night's colossal quiet, in heaven crowned. Flumen Tenebrarum. Richard Wilbur. CP-WilbR

This, no song of an ingénue. Ballade at Thirty-Five. Dorothy Parker. CP-ParkD

This noble soul, starting to move away. Petrarch. CP-Petra, *tr.* by J. G. Nichols

This Notebook. James Schuyler. CP-SchuJ

This now, this other story makes amends. Jochanan Hakkadosh. Robert Browning. CP-BroR2

This nutmeg stick of a boy in loose trousers! Notes from a Tunisian Journal. Rita Dove. SP-DoveR

This nycht betoir the dawing cleir. How [*or* Followis How] Dumbar wes Desyrd to be ane Freir. William Dunbar. CP-DunbW

This nycht in my sleip I wes agast. William Dunbar. CP-DunbW

This October. Halfway. A. R. Ammons. CP-AmmoA

This Octopus Exploits Women. James Fenton. SP-FentJ

This official bicentennial arts person programming. Bicentennial. John Ciardi. CP-CiarJ

This old man had lavender skin, a handkerchief. River Poem. James Merrill. SP-MerrJ

This old man is sly and wise. Homage to John Cowper Powys. Stevie Smith. CP-SmitS

This old monastery has seen. Charterhouse, The. "Rubén Dario." SP-DariR, *tr.* by Alberto Acereda

This old river town saw the. Chromo. Carl Sandburg. CP-SandC

This old woman who kept house for them. Tall Order, A. Raymond Carver. CP-CarvR

This one, / a common type. Song for Seven Parts of the Body. Maxine W. Kumin. SP-KumiM

This one is lovely still, and looks divine. Allegory. Charles Baudelaire. CP-BaudC, *tr.* by Walter Martin

This, one of our oldest tales. Falling Through the Ice. Wyatt Prunty. SP-PrunW

This one request I make to him that sits the clouds above. Love and Debt Alike Troublesome. Sir John Suckling. CP-SuckJ

This One Rhymes. James Laughlin. CP-LaugJ

This one teaches. My Comrades. Charles Bukowski. SP-BukC1

This one was no philanthropist. For the Grave of a Peace-Loving Man. Hans Magnus Enzensberger. SP-EnzeH, *tr.* by Hans Magnus Enzensberger *and* Michael Hamburger

This one we're in will have to. Dream Not of Other Worlds. James Laughlin. CP-LaugJ

This Only. Czeslaw Milosz. CP-MiloC; CP-MiloCN, *tr.* by Robert Hass

This out of within itself moo. E. E. Cummings. CP-CummE

This Pair. A. K. Ramanujan. CP-RamaA

This Pan is but an idle god, I guess. Pan. James Whitcomb Riley. CP-RileJ

This *papier-mâché*, which you see, my friends. Phasellus Ille. Ezra Pound. CP-PoEar

This passport your face (not you). When You Go Anywhere. William Stafford. SP-StafWW

This pen is where the writing flows in sight. Illustrative Lines. Robert Duncan. SP-DuncR

This person is so uncertain. Han-shan. CP-ColdM, *tr.* by Red Pine

This person would be an animal. What My House Would Be Like If It Were a Person. Denise Levertov. SP-LeveDL

This phoenix, so extravagantly plumed. Petrarch. CP-Petra, *tr.* by J. G. Nichols

This physical world has no two things alike. Awkward Comparison, An. Jelaluddin Rumi. SP-Rumi, *tr.* by Coleman Barks

This piece of food cannot be eaten. Jelaluddin Rumi. SP-Rumi, *tr.* by Coleman Barks

This pile was raised by Wolsey's impious hands. On the Burning of Whitehall in 1698. Jonathan Swift. CP-SwifJ

This Place in the Ways. Muriel Rukeyser. CP-RukeM

This place is a dream. Dream That Must Be Interpreted, The. Jelaluddin Rumi. SP-Rumi, *tr.* by Coleman Barks

This place is so much. Rain on South-East England. Donald Davie. CP-DaviDC

This place named you. Tomb Stone. James Dickey. CP-DickJ

This Place Rumord to Have Been Sodom. Robert Duncan. SP-DuncR

This place will not console us. Yehuda Amichai. SP-AmicYL, *tr. by* Benjamin Harshav *and* Barbara Harshav

This pleasant tale is like a little copse. Written on a Blank Space at the End of Chaucer's Tale of "The Floure and the Lefe" John Keats. CP-KeatJ

This plot of ground. Dedication for a Plot of Ground. William Carlos Williams. CP-WilW1

This Poem. Donald Hall. CP-HallD

This poem is about being middle class. Being Asked to Define Bourgeois Individuality. William Dickey. SP-DickW

This poem is an onion. Poem for the Governments, A. C. K. Williams. CP-WillC

This poem is concerned with language on a very plain level. Paradoxes and Oxymorons. John Ashbery. SP-AshbJ

This Poem Is for Bear. Gary Snyder. CP-SnydG *Fr.* Myths and Texts.

This Poem Is for Birds. Gary Snyder. CP-SnydG *Fr.* Myths and Texts.

This Poem Is for Deer. Gary Snyder. CP-SnydG *Fr.* Myths and Texts.

This poem is for my wife. Poem in Prose. Archibald MacLeish. CP-MacLA

This poem must be done to-day. Lapse, The. Paul Laurence Dunbar. CP-DunbP

This Poet. Charles Bukowski. SP-BukC1

This poetry is a picture or graph of a mind moving. Since You Ask Me. Philip Whalen. SP-WhalP

This pool in a pure frame. Reason and Nature. James Vincent Cunningham. CP-CunnJ

This porthole overlooks a sea. Bendix. John Updike. CP-UpdiJ

This posture and this manner suit. Grace. Laura Riding Jackson. CP-RidiL

This potion is love's portion. This herb. Robert Duncan. SP-DuncR *Fr.* Structure of Rime, The.

This poverty recognizes. Tenderloin. Thom Gunn. CP-GunnT

This Puzzles Me. Langston Hughes. CP-HughL; CP-HughL2

This quiet Dust was Gentlemen and Ladies. Cemetery, A. Emily Dickinson. CP-DickE

This quiet morning light. To Mark Anthony in Heaven. William Carlos Williams. CP-WilW1

This rain has stopped, and the moon has come out. Radio Waves. Raymond Carver. CP-CarvR

This rare and heavenly creature. Han-shan. CP-ColdM, *tr. by* Red Pine

This realm half sky half water. Longitude 170° West, Latitude 35° North. Gary Snyder. CP-SnydG

This red. Two Poems for Women. John Logan. CP-LogaJ

This resolve: with trouble's brow. Ageless Brow, An. Laura Riding Jackson. CP-RidiL

This reverend shadow cast that setting sun. Upon Bishop Andrewes's [*or* Andrewes His] Picture before His Sermons. Richard Crashaw. CP-CrasR

This rich Marble doth enter[r]. Epitaph on the Marchioness of Winchester, An. John Milton. CP-MiltJ

This Riddle rede or die. Riddle for Men, The. George Meredith. CP-MerG1

This road ends in a field of grain. Documentation. Michael Palmer. SP-PalmM

This road is a river, white. Adam in Winter. James Dickey. CP-DickJ

This rock and the dry birds. This as Including That. Wallace Stevens. CP-StevWP

This room for instance. Raymond Carver. CP-CarvR

This room, how well I know it. Afternoon Sun, The. Constantine P. Cavafy. CP-CavaC, *tr. by* Theoharis Constantine Theoharis

This room, / the circled wind. George Oppen. CP-OppGN

This rule of manners I will teach my guests. Good Manners at Meat. Robert Herrick. CP-HerrR

This Sabbath, as all others, finds. Non Sum Dignus. Josephine Jacobsen. CP-JacoJ

This saying good-by on the edge of the dark. Good-by and Keep Cold. Robert Frost. CP-FrosR

This scarcely uttered they advance, and straight. Virgil. CP-WorW2 *Fr.* Aeneid [*or* Eneados *or* Aeneis], The.

This sea, deep furrowed as the face of Time. Question, The. Dante Gabriel Rossetti. CW-RossD

This sea will never die, neither will it ever grow old. Middle of the World. D. H. Lawrence. CP-LawrD

This Section Is a Christmas Tree. Nicholas Vachel Lindsay. CP-LindV

This semi-permanent drunken coma is agreeable. On Hibernation in the Country. Alan Dugan. CP-DugaA

This severed / marble hand. Yannis Ritsos. SP-RitsY *Fr.* Paper Poems 2.

This shall be thy lullaby. Song to A.A. Emily Jane Brontë. CP-BronE

This shawl of hair and sighs. Behold the Woman. Thomas McGrath. SP-McGrT

This shining hour is an edifice. Ralph Waldo Emerson. CP-EmerR

This short-lived and this fragile happiness. Petrarch. CP-Petra, *tr. by* J. G. Nichols

This should be simple; if one's power were great. Edna St. Vincent Millay. CP-MillE

This side of the post. Parity. Olga Broumas. SP-BrouO

This Side of the Truth. Dylan Thomas. CP-ThomD

This silken wreath, which circles in mine arm. Upon a Ribbon [*or* Ribband]. Thomas Carew. CP-CareT

This silver anniversary much hair's gone from my head and I am the King of May. Return of Kral Majales. Allen Ginsberg. SP-GinsA

This singing / is a kind of dying. Fury of Guitars and Sopranos, The. Anne Sexton. SP-SextA *Fr.* Furies, The.

This single girl is two girls. Protean Maiden, The. Thomas Hardy. CP-HardT

This sky contemplated. Rainer Maria Rilke. CP-RilkFr, *tr. by* A. Poulin, Jr. *Fr.* Valaisian Quatrains, The.

This sky, for instance. Deschutes River. Raymond Carver. CP-CarvR

This slow Day moved along. Emily Dickinson. CP-DickE

This Soft October. James Schuyler. CP-SchuJ

This Solitude of Cataracts. Wallace Stevens. CP-StevW; CP-StevWP

This Song. Hayden Carruth. CP-CarHS

This song to the flower of Flaxmans joy. To Mrs Flaxman, 14 September 1800. William Blake. CP-BlakW

This soup is cold. Soup of Venus, The. James Tate. SP-TateJ

This South American up here on a Gugg. Interviewed by a Guggenheim Recipient. Charles Bukowski. SP-BukC2

This Space Available. Thomas Lux. SP-LuxT

This spark now set, retarded, yet forbears. Progress of the Spark, The. Rudyard Kipling. CP-KiplR *Fr.* Muse among the Motors, The.

This sparrow / who comes to sit at my window. Sparrow, The. William Carlos Williams. CP-WilW2

This spoonful of chocolate tapioca. Thinking of the Lost World. Randall Jarrell. CP-JarrR

This spring as it comes bursts up in bonfires green. Enkindled Spring, The. D. H. Lawrence. CP-LawrD

This spring the birds came back again too early. Returning Birds. Wisława Szymborska. SP-SzymW, *tr. by* Stanisław Barańczak *and* Clare Cavanagh

This statue, of excellent craftsmanship, of unusual stone. Niobe. Yannis Ritsos. SP-RitsY, *tr. by* Kimon Friar *and* Karelisa Hartigan

This statue of Liberty, busy man. Statue of Liberty, The. Thomas Hardy. CP-HardT

This Stone can tell the storie of my life. Upon the Lady Crew. Robert Herrick. CP-HerrR

This stone that is. For the Grave of Posterity. W. S. Merwin. SP-MerwW

This stone that rises before us. Epitaph for Isaac Albéniz. Federico García Lorca. CP-GarcF, *tr. by* Christopher Maurer

This strange thing happened to a painter once. Beatrice Signorini. Robert Browning. CP-BroR2; SP-BroR

This strange thing must have crept. Fork. Charles Simic. SP-SimiC; SP-SimiCE

This stranger in my blood, my skin. Tyrant of Syracuse. Archibald MacLeish. CP-MacLA

This Street Never Sleeps. Carl Sandburg. CP-SandC

This structure of ideas, these ghostly sequences. Bed of Old John Zeller, The. Wallace Stevens. CP-StevW; CP-StevWP

This Summer and Last. Thomas Hardy. CP-HardT

This Summer Day. Kenneth Patchen. CP-PatcK

This summer earth. Kenneth Patchen. CP-PatcK

This summer, under the constellation of the Lyre, we remain pensive. To Orpheus. Yannis Ritsos. SP-RitsY, *tr. by* Thanasis Maskaleris

This summer wind, with thee and me. A.G.A. to A.S. Emily Jane Brontë. CP-BronE

This sunlight shames November where he grieves. Autumn Idleness. Dante Gabriel Rossetti. CW-RossD *Fr.* House of Life, The.

This Sycamore, oft musical with bees. Inscription for a Fountain on a Heath. Samuel Taylor Coleridge. CP-ColeS; MW-ColeS

"This tabernacle" is a blissful trial. Emily Dickinson. SP-DickE

This that is tormented and very tired. Jelaluddin Rumi. SP-Rumi, *tr. by* Coleman Barks

This that lies heavy. This. Adam Zagajewski. SP-ZagaA, *tr. by* Renata Gorczynski

This, That, & the Other. Howard Nemerov. CP-NemeH

This that would greet—an hour ago. Emily Dickinson. CP-DickE

This the mortared stone. Prolegomenon to a Theodicy, A. Kenneth Rexroth. CP-RexrK

This Then—. Charles Bukowski. SP-BukC1

This, then, is the beast that has never actually been. Unicorn, The. Rainer Maria Rilke. CP-MuldP, *tr. by* Paul Muldoon

This, then, is the grave of my son. Nettles, The. Thomas Hardy. CP-HardT

This then is the point of my life. Point, A. Andrei Codrescu. SP-CodrA

This then shall be our April—this black heap. Winter Castle. Josephine Jacobsen. CP-JacoJ

This, then, the river he had to swim. Thomas at the Wheel. Rita Dove. SP-DoveR

This they know well: the Goddess yet abides. In Her Praise. Robert Graves. CP-GravR

This thing, that hath a code and not a core. Object, An. Ezra Pound. CP-PoEar;

SP-PounE

This thing that passes and remains. Air, The. Gabriela Mistral. SP-MistG, *tr. by* Maria Giachetti [*or* Jacketti]

This thing upon me is not death. Old Man, Dead in a Room. Charles Bukowski. SP-BukC2

This Time. Michael Palmer. SP-PalmM

This time has finished me. Retreat, The. Charles Bukowski. SP-BukC1

This time, I have left my body behind me, crying. Trying to Pray. James Wright. CP-WrigJ

This time of year a bumblebee's. Lonesome Valley. A. R. Ammons. CP-AmmoA

This time of year a twelvemonth past. A. E. Housman. CP-HousA

This Tokyo. Gary Snyder. CP-SnydG

This too I love. Flower, The. William Carlos Williams. CP-WilW2

This too is excessive, and that, and that. Nails, The. Yannis Ritsos. SP-RitsY, *tr. by* Kostas Myrsiades

This, too, is part of our still world. Vignette. Wallace Stevens. CP-StevWP

This Tower of Sun. James Vincent Cunningham. CP-CunnJ

This town has docks where channel boats come sidling. Arrivals, Departures. Philip Larkin. CP-LarkP

This town is haunted by some good deed. Aunt Mabel. William Stafford. SP-StafW; SP-StafWW

This tree had taken root in the far side of the garden. Tree, A. Yannis Ritsos. SP-RitsY, *tr. by* Kimon Friar

This tree has two million and seventy-five thousand leaves. Information. David Ignatow. SP-IgnaD

This tree, here fall'n, no common birth or death. On the Site of a Mulberry-Tree; Planted by Wm. Shakespeare, felled by the Rev. F. Gastrell. Dante Gabriel Rossetti. CW-RossD

This tree took root before Jerusalem. 10,000-Year-Old Tree Discovered Shades Two and Half Acres. Miller Williams. CP-WillM

This tress of hair my sweetheart sent to me. Tress of Hair, A. James Whitcomb Riley. CP-RileJ

This tributary verse receive, my fair. To a Young Lady on Her Birthday. Samuel Johnson. CP-JohnS

This tuft that thrives on saline nothingness. Air Plant, The. Hart Crane. CP-CranH

This twilight of two year[e]s, not past nor next. To the Countess of Bedford at New Year's Tide. John Donne. CP-DonnJ; MW-DonnJ

This ugly old crone. Age. Walter De la Mare. CP-DeLaW

This Uninhabited Island. Rudyard Kipling. CP-KiplR *Fr* Just-So Stories.

This urge, wrestle, resurrection of dry sticks. Cuttings. Theodore Roethke. CP-RoetT

This valley; as if a huge, dull, primordial axe. Grim Town in a Steep Valley. Thomas Lux. SP-LuxT

This vast inelegance may seem the blankest desolation. Wallace Stevens. CP-StevWP

This verse be thine, my friend, nor thou refuse. Epistle to Mr. Jervas, with Dryden's Translation of Fresnoy's *Art of Painting*. Alexander Pope. CP-PopeA

This votive pledge of fond esteem. Stanzas to a Lady, with the Poems of Camoëns. Lord Byron. CP-Byron

This wall interrupts the wind. Tossup. A. R. Ammons. CP-AmmoA

This warmish night of the thaw. In Memoriam. Hayden Carruth. CP-CarHS

This, Warren, is our trouble now. Brief Message. Allen Tate. CP-TateA

This was a Poet—It is That. Emily Dickinson. CP-DickE

This was childhood. Worms, The. Carolyn Kizer. CP-KizeC

This was her dream. Translation, A. Charles Olson. CP-OlsoC

This was in the White of the Year. Emily Dickinson. CP-DickE

This was mine, and I let it slip through my fingers. Some Old Tires. John Ashbery. SP-AshbJ

This was Mr Bleaney's room. He stayed. Mr Bleaney. Philip Larkin. CP-LarkP

This was my dream: I saw a Forest. Bad Dreams III. Robert Browning. CP-BroR2

This was not experience. Painted Cup, The. Michael Palmer. SP-PalmM

This was not love but love's true negative. Archibald MacLeish. CP-MacLA *Fr.* Happy Marriage, The.

This was the end and yet, another start. Merlin in the Cave: He Speculates without a Book. Thom Gunn. CP-GunnT

This was the first day that the leaves. Burning the Leaves. Howard Nemerov. CP-NemeH

This was the land's end: the last fingers, knuckled and rheumatic. Finisterre. Sylvia Plath. CP-PlatS

This was the summit of my views. Satire 2.6: "This was the summit of my views." Horace. SP-SmarC *Fr.* Satires.

This was the time of their heaviest migration. No Matter What, After All, and That Beautiful Word So. Hayden Carruth. CP-CarHS

This Was Told Me in Confidence. Ogden Nash. CP-NashO

This Was Your Place of Birth, This Daytime Palace. Philip Larkin. CP-LarkP

This was your very first wall, your crib against. Comes Winter, the Sea Hunting.

Norman Dubie. CP-DubiN

This water droplet, charity of the air. Man Seeking Experience Enquires His Way of a Drop of Water, The. Ted Hughes. SP-HughTN

This waverand warldis wretchidnes. William Dunbar. CP-DunbW

This wax-mannequin nude, the florist rose. Florist Rose, The. Robert Graves. CP-GravR

This way or that way, student, in the sprint. Student Dies in 100 Yard Dash. Howard Nemerov. CP-NemeH

This Way Out. Louis MacNeice. CP-MacNL

This Way Where November. Hart Crane. CP-CranH

This We Have Now. Jelaluddin Rumi. SP-Rumi, *tr. by* Coleman Barks

This week we / didn't meet. I. August Night. James Schuyler. CP-SchuJ

This West! this ocean! The bare. Seeing Her Leave. Donald Davie. CP-DaviDC

This wet morning a seasonal. To Record One Must be Unwary. Mona Van Duyn. SP-VanDM

This wet sack, wavering slackness. Macduff, Charles Tomlinson. CP-TomlC

This, which flickers at night. Little Testament. Eugenio Montale. CP-MontE, *tr. by* Jonathan Galassi

This which you call serenity or discipline, kindness or apathy. Reformation. Yannis Ritsos. SP-RitsY, *tr. by* Kimon Friar

This whitewashed house that stood waiting for the sailors lost at sea. Inexhaustible, The. Yannis Ritsos. SP-RitsY *Fr.* Wavering Scales, The.

This whole day have I followed in the rocks. Fergus and the Druid. William Butler Yeats. CP-YeatW

This wide, shallow bowl. Robert Creeley. SP-CreeR

This wild night, gathering the washing as if it were flowers. From the Roof. Denise Levertov. SP-LeveDP

This will be answered. Spanish Lie, The. Archibald MacLeish. CP-MacLA

This will happen now, and subsequently that. Intervention of the Gods, The. Constantine P. Cavafy. CP-CavaC, *tr. by* Theoharis Constantine Theoharis

This wind blows still in stone; blows. Greek Wind, The. Josephine Jacobsen. CP-JacoJ

This winter air is keen and cold. Le Jardin des Tuileries. Oscar Wilde. CP-WildO

This Winter Day. Maya Angelou. SP-AngeM

This winter's revolt of the unbellied trees. Tercets of the Triad. Allen Tate. CP-TateA

This, with a face. Item. William Carlos Williams. CP-WilW1

This woman cannot live more than one year. Where I? Robinson Jeffers. CP-JefR2

This woman! how shall I describe her. Chanson. William Carlos Williams. CP-WilW2

This woman is Black. Need: A Chorale for Black Woman Voices. Audre Lorde. SP-LordA

This woman mask that wears her to the bone. Contemporary Portrait. Archibald MacLeish. CP-MacLA

This woman with a dead face. Cold Front, A. William Carlos Williams. CP-WilW2

This woman, with the dear child-heart. This Dear Child-Hearted Woman That Is Dead. James Whitcomb Riley. CP-RileJ

This wood burns a dark. Dark Wood, Dark Water. Sylvia Plath. CP-PlatS

This Word Love. Raymond Carver. CP-CarvR

This World. Robert Creeley. SP-CreeR

This World. Czeslaw Milosz. CP-MiloCN, *tr. by* Robert Hass

This World Is Not Conclusion. Emily Dickinson. CP-DickE

This World is not Conclusion. This World Is Not Conclusion. Emily Dickinson. CP-DickE

This world is tedious. Ralph Waldo Emerson. CP-EmerR

This world knows them as blind people. Malebolge: Prince William Sound. Sam Hamill. SP-HamiS

This World Which Is Made of Our Love for Emptiness. Jelaluddin Rumi. SP-Rumi, *tr. by* Coleman Barks

This world's just mad enough to have been made. Creation Myth on a Moebius Band. Howard Nemerov. CP-NemeH

This wot all ye whom it concerns. Extempore Verses on Dining with Lord Daer. Robert Burns. CP-BurnR

This would be spring, if seasons could be found. Perhaps the Best Time. William Meredith. SP-MereW

This would not be the war we fought in. See, the foliage. Newsreel. Adrienne Rich. SP-RicA2 *Fr.* Shooting Script.

This wrecched worldes transmutacioun. Fortune. Geoffrey Chaucer. CP-ChauG

This yardful of the landlord's used cars. Autumn. Raymond Carver. CP-CarvR

This Year. Charles Olson. CP-OlsoC

This year again the bruise-colored oak. Seeing the Bones. Maxine W. Kumin. SP-KumiM

This year both our birthdays end in zero. Poem for Your Birthday. Carolyn Kizer. CP-KizeC

This year I traveled a long way. Jerusalem, 1967. Yehuda Amichai. SP-AmicY, *tr. by* Stephen Mitchell

This year I traveled far away. Jerusalem 1967. Yehuda Amichai. SP-AmicYL, *tr. by* Benjamin Harshav *and* Barbara Harshav

This Year is done. To Anna Eliza Austen. Fanny Knight. CP-AustJ

This year, maybe, do you think I can graduate? Deferred. Langston Hughes. CP-HughL; CP-HughL3

"This year she has changed greatly"—meaning you. Change. Robert Graves. CP-GravR

This year / that Valentine is / late. Louis Zukofsky. CP-ZukLS

This year the fourth without snow. Weather. Grace Paley. CP-PalGC

This yearning heart (Love! witness what I say). Love's Sanctuary. Samuel Taylor Coleridge. CP-ColeS

This year's grain being still unripe. Han-shan. CP-ColdM, *tr. by* Red Pine

This you have heard before. Through Bifocals. Donald Davie. CP-DaviDC

This, you were sure, whatever happened. Pair of Shoes, A. Theodore Weiss. SP-WeisT

This young dove I send you from the Turia. Sonnet in the Manner of Góngora in Which the Poet Sends His Beloved a Dove. Federico García Lorca. CP-GarcF, *tr. by* Angela Jaffray

This young question mark man. E. E. Cummings. CP-CummE

This youth too long has heard the break. Tale, A. Louise Bogan. CP-BogaL

This(a up green hugeness who and climbs). E. E. Cummings. CP-CummE

This(let's remember)day died again and. E. E. Cummings. CP-CummE

This(that / grey)white / (man)horse. E. E. Cummings. CP-CummE

Thistle. William Carlos Williams. CP-WilW1

Thistle, the nettle, the burdock, and belladonna, The. Czeslaw Milosz. CP-MiloCN, *tr. by* Robert Hass

Thistledown Night. Federico García Lorca. CP-GarcF, *tr. by* Jerome Rothenberg *Fr.* Summer Hours.

Thistles. Ted Hughes. SP-HughTN

Thither. Samuel Beckett. CP-BeckS

Thither as I look I see each result and glory retracing itself and nestling close, always obligated. Savantism. Walt Whitman. CP-WhitW

Tho' Artemisia talks, by fits. Artemisia. Alexander Pope. CP-PopeA

Tho blest with talents to attract and please! Poem on the Death of Richard Stockton, A. Elizabeth Graeme Fergusson. CP-StocA

Tho' gold and silk their charms unite. To Miss —: On Her Giving the Author a Gold and Silk Net-work Purse. Samuel Johnson. CP-JohnS

Tho' I get home how late—how late. Emily Dickinson. CP-DickE

Tho I steal sweet words from long ago. Quia Amore Langueo. Ezra Pound. CP-PoEar

Tho' I'm no Catholic. Catholic Bells, The. William Carlos Williams. CP-WilW1

Tho in a sort of summer the hard buds blossom. Technologies. George Oppen. CP-OppGN

Tho' my destiny be Fustian. Emily Dickinson. CP-DickE

Tho' [*or* Though] Grief and Fondness in my Breast rebel. London: A Poem. Samuel Johnson. CP-JohnS

Tho the body's heavy meat's sustained. Allen Ginsberg. SP-GinsA *Fr.* Reading Bai Juyi.

Tho' women's minds, like winter winds. Song: "Tho' women's minds, like winter winds." Robert Burns. CP-BurnR

Tho you have stop'd the muses tongue. Compos'd in a Dancing Room, December 69. Annis Boudinot Stockton. CP-StocA

Thomalin, why sytten we soe. March. Edmund Spenser. CP-Spens *Fr.* Shepheardes [*or* Shepeards *or* Shepherd's] Calender, The.

Thomas and Emma. Donald Davie. CP-DaviDC

Thomas at the Wheel. Rita Dove. SP-DoveR

Thomas Bewick. Thom Gunn. CP-GunnT

Thomas Chatterton. Dante Gabriel Rossetti. CW-RossD *Fr.* Five English Poets.

Thomas Earp. D. H. Lawrence. CP-LawrD

Thomas Hardy. Norman Dubie. CP-DubiN

Thomas Hardy. Walter De la Mare. CP-DeLaW

Thomas Hood. Edwin Arlington Robinson. CP-RobiE

Thomas Jefferson. Lorine Niedecker. CP-NiedL

Thomas Jefferson had red hair and a violin. Open Letter to the Poet Archibald MacLeish Who Has Forsaken His Massachusetts Farm to Make Propaganda for Freedom. Carl Sandburg. CP-SandC

Thomas Jefferson Inside. Lorine Niedecker. CP-NiedL

Thomas Love Peacock! Thomas Love Peacock! What Was in a Name. Carolyn Kizer. CP-KizeC

Thomas Mann. Wisława Szymborska. SP-SzymW, *tr. by* Stanislaw Barańczak *and* Clare Cavanagh

Thomas Mann. Wisława Szymborska. SP-SzymWM, *tr. by* Joanna Trzeciak

Thomas Merton and the Winter Marsh. Norman Dubie. CP-DubiN

Thomas Starr King. John Greenleaf Whittier. CP-WhitJ

Thomas the Pretender. James Whitcomb Riley. CP-RileJ

Thomas Tremble new-made me. Inscriptions for a Peal of Eight Bells. Thomas Hardy. CP-HardT

Thoreau, lank ghost, comes back to visit Concord. Walden 1950. Adrienne Rich. CP-RicAE

Thoreau loved the grayness of them, homespun. My Elusive Guest. Maxine W. Kumin. SP-KumiM

Thorkild's Song. Rudyard Kipling. CP-KiplR *Fr.* Puck of Pook's Hill.

Thorn, The. William Wordsworth. CP-WorW1; MW-WorW

Thorn, The. Langston Hughes. CP-HughL; CP-HughL3

Thorn, The. Walter De la Mare. CP-DeLaW

Thorn Forever in the Breast, A. Countee Cullen. CP-CullC

Thorn Merchant, The. Yusef Komunyakaa. CP-KomuY

Thorn Merchant's Daughter, The. Yusef Komunyakaa. CP-KomuY

Thorn Merchant's Mistress, The. Yusef Komunyakaa. CP-KomuY

Thorn Merchant's Right-Hand Man, The. Yusef Komunyakaa. CP-KomuY

Thorn Merchant's Son, The. Yusef Komunyakaa. CP-KomuY

Thorn Merchant's Wife, The. Yusef Komunyakaa. CP-KomuY

Thorns, The. Jones Very. CP-VeryJ

Thorsgill. Sir Walter Scott. SP-ScotW *Fr.* Rokeby.

Those antique virgins. Engravings of the Garden. Federico García Lorca. CP-GarcF, *tr. by* Jerome Rothenberg *Fr.* In the Garden of the Lunar Grapefruits.

Those beautiful days / when the city resembles a die, a fan, a bird song. Wet Picture. Jaroslav Seifert. SP-SeifJ, *tr. by* Ewald Osers

Those Blind from Birth. Robert Graves. CP-GravR

Those Born in the Years of Stagnation. Aleksandr Aleksandrovich Blok. SP-BlokA, *tr. by* Peter France *and* Jon Stallworthy

Those breathing Tokens of your kind regard. *sequel to* Gold and Silver Fishes in a Vase. William Wordsworth. CP-WorW2

Those Cambridge generations, Russell's, Keynes'. On Bertrand Russell's 'Portraits from Memory'. Donald Davie. CP-DaviDC

Those Cattle smaller than a Bee. Emily Dickinson. CP-DickE

Those clarities detached us, gave us form. Tourist and the Town, The. Adrienne Rich. CP-RicAE; SP-RicA2

Those Corridors. Czeslaw Milosz. CP-MiloC; CP-MiloCN, *tr. by* Robert Pinsky

Those Dancing Days Are Gone. William Butler Yeats. CP-YeatW

Those Days. Raymond Carver. CP-CarvR

Those days, having the morning clouds, and with no one. Peleg Lookout. William Stafford. SP-StafWW

Those days separate slowly. In Those Days, in This Time. Yehuda Amichai. SP-AmicYL, *tr. by* Benjamin Harshav *and* Barbara Harshav

Those days when I had money. Han-shan. CP-ColdM, *tr. by* Red Pine

Those days when Jesse B. Langston Hughes. Yusef Komunyakaa. CP-KomuY

Those dreams that on the silent night intrude. On Dreams. Jonathan Swift. CP-SwifJ

Those—dying then. Emily Dickinson. CP-DickE

Those empty (blind) trains. My Girl. James Tate. SP-TateJ

Those ends in War the best contentment bring. Pardons. Robert Herrick. CP-HerrR

Those envied places which do know her well. Day of Love, A. Dante Gabriel Rossetti. CW-RossD *Fr.* House of Life, The.

Those eyes appear to transmit energy. Looks. Thom Gunn. CP-GunnT

Those eyes of mine in nineteen-ten. 1910. Federico García Lorca. CP-GarcF, *tr. by* Greg Simon *and* Steven F. White

Those eyes of which so warmly I would speak. Petrarch. CP-Petra, *tr. by* J. G. Nichols

Those eyes that wounded me in such a way. Petrarch. CP-Petra, *tr. by* J. G. Nichols

Those fair—fictitious People. Emily Dickinson. CP-DickE

Those famous men of old, the Ogres. Ogres and Pygmies. Robert Graves. CP-GravR

Those fantastic forms, fang-sharp. City without Walls. W. H. Auden. CP-AudeW

Those final Creatures—who they are. Emily Dickinson. CP-DickE

Those five or six young guys. Blues. Derek Walcott. CP-WalcD

Those flaxen locks, those eyes of blue. To My Son. Lord Byron. CP-Byron

Those foolish moments of first love! Mistress of Poets, The. Jaroslav Seifert. SP-SeifJ, *tr. by* Ewald Osers

Those Garments lasting evermore. Cloaths for Continuance. Robert Herrick. CP-HerrR

Those great rough ranters, Branns. Simplification, A. Richard Wilbur. CP-WilbR

Those great sweeps of snow that stop suddenly six feet from the house. Snowbanks North of the House. Robert Bly. SP-BlyR

Those groans men use. Mutes, The. Denise Levertov. SP-LeveDP; SP-LeveDS

Those grooves in that forehead of sand-coloured flesh. Derek Walcott. CP-WalcD *Fr.* Midsummer.

Those hours when happy hours were my estate. Edna St. Vincent Millay. CP-MillE

Those ills that mortall men endure. Liberty. Robert Herrick. CP-HerrR

Those Images. William Butler Yeats. CP-YeatW

Those laden lilacs / at the lawn's end. Lilacs, The. Richard Wilbur. CP-WilbR

Those lights in the sky at night are not. To a Kid Who Believes in Astrology. Alan Dugan. CP-DugaA

Those lights, that plaza—I should know them all. In Time of Carnival. Adrienne

Rich. CP-RicAE

Those lines on your palm, they can be read. Turn Over Your Hand. William Stafford. SP-StafW; SP-StafWW

Those long uneven lines. MCMXIV. Philip Larkin. CP-LarkP

Those midland *a*'s. Class. Charles Tomlinson. CP-TomlC

Those not live yet. Emily Dickinson. CP-DickE

Those of you who auscultated the heart of the night. Nocturne: "Those of you who auscultated the heart of the night." "Rubén Dario." SP-DariR, *tr.* by Alberto Acereda *and* Will Derusha

Those old wooden logs. New Aqueduct, The. Jones Very. CP-VeryJ

Those picnics covered with sand. North Coast, The. Gary Snyder. CP-SnydG

"Those Platonists are a curse," he said. Statistics. William Butler Yeats. CP-YeatW

Those poor, arthritically swollen knees. With Her. Czeslaw Milosz. CP-MiloC; CP-MiloCN, *tr.* by Robert Hass

Those possesions short-liv'd are. Possesions. Robert Herrick. CP-HerrR

Those profiles, austere in the mine of the craters. Island (XII), The. Pablo Neruda. SP-NeruP *Fr.* Separate Rose, The.

Those random sparks from telegraph poles, horse. Game, A. Andrei Codrescu. SP-CodrA

Those rivers run from that land. Song: "Those rivers run from that land." Robert Creeley. CP-CreeR

Those Saints, which God loves best. Temptations. Robert Herrick. CP-HerrR

Those several times she cleaved my dark. Passage to Worship. Donald Hall. CP-HallD

Those silver clouds collected round the sun. Haunted Tree, To———, The. William Wordsworth. CP-WorW2

Those stars are the fleshed forebears. Fire-Eater. Ted Hughes. SP-HughTN

Those sufferings are over. Life Sentence. Adam Zagajewski. SP-ZagaA

Those sumptuous, lacquered oils, a renaissance. My Mother's Portrait. Eleanor Wilner. SP-WilnE

Those Tapers, which we set upon the grave. Tapers. Robert Herrick. CP-HerrR

Those that by bloody force. Treason Crime, The. Archibald MacLeish. CP-MacLA

Those that can give, open their hands this day. New Year's Sacrifice: To Lucinda, A. Thomas Carew. CP-CareT

Those that die seem near me. Emily Dickinson. SP-DickE

Those that go searching for love. Search for Love. D. H. Lawrence. CP-LawrD

Those that in blood such violent pleasure have. Ben Jonson. CP-JonsB

Those that leave us, possibly linger for awhile. Departures 2. Yannis Ritsos. SP-RitsY, *tr.* by N. C. Germanacos

Those things he pictured timidly while a schoolboy. Passing Through. Constantine P. Cavafy. CP-CavaC, *tr.* by Theoharis Constantine Theoharis

Those Times. Anne Sexton. CP-SextA

Those Two. Allen Ginsberg. SP-GinsA

Those two dark syllables, *begin*, / offer no sustenance. Miles Davis and Elizabeth Bishop Fake the Break. Charles Wright. SP-WrigCN

Those Upon Whom God Has Labored. Kenneth Patchen. CP-PatcK

Those Various Scalpels. Marianne Craig Moore. CP-MoorM

Those / various sounds consistently indistinct. Those Various Scalpels. Marianne Craig Moore. CP-MoorM

Those villages stricken with the melancholia of Sunday. Sabbaths, W.I. Derek Walcott. CP-WalcD

Those voices are sweetest which have forever. Sweet Voices. Constantine P. Cavafy. CP-CavaC, *tr.* by Theoharis Constantine Theoharis

Those waiting in line. Line. W. S. Merwin. SP-MerwWF

Those were not, it is certain, crimes just like ours. King Popiel. Czeslaw Milosz. CP-MiloC; CP-MiloCN

Those were the long afternoons when poetry left me. Long Afternoons. Adam Zagajewski. SP-ZagaA, *tr.* by Clare Cavanagh

Those white flecks cropping the ridges of Snowdon. Wales. Derek Walcott. CP-WalcD

Those Who Came Short. Robert Graves. CP-GravR

Those who cannot love the heavens or the earth. Chaff, The. W. S. Merwin. SP-MerwW

Those Who Come After. Eleanor Wilner. SP-WilnE

Those who come back from a number. Number, A. W. S. Merwin. SP-MerwW

Those who dare give nothing. On Giving. Robert Graves. CP-GravR

Those Who Do Not Dance. Gabriela Mistral. SP-MistG, *tr.* by Maria Giachetti [*or* Jacketti]

Those who don't like it say it's. Cello. Adam Zagajewski. SP-ZagaA, *tr.* by Clare Cavanagh

Those Who Fought for the Achaian Alliance. Constantine P. Cavafy. CP-CavaC, *tr.* by Theoharis Constantine Theoharis

Those who have been in the Grave the longest. Emily Dickinson. CP-DickE

Those who have lived here since before. False Portrait of D.B. as Niccolò Paganini. Michael Palmer. SP-PalmM

Those who have stayed so long. Old Couples. Hans Magnus Enzensberger. SP-EnzeH

Those who hold themselves above suicide. Their Heads Bent Toward Each Other Like Flowers. Tess Gallagher. SP-GallT

Those Who Ignore the Appropriate Time of Their Going. Tennessee Williams. CP-WillT

Those who leave home leave to be free. Shih-te. CP-ColdM, *tr.* by Red Pine

Those who leave home nowadays. Shih-te. CP-ColdM, *tr.* by Red Pine

Those who met by chance in the street, strangers, did not speak. Doubtful Encounters. Yannis Ritsos. SP-RitsY, *tr.* by Kostas Myrsiades

Those who rose up against arms so long ago rise up again. Conscientious Objection. Sam Hamill. SP-HamiS

Those who said God is praised. For the New Railway Station in Rome. Richard Wilbur. CP-WilbR

Those who say: 'For Chrissake', others who say: 'Get lost'. Customs Men, The. Arthur Rimbaud. CP-RimbA, *tr.* by Martin Sorrell

Those who say they knew you. Malcolm. Alice Walker. CP-WalkA

Those who straddle foaming sea-horses and ride into the sunrise. Moments of Dawn Riders. Carl Sandburg. CP-SandC

Those Who Wait. Federico García Lorca. CP-GarcF, *tr.* by Jerome Rothenberg *Fr.* Suite.

Those who went ahead. Paths and Thingscape. Margaret Atwood. SP-AtwM1

Those whom nor power, nor lying faith, nor toil. Fragments Supposed to Be Parts of Otho. Percy Bysshe Shelley. CP-ShelP

Those Winter Sundays. Robert Earl Hayden. CP-HaydR

Those [*or* Those] words were uttered as In [*or* in a] pensive mood. William Wordsworth. CP-WorW1; MW-WorW

Those Years. Yannis Ritsos. SP-RitsY, *tr.* by Kostas Myrsiades

Thou aged unreluctant earth who dost. Epithalamion: "Thou aged unreluctant earth who dost." E. E. Cummings. CP-CummE

Thou angel face!—like a small exquisite cage. Cage, The. Walter De la Mare. CP-DeLaW

Thou are not yet at home; perhaps thy feet. Thy Father's House. Jones Very. CP-VeryJ

Thou arguest wisely, with profoundest skill. Untimely Arguments. Jones Very. CP-VeryJ

Thou arrant robber, Death! On the Death of W. C. Paul Laurence Dunbar. CP-DunbP

"Thou art a fool," said my head to my heart. Retort. Paul Laurence Dunbar. CP-DunbP

Thou art a plant sprung up to wither never. To His Booke. Robert Herrick. CP-HerrR

Thou art come at length. Sitalkas. "H. D." CP-DoolH

Thou art fair, and few are fairer. To Sophia [Miss Stacey]. Percy Bysshe Shelley. CP-ShelP

Thou Art Fairer Than the Children of Men. Christina Georgina Rossetti. CP-RosC2

Thou Art Indeed Just, Lord. Gerard Manley Hopkins. CP-HopkG (Justus Quidem Tu Es, Domine.) CP-HopkG

Thou Art Like a Flower. Carl Sandburg. CP-SandC

Thou art more deadly than the Jew of old. Jew, The. Jones Very. CP-VeryJ

Thou art my Father Thou dost give me birth. Plant, The. Jones Very. CP-VeryJ

Thou art my God, sole object of my love. Translation of a Hymn of St. Francis Xavier. Saint Francis Xavier. CP-PopeA

Thou art my love. Intrigue. Stephen Crane. CP-CranS

Thou Art My Lute. Paul Laurence Dunbar. CP-DunbP

Thou Art Near at Hand, O Lord. Donald Davie. CP-DaviDC

Thou art not, as the Hindoos say. Nature Intelligible. Jones Very. CP-VeryJ

Thou Art Not Fair[e]. Thomas Campion. CP-CampT

Thou Art Not False, But Thou Art Fickle. Lord Byron. CP-Byron

Thou art not fayer for all thy red and white. Beautie Without Love Deformitie. Thomas Campion. CP-CampT

Thou art not lovelier than lilacs,—no. Edna St. Vincent Millay. CP-MillE

Thou art not, Penshurst, built to envious show. To Penshurst. Ben Jonson. CP-JonsB; SP-JonsB

Thou art not so black, as my heart. Jet Ring Sent, A. John Donne. CP-DonnJ; MW-DonnJ

Thou art not yet at home in thine own house. Absent, The. Jones Very. CP-VeryJ

Thou art sad, Castiglione. Scenes from Politian. Edgar Allan Poe. CP-PoeEd

Thou art silent: nailed high in the darkness. Silence. G. K. Chesterton. CP-ChesG

Thou art the First and Last, the End of all. Beginning and the End, The. Jones Very. CP-VeryJ

Thou art the soul of a summer's day. Song, A: "Thou art the soul of a summer's day." Paul Laurence Dunbar. CP-DunbP

Thou art; there is no stay but in Thy love. Rock, The. Jones Very. CP-VeryJ

Thou art to all lost love the best. To the Willow-Tree. Robert Herrick. CP-HerrR

Thou art too hard for me in Love. Love. George Herbert. CP-HerbG

Thou bay-crowned living one that oe'r the. Felicia Hemans. Elizabeth Barrett Browning. CP-BroEB

Thou bidd'st me mark how swells with rage. Arthur Hugh Clough. SP-ClouA

Thou bidst me change with every changing hour. Branch, The. Jones Very. CP-VeryJ

Thou bid'st me come away. To Death. Robert Herrick. CP-HerrR

Thou bid'st me come; I cannot come; for why. Another. Robert Herrick. CP-HerrR

Thou Blind Man's Mark. Sir Philip Sidney. SP-SidnP

Thou blind man's mark, thou fool's self-chosen snare. Thou Blind Man's Mark. Sir Philip Sidney. SP-SidnP

Thou brave, good woman! Loved of every one. Rosamond C. Bailey. James Whitcomb Riley. CP-RileJ

Thou call'st me effeminate, for I love women's joys. Manliness. John Donne. CP-DonnJ

Thou call'st me, little child. And a little child shall lead them. Isaiah 11.6. Jones Very. CP-VeryJ

Thou call'st me poet, as a term of shame. To My Lord Ignorant. Ben Jonson. CP-JonsB; SP-JonsB

Thou cam'st to cure me (Doctor) of my cold. Upon a Physitian. Robert Herrick. CP-HerrR

Thou canst not see him standing by. Foreboding. Walter De la Mare. CP-DeLaW

Thou Canst Read Nothing. Hart Crane. CP-CranH

Thou cheat'st us Ford, mak'st one seem[e] two by art. Upon Ford's Two Tragedies, "Loves Sacrifice" and "The Broken Heart" Richard Crashaw. CP-CrasR

Thou chid'st the wind, and snow, and sleet, and ice. Impatience. Jones Very. CP-VeryJ

Thou comest again, in bright scarlet drest. Return of the Columbine, The. Jones Very. CP-VeryJ

Thou dost exalt the humble; they shall be. Humble, The. Jones Very. CP-VeryJ

Thou dost make the pathway easy. Hymn: The Way of the Righteous Easy. Jones Very. CP-VeryJ

Thou dost prefer the song that rises pure. Sacrifice. Jones Very. CP-VeryJ

Thou dread, uncanny thing. Bat, The. James Whitcomb Riley. CP-RileJ

Thou drifting meadow of the air. Fog. Henry David Thoreau. CP-ThorH

Thou drowsy god, whose blurred eyes, half awink. Sleep. James Whitcomb Riley. CP-RileJ

Thou dusky spirit of the wood. Henry David Thoreau. CP-ThorH

Thou dwellest not, O Lord of all! Hymn for the House of Worship at Georgetown. John Greenleaf Whittier. CP-WhitJ

Thou fair-hair'd [or fair-haired] angel of the evening. To the Evening Star. William Blake. CP-BlakW

Thou fair yet lifeless leaf! on whom decay. Autumn Leaf, The. Jones Very. CP-VeryJ

Thou famished grave, I will not fill thee yet. Edna St. Vincent Millay. CP-MillE

Thou ferse god of armes, Mars the rede. Anelida and Arcite. Geoffrey Chaucer. CP-ChauG

Thou fill'st from the winged chalice of the soul. Mnemosyne. Dante Gabriel Rossetti. CW-RossD

Thou / firsting a hugeness of twi / -light. E. E. Cummings. CP-CummE

Thou flattering mark of friendship kind. To Mrs. C———. Robert Burns. CP-BurnR

Thou fool, in thy Phaeton towering. To the Honble Mr. R. M———, of P-nm-re, on His High Phaeton. Robert Burns. CP-BurnR

Thou foolish Hafiz! Say, do churls. Friendship. Hafiz. CP-EmerR

Thou for Christ hast waited long. Hymn: Waiting for Christ. Jones Very. CP-VeryJ

Thou, friend, wilt hear all censures; unto thee. Epigram to My Bookseller. Ben Jonson. CP-JonsB

Thou gav'st me leave to kiss. Chop-Cherry. Robert Herrick. CP-HerrR

Thou gav'st me many a fragrant flower. Gift, The. Jones Very. CP-VeryJ

'Thou Ghost,' I said, 'and is thy name To-day?'. Morrow's Message, The. Dante Gabriel Rossetti. CW-RossD Fr. House of Life, The.

Thou gladst my heart but not with oil and wine. Comfort. Jones Very. CP-VeryJ

Thou, God, Seest Me. Christina Georgina Rossetti. CP-RosC2

Thou great commandress, that dost move. New Years Gift. To the Queen, A. Thomas Carew. CP-CareT

Thou great offended God of love and kindness. Baccalaureate Hymn. Edna St. Vincent Millay. CP-MillE

Thou great proclaimer to the outward eye. Rail Road, The. Jones Very. CP-VeryJ

Thou had'st the wreath before, now take the Tree. Another ["Thou had'st the wreath before, now take the Tree"]. Robert Herrick. CP-HerrR

Thou hard, I will be blunt: Like widening. Matins. John Berryman. CP-BerrJ

Thou hast a lap full of seed. William Blake. CP-BlakW

Thou hast a moon for every cloudy night. Joy ("Thou hast a moon for every cloudy night"). Jones Very. CP-VeryJ

Thou hast begun well, Roe, which stand well too. To Sir Thomas Roe. Ben Jonson. CP-JonsB; SP-JonsB

Thou hast fallen in thine armor. To the Memory of Charles B. Storrs. John Greenleaf Whittier. CP-WhitJ

Thou hast left me ever, Jamie. Robert Burns. CP-BurnR

Thou hast made many Houses for the Dead. Bed-Man, or Grave-Maker, The. Robert Herrick. CP-HerrR

Thou hast no faith of him that hath none. Sir Thomas Wyatt. CP-WyatT

Thou hast no lightnings, O thou Just! Divine Justice Amiable. Jeanne Marie Bouvier de la Motte- Guyon. CP-CowpW

Thou hast no other hands than those that toil. Unfaithful Servants, The. Jones Very. CP-VeryJ

Thou hast / not foreign aggression. Memorial Day. Lorine Niedecker. CP-NiedL

Thou hast not left the rough-barked tree to grow. I Was Sick and in Prison. Jones Very. CP-VeryJ

Thou hast promis'd, Lord, to be. To God. Robert Herrick. CP-HerrR

Thou hast redeem'd us, Will; and future times. To My Friend Will. Davenant, on His Other Poems. Sir John Suckling. CP-SuckJ

Thou hast the art on't *Peter*; and canst tell. On St. *Peter* Casting Away His Nets at Our Saviours Call. Richard Crashaw. CP-CrasR

Thou hearst the hungry ravens when they cry. They Who Hunger. Jones Very. CP-VeryJ

Thou ill-formed offspring of my feeble brain. Author to Her Book, The. Anne Bradstreet. CP-BradA

Thou in the fields walk'st out thy supping hours. Liar, The. John Donne. CP-DonnJ; MW-DonnJ

Thou in whose swordgreat story shine the deeds. E. E. Cummings. CP-CummE

Thou indeed, little Swallow. Ode to the Swallow. Elizabeth Barrett Browning. CP-BroEB

Thou issuest from a fissure in the rock. Fragments from the "Christabel" Note-book. William Wordsworth. CP-WorW1

Thou Joy'st, Fond Boy. Thomas Campion. CP-CampT

Thou Knewest . . . Thou Oughtest Therefore. Christina Georgina Rossetti. CP-RosC2

Thou knowest all:—I seek in vain. True Knowledge, The. Oscar Wilde. CP-WildO

Thou know'st, my Julia, that it is thy turn. To Julia, the Flaminica Dialis, or Queen-Priest. Robert Herrick. CP-HerrR

Thou know'st not e'er the way to turn or go. To All. Jones Very. CP-VeryJ

Thou know'st not what thy Lord will say. Jones Very. CP-VeryJ

Thou large-brained woman and large-hearted man. To George Sand: A Desire. Elizabeth Barrett Browning. CP-BroEB

Thou, Liberty, thou art my theme. Fragment—on Glenriddel's Fox Breaking His Chain, A. Robert Burns. CP-BurnR

Thou Ling'ring Star. Robert Burns. CP-BurnR

(Song, A.) CP-BurnR

Thou little bud of being, Edith named. To Edith. Henry David Thoreau. CP-ThorH

Thou little kid didst play. Kid, The. William Blake. CP-BlakW

Thou little naked statuette. Lines: "Thou little naked statuette." James Whitcomb Riley. CP-RileJ

Thou living light that in thy rainbow hues. Fragment: To the Mind of Man. Percy Bysshe Shelley. CP-ShelP

Thou lookest up with meek, confiding eye. Wind-Flower, The. Jones Very. CP-VeryJ

Thou lovely and beloved, thou my love. Mid-Rapture. Dante Gabriel Rossetti. CW-RossD Fr. House of Life, The.

Thou lovely Fishermaiden. My Heart. Heinrich Heine. CP-MerG2

Thou lowest scoundrel of the scoundrel kind. Thomas Sheridan. CP-SherT Fr. Upon a Certain Bookseller, or Printer, in Utopia.

Thou, lytil quair, of mater miserabyll. Epistill, The: "Thou, lytil quair, of mater miserabyll." Sir David Lyndsay. SP-LyndD Fr. Dialog betwix Experience and ane Courteour, Ane.

Thou magic lyre, whose fascinating sound. Ode on the Marriage of a Friend. William Cowper. CP-CowpW

Thou maist be proud and be thou so for me. To a Disdaynefull Fayre. Robert Herrick. CP-HerrR

Thou mak'st me poor that I enriched by Thee. Star, The. Jones Very. CP-VeryJ

Thou mastering me. Wreck of the Deutschland, The. Gerard Manley Hopkins. CP-HopkG

Thou mayst of double ignorance boast. On One Ignorant and Arrogant. William Cowper. CP-CowpW

Thou mighty God of sea and land. Upon My Son Samuel His Going For England. Anne Bradstreet. CP-BradA

Thou mighty Lord and master of the Lyre. To Apollo. Robert Herrick. CP-HerrR

Thou more than most sweet glove. Glove, The. Ben Jonson. CP-JonsB Fr. Cynthia's Revels.

Thou Mother with Thy Equal Brood. Walt Whitman. CP-WhitW

Thou needst not flutter from thy half-built nest. Robin, The. Jones Very. CP-VeryJ

Thou needst not rest, the shining spheres are thine. Labor and Rest. Jones Very. CP-VeryJ

Thou, of all God's gifts the best. Bed, The. James Whitcomb Riley. CP-RileJ

Thou, of an independent mind. Poetical Inscription, for an Altar to Independence at Kerrouchtry, the Seat of Mr. Heron, Written in Summer 1795. Robert

Burns. CP-BurnR

Thou Orb Aloft Full-Dazzling. Walt Whitman. CP-WhitW

Thou our beloved and light of Earth hast crossed. Epitaph on the Tombstone of James Christopher Wilson. George Meredith. CP-MerG2

Thou Pain, the only guest of loathed constraint. Sir Philip Sidney. SP-SidnP

Thou Past! What art thou? whither dost thou lead. Past, The. Jones Very. CP-VeryJ

Thou pirate nested over Alde! George Meredith. CP-MerG2

Thou Poet, who, like any lark. Shoemaker, The. James Whitcomb Riley. CP-RileJ

Thou Power! who hast ruled me through infancy's days. Farewell to the Muse. Lord Byron. CP-Byron

Thou prayst not, save when in thy soul thou prayst. Jacob's Well. Jones Very. CP-VeryJ

Thou Reader. Walt Whitman. CP-WhitW

Thou readest, but each lettered word can give. Eye and Ear, The. Jones Very. CP-VeryJ

Thou ring that shalt my fair girl's finger bind. Elegy 2.15: "Thou ring that shalt my fair girl's finger bind." Ovid. CP-MarlC Fr. Elegies.

Thou ripenest the fruits with warmer air. Fruit, The. Jones Very. CP-VeryJ

Thou, run to the dry on this wayside bank. Empty Purse, The. George Meredith. CP-MerG1

Thou, run to the dry on this wayside bank. Empty Purse: A Sermon to our Later Prodigal Son, The. George Meredith. CP-MerG1

Thou sail'st with others, in this Argus here. No Shipwrack of Vertue. To a Friend. Robert Herrick. CP-HerrR

Thou saist [or sayest] Love[']s dart. To Oenone. Robert Herrick. CP-HerrR

Thou saist thou lov'st me Sapho; I say no. To Sapho. Robert Herrick. CP-HerrR

Thou say'st I'm dull; if edge-lesse so I be. To Perenna. Robert Herrick. CP-HerrR

Thou say'st [or saist] my lines are hard. To My Ill Reader. Robert Herrick. CP-HerrR

Thou seest me, Lucia, this year droop[e]. Crutches. Robert Herrick. CP-HerrR

Thou sent'st to me a True-love-knot; but I. Jimmall Ring, or True-Love-Knot, The. Robert Herrick. CP-HerrR

Thou shalt do what Thou wilt with thine own hand. Clay, The. Jones Very. CP-VeryJ

Thou shalt have one God only; who. Latest Decalogue, The. Arthur Hugh Clough. SP-ClouA

Thou shalt make thy house. Ralph Waldo Emerson. CP-EmerR

Thou shalt not All die; for while Love's fire shines. Upon Himself. Robert Herrick. CP-HerrR

Thou Shalt Not Kill. G. K. Chesterton. CP-ChesG

Thou Shalt Not Kill. Kenneth Rexroth. CP-RexrK

Thou shalt not laugh in this leaf, Muse, nor they. Satire 5. John Donne. MW-DonnJ Fr. Satires.

Thou shalt not live e'en by the bread alone. Temptation, The. Jones Very. CP-VeryJ

Thou shalt not love mee, neither shall these eyes. Dolus. Thomas Campion. CP-CampT

Thou shalt say to the eye of the woman stranger: Be the water. In Egypt. Paul Celan. SP-CelaP, tr. by John Felstiner

Thou shalt the mountain move; be strong in me. Mountain, The. Jones Very. CP-VeryJ

Thou Shepherd that dost Israel keep. Bible, O.T. See Give ear, O Shepherd of Israel, thou that leadest Joseph like a flock

Thou sinful Soul, how wilt thou feel. Christmas Canticle. Edna St. Vincent Millay. CP-MillE

Thou singest alone on the bare wintery bough. Winter Bird, The. Jones Very. CP-VeryJ

Thou sleepest fast and I with woeful heart. Sir Thomas Wyatt. CP-WyatT

Thou sleepest where the lilies fade. Buried. Christina Georgina Rossetti. CP-RosC3

Thou small, yet ever-bubbling spring. Cold Spring in North Salem, The. Jones Very. CP-VeryJ

"Thou solitary!" the Blackbird cried. Riddlers, The. Walter De la Mare. CP-DeLaW

Thou spak'st the word (thy word's a Law). Mark 10; The Blind Cured by the Word of Our Saviour. Bible, N.T. CP-CrasR Fr. St. Mark.

Thou splendor of the Father's glory. Splendor Paternae Gloriae. Saint Ambrose. CP-MertT

Thou springest from the ground, and may not I. Tent, The. Jones Very. CP-VeryJ

Thou standest in the greenwood now. To A.G.A. Emily Jane Brontë. CP-BronE

Thou steppest from thy splendour. Song: "Thou steppest from thy splendour." George Meredith. CP-MerG2

Thou still unravished [or unravish'd] bride of quietness. Ode on a Grecian Urn. John Keats. CP-KeatJ

Thou, strange maiden, I can see nought but the glistening. Witch II, The. D. H. Lawrence. CP-LawrD

Thou supreme Goddess! by whose power divine. Oedipus Tyrannus; or, Swellfoot the Tyrant. Percy Bysshe Shelley. CP-ShelP

Thou tellest truths unspoken yet by man. Violet, The. Jones Very. CP-VeryJ

Thou that hast given me back. Alma Sol Veneziae. Ezra Pound. CP-PoEar

Thou that hast giv'n so much to me. Gratefulness. George Herbert. CP-HerbG

Thou, that maks't gain thy end, and wisely well. To My Bookseller. Ben Jonson. CP-JonsB; SP-JonsB

Thou that on sin's wages starvest. Barnfloor and Winepress. Gerard Manley Hopkins. CP-HopkG

Thou, that wouldst find the habit of true passion. In Authorem. Ben Jonson. CP-JonsB

Thou think'st I flatter, when thy praise I tell. Non Est Mortale Quod Opto. Sir John Suckling. CP-SuckJ

Thou, thou that bear'st the sway. Hymne to Cupid, An. Robert Herrick. CP-HerrR

Thou to me art such a spring. Song: "Thou to me art such a spring." George Meredith. CP-McrG1

Thou tremblest O my love! thy hand in mine. Song: "Thou tremblest O my love! thy hand in mine." George Meredith. CP-MerG2

Thou trim'st a Prophets Tombe, and dost bequeath. Matthew 23; Yee Build the Sepulchres of the Prophets. Bible, N.T. CP-CrasR Fr. St. Matthew.

Thou unconverted saint. Morning. Henry David Thoreau. CP-ThorH

Thou vermin slander, bred in abject minds. Detraction Execrated. Sir John Suckling. CP-SuckJ

Thou wast all that [or that all] to me, love. To One in Paradise. Edgar Allan Poe. CP-PoeEd

Thou water turn'st to Wine (faire friend of Life). To Our Lord, upon the Water Made Wine. Richard Crashaw. CP-CrasR

Thou wert not, Cassius, and thou couldst not be. Otho. Percy Bysshe Shelley. CP-ShelP

Thou wert the morning star among the living. To Stella. Plato. CP-ShelP, tr. by Percy Bysshe Shelley

Thou which art I, ('tis nothing to be so[e]). Storm[e], The. John Donne. CP-DonnJ; MW-DonnJ

Thou who art dreary. End of Time, The. Christina Georgina Rossetti. CP-RosC3

Thou who condemnest Jewish hate. Self-Condemnation. George Herbert. CP-HerbG

Thou who didst hang upon a barren tree. Long Barren. Christina Georgina Rossetti. CP-RosC1

Thou who dost dwell and linger here below. Water-Course, The. George Herbert. CP-HerbG

Thou who first called me from the sleep of death. Father, The. Jones Very. CP-VeryJ

Thou who hast slept all night upon the storm. To the Man-of-War Bird. Walt Whitman. CP-WhitW

Thou, who in youthful vigour rich, and light. Inscription for a Seat by a Roadside, Half Way up a Steep Hill, Facing the South. William Wordsworth. CP-WorW1

Thou who keepst us each together. Hymn: "Thou who keepst us each together." Jones Very. CP-VeryJ

Thou who know'st all the sorrows of this earth. Hour-Glass, The. Walter De la Mare. CP-DeLaW

Thou who shalt stop, where Thames' translucent wave. On His Grotto at Twickenham. Alexander Pope. CP-PopeA

Thou, who survey'st these walls with curious eye. Translation of the Latin Epitaph on Sir Thomas Hanmer, Written by Doctor Freind, A. Samuel Johnson. CP-JohnS

Thou, who thy honour as thy God rever'st. Lines Sent to Sir John Whiteford, of Whiteford, Bart. with the Foregoing Poem. Robert Burns. CP-BurnR

Thou who wilt not love, do[e] this. Upon Some Women. Robert Herrick. CP-HerrR

Thou who with thy long hair. Hafiz. CP-EmerR Fr. Odes.

Thou whom chance may hither lead. Written in Friar's Carse Hermitage on the Banks of Nith—June—1788. Robert Burns. CP-BurnR

Thou whom I love, for whom I died. Take Care Of Him. Christina Georgina Rossetti. CP-RosC2

Thou, whom the former precepts have. Superliminare. George Herbert. CP-HerbG

Thou, whom these eyes saw never,—say friends true. Lines for the Tomb of Levi Lincoln Thaxter. Robert Browning. CP-BroR2

Thou, whose diviner soul hath caused [or caus'd] thee now. To Mr Tilman after He Had Taken Orders. John Donne. CP-DonnJ; MW-DonnJ

Thou whose spell can raise the dead. Saul. Lord Byron. CP-Byron

Thou, whose sweet youth and early hopes enhance. Perirrhanterium. George Herbert. CP-HerbG

Thou, whose sweet youth and early hopes inhance. Church-Porch, The. George Herbert. CP-HerbG

Thou wilt be near me Father, when I fail. Help. Jones Very. CP-VeryJ

Thou wilt my hands employ, though others find. Disciple, The. Jones Very. CP-VeryJ

Thou wilt not give me aught though I am poor. Fig Tree, The. Jones Very. CP-VeryJ

Thou wondrous Flower! in which, on grander scale. On Seeing the Victoria Regia in Bloom, at the Garden of J. Fisk Allen Esq. July 22d, 1853. Jones Very. CP-VeryJ

Thou wouldst be loved?—then let thy heart. To F—S S. O—D. Edgar Allan Poe. CP-PoeEd

Thou writes in Prose, how sweet all Virgins be. Upon Pearch. Robert Herrick. CP-HerrR

Though a wise man all pressures can sustaine. Vertue Is Sensible of Suffering. Robert Herrick. CP-HerrR

Though all our innocence cannot console us. Despairing of Understanding We Fall Into Decadence. Miller Williams. CP-WillM

Though all the Dead were all forgot. Memories. Rudyard Kipling. CP-KiplR

Though always one and the same, the one same who. Michelangelo Buonarroti. CP-Miche, *tr.* by John Frederick Nims

Though, at night, or anytime at all. LOVE 5. A. K. Ramanujan. CP-RamaA

Though authors are a dreadful clan. I Missed His Book, but I Read His Name. John Updike. CP-UpdiJ

Though aware of our rank and alert to obey orders. Ode: "Though aware of our rank and alert to obey orders." W. H. Auden. CP-AudeW

Though beauty be the mark of praise. Elegy, An: "Though beauty be the mark of praise." Ben Jonson. CP-JonsB

Though bent with age, to me. Michelangelo Buonarroti. CP-Miche, *tr.* by John Frederick Nims

Though between sullen hills. Shad-Time. Richard Wilbur. CP-WilbR

Though but a simple shelter. Emily Dickinson. SP-DickE

Though by well-warding many blowes w'ave past. Last Stroke Strike Sure, The. Robert Herrick. CP-HerrR

Though cats and birds be hardly friends. To Enid, Who Acted the Cat in Private Pantomime. G. K. Chesterton. CP-ChesG

Though Clock, / To tell how night draw[e]s hence, I've none. His Grange, or Private Wealth. Robert Herrick. CP-HerrR

Though countless as the Grains of Sand. Boethius. CP-JohnS *Fr.* Consolation of Philosophy, The ("De Consolacione Philosophie").

Though cruel Fate should bid us part. Northern Lass, The. Robert Burns. CP-BurnR

Though cruel seas like mountains fill the bay. Apple Island. Robert Graves. CP-GravR

Though Doctor Glen—the best of men. When Uncle Doc Was Young. James Whitcomb Riley. CP-RileJ

Though Dry, Not Dry. Donald Davie. CP-DaviDC

Though far from joy, my sorrowes are as far. Thomas Campion *and* Philip Rosseter. CP-CampT

Though fast youth's glorious fable flies. Lone Founts. Herman Melville. SP-MelvH

Though few, with noble purpose came. Hymn: "Though few, with noble purpose came." Jones Very. CP-VeryJ

Though fickle fortune has deceiv'd me. Robert Burns. CP-BurnR

Though flowers have perished at the touch. St. Martin's Summer. John Greenleaf Whittier. CP-WhitJ

Though for your sake I would not have you now. John Brown. Edwin Arlington Robinson. CP-RobiE

Though Frankinsense the *Deities* require. Meane in Our Meanes, A. Robert Herrick. CP-HerrR

Though from without no foes at all we feare. Cloathes, Are Conspirators. Robert Herrick. CP-HerrR

Though frost and snow locked [*or* lock'd] from mine eyes. To Saxham. Thomas Carew. CP-CareT

Though giant rains put out the sun. Deluge, The ("Though giant rains put out the sun"). G. K. Chesterton. CP-ChesG

Though God, as one that is an householder. Old and New Art (The Husbandmen). Dante Gabriel Rossetti. CW-RossD *Fr.* House of Life, The.

Though good things answer many good intents. Crosses. Robert Herrick. CP-HerrR

Though, happy muse, thou know my Digby well. Epigram to My Muse, the Lady Digby, on Her Husband, Sir Kenelm Digby, An. Ben Jonson. CP-JonsB

Though haunches of whales. Snowstorms in the Midwest. James Wright. CP-WrigJ

Though he checked the mist-net. Mist-Net, The. Paul Muldoon. CP-MuldP

Though her eye seek other forms. Ralph Waldo Emerson. CP-EmerR

Though hourely comforts from the Gods we see. Miseries. Robert Herrick. CP-HerrR

Though I am faithful to my loves lived through. Unknown Fair Faces. George Meredith. CP-MerG1

Though I am not the first in English terms. To France. Countee Cullen. CP-CullC

Though I am young, and cannot tell. Ben Jonson. CP-JonsB; SP-JonsB *Fr.* Sad Shepherd, The.

Though I at the time, had no one. More Love to His Life. Alice Walker. CP-WalkA

Though I be dead, and buried, yet I have. To the Countess of Bedford ("Though I be dead, and buried, yet I have"). John Donne. CP-DonnJ; MW-DonnJ

Though I beheld at first with blank surprise. To a Painter. William Wordsworth. CP-WorW2

Though I cannot always tell a fear. Entries for a Catalogue of Fears. A. K. Ramanujan. CP-RamaA

Though I cannot give thee fires. Short Hymne to Larr, A. Robert Herrick. CP-HerrR

Though I cannot your cruelty constrain. Sir Thomas Wyatt. CP-WyatT

Though I go drunken. Faithful One. Langston Hughes. CP-HughL; CP-HughL2

Though I Had Much More To Say. Kenneth Patchen. CP-PatcK

Though I have touched her flesh of moons. Modern Craft. Hart Crane. CP-CranH

Though I have tried to keep you from all blame. Petrarch. CP-Petra, *tr. by* J. G. Nichols

Though I must live here, and by force. To My Mistress[e] in My Absence. Thomas Carew. CP-CareT

Though I myself be bridled of my mind. Sir Thomas Wyatt. CP-WyatT

Though I prefer to charm my solitude with animals. Circe. Robert Stock. SP-StocR

Though I waste watches framing words to fetter. Revulsion. Thomas Hardy. CP-HardT

Though I'm modest as most. Available Now: Archaic Torsos of Both Sexes. Gregory Orr. SP-OrrG

Though in a little while. First Autumn, The. May Sarton. SP-SartM

Though In One Time. Laura Riding Jackson. CP-RidiL

Though in one time. Though In One Time. Laura Riding Jackson. CP-RidiL

Though it may seem rude. Ballad: "Though it may seem rude." Ben Jonson. CP-JonsB *Fr.* Masque of Augurs, The.

Though it's true we were young girls when we met. For Jan, in Bar Maria. Carolyn Kizer. CP-KizeC

Though jealous March, in marble skies. City's Spring, The. Thomas Merton. CP-MertT

Though joy attend Thee orient at the birth. To the Planet Venus, an Evening Star. William Wordsworth. CP-WorW2

Though joy is better than sorrow, joy is not great. Joy. Robinson Jeffers. CP-JefR1

Though leaves are many, the root is one. Coming of Wisdom with Time, The. William Butler Yeats. CP-YeatW

Though less for love than for the deep. Song for Young Lovers in a City. Edna St. Vincent Millay. CP-MillE

Though loath to grieve. Ode, Inscribed to W.H. Channing. Ralph Waldo Emerson. CP-EmerR

Though logic-choppers rule the town. Tom O'Roughley. William Butler Yeats. CP-YeatW

Though long it be, yeeres may repay the debt. Long Lookt for Comes at Last. Robert Herrick. CP-HerrR

Though love be gained only by truth in love. Love Gifts. Robert Graves. CP-GravR

Though love expels the ugly past. Freehold. Robert Graves. CP-GravR

Though love is the word a mother. Fatherhood. Donald Davie. CP-DaviDC

Though loves languish and sour. Prospect. Louis MacNeice. CP-MacNL

Though lumber was scarce, we found it. Courtship, The. James Dickey. CP-DickJ

Though many, many sheep I have. Lost Sheep, The. Jones Very. CP-VeryJ

Though many people still play the piano it's not. Piano & Everything Nice. Andrei Codrescu. SP-CodrA

Though many suns have risen and set. To May. William Wordsworth. CP-WorW2

Though mild clear weather. There Will Be No Peace. W. H. Auden. CP-AudeW

Though Miller lives in Arkansas. For Miller Williams. John Ciardi. CP-CiarJ

Though misfortunes my footsteps may ever attend. Song: "Though misfortunes my footsteps may ever attend." Jane Austen. CP-AustJ

Though most of them aren't much to write about. Beautiful Bowel Movement, The. John Updike. CP-UpdiJ

Though most that know me dare, I think, affirm. To My Dear Sister, the Author of these Poems. *Unknown.* CP-BradA

Though Mr. Ford can quite afford. Mr. Ford. G. K. Chesterton. CP-ChesG

Though narrow be that old Man's cares, and near. William Wordsworth. CP-WorW1

Though nature weigh our talents, and dispense. Conversation. William Cowper. CP-CowpW

Though neither thou doost keepe the Keyes of State. In Honour of the Author by *Tho: Campion* Doctor in Physicke. To the Reader. Thomas Campion. CP-CampT

Though no high-hung bells or din. Silver Jubilee, The. Gerard Manley Hopkins. CP-HopkG

Though no shyer than the others while her pitch is being checked she beams out at the audience. Prodigy, The. C. K. Williams. SP-WillC

Though not for common praise of him. Sainte-Nitouche. Edwin Arlington Robinson. CP-RobiE

Though now but marble are the marble urns. Postscript. Hart Crane. CP-CranH

Though now forever still. Voice of Peace, The. James Whitcomb Riley. CP-RileJ

Though now 'tis neither May nor June. [With Some Poems Sent to a Gentlewoman. II]. Richard Crashaw. CP-CrasR

Though oars are breaking the breathless gaze. Poem for Someone Killed in Spain, A. Randall Jarrell. CP-JarrR

Though of the sort there be that feign. Sir Thomas Wyatt. CP-WyatT

Though of weak faith, I believe in forces and powers. Powers. Czeslaw Milosz. CP-MiloC; CP-MiloCN, tr. by Robert Hass

Though once a puppy, and though Fop by name. Epitaph on Fop. William Cowper. CP-CowpW

Though once true lovers. Song: Though Once True Lovers. Robert Graves. CP-GravR

Though out of sight now, and as 'twere not the least to us. Paradox. Thomas Hardy. CP-HardT

Though pain be stark and bitter. Suffering. G. K. Chesterton. CP-ChesG

Though painters say Italian light does well. Going to Italy. Donald Davie. CP-DaviDC

Though Pulpits and the Desk May Fail. William Wordsworth. CP-WorW2

Though quite expensive, look, I've bought you this. Michelangelo Buonarroti. CP-Miche, tr. by John Frederick Nims

Though ready enough with beak and spurs. Cock in Pullet's Feathers. Robert Graves. CP-GravR

Though roused by that dark Vizir Riot rude. Priestley. Samuel Taylor Coleridge. CP-ColeS; MW-ColeS Fr. Effusions.

Though Shakespeare's Mermaid, ocean's mightiest daughter. On a Prohibitionist Poem. G. K. Chesterton. CP-ChesG

Though Sh——d-n will / Be Sh——d-n still. New Jingle on Tom Dingle, A. Unknown. CP-SherT

Though shouldered from the road I chose. Michelangelo Buonarroti. CP-Miche, tr. by John Frederick Nims

Though so fair, how soon they perish. Autumn Flowers, The. Jones Very. CP-VeryJ

Though some do grudge to see me joy. Sir Thomas Wyatt. CP-WyatT

Though tangled and twisted the course of true love. Rudyard Kipling. See Ere the steamer bore him Eastward, Sleary was engaged to marry

Though the air is full of singing. Silence, The. Wendell Berry. CP-BerrW

Though the Bold Wings of Poesy Affect. William Wordsworth. CP-WorW2

Though the Clerk of the Weather insist. Pebbles. Herman Melville. SP-MelvH

Though the crocuses poke up their heads in the usual places. Vernal Sentiment. Theodore Roethke. CP-RoetT

Though the day of my destiny's over. Stanzas to Augusta. Lord Byron. CP-Byron

Though the great song return no more. Nineteenth Century and After, The. William Butler Yeats. CP-YeatW

Though the great Waters sleep. Emily Dickinson. CP-DickE

Though the grey year scatter these deathy leaves. These Deathy Leaves. Allen Tate. CP-TateA

Though the little clouds ran southward still, the quiet autumnal. Autumn Evening. Robinson Jeffers. CP-JefR1

Though the moon beaming matronly and bland. To Lucia at Birth. Robert Graves. CP-GravR

Though the mountain's the same warm-tinted ivory. Presence. Denise Levertov. SP-LeveDS

Though the name of this place may make you to frown. Peg Ratcliff the Hostess's Invitation to Dean Swift. Unknown, sometimes at. to Thomas Sheridan. CP-SherT

Though the road lead nowhere. Song of Degrees, A. Howard Nemerov. CP-NemeH

Though the sky still was partly light. Saving, The. Robert Pinsky. CP-PinsR

Though the torrents from their fountains. Song for the Wandering Jew. William Wordsworth. CP-WorW1

Though the unseen may vanish, though insight fails. Plain Song for Comadre, A. Richard Wilbur. CP-WilbR

Though the whole heaven be one-eyed with the moon. End of Fear, The. G. K. Chesterton. CP-ChesG

Though the winds be dank. Meadow Lark, The. Paul Laurence Dunbar. CP-DunbP

Though there are always doctors who advise. Risk, The. Robert Graves. CP-GravR

Though there are wild dogs. Orpheus and Eurydice. Geoffrey Hill. CP-HillG

Though this the [or thy] port and I thy servant true. Sir Thomas Wyatt. CP-WyatT

Though thou art dead and gone from mortal sight. Lines on Reading the Death of Rev. Henry Ware, Jr. Jones Very. CP-VeryJ

Though thou beest all that Active Love. Another, to God. Robert Herrick. CP-HerrR

Though thou did'st hear the tempest from afar. To a Lady on Her Remarkable Preservation in an Hurricane in North-Carolina. Phillis Wheatley. CP-WheaP

Though thou hast passed thy summer standing, stay. Epithalamion: or, a Song. Ben Jonson. CP-JonsB

Though thou, indeed, hast quite forgotten ruth. Ballata: Of a continual Death in Love. Guido Cavalcanti. CW-RossD, tr. by Dante Gabriel Rossetti

Though thou walk through the Valley of the Shadow of Death. Emily Dickinson. SP-DickE

Though [or Tho] thou well dost wish me ill. Na Audiart. Ezra Pound. CP-PoEar; SP-PounE

Though to my feathers in the wet. Three Beggars, The. William Butler Yeats. CP-YeatW

Though unseen Poets, many and many a time. On My Songs. Wilfred Owen. CP-OwenW

Though Valentine brings love. Wallace Stevens. CP-StevWP

Though veiled in spires of myrtle wreath. Song: "Though veiled in spires of myrtle wreath." Samuel Taylor Coleridge. CP-ColeS

Though we are each unknown to ourself. Emily Dickinson. SP-DickE

Though we lie by their sides we may never know. Cider. Paul Muldoon. CP-MuldP

Though we may never be seen alive again. Lost in Ladispoli. Miller Williams. CP-WillM

Though years and years in dour allurement lapped. Michelangelo Buonarroti. CP-Miche, tr. by John Frederick Nims

Though you are in your shining days. Lover Pleads with His Friend for Old Friends, The. William Butler Yeats. CP-YeatW

Though You Are Young [or Yoong]. Thomas Campion. CP-CampT

Though you are young [or yoong] and I am old. Though You Are Young [or Yoong]. Thomas Campion. CP-CampT

Though you complain of me. Man to a Woman, A. William Carlos Williams. CP-WilW1

Though you, Diana-like, have liv'd still chaste. Lutea Allison. Sir John Suckling. CP-SuckJ

Though you know it anyhow. Tin Wedding Whistle. Ogden Nash. CP-NashO

Though you live in a little country. Here and Now, The. Theodore Weiss. SP-WeisT

Though you with line and color excel, securing. Michelangelo Buonarroti. CP-Miche, tr. by John Frederick Nims

Though your blind arrow, shot in time of need. Blind Arrow, A. Robert Graves. CP-GravR

Though your professions, ages and conditions. Love and Night. Robert Graves. CP-GravR

Though your sorrows not. E. E. Cummings. CP-CummE

Though your strangenesse frets my hart. Thomas Campion. CP-CampT

Though your wicked eyebrows seem. Song for an Afternoon. Charles Baudelaire. CP-BaudC, tr. by Walter Martin

Thought. D. H. Lawrence. CP-LawrD

Thought. Howard Nemerov. CP-NemeH

Thought. Walt Whitman. CP-WhitW

Thought, A. Samuel Taylor Coleridge. CP-ColeS

Thought, The. Consistency. Hans Magnus Enzensberger. SP-EnzeH, tr. by Michael Hamburger

Thought about Sheik Bedreddin, A. John Ciardi. CP-CiarJ

Thought and Reflections. G. K. Chesterton. CP-ChesG

   Comforting Reflection, A. CP-ChesG

   Singular Effects of Malediction. CP-ChesG

Thought as It Turns, A. Miller Williams. CP-WillM

Thought ay like a flower upon mine heart, A. Pain in Pleasure. Elizabeth Barrett Browning. CP-BroEB

Thought beneath so slight a film, The. Emily Dickinson. CP-DickE

Thought creeps along the baseboard of the dark mind, The. What Was the Throught. Robert Penn Warren. CP-WarrR

Thought does not crush to stone. Adamant, The. Theodore Roethke. CP-RoetT

Thought for a Lonely Death-Bed, A. Elizabeth Barrett Browning. CP-BroEB

Thought for a Sunshiny Morning. Dorothy Parker. CP-ParkD

Thought-Fox, The. Ted Hughes. SP-HughTN

Thought from Propertius, A. William Butler Yeats. CP-YeatW

Thought in Two Moods, A. Thomas Hardy. CP-HardT

Thought is false happiness: the idea. Crude Foyer. Wallace Stevens. CP-StevW; CP-StevWP

Thought is rapid, and so short the time, The. Petrarch. CP-Petra, tr. by J. G. Nichols

Thought is seldom itself. Thought. Howard Nemerov. CP-NemeH

Thought Is Superior. Stevie Smith. CP-SmitS

Thought looking out on thought. Opening of Eyes. Laura Riding Jackson. CP-RidiL

Thought may well be ever ranging. Arthur Hugh Clough. SP-ClouA

Thought of Columbus, A. Walt Whitman. CP-WhitW

Thought of Eve, within me, is a doll, The. Dolls. Wallace Stevens. CP-StevWP

Thought of Night. Heather McHugh. SP-McHuH

Thought of Something Else, The. Wendell Berry. CP-BerrW

Thought of Trees, The. Howard Nemerov. CP-NemeH

Thought of you is receding like a chambermaid given notice, The. In Memoriam. Joseph Brodsky. CP-BrodJ

Thought Revolved, A. Wallace Stevens. CP-StevW; CP-StevWP

Thought went up my mind today, A. Emily Dickinson. CP-DickE

Thoughtful brow and face—of sallow hue, A. Country Editor, The. James Whitcomb Riley. CP-RileJ

Thoughtful Lover, The. William Carlos Williams. CP-WilW2

Thoughtful of you, I was / anticipating change in. Rain (2). Robert Creeley. CP-CreeR

Thoughtful solitude / upon rosebush and stone, death and waking. Solitude. Federico García Lorca. CP-GarcF, tr. by William Bryant Logan

Thoughts. Dorothy Parker. CP-ParkD

Thoughts. Walt Whitman. CP-WhitW

Thoughts—I: Visages. Walt Whitman. CP-WhitW

Thoughts—6: "Of What I Write" Walt Whitman. CP-WhitW

Thoughts about the Christian Doctrine of Eternal Hell. Stevie Smith. CP-SmitS

Thoughts about the Person from Porlock. Stevie Smith. CP-SmitS

Thoughts and Desires. Jones Very. CP-VeryJ

Thoughts at Midnight. Thomas Hardy. CP-HardT

Thoughts came in to him—a convoy run, The. Yehuda Amichai. SP-AmicYL, tr. by Barbara Harshav and Benjamin Harshav Fr. Here We Loved.

Thoughts During an Air Raid. Stephen Spender. CP-SpenS

Thoughts fer the Discuraged Farmer. James Whitcomb Riley. CP-RileJ

Thoughts for a Speech of Lucifer, in the Tragedy of "Cain" Lord Byron. CP-Byron

Thoughts from Sophocles. Thomas Hardy. CP-HardT

Thoughts from Underground. Margaret Atwood. SP-AtwM1

Thoughts in a Zoo. Countee Cullen. CP-CullC

Thoughts moving / in her eyes. Ezra Pound. CP-PoEar

Thought[s] of a Briton on the Subjugation of Switzerland. William Wordsworth. CP-WorW1; MW-WorW

Thoughts of a Retired Diamond Cutter. Eleanor Wilner. SP-WilnE

Thoughts of a Young Girl. John Ashbery. SP-AshbJ

Thoughts of Home. Arthur Hugh Clough. SP-ClouA

Thoughts of Phena. Thomas Hardy. CP-HardT

Thoughts of the Time. Charles Olson. CP-OlsoC

Thoughts of you spatter my thought. Gambling. Kenneth Rexroth. CP-RexrK

Thoughts of Youth, The. James Whitcomb Riley. CP-RileJ

Thoughts on a Breath. Allen Ginsberg. CP-GinsA

Thoughts on a Pore Joke. James Whitcomb Riley. CP-RileJ

Thoughts on Looking at a Samuel Palmer Etching at the Tate. Gary Snyder. CP-SnydG

Thoughts on Looking into a Thicket. John Ciardi. CP-CiarJ

Thoughts on One's Head (In Plaster, with a Bronze Wash). William Meredith. SP-MereW

Thoughts on Saving the Manatee. Maxine W. Kumin. SP-KumiM

Thoughts on the Late War. James Whitcomb Riley. CP-RileJ

Thoughts on the Pythagorian System. Annis Boudinot Stockton. CP-StocA

Thoughts on the Run 1. Hans Magnus Enzensberger. SP-EnzeH, tr. by Rita Dove and Fred Viebahn

Thoughts on the Run 2. Hans Magnus Enzensberger. SP-EnzeH, tr. by Rita Dove and Fred Viebahn

Thoughts on the Run 3. Hans Magnus Enzensberger. SP-EnzeH, tr. by Rita Dove and Fred Viebahn

Thoughts on the Run 4. Hans Magnus Enzensberger. SP-EnzeH, tr. by Rita Dove and Fred Viebahn

Thoughts on the Seasons. William Wordsworth. CP-WorW2

Thoughts on the Works of Providence. Phillis Wheatley. CP-WheaP

Thoughts on Unpacking. Thom Gunn. CP-GunnT

Thoughts Sitting Breathing. Allen Ginsberg. CP-GinsA

Thoughts Suggested by a College Examination. Lord Byron. CP-Byron

Thoughts Suggested the Day Following, on the Banks of Nith, near the Poet's Residence. William Wordsworth. CP-WorW1

Thoughts, suggestions, aspirations, pictures. L of G. Walt Whitman. CP-WhitW

Thoughts Thought after a Bridge Party. Ogden Nash. CP-NashO

Thoughts Thought on an Avenue. Ogden Nash. CP-NashO

Thoughts Thought While Waiting for a Pronouncement from a Doctor, an Editor, a Big Executive, the Department of Internal Revenue or Any Other Momentous Pronouncer. Ogden Nash. CP-NashO

Thoughts to a Concerto of Telemann. Lawrence Ferlinghetti. SP-FerlL

Thoughts While Driving Home. John Updike. CP-UpdiJ

Thoughts While Reading The Sand Reckoner. James Tate. SP-TateJ

Thou's welcome, Wean! Mischanter fa' me. Poet's Welcome to His Love-Begotten Daughter [the First Instance that Entitled Him to the Venerable Appellation of Father], A. Robert Burns. CP-BurnR

Thousand and fifty-one waves, A. Numbers. Stevie Smith. CP-SmitS

Thousand and Second Night, The. James Merrill. SP-MerrJ

Thousand dangers of ruin has the street of love. Hafiz. CP-EmerR Fr. Odes.

Thousand doors ago, A. Young. Anne Sexton. CP-SextA; SP-SextA

Thousand housetops under the dome, A. London. G. K. Chesterton. CP-ChesG

Thousand leaves slant down across the rain, A. Requiem: "Thousand leaves slant down across the rain, A." Kenneth Rexroth. CP-RexrK

Thousand minstrels woke within me. Monadnoc. Ralph Waldo Emerson. CP-EmerR

Thousand perfect men and women appear, A. Offerings. Walt Whitman. CP-WhitW

Thousand plus a thousand: a winning-post, A. 2000. Primo Levi. CP-LeviP, tr. by Ruth Feldman

Thousand questions rise to my lips, A. Emily Dickinson. SP-DickE

Thousand sounds of happiness, A. Emily Jane Brontë. CP-BronE

Thousand sunsets behind tramcar wires in open skies of Warsaw, A. Moments Return, The. Allen Ginsberg. CP-GinsA

Thousands and thousands of hushed years ago. Silence. James Whitcomb Riley. CP-RileJ

Thousands each day passe by, which wee. Once Seen, and No More. Robert Herrick. CP-HerrR

Thousands of Days. Muriel Rukeyser. CP-RukeM

Thousands of sheep, soft-footed, black-nosed sheep—one by one going. Sheep. Carl Sandburg. CP-SandC

Thousandth Man, The. Rudyard Kipling. CP-KiplR

Thousandth Poem for Dylan Thomas, A. John Ciardi. CP-CiarJ

Thow that in hewin for our saluatioun. William Dunbar. CP-DunbW

Thracian parents, at his birth. Thracian, The. Vincent Bourne. CP-CowpW

Thracian, The. Vincent Bourne. CP-CowpW

Thrall. Carolyn Kizer. CP-KizeC

Thread, The. Denise Levertov. SP-LeveDP

Thread, The. W. S. Merwin. SP-MerwW

Thread of Life, The. Christina Georgina Rossetti. CP-RosC2

Thread was snapped too soon, A. Beyond the Dark Cedars. Kenneth Patchen. CP-PatcK

Thread with which he landed stuck to the bottom of the bathtub, The. Spider. Czeslaw Milosz. CP-MiloCN, tr. by Robert Hass

Threading. Yehuda Amichai. SP-AmicY, tr. by Stephen Mitchell

Threads our hands in blindness spin, The. Overruled. John Greenleaf Whittier. CP-WhitJ

Threads: Rosa Luxemburg from Prison. Jane Cooper. CP-CoopJ

Threadsuns / over the grayblack wasteness. Paul Celan. SP-CelaP, tr. by John Felstiner

Threat. Raymond Carver. CP-CarvR

Threat, The. Andrei Codrescu. SP-CodrA

Threat to a Fickle Lady. Dorothy Parker. CP-ParkD

Threatened. Alice Walker. CP-WalkA

Threatened by abundance, the ranchers. Killing the Calves. Robert Earl Hayden. CP-HaydR

Threatening Letter. Carolyn Kizer. CP-KizeC

Three. Carolyn Kizer. CP-KizeC Fr. Pro Femina.

Three. A. R. Ammons. CP-AmmoA

Three. Thom Gunn. CP-GunnT

Three. Tennessee Williams. CP-WillT

Three, The. James Dickey. CP-DickJ

3 A.M. John Updike. CP-UpdiJ

3 A. M. in a War Year. Mona Van Duyn. SP-VanDM

Three A.M., in Winter. Arthur Sze. SP-SzeA

3 a.m., September 1, 1969. Denise Levertov. SP-LeveDS

Three A.M. and Then Five. John Ciardi. CP-CiarJ

3 A.M. Kitchen: My Father Talking. Tess Gallagher. SP-GallT

3 A.M. The Girl with the Honey Colored Hair. William Carlos Williams. CP-WilW2

3 AM, the night is absolutely still. Night below Zero. Kenneth Rexroth. CP-RexrK

Three Americans. Lorine Niedecker. CP-NiedL

Three Angels. Adam Zagajewski. SP-ZagaA, tr. by Clare Cavanagh

Three angels came to the red red clay. From the Coptic. Stevie Smith. CP-SmitS

Three as a Magic Number. Alan Dugan. CP-DugaA

Three bags of gold, a fairytale. Fanny Howe. SP-HoweF Fr. Poem from a Single Pallet.

Three Balls. Carl Sandburg. CP-SandC

Three Baroque Meditations. Geoffrey Hill. CP-HillG

Three Beggars, The. William Butler Yeats. CP-YeatW

Three Bells, The. John Greenleaf Whittier. CP-WhitJ

Three Beyond. Donald Davie. CP-DaviDC

Three Bills. Randall Jarrell. CP-JarrR

Three Black Women. Muriel Rukeyser. CP-RukeM

Three blank walls, a barred window with no view. Philosopher, The. Robert Graves. CP-GravR

Three boats headed Northeast, moored. Waiting To Lean to the Master's Command. Richard Eberhart. CP-EberR

Three boys, American, in dungarees. February 22. John Updike. CP-UpdiJ

Three Brothers and the Chinese Princess, The. Jelaluddin Rumi. SP-Rumi, tr. by Coleman Barks

Three Bushes, The. William Butler Yeats. CP-YeatW

Three captains went to Indian wars. Casterbridge Captains, The. Thomas Hardy. CP-HardT

Three Carriers, The. Rainer Maria Rilke. CP-RilkFr, tr. by A. Poulin, Jr.

Three centuries now are gone. Rose. Walter De la Mare. CP-DeLaW

Three cheers for lusty winter. Parody of Alfred Austin. George Meredith. CP-MerG2

Three Cherry Trees, The. Walter De la Mare. CP-DeLaW

Three Children, The. Josephine Jacobsen. CP-JacoJ

Three Chinese in yellow coats stood on dunes, waist-high. Shipwreck. Norman Dubie. CP-DubiN

Three Chores. James Merrill. SP-MerrJ

Three Cities. Federico García Lorca. CP-GarcF, tr. by Cola Franzen

Three Conquistadors, The. G. K. Chesterton. CP-ChesG

Three Crepuscular Poems. Federico García Lorca. CP-GarcF, tr. by Jerome Rothenberg

Three / crimson / mongrels / bait. Another Ashtray. Louis Zukofsky. CP-ZukLS

Three damsels in the queen's chamber. Christmas Carol, A: "Three damsels in the queen's chamber." Algernon Charles Swinburne. SP-SwinA

Three Darknesses. Robert Penn Warren. CP-WarrR

Three-day-long rain from the east, A. Dark Day, The. William Carlos Williams. CP-WilW1

3 Days Ago. Philip Whalen. SP-WhalP

Three days back, first snow had fallen. Preternaturally Early Snowfall in Mating Season. Robert Penn Warren. CP-WarrR

Three days before, my soul reached such a place. Petrarch. CP-Petra, tr. by J. G. Nichols

Three days for an answer I have waited. Another Reply by the Dean. Jonathan Swift. CP-SwifJ

Three Days of Forest, a River, Free. Rita Dove. SP-DoveR

Three Dead Friends. James Whitcomb Riley. CP-RileJ

Three-Decker, The. Rudyard Kipling. CP-KiplR

Three Deer, Mount Rose, August 1995. Paul Muldoon. CP-MuldP

Three Deer One Coyote Running in the Snow. Gary Snyder. CP-SnydG

Three Desk Objects. Margaret Atwood. SP-AtwM1

Three Dimensions, The. Ralph Waldo Emerson. CP-EmerR

Three Disillusioning Witches, The. Federico García Lorca. CP-GarcF, tr. by Jerome Rothenberg Fr. In the Forest of the Lunar Grapefruits.

Three Dreams. A. K. Ramanujan. CP-RamaA

Three Eagles and the Sleepy Lion, The. George Meredith. CP-MerG2

Three Eggs Up. John Ciardi. CP-CiarJ

Three Elegiac Poems. Wendell Berry. CP-BerrW

Three Enemies, The. Christina Georgina Rossetti. CP-RosC1

Three Epigrams. Theodore Roethke. CP-RoetT

Three Epigrams. Ernesto Cardenal.
    "Shots were heard last night / Out by the burial ground." CP-MertT
    "Suddenly in the night the sirens." CP-MertT
    "We wake up with guns going off." CP-MertT

Three Epigrams. Jonathan Swift. CP-SwifJ

Three-Faced, The. Robert Graves. CP-GravR

Three faces in a single one. Narcissus in the Desert. Nicolas Calas. CP-WilW1

Three fairies by the Sangamon. Dancing for a Prize. Nicholas Vachel Lindsay. CP-LindV

Three fat flies copulate. Observatory. Yusef Komunyakaa. CP-KomuY

3 fat trout hang. Poem for Hemingway & W. C. Williams. Raymond Carver. CP-CarvR

Three Fatal[l] Sisters. Robert Herrick. CP-HerrR

Three Fish, The. Jelaluddin Rumi. SP-Rumi, tr. by Coleman Barks

Three Floors. Stanley Kunitz. CP-KunSC

Three-fold terror of love; a fallen flare, The. Mother of God, The. William Butler Yeats. CP-YeatW

Three for Children. Thom Gunn. CP-GunnT

345 W. 15th St. Allen Ginsberg. CP-GinsA

Three Fragments for Fishers of Destiny. Carl Sandburg. CP-SandC

Three Friends. Chuang Tzu. CP-MertT

Three Functions of Irony. Thomas McGrath. SP-McGrT

Three Gardens. James Schuyler. CP-SchuJ

Three Generations. K'o Chia Tsang. CP-WilW2

Three generations gone and I return. Search, The. Jorge Luis Borges. SP-BorgJ, tr. by Charles Tomlinson

Three Gentle Shepherds, The. Alexander Pope. CP-PopeA

Three Ghosts. Carl Sandburg. CP-SandC

Three gifts the dying left me. Hugh Stuart Boyd [Legacies]. Elizabeth Barrett Browning. CP-BroEB

Three Gipsies, The. Nikolaus Lenau. CP-MerG2

Three girls in a donkey cart are, The. Elegy to the Pulley of Superior Oblique. Norman Dubie. CP-DubiN

Three Graces, The. William Carlos Williams. CP-WilW2

Three Graves, The. William Wordsworth. CP-ColeS; CP-WorW1

Three Green Windows. Anne Sexton. CP-SextA

Three Gude Fellows Ayont Yon Glen. Robert Burns. CP-BurnR

Three Hermits, The. William Butler Yeats. CP-YeatW

Three Hills Look Different in the Moonshine. Carl Sandburg. CP-SandC

Three hours chain-smoking words. In the Evening. Adrienne Rich. CP-RicAE; SP-RicA2

Three hundred nights like three hundred walls. Parting. Jorge Luis Borges. SP-BorgJ, tr. by W. S. Merwin

3 in 1. Robert Creeley. CP-CreeR

Three in Transition. David Ignatow. SP-IgnaD

Three is a city of terror where. Fanny Howe. SP-HoweF Fr. O'Clock.

Three Jolly Hunters, The. James Whitcomb Riley. CP-RileJ

Three Kids. Richard Eberhart. CP-EberR

Three kids running down the meadow. Three Kids. Richard Eberhart. CP-EberR

Three Kinds of Pleasures. Robert Bly. SP-BlyR

Three Kings brought gifts to Him for whom. To E. H. and G. M. G. K. Chesterton. CP-ChesG

Three Kings, The. Adam Zagajewski. SP-ZagaA, tr. by Clare Cavanagh

Three Ladies, The. Robert Creeley. CP-CreeR

Three little birds in a row. Stephen Crane. CP-CranS

Three little children / On the wide wide earth. Christina Georgina Rossetti. CP-RosC2

Three Locked Hoops. Robert Graves. CP-GravR

Three Locutions Des Pierrots. Hart Crane. CP-CranH

Three looming poplars. Evening ("Three looming poplars"). Federico García Lorca. CP-GarcF, tr. by Alan S. Trueblood Fr. Andalusian Songs.

Three lost lights are blest by priests. Secular Signs. Thomas Merton. CP-MertT

Three lovely sisters working were. Parcæ, The; or, Three Dainty Destinies: The Armilet. Robert Herrick. CP-HerrR

Three Maidens, The. George Meredith. CP-MerG1

Three marble holes thumbed in the concrete road. Seamus Heaney. SP-HeanSO Fr. Squarings.

Three Marching Songs. William Butler Yeats. CP-YeatW

Three matches in a folder, you and me. Night-piece. James Vincent Cunningham. CP-CunnJ

Three Meditations. Denise Levertov. SP-LeveDP; SP-LeveDS

Three men on scaffolding scatter cornflakes down. Picture. Robert Pinsky. CP-PinsR

Three merry lads you own we are. Answer. George Rochfort. CP-SherT

Three messengers arrived, The. They went up the stairs. Strange Times. Yannis Ritsos. SP-RitsY, tr. by Kimon Friar

Three Moments. Christina Georgina Rossetti. CP-RosC3

Three months ago, I stabbed your cactus plant. Stalking Memory. Ai. SP-Ai

Three Monuments, The. William Butler Yeats. CP-YeatW

Three Moral Discoveries. Donald Davie. CP-DaviDC

Three Mornings. Philip Whalen. SP-WhalP

Three Movements. William Butler Yeats. CP-YeatW

Three Movements, The. Donald Hall. CP-HallD

Three Moves in six months and I remain. John Logan. CP-LogaJ

Three Nahuatl Poems. William Carlos Williams. CP-WilW2

Three Nuns. Christina Georgina Rossetti. CP-RosC3

Three Occasional Poems. W. H. Auden. CP-AudeW

Three Odes of Horace. Horace. CP-MacNL

Three of us sat. Triple Muse. Olga Broumas. SP-BrouO

Three old hermits took the air. Three Hermits, The. William Butler Yeats. CP-YeatW

Three on Luck. Robert Pinsky. CP-PinsR

Three-Part Song, A. Rudyard Kipling. CP-KiplR Fr. Puck of Pook's Hill.

Three Pastors in Berlin. Donald Davie. CP-DaviDC

Three-Penny Opera, The. Frank O'Hara. SP-OharF

Three people come where no people belong any more. Abandoned Ranch, Big Bend. Hayden Carruth. CP-CarHS

Three picture-drawn people stepped out of their frames. Family Portraits. Thomas Hardy. CP-HardT

Three Pieces on the Smoke of Autumn. Carl Sandburg. CP-SandC

Three pillows, end on end, rolled on a daybed. Robert Lowell. SP-LoweR Fr. Mexico.

Three Plum Buns. Christina Georgina Rossetti. CP-RosC2

3:00 p.m. Federico García Lorca. CP-GarcF, *tr. by* Jerome Rothenberg

Three Poems. Robert Penn Warren. CP-WarrR

Three Poems About Mark Twain. Nicholas Vachel Lindsay. CP-LindV

Three Poems for James Wright. Mary Oliver. SP-OlivM

Three Poems for Joanne. Gary Snyder. CP-SnydG

Three Poems for the New Year. Charles Wright.
  Three Poems for the New Year [1]. SP-WrigC
  Three Poems for the New Year [2]. SP-WrigC
  Three Poems for the New Year [3]. SP-WrigC

Three Poems for the New Year [1]. Charles Wright. SP-WrigC *Fr.* Three Poems for the New Year.

Three Poems for the New Year [2]. Charles Wright. SP-WrigC *Fr.* Three Poems for the New Year.

Three Poems for the New Year [3]. Charles Wright. SP-WrigC *Fr.* Three Poems for the New Year.

Three Poems from Michelangelo. Helen Pinkerton. CP-PinkH

Three Poems of Departure. Charles Wright. SP-WrigC

Three Poems of Incarnation. Kathleen Jessie Raine. SP-RainK

Three Poems on Aaron Siskind's Photographs. John Logan. CP-LoganJ

Three Poems on Illusion. Kathleen Jessie Raine. SP-RainK

Three Poems on Morris Graves' Paintings. John Logan. CP-LoganJ

Three Poems with Yevtushenko. James Dickey. CP-DickJ

Three Portraits with Shading. Federico García Lorca.
  Bacchus. CP-GarcF, *tr. by* Alan S. Trueblood
  Debussy. CP-GarcF, *tr. by* Alan S. Trueblood
  Juan Ramón Jiménez. CP-GarcF, *tr. by* Alan S. Trueblood
  Narcissus. CP-GarcF, *tr. by* Alan S. Trueblood
  Venus ("Dead maiden, The"). CP-GarcF, *tr. by* Alan S. Trueblood
  Verlaine. CP-GarcF, *tr. by* Alan S. Trueblood

Three Postcards from the Monastery. Thomas Merton. CP-MertT

Three Posthumous Poems. W. H. Auden. CP-AudeW
  Aubade: "At break of dawn." CP-AudeW
  Glad. CP-AudeW
  Minnelied. CP-AudeW

Three Praises. Margaret Atwood. SP-AtwM2

Three Prints of the Sky. Federico García Lorca. CP-GarcF, *tr. by* Jerome Rothenberg

Three prisoners—the biggest black. O My Name It Is Sam Hall. Randall Jarrell. CP-JarrR

Three Quatrains. Jelaluddin Rumi.
  "Let the lover be disgraceful, crazy." SP-Rumi
  "Night full of talking that hurts, A." SP-Rumi, *tr. by* Coleman Barks *and* John Moyne

Three Quatrains. Edwin Arlington Robinson. CP-RobiE

Three Realities, The. G. K. Chesterton. CP-ChesG

Three red foxes on my head, come down. False Youth: Autumn: Clothes of the Age. James Dickey. CP-DickJ

Three rompers run together, hand in hand. To ———: "Three rompers run together, hand in hand." Wilfred Owen. CP-OwenW

Three sang of love together: one with lips. Triad, A. Christina Georgina Rossetti. CP-RosC1

Three Seasons. Christina Georgina Rossetti. CP-RosC1

Three Seasons and a Gorilla. C. K. Williams. CP-WillC

Three Sentences for a Dead Swan. James Wright. CP-WrigJ

Three Sermons to the Dead. Laura Riding Jackson. CP-RidiL

Three Several Birds. James Whitcomb Riley. CP-RileJ

Three Shadows. Dante Gabriel Rossetti. CW-RossD

Three Shrines. Carl Sandburg. CP-SandC

Three shrines a woman has for a man. Three Shrines. Carl Sandburg. CP-SandC

Three sides, / four. Box, The. Robert Creeley. CP-CreeR

Three Sides of a Coin. Muriel Rukeyser. CP-RukeM

Three Singers to Young Blood, The. George Meredith. CP-MerG1

Three Singing Friends. James Whitcomb Riley. CP-RileJ

Three Sisters—and the youngest. Reflections. Walter De la Mare. CP-DeLaW

Three sisters, and there has been a quarrel. Afternoon Call, An. G. K. Chesterton. CP-ChesG

Three Sisters, The. Alfonso Cortes. CP-MertT

3/6/81, Amtrack. Andrei Codrescu. SP-CodrA

Three Skirmishes in the Endless Battle. James Laughlin. CP-LaugJ

Three Slants at New York. Carl Sandburg. CP-SandC

Three Small Parables for My Poet Friends. Stanley Kunitz. CP-KunSC

Three Songs. Thom Gunn.
  Baby Song. CP-GunnT
  Hitching into Frisco. CP-GunnT
  Sparrow. CP-GunnT

Three Songs. Gregory Orr. SP-OrrG

Three Songs. Louise Bogan. CP-BogaL

Three Songs. Hayden Carruth. CP-CarHS

Three Songs about Lynching. Langston Hughes.
  Flight. CP-HughL; CP-HughL1; CP-HughL2
  Lynching Song. CP-HughL; CP-HughL1; CP-HughL2
  Silhouette. CP-HughL

Three Songs for the Lute. Robert Graves. CP-GravR

Three Songs from "The Lamp and the Bell" Edna St. Vincent Millay. CP-MillE

Three Songs of Shattering. Edna St. Vincent Millay. CP-MillE

Three Songs to the One Burden. William Butler Yeats. CP-YeatW

Three Sonnets. William Carlos Williams. CP-WilW2

Three Sonnets for the Eyes. Elizabeth Bishop. CP-BishE

Three sophists came to greet the Consul. Enemies, The. Constantine P. Cavafy. CP-CavaC, *tr. by* Theoharis Constantine Theoharis

Three Sorts of Violence, The. William Meredith. SP-MereW

Three spirits came to me. April. Ezra Pound. SP-PounE

Three-spoked Wheel is relentless, The. Han-shan. CP-ColdM, *tr. by* Red Pine

Three Spring Notations on Bipeds. Carl Sandburg. CP-SandC

Three squirrels wound and sprung to this remitted. December 13, 1979. John Ciardi. CP-CiarJ

Three Stages. Christina Georgina Rossetti. CP-RosC3
  Pause of Thought, A. CP-RosC1

3 Stances. William Carlos Williams. CP-WilW2

Three Stanzas From Goethe. James Wright. CP-WrigJ

Three Steps to the Graveyard. James Wright. CP-WrigJ

Three stood listening to a fresh access, The. Snow. Robert Frost. CP-FrosR

Three stood outside TOC, The. Donut Dollies. Yusef Komunyakaa. CP-KomuY

Three Strangers, The. Walter De la Mare. CP-DeLaW

Three Students went over the Rhine one day. Landlady's Daughter, The. Ludwig Uhland. CP-MerG2

Three sunset eyes on a white plate. Three Eggs Up. John Ciardi. CP-CiarJ

Three tailors of Tooley Street wrote: We, the People. Three Ghosts. Carl Sandburg. CP-SandC

Three Talks on Civilization. Czeslaw Milosz. CP-MiloC; CP-MiloCN, *tr. by* Jan Darowski

Three Tall Men, The. Thomas Hardy. CP-HardT

Three Taverns, The. Edwin Arlington Robinson. CP-RobiE

Three thing[e]s there be[e] that prosper up apace. Sir Walter Ra[u]le[i]gh to His Son[ne]. Sir Walter Ralegh. CP-RaleW

Three Things. G. K. Chesterton. CP-ChesG

Three Things. Shmuel HaNagid. SP-HaNaS, *tr. by* Peter Cole

Three Things. William Butler Yeats. CP-YeatW

Three things make earth unquiet. Servant When He Reigneth, A. Rudyard Kipling. CP-KiplR

3:30 A.M. Conversation. Charles Bukowski. SP-BukC2

3,489 friendly people. Reflections in Sleepy Eye. Allen Ginsberg. CP-GinsA

Three times dark, first in the mind. Three as a Magic Number. Alan Dugan. CP-DugaA

Three Times I Came to Rome. Yehuda Amichai. SP-AmicYL, *tr. by* Benjamin Harshav *and* Barbara Harshav

Three Times In Love. Robert Graves. CP-GravR

Three times—we parted—Breath—and I. Emily Dickinson. CP-DickE

Three to thirteen my hair in braids, the clean. Body. Olga Broumas. SP-BrouO

Three Trees Were Cut Down. Federico García Lorca. CP-GarcF, *tr. by* Alan S. Trueblood *Fr.* Theories.

3/23/66. James Schuyler. CP-SchuJ

Three Types of Loss. Andrei Codrescu. SP-CodrA

Three Undated Fragments. John Keats. CP-KeatJ

Three Valentines. Elizabeth Bishop. CP-BishE

Three Valentines to the Wide World. Mona Van Duyn. SP-VanDM

Three very ancient faces stay with me. Elegy: "Three very ancient faces stay with me." Jorge Luis Borges. SP-BorgJ, *tr. by* Alastair Reid

Three Views of a Mother. John Ciardi. CP-CiarJ

Three Views of Horse. Clarence Major. SP-MajoC

Three Violins. Carl Sandburg. CP-SandC

Three violins are trying their hearts. Three Violins. Carl Sandburg. CP-SandC

Three Virgins at the break of day. Golden Net, The. William Blake. CP-BlakW

Three Voices. Adam Zagajewski. SP-ZagaA, *tr. by* Renata Gorczynski

Three Wagnerian Lyrics. Charles Tomlinson. CP-TomlC

Three walls around the town of Tela when I came. Ashurnatsirpal III. Carl Sandburg. CP-SandC

Three wealthy sisters swore they'd never part. E. E. Cummings. CP-CummE

Three weeks ago I went back. One for the Rose. Philip Levine. SP-LeviP

Three weeks now and the fog still clings to the white. San Pietro. Joseph Brodsky. CP-BrodJ, *tr. by* Barry Rubin

Three Weeks passed since I had seen Her. Emily Dickinson. CP-DickE

Three wide / Funnels raked aft, and the masts slanted, The. George Oppen. CP-

OppGN

Three Wishes, The. Billy Collins. SP-CollB

Three Women. Sylvia Plath. CP-PlatS

Three women / on a marriage bed. Snow White. Olga Broumas. SP-BrouO

Three Words Only. Robert Graves. CP-GravR

Three Worlds swarm with people, The. Han-shan. CP-ColdM, tr. by Red Pine

Three wrestle in the grass, The. Eclogue at Twilight. Yusef Komunyakaa. CP-KomuY

Three years ago, in the afternoons. Sitting Outside at the End of Autumn. Charles Wright. SP-WrigCN

Three years, now, the curve of Elizabeth Bridge. Over Elizabeth Bridge: a Circumvention. Charles Tomlinson. CP-TomlC

Three years she grew in sun and shower. William Wordsworth. MW-WorW Fr. Lucy.

Three Years Waiting. Robert Graves. CP-GravR

Three Young Tenneseans / Whom snobs called plebeians. Fourth Limick. Ogden Nash. CP-NashO

Threes. Carl Sandburg. CP-SandC

Threnodia Augustalis. John Dryden. CP-DryJ2

Threnody: "Christian coin, The." William Carlos Williams. CP-WilW2

Threnody for a Brown Girl. Countee Cullen. CP-CullC

Threnody: "Lilacs blossom just as sweet." Dorothy Parker. CP-ParkD

Threnody: "South-wind brings, The." Ralph Waldo Emerson. CP-EmerR

Threnos. Ezra Pound. CP-PoEar

Threshed corn lay piled like grit of ivory. Barn, The. Seamus Heaney. SP-HeanSO

Thresher Duck could o'er the Queen prevail, The. On Stephen Duck, the Thresher, and Favourite Poet. Jonathan Swift. CP-SwifJ

Threshing from left to right, whose. Flame. Charles Tomlinson. CP-TomlC

Threshold. Denise Levertov. SP-LeveDP

Threshold. Howard Nemerov. CP-NemeH

Threshold, The. Rudyard Kipling. CP-KiplR

Thrice, and above, blest (my soul's [or soules] half[e]) art thou. Country Life: To His Brother, M. Tho: Herrick. Robert Herrick. CP-HerrR

Thrice broken right. Collarbone. William Corbett. SP-CorbW

Thrice happie Roses, so much grac't, to have. Upon the Roses in Julias Bosome. Robert Herrick. CP-HerrR

Thrice happy they whose world is spanned. Verse with Allusions. Theodore Roethke. CP-RoetT

Thrice he came. Malacoda. Samuel Beckett. CP-BeckS

Thrice Toss[e] These Oaken Ashes in the Air [or Ayre]. Thomas Campion. CP-CampT

Thrice welcome from the Land of Flowers. Greeting, A. John Greenleaf Whittier. CP-WhitJ

Thrice welcome to thy sisters of the East. To Delaware. John Greenleaf Whittier. CP-WhitJ

Thrice, with a prophet's voice and prophet's power. To Mr. Congreve. Jonathan Swift. CP-SwifJ

Thrifty Lover, The. Marge Piercy. SP-PierM

Thrill came slowly like a Boon for, The. Emily Dickinson. CP-DickE

Thrill is gone, The. The fire's burnt out. Portrait, The. Charles Baudelaire. CP-BaudC, tr. by Walter Martin Fr. Phantom, A.

Thrise happie she that is so well assured. Sonnet 59. Edmund Spenser. CP-Spens Fr. Amoretti.

Thrive gentle plant! and weave a bow'r. On a Plant of Virgin's Bower. William Cowper. CP-CowpW

Thro' airy realms, he wings his instant flight. Phillis Wheatley. See Through airy roads he wings his instant flight

Thro' burden and heat of the day. Christina Georgina Rossetti. CP-RosC2

Thro' the rough ways of Life, with a patten on your Guard. On Capt. Foote's Marriage with Miss Patton. James Leigh Perrot. CP-AustJ

Thro' the vales to my love! Bride Song, A. Christina Georgina Rossetti. CP-RosC1

Thro' thickest glooms, look back, immortal Shade. Phillis Wheatley. See Through thickest glooms look back, immortal shade

Throe of Apocalypse. Laura Riding Jackson. CP-RidiL

Throe upon the features, A. Emily Dickinson. CP-DickE

Throned in the Sun's descending car. Cento Made By Wordsworth, A. William Wordsworth. CP-WorW2

Thrones, Powers, Dominions, Peoples, Kings. Our Fathers Also. Rudyard Kipling. CP-KiplR

Throng like shadowy caresses on the horizon. Great Sadnesses, The. Kenneth Patchen. CP-PatcK

Thronged boughs of the shadowy sycamore, The. Day-Dream, The. Dante Gabriel Rossetti. CW-RossD

Thronging the warped treadmill. Olive Groves of Thasos, The. Amy Clampitt. CP-ClamA

Through a Dark Wood. Robert Graves. CP-GravR

Through a drain grating, something. Key, The. Adrienne Rich. CP-RicAE

Through a Glass Darkly. Norman Dubie. CP-DubiN

Through a Glass Eye, Lightly. Carolyn Kizer. CP-KizeC

Through a glass greenly men as trees walking. Park, The. Louis MacNeice. CP-MacNL

Through a great lion's head clouded by mange. Mass Man. Derek Walcott. CP-WalcD

Through a hospital window. In a Hospital Garden. Randall Jarrell. CP-JarrR

Through a place in the roof the sun came down. Patience: In the Mill. James Dickey. CP-DickJ

Through a wide window all Somerset might look in. Under a Skylight. Donald Davie. CP-DaviDC

Through airy roads he wings his instant flight. Funeral Poem on the Death of C. E. an Infant of Twelve Months, A. Phillis Wheatley. CP-WheaP

Through all the night. To His Angrie God. Robert Herrick. CP-HerrR

Through all the town the busy triflers swarm. Phaedrus. CP-JohnS Fr. Fabulae.

Through Alpine meadows soft-suffused. Stanzas from the Grande Chartreuse. Matthew Arnold. SP-ArnoM

Through and through the inspired leaves. Book-Worms, The. Robert Burns. CP-BurnR

Through Bifocals. Donald Davie. CP-DaviDC

Through Binoculars. Charles Tomlinson. CP-TomlC

Through brush and love-vine, well blooded by blackberry thorn. Boy Wandering in Simms' Valley. Robert Penn Warren. CP-WarrR

Through centuries he lived in poverty. Good Man Has No Shape, The. Wallace Stevens. CP-StevW; CP-StevWP

Through Closed Eyes. Charles Tomlinson. CP-TomlC

Through cloudless skies, in silvery sheen. Stanzas: "Through cloudless skies, in silvery sheen." Lord Byron. CP-Byron

Through Cumbrian wilds, in many a mountain cove. William Wordsworth. CP-WorW1

Through customary for a woman. Charisma. Lewis Hyde. SP-BrouO, tr. by Olga Broumas

Through Death to Love. Dante Gabriel Rossetti. CW-RossD Fr. House of Life, The.

Through dreary winter had my soul endured. Wallace Stevens. CP-StevWP

Through every happy line I sing. All-Golden, The. James Whitcomb Riley. CP-RileJ

Through every precinct of the wintry city. Flight into Egypt, The. Thomas Merton. CP-MertT

Through fen and farmland walking. Song for a Summer's Day. Sylvia Plath. CP-PlatS

Through fire and flood this book has passed. Lines for Isaac Bradwell, of Indanoplis, Ind., County-Seat of Marion. James Whitcomb Riley. CP-RileJ

Through floods and flames to your retreat. On His Approaching Visit to Hayley. William Cowper. CP-CowpW

Through frost-thick weather. Vanity Fair. Sylvia Plath. CP-PlatS

Through Gripus Grounds let rich Pactolus roll. Boethius. CP-JohnS Fr. Consolation of Philosophy, The ("De Consolacione Philosophie").

Through heat and cold, and shower and sun. Drovers, The. John Greenleaf Whittier. CP-WhitJ

Through heaving heather, fallen stones. Stone Age Figure Far Below, A. Derek Mahon. CP-MahoD

Through her I swapped the Arno for the Sorgue. Petrarch. CP-Petra, tr. by J. G. Nichols

Through intricate motions ran. Stream and Sun at Glendalough. William Butler Yeats. CP-YeatW

Through lane it lay—through bramble. Emily Dickinson. CP-DickE

Through learned and laborious years. Outlaws, The. Rudyard Kipling. CP-KiplR

Through life's dull road, so dim and dirty. On My Thirty-third Birthday. Lord Byron. CP-Byron

Through Life's Dull Road, So Dim and Dirty. Lord Byron. See On My Thirty-third Birthday

Through light green haze, a rolling sea. Milan Cathedral. Herman Melville. SP-MelvH

Through many a year and many a vain assay. Michelangelo Buonarroti. CP-Miche, tr. by John Frederick Nims

Through many doors it's been—through. Journey, A. William Stafford. SP-StafWW

Through many nights of many years invincible. James Laughlin. CP-LaugJ

Through meadow and hedgerow, village and forest. Russia Comes Into Poland. Adam Zagajewski. SP-ZagaA, tr. by Renata Gorczynski, Benjamin Ivry and C. K. Williams

Through memory and actual. Stall. Heather McHugh. SP-McHuH

Through miles of mud we travelled, and by sick valleys. Of Grandcourt. Ivor Gurney. SP-GurnI

Through mud, fouled nuts, black grime. Removing the Plate of the Pump on the Hydraulic System of the Backhoe. Gary Snyder. CP-SnydG

Through my hemlocks and the spruce beyond. Aspect of the Air, An. John Ciardi. CP-CiarJ

Through my window and across the lawn. Endegeeste. Howard Nemerov. CP-

NemeH

Through Nightmare. Robert Graves. CP-GravR

Through pain the land of pain. Celebration of Failure. Laura Riding Jackson. CP-RidiL

Through portico of my elegant house you stalk. Conversation among the Ruins. Sylvia Plath. CP-PlatS

Through purblind night the wiper. Wiper, The. Louis MacNeice. CP-MacNL

Through rain falling on us no faster. Goodbye to Serpents. James Dickey. CP-DickJ

Through rifle sights. Roll Call. Yusef Komunyakaa. CP-KomuY

Through secret seas of blue and gold and skies of blood and fire. Literal Land, The. G. K. Chesterton. CP-ChesG

Through shattered galleries, 'mid roofless halls. Composed among the Ruins of a Castle in North Wales. William Wordsworth. CP-WorW2; MW-WorW

Through Sleepy-Land. James Whitcomb Riley. CP-RileJ

Through slits in the plantain leaf. Banks of a Stream Where Creatures Bathe. James Merrill. SP-MerrJ

Through snowy woods and shady. Seen by the Waits. Thomas Hardy. CP-HardT

Through storms you reach them and from storms are free. Enviable Isles, The. Herman Melville. SP-MelvH

Through summer-sparkling days, when skies were bright. Young Girl Singing, A. Marya Alexandrovna Zaturenska. SP-ZatuM

Through the ample open door of the peaceful country barn. Farm Picture, A. Walt Whitman. CP-WhitW

Through the arch of Elvira. Gacela of the Morning Market. Federico García Lorca. SP-GarcF, tr. by J. L. Gili and Stephen Spender

Through the Arch of Elvira. Ghazal of the Market in the Morning. Federico García Lorca. CP-GarcF, tr. by Christopher Maurer

Through the Boughs. Raymond Carver. CP-CarvR

Through the branches / hesitant. Captive. Federico García Lorca. CP-GarcF, tr. by Christopher Maurer

Through the branches of the laurel. Casida of the Dark Doves. Federico García Lorca. SP-GarcF, tr. by W. S. Merwin

Through the ceiling comes. Last Days of April, The. James Tate. SP-TateJ

Through the city flows a mighty river. Song about Girls, A. Jaroslav Seifert. SP-SeifJ, tr. by Ewald Osers

Through the Dark Sod—as Education. Emily Dickinson. CP-DickE

Through the dimness, curtains drawn, eyes closed. Verse for Urania. James Merrill. SP-MerrJ

Through the evening. Calling under the Breath, The. W. S. Merwin. SP-MerwW

Through the fog / The gulls. Poem: "Through the fog / The gulls." Thomas McGrath. SP-McGrT

Through the gate, where nowhere and night begin. At the Airport. Howard Nemerov. CP-NemeH

Through the goalposts of. Dropkick Me Jesus. James Laughlin. CP-LaugJ

Through the great sinful streets of Naples as I past. Easter Day. Naples, 1849. Arthur Hugh Clough. SP-ClouA

Through the green forest softly without a sound. Edna St. Vincent Millay. CP-MillE

Through the groves of Tamarit. Qasida of the Branches. Federico García Lorca. CP-GarcF, tr. by Catherine Brown Fr. Qasidas.

Through the high leafy branches. Autumnal. Denise Levertov. SP-LeveDL

Through the high window, upright rectangle of distance. Problem in Spatial Composition, A. Robert Penn Warren. CP-WarrR

Through the hours of yesternight. Emily Jane Brontë. CP-BronE

Through the Inner City to the Suburbs. Maya Angelou. SP-AngeM

Through the Junipers. William Stafford. SP-StafWW

Through the lanes. Procession. Federico García Lorca. SP-GarcF, tr. by Lysander Kemp Fr. Poem of the Saeta.

Through the laurel's branches. Qasida of the Dark Doves. Federico García Lorca. CP-GarcF, tr. by Catherine Brown Fr. Qasidas.

Through the left lashes of the left. War Duty. Alan Dugan. CP-DugaA

Through the long hall the shuttered windows shed. Panorama, The. John Greenleaf Whittier. CP-WhitJ

Through the Looking-Glass. W. H. Auden. CP-AudeW

Through the Metidja to Abd-el-Kadr. Robert Browning. CP-BroR1

Through the midnight streets of Babylon. Candles in Babylon. Denise Levertov. SP-LeveDL; SP-LeveDS

Through the open window he could see a flock of ducks. Sorrel. Raymond Carver. CP-CarvR

Through the Parklands, through the Parklands. Parklands, The. Stevie Smith. CP-SmitS

Through the Plagues of Egypt' we was chasin' Arabi. Jacket, The. Rudyard Kipling. CP-KiplR

Through the sea's crust of prisms looking up. Sea Burial. John Ciardi. CP-CiarJ

Through the shine, through the rain. Twilight Song. Edwin Arlington Robinson. CP-RobiE

Through the Smoke Hole. Gary Snyder. CP-SnydG

Through the soft evening air enwinding all. Italian Music in Dakota. Walt

Whitman. CP-WhitW

Through the strait-gate of passion. Paradise Re-entered. D. H. Lawrence. CP-LawrD

Through the strait pass of suffering. Emily Dickinson. CP-DickE

Through the streets of Marblehead. Landmarks, The. John Greenleaf Whittier. CP-WhitJ

Through the tasteless minute efficient room. E. E. Cummings. CP-CummE

Through the town-making stones I step lightly. Antipolis. James Dickey. CP-DickJ

Through the trees, with the moon underfoot. Owl King, The. James Dickey. CP-DickJ

Through the vaulted corridors. Corridor. Federico García Lorca. CP-GarcF, tr. by Jerome Rothenberg Fr. Palimpsests.

Through the water-eye of night. With the Huntress. George Meredith. CP-MerG1

Through the weeks of deep snow. Another Descent. Wendell Berry. CP-BerrW

Through the wide, grey loft window. Village Life, A. Derek Walcott. CP-WalcD

Through the world's low-water, the turn of the year. Child in the Crystal. Marya Alexandrovna Zaturenska. SP-ZatuM

Through thickest glooms look back, immortal shade. On the Death of Dr. Samuel Marshall. 1771. Phillis Wheatley. CP-WheaP

Through this my strong and new misaventure. Ballata: He perceives that his highest Love is gone from him. Guido Cavalcanti. CW-RossD, tr. by Dante Gabriel Rossetti

Through this sad winter as our crisis deepens. Lemuel Shaw's Meditation. Helen Pinkerton. CP-PinkH

Through those old Grounds of memory. Emily Dickinson. CP-DickE

Through throats where many rivers meet, the curlews cry. In the White Giant's Thigh. Dylan Thomas. CP-ThomD

Through thy battlements, Newstead, the hollow winds whistle. On Leaving Newstead Abbey. Lord Byron. CP-Byron

Through Thy clear spaces, Lord, of old. Invocation: "Through Thy clear spaces, Lord, of old." John Greenleaf Whittier. CP-WhitJ

Through Time. Michael Palmer. SP-PalmM

Through time their sharp features. Indians on Alcatraz, The. Paul Muldoon. CP-MuldP

Through torrid entrances, past icy poles. To Shakespeare. Hart Crane. CP-CranH

Through Two Points Only One Straight Line Can Pass. Yehuda Amichai. SP-AmicY, tr. by Stephen Mitchell

Through vaults of pain. Wasted Illness, A. Thomas Hardy. CP-HardT

Through Walls. Rae Armantrout. SP-ArmaA

Through weeds and thorns, and matted underwood. Picture, The. Samuel Taylor Coleridge. CP-ColeS

Through what doors will you enter, through what walls. Uninvited Guest, The. Marya Alexandrovna Zaturenska. SP-ZatuM

Through what extremes of passion. Hymn to Love Ended. William Carlos Williams. CP-WilW1

Through what fierce incarnations, furled. Beatific Vision, The. G. K. Chesterton. CP-ChesG

Through what transports of Patience. Emily Dickinson. CP-DickE

Through winter-time we call on spring. Wheel, The. William Butler Yeats. CP-YeatW

Through woods, Mme Une Telle, a trifle ill. Autumn Chapter in a Novel. Thom Gunn. CP-GunnT

Through your fine eyes I see such mellow light. Michelangelo Buonarroti. CP-Miche, tr. by John Frederick Nims

Throughout black winter the red haws withstood. Mayflower. Sylvia Plath. CP-PlatS

Throughout Our Lands. Czeslaw Milosz. CP-MiloC; CP-MiloCN, tr. by Peter Dale Scott

Throughout the field I find no grain. Winter in Durnover Field. Thomas Hardy. CP-HardT

Throughout the storm and party. Storm. Alice Walker. CP-WalkA

Throughout the world, if it were sought. Honesty. Sir Thomas Wyatt. CP-WyatT

Throw away thy rod. Discipline. George Herbert. CP-HerbG

Throw of the Dice, A. Stéphane Mallarmé. CP-MallS, tr. by Henry Weinfield

Throw of the dice / will never / even when launched in eternal, A. Throw of the Dice, A. Stéphane Mallarmé. CP-MallS, tr. by Henry Weinfield

Throw Pillows. Yehuda Amichai. SP-AmicYL, tr. by Benjamin Harshav and Barbara Harshav

Throw Roses. Carl Sandburg. CP-SandC

Throw roses on the sea where the dead went down. Throw Roses. Carl Sandburg. CP-SandC

Throw that ring / in the water. Marriage Vow. Federico García Lorca. CP-GarcF, tr. by Alan S. Trueblood Fr. Back of the World.

Throw your head back, child. Heaven's Carriage. Gabriela Mistral. SP-MistG, tr. by Maria Giachetti [or Jacketti]

Throwback, The. Paul Muldoon. CP-MuldP

Throwbacks. Carl Sandburg. CP-SandC

Throwing a careless pebble in the lake. Archibald MacLeish. CP-MacLA Fr.

Happy Marriage, The.

Throwing a Tree. Thomas Hardy. CP-HardT

Throwing away the Mail. Wendell Berry. CP-BerrW

Throwing Salt on a Path. Arthur Sze. SP-SzeA

Throwing the Apple. Richard Eberhart. CP-EberR

Throwing Yourself Away. Richard Eberhart. CP-EberR

Thrown a / -way It, A. E. E. Cummings. CP-CummE

Thrown Away. Rudyard Kipling. *Fr.* Plain Tales from the Hills.

Thru our kitchen window I see the house. Neighbors. George Oppen. CP-OppGN

Thrush. Paul Muldoon. CP-MuldP

Thrush, because I'd been wrong, A. On Having Mis-identified a Wild Flower. Richard Wilbur. CP-WilbR

Thrush in February, The. George Meredith. CP-MerG1

Thrush in the Gaelic Islands, The. Archibald MacLeish. CP-MacLA

Thrush Song at Dawn. Richard Eberhart. CP-EberR

Thrushes. Ted Hughes. SP HughTN

Thrushes sing as the sun is going, The. Proud Songsters. Thomas Hardy. CP-HardT

Thrusting its armoury of hot delight. Descartes and the Stove. Charles Tomlinson. CP-TomlC; SP-TomlC

Thud, thud, all the sores go blind. View From a Porch. Thomas Lux. SP-LuxT

Thugs of clumsy mutter shove upward leaving fat. Noise. E. E. Cummings. CP-CummE

Thule. Walter De la Mare. CP-DeLaW

Thumb, loose tooth of a horse. Bestiary for the Fingers of My Right Hand. Charles Simic. SP-SimiC; SP-SimiCE

Thump. Thump. The door / which never is knocked upon but cries. Door, The. Robert Creeley. CP-CreeR

Thumping old tunes give a voice to its whereabouts. Fairground. W. H. Auden. CP-AudeW

Thunder. Elizabeth Bishop. CP-BishE

Thunder and lightning. The veil of the temple rent. Burma. Paul Muldoon. CP-MuldP

Thunder by the Musician. Wallace Stevens. CP-StevW; CP-StevWP

Thunder in Tuscany. Charles Tomlinson. CP-TomlC; SP-TomlC

Thunder is all it is, and yet. Spring Thunder. Adrienne Rich. CP-RicAE

Thunder of the Rain God. House in Taos, A. Langston Hughes. CP-HughL; CP-HughL2

Thunder over the Nursery. Ogden Nash. CP-NashO

Thunder Storm, A. William Cowper. CP-CowpW

Thunderbolt strikes the ocean, The. Birth of Venus, The. Randall Jarrell. CP-JarrR

Thundercloud hung on the mantel of our summer, A. Waterloo. Robert Lowell. SP-LoweR

Thunderhead. Archibald MacLeish. CP-MacLA

Thundering, a throbbing sea. End of Childhood. Eugenio Montale. CP-MontE, *tr. by* Jonathan Galassi

Thunderstorm in Town, A. Thomas Hardy. CP-HardT

Thurber, they have come, the secret bearers. Elegy for James Thurber. Thomas Merton. CP-MertT

Thure Kumlien. Lorine Niedecker. CP-NiedL

Thursday. John Ciardi. CP-CiarJ

Thursday. Edna St. Vincent Millay. CP-MillE

Thursday. James Schuyler. CP-SchuJ

Thursday. William Carlos Williams. CP-WilW1

Thurso's Landing. Robinson Jeffers. CP-JefR2

Thus. Charles Simic. SP-SimiC; SP-SimiCE

Thus after plain repast each cheerful guest. Horace. CP-SherT *Fr.* Satires.

Thus, brother theologian, here you are. Poet at Seventy. Czeslaw Milosz. CP-MiloC; CP-MiloCN

Thus Cacus-like, His Calves He Backwards Pulls. Thomas Sheridan. CP-SherT

Thus crosslegged on round pillow sat in Teton Space. Mind Breaths. Allen Ginsberg. CP-GinsA; SP-GinsA

Thus desire / Becomes knowledge. Theological Question, The. George Oppen. CP-OppGN

Thus Did Great Socrates Improve the Mind. Thomas Sheridan. CP-SherT

Thus did you strive to vouchsafe James to Heaven. On the Same ["Thus did you strive to vouchsafe James to Heaven"]. John Milton. CP-MiltJ

Thus equal deaths are dealt, and equal chance. Mezentius and Lausus. Virgil. CP-DryJ2, *tr. by* John Dryden *Fr.* Aeneid (Dryden translation).

Thus, even with her tongue cut out, Philomel narrated her torments. Philomel. Yannis Ritsos. SP-RitsY, *tr. by* N. C. Germanacos

Thus Far So Nobly Advanced. Kenneth Patchen. CP-PatcK

Thus far, to March, into the dangerous year. Dangerous Year, The. John Berryman. CP-BerrJ

Thus, for a season, they fought it fair. Rudyard Kipling. CP-KiplR *Fr.* Plain Tales from the Hills.

Thus have I back again[e] to thy bright name. Apology [*or* Apologie] for the Foregoing Hymn[e], An. Richard Crashaw. CP-CrasR

Thus having said, forthwith on her way went quick-footed Iris. Achilles over the Trench. Homer. CP-MerG2 *Fr.* Iliad, The.

Thus Her Tale. Walter De la Mare. CP-DeLaW

Thus / Hides the. George Oppen. CP-OppGN

Thus I / Pass [*or* Passe] by. Upon His Departure Hence. Robert Herrick. CP-HerrR

Thus I Resolve. Thomas Campion. CP-CampT

Thus I resolve, and time hath taught me so. Thus I Resolve. Thomas Campion. CP-CampT

Thus I wrote in London, musing on my betters. Robert Browning. CP-BroR2

Thus like a sailor [*or* Sayler] by the tempest hurled [*or* hurl'd]. Lucretius. CP-DryJ2 *Fr.* De Rerum Natura (On the Nature of Things).

Thus long my grief has kept me dumb. Threnodia Augustalis. John Dryden. CP-DryJ2

Thus pious ignorance with dubious praise. To the Unknown Author of the following Poem, and that of *Absalom and Achitophel.* T. Adams. CP-DryJ2

Thus Puppies that Adore the Dark. Thomas Sheridan. CP-SherT

Thus said The Lord in the Vault above the Cherubim. Last Chantey, The. Rudyard Kipling. CP-KiplR

Thus says the prophet of the Turk. Love of the World Reproved, The. William Cowper. CP-CowpW

Thus she had lain Africa. Maya Angelou. SP-AngeM

Thus should have been our travels. Over 2000 Illustrations and a Complete Concordance. Elizabeth Bishop. CP-BishE

Thus spake great Bedel from his tomb. Lines Written on a Window in the Episcopal Palace at Kilmore. *Unknown, sometimes at. to* Thomas Sheridan. CP-SherT

Thus spoke to my Lady, the knight full of care. Grand Question Debated, The. Jonathan Swift. CP-SwifJ

Thus therefore, he who feels the fiery dart. Concerning the Nature of Love. Lucretius. CP-DryJ2 *Fr.* De Rerum Natura (On the Nature of Things).

Thus to be lost and thus to sink and die. To Constantia, Singing. Percy Bysshe Shelley. CP-ShelP

Thus Tophet look'd; so grinned the brawling fiend. Thomas Gray. *See* Such Tophet was; so looked the grinning fiend

Thus Truly. David Ignatow. SP-IgnaD

Thus was Italy mov'd—nor did the chief. Virgil. CP-CowpW *Fr.* Aeneid [*or* Eneados *or* Aeneis], The.

Thus will despair. Succubus, The. Robert Graves. CP-GravR

Thwarted. Tu Fu. CP-KizeC, *tr. by* Carolyn Kizer

Thwarted, old friend! Here we are, balked again! Thwarted. Tu Fu. CP-KizeC, *tr. by* Carolyn Kizer

Thweet Poethy! let me *lithp* forthwith. Smitten Purist, The. James Whitcomb Riley. CP-RileJ

Thy absence overflows the rose. Old Song. Hart Crane. CP-CranH

Thy azure robe, I did behold. Julia's Petticoat. Robert Herrick. CP-HerrR

Thy beauty fades and with it too my love. Sonnet, A: "Thy beauty fades and with it too my love." Jones Very. CP-VeryJ

Thy beauty hangs around thee like. Fragment: Beauty's Halo. Percy Bysshe Shelley. CP-ShelP

Thy Better Self. Jones Very. CP-VeryJ

Thy Brother's Blood. Jones Very. CP-VeryJ

Thy cheek is pale with thought, but not from woe. Sonnet, to the Same. Lord Byron. CP-Byron

Thy country, Wilberforce, with just disdain. To William Wilberforce, Esq. William Cowper. CP-CowpW

Thy country's curse is on thee, darkest crest. To the Lord Chancellor. Percy Bysshe Shelley. CP-ShelP

Thy Cross cruciferous doth flower in all. Bundle of Myrrh Is My Well-Beloved unto Me, A. Christina Georgina Rossetti. CP-RosC2

Thy cross is hard to bear it weighs me down. Task, The. Jones Very. CP-VeryJ

Thy Days Are Done. Lord Byron. CP-Byron

Thy dewy looks sink in my breast. Stanza, Written at Bracknell. Percy Bysshe Shelley. CP-ShelP

Thy elder care shall from thy careful face. Sir Philip Sidney. SP-SidnP *Fr.* Arcadia.

Thy error, Frémont, simply was to act. To John C. Frémont. John Greenleaf Whittier. CP-WhitJ

Thy face is a still white house of holy things. E. E. Cummings. CP-CummE

Thy face is far from this our war. To the True Romance. Rudyard Kipling. CP-KiplR

Thy fainting spouse, yet still Thy spouse. Christina Georgina Rossetti. CP-RosC2

Thy father all from thee, by his last will. Disinherited. John Donne. CP-DonnJ; MW-DonnJ

Thy Father's House. Jones Very. CP-VeryJ

Thy fingers make early flowers of. E. E. Cummings. CP-CummE; SP-CummE

Thy flattering picture, Phryne, is like thee. Phryne. John Donne. CP-DonnJ; MW-DonnJ

Thy foes to hunt, thy enviers to strike down. To the Shah, from Hafiz. Hafiz. CP-EmerR

Thy former coming was to cure. Christs Twofold Coming. Robert Herrick. CP-HerrR

Thy Friend and Thy Father's Friend Forget Not. Christina Georgina Rossetti. CP-RosC2

Thy friend, whom thy deserts to thee enchain[e]. To Mr C. B. John Donne. CP-DonnJ; MW-DonnJ

Thy Friendship oft has made my heart to ache [or ake]. To H[ayley]. William Blake. CP-BlakW

Thy functions are ethereal. On the Power of Sound. William Wordsworth. CP-WorW2; MW-WorW

Thy gift, if that it be of God. To a Dejected Poet. Ambrose Bierce. SP-BierA

Thy gifts are not the gifts that others give. Not as the World giveth. Jones Very. CP-VeryJ

Thy Gleeman Who Flattered Thee. Charles Olson. CP-OlsoC

Thy God was making hast into thy roofe. Matthew 8; I Am Not Worthy that Thou Should'st Come Under my Roofe. Bible, *N.T.* CP-CrasR *Fr.* St. Matthew.

Thy gracious ear, O Lord, encline. Bible, *O.T. See* Bow down thine ear, O Lord, hear me

Thy gracious ways, / O Lady of my heart, have. Canzone: Of Incense. Ezra Pound. CP-PoEar

Thy greatest knew thee, Mother Earth; unsoured. Spirit of Shakespeare, The. George Meredith. CP-MerG1

Thy Guardians are asleep. E.G. to M.R. Emily Jane Brontë. CP-BronE

Thy hands are washt, but o the waters spilt. To Pontius Washing His Hands. Richard Crashaw. CP-CrasR

Thy husband—poor, poor Heart!—is dead. Slow Nature, The. Thomas Hardy. CP-HardT

Thy husband to a banquet goes with me. Elegy 1.4: "Thy husband to a banquet goes with me." Ovid. CP-MarlC *Fr.* Elegies.

Thy knowledge cannot reach. Spiritual Birth, The. Jones Very. CP-VeryJ

Thy Land to favour graciously. Bible, *O.T. See* Lord, thou hast been favourable unto thy land

Thy lilies drink the dew, / Thy lambs the rill, and I will drink them too. Christina Georgina Rossetti. CP-RosC2

Thy little footsteps on the sands. To William Shelley. Percy Bysshe Shelley. CP-ShelP

Thy look of love has power to calm. To Harriet. Percy Bysshe Shelley. CP-ShelP

Thy lovely saints do bring Thee love, / Incense and joy and gold. Ransomed of the Lord, The. Christina Georgina Rossetti. CP-RosC2

Thy Name. Jones Very. CP-VeryJ

Thy name be hallowed, e'en thy Holy name. Hallowed be thy Name. Jones Very. CP-VeryJ

Thy Name, O Christ, as incense streaming forth. Christina Georgina Rossetti. CP-RosC2

Thy poems Hafiz shame the rose leaves. Hafiz. CP-EmerR *Fr.* Odes.

Thy praise or dispraise is to me alike. To Fool or Knave. Ben Jonson. CP-JonsB; SP-JonsB

Thy promise was to love me best. Sir Thomas Wyatt. CP-WyatT

Thy prophecies are but a lying tale. Aeschylus. CP-WildO *Fr.* Agamemnon.

Thy reliques, ROWE, to this fair Urn we trust. Epitaph Intended for Mr. Rowe, in Westminster Abbey. Alexander Pope. CP-PopeA

Thy rest has come thy long expected rest. Sabbath, The ("Thy rest has come thy long expected rest"). Jones Very. CP-VeryJ

Thy servant I am. Unfulfilling Brightnesses, The. Kenneth Patchen. CP-PatcK

Thy servant is in irons. Prisoner, The. Raissa Maritain. CP-MertT

Thy Servant Will Go and Fight with This Philistine. Christina Georgina Rossetti. CP-RosC2

Thy service Father! wants not aught beside. Eden. Jones Very. CP-VeryJ

Thy shadow, Earth, from Pole to Central Sea. At a Lunar Eclipse. Thomas Hardy. CP-HardT

Thy sins [or sinnes] and hairs [or haires] may no man equal[l] call. Licentious Person, A. John Donne. CP-DonnJ; MW-DonnJ

Thy songs O Hafiz. Hafiz. CP-EmerR *Fr.* Odes.

Thy sooty godhead I desire. To Vulcan. Robert Herrick. CP-HerrR

Thy soul / Grown delicate with satieties. O Atthis. Ezra Pound. SP-PounE

Thy soul shall find itself alone. Spirits of the Dead. Edgar Allan Poe. CP-PoeEd

Thy sting sufficeth, Death. If Heidegger first. Sonnet: "Thy sting sufficeth, Death. If Heidegger first." Hayden Carruth. CP-CarHS *Fr.* Sonnets.

Thy sudden terrors strike the world with dread. On the Great Earthquake in New Grenada. Jones Very. CP-VeryJ

Thy summer voice, Musketaquit. Two Rivers. Ralph Waldo Emerson. CP-EmerR

Thy sun is near meridian height. Written in the Gaaldine Prison Caves to A.G.A. Emily Jane Brontë. CP-BronE

Thy time is thee to wend. Interludium. Hart Crane. CP-CranH

Thy tones are silver melted into sound. To a Lady Playing the Harp. Paul Laurence Dunbar. CP-DunbP

Thy trespasses my heart has not forgiven. Forgive Me My Trespasses. Jones Very. CP-VeryJ

Thy various works, imperial queen, we see. On Imagination. Phillis Wheatley. CP-WheaP

Thy verse is "sad" enough, no doubt. To the Author of a Sonnet Beginning " 'Sad Is My Verse,' You Say, 'And Yet No Tear' " Lord Byron. CP-Byron

Thy way is simple for I am the light. I Am the Way. Jones Very. CP-VeryJ

Thy Will Be Done. John Greenleaf Whittier. CP-WhitJ

Thyestes. Seneca.

    "Climb at court for me that will." CP-MarvA, *tr. by* Andrew Marvell

Thyestes. Donald Davie. CP-DaviDC

Thyestes. Louis MacNeice. CP-MacNL

Thylacine, long thought to be extinct, The. Popular Revivals 1956. John Updike. CP-UpdiJ

Thyme. Louis Zukofsky. CP-ZukLS

Thyme Flowering among Rocks. Richard Wilbur. CP-WilbR

Thyrsis. Matthew Arnold. SP-ArnoM

Thyrsis, when we parted, swore. Song: "Thyrsis, when we parted, swore." Thomas Gray. CP-GrayT

Tibbie Dunbar. Robert Burns. CP-BurnR

Tibbie Fowler. Robert Burns. CP-BurnR

Tibby I hae seen the day. Song: "Tibby I hae seen the day." Robert Burns. CP-BurnR

Tiber, Nile, and Thames. Dante Gabriel Rossetti. CW-RossD

Tibia, tarsal, skull, and shin. Elegy for a Cave Full of Bones. John Ciardi. CP-CiarJ

Tibullus, whom I love and praise. Epistle 1.4: "Tibullus, whom I love and praise." Horace. SP-SmarC *Fr.* Epistles.

Tick / notch / fanrandole. For Clark Coolidge. Philip Whalen. SP-WhalP

Tick of time that stones the heads of kings, A. Blues for the Old Revolutionary Woman. Thomas McGrath. SP-McGrT

Ticker tapes roll down my sides, The. Along the Road. Mona Van Duyn. SP-VanDM

Tickets are expensive. So are the hotels. Abroad. Joseph Brodsky. CP-BrodJ *Fr.* Shorts.

Ticking—ticking—ticking of the clock!, The. Time. James Whitcomb Riley. CP-RileJ

Tidal Lagoon. W. S. Merwin. SP-MerwWF

Tide, The. Denise Levertov. SP-LeveDP

Tide, The. Jones Very. CP-VeryJ

Tide at Long Point, The. May Swenson. SP-SwenM

Tide goes down, uncovering its gifts, The. Promise, The. Charles Tomlinson. CP-TomlC

Tide goes up and down in the creek, The. Phenomena. John Updike. CP-UpdiJ

Tide-swell grinds crystal, under cliffs, The. Violet at Lough Aughresberg, A. Ted Hughes. SP-HughTN

Tide, the number 9 and creation, The. Discrete Gloss, A. Charles Olson. CP-OlsoC

Tides. Wallace Stevens. CP-StevWP

Tidewater Winter. Amy Clampitt. CP-ClamA

Tidings. Czeslaw Milosz. CP-MiloC; CP-MiloCN, *tr. by* Lillian Vallee

Tidings. Dan Pagis. SP-PagiD, *tr. by* Stephen Mitchell

Tie my hands, hang me up. S & M. Yusef Komunyakaa. CP-KomuY

Tie the Strings to my Life, My Lord. Emily Dickinson. CP-DickE

Tientai Mountains are my home, The. Han-shan. CP-ColdM, *tr. by* Red Pine

Tierra Del Fuego. Adam Zagajewski. SP-ZagaA, *tr. by* Clare Cavanagh

Tiger. Josephine Jacobsen. CP-JacoJ

Tiger, The. Robert Creeley. CP-CreeR

Tiger, The. Laura Riding Jackson. CP-RidiL

Tiger at the Movie-Show. Donald Davie. CP-DaviDC

Tiger came, A. Afternoon. Charles Olson. CP-OlsoC

Tiger in me I know late, not burning bright, The. Tiger, The. Laura Riding Jackson. CP-RidiL

Tiger in the tiger-pit, The. Lines for an Old Man. T. S. Eliot. CP-ElioT

Tiger kills hungry, The. The machine-guns. Tiger-Psalm. Ted Hughes. SP-HughTN

Tiger looks the younger and more male, The. Zambesi and Ranee. May Swenson. SP-SwenM

Tiger on Parade, The. Nicholas Vachel Lindsay. CP-LindV

Tiger-Psalm. Ted Hughes. SP-HughTN

Tiger shark, A. Mismatched Shoes. Yusef Komunyakaa. CP-KomuY

Tiger Skull. Charles Tomlinson. CP-TomlC

Tiger-Tiger. Rudyard Kipling. *Fr.* Second Jungle Book, The.

Tiger was his prototype, The. Tippoo's Tiger. Marianne Craig Moore. CP-MoorM

Tight. A. R. Ammons. CP-AmmoA

Tight-Rope Construction Surrounded by a Thousand Sonnets. Robert Stock. SP-StocR

Tight-socketed in space, they watch. Ponte Veneziano. Charles Tomlinson. CP-TomlC

Tightly-folded bud. Born Yesterday. Philip Larkin. CP-LarkP

Tightness and the nilness round that space, The. From the Frontier of Writing. Seamus Heaney. SP-HeanSO

Tightrope Walker, The. Yannis Ritsos. SP-RitsY, *tr. by* Christian McEwen *and* Nikos Tsingos

Tilda Trimpett and her seventh stage name. Starlet. John Ciardi. CP-CiarJ

Tiles of the swimming pool are azure, The. Lines Written in the Euganean Hills. Charles Tomlinson. CP-TomlC

Till all sweet gums and juices flow. Prince's Progress, The. Christina Georgina Rossetti. CP-RosC1

Till both my temples are completely white. Petrarch. CP-Petra, *tr. by* J. G. Nichols

Till dawn the wind drove round me. It is past. Dawn on the Night Journey. Dante Gabriel Rossetti. CW-RossD

Till Death—is narrow Loving. Emily Dickinson. CP-DickE

Till eight days like any happy fly. Course of a Life, The. Yehuda Amichai. SP-AmicY, *tr. by* Chana Bloch

Till I have peace with thee, war other men. Love's War. John Donne. MW-DonnJ *Fr.* Elegies.

Till I shall come again, let this suffice. Panegyric to Sir Lewis Pemberton, A. Robert Herrick. CP-HerrR

Till it has loved—no man or woman. Emily Dickinson. SP-DickE

Till Other Voices Wake Us. George Oppen. CP-OppGN

Till the Wind Gets Right. Paul Laurence Dunbar. CP-DunbP

Till they seemed to trip and trap. Ted Hughes.

Till thinking had worn out my enterprise. Spring Mountain Climb. Richard Eberhart. CP-EberR

Till Tomorrow. Christina Georgina Rossetti. CP-RosC2

Tillamook Burn, The. William Stafford. SP-StafWW

Tillaquils, The. Laura Riding Jackson. CP-RidiL

Tillie. Gertrude Stein. CP-SteiG

Tilter, the most may admire thee, though not I. To Sir Annual Tilter. Ben Jonson. CP-JonsB; SP-JonsB

Tilth. Robert Graves. CP-GravR

Tim and the Fables. Jonathan Swift. CP-SwifJ

"Dear Tim, no more such angry speeches." CP-SherT

Tim Murphy's gon' walkin' wid Maggie O'Neill. Circumstances Alter Cases. Paul Laurence Dunbar. CP-DunbP

Timber Moon. Carl Sandburg. CP-SandC

Timber Wings. Carl Sandburg. CP-SandC

Time. Yannis Ritsos. SP-RitsY *Fr.* Monovasia.

Time. Amy Clampitt. CP-ClamA

Time. Robert Graves. CP-GravR

Time. George Herbert. CP-HerbG

Time. Thomas Lux. SP-LuxT

Time. George Meredith. CP-MerG2

Time. James Merrill. SP-MerrJ

Time. Grace Paley.

Time. James Whitcomb Riley. CP-RileJ

Time. Percy Bysshe Shelley. CP-ShelP

Time. Jones Very. CP-VeryJ

Time, The. Robert Creeley. CP-CreeR

Time all of a sudden tightens the tether. Preface to the Past. Ogden Nash. CP-NashO

Time and again, time and again I tie. Edge, The. Louise Glück. SP-GlucL

Time and Sentiment. George Meredith. CP-MerG1

Time and Space decreed his lot. Inventor, The. Rudyard Kipling. CP-KiplR *Fr.* Muse among the Motors, The.

Time and Space Were Only Their Disguises. Philip Larkin. CP-LarkP

Time and the Thing-in-Itself in a Textbook. Randall Jarrell. CP-JarrR

Time and Time Again. A. K. Ramanujan. CP-RamaA

Time and time again we told them. Melted Money. Heather McHugh. SP-McHuH

Time as Hypnosis. Robert Penn Warren. CP-WarrR

Time,be kind;herself and i. E. E. Cummings. CP-CummE

Time Beneath, The. Laura Riding Jackson. CP-RidiL

Time Cannot Be Worn. Hart Crane. CP-CranH

Time cannot break the bird's wing from the bird. To a Young Poet. Edna St. Vincent Millay. CP-MillE

Time ("Can't live / mindless"). Robert Creeley. SP-CreeR

Time Capsule. William Stafford. SP-StafW

Time comes spirit weakens and goes blank apartments shuffled through and forgotten. Names, The. Allen Ginsberg. CP-GinsA; SP-GinsA

Time comes to go deeper, The. As I Lay Dying. Charles Bukowski. SP-BukC2

Time comes when you count the names—whether, The. Small Eternity. Robert Penn Warren. CP-WarrR

Time Defies and Betrays the Patricians. Shmuel HaNagid. SP-HaNaS, *tr. by* Peter Cole

Time does go on. Emily Dickinson. CP-DickE

Time does not bring relief; you all have lied. Edna St. Vincent Millay. CP-MillE

Time drops in decay. Moods, The. William Butler Yeats. CP-YeatW

Time Exposure. Josephine Jacobsen. CP-JacoJ

Time feels so vast that were it not. Emily Dickinson. CP-DickE

Time for a Smoke. Louis MacNeice. CP-MacNL

Time for the wood, the clay. Kept. Louise Bogan. CP-BogaL

Time grows dim. Time that was so long. For Mr. Death Who Stands with His Door Open. Anne Sexton. CP-SextA; SP-SextA

Time had come for me to establish peace, The. Petrarch. CP-Petra, *tr. by* J. G. Nichols

Time Has Come to Collect Evidence, The. Yehuda Amichai. SP-AmicYL, *tr. by* Benjamin Harshav *and* Barbara Harshav

Time has gone by, The. Never Born. Carl Sandburg. CP-SandC

Time Hinder Not Me; His Arms Reach Here and There. Muriel Rukeyser. CP-RukeM

Time in the seed that grief put down, return. Anniversary. Howard Nemerov. CP-NemeH

Time Is an Inclusion Series Said McTaggart. Kenneth Rexroth. CP-RexrK

Time is at an end, The. Ox-bow. Donald Davie. CP-DaviDC

Time is divided into. Time Is the Mercy of Eternity. Kenneth Rexroth. CP-RexrK

Time is hunger, space is cold. Great Prayer. Alfonso Cortes. CP-MertT, *tr. by* Thomas Merton

Time / is in night's colors. First/Last Meditation. Federico García Lorca. CP-GarcF, *tr. by* Jerome Rothenberg *Fr.* In the Forest of Clocks.

Time is not gone. Why the Face of a Clock is not Truly a Circle. Archibald MacLeish. CP-MacLA

Time is short and full. Emily Dickinson. SP-DickE

Time is slow. The light smooths surfaces, penetrates. Provincial Spring. Yannis Ritsos. SP-RitsY, *tr. by* N. C. Germanacos

Time is so long when a man is dead! Dead Lover, The. James Whitcomb Riley. CP-RileJ

"Time" is some sort of hindsight. Robert Creeley. CP-CreeR

Time is, The. Anger. Robert Creeley. CP-CreeR

Time is the Bound of things, where e're we go. Death Ends All Woe. Robert Herrick. CP-HerrR

Time Is the Late Train into Albany. John Ciardi. CP-CiarJ

Time Is the Mercy of Eternity. Kenneth Rexroth. CP-RexrK

Time Lapse with Tulips. Tess Gallagher. SP-GallT

Time lengthening, in the lengthening seemeth long. Christina Georgina Rossetti. CP-RosC2

Time like an ever-rolling stream. And Our Eternal Home. Donald Davie. CP-DaviDC

Time like glass. Void Only. Kenneth Rexroth. CP-RexrK

Time Long Past. Percy Bysshe Shelley. CP-ShelP

Time Marches On. Ogden Nash. CP-NashO

Time mocks but I would mock it. Way Out, A. Richard Eberhart. CP-EberR

Time ("Moment to / moment the"). Robert Creeley. CP-CreeR

Time moves in and out of me. Sonnet: "Time moves in and out of me." A. K. Ramanujan. CP-RamaA

Time, never wand'ring from his annual round. John Milton. *See* In his perpetual cycle Time, rolling back

Time: 1978. C. K. Williams. SP-WillC

Time: 1976. C. K. Williams. SP-WillC

Time now good-byes were said. Michelangelo Buonarroti. CP-Miche, *tr. by* John Frederick Nims

Time of Bees, A. Mona Van Duyn. SP-VanDM

Time of Clearer Twitterings. James Whitcomb Riley. CP-RileJ

Time of crisp and tawny leaves. Time of Clearer Twitterings. James Whitcomb Riley. CP-RileJ

Time of destruction. Of the most rigid powers of ascendance, A. Not Yet. Muriel Rukeyser. CP-RukeM

Time of Disturbance. Robinson Jeffers. CP-JefR3

Time of finks and nobles, A. Muriel Rukeyser. CP-RukeM

Time of gifts has come again, The. Pressed Gentian, The. John Greenleaf Whittier. CP-WhitJ

Time of school drags by with waiting, The. Childhood. Randall Jarrell. CP-JarrR

Time of the brown gold comes softly, The. Brown Gold. Carl Sandburg. CP-SandC

Time of the hawk counting chickens, of haystacks in, The. Season, A. Joseph Brodsky. CP-BrodJ

Time of the Missile. George Oppen. CP-OppGN

Time of Tree Cutting. W. S. Merwin. SP-MerwWF

Time of Waiting, A. Robert Graves. CP-GravR

Time of Waiting, The. Christina Georgina Rossetti. CP-RosC3

Time of year comes, The. Saturnalia. Thom Gunn. CP-GunnT

Time of year has grown indifferent, The. Man Whose Pharynx Was Bad, The. Wallace Stevens. CP-StevW; CP-StevWP

Time of Year, the Time of Day, The. Robert Pinsky. CP-PinsR

Time! on whose arbitrary wing. To Time. Lord Byron. CP-Byron

Time opens in a flower of bells. Hyacinth, The. Kathleen Jessie Raine. SP-RainK

Time Out. Robert Frost. CP-FrosR

Time ("Out window roof's slope"). Robert Creeley. SP-CreeR

Time Passes. Richard Eberhart. CP-EberR

Time Passes. Walter De la Mare. CP-DeLaW

Time passeth away with its pleasure and pain. Christina Georgina Rossetti. CP-RosC2

Time Passing, Beloved. Donald Davie. CP-DaviDC

Time Past, A. Denise Levertov. SP-LeveDL

Time-polished skulls of Yagan & Pemulwy. Protection of Moveable Cultural Heritage. Yusef Komunyakaa. CP-KomuY

Time, Real and Imaginary. Samuel Taylor Coleridge. MW-ColeS

Time ripening for the bow, she, lingered. Theodore Weiss. SP-WeisT *Fr.* Storeroom, The.

Time running beneath the pillow wakes. Disintegration. Philip Larkin. CP-LarkP

Time says hush. Gong of Time, The. Carl Sandburg. CP-SandC

Time seems not short: / If so I call to mind. Christina Georgina Rossetti. CP-RosC2

Time Spirals. Kenneth Rexroth. CP-RexrK

Time swings her burning hands. Way Down, The. Stanley Kunitz. CP-KunSC

Time tells them. They go along touching. Haycutters. William Stafford. SP-StafWW

Time, that is pleased to lengthen out the day. Edna St. Vincent Millay. CP-MillE

Time, that renews the tissues of this frame. Sonnet: "Time, that renews the tissues of this frame." Edna St. Vincent Millay. CP-MillE

Time the Bridegroom stayes from hence, The. Mora Sponsi, the Stay of the Bridegroome. Robert Herrick. CP-HerrR

Time the Hangman. William Carlos Williams. CP-WilW1

Time there was—as one may guess, A. Before Life and After. Thomas Hardy. CP-HardT

Time to Believe!, A. Kenneth Patchen. CP-PatcK

Time to Come. Ivor Gurney. SP-GurnI

Time to Come. Walt Whitman. CP-WhitW

Time to go. Robert Creeley. CP-CreeR

Time to grow old. Birthday. Robinson Jeffers. CP-JefR3

"Time to put off the world and go somewhere" Beggar to Beggar Cried. William Butler Yeats. CP-YeatW

Time to Stop. A. K. Ramanujan. CP-RamaA

Time to Talk, A. Robert Frost. CP-FrosR

Time to Tickle a Lizard, The. Lizard, The. Theodore Roethke. CP-RoetT

Time to Tinker 'Roun'! Paul Laurence Dunbar. CP-DunbP

Time wants to show you a different country. It's the one. Gift, The. William Stafford. SP-StafWW

Time was away and somewhere else. Meeting Point. Louis MacNeice. CP-MacNL

Time was, I walked in the February rain. Precession of the Equinoxes. Kenneth Rexroth. CP-RexrK

Time was my fire burned high, yes, even on ice. Michelangelo Buonarroti. CP-Miche, *tr. by* John Frederick Nims

Time was, not very long ago. Crime of 1903, The. Ambrose Bierce. SP-BierA

Time was. Time is. Time shall be. Solo for Saturday Night Guitar. Carl Sandburg. CP-SandC

Time was upon / The wing, to flie away. Upon Time. Robert Herrick. CP-HerrR

Time was when his half million drew. Bewick Finzer. Edwin Arlington Robinson. CP-RobiE

Time was when I was free as air. On a Goldfinch Starved to Death in His Cage. William Cowper. CP-CowpW

Time ("What happened to her"). Robert Creeley. CP-CreeR

Time will assuage. To the Reader. James Vincent Cunningham. CP-CunnJ

Time will come for these children, seated before their long black instruments, to strike the themes of love, The. Piano Practice at the Academy of the Holy Angels. Wallace Stevens. CP-StevWP

Time will come, The. Love after Love. Derek Walcott. CP-WalcD

Time will say nothing but I told you so. If I Could Tell You. W. H. Auden. CP-AudeW

Time X. James Tate. SP-TateJ

Time you tell us is the century and the day, The. In the Fullness of Time. Charles Tomlinson. CP-TomlC; SP-TomlC

Time you won your town the race, The. To an Athlete Dying Young. A. E. Housman. CP-HousA

Timeless / ly this / (merely and whose). E. E. Cummings. CP-CummE

Timeless Meeting. Robert Graves. CP-GravR

Timeless the pose as yesterday's caress. On Dieric Bouts's *Virgin and Child* (1460) in the California Palace of the Legion of Honor. Helen Pinkerton. CP-PinkH

Timeless, Twinned. Robert Penn Warren. CP-WarrR

Times, The. Lucille Clifton. SP-ClifL

Times are nightfall, look, their light grows less, The. Gerard Manley Hopkins. CP-HopkG

Times Are Tidy, The. Sylvia Plath. CP-PlatS

Times at Bellosguardo. Eugenio Montale. CP-MontE, *tr. by* Jonathan Galassi

Times Between, The. Wyatt Prunty. SP-PrunW

"Time's bitter flood!" Oh, that's all very well. In Exitum Cuiusdam. Ezra Pound. CP-PoEar

'Time's Conscience!' cried the allerion. For-ever Morning. Laura Riding Jackson. CP-RidiL

Time's Fool. John Updike. CP-UpdiJ

Time's greatest Mystery, the Word made man. Incarnation, The. Jones Very. CP-VeryJ

Time's House. Jones Very. CP-VeryJ

Times is mighty stirrin' 'mong de people up ouah way, De. How Lucy Backslid. Paul Laurence Dunbar. CP-DunbP

Times I've searched through southern pine groves, The. Royal Pavilion, The. Jaroslav Seifert. SP-SeifJ, *tr. by* Ewald Osers

Time's Revenges. Robert Browning. CP-BroR1

Time's sea hath been five years at its slow ebb. To ———: "Time's sea hath been five years at its slow ebb." John Keats. CP-KeatJ

Times-Square-Shoeshine-Composition. Maya Angelou. SP-AngeM

Times Square Water Music. Amy Clampitt. CP-ClamA

Times Table, The. Robert Frost. CP-FrosR

Time's wily Chargers will not wait. Emily Dickinson. CP-DickE

Times Worsen, The. Randall Jarrell. CP-JarrR

Timesweep. Carl Sandburg. CP-SandC

Timid muse reluctant to intrude, The. Epistle to General Washington [May 26, 1787]. Annis Boudinot Stockton. CP-StocA

Timing. A. R. Ammons. CP-AmmoA

Timing Her. Thomas Hardy. CP-HardT

Timolaos is the first musician. Timolaos the Syracusan. Constantine P. Cavafy. CP-CavaC, *tr. by* Theoharis Constantine Theoharis

Timolaos the Syracusan. Constantine P. Cavafy. CP-CavaC, *tr. by* Theoharis Constantine Theoharis

Timoleon. Herman Melville. SP-MelvH

Timor amoris conturbat me. James Laughlin. CP-LaugJ

Timor Dei. James Vincent Cunningham. CP-CunnJ

Timorous Hind, The. Samuel Taylor Coleridge. CP-ColeS

Tin bucket, A. Sketch for a Portrait of Henry Ford. William Carlos Williams. CP-WilW2

Tin Cup. Gregory Orr. SP-OrrG

Tin Fish. Rudyard Kipling. CP-KiplR

Tin-roofed shack by the railroad, The. Two Guitar Pieces. Philip Larkin. CP-LarkP

Tin shack, where my baby sleeps on his back. Everything: Eloy, Arizona, 1956. Ai. SP-Ai

Tin Wedding Whistle. Ogden Nash. CP-NashO

Tinder. Seamus Heaney. SP-HeanSO

Tinder, The. Thomas Carew. CP-CareT

Tingle: / a shaft must be imagined to. Getting Warm. Rae Armantrout. SP-ArmaA

Tingling Back, The. Karl Shapiro. SP-ShapK

Tiniest ones are the mightiest, The. Emily Dickinson. SP-DickE

Tinker, The. William Wordsworth. CP-WorW1; MW-WorW

Tinker Jack and the Tidy Wives. Sylvia Plath. CP-PlatS

Tinker out of Bedford, A. Holy War, The. Rudyard Kipling. CP-KiplR

Tinkers Song, The. Robert Herrick. CP-HerrR

Tinkle of Bells, A. James Whitcomb Riley. CP-RileJ

Tinkle on, O sweet guitar. To the Serenader. James Whitcomb Riley. CP-RileJ

Tinkling treble, / Rolling bass. Dream Boogie: Variation. Langston Hughes. CP-HughL; CP-HughL3

Tinsel glitter, and the specious mein, The. Phaedrus. CP-JohnS *Fr.* Fabulae.

Tinsel in February, tinsel in August. Pieces. Wallace Stevens. CP-StevW; CP-StevWP

Tint I cannot take—is best, The. Emily Dickinson. CP-DickE

Tiny Energies. Gary Snyder. CP-SnydG

Tiny fingers outspread. Failure, A. D. H. Lawrence. CP-LawrD

Tiny fish enjoy themselves, The. Little Fish. D. H. Lawrence. CP-LawrD

Tiny green birds skate over the surface of the room. Saturday Night in the Parthenon. Kenneth Patchen. CP-PatcK

Tiny immortal streams are on the move. Thaw. Philip Larkin. CP-LarkP

Tiny moon as small and white as a single jasmine flower, A. White Blossom, A.

D. H. Lawrence. CP-LawrD

Tiny orange-wing-tipped butterfly. Bixby Canyon Ocean Path Word Breeze. Allen Ginsberg. CP-GinsA

Tiny Place, A. Robert Creeley. CP-CreeR

Tiny queen, / Lelloine! Lelloine. James Whitcomb Riley. CP-RileJ

Tiny untamed window on the fifth. Rainer Maria Rilke. CP-RilkFr, *tr. by* A. Poulin, Jr. *Fr.* Windows, The.

Tip, The. Suite of Six Pieces for Siskind, A. John Logan. CP-LogaJ

Tippoo's Tiger. Marianne Craig Moore. CP-MoorM

Tips of celery. Farm, The. Robert Creeley. CP-CreeR

Tips of the reeds silver in sunlight. A cold wind. In the Bodies of Words. May Swenson. SP-SwenM

Tirade for the Next-to-Last Act. Nina Cassian. CP-KizeC, *tr. by* Carolyn Kizer

Tir'd with vain hopes, and with complaints as vain. For Sir W. Trumbull. Alexander Pope. CP-PopeA

Tired. Langston Hughes. CP-HughL; CP-HughL1

Tired agnostic longs for prayer, The. Agnostic, The. Edna St. Vincent Millay. CP-MillE

Tired banana & an empty mind, A. Dante's Tomb. John Berryman. CP-BerrJ

Tired Cupid, The. Walter De la Mare. CP-DeLaW

Tired of a landscape known too well when young. Story. Philip Larkin. CP-LarkP

Tired of the old descriptions of the world. Latest Freed Man, The. Wallace Stevens. SP-StevW; CP-SteVWP

Tired of the sad hospital and the fetid smell. Windows, The. Stéphane Mallarmé. CP-MallS, *tr. by* Henry Weinfield

Tired Out. James Whitcomb Riley. CP-RileJ

"Tired out!" Yet face and brow. Tired Out. James Whitcomb Riley. CP-RileJ

Tired. / Subterrene laughter synchronous. Ode on Independence Day, July 4th 1918. T. S. Eliot. SP-ElioT

Tires on Wet Asphalt at Night. Robert Penn Warren. CP-WarrR

Tires slowly came to a rubbery stop, The. Gazing Grain, The. John Ashbery. SP-AshbJ

Tiresias, having squinted into your ingle. Inquest. Robert Stock. SP-StocR

Tiriel. William Blake. CP-BlakW

Tirocinium; or, A Review of Schools. William Cowper. CP-CowpW

Tirsi, A. Christina Georgina Rossetti. CP-RosC3

'Tis a fine deceit. Hayden Carruth. CP-CarHS *Fr.* Bloomingdale Papers, The.

'Tis a Great Thing to Live. Jones Very. CP-VeryJ

'Tis a great thing to live. Not small the task. 'Tis a Great Thing to Live. Jones Very. CP VeryJ

'Tis a high stone pile. Sepulchre of the Books, The. Jones Very. CP-VeryJ

'Tis a known principle in War. Eyes, The. Robert Herrick. CP-HerrR

'Tis a May morning. Meditation on a Holiday. Thomas Hardy. CP-HardT

'Tis a new life—thoughts move not as they did. New Birth, The. Jones Very. CP-VeryJ

'Tis a record in heaven. You, that were. Eptiaph on Katherine, Lady Ogle. Ben Jonson. CP-JonsB

Tis a strange Place, this Limbo! not a Place. Limbo. Samuel Taylor Coleridge. CP-ColeS; MW-ColeS

'Tis all a great show. World, The ("'Tis all a great show"). Jones Very. CP-VeryJ

'Tis an old deserted homestead. Old Homestead, The. Paul Laurence Dunbar. CP-DunbP

'Tis Anguish grander than Delight. Emily Dickinson. CP-DickE

'Tis Art reclaims him! By those gifts of hers. Henry Irving. James Whitcomb Riley. CP-RileJ

Tis but a dog-like madness in bad Kings. Cruelty. Robert Herrick. CP-HerrR

'Tis customary as we part. Emily Dickinson. CP-DickE

'Tis Cypher lies beneath this crust. On an Insignificant. Samuel Taylor Coleridge. CP-ColeS

'Tis done:—I tow'r to that degree. On Taking a Batchelor's Degree. Christopher Smart. SP-SmarC

Tis done the world has vanished Christ remains. 'Tis Finished. Jones Very. CP-VeryJ

'Tis easier to pity those when dead. Emily Dickinson. CP-DickE

'Tis eight o'clock,—a clear March night. Idiot Boy, The. William Wordsworth. CP-WorW1; MW-WorW

'Tis Evanoe's, / A house not made with hands. House of Splendour, The. Ezra Pound. SP-PounE *Fr.* Und Drang.

'Tis evening now, the sun descends. Emily Jane Brontë. CP-BronE

'Tis evening, the black snail has got on his track. Evening. John Clare. SP-ClarJ

'Tis Ev'ning, my Sweet. To Electra. Robert Herrick. CP-HerrR

'Tis fine to play. Boy's Summer Song, A. Paul Laurence Dunbar. CP-DunbP

Tis finishd now the painful Conflicts o'er. Almira to Celadon, Founded on a Story in a Magazine. Annis Boudinot Stockton. CP-StocA

'Tis Finished. Jones Very. CP-VeryJ

'Tis five years since, "An end," said I. A. E. Housman. CP-HousA

'Tis Folly all—let me no more be told. Nativity, The. Jeanne Marie Bouvier de

la Motte- Guyon. CP-CowpW

'Tis forty to one. On Lord Carteret's Arms. Jonathan Swift. CP-SwifJ

'Tis Friendship's pledge, my young, fair FRIEND. To Chloris. Robert Burns. CP-BurnR

'Tis gone—with old belief and dream. Wishing-Gate Destroyed, The. William Wordsworth. CP-WorW2

'Tis good—the looking back on Grief. Emily Dickinson. CP-DickE

'Tis good to keep hinderward eyes. George Meredith. CP-MerG2

'Tis grown almost a danger to speak true. Epistle. To Katharine, Lady Aubigny. Ben Jonson. CP-JonsB

'Tis hard on Bagshot Heath to try. Ode to Sleep. Samuel Taylor Coleridge. CP-ColeS

'Tis hard to finde God, but to comprehend. God Not to be Comprehended. Robert Herrick. CP-HerrR

'Tis hard to say, if greater want of skill. Essay on Criticism, An. Alexander Pope. CP-PopeA

'Tis He Whose Yester-Evening's High Disdain. William Wordsworth. CP-WorW2

'Tis Heresie in others: In your face. Upon a Scarre in a Virgins Face. Robert Herrick. CP-HerrR

'Tis I have seen the coming man. George Meredith. CP-MerG2

'Tis just beyond mid-August. The summer has run mockingly away, as usual. Sometimes When Lovers Lie Quietly Together, Unexpectedly One of Them Will Feel the Other's Pulse. Hayden Carruth. CP-CarHS

'Tis known, at least it should be, that throughout. Beppo; a Venetian Story. Lord Byron. CP-Byron

'Tis liberty to serve one Lord; but he. Slavery. Robert Herrick. CP-HerrR

'Tis little I— could care for Pearls. Emily Dickinson. CP-DickE

'Tis midnight in the skies, my dear. George Meredith. CP-MerG2

'Tis moonlight, summer moonlight. Emily Jane Brontë. CP-BronE

Tis much among the filthy to be clean. Meane, The. Robert Herrick. CP-HerrR

'Tis murk upon the hills, but scarce a drop is flung. Windy Haymaking. George Meredith. CP-MerG2

'Tis mute, the word they went to hear on high Dodona mountain. Oracles, The. A. E. Housman. CP-HousA

'Tis my first night beneath the Sun. Emily Dickinson. CP-DickE

'Tis near the morning watch, the dim lamp burns. Morning Watch, The. Jones Very. CP-VeryJ

'Tis never or but seldom[e] known[e]. Power and Peace. Robert Herrick. CP-HerrR

'Tis "nine o'clock;" but few the summons heed. Nine O'Clock Bell, The. Jones Very. CP-VeryJ

Tis no discomfort in the world to fall. Comfort In Calamity. Robert Herrick. CP-HerrR

'Tis nobly done, a layman's creed professed. To Mr Dryden, on *Religio Laici*. Thomas Creech. CP-DryJ2

'Tis not a natural law alone. Dying Leaf, The. Jones Very. CP-VeryJ

'Tis not a thousand Bullocks thies. Cheerfulnesse in Charitie: or, The Sweet Sacrifice. Robert Herrick. CP-HerrR

'Tis not by water only but by blood. Christ, The. Jones Very. CP-VeryJ

'Tis not enough to overcome with arms. Outward Conquests Not Enough. Jones Very. CP-VeryJ

'Tis not ev'ry day that I. Not Every Day Fit for Verse. Robert Herrick. CP-HerrR

'Tis not for the unfeeling, the falsely refined. Farmer of Tilsbury Vale, The. William Wordsworth. CP-WorW1

'Tis not greatness they require. Sweetnesse in Sacrifice. Robert Herrick. CP-HerrR

'Tis not my voice now speaks; but as a bird. Nocturne: "'Tis not my voice now speaks; but as a bird." Walter De la Mare. CP-DeLaW

'Tis not that Dying hurts us so. Emily Dickinson. CP-DickE

'Tis not that I design to rob. Epistle to Robert Lloyd, Esq, An. William Cowper. CP-CowpW

'Tis not that Thou hast given to me. Immortal, The. Jones Very. CP-VeryJ

'Tis not the copious rains alone. Hymn: The Dew. Jones Very. CP-VeryJ

'Tis not the food, but the content. Content, Not Cates. Robert Herrick. CP-HerrR

'Tis not the lily-brow I prize. Song, ex improviso. Samuel Taylor Coleridge. CP-ColeS

'Tis not the swaying frame we miss. Emily Dickinson. CP-DickE

'Tis not the Walls, or purple, that defends. True Safety. Robert Herrick. CP-HerrR

'Tis not too late to build our young land right. To Reformers in Despair. Nicholas Vachel Lindsay. CP-LindV

Tis now dead night, and not a light on earth. To the Most Sacred Queen Anne. Thomas Campion. CP-CampT

'Tis now, since I sat[e] down before. Love's Siege. Sir John Suckling. CP-SuckJ

'Tis of the Father Hilary. World's Worth. Dante Gabriel Rossetti. CW-RossD

'Tis of the Father Hilary. Pax Vobis. Dante Gabriel Rossetti. CW-RossD

'Tis One by One—the Father counts. Emily Dickinson. CP-DickE

'Tis Opposites—entice. Emily Dickinson. CP-DickE

'Tis pleasant safely to behold from shore. Beginning of the Second Book, The. Lucretius. CP-DryJ2 *Fr.* De Rerum Natura (On the Nature of Things).

'Tis rent, the veil that parts the spirit world. Veil of the Temple, The. Jones Very. CP-VeryJ

Tis rumour'd, *Budgell* on a time. To Eustace Budgell, Esq., on His Translation of the Characters of Theophrastus. Alexander Pope. CP-PopeA

'Tis said, as Cupid danced [*or* danc't] among. How Roses Came Red. Robert Herrick. CP-HerrR

'Tis said that some have died for love. William Wordsworth. CP-WorW1; MW-WorW

'Tis said that to the brow of yon fair hill. Tradition of Oker Hill in Darley Dale, Derbyshire, A. William Wordsworth. CP-WorW2

'Tis Seasons since the Dimpled War. Emily Dickinson. CP-DickE

'Tis so appalling—it exhilirates. Emily Dickinson. CP-DickE

'Tis so much joy! 'Tis so much joy! Emily Dickinson. CP-DickE

'Tis spent—this burning day of June! Waggoner, The. William Wordsworth. CP-WorW1

'Tis spring; come out to ramble. Lent Lily, The. A. E. Housman. CP-HousA

'Tis still observ'd, that Fame ne'er sings. Fame. Robert Herrick. CP-HerrR

'Tis still observ'd, those men most valiant are. More Modest, More Manly. Robert Herrick. CP-HerrR

'Tis strange, the Miser should his Cares employ. Epistle IV, to Richard Boyle, Earl of Burlington. Alexander Pope. CP-PopeA

'Tis strange, what different thoughts inspire. Desire and Possession. Jonathan Swift. CP-SwifJ

'Tis Sunrise—Little Maid—Hast Thou. Emily Dickinson. CP-DickE

'Tis sweet to him, who all the week. Home-Sick. Samuel Taylor Coleridge. CP-ColeS

'Tis ten years since. Ten Years Since. Thomas Hardy. CP-HardT

'Tis the Chyrurgions praise, and height of Art. Lenitie. Robert Herrick. CP-HerrR

'Tis the clear light of love I praise. Canzon: The Spear. Ezra Pound. CP-PoEar

'Tis the middle of night by the castle clock. Christabel. Samuel Taylor Coleridge. CP-ColeS; MW-ColeS

'Tis the terror of tempest. The rags of the sail. Vision of the Sea, A. Percy Bysshe Shelley. CP-ShelP

'Tis the Witching Time [*or* Hour] of Night. John Keats. CP-KeatJ

'Tis the year's midnight, and it is the day's. Nocturnal[l] upon Saint Lucy's [*or* S. Lucy's *or* S. Lucies] Day, Being the Shortest Day, A. John Donne. CP-DonnJ; MW-DonnJ

'Tis thine, Constantius, to possess the skill. Ode to Constantius. Annis Boudinot Stockton. CP-StocA

'Tis time, I think, by Wenlock town. Wenlock Edge. A. E. Housman. CP-HousA

'Tis time this heart should be unmoved. On This Day I Complete My Thirty-sixth Year. Lord Byron. CP-Byron

'Tis to yourself I speak; you cannot know. Yourself. Jones Very. CP-VeryJ

'Tis true, dear[e] Ben, thy just chastizing [*or* chastising] hand. To Ben Jonson. Thomas Carew. CP-CareT

'Tis true, Idoloclastes Satyrane! Tombless Epitaph, A. Samuel Taylor Coleridge. CP-ColeS; MW-ColeS

'Tis true, I'm broke! Vows, oaths, and all I had. Elegy [*or* Elegie], An: "'Tis true, I'm broke! Vows, oaths, and all I had." Ben Jonson. CP-JonsB

'Tis true, my Lord, I gave my word. Seventh Epistle of the First Book of Horace Imitated, The. Alexander Pope. CP-PopeA

'Tis true that he is dead: but yet to choose. Elegy upon the Death of My Lord Francis Villiers, An. Andrew Marvell. CP-MarvA

'Tis true the wisdom that my mind exacts. My Theme: Continued. George Meredith. CP-MerG1

'Tis true—then why should I repine. In Sickness. Jonathan Swift. CP-SwifJ

'Tis true—They shut me in the Cold. Emily Dickinson. CP-DickE

'Tis true, 'tis day, what though it be? Break[e] of Day. John Donne. CP-DonnJ; MW-DonnJ

'Tis very fit the ambrosia of the gods. Henry David Thoreau. CP-ThorH

'Tis well, begone! your errand is perform'd. Agrippina. Thomas Gray. CP-GrayT

'Tis whiter than an Indian Pipe. Emily Dickinson. CP-DickE

Tis worse then barbarous cruelty to show. Pitie to the Prostrate. Robert Herrick. CP-HerrR

'Tis wretched in earnest to live like a mope. Ode 3.12: To Neobule. Horace. SP-SmarC *Fr.* Odes.

'Tis write on Paradise's gate. Hafiz. CP-EmerR *Fr.* Odes.

'Tis written by God's finger on our land. Freedom National, Slavery Sectional. Jones Very. CP-VeryJ

'Tis you, I think? Back from your week's work, Steve? One Who Married above Him. Thomas Hardy. CP-HardT

Titan! to whose immortal eyes. Prometheus. Lord Byron. CP-Byron

Titanettes, female fauna. Rubens' Women. Wisława Szymborska. SP-SzymW, *tr. by* Stanisław Barańczak *and* Clare Cavanagh

Tithe [*or* Tythe]: To the Bride, The. Robert Herrick. CP-HerrR

Tithonus. Alfred Tennyson. CP-TennA

Title divine—is mine! Emily Dickinson. CP-DickE

Title, The. William Carlos Williams. CP-WilW2

Title of Poet, The. Robert Graves. CP-GravR

Titmouse. Walter De la Mare. CP-DeLaW

Titmouse, The. Ralph Waldo Emerson. CP-EmerR

Tizdal my beautiful cat. Nodding. Stevie Smith. CP-SmitS

Tlanngershshsh! / Thrills of vibrant discord. Jazz, The. G. K. Chesterton. CP-ChesG

To. William Carlos Williams. CP-WilW1

To ———. William Wordsworth. *See* Sonnet: To———

To. Adam Zagajewski. SP-ZagaA, *tr. by* Renata Gorczynski

To ———. "Shu Ting." CP-KizeC, *tr. by* Carolyn Kizer *and* Y. H. Zhao

To a Bad Poet. Donald Davie. CP-DaviDC

To a Beautiful Quaker. Lord Byron. CP-Byron

To a Bed of Tulips. Robert Herrick. CP-HerrR

To a bell in Lincoln Cathedral. Oriental Visitor, An. Donald Davie. CP-DaviDC

To a Black Dancer in "The Little Savoy" Langston Hughes. *See* Midnight Dancer

To a Box Turtle. John Updike. CP-UpdiJ

To a Boy Whistling. James Whitcomb Riley. CP-RileJ

To a Bridegroom. Thomas Hardy. CP-HardT

To a Brother in the Mystery. Donald Davie. CP-DaviDC

To a Brown Girl. Countee Cullen. CP-CullC

To a Bully. Ambrose Bierce. SP-BierA

To a Butterfly. James Merrill. SP-MerrJ

To a Butterfly ("I've watched you now a full half-hour"). William Wordsworth. CP-WorW1; MW-WorW

To a Butterfly ("Stay near me—do not take thy flight!"). William Wordsworth. CP-WorW1; MW-WorW

To a Calvinist in Bali. Edna St. Vincent Millay. CP-MillE

To a Cape Ann Schooner. John Greenleaf Whittier. CP-WhitJ

To a Captious Critic. Paul Laurence Dunbar. CP-DunbP

To a Cat. Jorge Luis Borges. SP-BorgJ, *tr. by* Alastair Reid

To a Cat. John Keats. CP-KeatJ

   (To Mrs. Reynolds's Cat.) CP-KeatJ

To a Catherine Wheel. G. K. Chesterton. CP-ChesG

To a Censor. Ambrose Bierce. SP-BierA

To a Certain Cantatrice. Walt Whitman. CP-WhitW

To a Certain Civilian. Walt Whitman. CP-WhitW

To a Certain Friend. D. H. Lawrence. CP-LawrD

To a Certain Nation. G. K. Chesterton. CP-ChesG

To a Chameleon. Marianne Craig Moore. CP-MoorM

To a Child Dancing in the Wind. William Butler Yeats. CP-YeatW

To a Child in Calcutta. Galway Kinnell. SP-KinnGN

To a Child Trapped in a Barber Shop. Philip Levine. SP-LeviP

To a Child [Written in Her Album]. William Wordsworth. CP-WorW2

To a Chinese Woman. William Carlos Williams. CP-WilW2

To a Christian. Heather McHugh. SP-McHuH

To a City Sending Him Advertisements. Ezra Pound. CP-PoEar

To a Clergyman on the Death of His Lady. Phillis Wheatley. CP-WheaP

   (To the Rev. Mr. Pitkin, on the Death of His Lady.) CP-WheaP

To a Cloud. Jones Very. CP-VeryJ

To a Coin. Jorge Luis Borges. SP-BorgJ, *tr. by* Alastair Reid

To a Colleague. From the Country. Alan Dugan. CP-DugaA

To a Common Prostitute. Walt Whitman. CP-WhitW

To a Communist. Louis MacNeice. CP-MacNL

To a Composer. Arthur Sze. SP-SzeA

To a Comrade in Flanders. Wilfred Owen. CP-OwenW

To a Contemporary Bunkshooter. Carl Sandburg. CP-SandC

To a Convert. Yehuda Amichai. SP-AmicY, *tr. by* Chana Bloch

To a Creole Lady. Charles Baudelaire. CP-BaudC, *tr. by* Walter Martin

To a Critic. Samuel Taylor Coleridge. CP-ColeS

To A.D., Unreasonable, Distrustful of Her Own Beauty. Thomas Carew. CP-CareT

To a Dead Drunk. James Wright. CP-WrigJ

To a Dead Flame. John Updike. CP-UpdiJ

To a Dead Friend. Paul Laurence Dunbar. CP-DunbP

To a Dead Friend. Langston Hughes. CP-HughL; CP-HughL1

To a Dead Graduate Student. Thom Gunn. CP-GunnT

To a Dead Journalist. William Carlos Williams. CP-WilW1

To a Dead Man. Carl Sandburg. CP-SandC

To a Dead Vole. Stevie Smith. CP-SmitS

To a Defeated Savior. James Wright. CP-WrigJ

To a Dejected Poet. Ambrose Bierce. SP-BierA

To a Disdaynefull Fayre. Robert Herrick. CP-HerrR

To a Dog Injured in the Street. William Carlos Williams. CP-WilW2

To a Face in the Crowd. Robert Penn Warren. CP-WarrR

To a Fellow Poet. Joseph Brodsky. CP-BrodJ *Fr.* Shorts.

To a Fish Head Found on the Beach Near Málaga. Philip Levine. SP-LeviP

To a Foil'd European Revolutionaire. Walt Whitman. CP-WhitW

To a Freedom Fighter. Maya Angelou. SP-AngeM

To a Friend. Rainer Maria Rilke. CP-RilkFr, *tr. by* A. Poulin, Jr. *Fr.* Affectionate Taxes to France.

To a Friend. Matthew Arnold. SP-ArnoM

To a Friend. Robert Herrick. CP-HerrR

To a Friend. Ben Jonson. CP-JonsB; SP-JonsB

To a Friend. Howard Nemerov. CP-NemeH

To a Friend. John Greenleaf Whittier. CP-WhitJ

To a Friend. William Carlos Williams. CP-WilW1

To a Friend, an Epigram of Him. Ben Jonson. CP-JonsB; SP-JonsB

To a Friend, an Unhappy Poet. Miller Williams. CP-WillM

To a Friend and Fellow Poet. Hugh MacDiarmid. SP-MacDH

To a Friend [Charles Lamb] Who Had Declared His Intention of Writing No More Poetry. Samuel Taylor Coleridge. CP-ColeS

To a Friend, Composed near Calais, on the Road Leading to Ardres, August 7, 1802. William Wordsworth. MW-WorW

To a Friend Concerning Several Ladies. William Carlos Williams. CP-WilW1

To a Friend Estranged from Me. Edna St. Vincent Millay. CP-MillE

To a Friend Far Away. A. K. Ramanujan. CP-RamaA

To a Friend Going to Sea. Annis Boudinot Stockton. CP-StocA

To a Friend in Distress. William Cowper. CP-CowpW

To a Friend: In Memoriam. Joseph Brodsky. CP-BrodJ

To a Friend in Search of Rural Seclusion. Christopher Logue. SP-LoguC

To a Friend in Time of Trouble. Thom Gunn. CP-GunnT

To a Friend Lost. George Meredith. CP-MerG1

To a Friend, on Her Examination for the Doctorate in English. James Vincent Cunningham. CP-CunnJ

To a Friend Parting. Robert Penn Warren. CP-WarrR

To a Friend Who Had Been Much Abused in Many Inveterate Libels. Jonathan Swift. CP-SwifJ

To a Friend Who Had Persuaded Emelia to Marry, an Ode. Annis Boudinot Stockton. CP-StocA

To a Friend Who Sent Me Some Roses. John Keats. CP-KeatJ

To a Friend Whose Work Has Come to Nothing. William Butler Yeats. CP-YeatW

To a Friend Whose Work Has Come to Triumph. Anne Sexton. CP-SextA; SP-SextA

To a Friendly Dun. James Wright. CP-WrigJ

To a Fugitive. James Wright. CP-WrigJ

To A.G.A. Emily Jane Brontë. CP-BronE

To a Gentleman. Samuel Taylor Coleridge. *See* To William Wordsworth

To a Gentleman and Lady on the Death of the Lady's Brother and Sister, and a Child of the Name Avis, Aged One Year. Phillis Wheatley. CP-WheaP

To a Gentleman of the Navy. Phillis Wheatley. CP-WheaP

To a Gentleman on His Voyage to *Great-Britain* for the Recovery of His Health. Phillis Wheatley. CP-WheaP

To a Gentleman Who Had Sent Him a News-Paper, and Offered to Continue It Free of Expense. Robert Burns. CP-BurnR

To a Gentlewoman Objecting to Him His Grey Hairs. Robert Herrick. CP-HerrR

To a Gentlewoman on Just Dealing. Robert Herrick. CP-HerrR

To a Giraffe. Marianne Craig Moore. CP-MoorM

To a Girl in Malabar. Charles Baudelaire. CP-BaudC, *tr. by* Walter Martin

To a Girl Who Knew What Side Her Bread Was Buttered On. Audre Lorde. SP-LordA

To a Golden-Haired Girl in a Louisiana Town. Nicholas Vachel Lindsay. CP-LindV

To a Good man of most dear memory. Written after the Death of Charles Lamb. William Wordsworth. CP-WorW2

To a Haggis. Robert Burns. CP-BurnR

To a Hazel Tree. Czeslaw Milosz. CP-MiloCN, *tr. by* Robert Hass

To a high hill, that overlooks. Sunset in Haverhill, A. Jones Very. CP-VeryJ

To a Historian. Walt Whitman. CP-WhitW

To a Holy Roller. G. K. Chesterton. CP-ChesG

To a Hostess Saying Goodnight. James Wright. CP-WrigJ

To a Husband. Maya Angelou. SP-AngeM

To a Jilted Lover. Sylvia Plath. CP-PlatS

To a Jilted Swain. James Whitcomb Riley. CP-RileJ

To a Kid Who Believes in Astrology. Alan Dugan. CP-DugaA

To a Knot of Ungenerous Critics. Lord Byron. CP-Byron

To A. L.; Persuasions [*or* Perswasions] to Love. Thomas Carew. CP-CareT

To a Lady. Robert Burns. CP-BurnR

(To Miss Ainslie, in Chuch.) CP-BurnR

To a Lady. Lord Byron. CP-Byron

To a Lady. Lord Byron. CP-Byron

To a Lady. Lord Byron. CP-Byron

To a Lady. G. K. Chesterton. CP-ChesG

To a Lady. Samuel Taylor Coleridge. CP-ColeS

To a Lady[e]. William Dunbar. CP-DunbW

To a Lady. Thomas Hardy. CP-HardT

To a Lady. Dorothy Parker. CP-ParkD

To a Lady. Jonathan Swift. CP-SwifJ

To a Lady. William Wordsworth. CP-WorW2

To a Lady and Her Children, on the Death of Her Son and Their Brother. Phillis Wheatley. CP-WheaP

To a Lady in a Train. Stevie Smith. CP-SmitS

To a Lady, Not Yet Enjoyed by Her Husband. Thomas Carew. CP-CareT

To a Lady on Her Coming to North-America with Her Son, for the Recovery of Her Health. Phillis Wheatley. CP-WheaP

To a Lady on Her Remarkable Preservation in an Hurricane in *North-Carolina*. Phillis Wheatley. CP-WheaP

To a Lady on the Death of Her Husband. Phillis Wheatley. CP-WheaP
(To Mrs. Leonard, on the Death of Her Husband.) CP-WheaP

To a Lady on the Death of Three Relations. Phillis Wheatley. CP-WheaP

To a Lady Passing Time Better Left Unpassed. Ogden Nash. CP-NashO

To a Lady, Peruading Her to a Car. Rudyard Kipling. CP-KiplR *Fr.* Muse among the Motors, The.

To a Lady Playing and Singing in the Morning. Thomas Hardy. CP-HardT

To a Lady Playing the Harp. Paul Laurence Dunbar. CP-DunbP

To a Lady ["Star that beams on Anna's breast, The"]. William Cowper. CP-CowpW

To a Lady That Desired I Would Love Her. Thomas Carew. CP-CareT

To a Lady That Forbade to Love before Company. Sir John Suckling. CP-SuckJ

To a Lady Who Presented to the Author a Lock of Hair Braided with His Own, and Appointed a Night in December to Meet Him in the Garden. Lord Byron. CP-Byron

To a Lady with the Temple of Fame. Alexander Pope. CP-PopeA

To a Little Girl, One Year Old, in a Ruined Fortress. Robert Penn Warren. CP-WarrR

To a Little Lover-Lass, Dead. Langston Hughes. CP-HughL; CP-HughL1

To a Little Miss a Year Older than the One to Whom the Glass Was Promised, with a Toy Looking Glass. Annis Boudinot Stockton. CP-StocA

To a Little Miss, with a Toy Lookingglass. Annis Boudinot Stockton. CP-StocA

To a Locomotive in Winter. Walt Whitman. CP-WhitW

To a look in my son's eyes. Address. William Carlos Williams. CP-WilW2

To a Louse [On Seeing One on a Lady's Bonnet at Church]. Robert Burns. CP-BurnR

To a Love-Feast we both invited are. Parasceve, or Preparation, The. Robert Herrick. CP-HerrR

To a Loveless Lover. Laura Riding Jackson. CP-RidiL

To a Lovely Lady Gone to Theory. John Ciardi. CP-CiarJ

To a lovely mirtle bound. William Blake. *See* O, how sick and weary I

To a Lovely Old Bitch. William Carlos Williams. CP-WilW2

To A.M. George Meredith. CP-MerG2

To a Madonna. Charles Baudelaire. CP-BaudC, *tr. by* Walter Martin

To a Maid. Robert Herrick. CP-HerrR

To a Man. Maya Angelou. SP-AngeM

To a man and his wife. Ballad: "To a man and his wife." William Carlos Williams. CP-WilW2

To a Man Dying on His Feet. William Carlos Williams. CP-WilW2

To a Marsh Hawk in Spring. Henry David Thoreau. CP-ThorH

To a Maryland Editor, 1943. Lorine Niedecker. CP-NiedL

To a Mayd. Robert Herrick. CP-HerrR

To a mere. Frozen Lake, The. Stevie Smith. CP-SmitS

To a Mexican Pig-Bank. William Carlos Williams. CP-WilW1

To a Minor Poet of 1899. Jorge Luis Borges. SP-BorgJ, *tr. by* Charles Tomlinson

To a Minor Poet of the Greek Anthology. Jorge Luis Borges. SP-BorgJ, *tr. by* W. S. Merwin

To a Moth Seen in Winter. Robert Frost. CP-FrosR

To a Motherless Child. Thomas Hardy. CP-HardT

To a Mountain Daisy [On Turning One Down, with the Plough, in April—1786]. Robert Burns. CP-BurnR

To a Mouse; On Turning Her up in Her Nest, with the Plough, November, 1785. Robert Burns. CP-BurnR

To a Mouse says a Miser my dear Mr Mouse. Lucilius. *See* Asclepiades the Miser was horrified

To a Much Too Unfortunate Lady. Dorothy Parker. CP-ParkD

To a Musician. Edna St. Vincent Millay. CP-MillE

To a Nightingale ("In the bowers of the rising moon"). George Meredith. CP-MerG1

To a Nightingale ("O nightingale!"). George Meredith. CP-MerG2

To a Painter. Robert Burns. *See* To an Artist
To a Painter ("All praise the Likeness"). William Wordsworth. CP-WorW2
To a Painter ("Though I beheld at first"). William Wordsworth. CP-WorW2
To a Poet. Frank O'Hara. SP-OharF
To a Poet. Philip Whalen. SP-WhalP
To a Poet and a Lady. Paul Laurence Dunbar. CP-DunbP
To a Poet-Critic. James Whitcomb Riley. CP-RileJ
To a Poet on His Marriage. James Whitcomb Riley. CP-RileJ
To a Poet that Died Young. Edna St. Vincent Millay. CP-MillE
To a Poet Who Read in Gloucester Before the Cape Ann Historical Literary and Scientific Society. Charles Olson. CP-OlsoC
To a Poet, Who Would Have Me Praise Certain Bad Poets, Imitators of His and Mine. William Butler Yeats. CP-YeatW
To a Poetess. G. K. Chesterton. CP-ChesG
To a Poetical Trio in the City of Gotham. John Greenleaf Whittier. CP-WhitJ
To a Poor Old Woman. William Carlos Williams. CP-WilW1
To a President. Walt Whitman. CP-WhitW
To a Prize Bird. Marianne Craig Moore. CP-MoorM
To a Prodigal Old Maid. Allen Tate. CP-TateA
To a Pupil. Walt Whitman. CP-WhitW
To a Reason. Arthur Rimbaud. CP-RimbA, *tr.* by Martin Sorrell
To a Red-headed Beggar. Charles Baudelaire. CP-BaudC, *tr.* by Walter Martin
To a Red-Headed Do-Good Waitress. Alan Dugan. CP-DugaA
To a Romantic. Allen Tate. CP-TateA
To a Romantic Novelist. Allen Tate. CP-TateA
To A.S., 1830. Emily Jane Brontë. CP-BronE
To a Saxon Poet. Jorge Luis Borges. SP-BorgJ, *tr.* by Alastair Reid
To a Scholar in the Stacks. Howard Nemerov. CP-NemeH
To a Sea-Cliff. Thomas Hardy. CP-HardT
To a Severe Nun. Thomas Merton. CP-MertT
To a Sexton. William Wordsworth. CP-WorW1; MW-WorW
To a Shade. William Butler Yeats. CP-YeatW
To a Siberian Woodsman. Wendell Berry. CP-BerrW
To a Skull. James Whitcomb Riley. CP-RileJ
To a Sky-Lark. William Wordsworth. CP-WorW1
To a Skylark. George Meredith. CP-MerG1
To a Skylark. Percy Bysshe Shelley. CP-ShelP
To a Skylark. William Wordsworth. CP-WorW2
To a Snail. Marianne Craig Moore. CP-MoorM
To a Snake. Edna St. Vincent Millay. CP-MillE
To a Snow-Drop. William Wordsworth. CP-WorW2
To a Solitary Disciple. William Carlos Williams. CP-WilW1
To a Southern Statesman. John Greenleaf Whittier. CP-WhitJ
To a Sparrow. William Carlos Williams. CP-WilW2
To a Squirrel at Kyle-Na-No. William Butler Yeats. CP-YeatW
To a Staffordshireman, from a Devon Villa. Donald Davie. CP-DaviDC
To a Star. Percy Bysshe Shelley. CP-ShelP
To a Steam Roller. Marianne Craig Moore. CP-MoorM
To a Stranger. Walt Whitman. CP-WhitW
To a Stranger Born in Some Distant Country Hundreds of Years from Now. Billy Collins. SP-CollB
To a Stray Fowl. Henry David Thoreau. CP-ThorH
To a Suitor. Maya Angelou. SP-AngeM
To a Sword at York Minster. Jorge Luis Borges. SP-BorgJ, *tr.* by Charles Tomlinson
To a Teacher of French. Donald Davie. CP-DaviDC
To a Thinker. Robert Frost. CP-FrosR
To a Tolerant Mother. G. K. Chesterton. CP-ChesG
To a Tree. Elizabeth Bishop. CP-BishE
To a Tree in London. Thomas Hardy. CP-HardT
To a Troubled Friend. James Wright. CP-WrigJ
To a Turk. G. K. Chesterton. CP-ChesG
To a Vain Lady. Lord Byron. CP-Byron
To a Very Slow Air. Philip Larkin. CP-LarkP
To a Violet Found on All Saints' Day. Paul Laurence Dunbar. CP-DunbP
To a Visiting Poet in a College Dormitory. Carolyn Kizer. CP-KizeC
To a Waterbed. John Updike. SP-UpdiJ
To a Waterfowl. Donald Hall. CP-HallD
To a Weak Gamester in Poetry. Ben Jonson. CP-JonsB; SP-JonsB
To a Wealthy Man Who Promised a Second Subscription to the Dublin Municipal Gallery if It Were Proved the People Wanted Pictures. William Butler Yeats. CP-YeatW
To a Well-Named Dwelling. Thomas Hardy. CP-HardT
To a Western Boy. Walt Whitman. CP-WhitW
To a Woman. John Berryman. CP-BerrJ
To a Woman Seen Once. William Carlos Williams. CP-WilW2

To a woman that I knew. Her Eyes. John Crowe Ransom. SP-RansJ
To a Wood Thrush. William Carlos Williams. CP-WilW1
To a Woodpecker. William Carlos Williams. CP-WilW2
To a Wreath of Snow. Emily Jane Brontë. CP-BronE
To a Young American the Day after the Fall of Barcelona. John Ciardi. CP-CiarJ
To a Young Artist. Robinson Jeffers. CP-JefR1
To a Young Beauty. William Butler Yeats. CP-YeatW
To a Young Friend. Samuel Taylor Coleridge. CP-ColeS
To a Young Friend. William Cowper. CP-CowpW
To a Young Gentle-Woman, Councel Concerning Her Choice. Richard Crashaw. CP-CrasR
  (To [Mrs. M. R.] Councel Concerning Her Choise.) CP-CrasR
To a Young Girl. Edna St. Vincent Millay. CP-MillE
To a Young Girl. William Butler Yeats. CP-YeatW
To a Young Lady. Samuel Taylor Coleridge. CP-ColeS
To a Young Lady. William Cowper. CP-CowpW
  (Another [Addressed to a Young Lady].) CP-CowpW
To a Young Lady, *Miss Jessy L———, Dumfries; with Books which the Bard Presented Her*. Robert Burns. CP-BurnR
To a Young Lady [Miss Lavinia Poole] on Her Recovery from a Fever. Samuel Taylor Coleridge. CP-ColeS
To a Young Lady on Her Birthday. Samuel Johnson. CP-JohnS
To a Young Lady Who Had Been Reproached for Taking Long Walks in the Country. William Wordsworth. CP-WorW1
To a Young Lady Who Sent Me a Laurel Crown. John Keats. CP-KeatJ
To a Young Lady Who Stole a Pen. William Cowper. CP-CowpW
To a Young Poet. Edna St. Vincent Millay. CP-MillE
To a Young Poet Who Fled. John Logan. CP-LogaJ
To a Young Woman Dying at Weir. Norman Dubie. CP-DubiN
To a Young Wretch. Robert Frost. CP-FrosR
To a Youthful Friend. Lord Byron. CP-Byron
To Aberdein. William Dunbar. CP-DunbW
To Abide. Constantine P. Cavafy. CP-CavaC, *tr.* by Theoharis Constantine Theoharis
To actually see an actual marine monster. Dragons Are Too Seldom. Ogden Nash. CP-NashO
To Aeneas who closed his piano. Lorine Niedecker. CP-NiedL
To Ailsa Rock. John Keats. CP-KeatJ
To Alchemists. Ben Jonson. CP-JonsB; SP-JonsB
To Alexander Cunningham. Robert Burns. CP-BurnR
To Alexander Findlater. Robert Burns. CP-BurnR
To Alex. Smith, the "Glasgow Poet," on His Sonnet to "Fame" George Meredith. CP-MerG2
To Alfonso Cortes. Thomas Merton. CP-MertT
To Alfred Tennyson, My Grandson. Alfred Tennyson. CP-TennA
To Alice Dunbar. Paul Laurence Dunbar. CP-DunbP
To All. Jones Very. CP-VeryJ
To All Angels and Saints. George Herbert. CP-HerbG
To all except anguish. Emily Dickinson. SP-DickE
To All Gentleness. William Carlos Williams. CP-WilW2
To all our wounds, here, whatsoe'er they be. Christ. Robert Herrick. CP-HerrR
To all the spirits of Love that wander by. Supreme Surrender. Dante Gabriel Rossetti. CW-RossD *Fr.* House of Life, The.
To all those happy blessings which ye have. Sonnet 66. Edmund Spenser. CP-Spens *Fr.* Amoretti.
To all those I put off. For the Old Year. William Corbett. SP-CorbW
To all those million poems in the world. And Now Goodbye. Jaroslav Seifert. SP-SeifJ, *tr.* by Ewald Osers
To All, to Whom I Write. Ben Jonson. CP-JonsB; SP-JonsB
To all to whom this little book may come. Preface, A: "To all to whom this little book may come." Rudyard Kipling. CP-KiplR *Fr.* Land and Sea Tales.
To all who carve their love on a picnic table. Open Letter from a Constant Reader. Mona Van Duyn. SP-VanDM
To All Young Men That Love. Robert Herrick. CP-HerrR
To Allen Ginsberg. Czeslaw Milosz. CP-MiloCN, *tr.* by Robert Hass
To Almon Keefer. James Whitcomb Riley. CP-RileJ
To Alphonso [*or* Alfonso] Ferrabosco, on His Book. Ben Jonson. CP-JonsB; SP-JonsB
To Amanda—Who was Obliging Enough to Delight Her Friend with Singing Every Evening Two Songs Which She Was Very Fond Off. Annis Boudinot Stockton. CP-StocA
To Amaryllis love compels my way. Idyll 3: Amaryllis. Theocritus. CP-DryJ2 *Fr.* Idylls.
To an Actress. Thomas Hardy. CP-HardT
To an American Classicist. Donald Davie. CP-DaviDC
To an American Poet Just Dead. Richard Wilbur. CP-WilbR
To an American Publisher. Stevie Smith. CP-SmitS

To an Ancient. Robert Frost. CP-FrosR

To an Ancient Locust-Tree, Opposite Carltonville. Jones Very. CP-VeryJ

To an Apple. David Ignatow. SP-IgnaD

To an Artist. Robert Burns. CP-BurnR

(To a Painter.) CP-BurnR

To an Artist, to Take Heart. Louise Bogan. CP-BogaL

To an Athlete Dying Young. A. E. Housman. CP-HousA

To an Elder Poet. William Carlos Williams. CP-WilW1

To an Emigrant, Country is idle. Emily Dickinson. SP-DickE

To an Ex-Student. Alan Dugan. CP-DugaA

To an Importunate Ghost. James Whitcomb Riley. CP-RileJ

To an Imposter of Rosalind. Thomas Hardy. CP-HardT

To an Infant. Samuel Taylor Coleridge. MW-ColeS Fr. Effusions.

To an Ingrate. Paul Laurence Dunbar. CP-DunbP

To an Insolent Attorney. Ambrose Bierce. SP-BierA

To an Isle in the Water. William Butler Yeats. CP-YeatW

To an Oak at Newstead. Lord Byron. CP-Byron

To an Old Gipsy. Johann N. Vogl. CP-MerG2

To an Old Jaundiced Woman. William Carlos Williams. CP-WilW1

To an Old Philosopher in Rome. Wallace Stevens. CP-StevW; CP-StevWP

To an Old Poet in Peru. Allen Ginsberg. CP-GinsA

To an old soare a long cure must goe on. Great Maladies, Long Medicines. Robert Herrick. CP-HerrR

To an Unborn Pauper Child. Thomas Hardy. CP-HardT

To an Unfortunate Woman at the Theatre. Samuel Taylor Coleridge. CP-ColeS

To an Unfortunate Woman Whom the Author Had Known in the Days of Her Innocence. Samuel Taylor Coleridge. CP-ColeS

To an Unknown Direction. Yannis Ritsos. SP-RitsY, tr. by Minas Savvas

To an Unknown Poet. Countee Cullen. CP-CullC

To an Unknown Poet. Carolyn Kizer. CP-KizeC

To an Usherette. John Updike. CP-UpdiJ

To And. Robert Creeley. CP-CreeR

To Anna Akhmátova. Boris Leonidovich Pasternak. SP-WeisT, tr. by Theodore Weiss

To Anna Eliza Austen. Fanny Knight. CP-AustJ

To Anna Jean. Tennessee Williams. CP-WillT

To Anne. Lord Byron. CP-Byron

To Anne Bodham. William Cowper. CP-CowpW

To Annie. James Whitcomb Riley. CP-RileJ

To Another. Kenneth Rexroth. CP-RexrK

To Anthea ("Ah my Anthea!"). Robert Herrick. CP-HerrR

To Anthea ("Anthea I am going hence"). Robert Herrick. CP-HerrR

To Anthea ("Come Anthea, know thou this"). Robert Herrick. CP-HerrR

To Anthea ("If, deare Anthea, my hard fate it be"). Robert Herrick. CP-HerrR

To Anthea ("Let's call for Hymen if agreed thou art"). Robert Herrick. CP-HerrR

To Anthea ("Now is the time, when all the lights wax dim"). Robert Herrick. CP-HerrR

To Anthea ("Sick is Anthea, sickly is the spring"). Robert Herrick. CP-HerrR

To Anthea Lying in Bed. Robert Herrick. CP-HerrR

To Anthea, Who May Command Him Anything. Robert Herrick. CP-HerrR

To Antonio Machado. Denise Levertov. SP-LeveDS

To Antonius Julus, the Son of Mark Antony, tof the Triumvirate. Horace. See Odes

To Apollo ("Phœbus! when that I averse"). Robert Herrick. CP-HerrR

To Apollo ("Thou mighty lord"). Robert Herrick. CP-HerrR

To Aristius Fuscus. Horace. See Odes

To arrive / unexpectedly / from nowhere. Small Action Poem. Charles Tomlinson. CP-TomlC

To Art. Dante Gabriel Rossetti. CW-RossD

To Artemis. Hayden Carruth. CP-CarHS

To Artina. Langston Hughes. CP-HughL; CP-HughL3

To ask the hard question is simple. Question, The. W. H. Auden. CP-AudeW

To Aspasio. Annis Boudinot Stockton. CP-StocA

To Asra. Samuel Taylor Coleridge. CP-ColeS

To attain the highest good. Highest Good, The. James Whitcomb Riley. CP-RileJ

To attempt to speak of what has been. Emily Dickinson. SP-DickE

To Auden on His Fiftieth. Richard Eberhart. CP-EberR

To Aunt Rose. Allen Ginsberg. CP-GinsA; SP-GinsA

To Autumn. William Blake. CP-BlakW

To Autumn. Louise Glück. SP-GlucL

To Autumn. John Keats. CP-KeatJ

To Autumn. Thomas Kinsella. CP-KinsT

To Avis Keene. John Greenleaf Whittier. CP-WhitJ

To awaken in the arms of a friend. Survival. Rainer Maria Rilke. CP-RilkFr, tr. by A. Poulin, Jr.

To B.C. Sir John Suckling. CP-SuckJ

To B. R. Haydon. William Wordsworth. CP-WorW2; MW-WorW

To B.R. Haydon, On Seeing His Picture of Napoleon Buonaparte on the Island of St Helena. William Wordsworth. CP-WorW2

To B.R. Haydon, with a Sonnet Written on Seeing the Elgin Marbles. John Keats. CP-KeatJ

To Babylon's proud waters brought. Bible, O.T. See By the rivers of Babylon, there we sat down, yea, we wept, when [or then] we remembered Zion

To Bacchus, a Canticle. Robert Herrick. CP-HerrR

To Bake the Bread of Yearning. Yehuda Amichai. SP-AmicY, tr. by Stephen Mitchell

To barren heath, bleak moor, and quaking fen. Brownie's Cell, The. William Wordsworth. CP-WorW2

To be a Bell and Flower too. Emily Dickinson. SP-DickE

To be a boxer, or not to be there. Poetry Reading. Wisława Szymborska. SP-SzymW, tr. by Stanisław Barańczak and Clare Cavanagh

To be a child named after a star. Rijl. Tess Gallagher. SP-GallT

To be a giant and keep quiet about it. Trees. Howard Nemerov. CP-NemeH

To Be a Poet. Jaroslav Seifert. SP-SeifJ, tr. by Ewald Osers

To be a poet is no easy task. Prologue: "To be a poet is no easy task." Jaroslav Seifert. SP-SeifJ, tr. by Ewald Osers

To be a sweetness more desired than Spring. True Woman (Herself). Dante Gabriel Rossetti. CW-RossD Fr. House of Life, The.

To be a wholly worthy man. Simple Recipe, A. James Whitcomb Riley. CP-RileJ

To be able. To an Elder Poet. William Carlos Williams. CP-WilW1

To be able to forget is to be able to yield. Forget. D. H. Lawrence. CP-LawrD

To be adored by a proud Paladin. Beggar Maid and King Cophetua, The. Robert Graves. CP-GravR

To be alive—is Power. Emily Dickinson. SP-DickE

To be an ape in little of the mountain-making mother. On Building with Stone. Robinson Jeffers. CP-JefR1

To be an aristocrat of the sun. Aristocracy of the Sun. D. H. Lawrence. CP-LawrD

To be and not to be again! . . . Oh, lions born in cages! Fernando Pessoa. SP-PessF Fr. Absurd Hour.

To Be at All. Walt Whitman. CP-WhitW

To be backed. Fort Collins Remembered. Robert Creeley. SP-CreeR

To be, be thine. Arthur Hugh Clough. SP-ClouA

To be born famous, as your father's son. Troublesome Fame. Robert Graves. CP-GravR

To Be Called A Bear. Robert Graves. CP-GravR

To be carried / Good luck of skin. If I Yes. Olga Broumas. SP-BrouO

To Be Carved on a Stone at Thoor Ballylee. William Butler Yeats. CP-YeatW

To be certain we were to meet our Lost. Emily Dickinson. SP-DickE

To Be Charmed. Kenneth Patchen. CP-PatcK

To Be Closely Written on a Small Piece of Paper Which Folded into a Tight Lozenge Will Fit Any Girl's Locket. William Carlos Williams. CP-WilW1

To be constant through a lifetime. Gardens of the Savoy, The. Donald Davie. CP-DaviDC

To be dancer / of my own dismay. Dancing. Robert Creeley. CP-CreeR

To Be Dead. Randall Jarrell. CP-JarrR

To be discerned. Pentimento. Denise Levertov. SP-LeveDS

To Be Done in Winter. James Dickey. CP-DickJ

To Be Engraved on the Skull of a Cormorant. Charles Tomlinson. CP-TomlC; SP-TomlC

To Be Filed for Reference. Rudyard Kipling. Fr. Plain Tales from the Hills.

To be forgot by thee. Emily Dickinson. CP-DickE

To-Be-Forgotten, The. Thomas Hardy. CP-HardT

To be great, be whole; exclude. Fernando Pessoa. SP-PessF, tr. by Susan M. Brown and Edwin Honig

To Be Holy, Be Wholly Your Own. Kenneth Patchen. CP-PatcK

To be homeless is a pride. Jealous Man, A. Robert Graves. CP-GravR

To be human is more than to be divine. Emily Dickinson. SP-DickE

To be humble before other men is degrading, I am humble before no man. Tender Reverence. D. H. Lawrence. CP-LawrD

To Be Hungry Is to Be Great. William Carlos Williams. CP-WilW1

To be idiomatic in a vacuum. Poem: "To be idiomatic in a vacuum." Frank O'Hara. SP-OharF

To Be in Love. Gwendolyn Brooks. SP-BrooG

To Be in Love. Robert Graves. CP-GravR

To be in love is like going out- / side to see what kind of day. Business, The. Robert Creeley. CP-CreeR

To be less unworthy, my exalted lady. Michelangelo Buonarroti. CP-Miche, tr. by John Frederick Nims

To be like the water. Transients Welcome. Gregory Orr. SP-OrrG

To be lost for good to the gay self-esteem. As When the Mystic. Robert Graves. CP-GravR

To Be Merry. Robert Herrick. CP-HerrR

To be moved comes of want, tho[ugh] want be complete. 1892-1941. Louis Zukofsky. CP-ZukLS

To be near her is to be near the furnace. Fire Walker. Robert Graves. CP-GravR

To Be of Use. Marge Piercy. SP-PierM

To Be Poets. Robert Graves. CP-GravR

To be possessed by her is to possess—. Possessed. Robert Graves. CP-GravR

To Be Read Later On. Charles Tomlinson. SP-TomlC *Fr.* For A Granddaughter.

To be ready again if they find an owl, crows. Why the Sun Comes Up. William Stafford. SP-StafWW

To Be Recited to Flossie on Her Birthday. William Carlos Williams. CP-WilW2

To be remember'd thus is fame. Answer to Stanzas Addressed to Lady Hesketh. William Cowper. CP-CowpW

To be signallers and to be relieved two hours. Signallers. Ivor Gurney. SP-GurnI

To be singular under plural circumstances. Emily Dickinson. SP-DickE

To be so cold and yet not old. Eulenspiegelei. Stevie Smith. CP-SmitS

To be so poor. No earth, no abyss. Dante. Czeslaw Milosz. CP-MiloCN, *tr. by* Robert Hass

To Be Somebody. Langston Hughes. CP-HughL; CP-HughL2

To be struck by a taxicab. How Fortunate. James Laughlin. CP-LaugJ

To be Sung on the Fourth of July. Wyatt Prunty. SP-PrunW

To Be Sung on the Water. Louise Bogan. CP-BogaL

To Be Sung While Still Looking. W. S. Merwin. SP-MerwW

To Be Superior. D. H. Lawrence. CP-LawrD

To be the father of the fatherless. Sonnet to the Prince Regent. Lord Byron. CP-Byron

To be the only woman alive in a vast hive of death. Undead, The. Robert Graves. CP-GravR

To be well loved. Hazel Grove, The. Robert Graves. CP-GravR

To be wise the dull brain so earnestly throbs. Hafiz. CP-EmerR *Fr.* Odes.

To be with the one I love. Moon Conjunct Ace of Cups. Olga Broumas. SP-BrouO

To Be Written on the Mirror in Whitewash. Elizabeth Bishop. CP-BishE

To Beachey, 1912. Carl Sandburg. CP-SandC

To Beat the Child Was Bad Enough. Maya Angelou. SP-AngeM

To Beauty. Langston Hughes. CP-HughL1

To become the face of space. Arizona Highway. Charles Tomlinson. CP-TomlC

To Bed. Rita Dove. SP-DoveR

To bed, to bed: a storm is brewing. Window Pane, The. Robert Graves. CP-GravR

To begin, it begins. Journey, The. Sam Hamill. SP-HamiS

To Begin With. Raymond Carver. CP-CarvR

To begin with there are / No wild swans at Norfolk. Wild Swans at Norfolk, The. Hayden Carruth. CP-CarHS

To Beguile and Betray. Robert Graves. CP-GravR

To Belinda on the Rape of the Lock. Alexander Pope. CP-PopeA

To Belshazzar. Lord Byron. CP-Byron

To Ben Jonson. Thomas Carew. CP-CareT

To Benj. S. Parker. James Whitcomb Riley. CP-RileJ

To Benjamin Rudyerd. Ben Jonson. CP-JonsB; SP-JonsB

To Betsy Steiger. Rainer Maria Rilke. CP-RilkFr, *tr. by* A. Poulin, Jr.

To Bettine. Elizabeth Barrett Browning. CP-BroEB

To Betty the Grisette. Jonathan Swift. CP-SwifJ

To Bhain Campbell. John Berryman. CP-BerrJ

To Biancha. Robert Herrick. CP-HerrR

To Biancha, to Blesse Him. Robert Herrick. CP-HerrR

To Bliss Carman. James Whitcomb Riley. CP-RileJ

To Blossoms. Robert Herrick. CP-HerrR

To Bobbie. Robert Creeley. CP-CreeR

To Booker T. Washington. Paul Laurence Dunbar. CP-DunbP

To bow at the footlights / and sink into a curtsey. Smoke of Marijuana, The. Jaroslav Seifert. SP-SeifJ, *tr. by* Ewald Osers

To bow my body to the ground. It Does Me Good. James Laughlin. CP-LaugJ

To ———: "Bowers whereat, in dreams, I see, The." Edgar Allan Poe. CP-PoeEd

To Brain-Hardy. Ben Jonson. CP-JonsB; SP-JonsB

To Bread and Water none is poore. No Want Where There's Little. Robert Herrick. CP-HerrR

To break so vast a Heart. Emily Dickinson. CP-DickE

To break the pentameter, Pound's first heave. To a Bad Poet. Donald Davie. CP-DaviDC

To Bring the Dead to Life. Robert Graves. CP-GravR

To bug: an act of intelligence. To Try to Get Down One Citizen as Against Another. Charles Olson. CP-OlsoC

To burn is surely bad, to be. House of Fire. Theodore Weiss. SP-WeisT

To ———: "But once I dared to lift my eyes." Lord Byron. CP-Byron

To C.F.H. Thomas Hardy. CP-HardT

To C. T. Donald Davie. CP-DaviDC

To C. T. George Oppen. CP-OppGN

To call our sight Vision. I Am Not a Camera. W. H. Auden. CP-AudeW

To. Campiani Epigramma de Instituto Authoris. Thomas Campion. CP-CampT

To Captain Fryatt. G. K. Chesterton. CP-ChesG

To Captain G———, on Being Asked Why I Was Not to Be of the Party with Him and His Brother K-nm-re at Syme's. Robert Burns. CP-BurnR

To Captain H—D, of the 65th Regiment. Phillis Wheatley. CP-WheaP

To Captain Hungry. Ben Jonson. CP-JonsB; SP-JonsB

To Captain Mulzac. Langston Hughes. CP-HughL; CP-HughL2

To Captain Riddell. Robert Burns. CP-BurnR

To Cardinal Manning. George Meredith. CP-MerG1

To Carlyle. George Meredith. CP-MerG1

To Carmela Condón, Thanking Her for Some Dolls. Federico García Lorca. CP-GarcF, *tr. by* Christopher Maurer

To Carnations. Robert Herrick. CP-HerrR

To Caroline. Lord Byron. CP-Byron

To Carrey Clavel. Thomas Hardy. CP-HardT

To Carry the Child. Stevie Smith. CP-SmitS

To catch the meaning out of the air. Hardening into Print. Richard Eberhart. CP-EberR

To cause accord or to ag[g]re[e]. Sir Thomas Wyatt. CP-WyatT

To Cedars. Robert Herrick. CP-HerrR

To celebrate your brief life. To the Ghost of Marjorie Kinnan Rawlings. William Carlos Williams. CP-WilW2

To Celia, upon Love's Ubiquity. Thomas Carew. CP-CareT

To Censorious Courtling. Ben Jonson. CP-JonsB; SP-JonsB

To Certain "Brothers." Langston Hughes. CP-HughL; CP-HughL1

To Certain Critics. Countee Cullen. CP-CullC

To Certain English Poets. Donald Davie. CP-DaviDC

To Certain Intellectuals. Langston Hughes. CP-HughL; CP-HughL1

To Certain Journeymen. Carl Sandburg. CP-SandC

To Certain Negro Leaders. Langston Hughes. CP-HughL; CP-HughL1

To Certain Old Masters. Robert Penn Warren. CP-WarrR

To certain people there comes a day. Che Fece . . . Il Gran Rifiuto. Constantine P. Cavafy. CP-CavaC, *tr. by* Theoharis Constantine Theoharis

To Charles Cowden Clarke. John Keats. CP-KeatJ

To Charles Diodati. John Milton. CP-CowpW, *tr. by* William Cowper

To Charles Ford, Esq. on His Birthday. Jonathan Swift. CP-SwifJ

To Charles Sumner. John Greenleaf Whittier. CP-WhitJ

To Charles W. Felt Esq. On His New Type-Setting Machine. Jones Very. CP-VeryJ

To Chatterton. John Keats. CP-KeatJ

To Cherry-Blossomes. Robert Herrick. CP-HerrR

To Children. George Meredith. CP-MerG1

To Chloes breast young Cupid slily stole. William Blake. CP-BlakW

To Chloris. Robert Burns. CP-BurnR

To Christ. Robert Herrick. CP-HerrR

To Christina. John Milton. CP-CowpW

To Cipriano, in the Wind. Philip Levine. SP-LeviP

To claim, at a dead party, to have spotted a grackle. Lying. Richard Wilbur. CP-WilbR

To Clare Nicholl. G. K. Chesterton. CP-ChesG

To Clarinda. Robert Burns. CP-BurnR

To Clarinda. D. H. Lawrence. CP-LawrD

To cleanse his eyes, *Tom Brock* makes much adoe. Upon Brock. Robert Herrick. CP-HerrR

To Clement Edmonds, on His *Caesar's Commentaries* Observed, and Translated. Ben Jonson. CP-JonsB; SP-JonsB

To climb the belltower. Crystal Cage, The. Stanley Kunitz. CP-KunSC

To climb the intricate heights. Calliope. "H. D." CP-DoolH

To Clio, Muse of History. Howard Nemerov. CP-NemeH

To Close. William Carlos Williams. CP-WilW2

To Colonel Charles. George Meredith. CP-MerG1

To come back from the sweet South, to the North. Italia, Io Ti Saluto! Christina Georgina Rossetti. CP-RosC2

To come from Heaven is casual. Emily Dickinson. SP-DickE

To Come of Age. Robert Graves. CP-GravR

To come to the look in the sacrificer's eyes. Dura. Charles Olson. CP-OlsoC

To come to the river. Resolve, The. Denise Levertov. SP-LeveDP

To come unto our own. Emily Dickinson. SP-DickE

To conceive death as death. Death as Death. Laura Riding Jackson. CP-RidiL

To conclude, I announce what comes after me. So Long! Walt Whitman. CP-WhitW

To congratulate the Redeemed is perhaps superfluous. Emily Dickinson. SP-DickE

To Conquer Variety. Hart Crane. CP-CranH

To conquer'd men, some comfort 'tis to fall. Some Comfort in Calamity. Robert Herrick. CP-HerrR

To Constantia. Percy Bysshe Shelley. CP-ShelP

To Constantia, Singing. Percy Bysshe Shelley. CP-ShelP

To consummate / the inconsummate, and make of it. "To Work Is to Contradict Contradications, to Do Violence to Natural Violence." Robert Creeley. CP-CreeR

To Courtling. Ben Jonson. CP-JonsB; SP-JonsB

To Crickley. Ivor Gurney. SP-GurnI

To Critic[k]s. Robert Herrick. CP-HerrR

To cross a ferry that is no longer there. Crossing Brooklyn Ferry. Charles Tomlinson. CP-TomlC

To Crown[e] It. Robert Herrick. CP-HerrR

To cultivate in ev'ry noble mind. To the Rev. Dr. Thomas Amory on Reading His Sermons on Daily Devotion, in Which that Duty Is Recommended and Assisted. Phillis Wheatley. CP-WheaP

To Cupid. Robert Herrick. CP-HerrR

To Cyriack Skinner. John Milton. CP-MiltJ

(Sonnet 21.) CP-MiltJ

To D———. Lord Byron. CP-Byron

To D———, Dead by Her Own Hand. Howard Nemerov. CP-NemeH

To Daddy. Robert Lowell. SP-LoweR

To Daffodils [or Daffadills]. Robert Herrick. CP-HerrR

To Daisies, Not to Shut So Soon[c]. Robert Herrick. CP-HerrR

To Dan. Paul Laurence Dunbar. CP-DunbP

To Daphne and Virginia. William Carlos Williams. CP-WilW2

To Daunton Me. Robert Burns. CP-BurnR

To David, about His Education. Howard Nemerov. CP-NemeH

To-day a rude brief recitative. Song for All Seas, All Ships. Walt Whitman. CP-WhitW

To-day, across our fathers' graves. Veterans, The. Rudyard Kipling. CP-KiplR

To-day and Thee. Walt Whitman. CP-WhitW

To-day Death seems to me an infant child. Newborn Death ("To-day Death seems to me an infant child"). Dante Gabriel Rossetti. CW-RossD Fr. House of Life, The.

To-day, from each and all, a breath of prayer—a pulse of thought. Abraham Lincoln, Born Feb. 12, 1809. Walt Whitman. CP-WhitW

To day I climbed a handsome rounded hill. Henry David Thoreau. CP-ThorH

To-day the plant by Williams set. Spiritual Manifestation, A. John Greenleaf Whittier. CP-WhitJ

To-day, the social consciousness is mutilated. Fear of Society Is the Root of All Evil. D. H. Lawrence. CP-LawrD

To-day, This Insect. Dylan Thomas. CP-ThomD

To-day was a beautiful day, the sky was a brilliant. Louis MacNeice. CP-MacNL Fr. Autumn Journal.

To-day, with bending head and eyes, thou, too, Columbia. Dead Emperor, The. Walt Whitman. CP-WhitW

To Dean-bourn, a Rude River in Devon, by Which Sometimes He Lived. Robert Herrick. CP-HerrR

To Dean Inge Lecturing on Origen. Stevie Smith. CP-SmitS

To Dean Swift. Thomas Sheridan. CP-SherT

To Dean Swift. Jonathan Swift. CP-SwifJ

To Death. Robert Herrick. CP-HerrR

To Death. Robinson Jeffers. CP-JefR3

To Death. Percy Bysshe Shelley. CP-ShelP

To Death, of His Lady. François Villon. CW-RossD, tr. by Dante Gabriel Rossetti

To define the sea. Sea Change. Charles Tomlinson. CP-TomlC; SP-TomlC

To Delaware. John Greenleaf Whittier. CP-WhitJ

To Delia. William Cowper. CP-CowpW

To Delmore Schwartz. Robert Lowell. SP-LoweR

To Demosthenis. Unknown. CP-CowpW

To describe the clouds. Clouds. Wisława Szymborska. SP-SzymWM, tr. by Joanna Trzeciak

To Dewes. A Song. Robert Herrick. CP-HerrR

To di—without the Dying. Emily Dickinson. CP-DickE

To Dianeme. Robert Herrick. CP-HerrR

To Dianeme; a Ceremonie in Glocester. Robert Herrick. CP-HerrR

To die / And never know what killed you. Death in Africa. Langston Hughes. CP-HughL; CP-HughL2

To die be given us, or attain! Resignation. Matthew Arnold. SP-ArnoM

To die before it feared to die. Emily Dickinson. SP-DickE

To Die before One Wakes Must Be Glad. Alice Walker. CP-WalkA

To die is to be brought down among blacks. Off to the Cemetery. David Ignatow. SP-IgnaD

To die—takes just a little while. Emily Dickinson. CP-DickE

To Die, to Be Torn. Yehuda Amichai. SP-AmicYL, tr. by Benjamin Harshav and Barbara Harshav

To die unwrinkled near a breath of fire. Agony Among the Crowd, The. Nicolas Calas. CP-WilW2

To die with a forlorn hope, but soon to be raised. Survivor, The. Robert Graves. CP-GravR

To dig at Luxor, to peer. Hayden Carruth. CP-CarHS Fr. Bloomingdale Papers, The.

To disappear enhances. Emily Dickinson. CP-DickE

To distinctly English writers in England. Hugh MacDiarmid. SP-MacDH Fr. England Is Our Enemy.

To Dives (William Beckford). A Fragment. Lord Byron. CP-Byron

To divulge itself is Sorrow's Right. Emily Dickinson. SP-DickE

To do a magnanimous thing. Emily Dickinson. CP-DickE

To do some worthy deed of charity. To Rudyard Kipling. James Whitcomb Riley. CP-RileJ

To Doctor Alabaster. Robert Herrick. CP-HerrR

To Dr. Austin. William Cowper. CP-CowpW

To Dr. Blacklock. Robert Burns. CP-BurnR

To Dr. Darwin. William Cowper. CP-CowpW

To Dr. Delany, on the Libels Writ against Him. Jonathan Swift. CP-SwifJ

To Doctor Empiric[k]. Ben Jonson. CP-JonsB; SP-JonsB

To Dr. Helsham. Jonathan Swift. CP-SwifJ

To Dr. John MacKenzie. Robert Burns. CP-BurnR

To Dr Maxwell, on Miss Jessy Staig's Recovery. Robert Burns. CP-BurnR

To Doctor Rush Enclosing the Foregoing Ode of 1782. Annis Boudinot Stockton. CP-StocA

To Dr. Sheridan. Jonathan Swift. CP-SwifJ

To Doctor Smith on His Birth Day March 16th, 92. Annis Boudinot Stockton. CP-StocA

To Doctor Smith on His Birth Day March the 16th, 1790. Annis Boudinot Stockton. CP-StocA

To Dorothy Collins from G. K. Chesterton. G. K. Chesterton. CP-ChesG

To Dorothy Maynor. Langston Hughes. CP-HughL; CP-HughL2

To Dorothy— on Her Birthday—with Love. G. K. Chesterton. CP-ChesG

To Dorothy Wellesley. William Butler Yeats. CP-YeatW

To Dr. James Newton Matthews, Mason, Ill. Paul Laurence Dunbar. CP-DunbP

To draw no envy, Shakespeare, on thy name. To the Memory of My Beloved, the Author Mr [or Master] William Shakespeare: And What He Hath Left Us. Ben Jonson. CP-JonsB; SP-JonsB

To Draw the Warmth of Flesh from Subtle Graphite. Olga Broumas. SP-BrouO

To drift with every passion till my soul. Hélas! Oscar Wilde. CP-WildO

To drink in moderation, and to smoke. Party Knee. John Updike. CP-UpdiJ

To drive Paul out of any lumber camp. Paul's Wife. Robert Frost. CP-FrosR

To Dudley Fitts. John Ciardi. CP-CiarJ

To dwell in court, my freind, gife that thow list. William Dunbar. CP-DunbW

To E———. Lord Byron. CP-Byron

To E. B. B. Ezra Pound. CP-PoEar

To E. C. S. John Greenleaf Whittier. CP-WhitJ

To E. Fitzgerald. Alfred Tennyson. CP-TennA

To E. H. and G. M. G. K. Chesterton. CP-ChesG

To E. H. K. Paul Laurence Dunbar. CP-DunbP

To E.L., on His Travels in Greece. Alfred Tennyson. CP-TennA

To E. of D. with Six Holy Sonnets. John Donne. CP-DonnJ

To E. S. Salomon. Ambrose Bierce. SP-BierA

TO E. T.: 1917. Walter De la Mare. CP-DeLaW

To each captive and nobly gentle heart. Guido Cavalcanti. CP-CavaG, tr. by Marc Cirigliano

To earn it by disdaining it. Emily Dickinson. CP-DickE

To Earth. Hart Crane. CP-CranH

To Earthward. Robert Frost. CP-FrosR

To Ed Sissman. John Updike. CP-UpdiJ

To Edgar Wilson Nye. James Whitcomb Riley. CP-RileJ

To Edith. Henry David Thoreau. CP-ThorH

To Edmund Clarence Stedman. James Whitcomb Riley. CP-RileJ

To Edmund Clerihew Bentley. G. K. Chesterton. CP-ChesG

To Edward Alleyn. Ben Jonson. CP-JonsB; SP-JonsB

To Edward FitzGerald. Robert Browning. CP-BroR2

To Edward Noel Long, Esq. Lord Byron. CP-Byron

To Edward on the Death of His First Pony. James Austen. CP-AustJ

To Edward Williams. Percy Bysshe Shelley. CP-ShelP

To Ee Is Human. Ogden Nash. CP-NashO

To Electra. Robert Herrick. CP-HerrR

To Electra. Love Looks for Love. Robert Herrick. CP-HerrR

To Elinor Wylie. Edna St. Vincent Millay. CP-MillE

To Eliza. Lord Byron. CP-Byron

To Eliza Plucking Laurel in Mr Pope's Gardens. Samuel Johnson. CP-JohnS

To Elizabeth. James Whitcomb Riley. CP-RileJ

To Elizabeth, Countess of Rutland. Ben Jonson. CP-JonsB; SP-JonsB

To Ellen, at the South. Ralph Waldo Emerson. CP-EmerR

To Elsie. William Carlos Williams. CP-WilW1

To Elspeth. Dorothy Parker. CP-ParkD

To Emilia Viviani. Percy Bysshe Shelley. CP-ShelP

To Emily Dickinson. Hart Crane. CP-CranH

To Emma. Lord Byron. CP-Byron

To Emma. John Keats. CP-KeatJ

To Empty the Mind. Charles Olson. CP-OlsoC

To enact the evil or the good, waking, we say. Bad Dream, A. Kathleen Jessie Raine. SP-RainK

To end all carols, darling. Carol: "To end all carols, darling." Louis MacNeice. CP-MacNL

To end up alone. Poem for My 43rd Birthday. Charles Bukowski. SP-BukC2

To Endymion. Countee Cullen. CP-CullC

To English Connoisseurs. William Blake. CP-BlakW

To Englishmen. John Greenleaf Whittier. CP-WhitJ

To Enid the Huntress. G. K. Chesterton. CP-ChesG

To Enid, Who Acted the Cat in Private Pantomime. G. K. Chesterton. CP-ChesG

To Enjoy the Time. Robert Herrick. CP-HerrR

To enrich the earth I have sowed clover and grass. Enriching the Earth. Wendell Berry. CP-BerrW

To Enter That Rhythm Where the Self Is Lost. Muriel Rukeyser. CP-RukeM

To enter the real. Song: "To enter the real." Charles Tomlinson. SP-TomlC

To Enterprise. William Wordsworth. CP-WorW2

To erase the expression of coarse lust. Political Poem, A. Yehuda Amichai. SP-AmicYL, *tr.* by Benjamin Harshav *and* Barbara Harshav

To Eros. Wilfred Owen. CP-OwenW

To Esmé, Lord Aubigny. Ben Jonson. CP-JonsB; SP-JonsB

To E.T. Robert Frost. CP-FrosR

To Ethelinda. Christopher Smart. SP-SmarC

To Eustace Budgell, Esq., on His Translation of the Characters of Theophrastus. Alexander Pope. CP-PopeA

To Eva. Ralph Waldo Emerson. CP-EmerR

To Eva Descending the Stair. Sylvia Plath. CP-PlatS

To Evan. Richard Eberhart. CP-EberR

To Eve, Man's Dream of Wifehood as Described by Milton. Nicholas Vachel Lindsay. CP-LindV

To every creature / Adam gave its name. Ralph Waldo Emerson. CP-EmerR

To Every Seed His Own Body. Christina Georgina Rossetti. CP-RosC2

To every soul, howe'er obscure its birth. Soul's Opportunities, The. Jones Very. CP-VeryJ

To Evoke Posterity. Robert Graves. CP-GravR

To exist; to be among things. Monument. George Oppen. CP-OppGN

To F——. Edgar Allan Poe. CP-PoeEd

To F—S S. O—D. Edgar Allan Poe. CP-PoeEd

To F.S., who accused the Author of partiality in writing verses for F C Fowle, & not for him. Mrs. Austen. CP-AustJ

To fail (transitive and intransitive). Success Story. Philip Larkin. CP-LarkP

To Failure. Philip Larkin. CP-LarkP

To ———: "Fair Nature's priestesses! to whom." John Greenleaf Whittier. CP-WhitJ

To Faneuil Hall. John Greenleaf Whittier. CP-WhitJ

To Fanny. John Keats. CP-KeatJ

To Father O'Connor. G. K. Chesterton. CP-ChesG

To feel and speak the astonishing beauty of things—earth, stone and. Beauty of Things, The. Robinson Jeffers. CP-JefR3

To Fetch me Wine my *Lucia* went. Broken Christall, The. Robert Herrick. CP-HerrR

To fight aloud, is very brave. Emily Dickinson. CP-DickE

To fight history as it carries us. Phyllis Wounded. Marge Piercy. SP-PierM

To fill a Gap. Emily Dickinson. CP-DickE

To find a garden-tulip growing. Ages of Oath, The. Robert Graves. CP-GravR

To Find a Way. George Oppen. CP-OppGN

To find my home in one sentence, concise, as if hammered in metal. Czeslaw Milosz. CP-MiloC; CP-MiloCN, *tr.* by Robert Hass

To find that Tree of Life, whose Fruits did feed. To the King, To Cure the Evill. Robert Herrick. CP-HerrR

To find the Western path. Morning. William Blake. CP-BlakW

To Find[e] God. Robert Herrick. CP-HerrR

To Fine Grand. Ben Jonson. CP-JonsB; SP-JonsB

To Fine Lady Would-Be. Ben Jonson. CP-JonsB; SP-JonsB

To Fire. Gary Snyder. CP-SnydG

To Flaxman. William Blake. CP-BlakW

To F[laxman]. William Blake. CP-BlakW

To flee from memory. Emily Dickinson. CP-DickE

To fleece the Fleece from golden sheep. Scales of the Eyes, The. Howard Nemerov. CP-NemeH

To flex in the upper airs. Utterings. Donald Davie. CP-DaviDC

To fling my arms wide. Dream Variation[s]. Langston Hughes. CP-HughL; CP-HughL1

To Flood Stage Again. James Wright. CP-WrigJ

To Florence. Lord Byron. CP-Byron

To Florida. Louise Glück. SP-GlucL

To Flossie. William Carlos Williams. CP-WilW2

To Flowers. Robert Herrick. CP-HerrR

To Flowers from Italy in Winter. Thomas Hardy. CP-HardT

To Flush, My Dog. Elizabeth Barrett Browning. CP-BroEB

To follow the hard sunlight on the northern harbor. Muriel Rukeyser. CP-RukeM

To Fool or Knave. Ben Jonson. CP-JonsB; SP-JonsB

To ——— / For her this rhyme is penned, whose luminous eyes. Valentine, A. Edgar Allan Poe. CP-PoeEd

To Ford Madox Ford in Heaven. William Carlos Williams. CP-WilW2

To foreclose. Lorine Niedecker. CP-NiedL

To Foreign Lands. Walt Whitman. CP-WhitW

To forget you would be impossible. Emily Dickinson. SP-DickE

To forgive Enemies H[ayley] does pretend. On Hayley. William Blake. CP-BlakW

To form a just and finished piece. Directions for a Birthday Song. Jonathan Swift. CP-SwifJ

To Fortune. Samuel Taylor Coleridge. CP-ColeS

To Fortune. Robert Herrick. CP-HerrR

To France. Countee Cullen. CP-CullC

To Frances. G. K. Chesterton. CP-ChesG

To Francis Beaumont. Ben Jonson. CP-JonsB; SP-JonsB

To Frank O'Hara. James Schuyler. CP-SchuJ

To Frantz Fanon. Adrienne Rich. CP-RicAE

To Freda Spencer. G. K. Chesterton. CP-ChesG

To Fredrika Bremer. John Greenleaf Whittier. CP-WhitJ

To Friend-Tree of Counted Days. René Char. CP-WilW2

To Friends, for Good Health. Louis Zukofsky. CP-ZukLS

To fulfill the will of a powerless friend. Emily Dickinson. SP-DickE

To Fuzzy. James Tate. SP-TateJ

To G. G. John Greenleaf Whittier. CP-WhitJ

To Gary Snyder. Wendell Berry. CP-BerrW

To gather flowers Sappha went. Apron of Flowers, The. Robert Herrick. CP-HerrR

To Gather Something. Yehuda Amichai. SP-AmicYL, *tr.* by Benjamin Harshav *and* Barbara Harshav

To General Washington, An Epistle. Annis Boudinot Stockton. CP-StocA

To General Washington [Aug. 26, 1783]. Annis Boudinot Stockton. CP-StocA

To George B. Cheever. John Greenleaf Whittier. CP-WhitJ

To George, Earl Delawarr. Lord Byron. CP-Byron

To George Felton Mathew. John Keats. CP-KeatJ

To George Nim-Dan-Dean, Esq. upon His Incomparable Verses, &c. of August 2d, 1721. Thomas Sheridan. CP-SherT

To George Romney, Esq. William Cowper. CP-CowpW

To George Sand: A Desire. Elizabeth Barrett Browning. CP-BroEB

To George Sand: A Recognition. Elizabeth Barrett Browning. CP-BroEB

To Georgiana Augusta Wylie. John Keats. CP-KeatJ

To Gerhardt, There, among Europe's Things of Which He Has Written Us in His "Brief an Creely und Olson" Charles Olson. CP-OlsoC; SP-OlsoC

To get betimes in Boston town I rose this morning early. Boston Ballad [1854], A. Walt Whitman. CP-WhitW

To get into it / As it lies. Shirt. Charles Simic. SP-SimiC; SP-SimiCE

To get it all back and then to notice. End Games. Andrei Codrescu. SP-CodrA

To get out of thoughts about one's own person. Year 1900, The. Czeslaw Milosz. CP-MiloCN, *tr.* by Robert Hass

To get quicker through the day. Errand Boy 1, The. David Ignatow. SP-IgnaD

To Get the Final Lilt of Songs. Walt Whitman. CP-WhitW

To get thine ends, lay bashfulnesse aside. No Bashfulnesse in Begging. Robert Herrick. CP-HerrR

To get west you go east. Philip Levine. SP-LeviP *Fr.* Poem with No Ending, A.

To Giacomo Leopardi in the Sky. Charles Wright. SP-WrigC

To Giles Grotus, *vir amplissimus.* Capilupus Sends Greeting to Grotus. Ezra Pound. CP-PoEar

To give you back this wave. Wave, The. Adrienne Rich. SP-RicA2

To Gloriana. Nicholas Vachel Lindsay. CP-LindV

To Go. Heather McHugh. SP-McHuH

To Go By Singing. Wendell Berry. CP-BerrW

To go by the asters. Luxury. Denise Levertov. SP-LeveDP

To go in no direction. In No Direction. Robert Graves. CP-GravR

To go in the dark with a light is to know the light. To Know the Dark. Wendell Berry. CP-BerrW

To go there: do not fall asleep, your forehead. Neighborhood of Make-Believe,

The. Thomas Lux. SP-LuxT

To go to Lvov. Which station. Adam Zagajewski. SP-ZagaA, *tr. by* Renata Gorczynski

To go to the edge is to discover. Brazil. John Updike. CP-UpdiJ

To God. William Blake. CP-BlakW

To God: an Anthem, Sung in the Chapel at White-Hall, Before the King. Robert Herrick. CP-HerrR

To God, His Gift. Robert Herrick. CP-HerrR

To God, His Good Will. Robert Herrick. CP-HerrR

To God, in Time of Plundering. Robert Herrick. CP-HerrR

To God, on His Sickness[e]. Robert Herrick. CP-HerrR

To God or Man. Heather McHugh. SP-McHuH

To God our strength sing loud, and clear. Bible, *O.T. See* Sing aloud unto God our strength

To God: to illuminate all men. Beginning with Skid Road. Psalm III: "To God: to illuminate all men. Beginning with Skid Road." Allen Ginsberg. CP-GinsA

To good thou ask'st the way—enter the street. Way, The. Jones Very. CP-VeryJ

To Gottfried Benn. Frank O'Hara. SP-OharF

To Graham and Anna: from the Arctic Gate. Letter to Graham and Anna. Louis MacNeice. CP-MacNL

To grass, or leaf, or fruit, or wall. Snail, The. Vincent Bourne. CP-CowpW, *tr. by* William Cowper

To Gravina. William Cowper. CP-CowpW

To Greet a Letter Carrier. William Carlos Williams. CP-WilW1

To grip through the ground with your feet. Old Colonial Imperialist, An. Howard Nemerov. CP-NemeH

To Groom Idiot. Ben Jonson. CP-JonsB; SP-JonsB

To Groves. Robert Herrick. CP-HerrR

To Guido Cavalcanti. Ezra Pound. CP-PoEar

To H. C., Six Years Old. William Wordsworth. CP-WorW1; MW-WorW

To H. M. Howard Nemerov. CP-NemeH

To ———: "Had I a man's fair form, then might my sighs." John Keats. CP-KeatJ

To hang our head, ostensibly. Emily Dickinson. CP-DickE

To Harriet. Lord Byron. CP-Byron

To Harriet. Percy Bysshe Shelley. CP-ShelP

To Harriet Monroe. Richard Eberhart. CP-EberR

To Harriot all accomplish'd fair. Ode to Lady Harriot. Christopher Smart. SP-SmarC

To Harvey, Who Traced the Circulation. James Wright. CP-WrigJ

To Hattie—on Her Birthday. James Whitcomb Riley. CP-RileJ

To have a toothache and no competent dentist. Teacher's Vacation Lament in the Country. Alan Dugan. CP-DugaA

To have attained an endless, timeless meeting. Timeless Meeting. Robert Graves. CP-GravR

To have been Diogenes. Why not? Or de Sade. Sonnet: "To have been Diogenes. Why not? Or de Sade." Hayden Carruth. CP-CarHS *Fr.* Sonnets.

To have been the missing Hero. Emily Dickinson. SP-DickE

To Have Danced with Death. Yusef Komunyakaa. CP-KomuY

To Have Done Nothing. William Carlos Williams. CP-WilW1

To have had such Daughters is sanctity. Emily Dickinson. SP-DickE

To have it, sweetheart, is to know you have it. She to Him. Robert Graves. CP-GravR

To have known him, to have loved him. Monody. Herman Melville. SP-MelvH

To have seen Buenos Aires grow, grow and decline. Fame. Jorge Luis Borges. SP-BorgJ, *tr. by* Alastair Reid

To have someone of compatible mind. Sleeping With Friends. Miller Williams. CP-WillM

To have the whole air! Starting with a Line from Roethke. Jane Cooper. CP-CoopJ

To Have To. Heather McHugh. SP-McHuH

To have watched from one of your patios. South, The. Jorge Luis Borges. SP-BorgJ, *tr. by* W. S. Merwin

To have written then, when you writ, seemed to me. To the Countess of Bedford ("To have written then, when you writ, seemed to me"). John Donne. CP-DonnJ; MW-DonnJ

To have your face left overnight. Mask. Carl Sandburg. CP-SandC

To H[ayley]. William Blake. CP-BlakW

To Hayley. William Cowper. CP-CowpW

To Health. *Unknown.* CP-CowpW

To Hear an Oriole Sing. Emily Dickinson. CP-DickE

To hear her sing—to hear her sing. James Whitcomb Riley. CP-RileJ

To hear the clock strike, and strike away, in a still room. They Pass. Marya Alexandrovna Zaturenska. SP-ZatuM

To Heaven. Robert Herrick. CP-HerrR

To Heaven. Ben Jonson. CP-JonsB; SP-JonsB

To Hedli. Louis MacNeice. CP-MacNL

To Helen. Edgar Allan Poe. CP-PoeEd

To Helen Keller. Donald Davie. CP-DaviDC

To Hell wi' Happiness! Hugh MacDiarmid. SP-MacDH

To Hell with It. Frank O'Hara. SP-OharF

To hell with metric—I have read the lore of the ages. With Vengeance Like a Tiger Crawls. Charles Bukowski. SP-BukC2

To help our Bleaker Parts. Emily Dickinson. CP-DickE

To Hendrick Avercamp, mute. February 29, 1988. William Corbett. SP-CorbW

To Her. Paul Laurence Dunbar. CP-DunbP

To Her Again, She Burning in a Fever. Thomas Carew. *See* Song: To Her Again[e], She Burning in a Fe[a]ver

To her depths the sea has taken a sailor. Prayer: "To her depths the sea has taken a sailor." Constantine P. Cavafy. CP-CavaC, *tr. by* Theoharis Constantine Theoharis

To her derided Home. Emily Dickinson. CP-DickE

To Her Father, with Some Verses. Anne Bradstreet. CP-BradA

To Her in Absence; a Ship. Thomas Carew. CP-CareT

To Her Most Honored Father Thomas Dudley, Esquire, These Humbly Presented. Anne Bradstreet. CP-BradA

To hide a girl's blushes. Fan, The. Jaroslav Seifert. SP-SeifJ, *tr. by* Ewald Osers

To Hilaire Belloc. G. K. Chesterton. CP-ChesG

To him after long anguish. Renaissance. Hayden Carruth. CP-CarHS

To Him That Hath Shall Be Given. Jones Very. CP-VeryJ

To Him That Was Crucified. Walt Whitman. CP-WhitW

To him to whom Events and Omens. Emily Dickinson. SP-DickE

To Him Who bade the Heavens abide, yet cease not from their motion. Supports, The. Rudyard Kipling. CP-KiplR *Fr.* Debits and Credits.

To him who ever thought with love of me. Gerard Manley Hopkins. CP-HopkG

To him who fought for liberty. Secret of the Burning Stars, The. Pablo Antonio Cuadra. CP-MertT

To him who hath to him I love to give. Reward, The. Jones Very. CP-VeryJ

To him, who longs unto his CHRIST to go. Coming to Christ. Robert Herrick. CP-HerrR

To him who overcometh. Jones Very. CP-VeryJ

To him who overcometh I will give. To him who overcometh. Jones Very. CP-VeryJ

To His Angrie God. Robert Herrick. CP-HerrR

To His Book. Robert Herrick. CP-HerrR

To His Book[e]. Robert Herrick. CP-HerrR

(Another [To His Booke].) CP-HerrR

To His Book[e]. Robert Herrick. CP-HerrR

To His Booke. Robert Herrick. CP-HerrR

To His Brother in Law Master John Wingfield. Robert Herrick. CP-HerrR

To His Brother Nicolas Herrick. Robert Herrick. CP-HerrR

To His Children in Darkness. James Dickey. CP-DickJ

To His Closet-Gods. Robert Herrick. CP-HerrR

To His Conscience. Robert Herrick. CP-HerrR

To His Coy Mistress. Andrew Marvell. CP-MarvA

To His Cynical Mistress. Thom Gunn. CP-GunnT

To his deare Valentine, Mistresse Margaret Falconbrige. Robert Herrick. CP-HerrR

To His Deere God. Robert Herrick. CP-HerrR

To His Dying Brother, Master William Herrick. Robert Herrick. CP-HerrR

To His Ever-Loving God. Robert Herrick. CP-HerrR

To His Excellency General Washington. Phillis Wheatley. CP-WheaP

To His Excellency Our Lord Carteret, Lord Lieutenant of Ireland: The Humble Petition of Lord Viscount Mont-Cashel, and the Rest of His School-Fellows. Thomas Sheridan. CP-SherT

To his Faithfull Friend, Master John Crofts, Cup-bearer to the King. Robert Herrick. CP-HerrR

To His False Mistris. Robert Herrick. CP-HerrR

To His Father. John Milton. *See* To My Father

To his Friend, Master J. Jincks. Robert Herrick. CP-HerrR

To His Friend, on the Untunable Times. Robert Herrick. CP-HerrR

To His Friend the Author upon His *Richard.* Ben Jonson. CP-JonsB

To His Friend to Avoid Contention of Words. Robert Herrick. CP-HerrR

To His Girles. Robert Herrick. CP-HerrR

To his Girles who Would Have Him Sportfull. Robert Herrick. CP-HerrR

To His Grace the Archbishop of Dublin. Jonathan Swift. CP-SwifJ

To His Heart, Bidding It Have No Fear. William Butler Yeats. CP-YeatW

To His Honour the Lieutenant-Governor, on the Death of His Lady. *March* 24, 1773. Phillis Wheatley. CP-WheaP

To His Honour'd Friend, Sir Thomas Heale. Robert Herrick. CP-HerrR

To His Honoured and Most Ingenious Friend Mr. Charles Cotton. Robert Herrick. CP-HerrR

To His Honoured Friend, M. John Weare, Councellour. Robert Herrick. CP-HerrR

To His Honoured Friend, Sir John Mynts. Robert Herrick. CP-HerrR

To His Honoured Kinsman, Sir Richard Stone. Robert Herrick. CP-HerrR

To His Honoured Kinsman Sir William Soame. Robert Herrick. CP-HerrR

To his house the bodiless. Sculptor. Sylvia Plath. CP-PlatS

To His Household Gods. Robert Herrick. CP-HerrR

To His Jealous Mistress. Thomas Carew. CP-CareT

To His Kinsman, Master Thomas Herrick, Who Desired to Be in His Book. Robert Herrick. CP-HerrR

To His Kinsman, Sir Tho. Soame. Robert Herrick. CP-HerrR

To His Kinswoman, Mrs. Penelope Wheeler. Robert Herrick. CP-HerrR

To His Kinswoman, Mistresse Susanna Herrick. Robert Herrick. CP-HerrR

To His Lady, Then Mrs Cary. Ben Jonson. CP-JonsB; SP-JonsB

To His Learned Friend M. Jo. Harmar, Phisitian to to Colledge of Westminster. Robert Herrick. CP-HerrR

To His Love. G. K. Chesterton. CP-ChesG

To His Love. Ivor Gurney. SP-GurnI

To His Lovely Mistresses. Robert Herrick. CP-HerrR

To His Maid Prew. Robert Herrick. CP-HerrR

To His Mistress. Thomas Carew. CP-CareT

To His Mistress Going to Bed. John Donne. MW-DonnJ *Fr.* Elegies.

To His Mistress Objecting to Him Neither Toying or Talking. Robert Herrick. CP-HerrR

To His Mistress [*or* Mistris] Confined. James Shirley. CP-CareT

To His Mistress Retiring in Affection. Thomas Carew. CP-CareT

To His Mistress[e]. Robert Herrick. CP-HerrR

To His Mistress[es]. Robert Herrick. CP-HerrR

To His Mistresses. Robert Herrick. CP-HerrR

To His Much and Worthily Esteemed Friend the Author. Ben Jonson. CP-JonsB

To His Much Honoured the Lord Lepington upon His Translation of Malvezzi, His "Romulus" and "Tarquin" Sir John Suckling. CP-SuckJ

To His Muse. Robert Herrick. CP-HerrR

To His Muse, Another to the Same. Robert Herrick. CP-HerrR

To His Nephew, to Be Prosperous in His Art of Painting. Robert Herrick. CP-HerrR

To His Noble Friend, Mr Richard Lovelace, upon His Poems. Andrew Marvell. CP-MarvA

To His Paternall Countrey. Robert Herrick. CP-HerrR

To His Peculiar Friend M. Jo: Wicks. Robert Herrick. CP-HerrR

To His Peculiar Friend Master Thomas Shapcott, Lawyer. Robert Herrick. CP-HerrR

To His Peculiar Friend Sir Edward Fish, Knight Baronet. Robert Herrick. CP-HerrR

To His Rival. Sir John Suckling. CP-SuckJ

To His Savior [*or* Saviour]. The New Years [*or* yeers] Gift. Robert Herrick. CP-HerrR

To His Saviour. Robert Herrick. CP-HerrR

To His Saviour, a Child; a Present, by a Child. Robert Herrick. CP-HerrR

To His Saviours Sepulcher: His Devotion. Robert Herrick. CP-HerrR

To His Servant. Horace. *See* Odes

To his simplicity. Emily Dickinson. CP-DickE

To his Singular Friend, William Lithgow. *Unknown, sometimes at. to* Sir Walter Ralegh. CP-RaleW

To His Sister in Law, M. Susanna Herrick. Robert Herrick. CP-HerrR

To His Skeleton. Richard Wilbur. CP-WilbR

To his sweet Lute *Apollo* sung the motions of the Spheares. Thomas Campion. CP-CampT

To His Sweet Saviour. Robert Herrick. CP-HerrR

To His Tomb-Maker. Robert Herrick. CP-HerrR

To His Valentine, on S. Valentines Day. Robert Herrick. CP-HerrR

To His Verses. Robert Herrick. CP-HerrR

To His Watch. Gerard Manley Hopkins. CP-HopkG

To His Wife, in Her Illness. G. K. Chesterton. CP-ChesG

To His Worthy Friend Doctor Witty upon His Translation of the "Popular Errors" Andrew Marvell. CP-MarvA

To His Worthy Friend, M. Arthur Bartly. Robert Herrick. CP-HerrR

To his Worthy Friend M. John Hall, Student of Grayes-Inne. Robert Herrick. CP-HerrR

To Worthy Friend, M. Tho. Falconbirge. Robert Herrick. CP-HerrR

To His Worthy Kinsmen, Mr. Stephen Soame. Robert Herrick. CP-HerrR

To hold secure the province of Pure Art. Edna St. Vincent Millay. CP-MillE

To Homer. John Keats. CP-KeatJ

To Hook the Reader, You, John Murray. Lord Byron. CP-Byron

To Hope. John Keats. CP-KeatJ

To Hornet. Ben Jonson. CP-JonsB; SP-JonsB

To house the Hag, you must doe this. Another to Bring in the Witch. Robert Herrick. CP-HerrR

To house / these maddened times, these squalid. Building, A. Theodore Weiss.

SP-WeisT

To Hulme (T. E.) and Fitzgerald (A Certain). Ezra Pound. CP-PoeEar

To humble yourself before a radio on a Sunday. Ode (To Joseph Lesueur) on the Arrow That Flieth by Day. Frank O'Hara. SP-OharF

To Hunt. William Blake. CP-BlakW

To Hurl Haunting Memories. Yehuda Amichai. SP-AmicYL, *tr. by* Benjamin Harshav *and* Barbara Harshav

To hurt the Negro and avoid the Jew. University. Karl Shapiro. SP-ShapK

To I.F. William Wordsworth. CP-WorW2

To ———: "I fear thy kisses, gentle maiden." Percy Bysshe Shelley. CP-ShelP

To ———: "I heed not that my earthly lot." Edgar Allan Poe. CP-PoeEd

To ———: "I saw thee on thy bridal day." Edgar Allan Poe. CP-PoeEd

To Ianthe. Percy Bysshe Shelley. CP-ShelP

To ———: "If these brief Records, by the Muses' art." William Wordsworth. CP-WorW2

To Imagination. Emily Jane Brontë. CP-BronE

To imagine it, to believe it, bring to mind all. Placet Experiri. Mona Van Duyn. SP-VanDM

To imitate England. Fanny Howe. SP-HoweF *Fr.* Vineyard, The.

To —, in Her Seventieth Year. William Wordsworth. CP-WorW2

To Inez Milholland. Edna St. Vincent Millay. CP-MillE

To Inigo, Marquess Would Be, a Corollary. Ben Jonson. CP-JonsB

To insert myself into your story. Stéphane Mallarmé. CP-MallS, *tr. by* Henry Weinfield

To interrupt His Yellow Plan. Emily Dickinson. CP-DickE

To Ireland. Percy Bysshe Shelley. CP-ShelP

To Ireland in the Coming Times. William Butler Yeats. CP-YeatW

To Irene García. Federico García Lorca. CP-GarcF, *tr. by* Alan S. Trueblood *Fr.* Games.

To Isabelle Trumpy. Rainer Maria Rilke. CP-RilkFr, *tr. by* A. Poulin, Jr.

To Isherwood Dying. Thom Gunn. CP-GunnT

To Ishtar. Richard Wilbur. CP-WilbR

To Ivor Gurney. Charles Tomlinson. CP-TomlC; SP-TomlC

To J. H. Reynolds, Esq. John Keats. CP-KeatJ

To J. L. G. K. Chesterton. CP-ChesG

To J.M. George Meredith. CP-MerG1

To J. P. John Greenleaf Whittier. CP-WhitJ

To J. Q. Paul Laurence Dunbar. CP-DunbP

To J. S. [James Spedding]. Alfred Tennyson. CP-TennA

To J. S****. Robert Burns. *See* To James Smith

To J. W. Ralph Waldo Emerson. CP-EmerR

To James Newton Matthews. James Whitcomb Riley. CP-RileJ

To James Rice. John Keats. CP-KeatJ

To James Smith. Robert Burns. CP-BurnR

  (To J. S****.) CP-BurnR

To James T. Fields. John Greenleaf Whittier. CP-WhitJ

To James Whitcomb Riley. Rudyard Kipling. CP-KiplR

To Jane Addams at the Hague. Nicholas Vachel Lindsay. CP-LindV

To Jane; and in Imitation of Coleridge. Frank O'Hara. SP-OharF

To Jane: The Invitation. Percy Bysshe Shelley. CP-ShelP

To Jane: The keen stars were twinkling. Percy Bysshe Shelley. CP-ShelP

To Jane: The Recollection. Percy Bysshe Shelley. CP-ShelP

To Janus. Jonathan Swift. CP-SwifJ

To Jealousie. Robert Herrick. CP-HerrR

To Jean-Louis Vandoyer. Rainer Maria Rilke. CP-RilkFr, *tr. by* A. Poulin, Jr.

To Jenny came a gentle youth. Dance at the Phoenix, The. Thomas Hardy. CP-HardT

To Jerusalem. Constantine P. Cavafy. CP-CavaC, *tr. by* Theoharis Constantine Theoharis

  (Now they've come before Jerusalem.) CP-CavaC, *tr. by* Theoharis Constantine Theoharis

To Jesus on His Birthday. Edna St. Vincent Millay. CP-MillE

To Jesus, the Crown of my Hope. Longing To Be with Christ. William Cowper. CP-CowpW

To Joanna. William Wordsworth. CP-WorW1; MW-WorW

To Joel Chandler Harris. James Whitcomb Riley. CP-RileJ

To Johannes Brahms. Jorge Luis Borges. SP-BorgJ, *tr. by* Stephen Kessler

To John C. Frémont. John Greenleaf Whittier. CP-WhitJ

To John Donne ("Donne, the delight of Phoebus, and each Muse"). Ben Jonson. CP-JonsB; SP-JonsB

To John Donne ("Who shall doubt, Donne, where [*or* whe'er] I a poet be[e]"). Ben Jonson. CP-JonsB; SP-JonsB

To John Flaxman, 12 September 1800. William Blake. CP-BlakW

To John Johnson. William Cowper. CP-CowpW

To John Keats, Poet, at Springtime. Countee Cullen. CP-CullC

To John Kennedy. Robert Burns. CP-BurnR

To John Rouse. John Milton. CP-MiltJ

(Ode to Rouse.) CP-CowpW

To John Syme. Robert Burns. CP-BurnR

To John Taylor. Robert Burns. CP-BurnR
   (To Mr. John Taylor.) CP-BurnR

To join [or joyn] with them, who here confer. His Offering, with the Rest, at the Sepulcher. Robert Herrick. CP-HerrR

To Jos: Lo: Bishop of Exeter. Robert Herrick. CP-HerrR

To Juan at the Winter Solstice. Robert Graves. CP-GravR

To judge by what they wore on weekdays. Missing Persons. Miller Williams. CP-WillM

To Judith Asleep. John Ciardi. CP-CiarJ

To Judith, Taking Leave. Adrienne Rich. CP-RicAE; SP-RicA2

To Julia. Robert Herrick. CP-HerrR

To Julia, in Her Dawn, or Day-breake. Robert Herrick. CP-HerrR

To Julia in the Temple. Robert Herrick. CP-HerrR

To Julia, the Flaminica Dialis, or Queen-Priest. Robert Herrick. CP-HerrR

To justify God's ways to man. Just You Wait! Donald Davie. CP-DaviDC

To K. M. Walter De la Mare. See Horse in a Field

To Kate Bluestein. William Corbett. SP-CorbW

To Kathleen. Edna St. Vincent Millay. CP-MillE

To Keep a True Lent. Robert Herrick. CP-HerrR

To keep an eye on fables of the moon. Fables of the Moon. Richard Eberhart. CP-EberR

To keep my difficult life safe. Bank of the Future, The. Constantine P. Cavafy. CP-CavaC, tr. by Theoharis Constantine Theoharis

To keep the weakness secret. To deny it and break through. Muriel Rukeyser. CP-RukeM

To Kelly Miller, Jr. Paul Laurence Dunbar. CP-DunbP

To Kenya Tribesmen, the Turkana. Richard Eberhart. CP-EberR

To Kill in War Is Not Murder. Robinson Jeffers. CP-JefR3

To K[ing] Charles and Q[ueen] Mary, for the Loss of Their First-Born. An Epigram Consolatory. 1629. Ben Jonson. CP-JonsB

To King James ("How, best of kings, dost thou a scepter bear[e]!"). Ben Jonson. CP-JonsB; SP-JonsB

To King James ("That we the [or thy] loss might know, and thou our love"). Ben Jonson. CP-JonsB; SP-JonsB

To King James ("Who would not be thy subject, James, t'obey"). Ben Jonson. CP-JonsB; SP-JonsB

To kneel before some saintly shrine. Summer Pilgrimage, A. John Greenleaf Whittier. CP-WhitJ

To Know in Reverie the Only Phenomenology of the Absolute. Hayden Carruth. CP-CarHS

To know just how He suffered—would be dear. Emily Dickinson. CP-DickE

To know our destiny is to know the horror. Bweteen Hyssop and Axe. Robert Graves. CP-GravR

To Know Silence Perfectly. Carl Sandburg. CP-SandC

To know that there is shelter. Emily Dickinson. SP-DickE

To Know the Dark. Wendell Berry. CP-BerrW

To know the inhabiting reasons. For the Rebuilding of a House. Wendell Berry. CP-BerrW

To know, to esteem, to love,—and then to part. To Two Sisters. Samuel Taylor Coleridge. CP-ColeS

To know you better as you flee. Emily Dickinson. SP-DickE

To Kosciusko. John Keats. CP-KeatJ

To L. K. C. G. K. Chesterton. CP-ChesG

To L. K. C. from G. K. C. G. K. Chesterton. CP-ChesG

To L. Manlius Torquatus. Horace. See Odes

To La Contessa Bianzafior (Cent. XIV). Ezra Pound. CP-PoEar

To Lady Austen. William Cowper. CP-CowpW

To Lady Beaumont. William Wordsworth. CP-WorW1

To Lady Firebrace. Samuel Johnson. CP-JohnS

To Lady Jane. Nicholas Vachel Lindsay. CP-LindV

To Lalla, Reading My Verses Topsy-Turvy. Christina Georgina Rossetti. CP-RosC3

To Landrum Guy, Beginning to Write at Sixty. James Dickey. CP-DickJ

To Larr [or Lar]. Robert Herrick. CP-HerrR

To Laura. Annis Boudinot Stockton. CP-StocA

To Laura—a Card. Annis Boudinot Stockton. CP-StocA

To Laurels. Robert Herrick. CP-HerrR

To lay the logarithmic spiral on. Figures of Thought. Howard Nemerov. CP-NemeH

To lay the soul that loves him low. God Hides His People. Jeanne Marie Bouvier de la Motte- Guyon. CP-CowpW

To learn the Transport by the Pain. Emily Dickinson. CP-DickE

To leave a verse concerning the sad hour. To a Minor Poet of 1899. Jorge Luis Borges. SP-BorgJ, tr. by Charles Tomlinson

To leave the earth was my wish, and no will stayed my rising. Temple, A. Kenneth Patchen. CP-PatcK

To Leigh Hunt, Esq. John Keats. CP-KeatJ

To Leonainie. James Whitcomb Riley. CP-RileJ

To Leonora Singing at Rome. John Milton. See To the Same ["Another Leonora captured the poet Torquato"]

To Leonora Singing in Rome. John Milton. CP-MiltJ

To Lesbia. Lord Byron. CP-Byron

To Lesley. James Whitcomb Riley. CP-RileJ

To Let Go Or to Hold on—? D. H. Lawrence. CP-LawrD

To ———: "Let other bards of angels sing." William Wordsworth. CP-WorW2; MW-WorW

To Lettice, My Sister. D. H. Lawrence. See Brother and Sister

To Li Po. Tu Fu. CP-WilW2

To Liberty. Hart Crane. CP-CranH

To lie far off, in bed with a foul cough. Shift of Scene, A. Robert Graves. CP-GravR

To Life. Thomas Hardy. CP-HardT

To Like, to Love. Anne Sexton. CP-SextA

To Lindsay. Allen Ginsberg. CP-GinsA; SP-GinsA

To Listen. C. K. Williams. SP-WillC

To Liuba, Leaving. Eugenio Montale. CP-MontE, tr. by Jonathan Galassi

To Live Freely. Robert Herrick. CP-HerrR

To live illusionless, in the abandoned mine. Double Monologue. Adrienne Rich. CP-RicAE

To live lasts always, but to love. Emily Dickinson. SP-DickE

To Live Merrily, and To Trust to Good Verses. Robert Herrick. CP-HerrR

To live on charm, one must be courteous. She Bitches About Boys. Marilyn Hacker. SP-HackM

To live, to lie awake. Incipience. Adrienne Rich. SP-RicA2

To Lizbie Browne. Thomas Hardy. CP-HardT

To loll back, in a misty hammock, swung. Dream of Inspiration, A. James Whitcomb Riley. CP-RileJ

To Londoners. Donald Davie. CP-DaviDC

To ———: "Look at the fate of summer flowers." William Wordsworth. CP-WorW2

To look at the river made of time and water. Ars Poetica. Jorge Luis Borges. SP-BorgJ, tr. by W. S. Merwin

To look for meaning is as foolish as to find it. Lightly. David Ignatow. SP-IgnaD

To loose the button, is no lesse. Laxare Fibulam. Robert Herrick. CP-HerrR

To loosen with all ten fingers held wide and limber. Moss-Gathering. Theodore Roethke. CP-RoetT

To Lord Byron. John Keats. CP-KeatJ

To Lord Harley, since Earl of Oxford, on His Marriage. Jonathan Swift. CP-SwifJ

To Lord Palmerston. George Meredith. CP-MerG2

To Lord Thurlow. Lord Byron. CP-Byron

To lose one's faith—surpass. Emily Dickinson. CP-DickE

To Lose the Earth. Anne Sexton. CP-SextA

To lose thee—sweeter than to gain. Emily Dickinson. CP-DickE

To lose your hair, to lose you temper. Notice of Loss. Hans Magnus Enzensberger. SP-EnzeH

To Louisa in the Lane. Thomas Hardy. CP-HardT

To Louise. Paul Laurence Dunbar. CP-DunbP

To Love. Robert Herrick. CP-HerrR

To love a man wholly. Warning. Alice Walker. CP-WalkA

To Love and to the lovely eyes. Hymn: "To Love and to the lovely eyes." Charles Baudelaire. CP-BaudC, tr. by Walter Martin

To love love and not its meaning. Rape of the Swan, The. Archibald MacLeish. CP-MacLA

To love, one must slay. "H. D." CP-DoolH Fr. Electra-Orestes.

To love one woman, or to sit. Woman and Tree. Robert Graves. CP-GravR

To love poets / the vanishing fauna of Yellowstone Park. Red-Hot Fruit. Jaroslav Seifert. SP-SeifJ, tr. by Ewald Osers

To love thee Year by Year. Emily Dickinson. CP-DickE

To love you truly. Song: To Become Each Other. Robert Graves. CP-GravR

To Lu Chi. Howard Nemerov. CP-NemeH

To Lucasta, about That War. John Ciardi. CP-CiarJ

To Lucca Giordano. William Wordsworth. CP-WorW2

To Lucia at Birth. Robert Graves. CP-GravR

To Lucy, Countess of Bedford. Ben Jonson. CP-JonsB; SP-JonsB

To Lucy, Countess[e] of Bedford, with Mr. Donne's Satires [or Satyres]. Ben Jonson. CP-JonsB; SP-JonsB

To Lucy Larcom. John Greenleaf Whittier. CP-WhitJ

To Lyce, an Elderly Lady. Samuel Johnson. CP-JohnS

To Lydia Maria Child. John Greenleaf Whittier. CP-WhitJ

To M. Rainer Maria Rilke. CP-RilkFr, tr. by A. Poulin, Jr.

To M———. Lord Byron. CP-Byron

To M. E. W. G. K. Chesterton. CP-ChesG

To M. H. William Wordsworth. CP-WorW1; MW-WorW

To M. L. S——. Edgar Allan Poe. CP-PoeEd

To M.S.G. Lord Byron. CP-Byron

To Madame Alda, Singing a Song, in a White Gown. Wallace Stevens. CP-StevWP

To Madame du Châtelet. Voltaire. CP-WilbR

To Madame Jeanne-Renée Dubost. Rainer Maria Rilke. CP-RilkFr, tr. by A. Poulin, Jr.

To Madame the Baronness Renée De Brimont. Rainer Maria Rilke. CP-RilkFr, tr. by A. Poulin, Jr.

To Maecenas. Phillis Wheatley. CP-WheaP

To ——: "Maiden! with the fair brown tresses." John Greenleaf Whittier. CP-WhitJ

To maintain balance. One:Many. A. R. Ammons. CP-AmmoA

To make a final conquest of all me. Fair Singer, The. Andrew Marvell. CP-MarvA

To make a headway against the tide. Voyage, The. Richard Eberhart. CP-EberR

To make a prairie it takes a clover and one bee. Emily Dickinson. CP-DickE

To make an end of all this strife. Sir Thomas Wyatt. CP-WyatT

To make daylight. To put a mirror in front of the Thinker: to occasion Narcissus. Brief (Remembered) *Histoire* of Rejection, A. Andrei Codrescu. SP-CodrA

To make even Heaven more heavenly. Emily Dickinson. SP-DickE

To make her madrigal. Fistulae. Ezra Pound. CP-PoEar

To make it glad with a goodly crop. Answer, An. Christina Georgina Rossetti. CP-RosC3

To make it grow again like a wounded. Resurrected Christ, The. Rainer Maria Rilke. CP-RilkFr, tr. by A. Poulin, Jr.

To Make Much. George Oppen. CP-OppGN

To make One's Toilette—after Death. Emily Dickinson. CP-DickE

To make peace (borso / with the others,—or not too. Cantos, The. Robert Creeley. CP-CreeR

To make Routine a Stimulus. Emily Dickinson. CP-DickE

To make them moved, you should start from lightning. Dance of Words. Robert Graves. CP-GravR

To Make Words Sing. Langston Hughes. CP-HughL

To Manso. John Milton. *See* Manso

To Manuel Altolaguirre. Stephen Spender. CP-SpenS

To Manuel Mujica Lainez. Jorge Luis Borges. SP-BorgJ, tr. by Eric McHenry

To many men strange fates are given. From the Greek. Stevie Smith. CP-SmitS

To Marguerite—Continued. Matthew Arnold. SP-ArnoM *Fr.* Switzerland.

To Maria. Robert Burns. CP-BurnR

To Marie Laurencin. Rainer Maria Rilke. CP-RilkFr, tr. by A. Poulin, Jr.

To Marina. Kenneth Koch. CP-KochK

To Marina Zwetajewa-Efron. Rainer Maria Rilke. CP-RilkFr, tr. by A. Poulin, Jr.

To Marion. Lord Byron. CP-Byron

To Marjorie Rambeau; In "Daddy's Gone A-Hunting" Dorothy Parker. CP-ParkD

To Mark Anthony in Heaven. William Carlos Williams. CP-WilW1

To Market. C. K. Williams. CP-WillC

To Mary. William Cowper. CP-CowpW

To Mary. Louis MacNeice. CP-MacNL

To Mary——. Percy Bysshe Shelley. CP-ShelP

To Mary Boyle. Alfred Tennyson. CP-TennA

To Mary Church Terrell. Paul Laurence Dunbar. CP-DunbP

To [Mary Frogley]. John Keats. CP-KeatJ

To Mary, Lady Wroth ("How well, fair crown of your fair sex, might he"). Ben Jonson. CP-JonsB; SP-JonsB

To Mary, Lady Wroth ("Madam[e], had all antiquity [*or* antiquitie] been lost"). Ben Jonson. CP-JonsB; SP-JonsB

To Mary on Receiving Her Picture. Lord Byron. CP-Byron

To Mary Pridham. Samuel Taylor Coleridge. CP-ColeS

To Mary Rossetti. Christina Georgina Rossetti. CP-RosC3

To Mary Russell Mitford. Elizabeth Barrett Browning. CP-BroEB

To Mary Shelley. Percy Bysshe Shelley. CP-ShelP

To Mary Unwin. William Cowper. CP-CowpW
  (Sonnet to Mrs. Unwin.) CP-CowpW

To Mary, Who Died in This Opinion. Percy Bysshe Shelley. CP-ShelP

To Mary Wollstonecraft Godwin. Percy Bysshe Shelley. CP-ShelP

To Marygolds. Robert Herrick. CP-HerrR

To Massachusetts. John Greenleaf Whittier. CP-WhitJ

To Master Davenant for Absence. Sir John Suckling. CP-SuckJ
  (To Mr. Davenant for Absence.) CP-SuckJ

To M. Denham, on His Prospective Poem. Robert Herrick. CP-HerrR

To M. Henry Lawes, the Excellent Composer[.] of his Lyrics. Robert Herrick. CP-HerrR

To Master John Burges. Ben Jonson. CP-JonsB; SP-JonsB

To M. Kellam. Robert Herrick. CP-HerrR

To M. Laurence Swetnaham. Robert Herrick. CP-HerrR

To M. Leonard Willan His Peculiar Friend. Robert Herrick. CP-HerrR

To Master W. Montague. Thomas Carew. CP-CareT

To Matilda Betham from a Stranger. Samuel Taylor Coleridge. CP-ColeS

To Maude. Ambrose Bierce. SP-BierA

To May. William Wordsworth. CP-WorW2

To me, like hauntings of a vagrant breath. To E. H. K. Paul Laurence Dunbar. CP-DunbP

To me my Julia lately sent. Pomander Bracelet, The. Robert Herrick. CP-HerrR

To me, one silly task is like another. Cassandra. Louise Bogan. CP-BogaL

To me the A Major Concerto has been dearer. Hedger. Ivor Gurney. SP-GurnI

To me the disobedient. Fanny Howe. SP-HoweF *Fr.* Vineyard, The.

To Meadows [*or* Meddowes]. Robert Herrick. CP-HerrR

To meet and say farewell. Instead of a Farewell. A. K. Ramanujan. CP-RamaA

To Meet, or Otherwise. Thomas Hardy. CP-HardT

To Melpomene. William Wordsworth. CP-WorW1

To Memory. Buddhadeva Bose. CP-OppGN, tr. by George Oppen

To mend each tattered Faith. Emily Dickinson. CP-DickE

To Meng Hao-Jan. Li Po. CP-WilW2

To Mexico! To Mexico! Down the dovegray highway, past Atomic City. Ready to Roll. Allen Ginsberg. CP-GinsA

To Midnight Nan at Leroy's. Langston Hughes. CP-HughL; CP-HughL1

To Military Progress. Marianne Craig Moore. CP-MoorM

To Milton. Oscar Wilde. CP-WildO

To Mime. Ben Jonson. CP-JonsB; SP-JonsB

To Mimi Romanelli. Rainer Maria Rilke. CP-RilkFr, tr. by A. Poulin, Jr.

To Miss Ainslie, in Chuch. Robert Burns. *See* To a Lady

To Miss Bigg. Jane Austen. CP-AustJ

To Miss Creuzé. William Cowper. CP-CowpW

To Miss C*********, a Very Young Lady. Robert Burns. CP-BurnR

To Miss Ferrier. Robert Burns. CP-BurnR

To Miss Gage. Wallace Stevens. CP-StevWP

To Miss Graham of Fintray. Robert Burns. CP-BurnR

To Miss H—— with Some Music. Christopher Smart. SP-SmarC

To Miss Hickman Playing on the Spinet. Samuel Johnson. CP-JohnS

To Miss Isabella Macleod. Robert Burns. CP-BurnR

To Miss J. Austen. James Edward Austen-Leigh. CP-AustJ

To Miss Jane Austen the Reputed Author of Sense and Sensibility a Novel Lately Publish'd. James Austen. CP-AustJ

To Miss L———. Robert Burns. CP-BurnR

To Miss Macartney. William Cowper. CP-CowpW

To Miss Mary Britton. Paul Laurence Dunbar. CP-DunbP

To Miss Mary Stockton, an Epistle the 10th of Janu 78. Annis Boudinot Stockton. CP-StocA

To Miss Mary Stockton, an Epistle upon Some Gentleman Refusing to Admit Ladies of Their Circle into the Parlour till Supper Where They Met for Conversation and Business Once a Week. Annis Boudinot Stockton. CP-StocA

To Miss Nicola B. Rainer Maria Rilke. CP-RilkFr, tr. by A. Poulin, Jr.

To Miss —: On Her Giving the Author a Gold and Silk Net-work Purse. Samuel Johnson. CP-JohnS

To Miss —: On Her Playing upon the Harpsichord. Samuel Johnson. CP-JohnS

To Miss Sophy Giauque. Rainer Maria Rilke. CP-RilkFr, tr. by A. Poulin, Jr.

To Miss Unger. Robert Browning. CP-BroR2

To Mr. and Mrs.—, on the Death of Their Infant Son. Phillis Wheatley. CP-WheaP

To Mr B. B. John Donne. CP-DonnJ; MW-DonnJ

To Mr Ben Jonson in His Journey, by Mr Craven. Ben Jonson. CP-JonsB

To Mr C. B. John Donne. CP-DonnJ; MW-DonnJ

To Mr. Congreve. Jonathan Swift. CP-SwifJ

To Mr. Davenant for Absence. Sir John Suckling. *See* To Master Davenant for Absence

To Mr. Delany. Jonathan Swift. CP-SwifJ
  "You wonder now to see me write." CP-SherT

To Mr Dryden, on his Poem called *Religio Laici. Unknown.* CP-DryJ2

To Mr Dryden, on *Religio Laici.* Thomas Creech. CP-DryJ2

To Mr E. G. John Donne. CP-DonnJ; MW-DonnJ

To Mr. E——— on His Translation of and Commentaries on Martial. Robert Burns. *See* On Elphinston's Translation of Martial

To Mr Gavin Hamilton, Mauchline. Robert Burns. CP-BurnR

To Mr. Gay. Jonathan Swift. CP-SwifJ

To Mr. Gay, Congratulating Pope on Finishing His House and Gardens. Alexander Pope. CP-PopeA

To Mr. Graham of Fintry, On Being Appointed to My Excise Division. Robert Burns. CP-BurnR

To Mr. Harley's Surgeon. Jonathan Swift. CP-SwifJ

To Mr I. L ("Blessed [*or* Blesst] are your north parts, for all this long time").

John Donne. CP-DonnJ; MW-DonnJ

To Mr I. L ("Of that short Roll of friends writ in my heart"). John Donne. CP-DonnJ; MW-DonnJ

To Mr John Burges. Ben Jonson. CP-JonsB

To Mr. John Kennedy. Robert Burns. CP-BurnR

To Mr. John Moore, Author of the Celebrated Worm-Powder. Alexander Pope. CP-PopeA

To Mr. John Taylor. Robert Burns. *See* To John Taylor

To Mr Jonson upon these Verses. Ben Jonson. CP-JonsB

To Mr Joshua Sylvester. Ben Jonson. CP-JonsB; SP-JonsB

To Mr L. Maidwell on His New Method. John Dryden. CP-DryJ2

To Mr. Lawrence. John Milton. CP-MiltJ
 (Sonnet 20.) CP-MiltJ

To Mr Lewis Pintard on His Retirement at New Rochelle. Annis Boudinot Stockton. CP-StocA

To Mr. McMurdo, with a Pound of Lundiefoot Snuff. Robert Burns. CP-BurnR

To Mr. Murray. Lord Byron. CP-Byron
 (Strahan, Tonson, Lintot of the Times.) CP-Byron

To Mr. Newton. William Cowper. CP-CowpW

To Mr. Pye. Samuel Taylor Coleridge. CP-ColeS

To Mr R. W ("If, as mine is, thy life a slumber be"). John Donne. CP-DonnJ; MW-DonnJ

To Mr R. W ("Kindly I envy thy song's [*or* songs] perfection"). John Donne. CP-DonnJ; MW-DonnJ

To Mr R. W ("Muse not that by thy mind thy body is led"). John Donne. CP-DonnJ; MW-DonnJ

To Mr R. W ("Zealously my Muse doth salute all thee"). John Donne. CP-DonnJ; MW-DonnJ

To Mr. Roland Woodward. John Donne. CP-DonnJ; MW-DonnJ

To Mr S. B. John Donne. CP-DonnJ; MW-DonnJ

To Mr. S. McKenzie. Robert Burns. CP-BurnR

To Mr. Sheridan, upon His Verse, Written in Circles. Jonathan Swift. CP-SwifJ

To Mr Stockton on His Departure from America to England, 1769. Annis Boudinot Stockton. CP-StocA

To Mr T. W ("All hail, sweet poet, more full of more strong fire"). John Donne. CP-DonnJ; MW-DonnJ

To Mr T. W ("At once, from hence, my lines and I depart"). John Donne. CP-DonnJ; MW-DonnJ

To Mr T. W ("Haste thee harsh verse as fast as thy lame measure"). John Donne. CP-DonnJ; MW-DonnJ

To Mr T. W ("Pregnant again with th' old twins hope, and fear"). John Donne. CP-DonnJ; MW-DonnJ

To Mr. Thomas Southern, on His Birth-Day, 1742. Alexander Pope. CP-PopeA

To Mr Tilman after He Had Taken Orders. John Donne. CP-DonnJ; MW-DonnJ

To Mrs Alice Sutcliffe, on Her Divine *Meditations*. Ben Jonson. CP-JonsB

To Mrs Ann Flaxman. William Blake. CP-BlakW

To Mrs Butts. William Blake. CP-BlakW

To Mrs. C—— Robert Burns. CP-BurnR

To Mrs. Dacosta. Christopher Smart. SP-SmarC

To Mrs Flaxman, 14 September 1800. William Blake. CP-BlakW

To Mrs. Houghton of Bormount. Jonathan Swift. CP-SwifJ

To Mistress Katherine Bradshaw, the Lovely, That Crowned Him with Laurel. Robert Herrick. CP-HerrR

To Mistress Katherine Neville, on Her Green Sickness. Thomas Carew. CP-CareT

To Mrs. King. William Cowper. CP-CowpW

To Mrs. Leonard, on the Death of Her Husband. Phillis Wheatley. *See* To a Lady on the Death of Her Husband

To Mrs. M. B. on Her Birth-Day. Alexander Pope. CP-PopeA

To Mrs M. H. John Donne. CP-DonnJ; MW-DonnJ

To [Mrs. M. R.] Councel Concerning Her Choise. Richard Crashaw. *See* To a Young Gentle-Woman, Councel Concerning Her Choice

To Mrs Magdalen Herbert: of St. Mary Magdalen. John Donne. CP-DonnJ; MW-DonnJ

To Mrs. Newton. William Cowper. CP-CowpW

To Mrs Phillip Sidney. Ben Jonson. CP-JonsB; SP-JonsB

To Mrs Powel, an Ode. Annis Boudinot Stockton. CP-StocA

To Mrs. Professor in Defense of My Cat's Honor and Not Only. Czeslaw Milosz. CP-MiloCN, *tr. by* Robert Hass

To Mrs. Reynolds's Cat. John Keats. *See* To a Cat

To Mrs Rush, on Her Birth Day. Annis Boudinot Stockton. CP-StocA

To Mrs Thrale [on Her Thirty-fifth Birthday]. Samuel Johnson. CP-JohnS

To Mrs. Throckmorton. William Cowper. CP-CowpW

To Mistresse Amie Potter. Robert Herrick. CP-HerrR

To Mistresse Dorothy Parsons. Robert Herrick. CP-HerrR

To Mistresse Mary Willand. Robert Herrick. CP-HerrR

To Mitzi Mayfair. Toast to Floyd Collins, A. Miller Williams. CP-WillM

To Momus. Robert Herrick. CP-HerrR

To Monique and Blaise Briod. Rainer Maria Rilke. CP-RilkFr, *tr. by* A. Poulin, Jr.

To moralize the state, they drag out a man. Morning's News, The. Wendell Berry. CP-BerrW

To more than give names. Shorebird-Watching. Amy Clampitt. CP-ClamA

To Morning. William Blake. CP-BlakW

To-Morrow. Percy Bysshe Shelley. CP-ShelP

To-morrow I am going. George Meredith. CP-MerG2

To mortall men great loads alloted be. Poverty the Greatest Pack. Robert Herrick. CP-HerrR

To Motorists. Rudyard Kipling. CP-KiplR *Fr.* Muse among the Motors, The.

To mournful ditties, Clio, change thy note. Quibbling Elegy on the Worshipful Judge Boat, A. Jonathan Swift. CP-SwifJ

To move time back to where it was before I blundered. February 10, One Year Too Late. Charles Olson. CP-OlsoC

To Mr. Cyriack Skinner upon His Blindness. John Milton. CP-MiltJ
 (Sonnet 22.) CP-MiltJ

To Mr. H. Lawes On His Airs. John Milton. CP-MiltJ
 (Sonnet 13.) CP-MiltJ

To Mr. Newton [on His Return from Ramsgate]. William Cowper. CP-CowpW

To multiply the Harbors. Emily Dickinson. SP-DickE

To Music. Robert Herrick. CP-HerrR

To Music. Arthur Rimbaud. CP-RimbA, *tr. by* Martin Sorrell

To Music: A Song. Robert Herrick. CP-HerrR

To Music Bent Is My Retired Mind. Thomas Campion. CP-CampT
 (To Musicke bent is my retyred minde.) CP-CampT

To Music, to Becalm a Sweet-sick Youth. Robert Herrick. CP-HerrR

To Music, to Becalm His Fever. Robert Herrick. CP-HerrR

To ———: "Music, when soft voices die." Percy Bysshe Shelley. CP-ShelP

To Musicke bent is my retyred minde. Thomas Campion. *See* To Music Bent Is My Retired Mind

To my aunt blanche. Praise Song. Lucille Clifton. SP-ClifL

To My Baby Paul. Louis Zukofsky. CP-ZukLS

To my bedside reading, books of sublime artistry. Arthur Rimbaud. CP-RimbA, *tr. by* Martin Sorrell

To My Book. Ben Jonson. CP-JonsB; SP-JonsB

To My Bookseller. Ben Jonson. CP-JonsB; SP-JonsB

To My Brother George. John Keats. CP-KeatJ

To My Brother Hanson. W. S. Merwin. SP-MerwW

To My Brother: Killed: Hammont Wood: October, 1918. Louise Bogan. CP-BogaL

To My Brothers. John Keats. CP-KeatJ

To My Burrissa. Annis Boudinot Stockton. CP-StocA

To My Children, Fearing for Them. Wendell Berry. CP-BerrW

To My Chosen Friend the Learnèd Translator of Lucan, Thomas May, Esquire. Ben Jonson. CP-JonsB

To My Cousin (C.R.) Marrying My Lady (A.). Thomas Carew. CP-CareT

To My Daimon. James Vincent Cunningham. CP-CunnJ

To My Daimonion. Czeslaw Milosz. CP-MiloCN, *tr. by* Robert Hass

To My Daughter. Charles Tomlinson. SP-TomlC *Fr.* For A Granddaughter.

To My Daughter. Joseph Brodsky. CP-BrodJ

To My Daughter. Raymond Carver. CP-CarvR

To My Daughter. Stephen Spender. CP-SpenS

To My Daughter the Junkie on a Train. Audre Lorde. SP-LordA

To My Dear and Loving Husband. Anne Bradstreet. CP-BradA

To My Dear Friend Mr Congreve [on His Comedy Called "The Double-Dealer"]. John Dryden. SP-DrydJ

My dear Sir, and Warrior. Intermezzo. Thomas Kinsella. CP-KinsT

To My Dear Sister, the Author of these Poems. *Unknown*. CP-BradA

To My Dear Son, and Right-Learnèd Friend, Master Joseph Rutter. Ben Jonson. CP-JonsB

To My Dearest Cousin, on Her Removal of us from Silver End, to Weston. William Cowper. CP-CowpW

To My Dearest Sister M. Mercie Herrick. Robert Herrick. CP-HerrR

To My Dog. Dorothy Parker. CP-ParkD

To My Father. Jorge Luis Borges. SP-BorgJ, *tr. by* Willis Barnstone

To My Father. John Milton. CP-MiltJ
 (To His Father.) CP-CowpW

To My Father. Robert Pinsky. CP-PinsR

To My Father, Dying. Gregory Orr. SP-OrrG

To My Father's Violin. Thomas Hardy. CP-HardT

To My Fellow Artists. Christopher Logue. SP-LoguC

To My Fior-Di-Lisa. Christina Georgina Rossetti. CP-RosC3

To My First Love, My Mother. Christina Georgina Rossetti. CP-RosC2

To My Friend, behind Walls. Carolyn Kizer. CP-KizeC

To My Friend Butts I Write. William Blake. CP-BlakW
 (To Thomas Butts, 2 October 1800.) CP-BlakW

To My Friend Elizabeth. Christina Georgina Rossetti. CP-RosC3

To My Friend Ezra Pound. William Carlos Williams. CP-WilW2

To my Friend G.N. from Wrest. Thomas Carew. CP-CareT

To My Friend Mr J. Northleigh. John Dryden. CP-DryJ2

To My Friend on the Death of His Sister. John Greenleaf Whittier. CP-WhitJ

To My Friend the Late Beatrice Hastings. Hugh MacDiarmid. SP-MacDH

To My Friend Who Rhymes with Peace. Carolyn Kizer. CP-KizeC

To My Friend, Will. Davenant. Thomas Carew. CP-CareT

To My Friend Will. Davenant, on His Other Poems. Sir John Suckling. CP-SuckJ

To My Friend Will. Davenant, upon His Poem of "Madagascar" Sir John Suckling. CP-SuckJ

To My Friend (With an Identity Disc). Wilfred Owen. CP-OwenW

To My Friends. Aleksandr Aleksandrovich Blok. SP-BlokA, *tr. by* Peter France *and* Jon Stallworthy

To my Friends. Primo Levi. CP-LeviP, *tr. by* Ruth Feldman

To My God in His Sickness. Philip Levine. SP-LeviP

To My Godson, on His Christening. Mona Van Duyn. SP-VanDM

To My Good Master. James Whitcomb Riley. CP-RileJ

To My Greek. James Merrill. SP-MerrJ

To My Heart. Andrei Codrescu. SP-CodrA

To My Honourable Friend, Sr. Thomas Mounson, *Knight and Baronet*. Thomas Campion. CP-CampT

To My Honoured Friend, Master Thomas May, Upon His Comedy *The Heir*. Thomas Carew. CP-CareT

To My Honoured [*or* Honour'd] Kinsman, John Driden [of Chesterton in the County of Huntingdon, Esquire]. John Dryden. SP-DrydJ

To My Ill Reader. Robert Herrick. CP-HerrR

To My Inconstant Mistress [*or* Mistris]. Thomas Carew. CP-CareT

To My Inebriety. Robert Stock. SP-StocR

To My Lady. G. K. Chesterton. CP-ChesG

To My Lady E.C. at Her Going Out of England. Sir John Suckling. CP-SuckJ

To My Lady in a Distant Land That She Forget Me Not. James Laughlin. CP-LaugJ

To My Last Period. Lucille Clifton. SP-ClifL

To My Least Favorite Reviewer. Howard Nemerov. CP-NemeH

To My Lord Ignorant. Ben Jonson. CP-JonsB; SP-JonsB

To My L[ord] the King, on the Christening His Second Son James. Ben Jonson. CP-JonsB

To My Love, Combing Her Hair. Yehuda Amichai. SP-AmicY, *tr. by* Chana Bloch

To my love, combing her hair. To My Love, Combing Her Hair. Yehuda Amichai. SP-AmicY, *tr. by* Chana Bloch

To My Mere English Censurer. Ben Jonson. CP-JonsB; SP-JonsB

To My Mirtle. William Blake. CP-BlakW

To my mishap, alas, I find. Sir Thomas Wyatt. CP-WyatT

To My Mistress [*or* Mistris], I Burning in Love. Thomas Carew. CP-CareT

To My Mistress Sitting by a River's Side; an Eddy. Thomas Carew. CP-CareT

To My Mistress[e] in My Absence. Thomas Carew. CP-CareT

To My Mother. Walter De la Mare. CP-DeLaW

To My Mother. Eugenio Montale. CP-MontE, *tr. by* Jonathan Galassi

To My Mother. Edgar Allan Poe. CP-PoeEd

To My Mother on Her Birthday. Christina Georgina Rossetti. CP-RosC3

To My Much Honoured Friend, Henry, Lord Carey of Leppington, Upon His Translation of Malvezzi. Thomas Carew. CP-CareT

To My Muse. Ben Jonson. CP-JonsB; SP-JonsB

To My Old Faithful Servant: And (by His Continued Virtue) My Loving Friend: The Author of this Work, M[r] Rich[ard] Brome. Ben Jonson. CP-JonsB

To My Old Friend, William Leachman. James Whitcomb Riley. CP-RileJ

To My Old Schoolmaster. John Greenleaf Whittier. CP-WhitJ

To My Older Brother. Adam Zagajewski. SP-ZagaA, *tr. by* Clare Cavanagh

To My Pres- / sure Pump. Lorine Niedecker. CP-NiedL

To my quick ear the Leaves—conferred. Emily Dickinson. CP-DickE

To my revenge and to her desperate fears. Bubble; a Song, The. Robert Herrick. CP-HerrR

To My Rival. Thomas Carew. CP-CareT

To My Sister. James Whitcomb Riley. CP-RileJ

To My Sister. Theodore Roethke. CP-RoetT

To My Sister. John Greenleaf Whittier. CP-WhitJ

To My Sister. William Wordsworth. CP-WorW1

    (Lines Written at a Small Distance from my House, and Sent by my Little Boy to the Person to whom they are Addressed.) MW-WorW

To my sister journeying toward. No Harm Shall Come. Olga Broumas. SP-BrouO

To my sister Louise Vanaen de Voringhem:— her blue coif turned towards the North Sea. Devotions. Arthur Rimbaud. CP-RimbA, *tr. by* Martin Sorrell

To My Small / Electric Pump. Lorine Niedecker. CP-NiedL

To my small Hearth His fire came. Emily Dickinson. CP-DickE

To My Son. Lord Byron. CP-Byron

To My Students. John Ciardi. CP-CiarJ

To My Successor. George Herbert. CP-HerbG

To My Truly-Beloved Friend, Mr Browne: on His Pastorals. Ben Jonson. CP-JonsB

To My Valentines. Louis Zukofsky. CP-ZukLS

To My Wife. James Vincent Cunningham. CP-CunnJ

To My Wife. Philip Larkin. CP-LarkP

To My Wife: With a Copy of My Poems. Oscar Wilde. CP-WildO

To My Worthy and Honoured Friend, Mr George Chapman, on His Translation of Hesiod's *Works and Days*. Ben Jonson. CP-JonsB

To My Worthy Friend, Master Davenant Upon His Excellent Play, *The Just Italian*. Thomas Carew. CP-CareT

To My Worthy Friend, Master Edward Filmer, on His Work Published. Ben Jonson. CP-JonsB

To My Worthy Friend Master George Sands [*or* Sandys], on His Translation of the Psalms. Thomas Carew. CP-CareT

To My Worthy Friend, Mr. John Mounson, Sonne and Heyre to Sir Thomas Mounson, Knight and Baronet. Thomas Campion. CP-CampT

To My Worthy Friend, Mr. T.B. One of the People Called Quakers. Christopher Smart. SP-SmarC

To My Worthy Friend T S——, D. D. On His Incomparable Translation of and Notes on Persius. *Unknown*. CP-SherT

To Myrrha Hard-Hearted. Robert Herrick. CP-HerrR

To Myrtilla, On Easter Day. Dorothy Parker. CP-ParkD

To Myrto About Herself. Robert Graves. CP-GravR

To Myself, In an Album. Adam Zagajewski. SP-ZagaA, *tr. by* Renata Gorczynski, Benjamin Ivry *and* C. K. Williams

To Nancy F[laxman]. William Blake. CP-BlakW

To Nanine. Ambrose Bierce. SP-BierA

To Natalie Clifford Barney. Rainer Maria Rilke. CP-RilkFr, *tr. by* A. Poulin, Jr.

To Natty Bumppo. Thom Gunn. CP-GunnT

To Nature. Samuel Taylor Coleridge. CP-ColeS

To Night. Percy Bysshe Shelley. CP-ShelP

To-night, a first movement, a pulse. Act of Union. Seamus Heaney. SP-HeanSO

To-night, God knows what thing shall tide. Rudyard Kipling. CP-KiplR *Fr.* Plain Tales from the Hills.

To-night is so coarse with chocolate. Ode: "To-night is so coarse with chocolate." Louis MacNeice. CP-MacNL

To-night this sunset spreads two golden wings. Sunset Wings. Dante Gabriel Rossetti. CW-RossD

To night's order Over- / ridden, Over-. Paul Celan. SP-CelaP, *tr. by* John Felstiner

To Nigrovorine Who is Leaving. Rainer Maria Rilke. CP-RilkFr, *tr. by* A. Poulin, Jr.

To Nobodaddy. William Blake. CP-BlakW

To ——: "Not long ago, the writer of these lines." Edgar Allan Poe. CP-PoeEd

To notice other days were pages given. Jones Very. CP-VeryJ

To ——: "O dearer far than light and life are dear." William Wordsworth. CP-WorW2; MW-WorW

To obey me in my dreams. I Cannot Command You. James Laughlin. CP-LaugJ

To Odilon-Jean Périer. Rainer Maria Rilke. CP-RilkFr, *tr. by* A. Poulin, Jr.

To Oenone. Robert Herrick. CP-HerrR

To Oenone. Robert Herrick. CP-HerrR

To Oenone. Robert Herrick. CP-HerrR

To offer brave assistance. Emily Dickinson. CP-DickE

To Ogmian Hercules. Robert Graves. CP-GravR

To ——: "Oh! there are spirits of the air." Percy Bysshe Shelley. CP-ShelP

To ——: "Oh! well I know your subtle Sex." Lord Byron. CP-Byron

To Old Age. Walt Whitman. CP-WhitW

To Old-End Gatherer. Ben Jonson. CP-JonsB; SP-JonsB

To Oliver Wendell Holmes. John Greenleaf Whittier. CP-WhitJ

To—, on Her First Ascent to the Summit of Helvellyn. William Wordsworth. CP-WorW2

To One Awake. Robert Penn Warren. CP-WarrR

To One denied to drink. Emily Dickinson. CP-DickE

To one fair Lady out of Court. Challenge: A Court Ballad, The. Alexander Pope. CP-PopeA

To One in Paradise. Edgar Allan Poe. CP-PoeEd

To One "Investigated" by the Last Senate Committee, or the Next. John Ciardi. CP-CiarJ

To One No Longer Young. Jorge Luis Borges. SP-BorgJ, *tr. by* Alastair Reid

To One Not There. Countee Cullen. CP-CullC

To one of taste both flawless and robust. Michelangelo Buonarroti. CP-Miche, *tr. by* John Frederick Nims

To One Shortly to Die. Walt Whitman. CP-WhitW

To One that Desired Me Not to Name Him. Ben Jonson. CP-JonsB; SP-JonsB

To One That Desired to Know My Mistress [*or* Mistris]. Thomas Carew. CP-CareT

To One Who Has Been Long in City Pent. John Keats. CP-KeatJ

To One Who Might Have Borne a Message. Edna St. Vincent Millay. CP-MillE

To One Who Published in Print. Samuel Taylor Coleridge. CP-ColeS

To one who stood before the door, one. Paul Celan. SP-CelaP, *tr. by* John Felstiner

To One Who Went Too Far. Miller Williams. CP-WillM

To One Who, When I Praised My Mistress' Beauty, Said I Was Blind. Thomas Carew. CP-CareT

To one whose state is raised over all. Sir Philip Sidney. SP-SidnP *Fr.* Lady of May, The.

To———: "One word is too often profaned." Percy Bysshe Shelley. CP-ShelP

To Oneself. David Ignatow. SP-IgnaD

To Orpheus. Yannis Ritsos. SP-RitsY, *tr. by* Thanasis Maskaleris

To Others than You. Dylan Thomas. CP-ThomD

To Our Blessed Lord upon the Choice of His Sepulchre. Richard Crashaw. CP-CrasR

(Upon Our Saviour's Tomb[e] Wherein Never Man Was Laid.) CP-CrasR

To Our Lady of Vicarious Atonement. Ezra Pound. CP-PoEar

To Our Lord, upon the Water Made Wine. Richard Crashaw. CP-CrasR

To our senses, the elements are four. Four, The. D. H. Lawrence. CP-LawrD

To Outer Nature. Thomas Hardy. CP-HardT

To own a Susan of my own. Emily Dickinson. CP-DickE

To own the Art within the Soul. Emily Dickinson. CP-DickE

To Oxford. Gerard Manley Hopkins. CP-HopkG

To P.L., 1916–1937. Philip Levine. SP-LeviP

To P.O. Allen Ginsberg. CP-GinsA

To P.A. Labouchère Esq. George Meredith. CP-MerG2

To Paint a Water Lily. Ted Hughes. SP-HughTN

To paint the Fiend, *Pink* would the Devill see. Upon Pink an Ill-Fac'd Painter. Robert Herrick. CP-HerrR

To paint thy worth, if rightly I did know it. Poem Sent Me by Sir William Burlase, A. Ben Jonson. CP-JonsB

To Pansies. Robert Herrick. CP-HerrR

To Paris: Fear of the Heights Reached. Alan Dugan. CP-DugaA

To part is painful; nay, to bid adieu. Ancient Mansion, The. George Crabbe. SP-CrabG *Fr.* Posthumous Tales.

To pass through pain and not know it. Wave, A. John Ashbery. SP-AshbJ

To Patricia Gilgert Who Acted. G. K. Chesterton. CP-ChesG

To Paul now old enough to read. Lorine Niedecker. CP-NiedL

To pay his ransom Man must work. Ransom, The. Charles Baudelaire. CP-BaudC, *tr. by* Walter Martin

To Peg. Robert Stock. SP-StocR

To Pennsylvania. John Greenleaf Whittier. CP-WhitJ

To Penshurst. Ben Jonson. CP-JonsB; SP-JonsB

To people these lands with civil men. In a Brooklyn Park. Charles Tomlinson. CP-TomlC

To Perenna. Robert Herrick. CP-HerrR

To Perenna, A Mistresse. Robert Herrick. CP-HerrR

To Perilla. Robert Herrick. CP-HerrR

To Person Guilty ("Guilty, be wise; and though thou know'st the crimes"). Ben Jonson. CP-JonsB; SP-JonsB

To Person Guilty ("Guilty, because I bad[e] you late be wise"). Ben Jonson. CP-JonsB

To Pertinax Cob. Ben Jonson. CP-JonsB; SP-JonsB

To Peter on holy problems. Listen, Saints. Thomas Merton. CP-MertT

To Peter Stuart. Robert Burns. CP-BurnR

To Pfrimmer. Paul Laurence Dunbar. CP-DunbP

To Philip Bourke Marston, inciting me to Poetic Work. Dante Gabriel Rossetti. CW-RossD

To Phocas the Peasant. "Rubén Dario." SP-DariR, *tr. by* Alberto Acereda *and* Will Derusha

To Phyllis to Love and Live with Him. Robert Herrick. CP-HerrR

To Pia Di Valmarana. Rainer Maria Rilke. CP-RilkFr, *tr. by* A. Poulin, Jr.

To pile like Thunder to its close. Emily Dickinson. CP-DickE

To Pino. D. H. Lawrence. CP-LawrD

To Pius IX. John Greenleaf Whittier. CP-WhitJ

To Playwright. Ben Jonson. CP-JonsB; SP-JonsB

To please my Maria I take up my pen. To Miss Mary Stockton, an Epistle the 10th of Janu 78. Annis Boudinot Stockton. CP-StocA

To Plimmer, Verandah and Cello. George Meredith. CP-MerG2

To pluck down mine, Poll sets up new wits still. On Court-Parrot. Ben Jonson. CP-JonsB; SP-JonsB

To Poe: Over the Planet, Air Albany–Baltimore. Allen Ginsberg. CP-GinsA

To Poets' Worksheets in the Air-Conditioned Vault of a Library. Mona Van Duyn. SP-VanDM

To Pontius Washing His Blood-Stained Hands. Richard Crashaw. CP-CrasR

To Pontius Washing His Hands. Richard Crashaw. CP-CrasR

To popularize the mule, its neat exterior. Labors of Hercules, The. Marianne Craig Moore. CP-MoorM

To Portapovitch. Hart Crane. CP-CranH

To Posterity. Samuel Johnson. CP-JohnS

To Posterity. Louis MacNeice. CP-MacNL

To Posthumus. Horace. *See* Odes

To Prague. Jaroslav Seifert. SP-SeifJ, *tr. by* Ewald Osers

To praise men as good, and take them for such. Charity in Thought. Samuel Taylor Coleridge. CP-ColeS

To praise thy life, or waile thy worthie death. Epitaph upon the Right Honourable Sir Phillip Sidney, Knight: Lord Governor of Flushing, An. Edmund Spenser. CP-Spens *Fr.* Astrophel.

To praise thy life[,] or wail[e] thy worthy [*or* woorthie] death. Epitaph on Sir Philip Sidney. Sir Walter Ralegh. CP-RaleW

To prefer the nest in the linden. Hope. Randall Jarrell. CP-JarrR

To Primroses Filled with Morning Dew. Robert Herrick. CP-HerrR

To Prince Charles upon his coming to Exeter. Robert Herrick. CP-HerrR

To print our poems the propulsive cause. Fame Makes Us Forward. Robert Herrick. CP-HerrR

To protect the garden and watch over its fruits. Stroll in the Beautiful Gardens of the Valley of the Son of Hinnom, A. Yehuda Amichai. SP-AmicYL, *tr. by* Benjamin Harshav *and* Barbara Harshav

To Prowl the Plagiary. Ben Jonson. CP-JonsB; SP-JonsB

To public notice, with reluctance strong. Lines Written on a Blank Leaf in a Copy of the Author's Poem "The Excursion", upon Hearing of the Death of the Late Vicar of Kendal. William Wordsworth. CP-WorW2

To Puente Curvo on the Maldonado Spit in Uruguay. Pablo Neruda. SP-NeruP

To Punch. G. K. Chesterton. CP-ChesG

To purify their wine some people bleed. Epigram: "To purify their wine some people bleed." William Cowper. CP-CowpW

To Put It Simply. Robert Graves. CP-GravR

To Put One Brick upon Another. Philip Larkin. CP-LarkP

To put out the word, whore, thou dost me woo. To a Friend. Ben Jonson. CP-JonsB; SP-JonsB

To put this World down, like a Bundle. Emily Dickinson. CP-DickE

To Quilca. Jonathan Swift. CP-SherT; CP-SwifJ

To Quinbus Flestrin the Man-Mountain, a Lilliputian Ode. Alexander Pope. CP-PopeA

To R. B. Gerard Manley Hopkins. CP-HopkG

To R.H.H. with Daphne. George Meredith. CP-MerG2

To rail or jest, ye know I use it not. Sir Thomas Wyatt. CP-WyatT

To raise an iron tree. Calder, A. Karl Shapiro. SP-ShapK

To Raja Rao. Czeslaw Milosz. CP-MiloC; CP-MiloCN

To re-insert it in. Right Lads, The. Donald Davie. CP-DaviDC

To rebel is suitable philosophical tactics. Sonnet: "To rebel is suitable philosophical tactics." Hayden Carruth. CP-CarHS *Fr.* Sonnets.

To rebel. So I have saved my life, not once. Sonnet: "To rebel. So I have saved my life, not once." Hayden Carruth. CP-CarHS *Fr.* Sonnets.

To Record One Must Be Unwary. Mona Van Duyn. SP-VanDM

To Reformers in Despair. Nicholas Vachel Lindsay. CP-LindV

To Regain the Day Again. Nicolas Calas. CP-WilW2

To render it!—*this* moment. English Field in the Nuclear Age, An. Denise Levertov. SP-LeveDL

To Renton of Lamerton. Robert Burns. CP-BurnR

To rescue his truth, he spoke a thousand lies. Secret Pain of the Decor, The. Yannis Ritsos. SP-RitsY, *tr. by* Andonis Decavalles

To rest in love as a water bug rests on the surface, swinging to and fro. Life, The. David Ignatow. SP-IgnaD

To rest the weary nurse has gone. Isobel's Child. Elizabeth Barrett Browning. CP-BroEB

To Return to the Trees. Derek Walcott. CP-WalcD

To Rhea. Ralph Waldo Emerson. CP-EmerR

To Rhoda. G. K. Chesterton. CP-ChesG

To Rhoda, otherwise called Rohda. G. K. Chesterton. CP-ChesG

To Rich Givers. Walt Whitman. CP-WhitW

To Richard Brinsley Sheridan, Esq. Samuel Taylor Coleridge. CP-ColeS *Fr.* Effusions.

To Richard John Stockton Esqr, Inclosing the Preceding Elegy [Feb. 28, 1787]. Annis Boudinot Stockton. CP-StocA

To Riddel, much-lamented man. On Robert Riddel. Robert Burns. CP-BurnR

To ride in a buggy at dusk. Well-worn ruts. In a Buggy at Dusk. Czeslaw Milosz. CP-MiloC; CP-MiloCN, *tr. by* Robert Hass

To ride piggy-back. Slave. Langston Hughes. CP-HughL; CP-HughL3

To Rilke. Denise Levertov. SP-LeveDS

To Robbers furious, and to Lovers tame. Translation of Du Bellay's *Epigram on a Dog*. Samuel Johnson. CP-JohnS

To Robert Burns. James Whitcomb Riley. CP-RileJ

To Robert E. Symmes 1933 for a gift of resemblances. Michael Palmer. SP-PalmM

To Robert, Earl of Salisbury ("What need hast thou of me, or of my muse"). Ben Jonson. CP-JonsB; SP-JonsB

To Robert, Earl of Salisbury ("Who can consider thy right courses run"). Ben Jonson. CP-JonsB; SP-JonsB

To R***** G***** of F*****, Esq. Robert Burns. CP-BurnR

To Robt. Graham of Fintry Esqr, with a Request for an Excise Division. Robert Burns. CP-BurnR

To Robert Louis Stevenson. James Whitcomb Riley. CP-RileJ

To Robert Lowell. Czeslaw Milosz. CP-MiloCN, tr. by Robert Hass

To Robert Southey. Samuel Taylor Coleridge. CP-ColeS

To Robin Redbreast. Robert Herrick. CP-HerrR

To Robin Redbreast. George Meredith. CP-MerG1

To Robinson Jeffers. Czeslaw Milosz. CP-MiloC; CP-MiloCN, tr. by Richard Lourie

To Romance. Lord Byron. CP-Byron

To Ronge. John Greenleaf Whittier. CP-WhitJ

To Roosevelt. "Rubén Dario." SP-DariR, tr. by Alberto Acereda and Will Derusha

To Rosamounde. Geoffrey Chaucer. CP-ChauG

To Rosemary and Baies. Robert Herrick. CP-HerrR

To Roses in Julia's Bosome. Robert Herrick. CP-HerrR

To Rotha Q—. William Wordsworth. CP-WorW2

To rub it out, make it less virulent. Oleum Misericordiae. John Ashbery. SP-AshbJ

To Rudyard Kipling. James Whitcomb Riley. CP-RileJ

To Ruin. Robert Burns. CP-BurnR

To running through my. You've Set the Words. James Laughlin. CP-LaugJ

To S.H. William Wordsworth. CP-WorW2

To S. M. Edna St. Vincent Millay. CP-MillE

To S. M., a Young African Painter, on Seeing His Works. Phillis Wheatley. CP-WheaP

To S. V. B.—June 15, 1940. Edna St. Vincent Millay. CP-MillE

To safeguard man from wrongs, there nothing must. Distrust. Robert Herrick. CP-HerrR

To Salzilli, a Roman Poet, Being Ill. John Milton. CP-CowpW; CP-MiltJ
  (My halting Muse, that dragg'st by choice along.) CP-CowpW

To Samuel E. Sewall and Harriet W. Sewall. John Greenleaf Whittier. CP-WhitJ

To Santa Claus. James Whitcomb Riley. CP-RileJ

To Sapho. Robert Herrick. CP-HerrR

To Sappho. Robert Herrick. CP-HerrR

To Saxham. Thomas Carew. CP-CareT

To say great words of kings and life. Kings Are Gone, The. Charles Bukowski. SP-BukC2

To Say If You Love Someone. Kenneth Patchen. CP-PatcK

To Say It. Robert Creeley. SP-CreeR

To say it once held daisies and bluebells. Broken Bowl, The. James Merrill. SP-MerrJ

To say that he was unhappy is either to say too much. Epitaph for a Centaur. Joseph Brodsky. CP-BrodJ

To say what has to be said here. Communion 1. David Ignatow. SP-IgnaD

To School! Stevie Smith. CP-SmitS

To scream with pain, to cry, to summon help, to call. Let's Roar, Your Honor. Dale R. Carver. CP-CarvR

To See. Adam Zagajewski. SP-ZagaA, tr. by Clare Cavanagh

To see a woman long oppressed by fear. Sonnet: "To see a woman long oppressed by fear." Hayden Carruth. CP-CarHS Fr. Sonnets.

To see a World in a Grain of Sand. Auguries of Innocence. William Blake. CP-BlakW

To see both blended in one flood. Upon the Infant Martyrs. Richard Crashaw. CP-CrasR

To see clearly, not to be deceived. Private Eye, The. Howard Nemerov. CP-NemeH

To see her is a Picture. Emily Dickinson. CP-DickE

To See Him Again. Gabriela Mistral. SP-MistG, tr. by Maria Giachetti [or Jacketti]

To see is perhaps never quite the sorcery. Emily Dickinson. SP-DickE

To see that an ancestor has reappeared. Track, The. W. S. Merwin. SP-MerwW

To see that your famous beauty still endures. Michelangelo Buonarroti. CP-MicheE, tr. by John Frederick Nims

To See the Heron. Charles Tomlinson. CP-TomlC

To See the Light. Heather McHugh. SP-McHuH

To see the man who took care of our stock. Lorine Niedecker. CP-NiedL

To see the mother, naturing Nature, stand. Discouragement. Thomas Hardy. CP-HardT

To see the Summer Sky. Emily Dickinson. CP-DickE

To see the world the way a painter must. Conversing with Paradise. Howard Nemerov. CP-NemeH

To see this silken nakedness. Dancing Serpent, The. Charles Baudelaire. CP-BaudC, tr. by Walter Martin

To see you always bent over that work. Rose on Sunday. Rainer Maria Rilke. CP-RilkFr, tr. by A. Poulin, Jr.

To see you naked is to remember the Earth. Qasida of the Women Prone. Federico García Lorca. CP-GarcF, tr. by Catherine Brown Fr. Qasidas.

To see you naked is to remember the earth. Casida of the Reclining Woman. Federico García Lorca. SP-GarcF, tr. by W. S. Merwin

To see you one more time again. Great Indulgent Heart. Rainer Maria Rilke. CP-RilkFr

To seek each where where man doth live. Sir Thomas Wyatt. CP-WyatT

To seek of God more then we well can find. Sobriety in Search. Robert Herrick. CP-HerrR

To Seem the Stranger. Gerard Manley Hopkins. CP-HopkG

To seem the stranger lies nſy lot, my life. To Seem the Stranger. Gerard Manley Hopkins. CP-HopkG

To seize, to seize. Our Lady's Winter Words. Theodore Roethke. CP-RoetT

To sell me an old hound dog they'd tricked out to look like a. Yesterday They Tried. Kenneth Patchen. CP-PatcK

To sense / and sound. To My Small / Electric Pump. Lorine Niedecker. CP-NiedL

To serve a wench if any think it shame. Elegy 2.17: "To serve a wench if any think it shame." Ovid. CP-MarlC Fr. Elegies.

To Serve as an Epitaph for the Beautiful Madame B. Rainer Maria Rilke. CP-RilkFr, tr. by A. Poulin, Jr.

To Shakespeare. Hart Crane. CP-CranH

To Shakespeare. Thomas Hardy. CP-HardT

To show the laboring [or lab'ring] bosom's deep intent. To S. M., a Young African Painter, on Seeing His Works. Phillis Wheatley. CP-WheaP

To show us time, its passing and its change. Nature Teaches Us of Time and Its Duration. Jones Very. CP-VeryJ

To Sickness. Ben Jonson. CP-JonsB; SP-JonsB

To silence I open the inertia of fluid. Dirty Souls. Alfonso Cortes. CP-MertT

To Silvia. Robert Herrick. CP-HerrR

To Silvia to Wed. Robert Herrick. CP-HerrR

To Sincerity. Thomas Hardy. CP-HardT

To sing of wars, of captain[e]s, and of kings. Prologue, The. Anne Bradstreet. CP-BradA

To Sir Annual Tilter. Ben Jonson. CP-JonsB; SP-JonsB

To Sir Clipsebie Crew. Robert Herrick. CP-HerrR

To Sir Clipseby Crew. Robert Herrick. CP-HerrR

To Sir Cod. Ben Jonson. CP-JonsB; SP-JonsB

To Sir Edward Herbert. Ben Jonson. CP-JonsB; SP-JonsB

To Sir Edward Herbert, at Juliers [or Julyers]. John Donne. CP-DonnJ; MW-DonnJ

To Sir Francis Brian. Sir Thomas Wyatt. CP-WyatT Fr. Satires.

To Sir George Parrie, Doctor of the Civill Law. Robert Herrick. CP-HerrR

To Sir Godfrey Kneller, on His Painting for Me the Statues of Apollo, Venus and Hercules. Alexander Pope. CP-PopeA

To Sir Henry Cary. Ben Jonson. CP-JonsB; SP-JonsB

To Sir Henry Goodyer. John Donne. CP-DonnJ; MW-DonnJ

To Sir Henry Goodyere. Ben Jonson. CP-JonsB; SP-JonsB

To Sir Henry Nevil. Ben Jonson. CP-JonsB; SP-JonsB

To Sir Henry [or Henrie] Savile [upon His Translation of Tacitus]. Ben Jonson. CP-JonsB; SP-JonsB

To Sir Henry Vane the Younger. John Milton. CP-MiltJ
  (Sonnet 17.) CP-MiltJ

To Sir Henry Wotton, at His Going Ambassador to Venice. John Donne. CP-DonnJ; MW-DonnJ

To Sir Henry Wotton ("Here's no more news, than virtue, I may as well"). John Donne. CP-DonnJ; MW-DonnJ

To Sir Henry Wotton ("Sir, more than kisses, letters mingle souls"). John Donne. CP-DonnJ; MW-DonnJ

To Sir Horace Vere. Ben Jonson. CP-JonsB; SP-JonsB

To Sir John Berkeley, Governour of Exeter. Robert Herrick. CP-HerrR

To Sir John Fenn. William Cowper. CP-CowpW

To Sir John Radcliffe. Ben Jonson. CP-JonsB; SP-JonsB

To Sir Joshua Reynolds. William Cowper. CP-CowpW

To Sir Luckless Woo-All. Ben Jonson. CP-JonsB; SP-JonsB

To Sir Ra[l]ph Shelton. Ben Jonson. CP-JonsB; SP-JonsB

To Sir Robert Wroth. Ben Jonson. CP-JonsB; SP-JonsB

To Sir Thomas Overbury. Ben Jonson. CP-JonsB; SP-JonsB

To Sir Thomas Roe. Ben Jonson. CP-JonsB; SP-JonsB

To Sir William Jephson. Ben Jonson. CP-JonsB; SP-JonsB

To Sir William Uvedale. Ben Jonson. CP-JonsB; SP-JonsB

To sit and dream, to sit and read. To You. Langston Hughes. CP-HughL; CP-

HughL3

To sit on a chair, to eat from a table. Scherzo. Randall Jarrell. CP-JarrR

To sit on a hotel balcony in Jerusalem. Letter, A. Yehuda Amichai. SP-AmicY, *tr. by* Chana Bloch

To sit on History in an easy chair. Outside the Crowd. George Meredith. CP-MerG2

To Sleep. Robert Graves. CP-GravR

To Sleep. John Keats. CP-KeatJ

To Sleep. William Wordsworth. CP-WorW1

To sleep and forget everything for a few hours. Summer Fog. Raymond Carver. CP-CarvR

To sleep, even more be made of stone: how these. Michelangelo Buonarroti. CP-Miche, *tr. by* John Frederick Nims

To sleep here, I play dead. Ia Drang Valley. Yusef Komunyakaa. CP-KomuY

To Smile or Not to Smile. James Laughlin. CP-LaugJ

Tō So-kin of Rakuyō, ancient friend, Chancellor of Gen. Exile's Letter. Li Po. SP-PounE, *tr. by* Ezra Pound

To Soar in Freedom and in Fullness of Power. Walt Whitman. CP-WhitW

To Some I Have Talked with by the Fire. William Butler Yeats. CP-YeatW

To some it may well seem I pitch my style. Petrarch. CP-Petra, *tr. by* J. G. Nichols

To some it's a jewel in the belt of Alma Mater. Poet in Residence. Karl Shapiro. SP-ShapK

To Some Ladies. John Keats. CP-KeatJ

To some people / Love is given. Gifts. Langston Hughes. CP-HughL2

To Sophia [Miss Stacey], Percy Bysshe Shelley. CP-ShelP

To Speak. Denise Levertov. SP-LeveDP; SP-LeveDS

To Speak a Flower. Rainer Maria Rilke. CP-RilkFr, *tr. by* A. Poulin, Jr.

To speak in a flat voice. Speak. James Wright. CP-WrigJ

To speak of death is to deny it, is. Consolatio Nova. James Vincent Cunningham. CP-CunnJ

To speak of sorrow. To Speak. Denise Levertov. SP-LeveDP; SP-LeveDS

To Speak of Woe That Is in Marriage. Robert Lowell. SP-LoweR

To speak quietly at such a distance, to speak. Chocorua to Its Neighbor. Wallace Stevens. CP-StevW; CP-StevWP

To speak the prime word and vanish. Light Journal. Charles Wright. SP-WrigC

To speik of gift or almous deidis. William Dunbar. CP-DunbW

To speik of science, craft or sapience. William Dunbar. CP-DunbW

To spend unsolaced years of pain. Arthur Hugh Clough. SP-ClouA

To Spring. William Blake. CP-BlakW

To spring impetuously in air and remain. To Be in Love. Robert Graves. CP-GravR

To Springs and Fountains. Robert Herrick. CP-HerrR

To St. Michael, in Time of Peace. G. K. Chesterton. CP-ChesG

To stab my youth with desperate knives, to wear. Tædium Vitæ. Oscar Wilde. CP-WildO

To stand, in the shadow. Paul Celan. SP-CelaP, *tr. by* John Felstiner

To stand on common ground. Common Ground, A. Denise Levertov. SP-LeveDP; SP-LeveDS

To stand on the long field in fall. Harvest Home, A. Howard Nemerov. CP-NemeH

To Stand Up Straight. A. E. Housman. CP-HousA

To stand up straight and tread the turning mill. To Stand Up Straight. A. E. Housman. CP-HousA

To stand(alone)in some. E. E. Cummings. CP-CummE

To start, I have to draw blood. Un Poco Loco. Clarence Major. SP-MajoC

To start the world of old. It Is Almost the Year Two Thousand. Robert Frost. CP-FrosR

To start,to hesitateø stop. E. E. Cummings. CP-CummE; SP-CummE

To start with, it looked abstract. RomaI. Charles Wright. SP-WrigC

To Statecraft Embalmed. Marianne Craig Moore. CP-MoorM

To Stay Alive. David Ignatow. SP-IgnaD

To Stella. Plato. CP-ShelP, *tr. by* Percy Bysshe Shelley

To Stella. Jonathan Swift. CP-SwifJ

To Stella on Her Birthday, Written AD 1721–2. Jonathan Swift. CP-SwifJ

To Stella, Visiting Me in My Sickness. Jonathan Swift. CP-SwifJ

To Stella, Who Collected and Transcribed His Poems. Jonathan Swift. CP-SwifJ

To step over the low wall that divides. To the Sea. Philip Larkin. CP-LarkP

To still have footholds that are almost new. Child, The. Rainer Maria Rilke. CP-RilkFr, *tr. by* A. Poulin, Jr.

To S[tothar]d. William Blake. CP-BlakW

To Summer. William Blake. CP-BlakW

To sup with thee thou didst me home invite. Invitation, The. Robert Herrick. CP-HerrR

To Susan, Countess of Montgomery. Ben Jonson. CP-JonsB; SP-JonsB

To Swim, to Believe. Maxine W. Kumin. SP-KumiM

To Sycamores. Robert Herrick. CP-HerrR

To Symon Gray. Robert Burns. CP-BurnR

To T. H., a Lady Resembling My Mistress. Thomas Carew. CP-CareT

To T. H. The Amphora. Ezra Pound. CP-PoEar

To-ta Ti-om. Peter Blue Cloud. SP-BlueP

To taint th'attentive mind she tries. Ode 3.7: "To taint th'attentive mind she tries." Horace. CP-JohnS *Fr.* Odes.

To take the wrong road. Little Infinite Poem. Federico García Lorca. CP-GarcF, *tr. by* Greg Simon *and* Steven F. White

To talk about the green roof. Many Pages Must Be Thrown Away. Philip Whalen. SP-WhalP

To Tanya at Christmas. Wendell Berry. CP-BerrW

To Tell and Be Told. Robert Graves. CP-GravR

To tell my journeys where I daily walk. Journey, The. Jones Very. CP-VeryJ

To tell the Beauty would decrease. Emily Dickinson. CP-DickE

To tell the range of the English longbows. Palm Sunday. Paul Muldoon. CP-MuldP

To tell you the truth, the shoe pinched. Cinderella's Story. Mona Van Duyn. SP-VanDM

To Terraughty, on His Birth-Day. Robert Burns. CP-BurnR

To that charming. James Laughlin. CP-LaugJ

To that gaunt House of Art which lacks for naught. Athanasia. Oscar Wilde. CP-WildO

To That Most Splendid and Learned Gentleman, Sir Richard Bulstrode, on Account of the Sacred Poems Recently Written by Him. Unknown, *sometimes at. to* Thomas Sheridan. CP-SherT, *tr. by* Robert Hogan

To the aged, trembling, illiterate woman yesterday. Sonnet: "To the aged, trembling, illiterate woman yesterday." Hayden Carruth. CP-CarHS *Fr.* Sonnets.

To the Airport. Adrienne Rich. CP-RicAE

To the Algae. Charles Olson. CP-OlsoC

To the August Fallen. James Wright. CP-WrigJ

To the Author. Ben Jonson. CP-JonsB

To the Author of a Sonnet Beginning " 'Sad Is My Verse,' You Say, 'And Yet No Tear' " Lord Byron. CP-Byron

To the Author of "Tom Pun-Sibi Metamorphosed" Thomas Sheridan. CP-SherT

To the Author's Portrait. William Wordsworth. CP-WorW2

To the Babylonians. Howard Nemerov. CP-NemeH

To the Bartholdi Statue. Ambrose Bierce. SP-BierA

To the Beautiful Miss Eliza J———n, on Her Principles of Liberty and Equality. Robert Burns. CP-BurnR

To the belfry, one by one, went the ringers from the sun. Rhyme of the Duchess May. Elizabeth Barrett Browning. CP-BroEB

To the Bitter Sweet-heart: a Dream. Wilfred Owen. CP-OwenW

To the Bleeding Hearts Association of American Novelists. Howard Nemerov. CP-NemeH

To the Bluebell. Emily Jane Brontë. CP-BronE

To the bob-white's call. Red Lily, The. William Carlos Williams. CP-WilW1

To the Body. Allen Ginsberg. CP-GinsA

To the Boy with a Country. James Whitcomb Riley. CP-RileJ

To the bright east she flies. Emily Dickinson. CP-DickE

To the chief Chanters. God Saves the King. Donald Davie. CP-DaviDC

To the chopping-block, on which the farmer Sebastian split. Hands, The. Erich Arendt. CP-MuldP, *tr. by* Paul Muldoon

To the City of Bombay. Rudyard Kipling. CP-KiplR

To the Clock. Ralph Waldo Emerson. CP-EmerR

To the Cloud Juggler. Hart Crane. CP-CranH

To the Clouds. Gabriela Mistral. SP-MistG, *tr. by* Maria Giachetti [*or* Jacketti]

To the Clouds. William Wordsworth. CP-WorW1

To the cold, dark grave they go. Easter Ode, An. Paul Laurence Dunbar. CP-DunbP

To the Comet. Henry David Thoreau. CP-ThorH

To the Comic Spirit. George Meredith. CP-MerG1

To the Companions. Rudyard Kipling. CP-KiplR *Fr.* Debits and Credits.

To the Countess of Anglesey. Thomas Carew. CP-CareT

To the Countess of Bedford at New Year's Tide. John Donne. CP-DonnJ; MW-DonnJ

To the Countess of Bedford ("Honour is so sublime perfection"). John Donne. CP-DonnJ; MW-DonnJ

To the Countess of Bedford ("Madam, / Reason is our soul's left hand, Faith her right"). John Donne. CP-DonnJ; MW-DonnJ

To the Countess of Bedford ("Madam, / You have refined me, and to worthiest things"). John Donne. CP-DonnJ; MW-DonnJ

To the Countess of Bedford ("Though I be dead, and buried, yet I have"). John Donne. CP-DonnJ; MW-DonnJ

To the Countess of Bedford ("To have written then, when you writ, seemed to me"). John Donne. CP-DonnJ; MW-DonnJ

To the Countess of Blessington. Lord Byron. CP-Byron

To the Countess of Huntingdon ("Madam, / Man to God's image, Eve, to man's was made"). John Donne. CP-DonnJ; MW-DonnJ

To the Countess of Huntingdon ("That unripe side of earth, that heavy clime"). John Donne. CP-DonnJ; MW-DonnJ

To the Countess of Salisbury. John Donne. CP-DonnJ; MW-DonnJ

To the Cricket. James Whitcomb Riley. CP-RileJ

To the Cuckoo. William Wordsworth. CP-WorW1; MW-WorW

To the Cuckoo. William Wordsworth. CP-WorW2

To the Daisy ("Bright Flower! whose home is everywhere"). William Wordsworth. CP-WorW1; MW-WorW

To the Daisy ("In youth from rock to rock I went"). William Wordsworth. CP-WorW1; MW-WorW

To the Daisy ("Sweet Flower! belike one day to have"). William Wordsworth. CP-WorW1; MW-WorW

To the Daisy ("With little here to do or see"). William Wordsworth. CP-WorW1; MW-WorW

  (To the Same Flower [The Daisy].) CP-WorW1

To the Dark Mercedes of "El Palacio de Amor." Langston Hughes. CP-HughL; CP-HughL1

To the Dawn: Defiance. Ezra Pound. CP-PoEar

To the Dead Owner of a Gym. Thom Gunn. CP-GunnT

To the Dean. Thomas Sheridan. CP-SherT

To the Dean. William Carlos Williams. CP-WilW2

To the Dean of St. Patrick's ("Dear Dean, I'm in a sad condition"). Thomas Sheridan. CP-SherT

To the Dean of St. Patrick's ("Dear Sir, since you in humble wise"). Thomas Sheridan. CP-SherT

To the Dean of St. Patrick's ("Since your poetic prancer is turned into Cancer"). Thomas Sheridan. CP-SherT

To the Dean of St. Patrick's ("Sir, your Billingsgate Muse methinks does begin"). Thomas Sheridan. CP-SherT

To the Dean, when in England, in 1726. Thomas Sheridan. CP-SherT

To the Detracter. Robert Herrick. CP-HerrR

To the dim light and the large circle of shade. Sestina: Of the Lady Pietra degli Scrovigni. Dante Alighieri. CW-RossD, tr. by Dante Gabriel Rossetti

To The Discreet Reader: An Induction to Indiscretions. Robert Stock. SP-StocR

To the Dog Belvoir. Stevie Smith. CP-SmitS

To the Duke of Dorset. Lord Byron. CP-Byron

To the Earl of Burlington Asking Who Writ the Libels against Him. Alexander Pope. CP-PopeA

To the Earl of Clare. Lord Byron. CP-Byron

To the Earl of Oxford, Late Lord Treasurer. Jonathan Swift. CP-SwifJ

To the Earl of Peterborough. Jonathan Swift. CP-SwifJ

To the Earl of Roscommon, on His Excellent *Essay on Translated Verse*. John Dryden. CP-DryJ2

To the Earle of Westmerland. Robert Herrick. CP-HerrR

To the East and to the West. Walt Whitman. CP-WhitW

To the Eastern Shore. Paul Laurence Dunbar. CP-DunbP

To the Editor of *The Dublin Journal. Unknown, sometimes at. to* Thomas Sheridan. CP-SherT

To the Egyptian Mummy in the Etruscan Museum at Cortona. Charles Wright. SP-WrigCN

To the Empire of America, beneath the Western Hemisphere. Farewell to America. To Mrs. S. W. Phillis Wheatley. *See* Farewell[l] to America, A. To Mrs. S. W

To the Empress Josephine's Statue. Hart Crane. CP-CranH

To the End. Christina Georgina Rossetti. CP-RosC3

To the Etruscan Poets. Richard Wilbur. CP-WilbR

To the Evening Star. William Blake. CP-BlakW

To the Evening Star. Samuel Taylor Coleridge. CP-ColeS

To the Evening Star: Central Minnesota. James Wright. CP-WrigJ

To the Evening Star over Grasmere Water. William Wordsworth. CP-WorW1

To the faithful Absence is condensed presence. Emily Dickinson. SP-DickE

To the fateless ones. Fateless Ones, The. Kathleen Jessie Raine. SP-RainK

To the Fever, Not To Trouble Julia. Robert Herrick. CP-HerrR

To the Field Mice. Richard Eberhart. CP-EberR

To the Film Industry in Crisis. Frank O'Hara. SP-OharF

To the Fishermen. Jones Very. CP-VeryJ

To the Flamingos. Boy in the Roman Zoo. Archibald MacLeish. CP-MacLA

To the four corners of the earth they turn. Plague Column, The. Jaroslav Seifert. SP-SeifJ, tr. by Ewald Osers

To the galleys, thief, and sweat your soul out. Thief. Robert Graves. CP-GravR

To the Garden the World. Walt Whitman. CP-WhitW

To the Generous Reader. Robert Herrick. CP-HerrR

To the Genius of His House. Robert Herrick. CP-HerrR

To the German Language. Jorge Luis Borges. SP-BorgJ, tr. by Alastair Reid

To the Ghost of John Milton. Carl Sandburg. CP-SandC

To the Ghost of Marjorie Kinnan Rawlings. William Carlos Williams. CP-WilW2

To the Ghost of Martial. Ben Jonson. CP-JonsB; SP-JonsB

To the Girl Who Lives In a Tree. Audre Lorde. SP-LordA

To the God of all sure mercies let my blessing rise to-day. Cassandra Southwick. John Greenleaf Whittier. CP-WhitJ

To the God Who reigns on high. Hymn: "To the God Who reigns on high." Christina Georgina Rossetti. CP-RosC3

To the Governor & Legislature of Massachusetts. Howard Nemerov. CP-NemeH

To the Great Metropolis. Arthur Hugh Clough. SP-ClouA

To the grove, the meadow, the well. Pietro Metastasio. CP-WorW1

To the Halibut. William Cowper. *See* To the Immortal Memory of the Halibut on Which I Dined This Day, Monday, April 26, 1784

To the Hand. W. S. Merwin. SP-MerwW

To the Handsome Mistresse Grace Potter. Robert Herrick. CP-HerrR

To the Harbormaster. Frank O'Hara. SP-OharF

To the Heavens above us. Astrologer's Song, An. Rudyard Kipling. CP-KiplR

To the High and Noble Prince, George, Duke, Marquesse, and Earle of Buckingham. Robert Herrick. CP-HerrR

To the High-Flyers. Johann Gabriel Seidl. CP-MerG2

To the Highland Girl of Inversneyde. William Wordsworth. CP-WorW1

To the Holy Spirit. Wendell Berry. CP-BerrW

To the Honorable Mr. D. T. Thomas Sheridan. CP-SherT

To the Honble Mr. R. M——, of P-nm-re, on His High Phaeton. Robert Burns. CP-BurnR

To the honorable Senate and House. Belinda's Petition. Rita Dove. SP-DoveR

To the Honourable Col. Peter Schuyler. Annis Boudinot Stockton. CP-StocA

To the Hon.ble Commodore Hood on His Pardoning a Deserter. Phillis Wheatley. CP-WheaP

To the Hon. Mrs. George Lamb. Lord Byron. CP-Byron

To the Honourable T. H. Esq; on the Death of His Daughter. Phillis Wheatley. CP-WheaP

  (To the Hon'ble Thomas Hubbard, Esq; on the Death of Mrs. Thankfull Leonard.) CP-WheaP

To the Hon'ble Thomas Hubbard, Esq; on the Death of Mrs. Thankfull Leonard. Phillis Wheatley. *See* To the Honourable T. H. Esq; on the Death of His Daughter

To the Honoured, Master Endimion Porter. Robert Herrick. CP-HerrR

To the House. Robinson Jeffers. CP-JefR1

To the house on the grassy hill. Presence, The. Denise Levertov. SP-LeveDP

To the imagined lives. Inscription for a Monument. Wallace Stevens. CP-StevWP

To the Immaculate Virgin, on a Winter Night. Thomas Merton. CP-MertT

To the Immortal[l] Memory [*or* Memorie] and Friendship of That Noble Pair[e], Sir Lucius Cary and Sir H. [*or* Henry] Morison. Ben Jonson. CP-JonsB; SP-JonsB

To the Immortal Memory of the Halibut on Which I Dined This Day, Monday, April 26, 1784. William Cowper. CP-CowpW

  (To the Halibut.) CP-CowpW

To the Indians Who Died in Africa. T. S. Eliot. CP-ElioT

To the Infant Martyrs. Richard Crashaw. CP-CrasR

To—"The J. W. R. Literary Club." James Whitcomb Riley. CP-RileJ

To the Jesuits. G. K. Chesterton. CP-ChesG

To the Jewish People. Kenneth Patchen. CP-PatcK

To the Judge. James Whitcomb Riley. CP-RileJ

To the Judge of Right and Wrong. Choice, The. Rudyard Kipling. CP-KiplR

To the King. Robert Herrick. CP-HerrR

To the King and Queen[e], upon Their Unhappy Distances. Robert Herrick. CP-HerrR

To the King, at His Entrance into Saxham: By Master John Crofts. Thomas Carew. CP-CareT

To the King. On His Birthday. An Epigram Anniversary. Novem[ber] 19, 1632. Ben Jonson. CP-JonsB

To the King, To Cure the Evill. Robert Herrick. CP-HerrR

To the King, upon His Com[m]ing with His Army into the West. Robert Herrick. CP-HerrR

To the King, upon His Taking of Leicester. Robert Herrick. CP-HerrR

To the King, upon His Welcome to Hampton-Court. Robert Herrick. CP-HerrR

To the King's Most Excellent Majesty. 1768. Phillis Wheatley. CP-WheaP

  (To the King's Most Excellent Majesty on His Repealing the American Stamp Act.) CP-WheaP

To the King's Most Excellent Majesty on His Repealing the American Stamp Act. Phillis Wheatley. *See* To the King's Most Excellent Majesty. 1768

To the laboratory then I went. What little. Fragment: "To the laboratory then I went. What little." John Ciardi. CP-CiarJ

To the Lacedemonians. Allen Tate. SP-TateA

To the Ladies Who Saw Me Crowned. John Keats. CP-KeatJ

To the Lady Bedford. John Donne. CP-DonnJ; MW-DonnJ

To the Lady Crew, Upon the Death of her Child. Robert Herrick. CP-HerrR

To the Lady E.B. and the Hon. Miss P. William Wordsworth. CP-WorW2

To the Lady Elizabeth Queen of Bohemia. George Herbert. CP-HerbG

To the Lady Fleming on Seeing the Foundation Preparing for the Erection of Rydal Chapel, Westmoreland. William Wordsworth. CP-WorW2

To the Lady Margaret Ley. John Milton. CP-MiltJ
(Sonnet 10.) CP-MiltJ

To the Lady Mary Lowther. William Wordsworth. CP-WorW2

To the Lady Mary Villars, Governesse to the Princesse Henretta. Robert Herrick. CP-HerrR

To the Ladyes. Robert Herrick. CP-HerrR

To the Lark. Robert Herrick. CP-HerrR

To the Learnèd Critic. Ben Jonson. CP-JonsB; SP-JonsB

To the leaven'd soil they trod calling I sing for the last. Walt Whitman. CP-WhitW

To the legion of the lost ones, to the cohort of the damned. Gentlemen-Rankers. Rudyard Kipling. CP-KiplR

To the Little Fort of San Lazaro on the Ocean Front, Havana. Langston Hughes. CP-HughL; CP-HughL1

To the Little Spinners. Robert Herrick. CP-HerrR

To the Living. May Sarton.
"How faint the horn sounds in the mountain passes." SP-SartM

To the London Reader, on the Odcombian Writer, Polytopian Thomas the Traveller. Ben Jonson. CP-JonsB

To the Lord Chancellor. Percy Bysshe Shelley. CP-ShelP

To the Lord General Cromwell. John Milton. CP-MiltJ
(Sonnet 16.) CP MiltJ

To the Lord Hopton, on His Fight in Cornwall. Robert Herrick. CP-HerrR

To the lore of no manner of men. Burning Book [or the Contented Metaphysician], The. Edwin Arlington Robinson. CP-RobiE

To the Loud Wind. Donald Hall. CP-HallD

To the Mad Poets. Richard Eberhart. CP-EberR

To the Maid of Orleans. Edna St. Vincent Millay. CP-MillE

To the maiden. Stephen Crane. CP-CranS

To the Maids to Walke Abroad. Robert Herrick. CP-HerrR

To the Man in the Yellow Terry. Alice Walker. CP-WalkA

To the Man-of-War Bird. Walt Whitman. CP-WhitW

To the man with his jaw shot away, blood-badged. Protagonists. Richard Eberhart. CP-EberR

To the Mannequins. Howard Nemerov. CP-NemeH

To the Marquis of Dufferin and Ava. Alfred Tennyson. CP-TennA

To the meeting despair of eyes in the street, offer. Uncreating Chaos (Double Portrait in a Mirror), The. Stephen Spender. CP-SpenS

To the Memory Of. Philip Whalen. SP WhalP

To the Memory of Alpheus Crosby. Jones Very. CP-VeryJ

To the Memory of Charles B. Storrs. John Greenleaf Whittier. CP-WhitJ

To the Memory of John Wheelwright. Howard Nemerov. CP-NemeH

To the Memory of Mary Young. Paul Laurence Dunbar. CP-DunbP

To the Memory of Mr Oldham. John Dryden. CP-DryJ2; SP-DrydJ

To the Memory of Mrs. Lefroy. Jane Austen. CP-AustJ

To the Memory of My Beloved, the Author Mr [or Master] William Shakespeare: And What He Hath Left Us. Ben Jonson. CP-JonsB; SP-JonsB

To the Memory of My Dear and Ever Honored Father Thomas Dudley Esq. Who Deceased July 31, 1653, and of His Age 77. Anne Bradstreet. CP-BradA

To the Memory of My Dear Daughter in Law, Mrs. Mercy Bradstreet. Anne Bradstreet. CP-BradA

To the Memory of Raisley Calvert. William Wordsworth. CP-WorW1; MW-WorW

To the Memory of That Most Honoured Lady Jane, Eldest Daughter to Cuthbert, Lord Ogle: and Countess of Shrewsbury. Ben Jonson. CP-JonsB

To the Memory of the Rev. James Chisholm. Jones Very. CP-VeryJ

To the Memory of the Rev. James Flint, D. D. Jones Very. CP-VeryJ

To the Memory of the Unfortunate Miss Burns 1791. Robert Burns. CP-BurnR

To the Memory of Thomas Shipley. John Greenleaf Whittier. CP-WhitJ

To the Men of Kent (October, 1803). William Wordsworth. CP-WorW1; MW-WorW

To the Merchant[i]s of Edinburgh. William Dunbar. CP-DunbW

To the Merry Men of France. George Meredith. CP-MerG2

To the Miami. Paul Laurence Dunbar. CP-DunbP

To the microscopy of thinking small. Life-Size Is Too Large. Laura Riding Jackson. CP-RidiL

To the Misses Williams, On Seeing Their Beautiful Paintings of Wild Flowers. Jones Very. CP-VeryJ

To the mizen, the main, & the fore. Ralph Waldo Emerson. CP-EmerR

To the Moon. Thomas Hardy. CP-HardT

To the Moon. Rainer Maria Rilke. CP-RilkFr, tr. by A. Poulin, Jr.

To the Moon. Percy Bysshe Shelley. CP-ShelP

To the Moon. Philip Whalen. SP-WhalP

To the Moon (Composed by the Seaside,—on the Coast of Cumberland).

William Wordsworth. CP-WorW2

To the Moon (Rydal). William Wordsworth. CP-WorW2

To the Moonbeam. Percy Bysshe Shelley. CP-ShelP

To the Morn. Wallace Stevens. CP-StevWP

To the Morning. Satisfaction for Sleepe. Richard Crashaw. CP-CrasR

To the Most Accomplist Gentleman, Master Edward Norgate, Clark of the Signet to His Majesty. Robert Herrick. CP-HerrR

To the Most Accomplist Gentleman Master Michael Oulsworth. Robert Herrick. CP-HerrR

To the Most Comely and Proper M. Elizabeth Finch. Robert Herrick. CP-HerrR

To the Most Disconsolate Great Brittaine. Thomas Campion. CP-CampT

To the Most Fair and Lovely Mistress Anne Soame, Now Lady Abdie. Robert Herrick. CP-HerrR

To the Most High and Mighty Prince Charles. Thomas Campion. CP-CampT

To the Most Illustrious and Mighty Fredericke the Fift, Count Palantine of the Rhein. Thomas Campion. CP-CampT

To the Most Illustrious and Most Hopeful[l] Prince, Charles, Prince of Wales. Robert Herrick. CP-HerrR

To the Most Learned, Wise, and Arch-Antiquary, M. John Selden. Robert Herrick. CP-HerrR

To the Most Noble, and above His Titles, Robert, Earl of Somerset. Ben Jonson. CP-JonsB

To the Most Princely and Vertuous the Lady Elizabeth. Thomas Campion. CP-CampT

To The Most Sacred King James. Thomas Campion. CP-CampT

To the Most Sacred Queen Anne. Thomas Campion. CP-CampT

To the Most Virtuous Mistress Pot, Who Many Times Entertained Him. Robert Herrick. CP-HerrR

To the Mother. James Whitcomb Riley. CP-RileJ

To the Mountains. Henry David Thoreau. CP-ThorH

To the much-tossed Ulysses, never done. Ulysses. Robert Graves. CP-GravR

To the Muse. Aleksandr Aleksandrovich Blok. SP-BlokA, tr. by Peter France and Jon Stallworthy

To the Muse. Denise Levertov. SP-LeveDP

To the Muse. George Oppen. CP-OppGN

To the Muse. James Wright. CP-WrigJ

To the Muses. William Blake. CP-BlakW

To the Name above Every Name, the Name of Jesus, a Hymn. Richard Crashaw. CP-CrasR

To the New World. Randall Jarrell. CP-JarrR

To the New Year [For the Countess of Carlisle]. Thomas Carew. CP-CareT

To the Nieuport Scout. Geoffrey Hill. CP-HillG

To the Nightingale. Jorge Luis Borges. SP-BorgJ, tr. by Alastair Reid

To the Nightingale. William Cowper. CP-CowpW

To the Nightingale, and Robin-Red-Brest. Robert Herrick. CP-HerrR

To the Nile. John Keats. CP-KeatJ

To the Nile. Percy Bysshe Shelley. CP-ShelP

To the North. May Sarton. SP-SartM

To the Not Impossible Him. Edna St. Vincent Millay. CP-MillE

To the, O marcifull saliuiour myn, Iesus. Tabill of Confessioun, The. William Dunbar. CP-DunbW

To the Oak. "Shu Ting." CP-KizeC, tr. by Carolyn Kizer and Y. H. Zhao

To the old, long life and treasure. Song: "To the old, long life and treasure." Ben Jonson. CP-JonsB Fr. Gypsies Metamorphosed, The.

To the One in the Gray Coat. Robert Creeley. CP-CreeR

To the One of Fictive Music. Wallace Stevens. CP-StevW; CP-StevWP

To the Outer World. William Carlos Williams. CP-WilW1

To the Painter. Thomas Carew. CP-CareT

To the Painter, To Draw Him a Picture. Robert Herrick. CP-HerrR

To the Parliament. Ben Jonson. CP-JonsB; SP-JonsB

To the Passenger. Robert Herrick. CP-HerrR

To the Patron of Poets, M. End: Porter. Robert Herrick. CP-HerrR

To the Pay Toilet. Marge Piercy. SP-PierM

To the Peacock of France. Marianne Craig Moore. CP-MoorM

To the Pending Year. Walt Whitman. CP-WhitW

To the Pennsylvanians. William Wordsworth. CP-WorW2

To the Planet Venus. William Wordsworth. CP-WorW2

To the Planet Venus, an Evening Star. William Wordsworth. CP-WorW2

To the poet as a basement quilt, but perhaps. Or in My Throat. John Ashbery. SP-AshbJ

To the Poet, John Dyer. William Wordsworth. CP-WorW1

To the Poets. Howard Nemerov. CP-NemeH

To the Poets in New York. James Wright. CP-WrigJ

To the Poets: To Make Much of Life. George Oppen. CP-OppGN

To the poor (aux pauvres) crime alone (le crime seul) opens. Statue of Liberty. Karl Shapiro. SP-ShapK

To the President-elect. Joseph Brodsky. CP-BrodJ

To the President of the United States. Annis Boudinot Stockton. CP-StocA

To the Public. Louis MacNeice. CP-MacNL

To the Punks of Dawlish. Allen Ginsberg. CP-GinsA

To the Pure All Things Are Pure. Jones Very. CP-VeryJ

To the Queen. William Blake. *See* Dedication of the Illustrations to Blair's "Grave"

To the Queen. Alfred Tennyson. CP-TennA

To the Queen, an Apologie for the Length of the Following Panegyricke. Richard Crashaw. CP-CrasR

To the Queen of My Heart. Percy Bysshe Shelley. CP-ShelP

To the Queen, Upon her Numerous Progeny, a Panegyricke. Richard Crashaw. *See* Upon the Duke of *Yorke* his Birth a Panegyricke

To the Queene. Robert Herrick. CP-HerrR

To the Queen's Majesty. Richard Crashaw. CP-CrasR

To the Quick. Heather McHugh. SP-McHuH

To the Quiet Observer. James Whitcomb Riley. CP-RileJ

To the Rain. W. S. Merwin. SP-MerwW

To the Raphaelite Latinists. Ezra Pound. CP-PoEar

To the Reader. Charles Baudelaire. CP-BaudC, *tr.* by Walter Martin

To the Reader. Charles Baudelaire. CP-KunSC, *tr.* by Stanley Kunitz

To the Reader. Thomas Campion. CP-CampT

To the Reader. James Vincent Cunningham. CP-CunnJ

To the Reader ("Pray thee, take care, that tak'st my book[e] in hand"). Ben Jonson. CP-JonsB; SP-JonsB

To the Reader ("This figure, that thou here seest put"). Ben Jonson. CP-JonsB; SP-JonsB

To the Reader. Denise Levertov. SP-LeveDP

To the Reader at Parting. Walt Whitman. CP-WhitW

To the Reader of Master William Davenant's Play [*The Wits*]. Thomas Carew. CP-CareT

To the Reformers of England. John Greenleaf Whittier. CP-WhitJ

To the Republicans of North America. Percy Bysshe Shelley. CP-ShelP

To the Rev. W. J. Hort. Samuel Taylor Coleridge. CP-ColeS

To the Rev. Christopher Wordsworth, D.D., Master of Harrow School. William Wordsworth. CP-WorW2

To the Rev. Doctor Swift, Dean of St. Patrick's. A Birthday Poem. Nov. 30, 1736. Thomas Sheridan. CP-SherT

To the Rev. Dr. Thomas Amory on Reading His Sermons on Daily Devotion, in Which that Duty Is Recommended and Assisted. Phillis Wheatley. CP-WheaP

To the Rev. F. D. Maurice. Alfred Tennyson. CP-TennA

To the Rev. George Coleridge. Samuel Taylor Coleridge. CP-ColeS; MW-ColeS

To the Rev. John McMath, Inclosing a Copy of *Holy Willie's Prayer*, Which He Had Requested. Robert Burns. CP-BurnR

To the Rev. Mr. Newton. William Cowper. CP-CowpW

To the Rev. Mr. Pitkin, on the Death of His Lady. Phillis Wheatley. *See* To a Clergyman on the Death of His Lady

To the Rev. Mr. Powell. Christopher Smart. SP-SmarC

To the Reverend Shade of His Religious Father. Robert Herrick. CP-HerrR

To the Rev. [*or* Reverend] W. L. Bowles. Samuel Taylor Coleridge. MW-ColeS *Fr.* Effusions.

To the Rev. William Bull. William Cowper. CP-CowpW

To the Revolutionary Cadres of Balboa, Malibu & Santa Barbara. Philip Whalen. SP-WhalP

To the Right Gratious Prince, Lodwick, Duke of Richmond and Lenox. Robert Herrick. CP-HerrR

To the Right Hon. the Lord Chancellor (Bacon). George Herbert. CP-HerbG

To the Right Honorable the Lord Viscount Mont-Cassel. Thomas Sheridan. CP-SherT

To the Right Honl. William Legge, Earl of Dartmouth, His Majesty's Secretary of State for North America [variant 1]. Phillis Wheatley. *See* To the Right Honourable William, Earl of Dartmouth, His Majesty's Principal Secretary of State for North America

To the Right Honl. William Legge, Earl of Dartmouth, His Majesty's Secretary of State for North America [variant 2]. Phillis Wheatley. *See* To the Right Honourable William, Earl of Dartmouth, His Majesty's Principal Secretary of State for North America

To the Right Honourable, Both in Birth and Vertue, Francis, Earle of Cumberland. Thomas Campion. CP-CampT

To the Right Honourable Edward Earle of Dorset. Robert Herrick. CP-HerrR

To the Right Hon[oura]ble Hierome, L[ord] Weston. An Ode Gratulatory for His Return from His Embassy. 1632. Ben Jonson. CP-JonsB

To the Right Honourable Mildmay, Earl of Westmorland. Robert Herrick. CP-HerrR

To the Right Honourable, Philip, Earle of Pembroke, and Montgomerie. Robert Herrick. CP-HerrR

To the Right Honourable, the Lord High Treasurer of England. An Epistle Mendicant. 1631. Ben Jonson. CP-JonsB; SP-JonsB

To the Right Honourable, the Lord Treasurer of England. An Epigram. Ben Jonson. CP-JonsB

To the Right Honourable William, Earl of Dartmouth, His Majesty's Principal Secretary of State for North America. Phillis Wheatley. CP-WheaP

(To the Right Honl. William Legge, Earl of Dartmouth, His Majesty's Secretary of State for North America [variant 2].) CP-WheaP

To the Right, Noble, and Vertuous, Henry Lord Clifford, Sonne and Heyre to the Right Honourable, Francis, Earle of Cumberland. Thomas Campion. CP-CampT

To the Right Noble Tom, Tell-Troth of His Travels, the Coriat of Odcombe, and His Book Now Going to Travel. Ben Jonson. CP-JonsB

To the Right Person. Robert Frost. CP-FrosR

To the right the summer dawn wakes the leaves and mists and sounds. Ruts. Arthur Rimbaud. CP-RimbA, *tr.* by Martin Sorrell

To——— / The Ring is on my hand. Bridal Ballad. Edgar Allan Poe. CP-PoeEd

To the River ———. Edgar Allan Poe. CP-PoeEd

To the Road. Paul Laurence Dunbar. CP-DunbP

To the Roaring Wind. Wallace Stevens. CP-StevW; CP-StevWP

To the Rock that Will Be a Cornerstone of the House. Robinson Jeffers. CP-JefR1

To the Romantic Traditionists. Allen Tate. CP-TateA

To the Rose; a Song. Robert Herrick. CP-HerrR

To the Rose upon the Rood of Time. William Butler Yeats. CP-YeatW

To the Royal Academy. William Blake. CP-BlakW

To the Rulers. Howard Nemerov. CP-NemeH

To the sagging wharf. Summer's Dream, A. Elizabeth Bishop. CP-BishE

To the Salem Gazette, on the Completion of Its First Century. Jones Very. CP-VeryJ

To the Same. Lord Byron. CP-Byron

To the Same ("Another Leonora captured the poet Torquato"). John Milton. CP-MiltJ

(To Leonora Singing at Rome.) CP-CowpW

To the Same ("Why, credulous Naples, do you vaunt your clear-voiced Siren"). John Milton. CP-CowpW; CP-MiltJ

(Naples, too credulous, ah! boast no more.) CP-CowpW

To the Same. Thomas Sheridan. CP-SherT

To the Same [Alphonso Ferrabosco]. Ben Jonson. CP-JonsB; SP-JonsB

To the Same [Benjamin Rudyerd] ("If I would wish, for truth, and not for show"). Ben Jonson. CP-JonsB; SP-JonsB

To the Same [Benjamin Rudyerd] ("Writing thyself, or judging others' writ"). Ben Jonson. CP-JonsB; SP-JonsB

To the Same [Celia]. Ben Jonson. CP-JonsB; SP-JonsB, *tr.* by Ben Jonson *Fr.* Volpone.

To the Same Flower [The Daisy]. William Wordsworth. *See* To the Daisy ("With little here to do or see")

To the Same Flower [The Small Celandine]. William Wordsworth. CP-WorW1; MW-WorW

To the Same [John Lapraik]. Robert Burns. *See* Second Epistle to John Lapraik

To the Same, on the Author Being Threatened with His Resentment. Robert Burns. CP-BurnR *Fr.* Epigrams on Lord Galloway.

To the Same; on the Same. Ben Jonson. CP-JonsB

To the Same [Robert, Earl of Salisbury] [Upon the Accension of the Treasurership to Him]. Ben Jonson. CP-JonsB; SP-JonsB

To the Same Sir Cod. Ben Jonson. CP-JonsB; SP-JonsB

To the Same [Sir Henry Goodyere]. Ben Jonson. CP-JonsB; SP-JonsB

To the Same [Sir John Roe]. Ben Jonson. CP-JonsB; SP-JonsB

To the Same [Sir Luckless Woo-All]. Ben Jonson. CP-JonsB; SP-JonsB

To the Same [Sir Thomas Roe]. Ben Jonson. CP-JonsB; SP-JonsB

To the Scholars of Harvard. John Crowe Ransom. *See* Address to the Scholars of New England

To the Sea. Philip Larkin. CP-LarkP

To the Serenader. James Whitcomb Riley. CP-RileJ

To the Shade of Po Chü-I. William Carlos Williams. CP-WilW1

To the Shah, from Enweri. "Anvari." CP-EmerR

To the Shah, from Hafiz. Hafiz. CP-EmerR

To the She-Bear: *The 1st Song*. Charles Olson. CP-OlsoC

To the Sighing Strephon. Lord Byron. CP-Byron

To the Small Celandine. William Wordsworth. CP-WorW1; MW-WorW

To the Snake. Denise Levertov. SP-LeveDS

To the Son. Jorge Luis Borges. SP-BorgJ, *tr.* by Alastair Reid

To the Sons of Burns, after Visiting the Grave of Their Father. William Wordsworth. CP-WorW1

To the sound of trumpets rather than horns. Guido Orlandi. CP-CavaG, *tr.* by Marc Cirigliano

To the Sour[e] Reader. Robert Herrick. CP-HerrR

To the South. Paul Laurence Dunbar. CP-DunbP

To the south in the beginning of evening a dog. South. W. S. Merwin. SP-MerwW

To the Spade of a Friend (An Agriculturist). William Wordsworth. CP-WorW1

To the States. Walt Whitman. CP-WhitW

To the States, To Identify the 16th, 17th, or 18th Presidentiad. Walt Whitman. CP-WhitW

To the staunch Dust. Emily Dickinson. CP-DickE

To the Stone-Cutters. Robinson Jeffers. CP-JefR1

To the Story-Tellers. Robinson Jeffers. CP-JefR3

To the Sun. Kathleen Jessie Raine. SP-RainK

To the Sun-set Breeze. Walt Whitman. CP-WhitW

To the (Supposed) Patron. Geoffrey Hill. CP-HillG

To the Supreme Being. Michelangelo Buonarroti.

To the Swallow. Euenus. CP-CowpW, tr. by William Cowper

To the Swimmer. Countee Cullen. CP-CullC

To the Teumessian Vixen. Robert Graves. CP-GravR

To the Thawing Wind. Robert Frost. CP-FrosR

To the Thirty-Ninth Congress. John Greenleaf Whittier. CP-WhitJ

To the Three for Whom the Book. Countee Cullen. CP-CullC

To the Torrent at the Devil's Bridge, North Wales, 1824. William Wordsworth. CP-WorW2; MW-WorW

To the Translator of Lucan [or Lucan's Pharsalia, 1614]. Sir Walter Ralegh. CP-RaleW

To the True Romance. Rudyard Kipling. CP-KiplR

To the Tune of an Ancient Song. Kenneth Patchen. CP-PatcK

To the Tune of The Coventry Carol. Stevie Smith. CP-SmitS

To the University of Cambridge, in New-England. Phillis Wheatley. CP-WheaP (To the University of Cambridge, Wrote in 1767) CP-WheaP

To the University of Cambridge, Wrote in 1767. Phillis Wheatley. See To the University of Cambridge, in New-England

To the Unknown Author of the following Poem, and that of Absalom and Achitophel. T. Adams. CP-DryJ2

To the Unknown Goddess. Rudyard Kipling. CP-KiplR

To the Unknown Warrior. G. K. Chesterton. CP-ChesG

To the Unseeable Animal. Wendell Berry. CP-BerrW

To the Utilitarians. William Wordsworth. CP-WorW2

To the vast, shy light. Hovenweep. Kenneth Patchen. CP-PatcK

To the Virgin as She Now Stands to the Monk after a Beatles Movie. Andrei Codrescu. SP-CodrA

To the Virgins, to Make Much of Time. Robert Herrick. CP-HerrR

To the Visitant, from a Circle of Ladies, on Reading His Paper. No. 3, in the Pennsylvania Chronicle. Annis Boudinot Stockton. CP-StocA

To the Water Nymphs, Drinking at the Fountain. Robert Herrick. CP-HerrR

To the Weaver's Gin Ye Go. Robert Burns. CP-BurnR

To the Western Wind. Robert Herrick. CP-HerrR

To the Wife of a Sick Friend. Edna St. Vincent Millay. CP-MillE

To the Willow-Tree. Robert Herrick. CP-HerrR

To the winds give our banner! St. John. John Greenleaf Whittier. CP-WhitJ

To the Wine-God Merlus. James Whitcomb Riley. CP-RileJ

To the wonders of the Peak. Song of the Moon, A. Ben Jonson. CP-JonsB

To the World. Thomas Campion. CP-CampT

To the World [A Farewell for a Gentlewoman, Virtuous and Noble]. Ben Jonson. CP-JonsB; SP-JonsB

To the Worthy Author. Thomas Campion. CP-CampT

To the Worthy Author M[r] John Fletcher. Ben Jonson. CP-JonsB

To the Worthy Author on The Husband. Ben Jonson. CP-JonsB

To the Yew and Cypress to Grace His Funeral. Robert Herrick. CP-HerrR

To the Young Artist. Samuel Taylor Coleridge. CP-ColeS

To Thee, dear God of Mercy, both appeal. At the Close. George Meredith. CP-MerG1

To Thee, Lord, my cry I send. Bible, O.T. See Unto thee will I cry, O Lord my rock

To Thee, My Darling. Ambrose Bierce. SP-BierA

To thee, my way in epigrams seems new. To My Mere English Censurer. Ben Jonson. CP-JonsB; SP-JonsB

To Thee Old Cause. Walt Whitman. CP-WhitW

To thee, sweet Fop, these lines I send. Bounce to Fop. Alexander Pope. CP-SwifJ

To thee these first fruits of my growing death. Our Lord in His Circumcision to His Father. Richard Crashaw. CP-CrasR

To thee whom Albion's distant shore detains. By a Lady in America to Her Husband in England. Annis Boudinot Stockton. CP-StocA

To Thee whose eye all Nature owns. Chorus of the Pities. Thomas Hardy. CP-HardT Fr. Dynasts, The.

To their apartment deep. Emily Dickinson. CP-DickE

To their Excellencies the Lords Justices of Ireland. Mrs. Harris's Petition. Jonathan Swift. CP-SwifJ

To their grey heights they rise. Canna's Basalt Crags. Kathleen Jessie Raine. SP-RainK

To them I'm just a crazy nigger. Newport Beach, 1979. Yusef Komunyakaa. CP-KomuY

To them that knew her, there is vital flame. Lady C. M, The. George Meredith. CP-MerG1

To Them That Mourn. G. K. Chesterton. CP-ChesG

To them who crossed the flood. Inscription: "To them who crossed the flood." Herman Melville. SP-MelvH

To Theodore de Banville. Charles Baudelaire. CP-BaudC, tr. by Walter Martin

To these lovely moments. To Isabelle Trumpy. Rainer Maria Rilke. CP-RilkFr, tr. by A. Poulin, Jr.

To these whom death again did wed. Epitaph Upon Husband and Wife Who Died and Were Buried Together, An. Richard Crashaw. CP-CrasR

To things we are ghosts, soft shapes. Furniture, The. John Updike. CP-UpdiJ

To think of God is to disobey God. Fernando Pessoa. SP-PessF Fr. Keeper of Sheep, The.

To Think of the Life of a Man. Wendell Berry. CP-BerrW

To Think of Time. Walt Whitman. CP-WhitW

To think of you surcharged with. Loneliness. Kenneth Rexroth. CP-RexrK

To think that men of former days. Arthur Hugh Clough. SP-ClouA

To think that this meaningless thing was ever a rose. Summer Is Ended. Christina Georgina Rossetti. CP-RosC2

To think to know the country and not know. Hillside Thaw, A. Robert Frost. CP-FrosR

To thirst and find no fill—to wail and wander. Fragment: Igniculus Desiderii. Percy Bysshe Shelley. CP-ShelP

To this bridge the pale river and flickers away in images of blue. Summer, the Sacramento. Muriel Rukeyser. CP-RukeM

To this corner of Grant and Vallejo. Café Trieste: San Francisco. Joseph Brodsky. CP-BrodJ

To this sad shrine, whoe'er thou art! draw near. Epitaph on the Hon. Simon Harcourt. Alexander Pope. CP-PopeA

To this white Temple of my Heroes, here. To His Honoured Kinsman, Sir Richard Stone. Robert Herrick. CP-HerrR

To this World she returned. Emily Dickinson. CP-DickE

To Thom Gunn in Los Altos, California. Donald Davie. CP-DaviDC

To Thomas Atkins. Rudyard Kipling. CP-KiplR

To Thomas Butts, 2 October 1800. William Blake. See To My Friend Butts I Write

To Thomas Butts, 16 August 1803. William Blake. See O Why Was I Born With a Different Face?

To Thomas Butts, 22 November 1802. William Blake. See With Happiness Stretched [or stretched] across the Hills

To Thomas Clarkson, on the Final Passing of the Bill for the Abolition of the Slave Trade. March, 1807. William Wordsworth. CP-WorW1

To Thomas, Earl of Suffolk. Ben Jonson. CP-JonsB; SP-JonsB

To Thomas, Lord Chancellor. Ben Jonson. CP-JonsB; SP-JonsB

To Thomas Moore. Lord Byron. CP-Byron (My Boat Is on the Shore.) CP-Byron

To Thomas Palmer [on His Book "The Sprite of Trees and Herbs"]. Ben Jonson. CP-JonsB

To Thomas Sheridan. Patrick Delany. CP-SherT

To Thomas Sheridan. Jonathan Swift. CP-SherT, tr. by Robert Hogan

To Thomas Sheridan. Jonathan Swift. CP-SherT; CP-SwifJ

To Thomas Woolner. Dante Gabriel Rossetti. CW-RossD

To those who are isolate. Failed Spirit, The. Stevie Smith. CP-SmitS

To those who can estimate silence. Emily Dickinson. SP-DickE

To those who speak to the many deaf ears attend. Triad. Kathleen Jessie Raine. SP-RainK

To Those Who've Fail'd. Walt Whitman. CP-WhitW

To Those Without Pity. Edna St. Vincent Millay. CP-MillE

To ———: "Three rompers run together, hand in hand." Wilfred Owen. CP-OwenW

To throw yourself away. Throwing Yourself Away. Richard Eberhart. CP-EberR

To thy lover. Out of the Italian; a Song. Richard Crashaw. CP-CrasR

To Thyrza. Lord Byron. CP-Byron

To tie a girl up with string. Admonition. James Laughlin. CP-LaugJ

To Time. Lord Byron. CP-Byron

To Time it never seems that he is brave. I Could Give All to Time. Robert Frost. CP-FrosR

To ———: "Time's sea hath been five years at its slow ebb." John Keats. CP-KeatJ

To Tirzah. William Blake. CP-BlakW Fr. Songs of Experience.

To Toss the Troubled Night Long. D. H. Lawrence. CP-LawrD

To Toussaint L'Ouverture. William Wordsworth. CP-WorW1; MW-WorW

To tragedy I have no addiction. Emancipation of Mr. Poplin, or, Skoal to the Skimmerless. Ogden Nash. CP-NashO

To tragic verse while thou Achilles train't. Elegy 2.18: "To tragic verse while thou Achilles train't." Ovid. CP-MarlC Fr. Elegies.

To transmute crime to wisdom, & to stem. Ralph Waldo Emerson. CP-EmerR

To trap a chipmunk put a bait of nuts. Useless Knowledge. John Ciardi. CP-

CiarJ

To travel! Leave countries behind! Fernando Pessoa. SP-PessF, *tr. by* Susan M. Brown *and* Edwin Honig

To True Soldiers. Ben Jonson. CP-JonsB; SP-JonsB

To Try to Get Down One Citizen as Against Another. Charles Olson. CP-OlsoC

To try to speak, and miss the way. Emily Dickinson. CP-DickE

To Tui: Not to Hie Herself Off to Only God Knows How Dire & Pestilential a South Sea Island, But to Come With Us to Found Her Community in Brazil; Together with Some Preposterous Notes Toward an Ornithomancy of Lovingkindness. Robert Stock. SP-StocR

To turn a stone. High Noon at Los Alamos. Eleanor Wilner. SP-WilnE

To Two Sisters. Samuel Taylor Coleridge. CP-ColeS

To Ulysses. Alfred Tennyson. CP-TennA

To "Uncle Remus." James Whitcomb Riley. CP-RileJ

To understand / each other: anything. Their Attitudes Differ. Margaret Atwood. SP-AtwM1

To undertake is to achieve. Emily Dickinson. CP-DickE

To Unwin. William Cowper. CP-CowpW

To — Upon the Birth of Her First-Born Child, March, 1833. William Wordsworth. CP-WorW2

To Urania. Joseph Brodsky. CP-BrodJ, *tr. by* Joseph Brodsky

To urge, my loved Alphonso [*or* Alfonso], that bold fame. To Alphonso [*or* Alfonso] Ferrabosco, on His Book. Ben Jonson. CP-JonsB; SP-JonsB

To Vasko Popa In Rome. Charles Tomlinson. SP-TomlC

To venerate the simple days. Emily Dickinson. CP-DickE

To Venetian Artists. William Blake. CP-BlakW

To Victor Hugo of My Crow Pluto. Marianne Craig Moore. CP-MoorM

To Violets. Robert Herrick. CP-HerrR

To Virgil [*or* Vergil]. Alfred Tennyson. CP-TennA

To Virgins. Robert Herrick. CP-HerrR

To Vulcan. Robert Herrick. CP-HerrR

To W. S*****n, Ochiltree. Robert Burns. *See* To William Simpson, Ochiltree

To W. T. Scott. John Ciardi. CP-CiarJ

To W. Wordsworth. Samuel Taylor Coleridge. CP-ColeS

To wait an Hour—is long. Emily Dickinson. CP-DickE

To ———: " 'Wait, prithee, wait!' this answer Lesbia threw." William Wordsworth. CP-WorW2

To wake, and hear a cock. Dawn. Philip Larkin. CP-LarkP

To wake embedded in warm weight of limbs. Light, The. Carolyn Kizer. CP-KizeC

To wake the soul by tender strokes of art. Prologue to Mr. Addison's *Tragedy of Cato.* Alexander Pope. CP-PopeA

To Waken an Old Lady. William Carlos Williams. CP-WilW1

To walk anywhere in the world, to live. Walk in the Country, A. William Stafford. SP-StafWW

To Walk on Hills. Robert Graves. CP-GravR

To walk on hills is to employ legs. To Walk on Hills. Robert Graves. CP-GravR

To Walter de la Mare. T. S. Eliot. CP-ElioT

To wander through this living world. Remembrance. Langston Hughes. CP-HughL; CP-HughL2

To Wang Wei. Meng Hao Jan. CP-WilW2

To want is there to be where I am not. Sower, The. Jones Very. CP-VeryJ

To war they kept. Lorine Niedecker. CP-NiedL

To Warren Hastings. William Cowper. CP-CowpW

To watch the storms, and hear the sky. To Lady Austen. William Cowper. CP-CowpW

To wear the arctic fox. Arctic Ox, The. Marianne Craig Moore. CP-MoorM

To weary hearts, to mourning homes. Angel of Patience, The. John Greenleaf Whittier. CP-WhitJ

To wed good blood to bad blood to alleviate. Fathers, The. Charles Olson. CP-OlsoC

To Westward. John Ciardi. CP-CiarJ

To wet your eye withouten tear. Sir Thomas Wyatt. CP-WyatT

To what a cumbersome unwieldiness[e]. Love's Diet. John Donne. CP-DonnJ; MW-DonnJ

To what end serve the promises. Desdain. Sir John Suckling. CP-SuckJ

To what good, in the alleys of the lilacs. Last Looks at the Lilacs. Wallace Stevens. CP-StevW; CP-StevWP

To What Listens. Wendell Berry. CP-BerrW

To what purpose, April, do you return again? Spring. Edna St. Vincent Millay. CP-MillE

To What Purpose Is This Waste? Christina Georgina Rossetti. CP-RosC3

To What Serves Mortal Beauty? Gerard Manley Hopkins. CP-HopkG

To what summoned? And to whom? blindly, God almighty, through horizons of woolly haze. On the Road. Czeslaw Milosz. CP-MiloC; CP-MiloCN, *tr. by* Renata Gorczynski *and* Robert Hass

To ———: "When passion's trance is overpast." Percy Bysshe Shelley. CP-ShelP

To Where We Are. W. S. Merwin. SP-MerwW

To which as to a Reservoir. Emily Dickinson. SP-DickE

To Whoever is Reading Me. Jorge Luis Borges. SP-BorgJ, *tr. by* Alastair Reid

To whom a glass full of red wine. Hafiz. CP-EmerR *Fr.* Odes.

To whom / can I leave. Lorine Niedecker. CP-NiedL

To whom does the raggedy condor. Pablo Neruda. SP-NeruP *Fr.* Question Book.

To whom I owe the leaping delight. Dedication to My Wife, A. T. S. Eliot. CP-ElioT

To whom in summer long ago. Rhyme for a Parlour Game. G. K. Chesterton. CP-ChesG

To Whom It May Concern. James Vincent Cunningham. CP-CunnJ

To Whom It May Concern. Kenneth Patchen. CP-PatcK

To whom should I present this. Carmen 1. Catullus. CP-ZukLS *Fr.* Carmina.

To whom should I sue to ease my pain? Sir Thomas Wyatt. CP-WyatT

To whom the house of Montagu. Edna St. Vincent Millay. CP-MillE

To Whom the Mornings stand for Nights. Emily Dickinson. CP-DickE

To William Camden. Ben Jonson. CP-JonsB; SP-JonsB

To William Carlos Williams. Richard Eberhart. CP-EberR

To William Creech. Robert Burns. CP-BurnR

To William, Earl[e] of Pembroke. Ben Jonson. CP-JonsB; SP-JonsB

To William F. Bradbury. E. E. Cummings. CP-CummE

To William Godwin. Samuel Taylor Coleridge. CP-ColeS

To William H. Seward. John Greenleaf Whittier. CP-WhitJ

To William Hayley, Esq.: In Reply to His Solicitation to Write with Him in a Literary Work. William Cowper. CP-CowpW

To William Lloyd Garrison. John Greenleaf Whittier. CP-WhitJ

To William, Lord Mounteagle. Ben Jonson. CP-JonsB; SP-JonsB

To William Roe ("Roe (and my joy to name) th'art now, to go"). Ben Jonson. CP-JonsB; SP-JonsB

To William Roe ("When Nature bids us leave to live, 'tis late"). Ben Jonson. CP-JonsB; SP-JonsB

To William Shelley. Percy Bysshe Shelley. CP-ShelP

To William Simpson, Ochiltree. Robert Burns. CP-BurnR (To W. S*****n, Ochiltree.) CP-BurnR

To William Stewart. Robert Burns. CP-BurnR

To William Wilberforce, Esq. William Cowper. CP-CowpW (Sonnet to Wilberforce.) CP-CowpW

To William Wordsworth. Samuel Taylor Coleridge. CP-ColeS; MW-ColeS (To a Gentleman.) CP-ColeS

To win the battle of life you have to plan strategical as well as tactical. Caesar Knifed Again, or, Culture Biz Gets Hep, Boffs Profs. Ogden Nash. CP-NashO

To win the love of women one should first discover. Art of Love, The. Kenneth Koch. SP-KochK

To Wine. Louise Bogan. CP-BogaL

To Winter. William Blake. CP-BlakW

To wish and want and not obtain. Sir Thomas Wyatt. CP-WyatT

To Wish Myself Courage. William Carlos Williams. CP-WilW1

To wit, the lover said. News. Lorine Niedecker. CP-NiedL

To — With the Following Poem. Alfred Tennyson. CP-TennA

To Woman. Lord Byron. CP-Byron

To Women, as Far as I'm Concerned. D. H. Lawrence. CP-LawrD

To Women, to Hide Their Teeth, if They Be Rotten or Rusty. Robert Herrick. CP-HerrR

To Wordsworth. Percy Bysshe Shelley. CP-ShelP

To work a wonder, God would have her shown. Virgin Mary, The. Robert Herrick. CP-HerrR

"To Work Is to Contradict Contradications, to Do Violence to Natural Violence." Robert Creeley. CP-CreeR

To work it out even a thought better. At the Well. Robert Graves. CP-GravR

To worship / At the altar of Beauty. To Beauty. Langston Hughes. CP-HughL; CP-HughL1

To wreak what sweet revenge is his to wreak. Petrarch. CP-Petra, *tr. by* J. G. Nichols

To write a poem, perfect physical condition. Art of Poetry, The. Kenneth Koch. SP-KochK

To write a verse or two, is all the praise. Praise (1). George Herbert. CP-HerbG

To write down all I contain at this moment. Moment, The. Kathleen Jessie Raine. SP-RainK

To write one book in five years. Portrait. Carl Sandburg. CP-SandC

To Write One Song, I Said. Philip Larkin. CP-LarkP

To Yehosef, His Son. Shmuel HaNagid. SP-HaNaS, *tr. by* Peter Cole

To ———: "Yet look on me—take not thine eyes away." Percy Bysshe Shelley. CP-ShelP

To You. Langston Hughes. CP-HughL; CP-HughL3

To You. Kenneth Koch. SP-KochK

To You. Walt Whitman. CP-WhitW

To You Æmelia, lovely Virgin, sues. Poetical Correspondence between Palemon and Æmilia, A. Annis Boudinot Stockton. CP-StocA

To you, Fletcher, from my dark house asleep. One Dull Thing You Did Was to Die, Fletcher, The. John Ciardi. CP-CiarJ

To you, my true and faithful friend. To the Rev. Doctor Swift, Dean of St. Patrick's. A Birthday Poem. Nov. 30, 1736. Thomas Sheridan. CP-SherT

To you [or yow], my purse [or purs], and to non [or no or noon] other wight. Complaint of Chaucer to His Empty Purse, The. Geoffrey Chaucer. CP-ChauG

To you / Who are the. Rising Waters. Langston Hughes. CP-HughL; CP-HughL1

To you, whose virtues I must own. To Mr. Delany. Jonathan Swift. CP-SwifJ

To Young Pessimists. G. K. Chesterton. CP-ChesG

To your recital you were so beautiful. You Invited Me. James Laughlin. CP-LaugJ

To Youth. Robert Herrick. CP-HerrR

To Ysolt. For Pardon. Ezra Pound. CP-PoEar

To Yvor Winters, 1955. Thom Gunn. CP-GunnT

Toad, can die of Light, A. Emily Dickinson. CP-DickE

Toad the power mower caught, A. Death of a Toad, The. Richard Wilbur. CP-WilbR

Toadeater, The. Robert Burns. CP-BurnR

Toads. Philip Larkin. CP-LarkP

Toads Revisited. Philip Larkin. CP-LarkP

Toadstool comes up in a night, A. Christina Georgina Rossetti. CP-RosC2

Toast, A. Robert Burns. CP-BurnR

Toast, A. Louis MacNeice. CP-MacNL

Toast to Death, A. Robert Graves. CP-GravR

Toast to Floyd Collins, A. Miller Williams. CP-WillM

Tobacco Shop. Fernando Pessoa. SP-PessF, tr. by Susan M. Brown and Edwin Honig

Tobacco Shop Window, The. Constantine P. Cavafy. CP-CavaC, tr. by Theoharis Constantine Theoharis

Tobacconist of Eighth Street, The. Richard Eberhart. CP-EberR

Tobroken been the statutz hye in hevene. Lenvoy de Chaucer a Scogan. Geoffrey Chaucer. CP-ChauG

Toby to Aguecheek. Donald Davie. CP-DaviDC

Toccata of Galuppi's, A. Robert Browning. CP-BroR1; SP-BroR

Toccata's sails were up and set. Going Backward Going Forward. Richard Eberhart. CP-EberR

Today. Allen Ginsberg. CP-GinsA; SP-GinsA

Today. Langston Hughes. CP-HughL; CP-HughL2

Today. D. H. Lawrence. CP-LawrD

Today. Frank O'Hara. SP-OharF

Today. James Schuyler. CP-SchuJ

Today. Jones Very. CP-VeryJ

Today a kind of sound shadow lulls along the street. Our Way Those days before These Days. William Stafford. SP-StafWW

Today a woman signaled me in Hebrew. Threat. Raymond Carver. CP-CarvR

Today above the gull's call. Aubade: "Today above the gull's call." Louise Glück. SP-GlucL

Today, all at once, when the thread of my vision snapped. Elegy for Hassan Nasir. Faiz Ahmad Faiz. CP-KizeC, tr. by Carolyn Kizer

Today as I / Looked up at the sky's great face. Kathleen Jessie Raine. SP-RainK

Today as the news from Selma and Saigon. Monet's "Waterlilies." Robert Earl Hayden. CP-HaydR

Today, autumn. Fire of Despair Has Been Our Savior, The. Robert Bly. SP-BlyR

Today—because I must not lie to you. As I Would Wish You Birds. John Ciardi. CP-CiarJ

Today before a learn'd audience comes. Prologue Designed for the Play of Oedipus, Written in Greek, and Performed by Mr. Sheridan's Scholars, at the King's Inn Hall, on Tuesday the 10th of December, 1723, A. Thomas Sheridan. CP-SherT

Today being the day, what gift can I give. Birthday. David Ignatow. SP-IgnaD

Today, dear friend, this grey day. Confidence, A. William Carlos Williams. CP-WilW1

Today / Dr. William Carlos Williams. Credo ("Today / Dr. William Carlos Williams"). John Ciardi. CP-CiarJ

Today he'd be painting for the Central Committee, or Paramount. Visiting Ingres. Hans Magnus Enzensberger. SP-EnzeH, tr. by Michael Hamburger

Today How Many Hours. Pablo Neruda. SP-NeruP

Today I am at home. Few Sirens, A. Alice Walker. CP-WalkA

Today, I am dull, I am dull! Madrigal: "Today, I am dull, I am dull!" Tennessee Williams. CP-WillT

Today I Am Falling. James Tate. SP-TateJ

Today I am walking alone in a bare place. Late November in a Field. James Wright. CP-WrigJ

Today I asked Aileen. Destruction of Grief. Muriel Rukeyser. CP-RukeM

Today I go back to the sea. Return to Sea. Langston Hughes. CP-HughL; CP-HughL3

Today I / looked for myself. Concerning the Exclusions of the Object. A. R. Ammons. CP-AmmoA

Today I met Von Clausewitz. Great Men of Former Times, The. Thomas Merton. CP-MertT

Today I pass the time reading. Japan. Billy Collins. SP-CollB

Today I read nearly two pages. Fernando Pessoa. SP-PessF Fr. Keeper of Sheep, The.

Today I sat before the cliffs. Han-shan. CP-ColdM, tr. by Red Pine

Today I saw a picture of the cancer cells. Cancer Cells, The. Richard Eberhart. CP-EberR

Today I saw a woman wrapped in rags. At the Slackening of the Tide. James Wright. CP-WrigJ

Today I started late and quit early. Philip Whalen. SP-WhalP Fr. Scenes of Life at the Capital.

Today I trade my last unwise. How It Goes On. Maxine W. Kumin. SP-KumiM

Today I Was So Happy, So I Made this Poem. James Wright. CP-WrigJ

Today I will let the old boat stand. Waiting. Carl Sandburg. CP-SandC

Today I wished without mercy. All Day the Light Is Clear. Tess Gallagher. SP-GallT

Today, if a man does something pretentious and deliberate. Shows. D. H. Lawrence. CP-LawrD

Today I'm in a window mood. Rainer Maria Rilke. CP-RilkF1, tr. by A. Poulin, Jr. Fr. Windows, The.

Today in my heart. Autumn Song. Federico García Lorca. CP-GarcF, tr. by Catherine Brown

Today is almost over. Randall Jarrell. CP-JarrR

Today is the day they shipped. Loving the Killer. Anne Sexton. CP-SextA; SP-SextA

Today is Wednesday. Miller Williams. CP-WillM

Today Isn't Everything. Pablo Neruda. SP-NeruP

Today, it came to me. How you, my friends. To My Fellow Artists. Christopher Logue. SP-LoguC

Today, like every other day, we wake up empty. Jelaluddin Rumi. SP-Rumi, tr. by Coleman Barks

Today like yesterday. Monotony. Langston Hughes. CP-HughL; CP-HughL1

Today, lonely for my father, I saw. My Father's Wedding. Robert Bly. SP-BlyR

Today my poems seem / only the spells I muttered. Hayden Carruth. CP-CarHS Fr. Clay Hill Anthology, The.

Today old Janus opens the new year. New Year's Gift Sung to King Charles. 1635, A. Ben Jonson. CP-JonsB

Today on the lip of a bowl in the backyard. Caterpillar, The. Miller Williams. CP-WillM

Today or this noon. Emily Dickinson. CP-DickE

Today out of the window. Trembling of the Veil, The. Allen Ginsberg. CP-GinsA; SP-GinsA

Today outside your prison I stand. Message from the Wanderer, A. William Stafford. SP-StafWW

Today seventy tongues. Mist. W. S. Merwin. SP-MerwW

Today, should you let fall a glass it would. Tramontana at Lerici. Charles Tomlinson. CP-TomlC; SP-TomlC

Today small waves are rippling, crystal clear, upon the pebbles. Birth of Venus, The. William Carlos Williams. CP-WilW2

Today, society has sanctified. En Masse. D. H. Lawrence. CP-LawrD

Today the circus poster. Bells, The. Anne Sexton. CP-SextA

Today The Giant Weapon came. Giant Weapon, The. Kenneth Rexroth. CP-RexrK

Today the leaves cry, hanging on branches swept by wind. Course of a Particular, The. Wallace Stevens. CP-StevWP

Today the mountain. Effacement. Denise Levertov. SP-LeveDS

Today the sky is heavy like the thought of never making port. Fernando Pessoa. SP-PessF Fr. Absurd Hour.

Today the snow is drifting. Snow. Philip Levine. SP-LeviP

Today the water whitens over rocks. Letter. Wyatt Prunty. SP-PrunW

Today there is another marriage. Wedding on Cape Rosier, A. Richard Eberhart. CP-EberR

Today they cut down the oak. Stump. Donald Hall. CP-HallD

Today they invent. Portents. Thomas McGrath. SP-McGrT

Today: / This leafy apple-tree, gray. Kathleen Jessie Raine. SP-RainK

Today, three days before Christmas. Human, Avian, Vegetable, Blood. Kenneth Rexroth. CP-RexrK

Today we move in jade and cease with garnet. Sonnet: To Time. Sylvia Plath. CP-PlatS

Today we saw a tiger. Tiger, The. Robert Creeley. CP-CreeR

Today we were cleaning out the attic. Family Portrait, The. James Laughlin. CP-LaugJ

Today we woke up to a revolution of snow. Snow Day. Billy Collins. SP-CollB

Today we'd say she was depressed, clinically. Then. Emily's Mom. Thomas

Lux. SP-LuxT

Today, when I woke up, I asked myself. Winter Morning. Louise Glück. SP-GlucL

Today, while a steamshovel rooted in the cove. Subject of the Waves, A. May Swenson. SP-SwenM

Today, you threaten to leave me. Lie, The. Maya Angelou. SP-AngeM

Today's Burden. Christina Georgina Rossetti. CP-RosC2

Today's confident light / squanders the roses. Inside. Pablo Neruda. SP-NeruP

Today's your natal day. To My Mother on Her Birthday. Christina Georgina Rossetti. CP-RosC3

Toddlers under the cedar, mushrooms. Argyll Tour. Eugenio Montale. CP-MontE, tr. by Jonathan Galassi

Tod's Amendment. Rudyard Kipling. Fr. Plain Tales from the Hills.

Todtnauberg. Paul Celan. SP-CelaP, tr. by John Felstiner

Toe-Tag, The. Paul Muldoon. CP-MuldP

Toes, The. Raymond Carver. CP-CarvR

Together. G. K. Chesterton. CP-ChesG

Together. Rudyard Kipling. CP-KiplR

Together Again. William Stafford. SP-StafWW

Together in the pot. Soup, The. Charles Simic. SP-SimiCE

Together, keeping in line, slow as if hypnotised. Convoy. Louis MacNeice. CP-MacNL

Together, trustfully, through a dark wood. Through a Dark Wood. Robert Graves. CP-GravR

Together with my dead body shall they arise. Easter Tuesday. Christina Georgina Rossetti. CP-RosC2

Together with my stones. Shibboleth. Paul Celan. SP-CelaP, tr. by John Felstiner

Toil. James Whitcomb Riley. CP-RileJ

Toil. C. K. Williams. CP-WillC; SP-WillC

Toil and grow rich. Witch, The. William Butler Yeats. CP-YeatW

Tōji. Gary Snyder. CP-SnydG

Token, A. Robert Creeley. CP-CreeR

Token of friendship true and tried. Relic, The. John Greenleaf Whittier. CP-WhitJ

Toland's Invitation to Dismal to Dine with the Calves' Head Club. Jonathan Swift. CP-SwifJ

Told. Philip Levine. SP-LeviP

Told by "The Noted Traveler." James Whitcomb Riley. CP-RileJ Fr. Child-World, A.

Told me, "is no longer." "Poetry," John Wieners. William Corbett. SP-CorbW

Tolerable Wisdom, A. Derek Mahon. CP-MahoD

Tolerance. Thomas Hardy. CP-HardT

Tolerance. D. H. Lawrence. CP-LawrD

Toll, bell, toll. For hope is flying / Sighing from the earthbound soul. Christina Georgina Rossetti. CP-RosC2

Toll for the brave! On the Loss of the Royal George. William Cowper. CP-CowpW

Toll of the Roads, The. Stevie Smith. CP-SmitS

Tolling Bell. Robert Graves. CP-GravR

Tollund. Seamus Heaney. SP-HeanSO

Tollund Man, The. Seamus Heaney. SP-HeanSO

Tolstoy. William Carlos Williams. CP-WilW2

Tom. James Schuyler. CP-SchuJ

Tom and Dick had equal fame. Tom Mullinex and Dick. Jonathan Swift. CP-SwifJ

Tom at Cruachan. William Butler Yeats. CP-YeatW

Tom Blinks his Nose is full of wheales, and these. Upon Blinks. Robert Herrick. CP-HerrR

Tom Clark / Waco, Texas. Letter to Thomas Clark 22:VII:71 from Bolinas where He Sat beside Me to Help to Write it, The. Philip Whalen. SP-WhalP

Tom Deadlight. Herman Melville. SP-MelvH

Tom-Dobbin. Thom Gunn. CP-GunnT

Tom dreamed he was visiting. Tom's Dream. James Schuyler. CP-SchuJ

Tom Fool at Jamaica. Marianne Craig Moore. CP-MoorM

Tom, for a goose you keep but base quills. Sheridan, a Goose. Jonathan Swift. CP-SwifJ

Tom—garlanded with squat and surly steel. Tom's Garland: Upon the Unemployed. Gerard Manley Hopkins. CP-HopkG

Tom Grumblod's bridge has balusters set diagonally. Other Cambridge, The. John Berryman. CP-BerrJ

Tom is a man who yearns to have his friends about him. Feast of Friends, A. John Logan. CP-LogaJ

Tom Johnson's Quit. James Whitcomb Riley. CP-RileJ

Tom May's Death. Andrew Marvell. CP-MarvA

Tom Mooney! / Tom Mooney! Chant for Tom Mooney. Langston Hughes. CP-HughL; CP-HughL1

Tom Mullinex and Dick. Jonathan Swift. CP-SwifJ

Tom Noddy's body speaks, not so his mind. Dilemma, The. Robert Graves. CP-

GravR

Tom O'Roughley. William Butler Yeats. CP-YeatW

Tom Pun-Sibi Metamorphosed: Or, The Giber Gibed. William Tisdall. CP-SherT

Tom Pun-Sibi's Resurrection Disproved. Unknown. CP-SherT

T-m Punsibi gave us his Art. Laurence Whyte. CP-SherT Fr. Some Critical Annotations, on Various Subjects Which Have Been Handled by Several Authors.

Tom Punsibi's Farewell to the Muses. Unknown. CP-SherT

Tom Punsibi's Letter to Dean Swift. Thomas Sheridan. CP-SherT

Tom Raban. William Cowper. CP-CowpW

Tom shifts the Trenchers; yet he never can. Upon Trencherman. Robert Herrick. CP-HerrR

Tom the Lunatic. William Butler Yeats. CP-YeatW

Tom, Tom, the piper's son. Nursery Rhymes No. 2: Education. G. K. Chesterton. CP-ChesG

Tom Van Arden, my old friend. James Whitcomb Riley. CP-RileJ

Tom was a little merry grig. Tom Pun-Sibi Metamorphosed: Or, The Giber Gibed. William Tisdall. CP-SherT

Tomatoes squashes and cauliflowers intrigue me immensely. Best Side of Me, The. Andrei Codrescu. SP-CodrA

Tomb. Stéphane Mallarmé. CP-MallS, tr. by Henry Weinfield

Tomb at [or of] Akr Çaar, The. Ezra Pound. CP-PoEar; SP-PounE

Tomb Cover of Imam Riza. Unknown. CP-MertT

Tomb of a millionaire. Graceland. Carl Sandburg. CP-SandC

Tomb of Charles Baudelaire, The. Stéphane Mallarmé. CP-MallS, tr. by Henry Weinfield

Tomb of Edgar Poe, The. Stéphane Mallarmé. CP-MallS, tr. by Henry Weinfield

Tomb of Evrion. Constantine P. Cavafy. CP-CavaC, tr. by Theoharis Constantine Theoharis

Tomb of Iasis, The. Constantine P. Cavafy. CP-CavaC, tr. by Theoharis Constantine Theoharis

Tomb of Ignatios, The. Constantine P. Cavafy. CP-CavaC, tr. by Theoharis Constantine Theoharis

Tomb of Lanis, The. Constantine P. Cavafy. CP-CavaC, tr. by Theoharis Constantine Theoharis

Tomb of Stéphane Mallarmé, The. Charles Simic. SP-SimiC; SP-SimiCE

Tomb of the Grammarian Lysias. Constantine P. Cavafy. CP-CavaC, tr. by Theoharis Constantine Theoharis

Tomb Pond. Norman Dubie. CP-DubiN

Tomb Stone. James Dickey. CP-DickJ

Tombless Epitaph, A. Samuel Taylor Coleridge. CP-ColeS; MW-ColeS

Tombstone Told When She Died, The. Dylan Thomas. CP-ThomD

Tombstones in the Starlight. Dorothy Parker. CP-ParkD

Tome-Thoughts, from the Times. John Updike. CP-UpdiJ

Tomes. Billy Collins. SP-CollB

Tomlinson. Rudyard Kipling. CP-KiplR

Tommies in the Train. D. H. Lawrence. CP-LawrD

Tommy. Rudyard Kipling. CP-KiplR

Tommy is three and when he's bad. Red Roses. Anne Sexton. CP-SextA

Tommy Smith. James Whitcomb Riley. CP-RileJ

"Tommy" you was when it began. Service Man, The. Rudyard Kipling. CP-KiplR

Tommy's alluz playin' jokes. Thomas the Pretender. James Whitcomb Riley. CP-RileJ

Tommy's Pond. John Ciardi. CP-CiarJ

Tomorrow. Raymond Carver. CP-CarvR

Tomorrow. Peter Blue Cloud. SP-BlueP

Tomorrow. Donald Hall. CP-HallD

Tomorrow. Langston Hughes. CP-HughL; CP-HughL3

Tomorrow. David Ignatow. SP-IgnaD

Tomorrow. Charles Olson. CP-OlsoC

Tomorrow. Kenneth Patchen. CP-PatcK

Tomorrow. James Schuyler. CP-SchuJ

Tomorrow I'll begin to cook like Mother. How It Passes. Carolyn Kizer. CP-KizeC

Tomorrow is St. Valentine's: / tomorrow I'll think about. February 13, 1975. James Schuyler. CP-SchuJ

Tomorrow, Julia, I betimes must rise. Perfume, The. Robert Herrick. CP-HerrR

Tomorrow let loveless, let lover tomorrow make love. Vigil of Venus, The. Unknown. CP-TateA

Tomorrow may be. Tomorrow. Langston Hughes. CP-HughL; CP-HughL3

Tomorrow meet you? O not tomorrow. Gerard Manley Hopkins. CP-HopkG

Tomorrow, Partly Cloudy. Ogden Nash. CP-NashO

Tomorrow, since I have so few. Rooster. James Tate. SP-TateJ

Tomorrow the future will be here. Dime Found in the Snow, A. James Tate. SP-TateJ

"Tomorrow"—whose location. Emily Dickinson. CP-DickE

Tomorrow will have an island. Before night. Security. William Stafford. SP-

StafWW

Tomorrow's Envy of Today. Robert Graves. CP-GravR

Tomorrow's Seed. Langston Hughes. CP-HughL; CP-HughL3

Tomorrow's Song. Gary Snyder. CP-SnydG

Tomps 'ud allus haf to say. His Mother's Way. James Whitcomb Riley. CP-RileJ

Tom's a-Cold. Stephen Spender. CP-SpenS

Tom's Angel. Walter De la Mare. CP-DeLaW

Tom's Attempt to Seduce Big Brother Steve. James Schuyler. CP-SchuJ

Tom's Dream. James Schuyler. CP-SchuJ

Tom's Garland: Upon the Unemployed. Gerard Manley Hopkins. CP-HopkG

Tombstones, tombstones, standing like persons. Cemetary in Flaach. Rainer Maria Rilke. CP-RilkFr, *tr. by* A. Poulin, Jr.

Tone. Rae Armantrout. SP-ArmaA

Tone Poem, A. John Ashbery. SP-AshbJ

Tongue. Adam Zagajewski. SP-ZagaA, *tr. by* Clare Cavanagh

Tongue Is, The. Yusef Komunyakaa. CP-KomuY

Tongue of the waves tolled in the earth's bell, The. Want Bone, The. Robert Pinsky. CP-PinsR

Tongue—to tell Him I am true!, A. Emily Dickinson. CP-DickE

Tongues, The. George Oppen. CP-OppGN

Tonight. Charles Bukowski. SP-BukC1

Tonight again I watched that arrogant man Coriolanus, who was. He Did It to Please His Mother. James Laughlin. CP-LaugJ

Tonight as he is lying on his back. Silent Movie. Dan Pagis. SP-PagiD, *tr. by* Stephen Mitchell

Tonight / From the swaddled village, down the padded lane. Japanese River Tales. Ted Hughes. SP-HughTN

Tonight, grave sir, both my poor[e] house and I. Inviting a Friend to Supper. Ben Jonson. CP-JonsB; SP-JonsB

Tonight Hazard's father and stepmother are having. Politics. William Meredith. SP-MereW

Tonight I feel the stars are out. Black String of Days. Yusef Komunyakaa. CP-KomuY

Tonight I saw the marred and frosted moon. Shibboleth. Josephine Jacobsen. CP-JacoJ

Tonight I stay at the Summit Temple. Tennessee Williams. CP-WillT

Tonight I think of Boubouolina. Between Two Seas. Olga Broumas. SP-BrouO

Tonight I touch your breasts. No Love in This House. Yusef Komunyakaa. CP-KomuY

Tonight I watch my father's hair. Two Postures beside a Fire. James Wright. CP-WrigJ

Tonight, I write sadly. Write. Pablo Neruda. SP-LoguC, *tr. by* Christopher Logue *Fr.* Red Bird.

Tonight is clearer and colder. Yugao. Kenneth Rexroth. CP-RexrK

Tonight it is the wine (or not the wine). Excuse. Alice Walker. CP-WalkA

Tonight my heart makes. Rainer Maria Rilke. CP-RilkFr, *tr. by* A. Poulin, Jr. *Fr.* Orchards.

Tonight my love is sleeping cold. Requiescat. Dorothy Parker. CP-ParkD

Tonight, nothing is long enough—. Tunnel, The. Robert Creeley. CP-CreeR

Tonight, on the deck, the lights. Two Stories. Charles Wright. SP-WrigC

Tonight possibly they'll. One World. Robert Creeley. SP-CreeR

Tonight reality is in the rest. Money and Grass. David Ignatow. SP-IgnaD

Tonight the blessèd state, that long repose. De Quincey in Later Life. Derek Mahon. CP-MahoD

Tonight the moon is round golden entire. It. E. E. Cummings. CP-CummE

Tonight the waves march. Moonlight Night: Carmel. Langston Hughes. CP-HughL; CP-HughL2

Tonight, the young but rotten are on view. Young Hero Sings a Song of Self-Understanding, A. Christopher Logue. SP-LoguC *Fr.* Lily-White Boys, The.

Tonight, their simple church grown glamorous. Songs of Praise. Derek Mahon. CP-MahoD

Tonight there are only the winter stars. Dezembrum. Wallace Stevens. CP-StevW; CP-StevWP

Tonight There Is a Showing of Champion Lights. Thomas Merton. CP-MertT

Tonight there was something in the air. Rainer Maria Rilke. CP-RilkFr, *tr. by* A. Poulin, Jr. *Fr.* Orchards.

Tonight we are driving past Lac Qui Parle toward Boston. Driving toward Boston I Run across One of Robert Bly's Old Poems. Thomas McGrath. SP-McGrT

Tonight when all that flowers, on the air. Poem on Holy Saturday. Robert Stock. SP-StocR

Tonight / when you spread your pallet. Accident. Maya Angelou. SP-AngeM

Tonite all is well . . . What a / terrible future. I am twenty-three. Allen Ginsberg. CP-GinsA; SP-GinsA

Tonite I got hi in the window of my apartment. I Beg You Come Back & Be Cheerful. Allen Ginsberg. CP-GinsA

Tonite I walked out of my red apartment door on East tenth street's dusk. Mugging. Allen Ginsberg. CP-GinsA

Tonite I walked out of my red apartment door on East tenth street's dusk. Allen Ginsberg. SP-GinsA *Fr.* Mugging.

Too Anxious for Rivers. Robert Frost. CP-FrosR

Too Blue. Langston Hughes. CP-HughL; CP-HughL2

Too brief the sunlight when it smote. Twisted Tree, The. Marya Alexandrovna Zaturenska. SP-ZatuM

Too Busy. Paul Laurence Dunbar. *See* Get Somebody Else

Too calm to beg for pity yet too strained. Gaza. Jane Cooper. CP-CoopJ

Too cold almost for hope of spring. St. Valentine's Day 1881. Christina Georgina Rossetti. CP-RosC3

Too cold for joy, too cold for woe. George Meredith. CP-MerG2

Too cold is this. Emily Dickinson. CP-DickE

Too Dear, Too Vague. W. H. Auden. CP-AudeW

Too early fallen asleep here, I'm alive. Michelangelo Buonarroti. CP-Miche, *tr. by* John Frederick Nims

Too easy: to write of miracles, dreams where the famous give. Denise Levertov. SP-LeveDS

Too far away, O love, I know. Drunk. D. H. Lawrence. CP-LawrD

Too far for me to see. I Heard. Lorine Niedecker. CP-NiedL

Too few the mornings be. Emily Dickinson. CP-DickE

Too fierce the candlelight; your gentle voice. Measure of Casualness, A. Robert Graves. CP-GravR

Too frail for combat, he stands [*or* stood]. Aircraft. Rita Dove. SP-DoveR

Too frail to keep the lofty vow. Thoughts Suggested the Day Following, on the Banks of Nith, near the Poet's Residence. William Wordsworth. CP-WorW1

Too Full of Life. Charles Baudelaire. CP-BaudC, *tr. by* Walter Martin

Too good to be true—a city that empties. Rio de Janeiro. John Updike. CP-UpdiJ

Too happy Time dissolves itself. Emily Dickinson. CP-DickE

Too Late. Robert Browning. CP-BroR1

Too Late. Charles Bukowski. SP-BukC3

Too late, alas! the song. Rudyard Kipling. *See* What have we ever done to bear this grudge

Too late, and only because of what happened, we reread the poem and broke the code. Teachers, The. Gregory Orr. SP-OrrG

Too-Late Born, The. Archibald MacLeish. CP-MacLA

(Silent Slain, The.) CP-MacLA

Too late for Love to set my heart aflame. Michelangelo Buonarroti. CP-Miche, *tr. by* John Frederick Nims

Too late for peace. Devil As Friend, The. Laura Riding Jackson. CP-RidiL

Too late returns the measured sun and slow. Images on the Tomb. Robert Penn Warren. CP-WarrR

Too late the anxious fire came. Ralph Waldo Emerson. CP-EmerR

Too late, too late! I did not know my fairness. Beauty's Soliloquy during Her Honeymoon, A. Thomas Hardy. CP-HardT

Too limpid streets have grown narrow, The. Lament: "Too limpid streets have grown narrow, The." Tennessee Williams. CP-WillT

Too little. Door, The. Charles Tomlinson. CP-TomlC; SP-TomlC

Too little way the House must lie. Emily Dickinson. CP-DickE

Too long and quickly have I lived to vow. Transition. Dorothy Parker. CP-ParkD

Too long we lived for work and wages, we. Friedrich Hölderlin. SP-ZatuM, *tr. by* Marya Alexandrovna Zaturenska

Too many curds on the meat, too many dark cloth caps. Constant. Louis MacNeice. CP-MacNL

Too many echoes. Returning Home. "Shu Ting." CP-KizeC, *tr. by* Carolyn Kizer *and* Y. H. Zhao

Too many elegies. Too much memory. Smoke. Adam Zagajewski. SP-ZagaA, *tr. by* Clare Cavanagh

Too many olive trees in the valley. Yehuda Amichai. SP-AmicY, *tr. by* Stephen Mitchell

Too many years / Beatin' at the door. Down Where I Am. Langston Hughes. CP-HughL; CP-HughL3

Too much. Crunch, The. Charles Bukowski. SP-BukC1

Too much about death. Letter from a Reader. Adam Zagajewski. SP-ZagaA, *tr. by* Clare Cavanagh

Too much at first, too lavish—full moon. Venexia 1. Charles Wright. SP-WrigCN

Too much industry. Ruhr-Gebiet. Allen Ginsberg. CP-GinsA; SP-GinsA

Too much! the way he flaunts himself around. Michelangelo Buonarroti. CP-Miche, *tr. by* John Frederick Nims

Too Much to Hope. Denise Levertov. SP-LeveDL

Too much you mint me that cheating counterfeit. Aloof in Gaiety. D. H. Lawrence. CP-LawrD

Too old for love and still to love! Wild Old Wicked Man, The. Archibald MacLeish. CP-MacLA

Too pale! Too changed! Flowers to the House. Kenneth Patchen. CP-PatcK

Too peremptory a Courtship for Earth. Emily Dickinson. SP-DickE

Too poor for a bribe, and too proud to importune. Sketch of His Own Character. Thomas Gray. CP-GrayT

Too Pretty for Serious Business. Yusef Komunyakaa. CP-KomuY

Too proud to die; broken and blind he died. Elegy: "Too proud to die; broken and blind he died." Dylan Thomas. CP-ThomD

Too scanty 'twas to die for you. Emily Dickinson. CP-DickE

Too serious above his opened book. Tent, The. Wyatt Prunty. SP-PrunW

Too soon, too soon, a man will come. Two Horses Playing in the Orchard. James Wright. CP-WrigJ

Too soon you wearied of our tears. Darling Daughter of Babylon. Nicholas Vachel Lindsay. CP-LindV

Too Tenuous. Hayden Carruth. CP-CarHS

Too tight, it is running over. Fence Wire. James Dickey. CP-DickJ

Too tired to sleep I switch a picture on. Late Show. Miller Williams. CP-WillM

Too unfaithful mouth, my blunt will. Divine Disgrace. Rainer Maria Rilke. CP-RilkFr, tr. by A. Poulin, Jr.

Took. Kenneth Rexroth. CP-RexrK

Took my leave (last) five times before the end. In Memoriam (1914–1953). John Berryman. CP-BerrJ

Tool. W. S. Merwin. SP-MerwW

Tooling Up. A. R. Ammons. CP-AmmoA

Toomai of the Elephants. Rudyard Kipling. Fr. Jungle Book, The.

Toome. Seamus Heaney. SP-HeanSO

Toome Road, The. Seamus Heaney. SP-HeanSO

Tooth-Ache Cured by a Kiss, The. Thomas Carew. CP-CareT

Tooth upon Our Peace, A. Emily Dickinson. CP-DickE

Toothache Man. John Updike. CP-UpdiJ

Toothbrush lies in its case, The. Nocturne: Traveling Salesman in Hotel Bedroom. Robert Penn Warren. CP-WarrR

Tooting down the Gran Via. Madrid, May, 1977. Mona Van Duyn. SP-VanDM

Top of the fountain jet. Grand Design, The. Philip Whalen. SP-WhalP

Top of the mountain, The. Thinking. Robert Creeley. CP-CreeR

Top of the ridge is a cornfield, The. Cornfield Ridge and Stream. Carl Sandburg. CP-SandC

Top-turfy gimp fiery oes eyes. Queen Anne's Lace. Louis Zukofsky. CP-ZukLS

Topaz extra: that's *stoned*. School Daze. Andrei Codrescu. SP-CodrA

Tophet. Thomas Gray. CP-GrayT

(Thus Tophet look'd; so grinned the brawling fiend.) CP-GrayT

Topical questions. News of the World. Robert Creeley. SP-CreeR

Topics. James Merrill. SP-MerrJ

Topmost leaves of young oak. July 1968. Denise Levertov. SP-LeveDS

Topography of History, The. Thomas McGrath. SP-McGrT

Toppled wine-cup, A. Bits of Reminiscence. "Shu Ting." CP-KizeC, tr. by Carolyn Kizer and Y. H. Zhao

Tops. Philip Larkin. CP-LarkP

Tops heel and yaw. Tops. Philip Larkin. CP-LarkP

Tops of the higher peaks, The. Blues. Kenneth Rexroth. CP-RexrK

Tops of the midnight trees move helter-skelter. Window. Robert Lowell. SP-LoweR

Topsfield Fair. John Updike. CP-UpdiJ

Tor House. Robinson Jeffers. CP-JefR1

Torch, The. Walt Whitman. CP-WhitW

Torch and Crown, 1968. Robert Graves. CP-GravR

Torch-Bearers' Race, The. Robinson Jeffers. CP-JefR1

Torches in the windy corridors, The. Huon of Bordeaux. Robert Duncan. SP-DuncR

Tormented like your destiny. Sympathetic Horror. Charles Baudelaire. CP-BaudC, tr. by Walter Martin

Tormented with incessant pains. To Stella. Jonathan Swift. CP-SwifJ

Torn boughs trailing o'er the tusks aslant, The. Rudyard Kipling. CP-KiplR

Torn Down from Glory Daily. Anne Sexton. CP-SextA

Torn feet and cursed earth. Buna. Primo Levi. CP-LeviP, tr. by Ruth Feldman and Brian Swann

Torn Flower, The. Jones Very. CP-VeryJ

Torn from the dream-life, torn from the life-dream. Midnight Outcry. Robert Penn Warren. CP-WarrR

Torn from your parent bough. Leaf, The. Giacomo Leopardi. CW-RossD, tr. by Dante Gabriel Rossetti

Torn hillside with its crooked hands, The. Description of Some Confederate Soldiers, A. Randall Jarrell. CP-JarrR

Torn into light, you woke wriggling. How Much Earth. Philip Levine. SP-LeviP

Torn Letter, The. Thomas Hardy. CP-HardT

Torn Shades. Thomas Lux. SP-LuxT

Torn-up newspaper, The. Perfectly Free Association, A. Randall Jarrell. CP-JarrR

Torn wings of flame are wafting down the sky. Fall of Day, The. D. H. Lawrence. CP-LawrD

Tornado Warning. Karl Shapiro. SP-ShapK

Törnfallet. Joseph Brodsky. CP-BrodJ

Torpor and sloth, torpor and sloth. Procrastination Is All of the Time. Ogden Nash. CP-NashO

Torquato Tasso rests within this tomb. Gabriello Chiabrera. CP-WorW1

Torquemada. Stevie Smith. CP-SmitS

Torrent, The. Edwin Arlington Robinson. CP-RobiE

Torrent that rushes down. Song from *Puck Fair*. Muriel Rukeyser. CP-RukeM

Torso. Joseph Brodsky. CP-BrodJ, tr. by Howard Moss

Torso, The. Robert Duncan. SP-DuncR Fr. Passages.

Tortoise, The. Ogden Nash. CP-NashO

Tortoise, The. Dan Pagis. SP-PagiD, tr. by Stephen Mitchell

Tortoise Family Connections. D. H. Lawrence. CP-LawrD

Tortoise Gallantry. D. H. Lawrence. CP-LawrD

Tortoise is dreaming of a leaf of lettuce, The. Dream of the Old Tortoise, The. Wisława Szymborska. SP-SzymWM, tr. by Joanna Trzeciak

Tortoise-Shell. D. H. Lawrence. CP-LawrD

Tortoise Shout. D. H. Lawrence. CP-LawrD

Torture. Margaret Atwood. SP-AtwM2

Torture. Raymond Carver. CP-CarvR

Torture. Wisława Szymborska. SP-SzymWM, tr. by Joanna Trzeciak

Torture. Alice Walker. CP-WalkA

Tortured, The. May Sarton. SP-SartM

Tortured Heart. Arthur Rimbaud. CP-RimbA, tr. by Martin Sorrell

Tortures. Wisława Szymborska. SP-SzymW, tr. by Stanisław Barańczak and Clare Cavanagh

Toss, for John Cage, A. Charles Olson. CP-OlsoC

Tossed / by the muscular sea. Swimmers. May Swenson. SP-SwenM

Tossed [or Toss'd] in a troubled sea of griefs, I float. To Her in Absence; a Ship. Thomas Carew. CP-CareT

Tossing and Turning. John Updike. CP-UpdiJ

Tossing loneliness of many nights, The. Legende. Hart Crane. CP-CranH

Tossing spray of Cocheco's fall, The. How the Women Went from Dover. John Greenleaf Whittier. CP-WhitJ

Tossup. A. R. Ammons. CP-AmmoA

Total Harmony. Charles Baudelaire. CP-BaudC, tr. by Walter Martin

Total Parts of a World, The. Robert Creeley. CP-CreeR

Total stranger one black day, A. E. E. Cummings. CP-CummE

Total War. Langston Hughes. CP-HughL; CP-HughL3

Totally abashed and smiling. St. Paul and All That. Frank O'Hara. SP-OharF

Totally conscious, and apropos of nothing, you come to see me. Be Melting Snow. Jelaluddin Rumi. SP-Rumi, tr. by Coleman Barks

Totem. Sylvia Plath. CP-PlatS

Totem, The. Rudyard Kipling. CP-KiplR

Totonac and Colonial. Farewell to Baedeker. Robert Stock. SP-StocR

Tottering and elastic, middle name of Groan. Pedestrian. Thomas Lux. SP-LuxT

Tou Wan Speaks to Her Husband Liu Sheng. Rita Dove. SP-DoveR

Touch. Thom Gunn. CP-GunnT

Touch. Yusef Komunyakaa. CP-KomuY

Touch. D. H. Lawrence. CP-LawrD

Touch, The. Anne Sexton. CP-SextA

Touch-and-Go. Sylvia Plath. CP-PlatS

Touch and Go. Stevie Smith. CP-SmitS

Touch but thy lyre, my Harry, and I hear. To M. Henry Lawes, the Excellent Composer[,] of his Lyrics. Robert Herrick. CP-HerrR

Touch Comes. D. H. Lawrence. CP-LawrD

Touch gently / with the tips of their. Saleswomen in Bakery Shops. Mona Van Duyn. SP-VanDM

Touch it: it won't shrink like an eyeball. Life, A. Sylvia Plath. CP-PlatS

Touch lightly Nature's sweet Guitar. Emily Dickinson. CP-DickE

Touch Me. Stanley Kunitz. CP-KunSC

Touch me: it is the softness of good satin, and when you open me, what an unexpected rose! Fig, The. Gabriela Mistral. SP-MistG, tr. by Maria Giachetti [or Jacketti]

Touch me not forget me not, touch me forget me. Children's Games. Louis MacNeice. CP-MacNL

Touch My Shut Lips. Robert Graves. CP-GravR

Touch of flame—the illuminating fire—the loftiest look at last, The. Old Age's Lambent Peaks. Walt Whitman. CP-WhitW

Touch of Loving Hands, The. James Whitcomb Riley. CP-RileJ

Touch of Spring. John Updike. CP-UpdiJ

Touch of vocal flattery. Drowse Murmurs. Allen Ginsberg. CP-GinsA

Touch-up Man. Yusef Komunyakaa. CP-KomuY

Touched. Olga Broumas. SP-BrouO

Touched by fire, / Holding the light in my hand. Prometheus. Richard Eberhart. CP-EberR

Touched with the sin of false play, in his punk. On Captain Hazard the Cheater. Ben Jonson. CP-JonsB; SP-JonsB

Touches of her hands are like the fall, The. Dear Hands. James Whitcomb Riley. CP-RileJ

Touching. James Laughlin. CP-LaugJ

Touching Down. A. R. Ammons. CP-AmmoA

Touching "Never." Christina Georgina Rossetti. CP-RosC2

Touching sight, these relics rude, A. Indian Relics. Jones Very. CP-VeryJ

Touching the River. Thomas Kinsella. CP-KinsT

Touching you i say(it being Spring). E. E. Cummings. CP-CummE

Touching your goodness, I am like a man. Illiterate, The. William Meredith. SP-MereW

Touchstone. Robert Creeley. SP-CreeR

Touchstone—Watching Malvern, The. Ivor Gurney. SP-GurnI

Tough branch stems blue. Up in Michigan. Philip Whalen. SP-WhalP

Tough guy. Star of David. Cabdriver's Smile, The. Denise Levertov. SP-LeveDL

Tour, The. Rudyard Kipling. CP-KiplR *Fr.* Muse among the Motors, The.

Tour, The. Sylvia Plath. CP-PlatS

Tour 5. Robert Earl Hayden. CP-HaydR

Tour Guide. Yusef Komunyakaa. CP-KomuY

Tourist. Yehuda Amichai. SP-AmicYL, *tr. by* Benjamin Harshav *and* Barbara Harshav

Tourist and the Town, The. Adrienne Rich. CP-RicAE; SP-RicA2

Tourist Death. Archibald MacLeish. CP-MacLA

Tourist Eye. George Oppen. CP-OppGN

Tourist Poem. Alan Dugan. CP-DugaA

Touristic Note from the Gulf. Alan Dugan. CP-DugaA

Tourists. Yehuda Amichai. SP-AmicY, *tr by* Chana Bloch

Tourists. Yehuda Amichai. SP-AmicYL, *tr. by* Benjamin Harshav *and* Barbara Harshav

Tourists. D. H. Lawrence. CP-LawrD

Tourists at Ensenada. Thomas McGrath. SP-McGrT

Tourists in summer, looking at the view. Sand Man, The. Thom Gunn. CP-GunnT

Tourmaline plashing in a noose of reeds. Trasimene. Amy Clampitt. CP-ClamA

Tousled Pillow. Robert Graves. CP-GravR

Toussaint L'Ouverture. John Greenleaf Whittier. CP-WhitJ

Toussaint, the most unhappy man of men! To Toussaint L'Ouverture. William Wordsworth. CP-WorW1; MW-WorW

"*Tout ce qui existe est situé*" said max jacob and one day my situation. History of the Growth of Heaven, The ("'*Tout ce qui existe est situé*' said max jacob and one day my situation"). Andrei Codrescu. SP-CodrA

Tout Entouré de Mon Regard. Charles Tomlinson. CP-TomlC

Tow generations bridge or part us. Song: The Queen of Time. Robert Graves. CP-GravR

Tow Head on his skateboard. Skateboard. Thom Gunn. CP-GunnT

Toward a Definition of Marriage. Mona Van Duyn. SP-VanDM

Toward an Organic Philosophy. Kenneth Rexroth. CP-RexrK

Toward an Understanding. Heather McHugh. SP-McHuH

Toward August's end. Calendar. John Updike. CP-UpdiJ

Toward Climax. Gary Snyder. CP-SnydG

Toward countries that ripen the mustard. Runaway Sun. Pablo Neruda. SP-NeruP

Toward evening the wind changes. Boats. Net, The. Raymond Carver. CP-CarvR

Toward Home. Dan Pagis. SP-PagiD, *tr. by* Stephen Mitchell

Toward Rationality. Robert Penn Warren. CP-WarrR

Toward Saint Looey. James Tate. SP-TateJ

Towards the dawn, when *l'aura* (the mild breeze). Petrarch. CP-Petra, *tr. by* J. G. Nichols

Toward the End. William Stafford. SP-StafWW

Toward the end of April, for an idyllic. Isle of Wight, The. Amy Clampitt. CP-ClamA

Toward the End of 1969. Andrei Codrescu. SP-CodrA

Toward the end of the war, I brought from the Negev to the wine cellar. Itzhak's Last Kit Bag. Yehuda Amichai. SP-AmicYL, *tr. by* Benjamin Harshav *and* Barbara Harshav

Toward the person who has died. Dying Away. William Meredith. SP-MereW

Toward the Piraeus. "H. D." CP-DoolH

Toward the sun the drenched May-hedges lift. Incense Bearers, The. Ivor Gurney. SP-GurnI

Toward the Valley. Primo Levi. CP-LeviP, *tr. by* Ruth Feldman

Toward What? Yannis Ritsos. SP-RitsY, *tr. by* Kimon Friar

Toward world's end, through the bare. Magi, The. Louise Glück. SP-GlucL

Towards. Federico García Lorca. CP-GarcF, *tr. by* Jerome Rothenberg *Fr.* Return, The.

Towards. Thomas Lux. SP-LuxT

Towards a Relative Ending. Wyatt Prunty. SP-PrunW

Towards Autumn. Marilyn Hacker. SP-HackM

Towards Break of Day. William Butler Yeats. CP-YeatW

Towards Eternal Peace. Hans Magnus Enzensberger. SP-EnzeH

Towards nightfall when the wind. Winter Mask. Allen Tate. CP-TateA

Towards not being / anyone else's center. Movement. Denise Levertov. SP-LeveDL

Towards Simplicity. A. K. Ramanujan. CP-RamaA

Towards sleep I came. Bird Sanctuary. Derek Mahon. CP-MahoD

Towards the end he sailed into an extraordinary mildness. Herman Melville. W. H. Auden. CP-AudeW

Towards the Noel that morte saison. Villonaud for This Yule. Ezra Pound. CP-PoEar; SP-PounE

Towards the sun, towards the south-west. Eagle in New Mexico. D. H. Lawrence. CP-LawrD

Towards Tucson. James Vincent Cunningham. CP-CunnJ

Towards you. Towards. Thomas Lux. SP-LuxT

Tower. Federico García Lorca. CP-GarcF, *tr. by* Jerome Rothenberg *Fr.* In the Forest of the Lunar Grapefruits.

Tower. Langston Hughes. CP-HughL; CP-HughL1

Tower, The. William Butler Yeats. CP-YeatW

Tower, The. Randall Jarrell. CP-JarrR

Tower, The. Dan Pagis. SP-PagiD, *tr. by* Stephen Mitchell

Tower beyond Tragedy, The. Robinson Jeffers. CP-JefR1

Tower in tiers of architraves, The. Pisa's Leaning Tower. Herman Melville. SP-MelvH

Tower is broken, the house, The. La Torre. Charles Olson. CP-OlsoC

Tower of Babel. Thomas Merton. CP-MertT

Tower of Babel—A Morality, The. Thomas Merton. CP-MertT

Tower of Babel, The. Wisława Szymborska. SP-SzymW, *tr. by* Stanislaw Barańczak *and* Clare Cavanagh

Tower of Famine, The. Percy Bysshe Shelley. CP-ShelP

Tower of Love, The. Robert Graves. CP-GravR

Tower of the Spirit, The. Chuang Tzu. CP-MertT

Tower says: "up to here," The. Day Poems. Federico García Lorca. CP-GarcF, *tr. by* Jerome Rothenberg

Tower there is, where six Maidens do dwell, A. Six Maidens, The. Alexander Pope. CP-PopeA

Towering cliffs were the home I chose. Han-shan. CP-ColdM, *tr. by* Red Pine

Towering wall divides your house from mine, A. Wall, The. Robert Graves. CP-GravR

Towers look across. Prime. James McMichael. SP-McMiJ

Towers of God! Poets!" Rubén Dario." SP-DariR, *tr. by* Alberto Acereda *and* Will Derusha

Towers of Silence, The. Eleanor Wilner. SP-WilnE

Towers of Time, The. G. K. Chesterton. CP-ChesG

Towers that generations did combine, The. Van Buren. Ralph Waldo Emerson. CP-EmerR

Tower's the thing snatching his cowled eyes, The. Cathedral, The. Robert Stock. SP-StocR

Towers waited, shimmering just, The. Iphigenia, Setting the Record Straight. Eleanor Wilner. SP-WilnE

Towers, walls, thatched huts. Rainer Maria Rilke. CP-RilkR, *tr. by* A. Poulin, Jr. *Fr.* Valaisian Quatrains, The.

Towery city and branchy between towers. Duns Scotus's Oxford. Gerard Manley Hopkins. CP-HopkG

Town, The. Charles Olson. CP-OlsoC

Town, a town. George Oppen. CP-OppGN

Town and Country. James Whitcomb Riley. CP-RileJ

Town band, swaying dreamily on its feet, The. Siena in Sixty-Eight. Charles Tomlinson. SP-TomlC

Town Chief fasting for rain, The. Tewa Victories. Clarence Major. SP-MajoC

Town does not exist, The. Starry Night, The. Anne Sexton. CP-SextA; SP-SextA

Town Down the River, The. Edwin Arlington Robinson. CP-RobiE

Town Dump. Howard Nemerov. CP-NemeH

Town Eclogue, A. Jonathan Swift. CP-SwifJ

Town grows fiercer with heat!, The. Labour Battalion. D. H. Lawrence. CP-LawrD

Town has opened to the sun, The. Bombardment. D. H. Lawrence. CP-LawrD

Town in 1917. D. H. Lawrence. CP-LawrD

Town is never silent, The. No matter what time it is there is always someone talking. Silence. Andrei Codrescu. SP-CodrA

Town Karnteel, The. James Whitcomb Riley. CP-RileJ

Town Karnteel!—It's who'll reveal, The. Town Karnteel, The. James Whitcomb Riley. CP-RileJ

Town of American Visions, The. Nicholas Vachel Lindsay. CP-LindV

Town of Hill, The. Donald Hall. CP-HallD

Town of Scottsboro, The. Langston Hughes. CP-HughL; CP-HughL1

Town, the churchyard, and the setting sun, The. On Visiting the Tomb of Burns. John Keats. CP-KeatJ

Town where I was born, Radautz, in the county of Bukovina, The. Souvenir, The. Dan Pagis. SP-PagiD, *tr. by* Stephen Mitchell

Townend, 1976. Donald Davie. CP-DaviDC

Townhouse Interior with Cat. Amy Clampitt. CP-ClamA

Towns Become Jewels. Tennessee Williams. CP-WillT

Townspeople, those Dr. Williams loved and despised, The. Fourth. Hayden Carruth. CP-CarHS

Tow'r of brass, whose doors were barr'd, A. Ode 3.16: To Maecenas. Horace. SP-SmarC *Fr.* Odes.

Toy-Balloon, The. James Whitcomb Riley. CP-RileJ

Toy Bone, The. Donald Hall. CP-HallD

Toy Factory. Charles Simic. SP-SimiC; SP-SimiCE

Toy-Maker Ptolemy. Some Sort of Game. John Ciardi. CP-CiarJ

Toy Penny-Dog, The. James Whitcomb Riley. CP-RileJ

Toys. Rainer Maria Rilke. CP-RilkFr, *tr.* by A. Poulin, Jr.

Toys in a Field. Yusef Komunyakaa. CP-KomuY

Toys of an only God, The. Yehuda Amichai. SP-AmicY, *tr.* by Chana Bloch *Fr.* Songs of Zion the Beautiful.

Trace of a bite in Nowhere, The. Paul Celan. SP-CelaP, *tr.* by John Felstiner

Traces. A. K. Ramanujan. CP-RamaA

Traces of Living Things. Lorine Niedecker. CP-NiedL

Traces that met in the sand were erased. At the Seashore. Yehuda Amichai. SP-AmicYL, *tr.* by Benjamin Harshav *and* Barbara Harshav

Tracings around my edges, The? Nerve, The. Clarence Major. SP-MajoC

Track. Richard Eberhart. CP-EberR

Track, The. W. S. Merwin. SP-MerwW

Track across the desert runs vague toward the north star and then more firmly, The. Dead Men's Child, The. Robinson Jeffers. CP-JefR1

Track cuts west. Slant roof, sun-catcher, The. Muriel Rukeyser. CP-RukeM

Track of moonlight on a quiet lake, A. In Peace. John Greenleaf Whittier. CP-WhitJ

Track of the Deer, The. Charles Tomlinson. SP-TomlC

Track of the ermine, The. In the Snow. James Laughlin. CP-LaugJ

Track of the Master Builder, The. Marge Piercy. SP-PierM

Tracking through this. Love ("Tracking through this"). Robert Creeley. CP-CreeR

Trackless and lost between piss colored walls. His Wife at Bellevue. Marilyn Hacker. SP-HackM *Fr.* Navigators, The.

Tracks of rain and light linger in. Romance Moderne. William Carlos Williams. CP-WilW1

Tract. Paul Muldoon. CP-MuldP

Tract. William Carlos Williams. CP-WilW1

Tractatus. Derek Mahon. CP-MahoD

Tractor. Ted Hughes. SP-HughTN

Tractor stands frozen—an agony, The. Tractor. Ted Hughes. SP-HughTN

Tractor-trailer carrying two dozen crushed automobiles overtakes a tractor-trailer carrying a dozen new, A. Sheffield Ghazal 4: Driving West. Galway Kinnell. SP-KinnGN

Trade, The. Rudyard Kipling. CP-KiplR

Trade, The. Gary Snyder. CP-SnydG

Trade-wind jingles the rings in the nets around the racks by the docks on Indian River, The. Indian River. Wallace Stevens. CP-StevW; CP-StevWP

Trader I am to the African shore, A. Sweet Meat Has Sour Sauce. William Cowper. CP-CowpW

Traders, parsons, and stoolpigeons. Value Neuter. Kenneth Rexroth. CP-RexrK

Trades scant aware is plentiful. Zebrina etc. Louis Zukofsky. CP-ZukLS

Tradin' Joe. James Whitcomb Riley. CP-RileJ

Tradition. William Wordsworth. CP-WorW2 *Fr.* River Duddon [A Series of Sonnets], The.

Tradition. Lorine Niedecker. CP-NiedL

Tradition. Wallace Stevens. CP-StevWP

Tradition of Oker Hill in Darley Dale, Derbyshire, A. William Wordsworth. CP-WorW2

Tradition, thou art for suckling children. Stephen Crane. CP-CranS

Traditional Tune. Muriel Rukeyser. CP-RukeM

Traditionalist, The. Robert Graves. CP-GravR

Traditon, be thou mute! Oblivion, throw. In the Sound of Mull. William Wordsworth. CP-WorW2

Traditore, traduttore—spare us! Balancing Acts. Donald Davie. CP-DaviDC

Trafalgar Day. George Meredith. CP-MerG2

Traffic. Andrei Codrescu. SP-CodrA

Traffic. Donald Hall. CP-HallD

Traffic in Sheets. Ivor Gurney. SP-GurnI

Traffic Signals. Charles Bukowski. SP-BukC1

Traffic, the lion, the sophisticate. Lion, The. William Carlos Williams. CP-WilW2

Traffic, to speak from knowledge but begun. To the Great Metropolis. Arthur Hugh Clough. SP-ClouA

Traffic Victim Sends a Sonnet of Confused Thanks to God as the Sovereign Host, A. John Ciardi. CP-CiarJ

Trafficker. Carl Sandburg. CP-SandC

Tragedian to Tragedienne. Thomas Hardy. CP-HardT

Tragedie of the Cardinall, The. Sir David Lyndsay. SP-LyndD

Tragedy. D. H. Lawrence. CP-LawrD

Tragedy Comes to the Bad Lands. James Tate. SP-TateJ

Tragedy-Maker, The. John Ciardi. CP-CiarJ

Tragedy of Bricks, The. Galway Kinnell. SP-KinnGN

Tragedy of that moment, The. That Moment. Thomas Hardy. CP-HardT

Tragedy of Time, The. James Laughlin. CP-LaugJ

Tragedy seems to me a loud noise. Tragedy. D. H. Lawrence. CP-LawrD

Tragedy's Greatest Hits. James Tate. SP-TateJ

Tragic Detail. William Carlos Williams. CP-WilW2

Tragic man stares at the sun, The. Cloud Seeding. Howard Nemerov. CP-NemeH

Trail into Kansas, The. W. S. Merwin. SP-MerwW

Trail of Admiral Keppel, The. William Cowper. CP-CowpW

Trail to Cold Mountain is faint, The. Han-shan. CP-ColdM, *tr.* by Red Pine

Trailed and lagging grass, a pin-point island, A. Logic. Charles Tomlinson. CP-TomlC

Trailer, a bubble of aluminum and glass, The. Depth of Field, A. Norman Dubie. CP-DubiN

Trailing Arbutus, The. John Greenleaf Whittier. CP-WhitJ

Trailing the bill of a mallard. Fanny Howe. SP-HoweF *Fr.* Lines Out to Silence.

Trail's high up on the ridge, no one goes down, The. Love-Children. Robinson Jeffers. CP-JefR1

Train, The. Norman Dubie. CP-DubiN

Train, The. D. H. Lawrence. CP-LawrD

Train, The. Paul Muldoon. CP-MuldP

Train at Night, A. D. H. Lawrence. CP-LawrD

Train carries me swiftly by, yet, The. Landscape, Without Color. Charles Olson. CP-OlsoC

Train draws forth from the station-yard, The. Love the Monopolist. Thomas Hardy. CP-HardT

Train Going By. Robert Creeley. SP-CreeR

Train, in running across the weald, has fallen into a steadier stroke, The. Red Moon-Rise. D. H. Lawrence. CP-LawrD

Train leaps toward Italy, the French Riviera, The. Losing Track of Language. Amy Clampitt. CP-ClamA

Train-Misser, The. James Whitcomb Riley. CP-RileJ

Train of gay and clouded days, A. Life. Ralph Waldo Emerson. CP-EmerR

Train pursued by oleanders, A. Poems of the Hot Wind. Yehuda Amichai. SP-AmicYL, *tr.* by Benjamin Harshav *and* Barbara Harshav

Train Ride. Federico García Lorca. CP-GarcF, *tr.* by Jerome Rothenberg

Train Rising Out of the Sea. John Ashbery. SP-AshbJ

Train slows down, The. Arrival and Departure. Archibald MacLeish. CP-MacLA

Train Stop. Clarence Major. SP-MajoC

Train stopped in a field; the sudden silence, The. Opus Posthumous. Adam Zagajewski. SP-ZagaA, *tr.* by Clare Cavanagh

Train stops. The. Train Stop. Clarence Major. SP-MajoC

Train to Dublin. Louis MacNeice. CP-MacNL

Train Tune. Louise Bogan. CP-BogaL

Train went through a burial gate, A. Emily Dickinson. CP-DickE

Trained in tactics, war games, cold war, cold feet. Oh General, Oh Spy, Oh Bureaucrat! Wyatt Prunty. SP-PrunW

Training. Wilfred Owen. CP-OwenW

Training for Kid Aztec. Charles Bukowski. SP-BukC3

Trains. Andrei Codrescu. SP-CodrA

Trains came threading quietly through my dozing childhood. Trains in the Distance. Louis MacNeice. CP-MacNL

Trains in the Distance. Louis MacNeice. CP-MacNL

Trains pass and the trains pass, chains of lighted windows, The. Contact, A. Louis MacNeice. CP-MacNL

Trains run on emotion not. Trains. Andrei Codrescu. SP-CodrA

Traitoring *words*, tearing my thought across. John Berryman. *See* Treacherous *words,*—tearing my thought across

Traitors. D. H. Lawrence. CP-LawrD

Traitors tho' plumed & steel equipped. Ralph Waldo Emerson. CP-EmerR

Trajectory of a Scream. Robert Stock. SP-StocR

Trajectory of the Traveling Susan. Marge Piercy. SP-PierM

Trakl. Norman Dubie. CP-DubiN

Trala Trala Trala La-le-la. William Carlos Williams. CP-WilW2

Tramontana at Lerici. Charles Tomlinson. CP-TomlC; SP-TomlC

Tramp, The. John Clare. SP-ClarJ

Tramp thawing out, A. Sun Bathers, The. William Carlos Williams. CP-WilW1

Trampled yet red is the last of the embers. To Captain Fryatt. G. K. Chesterton. CP-ChesG

Tramps. Arthur Rimbaud. CP-RimbA, *tr.* by Martin Sorrell

Tramp's Refusal, The. Nicholas Vachel Lindsay. CP-LindV

Trampwoman's Tragedy, A. Thomas Hardy. CP-HardT

Trance. "H. D." CP-DoolH

Trance. Paul Muldoon. CP-MuldP

Trance, The. Stephen Spender. CP-SpenS

Tranced, The. Theodore Roethke. CP-RoetT

Tranced in the glamour of a dream. Loving Cup, The. James Whitcomb Riley. CP-RileJ

Tranquil sea behind the windowpanes, A. A poem expected. Extinction. Yannis Ritsos. SP-RitsY, *tr.* by Kimon Friar *and* Kostas Myrsiades

Tranquility at length, when autumn comes. Edna St. Vincent Millay. CP-MillE

Tranquillity! thou better name. Ode to Tranquillity. Samuel Taylor Coleridge. CP-ColeS

Transaction. A. R. Ammons. CP-AmmoA

Transatlantic. Joseph Brodsky. CP-BrodJ

Transcendence. Charles Baudelaire. CP-BaudC, *tr.* by Walter Martin

Transcendental Etude. Adrienne Rich. SP-RicA1; SP-RicA2

Transcendentalism: A Poem in Twelve Books. Robert Browning. CP-BroR1

Transcontinent. Donald Hall. CP-HallD

Transcribed Conversation in Praise of Cows. Alan Dugan. CP-DugaA

Transcription of Organ Music. Allen Ginsberg. CP-GinsA

Transcriptions from the "Anacreontea." Robert Browning. CP-BroR2

Transducer. A. R. Ammons. CP-AmmoA

Transfer. A. R. Ammons. CP-AmmoA

Transfer, The. Richard Eberhart. CP-EberR

Transference bird of little mind has risen high, The. Autumn. James Tate. SP-TateJ

Transfiguration, The. Robert Herrick. CP-HerrR

Transfiguration: Natura Naturans. Robert Stock. SP-StocR

Transfigured Bird. James Merrill. SP-MerrJ

Transfigured Life. Dante Gabriel Rossetti. CW-RossD *Fr.* House of Life, The.

Transformation. Raymond Carver. CP-CarvR

Transformation. Alan Dugan. CP-DugaA

Transformation. Richard Eberhart. CP-EberR

Transformation. Adam Zagajewski. SP-ZagaA, *tr.* by Clare Cavanagh

Transformation, The. John Logan. CP-LogaJ

Transformation and Disfiguration. Charles Bukowski. SP-BukC3

Transformation: For the Sacred Heart, The. Thomas Merton. CP-MertT

Transformation of objects in space, / or objects in time, The. Basic Dialogue. Charles Wright. SP-WrigCN

Transformations. Thomas Hardy. CP-HardT

Transformations. Stanley Kunitz. CP-KunSC

Transformations. D. H. Lawrence. CP-LawrD

Transformations. Jaroslav Seifert. SP-SeifJ, *tr.* by Ewald Osers

Transformed in show, but more transformed in mind. Sir Philip Sidney. SP-SidnP *Fr.* Arcadia.

Transgress, The. Muriel Rukeyser. CP-RukeM

Transgression, A. Seamus Heaney. SP-HeanSO

Transient Barracks. Randall Jarrell. CP-JarrR

Transients and Residents. Thom Gunn. CP-GunnT

Transients Welcome. Gregory Orr. SP-OrrG

Transit. John Berryman. CP-BerrJ

Transit. Adrienne Rich. SP-RicA1; SP-RicA2

Transit. Richard Wilbur. CP-WilbR

Transition. Lorine Niedecker. CP-NiedL

Transition. Dorothy Parker. CP-ParkD

Transitional. William Carlos Williams. CP-WilW1

Transitive body this fresco amen I mouth. Vowel Imprint. Olga Broumas. SP-BrouO

Translated from Ronsard. Pierre de Ronsard. CP-KeatJ, *tr.* by John Keats

Translated from Silence. Robert Stock. SP-StocR

Translating. A. R. Ammons. CP-AmmoA

Translating Anna Swir on an Island of the Caribbean. Czeslaw Milosz. CP-MiloCN, *tr.* by Robert Hass

Translating Footsteps. Yusef Komunyakaa. CP-KomuY

Translating the Birds. Charles Tomlinson. CP-TomlC

Translation. Carolyn Kizer. CP-KizeC

Translation. Howard Nemerov. CP-NemeH

Translation. Grace Paley. CP-PalGC

Translation. William Carlos Williams. CP-WilW2

Translation, A. James Laughlin. CP-LaugJ

Translation, A. Charles Olson. CP-OlsoC

Translation, The. Louis Zukofsky. CP-ZukLS

Translation from a Pantomime Version of Benserade's *Ballet de Cassandre*. Samuel Johnson. *See* I Am Cassander Come Down From the Sky

Translation from Anacreon. Lord Byron. CP-Byron

Translation from Catullus. Catullus. *See* Carmina

Translation from Horace. Lord Byron. CP-Byron

Translation from Petrarch. Petrarch. CP-WyatT

Translation from Pindar's Seventh Olympian, Epode III. Robert Browning. CP-BroR2

Translation from the Medea of Euripides. Lord Byron. CP-Byron

Translation from Vittorelli. Jacopo Vittorelli. CP-Byron, *tr.* by Lord Byron

Translation of a Celebrated Greek Song. William Wordsworth. CP-WorW1

Translation of a Distich on the Duke of Modena. Samuel Johnson. *See* Comets and Princes

Translation of a Greek Ode on Astronomy. Samuel Taylor Coleridge. CP-ColeS

Translation of a Hymn of St. Francis Xavier. Saint Francis Xavier. CP-PopeA

Translation of a Passage in Ottfried's Metrical Paraphrase of the Gospel. Samuel Taylor Coleridge. CP-ColeS

Translation of a Simile in Paradise Lost. John Milton. CP-CowpW

Translation of Addison's Pugmaiogeranomachia; The Battle of the Pygmies and Cranes. Samuel Johnson. CP-JohnS

Translation of Anacreon's *Dove* (Ode ix). Samuel Johnson. *See* Anacreon's Dove

Translation of Benserade's Verses *À Son Lit*. Isaac de Benserade. *See* Translation of Lines by Benserade

Translation of Dryden's Poem on Milton. John Dryden. CP-CowpW

Translation of Du Bellay's *Epigram on a Dog*. Samuel Johnson. CP-JohnS

Translation of Epitaph to Northcot. William Cowper. CP-CowpW

Translation of Horace "Epode the 2d" ("Beatus Ille"). Horace. CP-JohnS *Fr.* Epodes.

Translation of Horace: Epode xi. Horace. CP-JohnS *Fr.* Epodes.

Translation of Horace *Odes* IV vii ("Diffugere nives"), Horace. *See* Odes

Translation of Lines by Benserade. Isaac de Benserade. CP-JohnS, *tr.* by Samuel Johnson

(Translation of Benserade's Verses *À Son Lit*.) CP-JohnS, *tr.* by Samuel Johnson

Translation of Lines in Baretti's *Easy Phraseology*. Samuel Johnson. CP-JohnS

Translation of Part of the Dialogue Between Hector and Andromach; from the Sixth Book of Homer's *Iliad* (VI 390–502). Homer. CP-JohnS *Fr.* Iliad, The.

Translation of Prior's Chloe and Euphelia. Matthew Prior. CP-CowpW

Translation of the Beginning of *Rio Verde*. Samuel Johnson. CP-JohnS

Translation of the Epitaph on Virgil and Tibullus. Lord Byron. CP-Byron

Translation of the Famous Greek War Song *Deute Paides Tov Ellenon*. Lord Byron. CP-Byron

Translation of the Latin Epitaph on Sir Thomas Hanmer, Written by Doctor Freind, A. Samuel Johnson. CP-JohnS

Translation of the Romaic Song *Mpeno mes to periboli, Horaiotate Haide, k. t. l.* Lord Byron. CP-Byron

Translation of Verses to Lloyd. William Cowper. CP-CowpW

Translation of Virgil: Pastoral I. Virgil. CP-JohnS *Fr.* Pastorals.

Translation of Virgil: Pastoral V. Virgil. CP-JohnS *Fr.* Pastorals.

Translations. Adrienne Rich. SP-RicA2

Translations from Heine. Heinrich Heine. CP-PoEar, *tr.* by Ezra Pound

Translations from Metastasio. Pietro Metastasio. CP-JohnS *Fr.* La Clemenza di Tito.

Translations from Metastasio. Pietro Metastasio. CP-JohnS *Fr.* Adriano in Syria.

Translations from the *Medea* of Euripedes. Euripides. CP-JohnS *Fr.* Medea.

Translations from the Spanish. William Carlos Williams. CP-WilW1

Translations of Roy's Verses on Skaters. Samuel Johnson. CP-JohnS

Translator, The. Alexander Pope. CP-PopeA

Translyvania's Greek Revival Chapel. Graduate, The. Robert Lowell. SP-LoweR

Transparent tree, full of migrating birds on a blue morning. Seasons. Czeslaw Milosz. CP-MiloC; CP-MiloCN, *tr.* by Renata Gorczynski *and* Robert Hass

Transplanting. Theodore Roethke. CP-RoetT

Transport. William Meredith. SP-MereW

Transport one cannot contain, A. Emily Dickinson. CP-DickE

Transport or Slaves From Maryland to Mississippi, The. Rita Dove. SP-DoveR

Transport was what we'd come in search of. Ano Prinios. Amy Clampitt. CP-ClamA

Transport's mighty price is. Emily Dickinson. SP-DickE

Transposition. Yannis Ritsos. SP-RitsY, *tr.* by Kimon Friar *and* Kostas Myrsiades

Transpositions. Walt Whitman. CP-WhitW

TRANSVESTITE. Conditions That Prevail, The. Philip Whalen. SP-WhalP

Trap. A. R. Ammons. CP-AmmoA

Trap, A. In the Likeness of a Grasshopper. Ted Hughes. SP-HughTN

Trap, The. Robert Creeley. CP-CreeR

Trap, The. Robinson Jeffers. CP-JefR2

Trap, The. Nicholas Vachel Lindsay. CP-LindV

Trap, The. James Tate. SP-TateJ

Trap, of a Player turn'd a Priest now is. Upon Trap. Robert Herrick. CP-HerrR

Trap rises from the earth on a summer night, A. Yehuda Amichai. SP-AmicYL, *tr.* by Benjamin Harshav *and* Barbara Harshav

Trapped. Charles Bukowski. SP-BukC1

Trapped, blinded, led; and in the end betrayed. Minotaur, The. Muriel Rukeyser. CP-RukeM

Trapped in a dismal marsh, he told his troops. All Except Hannibal. Robert

Graves. CP-GravR

Trappers. C. K. Williams. CP-WillC

Trapper's Bride, The. Yusef Komunyakaa. CP-KomuY

Trappist Abbey: Matins, The. Thomas Merton. CP-MertT

Trappist Cemetery—Gethsemani, The. Thomas Merton. CP-MertT

Trappists, Working. Thomas Merton. CP-MertT

Trash. C. K. Williams. CP-WillC

Trash Book, The. James Schuyler. CP-SchuJ

Trasimene. Amy Clampitt. CP-ClamA

Trattoria in the *porto*, A. John Lennon in the Porto Santo Stefano. Lawrence Ferlinghetti. SP-FerlL

Traulus. Jonathan Swift. CP-SwifJ

(Trauma) Storm. Gregory Orr. SP-OrrG

Traumerai. Philip Larkin. CP-LarkP

Travail of Passion, The. William Butler Yeats. CP-YeatW

Travel. Edna St. Vincent Millay. CP-MillE

Travel Advisory for a Night Shift. Alan Dugan. CP-DugaA

Travel by Train. Yehuda Amichai. SP-AmicYL, *tr. by* Benjamin Harshav *and* Barbara Harshav

Travel Companion, The. Paul Celan. SP-CelaP, *tr. by* John Felstiner

Travel Elegy. Wisława Szymborska. SP-SzymW, *tr. by* Stanisław Barańczak *and* Clare Cavanagh

Travel Is Over. D. H. Lawrence. CP-LawrD

Travel, said he of the broken umbrella, enervates. Spirals. Lorine Niedecker. CP-NiedL

Travel, trouble, music, art. Faut de Mieux. Dorothy Parker. CP-ParkD

Travel why to Nature. Emily Dickinson. SP-DickE

Traveler. Grace Paley. CP-PalGC

Traveler. Adam Zagajewski. SP-ZagaA, *tr. by* Clare Cavanagh

Traveler, A. Denise Levertov. SP-LeveDS

Traveler, The. Maya Angelou. SP-AngeM

Traveler, The. Randall Jarrell. CP-JarrR

Traveler greets his new setting, The. Albi. Adam Zagajewski. SP-ZagaA, *tr. by* Clare Cavanagh

Travelers. C. K. Williams. SP-WillC

Travelers, The. Josephine Jacobsen. CP-JacoJ

Travelers in Erewhon. Kenneth Rexroth. CP-RexrK

Traveler's Rest. Ogden Nash. CP-NashO

Traveling. John Logan. CP-LogaJ

Traveling. W. S. Merwin. SP-MerwW

Travel[l]ing. Charles Simic. SP-SimiC

Traveling at Home. Wendell Berry. CP-BerrW

Traveling at thirty thousand feet, we see. Night Flight. Mary Oliver. SP-OlivM

Traveling Exhibit of Torture Instruments. Thomas Lux. SP-LuxT

Traveling Man, The. James Whitcomb Riley. CP-RileJ

Travel[l]ing Slaughterhouse. Charles Simic. SP-SimiC; SP-SimiCE

Traveling through Fog. Robert Earl Hayden. CP-HaydR

Traveling through the dark I found a deer. William Stafford. SP-StafW; SP-StafWW

Traveling Through the Yard. Rae Armantrout. SP-ArmaA

Traveller. Thomas Kinsella. CP-KinsT

Traveller, The. John Berryman. CP-BerrJ

Traveller, The. Robert Creeley. CP-CreeR

Traveller, The. Kathleen Jessie Raine. SP-RainK

Traveller, The. Allen Tate. CP-TateA

Traveller at the Depot, The. Jones Very. CP-VeryJ

Traveller at the depot waiting stands, The. Traveller at the Depot, The. Jones Very. CP-VeryJ

Traveller Born, A. Hart Crane. CP-CranH

Traveller-Heart, The. Nicholas Vachel Lindsay. CP-LindV

Traveller on the skirt of Sarum's Plain, A. Guilt and Sorrow; or Incidents upon Salisbury Plain. William Wordsworth. CP-WorW1

Traveller! on thy journey toiling. Fountain, The. John Greenleaf Whittier. CP-WhitJ

Traveller sees afar the mountain rise, The. Great Facts of Christ's History, The. Jones Very. CP-VeryJ

Traveller, the highway my guide, A. James Vincent Cunningham. CP-CunnJ

Traveller, this is no prison. Epitaph on Pursy. Henry David Thoreau. CP-ThorH

Traveller through Infinity, The. Samuel Taylor Coleridge. CP-ColeS

Travellers. Charles Baudelaire. CP-BaudC, *tr. by* Walter Martin

Travelling. Henry David Thoreau. CP-ThorH

Travelling. William Wordsworth. CP-WorW1; MW-WorW

Travelling, a man met a tiger, so . . . Good Taste. Christopher Logue. SP-LoguC

Travelling alone through Europe. Somewhere. John Updike. CP-UpdiJ

Travelling Companion, The. Thomas Kinsella. CP-KinsT

Travelling in the Family. Carlos Drummond de Andrade. CP-BishE

Travelling in trains of time, succession and causality. Halt, The. Kathleen Jessie Raine. SP-RainK

Travelling north day after day. Banquet, The. W. S. Merwin. SP-MerwWF

Travelling South. John Berryman. CP-BerrJ

Travelling to the Capital. Gary Snyder. CP-SnydG

Travelogue. George Oppen. CP-OppGN

Travelogue for Exiles. Karl Shapiro. SP-ShapK

Travels. Denise Levertov. SP-LeveDP

Travels of a Vigilante, The. Andrei Codrescu. SP-CodrA

Travels of Benjamin the Last, of Tudela, The. Yehuda Amichai. SP-AmicYL, *tr. by* Benjamin Harshav *and* Barbara Harshav

Travels of the Last Benjamin of Tudela. Yehuda Amichai. SP-AmicY, *tr. by* Stephen Mitchell

Trav'ller, regret not me; for thou shalt find. On a Good Man. *Unknown*. CP-CowpW

Tray. Robert Browning. CP-BroR2

Treacherous wind pipes a lewd song, The. Hafiz. CP-EmerR *Fr.* Odes.

Treacherous *words*,—tearing my thought across. Nowhere. John Berryman. CP-BerrJ

Treachery. Walter De la Mare. CP-DeLaW

Tread lightly, she is near. Requiescat. Oscar Wilde. CP-WildO

Tread, Sirs, as lightly as ye can. Upon an Old Man a Residenciarie. Robert Herrick. CP-HerrR

Treading More Water. Philip Whalen. SP-WhalP

Treading Water. Philip Whalen. SP-WhalP

Treason. Robert Herrick. CP-HerrR

Treason Crime, The. Archibald MacLeish. CP-MacLA

Treason of an accent, The. Emily Dickinson. CP-DickE

Treasure, The. Robinson Jeffers. CP-JefR1

Treasure and the Law, The. Rudyard Kipling. *Fr.* Puck of Pook's Hill.

Treasure of the Wise Man, The. James Whitcomb Riley. CP-RileJ

Treasure plies a feather, / Pleasure spreadeth wings. Lay Up for Yourselves Treasures in Heaven. Christina Georgina Rossetti. CP-RosC2

Treat me nice, Miss Mandy Jane. Plea, A. Paul Laurence Dunbar. CP-DunbP

Treaties. A. R. Ammons. CP-AmmoA

Treatise on Emptiness. Adam Zagajewski. SP-ZagaA, *tr. by* Clare Cavanagh

Treatise on Poetry, A. Czeslaw Milosz. CP-MiloCN, *tr. by* Robert Hass

Beautiful Times.

"Cabbies dozed under St. Mary's Tower." CP-MiloC, *tr. by* Robert Hass

Preface: "First, plain speech in the mother tongue." CP-MiloC, *tr. by* Robert Hass

Spirit of History, The.

"Under a linden tree, as before, daylight." CP-MiloC, *tr. by* Robert Hass

Treatment, The. Charles Olson. CP-OlsoC

Treaty. Josephine Jacobsen. CP-JacoJ

Treblinka Lights. Sam Hamill. SP-HamiS

Tree. Ted Hughes. SP-HughTN

Tree. Muriel Rukeyser. CP-RukeM

Tree. Charles Tomlinson. CP-TomlC

Tree. William Carlos Williams. CP-WilW1

Tree, A. Yannis Ritsos. SP-RitsY, *tr. by* Kimon Friar

Tree, The. John Ciardi. CP-CiarJ

Tree, The. Thomas Hardy. CP-HardT

Tree, The. Randall Jarrell. CP-JarrR

Tree, The. Gregory Orr. SP-OrrG

Tree, The. Ezra Pound. SP-PounE

Tree, The. Adrienne Rich. CP-RicAE

Tree, The. Charles Tomlinson. CP-TomlC

Tree, The ("I love thee when thy swelling buds appear"). Jones Very. CP-VeryJ

Tree, The ("I too will wait with thee returning spring"). Jones Very. CP-VeryJ

Tree and book and book and tree and book. Music we refuse to forget. Idem 3. Michael Palmer. SP-PalmM

Tree and Sky. William Carlos Williams. CP-WilW1

Tree and the Cloud, The. Donald Hall. CP-HallD

Tree and the Lady, The. Thomas Hardy. CP-HardT

Tree Angel. Josephine Jacobsen. CP-JacoJ

Tree at My Window. Robert Frost. CP-FrosR

Tree before my eyes bloomed into flame, The. Captain's Song, The. John Berryman. CP-BerrJ

Tree burial, you tell me, that's. Blue Dwarfs. Margaret Atwood. SP-AtwM2

Tree Ceremonies. Edna St. Vincent Millay. CP-MillE

Tree grew here before the grove, A. Han-shan. CP-ColdM, *tr. by* Red Pine

Tree has entered my hands, The. Girl, A. Ezra Pound. CP-PoEar

Tree House, The. Louise Glück. SP-GlucL

Tree in Pamela's Garden, The. Edwin Arlington Robinson. CP-RobiE

Tree in Spring, A. May Swenson. SP-SwenM

Tree in Winter. Emily Dickinson. CP-DickE

Tree is stiff, the branch, The. Tree. William Carlos Williams. CP-WilW1

Tree lay down, The. Hurricane, The. William Carlos Williams. CP-WilW2

Tree-leaves labour up and down. Nobody Comes. Thomas Hardy. CP-HardT

Tree, lifeless tree, / tree live green. Federico García Lorca. CP-GarcF, *tr.* by Alan S. Trueblood *Fr.* Andalusian Songs.

Tree Marriage. William Meredith. SP-MereW

Tree of blood soaks the morning, A. Adam. Federico García Lorca. CP-GarcF, *tr.* by Christopher Maurer

Tree of Faith its bare, dry boughs must shed, The. Adjustment. John Greenleaf Whittier. CP-WhitJ

Tree of Guilt, The. Louis MacNeice. CP-MacNL

Tree of Laughing Bells or The Wings of the Morning, The. Nicholas Vachel Lindsay. CP-LindV

Tree of Liberty, The. Robert Burns. CP-BurnR

Tree of Liberty, The. Jones Very. CP-VeryJ

Tree of Mystery, The. Samuel Taylor Coleridge. CP-ColeS

Tree of rivers flowing through our lives, A. Muriel Rukeyser. CP-RukeM

Tree of rivers seen and forgotten, The. Muriel Rukeyser. CP-RukeM

Tree of Song. Federico García Lorca. CP-GarcF, *tr.* by Alan S. Trueblood *Fr.* Games.

Tree Party. Louis MacNeice. CP-MacNL

Tree, says good Swedenborg, is a close relative of man, The. Into the Tree. Czeslaw Milosz. CP-MiloC; CP-MiloCN, *tr.* by Robert Hass

Tree-Sense. Laura Riding Jackson. CP-RidiL

Tree silhouettes of hickory and oak. On Blakelock's *Moonlit Landscape* in the de Young Museum, Helen Pinkerton. CP-PinkH

Tree Song, A. Rudyard Kipling. CP-KiplR *Fr.* Puck of Pook's Hill.

Tree Swallows. Richard Eberhart. CP-EberR

Tree-talk is breathing quielty today. Quiet Talk. Ivor Gurney. SP-GurnI

Tree Telling of Orpheus, A. Denise Levertov. SP-LeveDS

Tree that from its place. Walnut Tree. Rainer Maria Rilke. CP-RilkFr, *tr.* by A. Poulin, Jr.

Tree, the Bird, The. Theodore Roethke. CP-RoetT

Tree / The *tee* gives you leaves. Federico García Lorca. CP-GarcF, *tr.* by Jerome Rothenberg *Fr.* Capriccios.

Tree the tempest with a crash of wood, The. On a Tree Fallen across the Road. Robert Frost. CP-FrosR

Tree-Toad, The. James Whitcomb Riley. CP-RileJ

Tree, Tree. Federico García Lorca. SP-GarcF, *tr.* by J. L. Gili *and* Stephen Spender

Tree Trimming. John Ciardi. CP-CiarJ

Tree wanderer! Wheat rider! Wind! Linden Trees, The. Archibald MacLeish. CP-MacLA

Tree was wet with the moon's, The. Poem: "Tree was wet with the moon's, The." Alan Dugan. CP-DugaA

Treeful of Cleavage Flared Branching, A. A. R. Ammons. CP-AmmoA

Trees. Robert Creeley. CP-CreeR

Trees. Ted Hughes. SP-HughTN

Trees. Federico García Lorca. CP-GarcF, *tr.* by Catherine Brown

Trees. W. S. Merwin. SP-MerwWF

Trees. Howard Nemerov. CP-NemeH

Trees. William Carlos Williams. CP-WilW1

Trees, The. Philip Larkin. CP-LarkP

Trees, The. Adrienne Rich. CP-RicAE; SP-RicA1; SP-RicA2

Trees, The. William Carlos Williams. CP-WilW1

Trees along this city street, The. City Trees. Edna St. Vincent Millay. CP-MillE

Trees and Cattle. James Dickey. CP-DickJ

Trees are afraid of storms. Even oaks. Real People. William Stafford. SP-StafWW

Trees are afraid to put forth buds, The. Backward Spring, A. Thomas Hardy. CP-HardT

Trees are coming into leaf, The. Trees, The. Philip Larkin. CP-LarkP

Trees are crystal chandeliers, The. Homecoming. Jay Wright. SP-WrigJ

Trees are down all over the south of England, The. Hurricane and Charlotte Mew, The. Amy Clampitt. CP-ClamA

Trees are flowering, The. Japonica. Louise Glück. SP-GlucL

Trees are in their autumn beauty, The. Wild Swans at Coole, The. William Butler Yeats. CP-YeatW

Trees are never the same, The. Return, The. Thomas McGrath. SP-McGrT

Trees are sprayed, The. Awkward Silence. James Tate. SP-TateJ

Trees are tall gods, The. Epilogue: "Trees are tall gods, The." David Ignatow. SP-IgnaD

Trees are undressing, and fling in many places, The. Last Week in October. Thomas Hardy. CP-HardT

Trees at Night. Charles Simic. SP-SimiC; SP-SimiCE

Trees—being trees, the. Trees, The. William Carlos Williams. CP-WilW1

Trees bend down along the stream, The. Lazy Day, A. Paul Laurence Dunbar. CP-DunbP

Trees / breathing / air. Up in the Air. Robert Creeley. CP-CreeR

Trees by their yield. Gerard Manley Hopkins. CP-HopkG

Trees' Counselling, The. Christina Georgina Rossetti. CP-RosC3

Trees Eat Sunshine. John Updike. CP-UpdiJ

Trees fret fitfully and twist, The. On the Way. Thomas Hardy. CP-HardT

Trees full of snipers, the new kind, The. War. Lorine Niedecker. CP-NiedL

Tree's green explains what a light means, The. Notes for Echo Lake 5. Michael Palmer. SP-PalmM

Trees hang silent, The. No Word. Kenneth Rexroth. CP-RexrK

Trees hide the view from the window, The. Helen's House. Yannis Ritsos. SP-RitsY, *tr.* by Kimon Friar

Trees in groves / Kine in droves. Saadi. Ralph Waldo Emerson. CP-EmerR

Trees in Spring, The. Randall Jarrell. CP-JarrR

Trees in the Garden. D. H. Lawrence. CP-LawrD

Trees in the garden rained flowers, The. Stephen Crane. CP-CranS

Trees in time, The. On Looking for Models. Alan Dugan. CP-DugaA

Trees in trouble because of autumn, The. Reality of Peace, 1916. D. H. Lawrence. CP-LawrD

Trees inside are moving out into the forest, The. Trees, The. Adrienne Rich. CP-RicAE; SP-RicA1; SP-RicA2

Trees is bendin' in de sto'm, De. Plantation Melody, A. Paul Laurence Dunbar. CP-DunbP

Trees laid out. Homeland ("Trees laid out"). Federico García Lorca. CP-GarcF, *tr.* by Jerome Rothenberg *Fr.* Water Suite.

Tree's leaves may be ever so good, A. Leaves Compared with Flowers. Robert Frost. CP-FrosR

Trees like Tassels—hit—and swung, The. Emily Dickinson. CP-DickE

Trees Listening to Bach. James Merrill. SP-MerrJ

Trees of Life, The. Jones Very. CP-VeryJ

Trees of Madame Blavatsky, The. Norman Dubie. CP-DubiN

Trees of the Garden, The. Dante Gabriel Rossetti. CW-RossD *Fr.* House of Life, The.

Trees on the hospital lawn, The. University Hospital, Boston. Mary Oliver. SP-OlivM

Trees over the roof. Lorine Niedecker. CP-NiedL

Trees rise from the darkness of the world, The. In the Ward: The Sacred Wood. Randall Jarrell. CP-JarrR

Trees rise taller and taller, lifted, The. Corot. D. H. Lawrence. CP-LawrD

Trees shall rise around thy dwelling. Tenant, The. Jones Very. CP-VeryJ

Tree's streaming imitates light, A. Water gathers light behind the arm. Notes for Echo Lake 6. Michael Palmer. SP-PalmM

Trees that lift themselves like clouds. Quality of Genius, The. Denise Levertov. SP-LeveDL

Trees, the naked trees. Hayden Carruth. CP-CarHS *Fr.* Clay Hill Anthology, The.

Trees torpedoes Soviet galoshes. Christmas in New York. Andrei Codrescu. SP-CodrA

Trees turned around as if to quarrel with him, The. At the Death of a Mongolian Peasant. Norman Dubie. CP-DubiN

Trees / were in(give). E. E. Cummings. CP-CummE

Trees were plucked like iron bars, The. Jumbo. Wallace Stevens. CP-StevW; CP-StevWP

Trees! / Were you once arrows. Trees. Federico García Lorca. CP-GarcF, *tr.* by Catherine Brown

Trekking in Asia, spending nights in odd dwellings, in. Admonition, An. Joseph Brodsky. CP-BrodJ, *tr.* by George L. Kline

Tremble, Kings despised of man! Stanza from a Translation of the Marseillaise Hymn. Percy Bysshe Shelley. CP-ShelP

Tremble no more to hear my voice! Word from the Cannon's Mouth, A. George Meredith. CP-MerG2

Tremble, thou earth, at the Presence of the Lord. Earth Shall Tremble at the Look of Him, The. Christina Georgina Rossetti. CP-RosC2

'Tremble, thou earth!' th' anointed poet said. On the Power of the Supreme Being. Christopher Smart. SP-SmarC

Trembling before Thee we fall down to adore Thee. Epiphanytide. Christina Georgina Rossetti. CP-RosC2

Trembling of the Veil, The. Allen Ginsberg. CP-GinsA; SP-GinsA

Trembling water glimpsed through dark tangle, The. Water Colours. Ivor Gurney. SP-GurnI

Trembling / with delight. Soup ("Trembling / with delight"). Robert Creeley. CP-CreeR

Tremor. Federico García Lorca. CP-GarcF, *tr.* by Jerome Rothenberg *Fr.* Water Suite.

Trench Warfare. Charles Bukowski. SP-BukC1

Trencher-Knight, A. Ambrose Bierce. SP-BierA

Trenta-Sei of the Pleasure We Take in the Early Death of Keats, A. John Ciardi. CP-CiarJ

Tres tria, sed longe distantia sæcula, vates. Translation of Dryden's Poem on Milton. John Dryden. CP-CowpW

Trespass. Robert Frost. CP-FrosR

Trespass of my rustic Love, The. Emily Dickinson. SP-DickE

Tress of Hair, A. James Whitcomb Riley. CP-RileJ

Tresses, The. Thomas Hardy. CP-HardT

Trestle, The. Raymond Carver. CP-CarvR

Trestle and the Buck-Saw, The. James Whitcomb Riley. CP-RileJ

Trestle, The. W. S. Merwin. SP-MerwWF

Tretis [or Book] of the Tua Mariit Wemen [or Two Married Women] and the Wedo[w] [or Widow], The. William Dunbar. CP-DunbW

Trevenen. Donald Davie. CP-DaviDC

Treviso, the Pescheria. Donald Davie. CP-DaviDC

Triad. Robinson Jeffers. CP-JefR2

Triad. Kathleen Jessie Raine. SP-RainK

Triad, A. Christina Georgina Rossetti. CP-RosC1

Triad, The. William Wordsworth. CP-WorW2

Triad of British Evils, A. George Meredith. CP-MerG2

Triadic Node for Tim Reynold's Digestion. Robert Stock. SP-StocR

Trial, A. Alan Dugan. CP-DugaA

Trial, The. John Berryman. CP-BerrJ

Trial, The. Adam Zagajewski. SP-ZagaA, tr. by Renata Gorczynski

Trial and Death, a Double Feature. Howard Nemerov. CP-NemeH

Trial as a Stimulus. Emily Dickinson. SP-DickE

Trial by Existence, The. Robert Frost. CP-FrosR

Trial of Innocence. Robert Graves. CP-GravR

Trial of Man, The. Sylvia Plath. CP-PlatS

Trial of the Dead Cleopatra in Her Beautiful and Wonderful Tomb, The. Nicholas Vachel Lindsay. CP-LindV

Trial Run. Josephine Jacobsen. CP-JacoJ

Trial Run, A. Robert Frost. CP-FrosR

Trial Runs. Seamus Heaney. SP-HeanSO

Tribal Memories. Robert Duncan. SP-DuncR Fr. Passages.

Tribe of Templars, Play'rs, Apothecaries, The. Second Satire of the First Book of Horace Imitated, The. Alexander Pope. CP-PopeA

Tribes of Limbo, travellers report, The. Limbo Culture. W. H. Auden. CP-AudeW

Tribes of Rakala, The. Kenneth Patchen. CP-PatcK

Tributary Stream. William Wordsworth. CP-WorW2 Fr. River Duddon [A Series of Sonnets], The.

Tribute. Countee Cullen. CP-CullC

Tribute, The. "H. D." CP-DoolH

Tribute of His Home, The. James Whitcomb Riley. CP-RileJ

Tribute to Kafka for Someone Taken. Alan Dugan. CP-DugaA

Tribute to Neruda the Poet Collector of Seashells. William Carlos Williams. CP-WilW2

Tribute to the Angels. "H. D." CP-DoolH

Tribute to the Memory of the Same Dog. William Wordsworth. CP-WorW1

Tribute to the Painters. William Carlos Williams. CP-WilW2

Tribute to Wordsworth. Samuel Taylor Coleridge. CP-ColeS

Trick, The. Gregory Orr. SP-OrrG

Trick of finding what you didn't lose, The. E. E. Cummings. CP-CummE

Trick to Dull Our Bleeding, A. Charles Bukowski. SP-BukC2

Tricked by Eternity the Heart. Archibald MacLeish. CP-MacLA

Trickle Drops. Walt Whitman. CP-WhitW

Tricks. Yannis Ritsos. SP-RitsY, tr. by N. C. Germanacos

Tricks With Mirrors. Margaret Atwood. SP-AtwM1

Tricodon of Bruges, a Flemish. Annals. John Ciardi. CP-CiarJ

Tried always and Condemned by thee. Emily Dickinson. CP-DickE

Tried selling my pictures. In jail. Audubon. Lorine Niedecker. CP-NiedL

Tried to get into my head. Rodent, The. James Laughlin. CP-LaugJ

Triennial, The. Jones Very. CP-VeryJ

Trifle, A. Paul Muldoon. CP-MuldP

Trifle poor in the past, A. Han-shan. CP-ColdM, tr. by Red Pine

Trifler, The. Dorothy Parker. CP-ParkD

Trigg having turn'd his sute, he struts in state. Upon Trigg. Robert Herrick. CP-HerrR

Trigorin. Stephen Spender. CP-SpenS

Trill of thrushes, almost unnoticed, The. With the Gift of a Nootka Rose. Sam Hamill. SP-HamiS

Trilogy for X. Louis MacNeice. CP-MacNL

Trimountain. Ralph Waldo Emerson. CP-EmerR

Trinacria. Charles Olson. CP-OlsoC

Trinc: Praises II. Thomas McGrath. SP-McGrT

Trinitas. John Greenleaf Whittier. CP-WhitJ

Trinity. G. K. Chesterton. CP-ChesG

Trinity Churchyard. Muriel Rukeyser. CP-RukeM

Trinity Churchyard, Spring 1961. May Swenson. SP-SwenM

Trinity Place. Carl Sandburg. CP-SandC

Trinity Sunday. George Herbert. CP-HerbG

Trinity Sunday. Christina Georgina Rossetti. CP-RosC2

Trinkets, The. G. K. Chesterton. CP-ChesG

Trio. Carolyn Kizer. CP-KizeC

Trio of Love Songs. Sylvia Plath. CP-PlatS

Trio of Triolets, A. Gerard Manley Hopkins. CP-HopkG

Triolet: "Give back the heart that I gave." Dorothy Parker. CP-ParkD

Triolet: "I wish I were a jelly fish." G. K. Chesterton. CP-ChesG

Triolet: "It is never the cost of the gift." Dorothy Parker. CP-ParkD

Triolet, A: "You'll be returning, one day." Dorothy Parker. CP-ParkD

Triolets: "Herewith I send you my heart." Dorothy Parker. CP-ParkD

Trip. James Schuyler. CP-SchuJ

Trip, The. William Stafford. SP-StafWW

Trip on the Staten Island Ferry, A. Audre Lorde. SP-LordA

Trip: San Francisco. Langston Hughes. CP-HughL

Trip through Yucatán, A. Theodore Weiss. SP-WeisT

Trip to Four or Five Towns, A. John Logan. CP-LogaJ

Trip to Temple-Oge, Stephen's Green and the Bason, A: or, An Election of Dublin Beauties. Unknown, sometimes at. to Thomas Sheridan. CP-SherT

Trip to the Moon. Federico García Lorca. CP-GarcF, tr. by Greg Simon and Steven F. White

Triphammer Bridge. A. R. Ammons. CP-AmmoA

Triple Bronze. Robert Frost. CP-FrosR

Triple Fool, The. John Donne. CP-DonnJ; MW-DonnJ

Triple Muse. Olga Broumas. SP-BrouO

Triple Time. Philip Larkin. CP-LarkP

Triple World is a turning wheel, The. Shih-te. CP-ColdM, tr. by Red Pine

Triplex. "H. D." CP-DoolH

Trips to California. Robert Penn Warren. CP-WarrR

Triptych. Seamus Heaney. SP-HeanSO

Triptych. Alan Dugan. CP-DugaA

Triptych. Richard Eberhart. CP-EberR

Triptych, Middle Panel Burning. Thomas Lux. SP-LuxT

Tristan. Edna St. Vincent Millay. CP-MillE

Tristan and Iseult had nothing. Gregory Orr. SP-OrrG

Tristan and Isolde. Opera. T. S. Eliot. SP-ElioT

Tristan Corbière. T. S. Eliot. SP-ElioT

Triste Corbiére. Lawrence Ferlinghetti. SP-FerlL

Tristia. Osip Emilevich Mandelstam. CP-BrodJ, tr. by Joseph Brodsky

Tristia. Osip Emilevich Mandelstam. CP-KunSC, tr. by Stanley Kunitz

Tristium. Ovid.
   "Gainst Fate no counsell can prevaile." CP-RaleW

Tristram and Iseult. Matthew Arnold.
   Iseult of Brittany. SP-ArnoM

Tritemius of Herbipolis, one day. Gift of Tritemius, The. John Greenleaf Whittier. CP-WhitJ

Triumph. D. H. Lawrence. CP-LawrD

Triumph—may be of several kinds. Emily Dickinson. CP-DickE

Triumph of Achilles, The. Louise Glück. SP-GlucL

Triumph of Bullshit, The. T. S. Eliot. SP-ElioT

Triumph of Education, The. Howard Nemerov. CP-NemeH

Triumph of Heavenly Love Desired, The. Jeanne Marie Bouvier de la Motte Guyon. CP-CowpW

Triumph of Life, The. Percy Bysshe Shelley. CP-ShelP

Triumph of Man, The ("I plod and peer amid mean sounds and shapes"). G. K. Chesterton. CP-ChesG

Triumph of Man, The ("Say: Who is this that cometh royally"). G. K. Chesterton. CP-ChesG

Triumph of the Machine, The. D. H. Lawrence. CP-LawrD

Triumph of the Postmodern. Lawrence Ferlinghetti. SP-FerlL

Triumph of the Shell, The. Archibald MacLeish. CP-MacLA

Triumph of Time, The. Algernon Charles Swinburne. SP-SwinA

Triumphal March. Thomas McGrath. SP-McGrT

Triumphs of Owen, The. Thomas Gray. CP-GrayT

Triumphs of Science, and of Faith, The. Jones Very. CP-VeryJ

Trivial Details. Yannis Ritsos. SP-RitsY, tr. by Kimon Friar

Troades. Seneca.
   "Insulting chance ne'er call'd with louder voice." CP-JohnS

Trŏchĕe trĭps frŏm lŏng tŏ shŏrt. Metrical Feet. Samuel Taylor Coleridge. CP-ColeS; MW-ColeS

Trogger, The. Robert Burns. CP-BurnR

Troilus. Charles Olson. CP-OlsoC

Troilus and Cresida. William Wordsworth. CP-WorW1

Troilus and Cressida. John Dryden.
   (Song.) SP-DrydJ

Troilus and Criseyde [or Criseide]. Geoffrey Chaucer. CP-ChauG

Trojan camp the common danger shared, The. Nisus and Euryalus ("Trojan camp the common danger shared, The"). Virgil. CP-DryJ2, tr. by John

Dryden *Fr.* Aeneid (Dryden translation).

Trojan Women, The. Euripides.
  Aurora and Tithonus. CP-BroEB

Trojans. Constantine P. Cavafy. CP-CavaC, *tr. by* Theoharis Constantine Theoharis

Trolley-cars / are my inland waters. Twist, The. Charles Olson. SP-OlsoC *Fr.* Maximus Poems, The.

Trolley from Xochimilco, The. Norman Dubie. CP-DubiN

Trolley has stopped long since, The. Dump, The. Donald Hall. CP-HallD

Trolling for Blues. Richard Wilbur. CP-WilbR

Trolling the coho fly twenty feet behind the boat. Cutlery. Raymond Carver. CP-CarvR

Trolls, The. Louis MacNeice. CP-MacNL

Troll's Courtship. Louis MacNeice. CP-MacNL

Troll's Nosegay, The. Robert Graves. CP-GravR

Troop will be impatient; let us hie, The. Borderers, The. A Tragedy. William Wordsworth. CP-WorW1

Troopin'. Rudyard Kipling. CP-KiplR

Troopin', troopin', troopin' to the sea. Troopin'. Rudyard Kipling. CP-KiplR

Troops, The. Charles Bukowski. SP-BukC3

τροπη. Michael Palmer. SP-PalmM

Trophies. Muriel Rukeyser. CP-RukeM

Trophies of Peace. Herman Melville. SP-MelvH

Tropic. D. H. Lawrence. CP-LawrD

Tropic, indeed, a memory. Emily Dickinson. SP-DickE

Tropic Ritual. Denise Levertov. SP-LeveDL

Tropic Zone. Derek Walcott. CP-WalcD *Fr.* Midsummer.

Tropical Beetles. John Updike. CP-UpdiJ

Tropical Greenhouse. Dan Pagis. SP-PagiD, *tr. by* Stephen Mitchell

Tropics. Thomas Merton. CP-MertT

Trosachs, The. William Wordsworth. CP-WorW2

Trossachs, The. Sir Walter Scott. SP-ScotW *Fr.* Lady of the Lake, The.

Trossachs, The. Alexandre Dumas. SP-ScotW *Fr.* Lady of the Pearls, The.

Troth, and a grief, and a blessing, A. From the Headboard of a Grave in Paraguay. James Whitcomb Riley. CP-RileJ

Troth, Tom, I must confess I much admire. Upon T.C. Having the Pox. Sir John Suckling. CP-SuckJ

Troth with the Dead. D. H. Lawrence. CP-LawrD

Troths. Carl Sandburg. CP-SandC

Trouble. James Wright. CP-WrigJ

Trouble, A / archaically fettered. It Is a Living Coral. William Carlos Williams. CP-WilW1

Trouble about those that set up to be moral judges, The. Censors. D. H. Lawrence. CP-LawrD

Trouble in de Kitchen. Paul Laurence Dunbar. CP-DunbP

Trouble is there's, The. Connection, The. Charles Olson. CP-OlsoC

Trouble Making Trouble. A. R. Ammons. CP-AmmoA

Trouble, not of clouds, or weeping rain, A. On the Departure of Sir Walter Scott from Abbotsford, for Naples. William Wordsworth. CP-WorW2; MW-WorW

Trouble of a book is first to be, The. Troubles of a Book, The. Laura Riding Jackson. CP-RidiL

Trouble with a kitten is, The. Kitten, The. Ogden Nash. CP-NashO

Trouble with "In," The. Heather McHugh. SP-McHuH

Trouble with me is that whether I get love or not, The. On the Roof. C. K. Williams. CP-WillC

Trouble with my ex, The. Original Sin. James Vincent Cunningham. CP-CunnJ

Trouble with Reading, The. William Stafford. SP-StafWW

Trouble with the Times, The. Thomas McGrath. SP-McGrT

Trouble with tragedy is the fuss it makes, The. Nicolas-Sébastien Roch Chamfort. CP-BeckS

Trouble with Women Is Men, The. Ogden Nash. CP-NashO

Troubled Water. Langston Hughes. CP-HughL; CP-HughL3

Troubled Woman. Langston Hughes. CP-HughL; CP-HughL1

Troubles of a Book, The. Laura Riding Jackson. CP-RidiL

Troubles to win. Lorine Niedecker. CP-NiedL

Troubleshooting. William Stafford. SP-StafW; SP-StafWW

Troublesome Fame. Robert Graves. CP-GravR

Troublesome Reign, The. Geoffrey Hill. CP-HillG

Trough. David Ignatow. SP-IgnaD

Troughs of Sea. Robert Graves. CP-GravR

Trout, The. James Laughlin. CP-LaugJ

Trout let us say, A. Trout, The. James Laughlin. CP-LaugJ

Trout Map, The. Allen Tate. CP-TateA

Trouvée. Elizabeth Bishop. CP-BishE

Troy Town. Dante Gabriel Rossetti. CW-RossD

Truce. Charles Bukowski. SP-BukC3

Truce. Walter De la Mare. CP-DeLaW

Truce. Paul Muldoon. CP-MuldP

Truce for a Moment. Edna St. Vincent Millay. CP-MillE

Truce in Love Intreated. Thomas Carew. CP-CareT

Truce of Christmas, The. G. K. Chesterton. CP-ChesG

Truce of Piscataqua, The. John Greenleaf Whittier. CP-WhitJ

Truce of the Bear, The. Rudyard Kipling. CP-KiplR

Truck driver, second-floor roomer. Kitchen Chair Poem #5. Clarence Major. SP-MajoC

Truck-Garden Market-Day. Edna St. Vincent Millay. CP-MillE

Truck put me off on Fell. Hitching into Frisco. Thom Gunn. CP-GunnT *Fr.* Three Songs.

Trucker, A. Thom Gunn. CP-GunnT

Trucks and station wagons, VWs, old Chevys, Pintos. Traffic. Donald Hall. CP-HallD

Truco. Jorge Luis Borges. SP-BorgJ, *tr. by* Alastair Reid

Trudge, Body! Robert Graves. CP-GravR

Trudging to Eden, looking backward. Emily Dickinson. CP-DickE

True Account of Talking to the Sun at Fire Island, A. Frank O'Hara. SP-OharF

True and Faithful Inventory of the Goods Belonging to Dr. Swift, Vicar of Laracor; upon Lending His House to the Bishop of Meath, until His Own Was Built [*or* till His Palace Was Rebuilt], A. Jonathan Swift. CP-SherT

True Believer. Allen Tate. CP-TateA

True Confessional. Lawrence Ferlinghetti. SP-FerlL

True Confessions. Philip Whalen. SP-WhalP

True Conquerors. Walt Whitman. CP-WhitW

True Democracy. D. H. Lawrence. CP-LawrD

True Encounter, The. Edna St. Vincent Millay. CP-MillE

True Evil. Robert Graves. CP-GravR

True faith discovered was, The. Wisdom. William Butler Yeats. CP-YeatW

True Friendship. Robert Herrick. CP-HerrR

True genius, but true woman! dost deny. To George Sand: A Recognition. Elizabeth Barrett Browning. CP-BroEB

True harvests no mere intent may reap. Necessity of Faith, The. Wendell Berry. CP-BerrW

True-hearted friend of all true friendliness! Henry W. Grady. James Whitcomb Riley. CP-RileJ

True-hearted was he, the sad swain o' the Yarrow. Jessie—A New Scots Song. Robert Burns. CP-BurnR

True, I happen. So. Hayden Carruth. CP-CarHS *Fr.* Clay Hill Anthology, The.

True Illumination Is Habitude. Sam Hamill. SP-HamiS

True it is that Ambrosio Salinero. Gabriello Chiabrera. CP-WorW1

True Joy. Robert Graves. CP-GravR

True kindness is a pure divine affinity. Henry David Thoreau. CP-ThorH

True Knowledge, The. Oscar Wilde. CP-WildO

True Knowledge Necessary for the Voyage of Life. Jones Very. CP-VeryJ

True Light, The. Jones Very. CP-VeryJ

True Love. Robert Penn Warren. CP-WarrR

True Love at Last. D. H. Lawrence. CP-LawrD

True Love is founded in rocks of Remembrance. Love and Law. Nicholas Vachel Lindsay. CP-LindV

True love. Is it normal. Wisława Szymborska. SP-SzymW, *tr. by* Stanislaw Barańczak *and* Clare Cavanagh

True Lover, The. A. E. Housman. CP-HousA

True Lovers. G. K. Chesterton. CP-ChesG

True lovers in each happening of their hearts. E. E. Cummings. CP-CummE; SP-CummE

True Magic. Robert Graves. CP-GravR

True Man, The. Chuang Tzu. CP-MertT

True mirth resides not in the smiling skin. Mirth. Robert Herrick. CP-HerrR

True Nature of Time, The. Robert Penn Warren. CP-WarrR

True Night. Gary Snyder. CP-SnydG

True, noble words, which thrill the very soul. "It is vain to say, that this is the country of the 'white man.' It is the country of man." Charles Sumner. Jones Very. CP-VeryJ

True Numbers. Charles Olson. CP-OlsoC

True on the Plain I might have seen Salisbury Close. Regrets After Death. Ivor Gurney. SP-GurnI

True or False. John Ciardi. CP-CiarJ

True, our converse a stranger is to speech. Walden. Henry David Thoreau. CP-ThorH

True Pleasures. William Cowper. CP-CowpW *Fr.* Olney Hymns.

True / poet who could live and die. Cummings. Archibald MacLeish. CP-MacLA

True Religion, The. James Vincent Cunningham. CP-CunnJ

True rev'rence is (as Cassiodore doth prove). Reverence. Robert Herrick. CP-HerrR

True Safety. Robert Herrick. CP-HerrR

True Sensibility. G. K. Chesterton. CP-ChesG

True Stories. Margaret Atwood. SP-AtwM2

True Story, A. Christina Georgina Rossetti. CP-RosC3

True Story of God, A. Norman Dubie. CP-DubiN

True Story of What Happened, The. Miller Williams. CP-WillM

True Sympathy; or, Prevention of Cruelty to Teachers. G. K. Chesterton. CP-ChesG

True, the time, to one who does not love farce. Little Scraping, A. Robinson Jeffers. CP-JefR2

True, the walls fell. In Our Town. "H. D." CP-DoolH

True to your self, and sheets, you'l have me swear. To a Gentlewoman on Just Dealing. Robert Herrick. CP-HerrR

True Tyrant or the Spirit of Duty Rebuked, The. Stevie Smith. CP-SmitS

True Woman (Her Heaven). Dante Gabriel Rossetti. CW-RossD *Fr.* House of Life, The.

True Woman (Her Love). Dante Gabriel Rossetti. CW-RossD *Fr.* House of Life, The.

True Woman (Herself). Dante Gabriel Rossetti. CW-RossD *Fr.* House of Life, The.

True Worshipers, The. Jones Very. CP-VeryJ

Trueblue Gentleman, A. Kenneth Patchen. CP-PatcK

Truest Poetry Is the Most Feigning, The [or, Ars Poetica for Hard Times]. W. H. Auden. CP-AudeW

Truggin a Footman was; but now, growne lame. Upon Truggin. Robert Herrick. CP-HerrR

Truisms, The. Louis MacNeice. CP-MacNL

Truly Great, The. Stephen Spender. *See* I Think Continually of Those Who Were Truly Great

Truly Marvelous, The. James Whitcomb Riley. CP-RileJ

Truly the Light Is Sweet. Christina Georgina Rossetti. CP-RosC2

Truly we have not been here long—twelve hours. Thought as It Turns, A. Miller Williams. CP-WillM

Truly ye come of The Blood; slower to bless than to ban. England's Answer. Rudyard Kipling. CP-KiplR

Trümmerfrauen. Eleanor Wilner. SP-WilnE

Trumpet and drum, the old soldier said. Old Soldiers' Home, The. Howard Nemerov. CP-NemeH

Trumpet pealed thro' France. Then Italy. Massacre of Perugia, The. Christina Georgina Rossetti. CP-RosC3

Trumpet Player. Langston Hughes. CP-HughL; CP-HughL2

Trumpeters / from the Comandancia militar. Valle de Oaxaca. Charles Tomlinson. CP-TomlC; SP-TomlC

Trumpets. Rainer Maria Rilke. CP-RilkFr

Trumpets. Georg Trakl. CP-WrigJ

Trumpets blare "God Save the King," The. Eastbourne. Eugenio Montale. CP-MontE, *tr. by* Jonathan Galassi

Trumpet's voice, loud and authoritative, The. Reasons for Attendance. Philip Larkin. CP-LarkP

Truncated Bird, The. Richard Eberhart. CP-EberR

Trundled from / the strangeness of the sea. Sea-Elephant, The. William Carlos Williams. CP-WilWI

Truro Bear, The. Mary Oliver. SP-OlivM

Trust. D. H. Lawrence. CP-LawrD

Trust. John Greenleaf Whittier. CP-WhitJ

Trust adjusts her "Peradventure" Emily Dickinson. CP-DickE

Trust at least in this bird. Poem to Be Printed on a Very White Page. Robert Stock. SP-StocR

Trust in the Unexpected. Emily Dickinson. CP-DickE

Trust me Ladies, I will do. To the Ladyes. Robert Herrick. CP-HerrR

Trust me, the meed of praise, dealt thriftily. In a Letter to the Same [C. P.]. William Cowper. CP-CowpW

Trusting Heart, The. Dorothy Parker. CP-ParkD

Trusting the happy flower. Emily Dickinson. SP-DickE

Trusty as the stars. Emily Dickinson. CP-DickE

Truth. William Cowper. CP-CowpW

Truth. Geoffrey Chaucer. *See* Balade of Bon Conseill

Truth. Robert Herrick. CP-HerrR

Truth. Howard Nemerov. CP-NemeH

Truth. Robert Penn Warren. CP-WarrR

Truth. Adam Zagajewski. SP-ZagaA, *tr. by* Clare Cavanagh

Truth, The. Alfonso Cortes. CP-MertT

Truth, The. Richard Eberhart. CP-EberR

Truth, The. Randall Jarrell. CP-JarrR

Truth about Departures, The. W. S. Merwin. SP-MerwWF

Truth about Sisyphus is much more disagreeable than reports indicate, The. Prose Parables. Robert Stock. SP-StocR

Truth also is the pursuit of it. Leviathan. George Oppen. CP-OppGN

Truth and Divine Love Rejected by the World. Jeanne Marie Bouvier de la Motte Guyon. CP-CowpW

Truth and Error. Robert Herrick. CP-HerrR

Truth and Falsehood. Robert Herrick. CP-HerrR

Truth and Truthfulness. Miller Williams. CP-WillM

Truth by her own simplicity is known. Truth and Falsehood. Robert Herrick. CP-HerrR

Truth / gives heat. Lorine Niedecker. CP-NiedL

Truth—Goodness—Beauty—those celestial thrins. Henry David Thoreau. CP-ThorH

Truth in platonic ornaments bedeck'd. Boethius. CP-JohnS *Fr.* Consolation of Philosophy, The ("De Consolacione Philosophie").

Truth in Poetry. George Crabbe. SP-CrabG *Fr.* Village, The.

Truth is a golden thread seen here and there. Arthur Hugh Clough. SP-ClouA

Truth—is as old as God. Emily Dickinson. CP-DickE

Truth is best found out by the time, and eyes. Truth. Robert Herrick. CP-HerrR

Truth is eternal, and the son of heaven. Ode to Dr. William Sancroft. Jonathan Swift. CP-SwifJ

Truth is Forced, The. May Swenson. SP-SwenM

Truth is Hard. Shmuel HaNagid. SP-HaNaS, *tr. by* Peter Cole

Truth—is stirless, The. Emily Dickinson. CP-DickE

Truth is that there comes a time, The. Sad Strains of a Gay Waltz. Wallace Stevens. CP-StevW; CP-StevWP

Truth is the trial of itself. From *The Touchstone of Truth.* Ben Jonson. CP-JonsB

Truth is what you cannot tell. Truth. Robert Penn Warren. CP-WarrR

Truth kicks no sand into your eyes. What Is True. Ingeborg Bachmann. CP-KizeC, *tr. by* Carolyn Kizer

Truth Like the Belly of a Woman Turning, The. Gary Snyder. CP-SnydG

Truth-loving Persians do not dwell upon. Persian Version, The. Robert Graves. CP-GravR

Truth of my prologue is this: Down with sleazy romanticists!, The. Men (II), The. Pablo Neruda. SP-NeruP *Fr.* Separate Rose, The.

Truth of the Matter, The. Howard Nemerov. CP-NemeH

"Truth," said a traveller. Stephen Crane. CP-CranS

Truth the Dead Know, The. Anne Sexton. CP-SextA; SP-SextA

Truthful Song, The. Rudyard Kipling. CP-KiplR

Truth's in myth not fact, The. Poem: "Truth's in myth not fact, The." Gregory Orr. SP-OrrG

Try and trust Roger, was the word, but now. To the Right Noble Tom, Tell-Troth of His Travels, the Coriat of Odcombe, and His Book Now Going to Travel. Ben Jonson. CP-JonsB

Try as he will, no man breaks wholly loose. Virginity, The. Rudyard Kipling. CP-KiplR

Try It Suns. and Hols.; It's Closed Then. Ogden Nash. CP-NashO

Try subtlety. 'I was in love all May.' Tête à Tête. Thomas Kinsella. CP-KinsT

Try the might the Muse affords. Ralph Waldo Emerson. CP-EmerR

Try This on Your Piano [Whispers of Immortality]. T. S. Eliot. *See* Whispers of Immortality

Try to be yourself, they told the child. Polonius Passing Through a Stage. Howard Nemerov. CP-NemeH

Try to curry favor. Devotee's Complaint, A. A. K. Ramanujan. CP-RamaA

Try to keep them, poet. When They Surge, Excited. Constantine P. Cavafy. CP-CavaC, *tr. by* Theoharis Constantine Theoharis

Try to Praise the Mutilated World. Adam Zagajewski. SP-ZagaA, *tr. by* Clare Cavanagh

Try to remember, every April, not this one only. Talking to Oneself. Denise Levertov. SP-LeveDL; SP-LeveDS

Try to remember some details. Remember the clothing. Yehuda Amichai. SP-AmicY, *tr. by* Chana Bloch

Trying. Miller Williams. CP-WillM

Trying for a tigerish kind. Hazy Day in the Composition. Clarence Major. SP-MajoC

Trying to chop mother down is like. She Went to Stay. Robert Creeley. CP-CreeR

Trying to come out of it. Preparing to Leave Home. Jay Wright. SP-WrigJ

Trying to explain it to them. Esquimos Have No Word for "War," The. Mary Oliver. SP-OlivM

Trying to Feel Something. John Ciardi. CP-CiarJ

Trying to Get Even. Charles Bukowski. SP-BukC1

Trying to get "our men / back" and "our ship." Province, The. Robert Creeley. CP-CreeR

Trying to Hold It All Together. Richard Eberhart. CP-EberR

Trying to open locked doors with a sword, threading. Sojourn in the Whale. Marianne Craig Moore. CP-MoorM

Trying to Pray. James Wright. CP-WrigJ

Trying to protect his students' innocence. History Teacher, The. Billy Collins. SP-CollB

Trying to read in Nature's book. In Nine Sleep Valley. James Merrill. SP-MerrJ

Trying to read the news, after your visit. Winged Heart, The. Robert Graves. CP-GravR

Trying to Remember. Miller Williams. CP-WillM

Trying to Sleep. Gregory Orr. SP-OrrG

Trying to Sleep Late on a Saturday Morning in November. Raymond Carver. CP-CarvR

Trying to Talk with a Man. Adrienne Rich. SP-RicA1; SP-RicA2

Trying to Tell It. William Stafford. SP-StafWW

Trying to tell you how. When We Dead Awaken. Adrienne Rich. SP-RicA2

Trying to Tell You Something. Robert Penn Warren. CP-WarrR

Trying to think of. Rocks, The. Robert Creeley. CP-CreeR

Trying to understand myself, I fetch. Obiter Dicta. Donald Davie. CP-DaviDC

Trying to understand the words. Bird-Language. W. H. Auden. CP-AudeW

Trying to write a poem while it was still dark out. Caution. Raymond Carver. CP-CarvR

Tryst. Olga Broumas. SP-BrouO

Tryst, The. Walter De la Mare. CP-DeLaW

Tryst, The. Paul Laurence Dunbar. CP-DunbP

Tryst, The. James Tate. SP-TateJ

Tryst on Vinegar Hill. Robert Penn Warren. CP-WarrR

Tsankawi. Arthur Sze. SP-SzeA

Tsar, who knew you? Who. Hayden Carruth. CP-CarHS *Fr.* Clay Hill Anthology, The.

Tsier. Peter Blue Cloud. SP-BlueP

Tsokadze O Altitudo. John Updike. CP-UpdiJ

Tsushima Screen. Joseph Brodsky. CP-BrodJ

Tu Do Street. Yusef Komunyakaa. CP-KomuY

Tu Fu in English. William Corbett. SP-CorbW

Tu Fu, old and ravaged by consumption. Scrutability. Sam Hamill. SP-HamiS

Tu Fu to Li Po. Tu Fu. CP-KizeC, *tr.* by Carolyn Kizer

Tu scendi dalle stelle, O Re del Cielo. Christina Georgina Rossetti. CP-RosC3

Tub, A. Charles Simic. SP-SimiCE

Tuba's a sun & beneath it. Poem at the Fairground. Federico García Lorca. CP-GarcF, *tr.* by Jerome Rothenberg *Fr.* Fairs.

Tubes. Donald Hall. CP-HallD

Tübingen–Hamburg Schlafwagen. Allen Ginsberg. CP-GinsA

Tübingen, January. Paul Celan. SP-CelaP, *tr.* by John Felstiner

Tubs of / memory. Roof Garden. James Schuyler. CP-SchuJ

Tuck a child in his bed. Rainer Maria Rilke. CP-RilkFr, *tr.* by A. Poulin, Jr.

Tuck, Demitroïa, / Ariadne, and Froyja. George Meredith. CP-MerG2

Tuck, my treasure! Tuck, my pleasure! George Meredith. CP-MerG2

Tuck, sweet charmer, tell me why. George Meredith. CP-MerG2

Tuck, thou graceless sinner!—. George Meredith. CP-MerG2

Tuck! Tuck! Once you would flatter me. George Meredith. CP-MerG2

Tucson Gardens. Eleanor Wilner. SP-WilnE

Tuesday and Friday. Hero Sandwiches. Charles Tomlinson. CP-TomlC

Tuesday at 87 Rue de Rome. James Laughlin. CP-LaugJ

Tuesday in Holy Week. Christina Georgina Rossetti. CP-RosC2

Tuesday, June 4, 1991. Billy Collins. SP-CollB

Tuesday Night at the Savoy Ballroom. Yusef Komunyakaa. CP-KomuY

"Tuesday night, the schooner Weaver, of Glen Creek, N.J., went to pieces near Sandy Hook, and her entire crew were lost."—Transcript, March 22d. Jones Very. CP-VeryJ

Tuesday's Child. Tennessee Williams. CP-WillT

Tuft of Flowers, The. Robert Frost. CP-FrosR

Tuft of Kelp, The. Herman Melville. SP-MelvH

Tuft of Primroses, The. William Wordsworth. CP-WorW1

Tufts, follicles, grubstake. Vacant Lot with Pokeweed. Amy Clampitt. CP-ClamA

Tug against the river. George Oppen. CP-OppGN

Tugg Martin. James Whitcomb Riley. CP-RileJ

Tugg Martin's tough.—No doubt o' that! Tugg Martin. James Whitcomb Riley. CP-RileJ

Tugs of Hull, The. George Oppen. CP-OppGN

Tulip. Louis Zukofsky. CP-ZukLS

Tulip Bed, The. William Carlos Williams. CP-WilW1

Tulips. Sylvia Plath. CP-PlatS

Tulips, The. Denise Levertov. SP-LeveDP; SP-LeveDS

Tulips are too excitable, it is winter here, The. Tulips. Sylvia Plath. CP-PlatS

Tulsa. John Updike. CP-UpdiJ

Tumble me down, and I will sit. To Fortune. Robert Herrick. CP-HerrR

Tumbling-hair / picker of buttercups. E. E. Cummings. CP-CummE

Tumult and turmoil, trouble and toil. Peace I Leave wth You. Christina Georgina Rossetti. CP-RosC2

Tumulus of emeralds and of strangeness, A. At the Anonymous Tomb of Herrera y Reissig in the Cemetery of Montevideo. Federico García Lorca. CP-GarcF, *tr.* by Christopher Maurer

Tune for an Ill-Tempered Clavichord. Ogden Nash. CP-NashO

Tune for Festive Dances in the Nineteen Sixties, A. Thomas Merton. CP-MertT

Tune, in American Type. John Updike. CP-UpdiJ

Tune in to a raga. Assassination Raga. Lawrence Ferlinghetti. SP-FerlL

Tune Me, O Lord, into One Harmony. Christina Georgina Rossetti. CP-RosC2

Tune thy music[ke] to thy heart [*or* hart]. Heart's Music. Thomas Campion. CP-CampT

Tuned in Late One Night. William Stafford. SP-StafWW

Tuning the Sky. Susan Howe. SP-HoweS

Tunisian Nostalgia. Lawrence Ferlinghetti. SP-FerlL

Tunnel, The. Robert Creeley. CP-CreeR

Tunnel, The. Muriel Rukeyser. CP-RukeM

Tunnel, but the roof is green and some light, A. Black Road Over Which Green Trees Grow. Thomas Lux. SP-LuxT

Tunneling through the earth. Dreams ("Tunneling through the earth"). Robert Creeley. CP-CreeR

Tunnels. Yusef Komunyakaa. CP-KomuY

Tunstall Forest. Donald Davie. CP-DaviDC

Turf-Stacks. Louis MacNeice. *See* Among These Turf-Stacks

Turkey, The. Ogden Nash. CP-NashO

Turkey-Cock. D. H. Lawrence. CP-LawrD

Turkey in the Straw. William Carlos Williams. CP-WilW2

Turkey vulture, / a shy bird ungainly on the ground, The. Best Defense is Offensive, The. Marge Piercy. SP-PierM

Turmut-Hoeing. Ivor Gurney. SP-GurnI

Turn, The. Robert Creeley. CP-CreeR

Turn, The. Philip Whalen. SP-WhalP

Turn again, thou fair Eliza. Fair Eliza. Robert Burns. CP-BurnR

Turn all I touch to gold. Midas. Jones Very. CP-VeryJ

Turn back. Turn, young lady dear. Robber Bridegroom, The. Allen Tate. CP-TateA

Turn Back, You Wanton Flyer. Thomas Campion. CP-CampT (Turne Backe You Wanton Flier.) CP-CampT

Turn, / corazón! / turn. Towards. Federico García Lorca. CP-GarcF, *tr.* by Jerome Rothenberg *Fr.* Return, The.

Turn from that girl. I Shall Laugh Purely. Robinson Jeffers. CP-JefR3

Turn from the ocean now. In Between Stories. Jelaluddin Rumi. SP-Rumi, *tr.* by Coleman Barks

Turn into pearls. Things That Hurt Me. William Stafford. SP-StafWW

Turn me on your knees. C'mon Jack. Allen Ginsberg. CP-GinsA

Turn not from him, who asks of thee. Kind Words. Jones Very. CP-VeryJ

Turn not [to] the prophet's page, O Son! He knew. For The Holy Family, by Michelangelo, in the National Gallery. Dante Gabriel Rossetti. CW-RossD

Turn now and rise. Charles Olson. CP-OlsoC

Turn, now, tired mind, unto your rest. Forests. Walter De la Mare. CP-DeLaW

Turn O Libertad. Walt Whitman. CP-WhitW

Turn of head, that searching light, A. Brother and Sister. Walter De la Mare. CP-DeLaW

Turn of noontide has begun, The. Near Brussels—A Half-way Pause. Dante Gabriel Rossetti. CW-RossD

Turn of the Century, The. Wisława Szymborska. SP-SzymWM, *tr.* by Joanna Trzeciak

Turn of the Head, A. Denise Levertov. SP-LeveDP

Turn of the Moon. Robert Graves. CP-GravR

Turn of the Wheel. Carl Sandburg. CP-SandC

Turn of the wheel, I thrust, A. Twelve-Spoked Wheel Flashing, The. Marge Piercy. SP-PierM

Turn off the tap, Mahavveray, it's too cold here. Mahavveray. Louis MacNeice. CP-MacNL

Turn on my tongue, O Spanish verse; confirm. Ewigkeit. Jorge Luis Borges. CP-WilbR, *tr.* by Richard Wilbur

Turn on the prudent Ant thy heedless eyes. Paraphrase. Samuel Johnson. CP-JohnS

Turn out all the lights. Tanck's Song About Earl Hines. Hayden Carruth. CP-CarHS *Fr.* Songs About What Comes Down: The Complete Works of Mr. Septic Tanck.

Turn out the light, turn over, shut your eyes. City, City! Randall Jarrell. CP-JarrR

Turn out the lights around the statues. When in the Course of Human Events. Kenneth Patchen. CP-PatcK

Turn Over Your Hand. William Stafford. SP-StafW; SP-StafWW

Turn Right Next Corner / *The Biggest Little Town in Kansas*. Wichita Vortex Sutra. Allen Ginsberg. CP-GinsA

Turn the cadence the verse and the music, The. To Find a Way. George Oppen. CP-OppGN

Turn through his life, each word and deed. His Heart of Constant Youth. James Whitcomb Riley. CP-RileJ

Turn toward the holocaust, it approaches. Discipline, A. Wendell Berry. CP-BerrW

Turn we next to the dead. Matthew Arnold. SP-ArnoM *Fr.* Haworth Churchyard.

Turn ye turn ye who tread the wandring path. Path of Peace, The. Jones Very. CP-VeryJ

Turn your face this way. To a Skull. James Whitcomb Riley. CP-RileJ

Turnabout. Charles Bukowski. SP-BukC1

Turne all thy thoughts to eyes. Thomas Campion. CP-CampT

Turne Backe You Wanton Flier. Thomas Campion. *See* Turn Back, You Wanton Flyer

Turned away, sooner. Precursors. Hans Magnus Enzensberger. SP-EnzeH, *tr. by* Michael Hamburger

Turned Down. D. H. Lawrence. CP-LawrD

Turner. Kenneth Patchen. CP-PatcK

Turner's Seas. Kathleen Jessie Raine. SP-RainK

Turning. Adrienne Rich.
   "Whatever you are that has tracked us this far." SP-RicA1

Turning a Moment to Say So Long. A. R. Ammons. CP-AmmoA

Turning and turning in the widening gyre. Second Coming, The. William Butler Yeats. CP-YeatW

Turning around I see a flock of sheep. A. K. Ramanujan. CP-RamaA

Turning Away. James Dickey. CP-DickJ

Turning away from flowers, A. Lover. Yusef Komunyakaa. CP-KomuY

Turning climbing slowly in late spring among. Snowline. W. S. Merwin. SP-MerwWF

Turning clumsily into the embrace. One Incident of Many. William Dickey. SP-DickW

Turning from the waterhole I said Oh. A. R. Ammons. CP-AmmoA

Turning of the Babies in the Bed, The. Paul Laurence Dunbar. CP-DunbP

Turning / one wants it all—. Change. Robert Creeley. CP-CreeR

Turning Out the Bedside Lamp. Tennessee Williams. CP-WillT

Turning the corner I. Second Sight. W. S. Merwin. SP-MerwW

Turning the Garden in Middle Age. Maxine W. Kumin. SP-KumiM

Turning the Wheel. Adrienne Rich. SP-RicA2
   Turning the Wheel. SP-RicA1; SP-RicA2

Turning the Wheel. Adrienne Rich. SP-RicA1; SP-RicA2 *Fr.* Turning the Wheel.

Turning through a collection. Wes Hardin: From a Photograph. Raymond Carver. CP-CarvR

Turnip-Hoer, The. Thomas Hardy. CP-HardT

Turnip Vendor, The. Samuel Johnson. CP-JohnS
   (Burlesque Translation of Lines from Lope de Vega's *Arcadia*.) CP-JohnS

Turnpike, without history, a function, The. Bus. Denise Levertov. SP-LeveDL

Turns in a Worm's Lane. Ogden Nash. CP-NashO

Turnstone turned rover, A. Upon Learning That a Bird Exists Called the Turnstone. John Updike. CP-UpdiJ

Turquoise sea off Grottamare. Grottamare. Lawrence Ferlinghetti. SP-FerlL

Turtle, The. Mary Oliver. SP-OlivM

Turtle, The. Chuang Tzu. CP-MertT

Turtle, The. William Carlos Williams. CP-WilW2

Turtle Dove, The. Geoffrey Hill. CP-HillG

Turtle Goddess. Film, The. Denise Levertov. SP-LeveDP

Turtle in swamp. Ralph Waldo Emerson. CP-EmerR

Turtle lives 'twixt plated decks, The. Ogden Nash. CP-NashO

Turtles in this big green bowl are reduced by one, The. Death and the Turtle. Josephine Jacobsen. CP-JacoJ

Turtles on the ledges of July, The. Concord River. Adrienne Rich. CP-RicAE

Tuscan Brutus, The. Donald Davie. CP-DaviDC

Tuscan cypresses. Cypresses. D. H. Lawrence. CP-LawrD

Tuscan Morning. Donald Davie. CP-DaviDC

Tuscan thorn, A. Bus Song. William Corbett. SP-CorbW

Tuskegee Song. Paul Laurence Dunbar. CP-DunbP

Tuskegee, thou pride of the swift growing South. Tuskegee Song. Paul Laurence Dunbar. CP-DunbP

Tut-tut! give back the flags—how can you care. Confederate Flags, The. Ambrose Bierce. SP-BierA

Tutored Child, The. Stanley Kunitz. CP-KunSC

Tutorial. Ted Hughes. SP-HughTN *Fr.* Boom.

TV. Howard Nemerov. CP-NemeH

Tw / oo / ld / o / nce upo / n. E. E. Cummings. CP-CummE

Twa bonny [*or* bony] lads were Sandy and Jockie. Sandy and Jockie. Robert Burns. CP-BurnR

Twa Dogs, The. Robert Burns. CP-BurnR

'Twas a curious dream, good sooth! Dream of the Little Princess, The. James Whitcomb Riley. CP-RileJ

'Twas a Funny Little Fellow. Funny Little Fellow, The. James Whitcomb Riley. CP-RileJ

'Twas a long journey lay before us. Satire 1.5: "'Twas a long journey lay before us." Horace. CP-CowpW *Fr.* Satires.

'Twas a long Parting—but the time. Emily Dickinson. CP-DickE

'Twas a marvelous vision of Summer. Vision of Summer, A. James Whitcomb

Riley. CP-RileJ

'Twas a saying in use with the great Mr. Lowndes. Very Original Poem, Written with Even a Greater Endeavour than Ordinary after Intelligibility, and Hitherto Only Published on the First Leaf of the Author's Son's Account-Book. Robert Browning. CP-BroR2

'Twas a strange young man of the dreamy times. Strange Young Man, The. James Whitcomb Riley. CP-RileJ

'Twas a summer ago when he left me here. Lost Love, A. James Whitcomb Riley. CP-RileJ

'Twas a test I designed, in a quiet conceit. Test, A. James Whitcomb Riley. CP-RileJ

'Twas after dread Pultowa's day. Mazeppa. Lord Byron. CP-Byron

'Twas at the royal feast, for Persia won. Alexander's Feast; or, The Power of Music [*or* Musique]. John Dryden. SP-DrydJ

'Twas awkward, but it fitted me. Emily Dickinson. CP-DickE

'Twas Bedford Special Assize, one daft Midsummer's Day. Ned Bratts. Robert Browning. CP-BroR2; SP-BroR

'Twas but a hint of Spring—for still. Hint of Spring, A. James Whitcomb Riley. CP-RileJ

'Twas but a single Rose. Upon a Virgin Kissing a Rose. Robert Herrick. CP-HerrR

'Twas Cesars saying: Kings no lesse conquerers are. Counsell. Robert Herrick. CP-HerrR

'Twas comfort in her Dying Room. Emily Dickinson. CP-DickE

'Twas Crisis—All the length had passed. Emily Dickinson. CP-DickE

'Twas ev'n, the dewy fields were green. Song. On Miss W. A. Robert Burns. CP-BurnR

'Twas fighting for his Life he was. Emily Dickinson. CP-DickE

'Twas Fultah Fisher's boarding-house. Ballad of Fisher's Boardinghouse, The. Rudyard Kipling. CP-KiplR

'Twas Goethe taught us all / By diagnosis. Burlesque for Palgrave on the Pronunciation of "Metamorphosis." Robert Browning. CP-BroR2

'Twas here my summer paused. Emily Dickinson. CP-DickE

'Twas in a beauteous verdant shade. Vision, The. Annis Boudinot Stockton. CP-StocA

'Twas in a glimmering starlight. George Meredith. CP-MerG2

'Twas in a tavern that with old age stooped. Falstaff. Walter De la Mare. CP-DeLaW

'Twas in the glad season. Morning Dream, The. William Cowper. CP-CowpW

'Twas in the seventeen hunder year. Johnie B———'s Lament. Robert Burns. CP-BurnR *Fr.* Heron Ballads, 1795, The.

'Twas in the winter at the close of day. Pilgrim, The. Jones Very. CP-VeryJ

'Twas just at gnat and cobweb-time. Rift, The. Thomas Hardy. CP-HardT

'Twas just this time, last year, I died. Emily Dickinson. CP-DickE

'Twas later when the summer went. Emily Dickinson. CP-DickE

'Twas like a Maelstrom, with a notch. Final Inch, The. Emily Dickinson. CP-DickE

'Twas Love—not me. Emily Dickinson. CP-DickE

'Twas mercy brought me from my *Pagan* land. On Being Brought from Africa to America. Phillis Wheatley. CP-WheaP

'Twas my last waking thought, how it could be. Two Founts, The. Samuel Taylor Coleridge. CP-ColeS

'Twas my one Glory. Emily Dickinson. CP-DickE

'Twas my purpose, on a day. Figurative Description of the Procedure of Divine Love, A. Jeanne Marie Bouvier de la Motte Guyon. CP-CowpW

'Twas na her bonie blue e'e was my ruin. Song: "'Twas na her bonie blue e'e was my ruin." Robert Burns. CP-BurnR

'Twas night; her comrades gathered all. Geraldine. Emily Jane Brontë. CP-BronE

'Twas noontide of summer. Evening Star. Edgar Allan Poe. CP-PoeEd

'Twas not by strength of man, that Moses sought. Moses as Leader of Israel. Jones Very. CP-VeryJ

'Twas not Lov's Dart. Hymne to Sir Clipseby Crew, A. Robert Herrick. CP-HerrR

Twas not while England's sword unsheathed. American Rebellion, The. Rudyard Kipling. CP-KiplR

'Twas now the hour when Night had driven. From Anacreon. Lord Byron. CP-Byron

Twas on a lofty vase's side. Ode on the Death of a Favo[u]rite Cat, Drowned in a Tub [*or* Bowl] of Gold Fishes. Thomas Gray. CP-GrayT

'Twas on a Monday morning. Charlie He's My Darling. Robert Burns. CP-BurnR

Twas on a sunny summer day. Incident, An. Arthur Hugh Clough. SP-ClouA

'Twas on the good ship Dollymop. Isles of Jessamy, The. Christopher Logue. SP-LoguC

'Twas one of those dark, cloudy days. Emily Jane Brontë. CP-BronE

'Twas past ane o'clock in a cauld frosty morning. Cauld Frosty Morning. Robert Burns. CP-BurnR

'Twas sometime in the days of yore. Punegyric upon Tom Pun-sibi's *Ars Pun-*

ica, A. *Unknown.* CP-SherT

'Twas such a little little boat. Emily Dickinson. CP-DickE

'Twas Summer and the sun was mounted high. Ruined Cottage, The. William Wordsworth. MW-WorW

'Twas the apple that in Eden. Unlucky Apple, The. Paul Laurence Dunbar. CP-DunbP

'Twas the height of the fête when we quitted the riot. Moon-drowned. James Whitcomb Riley. CP-RileJ

'Twas the old—road—through pain. Emily Dickinson. CP-DickE

'Twas the voice of the sweet dove. Old Sweet Dove of Wiveton, The. Stevie Smith. CP-SmitS

'Twas the voice of the Wanderer, I heard her exclaim. Wanderer, The. Stevie Smith. CP-SmitS

'Twas thirty years ago. Henry David Thoreau. CP-ThorH

'Twas three an' thirty year ago. Rivals, The. Paul Laurence Dunbar. CP-DunbP

'Twas to greet the new rector I called here. Old Neighbour and the New, The. Thomas Hardy. CP-HardT

'Twas warm—at first—like Us. Emily Dickinson. CP-DickE

'Twas where the birch and sounding thong are plyed. Tale, A. Robert Burns. CP-BurnR

'Twas while the bush was burning, Moses saw. Moses at the Bush. Jones Very. CP-VeryJ

'Twas yesterday, at early dawn. M.G. For The U.S. Emily Jane Brontë. CP-BronE

'Twas yesterday such a black-dye-day. George Meredith. CP-MerG2

Tweedledee and Tweedledoom. Ogden Nash. CP-NashO

Twelfe Night, or King and Queene. Robert Herrick. CP-HerrR

Twelfth Morning; or What You Will. Elizabeth Bishop. CP-BishE

Twelfth Night. Louis MacNeice. CP-MacNL

Twell de Night Is Pas'. Paul Laurence Dunbar. CP-DunbP

Twelth Night, Gift Horses, and of Certain Reversals. Robert Stock. SP-StocR

Twelve, The. Aleksandr Aleksandrovich Blok. SP-BlokA, *tr. by* Peter France *and* Jon Stallworthy

Twelve, The. Allen Tate. CP-TateA

Twelve / a dozen. Ottffssente. Kenneth Rexroth. CP-RexrK

Twelve arrows, and a bow, and spear. Song: "Twelve arrows, and a bow, and spear." George Meredith. CP-MerG2

Twelve Articles. Jonathan Swift. CP-SwifJ

Twelve Dancing Princesses, The. Anne Sexton. CP-SextA

12:18 A.M. Charles Bukowski. SP-BukC1

Twelve Faces of the Emerald. Dan Pagis. SP-PagiD, *tr. by* Stephen Mitchell

Twelve Hours Out of New York After Twenty-Five Days at Sea. Gary Snyder. CP-SnydG

12 July 1980. Primo Levi. CP-LeviP, *tr. by* Ruth Feldman

12 June I've got three jobs. Crowded. Philip Whalen. SP-WhalP

Twelve Line Poem. William Carlos Williams. CP-WilW2

Twelve-noon whistle groans, The. Tragedy of Bricks, The. Galway Kinnell. SP-KinnGN

12 November 1948. Yannis Ritsos. SP-RitsY *Fr.* Exile's Journals 1.

Twelve O'Clock. Carolyn Kizer. CP-KizeC

Twelve o'clock. / Along the reaches of the street. Rhapsody on a Windy Night. T. S. Eliot. CP-ElioT; SP-ElioT

12 O'Clock News. Elizabeth Bishop. CP-BishE

Twelve people, most of us strangers, stand in a room. Eating the Pig. Donald Hall. CP-HallD

Twelve Poems from *The Keeper of the Flocks*. Fernando Pessoa. CP-MertT

Twelve Seasons. Donald Hall. CP-HallD

12. 6. 71. Louise Glück. SP-GlucL

Twelve snails went walking after night. Haughty Snail-King, The. Nicholas Vachel Lindsay. CP-LindV

Twelve Songs. W. H. Auden. CP-AudeW

Twelve Spartan virgins, noble, young and fair. Idyll 18: The Epithalamium of Helen and Menelaus. Theocritus. CP-DryJ2 *Fr.* Idylls.

Twelve-Spoked Wheel Flashing, The. Marge Piercy. SP-PierM

Twelve-Thousand-Day Honeymoon, The. Anne Sexton. CP-SextA

Twelve Years. Paul Celan. SP-CelaP, *tr. by* John Felstiner

Twelve years ago I came here. Burn, The. Galway Kinnell. SP-KinnGN

Twelve years to the day. Anniversary. Rita Dove. SP-DoveR

20th Street Spring. Grace Paley. CP-PalGC

Twentieth year is well-nigh past, The. To Mary. William Cowper. CP-CowpW

21. Lawrence Ferlinghetti. SP-FerlL

25. Lawrence Ferlinghetti. SP-FerlL

26. Lawrence Ferlinghetti. SP-FerlL

Twenty Bridges from Tower to Kew. River's Tale, The. Rudyard Kipling. CP-KiplR

28. Philip Levine. SP-LeviP

Twenty-eight, hairy belly hanging out. Bankruptcy. Raymond Carver. CP-CarvR

Twenty-eight years before on the living room couch he'd stared at me, I said.

Don't Grow Old. Allen Ginsberg. CP-GinsA *Fr.* Don't Grow Old.

25th Year of His Life, The. Constantine P. Cavafy. CP-CavaC, *tr. by* Theoharis Constantine Theoharis

21st Century Man. Richard Eberhart. CP-EberR

25 February 1944. Primo Levi. CP-LeviP, *tr. by* Ruth Feldman *and* Brian Swann

Twenty-Five Years. Adam Zagajewski. SP-ZagaA, *tr. by* Clare Cavanagh

24:IV:40075, 3:30 PM, N. of Coaldale, Nevada, a Glimpse through a Break in the Storm of the Summit of the White Mountains. O Mother Gaia. Gary Snyder. CP-SnydG

24 May 1950. Yannis Ritsos. SP-RitsY *Fr.* Exile's Journals 3.

24 November 1948. Yannis Ritsos. SP-RitsY *Fr.* Exile's Journals 2.

Twenty-four Years. Dylan Thomas. CP-ThomD

20:vii:58, On Which I Renounce the Notion of Social Responsiblity. Philip Whalen. SP-WhalP

Twenty men crossing a bridge. Metaphors of a Magnifico. Wallace Stevens. CP-StevW; CP-StevWP

Twenty men stand watching the muckers. Muckers. Carl Sandburg. CP-SandC

29 (A Dream in Two Parts). Ai. SP-Ai

29 Poems. Louis Zukofsky. CP-ZukLS

"Run on, you still dead to the sound of a name." CP-ZukLS

"Stubbing the cloud-fields—the searchlight, high." CP-ZukLS

29 Songs. Louis Zukofsky. CP-ZukLS

Twenty-one Love Poems. Adrienne Rich. SP-RicA1; SP-RicA2

21 November 1948. Yannis Ritsos. SP-RitsY *Fr.* Exile's Journals 1.

Twenty or more big cloth roses, pale rose or scarlet. Christmas Tree. Robert Lowell. SP-LowcR

27 June 1906, 2 P.M. Constantine P. Cavafy. CP-CavaC, *tr. by* Theoharis Constantine Theoharis

27 November 1948. Yannis Ritsos. SP-RitsY *Fr.* Exile's Journals 2.

26 January 1949. Yannis Ritsos. SP-RitsY *Fr.* Exile's Journals 2.

26 November 1948. Yannis Ritsos. SP-RitsY *Fr.* Exile's Journals 2.

Twenty-some years ago, I read Graham Stuart Thomas's. Horse-Chestnut Trees and Roses. James Schuyler. CP-SchuJ

Twenty Sonnets to Mary Queen of Scots. Joseph Brodsky. CP-BrodJ, *tr. by* Peter France

Twenty sparrows / on. Breakfast. William Carlos Williams. CP-WilW1

Twenty-third Psalm, The. George Herbert. CP-HerbG

23rd Street Runs into Heaven. Kenneth Patchen. CP-PatcK

23 January 1949. Yannis Ritsos. SP-RitsY *Fr.* Exile's Journals 2.

Twenty Three Point Prospectus for Small College in the Badlands. Thomas Merton. CP-MertT

.22. John Ciardi. CP-CiarJ

20–200 on 747. Heather McHugh. SP-McHuH

22,000 Dollars in 3 Months. Charles Bukowski. SP-BukC2

22,000 feet over Hazed square Vegetable planet Floor. Going to Chicago. Allen Ginsberg. CP-GinsA

Twenty-Two Tremblings of the Postulant. Jay Wright. SP-WrigJ

Twenty-Year Marriage. Ai. SP-Ai

Twenty-Year-Old Soldiers. Adam Zagajewski. SP-ZagaA, *tr. by* Clare Cavanagh

Twenty Years. Walt Whitman. CP-WhitW

Twenty Years Ago. D. H. Lawrence. CP-LawrD

Twenty years ago, you were the man. Momento Mori. Ai. SP-Ai

Twenty years, forty years, it's nothing. Cold Spring, The. Denise Levertov. SP-LeveDS

Twenty Years in the Valley. Dan Pagis. SP-PagiD, *tr. by* Stephen Mitchell

Twenty years step between. Stepmother: A Boy's Song. Yusef Komunyakaa. CP-KomuY

Twentyseven bums give a prostitute the once. E. E. Cummings. CP-CummE

'Twere sweet to have a comrade here. Dream of the City Shopwoman. Thomas Hardy. CP-HardT

Twi- / is -Light bird. E. E. Cummings. CP-CummE

Twice. Paul Muldoon. CP-MuldP

Twice. Christina Georgina Rossetti. CP-RosC1

Twice a week the winter thorough. A. E. Housman. CP-HousA

Twice, Away from Jack, I Thought of Him. John Ciardi. CP-CiarJ

Twice Born. Robert Penn Warren. CP-WarrR

Twice had Summer her fair Verdure. Emily Dickinson. CP-DickE

Twice has *Pudica* been a Bride, and led. Upon a Lady Faire, but Fruitlesse. Robert Herrick. CP-HerrR

Twice having seen your shingled heads adorable. Evening on Lesbos. Edna St. Vincent Millay. CP-MillE

Twice I woke up tonight and wandered to. On Love. Joseph Brodsky. CP-BrodJ, *tr. by* Daniel Weissbort

Twice I'd tried / to pass the / bastard outside. Arroyo Hondo. Charles Tomlinson. CP-TomlC

Twice in the past two weeks I think I met. Couple, The. Robert Lowell. SP-LoweR

Twice Lovely. Walter De la Mare. CP-DeLaW

Twice More. C. K. Williams. CP-WillC

Twice, now, I've gone back there, like a part-time ghost. Return to Marsh Street. Thomas McGrath. SP-McGrT

Twice now this woman for whom my unreasonable dislike. Emissary, The. Denise Levertov. SP-LeveDL

Twice Of The Same Fever. Robert Graves. CP-GravR

Twice one summer. Look Back. Gary Snyder. CP-SnydG

Twice or thrice had I loved thee. Air[e] and Angels. John Donne. CP-DonnJ; MW-DonnJ

Twice ten years old not fully told. Upon a Fit of Sickness, Anno 1632. Anne Bradstreet. CP-BradA

Twice this Christmas Day you tried. Amplitude. Tess Gallagher. SP-GallT

Twice you have been around the world. One Who Was Different, The. Randall Jarrell. CP-JarrR

Twickenham [or Twicknam] Garden. John Donne. CP-DonnJ; MW-DonnJ

Twig sprouteth, / The moth outeth, The. Are Ye Not Much Better Than They? Christina Georgina Rossetti. CP-RosC2

Twigs of the birch imprint the December sky, The. Prospect, The. Thomas Hardy. CP-HardT

Twigs stiffen / the fingers. Sense. Rae Armantrout. SP-ArmaA

Twilight. G. K. Chesterton. CP-ChesG

Twilight. Walter De la Mare. CP-DeLaW

Twilight. Paul Laurence Dunbar. CP-DunbP

Twilight. Robert Herrick. CP-HerrR

Twilight. D. H. Lawrence. CP-LawrD

Twilight. W. S. Merwin. SP-MerwWF

Twilight. Yannis Ritsos. SP-RitsY, tr. by Kimon Friar

Twilight. Wallace Stevens. CP-StevWP

Twilight. Walt Whitman. CP-WhitW

Twilight and little mountain. Lackawanna Twilight. Carl Sandburg. CP-SandC

Twilight approaches, with its last brief spot-lit. All That Is. Richard Wilbur. CP-WilbR

Twilight Calm. Christina Georgina Rossetti. CP-RosC1

Twilight Comes. Hayden Carruth. CP-CarHS

Twilight falls; I soften the dusting feathers, The. Sappho. James Wright. CP-WrigJ

Twilight is long fingers and black hair, The. Long Fingers. Allen Tate. CP-TateA

Twilight is no other thing (we say), The. Twilight. Robert Herrick. CP-HerrR

Twilight Land. John Logan. CP-LogaJ

Twilight leaned mirrored in a pool. Old Angler, The. Walter De la Mare. CP-DeLaW

Twilight Music. George Meredith. CP-MerG1

Twilight Night. Christina Georgina Rossetti. CP-RosC1

Twilight, no other thing is, Poets say. Twilight. Robert Herrick. CP-HerrR

Twilight of the dove, The. Unknown Street. Jorge Luis Borges. SP-BorgJ, tr. by Alexander Coleman

Twilight, old friend, has come back to the lower orchard. Vesper Journal. Charles Wright. SP-WrigC

Twilight on the Waste Lands. Donald Davie. CP-DaviDC

Twilight Song. Edwin Arlington Robinson. CP-RobiE

Twilight Song, A. Walt Whitman. CP-WhitW

Twilight stifled the valley wearily. Lityerses. Allen Tate. CP-TateA

Twilight Stories. James Whitcomb Riley. CP-RileJ

Twilight Sustenance Hiatus. James Tate. SP-TateJ

Twilight was a going of the gods: the air. Under the Moon's Reign. Charles Tomlinson. CP-TomlC

Twilights. James Wright. CP-WrigJ

Twilit snow. Silver Swan, The. Kenneth Rexroth. CP-RexrK

Twin Falls, The. James Dickey. CP-DickJ

Twin of Sleep, The. Robert Graves. CP-GravR

Twin spheres full of fur and noise. Poem: "Twin spheres full of fur and noise." Frank O'Hara. SP-OharF

Twin streaks twice higher than cumulus. Vapor Trails. Gary Snyder. CP-SnydG

Twined together and, as is customary. Never Such Love. Robert Graves. CP-GravR

Twinkletoes in the ballroom. Light Music. Derek Mahon. CP-MahoD

Twins. Charles Bukowski. SP-BukC1

Twins. Jane Cooper. CP-CoopJ

Twins. Robert Graves. CP-GravR

Twins, The. Robert Browning. CP-BroR1

Twins, The. Mona Van Duyn. SP-VanDM

Twins, The. James Whitcomb Riley. CP-RileJ

Twins, The. Karl Shapiro. SP-ShapK

Twintorette, A. James Whitcomb Riley. CP-RileJ

Twirling your blue skirts, travelling the sward. Blue Girls. John Crowe Ransom. SP-RansJ

Twirls on the tips of a carnation. Oriental Ballerina, The. Rita Dove. SP-DoveR

Twist, The. Charles Olson. SP-OlsoC Fr. Maximus Poems, The.

Twist me a crown of wind-flowers. Crown of Windflowers, A. Christina Georgina Rossetti. CP-RosC2

Twist ye, twine ye! even so. Spindle Song, The. Sir Walter Scott. SP-ScotW

Twist your fingers, cheery. New Song for Indiana Ophelias. Carl Sandburg. CP-SandC

Twisted and strange. Sailing Date. Langston Hughes. CP-HughL; CP-HughL2

Twisted body and whitesocked. Too Much to Hope. Denise Levertov. SP-LeveDL

Twisted Tree, The. Marya Alexandrovna Zaturenska. SP-ZatuM

Twisting, turning, A. Reflections on Milkweed. Peter Blue Cloud. SP-BlueP

'Twixt a smile and a tear. Twilight. Paul Laurence Dunbar. CP-DunbP

'Twixt Bedford Park and Westminster. Frances (A Fragment) ("'Twixt Bedford Park and Westminster"). G. K. Chesterton. CP-ChesG

'Twixt dream and wake we wandered on. Encounter, The. Walter De la Mare. CP-DeLaW

'Twixt Kings and Subjects ther[e]'s this mighty odds. Difference Betwixt King and Subjects, The. Robert Herrick. CP-HerrR

'Twixt Kings and Tyrants there's this difference known. Kings and Tyrants. Robert Herrick. CP-HerrR

'Twixt mt house and thy house the pathway is broad. Houses, The. Rudyard Kipling. CP-KiplR

'Twixt those twin worlds,—the world of Sleep, which gave. Percy Bysshe Shelley. Dante Gabriel Rossetti. CW-RossD Fr. Five English Poets.

Twixt Truth and Errour, there's this difference known. Truth and Error. Robert Herrick. CP-HerrR

Two. Carolyn Kizer. CP-KizeC Fr. Pro Femina.

Two. Robert Creeley. CP-CreeR

Two. David Ignatow. SP-IgnaD

TWO. Thomas Kinsella. CP-KinsT

Two. Yusef Komunyakaa. CP-KomuY

Two. Carl Sandburg. CP-SandC

Two. James Schuyler. CP-SchuJ

Two, The. Ivor Gurney. SP-GurnI

2 a.m. / December, and still no moon. Late Moon. Philip Levine. SP-LeviP

Two Amsterdams. Lawrence Ferlinghetti. SP-FerlL

Two and One Are a Problem. Ogden Nash. CP-NashO

2 and 2 are 4. Problems. Langston Hughes. CP-HughL

Two angels among the throng of angels. Vision, A. Denise Levertov. SP-LeveDP

Two Angels, The. John Greenleaf Whittier. CP-WhitJ

Two April Mornings, The. William Wordsworth. CP-WorW1; MW-WorW

Two Armies. Stephen Spender.

Two Artists. Denise Levertov. SP-LeveDL

Two Aspects of April. William Carlos Williams. CP-WilW1

Two at Norfolk. Wallace Stevens. CP-StevW; CP-StevWP

Two athletes / Are dancing in the cathedral. Spring Images. James Wright. CP-WrigJ

Two bad actors canonized by ballads. Villon/Leadbelly. Yusef Komunyakaa. CP-KomuY

Two beings were drifting. Destined Pair, The. Thomas Hardy. CP-HardT

Two bells six bells two bells six bells. Night Bells. Carl Sandburg. CP-SandC

Two Blackbirds, The. George Meredith. CP-MerG1

Two blue glasses of neat. Living in the Moment. Marilyn Hacker. SP-HackM

Two blushing roses, gathered recently. Petrarch. CP-Petra, tr. by J. G. Nichols

Two boats parked / and posing in. White Boat, Blue Boat. James Schuyler. CP-SchuJ

Two boats with nets lying off the sea-beach, quite still. Paumanok Picture, A. Walt Whitman. CP-WhitW

Two boys at the end of the full train. Brothers: Two Saltimbanques, The. John Logan. CP-LogaJ

Two boys down the road with a vegetable farm, The. Cow, The. W. S. Merwin. SP-MerwWF

Two Boys Went Into a Dream Diner. Allen Ginsberg. CP-GinsA

Two bres's, 'n' 'gongo 'brella. Little Cannibal's Bedtimesong. Kenneth Patchen. CP-PatcK

Two bricklayers are setting the walls. Bricklayer's Lunch Hour, The. Allen Ginsberg. CP-GinsA; SP-GinsA

Two British Airmen. Thomas Merton. CP-MertT

Two Brothers. Ai. SP-Ai

Two brothers, Oakes and Oliver. Two Gardens in Linndale. Edwin Arlington Robinson. CP-RobiE

Two brothers, Sleep and Death, they unblinkingly called, The. Nearly. Raymond Carver. CP-CarvR

Two Brothers went a journey hand in hand. Creed. George Meredith. CP-MerG2

Two brothers wisely kept apart, together are employ'd. Riddles: "Two brothers wisely kept apart, together are employ'd." James Leigh Perrot. CP-AustJ

Two bubbles found they had rainbows on their curves. Bubbles. Carl Sandburg. CP-SandC

Two Butterflies went out at Noon. Emily Dickinson. CP-DickE

Two, by themselves, each other, love and fear. Pyramus and Thisbe. John Donne. CP-DonnJ; MW-DonnJ

Two by two, past. Blessing the Animals. Yusef Komunyakaa. CP-KomuY

Two Camels. Robert Browning. CP-BroR2

Two Campers in Cloud Country. Sylvia Plath. CP-PlatS

Two Carriages. Raymond Carver. CP-CarvR

Two Cathedrals, The. Jorge Luis Borges. SP-BorgJ, tr. by Stephen Kessler

2 Chairs are empty in a sunlit room. Pastoral Jazz. Olga Broumas. SP-BrouO

Two Children. James Laughlin. CP-LaugJ

Two Children, The. Emily Jane Brontë. CP-BronE
  (A.E. and R.C.) CP-BronE

Two children bow their heads. Puzzle, The. Howard Nemerov. CP-NemeH

Two children, dressed in court costume. Old Picture, An. Howard Nemerov. CP-NemeH

Two Chorale-Preludes: On Melodies by Paul Celan. Geoffrey Hill. CP-HillG

Two Chorus's to the Tragedy of Brutus. Alexander Pope. CP-PopeA

Two Christmas-Cards. Robinson Jeffers. CP-JefR3

Two Christs were at Golgotha. Early Lynching. Carl Sandburg. CP-SandC

Two Cities. Marilyn Hacker. SP-HackM

Two Climbs. W. H. Auden. CP-AudeW

Two coins round my neck, warm coins, lonely. Soothsaying. Olga Broumas. SP-BrouO

Two college sophs of Cambridge growth. Cassinus and Peter. Jonathan Swift. CP-SwifJ

Two Comments on "Death's Chicken, Named Amelia." Alan Dugan. CP-DugaA

Two Conceits. Allen Tate. CP-TateA

Two Cranial Murals. Yusef Komunyakaa. CP-KomuY

Two crownèd Kings, and One that stood alone. Vision, A. Oscar Wilde. CP-WildO

Two Crucial Generations. Robert Graves. CP-GravR

Two cups / a given grace. Given Grace, A. Charles Tomlinson. CP-TomlC; SP-TomlC

Two days ago with dancing glancing hair. My Friend. Christina Georgina Rossetti. CP-RosC1

Two days behind the dust-storm—man's. Trips to California. Robert Penn Warren. CP-WarrR

Two days of fever! Too much, so I. Religion of My Time, The. Pier Paolo Pasolini. SP-PasoP, tr. by Norman MacAfee and Luciano Martinengo

Two days of listening to a police radio. Connections. Stephen Dobyns. SP-DoveR

Two days were walking down the street. Biography. William Stafford. SP-StafWW

Two days with one eye. Revelation. John Updike. CP-UpdiJ

Two Dedications. Donald Davie. CP-DaviDC

Two Deliberate Exercises. William Carlos Williams. CP-WilW2

Two Desert Fathers. Thomas Merton. CP-MertT

Two Devills at one blow thou hast laid flat. Luke 11; Upon the Dumbe Devill Cast Out, and the Slanderous Jewes Put to Silence. Bible, N.T. CP-CrasR Fr. St. Luke.

Two Disappeared into a House. Yehuda Amichai. SP-AmicY, tr. by Chana Bloch

Two Disciplines. Robert Graves. CP-GravR

Two Dogs Have I. Ogden Nash. CP-NashO

Two dogs / wait for the crumbs. Quarai. Charles Tomlinson. CP-TomlC

Two doors open directly onto the sky. School Holidays. Yannis Ritsos. SP-RitsY, tr. by Kimon Friar

Two doves upon the selfsame branch. Song: "Two doves upon the selfsame branch." Christina Georgina Rossetti. CP-RosC1

Two Dreams. Allen Ginsberg. CP-GinsA

Two Dry Poems. John Ciardi. CP-CiarJ

Two Early Poems. Tennessee Williams. CP-WillT

Two Easter Stanzas. Nicholas Vachel Lindsay. CP-LindV

Two Eclipses. Shmuel HaNagid. SP-HaNaS, tr. by Peter Cole

Two Egrets. John Ciardi. CP-CiarJ

Two Egyptian Portrait Masks. Robert Earl Hayden. CP-HaydR

2 8 3 2 5 6 7 4 5 4 9. Pablo Neruda. SP-NeruP

Two elderly orphans. Ironmonger's Shop, The. Hans Magnus Enzensberger. SP-EnzeH

Two Elizabeths, The. John Greenleaf Whittier. CP-WhitJ

Two Epigrams on Byron's Cain. William Wordsworth. CP-WorW2

Two Evening Moons. Federico García Lorca. CP-GarcF, tr. by Alan S. Trueblood Fr. Moon Songs.

Two evils, monstrous either one apart. Winter Remembered. John Crowe Ransom. SP-RansJ

Two executioners stalk along over the knolls, The. Throwing a Tree. Thomas Hardy. CP-HardT

Two eyes, two hands—. Gemini. Robert Creeley. CP-CreeR

Two-faced Janus, god of Time. To Janus. Jonathan Swift. CP-SwifJ

Two Fawns That Didn't See the Light This Spring. Gary Snyder. CP-SnydG

Two Figures in Dense Violet Night. Wallace Stevens. CP-StevW; CP-StevWP

Two Fires, The. Margaret Atwood. SP-AtwM1

Two Fish. Carl Sandburg. CP-SandC

Two fishes swimming in the sea. Laughing Blue Steel. Carl Sandburg. CP-SandC

Two flower-enfolding crystal vases she. Grace and Love. George Meredith. CP-MerG1

Two-Fold. D. H. Lawrence. CP-LawrD

Two-fold gift in this my volume lies, A. Phaedrus. CP-JohnS Fr. Fabulae.

Two for Gertrude Kasle. John Ciardi. CP-CiarJ

Two for History. Kenneth Patchen. CP-PatcK

Two Formal Elegies. Geoffrey Hill. CP-HillG

Two forms move among the dead, high sleep. Owl in the Sarcophagus, The. Wallace Stevens. CP-StevW; CP-StevWP

Two Forms of Insomnia. Jorge Luis Borges. SP-BorgJ, tr. by Alan S. Trueblood

Two Foscari, The. Lord Byron. CP-Byron

Two Founts, The. Samuel Taylor Coleridge. CP-ColeS

Two Fragments from Pausanias. James Laughlin. CP-LaugJ

Two Fragments on Sleep. D. H. Lawrence. CP-LawrD

Two Friends. David Ignatow. SP-IgnaD

Two Friends. Jelaluddin Rumi. SP-Rumi, tr. by Coleman Barks

Two from a pit. Flower, The. Carolyn Kizer. CP-KizeC

Two from Ireland. Donald Davie. CP-DaviDC

Two full generations. Song: Seven Fresh Years. Robert Graves. CP-GravR

Two Gardens in Linndale. Edwin Arlington Robinson. CP-RobiE

Two gazed into a pool, he gazed and she. Echo from Willowwood, An. Christina Georgina Rossetti. CP-RosC3

Two Gentlemen in Bonds. John Crowe Ransom. SP-RansJ

Two Ghosts Together. Kenneth Patchen. CP-PatcK

Two Girls. Federico García Lorca. CP-GarcF, tr. by Robert Nasatir

Two Girls. Howard Nemerov. CP-NemeH

Two girls discover. Secret, The. Denise Levertov. SP-LeveDP; SP-LeveDS

Two Girls Live in the Old House. Yehuda Amichai. SP-AmicYL, tr. by Benjamin Harshav and Barbara Harshav

Two girls one blond one latin with fixed hair. Girls Fighting, Broadway. Karl Shapiro. SP-ShapK

Two girls there are: within the house. Two Sisters of Persephone. Sylvia Plath. CP-PlatS

Two Goes into Two Once, If You Can Get It There. Ogden Nash. CP-NashO

Two grades above me, though two inches shorter. First Love. Robert Lowell. SP-LoweR

Two Guitar Pieces. Philip Larkin. CP-LarkP

Two Hands. Anne Sexton. CP-SextA

Two hands lie still, the hairy and the white. Love for a Hand. Karl Shapiro. SP-ShapK

Two Hangovers. James Wright. CP-WrigJ

Two Hatreds of Action. Alan Dugan. CP-DugaA

Two-Headed Poems. Margaret Atwood. SP-AtwM2

Two heavy trestles, and a board. My Table. William Butler Yeats. CP-YeatW Fr. Meditations in Time of Civil War.

Two Holidays. Heather McHugh. SP-McHuH

Two homecomings link my life. Homecomings. Pablo Neruda. SP-NeruP

Two hopes away from the battle, I had a vision of peace. Yehuda Amichai. SP-AmicY, tr. by Stephen Mitchell Fr. In a Right Angle: A Cycle of Quatrains.

Two hopes away from the battlefield, I had a vision of peace. Yehuda Amichai. SP-AmicYL, tr. by Barbara Harshav and Benjamin Harshav Fr. At Right Angles.

Two Hoppers. John Updike. CP-UpdiJ

Two-horse wagon was covered with tarpaulin stretched on boughs of hazel, A. Kazia. Czeslaw Milosz. CP-MiloCN, tr. by Robert Hass

Two horses in yellow light. August. Adrienne Rich. SP-RicA2

Two Horses Playing in the Orchard. James Wright. CP-WrigJ

Two Hours. John Ciardi. CP-CiarJ

Two Houses, The. Thomas Hardy. CP-HardT

Two houses joined, two poets to a play? Another Epilogue: "Two houses joined, two poets to a play?" Nathaniel Lee. CP-DryJ2 Fr. Duke of Guise, The.

Two hummingbirds as evanescent as. Vision. Richard Eberhart. CP-EberR

Two Humpties. Carl Sandburg. CP-SandC

200,000 rhododendron blossoms I estimate. Spring Notes from Robin Hill. Hayden Carruth. CP-CarHS

225 Pounds. Charles Bukowski. SP-BukC1

Two Illuminations, The. Muriel Rukeyser. CP-RukeM

Two Illustrations That the World Is What You Make of It. Wallace Stevens. CP-StevW; CP-StevWP

Two Immortals. Gary Snyder. CP-SnydG

Two in August. John Crowe Ransom. SP-RansJ

Two in the afternoon. The restlessness. Long Summers. Robert Lowell. SP-

LoweR

Two in the Campagna. Robert Browning. CP-BroR1; SP-BroR

Two in the plastic cockleshell. Mount Desert Island. George Oppen. CP-OppGN

Two in Twilight. Eugenio Montale. CP-MontE, tr. by Jonathan Galassi

Two instruments belong unto our God. Staffe and Rod, The. Robert Herrick. CP-HerrR

Two Intercepted Letters. Donald Davie. CP-DaviDC

Two Invocations of Death. Kathleen Jessie Raine. SP-RainK

Two Items. Carl Sandburg. CP-SandC

Two ivory women by a milky sea. Bathers, The. Hart Crane. CP-CranH

Two Japanese Poems. William Meredith. SP-MereW

Two kids, small. Robert Creeley. SP-CreeR

Two Kinds of Cause. Wyatt Prunty. SP-PrunW

Two Kinds of Deliverance. Mary Oliver. SP-OlivM

Two Kinds of Intelligence. Jelaluddin Rumi. SP-Rumi, tr. by Coleman Barks

Two Kings, The. William Butler Yeats. CP-YeatW

Two Kings and No-Form. Chuang Tzu. CP-MertT

Two Kopjes. Rudyard Kipling. CP-KiplR

Two ladies to the summit of my mind. Sonnet: Of Beauty and Duty. Dante Alighieri. CW-RossD, tr. by Dante Gabriel Rossetti

Two ladies walked on the soft green grass. Dream of Comparison, A. Stevie Smith. CP-SmitS

Two Leading Lights. Robert Frost. CP-FrosR

Two Legends. Ted Hughes. SP-HughTN Fr. Crow.

Two-legged. Heather McHugh. SP-McHuH

Two Lengths has every Day. Emily Dickinson. CP-DickE

Two Letters. Wallace Stevens. CP-StevWP

Two Letters on Samos. James Laughlin. CP-LaugJ

Two Limericks for the Elderly. John Updike.

Two Lines from the Brothers Grimm. Gregory Orr. SP-OrrG

Two Lips. Thomas Hardy. CP-HardT

Two Little Boots. Paul Laurence Dunbar. CP-DunbP

Two little girls, one fair, one dark. Lost Children, The. Randall Jarrell. CP-JarrR

2 little girls who live next door. You Can Take It with You. Josephine Jacobsen. CP-JacoJ

2 little whos / (he and she). E. E. Cummings. CP-CummE

Two Look at Two. Robert Frost. CP-FrosR

Two Lorries. Seamus Heaney. SP-HeanSO

Two Lovers and a Beachcomber by the Real Sea. Sylvia Plath. CP-PlatS

Two Lovers Murdered by a Partridge. Federico García Lorca. CP-GarcF, tr. by Greg Simon and Steven F. White

Two Loves. Richard Eberhart. CP-EberR

Two Loves. Heather McHugh. SP-McHuH

Two Loves, The. John Greenleaf Whittier. CP-WhitJ

Two Maidens, The. G. K. Chesterton. CP-ChesG

Two main diseases, con. Trial, A. Alan Dugan. CP-DugaA

Two Masks, The. George Meredith. CP-MerG1

Two Masks Unearthed in Bulgaria. William Meredith. SP-MereW

Two Memories. Hugh MacDiarmid. SP-MacDH

Two Men. Edwin Arlington Robinson. CP-RobiE

Two Men, The. Thomas Hardy. CP-HardT

Two men appear on a tractor. Poem about the Future. Hans Magnus Enzensberger. CP-EnzeH, tr. by Michael Hamburger

Two men came out of Shannon's, having known. Song at Shannon's, A. Edwin Arlington Robinson. CP-RobiE

Two men sat by a stone in what dim place. Night and the City. John Berryman. CP-BerrJ

Two men walked on the surface of the moon. 1971. Jorge Luis Borges. SP-BorgJ, tr. by Alastair Reid

Two Metaphysical Sonnets. Tennessee Williams. CP-WillT

Two minutes long it pitches through some bar. Elvis Presley. Thom Gunn. CP-GunnT

Two Mites, two drops (yet all her house and land). Widow[e]'s Mites, The. Richard Crashaw. CP-CrasR

Two Months. Rudyard Kipling. CP-KiplR

Two months of blood-summer were in store. Death. Thomas Kinsella. CP-KinsT

Two months old, already. Metempsychosis. Kenneth Rexroth. CP-RexrK

Two Moon Fantasies. Carl Sandburg. CP-SandC

Two morning stars, Venus and Jupiter. New Year's Dawn, 1947. Robinson Jeffers. CP-JefR3

Two Mothers lifting prayers unto one God. War. George Meredith. CP-MerG2

Two Motions. A. R. Ammons. CP-AmmoA

Two natives of the bare mountains appear in the doorway. Visitation. W. S. Merwin. SP-MerwWF

Two Neighbors. Carl Sandburg. CP-SandC

Two neighbours furiously dispute. Cause Won, The. Vincent Bourne. CP-CowpW

Two nights running I was out there. Mummies, The. Maxine W. Kumin. SP-KumiM

Two noble knights, whom true desire and zeal. Speech Presented unto King James at a Tilting in the Behalf of the Two Noble Brothers S[ir] Robert and S[ir] Henry Rich, Now Earls of Warwick and Holland, A. Ben Jonson. CP-JonsB

Two Nocturns. Carl Sandburg. CP-SandC

Two Norms. Federico García Lorca. CP-GarcF, tr. by Christopher Maurer

Two nudists of Dover. Third Limick. Ogden Nash. CP-NashO

Two nymphs, both nearly of an age. Judgment of the Poets, The. William Cowper. CP-CowpW

Two oaks lean apart for light, The. Couple of Trees, A. William Meredith. SP-MereW

Two of a thousand things, are disallow'd. Two Things Odious. Robert Herrick. CP-HerrR

Two, of course there are two. Death and Co. Sylvia Plath. CP-PlatS

Two of them were looking at the large wall map. Silent Agreement. Yannis Ritsos. SP-RitsY, tr. by Kimon Friar

Two Old Crows. Nicholas Vachel Lindsay. CP-LindV

Two old dancing shoes my grandfather. Genius. Philip Levine. SP-LeviP

Two old men. Lorine Niedecker. CP-NiedL

Two old men / meet at the lunch. Speeches. Donald Hall. CP-HallD

Two old, simple problems ever intertwined, The. Life and Death. Walt Whitman. CP-WhitW

Two omens seems propitious to my fame. To Sir John Fenn. William Cowper. CP-CowpW

Two on the stairs in a house where they had loved. In a Dark House. Muriel Rukeyser. CP-RukeM

Two or three angels. Stephen Crane. CP-CranS

Two or three lines across; the black ones, down. Crayon House. Muriel Rukeyser. CP-RukeM

Two or Three, or a Receipt to Make a Cuckold. Alexander Pope. CP-PopeA

Two or Three Posies. John Keats. CP-KeatJ

Two or three things in the past. Dancer. Langston Hughes. CP-HughL; CP-HughL3

Two Organs. John Berryman. CP-BerrJ

2 Outside, As Bones Break in My Kitchen. Charles Bukowski. SP-BukC2

Two Pair. Howard Nemerov. CP-NemeH

Two Pairs of Eyes. Eleanor Wilner. SP-WilnE

Two pale women cried, The. Parting-Scene, A. Thomas Hardy. CP-HardT

Two Palm Trees, The. Miguel Hernández. CP-MertT

Two Parables from "The Ocean of Story." James Laughlin. CP-LaugJ

Two Parents, The. Hugh MacDiarmid. SP-MacDH

Two-part book rejoicing in single garb. To John Rouse. John Milton. CP-MiltJ

Two Parted. Christina Georgina Rossetti. CP-RosC3

Two parts of us successively command. Hand and Tongue, The. Robert Herrick. CP-HerrR

Two Pendants: For the Ears. William Carlos Williams. CP-WilW2

Two people in a room, speaking harshly. Novella. Adrienne Rich. CP-RicAE; SP-RicA2

Two people meet. The sky turns winter. Glances. William Stafford. SP-StafWW

Two people saying goodbye / but not saying it. At the Gare Bruxelles-Midi. Lawrence Ferlinghetti. SP-FerlL

Two people wakened suddenly by an earthquake. Earthquake, The. Jane Cooper. CP-CoopJ

Two Performing Elephants. D. H. Lawrence. CP-LawrD

Two Photographs. Yehuda Amichai. SP-AmicY, tr. by Stephen Mitchell

Two Pieces after Suetonius. Robert Penn Warren. CP-WarrR

Two Poems. "Nikolai Nikolaevich Morshen." CP-WilbR

Two Poems. Czeslaw Milosz.

Conversation with Jeanne. CP-MiloCN

Poem for the End of the Century, A. CP-MiloCN

Two Poems. Howard Nemerov. CP-NemeH

Two Poems. Adrienne Rich. CP-RicAE

Two Poems. Rainer Maria Rilke. CP-RilkFr, tr. by A. Poulin, Jr.

Two Poems about Nothing. Gregory Orr. SP-OrrG

Two Poems about President Harding. James Wright. CP-WrigJ

Two Poems for Benn. John Ciardi. CP-CiarJ

Two Poems for Christmas, 1937. "H. D." CP-DoolH

Two Poems for Sub-Zero Times. Mona Van Duyn. SP-VanDM

Two Poems for Tanabata Matsuri. Sam Hamill. SP-HamiS

Two Poems for Women. John Logan. CP-LogaJ

Two Poems from The Two-Character Play. Tennessee Williams. CP-WillT

Two Poems from the War. Archibald MacLeish. CP-MacLA

Two Poems of Flight Sleep. James Dickey. CP-DickJ

Two Poems of Going Home. James Dickey. CP-DickJ

Two Poems of Greece. John Logan. CP-LogaJ

Two Poems of the Military. James Dickey. CP-DickJ

Two Poems on the Passing of an Empire. Derek Walcott. CP-WalcD

Two Poems on titles proposed by Octavio and Marie José Paz. Charles Tomlinson. CP-TomlC

Two Poems, with Birds. Mona Van Duyn. SP-VanDM

Two Poets by the Lake. Carolyn Kizer. CP-KizeC

Two Poets in Mexico. Yehuda Amichai. SP-AmicYL, tr. by Benjamin Harshav and Barbara Harshav

Two Poets of Croisic, The. Robert Browning. CP-BroR2

Two poets, (poets by report). To Dr. Darwin. William Cowper. CP-CowpW

Two poles, The. We didn't disagree. Echo ("Two poles, The. We didn't disagree"). Michael Palmer. SP-PalmM

Two Portraits of Sex. Philip Larkin. CP-LarkP

Two Possibilities. A. R. Ammons. CP-AmmoA

Two Postures beside a Fire. James Wright. CP-WrigJ

Two powder'd coxcombs wait at your command. Lines with Two Cockscombs. William Cowper. CP-CowpW

Two Preludes for La Push. John Logan. CP-LogaJ

Two Priests, The. Archibald MacLeish. CP-MacLA

Two prisoners slump like baskets of contraband rice, blue sky pushing past, The. Phantasmagoria. Yusef Komunyaaka. CP-KomuY

2 Propositions and 3 Proof. Charles Olson. CP-OlsoC

Two Pursuits. Christina Georgina Rossetti. CP-RosC3

Two Quatrains. Edwin Arlington Robinson. CP-RobiE

Two Quatrains for First Frost. Richard Wilbur. CP-WilbR

Two Quits and a Drum, and Elegy for Drinkers. Alan Dugan. CP-DugaA

Two Rabbins, The. John Greenleaf Whittier. CP-WhitJ

Two Races. Rudyard Kipling. CP-KiplR

Two Riddles. Charles Simic. SP-SimiC; SP-SimiCE

Two Riddles from Aldhelm. Richard Wilbur. CP-WilbR

Two rising flukes of green water. November 23, 1989. Norman Dubie. CP-DubiN

Two Rivers. Ralph Waldo Emerson. CP-EmerR

Two Rivulets. Walt Whitman. CP-WhitW

Two roads diverged in a yellow wood. Road Not Taken, The. Robert Frost. CP-FrosR

Two Romance Poems. George Oppen. CP-OppGN

Two Romantic Pieces. Hayden Carruth. CP-CarHS

Two Rosalinds, The. Thomas Hardy. CP-HardT

Two Rossettis (Brothers They), The. Christina Georgina Rossetti. CP-RosC1

Two Round Spaces on the Tombstone, The. Samuel Taylor Coleridge. CP-ColeS

Two Sailors Ashore. Federico García Lorca. SP-GarcF, tr. by Alan S. Trueblood Fr. Songs to End With.

Two Sailors on the Beach. Federico García Lorca. SP-GarcF, tr. by Donald Jenks

Two St. Petersburgs. Heather McHugh. SP-McHuH

Two Sayings, The. Elizabeth Barrett Browning. CP-BroEB

Two Scavengers in a Truck, Two Beautiful People in a Mercedes. Lawrence Ferlinghetti. SP-FerlL

Two Scenes. John Ashbery. SP-AshbJ

Two seated lovers form one shadow, dark. On Winslow Homer's Moonlight on Water (1895) in the Los Angeles County Museum of Art. Helen Pinkerton. CP-PinkH

Two Selves, The. David Ignatow. SP-IgnaD

Two separate divided silences. Severed Selves. Dante Gabriel Rossetti. CW-RossD Fr. House of Life, The.

Two Serenades. Thomas Hardy. CP-HardT

2 shes / both not quite / young perfectly. E. E. Cummings. CP-CummE

Two Ships. James Laughlin. CP-LaugJ

Two short, The. March. The Museum. Buffalo. de Chirico. John Logan. CP-LogaJ

Two shots down and I'm exalted. Untitled Poem: "Two shots down and I'm exalted." Alan Dugan. CP-DugaA

Two-Sided Man, The. Rudyard Kipling. CP-KiplR Fr. Kim.

Two Sides to an Outside: Meditation from Empson. Howard Nemerov. CP-NemeH

Two Sisters of Persephone. Sylvia Plath. CP-PlatS

Two Sketches. Elizabeth Barrett Browning. CP-BroEB

Two Soldiers, The. Thomas Hardy. CP-HardT

Two solemn soldiers helmeted. Gallery Walk: Fifteen Italian Drawings 1780–1890. John Logan. CP-LogaJ

Two Somewhat Different Epigrams. Langston Hughes. CP-HughL; CP-HughL3

Two Songs. W. H. Auden. CP-AudeW

Two Songs. Paul Laurence Dunbar. CP-DunbP

Two Songs. Adrienne Rich. CP-RicAE; SP-RicA2

Two Songs at the Marriage of the Lord Fauconberg and the Lady Mary Cromwell. Andrew Marvell. CP-MarvA

Two Songs for a Boss Named Mr. Longwell. Ogden Nash. CP-NashO

Two Songs for a Gunner. John Ciardi. CP-CiarJ

Two Songs [for Doreen]. Derek Mahon. CP-MahoD

Two Songs from a Play. William Butler Yeats. CP-YeatW Fr. Resurrection, The.

Two Songs from "The Hunted Revolutionaries." Thomas McGrath. SP-McGrT

Two Songs in a Stanza of Beddoes'. Richard Wilbur. CP-WilbR

Two Songs of a Fool. William Butler Yeats. CP-YeatW

Two Songs Rewritten for the Tune's Sake. William Butler Yeats. CP-YeatW

Two Sonnets. Allen Ginsberg. CP-GinsA

Two Sonnets. Edwin Arlington Robinson. CP-RobiE

Two Sonnets on Fame. John Keats.
  On Fame. CP-KeatJ
  On Fame ("How fever'd is the man who cannot look"). CP-KeatJ

Two Sonnets to the June-Bug. James Whitcomb Riley. CP-RileJ

Two Sonnets Whose Titles Came to Me Simultaneously. John Updike. CP-UpdiJ

Two Sons. Anne Sexton. CP-SextA

Two sons are gone. Later Still. Philip Levine. SP-LeviP

Two Sounds When We Sit by the Ocean. Robert Bly. SP-BlyR

Two Spanish cowhands from Monterey. Local Legend. Robinson Jeffers. CP-JefR3

Two Spirits[: An Allegory], The. Percy Bysshe Shelley. CP-ShelP

Two Spoons. James Laughlin. CP-LaugJ

Two Spring Charms. Unknown. CP-WrigJ, tr. by James Wright

Two States of Prayer. Thomas Merton. CP-MertT

Two statesmen met by moonlight. What the Moon Saw. Nicholas Vachel Lindsay. CP-LindV

Two Stick Drawings. Seamus Heaney. SP-HeanSO

Two stonebreakers in loincloths, The. Caste Wife Speaks to the Enigmatic Parabolas, The. Norman Dubie. CP-DubiN

Two Stories. Charles Wright. SP-WrigC

Two Strangers Breakfast. Carl Sandburg. CP-SandC

Two strings, one pierced cry. Variation on Pain. Rita Dove. SP-DoveR

Two Studies in Idealism: Short Survey of American and Human History. Robert Penn Warren. CP-WarrR

Two Styles in Love. A. K. Ramanujan. CP-RamaA

Two summers since, I saw at Lammas Fair. Phoebe Dawson. George Crabbe. SP-CrabG Fr. Parish Register, The.

Two Swede families live downstairs and an Irish policeman upstairs, and. House. Carl Sandburg. CP-SandC

Two swimmers wrestled on the spar. Emily Dickinson. CP-DickE

Two Tales of Liadoff. Wallace Stevens. CP-StevW; CP-StevWP

Two taxi drivers stopped for a red light. Madison and 42nd. Carl Sandburg. CP-SandC

Two that could not have lived their single lives. Two in August. John Crowe Ransom. SP-RansJ

Two theologues once, as they wended their way. Infralapsarian. Ambrose Bierce. SP-BierA

Two Thieves, The; or, the Last Stage of Avarice. William Wordsworth CP-WorW1; MW-WorW

Two thigh hills hold us at the fork. Song of the Tangle. Gary Snyder. CP-SnydG

Two things a man's built for, killing and you-know-what. Two Studies in Idealism: Short Survey of American and Human History. Robert Penn Warren. CP-WarrR

Two things do make society to stand. Society. Robert Herrick. CP-HerrR

Two things hast thou made known to half the nation. To One Who Published in Print. Samuel Taylor Coleridge. CP-ColeS

Two things I have never understood: first, the difference between. Will You Have Your Tedium Rare or Medium? Ogden Nash. CP-NashO

Two Things Odious. Robert Herrick. CP-HerrR

Two things possess the power. Langston Hughes. CP-HughL; CP-HughL1

Two things thou shalt not long for, if thou love a mind serene. From Ibn Jemin. Ibn-i-Yamin. CP-EmerR

Two Thoughts of Death. Countee Cullen. CP-CullC

Two Thoughts of Death. Christina Georgina Rossetti. CP-RosC3

2000. Primo Levi. CP-LeviP, tr. by Ruth Feldman

2527th Birthday of the Buddha. Yusef Komunyaaka. CP-KomuY

Two Times. Robert Creeley. CP-CreeR

Two Tortoiseshell Butterflies. Ted Hughes. SP-HughTN

Two Tramps in Mud Time. Robert Frost. CP-FrosR

Two Travellers perishing in Snow. Emily Dickinson. CP-DickE

Two Trees, The. Archibald MacLeish. CP-MacLA

Two Trees, The. William Butler Yeats. CP-YeatW

Two trunks like bodies, bodies like twined trunks. Philemon and Baucis. Thom Gunn. CP-GunnT

Two turtles aboard an ox cart. Han-shan. CP-ColdM, tr. by Red Pine

2:23 p.m. / The season glides to a click. Watching the Equinox Arrive in Charlottesville, September 1992. Charles Wright. SP-WrigCN

Two Types. Ambrose Bierce. SP-BierA

Two Variations. Denise Levertov. SP-LeveDP

Two Versions of "Knight, Death and the Devil." Jorge Luis Borges. SP-BorgJ, tr. by Stephen Kessler

Two Versions of the Same Poem. Wallace Stevens. CP-StevW; CP-StevWP

Two Views of a Cadaver Room. Sylvia Plath. CP-PlatS

Two Views of a Philosopher. Howard Nemerov. CP-NemeH

Two Views of Two Ghost Towns. Charles Tomlinson. CP-TomlC

Two Views of Withens. Sylvia Plath. CP-PlatS

Two Villages. Grace Paley. CP-PalGC

Two virtues ride, by stallion, by nag. Death of Myth-making, The. Sylvia Plath. CP-PlatS

Two Voices. Edna St. Vincent Millay. CP-MillE

Two Voices, The. Alfred Tennyson. CP-TennA

Two Voices are there; one is of the sea. Thought[s] of a Briton on the Subjugation of Switzerland. William Wordsworth. CP-WorW1; MW-WorW

Two Voices in a Meadow. Richard Wilbur. CP-WilbR

Two voices / took turns using my eyes. Double Voice, The. Margaret Atwood. SP-AtwM1

Two-Volume Novel. Dorothy Parker. CP-ParkD

Two W.P.A. men. Portrait of the Times, A. William Carlos Williams. CP-WilW2

Two wagons full of bricks. Rainer Maria Rilke. CP-RilkFr, tr. by A. Poulin, Jr. Fr. Orchards.

Two Walls. Robert Lowell. SP-LoweR

Two warriors sprang at one another, thrashed. Mortal Combat. Charles Baudelaire. CP-BaudC, tr. by Walter Martin

Two waters—squared. Fanny Howe. SP-HoweF Fr. Quietist, The.

Two Ways of Living and Dying. D. H. Lawrence. CP-LawrD

Two Ways of Looking in a Mirror. Robert Creeley. CP-CreeR

Two Ways of Running. Jelaluddin Rumi. SP-Rumi, tr. by Coleman Barks

Two ways only / For the weary lover. Nahoa Urn, for a Woman. Pablo Antonio Cuadra. CP-MertT

Two wedded Hearts, if e'er were such. Wedded Love. Samuel Taylor Coleridge. CP-ColeS

Two wedded lovers watched the rising moon. Song: "Two wedded lovers watched the rising moon." George Meredith. CP-MerG1

Two weeks from now. Table, The. Robert Creeley. SP-CreeR

Two well-assorted travellers use. Love and Thought. Ralph Waldo Emerson. CP-EmerR

Two went to pray? o rather say. Two Went Up into the Temple To Pray. Richard Crashaw. CP-CrasR

Two Went Up into the Temple To Pray. Richard Crashaw. CP-CrasR

Two—were immortal twice. Emily Dickinson. CP-DickE

Two were silent in a sunless church, The. Her Dilemma. Thomas Hardy. CP-HardT

Two white whales have been installed at. Wednesday at the Waldorf. May Swenson. SP-SwenM

Two Who Crossed a Line. Countee Cullen. CP-CullC

Two Who Crossed a Line (She Crosses). Countee Cullen. CP-CullC

Two Widows in Tashkent. Donald Davie. CP-DaviDC

Two Witches. Robert Frost. CP-FrosR

Two Witches, The. Robert Graves. CP-GravR

Two Wives. D. H. Lawrence. CP-LawrD

Two Wives, The. Thomas Hardy. CP-HardT

Two Women. James Dickey. CP-DickJ

Two Women. Carl Sandburg. CP-SandC

Two Women, The. G. K. Chesterton. CP-ChesG

Two Women and Their Fathers. Carl Sandburg. CP-SandC

Two women folding a double mystery. Pietà. Robert Stock. SP-StocR

Two women in their twenties do a drunken. Quality of Light, A. Yusef Komunyakaa. CP-KomuY

Two Women on the Potomac Parkway. Norman Dubie. CP-DubiN

Two women: one as good as bread. Ruby and Amethyst. Robert Graves. CP-GravR

Two women sit at a table by a window. Light breaks. After Twenty Years. Adrienne Rich. SP-RicA2

Two women stroll among the orange-trees. Mirror, The. Robert Duncan. SP-DuncR

Two Women Talking. Archibald MacLeish. CP-MacLA

Two wooden tubs of blue hydrangeas stand at the foot of the stone steps. Banal Sojourn. Wallace Stevens. CP-StevW; CP-StevWP

Two workmen were carrying a sheet of asbestos. Christo's. Paul Muldoon. CP-MuldP

Two Worlds. Raymond Carver. CP-CarvR

Two worlds are asleep, are sleeping, now, The. Old Man Asleep, An. Wallace Stevens. CP-StevW; CP-StevWP

Two X. E. E. Cummings. CP-CummE

Two Years. Muriel Rukeyser. CP-RukeM

Two-Years' Idyll, A. Thomas Hardy. CP-HardT

Two Years Later. William Butler Yeats. CP-YeatW

Two years we spent. Woods, The. Derek Mahon. CP-MahoD

Two Young Men, 23 to 24 Years Old. Constantine P. Cavafy. CP-CavaC, tr. by Theoharis Constantine Theoharis

Twofold. D. H. Lawrence. CP-LawrD

'Twould ease—a Butterfly. Emily Dickinson. CP-DickE

Tyanan Sculptor. Constantine P. Cavafy. CP-CavaC, tr. by Theoharis Constantine Theoharis

Tyger [or Tiger], The. William Blake. CP-BlakW Fr. Songs of Experience.

Tyger Tyger [or Tyger! Tyger! or Tiger! Tiger!] burning bright. Tyger [or Tiger], The. William Blake. CP-BlakW Fr. Songs of Experience.

Tyger's Letter to Caroline 1812. James Austen. CP-AustJ

Tying One On in Vienna. Carolyn Kizer. CP-KizeC Fr. Heine Journal, A.

Tympanum is worn thin, The. World's End. Laura Riding Jackson. CP-RidiL

Type of the antique Rome! Rich reliquary. Coliseum, The. Edgar Allan Poe. CP-PoeEd

Type of two mighty continents!—combining. Kossuth. John Greenleaf Whittier. CP-WhitJ

Typewriter's the Kind, The. Heather McHugh. SP-McHuH

Typical Affair, A. Allen Ginsberg. CP-GinsA

Typical Optical. John Updike. CP-UpdiJ

Tyrannic Love. John Dryden.
   Epilogue to Tyrannic[k] Love. SP-DrydJ

Tyranny of method! the outrageous smile. Third Elegy. The Fear of Form. Muriel Rukeyser. CP-RukeM

Tyrant Dying. Thomas Kinsella. CP-KinsT

Tyrant of Syracuse. Archibald MacLeish. CP-MacLA

Tyrant passed, and friendlier was his eye, The. Solon. George Meredith. CP-MerG1

Tyrant Who Rules the Homeless and Poor, The. Shmuel HaNagid. SP-HaNaS, tr. by Peter Cole

Tyson & Jo, Tyson & Jo. Death Ballad. John Berryman. CP-BerrJ

Tywater. Richard Wilbur. CP-WilbR

U

U.N. Headquarters in the High Commissioner's House in Jerusalem, The. Yehuda Amichai. SP-AmicY, tr. by Stephen Mitchell

U. S. 1946 King's X. Robert Frost. CP-FrosR

Ubi Ecclesia. G. K. Chesterton. CP-ChesG

Ubique. Rudyard Kipling. CP-KiplR

Udai Chand lay sick to death. Last Suttee, The. Rudyard Kipling. CP-KiplR

Udite, si dolgono mesti fringuelli. Christina Georgina Rossetti. CP-RosC3

Ugh! the planet screams. Morning. Allen Ginsberg. CP-GinsA

Ugliness. John Ciardi. CP-CiarJ

Ugly gargoyles peek out of your well-lit window. Via Funari. Joseph Brodsky. CP-BrodJ

Ugly look, close to tears, on a man's face. Skew Lines. Denise Levertov. SP-LeveDP

Ugly Secret, The. Robert Graves. CP-GravR

Ugly Sister. Philip Larkin. CP-LarkP

Ugly woman clutched, The. In Sisterly Fashion. William Carlos Williams. CP-WilW2

Ugolino. Dante Alighieri. SP-HeanSO, tr. by Seamus Heaney Fr. Divina Commedia.

Ugolino. Dante Alighieri. CP-ShelP Fr. Divina Commedia.

Uh! I sho am tired. Broke. Langston Hughes. CP-HughL; CP-HughL1

Uh, Philosophy. A. R. Ammons. CP-AmmoA

Ukraine held a referendum. Referendum. Adam Zagajewski. SP-ZagaA, tr. by Clare Cavanagh

Ulalume [or Ulalume—a Ballad]. Edgar Allan Poe. CP-PoeEd

Ulcerated tooth keeps me awake, there is. Letters from a Father. Mona Van Duyn. SP-VanDM

Ulster. Rudyard Kipling. CP-KiplR

Ultima Thule. Thomas Lux. SP-LuxT

Ultimate. G. K. Chesterton. CP-ChesG

Ultimate Act, The. Adrienne Rich. CP-RicAE

Ultimate Innocence. Yannis Ritsos. SP-RitsY, tr. by Kimon Friar and Kostas Myrsiades

Ultimate Poem, The. Robert Stock. SP-StocR

Ultimate Poem Is Abstract, The. Wallace Stevens. CP-StevW; CP-StevWP

Ultimate Problems. William Stafford. SP-StafW; SP-StafWW

Ultimate Reality. D. H. Lawrence. CP-LawrD

Ultimate Song. Richard Eberhart. CP-EberR

Ultimately the air. From Disaster. George Oppen. CP-OppGN

Ultimately, there should be a language. Ab Ovo. Joseph Brodsky. CP-BrodJ

Ultimatum. Countee Cullen. CP-CullC

Ultimatum. Langston Hughes. CP-HughL; CP-HughL3

Ultimatum. Philip Larkin. CP-LarkP

Ultimatum. Dorothy Parker. CP-ParkD

Ultimatum: Kid to Kid. Langston Hughes. CP-HughL; CP-HughL3

Ultimus Heroum: or, To the Most Learned, and to the Right Honourable, Henry, Marquesse of Dorchester. Robert Herrick. CP-HerrR

Uluru Wild Fig Song. Gary Snyder. CP-SnydG

Ulvade Texas to Nashville Tennessee. Picker. Miller Williams. CP-WillM

Ulysses. Robert Graves. CP-GravR

Ulysses. Alfred Tennyson. CP-TennA

Ulysses, much-experienced man. To Ulysses. Alfred Tennyson. CP-TennA

Umber was painting of a lion [or Lyon] fierce. Upon Umber: Epigram. Robert Herrick. CP-HerrR

Umbra. Thomas Campion. CP-CampT

Umbra. Alexander Pope. CP-PopeA

Umbrageous cedars murmuring symphonies. Hamlet. Walter De la Mare. CP-DeLaW

Umbrella, The. Donald Hall. CP-HallD

Umbrella from Piccadilly, An. Jaroslav Seifert. SP-SeifJ, tr. by Ewald Osers

Umbrian Dreams. Charles Wright. SP-WrigCN

Umbrian night. Assisi. Paul Celan. SP-CelaP, tr. by John Felstiner

Ume: Plum. Eleanor Wilner. SP-WilnE

Un-American Investigators. Langston Hughes. CP-HughL; CP-HughL3

Un Bel di Vedremo. Kenneth Rexroth. CP-RexrK

Un / der fog / 's / touch. E. E. Cummings. CP-CummE

Un Poco Loco. Clarence Major. SP-MajoC

Una. Ralph Waldo Emerson. CP-EmerR

Unable are the Loved to die. Emily Dickinson. CP-DickE

Unable to endure my world and calling the failure God, I will destroy yours. Savonarola. W. S. Merwin. SP-MerwW

Unable to sleep, I spend the predawn hours. November. Gregory Orr. SP-OrrG

Unable to sleep, or pray, I stand. Ice Storm. Robert Earl Hayden. CP-HaydR

Unacceptable, The. Yannis Ritsos. SP-RitsY, tr. by N. C. Germanacos

Unacceptable Man, The. Yannis Ritsos. SP-RitsY, tr. by Kimon Friar

Unaccomplished. Yannis Ritsos. SP-RitsY, tr. by Kimon Friar

Unaccustomed as I am. Confessio Amantis. James Laughlin. CP-LaugJ

Unaccustomed ripeness in the wood; An. Elizabeth. Robert Lowell. SP-LoweR

Unanswerable Question, The. James Laughlin. CP-LaugJ

Unanswered. Yannis Ritsos. SP-RitsY, tr. by Kimon Friar

Unanswered by Request. Ogden Nash. CP-NashO

Unanswering Correspondences, The. Kenneth Patchen. CP-PatcK

Unappeasable Host, The. William Butler Yeats. CP-YeatW

Unarguably there are spirits, ghosts, witches. Modern Superstition. Laura Riding Jackson. CP-RidiL

Unassimilable fact leads us on, The. Misfit, The. A. R. Ammons. CP-AmmoA

Unaware that the links of a continent. Quebec, rattling chains of Separatism. Peter Blue Cloud. SP-BlueP

Unbar the door, since thou the Opener art. Omar Khayyám. CP-EmerR

Un(bee)mo / vi / n(in)g. E. E. Cummings. CP-CummE

Unbelievable as an antique ritual. Ceremony By the Sea, A. Richard Eberhart. CP-EberR

Unbeliever, The. Elizabeth Bishop. CP-BishE

Unbiassed at least he was when he arrived on his mission. Partition. W. H. Auden. CP-AudeW

Unborn, The. Thomas Hardy. CP-HardT

Unborn Child, An. Derek Mahon. CP-MahoD

Unborn Song. Muriel Rukeyser. CP-RukeM

Unbrooding as an ox, he thrusts a bald. Force of Eloquence, The. Thomas Kinsella. CP-KinsT

Uncalendared Love. Robert Graves. CP-GravR

Uncertain lease—develops lustre. Emily Dickinson. CP-DickE

Uncertain light limns hills obscure and sere. On Goya's Duel with Cudgels (ca. 1820), a "Black Painting" in the Prado. Helen Pinkerton. CP-PinkH

Uncertain Obligations. Yannis Ritsos. SP-RitsY, tr. by Kimon Friar and Kostas Myrsiades

Uncertain of the Crime. Paul Éluard. CP-WilW2

Uncertain Season in High Country. Robert Penn Warren. CP-WarrR

Uncertain Skies. Charles Baudelaire. CP-BaudC, tr. by Walter Martin

Uncertain Solitude. Federico García Lorca. CP-GarcF, tr. by Christopher Maurer

Uncertainty in Blue. Yusef Komunyakaa. CP-KomuY

Uncertainty in Love. Samuel Taylor Coleridge. CP-ColeS

Unchanged within, to see all changed without. Duty Surviving Self-Love. Samuel Taylor Coleridge. CP-ColeS; MW-ColeS

Unchanging, The. Walter De la Mare. CP-DeLaW

Unchill'd I handle stinging snow. Pilate. Gerard Manley Hopkins. CP-HopkG

Uncle. Philip Levine. SP-LeviP

Uncle. James Tate. SP-TateJ

Uncle Ananias. Edwin Arlington Robinson. CP-RobiE

Uncle Dan'l in Town over Sunday. James Whitcomb Riley. CP-RileJ

Uncle Henry. W. H. Auden. CP-AudeW

Uncle Jim. Countee Cullen. CP-CullC

Uncle John, he makes me tired. Confidence, A. Paul Laurence Dunbar. CP-DunbP

Uncle Mart's Poem. James Whitcomb Riley. CP-RileJ Fr. Child-World, A.

Uncle Sam— / And old Jim Crow. Crow Goes, Too. Langston Hughes. CP-HughL; CP-HughL3

Uncle Sam / With old Jim Crow. Poem to Uncle Sam. Langston Hughes. CP-HughL; CP-HughL3

Uncle Sidney. James Whitcomb Riley. CP-RileJ

Uncle Sidney, when he was here. Squirt-Gun Uncle Maked Me, The. James Whitcomb Riley. CP-RileJ

Uncle Sidney's Logic. James Whitcomb Riley. CP-RileJ

Uncle Sidney's Rhymes. James Whitcomb Riley. CP-RileJ

Uncle Sidney's Views. James Whitcomb Riley. CP-RileJ

Uncle Speaks in the Drawing Room, The. Adrienne Rich. CP-RicAE; SP-RicA1

Uncle Tom is a legend and a dream. Uncle Tom ("Uncle Tom is a legend and a dream"). Langston Hughes. CP-HughL; CP-HughL2

Uncle Tom ("Uncle Tom is a legend and a dream"). Langston Hughes. CP-HughL; CP-HughL2

Uncle Tom, / When he was alive. Epitaph: "Uncle Tom, / When he was alive." Langston Hughes. CP-HughL; CP-HughL3

Uncle Tom ("Within— / The beaten pride"). Langston Hughes. CP-HughL; CP-HughL3

Uncle Torquemada. Torquemada. Stevie Smith. CP-SmitS

Uncle William, last July. Uncle William's Picture. James Whitcomb Riley. CP-RileJ

Uncle William's Picture. James Whitcomb Riley. CP-RileJ

Unclench Yourself. Marge Piercy. SP-PierM

Unclosing flowers are inflexible and have yielded nothing, The. For Those Who Have Not Eaten the Apple. Josephine Jacobsen. CP-JacoJ

Unclouded seas of bluebells have ebbed and passed, The. Campions. D. H. Lawrence. CP-LawrD

Uncomforted. James Whitcomb Riley. CP-RileJ

Uncompromising, The. Yannis Ritsos. SP-RitsY, tr. by Kimon Friar

Uncreating Chaos (Double Portrait in a Mirror), The. Stephen Spender. CP-SpenS

Uncreation. G. K. Chesterton. CP-ChesG

Uncreation, The. Robert Pinsky. CP-PinsR

Unctuous Platitudes. John Ashbery. SP-AshbJ

Uncut Diamond, The. Robert Graves. CP-GravR

Und Drang. Ezra Pound. CP-PoEar
   House of Splendour, The. SP-PounE

Undazzled, keen, / love sits. Charles Olson. CP-OlsoC

Unde Malum. Czeslaw Milosz. CP-MiloCN, tr. by Robert Hass

Undead, The. Robert Graves. CP-GravR

Undead, The. Richard Wilbur. CP-WilbR

Undead, The. C. K. Williams. CP-WillC

Under. Carl Sandburg. CP-SandC

Under a Certain Little Star. Wisława Szymborska. SP-SzymWM, tr. by Joanna Trzeciak

Under a daisied bank. Milkmaid, The. Thomas Hardy. CP-HardT

Under a Hat Rim. Carl Sandburg. CP-SandC

Under a lawne, than skyes more cleare. Upon Roses. Robert Herrick. CP-HerrR

Under a linden tree, as before, daylight. Czeslaw Milosz. CP-MiloC, tr. by Robert Hass Fr. Treatise on Poetry, A.

Under a low sky. Silence. William Carlos Williams. CP-WilW2

Under a lucky star I saw those eyes. Petrarch. CP-Petra, tr. by J. G. Nichols

Under a prairie fog moon. Pearl Horizons. Carl Sandburg. CP-SandC

Under a priceless sun. B.W.I. John Updike. CP-UpdiJ

Under a red face, black velvet shyness. Chicago Morning. Ted Berrigan. SP-BerrT

Under a round roof the flying. Still Turning. May Swenson. SP-SwenM

Under a Skylight. Donald Davie. CP-DaviDC

Under a Splendid Chestnut Tree. Philip Larkin. CP-LarkP

Under a spreading chestnut tree. Village Blacksmith, The. Henry Wadsworth Longfellow. SP-LongH

Under a starry sky I was taking a walk. Temptation. Czeslaw Milosz. CP-MiloC; CP-MiloCN, tr. by Lillian Vallee

Under a Telephone Pole. Carl Sandburg. CP-SandC

Under a Tree. Kenneth Patchen. CP-PatcK

Under a Tree. Richard Wilbur. CP-WilbR

Under an elm tree where the river reaches. Archibald MacLeish. CP-MacLA Fr. Happy Marriage, The.

Under an overwashed, stiff, gray. In the Missouri Ozarks. Mona Van Duyn. SP-VanDM

Under an undermined, and shot-bruised wall. Fall of a Wall. John Donne. CP-DonnJ; MW-DonnJ

Under apparel, apparel lies. One Self. Laura Riding Jackson. CP-RidiL

Under asters the color of my shadow. Sleeping Mountain, The. W. S. Merwin. SP-MerwW

Under Ben Bulben. William Butler Yeats. CP-YeatW

Under Black Leaves. W. S. Merwin. SP-MerwW

Under boughs of breathing May. Song: "Under boughs of breathing May." George Meredith. CP-MerG1

Under cerulean, amid her backyard's knobby rhubarb squats. My Cousin in April. Louise Glück. SP-GlucL

Under contract to the church he carves. Dollmaker, The. Robert Stock. SP-StocR

Under Cygnus. Richard Wilbur. CP-WilbR

Under dead leaves Tanya finds a tortoise. Berry Territory. Gary Snyder. CP-SnydG

Under dense fir boughs. Bower, The. Richard Eberhart. CP-EberR

Under every green tree, sex. Charles Olson. CP-OlsoC

Under glass: glass dishes that [or which] changed. Fundamental Project of Technology, The. Galway Kinnell. SP-KinnGN

Under High-Stoy Hill. Thomas Hardy. CP-HardT

Under his helmet, up against his pack. Asleep. Wilfred Owen. CP-OwenW

Under His Microscope. James Laughlin. CP-LaugJ

Under his view the wind. View, The. Howard Nemerov. CP-NemeH

Under House Arrest. Yusef Komunyakaa. CP-KomuY

Under how many suns have we embraced. Together. G. K. Chesterton. CP-ChesG

Under Ideal Conditions. William Corbett. SP-CorbW

Under its hangar the afternoon. Beautiful Aeroplane, The. Charles Tomlinson. CP-TomlC

Under ledges of snow outthrust from ledges. Seasons. Robert Penn Warren. CP-WarrR

Under Libra: Weights and Measures. James Merrill. SP-MerrJ

Under my bowels, yellow with smoke. Other, The. Anne Sexton. CP-SextA

Under my hat I custom you intricate, Ella. Homecoming. William Stafford. SP-StafWW

Under my window-ledge the waters race. Coole Park and Ballylee, 1931. William Butler Yeats. CP-YeatW

Under no hanging heaven-rooted tree. Stony Limits. Hugh MacDiarmid. SP-MacDH

Under Oblivion. Yannis Ritsos. SP-RitsY, tr. by Kimon Friar

Under One Small Star. Wisława Szymborska. SP-SzymW, tr. by Stanisław Barańczak and Clare Cavanagh

Under orders to shoot the spy, I discharged. Imaginary Universes. Allen Ginsberg. CP-GinsA

Under pure skies of April blue I stood. Cherry Trees, The. Walter De la Mare. CP-DeLaW

Under St Paul's. Donald Davie. CP-DaviDC

Under Saturn. William Butler Yeats. CP-YeatW

Under silver wing. Crossing Nation. Allen Ginsberg. CP-GinsA

Under Sirius. W. H. Auden. CP-AudeW

Under sky that is water. Fanny Howe. SP-HoweF Fr. O'Clock.

Under Soracte. Kenneth Rexroth. CP-RexrK

Under Stars. Tess Gallagher. SP-GallT

Under Taurus. Louise Glück. SP-GlucL

Under that benign calm eye that sees. Dream, The. Charles Tomlinson. CP-TomlC

Under that summer asphalt, under vistas. Capital, The. Adrienne Rich. CP-RicAE

Under the April Rain. Tennessee Williams. CP-WillT

Under the arch of Life, where love and death. Soul's Beauty. Dante Gabriel Rossetti. CW-RossD Fr. House of Life, The.

Under the Balcony. Oscar Wilde. CP-WildO

Under the Bell Jar. Howard Nemerov. CP-NemeH

Under the blue-grey twilight, heaped. Twilight. D. H. Lawrence. CP-LawrD

Under the bluffs of Oroville, blue cloud September skies. Beginning of a Poem of These States. Allen Ginsberg. CP-GinsA

Under the bluffs of Oroville, blue cloud September skies, entering. Beginning of a Long Poem of These States. Allen Ginsberg. CP-GinsA

Under the blunt pine / In the winter sun. Elias—Variations on a Theme. Thomas Merton. CP-MertT

Under the Bridge. Charles Tomlinson. CP-TomlC; SP-TomlC

Under the bronze crown. Baroque Wall-Fountain in the Villa Sciarra, A. Richard Wilbur. CP-WilbR

Under the Capitol Dome. Carl Sandburg. CP-SandC

Under the ceiling of metal stamped like plaster. Library Scene. Robert Pinsky. CP-PinsR

Under the cliff, green powdered in from the open. Exchanges. James Dickey. CP-DickJ

Under the cobbled bridge the white swans float. Swans on the River Ayr. Mary Oliver. SP-OlivM

Under the concrete benches. Weed Puller. Theodore Roethke. CP-RoetT

Under the cottonwoods. Overthrow, An. John Ciardi. CP-CiarJ

Under the cradle of the incense. Unmarried Woman at Mass, The. Federico García Lorca. CP-GarcF, tr. by Alan S. Trueblood Fr. Eros with a Cane.

Under the day's crust a half-eaten child. Pied Piper, The. John Ashbery. SP-AshbJ

Under the door in the wall. Door in the Wall, The. Charles Tomlinson. SP-TomlC

Under the east cliff the spring flows into the snow. After the Solstice. W. S. Merwin. SP-MerwW

Under the eglantine. Anything Is Beautiful If You Say It Is. Wallace Stevens. CP-StevW; CP-StevWP

Under the enormous pier-shadow. River Down Home, The. James Wright. CP-WrigJ

Under the ever-moving, mighty dreams. Whales. Kathleen Jessie Raine. SP-RainK

Under the eyes. Hustings, The. Charles Olson. CP-OlsoC

Under the familiar weight. New Year Letter. W. H. Auden. CP-AudeW

Under the Farm of All the Winds. Red Cross Warrior, The. G. K. Chesterton. CP-ChesG

Under the Floor. Ogden Nash. CP-NashO

Under the French horns of a November afternoon. Man in Blue, A. James Schuyler. CP-SchuJ

Under the glassy Christmas tree. Family, The. Donald Hall. CP-HallD

Under the Great Comedian's tomb the crowd. Parnell's Funeral. William Butler Yeats. CP-YeatW

Under the great hill sloping bare. King's Missive, The. John Greenleaf Whittier. CP-WhitJ

Under the green lamp-light her letter there. Letter of a Mother. Robert Penn Warren. CP-WarrR

Under the green leaf hangs a little pouch. Fig, The. May Sarton. SP-SartM

Under the green ledge. Kenneth Patchen. CP-PatcK

Under the green umbrellas. View of the Terrace, A. Adrienne Rich. CP-RicAE

Under the Grind. Marge Piercy. SP-PierM

Under the Hanger. James Schuyler. CP-SchuJ

Under the Harbour Bridge. Yusef Komunyakaa. CP-KomuY

Under the Harvest Moon. Carl Sandburg. CP-SandC

Under the hive-like dome the stooping haunted readers. British Museum Reading Room, The. Louis MacNeice. CP-MacNL

Under the houses there are immemorial graves. Perforation. Yannis Ritsos. SP-RitsY, tr. by N. C. Germanacos

Under the ivy bush / One sits sighing. Christina Georgina Rossetti. CP-RosC2

Under the killdeer cry. Our People. William Stafford. SP-StafWW

Under the Light, yet under. Emily Dickinson. CP-DickE

Under the lightly leaved. On the House of a Friend. John Logan. CP-LogaJ

Under the long dark boughs, like jewels red. Cherry Robbers. D. H. Lawrence. CP-LawrD

Under the Maud Moon. Galway Kinnell. SP-KinnGN

Under the Migrants. W. S. Merwin. SP-MerwW

Under the Mirabeau Bridge there flows the Seine. Mirabeau Bridge. Guillaume Apollinaire. CP-WilbR, tr. by Richard Wilbur

Under the Moon. William Butler Yeats. CP-YeatW

Under the moon my brother's body lay. Antigone. Howard Nemerov. CP-NemeH

Under the Moon's Reign. Charles Tomlinson. CP-TomlC

Under the Mountain. Louis MacNeice. CP-MacNL

Under the multiplications. New York. Federico García Lorca. CP-GarcF, tr. by Greg Simon and Steven F. White

Under the night window. Attic, The. Derek Mahon. CP-MahoD

Under the Nine Trees in January. Charles Wright. SP-WrigCN

Under the notion of a play, you see. Mr. Sheridan's Prologue to the Greek Play of Phaedra and Hippolytus; Designed to Have Been Spoke by a Boy of Six Years Old. Thomas Sheridan. CP-SherT

Under the Oak. D. H. Lawrence. CP-LawrD

Under the olive trees, from the ground. Coward, The. Stephen Spender. CP-SpenS

Under the Olives. Robert Graves. CP-GravR

Under the orange tree. Two Girls. Federico García Lorca. CP-GarcF, tr. by Robert Nasatir

Under the orchards, under. Vicenza. Kenneth Rexroth. CP-RexrK

Under the orchid, blooming as it bloomed. Subway from New Britain to the Bronx, The. Randall Jarrell. CP-JarrR

Under the peach trees, the ideograms the leaves throw. Ordinary Afternoon in Charlottesville, An. Charles Wright. SP-WrigCN

Under the pink quilted covers. Fortress, The. Anne Sexton. CP-SextA; SP-SextA

Under the pond, among rocks. Dragonfly, The. Howard Nemerov. CP-NemeH

Under the Pot. Robert Graves. CP-GravR

Under the rock on the trail. Arabian Ballad. Johann Wolfgang von Goethe. CP-EmerR

Under the rose-tree's dancing shade. Fantaisies Décoratives. Oscar Wilde. CP-

WildO

Under the Round Tower. William Butler Yeats. CP-YeatW

Under the second moon the. Time Spirals. Kenneth Rexroth. CP-RexrK

Under the separated leaves of shade. Man Meets a Woman in the Street, A. Randall Jarrell. CP-JarrR

Under the shadow of a cloud, the light. Lines on Leaving Appledore. John Greenleaf Whittier. CP-WhitJ

Under the shape of his sail, Ulysses. Presence of an External Master of Knowledge. Wallace Stevens. CP-StevWP

Under the shape of his sail, Ulysses. Sail of Ulysses, The. Wallace Stevens. CP-StevWP

Under the shuddering eyelid. Maudgalyâyana Saw Hell. Gary Snyder. CP-SnydG Fr. Myths and Texts.

Under the skin, / it's as if a woman. Whole. Rae Armantrout. SP-ArmaA

Under the Skin of It. Gary Snyder. CP-SnydG

Under the stone sky the water. Well, The. W. S. Merwin. SP-MerwW

Under the strained. Pietà. Louise Glück. SP-GlucL

Under the tall black sky you look out of your body. Endless. Muriel Rukeyser. CP-RukeM

Under the terrible north-light north-sea. Lakes of Värmland. James Dickey. CP-DickJ

Under the thunder-dark, the cicadas resound. Dark Summer. Louise Bogan. CP-BogaL

Under the too white marmoreal Lincoln Memorial. March 1, The. Robert Lowell. SP-LoweR

Under the trees. Running Water Music. Gary Snyder. CP-SnydG

Under the trimmed willows, where brown children. Trumpets. Georg Trakl. CP-WrigJ

Under the tropical moon. Mnemogasoline. Andrei Codrescu. SP-CodrA

Under the unreal helmet the severe. Two Versions of "Knight, Death and the Devil." Jorge Luis Borges. SP-BorgJ, tr. by Stephen Kessler

Under the very hills where at the first. Petrarch. CP-Petra, tr. by J. G. Nichols

Under the Viaduct, 1932. Rita Dove. SP-DoveR

Under the water tower at the edge of town. To the Evening Star: Central Minnesota. James Wright. CP-WrigJ

Under the Waterfall. Thomas Hardy. CP-HardT

Under the wave it is altogether still. Return of Aphrodite, The. May Sarton. SP-SartM

Under the Window: Ouro Prêto. Elizabeth Bishop. CP-BishE

Under the World There's a Lot of Ass, a Lot of Cunt. Allen Ginsberg. CP-GinsA; SP-GinsA

Under the wrath of my dear enemy. Petrarch. CP-Petra, tr. by J. G. Nichols

Under their great hats the women walk. Enthusiasm for Hats. Howard Nemerov. CP-NemeH

Under these hills too high and bare. Kathleen Jessie Raine. SP-RainK

Under this Marble, or under this Sill. Epitaph for One Who Would Not Be Buried in Westminster Abbey. Alexander Pope. CP-PopeA

Under this rain-wind the sombre magnificence of the coast. Solstice. Robinson Jeffers. CP-JefR2

Under this stone lie Dicky and Dolly. Elegy on Dicky and Dolly, An. Jonathan Swift. CP-SwifJ

Under this stone there lieth at rest. Epitaph of Sir Thomas Gravener, [Knight], An. Sir Thomas Wyatt. CP-WyatT

Under thy shadow may I lurk a while. St. Peter's Shadow. Richard Crashaw. CP-CrasR

Under various names, I have praised only you, rivers! Rivers ("Under various names, I have praised only you, rivers!"). Czeslaw Milosz. CP-MiloC; CP-MiloCN, tr. by Renata Gorczynski and Robert Hass

Under what conditions do you dream of the dead? Plotting with the Dead. Wisława Szymborska. SP-SzymW, tr. by Stanislaw Barańczak and Clare Cavanagh

Under what spell are we debased. Call, The. George Meredith. CP-MerG2

Under what withering leprous light. Towers of Time, The. G. K. Chesterton. CP-ChesG

Under Which Lyre, a Reactionary Tract for the Times. W. H. Auden. CP-AudeW

Under Willows. Christina Georgina Rossetti. CP-RosC3

Under Wrong Trees . . . or Freeing the Colonial Peoples. Stevie Smith. CP-SmitS

Under yonder beech-tree single on the green-sward. Love in the Valley. George Meredith. CP-MerG1

Under yonder beech-tree standing on the green-sward. George Meredith. See Under yonder beech-tree single on the green-sward

Under your illkempt yellow roses. Delia Rexroth ("Under your illkempt yellow roses"). Kenneth Rexroth. CP-RexrK

Under your Milky Way. Return of the Goddess [Artemis]. Robert Graves. CP-GravR

Undercliff Evening. Richard Eberhart. CP-EberR

Underground, The. Seamus Heaney. SP-HeanSO

Underground, The. Langston Hughes. CP-HughL; CP-HughL2

Underground, The. Thomas McGrath. SP-McGrT

Underground do you feel. What Do You Feel Underground? Gabriela Mistral. SP-MistG, tr. by Maria Giachetti [or Jacketti]

Underground grower, blind and a common brown, An. Potato. Richard Wilbur. CP-WilbR

Underground Stream, The. James Dickey. CP-DickJ

Underground System. Edna St. Vincent Millay. CP-MillE

Underground the Darkness Is the Light. Hayden Carruth. CP-CarHS

Undergrowth's a conveyance of butterflies, The. Hope's Okay. A. R. Ammons. CP-AmmoA

Undermining of the Defense Economy, The. James Wright. CP-WrigJ

Underneath. D. H. Lawrence. CP-LawrD

Underneath an old oak tree. Raven, The. Samuel Taylor Coleridge. CP-ColeS

Underneath its snowy bed. Hepatica in Winter, The. Jones Very. CP-VeryJ

Underneath my lids another eye has opened. From the Prison House. Adrienne Rich. SP-RicA2

Underneath the autumn sky. Veteran, The. Paul Laurence Dunbar. CP-DunbP

Underneath the broad hat is the face of the Ambassador. Ambassador, The. Stevie Smith. CP-SmitS

Underneath, the dunes. February Beach. A. R. Ammons. CP-AmmoA

Underneath the growing grass. Bourne, The. Christina Georgina Rossetti. CP-RosC1

Underneath the ice. Saffron. Stevie Smith. CP-SmitS

Underneath the leaves of life. Riddle, The. W. H. Auden. CP-AudeW

Underneath the tangled tree. Voices about the Princess Anemone. Stevie Smith. CP-SmitS

Underneath the tree on some. Like They Say. Robert Creeley. CP-CreeR

Undersea. A. R. Ammons. CP-AmmoA

Undersea Fragment in Colons. James Dickey. CP-DickJ

Understand me, dead is nothing. Lorine Niedecker. CP-NiedL

Understand me please there's no man underneath there's. Twice More. C. K. Williams. CP-WillC

Understand that they were sitting just inside the door. State of the Nation, The. Kenneth Patchen. CP-PatcK

Understand That This Is a Dream. Allen Ginsberg. CP-GinsA

Understanding. Constantine P. Cavafy. CP-CavaC, tr. by Theoharis Constantine Theoharis

Understanding. Yannis Ritsos. SP-RitsY, tr. by Kimon Friar

Understanding's copper coin, The. Hafiz. CP-EmerR Fr. Odes.

Understandings in Blue. Carl Sandburg. CP-SandC

Undertaker, who was with the local minister, The. Fall. John Updike. CP-UpdiJ

Undertakers, The. Rudyard Kipling. Fr. Second Jungle Book, The.

Undertakers, hearse drivers, grave diggers. To Certain Journeymen. Carl Sandburg. CP-SandC

Undertaker's Horse, The. Rudyard Kipling. CP-KiplR

Undertaking, The. John Donne. CP-DonnJ; MW-DonnJ

Undertaking, The. Louise Glück. SP-GlucL

Undertaking in New Jersey, The. George Oppen. CP-OppGN

Undertow. Langston Hughes. CP-HughL; CP-HughL3

Underwater brightness flows, An. Two in Twilight. Eugenio Montale. CP-MontE, tr. by Jonathan Galassi

Underwater eyes, an eel's. Otter, An. Ted Hughes. SP-HughTN

Underwear. Lawrence Ferlinghetti. SP-FerlL

Underworld of Dante, The. Dante Alighieri. CP-ClamA Fr. Divina Commedia.

Undesirable you may have been, untouchable. September Song. Geoffrey Hill. CP-HillG

Undine. Seamus Heaney. SP-HeanSO

Undine. Christina Georgina Rossetti. CP-RosC3

Undo time's work. R². Charles Olson. CP-OlsoC

Undoing the self is a hard road. Ostinato and Drone. Charles Wright. SP-WrigCN

Undone or done up with love. Carmen 100. Catullus. CP-ZukLS Fr. Carmina.

Undressing Justine. Czeslaw Milosz. CP-MiloCN, tr. by Robert Hass

Undressing of the Hanged Man, The. Yannis Ritsos. SP-RitsY, tr. by Kimon Friar and Kostas Myrsiades

Undue Significance a starving man attaches. Emily Dickinson. CP-DickE

Undulant across the slopes. Grasses. Amy Clampitt. CP-ClamA

Undying love to buy. His Confidence. William Butler Yeats. CP-YeatW

Une Présence Absolue. Hayden Carruth. CP-CarHS

Uneasiness in Fall. Robert Bly. See Silence

Uneasy a February afternoon. Remembering the Man. Miller Williams. CP-WillM

Unemployed. Stephen Spender. CP-SpenS

Unemployed, I recollect setting a plumb. Weather Shifts, The. Arthur Sze. SP-SzeA

Unending Rose, The. Jorge Luis Borges. SP-BorgJ, tr. by Alastair Reid

Unenlightened Face, The. James Laughlin. CP-LaugJ

Unerring tragedy of our lives is to sail, The. Splash, Flow. Arthur Sze. SP-SzeA

Unexpected angel glided down, An. Petrarch. CP-Petra, *tr.* by J. G. Nichols

Unexpected interest made him flush, The. Episode of Hands. Hart Crane. CP-CranH

Unexpected Meeting, An. Wisława Szymborska. SP-SzymW, *tr.* by Stanislaw Barańczak *and* Clare Cavanagh

Unexpectedly. Yannis Ritsos. SP-RitsY, *tr.* by Kimon Friar

Unexplorer, The. Edna St. Vincent Millay. CP-MillE

Unexpounded. Ambrose Bierce. SP-BierA

Unexpress'd, The. Walt Whitman. CP-WhitW

Unexpressed. Paul Laurence Dunbar. CP-DunbP

Unextinguished, The. Theodore Roethke. CP-RoetT

Unfaithful Servants, The. Jones Very. CP-VeryJ

Unfaithful Wife, The. Federico García Lorca. CP-GarcF, *tr.* by Will Kirkland

Unfaithfulness. Constantine P. Cavafy. CP-CavaC, *tr.* by Theoharis Constantine Theoharis

Unfamiliar Instrument. Yannis Ritsos. SP-RitsY, *tr.* by Andonis Decavalles

Unfathomable Sea! whose waves are years. Time. Percy Bysshe Shelley. CP-ShelP

Unfathomed deep, unfetter'd waste. Ocean. John Greenleaf Whittier. CP-WhitJ

Unfelt, unheard, unseen. Lines: "Unfelt, unheard, unseen." John Keats. CP-KeatJ

Unfinished Book of Kings. W. S. Merwin. SP-MerwW

Unfinished Business. Primo Levi. CP-LeviP, *tr.* by Ruth Feldman

Unfinished Dream, The. Walter De la Mare. CP-DeLaW

Unfinished History. Archibald MacLeish. CP-MacLA

Unfinished Poem. Philip Larkin. CP-LarkP

Unfinished (raw) hero—un–, The. Charles Olson. CP-OlsoC

"Unfinished," The. Frank O'Hara. SP-OharF

Unfold! Unfold! Theodore Roethke. CP-RoetT

Unfold Your Own Myth. Jelaluddin Rumi. SP-Rumi, *tr.* by Coleman Barks

Unfolded Out of the Folds. Walt Whitman. CP-WhitW

Unforeseen. Walter De la Mare. CP-DeLaW

Unforgiven. Sam Hamill. SP-HamiS

Unforgiven, The. Edwin Arlington Robinson. CP-RobiE

Unforgotten. Christina Georgina Rossetti. CP-RosC3

Unformed volcanic earth, a female thing, The. Robinson Jeffers. CP-JefR3

Unfortunate Coincidence. Dorothy Parker. CP-ParkD

Unfortunate human disorder, The. Han-shan. CP-ColdM, *tr.* by Red Pine

Unfortunate Lover, The. Andrew Marvell. CP-MarvA

Unfrocked Priest, The. William Carlos Williams. CP-WilW1

Unfulfilled to Observation. Emily Dickinson. CP-DickE

Unfulfilling Brightnesses, The. Kenneth Patchen. CP-PatcK

Unfunny uncles who insist. Exchanging Hats. Elizabeth Bishop. CP-BishE

Ungar and Rolfe. Herman Melville. SP-MelvH *Fr.* Clarel: A Poem and Pilgrimage in the Holy Land.

Ungrateful Garden, The. Carolyn Kizer. CP-KizeC

Ungratefulness. George Herbert. CP-HerbG

Unguent. Heather McHugh. SP-McHuH

Unhappy about some far off things. Stars Go Over the Lonely Ocean, The. Robinson Jeffers. CP-JefR3

Unhappy country what wings you have. Even here. Eagle Valor, Chicken Mind. Robinson Jeffers. CP-JefR3

Unhappy Dives! in an evil hour. To Dives (William Beckford). A Fragment. Lord Byron. CP-Byron

Unhappy Lot of all that shine in Courts. Samuel Johnson. CP-JohnS *Fr.* Irene.

Unhappy poets of a sunken prime! Point of Taste, The. George Meredith. CP-MerG1

Unhappy Souls. D. H. Lawrence. CP-LawrD

Unhappy State! with horrors still to strive. France. Ambrose Bierce. SP-BierA

Unhappy summer you. This Summer and Last. Thomas Hardy. CP-HardT

Unhappy time why have you built up your house. Air-Raid Rehearsals. Robinson Jeffers. CP-JefR2

Unharvested. Robert Frost. CP-FrosR

Unheard, The. James Whitcomb Riley. CP-RileJ

Unheard Melodies. Walter De la Mare. CP-DeLaW

Unheard, omnivorous, The. Air. Derek Walcott. CP-WalcD

Unhidden, The. Yannis Ritsos. SP-RitsY, *tr.* by N. C. Germanacos

Unicorn, The. Randall Jarrell. CP-JarrR

Unicorn, The. Rainer Maria Rilke. CP-MuldP, *tr.* by Paul Muldoon

Unicorn and the White Doe. Robert Graves. CP-GravR

Unicorn bred virtue for a light, The. Shield Against the Trampling Foe, A. Robert Stock. SP-StocR

Unicorn Defends Himself, The. Paul Muldoon. CP-MuldP

Unicorn is an easy prey: its horn, The. Hunting Manual. Eleanor Wilner. SP-WilnE

Unicorn with burning heart. Unicorn and the White Doe. Robert Graves. CP-GravR

Unicorns and cyclops. Fable: "Unicorns and cyclops." Federico García Lorca.

CP-GarcF, *tr.* by Alan S. Trueblood *Fr.* Theories.

Unicorns and cyclopses. Fable: "Unicorns and cyclopses." Federico García Lorca. SP-GarcF, *tr.* by Roy Campbell

Unidentified Flying Object. Robert Earl Hayden. CP-HaydR

Uniformly over the whole countryside. On What Planet. Kenneth Rexroth. CP-RexrK

Unifying Principle, The. A. R. Ammons. CP-AmmoA

Unimaginable beings. Harrow, The. Donald Davie. CP-DaviDC

Unintentional Paint. Carl Sandburg. CP-SandC

Uninterpreted. James Whitcomb Riley. CP-RileJ

Uninterrupted days occasion us. Towards a Relative Ending. Wyatt Prunty. SP-PrunW

Uninvited, The. Josephine Jacobsen. CP-JacoJ

Uninvited Guest, The. Marya Alexandrovna Zaturenska. SP-ZatuM

Union. Emily Dickinson. CP-DickE

Union. Langston Hughes. CP-HughL; CP-HughL1

Union, The. G. K. Chesterton. CP-ChesG

Union in Disseverance. George Meredith. CP-MerG1

Union of Women. Carolyn Kizer. CP-KizeC

Union Street: San Francisco, Summer 1975. Raymond Carver. CP-CarvR

Unique planets break. Place, The. Kenneth Rexroth. CP-RexrK

Unison, A. William Carlos Williams. CP-WilW2

Unit, like Death, for Whom? Emily Dickinson. CP-DickE

United Dames of America. Wallace Stevens. CP-StevW; CP-StevWP

United 555. Richard Eberhart. CP-EberR

United Front, The. William Carlos Williams. CP-WilW2

UN Headquarters in the High Commissioner's Residence in Jerusalem. Yehuda Amichai. SP-AmicYL, *tr.* by Benjamin Harshav *and* Barbara Harshav

United States, The. William Carlos Williams. CP-WilW2

United States of America is like a convention, The. Love and Money. Alan Dugan. CP-DugaA

United States to Old World Critics, The. Walt Whitman. CP-WhitW

Unity. Ralph Waldo Emerson. CP-EmerR

Unity complete, assured, and high, A. National Unity ("Unity complete, assured, and high, A"). Jones Very. CP-VeryJ

Unity with Nature. Samuel Taylor Coleridge. CP-ColeS

Universal Analogies. Charles Baudelaire. CP-BaudC, *tr.* by Walter Martin

Universal & Susquehanna Mercy Co. Dayton, O., The. Philip Whalen. SP-WhalP

Universal Prayer [Deo Opt. Max.], The. Alexander Pope. CP-PopeA

Universality of things, The. Eyeglasses, The. William Carlos Williams. CP-WilW1

Universe, The. Walter De la Mare. CP-DeLaW

Universe expands and contracts like a great heart, The. Great Explosion, The. Robinson Jeffers. CP-JefR3

Universe Flows, The. D. H. Lawrence. CP-LawrD

Universe has four large gates, The. Indian Image. Constantine P. Cavafy. CP-CavaC, *tr.* by Theoharis Constantine Theoharis

Universe is a form of a divine law, The. Father Reason. Jelaluddin Rumi. SP-Rumi, *tr.* by Coleman Barks

Universe is but the Thing of things, The. Accidentally on Purpose. Robert Frost. CP-FrosR

Universe is One Place. William Stafford. SP-StafWW

Universe / keeps them turning turning. Photograph. Lucille Clifton. SP-ClifL

Universe of course is infinite, The. Two Sides to an Outside: Meditation from Empson. Howard Nemerov. CP-NemeH

Universe-Solitude. Paul Éluard. CP-BeckS

Universe with its, The. Shoreless Tide, The. A. R. Ammons. CP-AmmoA

University. Karl Shapiro. SP-ShapK

University Hospital, Boston. Mary Oliver. SP-OlivM

University of the South, The. Donald Davie. CP-DaviDC

Unjeweled in black as ever comedienne. Words for Maria. James Merrill. SP-MerrJ

Unjust, The. Yannis Ritsos. SP-RitsY, *tr.* by Minas Savvas

Unjust decrees, that do at once exact. Song: "Unjust decrees, that do at once exact." Sir John Suckling. CP-SuckJ

Unjustly. Yannis Ritsos. SP-RitsY, *tr.* by Kostas Myrsiades

Unkept Good Fridays. Thomas Hardy. CP-HardT

Unkind Poem, An. Charles Bukowski. SP-BukC1

Unkindly May, An. Thomas Hardy. CP-HardT

Unkindness. George Herbert. CP-HerbG

Unknowable? Perhaps Not Altogether. John Berryman. CP-BerrJ

Unknowing. Thomas Hardy. CP-HardT

Unknown, The. Denise Levertov. SP-LeveDP

Unknown, The. William Carlos Williams. CP-WilW2

Unknown—a stranger in Antioch—the man from Edessa. That's the Man. Constantine P. Cavafy. CP-CavaC, *tr.* by Theoharis Constantine Theoharis

Unknown Citizen, The. W. H. Auden. CP-AudeW

Unknown Fair Faces. George Meredith. CP-MerG1

Unknown Forebear. W. S. Merwin. SP-MerwWF

Unknown Friends. James Whitcomb Riley. CP-RileJ

Unknown Girl in the Maternity Ward. Anne Sexton. CP-SextA; SP-SextA

Unknown is the largest need, The. Emily Dickinson. SP-DickE

Unknown One, The. Charles Simic. SP-SimiCE

Unknown river whose banks drip feathers, An. Kwashiorkor; Marasmus. Thomas Lux. SP-LuxT

Unknown Sailor, The. Miller Williams. CP-WillM

Unknown Street. Jorge Luis Borges. SP-BorgJ, *tr. by* Alexander Coleman

Unknown War, The. Carl Sandburg. CP-SandC

Unknown Woman's Afternoon. Rainer Maria Rilke. CP-RilkFr, *tr. by* A. Poulin, Jr.

Unlearning to Not Speak. Marge Piercy. SP-PierM

Unless. James Whitcomb Riley. CP-RileJ

Unless. Robert Penn Warren. CP-WarrR

Unless I yield my love to you, you swear. Mood. Dorothy Parker. CP-ParkD

Unless the soul, to vice a thrall. Boethius. CP-JohnS *Fr.* Consolation of Philosophy, The ("De Consolacione Philosophie").

Unless this is the shelf of whatever happens? John Ashbery. SP-AshbJ *Fr.* Fantasia on "The Nut-Brown Maid"

Unless, through blind desire which breaks the heart. Petrarch. CP-Petra, *tr. by* J. G. Nichols

Unless you come of the gipsy stock. Gipsy Vans. Rudyard Kipling. CP-KiplR *Fr.* Debits and Credits.

Unlesse there were consent twixt hell and heaven. Thomas Campion *and* Philip Rosseter. CP-CampT

Unlike Joubert. James Schuyler. CP-SchuJ

Unlike the ribald, whose licentious jest. Lucan. CP-JohnS *Fr.* Ad Pisonem.

Unlike virtue / style doesn't require any examples. Examples can use. À Francis Ponge. Andrei Codrescu. SP-CodrA

Unloved, The. Kathleen Jessie Raine. SP-RainK

Unlove's the heavenless hell and homeless home. E. E. Cummings. CP-CummE

Unluckily for a Death. Dylan Thomas. CP-ThomD

Unlucky Apple, The. Paul Laurence Dunbar. CP-DunbP

Unlucky the hero born. Times Are Tidy, The. Sylvia Plath. CP-PlatS

Unmanned ship—a bed. Fanny Howe. SP-HoweF *Fr.* O'Clock.

Unmapped Road. Robert Stock. SP-StocR

Unmarked Boxes. Jelaluddin Rumi. SP-Rumi, *tr. by* Coleman Barks

Unmarried, near-sighted, rather deaf. Maker, The. W. H. Auden. CP-AudeW

Unmarried Woman at Mass, The. Federico García Lorca. CP-GarcF, *tr. by* Alan S. Trueblood *Fr.* Eros with a Cane.

Unmeasured Tempo. Maya Angelou. SP-AngeM

Unmindful of the roses, / Unmindful of the thorns. One Sea-Side Grave. Christina Georgina Rossetti. CP-RosC2

Unmoving vault / receives their movement, The. At Wells: Polyphony. Charles Tomlinson. CP-TomlC

Unnamable River, The. Arthur Sze. SP-SzeA

Unnamed Lands. Walt Whitman. CP-WhitW

Unnamed Spell, The. Robert Graves. CP-GravR

Unnatural Deaths. Yusef Komunyakaa. CP-KomuY

Unnatural History of Peru, The. Kenneth Patchen. CP-PatcK

Unnatural Love. Allen Tate. CP-TateA

Unnatural Powers. Robinson Jeffers. CP-JefR3

Unnatural State of the Unicorn. Yusef Komunyakaa. CP-KomuY

Unnatural Unselection. Hayden Carruth. CP-CarHS

Unnoted as the setting of a star. Mulford. John Greenleaf Whittier. CP-WhitJ

Unnoticed woman from whose kind large flesh. E. E. Cummings. CP-CummE

Unnumbered herds flow like lichens, The. In a Clearing. W. S. Merwin. SP-MerwW

Unnumbered thoughts my brain a captive holds. Imitation of Sidney: To Stella. (Miss B?). Wallace Stevens. CP-StevWP

Unoccupied Zone, The. Louis Aragon. CP-MacNL

Unopened Song. Federico García Lorca. CP-GarcF, *tr. by* Jerome Rothenberg *Fr.* Moments of Song.

Unpacking in the raw new rooms, I clear. Thoughts on Unpacking. Thom Gunn. CP-GunnT

Unpardonable Sin, The. G. K. Chesterton. CP-ChesG

Unpardonable Sin, The. Nicholas Vachel Lindsay. CP-LindV

Unpenned Poem, The. Robert Graves. CP-GravR

Unpeopled, Conventional Rose-Garden, The. Kenneth Rexroth. CP-RexrK

Unperishing youth! / Thou leapest from forth. On a Cataract. Samuel Taylor Coleridge. CP-ColeS

Unplanted Primrose, The. Thomas Hardy. CP-HardT

Unpopular, Lonely and Loving. Stevie Smith. CP-SmitS

Unposted Letter. Robert Graves. CP-GravR

Unpredictable but Providential. W. H. Auden. CP-AudeW

Unpurged images of day recede, The. Byzantium. William Butler Yeats. CP-YeatW

Unquiet Childhood here by special grace. Infant M— M—, The. William Wordsworth. CP-WorW2

Unquiet Ones, The. Stanley Kunitz. CP-KunSC

Unquiet thought, whom at the first I bred. Sonnet 2. Edmund Spenser. CP-Spens *Fr.* Amoretti.

Unraveling a rope. Rope's End, The. Howard Nemerov. CP-NemeH

Unread Pages. Laura Riding Jackson. CP-RidiL

Unrealized. Thomas Hardy. CP-HardT

Unrefractory petalbent. Canvass. Lorine Niedecker. CP-NiedL

Unregarding. Walter De la Mare. CP-DeLaW

Unremitting Voice of Nightly Streams, The. William Wordsworth. CP-WorW2

Unresolved. Denise Levertov. SP-LeveDL

Unresolved Burdens. Primo Levi. CP-LeviP, *tr. by* Ruth Feldman

Unresponsible / people versus / serious. News, The. Robert Creeley. CP-CreeR

Unreturning, The. Wilfred Owen. CP-OwenW

Unreturning Hosts, The. Kenneth Patchen. CP-PatcK

Unrevealed, The. Jones Very. CP-VeryJ

Unrhymed, unrhythmical, the chatter goes. At the Party. W. H. Auden. CP-AudeW

Unripe Fruit, The. Jones Very. CP-VeryJ

Unripe harvest there hath none to reap it. Castle-Builder's World, A. Christina Georgina Rossetti. CP-RosC2

Unrisen splendour of the brightest sun. Fragment: "Unrisen splendour of the brightest sun." Percy Bysshe Shelley. CP-ShelP

Unrolling the black thread. Thread, The. W. S. Merwin. SP-MerwW

Unsaid. A. R. Ammons. CP-AmmoA

Unsaid Word, An. Adrienne Rich. CP-RicAE; SP-RicA1; SP-RicA2

Unsatisfactory Dream, The. James Laughlin. CP-LaugJ

Unscientific Postscript. Howard Nemerov. CP-NemeH

Unseasonable man, statue of ice. Epithalamion at the Marriage of the Earl of Somerset. John Donne. CP-DonnJ; MW-DonnJ

Unseemly are the open eyes. Sight. Dorothy Parker. CP-ParkD

Unseen, The. Robert Pinsky. CP-PinsR

Unseen at forest edge. Darwin's Dream. Clarence Major. SP-MajoC

Unseen Buds. Walt Whitman. CP-WhitW

Unselfish Husband, The. Ogden Nash. CP-NashO

Unsepulchred, 1914–1918, The. Marya Alexandrovna Zaturenska. SP-ZatuM

Unser Vater. Stevie Smith. CP-SmitS

Unsettled again and hearing Russian spoken. Hearing Russian Spoken. Donald Davie. CP-DaviDC

Unsettled Motorcyclist's Vision of His Death, The. Thom Gunn. CP-GunnT

Unsigned, almost unsent, and all unsaid. On a Letter. James Cunningham. CP-CunnJ

Unsleeping principle of delight that, The. Interjection #8: Or, Sometimes, Night. Robert Penn Warren. CP-WarrR

Unsnack your snood, madanna, for the stars. Late Hymn from the Myrrh-Mountain. Wallace Stevens. CP-StevW; CP-StevWP

Unsounded. Adrienne Rich. CP-RicAE

Unspeakable. Heather McHugh. SP-McHuH

Unspoken. James Whitcomb Riley. CP-RileJ

Unspotted lambs to follow the one Lamb. Christina Georgina Rossetti. CP-RosC2

Unstable dream[e] [*or* dreme], according [*or* accordyng] to the place. Sir Thomas Wyatt. CP-WyatT

Unstamped Letter in Our Rural Letter Box, An. Robert Frost. CP-FrosR

Unsteady Yellow. Tess Gallagher. SP-GallT

Unstill Universe. Lucio Piccolo. CP-TomlC

Unstrung. Eleanor Wilner. SP-WilnE

Unsung Heroes, The. Paul Laurence Dunbar. CP-DunbP

Unsupported by reason's enigma. Scheherazade. John Ashbery. SP-AshbJ

Unsuspected Blackcurrant river rolls. Blackcurrant River. Arthur Rimbaud. CP-RimbA, *tr. by* Martin Sorrell

Untamed. Yannis Ritsos. SP-RitsY, *tr. by* Kimon Friar

Untenable Situation, An. Pablo Neruda. SP-NeruP

Unthronged Oracle, The. Laura Riding Jackson. CP-RidiL

Until and i heard. E. E. Cummings. CP-CummE

Until at length the north winds blow. Henry David Thoreau. CP-ThorH

Until Daybreak. Yannis Ritsos. SP-RitsY, *tr. by* Kimon Friar

Until fall, a grasshopper / Chose to chirr. Grasshopper and the Ant, The. Jean de La Fontaine. CP-WilbR

Until I asked her to please stop doing it and was astonished to find that she not only could. My Mother's Lips. C. K. Williams. CP-WillC; SP-WillC

Until I stand on the January platform. Muriel Rukeyser. CP-RukeM

Until that child, one flight below, stops crying. White Ceiling, The. David Ignatow. SP-IgnaD

Until the crumpets and the christians. "Jesus, The." Langston Hughes. CP-HughL; CP-HughL3

Until the Day Break. Christina Georgina Rossetti. CP-RosC2

Until the Desert knows. Emily Dickinson. CP-DickE

Until thy feet have trod the Road. Comforters, The. Rudyard Kipling. CP-KiplR

Until tonight they were separate specialities. Story for Rose on the Midnight Flight to Boston, A. Anne Sexton. CP-SextA

Until We Both. Robert Graves. CP-GravR

Untilted. John Ashbery. SP-AshbJ

Untimely. Rudyard Kipling. CP-KiplR *Fr.* Debits and Credits.

Untimely Arguments. Jones Very. CP-VeryJ

Untimely Lost: Oliver Madox Brown. Born 1855; Died 1874. Dante Gabriel Rossetti. CW-RossD

Untitled. John Clare. SP-ClarJ *Fr.* Badger, The.

Untitled. Heather McHugh. SP-McHuH

Untitled: "I am fifty-two years old." Kenneth Rexroth. CP-RexrK

Untitled Blues; After a Photograph by Yevgeni Yevtushenko. Yusef Komunyakaa. CP-KomuY

Untitled Poem: "City is empty, like a dangerous area, The." Alan Dugan. CP-DugaA

Untitled Poem: "Consternation in household!" Alan Dugan. CP-DugaA

Untitled Poem: "Doctor and I have become intimate, The." Alan Dugan. CP-DugaA

Untitled Poem: "I love the way the heel of my hand feels." Alan Dugan. CP-DugaA

Untitled Poem: "I never saw any point." Alan Dugan. CP-DugaA

Untitled Poem: "I used to enjoy the night-time." Alan Dugan. CP-DugaA

Untitled Poem: "I'm in the house because." Alan Dugan. CP-DugaA

Untitled Poem: "I'm waiting for you, but not purely." Alan Dugan. CP-DugaA

Untitled Poem: "I've promised that I will not care about things." Alan Dugan. CP-DugaA

Untitled Poem: "Let them take to the air before." Alan Dugan. CP-DugaA

Untitled Poem: "Monarchs, the butterflies, are commanded, The." Alan Dugan. CP-DugaA

Untitled Poem: "Once on the beach at night I heard the waves." Alan Dugan. CP-DugaA

Untitled Poem: "Once, one of my students read a book we had." Alan Dugan. CP-DugaA

Untitled Poem: "One tries to be sober and respectable." Alan Dugan. CP-DugaA

Untitled Poem: "One used to be able to say." Alan Dugan. CP-DugaA

Untitled Poem: "Our German teacher used to say." Alan Dugan. CP-DugaA

Untitled Poem: "Patients in the waiting room, The." Alan Dugan. CP-DugaA

Untitled Poem: "Speciously individual." Alan Dugan. CP-DugaA

Untitled Poem: "Two shots down and I'm exalted." Alan Dugan. CP-DugaA

Untitled Poem: "What I remember most." Alan Dugan. CP-DugaA

Untitled Poem: "When the window glass blows in." Alan Dugan. CP-DugaA

Untitled Poem: "Who can abide whom or what? That's." Alan Dugan. CP-DugaA

Untitled Poem: "Why feel guilty because the death of a lover causes lust?" Alan Dugan. CP-DugaA

Untitled Poem in Two Parts. Alan Dugan. CP-DugaA

Untitled, 6 September 1969. Kenneth Rexroth. CP-RexrK

Unto a broken heart. Emily Dickinson. CP-DickE

Unto blest Melancholy's house one happy day. Son of Melancholy, The. Walter De la Mare. CP-DeLaW

Unto her wonderful, the night's own might. For Ysolt. The Triad of Dawn. Ezra Pound. CP-PoEar

Unto like Story—Trouble has incited me. Emily Dickinson. CP-DickE

"Unto me?" I do not know you. Emily Dickinson. CP-DickE

Unto my Books—so good to turn. Emily Dickinson. CP-DickE

Unto my thinking, thou beheld'st all worth. Sonnet: He interprets Dante's Dream, related in the first Sonnet of the Vita Nuova. Guido Cavalcanti. CW-RossD, *tr.* by Dante Gabriel Rossetti

Unto One of the Least of These. Miller Williams. CP-WillM

Unto Pastillus ranke Gorgonius came. Upon Gorgonius. Robert Herrick. CP-HerrR

Unto seventy years and seven. For a Lady Who Must Write Verse. Dorothy Parker. CP-ParkD

Unto that love must we through fire attain. Hueless Love, The. George Meredith. CP-MerG1

Unto the caitiff wretch whom long affliction holdeth. Sir Philip Sidney. SP-SidnP *Fr.* Arcadia.

Unto the Whole—how add? Emily Dickinson. CP-DickE

Unto thee i / burn incense. E. E. Cummings. CP-CummE

Unto thee, O Lord, do I lift up my soul. Psalm 25: "Unto thee, O Lord, do I lift up my soul." Bible, *O.T.* SP-SmarC *Fr.* Psalms.

Unto thee will I cry, O Lord my rock. Psalm 28: "Unto thee will I cry, O Lord my rock." Bible, *O.T.* SP-SidnP *Fr.* Psalms.

Unto whose use the pregnant suns are poised. Rudyard Kipling. CP-KiplR *Fr.* Kim.

Unto you is born a Saviour. Jones Very. CP-VeryJ

Untold Want, The. Walt Whitman. CP-WhitW

Untouched grandeur in the hinterlands. Life in the Boondocks. A. R. Ammons. CP-AmmoA

Untouched through all severity of cold. Filial Piety. William Wordsworth. CP-WorW2

Untoward Occurance at Embassy Poetry Reading. Marilyn Hacker. SP-HackM

Untruth is become the mode. Hafiz. CP-EmerR *Fr.* Odes.

Unused tent, The. Attic Which Is Desire, The. William Carlos Williams. CP-WilW1

Unusual Precautions. John Ashbery. SP-AshbJ

Unwandering, I can move. For Robert Bhain Campbell. James Dickey. CP-DickJ

Unwanted Memory. Clarence Major. SP-MajoC

Unwarned, catch into this. Eagle's Mile, The. James Dickey. CP-DickJ

Unwashed, unshat. Iceland Revisited. W. H. Auden. CP-AudeW

Unwillingly Miranda wakes. Lady Thinks She Is Thirty, A. Ogden Nash. CP-NashO

Unwin, I should but ill repay. To Unwin. William Cowper. CP-CowpW

Unwind my riddle. Stephen Crane. CP-CranS

Unwinged Ones, The. Ogden Nash. CP-NashO

Unwithered Garland, The. Stanley Kunitz. CP-KunSC

Unworthy of her Breast. Emily Dickinson. CP-DickE

Unworthy porter, bound in chains full sore. Elegy 1.6: "Unworthy porter, bound in chains full sore." Ovid. CP-MarlC *Fr.* Elegies.

Unwrap the dust from its mummycloths. Freeing of the Dust, The. Denise Levertov. SP-LeveDL; SP-LeveDS

Unwritten. G. K. Chesterton. CP-ChesG

Unwritten, The. W. S. Merwin. SP-MerwW

Unyielding in the pride of his defiance. Flying Dutchman, The. Edwin Arlington Robinson. CP-RobiE

Up. A. R. Ammons. CP-AmmoA

Up. James Schuyler. CP-SchuJ

Up a heavy wooded hill. Christmas Tree. Richard Eberhart. CP-EberR

Up against It. Eleanor Wilner. SP-WilnE

Up all night with a hundred dying chicks. Sam Hamill.

Up among the stucco pears, the iron vines. Dirge for a Town in France. Thomas Merton. CP-MertT

Up and be doing, all who have a hand. Call to National Service, A. Thomas Hardy. CP-HardT

Up and Down. James Merrill. SP-MerrJ

Up and Down. Stevie Smith. CP-SmitS

Up and Down Old Brandywine. James Whitcomb Riley. CP-RileJ

Up and down / she walks, listless. Rose, The. Robert Creeley. CP-CreeR

Up and down the small streets, in which. Widows, The. Donald Hall. CP-HallD

Up and down the village streets. Prophecy of Samuel Sewall, The. John Greenleaf Whittier. CP-WhitJ

Up and down / what falls. They Say. Robert Creeley. CP-CreeR

Up and Warn A' Willie. Robert Burns. CP-BurnR

Up at a Villa—Down in the City. Robert Browning. CP-BroR1; SP-BroR

Up at dawn. 7.IV.64. Gary Snyder. CP-SnydG

Up at La Serra. Charles Tomlinson. CP-TomlC; SP-TomlC

Up-Beat. Langston Hughes. CP-HughL; CP-HughL3

Up beyond sense and praise. Little Fanfare for Felix Magowan. James Merrill. SP-MerrJ

Up, black, striped and damasked like the chasuble. Skunk, The. Seamus Heaney. SP-HeanSO

Up came the young Centaur-colts from the plains they were fathered in. Centaurs, The. Rudyard Kipling. CP-KiplR *Fr.* Debits and Credits.

"Up, down, good, bad," said. Tubes. Donald Hall. CP-HallD

Up-end the rain stick and what happens next. Rain Stick, The. Seamus Heaney. SP-HeanSO

Up from Blood Bay are the hills. Wild Parrots of Blood Bay, The. Josephine Jacobsen. CP-JacoJ

Up from Lewes. Desert Storm. William Corbett. SP-CorbW

Up from many a sheeted valley. Margrave's Birthnight, The. Herman Melville. SP-MelvH

Up from oysters. Fish That Walked, The. Anne Sexton. CP-SextA

Up from the bronze, I saw. Roman Fountain. Louise Bogan. CP-BogaL

Up from the city street, as in any green wood. Travelers, The. Josephine Jacobsen. CP-JacoJ

Up from the Egg; the Confessions of a Nuthatch Avoider. Ogden Nash. CP-NashO

Up from the meadows rich with corn. Barbara Frietchie. John Greenleaf Whittier. CP-WhitJ

Up from the sea the wild north wind is blowing. Wind of March, The. John Greenleaf Whittier. CP-WhitJ

Up from the street and the crowds that went. Her Eyes. Edwin Arlington Robinson. CP-RobiE

Up from the valley. Now and Then. James Schuyler. CP-SchuJ

Up from the Wheelbarrow. Ogden Nash. CP-NashO

Up He Goes! D. H. Lawrence. CP-LawrD

Up Here. Robert Creeley. SP-CreeR

Up Here. James Tate. SP-TateJ

Up here among the gull cries. Magnolia Shoals. Sylvia Plath. CP-PlatS

Up here I love light, travel. Toward an Understanding. Heather McHugh. SP-McHuH

Up here we don't plant trees sometimes we take them down. For My Friend Who Planted a Tree for His Daughter Jane. Grace Paley. CP-PalGC

Up high the trail turns steep. Shih-te. CP-ColdM, *tr.* by Red Pine

Up I rose, my lads, an' i heard yer. Up He Goes! D. H. Lawrence. CP-LawrD

Up in Michigan. Philip Whalen. SP-WhalP

Up in northern California. Little Girls, The. Charles Bukowski. SP-BukC1

Up in Tentoleena Land. Christine's Song. James Whitcomb Riley. CP-RileJ

Up in the Air. Robert Creeley. CP-CreeR

Up in the air / among the Iroquois: no. Above Manhattan. Charles Tomlinson. CP-TomlC; SP-TomlC

Up in the high. Song: "Up in the high." D. H. Lawrence. CP-LawrD

Up in the Morning Early. Robert Burns. CP-BurnR

'Up in the pools,' they'd said, and 'Two miles upstream.' Milesian Encounter on the Sligachan. Ted Hughes. SP-HughTN

Up in the second balcony. Burlesque. Muriel Rukeyser. CP-RukeM

Up in the sky the star is waiting. Randall Jarrell. CP-JarrR

Up into the silence green. E. E. Cummings. CP-CummE

Up, Jack. Richard Wilbur. CP-WilbR

Up, laggards of Freedom!—our free flag is cast. Song for the Time, A. John Greenleaf Whittier. CP-WhitJ

Up Life's Hill with my little Bundle. Emily Dickinson. CP-DickE

Up, my drowsing eyes! / Up, my sinking heart! Vigil of all Saints. Christina Georgina Rossetti. CP-RosC2

Up my lads, and lift the ledgers, sleep and ease are o'er. Songs for the City. G. K. Chesterton. CP-ChesG

Up Naumkeck they sail, and far explore. Naumkeck River. Jones Very. CP-VeryJ

Up north here, in my own country, and free-. Long Summers. Robert Lowell. SP-LoweR

Up on a hill / the morning moon washed clean. Olive Grove, The. Arthur Sze. SP-SzeA

Up on the mountain where nobody is looking. Houses, The. W. S. Merwin. SP-MerwWF

Up past the burnt hills. Distance and the crowd. Muriel Rukeyser. CP-RukeM

Up public joy, remember. Ode, or Song, by All the Muses, An. Ben Jonson. CP-JonsB

Up Rising. Robert Duncan. SP-DuncR *Fr.* Passages.

Up rose the moon in glory. Despair. Christina Georgina Rossetti. CP-RosC3

Up Tail[e]s All. Robert Herrick. CP-HerrR

Up the chasm-walls of my bleeding heart. Hive, The. Hart Crane. CP-CranH

Up the Dark Valley. Thomas McGrath. SP-McGrT

Up the hillside, down the glen. Texas. John Greenleaf Whittier. CP-WhitJ

Up the old hill to the old house again. Long Race, The. Edwin Arlington Robinson. CP-RobiE

Up the path, past the iced birdbath and the black roses. Arrival. Josephine Jacobsen. CP-JacoJ

Up the road. Apple Core. Clarence Major. SP-MajoC

Up the street / go the four young blades. Ghazal of the Hundred-Year-Old Love. Federico García Lorca. CP-GarcF, *tr.* by Catherine Brown *Fr.* Ghazals.

Up the streets of Aberdeen. Barclay of Ury. John Greenleaf Whittier. CP-WhitJ

Up the verdantest of hills. Medieval Miniature, A. Wisława Szymborska. SP-SzymW, *tr.* by Stanisław Barańczak *and* Clare Cavanagh

Up the west slope before dark. Kin. W. S. Merwin. SP-MerwW

Up there day and nights for weeks they turn to water. School on the Roof, The. W. S. Merwin. SP-MerwWF

Up there, do you see alpine pastures for angels. Rainer Maria Rilke. CP-RilkFr, *tr.* by A. Poulin, Jr. *Fr.* Valaisian Quatrains, The.

Up there / in that diorama of morning. Song Thief, The. Yusef Komunyakaa. CP-KomuY

Up this high and far north. Further On. A. R. Ammons. CP-AmmoA

Up this pleasant stream let's row. Assabet, The. Henry David Thoreau. CP-ThorH

Up Thy Hill of Sorrows / Thou all alone. Good Friday Morning. Christina Georgina Rossetti. CP-RosC2

Up, Timothy, up with your staff and away! Childless Father, The. William Wordsworth. CP-WorW1; MW-WorW

Up to battle! Sons of Suli. Song to the Suliotes. Lord Byron. CP-Byron

Up to the moment of the yellow sunset. Gold of the Tigers, The. Jorge Luis Borges. SP-BorgJ, *tr.* by Alastair Reid

Up to the throne of God is borne. Labourer's Noon-Day Hymn, The. William Wordsworth. CP-WorW2

Up up and away! Hiway Poesy: L.A.–Albuquerque–Texas–Witchita. Allen Ginsberg. CP-GinsA

Up, up, lad, time's a-wastin', press the ignition. Ms. Found in a Quagmire. Ogden Nash. CP-NashO

Up! up! my friend, and clear your looks. William Wordsworth. *See* Up! up! my friend, and quit your books

Up! up! my friend, and quit your books. Tables Turned, The. William Wordsworth. CP-WorW1

Up, up, up—next step of the staircase. Fust and His Friends. Robert Browning. CP-BroR2

Up, up! ye dames, [and] ye lasses gay! Hunting Song. Samuel Taylor Coleridge. CP-ColeS; MW-ColeS *Fr.* Zapolya.

Up wi' the carls of Dysart. Hey Ca' thro'. Robert Burns. CP-BurnR

Up winding stair, / here, where, in what theater lost? Logic and The Magic Flute. Marianne Craig Moore. CP-MoorM

Up with me! up with me into the clouds! To a Sky-Lark. William Wordsworth. CP-WorW1

Up with the Quintill, that the Rout. Quintell, The. Robert Herrick. CP-HerrR

Up Your Yellow River. Charles Bukowski. SP-BukC1

Up, youths and virgins, up, and praise. Epithalamion: "Up, youths and virgins, up, and praise." Ben Jonson. CP-JonsB *Fr.* Haddington Masque, The.

Upbraiding, An. Thomas Hardy. CP-HardT

Upcountry. Adrienne Rich. SP-RicA1; SP-RicA2

Upended, it crouches on broken limbs. Poem: "Upended, it crouches on broken limbs." Charles Tomlinson. CP-TomlC

Upgrade, past snow-tangled bramble, past. Sila. Robert Penn Warren. CP-WarrR

Uphill. Christina Georgina Rossetti. CP-RosC1

Upland. A. R. Ammons. CP-AmmoA

Upland flocks grew starved and thinned, The. Lambs of Grasmere, 1860, The. Christina Georgina Rossetti. CP-RosC1

Uplands in May. Carl Sandburg. CP-SandC

Uplifted and waved till immobilized. Elephants. Marianne Craig Moore. CP-MoorM

Upon a bank, easeless with knobs of gold. Gloria Mundi. Walter De la Mare. CP-DeLaW

Upon a Black Twist, Rounding the Arm of the Countess of Carlisle. Robert Herrick. CP-HerrR

Upon a Bleare-Ey'd Woman. Robert Herrick. CP-HerrR

Upon a Certain Bookseller, or Printer, in Utopia. Thomas Sheridan. "Thou lowest scoundrel of the scoundrel kind." CP-SherT

Upon a Cheap Laundresse: Epigram. Robert Herrick. CP-HerrR

Upon a Cherrystone Sent to the Tip of the Lady Jemmonia Walgraves Eare. Robert Herrick. CP-HerrR

Upon a Child. Robert Herrick. *See* Here a pretty Baby lies

Upon a child. Robert Herrick. CP-HerrR
  (Upon a Child.) CP-HerrR

Upon a Child. An Epitaph. Robert Herrick. CP-HerrR

Upon a Child That Died [*or* Dyed]. Robert Herrick. CP-HerrR

Upon a Comely, and Curious Maide. Robert Herrick. CP-HerrR

Upon a Crooked Maid. Robert Herrick. CP-HerrR

Upon a day, came sorrow in to me. Sonnet: On the 9th of June 1290. Dante Alighieri. CW-RossD, *tr.* by Dante Gabriel Rossetti

Upon a Delaying Lady. Robert Herrick. CP-HerrR

Upon a Dying Lady. William Butler Yeats. CP-YeatW

Upon a Fit of Sickness, Anno 1632. Anne Bradstreet. CP-BradA

Upon a Flie. Robert Herrick. CP-HerrR

Upon a Free Maid, with a Foule Breath. Robert Herrick. CP-HerrR

Upon a Gentlewoman with a Sweet Voice. Robert Herrick. CP-HerrR

Upon a golden tray Salome brings. Salome. Constantine P. Cavafy. CP-CavaC, *tr.* by Theoharis Constantine Theoharis

Upon a Grave. Stevie Smith. CP-SmitS

Upon a Hoarse Singer. Robert Herrick. CP-HerrR

Upon a holy thursday their innocent faces clean. William Blake. CP-BlakW *Fr.* Island in the Moon, An.

Upon a House Shaken by the Land Agitation. William Butler Yeats. CP-YeatW

Upon a Lady Faire, but Fruitlesse. Robert Herrick. CP-HerrR

Upon a Lady That Dyed in Child-Bed, and Left a Daughter behind Her. Robert Herrick. CP-HerrR

Upon a Lilac Sea. Emily Dickinson. CP-DickE

Upon A.M. Sir John Suckling. CP-SuckJ

Upon a Maid. Robert Herrick. CP-HerrR

Upon a Maid That Died [*or* Dyed] the Day She Was Married [*or* Marryed]. Meleager. CP-HerrR, *tr.* by Robert Herrick

Upon a Maid[e]. Robert Herrick. CP-HerrR

Upon a Maide. Robert Herrick. CP-HerrR

Upon a Moebius strip. Moebius Strip, The. Charles Olson. CP-OlsoC

Upon a Mole in Celia's Bosom. Thomas Carew. CP-CareT
Upon a noon I pilgrimed through. Her Immortality. Thomas Hardy. CP-HardT
Upon a Painted Gentlewoman. Robert Herrick. CP-HerrR
Upon a peak in Darien. Sage of Darien, The. Ogden Nash. CP-NashO
Upon a Physitian. Robert Herrick. CP-HerrR
Upon a poet's page I wrote. Her Initials. Thomas Hardy. CP-HardT
Upon a Portrait. William Wordsworth. CP-WorW2
Upon a Ribbon [or Ribband]. Thomas Carew. CP-CareT
Upon a rock yet uncreate. Ralph Waldo Emerson. CP-EmerR
Upon a Sabbath-day it fell. Eve of St. Mark, The. John Keats. CP-KeatJ
Upon a Scarre in a Virgins Face. Robert Herrick. CP-HerrR
Upon a simmer Sunday morn. Holy Fair, The. Robert Burns. CP-BurnR
Upon a Sowre-Breath Lady. Robert Herrick. CP-HerrR
Upon a time, before the faery broods. Lamia. John Keats. CP-KeatJ
Upon a Venerable Rival. William Cowper. CP-CowpW
Upon a Virgin. Robert Herrick. CP-HerrR
Upon a Virgin Kissing a Rose. Robert Herrick. CP-HerrR
Upon a Wife That Dyed Mad with Jealousie. Robert Herrick. CP-HerrR
Upon a Young Mother of Many Children. Robert Herrick. CP-HerrR
Upon Adam Peapes. Robert Herrick. CP-HerrR
Upon an Eunuch: A Poet. Andrew Marvell. CP-MarvA
Upon an Old Man a Residenciarie. Robert Herrick. CP-HerrR
Upon an Old Woman. Robert Herrick. CP-HerrR
Upon Appleton House [To My Lord Fairfax]. Andrew Marvell. CP-MarvA
Upon Batt. Robert Herrick. CP-HerrR
Upon Ben Jo[h]nson. Robert Herrick. CP-HerrR
Upon Bice. Robert Herrick. CP-HerrR
Upon Bishop Andrewes's [or Andrewes His] Picture before His Sermons. Richard Crashaw. CP-CrasR
   (See here a Shadow from that setting Sunne.) CP-CrasR
Upon Blanch. Robert Herrick. CP-HerrR
Upon Blinks. Robert Herrick. CP-HerrR
Upon Blisse. Robert Herrick. CP-HerrR
Upon Boreman. Epig. Robert Herrick. CP-HerrR
Upon Bran. Robert Herrick. CP-HerrR
Upon Bridget. Robert Herrick. CP-HerrR
Upon Brock. Robert Herrick. CP-HerrR
Upon Buggins. Robert Herrick. CP-HerrR
Upon Bunce: Epigram. Robert Herrick. CP-HerrR
Upon Bungie. Robert Herrick. CP-HerrR
Upon Burr. Robert Herrick. CP-HerrR
Upon Candlemasse Day. Robert Herrick. CP-HerrR
Upon Case. Robert Herrick. CP-HerrR
Upon Center a Spectacle-Maker with a Flat Nose. Robert Herrick. CP-HerrR
Upon Chub. Robert Herrick. CP-HerrR
Upon Clunn. Robert Herrick. CP-HerrR
Upon Cob. Robert Herrick. CP-HerrR
Upon Cock. Robert Herrick. CP-HerrR
Upon Comely a Good Speaker but an Ill Singer. Robert Herrick. CP-HerrR
Upon Concluded Lives. Emily Dickinson. CP-DickE
Upon Coone. Robert Herrick. CP-HerrR
Upon Crab. Robert Herrick. CP-HerrR
Upon Craw. Robert Herrick. CP-HerrR
Upon Croot. Robert Herrick. CP-HerrR
Upon Cuffe. Epig. Robert Herrick. CP-HerrR
Upon Cupid. Robert Herrick. CP-HerrR
Upon Cuts. Robert Herrick. CP-HerrR
Upon Deb. Robert Herrick. CP-HerrR
Upon Dol. Robert Herrick. CP-HerrR
Upon Doll. Robert Herrick. CP-HerrR
Upon Dundrige. Robert Herrick. CP-HerrR
Upon Eeles. Robert Herrick. CP-HerrR
Upon Electra. Robert Herrick. CP-HerrR
Upon Electra's Teares. Robert Herrick. CP-HerrR
Upon Faunus. Robert Herrick. CP-HerrR
Upon First Reading the Immortal Literature of the World—. Charles Bukowski. SP-BukC3
Upon Flimsey: Epigram. Robert Herrick. CP-HerrR
Upon Flood, Or a Thankfull Man. Robert Herrick. CP-HerrR
Upon Fone a School-master. Epigram. Robert Herrick. CP-HerrR
Upon Ford's Two Tragedies, "Loves Sacrifice" and "The Broken Heart" Richard Crashaw. CP-CrasR
Upon Four Dismal Stories in the Doctor's Letter. Jonathan Swift. CP-SwifJ
Upon Franck. Robert Herrick. CP-HerrR
Upon Gander. Robert Herrick. CP-HerrR
Upon Glasco. Epig. Robert Herrick. CP-HerrR

Upon Glass: Epigram. Robert Herrick. CP-HerrR
Upon God. Robert Herrick. CP-HerrR
Upon Gorgonius. Robert Herrick. CP-HerrR
Upon Greedy. Robert Herrick. CP-HerrR
Upon Groynes. Robert Herrick. CP-HerrR
Upon Grubs. Robert Herrick. CP-HerrR
Upon Grudgings. Robert Herrick. CP-HerrR
Upon Gryll. Robert Herrick. CP-HerrR
Upon Gubbs. Robert Herrick. CP-HerrR
Upon Guesse. Robert Herrick. CP-HerrR
Upon Gut. Robert Herrick. CP-HerrR
Upon Hanch a Schoolmaster. Robert Herrick. CP-HerrR
Upon Happiness. James Thomson. CP-ThomD
Upon Her Almes. Robert Herrick. CP-HerrR
Upon Her Blush. Robert Herrick. CP-HerrR
Upon her breast her hands and hair. Caught in a Net. Nicholas Vachel Lindsay. CP-LindV
Upon her cheekes she wept, and from those showers. Upon Electra's Teares. Robert Herrick. CP-HerrR
Upon Her Eyes. Robert Herrick. CP-HerrR
Upon Her Feet. Robert Herrick. CP-HerrR
Upon her plodding palfrey. Ballad of a Wilful Woman. D. H. Lawrence. CP-LawrD
Upon her soothing breast. Emily Jane Brontë. CP-BronE
Upon Her Voice. Robert Herrick. CP-HerrR
Upon Her Weeping. Robert Herrick. CP-HerrR
Upon Himself. Robert Herrick. CP-HerrR
Upon Himselfe. Robert Herrick. CP-HerrR
Upon Himselfe Being Buried. Robert Herrick. CP-HerrR
Upon His Departure Hence. Robert Herrick. CP-HerrR
Upon His Eye-Sight Failing Him. Robert Herrick. CP-HerrR
Upon His Gray Haires. Robert Herrick. CP-HerrR
Upon His Julia. Robert Herrick. CP-HerrR
Upon his Kinswoman Mrs. M. S. Robert Herrick. CP-HerrR
Upon His Kinswoman Mistresse Bridget Herrick. Robert Herrick. CP-HerrR
Upon His Kinswoman Mistris Elizabeth Herrick. Robert Herrick. CP-HerrR
Upon his Saddle sprung a Bird. Emily Dickinson. CP-DickE
Upon His Sister-in-Law, Mistress Elizabeth Herrick. Robert Herrick. CP-HerrR
Upon His Spaniel[l] Tracie [or Tracy]. Robert Herrick. CP-HerrR
Upon His Verses. Robert Herrick. CP-HerrR
Upon Hog. Robert Herrick. CP-HerrR
Upon Horne. Robert Herrick. CP-HerrR
Upon Huncks: Epigram. Robert Herrick. CP-HerrR
Upon Irene. Robert Herrick. CP-HerrR
Upon Jack and Jill: Epigram. Robert Herrick. CP-HerrR
Upon Jollies Wife. Robert Herrick. CP-HerrR
Upon Jolly and Jilly. Robert Herrick. CP-HerrR
Upon Jone and Jane. Robert Herrick. CP-HerrR
Upon Judith. Robert Herrick. CP-HerrR
Upon Julia's Breasts. Robert Herrick. CP-HerrR
Upon Julia's Clothes. Robert Herrick. CP-HerrR
Upon Julia's Fall. Robert Herrick. CP-HerrR
Upon Julia's Haire, Bundled up in a Golden Net. Robert Herrick. CP-HerrR
Upon Julia's Haire Fill'd with Dew. Robert Herrick. See Dew Sat on Julia's Hair
Upon Julias Recovery. Robert Herrick. CP-HerrR
Upon Julia's Ribband. Robert Herrick. CP-HerrR
Upon Julia's Sweat. Robert Herrick. CP-HerrR
Upon Julia's Unlacing Her Self. Robert Herrick. CP-HerrR
Upon Julia's Voice. Robert Herrick. CP-HerrR
Upon Julia['s] Washing Herself in the River. Robert Herrick. CP-HerrR
Upon Kings. Robert Herrick. CP-HerrR
Upon L.M. Weeping. Sir John Suckling. CP-SuckJ
Upon Lazarus His Teares. Richard Crashaw. CP-CrasR
Upon Learning That a Bird Exists Called the Turnstone. John Updike. CP-UpdiJ
Upon Learning That a Town Exists in Virginia Called Upperville. John Updike. CP-UpdiJ
Upon Leech. Robert Herrick. CP-HerrR
Upon Letcher: Epigram. Robert Herrick. CP-HerrR
Upon Linnit. Robert Herrick. CP-HerrR
Upon Loach. Robert Herrick. CP-HerrR
Upon Looking into Sylvia Plath's Letters Home. John Updike. CP-UpdiJ
Upon Love. Robert Herrick. CP-HerrR
Upon Love, by Way of Question and Answer. Robert Herrick. CP-HerrR
Upon Lucia. Robert Herrick. CP-HerrR
Upon Lucia Dabled in the Deaw. Robert Herrick. CP-HerrR
Upon Lucie. Robert Herrick. CP-HerrR

Upon Luggs. Robert Herrick. CP-HerrR

Upon Lulls. Robert Herrick. CP-HerrR

Upon Lungs. Robert Herrick. CP-HerrR

Upon Lupes. Robert Herrick. CP-HerrR

Upon Luske. Robert Herrick. CP-HerrR

Upon Madam Ursly. Robert Herrick. CP-HerrR

Upon Magot a Frequenter of Ordinaries. Robert Herrick. CP-HerrR

Upon Man. Robert Herrick. CP-HerrR

Upon M. Ben Jo[h]nson: Epigram. Robert Herrick. CP-HerrR

Upon Master Fletchers Incomparable Playes. Robert Herrick. CP-HerrR

Upon Master W. Montague, His Return from Travel. Thomas Carew. *See* Upon Master Walter Montagu's Return from Travel

Upon Master Walter Montagu's Return from Travel. Thomas Carew. CP-CareT (Upon Master W. Montague, His Return from Travel.) CP-CareT

Upon M. William Lawes, the Rare Musitian. Robert Herrick. CP-HerrR

Upon me and my mackintosh. Happy Xmas, A ("Upon me and my mackintosh"). G. K. Chesterton. CP ChesG

Upon Mease. Robert Herrick. CP-HerrR

Upon Meeting Don L. Lee, in a Dream. Rita Dove. SP-DoveR

Upon Megg. Robert Herrick. CP-HerrR

Upon Mr. Sheridan's Turning Author, 1716. *Unknown.* CP-SherT

Upon Mrs. Anne Bradstreet, Her Poems, Etc. John Rogers. CP-BradA

Upon Mistress Elizabeth Wheeler under the Name of Amarillis. Robert Herrick. CP-HerrR

Upon Mistresse Susanna Southwell, Her Cheeks. Robert Herrick. CP-HerrR

Upon Much-More. Robert Herrick. CP-HerrR

Upon Mudge. Robert Herrick. CP-HerrR

Upon mutability—if it were possible. But you don't. Ovid, Old Buddy, I Would Discourse with You a While. Hayden Carruth. CP-CarHS

Upon my bed at early dawn. Cock-crowing. Henry David Thoreau. CP-ThorH

Upon My Daughter Hannah Wiggin her Recovery from a Dangerous Fever. Anne Bradstreet. CP-BradA

Upon My Dear and Loving Husband His Going into England. Anne Bradstreet. CP-BradA

Upon My Lady Carlisle's Walking in Hampton Court Garden. Sir John Suckling. CP-SuckJ

Upon My Life, Sir Nevis, I Am Piqued. John Keats. CP-KeatJ

Upon My Lord Brohall's Wedding. Sir John Suckling. CP-SuckJ

Upon My Lord Chief Justice's Election of My Lady Anne Wentworth [*or* A.W.] for His Mistress. Thomas Carew. CP-CareT

Upon My Son Samuel His Going For England. Anne Bradstreet. CP-BradA

Upon my throat your kisses blur their man. Meditation of My Lady of Sorrows. Kenneth Patchen. CP-PatcK

Upon Nis. Robert Herrick. CP-HerrR

Upon Nodes. Robert Herrick. CP-HerrR

Upon One-Fy'd Broomsted. Robert Herrick. CP-HerrR

Upon One Lillie, Who Marryed with a Maid Call'd Rose. Robert Herrick. CP-HerrR

Upon One Who Said She Was Alwayes Young. Robert Herrick. CP-HerrR

Upon Our Saviour's Tomb[e] Wherein Never Man Was Laid. Richard Crashaw. *See* To Our Blessed Lord upon the Choice of His Sepulchre

Upon Pagget. Robert Herrick. CP-HerrR

Upon Parrat. Robert Herrick. CP-HerrR

Upon Parson Beanes. Robert Herrick. CP-HerrR

Upon Parting. Robert Herrick. CP-HerrR

Upon Paske a Draper. Robert Herrick. CP-HerrR

Upon Patrick a Footman. Robert Herrick. CP-HerrR

Upon Paul. Robert Herrick. CP-HerrR

Upon Pearch. Robert Herrick. CP-HerrR

Upon Peason. Robert Herrick. CP-HerrR

Upon Pennie. Robert Herrick. CP-HerrR

Upon Perusing the "Epistle [To Sir George Howland Beaumont"] Thirty Years after Its Composition. William Wordsworth. CP-WorW2

Upon Pievish. Robert Herrick. CP-HerrR

Upon Pimpe. Robert Herrick. CP-HerrR

Upon Pink an Ill-Fac'd Painter. Robert Herrick. CP-HerrR

Upon Prickles. Robert Herrick. CP-HerrR

Upon Prig. Robert Herrick. CP-HerrR

Upon Prigg. Robert Herrick. CP-HerrR

Upon Prudence Baldwin Her Sickness[e]. Robert Herrick. CP-HerrR

Upon Prue [*or* Prew], His Maid. Robert Herrick. CP-HerrR

Upon Punchin. Robert Herrick. CP-HerrR

Upon Pusse and her Prentice. Robert Herrick. CP-HerrR

Upon Ralph. Robert Herrick. CP-HerrR

Upon Raspe. Robert Herrick. CP-HerrR

Upon Reape. Robert Herrick. CP-HerrR

Upon Reflection. Lawrence Ferlinghetti. SP-FerlL

Upon Rook: Epigram. Robert Herrick. CP-HerrR

Upon Roots. Robert Herrick. CP-HerrR

Upon Roses. Robert Herrick. CP-HerrR

Upon Rumpe. Robert Herrick. CP-HerrR

Upon Rush. Robert Herrick. CP-HerrR

Upon Sapho. Robert Herrick. CP-HerrR

Upon Sapho, Sweetly Playing, and Sweetly Singing. Robert Herrick. CP-HerrR

Upon Scobble [Epigram]. Robert Herrick. CP-HerrR

Upon seeing a Coloured Drawing of the Bird of Paradise in an Album. William Wordsworth. CP-WorW2

Upon Seeing An Ultrasound Photo of an Unborn Child. Thomas Lux. SP-LuxT

Upon Shark. Robert Herrick. CP-HerrR

Upon Shaving Off One's Beard. John Updike. CP-UpdiJ

Upon Shift. Robert Herrick. CP-HerrR

Upon Shopter. Robert Herrick. CP-HerrR

Upon Showbread [*or* Shewbread]: Epigram. Robert Herrick. CP-HerrR

Upon Sibb. Robert Herrick. CP-HerrR

Upon Sibilla. Robert Herrick. CP-HerrR

Upon Silvia, a Mistresse. Robert Herrick. CP-HerrR

Upon Sir John Lawrence's Bringing Water over the Hills [to My L. Middlesex His House at Witten]. Sir John Suckling. CP-SuckJ

Upon Skinns. Robert Herrick. CP-HerrR

Upon Skoles. Robert Herrick. CP-HerrR

Upon Skrew. Robert Herrick. CP-HerrR

Upon Skurffe. Robert Herrick. CP-HerrR

Upon Slouch. Robert Herrick. CP-HerrR

Upon Smeaton. Robert Herrick. CP-HerrR

Upon Snare, an Usurer. Robert Herrick. CP-HerrR

Upon Sneape. Robert Herrick. CP-HerrR

Upon Some Alterations in My Mistress, after My Departure into France. Thomas Carew. CP-CareT

Upon Some Distemper of Body. Anne Bradstreet. CP-BradA

Upon Some Women. Robert Herrick. CP-HerrR

Upon Spalt. Robert Herrick. CP-HerrR

Upon Spenke. Robert Herrick. CP-HerrR

Upon Spokes. Robert Herrick. CP-HerrR

Upon Spunge. Robert Herrick. CP-HerrR

Upon Spur. Robert Herrick. CP-HerrR

Upon Stealing a Crown when the Dean Was Asleep. Thomas Sheridan. CP-SherT

Upon Strut. Robert Herrick. CP-HerrR

Upon Sudds, a Laundress[e]. Robert Herrick. CP-HerrR

Upon T.C. Having the Pox. Sir John Suckling. CP-SuckJ

Upon Taking Hold. Robert Duncan. SP-DuncR

Upon Tap. Robert Herrick. CP-HerrR

Upon Teage. Robert Herrick. CP-HerrR

Upon Teares. Robert Herrick. CP-HerrR

Upon that face for which I sigh and pine. Petrarch. CP-Petra, *tr.* by J. G. Nichols

Upon that inward eye. Daffodils, The. Rae Armantrout. SP-ArmaA

Upon that night, when fairies light. Halloween. Robert Burns. CP-BurnR

Upon the Annunciation and Passion Falling upon One Day. 1608. John Donne. CP-DonnJ; MW-DonnJ

Upon the Asse That Bore Our Saviour. Richard Crashaw. CP-CrasR

Upon the Author. Patrick Delany. CP-SherT

Upon the Author. *Unknown.* CP-BradA

Upon the Author. By a Known Friend. Benjamin Woodbridge. CP-BradA

Upon the Author of the following Poem. Nahum Tate. CP-DryJ2

Upon the banners fluttering overhead. Children's Procession. Yehuda Amichai. SP-AmicY, *tr.* by Stephen Mitchell

Upon the birth of the Princesse Elizabeth. Richard Crashaw. CP-CrasR

Upon the Bishop of Lincolne's Imprisonment. Robert Herrick. CP-HerrR

Upon the Black Spots Worn, by My Lady D.E. Sir John Suckling. CP-SuckJ

Upon the Circumcision. John Milton. CP-MiltJ

Upon the coasters' spreading sails. Coasters, The. Jones Very. CP-VeryJ

Upon the dead grass. March Is a Light. William Carlos Williams. CP-WilW1

Upon the Death of a Freind. Richard Crashaw. CP-CrasR

Upon the Death of a Gentleman. Richard Crashaw. CP-CrasR

Upon the Death of His Sparrow; an Elegie. Robert Herrick. CP-HerrR

Upon the Death of Mister Herrys. Richard Crashaw. CP-CrasR

Upon the Death of the Lord Hastings. Andrew Marvell. CP-MarvA

Upon the Death of the Most Desired Mister Herrys. Richard Crashaw. CP-CrasR

Upon the decks they take beef tea. Passage Steamer. Louis MacNeice. CP-MacNL

Upon the Duke of *Yorke* his Birth a Panegyricke. Richard Crashaw. CP-CrasR (To the Queen, Upon her Numerous Progeny, a Panegyricke.) CP-CrasR

Upon the Ensuing Treatises [of Mr. Shelford]. Richard Crashaw. CP-CrasR

Upon the Faire Ethiopian Sent to a Gentlewoman. Richard Crashaw. CP-CrasR

Upon the fallen. In the 'Sconset Bus. William Carlos Williams. CP-WilW1

Upon the Feast of St Simon and St Jude. Samuel Johnson. CP-JohnS

Upon the First Sight of My Lady Seymour. Sir John Suckling. CP-SuckJ

Upon the gallows hung a wretch. Emily Dickinson. CP-DickE

Upon the Gunpowder Treason. Richard Crashaw. CP-CrasR

Upon the Hill and Grove at Bilbrough. Andrew Marvell. CP-MarvA

Upon the Horrid Plot Discovered by Harlequin the Bishop of Rochester's French Dog. Jonathan Swift. CP-SwifJ

Upon the Infant Martyrs. Richard Crashaw. CP-CrasR

Upon the Kings Coronation. Richard Crashaw. CP-CrasR

Upon the King's Sickness. Thomas Carew. CP-CareT

Upon the Lady Crew. Robert Herrick. CP-HerrR

Upon the landscape of his coming life. Untimely Lost: Oliver Madox Brown. Born 1855; Died 1874. Dante Gabriel Rossetti. CW-RossD

Upon the Last Day of His Forty-Ninth Year. John Updike. CP-UpdiJ

Upon the Late General Fast. March, 1832. William Wordsworth. CP-WorW2

Upon the lofty elm tree sprays. Vireo, The. Henry David Thoreau. CP-ThorH

Upon the Losse of His Finger. Robert Herrick. CP-HerrR

Upon the Loss[e] of His Mistresses. Robert Herrick. CP-HerrR

Upon the mountain of the young. I Heard a Hermit Speak. Adrienne Rich. CP-RicAE

Upon the mountain's Edge all lightly resting. Samuel Taylor Coleridge. *See* Upon the mountain's edge with light touch resting

Upon the mountain's edge with light touch resting. Sunset, A. Samuel Taylor Coleridge. CP-ColeS

Upon the Much Lamented, Mr. J. Warr. Robert Herrick. CP-HerrR

Upon the Nipples of Julia's Breast. Robert Herrick. CP-HerrR

Upon the Plymouth shore the wild rose blooms. Wild Rose of Plymouth, The. Jones Very. CP-VeryJ

Upon the Powder Day. Richard Crashaw. CP-CrasR

Upon the Rights of Man, at first, was built. Philanthropy Before Nationality. Jones Very. CP-VeryJ

Upon the road of my life. Stephen Crane. CP-CranS

Upon the room's / silence,i will sew. E. E. Cummings. CP-CummE

Upon the Roses in Julias Bosome. Robert Herrick. CP-HerrR

Upon the Same. Ausonius. CP-CrasR

Upon the Same. Robert Herrick. CP-HerrR

Upon the Sepulchre of our Lord. Richard Crashaw. CP-CrasR

Upon the Sickness of E.S. Thomas Carew. CP-CareT

Upon the Sight of a Beautiful Picture. William Wordsworth. CP-WorW1

Upon the Sight of the Portrait of a Female Friend. William Wordsworth. CP-WorW2

Upon the South Sea Project. Jonathan Swift. CP-SwifJ

Upon the table in their bowl. Disputants, The. William Carlos Williams. CP-WilW1

Upon the Thornes Taken Downe from Our Lords Head Bloody. Richard Crashaw. CP-CrasR

Upon the Translation of the Psalms by Sir Philip Sidney, and the Countess of Pembroke His Sister. John Donne. CP-DonnJ; MW-DonnJ

Upon the treacherous sands the horsemen ride. Horsemen on the Sands, The. Jones Very. CP-VeryJ

Upon the Troublesome Times. Robert Herrick. CP-HerrR

Upon the wall a face. Projected Slide of an Unknown Soldier. Margaret Atwood. SP-AtwM1

Upon the water in the boat. Arthur Hugh Clough. SP-ClouA

Upon this age, that never speaks its mind. Edna St. Vincent Millay. CP-MillE

Upon This Beach. Louis MacNeice. CP-MacNL

Upon this leafy bush. Linnet, The. Walter De la Mare. CP-DeLaW

Upon this line between adventure. Between Adventure. W. H. Auden. CP-AudeW

Upon this marble bust that is not I. To Inez Milholland. Edna St. Vincent Millay. CP-MillE

Upon this primrose hill. Primrose, The; Being at Montgomery Castle, upon the hill, on which it is situate. John Donne. CP-DonnJ; MW-DonnJ

Upon this scene, this show. Red Jacket (from Aloft). Walt Whitman. CP-WhitW

Upon those lips, those placid lips, I look. Upon the Sight of the Portrait of a Female Friend. William Wordsworth. CP-WorW2

Upon those stifling August nights. Little Passion, The ("Upon those stifling August nights"). T. S. Eliot. SP-ElioT *Fr.* Agony in the Garret, An.

Upon Time. Robert Herrick. CP-HerrR

Upon Tooly. Robert Herrick. CP-HerrR

Upon Trap. Robert Herrick. CP-HerrR

Upon Trencherman. Robert Herrick. CP-HerrR

Upon Trigg. Robert Herrick. CP-HerrR

Upon Truggin. Robert Herrick. CP-HerrR

Upon Tubbs. Robert Herrick. CP-HerrR

Upon Tuck. Robert Herrick. CP-HerrR

Upon Two Greene Apricockes Sent to Cowley by Sir Crashaw. Richard Crashaw. CP-CrasR

Upon Two Sisters. Sir John Suckling. CP-SuckJ

Upon Umber: Epigram. Robert Herrick. CP-HerrR

Upon Urles. Robert Herrick. CP-HerrR

Upon Ursley. Robert Herrick. CP-HerrR

Upon Venus Putting on Mars His Armes. Leonidas of Alexandria. CP-CrasR, *tr. by* Richard Crashaw

Upon Vinegar. Robert Herrick. CP-HerrR

Upon waking a nerve complains in the. Fortification, A. Margaret Atwood. SP-AtwM1

Upon William Tisdall, D. D. Thomas Sheridan. CP-SherT

Upon Woman and Mary. Robert Herrick. CP-HerrR

Upon Wrinkles. Robert Herrick. CP-HerrR

Upon Zelot. Robert Herrick. CP-HerrR

Upper Birch-Leaves, The. Thomas Hardy. CP-HardT

Upper Broadway. Adrienne Rich. SP-RicA2

Upright. A. R. Ammons. CP-AmmoA

Upriver Incident, The. Paul Muldoon. CP-MuldP

Uproot a plant—there's no way it can seal. Michelangelo Buonarroti. CP-Miche, *tr. by* John Frederick Nims

Uproot that burning tree of lightning struck veins. Few Ashes for Sunday Morning, A. Marge Piercy. SP-PierM

Uprooted, The. D. H. Lawrence. CP-LawrD

Uprose the King of Men with speed. Descent of Odin, The. Thomas Gray. CP-GrayT

Uprose, uprose, the stony fields uprose. Tree, the Bird, The. Theodore Roethke. CP-RoetT

Upshore from the cloud. By a Lake in Minnesota. James Wright. CP-WrigJ

Upside-down, he still. Shot, The. Dan Pagis. SP-PagiD, *tr. by* Stephen Mitchell

Upstairs. Carl Sandburg. CP-SandC

Upstairs Jenny crashed her car & became a living corpse, Jake sold grass. Charnel Ground, The. Allen Ginsberg. SP-GinsA

Upstate. Derek Walcott. CP-WalcD

Upstate New York. James Laughlin. CP-LaugJ

Upstream. Carl Sandburg. CP-SandC

Uptown. Allen Ginsberg. CP-GinsA; SP-GinsA

Uptown on Lenox Avenue. Prime. Langston Hughes. CP-HughL; CP-HughL3

Upward Moon and the Downward Moon, The. Robert Bly. SP-BlyR

Upwardness. Robert Penn Warren. CP-WarrR

Ur Burial. Richard Eberhart. CP-EberR

Urania. Mary Sidney, Countess of Montgomery Wroth. CP-WrotM

Uranium, with which we know. What It Could Be. Denise Levertov. SP-LeveDL

Uranus. Arthur Hugh Clough. SP-ClouA

Urban Convalescence, An. James Merrill. SP-MerrJ

Urban Renewal. Yusef Komunyakaa. CP-KomuY

Urbanal. Christopher Logue. SP-LoguC

Urbs Sacra Æterna. Oscar Wilde. CP-WildO

Urchin, The. Robinson Jeffers. CP-JefR3

Urge to Tell the Truth, The. Jane Cooper. CP-CoopJ

Urge to wander is, The. Leaving. Rae Armantrout. SP-ArmaA

Urged by your needs and my desire. Trial of Innocence. Robert Graves. CP-GravR

Urgent letter that I try to write, The. Night Letter. Stanley Kunitz. CP-KunSC

Urges, The. Andrei Codrescu. SP-CodrA

Uriel. Ralph Waldo Emerson. CP-EmerR

Urles had the Gout so, that he co'd not stand. Upon Urles. Robert Herrick. CP-HerrR

Urlicht. Charles Tomlinson. CP-TomlC

Urn-Burial and the Butterfly Migration. Amy Clampitt. CP-ClamA

Urn with a Political Profile. Pablo Antonio Cuadra. CP-MertT

Urns of stillness are empty, The. Darkness. Paul Celan. SP-CelaP, *tr. by* John Felstiner

Ursa Major ("Bear mother / gives suck to the stars"). Federico García Lorca. CP-GarcF, *tr. by* Jerome Rothenberg *Fr.* Night (Suite for Piano and Poet's Voice).

Ursa Major ("Makes me feel sad"). Federico García Lorca. CP-GarcF, *tr. by* Jerome Rothenberg *Fr.* Shadow.

Ursley, she thinks those Velvet Patches grace. Upon Ursley. Robert Herrick. CP-HerrR

Ursula, in a garden, found. Cy Est Pourtraicte, Madame Ste Ursule, et Les Unze Mille Vierges. Wallace Stevens. CP-StevW; CP-StevWP

Us. Andrei Codrescu. SP-CodrA

Us. George Oppen. CP-OppGN

Us. Anne Sexton. CP-SextA; SP-SextA

Us. Stephen Spender. CP-SpenS

Us: Colored. Langston Hughes. CP-HughL; CP-HughL3

Us farmers in the country, as the seasons go and come. James Whitcomb Riley. CP-RileJ

Us-folks is purty pore—but Ma. Dubious "Old Kriss," A. James Whitcomb Riley. CP-RileJ

Us if therefore must forget ourselves. E. E. Cummings. CP-CummE

Us parents mostly thinks our own's. What Little Saul Got, Christmas. James Whitcomb Riley. CP-RileJ

USA slowly lost its mandate, The. Tomorrow's Song. Gary Snyder. CP-SnydG

Use of Books, The. Thomas McGrath. SP-McGrT

Use the diamond point of grief. Diamond Point, The. Arthur Sze. SP-SzeA

Use will in man new grace reveal. Ralph Waldo Emerson. CP-EmerR

"Used Handkerchiefs 5¢." James Schuyler. CP-SchuJ

Used-to-Be, The. James Whitcomb Riley. CP-RileJ

Used to stumble, go down, bounce. Tanck's Song About Fear of Falling. Hayden Carruth. CP-CarHS *Fr.* Songs About What Comes Down: The Complete Works of Mr. Septic Tanck.

Used Up. Thomas McGrath. SP-McGrT

Useful and the sweet the fair and true, The. Good, The. Jones Very. CP-VeryJ

Usefulness of Art, The. Yannis Ritsos. SP-RitsY, *tr.* by Kimon Friar

Useless, The. Chuang Tzu. CP-MertT

Useless Knowledge. John Ciardi. CP-CiarJ

Useless Song. Federico García Lorca. CP-GarcF, *tr.* by Alan S. Trueblood *Fr.* Songs to End With.

Useless Song. Federico García Lorca. SP-GarcF, *tr.* by W. S. Merwin

Useless Tree, The. Chuang Tzu. CP-MertT

Useless Vigil, The. Gabriela Mistral. SP-MistG, *tr.* by Maria Giachetti [*or* Jacketti]

Useless Words. Carl Sandburg. CP-SandC

Uses. Anne Sexton. CP-SextA

Uses of Poetry. Lawrence Ferlinghetti. SP-FerlL

Uses of Poetry, The. William Carlos Williams. CP-WilW1

Uses of the Lost Poets. Thomas McGrath. SP-McGrT

Using an old water-stained. Thorn Merchant's Son, The. Yusef Komunyakaa. CP-KomuY

Using the gun mounts. Toys in a Field. Yusef Komunyakaa. CP-KomuY

Usual Prayer, A. John Berryman. CP-BerrJ

Usually at the helipad. Prisoners. Yusef Komunyakaa. CP-KomuY

Usurers of Heaven, The. William Carlos Williams. CP-WilW2

Usurper. Richard Eberhart. CP-EberR

Ut pictura . . . The confounding lips. Fan, The. Eugenio Montale. CP-MontE, *tr.* by Jonathan Galassi

Ut Queant. Paul the Deacon. CP-MertT

Uta Mound, The. Sam Hamill. SP-HamiS

Ute Mountain. Charles Tomlinson. CP-TomlC; SP-TomlC

Utensil. A. R. Ammons. CP-AmmoA

Utilitarian View of the Monitor's Fight, A. Herman Melville. SP-MelvH

Utmost sign of the inmost, The. G. K Chesterton. *See* Far in the sunlit eastward

Utmost type of the inmost, The. G. K. Chesterton. *See* Far in the sunlit eastward

Utopia. Wisława Szymborska. SP-SzymW, *tr.* by Stanisław Barańczak *and* Clare Cavanagh

Utopian Journey, A. Randall Jarrell. CP-JarrR

Utter indifference to your welfare, Caesar. Carmen 93. Catullus. CP-ZukLS *Fr.* Carmina.

Utter Rim, The. Robert Graves. CP-GravR

Utter the song, O my soul! the flight and return of Mohammed. Mahomet. Samuel Taylor Coleridge. CP-ColeS

Utterance. John Greenleaf Whittier. CP-WhitJ

Utterings. Donald Davie. CP-DaviDC

Utterly and amusingly I am pash. E. E. Cummings. CP-CummE

Uvedale, thou piece of the first times, a man. To Sir William Uvedale. Ben Jonson. CP-JonsB; SP-JonsB

Uxorem Crispinus habet; tamen indigus unam. In Crispinum. Thomas Campion. CP-CampT

V

V. Stevie Smith. CP-SmitS

V. B. Nimble, V. B. Quick. John Updike. CP-UpdiJ

V. B. Wigglesworth wakes at noon. V. B. Nimble, V. B. Quick. John Updike. CP-UpdiJ

V-J Day. John Ciardi. CP-CiarJ

V-Letter. Karl Shapiro. SP-ShapK

Vacancy in the Park. Wallace Stevens. CP-StevW; CP-StevWP

Vacancy in which, apparently, A. All is Emptiness, And I Must Spin. Thomas Kinsella. CP-KinsT

Vacant Day, The. Walter De la Mare. CP-DeLaW

Vacant Lot with Pokeweed. Amy Clampitt. CP-ClamA

Vacant Lot with Tumbleweed and Pigeons. Amy Clampitt. CP-ClamA

Vacant lots are occupied, the woods, The. Shillington. John Updike. CP-UpdiJ

Vacant Possession, A. James Fenton. SP-FentJ

Vacation. William Stafford. SP-StafWW

Vacation. Adam Zagajewski. SP-ZagaA, *tr.* by Renata Gorczynski, Benjamin Ivry *and* C. K. Williams

Vacation Trip. William Stafford. SP-StafW; SP-StafWW

Vacation? Well, our children took our love apart. Any Time. William Stafford. SP-StafW; SP-StafWW

Vachel, the stars are out. To Lindsay. Allen Ginsberg. CP-GinsA; SP-GinsA

Vacillation. William Butler Yeats. CP-YeatW

Vacuum, The. Howard Nemerov. CP-NemeH

Vade Mecum. Billy Collins. SP-CollB

Vagabond, A. James Tate. SP-TateJ

Vagabond is a newcomer, A. Vagabond, A. James Tate. SP-TateJ

Vagabonds. Langston Hughes. CP-HughL; CP-HughL2

Vagg Hollow. Thomas Hardy. CP-HardT

Vagrant, The. James Laughlin. CP-LaugJ

Vagrant at the Church Door, The. Jones Very. CP-VeryJ

Vagrants. Paul Laurence Dunbar. CP-DunbP

Vagrant's Song. Thomas Hardy. CP-HardT

Vague mist hanging 'round half the pages, A. Apparitions. Walt Whitman. CP-WhitW

Vague pearl, a wan pearl, A. Spells and Incantation (a Fragment). Wilfred Owen. CP-OwenW

Vague sea thuds against the marble cliffs, The. Time. Robert Graves. CP-GravR

Vaguely I hear the purple roar of the torn-down Third Avenue El. You Are Gorgeous and I'm Coming. Frank O'Hara. SP-OharF

Vagueness comes over everything, A. Fog. Amy Clampitt. CP-ClamA

Vaile, love, mine eyes, O hide from me. Thomas Campion. CP-CampT

Vaile thou thine eyes a while my Deare. Eclipse, The. Robert Herrick. CP-HerrR

Vain against him were hostile blows. Ralph Waldo Emerson. CP-EmerR

Vain and Careless. Robert Graves. CP-GravR

Vain Bards! I can discover all. Song of Taliesin. Taliesin. CP-EmerR

Vain Finding. Walter De la Mare. CP-DeLaW

Vain Gratuities. Edwin Arlington Robinson. CP-RobiE

Vain is the wish to try rhyming it, writing it! History of an Hour, The. Thomas Hardy. CP-HardT

Vain Life of Voltaire, The. Laura Riding Jackson. CP-RidiL

Vain man runs headlong, to caprice resign'd. Juvenal. CP-JohnS *Fr.* Satires.

Vain Men, Whose Follies. Thomas Campion. CP-CampT

Vain, proud, rebellious Prince, thy treacherous hair. Absalom. Walter De la Mare. CP-DeLaW

Vain Questioning. Walter De la Mare. CP-DeLaW

Vain Shadow, A. Christina Georgina Rossetti. CP-RosC2

Vain surety of man's mind so near to death. Marlowe. Robert Lowell. SP-LoweR

Vain Virtues. Dante Gabriel Rossetti. CW-RossD *Fr.* House of Life, The.

Vaine men, whose follies make a God of Love. Vain Men, Whose Follies. Thomas Campion. CP-CampT

Vainly the Tyrian Purple bright. Boethius. CP-JohnS *Fr.* Consolation of Philosophy, The ("De Consolacione Philosophie").

Vala; or The Four Zoas. William Blake. CP-BlakW

Valaisian Quatrains, The. Rainer Maria Rilke.
  "After a day of wind." CP-RilkFr, *tr.* by A. Poulin, Jr.
  "Ancient country with towers insisting." CP-RilkFr, *tr.* by A. Poulin, Jr.
  "As someone speaking of his mother." CP-RilkFr, *tr.* by A. Poulin, Jr.
  "Beautiful butterfly near, A." CP-RilkFr, *tr.* by A. Poulin, Jr.
  "Before you can count ten." CP-RilkFr, *tr.* by A. Poulin, Jr.
  Belltower's Song. CP-RilkFr, *tr.* by A. Poulin, Jr.
  "Country singing while working." CP-RilkFr, *tr.* by A. Poulin, Jr.
  "Even so, let us bring all that feeds." CP-RilkFr, *tr.* by A. Poulin, Jr.
  "Gentle curves along the ivy." CP-RilkFr, *tr.* by A. Poulin, Jr.
  "Here, all sings the life of yesterday." CP-RilkFr, *tr.* by A. Poulin, Jr.
  "Here the earth is surrounded." CP-RilkFr, *tr.* by A. Poulin, Jr.
  "Here the earth tells her story." CP-RilkFr, *tr.* by A. Poulin, Jr.
  "In the tall grass, a mauve rose." CP-RilkFr, *tr.* by A. Poulin, Jr.
  "Invisible almost shines, The." CP-RilkFr, *tr.* by A. Poulin, Jr.
  "Landscape stopped halfway." CP-RilkFr, *tr.* by A. Poulin, Jr.
  "Locusts have finished their ravage, The." CP-RilkFr, *tr.* by A. Poulin, Jr.
  "Not only the gaze of those." CP-RilkFr, *tr.* by A. Poulin, Jr.
  "Oh summer's happiness: the carillon chimes." CP-RilkFr, *tr.* by A. Poulin, Jr.
  "Oh those altars where fruit was placed." CP-RilkFr, *tr.* by A. Poulin, Jr.
  "Once again the hour's turning silver." CP-RilkFr, *tr.* by A. Poulin, Jr.
  "Proud crumbling of these towers." CP-RilkFr, *tr.* by A. Poulin, Jr.
  "Rather than evade itself." CP-RilkFr, *tr.* by A. Poulin, Jr.
  "Road that turns and plays." CP-RilkFr, *tr.* by A. Poulin, Jr.
  "Roads leading nowhere." CP-RilkFr, *tr.* by A. Poulin, Jr.

"Rose of light, a crumbling wall." CP-RilkFr, *tr.* by A. Poulin, Jr.

"Silent country whose prophets keep quiet." CP-RilkFr, *tr.* by A. Poulin, Jr.

"Simple stocky belfry that with a sower's gesture." CP-RilkFr, *tr.* by A. Poulin, Jr.

"Small clematis tumbles, The." CP-RilkFr, *tr.* by A. Poulin, Jr.

Small Fountain. CP-RilkFr, *tr.* by A. Poulin, Jr.

"So much solemn black." CP-RilkFr, *tr.* by A. Poulin, Jr.

"Such evening calm, such calm." CP-RilkFr, *tr.* by A. Poulin, Jr.

"This sky contemplated." CP-RilkFr, *tr.* by A. Poulin, Jr.

"Towers, walls, thatched huts." CP-RilkFr, *tr.* by A. Poulin, Jr.

"Up there, do you see alpine pastures for angels." CP-RilkFr, *tr.* by A. Poulin, Jr.

Valaisian Sky. CP-RilkFr, *tr.* by A. Poulin, Jr.

"What goddess, what god." CP-RilkFr, *tr.* by A. Poulin, Jr.

"Whole length of the dusty road, The." CP-RilkFr, *tr.* by A. Poulin, Jr.

"Wind that grips this country like a craftsman." CP-RilkFr, *tr.* by A. Poulin, Jr.

"Year turns on the pivot, The." CP-RilkFr, *tr.* by A. Poulin, Jr.

Valaisian Sky. Rainer Maria Rilke. CP-RilkFr, *tr.* by A. Poulin, Jr. *Fr.* Valaisian Quatrains, The.

Vale. John Ciardi. CP-CiarJ

Vale of Esthwaite, The. William Wordsworth. CP-WorW1

Vale of the Merrimac, The. John Greenleaf Whittier. CP-WhitJ

Valediction: "She went with morning on her lips." Tennessee Williams. CP-WillT

Valediction: "Their verdure dare not show . . . their verdure dare not show." Louis MacNeice. CP-MacNL

Valediction, A: Forbidding Mourning. John Donne. CP-DonnJ; MW-DonnJ

Valediction, A: "God be with thee, my beloved,—God be with thee!" Elizabeth Barrett Browning. CP-BroEB

Valediction, A: of My Name in the Window. John Donne. CP-DonnJ; MW-DonnJ

Valediction, A: of the Book. John Donne. CP-DonnJ; MW-DonnJ

Valediction, A: of Weeping. John Donne. CP-DonnJ; MW-DonnJ

Valediction, The: "Farewell, false hearts! whose best affections fail." William Cowper. CP-CowpW

Valediction Forbidding Mourning, A. Adrienne Rich. CP-RicAE; SP-RicA1; SP-RicA2

Valedictory Poem. Ralph Waldo Emerson. CP-EmerR

Valedictory Sonnet. William Wordsworth. CP-WorW2

Valenciennes. Thomas Hardy. CP-HardT

Valentine. Hayden Carruth. CP-CarHS

Valentine. Edna St. Vincent Millay. CP-MillE

Valentine. George Oppen. CP-OppGN

Valentine, A. Joseph Brodsky. CP-BrodJ *Fr.* Shorts.

Valentine, A. Emily Dickinson. CP-DickE

Valentine, A. Edgar Allan Poe. CP-PoeEd

Valentine, A. Wallace Stevens. CP-StevWP

Valentine, A. Louis Zukofsky. CP-ZukLS

Valentine, 1882, A. Christina Georgina Rossetti. *See* Valentine to My Mother, A

Valentine, 1877, A. Christina Georgina Rossetti. CP-RosC3

Valentine Gift, A. Charles Bukowski. SP-BukC3

Valentine of desire is pasted over my heart, The. Not Touching. Billy Collins. SP-CollB

Valentine to My Mother, A. Christina Georgina Rossetti. CP-RosC3 (Valentine, 1882, A.) CP-RosC3

Valentines From C.G.R. Christina Georgina Rossetti. CP-RosC3

Valentine's Night. D. H. Lawrence. CP-LawrD

Valentines to My Mother, 1880. Christina Georgina Rossetti. CP-RosC3 (1880.) CP-RosC3

Valestrieri. Charles Tomlinson. SP-TomlC

Valle de Oaxaca. Charles Tomlinson. CP-TomlC; SP-TomlC

Vallejo writing about. What They Want. Charles Bukowski. SP-BukC1

Valley, A. Primo Levi. CP-LeviP, *tr.* by Ruth Feldman

Valley and above it forests in autumn colors, A. This Only. Czeslaw Milosz. CP-MiloC; CP-MiloCN, *tr.* by Robert Hass

Valley Candle. Wallace Stevens. CP-StevW; CP-StevWP

Valley of Morning. Donald Hall. CP-HallD

Valley of the Black Pig, The. William Butler Yeats. CP-YeatW

Valley of the Fallen, The. Carolyn Kizer. CP-KizeC

Valley of the Shadow, The. Edwin Arlington Robinson. CP-RobiE

Valley of Unrest, The. Edgar Allan Poe. CP-PoeEd

Valley re-echoing with woes of mine. Petrarch. CP-Petra, *tr.* by J. G. Nichols

Valley rings with mirth and joy, The. Idle Shepherd-Boys, The; or, Dungeon-Ghyll Force. A Pastoral. William Wordsworth. CP-WorW1; MW-WorW

Valley-sleeper, the Children, the Snakes, and the Giant, The. Kenneth Patchen. CP-PatcK

Valley Song. Carl Sandburg. CP-SandC

Valley was swept with a blue broom to the west, The. Santa Fe Sketches. Carl Sandburg. CP-SandC

Valley Where I Don't Belong, A. Marge Piercy. SP-PierM

Valley's Singing Day, The. Robert Frost. CP-FrosR

Valmorbia, flowering clouds of plants. Eugenio Montale. CP-MontE, *tr.* by Jonathan Galassi

Valor in the dark. Emily Dickinson. SP-DickE

Valour and Innocence. Queen's Men, The. Rudyard Kipling. CP-KiplR

Valparaíso. Gabriela Mistral. SP-MistG, *tr.* by Maria Giachetti [*or* Jacketti]

Valparaíso is fading. Valparaíso. Gabriela Mistral. SP-MistG, *tr.* by Maria Giachetti [*or* Jacketti]

Valse, The. Paul Laurence Dunbar. CP-DunbP

Valse Triste et Sentimentale. Hans Magnus Enzensberger. SP-EnzeH

Valuable. Stevie Smith. CP-SmitS

Valuation. John Greenleaf Whittier. CP-WhitJ

Value in Mountains. Kenneth Rexroth. CP-RexrK

Value Neuter. Kenneth Rexroth. CP-RexrK

Value of Gold, The. Thom Gunn. CP-GunnT

Values are split, summer, the fierce. Pause, The. William Carlos Williams. CP-WilW2

Values in Use. Marianne Craig Moore. CP-MoorM

Valuta. Kenneth Rexroth. CP-RexrK

Vampire. Ted Hughes. SP-HughTN

Vampire. Paul Muldoon. CP-MuldP

Vampire, The. Charles Baudelaire. CP-BaudC, *tr.* by Walter Martin

Vampire, The. Rudyard Kipling. CP-KiplR

Vampirine Fair, The. Thomas Hardy. CP-HardT

Van Black, an Old Farmer in His Dell. Richard Eberhart. CP-EberR

Van Buren. Ralph Waldo Emerson. CP-EmerR

Van der Lubbe. Stephen Spender. CP-SpenS

Van Gogh. Lorine Niedecker. CP-NiedL

Van Gogh. Charles Tomlinson. CP-TomlC

Van Gogh could see. Lorine Niedecker. CP-NiedL

Van Gogh's Face. Adam Zagajewski. SP-ZagaA, *tr.* by Renata Gorczynski

Vana. Ezra Pound. CP-PoEar

Vanbrug's House. Jonathan Swift. CP-SwifJ

Vancouver. Donald Davie. CP-DaviDC

Vane on Hughley steeple, The. Hughley Steeple. A. E. Housman. CP-HousA

Vane, young in yeares, but in sage counsell old. To Sir Henry Vane the Younger. John Milton. CP-MiltJ

Vanguard of liberty, ye Men of Kent. To the Men of Kent (October, 1803). William Wordsworth. CP-WorW1; MW-WorW

Vanished. Emily Dickinson. CP-DickE

Vanished, The. Hans Magnus Enzensberger. SP-EnzeH, *tr.* by Rita Dove *and* Fred Viebahn

Vanished house that for an hour I knew, A. Souvenir. Edwin Arlington Robinson. CP-RobiE

Vanished Work. Hans Magnus Enzensberger. SP-EnzeH, *tr.* by Hans Magnus Enzensberger *and* Michael Hamburger

Vanishers, The. John Greenleaf Whittier. CP-WhitJ

Vanishing Institution, A. Kenneth Patchen. CP-PatcK

Vanishing Point, The. Miller Williams. CP-WillM

Vanishing Red, The. Robert Frost. CP-FrosR

Vanities. Elizabeth Barrett Browning. CP-BroEB

Vanity. G. K. Chesterton. CP-ChesG

Vanity. Robert Graves. CP-GravR

Vanity and gluttony were always her sins. Initiation. Czeslaw Milosz. CP-MiloC; CP-MiloCN, *tr.* by Robert Hass

Vanity Fair. Sylvia Plath. CP-PlatS

Vanity! hog-vanity, ape-lust. Vespers. John Berryman. CP-BerrJ

Vanity (like a belly / dancer's romance): just. Apple Uppfle. Robert Creeley. CP-CreeR

Vanity of All Worldly Things, The. Anne Bradstreet. CP-BradA

Vanity of Human Wishes, The; The Tenth Satire of Juvenal Imitated. Samuel Johnson. CP-JohnS

Vanity of Vanities. Christina Georgina Rossetti. CP-RosC1

Vanity of Vanities. Christina Georgina Rossetti. CP-RosC2

Vanity of vanities, the Preacher saith. One Certainty, The. Christina Georgina Rossetti. CP-RosC1

Vanity of Wealth, The. Samuel Johnson. CP-JohnS

Vanity [*or* Vanitie] (1). George Herbert. CP-HerbG

Vanity, saith the preacher, vanity! Bishop Orders His Tomb at Saint Praxed's Church, The. Robert Browning. CP-BroR1; SP-BroR

Vanity (2). George Herbert. CP-HerbG

Vanity, vanity, all is vanity. Ha! Original Sin! Ogden Nash. CP-NashO

Vanquished [*or* Vanquish'd] and weary was my soul in me. Sonnet: A Trance of Love. Cino da Pistoia. CW-RossD, *tr.* by Dante Gabriel Rossetti

Vantage Point, The. Robert Frost. CP-FrosR

Vapor Trail Reflected in the Frog Pond. Galway Kinnell. SP-KinnGN

Vapor Trails. Gary Snyder. CP-SnydG

Vaporetto. Adam Zagajewski. SP-ZagaA, *tr. by* Constantine P. Cavafy

Vaporish closeness of this two-month fog, The. 1930's. Robert Lowell. SP-LoweR

Vaquero. Paul Muldoon. CP-MuldP

Varennes. Ivor Gurney. SP-GurnI

Vari-Colored Song. Langston Hughes. CP-HughL; CP-HughL3

Variables of Green. Robert Graves. CP-GravR

Variant. John Ashbery. SP-AshbJ

Variant, The. Charles Simic. SP-SimiC; SP-SimiCE

Variant on a Scrap of Conversation. Charles Tomlinson. CP-TomlC

Variation ("Backwater of air, The"). Federico García Lorca. CP-GarcF, *tr. by* Jerome Rothenberg *Fr.* Backwaters.

Variation ("Facing the deserted fair"). Federico García Lorca. CP-GarcF, *tr. by* Jerome Rothenberg *Fr.* Fairs.

Variation, A. Robert Creeley. CP-CreeR

Variation, A. James Whitcomb Riley. CP-RileJ

Variation and Reflection on a Theme by Rilke. Denise Levertov. SP-LeveDS

Variation in V. Joseph Brodsky. CP-BrodJ

Variation: Ode to Fear. Robert Penn Warren. CP-WarrR

Variation on a Polish Folk Song. Marya Alexandrovna Zaturenska. SP-ZatuM

Variation on a Sentence. Louise Bogan. CP-BogaL

Variation on a Theme by Stevens. Alan Dugan. CP-DugaA

Variation on Gaining a Son. Rita Dove. SP-DoveR

Variation on Guilt. Rita Dove. SP-DoveR

Variation on Heraclitus. Louis MacNeice. CP-MacNL

Variation on Lines of Landor, A. Robert Browning. CP-BroR2

Variation on Pain. Rita Dove. SP-DoveR

Variation on Paz. Charles Tomlinson. CP-TomlC

Variation on the Word *Sleep*. Margaret Atwood. SP-AtwM2

Variation on Themes by Roethke and Eliot. Alan Dugan. CP-DugaA

Variation on "To Say to Go to Sleep," A. Randall Jarrell. CP-JarrR

Variation on "Winter's Onset from an Alienated Point of View." Alan Dugan. CP-DugaA

Variations. Robert Creeley. CP-CreeR

Variations. Randall Jarrell. CP-JarrR

Variations. Federico García Lorca. SP-GarcF, *tr. by* Lysander Kemp

Variations, Calypso and Fugue on a Theme of Ella Wheeler Wilcox. John Ashbery. SP-AshbJ

Variations Done for Gerald Van De Wiele. Charles Olson. CP-OlsoC; SP-OlsoC

Variations of Greek Themes. *Various authors*. CP-RobiE

Variations on a Summer Day. Wallace Stevens. CP-StevW; CP-StevWP

Variations on a Theme. Countee Cullen. CP-CullC

Variations on a theme. Josephine Jacobsen. CP-JacoJ

Variations on a Theme. Carl Sandburg. CP-SandC

Variations on a Theme by George Herbert. Marya Alexandrovna Zaturenska. SP-ZatuM

Variations on a Theme by William Carlos Williams. Kenneth Koch. SP-KochK

Variations on Pasternak's "Mein Liebchen, Was Willst Du Noch Mehr?" Frank O'Hara. SP-OharF

Variations on Variety. Josephine Jacobsen. CP-JacoJ

Variations: The Air Is Sweetest That a Thistle Guards. James Merrill. SP-MerrJ

Variations Within Instances. Robert Stock. SP-StocR

Varick Street. Elizabeth Bishop. CP-BishE

Varied colours are a fitful heap, The. Year's Sheddings, The. George Meredith. CP-MerG1

Variegated flowers, nuts, cockle-shells. Necklace, The. Robert Graves. CP-GravR

Various ills ordain'd to man by fate, The. Ovid. CP-JohnS *Fr.* Metamorphoses.

Varium et Mutabile. Sir Thomas Wyatt. CP-WyatT

Varus old crony had me visit his love. Catullus. *See* Alfenus Varus / buttonholes me

Vas en Afrique! Back to Africa! the butcher we used to / patronize in the rue Cadet market. Racists. C. K. Williams. SP-WillC

Vase, The. David Ignatow. SP-IgnaD

Vase, The. Gregory Orr. SP-OrrG

Vase of Life, The. Dante Gabriel Rossetti. CW-RossD *Fr.* House of Life, The.

Vase was made of clay, The. Elegy to the Sioux. Norman Dubie. CP-DubiN

Vast and grey, the sky. Desolate Field, The. William Carlos Williams. CP-WilW1

Vast Confusion, A. Lawrence Ferlinghetti. SP-FerlL

Vast oblong space. Chanting at the Crystal Sea. Susan Howe. SP-HoweSE

Vast, tremulous. I Sent Thee Late. Louis Zukofsky. CP-ZukLS

Vast unmapped badlands spread without a road. Lone Ranger, The. Donald Hall. CP-HallD

Vastest earthly Day, The. Emily Dickinson. CP-DickE

Vastness and Indifference of the World, The. Richard Eberhart. CP-EberR

Vatican Museum. Yannis Ritsos. SP-RitsY, *tr. by* Kostas Myrsiades

Vaudeville Dancer. Carl Sandburg. CP-SandC

Vaudois Teacher, The. John Greenleaf Whittier. CP-WhitJ

Vaudracour and Julia. William Wordsworth. CP-WorW1

Vault on the opal carpet of the sun. To Portapovitch. Hart Crane. CP-CranH

Vaunting Oak. John Crowe Ransom. SP-RansJ

   (He is a tower unleaning. But how he'll break.) SP-RansJ

Veal and mushrooms, wine, a too pungent salad. Joint. James Schuyler. CP-SchuJ

Vealers, The. Maxine W. Kumin. SP-KumiM

Vector Analysis. Philip Whalen. SP-WhalP

Veer-Voices: Two Sisters under Crows. James Dickey. CP-DickJ

Vegetable Garden, The. Wyatt Prunty. SP-PrunW

Vegetable King, The. James Dickey. CP-DickJ

Vegetables, The. James McMichael. SP-McMiJ

Vegetables please us with their modes and virtues, The. Praises. Thomas McGrath. SP-McGrT

Vegetarians, The. John Ashbery. SP-AshbJ

Vegetation. Kathleen Jessie Raine. SP-RainK

Vehicle: Absence. C. K. Williams. SP-WillC

Vehicle: Conscience. C. K. Williams. SP-WillC

Vehicle: Violence. C. K. Williams. SP-WillC

Veil, Rue Armantrout. SP-ArmaA

Veil, The. Walter De la Mare. CP-DeLaW

Veil of Light, The. Samuel Taylor Coleridge. CP-ColeS

Veil of Spirit, The. Samuel Taylor Coleridge. CP-ColeS

Veil of the Temple, The. Jones Very. CP-VeryJ

Veil them, cover them, wall them round. Rudyard Kipling. CP-KiplR *Fr.* Second Jungle Book, The.

Veil Upon the Heart, The. Jones Very. CP-VeryJ

Veil upon veil. Natura Naturans. Kathleen Jessie Raine. SP-RainK

Veils of clarity. Metric Figure. William Carlos Williams. CP-WilW1

Veins of other Flowers, The. Emily Dickinson. CP-DickE

Veins on the back of my hand (now that I'm old), The. Holy Rivers, The. James Laughlin. CP-LaugJ

Velvet Rocks. Richard Eberhart. CP-EberR

Velvet Roses. James Schuyler. CP-SchuJ

Vending Machine. Hans Magnus Enzensberger. SP-EnzeH

Venemous toung, tipt with vile adders sting. Sonnet 85. Edmund Spenser. CP-Spens *Fr.* Amoretti.

Veneris Venefica Agrestis. Lucio Piccolo. CP-TomlC, *tr. by* Charles Tomlinson

Venetian; all thy Colouring is no more. William Blake. CP-BlakW

Venetian Blind. Thom Gunn. CP-GunnT

Venetian Blind, The. Randall Jarrell. CP-JarrR

Venetian Dog. Charles Wright. SP-WrigCN

Venetian Pastoral, by Giorgone, in the Louvre, A. Dante Gabriel Rossetti. CW-RossD

Venetian Stanzas 1. Joseph Brodsky. CP-BrodJ, *tr. by* Jane Miller

Venetian Stanzas 2. Joseph Brodsky. CP-BrodJ, *tr. by* Jane Miller

Venexia 1. Charles Wright. SP-WrigCN

Venexia 2. Charles Wright. SP-WrigCN

Venez vite / Avec moi. Come. Stevie Smith. CP-SmitS

Vengeance. Grace Paley.

Vengeance Is Mine. D. H. Lawrence. CP-LawrD

Vengeance Is Mine, Saith the Lord. Donald Davie. CP-DaviDC

Vengeance is Sweet. Paul Laurence Dunbar. CP-DunbP

Vengeance of Apollo, The. Homer. CP-MerG2 *Fr.* Iliad, The.

Vengeful across the cold November moors. Pity of the Leaves, The. Edwin Arlington Robinson. CP-RobiE

Veni. Arthur Hugh Clough. SP-ClouA

Veni Coronaberis. Geoffrey Hill. CP-HillG

Veni Creator. Czeslaw Milosz. CP-MiloC; CP-MiloCN, *tr. by* Robert Pinsky

Venice. Lord Byron. CP-Byron

Venice. Raymond Carver. CP-CarvR

Venice. Herman Melville. SP-MelvH

Venice. Kenneth Rexroth. CP-RexrK

Venice. Charles Tomlinson. CP-TomlC; SP-TomlC

Venice dream of the mainland, A. Clarence Major. SP-MajoC

Venice: Lido. Joseph Brodsky. CP-BrodJ, *tr. by* Alan Myers

Venice, 182. John Berryman. CP-BerrJ

Venice portrait: he, The. Humanist, The. Geoffrey Hill. CP-HillG

Venice Revisited. Amy Clampitt. CP-ClamA

Venom. James Dickey. CP-DickJ

Venomous thorns that are so sharp and keen. Sir Thomas Wyatt. CP-WyatT

Venta! within thy sacred fane. James Austen. CP-AustJ

Ventriloquy / is the mother tongue. Attention. Rae Armantrout. SP-ArmaA

Venus ("Dead maiden, The"). Federico García Lorca. CP-GarcF, *tr. by* Alan S. Trueblood *Fr.* Three Portraits with Shading.

Venus ("Open sesame / by day"). Federico García Lorca. CP-GarcF, *tr. by* Jerome Rothenberg *Fr.* Night (Suite for Piano and Poet's Voice).

Venus. "Rubén Dario." SP-DariR, *tr. by* Alberto Acereda *and* Will Derusha

Venus. Charles Simic. SP-SimiCE

Venus, again[e] thou mov'st a war[re]. Ode 4.1: To Venus. Horace. CP-JonsB *Fr.* Odes.

Venus and the Ark. Anne Sexton. CP-SextA

Venus de Milo didn't have one, at least no pussy, The. Cunts. John Updike. CP-UpdiJ

Venus Emerging. Arthur Rimbaud. CP-RimbA, *tr. by* Martin Sorrell

Venus glows in the east. Work to Do Toward Town. Gary Snyder. CP-SnydG

Venus, in sport, to please therewith her dear. Sir Thomas Wyatt. CP-WyatT

Venus in the pale green sky. Hojoki. Kenneth Rexroth. CP-RexrK

Venus Over the Desert. William Carlos Williams. CP-WilW2

Venus seems my Mouse, A. My Mouse. Christina Georgina Rossetti. CP-RosC3

Venus Verticordia. Dante Gabriel Rossetti. CW-RossD

Venus Victrix. Dante Gabriel Rossetti. CW-RossD *Fr.* House of Life, The.

Venus When Young Choosing Death. Stevie Smith. CP-SmitS

Venus Will Now Say a Few Words. W. H. Auden. CP-AudeW

Venus's-flytraps. Yusef Komunyakaa. CP-KomuY

Venus's Looking-Glass. Christina Georgina Rossetti. CP-RosC1

Venus's Looking-glass. Louis Zukofsky. CP-ZukLS

Ver anni Lunaeque fuit, pars verna diei. Elegia I (1619). Thomas Campion. CP-CampT

Vera stopped at the flower called fireweed. Then. Grace Paley. CP-PalGC

Verandah. Derek Walcott. CP-WalcD

Verandahs, where the pages of the sea. Another Life. Derek Walcott. CP-WalcD

Veraniolus, / first of friends. Carmen 9. Catullus. CP-ZukLS *Fr.* Carmina.

Veranius of all my beloved friends. Catullus. *See* Veraniolus, / first of friends

Verba volant; verum: quid enim velocius illis? Thomas Campion. CP-CampT

Verbal Generation, The. John Ciardi. CP-CiarJ

Verbalist of Summer, The. Richard Eberhart. CP-EberR

Verbatim from Boileau. Alexander Pope. CP-PopeA

Verborum satis est; oneri sunt plura libello. Ad Librum. Thomas Campion. CP-CampT

Verdict, A. G. K. Chesterton. CP-ChesG

Verdicts, The. Rudyard Kipling. CP-KiplR

Verdun. Robert Lowell. SP-LoweR

Verily it snows. Emily Dickinson. SP-DickE

Veritable night, The. Rigamarole. William Carlos Williams. CP-WilW1

Verlaine. Federico García Lorca. CP-GarcF, *tr. by* Alan S. Trueblood *Fr.* Three Portraits with Shading.

Verlaine. Edwin Arlington Robinson. CP-RobiE

Vermeer. Howard Nemerov. CP-NemeH

Vermeer's little girl, now famous. Adam Zagajewski. SP-ZagaA, *tr. by* Clare Cavanagh

Vermont. Hayden Carruth. CP-CarHL

Vermont. John Updike. CP-UpdiJ

Vermont Apollinaire. William Corbett. SP-CorbW

Vermont Ballad: Change of Season. Robert Penn Warren. CP-WarrR

Vermont Diary, A. James Schuyler. CP-SchuJ

Vermont Idyll. Richard Eberhart. CP-EberR

Vermont Thaw. Robert Penn Warren. CP-WarrR

Verna diu saevas sensurunt pascua nubes. Inundatio Oxoniana. Gerard Manley Hopkins. CP-HopkG

Vernal Ode. William Wordsworth. CP-WorW2; MW-WorW

Vernal Sentiment. Theodore Roethke. CP-RoetT

Verona, late January. Mid-winter Snowfall in the Piazza Dante. Charles Wright. SP-WrigCN

Verona, Ohio / right 3 miles. Jaunt. Louis Zukofsky. CP-ZukLS

Veronica passes her cape between breath. For the Walking Dead. Yusef Komunyakaa. CP-KomuY

Veronica's Napkin. William Butler Yeats. CP-YeatW

Vers Démodé. Dorothy Parker. CP-ParkD

Versailles. Adrienne Rich. CP-RicAE

Verse, a breeze mid blossoms straying. Youth and Age. Samuel Taylor Coleridge. CP-ColeS; MW-ColeS

Verse Composed and Repeated by *Burns*, to the Master of the House, on Taking Leave at a Place in the Highlands, Where He Had Been Hospitably Entertained, A. Robert Burns. CP-BurnR

Verse for a Certain Dog. Dorothy Parker. CP-ParkD

Verse for Urania. James Merrill. SP-MerrJ

Verse from Defensio Secunda. John Milton. CP-MiltJ

Verse from Pro Populo Anglicano Defensio. John Milton. CP-MiltJ

Verse from the Advertisement to Blake's Exhibition of Paintings, 1809. William Blake. CP-BlakW

Verse Reporting Late Arrival at a Conclusion. Dorothy Parker. CP-ParkD

Verse with Allusions. Theodore Roethke. CP-RoetT

Verses. Robert Herrick. CP-HerrR

Verses: "I am a keeper of the law." Robert Burns. CP-BurnR

Verses: "I am confirm'd a woman can." Sir John Suckling. CP-SuckJ

Verses Addressed to J. Horne Tooke and the Company Who Met on 28 June 1796 to Celebrate His Poll at the Westminster Election. Samuel Taylor Coleridge. CP-ColeS

Verses After Which the Mourning Statue is Presumed to Speak. Robert Stock. SP-StocR

Verses for a Centennial. Archibald MacLeish. CP-MacLA

Verses Found in a Summer-House at Hales-Owen. Lord Byron. CP-Byron

Verses from an Old Tapestry. Jaroslav Seifert. SP-SeifJ, *tr. by* Ewald Osers

Verses from Quilica. Jonathan Swift. CP-SwifJ

Verses in Baretti's Commonplace Book. Samuel Johnson. CP-JohnS

    (Reply to Impromptu Verses by Baretti, A.) CP-JohnS

Verses in the Night. Dorothy Parker. CP-ParkD

Verses Intended to Be Written below a Noble Earl's Picture. Robert Burns. CP-BurnR

Verses Left by Mr. Pope, on His Lying in the Same Bed which Wilmot, the Celebrated Earl of Rochester, Slept in, at Adderbury, then Belonging to the Duke of Argyle, July 9th, 1739. Alexander Pope. CP-PopeA

Verses Left in a Window of Dublin Castle. Jonathan Swift. CP-SwifJ

Verses Made for the Women Who Cry Apples, etc. Jonathan Swift. CP-SwifJ Onyons. CP-SwifJ

    (Onions.) CP-SwifJ

Verses Made in Swift's Sleep. Jonathan Swift. CP-SwifJ

    (I Walk before No Man (Composed While Asleep).) CP-SwifJ

Verses Made up in a Dream. G. K. Chesterton. CP-ChesG

Verses Modelled on Pope. Samuel Johnson. *See* While Many a Merry Tale

Verses Occasioned by an & c. at the End of Mr. D'Urfy's Name in the Title to One of His Plays. Alexander Pope. CP-PopeA

Verses Occasioned by the Sudden Drying Up of St. Patrick's Well near Trinity College, Dublin. Jonathan Swift. CP-SwifJ

Verses on a Cat. Percy Bysshe Shelley. CP-ShelP

Verses on a Wooden Leg. *Unknown, sometimes at. to* Thomas Sheridan. CP-SherT

Verses on Games. Rudyard Kipling. CP-KiplR

Verses on I Know Not What. Jonathan Swift. CP-SwifJ

Verses on the Death of Dr. Swift, D.S.P.D. Jonathan Swift. CP-SwifJ

Verses on the Death of His Mother. Samuel Johnson. CP-JohnS

Verses on the Revival of the Order of the Bath. Jonathan Swift. CP-SwifJ

Verses on the Upright Judge. Jonathan Swift. CP-SwifJ

Verses Said to Be Written on the Union. Jonathan Swift. CP-SwifJ

Verses Spoken Extempore by Dean Swift on His Curate's Complaint of Hard Duty. Jonathan Swift. CP-SwifJ

Verses to Be Placed under the Picture of England's Arch-Poet: Containing a Compleat Catalogue of His Works. Alexander Pope. CP-PopeA

Verses to be Prefix'd before Bernard Lintot's New Miscellany. Alexander Pope. CP-PopeA

Verses to Rhyme with 'Rose.' Elizabeth Austen. CP-AustJ

Verses Trivocular. Samuel Taylor Coleridge. CP-ColeS

Verses Written at Bath on Finding the Heel of a Shoe. William Cowper. CP-CowpW

Verses Written for Student Antidraft Registration Rally 1980. Allen Ginsberg. CP-GinsA

Verses Written on a Window of the Inn at Carron. Robert Burns. CP-BurnR

Verses Written on One of the Windows at Delville. *Unknown, sometimes at. to* Thomas Sheridan. CP-SherT

Verses Wrote in a Lady's Ivory Table-Book. Jonathan Swift. CP-SwifJ

Verses you sent on the bottling your wine, The. Dr. Swift's Answer to Dr. Sheridan. Jonathan Swift. CP-SwifJ

Versi. Christina Georgina Rossetti. CP-RosC3

Versicles on Sign-Posts. Robert Burns. CP-BurnR

Versify it, Donald. Lost Bride, The. Donald Davie. CP-DaviDC

Version. Robert Frost. CP-FrosR

Version of Ossian's Address to the Sun, A. Lord Byron. CP-Byron

Version of the First Psalm, for the Use of a Young Lady, A. Alexander Pope. CP-PopeA

Versions. Robert Creeley. SP-CreeR

Vertical Man. Thomas Kinsella. CP-KinsT

Vertical plate serving us. Rainer Maria Rilke. CP-RilkFr, *tr. by* A. Poulin, Jr. *Fr.* Windows, The.

Vertigo. Adrienne Rich. CP-RicAE

Vertue. Robert Herrick. CP-HerrR

Vertue Best United. Robert Herrick. CP-HerrR

Vertue Is Sensible of Suffering. Robert Herrick. CP-HerrR

Vertue the Best Monument. *Unknown, sometimes at. to* Sir Walter Ralegh. CP-RaleW

Vertumnus. Joseph Brodsky. CP-BrodJ

Vertumnus and Pomona. Ovid. CP-PopeA *Fr.* Metamorphoses.

Vervain . . . basil . . . orison. Incantation. Walter De la Mare. CP-DeLaW

Very. Charles Bukowski. SP-BukC2

Very ancient olive trees, hollow twisted trunks. Leaving Monovasia. Yannis Ritsos. SP-RitsY *Fr.* Monovasia.

Very bitter were the sorrows. Lament of the Children of Israel in Rome. Randall Jarrell. CP-JarrR

Very cool that bed must be. There Remaineth Therefore a Rest. Christina Georgina Rossetti. CP-RosC3

Very Dove, A. Allen Ginsberg. CP-GinsA

Very dreamy self, A. Long Door. Andrei Codrescu. SP-CodrA

Very Early Morning Exercise, A. Kenneth Rexroth. CP-RexrK

Very felicitous eve, A. Delightful Evening. Wallace Stevens. CP-StevW; CP-StevWP

Very flatness / of portraits, The. Our Nature. Rae Armantrout. SP-ArmaA

Very Funny, Very Funny. Ogden Nash. CP-NashO

Very instant he has loosed his shot, The. Petrarch. CP-Petra, *tr. by* J. G. Nichols

"Very last time I ever was here, The," he said. Jubilate. Thomas Hardy. CP-HardT

Very Many People. Rudyard Kipling. CP-KiplR

Very Mournful Ballad, A. Lord Byron. CP-Byron

Very old are the woods. All That's Past. Walter De la Mare. CP-DeLaW

Very Old Song, A. "William Laird." CP-HerrR

Very old woman / Lives in yon house, A. Alone. Walter De la Mare. CP-DeLaW

Very Original Poem, Written with Even a Greater Endeavour than Ordinary after Intelligibility, and Hitherto Only Published on the First Leaf of the Author's Son's Account-Book. Robert Browning. CP-BroR2

Very proud / he barely asked directions. Black Prince, The. Alice Walker. CP-WalkA

Very reverend Dean Smedley, The. Dean Smedley Gone to Seek His Fortune. Jonathan Swift. CP-SherT; CP-SwifJ

Very Rich Hours, The. James McMichael. SP-McMiJ

Very Seldom. Constantine P. Cavafy. CP-CavaC, *tr. by* Theoharis Constantine Theoharis

Very Short Song, A. Dorothy Parker. CP-ParkD

Very Tall Boy, A. James Whitcomb Riley. CP-RileJ

Very Tree. Stanley Kunitz. CP-KunSC

Very Unclubbable Man, The. Ogden Nash. CP-NashO

Very Very Important. Carl Sandburg. CP-SandC

Very West-of-Wessex girl, A. West-of-Wessex Girl, The. Thomas Hardy. CP-HardT

Vesper Journal. Charles Wright SP-WrigC

Vesper out there, you vain knees can sure get up: Vesper, Olympus. Catullus. *See* Gather young men as the twilight gathers

Vespers. John Berryman. CP-BerrJ

Vespers. James McMichael. SP-McMiJ

Vespers. Paul Muldoon. CP-MuldP

Vessel blatting, A. Measure. Charles Olson. CP-OlsoC

Vessels. James Dickey. CP-DickJ

Vessels of heavenly medicine! may the breeze. Sonnet: On Launching Some Bottles Filled with Knowledge into the Bristol Channel. Percy Bysshe Shelley. CP-ShelP

Vessels of several. Gandhi's Gun (and Brecht's Vow). Denise Levertov. SP-LeveDS *Fr.* Staying Alive.

Vesta. John Greenleaf Whittier. CP-WhitJ

Veteran. Fanny Howe. SP-HoweF

Veteran, The. Paul Laurence Dunbar. CP-DunbP

Veteran, The. Dorothy Parker. CP-ParkD

Veteran Sirens. Edwin Arlington Robinson. CP-RobiE

Veterans, The. Rudyard Kipling. CP-KiplR

Vex'd elm-heads are pale with the view, The. Windy Day in Summer, A. Gerard Manley Hopkins. CP-HopkG

Vexilla Regis. Richard Crashaw. CP-CrasR

Via appia. James Dickey. CP-DickJ

Via Cigna. Primo Levi. CP-LeviP, *tr. by* Brian Swann

Via Crucis. Herman Melville. SP-MelvH *Fr.* Clarel: A Poem and Pilgrimage in the Holy Land.

Via Funari. Joseph Brodsky. CP-BrodJ

Via Portello. Donald Davie. CP-DaviDC

'Via Portello,' I wrote. Hardness of Light, The. Donald Davie. CP-DaviDC

Viable. A. R. Ammons. CP-AmmoA

Vibennius & son, renowned. Carmen 33. Catullus. CP-ZukLS *Fr.* Carmina.

Vibration. John Updike. CP-UpdiJ

Vibration of Justice. D. H. Lawrence. CP-LawrD

Vicar, The. George Crabbe. SP-CrabG *Fr.* Borough, The.

Vice of habit. Bread. Gabriela Mistral. SP-MistG, *tr. by* Maria Giachetti [*or* Jacketti]

Vicenza. Kenneth Rexroth. CP-RexrK

Vices. Robinson Jeffers. CP-JefR1

Viciousness in the kitchen! Lesbos. Sylvia Plath. CP-PlatS

Vicissitudes Experienced in the Christian Life, The. Jeanne Marie Bouvier de la Motte- Guyon. CP-CowpW

Vicissitudes of the Creator. Archibald MacLeish. CP-MacLA

Vickery's Mountain. Edwin Arlington Robinson. CP-RobiE

Victim, The. Thom Gunn. CP-GunnT

Victim not of an accident. Proposal for Recycling Wastes, A. Marge Piercy. SP-PierM

Victims, a Play for the Home, The. Muriel Rukeyser. CP-RukeM

Victor. W. H. Auden. CP-AudeW

Victor Dog, The. James Merrill. SP-MerrJ

Victor was a little baby. Victor. W. H. Auden. CP-AudeW

Victoria. Dorothy Parker. CP-ParkD

Victoria Clementina, negress. Exposition of the Contents of a Cab. Wallace Stevens. CP-StevWP

Victorian Eclogues. Ezra Pound. CP-PoEar

Victorian Rehearsal, A. Thomas Hardy. CP-HardT

Victoria's Secret. Billy Collins. SP-CollB

Victoria's Tears. Elizabeth Barrett Browning. CP-BroEB

"Victories," The. Rainer Maria Rilke. CP-RilkFr, *tr. by* A. Poulin, Jr.

Victorious and triumphal laurel-tree. Petrarch. CP-Petra, *tr. by* J. G. Nichols

Victors, The. Denise Levertov. SP-LeveDP

Victory. James Dickey. CP-DickJ

Victory, The. Laura Riding Jackson. CP-RidiL

Victory, The. Thomas Merton. CP-MertT

Victory Asleep. Rainer Maria Rilke. CP-RilkFr, *tr. by* A. Poulin, Jr.

Victory comes late. Emily Dickinson. CP-DickE

Victory Over Seville, The. Shmuel HaNagid. SP-HaNaS, *tr. by* Peter Cole

'Victory!' / So once more the cry must be. Wellington's Funeral. Dante Gabriel Rossetti. CW-RossD

Vidalia Potter (who often as not). Potter, Vidalia. Miller Williams. CP-WillM

Video Cuisine. Maxine W. Kumin. SP-KumiM

Vieil aller / vieux arrêts. Samuel Beckett. CP-BeckS

Vienna the Volk iss very lustig. Lustspiel. William Carlos Williams. CP-WilW2

Vietnam Addenda. Audre Lorde. SP-LordA

Vietnam eyes my children in the sandbox. Middle Age. A. K. Ramanujan. CP-RamaA

Vietnam Memorial. Karl Shapiro. SP-ShapK

View. Rae Armantrout. SP-ArmaA

View. William Carlos Williams. CP-WilW1

View, A. Mona Van Duyn. SP-VanDM

View, A. James Schuyler. CP-SchuJ

View, The. Robert Creeley. SP-CreeR

View, The. Philip Larkin. CP-LarkP

View, The. Czeslaw Milosz. CP-MiloC; CP-MiloCN, *tr. by* Lillian Vallee

View, The. Howard Nemerov. CP-NemeH

View, The. Charles Tomlinson. CP-TomlC

View Across the Roman Campagna. Elizabeth Barrett Browning. CP-BroEB

View by Color Photography on a Commercial Calendar. William Carlos Williams. CP-WilW2

View From a Porch. Thomas Lux. SP-LuxT

View from an Apartment. Michael Palmer. SP-PalmM

View from an Attic Window, The. Howard Nemerov. CP-NemeH

View from an Empty Chair. Tess Gallagher. SP-GallT

View from Charles Bridge. Jaroslav Seifert. SP-SeifJ, *tr. by* Ewald Osers

View from His Room. Clarence Major. SP-MajoC

View from Pisgah, The. Howard Nemerov. CP-NemeH

View from Rosehill Cemetery: Vicksburg. Alice Walker. CP-WalkA

View from the Hill. Joseph Brodsky. CP-BrodJ, *tr. by* Alan Myers

View from the Top of Black Comb. William Wordsworth. CP-WorW1

View is fine from fifty, The. View, The. Philip Larkin. CP-LarkP

View it, by day, from the back. Movie House. John Updike. CP-UpdiJ

View Mee, Lord. Thomas Campion. CP-CampT

View of a Lake. William Carlos Williams. CP-WilW1

View of a Pig. Ted Hughes. SP-HughTN

View of Delft, A. Adam Zagajewski. SP-ZagaA

View of Fujiyama after the War, A. James Dickey. CP-DickJ

View of Krakow, A. Adam Zagajewski. SP-ZagaA, *tr. by* Clare Cavanagh

View of Merton College, A. Adrienne Rich. CP-RicAE

View of the Brooklyn Bridge, A. William Meredith. SP-MereW

View of the Capitol from the Library of Congress. Elizabeth Bishop. CP-BishE

View of the Terrace, A. Adrienne Rich. CP-RicAE

View of winter trees. Jersey Lyric. William Carlos Williams. CP-WilW2

View to the North. May Swenson. SP-SwenM

View with a Flood. Joseph Brodsky. CP-BrodJ

View with a Grain of Sand. Wisława Szymborska. SP-SzymWM, *tr. by* Joanna Trzeciak

View with a Grain of Sand. Wisława Szymborska. SP-SzymW, *tr. by* Stanislaw Barańczak *and* Clare Cavanagh

Viewing Photographs of China. Arthur Sze. SP-SzeA

Viewless and invisible Consequence, The. Fragment: "Viewless and invisible Consequence, The." Percy Bysshe Shelley. CP-ShelP

Views and Spectacles. Theodore Weiss. SP-WeisT

Views of Myself. John Berryman. CP-BerrJ

Vigil. Raymond Carver. CP-CarvR

Vigil. Walter De la Mare. CP-DeLaW

Vigil, The. Jelaluddin Rumi. SP-Rumi, *tr. by* Coleman Barks

Vigil of all Saints. Christina Georgina Rossetti. CP-RosC2

Vigil of Corpus Christi, The. Thom Gunn. CP-GunnT

Vigil of St. Bartholomew. Christina Georgina Rossetti. CP-RosC2

Vigil of St. Peter. Christina Georgina Rossetti. CP-RosC2

Vigil of the Annunciation. Christina Georgina Rossetti. CP-RosC2

Vigil of the Presentation. Christina Georgina Rossetti. CP-RosC2

Vigil of Venus, The. *Unknown*. CP-TateA

  (Pervigilium Veneris.) CP-TateA

Vigil Strange I Kept on the Field One Night. Walt Whitman. CP-WhitW

Vigilant Woman, The. Gabriela Mistral. SP-MistG, *tr. by* Maria Giachetti [*or* Jacketti]

Vigilante. Yusef Komunyakaa. CP-KomuY

Vigils. Arthur Rimbaud. CP-RimbA, *tr. by* Martin Sorrell

Vignette. Wallace Stevens. CP-StevWP

Vignettes of the Wind. Federico García Lorca. CP-GarcF, *tr. by* Jerome Rothenberg

Vigor and majesty of the air, The. Light From Above. Richard Eberhart. CP-EberR

Viking Dublin: Trial Pieces. Seamus Heaney. SP-HeanSO

Villa Adriana. Adrienne Rich. CP-RicAE; SP-RicA2

Village, The. George Crabbe.

  Truth in Poetry. SP-CrabG

  (Rural Life.) SP-CrabG

Village Blacksmith, The. Henry Wadsworth Longfellow. SP-LongH

Village Improvement Parade, The. Nicholas Vachel Lindsay. CP-LindV

Village in East Anglia, A. Donald Hall. CP-HallD

Village in Late Summer. Carl Sandburg. CP-SandC

Village Life, A. Derek Walcott. CP-WalcD

Village of kite-flyers, we, A. Kites. Donald Davie. CP-DaviDC

Village of Reason, The. Michael Palmer. SP-PalmM

Village 104. James Tate. SP-TateJ

Village Priest, A. Norman Dubie. CP-DubiN

Village Tale, A. May Sarton. SP-SartM

Village, Town, City—Highway, Road, Path. A. R. Ammons. CP-AmmoA

Village Tudda, The. Kenneth Patchen. CP-PatcK

Villagers and Death, The. Robert Graves. CP-GravR

Villagers who gather round. Spiel of [the] Three Mountebanks. John Crowe Ransom. SP-RansJ

Villain at the Gallows tree, The. Pitiful Case, A. William Blake. CP-BlakW

Villain shows his indiscretion. Curtain. Paul Laurence Dunbar. CP-DunbP

Villains. Stevie Smith. CP-SmitS

Villanelle: "Christ is walking in your blood today." Richard Eberhart. CP-EberR

Villanelle: "Every day our bodies separate." Marilyn Hacker. SP-HackM

Villanelle for an Anniversary. Seamus Heaney. SP-HeanSO

Villanelle: Late Summer. Marilyn Hacker. SP-HackM

Villanelle of Change. Edwin Arlington Robinson. CP-RobiE

Villanelle of the Suicide's Mother. C. K. Williams. SP-WillC

Villanelle: The Psychological Hour. Ezra Pound. SP-PounE

Villon/Leadbelly. Yusef Komunyakaa. CP-KomuY

Villonaud for This Yule. Ezra Pound. CP-PoEar; SP-PounE

Villonauld, A. Ballad of the Gibbet. Ezra Pound. CP-PoEar

Vince Viet Cong! The testimony of walls. Tarquinia. Charles Tomlinson. CP-TomlC

Vindication of Jovan Babič, The. Donald Davie. CP-DaviDC

Vindictives, The. Robert Frost. CP-FrosR

Vine, The. Robert Herrick. CP-HerrR

Vine, The. Thomas Merton. CP-MertT

Vine and Clarel. Herman Melville. SP-MelvH *Fr.* Clarel: A Poem and Pilgrimage in the Holy Land.

Vine grows so many tendrils, The. Grisaille. Rainer Maria Rilke. CP-RilkFr, *tr. by* A. Poulin, Jr.

Vinea submittit capr(e)as non semper edulis. On a Beautiful Bar Butterfly in the Black Cat. Kenneth Rexroth. CP-RexrK

Vinegar is no other I define. Upon Vinegar. Robert Herrick. CP-HerrR

Vinegrowers dig up. Paul Celan. SP-CelaP, *tr. by* John Felstiner

Vines. Louis Zukofsky. CP-ZukLS

Vines tougher than wrists. Forcing House. Theodore Roethke. CP-RoetT

Vines with Their. Kenneth Patchen. CP-PatcK

Vineyard, The. Fanny Howe.

  "All night the rain." SP-HoweF

  "By a bottle of fatigued blue flowers." SP-HoweF

  "Fog grays the skyline." SP-HoweF

  "In a workplace torn by a union." SP-HoweF

  "Liberty for the few." SP-HoweF

  "Love's body and mouth lie down together." SP-HoweF

  "Now a daring blue heron." SP-HoweF

  "Our dreams of a land with vines." SP-HoweF

  "Owners over the ocean sailed, The." SP-HoweF

  "Red X, correction. Red check, yes." SP-HoweF

  "Self is a servant only, The." SP-HoweF

  "Since tears become stones." SP-HoweF

  "Some selves are generous." SP-HoweF

  "To imitate England." SP-HoweF

  "To me the disobedient." SP-HoweF

  "When home was a courthouse." SP-HoweF

  "When men wore overcoats down the stairs." SP-HoweF

Vineyard, The. Rudyard Kipling. CP-KiplR *Fr.* Debits and Credits.

Vineyard, The. W. S. Merwin. SP-MerwWF

Vineyard country, russet, reddish, carmine-brown in this season, The. December 1. Czeslaw Milosz. CP-MiloCN, *tr. by* Robert Hass

Vintagers, The. Paul Celan. SP-CelaP, *tr. by* John Felstiner

Viol lace each stilled note. Violet. Louis Zukofsky. CP-ZukLS

Violence. Allen Ginsberg. CP-GinsA

Violence. Adrienne Rich. CP-RicAE

Violence, The. David Ignatow. SP-IgnaD

Violence in the dream, violation of body and spirit; torment, mutiliation, butchery, debasement. Crime, The. C. K. Williams. SP-WillC

Violence threatens you no longer. Cliff Edge, The. Robert Graves. CP-GravR

Violent darkness claims us all, The. Two Songs from "The Hunted Revolutionaries" Thomas McGrath. SP-McGrT

Violent Hand, The. Stevie Smith. CP-SmitS

Violent order is disorder; and, A. Connoisseur of Chaos. Wallace Stevens. CP-StevW; CP-StevWP

Violent Pastoral. James Merrill. SP-MerrJ

Violently asleep in the old house. Blue Ghazals, The. Adrienne Rich. CP-RicAE; SP-RicA2

Violet. Louis Zukofsky. CP-ZukLS

Violet, The. Jones Very. CP-VeryJ

Violet and Jasper. Richard Wilbur. CP-WilbR

Violet at Lough Aughresberg, A. Ted Hughes. SP-HughTN

Violet hush: and sunbursts, A. Heather and Calendulas. James Schuyler. CP-SchuJ

Violet scent is sacred, The. Mariner, The. G. K. Chesterton. CP-ChesG

Violets. D. H. Lawrence. CP-LawrD

Violets. George Meredith. CP-MerG1

Violets are by my side, The. Emily Dickinson. SP-DickE

Violets for the Dead. D. H. Lawrence. CP-LawrD

Violin Debut. Lorine Niedecker. CP-NiedL

Violinist's shadow vanishes, The. Cadenza. Ted Hughes. SP-HughTN

Violins float in the sky. Europe, Late. Dan Pagis. SP-PagiD, *tr. by* Stephen Mitchell

Violins in Chaos? Philip Whalen. SP-WhalP

Violins tended to shriek, The. Triumph of the Postmodern. Lawrence Ferlinghetti. SP-FerlL

Viper-Man. Donald Davie. CP-DaviDC

Vipera Berus. Czeslaw Milosz. CP-MiloCN, *tr. by* Robert Hass

Vire will wind in other shadows. Saint-Lô. Samuel Beckett. CP-BeckS

Vireo, The. Henry David Thoreau. CP-ThorH

Virgils Gnat. Edmund Spenser. CP-Spens

Virgin, The. Richard Eberhart. CP-EberR

Virgin, The. Laura Riding Jackson. CP-RidiL

Virgin and Child, by Hans Memmeling, A; in the Academy of Bruges. Dante Gabriel Rossetti. CW-RossD

Virgin and Martyr. Howard Nemerov. CP-NemeH

Virgin Carrying a Lantern, The. Wallace Stevens. CP-StevW; CP-StevWP

Virgin in a Tree. Sylvia Plath. CP-PlatS

Virgin in crinoline. Paso. Federico García Lorca. SP-GarcF *Fr.* Poem of the Saeta.

Virgin Marie was (as I have read), The. Virgin Mary, The. Robert Herrick. CP-HerrR

Virgin Mary, The. Robert Herrick. CP-HerrR

Virgin Mary to the Child Jesus, The. Elizabeth Barrett Browning. CP-BroEB

Virgin Mirror. Robert Graves. CP-GravR

Virgin Mother, The. D. H. Lawrence. CP-LawrD

Virgin-Mother stood at distance (there), The. Observation. Robert Herrick. CP-HerrR

Virgin Mother walked barefoot, The. Begotten of the Spleen. Charles Simic. SP-SimiC; SP-SimiCE

Virgin Mule. Andrei Codrescu. SP-CodrA

Virgin poet was served up today, A. Epilogue, The: "Virgin poet was served up today, A." Thomas Southerne. CP-DryJ2 *Fr.* Loyal Brother, The.

Virgin, the, the Doe, and the Leper, The. Marya Alexandrovna Zaturenska. SP-ZatuM

Virgin with a Lamp. Marya Alexandrovna Zaturenska. SP-ZatuM

Virgin Youth. D. H. Lawrence. CP-LawrD

Virginal, A. Ezra Pound. CP-PoEar; SP-PounE

Virginal, vibrant, and beautiful dawn, The. Stéphane Mallarmé. CP-MallS, *tr. by* Henry Weinfield

Virginia Backyard: July. Gregory Orr. SP-OrrG

Virginia Britannia. Marianne Craig Moore. CP-MoorM

Virginia Reel. Charles Wright. SP-WrigC

Virginia Reel, A. Paul Laurence Dunbar. CP-DunbP

Virginia—the West. Walt Whitman. CP-WhitW

Virginia Woolf. James Schuyler. CP-SchuJ

Virginia Woolf Gathers Mushrooms. William Dickey. SP-DickW

Virginity, The. Rudyard Kipling. CP-KiplR

Virgin's Cradle-Hymn, The. Samuel Taylor Coleridge. CP-ColeS (Dormi, Jesu! Mater ridet.) CP-ColeS

Virgins promis'd when I died [*or* dy'd]. Epitaph upon a Child, An. Robert Herrick. CP-HerrR

Virgins, time-past, known were these. How Primroses Came Green. Robert Herrick. CP-HerrR

Virgule. Thomas Lux. SP-LuxT

Viridian and gamboge and vermilion. Song of the Man Forsaken and Obsessed. John Berryman. CP-BerrJ

Virtu. A. R. Ammons. CP-AmmoA

Virtue. Walter De la Mare. CP-DeLaW

Virtue. Kenneth Patchen. CP-PatcK

Virtue. William Carlos Williams. CP-WilW1

Virtue, beauty, and speech, did strike, wound, charm. Sir Philip Sidney. SP-SidnP *Fr.* Arcadia.

Virtue concealed within our breast. Part of the Ninth Ode of the Fourth Book of Horace. Jonathan Swift. CP-SwifJ

Virtue [*or* Vertue]. George Herbert. CP-HerbG

Virtue runs before the Muse. Loss and Gain. Ralph Waldo Emerson. CP-EmerR

Virtue, the greatest of all monarchies. Ode to the Honourable Sir William Temple. Jonathan Swift. CP-SwifJ

Virtues and Woes alike too great for man. With Fielding's *Amelia*. Samuel Taylor Coleridge. CP-ColeS

Virtues of Sid Hamet the Magician's Rod, The. Jonathan Swift. CP-SwifJ

Virtuoso, The. Stevie Smith. CP-SmitS

Virtuoso dog at midnight—wavering howl, A. Strange Song. Denise Levertov. SP-LeveDL

Virtuous Agent, The. William Carlos Williams. CP-WilW2

Virtuous girl wakes in the arms of her husband, The. Morning. Louise Glück. SP-GlucL

Virus, The. Robert Graves. CP-GravR

Virus and its hash of knobby aches, A. Plane Ticket. Robert Lowell. SP-LoweR

Visibility. Rae Armantrout. SP-ArmaA

Visible and Invisible. Helen Pinkerton. CP-PinkH

Visible, invisible. Jellyfish, A. Marianne Craig Moore. CP-MoorM

Visible sea at a distance from the shore, The. Seamus Heaney. SP-HeanSO *Fr.* Squarings.

Visible the Untrue, The. Hart Crane. CP-CranH

Vision. G. K. Chesterton. CP-ChesG

Vision. E. E. Cummings. CP-CummE

Vision. Richard Eberhart. CP-EberR

Vision. W. S. Merwin. SP-MerwWF

Vision. Robert Penn Warren. CP-WarrR

Vision, A. William Butler Yeats. All Souls' Night. CP-YeatW

Vision, A. Denise Levertov. SP-LeveDP

Vision, A. John Updike. CP-UpdiJ

Vision, A. Oscar Wilde. CP-WildO

Vision, The. Robert Burns. CP-BurnR

Vision, The. Robert Herrick. CP-HerrR

Vision, The. Robert Herrick. CP-HerrR

Vision, The. Annis Boudinot Stockton. CP-StocA

Vision and Prayer. Dylan Thomas. CP-ThomD

Vision and Prayer. Miller Williams. CP-WillM

Vision Beatific. Allen Tate. CP-TateA

Vision by Sweetwater. John Crowe Ransom. SP-RansJ

Vision is locked in stone. Lion and the Rose, The. May Sarton. SP-SartM

Vision like quanta shooting off any which way. Memory. Richard Eberhart. CP-EberR

Vision 1948. Allen Ginsberg. CP-GinsA

Vision of a haloed host, The. Ultimate. G. K. Chesterton. CP-ChesG

Vision of Belshazzar, The. Lord Byron. CP-Byron

Vision of Ben Jonson, on the Muses of His Friend M. Drayton, The. Ben Jonson. CP-JonsB

Vision of Delight, The. Ben Jonson. "Break, Fant'sy, from thy cave of cloud." CP-JonsB

Vision of Delight, The. Philip Whalen. SP-WhalP

Vision of Doom, A. Ambrose Bierce. SP-BierA

Vision of Echard, The. John Greenleaf Whittier. CP-WhitJ

Vision of Edens, A. G. K. Chesterton. CP-ChesG
   "In the ghostly virgin forests." CP-ChesG
   "In the inmost fieriest circle." CP-ChesG
   "In the mytic eastern forest." CP-ChesG
   "In the yellow mists of morning." CP-ChesG
   "Is the stern old story shattered." CP-ChesG
   "Mid the trunks and roots gigantic." CP-ChesG
   "One great plain and five great chieftains." CP-ChesG

Vision of Good Secrets, A. William Meredith. SP-MereW

Vision of Immortal Life has been fulfilled, The. Emily Dickinson. SP-DickE

Vision of Judgment, The. Lord Byron. CP-Byron

Vision of Poets, A. Elizabeth Barrett Browning. CP-BroEB

Vision of Rabbi Ben Issac, The. James Whitcomb Riley. CP-RileJ

Vision of Scotland, A. Hugh MacDiarmid. SP-MacDH

Vision of Sin, The. Alfred Tennyson. CP-TennA

Vision of Summer, A. James Whitcomb Riley. CP-RileJ

Vision of the Bodhisattvas, A. Philip Whalen. SP-WhalP

Vision of the Garden, A. James Merrill. SP-MerrJ

Vision of the Mermaids, A. Gerard Manley Hopkins. CP-HopkG

Vision of the Sea, A. Percy Bysshe Shelley. CP-ShelP

Vision of Three Angels Viewing the Progress of Socialism. Thomas McGrath. SP-McGrT

Vision Test, The. Mona Van Duyn. SP-VanDM

Vision through Timothy. Richard Eberhart. CP-EberR

Vision to Electra, The. Robert Herrick. CP-HerrR

Vision under the October Mountain: A Love Poem. Robert Penn Warren. CP-WarrR

Vision upon This Concei[p]t of the Faerie [*or* Faery] Queen[e], A. Sir Walter Ralegh. CP-RaleW *Fr.* Commendatory Verses to Edmund Spenser's Fairy Queen.

Vision will come—the Truth be revealed—but, The. Vision. Robert Penn Warren. CP-WarrR

Visionary, The. Emily Jane Brontë. CP-BronE

Visionary, The. Walter De la Mare. CP-DeLaW

Visionary and not believed. Frozen City, The. Howard Nemerov. CP-NemeH

Visionary Hope, The. Samuel Taylor Coleridge. CP-ColeS; MW-ColeS

Visions of Bellay, The. Joachim Du Bellay. CP-Spens

Visions of Daniel. Robert Pinsky. CP-PinsR

Visions of Daquqi, The. Jelaluddin Rumi. SP-Rumi, *tr. by* Coleman Barks

Visions of Mackenzie King, The. John Updike. CP-UpdiJ

Visions of Petrarch, The. Petrarch. CP-Spens

Visions of the Daughters of Albion. William Blake. CP-BlakW

Visions of the World's Vanity [*or* Vanitie]. Edmund Spenser. CP-Spens

Visit. A. R. Ammons. CP-AmmoA

Visit. Tu Fu. CP-WilW2

Visit, A. Denise Levertov. SP-LeveDL

Visit, The. Robert Creeley. SP-CreeR

Visit, The. Ralph Waldo Emerson. CP-EmerR

Visit, The. Ogden Nash. CP-NashO

Visit, The. William Carlos Williams. CP-WilW2

Visit (1). George Oppen. CP-OppGN

Visit (2). George Oppen. CP-OppGN

Visit From Dr. Fell, A. Ogden Nash. CP-NashO

Visit Home, A. William Stafford. SP-StafWW

Visit in Winter to the Temple of His Mystical Majesty, A. Tu Fu. CP-KizeC, *tr. by* Carolyn Kizer

Visit of the Gods, The. Samuel Taylor Coleridge. CP-ColeS

Visit of the Queen of Sheba, The. Yehuda Amichai. SP-AmicY, *tr. by* Stephen Mitchell

Visit to a Physicist. Dan Pagis. SP-PagiD, *tr. by* Stephen Mitchell

Visit to Aunt Francesca, A. John Ciardi. CP-CiarJ

Visit to Bill Merwin at His Hawaiian Home, A. John Logan. CP-LogaJ

Visit to Fadin. Eugenio Montale. CP-MontE, *tr. by* Jonathan Galassi

Visit to Mab, The. Nicholas Vachel Lindsay. CP-LindV

Visit to Rouen. Louis MacNeice. CP-MacNL

Visit to the Asylum, A. Edna St. Vincent Millay. CP-MillE

Visit to the Island of Lost Souls. Gregory Orr. SP-OrrG

Visit to the Painter Vladimír Komárek, A. Jaroslav Seifert. SP-SeifJ, *tr. by* Ewald Osers

Visit to Toronto, with Companions. Margaret Atwood. SP-AtwM1

Visitación! Visitación! October 17. Andrei Codrescu. SP-CodrA

Visitant. Seamus Heaney. SP-HeanSO

Visitant. Denise Levertov. SP-LeveDL

Visitant, The. Theodore Roethke. CP-RoetT

Visitation. Ai. SP-Ai

Visitation. Yusef Komunyakaa. CP-KomuY

Visitation. W. S. Merwin. SP-MerwWF

Visitation. Robert Stock. SP-StocR

Visitation, The. Robert Graves. CP-GravR

Visitations. Louis MacNeice. CP-MacNL

Visiting a Dead Man on a Summer Day. Marge Piercy. SP-PierM

Visiting Belfast at the end of June. Belfast on a Sunday Afternoon. Donald Davie. CP-DaviDC

Visiting Hour. Thomas Kinsella. CP-KinsT

Visiting Ingres. Hans Magnus Enzensberger. SP-EnzeH, *tr. by* Michael Hamburger

Visiting the Farallones. Robert Bly. SP-BlyR

Visitor, A. Mary Oliver. SP-OlivM

Visitor, The. Paul Laurence Dunbar. CP-DunbP

Visitor, The. James Laughlin. CP-LaugJ

Visitor, The. Li Po. CP-WilW2

Visitor in Marl, A. Emily Dickinson. CP-DickE

Visitors, a lost last remnant. Progress at Building Site With (Fewer) Pigeons. Amy Clampitt. CP-ClamA

Visitor's Guide to the Blue Planet, The. Miller Williams. CP-WillM

Visitors in room 8509, The. Moon of Mind Against the Wooden Louver, The. Olga Broumas. SP-BrouO

Visitors Laugh at Locksmiths or, Hospital Doors Haven't Got Locks Anyhow. Ogden Nash. CP-NashO

Visitors to the Black Belt. Langston Hughes. CP-HughL; CP-HughL2

Visits to St. Elizabeths. Elizabeth Bishop. CP-BishE

Visor'd. Walt Whitman. CP-WhitW

Vistas. Louis MacNeice. CP-MacNL

Visual Delight, A. Repent. Maxine W. Kumin. SP-KumiM

Vita. William Stafford. SP-StafWW

Vita Mea. Wallace Stevens. CP-StevWP

Vita Nuova. Stanley Kunitz. CP-KunSC

Vita Nuova. Oscar Wilde. CP-WildO

Vital Choice, The. George Meredith. CP-MerG1

Vital spark of heavenly [*or* heav'nly] flame! Ode: The Dying Christian to His Soul. Alexander Pope. CP-PopeA

Vitality. D. H. Lawrence. CP-LawrD

Vitamins and Roughage. Kenneth Rexroth. CP-RexrK

Vittoria Concluding the Opera of "Camilla." George Meredith. CP-MerG2

Vittoria's *Italia* Song. George Meredith. CP-MerG2

Vive morte ma seule saison. Samuel Beckett. CP-BeckS

Vivid and heavy, he strolls through dark brick kitchens. Composer's Winter Dream, The. Norman Dubie. CP-DubiN

Vivid in our immortal Group. Emily Dickinson. SP-DickE

Vivid to the myopic are the blue. Blue Eye, The. James Merrill. SP-MerrJ

Vividly gloomy, with bright darkling glows. Purple. Wilfred Owen. CP-OwenW

Vivitur Parvo Malè, Sed Canebat. Thomas Sheridan. CP-SherT, *tr. by* Robert Hogan

Vocabulary. Wisława Szymborska. SP-SzymW, *tr. by* Stanislaw Barańczak *and* Clare Cavanagh

Vocalism. Walt Whitman. CP-WhitW

Vocation. William Stafford. SP-StafW; SP-StafWW

Vocation: A Life: *Suite Based on Four Words from Willa Cather.* Jane Cooper. CP-CoopJ

Vocations. W. S. Merwin. SP-MerwW

Vocatus atque Non Vocatus. William Stafford. SP-StafWW

Vodka chased with coffee. Each morning. Cheers. Raymond Carver. CP-CarvR

Vodka, I hope you will note, is. John Ciardi. CP-CiarJ

Voice. W. S. Merwin. SP-MerwW

Voice, A. Margaret Atwood. SP-AtwM1

Voice, The. Charles Baudelaire. CP-BaudC, *tr. by* Walter Martin

Voice, The. Walter De la Mare. CP-DeLaW

Voice, The. Thomas Hardy. CP-HardT

Voice, The. Philip Levine. SP-LeviP

Voice, The. Theodore Roethke. CP-RoetT

Voice and Address. Michael Palmer. SP-PalmM

Voice and Violl, The. Robert Herrick. CP-HerrR

Voice flew out of the river as morning flew, A. Song: "Voice flew out of the river as morning flew, A." Muriel Rukeyser. CP-RukeM

Voice from Death, A. Walt Whitman. CP-WhitW

Voice from Leeds will rouse amain, A. Darwinians at Play. G. K. Chesterton. CP-ChesG

Voice from Pekin, A. Ambrose Bierce. SP-BierA

Voice from the Chorus, A. Aleksandr Aleksandrovich Blok. SP-BlokA, *tr. by* Peter France *and* Jon Stallworthy

Voice from the dark called out, A. Making Peace. Denise Levertov. SP-LeveDS

Voice from the Farm, A. James Whitcomb Riley. CP-RileJ

Voice from the old Hesperides. Dialogue. Marya Alexandrovna Zaturenska. SP-ZatuM

Voice from the other country, A. Voice, A. Margaret Atwood. SP-AtwM1

Voice from the Sea. Constantine P. Cavafy. CP-CavaC, *tr. by* Theoharis Constantine Theoharis

Voice from the Side of Etna, The; or, the Mad Monk. Samuel Taylor Coleridge. *See* Mad Monk, The

Voice from the Tomb (1). Stevie Smith. CP-SmitS

Voice from the Tomb (2). Stevie Smith. CP-SmitS

Voice from the Tomb (3). Stevie Smith. CP-SmitS

Voice from the Tomb (4). Stevie Smith. CP-SmitS

Voice from the Tomb (5). Stevie Smith. CP-SmitS

Voice from the World, A. Gerard Manley Hopkins. CP-HopkG

Voice from under the Table, A. Richard Wilbur. CP-WilbR

Voice grows thicker. Drunkard. Langston Hughes. CP-HughL; CP-HughL3

Voice in the Poplars, The. Jones Very. CP-VeryJ

Voice of a people suffering long. Jubilee Singers, The. John Greenleaf Whittier. CP-WhitJ

Voice of Age, The. Edwin Arlington Robinson. CP-RobiE

Voice of America. Miller Williams. CP-WillM

Voice of Freedom, The. Phillis Wheatley. CP-WheaP

Voice of God, The. Jones Very. CP-VeryJ

Voice of Jesus I. Rush singing, The. Poem Beginning "The" Louis Zukofsky. CP-ZukLS

Voice of Mankind, sing over land and sea. Hymn Exultant. James Whitcomb Riley. CP-RileJ

Voice of Nature in Youth and Age, The. Jones Very. CP-VeryJ

Voice of Peace, The. James Whitcomb Riley. CP-RileJ

Voice of Rock, The. Allen Ginsberg. CP-GinsA

Voice of St. Francis of Assisi, The. Nicholas Vachel Lindsay. CP-LindV

Voice of song from distant lands shall call, The. King of Sweden, The. William Wordsworth. CP-WorW1

Voice of the Ancient Bard, The. William Blake. CP-BlakW *Fr.* Songs of Experience.

Voice of the Banjo, The. Paul Laurence Dunbar. CP-DunbP

Voice of the Derwent, The. William Wordsworth. CP-WorW1 (Fragment: "Yet once again") CP-WorW1

Voice of the Dharma, The. Regarding Wave. Gary Snyder. CP-SnydG

Voice of the Holy Spirit, making known. Word, The. John Greenleaf Whittier. CP-WhitJ

Voice of the last cricket, The. Splinter. Carl Sandburg. CP-SandC

Voice of the Rain, The. Walt Whitman. CP-WhitW

Voice of the Thorn, The. Thomas Hardy. CP-HardT

Voice of Things, The. Thomas Hardy. CP-HardT

Voice said: "Follow, follow;" and I rose, A. Two Pursuits. Christina Georgina Rossetti. CP-RosC3

Voice said, "Hurl her down!", The. Lovely Shall Be Choosers, The. Robert Frost. CP-FrosR

Voice said, Look me in the stars, A. Question, A. Robert Frost. CP-FrosR

Voice sobs on colored sand, A. Cinque Terre. Kenneth Rexroth. CP-RexrK

Voice That Came with the Coots. Eugenio Montale. CP-MontE, *tr. by* Jonathan Galassi

Voice that spake to Abraham of old, The. Calling, The. Jones Very. CP-VeryJ

Voice that speaks when thou art in thy tomb, The. Word, The ("Voice that speaks when thou art in thy tomb, The"). Jones Very. CP-VeryJ

Voice that stands for Floods to me, The. Emily Dickinson. CP-DickE

Voice Ways. Robert Frost. CP-FrosR

Voice within my shadow wakened me, A. One Night. William Stafford. SP-StafWW

Voice You Hear When You Read Silently, The. Thomas Lux. SP-LuxT

Voiceless Child, The. Federico García Lorca. CP-GarcF, *tr. by* Alan S. Trueblood *Fr.* Back of the World.

Voiceless spirits, they who have given up, The. Hymn to the Living. Jones Very. CP-VeryJ

Voices. Constantine P. Cavafy. CP-CavaC, *tr. by* Theoharis Constantine Theoharis

Voices. G. K. Chesterton. CP-ChesG

Voices. Walter De la Mare. CP-DeLaW

Voices. Primo Levi. CP-LeviP, *tr. by* Ruth Feldman

Voices. Federico García Lorca. CP-GarcF, *tr. by* Christopher Maurer

Voices. Muriel Rukeyser. CP-RukeM

Voices. Wisława Szymborska. SP-SzymW, *tr. by* Stanisław Barańczak *and* Clare Cavanagh

Voices, The. James Laughlin. CP-LaugJ

Voices, The. James Whitcomb Riley. CP-RileJ

Voices, The. John Greenleaf Whittier. CP-WhitJ

Voices about the Princess Anemone. Stevie Smith. CP-SmitS

Voices against England in the Night. Stevie Smith. CP-SmitS

Voices crying in the wilderness. To Certain Negro Leaders. Langston Hughes. CP-HughL; CP-HughL1

Voices dispersed in the gardens long ago. Poems of Lies and Beauty. Yehuda Amichai. SP-AmicYL, *tr. by* Benjamin Harshav *and* Barbara Harshav

Voices from above and from beneath, / Voices of creation near and far, And There Was No More Sea. Christina Georgina Rossetti. CP-RosC2

Voices from dining room and hall off study. Domestic and Unavoidable. Lorine Niedecker. CP-NiedL

Voices from Lemnos. Sophocles. SP-HeanSO *Fr.* Philoctetes.

Voices from the Other World. James Merrill. SP-MerrJ

Voices from Things Growing in a Churchyard. Thomas Hardy. CP-HardT

Voices in Air. Marya Alexandrovna Zaturenska. SP-ZatuM

Voices mute for ever, or since yesterday, or just stilled; Voices. Primo Levi. CP-LeviP, *tr. by* Ruth Feldman

Voices, nicked into. Paul Celan. SP-CelaP, *tr. by* John Felstiner

Voices of death resounded. Death of Antonito el Camborio, The. Federico García Lorca. SP-GarcF, *tr. by* J. L. Gili *and* Stephen Spender

Voices of death were heard. Death of Little Tony Camborio, The. Federico García Lorca. CP-GarcF, *tr. by* Will Kirkland

Voices of Poor People. Czeslaw Milosz. CP-MiloC; CP-MiloCN

Voices of Waking. Muriel Rukeyser. CP-RukeM

Voices, such voices . . . They assail me now. Bella & Rosa. Donald Davie. CP-DaviDC

Voices to voices, lip to lip. E. E. Cummings. CP-CummE; SP-CummE

Void in Law. Elizabeth Barrett Browning. CP-BroEB

Void Only. Kenneth Rexroth. CP-RexrK

Voix Glauque. Lawrence Ferlinghetti. SP-FerlL

Vojo the night elevator man. Beautiful One, The. James Laughlin. CP-LaugJ

Vol de nuit: It's that French. Night Flight. Marge Piercy. SP-PierM

Vola, preghiera, e digli. Chiesa E Signore. Christina Georgina Rossetti. CP-RosC3

Volant Tribe of Bards on Earth Are Found, A. William Wordsworth. CP-WorW2

Volcanic Dirge & Co. Andrei Codrescu. SP-CodrA

Volcanic Venus. D. H. Lawrence. CP-LawrD

Volcano. Derek Walcott. CP-WalcD

Volcano in Kyushu, A. Gary Snyder. CP-SnydG

Volcanoes be in Sicily. Emily Dickinson. CP-DickE

Volkswagen. George Oppen. CP-OppGN

Volkswagen parked in the gap, The. Ireland. Paul Muldoon. CP-MuldP

Volpone. Ben Jonson.
  Fools. CP-JonsB
  "Had old Hippocrates, or Galen." CP-JonsB
  Song. To Celia ("Come my Celia, let us prove"). CP-JonsB; SP-JonsB, *tr. by* Ben Jonson
  To the Same [Celia]. CP-JonsB; SP-JonsB, *tr. by* Ben Jonson
  "You that would last long, list to my song." CP-JonsB

Voltaire at Ferney. W. H. Auden. CP-AudeW

Voltaire is born. Vain Life of Voltaire, The. Laura Riding Jackson. CP-RidiL

Voluble Wheel Chair, The. Ogden Nash. CP-NashO

Volume, The. Robert Pinsky. CP-PinsR

Voluntaries. Ralph Waldo Emerson. CP-EmerR

Volupté. Denise Levertov. SP-LeveDL

Volusian sheets / shit-shotten Annals. Carmen 36. Catullus. CP-ZukLS *Fr.* Carmina.

Vomit Express. Allen Ginsberg. SP-GinsA

Von Masoch met the Count de Sade. Encounter, The. Robert Graves. CP-GravR

Voortrekker, The. Rudyard Kipling. CP-KiplR

Voraciousness of that only gaze, The. Emily Dickinson. SP-DickE

Voracities and Verities Sometimes Are Interacting. Marianne Craig Moore. CP-MoorM

Votaries of Both Sexes Cry First to Venus. Stevie Smith. CP-SmitS

Voting in the Old North Church. Jones Very. CP-VeryJ

Votum. William Cowper. CP-CowpW

Vow. John Updike. CP-UpdiJ

Vow, A. Allen Ginsberg. CP-GinsA

Vow, The. Robert Graves. CP-GravR

Vow of Washington, The. John Greenleaf Whittier. CP-WhitJ

Vow to Mars, A. Robert Herrick. CP-HerrR

Vow to Minerva, A. Robert Herrick. CP-HerrR

Vow to Venus, A. Robert Herrick. CP-HerrR

Vowel Imprint. Olga Broumas. SP-BrouO

Vowels. Arthur Rimbaud. CP-RimbA, *tr. by* Martin Sorrell

Vowels ploughed into other: opened ground. Glanmore Sonnets. Seamus Heaney. SP-HeanSO

Vox Ecclesiae, Vox Christi. Dante Gabriel Rossetti. CW-RossD

Vox Humana. Thom Gunn. CP-GunnT

Voyage. Denise Levertov. SP-LeveDL

Voyage. Archibald MacLeish. CP-MacLA

Voyage. George Oppen. CP-OppGN

Voyage. Marya Alexandrovna Zaturenska. SP-ZatuM

Voyage, A. W. H. Auden. CP-AudeW

Voyage, The. Richard Eberhart. CP-EberR

Voyage Autour de Mes Cartes Postales. James Schuyler. CP-SchuJ

Voyage en Provence. Archibald MacLeish. CP-MacLA

Voyage from Stockholm to Take Advantage of Lower Prices on the Finnish Island of Åland. James Tate. SP-TateJ

Voyage of the Jettie. John Greenleaf Whittier. CP-WhitJ

Voyage of the Needle, The. James Dickey. CP-DickJ

Voyage of the "Ophir," The. George Meredith. CP-MerG2

Voyage of the soul is simply, The. Helmsman, The; an Ode. James Vincent Cunningham. CP-CunnJ

Voyage through the Low Countries, A. Two Amsterdams. Lawrence Ferlinghetti. SP-FerlL

Voyage to Arran, The. Sir Walter Scott. SP-ScotW *Fr.* Lord of the Isles, The.

Voyage to Cythera, A. Charles Baudelaire. CP-BaudC, *tr. by* Walter Martin

Voyage to the Moon. Archibald MacLeish. CP-MacLA

Voyage to the Moon. Robert Pinsky. CP-PinsR

Voyage West. Archibald MacLeish. CP-MacLA

Voyager. Carolyn Kizer. CP-KizeC

Voyager in gardens, The. Herbals. Federico García Lorca. CP-GarcF, *tr. by* Jerome Rothenberg

Voyager returned, but much perplexed, The. Who Did Not Die in Vain. Howard Nemerov. CP-NemeH

Voyager Takes Pause, A. Robert Stock. SP-StocR

Voyagers Song. Henry David Thoreau. CP-ThorH

Voyages. Hart Crane. CP-CranH

Voyages. Amy Clampitt. CP-ClamA

Voyages, The. Gregory Orr. SP-OrrG

Voyages always beginning, always ending, The. Departure of the Ships. Howard Nemerov. CP-NemeH

Voyageurs / sang, rowed. Lorine Niedecker. CP-NiedL

Voyeur. Czeslaw Milosz. CP-MiloCN, *tr. by* Robert Hass

Voyeur, The. Yehuda Amichai. SP-AmicYL, *tr. by* Benjamin Harshav *and* Barbara Harshav

Voyeur, The. Mona Van Duyn. SP-VanDM

Voznesensky's "Silent Tingling." Allen Ginsberg. CP-GinsA

V.R. 1819–1901. Thomas Hardy. CP-HardT

Vron Woods (North Wales), The. Denise Levertov. SP-LeveDL

Vsion of Labor, A: 1931. William Carlos Williams. CP-WilW2

Vuccerìa. James Fenton. SP-FentJ

Vulcan. George Oppen. CP-OppGN

Vulcan begat me. Minerva me taught. Sir Thomas Wyatt. CP-WyatT

Vulgar Nocturne. Arthur Rimbaud. CP-RimbA, *tr. by* Martin Sorrell

Vulgarised. G. K. Chesterton. CP-ChesG

Vulnerant Omnes, Ultima Necat. Constantine P. Cavafy. CP-CavaC, *tr. by* Theoharis Constantine Theoharis

Vulture. Robinson Jeffers. CP-JefR3

Vulture, The. Samuel Beckett. CP-BeckS *Fr.* Echo's Bones.

Vulture Peak: Gridhakuta Hill. Allen Ginsberg. CP-GinsA

Vultures. Margaret Atwood. SP-AtwM2

Vultures. Mary Oliver. SP-OlivM

Vultures at the zoo, The. Rain or Shine. Charles Bukowski. SP-BukC1

Vying is our trouble. Donald Davie. CP-DaviDC

W

W. E. B. DuBois at Harvard. Jay Wright. SP-WrigJ

W. H. *Eheu!*. Samuel Taylor Coleridge. CP-ColeS

W.H.W., Jr. E. E. Cummings. CP-CummE

W. S. Landor. Marianne Craig Moore. CP-MoorM

Waddling / madam star, The. E. E. Cummings. CP-CummE

Wade all life / backward to its / source which / runs too far / ahead. Next Year or I Fly My Rounds Tempestuous. Lorine Niedecker. CP-NiedL

Wade / through black jade. Fish, The. Marianne Craig Moore. CP-MoorM

Wadin' in de Crick. Paul Laurence Dunbar. CP-DunbP

Wading at Wellfleet. Elizabeth Bishop. CP-BishE

Wae Is My Heart. Robert Burns. CP-BurnR

Wae worth thy pow'r, thou cursed leaf! Lines Written on a Bank-Note. Robert Burns. CP-BurnR

Wafflebutt. John Ciardi. CP-CiarJ

Wage-Slaves, The. Rudyard Kipling. CP-KiplR

Wager, The. George Crabbe. SP-CrabG *Fr.* Tales.

Wages. Robert Herrick. CP-HerrR

Wages. D. H. Lawrence. CP-LawrD

Wages of Eloquence, The. Laura Riding Jackson. CP-RidiL

Wagging their hoary heads, glaring through their bright spectacles. Miching Mallecho. Robinson Jeffers. CP-JefR3

Waggoner, The. William Wordsworth. CP-WorW1

Wagner gave six concerts: five. Impromptu on Richard Wagner. Robert Browning. CP-BroR2

Wagon had stopped, facing from the sea, The. Idiot, The. Yannis Ritsos. SP-RitsY, *tr. by* Kimon Friar

Wagon trails stopped here, ditched, The. Tucson Gardens. Eleanor Wilner. SP-WilnE

Wagon Wheel Gap is a place I never saw. Localities. Carl Sandburg. CP-SandC

Wagons. A. R. Ammons. CP-AmmoA

Wagtail and Baby. Thomas Hardy. CP-HardT

Wagtail, The. Theodore Roethke. CP-RoetT

Waies, through which my weary steps I guyde, The. Book 6. Edmund Spenser. CP-Spens *Fr.* Faerie Queene, The.

Wail. Dorothy Parker. CP-ParkD

Wailing of a flute, a little drum. In Music. Czeslaw Milosz. CP-MiloCN, *tr. by* Robert Hass

Wain upon the northern steep, The. Astronomy. A. E. Housman. CP-HousA

Wait. Langston Hughes. CP-HughL; CP-HughL1

Wait. David Ignatow. SP-IgnaD

Wait. Galway Kinnell. SP-KinnGN

Wait. James Whitcomb Riley. CP-RileJ

Wait, The. Rainer Maria Rilke. CP-RilkFr, *tr. by* A. Poulin, Jr.

Wait for Me. Robert Creeley. CP-CreeR

Wait for Me. James Tate. SP-TateJ

Wait, for now. Wait. Galway Kinnell. SP-KinnGN

Wait for the morning:—it will come, indeed. James Whitcomb Riley. CP-RileJ

"Wait. Let me think a minute," you said. Wit, The. Elizabeth Bishop. CP-BishE

Wait Mister. Which way is home? Music Swims Back to Me. Anne Sexton. CP-SextA; SP-SextA

Wait not till I invite thee, but observe. Henry David Thoreau. CP-ThorH

Wait not till slaves pronounce the word. Henry David Thoreau. CP-ThorH

"Wait, prithee, wait!" this answer Lesbia threw. To ———: " 'Wait, prithee, wait!' this answer Lesbia threw." William Wordsworth. CP-WorW2

Wait till the Majesty of Death. Emily Dickinson. CP-DickE

Wait. / Wait. / Wait. Murder of Two Men by a Young Kid Wearing Lemon-colored Gloves, The. Kenneth Patchen. CP-PatcK

Waiter dropped a tray of glassware and, The. Spilled. Heather McHugh. SP-McHuH

Waiter in a California Vietnamese Restaurant. Clarence Major. SP-MajoC

Waiter waited, the cook ate, The. What Happened? What Do You Expect? Alan Dugan. CP-DugaA

Waiters' Ballet, The. James Laughlin. CP-LaugJ

Waiters / 'gliding' / with the accuracy. Ship's Waiters. Charles Tomlinson. CP-TomlC

Waitin' fer the Cat to Die. James Whitcomb Riley. CP-RileJ

Waiting. Raymond Carver. CP-CarvR

Waiting ("He pushes behind the words"). Robert Creeley. CP-CreeR

Waiting ("Were you counting the days"). Robert Creeley. SP-CreeR

Waiting. Walter De la Mare. CP-DeLaW

Waiting. Paul Laurence Dunbar. CP-DunbP

Waiting. Robert Frost. CP-FrosR

Waiting. Primo Levi. CP-LeviP, *tr. by* Ruth Feldman *and* Brian Swann

Waiting. Robert Pinsky. CP-PinsR

Waiting. Carl Sandburg. CP-SandC

Waiting. Robert Penn Warren. CP-WarrR

Waiting. William Carlos Williams. CP-WilW1

Waiting, The. John Greenleaf Whittier. CP-WhitJ

Waiting behind the cyclone fence. Exchange Student Awaits the Arrival of an African Princess, An. Yusef Komunyakaa. CP-KomuY

Waiting Both. Thomas Hardy. CP-HardT

Waiting Can Be Pretty Lousy. Kenneth Patchen. CP-PatcK

Waiting for a bus. Peace ("Waiting for a bus"). Robert Creeley. CP-CreeR

Waiting for a Bus "en Frente de la Iglesia." Robert Creeley. SP-CreeR

Waiting for a Tree through a Window. Yusef Komunyakaa. CP-KomuY

Waiting for Breakfast, While She Brushed Her Hair. Philip Larkin. CP-LarkP

Waiting for Ed to log on. Lines Written After Reading Frank O'Hara's "A Step Away from Them." William Corbett. SP-CorbW

Waiting for her in some small park. Justin. Thom Gunn. CP-GunnT

Waiting for Icarus. Muriel Rukeyser. CP-RukeM

Waiting for the Barbarians. Constantine P. Cavafy. CP-CavaC, *tr. by* Theoharis Constantine Theoharis

Waiting for the Chariot. Carl Sandburg. CP-SandC

Waiting for the Light. James Laughlin. CP-LaugJ

Waiting for the Paper to be Delivered. Miller Williams. CP-WillM

Waiting for Tu Fu. Charles Wright. SP-WrigCN

Waiting for when the sun an hour or less. In Santa Maria del Popolo. Thom Gunn. CP-GunnT

Waiting Head, The. Anne Sexton. CP-SextA

Waiting in Line. William Stafford. SP-StafW; SP-StafWW

Waiting in the Children's Hospital. Clarence Major. SP-MajoC

Waiting on the Corners. Donald Hall. CP-HallD

Waiting Rooms. John Updike. CP-DickE

Waiting Rooms. Howard Nemerov. CP-NemeH

Waiting / Seems to be most of everything. For Judith. John Ciardi. CP-CiarJ

Waiting To Lean to the Master's Command. Richard Eberhart. CP-EberR

Waiting to leave all day I hear the words. Gates, The. Muriel Rukeyser. CP-RukeM

Waiting to see if. Apocalypse Now. Robert Creeley. SP-CreeR

Waitress. Thom Gunn. CP-GunnT

Waitress. Karl Shapiro. SP-ShapK

Waitress, The. Billy Collins. SP-CollB

Wake. Langston Hughes. CP-HughL; CP-HughL2

Wake, The. Robert Herrick. CP-HerrR

Wake early to the early robin. Spring Song ("Wake early to the early robin"). John Ciardi. CP-CiarJ

Wake, friend, from forth thy lethargy; the drum. Epistle to a Friend, to Persuade [*or* Perswade] Him to the Wars [*or* Warres], An. Ben Jonson. CP-JonsB; SP-JonsB

Wake not for the world-heard thunder. A. E. Housman. CP-HousA

Wake on the train. Sheep Clouds. W. S. Merwin. SP-MerwWF

Wake! Our mirth begins to die. Ben Jonson. CP-JonsB *Fr.* Poetaster, The.

Wake, sisters, wake! the day-star shines. Hymn of the Dunkers. John Greenleaf Whittier. CP-WhitJ

Wake the serpent not—lest he. Fragment: "Wake the serpent not—lest he." Percy Bysshe Shelley. CP-ShelP

Wake: the silver dusk returning. Reveille. A. E. Housman. CP-HousA

Wake Up. Raymond Carver. CP-CarvR

Wake up. Things to Do in Tokyo. Robert Creeley. SP-CreeR

Wake up high up. Things To Do in New York (City). Ted Berrigan. SP-BerrT

Wake Up/Ring Out. Federico García Lorca. CP-GarcF, *tr. by* Jerome Rothenberg *Fr.* In the Garden of the Lunar Grapefruits.

Wakeful I think upon the suffering race. Freedmen of the Mississippi Valley, The. Jones Very. CP-VeryJ

Waken, lords and ladies gay. Hunting Song. Sir Walter Scott. SP-ScotW

Wakened lover speaks directly to the beloved, The. I Have Five Things to Say. Jelaluddin Rumi. SP-RumiJ, *tr. by* Coleman Barks

Wakening at noon I smelled airplanes and hay. Sonnet for Jane Freilicher, A. Frank O'Hara. SP-OharF

Wakening with the window over fields. Poem: "Wakening with the window over fields." Charles Tomlinson. CP-TomlC

Wakes that boats make, The. Ways, The. Louis Zukofsky. CP-ZukLS

Wakes wet; is promptly toileted. One-Year-Old, The. John Updike. CP-UpdiJ

Waking. Josephine Jacobsen. CP-JacoJ

Waking. Archibald MacLeish. CP-MacLA

Waking. James Tate. SP-TateJ

Waking, The. Galway Kinnell. SP-KinnGN

Waking, The. Theodore Roethke. CP-RoetT

Waking, The. Arthur Sze. SP-SzeA

Waking Alone. Anne Sexton. CP-SextA

Waking alone in a multitude of loves when morning's light. On the Marriage of a Virgin. Dylan Thomas. CP-ThomD

Waking an Angel. Philip Levine. SP-LeviP

Waking at 3 A.M. William Stafford. SP-StafWW

Waking before sunrise, in a house not my own. Mesopotamia. Raymond Carver. CP-CarvR

Waking Dream, A. Thom Gunn. CP-GunnT

Waking Dream about a Lost Child. William Meredith. SP-MereW

Waking each day, always. King of the Earthworms, The. Gregory Orr. SP-OrrG

Waking Early Sunday Morning. Robert Lowell. SP-LoweR

Waking Father, The. Paul Muldoon. CP-MuldP

Waking from a Dream. Miller Williams. CP-WillM

Waking from a Nap on the Beach. May Swenson. SP-SwenM

Waking from Sleep. Robert Bly. SP-BlyR

Waking half-drunk in a strange pad. North Beach Alba. Gary Snyder. CP-SnydG

Waking, he found himself in a train, andante. Slow Movement. Louis MacNeice. CP-MacNL

Waking / I was eating pears! Fruit, The. William Carlos Williams. CP-WilW2

Waking in a Newly Built House. Thom Gunn. CP-GunnT

Waking in New York. Allen Ginsberg. CP-GinsA

Waking in the Blue. Robert Lowell. SP-LoweR

Waking in the Dark. Adrienne Rich. SP-RicA1; SP-RicA2

Waking in Winter. Sylvia Plath. CP-PlatS

Waking into Sleep. Kenneth Patchen. CP-PatcK

Waking Jed. C. K. Williams. CP-WillC; SP-WillC

Waking late, still inside a humid. Virginia Backyard: July. Gregory Orr. SP-OrrG

Waking on the Seventh Day of Creation. Sabbath, The. W. H. Auden. CP-AudeW

Waking one morning / we cannot find. New Animals. Donald Hall. CP-HallD

Waking outside his Babylonian binge. Thousandth Poem for Dylan Thomas, A. John Ciardi. CP-CiarJ

Waking thickheaded by crow's light. Continuum. Adrienne Rich. CP-RicAE

Waking this Morning. Muriel Rukeyser. See This Morning

Waking to all that white, as week by week. Resumption, Or Possibly a Remission, A. Amy Clampitt. CP-ClamA

Waking to silence. Goodbye. Philip Levine. SP-LeviP

Waking to Tap of Hammer. Robert Penn Warren. CP-WarrR

Waking Up. Jorge Luis Borges. SP-BorgJ, tr. by Alastair Reid

Waking Up. Robert Pinsky. CP-PinsR

Waking up in my curtain-dark bedroom, I hear. Waking to Tap of Hammer. Robert Penn Warren. CP-WarrR

Waking up over the candy store together. First Early Mornings Together. Robert Pinsky. CP-PinsR

Waking was laughing then. Grammar Lesson. Stanley Kunitz. CP-KunSC

Waking Who Knows. George Oppen. CP-OppGN

Wal, Thanksgivin' do be comin' round. Ezra on the Strike. Ezra Pound. CP-PoEar

Waldeinsamkeit. Ralph Waldo Emerson. CP-EmerR

Walden. Henry David Thoreau. CP-ThorH

Walden 1950. Adrienne Rich. CP-RicAE

Walden Pond's crowded this Saturday afternoon, cars backed up to the main highway. Frontispiece. Yusef Komunyakaa. CP-KomuY

Wales. Derek Walcott. CP-WalcD

Wales Visitation. Allen Ginsberg. CP-GinsA; SP-GinsA

Walgh-Vogel, The. Richard Wilbur. CP-WilbR

Walk, A. Raymond Carver. CP-CarvR

Walk, A. G. K. Chesterton. CP-ChesG

Walk, A. Gary Snyder. CP-SnydG

Walk, The. Thomas Hardy. CP-HardT

Walk, The. Seamus Heaney. SP-HeanSO

Walk, The. James Schuyler. CP-SchuJ

Walk, The. Derek Walcott. CP-WalcD

Walk After Dark, A. W. H. Auden. CP-AudeW

Walk by the Charles, A. Adrienne Rich. CP-RicAE; SP-RicA2

Walk high on the bridge of Estador. Bridge of Estador, The. Hart Crane. CP-CranH

Walk in Harmony Grove, A. Jones Very. CP-VeryJ

Walk in Late Summer, A. Theodore Roethke. CP-RoetT

Walk in the Country, A. William Stafford. SP-StafWW

Walk in the Pastures, A. Jones Very. CP-VeryJ

Walk in this faithless grass with studious tread. Cold Pastoral. Allen Tate. CP-TateA

Walk on the delicate parts. Foot-Note, A. William Carlos Williams. CP-WilW1

Walk on the Water. Olga Broumas. SP-BrouO

Walk quietly around in. Ars Poetica. Donald Davie. CP-DaviDC

Walk right in / sit right down. Things To Do in Anne's Room. Ted Berrigan. SP-BerrT

Walk softly on my grave. Address, An. William Carlos Williams. CP-WilW2

Walk There. David Ignatow. SP-IgnaD

Walk through the Notebooks, A. Denise Levertov. SP-LeveDP

Walk to the well. Jelaluddin Rumi. SP-Rumi, tr. by Coleman Barks

Walk-up. W. S. Merwin. SP-MerwW

Walk Warily. D. H. Lawrence. CP-LawrD

Walk with Tom Jefferson, A. Philip Levine. SP-LeviP

Walked in the swamp. His cheek vermilion. Camoufleur. May Swenson. SP-SwenM

Walker. Alice Walker. CP-WalkA

Walkers with the Dawn. Langston Hughes. CP-HughL; CP-HughL1

Walking. Robert Creeley. CP-CreeR

Walking. Philip Whalen. SP-WhalP

Walking about the emptied house I. Measured Tread, A. Donald Davie. CP-DaviDC

Walking across the Atlantic. Billy Collins. SP-CollB

Walking After Supper. Miller Williams. CP-WillM

Walking along a beach on St. George Island. Woman with Dog. Miller Williams. CP-WillM

Walking along a street in a neighborhood. Housing. Grace Paley. CP-PalGC

Walking along Elm Road. Turn, The. Philip Whalen. SP-WhalP

Walking [or Talking] along in this not quite prose way. Near. William Stafford. SP-StafW; SP-StafWW

Walking around in the park. Toads Revisited. Philip Larkin. CP-LarkP

Walking around on our first day. Hat, The. Raymond Carver. CP-CarvR

Walking at night on asphalt campus. Death News. Allen Ginsberg. CP-GinsA

Walking away means. Purifying the Language of the Tribe. William Stafford. SP-StafW; SP-StafWW

Walking back to the farm from the depot. Table, The. Donald Hall. CP-HallD

Walking Basil. William Corbett. SP-CorbW

Walking beside a pile of unsorted keys. Apples. W. S. Merwin. SP-MerwWF

Walking beside the Kamogawa, Remembering Nansen and Fudo and Gary's Poem. Philip Whalen. SP-WhalP

Walking by lakeshore, feet in slush, it rains. Four Auguries. Margaret Atwood. SP-AtwM1

Walking by map, I chose unwonted ground. On the Hall at Stowey. Charles Tomlinson. CP-TomlC; SP-TomlC

Walking Chapultepec. Jay Wright. SP-WrigJ

Walking down a / walk, a stone. Pay. Robert Creeley. CP-CreeR

Walking down / backward, wall. Tiny Place, A. Robert Creeley. CP-CreeR

Walking down Madison, I suddenly stopped. Stared. Somewhere. Robert Penn Warren. CP-WarrR

Walking Down Westgate in the Fall. Howard Nemerov. CP-NemeH

Walking Home after the First Encounter. Gregory Orr. SP-OrrG

Walking Home at Night. Allen Ginsberg. CP-GinsA

Walking in a mountain meadow toward the north slope. Mushroom Hunting in the Jemez Mountains. Arthur Sze. SP-SzeA

Walking in February. Thin Ice. Gary Snyder. CP-SnydG

Walking in Paris. Anne Sexton. CP-SextA; SP-SextA

Walking in the flat Oxfordshire fields. Subjected Earth. Robinson Jeffers. CP-JefR2

Walking in the sky. Stephen Crane. CP-CranS

Walking in the Woods. Grace Paley. CP-PalGC

Walking into Autumn. W. S. Merwin. SP-MerwWF

Walking into Love. Marge Piercy. SP-PierM

Walking Man of Rodin, The. Carl Sandburg. CP-SandC

Walking north toward the point, I come on a dead seal. Dead Seal [near McClure's Beach], The. Robert Bly. SP-BlyR

Walking of the first wayfarer, The. Ode and Elegy of the Roads. Constantine P. Cavafy. CP-CavaC, tr. by Theoharis Constantine Theoharis

Walking / off street. Ciano's. Robert Creeley. SP-CreeR

Walking on the River Ice. Wendell Berry. CP-BerrW

Walking on Water. James Dickey. CP-DickJ

Walking one day in the park in winter. In the Park. Stevie Smith. CP-SmitS

Walking Song. Ivor Gurney. SP-GurnI

Walking street back here. Evening. Robert Creeley. SP-CreeR

Walking Swiftly. Robert Bly. SP-BlyR

Walking swiftly with a dreadful duchess. Infelice. Stevie Smith. CP-SmitS

Walking the Borders. William Stafford. SP-StafWW

Walking the Dog. Robert Creeley. CP-CreeR

Walking the Dog: A Diatribe. Mona Van Duyn. SP-VanDM

Walking the field. Acapulco. George Oppen. CP-OppGN

Walking the Fire Line. James Dickey. CP-DickJ

Walking the square in a tree-thick mountain town. For J. William Fulbright on the Day of His Death. Miller Williams. CP-WillM

Walking the village street, to watch the stars and find. Battalion Is Now On Rest, The. Ivor Gurney. SP-GurnI

Walking these woods and these unfriendly ways. Petrarch. CP-Petra, tr. by J. G. Nichols

Walking this field I remember. Premonition, The. Theodore Roethke. CP-RoetT

Walking thru twisted hollow pathways. Peter Blue Cloud. SP-BlueP

Walking to Bells. Charles Tomlinson. CP-TomlC

Walking to Sleep. Richard Wilbur. CP-WilbR

Walking to Work. Frank O'Hara. SP-OharF

Walking up from the barn to the house. Mara. Robinson Jeffers. CP-JefR3

Walking West. William Stafford. SP-StafWW

Walking with a virgin heart. Hills of May, The. Robert Graves. CP-GravR

Walking with Angels. Robert Stock. SP-StocR

Walking with you and another lady. Dream of Jealousy, A. Seamus Heaney. SP-HeanSO

Walks. W. H. Auden. CP-AudeW

Walks. Charles Tomlinson. SP-TomlC

Walks of our age, The. Walks. Charles Tomlinson. SP-TomlC

Wall. Gabriela Mistral. SP-MistG, *tr. by* Maria Giachetti [*or* Jacketti]

Wall, A. Robert Creeley. CP-CreeR

Wall, A. Charles Simic. SP-SimiC; SP-SimiCE

Wall, The. Robert Graves. CP-GravR

Wall, The. Yusef Komunyakaa. CP-KomuY

Wall, The. Louis MacNeice. CP-MacNL

Wall, The. Anne Sexton. CP-SextA

Wall, a bastion, A. St Luke. D. H. Lawrence. CP-LawrD

Wall, as I watched, came neck-high, The. Girl, The. William Carlos Williams. CP-WilW2

Wall Calender. Dan Pagis. SP-PagiD, *tr. by* Stephen Mitchell

Wall, Cave, and Pillar Statements, after Asōka. Alan Dugan. CP-DugaA

Wall is yellow, The. Yannis Ritsos. SP-RitsY *Fr.* Paper Poems 1.

Wall of a Museum, The. Czeslaw Milosz. CP-MiloCN, *tr. by* Robert Hass

Wall / one's up against, The. Robert Creeley. CP-CreeR

Wall Shadows. Carl Sandburg. CP-SandC

Wall street aflame, strategic police stations. Bicentennial. Robert Penn Warren. CP-WarrR

Wall was white, whitewash lime, The. Up against It. Eleanor Wilner. SP-WilnE

Wallabout Martyrs, The. Walt Whitman. CP-WhitW

Wallace Stevens Remembers Halloween. Wyatt Prunty. SP-PrunW

Wallace Stevens, what's he done? Rouse for Stevens, A. Theodore Roethke. CP-RoetT

Walled-in yard, a tree, a bit of sun in the morning hours on the wall, A. Prison Tree and the Women, The. Yannis Ritsos. SP-RitsY, *tr. by* Kimon Friar

Wallet stolen, so we must end our stay. Note of Thanks, A. Wyatt Prunty. SP-PrunW

Wallflower. Anne Sexton. CP-SextA

Wallflowers leaping on slope facing southeast. Late Snow. W. S. Merwin. SP-MerwWF

Wallowing in this bloody sty. Drunken Fisherman, The. Robert Lowell. SP-LoweR

Walls. Constantine P. Cavafy. CP-CavaC, *tr. by* Theoharis Constantine Theoharis

Walls. Robert Creeley. CP-CreeR

Walls. Langston Hughes. CP-HughL; CP-HughL2

Walls, The. Charles Bukowski. SP-BukC3

Walls and the dome of the evening, The. Earth's Festival, The ("Walls and the dome of the evening, The"). G. K. Chesterton. CP-ChesG

Walls constituting our / access to the property—, The. Way. Robert Creeley. CP-CreeR

Walls Do Not Fall, The. "H. D." CP-DoolH

Walls, except that they stretch through China. Variations on Pasternak's "Mein Liebchen, Was Willst Du Noch Mehr?" Frank O'Hara. SP-OharF

Walls, from its looted stones, defend. At the Hill Fort. Charles Tomlinson. CP-TomlC

Walls have been shaded for so many years, The. Soldier Walks under the Trees of the University, The. Randall Jarrell. CP-JarrR

Walls hold each other up when they meet. In a Corner. William Stafford. SP-StafWW

Walls join hands and, The. Present, The. W. S. Merwin. SP-MerwW

Walls, mounds, enclosing corrugations. Castle, The. Robert Graves. CP-GravR

Walls were thin, and when he left, The. Wedding Stop, The. Wyatt Prunty. SP-PrunW

Walnut, hickory, beechmast. Pig-song. Denise Levertov. SP-LeveDL

Walnut Tree. Rainer Maria Rilke. CP-RilkFr, *tr. by* A. Poulin, Jr.

Walpole talks of "a man and his price." Rudyard Kipling. *See* By the Laws of the Family Circle 'tis written in letters of brass

Walpole, traveling in the Alps. L'Inglese. John Ciardi. CP-CiarJ

Walrus stretches forth a wrinkled hand, The. Kingfisher's Boxing Gloves, The. James Fenton. SP-FentJ

Walt. Ted Hughes. SP-HughTN

Walt Whitman. "Rubén Dario." SP-DariR, *tr. by* Alberto Acereda *and* Will Derusha

Walt Whitman in the Civil War Hospitals. David Ignatow. SP-IgnaD

Walt Whitman noticed a group of them. Flies. Galway Kinnell. SP-KinnGN

Walt Whitman took the Earth to bed. Instances. John Ciardi. CP-CiarJ

Walt Whitman's Brain Dropped on Laboratory Floor. Thomas Lux. SP-LuxT

Walt, you shangied me to this. Kosmos. Yusef Komunyakaa. CP-KomuY

Walter Armistead. James Dickey. CP-DickJ

Walter Jenks' Bath. William Meredith. SP-MereW

Walter Rawley [*or* Ralegh *or* Rawely] of the Middle Temple, in Commendation of the Steel[e] Glass[e]. Sir Walter Ralegh. *See* In Commendation of George Gascoigne's Steel Glass

Walter Scott. James Schuyler. CP-SchuJ

Walton-on-the-Naze. G. K. Chesterton. CP-ChesG

Waltz, The. Lord Byron. CP-Byron

Waltz in the Branches. Federico García Lorca. CP-GarcF, *tr. by* Greg Simon *and* Steven F. White

Waltzer in the House, The. Stanley Kunitz. CP-KunSC

Wan enormous head bowed beside the hollow tree, The. Dream, The: A Reflection on Morris Graves's Paintings. John Logan. CP-LogaJ

Wan new garment of young green, A. Last Masquerade, The. G. K. Chesterton. CP-ChesG

Wan sky greener than the lawn, A. Vanity. G. K. Chesterton. CP-ChesG

Wan / Swan. Bereaved Swan, The. Stevie Smith. CP-SmitS

Wan-voiced, / flayed from the depths. Paul Celan. SP-CelaP, *tr. by* John Felstiner

Wand, The. Robert Graves. CP-GravR

Wand of gold from the reaper's moon, A. George Meredith. CP-MerG2

Wanda. Czeslaw Milosz. CP-MiloCN, *tr. by* Robert Hass

Wanda Telakowska (1905–1985), once a popular figure in artistic Warsaw. Wanda. Czeslaw Milosz. CP-MiloCN, *tr. by* Robert Hass

Wanda's Blues. Jane Cooper. CP-CoopJ

Wanda's daddy was a railroadman, she was his little wife. Wanda's Blues. Jane Cooper. CP-CoopJ

Wander, spirit?—I!. Which Way? Walter De la Mare. CP-DeLaW

Wander through expensive party not for me. Dream. Philip Whalen. SP-WhalP

Wander, you may wander. Sir John Mandeville and I Sat Up Talking. Robert Stock. SP-StocR

Wanderbush, you snare. Paul Celan. SP-CelaP, *tr. by* John Felstiner

Wanderer, A. Denise Levertov. SP-LeveDL

Wanderer, A. Adam Zagajewski. SP-ZagaA, *tr. by* Renata Gorczynski

Wanderer, The. W. H. Auden. CP-AudeW

Wanderer, The. Thomas Hardy. CP-HardT

Wanderer, The. Seamus Heaney. SP-HeanSO

Wanderer, The. Denise Levertov. SP-LeveDS

Wanderer, The. Stevie Smith. CP-SmitS

Wanderer Awaiting Preferment, The. William Stafford. SP-StafWW

Wanderer comes at last, A. Spirits Appeased, The. Denise Levertov. SP-LeveDS

Wanderer in our skies. Voyage to the Moon. Archibald MacLeish. CP-MacLA

Wanderer moon / smiling a. Summer Song. William Carlos Williams. CP-WilW1

Wanderer! that stoop'st so low, and com'st so near. To the Moon (Composed by the Seaside,—on the Coast of Cumberland). William Wordsworth. CP-WorW2

Wanderer, The: A Rococo Study. William Carlos Williams. CP-WilW1

Wanderer's Daysong. Denise Levertov. SP-LeveDL

Wanderers, The. Walter De la Mare. CP-DeLaW

Wanderers of the Pale Wood. Kenneth Patchen. CP-PatcK

Wandering among the chimneys. Gentle Negress, The. William Carlos Williams. CP-WilW2

Wandering at Morn. Walt Whitman. CP-WhitW

Wandering Cosmos, The. D. H. Lawrence. CP-LawrD

Wandering gadling in the summer tide, The. Sir Thomas Wyatt. CP-WyatT

Wandering in the dusk. Dusk. Langston Hughes. CP-HughL; CP-HughL2

Wandering Jew, The. James Whitcomb Riley. CP-RileJ

Wandering Jew, The. Edwin Arlington Robinson. CP-RobiE

Wandering Jew and the Heavenly Hosts, The. Robert Stock. SP-StocR

Wandering Jew's Soliloquy, The. Percy Bysshe Shelley. CP-ShelP

Wandering oversea dreamer. Prayer after World War. Carl Sandburg. CP-SandC

Wandering Scholar's Prayer to St. Catherine of Egypt, The. James Vincent Cunningham. CP-CunnJ

Wandering through cold streets tangled like old string. Brussels in Winter. W. H. Auden. CP-AudeW

Wandering Willie. George Meredith. CP-MerG2

Wandering world of rivers, A. Trinkets, The. G. K. Chesterton. CP-ChesG

Wanderings of Cain, The. Samuel Taylor Coleridge. CP-ColeS

Wanderings of Oisin, The. William Butler Yeats. CP-YeatW

Wanderings of the Tribe, The. Alí Chumacero. CP-WilW2

Wanderlust. Dorothy Parker. CP-ParkD

Wang Wei. Arthur Sze. SP-SzeA

Waning moon looks upward; this grey night, The. Nostalgia. D. H. Lawrence.

CP-LawrD

Waning Moon, The. Percy Bysshe Shelley. CP-ShelP

Wansfell! This Household Has a Favoured Lot. William Wordsworth. CP-WorW2

Want. Robert Herrick. CP-HerrR

Want Bone, The. Robert Pinsky. CP-PinsR

Want is a softer Wax, that takes thereon. Want. Robert Herrick. CP-HerrR

Want of Peace, The. Wendell Berry. CP-BerrW

Want to Be Whur Mother Is. James Whitcomb Riley. CP-RileJ

Want to trade me, do you, mistah? Oh, well, now, I reckon not. Dat Ol' Mare o' Mine. Paul Laurence Dunbar. CP-DunbP

Wanta / spendsix / dollars Kid. E. E. Cummings. CP-CummE

Wanting a Soul in the South. W. S. Merwin. SP-MerwW

Wanting I send you certain poems. Guido Cavalcanti. CP-CavaG, tr. by Marc Cirigliano

Wanting is—what? Robert Browning. CP-BroR2; SP-BroR

Wanting the Impossible. Carl Sandburg. CP-SandC

Wanting throat crown narcissus proves. Snowflake. Louis Zukofsky. CP-ZukLS

Wanting to Die. Anne Sexton. CP-SextA; SP-SextA

Wanting to save their fortunes for. Usurers of Heaven, The. William Carlos Williams. CP-WilW2

Wanting You. Robert Creeley. CP-CreeR

Wanton and lascivious eye. A. Eye, The. Robert Herrick. CP-HerrR

Wanton troopers riding by, The. Nymph Complaining for the Death of Her Faun [or Fawn], The. Andrew Marvell. CP-MarvA

Wanton Wenches doe not bring. To His Girles. Robert Herrick. CP-HerrR

Wantons we are; and though our words be such. Poets. Robert Herrick. CP-HerrR

Wants. Philip Larkin. CP-LarkP

Wants my son. White Lady. Lucille Clifton. SP-ClifL

Wap and rowe, wap and row. Reel o' Stumpie, The. Robert Burns. CP-BurnR

Wapiti, The. Ogden Nash. CP-NashO

War. Langston Hughes. CP-HughL; CP-HughL3

War. George Meredith. CP-MerG2

War. Lorine Niedecker. CP-NiedL

War. Grace Paley.

War. Arthur Rimbaud. CP-RimbA, tr. by Martin Sorrell

War. C. K. Williams. SP-WillC

War, A. Randall Jarrell. CP-JarrR

War, The. W. S. Merwin. SP-MerwW

War, The. Jones Very. CP-VeryJ

War against the Trees, The. Stanley Kunitz. CP-KunSC

War & Peace. Andrei Codrescu. SP-CodrA

War & Peace. Robert Creeley. SP-CreeR

War and Peace. Miller Williams. CP WillM

War and Silence. Robert Bly. SP-BlyR

War-Baby. D. H. Lawrence. CP-LawrD

War brings increase of crime; itself a sin. On the Increase in Crime Since the Late Civil War. Jones Very. CP-VeryJ

War broke: and now the Winter of the world. 1914. Wilfred Owen. CP-OwenW

War broke out in autumn, in the no-man's land. Yehuda Amichai. SP-AmicYL, tr. by Barbara Harshav and Benjamin Harshav Fr. Poems of the Land of Zion and Jerusalem.

War broke out in the fall, at the empty border. Yehuda Amichai. SP-AmicY, tr. by Chana Bloch Fr. Songs of Zion the Beautiful.

War chief danced the old way, The. At the Klamath Berry Festival. William Stafford. CP-StafWW

War Comes into my Room, The. Muriel Rukeyser. CP-RukeM

War Criminal. Donald Davie. CP-DaviDC

War Duty. Alan Dugan. CP-DugaA

War ends, and he's returning. Wife and Another, A. Thomas Hardy. CP-HardT

War games are over, The. We'll to the Woods No More, the Laurels Are Cut Down. May Sarton. SP-SartM

War God, The. Stephen Spender. CP-SpenS

War-Guilt Trials. Robinson Jeffers. CP-JefR3

War is a fevered god. Telesila. "H. D." CP-DoolH

War is far away, sweet, The. Sea Coming Indoors, The. Marilyn Hacker. SP-HackM

War Memorial, The. Amy Clampitt. CP-ClamA

War occurred in the vicinity, A. Fanny Howe. SP-HoweF Fr. O'Clock.

War of your great beauty is in all the skies, The. At Dawn. William Carlos Williams. CP-WilW1

War on the Mind in a Time of Love. Charles Olson. CP-OlsoC

War Poem for Diane di Prima. Philip Whalen. SP-WhalP

War Poet. Ivor Gurney. SP-GurnI

War Profit Litany. Allen Ginsberg. CP-GinsA

War Resisters' Song. Thomas McGrath. SP-McGrT

War shook the land where Levi dwelt. Field of Glory, The. Edwin Arlington Robinson. CP-RobiE

War Song. Dorothy Parker. CP-ParkD

War Song [to Englishmen], A. William Blake. CP-BlakW

War, the Destroyer. William Carlos Williams. CP-WilW2

War was not strife, The. Late War, The. D. H. Lawrence. CP-LawrD

War-Wife of Catknoll, The. Thomas Hardy. CP-HardT

War with England, The. Hugh MacDiarmid. "I was better with the sounds of the sea." SP-MacDH

War with Yadir, The. Shmuel HaNagid. SP-HaNaS, tr. by Peter Cole

War Wound, The. James Dickey. CP-DickJ

Waratah. Yusef Komunyakaa. CP-KomuY

Warble for Lilac-Time. Walt Whitman. CP-WhitW

Warble me now for joy of lilac-time (returning in reminiscence). Warble for Lilac-Time. Walt Whitman. CP-WhitW

Ward in the States, A. Randall Jarrell. CP-JarrR

Ward is barred with moonlight, The. Ward in the States, A. Randall Jarrell. CP-JarrR

Ward of the Law!—dread Shadow of a King! On the Death of His Majesty (George the Third). William Wordsworth. CP-WorW2

Warden, The. Stevie Smith. CP-SmitS

Wardraipper of Wenus boure, The. William Dunbar. CP-DunbW

Wardrobe towers above the table lamp, The. Madness, Allen Tate. CP-TateA

Wards, The. Muriel Rukeyser. CP-RukeM

Waring. Robert Browning. CP-BroR1

Warm air throbbing with locust songs. Summer Song. E. E. Cummings. CP-CummE

Warm, but stuffy in the middle. Manyone Flying. May Swenson. SP-SwenM

Warm day, early March. The buds preen, busting their shirtwaists. Still Life with Spring and Time to Burn. Charles Wright. SP-WrigCN

Warm Day in Winter, A. Paul Laurence Dunbar. CP-DunbP

Warm flute on the cold snow. Nine Variations in a Chinese Winter Setting. Charles Tomlinson. CP-TomlC; SP-TomlC

Warm gale, a dose of spring—revert to the pores. Catullus. See Now spring bursts

'Warm hands, cold heart' they say; and vice-versa. Hot Hands. Donald Davie. CP-DaviDC

Warm in her Hand these accents lie. Emily Dickinson. CP-DickE

Warm in the pool the wasted man. Slow Dialogue between Pain and Roosevelt. Muriel Rukeyser. CP-RukeM

Warm in the underbough of dark. Witches Waken the Natural World in Spring. James Wright. CP-WrigJ

Warm odor remained in the armpits of her coat, A. Remembrance. Yannis Ritsos. SP-RitsY, tr. by Kimon Friar

Warm Pastures. W. S. Merwin. SP-MerwWF

Warm pulse of the nation has grown chill, The. Morton. James Whitcomb Riley. CP-RileJ

Warm rains / wash away winter's. Hermaphroditic Telephones, The. William Carlos Williams. CP-WilW1

Warm. / See sun shine. 10:30 AM: Ralph Hotere's. Robert Creeley. SP-CreeR

Warm sun and chilly air, water is low and the creek is clear. Somebody Else's Problem Bothers Me. Philip Whalen. SP-WhalP

Warm sun is failing, the bleak wind is wailing, The. Autumn: A Dirge. Percy Bysshe Shelley. CP-ShelP

Warm sun, quiet air. Election Day. William Carlos Williams. CP-WilW2

Warm today in a field of crows. For Paolo and Andy. Michael Palmer. SP-PalmM

Warm wind, the leaves. 3 a.m., September 1, 1969. Denise Levertov. SP-LeveDS

Warm yellowy-green / In the blue serene. Upper Birch-Leaves, The. Thomas Hardy. CP-HardT

Warm'd by the summer sun's meridian ray. Upon Happiness. James Thomson. CP-ThomD

Warmed by her hand and shadowed by her hair. Love-Letter, The. Dante Gabriel Rossetti. CW-RossD Fr. House of Life, The.

Warmed over pine-cones. Fairy Song. Randall Jarrell. CP-JarrR

Warmth / is the way. Looking Out. Robert Creeley. CP-CreeR

Warmth of cows, The. Carol, A. Donald Hall. CP-HallD

Warning ("Daddy, / don't let your dog"). Langston Hughes. CP-HughL

Warning. Langston Hughes. See Roland Hayes Beaten (Georgia: 1942)

Warning. Wisława Szymborska. SP-SzymW, tr. by Stanislaw Barańczak and Clare Cavanagh

Warning. Alice Walker. CP-WalkA

Warning, A. Grace Paley. CP-PalGC

Warning, The. Robert Creeley. CP-CreeR

Warning, The. Henry Wadsworth Longfellow. SP-LongH

Warning, The. George Meredith. CP-MerG2

Warning and Reply. Emily Jane Brontë. CP-BronE

Warning: Augmented. Langston Hughes. CP-HughL; CP-HughL3

Warning: Children at Play. Howard Nemerov. CP-NemeH

Warning to Children. Robert Graves. CP-GravR

Warning to My Readers, A. Wendell Berry. CP-BerrW

Warning to Wives, A. Ogden Nash. CP-NashO

Warped this perhapsy. E. E. Cummings. CP-CummE

Warrant for Pablo Neruda, A. Thomas McGrath. SP-McGrT

Warre. Robert Herrick. CP-HerrR

Warren G. Harding invented the word "normalcy." Qualm. John Ashbery. SP-AshbJ

Warrior, The. Jones Very. CP-VeryJ

Warrior Who Went With a Crowd, my sand-painter grandfather. Navajo Setting the Record Straight. John Berryman. CP-BerrJ

Warrior by warriors smitten. To a Turk. G. K. Chesterton. CP-ChesG

Warrior is afraid, The. Verses Written for Student Antidraft Registration Rally 1980. Allen Ginsberg. CP-GinsA

Warriors and chiefs! should the shaft or the sword. Song of Saul before His Last Battle. Lord Byron. CP-Byron

Warriors of the North, The. Ted Hughes. SP-HughTN

Warrior's Prayer, The. Paul Laurence Dunbar. CP-DunbP

Wars. Carl Sandburg. CP-SandC

Wars, The. Pablo Neruda. SP-NeruP

Wars and of arms some sing, but I. Claudio Achillini. SP-ZatuM, *tr. by* Marya Alexandrovna Zaturenska

Wars in Sweden, The. Carolyn Kizer. CP-KizeC

Wars worse than civil on Thessalian plains. Lucan. CP-MarlC *Fr.* Civil War [Bellum Civile] *or* Pharsalia.

Wartime. Lorine Niedecker. CP-NiedL

Warwickshire. Donald Davie. CP-DaviDC

Wary of time O it seizes the soul tonight. Easter Eve 1945. Muriel Rukeyser. CP-RukeM

Was. Robert Creeley. CP-CreeR

Was 'a barbaric yawp.' Ned Skinner. Paul Muldoon. CP-MuldP

Was a Man. John Ciardi. CP-CiarJ

Was enabled to ride. Matchstick-Viewed-without-Regard-to-Its-Outer-Surface, A. Kenneth Patchen. CP-PatcK

Was Ever a Dream a Drum? Carl Sandburg. CP-SandC

Was He Married? Stevie Smith. CP-SmitS

Was I angry with Hayley who used me so ill. William Blake. CP-BlakW

Was I clever enough? Was I charming? Thoughts While Driving Home. John Updike. CP-UpdiJ

Was I never yet of your love grieved. Sir Thomas Wyatt. CP-WyatT

Was I too glib about eternal things. Sequel, The. Theodore Roethke. CP-RoetT

Was It. James Schuyler. CP-SchuJ

Was it a chance that made her pause. Guesses. Christina Georgina Rossetti. CP-RosC3

Was it a dream, or was it memory? Festivals, The. Robert Duncan. SP-DuncR

Was it a friend or foe that spread these lies? Dante Gabriel Rossetti. CW-RossD

Was it a long-lost recollection crawling. Problem of Autobiography / Vague Recollection or Dream? Robert Penn Warren. CP-WarrR

Was it a morning or an afternoon. Entretien dans un parc. T. S. Eliot. SP-ElioT

Was it always a dream then? Atget's Gardens. Eleanor Wilner. SP-WilnE

Was it an animal was it a bird? Lovepet, The. Ted Hughes. SP-HughTN

Was it difficult to escape. Graceful Exit, A. James Laughlin. CP-LaugJ

Was it ever possible they would renounce. Julian and the Antiochians. Constantine P. Cavafy. CP-CavaC, *tr. by* Theoharis Constantine Theoharis

Was it for mere existence, that we fought. Ends for Which a Nation Exists, The. Jones Very. CP-VeryJ

Was it for this I uttered prayers. Grown-up. Edna St. Vincent Millay. CP-MillE

Was it, I wondered, some freak. Hertfordshire. Donald Davie. CP-DaviDC

Was it in the misty twilight, or the midnight or the morning. Glamour. James Whitcomb Riley. CP-RileJ

Was it my forehead or my lips you kissed? Dialogue. Jaroslav Seifert. SP-SeifJ, *tr. by* Ewald Osers

Was It Not Curious? Stevie Smith. CP-SmitS

Was It One of the Long Hunters of Kentucky who Discovered Boone at Sunset? Robert Penn Warren. CP-WarrR

Was it the double of my dream. Towards Break of Day. William Butler Yeats. CP-YeatW

Was it the worke of Nature or of Art. Sonnet 21. Edmund Spenser. CP-Spens *Fr.* Amoretti.

Was it too quick to be true. It Can Happen. James Laughlin. CP-LaugJ

Was it wind off the dumps. Summer Home. Seamus Heaney. SP-HeanSO

Was it wise to count the ranks of teeth. George Meredith. CP-MerG2

Was it with the fields of green. Emily Jane Brontë. CP-BronE

Was it worms, having once bitten. Pear like a Potato, A. John Updike. CP-UpdiJ

Was lying in am lying on I is I am it surrounds. Notes for Echo Lake 9. Michael Palmer. SP-PalmM

Was never born, never. Garden, The. Federico García Lorca. CP-GarcF, *tr. by*

Jerome Rothenberg *Fr.* In the Garden of the Lunar Grapefruits.

Was never form and never face. Beauty. Ralph Waldo Emerson. CP-EmerR

Was not the lost dauphin, though handsome was only. Audubon: A Vision. Robert Penn Warren. CP-WarrR

"Was not" was all the Statement. Emily Dickinson. CP-DickE

Was pain within you then—a grinning thing. Dostoyevsky. Kenneth Patchen. CP-PatcK

Was probably brought to America. Plant Called Yarrow, The. Robert Stock. SP-StocR

Was she so chaste? She Rebukes Hippolyta. "H. D." CP-DoolH

Was sitting here, drinking a glass of. Not All That Bad. Charles Bukowski. SP-BukC3

Was *that* the landmark? What,—the foolish well. Landmark, The. Dante Gabriel Rossetti. CW-RossD *Fr.* House of Life, The.

Was the aim frustrated by force or guile. Malham Cove. William Wordsworth. CP-WorW2

Was the silkiest day of the young year. Day He Died, The. Ted Hughes. SP-HughTN

Was the Word and the Word was just. Thinking Friday Night with a Gothic Storm Going About Final Causes and Logos and Mitzi Mayfair. Miller Williams. CP-WillM

Was there a garden or was the garden a dream? Adam Cast Forth. Richard Eberhart. CP-EberR

Was There a Time. Dylan Thomas. CP-ThomD

Was there ever a cause too lost. Hannibal. Robert Frost. CP-FrosR

Was thirty when we met. I was. Pandora's Box, An Ode. Ted Berrigan. SP-BerrT

Was this His coming! I had hoped to see. Ave Maria Gratia Plena. Oscar Wilde. CP-WildO

Was Thy Wrath against the Sea? Christina Georgina Rossetti. CP-RosC2

Was very kind. When she regained. Raper from Passenack, The. William Carlos Williams. CP-WilW1

Was Yahweh chosen by the chosen people? Sonnet: "Was Yahweh chosen by the chosen people?" Hayden Carruth. CP-CarHS *Fr.* Sonnets.

Was yesterday. I went out in the yard. August First, 1974. James Schuyler. CP-SchuJ

Was your's a daddy. Question. D. H. Lawrence. CP-LawrD

Wasabi. Arthur Sze. SP-SzeA

Wash. John Updike. CP-UpdiJ

Wash clean the Vessell, lest ye soure. Sincerity. Robert Herrick. CP-HerrR

Wash Lowry's Reminiscence. James Whitcomb Riley. CP-RileJ

Wash me on home, mama. Gary Snyder. CP-SnydG *Fr.* Myths and Texts.

Wash of cold river. "H. D." CP-DoolH

Wash, the plunge / down, The. Sea, The. Robert Creeley. CP-CreeR

Wash your hands, or else the fire. Another to the Maids. Robert Herrick. CP-HerrR

Washback of the waters, swirl of time. Sea-Ruck. Richard Eberhart. CP-EberR

Washed into the doorway. Guest, The. Wendell Berry. CP-BerrW

Washer Womans Song, The. William Blake. CP-BlakW

Washerwoman. Carl Sandburg. CP-SandC

Washerwoman is a member of the Salvation Army, The. Washerwoman. Carl Sandburg. CP-SandC

Washing. Randall Jarrell. CP-JarrR

Washing hangs upon the line, A. Songs for a Colored Singer. Elizabeth Bishop. CP-BishE

Washing Kai in the sauna. Bath, The. Gary Snyder. CP-SnydG

Washing My Face. Gregory Orr. SP-OrrG

Washing the Corpse. Randall Jarrell. CP-JarrR

Washing the corpse, the boat, and her pine floors. Village Priest, A. Norman Dubie. CP-DubiN

Washing your feet is hard when you get fat. John Ciardi. CP-CiarJ

Washington. John Updike. CP-UpdiJ

Washington. Jones Very. CP-VeryJ

Washington Cathedral. Karl Shapiro. SP-ShapK

Washington in Love. John Berryman. CP-BerrJ

Washington Monument by Night. Carl Sandburg. CP-SandC

Washington: Tourist View. John Updike. CP-UpdiJ

Washington's Monument, February, 1885. Walt Whitman. CP-WhitW

Wasn't it a funny dream!—perfectly bewild'rin'! Dream-March. James Whitcomb Riley. CP-RileJ

Wasn't it a good time. When We First Played "Show." James Whitcomb Riley. CP-RileJ

Wasn't it pleasant, O brother mine. Out to Old Aunt Mary's. James Whitcomb Riley. CP-RileJ

Wasp, The. Ogden Nash. CP-NashO

Wassail for the New Year, A. George Meredith. CP-MerG2

Wassaile, The. Robert Herrick. CP-HerrR

Wassaile the Trees, that they may beare. Another. Robert Herrick. CP-HerrR

Waste Land, The. T. S. Eliot. CP-ElioT

Wasted arms, feeble knees. Don't Grow Old. Allen Ginsberg. SP-GinsA *Fr.* Don't Grow Old.

Wasted Days. Oscar Wilde. CP-WildO

Wasted Illness, A. Thomas Hardy. CP-HardT

Wasteland slips and crumbles past the threshold, The. At an Abandoned Shrine of Saint Mary Aegyptian. Robert Stock. SP-StocR

Waster, The. Rudyard Kipling. CP-KiplR

Watch, The. A. R. Ammons. CP-AmmoA

Watch, The. Robert Graves. CP-GravR

Watch, The. Robert Herrick. CP-HerrR

Watch a wild turkey come in to land. Birds, like Thoughts. John Ciardi. CP-CiarJ

Watch Any Day. W. H. Auden. CP-AudeW
    (Free One, A.) CP-AudeW

Watch any day his nonchalant pauses, see. Watch Any Day. W. H. Auden. CP-AudeW

Watch how the aspen leaf, pale and windless, waggles. Aspen Leaf in Windless World. Robert Penn Warren. CP-WarrR

Watch out for power. Admonitions to a Special Person. Anne Sexton. SP-SextA

Watch out for this peeled doorlight! In the Rain and the Sun. Thomas Merton. CP-MertT

Watch Out, Papa. Langston Hughes. CP-HughL; CP-HughL2

Watch people stop by bodies in funeral homes. On the Symbolic Consideration of Hands and the Significance of Death. Miller Williams. CP-WillM

Watch Repair. Charles Simic. SP SimiC; SP-SimiCE

Watch the great bough lashed by wind and rain. Is it. Ah, Anima! Robert Penn Warren. CP-WarrR

Watch the Lights Fade. Robinson Jeffers. CP-JefR3

Watch thou and fear; to-morrow thou shalt die. Choice, The ("Watch thou and fear; to-morrow thou shalt die"). Dante Gabriel Rossetti. CW-RossD *Fr.* House of Life, The.

Watch tower once for pirates. To the Little Fort of San Lazaro on the Ocean Front, Havana. Langston Hughes. CP-HughL; CP-HughL1

Watch yet a while, / Weep till that day shall dawn when thou shalt smile. Day Is At Hand, The. Christina Georgina Rossetti. CP-RosC2

Watch your footing down the iron steps. . . they ring. East Mauch Chunk - Jim Thorpe. William Corbett. SP-CorbW

Watched clock never moves, they said, A. Slow Starter, The. Louis MacNeice. CP-MacNL

Watched Example Never Boils, A. Ogden Nash. CP-NashO

Watched on the sandy, stony bottom of the stream. Motion for Motion. A. R. Ammons. CP-AmmoA

Watcher, The. Robert Bly. SP-BlyR

Watcher, The. Jorge Luis Borges. SP-BorgJ, *tr. by* Alastair Reid

Watcher, The. Kenneth Patchen. CP-PatcK

Watcher, The. Jones Very. CP-VeryJ

Watchers. W. S. Merwin. SP-MerwW

Watchers, The. W. H. Auden. CP-AudeW

Watchers, The. A. K. Ramanujan. CP-RamaA

Watchers, The. Christina Georgina Rossetti. CP-RosC3

Watchers, The. Muriel Rukeyser. CP-RukeM

Watchers, The. John Greenleaf Whittier. CP-WhitJ

Watcher's Regret, A. Thomas Hardy. CP-HardT

Watches of the Night, The. James Whitcomb Riley. CP-RileJ

Watchful. Stevie Smith. CP-SmitS

Watchfulness and sensation as John Keats. Memories of John Keats. Denise Levertov. SP-LeveDS

Watching a kettle boil, a puddle. John Ciardi. CP-CiarJ

Watching a tv show. Sword, The. Charles Bukowski. SP-BukC3

Watching, among the rifled branches, for the sun, our hero. Poem: "Watching, among the rifled branches, for the sun, our hero." Thomas Merton. CP-MertT

Watching baseball. Baseball Canto. Lawrence Ferlinghetti. SP-FerlL

Watching Dan- / cers on Skates. Lorine Niedecker. CP-NiedL

Watching Football on TV. Howard Nemerov. CP-NemeH

Watching hands transplanting. Transplanting. Theodore Roethke. CP-RoetT

Watching incredible kids. Kids / Seoul. Robert Creeley. SP-CreeR

Watching my paralytic friend. Figurehead, The. Karl Shapiro. SP-ShapK

Watching Neighbors' Children. Kenneth Patchen. CP-PatcK

Watching Sandhill Cranes. William Stafford. SP-StafWW

Watching Shoah in a Hotel Room in America. Adam Zagajewski. SP-ZagaA, *tr. by* Renata Gorczynski, Benjamin Ivry *and* C. K. Williams

Watching the dark my spirit rose in flood. Bach and the Sentry. Ivor Gurney. SP-GurnI

Watching the Equinox Arrive in Charlottesville, September 1992. Charles Wright. SP-WrigCN

Watching the famous eruption of a volcano on Heimaey, Iceland. Reprieve, The.

Hans Magnus Enzensberger. SP-EnzeH, *tr. by* Michael Hamburger

Watching the Jet Planes Dive. William Stafford. SP-StafW; SP-StafWW

Watching the mistlines flow slowly in. Mistlines. Charles Tomlinson. CP-TomlC

Watching the shied core. As Bad as a Mile. Philip Larkin. CP-LarkP

Watching the stream come spilling over its ledge. Silver Creek Falls. William Dickey. SP-DickW

Watching the tail end of a film running through the projector. Talking Picture, The. Philip Whalen. SP-WhalP

Watching the Waves. Sam Hamill. SP-HamiS

Watching the White Image, electric moon, white mist drifting over woods. In a Moonlit Hermit's Cabin. Allen Ginsberg. CP-GinsA

Watching the world from my peeled doorlight. Poem in the Rain and the Sun. Thomas Merton. CP-MertT

Watching two surfers walk toward the tide. Moment, The. Charles Tomlinson. CP-TomlC; SP-TomlC

Watching unto God in the Night-Season. Jeanne Marie Bouvier de la Motte-Guyon. CP CowpW

Watching You. James Schuyler. CP-SchuJ

Watching you in the mirror I wonder. Mirror, The. Louise Glück. SP-GlucL

Watching you sleep. Watching You. James Schuyler. CP-SchuJ

Watchmaker God. Robert Lowell. SP-LoweR

Watchman, The. Jones Very. CP-VeryJ

Watchman, What of the First First Lady? Ogden Nash. CP-NashO

Watchman, what of the night? Nachtwache. Primo Levi. CP-LeviP, *tr. by* Ruth Feldman

Water. Robert Creeley. CP-CreeR

Water. Ralph Waldo Emerson. CP-EmerR

Water. Ted Hughes. SP-HughTN

Water. Yusef Komunyakaa. CP-KomuY

Water. Philip Larkin. CP-LarkP

Water. Robert Lowell. SP-LoweR

Water. Wyatt Prunty. SP-PrunW

Water. Kathleen Jessie Raine. SP-RainK

Water. Anne Sexton. CP-SextA

Water. Gary Snyder. CP-SnydG

Water. Wisława Szymborska. SP-SzymW, *tr. by* Stanislaw Barańczak *and* Clare Cavanagh

Water. Wisława Szymborska. SP-SzymWM, *tr. by* Joanna Trzeciak

Water all around me. Question. Robert Creeley. SP-CreeR

Water and windmills, greenness, Islets green. Netherlands, The. Samuel Taylor Colcridge. CP-ColeS

Water Ballad. Samuel Taylor Coleridge. CP-ColeS

Water Buffalo. Yusef Komunyakaa. CP-KomuY

Water calmly flowing, / Sun-light deeply glowing. Earth and Heaven. Christina Georgina Rossetti. CP-RosC3

Water, cold, and sweet, and pure. Xenophanes. Louis Zukofsky. CP-ZukLS

Water-Color, A. James Whitcomb Riley. CP-RileJ

Water Colours. Ivor Gurney. SP-GurnI

Water-Course, The. George Herbert. CP-HerbG

Water drips, / a fissure of leaking. Water (2). Robert Creeley. CP-CreeR

Water flows, drenches the fields, flows, shines, The. Lyric Poem. Yannis Ritsos. SP-RitsY, *tr. by* Athan Anagnostopoulos

Water, for anguish of the solstice:—nay. Venetian Pastoral, by Giorgone, in the Louvre, A. Dante Gabriel Rossetti. CW-RossD

Water, for anguish of the solstice,—yea. Venetian Pastoral, by Giorgone, in the Louvre, A. Dante Gabriel Rossetti. CW-RossD

Water Fowl. William Wordsworth. CP-WorW1

Water from last night in the puddles. Deganya. Yehuda Amichai. SP-AmicYL, *tr. by* Benjamin Harshav and Barbara Harshav

Water from the sprinkler. Contingency. A. R. Ammons. CP-AmmoA

Water from Your Spring. Jelaluddin Rumi. SP-Rumi, *tr. by* Coleman Barks

Water-Front Streets. Langston Hughes. CP-HughL; CP-HughL1

Water-grass under had never waved, The. Rain Guitar, The. James Dickey. CP-DickJ

Water-hammer, the history of ice, The. Muriel Rukeyser. CP-RukeM

Water has flowed under the bridges. J.D.C., The: A Celebration. G. K. Chesterton. CP-ChesG

Water in the millrace, through a sluice of stone. Winter Landscape, with Rooks. Sylvia Plath. CP-PlatS

Water is deeper than the land, The. Emily Dickinson. SP-DickE

Water is green, The. The two boats out at a distance. These Untitled Little Verses in Which, at Dawn, Two Obscure Dutch Peasants Struggled with an Auburn Horse. Norman Dubie. CP-DubiN

Water is H_2O, hydrogen two parts, oxygen one. Third Thing, The. D. H. Lawrence. CP-LawrD

Water is heavy silver over stone. What Any Lover Learns. Archibald MacLeish. CP-MacLA

Water, is taught by thirst. Emily Dickinson. CP-DickE

Water itself is leaving the harbor, The. Hulk, The. W. S. Merwin. SP-MerwW

Water Jets. Federico García Lorca.

    Aside. CP-GarcF, *tr. by* Jerome Rothenberg

    Garden. CP-GarcF, *tr. by* Jerome Rothenberg

    Homeland ("Water jets in dreams"). CP-GarcF, *tr. by* Jerome Rothenberg

    Interior ("From my room I hear"). CP-GarcF, *tr. by* Jerome Rothenberg

    "Only right then it was!" CP-GarcF, *tr. by* Jerome Rothenberg

Water jets in dreams. Homeland ("Water jets in dreams"). Federico García Lorca. CP-GarcF, *tr. by* Jerome Rothenberg *Fr.* Water Jets.

Water Lace and White Eyes. Eleanor Wilner. SP-WilnE

Water-Lilies. E. E. Cummings. CP-CummE

Water Lilies: A Nocturne. Marya Alexandrovna Zaturenska. SP-ZatuM

Water Lily. Rainer Maria Rilke. CP-RilkFr, *tr. by* A. Poulin, Jr.

Water makes many Beds. Emily Dickinson. CP-DickE

Water Music. Hugh MacDiarmid.

    Water Music. SP-MacDH

    ("Wheesht, wheesht, Joyce, and let me hear.") SP-MacDH

Water Music. Hugh MacDiarmid. SP-MacDH *Fr.* Water Music.

Water Music. Robert Creeley. CP-CreeR

Water / neither knows / who drinks. Down Home. Robert Creeley. CP-CreeR

Water Night. Muriel Rukeyser. CP-RukeM

Water of Life. Hugh MacDiarmid. SP-MacDH

Water of the Suns, The. W. S. Merwin. SP-MerwW

Water on rocks the hiss of steam. Sweat Lodge—The Afterwards. Peter Blue Cloud. SP-BlueP

Water perfectly calm. Perfectly amazing. Wind. Raymond Carver. CP-CarvR

Water Picture. May Swenson. SP-SwenM

Water-poet lay down with flowers above, The. Room in Rome, A. Karl Shapiro. SP-ShapK

Water, salt, and the sun devour houses bit by bit. Knocking. Yannis Ritsos. SP-RitsY, *tr. by* Kimon Friar

Water Slide Along the Beach. Wyatt Prunty. SP-PrunW

Water Snake. Mary Oliver. SP-OlivM

Water Spirit's Song, The. Christina Georgina Rossetti. CP-RosC3

Water! / Star! / and somewhere near now nodding. Lao Tsze. Kenneth Patchen. CP-PatcK

Water still flows. Illegitimate Things. William Carlos Williams. CP-WilW2

Water Suite. Federico García Lorca.

    Acacia. CP-GarcF, *tr. by* Jerome Rothenberg

    Beehive. CP-GarcF, *tr. by* Jerome Rothenberg

    Curve. CP-GarcF, *tr. by* Jerome Rothenberg

    Homeland ("Trees laid out"). CP-GarcF, *tr. by* Jerome Rothenberg

    Tremor. CP-GarcF, *tr. by* Jerome Rothenberg

Water / taps its silver. Portico ("Water / taps its silver"). Federico García Lorca. CP-GarcF, *tr. by* Jerome Rothenberg *Fr.* Garden in Umber; or The Garden of the Brownhaired Girls.

Water that made the island, The. North Island Songs. Heather McHugh. SP-McHuH

Water turns / a long way down over the raw stone, The. You Are Happy. Margaret Atwood. SP-AtwM1

Water (2). Robert Creeley. CP-CreeR

Water understands / Civilization well, The. Water. Ralph Waldo Emerson. CP-EmerR

The ("Water / waiting far, The"). Robert Creeley. CP-CreeR

Water / waiting far, The. The ("Water / waiting far, The"). Robert Creeley. CP-CreeR

Water Walker. Richard Wilbur. CP-WilbR

Water wanted to live. How Water Began to Play. Ted Hughes. SP-HughTN

"Water" was her answer and I fell instantly and I knew self-destructively in love with her. Game, The. C. K. Williams. SP-WillC

Water, water I desire. Scar[e]-Fire, The. Robert Herrick. CP-HerrR

Water, Water I espie. His Misery in a Mistresse. Robert Herrick. CP-HerrR

Water, wind-impelled, advancing, The. Marine. Charles Tomlinson. CP-TomlC

Waterbird. May Swenson. SP-SwenM

Watercolor of Grantchester Meadows. Sylvia Plath. CP-PlatS

Watercourse dry of puddles, not a drop of water left, The. General Quiroga Rides to His Death in a Carriage. Jorge Luis Borges. SP-BorgJ, *tr. by* Alastair Reid

Waterfall, The. Amy Clampitt. CP-ClamA

Waterfall, The. Mary Oliver. SP-OlivM

Waterfall and the Eglantine, The. William Wordsworth. CP-WorW1; MW-WorW

Waterfall at Powerscourt, The. Donald Davie. CP-DaviDC

Waterfall sounds behind huts out of a comic opera, The. Winter Festival. Arthur Rimbaud. CP-RimbA, *tr. by* Martin Sorrell

Waterfalls in a Bank. A. K. Ramanujan. CP-RamaA

Watergaw, The. Hugh MacDiarmid. SP-MacDH

Watering Can. Czeslaw Milosz. CP-MiloCN, *tr. by* Robert Hass

Watering-Place Lady Inventoried, A. Thomas Hardy. CP-HardT

Watering the Horse. Robert Bly. SP-BlyR

Watering Trough. Maxine W. Kumin. SP-KumiM

Waterlily Fire. Muriel Rukeyser. SP-RukeM

Waterloo. Robert Lowell. SP-LoweR

Watermelons. Charles Simic. SP-SimiC; SP-SimiCE

Waters. Donald Hall. CP-HallD

Waters, The. W. S. Merwin. SP-MerwWF

Waters, The. Richard Wilbur. CP-WilbR

Waters are flashing, The. Fugitives, The. Percy Bysshe Shelley. CP-ShelP

Waters are loose: from Judith and the Larb. Schoolcraft's Diary Written on the Missouri: 1830. Robert Bly. SP-BlyR

Waters chased him as he fled, The. Emily Dickinson. CP-DickE

Waters come welling into this valley. After the Storm. Charles Tomlinson. CP-TomlC

Waters deep, the waters dark, The. Casting. Howard Nemerov. CP-NemeH

Waters, hypnotic, long after moonset, murmur. Dream. Robert E. Penn. CP-WarrR

Water's wide spread, The. From Sea Cliff, March. May Swenson. SP-SwenM

Watertowers. The. W. H. Auden. CP-AudeW

Waterwheel, The. Jelaluddin Rumi. SP-Rumi, *tr. by* Coleman Barks

Watteau. Derek Walcott. CP-WalcD *Fr.* Midsummer.

Waukrife Minnie, A. Robert Burns. CP-BurnR

Wave. Gary Snyder. CP-SnydG

Wave, A. John Ashbery. SP-AshbJ

Wave, The. Elizabeth Bishop. CP-BishE

Wave, The. W. S. Merwin. SP-MerwW

Wave, The. Adrienne Rich. SP-RicA2

Wave and the Dune, The. May Swenson. SP-SwenM

Wave broke in, and the star came up, The. Sea and Star. G. K. Chesterton. CP-ChesG

Wave in the round of the port-hole. Party on Shipboard. George Oppen. CP-OppGN

Wave is breaking on the shore, The. New Year, The. John Greenleaf Whittier. CP-WhitJ

Wave of an awful torrent, thronging down. Past and Coming Year, The. John Greenleaf Whittier. CP-WhitJ

Wave of sorrow. Island ("Wave of sorrow"). Langston Hughes. CP-HughL; CP-HughL2

Wave-shaped dune is still, The. Wave and the Dune, The. May Swenson. SP-SwenM

Wave sucks back and with the last of water, The. On Being Idolized. Robert Frost. CP-FrosR

Wave them / Flap white wings and yellow pinions. Fire. D. H. Lawrence. CP-LawrD

Wave withdrawing, The. "Dover Beach"—a Note to That Poem. Archibald MacLeish. CP-MacLA

Wavering his scums and incisions. Anatomy Lab. John Ciardi. CP-CiarJ

Wavering Scales, The. Yannis Ritsos.

    Inexhaustible, The. SP-RitsY

    Insufficiency. SP-RitsY

Waves are pressing up with force, The. George Meredith. CP-MerG2

Waves have frozen, The. Zero in the Cove. May Swenson. SP-SwenM

Waves of assault break on this rocky spur. On a Painting by Todd Price of the 16th Michigan Infantry on Little Round Top, July 2, 1863. Helen Pinkerton. CP-PinkH

Waves of their purposefulness go flooding through me, The. Covenanters, The. Hugh MacDiarmid. SP-MacDH

Waves on the Normandy coast jump heavily toward us, The. Normandy Beach. Miller Williams. CP-WillM

Waves / rhyme with sighs. Harmony. Federico García Lorca. CP-GarcF, *tr. by* Jerome Rothenberg *Fr.* Newton.

Waves rush up, pause, and drag pebbles back around. Two Sounds When We Sit by the Ocean. Robert Bly. SP-BlyR

Waving a flag I retreat a long way beyond. Remarks on My Character. William Stafford. SP-StafWW

Waving Adieu, Adieu, Adieu. Wallace Stevens. CP-StevW; CP-StevWP

Waving and Waving Goodbye. Charles Bukowski. SP-BukC1

Waving goodbye, from your banked hospital bed. Ted Hughes. SP-HughTN

Waving of a Hand, The. W. S. Merwin. SP-MerwWF

Waving slowly before me, pushed into the dark. Sickness. D. H. Lawrence. CP-LawrD

Waving to the Devil. Denise Levertov. SP-LeveDL

Waving whispering trees. Adieu. Dante Gabriel Rossetti. CW-RossD

Wax. Jelaluddin Rumi. SP-Rumi, *tr. by* Coleman Barks

Wax Candle, The. Jaroslav Seifert. SP-SeifJ, *tr. by* Ewald Osers

Wax Dummies. Yannis Ritsos. SP-RitsY, *tr. by* Andonis Decavalles

Wax, / to seal what's unwritten. With Letter and Clock. Paul Celan. SP-CelaP, *tr.*

by John Felstiner.
Way. Robert Creeley. CP-CreeR
Way, The. Rae Armantrout. SP-ArmaA
Way, The. Robert Creeley. CP-CreeR
Way, The. Robert Herrick. CP-HerrR
Way, The. Lying and Looking. May Swenson. SP-SwenM
Way, The. Jones Very. CP-VeryJ
Way a Child Might Believe, The. Olga Broumas. SP-BrouO
Way a crow, The. Dust of Snow. Robert Frost. CP-FrosR
Way a word does when, The. One Way. Howard Nemerov. CP-NemeH
Way! ah, who could tell, as well as thou, The. Hymn: I Am the Way. Jones Very. CP-VeryJ
Way Ahead, The. W. S. Merwin. SP-MerwW
Way at night these piping peepers, The. Peepers in Our Meadow, The. Archibald MacLeish. CP-MacLA
Way boxers postulate a feeling to label that with which they overcome the body's vile fears, The. Vehicle: Violence. C. K. Williams. SP-WillC
Way Down, The. Stanley Kunitz. CP-KunSC
Way Down South in Dixie. Song for a Dark Girl. Langston Hughes. CP-HughL; CP-HughL1
Way enchased with glass and beads, A. Temple, The. Robert Herrick. CP-HerrR
Way eyes turn, The. New Yorker, A. James Schuyler. CP-SchuJ
Way grapes will cast a green rail, The. Ode to the Spectral Thief, Alpha. Norman Dubie. CP-DubiN
Way, her father dead a day ago, the child goes in his closet, finds herself inside his closet, The. Vehicle: Absence. C. K. Williams. SP-WillC
Way Hope builds his House, The. Emily Dickinson. CP-DickE
Way I read a Letter's—this, The. Emily Dickinson. CP-DickE
Way I Write, The. William Stafford. SP-StafWW
Way in a Crowd. Robert Herrick. CP-HerrR
Way In, The. Charles Tomlinson. CP-TomlC; SP-TomlC
Way is full of genuine sacrifice, The. Of Being Woven. Jelaluddin Rumi. SP-Rumi, *tr.* by Coleman Barks
Way it came spinning onto the lawn, The. Seed. Amy Clampitt. CP-ClamA
Way It Is, The. Laura Riding Jackson. CP-RidiL
Way It Is, The. Denise Levertov. SP-LeveDL
Way It Is, The. Charles Simic. SP-SimiC
Way It Is, The. William Stafford. SP-StafWW
Way It Was, The. Yehuda Amichai. SP-AmicY, *tr.* by Chana Bloch
Way It Wuz, The. James Whitcomb Riley. CP-RileJ
Way light, The. Captain Diable's Receptionist. Yusef Komunyakaa. CP-KomuY
Way MacLane died, they set, The. Place of Value, The. Howard Nemerov. CP-NemeH
Way men live is a lie, The. Kenneth Patchen. CP-PatcK
Way of a World, The. Charles Tomlinson. CP-TomlC; SP-TomlC
Way of Life, A. Howard Nemerov. CP-NemeH
Way of love is not, The. Jelaluddin Rumi. SP-Rumi, *tr.* by Coleman Barks
Way of love is unlimited, The. Hafiz. CP-EmerR *Fr.* Odes.
Way of many ways: a god, A. Doctor Faustus. Geoffrey Hill. CP-HillG
Way of Pain, The. Wendell Berry. CP-BerrW
Way of the Conventicle of the Trees, The. Hayden Carruth. CP-CarHS
Way of the World, The. Christina Georgina Rossetti. CP-RosC3
Way of the World, The. Carl Sandburg. CP-SandC
Way on high burned white beneath the sun, The. Defeat. Walter De la Mare. CP-DeLaW
Way our American wildflowers hover, The. Fleckings, The. John Updike. CP-UpdiJ
Way Out, A. Richard Eberhart. CP-EberR
Way Out, The. D. H. Lawrence. CP-LawrD
Way out they are riding, it is an old. Herd, The. Robert Creeley. CP-CreeR
Way someone stays home, that's all, stays in the house, in the room, just stays, The. Race of the Flood, The. C. K. Williams. CP-WillC
Way sorrow enters the bone, The. Blue Rim of Memory, The. Denise Levertov. SP-LeveDL
Way spring comes this time, with a soft, The. Zalmoxis. Howard Nemerov. CP-NemeH
Way-Station. Archibald MacLeish. CP-MacLA
Way the Baby Came, The. James Whitcomb Riley. CP-RileJ
Way the Baby Woke, The. James Whitcomb Riley. CP-RileJ
Way the Cards Fall, The. Yusef Komunyakaa. CP-KomuY
Way the cooked shoes sizzle, The. Amanda Is Shod. Maxine W. Kumin. SP-KumiM
Way the dog trots out the front door, The. Dharma. Billy Collins. SP-CollB
Way the Roundness Feels, The. Clarence Major. SP-MajoC
Way "The Tennessee Waltz," The. Overhearing. Rae Armantrout. SP-ArmaA
Way the willow-bark, The. Braiding, The. Denise Levertov. SP-LeveDS
Way the world came swinging around my ears, The. Perennial Answer, The.

Adrienne Rich. CP-RicAE; SP-RicA2
Way these days she dresses with more attention to go out to pass the afternoon alone, The. Mirror, The. C. K. Williams. SP-WillC
Way through the woods is past trees, The. Walk There. David Ignatow. SP-IgnaD
Way Through The Woods, The. Rudyard Kipling. CP-KiplR
Way T'ings Come, De. Paul Laurence Dunbar. CP-DunbP
Way to Go. A. R. Ammons. CP-AmmoA
Way to Go, The. William Corbett. SP-CorbW
Way to hump a cow is not, The. E. E. Cummings. CP-CummE
Way to know the Bobolink, The. Emily Dickinson. CP-DickE
Way to Love God, A. Robert Penn Warren. CP-WarrR
Way to Make a Living, A. James Wright. CP-WrigJ
Way to the River leads past the names, The. W. S. Merwin. SP-MerwW
Way we get under cars and in, The. Just Right. C. K. Williams. CP-WillC
Way We Write Letters, The. Carolyn Kizer. CP-KizeC
Way West, Underground, The. Gary Snyder. CP-SnydG
Way you see it first is through, The. Secret Garden, The. Eleanor Wilner. SP-WilnE
Wayfarer / Perceiving the pathway to truth. The. Stephen Crane. CP-CranS
Ways. Langston Hughes. CP-HughL; CP-HughL1
Ways, The. Louis Zukofsky. CP-ZukLS
Ways about it, In fact, that only scratches the surface; for—well. There Are Two. Kenneth Patchen. CP-PatcK
Ways and Means. Richard Eberhart. CP-EberR
Ways and the Peoples, The. Randall Jarrell. CP-JarrR
Ways of Conquest. Denise Levertov. SP-LeveDL
Ways of Day. Robert Penn Warren. CP-WarrR
Ways to Live. William Stafford. SP-StafWW
Ways to say good-bye are going with him. Last Person to Speak His Language is Dying, The. Miller Williams. CP-WillM
WCW. A. R. Ammons. CP-AmmoA
We. Miller Williams. CP-WillM
We all are little infants. Nursery Rhyme, A. G. K. Chesterton. CP-ChesG
We all have moments with the dust. Emily Dickinson. SP-DickE
We all have our faults. Mine is trying to write poems. Singing Aloud. Carolyn Kizer. CP-KizeC
We all know about death that. In Death, Cannot Reach What Is Most Near. Allen Ginsberg. CP-GinsA
We all live / on islands. Poem for My Friend Peter at Pihana. John Logan. CP-LogaJ
We all possess the buddha of buddhas. Shih-te. CP-ColdM, *tr.* by Red Pine
We All Shall Rest at Last. Walt Whitman. CP-WhitW
We all traveled into that big room. How We Did It. Muriel Rukeyser. CP-RukeM
We all were watching the quiz on television. Singular Metamorphosis, A. Howard Nemerov. CP-NemeH
We Alone. Alice Walker. CP-WalkA
We alwus had to herd cattle. Mona Van Duyn. SP-VanDM
We and They. Rudyard Kipling. CP-KiplR *Fr.* Debits and Credits.
We Are. Maxine W. Kumin. SP-KumiM
We are a meadow where the bees hum. Bedtime. Denise Levertov. SP-LeveDP; SP-LeveDS
We are afraid that we have not lived. Calidus Juventa? Allen Tate. CP-TateA
We are again / walking in a / straight line—feet. For Betsy and Tom. Robert Creeley. CP-CreeR
We are all children to the past. Memoirs of Glückel of Hameln, The. Randall Jarrell. CP-JarrR
We are all docile Dough-Faces. Song for Certain Congressmen. Walt Whitman. CP-WhitW
We are all liars, because. Lies About Love. D. H. Lawrence. CP-LawrD
We are always saying / "Good-bye, good-bye!" Saying Good-bye. Thomas Hardy. CP-HardT
We are America. Firebombers, The. Anne Sexton. CP-SextA
We are an aging couple. Separate Rooms. David Ignatow. SP-IgnaD
We are approaching sleep: the chestnut blossoms in the mind. Awakening. Robert Bly. SP-BlyR
We are as clouds that veil the midnight moon. Mutability. Percy Bysshe Shelley. CP-ShelP
We are asleep under mirrors. What do I. Before the War. Marilyn Hacker. SP-HackM
We are being torn down. On a Dispossess Precept. 1. Alan Dugan. CP-DugaA
We are betrayed by what is false. Within. Anima. Richard Eberhart. CP-EberR
We are beyond the ways of the far ships. Landfall, The. Thomas Merton. CP-MertT
We are born at sunset and we die ere morn. Fernando Pessoa. SP-PessF *Fr.* 35 Sonnets.
We are born into life—it is sweet, it is strange. Rhapsody of Life's Progress, A. Elizabeth Barrett Browning. CP-BroEB

We are born with luck. Evil Seekers, The. Anne Sexton. CP-SextA

We are brought thick desserts, and we rarely refuse them. When We Pray Alone. Jelaluddin Rumi. SP-Rumi, tr. by Coleman Barks

We are budding, Master, budding. Master and the Leaves, The. Thomas Hardy. CP-HardT

We are children of our age. Children of Our Age. Wisława Szymborska. SP-SzymW, tr. by Stanislaw Barańczak and Clare Cavanagh

We are children of our era. Children of Our Era. Wisława Szymborska. SP-SzymWM, tr. by Joanna Trzeciak

We are Coheires with Christ; nor shall His own. Coheires. Robert Herrick. CP-HerrR

We are coming down the pike. Exodus. Carolyn Kizer. CP-KizeC

We are driven to odd attempts; once it would not have occurred to. Adrienne Rich. SP-RicA1; SP-RicA2 Fr. Shooting Script.

We are elements of design just now. Y Un Canción Por E. Andrei Codrescu. SP-CodrA

We are false and evanescent, and aware of our deceit. False Gods, The. Edwin Arlington Robinson. CP-RobiE

We are fishermen in a flat scene. Water. Anne Sexton. CP-SextA

We are free to find our own way. Off the Trail. Gary Snyder. CP-SnydG

We Are Getting to the End. Thomas Hardy. CP-HardT

We are given a chance. First Time, The. Robert Creeley. CP-CreeR

We are growing a bitter seed issue. Demands of Exile. Andrei Codrescu. SP-CodrA

We are happy all the time. Sweet Briars of the Stairways. Nicholas Vachel Lindsay. CP-LindV

We are happy in our way of life. Parergon. John Ashbery. SP-AshbJ

We are hard on each other. Margaret Atwood. SP-AtwM1

We are holiday weepers, engraving our names on every stone. In the Old City. Yehuda Amichai. SP-AmicY, tr. by Chana Bloch

We are involved in a transpersonified state. Chinese Nightingale. Ted Berrigan. SP-BerrT

We Are Leaves. James Schuyler. CP-SchuJ

We are like doves, well-paired. Green-Sailed Vessel, The. Robert Graves. CP-GravR

We are not a large concern, although compared. Promotion, The. Miller Williams. CP-WillM

We Are Not Always Glad When We Smile. James Whitcomb Riley. CP-RileJ

We are not born yet, and everything's crystal under our feet. California Dreaming. Charles Wright. SP-WrigC

We are not lovers. Man and Wife. Anne Sexton. CP-SextA

We are not often alone, we two. Voice, The. Walter De la Mare. CP-DeLaW

We are not so badly off, if we can. Realism. Czeslaw Milosz. CP-MiloCN, tr. by Robert Hass

We are not wasted. We are not left out. Welcome to Quetzalcoatl. D. H. Lawrence. CP-LawrD

We Are Not Worthy, Lord. Kenneth Patchen. CP-PatcK

We are now about to die the death of endeavour. We Are the Resurrection. Laura Riding Jackson. CP-RidiL

We are of those who tremble at Thy word. Christina Georgina Rossetti. CP-RosC2

We are one but we intended two. On the Sacrifice of a Siamese Twin at Birth. Miller Williams. CP-WillM

We are others and the earth. From the Distance. Wendell Berry. CP-BerrW

We are ourselves but carriers. Life. For a Woman with Child. James Vincent Cunningham. CP-CunnJ

We are out on the open road. On the March. D. H. Lawrence. CP-LawrD

We are partners in this bee. Plunging into the Improbable. Olga Broumas. SP-BrouO

We are pleased to present for your listening pleasure. We. Miller Williams. CP-WillM

We are returning to New England for two weeks! My sister. Photographer's Annual, The. Norman Dubie. CP-DubiN

We are ruled by thunderbolts, as Herakleitos said. Listen, Ianni. Sam Hamill. SP-HamiS

We Are Seven. William Wordsworth. CP-WorW1; MW-WorW

We are snatching our jewels from the frost. Emily Dickinson. SP-DickE

We are the antlers of that white animal. Afterwards. Muriel Rukeyser. CP-RukeM

We are the desperate. Vagabonds. Langston Hughes. CP-HughL; CP-HughL2

We are the hollow men. Hollow Men, The. T. S. Eliot. CP-ElioT

We are the lords of the cigarette. Song of the GIs & the MGs. James Laughlin. CP-LaugJ

We are the mirror as well as the face in it. Jelaluddin Rumi. SP-Rumi, tr. by Coleman Barks

We are the night ocean filled. Jelaluddin Rumi. SP-Rumi, tr. by Coleman Barks

We Are the Resurrection. Laura Riding Jackson. CP-RidiL

We are the river you spoke of, Heraclitus. Maker, The. Jorge Luis Borges. SP-BorgJ, tr. by Stephen Kessler

We are the seas through whom the great fish passed. Neruda, the Wine. Muriel Rukeyser. CP-RukeM

•We are the smirched. Queen Honor is the spotless. Honor Among Scamps. Nicholas Vachel Lindsay. CP-LindV

We Are Those People. Robinson Jeffers. CP-JefR3

We are three women eating out. Crêpes Flambeau. Tess Gallagher. SP-GallT

We are tired of your tiresome imitations of Mayakovsky. Answer to Voznesensky and Evtushenko. Frank O'Hara. SP-OharF

We are to be his victim after all. Petrarch. CP-Petra, tr. by J. G. Nichols

We are to tell one man tonight good-bye. Farewell to Miles. John Berryman. CP-BerrJ

We are too much on the outside. Whip, The. Charles Tomlinson. CP-TomlC

We Are Transmitters. D. H. Lawrence. CP-LawrD

We are trying to live. Rough Times. Marge Piercy. SP-PierM

We are two acquaintances on a train. Sunday Evening. Adrienne Rich. CP-RicAE

We are two countries girded for the war. Foreign Affairs. Stanley Kunitz. CP-KunSC

We are two lovers of no careless breed. To Be Poets. Robert Graves. CP-GravR

We are very slightly changed. General Summary, A. Rudyard Kipling. CP-KiplR

We Are Waiting. Yannis Ritsos. SP-RitsY, tr. by Thanasis Maskaleris

We are warned by slow footsteps. Second People, The. Kenneth Patchen. CP-PatcK

We are what we are made; each following day. Written in Naples, March, 1833. Ralph Waldo Emerson. CP-EmerR

We arrange and we compose. Rainer Maria Rilke. CP-RilkFr, tr. by A. Poulin, Jr. Fr. Orchards.

We asked for rain. It didn't flash and roar. Our Hold on the Planet. Robert Frost. CP-FrosR

We ate with steeps of sky about our shoulders. Terrace, The. Richard Wilbur. CP-WilbR

We be the Gods of the East. Rudyard Kipling. CP-KiplR Fr. Naulahka, The.

We Become New. Marge Piercy. SP-PierM

We—Bee and I—live by the quaffing. Emily Dickinson. CP-DickE

We began at The Silver Shadow. Butterfly-toed Shoes. Yusef Komunyakaa. CP-KomuY

We begin with the osprey who cries, "Clang, clang!" Marriage Song: "We begin with the osprey who cries, 'Clang, clang!'" Carolyn Kizer. CP-KizeC

We being not each other:without love. E. E. Cummings. CP-CummE

We believed in highdays then. Yuletide in a Younger World. Thomas Hardy. CP-HardT

We blame, nay we despise her paines. Out of Time, Out of Tune. Robert Herrick. CP-HerrR

We blench when maniacs to dance begin. Judex Jocosus. Ambrose Bierce. SP-BierA

We both are mortal; but thou, frailer creature. On a Very Old Glass. Jonathan Swift. CP-SwifJ

We boys are privates in our Regiment's ranks. Conclusion of a Compliment to the Captain. Robert Browning. CP-BroR2

We breed plants, order seeds from. Daily Life of the Worker Bee, The. Marge Piercy. SP-PierM

We buried her among the flowers. Song: "We buried her among the flowers." Christina Georgina Rossetti. CP-RosC3

We buried him high on a windy hill. Death of an Old Seaman. Langston Hughes. CP-HughL; CP-HughL1

We call for discipline not expecting applause. Higher Arguments in Favor of Discipline Derived from the Speech Before the Council of the Universal State in 2068. Czeslaw Milosz. CP-MiloC; CP-MiloCN, tr. by Robert Hass

We call it a grain of sand. View with a Grain of Sand. Wisława Szymborska. SP-SzymWM, tr. by Joanna Trzeciak

We call it a grain of sand. View with a Grain of Sand. Wisława Szymborska. SP-SzymW, tr. by Stanislaw Barańczak and Clare Cavanagh

We call material this fair world of ours. Revelation of the Spirit Through the Material World, The. Jones Very. CP-VeryJ

We call them beautiful. Turner's Seas. Kathleen Jessie Raine. SP-RainK

We call up the green to hide us. Summer Wish. Louise Bogan. CP-BogaL

We called him—with his three / chins, earnest. Rumour. Charles Tomlinson. CP-TomlC

We cam' na here to view your warks. Verses Written on a Window of the Inn at Carron. Robert Burns. CP-BurnR

We came behind him by the wall. Wood-Cutter, The. G. K. Chesterton. CP-ChesG

We came by night. Near Hartland. Charles Tomlinson. CP-TomlC

We came here to live in a small town. Main Street. Miller Williams. CP-WillM

We came over the moor-top. Great Carbuncle, The. Sylvia Plath. CP-PlatS

We came to the outer light down a ramp in the dark. Westland Row. Thomas Kinsella. CP-KinsT

We came to visit the cow. Freedom, New Hampshire. Galway Kinnell. SP-KinnGN

We came where the salmon were so many. That Morning. Ted Hughes. SP-HughTN

We can but follow to the Sun. Emily Dickinson. CP-DickE

We can do little for these living dead. Virus, The. Robert Graves. CP-GravR

We can endure that He should waste our lands. Indignation of a High-Minded Spaniard 1810. William Wordsworth. CP-WorW1

We can look into the stove tonight. Burning Oneself Out. Adrienne Rich. SP-RicA2

We can not weather all this gold. Late Spring. "H. D." CP-DoolH

We can see you even now, asleep. Cradle Song for Mercedes, in Death. Federico García Lorca. CP-GarcF, tr. by Christopher Maurer

We cannot believe for each other. Emily Dickinson. SP-DickE

We cannot go to the country. Raleigh Was Right. William Carlos Williams. CP-WilW2

We cannot live, except thus mutually. Love. Elizabeth Barrett Browning. CP-BroEB

We Can't Be Too Careful. D. H. Lawrence. CP-LawrD

We can't complain. Middle Class Blues. Hans Magnus Enzensberger. SP-EnzeH, tr. by Hans Magnus Enzensberger and Michael Hamburger

We carried 'em in on barrows and planks. With Military Honors. Tennessee Williams. CP-WillT

We caught lions copulating on the plains. Lions Copulating. Richard Eberhart. CP-EberR

We caught the tread of dancing feet. Harlot's House, The. Oscar Wilde. CP-WildO

We chanced in passing by that afternoon. Black Cottage, The. Robert Frost. CP-FrosR

We Christmas-carolled down the Vale, and up the Vale, and round the Vale. Rash Bride, The. Thomas Hardy. CP-HardT

We climb, the changes changing rapidly. Foliage Tour, The. Wyatt Prunty. SP-PrunW

We climbed by the old quarries to the wide highland of heath. Broadstone, The. Robinson Jeffers. CP-JefR2

We climbed that day. Glacier, The. Charles Tomlinson. CP-TomlC

We climbed the Capitol by moonlight, felt. Seamus Heaney. SP-HeanSO Fr. Squarings.

We climbed the hill to the carriages. Clarence Major. SP-MajoC

We climbed the steep ascent to heaven. Saddest Day, The. D. H. Lawrence. CP-LawrD

We Come Back. Kenneth Rexroth. CP-RexrK

"We come," he says, "to bury an empty shell." During a Funeral Service the Mind of the Young Preacher Wanders Again. Miller Williams. CP-WillM

We come into being in alien cities. Song of an Emigré. Adam Zagajewski. SP-ZagaA, tr. by Renata Gorczynski

We come to this country. To be Sung on the Fourth of July. Wyatt Prunty. SP-PrunW

We come to you, men of weak faith. Ode for the Eightieth Birthday of Pope John Paul II. Czeslaw Milosz. CP-MiloCN, tr. by Robert Hass

We consider / precedent to that Shekinah. She. Maiden, The. Robert Duncan. SP-DuncR

We consider the underlying fallacy of the plaintiff's argument. Plessy vs Ferguson: Theme and Variations. Thomas Merton. CP-MertT

We Continue. W. S. Merwin. SP-MerwW

"We could try it," / Ralph says to Harold. Green Door, The. James Schuyler. CP-SchuJ

We could weep for him. Bodo. Thomas Lux. SP-LuxT

We couldn't even keep the furnace lit! To Delmore Schwartz. Robert Lowell. SP-LoweR

We counted several flames in one small fire. Tranced, The. Theodore Roethke. CP-RoetT

We Cover Thee—Sweet Face. Emily Dickinson. CP-DickE

We credit most our sight; one eye doth please. Eyes before the Eares, The. Robert Herrick. CP-HerrR

We cross the prairie as of old. Kansas Emigrants, The. John Greenleaf Whittier. CP-WhitJ

We cross the Sacramento River at Colusa. River in the Valley. Gary Snyder. CP-SnydG

We crossed Champlain to Keeseville with our friends. Adirondacs, The. Ralph Waldo Emerson. CP-EmerR

We cry among the skyscrapers. Afraid. Langston Hughes. CP-HughL; CP-HughL1

We dance on Chilean earth. Chilean Earth. Gabriela Mistral. SP-MistG, tr. by Maria Giachetti [or Jacketti]

We dance round in a ring and suppose. Secret Sits, The. Robert Frost. CP-FrosR

We Defer Things. James Whitcomb Riley. CP-RileJ

We descended the first night from Europe riding the ship's sling. Coming Back to America. James Dickey. CP-DickJ

We did at last manage to get the eyes. Colony of the Sun, The. Kenneth Patchen. CP-PatcK

We did it before the mirror. Yehuda Amichai. SP-AmicYL, tr. by Benjamin Harshav and Barbara Harshav

We did not know the first thing about. Thinking about Bill, Dead of AIDS. Miller Williams. CP-WillM

We did our duty. We Have Done Our Duty. Yehuda Amichai. SP-AmicYL, tr. by Benjamin Harshav and Barbara Harshav

We Did What We Had To. Chana Bloch. SP-AmicY

We didn't know at the time. It was. Long Distance. William Stafford. SP-StafW; SP-StafWW

We die. Great Contemporary Discoveries. Archibald MacLeish. CP-MacLA

We Die Together. D. H. Lawrence. CP-LawrD

We die, / Welcoming Bluebeards to our darkening closets. Detached, The. Maya Angelou. SP-AngeM

We dine in a glade concealed in peach petals. In Dream's Wake. Ts'un Hsu Li. CP-WilW2

We do not bargain for delight; vitality. Ark: Angelus: Anvil. Kenneth Patchen. CP-PatcK

We do not care. Wisdom and War. Langston Hughes. CP HughL; CP HughL2

We do not curse thee, Waterloo! Ode from the French. Lord Byron. CP-Byron

We do not know the time we lose. Emily Dickinson. CP-DickE

We do not play on Graves. Emily Dickinson. CP-DickE

We do not see them come. Scala Coeli. Kathleen Jessie Raine. SP-RainK

We do not speak like Petrarch or wear a hat like Spenser. American Sonnet. Billy Collins. SP-CollB

We don't cry Tim and I. Emily Dickinson. CP DickE

We don't exist unless we are deeply and sensually in touch. Non-Existence. D. H. Lawrence. CP-LawrD

We don't go much on lawin'. Case in P'int, A. James Whitcomb Riley. CP-RileJ

We don't know how lovely the elements are. Elements, The. D. H. Lawrence. CP-LawrD

We don't lack people here on the Northern coast. Amusing Our Daughters. Carolyn Kizer. CP-KizeC

We don't need a face in the picture to know. Hands. W. H. Auden. CP-AudeW

We Don't Need to Leave Yet, Do We? Or, Yes We Do. Ogden Nash. CP-NashO

We don't see dew from this morning. Han-shan. CP-ColdM, tr. by Red Pine

We don't want to fight. On Benjamin Disraeli. Robert Browning. CP-BroR2

We dream—it is good we are dreaming. Emily Dickinson. CP-DickE

We drive between lakes just turning green. Driving through Minnesota during the Hanoi Bombings. Robert Bly. SP-BlyR

We drop in the evening like dew. Ecology, An. David Ignatow. SP-IgnaD

We drove through October, Grandmother pointing at cows. River Styx, Ohio, The. Mary Oliver. SP-OlivM

We dust the walls. Aus Einem April. Frank O'Hara. SP-OharF

We eat this body and remain ourselves. Air without Incense. Adrienne Rich. CP-RicAE

We enter this evening as we enter a quartet. Evening Music. May Sarton. SP-SartM

We entered silence / before the clock struck. Suspension. Audre Lorde. SP-LordA

We extend arms / infinitely long. Morning Shutters. Arthur Sze. SP-SzeA

We Field-Women. Thomas Hardy. CP-HardT

We fight for hours, through dinner, through the endless evening, who even knows now what about. Peace. C. K. Williams. SP-WillC

We finished clearing the last. Above Pate Valley. Gary Snyder. CP-SnydG

We fixed the ages of the irises at flower. To the Quick. Heather McHugh. SP-McHuH

We fling our being, Norman, hurl our full flesh. Word with Norman Rosten. Robert Stock. SP-StocR

We flung against their gods. After Troy. "H. D." CP-DoolH

We fly through a night of stars. Spiritual Explorations. Stephen Spender. CP-SpenS

We followed the narrow track, my love, we followed the narrow. Mudroom, The. Paul Muldoon. CP-MuldP

We forget sometimes that no matter what. Convivio. William Carlos Williams. CP-WilW2

We forgot where we came from. Our Jewish. Jews in the Land of Israel. Yehuda Amichai. SP-AmicY, tr. by Chana Bloch

We found him in that Far-away that yet to us seems near. Proem: "We found him in that Far-away that yet to us seems near." James Whitcomb Riley. CP-RileJ

We found them again under the rock, in the rock. Silent. Dead, The. Yannis Ritsos. SP-RitsY Fr. Monovasia.

We found this small, dry rise with a nice view. Middle-Class Vantage. Eleanor Wilner. SP-WilnE

We gave our craft to the slow-moving stream. Downstream ("We gave our craft to the slow-moving stream"). Thomas Kinsella. CP-KinsT

We gaze—nor grieve to think that we must die. Upon a Portrait. William Wordsworth. CP-WorW2

We give the world to understand. Drapier's Hill. Jonathan Swift. CP-SwifJ

We give thy natal day to hope. Our Country. John Greenleaf Whittier. CP-WhitJ

We give to chivalry a separate age. Chivalry. George Meredith. CP-MerG2

We go by detachments to the strange Home. Emily Dickinson. SP-DickE

We go down by the deserted mule-track. Retrospect, A: 1951-91. Charles Tomlinson. SP-TomlC

We go no more to Calverly's. Calverly's. Edwin Arlington Robinson. CP-RobiE

We Go Out Together. Kenneth Patchen. CP-PatcK

We go out together into the staring town. We Go Out Together. Kenneth Patchen. CP-PatcK

We go over to see the head of a woman. Balance and Beauty. Clarence Major. SP-MajoC

We go to gather berries of rain. One Morning in New Hampshire. May Swenson. SP-SwenM

We' got a' Uncle writes poetry-rhymes. Lisping in Numbers. James Whitcomb Riley. CP-RileJ

We got it up a-purpose, jes' fer little Johnts, you know. Little Johnts's Chris'mus. James Whitcomb Riley. CP-RileJ

We got rid of the big people. Before This. C. K. Williams. CP-WillC

We got up a Christmas-doin's. John Alden and Percilly. James Whitcomb Riley. CP-RileJ

We grant they're thine, those beauties all. Extempore—On Being Shown a Beautiful County Seat Belonging to the Same [Maxwell of Cardoness]. Robert Burns. CP-BurnR

We grow accustomed to the Dark. Emily Dickinson. CP-DickE

We had a fellow-Passenger who came. September 1, 1802. William Wordsworth. MW-WorW

We had a female Passenger who came. September 1, 1802. William Wordsworth. CP-WorW1

We had a guitar, a knife, three unmatched chairs. Other Man, The. Yannis Ritsos. SP-RitsY, *tr. by* Kimon Friar *and* Kostas Myrsiades

We had a motorbike all through the war. Motorbike, A. Ted Hughes. SP-HughTN

We had already left him. I walked the ice. Ugolino. Dante Alighieri. SP-HeanSO, *tr. by* Seamus Heaney *Fr.* Divina Commedia.

We had an hour. "—and on the way," she said. Rodin: The Cathedral. Miller Williams. CP-WillM

We had been in the tall grass for hours. At Midsummer. Norman Dubie. CP-DubiN

We had been wandering for many days. Bridal of Pennacook, The. John Greenleaf Whittier. CP-WhitJ

We had begun to think the winter would never end. Spring Revelations. John Logan. CP-LogaJ

We had codes. Scraps. Louise Glück. SP-GlucL

We had come from being kind. What Happened in the Camps. Kenneth Patchen. CP-PatcK

We had lived centuries apart. The imperial. Amelia. Eleanor Wilner. SP-WilnE

We had made love and I asked. It Was the First Time. James Laughlin. CP-LaugJ

We had not expected it, the whole street. Red Hook: December. George Oppen. CP-OppGN

We had our wells within our houses. Wells and People. Yannis Ritsos. SP-RitsY, *tr. by* Kimon Friar

We had ridden three days Eugenie and I. Who Shot Eugenie? Stevie Smith. CP-SmitS

We had seen bare land. Memory at 'The Modern.' George Oppen. CP-OppGN

We had to take the world as it was given. Ideal Landscape. Adrienne Rich. CP-RicAE; SP-RicA2

We hail our Jubilee to-day. Hymn, Sung at the Thompson Jubilee, at Barre, Jan. 12, 1854. Jones Very. CP-VeryJ

We hardly ever see the moon any more. Avenue A. Frank O'Hara. SP-OharF

We hate the Victorians so much. Deadly Victorians, The. D. H. Lawrence. CP-LawrD

We have a bat, one bat, that bug-surfs / our late-summer back yard. Meditation on Summer and Shapelessness. Charles Wright. SP-WrigCN

We Have a Beautiful Mother. Alice Walker. CP-WalkA

We have a huge barrel of wine, but no cups. Jelaluddin Rumi. SP-Rumi, *tr. by* Coleman Barks

We have a language that serves us more or less. For Rebecca, for Whom Nothing Has Been Written Page after Page. Miller Williams. CP-WillM

We have a lawn of moss. For Doreen. A Voice from the Garden. Donald Davie. CP-DaviDC

We Have a Map of the World. Alice Walker. CP-WalkA

We have a song for the death in her body. Ballad, A: "We have a song for the death in her body." Robert Creeley. CP-CreeR

We have all been in rooms. Adultery. James Dickey. CP-DickJ

We have all resigned ourselves. No More Than Is. Laura Riding Jackson. CP-RidiL

We have another Viceroy now,—those days are dead and done. Rudyard Kipling. *See* Delilah Aberyswith was a lady—not too young

We have been here quite a while. Dialogue. Carl Sandburg. CP-SandC

We have been looking at cars lately. Summer in Sacramento, A. Raymond Carver. CP-CarvR

We have been picketing Woolworth's. Poem, Small and Delible. Carolyn Kizer. CP-KizeC

We have been shown. Six Variations. Denise Levertov. SP-LeveDP

We have bit no forbidden apple. Renascence. D. H. Lawrence. CP-LawrD

"We have brought you," they said, "a map of the country." Have a Good Time. W. H. Auden. CP-AudeW

We have come back to the cold North. To the North. May Sarton. SP-SartM

We have come down by the moon brilliantly. Tenor Sax Taking the Breaks. Tennessee Williams. CP-WillT

We have cried in our despair. When Helen Lived. William Butler Yeats. CP-YeatW

We Have Done Our Duty. Yehuda Amichai. SP-AmicYL, *tr. by* Benjamin Harshav *and* Barbara Harshav

We have forgotten weather, by virtue of the protecting mass. Escape in Ice. Josephine Jacobsen. CP-JacoJ

We have found a certain heavy kind of wolf. Research Team in the Mountains, The. William Stafford. SP-StafW; SP-StafWW

We have gone out in boats upon the sea at night. Passage Over Water. Robert Duncan. SP-DuncR

We Have Gone Through Great Rooms Together. Carl Sandburg. CP-SandC

We Have Gone Too Far. D. H. Lawrence. CP-LawrD

We have gone too far; we do not know how to stop: impetus. Edna St. Vincent Millay. CP-MillE

We have heard of Quintia's beauty. To me she is tall, slender. Carmen 86. Catullus. CP-ZukLS *Fr.* Carmina.

We have heard of the undimmed air. Icarium Mare. Richard Wilbur. CP-WilbR

We have lived in that room larger than the world. Lyf so short . . . , The. William Stafford. SP-StafWW

We have loved each other in this time twenty years. Unfinished History. Archibald MacLeish. CP-MacLA

We have made a new surface of the earth. Rainer Maria Rilke. CP-RilkFr, *tr. by* A. Poulin, Jr. *Fr.* Fragments.

We have memorized America. Of History and Hope. Miller Williams. CP-WillM

We have met late—it is too late to meet. Denial, A. Elizabeth Barrett Browning. CP-BroEB

We have never quite starved, thanks to some God or other. Cretan Woman, The. Robinson Jeffers. CP-JefR3

We have no father and no mother. Thank You. Stevie Smith. CP-SmitS

We have no heart for the fishing—we have no hand for the oar. Dykes, The. Rudyard Kipling. CP-KiplR

We have no history. Ballad for Americans. Charles Olson. CP-OlsoC

We have no peanuts to eat so sad. Song for 2 Balalaikas on the Corner of 3rd & Market. Philip Whalen. SP-WhalP

We have no prairies. Bogland. Seamus Heaney. SP-HeanSO

We have no statutes here. Emily Dickinson. SP-DickE

We have not forgot the clanking of grey armors. Crusade. Robert Penn Warren. CP-WarrR

We Have Not Long to Love. Tennessee Williams. CP-WillT

We have now set forth, in our imperfect way. Epilogue: "We have now set forth, in our imperfect way." Thomas Hardy. CP-HardT *Fr.* Dynasts, The.

We have now won two world-wars; neither of which concerned us; we. So Many Blood-Lakes. Robinson Jeffers. CP-JefR3

We have often considered the wind. Why of the Wind, The. Laura Riding Jackson. CP-RidiL

We have opened the door. Dead Feast of the Kol-Folk, The. John Greenleaf Whittier. CP-WhitJ

We have reached the end of pastime, for always. End of Play. Robert Graves. CP-GravR

We have seen a house in the sleeping town. Death of the Horses by Fire. Tess Gallagher. SP-GallT

We have seen how dignity can be torn. Hard Death, A. May Sarton. SP-SartM

We have seen mighty men ballooning high. Warning, The. George Meredith. CP-MerG2

We have seen so much on earth and yet malachite mountains at sunset are greeted as always with a song and a low bow. Dithyramb. Czeslaw Milosz. CP-MiloC; CP-MiloCN, *tr. by* Peter Dale Scott

We Have Seen Thee, O Love. Algernon Charles Swinburne. SP-SwinA *Fr.* Atalanta in Calydon.

We have shown each other the tricks. To C. T. Donald Davie. CP-DaviDC

We have shut the doors behind us, and the velvet flowers of night. Hyde Park at Night, before the War. D. H. Lawrence. CP-LawrD

We have struck the regions wherein we are keel or reef. Zone. Louise Bogan. CP-BogaL

We have the looks you want. Purists Will Object. John Ashbery. SP-AshbJ

We have the picture of you in mind. Three Graces, The. William Carlos Williams. CP-WilW2

We have the waking of an eye. In the Dry. George Meredith. CP-MerG2

We have this way of talking, and we have another. Jelaluddin Rumi. SP-Rumi, *tr. by* Coleman Barks

We have thought long enough and talked long enough. Fanatic, The. G. K. Chesterton. CP-ChesG

We have tomorrow. Youth. Langston Hughes. CP-HughL

We have wept the bloods of countless ages. Tomorrow. Peter Blue Cloud. SP-BlueP

We have wintered the death of the old, cold year. Coming of May, The. E. E. Cummings. CP-CummE

We have written. Genius, The. William Carlos Williams. CP-WilW2

We have written to Giulia, saying. Gemona-del-Friuli, 1961–1976. Donald Davie. CP-DaviDC

We hear a song bird trilling. Nanine. Ambrose Bierce. SP-BierA

We hear about the ministers of state. Han-shan. CP-ColdM, *tr. by* Red Pine

We hear it but choose to ignore. Good News and Gospel. Philip Whalen. SP-WhalP

We hear nothing these days. Margaret Atwood. SP-AtwM1

We heard of that king & his building. Events in a Rustic Mirror. George Meredith. CP-MerG2

We held a meeting in Eureka. Arts Council Meets in Eureka, The. Gary Snyder. CP-SnydG

We Hesitate. John Ashbery. SP-AshbJ

We hibernate among the bricks. Interlude in London. T. S. Eliot. SP-ElioT

We hit like a hoof. Hands. Archibald MacLeish. CP-MacLA

We hold these truths to be self-evident. Decoy. John Ashbery. SP-AshbJ

We Hold These Truths to Be Self-Evident. Kenneth Patchen. CP-PatcK

We hunger for the iridescent shine of an abalone shell. Renga: "We hunger for the iridescent shine of an abalone shell." Arthur Sze. SP-SzeA

We hunted the mad bastard. As It Should Be. Derek Mahon. CP-MahoD

We hurry back to resume our awaited commissions. Men (XIX), The. Pablo Neruda. SP-NeruP *Fr.* Separate Rose, The.

We hurtle forward and seem to rise. Plane. W. S. Merwin. SP-MerwW

We ice skated once. Family. William Corbett. SP-CorbW

We immediately recognize the coconut palms. Coconut Palms, The. Gabriela Mistral. SP-MistG, *tr. by* Maria Giachetti [*or* Jacketti]

We in all lights are coming. Dark Ones. James Dickey. CP-DickJ

We in our season like progress and inventions. Parallel Invention. Muriel Rukeyser. CP-RukeM

We inherited more than body language. De Síntoma Profundo. Yusef Komunyakaa. CP-KomuY

We Interrupt to Bring You. William Stafford. SP-StafWW

We introduce ourselves. Emily Dickinson. CP-DickE

We invented one. Nymph to Narcissus, The. Heather McHugh. SP-McHuH

We is gathahed hyeah, my brothahs. Ante-Bellum Sermon, An. Paul Laurence Dunbar. CP-DunbP

We join the animals. Heroic Sculpture. Frank O'Hara. SP-OharF

We keep forgetting the world is alive. What's New? Philip Whalen. SP-WhalP

We keep forgetting where we came from. Our Jewish names. Jews in the Land of Israel. Yehuda Amichai. SP-AmicYL, *tr. by* Benjamin Harshav *and* Barbara Harshav

We kissed at the barrier; and passing through. On the Departure Platform. Thomas Hardy. CP-HardT

We knew all that before your tender coming. Loss. Rainer Maria Rilke. CP-RilkFr, *tr. by* A. Poulin, Jr.

We knew. / Anne to come. New. Gertrude Stein. CP-SteiG

We knew him first as a pious reputation. Administrator. Thomas Kinsella. CP-KinsT

We knew him when he was dressed, austere, collected. Maturity. Yannis Ritsos. SP-RitsY, *tr. by* Gwendolyn MacEwen *and* Nikos Tsingos

We knew how to order. Just the dash. Gay Chaps at the Bar. Gwendolyn Brooks. SP-BrooG *Fr.* Gay Chaps at the Bar.

We knew it was not a valid thing. Poor Man and a Lady, A. Thomas Hardy. CP-HardT

We knew not that we were to live. Emily Dickinson. CP-DickE

We knew the world backwards and forwards. Wisława Szymborska. SP-SzymWM, *tr. by* Joanna Trzeciak

We knew thee of old. Ode to Liberty. Rudyard Kipling. CP-KiplR

We know everything we read a lot. Adam Zagajewski. SP-ZagaA, *tr. by* Renata Gorczynski

We know him—Law and Order League. Lorine Niedecker. CP-NiedL

We know not a voice of that River, / If vocal or silent it be. Whitsun Monday. Christina Georgina Rossetti. CP-RosC2

We know not when, we know not where. Christina Georgina Rossetti. CP-RosC2

We know, O faltering heart. Wait. James Whitcomb Riley. CP-RileJ

We know the Rocket's upward whizz. Bonfires, The. Rudyard Kipling. CP-KiplR

We know the scene: the room, variously furnished. Annunciation. Denise Levertov. SP-LeveDS

We know the story. Generation. Rae Armantrout. SP-ArmaA

We know the story. The children. Remembering the Children of Auschwitz.

We know those tales of gods in hot pursuit. Under a Tree. Richard Wilbur. CP-WilbR

We know we're not allowed to use your name. Soul, The. Adam Zagajewski. SP-ZagaA, *tr. by* Clare Cavanagh

We last of Yugo-Slav. Well-found Poem. Donald Davie. CP-DaviDC

We laugh, we frown, our fingers twitch. Ageless Reason. Robert Graves. CP-GravR

We laughed when he sat down at the piano. "You've Tried the World, Try Jesus." Robert Creeley. CP-CreeR

We lay beneath the alder tree. What Must. Archibald MacLeish. CP-MacLA

We lay / deep in the maquis as you. Paul Celan. SP-CelaP, *tr. by* John Felstiner

We lay red roses on his grave. Paul Laurence Dunbar. Robert Earl Hayden. CP-HaydR

We lead our real lives. Barbarity, A. George Oppen. CP-OppGN

We lean outdoors toward. Heart's Noise. Rainer Maria Rilke. CP-RilkFr, *tr. by* A. Poulin, Jr.

We lean'd beneath the purple vine. Rhine-Land. George Meredith. CP-MerG2

We leaned against the rain-spitted. Native Wisdom. Thomas Kinsella. CP-KinsT

We learn in the Retreating. Emily Dickinson. CP-DickE

We learned the Whole of Love. Emily Dickinson. CP-DickE

We Leave You Pleasure. Kenneth Patchen. CP-PatcK

We lent to Alexander the strength of Hercules. Parade-Song of the Camp Animals. Rudyard Kipling. CP-KiplR *Fr.* Jungle Book, The.

We lie like the gods. Perfect Love Casteth Out Everything. Randall Jarrell. CP-JarrR

We like a Hairbreadth 'scape. Emily Dickinson. CP-DickE

We like March. Emily Dickinson. CP-DickE

We like March—his shoes are Purple. Emily Dickinson. CP-DickE

We liked its name: those ones, feminine plural. Celles. Marilyn Hacker. SP-HackM

We lit a fire with some dry twigs. 17 November 1948. Yannis Ritsos. SP-RitsY, *tr. by* Minas Savvas *Fr.* Exile's Journals 1.

We live beneath / a giant mirror. Giant Mirror, The. Federico García Lorca. CP-GarcF, *tr. by* Jerome Rothenberg *Fr.* Mirror Suite.

We live by Faith; but Faith is not the slave. Requirement. John Greenleaf Whittier. CP-WhitJ

We live by love, but not by love alone. Oysters and Hermits. Donald Hall. CP-HallD

We live in a constellation. July Mountain. Wallace Stevens. CP-StevWP

We live in crystal / cells. Beehive. Federico García Lorca. CP-GarcF, *tr. by* Jerome Rothenberg *Fr.* Water Suite.

We live in history, says one. Talk in the Dark. Denise Levertov. SP-LeveDL

We live in the world of the voice, / not in the world of the word. Absence Inside an Absence. Charles Wright. SP-WrigCN

We live in this flat blue basin. Invitation. William Carlos Williams. CP-WilW1

We live on an ancient bartering ground. Memories of Muzot. Rainer Maria Rilke. CP-RilkFr, *tr. by* A. Poulin, Jr.

We live our lives of human passions. Sojourns in the Parallel World. Denise Levertov. SP-LeveDS

We live the lives our parents never knew. Ghosts. Derek Mahon. CP-MahoD

We lived deep in a land of optative moods. From the Canton of Expectation. Seamus Heaney. SP-HeanSO

We lived in a city tinted the color of frozen vodka. Photograph, A. Joseph Brodsky. CP-BrodJ

We lived understanding little and craving. Lightning. Adam Zagajewski. SP-ZagaA, *tr. by* Renata Gorczynski

We look for her that sunlike stood. France. George Meredith. CP-MerG1

We look for her that sunlike stood. George Meredith. CP-MerG1 *Fr.* France.

We look out at them on clear nights, thrilled. Examples of Created Systems. William Meredith. SP-MereW

We look up at her. Sheelagh na Gig. Seamus Heaney. SP-HeanSO

We looked at Matthew's child, our granddaughter. Grandparents. Stephen Spender. CP-SpenS

We looked at the hawthorn with the helpless joy. Trees in Spring, The. Randall Jarrell. CP-JarrR

We looked for the tide, for the full river. Severnside. Charles Tomlinson. CP-TomlC

We looked, we loved, and therewith instantly. Pure Death. Robert Graves. CP-GravR

We loosen the coping-stone that has sealed for years. Well, The. Charles Tomlinson. SP-TomlC

We lose—because we win. Emily Dickinson. CP-DickE

We love each other very dearly. E. E. Cummings. CP-CummE

We love Paris. Migration of Cities, The. Thomas McGrath. SP-McGrT

We love the venerable house. Hymn Sung at the Second Church, Boston, at the Ordination of Rev. Chandler Robbins. Ralph Waldo Emerson. CP-EmerR

We Love This Body. Robert Bly. SP-BlyR

We love to think of Alan Gaylord. Clerihew for Alan Gaylord, A. Richard

Eberhart. CP-EberR

We love your dear old face and voice. To "Uncle Remus." James Whitcomb Riley. CP-RileJ

We Loved Here. Yehuda Amichai.

   "In the long nights our room was closed off and." SP-AmicY, *tr. by* Stephen Mitchell

   "Lips of dead men whisper where they lie, The." SP-AmicY, *tr. by* Stephen Mitchell

   "My father spent four years inside their war." SP-AmicY, *tr. by* Stephen Mitchell

   "Preface first: the two of them, the brittle, A." SP-AmicY, *tr. by* Stephen Mitchell

We Lying by Seasand. Dylan Thomas. CP-ThomD

We made all possible preparations. Let History Be My Judge. W. H. Auden. CP-AudeW

We made strong poems for each other. Neighbors. Audre Lorde. SP-LordA

We make our meek adjustments. Chaplinesque. Hart Crane. CP-CranH

We Make Our Vows Together with All Beings. Gary Snyder. CP-SnydG

We make ourselves a place apart. Revelation. Robert Frost. CP-FrosR

We marched, and saw a company of Canadians. Canadians. Ivor Gurney. SP-GurnI

We marked the pitch: four jackets for four goalposts. Markings. Seamus Heaney. SP-HeanSO

We may idealize the chief of men. Doctor, The. James Whitcomb Riley. CP-RileJ

We may not always rate. Laws Can Say, The. Louis Zukofsky. CP-ZukLS

We may well ask now: "Where are the lilacs?" Yes . . . . Lament for Pablo Neruda. Thomas McGrath. SP-McGrT

We measured the place, flung the dead in lime. Sluggishly. Yannis Ritsos. SP-RitsY, *tr. by* Kostas Myrsiades

We meet again: but all around. J.D.C., The: A Reunion. G. K. Chesterton. CP-ChesG

We meet, eating, smoking. William Dickey. SP-DickW *Fr.* In The Dreaming.

We meet in an evil land. Rudyard Kipling. CP-KiplR *Fr.* Naulahka, The.

We meet in joy, tho' we part in sorrow. Martyrs' Song. Christina Georgina Rossetti. CP-RosC1

We meet no Stranger. Emily Dickinson. SP-DickE

We meet not as we parted. Lines: "We meet not as we parted." Percy Bysshe Shelley. CP-ShelP

We merit all we suffer, and by far. Sufferings. Robert Herrick. CP-HerrR

We met as Sparks—Diverging Flints. Emily Dickinson. CP-DickE

We met, hand to hand. Twilight Night. Christina Georgina Rossetti. CP-RosC1

We Met in a Dream. James Laughlin. CP-LaugJ

We met the British in the dead of winter. Meeting the British. Paul Muldoon. CP-MuldP

We met where people like us meet. Elegy for a Writer. Eleanor Wilner. SP-WilnE

We might have foreseen it. Wheelers and Dealers: The Theory of Games. George Oppen. CP-OppGN

We might have guessed it would end in argument. Portrait of the Artist, A. Thomas Kinsella. CP-KinsT

We miss a Kinsman more. Emily Dickinson. CP-DickE

We miss Her, not because We see. Emily Dickinson. CP-DickE

We miss you,jack—tactfully you(with one cocked). E. E. Cummings. CP-CummE

We move as dragons in the lethargy. Albigenses, The. Robert Duncan. SP-DuncR

We move on; but does the weight. Heavy Dead, The. Rainer Maria Rilke. CP-RilkFr, *tr. by* A. Poulin, Jr.

We moved down the valley. Forms of Knowledge, The. Kenneth Patchen. CP-PatcK

We moved like fingers. San Francisco Poem. John Logan. CP-LogaJ

We moved to be happy. Fanny Howe. SP-HoweF *Fr.* Q.

We moved with pensive paces. Noble Lady's Tale, The. Thomas Hardy. CP-HardT

We must admire her perfect aim. Colder the Air, The. Elizabeth Bishop. CP-BishE

We must anticipate the dawn one day. Roe Deer, The. Charles Tomlinson. CP-TomlC

We must at times acknowledge on the balance sheet. To The Discreet Reader: An Induction to Indiscretions. Robert Stock. SP-StocR

We must be careful what we say. Emily Dickinson. SP-DickE

We must be less than Death. Emily Dickinson. SP-DickE

We Must Be Polite. Carl Sandburg. CP-SandC

We Must Be Slow. Kenneth Patchen. CP-PatcK

We must be slow and delicate; return. My Generation Reading the Newspapers. Kenneth Patchen. CP-PatcK

We must be the only ones. After the Flood, We. Margaret Atwood. SP-AtwM1

We Must Believe. James Whitcomb Riley. CP-RileJ

We must believe that all is well. Rainer Maria Rilke. CP-RilkFr, *tr.* by A. Poulin, Jr. *Fr.* Affectionate Taxes to France.

We must bring no Twilight. Emily Dickinson. SP-DickE

We must dream inwards, and we must dream. Variation on Paz. Charles Tomlinson. CP-TomlC

We must get home! How could we stray like this? James Whitcomb Riley. CP-RileJ

We must go back and find a trail on the ground. Watching the Jet Planes Dive. William Stafford. SP-StafW; SP-StafWW

We must lie long in the weeds. Way We Write Letters, The. Carolyn Kizer. CP-KizeC

We Must Make a Kingdom of It. Gregory Orr. SP-OrrG

We must not honor a girl of Minnie's kind. Moments of Minnie. John Crowe Ransom. SP-RansJ

We must say it all, and as clearly. Each One, Pull One. Alice Walker. CP-WalkA

We must see, we must know. Slop Barrel, The. Philip Whalen. SP-WhalP

We must sit down. Councils. Marge Piercy. SP-PierM

We must work & play and John Jacob Niles. Home Ballad, The. John Berryman. CP-BerrJ

We Mutually Pledge to Each Other. Kenneth Patchen. CP-PatcK

We need a private bush. Somehow. Marge Piercy. SP-PierM

We need more reverence in this froward age. Reverence. Jones Very. CP-VeryJ

We need some rallying point round which. George Meredith. CP-MerG2

We need the ceremony of one another. Hazard Faces a Sunday in the Decline. William Meredith. SP-MereW

We need to discover America. National Anthem; Imitation of Carlos Drummond de Andrade's *"Hino Nacional."* Robert Stock. SP-StocR

We needs must love the highest when we see it. Friend, The. Stevie Smith. CP-SmitS

We never believed in safety. For Jan as the End Draws Near. Carolyn Kizer. CP-KizeC

We never discuss tenancy. Petite Madeleine. Andrei Codrescu. SP-CodrA

We Never Know. Yusef Komunyakaa. CP-KomuY

We never know how high we are. Emily Dickinson. CP-DickE

We never know we go when we are going. Emily Dickinson. CP-DickE

We never liked the demi-gods, the gods, the super-heroes, the over-complicated myth. Apples of the Hesperides 1, The. Yannis Ritsos. SP-RitsY, *tr. by* Gwendolyn MacEwen *and* Nikos Tsingos

We never made it. Time and time again. Derbyshire. Donald Davie. CP-DaviDC

We never sang together. On the Tune Called the Old-Hundred-and-Fourth. Thomas Hardy. CP-HardT

We never saw you, like our sires. Dead Hero, The. G. K. Chesterton. CP-ChesG

We never see him now, except at dinner. Robert Lowell. SP-LoweR

We never would have loved had love not struck. Under the Olives. Robert Graves. CP-GravR

We now, held in captivity. Rudyard Kipling. CP-KiplR

We of the New World clasp hands with the Old. Tennyson. James Whitcomb Riley. CP-RileJ

We open infant eyes. Dear Friends and Gentle Hearts. Countee Cullen. CP-CullC

We outgrow love like other things. Emily Dickinson. CP-DickE

We overstate the ills of life, and take. Exaggeration. Elizabeth Barrett Browning. CP-BroEB

We pace each other for a long time. Iva's Pantoum. Marilyn Hacker. SP-HackM

We park and stare. A full sky of the stars. Death of the Sheriff, The. Robert Lowell. SP-LoweR

We parted where the old gas-lamp still burned. Afterthoughts. Edwin Arlington Robinson. CP-RobiE

We passed the ice of pain. Moment, The. Theodore Roethke. CP-RoetT

We passed their graves. Peace. Langston Hughes. CP-HughL; CP-HughL3

We passed where flag and flower. Middle-Age Enthusiasms. Thomas Hardy. CP-HardT

We pattern our Heaven. Earthworm. John Updike. CP-UpdiJ

We physicians watch the juices rise. Lorine Niedecker. CP-NiedL

We picked flints. Tinder. Seamus Heaney. SP-HeanSO

We pierce tongue. Woebegone. Yusef Komunyakaa. CP-KomuY

We pitied our uncle, the odd face. Writing It Down. William Stafford. SP-StafWW

We plan in partial sleep. End of the Line, The. James Tate. SP-TateJ

We play at Paste. Emily Dickinson. CP-DickE

We pledged our hearts, my love and I. Exchange, The. Samuel Taylor Coleridge. CP-ColeS

We praise not now the poet's art. Bryant on His Birthday. John Greenleaf Whittier. CP-WhitJ

We pray 'gainst Warre, yet we enjoy no Peace. Things of Choice, Long a Comming. Robert Herrick. CP-HerrR

We pray most earnestly: our breath. Josephine Jacobsen. CP-JacoJ

We pray—to Heaven. Emily Dickinson. CP-DickE

We press our lips to the enameled rim of the cups. Morning, Thinking of Empire. Raymond Carver. CP-CarvR

We prop him up. Good Joe. Yusef Komunyakaa. CP-KomuY

We pulled for you when the wind was against us and the sails were low. Song of the Galley-Slaves. Rudyard Kipling. CP-KiplR

We put down our popguns. Looking for Choctaw. Yusef Komunyakaa. CP-KomuY

We put the mountains in the valleys. On the Liquidation of Zoology. Alan Dugan. CP-DugaA

We put up our tent while the dark closed in. Camping in Madera Canyon. May Swenson. SP-SwenM

We reach a place without a border. Midway the Journey of This Life. Eleanor Wilner. SP-WilnE

We reach for destinies beyond. Beyond What. Alice Walker. CP-WalkA

We reach the utmost limit of the earth. Prometheus Bound. Aeschylus. CP-BroEB, *tr. by* Elizabeth Barrett Browning

We reached the sea in early afternoon. Day Trip to Donegal. Derek Mahon. CP-MahoD

We read and hear about you every day. To the Rulers. Howard Nemerov. CP-NemeH

We read how Faunus, he the shepheards God. Upon Faunus. Robert Herrick. CP-HerrR

We read in a tremendous Book. Emily Dickinson. SP-DickE

We read of kings and gods that kindly took. Cruel Mistress, A. Thomas Carew. CP-CareT

We read the letters of the dead like helpless gods. Letters of the Dead, The. Wisława Szymborska. SP-SzymW, *tr. by* Stanislaw Barańczak *and* Clare Cavanagh

We read the tulips, we read. Reading Flowers. Rainer Maria Rilke. CP-RilkFr, *tr. by* A. Poulin, Jr.

We read the words but know them not. Emily Dickinson. SP-DickE

We Real Cool. Gwendolyn Brooks. SP-BrooG

We reckon Cooke our best chemist alive. Research and Development: Classified. Robert Graves. CP-GravR

We regretted the rain. Japanese Prints. May Sarton. SP-SartM

We remind her we love her. Emily Dickinson. SP-DickE

We resolve to think of ourselves. Testament, A. Robert Creeley. CP-CreeR

We return from the field. The wind. Autumn in Norenskaia. Joseph Brodsky. CP-BrodJ, *tr. by* Daniel Weissbort

We Rise on Sun Beams and Fall in the Night. Allen Ginsberg. CP-GinsA

We roam afar, o'er sea and land. Woodwax in Bloom, The. Jones Very. CP-VeryJ

We rode across the level plain. Guide, The. James Whitcomb Riley. CP-RileJ

"We rode out the depression on technique." How gratifying, how rare. "Sure," Said Benny Goodman. Hayden Carruth. CP-CarHS

We roll apart, lie side by side. Concrete. David Ignatow. SP-IgnaD

We rolled apart on the forest floor. Existence Before Essence. Hayden Carruth. CP-CarHS

We run, / We run. Shadows. Langston Hughes. CP-HughL; CP-HughL1

We sad, despondent quills. Guido Cavalcanti. CP-CavaG, *tr. by* Marc Cirigliano

"We," said my young radical neighbor, smashing my window. Encounter. John Ciardi. CP-CiarJ

We sail out of season into an oyster-gray wind. Crossing the Atlantic. Anne Sexton. CP-SextA

We sat across the table. Friend, The. Marge Piercy. SP-PierM

We sat and talked. It was June, and the summer light. Horse in a Field. Walter De la Mare. CP-DeLaW

We Sat at the Window. Thomas Hardy. CP-HardT

We sat beneath the humming pines. George Meredith. CP-MerG2

We sat by the shore. Philip Levine. SP-LeviP *Fr.* Poem with No Ending, A.

We sat face to face at the kitchen table. Thomas Kinsella. CP-KinsT

We sat in the room. Outside the Casement. Thomas Hardy. CP-HardT

We Sat Smoking at a Table. May Sarton. SP-SartM

We sat together at one summer's end. Adam's Curse. William Butler Yeats. CP-YeatW

We sat together, last May-day, and talked. Within the Gate. John Greenleaf Whittier. CP-WhitJ

We sat with the banqueting-party. At a Fashionable Dinner. Thomas Hardy. CP-HardT

We sat within the farm-house old. Fire of Drift-Wood, The. Henry Wadsworth Longfellow. SP-LongH

We sate down and wept by the waters. By the Rivers of Babylon We Sat Down and Wept. Lord Byron. CP-Byron

We sauntered amidst miracles. Ralph Waldo Emerson. CP-EmerR

We saw a grand piano fall off a roof. Empirical Scene. Alan Dugan. CP-DugaA

We Saw Beyond Our Seeming. Maya Angelou. SP-AngeM

We saw leaves go to glory. November. Robert Frost. CP-FrosR

We saw nothing but change in all the ways we went. Nothing But Change. Richard Eberhart. CP-EberR

"We saw reindeer / browsing," a friend who'd been in Lapland, said. Rigorists. Marianne Craig Moore. CP-MoorM

We saw the slow tides go and come. Sea Dream, A. John Greenleaf Whittier. CP-WhitJ

We saw the smoke. The blue skull of the sky. Death of a Bomber. John Ciardi. CP-CiarJ

We say and we say and we say. We Defer Things. James Whitcomb Riley. CP-RileJ

We say: I dreamt, and not: I lied. Lies 3. Rainer Maria Rilke. CP-RilkFr, *tr. by* A. Poulin, Jr.

We say, "It rains." Slow of belief the Age. Hath the Rain a Father? Or Who Hath Begotten the Drops of Dew? Job 38:28. Jones Very. CP-VeryJ

We say that some are mad. In fact. Little Poem, A. Miller Williams. CP-WillM

We say the sea is lonely; better say. Open Sea, The. William Meredith. SP-MereW

We Say We Shall Not Meet. Thomas Hardy. CP-HardT

We secretly hate one another. To My Friends. Aleksandr Aleksandrovich Blok. SP-BlokA, *tr. by* Peter France *and* Jon Stallworthy

We see—Comparatively. Emily Dickinson. CP-DickE

We see it every day from. Will We Ever Go to the Lighthouse? James Laughlin. CP-LaugJ

We see not, know not; all our way. Thy Will Be Done. John Greenleaf Whittier. CP-WhitJ

We see the farther in the far. George Meredith. CP-MerG2

We see the *planet* fall. Henry David Thoreau. CP-ThorH

We See the Spring Breaking across Rough Stone. Philip Larkin. CP-LarkP

We see us as we truly behave. Two Scenes. John Ashbery. SP-AshbJ

We send the Wave to find the Wave. Emily Dickinson. CP-DickE

We set great wreaths of brightness on the graves of the passionate. Song for Dead Children. Muriel Rukeyser. CP-RukeM

We settle deep in this our second mine. Buried Talents, The. Robert Stock. SP-StocR

We shall break out. Meteorologist, September. Donald Davie. CP-DaviDC

We shall come tomorrow morning, who were not to have her love. Emily Hardcastle, Spinster. John Crowe Ransom. SP-RansJ

We shall find the Cube of the Rainbow. Emily Dickinson. CP-DickE

We shall have our little day. Recurrence. Dorothy Parker. CP-ParkD

We shall love each other in bed, parlor, and kitchen. Each of Us. David Ignatow. SP-IgnaD

We shall never be one mummy only. From the French (2). Stevie Smith. CP-SmitS

We shall not always plant while others reap. From the Dark Tower. Countee Cullen. CP-CullC

We shall see her no more. Rejected Member's Wife, The. Thomas Hardy. CP-HardT

We shall sleep-out together through the dark. Ararat. Charles Tomlinson. SP-TomlC

We shopped for dresses which were always wrong. Fourteen. Marilyn Hacker. SP-HackM

We should guard our dead and their power, lest at some hour. Graves of Our Ancestors, The. Yannis Ritsos. SP-RitsY, *tr. by* Kimon Friar *and* Karelisa Hartigan

We should have a land of sun. Our Land. Langston Hughes. CP-HughL; CP-HughL1

We should not carve in stone. If putty fails. Lines to the Statue of Ferdinand Foch. G. K. Chesterton. CP-ChesG

We should not mind if on our ear there fell. Henry David Thoreau. CP-ThorH

We should not mind so small a flower. Emily Dickinson. CP-DickE

We shun because we prize her Face. Emily Dickinson. CP-DickE

We shun it ere it comes. Emily Dickinson. CP-DickE

We sipped tea. Politely musing. Projectile, The. Raymond Carver. CP-CarvR

We sit at a sidewalk table. Firebreathers at the Café Deux Magots, The. Miller Williams. CP-WillM

We sit balanced. Peter Blue Cloud. SP-BlueP

We sit indoors and talk of the cold outside. There Are Roughly Zones. Robert Frost. CP-FrosR

We six pile in, the engine churning ink. Nigger Song: An Odyssey. Rita Dove. SP-DoveR

We slapped the smirking mother. Learners, The. Mona Van Duyn. SP-VanDM

We slept naked. Gradualism. Kenneth Rexroth. CP-RexrK

We slip into Tientai caves. Shih-te. CP-ColdM, *tr. by* Red Pine

We slung do out of the rosy alligator. Makers, The. A. R. Ammons. CP-AmmoA

We smile at astrological hopes. For the Conjunction of Two Planets. Adrienne Rich. CP-RicAE; SP-RicA2

We smile at each other. Conversation. Ai. SP-Ai

We sow the glebe, we reap the corn. Human Life's Mystery. Elizabeth Barrett Browning. CP-BroEB

We speak the verses out of Mark. Maundy Thursday's Candles. Donald Hall. CP-HallD

We spend our lives in learning pilotage. Wisdom of Eld, The. George Meredith. CP-MerG1

We spent together was like. First Night, The. James Laughlin. CP-LaugJ

We spoke last evening of your work and mine. Alike and Yet Unlike: General Richard Taylor Writes to Henry Adams. Helen Pinkerton. CP-PinkH

We sprang for the side-holts—my gripsack and I. Another Ride from Ghent to Aix. James Whitcomb Riley. CP-RileJ

We spurred our parents to the kiss. Children of Darkness. Robert Graves. CP-GravR

We squat upon the beach of love. Lawrence Ferlinghetti. SP-FerlL

We stand around the burning oil drum. Near Klamath. Raymond Carver. CP-CarvR

We stand in line all morning long to see it. Most Expensive Picture in the World, The. Howard Nemerov. CP-NemeH

We started our house midway through the Cultural Revolution. Building. Gary Snyder. CP-SnydG

We started to walk but it was wading-slow. Eel. Muriel Rukeyser. CP-RukeM

We stayed the night in the pathless gorge of Ventana Creek, up th east. Oh, Lovely Rock. Robinson Jeffers. CP-JefR2

We step out on the green rectangle. On the Tennis Court at Night. Galway Kinnell. SP-KinnGN

We still remain we. New Eternity, The. Robert Graves. CP-GravR

We stood around the raw new-planted garden. Divining Water. Muriel Rukeyser. CP-RukeM

We stood at the back door. And the Trains Go On. Philip Levine. SP-LeviP

We stood by a pond that winter day. Neutral Tones. Thomas Hardy. CP-HardT

We stood by the library. It was an August night. Dedication, A: "We stood by the library. It was an August night." William Stafford. SP-StafWW; SP-StafWW

We stood in a wide-legged. Mumble Peg. Yusef Komunyakaa. CP-KomuY

We stood in the garden alone. George Meredith. CP-MerG2

We stood so the day slanted. Seasons between Yes & No. Yusef Komunyakaa. CP-KomuY

We Stood There Singing. Maxine W. Kumin. SP-KumiM

We stood together, side by side, rooted. Iron Palace. Robert Graves. CP-GravR

We stopped at her hut. Ballad of Ballymote, The. Tess Gallagher. SP-GallT

We stopped, ventured a glance. Glacier, The. Primo Levi. CP-LeviP, tr. by Ruth Feldman and Brian Swann

We strike camp on that portion of road completed. Corduroy Road. Rita Dove. SP-DoveR

We stripped in the first warm spring night. Belle Isle, 1949. Philip Levine. SP-LeviP

We swallow the odors of Southern cities. Georgia Song, A. Maya Angelou. SP-AngeM

We talk about it, but do we know? Great Pardon, The. Rainer Maria Rilke. CP-RilkFr, tr. by A. Poulin, Jr.

We talk about this film. Iron Mike. Charles Bukowski. SP-BukC1

We talk of taxes, and I call you friend. Edna St. Vincent Millay. CP-MillE

We talked as Girls do. Emily Dickinson. CP-DickE

We talked of things but all the time we wanted each other. And What with the Blunders. Kenneth Patchen. CP-PatcK

We talked [or talk'd] with open heart, and tongue. Fountain, The. William Wordsworth. CP-WorW1; MW-WorW

We talked sports. My Father-in-Law's Coat. William Corbett. SP-CorbW

We talked the last of the mild. Theodore Weiss. SP-WeisT Fr. Polish Question, The.

We talked with each other about each other. Emily Dickinson. CP-DickE

We tattered rhymers of the trade. Three Realities, The. G. K. Chesterton. CP-ChesG

"We thank thee Oh Father" for these strange Minds. Emily Dickinson. SP-DickE

We that ar heir in hevynnis glorie. Dumbaris Dirige to the King. William Dunbar. CP-DunbW

We that have done and thought. Spilt Milk. William Butler Yeats. CP-YeatW

We that were wood / when that a wide wood was. Susan Howe. SP-HoweS

We, the befallen fates. Fates and the Mothers, The. Laura Riding Jackson. CP-RidiL

We, the old children, are now old again. Borrowed Ones, The. Tess Gallagher. SP-GallT

We think of time past. Geography of Time, The. Miller Williams. CP-WillM

We thirst at first—'tis Nature's Act. Thirst. Emily Dickinson. CP-DickE

We thought at first it was a body. Morning Coffee. Thomas Kinsella. CP-KinsT

We thought it would come, we thought the Germans would come. Curator, The. Miller Williams. CP-WillM

We thought our arms. Natural History. Eleanor Wilner. SP-WilnE

We thought we ranked above the chance of ill. Covenant, The. Rudyard Kipling. CP-KiplR

We Three. Jelaluddin Rumi. SP-Rumi, tr. by Coleman Barks

We three park by the Big Sur Road. Big Sur: Partington Cove. John Logan. CP-LogaJ

We tied branches to our helmets. Camouflaging the Chimera. Yusef Komunyakaa. CP-KomuY

We to Sigh Instead of Sing. James Whitcomb Riley. CP-RileJ

We to your story, game and smugness, do add. Tomorrow. Kenneth Patchen. CP-PatcK

We told of him as one who should have soared. Discovery. Edwin Arlington Robinson. CP-RobiE

We, Too. Langston Hughes. CP-HughL; CP-HughL3

We Too Had Known Golden Hours. W. H. Auden. CP-AudeW

We too, we too, descending once again. Too-Late Born, The. Archibald MacLeish. CP-MacLA

We Took the Town After a Heavy Bombing. Fernando Pessoa. SP-PessF, tr. by Susan M. Brown and Edwin Honig

We tossed our beer cans down among the rocks. Fishermen, The. James Wright. CP-WrigJ

We touch them at the raw turns. Melancholy of Storm Windows, The. John Updike. CP-UpdiJ

We trace the pow'r of Death from tomb to tomb. To a Lady on the Death of Three Relations. Phillis Wheatley. CP-WheaP

We transients, we deadbeats: we blunder about. Men (IV), The. Pablo Neruda. SP-NeruP Fr. Separate Rose, The.

We traveled down to see your house. Failed Tribute to the Stonemason of Tor House, Robinson Jeffers. James Tate. SP-TateJ

We treat each other with exceeding courtesy. Unexpected Meeting, An. Wisława Szymborska. SP-SzymW, tr. by Stanisław Barańczak and Clare Cavanagh

We trenched, we trumpeted and drummed. Valenciennes. Thomas Hardy. CP-HardT

We Trust not to the multitude in Warre. Multitude. Robert Herrick. CP-HerrR

We turn not older with years. Emily Dickinson. SP-DickE

We turn off. To Bed. Rita Dove. SP-DoveR

We turn the corner of the street. Fourth Caprice in Montparnasse. T. S. Eliot. SP-ElioT

We turn to history looking. Desolate Light. Denise Levertov. SP-LeveDL

We turned hearing the same note. Shore. W. S. Merwin. SP-MerwW

We twin cherubs above the Mercy Seat. Sun-Face and Moon-Face. Robert Graves. CP-GravR

We Two. "H. D." CP-DoolH

We two are last in Hell: what may we fear[e]. Barley-Break; or, Last in Hell. Robert Herrick. CP-HerrR

We Two Boys Together Clinging. Walt Whitman. CP-WhitW

We, two elementals, woman and man. Meeting, The. Robert Graves. CP-GravR

We Two, How Long We Were Fool'd. Walt Whitman. CP-WhitW

We two kept house, the Past and I. Ghost of the Past, The. Thomas Hardy. CP-HardT

We two stood simply friend-like side by side. Inapprehensiveness. Robert Browning. CP-BroR2

We two that planets erst had been. Love. Henry David Thoreau. CP-ThorH

We used to go to Froom-hill Barrow. Seeing the Moon Rise. Thomas Hardy. CP-HardT

We vainly wrestle with the blind belief. Robert Frost. CP-FrosR

We violets white and blue. George Meredith. CP-MerG2

We voted 'em in, and we'll vote 'em out! Flapper Vote. D. H. Lawrence. CP-LawrD

We wait beneath the furnace-blast. Ein Feste Burg Ist Unser Gott. John Greenleaf Whittier. CP-WhitJ

We wait to see you nail. Recital of Water over Stones. Yusef Komunyakaa. CP-KomuY

We waited for the sun. In the Garden. Thomas Hardy. CP-HardT

We wake to double blue. Early Morning: Cape Cod. May Swenson. SP-SwenM

We wake up with guns going off. Ernesto Cardenal. CP-MertT Fr. Three Epigrams.

We Walk. James Schuyler. CP-SchuJ

We walk on / an unsilvered. Earth ("We walk on / an unsilvered"). Federico García Lorca. CP-GarcF, tr. by Jerome Rothenberg Fr. Mirror Suite.

We walk through a yellow-ocher adobe house. Silence, The. Arthur Sze. SP-SzeA

We walk up Madison. It is the end. On Madison. Charles Tomlinson. CP-TomlC

We walked beside the sea. Sea-side walk, A. Elizabeth Barrett Browning. CP-BroEB

We walked [or walk'd] along, while bright and red. Two April Mornings, The. William Wordsworth. CP-WorW1; MW-WorW

We walked under cliffs where the Upward and Downward are. Fifth Dimension. Kenneth Patchen. CP-PatcK

We walked very slowly down the concrete. Generation, The. Adam Zagajewski. SP-ZagaA, tr. by Renata Gorczynski

We walked where Victor Jove was shrined awhile. Rome: On the Palatine. Thomas Hardy. CP-HardT

We wandered diligently and widely. Mountain Lovers. Robert Graves. CP-GravR

We wandered hours amid a lovely scene. On visiting the beautiful estate of H. H. Hunnewell, Esq., at Wellesley. Jones Very. CP-VeryJ

We wanted something: a nude instance. Nature Poem: Demanding Stiff

Sentences. James Tate. SP-TateJ

We wanted to confess our sins but there were no takers. At a Certain Age. Czeslaw Milosz. CP-MiloCN, *tr. by* Robert Hass

We watch through the shop-front while. Blackie, The Electric Rembrandt. Thom Gunn. CP-GunnT

We watched Baghdad's skyline. Dolphy's Aviary. Yusef Komunyakaa. CP-KomuY

We watched the selfsame scene on that long drive. Alike and Unlike. Thomas Hardy. CP-HardT

We watched you building, stone by stone. Escape, The. G. K. Chesterton. CP-ChesG

We wave a handkerchief. Song: "We wave a handkerchief." Jaroslav Seifert. SP-SeifJ, *tr. by* Ewald Osers

We, we children, why our lives are circumscribed, circumferential. Unusual Precautions. John Ashbery. SP-AshbJ

We wear our sober Dresses when we die. Emily Dickinson. CP-DickE

We Wear the Mask. Paul Laurence Dunbar. CP-DunbP

We welcome to our Hall and Fair. Welcome Written for the Essex Institute Fair, Held at Salem Sept. 4th, 1860. Jones Very. CP-VeryJ

We welcome, with the opening year. Original Hymn ("We welcome, with the opening year"). Jones Very. CP-VeryJ

We welcomed the breeze. Lies of the Poem. Michael Palmer. SP-PalmM

We went a day's excursion to the stream. Best Times. Thomas Hardy. CP-HardT

We went our Christmas rounds once more. Paphian Ball, The. Thomas Hardy CP-HardT

We went there on the train. *They had big barges that they towed.* Protocols. Randall Jarrell. CP-JarrR

We went to sleep as if it were a country. Emily Dickinson. SP-DickE

We went to the park. Some Objects of Wood and Stone. Margaret Atwood. SP-AtwM1

We went up the hill to view our land. Our Land. Yannis Ritsos. SP-RitsY, *tr. by* Andonis Decavalles

We were a band of kids willing to learn something. Queer Client and the Forest-Inn, The. Kenneth Patchen. CP-PatcK

We were all one heart and one race. Declaration of London, The. Rudyard Kipling. CP-KiplR

We were almost unreal. Genealogy. Yusef Komunyakaa. CP-KomuY

We were alone one night on a long. Once in the 40s. William Stafford. SP-StafWW

We were annihilated there in Salamis. Naval Battle, The. Constantine P. Cavafy. CP-CavaC, *tr. by* Theoharis Constantine Theoharis

We were apart, yet, day by day. Isolation: To Marguerite. Matthew Arnold. SP-ArnoM *Fr.* Switzerland.

We were at the faculty dining table. Father in a Dream. Robert Lowell. SP-LoweR

We were bound on the wheel of an endless conversation. Adrienne Rich. SP-RicA1; SP-RicA2 *Fr.* Shooting Script.

We were drinking vodka together, Brodsky, Venclova. At Yale. Czeslaw Milosz. CP-MiloCN, *tr. by* Robert Hass

We were driving the river road. Looking across the River. William Stafford. SP-StafW; SP-StafWW

We were entwined in red rings. Kin. Maya Angelou. SP-AngeM

We were five at the craps table. Blood. Raymond Carver. CP-CarvR

We were hiding / Somewhere in the Alps. Alpine. George Oppen. CP-OppGN

We were in a room that was once an attic. Amiel's Leg. Thomas Lux. SP-LuxT

We were in bed and. 225 Pounds. Charles Bukowski. SP-BukC1

We were in Rome not far from the Piazza di Spagna. Restoration of the Pictures, The. Raissa Maritain. CP-MertT

We were joined at the hip. We were joined at the hip. Lag. Paul Muldoon. CP-MuldP

We were like children who didn't want to. Memory of Love—Terms and Conditions. Yehuda Amichai. SP-AmicYL, *tr. by* Benjamin Harshav *and* Barbara Harshav

We were not ever of their feline race. Frightened Men. Robert Graves. CP-GravR

We were on the pier, you desiring. Under Taurus. Louise Glück. SP-GlucL

We were riding through frozen fields in a wagon at dawn. Encounter. Czeslaw Milosz. CP-MiloC; CP-MiloCN, *tr. by* Lillian Vallee

We were singing one day about justice. Learning, Any Time. William Stafford. SP-StafWW

We were starving. Sweaty Day in August, A. Charles Bukowski. SP-BukC3

We were supposed to do a job in Italy. What He Thought. Heather McHugh. SP-McHuH

We were taken from the ore-bed and the mine. Secret of the Machines, The. Rudyard Kipling. CP-KiplR

We were talking of O'Hara. In Memory of George Oppen. Charles Tomlinson. SP-TomlC

We were taught the very same things: respect for the church. Men (IX), The. Pablo Neruda. SP-NeruP *Fr.* Separate Rose, The.

We were the barbarians. Barbarians. Adam Zagajewski. SP-ZagaA, *tr. by* Clare Cavanagh

We were The Hottentot Venus. Boys in Dresses. Yusef Komunyakaa. CP-KomuY

We were the pioneers. Inheritors. Tennessee Williams. CP-WillT

We were trying to put the roots back. Re-Rooting. Denise Levertov. SP-LeveDL

We were two lovers; let me lie by her. Bifurcation. Robert Browning. CP-BroR2

We were very tired, we were very merry. Recuerdo. Edna St. Vincent Millay. CP-MillE

We were walking through the bees. Calm, The. Tess Gallagher. SP-GallT

We were wrong to think. Form. Heather McHugh. SP-McHuH

We western fellow students salute with Calypso anthems. Western Fellow Students Salute with Calypso Anthems the Movie Career of Robert Lax. Thomas Merton. CP-MertT

We which were Ovid's five books now are three. Elegy 1.1: "We which were Ovid's five books now are three." Ovid. CP-MarlC *Fr.* Elegies.

Who are old, old and gay. Faery Song, A. William Butler Yeats. CP-YeatW

We who are strangers now, after our years of easy friendship. Bangla Desh: 3. Faiz Ahmad Faiz. CP-KizeC, *tr. by* Carolyn Kizer

We who have lived too long among your wicked children. Pilgrims' Song. Thomas Merton. CP-MertT

We / Who have nothing to lose. Black Dancers. Langston Hughes. CP-HughL; CP-HughL1

We who have seen Italia in the throes. Centenary of Garibaldi, The. George Meredith. CP-MerG?

We who must act as handmaidens. Muse of Water, A. Carolyn Kizer. CP-KizeC

We who praise poets with our labouring pen. Ivor Gurney. SP-GurnI

We Who Prayed and Wept. Wendell Berry. CP-BerrW

We who prayed and wept. We Who Prayed and Wept. Wendell Berry. CP-BerrW

We who survived the war and took to wife. Thirtieth Anniversary Report of the Class of '41. Howard Nemerov. CP-NemeH

We whom great mercy holds in fear. Port of London Authority, The. G. K. Chesterton. CP-ChesG

We, whose lungs fill with the sweetness of day. Child of Europe. Czeslaw Milosz. CP-MiloC; CP-MiloCN, *tr. by* Jan Darowski

We will be leaving now in less than a week. Ferry Port. W. S. Merwin. SP-MerwWF

We will call today. Michael Palmer. SP-PalmM

We will dream our siesta. Mayten, The. Gabriela Mistral. SP-MistG, *tr. by* Maria Giachetti [*or* Jacketti]

We will have to go away, said the girls in the circus. Circus, The. Kenneth Koch. SP-KochK

We will not go out to hear the "mysterious and private." Poem: "We will not go out to hear the 'mysterious and private.'" Michael Palmer. SP-PalmM

We will not let thee be, for thou art ours. To a Certain Nation. G. K. Chesterton. CP-ChesG

We will see no more. Requiem: "We will see no more." Wendell Berry. CP-BerrW

We will take you and kill you. Expendable. Langston Hughes. CP-HughL; CP-HughL3

We Will Taste the Islands and the Sea. Charles Bukowski. SP-BukC1

We will tell no more than a little. Foreword. W. S. Merwin. SP-MerwW

We will weep / yet not weep together. Kisses Forgotten. Carl Sandburg. CP-SandC

We will write a / simple epic of. June 6, 1970. Robert Creeley. CP-CreeR

We wish like the glass. Hafiz. CP-EmerR *Fr.* Odes.

We with our Fair pitched among the feathery clover. Individualist Speaks, The. Louis MacNeice. CP-MacNL

We wondered what our walk should mean. Peace Walk. William Stafford. SP-StafW; SP-StafWW

We work here together. Pine Planters, The. Thomas Hardy. CP-HardT

We would climb the highest dune. With Kit, Age 7, at the Beach. William Stafford. SP-StafW; SP-StafWW

We would do nought but good. Hafiz. CP-EmerR *Fr.* Odes.

We would get a map of our farm as big. Fiction. William Stafford. SP-StafWW

We Would Refer You to Our Service Department, If We Had One. Ogden Nash. CP-NashO

We would'nt mind the sun, dear. Emily Dickinson. SP-DickE

Weak and irresolute is man. Human Frailty. William Cowper. CP-CowpW

Weak is the will of Man, his judgement blind. William Wordsworth. CP-WorW1

Weak Mind in the Mountains, A. Wallace Stevens. CP-StevW; CP-StevWP

Weak Monk, The. Stevie Smith. CP-SmitS

Weaker and weaker, the sunlight falls. Lebensweisheitspielerei. Wallace Stevens. CP-StevW; CP-StevWP

Weakest Thing, The. Elizabeth Barrett Browning. CP-BroEB

Weald is good, the Downs are best, The. Run of the Downs, The. Rudyard Kipling. CP-KiplR

Wealth. Ralph Waldo Emerson. CP-EmerR

Wealth. Langston Hughes. CP-HughL; CP-HughL2

Wealth. D. H. Lawrence. CP-LawrD

Wealth and dominion fade into the mass. Fragment: Amor Aeternus. Percy Bysshe Shelley. CP-ShelP

Wealth and position attract distant kin. Han-shan. CP-ColdM, *tr. by* Red Pine

Wealth of the Destitute, The. Denise Levertov. SP-LeveDL

Wean Yourself. Jelaluddin Rumi. SP-Rumi, *tr. by* Coleman Barks

Weaned from life and torn away. Emily Jane Brontë. CP-BronE

Weapon, The. Hugh MacDiarmid. SP-MacDH

Weapon shapely, naked, wan. Song of the Broad-Axe [*or* Broad-Ax]. Walt Whitman. CP-WhitW

Wear it / Like a banner. Color. Langston Hughes. CP-HughL; CP-HughL3

Wear the Gown, and wear the Hat. On Hearing Miss Thrale Deliberate about Her Hat. Samuel Johnson. CP-JohnS

Wear the weight of equinoctial evening. September 21. Adrienne Rich. CP-RicAE

Wearied by wind and wave death goes. From the Saddle. Ezra Pound. CP-PoEar

Wearied of sinning, wearied of repentance. For Thine Own Sake, O My God. Christina Georgina Rossetti. CP-RosC2

Wearied Pilgrim, I have wandred here, A. On Himself. Robert Herrick. CP-HerrR

Wearied with saying grace and prayer. Dan Jackson's Reply. Jonathan Swift. CP-SwifJ

Wearing a flowered nightgown. Shopping in Ferney with Voltaire. Maxine W. Kumin. SP-KumiM

Wearing of the Green, The. Donald Davie. CP-DaviDC

Wearing that same black dress. Women You Are Accustomed To, The. Lucille Clifton. SP-ClifL

Weary already, weary miles to-night. Match with the Moon, A. Dante Gabriel Rossetti. CW-RossD

Weary and Heavy Laden, The. Jones Very. CP-VeryJ

Weary and weak,—accept my weariness. I Will Arise. Christina Georgina Rossetti. CP-RosC2

Weary Blues, The. Langston Hughes. CP-HughL; CP-HughL1

Weary fa' you, Duncan Gray. Duncan Gray ["Weary fa' you, Duncan Gray"]. Robert Burns. CP-BurnR

Weary faces, weary hands. Unjustly. Yannis Ritsos. SP-RitsY, *tr. by* Kostas Myrsiades

Weary in Well-Doing. Christina Georgina Rossetti. CP-RosC1

Weary of bitter sleep in which my indolence. Stéphane Mallarmé. CP-MallS, *tr. by* Henry Weinfield

Weary of his Spanish homeland, an aging soldier of the king's army sought. Parable of Cervantes and Don Quixote. Jorge Luis Borges. SP-BorgJ

Weary of jangling noises never stilled. Story of Ida, The. John Greenleaf Whittier. CP-WhitJ

Weary of myself, and sick of asking. Self-Dependence. Matthew Arnold. SP-ArnoM

Weary of the world's guileful inconstancy. Bacchic. Constantine P. Cavafy. CP-CavaC, *tr. by* Theoharis Constantine Theoharis

Weary Pund o' Tow, The. Robert Burns. CP-BurnR

Weary salt said: Here, The. Yehuda Amichai. SP-AmicYL *Fr.* Poems on the Shore of Caesarea.

Weary tourists seek illuminations, The. Sénanque. Adam Zagajewski. SP-ZagaA, *tr. by* Clare Cavanagh

Weary Walker, The. Thomas Hardy. CP-HardT

Weasel Snout. William Carlos Williams. CP-WilW1

Weather. Joseph Brodsky. CP-BrodJ *Fr.* Shorts.

Weather. Grace Paley. CP-PalGC

Weather. May Swenson. SP-SwenM

Weather, The. David Ignatow. SP-IgnaD

Weather came over this low knoll, west to east, The. On Jenkins' Hill. William Meredith. SP-MereW

Weather in the drawing-room, The. Ceremony and Vision. John Berryman. CP-BerrJ

Weather is changing. The mountainous temperate climate, The. Late August. Marilyn Hacker. SP-HackM

Weather is like Africa, The. Emily Dickinson. SP-DickE

Weather is sharp, The. Music in a Snowy Street. Thomas Hardy. CP-HardT

Weather is so very mild, The. Watched Example Never Boils, A. Ogden Nash. CP-NashO

Weather of flashes, fragments, A. In October. Charles Tomlinson. CP-TomlC

Weather of living in an island, The. Emigrant, to the Receding Shore. Donald Davie. CP-DaviDC

Weather of Olympus, The. Robert Graves. CP-GravR

Weather of Six Mornings, The. Jane Cooper. CP-CoopJ

Weather of the World, The. Howard Nemerov. CP-NemeH

Weather of this winter night, my dream-wife, The. James Merrill. *See* Weather of this winter night, my mistress, The.

Weather of this winter night, my mistress, The. Childlessness. James Merrill. SP-MerrJ

Weather releases him from the tyranny of rooms. Weatherman. Charles Tomlinson. CP-TomlC

Weather Report. Charles Bukowski. SP-BukC1

Weather Report. William Stafford. SP-StafW; SP-StafWW

Weather Report. Robert Penn Warren. CP-WarrR

Weather Shifts, The. Arthur Sze. SP-SzeA

Weather the frost, stir. Rose-hips. Charles Tomlinson. CP-TomlC

Weather wears many dresses. Weather. Joseph Brodsky. CP-BrodJ *Fr.* Shorts.

Weather wept, and all the trees bent down, The. Shimmer of Evil, The. Theodore Roethke. CP-RoetT

Weathercock on the Cathedral of Quito, The. Jorge Carrera Andrade. CP-MertT

Weathercocks, The. Charles Tomlinson. CP-TomlC; SP-TomlC

Weathering Out. Rita Dove. SP-DoveR

Weatherman. Charles Tomlinson. CP-TomlC

Weatherman. Miller Williams. CP-WillM

Weathers [*or* Weather]. Thomas Hardy. CP-HardT

Weather's a funny. Eye o' the Storm. Robert Creeley. SP-CreeR

Weather's changes are the private rites, The. Walking Down Westgate in the Fall. Howard Nemerov. CP-NemeH

Weathervane. Federico García Lorca. CP-GarcF, *tr. by* Catherine Brown

Weave In, My Hardy Life. Walt Whitman. CP-WhitW

Weaving / between assorted terrors. Lenox Avenue Bar. Langston Hughes. CP-HughL; CP-HughL3

Weaving Love-Knots. Hsüeh T'ao. CP-KizeC, *tr. by* Carolyn Kizer

Weazened Irrefutable unastonished. E. E. Cummings. CP-CummE

Web. Denise Levertov. SP-LeveDS

Web, The. Jorge Luis Borges. SP-BorgJ, *tr. by* Alastair Reid

Web, The. Robert Earl Hayden. CP-HaydR

Web, The. W. S. Merwin. SP-MerwW

Web, The. / daily spreads the fabulous tales she's drunk. Theodore Weiss. SP-WeisT *Fr.* Storeroom, The.

Web One Weaves of Italy, The. Marianne Craig Moore. CP-MoorM

Webs. Carl Sandburg. CP-SandC

Webs of misery spread in the brain. Phoenix and the Tortoise, The. Kenneth Rexroth. CP-RexrK

Webster. Ralph Waldo Emerson. CP-EmerR

Webster was much possessed by death. Whispers of Immortality. T. S. Eliot. CP-ElioT; SP-ElioT

We'd break the city's unfeeling clutch. Cassandra Drops into Verse. Dorothy Parker. CP-ParkD

We'd build a little bungalow. Day-Dreams. Dorothy Parker. CP-ParkD

We'd dance, with grapes in our wind-tossed hair. Song of the Conventions. Dorothy Parker. CP-ParkD

We'd found the old Boche dug-out, and he knew. Sentry, The. Wilfred Owen. CP-OwenW

We'd had any number of joints and some. Trying to Get Even. Charles Bukowski. SP-BukC1

We'd have danced. Badlands, The. Lorine Niedecker. CP-NiedL

We'd loved, we two, some while. Fight on Durnover Moor, The. Thomas Hardy. CP-HardT

We'd rather have the iceberg than the ship. Imaginary Iceberg, The. Elizabeth Bishop. CP-BishE

We'd talked long into the night. At Midnight. Adam Zagajewski. SP-ZagaA, *tr. by* Renata Gorczynski, Benjamin Ivry *and* C. K. Williams

We'd want a little mercy, a little. Rainer Maria Rilke. CP-RilkFr, *tr. by* A. Poulin, Jr. *Fr.* Fragments.

Wedded Love. Samuel Taylor Coleridge. CP-ColeS

(Builder left one narrow rent, The.) CP-ColeS

Wedding, A. James Tate. SP-TateJ

Wedding, The. James Dickey. SP-DickJ

Wedding, The. Richard Eberhart. CP-EberR

Wedding, The. Robert Graves. CP-GravR

Wedding Day. Seamus Heaney. SP-HeanSO

Wedding in War-Time, A. G. K. Chesterton. CP-ChesG

Wedding Morn. D. H. Lawrence. CP-LawrD

Wedding Morning. Thomas Kinsella. CP-KinsT

Wedding Morning, The. Thomas Hardy. CP-HardT

Wedding Night, The. Anne Sexton. CP-SextA

Wedding of the Rose and the Lotus, The. Nicholas Vachel Lindsay. CP-LindV

Wedding on Cape Rosier, A. Richard Eberhart. CP-EberR

Wedding Party. Donald Hall. CP-HallD

Wedding Party, The. Norman Dubie. CP-DubiN

Wedding Photograph, The. Stevie Smith. CP-SmitS

Wedding Postponed. Carl Sandburg. CP-SandC

Wedding Presents. Muriel Rukeyser. CP-RukeM

Wedding-Ring. Denise Levertov. SP-LeveDL; SP-LeveDS

Wedding Ring Dance, The. Anne Sexton. CP-SextA

Wedding Stop, The. Wyatt Prunty. SP-PrunW

Wedding Toast, A. Richard Wilbur. CP-WilbR

Wedding-Wind. Philip Larkin. CP-LarkP

Wedge, The. Gregory Orr. SP-OrrG

Wedged in by earthworks. Merely to Know. Adrienne Rich. CP-RicAE; SP-RicA2

Wedlock. D. H. Lawrence. CP-LawrD

Wedlock, The. Anne Sexton. CP-SextA

Wednesday. Philip Levine. SP-LeviP

Wednesday at the Waldorf. May Swenson. SP-SwenM

Wednesday in Holy Week. Christina Georgina Rossetti. CP-RosC2

Wednesday Matinee. Ogden Nash. CP-NashO

Wednesday Night Prayer Meeting. Jay Wright. SP-WrigJ

Wednesday nights. Original Sin. Miller Williams. CP-WillM

Wednesday of Holy Week, 1940. Kenneth Rexroth. CP-RexrK

Wee, modest, crimson-tipped flow'r. To a Mountain Daisy [On Turning One Down, with the Plough, in April—1786]. Robert Burns. CP-BurnR

Wee people / dwelling / between serene. E. E. Cummings. CP-CummE

Wee, sleeket [or sleekit], cow'rin' [or cowran], tim'rous beastie. To a Mouse; On Turning Her up in Her Nest, with the Plough, November, 1785. Robert Burns. CP-BurnR

Wee wee husband, / Give me some money. Christina Georgina Rossetti. CP-RosC2

Wee Willie Gray. Robert Burns. CP-BurnR

Weed, The. Elizabeth Bishop. CP-BishE

Weed bends, The. Definitions. A. R. Ammons. CP-AmmoA

Weed, moss-weed. Sea Iris. "H. D." CP-DoolH

Weed Puller. Theodore Roethke. CP-RoetT

Weeds. James Dickey. CP-DickJ

Weeds. Edna St. Vincent Millay. CP-MillE

Weeds. Carl Sandburg. CP-SandC

Weeds. Louis Zukofsky. CP-ZukLS

Weeds, The. Gregory Orr. SP-OrrG

Weeds, The. / I'll cut my right hand off. Omega. Federico García Lorca. CP-GarcF, tr. by Greg Simon and Steven F. White

Weeds as Partial Survivors. Alan Dugan. CP-DugaA

Week, A. Thomas Hardy. CP-HardT

Week ago on longer clocks than ours, A. Possibilities. John Ciardi. CP-CiarJ

Week in August you come home, The. Family Reunion. Maxine W. Kumin. SP-KumiM

Week is dealt out like a hand, The. Hope. Randall Jarrell. CP-JarrR

Week That Was, The. John Ciardi. CP-CiarJ

Week the latest rocket went, The. Discovery. Amy Clampitt. CP-ClamA

Week waiting for you to be born I read, The. For My Daughter When She Can Read. Thomas Lux. SP-LuxT

Weekend Bathers. Kenneth Patchen. CP-PatcK

Weekend Glory. Maya Angelou. SP-AngeM

Weeknight Service. D. H. Lawrence. CP-LawrD

Weeks go by, The. I shelve them. Firstborn. Louise Glück. SP-GlucL

Weeks hitting the road, one fasting in the bathtub. Returning Turtle. Robert Lowell. SP-LoweR

Weeks of wild delirium past. Rosina. Emily Jane Brontë. CP-BronE

We[e]lcome! but yet no entrance, till we bless[e]. Entertainment, or Porch-Verse, at the Marriage of Mr. Henry Northleigh [or Hen. Northly] and the Most Witty Mrs. Lettice Yard, The. Robert Herrick. CP-HerrR

Weep, and weep long, but do not weep for me. To a Troubled Friend. James Wright. CP-WrigJ

Weep, daughter of a royal line. Lines to a Lady Weeping. Lord Byron. CP-Byron

Weep him dead and mourn as you may. Keen. Edna St. Vincent Millay. CP-MillE

Weep, ladies; as you weep, let Love weep too. Petrarch. CP-Petra, tr. by J. G. Nichols

Weep no more, thou weary one. Irrevocable, The. Walter De la Mare. CP-DeLaW

Weep not, belovèd Friends! nor let the air. Gabriello Chiabrera. CP-WorW1

Weep not, my dear, for I shall go. Parting, Celia Weeps. Thomas Carew. CP-CareT

Weep not, nor backward turn your beams. Lover, upon an Accident Necessitating His Departure, Consults with Reason, A. Thomas Carew. CP-CareT

Weep not, you who love her. Threnody for a Brown Girl. Countee Cullen. CP-CullC

Weep now, my eyes; accompany my heart. Petrarch. CP-Petra, tr. by J. G. Nichols

Weep[e] with me, all you that read. Epitaph on S. P. [or Salomon Pavy], a Child of Q[ueen] El[izabeth's] Chapel. Ben Jonson. CP-JonsB; SP-JonsB

Weep yet a while / Weep till that day shall dawn when thou shalt smile. Heart Knoweth Its Own Bitterness, The. Christina Georgina Rossetti. CP-RosC3

Weepe for the dead, for they have lost this light. On Himselfe. Robert Herrick. CP-HerrR

Weeper, The. Richard Crashaw. CP-CrasR

Weeper in Jalisco. Charles Tomlinson. CP-TomlC

Weepies, The. Paul Muldoon. CP-MuldP

Weeping. Alexander Pope. CP-PopeA

Weeping, The. John Logan. CP-LogaJ

Weeping Burgher, The. Wallace Stevens. CP-StevW; CP-StevWP

Weeping Cherry, The. Robert Herrick. CP-HerrR

Weeping Pleiads wester, The. Sappho. CP-HousA, tr. by A. E. Housman

Weeping Saviour, The. Elizabeth Barrett Browning. CP-BroEB

Weeping Woman. Denise Levertov. SP-LeveDL

Weicht zacht gemeine herren geuze zein. On Himself. G. K. Chesterton. CP-ChesG

Weigh all my faults and follies righteously. Christina Georgina Rossetti. CP-RosC2

Weigh me the fire; or canst thou find. To Find[e] God. Robert Herrick. CP-HerrR

Weighed down by its dense bones. Thoughts on Saving the Manatee. Maxine W. Kumin. SP-KumiM

Weighing In. Seamus Heaney. SP-HeanSO

Weight him down, O side-stars, with the great weightings of the end. Madame La Fleurie. Wallace Stevens. CP-StevW; CP-StevWP

Weight of the world, The. Song: "Weight of the world, The." Allen Ginsberg. CP-GinsA; SP-GinsA

Weight of years is on the pile, The. Hymn, Sung at the Dedication of the New Stone Church of the North Society in Salem June 22d, 1836. Jones Very. CP-VeryJ

Weight with Needles on the pounds, A. Emily Dickinson. CP-DickE

Weights, the secret. Mathematical Secret, and the Apron, The. Charles Olson. CP-OlsoC

Weird, flat seeming. Seoul Sounds. Robert Creeley. SP-CreeR

Weird-looking, sturdy types. Many of them have exploited your worlds. Parade. Arthur Rimbaud. CP-RimbA, tr. by Martin Sorrell

"Weiss," a new anthology observes. Library Revisited, The. Theodore Weiss. SP-WeisT

Weland's Sword. Rudyard Kipling. Fr. Puck of Pook's Hill.

Welcome. Thomas Merton. CP-MertT

Welcome, The. James Laughlin. CP-LaugJ

Welcome Address. Paul Laurence Dunbar. CP-DunbP

Welcome all that [or who] lead or follow. Over the Door at the Entrance into the Apollo. Ben Jonson. CP-JonsB

Welcome, Brazilian brother—thy ample place is ready. Christmas Greeting, A. Walt Whitman. CP-WhitW

Welcome dear feast of Lent: who loves not thee. Lent. George Herbert. CP-HerbG

Welcome Death. D. H. Lawrence. CP-LawrD

Welcome, deep WILEY! from the sylvan dells. Prologue to Wiley on November 17, 1941. Randall Jarrell. CP-JarrR

Welcome, eccentric life. By Lamplight. Stanley Kunitz. CP-KunSC

Welcome! Enter! This is the Inn at the Cross Roads. Hospital. Walter De la Mare. CP-DeLaW

Welcome from War. Muriel Rukeyser. CP-RukeM

Welcome, Great Cesar, welcome now you are. To the King, upon His Welcome to Hampton-Court. Robert Herrick. CP-HerrR

Welcome Home. Thomas Hardy. CP-HardT

Welcome home again, brave seaman! with thy thoughtful brow and gray. Branded Hand, The. John Greenleaf Whittier. CP-WhitJ

Welcome home ye lads of the eighth army. Trial Runs. Seamus Heaney. SP-HeanSO

Welcome Joy, and Welcome Sorrow. John Keats. CP-KeatJ

Welcome, maids of honor. To Violets. Robert Herrick. CP-HerrR

Welcome me, if you will. For James Dean. Frank O'Hara. SP-OharF

Welcome Morning. Anne Sexton. CP-SextA

Welcome, most welcome to our Vow[e]s and us. To the King, upon His Com[m]ing with His Army into the West. Robert Herrick. CP-HerrR

Welcome my Griefe, my Joy; how deare's. John 16; Verily I Say unto You, Yee Shall Weep and Lament. Bible, N.T. CP-CrasR Fr. St. John.

Welcome, old swede. Survival Poem, The. Maxine W. Kumin. SP-KumiM

Welcome once more the suns refulgent ray. On Doctor Rushes Birth Day the 5th of January—after Ten Days Thick Fog. Annis Boudinot Stockton. CP-StocA

Welcome stranger to this place. Song 1st By a Shepherd. William Blake. CP-BlakW

Welcome sweet and sacred cheer. Banquet, The. George Herbert. CP-HerbG

Welcome sweet flower, that scent'st the morn. Houstonia, The. Jones Very. CP-VeryJ

Welcome television to this rug-ruined room. Fanny Howe. SP-HoweF Fr. O'Clock.

Welcome the Wrath. Stanley Kunitz. CP-KunSC

Welcome, thrice welcome to thy native Place! Mary Gulliver to Capt. Lemuel Gulliver. John Gay *and* Alexander Pope. CP-PopeA

Welcome to Lowell, A. John Greenleaf Whittier. CP-WhitJ

Welcome to Quetzalcoatl. D. H. Lawrence. CP-LawrD

Welcome to Sack, The. Robert Herrick. CP-HerrR

Welcome to this my college [*or* colledge], and though late. To His Kinsman, Master Thomas Herrick, Who Desired to Be in His Book. Robert Herrick. CP-HerrR

Welcome to what. Visitor's Guide to the Blue Planet, The. Miller Williams. CP-WillM

Welcome, welcome, little star! White Dwarf. John Updike. CP-UpdiJ

Welcome What Comes. Robert Herrick. CP-HerrR

Welcome Written for the Essex Institute Fair, Held at Salem Sept. 4th, 1860. Jones Very. CP-VeryJ

Well. Heather McHugh. SP-McHuH

Well. Charles Olson. CP-OlsoC

Well. Alice Walker. CP-WalkA

Well, The. Denise Levertov. SP-LeveDP

Well, The. W. S. Merwin. SP-MerwW

Well, The. Adrienne Rich. CP-RicAE

Well, The. Charles Tomlinson. CP-TomlC; SP-TomlC

Well All Right. James Laughlin. CP-LaugJ

Well, as Kavanagh said, we have lived. Singing School. Seamus Heaney. SP-HeanSO

We'll be careful. Crossing. Rae Armantrout. SP-ArmaA

Well, beat on, beat on. Hayden Carruth. CP-CarHS *Fr.* Clay Hill Anthology, The.

Well-Beloved, The. Thomas Hardy. CP-HardT

Well, Bokardo, here we are. Bokardo. Edwin Arlington Robinson. CP-RobiE

Well, death's been here. Live. Anne Sexton. CP-SextA; SP-SextA

Well Dennis O'Grady. Thom Gunn. CP-GunnT

We'll die / soon enough. Robert Creeley. CP-CreeR

Well Disciplined Bargeman, The. William Carlos Williams. CP-WilW2

Well Dressed Man with a Beard, The. Wallace Stevens. CP-StevW; CP-StevWP

Well, everyone wants to know, of course, that's. Septic Tanck. Hayden Carruth. CP-CarHS

Well-found Poem. Donald Davie. CP-DaviDC

Well girl, goodbye. To My Last Period. Lucille Clifton. SP-ClifL

We'll go out before breakfast, and get. Instant, The. Denise Levertov. SP-LeveDS

We'll go out to the open spaces. Song of the Wilderness. Dorothy Parker. CP-ParkD

Well God is / love. Calypsos. William Carlos Williams. CP-WilW2

Well, good evening; the two of them again, face to face. His Lamp toward Daybreak. Yannis Ritsos. SP-RitsY, *tr. by* Kimon Friar

Well, good. You got here. Let me take your things. Art Photographer Puts His Model at Ease, The. Miller Williams. CP-WillM

Well hast thou spoken—and yet not taught. My Comforter. Emily Jane Brontë. CP-BronE

Well have I loved ye, / little songs of mine. Envoi: "Well have I loved ye, / little songs of mine." Ezra Pound. CP-PoEar

Well have yon Railway Labourers to THIS ground. At Furness Abbey. William Wordsworth. CP-WorW2

Well he saw man created according. Swedenborg. Lorine Niedecker. CP-NiedL

Well. / He was a poet. Well. Alice Walker. CP-WalkA

Well, he was drunk. That much was clear. Archibald MacLeish. CP-MacLA *Fr.* Happy Marriage, The.

Well, here I am thirty-eight. Not George Washington's, Not Abraham Lincoln's, but Mine. Ogden Nash. CP-NashO

Well here's a salute to. James Laughlin. CP-LaugJ *Fr.* America I Love You.

We'll Hide the Couper behint the Door. Robert Burns. CP-BurnR

Well Hung. Hugh MacDiarmid. SP-MacDH

Well, I am sorry to admit. Month of Saints, A. John Logan. CP-LogaJ

Well I can see you now. Bob Visits Friends. Grace Paley. CP-PalGC

Well I have and in fact. On Being Asked to Write a Poem Against the War in Vietnam. Hayden Carruth. CP-CarHS

"Well, I have had a happy life," said Hazlitt. Boyg, Peer Gynt, the One Only One, The. Randall Jarrell. CP-JarrR

Well, I have lost you; and I lost you fairly. Edna St. Vincent Millay. CP-MillE

Well, I know / You had a hard time in your life. Abe Lincoln. Langston Hughes. CP-HughL; CP-HughL3

Well, I may now receive, and die: my sin. Satire 4. John Donne. MW-DonnJ *Fr.* Satires.

Well I remember him long years ago. Capt. Samuel Cook. Jones Very. CP-VeryJ

Well I remember once, Papa. Dirt & Slime. James Edward Austen-Leigh. CP-AustJ

Well I remember the pigeons in the sunny arbour. Pigeons, The. Edna St.

Vincent Millay. CP-MillE

Well, I still have a train ticket valid. Poor Washed Up by Chicago Winter, The. James Wright. CP-WrigJ

Well; if ever I saw another man since my mother bound my head. Mary the Cook-Maid's Letter to Dr. Sheridan. Jonathan Swift. CP-SwifJ

Well if he treats me like a young girl still. Ms. Lot. Muriel Rukeyser. CP-RukeM

Well, if it be my time to quit the stage. Satire IV of Dr. John Donne, Versified. Alexander Pope. CP-PopeA

Well! If the Bard was weather-wise, who made. Dejection: An Ode. Samuel Taylor Coleridge. CP-ColeS; MW-ColeS

Well! if the Bard was weatherwise, who made. Letter to Sara Hutchinson. Samuel Taylor Coleridge. CP-ColeS

Well, if you wilt, then, ask me. Philosophical Fantasy, A. Thomas Hardy. CP-HardT

Well, is it not the virtue of art. Theory of Repetition, The. Theodore Weiss. SP-WeisT *Fr.* Polish Question, The.

Well is this place a cemetery called. Cemetery of Harmony Grove, The. Jones Very. CP-VeryJ

Well, / it is better. Ode on Necrophilia. Frank O'Hara. SP-OharF

Well, it's enough to turn his head to have a feller's name. To—"The J. W. R. Literary Club." James Whitcomb Riley. CP-RileJ

Well / it's interesting what does go on. Minor Impulse to Complain, A. Charles Bukowski. SP-BukC2

Well, it's still the loveliest meadow in all Vermont. My Meadow. Hayden Carruth. CP-CarHS

Well, Jim says that the couplet at the end. Sonnet: "Well, Jim says that the couplet at the end." Hayden Carruth. CP-CarHS *Fr.* Sonnets.

Well-lit, The. Venus. Charles Simic. SP-SimiCE

Well, Lizzie Anderson! seventeen men—and. To a Friend. William Carlos Williams. CP-WilW1

We'll love each other if you choose. Rondel: "We'll love each other if you choose." Stéphane Mallarmé. CP-MallS, *tr. by* Henry Weinfield

Well may my Book come forth like Public [*or* Publique] Day. To the Most Illustrious and Most Hopeful[l] Prince, Charles, Prince of Wales. Robert Herrick. CP-HerrR

Well may the continental eagles scream. To Lord Palmerston. George Meredith. CP-MerG2

Well mayst thou halt—and gaze with brightening eye! Admonition. William Wordsworth. CP-WorW1

Well meaning readers! you that come as friends [*or* freinds]. Flaming Heart, The. Richard Crashaw. CP-CrasR

We'll meet in Madrid. Once We Meant It. Thomas McGrath. SP-McGrT

Well, mind, here we have. Promenade. William Carlos Williams. CP-WilW1

Well! my lov'd Niece, I hear the bustle's o'er. Poetical Epistle, Addressed by a Lady of New-Jersey, to Her Niece, upon Her Marriage, in This City, A. Annis Boudinot Stockton. CP-StocA

Well, my poor man. Archeology. Wisława Szymborska. SP-SzymW, *tr. by* Stanislaw Barańczak *and* Clare Cavanagh

Well, narrower draw the circle round. Douglas's Ride. Emily Jane Brontë. CP-BronE

Well-nigh the voyage now is overpast. Michelangelo Buonarroti. CP-WorW1

We'll not begin again to love. Song to Aurore. Thomas Hardy. CP-HardT

Well, / now some eat to forget and some drink to forget and some. Now. Charles Bukowski. SP-BukC3

Well, nuncle, this plainly won't do. Floral Decorations for Bananas. Wallace Stevens. CP-StevW; CP-StevWP

Well of Loch Maree, The. John Greenleaf Whittier. CP-WhitJ

Well-Ordered Life, The. Miller Williams. CP-WillM

We'll pass without the parting. Emily Dickinson. CP-DickE

Well, Paul, when you were nine. Poem for My Son. John Logan. CP-LogaJ

Well *Peter* dost thou wield thy active sword. On Saint Peter Cutting of Malchus His Eare. Richard Crashaw. CP-CrasR

Well, Ralph, howe'er you're pleased to strive. Tom Pun-Sibi's Resurrection Disproved. *Unknown.* CP-SherT

Well reason they, who from the birds, and flowers. Nature Teaches Only Love. Jones Very. CP-VeryJ

Well rising without sound, The. William Stafford. SP-StafW; SP-StafWW

Well, sainthood's a bottomless pity, / as some wag once said, so. Holy Ghost Asketh for Us with Mourning and Weeping Unspeakable, The. Charles Wright. SP-WrigCN

Well sang the Bard who called the grave, in strains. Earl of Breadalbane's Ruined Mansion, and Family Burial-Place, near Killin, The. William Wordsworth. CP-WorW2

Well-shadow'd landskip, fare ye well. Sir John Suckling. *See* Well-shadowed landscape, fare ye well!

Well-shadowed landscape, fare ye well! Farewell to Love. Sir John Suckling. CP-SuckJ

Well, she told me I had an aura. "What?" I said. Sonnet: "Well, she told me I had an aura. 'What?' I said." Hayden Carruth. CP-CarHS

Well, son, I'll tell you. Mother to Son. Langston Hughes. CP-HughL; CP-

HughL1

Well speed they mission, bold Iconoclast! Men of Old, The. John Greenleaf Whittier. CP-WhitJ

We'll take refuge in bells, in the swinging bells. Bells, The. Adam Zagajewski. SP-ZagaA, *tr.* by Renata Gorczynski, Benjamin Ivry *and* C. K. Williams

Well, that old big fat man. Mona Van Duyn. SP-VanDM

Well, that was Saturday, day before Easter. Mona Van Duyn. SP-VanDM

Well, that's Pretty Boy Emeritus. Thorn Merchant's Right-Hand Man, The. Yusef Komunyakaa. CP-KomuY

Well, the brilliance is gone. Paraphrase from Notebooks. Howard Nemerov. CP-NemeH

Well, the grass is a pleasant thing. Latesummer Blues. Kenneth Patchen. CP-PatcK

Well the hearts are—is. Multiples. Michael Palmer. SP-PalmM

Well then, a man has got to stop somewhere. Tale. Howard Nemerov. CP-NemeH

Well, then, I hate Thee, unrighteous picture. Stephen Crane. CP-CranS

Well then, poor G——— lies under ground! Epitaph: "Well then, poor G——— lies under ground!" Alexander Pope. CP-PopeA

Well then, the promised [*or* promis'd] hour is come at last. To My Dear Friend Mr Congreve [on His Comedy Called "The Double-Dealer"]. John Dryden. SP-DrydJ

Well they are gone, and here must I remain. This Lime-Tree Bower My Prison. Samuel Taylor Coleridge. CP-ColeS; MW-ColeS

Well, they loaded him with armor and left him. Childe Horvald to the Dark Tower Came. John Ciardi. CP-CiarJ

Well, they rocked him with road-apples. Not a Movie. Langston Hughes. CP-HughL, CP-HughL3

"Well," they were saying, "The war's over." Memorial Day. John Ciardi. CP-CiarJ

Well they'd made up their minds to be everywhere because why not. Last One, The. W. S. Merwin. SP-MerwW

Well! Thou Art Happy. Lord Byron. CP-Byron

Well, though it seems. Liddell and Scott. Thomas Hardy. CP-HardT

Well thought! who would not rather hear. To James T. Fields. John Greenleaf Whittier. CP-WhitJ

Well, 'tis as Bickerstaff had guessed. Elegy On the Supposed Death of Mr. Partridge, the Almanac Maker. Jonathan Swift. CP-SwifJ

Well-to-Do Invalid, A. Randall Jarrell. CP-JarrR

We'll to the woods no more. A. E. Housman. CP-HousA

We'll to the Woods No More, the Laurels Are Cut Down. May Sarton. SP-SartM

Well upon the Brook, The. Emily Dickinson. CP-DickE

Well was dry beside the door, The. Going for Water. Robert Frost. CP-FrosR

Well Water. Randall Jarrell. CP-JarrR

Well, well, little poet! For a Critic Who Tries to Write Poems. Thomas McGrath. SP-McGrT

Well/Well/Not-At-All. Hart Crane. CP-CranH

Well, well, well, so this is summer, isn't that *mirabile dictu.* September Is Summer, Too. Ogden Nash. CP-NashO

Well, what shall I do today? On Waking to the Third Rainy Morning of a Long Week End. Ogden Nash. CP-NashO

Well, why did he do it *then?* I can say. Winter's Tale. Josephine Jacobsen. CP-JacoJ

Well, World, you have kept faith with me. He Never Expected Much. Thomas Hardy. CP-HardT

Well-Worn Story, A. Dorothy Parker. CP-ParkD

Well, ya better mail one to M.S. or she'll prob. What to Do with Contributor's Copies? Charles Bukowski. SP-BukC2

Well, you shall have that song which Leonard wrote. Golden Year, The. Alfred Tennyson. CP-TennA

Welladay! / Here I lay. Worn-out Pencil, A. James Whitcomb Riley. CP-RileJ

Wellfleet: The House. Richard Wilbur. CP-WilbR

Wellfleet Whale, The. Stanley Kunitz. CP-KunSC

Well)here's looking at ourselves. E. E. Cummings. CP-CummE

Welling and flowing and fastening, too. Window: Thing as Participle. Heather McHugh. SP-McHuH

Wellington's Funeral. Dante Gabriel Rossetti. CW-RossD

Wells. Donald Hall. CP-HallD

Wells and People. Yannis Ritsos. SP-RitsY, *tr.* by Kimon Friar

Well's pulley creaks, The. Eugenio Montale. CP-MontE, *tr.* by Jonathan Galassi

Wellsian Futures. D. H. Lawrence. CP-LawrD

Wellspring Rushes, The. Paul Celan. SP-CelaP, *tr.* by John Felstiner

Welsh Incident. Robert Graves. CP-GravR

Welsh Marches, The. A. E. Housman. CP-HousA

Weltering London ways where children weep, The. John Keats. Dante Gabriel Rossetti. CW-RossD *Fr.* Five English Poets.

Weltschmertz. Paul Laurence Dunbar. CP-DunbP

W'en daih's chillun in de house. Old Front Gate, The. Paul Laurence Dunbar. CP-DunbP

W'en de clouds is hangin' heavy in de sky. My Sweet Brown Gal. Paul Laurence Dunbar. CP-DunbP

W'en de colo'ed ban' comes ma'chin' down de street. Colored Band, The. Paul Laurence Dunbar. CP-DunbP

W'en de evenin' shadders. Boogah Man, The. Paul Laurence Dunbar. CP-DunbP

W'en de snow's a-fallin'. Grievance, A. Paul Laurence Dunbar. CP-DunbP

W'en de sun's gone down, an' de moon is riz. Bin a-Fishin'. James Whitcomb Riley. CP-RileJ

W'en I git up in de mo'nin' an' de clouds is big an' black. Fishing. Paul Laurence Dunbar. CP-DunbP

W'en I Gits Home. Paul Laurence Dunbar. CP-DunbP

W'en us fellers stomp around, makin' lots o' noise. When a Feller's Itchin' to be Spanked. Paul Laurence Dunbar. CP-DunbP

W'en you full o' worry. Advice. Paul Laurence Dunbar. CP-DunbP

Wenas Ridge. Raymond Carver. CP-CarvR

Wendigo, The. Ogden Nash. CP-NashO

Wendy out her black eyes on me. Sweeping Wendy: Study in Fugue. Carl Sandburg. CP-SandC

Wenlock Edge. A. E. Housman. CP-HousA

Went up a year this evening! Emily Dickinson. CP-DickE

Went up the steep stone hill, thinking. Squaw Lilies: Some Notes. Margaret Atwood. SP-AtwM2

Went weeping, little bones. But where? I Cry, Love! Love! Theodore Roethke. CP-RoetT

Went with us to the beach. Blue towel, A. James Schuyler. CP-SchuJ

Went you to conquer? and have so much lost. H. W. in Hibernia Belligeranti. John Donne. CP-DonnJ; MW-DonnJ

Wer, wenn ich schriee, hörte mich denn aus der *Engel.* Answer to the Rilke Question. Alan Dugan. CP-DugaA

We're all Americans, except the Doc. Mad Negro Soldier Confined at Munich, A. Robert Lowell. SP-LoweR

We're All in the Telephone Book. Langston Hughes. CP-HughL

We're both in Greenville, but a state apart. Letter from Goose Creek: April. Marilyn Hacker. SP-HackM

Were *Death* an *evil,* would *I* let thee *live?* Thoughts for a Speech of Lucifer, in the Tragedy of "Cain." Lord Byron. CP-Byron

We're Extremely Fortunate. Wisława Szymborska. SP-SzymW, *tr.* by Stanislaw Barańczak *and* Clare Cavanagh

We're flattered they come so close. Animal Song. Heather McHugh. SP-McHuH

We're foot—slog—slog—slog—sloggin' over Africa. Boots. Rudyard Kipling. CP-KiplR

Were I myself more blithe. Song: "Were I myself more blithe." Robert Creeley. CP-CreeR

Were I that wandering citizen whose city is the world. English Graves, The. G. K. Chesterton. CP-ChesG

Were I to cut my hand. Dangerous Gift, The. Robert Graves. CP-GravR

Were I to give thee *Baptime,* I wo'd chuse. To His Muse. Robert Herrick. CP-HerrR

Were I with you or you with me. Arthur Hugh Clough. SP-ClouA

We're in the Great Place, Fable Place, Beulah, Man wedded to Earth, Planet of green Grass. Falling Asleep in America. Allen Ginsberg. CP-GinsA

Were it but Me that gained the Height. Emily Dickinson. CP-DickE

Were it indeed an accident of birth. Blemish. Paul Muldoon. CP-MuldP

Were it to be the last. Emily Dickinson. CP-DickE

Were it true that, besides my own, another's arms. Michelangelo Buonarroti. CP-Miche, *tr.* by John Frederick Nims

We're marchin' on relief over Injia's sunny plains. Route Marchin'. Rudyard Kipling. CP-KiplR

"We're married," said Eddie. Newlyweds, The. John Updike. CP-UpdiJ

Were men of such importance as they deem. George Meredith. CP-MerG2

Were My Bosom As False As Thou Deem'st It to Be. Lord Byron. CP-Byron

Were My Heart as Some Men's Are. Thomas Campion. CP-CampT

Were nature mortal lady. Emily Dickinson. CP-DickE

We're not going to die. For My Daughter in Reply to a Question. David Ignatow. SP-IgnaD

We're not so old in the Army List. Irish Guards, The. Rudyard Kipling. CP-KiplR

Were one allowed to kill himself right here. Michelangelo Buonarroti. CP-Miche, *tr.* by John Frederick Nims

Were really one problem: the God he chose. Job's Problems. Thomas Lux. SP-LuxT

We're [*or* We are] related—you and I. Brothers. Langston Hughes. CP-HughL; CP-HughL2; CP-HughL3

We're the Twins from Aunt Marrin's. Twins, The. James Whitcomb Riley. CP-RileJ

Were the Velocity of Affection. Emily Dickinson. SP-DickE

Were there, below, a spot of holy ground. Descriptive Sketches Taken During a Pedestrian Tour among the Alps. William Wordsworth. CP-WorW1

Were there no rain there would be little noise. Code, The. John Updike. CP-

UpdiJ

Were there not a Matter known. Passion. Robert Herrick. CP-HerrR

Were there too many revolving mirrors? Air Circus. Carl Sandburg. CP-SandC

Were they shepherds, who sat all day. Death Of A.G.A, The. Emily Jane Brontë. CP-BronE

Were they that named you, prophets? Did they see. To Susan, Countess of Montgomery. Ben Jonson. CP-JonsB; SP-JonsB

Were we now to fall. Mechanic, The. Robert Creeley. CP-CreeR

Were you but lying cold and dead. He Wishes His Beloved Were Dead. William Butler Yeats. CP-YeatW

Were you counting the days. Waiting ("Were you counting the days"). Robert Creeley. SP-CreeR

Were you to break the vow we swore together. Court of Love, A. Robert Graves. CP-GravR

Were you to cross the world, my dear. Distance. Dorothy Parker. CP-ParkD

We're your grandparents. Comedy of Thirst. Arthur Rimbaud. CP-RimbA, *tr.* by Martin Sorrell

Wereman, The. Margaret Atwood. SP-AtwM1

Werewife, The. James Whitcomb Riley. CP-RileJ

Werewolf Movies. Margaret Atwood. SP-AtwM2

Werner; or, The Inheritance. Lord Byron. CP-Byron

Wert Thou but ill—that I might show thee. Emily Dickinson. CP-DickE

Wes Hardin: From a Photograph. Raymond Carver. CP-CarvR

Wess he says, and sort o grins, "Art and Poetry is twins!" Art and Poetry. James Whitcomb Riley. CP-RileJ

Wessex Guidebook. Louis MacNeice. CP-MacNL

Wessex Heights. Thomas Hardy. CP-HardT

West. Federico García Lorca. CP-GarcF, *tr.* by Jerome Rothenberg *Fr.* Cross.

West. Charles Olson. CP-OlsoC

West. George Oppen. CP-OppGN

West, The. A. E. Housman. CP-HousA

West and away the wheels of darkness roll. Revolution. A. E. Housman. CP-HousA

West Branch Ponds, Kokadjo, Maine. Mona Van Duyn. SP-VanDM

West Country Song. Edna St. Vincent Millay. CP-MillE

West Gloucester. Charles Olson. SP-OlsoC *Fr.* Maximus Poems, The.

West Is the Best and the Future Is Near, The. Andrei Codrescu. SP-CodrA

West light flat on trees. Way to Go. A. R. Ammons. CP-AmmoA

West of Here. William Stafford. SP-StafWW

West-of-Wessex Girl, The. Thomas Hardy. CP-HardT

West of your city into the fern. Midwest. William Stafford. SP-StafWW

West pink, The. Intended Angle of Vision Is from My Kitchen, The. Charles Olson. CP-OlsoC

West-Running Brook. Robert Frost. CP-FrosR

West Texas. Langston Hughes. CP-HughL; CP-HughL2

West Village by then was changing; before long, The. Hedge of Rubber Trees. A. Amy Clampitt. CP-ClamA

West Virginia. Muriel Rukeyser. CP-RukeM

West Virginia's Auburn. Donald Davie. CP-DaviDC

West was getting out of gold, The. Looking for a Sunset Bird in Winter. Robert Frost. CP-FrosR

West Wind. Kenneth Koch. SP-KochK

West window is a panel of marching onions, The. Panels. Carl Sandburg. CP-SandC

Westering. Seamus Heaney. SP-HeanSO

Western Air boat bouncing. Over Laramie. Allen Ginsberg. CP-GinsA

Western Approaches, The. Howard Nemerov. CP-NemeH

Western Ballad, A. Allen Ginsberg. CP-GinsA; SP-GinsA

Western clouds a deepening gloom display, The. William Wordsworth. CP-WorW1

Western Country. W. S. Merwin. SP-MerwW

Western Fellow Students Salute with Calypso Anthems the Movie Career of Robert Lax. Thomas Merton. CP-MertT

Western Invention of Lyrical Nature, The. Gregory Orr. SP-OrrG

Western Landscape. Louis MacNeice. CP-MacNL

Western waves of ebbing day, The. Trossachs, The. Sir Walter Scott. SP-ScotW *Fr.* Lady of the Lake, The.

Western waves of ebbing day, The. Trossachs, The. Alexandre Dumas. SP-ScotW *Fr.* Lady of the Pearls, The.

Western wind is blowing fair, The. Serenade: "Western wind is blowing fair, The." Oscar Wilde. CP-WildO

Westland Row. Thomas Kinsella. CP-KinsT

Westmoreland Girl, The. William Wordsworth. CP-WorW2

Westmorland. Donald Davie. CP-DaviDC

Westphalian Song. *Unknown.* CP-ColeS, *tr.* by Samuel Taylor Coleridge

Westward. Amy Clampitt. CP-ClamA

Westward from Sète / As I went long before. Word of Mouth. Muriel Rukeyser. CP-RukeM

Westward I had expected reminders: somewhere in the Dakotas' carpet. To Westward. John Ciardi. CP-CiarJ

Westward Mother-mountains drift Pacific, green-sloped canyons vaster than Mexico City. Past Silver Durango Over Mexic Sierra-Wrinkles. Allen Ginsberg. CP-GinsA

Westward on the high-hilled plains. A. E. Housman. CP-HousA

"Westward the course of empire takes its way." Welcome Address. Paul Laurence Dunbar. CP-DunbP

Westward the Great Plains are lifting, as you. Going West. Robert Penn Warren. CP-WarrR

Wet almond-trees, in the rain. Bare Almond-Trees. D. H. Lawrence. CP-LawrD

Wet August, A. Thomas Hardy. CP-HardT

Wet Casements. John Ashbery. SP-AshbJ

Wet dawn inks are doing their blue dissolve, The. Winter Trees. Sylvia Plath. CP-PlatS

Wet heat drifts through the afternoon. Ann Arbor Variations. Frank O'Hara. SP-OharF

Wet hitching post of the quay: a sulky hackney, The. Venetian Stanzas 1. Joseph Brodsky. CP-BrodJ, *tr.* by Jane Miller

Wet Litany, The. Rudyard Kipling. CP-KiplR

Wet Night, A. Thomas Hardy. CP-HardT

Wet Nurse. Yusef Komunyakaa. CP-KomuY

Wet Picture. Jaroslav Seifert. SP-SeifJ, *tr.* by Ewald Osers

Wet sheet and a straining sail, A. Chantey. Dorothy Parker. CP-ParkD

Wet skeletons play wet harmonicas in the electric. Ballad of the Typist. Andrei Codrescu. SP-CodrA

Wet / the tide out. March Here. James Schuyler. CP-SchuJ

Wet Time, A. Wendell Berry. CP-BerrW

Wet umbrella is open in the tub, A. It's midnight. Descent into the Hours of the Peregrine. Norman Dubie. CP-DubiN

Wet-Weather Talk. James Whitcomb Riley. CP-RileJ

Wether Contempt or pity most I feel. Impromptu on Hearing that a Print of the Guliteene with Our Beloved Presidents Figure under It Was Executed in Mr Genets Family—under His Sanction. Annis Boudinot Stockton. CP-StocA

Wetness of that street, the light, The. Place, A. Robert Creeley. CP-CreeR

We)under)over,the thing of floating Of. E. E. Cummings. CP-CummE

We've all been off some little while—some one place, some another. Old High School and the New, The. Paul Laurence Dunbar. CP-DunbP

We've been here alone for days. Origins. Jay Wright. SP-WrigJ

We've belled you, baby. Because the countryside here. To My Godson, on His Christening. Mona Van Duyn. SP-VanDM

We've come again to that knee of seacoast. Meadowsounds. Jelaluddin Rumi. SP-Rumi, *tr.* by Coleman Barks

We've drunk to the Queen—God bless her! Native-Born, The. Rudyard Kipling. CP-KiplR

We've forgotten so well. Rainer Maria Rilke. CP-RilkFr, *tr.* by A. Poulin, Jr. *Fr.* Orchards.

We've fought with many men acrost the seas. Fuzzy-Wuzzy. Rudyard Kipling. CP-KiplR

We've gone through two thirds. November Late. Theodore Weiss. SP-WeisT

We've got a change of government. Change of Government. D. H. Lawrence. CP-LawrD

We've got the cholera in camp—it's worse than forty fights. Cholera Camp. Rudyard Kipling. CP-KiplR

We've made a child. Audre Lorde. *See* Now we've made a child

We've made a great mess of love. Mess of Love, The. D. H. Lawrence. CP-LawrD

We've our business to attend Day's duties. Bending the Bow. Robert Duncan. SP-DuncR

We've plodded through a weird and weary time. Metamorphosis. E. E. Cummings. CP-CummE

We've rode and fought and ate and drunk as rations come to hand. Parting of the Columns, The. Rudyard Kipling. CP-KiplR

We've sent our little Cupids all ashore. Second Voyage, The. Rudyard Kipling. CP-KiplR

We've walked the grounds. Monastery at Vršac, The. Charles Wright. SP-WrigC

We've written our wills so beautifully. 24 May 1950. Yannis Ritsos. SP-RitsY *Fr.* Exile's Journals 3.

Wha, in a brulzie, will first cry a parley? Bannocks o' Bear-Meal. Robert Burns. CP-BurnR

Wha Is That at My Bower-Door? Robert Burns. CP-BurnR

Wha kens on whatna Bethlehems. Innumerable Christ, The. Hugh MacDiarmid. SP-MacDH

Wha looks on water and's no' affected yet. Water of Life. Hugh MacDiarmid. SP-MacDH

Wha will buy my Troggin. Buy Braw Troggin. An Excellent New Song. Robert Burns. CP-BurnR *Fr.* Heron Ballads, 1795, The.

Whale. Anne Sexton. CP-SextA; SP-SextA

Whale, The. Theodore Roethke. CP-RoetT

Whale butting through scarps of moving marble, The. Explorations. Louis MacNeice. CP-MacNL

Whale on the beach, you dinosaur. Whale. Anne Sexton. CP-SextA; SP-SextA

Whaleboat Sturck, The. A. R. Ammons. CP-AmmoA

Whalen, curious vulture. Sinecure for P. Whalen, A. Gary Snyder. CP-SnydG

Whaler's Wife, The. Thomas Hardy. CP-HardT

Whales. Kathleen Jessie Raine. SP-RainK

Whales and fish / sailing. Wood Whittler, The. Arthur Sze. SP-SzeA

Whales have calves / Cats have kittens. Guppy, The. Ogden Nash. CP-NashO

Wha'll M-w Me Now. Robert Burns. CP-BurnR

Wham will we send to London town. Robert Burns. CP-BurnR *Fr.* Heron Ballads, 1795, The.

WHAMP WHAMP WHAMP. Growing and Changing. Philip Whalen. SP-WhalP

Whan that Aprille with his shoures soote. Chaucer. Ted Hughes. SP-HughTN

Whare are you gaun, my bony lass. Waukrife Minnie, A. Robert Burns. CP-BurnR

Whare hae ye been sae braw, lad! Killiecrankie. Robert Burns. CP-BurnR

Whare live ye my bonie lass. My Collier Laddie. Robert Burns. CP-BurnR

Wharf, The. W. S. Merwin. SP-MerwW

What. James Schuyler. CP-SchuJ

What? Langston Hughes. CP-HughL
    (White Felts in Fall.) CP-HughL2

What? Walter De la Mare. CP-DeLaW

What? Christina Georgina Rossetti. CP-RosC3

What a beautiful young man. Portrait. Alan Dugan. CP-DugaA

What a calamity, given how ready you are. Satrapy, The. Constantine P. Cavafy. CP CavaC, *tr. by* Theoharis Constantine Theoharis

What a chance I had! I should have, while i could. Michelangelo Buonarroti. CP-Miche, *tr. by* John Frederick Nims

What a Circus. Alan Dugan. CP-DugaA

What a complicated mess in this little country. Yehuda Amichai. SP-AmicY, *tr. by* Chana Bloch

What a curious rendezvous: through mean sleet. Elective Affiniites. Josephine Jacobsen. CP-JacoJ

What a Dead Man Said. James Whitcomb Riley. CP-RileJ

What a dream of a landscape! Landscape with Figures. Howard Nemerov. CP-NemeH

What a fair and happy place. Columbian's Song, The. Walt Whitman. CP-WhitW

What a flimsy shred of the world. Split Second. Denise Levertov. SP-LeveDL

What a furious grandmother. My Rebel Grandmother. John Logan. CP-LogaJ

What a girl called "the dailiness of life" Well Water. Randall Jarrell. CP-JarrR

What a grand time was the war! World War II. Langston Hughes. CP-HughL; CP-HughL3

What a Hazard a Letter is! Emily Dickinson. SP-DickE

What a hot day it is! for. Terrestrial Cuckoo, A. Frank O'Hara. SP-OharF

What a jewel the view. Butcher!, Borges, What a Shock!, The. Alan Dugan. CP-DugaA

What a lovely, brilliant fire. Autumn Fire. Rainer Maria Rilke. CP-RilkFr, *tr. by* A. Poulin, Jr.

What a man on a bald mountain in Jerusalem! Yehuda Amichai. SP-AmicYL, *tr. by* Benjamin Harshav *and* Barbara Harshav

What a message! what a picture! Postcard from John Ashbery, A. Frank O'Hara. SP-OharF

What a pity, when a man looks at himself in the glass. Man's Image. D. H. Lawrence. CP-LawrD

What a pretty tale you told me. Robert Browning. CP-BroR2

What a proud dreamhorse pulling(smoothloomingly)through. E. E. Cummings. CP-CummE; SP-CummE

What a rough night! It's either no dreams at all. Road, The. Raymond Carver. CP-CarvR

What a scurvy mind. Observer, The. William Carlos Williams. CP-WilW2

What a sound his. C. K. Williams. CP-WillC

What a strange feeling all the years to carry. Re-interment: Recollection of a Grandfather. Robert Penn Warren. CP-WarrR

What a sweet smell rises. Laying the Dust. Denise Levertov. SP-LeveDS

What a team. He Has Beaten about the Bush Long Enough. William Carlos Williams. CP-WilW2

What a thrill. Cut. Sylvia Plath. CP-PlatS

What a traffick amongst limbs and loins. Picture, The. Charles Olson. CP-OlsoC

What a way to spend the golden years, Tomasito! Poem—Unfinished Poem. Thomas McGrath. SP-McGrT

What a wild room / We enter, when the gloom. Man-Made World, A. Stephen Spender. CP-SpenS

What a woman!—hooks men like rugs. Lorine Niedecker. CP-NiedL

What a Wonder Among the Instruments Is the Walloping Tramboone! Hayden Carruth. CP-CarHS

What a wonderful thing has come to pass. One of the Crowd on the Shore Tells How It Was. Miller Williams. CP-WillM

What about all this writing? Young Love. William Carlos Williams. CP-WilW1

What About It? Philip Whalen. SP-WhalP

What about measure, I learnt. Peri Poietikes. Louis Zukofsky. CP-ZukLS

What about the people who came to my father's office. Questions, The. Robert Pinsky. CP-PinsR

What Ails My Fern? James Schuyler. CP-SchuJ

What Ails Thee? D. H. Lawrence. CP-LawrD

What ails ye now, ye lousy b———h. Robert Burns' Answer [to Epistle from a Taylor]. Robert Burns. CP-BurnR

What! alive and so bold, O Earth? Lines Written on Hearing the News of the Death of Napoleon. Percy Bysshe Shelley. CP-ShelP

What all the books of ages paint, I have. Ralph Waldo Emerson. CP-EmerR

What Almost Every Woman Knows Sooner or Later. Ogden Nash. CP-NashO

What Am I After All. Walt Whitman. CP-WhitW

What am I doing here. Language of the Country. Hans Magnus Enzensberger. SP-EnzeH, *tr. by* Michael Hamburger

What am I doing here? Birthday. May Swenson. SP-SwenM

What am I? Nosing here, turning leaves over. Wodwo. Ted Hughes. SP-HughTN

What, Amicus, constitutes mastery? Master at a Mediterranean Port, The. Howard Nemerov. CP-NemeH

What an amazing thing to watch a man. Wrestling with Angels. Robert Stock. SP-StocR

What ancestor of mine in wet Wales or wild Scotland. Patronymic. Robinson Jeffers. CP-JefR3

What, and how great, the Virtue and the Art. Second Satire of the Second Book of Horace Imitated, The. Alexander Pope. CP-PopeA

What angel rolled it? Field in New England, A. Gregory Orr. SP-OrrG

What anger in my hard-won bones. Spring People. Audre Lorde. SP-LordA

What Any Lover Learns. Archibald MacLeish. CP-MacLA

What Appears to Be Yours. Frank O'Hara. SP-OharF

What are all the flowers. Ralph Waldo Emerson. CP EmerR

What are Cities For? Robinson Jeffers. CP-JefR2

What are days for? Days. Philip Larkin. CP-LarkP

What Are Heavy? Christina Georgina Rossetti. CP-RosC2

What are his machines. New England Capitalist. Ralph Waldo Emerson. CP-EmerR

What are little boys made of? Cosmic Factories, The. G. K. Chesterton. CP-ChesG

What are our patches, tatters, raggs, and rents. Raggs. Robert Herrick. CP-HerrR

What are ruins to us. At Lindos. May Sarton. SP-SartM

"What are the bugles blowin' for?" said Files-on-Parade. Danny Deever. Rudyard Kipling. CP-KiplR

What Are the Gods? D. H. Lawrence. CP-LawrD

What are the hills of Ross-shire like? Ross-shire Hills, The. Hugh MacDiarmid. SP-MacDH

What are the islands to me. Islands, The. "H. D." CP-DoolH

What are the major men? All men are brave. Paisant Chronicle. Wallace Stevens. CP-StevW; SP-StevWP

What are the marks of the enemy? / He has no wit. Thomas Merton. CP-MertT

What are the signs of life? the breath, the pulse. For a Song of the Languagers. Robert Duncan. SP-DuncR

What are the springs of sleep? What is the motion. Causerie. Allen Tate. CP-TateA

What are the things that make life bright? To J. Q. Paul Laurence Dunbar. CP-DunbP

What are the two poor children thinking there. REM Sleep. William Meredith. SP-MereW

What Are the Wild Waves Saying? D. H. Lawrence. CP-LawrD

What, are there gods? herself she hath forswore. Elegy 3.3: "What, are there gods? herself she hath forswore." Ovid. CP-MarlC *Fr.* Elegies.

What Are These. Shmuel HaNagid. SP-HaNaS, *tr. by* Peter Cole

What are these elations I have. Descent of Winter, The. William Carlos Williams. CP-WilW1

What are these lovely ones, yea, what are these? Christina Georgina Rossetti. CP-RosC2

What are these objects everyone speaks of? Why is it that not one day can pass. In the Supermarket. Andrei Codrescu. SP-CodrA

What are these presents Look how many. Give and Take. William Meredith. SP-MereW

What are these songs. Louis Zukofsky. CP-ZukLS

What are these very desolate ones. So It Ends. Kenneth Patchen. CP-PatcK

What are those of the known but to ascend and enter the Unknown? Portals. Walt Whitman. CP-WhitW

What are to me those honours or renown. Last Words on Greece. Lord Byron. CP-Byron

What are we doing gathered in the bazaar, and waiting? Waiting for the Barbarians. Constantine P. Cavafy. CP-CavaC, *tr. by* Theoharis Constantine

Theoharis

What are we set on earth for? Say, to toil. Work. Elizabeth Barrett Browning. CP-BroEB

What are we to do with this hour of the evening. Sunset: The Canary Islands. Miller Williams. CP-WillM

What Are Years? Marianne Craig Moore. CP-MoorM

What *are* you, apple! There are men. Still Life. Buddhadeva Bose. CP-OppGN, *tr. by* George Oppen

What are you but a drifting crowd? Ode for You. Philip Whalen. SP-WhalP

What are you doing. Levitation. A. R. Ammons. CP-AmmoA

What are you doing? Plus Ça Change. Philip Whalen. SP-WhalP

What are you doing, dear Ingelo, a deserter to the northern zone. Letter to Doctor Ingelo, A. Andrew Marvell. CP-MarvA

What are you doing here, poet, on the ruins. In Warsaw. Czeslaw Milosz. CP-MiloC; CP-MiloCN, *tr. by* Robert Hass *and* Madeline Levine

What are you doing outside my walls. New Dawn's Business, The. Thomas Hardy. CP-HardT

What are you doing today, brother? Poem Written after Reading Certain Poets Sired by the English School and Bitched by the C.P. Kenneth Patchen. CP-PatcK

What are you doing up, my cat. Intruding. Marge Piercy. SP-PierM

What are you doing with all those paper. She Said. Charles Bukowski. SP-BukC3

What are you hiding under your hump? Pablo Neruda. SP-NeruP *Fr.* Question Book.

What are you looking for. On a Shell-strewn Beach. Kathleen Jessie Raine. SP-RainK

What Are You Smiling About. James Laughlin. CP-LaugJ

What are you still, still thinking. Moth-Signal, The. Thomas Hardy. CP-HardT

What Are You Studying, These Days? Philip Whalen. SP-WhalP

What armies ride November clouds. These Years a Winter. Thomas Merton. CP-MertT

What art and anti-art to lead us by the sharpness. Semite. George Oppen. CP-OppGN

What art thou, Presumptuous, who profanest. Fragment: The False Laurel and the True. Percy Bysshe Shelley. CP-ShelP

"What art thou thinking of," said the Mother. Mother and Child. Christina Georgina Rossetti. CP-RosC3

What avails it me. Ralph Waldo Emerson. CP-EmerR

What be those crowned forms high over the sacred fountain? Parnassus. Alfred Tennyson. CP-TennA

What beauty would have lovely styled. Epitaph, An: "What beauty would have lovely styled." Ben Jonson. CP-JonsB

What beckoning [*or* beck'ning] ghost, along the moonlight shade. Elegy to the Memory of an Unfortunate Lady. Alexander Pope. CP-PopeA

What began as death's avenue. At Père Lachaise. Mona Van Duyn. SP-VanDM

What being in rank-old nature should earlier have that breath been. Gerard Manley Hopkins. CP-HopkG

What Best I See in Thee. Walt Whitman. CP-WhitW

What bird would light. Lorine Niedecker. CP-NiedL

What body can be ploughed. Chanson un Peu Naïve. Louise Bogan. CP-BogaL

What boots it on the Gods to call? Recantation, A. Rudyard Kipling. CP-KiplR

What boots it, thy virtue. Tact. Ralph Waldo Emerson. CP-EmerR

What bothers me most about. Junk Collector, The. James Laughlin. CP-LaugJ

What bright soft thing is this? Tear[e], The. Richard Crashaw. CP-CrasR

What can a man do that a beast cannot. In Shame and Humiliation. James Wright. CP-WrigJ

What can a young lassie, what shall a young lassie. Robert Burns. CP-BurnR

"What can I do for you?" she asked gently. Wild Cyclamen. Robert Graves. CP-GravR

What can I do in Poetry. Departure of the Good Daemon, The. Robert Herrick. CP-HerrR

What Can I Do to Drive Away. John Keats. CP-KeatJ

What can I do with this bayonet? Bayonet. Anne Sexton. CP-SextA

What can i promise to be is water. Further Note to Clark. Lucille Clifton. SP-ClifL

What can I tell you? Though your quarry. Rune. Paul Muldoon. CP-MuldP

What can it mean to endure. Pablo Neruda. SP-NeruP *Fr.* Question Book.

What can lambkins do. Chill, A. Christina Georgina Rossetti. CP-RosC1

What can my Kellam drink his Sack. To M. Kellam. Robert Herrick. CP-HerrR

What can occur / invests the weather, also. To Bobbie. Robert Creeley. CP-CreeR

What can purge my heart. Song for Billie Holiday. Langston Hughes. CP-HughL; CP-HughL2

What can the cause be, when the king hath [*or* K. have] given. Epigram. To the Household. 1630, An. Ben Jonson. CP-JonsB

What can the spirit believe? Young Girl, The. Theodore Roethke. CP-RoetT

What can the white man say to the black woman? Right to Life, The: What Can the White Man Say to the Black Woman? Alice Walker. CP-WalkA

What Can We Not Ask? Robert Graves. CP-GravR

What can we say of the night? Far Rockaway Night Till Morning. Carl Sandburg. CP-SandC

What can you do with this. Continuo, The. W. S. Merwin. SP-MerwW

What can you say about Pennsylvania. Returning Native. John Updike. CP-UpdiJ

What Cannot Be. Constantine P. Cavafy. CP-CavaC, *tr. by* Theoharis Constantine Theoharis

What care I if good God be. Egocentric. Stevie Smith. CP-SmitS

What care I, so they stand the same. Merops. Ralph Waldo Emerson. CP-EmerR

What care the Dead, for Chanticleer. Emily Dickinson. CP-DickE

What catches the eye the quick hand reaches toward. Consciousness. Robinson Jeffers. CP-JefR1

What cave are you in, hiding, rained on? Man Writes to a Part of Himself, A. Robert Bly. SP-BlyR

What charming peals are these. To My Worthy Friend, Master Edward Filmer, on His Work Published. Ben Jonson. CP-JonsB

What cheer, O Ren Jaldain? Down in the Lone Valley. Kenneth Patchen. CP-PatcK

What chores these churls do put upon the great. Edna St. Vincent Millay. CP-MillE

What Chris'mas Fetched the Wigginses. James Whitcomb Riley. CP-RileJ

What clamped us together? When each night fell we lay down. Remembering Old Wars. Thomas Kinsella. CP-KinsT

What coarse god. Ovid in Tomis. Derek Mahon. CP-MahoD

What common language to unravel? Paterson: The Falls. William Carlos Williams. CP-WilW2

What conscience, say, is it in thee. To Oenone. Robert Herrick. CP-HerrR

What constitutes the training of the hand? Sentences. Czeslaw Milosz. CP-MiloC; CP-MiloCN, *tr. by* Lillian Vallee

What could be more endearing, on a long, too quiet, lonely evening in an unfamiliar house. Time: 1978. C. K. Williams. SP-WillC

What Could Hold Us. Heather McHugh. SP-McHuH

What could I do with a man? Young Farm Woman Alone. Ai. SP-Ai

What could she say to the fantastic foolybear. Lawrence Ferlinghetti. SP-FerlL

What could / they give me I. They. Robert Creeley. CP-CreeR

What could those Three. Rainer Maria Rilke. CP-RilkFr, *tr. by* A. Poulin, Jr. *Fr.* Affectionate Taxes to France.

What could we say to you. Or Else. Heather McHugh. SP-McHuH

What Counts. Yusef Komunyakaa. CP-KomuY

What crowd is this in Catknoll Street. War-Wife of Catknoll, The. Thomas Hardy. CP-HardT

What crowd is this? what have we here! we must not pass it by. Star-Gazers. William Wordsworth. CP-WorW1; MW-WorW

What cry of peach blossoms. Peach Blossoms. Carl Sandburg. CP-SandC

What curious things we said. Intra Sepulchrum. Thomas Hardy. CP-HardT

What dat scratchin' at de kitchen do'? When de Folks Is Gone. James Whitcomb Riley. CP-RileJ

What dawn-pulse at the heart of heaven, or last. Beauty's Pageant. Dante Gabriel Rossetti. CW-RossD *Fr.* House of Life, The.

What day was that which, all sad haps to bring. Elegy 3.11: "What day was that which, all sad haps to bring." Ovid. CP-MarlC *Fr.* Elegies.

What death is worse than this? Sir Thomas Wyatt. CP-WyatT

What death means is not this. Canticle. Wendell Berry. CP-BerrW

What delightful hosts are they. Parting Guest, A. James Whitcomb Riley. CP-RileJ

What demented malice, my silly Ravidus. Catullus. *See* Whatever could have possessed you

What demon lurked among those olive-trees. Tower of Love, The. Robert Graves. CP-GravR

What did he do except lie. Banneker. Rita Dove. SP-DoveR

What Did I Dream? Robert Graves. CP-GravR

What did I think I was bringing her into? Circus. Heather McHugh. SP-McHuH

What Did It mean? Thomas Hardy. CP-HardT

What did Klimt mean by. Kiss, The. James Laughlin. CP-LaugJ

What Did She Know, When Did She Know It. Lucille Clifton. SP-ClifL

What did that old philosopher say? Lovable Babblers. Carl Sandburg. CP-SandC

What did the day bring? Letter from a Coward to a Hero. Robert Penn Warren. CP-WarrR

What Did the Man Do with the Clouds? C. K. Williams. CP-WillC

What did the man who burned to death. Yehuda Amichai. SP-AmicY, *tr. by* Chana Bloch *Fr.* Songs of Zion the Beautiful.

What did the poem say that day. Four Short Pieces. Grace Paley. CP-PalGC

What did They do since I saw Them? Emily Dickinson. CP-DickE

What did we want with the golden fleece?—a new trial—perhaps the greatest. Golden Fleece, The. Yannis Ritsos. SP-RitsY, *tr. by* Kimon Friar *and* Karelisa Hartigan

What did you do? Cannot you let me know? Reluctant Confession. Thomas Hardy. CP-HardT

What did you do for the holiday? Eclogue between the Motherless. Louis MacNeice. CP-MacNL

What did you do with my heart. In the Salzkammergut. James Laughlin. CP-LaugJ

What did you eat? Who did you call? Oh, exquisite asparagus. Evening Particulier. Andrei Codrescu. SP-CodrA

What Did You Say? Robert Graves. CP-GravR

What did you say? Which? Walter De la Mare. CP-DeLaW

What did you say to me. Bird, The. Robert Creeley. CP-CreeR

What did you see, Cromarty, by the house. Seeing. Archibald MacLeish. CP-MacLA

What dire offense from amorous [or am'rous] causes springs. Rape of the Lock, The; an Heroi-Comical Poem. Alexander Pope. CP-PopeA

What do a few crimes. Adultery. Alan Dugan. CP-DugaA

What do I care. Pursuit. "H. D." CP-DoolH

What Do I Care? D. H. Lawrence. CP-LawrD

What do I catch upon the night-wind, husband? Sound in the Night, A. Thomas Hardy. CP-HardT

What Do I Give You? Muriel Rukeyser. CP-RukeM

What do I remember of my visit to Ravenna? Firstly. Ravenna. Louis MacNeice. CP-MacNL

What do I want in these rooms papered with visions of money? Paterson. Allen Ginsberg. CP-GinsA; SP-GinsA

What do the stars do / Up in the sky. Christina Georgina Rossetti. CP-RosC2

What do they matter now, the deprivations. Page to Commemorate Colonel Suárez, Victor at Junín, A. Jorge Luis Borges. SP-BorgJ, tr. by Alastair Reid

What do they mean to us, my heart, the sheets of blood. Arthur Rimbaud. CP-RimbA, tr. by Martin Sorrell

What do they think has happened, the old fools. Old Fools, The. Philip Larkin. CP-LarkP

What do they think of themselves. Little Whale Song. Ted Hughes. SP-HughTN

What Do We See? Muriel Rukeyser. CP-RukeM

What do we see / In the perfect thing? Is our seeing. Images of Perfection. Charles Tomlinson. CP-TomlC; SP-TomlC

What do you body want? Food? Food? Body Blues. Andrei Codrescu. SP-CodrA

What do you do if you meet a witch? Working World's Bloody Flux, The. Alan Dugan. CP-DugaA

What do you do when you've wedded a girl all legal and lawful. Aside to Husbands. Ogden Nash. CP-NashO

What Do You Feel Underground? Gabriela Mistral. SP-MistG, tr. by Maria Giachetti [or Jacketti]

What do you hear up here? September Mendocino. Clarence Major. SP-MajoC

What do you know about it? the Architect said. Controversy, The. William Carlos Williams. CP-WilW2

What do you know about people who go about. Song of the Conspirators. G. K. Chesterton. CP-ChesG

What do you know of America? I asked a little Russian schoolgirl. Muriel Rukeyser. CP-RukeM

What do you look for down there. Absent-Minded Are Always to Blame, The. Adrienne Rich. CP-RicAE

"What do you make so fair and bright?" Cloak, the Boat, and the Shoes, The. William Butler Yeats. CP-YeatW

What do you remember thinking back. Ever Since. Archibald MacLeish. CP-MacLA

What do you see in that time-touched stone. In the British Museum. Thomas Hardy. CP-HardT

What do you see in Vagg Hollow. Vagg Hollow. Thomas Hardy. CP-HardT

What do you so regret, my lady. Lady of Forebodings, The. Thomas Hardy. CP-HardT

What / do you think it is. Robert Creeley. CP-CreeR

What do you think, my soul? Will there be peace? Petrarch. CP-Petra, tr. by J. G. Nichols

What do you want. Speech at Soli, The. George Oppen. CP-OppGN

What do you / want, love. To be. Song: "What do you / want, love. To be." Robert Creeley. CP-CreeR

What do you write? Muriel Rukeyser. CP-RukeM

What doating bigot to his faults so blind. Satire 1.1: "What doating bigot to his faults so blind." Horace. CP-JohnS Fr. Satires.

What, doctor, if great Carteret condescends. Letter of Advice to the Reverend Dr. D-la-y, Humbly Proposed to the Consideration of a Certain Great Lord, A. Unknown, sometimes at. to Thomas Sheridan. CP-SherT

What does he think about. Bootblack, The. Charles Tomlinson. CP-TomlC

What does it matter? you ask. What Ovid Taught Me. Alice Walker. CP-WalkA

What Does It Mean. Czeslaw Milosz. CP-MiloC; CP-MiloCN

What does it mean, I ask myself, while I am mowing. Distance. Maxine W. Kumin. SP-KumiM

What does it mean? Lord knows; least of all I. Apology for Using the Word "Heart" in Too Many Poems, An. Hayden Carruth. CP-CarHS

What does little Ernest croon. E. E. Cummings. CP-CummE

What does not change / is the will to change. Kingfishers, The. Charles Olson. CP-OlsoC; SP-OlsoC

What does serpent mean? Fanny Howe. SP-HoweF Fr. Quietist, The.

What Does She See When She Shuts Her Eyes. Gertrude Stein. CP-SteiG

What Does She Want? D. H. Lawrence. CP-LawrD

What does she want from us, life whose every mortal moment. Menace. Rainer Maria Rilke. CP-RilkFr

What Does the Bee Do? Christina Georgina Rossetti. CP-RosC2

What does the donkey bray about? Christina Georgina Rossetti. CP-RosC2

What does the hangman think about. Hangman at Home, The. Carl Sandburg. CP-SandC

What does the horse give you. Horse. Louise Glück. SP-GlucL

What does the song hope for? And his moved hands. Orpheus. W. H. Auden. CP-AudeW

What does the storm say? What the trees wish. Ways and the Peoples, The. Randall Jarrell. CP-JarrR

What does the veery say, at dusk in shad-thicket? Code Book Lost. Robert Penn Warren. CP-WarrR

What does this day bestow? Kathleen Jessie Raine. SP-RainK

What Does This Mean? Sir Thomas Wyatt. CP-WyatT

What does / wisdom say. Golden Mean, The. A. R. Ammons. CP-AmmoA

What doest thou here, Elijah? Ghost of Abel, The. William Blake. CP-BlakW

What dost thou here far from thy native place? Banquo. Walter De la Mare. CP-DeLaW

What doth he ask? Hero, The. Henry David Thoreau. CP-ThorH

What doth this noise of thoughts within my heart. Family [or Familie], The. George Herbert. CP-HerbG

What dreams we have and how they fly. Dreams. Paul Laurence Dunbar. CP-DunbP

What dreams you must have had last night. Dream, The. Randall Jarrell. CP-JarrR

What Ducks Require. John Crowe Ransom. SP-RansJ

What else is left to people nowadays. Dome of the Observatory, The. Jaroslav Seifert. SP-SeifJ, tr. by Ewald Osers

What, Enid, was your soul's mystic hour? Enid, An Invitation. G. K. Chesterton. CP-ChesG

What Entanglement in This Small Country. Yehuda Amichai. SP-AmicYL, tr. by Benjamin Harshav and Barbara Harshav

What ever man he be, whose heavie minde. Daphnaïda. Edmund Spenser. CP-Spens

What ever men for Loyalty pretend. Distrust. Robert Herrick. CP-HerrR

What ever story of their crueltie. On the Still Surviving Markes of Our Saviours Wounds. Richard Crashaw. CP-CrasR

What evil coil of fate has fastened me. Ivor Gurney. SP-GurnI

What face, in the water. Lament: "What face, in the water." William Carlos Williams. CP-WilW2

What fair pomp have I spied of glittering ladies. What Fair[e] Pomp[e]. Thomas Campion. CP-CampT

What Fair[e] Pomp[e]. Thomas Campion. CP-CampT
(Canto Secundo.) CP-CampT

What faire pompe have I spide of glittering Ladies. Thomas Campion. See What fair pomp have I spied of glittering ladies

What fate decreed, Time now ha's made us see. To Prince Charles upon his coming to Exeter. Robert Herrick. CP-HerrR

What fate of mine, what trickery, what force. Petrarch. CP-Petra, tr. by J. G. Nichols

What fear is mine when I recall that day. Petrarch. CP-Petra, tr. by J. G. Nichols

What Fears, what Terrors does thy Gift create! On a Lady's Presenting a Sprig of Myrtle to a Gentleman. Samuel Johnson. CP-JohnS

What Fifty Said. Robert Frost. CP-FrosR

What file's incessant bite. Michelangelo Buonarroti. CP-Miche, tr. by John Frederick Nims

What fire has blackened to sleeping. Sculpture in Soil. Peter Blue Cloud. SP-BlueP

What flag will fly for me. August 19th. Langston Hughes. CP-HughL; CP-HughL1

What flecks the outer gray beyond. Dead Ship of Harpswell, The. John Greenleaf Whittier. CP-WhitJ

What flies forever and rests never? The Wind. So say Senegalese. Maybe. Riddles and Whims. Carl Sandburg. CP-SandC

What flowing central forces, say. Ralph Waldo Emerson. CP-EmerR

What fool would feel. Naked. William Carlos Williams. CP-WilW1

What forced labor / for Hitler in Hell? Pablo Neruda. SP-NeruP Fr. Question Book.

What freedom's not some under's mere above. E. E. Cummings. CP-CummE; SP-CummE

What from this barren being do we reap. Ralph Waldo Emerson. CP-EmerR

What, Gellius, of the man. Carmen 88. Catullus. CP-ZukLS Fr. Carmina.

What General has a good army in himself, has a good army. Leaflets. Walt

Whitman. CP-WhitW

What generations could have dreamed. Pedestrian. George Oppen. CP-OppGN

What gentle echoes. Massachusetts. Robert Creeley. CP-CreeR

What gentle ghost, besprent with April dew. Elegy [or Elegie] on the Lady Jane Pawlet [or Paulet], [Marchioness of Winton], An. Ben Jonson. CP-JonsB

What Gets Away. William Stafford. SP-StafWW

What Gets You. "Rubén Dario." SP-DariR, tr. by Alberto Acereda and Will Derusha

What Ghosts Can Say. Adrienne Rich. CP-RicAE

What ghosts of cuckoo-spit and dew. Louis MacNeice. CP-MacNL Fr. Jigsaws.

What girl but, having gathered flowers. Humility. Robert Browning. CP-BroR2

What Gives. Richard Eberhart. CP-EberR

What gives it power makes it change its mind. Beautiful Lawn Sprinkler, The. Howard Nemerov. CP-NemeH

What glories would we? Motions of the soul? Renewal, The. Theodore Roethke. CP-RoetT

What glory, this, for Herodis Attikos. Herodis Attikos. Constantine P. Cavafy. CP-CavaC, tr. by Theoharis Constantine Theoharis

What God gives, and what we take. Grace for Children, A. Robert Herrick. CP-HerrR

What God Is. Robert Herrick. CP-HerrR

What God is like to him I serve? Anne Bradstreet. CP-BradA

What God, what Genius did the Pencil move. To Sir Godfrey Kneller, on His Painting for Me the Statues of Apollo, Venus and Hercules. Alexander Pope. CP-PopeA

What goddess, what god. Rainer Maria Rilke. CP-RilkFr, tr. by A. Poulin, Jr. Fr. Valaisian Quatrains, The.

What goes on in the pauses. Torture. Margaret Atwood. SP-AtwM2

What golden splendent star is this so bright. In Praise of the Author, Mistress Anne Bradstreet, Virtue's True and Lively Pattern. Unknown. CP-BradA

What good are children anyhow? Children. Carolyn Kizer. CP-KizeC

What good is life without music. Read the Great Poets. James Tate. SP-TateJ

What Good Shall My Life Do Me? Christina Georgina Rossetti. CP-RosC2

What Good Shall My Life Do Me? Christina Georgina Rossetti. CP-RosC3

What good, what profit did fortune seek. Poet and the Muse, The. Constantine P. Cavafy. CP-CavaC, tr. by Theoharis Constantine Theoharis

What Got him was Noth. E. E. Cummings. CP-CummE

What Grandpa Mouse Said. Nicholas Vachel Lindsay. CP-LindV

What great genius invented the waiting room? Waiting Rooms. Howard Nemerov. CP-NemeH

What Greece, when learning flourished [or flourish'd], only [or onle] knew. Prologue to the University of Oxford, 1673. John Dryden. SP-DrydJ

What had he done. Case History. A. K. Ramanujan. CP-RamaA

What Had to Go. Charles Olson. CP-OlsoC

What Happened. Rudyard Kipling. CP-KiplR

What Happened Here Before. Gary Snyder. CP-SnydG

What Happened in the Camps. Kenneth Patchen. CP-PatcK

What happened? The stone stepped from the mountain. Paul Celan. SP-CelaP, tr. by John Felstiner

What happened to her. Time ("What happened to her"). Robert Creeley. CP-CreeR

What happened to me. All Wars Are Holy. Andrei Codrescu. SP-CodrA

What Happened? What Do You Expect? Alan Dugan. CP-DugaA

What happens afterwards, none need enquire. Conjunction. Robert Graves. CP-GravR

What happens I wonder to. Two Ships. James Laughlin. CP-LaugJ

What happens is, the kind of snow that sweeps. For a Lost Child. William Stafford. SP-StafW; SP-StafWW

What happens to a dream deferred? Harlem ("What happens to a dream deferred?"). Langston Hughes. CP-HughL; CP-HughL3 Fr. Lenox Avenue Mural.

What happens to little cats? Little Cats. Langston Hughes. CP-HughL; CP-HughL3

What happens / to the leaves after. Roses, Late Summer. Mary Oliver. SP-OlivM

What Harbinger? Denise Levertov. SP-LeveDS

What harts content can he finde. Thomas Campion and Philip Rosseter. CP-CampT

What Harvest Half So Sweet Is. Thomas Campion. CP-CampT

What has availed. Question and Answer. Robert Penn Warren. CP-WarrR

What / has happened. Here ("What / has happened"). Robert Creeley. CP-CreeR

What has happened here will do. Boundary. Adrienne Rich. CP-RicAE

What has happened in the world? Volcanic Venus. D. H. Lawrence. CP-LawrD

What has happened to the young men of Eng.? Eng. Stevie Smith. CP-SmitS

What has it come to, Dr. Y. Anne Sexton. SP-SextA Fr. Letters to Dr. Y.

What has just happened between the lovers. Waking, The. Galway Kinnell. SP-KinnGN

What has killed mankind—for the bulk of mankind is dead—is lies. Poison. D. H. Lawrence. CP-LawrD

What has this bugbear death to frighten man. Against the Fear of Death. Lucretius. CP-DryJ2, tr. by John Dryden Fr. De Rerum Natura (On the Nature of Things).

What hasn't happened. Song / for Sanna. Olga Broumas. SP-BrouO

What hast thou, O my soul, with paradise? Blandula, Tenulla [or Tenella], Vagula. Ezra Pound. CP-PoEar; SP-PounE

What Hath God Wrought! Christina Georgina Rossetti. CP-RosC2

What hath God wrought? What hath God wrought? First Telegraphic Message, The. Jones Very. CP-VeryJ

"What have I earned for all that work," I said. People, The. William Butler Yeats. CP-YeatW

What Have I Learned. Gary Snyder. CP-SnydG

What have I learned that can keep me. Reading at Night. David Ignatow. SP-IgnaD

What have I saved out of a morning? Moon Riders. Carl Sandburg. CP-SandC

What have I to do with Arras. Wallace Stevens. CP-StevWP

What have I to regret. Kathleen Jessie Raine. SP-RainK

What have I to say to you? Love Song: First Version, 1915, A. William Carlos Williams. CP-WilW1

What have the clouds been up to today? You can't. No Praise, No Blame. William Stafford. SP-StafWW

What have they done to our dollar, darling. On the Recently Minted Hundred-Cent Piece. John Updike. CP-UpdiJ

What Have They Done to You? D. H. Lawrence. CP-LawrD

What have they done to you, all-conquering love? Observations of P. Ovidus Naso on the Incidence of Sex in the Contemporary Novel. Archibald MacLeish. CP-MacLA

What have we but an empty song? Empty Song, The. James Whitcomb Riley. CP-RileJ

What have we done this winter to deserve. Fly. John Updike. CP-UpdiJ

What have we ever done to bear this grudge. Plea of the Simla Dancers, The. Rudyard Kipling. CP-KiplR

What Have You Brought Home from the Wars? Muriel Rukeyser. CP-RukeM

What have you left for us to say to you? Letter to the Old Men. Kenneth Patchen. CP-PatcK

What have you looked at, Moon. To the Moon. Thomas Hardy. CP-HardT

What he dreamt of as a support had day by day removed. Stages of Ignorance. Yannis Ritsos. SP-RitsY, tr. by Kimon Friar and Kostas Myrsiades

What he holds to / is a cross. Women, The. Robert Creeley. CP-CreeR

What, he on whom our voices unanimously ran. Pope and the Net, The. Robert Browning. CP-BroR2

What He Thought. Heather McHugh. SP-McHuH

What He—who, 'mid the kindred throng. Effusion in the Pleasure-Ground on the Banks of the Bran, Near Dunkeld. William Wordsworth. CP-WorW2

What heartbeats, lisping like a lizard in a broken cistern. Ode to the Present Century. Thomas Merton. CP-MertT

What Heavenly Smiles! O Lady Mine. William Wordsworth. CP-WorW2

What Hell Is. Heather McHugh. SP-McHuH

What helps it woman to be free from war. Elegy 2.14: "What helps it woman to be free from war." Ovid. CP-MarlC Fr. Elegies.

What here we hope for, we shall once inherit. Faith. Robert Herrick. CP-HerrR

What hill can ever hold us? Cats and a Cock. Muriel Rukeyser. CP-RukeM

What ho! the wind is up and eloquent. Tally-Ho. Ezra Pound. CP-PoEar

What horror to awake at night. Lorine Niedecker. CP-NiedL

What hurrying human tides, or day or night! Broadway. Walt Whitman. CP-WhitW

What I am is not important, whether I live or die. Children in Exile. James Fenton. SP-FentJ

What I am not, and what I fain would be. Epistle to Master Arth[ur] Squib, An. Ben Jonson. CP-JonsB

What I am now is the cock. What Must I Do To Be Lost? C. K. Williams. CP-WillC

What I am saying now was said before. Sonnet: "What I am saying now was said before." Countee Cullen. CP-CullC

What I Can Do. Raymond Carver. CP-CarvR

What I can do—I will. Emily Dickinson. CP-DickE

What I did I did. Letter to Her. Robert Bly. SP-BlyR

What I did not say the other day to you for today. Or a Valentine. Louis Zukofsky. CP-ZukLS

What I Did on a Rainy Day. May Swenson. SP-SwenM

What, I disturb thee at thy morning-meal. Cherries. Robert Browning. CP-BroR2

What I do is / our secret. Afterschool Lessons from a Hitman. Ai. SP-Ai

What I Expected. Stephen Spender. CP-SpenS

What I fancy, I approve. No Loathsomnesse in Love. Robert Herrick. CP-HerrR

What I had witnessed had been lived through. Shadowing the Ground. David Ignatow. SP-IgnaD

What I have to tell you is the rain. Caligula in Blue. Wyatt Prunty. SP-PrunW

What I hear is not only water but stones. Tassajara. Philip Whalen. SP-WhalP

What I hear mostly, sitting on this porch. Talking to Himself He Gets a Few

Things Settled in His Mind. Miller Williams. CP-WillM

What I Know About Life. Ogden Nash. CP-NashO

What I Learned from Jeanne Hersch. Czeslaw Milosz. CP-MiloCN, *tr. by* Robert Hass

What I like is when. Hacienda. Charles Tomlinson. SP-TomlC

What I look at amazes me. What I love scares me. Sometimes I'm a nun. Origin of Electricity, The. Andrei Codrescu. SP-CodrA

What I love about this little leaning mark. Virgule. Thomas Lux. SP-LuxT

What I must not forget. Many Mansions, The. Denise Levertov. SP-LeveDL

What I remember most. Untitled Poem: "What I remember most." Alan Dugan. CP-DugaA

What I remember most was not. Lamplighter: 1914. Stanley Kunitz. CP-KunSC

What I Remember the Writers Telling Me When I Was Young. William Meredith. SP-MereW

What I saw in his head. Friend, The. Robert Creeley. CP-CreeR

What I saw on his face scared me—ants. Rape in the Engineering Building. James Tate. SP TateJ

What I See. Muriel Rukeyser. CP-RukeM

What I see not, I better see. Emily Dickinson. CP-DickE

What I See When I Drive to Work. Thomas Lux. SP-LuxT

What I Think. Langston Hughes. CP-HughL; CP-HughL3

What I Think When I Ride the Train. Lucille Clifton. SP-ClifL

What I took in my hand. Son: "What I took in my hand." Robert Creeley. CP-CreeR

What I want from God, feared to be. Breath. Heather McHugh. SP-McHuH

What I want? green. Vector Analysis. Philip Whalen. SP-WhalP

What I want in heart. But of Life? Kenneth Patchen. CP-PatcK

What I Want to Say. Mona Van Duyn. SP-VanDM

What I was would not work. Encounter in the Cage Country. James Dickey. CP-DickJ

What, I wonder, were we hurrying to. Leaving Church Early. John Updike. CP-UpdiJ

What I'd Like to Do. Allen Ginsberg. CP-GinsA

What I'd like to know is. Kenneth Patchen. CP-PatcK

What idiocy could transform the moon, that old sea-overgrown. Not the Moon. Margaret Atwood. SP-AtwM2

What If a Day [*or* a Month or a Year]. Thomas Campion. CP-CampT

What If a Much of a Which of a Wind. E. E. Cummings. CP-CummE; SP-CummE

What if a much of a which of a wind. What If a Much of a Which of a Wind. E. E. Cummings. CP-CummE; SP-CummE

What if his glance is bold and free. To a Brown Girl. Countee Cullen. CP-CullC

What if I bade you leave. Those Images. William Butler Yeats. CP-YeatW

What if I came down now out of these. Contemporary, A. W. S. Merwin. SP-MerwWF

What if I say I shall not wait! Emily Dickinson. CP-DickE

What if I told you the truth? What if I could? Lament for the Makers. Robert Pinsky. CP-PinsR

What if it should turn out eternity. Steeple on the House, A. Robert Frost. CP-FrosR

What if our numbers barely could defy. William Wordsworth. CP-WorW1

What if Prince Paris, after taking thought. Judgement of Paris. Robert Graves. CP-GravR

What if the ethical gunmen isolated evil. How Humble We Were before This. C. K. Williams. CP-WillC

What if the poet in a moment of terror. Helmet of Goliath, The. Robert Duncan. SP-DuncR

What if the psychologians, those grand old frauds. Sonnet: "What if the psychologians, those grand old frauds." Hayden Carruth. CP-CarHS *Fr.* Sonnets.

What if the revolution comes and I'm in it and my job. Rabbit Fights for His Life the Leopard Eats Lunch, The. C. K. Williams. CP-WillC

What if the wild confinement were empty. City after Noon, The. Thomas Merton. CP-MertT

What if the wind do howl without. Right's Security. Paul Laurence Dunbar. CP-DunbP

What if the world's corruption nears. Ultimate Act, The. Adrienne Rich. CP-RicAE

What if, then. One Year Later. Lucille Clifton. SP-ClifL

What if there were no sea. Helen Groves. Olga Broumas. SP-BrouO

What if this century doesn't end. What If (This Week). Grace Paley. CP-PalGC

What If (This Week). Grace Paley. CP-PalGC

What if to edge of dream. Owl, The. Walter De la Mare. CP-DeLaW

What if we two should move. Invitation to a Voyage. Charles Baudelaire. CP-BaudC, *tr. by* Walter Martin

What I'm saying isn't exactly news. Gregory Orr. SP-OrrG

What I'm trying to say is that if an experience is. Around the Fire. Ted Berrigan. SP-BerrT

What image of a higher, holier day. Each Day a Prophecy. Jones Very. CP-VeryJ

What in your handsome face I see, my lord. Michelangelo Buonarroti. CP-Miche, *tr. by* John Frederick Nims

What indeed is Earth but a Nest. Emily Dickinson. SP-DickE

What Inn is this. Emily Dickinson. CP-DickE

What intuition named thee? Robert Burns Wilson. James Whitcomb Riley. CP-RileJ

What Is a Buslus? G. K. Chesterton. CP-ChesG

What is a day, what is a yeere. *Unknown*. CP_CampT, *tr. by* Thomas Campion

What is a Jew in solitude? Yom Kippur 1984. Adrienne Rich. SP-RicA1

What is a kiss[e]? Why this, as some approve. Kiss[e], A. Robert Herrick. CP-HerrR

What Is a Man to Do? D. H. Lawrence. CP-LawrD

What is a man worth? Buyers and Sellers. Carl Sandburg. CP-SandC

What is / a / voyage / ? E. E. Cummings. CP-CummE

What is a What Not. What Nots? Hart Crane. CP-CranH

What is a woman that you forsake her. Harp Song of the Dane Women. Rudyard Kipling. CP-KiplR *Fr.* Puck of Pook's Hill.

What Is a Word? Jones Very. CP-VeryJ

What is a word? A spirit-birth. What Is a Word? Jones Very. CP-VeryJ

What is Africa to me. Heritage. Countee Cullen. CP-CullC

What Is and Is Not. C. K. Williams. CP-WillC

What is beheld through glass seems glass. Prisms. Laura Riding Jackson. CP-RidiL

What is better than leaving a bar. Swing Shift Blues. Alan Dugan. CP-DugaA

What is beyond reproof / Is done in this building. Thomas Merton. CP MertT

What Is Bibbidi-Bobbidi-Boo in Sanskrit? Ogden Nash. CP-NashO

What is death, I ask. Hurry Up Please It's Time. Anne Sexton. CP-SextA

What is dying all over the world. Door, A ("What is dying all over the world"). W. S. Merwin. SP-MerwW

What is God, we shall never know! Song of Don Ramon, The. D. H. Lawrence. CP-LawrD

What is good for a bootless bene? Force of Prayer, The; or, The Founding of Bolton Priory; A Tradition. William Wordsworth. CP-WorW1

What is good? Garlic. A leg of lamb on a spit. In Common. Czeslaw Milosz. CP-MiloCN, *tr. by* Robert Hass

What is green in me. Stepping Westward. Denise Levertov. SP-LeveDP

What is happening to me now that loved faces. Childhood in Jacksonville, Florida. Jane Cooper. CP-CoopJ

What is hard to hide? the Fire! Confession. Johann Wolfgang von Goethe. CP-MerG2

What Is He? D. H. Lawrence. CP-LawrD

What is he buzzing in my ears? Confessions. Robert Browning. CP-BroR1; SP-BroR

What is heaven? 'tis a country. Heaven. Christina Georgina Rossetti. CP-RosC3

What is important about Tarzan is muscles, he is. You White Cunning Devils. William Dickey. SP-DickW

What is insomnia? Two Forms of Insomnia. Jorge Luis Borges. SP-BorgJ, *tr. by* Alan S. Trueblood

What is it about people that makes me sigh. Han-shan. CP-ColdM, *tr. by* Red Pine

What is it? An airplane at dawn. No. Yehuda Amichai. SP-AmicYL, *tr. by* Benjamin Harshav *and* Barbara Harshav

What is it? An old shed for tools. Yehuda Amichai. SP-AmicYL, *tr. by* Benjamin Harshav *and* Barbara Harshav

What is it Braque. Miracle of the Bottle and the Fishes, The. Charles Tomlinson. SP-TomlC

What is it doing there, this house in the quarry? House in the Quarry, The. Charles Tomlinson. SP-TomlC

What is it, fool, in the tall stars you'd find. Astrologer, The. Sir Thomas More. CP-CunnJ, *tr. by* James Vincent Cunningham

What is it for / this form of saying, truce. Ars Poetica. Charles Tomlinson. CP-TomlC

What is it, Gwen, my girl? why do you hover and haunt me? St. Winefred's Well. Gerard Manley Hopkins. CP-HopkG

What is it I am waiting for? Guinevere. James Whitcomb Riley. CP-RileJ

What is it I most want in all the world? To Tell and Be Told. Robert Graves. CP-GravR

What is it in old fiddle-chunes. My Dancin'-Days Is Over. James Whitcomb Riley. CP-RileJ

What is it, it does not. Margaret Atwood. SP-AtwM1

What is it Jesus saith unto the soul? Christina Georgina Rossetti. CP-RosC2

What Is It Makes One Girl. James Laughlin. CP-LaugJ

What is it that all men possesse, among themselves conversing? Thomas Campion. CP-CampT

What is it that goes round and round the house. Riddle, The. Louis MacNeice. CP-MacNL

What is it that tells my soul the Sun is setting? William Wordsworth. CP-WorW1

What is it this time the dark barn again. Ted Hughes. SP-HughTN *Fr.* Sheep.

What is it to educate a human soul? Education. Jones Very. CP-VeryJ

What is it to forgive? Not for Charity. James Vincent Cunningham. CP-CunnJ

What is it to grow old? Growing Old. Matthew Arnold. SP-ArnoM

What is it to look into a human eye. Name-Day Night. Charles Olson. CP-OlsoC

What is it to sail. Ralph Waldo Emerson. CP-EmerR

What is it we want: not battleships. Pick Up the Evening Paper. Kenneth Patchen. CP-PatcK

What is it you're mumbling, old Father, my Dad? By the Exeter River. Donald Hall. CP-HallD

What Is Life? Samuel Taylor Coleridge. CP-ColeS; MW-ColeS

What is life? Life is stepping down a step or sitting in a chair. You and Me and P.B. Shelley. Ogden Nash. CP-NashO

What is life that we should love it. Present and Future. Christina Georgina Rossetti. CP-RosC3

What is love—. Robert Creeley. CP-CreeR

What is Love? Robert Graves. CP-GravR

What is man that you should weigh. Levity. Donald Davie. CP-DaviDC

What Is Man Without an Income. D. H. Lawrence. CP-LawrD

What is meant by a "true man?" True Man, The. Chuang Tzu. CP-MertT

What Is Modern. W. S. Merwin. SP-MerwWF

What is more gentle than a wind in summer? Sleep and Poetry. John Keats. CP-KeatJ

What is named. Need for Dictionaries II, The. Thomas McGrath. SP-McGrT

What is our innocence. What Are Years? Marianne Craig Moore. CP-MoorM

What Is Our Life? Sir Walter Ralegh. CP-RaleW

   (On the Life of Man.) CP-RaleW

What is our life? a play of passion. What Is Our Life? Sir Walter Ralegh. CP-RaleW

What is—"Paradise." Emily Dickinson. CP-DickE

What Is Pink? Christina Georgina Rossetti. CP-RosC2

What Is Poetry. John Ashbery. SP-AshbJ

WHAT IS PRUDERY? / 'Tis a Beldam. Answer to the Following Question of Mrs. Howe. Alexander Pope. CP-PopeA

What is reality? Self in 1958. Anne Sexton. CP-SextA; SP-SextA

What is recorded. Park, The. Andrei Codrescu. SP-CodrA

What is required of us is the recognition of the frontiers. Geography of this Time. Archibald MacLeish. CP-MacLA

What is she, while I live?—. Other, The. Theodore Roethke. CP-RoetT

What Is She Writing? Perhaps It Will Be Good. Stevie Smith. CP-SmitS

What is so strange about a tree alone in an open field? Hunting Pheasants in a Cornfield. Robert Bly. SP-BlyR

What is sometimes called a / tongue of flame. Autumn. Grace Paley. CP-PalGC

What is strictly fiercely and wholly dies. E. E. Cummings. CP-CummE

"What is that flower?" we asked right away. What a sight! Postcards from Cape Split. Mona Van Duyn. SP-VanDM

What is that shining. Dead from Love. Federico García Lorca. CP-GarcF, *tr. by* Will Kirkland

What is that smoke that ever still. Emily Jane Brontë. CP-BronE

What is that sound, like a foghorn but no sea near? Ode to Innocence. Eleanor Wilner. SP-WilnE

What Is That to Thee? Follow Thou Me. Christina Georgina Rossetti. CP-RosC2

What Is the Beautiful? Kenneth Patchen. CP-PatcK

What is the beginning? Love. What the course? Love still. Christina Georgina Rossetti. CP-RosC2

What is the boy now, who has lost his ball. Ball Poem, The. John Berryman. CP-BerrJ

What is the form is the gro- / tesquerie—the accident. Place, The ("What is the form is the gro- / tesquerie—the accident"). Robert Creeley. CP-CreeR

What is the head. Some Last Questions. W. S. Merwin. SP-MerwW

What is the heavy, hot hand. Loss. D. H. Lawrence. CP-LawrD

What is the matter? And why do you turn. Petrarch. CP-Petra, *tr. by* J. G. Nichols

What is the misery in one that turns one with gladness. Grace Abounding. A. R. Ammons. CP-AmmoA

What is the moral? Who rides may read. Winners, The. Rudyard Kipling. CP-KiplR *Fr.* Story of the Gadsbys, The.

What is the name of King Ringang's daughter? Beauty Rohtraut. Eduard Friedrich Mörike. CP-MerG1, *tr. by* George Meredith

What Is the Need. James Laughlin. CP-LaugJ

What is the noise that shakes the night. Christmas in the Elgin Room. Thomas Hardy. CP-HardT

What is the number of your days? I've counted them. Crow's Song 2, The. Primo Levi. CP-LeviP, *tr. by* Ruth Feldman *and* Brian Swann

What is the point. Songless. Alice Walker. CP-WalkA

What is the reason Coone so dully smels? Upon Coone. Robert Herrick. CP-HerrR

What is the saddest thing in the world. Han-shan. CP-ColdM, *tr. by* Red Pine

What is the skill of this waking? Heard the singing. For Kayle Boyle. Muriel Rukeyser. CP-RukeM

What is the song the children sing. Counting-Out Song, A. Rudyard Kipling. CP-KiplR *Fr.* Land and Sea Tales.

What is the sorriest thing that enters Hell? Vain Virtues. Dante Gabriel Rossetti. CW-RossD *Fr.* House of Life, The.

What Is the Time?; or, St. Hugh of Lincoln. Stevie Smith. CP-SmitS

What is the use of being sagacious. Sagacity. Richard Eberhart. CP-EberR

What is the voice that speaks? Oh, tongue. Robert Penn Warren. CP-WarrR

What Is the Word? Jones Very. CP-VeryJ

What is the word? I often hear men say. What Is the Word? Jones Very. CP-VeryJ

What is the world, O soldiers? Napoleon. Walter De la Mare. CP-DeLaW

What is there for us two. Fifty-Fifty. Carl Sandburg. CP-SandC

What is there in the universal Earth. To the Ladies Who Saw Me Crowned. John Keats. CP-KeatJ

What is there in the vale of life. Love Abused. William Cowper. CP-CowpW

What is there which so approaches an art form in its stubborn patience, its devotion to technique. Resentment. C. K. Williams. SP-WillC

What is there within this beggar lad. Beggar Boy. Langston Hughes. CP-HughL; CP-HughL1

What is this above thy head, / O Man? Christina Georgina Rossetti. CP-RosC2

What is this, behind this veil, is it ugly, is it beautiful? Birthday Present, A. Sylvia Plath. CP-PlatS

What is this creature who must sweat all day. Riddle the Sphinx Forgot, A. Howard Nemerov. CP-NemeH

What is this strange and uncouth thing? Cross[e], The. George Herbert. CP-HerbG

What is this vengeful thing. Timor amoris conturbat me. James Laughlin. CP-LaugJ

What is this whiteness on the field? Grace Paley. CP-PalGC

What is thy mouth to me? E. E. Cummings. CP-CummE

What is to be born already fidgets in the stem. Christmas Card, After the Assassinations, A. Mona Van Duyn. SP-VanDM

What is to start? As Many Questions As Answers. Laura Riding Jackson. CP-RidiL

What Is True. Ingeborg Bachmann. CP-KizeC, *tr. by* Carolyn Kizer

What is truth? says Pilate. Louis MacNeice. CP-MacNL

What is unseen. Vision. W. S. Merwin. SP-MerwWF

What is war. War, the Destroyer. William Carlos Williams. CP-WilW2

What is Worthless? Robinson Jeffers. CP-JefR3

What islands known, what passages discovered. Ship's Log. Archibald MacLeish. CP-MacLA

What is't, fine Grand, makes thee my friendship fly. To Fine Grand. Ben Jonson. CP-JonsB; SP-JonsB

What is't that wasts a Prince? example showes. Flatterie. Robert Herrick. CP-HerrR

What It Could Be. Denise Levertov. SP-LeveDL

What it is, the literal size / incorporates. Riddle, The. Robert Creeley. CP-CreeR

What it makes minus is small things. Talking Back (To W. H. Auden). William Meredith. SP-MereW

What it must be like to be an angel. Parents. William Meredith. SP-MereW

What It Really Means. Alan Dugan. CP-DugaA

What it was struck the terror into me? Imperante Augusto Natus Est. Robert Browning. CP-BroR2

What Jesus Runs Away From. Jelaluddin Rumi. SP-Rumi, *tr. by* Coleman Barks

What jungle tree have you slept under. Nude Young Dancer. Langston Hughes. CP-HughL; CP-HughL1

What just excuse had agèd Time. Ben Jonson. CP-JonsB *Fr.* Love Freed from Ignorance and Folly.

What, keep love in *perspective?*—that old lie. In Perspective. Robert Graves. CP-GravR

What Kind of a Guy Was He? Howard Nemerov. CP-NemeH

"What kind of a person are you," I heard them say to me. Yehuda Amichai. SP-AmicYL, *tr. by* Benjamin Harshav *and* Barbara Harshav

"What kind of man are you?" people ask me. Yehuda Amichai. SP-AmicY, *tr. by* Chana Bloch

What kind of man I was to be you've known since the beginning. Alcoholic Enters the Gates of Heaven, An. Czeslaw Milosz. CP-MiloCN, *tr. by* Robert Hass

What Kind of Mistress[e] He Would Have. Robert Herrick. CP-HerrR

What kind of people / Are these? Some stammer. Love Poem in Twos and Threes. Robert Bly. SP-BlyR

What kind of woman goes searching and searching? Searching / Not Searching. Muriel Rukeyser. CP-RukeM

What laid, I said. Rhyme. Louise Bogan. CP-BogaL

What large, dark hands are those at the window. Love On the Farm. D. H. Lawrence. CP-LawrD

What lasts is what you start with. Journal of Southern Rivers, A. Charles Wright. SP-WrigC

What lay beyond those blowing beaches. Perseus Airborne. Amy Clampitt. CP-ClamA

What leaf-fringed legend haunts. Tempe in the Rain. Amy Clampitt. CP-ClamA

What leafless tree plunging. Conversion of Brother Lawrence. Denise Levertov. SP-LeveDS

What length of verse can serve brave *Mopsa*'s good to show? Sir Philip Sidney. SP-SidnP *Fr.* Arcadia.

What lies youth tells itself all from the need. Goodbye. Robert Penn Warren. CP-WarrR

What Life is that, which, like the Spring. Hymn: The New Life of Humanity. Jones Very. CP-VeryJ

What lifts the heron leaning on the air. Snowy Heron. John Ciardi. CP-CiarJ

What light hath passed us in the silent ways? Prologue, A: "What light hath passed us in the silent ways?" Ezra Pound. CP-PoEar

What light will, in your eyes, like an archangel. Holy Communion: the City. Thomas Merton. CP-MertT

What links are ours with orbs that are. Meditation under Stars. George Meredith. CP-MerG1

What Little Saul Got, Christmas. James Whitcomb Riley. CP-RileJ

What lively lad most pleasured me. Last Confession, A. William Butler Yeats. CP-YeatW

What lovelier forms things wear. Hafiz. CP-EmerR *Fr.* Odes.

What lovely things / Thy hand hath made. Scribe, The. Walter De la Mare. CP-DeLaW

What made that mirth last night? the neighbours say. Upon Bran. Robert Herrick. CP-HerrR

What made the place a landscape of despair. Claus von Stauffenberg. Thom Gunn. CP-GunnT

What Magic Drum? William Butler Yeats. CP-YeatW

What makes a young man grieve. Han-shan. CP-ColdM, *tr.* by Red Pine

What makes it hard to understand. George Meredith. CP-MerG2

What makes my bed seem hard seeing it is soft? Elegy 1.2: "What makes my bed seem hard seeing it is soft?" Ovid. CP-MarlC, *tr.* by Christopher Marlowe *Fr.* Elegies.

What makes people unsatisfied. Courage. D. H. Lawrence. CP-LawrD

What makes you come *here* fer, Mister. Prior to Miss Belle's Appearance. James Whitcomb Riley. CP-RileJ

What makes your voice so flat. Delete the Inapplicable. Hans Magnus Enzensberger. SP-EnzeH, *tr.* by Michael Hamburger

What Malvern is the day is, and its touchstone. Touchstone—Watching Malvern, The. Ivor Gurney. SP-GurnI

What man are you that dares to come this way, Sir? Sheridan's Masterpiece, or, Tom Pun-Sibi's Folly Complete, *Alexander's Overthrow, or The Downfall of Babylon*, as It Was Acted at Mr. Lyddal's in Dame Street, December 11th, 1721. *Unknown, sometimes at. to* Thomas Sheridan. CP-SherT

What man could do. Crowded Countries of the Bomb, The. George Oppen. CP-OppGN

What Man could esteem, or what Woman could love. Epitaph on R. Muir. Robert Burns. CP-BurnR

What man could stomach the sight. Carmen 29. Catullus. CP-ZukLS *Fr.* Carmina.

What man has done to woman and man. Traveling Exhibit of Torture Instruments. Thomas Lux. SP-LuxT

What man is he that yearneth. Chorus: "What man is he that yearneth." Sophocles. CP-HousA *Fr.* Oedipus at Colonus.

What man that sees the ever-whirling wheele. Book 7. Edmund Spenser. CP-Spens *Fr.* Faerie Queene, The.

What man will now take liberal arts in hand. Elegy 3.7: "What man will now take liberal arts in hand." Ovid. CP-MarlC *Fr.* Elegies.

What manner of building shall we build? Architecture. Wallace Stevens. CP-StevWP

What? Mars his sword? faire Cytherea say. Upon Venus Putting on Mars His Armes. Leonidas of Alexandria. CP-CrasR, *tr.* by Richard Crashaw

What Mary is when she a little smiles. Dante Alighieri. CP-ShelP *Fr.* La Vita Nuova.

What masque of what old wind-withered New-Year. For Spring, by Sandro Botticelli, in the Accademia of Florence. Dante Gabriel Rossetti. CW-RossD

What matter that you understood no word! Ribh in Ecstasy. William Butler Yeats. CP-YeatW

What Matter the Pangs of a Husband and Father. Lord Byron. CP-Byron

What Matters. James Laughlin. CP-LaugJ

What Matters. D. H. Lawrence. CP-LawrD

What matters that I stormed and swore? For an Anarchist. Countee Cullen. CP-CullC

What may be born of the anxious union. On a New Generation. Laura Riding Jackson. CP-RidiL

What may I do to make you glad. Poet's Wooing, A. James Whitcomb Riley. CP-RileJ

What may we chant, O thou within this tomb? Outlines for a Tomb. Walt Whitman. CP-WhitW

What meanes this folly, now to brave it so. Thomas Campion. CP-CampT

What means [*or* meaneth *or* menethe] this when I lie [*or* lye] alone. What Does This Mean? Sir Thomas Wyatt. CP-WyatT

What men gain fairly—that they should possess. Fragment: "What men gain fairly—that they should possess." Percy Bysshe Shelley. CP-ShelP

What merriment has taen the whigs. German Lairdie, The. Robert Burns. CP-BurnR

What message from imagined Paradise. Kathleen Jessie Raine. SP-RainK

What mighty princes poets are! those things. To My Friend Will. Davenant, upon His Poem of "Madagascar." Sir John Suckling. CP-SuckJ

What Miracles the News is! Emily Dickinson. SP-DickE

What mischief cleaves to unsubdued regret. Composed by the Sea-Shore. William Wordsworth. CP-WorW2

What Montezuma Fed Cortés and His Men. Thomas Lux. SP-LuxT

What more can we say? What can we do? We found the old again. Deceptive Discoveries. Yannis Ritsos. SP-RitsY *Fr.* Monovasia.

What more delightful than to wander forth. Jones Very. CP-VeryJ

What more is there to love than that I have loved? Montrachet-le-Jardin. Wallace Stevens. CP-StevW; CP-StevWP

What Must. Archibald MacLeish. CP-MacLA

What must a man do to be at home in the world? Silence, The. Wendell Berry. CP-BerrW

What Must I Do To Be Lost? C. K. Williams. CP-WillC

What My Child Learns of the Sea. Audre Lorde. SP-LordA

What! my friend! you're surely daft. Glee. George Meredith. CP-MerG2

What my hand follows on your body. Beneath My Hand and Eye the Distant Hills, Your Body. Gary Snyder. CP-SnydG

What My House Would Be Like If It Were a Person. Denise Levertov. SP-LeveDL

What mystery is it? The morning as rare. Autumnal Tonic, An. James Whitcomb Riley. CP-RileJ

What mystery pervades a well! Emily Dickinson. CP-DickE

What name could. Stormy. William Carlos Williams. CP-WilW2

What name do I have for you? Just Walking Around. John Ashbery. SP-AshbJ

What nature, alas! has denied. Winter Nosegay, The. William Cowper. CP-CowpW

What need hast thou of me, or of my muse. To Robert, Earl of Salisbury ("What need hast thou of me, or of my muse"). Ben Jonson. CP-JonsB; SP-JonsB

What need of clamorous bells, or ribands gay. Composed on the Eve of the Marriage of a Friend in the Vale of Grasmere, 1812. William Wordsworth. CP-WorW1

What need? This strange desire for something which desire. Roses of Life, The. Kenneth Patchen. CP-PatcK

What need we marry Women, when. Women Uselesse. Robert Herrick. CP-HerrR

What need you, being come to sense. September 1913. William Butler Yeats. CP-YeatW

What needest thou?—a few brief hours of rest. Vain Questioning. Walter De la Mare. CP-DeLaW

What needeth these threnning words and wasted wind? Sir Thomas Wyatt. CP-WyatT

What needs complaints. Comfort to a Youth That Had Lost His Love. Robert Herrick. CP-HerrR

What needs my *Shakespear[e]* for his honour'd [*or* honoured *or* honored] Bones. On Shakespear[e]. John Milton. CP-MiltJ

What needs this din about the town o' Lon'on. Scots Prologue, *For Mrs. Sutherland's Benefit Night*, Spoken at the Theatre Dumfries. Robert Burns. CP-BurnR

What needs to be done? Writing a Résumé. Wisława Szymborska. SP-SzymW, *tr.* by Stanisław Barańczak *and* Clare Cavanagh

What never is but only is to be. Indifference of the Heavens, The. Samuel Taylor Coleridge. CP-ColeS

What never was no, & still will be. Ralph Waldo Emerson. CP-EmerR

What new element before us unborn in nature? Is there a new thing under the Sun? Plutonian Ode. Allen Ginsberg. CP-GinsA; SP-GinsA

What News, What News? Queen Orraca. Lord Byron. CP-Byron

What! no more favours? Not a ribbon more. To a Lady That Forbade to Love before Company. Sir John Suckling. CP-SuckJ

What, No Oysters? Ogden Nash. CP-NashO

What no, Perdy [*or* Perdie *or* perdie][!] ye may be sure[!]. No! Indeed. Sir Thomas Wyatt. CP-WyatT

What, No Sheep? Ogden Nash. CP-NashO

What not to do for him. Accomplishment. Tess Gallagher. SP-GallT

What Nots? Hart Crane. CP-CranH

What nourishes the polar star? Thoughts While Reading *The Sand Reckoner*. James Tate. SP-TateJ

What, now, in the eighties! Smoking Pot on the Bus. Thom Gunn. CP-GunnT

What now, O Man! thou dost, or mean'st to do. For a Market-Clock. Samuel

Taylor Coleridge. CP-ColeS

What now we like, anon we disapprove. Change Gives Content. Robert Herrick. CP-HerrR

What number do you start with. By the Numbers. James Laughlin. CP-LaugJ

What Odd Expedients. Robinson Jeffers. CP-JefR3

What of her glass without her? The blank grey. Without Her. Dante Gabriel Rossetti. CW-RossD *Fr.* House of Life, The.

What of It? Robinson Jeffers. CP-JefR3

What of Our Country? is the word. Jones Very. CP-VeryJ

What of the Day? John Greenleaf Whittier. CP-WhitJ

What of the end, Pandora? Was it thine. Pandora. Dante Gabriel Rossetti. CW-RossD

What of the faith and fire within us. Men Who March Away. Thomas Hardy. CP-HardT

What of the hunting, hunter bold? Rudyard Kipling. CP-KiplR *Fr.* Second Jungle Book, The.

What of the Night? Stanley Kunitz. CP-KunSC

What of the Night? Jones Very. CP-VeryJ

What of the night? O watchman! tell. What of the Night? Jones Very. CP-VeryJ

What of the structure of Rime? I said. Robert Duncan. SP-DuncR *Fr.* Structure of Rime, The.

'What of vile dust?' the preacher said. Praise of Dust, The. G. K. Chesterton. CP-ChesG

What offspring other men have got. Upon His Verses. Robert Herrick. CP-HerrR

What "Old Santa" Overheard. James Whitcomb Riley. CP-RileJ

What once was great, now appeared small. Czeslaw Milosz. CP-MiloC; CP-MiloCN

What other woman could be loved like you. Soul-Light. Dante Gabriel Rossetti. CW-RossD *Fr.* House of Life, The.

What others have cheapnesse seene, and ease. To His Brother Nicolas Herrick. Robert Herrick. CP-HerrR

What over and which under. E. E. Cummings. CP-CummE

What Ovid Taught Me. Alice Walker. CP-WalkA

What pain, to wake and miss you! Quite Forsaken. D. H. Lawrence. CP-LawrD

What part does that old man. Old Comedian, The. James Laughlin. CP-LaugJ

What passing-bells for these who die as cattle? Anthem for Doomed Youth. Wilfred Owen. CP-OwenW

What Patron could I chuse, great *Lord*, but you? To the Right Honourable, Both in Birth and Vertue, Francis, Earle of Cumberland. Thomas Campion. CP-CampT

What pitying messenger, what angel was. Petrarch. CP-Petra, *tr. by* J. G. Nichols

What Place Is Besieged? Walt Whitman. CP-WhitW

What place is this. At the Centre. Thom Gunn. CP-GunnT

What place is this? / All's strange to me, and I. Heresy. Walter De la Mare. CP-DeLaW

What place so strange,—though unrevealèd snow. Memorial Thresholds. Dante Gabriel Rossetti. CW-RossD *Fr.* House of Life, The.

What Plagues, what Tortures are in store for thee. Samuel Johnson. CP-JohnS *Fr.* Irene.

What pleasanter task for All Fools' Day than going over all the. Raven, Don't Stay Away from My Door—A Chant for April First. Ogden Nash. CP-NashO

What pleased him more. Days of Yore, The. Stevie Smith. CP-SmitS

What Poems Are For. Heather McHugh. SP-McHuH

What pomposity. Reflections. Robert Creeley. SP-CreeR

What portents, from what distant region, ride. On the Ice Islands Seen Floating in the German Ocean. William Cowper. CP-CowpW

What potion's to be found, distilled from herbs. Following the Formulas of Ancient Greco-Syrian Magicians. Constantine P. Cavafy. CP-CavaC, *tr. by* Theoharis Constantine Theoharis

What profane character uttered such blasphemy? Word and Silence. Constantine P. Cavafy. CP-CavaC, *tr. by* Theoharis Constantine Theoharis

What Quetzalcoatl Saw in Mexico. D. H. Lawrence. CP-LawrD

What rage is this? What furo[u]r of what kind [*or* kynd]? Sir Thomas Wyatt. CP-WyatT

What rattles in the dark? The blinds at Brewster? In Limbo. Richard Wilbur. CP-WilbR

What Redress. James Whitcomb Riley. CP-RileJ

What remained of the Army. Bluebird Houses. James Tate. SP-TateJ

What rhymes are thine which I have ta'en from thee. Sonnet: He owes nothing to Guido as a Poet. Cino da Pistoia. CW-RossD, *tr. by* Dante Gabriel Rossetti

What rich joke does. Natural Question. John Updike. CP-UpdiJ

What Riddle Asked the Sphinx. Archibald MacLeish. CP-MacLA

What rider spurs him from the darkening east. Edna St. Vincent Millay. CP-MillE

What right has anyone to say. Poet to Patron. Langston Hughes. CP-HughL; CP-HughL1

What rime, what tinsel pure and chill. Man Coming of Age. Robert Penn

Warren. CP-WarrR

What rural beauties deck this charming seat. Impromptu Written with a Pencil in a Chinese Temple in the Garden of Mr Elisha Boudinot. Annis Boudinot Stockton. CP-StocA

What! Salomon! such words from you. To E. S. Salomon. Ambrose Bierce. SP-BierA

What Sappho Would Have Said Had Her Leap Cured Instead of Killing Her. Christina Georgina Rossetti. CP-RosC3

What Savage Blossom. Edna St. Vincent Millay. CP-MillE

"What say I?"—not a syllable further in prose. Fragment of an Epistle to Thomas Moore. Lord Byron. CP-Byron

What say you, critic, now you have become. Camelus Saltat. George Meredith. CP-MerG1

What says the sea, little shell? Stephen Crane. CP-CranS

What says the wind to the waving trees? Secret, The. Paul Laurence Dunbar. CP-DunbP

What seas what shores what grey rocks and what islands. Marina. T. S. Eliot. CP-ElioT

What seclusion has the sage gone to. If Actually Dead. Constantine P. Cavafy. CP-CavaC, *tr. by* Theoharis Constantine Theoharis

What seems a soul where Love's outside the porch. Response to a Translation by Longfellow. Robert Browning. CP-BroR2

What Semiramis Said. Nicholas Vachel Lindsay. CP-LindV

What shakes the eye but the invisible? Decision, The. Theodore Roethke. CP-RoetT

What shall a poor girl do. Cappadocian Song. Hayden Carruth. CP-CarHS

What shall be said of this embattled day. Parted Love. Dante Gabriel Rossetti. CW-RossD *Fr.* House of Life, The.

What shall I bring you? Colour, The. Thomas Hardy. CP-HardT

What Shall I Do for the Land that Bred Me. Gerard Manley Hopkins. CP-HopkG

What shall I do now—it whimpers so. Emily Dickinson. CP-DickE

What shall I do when the Summer troubles. Emily Dickinson. CP-DickE

What shall I do with my friends. Trees. Robert Creeley. CP-CreeR

What shall I do with this absurdity. Tower, The. William Butler Yeats. CP-YeatW

What shall I leave my son. Testament. Langston Hughes. CP-HughL; CP-HughL3

What shall I render to thy Name. In Thankful[l] Remembrance for My Dear Husband['']s Safe Arrival[l]. Anne Bradstreet. CP-BradA

What shall I say, because talk I must? Yellow Flower, The. William Carlos Williams. CP-WilW2

What shall I say, dear friends, to whom I owe. Farewell, A: "What shall I say, dear friends, to whom I owe." John Greenleaf Whittier. CP-WhitJ

What shall I say to Walt Whitman tonight? Centennial For Whitman. Richard Eberhart. CP-EberR

What shall I wish him? Strength and health. Lines Written in an Album. John Greenleaf Whittier. CP-WhitJ

What shall the feast be called this year. Christmas, 1937. Laura Riding Jackson. CP-RidiL

What shall the world do with its children? Romans Angry about the Inner World. Robert Bly. SP-BlyR

What shall we add now? He is dead. Died. Elizabeth Barrett Browning. CP-BroEB

What shall we do with Margery? Margery. Christina Georgina Rossetti. CP-RosC3

What shall we know we don't know. Somebody Died. Robert Creeley. CP-CreeR

What shall we say? In quietude. Emerson. James Whitcomb Riley. CP-RileJ

What shall we say of her. Old Tale, An. Marya Alexandrovna Zaturenska. SP-ZatuM

What shall we say of the soldier, Grant. Grant. James Whitcomb Riley. CP-RileJ

What shall we say of this curious young man? Lord Mope. Stevie Smith. CP-SmitS

What She Could Not Tell Him. Denise Levertov. SP-LeveDL

What she made in her body is broken. Poem for J. Wendell Berry. CP-BerrW

What she refused him—in the name of love. Love as Lovelessness. Robert Graves. CP-GravR

What she remembers. Mother of the Groom. Seamus Heaney. SP-HeanSO

What Ship Puzzled at Sea. Walt Whitman. CP-WhitW

What should a man do but love excellence. Speech to the Detractors. Archibald MacLeish. CP-MacLA

What should I be but a prophet and a liar. Singing-Woman from the Wood's Edge, The. Edna St. Vincent Millay. CP-MillE

What should I do? Love, what do you advise? Petrarch. CP-Petra, *tr. by* J. G. Nichols

What should I say. Sir Thomas Wyatt. CP-WyatT

What should I say of Henry Miller. To the Dean. William Carlos Williams. CP-WilW2

What should one. Picture of J. T. in a Prospect of Stone, The. Charles

Tomlinson. CP-TomlC; SP-TomlC

What should the young / man say, because he is buying. Lover, The. Robert Creeley. CP-CreeR

What should we be without the sexual myth. Men Made out of Words. Wallace Stevens. CP-StevW; CP-StevWP

What shul these clothes thus manyfold. Proverbs: "What shul these clothes thus manyfold." Geoffrey Chaucer. CP-ChauG

What sight so lured him through the fields he knew. Far-Far-Away. Alfred Tennyson. CP-TennA

What sign do you give, O Swan, with your curving neck. "Rubén Dario." SP-DariR, tr. by Alberto Acereda and Will Derusha

What silk steeped in the balms of time. Stéphane Mallarmé. CP-MallS, tr. by Henry Weinfield

What / singular upright flourishing. Numbers. Robert Creeley. CP-CreeR

What siren zooming is sounding our coming. Exiles, The. W. H. Auden. CP-AudeW

What slender youth bedewed [or bedew'd] with liquid odours. Ode 1.5: "What slender youth bedewed [or bedew'd] with liquid odours." Horace. CP-MiltJ, tr. by John Milton Fr. Odes.

What small grace comes must. Medium. A. R. Ammons. CP-AmmoA

What Smith Knew about Farming. James Whitcomb Riley. CP-RileJ

What smouldering senses in death's sick delay. Kiss, The. Dante Gabriel Rossetti. CW-RossD Fr. House of Life, The.

What? So Soon! Langston Hughes. CP-HughL; CP-HughL3

What Soft—Cherubic Creatures. Emily Dickinson. CP-DickE

What solitude I've / finally inherited. Allen Ginsberg. SP-GinsA Fr. Siesta in Xbalba.

What some mistake for me meditating. Stupor at the End of May. Andrei Codrescu. SP-CodrA

What soothes the angry snail? Eine Kleine Snailmusik. May Sarton. SP-SartM

What sort of man is coming. Lady's Second Song, The. William Butler Yeats. CP-YeatW

What sound awakened me, I wonder. Deserter, The. A. E. Housman. CP-HousA

What Splendid Birthdays. Kenneth Patchen. CP-PatcK

What splendour of imperial station man. Milton. George Meredith. CP-MerG2

What State Street Said to South Carolina, and What South Carolina Said to State Street. John Greenleaf Whittier. CP-WhitJ

What strange disorder often springs. To the Honorable Mr. D. T. Thomas Sheridan. CP-SherT

What stranger passion. Rainer Maria Rilke. CP-RilkFr, tr. by A. Poulin, Jr. Fr. Fragments.

What strikes the eye hurts, what one hears is a lie. Soviet Souvenir. Ted Berrigan. SP-BerrT

What strong allurement draws, what spirit guides. To the Planet Venus. William Wordsworth. CP-WorW2

What succour can I hope the Muse will send. To the Morning. Satisfaction for Sleepe. Richard Crashaw. CP-CrasR

What summer hasn't shaken. Whoosh. Heather McHugh. SP-McHuH

What suns had to rise and set. Three Desk Objects. Margaret Atwood. SP-AtwM1

What Survives. Rainer Maria Rilke. CP-RilkFr

What sweeter music[k] can we bring. Christmas Caroll Sung to the King in the Presence at White-Hall, A. Robert Herrick. CP-HerrR

What sweeter Shelter than the Hearts. Emily Dickinson. SP-DickE

What syllable are you seeking. To the Roaring Wind. Wallace Stevens. CP-StevW; CP-StevWP

What teares (Deare Prince) can serve to water all. Songe Made by Sir Walter Rawley, A. Unknown, sometimes at. to Sir Walter Ralegh. CP-RaleW

What tenements of clover. Emily Dickinson. CP-DickE

What the actors say in the play. Questions, The. James Laughlin. CP-LaugJ

What the Animals Did. James Laughlin. CP-LaugJ

What the Bird with the Human Head Knew. Anne Sexton. CP-SextA

What the Birds Said. John Greenleaf Whittier. CP-WhitJ

What the birds say / is colored. Shade. "Internal and External Forms." Donald Hall. CP-HallD

What the blind lost when radio. After the Revolution for Jesus a Secular Man [or the Associate Professor] Prepares His Final Remarks. Miller Williams. CP-WillM

What the Bones Know. Carolyn Kizer. CP-KizeC

What the Clown Said. Nicholas Vachel Lindsay. CP-LindV

What the Coal-Heaver Said. Nicholas Vachel Lindsay. CP-LindV

What the cosmologist meant by what constitutes. Americans, The. Charles Olson. CP-OlsoC

What the Deceased Had to Say about Himself. Nicanor Parra. CP-MertT

What the Doctor Said. Raymond Carver. CP-CarvR

What the Earth Asked Me. James Wright. CP-WrigJ

What the eye sees is a dream of sight. To the Hand. W. S. Merwin. SP-MerwW

What the Finger Writes. Alice Walker. CP-WalkA

What the Forester Said. Nicholas Vachel Lindsay. CP-LindV

What the Ghost of the Gambler Said. Nicholas Vachel Lindsay. CP-LindV

What the gods enact we interrupt. Interruption. Constantine P. Cavafy. CP-CavaC, tr. by Theoharis Constantine Theoharis

What the Gray-Winged Fairy Said. Nicholas Vachel Lindsay. CP-LindV

What the Grecian Earns. Kenneth Patchen. CP-PatcK

What the Hell, Rage, Give in to Natural Graces. Alan Dugan. CP-DugaA

What the Hyena Said. Nicholas Vachel Lindsay. CP-LindV

What the Indians. Control Burn. Gary Snyder. CP-SnydG

What the Joree Said, The Joree Being Only a Bird. Robert Penn Warren. CP-WarrR Fr. Prognosis: A Short Story, the End of Which You Will Know Soon Enough.

What the Light Was Like. Amy Clampitt. CP-ClamA

What the Miner in the Desert Said. Nicholas Vachel Lindsay. CP-LindV

What the Moon Saw. Nicholas Vachel Lindsay. CP-LindV

What the Motorcycle Said. Mona Van Duyn. SP-VanDM

What the mouth sings, the soul must learn to forgive. What the Water Knows. Sam Hamill. SP-HamiS

What the Old Women Say. Archibald MacLeish. CP-MacLA

What the Owl Sees. Marge Piercy. SP-PierM

What the Pencil Writes. James Laughlin. CP-LaugJ

What the People Said. Rudyard Kipling. CP-KiplR

What the Poet is Told on the Subject of Flowers. Arthur Rimbaud. CP-RimbA, tr. by Martin Sorrell

What the pulse flashes. Systemic. Rae Armantrout. SP-ArmaA

What the Rattlesnake Said. Nicholas Vachel Lindsay. CP-LindV

What the Scarecrow Said. Nicholas Vachel Lindsay. CP-LindV

What the Seer Said. Jane Cooper. CP-CoopJ

What the Sexton Said. Nicholas Vachel Lindsay. CP-LindV

What the Snow Man Said. Nicholas Vachel Lindsay. CP-LindV

What the Traveller Said at Sunset. John Greenleaf Whittier. CP-WhitJ

What the Voice Said. John Greenleaf Whittier. CP-WhitJ

What the Water Knows. Sam Hamill. SP-HamiS

What the Well-Read Patient Is Talking About, or, Look, Ma, What I Got! Ogden Nash. CP-NashO

What the White Had to Say. Charles Simic. SP-SimiCE

What the White Had to Say. Charles Simic. SP-SimiC

What the Wind Said. James Whitcomb Riley. CP-RileJ

What the words, / abstracted, tell. Phone. Robert Creeley. CP-CreeR

What Then? William Butler Yeats. CP-YeatW

What Then Is Evil? D. H. Lawrence. CP-LawrD

What Then Is Love But Mourning? Thomas Campion. CP-CampT
  (What thing is love but mourning?) CP-CampT

What There Is. Kenneth Patchen. CP-PatcK

What there is as a surround to our figures. Pleasure Island. W. H. Auden. CP-AudeW

What They Call Red Cherry Pie. Wallace Stevens. CP-StevWP

What they did. At Eleusis. "H. D." CP-DoolH

What They Said. James Whitcomb Riley. CP-RileJ

What They Said. Muriel Rukeyser. CP-RukeM

What they say on the quay is. On the Quay. Theodore Roethke. CP-RoetT

What they undertook to do. Gratitude to the Unknown Instructors. William Butler Yeats. CP-YeatW

What They Want. Charles Bukowski. SP-BukC1

What thing is love but mourning? Thomas Campion. See What Then Is Love But Mourning?

What thing is that that I both have and lack. Sir Thomas Wyatt. CP-WyatT

What thing is this that, built of salt and lime. Fatal Interview. Edna St. Vincent Millay. CP-MillE

What thing unto mine ear. Stream's Secret, The. Dante Gabriel Rossetti. CW-RossD

What things for dream there are when specter-like. Waiting. Robert Frost. CP-FrosR

What things I have missed today, I know very well. Yesterday Lost. Ivor Gurney. SP-GurnI

What Think You I Take My Pen in Hand? Walt Whitman. CP-WhitW

What This Mode of Motion Said. A. R. Ammons. CP-AmmoA

What tho the lotus bloom / This our Fenicé. Lotus-Bloom. Ezra Pound. CP-PoEar

What though around thee blazes. To Massachusetts. John Greenleaf Whittier. CP-WhitJ

What though, for showing truth to flatter'd [or flattered] state. Written on the Day That Mr. Leigh Hunt Left Prison. John Keats. CP-KeatJ

What though green leaves only witness. Wreath for a Bridal. Sylvia Plath. CP-PlatS

What though my harp, and viol[l] be. To God, on His Sickness[e]. Robert Herrick. CP-HerrR

What though Reason forged your scheme? Reasonable Constitution, A. Herman Melville. SP-MelvH

What though the Accused, upon his own appeal. Humanity. William Wordsworth. CP-WorW2

What though the chilly wide-mouth'd quacking chorus. Lines to a Comic Author, on an Abusive Review. Samuel Taylor Coleridge. CP-ColeS

What though the Heaven be lowring now. Hope Well and Have Well: or, Faire after Foule Weather. Robert Herrick. CP-HerrR

What though the sea be calme? Trust to the shore. Safety on the Shore. Robert Herrick. CP-HerrR

What though, while the wonders of nature exploring. To Some Ladies. John Keats. CP-KeatJ

What thoughts I have of you tonight, Walt Whitman, for I walked down the sidestreets. Supermarket in California, A. Allen Ginsberg. CP-GinsA; SP-GinsA

What throws you out is what drags you in. Overboard. May Swenson. SP-SwenM

What time are the big people. Big People, The. César Vallejo. CP-WrigJ

What time I lay these rhymes anear thy feet. To Mary Russell Mitford. Elizabeth Barrett Browning. CP-BroEB

What time is it i wonder never mind. E. E. Cummings. CP-CummE

What time is it?it is by every star. E. E. Cummings. CP-CummE

"What time is it?" "Oh yes, I'm so happy." Tower of Babel, The. Wisława Szymborska. SP-SzymW, tr. by Stanisław Barańczak and Clare Cavanagh

What time is it? Raphael, says Vasari. Reading on the Beach. Josephine Jacobsen. CP-JacoJ

What time is it? Yes. Tailpiece. William Carlos Williams. CP-WilW2

What time of day is it? After Reading H.D.'s *Hermetic Definitions*. Robert Duncan. SP-DuncR

What time the bittern, solitary bird. Noon. Henry David Thoreau. CP-ThorH

What Time the sun to dark is trod. Praise. G. K. Chesterton. CP-ChesG

What times of sweetnesse this faire day fore-shows. Upon One Lillie, Who Marryed with a Maid Call'd Rose. Robert Herrick. CP-HerrR

What title best befits the man. James Whitcomb Riley. CP-RileJ

What to Do? Christina Georgina Rossetti. CP-RosC3

What to Do until the Doctor Goes or It's Tomorrow Than You Think. Ogden Nash. CP-NashO

What to do / when the days' heavy heart. Peace. Ted Berrigan. SP-BerrT

What to do with a day. Satisfaction Coal Company, The. Rita Dove. SP-DoveR

What to Do with Contributor's Copies? Charles Bukowski. SP-BukC2

What to say. Thinking of Walter Benjamin. Robert Creeley. SP-CreeR

What to say when the spider. Elegy in a Spider's Web. Laura Riding Jackson. CP-RidiL

What to Think When It Rains Blood. Thomas Merton. CP-MertT

What tongue can her perfections tell. What Tongue Can Her Perfections Tell? Sir Philip Sidney. SP-SidnP *Fr.* Arcadia.

What Tongue Can Her Perfections Tell? Sir Philip Sidney. SP-SidnP *Fr.* Arcadia.

What touched me most. James Laughlin. CP-LaugJ

What tree may not the fig be gathered from? Wild Grapes. Robert Frost. CP-FrosR

What troubled eyes you have!—à *moitié*. Uncertain Skies. Charles Baudelaire. CP-BaudC, tr. by Walter Martin

What Troubles I Have Seen in Birdlegged Spring. Thomas Merton. CP-MertT

What Twigs We held by. Emily Dickinson. CP-DickE

What two brave perils of the private sword. On Sir John Roe ("What two brave perils of the private sword"). Ben Jonson. CP-JonsB; SP-JonsB

What use is it to slumber here. Emily Jane Brontë. CP-BronE

What vaileth [*or* 'vaileth] truth [*or* trouth]? or by it to take pain [*or* payn]? Sir Thomas Wyatt. CP-WyatT

What Virginia Said. Charles Tomlinson. CP-TomlC

What virtue or what mental grace. Friendship. William Cowper. CP-CowpW

What voice at Moth-Hour did I hear calling. Robert Penn Warren. CP-WarrR

What voice did on my spirit fall. Peschiera. Arthur Hugh Clough. SP-ClouA

What voice is that I hear. Sorcery. Walter De la Mare. CP-DeLaW

What waiting in the halls. Passage, The. Robert Creeley. CP-CreeR

What was a mountain and afterward air and later a star. Wisdom. Yannis Ritsos. SP-RitsY, tr. by Kimon Friar and Kostas Myrsiades

What was dear to Pan is dear to him no more. Ivor Gurney. SP-GurnI

What Was Going On. Eleanor Wilner. SP-WilnE

What was he doing, the great god Pan. Musical Instrument, A. Elizabeth Barrett Browning. CP-BroEB

What was her beauty in our first estate. She. Richard Wilbur. CP-WilbR

What *Was* Her Name. John Ciardi. CP-CiarJ

What Was in a Name. Carolyn Kizer. CP-KizeC

What was in that candle's light. Water from Your Spring. Jelaluddin Rumi. SP-RumI, tr. by Coleman Barks

What was it we should strike the road again? Castara Victrix. Gerard Manley Hopkins. CP-HopkG

What was it? What was it? Woman as Market. Muriel Rukeyser. CP-RukeM

What was left before crumbling. For George (I). Grace Paley. CP-PalGC

What Was Left Over. Eleanor Wilner. SP-WilnE

What was longed for and, once, certain. Randall Jarrell. CP-JarrR

What Was Lost. William Butler Yeats. CP-YeatW

What was lost is found. Secret Waters, The. D. H. Lawrence. CP-LawrD

What was my crime, youthful most gentle god. On Sleep. Publius Papinius Statius. CP-CunnJ *Fr.* Sylvae [*or* Silvae].

What was once an island with birds. Poem: "What was once an island with birds." Alan Dugan. CP-DugaA

What was she doing when it blew in. Detective, The. Sylvia Plath. CP-PlatS

What was the blond child building. Builder of Houses, The. Jane Cooper. CP-CoopJ

What was the matter with life on my shoulder. Death of a Favorite Bird. W. S. Merwin. SP-MerwW

What was the message of the burned man? Yehuda Amichai. SP-AmicYL, tr. by Barbara Harshav *and* Benjamin Harshav *Fr.* Poems of the Land of Zion and Jerusalem.

What was the name you called me? Evening Waterfall. Carl Sandburg. CP-SandC

What was the need like driving rain. Round. Robert Pinsky. CP-PinsR

What was the promise that smiled from the maples at evening? Promises. Robert Penn Warren. CP-WarrR

What Was the Throught. Robert Penn Warren. CP-WarrR

What was't that fell but now. On Gelli-Flowers Begotten. Robert Herrick. CP-HerrR

What waste in the labour of Chariot and Steed! On Seeing Some Tourists of the Lakes Pass by Reading; a Practice Very Common. William Wordsworth. CP-WorW1

What we are / given. C. K. Williams. CP-WillC; SP-WillC

What we do best is breed. Christening, A. Donald Davie. CP-DaviDC

What we do not know of ourselves. A B Cs (2). Charles Olson. CP-OlsoC

What we failed to see. Old Man's Beard. Charles Tomlinson. CP-TomlC

What we go out for. Far Out, Far In. Theodore Weiss. SP-WeisT

What we have been becomes. Anniversary, An. Wendell Berry. CP-BerrW

What we have done to celebrate. Twelfth Night, Gift Horses, and of Certain Reversals. Robert Stock. SP-StocR

What we need is one of those gods. Little Shirt, The. C. K. Williams. CP-WillC

What we see here in the sand dunes of the white moon alone with. Dunes. Carl Sandburg. CP-SandC

What We See Is What We Think. Wallace Stevens. CP-StevW; CP-StevWP

What we see we know somewhat. Emily Dickinson. CP-DickE

What We Think We Know. Thomas McGrath. SP-McGrT

What we, when face to face we see. Arthur Hugh Clough.
  "What we, when face to face we see." SP-ClouA

What went ye out to see? a shaken reed? John. Jones Very. CP-VeryJ

What were our Forefathers trying to find. Quest of the Fathers, The. James Whitcomb Riley. CP-RileJ

What Were They Like? Denise Levertov. SP-LeveDP

What were we playing? Was it prisoner's base? Running. Richard Wilbur. CP-WilbR

What were we thinking of, / where were we trying to go. Sprung Narratives. Charles Wright. SP-WrigCN

What were you like when you were a little girl, down there in Montevideo. Your Early Life. James Laughlin. CP-LaugJ

What wholly blameless fun. Dutch Courtyard, A. Richard Wilbur. CP-WilbR

What Why When How Who. Robert Pinsky. CP-PinsR

What Wild Dawns There Were. Denise Levertov. SP-LeveDS

What Will Be, Is. Robert Graves. CP-GravR

What Will Happen. George Oppen. CP-OppGN

What will his crimes become, now that her hands. Long Novel, A. John Ashbery. SP-AshbJ

What Will I Do Gin My Hoggie Die. Robert Burns. CP-BurnR

What will it be, O my soul, what will it be. Christina Georgina Rossetti. CP-RosC3

What will our reputations be? Poetical Remains. Archibald MacLeish. CP-MacLA

What will the Poles think of my hat. Pablo Neruda. SP-NeruP *Fr.* Question Book.

What will / the shame be. Shame, The. Robert Creeley. CP-CreeR

What will ye (my poor Orphans) do. To His Verses. Robert Herrick. CP-HerrR

What will you give me for my pound? Christina Georgina Rossetti. CP-RosC2

What will you say, hermetic soul? Resigned. Charles Baudelaire. CP-BaudC, tr. by Walter Martin

What winter floods, what showers of spring. Emily Jane Brontë. CP-BronE

What Wisdome, Learning, Wit, or Worth. Upon the Much Lamented, Mr. J. Warr. Robert Herrick. CP-HerrR

What with hounds and friends and, in the winter. Pushkin. A Didactic Poem. Donald Davie. CP-DaviDC

What woman hugs her infant there? Nativity, A. William Butler Yeats. CP-YeatW

What wonder that—seeing how, beside your fire. Michelangelo Buonarroti. CP-Miche, *tr.* by John Frederick Nims

What word have you, interpreters, of men. Of Heaven Considered as a Tomb. Wallace Stevens. CP-StevW; CP-StevWP

What word is that that changeth not. Sir Thomas Wyatt. CP-WyatT

What words can make / seems next to nothing now. Dedication in These Days. Hayden Carruth. CP-CarHS

What would a baby be. Human Song. Robert Creeley. SP-CreeR

What would best please our friend, in token of. Oscar C. McCulloch. James Whitcomb Riley. CP-RileJ

What would I do without this world faceless incurious. Samuel Beckett. CP-BeckS

What Would I Give? Christina Georgina Rossetti. CP-RosC1

What would I give to see his face? Emily Dickinson. CP-DickE

What would it profit you, now as good as dead, if Monday came. Sick Man in the Sun. Pablo Neruda. SP-NeruP

What would the body of Saint Francis be like? Body, The. Gabriela Mistral. SP-MistG, *tr.* by Maria Giachetti [*or* Jacketti]

What would we give. August. Lucille Clifton. SP-ClifL

What would ye more of me, your slave, require. Sir Thomas Wyatt. CP-WyatT

What Would You Do If You Lost It. Allen Ginsberg. CP-GinsA

What Would You Fight For? D. H. Lawrence. CP-LawrD

What? Writing in the Dining Room? Philip Whalen. SP-WhalP

What years of the other times, what centuries. Message from Abroad. Allen Tate. CP-TateA

What years, what hours, has spider contemplation spun. Problem of Knowledge. Robert Penn Warren. CP-WarrR

"What you are stepping westward?"—"Yea." Stepping Westward. William Wordsworth. CP-WorW1; MW-WorW

What you give me I cheerfully accept. To Rich Givers. Walt Whitman. CP-WhitW

What you give me is. Love Poem: "What you give me is." Denise Levertov. SP-LeveDL

What you have given me. February 14. William Meredith. SP-MereW

What you have to know. Associate Professor (Mad Scientist) to (His Love) His Student in Physics 100 Lab. Miller Williams. CP-WillM

What you hold. To Be Done in Winter. James Dickey. CP-DickJ

What you knew of me. Eugenio Montale. CP-MontE, *tr.* by Jonathan Galassi

What you know of me. Sign ("What you know of me"). Robert Creeley. CP-CreeR

What you love is gone; the worst have got it. Aban Kavost and Ivar Oakeson. Robert Bly. SP-BlyR

What you may cluster 'round the knees of space. To the Cloud Juggler. Hart Crane. CP-CranH

What you may yank up *readiest* Yank. Pillar and the Post, The. Hart Crane. CP-CranH

What You Need for Painting. Raymond Carver. CP-CarvR

What You Need to Know for Fishing. Raymond Carver. CP-CarvR

What you see is what you see. Horse With Greenblue Eyes, A. Charles Bukowski. SP-BukC1

What You Should Know to Be a Poet. Gary Snyder. CP-SnydG

What You Up To? Allen Ginsberg. SP-GinsA

What You Waited For. Marge Piercy. SP-PierM

What you wanted I told you. Rant, A. Frank O'Hara. SP-OharF

What you wouldn't have suspected. Song of the Motionless Gardener. Federico García Lorca. CP-GarcF, *tr.* by Jerome Rothenberg *Fr.* In the Garden of the Lunar Grapefruits.

What you wrote to know. Littleton Whale, The. Charles Tomlinson. CP-TomlC; SP-TomlC

What, younger, felt. Myself. Robert Creeley. SP-CreeR

What you're holding now in your hand is almost white. Blank Sheet, The. Hans Magnus Enzensberger. SP-EnzeH, *tr.* by Michael Hamburger

What'd you throw it on the floor for? Riddle: "What'd you throw it on the floor for?" Robert Creeley. SP-CreeR

Whate'er I ask I know I have from Thee. Good Gift, The. Jones Very. CP-VeryJ

Whate'er I be, old England is my dam! Old Chartist, The. George Meredith. CP-MerG1

Whate'er is Born of Mortal Birth. To Tirzah. William Blake. CP-BlakW *Fr.* Songs of Experience.

Whateer is done to her she cannot know. On the Virginity of the Virgin Mary & Johanna Southcott. William Blake. CP-BlakW

Whate'er thou wouldst receive at others' hands. Charity. Jones Very. CP-VeryJ

Whate'er we leave to God, God does. Inspiration. Henry David Thoreau. CP-ThorH

Whate'er your predecessors taught us. Letter to the Reverend Dr. Sheridan, A. Jonathan Swift. CP-SwifJ

Whatever a man of the sons of men. Les Noyades. Algernon Charles Swinburne. SP-SwinA

Whatever awaits us of Doom or Home. Emily Dickinson. SP-DickE

Whatever became of that brass ring. Brass Ring, The. Raymond Carver. CP-CarvR

Whatever comes, comes from a need. Joy at Sudden Disappointment. Jelaluddin Rumi. SP-Rumi, *tr.* by Coleman Barks

Whatever comes, let's be content withall. Welcome What Comes. Robert Herrick. CP-HerrR

Whatever constitutes. Act of Love, The. Robert Creeley. CP-CreeR

Whatever contribution I was to make to living. David Ignatow. SP-IgnaD

Whatever could have possessed you. Carmen 40. Catullus. CP-ZukLS *Fr.* Carmina.

Whatever course of Life great Jove allots. Festina Lentè. Samuel Johnson. CP-JohnS

Whatever else they say of me. As for Me, I'm a Patriot. D. H. Lawrence. CP-LawrD

Whatever else we learned. Homecoming: Anse La Raye. Derek Walcott. CP-WalcD

Whatever else you come to be. For Reuben, at Twelve Months. Miller Williams. CP-WillM

Whatever Happened? Philip Larkin. CP-LarkP

Whatever happens. Whatever. Prayer. Galway Kinnell. SP-KinnGN

Whatever I hold in my hand, a stylus, reed, quill or a ballpoint. From the Rising of the Sun. Czeslaw Milosz. CP-MiloC; CP-MiloCN

Whatever I talk about is yesterday. Talking. W. S. Merwin. SP-MerwWF

Whatever is before goes behind. Room. Laura Riding Jackson. CP-RidiL

Whatever is here, it is. Confessions of the Life Artist. Thom Gunn. CP-GunnT

Whatever is to become of me. Wind, The. Robert Creeley. CP-CreeR

Whatever it is, it all comes down to this. October 1950. Paul Muldoon. CP-MuldP

Whatever it is, it's a passion. Love in America. Marianne Craig Moore. CP-MoorM

Whatever it is—she has tried it. Emily Dickinson. CP-DickE

Whatever it is that jigs and gleams. Indian Village. Louis MacNeice. CP-MacNL

Whatever It Is, Wherever You Are. John Ashbery. SP-AshbJ

Whatever it may be whoever it may be. Patna-Benares Express. Allen Ginsberg. CP-GinsA; SP-GinsA

Whatever it was gone wrong inside his head. At Three Every Thursday Afternoon. Miller Williams. CP-WillM

Whatever it was: the grains of the glacier caked in the boot-cleats. Adrienne Rich. SP-RicA1; SP-RicA2 *Fr.* Shooting Script.

Whatever last slump of flesh. Faint Praise. C. K. Williams. CP-WillC

Whatever Man Makes. D. H. Lawrence. CP-LawrD

Whatever may be going through our heads. Sarabande. Howard Nemerov. CP-NemeH

Whatever pops into your head, and whitely. Minneapolis Story. Robert Penn Warren. CP-WarrR

Whatever roams the air is traveling. Phaneron. Muriel Rukeyser. CP-RukeM

Whatever roams the air is traveling. Muriel Rukeyser. CP-RukeM

Whatever sleeping in the world awakes. Creation of Anguish. Howard Nemerov. CP-NemeH

Whatever slid into my mother's room that. Moonchild. Lucille Clifton. SP-ClifL

Whatever stops is death, and is our death. Fernando Pessoa. SP-PessF, *tr.* by Susan M. Brown *and* Edwin Honig

Whatever the eye finds lovely, in a flash. Michelangelo Buonarroti. CP-Miche, *tr.* by John Frederick Nims

"Whatever the weather may be," says he. James Whitcomb Riley. CP-RileJ

Whatever this is of nature, the peach tree. Late Peaches. John Ciardi. CP-CiarJ

Whatever was living is dead. Poem: "Whatever was living is dead." Alan Dugan. CP-DugaA

Whatever we are, we're torn like strips. Good-bye. Wyatt Prunty. SP-PrunW

Whatever we do to a landscape—even to look—damages it. Extinct Vertebrate, An. Robinson Jeffers. CP-JefR3

Whatever we do, whether we light. Dilemma. David Ignatow. SP-IgnaD

Whatever went wrong, that week, was more than weather. Hairline Fracture, A. Amy Clampitt. CP-ClamA

Whatever wonder is found. Petrarch. CP-Petra, *tr.* by J. G. Nichols

Whatever you are that has tracked us this far. Adrienne Rich. SP-RicA1 *Fr.* Turning.

Whatever you have to say, leave. These Days. Charles Olson. CP-OlsoC

Whatever You Now Are. Robert Penn Warren. CP-WarrR

Whatever you say, paola francesca di virgine. Testing. Testing. Andrei Codrescu. SP-CodrA

Whatever You Say Say Nothing. Seamus Heaney.
   "I'm writing this just after an encounter." SP-HeanSO
   "'Religion's never mentioned here,' of course." SP-HeanSO
   "This morning from a dewy motorway." SP-HeanSO

Whatever your mirrors tell you, morning and evening. Poem for a Soldier's Girl. John Ciardi. CP-CiarJ

Whatever's merely wilful, / and not miraculous. E. E. Cummings. CP-CummE

Whatnot, The. John Logan. CP-LogaJ

What's a virgin? Conversation with a Dirty-Minded Little Girl. Alan Dugan. CP-DugaA

What's all this hubbub and yelling. Armistice Day, 1918. Robert Graves. CP-GravR

What's bad about all. Luck. Charles Bukowski. SP-BukC1

What's become of Waring. Waring. Robert Browning. CP-BroR1

What's coming up? Federico García Lorca. CP-GarcF, *tr. by* Jerome Rothenberg *Fr.* Suite.

What's Dead? Allen Ginsberg. CP-GinsA

What's Fame with Men, by Custom of the Nation. To a Lady with the Temple of Fame. Alexander Pope. CP-PopeA

What's Familiar is Sometimes Distanced. Shmuel HaNagid. SP-HaNaS, *tr. by* Peter Cole

What's filling up the mirror? O, it is not I. Fat Man in the Mirror, The. Robert Lowell. SP-LoweR

What's for Dinner. Robert Creeley. CP-CreeR

What's gone. B.B. Robert Creeley. SP-CreeR

What's got by Justice is establisht sure. Rapine Brings Ruine. Robert Herrick. CP-HerrR

What's greater, Pebble or Pond? Once More, the Round. Theodore Roethke. CP-RoetT

What's happening continues. Congress of Vienna, The. Philip Whalen. SP-WhalP

What's in a Name? Christina Georgina Rossetti. CP-RosC2

What's in a Name? Here's What's in a Name, or, I Wonder What Became of John and Mary. Ogden Nash. CP-NashO

What's in a Name? Some Letter I Always Forget. Ogden Nash. CP-NashO

What's in a name *that's*. Petunia. Louis Zukofsky. CP-ZukLS

What's in My Journal. William Stafford. SP-StafWW

"What's in the paper?" O, it's dev'lish dull. Something in the Papers. Ambrose Bierce. SP-BierA

What's in this grave is worth your tear. For Myself. Countee Cullen. CP-CullC

What's in those pills? / After lunch and I can. What. James Schuyler. CP-SchuJ

What's it like? Late Train, The. Theodore Weiss. SP-WeisT

What's it like? You take it from me. Capper Kaplinski at the North Side Cue Club. Hayden Carruth. CP-CarHS

What's left of all those beautiful moments? Song of the Sweepings. Jaroslav Seifert. SP-SeifJ, *tr. by* Ewald Osers

What's missing is the eyeballs. "Daddy" Warbucks. Anne Sexton. CP-SextA

What's New? Philip Whalen. SP-WhalP

What's Next on the Agenda, Mr. Williams? Tennessee Williams. CP-WillT

What's perceived. Occasional Dilemmas. Philip Whalen. SP-WhalP

What's riches to him. Peacock, The. William Butler Yeats. CP-YeatW

What's Sane and What Isn't. D. H. Lawrence. *See* Bawdy Can Be Sane

What's strange about it? I didn't like the sky. Old Mole. Primo Levi. CP-LeviP, *tr. by* Ruth Feldman

What's sweeter than at the end of a summer's day. Thanksgiving. Kenneth Koch. SP-KochK

What's That. Anne Sexton. CP-SextA; SP-SextA

What's that? / An egg? Whoroscope. Samuel Beckett. CP-BeckS

What's that approaching like dusk like poverty. Ballad: "What's that approaching like dusk like poverty." Charles Simic. SP-SimiC; SP-SimiCE

What's That Smell in the Kitchen? Marge Piercy. SP-PierM

"What's that tapping at night: tack, tack." Three Tall Men, The. Thomas Hardy. CP-HardT

What's that that hirples at my side? Heriot's Ford. Rudyard Kipling. CP-KiplR *Fr.* Light That Failed, The.

What's that we see from far? the spring of Day. Nuptiall Song, or Epithalamie, on Sir Clipseby Crew and His Lady, A. Robert Herrick. CP-HerrR

What's the balm. Poem: "What's the balm." Alan Dugan. CP-DugaA

What's the best life for a man? Robinson Jeffers. CP-JefR3

What's the best thing in the world? Best Thing in the World, The. Elizabeth Barrett Browning. CP-BroEB

What's the good of a man. Glimpses. D. H. Lawrence. CP-LawrD

What's the good of going to Ridgeway. Old Excursions. Thomas Hardy. CP-HardT

What's the Matter, Haven't You Got Any Sense of Humor? Ogden Nash. CP-NashO

What's the Riddle. Randall Jarrell. CP-JarrR

What's the Use. Paul Laurence Dunbar. CP-DunbP

What's the Use. Ogden Nash. CP-NashO

What's the Use? Yannis Ritsos. SP-RitsY, *tr. by* N. C. Germanacos

What's the use of so many quarrels, lawsuits and wars? Dromedary, The. Primo Levi. CP-LeviP, *tr. by* Ruth Feldman

What's the worst that could happen? About. Rae Armantrout. SP-ArmaA

What's there to praise. Use of Books, The. Thomas McGrath. SP-McGrT

What's There to Tell? Thomas Hardy. CP-HardT

What's this? A dish for fat lips. Shape of the Fire, The. Theodore Roethke. CP-RoetT

What's this crying for. Han-shan. CP-ColdM, *tr. by* Red Pine

What's of death, from you who never will die? Edna St. Vincent Millay. CP-MillE

What's to Be Done. D. H. Lawrence. CP-LawrD

What's to be said. Last Mile, The. Robert Creeley. SP-CreeR

What's to be said. Robert Creeley. CP-CreeR

What's to become of her, long years from now. Michelangelo Buonarroti. CP-Miche, *tr. by* John Frederick Nims

What's to become of me? What's this you're doing. Michelangelo Buonarroti. CP-Miche, *tr. by* John Frederick Nims

What's written goes hollow, what's. Paul Celan. SP-CelaP, *tr. by* John Felstiner

What's Wrong. D. H. Lawrence. CP-LawrD

What's wrong with American literature? Question and Answer. William Carlos Williams. CP-WilW1

What's Wrong with Pindar. Charles Olson. CP-OlsoC

What's wrong with you-zie? Her-zie. Stevie Smith. CP-SmitS

Whatsoever Is Right, That Shall Ye Receive. Christina Georgina Rossetti. *See* Heart Knoweth Its Own Bitterness, The

Whatsoever thing I see. Love Dislikes Nothing. Robert Herrick. CP-HerrR

Wheat is threshed and cut the heavy clover. August Revival: Crosby Junction. Robert Penn Warren. CP-WarrR

Wheel, The. Wendell Berry. CP-BerrW

Wheel, The. Robert Earl Hayden. CP-HaydR

Wheel, The. William Butler Yeats. CP-YeatW

Wheel King, The. Howard Nemerov. CP-NemeH

Wheel me gently to the garage, since my car and I must part. Dying Chauffer, The. Rudyard Kipling. CP-KiplR *Fr.* Muse among the Motors, The.

Wheel of Fortune, The. Thom Gunn. CP-GunnT

Wheel Revolves, The. Kenneth Rexroth. CP-RexrK

Wheelbarrow's tire is flat, muddy ground now sets. Winter, The ("Wheelbarrow's tire is flat, muddy ground now sets"). Philip Whalen. SP-WhalP

Wheelchair Butterfly, The. James Tate. SP-TateJ

Wheelers and Dealers: The Theory of Games. George Oppen. CP-OppGN

Wheeling, the careening. Edge of the Hurricane, The. Amy Clampitt. CP-ClamA

Wheels and galleries of the control of tears. Muriel Rukeyser. CP-RukeM

Wheels of Fortune. Federico García Lorca.
  Fan. CP-GarcF, *tr. by* Jerome Rothenberg
  Roulette. CP-GarcF, *tr. by* Jerome Rothenberg

Wheels of the Trains, The. W. S. Merwin. SP-MerwW

Wheels within Wheels. Seamus Heaney. SP-HeanSO

Wheels within wheels, the wheels for ever turning. Song of the Wheel, The. G. K. Chesterton. CP-ChesG

Wheesht, Wheesht. Hugh MacDiarmid. SP-MacDH

Wheesht, wheesht, Joyce, and let me hear. Hugh MacDiarmid. *See* Archin' here and arrachin there

Whelks. Mary Oliver. SP-OlivM

Whelped from blackness by a pressure of rocks. Oasis. Alan Dugan. CP-DugaA

When. James Dickey. CP-DickJ

When. C. K. Williams. SP-WillC

When a bar of pure silver or ignot of gold. Flatting Mill, The. William Cowper. CP-CowpW

When a bird flips his tail in getting his balance on a tree. Many Mansions. D. H. Lawrence. CP-LawrD

When a blizzard powders the harbor, when the creaking pine. North Baltic. Joseph Brodsky. CP-BrodJ

When a child turned in a false. On an Accident: On a Newspaper Story. Alan Dugan. CP-DugaA

When a chile gets to be thirteen. Mystery. Langston Hughes. CP-HughL; CP-HughL3

When a common noun becomes a Proper One. Capitals. Howard Nemerov. CP-NemeH

When a cuckoo comes to the village. Immortal Prankster. Charles Simic. SP-SimiCE

When a daffadill [*or* daffodil] I see. Divination by a Daffadill [*or* Daffodil]. Robert Herrick. CP-HerrR

When a dark-eyed dawn. Vagrant's Song. Thomas Hardy. CP-HardT

When a daughter tries suicide. Risk, The. Anne Sexton. CP-SextA

When a Feller's Itchin' to be Spanked. Paul Laurence Dunbar. CP-DunbP

When a friend calls to me from the road. Time to Talk, A. Robert Frost. CP-FrosR

When a goat likes a book, the whole book is gone. Trouble with Reading, The. William Stafford. SP-StafWW

When a Hideous Man. Chuang Tzu. CP-MertT

When a holy black Suede, the Son of Bob. Windsor Prophecy, The. Jonathan Swift. CP-SwifJ

When a live flower, a single name of names. Desert Fringe. Robert Graves. CP-GravR

When a lover clasps his fairest. Fragment: "When a lover clasps his fairest." Percy Bysshe Shelley. CP-ShelP

When a lover hies abroad. Rudyard Kipling. CP-KiplR *Fr.* Naulahka, The.

When a Lover is a Beggar. Emily Dickinson. CP-DickE

When a magnet is / struck by a hammer. Simple Experiment, A. Muriel Rukeyser. CP-RukeM

When a man can love no more. Basta! D. H. Lawrence. CP-LawrD

When a man dies angels tick. John Ciardi. CP-CiarJ

When a man grows older, his life becomes less dependent. All These Make a Dance Rhythm. Yehuda Amichai. SP-AmicY, *tr. by* Chana Bloch

When a man had gone. Unfrocked Priest, The. William Carlos Williams. CP-WilW1

When a Man Hath No Freedom to Fight for at Home. Lord Byron.

When a man is away from his homeland for a long time. Yehuda Amichai. SP-AmicYL, *tr. by* Benjamin Harshav *and* Barbara Harshav

When a man starts out with nothing. Freedom's Plow. Langston Hughes. CP-HughL; CP-HughL2

When a mans Faith is frozen up, as dead. Lamp, The. Robert Herrick. CP-HerrR

When a man's far away from his country for a long time. Yehuda Amichai. SP-AmicY, *tr. by* Chana Bloch

When a mounting skylark sings / In the sunlit summer morn. Heaven Is Heaven. Christina Georgina Rossetti. CP-RosC2

When a night in November. On One Who Lived and Died Where He Was Born. Thomas Hardy. CP-HardT

When a people reach the top of a hill. Stephen Crane. CP-CranS

When a Polish romantic is sitting on the papal throne. Selecting Iwaszkiewicz's Poems for an Evening of His Poetry at the National Theater in Warsaw. Czeslaw Milosz. CP-MiloCN, *tr. by* Robert Hass

When a Roman was dying, the next man or kin. Upon William Tisdall, D. D. Thomas Sheridan. CP-SherT

When a sister, born for each strong month-brother. Ad Mariam. Gerard Manley Hopkins. CP-HopkG

When a tree falls. Cycles of Strangeness. Laura Riding Jackson. CP-RidiL

When a tree falls in a forest. Bedtime Story. Charles Simic. SP-SimiC; SP-SimiCE

When a woman looks up at you with a twist about her eyes. Made to Order Smile, The. Paul Laurence Dunbar. CP-DunbP

When Abraham Lincoln was shoveled into the tombs. Cool Tombs. Carl Sandburg. CP-SandC

When Abu Bakr met Muhammad, he said. Polishing the Mirror. Jelaluddin Rumi. SP-Rumi, *tr. by* Coleman Barks

When Achilles fought and fell. Randall Jarrell. CP-JarrR

When Achilles with his short sword pierced the breast of Penthesilea. Achilles. Penthesilea. Zbigniew Herbert. CP-BrodJ, *tr. by* Joseph Brodsky

When Adam walked in Eden young. A. E. Housman. CP-HousA

When Adam went from Paradise. On Righteous Indignation. G. K. Chesterton. CP-ChesG

When, after a long life, it falls out. Czeslaw Milosz. CP-MiloC; CP-MiloCN, *tr. by* Robert Hass

When after hours of walking. Outing with a Woman. Yehuda Amichai. SP-AmicYL, *tr. by* Benjamin Harshav *and* Barbara Harshav

When after many Lustrs thou shalt be. To His Worthy Friend, M. Arthur Bartly. Robert Herrick. CP-HerrR

When after supper Tatyana Ivanovna sat quietly down. Smoke and Deception. Raymond Carver. CP-CarvR

When after the screens of the evening of defeat. Willkie in the *Gulliver*. Muriel Rukeyser. CP-RukeM

When Age Comes On. James Whitcomb Riley. CP-RileJ

When Age or Chance has made me blind. Being Once Blind, His Request to Biancha. Robert Herrick. CP-HerrR

When Alberta swims the whole night in the creek behind the house. Alberta. Andrei Codrescu. SP-CodrA

When Alexander Pope strolled in the city. Mr. Pope. Allen Tate. CP-TateA

When all analogies are broken. In the Black Museum. Howard Nemerov. CP-NemeH

When all around grew drear and dark. Stanzas to Augusta. Lord Byron. CP-Byron

When all Birds els[e] do of their music[k] fail[e]. Money Makes the Mirth. Robert Herrick. CP-HerrR

When all else fails, To a Friend in Search of Rural Seclusion. Christopher Logue. SP-LoguC

When all I wanted was to sing. Rainer Maria Rilke. CP-RilkFr, *tr. by* A. Poulin, Jr. *Fr.* Fragments.

When All Is Done. Paul Laurence Dunbar. CP-DunbP

When all is over and you march for home. Spoils. Robert Graves. CP-GravR

When all my days are ending. Second Childhood, A. G. K. Chesterton. CP-ChesG

When All My Five and Country Senses See. Dylan Thomas. CP-ThomD

When all my hours are mine. Preoccupation's Gift. Donald Davie. CP-DaviDC

When all / My waterfall. Her Time. Theodore Roethke. CP-RoetT

When all the flowers were full and fair. Artist, The. G. K. Chesterton. CP-ChesG

When all the follies here provoke. Inscribed in a Copy of "Greybeards at Play" G. K. Chesterton. CP-ChesG

When all the overwork of life. Heart Knoweth Its Own Bitterness, The. Christina Georgina Rossetti. CP-RosC2

When all the snow has melted. Thaw, The. Primo Levi. CP-LeviP, *tr. by* Ruth Feldman

When all the world was younger. Song: "When all the world was younger." Dorothy Parker. CP-ParkD

When all the world would keep a matter hid. Fabulists, The. Rudyard Kipling. CP-KiplR

When all their blooms the meadows flaunt. May. Ralph Waldo Emerson. CP-EmerR

When all things forget color and shape. Mirror's Mission, The. Jorge Carrera Andrade. CP-MertT

When all this is over we'll find outselves. Betrothal / the Bride's Lament. Olga Broumas. SP-BrouO

When all turned to altitude. Pablo Neruda. SP-NeruP *Fr.* Skystones.

When all within is peace. Song: "When all within is peace." William Cowper. CP-CowpW

When all works that have. Fool by the Roadside, The. William Butler Yeats. CP-YeatW

When along the pavement, Submergence. D. H. Lawrence. CP-LawrD

When Americans say a man. Language Lesson 1976. Heather McHugh. SP-McHuH

When an act of kindness is not done. Story, A. Miller Williams. CP-WillM

When an archer is shooting for nothing. Need to Win, The. Chuang Tzu. CP-MertT, *tr. by* Thomas Merton

When an auctioneer's seen with a good-looking boy. Carmen 106. Catullus. CP-ZukLS *Fr.* Carmina.

When an hour is harmonious. Swinging Bridge, The. Richard Eberhart. CP-EberR

When an old man takes a young wife. Han-shan. CP-ColdM, *tr. by* Red Pine

When Anaxagoras says: Even snow is black! Anaxagoras. D. H. Lawrence. CP-LawrD

When ancient girl is garbed in spite. Smile, The. Stevie Smith. CP-SmitS

When and Why. Robert Graves. CP-GravR

When anger comes to the coast of our desolate country. Peril, The. Thomas Merton. CP-MertT

When any mortal(even the most odd). E. E. Cummings. CP-CummE

When April with her wild blue eye. Death of Winter, The. George Meredith. CP-MerGi

When as Leander young was drown'd. Leanders Obsequies. Robert Herrick. CP-HerrR

When, as the captive of Your own invincible consent. Freedom as Experience. Thomas Merton. CP-MertT

When Asked to Lie Down on the Altar. Eleanor Wilner. SP-WilnE

When at a desperate plight. In Isolation. Josephine Jacobsen. CP-JacoJ

When at last he was well enough to take the sun. Leg in a Plaster Cast, A. Muriel Rukeyser. CP-RukeM

When at last you came down from your hills. Kali. Sam Hamill. SP-HamiS

When at the end of *Don Pasquale*. Seductive Piece of Business, A. Randall Jarrell. CP-JarrR

When August days are hot an' dry. In August. Paul Laurence Dunbar. CP-DunbP

When Aulus, the nocturnal thief, made prize. On a Thief. *Unknown*. CP-CowpW

When Autumn shakes the rambo-tree. Rambo-Tree, The. James Whitcomb Riley. CP-RileJ

When Baby Played. James Whitcomb Riley. CP-RileJ

When Baby Slept. James Whitcomb Riley. CP-RileJ

When Baby Woke. James Whitcomb Riley. CP-RileJ

When Bacchus first beheld the desolate. How Bacchus Finds Ariadne Sleeping. Nonnus. CP-BroEB *Fr.* Dionysiaca.

When battles were fought / With a chivalrous sense of Should and Ought. Then and Now. Thomas Hardy. CP-HardT

When beasts could speak, (the learned say). Beasts' Confession to the Priest, The. Jonathan Swift. CP-SwifJ

When beauty breaks and falls asunder. Juan's Song. Louise Bogan. CP-BogaL

When Bells stop ringing—Church—begins. Emily Dickinson. CP-DickE

When Berthe Soucaret, / a Creole girl from Guadeloupe. Berthe Soucaret. Jaroslav Seifert. SP-SeifJ, *tr. by* Ewald Osers

When Bess gave her Dollies a tea, said she. Company Manners. James Whitcomb Riley. CP-RileJ

When Bessie Died. James Whitcomb Riley. CP-RileJ

When birds sang this spring. Han-shan. CP-ColdM, *tr. by* Red Pine

When biting *Boreas*, fell and doure. Winter Night, A. Robert Burns. CP-BurnR

When blackguards and murderers. In Chains. William Carlos Williams. CP-WilW2

When blessed Marie [*or* Mary] wip'd her Saviours [*or* Saviour's] feet. Mary [*or* Marie] Magdalene. George Herbert. CP-HerbG

When blithely Love would lift me up to heaven. Michelangelo Buonarroti. CP-Miche, *tr. by* John Frederick Nims

When books have all seized up like the books in graveyards. To Posterity. Louis MacNeice. CP-MacNL

When branches bend in fruitful stupor. Not Even for Brunch. Ogden Nash. CP-NashO

When breathless noon hath paused on hill and vale. Henry David Thoreau. CP-ThorH

When breathless queens release their panthers. Winter Poem. Kenneth Patchen. CP-PatcK

When brightest colours seem but dull in hue. L'Art. Ezra Pound. CP-PoEar

When brown folk lived a distance. Lorine Niedecker. CP-NiedL

When buds of palm do burst and spread. Song: Spring. George Meredith. CP-MerG1

When Bunyan swung his whopping axe. Folk Tune. Richard Wilbur. CP-WilbR

When but a little boy, it seemed. Sad Perversity. James Whitcomb Riley. CP-RileJ

When by a generous Public's kind acclaim. Prologue: "When by a generous Public's kind acclaim." Robert Burns. CP-BurnR

When by my solitary hearth I sit. To Hope. John Keats. CP-KeatJ

When by the labour of my 'ands. Half-Ballad of Waterval. Rudyard Kipling. CP-KiplR

When by thy scorn[e], O murderess[e] [*or* murd'ress *or* murdress], I am dead. Apparition, The. John Donne. CP-DonnJ; MW-DonnJ

When by Zeus relenting the mandate was revoked. Phoebus with Admetus. George Meredith. CP-MerG1

When Caesar Fell. Edna St. Vincent Millay. CP-MillE

When chapman [*or* chapmen] billies leave the street. Tam o' Shanter; A Tale. Robert Burns. CP-BurnR

When chill November's surly blast. Man Was Made to Mourn, a Dirge. Robert Burns. CP-BurnR

When chirping crickets fainter cry. Home at Night. James Whitcomb Riley. CP-RileJ

When Chloë flies on silken wings. Chloë's Poem. John Updike. CP-UpdiJ

When Christ, the seaman, was aboard. Ode to Admiral Sir George Pocock. Christopher Smart. SP-SmarC

When Christ went up to Heaven the Apostles stayed. Ascension Day. Christina Georgina Rossetti. CP-RosC2

When Chub brings in his harvest, still he cries. Upon Chub. Robert Herrick. CP-HerrR

When citied day with the sonorous homes. E. E. Cummings. CP-CummE

When class was in the garden at Greylands. Thomas Merton. CP-MertT

When Cleopatra was made a Guide. G. K. Chesterton. CP-ChesG

When cockle takes over it's. Cockle. Louis Zukofsky. CP-ZukLS

When cold, I huddle up, foetal, cross. Christmas Eve. A. R. Ammons. CP-AmmoA

When cold November sits among the reeds like an unlucky fisher. Regret, The. Thomas Merton. CP-MertT

When Coldness Wraps This Suffering Clay. Lord Byron. CP-Byron

When comes the lighted day for men to read. Hawarden. George Meredith. CP-MerG1

When comes the sun to visit thee at morn. Day not for Gain, The. Jones Very. CP-VeryJ

When Confucius was visiting the state of Chu. Confucius and the Madman. Chuang Tzu. CP-MertT

When Continents expire. Emily Dickinson. SP-DickE

When Corydon went to the fair. Song: "When Corydon went to the fair." Jane Austen. CP-AustJ

When country fiddlers held a convention in. Hell on the Wabash. Carl Sandburg. CP-SandC

When country roads begin to thaw. When Early March Seems Middle May. James Whitcomb Riley. CP-RileJ

When Crow was white he decided the sun was too white. Crow's Fall. Ted Hughes. SP-HughTN

When Cupid did his grandsire Jove entreat. On Mrs. Biddy Floyd. Jonathan Swift. CP-SwifJ

When daring Blood his rents to have regained. Bludius et Corona [Blood and the Crown]. Andrew Marvell. CP-MarvA

When dark and deafening skies are bowed. Deluge, The ("When dark and deafening skies are bowed"). G. K. Chesterton. CP-ChesG

When darkness settles itself. Within the Seasons. Peter Blue Cloud. SP-BlueP

When dawn lights the sky. Lonely Nocturne. Langston Hughes. CP-HughL; CP-HughL3

When dawn's pink fingers probe licentious beds. Spiritual Dawn. Charles Baudelaire. CP-BaudC, *tr. by* Walter Martin

When / (day's amazing murder with). E. E. Cummings. CP-CummE

When days are short. Her Sadness. Denise Levertov. SP-LeveDL

When days of Beauty deck the earth. Emily Jane Brontë. CP-BronE

When de Co'n Pone's Hot. Paul Laurence Dunbar. CP-DunbP

When de fiddle gits to singin' out a ol' Vahginny reel. Angelina. Paul Laurence Dunbar. CP-DunbP

When de Folks Is Gone. James Whitcomb Riley. CP-RileJ

When Dead. Thomas Hardy. CP-HardT

When dear Clarinda, matchless fair. Answer to the Foregoing—Extempore [Clarinda]. Robert Burns. CP-BurnR

When, dearest, I but think on [*or* of] thee. Song: "When, dearest, I but think on [*or* of] thee." Sir John Suckling *and* Owen Feltltham. CP-SuckJ

When Death Came April Twelve 1945. Carl Sandburg. CP-SandC

When Death Comes. Mary Oliver. SP-OlivM

When death draws down the blinds in this old house. Reflections in an Old House. Allen Tate. CP-TateA

When death shall part us from these kids. Dialogue between Thyrsis and Dorinda, A. Andrew Marvell. CP-MarvA

When Death was on thy drums, Democracy. Revolutionist, The: or Lines to a Statesman. G. K. Chesterton. CP-ChesG

When death's dark stream I ferry o'er. Verse Composed and Repeated by *Burns*, to the Master of the House, on Taking Leave at a Place in the Highlands, Where He Had Been Hospitably Entertained, A. Robert Burns. CP-BurnR

When Delia fair defleas her bitch. Lines Upon Delia And to the Chevaliers of the Cordon Bleu. Robert Stock. SP-StocR

When Denmark's raven soar'd on high. Thorsgill. Sir Walter Scott. SP-ScotW *Fr.* Rokeby.

When descends on the Atlantic. Seaweed. Henry Wadsworth Longfellow. SP-LongH

When despair for the world grows in me. Peace of Wild Things, The. Wendell Berry. CP-BerrW

When devils bite. Ralph Waldo Emerson. CP-EmerR

When Dey 'Listed Colored Soldiers. Paul Laurence Dunbar. CP-DunbP

When Diamonds are a Legend. Emily Dickinson. CP-DickE

When Dickens first dawned on us . . . . Hey! to wake. St. Lirriper. James Whitcomb Riley. CP-RileJ *Fr.* Child-World, A.

When Dicky was sick. Little Dick and the Clock. James Whitcomb Riley. CP-RileJ

When did I ever deny, though this was fleeting. Edna St. Vincent Millay. CP-MillE

When did you begin your quest? Absences. James Tate. SP-TateJ

When did you start your tricks. Mosquito, The. D. H. Lawrence. CP-LawrD

When Dido feasted first the wandering Trojan knight. Iopas's Song. Sir Thomas Wyatt. CP-WyatT

When do I see thee most, beloved one? Lovesight. Dante Gabriel Rossetti. CW-RossD *Fr.* House of Life, The.

When do poppies bloom I ask myself, stopping again. Charles Olson. SP-OlsoC *Fr.* Maximus Poems, The.

When do we live again Ann. Lorine Niedecker. CP-NiedL

When doctors with tirades on Tea affright us. Classicality Applied to Tea-Dealing: A Fancy Inspired by Westbourne Grove. Robert Browning. CP-BroR2

When does a town become a city? This. Townend, 1976. Donald Davie. CP-DaviDC

When does the butterfly read. Pablo Neruda. SP-NeruP *Fr.* Question Book.

When Does the Play Begin? James Laughlin. CP-LaugJ

When, doff'd his casque, he felt free air. Death of Marmion, The. Sir Walter Scott. SP-ScotW *Fr.* Marmion.

When Doris Danced. Richard Eberhart. CP-EberR

When down I went to the rust-red quarry. Wedding, The. Robert Graves. CP-GravR

When Dragon-fly would fix his wings. Flower of Mending, The. Nicholas Vachel Lindsay. CP-LindV

When Dryden's fool, "unknowing what he sought." Verses Found in a Summer-House at Hales-Owen. Lord Byron. CP-Byron

When Early March Seems Middle May. James Whitcomb Riley. CP-RileJ

When early morn walks forth in sober grey. Song: "When early morn walks forth in sober grey." William Blake. CP-BlakW

When earth and all her seers were sad. Child, The. G. K. Chesterton. CP-ChesG

When Earth's Last Picture Is Painted. Rudyard Kipling. *See* L'Envoi

When Earth's last picture is painted, and the tubes are twisted and dried. L'Envoi. Rudyard Kipling. CP-KiplR

When earth's last thesis is copied. Logical Conclusion, The. Ezra Pound. CP-PoEar

When Eighty-five was seven month auld. Mauchline Wedding, The. Robert Burns. CP-BurnR

When energising objects men pursue. Parenthetical Address. Lord Byron. CP-Byron

When England did enjoy her halcyon days. Elegy Upon that Honorable and Reknowned Knight Sir Philip Sydney, An. Anne Bradstreet. CP-BradA

When ere I go, or what so ere befalls. To My Dearest Sister M. Mercie Herrick.

Robert Herrick. CP-HerrR

When ere my heart, Love's warmth, but entertaines. Against Love. Robert Herrick. CP-HerrR

When Etna basks and purrs. Emily Dickinson. CP-DickE

When Eurydice saw him. Gregory Orr. SP-OrrG

When Eve ate the apple / My woes began. Ineffable, The. Richard Eberhart. CP-EberR

When evening had flowed between house. One Time. William Stafford. SP-StafWW

When Evening Shadows Fall. James Whitcomb Riley. CP-RileJ

When ever'thing's a-goin' like she's got-a-goin' now. Hoosier Spring-Poetry. James Whitcomb Riley. CP-RileJ

When everyone else dropped in a handful of dirt. Elegy for a Sweet Sharpy. John Ciardi. CP-CiarJ

When everything that can fall has fallen. Guide, The. Ted Hughes. SP-HughTN

When everything was fine. Poem for the End of the Century, A. Czeslaw Milosz. CP-MiloCN *Fr.* Two Poems.

When everything was over. Child Poems. "H. D." CP-DoolH

When eyeless fish meet her on. Goddess, The. Thom Gunn. CP-GunnT

When eyes that cast about the heights of heaven. Gerard Manley Hopkins. CP-HopkG

When faces called flowers float out of the ground. E. E. Cummings. CP-CummE; SP-CummE

When factious rage to cruel exile drove. Prologue to the Duchess. John Dryden. CP-DryJ2

When faint and sad o'er Sorrow's desart wild. Monody on the Death of Chatterton. Samuel Taylor Coleridge. CP-ColeS

When Faith and Love which parted from thee never. Sonnet: On the Religious Memorie of Mrs. Catherine Thomason My Christian Friend Deceas'd Decem. 1646. John Milton. CP-MiltJ

When faith in black candles. Number. Langston Hughes. CP-HughL; CP-HughL3

When, far and wide, swift as the beams of the moon. *see also* On a Celebrated Event in Ancient History. William Wordsworth. CP-WorW1

When feare admits no hope of safety, then. No Danger to Men Desperate. Robert Herrick. CP-HerrR

When fears and sorrows me beset. For the Restoration of My Dear Husband from a Burning Ague. Anne Bradstreet. CP-BradA

When Fergus woke crying at night. Olive Wood Fire, The. Galway Kinnell. SP-KinnGN

When fierce conflicting passions urge. Translation from the Medea of Euripides. Lord Byron. CP-Byron

When first by Eden Tree. Song of the Fifth River. Rudyard Kipling. CP-KiplR *Fr.* Puck of Pook's Hill.

When first, descending from the moorlands. Extempore Effusion upon the Death of James Hogg. William Wordsworth. CP-WorW2; MW-WorW

When first Diana leaves her Bed. Progress of Beauty, The. Jonathan Swift. CP-SwifJ

When first, fair mistress, I did see your face. To B.C. Sir John Suckling. CP-SuckJ

When first I came to Stewart Kyle. Fragment, A: "When first I came to Stewart Kyle." Robert Burns. CP-BurnR

When first I find those Numbers thou do'st write. To His Learned Friend M. Jo. Harmar, Phisitian to to Colledge of Westminster. Robert Herrick. CP-HerrR

When first I journeyed hither, to a home. William Wordsworth. MW-WorW

When first I saw our banner wave. Astræa at the Capitol. John Greenleaf Whittier. CP-WhitJ

When first I saw thee 'neath the silver mist. Canzon: The Vision. Ezra Pound. CP-PoEar

When first mine eyes did view and mark. Sir Thomas Wyatt. CP-WyatT

When first my brave Johnie lad came to this town. Cock up Your Beaver. Robert Burns. CP-BurnR

When first my lines [*or* verse] of heavenly [*or* heav'nly] joy[e]s made mention. Jordan (2). George Herbert. CP-HerbG

When first, my lord, I saw you back your horse. Epigram. To William, Earl of Newcastle, An. Ben Jonson. CP-JonsB

When first my way to fair I took. A. E. Housman. CP-HousA

When first of wise old Johnson taught. At Cheshire Cheese. Paul Laurence Dunbar. CP-DunbP

When first that horse, within whose populous womb. Death's Songsters. Dante Gabriel Rossetti. CW-RossD *Fr.* House of Life, The.

When first the peasant, long inclin'd to roam. Young Author, The. Samuel Johnson. CP-JohnS

When first thou didst entice to thee my heart. Affliction (1). George Herbert. CP-HerbG

When first thy sweet and gracious eye. Glance, The. George Herbert. CP-HerbG

When first we came together. Our Self. Robert Graves. CP-GravR

When First We Faced, and Touching Showed. Philip Larkin. CP-LarkP

When first we knew it, gibbet-bare. Tree of Guilt, The. Louis MacNeice. CP-MacNL

When first we saw the apple tree. Apple Tree, The. Dorothy Parker. CP-ParkD

When first you fluttered on this scene. Hundred Years Since, A. Thomas Hardy. CP-HardT

When fishes flew and forests walked. Donkey, The. G. K. Chesterton. CP-ChesG

When fishes set umbrellas up. Christina Georgina Rossetti. CP-RosC2

When fishes set umbrellas up / If the rain-drops run. When fishes set umbrellas up. Christina Georgina Rossetti. CP-RosC2

When flowing garments I behold. Leprosie in Cloathes. Robert Herrick. CP-HerrR

When foes are o'ercome, we preserve them from slaughter. Serious Poem upon William Wood, A. Jonathan Swift. CP-SwifJ

When, foot to wheel and back to wind. In the Matter of One Compass. Rudyard Kipling. CP-KiplR

When for a long time I contemplate this box. Casket of Pandora, The. Marya Alexandrovna Zaturenska. SP-ZatuM

When, for the fifteenth year, Tiberius Caesar. St. John Baptist. Thomas Merton. CP-MertT

When for the Thorns with which I long, too long. Coronet, The. Andrew Marvell. CP-MarvA

When formerly we thought, Dear. Looking Back. Thomas Hardy. CP-HardT

When France got free Europe 'twixt Fools & Knaves. William Blake. CP-BlakW

When Freedom, on her natal day. Moral Warfare, The. John Greenleaf Whittier. CP-WhitJ

When French monks stole the bones. On a Travel Story from Wormwood Valley. Alan Dugan. CP-DugaA

When Fresh, It Was Sweet. William Carlos Williams. CP-WilW1

When friendly summer calls again. Summer Schemes. Thomas Hardy. CP-HardT

When Friendship or Love our sympathies move. Tear, The. Lord Byron. CP-Byron

When / from a sidewalk. E. E. Cummings. CP-CummE

When from his cave, young Mao in his youthful mind. Cultural Evolution. Carolyn Kizer. CP-KizeC

When from the curve of the wood's edge does grow. Ivor Gurney. SP-GurnI

When, from the heart where Sorrow sits. Impromptu, in Reply to a Friend. Lord Byron. CP-Byron

When from thee, weeping I removed. Exile's Return, The. Elizabeth Barrett Browning. CP-BroEB

When from their sight the Savior went. Hymn: The Promise of the Spirit. Jones Very. CP-VeryJ

When from your sleepy mind the day's burden. Secret Theatre. Robert Graves. CP-GravR

When frost's all on our winder, an' the snow's. Climatic Sorcery. James Whitcomb Riley. CP-RileJ

When fruit-filled Tuscia should a wife give me. Elegy 3.12: "When fruit-filled Tuscia should a wife give me." Ovid. CP-MarlC *Fr.* Elegies.

When G——le Has Her Mind at Ease. Thomas Sheridan. CP-SherT

When getting my nose in a book. Study of Reading Habits. A. Philip Larkin. CP-LarkP

When glad vacation time began. Visit to Mab, The. Nicholas Vachel Lindsay. CP-LindV

When gloaming droops / To the raven's croak. Captive, The. Walter De la Mare. CP-DeLaW

When God at first made man. Pulley, The. George Herbert. CP-HerbG

When god decided to invent. E. E. Cummings. CP-CummE; SP-CummE

When God, disgusted with man. Crow Blacker than Ever. Ted Hughes. SP-HughTN

When God Lets My Body Be. E. E. Cummings. CP-CummE; SP-CummE

When god lets my body be. When God Lets My Body Be. E. E. Cummings. CP-CummE; SP-CummE

When God scooped up a handful of dust. They Ask: Is God, Too, Lonely? Carl Sandburg. CP-SandC

When God turned back eternity and was young. Little Litany, A. G. K. Chesterton. CP-ChesG

When God was born in Bethlehem. Christmas Rhyme, A. G. K. Chesterton. CP-ChesG

When God was learning to draw the human face. Two Masks Unearthed in Bulgaria. William Meredith. SP-MereW

When God's parachute failed. Religion Back Home. William Stafford. SP-StafWW

When Goethe becomes an Apollo, he becomes a plaster cast. Goethe and Pose. D. H. Lawrence. CP-LawrD

When Golda Meir Was in Africa. Alice Walker. CP-WalkA

When Golden Flies Upon My Carcass Come. Richard Eberhart. CP-EberR

"When good people die they become worms in Detroit," they say. Accommodation to Detroit. Alan Dugan. CP-DugaA

When great Nature sighs, we hear the winds. Breath of Nature, The. Chuang Tzu. CP-MertT, *tr. by* Thomas Merton

When green buds hang in the elm. A. E. Housman. CP-HousA

When green buds hang in the elm like dust. When green buds hang in the elm.

A. E. Housman. CP-HousA

When *Guilford* good our Pilot stood. Fragment, A: "When *Guilford* good our Pilot stood." Robert Burns. CP-BurnR

When guns fall silent for an hour. Edge, The. Yusef Komunyakaa. CP-KomuY

When H—y finds out what you cannot do. On H[ayle]ys Friendship. William Blake. CP-BlakW

When hair falls off and eyes blur And. E. E. Cummings. CP-CummE

When Hamlet had sunk to the moist ground. Hamlet Father, The. Richard Eberhart. CP-EberR

When hard luck overtakes you. Hard Luck. Langston Hughes. CP-HughL; CP-HughL1

When Harry Wylie saw his father's ghost. What Ghosts Can Say. Adrienne Rich. CP-RicAE

When Haughty Expectations Prostrate Lie. William Wordsworth. CP-WorW2

When have I last looked on. Lines Written in Dejection. William Butler Yeats. CP-YeatW

When, having entered. George Oppen. CP-OppGN

When having something to do. Coda: Song. Ted Berrigan. SP-BerrT

When he and I. Robert Creeley. CP-CreeR

When he began to witness, it was not to a journey. Muriel Rukeyser. CP-RukeM

When he brings home a whale. Naughty Boy. Robert Creeley. CP-CreeR

When he came back from saying good-bye. Condolence. Donald Davie. CP-DaviDC

When he came to he knew. After the Crash. Louis MacNeice. CP-MacNL

When he came to my house months ago to measure. Lemonade. Raymond Carver. CP-CarvR

When he closed his eyes he could remember nothing of that summer. Plaster Model. Yannis Ritsos. SP-RitsY, *tr. by* Kimon Friar

When he considered his linguistic fallacy. Man's Type. Richard Eberhart. CP-EberR

When he goes out in the morning. Companions, The. Wendell Berry. CP-BerrW

When he got into bed. Damon & Pythias. Robert Creeley. CP-CreeR

When he had carried to term the sacred poem. Aftermath. Howard Nemerov. CP-NemeH

When he kissed my nipple. After Thoughts. Allen Ginsberg. CP-GinsA

When he lies in the night away from her. Jealous Lovers, The. Donald Hall. CP-HallD

When he lit the candles there. Young Churchwarden, The. Thomas Hardy. CP-HardT

When he lost his way in the Hagodah. Seder Night. Amy Clampitt. CP-ClamA

When he protested, not too solemnly. Erasmus. Edwin Arlington Robinson. CP-RobiE

When he pushed his bush of black hair off his brow. Sicilian Cyclamens. D. H. Lawrence. CP-LawrD

When he sensed her hand on his shoulder. To an Unknown Direction. Yannis Ritsos. SP-RitsY, *tr. by* Minas Savvas

When he stands in the judgement place. Stone Verdict, The. Seamus Heaney. SP-HeanSO

When he was a little boy. Protestant Easter. Anne Sexton. CP-SextA; SP-SextA

When he was here alive, Eileen. Lisette and Eileen. Edwin Arlington Robinson. CP-RobiE

When he, who is the unforgiven. Unforgiven, The. Edwin Arlington Robinson. CP-RobiE

When he who owns a house has come to thee. Removal, The. Jones Very. CP-VeryJ

When He Would Have His Verses Read. Robert Herrick. CP-HerrR

When heat leaves the walls at last. Adrienne Rich. SP-RicA1 *Fr.* Darklight.

When heaven confirmed your brilliance, most of all. Michelangelo Buonarroti. CP-Miche, *tr. by* John Frederick Nims

When heavy, threatening skies weigh like a lid. Black Bile ("When heavy, threatening skies weigh like a lid"). Charles Baudelaire. CP-BaudC, *tr. by* Walter Martin

When he'd exhaust everything around him and inside himself. One Word. Yannis Ritsos. SP-RitsY, *tr. by* Kostas Myrsiades

When Helen Lived. William Butler Yeats. CP-YeatW

When her grave opened its ugly mouth. Error, The. Ted Hughes. SP-HughTN

When hermits hide from society. Han-shan. CP-ColdM, *tr. by* Red Pine

When he's returned I'll tell him——oh. A. J. J. A. E. Housman. CP-HousA

When hides the sun behind the hills. Stock-Gilly Flowers, The. Jones Very. CP-VeryJ

When his boat snapped loose. Long Boat, The. Stanley Kunitz. CP-KunSC

When His Excellency Prince Norodom Chantaraingsey. Dead Soldiers. James Fenton. SP-FentJ

When his hour for death had come. Osceola. Walt Whitman. CP-WhitW

When his machine was running right. Jack-Off of the Graveyard Shift, The. Alan Dugan. CP-DugaA

When his mother called for the second time. Where the Groceries Went. Raymond Carver. CP-CarvR

When his small skiff returned alone. Portrait of the Man Who Drowned Wearing

His Best Suit and Shoes. Thomas Lux. SP-LuxT

When home was a courthouse. Fanny Howe. SP-HoweF *Fr.* Vineyard, The.

When Hope but made Tranquillity be felt. Hope and Tranquillity. Samuel Taylor Coleridge. CP-ColeS

When hope was flourishing. Petrarch. CP-Petra, *tr. by* J. G. Nichols

When Horse and Rider each can trust the other everywhere. Together. Rudyard Kipling. CP-KiplR

When Howitzers Began. Hayden Carruth. CP-CarHS

When human beings found out about death. Dog Was Crying Tonight in Wicklow Also, A. Seamus Heaney. SP-HeanSO

When human curses reach angelic ears. Saint Peter's Denial. Charles Baudelaire. CP-BaudC, *tr. by* Walter Martin

When human touch (as monkish books attest). St Catherine of Ledbury. William Wordsworth. CP-WorW2

When I a ship see on the Seas. Way, The. Robert Herrick. CP-HerrR

When I a verse shall make. His Prayer to Ben Jonson. Robert Herrick. CP-HerrR

When I a winsome babe did creep. Pappy Wants a Poppy. Ogden Nash. CP-NashO

When I Am a Cup. "H. D." CP-DoolH

When I am alone I am happy. Waiting. William Carlos Williams. CP-WilW1

When I am clothed I am a moral man. Moral Clothing. D. H. Lawrence. CP-LawrD

When I am covered with the dust of peace. Ivor Gurney. SP-GurnI

When I am dead, and Doctors know not why. Damp[e], The. John Donne. CP-DonnJ; MW-DonnJ

When I am dead, even then. Then. Muriel Rukeyser. CP-RukeM

When I am dead, it will not be. Two Thoughts of Death. Countee Cullen. CP-CullC

When I am dead, my dearest. Song: "When I am dead, my dearest." Christina Georgina Rossetti. CP-RosC1

When I Am Dead, My Dearest. Miller Williams. CP-WillM

When I am feeling depressed and anxious sullen. Poem: "When I am feeling depressed and anxious sullen." Frank O'Hara. SP-OharF

When I am gone. Ute Mountain. Charles Tomlinson. CP-TomlC; SP-TomlC

When i am in boston,i do not speak. E. E. Cummings. CP-CummE

When I am in hell or some such place. One Ralph Blossom Soliloquizes. Thomas Hardy. CP-HardT

When I am not dead I. John Ciardi. CP-CiarJ

When I am old. One of These Days. Lawrence Ferlinghetti. SP-FerlL

When I am old. Therefore. Grace Paley. CP-PalGC

When I am old, and comforted. Afternoon. Dorothy Parker. CP-ParkD

When I am old / I will not have you look apart. In Tempore Senectutis ("When I am old / I will not have you look apart"). Ezra Pound. CP-PoEar

When I am riding round the ring no longer. Circus-Rider to Ringmaster. Thomas Hardy. CP-HardT

When I am sick and tired it is God's will. Who Have a Form of Godliness. Christina Georgina Rossetti. CP-RosC3

When I am the sky. Cancion: "When I am the sky." Denise Levertov. SP-LeveDL

When I am with you, we stay up all night. Jelaluddin Rumi. SP-Rumi, *tr. by* Coleman Barks

When I asked the very old man. Quotations. George Oppen. CP-OppGN

When I attain to utter forth in verse. Insufficiency. Elizabeth Barrett Browning. CP-BroEB

When I attained enlightenment. Testimony of J. Robert Oppenheimer, The. Ai. SP-Ai

When I awoke on the morning. On Reaching the Age of Two Hundred. Donald Hall. CP-HallD

When I awoke, the glancing day looked gay. Promisers, The. Wilfred Owen. CP-OwenW

When I awoke with cold. Coffee. James Vincent Cunningham. CP-CunnJ

When I banged my head on the door, I screamed. Yehuda Amichai. SP-AmicY, *tr. by* Chana Bloch

When I become the land, when they will build. One Forever Alien. Howard Nemerov. CP-NemeH

When I began to grow old I searched out the Land. What About It? Philip Whalen. SP-WhalP

When I begin to send out sighs and call. Petrarch. CP-Petra, *tr. by* J. G. Nichols

When I beheld the Poet blind, yet bold. On Mr Milton's "Paradise Lost." Andrew Marvell. CP-MarvA

When I behold a forrest spread. Art above Nature, to Julia. Robert Herrick. CP-HerrR

When I behold, by warrant from thy pen. To My Friend, Will. Davenant. Thomas Carew. CP-CareT

When I behold how black, immortal ink. Silet. Ezra Pound. CP-PoEar

When I behold that beauties wonderment. Sonnet 24. Edmund Spenser. CP-Spens *Fr.* Amoretti.

When I behold Thee, almost slain. His Anthem, to Christ on the Crosse. Robert Herrick. CP-HerrR

When I but think upon the great dead days. Piere Vidal Old. Ezra Pound. CP-PoEar

When I Buy Pictures. Marianne Craig Moore. CP-MoorM

When I Came Back. Bogomil Gjuzel. CP-KizeC, *tr.* by Carolyn Kizer

When I came back from my last dream, when I. Alarm, The. James Wright. CP-WrigJ

When I Came Back to Fleet Street. G. K. Chesterton. CP-ChesG

When I came down from the sky above Palmyra. Winter Light. Eugenio Montale. CP-MontE, *tr.* by Jonathan Galassi

When I came from my mother's womb. Mars. Howard Nemerov. CP-NemeH

When I came into pleasure's house. And I Reclined and Lay on Their Beds. Constantine P. Cavafy. CP-CavaC, *tr.* by Theoharis Constantine Theoharis

When I came last to Ludlow. Friends. A. E. Housman. CP-HousA

When I came up to bed all. You Were Asleep. James Laughlin. CP-LaugJ

When I can hold a stone within my hand. Rumination. Richard Eberhart. CP-EberR

When I can't bear to watch birds play. Han-shan. CP-ColdM, *tr.* by Red Pine

When I carefully consider the curious habits of dogs. Meditatio. Ezra Pound. SP-PounE

When I carry my little son in the cold. Poem: "When I carry my little son in the cold." Thomas McGrath. SP-McGrT

When I come back I find. After a Storm. W. S. Merwin. SP-MerwWF

When I come home in the city and see the young roaches. Standing Nowhere. W. S. Merwin. SP-MerwWF

When I come in f'om de c'on-fiel' aftah wo'kin ha'd all day. At Candle-Lightin' Time. Paul Laurence Dunbar. CP-DunbP

When I come near the red peony flower. At the Time of Peony Blossoming. Robert Bly. SP-BlyR

When I consider. Milton Über Alles. Robert Creeley. SP-CreeR

When I consider (Dearest) thou dost stay. To His Kinswoman, Mistresse Susanna Herrick. Robert Herrick. CP-HerrR

When I consider how my life is spent. Reminiscent Reflection. Ogden Nash. CP-NashO

When I consider men of golden talents. So That's Who I Remind Me Of. Ogden Nash. CP-NashO

When I consider mighty nations' fate. Reflections on the History of Nations. Jones Very. CP-VeryJ

When I consider, pro and con. Searched Soul, The. Dorothy Parker. CP-ParkD

When I consider the children of the middle class. World as Will and Representation, The. Hayden Carruth. CP-CarHS

When I considered it too closely, when I wore it like an element and smelt it like water. Meditation on Saviors. Robinson Jeffers. CP-JefR1

When I count the seeds. Emily Dickinson. CP-DickE

When I departed am, ring thou my knell. To the Nightingale, and Robin-Red-Brest. Robert Herrick. CP-HerrR

When I did goe from thee, I felt that smart. His Parting from Mistress Dorothy Keneday. Robert Herrick. CP-HerrR

When I die choose a star. For My Daughter. David Ignatow. SP-IgnaD

When I die, I will see the lining of the world. Meaning. Czeslaw Milosz. CP-MiloCN, *tr.* by Robert Hass

When I die, oh lay me low. Sir Eustace Grey. Christina Georgina Rossetti. CP-RosC3

When I died, love, when I died. Western Ballad, A. Allen Ginsberg. CP-GinsA; SP-GinsA

When I died [*or* dyed] last, and, dear[e], I die [*or* dye]. Legacy [*or* Legacie], The. John Donne. CP-DonnJ; MW-DonnJ

When I died the devils tortured me with icepicks and pliers. Against France: On the Algerian Pleasures of Entity. Alan Dugan. CP-DugaA

When I do mock the blackness of the night. James Whitcomb Riley. CP-RileJ

When I don't know, don't know. Paul Celan. SP-CelaP, *tr.* by John Felstiner

When I dream that you love me, you'll surely forgive. To M.S.G. Lord Byron. CP-Byron

When I drink. Contagion. James Tate. SP-TateJ

When I drive, every bridge is. Together Again. William Stafford. SP-StafWW

When I drop four cubes of ice. Sympathy in White Major. Philip Larkin. CP-LarkP

When I entertained evil. Evil. Richard Eberhart. CP-EberR

When I face north a lost Cree. Returned to Say. William Stafford. SP-StafW; SP-StafWW

When I first reached this country. Thoughts from Underground. Margaret Atwood. SP-AtwM1

When I first saw her. Gregory Orr. SP-OrrG

When I first started out to make what later became known as Hayden's Runaway. Underground the Darkness Is the Light. Hayden Carruth. CP-CarHS

When I flew into Russia I said to my friend. Willkie: Words from Russia. Muriel Rukeyser. CP-RukeM

When I get to be a colored composer. Langston Hughes. *See* When I get to be a composer

When I get to be a composer. Daybreak in Alabama. Langston Hughes. CP-HughL; CP-HughL2; CP-HughL3

When I get up he has been long at work. Willingly. Tess Gallagher. SP-GallT

When I go back of my head. Landscape with Figures. A. R. Ammons. CP-AmmoA

When I go free. Little Salamander, The. Walter De la Mare. CP-DeLaW

When I go home, the old are older. My Home Town. Tu Fu. CP-KizeC, *tr.* by Carolyn Kizer

When I go up through the mowing field. Late Walk, A. Robert Frost. CP-FrosR

When I go West you wear a marshal's star. Cops and Robbers. Donald Hall. CP-HallD

When I goe Hence ye Closet-Gods, I feare. To His Closet-Gods. Robert Herrick. CP-HerrR

When I got past relevance. Bourn. A. R. Ammons. CP-AmmoA

When I got word of the calamity, that Myris was dead. Myris: Alexandria, 340 A.D. Constantine P. Cavafy. CP-CavaC, *tr.* by Theoharis Constantine Theoharis

When I had been born eight years I was born again. And When in Scenes of Glory. Miller Williams. CP-WillM

When I had read your holy *Meditations*. To Mrs Alice Sutcliffe, on Her Divine *Meditations*. Ben Jonson. CP-JonsB

When I had spread it all on linen cloth. Wife's Tale, The. Seamus Heaney. SP-HeanSO

When I have a stomachache, I feel like. Yehuda Amichai. SP-AmicY, *tr.* by Chana Bloch

When I have borne in memory what has tamed. William Wordsworth. CP-WorW1; MW-WorW

When I Have Fears [That I May Cease to Be]. John Keats. CP-KeatJ

When I have seen the Sun emerge. Emily Dickinson. CP-DickE

When I have stared for some time fixedly. Petrarch. CP-Petra, *tr.* by J. G. Nichols

When I have struggled through three hundred years. Ballad of the Scholar's Lament. E. E. Cummings. CP-CummE

When i have thought of you somewhat too. E. E. Cummings. CP-CummE

When I hear a man spouting about humility, today. Humility Mongers. D. H. Lawrence. CP-LawrD

When I hear somebody complain of being lonely. Lonely, Lonesome, Loney—O! D. H. Lawrence. CP-LawrD

When I hear you attractively speak out. Petrarch. CP-Petra, *tr.* by J. G. Nichols

When I hear you express an affection so warm. To Caroline. Lord Byron. CP-Byron

When I Heard At The Close Of The Day. Walt Whitman. CP-WhitW

When I heard Monica's. Cider 5¢ A Glass. Donald Hall. CP-HallD

When I heard the call of the osprey. Ospreys in Cry. Richard Eberhart. CP-EberR

When I Heard the Learn'd Astronomer. Walt Whitman. CP-WhitW

When I hoked there, I would find Terminus. Seamus Heaney. SP-HeanSO

When I hoped I feared. Emily Dickinson. CP-DickE

When I hoped, I recollect. Emily Dickinson. CP-DickE

When I hug you, you are light as a grasshopper. For Jeriann's Hands. Marge Piercy. SP-PierM

When I know what people think of me. End, The. Robert Creeley. CP-CreeR

When I landed in the republic of conscience. From the Republic of Conscience. Seamus Heaney. SP-HeanSO

When I last wrote / I was so hung up with old guilt. Letter to a Young Father in Exile. John Logan. CP-LogaJ

When I left Rome for Lalage's sake. Rimini. Rudyard Kipling. CP-KiplR *Fr.* Puck of Pook's Hill.

When I lie down to love. Old Dwarf Heart. Anne Sexton. CP-SextA; SP-SextA

When I lie down to sleep dream the Wishing Well it rings. I Am a Victim of Telephone. Allen Ginsberg. CP-GinsA; SP-GinsA

When I lie on the ground. Antaeus. Seamus Heaney. SP-HeanSO

When I lie where shades of darkness. Fare Well. Walter De la Mare. CP-DeLaW

When I look back and see how the swift years. Petrarch. CP-Petra, *tr.* by J. G. Nichols

When I look for you everything falls silent. Search, The. W. S. Merwin. SP-MerwW

When I look forth at dawning, pool. Nature's Questioning. Thomas Hardy. CP-HardT

When I looked at the tree the bough was still shaking. Tree, The. Randall Jarrell. CP-JarrR

When I looked out the win- / dow I thought it had snowed. Snow in May. James Laughlin. CP-LaugJ

When I looked up at my love-birds. Her Love-Birds. Thomas Hardy. CP-HardT

When I lose my center. Decipherings. Denise Levertov. SP-LeveDS

When I love, (as some have told). Hymne to the Graces, A. Robert Herrick. CP-HerrR

When I made answer, I began: 'Alas!'. Francesca da Rimini. Dante Alighieri. CW-RossD *Fr.* Divina Commedia.

When I meet the morning beam. Immortal Part, The. A. E. Housman. CP-HousA

When I meet the skier she is always. Transit. Adrienne Rich. SP-RicA1; SP-RicA2

When I Met My Muse. William Stafford. SP-StafWW

When I move / Into a neighborhood. Restrictive Covenants. Langston Hughes. CP-HughL; CP-HughL2

When I must come to you, O my God, I pray. Prayer to Go to Paradise with the Donkeys, A. Francis Jammes. CP-WilbR, *tr.* by Richard Wilbur

When I no longer have your heart. Walker. Alice Walker. CP-WalkA

When I of Villars doe but heare the name. To the Lady Mary Villars, Governesse to the Princesse Henretta. Robert Herrick. CP-HerrR

When I opened your book. Double Rainbow, The. Charles Tomlinson. CP-TomlC

When I pass'd through a populous city. Throughout Our Lands. Czeslaw Milosz. CP-MiloC; CP-MiloCN, *tr.* by Peter Dale Scott

When I peered out, he had nine nights to spare. Drugs Alcohol Little Sister. John Berryman. CP-BerrJ

When I Peruse the Conquer'd Fame. Walt Whitman. CP-WhitW

When I play on my fiddle in Dooney. Fiddler of Dooney, The. William Butler Yeats. CP-YeatW

When I ponder lovely ladies. Rhyme of an Involuntary Violet. Dorothy Parker. CP-ParkD

When I press my hand to my chest. Dove in the Eaves, A. Jelaluddin Rumi. SP-Rumi, *tr.* by Coleman Barks

When I put her out, once, by the garbage pail. Geranium, The. Theodore Roethke. CP-RoetT

When I reached his place. It Was All Very Tidy. Robert Graves. CP-GravR

When I reached the sea. Identities. Paul Muldoon. CP-MuldP

When I Read John Wieners's Selected Poems. William Corbett. SP-CorbW

When I read poems to the art students. Marilyn Hacker. SP-HackM *Fr.* Taking Notice.

When I Read Shakespeare. D. H. Lawrence. CP-LawrD

When I Read the Book. Walt Whitman. CP-WhitW

When I remember bygone days. Middle, The. Ogden Nash. CP-NashO

When I remember, friend, whom lost I call. To a Friend Lost. George Meredith. CP-MerG1

When I remember that letter of Pliny's. Pliny—9, 36—Lampridius—29. Kenneth Rexroth. CP-RexrK

When I remember your love. Jelaluddin Rumi. SP-Rumi, *tr.* by Coleman Barks

When I returned from lovers' lane. Kimono, The. James Merrill. SP-MerrJ

When I returned from you in the blue of midnight. Cézanne. John Ciardi. CP-CiarJ

When I Returned They Told Me There's No. Yehuda Amichai. SP-AmicYL, *tr.* by Benjamin Harshav *and* Barbara Harshav

When I returned with drinks and nuts my friend. Friend of the Fourth Decade, The. James Merrill. SP-MerrJ

When I rolled three 7's. Situation. Langston Hughes. CP-HughL; CP-HughL3

When I Roved a Young Highlander. Lord Byron. CP-Byron

When I saw. William Carlos Williams. CP-WilW1 *Fr.* Paterson.

When I saw her straying a little dazed through her untidy house. Spanish Wife, The. D. H. Lawrence. CP-LawrD

When I saw how man's spirit against his night. Prometheus Passes the Toast. Robert Stock. SP-StocR

When I saw that clumsy crow. Night Crow. Theodore Roethke. CP-RoetT

When I saw the fox, it was kneeling. Fox, The. Charles Tomlinson. CP-TomlC

When I search the past for you. Heloise. Ted Berrigan. SP-BerrT

When I see a cockroach. Cockroach. Charles Simic. SP-SimiCE

When I see a couple of kids. High Windows. Philip Larkin. CP-LarkP

When I see a Rubens Rembrandt [or] Correggio. William Blake. CP-BlakW

When I see a young tree. My Lady Is Compared to a Young Tree. Nicholas Vachel Lindsay. CP-LindV

When I see birches bend to left and right. Birches. Robert Frost. CP-FrosR

When I see fish swimming in schools. With Others. David Ignatow. SP-IgnaD

When I see the great cities. City-Life. D. H. Lawrence. CP-LawrD

When I see the ignoble procession. Ignoble Procession, The. D. H. Lawrence. CP-LawrD

When I see the room it hurts me. Musical Incident, A. Thomas Hardy. CP-HardT

When I see thee as some poor song-bird. Scriptor Ignotus. Ezra Pound. CP-PoEar

When I see you and how you are. Wax. Jelaluddin Rumi. SP-Rumi, *tr.* by Coleman Barks

When I see you in the first light, again. Mirror, The. Robert Creeley. CP-CreeR

When I see your face, the stones start spinning! Great Wagon, A. Jelaluddin Rumi. SP-Rumi, *tr.* by Coleman Barks

When I see your picture in its frame. As If You Had Never Been. Richard Eberhart. CP-EberR

When I Set Fire to the Reed Patch. A. R. Ammons. CP-AmmoA

When I Set Out for Lyonnesse. Thomas Hardy. CP-HardT

When I shall marry, if I do not find. Married Woman, A. Thomas Carew. CP-CareT

When I shall sin, pardon my trespasse here. Gods Pardon. Robert Herrick. CP-HerrR

When I sit before a paper. After All, What Else Is There to Say? Allen Ginsberg. CP-GinsA

When I sold my fake Vermeers to Goering. Forger, The. Derek Mahon. CP-MahoD

When I spread out my hand here today. Sitting by a Bush in Broad Sunlight. Robert Frost. CP-FrosR

When I stand in the center of that man's madness. Reflection by a Mailbox. Stanley Kunitz. CP-KunSC

When I studied my A-B-C's. Kids in School with Me, The. Langston Hughes. CP-HughL

When I suspect I'm a character in a novel. Learning to Read. Miller Williams. CP-WillM

When I take your hand. Sometimes. Thomas McGrath. SP-McGrT

When I Think about Myself. Maya Angelou. SP-AngeM

When I think of all the centuries long dead. Wallace Stevens. CP-StevWP

When I think of death. Bop Lyrics. Allen Ginsberg. CP-GinsA

When I think of him, midnight. One Soldier. Muriel Rukeyser. CP-RukeM

When I think of how the light touches him. Photograph and Pearls. Tennessee Williams. CP-WillT

When I Think of Myself Dead. Charles Bukowski. SP-BukC1

When I think of the liberation of Palestine. Israel. Karl Shapiro. SP-ShapK

When I think of the little children learning. Cairn, The. Edna St. Vincent Millay. CP-MillE

When I think of you. Christmas Syllabics for a Wife. Donald Davie. CP-DaviDC

When I through all my many poems look. To the Most Virtuous Mistress Pot, Who Many Times Entertained Him. Robert Herrick. CP-HerrR

When I throw back my head and howl. Life with a Hole in It, The. Philip Larkin. CP-LarkP

When I thy parts runne o're, I can't espie. To Perenna. Robert Herrick. CP-HerrR

When I thy singing next shall heare. Againe. Robert Herrick. CP-HerrR

When I too long have looked upon your face. Edna St. Vincent Millay. CP-MillE

When I took a job teaching in Massachusetts. To the Governor & Legislature of Massachusetts. Howard Nemerov. CP-NemeH

When I turn my head in the afternoon. Coming Back in the Spring. W. S. Merwin. SP-MerwWF

When I wake, I hear sheep eating apple peels just. Walking Swiftly. Robert Bly. SP-BlyR

When I wake next. Places ("When I wake next"). Robert Creeley. CP-CreeR

When I wake up. Remote House. Hans Magnus Enzensberger. SP-EnzeH, *tr.* by Michael Hamburger

When I walked my nazi girlfriend. Memories of 1936–7. Alan Dugan. CP-DugaA

When I walked roseless tracks and wide. Before Knowledge. Thomas Hardy. CP-HardT

When I want to tell of the laughing throne. Old Flag. W. S. Merwin. SP-MerwW

When I was a boy, a relative. Way to Make a Living, A. James Wright. CP-WrigJ

When I was a boy and a man would die. June Twenty, *Three Days After.* Miller Williams. CP-WillM

When I was a boy here. Horses. Wendell Berry. CP-BerrW

When I was a boy I saw the world I was in. Old-Time Childhood in Kentucky. Robert Penn Warren. CP-WarrR

When I was a boy, I used to go to bed. Remorse for Time, The. Howard Nemerov. CP-NemeH

When I was a callant, born far hence. Inkidoo and the Queen of Babel. Robert Graves. CP-GravR

When I Was a Child. Yehuda Amichai. SP-AmicY, *tr.* by Stephen Mitchell

When I was a child. Autobiographia Literaria. Frank O'Hara. SP-OharF

When I was a child. Witch's Life, The. Anne Sexton. SP-SextA

When I was a child, I came to worship tigers with a passion. Dreamtigers. Jorge Luis Borges. SP-BorgJ, *tr.* by Alastair Reid

When I was a child, I thought. Best Society. Philip Larkin. CP-LarkP

When I was a chile we used to play. Children's Rhymes ("When I was a chile we used to play"). Langston Hughes. CP-HughL; CP-HughL3

When I was a girl in Los Angeles we'd go gleaning. Gleaning. Randall Jarrell. CP-JarrR

When I was a kid. Train Going By. Robert Creeley. SP-CreeR

When I was a King and a Mason—a Master proven and skilled. Palace, The. Rudyard Kipling. CP-KiplR

When I was a little boy, long ago. Little Man in the Tin-Shop, The. James Whitcomb Riley. CP-RileJ

When I was a mailman. Famous Writer, The. Charles Bukowski. SP-BukC3

When I was a windy boy and a bit. Lament: "When I was a windy boy and a bit." Dylan Thomas. CP-ThomD

When I was about eight, I once stabbed somebody, another kid, a little girl. Blades. C. K. Williams. CP-WillC; SP-WillC

When I was about ten. Making Beasts. Gregory Orr. SP-OrrG

When I was alive—only glimpses. Gregory Orr. SP-OrrG

When I Was Asked How I Could Leave Vermont in the Middle of October. Grace Paley. CP-PalGC

When I was bold, when I was bold. Liebestod. Dorothy Parker. CP-ParkD

When I was born. Day's Ration, The. Ralph Waldo Emerson. CP-EmerR

When I was born I saw. Saving Just the Real. Clarence Major. SP-MajoC

When I was born, my mother taped my ears. Youth's Progress. John Updike. CP-UpdiJ

When I was born, one of the crooked. Seven-Sided Poem. Carlos Drummond de Andrade. CP-BishE, tr. by Elizabeth Bishop

When I was born the row began. Birthright. Louis MacNeice. CP-MacNL

When I was but a boy. Epstein, Spare That Yule Log! Ogden Nash. CP-NashO

When I was but a little thing of two, or maybe three. Grandfather Said It. Dorothy Parker. CP-ParkD

When I was changed from a feeble cosmopolite. Serpent. Robert Lowell. SP-LoweR

When I was dangerous tracers leaped from me. Two Songs for a Gunner. John Ciardi. CP-CiarJ

When I was dead, my spirit turned. At Home. Christina Georgina Rossetti. CP-RosC1

When I Was Drunk and Disorderly the Boston Policeman Told Me. Alan Dugan. CP-DugaA

When I was employed at Cooperative Fashions, In spite of the. Hell is Graduated. Max Jacob. CP-BishE

When I was first born. Let Me Be. Philip Levine. SP-LeviP

When I was five and said I'd seen an angel. Cousins, Brothers, Sisters. Wyatt Prunty. SP-PrunW

When I was four my father went to Scotland. Truth, The. Randall Jarrell. CP-JarrR

When I was home de. Po' Boy Blues. Langston Hughes. CP-HughL; CP-HughL1

When I Was Home Last Christmas. Randall Jarrell. CP-JarrR

When I Was in Trouble I Called upon the Lord. Christina Georgina Rossetti. CP-RosC2

When I was ist a Brownie—a weenty-teenty Brownie. Bee-Bag, The. James Whitcomb Riley. CP-RileJ

When I was just a youngster. Your Lead, Partner, I Hope We've Read the Same Book. Ogden Nash. CP-NashO

When I was just as far as I could walk. Telephone, The. Robert Frost. CP-FrosR

When I was known as Aphrodite, men. Milady Reflects. John Updike. CP-UpdiJ

When I was little and had. Sweet Kiss, A. James Laughlin. CP-LaugJ

When I was little, when. Poplar's Shadow, The. May Swenson. SP-SwenM

When I was nine years old, in 1889. John L. Sullivan, the Strong Boy of Boston. Nicholas Vachel Lindsay. CP-LindV

When I was one-and-twenty. A. E. Housman. CP-HousA

When I was past such thinking / you came as a song when I had. You Came as a Thought. James Laughlin. CP-LaugJ

When I was Saul, and sat among the cloaks. St. Paul. Thomas Merton. CP-MertT

When I was seventeen or so. Eheu! Fugaces, or, What a Difference a Lot of Days Make. Ogden Nash. CP-NashO

When I was sleeping this morning one of my feet. Last, The. C. K. Williams. CP-WillC

When I was small, a Woman died. Emily Dickinson. CP-DickE

When I was small and stayed quiet. Animals from Mountains. W. S. Merwin. SP-MerwW

When I was told, as Delta children were. Ruby Tells All. Miller Williams. CP-WillM

When I was young and bold and strong. Veteran, The. Dorothy Parker. CP-ParkD

When I was young and full of faith. Hesitating Veteran, The. Ambrose Bierce. SP-BierA

When I was young and full of shame. Sisyphus. Maxine W. Kumin. SP-KumiM

When I was young and returning from. Atlantic City 1939. Maxine W. Kumin. SP-KumiM

When I was young I believed in intellectual conversation. In the Men's Room(s). Marge Piercy. SP-PierM

When I was young / I fell in love. Two Poems about Nothing. Gregory Orr. SP-OrrG

When I was young I longed for Love. Vengeance is Sweet. Paul Laurence Dunbar. CP-DunbP

When I was young I looked high and low for a father. For His Father. William Meredith. SP-MereW

When I was young I often heard. Go to the Wall. Christopher Logue. SP-LoguC Fr. Lily-White Boys, The.

When I was young, I used to. Men. Maya Angelou. SP-AngeM

When I was young in school in Switzerland, about the time of the Boer. End of the World. Robinson Jeffers. CP-JefR3

When I was young, just starting at our game. To My Least Favorite Reviewer. Howard Nemerov. CP-NemeH

When I was young my teachers were the old. What Fifty Said. Robert Frost. CP-FrosR

When I was young, the country was young too. My father. Yehuda Amichai. SP-AmicYL, tr. by Benjamin Harshav and Barbara Harshav

When I was young, the whole country was young. And my father. Yehuda Amichai. SP-AmicY, tr. by Chana Bloch

When I was young the world was fair. Macrobian. Ambrose Bierce. SP-BierA

When I was young, we dwelt in a vale. In a Vale. Robert Frost. CP-FrosR

When I was young with mysteries. Solitude Calls the Man. G. K. Chesterton. CP-ChesG

When I was younger. Pastoral: "When I was younger." William Carlos Williams. CP-WilW1

When I Watch the Living Meet. A. E. Housman. CP-HousA

When I weekly knew. Quid Hic Agis? Thomas Hardy. CP-HardT

When I went inside, the manager said, "You don't want to live here, kid." Hotel St. Louis, New York City, Fall 1969. Gregory Orr. SP-OrrG

When I went into my room, at mid-morning. Man and Bat. D. H. Lawrence. CP-LawrD

When I went out to kill myself, I caught. Saint Judas. James Wright. CP-WrigJ

When I went there first. Three Steps to the Graveyard. James Wright. CP-WrigJ

When I Went to the Circus. D. H. Lawrence. CP-LawrD

When I Went to the Film. D. H. Lawrence. CP-LawrD

When I went to the scientific doctor. Scientific Doctor, The. D. H. Lawrence. CP-LawrD

When I went to Zuni. Three A.M., in Winter. Arthur Sze. SP-SzeA

When I wish I was rich, then I know I am ill. Riches. D. H. Lawrence. CP-LawrD

When I woke. Dylan Thomas. CP-ThomD

When I woke, the lake-lights were quivering on the wall. Coming Awake. D. H. Lawrence. CP-LawrD

When I woke up this morning. Lost Love, The. Randall Jarrell. CP-JarrR

When I woke up to the snow. Kathleen Jessie Raine. SP-RainK

When I woke up with my head in the fireplace. Untitled Poem in Two Parts. Alan Dugan. CP-DugaA

When I would image her features. George Meredith. CP-MerG1

When I would know thee Goodyere, my thought looks. To the Same [Sir Henry Goodyere]. Ben Jonson. CP-JonsB; SP-JonsB

When I would muse in boyhood. A. E. Housman. CP-HousA

When I would sing of crooked streams and fields. Song, The. Jones Very. CP-VeryJ

When I write poems, I need to be near grass that no one else sees. Grass from Two Years. Robert Bly. SP-BlyR

When I Wrote a Little. Hayden Carruth. CP-CarHS

When I wrote of the women in their dances and wildness. Poem as Mask, The. Muriel Rukeyser. CP-RukeM

When I wrote the abstract of Heaven. Evaluation Under a Pine Tree, Lying On Pine Needles, An. Richard Eberhart. CP-EberR

When I wuz ist a little bit o' weenty-teenty kid. Impromptu Fairy-Tale, An. James Whitcomb Riley. CP-RileJ

When I'd win the fight. Happiness. Yusef Komunyakaa. SP-KomuY

When if ever life is sweet. St. Elizabeth of Hungary. Christina Georgina Rossetti. CP-RosC3

When I'm by myself / your ten years stay with me. Little Stanton. Federico García Lorca. CP-GarcF, tr. by Greg Simon and Steven F. White

When I'm Missing You. James Laughlin. CP-LaugJ

When in eternity the light. Hafiz. CP-EmerR Fr. Odes.

When in from Delos came the gold. White Lights, The. Edwin Arlington Robinson. CP-RobiE

When in our blithest youth we sing. Youth and Age. James Whitcomb Riley. CP-RileJ

When in Rome—Apologia. Yusef Komunyakaa. CP-KomuY

When in some cove I lie. Henry David Thoreau. CP-ThorH

When in still air and still in summertime. Threshold. Howard Nemerov. CP-NemeH

When in that gold. Listening to Foxhounds. James Dickey. CP-DickJ

When in the Antique age of bow and spear. On the Same Occasion [on Seeing the Foundation Preparing for the Erection of Rydal Chapel]. William Wordsworth. CP-WorW2

When in the brazen leaves of Fame. On the Duke of Buckingham. Thomas Carew. CP-CareT

When in the Course of Human Events. Kenneth Patchen. CP-PatcK

When, in the dark, the frost cracks on the window. Winter's Night, The. Thomas Merton. CP-MertT

When, in the darkness of his dream. Legendary Progress. Thomas McGrath. SP-McGrT

When in the evening, she returned from the riverbank to the seafaring town. At Nausicä's House. Yannis Ritsos. SP-RitsY, *tr.* by Kimon Friar

When in the history books. Jaroslav Seifert. SP-SeifJ, *tr.* by Ewald Osers

When in the mask of night there shone that cut. Landing on the Moon. May Swenson. SP-SwenM

When in the Soul of the Serene Disciple. Thomas Merton. CP-MertT

When in the widening circle of rebirth. Fernando Pessoa. SP-PessF *Fr.* 35 Sonnets.

When in their ignorance and haste the skies must fall. Spring Storm. Thomas Merton. CP-MertT

When in thy breast the virtues all reside. To a Friend Who Had Persuaded Emelia to Marry, an Ode. Annis Boudinot Stockton. CP-StocA

When in your middle years. Lights in the Sky are Stars, The. Kenneth Rexroth. CP-RexrK

When infant voices lisp thy honourd name. To General Washington, An Epistle. Annis Boudinot Stockton. CP-StocA

When into the night the yellow light is roused like dust above the towns. Piccadilly Circus at Night. D. H. Lawrence. CP-LawrD

When is a man not a man? Gentleman, The. D. H. Lawrence. CP-LawrD

When Israel Came Out of Egypt. Arthur Hugh Clough. SP-ClouA

When Israel, of the Lord beloved [*or* belov'd]. Rebecca's Hymn. Sir Walter Scott. SP-ScotW *Fr.* Ivanhoe.

When Israel out of Egypt came. A. E. Housman. CP-HousA

When Israel's Daughters mourn'd their past Offences. Epigram in a Maid of Honour's Prayer-Book. Alexander Pope. CP-PopeA

When Israel's ruler on the royal bed. Hymn to the Supreme Being. Christopher Smart. SP-SmarC

When it comes down to it. Reckless Head. Ted Hughes. SP-HughTN

When it comes down turning. Snow. Adrienne Rich. CP-RicAE

When it comes to sentiment, as it will, you can't compete. Differences, The. Andrei Codrescu. SP-CodrA

When it dawned, the silence was heavy amidst the smoking ruins. After the Fire. Yannis Ritsos. SP-RitsY, *tr.* by Minas Savvas

When It Happens. A. K. Ramanujan. CP-RamaA

When it is cold it stinks, and not till then. Samuel Beckett's Dublin. Donald Davie. CP-DaviDC

When it is finally ours, this freedom, this liberty, this beautiful. Frederick Douglass. Robert Earl Hayden. CP-HaydR

When it is not yet day. Looking for Mushrooms at Sunrise. W. S. Merwin. SP-MerwW

When It Is Over. Edna St. Vincent Millay. CP-MillE

When it is sensation time at the home. Song: Sensation Time at the Home, A. Thomas Merton. CP-MertT

When it is spring, / When the huge bulls roam in their pens. Spring: Monastery Farm. Thomas Merton. CP-MertT

When it rains, and with the rain. James Whitcomb Riley. CP-RileJ

When it was day, we heard the panes of windows. Song, A: "When it was day, we heard the panes of windows." Thomas Merton. CP-MertT

When it was found a fault. Scythian Charioteers, The. Donald Davie. CP-DaviDC

When it's Christmas we're all of us magi. December 24, 1971. Joseph Brodsky. CP-BrodJ, *tr.* by Alan Myers

When it's cold and raining. Freshness, The. Jelaluddin Rumi. SP-Rumi, *tr.* by Coleman Barks

"When it's *got* to be,"—like I always say. It's *Got* to Be. James Whitcomb Riley. CP-RileJ

When it's night, and no light, too. In the Night. James Whitcomb Riley. CP-RileJ

When it's your own pain, you notice it. Hunger. William Stafford. SP-StafWW

When I've made a million dollars—it may take a year or two. And Oblige. Dorothy Parker. CP-ParkD

When Jacob rolled the stone off the well. Biblical Meditations. Yehuda Amichai. SP-AmicYL, *tr.* by Benjamin Harshav *and* Barbara Harshav

When Jane was absent Edgar's eye. Ralph Waldo Emerson. CP-EmerR

When Januar' wind war blawing cauld. Lass That Made the Bed for Me, The. Robert Burns. CP-BurnR

When jessie's fever went up god got farther away so he could see better. Next to the Last Poem about God, The. C. K. Williams. CP-WillC

When Jesus commanded us to love our neighbor. Commandments. D. H. Lawrence. CP-LawrD

When Jesus died at Calvary. Ballad of the Two Thieves. Langston Hughes. CP-HughL; CP-HughL3

When Jesus' friend had ceased to be. Weeping Saviour, The. Elizabeth Barrett Browning. CP-BroEB

When Jesus got my broken back for Christmas, Juniors. Carol, A: "When Jesus got my broken back for Christmas, Juniors." Thomas Merton. CP-MertT

When Jesus walked into the wilderness. Jesus Walking. Anne Sexton. CP-SextA

When Jill complain[e]s to Jack for want of meat[e]. Upon Jack and Jill: Epigram. Robert Herrick. CP-HerrR

When Johnny (Chapman) Appleseed. Lorine Niedecker. CP-NiedL

When Juan went down below and paid the fee. Don Juan in the Underworld. Charles Baudelaire. CP-BaudC, *tr.* by Walter Martin

When Julia blushes, she do's show. Upon Her Blush. Robert Herrick. CP-HerrR

When Julia chid, I stood as mute the while. Teares are Tongues. Robert Herrick. CP-HerrR

When Julius Fabricius, Sub-Prefect of the Weald. Land, The. Rudyard Kipling. CP-KiplR

When June is here—what art have we to sing. James Whitcomb Riley. CP-RileJ

When Kai is born. Not Leaving the House. Gary Snyder. CP-SnydG

When Katie walks, this simple pair accompany her side. Emily Dickinson. CP-DickE

When Klopstock England defied. William Blake. CP-BlakW

When Knowledge Went North. Chuang Tzu. CP-MertT

When L———lles thought fit from this world to depart. On Captn. L———lles. Robert Burns. CP-BurnR

When labor is light and the morning is fair. Riding to Town. Paul Laurence Dunbar. CP-DunbP

When lads were home from labour. Fancy's Knell. A. E. Housman. CP-HousA

When last before her people's face her own fair face she bent. Crowned and Wedded. Elizabeth Barrett Browning. CP-BroEB

When last I went riding. Lyme Regis Sed Sine Regina. G. K. Chesterton. CP-ChesG

When late (grave Palmer) these thy graffs [*or* grafts] and flowers. To Thomas Palmer [on His Book "The Sprite of Trees and Herbs"]. Ben Jonson. CP-JonsB

When, lately *Stella's* form display'd. Stella in Mourning. Samuel Johnson. CP-JohnS

When Laura smiles her sight revives both night and day. Thomas Campion *and* Philip Rosseter. CP-CampT

When Lawes full power have to sway, we see. Lawes. Robert Herrick. CP-HerrR

When Lawyers strive to heal a breach. Sergeant's Song, The. Thomas Hardy. CP-HardT

When Learning's Triumph o'er her barb'rous [*or* barbarous] Foes. Prologue Spoken by Mr[.] Garrick at the Opening of the Theatre in Drury Lane, 1747. Samuel Johnson. CP-JohnS

When leaving the primrose, bayberry dunes, seaward. Constant, The. A. R. Ammons. CP-AmmoA

When left the sun the distant west. Sunset, The. Jones Very. CP-VeryJ

When liberty is headlong girl. Liberty. Archibald MacLeish. CP-MacLA

When *Libra, Solidus, Denarius*. £ S. D. Robert Graves. CP-GravR

When Lide married *him*—w'y, she had to jes' dee-fy. James Whitcomb Riley. CP-RileJ

When Life Begins. Robert Penn Warren. CP-WarrR

When life contracts into a vulgar span. Greece. Henry David Thoreau. CP-ThorH

When life is quite through with. E. E. Cummings. CP-CummE

When life, love, poems. With Warm Regards to Miss Moore and Mr. Ransom. Mona Van Duyn. SP-VanDM

When Lightning Struck, 1. Andrei Codrescu. SP-CodrA

When Lightning Struck, 2. Andrei Codrescu. SP-CodrA

When lights are low, and the day has died. Song of the Open Country. Dorothy Parker. CP-ParkD

When, Like a Running Grave. Dylan Thomas. CP-ThomD

WHEN like faint music through a velvet-curtained door. Ave Atque Vale. Tennessee Williams. CP-WillT

When lions in the deserts quit their prey. Epistle—To Lucius. Annis Boudinot Stockton. CP-StocA

When little birds complaining, or green leaves. Petrarch. CP-Petra, *tr.* by J. G. Nichols

When little boys grown [*or* grow] patient at last, weary. Death of Little Boys. Allen Tate. CP-TateA

When Little Claude was naughty wunst. Naughty Claude. James Whitcomb Riley. CP-RileJ

When little Dickie Swope's a man. Impetuous Resolve, An. James Whitcomb Riley. CP-RileJ

When little Elizabeth whispers. Her Lonesomeness. James Whitcomb Riley. CP-RileJ

When little hills like lambs did skip. Fair Haven ("When little hills like lambs did skip"). Henry David Thoreau. CP-ThorH

When little more than boy in age. William Cowper. CP-CowpW

When little 'Pollus Morton he's. Penalty of Genius, The. James Whitcomb Riley. CP-RileJ

When Loneliness Is a Man. Yusef Komunyakaa. CP-KomuY

When long sequester'd from his throne. On the Queens's Visit to London. William Cowper. CP-CowpW

When looking at that picture, all the past. Dedicated to Dear Nana Clarke. E. E. Cummings. CP-CummE

When looking in a pool on a quiet day. Comment on the Relevance of Modern Science to the Everyday Lives of the Larger Animals, A. Eleanor Wilner. SP-WilnE

When, looking on the present face of things. October, 1803 ("When, looking on the present face of things"). William Wordsworth. CP-WorW1; MW-WorW

When Lord Love makes her cast her glances down. Petrarch. CP-Petra, *tr. by* J. G. Nichols

When Love at first did move. Ben Jonson. CP-JonsB *Fr.* Masque of Beauty, The.

When Love Becomes Words. Laura Riding Jackson. CP-RidiL

When love, exaltation, the holy awe. Face. Denise Levertov. SP-LeveDL

When love is a shimmering curtain. On Diverse Deviations. Maya Angelou. SP-AngeM

When love is for- / bidden, it / is the most! Now Then. Robert Creeley. CP-CreeR

When Love Is Not. Robert Graves. CP-GravR

When Love, puffed up with rage of high disdain. Sir Philip Sidney. SP-SidnP

When Love was born of heavenly line. Birth of Love, The. William Wordsworth. CP-WorW1

When love would strike th' offending fair. Of Her Sighing. Alexander Pope. CP-PopeA

When Lucifer was undefiled. Last Song of Lucifer, The. Nicholas Vachel Lindsay. CP-LindV

When lyart leaves bestrow the yird. Jolly Beggars, The. Robert Burns. CP-BurnR

When M-r-ne, deceased, to the devil went down. On J-hn M-r-ne, Laird of L-gg-n. Robert Burns. CP-BurnR

When ma man looks at me. Ma Man. Langston Hughes. CP-HughL; CP-HughL1

When mack smacked phyllis on the snout. Adhuc sub Judice Lis. E. E. Cummings. CP-CummE

When Maimie married Charley Brown. James Whitcomb Riley. CP-RileJ

When Malindy Sings. Paul Laurence Dunbar. CP-DunbP

When man, born 'mid luxuriant Tropic bowers. Man's First Experience of Winter. Jones Very. CP-VeryJ

When Man Enters Woman. Anne Sexton. CP-SextA; SP-SextA

When Man, expell'd from Eden's bowers. To a Lady. Lord Byron. CP-Byron

When man is punisht, he is plagued still. Will the Cause of Woe, The. Robert Herrick. CP-HerrR

When Man rose up out of the red mountains. Return of Eve, The. G. K. Chesterton. CP-ChesG

When March blows, and Monday's linen is shown. Ivor Gurney. SP-GurnI

When March went out a lion or a lamb. Lines to a Young Lady Born Before April Fools' Day. G. K. Chesterton. CP-ChesG

When Mary cam over the Border. Bonie Mary. Robert Burns. CP-BurnR

When Mary first came to present the Christ Child. Nunc Dimittis. Joseph Brodsky. CP-BrodJ, *tr. by* George L. Kline

When Master Tung was young. Han-shan. CP-ColdM, *tr. by* Red Pine

When maukin bucks at early f—s. Ode to Spring. Robert Burns. CP-BurnR

When May arrived at last. Our Lady of Žižkov. Jaroslav Seifert. SP-SeifJ, *tr. by* Ewald Osers

When May is painting with her colours gay. Fragment: May the Limner. Percy Bysshe Shelley. CP-ShelP

When Me an' my Ma an' Pa went to the Fair. Goin' to the Fair. James Whitcomb Riley. CP-RileJ

When memory directs. In the Cemetery. Constantine P. Cavafy. CP-CavaC, *tr. by* Theoharis Constantine Theoharis

When Memory is full. Emily Dickinson. CP-DickE

When Memory, with gentle hand. When Mother Combed My Hair. James Whitcomb Riley. CP-RileJ

When men a dangerous disease did 'scape. To Doctor Empiric[k]. Ben Jonson. CP-JonsB; SP-JonsB

When men and women marry. Shih-te. CP-ColdM, *tr. by* Red Pine

When men are made in bottles. Wellsian Futures. D. H. Lawrence. CP-LawrD

When Men Can't Trust Hands with Wood. Yusef Komunyakaa. CP-KomuY

When Men Got to the Summit. Ted Hughes. SP-HughTN

When men see Han-Shan. Gary Snyder. CP-SnydG

When men think they are like gods. Men Like Gods. D. H. Lawrence. CP-LawrD

When men turn mob. Music and Drum. Archibald MacLeish. CP-MacLA

When men wore overcoats down the stairs. Fanny Howe. SP-HoweF *Fr.* Vineyard, The.

When Mercury and Love and Death. Emasculation. D. H. Lawrence. CP-LawrD

When mid-autumn's moan shook the night-time. Mother Mourns, The. Thomas Hardy. CP-HardT

When midnight comes a host of dogs and men. Badger. John Clare. SP-ClarJ

When midnight occupied the porches of the Poet's reason. Holy Child's Song, The. Thomas Merton. CP-MertT

When Mill first came to court, the unprofiting fool. On Mill, My Lady's Woman. Ben Jonson. CP-JonsB; SP-JonsB

When Miriam Tazewell heard the tempest bursting. Miriam Tazewell. John Crowe Ransom. SP-RansJ

When mirth sways like a mast. Fanny Howe. SP-HoweF *Fr.* Introduction to the World.

When Mr. Apollinax visited the United States. Mr. Apollinax. T. S. Eliot. CP-ElioT

When Mrs. Welch's chimney smokes. Jonathan Swift. CP-SwifJ

When M'Liss went away from the old home. M'Liss and Louie. Carl Sandburg. CP-SandC

When moiling seems at cease. According to the Mighty Working. Thomas Hardy. CP-HardT

When Moses in Horeb struck the rock. On Certain Wits. Howard Nemerov. CP-NemeH

When Moses sat. Giving of the Torah, The. Yehuda Amichai. SP-AmicYL, *tr. by* Benjamin Harshav *and* Barbara Harshav

When Most Men Die. D. H. Lawrence. CP-LawrD

When Mother Clud had rose from play. History of Vanbrug's House, The. Jonathan Swift. CP-SwifJ

When Mother Combed My Hair. James Whitcomb Riley. CP-RileJ

When Mother Nature filled the early world. Giantess, The. Charles Baudelaire. CP-BaudC, *tr. by* Walter Martin

When mountain rocks and leafy trees. Nature's Lineaments. Robert Graves. CP-GravR

When muckers pimps and tratesmen. E. E. Cummings. CP-CummE

When Munson was in Paris Harold Crane. Lines Against A Loved American Poet After Hearing An Irish One's Nickman. John Logan. CP-LogaJ

When music captivates me like the sea. Music. Charles Baudelaire. CP-BaudC, *tr. by* Walter Martin

When music sounds, gone is the earth I know. Music. Walter De la Mare. CP-DeLaW

When my abodes prefixed time is spent. Sonnet 46. Edmund Spenser. CP-Spens *Fr.* Amoretti.

When my arms wrap you round I press. He Remembers Forgotten Beauty. William Butler Yeats. CP-YeatW

When my body leaves me. Gone Away. Denise Levertov. SP-LeveDP

When my contemporaries were driving. Private Man on Public Men, A. Thomas Hardy. CP-HardT

When my date's done, and my gray age must die. To the Earle of Westmerland. Robert Herrick. CP-HerrR

When my devotions could not pierce. Denial[l]. George Herbert. CP-HerbG

When My Dreams Come True. James Whitcomb Riley. CP-RileJ

When my dreams showed signs. North American Time. Adrienne Rich. SP-RicA1; SP-RicA2

When my eyes are weeds. August. Dorothy Parker. CP-ParkD

When my father died I saw a narrow valley. Strawberries. W. S. Merwin. SP-MerwWF

When my father had been dead a week. White Apples. Donald Hall. CP-HallD

When my 1st is a task to a young girl of spirit. Riddles: "When my 1st is a task to a young girl of spirit." Jane Austen. CP-AustJ

When my friend John Dugan, the carpenter. Powder-Monkey. Raymond Carver. CP-CarvR

When, My Friends, I Was in Love. Constantine P. Cavafy. CP-CavaC, *tr. by* Theoharis Constantine Theoharis

When my grave is broke up again[e]. Relic, The. John Donne. CP-DonnJ; MW-DonnJ

When my hair was first trimmed across my forehead. Long Banister Lane. Li Po. CP-WilW2

When My Heart Is Vexed, I Will Complain. Christina Georgina Rossetti. CP-RosC1

When My Heart Is Vexed I Will Complain. Christina Georgina Rossetti. CP-RosC2

When my life his pillar has raised to heaven. Sapphics. E. E. Cummings. CP-CummE

When my little son leaps in my sight. George Meredith. CP-MerG2

When my love came home to me. In the Lane. Christina Georgina Rossetti. CP-RosC3

When my love comes to see me it's. E. E. Cummings. CP-CummE

When my mother. Four Years Later. Robert Creeley. SP-CreeR

When my mother snapped open her flimsy parasol. Brazil. Paul Muldoon. CP-MuldP

When my off'ring next I make. Frankincense, The. Robert Herrick. CP-HerrR

When my passion—that with two glowing spurs. Petrarch. CP-Petra, *tr. by* J. G. Nichols

When my sensational moments are no more. E. E. Cummings. CP-CummE

When my soul was raging, a flock of birds which whir up. Quail. Charles Olson. CP-OlsoC

When my thought strays to you, it becomes perfumed. Autumn Verses. "Rubén Darío." SP-DariR, *tr. by* Alberto Acereda *and* Will Derusha

When my Uncle came to visit us. Wouldn't You Be after a Jaunt of 964,000,000,000,000 Million Miles? Kenneth Patchen. CP-PatcK

When my wife said, "Oh angel, angel, angel, you'll save me" in her sleep. Religious Question. Alan Dugan. CP-DugaA

When mynahs scream in the cages. On the Very Possible Jaundice of an Unborn Daughter. A. K. Ramanujan. CP-RamaA

When Nations grow Old. The Arts grow Cold. William Blake. CP-BlakW

When Nature bids us leave to live, 'tis late. To William Roe ("When Nature bids us leave us leave to live, 'tis late"). Ben Jonson. CP-JonsB; SP-JonsB

When Nature her great Masterpiece designed. To Robt. Graham of Fintry Esqr, with a Request for an Excise Division. Robert Burns. CP-BurnR

When nature once in lustful hot undress. Giantess, The. Charles Baudelaire. SP-ShapK

When Nellie, my old pussy. Theory of Prosody, A. Philip Levine. SP-LeviP

When night believes itself alone. Five Women Bathing in Moonlight. Richard Wilbur. CP-WilbR

When night comes black. Shrike, The. Sylvia Plath. CP-PlatS

When night comes down upon the Chesapeake. Night on the Chesapeake. Paul Laurence Dunbar. CP-DunbP

When Night is almost done. Emily Dickinson. CP-DickE

When night slinks, like a puma, down the sky. Street Lamps. Philip Larkin. CP-LarkP

When night was lifting. At Waking. Thomas Hardy. CP-HardT

When no one listens. Stranger. Thomas Merton. CP-MertT

When no resolution in justice can be attained. Athena's Vote. Constantine P. Cavafy. CP-CavaC, tr. by Theoharis Constantine Theoharis

When noon-time comes the whistle blows. Nuptials. Allen Tate. CP-TateA

When not disintricating the Yi Ching's knots. Anacreontic for a Chinese Scholar. Robert Stock. SP-StocR

When November stripped. Configurations. A. R. Ammons. CP-AmmoA

When nuts behind the hazel-leaf. Song: Autumn. George Meredith. CP-MerG1

When Oats Were Reaped. Thomas Hardy. CP-HardT

When ocean-clouds over inland hills. Misgivings. Herman Melville. SP-MelvH

When o'er the Aegean vast he sails. Ode 2.16: To Grosphus. Horace. SP-SmarC Fr. Odes.

When o'er the hill the eastern star. Lea-Rig, The. Robert Burns. CP-BurnR

When oer the world the son of genius rose. Poem on Eloquence by R. W. Emerson. Ralph Waldo Emerson. CP-EmerR

When of tender mind and body. Bridge of Lodi, The. Thomas Hardy. CP-HardT

When of your eyes one smile entirely brings down. E. E. Cummings. CP-CummE

When Old Folks they wuz young like us. Best Times, The. James Whitcomb Riley. CP-RileJ

When old Grimes died, he left a son. Young Grimes. Walt Whitman. CP-WhitW

When Old Jack died, we stayed from school (they said). James Whitcomb Riley. CP-RileJ

When old women say, it smells of snow. Northern Exposure. Charles Simic. SP-SimiC; SP-SimiCE

When 'Omer Smote 'Is Bloomin' Lyre. Rudyard Kipling. CP-KiplR

When on fair Celia I did spy. Mistake, The. Thomas Carew. CP-CareT

When on my day of life the night is falling. At Last. John Greenleaf Whittier. CP-WhitJ

When on my faithful charger. Song: "When on my faithful charger." George Meredith. CP-MerG2

When on the altar of my hand. In the Person of a Lady To Her Inconstant Servant. Thomas Carew. CP-CareT

When on the cliffs we met, by chance. Recognition. Robert Graves. CP-GravR

When on the coral-red steps of old brownstones. Summer: West Side. John Updike. CP-UpdiJ

When on the primal peaceful blank profound. Uranus. Arthur Hugh Clough. SP-ClouA

When, on your dangerous mission gone. Confidential Instructions. Stanley Kunitz. CP-KunSC

When, once enmeshed in the motions of their legs. Day of Generation. Czeslaw Milosz. CP-MiloC; CP-MiloCN

When once the sin has fully acted been. Sin Seen. Robert Herrick. CP-HerrR

When once the Soule has lost her way. Soule, The. Robert Herrick. CP-HerrR

When Once the Twilight Locks No Longer. Dylan Thomas. CP-ThomD

When One Age Goes with It Suddenly Its Errors Evaporate. Charles Olson. CP-OlsoC

When One has given up One's life. Emily Dickinson. CP-DickE

When One Has Lived a Long Time Alone. Galway Kinnell. SP-KinnGN

When one is lonely (and You). Minnelied. W. H. Auden. CP-AudeW Fr. Three Posthumous Poems.

When one is past, another care we have. Sorrows Succeed. Robert Herrick. CP-HerrR

When one more means on less, you are a drudge. Fanny Howe. SP-HoweF Fr. O'Clock.

When one of my oldest and dearest friends died and another friend called to console me. Call, The. C. K. Williams. SP-WillC

When one of them passed through Selefkia's market. One of Their Gods. Constantine P. Cavafy. CP-CavaC, tr. by Theoharis Constantine Theoharis

When one thing presses on another. Impingement Sydrome. Thomas Lux. SP-LuxT

When open trucks with German prisoners in them. Wiedersehen. Miller

Williams. CP-WillM

When other Ladies to the Groves go down. Epigram: "When other Ladies to the Groves go down." Alexander Pope. CP-PopeA

When others gain much by the present cast. Gain and Gettings. Robert Herrick. CP-HerrR

When Our Baby Died. James Whitcomb Riley. CP-RileJ

When our brother Fire was having his dog's day. Brother Fire. Louis MacNeice. CP-MacNL

When our hands touched, my darling, suddenly I heard. Sentimental Delusion, A. Mona Van Duyn. SP-VanDM

When our privacy starts over again. Early Spring Between Madison and Bellingham. Robert Bly. SP-BlyR

When out of all the ladies in her sphere. Petrarch. CP-Petra, tr. by J. G. Nichols

When out of bed my love doth spring. Upon Electra. Robert Herrick. CP-HerrR

When over the fair fame of friend or foe. Let Something Good Be Said. James Whitcomb Riley. CP-RileJ

When over the flowery, sharp pasture's. Flowers by the Sea. William Carlos Williams. CP-WilW1

When overwhelmed to know. Emily Dickinson. SP-DickE

When Owen Roe. Commodore Barry. Donald Davie. CP-DaviDC

When painfully athwart my brain. Play-Ground, The. Walt Whitman. CP-WhitW

When pale famine fed on thee. To the Most Disconsolate Great Brittaine. Thomas Campion. CP-CampT

When panting sighs the bosom fill. Arthur Hugh Clough. SP-ClouA

When Parnell's Irish in the House. Wilfred Owen's Photographs. Ted Hughes. SP-HughTN

When parsing warmths of dusk construe. E. E. Cummings. CP-CummE

When passion's trance is overpast. To ———: "When passion's trance is overpast." Percy Bysshe Shelley. CP-ShelP

When pavements were blown up, exposing wires. Epilogue to a Human Drama. Stephen Spender. SP-SpenS

When people are born. People. Miller Williams. CP-WillM

When people are dead and peaceless. Dead People. D. H. Lawrence. CP-LawrD

When people aren't asking questions. More About People. Ogden Nash. CP-NashO

When people bandy about bright sayings they like to attribute. There Were Giants in Those Days or Maybe There Weren't. Ogden Nash. CP-NashO

When people tell me French is difficult, I show my dimple. What Is Bibbidi-Bobbidi-Boo in Sanskrit? Ogden Nash. CP-NashO

When Peter Jackson Preached in the Old Church. Nicholas Vachel Lindsay. CP-LindV

When Philoctetes in the Lemnian Isle. William Wordsworth. CP-WorW2

When Phoebus was am'rous, and lon'g to be rude. Apollo and Daphne. Christopher Smart. SP-SmarC

When Phyllis sighs and from her eyes. Response. Paul Laurence Dunbar. CP-DunbP

When Pimpes feet sweat (as they doe often use). Upon Pimpe. Robert Herrick. CP-HerrR

When pimps out of loneliness cry. Sliver of Sermon. Langston Hughes. CP-HughL; CP-HughL3

When plans were announced to tear down. Condo Moon. John Updike. CP-UpdiJ

When Polly's reddening hand. Three Chores. James Merrill. SP-MerrJ

When pre-pubescent I felt. Thanksgiving, A. W. H. Auden. CP-AudeW

When Princes and Prelates and het-headed zealots. Why Should Na Poor Folk Mowe. Robert Burns. CP-BurnR

When psalms surprise me with their music. Psalm, A: "When psalms surprise me with their music." Thomas Merton. CP-MertT

When Queen Djenira slumbers through. Queen Djenira. Walter De la Mare. CP-DeLaW

When questioned by re-. James Laughlin. CP-LaugJ Fr. America I Love You.

When Rahman rides a dead haste in a dusty wind. A. R. Ammons. CP-AmmoA

When rain, (sings light) rain has devoured my house. Song: "When rain, (sings light) rain has devoured my house." Thomas Merton. CP-MertT

When rain whom fear. E. E. Cummings. CP-CummE

When rainy-greener shoots the grass. Sis Rapalye. James Whitcomb Riley. CP-RileJ

When recently, at the same time against the King and the British lords. On the Gunpowder Plot. John Milton. CP-MiltJ

When reeds are dead and a straw to thatch the marshes. Death of Autumn, The. Edna St. Vincent Millay. CP-MillE

When Romans gambled in the clash of lancelight. Sponge Full of Vinegar, The. Thomas Merton. CP-MertT

When, Rome, I read thee in thy mighty pair. To My Chosen Friend the Learnèd Translator of Lucan, Thomas May, Esquire. Ben Jonson. CP-JonsB

When Rome was rotten-ripe to her fall. Pirates in England, The. Rudyard Kipling. CP-KiplR

When Roses cease to bloom, Sir. Emily Dickinson. CP-DickE

When rosy May comes in wi' flowers. Gardener wi' His Paddle—or, The

Gardener's March, The. Robert Burns. CP-BurnR

When Ruth was left half desolate. Ruth [or, The Influences of Nature]. William Wordsworth. CP-WorW1

When sages speak of the freedom of the will. Philosophy. Howard Nemerov. CP-NemeH

When Sam'l Sings. Paul Laurence Dunbar. CP-DunbP

When Samson set my brush afire. Fox-Hunting. Rudyard Kipling. CP-KiplR

When Sarah Pierrepont let her spirit rage. Address to the Scholars of New England. John Crowe Ransom. SP-RansJ

When Sarah wrote Peter how she slept. Sarah's Letter to Peter. Carl Sandburg. CP-SandC

When Satan Fell. D. H. Lawrence. CP-LawrD

When science starts to be interpretive. Self-Protection. D. H. Lawrence. CP-LawrD

When serpents bargain for the right to squirm. E. E. Cummings. CP-CummE; SP-CummE

When sets the sun, the traveller waits for light. Light of Freedom Necessary to National Progress, The. Jones Very. CP-VeryJ

When Severn's Sweeping Flood Had Overthrown. William Wordsworth. CP-WorW2

When shall I behold again the cold limbed bare breasted. Return. Archibald MacLeish. CP-MacLA

When shall I see the half-moon sink again. End of Another Home Holiday. D. H. Lawrence. CP-LawrD

When shall that fuel fed fire grown fatter. Humane Materialist at the Burning of a Heretic, The. Stevie Smith. CP-SmitS

When shall we learn, what should be clear as day. Canzone: "When shall we learn, what should be clear as day." W. H. Auden. CP-AudeW

When she arrives where greatest beauty is. Petrarch. CP-Petra, tr. by J. G. Nichols

When She Cam Ben She Bobbed. Robert Burns. CP-BurnR

When she came on, you couldn't keep your seat. He Hears That His Beloved Has Become Engaged. Philip Larkin. CP-LarkP

When she came suddenly in. Door, The. Robert Graves. CP-GravR

When she came to me that night in Damascus Street. Longbones. Paul Muldoon. CP-MuldP

When she cannot be sure. Woman Alone, A. Denise Levertov. SP-LeveDL; SP-LeveDS

When she cocks her head. Thorn Merchant's Daughter, The. Yusef Komunyakaa. CP-KomuY

When she comes home again! A thousand ways. James Whitcomb Riley. CP-RileJ

When she gives a "psychic reading" Crepe de Chine. Tennessee Williams. CP-WillT

When she had her stroke the china dogs. Louis MacNeice. CP-MacNL Fr. Kingdom, The.

When she hoiked it off. Sky-Woman. Paul Muldoon. CP-MuldP

When she left me. Still Life. A. K. Ramanujan. CP-RamaA

When she married years ago. Italian Garden, The. William Carlos Williams. CP-WilW2

When she rises in the morning. Gloire de Dijon. D. H. Lawrence. CP-LawrD

When she sensed that her hour had come, she called her two sons and made her will. Country Woman. Yannis Ritsos. SP-RitsY, tr. by Kimon Friar

When she speaks it is like coming onto a grave. Gray Eyes. Tess Gallagher. SP-GallT

When she was alone in her cell, she didn't exist. Fanny Howe. SP-HoweF Fr. Quietist, The.

When she was four or five. Looking for a Cousin on a Swing. A. K. Ramanujan. CP-RamaA

When she was in the strangers' house. Daughter (1), A. Denise Levertov. SP-LeveDL

When she was young she wanted. Stanzas: Old Age and the Conventions of Retirement Have Driven My Friends from the Work They Love. Grace Paley. CP-PalGC

When she woke up. Sleeping Beauty. Lucille Clifton. SP-ClifL

When she's asleep and wakes for a moment. Infantile Language, The. James Laughlin. CP-LaugJ

When shrouded by the darkness of the earth. Christ's Capture in the Garden: A Paraphrase. Jones Very. CP-VeryJ

When sick of life and all the world. I Will Lift Up Mine Eyes unto the Hills. Christina Georgina Rossetti. CP-RosC2; CP-RosC3

When silly Sol in winter roisters. Song of the Open Fireplace. John Updike. CP-UpdiJ

When silver Snow decks Susan's clothes. Blind-Man's Buff. William Blake. CP-BlakW

When silver snow decks Sylvio's cloaths [or clothes]. Song 3rd By an Old Shepherd. William Blake. CP-BlakW

When simple *Macer*, now of high renown. Macer: A Character. Alexander Pope. CP-PopeA

When Sir Gawain was led to his bridal-bed. Song of Courtesy, The. George Meredith. CP-MerG1

When Sir [or Sr] Joshua Reynolds died. Sir Joshua Reynolds. William Blake. CP-BlakW

When slow Disease, with all her host of pains. Childish Recollections. Lord Byron. CP-Byron

When slow from pensive twilight's latest gleams. William Wordsworth. CP-WorW1

When smoke stood up from Ludlow. A. E. Housman. CP-HousA

When snow. Engagement, The. May Swenson. SP-SwenM

When snow falls on Franklin Park. Fanny Howe. SP-HoweF Fr. Robeson Street.

When snow is here, and the trees look weird. Brave Refrain, A. James Whitcomb Riley. CP-RileJ

When snow like sheep lay in the fold. In Memory of Jane Fraser [or Frazer]. Geoffrey Hill. CP-HillG

When snows begin to fill the park. Seasonless, The. James Wright. CP-WrigJ

When soft September brings again. Pont-Y-Wern. Arthur Hugh Clough. SP-ClouA

When soft winds and sunny skies. Fragment: "When soft winds and sunny skies." Percy Bysshe Shelley. CP-ShelP

When solemnly sentimental sanity. Variations Within Instances. Robert Stock. SP-StocR

When solitaries draw close, releasing. About Political Action in Which Each Individual Acts from the Heart. Denise Levertov. SP-LeveDL

When some beloved voice that was to you. Substitution. Elizabeth Barrett Browning. CP-BroEB

When some beloveds, 'neath whose eyelids lay. Bereavement. Elizabeth Barrett Browning. CP-BroEB

When some proud son of man returns to earth. Inscription on the Monument of a Newfoundland Dog. Lord Byron. CP-Byron

When some shall say, Faire once my Silvia was. Upon Silvia, a Mistresse. Robert Herrick. CP-HerrR

When some were happy as the grass was green. Dissentient Voice, A. Donald Davie. CP-DaviDC

When someone died, for miles around. Come into My Parlour. Paul Muldoon. CP-MuldP

When sorrow lays us low. Shinto. Jorge Luis Borges. SP-BorgJ, tr. by Hoyt Rogers

When sorrows had begirt me round. For Deliverance from a Fever. Anne Bradstreet. CP-BradA

When, soul in soul reflected. Unknowing. Thomas Hardy. CP-HardT

When soul love & scrunch love. Party on Olympus, The. James Laughlin. CP-LaugJ

When speaking of people and their beliefs I wear my belief on my sleeve. Seeing Eye to Eye Is Believing. Ogden Nash. CP-NashO

When spring-time flushes the desert grass. Ballad of the King's Jest, The. Rudyard Kipling. CP-KiplR

When, staunchly entering port. Beauty of the Ship, The. Walt Whitman. CP-WhitW

When Stella strikes the tuneful String. To Miss —: On Her Playing upon the Harpsichord. Samuel Johnson. CP-JohnS

When storms arise. Hymn: "When storms arise." Paul Laurence Dunbar. CP-DunbP

When stormy day is cold & gray. George Meredith. CP-MerG2

When stretch'd on one's bed. Jane Austen. CP-AustJ

When strife is a thing of two. Strife. D. H. Lawrence. CP-LawrD

When Structure Fails Rhyme Attempts to Come to the Rescue. William Carlos Williams. CP-WilW2

When stupid people read my poems. Han-shan. CP-ColdM, tr. by Red Pine

When success exalts thy lot. Ralph Waldo Emerson. CP-EmerR

When suddenly Saint Martin shunts his embers. Iris. Eugenio Montale. CP-MontE, tr. by Jonathan Galassi

When Sue Wears Red. Langston Hughes. CP-HughL; CP-HughL1

When summer came, we locked up our lives and fled. Gentle Snorer, The. Mona Van Duyn. SP-VanDM

When Summer hath her noon, it likes me lie. Sonnet of the August Calm. Ezra Pound. CP-PoEar

When summer heat has drowsed the day. Memory. Walter De la Mare. CP-DeLaW

When summer months branch backward. Lac into Seal. A. K. Ramanujan. CP-RamaA

When summer shone / Its sweetest on. Faithful Swallow, The. Thomas Hardy. CP-HardT

When summer time has come, and all. In Summer Time. Paul Laurence Dunbar. CP-DunbP

When summer used to linger. Song: "When summer used to linger." Dorothy Parker. CP-ParkD

When summer's end is nighing. A. E. Housman. CP-HousA

When sun, light handed, sows this Indian water. Aubade: Lake Erie. Thomas Merton. CP-MertT

When sunset, a brass gong. Saddhu of Couva, The. Derek Walcott. CP-WalcD

When Susanna Jones wears red. When Sue Wears Red. Langston Hughes. CP-HughL; CP-HughL1

When Susan's work was done, she'd [*or* she would] sit. Old Susan. Walter De la Mare. CP-DeLaW

When svelte the dawn reflected in the west. Aube of the West Dawn. Venetian June. Ezra Pound. CP-PoEar

When Sweeney heard the shouts of the soldiers and the big noise. Sweeney in Flight. Seamus Heaney. SP-HeanSO

When that day comes, whose evening sayes I'm gone. His Sailing from Julia. Robert Herrick. CP-HerrR

When that dead-certainty appals my thought. Death, from a Distance. Jorge Guillén. CP-WilbR

When that dead face, bowered in the furthest years. Love-Moon, The. Dante Gabriel Rossetti. CW-RossD *Fr.* House of Life, The.

When that I call unto my mind. Sir Thomas Wyatt. CP-WyatT

When that jackbooted choreography. Marilyn Hacker. SP-HackM *Fr.* Taking Notice.

When that planet which divides the hours. Petrarch. CP-Petra, *tr. by* J. G. Nichols

When that prime heroine of our nation, Alice. Alice. Robert Graves. CP-GravR

When that rich soul[e] which to her heaven is gone. Anatomy [*or* Anatomie] of the World, An: The First Anniversary. John Donne. CP-DonnJ; MW-DonnJ

When that tree moves from where it ought to be. Petrarch. CP-Petra, *tr. by* J. G. Nichols

When that with meat and drink they had fulfilled. When the Journey Was Intended to the City. Rudyard Kipling. CP-KiplR *Fr.* Muse among the Motors, The.

When the air was damp. Tresses, The. Thomas Hardy. CP-HardT

When the albums of this century's intermingling. Island Sun. John Updike. CP-UpdiJ

When the alcoholic passed the crucial point. Point of No Return. Robert Graves. CP-GravR

When the 'arf-made recruity goes out to the East. Young British Soldier, The. Rudyard Kipling. CP-KiplR

When the Armies Passed. Langston Hughes. CP-HughL; CP-HughL2

When the Assault Was Intended to the City. John Milton. CP-MiltJ (Sonnet 8.) CP-MiltJ

When the Astronomer stops seeking. Emily Dickinson. CP-DickE

When the autumn roses. Song-Day in Autumn. D. H. Lawrence. CP-LawrD

When the badger glimmered away. Badgers, The. Seamus Heaney. SP-HeanSO

When the bare feet of the baby beat across the grass. D. H. Lawrence. *See* When the white feet of the baby beat across the grass

When the barn catches fire. Longing to Be Saved, The. Maxine W. Kumin. SP-KumiM

When the beautiful cellist Jacqueline DuPré. Lament for Cellists and Jacqueline DuPré. Alan Dugan. CP-DugaA

When the bee lands the. Transfer. A. R. Ammons. CP-AmmoA

When the bees are humming in the honeysuckle vine. Love's Seasons. Paul Laurence Dunbar. CP-DunbP

When the bells justle in the tower. A. E. Housman. CP-HousA

When the Berry Bush Dies I'll Swim Down the Green River with My Hair on Fire. Charles Bukowski. SP-BukC2

When the birds are singing in the bushes. Evening Bird Song. Richard Eberhart. CP-EberR

When the birds begin to walk. Signs. Lucille Clifton. SP-ClifL

When the black snake. Black Snake, The. Mary Oliver. SP-OlivM

When the blackberries hang. August. Mary Oliver. SP-OlivM

When the blest seed of *Terah's* faithfull Son. Paraphrase on Psalm 114, A. John Milton. CP-MiltJ

When the body might free, and there was use in walking. Ivor Gurney. SP-GurnI

When the boys came home, everything stopped. Bird Frau, The. Rita Dove. SP-DoveR

When the British warrior queen. Boadicea: An Ode. William Cowper. CP-CowpW

When the cabin port-holes are dark and green. Fifty North and Forty West. Rudyard Kipling. CP-KiplR *Fr.* Just-So Stories.

When the candle has burned out. Rainer Maria Rilke. CP-RilkFr, *tr. by* A. Poulin, Jr. *Fr.* Orchards.

When the car at night. Insight. Mona Van Duyn. SP-VanDM

When the cataract dries up, my dear. Note, A. William Carlos Williams. CP-WilW2

When the charge of election bribery was brought against an Illinois. Implications. Carl Sandburg. CP-SandC

When the children of Israel, when the noble tribes of Jacob. Psalm 114. John Milton. CP-MiltJ

When the Christians brought him out to hang him. 27 June 1906, 2 P.M. Constantine P. Cavafy. CP-CavaC, *tr. by* Theoharis Constantine Theoharis

When the circumstance takes. Then One. A. R. Ammons. CP-AmmoA

When the clever man asks the perfect boon. Mythologies 2. A. K. Ramanujan. CP-RamaA

When the clock struck at a goodly distance from his window. Knowledge of the Ambiguous. Yannis Ritsos. SP-RitsY, *tr. by* Kimon Friar

When the clock-tick fades. Sound of Time, The. Charles Tomlinson. CP-TomlC

When the cloud shut down on the morning shine. Occultation, The. Thomas Hardy. CP-HardT

When the cold comes. Where? When? Which? Langston Hughes. CP-HughL; CP-HughL3

When the colossus of the will's dominion. Villa Adriana. Adrienne Rich. CP-RicAE; SP-RicA2

When the colossuses multiplied, / walked upright into their own. Island (VII), The. Pablo Neruda. SP-NeruP *Fr.* Separate Rose, The.

When the corn stands yellow in September. Harvest. Carl Sandburg. CP-SandC

When the corn's all cut and the bright stalks shine. Corn-Stalk Fiddle, The. Paul Laurence Dunbar. CP-DunbP

When the cows come home the milk is coming. Christina Georgina Rossetti. CP-RosC2

When the crew from the tele- / phone company came to replace. Problem Struck Me, The. James Laughlin. CP-LaugJ

When the crickets. Louis Zukofsky. CP-ZukLS

When the cuckoo, the cow, and the coffe-plant chipped the. Him with His Tail in His Mouth. D. H. Lawrence. CP-LawrD

When the dark dawn humped off to die. Little Girl on Her Way to School, A. James Wright. CP-WrigJ

When the darkened Fifties dip to the North. Song of the Wise Children. Rudyard Kipling. CP-KiplR

When the dawn split with sudden gold. Gate of Everywhere, The. G. K. Chesterton. CP-ChesG

When the days grow teeth at last and games. Letter to the Young Men, A. Kenneth Patchen. CP-PatcK

When the dentist adjusts his drill. Variation: Ode to Fear. Robert Penn Warren. CP-WarrR

When the departing sun resigns. Ode on a Lady Leaving Her Place of Abode; Almost Impromptu, An. Samuel Johnson. CP-JohnS

When the Devil Was Sick Could He Prove It? Ogden Nash. CP-NashO

When the dim light, at Lauds, comes strike her window. Aubade—the Annunciation. Thomas Merton. CP-MertT

When the dirty snow buries your treasures. Europe in Winter. Adam Zagajewski. SP-ZagaA, *tr. by* Clare Cavanagh

When the drums begin to beat. Juggler's Song, The. Rudyard Kipling. CP-KiplR *Fr.* Kim.

When the Dumb Speak. Robert Bly. SP-BlyR

When the eagle soared clear through a dawn distilling of emerald. Crow and the Birds. Ted Hughes. SP-HughTN

When the earth was sick and the skies were grey. Rudyard Kipling. CP-KiplR *Fr.* Plain Tales from the Hills.

When the elephant's-ear in the park. Tea. Wallace Stevens. CP-StevW; CP-StevWP

When the eleventh hour / Unbars the burning west. Fall of Night, The. Thomas Merton. CP-MertT

When the exposed spirit, busy in daytime. Night-Music. Muriel Rukeyser. CP-RukeM

When the eye hardly sees. Long Looked For. Christina Georgina Rossetti. CP-RosC3

When the eye of day is shut. A. E. Housman. CP-HousA

When the face is struck. Firescreen at Mount Vernon, A. William Meredith. SP-MereW

When the farmer, from his fields. Forsaken Harvest Field, The. Jones Very. CP-VeryJ

When the field is cold, Lord. Crows. Arthur Rimbaud. CP-RimbA, *tr. by* Martin Sorrell

When the first signs go on. Ernesto Cardenal. CP-MertT *Fr.* Gethsemani, KY.

When the first tree was level with the ground. Petrarch. CP-Petra, *tr. by* J. G. Nichols

When the Five Prominent Poets. Josephine Jacobsen. CP-JacoJ

When the flaming lute-thronged angelic door is wide. Travail of Passion, The. William Butler Yeats. CP-YeatW

When the flush of a new-born sun fell first on Eden's green and gold. Conundrum of the Workshops, The. Rudyard Kipling. CP-KiplR

When the Flyin' Scot. Uncle Henry. W. H. Auden. CP-AudeW

When the footbridge washes away. Roadway, The. Adrienne Rich. CP-RicAE

When the forests have been destroyed their darkness remains. Asians Dying, The. W. S. Merwin. SP-MerwW

When the front-end loader ran over my wife's Montauk daisies. On Flowers. On Negative Evolution. Alan Dugan. CP-DugaA

When the Frost Is on the Punkin. James Whitcomb Riley. CP-RileJ

When the frost is on the punkin and the fodder's in the shock. When the Frost Is on the Punkin. James Whitcomb Riley. CP-RileJ

When the full fields begin to smell of sunrise. Trappist Abbey: Matins, The. Thomas Merton. CP-MertT

When the Full-Grown Poet Came. Walt Whitman. CP-WhitW

When the Future Is Black. Heather McHugh. SP-McHuH

When the Gentle were dead these inherited their coats. Crows on the North Slope. W. S. Merwin. SP-MerwW

When the Glass of My Body Broke. Anne Sexton. CP-SextA

When the gleeful Spring on dancing feet. Ballad of Smiles and Tears, The. Lee O. Harris. CP-RileJ

When the gnats dance at evening. Gnat-Psalm. Ted Hughes. SP-HughTN

When the God of Merrie Love. Thomas Campion. CP-CampT

When the Great Ark. Rudyard Kipling. CP-KiplR

When the great dust. Fittest, The. Josephine Jacobsen. CP-JacoJ

When the great Kings return to clay. Burial, The. Rudyard Kipling. CP-KiplR

When the great nothingness was everything. Mystery of the Abstract. Richard Eberhart. CP-EberR

When the great ship ran madly towards the rocks. Gorgon Mask. Robert Graves. CP-GravR

When the Greek sea. Sometimes, as a Child. Olga Broumas. SP-BrouO

When the Green Gits Back in the Trees. James Whitcomb Riley. CP-RileJ

When the grey geese heard the Fool's tread. Flight, The. Rudyard Kipling. CP-KiplR

When the grey stranger shows up in your dream. Nightmare. Howard Nemerov. CP-NemeH

When the half-body dies its frightful death. Resurrection of the Right Side. Muriel Rukeyser. CP-RukeM

When the hamlet hailed a birth. Mad Judy. Thomas Hardy. CP-HardT

When the Head of Bran / Was firm on British shoulders. Head of Bran the Blest, The. George Meredith. CP-MerG1

When the Hearse Comes Back. James Whitcomb Riley. CP-RileJ

When the hero of the threshold enters our lives and our houses. Hero Speech. Muriel Rukeyser. CP-RukeM

When the Himalayan peasant meets the he-bear in his pride. Female of the Species, The. Rudyard Kipling. CP-KiplR

When the historical process breaks down and armies organize with. Age of Anxiety, The. W. H. Auden. CP-AudeW

When the Horizon Is Gone. W. S. Merwin. SP-MerwW

When the Hounds of Spring. Algernon Charles Swinburne. SP-SwinA *Fr.* Atalanta in Calydon.

When the hounds of spring are on winter's traces. When the Hounds of Spring. Algernon Charles Swinburne. SP-SwinA *Fr.* Atalanta in Calydon.

When the ice starts to shiver. On Edges. Adrienne Rich. CP-RicAE; SP-RicA1; SP-RicA2

When the immense drugged universe explodes. Ecstasy of Chaos. Robert Graves. CP-GravR

When the inmate stirs, the birds retire discreetly. Bird-Scene at a Rural Dwelling, A. Thomas Hardy. CP-HardT

When the Journey Was Intended to the City. Rudyard Kipling. CP-KiplR *Fr.* Muse among the Motors, The.

When the jury files in to deliver a verdict after weeks of direct and cross. Lawyer. Carl Sandburg. CP-SandC

When the King sat down to the feast and the golden lid revealed. Thyestes. Louis MacNeice. CP-MacNL

When the lad for longing sighs. A. E. Housman. CP-HousA

When the lamp glowed. Bye-Child. Seamus Heaney. SP-HeanSO

When the lamp is shattered [*or* shatter'd]. Lines: "When the lamp is shattered [*or* shatter'd]." Percy Bysshe Shelley. CP-ShelP

When the large frame of the window collapses in the fire. Wedding Party, The. Norman Dubie. CP-DubiN

When the last man living. Last Man Living, The. Langston Hughes. CP-HughL; CP-HughL3

When the last song. Keeper of the Vigil. Yusef Komunyakaa. CP-KomuY

When the last sunshine of expiring day. Monody on the Death of the Right Hon. R. B. Sheridan. Lord Byron. CP-Byron

When the lids of dusk are falling. To Annie. James Whitcomb Riley. CP-RileJ

When the lieutenant of the Guardia de Asalto. On the Murder of Lieutenant José Del Castillo by the Falangist Bravo Martinez, July 12, 1936. Philip Levine. SP-LeviP

When the light falls, it falls on her. Stanley Kunitz. CP-KunSC

When the light leaves. Night Time. Robert Creeley. SP-CreeR

When the light spine of a society. For the Spanish Poet Miguel Hernandez. Thomas Merton. CP-MertT

When the light was shutting down on you. Reading Aloud. Tess Gallagher. SP-GallT

When the lips / And the body. Sleep. Langston Hughes. CP-HughL; CP-HughL2

When the lithe moonlight silently. Nocturne: "When the lithe moonlight silently." E. E. Cummings. CP-CummE

When the little girl was told that the sun someday. Saving Way, The. Hayden Carruth. CP-CarHS

When the little sow piglet squirmed free. Sow Piglet's Escapes, The. Galway Kinnell. SP-KinnGN

When the Lord Is With You. Shmuel HaNagid. SP-HaNaS, *tr. by* Peter Cole

When the Lord was a man of war and sailed out. Life and Death of the Cantata System, The. Alan Dugan. CP-DugaA

When the lovely bride and groom came out onto the grand front steps. Report on a Happening in Washington Square San Francisco, A. Lawrence Ferlinghetti. SP-FerlL

When the Macedonians forsook him. King Dimitrios. Constantine P. Cavafy. CP-CavaC, *tr. by* Theoharis Constantine Theoharis

When the maiden leaves off teasing. Gallant's Song. Thomas Hardy. CP-HardT

When the man is busy. Revolution Is One Form of Social Change. Audre Lorde. SP-LordA

When the Master was calling the roll. Anseo. Paul Muldoon. CP-MuldP

When the moon comes out. Full Moon. Federico García Lorca. CP-GarcF, *tr. by* Jerome Rothenberg *Fr.* Sublunar Cantos.

When the moon falls on a man's blood. Moon Memory. D. H. Lawrence. CP-LawrD

When the moon is full. Anniversary of My Father's Death, The. Yehuda Amichai. SP-AmicYL, *tr. by* Benjamin Harshav *and* Barbara Harshav

When the moon rises. Moon Rising, The. Federico García Lorca. SP-GarcF, *tr. by* Lysander Kemp

When the moon rises and women in flowery dresses are strolling. Czeslaw Milosz. CP-MiloC; CP-MiloCN, *tr. by* Robert Pinsky

When the moon was a hammock of gold. Moon Hammock. Carl Sandburg. CP-SandC

When the morning swoons in its highest heat. Ballade of the Coming Rain, The. James Whitcomb Riley. CP-RileJ

When the morning was waking over the war. Among Those Killed in the Dawn Raid Was a Man Aged a Hundred. Dylan Thomas. CP-ThomD

When the motorcade rolled to a halt, Quang Duc. 2527th Birthday of the Buddha. Yusef Komunyakaa. CP-KomuY

When the moviehouse lights click off and images flicker-dance against the white walls, I hear Billie's whispered lament. Summer Night in Hanoi, A. Yusef Komunyakaa. CP-KomuY

When the music is going strong. Children's Games. Miller Williams. CP-WillM

When the neighbor's outhouse went by. Surviving the Hurricane. Alan Dugan. CP-DugaA

When the new frogs in their exuberant arrivals. On Returning to a Lake in Spring. Richard Eberhart. CP-EberR

When the Night Puts Twenty Veils. Philip Larkin. CP-LarkP

When the night winds whistle through the trees and blow the crisp brown leaves a-crackling down. Thanksgiving Time. Langston Hughes. CP-HughL

When the nightingale to his mate. Alba ("When the nightingale to his mate"). Ezra Pound. SP-PounE *Fr.* Langue d'Oc.

When the night's coming and the last light falls. Ancestors, The. Allen Tate. CP-TateA

When the Nomads Come Over the Hill. James Tate. SP-TateJ

When the north and the east crawled with armed tribes toward mindless wars. At the Birth of an Age. Robinson Jeffers. CP-JefR2

When the nurses, interns, doctors came running full tilt down the hall. Medicine ("When the nurses, interns, doctors came running full tilt down the hall"). Carolyn Kizer. CP-KizeC

When the occasioner of my many a sigh. Michelangelo Buonarroti. CP-Miche, *tr. by* John Frederick Nims

When the odds are long. When You Say That, Smile! or All Right Then, Don't Smile. Ogden Nash. CP-NashO

When the old junk man Death. Question ("When the old junk man Death"). Langston Hughes. CP-HughL; CP-HughL1

When the Old Man Smokes. Paul Laurence Dunbar. CP-DunbP

When the old man who had bought all his wives. Old Man. John Ciardi. CP-CiarJ

When the old servant reveals she is the mother. Night at the Opera, A. Charles Tomlinson. CP-TomlC

When the ox-horn sounds in the buried hills. Second Psalm: The Signals. W. S. Merwin. SP-MerwW

When the pain of the world finds words. Words. W. S. Merwin. SP-MerwW

When the patient, shining with pain. Crow's Battle Fury. Ted Hughes. SP-HughTN

When the people knew you. Lonely Particular. Alice Walker. CP-WalkA

When the pistol muzzle oozing blue vapour. That Moment. Ted Hughes. SP-HughTN *Fr.* Crow.

When the planes come in all night, and the lights reach, wavering. Learners, The. Randall Jarrell. CP-JarrR

When the plowblade struck. Yellowjackets. Yusef Komunyakaa. CP-KomuY

When the Poet comes, by sovereign decree. Benediction. Charles Baudelaire. CP-BaudC, *tr. by* Walter Martin

When the poet was dying of cancer. On the Death of Norman Dukes. Alan Dugan. CP-DugaA

When the poor guy saw her pass. "Rubén Dario." SP-DariR, *tr. by* Alberto Acereda *and* Will Derusha

When the Present has latched its postern behind my tremulous stay. Afterwards.

Thomas Hardy. CP-HardT

When the proficient poison of pure sleep. E. E. Cummings. CP-CummE

When the prophet, a complacent fat man. Stephen Crane. CP-CranS

When the Prophet's ray of intelligence. Why Wine Is Forbidden. Jelaluddin Rumi. SP-Rumi, *tr.* by Coleman Barks

When the Pulitzers showered on some dope. Words for Hart Crane. Robert Lowell. SP-LoweR

When the purple twilight is unbound. "Fair Helena" by Rackham. Ezra Pound. CP-PoEar

When the Queen of Sheba came to Solomon. Sheba's Throne. Jelaluddin Rumi. SP-Rumi, *tr.* by Coleman Barks

When the rain is over / I go to the woods. Dreams. Mary Oliver. SP-OlivM

When the rain stops. Midnight. Robert Creeley. CP-CreeR

When the rain struck the windowpane with one of it fingers. Final Agreement. Yannis Ritsos. SP-RitsY, *tr.* by Kimon Friar

When the rattlesnake bit, I lay. Poisoned Man, The. James Dickey. CP-DickJ

When the reaper's task was ended, and the summer wearing late. Swan Song of Parson Avery, The. John Greenleaf Whittier. CP-WhitJ

When the red pond fills fish appear. Ayers Rock / Uluru Song. Allen Ginsberg. CP-GinsA; SP-GinsA

When the Ripe Fruit Falls. D. H. Lawrence. CP-LawrD

When the roast smoked in the oven, belching out darkness. Gnomic Verses. Ezra Pound. CP-PoEar

When the robust and Brass-bound Man commissioned first for sea. Poseidon's Law. Rudyard Kipling. CP-KiplR

When the rookery of women. Amazons. Lucille Clifton. SP-ClifL

When the rooster jumps up on the windowsill. Cuba, 1962. Ai. SP-Ai

When the rose is faded. Walter De la Mare. CP-DeLaW

When the runner's whistle lights the last miles of darkness. Soldier [T. P.]. Randall Jarrell. CP-JarrR

When the Russian Tanks Roll Westward. Philip Larkin. CP-LarkP

When the Saints Come Marching In. Audre Lorde. SP-LordA

When the scrapers of the. Many Hats. Carl Sandburg. CP-SandC

When the sea is calm I wade. Sea, The. May Swenson. SP-SwenM

When the sea is everywhere. North Atlantic. Carl Sandburg. CP-SandC

When the sea pours out under the bridge. Froth. Richard Eberhart. CP-EberR

When the serpent emerged, earth-bowel brown. Horrible Religious Error, A. Ted Hughes. SP-HughTN

When the shadow menaced with its fatal law. Stéphane Mallarmé. CP-MallS, *tr.* by Henry Weinfield

When the shadow of the sparrowhawk passes over. Freezing. William Meredith. SP-MereW

When the she-leopard stalks and pounces on. Catchment. Maxine W. Kumin. SP-KumiM

When the shining boughs are bare. Song: The Wren. George Meredith. CP-MerG2

When the Shoe Fits. Chuang Tzu. CP-MertT

When the shoe strings break. Blues, The. Langston Hughes. CP-HughL

When the snow falls the flakes. Dance, The. William Carlos Williams. CP-WilW2

When the snow melts. 30 November 1948. Yannis Ritsos. SP-RitsY *Fr.* Exile's Journals 2.

When the soft hand of sleep had closed the latch. Ode: 1814. William Wordsworth. CP-WorW2

When the soprano sang. Broken Hearted Soprano. Carl Sandburg. CP-SandC

When the sound of forest leaves is like the sleep-talk. Vessels. James Dickey. CP-DickJ

When the Sparrow Flies. Stevie Smith. CP-SmitS

When the spear of Diomedes, guided by the hand of the goddess. Conjunction "Or," The. Yannis Ritsos. SP-RitsY, *tr.* by Kimon Friar

When the spent day begins to frail. E. E. Cummings. CP-CummE

When the spent sun throws up its rays on cloud. Acceptance. Robert Frost. CP-FrosR

When the spring comes round, and a certain day. Joys of Memory. Thomas Hardy. CP-HardT

When the stern god. Mythic Fragment. Louise Glück. SP-GlucL

When the stones burst into flame. Kenneth Patchen. CP-PatcK

When the storm passed. Ithaca, N.Y. A. R. Ammons. CP-AmmoA

When the streetcar stalled on Joy Road. On the Birth of Good & Evil During the Long Winter of '28. Philip Levine. SP-LeviP

When the stuffed prophets quarrel, when the sawdust comes. Roosevelt. Nicholas Vachel Lindsay. CP-LindV

When the Summer fields are mown. Aftermath. Henry Wadsworth Longfellow. SP-LongH

When the sun / falls behind the sumac. Loss. A. R. Ammons. CP-AmmoA

When the sun gets low, in winter. Human Things. Howard Nemerov. CP-NemeH

When the sun shouts and people abound. Summer Holiday. Robinson Jeffers. CP-JefR1

When the sun sinks his golden chariot. Petrarch. CP-Petra, *tr.* by J. G. Nichols

When the sun went down and the night came on. Watch, The. A. R. Ammons. CP-AmmoA

When the swans turned my sister into a swan. Black Swan, The. Randall Jarrell. CP-JarrR

When the tall puffy. Couplet. Donald Hall. CP-HallD

When the thorn on the down. Voice of the Thorn, The. Thomas Hardy. CP-HardT

When the thunder stalks the sky. Summer Serenade. Ogden Nash. CP-NashO

When the tide was out. Ship Burning and a Comet All in One Day, A. Richard Eberhart. CP-EberR

When the time has arrived. Trala Trala Trala La-le-la. William Carlos Williams. CP-WilW2

When the toads begin to ring. Henry David Thoreau. CP-ThorH

When the tooth cracks—zing!—it. Robert Penn Warren. CP-WarrR

When the torch is taken / And the room is dark. Seneca. Thomas Merton. CP-MertT

When the train whistles, it wants to say. See-er of Cities, The. Randall Jarrell. CP-JarrR

When the trains go by. Waiting. Robert Pinsky. CP-PinsR

When the tree-sparrows with no sound through the pearl-pale air. Edna St. Vincent Millay. CP-MillE

When the trees do laugh with our merry wit. Song 2nd By a Young Shepherd. William Blake. CP-BlakW

When the true things meet us at the place we reach, they are all. Muriel Rukeyser. CP-RukeM

When the two fish spoke. Two Fish. Carl Sandburg. CP-SandC

When the urge to strip becomes too much i rub against a tree. Urges, The. Andrei Codrescu. SP-CodrA

When the vain triumph of the imperial lord. Condolatory Address. Lord Byron. CP-Byron

When the vein of jade is opened. Green Connection, The. Eleanor Wilner. SP-WilnE

When the voices of children are heard on the green / And whisperings [*or* whisprings] are in the dale. Nurse's Song. William Blake. CP-BlakW *Fr.* Songs of Experience.

When the walls were red. Ageing House, The. Thomas Hardy. CP-HardT

When the War Is Over. W. S. Merwin. SP-MerwW

When the wasting embers redden the chimney-breast. Night in the Old Home. Thomas Hardy. CP-HardT

When the Watchman Saw the Light. Constantine P. Cavafy. CP-CavaC, *tr.* by Theoharis Constantine Theoharis

When the waters' countenance. Wet Litany, The. Rudyard Kipling. CP-KiplR

When the Waters were dried an' the Earth did appear. Sappers. Rudyard Kipling. CP-KiplR

When the white feet of afternoon. Lines Written in Dejection. G. K. Chesterton. CP-ChesG

When the white feet of the baby beat across the grass. Baby Running Barefoot. D. H. Lawrence. CP-LawrD

When the white fog burns off. Depths, The. Denise Levertov. SP-LeveDP

When the white folks get through. Office Building: Evening. Langston Hughes. CP-HughL; CP-HughL3

When the white stars talk together like sisters. Christmas Card, A. Thomas Merton. CP-MertT

When the wild strawberry leaves turn. Grace Paley. CP-PalGC

When the Wind. Stevie Smith. CP-SmitS

When the wind blows her veil. Birdcage Walk. D. H. Lawrence. CP-LawrD

When the wind ended and we came down. Whispered into the Ground. William Stafford. SP-StafWW

When the wind works against us in the dark. Storm Fear. Robert Frost. CP-FrosR

When the window glass blows in. Untitled Poem: "When the window glass blows in." Alan Dugan. CP-DugaA

When the windows of the West Side clash like cymbals in the setting sunlight. Hymn of Not Much Praise for New York City. Thomas Merton. CP-MertT

When the witches' coven across the street. Suburban Exorcism. Alan Dugan. CP-DugaA

When the woman's face contorted and she clutched the railing for support, we knew she would die. Fiction ("When the woman's face contorted and she clutched the railing for support, we knew she would die"). Rae Armantrout. SP-ArmaA

When the words *would with not and*. Song, The. George Oppen. CP-OppGN

When the World Bu'sts Through. James Whitcomb Riley. CP-RileJ

When the world grows old by the chimney side. Peal of the Bells, The. Henry David Thoreau. CP-ThorH

When the world has been reduced to a single dark wood for our four astonished eyes. Phrases ("When the world has been reduced to a single dark wood for our four astonished eyes"). Arthur Rimbaud. CP-RimbA, *tr.* by Martin Sorrell

When the world takes over for us. Lear. William Carlos Williams. CP-WilW2

When the Year Grows Old. Edna St. Vincent Millay. CP-MillE

When the young man reaches his full height. Muriel Rukeyser. CP-RukeM

When/Then. Adrienne Rich. SP-RicA2

When there are so many we shall have to mourn. In Memory of Sigmund Freud. W. H. Auden. CP-AudeW

When there was air, when you could. Remembering. William Stafford. SP-StafW; SP-StafWW

When there were no depths. I Weep, Fountain of Jazer. Charles Olson. CP-OlsoC

When there were two of us. Wedge, The. Gregory Orr. SP-OrrG

When these, and such, their voices have employed. To His Friend the Author upon His *Richard*. Ben Jonson. CP-JonsB

When Theseus went down. Ariadne and the Minotaur. Charles Tomlinson. CP-TomlC; SP-TomlC

When Thetis and Peleus were married. Unfaithfulness. Constantine P. Cavafy. CP-CavaC, *tr. by* Theoharis Constantine Theoharis

When they are grown. For All Our Great-Grandchildren. Miller Williams. CP-WillM

When they bring in the Dish. Holy Grail, The. Andrei Codrescu. SP-CodrA

When they came near. Names, The. Robert Creeley. CP-CreeR

When they caressed. Her Lament. Denise Levertov. SP-LeveDL

When they come back—if Blossoms do. Emily Dickinson. CP-DickE

When they did greet me Father, sudden Awe. Sonnet on Receiving a Letter Informing Me of the Birth of a Son. Samuel Taylor Coleridge. CP-ColeS

When they killed my mother it made me nervous. State, The. Randall Jarrell. CP-JarrR

When they mow the fields, I see the world reformed. 7/16/68: ii. Adrienne Rich. CP-RicAE *Fr.* Ghazals: Homage to Ghalib,

When they needed a foreign part. Grace. William Meredith. SP-MereW

When they put him in rompers the habits. Habits, The. Louis MacNeice. CP-MacNL

When they removed the bandages. Judgment. Eleanor Wilner. SP-WilnE

When they said *Carrickfergus* I could hear. Singer's House, The. Seamus Heaney. SP-HeanSO

When they said I must leave hell. Gregory Orr. SP-OrrG

When they shook the box, and poured out its chances. For a Daughter Gone Away. William Stafford. SP-StafWW

When They Surge, Excited. Constantine P. Cavafy. CP-CavaC, *tr. by* Theoharis Constantine Theoharis

When they swoop on you hobbled there. Quatrains for Ishi. Yusef Komunyakaa. CP-KomuY

When they tell me that my body. Donor. Lucille Clifton. SP-ClifL

When they torture your mother. Torture. Alice Walker. CP-WalkA

When they turn the sun. Yellow. Anne Sexton. CP-SextA

When They Were Come unto the Faery's Court. John Keats. CP-KeatJ

When they're decent about women, they're frightful about. What Do We See? Muriel Rukeyser. CP-RukeM

When thin-strewn memory I look through. Miss Loo. Walter De la Mare. CP-DeLaW

When things get very bad, they pass beyond tragedy. At Last. D. H. Lawrence. CP-LawrD

When This Clangor in the Brain. Adrienne Rich. CP-RicAE

When this fly lived, she used to play. Fly That Flew into My Mistress'[s] Eye, A. Thomas Carew. CP-CareT

When this hand is gone to earth. Artifact. Muriel Rukeyser. CP-RukeM

When this is the thing you put on. Armor. James Dickey. CP-DickJ

When this old body. Grace Paley. CP-PalGC

When this yokel comes maundering. Plot Against the Giant, The. Wallace Stevens. CP-StevW; CP-StevWP

When those of us who seem. Marriages. Philip Larkin. CP-LarkP

When thou art dead,dead,and far from the splendid sin. E. E. Cummings. CP-CummE

When thou art done thy toil, anew art born. Settler, The. Jones Very. CP-VeryJ

When thou art little as I am, mother. Karma. Walter De la Mare. CP-DeLaW

When thou do'st play, and sweetly sing. Upon Sapho, Sweetly Playing, and Sweetly Singing. Robert Herrick. CP-HerrR

When thou goest through the Waters. Emily Dickinson. SP-DickE

When thou hast taken thy last applause,and when. E. E. Cummings. CP-CummE

When Thou Must Home. Propertius. CP-CampT, *tr. by* Thomas Campion

When thou must home to shades of underground [*or* under ground]. When Thou Must Home. Propertius. CP-CampT, *tr. by* Thomas Campion

When thou, poor[e] excommunicate. To My Inconstant Mistress [*or* Mistris]. Thomas Carew. CP-CareT

When thou sittest moping. Ralph Waldo Emerson. CP-EmerR

When thou to my true-love [*or* true love] com'st. Westphalian Song. *Unknown*. CP-ColeS, *tr. by* Samuel Taylor Coleridge

When Thou wast taken, Lord, I oft have read. His Words to Christ, Going to the Cross. Robert Herrick. CP-HerrR

When thoughtlessly two lamps were burned. Song: We Have No Ship at Sea. Jones Very. CP-VeryJ

When through some lacuna, chink, or interstice. Outer Bar, The. Amy Clampitt. CP-ClamA

When Thurlow This Damn'd Nonsense Sent. Lord Byron. CP-Byron

When thy soul / Is filled with a just image fear not thou. Ralph Waldo Emerson. CP-EmerR

When time delicately is sponging sum after. E. E. Cummings. CP-CummE

When time had got his hair and made him well. Homage to a Rake-Hell. William Meredith. SP-MereW

When Time, or soon or late, shall bring. Euthanasia. Lord Byron. CP-Byron

When time was young, and the world in infancy. Four[e] Monarchies, The. Anne Bradstreet. CP-BradA

When times are troubled, then forbeare; but speak. Speake in Season. Robert Herrick. CP-HerrR

When to a House I come, and see. Leprosie in Houses. Robert Herrick. CP-HerrR

When, to disarm suspicious minds at lunch. Household, A. W. H. Auden. CP-AudeW

When to Her Lute. Thomas Campion. CP-CampT

When to Mediterranean the birds' thoughts turn. Here, If Forlorn. Ivor Gurney. SP-GurnI

When to my house you come, dear Dean. Tom Punsibi's Letter to Dean Swift. Thomas Sheridan. CP-SherT

When to my melancholy. Revivals. Denise Levertov. SP-LeveDP

When to sweet music my lady is dancing. Valse, The. Paul Laurence Dunbar. CP-DunbP

When to that beauty that I saw before. Michelangelo Buonarroti. CP-Miche, *tr. by* John Frederick Nims

When, to the attractions of the busy world. William Wordsworth. CP-WorW1

When, to the inward darkness of my mind. Twilight. Walter De la Mare. CP-DeLaW

When, to their airy hall, my fathers' voice. Fragment, A: "When, to their airy hall, my fathers' voice." Lord Byron. CP-Byron

When to thy Porch I come, and (ravisht) see. To the Honoured, Master Endimion Porter. Robert Herrick. CP-HerrR

When toward noon a Greek youth stood in the center. Ancient Amphitheater. Yannis Ritsos. SP-RitsY, *tr. by* Kimon Friar

When, towards the summer's close. Yellow-Hammer, The. Thomas Hardy. CP-HardT

When Trakl crossed over, the angels. There. Gregory Orr. SP-OrrG

When true love broke my heart in half. Surly One, The. Theodore Roethke. CP-RoetT

When Tu Fu was a small boy. For the Chinese Actress, Gardenia Chang. Kenneth Rexroth. CP-RexrK

When twilight comes, before it gets too late. Evening Walk in France. May Sarton. SP-SartM

When twilight darkens, and one by one. Evening. Walter De la Mare. CP-DeLaW

When two little boys—renowned but for noise. Hik-Tee-Dik. James Whitcomb Riley. CP-RileJ

When Two Suns Do Appear. Sir Philip Sidney. SP-SidnP *Fr.* Arcadia.

When two suns do appear. When Two Suns Do Appear. Sir Philip Sidney. SP-SidnP *Fr.* Arcadia.

When two take gas. Moving Picture. David Ignatow. SP-IgnaD

When two times two was three. Chicken Without a Head, The. Charles Simic. SP-SimiC; SP-SimiCE

When Ulysses braved the wine-dark sea. Making the Move. Paul Muldoon. CP-MuldP

When Uncle David fell in the First World War. Two Photographs. Yehuda Amichai. SP-AmicY, *tr. by* Stephen Mitchell

When Uncle Doc Was Young. James Whitcomb Riley. CP-RileJ

When Uncle Sidney he comes here. Doodle-Bug's Charm, The. James Whitcomb Riley. CP-RileJ

When unto nights of autumn do complain. E. E. Cummings. CP-CummE

When up aloft / I fly and fly. Robin, The. Thomas Hardy. CP-HardT

When vain desire at last and vain regret. One Hope, The. Dante Gabriel Rossetti. CW-RossD *Fr.* House of Life, The.

When Victor Emanuel the King. Sword of Castruccio Castracani, The. Elizabeth Barrett Browning. CP-BroEB

When Walking. Stevie Smith. CP-SmitS

When was it that we swore to love for ever? Rose, The. Robert Graves. CP-GravR

When was the last time. Sun Tan at Dusk. James Wright. CP-WrigJ

When was the last time I cried. Time Has Come to Collect Evidence, The. Yehuda Amichai. SP-AmicYL, *tr. by* Benjamin Harshav *and* Barbara Harshav

When was there contract better driven by Fate? On the Union. Ben Jonson. CP-JonsB; SP-JonsB

When was when. Fanny Howe. SP-HoweF *Fr.* O'Clock.

When Watchful came to me he said. Watchful. Stevie Smith. CP-SmitS

When water is so clear it sparkles. Han-shan. CP-ColdM, *tr.* by Red Pine

When water turns ice does it remember. Metamorphosis. Carl Sandburg. CP-SandC

When we are going toward someone we say. Simple-Song. Marge Piercy. SP-PierM

When we are old and these rejoicing veins. Edna St. Vincent Millay. CP-MillE

When we as strangers sought. At an Inn. Thomas Hardy. CP-HardT

When we came out of the wood. Attack, The. D. H. Lawrence. CP-LawrD

When we can all so excellently give. Sonnet: "When we can all so excellently give." Edwin Arlington Robinson. CP-RobiE

When we climbed the slopes of the cutting. Railway Children, The. Seamus Heaney. SP-HeanSO

When We Dead Awaken. Adrienne Rich. SP-RicA2

When we die / we'll take with us. Memento ("When we die / we'll take with us"). Federico García Lorca. CP-GarcF, *tr.* by Jerome Rothenberg *Fr.* Shadow.

When we do give, Alphonso [*or* Alfonso], to the light. To the Same [Alphonso Ferrabosco]. Ben Jonson. CP-JonsB; SP-JonsB

When we drove up to the curb the woman. On Earth. Olga Broumas. SP-BrouO

When we entered the waters of Caesarea. Caesarea. Czeslaw Milosz. CP-MiloC; CP-MiloCN, *tr.* by Lillian Vallee

When we finally tracked him down, the old man (not really all that very old, we thought). Rungs. C. K. Williams. SP-WillC

When we [first] moved here, pulled. Oregon Message, An. William Stafford. SP-StafW; SP-StafWW

When We First Played "Show." James Whitcomb Riley. CP-RileJ

When we 'gainst Satan stoutly fight, the more. Satan. Robert Herrick. CP-HerrR

When we get back, the wagon will be gone. Refusal, The. James Wright. CP-WrigJ

When we get out of the glass bottles of our ego. Escape. D. H. Lawrence. CP-LawrD

When we have ceased to care. Emily Dickinson. CP-DickE

When we have gone the stone will stop singing. April. W. S. Merwin. SP-MerwW

When we have thrown off this old suit. Question Whither, The. George Meredith. CP-MerG1

When we hear Uncle Sidney tell. Good, Old-fashioned People, The. James Whitcomb Riley. CP-RileJ

When we last met at Pinoli's winter roared with snow and sleet. J.D.C.: Ode; On the Second Annual Assembly of the Junior Debating Club, 1900. G. K. Chesterton. CP-ChesG

When we lay where Budmouth Beach is. Budmouth Dears. Thomas Hardy. CP-HardT *Fr.* Dynasts, The.

When we learn. It Is the Season. Josephine Jacobsen. CP-JacoJ

When we locked up the house at night. Locked Out. Robert Frost. CP-FrosR

When we look at things in the light of Tao. Great and Small. Chuang Tzu. CP-MertT

When We Look Up. Denise Levertov. SP-LeveDS *Fr.* During the Eichmann Trial.

When we make love you em- / body whatever was beauti-. Love Is Cumulative. James Laughlin. CP-LaugJ

When we met. Awakening, The. Alice Walker. CP-WalkA

When We Pray Alone. Jelaluddin Rumi. SP-Rumi, *tr.* by Coleman Barks

When We Say Goodbye. Thomas McGrath. SP-McGrT

When we see. Removal, The. W. S. Merwin. SP-MerwW

When we speak of freedom. On the Way Back. Bogomil Gjuzel. CP-KizeC, *tr.* by Carolyn Kizer

When we speak / of those musket-draped. Crispus Attucks. Jay Wright. SP-WrigJ

When we stand on the tops of Things. Emily Dickinson. CP-DickE

When we start breaking up in the wet darkness. Consolations of Philosophy. Derek Mahon. CP-MahoD

When we stop, / a green snake starts again. Greenness Taller Than Gods, A. Yusef Komunyakaa. CP-KomuY

When we stop where you lived, the house. Disappearances in the Guarded Sector. Tess Gallagher. SP-GallT

When we that wore the myrtle wear the dust. Edna St. Vincent Millay. CP-MillE

When we three meet? Ah! friend of mine. James Whitcomb Riley. CP-RileJ

When We Two Parted. Lord Byron. CP-Byron

When we went hunting the Dragon. Hunting of the Dragon, The. G. K. Chesterton. CP-ChesG

When we were boys (I was). Digging Down to China. James Laughlin. CP-LaugJ

When We Were Children. Louis MacNeice. CP-MacNL

When we were children said. Jemez. Charles Tomlinson. CP-TomlC

When we were fleeing the burning city. Flight. Czeslaw Milosz. CP-MiloC; CP-MiloCN, *tr.* by John Carpenter *and* Bogdana Carpenter

When We Were Here Together. Kenneth Patchen. CP-PatcK

When we were sitting side by. Last Caress, The. James Laughlin. CP-LaugJ

When We Were Very Sore; Lines on Discovering that You Have Been Advertised as America's A.A. Milne. Dorothy Parker. CP-ParkD

When we were young, because we. Illusion. Kenneth Rexroth. CP-RexrK

When Wearily We Shrink Away. Thomas Hardy. CP-HardT

When weary with the long day's care. To Imagination. Emily Jane Brontë. CP-BronE

When weenty-teenty Baby slept. When Baby Slept. James Whitcomb Riley. CP-RileJ

When weenty-teenty Baby woke. When Baby Woke. James Whitcomb Riley. CP-RileJ

When, well or ill, the task is done. From Where? A. K. Ramanujan. CP-RamaA

When well we speak, & nothing do that's good. Chewing [of] the Cud, The. Robert Herrick. CP-HerrR

When what has helped us has helped us enough. Place of Backs, The. W. S. Merwin. SP-MerwW

When what hugs stopping earth than silent is. E. E. Cummings. CP-CummE

When what is lov'd, is Present, love doth spring. Presence and Absence. Robert Herrick. CP-HerrR

When what's-his-name the quadriplegic got. Hard-on Death. Alan Dugan. CP-DugaA

When, when & whenever. Last Poem to Be Written, The. James Laughlin. CP-LaugJ

When white haired. Prayer. William Corbett. SP-CorbW

When wickedness is broken as a tree / Paradise comes to light, ah holy land! Christina Georgina Rossetti. CP-RosC2

When wild War's deadly blast was blawn. Robert Burns. CP-BurnR

When will that voice come? Drawn from the air in that drab room. Séance, The. Marya Alexandrovna Zaturenska. SP-ZatuM

When will the bell ring, and end this weariness? Last Lesson of the Afternoon. D. H. Lawrence. CP-LawrD

When will the day bring its pleasure? Until the Day Break. Christina Georgina Rossetti. CP-RosC2

When will the treadmill of life and death stop. Han-shan. CP-ColdM, *tr.* by Red Pine

When Will was at home in his palace of zinc. George Meredith. CP-MerG2

When will you ever, Peace, wild wooddove, shy wings shut. Peace. Gerard Manley Hopkins. CP-HopkG

When will you learn, my self, to be. Leaf and the Tree, The. Edna St. Vincent Millay. CP-MillE

When Willie Crosby died I thought too much. Survival in Missouri. John Ciardi. CP-CiarJ

When Wilt Thou Teach the People? D. H. Lawrence. CP-LawrD

When wilt thou wake, O Mother, wake and see. Sleep-Worker, The. Thomas Hardy. CP-HardT

When Winchester races first took their beginning. Written at Winchester on Tuesday the 15th July 1817. Jane Austen. CP-AustJ

When wind and rain were like a cloak a-blow. G. K. Chesterton. *See* Wrapped in the windy rains that pelt and blow

When wind and winter turn our vineyard. Vine, The. Thomas Merton. CP-MertT

When Winds and Seas do rage. Goodnesse of His God, The. Robert Herrick. CP-HerrR

When winds that move not its calm surface sweep. Ocean, The. Moschus. CP-ShelP, *tr.* by Percy Bysshe Shelley

When winter covering all the ground. When Winter Darkening All Around. Paul Laurence Dunbar. CP-DunbP

When Winter Darkening All Around. Paul Laurence Dunbar. CP-DunbP

When Winter fringes every bough. Fair Haven ("When Winter fringes every bough"). Henry David Thoreau. CP-ThorH

When winter's glaze is lifted from the greens. Sometime Sportsman Greets the Spring, The. John Updike. CP-UpdiJ

When wise Lord Berkeley first came here. Discovery, The. Jonathan Swift. CP-SwifJ

When wise Ulysses from his native Coast. Argus. Alexander Pope. CP-PopeA

When wit and genius meet their doom. On the Same. William Cowper. CP-CowpW

When wit, and learning are so hardly set. To Mr Ben Jonson in His Journey, by Mr Craven. Ben Jonson. CP-JonsB

When with a clanking chain a master locks. Michelangelo Buonarroti. CP-Miche, *tr.* by John Frederick Nims

When, with a pain he desires to explain to his servitors, Baby. Nurses, The. Rudyard Kipling. CP-KiplR *Fr.* Land and Sea Tales.

When with day's woes night haunts wake-weary eyes. Prayer, A. Walter De la Mare. CP-DeLaW

When with pale cheek and sunken eye I sang. Henry David Thoreau. CP-ThorH

When with the Virgin morning thou dost rise. Matins [*or* Mattens], or Morning Prayer. Robert Herrick. CP-HerrR

When women stop carrying. Beginning, A. Charles Bukowski. SP-BukC3

When words we want, Love teacheth to endite. Writing. Robert Herrick. CP-HerrR

When, wounded by her anger at some trifle. Pearl, The. Robert Graves. CP-

GravR

When, wrapt in self, the soul grows dull. Nature's Help for the Soul. Jones Very. CP-VeryJ

When wrath & terror changed Jove's regal port. Ralph Waldo Emerson. CP-EmerR

When ye say to Tabaqui, "My Brother!" when ye call the Hyena to meat. Rudyard Kipling. CP-KiplR *Fr.* Second Jungle Book, The.

When ye stood up in the house. Fourfold Aspect, The. Elizabeth Barrett Browning. CP-BroEB

When you and I on the Palos Verdes cliff. Shane O'Neill's Cairn. Robinson Jeffers. CP-JefR2

When you and I were all. Randall Jarrell. CP-JarrR

When you and I were young, the days. Retrospection. Paul Laurence Dunbar. CP-DunbP

When you and my true lover meet. Lady's Third Song, The. William Butler Yeats. CP-YeatW

When you appeared it was as if. Happenstance. Rita Dove. SP-DoveR

When you are come by ways emptied of light. Art. Allen Tate. CP-TateA

When you are dead, and your disturbing eyes. Edna St. Vincent Millay. CP-MillE

When you are far away. James Laughlin. CP-LaugJ

When you are gone, there is nor bloom nor leaf. Little Words. Dorothy Parker. CP-ParkD

When you are Mistresse of the song. To the Queen, an Apologie for the Length of the Following Panegyricke. Richard Crashaw. CP-CrasR

When You Are Old. Pierre de Ronsard. CP-ChesG, *tr. by* G. K. Chesterton

When You Are Old. William Butler Yeats. CP-YeatW

When you are old and beautiful. At Majority. Adrienne Rich. CP-RicAE

When you are old as I now am. Serpent's Tail. Robert Graves. CP-GravR

When you are old, when candle and evening cloud. When You Are Old. Pierre de Ronsard. CP-ChesG, *tr. by* G. K. Chesterton

When you are silent, shining host by guest. E. E. Cummings. CP-CummE

When you are with everyone but me. Jelaluddin Rumi. SP-Rumi, *tr. by* Coleman Barks

When You Asked for It. Kenneth Rexroth. CP-RexrK

When you began your story all its words. To a Scholar in the Stacks. Howard Nemerov. CP-NemeH

When you break your leg. Prayer Blues. Allen Ginsberg. SP-GinsA

When you came and you talked and you read with your. For William Carlos Williams. Galway Kinnell. SP-KinnGN

When you came in the office saying "Hi." Sexist Lament: Ruin by Monitor. Alan Dugan. CP-DugaA

When you came over the top of the world. On the Downs. G. K. Chesterton. CP-ChesG

When you can no longer / eat. Attentiveness. Alice Walker. CP-WalkA

When you climb up to the middle classes. Climbing Up. D. H. Lawrence. CP-LawrD

When you come, as you soon must, to the streets of our city. Advice to a Prophet. Richard Wilbur. CP-WilbR

When you come / Every evening. Exchange of Gifts, An. May Sarton. SP-SartM

When You Come Past My Window. "Shu Ting." CP-KizeC, *tr. by* Carolyn Kizer *and* Y. H. Zhao

When you come to London Town. London Stone. Rudyard Kipling. CP-KiplR

When You Come to Me. Maya Angelou. SP-AngeM

When you consider the radiance, that it does not withhold. City Limits, The. A. R. Ammons. CP-AmmoA

When You Danced. James Laughlin. CP-LaugJ

When you discover. For Those Whom the Gods Love Less. Denise Levertov. SP-LeveDS

When you do say hello I am never sure. Progress Report. Audre Lorde. SP-LordA

When you feel your lips becoming infinite. Jelaluddin Rumi. SP-Rumi, *tr. by* Coleman Barks

When you first introduced me to your nurse. Well-to-Do Invalid, A. Randall Jarrell. CP-JarrR

When you get there, it will be the same life. Passport. Sam Hamill. SP-HamiS

When You Go Anywhere. William Stafford. SP-StafWW

When you go away the wind clicks around to the north. W. S. Merwin. SP-MerwW

When you go to the fair. All Night Fair. Federico García Lorca. CP-GarcF, *tr. by* Jerome Rothenberg *Fr.* Fairs.

When you ground the lenses and the moons swam free. Emancipators, The. Randall Jarrell. CP-JarrR

When you happened to sprain your wrist or ankle. Glanders. Paul Muldoon. CP-MuldP

When you have nothing more to say, just drive. Peninsula, The. Seamus Heaney. SP-HeanSO

When you hear it languishing. Oxford Voice, The. D. H. Lawrence. CP-LawrD

When you imagine trumpet-faced musicians. Homage to Literature. Muriel Rukeyser. CP-RukeM

When you invent an all. Against Veils on Exodus 33:23 and 34:33. Alan Dugan. CP-DugaA

When you kissed me it was as if. Pencil Sketch of Self & Other. Jane Cooper. CP-CoopJ

When you look at a picture you always can see. William Blake. CP-BlakW

When you look down from the airplane you see lines. Field and Forest. Randall Jarrell. CP-JarrR

When you paced forth, to await maternity. At a Bridal. Thomas Hardy. CP-HardT

When you plunged. Otter, The. Seamus Heaney. SP-HeanSO

When You Point Your Finger. Alfonso Cortes. CP-MertT

When you put on that inmost ring. Felled Elm and She, The. Thomas Hardy. CP-HardT

When you put your legs up / against the wall after we. Why. James Laughlin. CP-LaugJ

When you rang at Dick Mid's Place. E. E. Cummings. CP-CummE

When you recall me in that land. Song to No Music, A. Joseph Brodsky. CP-BrodJ, *tr. by* David Rigsbee

When you remember me, my child. Mississippi Winter II. Alice Walker. CP-WalkA

When you roll along admiring the view. Voluble Wheel Chair, The. Ogden Nash. CP-NashO

When you said "accidental" / I thought it was that you were formal. Je Vois dans le Hasard Tous les Biens Que J'espere. Robert Creeley. CP-CreeR

When you sat, far-eyed and cold, in the basalt throne. Seamus Heaney. SP-HeanSO *Fr.* Squarings.

When You Say That, Smile! or All Right Then, Don't Smile. Ogden Nash. CP-NashO

When you see me sitting quietly. On Aging. Maya Angelou. SP-AngeM

When you see them. Take Time Out. Maya Angelou. SP-AngeM

When you shall arrive. Paul. William Carlos Williams. CP-WilW2

When you sleep and know it not. Song of the Grey Dog, The. D. H. Lawrence. CP-LawrD

When you slowly emerged from the den of Time. Plaint to Man, A. Thomas Hardy. CP-HardT

When You Speak to Me. Tess Gallagher. SP-GallT

When you take her into your wounded embrace, a bra clasp unhooks itself. Phantom Limbs. Yusef Komunyakaa. CP-KomuY

When you, that at this moment are to me. Edna St. Vincent Millay. CP-MillE

When you the sun-burnt pilgrim see. Good Counsel to a Young Maid. Thomas Carew. CP-CareT

When you think of the distances. Distances, The. W. S. Merwin. SP-MerwW

When you think strong enough, you get something. Six, The. James Dickey. CP-DickJ

When you thrill with joy. Watch Out, Papa. Langston Hughes. CP-HughL; CP-HughL2

When you told me that he was in jail. Marilyn Hacker. SP-HackM *Fr.* Navigators, The.

When you turn the corner. Final Curve. Langston Hughes. CP-HughL; CP-HughL2

When you visit the Humans. Observe Details. Christopher Logue. SP-LoguC

When you wake to the dream of now. Dream of Now, The. William Stafford. SP-StafWW

When you walked in with your suitcase, leaving. Rosy. Louise Glück. SP-GlucL

When you went away it was morning. E. E. Cummings. CP-CummE

When you went, how was it you carried with you. Grey Evening. D. H. Lawrence. CP-LawrD

When you were explaining America, Robert, you did not. Pastor Errante. Donald Davie. CP-DaviDC

When you were little, wind tailed you. Poem for Karl Wallenda, Aerialist Supreme. Raymond Carver. CP-CarvR

When / you were small, I. C. K. Williams. CP-WillC

When you wrote to tell me of your arrival. Charles Tomlinson. SP-TomlC *Fr.* Winter Journey.

When young I scribbled, boasting, on my wall. Summing-up, The. Stanley Kunitz. CP-KunSC

When, young, I slept in a cold bed. Dream Range, The. Thomas McGrath. SP-McGrT

When young spring comes. Poem: "When young spring comes." Langston Hughes. CP-HughL; CP-HughL1

When your beauty is grown old in all men's songs. Laudantes Decem Pulchritudinis Johannae Templi. Ezra Pound. CP-PoEar

When your honest redskin toma. E. E. Cummings. CP-CummE

When your lobster was lifted out of the tank. Something Else. Paul Muldoon. CP-MuldP

When your loud axe's echo on the ponds, at early morning. St. Alberic. Thomas Merton. CP-MertT

When your soft welcomings were said. On a Discovered Curl of Hair. Thomas

Hardy. CP-HardT

When your sperm enters me, it is altered. Adrienne Rich. CP-RicAE

When your "Uncle Jim" was younger. To Hattie—on Her Birthday. James Whitcomb Riley. CP-RileJ

When your voice breaks. Grief. Denise Levertov. SP-LeveDL

When your widow had left the graveside. Ritual of Memories, The. Tess Gallagher. SP-GallT

When you're desperate ride. Shmuel HaNagid. SP-HaNaS, *tr.* by Peter Cole

When You're Lost in Juarez, in the Rain, and It's Eastertime Too. Charles Wright. SP-WrigCN

When you're ready to sell your diamonds. Commercial Variations. Frank O'Hara. SP-OharF

When you've shouted "Rule Britania," when you've sung "God Save the Queen." Absent-Minded Beggar, The. Rudyard Kipling. CP-KiplR

Whenas in silks my Julia goes. Upon Julia's Clothes. Robert Herrick. CP-HerrR

Whence are ye, vague desires. Arthur Hugh Clough. SP-ClouA

Whence came his feet into my field, and why? He and I. Dante Gabriel Rossetti. CW-RossD *Fr.* House of Life, The.

Whence came this morn, this glorious morn. This Morn. Jones Very. CP-VeryJ

Whence come you, all of you so sorrowful? Sonnet: To certain Ladies; when Beatrice was lamenting her Father's Death. Dante Alighieri. CW-RossD, *tr.* by Dante Gabriel Rossetti

Whence comes solace?—Not from seeing. On a Fine Morning. Thomas Hardy. CP-HardT

Whence comes that small continuous silence. Swallows Flown. Walter De la Mare. CP-DeLaW

Whence comes those many-colored birds. Birds of Passage, The. Jones Very. CP-VeryJ

Whence comest thou, Gehazi. Gehazi. Rudyard Kipling. CP-KiplR

Whence deathless *Kit-Cat* took its Name. Epigram on the Toasts of the Kit-Cat Club, Anno 1716. Alexander Pope. CP-PopeA

Whence did all that fury come? Stick of Incense, A. William Butler Yeats. CP-YeatW

Whence didst thou spring, or art thou yet unborn. Field and Wood, The. Jones Very. CP-VeryJ

Whence Had They Come? William Butler Yeats. CP-YeatW

Whence is it, that amaz'd I hear. To the Nightingale. William Cowper. CP-CowpW

Whence that low voice?—A whisper from the heart. William Wordsworth. CP-WorW2 *Fr.* River Duddon [A Series of Sonnets], The.

Whence the brooch of burning gold. Brooch of Lorn, The. Sir Walter Scott. SP-ScotW *Fr.* Lord of the Isles, The.

Whene'er I view those lips of thine. To M.S.G. Lord Byron. CP-Byron

Whene'er the mist, that stands 'twixt God and thee. Reason. Samuel Taylor Coleridge. CP-ColeS

Whene'er this Stone, now hid beneath the Lake. To Posterity. Samuel Johnson. CP-JohnS

Whenever Cold Mountain stops to visit. Feng-kan. CP-ColdM, *tr.* by Red Pine

Whenever her white foot moves through the green. Petrarch. CP-Petra, *tr.* by J. G. Nichols

Whenever I am got under my gravestone. Soliloquy: "Whenever I am got under my gravestone." Ted Hughes. SP-HughTN

Whenever I behold an asp. Asp, The. Ogden Nash. CP-NashO

Whenever I do not create. Beast. Alice Walker. CP-WalkA

Whenever I go by there nowadays. Tavern, The. Edwin Arlington Robinson. CP-RobiE

Whenever I go there everything is changed. W. S. Merwin. SP-MerwW

Whenever I have an appointment to see the assistant. Poem for Benn's Graduation from High School, A. John Ciardi. CP-CiarJ

Whenever I look you are islands. Islands. W. S. Merwin. SP-MerwWF

Whenever I plunge my arm, like this. Under the Waterfall. Thomas Hardy. CP-HardT

Whenever I See Beauty I See Death. Richard Eberhart. CP-EberR

Whenever I talk of my art. Resolutions. Donald Davie. CP-DaviDC

Whenever I waken and this animal. Happiness. John Ciardi. CP-CiarJ

Whenever Love makes his assaults on me. Petrarch. CP-Petra, *tr.* by J. G. Nichols

Whenever my gentle faithful comforter. Petrarch. CP-Petra, *tr.* by J. G. Nichols

Whenever my past unrolls before these eyes. Michelangelo Buonarroti. CP-Miche, *tr.* by John Frederick Nims

Whenever poets want to give you the idea that something is par-. Don't Cry, Darling, It's Blood All Right. Ogden Nash. CP-NashO

Whenever remembrance of the one I love. Michelangelo Buonarroti. CP-Miche, *tr.* by John Frederick Nims

Whenever Richard Cory went down town [*or* downtown]. Richard Cory. Edwin Arlington Robinson. CP-RobiE

Whenever Richard Gallup is dissevered. Poem in the Traditional Manner. Ted Berrigan. SP-BerrT *Fr.* Sonnets, The.

Whenever the landlord and landlady get. Buffalo Bill. Charles Bukowski. SP-

BukC2

Whenever we're left alone in the room she performs. Gloria's Clues. Yusef Komunyakaa. CP-KomuY

Whenever you are thought, the mind. Few and Simple. W. H. Auden. CP-AudeW

"Whenever you dress me dolls, mammy" Dolls, The. Thomas Hardy. CP-HardT

Whenever you wake, you will find journeying. Voices of Waking. Muriel Rukeyser. CP-RukeM

When's the Last Boat to Alcatraz? Peter Blue Cloud. SP-BlueP

Where. Wendell Berry. CP-BerrW

Where. Heather McHugh. SP-McHuH

Where? Walter De la Mare. CP-DeLaW

Where a faint light shines alone. Dark House, The. Edwin Arlington Robinson. CP-RobiE

—Where a heavy. Bastard Peace, A. William Carlos Williams. CP-WilW1

Where a naked man, asleep, is strapped. Edward Kienholz: *The State Hospital.* Paul Muldoon. CP-MuldP

Where a Poet's From. Archibald MacLeish. CP-MacLA

Where a river roars in rapids. Our Guardian Angels and Their Children. Nicholas Vachel Lindsay. CP-LindV

Where a river touches an island. Stillborn. William Stafford. SP-StafWW

Where aerial gunnery was, you think at first a cadaver. Gila Bend. James Dickey. CP-DickJ

Where all is black. Nature and Man. George Meredith. CP-MerG2

Where American magazines. Aging Painter Sits Where the Great Tower Heaves Down Midnight. Robert Penn Warren. CP-WarrR

Where and to whom. Two Sons. Anne Sexton. CP-SextA

Where and when exactly did we first have sex? History. Paul Muldoon. CP-MuldP

Where are all thy beauties now, all hearts enchaining? [*or* harts enchayning?]. Thomas Campion. CP-CampT

Where are my children, whom from youth I raised. Rachel. Jones Very. CP-VeryJ

Where are my pretty ones! My Pretty Animals. Kenneth Patchen. CP-PatcK

Where are the centuries, where is the dream. Instant, The. Jorge Luis Borges. SP-BorgJ, *tr.* by Alastair Reid

Where are the heroes of the rain? There's a live one carrying a. Deadlines. James Tate. SP-TateJ

Where are the horses of the sun? Charioteer of Delphi, The. James Merrill. SP-MerrJ

Where are the joys I have met in the morning. Fair Jenny. Robert Burns. CP-BurnR

Where are the merchants and the money-lenders. Death. Thomas Merton. CP-MertT

Where are the poems? Why do I now write none? At the Gate. Robert Graves. CP-GravR

Where are the songs I used to know. Key-Note, The. Christina Georgina Rossetti. CP-RosC2

Where are the women who, *entre deux guerres.* Ballad of Ladies Lost and Found. Marilyn Hacker. SP-HackM

Where are they going. Home Home Home. Lawrence Ferlinghetti. SP-FerlL

Where are they going, the girls with little curls. Sarcophagi. Eugenio Montale. CP-MontE, *tr.* by Jonathan Galassi

Where are they gone that did delight in honour. In October. G. K. Chesterton. CP-ChesG

Where are they, not those young men, not those. Lost Romans, The. Muriel Rukeyser. CP-RukeM

Where are they now, those wanton Boys? Sequel to *Beggars* Composed Many Years After. William Wordsworth. CP-WorW2; MW-WorW

Where are they—the Afterwhiles. Afterwhiles. James Whitcomb Riley. CP-RileJ

Where are they?—the friends of my childhood enchanted. Boys, The. James Whitcomb Riley. CP-RileJ

Where Are Those High and Haunting Skies. Richard Eberhart. CP-EberR

Where are those honours, Ida! once you own. On a Change of Masters at a Great Public School. Lord Byron. CP-Byron

Where Are We? Jelaluddin Rumi. SP-Rumi, *tr.* by Coleman Barks

Where are we going? where are we going. Song of Slaves in the Desert. John Greenleaf Whittier. CP-WhitJ

Where are we, / Mary, where are we? Bahamas. George Oppen. CP-OppGN

Where are ye, ye who mocked my arm of late. Warrior, The. Jones Very. CP-VeryJ

Where Are You Going? Stevie Smith. CP-SmitS

Where are you going to-night, to-night. John Evereldown. Edwin Arlington Robinson. CP-RobiE

Where are you now—. Face of the Precipice is Black with Lovers, The. Thomas McGrath. SP-McGrT

Where are you now, partisans of all the valleys. Partisan. Primo Levi. CP-LeviP, *tr.* by Ruth Feldman

Where are you taking me from here? Where does this road go? Tell me.

Unanswered. Yannis Ritsos. SP-RitsY, *tr. by* Kimon Friar

Where are your monuments, your battles, martyrs? Sea is History, The. Derek Walcott. CP-WalcD

Where art thou, beloved To-morrow? To-Morrow. Percy Bysshe Shelley. CP-ShelP

Where art thou friend, whom I shall never see. Gerard Manley Hopkins. CP-HopkG

Where art thou, genius? I should use. Ode to James, Earl of Desmond, An. Ben Jonson. CP-JonsB

Where art thou, my beloved Son. Affliction of Margaret, The. William Wordsworth. CP-WorW1

Where art thou Sol, while thus the blind-fold Day. On a Foule Morning, Being Then to Take a Journey. Richard Crashaw. CP-CrasR

Where art thou / Thou beautiful dream. Ralph Waldo Emerson. CP-EmerR

Where? / At night in crumbling rockmass. Paul Celan. SP-CelaP, *tr. by* John Felstiner

Where-Away. James Whitcomb Riley. CP-RileJ

Where be the temples which in Britain's Isle. Artegal and Elidure. William Wordsworth. CP-WorW2

Where Be You [*or* Ye] Going, You [*or* Ye] Devon Maid? John Keats. CP-KeatJ

Where beams the sun the brightest. To A.S., 1830. Emily Jane Brontë. CP-BronE

Where bells no more affright the morn. Emily Dickinson. CP-DickE

Where Blackmoor was, the road that led. Geographical Knowledge. Thomas Hardy. CP-HardT

Where braving angry Winter's storms. Robert Burns. CP-BurnR

Where, but here / would you. Matachines, The. Charles Tomlinson. CP-TomlC

Where can I shit. Old Dog's Song, The. Grace Paley. CP-PalGC

Where can the heart be hidden in the ground. Edna St. Vincent Millay. CP-MillE

Where Can They Have Gone? Jorge Luis Borges. SP-BorgJ, *tr. by* Eric McHenry

Where Cart rins rowin to the sea. Gallant Weaver, The. Robert Burns. CP-BurnR

Where ceaseless Spring her garland twines. Kinsman. John Greenleaf Whittier. CP-WhitJ

Where choked by hairy cactus-fingers. Trinity. G. K. Chesterton. CP-ChesG

Where clouds and mountains are piled to the sky. Han-shan. CP-ColdM, *tr. by* Red Pine

Where Cold Mountain dwells in peace. Han-shan. CP-ColdM, *tr. by* Red Pine

Where contemplation finds her sacred spring. To a Clergyman on the Death of His Lady. Phillis Wheatley. CP-WheaP

Where, Corinth, charm incarnate, are your shrines? Antipater of Sidon. "H. D." CP-DoolH

Where death has uttered an apocalypse. Cacti. Tennessee Williams. CP-WillT

Where death / Stretches its wide horizons. There. Langston Hughes. CP-HughL; CP-HughL2

Where Depths Are Surfaces. Donald Davie. CP-DaviDC

Where did doves perch before there were telephone wires? Damnation of Doves, A. John Ciardi. CP-CiarJ

Where did Love ever get the gold, to give. Petrarch. CP-Petra, *tr.* by J. G. Nichols

Where did the custom come from, anyway. Law of the Perverse, The. James Whitcomb Riley. CP-RileJ

Where did these enormous children come from. Parents' Pantoum. Carolyn Kizer. CP-KizeC

Where did we stop? In dead summer, that is. Kindness, A. William Dickey. SP-DickW

Where did you suppose the moths went. Peril. W. S. Merwin. SP-MerwW

Where did your words go. To Cipriano, in the Wind. Philip Levine. SP-LeviP

Where didst thou find, young Bard, thy sounding lyre? Sonnet: "Where didst thou find, young Bard, thy sounding lyre?" John Keats. CP-KeatJ

Where Dino Campana once tried to sell his sad poems. With Simic and Marinetti at the Giubbe Rosse. Charles Wright. SP-WrigCN

Where dips the rocky highland. Stolen Child, The. William Butler Yeats. CP-YeatW

Where do our thoughts meet. Our Meetings. James Laughlin. CP-LaugJ

Where do the hours of a city begin and end. Counting Houses, The. W. S. Merwin. SP-MerwWF

Where do these / invisible seeds. Advantage, The. Charles Olson. CP-OlsoC

Where do they come from? Those whom we so much dread. They. W. H. Auden. CP-AudeW

Where do they find the answers? Neighbors. David Ignatow. SP-IgnaD

Where do you go when you go to sleep. Through Sleepy-Land. James Whitcomb Riley. CP-RileJ

Where do you think, serpent. Bagatelles the Madrigals, The. Wallace Stevens. CP-StevW; CP-StevWP

Where do you want me to go? Orphan Song. Rainer Maria Rilke. CP-RilkFr

Where does Cinderella sleep? Parvenu. Nicholas Vachel Lindsay. CP-LindV

Where does one look. Dialogue with La Mettrie, A. John Logan. CP-LogaJ

Where does she go. Nameless Voyage, The. James Laughlin. CP-LaugJ

Where does spirit live? Inside or outside. Seamus Heaney. SP-HeanSO *Fr.* Squarings.

Where does the sadness come from? The great Seychellesan tortoise that heaved its. Cross My Heart and Hope to Die, It Was the Very Same Song Exactly. Hayden Carruth. CP-CarHS

Where does this strange black tide, this tidal wave. Ever the Same. Charles Baudelaire. CP-BaudC, *tr. by* Walter Martin

Where dost [*or* do'st] thou careless[e] lie. Ode to Himself, An. Ben Jonson. CP-JonsB; SP-JonsB

Where Dream Begins. May Sarton. SP-SartM

Where droop the little ivy shoots. In a Churchyard. James Schuyler. CP-SchuJ

Where ends our chancel in a vaulted space. Vicar, The. George Crabbe. SP-CrabG *Fr.* Borough, The.

Where eons back, earth slipped and cracked. Synonyms. Robert Penn Warren. CP-WarrR

Where ever Nodes do's in the Summer come. Upon Nodes. Robert Herrick. CP-HerrR

Where every bird is bold to go. Emily Dickinson. CP-DickE

Where Every Prospect. Kenneth Patchen. CP-PatcK

Where Everything Is Music. Jelaluddin Rumi. SP-Rumi, *tr. by* Coleman Barks

Where faces are hueless, where eyelids are dewless. Requiem: "Where faces are hueless, where eyelids are dewless." George Meredith. CP-MerG1

Where far in forest I am laid. Riddle, A. Richard Wilbur. CP-WilbR

Where giant wordlings interrupt the stuttering machine-gun wit. Descriptions of Imaginary Poetries. Robert Duncan. SP-DuncR

Where God in mercy, there write down thy fears. Gods Mirth, Mans Mourning. Robert Herrick. CP-HerrR

Where grac'd with many a classic spoil. Absence. Samuel Taylor Coleridge. CP-ColeS

Where gray walks slope through shadows shaped like lace. Duet, with Muffled Brake Drums. John Updike. CP-UpdiJ

Where had her sweetness gone? Quarrel in Old Age. William Butler Yeats. CP-YeatW

Where had I heard this wind before. Bereft. Robert Frost. CP-FrosR

Where has Maid Quiet gone to. Maid Quiet. William Butler Yeats. CP-YeatW

Where has the sun a home? didst thou e'er trace. Sun, The. Jones Very. CP-VeryJ

Where hast thou been my brother? thou art torn. Prodigal, The. Jones Very. CP-VeryJ

Where hast thou been roaming. Homeless Wind, The. Jones Very. CP-VeryJ

Where hast thou been since round the walls of Troy. New Helen, The. Oscar Wilde. CP-WildO

Where hast thou floated, in what seas pursued. To the Immortal Memory of the Halibut on Which I Dined This Day, Monday, April 26, 1784. William Cowper. CP-CowpW

Where have I "heard" a silence before. Glen of Silence, The. Hugh MacDiarmid. SP-MacDH

Where have I lost my way among money and horses? Lament of a New England Mother, The. Richard Eberhart. CP-EberR

Where have the people gone. From Spain to Alabama. Langston Hughes. CP-HughL; CP-HughL2

Where have these hands been. Musician. Louise Bogan. CP-BogaL

Where have you been this while away. Widow's Party, The. Rudyard Kipling. CP-KiplR

Where he stood in boots in water to his calves. Fishvendor, The. William Meredith. SP-MereW

Where Helen Lies. Robert Burns. CP-BurnR

Where He's Staying Now. William Meredith. SP-MereW

Where history was. Sightseers. Howard Nemerov. CP-NemeH

Where holy ground begins, unhallowed ends. Parsonage in Oxfordshire, A. William Wordsworth. CP-WorW2

Where Humber pours his rich commercial stream. Tale, Founded on a Fact, A. William Cowper. CP-CowpW

Where hundreds of frogs. West Branch Ponds, Kokadjo, Maine. Mona Van Duyn. SP-VanDM

Where I? Robinson Jeffers. CP-JefR2

Where I grew up, I used to see. Rabbi, The. Robert Earl Hayden. CP-HaydR

Where I have been. Henry David Thoreau. CP-ThorH

Where I have lost, I softer tread. Emily Dickinson. CP-DickE

Where I Live. Billy Collins. SP-CollB

Where I Live in This Honorable House of the Laurel Tree. Anne Sexton. CP-SextA

Where I Sit Writing My Letter. Ted Hughes. SP-HughTN

Where I spat in the harbor the oranges were bobbing. Metamorphoses, The. Randall Jarrell. CP-JarrR

Where I walk is with her. Goddess. Philip Whalen. SP-WhalP

Where I waved at the sky. Balance Wheel, The. Anne Sexton. SP-SextA

Where / if it's not too much to ask. Carmen 55. Catullus. CP-ZukLS *Fr.* Carmina.

Where in the world is Helen gone. Gone Ladies. François Villon. SP-LoguC, *tr.*

by Christopher Logue

Where Innocent Bright-Eyed Daisies Are. Christina Georgina Rossetti. CP-RosC2

Where is Alex, keeper of horses? Alex. Mary Oliver. SP-OlivM

Where is David?.Oh God's people. In Which Roosevelt Is Compared to Saul. Nicholas Vachel Lindsay. CP-LindV

Where is he now, in his soiled shirt reeking of garlic. For Pao-Chin, a Boatman on the Yellow Sea. Edna St. Vincent Millay. CP-MillE

Where is he taking us. Eros. "H. D." CP-DoolH

Where is little Marjorie? Little Marjorie. James Whitcomb Riley. CP-RileJ

Where is love when love is not? When Love Is Not. Robert Graves. CP-GravR

Where is my love! I cried. Ballad of Love. E. E. Cummings. CP-CummE

Where is my love— / In silence and shadow she lies. Where? Walter De la Mare. CP-DeLaW

Where is my mother? Bothering Me at Last. David Ignatow. SP-IgnaD

Where is Skrymir? Giant Skrymir? Ralph Waldo Emerson. CP-EmerR

Where Is Tao? Chuang Tzu. CP-MertT

Where is that Helen, who could occupy. Double Ballade of Newfangled Ladies, A. Robert Stock. SP-StocR

Where is that holy fire, which verse is said. Sappho to Philaenis. John Donne. MW-DonnJ *Fr.* Elegies.

Where is that sugar, Hammond. Early Evening Quarrel. Langston Hughes. CP-HughL; CP-HughL2

Where is that woman of the west. Woman Who Went East, The. Thomas Hardy. CP-HardT

Where is the Black Beast? Black Beast, The. Ted Hughes. SP-HughTN

Where is the child that I was. Pablo Neruda. SP-NeruP *Fr.* Question Book.

Where is the forehead that with one slight shake. Petrarch. CP-Petra, *tr.* by J. G. Nichols

Where is the grave of Sir Arthur O'Kellyn? Knight's Tomb, The. Samuel Taylor Coleridge. CP-ColeS; MW-ColeS

Where is the Jack that built the house. Château Jackson. Louis MacNeice. CP-MacNL

Where is the Jim Crow section. Merry-Go-Round. Langston Hughes. CP-HughL; CP-HughL2; CP-HughL3

Where is the marvelous thief. Dirge for the Proud World. Thomas Merton. CP-MertT

Where is the prisoner? Two Foscari, The. Lord Byron. CP-Byron

Where Is the Real Non-Resistant? Nicholas Vachel Lindsay. CP-LindV

Where is the sky born? Climate and Lyre. Radovan Pavlovski. CP-KizeC, *tr.* by Carolyn Kizer

Where is the sky hurrying to. Coeur Simple. Stevie Smith. CP-SmitS

Where is the time to light a cigarette. Yannis Ritsos. SP-RitsY *Fr.* Second Series.

Where is the toothed estuary the toothed. Ōkeanos and the Golden Sickle. Kenneth Rexroth. CP-RexrK

Where is the truth to indulge my heart. Seven Years. Robert Graves. CP-GravR

Where is the written doe headed, through these written woods? Joy of Writing, The. Wisława Szymborska. SP-SzymWM, *tr.* by Joanna Trzeciak

Where Is Thy Victory? Walter De la Mare. CP-DeLaW

Where is your scorn now? To My Father, Dying. Gregory Orr. SP-OrrG

Where it says snow. Errata. Charles Simic. SP-SimiC; SP-SimiCE

Where It Was at Back Then. Anne Sexton. CP-SextA; SP-SextA

Where I've Been All My Life. Carolyn Kizer. CP-KizeC

Where Knock Is Open Wide. Theodore Roethke. CP-RoetT

Where lately harboured many a famous whore. On the New Hot-House. Ben Jonson. CP-JonsB; SP-JonsB

Where lies the land to which the ship would go? Arthur Hugh Clough. SP-ClouA *Fr.* Songs in Absence.

Where lies the Land to which yon Ship must go? William Wordsworth. CP-WorW1; MW-WorW

Where Lies the Truth? Has Man in Wisdom's Creed. William Wordsworth. CP-WorW2

Where, like a pillow on a bed. Ecstasy, The. John Donne. CP-DonnJ; MW-DonnJ

Where love begins, there dead thy first desire. Another. Robert Herrick. CP-HerrR

Where love is, there comes sorrow / Today or else tomorrow. Christina Georgina Rossetti. CP-RosC2

Where lovers go to learn. Love Is a School. James Laughlin. CP-LaugJ

Where man's profane and tainting hand. Fragment of a Sonnet: Farewell to North Devon. Percy Bysshe Shelley. CP-ShelP

Where might there be a refuge for me. Tell Me, Tell Me. Marianne Craig Moore. CP-MoorM

Where most surely comes a day. Day. Langston Hughes. CP-HughL; CP-HughL1

Where my imaginary line. Beech. Robert Frost. CP-FrosR

Where my love lives is nowhere in my heart. Michelangelo Buonarroti. CP-Miche, *tr.* by John Frederick Nims

Where my stag-antlered love moves. Kenneth Patchen. CP-PatcK

Where Neither Rust Nor Moth Doth Corrupt. Christina Georgina Rossetti. CP-RosC2

Where never tempest heaveth, / Nor sorrow grieveth. Christina Georgina Rossetti. CP-RosC2

Where no question possibly remains—someone crying, someone dead—blame asks: whose fault? Blame. C. K. Williams. SP-WillC

Where no tree nor grass can grow. On a Lichen from North Cape: Gathered by Mr. J. M. Richards, July 3d, 1874. Jones Very. CP-VeryJ

Where Nothing Is Hidden. David Ignatow. SP-IgnaD

Where now has our young Adam. Nocturne: "Where now has our young Adam." John Crowe Ransom. SP-RansJ

Where now is the memory. To a Minor Poet of the Greek Anthology. Jorge Luis Borges. SP-BorgJ, *tr.* by W. S. Merwin

Where now shall I begin this Spacious Feild. Atheism. Phillis Wheatley. CP-WheaP

Where now the huts are empty. What the Ghost of the Gambler Said. Nicholas Vachel Lindsay. CP-LindV

Where O America are you. After Dead Souls. Allen Ginsberg. CP-GinsA

Where o where is the message which today. Hafiz. CP-EmerR *Fr.* Odes.

Where once I loved my flesh. Progress of the Soul, The. Thomas McGrath. SP-McGrT

Where Once the Waters of Your Face. Dylan Thomas. CP-ThomD

Where once we danced, where once we sang. Ancient to Ancients, An. Thomas Hardy. CP-HardT

Where others love, and praise my Verses; still. To the Detracter. Robert Herrick. CP-HerrR

Where, over heathen doom-rings and gray stones of the Horg. King Volmer and Elsie. John Greenleaf Whittier. CP-WhitJ

Where people live on earth there is a kind. Of Kindness. William Meredith. SP-MereW

Where Pleasures rule a Kingdome, never there. Pleasures Pernicious. Robert Herrick. CP-HerrR

Where Roses would not dare to go. Emily Dickinson. CP-DickE

Where run your colts at pasture? White Horses. Rudyard Kipling. CP-KiplR

Where sanity is. God. D. H. Lawrence. CP-LawrD

Where Service Is Needed. Langston Hughes. CP-HughL; CP-HughL3

Where shall I find a white rose blowing? Christina Georgina Rossetti. CP-RosC2

Where shall I find you. Sub Terra. William Carlos Williams. CP-WilW1

Where shall I have at mine own will. Sir Thomas Wyatt. CP-WyatT

Where shall I refuge seeke, if you refuse mee? Thomas Campion. CP-CampT

Where shall the lover rest. Fitz-Eustace's Song. Sir Walter Scott. SP-ScotW *Fr.* Marmion.

Where shall we go? Hounded Lovers, The. William Carlos Williams. CP-WilW2

Where Shall We Land? James Whitcomb Riley. CP-RileJ

Where She Her Sacred Bower Adorns. Thomas Campion. CP-CampT

(Where shee her sacred bowre adornes.) CP-CampT

Where she was burned the early market. Visit to Rouen. Louis MacNeice. CP-MacNL

Where shee her sacred bowre adornes. Thomas Campion. *See* Where She Her Sacred Bower Adorns

Where Ships of Purple—gently toss. Emily Dickinson. CP-DickE

Where should he seek, to go away. Mark, The. Louise Bogan. CP-BogaL

Where sunless rivers weep. Dream Land. Christina Georgina Rossetti. CP-RosC1

Where the arrows. Wintergreen Ridge. Lorine Niedecker. CP-NiedL

Where the bay flashed, and an unrecorded number. Thermopylae. Amy Clampitt. CP-ClamA

Where the Breath Is. Adam Zagajewski. SP-ZagaA

Where the cedar leaf divides the sky. Passage. Hart Crane. CP-CranH

Where the Children Used to Play. James Whitcomb Riley. CP-RileJ

Where the cities end, the. Transcontinent. Donald Hall. CP-HallD

Where the city's ceaseless crowd moves on the livelong day. Sparkles from the Wheel. Walt Whitman. CP-WhitW

Where the cruel swan. In the Park at Caserta. Eugenio Montale. CP-MontE, *tr.* by Jonathan Galassi

Where the drowsy landscape draws. Terraces of Light. Marya Alexandrovna Zaturenska. SP-ZatuM

Where the East wind is brewed fresh and fresh every morning. North Sea Patrol, The. Rudyard Kipling. CP-KiplR

Where the elevated subway slows down. Punch Minus Judy. Charles Simic. SP-SimiCE

Where the flickering river loiters. Man at Play on the River, A. D. H. Lawrence. CP-LawrD

Where the fungus broad & red. Ralph Waldo Emerson. CP-EmerR

Where the Great Lake's sunny smiles. Grave by the Lake, The. John Greenleaf Whittier. CP-WhitJ

Where the Groceries Went. Raymond Carver. CP-CarvR

Where the Hayfields Were. Archibald MacLeish. CP-MacLA

Where the hillside stream unearths itself. Confluence. Charles Tomlinson. CP-TomlC

Where the living with effort go. White Ship, The. Geoffrey Hill. CP-HillG

Where the lizard ran to its little prey. Range in the Desert, The. Randall Jarrell. CP-JarrR

Where the minnows trace. Narcissus. D. H. Lawrence. CP-LawrD

Where the mire was thick from winter sledges. Ivor Gurney. SP-GurnI

Where the moonlit spring descends. Autumn Quarries. Eugenio Montale. CP-MontE, *tr.* by Jonathan Galassi

Where the path closed / down and over. Egrets. Mary Oliver. SP-OlivM

Where the pavement had turned into tufts of grass. Merry-Go-Round with White Swan. Jaroslav Seifert. SP-SeifJ, *tr.* by Ewald Osers

Where the Picnic Was. Thomas Hardy. CP-HardT

Where the pool unfurls its undercloud. Ophelia. Ted Hughes. SP-HughTN

Where the quiet-colo[u]red end of evening smiles. Love among the Ruins. Robert Browning. CP-BroR1; SP-BroR

Where the railroad meets the sea. Pride's Crossing. James Tate. SP-TateJ

Where the Rainbow Ends. Robert Lowell. SP-LoweR

Where the ranch-house disappeared its garden. Under the Bridge. Charles Tomlinson. CP-TomlC; SP-TomlC

Where the remote *Bermudas* ride. Bermudas. Andrew Marvell. CP-MarvA

Where the road came, no longer bearing men. Supplanting, The. Wendell Berry. CP-BerrW

Where the sally tree went pale in every breeze. Field Work. Seamus Heaney. SP-HeanSO

Where the slow river. Leda. "H. D." CP-DoolH

Where the sober-coloured cultivator smiles. Tale of Two Cities, A. Rudyard Kipling. CP-KiplR

Where the Southern cross the Yellow Dog. Poem Almost Wholly in My Own Manner. Charles Wright. SP-WrigCN

Where the tennis court once was. Eugenio Montale. CP-MontE, *tr.* by Jonathan Galassi

Where the three magenta. Man in Black. Sylvia Plath. CP-PlatS

Where the Treasure is. Emily Dickinson. SP-DickE

Where the trees rise like cliffs, proud and blue-tinted in the distance. Guards. D. H. Lawrence. CP-LawrD

Where the two rivers come together—one cold. At the Confluence of the Colorado and the Little Colorado. William Meredith. SP-MereW

Where the wheel of light is turned. Pole Star for This Year. Archibald MacLeish. CP-MacLA

Where the white bridge rears up its stamping arches. In Memory of the Spanish Poet Federico Garcia Lorca. Thomas Merton. CP-MertT

Where the wife is scouring the frying pan. Land of Little Sticks, 1945. James Tate. SP-TateJ

Where the wind. Footprints on the Glacier. W. S. Merwin. SP-MerwW

Where the wings of a sunny Dome expand. America. Herman Melville. SP-MelvH

Where the word, that was undying, fell. Paul Celan. SP-CelaP, *tr.* by John Felstiner

Where Their Worm Dieth Not, and the Fire Is Not Quenched. Christina Georgina Rossetti. CP-RosC2

Where then shall hope and fear their objects find? Additional Poem, An. John Ashbery. SP-AshbJ

Where there is no Vision. Vision. G. K. Chesterton. CP-ChesG

Where there is personal liking we go. Hero, The. Marianne Craig Moore. CP-MoorM *Fr.* Part of a Novel, Part of a Poem, Part of a Play.

Where there was nothing. Widdop. Ted Hughes. SP-HughTN

Where there's a telephone there's a woman to be talking on it. Palimpsest. Philip Whalen. SP-WhalP

Where There's a Will, There's Velleity. Ogden Nash. CP-NashO

Where They Lived. Thomas Hardy. CP-HardT

Where they once dug for money. Old Marlborough Road, The. Henry David Thoreau. CP-ThorH

Where They'd Lived. Raymond Carver. CP-CarvR

Where this floated up from, or why. Woolworth's, 1954. Raymond Carver. CP-CarvR

Where this man walks his fences. Relearning the Language of April. Maxine W. Kumin. SP-KumiM

Where this one dwells and that, thou know'st it well. Narrow Way, The. Jones Very. CP-VeryJ

Where those stone waterpots stood round the wall. Spilth. G. K. Chesterton. CP-ChesG

Where Thou art—that—is Home. Emily Dickinson. CP-DickE

Where thou dwellest, in what Grove. Birds, The. William Blake. CP-BlakW

Where thou hast been once well received. Sick, The. Jones Very. CP-VeryJ

Where Three Roads Joined. Thomas Hardy. CP-HardT

Where Time the measure of his hours. Star of Bethlehem, The. John Greenleaf Whittier. CP-WhitJ

Where to Turn When Sorrow Comes like a Black Bull in Your Dreams. Miller Williams. CP-WillM

Where true Love burns Desire is Love's pure flame. Desire. Samuel Taylor Coleridge. CP-ColeS

Where twigs are breaking stones. Fanny Howe. SP-HoweF *Fr.* O'Clock.

Where Two O'clock Came From. Kenneth Patchen. CP-PatcK

Where two or three were flung together, or fifty. March 2, The. Robert Lowell. SP-LoweR

Where, vomit-yellow, the lichen crawls. Why You Climbed Up. Robert Penn Warren. CP-WarrR

"Where was he wounded?" You don't know. Yehuda Amichai. SP-AmicYL, *tr.* by Barbara Harshav *and* Benjamin Harshav *Fr.* Poems of the Land of Zion and Jerusalem.

Where was my gentle gaurdian where. After a Night of Perplexing Dreams. Annis Boudinot Stockton. CP-StocA

Where Water Comes Together with Other Water. Raymond Carver. CP-CarvR

Where waterfalls in shining folds. Italian Garden. May Sarton. SP-SartM

Where We Are. William Stafford. SP-StafWW

Where we are there must. Robert Creeley. CP-CreeR

Where We Belong, A Duet. Maya Angelou. SP-AngeM

Where we made the fire. Where the Picnic Was. Thomas Hardy. CP-HardT

Where we owe so much it defies Money. Emily Dickinson. SP-DickE

Where we went in the boat was a long bay. Mediterranean, The. Allen Tate. CP-TateA

Where were the greenhouses going. Big Wind. Theodore Roethke. CP-RoetT

Where were ye all? and where wert thou? Emily Jane Brontë. CP-BronE

Where were ye, nymphs, when the remorseless deep. Dog—An Idyllium, The. William Wordsworth. CP-WorW1

Where were you last night? I watched at the gate. Last Night. Christina Georgina Rossetti. CP-RosC3

Where? When? Which? Langston Hughes. CP-HughL; CP-HughL3

Where white clouds form high rugged crags. Han-shan. CP-ColdM, *tr.* by Red Pine

Where wildered anemones hay-lei moony. Grape-Hyacinth. Louis Zukofsky. CP-ZukLS

Where will they stop, those breathing powers. Devotional Incitements. William Wordsworth. CP-WorW2

Where will we be when these flowers turn into fruit. Between. Yehuda Amichai. SP-AmicY, *tr.* by Chana Bloch

Where will you be tonight? Past Lisbon, flying. Muriel Rukeyser. CP-RukeM

Where would I be if not for your wild heart? Wild Heart. Gregory Orr. SP-OrrG

Where would I go from Thee? Thou lov'st me here. Whither Shall I Go from Thy Spirit. Jones Very. CP-VeryJ

Where wrought iron spears. Goodbye, Post Office Square. Fanny Howe. SP-HoweF

Where you are. Ancient Wisdom Speaks. "H. D." CP-DoolH

Where you are rigidly anchored. Landfall, Grenada. Derek Walcott. CP-WalcD

Where you begin. Lackawanna. W. S. Merwin. SP-MerwW

Where you dream of water. For an Anniversary. Robert Creeley. CP-CreeR

Where you fall after the sharp shot. Capercaillie, The. Eugenio Montale. CP-MontE, *tr.* by Jonathan Galassi

Whereas at morning in a jeweled crown. Edna St. Vincent Millay. CP-MillE

Whereas by dark really released,the modern. E. E. Cummings. CP-CummE

Whereas the man who hits. Carnival, The. Robert Creeley. CP-CreeR

Whereat—the King unthroned, the God. Actfive. Archibald MacLeish. CP-MacLA

Where'd all the music. Ode to Music, The. Philip Whalen. SP-WhalP

Where'er I find the Good, the True, the Fair. Philosophical Trinity, The. Samuel Taylor Coleridge. CP-ColeS

Where'er thou sail'st who sailed with me. Henry David Thoreau. CP-ThorH

Wherefore do thy sad numbers flow. Grief Engrossed. Thomas Carew. CP-CareT

Wherefore the praise, the pause. Wages of Eloquence, The. Laura Riding Jackson. CP-RidiL

Wherein are words sublime or noble? What. Karenge Ya Marenge. Countee Cullen. CP-CullC

Wherein is Moscow's dignity. Men, The. William Carlos Williams. CP-WilW1

Wherein the Maker's Right Hand Moralizes the Way to a Familiar but Rare Felicity, Whatwhile the Left Hand Seemingly Knoweth Not Its Brother's Ambages and So Falleth in the Way of an Undiscerning Subtraction. Robert Stock. SP-StocR

Wherelings whenlings / (daughters of if but offspring of hopefear). E. E. Cummings. CP-CummE

Where's a boy a-goin'. When the World Bu'sts Through. James Whitcomb Riley. CP-RileJ

Where's Agnes? Elizabeth Barrett Browning. CP-BroEB

Where's he born? Where a Poet's From. Archibald MacLeish. CP-MacLA

Where's Jack Was / General Was. E. E. Cummings. CP-CummE

Where's Madge then / Madge and her men? E. E. Cummings. CP-CummE

Where's that Coy Gazelle. Shmuel HaNagid. SP-HaNaS

Where's the lamp that Hero lit. Song of Travel, A. Rudyard Kipling. CP-KiplR

Where's the need of singing now? Momus. Edwin Arlington Robinson. CP-RobiE

Where's the Poet? Show Him! Show Him. John Keats. CP-KeatJ

Where's this barn's house? It never had a house. Old Barn at the Bottom of the Fogs, The. Robert Frost. CP-FrosR

Wheresoe'er I turn my View. Lines on Thomas Warton's Poems. Samuel Johnson. CP-JohnS

Whereto shall we liken this Blessed Mary Virgin. Feast of the Annunciation. Christina Georgina Rossetti. CP-RosC2

Whereupon i seize a train and suddenly i am in Paris toward night, in Mai. Rain Is a Handsome Animal, The. E. E. Cummings. CP-CummE

Wherever. Czeslaw Milosz. CP-MiloCN, *tr.* by Tony Milosz

Wherever. Muriel Rukeyser. CP-RukeM

Wherever he looks, standing still in the city. Coupling. David Ignatow. SP-IgnaD

Wherever he may go, by sea or land. Lid, The. Charles Baudelaire. CP-BaudC, *tr.* by Walter Martin

Wherever I am, and whatever I do. Song: "Wherever I am, and whatever I do." John Dryden. SP-DrydJ *Fr.* Conquest of Granada, The.

Wherever I am, at whatever place on earth, I hide from people the conviction. Wherever. Czeslaw Milosz. CP-MiloCN, *tr.* by Tony Milosz

Wherever I am becomes an end. Orpheus (2). Fanny Howe. SP-HoweF *Fr.* Q.

Wherever I surface I reinvent. April Interval. Marilyn Hacker. SP-HackM

Wherever I turn my eyes or let them rest. Petrarch. CP-Petra, *tr.* by J. G. Nichols

Wherever I walked I went green among young growing. Trinity Churchyard. Muriel Rukeyser. CP-RukeM

Wherever the dead are, there they are and. Creation. Kenneth Patchen. CP-PatcK

Wherever we may be. Song: Wherever We May Be. Robert Graves. CP-GravR

Wherever we walk, we walk. Softly. Josephine Jacobsen. CP-JacoJ

Wherever you turn. Inside Chapultepec Castle. Jay Wright. SP-WrigJ

Whether all towns and all who live in them. Tasker Norcross. Edwin Arlington Robinson. CP-RobiE

Whether away my sweetest deerest? Thomas Campion. CP-CampT

Whether he will go on singing. Orpheus (2). Margaret Atwood. SP-AtwM2

Whether I am happy or unhappy I do not question. Addition. Constantine P. Cavafy. CP-CavaC, *tr.* by Theoharis Constantine Theoharis

Whether I was my selfe, or else did see. School or Perl of Putney, the Mistress of All Singular Manners, Mistresse Portman, The. Robert Herrick. CP-HerrR

Whether in the world below or above. Beyond. Robert Creeley. SP-CreeR

Whether it is a speaker, taut on a platform. Metaphor to Action. Muriel Rukeyser. CP-RukeM

Whether it is possible to become lost. How To Tell One Country from Another. Margaret Atwood. SP-AtwM2

Whether it was your way of walking. Your Private Way. Robert Graves. CP-GravR

Whether it's sunny or not, it's sure. Poem about Morning. William Meredith. SP-MereW

Whether my bark went down at sea. Emily Dickinson. CP-DickE

Whether my day is day for you. Ladder, The. Kenneth Patchen. CP-PatcK

Whether my Lady will to hear of me. Leviora. Ezra Pound. CP-PoEar

Whether on Ida's shady brow. To the Muses. William Blake. CP-BlakW

Whether one walks around the hill, or over. There Was Glass and There Are Stars. Randall Jarrell. CP-JarrR

Whether or Not. D. H. Lawrence. CP-LawrD

Whether or not, it is no question now. Entrance. Kenneth Rexroth. CP-RexrK

Whether or not the light I long for, sent. Michelangelo Buonarroti. CP-Miche, *tr.* by John Frederick Nims

Whether or not you like it is not my. Poetry. John Ciardi. CP-CiarJ

Whether partial or supreme. Hymn Directed Somewhere Toward the Pantheon. Robert Stock. SP-StocR

Whether sooner or later. Later or Sooner. Richard Eberhart. CP-EberR

Whether that soul which now comes up to you. Hymn to the Saints, and to Marquis Hamilton, An. John Donne. CP-DonnJ; MW-DonnJ

Whether the fruitful Nile, or Tyrian shore. To the Earl of Roscommon, on His Excellent *Essay on Translated Verse*. John Dryden. CP-DryJ2

Whether the moorings are invisible. Conversation. John Berryman. CP-BerrJ

Whether the rain comes down. Reverie and Invocation. William Carlos Williams. CP-WilW2

Whether the State can loose and bind. MacDonough's Song. Rudyard Kipling. CP-KiplR

Whether There Is Enjoyment in Bitterness. Thomas Merton. CP-MertT

Whether There Is Sorrow in the Demons. John Berryman. CP-BerrJ

Whether they be followed. Last Letters, The. Theodore Weiss. SP-WeisT

Whether they have forgotten. Emily Dickinson. CP-DickE

Whether to sally and see thee, girl of my dreams. To Meet, or Otherwise. Thomas Hardy. CP-HardT

Whether to *use* time, or to *kill* time, either. Moment. Robert Creeley. CP-CreeR

Whether to wend through straight streets strictly. Advertisement, The. Rudyard Kipling. CP-KiplR *Fr.* Muse among the Motors, The.

Whether we've far withdrawn. Farewell. Henry David Thoreau. CP-ThorH

Whether you fished me bravely out of the Pacific. Elegy: "Whether you fished

me bravely out of the Pacific." Joseph Brodsky. CP-BrodJ

Which? Robert Browning. CP-BroR2

Which? Walter De la Mare. CP-DeLaW

Which ane, an' which ane. James Whitcomb Riley. CP-RileJ

Which eye's his eye? Gentleman of Shalott, The. Elizabeth Bishop. CP-BishE

Which in a dry season might. Echo. Michael Palmer. SP-PalmM

Which is best? Heaven. Emily Dickinson. CP-DickE

Which is like a stock room anyway. In an Automotive Store. Charles Olson. CP-OlsoC

Which is my little boy, which is he. Tennessee Williams. CP-WillT

Which is real— / This bottle of indigo glass in the grass. Indigo Glass in the Grass, The. Wallace Stevens. CP-StevWP

Which is the best—the Moon or the Crescent? Emily Dickinson. CP-DickE

Which is the day I have decided to understand. Today is Wednesday. Miller Williams. CP-WillM

Which is the very. E. E. Cummings. CP-CummE

Which is the weakest thing of all. Weakest Thing, The. Elizabeth Barrett Browning. CP-BroEB

Which Is to Say. Robert Creeley. SP-CreeR

Which is worse the lieutenant raising his rifle. Poor Hope. C. K. Williams. CP-WillC

Which is worth more, a crowd of thousands. Jelaluddin Rumi. SP-Rumi, *tr.* by Coleman Barks

Which it / was, form, The. Robert Creeley. CP-CreeR

Which misses most. Emily Dickinson. CP-DickE

Which of my cities will I die in? Web, The. Jorge Luis Borges. SP-BorgJ, *tr.* by Alastair Reid

Which of the fairest three. Apollo to the Graces. John Keats. CP-KeatJ

Which of thy names I take, not only bears. To Sir Horace Vere. Ben Jonson. CP-JonsB; SP-JonsB

Which of us will be left then. In the Year 2020. Raymond Carver. CP-CarvR

Which reminds me. Some Picnic. Charles Bukowski. SP-BukC1

Which Reminds Me. A. K. Ramanujan. CP-RamaA

Which resounds. Re-sounds. Where first would follow. Echo. Michael Palmer. SP-PalmM

Which seems so barren once gave birth. Earth, The. Henry David Thoreau. CP-ThorH

Which time is the real time. Properate Tempus. James Laughlin. CP-LaugJ

Which usually. History. A. K. Ramanujan. CP-RamaA

Which Way? Walter De la Mare. CP-DeLaW

Which way and whence the lightning flew. Ben Jonson. CP-JonsB *Fr.* Masque of Augurs, The.

Whichever Stone You Lift. Paul Celan. SP-CelaP, *tr.* by John Felstiner

Whichever way you turn. Mexican Girls, The. Charles Bukowski. SP-BukC2

Whiffletree. Carl Sandburg. CP-SandC

Whiffs of the Ohio River at Cincinnati. Carl Sandburg. CP-SandC

While a once world slips from. E. E. Cummings. CP-CummE

While an intrinsic ardor bids me write. Phillis Wheatley. *See* While an intrinsic ardor prompts to write

While an intrinsic ardor prompts to write. To the University of Cambridge, in New-England. Phillis Wheatley. CP-WheaP

While Anna's Peers and Early Playmates Tread. William Wordsworth. CP-WorW2

While *any* day was notable and dear. Prospective Visit, A. James Whitcomb Riley. CP-RileJ *Fr.* Child-World, A.

While any two are talking, one. Small Garden Near a Field. Tess Gallagher. SP-GallT

While Asters— / On the Hill. Emily Dickinson. CP-DickE

While at her bedroom window once. Keys of Morning, The. Walter De la Mare. CP-DeLaW

While at the stook the shearers cow'r. To the Rev. John McMath, Inclosing a Copy of *Holy Willie's Prayer*, Which He Had Requested. Robert Burns. CP-BurnR

While Beams of Orient Light Shoot Wide and High. William Wordsworth. CP-WorW2

While Beast instructs his fair, and innocent wife. On Sir Voluptuous Beast. Ben Jonson. CP-JonsB; SP-JonsB

While behind All, Firm and Erect. Walt Whitman. CP-WhitW

While briers an' woodbines budding green. Epistle to John Lapraik. Robert Burns. CP-BurnR

While Celia's tears make sorrow bright. Weeping. Alexander Pope. CP-PopeA

While Christ lay dead the widowed world / Wore willow green for hope undone. Our Church Palms are Budding Willow Twigs. Christina Georgina Rossetti. CP-RosC2

While Cigarettes to Ashes Turn. James Whitcomb Riley. CP-RileJ

While deep in love with one another. Pride of Progeny. Robert Graves. CP-GravR

While deep you mourn beneath the cypress-shade. To the Honourable T. H. Esq; on the Death of His Daughter. Phillis Wheatley. CP-WheaP

While discovery is the fact. Fact, The. Laura Riding Jackson. CP-RidiL

While Drawing in a Churchyard. Thomas Hardy. CP-HardT

While drinking from this cup perhaps. For Monique. Rainer Maria Rilke. CP-RilkFr, tr. by A. Poulin, Jr.

While Europe's eye is fixed on mighty things. Rights of Woman—Spoken by Miss Fontenelle on Her Benefit Night, The. Robert Burns. CP-BurnR

While ever at my back I hear Time's winged chariot. Compulsive Obligatory Paranoia Flashes. Philip Whalen. SP-WhalP

While everyone else is laughing & drinking. Carmen 12. Catullus. CP-ZukLS Fr. Carmina.

While faith forecasts millenial years. Age of the Antonines, The. Herman Melville. SP-MelvH

While Fame Is Young, Too Weak to Fly Away. Unknown, sometimes at. to Thomas Sheridan. CP-SherT

While Fate permits us, let's be merry. To Enjoy the Time. Robert Herrick. CP-HerrR

While flowing rivers yield a blameless sport. Written upon a Blank Leaf in "The Compleat Angler" William Wordsworth. CP-WorW2

While Footman-like He Waits in Every Hall. Thomas Sheridan. CP-SherT

While from the purpling east departs. Ode Composed on May Morning. William Wordsworth. CP-WorW2

While furie gallops on the way. Ovid. CP-RaleW Fr. Remediae Amoris.

While he looks into the eyes of women. Bran. Paul Muldoon. CP-MuldP

While he was dying of. Unspeakable. Heather McHugh. SP-McHuH

While he was here with breath and bone. Casual Acquaintance, The. Thomas Hardy. CP-HardT

While I can watch the gusty grass at play. Rival, A. G. K. Chesterton. CP-ChesG

While I, from that reed-throated whisperer. William Butler Yeats. CP-YeatW

While I lay sleeping my heart awoke. Dreamer, The. Robert Pinsky. CP-PinsR

While I live. David Ignatow. SP-IgnaD

While I sit at the door. Eve. Christina Georgina Rossetti. CP-RosC1

While I still keep you turned, though tired, my eyes. Petrarch. CP-Petra, tr. by J. G. Nichols

While I stood here, in the open, lost in myself. Milkweed. James Wright. CP-WrigJ

While I stood listening, discreetly dumb. Growth of "Lorraine," The. Edwin Arlington Robinson. CP-RobiE

While I was building neat. It Is Dangerous to Read Newspapers. Margaret Atwood. SP-AtwM1

While I was / Sitting on the porch, involved in air. Learning from Nature. Richard Eberhart. CP-EberR

While I watch the Christmas blaze. Reminder, The. Thomas Hardy. CP-HardT

While I write war tells me truth; as for brave. Ivor Gurney. SP-GurnI

While I wrought out these fitful Danaan dreams. To Some I Have Talked with by the Fire, William Butler Yeats. CP-YeatW

While intently on ourselves we look. In the Sap. George Meredith. CP-MerG2

While it is alive. Emily Dickinson. CP-DickE

While it is so that you. Transcribed Conversation in Praise of Cows. Alan Dugan. CP-DugaA

While its owner looks away I touch the rabbit. Farewell, Age Ten, A. William Stafford. SP-StafWW

While Janet eyes the Lanthorn's Magic. George Meredith. CP-MerG2

While keeping circumference. Extra-Terrestrial Function of Spokes. Robert Stock. SP-StocR

While labouring thousands ply their task. Veni. Arthur Hugh Clough. SP-ClouA

While larks with little wing. Phillis the Fair. Robert Burns. CP-BurnR

While leanest beasts in pastures feed. Supreme Fortune Falls Soonest. Robert Herrick. CP-HerrR

While Love Is Unfashionable. Alice Walker. CP-WalkA

While, Lydia, I was lov'd of thee. Ode 3.9: Dialogue between Horace and Lydia, A ("Donec gratus eram"). Horace. CP-HerrR, tr. by Robert Herrick Fr. Odes.

While Many a Merry Tale. Samuel Johnson. CP-JohnS

(Verses Modelled on Pope.) CP-JohnS

While Marquis De Sade had himself buggered. East[ern] European Cooking. Charles Simic. SP-SimiC; SP-SimiCE

While maudlin Whigs deplored [or deplor'd] their Cato's Fate. On a Lady Who P-ssed [or P———st] at the Tragedy of Cato. Alexander Pope. CP-PopeA

While men, in War's dread service, tax their powers. To Charles W. Felt Esq. On His New Type-Setting Machine. Jones Very. CP-VeryJ

While men with ceaseless strife, in Church and State. Finishing the Work. Jones Very. CP-VeryJ

While Merlin paced the Cornish sands. Egyptian Maid; or, The Romance of the Water Lilly, The. William Wordsworth. CP-WorW2

While my father walked through mud. 1905. David Ignatow. SP-IgnaD

While my poor heart was being eaten still. Petrarch. CP-Petra, tr. by J. G. Nichols

While my wife at my side lies slumbering, and the wars are over long. Artilleryman's Vision, The. Walt Whitman. CP-WhitW

While my young cheek retains its healthful hues. Sonnet to William Linley. Samuel Taylor Coleridge. CP-ColeS

While Nature mocks her truth with mimic shows. George Meredith. CP-MerG2

While Nature still delays her flowers to bring. On the Wild Flowers of the Art Exhibition. Jones Very. CP-VeryJ

While new-ca'd kye rowte at the stake. Second Epistle to John Lapraik. Robert Burns. CP-BurnR

While not a leaf seems faded; while the fields. September, 1815. William Wordsworth. CP-WorW2; MW-WorW

While Not the Past Forgetting. Walt Whitman. CP-WhitW

While now at poise the wings of shade. Mortmain Reappears. Herman Melville. SP-MelvH Fr. Clarel: A Poem and Pilgrimage in the Holy Land.

While now, to serve the pilgrim train. Vine and Clarel. Herman Melville. SP-MelvH Fr. Clarel: A Poem and Pilgrimage in the Holy Land.

While others chant of gay Elysian scenes. To a Gentleman on His Voyage to Great-Britain for the Recovery of His Health. Phillis Wheatley. CP-WheaP

While others go to Church. Emily Dickinson. SP-DickE

While others waged war. Death of a Pianist. Adam Zagajewski. SP-ZagaA, tr. by Clare Cavanagh

While people live the life. Two Ways of Living and Dying. D. H. Lawrence. CP-LawrD

While poring Antiquarians search the ground. Roman Antiquities Discovered at Bishopstone, Herefoirshire. William Wordsworth. CP-WorW2

While Prose-work and rhymes. Ballad, A: "While Prose-work and rhymes." Robert Burns, CP-BurnR

While Psyche wept upon the rock forsaken. Psyche Wafted by Zephyrus. Elizabeth Barrett Browning. CP-BroEB

While raging tempests shake the shore. Ode to Neptune. Phillis Wheatley. CP-WheaP

While rain, with eve in partnership. Beyond the Last Lamp. Thomas Hardy. CP-HardT

While rashly her womb's burden she casts out. Elegy 2.13: "While rashly her womb's burden she casts out." Ovid. CP-MarlC Fr. Elegies.

While roses are so red. Beauty Is Vain. Christina Georgina Rossetti. CP-RosC1

While roses bloomed along the plain. Elyas Yusof Nezami Ganjavi]. CP-EmerR

While she sits. Young Woman at a Window. William Carlos Williams. CP-WilW1

While skies glint bright with bluest light. Song—for November. James Whitcomb Riley. CP-RileJ

While snow fell carelessly. Crack, The. Denise Levertov. SP-LeveDP

While spoon-feeding him with one hand. Parkinson's Disease. Galway Kinnell. SP-KinnGN

While, Stella, to your lasting praise. To Stella on Her Birthday, Written AD 1721–2. Jonathan Swift. CP-SwifJ

While still in the bookshop on Rua Carioca. Selected Poems of Mañuel Bandeira, The. Robert Stock. SP-StocR

While sun and sea—and I, and I, Island, The. Randall Jarrell. CP-JarrR

While that my soul repairs to her devotion. Church Monuments. George Herbert. CP-HerbG

While the bell awakens its voice clear and bright. Bell-Ringer, The. Stéphane Mallarmé. CP-MallS, tr. by Henry Weinfield

While the carrots sang arias into the holy earth. Passion of the Mad Rabbit, The. Anne Sexton. CP-SextA

While the Chosen People. Sleep in Jerusalem. Yehuda Amichai. SP-AmicYL, tr. by Benjamin Harshav and Barbara Harshav

While the clocks of the midnight hours are squandering. Dream, The. Jorge Luis Borges. SP-BorgJ, tr. by Alastair Reid

While the far farewell music thins and fails. Departure. Thomas Hardy. CP-HardT

While the frozen armies trembled. Autobiographies. Derek Mahon. CP-MahoD

While the house was away. Taker, The. Anne Sexton. CP-SextA

While the hum and the hurry. Under a Hat Rim. Carl Sandburg. CP-SandC

While the inimitable roof of the Louvre rises. Inscribenda Luparae [To Be Written on the Louvre]. Andrew Marvell. CP-MarvA

While the light of Canaletto. On a Flyleaf of Rime—Gaspara Stampa. Kenneth Rexroth. CP-RexrK

While the milder Fates consent. Lyric to Mirth, A. Robert Herrick. CP-HerrR

While the Musician Played. James Whitcomb Riley. CP-RileJ

While the nation welcomes home its heroes. Yellow Ribbons, Madness, Victory. Sam Hamill. SP-HamiS

While the Poor gather round, till the end of time. Countess' Pillar. William Wordsworth. CP-WorW2

While the red mouths of machine-guns spit blood. Evil. Arthur Rimbaud. CP-RimbA, tr. by Martin Sorrell

While the snaffle holds or the long-neck stings. Rudyard Kipling. CP-KiplR Fr. Plain Tales from the Hills.

While the south rains, the north. Sled Burial, Dream Ceremony. James Dickey. CP-DickJ

While the summer's growth kept me. Heron, The. Wendell Berry. CP-BerrW

While the train waited for an hour in Troy. Home for the Holidays. Howard

Nemerov. CP-NemeH

While the years were mine. I walked the high country. Arrival. William Stafford. SP-StafWW

While they were out buying Easter hats. Nude Tango. Yusef Komunyakaa. CP-KomuY

While they were squatting stark naked. Ducking Stool, The. Paul Muldoon. CP-MuldP

While thirteen moons saw smoothly run. Stanzas Subjoined to the Yearly Bill of Mortality of the Parish of All Saints, Northampton; for the Year 1787. William Cowper. CP-CowpW

While this America settles in the mould of its vulgarity, heavily thickening to empire. Shine, Perishing Republic. Robinson Jeffers. CP-JefR1

While thou didst keep thy candor undefil'd. To His Booke. Robert Herrick. CP-HerrR

While three hundred Americans died in flight. John Finley. Richard Eberhart. CP-EberR

While thus you mourn beneath the Cypress shade. Phillis Wheatley. *See* While deep you mourn beneath the cypress-shade

While virgin Spring, By Eden's flood. Address, to the Shade of Thomson, on Crowning His Bust, at *Ednam, Roxburgh-shire*, with Bays. Robert Burns. CP-BurnR

While waiting for my body to stuff itself. Spirit. Boris Christov. CP-PinsR, *tr. by* Robert Pinsky

While waiting for the falling ball. Ball, The. Rainer Maria Rilke. CP-RilkFr, *tr. by* A. Poulin, Jr.

While we lie in the road to block traffic from the air-force base. Distance, The. Denise Levertov. SP-LeveDL

While we sleep. Tide, The. Denise Levertov. SP-LeveDP

While we slept. Ground Zero [June 1982]. William Stafford. SP-StafWW

While we slumber and sleep / The sun leaps up from the deep. Song of Flight, A. Christina Georgina Rossetti. CP-RosC2

While we talk. At the Same Time. W. S. Merwin. SP-MerwW

While we were fearing it, it came. Emily Dickinson. CP-DickE

While we who wished to help stood helplessly by. Grave, A. James Schuyler. CP-SchuJ

While winds frae off Ben-Lomond blaw. Epistle to Davie, a Brother Poet. Robert Burns. CP-BurnR

While with Ambition's hectic flame. Singer, The. James Whitcomb Riley. CP-RileJ

While wordlessly admiring an ancient wall. Logos. Robert Stock. SP-StocR

While yet Rolfe's foot in stirrup stood. Inscription, The: "While yet Rolfe's foot in stirrup stood." Herman Melville. SP-MelvH *Fr.* Clarel: A Poem and Pilgrimage in the Holy Land.

While you, great Patron of Mankind! sustain. First Epistle of the Second Book of Horace Imitated, The. Alexander Pope. CP-PopeA

While you stood talking at the counter, cutting. Sonnet: "While you stood talking at the counter, cutting." Hayden Carruth. CP-CarHS *Fr.* Sonnets.

While you walk the water's edge. Beach Glass. Amy Clampitt. CP-ClamA

While you were absent in the lavatory. T. S. Eliot. SP-ElioT

While you were promised to me. Song: The Promise. Robert Graves. CP-GravR

While you were singing, fall arrived. Fly, The. Joseph Brodsky. CP-BrodJ, *tr. by* Jane Miller

Whiles I admire, thy first and second wayes. To his Singular Friend, William Lithgow. *Unknown, sometimes at. to* Sir Walter Ralegh. CP-RaleW

Whilst I disdain the populace. Ibn-i-Yamin. CP-EmerR

Whilst, Lydia, I was loved of thee. Ode 3.9: To Lydia. Dialogue of Horace and Lydia. Horace. CP-JonsB *Fr.* Odes.

Whilst pale Anxiety, corrosive Care. On the Prospect of Establishing a Pantisocracy in America. Samuel Taylor Coleridge. CP-ColeS

Whilst thus the darlings of the gods. Third Song, The. Thomas Carew. CP-CareT *Fr.* Carew's Masque.

Whilst thy weighed judgments [*or* weigh'd judgements], Egerton, I hear[e]. To Thomas, Lord Chancellor. Ben Jonson. CP-JonsB; SP-JonsB

Whilst yet to prove. Farewell to Love. John Donne. CP-DonnJ; MW-DonnJ

Whilst you three merry poets traffic. On Dan Jackson's Picture. Jonathan Swift. CP-SwifJ

Whim. Paul Muldoon. CP-MuldP

Whim of Time, the general arbiter, A. In 1929. Stephen Spender. CP-SpenS

Whimper of Sympathy. George Meredith. CP-MerG1

Whimsicality is a thing in itself. Triptych. Richard Eberhart. CP-EberR

Whinlands. Seamus Heaney. SP-HeanSO

Whip, The. Robert Creeley. CP-CreeR

Whip, The. Edwin Arlington Robinson. CP-RobiE

Whip, The. Charles Tomlinson. CP-TomlC

Whip it to a jelly! Rent-Party Shout: For a Lady Dancer. Langston Hughes. CP-HughL; CP-HughL1

Whip-Poor-Will. Donald Hall. CP-HallD

Whip-Poor-Will and Katy-Did. Paul Laurence Dunbar. CP-DunbP

Whipped creams and the Blue Danube. Agenda. Wallace Stevens. CP-StevWP

Whipper-In, The. Thomas Hardy. CP-HardT

Whipping, The. Robert Earl Hayden. CP-HaydR

Whipping the face. Europe, with all her winds. Jetty. Dover, The. Muriel Rukeyser. CP-RukeM

Whippoorwill in the Woods, A. Amy Clampitt. CP-ClamA

Whippoorwill this / moonday into. E. E. Cummings. CP-CummE

Whips. Robert Herrick. CP-HerrR

Whirl-blast from behind the hill, A. William Wordsworth. CP-WorW1

Whirl up, sea. Oread. "H. D." CP-DoolH

Whirl, whorl, or wharve! The world. Reel. John Updike. CP-UpdiJ

Whirl Wind Must, The. George Oppen. CP-OppGN

Whirled dust, world dust. Falling Leaves. Kathleen Jessie Raine. SP-RainK

Whirligigs of wind stir up the dust. Arsenio. Eugenio Montale. CP-MontE, *tr. by* Jonathan Galassi

Whirls. Carl Sandburg. CP-SandC

Whirlwind in the fields, A. Interference. A. R. Ammons. CP-AmmoA

Whiskey-colored sun, The. Skimpy Day at the Solstice. Marge Piercy. SP-PierM

Whiskey on your breath, The. My Papa's Waltz. Theodore Roethke. CP-RoetT

Whisper, The. Denise Levertov. SP-LeveDP

Whispered at the Church-Opening. Thomas Hardy. CP-HardT

Whispered in Winter. William Stafford. SP-StafWW

Whispered into the Ground. William Stafford. SP-StafWW

Whispered to a Girl. Federico García Lorca. CP-GarcF, *tr. by* Alan S. Trueblood *Fr.* Games.

Whispered to Lucifer. Lucille Clifton. SP-ClifL

Whispering Gallery, The. Yusef Komunyakaa. CP-KomuY

Whispering to each handhold, "I'll be back" After Arguing against the Contention That Art Must Come from Discontent. William Stafford. SP-StafWW

Whispering to themselves apart. What They Said. James Whitcomb Riley. CP-RileJ

Whispers. Charles Simic. SP-SimiCE

Whispers in the Next Room. Charles Simic. SP-SimiC

Whispers of Heavenly Death. Walt Whitman. CP-WhitW

Whispers of Immortality. T. S. Eliot. CP-ElioT; SP-ElioT
(Try This on Your Piano [Whispers of Immortality].) SP-ElioT

Whispers of maroon came on the little river. Maroon with Silver Frost. Carl Sandburg. CP-SandC

Whispers / Of springtime. Fragments: "Whispers / Of springtime." Langston Hughes. CP-HughL2

Whistle, The. Yusef Komunyakaa. CP-KomuY

Whistle. A Ballad, The. Robert Burns. CP-BurnR

Whistle, and I'll Come to You, My Lad. Robert Burns. CP-BurnR
(Song.) CP-BurnR

Whistle o'er the Lave o't. Robert Burns. CP-BurnR

Whistle of the 3 A.M. Robert Penn Warren. CP-WarrR

Whistle or Hoot. David Ignatow. SP-IgnaD

Whistle us something old, you know! Stanzas for a New Song. James Whitcomb Riley. CP-RileJ

Whistlers. Grace Paley.

Whistling from Aconcagua, A. Clover Patch. Gabriela Mistral. SP-MistG, *tr. by* Maria Giachetti [*or* Jacketti]

Whistling Girl, The. Dorothy Parker. CP-ParkD

with music. Paul Laurence Dunbar. CP-DunbP

"Whistling Wings." Jesus Christ. Whistling Wings or White Turtle in the Watertree. John Logan. CP-LogaJ

Whistling Wings or White Turtle in the Watertree. John Logan. CP-LogaJ

Whit Monday. Louis MacNeice. CP-MacNL

Whitby-sur-Moyola. Seamus Heaney. SP-HeanSO

White. Yannis Ritsos. SP-RitsY *Fr.* Monovasia.

White. Amy Clampitt. CP-ClamA

White. Paul Muldoon. CP-MuldP

White. James Schuyler. CP-SchuJ

White. Charles Simic. SP-SimiC

White, a shingled path. Icos. Charles Tomlinson. CP-TomlC

White Album. Federico García Lorca.
Fifth Page. CP-GarcF, *tr. by* Jerome Rothenberg
Final Page. CP-GarcF, *tr. by* Jerome Rothenberg
First Page. CP-GarcF, *tr. by* Jerome Rothenberg
Fourth Page. CP-GarcF, *tr. by* Jerome Rothenberg
Second Page. CP-GarcF, *tr. by* Jerome Rothenberg
Third Page. CP-GarcF, *tr. by* Jerome Rothenberg

White almonds of a statue stare, The. From This Far. Derek Walcott. CP-WalcD

White / among the green pads. Lorine Niedecker. CP-NiedL

White-and-black sine, The. Eugenio Montale. CP-MontE, *tr. by* Jonathan Galassi

White and yellow were the flowers. Arabella. Stevie Smith. CP-SmitS

White Apples. Donald Hall. CP-HallD

White as an Indian Pipe. Emily Dickinson. CP-DickE

White as the snow on mountaintop. Lament of a Graying Woman. Cho Wen-chun. CP-WilW2

White as Zenobias teeth, the which the Girles. Candor of Julias Teeth, The. Robert Herrick. CP-HerrR

White Ash. Carl Sandburg. CP-SandC

White barns this morning match the trees. Iowa. John Updike. CP-UpdiJ

White bed against a gray wall. Above the bedcovers, a dance begins. Trip to the Moon. Federico García Lorca. CP-GarcF, *tr. by* Greg Simon *and* Steven F. White

White Begonia. Louis Zukofsky. CP-ZukLS

White Birds, The. William Butler Yeats. CP-YeatW

White Blossom, A. D. H. Lawrence. CP-LawrD

White & blue my breathing lady leans. Venice, 182. John Berryman. CP-BerrJ

White Boat, Blue Boat. James Schuyler. CP-SchuJ

White bone found. Bone Dreams. Seamus Heaney. SP-HeanSO

White bone in the yellow flats of sun. Columns of the Parthenon, The. Donald Hall. CP-HallD

White butterfly, A. Graceful Bastion, The. William Carlos Williams. CP-WilW2

White Ceiling, The. David Ignatow. SP-IgnaD

White chocolate jar full of petals, The. Chez Jane. Frank O'Hara. SP-OharF

White City, A. James Schuyler. CP-SchuJ

White cloud bearing to me the darkness of my mind, The. Wall and Cloud. James Dickey. CP-DickJ

White cloud / wind-worn. Glacier Country. Peter Blue Cloud. SP-BlueP

White clouds, whose shadows haunt the deep. Summer by the Lakeside. John Greenleaf Whittier. CP-WhitJ

White coats / White aprons. Interne at Provident. Langston Hughes. CP-HughL; CP-HughL2

White Cockade, The. Robert Burns. CP-BurnR

White cock's tail, The. Ploughing on Sunday. Wallace Stevens. CP-StevW; CP-StevWP

White-collar man blue-collar / Man I am a no-collar man. Solitary Life. Thomas Merton. CP-MertT

White Corn Sister. Peter Blue Cloud. SP-BlueP

White crane carries a bitter flower, A. Han-shan. CP-ColdM, *tr. by* Red Pine

White dawn. Stillness. When the rippling began. Tree Telling of Orpheus, A. Denise Levertov. SP-LeveDS

White day, black river. Predicter of Famine, The. William Carlos Williams. CP-WilW2

White decorators interested in Art. Nights of 1965: the Old Reliable. Marilyn Hacker. SP-HackM

White Doe of Rylstone, The; or, The Fate of the Nortons. William Wordsworth. CP-WorW1

White dory, face down, its rusted keel staining, A. Tropic Zone. Derek Walcott. CP-WalcD *Fr.* Midsummer.

White Dove and the Snow, The. Jones Very. CP-VeryJ

White dove cooeth in her downy nest, The. Whitsun Eve. Christina Georgina Rossetti. CP-RosC3

White dove has landed me, A. Leaving a Dove. Eugenio Montale. CP-MontE, *tr. by* Jonathan Galassi

White Dress, The. Marya Alexandrovna Zaturenska. SP-ZatuM

White Dwarf. John Updike. CP-UpdiJ

White Feather. John Berryman. CP-BerrJ

White Felts in Fall. Langston Hughes. *See* What?

White Field, The. Raymond Carver. CP-CarvR

White, flipping. Trap. A. R. Ammons. CP-AmmoA

White Flowers. Mary Oliver. SP-OlivM

White flowers among white stones. Sound of Rapids of Laramie River in Late August. W. S. Merwin. SP-MerwWF

White fog lifting and falling on mountain-brow. Wales Visitation. Allen Ginsberg. CP-GinsA; SP-GinsA

"White folks is white," says Uncle Jim. Uncle Jim. Countee Cullen. CP-CullC

White folks, / You better get some new jive. Get Up Off That Old Jive. Langston Hughes. CP-HughL; CP-HughL3

WHITE FOOLSCAP / Book of Cordelia. Susan Howe. SP-HoweS

White founts falling in the courts of the sun. Lepanto. G. K. Chesterton. CP-ChesG

White. From the / Under arm of T. George Oppen. CP-OppGN

White girl lay on the grass, A. Mythological Introduction. Philip Larkin. CP-LarkP

White girls lift their heads like trees, The. Song for Our Lady of Cobre. Thomas Merton. CP-MertT

White Goddess, The. Robert Graves. CP-GravR

White guardians of the universe of sleep. E. E. Cummings. CP-CummE

White-Haired Girl. Archibald MacLeish. CP-MacLA

White-Haired, I Walk in on My Parents. David Ignatow. SP-IgnaD

White Hands. Carl Sandburg. CP-SandC

White haze over Manhattan's towers. Swirls of Black Dust on Avenue D. Allen Ginsberg. CP-GinsA

White hen sitting / On white eggs three, A. Christina Georgina Rossetti. CP-RosC2

White Horse. Charles Olson. CP-OlsoC

White Horse, The. D. H. Lawrence. CP-LawrD

White Horse, The. Jones Very. CP-VeryJ

White horse dissected in two by the blue shadow of a cypress tree, A. Noon. Yannis Ritsos. SP-RitsY, *tr. by* Minas Savvas

White Horses. Rudyard Kipling. CP-KiplR

White house is silent, The. Arriving in the Country Again. James Wright. CP-WrigJ

White houses bank the hill. Rooftop, The. Thom Gunn. CP-GunnT

White in the moon the long road lies. A. E. Housman. CP-HousA

White Innocence, that now liest spread. To Mistress Katherine Neville, on Her Green Sickness. Thomas Carew. CP-CareT

White Iris, The. Philip Levine. SP-LeviP

White is right, / Yellow mellow. Argument ("White is right, / Yellow mellow"). Langston Hughes. CP-HughL; CP-HughL3

White Island. Robert Herrick. CP-HerrR

White Lady. Lucille Clifton. SP-ClifL

White Lady. Yusef Komunyakaa. CP-KomuY

White Lady, The. Dorothy Parker. CP-ParkD

White light is artificial, and hygienic as heaven, The. Surgeon at 2 A.M, The. Sylvia Plath. CP-PlatS

White Lights, The. Edwin Arlington Robinson. CP-RobiE

White light's wet glaze on asphalt city floor. Studying the Signs. Allen Ginsberg. CP-GinsA

White Lily. Rainer Maria Rilke. CP-RilkFr, *tr. by* A. Poulin, Jr.

White lily, just by dint of being. White Lily. Rainer Maria Rilke. CP-RilkFr, *tr. by* A. Poulin, Jr.

White lions are roaring on the water. Kenneth Patchen. CP-PatcK

White Man. Langston Hughes. CP-HughL; CP-HughL1

White-maned, wide-throated, the heavy-shouldered children of the wind leap at the sea-cliff. Granite and Cypress. Robinson Jeffers. CP-JefR1

White Man's Burden, The. Rudyard Kipling. CP-KiplR

White man's soul, it thirsts for gain, The. Indian's Retort, The. Jones Very. CP-VeryJ

(WHITE MARBLE) leaf frame shadow leaf. Susan Howe. SP-HoweS

White marble pillars in the Rector's courtyard. Eroica. Allen Ginsberg. CP-GinsA

White mares lashed to the sulky carriages. In Ohio. James Wright. CP-WrigJ

White Mind and Roses. Heather McHugh. SP-McHuH

White Moon comes in on a baby face. Baby Face. Carl Sandburg. CP-SandC

White moon, star-strewn sky. Torquato Tasso. SP-ZatuM, *tr. by* Marya Alexandrovna Zaturenska

White morning flows into the mirror. Parting: II, The. Adrienne Rich. CP-RicAE; SP-RicA2

White moth to the closing vine, The. Gipsy Trail, The. Rudyard Kipling. CP-KiplR

White Negress. Yehuda Amichai. SP-AmicYL, *tr. by* Benjamin Harshav *and* Barbara Harshav

White Negress, The. Karl Shapiro. SP-ShapK

White Night. Kadya Molodovsky. CP-RicAE; SP-RicA2

White Night. Mary Oliver. SP-OlivM

White Night. Boris Leonidovich Pasternak. CP-MahoD, *tr. by* Derek Mahon

White Night. Adrienne Rich. SP-RicA2

White night roared with a huge north-wind, The. Ballade: "White night roared with a huge north-wind, The." E. E. Cummings. CP-CummE

White, O white face. Prayer: "White, O white face." "H. D." CP-DoolH

White of her Colonial, The. Archibald MacLeish. CP-MacLA *Fr.* Happy Marriage, The.

White on white. Yannis Ritsos. SP-RitsY *Fr.* Paper Poems 1.

White Ones, The. Langston Hughes. CP-HughL; CP-HughL1

White orchids along the window. Original Memory. Arthur Sze. SP-SzeA

White Owl Flies Into and Out of the Field. Mary Oliver. SP-OlivM

White Page, The. "Rubén Dario." SP-DariR, *tr. by* Alberto Acereda *and* Will Derusha

White paint splotches on blue head bandanas. Painting the North San Juan School. Gary Snyder. CP-SnydG

White Pass Ski Patrol. John Logan. CP-LogaJ

White Pines, Felled 1984. Richard Eberhart. CP-EberR

White pool, draining out beneath a star-apple. Lines to a White Persian Sleeping. Robert Stock. SP-StocR

White Poppy, heavy with dreams. Planh. Ezra Pound. CP-PoEar

White, pure-cotton angel, A. Angel. Joseph Brodsky. CP-BrodJ

White River, because white sand. White River Ode. Philip Whalen. SP-WhalP

White River Ode. Philip Whalen. SP-WhalP

White Rose. "H. D." CP-DoolH

White Rose. César Vallejo. CP-WrigJ

White rose my soul, The. Dedication: "White rose my soul, The." E. E. Cummings. CP-CummE

White rose your sea shell. Decenber. William Carlos Williams. CP-WilW2

White Roses. John Ashbery. SP-AshbJ

White roses, tiny and old, flare among thorns. Old Roses. Donald Hall. CP-HallD

White rows of suburbs alternate with trees. Boy or Girl. John Ciardi. CP-CiarJ

White Satyr. Federico García Lorca. CP-GarcF, tr. by Jerome Rothenberg Fr. In the Garden of the Lunar Grapefruits.

White Seal, The. Rudyard Kipling. Fr. Jungle Book, The.

White Ship, The. Geoffrey Hill. CP-HillG

White Ship, The. Dante Gabriel Rossetti. CW-RossD

White Shoulders. Paul Muldoon. CP-MuldP

White Shoulders. Carl Sandburg. CP-SandC

White Shroud. Allen Ginsberg. SP-GinsA

White-sided flowers are thrusting up on the hillside. Hawaii Dantesca. Charles Wright. SP-WrigC

White sky, over the hemlocks bowed with snow. Buck in the Snow, The. Edna St. Vincent Millay. CP-MillE

White Smell. Federico García Lorca. CP-GarcF, tr. by Jerome Rothenberg Fr. In the Garden of the Lunar Grapefruits.

White Snake, The. Anne Sexton. CP-SextA

White spire, / Its peak encircled, A. Shell, The. Charles Tomlinson. CP-TomlC

White spot of a Flicker, The. Tiny Energies. Gary Snyder. CP-SnydG

White Stag, The. Ezra Pound. CP-PoEar; SP-PounE

White suffused with red. Crimson Cyclamen, The. William Carlos Williams. CP-WilW1

White Summer Flower. W. S. Merwin. SP-MerwWF

White sunshine on sweating skulls. Anti-Vietnam War Peace Mobilization. Allen Ginsberg. CP-GinsA

White-Tailed Hornet, The. Robert Frost. CP-FrosR

White, the silent stars, The. Poem: 1939. Thomas Merton. CP-MertT

White, these villages. White. In Connecticut. Charles Tomlinson. CP-TomlC

White though ye be, yet, lillies, know. How Lillies Came White. Robert Herrick. CP-HerrR

White Thought, The. Stevie Smith. CP-SmitS

White Tintoretto clouds beneath my naked feet. Strand, The. Louis MacNeice. CP-MacNL

White tortoise, / sleeping moon. Song for the Moon. Federico García Lorca. CP-GarcF, tr. by Catherine Brown

White Troops Had Their Orders but the Negroes Looked Like Men. Gwendolyn Brooks. SP-BrooG

White Van, The. Charles Tomlinson. CP-TomlC

White violet, The. Sea Violet. "H. D." CP-DoolH

White walls of this airy house assume, The. Flower-Arranging Summer, A. May Sarton. SP-SartM

White-washed monastery where we sat, The. October in Hyde Park. Derek Mahon. CP-MahoD

White Water Lily, The. Stéphane Mallarmé. CP-MallS, tr. by Henry Weinfield

White whisk and sandalwood handle. Han-shan. CP-ColdM, tr. by Red Pine

White, white in that dawnlight, the world was exploding, white. Time as Hypnosis. Robert Penn Warren. CP-WarrR

White winter sun struck its stroke on the bridge, The. Thing Unplanned, The. Thomas Hardy. CP-HardT

White Witch, The. G. K. Chesterton. CP-ChesG

White Witchcraft. Robert Browning. CP-BroR2

White with daisies and red with sorrel. Weeds. Edna St. Vincent Millay. CP-MillE

White workers of the South. Open Letter to the South. Langston Hughes. CP-HughL; CP-HughL1

White World. "H. D." CP-DoolH

Whitegray of a / steeply caved. Paul Celan. SP-CelaP, tr. by John Felstiner

Whitelight. Carl Sandburg. CP-SandC

Whitely, while benzine / Rinsings from the moon. Lachrymae Christi. Hart Crane. CP-CranH

Whiteness. Czeslaw Milosz. CP-MiloC; CP-MiloCN, tr. by Richard Lourie

Whiteness being what I remember. Whiteness I Remember. Sylvia Plath. CP-PlatS

Whiteness I Remember. Sylvia Plath. CP-PlatS

Whiteness most white. Ah, to be clean again. They Shall Be as White as Snow. Christina Georgina Rossetti. CP-RosC2

Whiteness near and far, The. From a Notebook. James Merrill. SP-MerrJ

Whiteness of silence, in silence of squadrons, The. Snowfall. Robert Penn Warren. CP-WarrR

Whitening upward. Beaten Path, A. G. K. Chesterton. CP-ChesG

Whiteout. Arthur Sze. SP-SzeA

Whiter bone: / the sea-voice, A. Sea Poem. Charles Tomlinson. CP-TomlC; SP-TomlC

Whiter / than the crust. Wind Sleepers, The. "H. D." CP-DoolH

Whitewash. Yannis Ritsos. SP-RitsY, tr. by N. C. Germanacos

Whitewashed room, roof, The. To P.O. Allen Ginsberg. CP-GinsA

Whitewashed Wall, The. Thomas Hardy. CP-HardT

Whiteweed, The. Jones Very. CP-VeryJ

Whither are all her false oathes blowne. To His False Mistris. Robert Herrick. CP-HerrR

Whither away delight? Glimpse, The. George Herbert. CP-HerbG

Whither bound, water? Federico García Lorca. CP-GarcF, tr. by Alan S. Trueblood Fr. Songs to End With.

Whither dost thou whorry me. To Bacchus, a Canticle. Robert Herrick. CP-HerrR

Whither he went I may not follow him. His eyes. Idyl for Glaucus, An. Ezra Pound. CP-PoEar

Whither is fled the Secretary Bird? To Freda Spencer. G. K. Chesterton. CP-ChesG

Whither, mad maiden, wilt thou roame? To His Muse. Robert Herrick. CP-HerrR

Whither, O Cloud! with richest treasures fraught. To a Cloud. Jones Very. CP-VeryJ

Whither, O, whither art thou fled. Search, The. George Herbert. CP-HerbG

Whither? Say, whither shall I fly. Frozen Zone; or, Julia Disdainful, The. Robert Herrick. CP-HerrR

Whither Shall I Go from Thy Spirit. Jones Very. CP-VeryJ

Whither the Tribes Go Up, Even the Tribes of the Lord. Christina Georgina Rossetti. CP-RosC2

Whitheraways!—That's what I'll have to call, The. Whitheraways, The. James Whitcomb Riley. CP-RileJ

Whitheraways, The. James Whitcomb Riley. CP-RileJ

Whitman in Black. Ted Berrigan. SP-BerrT

Whitman took the cars. Empathy and New Year. James Schuyler. CP-SchuJ

Whitshed's Motto on His Coach. Jonathan Swift. CP-SwifJ

Whitsun. Sylvia Plath. CP-PlatS

Whitsun Canticle, A. Thomas Merton. CP-MertT

Whitsun Day. Christina Georgina Rossetti. CP-RosC2

Whitsun Eve. Christina Georgina Rossetti. CP-RosC2

Whitsun Eve. Christina Georgina Rossetti. CP-RosC3

Whitsun Monday. Christina Georgina Rossetti. CP-RosC2

Whitsun Tuesday. Christina Georgina Rossetti. CP-RosC2

Whitsun Weddings, The. Philip Larkin. CP-LarkP

Whitsunday. George Herbert. CP-HerbG

Whitsunday in Kirchstetten. W. H. Auden. CP-AudeW

Whittier. Paul Laurence Dunbar. CP-DunbP

Whittier—at Newburyport. James Whitcomb Riley. CP-RileJ

Whittle me down. Bitter Brew. Langston Hughes. CP-HughL; CP-HughL3

Whittled crystal: fissured, The. Head Hewn with an Axe. Charles Tomlinson. CP-TomlC; SP-TomlC

Who. Allen Ginsberg. CP-GinsA

Who. Laura Riding Jackson. CP-RidiL

Who. Charles Olson. CP-OlsoC

Who? Walter De la Mare. CP-DeLaW

Who? Alice Walker. CP-WalkA

Who abdicated Ambush. Emily Dickinson. CP-DickE

Who after his transgression doth repent. Penitence. Robert Herrick. CP-HerrR

Who after this would commit his thoughts to babbling paper. Illustrissimo Viro Domino Lanceloto Josepho de Maniban Grammatomanti [To That Renowned Man Lord Lancelot Joseph de Maniban Graphologist]. Andrew Marvell. CP-MarvA

Who am I? Big-Timer, The. Langston Hughes. CP-HughL; CP-HughL1

Who Am I? Carl Sandburg. CP-SandC

Who am I but the Frog!—the Frog! Frog, The. James Whitcomb Riley. CP-RileJ

Who am I here in this cool cathedral and who. Gothic, The. Adam Zagajewski. SP-ZagaA, tr. by Renata Gorczynski, Benjamin Ivry and C. K. Williams

Who am I? I have pondered with my peers. James Vincent Cunningham. CP-CunnJ

Who am I? Saliva. Milarepa Taste. Allen Ginsberg. CP-GinsA; SP-GinsA

Who am I, who. Self. Kathleen Jessie Raine. SP-RainK

Who / am I—. Intervals. Robert Creeley. CP-CreeR

Who are these people at the bridge to meet me? They are the villagers. Bee Meeting, The. Sylvia Plath. CP-PlatS

Who are these strange faces in Mexico? What Quetzalcoatl Saw in Mexico. D. H. Lawrence. CP-LawrD

Who / are these two women, walking. Operations: Desert Shield, Desert Storm. Eleanor Wilner. SP-WilnE

Who are these? Why sit they here in twilight? Mental Cases. Wilfred Owen. CP-OwenW

Who are we now, who are we ever. Jack of Hearts, The. Lawrence Ferlinghetti.

SP-FerlL

'Who are we waiting for?' *'Soup* burnt?' ' . . . Eight—.' Feckless Dinner-Party, The. Walter De la Mare. CP-DeLaW

Who are we? Why are we here. Sea, That Has No Ending, The. Stanley Kunitz. CP-KunSC

Who are you? You and I. Tennessee Williams. CP-WillT

Who are you dusky woman, so ancient hardly human. Ethiopia Saluting the Colors. Walt Whitman. CP-WhitW

Who are you,little i. E. E. Cummings. CP-CummE

Who are you that the whole world's song. To Our Lady of Vicarious Atonement. Ezra Pound. CP-PoEar

Who are you? Who am I? Haunted. Growing. Kenneth Rexroth. CP-RexrK

Who / Are you / Who is born. Vision and Prayer. Dylan Thomas. CP-ThomD

Who art thou that comest with a stedfast face. I Have Fought a Good Fight. Christina Georgina Rossetti. CP-RosC3

Who(at / her nons- / elf). E. E. Cummings. CP-CummE

Who Be Kind To. Allen Ginsberg. CP-GinsA; SP-GinsA

Who beckons the green ivy up. Miracle, The. Walter De la Mare. CP-DeLaW

Who before dying demands not rebirth. E. E. Cummings. CP-CummE

Who begs to die for feare of humane need. Need. Robert Herrick. CP-HerrR

Who bides his time, and day by day. James Whitcomb Riley. CP-RileJ

Who but hails the sight with pleasure. Hint from the Mountains for Certain Political Pretenders. William Wordsworth. CP-WorW2

Who but Is Pleased to Watch the Moon on High. William Wordsworth. CP-WorW2

Who but the Goddess? All that is. To Memory. Buddhadeva Bose. CP-OppGN, *tr. by* George Oppen

Who but the Lord? Langston Hughes. CP-HughL; CP-HughL3

Who call her Mother and who calls her Wife. M. M. George Meredith. CP-MerG1

"Who called?" I said, and the words. Echo. Walter De la Mare. CP-DeLaW

Who Called Love Conquering. Philip Larkin. CP-LarkP

Who Called That Robin a Piccolo Player? Ogden Nash. CP-NashO

Who calleth?—Thy Father calleth. Master Is Come, and Calleth for Thee, The. Christina Georgina Rossetti. CP RosC1

Who calls her two-faced? Faces, she has three. Three-Faced, The. Robert Graves. CP-GravR

Who can abide whom or what? That's. Untitled Poem: "Who can abide whom or what? That's." Alan Dugan. CP-DugaA

Who can believe with common sense. Epigram on Fasting. Jonathan Swift. CP-SwifJ

Who / can blame her for hunkering. Fox. Lucille Clifton. SP-ClifL

Who can consider thy right courses run. To Robert, Earl of Salisbury ("Who can consider thy right courses run"). Ben Jonson. CP-JonsB; SP-JonsB

Who can doubt that all the world's a zoo. Monkey's Address to Others of His Kind, A. Robert Stock. SP-StocR

Who can ever praise enough. Price, The. W. H. Auden. CP-AudeW

Who can know more deeply than I your loneliness there? Fragment: "Who can know more deeply than I your loneliness there?" Hayden Carruth. CP-CarHS

Who can persuade the sea. Pablo Neruda. SP-NeruP *Fr.* Question Book.

Who can pick up the weight of Britain. Imago. Wallace Stevens. CP-StevW; CP-StevWP

Who can surrender to Christ, dividing his best with the stranger. Where Is the Real Non-Resistant? Nicholas Vachel Lindsay. CP-LindV

Who can tell who was born of what? Doorstep, Lightning, Waif-Dreaming. James Dickey. CP-DickJ

Who can think of the sun costuming clouds. Fading of the Sun, A. Wallace Stevens. CP-StevW; CP-StevWP

Who cantereth forth in the night so late. Witch of Erkmurden, The. James Whitcomb Riley. CP-RileJ

Who cares / About the hurt in your heart? Hurt. Langston Hughes. CP-HughL; CP-HughL1

Who cares for earthly bread tho' white? Christina Georgina Rossetti. CP-RosC2

Who Cares, Long as It's B-Flat. Hayden Carruth. CP-CarHS

Who challenged my soldier mother? Catechism, A. William Stafford. SP-StafW; SP-StafW

Who chides the tears that weep so dear a head? Ode 1.24: "Who chides the tears that weep so dear a head?" Horace. CP-CummE *Fr.* Odes.

Who comes is occupied. George Oppen. CP-OppGN

Who compares a poem. Hafiz. CP-EmerR *Fr.* Odes.

Who could be ill in March. Emily Dickinson. SP-DickE

Who could be motherless. Emily Dickinson. SP-DickE

Who could believe an ant in theory? Credibility. John Ciardi. CP-CiarJ

Who could have believed it? This is hell and I am looking out upon grass and trees. David Ignatow. SP-IgnaD

Who could have figured, when the harnesses improved. Wide Prospect, The. Randall Jarrell. CP-JarrR

Who could have thought that men and women could feel. Old Paintings on

Italian Walls. Kathleen Jessie Raine. SP-RainK

Who could possibly approve of Metternich. Pseudo-Questions. W. H. Auden. CP-AudeW

Who could say that he saw you, and when? On the Death of José de Ciria y Escalante. Federico García Lorca. CP-GarcF, *tr. by* Christopher Maurer

Who Court obtain within Himself. Emily Dickinson. CP-DickE

Who cries all art is a fraud & Genius a trick. William Blake. *See* Having given great offence by writing in Prose

Who cut down the moon's / stem? Acacia. Federico García Lorca. CP-GarcF, *tr. by* Jerome Rothenberg *Fr.* Garden in Umber; or The Garden of the Brownhaired Girls.

Who cut down the moon's / stem? Acacia. Federico García Lorca. CP-GarcF, *tr. by* Jerome Rothenberg *Fr.* Water Suite.

Who dares affirm this is no pious age. Epilogue to a Play for the Benefit of the Weavers in Ireland, An. Jonathan Swift. CP-SwifJ

Who dares deny, that all first fruits are due. To K[ing] Charles and Q[ueen] Mary, for the Loss of Their First-Born, An Epigram Consolatory. 1629. Ben Jonson. CP-JonsB

Who dat knockin' at de do'? Encouragement. Paul Laurence Dunbar. CP-DunbP

Who decided what is useful in its beauty. Looking at Quilts. Marge Piercy. SP-PierM

Who decorated last night's dream. Large Opera Singer, The. James Laughlin. CP-LaugJ

Who dedicates himself to the glass. Hafiz. CP-EmerR *Fr.* Odes

Who did he talk to. Notes for Echo Lake 4. Michael Palmer. SP-PalmM

Who Did Not Die in Vain. Howard Nemerov. CP-NemeH

Who Did Which? or Who Indeed? Ogden Nash. CP-NashO

Who died on the wires, and hung there, one of two. Silent One, The. Ivor Gurney. SP-GurnI *Fr.* Silent One, The.

Who do you think stands watching. Everlasting Flowers. D. H. Lawrence. CP-LawrD

Who does not blush when charged with selfish views? Against Interested Love. William Cowper. CP-CowpW

Who does not sit in the seat of the scoffer. Blessed Is the Man. Marianne Craig Moore. CP-MoorM

Who dreamed [*or* dream'd] that beauty passes like a dream? Rose of the World, The. William Butler Yeats. CP-YeatW

Who Edmond[e]s, reads thy book, and doth not see. To the Same; on the Same. Ben Jonson. CP-JonsB

Who enters this / kingdom. And. Laughing. Robert Creeley. CP-CreeR

Who equallest the coward's haste. Henry David Thoreau. CP-ThorH

Who ere she[e] be[e]. Wishes. To His (Supposed) Mistress[e]. Richard Crashaw. CP-CrasR

Who even dead, yet hath his mind entire! Canto 47: "Who even dead, yet hath his mind entire!" Ezra Pound. SP-PounE *Fr.* Cantos.

Who ever saw me / cutting stalks, threshing chaff from the wheat? Negative Hands. Pablo Neruda. SP-NeruP

Who ever suffered as I from separation? Hafiz. CP-EmerR *Fr.* Odes.

Who extols a wilderness? Love Defended. Christina Georgina Rossetti. CP-RosC3

Who fancied what a pretty sight. William Wordsworth. CP-WorW1; MW-WorW

Who fights behind a shield. Trinacria. Charles Olson. CP-OlsoC

Who for their living lived. Unnatural History of Peru, The. Kenneth Patchen. CP-PatcK

Who formes a Godhead out of Gold or Stone. Devotion Makes the Deity. Robert Herrick. CP-HerrR

Who gave me grassy Lawns for miry ways. To My Dearest Cousin, on Her Removal of us from Silver End, to Weston. William Cowper. CP-CowpW

Who gave thee, O Beauty. Ode to Beauty. Ralph Waldo Emerson. CP-EmerR

Who gave thy cheek the mixed tint. Hafiz. CP-EmerR *Fr.* Odes.

Who gave us flowers? Purple Anemones. D. H. Lawrence. CP-LawrD

Who gets up early to discover the moment light begins? Unfold Your Own Myth. Jelaluddin Rumi. SP-Rumi, *tr. by* Coleman Barks

Who Giants know, with lesser Men. Emily Dickinson. CP-DickE

Who gives and hides the giving hand. Giving and Taking. John Greenleaf Whittier. CP-WhitJ

Who gives him the Bath? New Knighthood, The. Rudyard Kipling. CP-KiplR

Who Goes Home? G. K. Chesterton. CP-ChesG

Who goes to dine must take his Feast. Emily Dickinson. CP-DickE

Who Goes with Fergus? William Butler Yeats. CP-YeatW

Who grieve now at my grave, in vain they pray. Michelangelo Buonarroti. CP-Miche, *tr. by* John Frederick Nims

Who has gone farthest? for I would go farther. Excelsior. Walt Whitman. CP-WhitW

Who has more fun in bed, men or women. On a Myth. On a Conventional Wisdom. Alan Dugan. CP-DugaA

Who has not been. Who? Alice Walker. CP-WalkA

Who has not found the Heaven—below. God's Residence. Emily Dickinson. CP-DickE

Who has not left home and walked. Ed. William Corbett. SP-CorbW

Who has not seen Brancusi's White Negress? White Negress, The. Karl Shapiro. SP-ShapK

Who has not *wanted* does not guess. Unless. James Whitcomb Riley. CP-RileJ

Who Has Seen the Wind? Christina Georgina Rossetti. CP-RosC2

Who has told you what discoveries. Basics. James Dickey. CP-DickJ

Who hasn't been frustrated. Plea for Mercy, A. William Carlos Williams. CP-WilW2

Who hath desired the Sea?—the sight of salt water unbounded. Sea and the Hills, The. Rudyard Kipling. CP-KiplR

Who Hath Despised the Day of Small Things? Christina Georgina Rossetti. CP-RosC2

Who Hath Ears to Hear Let Him Hear! Jones Very. CP-VeryJ

Who Hath Given, Man Speech? Algernon Charles Swinburne. SP-SwinA *Fr.* Atalanta in Calydon.

Who hath he[a]rd of such[e] cruelty before. Sir Thomas Wyatt. CP-WyatT

Who hath not glow'd above the page where fame. Address Intended to be Recited at the Caledonian Meeting. Lord Byron. CP-Byron

Who Have a Form of Godliness. Christina Georgina Rossetti. CP-RosC3

Who have been lonely once. Careless Love. Stanley Kunitz. CP-KunSC

Who have survived the time extreme. Last Fellows. Laura Riding Jackson. CP-RidiL

Who he was, remained an open question. Question of Identity, A. Stephen Spender. CP-SpenS

Who hears of Helen's Tower, may dream perchance. Helen's Tower. Robert Browning. CP-BroR2

Who hears that whistle blowing? Little Black Train, The. Kenneth Patchen. CP-PatcK

Who hears the humming. Breath. Philip Levine. SP-LeviP

Who hears the parson. Henry David Thoreau. CP-ThorH

Who hock in toss regret. Hyacinth. Louis Zukofsky. CP-ZukLS

Who hurt you so. Edna St. Vincent Millay. CP-MillE

Who in One Lifetime. Muriel Rukeyser. CP-RukeM

Who, in the dark, has cast the harbor-chain? Putting to Sea. Louise Bogan. CP-BogaL

Who in the Hell is Tom Jones? Charles Bukowski. SP-BukC1

Who in the Realm to-day lays down dear life for the sake of a land more dear? Dead King, The [Edward VII; 1910]. Rudyard Kipling. CP-KiplR

Who includes diversity and is Nature. Kosmos. Walt Whitman. CP-WhitW

Who Is at My Window. Denise Levertov. SP-LeveDP

Who is ever quite without his landscape. Detective Story. W. H. Auden. CP-AudeW

Who is he? Despair. Anne Sexton. CP-SextA

Who is it beside me, who is here beside me, in the hollow hill? In the Hill at Newgrange. Robinson Jeffers. CP-JefR2

Who is it calling by the darkened river. Voices. Walter De la Mare. CP-DeLaW

Who is it seeks my Pillow Nights. Emily Dickinson. CP-DickE

Who is luckiest in this whole orchestra? The reed. Constant Conversation. Jelaluddin Rumi. SP-Rumi, *tr. by* Coleman Barks

Who is my father in this world, in this house. Irish Cliffs of Moher, The. Wallace Stevens. CP-StevW; CP-StevWP

Who Is Now Reading This? Walt Whitman. CP-WhitW

Who is she coming, that the roses bend. Sonnet: Chi È Questa? Ezra Pound. CP-PoEar

Who is she coming, whom all gaze upon. Sonnet: A Rapture concerning his Lady. Guido Cavalcanti. CW-RossD, *tr. by* Dante Gabriel Rossetti

Who is speaking? Who has spoken? As We Read Burns. James Whitcomb Riley. CP-RileJ

Who is that blue / Dark, dreamer dreaming / Of me? To Harvey, Who Traced the Circulation. James Wright. CP-WrigJ

Who is that man with the handshake? Don't you know. Satirist, The. Louis MacNeice. CP-MacNL

Who is that well-dressed handsome man? Man With Two New Suits, The. Ogden Nash. CP-NashO

Who Is the Child. James Laughlin. CP-LaugJ

Who is the Chinese poet. Of Small Delights in Idleness. William Corbett. SP-CorbW

Who is the East? Yellow Man, Purple Man. Emily Dickinson. CP-DickE

Who is the happy warrior? Who is he. Character of the Happy Warrior. William Wordsworth. CP-WorW1

Who is the honest man? Constancy. George Herbert. CP-HerbG

Who is the lover of the world?: him choose. Scorn of God, The. G. K. Chesterton. CP-ChesG

Who is the man that stands against this bridge. For Danton. Charles Tomlinson. CP-TomlC; SP-TomlC

Who is the person who's in. Qui Nunquam Amavit. James Laughlin. CP-LaugJ

Who is the shroudy stranger of the night. Please Open the Window and Let Me In. Allen Ginsberg. CP-GinsA

Who is the ugly one slump-slopping down the street? Homage to Theodore Dreiser. Robert Penn Warren. CP-WarrR

Who is there. Choros Translations. Euripides. CP-DoolH *Fr.* Bacchae.

Who is this / dai / nty mademoiselle. E. E. Cummings. CP-CummE

Who is this poor dreamer. Han-shan. CP-ColdM, *tr. by* Red Pine

Who is this that comes in splendour, coming from the blazing East? Airy Christ, The. Stevie Smith. CP-SmitS

Who is this that cometh up not alone. Bride Song. Christina Georgina Rossetti. CP-RosC2

Who is this who came. Guido Cavalcanti. CP-CavaG, *tr. by* Marc Cirigliano

Who Is This Who Howls and Mutters? Stevie Smith. CP-SmitS

Who is three comes down / the stairs reciting the. James My Namesake. James Laughlin. CP-LaugJ

Who It Is. W. S. Merwin. SP-MerwW

Who it is who sits. Babe, The. Charles Olson. CP-OlsoC

Who Kill'd John Keats? Lord Byron. CP-Byron

Who Killed Lawless Lean? Stevie Smith. CP-SmitS

'Who knocks?' 'I, who was beautiful.' Ghost, The. Walter De la Mare. CP-DeLaW

Who knows. Light in the Eyes, The. Miller Williams. CP-WillM

Who Knows? Nicholas Vachel Lindsay. CP-LindV

Who knows? God knows: and what He knows / Is well and best. Take No Thought for The Morrow. Christina Georgina Rossetti. CP-RosC2

Who knows his will? Meditation on a Memoir. James Vincent Cunningham. CP-CunnJ

Who knows how deep the Heart is. Emily Dickinson. SP-DickE

Who knows how the Wag-tail woos? Wagtail, The. Theodore Roethke. CP-RoetT

Who knows how to catch rats. Shih-te. CP-ColdM, *tr. by* Red Pine

Who knows if the moon's. E. E. Cummings. CP-CummE; SP-CummE

Who knows the heart of the Christian? How does he reason? Hadramauti. Rudyard Kipling. CP-KiplR *Fr.* Plain Tales from the Hills.

Who knows this or that? Limits. Ralph Waldo Emerson. CP-EmerR

Who knows what I know. Night's Nothings Again. Carl Sandburg. CP-SandC

Who knows where our hearts go. Emily Dickinson. SP-DickE

Who knows whether the sea heals or corrodes? Plague of Dead Sharks. Alan Dugan. CP-DugaA

Who lay against the sea, and fled. Sea, The. Dorothy Parker. CP-ParkD

Who leads a happy life. Tinker, The. William Wordsworth. CP-WorW1; MW-WorW

Who Learns My Lesson Complete. Walt Whitman. CP-WhitW

Who lies dead in the sea. Wallace Stevens. CP-StevWP

Who lies with his milk-white maiden. Song of Praise. Countee Cullen. CP-CullC

Who list his wealth and ease retain. Sir Thomas Wyatt. CP-WyatT

Who listens, when in the concert-hall. Kathleen Jessie Raine. SP-RainK

Who live under the shadow of a war. Shadow of War. Stephen Spender. CP-SpenS

Who lived at the top end of our street. Retired Colonel, The. Ted Hughes. SP-HughTN

Who lives by wisdom and to others gives. James Vincent Cunningham. CP-CunnJ

Who lives in the biggest, whitest house in town? Beautiful Funerals. James Schuyler. CP-SchuJ

Who lives o on Helicon hill. Catullus. *See* Hill (breeder) of Helicon

Who lives where beggars rarely speed. My Mary. John Clare. CP-MacNL

Who long for rest, who look for pleasure. Penmaen Pool. Gerard Manley Hopkins. CP-HopkG

Who, looking backward from his manhood's prime. Reward, The. John Greenleaf Whittier. CP-WhitJ

Who loved more? William Carlos Williams. William Carlos Williams. Robert Lowell. SP-LoweR

Who loves beauty / veil her statues. Carmen 3. Catullus. CP-ZukLS *Fr.* Carmina.

Who loves his friend with his heart of hearts. Sadi. CP-EmerR

Who loves me here and has my love. Daphne. Gerard Manley Hopkins. CP-HopkG

Who loves to peer up at the morning sun. On "The Story of Rimini" John Keats. CP-KeatJ

Who loves you most. Emily Dickinson. SP-DickE

Who Made Her. Heather McHugh. SP-McHuH

Who made the world? Summer Day, The. Mary Oliver. SP-OlivM

Who made these flowers, I asked a child. Child's Answer, The. Jones Very. CP-VeryJ

Who made you come and find the door to there? William Dickey. SP-DickW *Fr.* Part Song, With Concert of Recorders.

Who makes the past, a pattern for next year. To Sir Henry Goodyer. John Donne. CP-DonnJ; MW-DonnJ

Who Makes These Changes? Jelaluddin Rumi. SP-Rumi, *tr.* by Coleman Barks

Who may do most, do's least: The bravest will. More Mighty, the More Merciful, The. Robert Herrick. CP-HerrR

Who may tell the tale. Tailpiece. Samuel Beckett. CP-BeckS

Who "meddled" with the costly Hearts. Emily Dickinson. SP-DickE

Who modelled your head of terracotta? Earthenware Head, The. Ted Hughes. SP-HughTN

Who murmurs, hither, hither: who. With the Persuader. George Meredith. CP-MerG1

Who never lost, are unprepared. Emily Dickinson. CP-DickE

Who never wanted—maddest Joy. Emily Dickinson. SP-DickE

Who now calls on thee, Nevil, is a muse. To Sir Henry Nevil. Ben Jonson. CP-JonsB; SP-JonsB

Who, now, put dreams into thy slumbering mind? Death-Dream, The. Walter De la Mare. CP-DeLaW

Who now reads Thomson or Collins? Surrey. Donald Davie. CP-DaviDC

Who now remembers Almack's balls. Reminiscences of a Dancing Man. Thomas Hardy. CP-HardT

Who, now, seeing Her so. Et in Arcadia Ego. W. H. Auden. CP-AudeW

Who, now, when evening darkens the water and the stream is dull. To a Musician. Edna St. Vincent Millay. CP-MillE

Who now will praise the Wizard in the street. Wizard in the Street, The. Nicholas Vachel Lindsay. CP-LindV

Who occupies this House? Emily Dickinson. CP-DickE

Who often found their way to pleasant meadows. Elegy for Minor Poets. Louis MacNeice. CP-MacNL

Who on earth is that. Han-shan. CP-ColdM, tr. by Red Pine

Who on your breast pillows his head now. Lost Jewel, A. Robert Graves. CP-GravR

Who owns the earth, you. Incorporeal Ruler. Adam Zagajewski. SP-ZagaA, tr. by Renata Gorczynski, Benjamin Ivry and C. K. Williams

'Who owns these lands?' the Pilgrim said. Staff and Scrip, The. Dante Gabriel Rossetti. CW-RossD

Who owns these scrawny little feet? Death. Examination at the Womb-Door. Ted Hughes. SP-HughTN

Who peered from the invisible world. Seven Forbidden Words. Michael Palmer. SP-PalmM

Who plants an Olive, but to eate the Oile? Recompence. Robert Herrick. CP-HerrR

Who plots, then, the lines. Le Fou. Robert Creeley. CP-CreeR

Who ponders National events shall find. In Allusion to Various Recent Histories and Notices of the French Revolution, Continued. William Wordsworth. CP-WorW2

Who prop, thou ask'st, in these bad days, my mind? To a Friend. Matthew Arnold. SP-ArnoM

Who put this pit-head wheel. On the Reservations. Ted Hughes. SP-HughTN

Who put up that cage? Money, Politics, Love, and Glory. Carl Sandburg. CP-SandC

Who puts off shift. My Naked Aunt. Archibald MacLeish. CP-MacLA

Who, railing, drives the Lazar from his door. Biting of Beggars. Robert Herrick. CP-HerrR

Who rashly strove thy Image to portray? Upon seeing a Coloured Drawing of the Bird of Paradise in an Album. William Wordsworth. CP-WorW2

Who read a chapter when they rise. Charms and Knots. George Herbert. CP-HerbG

Who reads my book reads all my life. Marya Alexandrovna Zaturenska. SP-ZatuM Fr. Madness of Jean-Jacques Rousseau, The.

Who read'st this Book, that I have writ. To Momus. Robert Herrick. CP-HerrR

Who recalls the twilight and the rangèd tents in order. Dirge of Dead Sisters. Rudyard Kipling. CP-KiplR

Who released to Salmasius his "hundred" Verse from Pro Populo Anglicano Defensio. John Milton. CP-MiltJ

Who remembers him also, he thinks. For a Friend. Robert Creeley. CP-CreeR

Who remembers now the backyards of our innocence. Letter for Those Who Grew Up Together. John Ciardi. CP-CiarJ

Who remembers the Great Flood? The scope. Cheville. Hugh MacDiarmid. SP-MacDH

Who represents my body in Pentagon? Who spends. Pentagon Exorcism. Allen Ginsberg. CP-GinsA

Who rides by night on horseback, come the day. Michelangelo Buonarroti. CP-Miche, tr. by John Frederick Nims

Who rises on the banks of Seine. Ode: "Who rises on the banks of Seine." William Wordsworth. CP-WorW2

Who royally bedded. Hafiz. CP-EmerR Fr. Odes.

Who rules the duller earth, the wind-swolne streames. Ode 3.4: "Who rules the duller earth, the wind-swolne streames." Horace. CP-RaleW Fr. Odes.

Who Runs America? Allen Ginsberg. CP-GinsA

Who Said It Was Simple. Audre Lorde. SP-LordA

Who saith our times nor have, nor can. Ode Allegoric. Ben Jonson. CP-JonsB

Who Santy Claus Wuz. James Whitcomb Riley. CP-RileJ

Who saw no Sunrise cannot say. Emily Dickinson. CP-DickE

Who saw the hid beginnings. Ralph Waldo Emerson. CP-EmerR

Who say[e]s that fictions on[e]ly and false hair. Jordan (1). George Herbert. CP-HerbG

Who says I shall not straighten till I bend. Under Cygnus. Richard Wilbur. CP-WilbR

Who says my hea't ain't true to you? Protest. Paul Laurence Dunbar. CP-DunbP

Who says, she is in danger. Song: "Who says, she is in danger." George Meredith. CP-MerG2

Who says that all must vanish? What Survives. Rainer Maria Rilke. CP-RilkFr

Who says that Giles and Joan at discord be? On Giles and Joan. Ben Jonson. CP-JonsB; SP-JonsB

Who Says Words with My Mouth. Jelaluddin Rumi. SP-Rumi, tr. by Coleman Barks and John Moyne

Who scans the bright machinery of the skies. Carmen 66. Catullus. CP-ZukLS Fr. Carmina.

Who scatters tares shall reap no wheat. Rogationtide. Christina Georgina Rossetti. CP-RosC2

Who sees inside from outside? Jelaluddin Rumi. SP-Rumi, tr. by Coleman Barks

Who shall bridle the winds, in their seven directions. Winter Afternoon. Thomas Merton. CP-MertT

Who shall decide, when Doctors disagree. Epistle III, to Allen Lord Bathurst. Alexander Pope. CP-PopeA

Who Shall Deliver Me? Christina Georgina Rossetti. CP-RosC1

Who Shall Doubt. George Oppen. CP-OppGN

Who shall doubt, Donne, where [or whe'er] I a poet be[e]. To John Donne ("Who shall doubt, Donne, where [or whe'er] I a poet be[e]"). Ben Jonson. CP-JonsB; SP-JonsB

Who shall my wandering thoughts steady & fix. Christina Georgina Rossetti. CP-RosC3

Who shall say what is said in me. Dante Gabriel Rossetti. CW-RossD

Who shall tell the lady's grief. On the Death of a Cat. Christina Georgina Rossetti. CP-RosC3

Who shall tell what did befall. Wealth. Ralph Waldo Emerson. CP-EmerR

Who shall we send to fetch him away. Choosers, The. Stevie Smith. CP-SmitS

Who sharpens every dull. E. E. Cummings. CP-CummE

Who Shot Eugenie? Stevie Smith. CP-SmitS

Who showed me. To Flossie. William Carlos Williams. CP-WilW2

Who sits with the King in His Throne? Not a slave but a Bride. Christina Georgina Rossetti. CP-RosC2

Who slays the Spanish sun. Charles Olson. CP-OlsoC

Who standeth at the gate? —A woman old. Behold, I stand at the door and knock. Christina Georgina Rossetti. CP-RosC3

Who stands on that cliff, like a figure of stone. Mogg Megone. John Greenleaf Whittier. CP-WhitJ

Who stands, the crux left of the watershed. Watertowers, The. W. H. Auden. CP-AudeW

Who stays in the city in August? August. Primo Levi. CP-LeviP, tr. by Ruth Feldman

Who swerves from innocence, who makes divorce. William Wordsworth. CP-WorW2 Fr. River Duddon [A Series of Sonnets], The.

Who takes the Cold Mountain Road. Han-shan. CP-ColdM, tr. by Red Pine

Who takes thy volume to his virtuous hand. To His Much and Worthily Esteemed Friend the Author. Ben Jonson. CP-JonsB

Who talks of Plato's spindle. His Bargain. William Butler Yeats. CP-YeatW

Who Taught Caddies to Count? or A Burnt Golfer Fears the Child. Ogden Nash. CP-NashO

Who taught thee conflict with the pow'rs of night. On the Death of a Young Gentleman. Phillis Wheatley. CP-WheaP

Who that can feel the gentleness of Death. Gentleness of Death, The. George Meredith. CP-MerG2

Who, then, is child. Care in Calling. Laura Riding Jackson. CP-RidiL

Who, then, was Cestius. Rome: At the Pyramid of Cestius near the Graves of Shelley and Keats. Thomas Hardy. CP-HardT

Who / threw the silver dollar up into the tree? E. E. Cummings. CP-CummE

Who to the North, or South, doth set. Observation. Robert Herrick. CP-HerrR

Who told my mother of my shame. Sister Maude. Christina Georgina Rossetti. CP-RosC1

Who told you / you were visible? Plan, The. Rae Armantrout. SP-ArmaA

Who tracks this author's, or translator's pen. On the Author, Work, and Translator. Ben Jonson. CP-JonsB

Who Understands Who Anyhow? Ogden Nash. CP-NashO

Who violates the Customes, hurts the Health. Lawes. Robert Herrick. CP-HerrR

Who, Virtue, can thy power forget. Ben Jonson. CP-JonsB Fr. Masque of Queens, The.

Who Wakes. May Sarton. SP-SartM

Who walks on white feet turned. For a Lady of Whom I Speak. Charles Olson. CP-OlsoC

Who Walks There? Kenneth Patchen. CP-PatcK

Who wants action. Promise, A. Charles Olson. CP-OlsoC

Who wants my jellyfish? Jellyfish, The. Ogden Nash. CP-NashO

Who wants to see what can be done by Nature. Petrarch. CP-Petra, *tr. by* J. G. Nichols

Who wants to show everything. Who Is the Child. James Laughlin. CP-LaugJ

Who was born January first. Birthday Book, A. Gertrude Stein. CP-SteiG

Who was born too soon? I will tell you who was born too soon. All, All Are Gone, the Old Familiar Quotations. Ogden Nash. CP-NashO

Who was Mary Shelley? Lorine Niedecker. CP-NiedL

Who was the great devil who, we are told, was judged worthy beyond others in the veneration of all? Idol of Sarapis, The. Clement of Alexandria. CP-MertT *Fr.* Diatribe Against the Old Gods.

Who was there had seen us. Dark Girl's Rhyme, The. Dorothy Parker. CP-ParkD

Who weeps for strangers? Many wept. Elegiac Stanzas Composed in the Churchyard of Grasmere. William Wordsworth. CP-WorW1

Who were so dark of heart they might not speak. E. E. Cummings. CP-CummE

Who were "the Father and the Son" Emily Dickinson. CP-DickE

Who were the twain that trod this track. Jog-Trot Pair, A. Thomas Hardy. CP-HardT

Who whispered in your ear that secret. Interval. Fernando Pessoa. SP-PessF, *tr. by* Susan M. Brown *and* Edwin Honig

Who whispered, souls have shapes? My Sisters. Stanley Kunitz. CP-KunSC

Who Whistled for the Wind, That It Should Break. Philip Larkin. CP-LarkP

Who Will Endure. W. H. Auden. CP-AudeW
(No Change of Place.) CP-AudeW

Who will ever see happy men and women. Happy Men and Women. Rainer Maria Rilke. CP-RilkFr, *tr. by* A. Poulin, Jr.

Who will forgive me for the things I do? My Friend, My Friend. Anne Sexton. SP-SextA

Who will go drive with Fergus now. Who Goes with Fergus? William Butler Yeats. CP-YeatW

Who will honor the city without a name. City without a Name. Czeslaw Milosz. CP-MiloC; CP-MiloCN, *tr. by* Renata Gorczynski, Robert Hass *and* Robert Pinsky

Who will, may hear Sordello's story told. Sordello. Robert Browning. CP-BroR1

Who will not honour Noble Numbers, when. Verses. Robert Herrick. CP-HerrR

Who will protect you from the thrust of wings. To My Friend, behind Walls. Carolyn Kizer. CP-KizeC

Who will slacken the mental strain. Ballade of a Not Insupportable Loss. Dorothy Parker. CP-ParkD

Who will take away. Spell Against Sorrow. Kathleen Jessie Raine. SP-RainK

Who Will Take Over the Universe? Allen Ginsberg. CP-GinsA

Who will wed the Dowager's youngest daughter. Romance of a Youngest Daughter. John Crowe Ransom. SP-RansJ

Who with a little cannot be content. Again. Robert Herrick. CP-HerrR

Who, with dull mind, can view man's wondrous frame. Know Thyself: Suggested by Hearing Dr. A. E. Miller's Lectures on the Human Body. Jones Very. CP-VeryJ

Who with thy leaves shall wipe (at need). To His Book[e]. Robert Herrick. CP-HerrR

Who would be / A merman gay. Merman, The. James Whitcomb Riley. CP-RileJ

Who would have ever thought. Sir Thomas Wyatt. CP-WyatT

Who would have thought. Old Likeness, An. Thomas Hardy. CP-HardT

Who would here sojourn for an outstreched spell. Thoughts from Sophocles. Thomas Hardy. CP-HardT

Who would I show it to. Elegy: "Who would I show it to." W. S. Merwin. SP-MerwW

Who would love you. Happy Man, The. Robert Creeley. CP-CreeR

Who would not be thy subject, James, t'obey. To King James ("Who would not be thy subject, James, t'obey"). Ben Jonson. CP-JonsB; SP-JonsB

Who would not laugh, if Lawrence, hired to grace. Hints from Horace. Lord Byron. CP-Byron

Who would want to become his admirers? Letter for the End. Wyatt Prunty. SP-PrunW

Who would wish back the Saints upon our rough. Christina Georgina Rossetti. CP-RosC2

Who writes my poems. Person, The. James Laughlin. CP-LaugJ

Who wrote / in the great world. In Memoriam Charles Reznikoff. George Oppen. CP-OppGN

Who you gonna put in it? Air Raid over Harlem. Langston Hughes. CP-HughL; CP-HughL1

Who'd Want to Be a Man? Gregory Orr. SP-OrrG

Who'd want to be the biggest one. Big Ideas among Earthlings. Heather McHugh. SP-McHuH

Whoe doesn't love / roses, and who. Hummingbird Pauses at the Trumpet Vine. Mary Oliver. SP-OlivM

Whoe'er he be that sojourns here. Epigram: "Whoe'er he be that sojourns here." Robert Burns. CP-BurnR

Who'er thou art, O reader, know. On Wee Johnie. Robert Burns. CP-BurnR

Whoe're thou art whom this fair statue charms. On the Statue of *Cleopatra*, Made into a Fountain by *Leo* the Tenth. Baldassare, Count of Novilara Castiglione. CP-PopeA

Whoever desires to strengthen his spirit. Becoming Stronger. Constantine P. Cavafy. CP-CavaC, *tr. by* Theoharis Constantine Theoharis

Whoever despises the clitoris despises the penis. Speed of Darkness, The. Muriel Rukeyser *and* Leif Sjoberg. CP-RukeM

Whoever disenchants. Emily Dickinson. CP-DickE

Whoever embraces a woman is Adam. The woman is Eve. Happiness. Jorge Luis Borges. SP-BorgJ, *tr. by* Stephen Kessler

Whoever has Cold Mountain's poems. Han-shan. CP-ColdM, *tr. by* Red Pine

Whoever has drowned and awhile entered. True Joy. Robert Graves. CP-GravR

Whoever he be, would write a story at. To the London Reader, on the Odcombian Writer, Polytopian Thomas the Traveller. Ben Jonson. CP-JonsB

Whoever is able will pursue the plainly. Giant's Ring, The. Robinson Jeffers. CP-JefR2

Whoever lives beside a mountain knows. Burden. Richard Eberhart. CP-EberR

Whoever loves, if he do not propose. Love's Progress. John Donne. MW-DonnJ *Fr.* Elegies.

Whoever [*or* Who ever] comes to shroud me, do not harm[e]. Funeral[l], The. John Donne. CP-DonnJ; MW-DonnJ

Whoever [*or* Who ever] guesses, thinks, or dream[e]s he know[e]s. Curse, The. John Donne. CP-DonnJ; MW-DonnJ

Whoever pleaseth to inquire. On the Little House by the Churchyard of Castleknock. Jonathan Swift. CP-SwifJ

Whoever quite expected it would change. Queen Anne's Lace. Robert Stock. SP-StocR

Whoever runs into a ghost or spirit. Han-shan. CP-ColdM, *tr. by* Red Pine

Whoever swings an ax. Ax. Charles Simic. SP-SimiC; SP-SimiCE

Whoever vies with Pindar's strain. Horace. *See* Pindar is imitable by none

Whoever wants to make it. Paradise of Squares. Nicanor Parra. CP-MertT

Whoever was the cause your tears were shed. Upon L.M. Weeping. Sir John Suckling. CP-SuckJ

Whoever with the compasses of his eyes. Waitress. Karl Shapiro. SP-ShapK

Whoever You Are Holding Me Now in Hand. Walt Whitman. CP-WhitW

Whoever you are, I fear you are walking the walks of dreams. To You. Walt Whitman. CP-WhitW

Whoever you are, this poem is clearly about you. Garland for You. Robert Penn Warren. CP-WarrR

Whoever you are, you have the number you dialed. Hello. Miller Williams. CP-WillM

Whoever you may be, however endowed. Walking with Angels. Robert Stock. SP-StocR

Who(is?are)who. E. E. Cummings. CP-CummE

Whole. Rae Armantrout. SP-ArmaA

Whole blear world, The. Sunset. Allen Ginsberg. CP-GinsA

Whole city, The. Nation. George Oppen. CP-OppGN

Whole countryside deployed on the hills of heather, an army with, The. Shooting Season. Robinson Jeffers. CP-JefR2

Whole day long, under the walking sun, The. Sleeping Giant, The. Donald Hall. CP-HallD

Whole green sky is dying, The. The last tree flares. On a Line from Valéry. Carolyn Kizer. CP-KizeC

Whole Gulfs—of Red—and Fleets—of Red. Emily Dickinson. CP-DickE

Whole Half, The. A. R. Ammons. CP-AmmoA

Whole Head Is Sick, and the Whole Heart Faint, The. Christina Georgina Rossetti. CP-RosC3

Whole idea of it makes me feel, The. On Turning Ten. Billy Collins. SP-CollB

Whole is by breaking and by mending. Autobiography of the Present. Laura Riding Jackson. CP-RidiL

Whole length of the dusty road, The. Rainer Maria Rilke. CP-RilkFr, *tr. by* A. Poulin, Jr. *Fr.* Valaisian Quatrains, The.

Whole length of the seashore was strewn with dried fish, The. Exonerated. Yannis Ritsos. SP-RitsY, *tr. by* Kimon Friar *and* Kostas Myrsiades

Whole Love. Robert Graves. CP-GravR

Whole lower panel of the chain-link fence girdling my old grammar school playground, The. Soon. C. K. Williams. CP-WillC

Whole murky forest is one, The. Overview. Federico García Lorca. CP-GarcF, *tr. by* Jerome Rothenberg *Fr.* In the Forest of Clocks.

Whole night in form the whorl on earth. Pamphylian. Louis Zukofsky. CP-ZukLS

Whole night rests, The. Rainer Maria Rilke. CP-RilkFr, *tr. by* A. Poulin, Jr. *Fr.* Orchards.

Whole of appearance is a toy, The. For this. Dove in the Belly, The. Wallace Stevens. CP-StevW; CP-StevWP

Whole of creation shall come to his funeral, The. Absolutely Vernal. Charles Olson. CP-OlsoC

Whole of it came not at once, The. Emily Dickinson. CP-DickE

Whole process is a lie, The. Ivy Crown, The. William Carlos Williams. CP-WilW2

Whole Question, The. Robert Penn Warren. CP-WarrR

Whole rich process of twined opposites, The. To a Dead Graduate Student. Thom Gunn. CP-GunnT

Whole section of the city I live in has been urban renewed, some of it torn down, A. Bread. C. K. Williams. CP-WillC; SP-WillC

Whole terrace, The. St. Catherine's Clock. Thomas Kinsella. CP-KinsT

Whole towns shut down. Late Snow & Lumber Strike of the Summer of Fifty-four, The. Gary Snyder. CP-SnydG

Whole / Weight of / Everything, The. For Creely's Ear. Allen Ginsberg. CP-GinsA

Whole white world is ours, The. White World. "H. D." CP-DoolH

Whole Works, The. Federico García Lorca. CP-GarcF, tr. by Jerome Rothenberg Fr. Night (Suite for Piano and Poet's Voice).

Whole World, The. Charles Olson. CP-OlsoC

Whole world seated / at table, The. Sitting Down. Pablo Neruda. SP-NeruP

Wholeness. Chuang Tzu. CP-MertT

Wholesome. William Meredith. SP-MereW

Who'll that be. Kenneth Patchen. CP-PatcK

Wholly absorbed / into my own conduits to. Charles Olson. SP-OlsoC Fr. Maximus Poems, The.

Wholly from idiosyncratic reasons, my feet. Narcissus Unbound. William Dickey. SP-DickW

Wholly Unscholastic Opinion, A. James Whitcomb Riley. CP-RileJ

Whom are you carrying. João Cabral de Melo Neto. CP-BishE Fr. Death and Life of a Severino, The.

Whom bomb? Hum Bom! Allen Ginsberg. CP-GinsA

Whom can I ask / what I meant to achieve in this world? Pablo Neruda. SP-NeruP Fr. Question Book.

Whom can we love in all these little wars? Meteors. Jane Cooper. CP-CoopJ

Whom do I give my neat little volume. Catullus. See To whom should I present this

Whom do you love, she said, when you look out. Archibald MacLeish. CP-MacLA Fr. Happy Marriage, The.

Whom I have trusted to no end (Rufus). Carmen 77. Catullus. CP-ZukLS Fr. Carmina.

Whom I saw in a Dream Push Baby N. To the Dog Belvoir. Stevie Smith. CP-SmitS

Whom impious Rome had just marked out for her curses. On the Same ["Whom impious Rome had just marked out for her curses"]. John Milton. CP-MiltJ

Whom seek you here, sweet Mistress Fell? Mistress Fell. Walter De la Mare. CP-DeLaW

Whom sho'd I feare to write to, if I can. To Jos: Lo: Bishop of Exeter. Robert Herrick. CP-HerrR

Whom the gods love, die young. Old Men. D. H. Lawrence. CP-LawrD

Whom the Lord Loveth He Chasteneth. Christina Georgina Rossetti. CP-RosC2

Whom the untaught Shepherds call. Songs of the Pixies. Samuel Taylor Coleridge. CP-ColeS; MW-ColeS

"Whomever," this is for you! San Francisco for Whomever. Andrei Codrescu. SP-CodrA

Whoosh. Heather McHugh. SP-McHuH

Whore moves a basin of green antiseptic water, A. After Three Photographs of Brassaï. Norman Dubie. CP-DubiN

Whorls. William Meredith. SP-MereW

Whoroscope. Samuel Beckett. CP-BeckS

Who's coming to finish Love's temple? Rainer Maria Rilke. CP-RilkFr, tr. by A. Poulin, Jr. Fr. Orchards.

Who's in the Next Room? Thomas Hardy. CP-HardT

Who's killed the leaves? Leaves. Ted Hughes. SP-HughTN

Who's most afraid of death?thou. E. E. Cummings. CP-CummE

Who's she, / that one in your arms. Interrogation of the Man of Many Hearts, The. Anne Sexton. CP-SextA

Who's that? Walter De la Mare. CP-DeLaW

Who's this out there. Lines: "Who's this out there." A. K. Ramanujan. CP-RamaA

Who's this that draws me forcibly to you? Michelangelo Buonarroti. CP-Miche, tr. by John Frederick Nims

Who's Who. W. H. Auden. CP-AudeW

Whose are the little beds, I asked. Emily Dickinson. CP-DickE

Whose are these(wraith a clinging with a wraith). E. E. Cummings. CP-CummE

Whose cheek is this? Emily Dickinson. CP-DickE

Whose child is this they bring. Christening, The. Thomas Hardy. CP-HardT

Whose head befringed with bescattered tresses. Descripcion; of a Woman, The. Robert Herrick. CP-HerrR

Whose hoax to put up with, outstare, protest patience. Catullus. See What man could stomach the sight

Whose is my pain, if I reject it. Pain Is an Eagle Clinging to Your Name. Pablo Antonio Cuadra. CP-MertT

Whose is that noble dauntless brow? Verses Intended to Be Written below a Noble Earl's Picture. Robert Burns. CP-BurnR

Whose is the love that gleaming through the world. Queen Mab. Percy Bysshe Shelley. CP-ShelP

Whose little lady is you, chile. Possession. Paul Laurence Dunbar. CP-DunbP

Whose love is given over-well. Partial Comfort. Dorothy Parker. CP-ParkD

Whose minds like horse or ox. Learned Men, The. Archibald MacLeish. CP-MacLA

Whose Pink career may have a close. Emily Dickinson. CP-DickE

Whose Timeless Reach. A. R. Ammons. CP-AmmoA

Whose tongues are twisted and whose hearts are shrunk. For Jordan With Love the Eighth Year of the Slaughter: A Minuet for Army Boots and Orchestra. Miller Williams. CP-WillM

Whose west walls take the sunset like a blow. House, The. James Merrill. SP-MerrJ

Whose wine shop is this aglow. Han-shan. CP-ColdM, tr. by Red Pine

Whose woods these are I think I know. Stopping by Woods on a Snowy Evening. Robert Frost. CP-FrosR

Whose work could this be, Chapman, to refine. To My Worthy and Honoured Friend, Mr George Chapman, on His Translation of Hesiod's Works and Days. Ben Jonson. CP-JonsB

Whoso alas is young. Ralph Waldo Emerson. CP-EmerR

Whoso for hours or lengthy days. Eunice. Thomas Hardy. CP-HardT

Whoso hath anguish is not dead in sin. Subject To Like Passions as We Are. Christina Georgina Rossetti. CP-RosC2

Whoso List to Hunt. Sir Thomas Wyatt. CP-WyatT

Whoso list to hunt, I know where is an hind. Whoso List to Hunt. Sir Thomas Wyatt. CP-WyatT

Whozat Jimmie Berman. Jimmy Berman Rag. Allen Ginsberg. SP-GinsA

Whut dat you whisperin' keepin' f'om me? News, The. Paul Laurence Dunbar. CP-DunbP

"Whut do you spose thet thing is," Oi said. "Whut?" Sonnet: "'Whut do you spose thet thing is,' Oi said. "Whut?" Hayden Carruth. CP-CarHS

Whut time 'd dat clock strike? At Night. Paul Laurence Dunbar. CP-DunbP

Whut you say, dah? huh, uh! chile. Cabin Tale, A. Paul Laurence Dunbar. CP-DunbP

Why. Richard Eberhart. CP-EberR

Why. James Laughlin. CP-LaugJ

Why. Hugh MacDiarmid. SP-MacDH

Why. Czeslaw Milosz. CP-MiloCN, tr. by Robert Hass

Why—? D. H. Lawrence. CP-LawrD

Why? Christina Georgina Rossetti. CP-RosC2

Why am I loth to leave this earthly scene? Stanzas on the Same Occasion [in the Prospect of Death]. Robert Burns. CP-BurnR

Why am I not myself these many days. Evangelist's Wife, An. Edwin Arlington Robinson. CP-RobiE

Why am I so angry at Kissinger? Tübingen–Hamburg Schlafwagen. Allen Ginsberg. CP-GinsA

Why am I so troubled. Han-shan. CP-ColdM, tr. by Red Pine

Why am I / the laggard, as if. Same. Robert Creeley. CP-CreeR

Why Are the Clergy . . . ? Stevie Smith. CP-SmitS

Why are the stamps adorned with kings and presidents? Power to the People. Howard Nemerov. CP-NemeH

Why are these pipples taking their hets off? ? E. E. Cummings. CP-CummE

Why are they written—all these lovers' rhymes? James Whitcomb Riley. CP-RileJ

Why are women so energetic? Energetic Women. D. H. Lawrence. CP-LawrD

Why are you so bent down before your time. Old Workman, The. Thomas Hardy. CP-HardT

Why art thou not awake my son? Call, The ("Why art thou not awake my son?"). Jones Very. CP-VeryJ

Why art thou silent and invisible. To Nobodaddy. William Blake. CP-BlakW

Why Art Thou Silent [Is Thy Love a Plant]. William Wordsworth. CP-WorW2

Why, as I was walking up the hill. Rich Interior, After Thomas Mann. Philip Whalen. SP-WhalP

Why ask to know the date—the clime? Emily Jane Brontë. CP-BronE

Why ask to know what date, what clime? Emily Jane Brontë. CP-BronE

Why Be at Pains? Thomas Hardy. CP-HardT

"Why?" Because all I haply can and do. Why I Am a Liberal. Robert Browning. CP-BroR2

Why Boy Came to Lonely Place. Robert Penn Warren. CP-WarrR

Why Brownlee Left. Paul Muldoon. CP-MuldP

Why Brownlee left, and where he went. Why Brownlee Left. Paul Muldoon. CP-MuldP

Why, by an ingrained habit, deviate. With the Grain. Donald Davie. CP-DaviDC

Why can I never when I think about it. For My Mother in Her First Illness, from a Window Overlooking Notre Dame. Jane Cooper. CP-CoopJ

Why cannot I make plain, to sinful men. Veil Upon the Heart, The. Jones Very. CP-VeryJ

Why cannot the one good. War God, The. Stephen Spender. CP-SpenS

Why can't I be happy. Lorine Niedecker. CP-NiedL

Why Can't I Leave You? Ai. SP-Ai

Why can't we suffocate the worm Remorse. Irreparable, The. Charles Baudelaire. CP-BaudC, *tr.* by Walter Martin

Why come you out to me with clubs and staves. Behold He Is at Hand That Doth Betray Me. Jones Very. CP-VeryJ

Why complain, brothers, to you, my writing. Sonnet: "Why complain, brothers, to you, my writing." Hayden Carruth. CP-CarHS *Fr.* Sonnets.

Why couldn't you have. Cordelia. James Laughlin. CP-LaugJ

Why covet what eye cannot see. Out Of Bounds. Walter De la Mare. CP-DeLaW

Why, credulous Naples, do you vaunt your clear-voiced Siren. To the Same ["Why, credulous Naples, do you vaunt your clear-voiced Siren"]. John Milton. CP-CowpW; CP-MiltJ

Why decide in advance what to do. Eucalyptus trees their shiny. Many Colored Squares. Philip Whalen. SP-WhalP

Why deck with flow'rs these humble mounds? Memorial Day. Paul Laurence Dunbar. CP-DunbP

Why did all manly gifts in Webster fail? Webster. Ralph Waldo Emerson. CP-EmerR

Why did baby die. Christina Georgina Rossetti. CP-RosC2

Why did baby die, / Making Father sigh. Why did baby die. Christina Georgina Rossetti. CP-RosC2

Why did he write to her. One Parting. Carl Sandburg. CP-SandC

Why Did I Dream of You Last Night? Philip Larkin. CP-LarkP

Why Did I Laugh Tonight? John Keats. CP-KeatJ

Why did I print upon myself the names. Requiem for the Death of a Boy. Randall Jarrell. CP-JarrR

Why Did I Sketch. Thomas Hardy. CP-HardT

Why did I wake that night, all the house at rest? Moonlight's Dream, The. Robert Penn Warren. CP-WarrR

Why did Massenet compose *Thaïs*? Greetings from the Chateau. James Schuyler. CP-SchuJ

Why did that man. Park ("Why did that man"). Robert Creeley. SP-CreeR

Why did the woman want to kill one dog? Village Tale, A. May Sarton. SP-SartM

Why did we meet long years of yore? Because. James Whitcomb Riley. CP-RileJ

Why did you elude me last night. Unsatisfactory Dream, The. James Laughlin. CP-LaugJ

Why did you flutter in vain hope, poor bird. Cage, The. Walter De la Mare. CP-DeLaW

Why did you give no hint that night. Going, The. Thomas Hardy. CP-HardT

Why did you go. E. E. Cummings. CP-CummE

Why did you kiss the girl who cried. What the Earth Asked Me. James Wright. CP-WrigJ

Why did you melt your waxen man. Sister Helen. Dante Gabriel Rossetti. CW-RossD

Why did you stay away. Way the Cards Fall, The. Yusef Komunyakaa. CP-KomuY

Why didn't you say you was promised, Rose-Ann. Rose-Ann. Thomas Hardy. CP-HardT

Why, disease, dost thou molest. To Sickness. Ben Jonson. CP-JonsB; SP-JonsB

Why Do I. Stevie Smith. CP-SmitS

Why Do I? Thomas Hardy. CP-HardT

Why do I deny manna to another? Sather Gate Illumination. Allen Ginsberg. CP-GinsA

Why do I fear the true winter death to come. Winter, The ("Why do I fear the true winter death to come"). Philip Whalen. SP-WhalP

Why do I go on doing these things? Why Do I? Thomas Hardy. CP-HardT

Why do I hate that lone green dell? Emily Jane Brontë. CP-BronE

Why do I have to make. Are We Through Talking, I Hope? John Ciardi. CP-CiarJ

Why do I imagine the death of Mandelstam. Preparing for Exile. Derek Walcott. CP-WalcD

Why do I languish thus, drooping and dull. Dulness[e]. George Herbert. CP-HerbG

Why do I live among the green mountains? Poet's Laughter. Archibald MacLeish. CP-MacLA

Why do I love the sound of children's voices in unknown games. American Twilight. Charles Wright. SP-WrigCN

"Why do I love" You, Sir? Emily Dickinson. CP-DickE

Why do I remember you. Little Doncella, The. Federico García Lorca. CP-GarcF, *tr.* by Jerome Rothenberg *Fr.* Secrets.

Why do I see the power of Genius droop. Lines on Hearing of the Death of Doctor Franklin. Annis Boudinot Stockton. CP-StocA

Why do I see these empty boats, sailing on airy seas? Empty Boats, The. Nicholas Vachel Lindsay. CP-LindV

Why do I still run. Weeping, The. John Logan. CP-LoganJ

Why do I still wake up and not know?—though later. Recollection in Upper Ontario, from Long Before. Robert Penn Warren. CP-WarrR

Why do I want to go away? Tennessee Williams. CP-WillT

Why do I write today? Apology. William Carlos Williams. CP-WilW1

Why / do the / fingers. E. E. Cummings. CP-CummE

Why do the Gentiles tumult, and the Nations. Psalm 2: "Why do the heathen rage." Bible, *O.T. Fr.* Psalms.

Why do the Muses thus neglect to come? On the Death of General Montgomery. Annis Boudinot Stockton. CP-StocA

Why do they ring that bell. Signal, The. Archibald MacLeish. CP-MacLA

Why—do they shut Me out of Heaven? Emily Dickinson. CP-DickE

Why do we bother with the rest of the day. Morning. Billy Collins. SP-CollB

Why do we labor at the poem. Reasons for Music. Archibald MacLeish. CP-MacLA

Why do we mourn that heaven should claim. Lines on the Death of Mrs Petit of Philadelphia. Annis Boudinot Stockton. CP-StocA

Why do we waste so much time in arguing? Sushi. Paul Muldoon. CP-MuldP

Why do you dig like long-clawed scavengers. Verlaine. Edwin Arlington Robinson. CP-RobiE

Why do you fly from the drowned shores of Galilee. Quickening of St. John the Baptist, The. Thomas Merton. CP-MertT

Why do you follow me? Daphne. Edna St. Vincent Millay. CP-MillE

Why do you groan under graven tables. Raid, A. G. K. Chesterton. CP-ChesG

Why do you harbour that great cheval-glass. Cheval-Glass, The. Thomas Hardy. CP-HardT

Why do you listen, trees? Farm, The. Archibald MacLeish. CP-MacLA

Why Do You Never Enter My Dreams. James Laughlin. CP-LaugJ

Why do you not steer straight, my love, she cried. Advice. Ivor Gurney. SP-GurnI

Why do you play such dreary music. Radio. Frank O'Hara. SP-OharF

Why Do You Rage? Stevie Smith. CP-SmitS

Why do you seek the sun. Queen of Bubbles, The. Nicholas Vachel Lindsay. CP-LindV

Why do you sit, o pale thin man. Penance. Thomas Hardy. CP-HardT

Why do you spurt and sprottle. Rabbit Snared in the Night. D. H. Lawrence. CP-LawrD

Why do you stand in the dripping rye. Woman in the Rye, The. Thomas Hardy. CP-HardT

Why do you stay there in the wood? Hunter, The. Kenneth Patchen. CP-PatcK

Why do you strive for greatness, fool? Stephen Crane. CP-CranS

Why do you talk so much. For Robert Frost. Galway Kinnell. SP-KinnGN

Why do you weep there, O sweet lady. Memorial Brass, The: 186–. Thomas Hardy. CP-HardT

Why doe not all fresh maids appeare. Upon the Death of His Sparrow; an Elegie. Robert Herrick. CP-HerrR

Why do[e] ye weep, sweet babes? To Primroses Filled with Morning Dew. Robert Herrick. CP-HerrR

Why does she turn in that soft shy way. Whitewashed Wall, The. Thomas Hardy. CP-HardT

Why Does She Weep? D. H. Lawrence. CP-LawrD

Why does the sea burn? Why do the hills cry? Zaydee. Philip Levine. SP-LeviP

Why does the sea moan evermore? By the Sea. Christina Georgina Rossetti. CP-RosC1

Why does the Sun in usual splendor rise. Short Elegy to the Memory of Her Husband, A. Annis Boudinot Stockton. CP-StocA

Why does the thin grey strand. Sorrow. D. H. Lawrence. CP-LawrD

Why does this written doe bound through these written woods? Joy of Writing, The. Wisława Szymborska. SP-SzymW, *tr.* by Stanislaw Barańczak *and* Clare Cavanagh

Why / don't / be / sil / ly. E. E. Cummings. CP-CummE

Why don't people leave off being lovable. Elemental. D. H. Lawrence. CP-LawrD

Why don't we board a train and go off to Persia? Anti-Shenandoah: Two Skits and a Chorus. Joseph Brodsky. CP-BrodJ

Why don't you like the wild cry of the madmen. Old Dichotomy: Choosing Sides. Richard Eberhart. CP-EberR

Why Don't You Write for Me? John Ciardi. CP-CiarJ

Why dost thou dally, Death, and tarry on the way? Come, Death (1). Stevie Smith. CP-SmitS

Why dost thou haste away. Madrigal. Sir Philip Sidney. SP-SidnP *Fr.* Arcadia.

Why dost thou sound, my dear[e] Aurelian. In Answer of an Elegiacal[l] Letter, Upon the Death of the King of Sweden [from Aurelian Townsend, Inviting Me to Write on That Subject]. Thomas Carew. CP-CareT

Why do'st thou wound, & break my heart? His Covenant or Protestation to Julia. Robert Herrick. CP-HerrR

Why dost Thou wound my wounds, o Thou that passest by. Luke 10; And a Certaine Priest Comming that Way Looked on Him and Passed by. Bible, *N.T.* CP-CrasR *Fr.* St. Luke.

Why d'you ask me to scribble in verse. Bouts-Rimeés (Written at Chawton

Cottage, 1820). George Knight. CP-AustJ

Why ease the tension of this wild desire. Michelangelo Buonarroti. CP-Miche, *tr. by* John Frederick Nims

Why East Wind Chills. Dylan Thomas. CP-ThomD

Why Else but to Forestall This Hour. Adrienne Rich. CP-RicAE

Why extremely do we observe more of. Sonnet: "Why extremely do we observe more of." Hayden Carruth. CP-CarHS *Fr.* Sonnets.

Why Fades a Dream? Paul Laurence Dunbar. CP-DunbP

Why fails my pulse, as from yon holy tower. Poem on the Death of Mrs. Smith, A. Mary Field Stockton Harrison. CP-StocA

Why fallen so soon asleep? Not hard to tell. Michelangelo Buonarroti. CP-Miche, *tr. by* John Frederick Nims

Why fear to die. Ralph Waldo Emerson. CP-EmerR

Why Fear to Die? Sir Philip Sidney. SP-SidnP *Fr.* Arcadia.

Why feel guilty because the death of a lover causes lust? Untitled Poem: "Why feel guilty because the death of a lover causes lust?" Alan Dugan. CP-DugaA

Why Flowers Change Color. Robert Herrick. CP-HerrR

Why forms discuss, if that the soul is fled? Communion, The. Jones Very. CP-VeryJ

Why from the danger did mine eyes not start [*or* did not mine eyes start]. Sonnet: Of his Pain from a new Love. Guido Cavalcanti. CW-RossD, *tr. by* Dante Gabriel Rossetti

Why from this her and him. E. E. Cummings. CP-CummE

Why gird at Lollius if he care. Lollius. Rudyard Kipling. CP-KiplR

Why go the east road now? By Henstridge Cross at the Year's End. Thomas Hardy. CP-HardT

Why go to Saint-Juliot? What's Juliot to me? Dream or No, A. Thomas Hardy. CP-HardT

Why God Permits Evil: For Answers to This Question of Interest to Many Write Bible Answers, Dept. E-7. Miller Williams. CP-WillM

Why has my Anna thus forgot her friend? Tears of Friendship. Elegy the Third.—To a Friend Just Married, and Who Had Promised to Write, on Parting, but Had Neglected It. Annis Boudinot Stockton. CP-StocA

Why has Spring one syllable less. What's in a Name? Christina Georgina Rossetti. CP-RosC2

Why hasn't it risen, the powerful hymn? Why. Czeslaw Milosz. CP-MiloCN, *tr. by* Robert Hass

Why hast thou tarried till the eleventh hour. Last, The. Jones Very. CP-VeryJ

Why hath the rose faded and fallen, yet these eyes have not seen. Awake! Walter De la Mare. CP-DeLaW

Why have I wandered the asphalt of midnight and not known why? Robert Penn Warren. CP-WarrR

Why have such scores of lovely, gifted girls. Slice of Wedding Cake, A. Robert Graves. CP-GravR

Why have you made life so intolerable. To God. Ivor Gurney. SP-GurnI

Why Have You Sought? "H. D." CP-DoolH

Why heard, amidst these shades, the tongue of time. On Hearing the Clock Strike, in Harmony Grove. Jones Very. CP-VeryJ

Why hold that poets are so sensitive? To the Public. Louis MacNeice. CP-MacNL

Why honor the new men. Ralph Waldo Emerson. CP-EmerR

Why, how now dapper black. Beau's Reply to the Five Ladies' Answer, The. Jonathan Swift. CP-SwifJ

Why, how now, saucy Tom. Bowles and Campbell. Lord Byron. CP-Byron

Why hurry when you're so well defended? Snail, The. Primo Levi. CP-LeviP, *tr. by* Ruth Feldman

Why I Am a Liberal. Robert Browning. CP-BroR2

Why I Am a Poet. William Stafford. SP-StafWW

Why I Am Happy. William Stafford. SP-StafWW

Why I Am Not a Painter. Frank O'Hara. SP-OharF

Why I Meditate. Allen Ginsberg. SP-GinsA

Why, I saw you with the sexton, outside the church-door. She Saw Him, She Said. Thomas Hardy. CP-HardT

Why I tie [*or* tye] about thy wrist. Bracelet to Julia, The. Robert Herrick. CP-HerrR

Why I Turned Vegetarian. Rita Dove. SP-DoveR

Why I Voted the Socialist Ticket. Nicholas Vachel Lindsay. CP-LindV

Why I Will Not Get Out of Bed. James Tate. SP-TateJ

Why I Write Not of Love. Ben Jonson. CP-JonsB; SP-JonsB

Why if it be so, for the dismal morn. Gerard Manley Hopkins. CP-HopkG

Why in my heart, O Grief. Disguise, The. Walter De la Mare. CP-DeLaW

Why in the world did Perilámpes, that man of taste, want to carry off. Peacocks of Perilampes, The. Yannis Ritsos. SP-RitsY, *tr. by* Kimon Friar

Why Is God Love, Jack? Allen Ginsberg. CP-GinsA

Why is it Nobleness makes us ashamed. Emily Dickinson. SP-DickE

Why is it said thou canst not live. Love. Percy Bysshe Shelley. CP-ShelP

Why is it so hard to start exactly where I'm at? Selavie. Andrei Codrescu. SP-CodrA

Why is it that whenever I talk with the duchess. Complaint. Richard Wilbur. CP-WilbR

Why is it, when I am in Rome. On Being a Woman. Dorothy Parker. CP-ParkD

"Why is my District death-rate low?" Rudyard Kipling. *See* It was an August evening and, in snowy garments clad

Why is our soul sometimes so weary. Rainer Maria Rilke. CP-RilkFr, *tr. by* A. Poulin, Jr. *Fr.* Fragments.

Why is the child so pale. Louise. Stevie Smith. CP-SmitS

Why is the universe mysterious? Questions. Howard Nemerov. CP-NemeH

Why is the word pretty so underrated? Pretty. Stevie Smith. CP-SmitS

Why / is what i ask myself. Hag Riding. Lucille Clifton. SP-ClifL

Why it has to be December. Iron. Adam Zagajewski. SP-ZagaA, *tr. by* Renata Gorczynski

Why it was necessary to fumble out of the dark. Travelling Companion, The. Thomas Kinsella. CP-KinsT

Why lie to you so much, O child, in your first soft nest? Lying to a Child. Rainer Maria Rilke. CP-RilkFr

Why listen, even the water is sobbing for something. Maid's Thought, The. Robinson Jeffers. CP-JefR1

Why Log Truck Drivers Rise Earlier Than Students of Zen. Gary Snyder. CP-SnydG

Why look we to the distant past to learn. Teaching of History Confirmed, The. Jones Very. CP-VeryJ

Why, Madam, will ye longer weep. To the Lady Crew, Upon the Death of her Child. Robert Herrick. CP-HerrR

Why make it doubt—it hurts it so. Emily Dickinson. CP-DickE

Why make so much of fragmentary blue. Fragmentary Blue. Robert Frost. CP-FrosR

Why marry ogre. Marriage Counsel. John Updike. CP-UpdiJ

Why me? Pili's Wall. Philip Levine. SP-LeviP

Why, Minstrel, These Untuneful Murmurings. William Wordsworth. CP-WorW2

Why must itself up every of a park. E. E. Cummings. CP-CummE

Why nag at the ideas of Hercules, Don Don? New England Verses. Wallace Stevens. CP-StevW; CP-StevWP

Why need I say, Louisa dear! To a Young Lady [Miss Lavinia Poole] on Her Recovery from a Fever. Samuel Taylor Coleridge. CP-ColeS

Why Not? James Laughlin. CP-LaugJ

Why not make them. Buildings. Robert Creeley. SP-CreeR

Why not merely the despaired of. Cascando. Samuel Beckett. CP-BeckS

Why not my father said so. My Father Said. Grace Paley. CP-PalGC

Why not ride / with pleasure. Some Afternoon. Robert Creeley. CP-CreeR

Why of the sheep do you not learn peace? Answer to the Parson, An. William Blake. CP-BlakW

Why of the Weather, The. Robert Graves. CP-GravR

Why of the Wind, The. Laura Riding Jackson. CP-RidiL

Why only at long last, why next to never. Michelangelo Buonarroti. CP-Miche, *tr. by* John Frederick Nims

Why Paint? Andrei Codrescu. SP-CodrA

Why, Pigot, complain of this damsel's disdain. Reply to Some Verses of J.M.B. Pigot, Esq., on the Cruelty of His Mistress. Lord Byron. CP-Byron

Why pluck their flowers? Each might have been. Blueberry Blossoms, The. Jones Very. CP-VeryJ

Why presumes thy pride on that, that must so private be. Thomas Campion. CP-CampT

Why readest thou? thou canst not gain the life. To Him That Hath Shall Be Given. Jones Very. CP-VeryJ

Why reclining, interrogating? why myself and all drowsing? To the States, To Identify the 16th, 17th, or 18th Presidentiad. Walt Whitman. CP-WhitW

Why Repeat the Sins. Shmuel HaNagid. SP-HaNaS, *tr. by* Peter Cole

Why rings not back the welcome shout. Frozen Ship, The. Jones Very. CP-VeryJ

Why rouse from thy long winter sleep? Queen Wasp, A. Walter De la Mare. CP-DeLaW

Why say "death"? Death is neither harsh nor kind. Presence, The. Robert Graves. CP-GravR

Why say to them. Robert Creeley. CP-CreeR

Why seek to alter people, why not leave them alone? Mills of God, The. D. H. Lawrence. CP-LawrD

Why seraphim like lutanists arranged. Evening without Angels. Wallace Stevens. CP-StevW; CP-StevWP

Why, Sergeant, stray on the Ivel Way. San Sebastian. Thomas Hardy. CP-HardT

Why shall I keep the old name? Blacklisted. Carl Sandburg. CP-SandC

Why She Moved House. Thomas Hardy. CP-HardT

Why sho'd we covet much, when as we know. Not to Covet Much Where Little is the Charge. Robert Herrick. CP-HerrR

Why should dull Art, which is wise Nature's ape. Divine Love, A. Thomas Carew. CP-CareT

Why should I be bound to thee. To My Mirtle. William Blake. CP-BlakW

Why should I be wondering. Hummingbird Woman. Carl Sandburg. CP-SandC

Why should I blame her that she filled my days. No Second Troy. William

Butler Yeats. CP-YeatW

Why should I call Thee Lord, Who art my God? After Communion. Christina Georgina Rossetti. CP-RosC1

Why should I care for the Ages. Novelty, A. G. K. Chesterton. CP-ChesG

Why Should I Care for the Men of Thames? William Blake. CP-BlakW (Thames.) CP-BlakW

Why should I have returned? Noah's Raven. W. S. Merwin. SP-MerwW

Why should I keep holiday. Compensation. Ralph Waldo Emerson. CP-EmerR

Why should I let the toad work. Toads. Philip Larkin. CP-LarkP

Why should I live. Ralph Waldo Emerson. CP-EmerR

Why should I seek for love or study it? Ribh Considers Christian Love Insufficient. William Butler Yeats. CP-YeatW

Why should I vaunt as stars that flame. Evolutionist to His Lady, The. G. K. Chesterton. CP-ChesG

Why should I, who know the cost so well. Sale, The. William Carlos Williams. CP-WilW2

Why should I wish you wise? Merciless Madrigal. Charles Baudelaire. CP-BaudC, tr. by Walter Martin

Why should it be *my* loneliness. Tell Me. Langston Hughes. CP-HughL; CP-HughL3

Why should my anxious breast repine. L'Amitié Est L'Amour Sans Ailes. Lord Byron. CP-Byron

Why Should Na Poor Folk Mowe. Robert Burns. CP-BurnR

Why should the hearts of you purists bear. Shmuel HaNagid. SP-HaNaS, tr. by Peter Cole

Why should their foolish bands, their hopeless hearses. Gerard Manley Hopkins. CP-HopkG

Why should this flower delay so long. Last Chrysanthemum, The. Thomas Hardy. CP-HardT

Why should we defer our joys? Dule of a Dewsbury Matron. Donald Davie. CP-DaviDC

Why should we hurry—why indeed? Emily Dickinson. CP-DickE

Why should we reck of hours that rend. Marriage Song, A. G. K. Chesterton. CP-ChesG

Why should we set these hearts of ours above. Fragment: "Why should we set these hearts of ours above." Dorothy Parker. CP-ParkD

Why should we speak?—he said—What's the use of many explanations. Relation of the Unrelated, The. Yannis Ritsos. SP-RitsY, tr. by Kimon Friar

Why should we weep or mourn, Angelic boy. Sonnet: "Why should we weep or mourn, Angelic boy." William Wordsworth. CP-WorW2

Why should we worry about to-morrow. For a Berry Voice. Ezra Pound. CP-PoEar

Why should you believe in magic. Consumed. James Tate. SP-TateJ

Why Shouldn't I. James Laughlin. CP-LaugJ

Why sing, amidst the strife which reigns around? Poet's Plea, The. Jones Very. CP-VeryJ

Why Sleeps the future, as a snake enrolled. Conclusion: "Why Sleeps the future, as a snake enrolled." William Wordsworth. CP-WorW2 Fr. Ecclesiastical Sonnets.

Why so often, silent one. Musing Maiden, The. Thomas Hardy. CP-HardT

Why so slowly do you move. Delaying Bride, The. Robert Herrick. CP-HerrR

Why so swift thou hurrying tide. Youth and the Stream, The. Jones Very. CP-VeryJ

Why Some Look up to Planets and Heroes. Thomas Merton. CP-MertT

Why some people be mad at me sometimes. Lucille Clifton. SP-ClifL

Why spatter me, you madly babbling bard. Cur Me Bespateras, Blaterans Furiosè Poeta. Thomas Sheridan. CP-SherT, tr. by Robert Hogan

Why speak of memory and death. Two Views of Two Ghost Towns. Charles Tomlinson. CP-TomlC

Why speak of the use / of poetry? Poetry. Hayden Carruth. CP-CarHS Fr. Clay Hill Anthology, The.

Why stand'st thou here alone, when all thy mates. To an Ancient Locust-Tree, Opposite Carltonville. Jones Very. CP-VeryJ

Why Steals the big drop from my Eye? Anniversary Elegy on the Death of Mr Stockton the 28th of Feb 1783. Annis Boudinot Stockton. CP-StocA

Why stirs, with sad alarm, the heart. Farewell Song. Paul Laurence Dunbar. CP-DunbP

"Why? Tell me why?" he said in dismay to Corrigan. Colloquy. Josephine Jacobsen. CP-JacoJ

Why that wild poet came to me to damn me. Lycambes Talks to John. Allen Tate. CP-TateA

Why the Face of a Clock is not Truly a Circle. Archibald MacLeish. CP-MacLA

Why the full heart is speechless. Emily Dickinson. SP-DickE

Why the Postman Has to Ring Twice, or, Yellow Envelope, Where Have You Gone? Ogden Nash. CP-NashO

Why the Question? Yannis Ritsos. SP-RitsY, tr. by N. C. Germanacos

Why the Soup Tastes Like the *Daily News*. Marge Piercy. SP-PierM

Why the Sun Comes Up. William Stafford. SP-StafWW

Why the Telephone Wires Dip and the Poles Are Cracked and Crooked. John

Updike. CP-UpdiJ

Why the Thief ingredient accompanies all Sweetness. Emily Dickinson. SP-DickE

Why, then, if love is all there is need to give. Argument, The. Walter De la Mare. CP-DeLaW

Why, then, weep not. This Dusky Faith. Edna St. Vincent Millay. CP-MillE

Why there are black half-donuts beneath each eye. At Least Let Me Explain. Thomas Lux. SP-LuxT

Why There Is No Class Solidarity in America I Read It In *The Times*. Aug. 2, 1987. Alan Dugan. CP-DugaA

Why this Flower is now call'd so. How the Wall-Flower Came First, and Why So Called. Robert Herrick. CP-HerrR

Why this man gelded Martial[l] I muse. Raderus. John Donne. CP-DonnJ; MW-DonnJ

Why this preoccupation, soul, with Death. Sonnet Dialogue. Countee Cullen. CP-CullC

Why? thou great ruler of Olympus, why. Lucan. CP-SherT Fr. Civil War [Bellum Civile] or Pharsalia.

Why, Tityrus! But you've forgotten me. Build Soil. Robert Frost. CP-FrosR

Why toll the bell today. Henry David Thoreau. CP-ThorH

Why urge the long, unequal fight. Voices, The. John Greenleaf Whittier. CP-WhitJ

Why vainly do I hither fly. Lament of Professor Turbojet, The. James Laughlin. CP-LaugJ

Why wait for Death to mow? Body and Soul. "H. D." CP-DoolH

Why Wait for Science. Robert Frost. CP-FrosR

Why wait? The squirrel beats his torch-tail. Eugenio Montale. CP-MontE, tr. by Jonathan Galassi

Why walkes Nick Flimsey like a Male-content? Upon Flimsey: Epigram. Robert Herrick. CP-HerrR

Why wanders my friend in this grove? Annis Boudinot Stockton. CP-StocA

Why want to go afar. Expostulation, An. Thomas Hardy. CP-HardT

Why was Cupid a Boy. William Blake. CP-BlakW

Why was I born if I have to die. Buzz. David Ignatow. SP-IgnaD

Why was it Bavaria? The house in the forest. To Know in Reverie the Only Phenomenology of the Absolute. Hayden Carruth. CP-CarHS

Why was it that the thunder voice of Fate. Robert Gould Shaw. Paul Laurence Dunbar. CP-DunbP

Why was it the apple. Question. Federico García Lorca. CP-GarcF, tr. by Jerome Rothenberg Fr. Newton.

Why We Are Going Back to Paradise Island. Marilyn Hacker. SP-HackM

Why weep ye by the tide, ladie? Jock of Hazeldean. Sir Walter Scott. SP-ScotW

'Why weeps my Boy?' His Father said. To Edward on the Death of His First Pony. James Austen. CP-AustJ

Why weeps the muse for England? What appears. Expostulation. William Cowper. CP-CowpW

Why were you born when the snow was falling? Dirge, A: "Why were you born when the snow was falling?" Christina Georgina Rossetti. CP-RosC1

Why weren't my eyes blinded. Guido Cavalcanti. CP-CavaG, tr. by Marc Cirigliano

Why, when it was all over, did I hold on to them? Old Icons, The. Seamus Heaney. SP-HeanSO Fr. Sweeney Redivivus.

Why, who makes much of a miracle? Miracles. Walt Whitman. CP-WhitW

Why why / How many winds make wonderful. E. E. Cummings. CP-CummE

Why, why tell thy lover. Fragment: "Why, why tell thy lover." Robert Burns. CP-BurnR

Why will you vex me with. To His Skeleton. Richard Wilbur. CP-WilbR

Why, William, on that old grey [or gray] stone. Expostulation and Reply. William Wordsworth. CP-WorW1; MW-WorW

Why wilt thou cast the roses from thine hair? Mary Magdalene at the Door of Simon the Pharisee. Dante Gabriel Rossetti. CW-RossD

Why wilt thou take my heart? It fawnlike flies. Hunter, The. Walter De la Mare. CP-DeLaW

Why Wine Is Forbidden. Jelaluddin Rumi. SP-Rumi, tr. by Coleman Barks

Why wore th'Egyptians Jewells in the Eare? Eare-rings. Robert Herrick. CP-HerrR

Why would she come to him. Versions. Robert Creeley. SP-CreeR

Why would they want one another. Aging Lovers, The. John Ciardi. CP-CiarJ

Why wouldn't she entertain her nephew? Lost in Translation. Carolyn Kizer. CP-KizeC

Why Write. Andrei Codrescu. SP-CodrA

Why, ye tenants of the lake. On Scaring Some Waterfowl in Loch Turit, a Wild Scene among the Hills of Oughtertyre. Robert Burns. CP-BurnR

Why yet, my noble hearts, they cannot say. Speech According to Horace, A. Ben Jonson. CP-JonsB; SP-JonsB

Why You Climbed Up. Robert Penn Warren. CP-WarrR

Why'n't you bring me. To Greet a Letter-Carrier. William Carlos Williams. CP-WilW1

Wichita Vortex Sutra. Allen Ginsberg. CP-GinsA

"Kansas! Kansas! Shuddering at last!" SP-GinsA

Wicked and corrupt. Evangelie, or, The Figure of Literary Corruption, Seeking Glory Not Truth. Stevie Smith. CP-SmitS

Wicked and the base do compass round, The. Fear not: for they that are with us are more than they that are with them. 2 Kings 6:16. Jones Very. CP-VeryJ

Wicked man is bad enough on earth, A. John Lackland. George Meredith. CP-MerG1

Wicked old women with candles and sheets. Yannis Ritsos. SP-RitsY *Fr.* Paper Poems 2.

Wicker Basket, A. Robert Creeley. CP-CreeR

Widdop. Ted Hughes. SP-HughTN

Wide and womanly city, The. Concepción. Gabriela Mistral. SP-MistG, *tr. by* Maria Giachetti [*or* Jacketti]

Wide Awake, Full of Love. William Carlos Williams. CP-WilW2

Wide cathedral aisles are lone, The. Emily Jane Brontë. CP-BronE

Wide-eyed. Arthur Rimbaud. CP-RimbA, *tr. by* Martin Sorrell

Wide Land, The. A. R. Ammons. CP AmmoA

Wide Place in the Road. Miller Williams. CP-WillM

Wide Prospect, The. Randall Jarrell. CP-JarrR

Wide River. Langston Hughes. CP-HughL; CP-HughL1

Wide though the interrupt be that divides us, runers and counters. Aliens, The. W. H. Auden. CP-AudeW

Wide, wide in the rose's side. Kenneth Patchen. CP-PatcK

Wide windy reaches of high stubble field. Californian Summer Pictures. Ambrose Bierce. SP-BierA

Widener Library, Reading Room. John Updike. CP-UpdiJ

Widest prairies have electric fences, The. Wires. Philip Larkin. CP-LarkP

Widgeon. Seamus Heaney. SP-HeanSO

Widow. Sylvia Plath. CP-PlatS

Widow, The. Walter De la Mare. CP-DeLaW

Widow, The. W. S. Merwin. SP-MerwW

Widow, The. Wallace Stevens. CP-StevWP

Widow, The. Jones Very. CP-VeryJ

Widow, The. Miller Williams. CP-WillM

Widow. William Stafford. SP-StafWW

Widow at Windsor, The. Rudyard Kipling. CP-KiplR

Widow Betrothed, The. Thomas Hardy. CP-HardT

Widow in Wintertime, A. Carolyn Kizer. CP-KizeC

Widow kept a favourite cat, A. Fable of the Widow and Her Cat, A. Jonathan Swift. CP-SwifJ

Widow of Naim, The. Thomas Merton. CP-MertT

Widow of the Beast of Ingolstadt, The. Norman Dubie. CP-DubiN

Widow on Windmere Side, The. William Wordsworth. CP-WorW2

Widow Speaks to the Auroras of a December Night, A. Norman Dubie. CP-DubiN

Widow Woman. Langston Hughes. CP-HughL; CP-HughL2

Widower. Donald Davie. CP-DaviDC

Widower, The. Rudyard Kipling. CP-KiplR

Widowers. Donald Davie. CP-DaviDC

Widower's Monologue. Alí Chumacero. CP-WilW2

Widow[e]'s Mites, The. Richard Crashaw. CP-CrasR

Widowhood or The Home-Coming of Lady Ross. Stevie Smith. CP-SmitS

Widows, The. Donald Hall. CP-HallD

Widow's Halloween, The. Wyatt Prunty. SP-PrunW

Widow's Lament in Springtime, The. William Carlos Williams. CP-WilW1

Widow's Party, The. Rudyard Kipling. CP-KiplR

Widow's Song, The. Randall Jarrell. CP-JarrR

Widow's Tears [*or* Widdowes Teares]: or, Dirge of Dorcas, The. Robert Herrick. CP-HerrR

Wiedersehen. Miller Williams. CP-WillM

Wife, The. Robert Creeley. CP-CreeR

Wife and Another, A. Thomas Hardy. CP-HardT

Wife and child and soup being brought. Workman's Wife, The. Stéphane Mallarmé. CP-MallS *Fr.* Street Songs.

Wife and child and soup being brought. Workman's Wife, The. Stéphane Mallarmé. CP-MallS, *tr. by* Henry Weinfield

Wife—at Daybreak I shall be, A. Emily Dickinson. CP-DickE

Wife being absent, I could find. Rosalind. George Meredith. CP-MerG2

Wife-Blessed, The. James Whitcomb Riley. CP-RileJ

Wife Comes Back, A. Thomas Hardy. CP-HardT

Wife got tired of weaving, The. Han-shan. CP-ColdM, *tr. by* Red Pine

Wife Hits Moose. Thomas Lux. SP-LuxT

Wife in London, A. Thomas Hardy. CP-HardT

Wife of Bath, The. Geoffrey Chaucer. CP-PopeA *Fr.* Canterbury Tales, The.

Wife of Flanders, The. G. K. Chesterton. CP-ChesG

Wife of Manoah to Her Husband, The. John Greenleaf Whittier. CP-WhitJ

Wife of the clown, The. Thirty-Three Ring Circus, The. John Logan. CP-LogaJ

Wife of the Friend of those I most revere. To Mrs Butts. William Blake. CP-BlakW

Wife to Husband. Christina Georgina Rossetti. CP-RosC1

Wife: We'll gather all the people together. Family Statements. Alan Dugan. CP-DugaA

Wifebeater, The. Anne Sexton. CP-SextA

Wife's Tale, The. Seamus Heaney. SP-HeanSO

Wigging in, wigging out: / when I stop to think. Trip. James Schuyler. CP-SchuJ

Wigs and Beards. Robert Graves. CP-GravR

Wilbur Wright is racing the locomotive. Photograph, U.S. Army Flying School, College Park, Maryland, 1909. Maxine W. Kumin. SP-KumiM

Wild, The. Wendell Berry. CP-BerrW

Wild air, world-mothering air. Blessed Virgin Compared to the Air We Breathe, The. Gerard Manley Hopkins. CP-HopkG

Wild and wavy event, The. Lorine Niedecker. CP-NiedL

Wild and wicked gunman—one who held a gang in thrall, A. Gunman and the Débutante, The. Dorothy Parker. CP-ParkD

Wild Anemone, The. James Laughlin. CP-LaugJ

Wild-bear chase, didst never see?, A. Bear Hunt, The. Abraham Lincoln. CP-LincA

Wild bee reels from bough to bough, The. Her Voice. Oscar Wilde. CP-WildO

Wild Birds, The. Randall Jarrell. CP-JarrR

Wild Blessings. Lucille Clifton. SP-ClifL

Wild blue and wild green. Round of Colors. Gabriela Mistral. SP-MistG, *tr. by* Maria Giachetti [*or* Jacketti]

Wild Blue sky abreast of Winds, A. Emily Dickinson. CP-DickE

Wild Boar Clough. Donald Davie. CP-DaviDC

Wild boars come down by night. At the Autumn Equinox. Charles Tomlinson. SP-TomlC

Wild-cat, gnat and I. Edna St. Vincent Millay. CP-MillE

Wild Cheese, The. James Tate. SP-TateJ

Wild cherries ripen, black and fat, The. Fall. Wendell Berry. CP-BerrW

Wild cherries sprout on slim. Adam Zagajewski. SP-ZagaA, *tr. by* Renata Gorczynski, Benjamin Ivry *and* C. K. Williams

Wild Common, The. D. H. Lawrence. CP-LawrD

Wild Cyclamen. Robert Graves. CP-GravR

Wild Dog, The. Stevie Smith. CP-SmitS

Wild Dreams of a New Beginning. Lawrence Ferlinghetti. SP-FerlL

Wild Duck's Nest, The. William Wordsworth. CP-WorW2

Wild Ducks, People and Distances. Wallace Stevens. CP-StevW; CP-StevWP

Wild Edge, The. Gary Snyder. CP-SnydG

Wild Eggs. James Schuyler. CP-SchuJ

Wild flower in the weeds, A. Tale of Courtship. John Logan. CP-LogaJ *Fr.* Epilogue, Songs of the Spouses, Complaint of Love.

Wild Flower's Song, The. William Blake. CP-BlakW

Wild garlic flowers. Fanny Howe. SP-HoweF *Fr.* O'Clock.

Wild Gazelle, The. Lord Byron. CP-Byron

Wild Geese. Mary Oliver. SP-OlivM

Wild Geese, The. Wendell Berry. CP-BerrW

Wild Geranium. Louis Zukofsky. CP-ZukLS

Wild Grapes. Robert Frost. CP-FrosR

Wild Heart. Gregory Orr. SP-OrrG

Wild Honeysuckle. Louis Zukofsky. CP-ZukLS

Wild Horse Love. William Stafford. SP-StafWW

Wild Horses, The. Wyatt Prunty. SP-PrunW

Wild Jackass, The. Ogden Nash. CP-NashO

Wild Life and Tamed Life. Richard Eberhart. CP-EberR

Wild Life Cameo, Early Morn. Lawrence Ferlinghetti. SP-FerlL

Wild Life Studies. James Fenton. Wild Ones[, The]. SP-FentJ

Wild Nights—Wild Nights! Emily Dickinson. CP-DickE

Wild Oats. Philip Larkin. CP-LarkP

Wild Oats. Robert Penn Warren. CP-WarrR

Wild Old Wicked Man, The. Archibald MacLeish. CP-MacLA

Wild Old Wicked Man, The. William Butler Yeats. CP-YeatW

Wild Ones[, The]. James Fenton. SP-FentJ *Fr.* Wild Life Studies.

Wild Orchard. William Carlos Williams. CP-WilW1

Wild Orphan. Allen Ginsberg. CP-GinsA

Wild, pale, and wonder-stricken, even as one. Ginevra. Percy Bysshe Shelley. CP-ShelP

Wild Parrots of Blood Bay, The. Josephine Jacobsen. CP-JacoJ

Wild patience has taken me this far, A. Integrity. Adrienne Rich. SP-RicA1; SP-RicA2

Wild Peace. Yehuda Amichai. SP-AmicYL, *tr. by* Benjamin Harshav *and* Barbara Harshav

Wild poppy-flower, A. Poppy Flower. Langston Hughes. CP-HughL; CP-HughL2

Wild red-wing black-, The. Red-Wing Blackbird, The. William Carlos Williams. CP-WilW2

Wild Redbreast! hadst thou at Jemima's lip. In the Woods of Rydal. William Wordsworth. CP-WorW2

Wild Rose, The. George Meredith. CP-MerG2

Wild Rose and the Snowdrop, The. George Meredith. CP-MerG1

Wild Rose of Plymouth, The. Jones Very. CP-VeryJ

Wild Sky, The. Adrienne Rich. CP-RicAE

Wild strawberries. Lorine Niedecker. CP-NiedL

Wild strawberry, set apart, The. Gabriela Mistral. SP-MistG, tr. by Maria Giachetti [or Jacketti]

Wild Swans. Edna St. Vincent Millay. CP-MillE

Wild Swans at Coole, The. William Butler Yeats. CP-YeatW

Wild Swans at Norfolk, The. Hayden Carruth. CP-CarHS

Wild Swans of Inverane, The. Richard Eberhart. CP-EberR

Wild Things in Captivity. D. H. Lawrence. CP-LawrD

Wild time *liveforever* horsethyme ice. Liveforever. Louis Zukofsky. CP-ZukLS

Wild trees have bought me. Song: "Wild trees have bought me." Audre Lorde. SP-LordA

Wild warblers are warbling in the jungle, The. Meditation Celestial & Terrestrial. Wallace Stevens. CP-StevW; CP-StevWP

Wild, wild the storm, and the sea high running. Patrolling Barnegat. Walt Whitman. CP-WhitW

Wild winds weep, The. Mad Song. William Blake. CP-BlakW

Wild with ego, wild with world-blame. Interjection #5: Solipsism and Theology. Robert Penn Warren. CP-WarrR

Wild woods, your green cathedrals chill the bone! Obsession. Charles Baudelaire. CP-BaudC, tr. by Walter Martin

Wild(at our first)beasts uttered human words. E. E. Cummings. CP-CummE

Wilderness. Lorine Niedecker. CP-NiedL

Wilderness, The. Kathleen Jessie Raine. SP-RainK

Wilderness, The. Edwin Arlington Robinson. CP-RobiE

Wilderness. Carl Sandburg. CP-SandC

Wildflower, The. William Carlos Williams. CP-WilW1

Wildflowers withering with the same death. Mountain: One from Bryant. Muriel Rukeyser. CP-RukeM

Wilding little stubble flower, A. George Meredith. CP-MerG2

Wildly bound the bells this morning. Tarrying Bridegroom, The. Thomas Hardy. CP-HardT

Wildly dissimilar. Scribe. "H. D." CP-DoolH

Wildly round our woodland quarters. Lumbermen, The. John Greenleaf Whittier. CP-WhitJ

Wildness of nature is in Florida. Opposition. Richard Eberhart. CP-EberR

Wildness of the flower is all in the tone, The. Fanny Howe. SP-HoweF Fr. Poem from a Single Pallet.

Wildness sleeps upon the mountain. Fisher Cat, The. Richard Eberhart. CP-EberR

Wildpeace. Yehuda Amichai. SP-AmicY, tr. by Chana Bloch

Wildrose. Robert Lowell. SP-LoweR

Wilds horrid and dark with o'ershadowing trees. Scenes Favourable to Meditation. Jeanne Marie Bouvier de la Motte- Guyon. CP-CowpW

Wildwest. Archibald MacLeish. CP-MacLA

Wiles, guiles, smiles, gold and pearls, her gala ways. Michelangelo Buonarroti. CP-Miche, tr. by John Frederick Nims

Wilfred Owen's Photographs. Ted Hughes. SP-HughTN

Wilful-Missing. Rudyard Kipling. CP-KiplR

Wilful we are, in our infirmity. Sermon of the Rose, The. James Whitcomb Riley. CP-RileJ

Will, The. John Donne. CP-DonnJ; MW-DonnJ

Will, The. James Merrill. SP-MerrJ

Will, The. Jones Very. CP-VeryJ

Will. Alfred Tennyson. CP-TennA

Will. Alice Walker. CP-WalkA

Will bring a mouse it has. You Know How a Cat. James Laughlin. CP-LaugJ

Will Consider Situation. Ogden Nash. CP-NashO

Will Dallas grow, or wither? Fear Not. Gary Snyder. CP-SnydG

Will Ever? Stevie Smith. CP-SmitS

Will Faulkner, Will Faulkner. Ballad of the Corn-Cob and the Lie, The. Archibald MacLeish. CP-MacLA

Will I! Will You Write Me a Christmas Poem? Lorine Niedecker. CP-NiedL

Will i ever forget that precarious moment? E. E. Cummings. CP-CummE

Will I have expressed it before I leave. Rainer Maria Rilke. CP-RilkFr, tr. by A. Poulin, Jr. Fr. Affectionate Taxes to France.

Will I have some mo' dat pie? Reluctance. Paul Laurence Dunbar. CP-DunbP

Will is always near, dear, the. Emily Dickinson. SP-DickE

Will it be one of those. Viper-Man. Donald Davie. CP-DaviDC

Will it last? he says. Snowflake Which Is Now and Hence Forever, The. Archibald MacLeish. CP-MacLA

Will it never be possible. Portrait in Greys, A. William Carlos Williams. CP-WilW1

Will Makes the Work, or Consent Makes the Cure, The. Robert Herrick. CP-HerrR

Will Man Ever Face Fact and Not Feel Flat? Stevie Smith. CP-SmitS

Will never say of us. Those Who Come After. Eleanor Wilner. SP-WilnE

Will no one say hush! to thee. Poor Bit of a Wench! D. H. Lawrence. CP-LawrD

Will Not Come Back. Robert Lowell. SP-LoweR

Will not some dozen sacks of rags. Marianne Moore. William Carlos Williams. CP-WilW1

Will o' the Wisp. George Meredith. CP-MerG1

Will-o'-the-wisp dusts the street with powder, A. Costa San Giorgio. Eugenio Montale. CP-MontE, tr. by Jonathan Galassi

Will of the Lord Be Done, The. Christina Georgina Rossetti. CP-RosC2

Will out of the kindness of their hearts a few philosophers tell me. E. E. Cummings. CP-CummE

Will people accept them? Tenzone. Ezra Pound. SP-PounE Fr. Contemporania.

Will perch on your left epaulette. Destroying Angel, The. Paul Muldoon. CP-MuldP

Will prayer temper the wind to the shorn lamb? Two Dry Poems. John Ciardi. CP-CiarJ

'Will sprawl, now that the heat of day is best. Caliban upon Setebos; or, Natural Theology in the Island. Robert Browning. CP-BroR1; SP-BroR

Will suddenly trees leap up from winter and will. E. E. Cummings. CP-CummE

Will: termite mothers. Charles Olson. CP-OlsoC

Will the Cause of Woe, The. Robert Herrick. CP-HerrR

Will the day be bright or cloudy? Emily Jane Brontë. CP-BronE

Will the moment come again. Why the Question? Yannis Ritsos. SP-RitsY, tr. by N. C. Germanacos

Will: the rat. Charles Olson. CP-OlsoC

Will there really be a "Morning"? Emily Dickinson. See Will there really be a "morning"?

Will there really be a "morning"? Morning. Emily Dickinson. CP-DickE

Will These Hands Ne'er Be Clean? Christina Georgina Rossetti. CP-RosC3

Will they gape for the husks that ye proffer. Rudyard Kipling. CP-KiplR Fr. Naulahka, The.

Will they have children? Will they have more children? Neighbors. James Tate. SP-TateJ

Will they occur. Brasilia. Sylvia Plath. CP-PlatS

Will those who praise things go to paradise. Rainer Maria Rilke. CP-RilkFr, tr. by A. Poulin, Jr. Fr. Fragments.

Will To, The. Charles Olson. CP-OlsoC

Will To Be Working, A. Robert Herrick. CP-HerrR

Will to Change, The. Adrienne Rich. CP-RicAE

Will used a broken pen, must have broken many. Broken Pen, The. Richard Eberhart. CP-EberR

Will V-Day Be Me-Day Too? Langston Hughes. CP-HughL; CP-HughL2

Will We Ever Go to the Lighthouse? James Laughlin. CP-LaugJ

Will we make it to 2000? Young and the Old, the. Richard Eberhart. CP-EberR

Will we speak to each other. Answer, The. Robert Creeley. CP-CreeR

Will Whistle. George Meredith. CP-MerG2

Will ye go to the Highlands Leezie Lindsay. Leezie Lindsay. Robert Burns. CP-BurnR

Will ye go to the Indies, my Mary. Song: "Will ye go to the Indies, my Mary." Robert Burns. CP-BurnR

Will ye heare, what I can say. Upon His Julia. Robert Herrick. CP-HerrR

Will ye see what wonders love hath wrought? Sir Thomas Wyatt. CP-WyatT

Will you be dust. Love: "Will you be dust." Robert Creeley. SP-CreeR

Will you be there? my yearning heart has cried. Christina Georgina Rossetti. CP-RosC3

Will you be well will you be well. More Grammar for a Sentence. Gertrude Stein. CP-SteiG

Will you conquer my heart with your beauty, my soul going out from afar? To the Unknown Goddess. Rudyard Kipling. CP-KiplR

Will you dance at my doorway. Seven. Thomas Kinsella. CP-KinsT

Will you eat water melon. Among the Cypresses at the End of the Way of the Cross. Kenneth Rexroth. CP-RexrK

Will you give yourself airs. Her face the Book of—Love Delights in—Praises. Louis Zukofsky. CP-ZukLS

Will you glimmer on the sea? Moonrise. "H. D." CP-DoolH

Will You Have Your Tedium Rare or Medium? Ogden Nash. CP-NashO

Will you hear my story also. Donald. Robert Browning. CP-BroR2; SP-BroR

Will you live long enough to sit in the shade. Dalhousie Farm. William Meredith. SP-MereW

Will you please rush down and see. To Close. William Carlos Williams. CP-WilW2

Will you still lament and rayse. Parkinsons Shade to the House of Mr. Pallauicine Taking His Death Ill. Robert Herrick. CP-HerrR

Will you teach a. E. E. Cummings. CP-CummE

Will you turn a deaf ear. Questioner Who Sits So Sly, The. W. H. Auden. CP-AudeW

Will you write in a new book. Request. Richard Eberhart. CP-EberR

Will You Write Me a Christmas Poem? Lorine Niedecker. CP-NiedL

Willed down, waited for, in place at last and for good. Settle Bed, The. Seamus Heaney. SP-HeanSO

Willets, The. May Swenson. SP-SwenM

Willful Homing. Robert Frost. CP-FrosR

William Adams Delano. Archibald MacLeish. CP-MacLA

William Bartram how many. Other Travelers to the River. W. S. Merwin. SP-MerwW

William Blake. Dante Gabriel Rossetti. CW-RossD *Fr.* Five English Poets.

William Blake. Allen Tate. CP-TateA

William Bond. William Blake. CP-BlakW

William Brown. James Whitcomb Riley. CP-RileJ

William Carlos Williams. Robert Lowell. SP-LoweR

William Carlos Williams had finished. Physical Moon beyond Paterson, A. Norman Dubie. CP-DubiN

William Cowper Esqre. William Blake. CP-BlakW

William Cullen Bryant. Jones Very. CP-VeryJ

William Dewy, Tranter Reuben, Farmer Ledlow late at plough. Friends Beyond. Thomas Hardy. CP-HardT

William does thy frigid soul. Ralph Waldo Emerson. CP-EmerR

William F. Smith. Ambrose Bierce. SP-BierA

William Forster. John Greenleaf Whittier. CP-WhitJ

William Francis Bartlett. John Greenleaf Whittier. CP-WhitJ

William McKinley. James Whitcomb Riley. CP-RileJ

William, my teacher, my friend! dear William and dear Dorothea! Hexameters. Samuel Taylor Coleridge. CP-ColeS

William of Orange. G. K. Chesterton. CP-ChesG

William Pinkney Fishback. James Whitcomb Riley. CP-RileJ

William Rufus and the Jew. Ralph Waldo Emerson. CP-EmerR

William Shakespeare to Mrs Anne, Regular Servant to the Rev. Mr Precentor of York. Thomas Gray. CP-GrayT

William the Norman was brave in the field. Succession of Kings, The. Christina Georgina Rossetti. CP-RosC3

William was once a bashful youth. Of Himself. William Cowper. CP-CowpW

Williams: An Essay. Denise Levertov. SP-LeveDL; SP-LeveDS

Williams Avenue Zionist Church, The. Russia. William Carlos Williams. CP-WilW2

Willie. Maya Angelou. SP-AngeM

Willie Brew'd [*or* Brewed] a Peck o' Maut. Robert Burns. CP-BurnR

Willie Francis and the Electric Chair. Charles Olson. CP-OlsoC

Willie Henderson, Massachusetts-born, painted and dreamed in Chicago. Scripture. Carl Sandburg. CP-SandC

Willie was a man without fame. Willie. Maya Angelou. SP-AngeM

Willie Wastle dwalt [*or* dwals] on Tweed. Sic a Wife as Willie Had. Robert Burns. CP-BurnR

Willing pitifully to bewitch. E. E. Cummings. CP-CummE

Willing Prisoner to His Mistress, The. Thomas Carew. *See* Song: The Willing Prisoner to His Mistress

Willing to die, / you give up. Poem: "Willing to die, / you give up." Wendell Berry. CP-BerrW

Willingly. Tess Gallagher. SP-GallT

Willis, I didn't want you here today:. Self-Seeker, The. Robert Frost. CP-FrosR

Willkie in the *Gulliver.* Muriel Rukeyser. CP-RukeM

Willkie—Stopless Falling through Air. Muriel Rukeyser. CP-RukeM

Willkie: Words from Russia. Muriel Rukeyser. CP-RukeM

Willow. Federico García Lorca. CP-GarcF, *tr. by* Jerome Rothenberg *Fr.* Shadow.

Willow. James Merrill. SP-MerrJ

Willow, The. Walter De la Mare. CP-DeLaW

Willow, The. Dorothy Parker. CP-ParkD

Willow Garland, The. Robert Herrick. CP-HerrR

Willow Poem. William Carlos Williams. CP-WilW1

Willow soon, and vine. Valentine, A. Wallace Stevens. CP-StevWP

Willows carried a slow sound, The. Repose of Rivers. Hart Crane. CP-CranH

Willows grow dark like mist, The. Han-shan. CP-ColdM, *tr. by* Red Pine

Willows in the wind act out "afraid." Charades. William Stafford. SP-StafWW

Willows never forget how it feels. Climbing along the River. William Stafford. SP-StafWW

Willows of Massachusetts, The. Denise Levertov. SP-LeveDP

Willoware Cup. James Merrill. SP-MerrJ

Willowwood ("And now Love sang: but his was such a song"). Dante Gabriel Rossetti. CW-RossD *Fr.* House of Life, The.

Willowwood ("I sat with Love upon a woodside well"). Dante Gabriel Rossetti. CW-RossD *Fr.* House of Life, The.

Willowwood ("O ye, all ye that walk in Willowwood"). Dante Gabriel Rossetti. CW-RossD *Fr.* House of Life, The.

Willowwood ("So sang he: and as meeting rose and rose"). Dante Gabriel Rossetti. CW-RossD *Fr.* House of Life, The.

Wills of the Wisp, The. Samuel Taylor Coleridge. CP-ColeS

Willy is a silly boy. Lament of a Vanquished Beau, The. Langston Hughes. CP-HughL

Willy Lyons. James Wright. CP-WrigJ

Willy Wet-Leg. D. H. Lawrence. CP-LawrD

Wilson. John Greenleaf Whittier. CP-WhitJ

Wilson and Pilcer and Snack stood before the zoo elephant. Elephants Are Different to Different People. Carl Sandburg. CP-SandC

Wilson in Hell. Robinson Jeffers. CP-JefR3

Wilt thou be my Dearie. Robert Burns. CP-BurnR

Wilt thou forget the happy hours. Past, The. Percy Bysshe Shelley. CP-ShelP

Wilt thou forgive that sin[ne] where I begun[ne]. Hymn[e] to God the Father, A. John Donne. CP-DonnJ; MW-DonnJ

Wilt thou life's best elixir drain? Fayzi. CP-EmerR

Wilt thou my true Friend be? True Friendship. Robert Herrick. CP-HerrR

Wilt thou never come again. Phantom, The. Walter De la Mare. CP-DeLaW

Wilt Thou not visit me? Prayer, The ("Wilt Thou not visit me?"). Jones Very. CP-VeryJ

Wiltshire. Donald Davie. CP-DaviDC

Win' a-blowin' gentle so de san' lay low. Florida Night, A. Paul Laurence Dunbar. CP-DunbP

Win' is blowin' wahmah, De. Christmas Folksong, A. Paul Laurence Dunbar. CP-DunbP

Win' is hollahin' "Daih you,"De. Little Christmas Basket, A. Paul Laurence Dunbar. CP-DunbP

Winchester: The Autumn Equinox. Amy Clampitt. CP-ClamA

Wind. Raymond Carver. CP-CarvR

Wind. James Fenton. SP-FentJ

Wind. Ted Hughes. SP-HughTN

Wind. Kathleen Jessie Raine. SP-RainK

Wind. Charles Tomlinson. CP-TomlC

Wind. John Updike. CP-UpdiJ

Wind had blown the leaves away and left, The. Last Metaphor, The. Robert Penn Warren. CP-WarrR

Wind had taken the tree-tops, The. Two Maidens, The. G. K. Chesterton. CP-ChesG

Wind-haired, mufflered. Exile. Derek Walcott. CP-WalcD

Wind, and all the midges in the air. View of Fujiyama after the War, A. James Dickey. CP-DickJ

Wind and Gibbon. Robert Penn Warren. CP-WarrR

Wind and the Rain, The. Robert Frost. CP-FrosR

Wind and the Sea, The. Paul Laurence Dunbar. CP-DunbP

Wind and Tree. Paul Muldoon. CP-MuldP

Wind and Window Flower. Robert Frost. CP-FrosR

Wind arrow, wind rose, the wind currents in air. Muriel Rukeyser. CP-RukeM

Wind at first light, A. On the Mountain. W. S. Merwin. SP-MerwWF

Wind at Night. Adam Zagajewski. SP-ZagaA, *tr. by* Renata Gorczynski, Benjamin Ivry *and* C. K. Williams

Wind at Penistone, The. Donald Davie. CP-DaviDC

Wind-bags, The. Hugh MacDiarmid. SP-MacDH

Wind begun to knead the Grass, The. Emily Dickinson. CP-DickE

Wind begun to rock the Grass, The. Emily Dickinson. *See* Wind begun to knead the Grass, The

Wind billowing out the seat of my britches, The. Child on Top of a Greenhouse. Theodore Roethke. CP-RoetT

Wind blew all my wedding-day, The. Wedding-Wind. Philip Larkin. CP-LarkP

Wind blew and carried the clouds, The. Peacock, The. Gabriela Mistral. SP-MistG, *tr. by* Maria Giachetti [*or* Jacketti]

Wind blew hollow frae the hills, The. Lament for James, Earl of Glencairn. Robert Burns. CP-BurnR

Wind blew out from Bergen from the dawning to the day, The. Last Hero, The. G. K. Chesterton. CP-ChesG

Wind blew, The. Some days, rain. Generation Before, The. Robert Pinsky. CP-PinsR

Wind Blew Words, The. Thomas Hardy. CP-HardT

Wind Bloweth Where It Listeth, The. Countee Cullen. CP-CullC

Wind blows. The corn leans. The corn leaves go rustling. The march, The. Ripe Corn. Carl Sandburg. CP-SandC

Wind came across the corn laughing, The. Corn Prattlings. Carl Sandburg. CP-SandC

Wind came every night like an animal, The. Old Hamer Place. William Stafford. SP-StafWW

Wind came in for several thousand miles all night, The. On an East Wind from the Wars. Alan Dugan. CP-DugaA

Wind came in red, The. Vignettes of the Wind. Federico García Lorca. CP-GarcF, tr. by Jerome Rothenberg

Wind came up from the black streets my childhood knew, The. Pilgrimage. Marya Alexandrovna Zaturenska. SP-ZatuM

Wind-claps of soot and snow. Barnsley, 1966. Donald Davie. CP-DaviDC

Wind comes from the north, The. Suspense. D. H. Lawrence. CP-LawrD

Wind Coming Down From, The. A. R. Ammons. CP-AmmoA

Wind converses before the windows, The. Assistance. Yannis Ritsos. SP-RitsY, tr. by Kimon Friar

Wind didn't come from the Orchard—today, The. Emily Dickinson. CP-DickE

Wind drew off, The. Emily Dickinson. CP-DickE

Wind finds the northwest gap, fall comes. Heart of Autumn. Robert Penn Warren. CP-WarrR

Wind flapped loose, the wind was still, The. Woodspurge, The. Dante Gabriel Rossetti. CW-RossD

Wind. Flower. Pretty village. For the Mother of My Mother's Mother. Kenneth Patchen. CP-PatcK

Wind-Flower, The. Jones Very. CP-VeryJ

Wind frightens my dog, but I bathe in it, The. April Gale. Ivor Gurney. SP-GurnI

Wind from a Wing, A. William Stafford. SP-StafWW

Wind from off the sea says nothing new, The. Marrow, The. Theodore Roethke. CP-RoetT

Wind from the northwestern quarter is lifting him high above. Hawk's Cry in Autumn, The. Joseph Brodsky. CP-BrodJ, tr. by Joseph Brodsky and Alan Myers

Wind From Variable Directions. Dan Pagis. SP-PagiD, tr. by Stephen Mitchell

Wind Gust. Federico García Lorca. CP-GarcF, tr. by Jerome Rothenberg Fr. Return, The.

Wind has at last got into the clock, The. Wind, the Clock, the We, The. Laura Riding Jackson. CP-RidiL

Wind has blown the rain away and blown, A. E. E. Cummings. CP-CummE

Wind Has Such a Rainy Sound, The. Christina Georgina Rossetti. CP-RosC2

Wind has such a rainy sound, The. Wind Has Such a Rainy Sound, The. Christina Georgina Rossetti. CP-RosC2

Wind has swept from the wide atmosphere, The. Summer Evening Churchyard, A. Percy Bysshe Shelley. CP-ShelP

Wind high along the headland, The. Admission. A. R. Ammons. CP-AmmoA

Wind Horses. Carl Sandburg. CP-SandC

Wind, I hear it sighing, The. Emily Jane Brontë. CP-BronE

Wind I know blows dirt, A. Conditioned Air, A. Donald Davie. CP-DaviDC

Wind in the ash-tree sounds like surf on the shore at Truro, The. Memory of Cape Cod. Edna St. Vincent Millay. CP-MillE

Wind in the fleece of ivy. Gorge, The. Charles Tomlinson. CP-TomlC

Wind in the Mirror. Robert Stock. SP-StocR

Wind in the Street. Thom Gunn. CP-GunnT

Wind in the Sunporch, The. Josephine Jacobsen. CP-JacoJ

Wind inclines the cedars and lets, The. Jersey Cedars. A. R. Ammons. CP-AmmoA

Wind Increases, The. William Carlos Williams. CP-WilW1

Wind is a Lady with, The. E. E. Cummings. CP-CummE

Wind is blowing, A. The book being written. Novel, The. Denise Levertov. SP-LeveDP

Wind is east but the hot weather continues, The. American Letter. Archibald MacLeish. CP-MacLA

Wind is East, the wind is West, The. Stave of Roving Tim, A. George Meredith. CP-MerG1

Wind is level now, The. But pails of rain. Bahia, Brazil. Raymond Carver. CP-CarvR

Wind is now thy organist;—a clank, The. Composed in Roslin Chapel, During a Storm. William Wordsworth. CP-WorW2

Wind is out in its rage tonight, The. Fisher Child's Lullaby, The. Paul Laurence Dunbar. CP-DunbP

Wind is ruffling the tawny pelt, A. Far Cry from Africa, A. Derek Walcott. CP-WalcD

Wind is the Wall of the Year. Marge Piercy. SP-PierM

Wind lifts lightly. Robert Creeley. SP-CreeR

Wind Makes Up, A. George Oppen. CP-OppGN

Wind meets me at Penistone, The. Wind at Penistone, The. Donald Davie. CP-DaviDC

Wind might blow a lotus petal, A. History. William Carlos Williams. CP-WilW1

Wind mills churn on Windy City's. Written on Hotel Napkin: Chicago Futures. Allen Ginsberg. CP-GinsA

Wind of March, The. John Greenleaf Whittier. CP-WhitJ

Wind of the sea. Sea-Choros. Euripides. CP-DoolH Fr. Hecuba.

Wind of the Village. William Carlos Williams. CP-WilW1

Wind of what memory, from what life did the wind, The. Rainer Maria Rilke. CP-RilkFr, tr. by A. Poulin, Jr. Fr. Fragments.

Wind on Crow Hill was her darling, The. Emily Brontë. Ted Hughes. SP-

Wind on the Crescent. Eugenio Montale. CP-MontE, tr. by Jonathan Galassi

Wind on the Lyre. George Meredith. CP-MerG1

Wind on the Way, The. Carl Sandburg. CP-SandC

Wind out of freezing Europe. A mean snow. Bringing in New Couples. Ted Hughes. SP-HughTN

Wind passed over my mind, A. Image-Maker, The. Stanley Kunitz. CP-KunSC

Wind picks up, the dark is torn to shreds, The. Promenade. Eugenio Montale. CP-MontE, tr. by Jonathan Galassi

Wind rests its cheek upon the ground and feels the cool damp, The. Hymn to Life. James Schuyler. CP-SchuJ

Wind rocks the car. / We sit parked by the river. Like This Together. Adrienne Rich. CP-RicAE; SP-RicA1; SP-RicA2

Wind rose at night, The. Wind at Night. Adam Zagajewski. SP-ZagaA, tr. by Renata Gorczynski, Benjamin Ivry and C. K. Williams

Wind / rounding the gap, The. Joshua Tree. A. R. Ammons. CP-AmmoA

Wind runs free across our plains, The. For Adolf Eichmann. Primo Levi. CP-LeviP, tr. by Ruth Feldman and Brian Swann

Wind scatters the fragrance of the willows over the shop. In the Wineshop of Chinling. Li Po. CP-WilW2

Wind-scraped headland, a sludgy, dishwater sea, A. Derek Walcott. CP-WalcD Fr. Midsummer.

Wind scruffing in the bay, The. Green and White. Wendell Berry. CP-BerrW

Wind & sea are as playmates. George Meredith. CP-MerG2

Wind shall lull us yet, The. From the Antique. Christina Georgina Rossetti. CP-RosC3

Wind Shifts, The. Wallace Stevens. CP-StevW; CP-StevWP

Wind Sings Welcome in Early Spring, The. Carl Sandburg. CP-SandC

Wind, sink to rest in the heather. Emily Jane Brontë. CP-BronE

Wind Sleepers, The. "H. D." CP-DoolH

Wind Song. Carl Sandburg. CP-SandC

Wind sounds only in opposing straits, The. Finite and Infinite. Elizabeth Barrett Browning. CP-BroEB

Wind Sprang Up at Four o'Clock, The. T. S. Eliot. CP-ElioT

Wind stops, the wind begins, The. Sand Scribblings. Carl Sandburg. CP-SandC

Wind-Struck Music, The. Robinson Jeffers. CP-JefR2

Wind Suffers of Blowing, The. Laura Riding Jackson. CP-RidiL

Wind sways the pines, A. Dirge in Woods. George Meredith. CP-MerG1

Wind—tapped like a tired Man, The. Wind's Visit, The. Emily Dickinson. CP-DickE

Wind, taut as piano wire, The. Regeneration, The. Jay Wright. SP-WrigJ

Wind tears up the sun, The. Poem: "Wind tears up the sun, The." James Schuyler. CP-SchuJ

Wind, that beats the mountain, blows, The. To J. S. [James Spedding]. Alfred Tennyson. CP-TennA

Wind that blows these words to you, The. Beyond Howth Head. Derek Mahon. CP-MahoD

Wind that grips this country like a craftsman. Rainer Maria Rilke. CP-RilkFr, tr. by A. Poulin, Jr. Fr. Valaisian Quatrains, The.

Wind that rose, A. Emily Dickinson. CP-DickE

Wind, The. Robert Creeley. CP-CreeR

Wind, The. Emily Dickinson. CP-DickE

Wind, The. Rainer Maria Rilke. CP-RilkFr, tr. by A. Poulin, Jr.

Wind, the Clock, the We, The. Laura Riding Jackson. CP-RidiL

Wind, the Rascal, The. D. H. Lawrence. CP-LawrD

Wind, the season-climate mixer. Clear and Colder. Robert Frost. CP-FrosR

Wind thrashes the maple seed-pods, The. John Ashbery. SP-AshbJ Fr. Skaters, The.

Wind told the little leaves to hurry, The. Chase, The. Paul Laurence Dunbar. CP-DunbP

Wind took off with the sunset, The. Egg-Shell, The. Rudyard Kipling. CP-KiplR

Wind took up the Northern Things, The. Emily Dickinson. CP-DickE

Wind, transparent, cannot displace, The. Antigua. John Updike. CP-UpdiJ

Wind-wafted from the sunset, o'er the swell. Isle's Enchantress, The. Robert Browning. CP-BroR2

Wind was rough which tore, The. Emily Jane Brontë. CP-BronE

Wind, wave, and bark, bear Euthukles and me. Aristophanes' Apology. Robert Browning. CP-BroR2

Wind went over, The. Mission. A. R. Ammons. CP-AmmoA

Wind whines in the elevator shaft, The. The houseless. Prairie, The. Amy Clampitt. CP-ClamA

Wind won't come to draw smiles in the sand of dreams, The. Elegy: "Wind won't come to draw smiles in the sand of dreams, The." Yehuda Amichai. SP-AmicY, tr. by Stephen Mitchell

Wind wore me north, London I left a year, The. London. Randall Jarrell. CP-JarrR

Wind World. William Stafford. SP-StafW

Wind your thread. Rocking Woman, The. William Carlos Williams. CP-WilW2

HughTN

Windflower. Louis Zukofsky. CP-ZukLS

Windflower Leaf. Carl Sandburg. CP-SandC

Windflower overworld selvageflame sun coddle. Windflower. Louis Zukofsky. CP-ZukLS

Windhover, The. Gerard Manley Hopkins. CP-HopkG

Winding grain. Old Rotting Tree Trunk Down. Gary Snyder. CP-SnydG

Winding Up. Derek Walcott. CP-WalcD

Winding way the serpent takes, The. Norembega. John Greenleaf Whittier. CP-WhitJ

Window. Robert Creeley. SP-CreeR

Window. Robert Lowell. SP-LoweR

Window. Czeslaw Milosz. CP-MiloC; CP-MiloCN, *tr. by* Lillian Vallee

Window. Robert Pinsky. CP-PinsR

Window. Carl Sandburg. CP-SandC

Window, A. Denise Levertov. SP-LeveDP

Window, The. Louis MacNeice. CP-MacNL

Window, The. Rainer Maria Rilke. CP-RilkFr, *tr. by* A. Poulin, Jr. *Fr.* Orchards.

Window, The. Raymond Carver. CP-CarvR

Window, The. Robert Creeley. CP-CreeR

Window, The. Robert Creeley. CP-CreeR

Window, The. Walter De la Mare. CP-DeLaW

Window, a wide pane in the bare, The. Waking in a Newly Built House. Thom Gunn. CP-GunnT

Window bars are spider webs, The. Hall Five. Hayden Carruth. CP-CarllS *Fr.* Bloomingdale Papers, The.

Window here is hung in the west wall, The. Evening: A Studio in Rome. Miller Williams. CP-WillM

Window, how you add the sense. Rainer Maria Rilke. CP-RilkFr, *tr. by* A. Poulin, Jr. *Fr.* Windows, The.

Window in the Slums, A. Wallace Stevens. CP-StevWP

Window, just how long have we. Rainer Maria Rilke. CP-RilkFr, *tr. by* A. Poulin, Jr. *Fr.* Windows, The.

Window of the Woman Burning, The. Marge Piercy. SP-PierM

Window on Birds' Wings. Jaroslav Seifert. SP-SeifJ, *tr. by* Ewald Osers

Window Pane, The. Robert Graves. CP-GravR

Window Poems. Wendell Berry. CP-BerrW

Window screen, The. Sunday Rain. John Updike. CP-UpdiJ

Window showed a willow in the west, The. Elegy in a Firelit Room. James Wright. CP-WrigJ

Window Sill, The. Robert Graves. CP-GravR

Window: Thing as Participle. Heather McHugh. SP-McHuH

Window was made of ice with bears lumbering across it, The. Bad Dream. Louis MacNeice. CP-MacNL

Window Washer. Charles Simic. SP-SimiC; SP-SimiCE

Window Washer, The. Wyatt Prunty. SP-PrunW

Window we so often look for. Rainer Maria Rilke. CP-RilkFr, *tr. by* A. Poulin, Jr. *Fr.* Windows, The.

Window woman whose dress has been hung and draped, The. Stage Directions. Lorine Niedecker. CP-NiedL

Windowglass, warmed plush, a sneeze. Flèche d'Or. James Merrill. SP-MerrJ

Windowjarring gusts again. Monday. A. R. Ammons. CP-AmmoA

Windows. Randall Jarrell. CP-JarrR

Windows, The. Rainer Maria Rilke.

  "Aren't you our geometry." CP-RilkFr, *tr. by* A. Poulin, Jr.

  "From the back of the room, the bed, only a pallor spread." CP-RilkFr, *tr. by* A. Poulin, Jr.

  "It's because I saw you." CP-RilkFr, *tr. by* A. Poulin, Jr.

  "It's enough that on a balcony." CP-RilkFr, *tr. by* A. Poulin, Jr.

  "She spends anxious hours." CP-RilkFr, *tr. by* A. Poulin, Jr.

  "She was in a window mood that day." CP-RilkFr, *tr. by* A. Poulin, Jr.

  "Sigh, sigh, pure sigh!" CP-RilkFr, *tr. by* A. Poulin, Jr.

  "Tiny untamed window on the fifth." CP-RilkFr, *tr. by* A. Poulin, Jr.

  "Today I'm in a window mood." CP-RilkFr, *tr. by* A. Poulin, Jr.

  "Vertical plate serving us." CP-RilkFr, *tr. by* A. Poulin, Jr.

  "Window, how you add the sense." CP-RilkFr, *tr. by* A. Poulin, Jr.

  "Window, just how long have we." CP-RilkFr, *tr. by* A. Poulin, Jr.

  "Window we so often look for." CP-RilkFr, *tr. by* A. Poulin, Jr.

  "You propose I wait, strange window." CP-RilkFr, *tr. by* A. Poulin, Jr.

  "You window, O waiting's measure." CP-RilkFr, *tr. by* A. Poulin, Jr.

Windows, The. Constantine P. Cavafy. CP-CavaC, *tr. by* Theoharis Constantine Theoharis

Windows, The. George Herbert. CP-HerbG

Windows, The. Stéphane Mallarmé. CP-MallS, *tr. by* Henry Weinfield

Windows, The. W. S. Merwin. SP-MerwWF

Windows flash in Taunton town, The. Monmouth. George Meredith. CP-MerG2

Windows go orange in the slowly. E. E. Cummings. CP-CummE

Windows I see into, The. Ugliness. John Ciardi. CP-CiarJ

Windows of the Summer Vacation Houses, The. Raymond Carver. CP-CarvR

Windows wide through day and night, The. Last Days at Teddington. Thom Gunn. CP-GunnT

Windowscape. Louis MacNeice. CP-MacNL

Winds. Kathleen Jessie Raine. SP-RainK

Winds, The. William Carlos Williams. CP-WilW1 *Fr.* Folded Skyscraper, A.

Winds are cold, the days are dark, The. Ralph Waldo Emerson. CP-EmerR

Winds are out with loud increasing shout, The. Autumn Days. Jones Very. CP-VeryJ

Winds blow the open grasy places bleak. Atmosphere. Robert Frost. CP-FrosR

Wind's Body, The. Yannis Ritsos. SP-RitsY, *tr. by* Kimon Friar

Winds from Cook's Strait cannot blow. Trevenen. Donald Davie. CP-DaviDC

Wind's hand, The. Whole Works, The. Federico García Lorca. CP-GarcF, *tr. by* Jerome Rothenberg *Fr.* Night (Suite for Piano and Poet's Voice).

Winds have talked with him confidingly, The. Longfellow. James Whitcomb Riley. CP-RileJ

Winds light & variable break. Pluralist. A. R. Ammons. CP-AmmoA

Winds of hatred blow, The. Lull. Theodore Roethke. CP-RoetT

Winds of heaven trample down the pines, The. Science. Ambrose Bierce. SP-BierA

Winds of Orisha, The. Audre Lorde. SP-LordA

Winds of the World, give answer! They are whimpering to and fro. English Flag, The. Rudyard Kipling. CP-KiplR

Winds on the stems make them creak like manmade things. Stalin. Robert Lowell. SP-LoweR

Winds out of the west land blow, The. A. E. Housman. CP-HousA

Wind's Prophecy, The. Thomas Hardy. CP-HardT

Winds sing to us where we lie, The. Let Them Rejoice in Their Beds. Christina Georgina Rossetti. CP-RosC3

Wind's Visit, The. Emily Dickinson. CP-DickE

Winds / which blew my daughter, The. Charles Olson. CP-OlsoC

Windshield, The. Charles Tomlinson. CP-TomlC

Windsor-Forest [*or* Windsor Forest]. Alexander Pope. CP-PopeA

Windsor Poetics. Lord Byron. CP-Byron

Windsor Prophecy, The. Jonathan Swift. CP-SwifJ

Windswept gallery, A. With its telephones. Crossing the Line. Paul Muldoon. CP-MuldP

Windy City, The. Carl Sandburg. CP-SandC

Windy Day, A. James Whitcomb Riley. CP-RileJ

Windy Day in Summer, A. Gerard Manley Hopkins. CP-HopkG

Windy gentlemen wreathing a long verandah. Prometheus in Straits. John Crowe Ransom. SP-RansJ

Windy Haymaking. George Meredith. CP-MerG2

Windy Night. Charles Bukowski. CP-BukC3

Windy shell singing upon the shore, A. To What Purpose Is This Waste? Christina Georgina Rossetti. CP-RosC3

Windy Trees. A. R. Ammons. CP-AmmoA

Wine. Raymond Carver. CP-CarvR

Wine, The. W. S. Merwin. SP-MerwWF

Wine and a bobwhite / And the afternoon sun. O Sweet Irrational Worship. Thomas Merton. CP-MertT

Wine and oil gleaming within their heads. Double Ode. Muriel Rukeyser. CP-RukeM

Wine and Water. G. K. Chesterton. CP-ChesG

Wine Bowl. "H. D." CP-DoolH

Wine can dress up the lowest cabaret. Poison. Charles Baudelaire. CP-BaudC, *tr. by* Walter Martin

Wine comes in at the mouth. Drinking Song, A. William Butler Yeats. CP-YeatW

Wine-Drinkers, The. Tennessee Williams. CP-WillT

Wine-drinkers sit on the porte cochère in the sun, The. Wine-Drinkers, The. Tennessee Williams. CP-WillT

Wine from These Grapes. Edna St. Vincent Millay. CP-MillE

Wine-maiden / Of the jazz-tuned night. Midnight Dancer. Langston Hughes. CP-HughL

Wine Menagerie, The. Hart Crane. CP-CranH

Wine-O. Langston Hughes. CP-HughL; CP-HughL3

Wine of August was spilled on the face of the girl, but, The. Elegy on an Abandoned Village. Yehuda Amichai. SP-AmicY, *tr. by* Stephen Mitchell

Wine of Cyprus. Elizabeth Barrett Browning. CP-BroEB

Wine of the grey sky. Idyl: "Wine of the grey sky." William Carlos Williams. CP-WilW1

Wine of the Solitary Man, The. Charles Baudelaire. CP-BaudC, *tr. by* Walter Martin

Wine of wisdom is so cold, The. Shih-te. CP-ColdM, *tr. by* Red Pine

Wine resembles the Lord Jesus. Hafiz. CP-EmerR *Fr.* Odes.

Wine sleeps in casks of Rhine oak. Mittelbergheim. Czeslaw Milosz. CP-MiloC; CP-MiloCN, *tr. by* Richard Lourie

Wine we really drink is our own blood, The. Jelaluddin Rumi. SP-Rumi, *tr. by* Coleman Barks

Wing Wong,uninterred at twice. E. E. Cummings. CP-CummE

Winged Hats, The. Rudyard Kipling. *Fr.* Puck of Pook's Hill.

Winged Heart, The. Robert Graves. CP-GravR

Winged Hours. Dante Gabriel Rossetti. CW-RossD *Fr.* House of Life, The.

Winged Rock. Robinson Jeffers. CP-JefR2

Winged Seed. Rainer Maria Rilke. CP-RilkFr, *tr. by* A. Poulin, Jr.

Wingéd shadow with the self within, The. Plane. Howard Nemerov. CP-NemeH

Winged spark doth soar about, A. Emily Dickinson. CP-DickE

Winged Victory. Eleanor Wilner. SP-WilnE

Wingfoot Lake. Rita Dove. SP-DoveR

Wings, The. Denise Levertov. SP-LeveDP; SP-LeveDS

Wings filmed, the threads of knowledge thicken. Jam Trap, The. Charles Tomlinson. CP-TomlC

Wings in the Pedlar's Pack. Denise Levertov. SP-LeveDS

Wings lacking a trunk, The. Idea of Flying, The. Donald Hall. CP-HallD

Wings Lifted over the Black Pit. Allen Ginsberg. CP-GinsA

Wings of Time are black and white, The. Compensation. Ralph Waldo Emerson. CP-EmerR

Wings whirr by moon and midnight. Pablo Neruda. SP-LoguC, *tr. by* Christopher Logue *Fr.* Red Bird.

Wingtip. Carl Sandburg. CP-SandC

Winked too much and were afraid of snakes. Monkeys, The. Marianne Craig Moore. CP-MoorM

Winnah, The! pure as snow. Aftermath, The. William Carlos Williams. CP-WilW2

Winner, The. Robert Creeley. SP-CreeR

Winners, The. Rudyard Kipling. CP-KiplR *Fr.* Story of the Gadsbys, The.

Winnie Mandela We Love You. Alice Walker. CP-WalkA

Winsome Woman, A. Thomas Hardy. CP-HardT

Wintah, summah, snow er shine. Song: "Wintah, summah, snow er shine." Paul Laurence Dunbar. CP-DunbP

Wintah time hit comin'. Plantation Child's Lullaby, The. Paul Laurence Dunbar. CP-DunbP

Winter. Charles Bukowski. SP-BukC1

Winter. Paul Celan. SP-CelaP, *tr. by* John Felstiner

Winter. Robert Creeley. SP-CreeR

Winter. A. E. Housman. CP-HousA

Winter. Philip Larkin. CP-LarkP

Winter. Walter De la Mare. CP-DeLaW

Winter. Czeslaw Milosz. CP-MiloC; CP-MiloCN, *tr. by* Robert Hass

Winter. Pablo Neruda. SP-NeruP

Winter. Mary Oliver. SP-OlivM

Winter. Adrienne Rich. CP-RicAE

Winter. Rainer Maria Rilke. CP-RilkFr, *tr. by* A. Poulin, Jr.

Winter. Dante Gabriel Rossetti. CW-RossD

Winter. Charles Tomlinson. CP-TomlC

Winter ("There is a winter in the godless heart"). Jones Very. CP-VeryJ

Winter. William Carlos Williams. CP-WilW1

Winter, The ("Wheelbarrow's tire is flat, muddy ground now sets"). Philip Whalen. SP-WhalP

Winter, The ("Why do I fear the true winter death to come"). Philip Whalen. SP-WhalP

Winter, a Dirge. Robert Burns. CP-BurnR

Winter; a short walk from the 10th St. Pier. Hudson Letter, The. Derek Mahon. CP-MahoD

Winter After, The. Charles Olson. CP-OlsoC

Winter Afternoon. Thomas Merton. CP-MertT

Winter Afternoon. Grace Paley. CP-PalGC

Winter Afternoons in the V & A, Pre-W.W. II. Denise Levertov. SP-LeveDL

Winter at the Inn. Kenneth Patchen. CP-PatcK

Winter Bells. Wallace Stevens. CP-StevW; CP-StevWP

Winter Bird, The. Jones Very. CP-VeryJ

Winter Burial, A. Amy Clampitt. CP-ClamA

Winter came as it does in this valley. It Was Winter. Czeslaw Milosz. CP-MiloC; CP-MiloCN, *tr. by* Renata Gorczynski, Robert Hass *and* Robert Pinsky

Winter Carol. May Sarton. SP-SartM

Winter Castle. Josephine Jacobsen. CP-JacoJ

Winter. Cold like a carved thing outside the window glass. Drone and Ostinato. Charles Wright. SP-WrigCN

Winter comes but once a year but it lasts for most of it. Summergreen for President. Ogden Nash. CP-NashO

Winter Comes to a Lot of Places in August. Charles Bukowski. SP-BukC2

Winter crisp and the brittleness of snow. Words for Love. Ted Berrigan. SP-BerrT

Winter, / damn, / again. C. K. Williams. CP-WillC

Winter Dawn. D. H. Lawrence. CP-LawrD

Winter Day in Ohio, A. James Wright. CP-WrigJ

Winter deepening, the hay all in, The. Sonnet: "Winter deepening, the hay all in, The." Richard Wilbur. CP-WilbR

Winter Dream. Arthur Rimbaud. CP-RimbA, *tr. by* Martin Sorrell

Winter Dreams. Robert Penn Warren. CP-WarrR

Winter Dusk. Walter De la Mare. CP-DeLaW

Winter Eden, A. Robert Frost. CP-FrosR

Winter Encounters. Charles Tomlinson. CP-TomlC; SP-TomlC

Winter Evening. John Clare. SP-ClarJ

Winter evening at the cottage by the bay, A. Seagull, The. Norman Dubie. CP-DubiN

Winter evening settles down, The. Preludes. T. S. Eliot. CP-ElioT; SP-ElioT

Winter Exercise. Howard Nemerov. CP-NemeH

Winter Fancies. James Whitcomb Riley. CP-RileJ

Winter Festival. Arthur Rimbaud. CP-RimbA, *tr. by* Martin Sorrell

Winter for an Untenable Situation. Alan Dugan. CP-DugaA

Winter Gale. Alan Dugan. CP-DugaA

Winter Garden. Eleanor Wilner. SP-WilnE

Winter garden in an alder swamp, A. Winter Eden, A. Robert Frost. CP-FrosR

Winter Gold. Carl Sandburg. CP-SandC

Winter has arrived. Frozen sparrows. Snowy Weather. Yannis Ritsos. SP-RitsY, *tr. by* Kostas Myrsiades

Winter has come. Tanka: "Winter has come." James Laughlin. CP-LaugJ

Winter has spent this snow. M.B. William Carlos Williams. CP-WilW1

Winter: He Shapes Up. William Meredith. SP-MereW

Winter Heavens. George Meredith. CP-MerG1

Winter in Durnover Field. Thomas Hardy. CP-HardT

Winter in Istanbul. Andrei Codrescu. SP-CodrA

Winter in the Boulevard. D. H. Lawrence. CP-LawrD

Winter in the Country. Mary Oliver. SP-OlivM

Winter in the country, Southampton, pale horse. Frank O'Hara. Ted Berrigan. SP-BerrT

Winter Insomnia. Raymond Carver. CP-CarvR

Winter is almost upon us. Under the Migrants. W. S. Merwin. SP-MerwW

Winter Is Another Country. Archibald MacLeish. CP-MacLA

Winter is cold-hearted. Summer. Christina Georgina Rossetti. CP-RosC1

Winter is fallen early. Children of Stare, The. Walter De la Mare. CP-DeLaW

Winter is good—his Hoar Delights. Emily Dickinson. CP-DickE

Winter is inventory time. Poor Man's Riches 1, A. A. K. Ramanujan. CP-RamaA

Winter is long in this climate. March. William Carlos Williams. CP-WilW1

Winter is to come, A. Way Ahead, The. W. S. Merwin. SP-MerwW

Winter is white on turf and tree. Seasons of Her Year, The. Thomas Hardy. CP-HardT

Winter It Is Past, The. Robert Burns. CP-BurnR

Winter Journey. Charles Tomlinson.

  "When you wrote to tell me of your arrival." SP-TomlC

Winter Kill. Richard Eberhart. CP-EberR

Winter landscape hangs in balance now, The. Prologue to Spring. Sylvia Plath. CP-PlatS

Winter Landscape near Ely, A. Donald Davie. CP-DaviDC

Winter Landscape, with Rooks. Sylvia Plath. CP-PlatS

Winter Landscapes. Donald Davie. CP-DaviDC

Winter Light. Eugenio Montale. CP-MontE, *tr. by* Jonathan Galassi

Winter Lightning, The. Howard Nemerov. CP-NemeH

Winter-Lull. D. H. Lawrence. CP-LawrD

Winter Mask. Allen Tate. CP-TateA

Winter Melody. Wallace Stevens. CP-StevWP

Winter Milk. Carl Sandburg. CP-SandC

Winter Moon. Langston Hughes. CP-HughL; CP-HughL1

Winter Morning. Louise Glück. SP-GlucL

Winter Music. John Ciardi. CP-CiarJ

Winter: My Secret. Christina Georgina Rossetti. CP-RosC1

Winter Night. Edna St. Vincent Millay. CP-MillE

Winter Night. Charles Simic. SP-SimiC; SP-SimiCE

Winter Night, A. Robert Burns. CP-BurnR

Winter Night, A. Georg Trakl. CP-WrigJ

Winter Night, The. Jones Very. CP-VeryJ

Winter Night in Woodland. Thomas Hardy. CP-HardT

Winter-night now well-nigh worn away, The. Salad, The. William Cowper. CP-CowpW

Winter Night Poem for Mary. Wendell Berry. CP-BerrW

Winter Nightfall. Wendell Berry. CP-BerrW

Winter Nocturne. Philip Larkin. CP-LarkP

Winter Nosegay, The. William Cowper. CP-CowpW

Winter Ocean. John Updike. CP-UpdiJ

Winter on the River. William Meredith. SP-MereW

Winter over, ice-bound. Thaw. A. R. Ammons. CP-AmmoA

Winter owl banked just in time to pass, The. Questioning Faces. Robert Frost. CP-FrosR

Winter Palace, The. Philip Larkin. CP-LarkP

Winter Paradise. Kathleen Jessie Raine. SP-RainK

Winter ("Perils of the ocean safely o'er, The"). Jones Very. CP-VeryJ

Winter-Piece. Charles Tomlinson. CP-TomlC; SP-TomlC

Winter-Piece to a Friend Away, A. John Berryman. CP-BerrJ

Winter Poem. Robert Bly. SP-BlyR

Winter Poem. Kenneth Patchen. CP-PatcK

Winter Quiet. William Carlos Williams. CP-WilW1

Winter Rain. Christina Georgina Rossetti. CP-RosC1

Winter Rain, The. Wendell Berry. CP-BerrW

Winter Rain, The. Jones Very. CP-VeryJ

Winter Remembered. John Crowe Ransom. SP-RansJ

Winter River. Thomas Lux. SP-LuxT

Winter Road, The. Jane Cooper. CP-CoopJ

Winter Roads. Thomas McGrath. SP-McGrT

Winter rose I saw, The. Marya Alexandrovna Zaturenska. SP-ZatuM

Winter Roses. John Greenleaf Whittier. CP-WhitJ

Winter Saint, A. R. Ammons. CP AmmoA

Winter Scene. A. R. Ammons. CP-AmmoA

Winter Ship, A. Sylvia Plath. CP-PlatS

Winter Shiver. Stéphane Mallarmé. CP-MallS, tr. by Henry Weinfield

Winter Smoke Is Blue and Bitter. Tennessee Williams. CP-WillT

Winter Solstice. Charles Olson. CP-OlsoC

Winter Solstice. Kathleen Jessie Raine. SP-RainK

Winter-Song. Paul Laurence Dunbar. CP-DunbP

Winter Song. Carolyn Kizer. CP-KizeC

Winter Song. William Meredith. SP-MereW

Winter Song. Wilfred Owen. CP-OwenW

Winter Spring. Richard Wilbur. CP-WilbR

Winter stops by for a visit each year. Over in Montana. William Stafford. SP-StafWW

Winter, summer, on the roof of Atreus's house. When the Watchman Saw the Light. Constantine P. Cavafy. CP-CavaC, tr. by Theoharis Constantine Theoharis

Winter Sunset. William Carlos Williams. CP-WilW1

Winter Swan. Louise Bogan. CP-BogaL

Winter Sweetness. Langston Hughes. CP-HughL

Winter Syntax. Billy Collins. SP-CollB

Winter Talent, A. Donald Davie. CP-DaviDC

Winter, that coils in the thickets now. Deciduous Branch. Stanley Kunitz. CP-KunSC

Winter, that is a fireless room. Girl's Song. Louise Bogan. CP-BogaL

Winter-time, er Summer-time. What Chris'mas Fetched the Wigginses. James Whitcomb Riley. CP-RileJ

Winter Trees. Sylvia Plath. CP-PlatS

Winter Trees. William Carlos Williams. CP-WilW1

Winter Trout. James Dickey. CP-DickJ

Winter Tuesday, the city pouring fire, A. Coming Home, Detroit, 1968. Philip Levine. SP-LeviP

Winter twilight. She comes out of the lab-. Frame. Adrienne Rich. SP-RicA2

Winter under cultivation. Emily Dickinson. CP-DickE

Winter Verse for His Sister. William Meredith. SP-MereW

Winter was mild that year. For Gabriela Münter. Adam Zagajewski. SP-ZagaA, tr. by Clare Cavanagh

Winter Weather. Carl Sandburg. CP-SandC

Winter Wheat: Oklahoma. Robert Penn Warren. CP-WarrR

Winter when no flower. Thomas Jefferson Inside. Lorine Niedecker. CP-NiedL

Winter will bar the swimmer soon. Swimming Chenango Lake. Charles Tomlinson. CP-TomlC; SP-TomlC

Winter will be feasts and fires in the shut houses. Fall in Corrales. Richard Wilbur. CP-WilbR

Winter will make white circles. Future, The. Gabriela Mistral. SP-MistG, tr. by Maria Giachetti [or Jacketti]

Winter wind is loud and wild, The. I.M. to I.G. Emily Jane Brontë. CP-BronE

Winter with the Gulf Stream. Gerard Manley Hopkins. CP-HopkG

Winter without / And warmth within. Winter Fancies. James Whitcomb Riley. CP-RileJ

Winter Words. Philip Levine. SP-LeviP

Winter-Worship. Charles Wright. SP-WrigCN

Wintergreen Ridge. Lorine Niedecker. CP-NiedL

Wintering. Sylvia Plath. CP-PlatS

Winterlong, off La Manche, wind leaning. Gray stones of the gray. Flaubert in

Egypt. Robert Penn Warren. CP-WarrR

Winterpig. Denise Levertov. SP-LeveDL

Winter's Approach. Paul Laurence Dunbar. CP-DunbP

Winters are so short, The. Emily Dickinson. CP-DickE

Winter's Day, A. Paul Laurence Dunbar. CP-DunbP

Winter's Evening, A. William Wordsworth. CP-WorW1

Winters know / Easily to shed the snow. Nature 1. Ralph Waldo Emerson. CP-EmerR

Winter's latest snowflake is the snowdrop flower. 1886, St. Valentine's Day. Christina Georgina Rossetti. CP-RosC3

Winter's Night, The. Thomas Merton. CP-MertT

Winter's Onset from an Alienated Point of View. Alan Dugan. CP-DugaA

Winter's Tale. Josephine Jacobsen. CP-JacoJ

Winter's Tale, A. D. H. Lawrence. CP-LawrD

Winter's Tale, A. Sylvia Plath. CP-PlatS

Winter's Tale, A. Wyatt Prunty. SP-PrunW

Winter's Tale, A. Dylan Thomas. CP-ThomD

Winter's Tale, The. Randall Jarrell. CP-JarrR

Winter's Tale, by a Wife, A. Mona Van Duyn. SP-VanDM

Winter's Talents. Donald Davie. CP-DaviDC

Winter's total silence. Rainer Maria Rilke. CP-RilkFr, tr. by A. Poulin, Jr. Fr. Orchards.

Winter's Walk, The. Samuel Johnson. CP-JohnS

Wintertime nighs. In Tenebris. Thomas Hardy. CP-HardT

Winthrop's Fleet. Jones Very. CP-VeryJ

Wintry boughs against a wintry sky; / Yet the sky is partly blue. There Is a Budding Morrow in Midnight. Christina Georgina Rossetti. CP-RosC2

Wintry haw is burning out of season, The. Haw Lantern, The. Seamus Heaney. SP-HeanSO

Wintry Sonnet, A. Christina Georgina Rossetti. CP-RosC2

Wintry West extends his blast, The. Winter, a Dirge. Robert Burns. CP-BurnR

Wiper, The. Louis MacNeice. CP-MacNL

Wire. Paul Muldoon. CP-MuldP

Wire. Louis Zukofsky. CP-ZukLS

Wire cage flues / on / the roofs. Wire. Louis Zukofsky. CP-ZukLS

Wired up at the ankles and one wrist. Heart Test with an Echo Chamber. Margaret Atwood. SP-AtwM2

Wires. Philip Larkin. CP-LarkP

Wires of the Night, The. Billy Collins. SP-CollB

Wisdom. Robert Creeley. CP-CreeR

Wisdom. Langston Hughes. CP-HughL; CP-HughL2

Wisdom. Thomas Merton. CP-MertT

Wisdom. Dorothy Parker. CP-ParkD

Wisdom. Yannis Ritsos. SP-RitsY, tr. by Kimon Friar and Kostas Myrsiades

Wisdom. Christina Georgina Rossetti. CP-RosC2
(Yea, the Sparrow Hath Found Her an House.) CP-RosC2

Wisdom. William Butler Yeats. CP-YeatW

Wisdom and Spirit of the universe! Influence of Natural Objects [in Calling Forth and Strengthening the Imagination in Boyhood and Early Youth]. William Wordsworth. CP-WorW1 Fr. Prelude, The; Growth of a Poet's Mind [1850 vers.].

Wisdom and War. Langston Hughes. CP-HughL; CP-HughL2

Wisdom Cometh with the Years. Countee Cullen. CP-CullC

Wisdom is having things right in your life. Little Ways that Encourage Good Fortune, The. William Stafford. SP-StafWW

Wisdom, Madam, of your private life, The. Epigram. To the Honoured——, Countess of——, An. Ben Jonson. CP-JonsB

Wisdom of Eld, The. George Meredith. CP-MerG1

Wisdom of Insecurity, The. Richard Eberhart. CP-EberR

Wisdom set apart from all desire. Guillaume de Lorris Belated. Ezra Pound. CP-PoEar

Wisdom Unapplied. Elizabeth Barrett Browning. CP-BroEB

Wise, The. Countee Cullen. CP-CullC

Wise and Foolish Virgins, The. Rainer Maria Rilke. CP-RilkFr, tr. by A. Poulin, Jr.

Wise, and many-headed bench, that sits, The. To the Worthy Author M[r] John Fletcher. Ben Jonson. CP-JonsB

Wise are ye, O ancient woods! Woods. Ralph Waldo Emerson. CP-EmerR

Wise Brothers, The. Edwin Arlington Robinson. CP-RobiE

Wise child is born, The. Hayden Carruth. CP-CarHS Fr. Clay Hill Anthology, The.

Wise have known themselves, The. Some few. Gnothi Seauton. James Vincent Cunningham. CP-CunnJ

Wise house, and / man to know it. For a Bus on Its Side and the Man Inside It. Robert Creeley. CP-CreeR

Wise man isn't greedy, A. Han-shan. CP-ColdM, tr. by Red Pine

Wise Men. Langston Hughes. CP-HughL; CP-HughL1

Wise Men, The. G. K. Chesterton. CP-ChesG

Wise Men in Their Bad Hours. Robinson Jeffers. CP-JefR1

Wise men patience never want. Thomas Campion. CP-CampT

Wise nature here has done her kindest part. Annis Boudinot Stockton. CP-StocA

Wise ones you ignore me. Han-shan. CP-ColdM, *tr. by* Red Pine

Wise pretend to make it clear, The. Answer to Dr. Delany, The. Jonathan Swift. CP-SwifJ

Wise Rochefoucauld a maxim writ. Life and Genuine Character of Dr Swift, The. Jonathan Swift. CP-SwifJ

Wise Sense Imminent Events, The. Constantine P. Cavafy. CP-CavaC, *tr. by* Theoharis Constantine Theoharis

Wise understand the maker of parables, The. Shmuel HaNagid. SP-HaNaS, *tr. by* Peter Cole

Wisely each state for its own rights contends. State Rights. Jones Very. CP-VeryJ

Wisest and fairest messenger of God. Litanies to Satan. Charles Baudelaire. CP-BaudC, *tr. by* Walter Martin

Wisest of sparrows that sparrow which sitteth alone. Wisdom. Christina Georgina Rossetti. CP-RosC2

Wish. W. S. Merwin. SP-MerwW

Wish, A. G. K. Chesterton. CP-ChesG

Wish, A. Samuel Taylor Coleridge. CP-ColeS

Wish, A. Robert Creeley. CP-CreeR

Wish, A. Ivor Gurney. SP-GurnI

Wish for a Young Wife. Theodore Roethke. CP-RoetT

Wish for Dreamful Sleep, A. Samuel Taylor Coleridge. CP-ColeS

Wish for Unconsciousness, A. Thomas Hardy. CP-HardT

Wish: Metamorphosis to Heraldic Emblem. Margaret Atwood. SP-AtwM1

Wish of To-day, The. John Greenleaf Whittier. CP-WhitJ

Wish on a Wedding Day Morning, The. Annis Boudinot Stockton. CP-StocA

Wish to Be Believed, The. Mona Van Duyn. SP-VanDM

Wish to Be Generous, The. Wendell Berry. CP-BerrW

Wish to Comply, A. Robert Frost. CP-FrosR

Wish to Miss Hannah Stockton, The. Annis Boudinot Stockton. CP-StocA

Wish we could talk today. Remembering Williams. Charles Tomlinson. CP-TomlC

Wishbone, The. Paul Muldoon. CP-MuldP

Wished-For Song, A. Jelaluddin Rumi. SP-Rumi, *tr. by* Coleman Barks

Wishes. Andrei Codrescu. SP-CodrA

Wishes. Robert Creeley. SP-CreeR

Wishes for Sons. Lucille Clifton. CP-ClifL

Wishes left on your lips. Wistful. Carl Sandburg. CP-SandC

Wishes on this child's mouth, The. Helga. Carl Sandburg. CP-SandC

Wishes: Sonnet. Christina Georgina Rossetti. CP-RosC3

Wishes. To His (Supposed) Mistress[e]. Richard Crashaw. CP-CrasR

Wishfully I look and languish. Robert Burns. *See* Bonnie [*or* Bonny] Wee Thing, The

Wishing Bridge, The. John Greenleaf Whittier. CP-WhitJ

Wishing-Caps, The. Rudyard Kipling. CP-KiplR *Fr.* Kim.

Wishing-Gate, The. William Wordsworth. CP-WorW2

Wishing-Gate Destroyed, The. William Wordsworth. CP-WorW2

Wishing More Dear. Laura Riding Jackson. CP-RidiL

Wishing Tree, The. Seamus Heaney. SP-HeanSO

Wisp & meteor nightly falling. Ralph Waldo Emerson. CP-EmerR

Wistful. Carl Sandburg. CP-SandC

Wistful Lady, The. Thomas Hardy. CP-HardT

Wistful, / they speak of / satis- / faction, love. People, The. Robert Creeley. CP-CreeR

The(/ Wistfully / dead seem generous)don't. E. E. Cummings. CP-CummE

Wit, The. Elizabeth Bishop. CP-BishE

Wit in fools has something shocking. Long after Chamfort. Nicolas-Sébastien Roch Chamfort. CP-BeckS

Wit Punisht, Prospers Most. Robert Herrick. CP-HerrR

Wit, weight, or wealth there was not. Experience, An. Thomas Hardy. CP-HardT

Witch, The. Primo Levi. CP-LeviP, *tr. by* Ruth Feldman *and* Brian Swann

Witch, The. William Butler Yeats. CP-YeatW

Witch I, The. D. H. Lawrence. CP-LawrD

Witch II, The. D. H. Lawrence. CP-LawrD

Witch Doctor. Robert Earl Hayden. CP-HaydR

Witch of Atlas, The. Percy Bysshe Shelley. CP-ShelP

Witch of Erkmurden, The. James Whitcomb Riley. CP-RileJ

Witch of Wenham, The. John Greenleaf Whittier. CP-WhitJ

Witch that came (the withered hag), The. Provide, Provide. Robert Frost. CP-FrosR

Witch-Wife. Edna St. Vincent Millay. CP-MillE

Witchcraft by a Picture. John Donne. CP-DonnJ; MW-DonnJ

Witchcraft has not a Pedigree. Emily Dickinson. CP-DickE

Witchcraft was hung, in History. Emily Dickinson. CP-DickE

Witches. Ted Hughes. SP-HughTN

Witches' Charms, The. Ben Jonson. *Fr.* Masque of Queens, The.

Witches Waken the Natural World in Spring. James Wright. CP-WrigJ

Witch's Life, The. Anne Sexton. CP-SextA

With a Changing Key. Paul Celan. SP-CelaP, *tr. by* John Felstiner

With a Child All Day. James Tate. SP-TateJ

With a Child-Book. James Whitcomb Riley. CP-RileJ

With a cold and wintry noon-light. At Washington. John Greenleaf Whittier. CP-WhitJ

With a Copy of 'A House of Pomegranates'. Oscar Wilde. CP-WildO

With a Copy of Stevens' *Harmonium*. J. V. Cunningham. CP-CunnJ

With a dry eye, she. For Sappho, Back. Charles Olson. CP-OlsoC; SP-OlsoC

With a Gift of Rings. Robert Graves. CP-GravR

With a glass of / boiled water. Deaths. Denise Levertov. SP-LeveDP

With a glory of winter sunshine. Poet and the Children, The. John Greenleaf Whittier. CP-WhitJ

With a Guitar, to Jane. Percy Bysshe Shelley. CP-ShelP

With a half-glance upon the sky. Character, A. Alfred Tennyson. CP-TennA

With a happy heart. Jake Flower, The. Clarence Major. SP-MajoC

With a hey! and a hi! and a hey-ho glee! Christmas Glee, A. James Whitcomb Riley. CP-RileJ

With a hey! and a hi! and a hey-ho rhyme! Some Songs after Master-Singers. James Whitcomb Riley. CP-RileJ

With a lantern that wouldn't burn. Draft Horse, The. Robert Frost. CP-FrosR

With a lily in your hand. Curve. Federico García Lorca. CP-GarcF, *tr. by* Jerome Rothenberg *Fr.* Water Suite.

With a Machet Across My Knees. Robert Stock. SP-StocR

With a pale green curly. Love of Lettuce, The. Marge Piercy. SP-PierM

With a pert moustache and a ready candid smile. Mixer, The. Louis MacNeice. CP-MacNL

With a Photograph to Zell, Now Bound for Spain. Hart Crane. CP-CranH

With a Picture Sent to a Friend. Richard Crashaw. CP-CrasR

With a pocketful of stones. For the Recorder of Suicides. Jane Cooper. CP-CoopJ

With a quick / jump he caught. Hello. Robert Creeley. CP-CreeR

With a Rose, to Brunhilde. Nicholas Vachel Lindsay. CP-LindV

With a Small Present. William Wordsworth. CP-WorW2

With a southwest wind blowing late August. Wedding, The. Richard Eberhart. CP-EberR

With a spoon. King of Harlem, The. Federico García Lorca. SP-GarcF, *tr. by* J. L. Gili *and* Stephen Spender

With a spoon / he dug out the crocodiles' eyes. King of Harlem, The. Federico García Lorca. CP-GarcF, *tr. by* Greg Simon *and* Steven F. White

With a stick and a leather glove. Evening with the Master, An. Charles Simic. SP-SimiCE

With a sudden, sweet surprise. Ship Rock. Jones Very. CP-VeryJ

With a sweeter voice than birds. Autumnal Extravaganza, An. James Whitcomb Riley. CP-RileJ

With a Telescope Rod on Cowiche Creek. Raymond Carver. CP-CarvR

With a tiny bird whistle. Evening with the Master, An. Charles Simic. SP-SimiC

With a Wave of Her Old Hand. Kathleen Jessie Raine. SP-RainK

With a whirl of thought oppressed. Day of Judgement, The. Jonathan Swift. CP-SwifJ

With a Wife. Gertrude Stein. CP-SteiG

With Age Wisdom. Archibald MacLeish. CP-MacLA

With aimless feet, along the verge. Basilica. Ambrose Bierce. SP-BierA

With aimless fury hurries on its path. On the Late Tornado, at Wallingford, Conn. Jones Very. CP-VeryJ

With Alfred and St. Louis he doth win. Emperor Frederick of Our Time, The. George Meredith. CP-MerG1

With all I know. There ("With all I know"). Robert Creeley. SP-CreeR

With all my heart I love you; if not so. Michelangelo Buonarroti. CP-Miche, *tr. by* John Frederick Nims

With all my questions. God-Monger, The. Anne Sexton. CP-SextA; SP-SextA

With all my thoughts I went. Paul Celan. SP-CelaP, *tr. by* John Felstiner

With all the powres my poor heart hath. Adoro Te. The Hymn of Saint Thomas in Adoration of the Blessed Sacrament. Richard Crashaw. CP-CrasR

With All the Rigor of Pity. Yehuda Amichai. SP-AmicYL, *tr. by* Benjamin Harshav *and* Barbara Harshav

With all this clamour for progress. Homage to Clichés. Louis MacNeice. CP-MacNL

With all those I love. From a Long Way Out of Pah-Gatzin-Kay. Thomas McGrath. SP-McGrT

With all thy Countries Blessings on thy head. To General Washington [Aug. 26, 1783]. Annis Boudinot Stockton. CP-StocA

With All Thy Gifts. Walt Whitman. CP-WhitW

With an easiness we almost learn. Name, The. Wyatt Prunty. SP-PrunW

With Antecedents. Walt Whitman. CP-WhitW

With armloads of lignum vitae, hands frightened over mouths, kinfolk gape at the paradox. Pushing in All the Buttons. Yusef Komunyakaa. CP-KomuY

With B.E.F. June 10. Dear Wife. Letter, The. Wilfred Owen. CP-OwenW

With banners furled, and [or the] clarions mute. Night-March, The. Herman Melville. SP-MelvH

With beasts and gods, above, the wall is bright. Children Selecting Books in a Library. Randall Jarrell. CP-JarrR

With beauty, with pleasure surrounded, to languish. Amatory Lines. Thomas Gray. CP-grayT

With bells for hooves in sounding streets. Lawrence Ferlinghetti. SP-FerlL

With Bernard de Mandeville. Robert Browning. CP-BroR2

With Best Wishes. Dorothy Parker. CP-ParkD

With big breasts. Girl, The. William Carlos Williams. CP-WilW1

With bits of pale colored chalk. Ghosts on the Northern Land of Ur. Norman Dubie. CP-DubiN

With blackest moss the flower-pots [or flowerpots]. Mariana. Alfred Tennyson. CP-TennA

With blameless carriage, I lived [or liv'd] here. Epitaph upon a Sober Matron, An. Robert Herrick. CP-HerrR

With bold, unblushing front the Giant Wrong. Goliath. Jones Very. CP-VeryJ

With Bruce and Ronald bides the tale. Loch Coruisk. Sir Walter Scott. SP-ScotW Fr. Lord of the Isles, The.

With Buck still tied to the log, on comes the light. Double Feature. Theodore Roethke. CP-RoetT

With business haste, or with a worldly mind. Pleasure ("With business haste, or with a worldly mind"). Jones Very. CP-VeryJ

With careful step to keep his balance up. Braggart. John Clare. SP-ClarJ

With changeful sound life beats upon the ear. Silence. Walter De la Mare. CP-DeLaW

With Charles Avison. Robert Browning. CP-BroR2

With Christopher Smart. Robert Browning. CP-BroR2

With cicada's nymphal skin. Largess, The. Richard Eberhart. CP-EberR

With clearer light, Cross of the South, shine forth. Freedom in Brazil. John Greenleaf Whittier. CP-WhitJ

With closer clutch for that which remains. Emily Dickinson. SP-DickE

With conscience cocked to listen for the thunder. Luther. W. H. Auden. CP-AudeW

With copious eulogy in prose or rhyme. Elegiac Musings in the Grounds of Coleorton Hall, the Seat of the Late Sir G.H. Beaumont, BART. William Wordsworth. CP-WorW2

With crayons and pieces of paper. Room, The. Gregory Orr. SP-OrrG

With cunning plates the polished leaves were decked. "Book of Gems," The. Henry David Thoreau. CP-ThorH

With Dad gone, Mom and I worked. Adolescence—III. Rita Dove. SP-DoveR

With daily ebb and flow. Tide, The. Jones Very. CP-VeryJ

With Daniel Bartoli. Robert Browning. CP-BroR2

With Deep Repentance for My Wasted Days. Gaspara Stampa. SP-ZatuM, tr. by Marya Alexandrovna Zaturenska

With defective thyroid glands. Bill's. Clarence Major. SP-MajoC

With difficulty I read what's on this ancient stone. In the Month of Athyr. Constantine P. Cavafy. CP-CavaC, tr. by Theoharis Constantine Theoharis

With dog and catalpa, panicles. She Who Hits at Will. Charles Olson. CP-OlsoC

With Donne, whose muse on dromedary trots. On Donne's Poetry. Samuel Taylor Coleridge. CP-ColeS; MW-ColeS

With Drake in the Tropics. Rudyard Kipling. CP-KiplR

With dread she heard the letter. Crosspurposes. Denise Levertov. SP-LeveDL

With each journey it gets. Truth about Departures, The. W. S. Merwin. SP-MerwW

With each recurrence of this glorious morn. Composed in One of the Valleys of Westmoreland, on Easter Sunday. William Wordsworth. CP-WorW2

With Eddie and Nancy in Arezzo at the Caffè Grande. Charles Wright. SP-WrigCN

With evening. Patio. Jorge Luis Borges. SP-BorgJ, tr. by Robert Fitzgerald

With ever one fear at the heart o' me. At the Heart o' Me. Ezra Pound. CP-PoEar

With every other strategem. Having Failed. James Laughlin. CP-LaugJ

With every wife he can and you know why? James Vincent Cunningham. CP-CunnJ

With eye and with gesture. Stephen Crane. CP-CranS

With Eyes at the Back of Our Heads. Denise Levertov. SP-LeveDS

With eyes that have found the rain and first stars. For Robert, Son of Man. Miller Williams. CP-WillM

With favour and fortune fastidiously blessed [or blest]. Character of Sir Robert Walpole, The. Jonathan Swift. CP-SwifJ

With fear I trembled in the House of Life. Vita Mea. Wallace Stevens. CP-StevWP

With Fielding's Amelia. Samuel Taylor Coleridge. CP-ColeS

With fifty years between you and your well-kept wedding vow. Golden Wedding of Longwood, The. John Greenleaf Whittier. CP-WhitJ

With flag unfurled along the shore they sail. Landing, The. Jones Very. CP-VeryJ

With flecks of web like foam. Spelunker. Robert Pinsky. CP-PinsR

With focus sharp as Flemish-painted face. Dome of Sunday, The [or A]. Karl Shapiro. SP-ShapK

With food in which Lord Love seems to abound. Petrarch. CP-Petra, tr. by J. G. Nichols

With Francis Furini. Robert Browning. CP-BroR2

With Frank and George at Lexington. James Schuyler. CP-SchuJ

With frontier strength ye stand your ground. Mountains in the Horizon, The. Henry David Thoreau. CP-ThorH

With gentlest tears, no less than jubilee. Eugene Field. James Whitcomb Riley. CP-RileJ

With George Bubb Dodington. Robert Browning. CP-BroR2

With Gerard de Lairesse. Robert Browning. CP-BroR2

With ginger hair dragged over. Art Student. Stephen Spender. CP-SpenS

With God. Olga Broumas. SP-BrouO

With golden Censers, and with Incense, here. To God. Robert Herrick. CP-HerrR

With golden mantle, rings, and necklace fair. Dante Gabriel Rossetti. CW-RossD

With great love the people. They Are All Dice. Yehuda Amichai. SP-AmicY, tr. by Chana Bloch

With great satisfaction I take. What the Deceased Had to Say about Himself. Nicanor Parra. CP-MertT

With gypsies and sailors. Farewell, A. Langston Hughes. CP-HughL; CP-HughL1

With half an eye. Answer to Delany's Riddle, The. Jonathan Swift. CP-SwifJ

With hands in pocket hid and buttoned up. Clown, The. John Clare. SP-ClarJ

With Happiness Stretched [or stretched] across the Hills. William Blake. CP-BlakW

(To Thomas Butts, 22 November 1802.) CP-BlakW

With haste, with the haggard color. Woman on the Stair, The. Archibald MacLeish. CP-MacLA

With heads like chessmen, bishop or queen. Another Cold May. Louis MacNeice. CP-MacNL

With heart of sulphur, flesh of tinder too. Michelangelo Buonarroti. CP-Miche, tr. by John Frederick Nims

With heavy eyelids I am still in love. Ballroom Dark. Clarence Major. SP-MajoC

With heedless feet on fires you go. Ode 2.1: "With heedless feet on fires you go." Horace. CP-JohnS Fr. Odes.

With Her. Czeslaw Milosz. CP-MiloC; CP-MiloCN, tr. by Robert Hass

With her face between his hands! James Whitcomb Riley. CP-RileJ

With Her in an Apple. Yehuda Amichai. SP-AmicYL, tr. by Benjamin Harshav and Barbara Harshav

With Her Lips Only. Robert Graves. CP-GravR

With higher thoughts, O God, uplift. Things Unseen. Jones Very. CP-VeryJ

With his eyes closed, in the sun: naked. Seaweed and salt. Stripped Naked. Yannis Ritsos. SP-RitsY, tr. by Kimon Friar

With his heart. Who'd Want to Be a Man? Gregory Orr. SP-OrrG

With his shopping cart, his bags of booty and his wine, I'd always found him inoffensive. Harm. C. K. Williams. SP-WillC

With holy earnest eyes enshrined. St. Thérèse. George Meredith. CP-MerG2

With Horace I take my stand beside the rocks. David Ignatow. SP-IgnaD

With horses' hooves clattering. Sigismundo Malatesta Brings His Favorite Philosopher's Bones to Italy. Robert Stock. SP-StocR

With huge jowls that wobble with sad o. Sorrow, The. C. K. Williams. CP-WillC

With Husky-Haughty Lips, O Sea! Walt Whitman. CP-WhitW

With Ignorance. C. K. Williams. CP-WillC; SP-WillC

With inauspicious love a wretched swain. Idyll 23: The Despairing Lover. Theocritus. CP-DryJ2 Fr. Idylls.

With innocent wide penguin eyes, three. Bird-witted. Marianne Craig Moore. CP-MoorM

With its baby rivers and little towns, each with its abbey or its cathedral. England. Marianne Craig Moore. CP-MoorM

With its burden of dreams. Sleep. James Schuyler. CP-SchuJ

With its cloud of skirmishers in advance. Army Corps on the March, An. Walt Whitman. CP-WhitW

With Janice. Kenneth Koch. SP-KochK

With joy she showed the traveller Macy's. 34th Street Song. Grace Paley. CP-PalGC

With Kit, Age 7, at the Beach. William Stafford. SP-StafW; SP-StafWW

With leaves below and leaves above. Bay Combe. G. K. Chesterton. CP-ChesG

With Leopards for Playmates, the beautiful Child. Emily Dickinson. SP-DickE

With Letter and Clock. Paul Celan. SP-CelaP, tr. by John Felstiner

With Life and Death I walked when Love appeared. Hymn to Colour. George Meredith. CP-MerG1

With little here to do or see. To the Daisy ("With little here to do or see"). William Wordsworth. CP-WorW1; MW-WorW

With love exceeding a simple love of the things. Melampus. George Meredith. CP-MerG1

With madness seized men their own works destroy. Destruction of Public Property by Mobs, The. Jones Very. CP-VeryJ

With masts sung earthward. Paul Celan. SP-CelaP, *tr.* by John Felstiner

With me retire and leave the pomp of courts. Virgil. CP-JohnS *Fr.* Eclogues.

With Mercy for the Greedy. Anne Sexton. CP-SextA; SP-SextA

With Military Honors. Tennessee Williams. CP-WillT

With much of time and life gone, all the more. Michelangelo Buonarroti. CP-Miche, *tr.* by John Frederick Nims

With Music and Poetry Equally Blessed. George Rochfort. CP-SherT

With my back to the insane world. David Ignatow. SP-IgnaD

With my brother I ran. Great Wave, The. Denise Levertov. SP-LeveDL

With My Crowbar Key. William Stafford. SP-StafWW

With my deep sighs I fill the ambient air. Petrarch. CP-Petra, *tr.* by J. G. Nichols

With my eyes turned to the sky. Love Poem for the Forty-Second Street Library. David Ignatow. SP-IgnaD

With my long-honoured, dear, and cruel lord. Petrarch. CP-Petra, *tr.* by J. G. Nichols

With my looks I am bound to look simple or fast I would rather look simple. Magna Est Veritas. Stevie Smith. CP-SmitS

With My Mother. Yehuda Amichai. SP-AmicYL, *tr.* by Benjamin Harshav *and* Barbara Harshav

With My Third Eye. James Laughlin. CP-LaugJ

With my whole body I taste these peaches. Dish of Peaches in Russia, A. Wallace Stevens. CP-StevW; CP-StevWP

With my words. His Grief. Gregory Orr. SP-OrrG

With narrow view each state its own would claim. Rights of Man, The. Jones Very. CP-VeryJ

With Neighbors One Afternoon. William Stafford. SP-StafWW

With neither bones nor skin. Round Fish, The. Eleanor Wilner. SP-WilnE

With no less joy than grief and consternation. Michelangelo Buonarroti. CP-Miche, *tr.* by John Frederick Nims

With no one to talk to, he talked to the five fish. Unto One of the Least of These. Miller Williams. CP-WillM

With no poetic ardour fir'd. Verses Left by Mr. Pope, on His Lying in the Same Bed which Wilmot, the Celebrated Earl of Rochester, Slept in, at Adderbury, then Belonging to the Duke of Argyle, July 9th, 1739. Alexander Pope. CP-PopeA

With no regret, not envying anyone. Petrarch. CP-Petra, *tr.* by J. G. Nichols

With no rich viands overcharg'd, I send. John Milton. *See* On an empty stomach I send you a wish for health

With noble and strange devices Man hath-spanned. Bridge, The. Walter De la Mare. CP-DeLaW

With noises meaningful and vague as ever. Pleasure Pier. Robert Pinsky. CP-PinsR

With not-quite truth. Czeslaw Milosz. CP-MiloC; CP-MiloCN, *tr.* by Robert Hass

With nothing else for speech. Fan, A; of Madame Mallarmé. Stéphane Mallarmé. CP-MallS, *tr.* by Henry Weinfield

With ocean shell clasped to his breast. Indian Remains. Jones Very. CP-VeryJ

With oil that streaks streets a magic color. Ballade of Poisons. Allen Ginsberg. CP-GinsA

With old hours all belfry heads. Ding-Donging. Laura Riding Jackson. CP-RidiL

With one black shadow at its feet. Mariana in the South. Alfred Tennyson. CP-TennA

With one dear friend we go up the highest mountain. Mountain Days. W. S. Merwin. SP-MerwWF

With only his dim lantern. Charles Simic. *See* With only his dim [*or* feeble] lantern

With only his dim [*or* feeble] lantern. Charon's Cosmology. Charles Simic. SP-SimiC; SP-SimiCE

With open arms the water runs in to the wheel. To Where We Are. W. S. Merwin. SP-MerwW

With other women I beheld my love. Ballata: Of his Lady among other Ladies. Guido Cavalcanti. CW-RossD, *tr.* by Dante Gabriel Rossetti

With Others. David Ignatow. SP-IgnaD

With outward impulse, running to and fro. Inward Direction. Jones Very. CP-VeryJ

With outward signs, as well as inward life. First Atlantic Telegraph, The. Jones Very. CP-VeryJ

With pale green hopes and the gay colors flying. Parthenia. Allen Tate. CP-TateA

With Pantheist energy of will. Venice. Herman Melville. SP-MelvH

With paste of almonds Syb her hands doth scour[e]. Upon Sibilla. Robert Herrick. CP-HerrR

With Pegasus upon a day. To John Taylor. Robert Burns. CP-BurnR

With Pinions of Disdain. Emily Dickinson. CP-DickE

With prayer-plant eyes annually winter-leggy. Zinnia. Louis Zukofsky. CP-ZukLS

With prune-dark eyes, thick lips, jostling each other. Refugees. Louis MacNeice. CP-MacNL

With reeds and bird-lime from the desert air. On a Fowler. Isidorus. CP-CowpW,

tr. by William Cowper

With Ropes of Hemp. A. R. Ammons. CP-AmmoA

With Rue My Heart Is Laden. A. E. Housman. CP-HousA

With sacrifice before the rising morn. Laodamia. William Wordsworth. CP-WorW2

With sagest craft Arachne worked. Garden Idyl, A. George Meredith. CP-MerG1

With saintly grace and reverent tread. Presentiment. Ambrose Bierce. SP-BierA

With Scindia to Delhi. Rudyard Kipling. CP-KiplR

With scissors she snipped the blue. Walking Home after the First Encounter. Gregory Orr. SP-OrrG

With seed the sowers scatter. A. E. Housman. CP-HousA

With serving still. His Reward. Sir Thomas Wyatt. CP-WyatT

With Shakspeare's manhood at a boy's wild heart. Thomas Chatterton. Dante Gabriel Rossetti. CW-RossD *Fr.* Five English Poets.

With sharp lights winking. Thinking Back Toward Christmas: A Statement for the Virgin. William Carlos Williams. CP-WilW2

With Ships the sea was sprinkled far and nigh. William Wordsworth. CP-WorW1; MW-WorW

With sick and famished [*or* famisht] eyes. Longing. George Herbert. CP-HerbG

With sickness and with famine they contend. Sickness. Jones Very. CP-VeryJ

With sights of beauty rare. Voice of Nature in Youth and Age, The. Jones Very. CP-VeryJ

With Simic and Marinetti at the Giubbe Rosse. Charles Wright. SP-WrigCN

With sleep-crowned eyes I / see the morning sunlight. Sleep-Gummed Eyes. James Schuyler. CP-SchuJ

With sleepless toil on land and wave. Force and His Master. George Meredith. CP-MerG2

With sombre mien, the Evening Grey. Farewell to Arcady. Paul Laurence Dunbar. CP-DunbP

[With Some Poems Sent to a Gentlewoman]. I]. Richard Crashaw. CP-CrasR

[With Some Poems Sent to a Gentlewoman. II]. Richard Crashaw. CP-CrasR

With song elate we celebrate. Poor Student, The. James Whitcomb Riley. CP-RileJ

With sorrow that the Joy is past. Emily Dickinson. SP-DickE

With splendour of a silver day. Night of Frost in May. George Meredith. CP-MerG1

With spring-like mildness passeth, day by day. On the Late Mild Winter. Jones Very. CP-VeryJ

With stammering lips and insufficient sound. Soul's Expression, The. Elizabeth Barrett Browning. CP-BroEB

With Stars. Tess Gallagher. SP-GallT

With stealthy whistle of wing. Crossing, The. May Swenson. SP-SwenM

With sturdy blows the echoing woods resound. Location. Jones Very. CP-VeryJ

With subtle poise he grips his tray. Atlantic City Waiter. Countee Cullen. CP-CullC

With such a firm grip on the Muse's curls. To Theodore de Banville. Charles Baudelaire. CP-BaudC, *tr.* by Walter Martin

With sweet surprise, as when one finds a flower. On Finding the Truth. Jones Very. CP-VeryJ

With sweetness unabated. Emily Dickinson. CP-DickE

With tall and silent trees to guard its mounts. On Combe Bottom: Surrey. George Meredith. CP-MerG2

With Tewksbury and Barnet heath. Battle of Stone River, Tennessee. Herman Melville. SP-MelvH

With that same imprecise smile in his eyes. Transposition. Yannis Ritsos. SP-RitsY, *tr.* by Kimon Friar *and* Kostas Myrsiades

With the actual the illusory. Orford. Boris Leonidovich Pasternak. CP-DaviDC, *tr.* by Donald Davie

With the bias of one disobediant to death. Biased Man, The. Yannis Ritsos. SP-RitsY, *tr.* by N. C. Germanacos

With the blue-dark dome old-starred at night, green boat-lights purring over water, Galilee Shore. Allen Ginsberg. CP-GinsA

With the boys busy. Philomena Andronico. William Carlos Williams. CP-WilW2

With the Caribou. Maxine W. Kumin. SP-KumiM

With the collapse of the vocal chords and through. Ode to Laryngitis. Andrei Codrescu. SP-CodrA

With the Current. James Whitcomb Riley. CP-RileJ

With the effect almost of carving the hillside. Donald Davie. CP-DaviDC

With the face goes a mirror. Laura Riding Jackson. CP-RidiL

With the frenzy of an old snake shedding its skin. Derek Walcott. CP-WalcD *Fr.* Midsummer.

With the fury of cinders, with the despair of dusty. Warrant for Pablo Neruda, A. Thomas McGrath. SP-McGrT

With the Gift of a Lion's Claw. Robert Graves. CP-GravR

With the Gift of a Nootka Rose. Sam Hamill. SP-HamiS

With the Grain. Donald Davie. CP-DaviDC

With the great thought, thy Country's cause, its life. Crisis, The. Jones Very. CP-VeryJ

With the help of three dwarfs from a nearby world. I Suddenly Became

Conscious That This Thing Was Looking at Me Intently. Kenneth Patchen. CP-PatcK

With the Herring Fishers. Hugh MacDiarmid. SP-MacDH

With the Huntress. George Meredith. CP-MerG1

With the key of the secret he marches faster. Ralph Waldo Emerson. CP-EmerR

With the Lark. Paul Laurence Dunbar. CP-DunbP

With the motion of angels, out of. In the Mountains. Robert Penn Warren. CP-WarrR

With the old kindness, the old distinguished grace. Upon a Dying Lady. William Butler Yeats. CP-YeatW

With the persecuted in late, un- / silenced. Paul Celan. SP-CelaP, *tr. by* John Felstiner

With the Persuader. George Meredith. CP-MerG1

With the same letter heaven and home begin. Home and Heaven. Jones Very. CP-VeryJ

With the shouting, the noise, the beautiful multicolored garments. After the Ceremony. Yannis Ritsos. SP-RitsY, *tr. by* Kimon Friar

With the smell of firebombing. Waiter in a California Vietnamese Restaurant. Clarence Major. SP-MajoC

With the spirit Christians sung. Congregational Singing. Jones Very. CP-VeryJ

With the spring flowers I likewise am. Bird, the Bird, the Bird, The. Robert Creeley. CP-CreeR

With the stampeding hiss and scurry of green lemmings. Derek Walcott. CP-WalcD *Fr.* Midsummer.

With the storm moved on the next town. Centipede. Rita Dove. SP-DoveR

With the sun half way down the tall pines. River Water Music. Richard Eberhart. CP-EberR

With the Sun's Fire. David Ignatow. SP-IgnaD

With the World in My Blood Stream. Thomas Merton. CP-MertT

With the years—he says—colors abandon me, I abandon them. Experiences. Yannis Ritsos. SP-RitsY, *tr. by* N. C. Germanacos

With the years, purely by chance, with nothing in mind, they replaced. Whitewash. Yannis Ritsos. SP-RitsY, *tr. by* N. C. Germanacos

With thee—in the Desert. Emily Dickinson. CP-DickE

With their backs to the sea two fiddlers stand. At the Aquatic Sports. Thomas Hardy. CP-HardT

With their money they bought ignorance. Killers. Alice Walker. CP-WalkA

With their respective lions. Sea Unicorns and Land Unicorns. Marianne Craig Moore. CP-MoorM

With their throb and yearn, their sad. Exeunt the Viols. Rita Dove. SP-DoveR

With them there rode a lustie Engineere. Justice's Tale, The. Rudyard Kipling. CP-KiplR *Fr.* Muse among the Motors, The.

With these moody negations / I said goodbye to the mirrors. Conditions. Pablo Neruda. SP-NeruP

With These Stones. Yannis Ritsos. SP-RitsY, *tr. by* Kimon Friar

With this body worship her. Cross-Legged, the Spider and the Web. Charles Olson. CP-OlsoC; SP-OlsoC

With this you trim it. Do it right and it'll fly. Two Poems of Flight Sleep. James Dickey. CP-DickJ

With those that bred, with those that loosed the strife. General Joubert. Rudyard Kipling. CP-KiplR

With thy small stock, why art [*or are*] thou venturing [*or* vent'ring] still. To a Weak Gamester in Poetry. Ben Jonson. CP-JonsB; SP-JonsB

With time and fatigue—he said—words die too. Need to Express. Yannis Ritsos. SP-RitsY, *tr. by* Andonis Decavalles

With treading of Night as a vintage. Twilight. G. K. Chesterton. CP-ChesG

With troubled heart and trembling hand I write. In Memory of My Dear Grandchild Anne Bradstreet Who Deceased June 20, 1669, Being Three Years and Seven Months Old. Anne Bradstreet. CP-BradA

With Trumpets and Zithers. Czeslaw Milosz. CP-MiloC; CP-MiloCN

With two spurs or one; no great matter which. Cantab, The. Vincent Bourne. CP-CowpW

With two strange fires of equal heat possessed [*or* possest]. Love and Jealousy. Sir Philip Sidney. SP-SidnP *Fr.* Arcadia.

With two white roses on her breasts. Brown Girl Dead, A. Countee Cullen. CP-CullC

With us there rade a Maister-Cook that came. Master-Cook, The. Rudyard Kipling. CP-KiplR *Fr.* Land and Sea Tales.

With *Usura.* Canto 45: "With *Usura.*" Ezra Pound. SP-PounE *Fr.* Cantos.

With Vengeance Like a Tiger Crawls. Charles Bukowski. SP-BukC2

With Warm Regards to Miss Moore and Mr. Ransom. Mona Van Duyn. SP-VanDM

With warning hand I mark Time's rapid flight. Inscriptions. John Greenleaf Whittier. CP-WhitJ

With what delight I view each line. On Reading a Letter. Jane Anna Elizabeth Austen. CP-AustJ

With what I got out. Charles Olson. CP-OlsoC

With what joy I am carrying. Wine, The. W. S. Merwin. SP-MerwWF

With what joy / I left home to deposit one thousand, one hundred and nineteen.

Middle-Age Poem. Grace Paley. CP-PalGC

With what painful deliberation he comes down the stair. English Cocker: Old and Blind. Robert Penn Warren. CP-WarrR

With what panache, he said. Lions, The. Robert Earl Hayden. CP-HaydR

With what thou gavest me, O Master. Equipment. Paul Laurence Dunbar. CP-DunbP

With white frost gone. Strumpet Song. Sylvia Plath. CP-PlatS

With whom / do you leave yourself. Articulation. Rae Armantrout. SP-ArmaA

With Whom Is No Variableness, Neither Shadow of Turning. Arthur Hugh Clough. SP-ClouA

With wide cool eyes she gazes on mankind. Girl and Scarecrow. Marya Alexandrovna Zaturenska. SP-ZatuM

With wine and lostness, with. Paul Celan. SP-CelaP, *tr. by* John Felstiner

With wisdom far beyond her years. How Mary Grew. John Greenleaf Whittier. CP-WhitJ

With women unlike Marie no holds are barred. Hung Wu Vase, The. Robert Graves. CP-GravR

With wood from a hundred-year-old tree. Five Enemies, The. Chuang Tzu. CP-MertT

With words, with appearance, and with manners. Aimilianos Monai, Alexandrian, 628–655 A.D.. Constantine P. Cavafy. CP-CavaC, *tr. by* Theoharis Constantine Theoharis

With you for mast and sail and flag. Narrow Sea, The. Robert Graves. CP-GravR

With you it is still the middle of the night. Lag, The. Adrienne Rich. CP-RicAE

With you, my heart is quiet here. Thin Edge, The. Dorothy Parker. CP-ParkD

With you to Bideford. Admiral to His Lady, The. Donald Davie. CP-DaviDC

Withal a meagre [*or* meager] man was Aaron Stark. Aaron Stark. Edwin Arlington Robinson. CP-RobiE

Withdrawal of the Fuel of Rapture, The. Emily Dickinson. SP-DickE

Withdrawn to a third your size, and frowning doubts. Angling. Robert Lowell. SP-LoweR

Wither'd with yeeres, and bed-rid *Mumma* lyes. Upon a Bleare-Ey'd Woman. Robert Herrick. CP-HerrR

Withered Leaf—seen on a Poet's Table, A. Jones Very. CP-VeryJ

Withered silence filled my chest of sorrow, A. Debt. Allen Tate. CP-TateA

Withered Tree, The. Jones Very. CP-VeryJ

Withering and keen the winter comes. January: A Winters Day. John Clare. SP-ClarJ *Fr.* Shepherd's [*or* Shepheards] Calendar, The.

Withering of the Boughs, The. William Butler Yeats. CP-YeatW

Within a churchyard, on a recent grave. Caged Goldfinch, The. Thomas Hardy. CP-HardT

Within,a coldly echoing floor:a terror. Death's Chimney. E. E. Cummings. CP-CummE

Within a copse, I met a shepherd-maid. Ballata: Concerning a Shepherd-maid. Guido Cavalcanti. CW-RossD, *tr. by* Dante Gabriel Rossetti

Within a London garret high. Garret, The. Paul Laurence Dunbar. CP-DunbP

Within a low wall falling away. Jewish Graveyards, Italy. Philip Levine. SP-LeviP

Within a Quad. John Updike. CP-UpdiJ

Within a shadowland of trees. Reflections in a Forest. W. H. Auden. CP-AudeW

Within a Temple of the Toes. Phantasy. George Meredith. CP-MerG1

Within her gilded cage confined. Contrast; the Parrot and the Wren, The. William Wordsworth. CP-WorW2

Within my breast I never thought it gain. Sir Thomas Wyatt. CP-WyatT

Within my four provisional walls. Camera Obscura. Hans Magnus Enzensberger. SP-EnzeH, *tr. by* Michael Hamburger

Within my Garden, rides a Bird. Emily Dickinson. CP-DickE

Within my house the gray ghost Peace has lain. Quiet House, The. Marya Alexandrovna Zaturenska. SP-ZatuM

Within my mind two spirits strayed. Wanderers, The. Walter De la Mare. CP-DeLaW

Within my reach! Emily Dickinson. CP-DickE

Within our happy Castle there dwelt One. Stanzas Written in My Pocket-Copy of Thomson's "Castle of Indolence." William Wordsworth. CP-WorW1; MW-WorW

Within Reason. Robert Graves. CP-GravR

Within that little Hive. Emily Dickinson. CP-DickE

Within— / The beaten pride. Uncle Tom ("Within— / The beaten pride"). Langston Hughes. CP-HughL; CP-HughL3

Within the circles of our lives. Song (4). Wendell Berry. CP-BerrW

Within the city of the burning cloud. Open the Gates. Stanley Kunitz. CP-KunSC

Within the coziest corner of my dreams. Laughter. James Whitcomb Riley. CP-RileJ

Within the Dream You Said. Philip Larkin. CP-LarkP

Within the Gate. John Greenleaf Whittier. CP-WhitJ

Within the gentle heart Love shelters him. Canzone: Of the Gentle Heart. Guido Guinicelli. CW-RossD, *tr. by* Dante Gabriel Rossetti

Within the grated dungeon of the eye. Among the Gods. Stanley Kunitz. CP-

KunSC

Within the House of the Soul the Passions go about. In the House of the Soul. Constantine P. Cavafy. CP-CavaC, *tr. by* Theoharis Constantine Theoharis

Within the limestone mantle of the shelf. Limits. Howard Nemerov. CP-NemeH

Within the mind strong fancies work. Pass of Kirkstone, The. William Wordsworth. CP-WorW2; MW-WorW

Within the Seasons. Peter Blue Cloud. SP-BlueP

Within the sitting-room, the company. Evening Company, The. James Whitcomb Riley. CP-RileJ *Fr.* Child-World, A.

Within the Veil. Christina Georgina Rossetti. CP-RosC3

Within the waxen lotus gleams the jewel. Elegy and Nocturne for Lora Baxter. Marya Alexandrovna Zaturenska. SP-ZatuM

Within the wires of the post, unloading the cans of garbage. Prisoners. Randall Jarrell. CP-JarrR

Within the yellow ring of flame. Burnt Dancer, The. T. S. Eliot. SP-ElioT

Within these circling Hollies Woodbine-clad. Angel Visitant, An. Samuel Taylor Coleridge. CP-ColeS

Within this grave lie. Epitaph: "Within this grave lie." Langston Hughes. CP-HughL1

Within this restless, hurried, modern world. My Voice. Oscar Wilde. CP-WildO

Within this sober frame expect. Upon Appleton House [To My Lord Fairfax]. Andrew Marvell. CP-MarvA

Within this tomb our handsome Braccio's laid. Michelangelo Buonarroti. CP-Miche, *tr. by* John Frederick Nims

Within those walls, and near that house of glass. Epigram on School Days. Robert Browning. CP-BroR2

Within thy Grave! Emily Dickinson. CP-DickE

Within, walls white as canvas stretched to stain. Streets of Pearl and Gold. Carolyn Kizer. CP-KizeC

Without. Gary Snyder. CP-SnydG

Without a Counterpart. Thom Gunn. CP-GunnT

Without a Mirror Now. Yannis Ritsos. SP-RitsY, *tr. by* Kimon Friar *and* Kostas Myrsiades

Without a raincoat. Saint Monday. Alan Dugan. CP-DugaA

Without a smile—Without a Throe. Emily Dickinson. CP-DickE

Without a stone to mark the spot. To Thyrza. Lord Byron. CP-Byron

Without an end the world had seemed. African's First Sight of the Ocean, The. Jones Very. CP-VeryJ

Without being less venerable. Rainer Maria Rilke. CP-RilkFr, *tr. by* A. Poulin, Jr. *Fr.* Orchards.

Without Benefit of Clergy. Rudyard Kipling. *Fr.* Life's Handicap.

Without Benefit of Declaration. Langston Hughes. CP-HughL; CP-HughL3

Without Ceremony. Thomas Hardy. CP-HardT

Without Commercials. Alice Walker. CP-WalkA

Without dressmakers to connect. Because of Clothes. Laura Riding Jackson. CP-RidiL

Without End. Adam Zagajewski. SP-ZagaA, *tr. by* Renata Gorczynski

Without excess (no galaxies). Civilities of Lamplight. Charles Tomlinson. CP-TomlC; SP-TomlC

Without expectation. Summer Oracle. Audre Lorde. SP-LordA

Without Form. Adam Zagajewski. SP-ZagaA, *tr. by* Renata Gorczynski, Benjamin Ivry *and* C. K. Williams

Without Her. Dante Gabriel Rossetti. CW-RossD *Fr.* House of Life, The.

Without him near, completing her, she feels. Theodore Weiss. SP-WeisT *Fr.* Storeroom, The.

Without me divided, fair ladies I ween. Charade: "Without me divided, fair ladies I ween." Charles John Austen. CP-AustJ

Without meaning to, they watch him play. Child, The. Randall Jarrell. CP-JarrR

Without millions of pennies and millions of men. Victory, The. Laura Riding Jackson. CP-RidiL

Without my melancholia I am lonely. After the Shrink. Alice Walker. CP-WalkA

Without, Not within Her. Thomas Hardy. CP-HardT

Without Notice Beforehand. Carl Sandburg. CP-SandC

Without other cost than breath. Quality of Heaven, The. William Carlos Williams. CP-WilW2

Without Recrimination. David Ignatow. SP-IgnaD

Without regard, without pity, without shame. Walls. Constantine P. Cavafy. CP-CavaC, *tr. by* Theoharis Constantine Theoharis

Without Regret. Eleanor Wilner. SP-WilnE

Without remorse, without regret, without fear, without envy. Flowing of the River, The. Marya Alexandrovna Zaturenska. SP-ZatuM

Without saddle, without stirrup. Sweetheart of the Csikos, The. Johann N. Vogl. CP-MerG2

Without self-mutilation there can be no withdrawing from our fellows. George Oppen. CP-OppGN

Without sexual attraction, there is. David Ignatow. SP-IgnaD

Without shedding of blood there is no remission of sin. Shedding of Blood. D. H. Lawrence. CP-LawrD

Without the Cane and the Derby. Carl Sandburg. CP-SandC

Without the grand old British Museum. Serena I. Samuel Beckett. CP-BeckS

Without the mercy of / your eyes your. E. E. Cummings. CP-CummE

Without the red splashed through the yellow. Arriving Uninvited. Clarence Major. SP-MajoC

Without the Season of Structure, Modes Lie Like Gods Thrown Down, Helpless Before the Newness Upsets Genesis When the Young Men Pour In. Charles Olson. CP-OlsoC

Without the wax, what can one do? Street Songs. Stéphane Mallarmé. CP-MallS

Without the wax, what can one do? Shoemaker, The. Stéphane Mallarmé. CP-MallS *Fr.* Street Songs.

Without the wax, what can one do? Shoemaker, The. Stéphane Mallarmé. CP-MallS, *tr. by* Henry Weinfield

Without this—there is nought. Emily Dickinson. CP-DickE

Witley Court. James Schuyler. CP-SchuJ

Witness. Amy Clampitt. CP-ClamA

Witness. Donald Davie. CP-DaviDC

Witness. Denise Levertov. SP-LeveDS

Witness. William Stafford. SP-StafWW

Witness all: that unrepenting. Desecraters, The. G. K. Chesterton. CP-ChesG

Witness now this trust! the rain. Possessions. Hart Crane. CP-CranH

Witness, the Darling, The. Jelaluddin Rumi. SP-Rumi, *tr. by* Coleman Barks

Witness thou / The dear companion of my lonely walk. Fragment: "Witness thou / The dear companion of my lonely walk." William Wordsworth. CP-WorW1

Witness, would you. Keller Gegen Dom. William Carlos Williams. CP-WilW1

Witnesses. W. S. Merwin. SP-MerwW

Witnesses, The. W. H. Auden. CP-AudeW

Witnesses, The. Charles Tomlinson. CP-TomlC

Witnesses Everywhere. Yannis Ritsos. SP-RitsY, *tr. by* Kimon Friar *and* Kostas Myrsiades

Wits, The; A Session[s] of the Poets. Sir John Suckling. CP-SuckJ

Wives; A Hymn of Hate. Dorothy Parker. CP-ParkD

Wives in the Sere. Thomas Hardy. CP-HardT

Wives of the black-sailed seminarians, The. 20th Street Spring. Grace Paley. CP-PalGC

Wives on day-coaches traveling with a baby. Good-bye, Wendover; Good-bye, Mountain Home. Randall Jarrell. CP-JarrR

Wizard in the Street, The. Nicholas Vachel Lindsay. CP-LindV

Wizard Wind, The. Nicholas Vachel Lindsay. CP-LindV

Wm. Brazier. Robert Graves. CP-GravR

Wm. Yates, colored. Sick African. William Carlos Williams. CP-WilW1

Wo is me woe's me when I think. Michelangelo Buonarroti. CP-EmerR

Wobbly Top, A. A. K. Ramanujan. CP-RamaA

Wo'd I see Lawn, clear as the Heaven, and thin? Lawne, The. Robert Herrick. CP-HerrR

Wo'd I wooe, and wo'd I winne. To Biancha, to Blesse Him. Robert Herrick. CP-HerrR

Wo'd ye oyle of Blossoms get? Upon Julia's Sweat. Robert Herrick. CP-HerrR

Wodwo. Ted Hughes. SP-HughTN

Woe. D. H. Lawrence. CP-LawrD

Woe! Czeslaw Milosz. CP-MiloCN, *tr. by* Robert Hass

Woe alas my guilty hand. William Blake. *See* Little Fly

Woe for the day; Regina's pride. Emily Jane Brontë. CP-BronE

Woe for the young who say that life is long. Whole Head Is Sick, and the Whole Heart Faint, The. Christina Georgina Rossetti. CP-RosC3

Woe, he went galloping into the war. Rosny. Robert Browning. CP-BroR2

Woe is me! an old man said. Last *Complaint*, The. Christina Georgina Rossetti. CP-RosC3

Woe the earth is tiny in the brochures. Purgatorio. Hans Magnus Enzensberger. SP-EnzeH, *tr. by* Michael Hamburger

Woe unto Thee! Donald Davie. CP-DaviDC

Woe unto them that keep a God like a silk hat, that believe not in God, but in a God. Some Prophecies. G. K. Chesterton. CP-ChesG

Woe, woe to them, who (by a ball of strife). To the King and Queen[e], upon Their Unhappy Distances. Robert Herrick. CP-HerrR

Woebegone. Yusef Komunyakaa. CP-KomuY

Wokanmagulli. Yusef Komunyakaa. CP-KomuY

Woke up early this morning and from my bed. Grief. Raymond Carver. CP-CarvR

Woke up feeling anxious and bone-lonely. White Field, The. Raymond Carver. CP-CarvR

Woke up this morning. Christopher Logue. SP-LoguC

Woke up this morning with. Rain. Raymond Carver. CP-CarvR

Woken, I lay in the arms of my own warmth and listened. First Things First. W. H. Auden. CP-AudeW

Wolf. Peter Blue Cloud. SP-BlueP

Wolf, A. Paul Éluard. CP-WilW2

Wolf and the Lamb Shall Feed Together, The. Jones Very. CP-VeryJ

"Wolf!" cried my cunning heart. True Encounter, The. Edna St. Vincent Millay. CP-MillE

Wolf-cub at even lay hid in the corn, The. Rudyard Kipling. CP-KiplR *Fr.* Light That Failed, The.

Wolf Knife. Donald Hall. CP-HallD

Wolf Moon. Mary Oliver. SP-OlivM

Wolf of winter, The. Kenneth Patchen. CP-PatcK

Wolf, why heeds he not the sportive lamb, The. Wolf and the Lamb Shall Feed Together, The. Jones Very. CP-VeryJ

Wolf with its belly stitched full of big pebbles, The. February. Ted Hughes. SP-HughTN

Wolfe demanded during dying. Emily Dickinson. CP-DickE

Wolfe Tone. Seamus Heaney. SP-HeanSO

Wolf's cousin, The. Night Patrol. Josephine Jacobsen. CP-JacoJ

Wolf's Hour. Tennessee Williams. CP-WillT

Wolfsbeau. Paul Celan. SP-CelaP, *tr. by* John Felstiner

Wolves. Louis MacNeice. CP-MacNL

Wolves, The. Allen Tate. CP-TateA

Wolves in the Zoo. Howard Nemerov. CP-NemeH

Woman. Randall Jarrell. CP-JarrR

Woman, A. Robert Pinsky. CP-PinsR

Woman, A. John Greenleaf Whittier. CP-WhitJ

Woman, The. Robert Creeley. CP-CreeR

Woman, The. Denise Levertov. SP-LeveDL; SP-LeveDS

Woman Alone, A. Denise Levertov. SP-LeveDL; SP-LeveDS

Woman and child running / in a field A man planted. Mother-Right. Adrienne Rich. SP-RicA2

Woman and Emblems. Muriel Rukeyser. CP-RukeM

Woman and the Wife, The. Edwin Arlington Robinson. CP-RobiE

Woman and Tree. Robert Graves. CP-GravR

Woman are books in which we often spy. Sarcasm against the Ladies in a Newspaper, A; An Impromptu Answer. Annis Boudinot Stockton. CP-StocA

Woman as Market. Muriel Rukeyser. CP-RukeM

Woman asked us in for pie, The. Started. Next Door. Raymond Carver. CP-CarvR

Woman asks me. Guido Cavalcanti. CP-CavaG, *tr. by* Marc Cirigliano

Woman at Her Mirror. Rainer Maria Rilke. CP-RilkFr, *tr. by* A. Poulin, Jr.

Woman at the checkstand, The. How Much Can It Hurt? Philip Levine. SP-LeviP

Woman at the Piano. Marya Alexandrovna Zaturenska. SP-ZatuM

Woman at the Washington Zoo, The. Randall Jarrell. CP-JarrR

Woman Bathing. Raymond Carver. CP-CarvR

Woman Bewildered, The. Robert Bly. SP-BlyR

Woman, caught in a homeland-trap of the Chosen People: you, A. National Thoughts. Yehuda Amichai. SP-AmicY, *tr. by* Stephen Mitchell

Woman dancing with hair. Window of the Woman Burning, The. Marge Piercy. SP-PierM

Woman Dead in Her Forties, A. Adrienne Rich. SP-RicA2

Woman dealing with matters of the past, A. Voyeur, The. Yehuda Amichai. SP-AmicYL, *tr. by* Benjamin Harshav *and* Barbara Harshav

Woman, destitute, and taking cover, A. Oldest Desire, The. Eleanor Wilner. SP-WilnE

Woman dreamed, A. Primitive. George Oppen. CP-OppGN

Woman Driving, A. Thomas Hardy. CP-HardT

Woman-Enough. Tess Gallagher. SP-GallT

Woman every night, A. Universe-Solitude. Paul Éluard. CP-BeckS

Woman! experience might have told me. To Woman. Lord Byron. CP-Byron

Woman exposed as rock, A. Aphrodite. Louise Glück. SP-GlucL

Woman fears for man, he goes. Abel's Bride. Denise Levertov. SP-LeveDP

Woman for whom the great gods might strive! A. Chosen, The. Thomas Hardy. CP-HardT

Woman from the River. W. S. Merwin. SP-MerwW

Woman had done hin wrong, The. Without the Cane and the Derby. Carl Sandburg. CP-SandC

Woman has given me strength and affluence, A. Manifesto. D. H. Lawrence. CP-LawrD

Woman Homer Sung, A. William Butler Yeats. CP-YeatW

Woman, I Got the Blues. Yusef Komunyakaa. CP-KomuY

Woman I have never seen before, A. Transit. Richard Wilbur. CP-WilbR

Woman I Met, The. Thomas Hardy. CP-HardT

Woman, I return to you. Naming the Beast. Sam Hamill. SP-HamiS

Woman in a psychiatric ward, A. Pulse, The. Arthur Sze. SP-SzeA

Woman in Front of a Bank, A. William Carlos Williams. CP-WilW2

Woman in middle life. Lorine Niedecker. CP-NiedL

Woman in Sunshine, The. Wallace Stevens. CP-StevW; CP-StevWP

Woman in the Ordinary, The. Marge Piercy. SP-PierM

Woman in the Room, The. Miller Williams. CP-WillM

Woman in the Rye, The. Thomas Hardy. CP-HardT

Woman in the shape of a monster, A. Planetarium. Adrienne Rich. CP-RicAE; SP-RicA1; SP-RicA2

Woman in the spiked device, The. Women's Issue, A. Margaret Atwood. SP-AtwM2

Woman invented fire and called it, A. Grace Paley. CP-PalGC

Woman Is Not, A. Woman Is Not a Potted Plant, A. Alice Walker. CP-WalkA

Woman is not a pear tree, A. Right to Life. Marge Piercy. SP-PierM

Woman Is Not a Potted Plant, A. Alice Walker. CP-WalkA

Woman is perfected, The. Edge. Sylvia Plath. CP-PlatS

Woman is reading a poem on the street, A. Hug, The. Tess Gallagher. SP-GallT

Woman is sitting in a doorway, A. First. Clarence Major. SP-MajoC

Woman Looking at a Vase of Flowers. Wallace Stevens. CP-StevW; CP-StevWP

Woman Makes Peace with Her Faulty Heart, The. Margaret Atwood. SP-AtwM2

Woman Mc. Maya Angelou. SP AngeM

Woman Meets an Old Lover, A. Denise Levertov. SP-LeveDL

"Woman," men say of him, and women, "Man." To Be Dead. Randall Jarrell. CP-JarrR

Woman Mourned by Daughters, A. Adrienne Rich. CP-RicAE; SP-RicA2

Woman much missed, how you call to me, call to me. Voice, The. Thomas Hardy. CP-HardT

Woman named Tomorrow, The. Four Preludes on Playthings of the Wind. Carl Sandburg. CP-SandC

Woman neither young nor old, she moves, A. My Mother's Life. William Meredith. SP-MereW

"Woman never agreed to it! A" said my knowing friend to me. Elopement, The. Thomas Hardy. CP-HardT

Woman / of bronze / unhappy, A. E. E. Cummings. CP-CummE.

Woman of Greece. Robert Graves. CP-GravR

Woman of the house, The. Leaving an Island. Paul Muldoon. CP-MuldP

Woman of the more primitive tribes, A. Food. Josephine Jacobsen. CP-JacoJ

Woman on the fourth floor said You slut! don't you knock on my, The. On the Fourth Floor. Grace Paley. CP-PalGC

Woman on the Stair, The. Archibald MacLeish. CP-MacLA

Woman Poet and Man Poet. Robert Graves. CP-GravR

Woman power / is / Black power. NOW. Audre Lorde. SP-LordA

Woman Pulls the Wires. Ogden Nash. CP-NashO

Woman, reviling term. Rhythms of Love. Laura Riding Jackson. CP-RidiL

Woman riding the two mares of her thighs, Steamboat Whistle, The. Archibald MacLeish. CP-MacLA

Woman, said Diane, speaking wisely, A. George Oppen. CP-OppGN

Woman sails, man must row. Sail and Oar. Robert Graves. CP-GravR

Woman Says, The. Grace Paley. CP-PalGC

Woman says read me, The. Woman Says, The. Grace Paley. CP-PalGC

Woman scaly & a Man all Hairy, A. William Blake. CP-BlakW

Woman Selling Aromatic Herbs, The. Stéphane Mallarmé. CP-MallS *Fr.* Street Songs.

Woman Selling Aromatic Herbs, The. Stéphane Mallarmé. CP-MallS, *tr. by* Henry Weinfield

Woman shakes a blanket from the window, The. Forged Passport. Yannis Ritsos. SP-RitsY, *tr. by* Kimon Friar

Woman singeth at her spinning-wheel, The. Work and Contemplation. Elizabeth Barrett Browning. CP-BroEB

Woman Sings a Song for a Soldier Come Home, A. Wallace Stevens. CP-StevW; CP-StevWP

Woman sinks to sink it in the sea, A. Heart Believes with Blows. Olga Broumas. SP-BrouO

Woman sits on the one rock, A. At Pointe de Rompe Talon. Clarence Major. SP-MajoC

Woman Skating. Margaret Atwood. SP-AtwM1

Woman smells like fresh-plowed ground, A. Could She See the Whole Real World with Her Ghost Breast Eyes Shut under a Blouse Lid? Gary Snyder. CP-SnydG

Woman standing in the doorway, A. Evening Song. Langston Hughes. CP-HughL; CP-HughL3

Woman stepped out of no, A. House of Snow, A. Yusef Komunyakaa. CP-KomuY

Woman stood before the table, The. Her sad hands. Miniature. Yannis Ritsos. SP-RitsY, *tr. by* Kimon Friar

Woman that disappeared beyond, The. Yehuda Amichai. SP-AmicYL *Fr.* Poems on the Shore of Caesarea.

Woman That Had More Babies than That, The. Wallace Stevens. CP-StevWP

Woman, that you know of death is a blessing. Blessing. David Ignatow. SP-IgnaD

Woman, then, while writhing on the bed, The. Metamorphoses of the Vampire. Charles Baudelaire. CP-BaudC, *tr. by* Walter Martin

Woman Thing, The. Audre Lorde. SP-LordA

Woman to the man, The. Welcome from War. Muriel Rukeyser. CP-RukeM

Woman told a man, A. Up Your Yellow River. Charles Bukowski. SP-BukC1

Woman Unconscious, A. Ted Hughes. SP-HughTN

Woman unlike myself is running, A. My Dream About Time. Lucille Clifton. SP-ClifL

Woman Waiting. Mona Van Duyn. SP-VanDM

Woman Waits for Me, A. Walt Whitman. CP-WhitW

Woman waking behind grimed blinds slatted across a courtyard, A. Adrienne Rich. SP-RicA1 *Fr.* Shooting Script.

Woman Walking. William Carlos Williams. CP-WilW1

Woman walks by and I look at her and know that her existence is, A. Notations from a Muddled Indolence. Charles Bukowski. SP-BukC2

Woman wants monogamy. General Review of the Sex Situation. Dorothy Parker. CP-ParkD

Woman was made for man's delight. Helpmeet For Him, A. Christina Georgina Rossetti. CP-RosC2

Woman was playing, A. At the Piano. Thomas Hardy. CP-HardT

Woman was still lying in bed, The. He. Exhibits. Yannis Ritsos. SP-RitsY, *tr. by* Kostas Myrsiades

Woman! When I Behold Thee Flippant, Vain. John Keats. CP-KeatJ

Woman Who Blamed Life on a Spaniard, The. Wallace Stevens. CP-StevWP

Woman Who Could Not Live With Her Faulty Heart, The. Margaret Atwood. SP-AtwM2

Woman who has grown old, The. Crows, The. Louise Bogan. CP-BogaL

Woman Who Laughed on Calvary. Heather McHugh. SP-McHuH

Woman who lived, A. Moon, The. Donald Hall. CP-HallD

Woman who looks like my mother sees a man who looks like me, A. Four Resurrections in the Valley of the Ghosts. Yehuda Amichai. SP-AmicYL, *tr. by* Benjamin Harshav *and* Barbara Harshav

Woman / who loves a woman, A. Rapunzel. Anne Sexton. CP-SextA; SP-SextA

Woman Who Raised Goats, The. Tess Gallagher. SP-GallT

Woman Who Went East, The. Thomas Hardy. CP-HardT

Woman who writes feels too much, A. Black Art, The. Anne Sexton. CP-SextA; SP-SextA

Woman whose existence is indifferent to yours, A. Emblem. Olga Broumas. SP-BrouO

Woman whose hut was mumbled by termites, The. Life in the Forest. Denise Levertov. SP-LeveDL

Woman with a Past. Carl Sandburg. CP-SandC

Woman with Child. Olga Broumas. SP-BrouO

Woman with Dog. Miller Williams. CP-WillM

Woman with Girdle. Anne Sexton. CP-SextA

Woman with her forests, moons, flowers, waters. At Best, Poets. Robert Graves. CP-GravR

Woman with one glass eye, The. Orbit. Heather McHugh. SP-McHuH

Woman with Umbrella. Lorine Niedecker. CP-NiedL

Woman Work. Maya Angelou. SP-AngeM

Womanhood, The. Gwendolyn Brooks. SP-BrooG

Womanly Noblesse. Geoffrey Chaucer. CP-ChauG

Woman's beauty, new, A. Michelangelo Buonarroti. CP-Miche. *tr. by* John Frederick Nims

Woman's breasts, A. St. Valentine. William Carlos Williams. CP-WilW2

Woman's Constancy. John Donne. CP-DonnJ; MW-DonnJ

Woman's Constancy. Sir John Suckling. CP-SuckJ

Woman's Fancy, A. Thomas Hardy. CP-HardT

Woman's figure, on a ground of night, A. Suspense. James Whitcomb Riley. CP-RileJ

Woman's friendship! God whom I trust in, A. Satirical Shrub, A. Ben Jonson. CP-JonsB

Woman's Last Word, A. Robert Browning. CP-BroR1

Woman's Nipples Is the Rose of the World, A. Charles Olson. CP-OlsoC

Woman's sho' a cur'ous critter. Turning of the Babies in the Bed, The. Paul Laurence Dunbar. CP-DunbP

Woman's Shortcomings, A. Elizabeth Barrett Browning. CP-BroEB

Woman's Trust, A. Thomas Hardy. CP-HardT

Womb / Rattles its pod, the moon, The. Childless Woman. Sylvia Plath. CP-PlatS

Wombat, The. Ogden Nash. CP-NashO

Wombwell on Strike. Donald Davie. CP-DaviDC

Women. Louise Bogan. CP-BogaL

Women. Robert Creeley. SP-CreeR

Women. Adrienne Rich. CP-RicAE; SP-RicA2

Women, The. Robert Creeley. CP-CreeR

Women; A Hate Song. Dorothy Parker. CP-ParkD

Women, although they ne're so goodly make it. Deniall in Women No Disheartning to Men. Robert Herrick. CP-HerrR

Women and Masks. Gábor Devecseri. CP-GravR

Women and Roses. Robert Browning. CP-BroR1

Women and War. Donald Davie. CP-DaviDC

Women are dancing around a fire. Message Hidden in an Empty Wine Bottle that I Threw into a Gully of Maple Trees One Night at an Indecent Hour, A. James Wright. CP-WrigJ

Women are the makers of the men, The. Fable. Heather McHugh. SP-McHuH

Women are very distant. Their bedsheets smell of good-night. Yannis Ritsos. SP-RitsY, *tr. by* Kimon Friar

Women at Point Sur, The. Robinson Jeffers. CP-JefR1

Women ben full of ragerie. Imitation of Chaucer. Alexander Pope. CP-PopeA

Women, clients, and slaves wept, The. Autumn at Baiae: For Cavafy. Alan Dugan. CP-DugaA

Women don't know how to love. Me. Charles Bukowski. SP-BukC1

Women don't want wistful. Women Want Fighters for Their Lovers. D. H. Lawrence. CP-LawrD

Women from Algiers sit. Divine Law: A Blue Beach Sermon. Clarence Major. SP-MajoC

Women had been sent away so there would be no scenes, The. Scenes from a Death. Heather McHugh. SP-McHuH

Women have loved before as I love now. Edna St. Vincent Millay. CP-MillE

Women have no wilderness in them. Women. Louise Bogan. CP-BogaL

Women in anger, it seems, become theatrical. Sonnet: "Women in anger, it seems, become theatrical." Hayden Carruth. CP-CarHS *Fr.* Sonnets.

Women in their marble glory still, The. Klimt and Schiele Confront the Cunt. John Updike. CP-UpdiJ

Women leaving an odor behind them. Parenthesis. Federico García Lorca. CP-GarcF, *tr. by* Jerome Rothenberg *Fr.* In the Garden of the Lunar Grapefruits.

Women like new brooms. Hayden Carruth. CP-CarHS *Fr.* Clay Hill Anthology, The.

Women mould a core of clay and straw, The. Difference, The. A. K. Ramanujan. CP-RamaA

Women mourners were giving their sister to fire. On Parting with My Wife, Janina. Czeslaw Milosz. CP-MiloC; CP-MiloCN, *tr. by* Robert Hass

"Women of Color" Have Rarely Had the Opportunity to Write about Their Love Affairs. Alice Walker. CP-WalkA

Women of night life amid the lights. It Is Much. Carl Sandburg. CP-SandC

Women of Samos are lost in love for me. Ibycus of Samos. Robert Graves. CP-GravR

Women of the city where I was forgotten, The. François Villon Forgotten. Carl Sandburg. CP-SandC

Women of Trachis. Sophocles.

  "PHOEBUS, Phoebus, ere thou slay." SP-PounE, *tr. by* Ezra Pound

Women on a Bus. Randall Jarrell. CP-JarrR

Women sit or move to and fro, some old, some young. Beautiful Women. Walt Whitman. CP-WhitW

Women Talking. Eleanor Wilner. SP-WilnE

Women Uselesse. Robert Herrick. CP-HerrR

Women Want Fighters for Their Lovers. D. H. Lawrence. CP-LawrD

Women Washing Their Hair. Carl Sandburg. CP-SandC

Women were singing by the spiked wall, The. Ode to the Most Holy Sacrament of the Altar. Federico García Lorca. CP-GarcF, *tr. by* Greg Simon *and* Steven F. White

Women / who build nations. Seventh Sign, The. Audre Lorde. SP-LordA

Women who were turned inside-out. Love. Gary Snyder. CP-SnydG

Women with hats like the rear ends of pink ducks. To a Waterfowl. Donald Hall. CP-HallD

Women You Are Accustomed To, The. Lucille Clifton. SP-ClifL

Women your age have decided. Suzy. William Carlos Williams. CP-WilW2

Women's Issue, A. Margaret Atwood. SP-AtwM2

Women's Laughter. Marge Piercy. SP-PierM

Women's Prison, The: El Salvador / The Ballad of Visiting Day. Grace Paley. CP-PalGC

Women's Tug of War at Lough Arrow. Tess Gallagher. SP-GallT

Wonder. Maya Angelou. SP-AngeM

Wonder. Langston Hughes. CP-HughL; CP-HughL3

Wonder. Yannis Ritsos. SP-RitsY, *tr. by* Minas Savvas

Wonder / And pain. Juliet. Langston Hughes. CP-HughL

Wonder as of old things. Uplands in May. Carl Sandburg. CP-SandC

WONDER BAR / WISHING WELL. Neon Signs. Langston Hughes. CP-HughL; CP-HughL3

Wonder if / you're gross. Miss. A. R. Ammons. CP-AmmoA

Wonder is mine as she counts, The. Old. David Ignatow. SP-IgnaD

Wonder—is not precisely Knowing. Emily Dickinson. CP-DickE

Wonder not if I stay not here. To Master Davenant for Absence. Sir John Suckling. CP-SuckJ

Wonder not much, if thus amaz'd I look. Upon the First Sight of My Lady Seymour. Sir John Suckling. CP-SuckJ

Wonder not, though I am blind. To One Who, When I Praised My Mistress' Beauty, Said I Was Blind. Thomas Carew. CP-CareT

Wonder of cherries, The. About Money. David Ignatow. SP-IgnaD

Wonder of light is your familiar tale, The. Sonnet to Beauty. Allen Tate. CP-TateA

Wonder / once / whence / *mulier*. Translation, The. Louis Zukofsky. CP-ZukLS

"Wonder whether you or they hold the rights" and would you. Life of Literature, The. Philip Whalen. SP-WhalP

Wonderful Baker, The. Yehuda Amichai. SP-AmicYL, *tr. by* Benjamin Harshav *and* Barbara Harshav

Wonderful bears that walked my room all night. Bears. Adrienne Rich. CP-RicAE; SP-RicA2

Wonderful creatures! And Thus with All Praise. William Carlos Williams. CP-WilW1

Wonderful freshness, air, A. Light from Canada. James Schuyler. CP-SchuJ

Wonderful Man, Part the Third. *Unknown, sometimes at. to* Thomas Sheridan. CP-SherT

Wonderful Musician, The. Anne Sexton. CP-SextA

Wonderful Spiritual Women. D. H. Lawrence. CP-LawrD

Wonderful thoughtful women who make such good companions to a man, The. Wonderful Spiritual Women. D. H. Lawrence. CP-LawrD

Wonderful time—the War, A. Green Memory. Langston Hughes. CP-HughL; CP-HughL3

Wonderful workings of the world: wonderful, The. Cut the Grass. A. R. Ammons. CP-AmmoA

Wonderful World. James Schuyler. CP-SchuJ

Wondering long, how I could harmless see. Love's Burning-Glass. Sir John Suckling. CP-SuckJ

Wondering what to take seriously. East Sixty-seventh Street. John Ciardi. CP-CiarJ

Wonders are many and none is more wonderful than man. Glengormley. Derek Mahon. CP-MahoD

Wondrous the Gods, more wondrous are the Men. Compliment to the Ladies, A. William Blake. CP-BlakW

Wong, goes the bell in the head of the maid. Gifts of Percussion. Andrei Codrescu. SP-CodrA

Won't It Be Strange—? D. H. Lawrence. CP-LawrD

Won't our life be a tunnel. Pablo Neruda. SP-NeruP *Fr.* Question Book.

Woo me now & you'll win me. Song: "Woo me now & you'll win me." George Meredith. CP-MerG2

Wood, A. W. S. Merwin. SP-MerwW

Wood, A. Richard Wilbur. CP-WilbR

Wood, The. Paul Muldoon. CP-MuldP

Wood, an Insect. Jonathan Swift. CP-SwifJ

Wood-Cutter, The. G. K. Chesterton. CP-ChesG

Wood Dove at Sandy Spring, The. Archibald MacLeish. CP-MacLA

Wood-doves are singing along the Perkiomen, The. Thinking of a Relation between the Images of Metaphors. Wallace Stevens. CP-StevW; CP-StevWP

Wood Fire, The. Thomas Hardy. CP-HardT

Wood Giant, The. John Greenleaf Whittier. CP-WhitJ

Wood lark whistles. Hogs carry straw. Under the Hanger. James Schuyler. CP-SchuJ

Wood-Pile, The. Robert Frost. CP-FrosR

Wood Road, The. Edna St. Vincent Millay. CP-MillE

Wood-sorrel lady's-sorrel 3-hearts tow ox. Oxalis. Louis Zukofsky. CP-ZukLS

Wood that can learn is no good for a bow. Sparkle Depends on Flaws in the Diamond, The. William Stafford. SP-StafWW

Wood was rather old and dark, The. Little Boy Lost. Stevie Smith. CP-SmitS

Wood Weasel, The. Marianne Craig Moore. CP-MoorM

Wood Whittler, The. Arthur Sze. SP-SzeA

Woodcarver, The. Chuang Tzu. CP-MertT

Woodchucks. Maxine W. Kumin. SP-KumiM

Woodcut. Thomas McGrath. SP-McGrT

Woodcut, A. Denise Levertov. SP-LeveDS

Woodcutter. Federico García Lorca. CP-GarcF, *tr. by* Jerome Rothenberg *Fr.* Secrets.

Woodcutter. Song of the Barren Orange Tree. Federico García Lorca. SP-GarcF, *tr. by* W. S. Merwin

Woodcutter. / Cut down my shadow. Song of the Dead Orange Tree. Federico García Lorca. CP-GarcF, *tr. by* Alan S. Trueblood *Fr.* Songs to End With.

Woodcutting on Lost Mountain. Tess Gallagher. SP-GallT

Wooden Buildings. John Ashbery. SP-AshbJ

Wooden Darning Egg, A. John Updike. CP-UpdiJ

Wooden Heart. Primo Levi. CP-LeviP, *tr. by* Ruth Feldman

Wooden Horses. Federico García Lorca. CP-GarcF, *tr. by* Jerome Rothenberg *Fr.* Fairs.

Wooden Mirror, The. John Logan. CP-LogaJ

Wooden Spring. Muriel Rukeyser. CP-RukeM

Woodland Peace. George Meredith. CP-MerG1

Woodland Song. Dorothy Parker. CP-ParkD

Woodlark, The. Gerard Manley Hopkins. CP-HopkG

Woodlot, The. Amy Clampitt. CP-ClamA

Woodman and Echo. George Meredith. CP-MerG1

Woodman and the Nightingale, The. Percy Bysshe Shelley. CP-ShelP

Woodman whose rough heart was out of tune, A. Woodman and the Nightingale, The. Percy Bysshe Shelley. CP-ShelP

Woodnotes I ("For this present, hard"). Ralph Waldo Emerson. CP-EmerR

Woodnotes II ("As sunbeams stream through liberal space"). Ralph Waldo Emerson. CP-EmerR

Woodpecker, The. William Carlos Williams. CP-WilW2

Woodpecker in his red cap suddenly brought back, A. Stary Sacz. Adam Zagajewski. SP-ZagaA, *tr. by* Clare Cavanagh

Woodpigeons at Raheny. Donald Davie. CP-DaviDC

Woodrow Wilson. Robinson Jeffers. CP-JefR1

Woods. Wendell Berry. CP-BerrW

Woods. Ralph Waldo Emerson. CP-EmerR

Woods. Louis MacNeice. CP-MacNL

Woods, The. Josephine Jacobsen. CP-JacoJ

Woods, The. Derek Mahon. CP-MahoD

Woods and springs make me smile. Shih-te. CP-ColdM, *tr. by* Red Pine

Woods are bronzed with autumn, The. Autumn, The. G. K. Chesterton. CP-ChesG

Woods are dark, tempt not its ways!, The. Boy's Death, The. Ludwig Uhland CP-MerG2

Woods are lapped in snow, The. Snowy Woods, The. Marya Alexandrovna Zaturenska. SP-ZatuM

Woods are preparing to wait out winter, The. View, The. Charles Tomlinson. CP-TomlC

"Woods" at Midnight, The. Andrei Codrescu. SP-CodrA

Woods at Night, The. May Swenson. SP-SwenM

Woods decay, the woods decay and fall, The. Tithonus. Alfred Tennyson. CP-TennA

Woods in Spring. Gerard Manley Hopkins. CP-HopkG

Woods is shining this morning, The. Grace. Wendell Berry. CP-BerrW

Woods of Arcady are dead, The. Song of the Happy Shepherd, The. William Butler Yeats. CP-YeatW

Woods of Westermain, The. George Meredith. CP-MerG1

Woods were still. No breath of air, The. Dreamer, The. Walter De la Mare. CP-DeLaW

Woods, you need not frown on me. Emily Jane Brontë. CP-BronE

Woodsmen blow their horns, and close the day, The. Fair in the Woods, The. Thom Gunn. CP-GunnT

Woodsmoke and a distant loudspeaker. Yaddo: The Grand Manor. Sylvia Plath. CP-PlatS

Woodsmoke at 70. Hayden Carruth. CP-CarHS

Woodspurge, The. Dante Gabriel Rossetti. CW-RossD

Woodsroad, The. A. R. Ammons. CP-AmmoA

Woodthrush, The. William Carlos Williams. CP-WilW2

Woodwax. The. Jones Very. CP-VeryJ

Woodwax in Bloom, The. Jones Very. CP-VeryJ

Woodwind whistles down the shore, The. September in Gt. Yarmouth. Derek Mahon. CP-MahoD

Wooing, A. Langston Hughes. CP-HughL; CP-HughL1

Wooing, The. Paul Laurence Dunbar. CP-DunbP

Wool white horses and their heads sag and roll. Sky Talk. Carl Sandburg. CP-SandC

Woolen socks, woolen socks! Shinking Song. Ogden Nash. CP-NashO

Woolly-cheeked wink flasher. Gray, Intermittently Blue, Eyed Hero. James Schuyler. CP-SchuJ

Woolly dog, A. From the Italian. Stevie Smith. CP-SmitS

Woolner, to-night it snows for the first time. To Thomas Woolner. Dante Gabriel Rossetti. CW-RossD

Woolworth's. Donald Hall. CP-HallD

Woolworth's, 1954. Raymond Carver. CP-CarvR

Worcestershire. Donald Davie. CP-DaviDC

Word. Stephen Spender. CP-SpenS

Word, A. G. K. Chesterton. CP-ChesG

Word, A. Jones Very. CP-VeryJ

Word, The. Robert Graves. CP-GravR

Word, The. Stevie Smith. CP-SmitS

Word, The. John Greenleaf Whittier. CP-WhitJ

Word, The ("Voice that speaks when thou art in thy tomb, The"). Jones Very. CP-VeryJ

Word, The ("Word! it cannot fail; it ever speaks, The"). Jones Very. CP-VeryJ

Word, The ("Word where is it? hath it voice, The"). Jones Very. CP-VeryJ

Word—a Responsory, The. Thomas Merton. CP-MertT

Word about going-to-the-depths, The. Paul Celan. SP-CelaP, *tr. by* John Felstiner

Word about Winter, A. Ogden Nash. CP-NashO

Word and Silence. Constantine P. Cavafy. CP-CavaC, *tr. by* Theoharis Constantine Theoharis

Word Basket Woman. Gary Snyder. CP-SnydG

Word bites like a fish, The. Word. Stephen Spender. CP-SpenS

Word came down to Dives in Torment where he lay, The. Peace of Dives, The. Rudyard Kipling. CP-KiplR

Word came forth in Galilee, a word like to a star, A. Word, A. G. K. Chesterton. CP-ChesG

Word, defining, muzzles, The; the drawn line. Poems, Potatoes. Sylvia Plath. CP-PlatS

Word does not share, The. Tree, The. Gregory Orr. SP-OrrG

Word "dream" is technical and means nothing, The. View from an Apartment. Michael Palmer. SP-PalmM

Word dropped careless on a Page, A. Emily Dickinson. CP-DickE

Word for Spring, A. Sam Hamill. SP-HamiS

Word for the Dumb, A. Christina Georgina Rossetti. CP-RosC3

Word for the Hour, A. John Greenleaf Whittier. CP-WhitJ

Word for Today is "panoptic," which the goddamn, The. Sonnet: "Word for Today is 'panoptic,' which the goddamn, The." Hayden Carruth. CP-CarHS *Fr.* Sonnets.

Word forms / on the left: you must, The. A B Cs. Charles Olson. CP-OlsoC

Word from the Cannon's Mouth, A. George Meredith. CP-MerG2

Word goes forth! I see its conquering way, The. White Horse, The. Jones Very. CP-VeryJ

Word had me, The. Yannis Ritsos. SP-RitsY *Fr.* Paper Poems 2.

Word has been abroad, is back, with a tanned look, The. Annunciations. Geoffrey Hill. CP-HillG

Word in Edgeways, A. Charles Tomlinson. CP-TomlC

Word in the bread feeds me, The. Rune. Muriel Rukeyser. CP-RukeM

Word in the hand is the sound in the eye is the sight in the, The. Writing as Writing. Robert Duncan. SP-DuncR

Word is, The. Motion. A. R. Ammons. CP-AmmoA

Word is coming up on the screen, give me a moment, A. Michael Palmer. SP-PalmM

Word is dead, A. Emily Dickinson. CP-DickE

Word is dead, A. Word is dead, A. Emily Dickinson. CP-DickE

Word is unspoken, The. Word, The. Robert Graves. CP-GravR

Word is writ that he who runs may read, The. Booker T. Washington. Paul Laurence Dunbar. CP-DunbP

Word! it cannot fail; it ever speaks, The. Word, The ("Word! it cannot fail; it ever speaks, The"). Jones Very. CP-VeryJ

Word *lassitude,* for instance, The. Fool's Paradise. Charles Simic. SP-SimiCE

Word Made Flesh. Kathleen Jessie Raine. SP-RainK

Word made Flesh is seldom, A. Emily Dickinson. CP-DickE

Word must fall; but where the well-tilled ground, The. Good Ground, The. Jones Very. CP-VeryJ

Word of a snail on the plate of a leaf, The? Couriers, The. Sylvia Plath. CP-PlatS

Word of God doth sanction nothing ill, The. Bible Does Not Sanction Polygamy, The. Jones Very. CP-VeryJ

Word of Godspeed and good cheer, A. Christmas Greeting. James Whitcomb Riley. CP-RileJ

Word of Mouth. Muriel Rukeyser. CP-RukeM

Word of the Lord by night, The. Boston Hymn. Ralph Waldo Emerson. CP-EmerR

Word of wax. / Forget your word of wax. Federico García Lorca. CP-GarcF, *tr. by* Christopher Maurer

Word on Statistics, A. Wisława Szymborska. SP-SzymWM, *tr. by* Joanna Trzeciak

Word on the Quick and Modern Poem-Makers, A. Charles Bukowski. SP-BukC2

Word on Wind, A. Ogden Nash. CP-NashO

Word over all, beautiful as the sky. Reconciliation. Walt Whitman. CP-WhitW

Word sounds like the thing. Onomatopoeia. Thomas Lux. SP-LuxT

Word sticks in the wind's throat, A. Apology. Richard Wilbur. CP-WilbR

Word that burned into a page, The. Ideal and the Real, The. Richard Eberhart. CP-EberR

Word the Gospel brought was love and peace, The. Gospel the Reconciling Power, The. Jones Very. CP-VeryJ

Word Thrum, The. Grace Paley. CP-PalGC

Word to the Unwise, A. Ambrose Bierce. SP-BierA

Word traps catch big bears in silence. Winter Kill. Richard Eberhart. CP-EberR

Word where is it? hath it voice, The. Word, The ("Word where is it? hath it voice, The"). Jones Very. CP-VeryJ

Word whose breath is the world-circling atmosphere. Word Made Flesh. Kathleen Jessie Raine. SP-RainK

Word with José Rodríguez-Feo, A. Wallace Stevens. CP-StevW; CP-StevWP

Word with Norman Rosten. Robert Stock. SP-StocR

Word with You, A. Elizabeth Bishop. CP-BishE

Word you created. Glukapikron. Gregory Orr. SP-OrrG

Words. Rae Armantrout. SP-ArmaA

Words. W. H. Auden. CP-AudeW

Words. Robert Creeley. CP-CreeR

Words. Richard Eberhart. CP-EberR

Words. Thom Gunn. CP-GunnT

Words. Philip Levine. SP-LeviP

Words. Robert Lowell. SP-LoweR

Words. W. S. Merwin. SP-MerwW

Words. Grace Paley.

Words. Sylvia Plath. CP-PlatS

Words. Anne Sexton. CP-SextA

Words. Miller Williams. CP-WillM

Words. William Butler Yeats. CP-YeatW

Words again, rehearsal. Corn Close. Robert Creeley. SP-CreeR

Words and Music. Samuel Beckett. Song: "Age is when to a man." CP-BeckS

Words are a beautiful music, The. Water Music. Robert Creeley. CP-CreeR

Words are much like stones. You can build. Moderation. Yannis Ritsos. SP-RitsY, *tr. by* Andonis Decavalles

Words are really tiny. Muffled by a Belt across the Mouth. Andrei Codrescu. SP-CodrA

Words as plain as hen-birds' wings. Modesties. Philip Larkin. CP-LarkP

Words beget Anger: Anger brings forth blowes. To His Friend to Avoid Contention of Words. Robert Herrick. CP-HerrR

Words cannot utter / Christ His returning. Easter Day. Christina Georgina Rossetti. CP-RosC2

Words Continue Their Journey, The. Margaret Atwood. SP-AtwM2

Words fail me. The ocean traveling stone. Inlet, The. Louise Glück. SP-GlucL

Words for a Nursery. Sylvia Plath. CP-PlatS

Words, for alas my trade is words, a barren burst of rhymes. To M. E. W. G. K. Chesterton. CP-ChesG

Words for Hart Crane. Robert Lowell. SP-LoweR

Words for Love. Ted Berrigan. SP-BerrT

Words for Maria. James Merrill. SP-MerrJ

Words for Muffin, a Guinea Pig. Robert Lowell. SP-LoweR

Words for Some Ash. Thom Gunn. CP-GunnT

Words for the Madrigalist. Charles Tomlinson. CP-TomlC

Words for the Unknown Makers. Stanley Kunitz. CP-KunSC

Words for the Wind. Theodore Roethke. CP-RoetT

Words from a Totem Animal. W. S. Merwin. SP-MerwW

Words from the mirror softly pass. Lament of the Looking-Glass, The. Thomas Hardy. CP-HardT

Words from their root their quantity. Thomas Sheridan. CP-SherT *Fr.* Of Prosody.

Words have another shell. Yannis Ritsos. SP-RitsY *Fr.* Paper Poems 1.

Words Heard, by Accident, over the Phone. Sylvia Plath. CP-PlatS

Words I give thee they are not thine own, The. Promise, The ("Words I give thee they are not thine own, The"). Jones Very. CP-VeryJ

Words, idle words, are what people's social life contains a goodly store of. I'll Write Their Number Down When We Get Home. Ogden Nash. CP-NashO

Words in a Certain Appropriate Mode. Hayden Carruth. CP-CarHS

Words in the Mourning Time. Robert Earl Hayden. CP-HaydR

Words in Time. Archibald MacLeish. CP-MacLA

Words into Words Won't Go. Clarence Major. SP-MajoC

Words Like Freedom. Langston Hughes. *See* Refugee in America

Words Lying Idle, The. William Carlos Williams. CP-WilW2

Words of Comfort to Be Scratched on a Mirror. Dorothy Parker. CP-ParkD

Words of the Preacher, The. Stanley Kunitz. CP-KunSC

Words on the Window-Pane. Dante Gabriel Rossetti. CW-RossD

Words Rising. Robert Bly. SP-BlyR

Words say, mispell and mispell your name. Michael Palmer. SP-PalmM

Words that come in smoke and go. Notes for Echo Lake 3. Michael Palmer. SP-PalmM

Words that come unuttered by the breath, The. Apostles, The. Jones Very. CP-VeryJ

Words the happy say, The. Emily Dickinson. CP-DickE

Words, the Words, the Words, The. William Carlos Williams. CP-WilW2

Words to be Spoken. Archibald MacLeish. CP-MacLA

Words we might else have been compelled to say. Lines to the Memory of James Dow. Robert Browning. CP-BroR2

Words will one day come, The. Movie Run Backward, The. Robert Creeley. SP-CreeR

Words words like steel. Itch, Come and Gone. Charles Bukowski. SP-BukC2

Words, words, such deeds words, come. Theodore Weiss. SP-WeisT *Fr.* Polish Question, The.

Words Written Near a Candle. Tess Gallagher. SP-GallT

Words you said grow faint, The. Faithless. Walter De la Mare. CP-DeLaW

Wordsworth. John Greenleaf Whittier. CP-WhitJ

Wordsworth upon Helvellyn! Let the cloud. On a Portrait of Wordsworth by B. R. Haydon. Elizabeth Barrett Browning. CP-BroEB

Work. Elizabeth Barrett Browning. CP-BroEB

Work. Raymond Carver. CP-CarvR

Work. Andrei Codrescu. SP-CodrA

Work. Yusef Komunyakaa. CP-KomuY

Work. D. H. Lawrence. CP-LawrD

Work. C. K. Williams. SP-WillC

Work, The. Primo Levi. CP-LeviP, tr. by Ruth Feldman

Work and Contemplation. Elizabeth Barrett Browning. CP-BroEB

Work & the Labor, The. Andrei Codrescu. SP-CodrA

Work Drafts. Robert Graves. CP-GravR

Work, for the Day Is Coming. Muriel Rukeyser. CP-RukeM

Work Gangs. Carl Sandburg. CP-SandC

Work Gloves. Gregory Orr. SP-OrrG

Work? / I don't have to work. Necessity. Langston Hughes. CP-HughL; CP-HughL3

Work in the loss of mass, The. Muriel Rukeyser. CP-RukeM

Work is a bleak redeemer. Emily Dickinson. SP-DickE

Work is done; now let my Lawrell be, The. To God. Robert Herrick. CP-HerrR

Work is done, The. The hammer is laid down. Fernando Pessoa. SP-PessF Fr. Inscriptions.

Work is heavy, The. I see. To the Shade of Po Chü-I. William Carlos Williams. CP-WilW1

Work of Artifice, A. Marge Piercy. SP-PierM

Work of Creation, The. D. H. Lawrence. CP-LawrD

Work of Happiness, The. May Sarton. SP-SartM

Work of Her that went, The. Emily Dickinson. CP-DickE

Work-Room. Robert Graves. CP-GravR

Work Song. Wendell Berry. CP-BerrW

Work-table, litter, books and standing lamp. Night Sweat. Robert Lowell. SP-LoweR

Work to Do Toward Town. Gary Snyder. CP-SnydG

Work without Hope. Samuel Taylor Coleridge. CP-ColeS; MW-ColeS

Workbox, The. Thomas Hardy. CP-HardT

Work'd into sudden rage by wintry show'rs. Homer. CP-JohnS Fr. Iliad, The.

Work[e] is done: young men, and maidens set, The. On Himselfe. Robert Herrick. CP-HerrR

Worker in Mirror, at his Bench. Thomas Kinsella. CP-KinsT

Workers. Arthur Rimbaud. CP-RimbA, tr. by Martin Sorrell

Workers fly back and forth like piston-rods. Men Like Gods. G. K. Chesterton. CP-ChesG

Workers have themselves become the Cid Campeador, The. Major Road Ahead. Hugh MacDiarmid. SP-MacDH Fr. Battle Continues, The.

Workers Rose on May Day or Postcript to Karl Marx, The. Audre Lorde. SP-LordA

Workin' Man. Langston Hughes. CP-HughL; CP-HughL1

Working Day, A. Theodore Weiss. SP-WeisT

Working Day, The. Kenneth Rexroth. CP-RexrK

Working for Profit. Andrei Codrescu. SP-CodrA

Working Girls. Carl Sandburg. CP-SandC

Working girls in the morning are going to work, The. Working Girls. Carl Sandburg. CP-SandC

Working man appeared in the street, A. Lorine Niedecker. CP-NiedL

Working Man, The. D. H. Lawrence. CP-LawrD

Working night shift. Soliloquy: Man Talking to a Mirror. Yusef Komunyakaa. CP-KomuY

Working on the '58 Willys Pickup. Gary Snyder. CP-SnydG

Working Outdoors in Winter. John Updike. CP-UpdiJ

Working Principle, A. David Ignatow. SP-IgnaD

Working Still. A. R. Ammons. CP-AmmoA

Working the Block. Eleanor Wilner. SP-WilnE

Working through sonnet forms, he turns. Poetry and Our City. A. K. Ramanujan. CP-RamaA

Working with Tools. A. R. Ammons. CP-AmmoA

Working World's Bloody Flux, The. Alan Dugan. CP-DugaA

Workingman with hand so hairy-sturdy. E. E. Cummings. CP-CummE

Workman. George Oppen. CP-OppGN

Workman shall not always work; who builds, The. Laborers, The. Jones Very. CP-VeryJ

Workman's Wife, The. Stéphane Mallarmé. CP-MallS Fr. Street Songs.

Workman's Wife, The. Stéphane Mallarmé. CP-MallS, tr. by Henry Weinfield

Works of ancient bards divine, The. Retaliation. William Cowper. CP-CowpW

Workshop. Billy Collins. SP-CollB

World. A. R. Ammons. CP-AmmoA

World, The. Czeslaw Milosz. CP-MiloC; CP-MiloCN

World, The. Robert Creeley. CP-CreeR

World, The. George Herbert. CP-HerbG

World, The. David Ignatow. SP-IgnaD

World, The. Kathleen Jessie Raine. SP-RainK

World, The. Christina Georgina Rossetti. CP-RosC1

World, The ("End of all thou seest is near, The"). Jones Very. CP-VeryJ

World, The ("'Tis all a great show"). Jones Very. CP-VeryJ

World alive with love, where leaves tremble, The. Childhood's End. Denise Levertov. SP-LeveDS

World and all its fables long ago, The. Michelangelo Buonarroti. CP-Miche, tr. by John Frederick Nims

World and I, The. Laura Riding Jackson. CP-RidiL

World and the Child, The. James Merrill. SP-MerrJ

World around her like a shadow, A. O Western Wind. George Oppen. CP-OppGN

World around us speaks in code, The. Breaking the Code. Robert Penn Warren. CP-WarrR

World as Brueghel Imagined It, The. Howard Nemerov. CP-NemeH

World as Meditation, The. Wallace Stevens. CP-StevW; CP-StevWP

World as we reach stretches, The. Upon Taking Hold. Robert Duncan. SP-DuncR

World as Will and Representation, The. Hayden Carruth. CP-CarrHS

World at his feet, Carpet Not Bought, A. James Merrill. SP-MerrJ

World at Large, The. James McMichael. SP-McMiJ

World atop Maine and our heads is north, The. My Heavenly Shiner (Elizabeth). Robert Lowell. SP-LoweR

World autumn, The. Louis Zukofsky. CP-ZukLS

World Away, A. Charles Baudelaire. CP-BaudC, tr. by Walter Martin

World begins, The. 32 Adults. Heather McHugh. SP-McHuH

World begins again!, The. Birds, The. William Carlos Williams. CP-WilW1

World below the Brine, The. Walt Whitman. CP-WhitW

World Book Salesman, The. Raymond Carver. CP-CarvR

World Breaking Apart. Louise Glück. SP-GlucL

World carpet, robe, every leaf. Before It Burned over: A Sioux Grass Chant. William Stafford. SP-StafWW

World Contracted to a Recognizable Image, The. William Carlos Williams. CP-WilW2

World discernes it selfe, while I the world behold, The. Ovid. CP-RaleW Fr. Metamorphoses.

World ends at the barriers of snow, The. Barrier Snow. Robert Stock. SP-StocR

World-famous golden-thighed Pythagoras. Line of Verse of Yeats, A. Richard Eberhart. CP-EberR

World—feels Dusty, The. Flags Vex a Dying Face. Emily Dickinson. CP-DickE

World full of successful people's, A. Darlings. Charles Bukowski. SP-BukC3

World gets worse, The. Horse Power. Andrei Codrescu. SP-CodrA

World goes none the lamer, The. A. E. Housman. CP-HousA

World goes on quite happily, The. Casino Pierre. Andrei Codrescu. SP-CodrA

World has billions of people, The. Shih-te. CP-ColdM, tr. by Red Pine

World has its know-it-alls, The. Shih-te. CP-ColdM, tr. by Red Pine

World has many seas, Mediterranean, Atlantic, but here is the shore of the one ocean, The. Contrast. Robinson Jeffers. CP-JefR1

World has never known me bid them hear, The. Preacher, The. Jones Very. CP-VeryJ

World hath set its heavy yoke, The. Rudyard Kipling. CP-KiplR Fr. Plain Tales from the Hills.

World I did not wish to enter, A. Necessitarian's Epitaph, A. Thomas Hardy. CP-HardT

World: / Image on water, waves. Kathleen Jessie Raine. SP-RainK

World in a / plastic octa- / gon from a. Kiki. Robert Creeley. CP-CreeR

World is a beautiful place, The. Lawrence Ferlinghetti. SP-FerlL

World is a beautiful place, The. 25. Lawrence Ferlinghetti. SP-FerlL

World is a bride superbly dressed, The. Hafiz. CP-EmerR Fr. Odes.

World Is a Bundle of Hay, The. Lord Byron. CP-Byron

World is a painted memory, where coloured shapes, The. Dreams Old and Nascent: Nascent. D. H. Lawrence. CP-LawrD

World Is a Round Earthenware Plate, The. Pablo Antonio Cuadra. CP-MertT

World is a snob, and the man who wins, The. For the Man Who Fails. Paul Laurence Dunbar. CP-DunbP

World is an invention of the spirit the spirit, The. Revisionist Poem—Octavio Paz. Thomas McGrath. SP-McGrT

World is charged with the grandeur of God, The. God's Grandeur. Gerard Manley Hopkins. CP-HopkG

World is come upon me, I used to keep it a long way off, The. Deserter, The. Stevie Smith. CP-SmitS

World is dreary / And I'm weary, The. To Mary Shelley. Percy Bysshe Shelley. CP-ShelP

"World is dull," I cried in my despair, The. Tempora Mutantur. Ambrose Bierce.

SP-BierA

World is everything that is the case, The. Brief Lives. Donald Hall. CP-HallD

World is everything that is the case, The. Tractatus. Derek Mahon. CP-MahoD

World is full of busy people, The. Han-shan. CP-ColdM, *tr. by* Red Pine

World is full of colored, The. Song: "World is full of colored, The." Alice Walker. CP-WalkA

World is full of different fates, The. George Meredith. CP-MerG2

World is full of loss; bring, wind, my love, The. Song: "World is full of loss; bring, wind, my love, The." Muriel Rukeyser. CP-RukeM

World is full of mostly invisible things, The. To David, about His Education. Howard Nemerov. CP-NemeH

World is kaleidoscopic, ever changing, The. Stopping a Kaleidoscope. Richard Eberhart. CP-EberR

World is made of less and less, The. Wanting a Soul in the South. W. S. Merwin. SP-MerwW

World is made up of cab drivers, The. Simulacrum. David Ignatow. SP-IgnaD

World is moving, moving still, towards further democracy, The. Future Relationships. D. H. Lawrence. CP-LawrD

World is my dream, says the wise child, The. Solipsism. Karl Shapiro. SP-ShapK

World is never ready, The. Tale Begun, A. Wisława Szymborska. SP-SzymW, *tr. by* Stanislaw Barańczak *and* Clare Cavanagh

World Is Not a Meditation, The. Eleanor Wilner. SP-WilnE

World is / not with us enough, The. O Taste and See. Denise Levertov. SP-LeveDP; SP-LeveDS

World is now our dwelling-place, The. From the Original Draft of the Poem to William Shelley. Percy Bysshe Shelley. CP-ShelP

World is ours till sunset, The. Song of the Children, The. G. K. Chesterton. CP-ChesG

World is round, The. Modulations for Solo Voice. Denise Levertov. SP-LeveDL

World is so difficult to give up, The. World, The. David Ignatow. SP-IgnaD

World is that map's white blotch, no charted coast, The. Empty White Blotch on Map of Universe: A Possible View. Robert Penn Warren. CP-WarrR

World is too much with us; late and soon, The. William Wordsworth. CP-WorW1; MW-WorW

World is too much with us, The. Escape, The. James Laughlin. CP-LaugJ

World is turned ag'in' me, The. Johnson's Boy. James Whitcomb Riley. CP-RileJ

World is very big, and we, The. E. E. Cummings. CP-CummE

World is woven all of dream and error, The. Fernando Pessoa. SP-PessF *Fr.* 35 Sonnets.

World is young, the world is well, The. George Meredith. CP-MerG2

World Isn't a Wedding of the Artists of Yesterday, The. Norman Dubie. CP-DubiN

World looks not the wider for thy travel, The. Sayings. Jones Very. CP-VeryJ

World made penniless by that departure. Emily Dickinson. CP-DickE

World Narrowed to a Point, The. William Carlos Williams. CP-WilW2

World of change & loss, a world of death, A. February 14. 1883. Christina Georgina Rossetti. CP-RosC3

World of Dreams, The. George Crabbe. SP-CrabG

World of God has turned its two stone faces, The. To a Brother in the Mystery. Donald Davie. CP-DaviDC

World of snowy hills set aloft in a golden sky, A. Book of Wild Pictures, A. G. K. Chesterton. CP-ChesG

World of storm, A. Come in Go Out. May Swenson. SP-SwenM

World of the Perfect Tear, The. Thomas McGrath. SP-McGrT

World of the Salamanders, The. Marya Alexandrovna Zaturenska. SP-ZatuM

World of Words, The. Hugh MacDiarmid.
   "Ah, Joyce, this is our task." SP-MacDH

World outside is dark; my fire burns low, The. Passing of the Year, The. E. E. Cummings. CP-CummE

World Outside, The. Denise Levertov. SP-LeveDP

World pours in / on wings of song, The. Mary's Fancy. Robert Creeley. CP-CreeR

World-Soul, The. Ralph Waldo Emerson. CP-EmerR

World—stands—solemner—to me, The. Emily Dickinson. CP-DickE

World State, The. G. K. Chesterton. CP-ChesG

World Take Good Notice. Walt Whitman. CP-WhitW

World-Telegram. John Berryman. CP-BerrJ

World, that cannot deeme of worthy things, The. Sonnet 84. Edmund Spenser. CP-Spens *Fr.* Amoretti.

World *the fog.* Natural, The. George Oppen. CP-OppGN

World; The Lovers; Falling Stars, The. Thomas McGrath. SP-McGrT

World the window held, The. Bar and Grill. Heather McHugh. SP-McHuH

World to be stuttered after. Paul Celan. SP-CelaP, *tr. by* John Felstiner

World to Do, A. Theodore Weiss. SP-WeisT

World values books, and thinks that in so doing, The. Duke Hwan and the Wheelwright. Chuang Tzu. CP-MertT

World vibrates, my sleepless nights, The. Vibration. John Updike. CP-UpdiJ

World War. Richard Eberhart. CP-EberR

World War II. Troops, The. Charles Bukowski. SP-BukC3

World War II. Langston Hughes. CP-HughL; CP-HughL3

World was made by someone else, The. Creator. Archibald MacLeish. CP-MacLA

World was wrought with a mixture of dirt, water, fire, The. Axiom. Joseph Brodsky. CP-BrodJ, *tr. by* Jonathan Aaron

World,—what a world, ah me! / Mouldy, worm-eaten, grey. Vain Shadow, A. Christina Georgina Rossetti. CP-RosC2

World where the dead live is a dry heart, The. Life of the Dead, The. Laura Riding Jackson. CP-RidiL

World Whose Sun Retreats Before the Brave, A. Kenneth Patchen. CP-PatcK

World-wide dusk. Black Seed. Langston Hughes. CP-HughL; CP-HughL1

World Will Little Note, The. Kenneth Patchen. CP-PatcK

"World Without Objects Is a Sensible Emptiness, A." Richard Wilbur. CP-WilbR

World without Peculiarity. Wallace Stevens. CP-StevW; CP-StevWP

World, World—. George Oppen. CP-OppGN

World world world / I sit in my room. Europe! Europe! Allen Ginsberg. CP-GinsA

World world world world / and the face grave. Enueg II. Samuel Beckett. CP-BeckS

World would rather *see* hope than just hear, The. Smiles. Wisława Szymborska. SP-SzymW, *tr. by* Stanislaw Barańczak *and* Clare Cavanagh

World / you know as / one piece after, The. Sunset. Robert Creeley. CP-CreeR

Worldly Failure. Richard Eberhart. CP-EberR

Worldly people make me sigh. Shih-te. CP-ColdM, *tr. by* Red Pine

Worlds. Federico García Lorca. CP-GarcF, *tr. by* Jerome Rothenberg *Fr.* Countries.

Worlds. Richard Wilbur. CP-WilbR

World's Advance, The. George Meredith. CP-MerG1

World's as the world is; the nations rearm and prepare to change; the, The. Night Without Sleep. Robinson Jeffers. CP-JefR2

World's Convention, The. John Greenleaf Whittier. CP-WhitJ

World's End. Laura Riding Jackson. CP-RidiL

World's Fair. John Berryman. CP-BerrJ

Worlds fly past. Years fly past. The empty. Aleksandr Aleksandrovich Blok. SP-BlokA, *tr. by* Peter France *and* Jon Stallworthy

World's Greatest Tricycle-Rider, The. C. K. Williams. CP-WillC; SP-WillC

World's Harmonies, The. Christina Georgina Rossetti. CP-RosC3

Worlds light shines; shine as it will, The. John 3; But Men Loved Darknesse Rather than Light. Bible, *N.T.* CP-CrasR, *tr. by* Richard Crashaw *Fr.* St. John.

World's light shines; shine as it will, The. But Men loved Darknesse[e] Rather Than [*or* Then] Light. Richard Crashaw. CP-CrasR

World's lopsided. Survey of the Whole. May Swenson. SP-SwenM

World's Miser, The. G. K. Chesterton. CP-ChesG

World's / not wanton, The. Implosions. Adrienne Rich. CP-RicAE; SP-RicA1; SP-RicA2

World's Prose, The. Adam Zagajewski. SP-ZagaA, *tr. by* Clare Cavanagh

World's Wanderers, The. Percy Bysshe Shelley. CP-ShelP

World's Wonders, The. Robinson Jeffers. CP-JefR3

World's Worth. Dante Gabriel Rossetti. CW-RossD

Worm, The. Jones Very. CP-VeryJ

Worm artist, The. Earth Worm, The. Denise Levertov. SP-LeveDP

Worm Either Way. D. H. Lawrence. CP-LawrD

Worm / In an otherwise, A. Interlude. Charles Simic. SP-SimiC; SP-SimiCE

Worm Turns, The. D. H. Lawrence. CP-LawrD

Worms, The. Carolyn Kizer. CP-KizeC

Worms and the Wind. Carl Sandburg. CP-SandC

Worms at Heaven's Gate, The. Wallace Stevens. CP-StevW; CP-StevWP

Worm's Waking, The. Jelaluddin Rumi. SP-Rumi, *tr. by* Coleman Barks

Worms would rather be worms. Worms and the Wind. Carl Sandburg. CP-SandC

Wormwood. Thomas Kinsella. CP-KinsT

Worn on the. Kenneth Patchen. CP-PatcK

Worn Out. Paul Laurence Dunbar. CP-DunbP

Worn-out Pencil, A. James Whitcomb Riley. CP-RileJ

Worriation. Langston Hughes. CP-HughL; CP-HughL3

Worry. Robert Creeley. SP-CreeR

Worry and low murmur, The. Kettle Song. Ivor Gurney. SP-GurnI

Worry hedges my days. On Not Deserving. Donald Davie. CP-DaviDC

"Worse than the sunflower," she had said. Ecclesiast, The. John Ashbery. SP-AshbJ

Worse things could happen, life is insecure. First Things. Robert Lowell. SP-LoweR

Worsening Situation. John Ashbery. SP-AshbJ

Worship. G. K. Chesterton. CP-ChesG

Worship. Ralph Waldo Emerson. CP-EmerR

Worship. D. H. Lawrence. CP-LawrD

Worship. John Greenleaf Whittier. CP-WhitJ

Worship ("But, still preserved by pious care behold"). Jones Very. CP-VeryJ

Worship declines; nor hidden is the cause. On the Neglect of Public Worship. Jones Very. CP-VeryJ

Worship God. Christina Georgina Rossetti. CP-RosC2

Worship of Nature, The. John Greenleaf Whittier. CP-WhitJ

Worship ("There is no worship now—the idol stands"). Jones Very. CP-VeryJ

Worship this world of watercolor mood. April Aubade. Sylvia Plath. CP-PlatS

Worshipping same / they squirm and they spawn. E. E. Cummings. CP-CummE

Worst and the Best, The. Charles Bukowski. SP-BukC1

Worst conspired, their differences sunk, The. Court Revolt, The. Thom Gunn. CP-GunnT

Worst of It, The. Robert Browning. CP-BroR1

Worst of it is, The. Modern Problems. D. H. Lawrence. CP-LawrD

Worst of the younger generation, those Latter-Day sinners, The. Latter-Day Sinners. D. H. Lawrence. CP-LawrD

Worst Poems Make the Best "Poems," The. Andrei Codrescu. SP-CodrA

Worst side of it all, The. White Roses. John Ashbery. SP-AshbJ

Worst Sinner, Jonathan Edwards' God, The. Robert Lowell. SP-LoweR

Wortermelon Time. James Whitcomb Riley. CP-RileJ

Worth no more than a man's hard pride. Question Is, Who Is Afraid of What, The? Kenneth Patchen. CP-PatcK

Worthless and wealthy, decrepit and young. Black Bile ("Worthless and wealthy, decrepit and young"). Charles Baudelaire. CP-BaudC, *tr. by* Walter Martin

Worthlessness of Earthly things, The. Emily Dickinson. CP-DickE

Worthy art Thou, O Lord of praise! Deliverance from a Fit of Fainting. Anne Bradstreet. CP-BradA

Wot makes the soldier's 'eart to penk, wot makes 'im to perspire! Oonts. Rudyard Kipling. CP-KiplR

Would a man 'scape the rod? Ben Karshook's Wisdom. Robert Browning. CP-BroR2

Would any one the true cause find. Out of the Italian. Ammianus Marcellinus. CP-CrasR

Would-Be Merman, The. Nicholas Vachel Lindsay. CP-LindV

Would God I knew there were a God to thank. Dante Gabriel Rossetti. CW-RossD

Would God, my Burges, I could think. To Mr John Burges. Ben Jonson. CP-JonsB

Would God your health were as this month of May. English May. Dante Gabriel Rossetti. CW-RossD

Would he be the one. Guest, The. Charles Simic. SP-SimiCE

Would he might come. La Gretchen de Nos Jours (I). Stevie Smith. CP-SmitS

Would I could cast a sail on the water. Collarbone [*or* Collar-Bone] of a Hare, The. William Butler Yeats. CP-YeatW

Would I might stay those features as they pass. Portrait, The. Jones Very. CP-VeryJ

Would it were anything but merely voice! King and No King. William Butler Yeats. CP-YeatW

Would it were I had been false, not you! Worst of It, The. Robert Browning. CP-BroR1

Would my Delia know if I love, let her take. Symptoms of Love, The. William Cowper. CP-CowpW

Would [*or* Wo'd] ye[e] have fresh cheese and cream? Fresh Cheese and Cream. Robert Herrick. CP-HerrR

Would Prometheus, cursing on his rock. Or Consider Prometheus. Amy Clampitt. CP-ClamA

Would / That I were a jewel. Songs to the Dark Virgin. Langston Hughes. CP-HughL; CP-HughL1

Would that I were a turnip white. Christina Georgina Rossetti. CP-RosC3

"Would that I'd not drawn breath here!" some one said. In Time of Wars and Tumults. Thomas Hardy. CP-HardT

Would that my lips might pour out in thy praise. Ditty of No Tone, A. James Whitcomb Riley. CP-RileJ

Would that the structure brave, the manifold music I build. Abt Vogler. Robert Browning. CP-BroR1

Would that the winds might only blow. Becalmed. James Whitcomb Riley. CP-RileJ

Would that young Amenophis Fourth returned. Litany of the Heroes. Nicholas Vachel Lindsay. CP-LindV

Would we were blind with Milton, and we sang. Invocation for "The Map of the Universe" Nicholas Vachel Lindsay. CP-LindV

Would—would that there were. In a Library. Walter De la Mare. CP-DeLaW

Would you be an angel. Something of a Departure. Paul Muldoon. CP-MuldP

Would you believe me. Family, A. W. S. Merwin. SP-MerwWF

Would you believe, when you this Monsieur see. On English Monsieur. Ben Jonson. CP-JonsB; SP-JonsB

Would you call upon the people; in what ear shall it be told? Appeal of the Peers, The. G. K. Chesterton. CP-ChesG

Would you care to explain. Something to Say. Robert Graves. CP-GravR

Would You Go to the House by the True Gate. Lord Byron. CP-Byron

Would you have me peel an orange and. Swans Walk My Brain in April It Rains, The. Charles Bukowski. SP-BukC2

Would you hope to gain my heart. Translations from Metastasio. Pietro Metastasio. CP-JohnS *Fr.* La Clemenza di Tito.

Would you know what joy is hid. Ralph Waldo Emerson. CP-EmerR

Would you know what's soft? I dare. James Shirley. CP-CareT

Would you like summer? Taste of ours. Emily Dickinson. CP-DickE

Would you like to throw a stone at me? Peach. D. H. Lawrence. CP-LawrD

Would you not like a broomstick? As for me. Johann Wolfgang von Goethe. CP-ShelP *Fr.* Faust.

Would you rise in the church, be stupid and dull. Advice to a Parson. Jonathan Swift. CP-SwifJ

Would you see what I'm like. Directions for Finding the Bard. Dorothy Parker. CP-ParkD

Would you that Delville I describe? Description of Doctor Delany's Villa, A. Thomas Sheridan. CP-SherT

Wouldn't You Be after a Jaunt of 964,000,000,000,000 Million Miles? Kenneth Patchen. CP-PatcK

Wouldst thou be gathered to Christ's chosen flock. Inscription on a Rock at Rydal Mount. William Wordsworth. CP-WorW2

Wouldst thou be taught, when sleep has taken flight. Cuckoo-Clock, The. William Wordsworth. CP-WorW2

Wouldst thou behold my features cleanse thy heart. Seed, The. Jones Very. CP-VeryJ

Wouldst thou give me a heavy jewelled crown. Christina Georgina Rossetti. CP-RosC3

Wouldst thou hear what man can say. Epitaph on Elizabeth, L. H. Ben Jonson. CP-JonsB; SP-JonsB

Would'st thou then happy be. Self to self. Walter De la Mare. CP-DeLaW

Wouldst thou to some stedfast Seat. Boethius. CP-JohnS *Fr.* Consolation of Philosophy, The ("De Consolacione Philosophie").

Wound, The. Louise Glück. SP-GlucL

Wound, The. Thom Gunn. CP-GunnT

Wound, The. Thomas Hardy. CP-HardT

Wound-Dresser, The. Walt Whitman. CP-WhitW

Wound is open, The. Grandfather, Your Wound. Anne Sexton. CP-SextA

Wound kills that does not bleed, The. Woman Sings a Song for a Soldier Come Home, A. Wallace Stevens. CP-StevW; CP-StevWP

Wounded Bullfighter, The. Clarence Major. SP-MajoC

Wounded cow lay down, The. Cow. Federico García Lorca. CP-GarcF, *tr. by* Greg Simon *and* Steven F. White

Wounded Cupid, The. Robert Herrick. CP-HerrR

Wounded Deer Leaps Highest, A. Emily Dickinson. CP-DickE

Wounded Heart, The. Robert Herrick. CP-HerrR

Wounded I sing, tormented I indite. Joseph's Coat. George Herbert. CP-HerbG

Wounded Pigeon, The. Jones Very. CP-VeryJ

Wounds of Love. Federico García Lorca. CP-GarcF, *tr. by* Angela Jaffray

Wovoka's Witness. William Stafford. SP-StafWW

Wow, but your letter made me vauntie! To Dr. Blacklock. Robert Burns. CP-BurnR

Wraith. Edna St. Vincent Millay. CP-MillE

Wraith, The. Paul Laurence Dunbar. CP-DunbP

Wraith of Summer-Time, A. James Whitcomb Riley. CP-RileJ

Wrangdillion, A. James Whitcomb Riley. CP-RileJ

Wrapped in a yielding air, beside. As He Is. W. H. Auden. CP-AudeW

Wrapped in the dark-red mantle of warm memories. After All Saints' Day. D. H. Lawrence. CP-LawrD

Wrapped in the windy rains that pelt and blow. Benediction, A. G. K. Chesterton. CP-ChesG

Wrapped like a sprained ankle from head to toe. To the Egyptian Mummy in the Etruscan Museum at Cortona. Charles Wright. SP-WrigCN

Wrathful East of smoke and iron, The. Ode to the Setting Sun. Allen Ginsberg. CP-GinsA

Wrathful mastodon is tearing, The. Why Paint? Andrei Codrescu. SP-CodrA

Wre drink in the mountains while the flowers bloom. Drinking Together. Li Po. CP-WilW2

Wreath, A. George Herbert. CP-HerbG

Wreath, A. Yannis Ritsos. SP-RitsY, *tr. by* Edmund Keeley

Wreath, The. Robert Graves. CP-GravR

Wreath for a Bridal. Sylvia Plath. CP-PlatS

Wreath for Alexandra Molostvova, A. Tennessee Williams. CP-WillT

Wreath is plaited wicker: the green varnish, The. Place of Death, The. Randall Jarrell. CP-JarrR

Wreath of banquet overnight lay withered on the neck, The. With Scindia to Delhi. Rudyard Kipling. CP-KiplR

Wreath of Women. Muriel Rukeyser. CP-RukeM

Wreathe no more lilies in my hair. Summer Is Ended, The. Christina Georgina Rossetti. CP-RosC3

Wreathèd garland of deservèd praise, A. Wreath, A. George Herbert. CP-HerbG

Wreaths. Geoffrey Hill. CP-HillG

Wreck, The. Walter De la Mare. CP-DeLaW

Wreck of Rivermouth, The. John Greenleaf Whittier. CP-WhitJ

Wreck of the Circus Train, The. Hayden Carruth. CP-CarHS

Wreck of the Deutschland, The. Gerard Manley Hopkins. CP-HopkG

Wreck of the *Hesperus*, The. Henry Wadsworth Longfellow. SP-LongH

Wreck of the *Swan*, The. Hugh MacDiarmid. SP-MacDH

Wreck of the Thresher, The (Lost at Sea, April 10, 1963). William Meredith. SP-MereW

Wreckage, The. Donald Hall. CP-HallD

Wreckage of Europe or the birth of Africa, The. To Lose the Earth. Anne Sexton. CP-SextA

Wrecks dissolve above us; their dust drops down from afar, The. Deep-Sea Cables, The. Rudyard Kipling. CP-KiplR

Wren and Barry, Rennie and Mylne and Dance. Under St Paul's. Donald Davie. CP-DaviDC

Wren-song in trellis: a light ecstasy of butterflies courting. Light Poem. Theodore Roethke. CP-RoetT

Wrens and robins in the hedge. Christina Georgina Rossetti. CP-RosC2

Wrens have troubles like us. The house of a wren will not run itself, The. People of the Eaves, I Wish You Good Morning. Carl Sandburg. CP-SandC

Wren's Nest, A. William Wordsworth. CP-WorW2

Wren's Nest, The. Robert Burns. CP-BurnR

Wressley of the Foreign Office. Rudyard Kipling. *Fr.* Plain Tales from the Hills.

Wrested from Mirrors. Nicolas Calas. CP-WilW2

Wrestlers on the Vase, The. Charles Tomlinson. CP-TomlC

Wrestling. Thom Gunn. CP-GunnT

Wrestling Match, The. Robert Penn Warren. CP-WarrR

Wrestling with Angels. Robert Stock. SP-StocR

Wretch that often has deceiv'd, The. Phaedrus. CP-JohnS *Fr.* Fabulae.

Wretched and foolish jealousy [*or* jealousie]. Against Jealousy [*or* Jealousie]. Ben Jonson. CP-JonsB

Wretched are the poor in spirit, for under the earth they will be as they are on earth. Fragments from an Apocryphal Gospal. Jorge Luis Borges. SP-BorgJ, *tr. by* Stephen Kessler

Wretched Woman. Stevie Smith. CP-SmitS

Wring the swan's neck, seeking. Craving. Denise Levertov. SP-LeveDL

Wrinkles no more are, or no lesse. Upon Wrinkles. Robert Herrick. CP-HerrR

Wrists web rythms / And the poke. Of an Evening Pulling Off a Little Experience (with the english language). Hart Crane. CP-CranH

Writ, The. Charles Olson. CP-OlsoC

Writ in between the lines of his life-deed. John Brown. James Whitcomb Riley. CP-RileJ

Write a giggly ode about. Citizen. Robert Creeley. CP-CreeR

Write in air. Cheap Thrill. Robert Creeley. SP-CreeR

Write me a rhyme of the present time. Job Work. James Whitcomb Riley. CP-RileJ

Write me when this geste, our life is done. In Epitaphium. Ezra Pound. CP-PoEar

Write on My Tomb. James Laughlin. CP-LaugJ

Write this down. Write it. In ordinary ink. Starvation Camp at Jasło. Wisława Szymborska. SP-SzymWM, *tr. by* Joanna Trzeciak

Write this. We have burned all their villages. Sun. Michael Palmer. SP-PalmM

Write your wishes. Corn Hut Talk. Carl Sandburg. CP-SandC

Writer, A. Philip Larkin. CP-LarkP

Writer, The. Muriel Rukeyser. CP-RukeM

Writer, The. Richard Wilbur. CP-WilbR

Writers. Dan Pagis. SP-PagiD, *tr. by* Stephen Mitchell

Writer's Prologue to a Play in Verse. William Carlos Williams. CP-WilW2

Writhe and / gape of tortured. E. E. Cummings. CP-CummE

Writhing vines were her only apparel. Virtue. Kenneth Patchen. CP-PatcK

Writin' Back to the Home Folks. James Whitcomb Riley. CP-RileJ

Writing. Rae Armantrout. SP-ArmaA

Writing. Robert Herrick. CP-HerrR

Writing. Howard Nemerov. CP-NemeH

Writing a Résumé. Wisława Szymborska. SP-SzymW, *tr. by* Stanisław Barańczak *and* Clare Cavanagh

Writing as Writing. Robert Duncan. SP-DuncR

Writing in the Dark. Denise Levertov. SP-LeveDL

Writing Is a State of Trance. Charles Bukowski. SP-BukC3

Writing is brief and fleeting. Emily Dickinson. SP-DickE

Writing It Down. William Stafford. SP-StafWW

Writing Life, The. Charles Wright. SP-WrigCN

Writing on a Fallen Leaf, The. W. S. Merwin. SP-MerwW

Writing on Sand. Charles Tomlinson. CP-TomlC; SP-TomlC

Writing thyself, or judging others' writ. To the Same [Benjamin Rudyerd] ("Writing thyself, or judging others' writ"). Ben Jonson. CP-JonsB; SP-JonsB

Writing to Aaron. Denise Levertov. SP-LeveDL

Writings left behind by those your dread, The. You Are Not the Others. Jorge Luis Borges. SP-BorgJ, *tr. by* Eric McHenry

Writings of light assault the darkness, more prodigious than meteors. Boast of Quietness. Jorge Luis Borges. SP-BorgJ, *tr. by* Stephen Kessler

Writings of the Mystics, The. Charles Simic. SP-SimiC; SP-SimiCE

Written after Leaving Her at New Burns. William Cowper. CP-CowpW

Written after Reading an Item in the Paper about a Young Lady Who Went Mad upon Forsaking Her Lover. He Is Here Assumed to Speak. Kenneth Patchen. CP-PatcK

Written After Swimming from Sestos to Abydos. Lord Byron. CP-Byron

Written after the Death of Charles Lamb. William Wordsworth. CP-WorW2

see also Inscription in the Grounds of Coleorton, the Seat of Sir George Beaumont, BART., Leicestershire *and* Inscription in a Garden of the Same. William Wordsworth. CP-WorW1

Written at Winchester on Tuesday the 15th July 1817. Jane Austen. CP-AustJ

Written for a Musician. Nicholas Vachel Lindsay. CP-LindV

Written in a Book Abandoned on the Trip. Fernando Pessoa. SP-PessF, *tr. by* Susan M. Brown *and* Edwin Honig

Written in a Copy of Swift's Poems, for Wayne Burns. James Wright. CP-WrigJ

Written in a Grotto. William Wordsworth. CP-WorW1

Written in a Quarrel. William Cowper. CP-CowpW

Written in a Volume of Goethe. Ralph Waldo Emerson. CP-EmerR

Written in an old Aeolian dialect. Palimpsest: "Written in an old Aeolian dialect." "Rubén Dario." SP-DariR, *tr. by* Alberto Acereda *and* Will Derusha

Written in Aspin Castle. Emily Jane Brontë. CP-BronE

Written in Bunner's "Airs from Arcady" James Whitcomb Riley. CP-RileJ

Written in Disgust of Vulgar Superstition. John Keats. CP-KeatJ

Written in Friar's Carse Hermitage on the Banks of Nith—June—1788. Robert Burns. CP-BurnR

Written in Germany on One of the Coldest Days of the Century. William Wordsworth. CP-WorW1

Written in "Letters to an Italian Nun and an English Gentleman: by J.J. Rousseau: Founded on Facts." Lord Byron. CP-Byron

Written in London, September, 1802. William Wordsworth. CP-WorW1; MW-WorW

Written in March [While Resting on the Bridge at the Foot of Brother's Water]. William Wordsworth. CP-WorW1; MW-WorW

Written in Mrs Field's Album opposite a Pen-and-Ink Sketch in the Manner of a Rembrandt Etching Done by Edmund Field. William Wordsworth. CP-WorW2

Written in My Dream by W. C. Williams. Allen Ginsberg. SP-GinsA

Written in Naples, March, 1833. Ralph Waldo Emerson. CP-EmerR

Written in Pencil in the Sealed Railway-Car. Dan Pagis. SP-PagiD, *tr. by* Stephen Mitchell

Written in Sickness. Ralph Waldo Emerson. CP-EmerR

Written in the Gaaldine Prison Caves to A.G.A. Emily Jane Brontë. CP-BronE

Written in the Strangers' Book at "The Station," Opposite Bowness. William Wordsworth. CP-WorW2

Written in Very Early Youth. William Wordsworth. CP-WorW1

Written in Water. Amy Clampitt. CP-ClamA

Written Next to a Blue Flower. Pablo Antonio Cuadra. CP-MertT

Written on a Blank Space at the End of Chaucer's Tale of "The Floure and the Lefe." John Keats. CP-KeatJ

Written on Hotel Napkin: Chicago Futures. Allen Ginsberg. CP-GinsA

Written on Returning to the P. of I. on the 10th of January, 1827. Emily Jane Brontë. CP-BronE

Written on the Day That Mr. Leigh Hunt Left Prison. John Keats. CP-KeatJ

Written on the Stub of the First Paycheck. William Stafford. SP-StafW *Fr.* Move to California, The.

Written structure. George Oppen. CP-OppGN

Written the Day I Was to Begin a Residency at the State Penitentiary. Arthur Sze. SP-SzeA

Written to Music. Kenneth Rexroth. CP-RexrK

Written under the Picture of the Celebrated Miss Burns. Robert Burns. CP-BurnR

Written upon a Blank Leaf in "The Compleat Angler" William Wordsworth. CP-WorW2

Written, verse or prose, was of no consequence, The. Stanzas for Mary Stuart. Derek Mahon. CP-MahoD

Written with a Pencil over the Chimney-Piece, in the Parlour of the Inn at Kenmore, Taymouth. Robert Burns. CP-BurnR

Written with a Pencil, Standing by the Fall of Fyers, near Loch-Ness. Robert Burns. CP-BurnR

Written with a Pencil upon a Stone in the Wall of the House (an Out-House), on the Island at Grasmere. William Wordsworth. CP-WorW1

Written with a Slate Pencil on a Stone, on the Side of the Mountain of Black Comb. William Wordsworth. CP-WorW1

Written with a Slate Pencil upon a Stone, the Largest of a Heap Lying near a Deserted Quarry, upon One of the Islands at Rydal. William Wordsworth. CP-WorW1; MW-WorW

Wrong Door, The. William Carlos Williams. CP-WilW2

Wrong has a twisty look like wrung misprinted. Ritornello. Charles Tomlinson. CP-TomlC

Wrong Kind of Insurance, The. John Ashbery. SP-AshbJ

Wrong look into heavy stone, A. Tapestry and Sail. James Dickey. CP-DickJ

Wrong Number. Charles Bukowski. SP-BukC2

Wrong Train. Ted Berrigan. SP-BerrT

Wrong'd, yet not daring to expresse my paine. Virgils Gnat. Edmund Spenser. CP-Spens

Wrongs if neglected, vanish in short time. Anger. Robert Herrick. CP-HerrR

Wrote Bernard of Cluny (al - / most 3000 lines of it with). De Contemptu Mundi. James Laughlin. CP-LaugJ

Wrote on the Blank Leaf of a Copy of My First Edition, Which I Sent to an Old Sweetheart, Then Married. Robert Burns. CP-BurnR

Wrote This Last Night. Allen Ginsberg. CP-GinsA

Wrought iron of the gate at Pierson College, The. Pierson College. Czeslaw Milosz. CP-MiloCN, tr. by Robert Hass

Wunst I sassed my Pa, an' he. Runaway Boy, The. James Whitcomb Riley. CP-RileJ

Wunst I tooked our pepper-box lid. Some Scattering Remarks of Bub's. James Whitcomb Riley. CP-RileJ

Wunst we went a-fishin'—Me. Fishing Party, The. James Whitcomb Riley. CP-RileJ

Wunzt, 'way West in Illinoise. Bear Family, A. James Whitcomb Riley. CP-RileJ

Wuthering Heights. Sylvia Plath. CP-PlatS

WWI. Miller Williams. CP-WillM

W'y, one time wuz a little-weenty dirl. Maymie's Story of Red Riding-Hood. James Whitcomb Riley. CP-RileJ Fr. Child-World, A.

W'y, wunst they wuz a Little Boy went out. Bear Story, The. James Whitcomb Riley. CP-RileJ Fr. Child-World, A.

Wyeth's Mild Cans. Richard Wilbur. CP-WilbR

Wyncote, Pennsylvania: A Gloss. Thomas Kinsella. CP-KinsT

Wyoming. Clarence Major. SP-MajoC

Wystan Auden. James Schuyler. CP-SchuJ

X

"X" Louis Zukofsky. CP-ZukLS

X out the rondure of. Object. A. R. Ammons. CP-AmmoA

X Ray. Arthur Sze. SP-SzeA

X-Ray Waiting Room in the Hospital, The. Randall Jarrell. CP-JarrR

X to the Nth. Charles Olson. CP-OlsoC

X, whom society's most mild command. Nonconformist, The. Donald Davie. CP-DaviDC

Xenia ("And / Unto thine eyes my heart"). Ezra Pound. CP-PoEar

Xenia ("Come let us play with our own toys"). Ezra Pound. CP-PoEar

Xenia ("Out of the overhanging gray mist"). Ezra Pound. CP-PoEar

Xenophanes. Ralph Waldo Emerson. CP-EmerR

Xenophanes. Louis Zukofsky. CP-ZukLS

Xenophanes, the Monist of Colophon. Thomas Hardy. CP-HardT

Xenophobia. Rae Armantrout. SP-ArmaA

Xerox the Spirit and Be Well. Andrei Codrescu. SP-CodrA

Xeroxed on brainmatter. Tongue Is, The. Yusef Komunyakaa. CP-KomuY

Xmas. Robert Creeley. CP-CreeR

Xmas Carol, A. G. K. Chesterton.

Xmas Coming. Kenneth Rexroth. CP-RexrK

Xmas Day. G. K. Chesterton. CP-ChesG

Xmas Gift. Allen Ginsberg. CP-GinsA; SP-GinsA

Xmas Poem: Bolinas. Robert Creeley. CP-CreeR

Xylophone, triangle, marimba, soprano, violin. Rehearsal, The. Arthur Sze. SP-SzeA

Y

Y is a WELL KNOWN ATHLETE'S BRIDE. E. E. Cummings. CP-CummE

Y mae'n llewyn yma'n llon. Cywydd. Gerard Manley Hopkins. CP-HopkG

Y Un Canción Por E. Andrei Codrescu. SP-CodrA

Yacht for Sale. Archibald MacLeish. CP-MacLA

Yachts, The. William Carlos Williams. CP-WilW1

Yaddo Letter, The. Derek Mahon. CP-MahoD

Yaddo: The Grand Manor. Sylvia Plath. CP-PlatS

Yadwigha, on a Red Couch, among Lilies. Sylvia Plath. CP-PlatS

Yadwigha, the literalists once wondered how you. Yadwigha, on a Red Couch, among Lilies. Sylvia Plath. CP-PlatS

Yah. Robert Creeley. SP-CreeR

Yahoo's Overthrow, The. Jonathan Swift. CP-SwifJ

Yak, The. Theodore Roethke. CP-RoetT

Yakka-hoola-hikki-doola. Well/Well/Not-At-All. Hart Crane. CP-CranH

Yankee Doodle. Nicholas Vachel Lindsay. CP-LindV

Yankee Girl, The. John Greenleaf Whittier. CP-WhitJ

Yánnina. James Merrill. SP-MerrJ

Yard, The. Yannis Ritsos. SP-RitsY, tr. by Andonis Decavalles

Yard has sopped into its green-grizzled self its new year whiteness, The. In January. James Schuyler. CP-SchuJ

Yard Journal. Charles Wright. SP-WrigC

Yard Work. Charles Wright. SP-WrigCN

Yardley Oak. William Cowper. CP-CowpW

Yarrow. Paul Muldoon. CP-MuldP

Yarrow. Louis Zukofsky. CP-ZukLS

Yarrow Revisited. William Wordsworth. CP-WorW2; MW-WorW

Yarrow Unvisited [1803]. William Wordsworth. CP-WorW1; MW-WorW

Yarrow Visited [September, 1814]. William Wordsworth. CP-WorW2, MW-WorW

Yase: September. Gary Snyder. CP-SnydG

Yaupon. Louis Zukofsky. CP-ZukLS

Y'ave laught enough (sweet) vary now your Text. Laugh and Lie Downe. Robert Herrick. CP-HerrR

Yawn, A. Christina Georgina Rossetti. CP-RosC3

Yawning, sunned concave, A. Sheep-Boy, The. Thomas Hardy. CP-HardT

Ye Are Come unto Mount Sion. Christina Georgina Rossetti. CP-RosC2

Ye banks and braes and streams around. Highland Mary. Robert Burns. CP-BurnR

Ye banks and braes o' bonie [or bonnie] Doon. Banks o' Doon, The ("Ye banks and braes o' bonie [or bonnie] Doon"). Robert Burns. CP-BurnR

Ye beauties! O how great the sun. On a Bed of Guernsey Lilies. Christopher Smart. SP-SmarC

Ye blind, ye deaf, ye mute! Ho, here's healing! Lines for a Hospital. Countee Cullen. CP-CullC

Ye blood-red spears-men of the dawn's array. To the Dawn: Defiance. Ezra Pound. CP-PoEar

Ye blooming train who give despair or joy. Epilogue to *The Distrest Mother*, An. Samuel Johnson. CP-JohnS

Ye Clouds! that far above me float and pause. France: An Ode. Samuel Taylor Coleridge. CP-ColeS; MW-ColeS

Ye Cupids, droop each little head. Catullus. See Who loves beauty / veil her statues

Ye damnable dunces, ye criblers, what mean ye. Answer to the Christmas-Box, An. Unknown, sometimes at. to Thomas Sheridan. CP-SherT

Ye distant spires, ye antique towers. Ode on a Distant Prospect of Eton College. Thomas Gray. CP-GrayT

Ye do command me to all virtue ever. Henry David Thoreau. CP-ThorH

Ye Dorian woods and waves, lament aloud. Moschus. CP-ShelP Fr. Lament for Bion.

Ye elms that wave on Malvern Hill. Malvern Hill. Herman Melville. SP-MelvH

Ye fellowship that sing the woods and spring. To the Raphaelite Latinists. Ezra Pound. CP-PoEar

Ye flags of Piccadilly, / Where I posted up and down. Arthur Hugh Clough. SP-ClouA

Ye flaming Powers, and winged Warrio[u]rs bright. Upon the Circumcision. John Milton. CP-MiltJ

Ye flowery banks o' bon[n]ie Doon. Banks o' Doon, The ("Ye flowery banks o' bon[n]ie Doon"). Robert Burns. CP-BurnR

Ye gallants bright I red you right. Beware o' Bonie Ann. Robert Burns. CP-BurnR

Ye Gave Me No Meat. Jones Very. CP-VeryJ

Ye gentle visitations of calm thought. Fragment: "Ye gentle visitations of calm thought." Percy Bysshe Shelley. CP-ShelP

Ye glitt'ring Train! whom Lace and Velvet bless. Samuel Johnson. CP-JohnS Fr. Irene.

Ye Goat-herd Gods. Sir Philip Sidney. SP-SidnP Fr. Arcadia.

Ye [or you] goat-herd gods, that love the grassy mountains. Ye Goat-herd Gods. Sir Philip Sidney. SP-SidnP Fr. Arcadia.

Ye gods that have a home beyond the world. Chorus of Old Men in "Ægeus", The. Edwin Arlington Robinson. CP-RobiE

Ye hasten to the grave! What seek ye there. Sonnet: "Ye hasten to the grave! What seek ye there." Percy Bysshe Shelley. CP-ShelP

Ye have been fresh and green. To Meadows [or Meddowes]. Robert Herrick. CP-HerrR

Ye Have Forgotten the Exhortation. Christina Georgina Rossetti. CP-RosC3

Ye have Grace. Ralph Waldo Emerson. CP-EmerR

Ye have hoarded up treasure in the last days.—James 5:3. Jones Very. CP-VeryJ

Ye heavenly spirites, whose ashie cinders lie. Ruins of Rome. Joachim Du Bellay. CP-Spens, *tr. by* Edmund Spenser

Ye intelligences, turning the third sphere. Banqauet, The. Dante Alighieri. CP-NemeH, *tr. by* Howard Nemerov *Fr.* Convito.

Ye Irish Lords, ye *knights* an' *squires.* Author's Earnest Cry and Prayer, to the Right Honorable and Honorable, the Scotch Representatives in the House of Commons, The. Robert Burns. CP-BurnR

Ye Jacobites By Name. Robert Burns. CP-BurnR

Ye jovial boys who love the joys. Fornicator. A New Song, The. Robert Burns. CP-BurnR

Ye juster Powers of Love and Fate. Invocation, The: "Ye juster Powers of Love and Fate." Sir John Suckling. CP-SuckJ

Ye kings, in wisdom, sense and power, supreme. Imitation of Juvenal — Satire VIII. William Wordsworth. CP-WorW1

Ye know my heart, my lady dear. Sir Thomas Wyatt. CP-WyatT

Ye ladies, walking past me piteous-eyed. Sonnet: To the same Ladies; with their Answer. Dante Alighieri. CW-RossD, *tr. by* Dante Gabriel Rossetti

Ye learned sisters which have oftentimes. Epithalamion: "Ye learned sisters which have oftentimes." Edmund Spenser. CP-Spens

Ye Lime-trees, ranged before this hallowed Urn. *see also* Inscription in the Grounds of Coleorton, the Seat of Sir George Beaumont, BART., Leicestershire *and* Inscription in a Garden of the Same. William Wordsworth. CP-WorW1

Ye Linnets, let us try, beneath this grove. God Neither Known Nor Loved by the World. Jeanne Marie Bouvier de la Motte- Guyon. CP-CowpW

Ye living Lamps, by whose dear light. Mower to the Glowworms [*or* Glow-Worms *or* Glo-Worms], The. Andrew Marvell. CP-MarvA

Ye living powers enclosed in stately shrine. Sir Philip Sidney. SP-SidnP *Fr.* Arcadia.

Ye Lords and Commons, Men of Wit. Sandys's Ghost, or a Proper New Ballad on the New Ovid's Metamorphosis as it Was Intended to Be. Alexander Pope. CP-PopeA

Ye maggots, feed on Willie's brains. Epitaph for William Nicol. Robert Burns. CP-BurnR

Ye martial pow'rs, and all ye tuneful nine. Goliath of Gath. Phillis Wheatley. CP-WheaP

Ye may simper, blush, and smile. To Cherry-Blossomes. Robert Herrick. CP-HerrR

Ye men of wit and wealth, why all this sneering. Lines *Written on a Window, at the King's Arms Tavern, Dumfries.* Robert Burns. CP-BurnR

Ye noble Lords who bravely fight. George Meredith. CP-MerG2

Ye now are panting up life's hill! Address to the Sons of Burns, after Visiting Their Father's Grave (August 14th, 1803). William Wordsworth. MW-WorW

Ye nymphs! if e'er your eyes were red. On the Lamented Death of Mrs. Throckmorton's Bullfinch. William Cowper. CP-CowpW

Ye nymphs of Himera (for ye have shed). John Milton. *See* Nymphs of Himera—for you remember Daphnis and Hylas

Ye Nymphs of Solyma! begin the song. Messiah [a Sacred Eclogue, in Imitation of Virgil's Pollio]. Alexander Pope. CP-PopeA

Ye nymphs, the charge is royal. Song: "Ye nymphs, the charge is royal." John Dryden. CP-DryJ2 *Fr.* Albion and Albanius.

Ye nymphs whom starry rays invest. To Lyce, an Elderly Lady. Samuel Johnson. CP-JohnS

Ye old mule, that thin[c]k your self so fair [*or* fayre]. Sir Thomas Wyatt. CP-WyatT

Ye old-time stave that pealth out. For This Christmas. James Whitcomb Riley. CP-RileJ

Ye paltry [*or* paultry] underlings of state. On the Irish Club. Jonathan Swift. CP-SwifJ

Ye patriot Crouds, who burn for *England's* Fame. New Prologue Spoken at the Representation of *Comus.* A. Samuel Johnson. CP-JohnS

Ye poets ragged and forlorn. Advice to the Grub Street Verse-Writers. Jonathan Swift. CP-SwifJ

Ye sacred Nurseries of blooming Youth! Oxford, May 30, 1820. William Wordsworth. CP-WorW2

Ye scenes of my childhood, whose loved recollection. On a Distant View of the Village and School of Harrow on the Hill. Lord Byron. CP-Byron

Ye Scholar. James Whitcomb Riley. CP-RileJ

Ye sister pow'rs, who o'er the sacred groves. John Milton. *See* Say, goddesses, guardians of the sacred groves

Ye sons of Athens, grant me one request. Prologue to *Hippolytus,* Spoken by a Boy of Six Years Old. Richard Helsham. CP-SherT

Ye Sons of Levi, Church Divines. Poem, A: "Ye Sons of Levi, Church Divines." Samuel Owens. CP-SherT

Ye sons of old Killie, assembled by Willie. Sons of Old Killie, The. Robert Burns. CP-BurnR

Ye sorrowing people! who from bondage fly. Fugitive Slaves, The. Jones Very. CP-VeryJ

Ye souls unus'd to lofty verse. Nose, The. Samuel Taylor Coleridge. CP-ColeS

Ye stars in ye skies seem twinkling. Edge of the Wind, The. James Whitcomb Riley. CP-RileJ

Ye Storms, resound the praises of your King! On the Same Occasion. William Wordsworth. CP-WorW2

Ye that a thousand earth-spins. For the Triumph of the Arts. Ezra Pound. CP-PoEar

Ye That Fear Him, Both Small and Great. Christina Georgina Rossetti. CP-RosC2

Ye that nourish hopes of fame! Teaching of the Blows of Fortune, The. George Meredith. CP-MerG2

Ye that when surges covered the stars. Uncreation. G. K. Chesterton. CP-ChesG

Ye true "Loyal Natives", attend to my song. Extempore [on the *Loyal Natives'* Verses]. Robert Burns. CP-BurnR

Ye vales and hills whose beauty hither drew. Inscription for a Monument in Crossthwaite Curch, in the Vale of Keswick. William Wordsworth. CP-WorW2

Ye watch the appearance of the earth and sky. Meteorologists, The. Jones Very. CP-VeryJ

Ye who against the evils of our lot. Be of Good Courage. Jones Very. CP-VeryJ

Ye who behold the State in grandeur rise. Appeal. Jones Very. CP-VeryJ

Ye who have passed Death's haggard hills; and ye. Trees of the Garden, The. Dante Gabriel Rossetti. CW-RossD *Fr.* House of Life, The.

Ye who intelligent the Third Heaven move. First Canzone of the Convito, The. Dante Alighieri. CP-ShelP, *tr. by* Percy Bysshe Shelley

Ye, who with buoyant spirits blessed. Inscription for a Seat by the Pathway Side Ascending to Windy Brow. William Wordsworth. CP-WorW1

Ye wise, instruct me to endure. On Censure. Jonathan Swift. CP-SwifJ

Ye wise philosophers! explain. Upon the South Sea Project. Jonathan Swift. CP-SwifJ

Ye woodland choirs come consecrate the lay. Epithalamium, The: "Ye woodland choirs come consecrate the lay." Annis Boudinot Stockton. CP-StocA

Yea, as I sit here, crutched, and cricked, and bent. Panthera. Thomas Hardy. CP-HardT

Yea, blessed and holy is he that hath part in the First / Resurrection! Christina Georgina Rossetti. CP-RosC2

Yea, I Have a Goodly Heritage. Christina Georgina Rossetti. CP-RosC3

Yea, I have put thee from me utterly. Dictum. Countee Cullen. CP-CullC

Yea, if Thou wilt, Thou canst put up Thy sword. Christina Georgina Rossetti. CP-RosC2

Yea, the Sparrow Hath Found Her an House. Christina Georgina Rossetti. *See* Wisdom

Yea, we go down to sea in ships. At Sea. James Whitcomb Riley. CP-RileJ

Year, The. Czeslaw Milosz. CP-MiloC; CP-MiloCN, *tr. by* Richard Lourie

Year, The. Carl Sandburg. CP-SandC

Year a bird flies against the drum, The. For Now. W. S. Merwin. SP-MerwW

Year after year the moon. Song of the Forsaken Lilac Tree. Marya Alexandrovna Zaturenska. SP-ZatuM

Year after your death, dear Y. Z., A. Elegy for Y. Z. Czeslaw Milosz. CP-MiloC; CP-MiloCN, *tr. by* Robert Hass

Year Afterwards, A. Christina Georgina Rossetti. CP-RosC3

Year ago I breathed the Italian air, A. Ravenna. Oscar Wilde. CP-WildO

Year ago tonight my father died, A. For My Father. Christopher Logue. SP-LoguC

Year ago you swore, fond she!, A. Endorsement to the Deed of Separation, in the April of 1816. Lord Byron. CP-Byron

Year burns an icon, The. 1984. Yusef Komunyakaa. CP-KomuY

Year draws down, The. In the meadows. Advent. Kenneth Rexroth. CP-RexrK

Year dulls toward its eaves-dripping end, The. Late Subterfuge. Robert Penn Warren. CP-WarrR

Year: 452. The Place: the southern, The. Encounter, An. W. H. Auden. CP-AudeW

Year goes by very fast but it takes a long time, The. Morning Walk, A. Philip Whalen. SP-WhalP

Year had flown, and o'er the sea away, A. Iseult of Brittany. Matthew Arnold. SP-ArnoM *Fr.* Tristram and Iseult.

Year has become heavy, will you dare, The. Dark Year, The. Marya Alexandrovna Zaturenska. SP-ZatuM

Year has cast its cloak away, The. Rondeau: "Year has cast its cloak away, The." Charles, Duc d' Orléans. CP-WilbR

Year has come to us as though out of hiding, A. Early January. W. S. Merwin. SP-MerwW

Year in its cold beginning, The. Gift-Poem. Muriel Rukeyser. CP-RukeM

Year in, year out, most of us do our best. Fifty. Miller Williams. CP-WillM

Year Is a Great Circle or the Year Is a Great Mistake, The. Charles Olson. CP-OlsoC

Year 1900, The. Czeslaw Milosz. CP-MiloCN, *tr. by* Robert Hass

Year 1934, The. Jaroslav Seifert. SP-SeifJ, *tr. by* Ewald Osers

Year of griefs being through, they had to merge, The. Blank, A. Thom Gunn. CP-GunnT

Year of Meteors(1859–60). Walt Whitman. CP-WhitW

Year of the Child, The. Robert Earl Hayden. CP-HaydR

Year of the Sloes, for Ishi, The. Paul Muldoon. CP-MuldP

Year on one line, A. Organic Form. Sam Hamill. SP-HamiS

Year or two, and grey Euripides, A. Baccalaureate. Archibald MacLeish. CP-MacLA

Year passes behind me, A. Speech of the Mother, from "The Middle of the Air" Muriel Rukeyser. CP-RukeM

Year Round. Langston Hughes. CP-HughL

Year still a child, The. Dead Hive, The. W. S. Merwin. SP-MerwW

Year stood at its equinox, The. Milking-Maid, The. Christina Georgina Rossetti. CP-RosC1

Year That Trembled and Reel'd beneath Me. Walt Whitman. CP-WhitW

Year the head / went out into a, The. 1971. Robert Creeley. CP-CreeR

Year the Prince Imperial was born, The. Recollection. Arthur Rimbaud. CP-RimbA, *tr. by* Martin Sorrell

Year They Outlawed Baseball, The. Miller Williams. CP-WillM

Year they outlawed baseball, The. Year They Outlawed Baseball, The. Miller Williams. CP-WillM

Year this truck was made, The. Working on the '58 Willys Pickup. Gary Snyder. CP-SnydG

Year turns on the pivot, The. Rainer Maria Rilke. CP-RilkFr, *tr. by* A. Poulin, Jr. *Fr.* Valaisian Quatrains, The.

Year turns. The wolf takes back her tit, The. Saturnalia. Louise Glück. SP-GlucL

Year was river-throated, with the stare of legend, The. Mother Garden's Round. Muriel Rukeyser. CP-RukeM

Yearly Distress, The. William Cowper. CP-CowpW

Yearly, with tent and rifle, our careless white men go. Truce of the Bear, The. Rudyard Kipling. CP-KiplR

Yearning for the time, trembling with the hope of Isabel. Homage to Herman Melville. John Logan. CP-LogaJ

Yearning yet chaste eyes she held upon, The. Petrarch. CP-Petra, *tr. by* J. G. Nichols

Years. Sylvia Plath. CP-PlatS

Years, The. Gary Snyder. CP-SnydG

Years after. Cat Ghosts. W. S. Merwin. SP-MerwW

Years after surviving. Word Basket Woman. Gary Snyder. CP-SnydG

Years ago, as dusk seeped from the blue. Lost Children, The. Gregory Orr. SP-OrrG

Years ago I lost. Unquiet Ones, The. Stanley Kunitz. CP-KunSC

Years ago it was easy to dream of wolves. Dream Dogs. Andrei Codrescu. SP-CodrA

Years ago—it would have been 1956 or 1957—when I was a teenager. Some Prose on *Poetry*. Raymond Carver. CP-CarvR

Years ago, while we were settling in. Stranger, The. Thomas Kinsella. CP-KinsT

Years ago, who sang in the towers? Prisoners. Rainer Maria Rilke. CP-RilkFr, *tr. by* A. Poulin, Jr.

Years are but half a score, The. On the Big Horn. John Greenleaf Whittier. CP-WhitJ

Years are many since his hand, The. William Forster. John Greenleaf Whittier. CP-WhitJ

Years are many since, in youth and hope, The. Miriam. John Greenleaf Whittier. CP-WhitJ

Years are passing, The. On the palace's pumice façade appears. Afterword. Joseph Brodsky. CP-BrodJ, *tr. by* Jamey Gambrell

Years As Catches, The. Robert Duncan. SP-DuncR

Year's Awakening, The. Thomas Hardy. CP-HardT

Year's before action when the wish alone. Course. Muriel Rukeyser. CP-RukeM

Year's "Casualties", A. Ambrose Bierce. SP-BierA

Years did I vainly seek the good Lord's grace. Anselmo. James Whitcomb Riley. CP-RileJ

Year's doors open, The. January First. Octavio Paz. CP-BishE

Year's End. Jorge Luis Borges. SP-BorgJ, *tr. by* W. S. Merwin

Year's End. Richard Wilbur. CP-WilbR

Years / Fall like dry leaves, The. New Year. Langston Hughes. CP-HughL; CP-HughL1

Years from now. Early One Summer. W. S. Merwin. SP-MerwW

Years gone by in Chicago once. Algeria. Hayden Carruth. CP-CarHS

Years grow small and gray, The. Reflections On a Centaur. Marya Alexandrovna Zaturenska. SP-ZatuM

Years Had Worn Their Season's Belt, The. George Meredith. CP-MerG2

Years have gathered grayly, The. In a Eweleaze near Weatherbury. Thomas Hardy. CP-HardT

Years have gone, The. It is spring. Andrée Rexroth ("Years have gone, The. It is spring"). Kenneth Rexroth. CP-RexrK

Years later what they talked about was. Old Cadets, The. Wyatt Prunty. SP-PrunW

Years long in the insanities of adolescence. Autobiography of a Comedian. John Ciardi. CP-CiarJ

Years. Many years. Friends laugh, including. Essay on Love. Hayden Carruth. CP-CarHS

Years of Loss, The. David Ignatow. SP-IgnaD

Years of the Dog. Archibald MacLeish. CP-MacLA

Years of the Modern. Walt Whitman. CP-WhitW

Year's run out, The. Timing. A. R. Ammons. CP-AmmoA

Years seem to tumble, The. Years, The. Gary Snyder. CP-SnydG

Year's Sheddings, The. George Meredith. CP-MerG1

Years since (but names to me before). Singer, The. John Greenleaf Whittier. CP-WhitJ

Year's Spinning, A. Elizabeth Barrett Browning. CP-BroEB

Years that did not count—Civilians in the towns, The. Hiatus. Louis MacNeice. CP-MacNL

Years that since we met have flown, The. Autograph, An. John Greenleaf Whittier. CP-WhitJ

Year's Windfalls, A. Christina Georgina Rossetti. CP-RosC1

Yeats had his Sato's sword, a true blade dipped. With a Machet Across My Knees. Robert Stock. SP-StocR

Yeats said, *To those who see spirits, human skin*. Seamus Heaney. SP-HeanSO *Fr.* Squarings.

Yee pretty Huswives, wo'd ye know. To the Little Spinners. Robert Herrick. CP-HerrR

Ye[e] silent shades, whose each tree here. To Groves. Robert Herrick. CP-HerrR

Yehuda Ha-Levi. Yehuda Amichai. SP-AmicY, *tr. by* Stephen Mitchell

Yell'ham-Wood's Story. Thomas Hardy. CP-HardT

Yellow. Robert Creeley. CP-CreeR

Yellow. Josephine Jacobsen. CP-JacoJ

Yellow. Anne Sexton. CP-SextA

Yellow Afternoon. Wallace Stevens. CP-StevW; CP-StevWP

Yellow and pale as ripened corn. Lines for a Painting by Leighton. Robert Browning. CP-BroR2

Yellow became alive. Yellow. Josephine Jacobsen. CP-JacoJ

Yellow Bicycle. Czeslaw Milosz. CP-MiloC; CP-MiloCN, *tr. by* Robert Hass

Yellow Book, The. Derek Mahon. CP-MahoD

Yellow Cab. Charles Bukowski. SP-BukC1

Yellow Cars. William Stafford. SP-StafWW

Yellow Chimney, The. William Carlos Williams. CP-WilW2

Yellow Christ, The; after Gauguin. John Logan. CP-LogaJ

Yellow Dog Café. Yusef Komunyakaa. CP-KomuY

Yellow dust on a bumble. Troths. Carl Sandburg. CP-SandC

Yellow Emperor went wandering, The. Lost Pearl, The. Chuang Tzu. CP-MertT

Yellow Evening Star. Carl Sandburg. CP-SandC

Yellow eye meets mine, A. Coyote in the Zoo, The. William Stafford. SP-StafWW

Yellow fingers / lift a match to. Match. Donald Hall. CP-HallD

Yellow flower / (Light and spirit), A. Song for Nobody. Thomas Merton. CP-MertT

Yellow Flower, The. William Carlos Williams. CP-WilW2

Yellow Flowers. James Schuyler. CP-SchuJ

Yellow flowers, yellow flowers. Descendant of Solomon and the Queen of Sheba. Clarence Major. SP-MajoC

Yellow goat in winter sunlight, The. Arkhangel'sk. Norman Dubie. CP-DubiN

Yellow-Hammer, The. Thomas Hardy. CP-HardT

Yellow, hurt light shivering over New York, A. Robert Stock. SP-StocR *Fr.* Separation.

Yellow leaf, from the darkness, A. Brooding Grief. D. H. Lawrence. CP-LawrD

Yellow leaves speak early November's heart on the river. Prairie Woodland. Carl Sandburg. CP-SandC

Yellow lion shakes the ground, The. Man and the Lion. Josephine Jacobsen. CP-JacoJ

Yellow-lit Budweiser signs over oaken bars. Uptown. Allen Ginsberg. CP-GinsA; SP-GinsA

Yellow Man, Purple Man. Emily Dickinson. CP-DickE

Yellow Newspaper and a Wooden Leg. James Tate. SP-TateJ

Yellow of the Mask, The. Charles Olson. CP-OlsoC

Yellow Pitcher Plant. Thom Gunn. CP-GunnT

Yellow Ribbons, Madness, Victory. Sam Hamill. SP-HamiS

Yellow River is boundless, The. Han-shan. CP-ColdM, *tr. by* Red Pine

Yellow Rose, A. Jorge Luis Borges. SP-BorgJ, *tr. by* Ken Krabbenhoft

Yellow scarf runs through his fingers, A. Courtship, Diligence. Rita Dove. SP-DoveR

Yellow Season, The. William Carlos Williams. CP-WilW2

Yellow Stones—Sea of Majestic Doves. Kenneth Patchen. CP-PatcK

Yellow sun steps over the mountain-top, The. Bad Beginning, A. D. H. Lawrence. CP-LawrD

Yellow Tree Peony, The. William Carlos Williams. CP-WilW2

Yellow trees bend over broken glass. It Does Not Follow, but When in the Street. A. K. Ramanujan. CP-RamaA

Yellow Violets, The. Jones Very. CP-VeryJ

Yellow, yellow, yellow, yellow! Primrose. William Carlos Williams. CP-WilW1

Yellowbird, The. James Whitcomb Riley. CP-RileJ

Yellowjacket. Peter Blue Cloud. SP-BlueP

Yellowjackets. Yusef Komunyakaa. CP-KomuY

Yeou taught men to break branches. Canto 53: "Yeou taught men to break branches." Ezra Pound. SP-PounE *Fr.* Cantos.

Yes. Wyatt Prunty. SP-PrunW

Yes. William Stafford. SP-StafWW

Yes, a long cool vindt is pacing over the plains and beside it Captain. Captain Bada. Frank O'Hara. SP-OharF

Yes. After all my arguments with myself. Sonnet: "Yes. After all my arguments with myself." Hayden Carruth. CP-CarHS *Fr.* Sonnets.

Yes and It's Hopeless. Allen Ginsberg. CP-GinsA

Yes And No. Laura Riding Jackson. CP-RidiL

Yes and No. Ogden Nash. CP-NashO

Yes and no then yes and no. Music Rewritten. Michael Palmer. SP-PalmM

Yes and when the warm unseasonable weather. Memory Green. Archibald MacLeish. CP-MacLA

Yes at first you / go down smooth as. Margaret Atwood. SP-AtwM1

Yes, Barcelona is three thousand miles. Reply to S. K. John Ciardi. CP-CiarJ

"Yes, But . . ." Theodore Weiss. SP-WeisT

Yes but even / 4 or(&). E. E. Cummings. CP-CummE

Yes but / it's October and the leaves. Here & Now. A. R. Ammons. CP-AmmoA

Yes but your sweetness. Echo ("Yes but your sweetness"). Robert Creeley. CP-CreeR

Yes, contumelious fair, you scorn. Author Apologizes to a Lady, for His Being a Little Man, The. Christopher Smart. SP-SmarC

—Yes for a time they held as well. Gerard Manley Hopkins. CP-HopkG

Yes! full surely 'twas the Echo. William Wordsworth. *See* Yes, it was the mountain Echo

Yes, he is here in this. At David's Grave. Denise Levertov. SP-LeveDS

Yes, he was that, or that, as you prefer. T. A. H. Ambrose Bierce. SP-BierA

Yes, holy be thy resting place. Emily Jane Brontë. CP-BronE

Yes! hope may with my strong desire keep pace. Love's Justification. Michelangelo Buonarroti. CP-WorW1, *tr. by* William Wordsworth

"Yes," I answered you last night. Lady's "Yes," The. Elizabeth Barrett Browning. CP-BroEB

Yes, I beheld th' Athenian Queen. On Receiving from the Right Hon. the Lady Frances Shirley a Standish and Two Pens. Alexander Pope. CP-PopeA

Yes, I being / the terrible puppet of my dreams, shall. Visible the Untrue, The. Hart Crane. CP-CranH

Yes, I have a thousand tongues. Stephen Crane. CP-CranS

Yes, I have seen their eyes. In peaceful gardens. Eighth Elegy. Children's Elegy. Muriel Rukeyser. CP-RukeM

Yes, I know. February 17th. Anne Sexton. CP-SextA

Yes, I Know. Stevie Smith. CP-SmitS

Yes, I know all that, I should be modern. Conventions of Despair. A. K. Ramanujan. CP-RamaA

Yes, I know his new poems. Simeon. Constantine P. Cavafy. CP-CavaC, *tr. by* Theoharis Constantine Theoharis

Yes, I loved him all to well. Eva. Christina Georgina Rossetti. CP-RosC3

Yes, I only got here on my own. On My Own. Philip Levine. SP-LeviP

Yes! I perceive it's to your Love. Letter's Triumph, The. Thomas Hardy. CP-HardT

Yes I remember those days. Those Days. Raymond Carver. CP-CarvR

Yes, I too could face death and never shrink. Christina Georgina Rossetti. CP-RosC3

Yes, I'd like a pair of *Bicos de Lacre*. Dear Elizabeth. May Swenson. SP-SwenM

Yes I'm a dope fiend, I dont believe your laws. Dope Fiend Blues. Allen Ginsberg. SP-GinsA

Yes, I'm the lady he wrote the sonnets to. Long View from the Suburbs. Jane Cooper. CP-CoopJ

Yes in a circle the imagined train. Michael Palmer. SP-PalmM

Yes! in the sea of life enisled. To Marguerite—Continued. Matthew Arnold. SP-ArnoM *Fr.* Switzerland.

Yes is a pleasant country. E. E. Cummings. CP-CummE; SP-CummM

Yes it *is* sex and money that matters, a long canyon wind effects. Dear M. Michael Palmer. SP-PalmM

Yes, it is the same Schopenhauer (1788). Schopenhauer's Crying. Adam Zagajewski. SP-ZagaA, *tr. by* Renata Gorczynski

Yes, it is there, the city full of music. It Is There. Muriel Rukeyser. CP-RukeM

Yes, it was the mountain Echo. William Wordsworth. CP-WorW1

Yes it was the prince's kiss. Fable: "Yes it was the prince's kiss." Muriel Rukeyser. CP-RukeM

Yes. / It's May 20th and the leaves. Leaves That Talk. Anne Sexton. CP-SextA

Yes, it's true, Berenike. Not more calm. Rite, The. Czeslaw Milosz. CP-MiloCN, *tr. by* Robert Hass

Yes, I've lived a good life—cows, the soil. Regards to Mr. Glover. Lorine Niedecker. CP-NiedL

Yes, let them gather! Summon forth. World's Convention, The. John Greenleaf Whittier. CP-WhitJ

Yes, let's face it Handspring, my Aurelius, good old friend. Girls as Windmills. James Laughlin. CP-LaugJ

Yes Log, The. Andrei Codrescu. SP-CodrA

Yes, my ha't 's ez ha'd ez stone. Coquette Conquered, A. Paul Laurence Dunbar. CP-DunbP

Yes, My life was short, yes, I loved. Franz Schubert: A Press Conference. Adam Zagajewski. SP-ZagaA, *tr. by* Renata Gorczynski

Yes, my love, I think about you. Thoughts. Dorothy Parker. CP-ParkD

Yes, noble old Warrior! this heart has beat high. British Stripling's War-Song, The. Samuel Taylor Coleridge. CP-ColeS

Yes, now I go ahead. Violins in Chaos? Philip Whalen. SP-WhalP

Yes, our election's past, and we've been free. Election, The. George Crabbe. SP-CrabG *Fr.* Borough, The.

Yes, pile the marble o'er him! It is well. Leggett's Monument. John Greenleaf Whittier. CP-WhitJ

"Yes," said the sister with the little pinched face. Drunkard's Funeral, The. Nicholas Vachel Lindsay. CP-LindV

Yes; She is Safely laid beneath the sod. Lines on Seeing Mrs Elizabeth Witherspoon Put in the Grave. Annis Boudinot Stockton. CP-StocA

Yes she was sweet and elegant and fair. Fragment on Hearing the Account of Mrs Ramseys Death. Annis Boudinot Stockton. CP-StocA

Yes; since she knows not need. Rake-hell Muses. Thomas Hardy. CP-HardT

Yes; such it was. Two-Years' Idyll, A. Thomas Hardy. CP-HardT

Yes; thank my stars! as early as I knew. Satire II of Dr. John Donne, Versified. Alexander Pope. CP-PopeA

Yes, that was a Sunless bad Friday. Reply of the County of Surrey to the Poet's Pathetic Address in Dispraise of Jean. George Meredith. CP-MerG2

Yes,—the bee sings—I confess it. To a Poet-Critic. James Whitcomb Riley. CP-RileJ

Yes, the Dead Speak to Us. Carl Sandburg. CP-SandC

Yes, the Mystery. May Swenson. SP-SwenM

Yes, then, always, as the rain, a star. Billion Freedoms, The. Kenneth Patchen. CP-PatcK

Yes, there is one thing braver than all flowers. Immortal. William Carlos Williams. CP-WilW1

Yes, these are the dog-days, Fortunatus. Under Sirius. W. H. Auden. CP-AudeW

Yes, they are alive and can have those colors. Blessing in Disguise, A. John Ashbery. SP-AshbJ

Yes, they remember you. William Dickey. SP-DickW *Fr.* At Your Old House.

Yes they set the house on fire, my father. Dream in Which the Routine Quality of My Imagination Is Fully Exposed. Jane Cooper. CP-CoopJ

Yes, this family portrait. Family Portrait. Carlos Drummond de Andrade. CP-BishE

Yes, this is how it was to have been born. Upon Looking into Sylvia Plath's *Letters Home*. John Updike. CP-UpdiJ

Yes. This Is the Call of Inspiration. Aleksandr Aleksandrovich Blok. SP-BlokA, *tr. by* Peter France *and* Jon Stallworthy

Yes! Thou Art Fair, Yet Be Not Moved. William Wordsworth. CP-WorW2

Yes tis an easy thing to view. Ode, An: "Yes tis an easy thing to view." Annis Boudinot Stockton. CP-StocA

Yes! Toss the words on the table. Games. Yehuda Amichai. SP-AmicYL, *tr. by* Benjamin Harshav *and* Barbara Harshav

Yes, we are all. L'Esprit de Géométrie et L'Esprit de Finesse. James Vincent Cunningham. CP-CunnJ

Yes – we excel in arts and arms. Story of a Cock and a Bull, A. Christopher Smart. SP-SmarC

Yes, we have liv'd—one pang, and then we part! Epitaph on Dr. Francis Atterbury, Bishop of Rochester, Who Died in Exile at Paris, 1732; a Dialogue. Alexander Pope. CP-PopeA

Yes; we'll pic-nic in the woods. George Meredith. CP-MerG2

Yes; we'll wed, my little fay. Conformers, The. Thomas Hardy. CP-HardT

Yes! we've our Borough-vices, and I know. Poor and Their Dwellings, The. George Crabbe. SP-CrabG *Fr.* Borough, The.

Yes. Whý do we áll, séeing of a soldier, bless him? bléss. Soldier, The. Gerard Manley Hopkins. CP-HopkG

Yes! wisdom shines in all his mien. R. C. Dallas. Lord Byron. CP-Byron

Yes, yes, and there is even a photograph. Meditation on a News Item. John Updike. CP-UpdiJ

Yes; yes; I am old. In me appears. Aged Newspaper Soliloquizes, The. Thomas Hardy. CP-HardT

Yes, yes—it's me. Sit down for a while. Nobody comes around anymore. I'm starting. Helen. Yannis Ritsos. SP-RitsY, *tr. by* Gwendolyn MacEwen *and* Nikos Tsingos

Yes, yes! that boon, life's richest treat. Improvisatore, The. Samuel Taylor Coleridge. CP-ColeS; MW-ColeS

Yes, you despise the man to Books confin'd. Epistle I, to Sir Richard Temple, Lord Cobham. Alexander Pope. CP-PopeA

Yes, you have it; I can see. Partnership. Edwin Arlington Robinson. CP-RobiE

Yes, your childhood: now a fable of fountains. Your Childhood in Menton. Federico García Lorca. CP-GarcF, tr. by Greg Simon and Steven F. White

Yes, your childhood now a legend of fountains. Your Childhood in Menton. Federico García Lorca. SP-GarcF, tr. by Edwin Honig

Yes; your up-dated modern page. Jubilee of a Magazine, The. Thomas Hardy. CP-HardT

Yes, you're still a little eccentric. Sagittarius Approaching Thirty-Five. Yusef Komunyakaa. CP-KomuY

Yessir they're all named. Go West Young Man. James Laughlin. CP-LaugJ

"Yessuh, here 'tis," Bumbo said, handing reins to the mister. October Picnic Long Ago. Robert Penn Warren. CP-WarrR

Yesterday. Raymond Carver. CP-CarvR

Yesterday. W. S. Merwin. SP-MerwWF

Yesterday, against admonishment. Father's Song. Gregory Orr. SP-OrrG

Yesterday and Today. Langston Hughes. CP-HughL; CP-HughL2

Yesterday and Tomorrow. Paul Laurence Dunbar. CP-DunbP

Yesterday doth never smile. Nun's Aspiration. Ralph Waldo Emerson. CP-EmerR

Yesterday, / from sudden red lily. Message. Philip Whalen. SP-WhalP

Yesterday he was nowhere to be found. New Foal. Ted Hughes. SP-HughTN

Yesterday I dressed in a dead man's. Yesterday. Raymond Carver. CP-CarvR

Yesterday I felt this ode. Ode to Laziness. Pablo Neruda. CP-WilN2, tr. by William Carlos Williams

Yesterday I found my pipe while pondering a long evening of work. Pipe, The. Stéphane Mallarmé. CP-MallS, tr. by Henry Weinfield

Yesterday I held your hand. Yesterday and Tomorrow. Paul Laurence Dunbar. CP-DunbP

Yesterday I saw a face. Horse of Desire, The. Robert Bly. SP-BlyR

Yesterday I wanted to. For Love. Robert Creeley. CP-CreeR

Yesterday, in a big market, I made seven thousand dollars. Back through the Looking Glass to This Side. John Ciardi. CP-CiarJ

Yesterday in Chicago for the moment. Revisit to the Room of a Saint. John Logan. CP-LogaJ

Yesterday is History. Emily Dickinson. CP-DickE

Yesterday, just before the first frost of the season. Field Pansy, The. Amy Clampitt. CP-ClamA

Yesterday, Licinius, what a day it was. Catullus. See Other day we spent, The

Yesterday Lost. Ivor Gurney. SP-GurnI

Yesterday morning enormous the moon hung low on the ocean. Their Beauty Has More Meaning. Robinson Jeffers. CP-JefR3

Yesterday Mrs. Friar phoned. "Mr. Ciardi" Suburban. John Ciardi. CP-CiarJ

Yesterday, snow was falling and all was chaos. Raymond Carver. CP-CarvR

Yesterday. / (Stars / blue). Song with Movement. Federico García Lorca. CP-GarcF, tr. by Alan S. Trueblood Fr. Theories.

Yesterday the fields were only grey with scattered snow. Winter's Tale, A. D. H. Lawrence. CP-LawrD

Yesterday, the man who calls himself "Our Father" Prisoner, The. Ai. SP-Ai

Yesterday They Tried. Kenneth Patchen. CP-PatcK

Yesterday, Today, and Forever. Emily Dickinson. SP-DickE

Yesterday, walking in a remote quarter. Before the House. Constantine P. Cavafy. CP-CavaC, tr. by Theoharis Constantine Theoharis

Yesterday was so long ago. Han-shan. CP-ColdM, tr. by Red Pine

Yesterdays. Jorge Luis Borges. SP-BorgJ, tr. by Stephen Kessler

Yesterday's norm encountered. Two Norms. Federico García Lorca. CP-GarcF, tr. by Christopher Maurer

Yesterday's sundown was very beautiful—I know it is out of fashion to. Ocean's Tribute, The. Robinson Jeffers. CP-JefR3

Yestreen I had a pint o' wine. Anna. Robert Burns. CP-BurnR

Yet a Little While. Christina Georgina Rossetti. See Heaven Is Not Far

Yet A Little While. Christina Georgina Rossetti. CP-RosC2

Yet a Little While. Christina Georgina Rossetti. CP-RosC3

Yet all comes out of this, that one door. Hafiz. CP-EmerR Fr. Odes.

Yet are they here the same unbroken knot. Gypsies. William Wordsworth. CP-WorW1

Yet at the last, ere our spearmen had found him. Rudyard Kipling. CP-KiplR Fr. Light That Failed, The.

Yet Dish. Gertrude Stein. CP-SteiG

Yet Do I Marvel. Countee Cullen. CP-CullC

Yet earth was very good in days of old, / And earth is lovely still. Sexagesima. Christina Georgina Rossetti. CP-RosC2

Yet from the antique heights or deeps of what. Front Door Soliloquy. Robert Graves. CP-GravR

Yet Gentle Will the Griffin Be. Nicholas Vachel Lindsay. CP-LindV Fr. Poems about the Moon.

Yet had I not much. That I Had Had Courage When Young. Hayden Carruth. CP-CarHS

Yet in an hour to come, disdainful dust. Edna St. Vincent Millay. CP-MillE

Yet in April, between the lines. Poor Man's Riches 2, A. A. K. Ramanujan. CP-RamaA

Yet in the end, defeated too, worn out and ready to fall. Oak-Leaves, The. Edna St. Vincent Millay. CP-MillE

Yet let us Thank the purblind race. Henry David Thoreau. CP-ThorH

Yet like grandfather. Extended Family. A. K. Ramanujan. CP-RamaA

Yet look on me—take not thine eyes away. To ———: "Yet look on me—take not thine eyes away." Percy Bysshe Shelley. CP-ShelP

Yet mystery is better than the light. Wallace Stevens. CP-StevWP

Yet Not to Listen to That Sung Nothing. John Ciardi. CP-CiarJ

Yet once again do I behold the forms. Voice of the Derwent, The. William Wordsworth. CP-WorW1

Yet once again, ye banks and bowery nooks. July's Farewell. Arthur Hugh Clough. SP-ClouA

Yet Once More. Jones Very. CP-VeryJ

Yet once more, O ye Laurels and once more. Lycidas. John Milton. CP-MiltJ

Yet see (may as I do) a confect of my cure—a dolor. Catullus. See Although entangled in prolonged grief

Yet sometimes to the sorrow stricken. Ralph Waldo Emerson. CP-EmerR

Yet though thou fetch thy pedegree so farre. Sir Walter Ralegh. CP-RaleW

Yet undone, become the unwritten, The. When Love Becomes Words. Laura Riding Jackson. CP-RidiL

Yet Unsayable, The. Robert Graves. CP-GravR

Yet what is this? the spring returns. George Meredith. CP-MerG2

Yet womanhood you reverence. Lady and the Painter, The. Robert Browning. CP-BroR2

Yet, yet, Biscayans! we must meet our Foes. Feelings of a Noble Biscayan at One of Those Funerals 1810. William Wordsworth. CP-WorW1

Yet, Yet Ye Downcast Hours. Walt Whitman. CP-WhitW

Yeti Poet Returns to His Village to Tell His Story, The. Lucille Clifton. SP-ClifL

Yevtushenko, Voznesensky and I. Dream, A. Charles Tomlinson. CP-TomlC

Yew-Tree on the Downs, The. D. H. Lawrence. CP-LawrD

Yew-Trees. William Wordsworth. CP-WorW1; MW-WorW

Yew's black fingers wag, The. Little Fugue. Sylvia Plath. CP-PlatS

Yggdrasill. Paul Muldoon. CP-MuldP

YgUDuh / ydoan / yunnuhstan. E. E. Cummings. CP-CummE

Yiddishe Kopf. Allen Ginsberg. SP-GinsA

Yield all, my love; but be withal as coy. Upon A.M. Sir John Suckling. CP-SuckJ

Yield to the tantalizing mechanism. Swan Ritual, The. A. R. Ammons. CP-AmmoA

Yillow, yillow, yillow, / Old worm, my pretty quirk. Metamorphosis. Wallace Stevens. CP-StevW; CP-StevWP

Yin and Yang. Kenneth Rexroth. CP-RexrK

Yippee! she is shooting in the harbor! he is jumping. Blocks. Frank O'Hara. SP-OharF

Ylladmar. James Whitcomb Riley. CP-RileJ

Yo, Dan, just give a look at this repulsive creature. In Hell with Virg and Dan. Carolyn Kizer. CP-KizeC

Yogi sits on the burning rock, a drying skin, The. Maya. Eleanor Wilner. SP-WilnE

Yoke, The. Jones Very. CP-VeryJ

Yokimura. Czeslaw Milosz. CP-MiloCN, tr. by Robert Hass

Yoko. Thom Gunn. CP-GunnT

Yom Kippur. Yehuda Amichai. SP-AmicYL, tr. by Benjamin Harshav and Barbara Harshav

Yom Kippur 1984. Adrienne Rich. SP-RicA1

Yom Kippur without my father and mother. Yehuda Amichai. SP-AmicY, tr. by Chana Bloch

Yom Kippur without my father and without my mother. Yom Kippur. Yehuda Amichai. SP-AmicYL, tr. by Benjamin Harshav and Barbara Harshav

Yon Far Country. A. E. Housman. CP-HousA

Yon flakes that fret the eastern sky. A. E. Housman. CP-HousA

Yon wild, mossy mountains sae lofty and wide. Robert Burns. CP-BurnR

Yonder. Richard Eberhart. CP-EberR

Yonder. James Tate. SP-TateJ

Yonder beyond all hopes of access. Gorge, The. Robert Graves. CP-GravR

Yonder deadfromtheneckup graduate of a. E. E. Cummings. CP-CummE

Yonder see the morning blink. A. E. Housman. CP-HousA

"Yonder," they told him, "things are not the same." By No Means Native. Adrienne Rich. CP-RicAE

Yonder's the man with his life in his hand. Atkins. George Meredith. CP-MerG2

Yonnondio. Walt Whitman. CP-WhitW

Yorkshire. Donald Davie. CP-DaviDC

Yorktown. John Greenleaf Whittier. CP-WhitJ

You. W. H. Auden. CP-AudeW

You. Charles Bukowski. SP-BukC1

You. Norman Dubie. CP-DubiN

You. David Ignatow. SP-IgnaD

You. D. H. Lawrence. CP-LawrD

"You acted unwisely," I cried, "as you see." Lacking Factor, A. Ambrose Bierce. SP-BierA

You, after all, were good. Afterthoughts of Donna Elvira. Carolyn Kizer. CP-KizeC

You again, you rising. Rainer Maria Rilke. CP-RilkFr, *tr. by* A. Poulin, Jr. *Fr.* Roses, The.

You: air-driven reft from the tuber-bitten soil. Adrienne Rich. SP-RicA1 *Fr.* Contradictions: Tracking Poems.

You All Know the Story of the Other Woman. Anne Sexton. CP-SextA; SP-SextA

You, all of you who know how to bless. Rainer Maria Rilke. CP-RilkFr, *tr. by* A. Poulin, Jr. *Fr.* Fragments.

You all your Youth observd the Golden Rule. To S[tothar]d. William Blake. CP-BlakW

You Also, Gaius Valerius Catullus. Archibald MacLeish. CP-MacLA

You always are making a god of your spouse. To Mrs. Houghton of Bormount. Jonathan Swift. CP-SwifJ

You always read about it. Cinderella. Anne Sexton. CP-SextA

You and Art. William Stafford. SP-StafWW

You and I. Tennessee Williams. CP-WillT

You and I, and that night, with its perfume and glory! That Night. James Whitcomb Riley. CP-RileJ

You and I Are Disappearing. Yusef Komunyakaa. CP-KomuY

You and Me and P.B. Shelley. Ogden Nash. CP-NashO

You, Andrew Marvell. Archibald MacLeish. CP-MacLA

You are a cousin of mine. Seamless Garment, The. Hugh MacDiarmid. SP-MacDH

You are a friend then, as I make it out. Ben Jonson Entertains a Man from Stratford. Edwin Arlington Robinson. CP-RobiE

You are a lord, an earl[e], nay more, a man. To the Right Honourable Mildmay, Earl of Westmorland. Robert Herrick. CP-HerrR

You are a roast beef I have purchased. Buying the Whore. Anne Sexton. CP-SextA

You are a sunrise. To a Golden-Haired Girl in a Louisiana Town. Nicholas Vachel Lindsay. CP-LindV

You are a tulip seen today. Meditation for His Mistress[e], A. Robert Herrick. CP-HerrR

You are a typical American woman. Fertile. William Carlos Williams. CP-WilW2

You are already. Touch. Thom Gunn. CP-GunnT

You are always / with me. Words. Robert Creeley. CP-CreeR

You are as faithless as a Carthaginian. Satire on an Inconstant Lover, A. Jonathan Swift. CP-SwifJ

You are as gold. Song: "You are as gold." "H. D." CP-DoolH

You are beside me like a wall; I touch you with my fingers and. Adrienne Rich. SP-RicA2 *Fr.* Shooting Script.

You are brief and frail and blue. Sweet Violets. Dorothy Parker. CP-ParkD

You are clear / O rose, cut in rock. Garden. "H. D." CP-DoolH

You are ever / in my thoughts. Roxy. James Schuyler. CP-SchuJ

You are falling asleep and I sit looking at you. After Dark. Adrienne Rich. CP-RicAE; SP-RicA1; SP-RicA2

You are falling in love again. This time. Torture. Raymond Carver. CP-CarvR

You are famous in my mind. Before the Big Storm. William Stafford. SP-StafWW

You are forever April. Song: "You are forever April." William Carlos Williams. CP-WilW2

You Are Gorgeous and I'm Coming. Frank O'Hara. SP-OharF

You are granite. Granite and Wineglass. Jelaluddin Rumi. SP-Rumi, *tr. by* Coleman Barks

You Are Happy. Margaret Atwood. SP-AtwM1

You are hearing a distant, almost familiar, French cradlesong. Elegies for the Ocher Deer on the Walls at Lascaux. Norman Dubie. CP-DubiN

You are here now. Sleeping Fury, The. Louise Bogan. CP-BogaL

You are home and the sound of your steps to the running water. Contemplation, The. Olga Broumas. SP-BrouO

You are in a barbed land and you are NOT dying. Politics. Andrei Codrescu. SP-CodrA

You Are in Bear Country. Maxine W. Kumin. SP-KumiM

You are in for another surprise too. Through Time. Michael Palmer. SP-PalmM

You are invulnerable. Have they not granted you. To Whoever is Reading Me. Jorge Luis Borges. SP-BorgJ, *tr. by* Alastair Reid

"You are large, Father Graham," the young fan opined. Jolly Greene Giant, The. John Updike. CP-UpdiJ

You are late for your train. Santa Maria Dei Frari. Clarence Major. SP-MajoC

You are like a warm dark dusk. Young Negro Girl. Langston Hughes. CP-HughL; CP-HughL2

You are like me born at the end of the year. Born in December. Muriel Rukeyser. CP-RukeM

You are like the moon except. From the Persian (2). Kenneth Rexroth. CP-RexrK

You are like the snow only. E. E. Cummings. CP-CummE

You are lovely as a river. Flowing River, A. William Carlos Williams. CP-WilW2

You are made of almost nothing. Dragonfly, The. Louise Bogan. CP-BogaL

You are most illustrious. Emily Dickinson. SP-DickE

You are my friend. Lorine Niedecker. CP-NiedL

You Are My Future. James Laughlin. CP-LaugJ

You are my shadow in the picture. Lines for Michael in the Picture. John Logan. CP-LogaJ

You Are My Silent Brethren. Adam Zagajewski. SP-ZagaA, *tr. by* Clare Cavanagh

You are no friend of mine. To Certain Intellectuals. Langston Hughes. CP-HughL; CP-HughL1

You are not going to,dear. You are not going to and. E. E. Cummings. CP-CummE

You are not looking at all well, my dear. Doctor, The. Stevie Smith. CP-SmitS

"You are not pregnant," said the man. All the Little Animals. Muriel Rukeyser. CP-RukeM

You are not random picked. I tell you you. Lofty in the Palais de Danse. Thom Gunn. CP-GunnT

You Are Not the Others. Jorge Luis Borges. SP-BorgJ, *tr. by* Eric McHenry

You are old, Father William, and though one would think. Father William. Lee O. Harris. CP-RileJ

You are only one of many. One of Many. Stevie Smith. CP-SmitS

You are reading me now and thanks. I know I feel a bit better. I'm a Depressed Poem. David Ignatow. SP-IgnaD

You are served "duck soup" and nothing more. But you. At Noon. Raymond Carver. CP-CarvR

You are sick, that's sure—they say. Robert Browning. CP-BroR2

You are so beautiful and I am a fool. Nightclub. Billy Collins. SP-CollB

You are so interested in yourself. To a Certain Friend. D. H. Lawrence. CP-LawrD

You are so small and slight in the rain. A small target. Yehuda Amichai. SP-AmicY, *tr. by* Chana Bloch

You are such a well-rounded sponge. Sediment. David Ignatow. SP-IgnaD

You are supposed to stay still. It won't. Inheriting the Earth: Quail. William Stafford. SP-StafWW

You Are That Frail. Hart Crane. CP-CranH

You are the black prince of bananas. American Tourist to a Guatemalan Tarantula. Alan Dugan. CP-DugaA

You are the bright bird. Haiku: "You are the bright bird." Robert Stock. SP-StocR

You are the center about. Mei Axis Mundi. James Laughlin. CP-LaugJ

You are the dark song / of the morning. Rage. Mary Oliver. SP-OlivM

You are the king's son. Judge a Moth by the Beauty of Its Candle. Jelaluddin Rumi. SP-Rumi, *tr. by* Coleman Barks

You are the love spider. Arachne. James Laughlin. CP-LaugJ

You are the man. Wilderness. Lorine Niedecker. CP-NiedL

You are the one man. For a Friend. Robert Creeley. CP-CreeR

You are the owner of one complete thought. Voice and Address. Michael Palmer. SP-PalmM

You are the problem I propose. Metaphysical Amorist, The. James Vincent Cunningham. CP-CunnJ

You are the *rose of Sharon, the lily of the valleys*. Hymn to a Masseuse. Yehuda Amichai. SP-AmicYL, *tr. by* Benjamin Harshav *and* Barbara Harshav

You are the sun / in reverse, all energy. Margaret Atwood. SP-AtwM1

You are the third term. One-Breath Song. Yusef Komunyakaa. CP-KomuY

You are / their sister. Admonition. Eleanor Wilner. SP-WilnE

You are there because it surrounds you. "Music" by David Hume. Michael Palmer. SP-PalmM

You are tired, / (I think). E. E. Cummings. CP-CummE

You are to me, love, half family half tree. She. Charles Olson. CP-OlsoC

You are too young, and I am scared to touch you. Valentine, A. Joseph Brodsky. CP-BrodJ *Fr.* Shorts.

You are walking / down the corridor. A man. Pornographic Poem. Marilyn Hacker. SP-HackM

You are walking in the grounds. Belated Birthday Poem, A. James Schuyler. CP-SchuJ

You are writing a love scene. Blue Stones, The. Raymond Carver. CP-CarvR

You are younger than I am, you are. Girl and Horse, 1928. Margaret Atwood. SP-AtwM1

You Ask for a "Volume of Nonsense" Lord Byron. CP-Byron

You ask for love but what you want is healing. Twins. Jane Cooper. CP-CoopJ

You ask how long I'll stay from thee. Impromptu on Parting from Elizabeth MacFadden, An. *Unknown, sometimes at. to* Thomas Sheridan. CP-SherT

You ask me, brothers, why I flinch. Time Marches On. Ogden Nash. CP-NashO

You ask me how Contempt who claims to sleep. Epigram: "You ask me how Contempt who claims to sleep." James Vincent Cunningham. CP-CunnJ

You ask me how I write. I'll tell you, but let this be confidential. For a Literary Survey. Dan Pagis. SP-PagiD, *tr. by* Stephen Mitchell

You ask me how to pray to someone who is not. On Prayer. Czeslaw Milosz. CP-MiloC; CP-MiloCN, *tr. by* Robert Hass

You ask me, Russell, why we fought and why. Melville's Letter to William Clark Russell. Helen Pinkerton. CP-PinkH

You ask me what I'm doing, now I'm free. Jubilación. Charles Tomlinson. SP-TomlC

You ask me what is Genius? 'tis that. George Meredith. CP-MerG2

You ask me why I bear such rage in heart. Antéros. Gérard de Nerval. CP-WilbR

You ask what I have found, and far and wide I go. Curse of Cromwell, The. William Butler Yeats. CP-YeatW

You ask why I am sad to-day. Weltschmertz. Paul Laurence Dunbar. CP-DunbP

You Ask Why Sometimes I Say Stop. Marge Piercy. SP-PierM

You ask[e] me what I do[e], and how I live? His Answer to a Friend. Robert Herrick. CP-HerrR

You asked me if I wrote now? Emily Dickinson. SP-DickE

You asked me to come:it was raining a little. E. E. Cummings. CP-CummE

You asked me what is the good of reading the Gospels in Greek. Readings. Czeslaw Milosz. CP-MiloC; CP-MiloCN, *tr. by* Lillian Vallee

You asked what. Hosts, The. W. S. Merwin. SP-MerwWF

You ate and drank your fill. You arrived here. Travels of Benjamin the Last, of Tudela, The. Yehuda Amichai. SP-AmicYL, *tr. by* Benjamin Harshav *and* Barbara Harshav

You ate and were filled, you came. Travels of the Last Benjamin of Tudela. Yehuda Amichai. SP-AmicY, *tr. by* Stephen Mitchell

You ("Back and forth across"). Robert Creeley. CP-CreeR

You bail, already the boat lists. Moiré. Eugenio Montale. CP-MontE, *tr. by* Jonathan Galassi

You be like you, ever. Paul Celan. SP-CelaP, *tr. by* John Felstiner

You beastly child, I wish you had miscarried. Lightly Bound. Stevie Smith. CP-SmitS

You beauty, O you beauty! Invocation to the Moon. D. H. Lawrence. CP-LawrD

You, because you love me, hold. Old Song and Dance, The. Kenneth Rexroth. CP-RexrK

You Begin. Margaret Atwood. SP-AtwM2

You being in love. E. E. Cummings. CP-CummE

You believe another life will come. Between You and Me. Sam Hamill. SP-HamiS

You Bet Travel Is Broadening. Ogden Nash. CP-NashO

You better not fool with a Bumblebee! Bumblebee, The. James Whitcomb Riley. CP-RileJ

You better sure shall live, not evermore. Sir Philip Sidney. SP-SidnP

You bid me hold my peace. Worn Out. Paul Laurence Dunbar. CP-DunbP

You bid me write t'amuse the tedious hours. Elegy 5.12: "You bid me write t'amuse the tedious hours." Ovid. CP-CowpW *Fr.* Elegies.

You bind me, and I tear away in a rage to open out. I'm Not Saying This Right. Jelaluddin Rumi. SP-Rumi, *tr. by* Coleman Barks

You birds stay out all night. Envy of Natural Formal Liberties, An. Alan Dugan. CP-DugaA

You blame me that I ran away? Arcades Ambo. Robert Browning. CP-BroR2

You Boston folks & Roxbury people. Henry David Thoreau. CP-ThorH

You break pebbles for your sins. Roadmender, The. Stéphane Mallarmé. CP-MallS *Fr.* Street Songs.

You break pebbles for your sins. Roadmender, The. Stéphane Mallarmé. CP-MallS, *tr. by* Henry Weinfield

You bring me good news from the clinic. Face Lift. Sylvia Plath. CP-PlatS

You bring me Ocean Star a dreaming Song. This Summer Day. Kenneth Patchen. CP-PatcK

You, browed maiden, your eyes' bright pictures have caught me. Witch I, The. D. H. Lawrence. CP-LawrD

You call: / guarded voices. O. Janis Joplin's Dead: Long Live Pearl. James Schuyler. CP-SchuJ

You call it fate? Comment against Lamp Post. Langston Hughes. CP-HughL3

You call it, "Love lies bleeding,"—so you may. Love Lies Bleeding. William Wordsworth. CP-WorW2

You call me Mad tis Folly to do so. To F[laxman]. William Blake. CP-BlakW

You call me sane, insane—I tell you men. Murderess, The. Louise Glück. SP-GlucL

You call yourself a man. Mary, Pity Women! Rudyard Kipling. CP-KiplR

You called yourself a dishwater blond. What You Waited For. Marge Piercy. SP-PierM

You Came as a Thought. James Laughlin. CP-LaugJ

You came back to us in a dream and we were not here. Come Back. W. S. Merwin. SP-MerwW

You came from the Aztecs. Aztec. Carl Sandburg. CP-SandC

You came in / and the rooms were empty. Rapture The. Theodore Weiss. SP-WeisT

You came in out of the night. Francesca. Ezra Pound. CP-PoEar

You came suddenly into my heart. Little Heartsong, A. James Laughlin. CP-LaugJ

You came with a cello in one hand. Left-Handed Cellist, The. Rita Dove. SP-DoveR

You can accomplish it rather easily—it's enough. More Sufficient, The. Yannis Ritsos. SP-RitsY, *tr. by* Edmund Keeley

You Can Be a Republican, I'm a Genocrat. Ogden Nash. CP-NashO

You can beat me, beat me! beat me, said the demon who stood. Patience of an Angel. Max Jacob. CP-BishE

You can catch the wind. Free Man. Langston Hughes. CP-HughL; CP-HughL2

You can count on anything, but you can't count on impulse. Impulse. D. H. Lawrence. CP-LawrD

You can / die for it— / an idea. Sunrise. Mary Oliver. SP-OlivM

You Can Have It. Philip Levine. SP-LeviP

You can hurry the pictures toward you but. Lamp, The. Charles Olson. CP-OlsoC; CP-OlsoC

You can lead a horse to water but you can't make it hold. Symposium. Paul Muldoon. CP-MuldP

You can pull off back roads. When Men Can't Trust Hands with Wood. Yusef Komunyakaa. CP-KomuY

You Can Rely on Him. Yehuda Amichai. SP-AmicY, *tr. by* Chana Bloch

You Can Rely on Him. Yehuda Amichai. SP-AmicYL, *tr. by* Benjamin Harshav *and* Barbara Harshav

You can scarcely grant me now. As a Less than Robber. Robert Graves. CP-GravR

You can see mountains propped there. Home State. William Stafford. SP-StafW

You can see that. Service. W. S. Merwin. SP-MerwWF

You can see them from the railings. St. Michael. Federico García Lorca. CP-GarcF, *tr. by* Christopher Maurer

You can see them from the road: go far and deep. Charleston Plantations. May Sarton. SP-SartM

You Can Start the Poetry Now, Or: News from Crazy Horse. Thomas McGrath. SP-McGrT

You Can Take It with You. Josephine Jacobsen. CP-JacoJ

You can talk about. Visitors to the Black Belt. Langston Hughes. CP-HughL; CP-HughL2

You can watch the sky from here, a fabled tower. Renegade. Eleanor Wilner. SP-WilnE

You cannot come to unity and remain material. Guide. A. R. Ammons. CP-AmmoA

You cannot make Remembrance grow. Emily Dickinson. CP-DickE

You cannot put a big load in a small bag. Symphony for a Sea Bird. Chuang Tzu. CP-MertT

You cannot put a Fire out. Emily Dickinson. CP-DickE

You cannot take itself. Emily Dickinson. CP-DickE

You cannot think my heart so tough. Lines to an Old Pro-Boer Who Asked for a Contribution to a Peace Periodical. G. K. Chesterton. CP-ChesG

You can't come in! *(Knock, knock)* The store is closed! Masque of Mercy, A. Robert Frost. CP-FrosR

You can't come with us. Another Day (You can't come). Muriel Rukeyser. CP-RukeM

You can't count. Yannis Ritsos. SP-RitsY *Fr.* Paper Poems 1.

You can't keep all the past in a backpack or purse. Memory. Miller Williams. CP-WillM

You can't look at yourself. Great Sadness, The. Federico García Lorca. CP-GarcF, *tr. by* Jerome Rothenberg *Fr.* Night (Suite for Piano and Poet's Voice).

You can't move an inch, my dear Marcus Emilius. Voices. Wisława Szymborska. SP-SzymW, *tr. by* Stanislaw Barańczak *and* Clare Cavanagh

You can't remember, giving a day. Dreams. James Schuyler. CP-SchuJ

You can't say it that way any more. And "Ut Pictura Poesis" Is Her Name. John Ashbery. SP-AshbJ

You can't sleep here. Drama for Winter Night (Fifth Avenue). Langston Hughes. CP-HughL; CP-HughL1

You can't win, you can't draw. 2. Comment on "Business Jacob, the Angel Wrestler." Alan Dugan. CP-DugaA

You carry flowers in a jug of green wine. Strawberries in Wooden Bowls. Arthur Sze. SP-SzeA

You carry the load of heavy buttocks and your eyes are light. Yehuda Amichai. SP-AmicYL, *tr. by* Benjamin Harshav *and* Barbara Harshav

You Carry the Weight of Heavy Buttocks. Yehuda Amichai. SP-AmicY, *tr. by* Chana Bloch

You celebrate with kisses the good fortune. Mankind and Ocean. Robert Graves.

CP-GravR

You centered in on one you could not stand. Man Who Was Pregnant with Envy, The. Robert Stock. SP-StocR

You charmed [or charm'd] me not with that fair face. Song: "You charmed [or charm'd] me not with that fair face." John Dryden. SP-DrydJ *Fr.* Evening's Love, An.

You chose a lion to be your lover—. Lion Lover. Robert Graves. CP-GravR

You clamber up rock, crash thicket, leap. Dreaming in Daylight. Robert Penn Warren. CP-WarrR

You climb three "golden steps" Always Another Viewpoint. Kenneth Patchen. CP-PatcK

You come along . . . tearing your shirt . . . yelling about Jesus. To a Contemporary Bunkshooter. Carl Sandburg. CP-SandC

You come down to a time. Myth & Ritual. Howard Nemerov. CP-NemeH

You come from poets, kings, bankrupts, preachers. For My Son. Muriel Rukeyser. CP-RukeM

You come from some other forest. Little Horse. W. S. Merwin. SP-MerwW

You come in late, wiping your lips. Other, The. Sylvia Plath. CP-PlatS

You come to fetch me from my work tonight. Putting in the Seed. Robert Frost. CP-FrosR

You Communists and Republicans! Approaching Hour, The. William Carlos Williams. CP-WilW2

You constituted Time. Emily Dickinson. CP-DickE

You could be sitting now in a carrel. Late Aubade, A. Richard Wilbur. CP-WilbR

You could be the beginning of treated birds. To a Lovely Lady Gone to Theory. John Ciardi. CP-CiarJ

You could die before me. During a Son's Dangerous Illness. Denise Levertov. SP-LeveDS

You could do everything. Which Is to Say. Robert Creeley. SP-CreeR

You could go on / talking to an imaginary. Wisdom. Robert Creeley. CP-CreeR

You could go to the Underground's platform. Bombings. Lorine Niedecker. CP-NiedL

You could put an X here. This Space Available. Thomas Lux. SP-LuxT

You could put silver dollars on my eyes. Audit at Key West. John Ciardi. CP-CiarJ

You could scream. Calling to Order. Czeslaw Milosz. CP-MiloC; CP-MiloCN, *tr. by* Lillian Vallee

You could see when I met you. Guido Cavalcanti. CP-CavaG, *tr. by* Marc Cirigliano

You could stop the factory whistles blowing. If You Would. Langston Hughes. CP-HughL; CP-HughL3

You could then, my heart, wit, eye, mean in proposing love our aim. Catullus. *See* Joy of my life! you tell me this

You couldn't get it. Davao Insular Hotel. Robert Creeley. SP-CreeR

You couldn't pack a Broadwood half a mile. Song of the Banjo, The. Rudyard Kipling. CP-KiplR

You crash over the trees. Storm. "H. D." CP-DoolH

You cross the ramp, its sure suspension. Still Moment at Dun Laoghaire. Tess Gallagher. SP-GallT

You Damned Blockheaded Irishman. To Anna Jean. Tennessee Williams. CP-WillT

You danced ahead of me, I took. For Bet. Denise Levertov. SP-LeveDS

You dazzle me. You are beautiful in passing. Comb, The. Hans Magnus Enzensberger. SP-EnzeH, *tr. by* Michael Hamburger

You delight, / So it would seem. Note to All Nazis Fascists and Klansmen. Langston Hughes. CP-HughL; CP-HughL2

You did it / it was you who started the countdown. Margaret Atwood. SP-AtwM1

You did not clock the turning of the leaves. Return. Audre Lorde. SP-LordA

You did not come. Broken Appointment, A. Thomas Hardy. CP-HardT

You did not come to Rome to dream. Rafael Alberti. CP-MertT *Fr.* Roman Nocturnes.

You did not know she was eternal? There. Kenneth Rexroth. CP-RexrK

You did not walk with me. Walk, The. Thomas Hardy. CP-HardT

You did not want to be Christlike. Though your Father. Being Christlike. Ted Hughes. SP-HughTN

You didn't take off your socks! Take Off Your Socks!! James Laughlin. CP-LaugJ

You didn't think you. Robert Creeley. SP-CreeR

You Didn't Understand. Constantine P. Cavafy. CP-CavaC, *tr. by* Theoharis Constantine Theoharis

You died. And because you were Greek they gave you. None. Hayden Carruth. CP-CarHS

You died, and made but little of it! After the Death of a Friend. Thomas Hardy. CP-HardT

You do not always know what I am feeling. For Grace, after a Party. Frank O'Hara. SP-OharF

You do not come dramatically, with dragons. To Failure. Philip Larkin. CP-

LarkP

You do not do, you do not do. Daddy. Sylvia Plath. CP-PlatS

You do not have to be good. Wild Geese. Mary Oliver. SP-OlivM

You do not know my pride. Kind of Scorn, A. Nicholas Vachel Lindsay. CP-LindV

You do not recognize me, but it's me all the same. To a Hazel Tree. Czeslaw Milosz. CP-MiloCN, *tr. by* Robert Hass

You do not understand her evil mood. Woman Who Blamed Life on a Spaniard, The. Wallace Stevens. CP-StevWP

You do understand I've waited long enough. Complaint: To the Muse. Philip Whalen. SP-WhalP

You, Doctor Martin. Anne Sexton. CP-SextA; SP-SextA

You, Doctor Martin, walk. You, Doctor Martin. Anne Sexton. CP-SextA; SP-SextA

You dont believe I wont attempt to make ye. William Blake. CP-BlakW

You don't find it for yourself. Someone takes you. Rainbow Grocery, The. William Dickey. SP-DickW

You don't know anything about city life. Monologue for a Sixth Avenue Screamer. Alan Dugan. CP-DugaA

You Don't Know the End. William Stafford. SP-StafWW

You don't know what love is Bukowski said. Raymond Carver. CP-CarvR

You don't look at all well, quite loin de l'être in fact. Loin de l'Être. Stevie Smith. CP-SmitS

You don't need to study any ponderous tome. I Know You'll Like Them. Ogden Nash. CP-NashO

You don't say / it is no / answer—you. Little Time—and Place. Robert Creeley. CP-CreeR

You don't see the moon. Moon at the Fair, A. Federico García Lorca. CP-GarcF, *tr. by* Jerome Rothenberg *Fr.* Fairs.

You don't survive in me. Interior Portrait. Rainer Maria Rilke. CP-RilkFr, *tr. by* A. Poulin, Jr. *Fr.* Orchards.

You don't think anything that I know of. Birdie. W. S. Merwin. SP-MerwWF

"You dream," he said, "because of the child." Dream, The. Stephen Spender. CP-SpenS

You dream someone is leaving you, though he says kindly, *It's not that you're cold.* Estrangement. Jane Cooper. CP-CoopJ

You drifted from across the sea. *Bui Doi*, Dust of Life. Yusef Komunyakaa. CP-KomuY

You drink a bitter draught. To a Freedom Fighter. Maya Angelou. SP-AngeM

You drive, the road aims for a mountain. View, A. Mona Van Duyn. SP-VanDM

You drunken / tottering. Drunkard, The. William Carlos Williams. CP-WilW1

You dweller in the dark cabin. Hymn from a Watermelon Pavilion. Wallace Stevens. CP-StevW; CP-StevWP

You dynamiting the structure of our loves. Theory of Flight. Muriel Rukeyser. CP-RukeM

You encounter a mirror and look away too late. Encounters. Dan Pagis. SP-PagiD, *tr. by* Stephen Mitchell

You entrusted the boy to me. He has died. Letter from Mexico (Vera Cruz, 10 February, 186–). Tristan Corbière. SP-MereW, *tr. by* William Meredith

You expect to see swirling chunks of ice. Whiteout. Arthur Sze. SP-SzeA

You expected a hermit to live in the wilderness. Hermitage. Wisława Szymborska. SP-SzymW, *tr. by* Stanisław Barańczak *and* Clare Cavanagh

You exquisite chunk of mud. K. McB. William Carlos Williams. CP-WilW1

You Eyes, you large and all-inquiring Eyes. For Arvia. Edwin Arlington Robinson. CP-RobiE

You, Failed Pronoun. Eleanor Wilner. SP-WilnE

You Felons on Trial in Courts. Walt Whitman. CP-WhitW

You Felt the Fear of Death. Shmuel HaNagid. SP-HaNaS, *tr. by* Peter Cole

You fit into me. Margaret Atwood. SP-AtwM1

You float inside your water. Fanny Howe. SP-HoweF *Fr.* O'Clock.

You flung your taunt across the wave. To Englishmen. John Greenleaf Whittier. CP-WhitJ

You-folks rickollect, I know. Boys of the Old Glee Club, The. James Whitcomb Riley. CP-RileJ

You force me to touch. Finished. Ai. SP-Ai

You fret how few now read what's hard to write. To a Friend, an Unhappy Poet. Miller Williams. CP-WillM

You full-blooming moon! Old Gods, The. Carolyn Kizer. CP-KizeC *Fr.* Heine Journal, A.

You gave, but will not give again. To a Wealthy Man Who Promised a Second Subscription to the Dublin Municipal Gallery if It Were Proved the People Wanted Pictures. William Butler Yeats. CP-YeatW

You gave me gifts, God-Enchanter. Thankfulness. Czeslaw Milosz. CP-MiloC; CP-MiloCN, *tr. by* Robert Hass

You get sent to the workhouse because you worked. Deadhouse at the Workhouse, The. Thomas Lux. SP-LuxT

You get to see all kinds of life. Friend Says of Job. Robert Creeley. SP-CreeR

You give me only what you're glutted with. Michelangelo Buonarroti. CP-Miche, *tr. by* John Frederick Nims

You give no hint how shy you really are, so thoroughly your warm and welcoming temperament masks. Fifteen. C. K. Williams. SP-WillC

You give quite a party, old Cocky. Punch Rubicundus. Thom Gunn. CP-GunnT

You give to brooks a tune. Afield. Wallace Stevens. CP-StevWP

You go away for a trip, either business or pleasure. Name Is Too Familiar, The. Ogden Nash. CP-NashO

You go down shade to the river, where naked men sit on flat brown rocks, to watch the ferry, in the sun. Elephant. D. H. Lawrence. CP-LawrD

You go for these wenches, she said. Pacific Telephone. Charles Bukowski. SP-BukC1

You go into a store and select half-a-dozen shirts and charge them. Friendly Touch, The. Ogden Nash. CP-NashO

You go to school to learn to. Thomas Lux. SP-LuxT

You, going along the path. Cyclops. Margaret Atwood. SP-AtwM1

You goodly pines, which still with brave ascent. Sir Philip Sidney. SP-SidnP *Fr.* Arcadia.

You grin like a grape. Child Stealer. Yusef Komunyakaa. CP-KomuY

You, guitar-shaped affair with tousled squalor. Minefield Revisited. Joseph Brodsky. CP-BrodJ

You gulp your breakfast and glance at the clock. Everybody Eats Too Much Anyhow. Ogden Nash. CP-NashO

You had everything to rattle the men who wrote. Margaret Fuller Drowned. Robert Lowell. SP-LoweR

You had fallen asleep beside. Atman of Sleep, The. James Laughlin. CP-LaugJ

You Had Me. Gabriela Mistral. SP-MistG, *tr. by* Maria Giachetti [*or* Jacketti]

You had to strip off Germany. Descent. Ted Hughes. SP-HughTN

You had *your* crowd. Good Time Girl. Charles Bukowski. SP-BukC3

You had your own reasons for getting. New Personal Poem. Ted Berrigan. SP-BerrT

You hand me a cup of water. It Breaks. Marge Piercy. SP-PierM

You hang at dawn, they said. Hostage, The. Stevie Smith. CP-SmitS

You, Hart Crane. Charles Olson. CP-OlsoC

You Hated Spain. Ted Hughes. SP-HughTN

You have ask'd for a verse—the request. To the Countess of Blessington. Lord Byron. CP-Byron

You have beaten me with swords. Ariadne. "H. D." CP-DoolH

You have been a fisherman. Lives. Lucille Clifton. SP-ClifL

You have been living now for a long time and there is nothing you do not know. Sortes Vergilianae. John Ashbery. SP-AshbJ

You have beheld a smiling Rose. Lilly in a Christal, The. Robert Herrick. CP-HerrR

You have betrayed me, Eros. Reproach, The. Louise Glück. SP-GlucL

You have broken the path of the dragonfly. Pearls. Rita Dove. SP-DoveR

You have come between me and the terrifying presence. Love Song: "You have come between me and the terrifying presence." William Carlos Williams. CP-WilW1

You have come your way, I have come my way. Fronleichnam. D. H. Lawrence. CP-LawrD

You have denied hard fact, or never tried. Epitaph on a Philosopher the Reports of Whose Death Have Been Grossly Minimized. Howard Nemerov. CP-NemeH

You have experienced Sanctity. Emily Dickinson. SP-DickE

You have forty-nine days between. In the Park. Maxine W. Kumin. SP-KumiM

You have gone and will not be returning. Introduction to the Second Book of Poems. Aleksandr Aleksandrovich Blok. SP-BlokA, *tr. by* Peter France *and* Jon Stallworthy

You have heard "A Spanish Lady." Armenian Lady's Love, The. William Wordsworth. CP-WorW2

You have here no otherness. James Vincent Cunningham. CP-CunnJ

You have, in a sense. Trip through Yucatán, A. Theodore Weiss. SP-WeisT

You have lived long but over-lonely. Advent of Summer. Robert Graves. CP-GravR

You have loved forty women, but you have only one thumb. Personality. Carl Sandburg. CP-SandC

You have millions. We are numberless. Scythians, The. Aleksandr Aleksandrovich Blok. SP-BlokA, *tr. by* Peter France *and* Jon Stallworthy

You Have More Freedom in a House. Ogden Nash. CP-NashO

You have more'n likely noticed. Perversity. James Whitcomb Riley. CP-RileJ

You have my. Marriage, The. Denise Levertov. SP-LeveDS

You have no word for soldiers to enjoy. Looking. Gwendolyn Brooks. SP-BrooG

You have nor face nor hands. Robert Creeley. CP-CreeR

You have not heard my love's dark throat. Song of Praise, A. Countee Cullen. CP-CullC

You have noticed the curious increasing exasperation. Nerves. Robinson Jeffers. CP-JefR3

You have now come with me, I have now come with you. Poet: A Lying Word. Laura Riding Jackson. CP-RidiL

You have now fallen three times in love. Three Times In Love. Robert Graves. CP-GravR

You have only to wait, they will find you. Messengers. Louise Glück. SP-GlucL

You Have Pissed Your Life. William Carlos Williams. CP-WilW1

You have probably come across. Earthling. Billy Collins. SP-CollB

You have put your two hands upon me, and your mouth. Betrothed. Louise Bogan. CP-BogaL

You have red toenails, chestnut. Leda and Her Swan. Olga Broumas. SP-BrouO

You have said what you are. Jelaluddin Rumi. SP-Rumi, *tr. by* Coleman Barks

You have seen a plough. Lines. Charles Tomlinson. CP-TomlC

You have seen better days, dear? So have I. Prince Hohenstiel-Schwangau, Saviour of Society. Robert Browning. CP-BroR1

You have seen her in the procession, but alone. Virgin with a Lamp. Marya Alexandrovna Zaturenska. SP-ZatuM

You have seen us come from nothing. Chorale, The. Christopher Logue. SP-LoguC *Fr.* Lily-White Boys, The.

You have Sir said it well but I have if. Aeneas at New York. Allen Tate. CP-TateA

You have skin pale like a snowdrop. Jaroslav Seifert. SP-SeifJ, *tr. by* George Gibian

You have spoken the answer. Answer, The. Carl Sandburg. CP-SandC

You have such a way of talking of Him! Gothic Candor. William Carlos Williams. CP-WilW2

You have the body, blood and bone. Habeas Corpus. Kenneth Rexroth. CP-RexrK

You have the tender advantage over us. Rainer Maria Rilke. CP-RilkFr, *tr. by* A. Poulin, Jr. *Fr.* Fragments.

You have to admire the workmanship of cousins. Sperm. Maxine W. Kumin. SP-KumiM

You have used a word. And When Freedom Is Achieved. Kenneth Patchen. CP-PatcK

You have wandered widely through your own mind. Within Reason. Robert Graves. CP-GravR

You have your hat and coat on and she says she will be right down. Evening Out, The. Ogden Nash. CP-NashO

You have your language too. Wellfleet Whale, The. Stanley Kunitz. CP-KunSC

You haven't / fucked for months now. Robert Creeley. CP-CreeR

You having turned from me. 12. 6. 71. Louise Glück. SP-GlucL

You hear a woman say: I love my husband dearly. Emotional Lies. D. H. Lawrence. CP-LawrD

You hear my step. To His Children in Darkness. James Dickey. CP-DickJ

You hear the long roll of the plunging ground. Prayer in My Sickness, A. James Wright. CP-WrigJ

You heard your voice saying: *thanks.* Thanksgiving. Yannis Ritsos. SP-RitsY, *tr. by* Kostas Myrsiades

You, Helen, who see the stars. Appeal, The. D. H. Lawrence. CP-LawrD

You, hiding there in your words. Book, The. Adrienne Rich. CP-RicAE; SP-RicA2

You hitched a thousand miles. August on Sourdough, a Visit from Dick Brewer. Gary Snyder. CP-SnydG

You hold your eager head. To a Romantic. Allen Tate. CP-TateA

You hold your hands up to the light. Going Out. Gregory Orr. SP-OrrG

You Home-Folks:—Aid your grateful guest. Proem to "Home-Folks" James Whitcomb Riley. CP-RileJ

You hosts are almost glad he gate-crashed: see. Vampire. Ted Hughes. SP-HughTN

You—hotblooded, hasty, course. Pearl Oyster. Primo Levi. CP-LeviP, *tr. by* Ruth Feldman

You hunted me with all the pack. Quarry, The. Walter De la Mare. CP-DeLaW

You identify / with the body's. My Associates. Rae Armantrout. SP-ArmaA

You, if you were sensible. Under the Oak. D. H. Lawrence. CP-LawrD

You in a tallness slenderly, as a lone. Sonnet: "You in a tallness slenderly, as a lone." Hayden Carruth. CP-CarHS *Fr.* Sonnets.

You in I'm not talking about. I Want to Breathe. James Laughlin. CP-LaugJ

You in the flesh and here. Bad Dreams II. Robert Browning. CP-BroR2

You in the hammock; and I, near by. In the Afternoon. James Whitcomb Riley. CP-RileJ

You / in win / ter who sit. E. E. Cummings. CP-CummE

You in your house among your roommate's plants. Letter. Denise Levertov. SP-LeveDL

You innocents who want to play the clown. Speech to the Student Clowns at the Circus Clown School at Sarasota, Florida. Alan Dugan. CP-DugaA

You intend no doubt. Gift. Alice Walker. CP-WalkA

You invaded my country by accident. Ways of Conquest. Denise Levertov. SP-LeveDL

You, invincibly yourself. Apology. Adrienne Rich. CP-RicAE

You Invited Me. James Laughlin. CP-LaugJ

You, island in this page. Michael Palmer. SP-PalmM

You just maturing youth! You male or female! Poem of Remembrances for a Girl or a Boy of These States. Walt Whitman. CP-WhitW

You keep me waiting in a truck. Twenty-Year Marriage. Ai. SP-Ai

You keep the cold from the body, the cold from the mind. Tolerable Wisdom, A. Derek Mahon. CP-MahoD

You kin boast about yer cities, and their stiddy growth and size. Little Town o' Tailholt, The. James Whitcomb Riley. CP-RileJ

You kin talk about yer anthems. Ol' Tunes, The. Paul Laurence Dunbar. CP-DunbP

You know and I know what breeds in the dark. Elegy for the Face at Your Elbow. John Ciardi. CP-CiarJ

You know da vinci's painting of. Name Day, A. James Schuyler. CP-SchuJ

You know, death does not exist—he told her. Almost Complete. Yannis Ritsos. SP-RitsY, *tr. by* Kostas Myrsiades

You know, he said, they used to make. Lorine Niedecker. CP-NiedL

You Know How a Cat. James Laughlin. CP-LaugJ

You know how the mad come into a room. Beanstalk Country, The. Tennessee Williams. CP-WillT

You know: I'm going to lose you again. Eugenio Montale. CP-MontE, *tr. by* Jonathan Galassi

You know in the muddy pond the fish is there. Trying to Remember. Miller Williams. CP-WillM

You know / it was very good. Miracle is the Shortest Time, The. Charles Bukowski. SP-BukC3

You know, my friends, with what a brave carouse. Bride, The. Ambrose Bierce. SP-BierA

You know, my Lord, that I too know you know. Michelangelo Buonarroti. CP-Miche, *tr. by* John Frederick Nims

You know my story. Round Midnight. Clarence Major. SP-MajoC

You know our office on the 18th. Above the City. James Laughlin. CP-LaugJ

"You know," she said, "you were at." Sexpot. Charles Bukowski. SP-BukC1

You know that comical. Hunting Dog, The. James Laughlin. CP-LaugJ

You know that moment of twilight in summer. Twilight. Yannis Ritsos. SP-RitsY, *tr. by* Kimon Friar

You know that Portrait in the Moon. Emily Dickinson. CP-DickE

You know the bloom, unearthly white. Evening Primrose, The. Dorothy Parker. CP-ParkD

You know the brick path in back of the house. Directions. Billy Collins. SP-CollB

You know the scene. You read it in a book. Literal Dream. Robert Penn Warren. CP-WarrR

You know there is not much. To a Friend Concerning Several Ladies. William Carlos Williams. CP-WilW1

You know those windless summer evenings, swollen to stasis. Cicadas. Richard Wilbur. CP-WilbR

You know, verse. Charles Olson. CP-OlsoC

You know we French stormed [*or* storm'd] Ratisbon. Incident of the French Camp. Robert Browning. CP-BroR1

You know what it is to be born alone. Baby Tortoise. D. H. Lawrence. CP-LawrD

You lament your lot at the bottom of an abyss. Consolations for Double Bass. Charles Tomlinson. CP-TomlC

You laugh / Because I'm poor and black and funny. Black Clown, The. Langston Hughes. CP-HughL; CP-HughL1

You laughed with an open mouth. Repealer, The: "You're Too Wild" Alan Dugan. CP-DugaA

You lay in the nest of your real death. Elizabeth Gone. Anne Sexton. CP-SextA; SP-SextA

You learned Lear's *Nonsense Rhymes* by heart, not rote. Plea to Boys and Girls, A. Robert Graves. CP-GravR

You left a trail of bad checks in forty-six states. Ansel Adams Card, The. Arthur Sze. SP-SzeA

You left me gasping on the shore. Epithalamion: "You left me gasping on the shore." Carolyn Kizer. CP-KizeC

You left me—Sire—two Legacies. Emily Dickinson. CP-DickE

You let down, from arched. Family Affairs. Maya Angelou. SP-AngeM

You lie amid a great listening. Paul Celan. SP-CelaP, *tr. by* John Felstiner

You lie packed. Self-Portrait 1. William Carlos Williams. CP-WilW1

You lie there, Anna. Grave by a Holm-Oak. Stevie Smith. CP-SmitS

You lied to your mother, you told her you didn't do it. Opusthirteen. Hayden Carruth. CP-CarHS

You like it under the trees in autumn. Motive for Metaphor, The. Wallace Stevens. CP-StevW; CP-StevWP

You like the state of West Virginia very much, do you not? Statement: Philippa Allen. Muriel Rukeyser. CP-RukeM

You like to hear about gold. Vindictives, The. Robert Frost. CP-FrosR

You Lingering Sparse Leaves of Me. Walt Whitman. CP-WhitW

You little scribbling beau. Five Ladies' Answer to the Beau, with the Wig and Wings at His Head, The. Thomas Sheridan. CP-SherT

You live in your permanent home. Elizabeth Swados. Yehuda Amichai. SP-AmicYL, *tr. by* Benjamin Harshav *and* Barbara Harshav

You lofty poplars—humans of this earth! Landscape. Paul Celan. SP-CelaP, *tr.*

by John Felstiner

You look at me with children. Johann. Alice Walker. CP-WalkA

"You look like a widdower, " she said. In a London Flat. Thomas Hardy. CP-HardT

You look, my Joseph, I should something say. To My Dear Son, and Right-Learnèd Friend, Master Joseph Rutter. Ben Jonson. CP-JonsB

You look out and you see people. Song: "You look out and you see people." Robert Creeley. CP-CreeR

You Look Through Open Eyes. Shmuel HaNagid. SP-HaNaS, *tr. by* Peter Cole

You loomed like Merlin. Gold. Paul Muldoon. CP-MuldP

You, Lord, are all my guide. Where I still fail. Sierra Nevada Hike. Helen Pinkerton. CP-PinkH

You love all, you say. May's Love. Elizabeth Barrett Browning. CP-BroEB

You, love, and I. Counting the Beats. Robert Graves. CP-GravR

You love me strangely, and in strangeness. Strangeness. Robert Graves. CP-GravR

You love me—you are sure. Emily Dickinson. CP-DickE

You love the Lord—you cannot see. Emily Dickinson. CP-DickE

You love your dog and carve his steaks. So You Put the Dog to Sleep. Thomas Lux. SP-LuxT

You loved me not at all, but let it go. Edna St. Vincent Millay. CP-MillE

You loved the daughter of Don Manrique? Night-Scene, The. Samuel Taylor Coleridge. CP-ColeS

You lucky to be a spider. 403 Blues. Langston Hughes. CP-HughL; CP-HughL2

You made algebra: his tastes in food. Marilyn Hacker. SP-HackM *Fr.* Navigators, The.

You made healing as you wanted us to make bread and poems. Mendings. Muriel Rukeyser. CP-RukeM

You Made Me in Your Last a Goose. Thomas Sheridan. CP-SherT

You make me jes' a little nervouser. Two Sonnets to the June-Bug. James Whitcomb Riley. CP-RileJ

"You make me sick!" this, with rancor, vehemence, disgust—again, "You hear me? *Sick!*" Kin. C. K. Williams. SP-WillC

You make me walk my town, its terrible. It Still Happens Now. William Stafford. SP-StafWW

You make us want to stay alive, Suzanne. Suzanne. John Logan. CP-LogaJ

You May All Go Home Now. Kenneth Patchen. CP-PatcK

You may be right: 'How can I dare to feel?' Rejoinder to a Critic. Donald Davie. CP-DaviDC

You may have a hoof. Falling: 2. Rae Armantrout. SP-ArmaA

You may have all things from me, save my breath. Fifteenth Farewell. Louise Bogan. CP-BogaL

You may have heard, it's the custom for kings. Childhood Friends. Jelaluddin Rumi. SP-Rumi, *tr. by* Coleman Barks

You may have met a man—quite young. So Various. Thomas Hardy. CP-HardT

You may have seen, in road or street. Calf, The. Thomas Hardy. CP-HardT

You may "have" sex. Disown. Rae Armantrout. SP-ArmaA

You may not remember whether. James Whitcomb Riley. CP-RileJ

You may safely. Paul Celan. SP-CelaP, *tr. by* John Felstiner

You may say this is no poem. May 1943. "H. D." CP-DoolH

You may smell the breath of the gods in the common roses. Cabbage-Roses. D. H. Lawrence. CP-LawrD

You may talk o' gin and [*or* an'] beer. Gunga Din. Rudyard Kipling. CP-KiplR

You may vow Ile not forgett. His Mistris to Him at His Farwell. Robert Herrick. CP-HerrR

You may walk among fuchsias unloud. Vision Beatific. Allen Tate. CP-TateA

You may write me down in history. Still I Rise. Maya Angelou. SP-AngeM

You mean that, halfway through. Chess 2. Primo Levi. CP-LeviP, *tr. by* Ruth Feldman

You might as well haul up. Epitaph for Fire and Flower. Sylvia Plath. CP-PlatS

You Might Get in Trouble. Allen Ginsberg. CP-GinsA

You might not be in love with me. Comforting Reflection, A. G. K. Chesterton. CP-ChesG *Fr.* Thought and Reflections.

You might not know I remembered you. Emily Dickinson. SP-DickE

You might not know this old tree by its bark. Black Birch in Winter, A. Richard Wilbur. CP-WilbR

You mince, you start. Young Cat and the Chrysanthemums, The. William Carlos Williams. CP-WilW1

You miss the garden. Empty Garlic, An. Jelaluddin Rumi. SP-Rumi, *tr. by* Coleman Barks

You Mock Me Now in Your Youth. Shmuel HaNagid. SP-HaNaS, *tr. by* Peter Cole

You mocked me that hot day at Carcassonne. Dear Jool, I Miss You in Saint-Saturnin. Marilyn Hacker. SP-HackM

You, Morningtide Star, now are steady-eyed, over the east. Lying Awake. Thomas Hardy. CP-HardT

You must agree that Rubens was a Fool. To English Connoisseurs. William Blake. CP-BlakW

You must fuse mind and wit with all the senses. Sense of Truth. D. H.

Lawrence. CP-LawrD

You Must Have Some Idea Where They've Gone. Kenneth Patchen. CP-PatcK

You must live through the time when everything hurts. Double Shame, The. Stephen Spender. CP-SpenS

You must not call me Maggie, you must not call me Dear. Maggie a Lady. Christina Georgina Rossetti. CP-RosC1

You must not only aim aright. Henry David Thoreau. CP-ThorH

You Must Not Show Weakness. Yehuda Amichai. SP-AmicYL, *tr. by* Benjamin Harshav *and* Barbara Harshav

You mustn't groom an Arab with a file. Moral, The. Rudyard Kipling. CP-KiplR *Fr.* Muse among the Motors, The.

You Mustn't Show Weakness. Yehuda Amichai. SP-AmicY, *tr. by* Chana Bloch

You mustn't swim till you're six weeks old. Rudyard Kipling. CP-KiplR *Fr.* Jungle Book, The.

You, my friends, and you strangers, all of you. Sheep in the Ruins, The. Archibald MacLeish. CP-MacLA

You, my friends, wherever you are. Appeal, An. Czeslaw Milosz. CP-MiloC; CP-MiloCN, *tr. by* Robert Hass

You name is Nothing. God without being, sly. Romantic Eros, The. Helen Pinkerton. CP-PinkH

You named those lies clustered. Blasphemy. Yusef Komunyakaa. CP-KomuY

You need a garden / and a bad heart. Bad Heart. Federico García Lorca. CP-GarcF, *tr. by* Christopher Maurer

You need not speak, if that be shame. Damask. Wallace Stevens. CP-StevWP

You need some. Old Indian Belief. A. K. Ramanujan. CP-RamaA

You need the untranslatable ice to watch. Appendix to the Anniad. Gwendolyn Brooks. SP-BrooG

You never come back. Mill-Doors. Carl Sandburg. CP-SandC

You never got to recline. For Mother on Father's Day. James Tate. SP-TateJ

You never heard of me, I dare. Voice from the Tomb (5). Stevie Smith. CP-SmitS

You never saw it used but still can hear. Riddle, The. Seamus Heaney. SP-HeanSO

You no / tice / nobod / y wants. E. E. Cummings. CP-CummE

You on the Tower. Thomas Hardy. CP-HardT

You, once a belle in Shreveport. Snapshots of a Daughter-in-Law. Adrienne Rich. CP-RicAE; SP-RicA1; SP-RicA2

You open your. Travelers in Erewhon. Kenneth Rexroth. CP-RexrK

You or You. Laura Riding Jackson. CP-RidiL

You ought to have seen what I saw on my way. Blueberries. Robert Frost. CP-FrosR

You ought to see him there in the backyard. Clutter of Silence: Invention for Two Voices. Miller Williams. CP-WillM

You out there, so secret. Poem: "You out there, so secret." Thomas McGrath. SP-McGrT

You overshadow them, you put to shame. Berthe's Eyes. Charles Baudelaire. CP-BaudC, *tr. by* Walter Martin

You peculiar pink stinks been crowdin'. Message from the Assistant Chief of the Fly People, A. Kenneth Patchen. CP-PatcK

You people are dead. Estais Muertos. César Vallejo. CP-MertT

You pick me up, a coin someone has lost. New Lover, A. Dan Pagis. SP-PagiD, *tr. by* Stephen Mitchell

You pick one up along the shore. Shells. Howard Nemerov. CP-NemeH

You picked a gentian. Bavarian Gentian, The. James Laughlin. CP-LaugJ

You picked up little, had small need. Seizure of the World. Laura Riding Jackson. CP-RidiL

You pillars of light mournful and beautiful. Island (XVII), The. Pablo Neruda. SP-NeruP *Fr.* Separate Rose, The.

You point to / Antares. Antares. Arthur Sze. SP-SzeA

You poured fine sand on me, your swimsuit. Sea Change. Olga Broumas. SP-BrouO

You prayer-, you blasphemy-, you. Wellspring Rushes, The. Paul Celan. SP-CelaP, *tr. by* John Felstiner

You prepare for one sorrow. Oddjob, a Bull Terrier. Derek Walcott. CP-WalcD

You promise me when certain things are done. Prospect, The. Adrienne Rich. CP-RicAE

You promised to send me some violets. Did you forget? Letter from Town: The Almond-Tree. D. H. Lawrence. CP-LawrD

You propose I wait, strange window. Rainer Maria Rilke. CP-RilkFr, *tr. by* A. Poulin, Jr. *Fr.* Windows, The.

You punched a hole in the paper. Yannis Ritsos. SP-RitsY *Fr.* First Series.

You pursue the matter. Conversation, The. Thom Gunn. CP-GunnT

You put on my clothes. Recognition, The. Wendell Berry. CP-BerrW

You put the house about my body. Who Made Her. Heather McHugh. SP-McHuH

You raise / your face from mine, parting. Four Beginnings / for Kyra. Olga Broumas. SP-BrouO

You reach me out of the age of the air. To the Rain. W. S. Merwin. SP-MerwW

You read the clicking keys as gibberish. Analogue. Howard Nemerov. CP-

NemeH

You read the New York Times. Alfred Corning Clark. Robert Lowell. SP-LoweR

You, reading over my shoulder, peering beneath. Reader over My Shoulder, The. Robert Graves. CP-GravR

You Reading This, Be Ready. William Stafford. SP-StafWW

You recognize it like. Dolly. Thom Gunn. CP-GunnT

You refilled my life. Motherhood. Rainer Maria Rilke. CP-RilkFr, *tr. by* A. Poulin, Jr.

You refuse to own / yourself, you permit. Margaret Atwood. SP-AtwM1

You reject the rainbow. Dream of Hell, A. Robert Graves. CP-GravR

You remember down at Florence our Cascine. Dance, The. Elizabeth Barrett Browning. CP-BroEB

You remember Rossignano. Hyphens. Donald Davie. CP-DaviDC

You remember that village where the border ran. Boundary Commission, The. Paul Muldoon. CP-MuldP

You revel in my torments, only you. Michelangelo Buonarroti. CP-Miche, *tr. by* John Frederick Nims

You & Rimbaud. I Believe in You. Charles Olson. CP-OlsoC

You rise like a mountain over the white building. Quarrel with a Cloud. Richard Eberhart. CP-EberR

You rose from our embrace and the small light spread. Sonnet: "You rose from our embrace and the small light spread." Hayden Carruth. CP-CarHS *Fr.* Sonnets.

You ruffled black blossom. Turkey-Cock. D. H. Lawrence. CP-LawrD

You said: I will go to another land, I will go to another sea. City, The. Constantine P. Cavafy. CP-CavaC, *tr. by* Theoharis Constantine Theoharis

You said Is / there anything which. E. E. Cummings. CP-CummE

You said that I "was Great"—one Day. Emily Dickinson. CP-DickE

You said that you loved the lark more than any other bird because of tis straight flight toward the sun. Lark, The. Gabriela Mistral. SP-MistG, *tr. by* Maria Giachetti [*or* Jacketti]

You said the anger would come back. Again and Again and Again. Anne Sexton. CP-SextA

You said, "Who's at the door?" Talking through the Door. Jelaluddin Rumi. SP-Rumi, *tr. by* Coleman Barks

You said you got to go home & feed your pussycat. Pussy Blues. Allen Ginsberg. CP-GinsA

You said you would kill it this morning. Pheasant. Sylvia Plath. CP-PlatS

You sang the song of rare delight. To Benj. S. Parker. James Whitcomb Riley. CP-RileJ

You sat in the tub. Swimmer, The. Louise Glück. SP-GlucL

You saw the sunlight ripen upon the wall. Grace in the Fore Street. Donald Davie. CP-DaviDC

You / say. On Being Out-Classed by Class. Alan Dugan. CP-DugaA

You say / A miracle from Heaven. Michael Palmer. SP-PalmM

You say, as I have often given tongue. To a Poet, Who Would Have Me Praise Certain Bad Poets, Imitators of His and Mine. William Butler Yeats. CP-YeatW

You say grace before meals. Grace, A. G. K. Chesterton. CP-ChesG

You say Hello and part of what you spend. Entropy. Miller Williams. CP-WillM

You say I love not, 'cause I do not play. To His Mistress Objecting to Him Neither Toying or Talking. Robert Herrick. CP-HerrR

You say I must write *another* book? But I've just written this one. To an American Publisher. Stevie Smith. CP-SmitS

You say I O.K.ed. Madam and the Phone Bill. Langston Hughes. CP-HughL; CP-HughL2

You say: / I open my eyes and see what is there. Appearances. Hans Magnus Enzensberger. SP-EnzeH, *tr. by* Michael Hamburger

You say love is this, love is that. Memory of April. William Carlos Williams. CP-WilW1

You say "no" with your body, and *no*. To Nigrovorine Who is Leaving. Rainer Maria Rilke. CP-RilkFr, *tr. by* A. Poulin, Jr.

You say, O Sage, when weather-checked. Child and the Sage, The. Thomas Hardy. CP-HardT

You say reserve & modesty he has. On Stothard. William Blake. CP-BlakW

You say: "Since life is cruel enough at best." Edna St. Vincent Millay. CP-MillE

You say that spite avails her nothing, that. Good Man, Bad Woman. Wallace Stevens. CP-StevWP

You say their Pictures well Painted be. William Blake. CP-BlakW

You say this is the iris? Wallace Stevens. CP-StevWP

You say, to me-wards your affection's strong. Love Me Little, Love Me Long. Robert Herrick. CP-HerrR

You say y'are sweet; how sho'd we know. On a Perfum'd Lady. Robert Herrick. CP-HerrR

You say y'are young; but when your Teeth are told. Upon One Who Said She Was Alwayes Young. Robert Herrick. CP-HerrR

You say you are holy. Stephen Crane. CP-CranS

You say you love, and yet your eye. To Caroline. Lord Byron. CP-Byron

You say you love; but with a voice. Stanzas: "You say you love; but with a voice." John Keats. CP-KeatJ

You say, you love me; that I thus must prove. To a Maid. Robert Herrick. CP-HerrR

You say you want this story. Interview with a Policeman. Ai. SP-Ai

You say you'l kiss me, and I thank you for it. Upon a Free Maid, with a Foule Breath. Robert Herrick. CP-HerrR

You scarcely need my tardy thanks. My Namesake. John Greenleaf Whittier. CP-WhitJ

You scream, waking from a nightmare. Little Sleep's-Head Sprouting Hair in the Moonlight. Galway Kinnell. SP-KinnGN

You see a man / trying to think. Ghost of a Chance. Adrienne Rich. CP-RicAE; SP-RicA1; SP-RicA2

You see before you an icing of skin. Root Canal, The. Marge Piercy. SP-PierM

You see here. Lorine Niedecker. CP-NiedL

You see I cannot see—your lifetime. Emily Dickinson. CP-DickE

You see, I did not want to leave. Staying Awake. John Logan. CP-LogaJ

You see me—one who goes crying. Guido Cavalcanti. CP-CavaG, tr. by Marc Cirigliano

You see no beauty in the parched parade. Prophecy. Robert Penn Warren. CP-WarrR

You see the jerked. Robert Creeley. CP-CreeR

You see them everywhere, the grinning martyrs. Orthodontia. John Updike. CP-UpdiJ

You see them vanish in their speeding cars. Fugue. Howard Nemerov. CP-NemeH

You see, they have no judgment. Drowned Children, The. Louise Glück. SP-GlucL

You see this dog. Flush or Faunus. Elizabeth Barrett Browning. CP-BroEB

You see this gentle streame, that glides. Proof to No Purpose. Robert Herrick. CP-HerrR

You see we keep a jealous Heart. Emily Dickinson. SP-DickE

You seem to cast, my vent'rous book. Epistle 1.20: "You seem to cast, my vent'rous book." Horace. SP-SmarC Fr. Epistles.

You send me your poems. Conspiracy, The. Robert Creeley. CP-CreeR

You senses, never still, but shrill as children. Holy Sacrament of the Altar, The. Thomas Merton. CP-MertT

You serve the best wines always, my dear sir. Martial. CP-CunnJ, tr. by James Vincent Cunningham and J. V. Cunningham

You set out on a morning bright. Clarence Major. SP-MajoC

You shadow and flame. Valentine's Night. D. H. Lawrence. CP-LawrD

You Shall Above All Things Be Glad and Young. E. E. Cummings. CP-CummE; SP-CummE

You shall be, my dear. Well Hung. Hugh MacDiarmid. SP-MacDH

You Shall Have Homes. Carl Sandburg. CP-SandC

You shall have peace with night and sleep. Peace, Night, Sleep. Carl Sandburg. CP-SandC

You shall hear how Hiawatha. Hiawatha's Fasting. Henry Wadsworth Longfellow. SP-LongH Fr. Song of Hiawatha, The.

You shall not be overbold. Titmouse, The. Ralph Waldo Emerson. CP-EmerR

You shall not love me for what daily spends. Ralph Waldo Emerson. CP-EmerR

You shall sing my songs, O earth. E. E. Cummings. CP-CummE

You Shall Want Nothing Fit for Mortal Man. Thomas Sheridan. CP-SherT

You should have seen them, small and wild. Geography Lesson, The. Paul Muldoon. CP-MuldP

You show me the poems of some woman. Translations. Adrienne Rich. SP-RicA2

You sicken me with lies. To Certain "Brothers." Langston Hughes. CP-HughL; CP-HughL1

You simply go out and shut the door. Locking Yourself Out, Then Trying to Get Back In. Raymond Carver. CP-CarvR

You sing, and the gift of State's applause. To a Poet and a Lady. Paul Laurence Dunbar. CP-DunbP

You sit beside the bed. Bedside. Margaret Atwood. SP-AtwM2

You sit by the bed. Learning. Miller Williams. CP-WillM

You sit here on solid sand banks trying to figure. Daybreak. James Dickey. CP-DickJ

You sit in this hard bright room with your abstract. One and Two. Tennessee Williams. CP-WillT

You sit on the couch. I've Seen Too Many Glazed-Eyed Bums Sitting under a Bridge Drinking Cheap Wine. Charles Bukowski. SP-BukC1

You sit talking in all earnestness to a woman. Drawing-Room. D. H. Lawrence. CP-LawrD

You sit there because I like to look at you. Another Day (You sit there). Muriel Rukeyser. CP-RukeM

You slapped my face. Short Poem. William Carlos Williams. CP-WilW2

You sleep in a room with bluegreen curtains. In the Wake of Home. Adrienne Rich. SP-RicA1; SP-RicA2

You sleep too well—too far away. TO E. T.: 1917. Walter De la Mare. CP-DeLaW

You sleeping I bend to cover. Night-Pieces: For a Child. Adrienne Rich. CP-RicAE; SP-RicA2

"You slut," he flung at her. Blue Maroons. Carl Sandburg. CP-SandC

You smile and you smoke your cigar, my boy. My Boy. James Whitcomb Riley. CP-RileJ

You smile upon your friend to-day. A. E. Housman. CP-HousA

You Smoke a Cigarette. Charles Bukowski. SP-BukC2

You soda crackers! I remember. Soda Crackers. Raymond Carver. CP-CarvR

You Sort Old Letters. Robert Penn Warren. CP-WarrR

You—Spanish-speaking. Hayden Carruth. CP-CarHS Fr. Clay Hill Anthology, The.

You speak. You say: Today's character is not. As You Leave the Room. Wallace Stevens. CP-StevWP

You splice together two broomsticks, then reef. Sonnet at Easter. Howard Nemerov. CP-NemeH

You spoke of "Hope" surpassing "Home." Emily Dickinson. SP-DickE

You spoke of spring and summer. Of the Seasons. May Sarton. SP-SartM

You spring from a fantasy. You. David Ignatow. SP-IgnaD

You stand alone in the empty street. Beginning. Gregory Orr. SP-OrrG

You stand as rocks stand. Portland, 1968. Louise Glück. SP-GlucL

You stand before the dark / Wet night of leaves. To Alfonso Cortes. Thomas Merton. CP-MertT

You stand behind the old black mare. Why Can't I Leave You? Ai. SP-Ai

You stand like a twin-headed bird. Arse Poetica. Sam Hamill. SP-HamiS

You stand near the window as lights wink. 23rd Street Runs into Heaven. Kenneth Patchen. CP-PatcK

You stand thinking of great principles. Great Principles Are Thrown Down by Time. Richard Eberhart. CP-EberR

You stared out of the window at [or on] the emptiness. To Manuel Altolaguirre. Stephen Spender. CP-SpenS

You steal into my room. Sleeping Beauty. Ai. SP-Ai

You stop at the end of the lane, where the birches grow. John's Birches. Robert Penn Warren. CP-WarrR

You strolled in the open, leisurely and alone. To the Poets in New York. James Wright. CP-WrigJ

You strop my anger, especially. To the Pay Toilet. Marge Piercy. SP-PierM

You suit me well, for you can make me laugh. To a Prize Bird. Marianne Craig Moore. CP-MoorM

You sullen pig of a man. Libertad! Igualdad! Fraternidad! William Carlos Williams. CP-WilW1

You Sweep the Floor. Jelaluddin Rumi. SP-Rumi, tr. by Coleman Barks

You take a rock, your hand is hard. Constructive. Heather McHugh. SP-McHuH

You take my hand and. Margaret Atwood. SP-AtwM1

You take off, we take off, they take off. Clothes. Wisława Szymborska. SP-SzymW, tr. by Stanislaw Barańczak and Clare Cavanagh

You take the dollar. For One Moment. David Ignatow. SP-IgnaD

You take this pill, a new world. RX Creative Writing: Identity. William Stafford. SP-StafWW

You talk like / they don't kick. Comment on Curb. Langston Hughes. CP-HughL; CP-HughL3 Fr. Lenox Avenue Mural.

You Taught Me. Thomas McGrath. SP-McGrT

You taught me Waiting with Myself. Emily Dickinson. CP-DickE

You tell me every man has a soul to save? Souls to Save. D. H. Lawrence. CP-LawrD

You tell me I am wrong. Pomegranate. D. H. Lawrence. CP-LawrD

You tell me that I love myself. Flattery. William Carlos Williams. CP-WilW2

You tell me that the world is fair, in spite. Fair World Tho' a Fallen, A. Christina Georgina Rossetti. CP-RosC3

You tell me this is God? Stephen Crane. CP-CranS

You tell these young spratasses around here. Pa McCabe. Hayden Carruth. CP-CarHS

You that a stranger in mid-Rome seek Rome. Rome. "Panormitanus." CP-CunnJ, tr. by James Vincent Cunningham

You that are she and you, that's double she. To the Lady Bedford. John Donne. CP-DonnJ; MW-DonnJ

You that are sprung of northern stock. To a Calvinist in Bali. Edna St. Vincent Millay. CP-MillE

You that come to birth and bring the mysteries. Jelaluddin Rumi. SP-Rumi, tr. by Coleman Barks

You, that decipher out the fate. Mourning. Andrew Marvell. CP-MarvA

You that go forth upon the buried cities. Buried City, The. G. K. Chesterton. CP-ChesG

You that have snarled through the ages, take your answer and go. Pessimist, The. G. K. Chesterton. CP-ChesG

You that in love find[e] luck[e] and [h]abunda[u]nce. May Time. Sir Thomas Wyatt. CP-WyatT

You that in vain would front the coming order. Old King's New Jester, The. Edwin Arlington Robinson. CP-RobiE

You that know the way. Lemuel's Blessing. W. S. Merwin. SP-MerwW

You that love lovers. Music Master. Jelaluddin Rumi. SP-Rumi, *tr. by* Coleman Barks

You that think Love can convey. Celia Singig. Thomas Carew. CP-CareT

You that will a wonder know. In Praise of His Mistress. Thomas Carew. CP-CareT

You that would bite the whole pie and. Vengeance Is Mine, Saith the Lord. Donald Davie. CP-DaviDC

You that would last long, list to my song. Ben Jonson. CP-JonsB *Fr.* Volpone.

You that would read the Bible, turn all. Thomas Sheridan. CP-SherT

You! the last Polish poet!—drunk, he embraced me. 1945. Czeslaw Milosz. CP-MiloC; CP-MiloCN, *tr. by* Robert Hass

You the very old, I have come. Waiting in Line. William Stafford. SP-StafW; SP-StafWW

You, the woman; I, the man; this, the world. Character of Love Seen as a Search for the Lost, The. Kenneth Patchen. CP-PatcK

You, there with your chin in your hand. Autumn Poem, The. "Rubén Dario." SP-DariR, *tr. by* Alberto Acereda *and* Will Derusha

You think a life can end? For the Anniversary of my Mother's Death. Archibald MacLeish. CP-MacLA

You think Fuseli is not a Great Painter. I'm glad. To Hunt. William Blake. CP-BlakW

You think I am your servant but you are wrong. Drawing Board, The. Derek Mahon. CP-MahoD

You think in the circle. Robert Creeley. CP-CreeR

You think it horrible that lust and rage. Spur, The. William Butler Yeats. CP-YeatW

You think it is a sorry thing. Blind. James Whitcomb Riley. CP-RileJ

You think them "out of reach," your dead? Out of Reach. James Whitcomb Riley. CP-RileJ

You Think There's No Hell That Will Hold You. Shmuel HaNagid. SP-HaNaS, *tr. by* Peter Cole

You Think They Are Permanent But They Pass. Richard Eberhart. CP-EberR

You think we don't have messages in Kentucky? Here is one I got by hounds, on the day of a blizzard. Message to Be Inscribed on Mark Van Doren's Hamilton Medal. Thomas Merton. CP-MertT

You think you remember but. Interdiction, The. James Laughlin. CP-LaugJ

You thought it heartless. Of Grief. May Sarton. SP-SartM

"You thought we knew," she said, "but we were wrong." Woman and the Wife, The. Edwin Arlington Robinson. CP-RobiE

You three:—my wife. Louis Zukofsky. CP-ZukLS

You, to whom I don't confide. Song: "You, to whom I don't confide." Rainer Maria Rilke. CP-RilkFr, *tr. by* A. Poulin, Jr.

You told me, I remember, glory, built. Table Talk. William Cowper. CP-CowpW

You told me resurrection in images of roots. Loan, The. Muriel Rukeyser. CP-RukeM

You told me: they all went in and saw the glass. Junk-Heap at Murano. Muriel Rukeyser. CP-RukeM

You too got tired of being an advertisement. Yehuda Amichai. SP-AmicY, *tr. by* Stephen Mitchell

You, too, my brother in your hour of Spring. Pietro Bembo. SP-ZatuM, *tr. by* Marya Alexandrovna Zaturenska

You took gospel what I said. Catch with Reuben. Miller Williams. CP-WillM

You took it in / at a glance: the March. Windshield, The. Charles Tomlinson. CP-TomlC

You tourist composed upon that fence. Baler, The. Hayden Carruth. CP-CarHS

You travel a path on paper. Fanny Howe. SP-HoweF *Fr.* O'Clock.

You try to beat loneliness. Tenebrae. Yusef Komunyakaa. CP-KomuY

You try to fix your mind upon his death. For W———, Who Commanded Well. Howard Nemerov. CP-NemeH

You turn into a plant on the coasts of time. Man from Ecuador beneath the Eiffel Tower, A. Jorge Carrera Andrade. CP-MertT

You turn your back, you turn your back. To Carrey Clavel. Thomas Hardy. CP-HardT

You two sit at the table late, each, now and then. After the Dinner Party. Robert Penn Warren. CP-WarrR

You understand both Adolphe and Fabrice. Birthday Poem. Thom Gunn. CP-GunnT

You understand the colors on the hillside have faded. Crucifixion. Hayden Carruth. CP-CarHS

You use your mind. To Military Progress. Marianne Craig Moore. CP-MoorM

You used to wear dungarees & blue workshirt. Brooklyn College Brain. Allen Ginsberg. CP-GinsA

You uterus / you have been patient. Poem to My Uterus. Lucille Clifton. SP-ClifL

You, vanquished and expelled. Czeslaw Milosz. CP-MiloCN, *tr. by* Robert Hass

You vines wreathe sands printless. Vines. Louis Zukofsky. CP-ZukLS

You visit me in an apple. With Her in an Apple. Yehuda Amichai. SP-AmicYL, *tr. by* Benjamin Harshav *and* Barbara Harshav

You visit me inside the apple. Inside the Apple. Yehuda Amichai. SP-AmicY, *tr.*

by Chana Bloch

You wake, all windows blind—embattled sprays. Winter-Piece. Charles Tomlinson. CP-TomlC; SP-TomlC

You wake tired, in the cabin light has filled. To a Friend in Time of Trouble. Thom Gunn. CP-GunnT

You walk on. Door, A ("You walk on"). W. S. Merwin. SP-MerwW

You walk, / you get muddy. In Motion. Federico García Lorca. CP-GarcF, *tr. by* Jerome Rothenberg *Fr.* Return, The.

You walked in front of me. Orpheus (1). Margaret Atwood. SP-AtwM2

You walked the length of Italy. Catherine of Siena. Rita Dove. SP-DoveR

You want something; that's the pretext. I recently abandoned a dream marrative called "Mark" Birthmark: The Pretext. Rae Armantrout. SP-ArmaA

You want to go back. Margaret Atwood. SP-AtwM1

You wanted me to tell you. Idyll: "You wanted me to tell you." Federico García Lorca. CP-GarcF, *tr. by* Alan S. Trueblood *Fr.* Love.

You wanted to compare, and there. Amazon Twins. Olga Broumas. SP-BrouO

You washed the fruit. Yehuda Amichai. SP-AmicY, *tr. by* Stephen Mitchell *Fr.* Summer or Its End.

You watch the night for images of death. According to His Seasons. Howard Nemerov. CP-NemeH

You watched the slender narcissus wilt. Elegy for Integral Domains, The. Norman Dubie. CP-DubiN

You waves, though you dance at my feet like children at play. Meditation of the Old Fisherman, The. William Butler Yeats. CP-YeatW

"You!" we chanted together. "How long has it been?" At O'Hare. John Ciardi. CP-CiarJ

You weep whole heartedly—your shining tears. Stolen Jewel. Robert Graves. CP-GravR

You were a beautiful child. Oaxaca 1925. Kenneth Rexroth. CP-RexrK

You were a child and I your veteran. Child with Veteran. Robert Graves. CP-GravR

You were a girl of satin and gauze. Wheel Revolves, The. Kenneth Rexroth. CP-RexrK

You were a haven once, my little room. Petrarch. CP-Petra, *tr. by* J. G. Nichols

You were a princess, lost; I. School Play. William Stafford. SP-StafWW

You Were Asleep. James Laughlin. CP-LaugJ

You were asleep. I wake you. Poem: "You were asleep. I wake you." Jorge Luis Borges. SP-BorgJ, *tr. by* Alastair Reid

You were begotten in a vague war. History Lesson. Maxine W. Kumin. SP-KumiM

You were born in the Spring. To Mary Rossetti. Christina Georgina Rossetti. CP-RosC3

You were both quiet, looking out over the water. Swans. Louise Glück. SP-GlucL

You were by my side, though I could not see you. Prohibition, The. Robert Graves. CP-GravR

You were dead, / Eloísa. Final Page. Federico García Lorca. CP-GarcF, *tr. by* Jerome Rothenberg *Fr.* White Album.

You were first. Behold the Lamb. Paul Muldoon. CP-MuldP

You were forever finding some new play. Exposed Nest, The. Robert Frost. CP-FrosR

You were here at his young beginning. End of the Year 1912. Thomas Hardy. CP-HardT

You were here on earth, in cities. Sad Dust Glories. Allen Ginsberg. CP-GinsA

You were like a religious fanatic. God, The. Ted Hughes. SP-HughTN

You were my beginning and again I am with you, here, where I learned the four quarters of the globe. In Szetejnie. Czeslaw Milosz. CP-MiloCN, *tr. by* Robert Hass

You were my death. Paul Celan. SP-CelaP, *tr. by* John Felstiner

You were my mother, thorn apple bush. Graves, The. Lorine Niedecker. CP-NiedL *Fr.* Element Mother, The.

You were never told, Mother, how old Illya was drunk. Czar's Last Christmas Letter, The: A Barn in the Urals. Norman Dubie. CP-DubiN

You were out when I called. Speech for Auden. Alan Dugan. CP-DugaA

You were rose color. Fright in the Dining Room. Federico García Lorca. CP-GarcF, *tr. by* Alan S. Trueblood *Fr.* Eros with a Cane.

You were rotten. To an Apple. David Ignatow. SP-IgnaD

You were silver-quiffed and tall. In Memory. Thomas Kinsella. CP-KinsT

You were so jealous of our nursemaid's love. Charles Baudelaire. CP-BaudC, *tr. by* Walter Martin

You were the last bulwark of my dreams. Bulwark. Langston Hughes. CP-HughL; CP-HughL1

You were the last to love America; too grim. Letter to Those Who Are About to Die. Kenneth Patchen. CP-PatcK

You were the one for skylights. I opposed. Skylight, The. Seamus Heaney. SP-HeanSO *Fr.* Glanmore Revisited.

You Were the Sort that Men Forget. Thomas Hardy. CP-HardT

You were to leave and being all but gone. Departure. Charles Tomlinson. CP-TomlC

You were unreasonably kind. S. Dead. Marge Piercy. SP-PierM

You Were Wearing. Kenneth Koch. SP-KochK

"You! What d'you mean by this?" I rapped. Inspection. Wilfred Owen. CP-OwenW

You which could grin three smiles into a dead. E. E. Cummings. CP-CummE

You White Cunning Devils. William Dickey. SP-DickW

You who always gaze horizontally should know. It Exists. Yannis Ritsos. SP-RitsY, tr. by Kostas Myrsiades

You who are bent, and bald, and blind. Wanderings of Oisin, The. William Butler Yeats. CP-YeatW

You who are so mighty. Appeal. William Carlos Williams. CP-WilW1

You, who are touched not by our mortal ways. Maestro di Tocar. Ezra Pound. CP-PoEar

You who can hear in scattered rhymes the sound. Petrarch. CP-Petra, tr. by J. G. Nichols

You who celebrate bygones. To a Historian. Walt Whitman. CP-WhitW

You who come after us. Only the Red Fox, Only the Crow. Charles Olson. CP-OlsoC

You who come and go. Reflections. Federico García Lorca. CP-GarcF, tr. by Jerome Rothenberg Fr. In the Forest of the Lunar Grapefruits.

You, who confess that you are poor. Hymn: Christ's Invitation in the Apocalypse. Jones Very. CP-VeryJ

You who, conspicuous with your shining mace, were accustomed. Elegy 2: On the Death of the Beadle of Cambrdige University. John Milton. CP-CowpW; CP-MiltJ

You, who contain augmented tears, explosions. To the Empress Josephine's Statue. Hart Crane. CP-CranH

You who demanded of God the law. Concerning Food. Laura Riding Jackson. CP-RidiL

You who desired so much—in vain to ask. To Emily Dickinson. Hart Crane. CP-CranH

You who follow Henry Thoreau. Fish is the Flower of Water, A. Charles Olson. CP-OlsoC

You who gave me birth between your sturdy legs. And Rest. David Ignatow. SP-IgnaD

You who go out on schedule. Two Variations. Denise Levertov. SP-LeveDP

You who had the sense. Invitation. William Carlos Williams. CP-WilW1

You who have spoken words in the earth. Reproach to Dead Poets. Archibald MacLeish. CP-MacLA

You who in water move as one. You Who Swim. John Updike. CP-UpdiJ

You who live secure. Shemà. Primo Levi. CP-LeviP, tr. by Ruth Feldman and Brian Swann

You who looked on passed ages as a glass. Christina Georgina Rossetti. CP-RosC3

You who see our homes at night. Tierra Del Fuego. Adam Zagajewski. SP-ZagaA, tr. by Clare Cavanagh

You who seek the truth. Yannis Ritsos. SP-RitsY Fr. Paper Poems 2.

You Who Swim. John Updike. CP-UpdiJ

You who think I find words for everything. Adrienne Rich. SP-RicA1 Fr. Contradictions: Tracking Poems.

You who to the rounded prime. To Joel Chandler Harris. James Whitcomb Riley. CP-RileJ

You Who Were Made for This Music. Louis Zukofsky. CP-ZukLS

You who were made for this music. You Who Were Made for This Music. Louis Zukofsky. CP-ZukLS

You who wronged a simple man. Czeslaw Milosz. CP-MiloC; CP-MiloCN, tr. by Richard Lourie

You Who'd Be Wise. Shmuel HaNagid. SP-HaNaS, tr. by Peter Cole

You whom I could not save. Dedication: "You whom I could not save." Czeslaw Milosz. CP-MiloC; CP-MiloCN

You whom the kings saluted; who refused not. To the Unknown Warrior. G. K. Chesterton. CP-ChesG

You whose name is aggressor and devourer. Czeslaw Milosz. CP-MiloCN, tr. by Robert Hass

You who've pierced my eyes to my heart. Guido Cavalcanti. CP-CavaG, tr. by Marc Cirigliano

You? Why you're. Fond Farewell, A. William Carlos Williams. CP-WilW2

You will be aware of an absence, presently. For a Fatherless Son. Sylvia Plath. CP-PlatS

You will be walking some night. Do Not Be Ashamed. Wendell Berry. CP-BerrW

You will cherish Beauty, God's shadow over the universe. Artist's Decalogue, The. Gabriela Mistral. SP-MistG, tr. by Maria Giachetti [or Jacketti]

You will come one day in a waver of love. Dream Girl. Carl Sandburg. CP-SandC

You will excuse me, I suppose. To the Dean, when in England, in 1726. Thomas Sheridan. CP-SherT

You will find it is. Émigré. W. S. Merwin. SP-MerwWF

You will find me drinking rum. Logical Vegetarian, The. G. K. Chesterton. CP-ChesG

You will hammer silver into a heart. Silver Trade, The. Arthur Sze. SP-SzeA

You will have to wait. Until it. Until. Waiting. Robert Penn Warren. CP-WarrR

You will like their upstairs. Reunion, A. James Schuyler. CP-SchuJ

You will never be alone, you hear so deep. Assurance. William Stafford. SP-StafWW

You will never be here. Robert Creeley. CP-CreeR

You will never understand how much I love you. Beloved Sleeps on the Poet's Breast, The. Federico García Lorca. CP-GarcF, tr. by Angela Jaffray

You will not forswear the bargainings. Quality of Mercy. Allen Tate. CP-TateA

You will not haunt the rue Vavin. To S. V. B.—June 15, 1940. Edna St. Vincent Millay. CP-MillE

You will remember little of yourself. You ("You will remember little of yourself"). Robert Creeley. SP-CreeR

You will see this big-jawed man walking up and down. Explorer on Main Street, The. Richard Eberhart. CP-EberR

You will someday. What This Mode of Motion Said. A. R. Ammons. CP-AmmoA

You Will Speak. Yehuda Amichai. SP-AmicYL, tr. by Benjamin Harshav and Barbara Harshav

You will walk toward the mirror. Your Life. William Stafford. SP-StafWW

You window, O waiting's measure. Rainer Maria Rilke. CP-RilkFr, tr. by A. Poulin, Jr. Fr. Windows, The.

You wished to die entirely and for good. To My Father. Jorge Luis Borges. SP-BorgJ, tr. by Willis Barnstone

You with no fear of dying. Snow, The. W. S. Merwin. SP-MerwWF

You with the beard as red as Barbarossa's. For My Great-Grandfather: A Message Long Overdue. Maxine W. Kumin. SP-KumiM

You with your wings like spatulas. Gull. Anne Sexton. CP-SextA

You won not verses, Madam, you won me. Epistle. To My Lady Covell. Ben Jonson. CP-JonsB

You wonder now to see me write. Jonathan Swift. CP-SherT Fr. To Mr. Delany.

You wonder who this is! And, why I name. On the Town's Honest Man. Ben Jonson. CP-JonsB; SP-JonsB

You wonder Who this Thing has writ. To the Earl of Burlington Asking Who Writ the Libels against Him. Alexander Pope. CP-PopeA

You wonder why Drab sells her love for gold? Epigram: "You wonder why Drab sells her love for gold?" James Vincent Cunningham. CP-CunnJ

You won't become a gourmet cook. Lines Written in the Fannie Farmer Cookbook. Elizabeth Bishop. CP-BishE

You won't recall the house of the customs men. House of the Customs Men, The. Eugenio Montale. CP-MontE, tr. by Jonathan Galassi

You wore the same quite correct clothing. Amitites. Ezra Pound. SP-PounE

You would be courted, dear, and I would love you. Martial. CP-CunnJ, tr. by James Vincent Cunningham

You would hoist an old hat on the tines of a fork. Bat on the Road, A. Seamus Heaney. SP-HeanSO

You would like to hear how it is in old age? New Province, A. Czeslaw Milosz. CP-MiloCN, tr. by Robert Hass

You would not think the room. Eight Observations on the Nature of Eternity. Charles Tomlinson. CP-TomlC

You would not want too reserved a speaker. Some Shadows. William Stafford. SP-StafW; SP-StafWW

You would think I'd be a specialist in contemporary. Put-Down Come On, The. A. R. Ammons. CP-AmmoA

You would think that the little birches. Mud. Maxine W. Kumin. SP-KumiM

You would think the fury of aerial bombardment. Fury of Aerial Bombardment, The. Richard Eberhart. CP-EberR

You would think with so much going on outside. Studio, The. Derek Mahon. CP-MahoD

You Wouldn't Say They Didn't Get Along Exactly. Miller Williams. CP-WillM

You wouldn't / walk alone. That's. But. Robert Creeley. CP-CreeR

You wound my soul with a thousand spears. Nonette. Langston Hughes. CP-HughL; CP-HughL1

You write, you tell me, for posterity. Martial. CP-CunnJ, tr. by James Vincent Cunningham

You, you are all unloving, loveless, you. Sea, The. D. H. Lawrence. CP-LawrD

You ("You will remember little of yourself"). Robert Creeley. SP-CreeR

You you you. First Launching. Federico García Lorca. CP-GarcF, tr. by Jerome Rothenberg Fr. Barrage of Firework Poems on the Occasion of the Poet's Birthday.

You'd be surprised how much, at. Bamberg. Randall Jarrell. CP-JarrR

You'd be surprised how short the roads. Windy Trees. A. R. Ammons. CP-AmmoA

You'd dozed in front of the TV. Old Days, The. Raymond Carver. CP-CarvR

You'd have men's hearts up from the dust. Near Perigord. Ezra Pound. SP-PounE

You'd look right with a wolf from Tambov. Arrow in the Wall, An. Andrey Andreievich Voznesensky. CP-WilbR

You'd never have thought the Queen was Helen's sister—Troy's burning-flower from Sparta, the beautiful sea-flower. Tower beyond Tragedy, The. Robinson Jeffers. CP-JefR1

You'd think we would have had enough. Flight of the Reader, The. Billy Collins. SP-CollB

You'd think we'd have them down by now. Funerals, The. Wyatt Prunty. SP-PrunW

You'd think, with all the age and sense. Temptress, The. Dorothy Parker. CP-ParkD

Youful / larger / of smallish). E. E. Cummings. CP-CummE

You'll always be my friend. More Girl than Boy. Yusef Komunyakaa. CP-KomuY

You'll be / coming home alone on the AA. Prayer for my Daughter. Marilyn Hacker. SP-HackM

You'll be returning, one day. Triolet, A: "You'll be returning, one day." Dorothy Parker. CP-ParkD

You'll be wonderin' whut's de reason. Expectation. Paul Laurence Dunbar. CP-DunbP

You'll find—it when you try to die. Emily Dickinson. CP-DickE

You'll have a gosling, call it Dan. Last Speech and Dying Words of Daniel Jackson, The. Thomas Sheridan. CP-SherT

You'll have to rethink the whole question. This. Whole Question, The. Robert Penn Warren. CP-WarrR

You'll know Her—by Her Foot. Emily Dickinson. CP-DickE

You'll know it—as you know 'tis Noon. Emily Dickinson. CP-DickE

You'll love me. Going Home. Robert Creeley. SP-CreeR

You'll not forget these rocks and what I told you? Dialogue on the Headland. Robert Graves. CP-GravR

You'll outlast me, good old concrete. Ode to Concrete. Joseph Brodsky. CP-BrodJ

You'll take back your Grand-duke? August Voice, An. Elizabeth Barrett Browning. CP-BroEB

You'll wait a long, long time for anything much. On Looking Up by Chance at the Constellations. Robert Frost. CP-FrosR

Young. Anne Sexton. CP-SextA; SP-SextA

Young. William Stafford. SP-StafWW

Young Abdul scorched in fire of a desert sun. True Believer. Allen Tate. CP-TateA

Young Adam surely must. Footnote on the Invention of Small Pleasures. Miller Williams. CP-WillM

Young, ambitious baker in a T-shirt (daubs of flour), A. Bakery. Adam Zagajewski. SP-ZagaA, tr. by Clare Cavanagh

Young and Simple though I Am. Thomas Campion. CP-CampT

Young and souple was I, when I lap the dyke. Broom Besoms ["Young and souple was I, when I lap the dyke"]. Robert Burns. CP-BurnR

Young and the Old, the. Richard Eberhart. CP-EberR

Young and Their Moral Guardians, The. D. H. Lawrence. CP-LawrD

Young Antiochian said to the king, The. Before Antiochus Epiphanis. Constantine P. Cavafy. CP-CavaC, tr. by Theoharis Constantine Theoharis

Young Are Not Greedy, The. D. H. Lawrence. CP-LawrD

Young Are Not Mean in Material Things, The. D. H. Lawrence. CP-LawrD

Young Author, The. Samuel Johnson. CP-JohnS

Young Birch, A. Robert Frost. CP-FrosR

Young body, light, A. To Beat the Child Was Bad Enough. Maya Angelou. SP-AngeM

Young Braccio's buried here. To mend a lack. Michelangelo Buonarroti. CP-MicheI, tr. by John Frederick Nims

Young Bride. Langston Hughes. CP-HughL; CP-HughL1

Young British Soldier, The. Rudyard Kipling. CP-KiplR

Young Bullfrogs. Carl Sandburg. CP-SandC

Young Calidore is paddling o'er the lake. Calidore. A Fragment. John Keats. CP-KeatJ

Young captain of a crazy bark! Last Contention, The. George Meredith. CP-MerG1

Young Cat and the Chrysanthemums, The. William Carlos Williams. CP-WilW1

Young child, Christ, is straight and wise, The. Child. Carl Sandburg. CP-SandC

Young Churchwarden, The. Thomas Hardy. CP-HardT

Young cock in his plebe strut, A. Come Morning. John Ciardi. CP-CiarJ

Young Cordwainer, The. Robert Graves. CP-GravR

Young Couple. Arthur Rimbaud. CP-RimbA, tr. by Martin Sorrell

Young Dancers, The. Marya Alexandrovna Zaturenska. SP-ZatuM

Young Dead Soldiers, The. Archibald MacLeish. CP-MacLA

Young Death. Christina Georgina Rossetti. CP-RosC3

Young doctor dreamed of revolution, The. Poetry as Continuity. Jane Cooper. CP-CoopJ

Young dog runs and leaps, The. Toss, for John Cage, A. Charles Olson. CP-OlsoC

Young Drummer Boy of Libby Prison: An Incident Related by Capt. James Hussey, The. Jones Very. CP-VeryJ

Young elm that must be cut, The. Living While It May. Denise Levertov. SP-LeveDP

Young England—What Is Then Become of Old. William Wordsworth. CP-WorW2

Young Farm Woman Alone. Ai. SP-Ai

Young Fathers. D. H. Lawrence. CP-LawrD

Young Fir-Wood, A. Dante Gabriel Rossetti. CW-RossD

Young Fire Eaters of Mexico City, The. Raymond Carver. CP-CarvR

Young Gal's Blues. Langston Hughes. CP-HughL; CP-HughL1

Young, gentle, and candid lover that I am. Sonnet 6: "Young, gentle, and candid lover that I am." John Milton. CP-CowpW; CP-MiltJ

Young German poked his head, The. Rare Gist, The. William Carlos Williams. CP-WilW2

Young Girl, A. Walter De la Mare. CP-DeLaW

Young Girl, The. Theodore Roethke. CP-RoetT

Young Girl, The. Niccolò Tommaseo. CW-RossD, tr. by Dante Gabriel Rossetti

Young girl found me at the track, The. On Being Recognized. Charles Bukowski. SP-BukC3

Young girl in a wheelchair, A. Chekhov on the West Heath. Denise Levertov. SP-LeveDL; SP-LeveDS

Young girl jogging in mittens and skimpy gym shorts through a freezing rainstorm up our block, The. Fat. C. K. Williams. SP-WillC

Young Girl of the Mississippi Valley, The. Muriel Rukeyser. CP-RukeM

Young Girl Singing, A. Marya Alexandrovna Zaturenska. SP-ZatuM

Young girl to marry. Lorine Niedecker. CP-NiedL

Young Girls, The. Raymond Carver. CP-CarvR

Young girls look up, The. Young Watch Us, The. Donald Hall. CP-HallD

Young girls wear flowers, / Young brides a flowery wreath. Flowers Appear on the Earth, The. Christina Georgina Rossetti. CP-RosC2

Young Glass-Stainer, The. Thomas Hardy. CP-HardT

Young Greek, Killed In The Wars, A. Richard Eberhart. CP-EberR

Young Grimes. Walt Whitman. CP-WhitW

Young Grimshaw. Robert Stock. SP-StocR

Young, having risen early, had gone, The. Guardians, The. Geoffrey Hill. CP-HillG

Young Hero Sings a Song of Self-Understanding, A. Christopher Logue. SP-LoguC Fr. Lily-White Boys, The.

Young Highland Rover, The. Robert Burns. CP-BurnR

Young Housewife, The. William Carlos Williams. CP-WilW1

Young Hunter, The. Richard Eberhart. CP-EberR

Young I drank beer & vomited green bile. Maturity. Allen Ginsberg. SP-GinsA

Young I was, but [or who] now am old. On Himselfe. Robert Herrick. CP-HerrR

Young in Fall I said: the birds. Lorine Niedecker. CP-NiedL

Young Instructor Talks to Himself Winding Up the Semester, The. Miller Williams. CP-WillM

Young is the blood that yonder. A. E. Housman. CP-HousA

Young Jockey was the blythest lad. Robert Burns. CP-BurnR

Young Lady of Tolosa, A. Guido Cavalcanti. CP-CavaG, tr. by Marc Cirigliano

Young lady opposite, The. Pastoral: "Young lady opposite, The." Ezra Pound. CP-PoEar

Young lady, The. Song of China in Europe. Federico García Lorca. CP-GarcF, tr. by Alan S. Trueblood Fr. Songs for Children.

Young lass, A. Spring Song. Li Po. CP-WilW2

Young Laundryman, The. William Carlos Williams. CP-WilW1

Young Love. Andrew Marvell. CP-MarvA

Young Love. William Carlos Williams. CP-WilW1

Young Love lies sleeping. Dream-Love. Christina Georgina Rossetti. CP-RosC1

Young m / oon:be kind to olde. E. E. Cummings. CP-CummE

Young Mage, The. Louise Bogan. CP-BogaL

Young Man, a Writer—in His 24th Year, A. Constantine P. Cavafy. CP-CavaC, tr. by Theoharis Constantine Theoharis

Young man, all mixed up, The. Hostage, The. Theodore Weiss. SP-WeisT

Young man, alone, on the high bridge over the Tagus, A. High Bridge above the Tagus River at Toledo, The. William Carlos Williams. CP-WilW2

Young man carrying a battered straw suit-case, A. Such Counsels You Gave to Me. Robinson Jeffers. CP-JefR2

Young man said to me, A. Ultimate Reality. D. H. Lawrence. CP-LawrD

Young man seated at his table, A. Lack of Repose, The. Wallace Stevens. CP-StevW; CP-StevWP

Young / man sitting, The. E. E. Cummings. CP-CummE

Young man studied letters and arms, A. Shih-te. CP-ColdM, tr. by Red Pine

Young man, the world's outside that door. Interview, An. Howard Nemerov. CP-NemeH

Young Man Travelling, A. Denise Levertov. SP-LeveDL

Young man who becomes an old man, The. Beautiful Morning. James Laughlin. CP-LaugJ

Young man with bright eyes, dark skin, The. Sisters of Charity. Arthur Rimbaud. CP-RimbA, tr. by Martin Sorrell

Young man with the guitar, testing new riffs, The. Song: The Young Man with the Guitar, Testing. Hayden Carruth. CP-CarHS

Young Man's Epigram on Existence, A. Thomas Hardy. CP-HardT

Young Man's Exhortation, A. Thomas Hardy. CP-HardT

Young man's numinous eye is like the sun, The. Death of Alexander. Robert Lowell. SP-LoweR

Young Man's Song. William Butler Yeats. CP-YeatW

Young Matrons Dancing. John Updike. CP-UpdiJ

Young Men, The. Muriel Rukeyser. CP-RukeM

Young Men at the Manor. Rudyard Kipling. *Fr.* Puck of Pook's Hill.

Young Men Aye Were Fickle Found Since Summer Trees Were Leafy. Christina Georgina Rossetti. CP-RosC3

Young men go walking in the woods. Pediment of Appearance, The. Wallace Stevens. CP-StevW; CP-StevWP

Young men, having no real joy in life and no hope in the future. Young Fathers. D. H. Lawrence. CP-LawrD

Young men late in the night. Witnesses, The. W. H. Auden. CP-AudeW

Young Men of Sidon (400 A.D.). Constantine P. Cavafy. CP-CavaC, *tr. by* Theoharis Constantine Theoharis

Young men waking at daybreak may be frightened at being. Tennessee Williams. CP-WillT

Young mouth laughs at a gift, A. Her Words. Theodore Roethke. CP-RoetT

Young Negro Girl. Langston Hughes. CP-HughL; CP-HughL2

Young Nun at Bread Loaf. Maxine W. Kumin. SP-KumiM

Young Oak! when I planted thee deep in the ground. To an Oak at Newstead. Lord Byron. CP-Byron

Young Old Man, The. James Whitcomb Riley. CP-RileJ

Young ones go away to school, The. Lorine Niedecker. CP-NiedL

Young or old / What was I but a story told. Kathleen Jessie Raine. SP-RainK

Young Pat was heir to fourscore cows. Paddy's Choice. *Unknown, sometimes at. to* Thomas Sheridan. CP-SherT

Young Peggy blooms our bonniest lass. Song. On Miss P——— K———, A. Robert Burns. CP-BurnR

Young Philiper Flash was a promising lad. Philiper Flash. James Whitcomb Riley. CP-RileJ

Young Poet, A. Frank O'Hara. SP-OharF

Young poet Evmenis, The. First Step, The. Constantine P. Cavafy. CP-CavaC, *tr. by* Theoharis Constantine Theoharis

Young Princess, The. George Meredith. CP-MerG1

Young Prostitute. Langston Hughes. CP-HughL; CP-HughL1

Young Queen, The. Elizabeth Barrett Browning. CP-BroEB

Young Queen, The. Rudyard Kipling. CP-KiplR

Young queen Nature, ever sweet and fair, The. Nature and Art. Paul Laurence Dunbar. CP-DunbP

Young Rabbits. John Clare. SP-ClarJ

Young Reynard. George Meredith. CP-MerG1

Young rice plants are just being. Heart's Garden, the Garden's Heart, The. Kenneth Rexroth. CP-RexrK

Young Sailor. Langston Hughes. CP-HughL; CP-HughL1

Young Sea. Carl Sandburg. CP-SandC

Young Sensitive one summer on the Cape. James Vincent Cunningham. CP-CunnJ

Young Sibyl, The. Robert Graves. CP-GravR

Young Singer. Langston Hughes. CP-HughL; CP-HughL1

Young skunk. Shu Swamp, Spring. May Swenson. SP-SwenM

Young soldier lies in spring, cut off from his name, A. Yehuda Amichai. SP-AmicYL, *tr. by* Benjamin Harshav *and* Barbara Harshav *Fr.* At Right Angles.

Young soldier lies in the springtime, cut off from his name, A. Yehuda Amichai. SP-AmicY, *tr. by* Stephen Mitchell *Fr.* In a Right Angle: A Cycle of Quatrains.

Young Soldier with Bloody Spurs, The. D. H. Lawrence. CP-LawrD

Young Son, The. John Ashbery. SP-AshbJ

Young Sycamore. William Carlos Williams. CP-WilW1

Young then, / we were bored already. Epitaph: "Young then, / we were bored already." Eleanor Wilner. SP-WilnE

Young thing in spring green slippers, stockings, A. Whiffs of the Ohio River at Cinncinnati. Carl Sandburg. CP-SandC

Young to-day are born prisoners, The. Poor Young Things. D. H. Lawrence. CP-LawrD

Young, twenty-eight, in a Tinean ship. In the Port. Constantine P. Cavafy. CP-CavaC, *tr. by* Theoharis Constantine Theoharis

Young Usurper, The. George Meredith. CP-MerG1

Young Want to Be Just, The. D. H. Lawrence. CP-LawrD

Young was the green world's chart. Heirs of the Ages, The. G. K. Chesterton. CP-ChesG

Young Watch Us, The. Donald Hall. CP-HallD

Young Wife, A. D. H. Lawrence. CP-LawrD

Young Woman. Robert Creeley. CP-CreeR

Young Woman. Howard Nemerov. CP-NemeH

Young Woman at a Window. William Carlos Williams. CP-WilW1

Young woman — dark lovely angry. Clarence Major. SP-MajoC

Young Woman's Song. John Berryman. CP-BerrJ

Younger Set, The; A Hymn of Hate. Dorothy Parker. CP-ParkD

Younger Sister, Going Swimming. Margaret Atwood. SP-AtwM1

Youngest Son, The. Theodore Weiss. SP-WeisT

Your absence has gone through me. Separation. W. S. Merwin. SP-MerwW

Your affair, my dear, need not be a mess. James Vincent Cunningham. CP-CunnJ

Your air, your bearing, and your grace. Too Full of Life. Charles Baudelaire. CP-BaudC, *tr. by* Walter Martin

Your anger charms me. Hyacinth. "H. D." CP-DoolH

Your ashes will not stir, even on this high ground. In Carrowdore Churchyard. Derek Mahon. CP-MahoD

Your baby grows a tooth, then two. Little Tooth, A. Thomas Lux. SP-LuxT

Your beauty an angel's, Lady, you were meant. Michelangelo Buonarroti. CP-Miche, *tr. by* John Frederick Nims

Your beauty is a thunder. Black Ode. Maya Angelou. SP-AngeM

Your beauty, Love, stuns mortal reckonings. Michelangelo Buonarroti. CP-Miche, *tr. by* John Frederick Nims

Your beauty, which I lost sight of once. Love Song. Denise Levertov. SP-LeveDP

Your / being over there tonight. Paul Celan. SP-CelaP, *tr. by* John Felstiner

Your billet, Sir, I grant receipt. To Renton of Lamerton. Robert Burns. CP-BurnR

Your birthday comes to tell me this. E. E. Cummings. CP-CummE

Your Birthday in the California Mountains. Kenneth Rexroth. CP-RexrK

Your Birthday in Wisconsin You Are 140. John Berryman. CP-BerrJ

Your blood mixed with air. Milkweed. Peter Blue Cloud. SP-BlueP

Your body is white like sand. Poems for a Woman. Yehuda Amichai. SP-AmicY, *tr. by* Stephen Mitchell

Your body may be a sack. Dancer's Reply, The. Howard Nemerov. CP-NemeH

Your body, / measured out by moans. Death of an Unfamiliar Sister, The. Jay Wright. SP-WrigJ

Your body tolls the hour. Glass, The. Carolyn Kizer. CP-KizeC

Your bony head, Jazbo, O dock walloper. Singing Nigger. Carl Sandburg. CP-SandC

Your bony white bowed back, in a singlet. Memory, A. Ted Hughes. SP-HughTN

Your book affords. Acknowledgement. James Vincent Cunningham. CP-CunnJ

Your bow swept over a string, and a long low note quivered to the air. Jan Kubelik. Carl Sandburg. CP-SandC

Your boyhood years waited for you in forgotten corners. Remembrances. Yannis Ritsos. SP-RitsY *Fr.* Monovasia.

Your breast against mine. Nina Answers Back. Arthur Rimbaud. CP-RimbA, *tr. by* Martin Sorrell

Your breasts / sliced-off The scars. Woman Dead in Her Forties, A. Adrienne Rich. SP-RicA2

Your brother brings you home from hunting. One Man Down. Ai. SP-Ai

Your brother has a falcon. Christina Georgina Rossetti. CP-RosC2

Your brother will trim my hedges! Eavesdropper. Sylvia Plath. CP-PlatS

Your camera / has caught it all, the lit. Snapshot. Charles Tomlinson. SP-TomlC

Your cat disguise makes me scream i suspect. Love & the Documents. Andrei Codrescu. SP-CodrA

Your Childhood in Menton. Federico García Lorca. SP-GarcF, *tr. by* Edwin Honig

Your Childhood in Menton. Federico García Lorca. SP-GarcF, *tr. by* Greg Simon *and* Steven F. White

Your claims to immortality were two. To an Ancient. Robert Frost. CP-FrosR

Your clear eye is the one absolutely beautiful thing. Child. Sylvia Plath. CP-PlatS

Your coming is a symptom of Summer. Emily Dickinson. SP-DickE

Your cottage, Furius, sheltered. Carmen 26. Catullus. CP-ZukLS *Fr.* Carmina.

Your Country. Andrei Codrescu. SP-CodrA

Your curls fall down on your. I Love the Way. James Laughlin. CP-LaugJ

Your daisies have come. Break Away, The. Anne Sexton. CP-SextA

Your dark eyes will never need to understand. Picture of a Black Child with a White Doll. Thomas Merton. CP-MertT

Your daughters / Zeus, provider. Zeus-Provider. "H. D." CP-DoolH *Fr.* Temple of the Sun.

Your death, dear Lady, was quite cold. Elegy for Eugenesis. Allen Tate. CP-TateA

Your delicious-looking rum cake, covered with. Earwigs. Raymond Carver. CP-CarvR

Your depth knows no bounds. Pain, The. Shmuel HaNagid. SP-HaNaS, *tr. by* Peter Cole

Your dream pulsed in the depths of time. Twenty-Five Years. Adam Zagajewski. SP-ZagaA, *tr. by* Clare Cavanagh

Your dust will be upon the wind. What the Sexton Said. Nicholas Vachel Lindsay. CP-LindV

Your dying was a difficult enterprise. Lament: "Your dying was a difficult enterprise." Thom Gunn. CP-GunnT

Your Early Life. James Laughlin. CP-LaugJ

Your electric hair's beautiful gold as Blake's Glad Day boy. To the Punks of Dawlish. Allen Ginsberg. CP-GinsA

Your enchantment / enchains me, stretched. Poem: "Your enchantment / enchains me, stretched." James Schuyler. CP-SchuJ

Your Error. James Laughlin. CP-LaugJ

Your erudition. Lorine Niedecker. CP-NiedL

Your exact errors make a music. You and Art. William Stafford. SP-StafWW

Your eye-light wanes with an ail of care. Every Artemisia. Thomas Hardy. CP-HardT

Your Eyes. James Laughlin. CP-LaugJ

Your eyes and the valley are memories. Valley Song. Carl Sandburg. CP-SandC

Your eyes are dark and luminous and. Two Pairs of Eyes. Eleanor Wilner. SP-WilnE

Your eyes are widely open flowers. Mysteries. Alice Walker. CP-WalkA

Your eyes change. Definitions of Old Age. Archibald MacLeish. CP-MacLA

Your eyes of draiad speak. Your Eyes. Charles Olson. CP-OlsoC

"Your eyes that once were never weary of mine." Ephemera. William Butler Yeats. CP-YeatW

Your eyes withstood great cold. I Sat in the Happiness. Yehuda Amichai. SP-AmicYL, tr. by Benjamin Harshav and Barbara Harshav

Your face did not rot. Lost Pilot, The. James Tate. SP-TateJ

Your face is like a chamber where a king. Edna St. Vincent Millay. CP-MillE

Your face is still so beautiful. In Half Darkness. James Laughlin. CP-LaugJ

Your Face on the Dog's Neck. Anne Sexton. CP-SextA; SP-SextA

Your face scrapes my sleep tonight. Letter to be Disguised as a Gas Bill. Marge Piercy. SP-PierM

Your face was hidden in the leaves. Wreath, A. Yannis Ritsos. SP-RitsY, tr. by Edmund Keeley

Your face Your tongue Your wit. In the Grace of Wit, of Tongue and Face. Sir Walter Ralegh. CP-RaleW

Your fair looks urge my desire. Be Wise, and Fly Not. Thomas Campion. CP-CampT

Your Fair[e] Look[e]s Inflame [My Desire]. Thomas Campion. CP-CampT

Your faire lookes urge my desire. Thomas Campion. See Your fair looks urge my desire

Your father had gangrene and. Moenkopi. Arthur Sze. SP-SzeA

Your father to me in your eighth summer. Lorine Niedecker. CP-NiedL

Your father waits inside. What Hell Is. Heather McHugh. SP-McHuH

Your fine white hand is Heaven's gift. Merciful Hand, The. Nicholas Vachel Lindsay. CP-LindV

Your fingers touch me like a bird's wing. Bird of Endless Time, The. James Laughlin. CP-LaugJ

Your Flight. Eugenio Montale. CP-MontE, tr. by Jonathan Galassi

Your flight, then, didn't fade out. Palio. Eugenio Montale. CP-MontE, tr. by Jonathan Galassi

Your friends come fondly to your living room. Birthday Card for a Psychiatrist. Mona Van Duyn. SP-VanDM

Your friendship much can make me blest. Interpolation. Robert Burns. CP-BurnR

Your frosty hands. Cats' Month, The. William Carlos Williams. CP-WilW1

Your German. Shibboleth. Ted Hughes. SP-HughTN

Your ghost will walk, you lover of trees. De Gustibus. Robert Browning. CP-BroR1

Your gift of life was idleness. Kathleen Jessie Raine. SP-RainK

Your gift to me was a gray stone cast upon a wild shore, traced over. Soliloquy Upon Love. Kathleen Jessie Raine. SP-RainK

Your gift to me was like a girl. Gift, The. John Logan. CP-LogaJ

Your Gifts are from the Sky. Emily Dickinson. SP-DickE

Your gold cloud, towering far above me. Gold Cloud. Robert Graves. CP-GravR

Your Golden Wedding!—fifty years. Golden Wedding, A. James Whitcomb Riley. CP-RileJ

Your grandad worked the signals. Northern Metres. Donald Davie. CP-DaviDC

Your great-grandfather was. Things of the Past. Theodore Weiss. SP-WeisT

Your great horse of a dog has been sick. Housed (A Report on a Visiting Dog). William Meredith. SP-MereW

Your great mistake is to disregard the satire. Mute Phenomena, The. Gérard de Nerval. CP-MahoD, tr. by Derek Mahon

Your grief for what you've lost lifts a mirror. Birdwings. Jelaluddin Rumi. SP-Rumi, tr. by Coleman Barks

Your grieving moonlight face looks down. Reproach. Robert Graves. CP-GravR

Your hand, my wonder, is now icy cold. Statue of a Couple. Czeslaw Milosz. CP-MiloC; CP-MiloCN

Your hand rigid, curled into its final shape. Sliding Away. Arthur Sze. SP-SzeA

Your hand was trying the keyboard. Eugenio Montale. CP-MontE, tr. by Jonathan Galassi

Your hands easy. Remembrance. Maya Angelou. SP-AngeM

Your hands lie open in the long fresh grass. Silent Noon. Dante Gabriel Rossetti. CW-RossD Fr. House of Life, The.

Your hands / make Pallas wonder. Myrtle Bough. "H. D." CP-DoolH

Your hawk today floated the loft of air. Red-Tailed Hawk. Helen Pinkerton. CP-PinkH

Your hay it is mowed, and your corn is reaped. Harvest Home. John Dryden. SP-DrydJ Fr. King Arthur.

Your health, Master Willow. Contrive me a bat. Tree Party. Louis MacNeice. CP-MacNL

Your heart plays hide-and-seek. Yehuda Amichai. SP-AmicYL Fr. Six Poems for Tamar.

Your heart was handed over. Foxgloves. Carl Sandburg. CP-SandC

Your Height Is Ours. James Whitcomb Riley. CP-RileJ

Your homecoming will be my homecoming. E. E. Cummings. CP-CummE

Your honest heart of duty, Worden. In the Turret. Herman Melville. SP-MelvH

Your hooves have stamped at the black margin of the wood. On a Picture of a Black Centaur by Edmund Dulac. William Butler Yeats. CP-YeatW

Your house of hair and lady's hand. Enigma in the Last Mercury Explained, The. Unknown, sometimes at. to Thomas Sheridan. CP-SherT

Your Ibsen volumes, violet-spined. Juvenilia. Adrienne Rich. CP-RicAE; SP-RicA2

Your intelligence is always with you. Body Intelligence. Jelaluddin Rumi. SP-Rumi, tr. by Coleman Barks

Your jar of Virginny. Poor Honest Men. Rudyard Kipling. CP-KiplR

Your kindness to me, and the ways of fate. Michelangelo Buonarroti. CP-Miche, tr. by John Frederick Nims

Your Labours are performed, your Bye-works too. To Ogmian Hercules. Robert Graves. CP-GravR

Your lance / will never wound. Road, The. Federico García Lorca. CP-GarcF, tr. by Catherine Brown

Your lashes leave me naked in the square. Barren. Audre Lorde. SP-LordA

Your Last Drive. Thomas Hardy. CP-HardT

Your laughter likes grapes. Yehuda Amichai. SP-AmicYL Fr. Six Poems for Tamar.

Your Lead, Partner, I Hope We've Read the Same Book. Ogden Nash. CP-NashO

Your Letter. Adrienne Rich. CP-RicAE

Your letter came.—Glutted the earth & cold. Winter-Piece to a Friend Away, A. John Berryman. CP-BerrJ

Your letter describes / what you see from your window. You chose. Letter to an English Poet. Donald Hall. CP-HallD

Your letter reached me. Idiotic and Politic. Jay Wright. SP-WrigJ

Your letter wrecked my day. My Sister's Letter. Bogomil Gjuzel. CP-KizeC, tr. by Carolyn Kizer

Your Life. William Stafford. SP-StafWW

Your Life and Death, Father. Yehuda Amichai. SP-AmicYL, tr. by Benjamin Harshav and Barbara Harshav

Your lists of victims dear. Becoming Somebody Else. C. K. Williams. CP-WillC

Your little mental gallantries. Emily Dickinson. SP-DickE

Your little voice / Over the wires came leaping. E. E. Cummings. CP-CummE

Your looks so often cast. Sir Thomas Wyatt. CP-WyatT

Your Love. James Laughlin. CP-LaugJ

Your love my dearest Phylonella. Amo Amas Amat. James Laughlin. CP-LaugJ

Your love to me was like an unread book. Bright Bindings. Countee Cullen. CP-CullC

Your Loved Ones Depress You. Shmuel HaNagid. SP-HaNaS, tr. by Peter Cole

Your lovely eyes, now bent. Michelangelo Buonarroti. CP-Miche, tr. by John Frederick Nims

Your lovely hands. Paterson. William Carlos Williams. CP-WilW1 Fr. Paterson.

Your lugs shopping bags of sweet corn. Introducing the Fathers. Maxine W. Kumin. SP-KumiM

Your lungs fill & spread themselves. Flying Inside Your Own Body. Margaret Atwood. SP-AtwM2

Your Manuscript Shines. Shmuel HaNagid. SP-HaNaS, tr. by Peter Cole

Your Marceau card. Dear Joe. William Corbett. SP-CorbW

Your merciful, sweet care. Michelangelo Buonarroti. CP-Miche, tr. by John Frederick Nims

Your midriff sags toward your knees. Woman with Girdle. Anne Sexton. CP-SextA

Your mind and you are our Sargasso Sea. Portrait d'une Femme. Ezra Pound. CP-PoEar; SP-PounE

Your mind was wrought in cosmic solitude. John Milton. Allen Tate. CP-TateA

Your mistress [or mistris], that you follow whores, still taxeth you. Self[e] Accuser, A. John Donne. CP-DonnJ; MW-DonnJ

Your Momma kissed the chauffeur. Thirteens (White), The. Maya Angelou. SP-AngeM

Your Momma took to shouting. Thirteens (Black), The. Maya Angelou. SP-

AngeM

Your most recent acquisition, Flavius. Carmen 6. Catullus. CP-ZukLS *Fr.* Carmina.

Your mother combs your hair. Girl Child. Peter Blue Cloud. SP-BlueP

Your mother shows me a photograph of you got up in lace. White. Paul Muldoon. CP-MuldP

Your mother, whom the mirror-world has claimed. Tutored Child, The. Stanley Kunitz. CP-KunSC

Your mother's soul hovers ahead. Travel Companion, The. Paul Celan. SP-CelaP, *tr. by* John Felstiner

Your name scrawled on a bit of paper moves me. What the Finger Writes. Alice Walker. CP-WalkA

Your neghbors in the country, whare you come from, hain't fergot! Lines to Perfesser John Clark Ridpath. James Whitcomb Riley. CP-RileJ

Your News and review, Sir, I've read through and through, Sir. To Captain Riddell. Robert Burns. CP-BurnR

Your nipples go to war. War & Peace. Andrei Codrescu. SP-CodrA

YOUR NUMBER'S COMING OUT! Blues in Stereo. Langston Hughes. CP-HughL; CP-HughL3

Your nurse could only speak Italian. Sailing Home from Rapallo. Robert Lowell. SP-LoweR

Your pain still hangs in air. Memory Unsettled. Thom Gunn. CP-GunnT

Your pardon, my friend, if my rhymes did offend. To the Sighing Strephon. Lord Byron. CP-Byron

Your patience, Sirs. The Devil took me up. Rudyard Kipling. CP-KiplR *Fr.* Naulahka, The.

Your pencil will do particles and waves—. Drawing Lessons. Howard Nemerov. CP-NemeH

Your perch is the branch. To a Sparrow. William Carlos Williams. CP-WilW2

Your picture smiles as first it smiled. Amulet, The. Ralph Waldo Emerson. CP-EmerR

Your Poem must eternal be. To Mr. Pye. Samuel Taylor Coleridge. CP-ColeS

"Your poems about the girls will still be around." Tonight. Charles Bukowski. SP-BukC1

Your presence like a benison to me. To Her. Paul Laurence Dunbar. CP-DunbP

Your Private Way. Robert Graves. CP-GravR

Your pubic hair is the apex of a lovely. Architecture. Andrei Codrescu. SP-CodrA

Your quatrain is a chariot drawn by wild. Salvador Díaz Mirón. "Rubén Dario." SP-DariR, *tr. by* Alberto Acereda *and* Will Derusha

Your rags are due to your past deeds. Han-shan. CP-ColdM, *tr. by* Red Pine

Your relentless Music. Emily Dickinson. SP-DickE

Your Riches—taught me—Poverty. Emily Dickinson. CP-DickE

Your riddle does feed though it never could eat. Directions for Laughing. *Unknown, sometimes at. to* Thomas Sheridan. CP-SherT

Your Sacred Idiot with Me. Olga Broumas. SP-BrouO

Your silence a ship, each sail taut in the wind. Fernando Pessoa. SP-PessF *Fr.* Absurd Hour.

Your silence against my shoulder. Tanck's Song About Silence. Hayden Carruth. CP-CarHS *Fr.* Songs About What Comes Down: The Complete Works of Mr. Septic Tank.

Your skin like dawn. Passing Time. Maya Angelou. SP-AngeM

Your slender feet as nimble as your hands. To a Girl in Malabar. Charles Baudelaire. CP-BaudC, *tr. by* Walter Martin

Your smile, delicate. Woman Me. Maya Angelou. SP-AngeM

Your smiling, or the hope, the thought of it. Simile for Her Smile, A. Richard Wilbur. CP-WilbR

Your son presses against me. Apple Trees, The. Louise Glück. SP-GlucL

Your song where you lie long dead on the shore of a Spanish river. Segre Song. Muriel Rukeyser. CP-RukeM

Your songs? / Oh! The little mothers. Famam Librosque Cano. Ezra Pound. CP-PoEar

Your songs, when you sing them with your two eyes closed. At the Wellhead. Seamus Heaney. SP-HeanSO

Your Soul Shines. Alice Walker. CP-WalkA

Your special witness, as I recollect. Selina, Countess of Huntingdon. Donald Davie. CP-DaviDC

Your spoken words are roses fine and sweet. Roses and Pearls. Paul Laurence Dunbar. CP-DunbP

Your stature is modelled. Contest, The. "H. D." CP-DoolH

Your Steventon Friends. Epistle to G. East Esq. Mrs. Austen. CP-AustJ

Your Subjects hope. Phillis Wheatley. *See* Your subjects hope, dread Sire

Your subjects hope, dread Sire. To the King's Most Excellent Majesty. 1768. Phillis Wheatley. CP-WheaP

Your sudden laugh restored felicity. Laugh, The. Robert Graves. CP-GravR

Your tear-wracked family bedside: elderly grandchildren. Pecked to Death by Swans. Thomas Lux. SP-LuxT

Your telephone call broke in. Adam Zagajewski. SP-ZagaA, *tr. by* Renata Gorczynski

Your temples, where the hair crowded in. Tender Place, The. Ted Hughes. SP-HughTN

Your thighs are appletrees. Portrait of a Lady. William Carlos Williams. CP-WilW1

Your thoughts don't have words every day. Emily Dickinson. CP-DickE

Your thoughts make shape like snow; in one night only. To a Communist. Louis MacNeice. CP-MacNL

Your tits are rosy in the dawn. Alba. Robert Creeley. CP-CreeR

Your toothbrush won't remember your mouth. And Then. Miller Williams. CP-WillM

Your touch is gentle on. Memory Piece / for Baby Jane. Olga Broumas. SP-BrouO

Your trail runs to the westward. To James Whitcomb Riley. Rudyard Kipling. CP-KiplR

Your train leaves at eleven-forty-five and it is now but eleven. Dr. Fell and Points West. Ogden Nash. CP-NashO

Your tree—your oak. Ted Hughes. SP-HughTN

Your troubles shrink not, though I feel them less. Confession to a Friend in Trouble, A. Thomas Hardy. CP-HardT

Your turn. Grass of confusion. Journal for My Daughter. Stanley Kunitz. CP-KunSC

Your unhappy and silly youth. Youth. Czeslaw Milosz. CP-MiloCN, *tr. by* Robert Hass

Your verses, Doctor, crawl on gouty feet. Now to Lampoon Myself for My Presumption. Thomas Sheridan. CP-SherT

Your verses were commended, as 'tis true. To Mr Jonson upon these Verses. Ben Jonson. CP-JonsB

Your violin! Ah me! James Whitcomb Riley. CP-RileJ

Your voice always whacked me right on the funny bone. Burying Blues for Janis. Marge Piercy. SP-PierM

Your voice at times a fist. To a Husband. Maya Angelou. SP-AngeM

Your voice comes to me, George, on the winter night. Questions. Hayden Carruth. CP-CarHS

Your voice watered the dune of my breast. Poet Speaks with His Beloved on the Telephone, The. Federico García Lorca. CP-GarcF, *tr. by* Angela Jaffray

Your voice, with clear location of June days. June Light. Richard Wilbur. CP-WilbR

Your western heads here cast on money. Coin, A. Carl Sandburg. CP-SandC

Your white shoulders. White Shoulders. Carl Sandburg. CP-SandC

Your whitelight flashes the frost tonight. Whitelight. Carl Sandburg. CP-SandC

Your whole age sits between what you hear. Sibyl. W. S. Merwin. SP-MerwW

"Your wife," the doctor said. Mr. and Mrs. Billings. Donald Hall. CP-HallD

Your wife's forty-five. Gift Horse. Yusef Komunyakaa. CP-KomuY

Your windfall at fifteen your Steinway grand. Solfeggietto. Adrienne Rich. SP-RicA1

"Your wish came true." Robert Creeley. CP-CreeR

Your wooden shaft has vanished; so has the body. Persian Arrow. Joseph Brodsky. CP-BrodJ

Your Years Are Sleep. Shmuel HaNagid. SP-HaNaS, *tr. by* Peter Cole

Your yes her no, your no her yes. The words. Red Loves Kit. Wallace Stevens. CP-StevWP

You're. Sylvia Plath. CP-PlatS

You're. James Schuyler. CP-SchuJ

You're a beast, she said. You. Charles Bukowski. SP-BukC1

You're allowed to write everything. Small Poetics, A. Dan Pagis. SP-PagiD, *tr. by* Stephen Mitchell

You're among them. Saigon Bar Girls, 1975. Yusef Komunyakaa. CP-KomuY

You're dead, what can I do for you? For John Berryman. David Ignatow. SP-IgnaD

You're entangled with someone more famous than you. Second Time Around. Carolyn Kizer. SP-KizeC

You're getting fat. Dear. Robert Creeley. SP-CreeR

You're grayer than one would have thought you. At a "National Encampment." Ambrose Bierce. SP-BierA

You're here again, old friend. Bennelong's Blues. Yusef Komunyakaa. CP-KomuY

You're looking at a chopper. Peace ("You're looking at a chopper"). Robert Creeley. SP-CreeR

You're more jive than Pigmeat. Crack. Yusef Komunyakaa. CP-KomuY

You're my friend: / I was the man the Duke spoke to. Flight of the Duchess, The. Robert Browning. CP-BroR1

You're not asleep? Masque of Reason, A. Robert Frost. CP-FrosR

You're not dead and I'm not dead. Haydn, Opus 76, Number 5. Yehuda Amichai. SP-AmicYL, *tr. by* Benjamin Harshav *and* Barbara Harshav

You're not going yet? I must; I have to work. This Way Out. Louis MacNeice. CP-MacNL

You're not really hermits. Han-shan. CP-ColdM, *tr. by* Red Pine

You're perfect as an autumn day, and yet. Conversation. Charles Baudelaire. CP-BaudC, *tr. by* Walter Martin

You're right—"the way is narrow." Emily Dickinson. CP-DickE

You're sick. Run-Through, The. A. R. Ammons. CP-AmmoA

You're sitting here with us, but you're also out walking. Diver's Clothes Lying Empty, The. Jelaluddin Rumi. SP-Rumi, *tr.* by Coleman Barks

You're small and thin in the rain. A small target. Yehuda Amichai. SP-AmicYL, *tr.* by Benjamin Harshav *and* Barbara Harshav

You're song, / a wished-for song. Wished-For Song, A. Jelaluddin Rumi. SP-Rumi, *tr.* by Coleman Barks

You're sucking / for a bruise. Harry. Robert Creeley. CP-CreeR

You're the can and I'm the salmon. Dialogue between Soul and Body, A. Randall Jarrell. CP-JarrR

You're too late. Blues, The. Lord Byron. CP-Byron

You're too young for this. I was twenty. Stripper, The. Miller Williams. CP-WillM

You're touched by all that touches us. Rainer Maria Rilke. CP-RilkFr, *tr.* by A. Poulin, Jr. *Fr.* Roses, The.

You're trapped, my tongue, and bound. Shmuel HaNagid. SP-HaNaS, *tr.* by Peter Cole

You're two, that's great. C. K. Williams. CP-WillC

You're very quick on your feet, Achilles. Tortoise, The. Dan Pagis. SP-PagiD, *tr.* by Stephen Mitchell

You're welcome to Despots, Dumourier. Address to General Dumourier. Robert Burns. CP-BurnR

You're Welcome, Willie Stewart. Robert Burns. CP-BurnR

You're wondering if I'm lonely. Song: "You're wondering if I'm lonely." Adrienne Rich. SP-RicA2

Your Eyes. Charles Olson. CP-OlsoC

Yours. C. K. Williams. CP-WillC; SP-WillC

Yours is the music for no instrument. E. E. Cummings. CP-CummE

Yours is the sea. Abalone. Peter Blue Cloud. SP-BlueP

Yours is the shame and sorrow. D. H. Lawrence. *See* Yours is the sullen sorrow

Yours is the sullen sorrow. Last Words to Miriam. D. H. Lawrence. CP-LawrD

Yours Next. Louis MacNeice. CP-MacNL

Yours received : those cursory notes. Epistle to Simon Perchik. Robert Stock. SP-StocR

Yours this moment I unseal. Extempore Reply to an Invitation. Robert Burns. CP-BurnR

Yours was the original freak-out: Samuel Beckett's. To Helen Keller. Donald Davie. CP-DaviDC

Yourself. Jones Very. CP-VeryJ

Yourself, myself and our togetherness. Three Locked Hoops. Robert Graves. CP-GravR

Yourself walked in the room tonight. Away. Robert Creeley. CP-CreeR

Youth. William Corbett. SP-CorbW

Youth. Langston Hughes. CP-HughL
   (Poem.) CP-HughL1

Youth. Czeslaw Milosz. CP-MiloCN, *tr.* by Robert Hass

Youth. Arthur Rimbaud. CP-RimbA, *tr.* by Martin Sorrell

Youth. James Wright. CP-WrigJ

Youth and Age. Samuel Taylor Coleridge. CP-ColeS; MW-ColeS

Youth, and Age. Robert Herrick. CP-HerrR

Youth and Age. James Whitcomb Riley. CP-RileJ

Youth and Age. William Butler Yeats. CP-YeatW

Youth and Art. Robert Browning. CP-BroR1; SP-BroR

Youth and Beauty. William Carlos Williams. CP-WilW1

Youth and Lordship. *Unknown.* CW-RossD, *tr.* by Dante Gabriel Rossetti

Youth and the Stream, The. Jones Very. CP-VeryJ

Youth brings us toward three things. Shmuel HaNagid. SP-HaNaS, *tr.* by Peter Cole

Youth, Day, Old Age and Night. Walt Whitman. CP-WhitW

Youth, divine treasure. Song of Autumn in Springtime. "Rubén Dario." SP-DariR, *tr.* by Alberto Acereda *and* Will Derusha

Youth from the capital rides by the east of the city, The. Youth on Horseback, The. Li Po. CP-WilW2

Youth in Age. George Meredith. CP-MerG2

Youth in apparel that glittered, A. Stephen Crane. CP-CranS

Youth in Memory. George Meredith. CP-MerG1

Youth is the ruggedest burden that can score. Septuagenarian, The. Robert Graves. CP-GravR

Youth is the time when hearts are large. On the Slain Collegians. Herman Melville. SP-MelvH

Youth, large, lusty, loving—youth full of grace, force, fascination. Youth, Day, Old Age and Night. Walt Whitman. CP-WhitW

Youth, like Indian Summer. Emily Dickinson. SP-DickE

Youth looked into the running stream, A. Boy's Dream, The: A Ballad. Jones Very. CP-VeryJ

Youth Mowing, A. D. H. Lawrence. CP-LawrD

Youth must be wanton, youth must be quick. Tennessee Williams. CP-WillT *Fr.*

Night of the Iguana, The.

Youth, Nature, and Relenting Jove. Lord Byron. CP-Byron

Youth of delight, come hither. Voice of the Ancient Bard, The. William Blake. CP-BlakW *Fr.* Songs of Experience.

Youth of Nature, The. Matthew Arnold. SP-ArnoM

Youth on Horseback, The. Li Po. CP-WilW2

Youth Sings a Song of Rosebuds. Countee Cullen. CP-CullC

Youth Stares at Minoan Sunset. Robert Penn Warren. CP-WarrR

Youth that trafficked long with Death. Expert, The. Rudyard Kipling. CP-KiplR

Youth the color of the hills laughed delighted at his Vanity, The. Allen Ginsberg. SP-GinsA *Fr.* Contest of Bards.

Youth walks up to the white horse, to put its halter on, The. White Horse, The. D. H. Lawrence. CP-LawrD

Youth went faring up and down, A. Wooing, The. Paul Laurence Dunbar. CP-DunbP

Youth Who Carried a Light, The. Thomas Hardy. CP-HardT

Youth who scarce had seen his twentieth year, A. Character of Wallenstein, The. Samuel Taylor Coleridge. CP-ColeS *Fr.* Death of Wallenstein, The.

Youthful Patriot, The. James Whitcomb Riley. CP-RileJ

Youthful Picnic Long Ago: Sad Ballad on Box. Robert Penn Warren. CP-WarrR

Youthful Press, The. James Whitcomb Riley. CP-RileJ

Youthful Quest, The. George Meredith. CP-MerG1

Youthful Truth-Seeker, Half-Naked, at Night, Running down Beach South of San Francisco. Robert Penn Warren. CP-WarrR

Youth's Antiphony. Dante Gabriel Rossetti. CW-RossD *Fr.* House of Life, The.

Youth's Progress. John Updike. CP-UpdiJ

Youth's Spring-Tribute. Dante Gabriel Rossetti. CW-RossD *Fr.* House of Life, The.

You've a manner all so mellow. My Old Friend. James Whitcomb Riley. CP-RileJ

You've climbed the mountain. At its top. To the President-elect. Joseph Brodsky. CP-BrodJ

You've dressed yourself so white for it! And you poise. Saying of Farewell, A. James Dickey. CP-DickJ

You've got another love / and I know it. Poor Girl. Maya Angelou. SP-AngeM

"You've got to cross that lonesome valley" and. Handshake, the Entrance, The. John Berryman. CP-BerrJ

You've got to fuck a great many women. How to Be a Great Writer. Charles Bukowski. SP-BukC1

You've gotten in through the transom. To a Child Trapped in a Barber Shop. Philip Levine. SP-LeviP

You've heard about the qualities of Bilal. New Moon, Hilal. Jelaluddin Rumi. SP-Rumi, *tr.* by Coleman Barks

You've lost the clue—somewhere. Labyrinth. Eleanor Wilner. SP-WilnE

You've lost your religion, the Rabbi said. Debate with the Rabbi. Howard Nemerov. CP-NemeH

You've made the loveliest face, O Death, turn pale. Petrarch. CP-Petra, *tr.* by J. G. Nichols

You've named a tree for me? It isn't nothing. Eugenio Montale. CP-MontE, *tr.* by Jonathan Galassi

You've never seen such a flat black ocean. Rainy Season, The. Clarence Major. SP-MajoC

You've only just heard? Paid on Both Sides. W. H. Auden. CP-AudeW

You've seen a herd of goats. Lame Goat, The. Jelaluddin Rumi. SP-Rumi, *tr.* by Coleman Barks

You've seen a strawberry. Nevertheless. Marianne Craig Moore. CP-MoorM

You've seen Balloons set—Haven't You? Emily Dickinson. CP-DickE

You've seen them, these semi-urban birds. Crows of Boston and New York, The. Thomas Lux. SP-LuxT

You've Set the Words. James Laughlin. CP-LaugJ

You've so distracted me. Jelaluddin Rumi. SP-Rumi, *tr.* by Coleman Barks

You've so filled my mind with pain. Guido Cavalcanti. CP-CavaG, *tr.* by Marc Cirigliano

You've taken my blues and gone. Note on Commercial Theatre. Langston Hughes. CP-HughL; CP-HughL2

"You've Tried the World, Try Jesus." Robert Creeley. CP-CreeR

You've wanted to hear my voice so hear me now. Out of a Clear Sky. Miller Williams. CP-WillM

Ypres—Minsterworth. Ivor Gurney. SP-GurnI

Yucca clump, The. Yucca Moth, The. A. R. Ammons. CP-AmmoA

Yucca Moth, The. A. R. Ammons. CP-AmmoA

Yugao. Kenneth Rexroth. CP-RexrK

Yuletide in a Younger World. Thomas Hardy. CP-HardT

Yup, our disgraces are. Asymptotes. Charles Olson. CP-OlsoC

Z

Za Ki Tan Ke Parlay Lot. Audre Lorde. SP-LordA

Zaccheus he / Did climb the tree. Sycamore. Robert Frost. CP-FrosR

Zaddik, you showed me. Letter to William Kinter of Muhlenberg, A. Denise Levertov. SP-LeveDP

Zalmoxis. Howard Nemerov. CP-NemeH

Zambesi and Ranee. May Swenson. SP-SwenM

Zamboni's Law. Wyatt Prunty. SP-PrunW

Zander on God. Howard Nemerov. CP-NemeH

Zapolya. Samuel Taylor Coleridge.
  Hunting Song. CP-ColeS; MW-ColeS
  Song: "Sunny shaft did I behold, A." CP-ColeS; MW-ColeS

Zara. Christina Georgina Rossetti. CP-RosC3

Zaydee. Philip Levine. SP-LeviP

Zdziechowski. Czeslaw Milosz. CP-MiloCN, *tr. by* Robert Hass

Zeal Required in Love. Robert Herrick. CP-HerrR

Zealously my Muse doth salute all thee. To Mr R. W ("Zealously my Muse doth salute all thee"). John Donne. CP-DonnJ; MW-DonnJ

Zebrina etc. Louis Zukofsky. CP-ZukLS

Zeno. Randall Jarrell. CP-JarrR

Zéphyrine Drouhin / lines out her. Like Lorraine Ellison. James Schuyler. CP-SchuJ

Zeppelin Factory, The. Rita Dove. SP-DoveR

Zermatt: To the Matterhorn. Thomas Hardy. CP-HardT

Zero. Tess Gallagher. SP-GallT

Zero, a nothing, A. Armies of the Plain. George Oppen. CP-OppGN

Zero at the Bone. Eleanor Wilner. SP-WilnE

Zero built a nest. Fanny Howe. SP-HoweF *Fr.* Quietist, The.

Zero burped by, A. Figuring. Charles Simic. SP-SimiC; SP-SimiCE

Zero in the Cove. May Swenson. SP-SwenM

Zeroes—taught us—Phosphorus, The. Emily Dickinson. CP-DickE

Zeus' Couchmate,—who of mortals knows not me. Herakles. Robert Browning. CP-BroR2

Zeus grieves mightily. Patroklos. Funeral of Sarpedon, The ("Zeus grieves mightily. Patroklos"). Constantine P. Cavafy. CP-CavaC, *tr. by* Theoharis Constantine Theoharis

Zeus himself could not undo the web. Labyrinth, The. Jorge Luis Borges. SP-BorgJ, *tr. by* Stephen Kessler

Zeus Is Dead. Clement of Alexandria. CP-MertT *Fr.* Diatribe Against the Old Gods.

Zeus is snake no longer, nor swan, nor eagle. Zeus Is Dead. Clement of Alexandria. CP-MertT *Fr.* Diatribe Against the Old Gods.

Zeus lies in Ceres' bosom. Canto 81: "Zeus lies in Ceres' bosom." Ezra Pound. SP-PounE *Fr.* Cantos.

Zeus over Redeye. Robert Earl Hayden. CP-HaydR

Zeus-Provider. "H. D." CP-DoolH *Fr.* Temple of the Sun.

Zeus was once overheard to shout at Hera. Weather of Olympus, The. Robert Graves. CP-GravR

Zhivago with a fine moustache. No Heroics, Please. Raymond Carver. CP-CarvR

Zikr. Jelaluddin Rumi. SP-Rumi, *tr. by* Coleman Barks

Zinc roofs in the moonlight, The. Ernesto Cardenal. CP-MertT *Fr.* Gethsemani, KY.

Zinnia. Louis Zukofsky. CP-ZukLS

Zinnias. Robert Earl Hayden. CP-HaydR

Zion. Donald Davie. CP-DaviDC

Zion. Rudyard Kipling. CP-KiplR

Zion Said. Christina Georgina Rossetti. CP-RosC3

Zip! Donald Davie. CP-DaviDC

ZIP Code Ode. John Updike. *See* Hymn to These Newly Abbreviated States

Zip! . . . / Did you just close. Capriccio ("Zip! . . . / Did you just close"). Federico García Lorca. CP-GarcF, *tr. by* Jerome Rothenberg *Fr.* Barrage of Firework Poems on the Occasion of the Poet's Birthday.

Zipangu. Charles Tomlinson. SP-TomlC

Zither and books are up to you. Han-shan. CP-ColdM, *tr. by* Red Pine

Zmyrna, my own Cinna, nine harvests passed making his hymn. Catullus. *See* Nine harvests & nine winters since its inception

Zodiac, The. James Dickey. CP-DickJ

Zodiac, The. Donald Davie. CP-DaviDC

Zodiac towel wipes the hands, The. Designs. Andrei Codrescu. SP-CodrA

Zodiacal Light, The. Jones Very. CP-VeryJ

Zola. Edwin Arlington Robinson. CP-RobiE

Zone. A. R. Ammons. CP-AmmoA

Zone. Guillaume Apollinaire. CP-BeckS, *tr. by* Samuel Beckett

Zone. Louise Bogan. CP-BogaL

Zone of Silence. Czeslaw Milosz. CP-MiloCN, *tr. by* Robert Hass

Zoo, The. John Logan. CP-LogaJ

Zoo, The. Stevie Smith. CP-SmitS

Zoo Bats. John Updike. CP-UpdiJ

Zoo Gardens Revisited. A. K. Ramanujan. CP-RamaA

Zoo Keeper's Wife. Sylvia Plath. CP-PlatS

Zorro Man, A. Maya Angelou. SP-AngeM

Zucca, The. Percy Bysshe Shelley. CP-ShelP

Zulu Girl, The. George Oppen. CP-OppGN

Zulus Live in Land without a Square. John Updike. CP-UpdiJ

Zurich, at the Stork. Paul Celan. SP-CelaP, *tr. by* John Felstiner

Zzzzzzzzzzzz. Andrei Codrescu. SP-CodrA

Zzzzzzzzzzzz / (Buzzing outside / the window). Fly. Federico García Lorca. CP-GarcF, *tr. by* Christopher Maurer

AUTHOR INDEX

Pseudonymous names are enclosed in quotation marks.

A

Abu Nadhar 'Abdu'l 'Aziz (Adsched of Meru) (*fl.* **11th cent.)**
Color, taste, and smell, smaragdus, sugar, and musk.

Achillini, Claudio (1614–40)
Wars and of arms some sing, but I.

Achterberg, Gerrit (1905–62)
Accountability.
City.
Dwingelo.
Eben Haëzer.
Statue.

Adams, T.
To the Unknown Author of the following Poem, and that of *Absalom and Achitophel*.

Aeschylus (525–456 B.C.)
Agamemnon, *sels.*
Prometheus Bound.
Seven against Thebes, The, *sels.*

Agathias (Agathias Scholasticus) (536–82)
Epigram on Plutarch, An.

Ai (Florence Anthony) (b. 1947)
Abortion.
Afterschool Lessons from a Hitman.
Antihero, The.
Back in the World.
Blood in the Water.
Blue Suede Shoes.
Boys and Girls, Lenny Bruce, or Back from the Dead.
Capture.
Chance.
Charisma.
Child Beater.
Cockfighter's Daughter, The.
Conversation.
Country Midwife, The: A Day.
Cruelty.
Cuba, 1962.
Detective, The.
Elegy: "Hundreds of flies."
Everything: Eloy, Arizona, 1956.
False Witness.
Finished.
Flashback.
General George Armstrong Custer: My Life in the Theater.
Gilded Man, The.
Go.
Good Shepherd, The: Atlanta, 1981.
Greed.
Hangman.
Hitchhiker, The.
Hoover, Edgar J.
Hoover Trismegistus.
I Can't Get Started.
I Have Got to Stop Loving You. So I Have Killed My Black Goat.
Ice.
Interview with a Policeman.
Jack Ruby on Ice.
James Dean.
Jimmy Hoffa's Odyssey.
Journalist, The.
Kid, The.
Killing Floor.
Knock, Knock.
Life Story.
Miracle in Manila.

Momento Mori.
More.
Mother's Tale, The.
Nothing but Color.
One Man Down.
Oswald Incognito & Astral Travels.
Paparazzi, The.
Passing Through.
Penis Envy.
Pentecost.
Priest's Confession, The.
Prisoner, The.
Rapture.
Ravine, The.
Reunions with a Ghost.
Riot Act, April 29, 1992.
Rwanda.
She Didn't Even Wave.
Sleeping Beauty.
Stalking Memory.
Star Vehicle (My Senior Year in High School).
Sweet, The.
Talking to His Reflection in a Shallow Pond.
Tenant Farmer, The.
Testimony of J. Robert Oppenheimer, The.
29 (A Dream in Two Parts).
Twenty-Year Marriage.
Two Brothers.
Visitation.
Why Can't I Leave You?
Young Farm Woman Alone.

Akhmatova, Anna Andreyevna (Anna Andreyevna Gorenko) (1889–1966)
Cleopatra.
Dante.
Lot's Wife.

Alberti, Rafael (b. 1902)
Roman Nocturnes, *sels.*

Albinovanus Pedo (*fl.* **early 1st cent.)**
Plants and trees made poore and old, The.

Albizzi, Niccolò degli (*fl.* **13th cent.)**
Prolonged Sonnet: When the Troops were Returning from Milan.

Alcayaga, Lucila Godoy *See* **Mistral, Gabriela**

Alcman (*fl.* **7th cent. B.C.)**
Astymelusa.

Ambrose, Saint (c.340–97)
Aeterne Rerum Conditor.
Gloria in Excelsis, The.
Splendor Paternae Gloriae.

Amichai [*or* Amikhai], Yehuda (b. 1924)
Aching bones of lovers, The.
Advice for Good Love.
Advice of good love: do not love.
Again, a Love Is Finished.
Aged Parents, The.
Akhziv.
All the Generations before Me.
All These Make a Dance Rhythm.
Almost a Love Poem.
Among the Stars You May Be right.
And After All That—the Rain.
And as Far as Abu Ghosh.
And I am always like this fleeing from hurt and pain.
And That Is Your Glory.
And the Migration of My Parents.
And This Is Your Glory.
And We Shall Not Get Excited.
Anniversaries of Love.
Anniversaries of War.

Anniversary of My Father's Death, The.
Arab Shepherd Is Searching for His Goat on Mount Zion, An.
Arab Shepherd Seeks a Kid on Mount Zion, A.
As at Funerals.
As for the World.
As It Was.
Ashkelon.
At Right Angles, *sels.*
At the Beach.
At the Maritime Museum.
At the Monastery of Latroun.
At the Seashore.
At the University of New Orleans.
Autobiography in the Year 1952.
Autobiography, 1952.
Autumn Is Near and Memory of My Parents.
Autumn Rain in Tel Aviv.
Ballad in the Streets of Buenos Aires.
Ballad of the Washed Hair.
Beautiful Are the Families of Jerusalem.
Bedouin Goes North, A.
Bedouin in Love.
Before.
Beginning of Autumn in the Hills of Ephraim.
Beit Guvrin.
Between.
Biblical Meditations.
Birthday.
Body Is the Cause of Love, The.
Both Together and Each Apart.
Box, The.
Bride Without a Dowry, A.
Bull Returns, The.
Caffè Dante in New York—1.
Caffè Dante in New York—2.
Caffè Dante in New York—3.
Changes, Mistakes, Loves.
Child is Something Else Again, A.
Children's Procession.
Closing the Jaffa Port.
Course of a Life, The.
Czech Refugee in London, A.
Dangerous Country.
Death of Assia G., The.
Deganya.
Deir Ayub, a Heap of Watermelons and the Rest of My Life.
Dennis Was Very Sick.
Diameter of the Bomb, The.
Do Not Accept.
Dog After Love, A.
Don't Prepare for Tomorrow.
Door of the house opened by mistake, The.
Early in the morning, you lean on the wall of an old house.
Ecology of Jerusalem.
Elecampane, Jasmine, Vine, and Oleander.
Elegies on the War Dead, *sels.*
Elegy on an Abandoned Village.
Elegy on the Lost Child.
Elegy: "Wind won't come to draw smiles in the sand of dreams, The."
Elizabeth Swados.
End of Elul.
End of Summer in the Judean Mountains.
End of the Archaeological Season in Eyn Gedi.
Eternal Mystery, The.
Eternal Window, An.
Eve of Rosh Hashanah, The.
Evening hours of the soul.
Evening is lying at the horizon, donating

blood, The.
Evidence.
Eyn Gedi Preserve.
Fall in Connecticut.
False Interpretation.
Family.
Farewell.
Farewell: "Fare thee well, it was your face, and now the face of memory."
Fields of Sunflowers.
First Rain on a Burned Car.
First Rain, The.
Flock of Sheep Near the Airport, A.
Flowers in a Room.
For My Birthday.
For My Mother.
Forecast.
Forgetting Someone.
Four Resurrections in the Valley of the Ghosts.
From All the Spaces.
From Jerusalem to the Sea and Back.
From Man You Came and to Man You Shall Return.
From the Book of Esther I Filtered the Sediment.
From the Scroll of Esther, I filtered out the sediment.
Games.
Gifts of Love.
Girl Goes Out in the Morning Like a Knight, A.
Giving of the Torah, The.
God Full of Mercy.
God Has Pity on Kindergarten Children.
God Takes Pity on Kindergarten Children.
Gods Come and Go, Prayers Remain Forever.
God's Hand in the World.
Good Time, A.
Great Calm: Questions and Answers.
Great Fatigue.
Great Tranquillity: Questions and Answers, A.
Greatest Desire of All, The.
Greatest Desire, The.
Hadera.
Half-Sized Violin.
Half the People in the World.
Hamadiya.
Hamadiya, Memory of Bliss.
Haydn, Opus 76, Number 5.
"He left two sons," they say.
Heart Is a Corrupt Stage Director, The.
Herbal Tea.
Here.
Here.
Here We Loved, *sels.*
Hirbet Sayid.
History.
"History's Wings Beating," They Used to Say.
Hour of Grace, An.
How did a banner begin? Let's assume there was something whole.
How goodly are your tents, Jacob. Even when there are no.
How Much Time.
Huleikat—The Third Poem about Dicky.
Human Bodies.
Hymn for Independence Day, A. So distant.
Hymn to a Masseuse.
Hymn to Summer.
Hymn to the Lovely Couple Varda and Schimmel.
I Am a Poor Prophet.
I Am Big and Fat.
I am like a leaf that knows its limits.
I am the figure of a Jewish father with a sack on his back, returning.
I Dreamed.
I Feel Just Fine in My Pants.
I Guard the Children.
I Have Dead People.
I Know a Man.
I Lost My Identity Card.
I love these people in their tall house.
I Sat in the Happiness.
I Told You It Would Be So—And You Didn't Believe.

I Walked Past a House Where I Lived Once.
I Want to Confuse the Bible.
I Want to Die in My Own Bed.
I Was the Moon.
I Was Waiting for My Girl and Her Steps Were Absent.
I was weaned from the curse of Adam.
I Will Have to Begin.
Ibn Gabirol.
Ibn Gabirol.
If My Belly Aches.
If Now in the Middle of My Life.
I'm in Great Trouble.
In a Foreign Country.
In a Leap Year.
In a Right Angle: A Cycle of Quatrains, *sels.*
In My Childhood.
In My Worst Dreams.
In the Full Severity of Mercy.
In the Garden, at the White Table.
In the garden, at the white table.
In the Jerusalem Mountains.
In the Middle of This Century.
In the Morning It Was Still Night.
In the Old City.
In the Room.
In this valley, where many waters.
In Those Days, in This Time.
Indian Summer in Princeton.
Inside the Apple.
Instead of a Love Poem.
Instead of Words.
Instructions for Her Voyage.
Itzhak's Last Kit Bag.
I've Already Been Weaned.
I've Grown Very Hairy.
Jacob and the Angel.
Jasmine.
Jerusalem.
Jerusalem 1967.
Jerusalem Ecology.
Jerusalem Is Full of Used Jews.
Jerusalem, 1985.
Jerusalem the cradle city that rocks me.
Jerusalem's Suicide Attempts.
Jews in the Land of Israel.
Jews, The.
Karl Marx, cold mark that you are.
Kibbutz Gevaram.
Land Knows, The.
Language School.
Last Word Is Captain, The.
Late in my life, I come to you.
Late Marriage.
Laundry Cellar, The.
Let the Coin Decide.
Letter, A.
Letter of Recommendation, A.
Life.
Like the Inner Wall of a House.
Like the Streams in the Negev.
Little Ruth.
Look: Thoughts and Dreams.
Lost Objects.
Lots of Grapes.
Love Is Finished Again.
Love of Jerusalem.
Love of the Land.
Love Poem: "People use each other."
Love Song: "This is how it started: suddenly it felt."
Lullaby 1957.
Luxury.
Man crossing the field was a Chief Rabbi, The.
Man in His Life, A.
Man Like That on a Bald Mountain in Jerusalem, A.
Man with Knapsack.
Man's Soul, A.
Mark Them with Signs.
Mayor.
Mayor, The.
Memory of Love—Image.
Memory of Love—Opening the Will.
Memory of Love—Terms and Conditions.
Mission.

Modern Girl, A.
Museum at Akhziv.
Mutual Lullaby, A.
My Child Wafts Peace.
My Children.
My Father in a White Space Suit.
My Father on Passover Eve.
My Father's Death.
My First Days in New York.
My former student is in the traffic police.
My Friend the Philosopher and Hanukah.
My friend, what you're doing now.
My God, the soul you gave me.
My Mother Baked the Whole World for Me.
My Mother Comes From the Days.
My Mother Died on Shavuot.
My Mother Once Told Me.
My Mother's Death and the Lost Battles for the Future of Her Children.
My Sleep.
My Son.
My Son, My Son, My Head, My Head.
My son, the softness of your face already shows.
My son was born in Asuta hopital and since then.
Name of the Place "Trieste," The.
National Thoughts.
Near the Wall of a House.
1978 Reunion of Palmach Veterans at Ma-ayan Harod.
1924.
1924.
North of Beer Sheba.
North of San Francisco.
Not like a Cypress.
Now in the Din.
Now in the Storm.
Now She's Breathing.
Now That the Water Presses Hard.
Now the Lifeguards Have All Gone Home.
Now to Break.
NYU.
Of a Vanished Kingdom.
Of Three or Four in a Room.
Oh, my old, venerable teacher, life.
Oleander.
On Mount Muhraka.
On My Birthday.
On Some Other Planet You May Be Right.
On the Day I Left.
On the Day My Daughter Was Born No One Died.
On the Day My Daughter Was Born Not a Single Person Died.
On the Wide Stairs—Lurking for Happiness.
On this evening, I think again.
Open Closets Are Sad.
Open Internalized.
Orchard.
Out of Three or Four People in a Room.
Outing with a Woman.
Pace Like That, A.
Parents Left the Child, The.
Peace of Mind, Peace of Mind.
People in the Dark Always See.
People with No Future Love.
Pinecones on the Tree Above.
Pity, A. We Were Such a Good Invention.
Pity, We Were a Good Invention.
Place Where I Never Was, The.
Place Where We Are Right, The.
Placenta of Love, A.
Poem about Repairs to My House.
Poem: "As at the beginning of birth."
Poem for Arbor Day.
Poem of Spring.
Poem Without an End.
Poems along the Hudson River.
Poems for a Woman.
Poems from Buenos Aires.
Poems of Akhziv.
Poems of continuity, mines and graves.
Poems of Lies and Beauty.
Poems of Resigning.
Poems of Spring in the Appalachian

Mountains.
Poems of the Hot Wind.
Poems of the Land of Zion and Jerusalem, *sels.*
Poems on the Shore of Caesarea, *sels.*
Poems to a Girl on the Seashore.
Political Poem, A.
Precise Woman, A.
Psalm: "Psalm on the day, A."
Quiet Joy, A.
Rabbi Nakhman of Bratslav.
Radius of the bomb was twelve inches, The.
Rain on the Battlefield.
Ramatayim.
Real Hero of the Sacrifice of Isaac, The.
Real Hero, The.
Relativity.
Release Her.
Resurrection.
Rosebush Hangs over the Wall, A.
Ruhama.
"Rustle of History's Wings," as They Used to
 Say Then, The.
Sadness of Eyes and Descriptions of a Voyage.
Same Embroidery, the Same Pattern, The.
Sandals.
Sea and the Shore, The.
Season of Recognition.
Seven Laments for the War-Dead.
Sharm A-Sheikh.
Sheepskin Coat.
Shifra and Batya promised.
Shore of Ashkelon, The.
Signs and Evidence in the Orchard of Gan-
 Hayim.
Since Then.
Six Poems for Tamar, *sels.*
Sleep in Jerusalem.
Smell of Gasoline Ascends in My Nose, The.
Smell of Gasoline in My Nose, The.
So I Went Down to the Ancient Harbor.
Soldiers in the grave say: you, up there, The.
Somber Spring.
Someplace.
Song of Lies on Sabbath Eve, A.
Songs of Continuity.
Songs of Zion the Beautiful, *sels.*
Sonnet from the Voyage.
Sort of an Apocalypse.
State of Affairs.
Statistics.
Stewardess.
Straight from Prejudice.
Stroll in the Beautiful Gardens of the Valley of
 the Son of Hinnom, A.
Such as Sorrow.
Suflah Spring in the Judean Mountains.
Summer Begins.
Summer Evening at the Window with Psalms.
Summer Evening in the Jerusalem Mountains.
Summer Night in the King David Hotel.
Summer or Its End, *sels.*
Summer Rest and Words.
Support for My Breathing.
Surplus of Flowers in the World.
Sweet Breakdowns of Abigail, The.
Sweet Voice from the Kibbutz, The.
Synagogue in Firenze, The.
Takis Sinopolus, Greek Poet.
Temporary Poem of My Time.
Then I went down to the ancient port: human
 actions.
There Are Candles That Remember.
These words, like heaps of feathers.
They Are All Dice.
They Lied to Us.
This Is the Life of Promises.
This Place.
Threading.
Three Times I Came to Rome.
Through Two Points Only One Straight Line
 Can Pass.
Throw Pillows.
Time Has Come to Collect Evidence, The.
To a Convert.
To Bake the Bread of Yearning.
To Die, to Be Torn.

To Gather Something.
To Hurl Haunting Memories.
To My Love, Combing Her Hair.
Too Many.
Tourist.
Tourists.
Trap rises from the earth on a summer night,
 A.
Travel by Train.
Travels of Benjamin the Last, of Tudela, The.
Travels of the Last Benjamin of Tudela.
Try to Remember Some Details.
Two Disappeared into a House.
Two Girls Live in the Old House.
Two Photographs.
Two Poets in Mexico.
U.N. Headquarters in the High Commissioner's
 House in Jerusalem, The.
UN Headquarters in the High Commissioner's
 Residence in Jerusalem.
Visit of the Queen of Sheba, The.
Voyeur, The.
Way It Was, The.
We Did It.
We Did What We Had To.
We Have Done Our Duty.
We Loved Here, *sels.*
What a Complicated Mess.
What a man on a bald mountain in Jerusalem!
What Entanglement in This Small Country.
What is it? An airplane at dawn. No.
What is it? An old shed for tools.
What Kind of a Person.
What Kind of Man.
When a man is away from his homeland for a
 long time.
When a Man's Far Away from His Country.
When I Banged My Head on the Door.
When I Have a Stomachache.
When I Returned They Told Me There's No.
When I Was a Child.
When I was young, the country was young too.
 My father.
When I Was Young, the Whole Country Was
 Young.
White Negress.
Wild Peace.
With All the Rigor of Pity.
With Her in an Apple.
With My Mother.
Wonderful Baker, The.
Yehuda Ha-Levi.
Yom Kippur.
You Are So Small and Slight in the Rain.
You Can Rely on Him.
You carry the load of heavy buttocks and your
 eyes are light.
You Carry the Weight of Heavy Buttocks.
You Must Not Show Weakness.
You Too Got Tired.
You Will Speak.
Your Life and Death, Father.
You're small and thin in the rain. A small
 target.

Ammianus Marcellinus (c.330–c.400)
Out of the Italian.

Ammons, A. R. (Archie Randolph) (1926–2001)
Account, The.
Admission.
After Yesterday.
Alternatives.
Anxiety.
Apologia pro Vita Sua.
April.
Arc Inside and Out, The.
At Dawn in 1098.
Attention.
Auto Mobile.
Autumn Song.
Back Country.
Banking.
Batsto.
Bay Bank.
Bearing Mercy.
Bees Stopped.
Belief.

Body Politic.
Bourn.
Breaks.
Bridge.
Brooks & Other Notions.
Butterflyweed.
Cascadilla Falls.
Catalyst.
Celestial.
Center.
Chaos Staggered Up the Hill.
Chasm.
Choice.
Christmas Eve.
Circles.
City Limits, The.
Civics.
Clarity.
Classic.
Clearing.
Clearing the Dark Symbiosis.
Cleavage.
Close-up.
Come Prima.
Coming To.
Coming to Sumer.
Communication.
Composing.
Concentrations.
Concerning the Exclusions of the Object.
Configurations.
Confirmers, The.
Conserving the Magnitude of Uselessness.
Consignee.
Consignor.
Constant, The.
Contingency.
Convergence.
Coon Song.
Correction.
Corsons Inlet.
Cougar.
Countering.
Crevice.
Crippled Angel, A.
Cut the Grass.
Dark Song.
Day.
Definitions.
Delaware Water Gap.
Devising.
Discoverer.
Dominion.
Doubling the Nerve.
Doxology.
Driving Through.
Dropping Eyelids Among the Aerial Ash.
Drought.
Dunes.
Dying in a Mirthful Place.
Early Morning in Early April.
Elegy for a Jet Pilot.
Emplacement.
Eolith.
Epiphany.
Equinox.
Essay on Poetics.
Eternal City, The.
Even.
Event.
Exotic.
Expressions of Sea Level.
Extremes and Moderations.
Eyesight.
Fall Creek.
Fall, The.
Father.
February Beach.
First Carolina Said-Song.
Foot-Washing, The.
Four Motions for the Pea Vines.
Further On.
Gain.
Garden.
Gilgamesh Was Very Lascivious.
Glass.
Golden Mean, The.

Grace Abounding.
Grass Miracles, The.
Grassy Sound.
Gravelly Run.
Ground Tide.
Guide.
Guitar Recitativos.
Halfway.
Hardweed Path Going.
Having Been Interstellar.
He Held Radical Light.
He Said.
Heat.
Height.
Help.
Here & Now.
Hibernaculum.
High & Low.
High Surreal.
Hippie Hop.
Holding On.
Holly.
Hope's Okay.
Hosts.
Hymn 2: "So when the year had come full round."
Hymn 3: "In the hour of extreme."
Hymn 4: "I hold you responsible for."
Hymn 5: "Assure us you side with order: throw."
Hymn: "I know if I find you I will have to leave the earth."
I Assume the World Is Curious about Me.
I Broke a Sheaf of Light.
I Came in a Dark Woods upon.
I Came upon a Plateau.
I Struck a Diminished Seventh.
I Went out to the Sun.
Identity.
If Anything Will Level with You Water Will.
Image.
Imagined Land, The.
Impulse.
In Strasbourg in 1349.
In the Wind My Rescue Is.
Increment.
Interference.
Interval.
Involved.
Ithaca, N.Y.
Jersey Cedars.
Joshua Tree.
Jungle Knot.
Kind.
King of Ice, The.
Landscape with Figures.
Laser.
Late Romantic.
Left.
Levitation.
Libation.
Life in the Boondocks.
Limit, The.
Lines.
Lion::Mouse.
Locus.
Loft.
Lollapalooza: 22 February.
Lonely Splendor.
Lonesome Valley.
Look for My White Self.
Looking Over the Acreage.
Loss.
Love Song: "Like the hills under dusk you."
Love Song: "Rings of birch bark."
Makers, The.
Making.
Making Waves.
Mansion.
March Song.
Mark, The.
Mays Landing.
Mean.
Mechanics.
Mechanism.
Mediation.

Medicine for Tight Spots.
Medium.
Meteorology.
Mid-August.
Mirrorment.
Misfit, The.
Miss.
Mission.
Moment.
Monday.
Money.
Motion.
Motion for Motion.
Mountain Liar.
Mountain Talk.
Mule Song.
Muse.
My Dice Are Crystal.
Needs.
Nelly Myers.
Next Day, The.
North Jersey.
Nucleus.
Object.
Ocean City.
Off.
Offset.
One Composing.
One:Many.
One More Time.
Open.
Orientale.
Passage.
Path.
Peak.
Peracute Lucidity.
Periphery.
Phase.
Photosynthesis.
Play.
Plexus.
Plunder.
Pluralist.
Poetics.
Positions.
Possibility Along a Line of Difference.
Precursors.
Prodigal.
Project.
Prospecting.
Put-Down Come On, The.
Quince Bush, The.
Rack.
Raft.
Reassessing.
Recovery.
Rectitude.
Reflective.
Renovating.
Requiem: "Strawberries along the roadbank in the hills bloomed, The."
Return.
Reversal.
Reward.
Right On.
Risks and Possibilities.
Ritual for Eating the World.
River.
Rome Zoo.
Round.
Run-Through, The.
Runoff.
Russet Gold.
Saliences.
Sap Is Gone Out of the Trees, The.
Satyr Formalist.
Saying.
Schooling.
Script.
Second Carolina Said-Song.
Self-Portrait.
September Drift.
Sharp Lookout.
Ship.
Shore Fog.
Shoreless Tide, The.

Silver.
Sitting Down, Looking Up.
Small Song.
Snow Log.
Snow Whirl.
So I Said I Am Ezra.
Some Months Ago.
Song: "Merging into place against a slope of trees."
Sorting.
Space Travel.
Spaceship.
Sphere.
Spiel.
Spindle.
Spinejacking.
Spring Coming.
Spring Song.
Square.
Staking Claim.
Still.
Storm.
Strait, The.
Street Song.
Sumerian.
Summer Session.
Swan Ritual, The.
Symmetry of Thought, A.
Terminus.
Terrain.
Thaw.
Then One.
This Black Rich Country.
This Bright Day.
Three.
Tight.
Timing.
Tooling Up.
Tossup.
Touching Down.
Transaction.
Transducer.
Transfer.
Translating.
Trap.
Treaties.
Treeful of Cleavage Flared Branching, A.
Triphammer Bridge.
Trouble Making Trouble.
Turning.
Turning a Moment to Say So Long.
Two Motions.
Two Possibilities.
Uh, Philosophy.
Undersea.
Unifying Principle, The.
Unsaid.
Up.
Upland.
Upright.
Utensil.
Viable.
Village, Town, City—Highway, Road, Path.
Virtu.
Visit.
WCW.
Wagons.
Watch, The.
Way to Go.
Whaleboat Sturck, The.
What This Mode of Motion Said.
When I Set Fire to the Reed Patch.
When Rahman Rides.
Whole Half, The.
Whose Timeless Reach.
Wide Land, The.
Wind Coming Down From, The.
Windy Trees.
Winter Saint.
Winter Scene.
With Ropes of Hemp.
Woodsroad, The.
Working Still.
Working with Tools.
World.
Yucca Moth, The.

Zone.

Angelou, Maya (b. 1928)
Accident.
Africa.
After.
Ain't That Bad.
Alone.
America.
Amoebaean for Daddy.
Arrival.
Artful Pose.
Avec Merci, Mother.
Awaking in New York.
Black Ode.
Brief Innocence.
Bump d'Bump.
Caged Bird.
California Prodigal.
Call Letters: Mrs. V.B.
Calling of Names, The.
Changes.
Chicken-Licken.
Child Dead in Old Seas.
Come, And Be My Baby.
Communication I.
Communication II.
Conceit, A.
Contemporary Announcement.
Country Lover.
Couple, The.
Detached, The.
Elegy: "I lay down in my grave."
Faces.
Family Affairs.
For Us, Who Dare Not Dare.
Gamut, The.
Georgia Song, A.
Good Woman Feeling Bad, A.
Greyday.
Harlem Hopscotch.
Health-Food Diner, The.
Here's to Adhering.
How I Can Lie to You.
I Almost Remember.
Impeccable Conception.
In a Time.
In Retrospect.
Insomniac.
John J.
Junkie Monkey Reel.
Just for a Time.
Just Like Job.
Kin.
Kind of Love, Some Say, A.
Lady Luncheon Club.
Last Decision, The.
Late October.
Lesson, The.
Let's Majeste.
Letter to an Aspiring Junkie.
Lie, The.
Life Doesn't Frighten Me.
Little Girl Speakings.
Lord, in My Heart.
Martial Choreograph.
Memory, The.
Men.
Miss Scarlet, Mr. Rhett and other Latter-Day
　　Saints.
Momma Welfare Roll.
Mothering Blackness, The.
Mourning Grace.
My Arkansas.
My Guilt.
My Life Has Turned to Blue.
No Loser, No Weeper.
No No No No.
Now Long Ago.
On a Bright Day, Next Week.
On Aging.
On Diverse Deviations.
On Reaching Forty.
On Working White Liberals.
One More Round.
Passing Time.
Phenomenal Woman.

Pickin Em Up and Layin Em Down.
Plagued Journey, A.
Poor Girl.
Prelude to a Parting.
Prescience.
Prisoner.
Pusher, The.
Recovery.
Refusal.
Remembering.
Remembrance.
Request.
Reverses.
Riot: 60's.
Senses of Insecurity.
Sepia Fashion Show.
Shaker, Why Don't You Sing?
Singer Will Not Sing, The.
Slave Coffle.
Song for the Old Ones.
Sounds Like Pearls.
Southeast Arkanasia.
Starvation.
Still I Rise.
Take Time Out.
Tears.
Telephone, The.
Thank You, Lord.
They Went Home.
Thirteens (Black), The.
Thirteens (White), The.
This Winter Day.
Through the Inner City to the Suburbs.
Times-Square-Shoeshine-Composition.
To a Freedom Fighter.
To a Husband.
To a Man.
To a Suitor.
To Beat the Child Was Bad Enough.
Traveler, The.
Unmeasured Tempo.
We Saw Beyond Our Seeming.
Weekend Glory.
When I Think about Myself.
When You Come to Me.
Where We Belong, A Duet.
Willie.
Woman Me.
Woman Work.
Wonder.
Zorro Man, A.

Anthony, Florence *See* **Ai**

**"Anvari" (Awhad ad-Din 'Ali ibn Vahid ad-Din
　　Muhammad Khavarani) (1126?–90?)**
Body and Soul.
O'er the garden water goes the wind alone.
Shah Sandschar, whose lowest slave.
To the Shah, from Enweri.

Apollinaire, Guillaume (1880–1918)
Annie.
Autumn.
Autumn Crocuses.
Mirabeau Bridge.
Mountebanks.
Pretty Redhead, The.
Rhenish Night.
Zone.

Aragon, Louis (1897–1982)
Lilacs and the Roses, The.
Red Front, The.
Richard Coeur-de-Lion.
Unoccupied Zone, The.

Arbiter, Caius Petronius *See* **Petronius Arbiter,**

Archpoet, The (c.1130–c.65)
Confession of Bishop Golias, The.

Arendt, Erich
Hands, The.

Ariosto, Ludovico (1474–1533)
Night and Day.
Orlando Furioso, *sels.*

Aristophanes (c.450–c.385 B.C.)
Clouds, The, *sels.*

Armantrout, Rae (b. 1947)
About.
Admission.

Anti-Short Story.
Articulation.
As We're Told.
Attention.
Birthmark: The Pretext.
Book, The.
Confidential.
Context.
Counter.
Covers.
Creation, The.
Crossing.
Daffodils, The.
Disown.
Double.
Dusk.
Engines.
Extremities.
Falling: 1.
Falling: 2.
Fiction ("Excitement of being someone else
　　about whom").
Fiction ("When the woman's face contorted
　　and she clutched the railing for support, we
　　knew she would die").
Garden, The.
Generation.
Getting Warm.
Grace.
Greeting.
Here.
Home Federal.
Inside Out.
Language of Love.
Leaving.
Light.
Manufacturing.
My Associates.
My Problem.
Native.
Natural History.
Near Rhyme.
Necromance.
Ongoing.
Our Nature.
Over.
Overhearing.
Piecemeal.
Plan, The.
Plot, The.
Postcards.
Precedence.
Pulse, A.
Purpose.
Qualia.
Rehearsal.
Sense.
Sets.
Single Most.
Statement.
Story, A.
Systemic.
Theories.
Through Walls.
Tone.
Traveling Through the Yard.
Veil.
View.
Visibility.
Way, The.
Whole.
Words.
Writing.
Xenophobia.

Arnold, Matthew (1822–88)
Buried Life, The.
Dover Beach.
Empedocles on Etna.
Forsaken Merman, The.
Growing Old.
Haworth Churchyard, *sels.*
In Harmony with Nature.
In Utrumque Paratus.
Memorial Verses.
Quiet Work.
Requiescat.

Resignation.
Scholar Gypsy, The.
Self-Dependence.
Shakespeare.
Sick King in Bokhara, The.
Sohrab and Rustum, *sels.*
Stanzas from the Grande Chartreuse.
Stanzas in Memory of the Author of
    "Obermann."
Summer Night, A.
Switzerland, *sels.*
Thyrsis.
To a Friend.
Tristram and Iseult, *sels.*
Youth of Nature, The.

Arouet, François Marie *See* **Voltaire**

Ashbery, John (b. 1927)
Absence of a Noble Presence, The.
Additional Poem, An.
And I'd Love You to Be in It.
And Others, Vaguer Presences.
And "Ut Pictura Poesis" Is Her Name.
And You Know.
Another Chain Letter.
As One Put Drunk into the Packet-Boat.
As We Know.
As You Came from the Holy Land.
At North Farm.
At the Inn.
Bird's-Eye View of the Tool and Die Co.
Blessing in Disguise, A.
Blue Sonata.
Boy, A.
Bungalows, The.
Business Personals.
Chateau Hardware, The.
Clepsydra.
Couple in the Next Room, The.
Crazy Weather.
Daffy Duck in Hollywood.
Darlene's Hospital.
Decoy.
Ecclesiast, The.
Errors.
Fantasia on "The Nut-Brown Maid," *sels.*
Farm Implements and Rutabagas in a
    Landscape.
Faust.
Flowering Death.
For John Clare.
Forties Flick.
Friends.
Frontispiece.
Gazing Grain, The.
Glazunoviana.
Grand Galop.
Grapevine, The.
Haunted Landscape.
He.
Here Everything Is Still Floating.
Hop o' My Thumb.
Houseboat Days.
How Much Longer Will I Be Able to Inhabit
    the Divine Sepulcher.
Ice-Cream Wars, The.
If the Birds Knew.
Illustration.
Instruction Manual, The.
Into the Dusk-Charged Air.
It Was Raining in the capital.
Ivory Tower, The.
Just Walking Around.
Lament Upon the Waters, The.
Landscape (After Baudelaire).
Last Month.
Last World, A.
Late Echo.
Le Livre Est sur la Table.
Leasing of September, The.
Litany.
Lonedale Operator, The.
Long Novel, A.
Love Poem, A.
Many Wagons Ago.
Märchenbilder.
Mixed Feelings.

More Pleasant Adventures.
My Erotic Double.
New Realism, The, *sels.*
Oleum Misericordiae.
On the Towpath.
Ongoing Story, The.
Or in My Throat.
Other Cindy, The.
Other Tradition, The.
Otherwise.
Our Youth.
Painter, The.
Paradoxes and Oxymorons.
Parergon.
Picture of Little J. A. in a Prospect of Flowers,
    The.
Pied Piper, The.
Plainness in Diversity.
Plural of "Jack-in-the-Box," The.
Popular Songs.
Punishing the Myth.
Purists Will Object.
Pursuit of Happiness, The.
Pyrography.
Qualm.
Recent Past, The.
Rivers and Mountains.
Saying It to Keep It from Happening.
Scheherazade.
Self-Portrait in a Convex Mirror.
Silhouette.
Skaters, The, *sels.*
Some Old Tires.
Some Trees.
Some Words.
Something Similar.
Song: "Song tells us of our old way of living,
    The."
Songs We Know Best, The.
Sonnet: "Each servant stamps the reader with a
    look."
Soonest Mended.
Sortes Vergilianae.
Spring Day.
Street Musicians.
Summer.
Syringa.
System, The.
Tapestry.
Task, The.
Thank You for Not Cooperating.
Their Day.
37 Haiku.
This Configuration.
Thoughts of a Young Girl.
Tone Poem, A.
Train Rising Out of the Sea.
Two Scenes.
Unctuous Platitudes.
Untilted.
Unusual Precautions.
Variant.
Variations, Calypso and Fugue on a Theme of
    Ella Wheeler Wilcox.
Vegetarians, The.
Wave, A.
We Hesitate.
Wet Casements.
What Is Poetry.
Whatever It Is, Wherever You Are.
White Roses.
Wooden Buildings.
Worsening Situation.
Wrong Kind of Insurance, The.
Young Son, The.

Atwood, Margaret (b. 1939)
After all you are quite.
After Heraclitus.
After the agony in the guest / bedroom, you
    lying by the.
After the Flood, We.
Against Still Life.
Aging Female Poet on Laundry Day.
Aging Female Poet Reads Little Magazines.
Aging Female Poet Sits on the Balcony.
All Bread.

Alternate Thoughts from Underground.
Anchorage.
Animals in That Country, The.
Another Elegy.
At first I was given centuries.
At the Tourist Centre in Boston.
Axiom.
Backdrop Addresses Cowboy.
Bad Mouth.
Bedside.
Beyond truth, / tenacity: of those.
Blue Dwarfs.
Boat, A.
Book of Ancestors.
Buffalo in Compound: Alberta.
Bus along St Clair: December, A.
Bus to Alliston, Ontario, The.
Carrying Food Home in Winter.
Charivari.
Christmas Carols.
Circe / Mud Poems.
Circle Game, The.
City Planners, The.
Comic Books vs. History.
Conversation, A.
Cyclops.
Daguerreotype Taken in Old Age.
Death of a Young Son by Drowning.
Deaths of the Other Children, The.
Departure from the Bush.
Digging.
Disembarking at Quebec.
Double Voice, The.
Dream 1: the Bush Garden.
Dream 3: Night Bear Which Frightened Cattle.
Dream 2: Brian the Still-Hunter.
Dreams of the Animals.
Eating Fire.
Eating Snake.
1837 War in Retrospect.
Elegy for the Giant Tortoises.
Eurydice.
Eventual Proteus.
Explorers, The.
First Neighbours.
Fishing for Eel Totems.
Five Poems for Dolls.
Five Poems for Grandmothers.
Flying Inside Your Own Body.
Fortification, A.
Foundling, A.
Four Auguries.
Four Small Elegies.
Further Arrivals.
Galiano Coast: Four Entrances.
Game after Supper.
Georgia Beach.
Girl and Horse, 1928.
Habitation.
Head against White.
Heart Test with an Echo Chamber.
Hesitations Outside the Door.
Highest Altitude.
How To Tell One Country from Another.
I am sitting on the / edge of the impartial.
I can't tell you my name.
I look up, you are standing.
I see you fugitive, stumbling across the prairie.
Immigrants, The.
Interlunar.
Is/Not / Not.
It Is Dangerous to Read Newspapers.
Journey to the Interior.
Keep.
Landcrab I.
Landcrab II.
Landlady, The.
Last Day.
Late August.
Later in Belleville: Career.
Letter from Persephone.
Looking in a Mirror.
Lying here, everything in me.
Machine. Gun. Nest.
Marrying the Hangman.
Marsh, Hawk.

Metempsychosis.
Midwinter, Presolstice.
Migration: C.P.R.
More and More.
Morning, A.
Mothers.
Mushrooms.
My beautiful wooden leader.
Newsreel: Man and Firing Squad.
Night Poem.
Nightshade on the Way to School.
No Name.
Not the Moon.
Notes towards a Poem That Can Never Be
   Written.
Nothing.
November.
Orpheus (1).
Orpheus (2).
Out.
Paper Bag, A.
Paths and Thingscape.
Place: Fragments, A.
Planters, The.
Porcupine Meditation.
Porcupine Tree.
Postcard.
Pre-Amphibian.
Precognition.
Procedures for Underground.
Progressive Insanities of a Pioneer.
Projected Slide of an Unknown Soldier.
Psalm to Snake.
Quattrocento.
Red Shirt, A.
Reincarnation of Captain Cook, The.
Rest, The.
Resurrection.
Robber Bridegroom, The.
Roominghouse, Winter.
Settlers, The.
She.
She Considers Evading Him.
Small Cabin, The.
Snake Woman.
Solipsism While Dying.
Solstice Poem.
Some Objects of Wood and Stone.
Songs of the Transformed.
Soul, Geologically, A.
Speeches for Dr Frankenstein.
Spring again, can I stand it.
Squaw Lilies: Some Notes.
Sunday Drive, A.
Sunset II.
Their Attitudes Differ.
There Is Only One of Everything.
They Are Hostile Nations.
They Eat Out.
They were all inaccurate.
This is a mistake, / these arms and legs.
This Is a Photograph of Me.
Thoughts from Underground.
Three Desk Objects.
Three Praises.
Torture.
Tricks With Mirrors.
True Stories.
Two Fires, The.
Two-Headed Poems.
Variation on the Word *Sleep*.
Visit to Toronto, with Companions.
Voice, A.
Vultures.
We are hard on each other.
We hear nothing these days.
Wereman, The.
Werewolf Movies.
What is it, it does not.
Wish: Metamorphosis to Heraldic Emblem.
Woman Makes Peace with Her Faulty Heart,
   The.
Woman Skating.
Woman Who Could Not Live With Her Faulty
   Heart, The.
Women's Issue, A.

Words Continue Their Journey, The.
Yes at first you / go down smooth as.
You Are Happy.
You are the sun / in reverse, all energy.
You Begin.
You did it / it was you who started the
   countdown.
You Fit into Me.
You refuse to own / yourself, you permit.
You take my hand and.
You want to go back.
Younger Sister, Going Swimming.

Auden, W. H. (Wystan Hugh) (1907–73)
A. E. Housman.
Academic Graffiti.
Address to the Beasts.
Adolescence.
After Reading a Child's Guide to Modern
   Physics.
Age of Anxiety, The.
Aliens, The.
Alone.
Amor Loci.
Another Time.
Anthem for St. Cecilia's Day.
Anthem: "Let us praise our Maker, with true
   passion extol Him."
Archaeology.
Art of Healing, The.
As He Is.
As I Walked Out One Evening.
Ascension Day, 1964.
At the Grave of Henry James.
At the Party.
Atlantis.
Aubade: "Beckoned anew to a World."
August 1968.
Bad Night, A.
Bathtub Thoughts.
Bestiaries Are Out.
Between Adventure.
Bird-Language.
Blessed Event.
Bonfires, The.
Bride in the 30's, A.
Brussels in Winter.
Bucolics.
Canzone: "When shall we learn, what should
   be clear as day."
Capital, The.
Casino.
Cattivo Tempo.
Change of Air, A.
Chimaeras, The.
Circe.
City without Walls.
Clocks cannot tell our time of day.
Composer, The.
Consider.
Contrast, A.
Council, The.
Curse, A.
Dame Kind.
Danse Macabre.
Dark Years, The.
Death's Echo.
Decoys, The.
Detective Story.
Diaspora.
Dichtung und Wahrheit.
Doggerel by a Senior Citizen.
Dover.
Duet, The.
Easy Knowledge.
Edward Lear.
Eleven Occasional Poems.
Encounter, An.
Epigoni, The.
Epistle to a Godson.
Epitaph on a Tyrant.
Et in Arcadia Ego.
Exiles, The.
Fairground.
Fall of Rome, The.
Family Ghosts.
Few and Simple.

First Things First.
Five Songs.
Fleet Visit.
For the Time Being; a Christmas Oratorio.
Forty Years On.
Friday's Child.
Gare du Midi.
Garrison, The.
Good-Bye to the Mezzogiorno.
Half Way.
Hammerfest.
Hands.
Happy Ending.
Have a Good Time.
Healthy Spot, A.
Heard and Seen.
Heavy Date.
Hell.
Herman Melville.
Hidden Law, The.
His Excellency.
History of Science, The.
History of Truth, The.
Homage to Clio.
Horae Canonicae.
Horatians, The.
Household, A.
Hunting Season.
I Am Not a Camera.
Iceland Revisited.
If I Could Tell You.
In Due Season.
In Memory of Ernst Toller.
In Memory of Sigmund Freud.
In Memory of W. B. Yeats.
In Praise of Limestone.
In Schrafft's.
In Sickness and in Health.
In Transit.
Insignificant Elephants.
Ischia.
Island Cemetery, An.
James Honeyman.
Journey to Iceland.
Kairos and Logos.
Lady[,] Weeping at the Crossroads.
Law like Love.
Leap Before You Look.
Legend.
Lesson, The.
Let History Be My Judge.
Letter, The.
Letter to Lord Byron.
Like a Vocation.
Limbo Culture.
Loneliness.
Love Feast, The.
Lullaby: "Din of work is subdued, The."
Lullaby: "Lay your sleeping head, my love."
Luther.
Maker, The.
Makers of History.
Man of La Mancha, *sels.*
Managers, The.
Many Happy Returns.
Marginalia.
May.
Maze, The.
Meiosis.
Memorial for the City.
Merax & Mullin.
Miss Gee.
Missing.
Misunderstanding, A.
Model, The.
Montaigne.
Moon Landing.
More Loving One, The.
Mundus et Infans.
Musée des Beaux Arts.
Music Is International.
Natural Linguistics.
Never Stronger.
New Year Greeting, A.
New Year Letter.
Night Mail, The.

1929.
No, Plato, No.
Nocturne: "Appearing unannounced, the
   moon."
Nocturne: "Do squamous and squiggling fish."
Not in Baedeker.
Novelist, The.
Numbers and Faces.
Nursery Rhyme.
O What Is That Sound [Which So Thrills the
   Ear].
Objects.
Ode: "Though aware of our rank and alert to
   obey orders."
Ode to Gaea.
Ode to Terminus.
Ode to the Diencephalon.
Ode to the Medieval Poets.
Old Man's Road, The.
Old People's Home.
On Sunday Walks.
On the Circuit.
On This Island.
One Circumlocution.
Orpheus.
Our Bias.
Our Hunting Fathers.
Oxford.
Paid on Both Sides.
Partition.
Paysage Moralisé.
Permanent Way, A.
Pleasure Island.
Posthumous Letter to Gilbert White.
Precious Five.
Price, The.
Profile.
Progress?
Prologue at Sixty.
Prophets, The.
Pseudo-Questions.
Quest, The.
Question, The.
Question, The: "All of us believe."
Questioner Who Sits So Sly, The.
Reflections in a Forest.
Riddle, The.
Rimbaud.
River Profile.
Rois Fainéants.
Sabbath, The.
Schoolchildren.
Sea and the Mirror, The.
Secondary Epic.
Secret Agent, The.
Secrets.
Shield of Achilles, The.
Shock, A.
Short Ode to the Cuckoo.
Shorts I.
Shorts II [1958–1971].
Shorts [1927–1932].
Shorts [1939–1947].
Shorts [1948–1957].
Shorts [1972–1973].
Since.
Six Commissioned Texts.
Smelt and Tasted.
Song, The: "So large a morning[,] so itself[,] to
   lean."
Sonnets from China.
Stark bewölkt.
Summer Night, A.
Symmetries & Asymmetries.
T the Great.
Talking to Dogs.
Talking to Mice.
Talking to Myself.
Taller To-day.
Ten Songs.
Thank You, Fog.
Thanksgiving, A.
Thanksgiving for a Habitat.
Their Lonely Betters.
There Will Be No Peace.
They.

This Loved One.
This Lunar Beauty.
Three Occasional Poems.
Three Posthumous Poems.
Through the Looking-Glass.
Too Dear, Too Vague.
Truest Poetry Is the Most Feigning, The [or,
   Ars Poetica for Hard Times].
Twelve Songs.
Two Climbs.
Two Songs.
Uncle Henry.
Under Sirius.
Under Which Lyre, a Reactionary Tract for the
   Times.
Unknown Citizen, The.
Unpredictable but Providential.
Venus Will Now Say a Few Words.
Victor.
Voltaire at Ferney.
Voyage, A.
Walk After Dark, A.
Walks.
Wanderer, The.
Watch Any Day.
Watchers, The.
Watertowers, The.
We Too Had Known Golden Hours.
Whitsunday in Kirchstetten.
Who Will Endure.
Who's Who.
Witnesses, The.
Words.
You.

Ausonius (Decimus Magnus Ausonius) (c.310–95)
I am that Dido which thou here do'st see.
On Nanus Mounted on an Ant.
Out of Catullus.
Upon the Same.

Ausonius, Decimus Magnus *See* **Ausonius**

Austen, Caroline Mary Craven (1805–80)
Noun Verse.

Austen, Cassandra Elizabeth (1773–1845)
Charades: "Should you chance to suffer thirst."
Verses to Rhyme with 'Rose'

Austen, Charles John (1779–1852)
Charade: "Without me divided, fair ladies I
   ween."

Austen, Elizabeth
Verses to Rhyme with 'Rose'

Austen, Francis William (1773–1865)
Charade: "By my 1st you may travel with
   safety & speed."

Austen, Henry Thomas (1771–1850)
Charade: "I with a Housemaid once was curst."
Godmersham The Temple of Delight.

Austen, James (1765–1819)
Address to Tyger.
Charade: "In my first that he may not be tardy
   & late."
Epilogue to the Sultan.
To Edward on the Death of His First Pony.
To Miss Jane Austen the Reputed Author of
   Sense and Sensibility a Novel Lately
   Publish'd.
Tyger's Letter to Caroline 1812.
Venta! within Thy Sacred Fane.

Austen, Jane (1775–1817)
Alas! Poor Brag, thou Boastful Game!
Between Session & Session.
Emma, *sels.*
Epitaph: "Here lies our freind who having
   promis-ed."
In Measured Verse.
I've a Pain in My Head.
Lines *Supposed* to Have Been Sent to an
   Uncivil Dress Maker.
Lines Written by Jane Austen for the
   Amusement of a Niece.
My Dearest Frank.
Ode to Pity.
Oh! Mr. Best, You're Very Bad.
On Sir Home Popham's Sentence—April 1807.

On the Marriage of Miss Camilla Wallop & the
   Revd. [Henry] Wake.
On the Marriage of Mr. Gell of East Bourn to
   Miss Gill.
Riddles: "When my 1st is a task to a young
   girl of spirit."
Song: "I am going to have my dinner."
Song: "I go to Town."
Song: "That Damon was in love with me."
Song: "Though misfortunes my footsteps may
   ever attend."
Song: "When Corydon went to the fair."
This Little Bag.
To Miss Bigg.
To the Memory of Mrs. Lefroy.
Verses to Rhyme with 'Rose'
When Stretch'd on One's Bed.
Written at Winchester on Tuesday the 15th
   July 1817.

**Austen, Jane Anna Elizabeth (Anna Lefroy)
(1793–1872)**
On Reading a Letter.

Austen-Leigh, James Edward (1798–1874)
Dirt & Slime.
Lines Addressed to his Father on Making Him
   a Present of a Knife.
To Miss J. Austen.

Austen, Mrs. (1739–1827)
Bouts-Rimeés (Written at Chawton Cottage,
   1820).
Dialogue between Death and Mrs A.
Epistle to G. East Esq.
Fables: "Cock was working very hard, A."
Humble Petition of Rd Buller & W.
   Goodenough, The.
I Hope, My Anna.
I Send You Here.
Miss Green's Reply.
Receipt for a Pudding, A.
Riddles and Charades.
To F.S., who accused the Author of partiality
   in writing verses for F C Fowle, & not for
   him.
Verses to Rhyme with 'Rose.'

Automedon (*fl.* c.6th cent. B.C.)
On life, on morals, be thy thoughts employ'd.

B

Bachmann, Ingeborg (1926–73)
Maryam.
What Is True.

Bandeira, Manuel (1886–1968)
Brazilian Tragedy.
My Last Poem.

Bassani, Giorgio (1916–2000)
Idyll: "As a horn of the high moon veers in
   clear skies over Main Street."
Looking Out from Ferrara.

Basualto, Neftalí Ricardo Reyes *See* **Neruda,
Pablo**

Baudelaire, Charles (1821–67)
Abel and Cain.
Abyss, The.
Affronted Moon, The.
Albatross, The.
Alchemist of Sorrows, The.
Allegory.
Autumn Sonnet.
Bad Luck.
Bad Monk, The.
Balcony,The.
Beauty.
Benediction.
Berthe's Eyes.
Black Bile ("No writing-desk crammed full of
   music, twine").
Black Bile ("Pluvius, venting spleen on all
   enclaves").
Black Bile ("When heavy, threatening skies
   weigh like a lid").
Black Bile ("Worthless and wealthy, decrepit
   and young").

Blind, The.
Burial, A.
Carefree Corpse, The.
Carrion.
Carrion, A.
Cask of Hate, The.
Cat.
Cats.
Clock, The.
Concerning a Jackass.
Confession.
Conversation.
Correspondences.
Cracked Bell, The.
Cupid & Skull.
Curious Man's Dream, A.
Damned Women ("Half-hidden in the dying
   light's caress").
Damned Women ("Like ruminating cattle on
   the sand").
Dancing Death.
Dancing Serpent, The.
Death of Artists, The.
Death of Lovers, The.
Death of the Poor, The.
Death to the Poor.
Debut of the Dancer, A. B., The.
Desire for Oblivion.
Don Juan in the Underworld.
End of the Day, The.
Enemy, The.
Epigraph for a Condemned Book.
Evening Harmony.
Ever the Same.
Examination of Conscience, The.
Exotic Scent.
Fantastic Engraving, A.
First Light.
Fountain of Blood.
Games of Chance.
Giantess, The.
Girandole, The.
Guiding Lights, The.
Her Hair.
Hymn to Beauty.
Hymn: "To Love and to the lovely eyes."
I Haven't Forgotten.
I love the thought of Ages of Undress.
I love you as I love the night itself.
Ideal, The.
In glistening shot-silk she seems to wind.
In Praise of My Françoise.
Invitation to a Voyage.
Irreparable, The.
Jewels.
Laments of an Icarus, The.
Landscape.
Last Light.
Last Rays of the Romantic Sun.
Lesbos.
Lethe.
Lid, The.
L'Invitation au Voyage.
Litanies to Satan.
Little Old Women, The.
Lively Watering Hole, A.
Living Dead, The.
Living Torch, The.
'Lola de Valence' by Manet.
Love of Artifice, The.
Lover's Wine.
Man and Sea.
Martyr, A.
Mask, The.
Meditation.
Melancholy Moon, The.
Mercenary Muse, The.
Merciless Madrigal.
Metamorphoses of the Vampire.
Mist and Rain.
Mortal Combat.
Murderer's Wine.
Music.
My Beatrice.
Obsession.
On a Portrait of Honoré Daumier.

One night I had some ghastly jewish whore.
Out of the Blue.
Out of the Depths I Called to Thee.
Owls.
Pagan's Prayer, The.
Parisian Dream.
Passing Glance, A.
Perfume-flask, The.
Phantom, A.
Pipe.
Point of No Return, The.
Poison.
Possessed.
Posthumous Remorse.
Posthumous Work.
Previous Existence.
Promise in a Pair of Eyes, The.
Proud Ship, The.
Punishment of Pride.
Ragpickers' Wine.
Ransom, The.
Rara Avis.
Rebel, The.
Restless and Sad.
Reversibility.
Roving Gypsies.
Ruin.
Saint Peter's Denial.
Self-Tormentor, The.
Serpent's Tooth, The.
Seven Old Men, The.
Sick Muse, The.
Sisina.
Sisters of Mercy.
Song for an Afternoon.
Song of Autumn.
Spirit of the Wine, The.
Spiritual Dawn.
Still Unsatisfied.
Sun, The.
Swan, The.
Sympathetic Horror.
'Tasso in Prison' by Delacroix.
These line I give to you in hopes my name.
To a Creole Lady.
To a Girl in Malabar.
To a Madonna.
To a Red-headed Beggar.
To the Reader.
To Theodore de Banville.
Too Full of Life.
Total Harmony.
Transcendence.
Travellers.
Uncertain Skies.
Universal Analogies.
Vampire, The.
Voice, The.
Voyage to Cythera, A.
What will you say, hermetic soul? Resigned.
When boredom gnaws your soul.
Wine of the Solitary Man, The.
World Away, A.
You were so jealous of our nursemaid's love.

Beccadelli, Antonio *See* **"Panormitanus"**
Beck, Karl (1817–79)
   Hungarian Horse-Herd, The.
Beckett, Samuel (1906–89)
   À elle l'acte calme.
   À l'instant de s'entendre dire.
   À peine à bien mené.
   Ainsi a-t-on beau.
   Alba.
   Arènes de Lutèce.
   Ascension.
   Bois seul.
   Bon bon il est un pays.
   Cascando.
   Ce qu'a de pis.
   Ce qu'ont les yeux.
   Chaque jour envie.
   Da Tagte Es.
   D'abord / à plat sur du dur.
   De pied ferme.
   Dieppe.
   Dieppe.

Dortmunder.
D'où / la voix qui dit.
Dread Nay.
Echo's Bones, *sels.*
Écoute-les / s'ajouter.
Elles viennent.
En face.
Enueg II.
Enueg I.
Être là sans mâchoires sans dents.
Fin fond du néant.
Fleuves et océans.
Flux cause.
Fous qui disiez.
Gnome.
Home Olga.
Hors crâne seul dedans.
Imagine si ceci.
Je suis ce cours de sable qui glisse.
Je voudrais que mon amour meure.
Jusque dans la caverne ciel et sol.
Lueurs lisières.
Malacoda.
Mort de A.D.
Morte parmi.
Mots survivants.
Mouche, La.
Musique de l'indifférence.
My way is in the sand flowing.
Ne manquez pas à Stuttgart.
Ne manquez pas à Tanger.
Noire soeur.
Nuit qui fais tant.
Nuit venue où l'âme allait, La.
Ooftish.
Pas à pas.
Pas davantage.
Plus loin un autre commémore.
Poem: "I would like my love to die."
Que ferais-je sans ce monde sans visage sans
   questions.
Rentrer / À la nuit.
Rêve / sans fin.
Rien nul / n'aura été.
Roundelay: "On all that strand."
Rue de Vaugirard.
Saint-Lô.
Samedi répit.
Sanies I.
Sanies II.
Serena I.
Serena III.
Serena II.
Silence tel que ce qui fut.
Sitôt sorti de l'ermitage.
Something There.
Somme toute / tout compte fait.
Son ombre une nuit.
Tailpiece.
They come.
Thither.
Vieil aller / vieux arrêts.
Vive morte ma seule saison.
What would I do without this world faceless
   incurious.
Whoroscope.
Words and Music, *sels.*

Begley, T.
   Digestibles of Sun.
   Helen Groves.
   Insomniac of a Zen-Garden Fruit.
   Photovoltaic.
   Sappho's Gymnasium.
   Vowel Imprint.
   Your Sacred Idiot with Me.
"Bell, Ellis" *See* **Brontë, Emily Jane**
Bembo, Pietro (1470–1547)
   On Raphael.
   You, too, my brother in your hour of Spring.
Benserade, Isaac de (*fl.* c.1650)
   Translation of Lines by Benserade.
Berrigan, Ted (1934–83)
   After Peire Vidal, & Myself.
   American Express.
   Ann Arbor Song.

Around the Fire.
Bean Spasms.
Certain Slant of Sunlight, A.
Chicago English Afternoon.
Chicago Morning.
Chinese Nightingale.
Coda: Song.
Cranston Near the City Line.
Crystal.
Dinner at George & Katie Schneeman's.
Epithalamion: "Pussy put her paw into the pail of paint."
February Air.
For You.
44th Birthday Evening, at Harris's.
Frank O'Hara.
Heloise.
I Heard Brew Moore Say, One Day.
In Anselm Hollo's Poems.
In the 51st State.
It's Important.
Lady.
Last Poem.
Many Happy Returns.
New Personal Poem.
Old-Fashioned Air.
Orange Clock, An.
Pandora's Box, An Ode.
Paul Blackburn.
Peace.
People Who Died.
Poem: "Of morning, Iowa City, blue."
Red Shift.
Sandy's Sunday Best.
Scorpio.
She.
She (Not to be confused with she, a girl).
So Going Around Cities.
Something Amazing Just Happened.
Sonnets, The, *sels.*
Soviet Souvenir.
Tambourine Life.
Things To Do in Anne's Room.
Things To Do in New York (City).
Things To Do in Providence.
Whitman in Black.
Words for Love.
Wrong Train.

Berry, Wendell (b. 1934)
Adze, The.
Against the War in Vietnam.
Air and Fire.
Anger against Beasts.
Anniversary, An.
Another Descent.
April Woods: Morning.
Architecture, An.
Aristocracy, The.
Arrival, The.
At a Country Funeral.
Autumn Burning, An.
Awake at Night.
Before Dark.
Below.
Bird Killer, The.
Birth (Near Port William), The.
Boone.
Breaking.
Broken Ground, The.
Canticle.
Clear Days, The.
Clearing, The.
Cold Pane, The.
Cold, The.
Companions, The.
Contrariness of the Mad Farmer, The.
Country of Marriage, The.
Creation Myth.
Current, The.
Dance, A.
Dance, The.
Dark with power.
Design of a House, The.
Desolation.
Discipline, A.
Do Not Be Ashamed.

Dream, The.
Earth and Fire.
Elegy: "To be at home on its native ground."
Elegy: "All day our eyes could find no resting place."
Enriching the Earth.
Envoy: "Love, all day there has been at the edge of my mind."
Except.
Fall.
Falling Asleep.
Familiar, The.
Farmer Among the Tombs, The.
Farmer and the Sea, The.
Farmer, Speaking of Monuments, The.
Fear of Darkness, The.
Fear of Love, The.
February 2, 1968.
Finches, The.
First, The.
For the Future.
For the Hog Killing.
For the Rebuilding of a House.
Forty Years.
From the Crest.
From the Distance.
Gathering, The.
Gift of Gravity, The.
Goods.
Grace.
Grandmother, The.
Green and White.
Grief.
Guest, The.
Handing Down, The.
Her First Calf.
Heron, The.
Hidden Singer, The.
History.
Homecoming, A.
Horses.
In Memory: Stuart Egnal.
In Rain.
In This World.
Independence Day.
July, 1773.
Kentucky River Junction.
Law That Marries All Things, The.
Letter.
Lilies, The.
Long Hunter, The.
Mad Farmer in the City, The.
Mad Farmer Manifesto: the First Amendment, The.
Mad Farmer Revolution, The.
Mad Farmer's Love Song, The.
Man Born to Farming, The.
Man Walking and Singing, A.
Manifesto: the Mad Farmer Liberation Front.
March Snow.
March 22, 1968.
Marriage.
Marriage, an Elegy, A.
May Song.
Meadow, The.
Meditation in the Spring Rain.
Meeting, A.
Morning's News, The.
Music, A.
My Great-Grandfather's Slaves.
Necessity of Faith, The.
New Roof, The.
Observance.
October 10.
Old Elm Tree by the River, The.
On the Hill Late at Night.
Our Children, Coming of Age.
Passing the Strait.
Peace of Wild Things, The.
Plan, The.
Planting Crocuses.
Planting Trees.
Poem for J.
Poem of Thanks, A.
Poem: "Willing to die, / you give up."
Porch over the River, The.

Praise.
Praise, A.
Prayer after Eating.
Prayers and Sayings of the Mad Farmer.
Purification, A.
Rain.
Recognition, The.
Requiem: "We will see no more."
Returning.
Ripening.
Rising.
River Bridged and Forgot, The.
Satisfactions of the Mad Farmer, The.
Seeds, The.
September 2, 1969.
Setting Out.
Seventeen Years.
Silence, The ("What must a man do to be alone in the world?").
Silence, The ("Though the air is full of singing").
Sleep.
Slip, The.
Snake, The.
Song (1).
Song (2).
Song (3).
Song (4).
Song: "I tell my love in rhyme."
Song in a Year of Catastrophe.
Song Sparrow Singing in the Fall, A.
Sorrel Filly, The.
Sowing.
Sparrow.
Springs, The.
Standing Ground, A.
Star, The.
Stay Home.
Stones, The.
Strait, The.
Supplanting, The.
Sycamore, The.
Testament.
Thief, The.
Thought of Something Else, The.
Three Elegiac Poems.
Throwing away the Mail.
To a Siberian Woodsman.
To Gary Snyder.
To Go By Singing.
To Know the Dark.
To My Children, Fearing for Them.
To Tanya at Christmas.
To the Holy Spirit.
To the Unseeable Animal.
To Think of the Life of a Man.
To What Listens.
Traveling at Home.
Walking on the River Ice.
Want of Peace, The.
Warning to My Readers, A.
Way of Pain, The.
We Who Prayed and Wept.
Wet Time, A.
Wheel, The.
Where.
Wild Geese, The.
Wild, The.
Window Poems.
Winter Night Poem for Mary.
Winter Nightfall.
Winter Rain, The.
Wish to Be Generous, The.
Woods.
Work Song.

Berryman, John (1914–72)
American Lights, Seen from Off Abroad.
Amos.
Ancestor.
Animal Trainer, The.
Antitheses.
Apparition, The.
At Chinese Checkers.
Away.
Back.
Ball Poem, The.

Beethoven Triumphant.
Black Book, The, *sels.*
Boston Common.
Cadenza on Garnette.
Canto Amor.
Captain's Song, The.
Caravan.
Ceremony and Vision.
Certainty Before Lunch.
Cloud and Flame.
Communist.
Compline.
Conversation.
Crisis.
Curse, The.
Damn You, Jim D., You Woke Me Up.
Damned.
Dangerous Year, The.
Dante's Tomb.
Death Ballad.
Defensio in Extremis.
Desire Is a World by Night.
Desires of Men and Women.
Despair.
Disciple, The.
Dispossessed, The.
Down & Back.
Drugs Alcohol Little Sister.
Drunks.
Ecce Homo.
Eleven Addresses to the Lord.
Enemies of the Angels, The.
Epilogue: "He died in December. He must
   descend."
Facts & Issues, The.
Fare Well.
Farewell to Miles.
First Night at Sea.
Form, The.
Formal Elegy.
Freshman Blues.
Friendless.
Gislebertus' Eve.
Handshake, the Entrance, The.
Have a Genuine American Horror-&-Mist on
   the Rocks.
He Resigns.
Heaven.
Hell Poem, The.
Hello.
Henry by Night.
Her & It.
Heroes, The.
Homage to Mistress Bradstreet.
Home Ballad, The.
How Do You Do, Dr Berryman, Sir?
Huddle of Need, A.
I Know.
Images of Elspeth.
In & Out.
In Memoriam (1914–1953).
Interstitial Office.
King David Dances.
Lauds.
Letter to His Brother.
Lightning, The.
Lines to Mr Frost.
London.
Long Home, The.
Matins.
Meditation.
Meeting.
Message.
Minnesota Thanksgiving.
Monkhood.
Moon and the Night and the Men, The.
My Special Fate.
Mysteries, The.
Narcissus Moving.
Navajo Setting the Record Straight.
New Year's Eve.
Night and the City.
Nineteen Thirty-Eight.
No.
Nones.
Not to Live.

Note to Wang Wei.
Nowhere.
Of Suicide.
Old Man Goes South Again Alone.
Olympus.
On the London Train.
1 September 1939.
Opus Dei.
Other Cambridge, The.
Overseas Prayer.
Pacifist's Song, The.
Parting as Descent.
Poem for Bhain, A.
Poet's Final Instructions, The.
Point of Age, A.
Possessed, The.
Prayer After All, A.
Prayer of the Middle-Aged Man, The.
Prime.
Professor's Song, A.
Purgatory.
Recovery.
Relations.
River Rouge, 1932.
Rock-Study with Wanderer.
Sanctuary.
Scholars at the Orchid Pavilion.
Scots Poem.
Search, The.
Sext.
Shirley & Auden.
Somber Prayer.
Song from "Cleopatra."
Song of the Bridegroom, The.
Song of the Demented Priest, The.
Song of the Man Forsaken and Obsessed.
Song of the Tortured Girl, The.
Song of the Young Hawaiian, The.
Sonnets to Chris.
Spinning Heart, The.
Statue, The.
Surviving Love.
Sympathy, A Welcome, A.
Tampa Stomp.
Tea.
Terce.
Thanksgiving: Detroit.
They Have.
To a Woman.
To Bhain Campbell.
Transit.
Traveller, The.
Travelling South.
Trial, The.
Two Organs.
Unknowable? Perhaps Not Altogether.
Usual Prayer, A.
Venice, 182.
Vespers.
Views of Myself.
Washington in Love.
Whether There Is Sorrow in the Demons.
White Feather.
Winter-Piece to a Friend Away, A.
World-Telegram.
World's Fair.
Young Woman's Song.
Your Birthday in Wisconsin You Are 140.
**Bertrans [or Bertran or Bertrand] de Born (*fl.*
  12th cent.)**
   Planh for the Young English King.
Bible, *N.T.*
   St. John, *sels.*
   St. Luke, *sels.*
   St. Mark, *sels.*
   St. Matthew, *sels.*
Bible, *O.T.*
   Psalms, *sels.*
Bierce, Ambrose (1842–c.1914)
   Abracadabra.
   After Portsmouth.
   Another Way.
   At a "National Encampment."
   Basilica.
   Binnacle, The.
   Bride, The.

Californian Summer Pictures.
Christian.
Compliance.
Confederate Flags, The.
Contentment.
Controversy.
Creation.
Crime of 1903, The.
Cynic perforce from studying mankind.
Death of Grant, The.
Devil's Dictionary, The, *sels.*
Eastern Question, The.
Error, An.
Fair Division, A.
False Prophecy, A.
Finis Æternitatis.
For those this mausoleum is erected.
France.
Genesis.
George Perry here is stiff and stark.
Geotheos.
Golden Age, The.
Grape.
Growler, A.
Guest, A.
Here lies the last of Deacon Fitch.
Here Salomon's body reposes.
Here Stanford lies, who thought it odd.
Hesitating Veteran, The.
How Blind Is He.
Humility.
In Memoriam.
Inauspiciously.
Incurable.
Infralapsarian.
Insectivora.
Invocation.
J.F.B.
Judex Jocosus.
Judex Judicatus.
King of Bores, The.
Lacking Factor, A.
Law.
Literary Method, A.
Loring Pickering.
Macrobian.
Matter for Gratitude.
McAllister, of talents rich and rare.
Montefiore.
Mormon Question, The.
My Day of Life.
Mystery, A.
Nanine.
New Decalogue, The.
Novum Organum.
On Stone.
One Morning.
Oneiromancy.
Passing Show, The.
Perverted Village, The.
Political Economy.
Possibility, A.
Presentiment.
Pun, The.
Rational Anthem, A.
Reminded.
Right.
Rosalie.
Saith the Czar.
Science.
Serenade: "Listen, maiden, to my strain."
Something in the Papers.
Statesmen, The.
Strained Relations.
Study in Gray, A.
Substance or Shadow.
T. A. H.
Tempora Mutantur.
To a Bully.
To a Censor.
To a Dejected Poet.
To an Insolent Attorney.
To E. S. Salomon.
To Maude.
To Nanine.
To the Bartholdi Statue.

To Thee, My Darling.
Trencher-Knight, A.
Two Types.
Unexpounded.
Vision of Doom, A.
Voice from Pekin, A.
William F. Smith.
Word to the Unwise, A.
Year's "Casualties", A.
Big Stick *See* **Feng-kan (Big Stick)**
Bion (c.315–255 B.C.)
Fragment of the Elegy on the Death of Adonis.
Lament for Adonis.
Bishop, Elizabeth (1911–79)
Anaphora.
Argument.
Armadillo, The.
Arrival at Santos.
At the Fishhouses.
Behind Stowe.
Bight, The.
Brazil, January 1, 1502.
Britannia Rules the Waves.
Burglar of Babylon, The.
Cape Breton.
Casabianca.
Chemin de Fer.
Cirque d'Hiver.
Cold Spring, A.
Colder the Air, The.
Cootchie.
Crusoe in England.
Electrical Storm.
End of March, The.
Exchanging Hats.
Faustina, or Rock Roses.
Filling Station.
First Death in Nova Scotia.
Fish, The.
Five Flights Up.
Flood, The.
Florida.
For C.W.B.
Four Poems.
From the Country to the City.
From Trollope's Journal.
Gentleman of Shalott, The.
Going to the Bakery.
Hanging of the Mouse, The.
House Guest.
Hymn to the Virgin.
Imaginary Iceberg, The.
Imber Nocturnus.
In the Waiting Room.
Insomnia.
Invitation to Miss Marianne Moore.
Jerónimo's House.
Large Bad Picture.
Late Air.
Letter to N.Y.
Lines Written in the Fannie Farmer Cookbook.
Little Exercise.
Love Lies Sleeping.
Lullaby for the Cat.
Man-Moth, The.
Manners.
Manuelzinho.
Map, The.
Miracle for Breakfast, A.
Monument, The.
Moose, The.
Mountain, The.
Night City.
North Haven.
Norther—Key West, A.
One Art.
Over 2000 Illustrations and a Complete
 Concordance.
Paris, 7 A.M.
Pink Dog.
Pleasure Seas.
Poem: "About the size of an old-style dollar
 bill."
Prodigal, The.
Quai d'Orléans.
Questions of Travel.

Rainy Season; Sub-Tropics.
Reprimand, The.
Riverman, The.
Roosters.
Sandpiper.
Santarém.
Seascape.
Sestina: "September rain falls on the house."
Shampoo, The.
Sleeping on the Ceiling.
Sleeping Standing Up.
Some Dreams They Forgot.
Song for the Rainy Season.
Song: "Summer is over upon the sea."
Songs for a Colored Singer.
Sonnet: "Caught—the bubble."
Sonnet: "I am in need of music that would
 flow."
Squatter's Children.
Summer's Dream, A.
Sunday at Key West.
Sunday, 4 A.M.
Thank-You Note.
Three Sonnets for the Eyes.
Three Valentines.
Thunder.
To a Tree.
To Be Written on the Mirror in Whitewash.
Trouvée.
Twelfth Morning; or What You Will.
12 O'Clock News.
Unbeliever, The.
Under the Window: Ouro Prêto.
Varick Street.
View of the Capitol from the Library of
 Congress.
Visits to St. Elizabeths.
Wading at Wellfleet.
Wave, The.
Weed, The.
Wit, The.
Word with You, A.
Blake, William (1757–1827)
Advice of the Popes Who Succeeded the Age
 of Rafael.
All Pictures thats Panted with sense & with
 Thought.
All Religions Are One.
America: A Prophecy.
Ancient Proverb, An.
And his legs carried it like a long fork.
And in Melodious Accents I.
Angel, The.
Anger & Wrath my bosom rends.
Another [Epitaph]: "Here lies John Trot, the
 Friend of all mankind."
Answer to the Parson, An.
Are not the joys of morning sweeter.
Around the Springs of Gray my wild root
 weaves.
Auguries of Innocence.
Beneath the white thorn lovely May.
Birds, The.
Blakes apology for His Catalogue.
Blind-Man's Buff.
Book of Ahania, The.
Book of Los, The.
Book of Thel, The.
Book of Urizen [*or* First Book of Urizen], The.
Call that the Public Voice which is their Error.
Caverns of the Grave [I've Seen], The.
Compliment to the Ladies, A.
Cosway Frazer & Baldwin of Egypts Lake.
Cradle Song, A: "Sleep, sleep, beauty bright."
Cripple every step Drudges & labours, The.
Cr[omek] loves artists as he loves his Meat.
Cromek Speaks.
Crystal Cabinet, The.
Cunning sures & the Aim at yours, The.
Day.
Dedication of the Illustrations to Blair's
 "Grave."
Each Man is in His Spectres power.
English Encouragement of Art Cromeks
 Opinions Put Into Rhyme.
Epitaph, An: "Come knock your heads against

 this stone."
Epitaph, An: "I was buried near this dyke [*or*
 Dike]."
Errors of a Wise Man make your Rule, The.
Europe; A Prophecy.
Everlasting Gospel, The.
Fair Elenor.
Fairy skipd [*or* leapt] upon my knee, A.
Fairy, The.
Fayette beside King Lewis stood.
Florentine Ingratitude.
Fox, the owl, the spider, and the mole, The.
French Revolution, The.
From Cratetos.
Gates of Paradise, The.
Ghost of Abel, The.
Give pensions to the Learned Pig.
Gnomic Verses.
Golden Net, The.
Great Men & Fools do often me Inspire.
Grey Monk, The.
Grown old in Love from Seven till Seven
 times Seven.
Gwin, King of Norway.
He is a Cock would.
Hebrew Nation did not write it, The.
Her Whole Life Is an Epigram.
Hes a Blockhead who wants a proof of what
 he Cant Percieve.
How came pride in Man.
How Sweet I Roamed [*or* Roam'd] from Field
 to Field.
How to Know Love from Deceit.
Human Image, The.
I am no Homers Hero You all know.
I feard the fury [*or* roughness] of my wind.
I found them blind, I taught them how to see.
I heard an Angel singing.
I laid me down upon a bank.
I rose up at the dawn of day.
I Rubens am a Statesman & a Saint.
I Saw a Chapel All of Gold.
I told my love I told my love.
I will tell you what Joseph of Arimathea.
If I eer Grow to a Mans Estate.
If it is True What the Prophets write.
If Men will act like a maid smiling over a
 Churn.
If you play a Game of Chance know before
 you begin.
If you trap the moment before its ripe.
Imitation of Spen[s]er, An.
In a Myrtle [*or* Mirtle] Shade.
In a Wife I Would Desire.
Island in the Moon, An, *sels.*
Jerusalem.
Kid, The.
King Edward the Third.
Lacedemonian Instruction.
Land of Dreams, The.
Let the Brothels of Paris be opened.
Long John Brown & Little Mary Bell.
[Look Flaxman & Stothard do] old
 acquaintance well.
Love's Secret.
Mad Song.
Madman I have been calld Fool they call thee.
Marriage.
Marriage of Heaven and Hell, The.
Mary.
Mental Traveller, The.
Merlins Prophecy.
Milton.
Mr Cromek to Mr Stothard.
Mr Stothard to Mr Cromek.
Mock On, Mock On, Voltaire, Rousseau.
Morning.
Motto to the Songs of Innocence & of
 Experience.
Mr. Cromek [*or* On Cromek].
My Spectre around Me Night and Day.
My title as an Genius thus is provd.
Nail his neck to the cross nail it with a nail.
No real Style of Colouring ever appears.
Now Art has lost its mental Charms.
O dear Mother outline of knowledge most

sage.
O Lapwing!
O Reader behold the Philosophers Grave.
O Why Was I Born With a Different Face?
Of H[ayle]s birth this was the happy lot.
Old Maid Early, An.
On Flaxman and Stothard.
On Hayley.
On H[ayley] the Pick Thank.
On H[ayle]ys Friendship.
On Sir Joshua Reynolds.
On Stothard.
On the Great Encouragement Given By
   English Nobility & Gentry to Correggio
   Rubens Rembrandt Reynolds Gainsborough
   Catalani Ducrowe & Dilbury Doodle.
On the Venetian Painter.
On the Virginity of the Virgin Mary & Johanna
   Southcott.
Orator Prigg.
Pair of Stays to mend the Shape, A.
P[hillips] loved me, not as he loved his
   Friends.
Pitiful Case, A.
Pretty Epigram for [Those] the Entertainment
   of Those Who [Pay] Have Paid Great Sums
   in the Venetian & Flemish Ooze, A.
Prologue, Intended for a Dramatic Piece of
   King Edward the Fourth.
Prologue to King John.
Rafael Sublime Majestic Graceful Wise.
Reveal the dragon thro' the human; coursing
   swift as fire.
Riches.
Several Questions Answered.
Silent Silent Night.
Since all the Riches of this World.
Sir Jo[s]hua praised Rubens with a Smile.
Sir Joshua Praises Michael Angelo.
Sir Joshua Reynolds.
Smile, The.
Soft Snow.
Some look. to see the sweet Outlines.
Some Men created for destruction come.
Some people admire the work of a Fool.
Song 1st By a Shepherd.
Song: "Fresh from the dewy hill, the merry
   year."
Song: "I love the jocund dance."
Song: "Love and harmony combine."
Song: "Memory, hither come."
Song: "My silks and fine array."
Song of Los, The.
Song 2nd By a Young Shepherd.
Song 3rd By an Old Shepherd.
Song: "When early morn walks forth in sober
   grey."
Songs of Experience, sels.
Songs of Innocence.
S[tothard] in Childhood on the Nursery floor.
Sussex Men are Noted Fools, The.
Swelld limbs with no outline that you can
   descry.
Terror in the house does roar.
There Is No Natural Religion.
These are the Idiots chiefest arts.
Thou hast a lap full of seed.
Tiriel.
To Autumn.
To Chloes breast young Cupid slily stole.
To English Connoisseurs.
To Flaxman.
To F[laxman].
To God.
To H[ayley].
To Hunt.
To John Flaxman, 12 September 1800.
To Mrs Ann Flaxman.
To Mrs Butts.
To Mrs Flaxman, 14 September 1800.
To Morning.
To My Friend Butts I Write.
To My Mirtle.
To Nancy F[laxman].
To Nobodaddy.
To Spring.

To S[tothar]d.
To Summer.
To the Evening Star.
To the Muses.
To the Royal Academy.
To Venetian Artists.
To Winter.
Vala; or The Four Zoas.
Venetian; all thy Colouring is no more.
Verse from the Advertisement to Blake's
   Exhibition of Paintings, 1809.
Visions of the Daughters of Albion.
War Song [to Englishmen], A.
Was I angry with Hayley who used me so ill.
Washer Womans Song, The.
When France got free Europe 'twixt Fools &
   Knaves.
When I see a Rubens Rembrandt [or]
   Correggio.
When Klopstock England Defied.
When Nations grow Old. The Arts grow Cold.
When you look at a picture you always can
   see.
Why Should I Care for the Men of Thames?
Why was Cupid a Boy.
Wild Flower's Song, The.
William Bond.
William Cowper Esqre.
With Happiness Stretched [or stretched] across
   the Hills.
Woman scaly & a Man all Hairy, A.
You dont believe I wont attempt to make ye.
You say their Pictures well Painted be.

Bloch, Chana (b. 1940)
We Did What We Had To.

Blok, Aleksandr Aleksandrovich (1880–1921)
Accordeon.
Among the Admirers of Carmen.
Artist, The.
As the Ocean Changes Colour.
Autumn Day.
Autumn Freedom.
Caught by the Blizzard.
Chivalry.
Commander's Footsteps, The.
Dances of Death, sels.
Dances of Death.
Do You Remember.
Earth's Heart Is Growing Cold Again.
Factory, The.
Florence.
Girl Was Singing, A.
Hard to Be Moving among Them.
I Am Nailed to a Bar with Liquor.
I Enter the Dark Church Slowly.
I Seek Salvation.
I Sense Your Coming.
I Want to Live.
Illusion.
Impulses of Youth, The.
Intellect Cannot Measure the Divine, The.
Introduction to the Second Book of Poems.
Kite, The.
Little Priest of the Fen, The.
O Spring without End.
O What is the Setting Sun's Radiance to Me.
On the Field of Kulikovo.
Ravenna.
Red Glow in the Sky, A.
Retribution, sels.
Russia ("Even sleeping you astonish me").
Russia ("Again, as in the golden age").
Russia and I.
Scythians, The.
Shamelessly, Endlessly Sinning.
She Came in from the Frost.
Snow Wine.
Song of the Wind, The.
Stranger, The.
They Do Not Trade, Sleep, or Remember.
Those Born in the Years of Stagnation.
To My Friends.
To the Muse.
Twelve, The.
Voice from the Chorus, A.
Worlds Fly Past.

Yes. This Is the Call of Inspiration.

Blue Cloud, Peter (b. 1933)
Abalone.
Alcatraz.
At Bald Rock with Old John.
Autumn Morning.
Backward Dancer.
Bear: A Totem Dance As Seen by Raven.
Being Forever.
Brief History (June–December 1994).
Camp.
Chokecherries.
Crazy Horse Monument.
Crow.
Crow's Flight.
Dawn.
Death Chant.
Dedication of a Roundhouse.
Deeper Than a Dream.
Descent.
Dogwood Blossoms.
Earth and Creation.
Expedition.
Fallen Oak, A.
First Brother.
First Light.
For a Child.
For a Dog-killed Doe.
For Ace.
Gentle Earthquake, A.
Gift of Stone.
Girl Child.
Glacier Country.
Grandma Marie Potts.
Hobo Bird.
Hunt, Its Chant, A.
Hurricane Andrew.
Incense.
Little Fawn.
Meditation of Leaves, A.
Milkweed.
Night Room Composition.
Old Friends.
Old man's lazy, The.
Old Tom would tell us.
Pomo Basketmaker.
Quebec, rattling chains of Separatism.
Red-winged Blackbird.
Reflections on Milkweed.
Reflections on the St. Lawrence Seaway.
Road 37C.
Sandhills That None May Visit.
Sculpture in Soil.
Searching for Eagles.
Shady Creek.
Storm Mountain Face.
Sweat Lodge—The Afterwards.
Sweet Corn.
Sweetgrass.
To-ta Ti-om.
Tomorrow.
Tsier.
Walking thru twisted hollow pathways.
We sit balanced.
When's the Last Boat to Alcatraz?
White Corn Sister.
Within the Seasons.
Wolf.
Yellowjacket.

Bly, Robert (b. 1926)
Aban Kavost and Ivar Oakeson.
After Drinking All Night with a Friend, We Go
   Out in a Boat at Dawn to See Who Can
   Write the Best Poem.
After Long Busyness.
After Working.
Ant Mansion, The.
Ants.
As the Asian War Begins.
Asian Peace Offers Rejected without
   Publication.
At a March against the Vietnam War.
At Midocean.
At the Time of Peony Blossoming.
August Rain.
Awakening.

Bouquet of Ten Roses, A.
Calm Day at Drake's Bay.
Caterpillar, A.
Chinese Tomb Guardians.
Christmas Eve Service at Midnight at St.
    Michael's.
Conversation, A.
Conversation with a Holy Woman Not Seen for
    Many Years.
Cornpicker Poem.
Counting Small-Boned Bodies.
Crazy Carlson's Meadow.
Cry Going Out over Pastures, The.
Danger of Loss, The.
Dawn in Threshing Time.
Dead Seal [near McClure's Beach], The.
December 23, 1926.
Defeated.
Digging Worms.
Dream of a Brother, A.
Dream of Retarded Children, A.
Dream of What Is Missing, A.
Dream on the Night of First Snow, A.
Dried Sturgeon, The.
Driving through Minnesota during the Hanoi
    Bombings.
Driving toward the Lac Qui Parle River.
Early Spring Between Madison and
    Bellingham.
Empty Place, An.
Evening When the Full Moon Rose as the Sun
    Set, An.
Executive's Death, The.
Falling Asleep.
Ferns.
Fifty Males Sitting Together.
Finding the Father.
Fire of Despair Has Been Our Savior, The.
For My Son Noah, Ten Years Old.
Four Seasons in American Woods, *sels.*
Four Ways of Knowledge.
Getting Up Late.
Glimpse of the Waterer.
Good Silence, The.
Grass from Two Years.
Hatred of Men with Black Hair.
Hawk, The.
Hockey Poem, The.
Hollow Tree, A.
Home in Dark Grass, A.
Horse of Desire, The.
Hunting Pheasants in a Cornfield.
In Mourning for Betrayal.
In Rainy September.
In the Month of May.
Indigo Bunting, The.
Johnson's Cabinet Watched by Ants.
July Morning.
Kennedy's Inauguration.
Kneeling Down to Look [*or* Peer] into a
    Culvert.
Late Moon.
Letter to Her.
Listening to the Köln Concert.
Loon's Cry, The.
Love Poem in Twos and Threes.
Man and a Woman Sit Near Each Other.
Man Locked Inside the Oak, The.
Man Writes to a Part of Himself, A.
Meditation on Philosophy, A.
My Father's Wedding.
Near the Giant's House.
Night.
Night Frogs.
Night of First Snow.
November Day at McClure's Beach.
Old Boards.
On a Ferry across Chesapeake Bay.
Opening the Door of a Barn I Thought Was
    Empty on New Year's Eve.
Orchard Keeper, The.
Origin of the Praise of God, The.
"Out of the Rolling Ocean, the Crowd . . ."
Out Picking up Corn.
Pilgrim Fish Heads.
Poem in Three Parts.

Praise for All Dancers.
Prodigal Son, The.
Reading in Fall Rain.
Romans Angry about the Inner World.
Schoolcraft's Diary Written on the Missouri:
    1830.
Silence.
Sitting on Some Rocks in Shaw Cove.
Six Winter Privacy Poems.
Snow Geese.
Snowbanks North of the House.
Snowfall in the Afternoon.
Solitude Late at Night in the Woods.
Starfish, The.
Surprised by Evening.
Teeth Mother Naked at Last, The.
Three Kinds of Pleasures.
Two Sounds When We Sit by the Ocean.
Upward Moon and the Downward Moon, The.
Visiting the Farallones.
Waking from Sleep.
Walking Swiftly.
War and Silence.
Watcher, The.
Watering the Horse.
We Love This Body.
When the Dumb Speak.
Winter Poem.
Woman Bewildered, The.
Words Rising.

Boethius (Anicius Manlius Severinus Boethius)
(480–524)
    Consolation of Philosophy, The ("De
      Consolacione Philosophie").

Bogan, Louise (1897–1970)
    Ad Castitatem.
    Alchemist, The.
    Animal, Vegetable and Mineral.
    At a Party.
    Baroque Comment.
    Betrothed.
    Cartography.
    Cassandra.
    Changed Woman, The.
    Chanson un Peu Naïve.
    Come, Break with Time.
    Come, Sleep.
    Crossed Apple, The.
    Crows, The.
    Cupola, The.
    Daemon, The.
    Dark Summer.
    Didactic Piece.
    Division.
    Dragonfly, The.
    Dream, The.
    Drum, The.
    Evening in the Sanitarium.
    Evening-Star.
    Exhortation.
    Feuer-Nacht.
    Fiend's Weather.
    Fifteenth Farewell.
    For a Marriage.
    Frightened Man, The.
    Girl's Song.
    Heard by a Girl.
    Henceforth, from the Mind.
    Homunculus.
    Hypocrite Swift.
    I Saw Eternity.
    If We Take All Gold.
    Italian Morning.
    Juan's Song.
    July Dawn.
    Kept.
    Knowledge.
    Last Hill in a Vista.
    Late.
    M., Singing.
    Man Alone.
    March Twilight.
    Mark, The.
    Medusa.
    Meeting, The.
    Memory.

    Men Loved Wholly Beyond Wisdom.
    Morning.
    Musician.
    My Voice Not Being Proud.
    Night.
    Old Countryside.
    Packet of Letters.
    Poem in Prose.
    Portrait.
    Putting to Sea.
    Question in a Field.
    Rhyme.
    Roman Fountain.
    Romantic, The.
    St. Christopher.
    Second Song.
    Several Voices Out of a Cloud.
    Short Summary.
    Simple Autumnal.
    Single Sonnet.
    Sleeping Fury, The.
    Solitary Observation Brought Back from a
      Sojourn in Hell.
    Song for a Lyre.
    Song for a Slight Voice.
    Song for the Last Act.
    Song: "It is not now I learn."
    Sonnet: "Dark, underground, is furnished with
      the bone."
    Sonnet: "Since you would claim the sources of
      my thought."
    Sorcerer's Daughter, The.
    Spirit's Song.
    Stanza: "No longer burn the hands that seized."
    Statue and Birds.
    Sub Contra.
    Summer Wish.
    Tale, A.
    Tears in Sleep.
    Three Songs.
    To an Artist, to Take Heart.
    To Be Sung on the Water.
    To My Brother: Killed: Hammont Wood:
      October, 1918.
    To Wine.
    Train Tune.
    Variation on a Sentence.
    Winter Swan.
    Women.
    Young Mage, The.
    Zone.

Boileau-Despéaux, Nicolas (1636–1711)
    Art of Poetry, The.

Borges, Jorge Luis (1899–1986)
    Accomplice, The.
    Adam Cast Forth.
    Adam Is Your Ashes.
    Adrogué.
    Afternoon, The.
    Alchemist, The.
    Alexander Selkirk.
    Alexandria, A.D. 641.
    Alhambra.
    Anticipation of Love.
    Ariosto and the Arabs.
    Ars Poetica.
    Baltasar Gracián.
    Baruch Spinoza.
    Benares.
    Beppo.
    Blade in the Northside, A.
    Blind Man, A.
    Boast of Quietness.
    Borges and I.
    Borges, The.
    Break of Day.
    Browning Resolves to Be a Poet.
    Bust of Janus Speaks, A.
    Cambridge.
    Camden, 1892.
    Causes, The.
    Chess.
    Christ on the Cross.
    Cloisters, The.
    Clouds ("High in the air these placid

mountains or").
Clouds ("There cannot be a single thing which is").
Compass.
Conjectural Poem.
Cyclical Night, The.
Dagger, The.
Deathwatch on the Southside.
Descartes.
Dream.
Dream of Pedro Henríquez Ureña, The.
Dream, The.
Dreamtigers.
1891.
Elegy for a Park.
Elegy: "Oh destiny of Borges."
Elegy: "Three very ancient faces stay with me."
Emanuel Swedenborg.
Embarking on the Study of Anglo-Saxon Grammer.
Emerson.
Empty Drawing Room.
Enigmas, The.
Epilogue: "Now that the number of steps you were given."
Everness.
Everness.
Everything and Nothing.
Ewigkeit.
Exile (1977), The.
Fame.
Flow of Memories, The.
For a Version of I Ching.
For Leopoldo Lugones.
Fragments from an Apocryphal Gospal.
General Quiroga Rides to His Death in a Carriage.
Gold of the Tigers, The.
Golem, The.
Guardian of the Books, The.
Gunnar Thorgilsson (1816-1879).
Happiness.
Hengist Wants Men (A.D. 449).
Herman Melville.
His End and His Beginning.
History of the Night.
Hourglass, The.
I.
I Am.
I Am Not Even Dust.
Iceland.
In Praise of Darkness.
Inferno 5, 129.
Inscription on Any Tomb.
Instant, The.
Invocation to Joyce.
Iron Coin, The.
James Joyce.
John I:14.
Jonathan Edwards.
June, 1968.
Just, The.
Labyrinth, The.
Leaves of the Cypress, The.
Limit, The.
Limits.
Lines That Could Have Been Written and Lost Round About 1922.
Luke 23.
Maker, The ("We are the river you spoke of, Heraclitus").
Maker, The ("He had never dwelled on the pleasures of memory").
Manuscript Found in a Book of Joseph Conrad.
Matthew 25:30.
Mexico.
Milonga of Albornoz.
Milonga of Don Nicanor Paredes.
Milonga of Manuel Flores.
Mirror, The.
Mirrors.
Moon, The ("The story goes that in those far off times").
Moon, The ("There is such loneliness in that gold").

Morning of 1649, A.
Museum.
Music Box.
My Last Tiger.
My Whole Life.
Mythical Founding of Buenos Aires, The.
New England, 1967.
Nightmare.
1971.
1972.
1964.
Northern Suburb.
Nostalgia for the Present.
Note for a Fantastic Story.
Ode Written in 1966.
Odyssey, Book Twenty-three.
Oedipus and the Enigma.
Of Heaven and Hell.
On Acquiring an Encyclopedia.
Other Tiger, The.
Page to Commemorate Colonel Suárez, Victor at Junín, A.
Palace, The.
Parable of Cervantes and Don Quixote.
Parable of the Palace.
Paradiso 31, 108.
Paris, 1856.
Parting.
Patio.
Poem of Quantity.
Poem of the Fourth Element.
Poem of the Gifts.
Poem Written in a Copy of Beowulf.
Poem: "You are asleep. I wake you."
Poet of the Thirteenth Century, A.
Ragnarök.
Rain.
Readers.
Recoleta Cemetary.
Remorse.
Remorse for Any Death.
Rose and Milton, A.
Rubaíyát.
Saturday, A.
Saxon (A.D. 449), A.
Sea, The.
Search, The.
Sepulchral Inscription.
Shinto.
Simplicity.
Soldier of Urbina, A.
Someone.
South, The.
Spinoza.
Stranger, The.
Street with a Pink Corner Store.
Streets, The.
Suicide, The.
Sunset over Villa Ortúzar.
Susana Bombal.
Talismans.
Tankas.
Texas.
That Man.
Things.
Things ("Fallen volume, hidden by the others, The").
Things That Might Have Been.
To a Cat.
To a Coin.
To a Minor Poet of 1899.
To a Minor Poet of the Greek Anthology.
To a Saxon Poet.
To a Sword at York Minster.
To Johannes Brahms.
To Manuel Mujica Lainez.
To My Father.
To One No Longer Young.
To the German Language.
To the Nightingale.
To the Son.
To Whoever is Reading Me.
Truco.
Two Cathedrals, The.
Two Forms of Insomnia.
Two Versions of "Knight, Death and the

Devil."
Unending Rose, The.
Unknown Street.
Waking Up.
Watcher, The.
Web, The.
Where Can They Have Gone?
Year's End.
Yellow Rose, A.
Yesterdays.
You Are Not the Others.

Bose, Buddhadeva
Dog, The.
Still Life.
To Memory.

Bourne, Vincent (1695–1747)
Ænigma, An.
Cantab, The.
Cause Won, The.
Cricket, The.
Denner's Old Woman.
Familiarity Dangerous.
Glow-worm, The.
Innocent Thief, The.
Invitation to the Redbreast.
Jackdaw, The.
Manual, A.
Maze, The.
No Sorrow Peculiar to the Sufferer.
Ode on the Death of a Lady.
On the Picture of a Sleeping Child.
Parrot, The.
Reciprocal Kindness the Primary Law of Nature.
Silk Worm, The.
Snail, The.
Sparrows Self-Domesticated.
Strada's Nightingale.
Tears of a Painter, The.
Thracian, The.

Bowdoin, James
Rebus, by I. B., A.

Boyd, Mark Alexander (1563–1601)
Cupid and Venus.

"Boyd, Nancy" See **Millay, Edna St. Vincent**

Bradstreet, Anne (c.1612–72)
Another.
As spring the winter doth succeed.
As Weary Pilgrim, Now at Rest.
Author to Her Book, The.
Before the Birth of One of Her Children.
Contemplations.
David's Lamentation for Saul and Jonathan.
Deliverance from a Fit of Fainting.
Dialogue between Old England and New, A.
Elegy Upon that Honorable and Reknowned Knight Sir Philip Sydney, An.
Epitaph on my Dear and Ever Honored Mother Mrs. Dorothy Dudley.
Flesh and the Spirit, The.
For Deliverance from a Fever.
For the Restoration of My Dear Husband from a Burning Ague.
Four Elements, The.
Four Seasons of the Year, The.
Four[e] Monarchies, The.
From Another Sore Fit.
Here Follows Some Verses upon the Burning of Our House [July 10th, 1666. Copied Out of a Loose Paper].
In Honor of Du Bartas, 1641.
In Honour of that High and Mighty Princess Queen Elizabeth of Happy Memory.
In Memory of My Dear Grandchild Anne Bradstreet Who Deceased June 20, 1669, Being Three Years and Seven Months Old.
In Memory of My Dear Grandchild Elizabeth Bradstreet Who Deceased August, 1665, Being a Year and Half Old.
In My Solitary Hours in My Dear Husband His Absence.
In Reference to Her Children, 23 June, 1659 [or 1659].
In Thankful Acknowledgement for the Letters I Received from My Husband Out Of

England.
In Thankful[l] Remembrance for My Dear
   Husband[']s Safe Arrival[l].
Letter to Her Husband, Absent upon Public[k]
   Employment, A.
My soul, rejoice thou in thy God.
My thankful heart with glorying tongue.
Occasional Meditations: "By night, when
   others soundly slept."
Of the Four Ages of Man.
Of the Four Humors in Man's Constitution.
On My Dear Grandchild Simon Bradstreet,
   [Who Died on 16TH November, 1669,
   Being But A Month And One Day Old].
On My Son's Return Out of England.
Prologue, The.
To Her Father, with Some Verses.
To Her Most Honored Father Thomas Dudley,
   Esquire, These Humbly Presented.
To My Dear and Loving Husband.
To the Memory of My Dear and Ever Honored
   Father Thomas Dudley Esq. Who Deceased
   July 31, 1653, and of His Age 77.
To the Memory of My Dear Daughter in Law,
   Mrs. Mercy Bradstreet.
Upon a Fit of Sickness, Anno 1632.
Upon My Daughter Hannah Wiggin her
   Recovery from a Dangerous Fever.
Upon My Dear and Loving Husband His
   Going into England.
Upon My Son Samuel His Going For England.
Upon Some Distemper of Body.
Vanity of All Worldly Things, The.
What God is like to him I serve?

Brecht, Bertolt (1898–1956)
Legend of the Dead Soldier, The.

Bremon, Peire
From Syria.

Bridges, Robert (1844–1930)
Incomplete Latin Version of "In all things
   beautiful" by Robert Bridges.

Brodsky, Joseph
Ab Ovo.
Admonition, An.
After Us.
Afterword.
Allenby Road.
Angel.
Anno Domini.
Anthem: "Praised be the climate."
Anti-Shenandoah: Two Skits and a Chorus.
At a Lecture.
At Carol Willink's Exhibition.
At the City Dump in Nantucket.
At the Helmet and Sword.
August Rain.
Autumn evening in the modest square, An.
Autumn in Norenskaia.
Axiom.
Belfast Tune.
Berlin Wall Tune, The.
Blues.
Bosnia Tune.
Brise Marine.
Bust of Tiberius, The.
Butterfly, The.
Cabbage and Carrot.
Café Trieste: San Francisco.
Cappadocia.
Centaurs 1.
Centaurs 2.
Centaurs 3.
Centaurs 4.
Classical ballet, let's say, is beauty's keep, The.
Clouds.
Constancy.
Daedalus in Sicily.
December in Florence.
December 24, 1971.
Dutch Mistress.
Eclogue 4: Winter.
Eclogue 5: Summer.
Elegy: "About a year has passed. I've returned
   to the place of battle."
Elegy: For Robert Lowell.
Elegy: "Sweetheart, losing your looks, go to

live in a village."
Elegy: "Whether you fished me bravely out of
   the Pacific."
End of a Beautiful Era, The.
Epitaph for a Centaur.
Ex Voto.
Exeter Revisited.
Fifth Anniversary, The.
Fin de Siècle.
Flourish.
Fly, The.
Folk Tune.
Footnote to Weather Forecasts, A.
Fossil Unwound.
Funeral of Bobò, The.
Funeral of Bobò, The.
Galatea Encore.
Gorbunov and Gorchakov.
Hawk's Cry in Autumn, The.
History of the Twentieth Century (A
   Roadshow).
Homage to Chekhov.
Homage to Girolamo Marcello.
Homage to Yalta.
I Sit by the Window.
In England.
In Front of Casa Marcello.
In Italy.
In Memoriam.
In Memory of Clifford Brown.
In the Lake District.
Infinitive.
Ischia in October.
Kellomäki.
Kolo.
Lagoon.
Letter to an Archaeologist.
Letters from the Ming Dynasty.
Letters to a Roman Friend.
Lines for the Winter Recess.
Lines on the Winter Campaign, 1980.
Lithuanian Divertissement.
Lithuanian Nocturne.
Love Song: "If you were drowning, I'd come
   to the rescue."
Lullaby: "Birth I gave you in a desert."
Lullaby of Cape Cod.
Martial Law Carol, A.
May 24, 1980.
Mexican Divertimento.
Minefield Revisited.
Nativity.
Nature Morte.
Near Alexandria.
New Jules Verne, The.
New Life.
MCMXCV.
MCMXCIV.
1972.
North Baltic.
North of Delphi.
Nunc Dimittis.
October Tune.
Ode to Concrete.
Odysseus to Telemachus.
On Love.
On the Death of Zhukov.
Once More by the Potomac.
Part of Speech, A.
Persian Arrow.
Photograph, A.
Plato Elaborated.
Polar Explorer, A.
Polonaise: A Variation.
Porta San Pancrazio.
Portrait of Tragedy.
Postcard, A.
Postcard from Lisbon.
Residence, The.
Reveille.
Rio Samba.
Robinsonade.
Roman Elegies.
Rustle of Acacias, The.
San Pietro.
Season, A.

Seaward.
Second Christmas by the shore, A.
Seven Strophes.
Shorts, *sels.*
Six Years Later.
So Forth.
Song, A: "I wish you were here, dear."
Song of Welcome.
Song to No Music, A.
Star of the Nativity.
Strophes: "Like a glass whose imprint."
Swiss Blue.
Tale, A.
Taps.
Thames at Chelsea, The.
To a Friend: In Memoriam.
To My Daughter.
To the President-elect.
To Urania.
Törnfallet.
Torso.
Transatlantic.
Tsushima Screen.
Twenty Sonnets to Mary Queen of Scots.
Variation in V.
Venetian Stanzas 1.
Venetian Stanzas 2.
Venice: Lido.
Vertumnus.
Via Funari.
View from the Hill.
View with a Flood.

Brontë, Emily Jane ("Ellis Bell") (1818–48)
A.G.A. to A.E.
A.G.A. to A.S
A.S. to G.S
Alcona, in its changing mood.
All day I've toiled, but not with pain.
All hushed and still within the house.
Alone I sat; the summer day.
And first an hour of mournful musing.
And like myself lone, wholly lone.
And now the house-dog stretched once more.
Anticipation.
At such a time, in such a spot.
Awaking morning laughs from heaven.
Away, away, resign me now.
Aye there it is! It wakes tonight.
Battle had passed from the height, The.
Blue bell is the sweetest flower, The.
But the hearts that once adored me.
Castle Wood.
Coldly, bleakly, drearily.
Come hither, child—who gifted thee.
Come, walk with me.
Companions, all day long we've stood.
D.G.C. to J.A.
Darkness was overtraced on every face.
Day Dream, A.
Death.
Death Of A.G.A., The.
Death Scene, A.
Deep, deep down in the silent grave.
Douglas's Ride.
E.G. to M.R.
E.W. to A.G.A.
Evening Sun, The.
F. de Samara to A. G. A.
Fair sinks the summer evening now.
Far, far away is mirth withdrawn.
Farewell To Alexandria, A.
From a Dungeon Wall in the Southern College.
From our evening fireside now.
Geraldine.
Gleneden's Dream.
God of Visions.
H.A. and A.S
Had there been falsehood in my breast.
Harp of wild and dream-like strain.
Heaven's glory shone where he was laid.
Here, with my knee upon thy stone.
'High waving heather.'
His land may burst the galling chain.
Hope.
How Clear She Shines!
How golden bright from earth and heaven.

How long will you remain? The midnight hour.
How loud the storm sounds round the Hall!
How still, how happy! These [or Those] are
    words.
I am the only being whose doom.
I gazed upon the cloudless moon.
I gazed within thine earnest eyes.
I know not how it falls on me.
I.M. to I.G.
I paused on the threshold, I turned to the sky.
I saw thee, child, one summer's day.
I see around me tombstones grey.
I would have touched the heavenly key.
 Iernë's eyes were glazed and dim.
If grief for grief can touch thee.
I'll come when thou art saddest.
I'm happiest when most away.
I'm standing in the forest now.
In dungeons dark I cannot sing.
Inspiring music's thrilling sound, The.
It is not pride, it is not shame.
It is too late to call thee now.
It was night, and on the mountains.
It will not shine again.
It's over now; I've known it all.
I've been wandering in the greenwoods.
Julian M. and A.G. Rochelle.
Lady, in your Palace Hall.
Lady to Her Guitar, The.
Lines by Claudia.
Lines: "Far away is the land of rest."
Lines: "I die; but when the grave shall press."
Lines: "Soft unclouded blue of air, The."
Little while, a little while, A.
Lonely at her window sitting.
Long Neglect Has Worn Away.
Loud without the wind was roaring.
Love and Friendship.
M.A. Written on the Dungeon Wall.
M. Douglas to E.R. Gleneden.
M.G. For The U.S
May flowers are opening.
Methinks this heart should rest awhile.
Mild the mist upon the hill.
Month after month, year after year.
Morning Star, The.
My Comforter.
Night of storms has passed, The.
Night was dark, yet winter breathed, The.
Night Wind, The.
No Coward Soul is Mine.
None but one beheld him dying.
None of my kindred now can tell.
Not a vapour had stained the breezeless blue.
Not many years but long enough to see.
Now trust a heart that trusts in you.
O come again; what chains withhold.
O come with me, thus ran the song.
O Dream, where art thou now?
O evening, why is thy light so sad?
O God of heaven! the dream of horror.
O hinder me by no delay.
O mother, I am not regretting.
O wander not so far away!
Old church tower and garden wall, The.
Old Hall of Elbë, ruined, lonely now.
Old Stoic, The.
On the Fall of Zalona.
Only some spires of bright green grass.
Organ swells, the trumpets sound, The.
Philosopher, The.
Prisoner, The.
Redbreast, Early in the morning.
Remembrance.
Rodric Lesley. 1830.
Rosina.
Self-Interrogation.
Shall Earth no more inspire thee.
She dried her tears, and they did smile.
Shed no tears o'er that tomb.
Sleep brings no joy to me.
Sleep Not, Dream Not.
Song.
Song By J. Brenzaida To G.S
Song by Julius Angora.
Song By Julius Brenzaida To G.S

Song: "King Julius left the south country."
Song: "Linnet in the rocky dells, The."
Song: "O between distress and pleasure."
Song to A.A.
Spellbound.
Stanzas: "I'll not weep that thou art going to
    leave me."
Stanzas: "Often rebuked, yet always back
    returning."
Stanzas to————.
Starry night shall tidings bring, The.
Stars.
Start not! upon the minister wall.
Still as she looked the iron clouds.
Still beside that dreary water.
Strong I stand, though I have borne.
Sudden chasm of ghastly light, A.
Sun Has Set, The.
Sympathy.
Tell me, tell me, smiling child.
That dreary lake, that midnight sky.
That wind, I used to hear it swelling.
There are two trees in a lonely field.
There let thy bleeding branch atone.
There shines the moon, at noon of night.
There swept adown that dreary glen.
There was a time when my cheek burned.
Thousand sounds of happiness, A.
Through the hours of yesternight.
'Tis evening now, the sun descends.
'Tis moonlight, summer moonlight.
To A.G.A.
To A.S., 1830.
To a Wreath of Snow.
To Imagination.
To the Bluebell.
'Twas one of those dark, cloudy days.
Two Children, The.
Two Children, The.
Upon her soothing breast.
Visionary, The.
Warning and Reply.
Was it with the fields of green.
Weaned from life and torn away.
What is that smoke that ever still.
What use is it to slumber here.
What winter floods, what showers of spring.
When days of Beauty deck the earth.
Where were ye all? and where wert thou?
Why ask to know the date—the clime?
Why ask to know what date, what clime?
Why do I hate that lone green dell?
Wide cathedral aisles are lone, The.
Will the day be bright or cloudy?
Wind, I hear it sighing, The.
Wind, sink to rest in the heather.
Wind was rough which tore, The.
Woe for the day; Regina's pride.
Woods, you need not frown on me.
Written in Aspin Castle.
Written in the Gaaldine Prison Caves to
    A.G.A.
Written on Returning to the P. of I. on the 10th
    of January, 1827.
Yes, holy be thy resting place.

Brooke, Henry (1703?–83)
Quilca House to the Dean.

Brooks, Gwendolyn (1917–2000)
Anniad, The.
Appendix to the Anniad.
Ballad of Rudolph Reed, The.
Bean Eaters, The.
Bronzeville Man with a Belt in the Back.
Bronzeville Mother Loiters in Mississippi, A.
    Meanwhile, a Mississippi Mother Burns
    Bacon.
Bronzeville Woman in a Red Hat.
Catch of Shy Fish, A.
Chicago *Defender* Sends a Man to Little Rock,
    The.
Crazy Woman, The.
Empty Woman, The.
Firstly Inclined to Take What It Is Told.
Flags.
Gay Chaps at the Bar.
God Works in a Mysterious Way.

In Emanuel's Nightmare: Another Coming of
    Christ.
In Honor of David Anderson Brooks, My
    Father.
Jessie Mitchell's Mother.
Langston Hughes.
Last Quatrain of the Ballad of Emmett Till,
    The.
Looking.
Love Note I: Surely.
Lovely Love, A.
Lovers of the Poor, The.
Man of the Middle Class, A.
Mentors.
Mrs. Small.
My Dreams, My Works Must Wait Till after
    Hell.
My Little 'Bout-Town Gal Has Gone.
"Negro" Hero.
Notes from the Childhood and the Girlhood.
Of Robert Frost.
Old Mary.
Penitent Considers Another Coming of Mary,
    A.
Piano after War.
Progress, The.
Riders to the Blood-Red Wrath.
Still Do I Keep My Look, My Identity . . . .
Street in Bronzeville, A.
"Strong Men, Riding Horses."
Sundays of Satin-Legs Smith, The.
Sunset of the City, A.
To Be in Love.
We Real Cool.
White Troops Had Their Orders but the
    Negroes Looked Like Men.
Womanhood, The.

Broumas, Olga (b. 1949)
Absence of Noise Presence of Sound.
After Lunch.
After *The Little Mariner*.
Amazon Twins.
Amberose Triste.
Aphrodite.
Artemis.
Attitude.
Aubade: "She wakes having flown."
Away from Water.
Backgammon.
Banner.
Beauty and the Beast.
Before the Elegy.
Betrothal / the Bride's Lament.
Between Two Seas.
Bitterness.
Black Holes, Black Stockings, *sels*.
Blockade.
Blues / for J.C.
Body.
Body and Soul.
Bride.
Buenos Días.
By Whose Hand.
Calypso.
Caritas.
Choir, The.
Cinderella.
Circe.
Contemplation, The.
Continuo, The.
Dactyls.
Days of Argument and Blossom.
Demeter.
Diagram of Abandoned Mosque.
Digestibles of Sun.
Easter.
Elegy: "Somebody left the world last night, I
    felt it."
Emblem.
Epithalamion: "Our mound of earth dug up."
Eros.
Etymology.
Evensong.
Eye of Heart.
Family.
Fast.

Field.
Five Interior Landscapes.
Flower Parry.
For Every Heart.
Foreigner.
Four Beginnings / for Kyra.
Grace.
Heart Believes with Blows.
Helen Groves.
Home Movies.
Host.
If I Yes.
Imaginary Sufi Garden.
Innocence.
Insomniac of a Zen-Garden Fruit.
Instruction.
Io.
Ithaca: Little Summer in Winter.
Jewel Lotus Harp.
Joinery.
Knife & the Bread, The.
Landscape with Angels.
Landscape with Driver.
Landscape with Leaves and Figure.
Landscape with Mantra.
Landscape with Next of Kin.
Landscape with Poets.
Landscape Without Touch.
Lark.
Leda and Her Swan.
Lenten.
Little Red Riding Hood.
Love Lines.
Lullaby: "I see you, centered."
Lumens.
Lying In.
Maenad.
Massacre, The.
Masseuse, The.
Memory Piece / for Baby Jane.
Mercy.
Mitosis.
Moon Conjunct Ace of Cups.
Moon of Mind Against the Wooden Louver,
    The.
Mornings Remembering Last Nights.
Mosaic.
Namaste.
Native.
Next to the *Café Chaos.*
No Harm Shall Come.
Ode: "Ask me no more."
Offertory.
On Earth.
Oregon Landscape with Lost Lover.
Out of Mind.
P.S.
Paper Flute.
Parity.
Pastoral Jazz.
Pealing, The.
Perennial.
Périsprit.
Photo Genic.
Photovoltaic.
Plunging into the Improbable.
Prayer with Martial Stance.
Rapunzel.
Roadside.
Rumpelstiltskin.
Sappho's Gymnasium.
Sea Change.
She Loves.
Sleeping Beauty.
Snow White.
Sometimes, as a Child.
Song / for Sanna.
Soothsaying.
Stars in Your Name.
Still Life.
Sugar.
Sweeping the Garden.
Thetis.
To Draw the Warmth of Flesh from Subtle
    Graphite.
Touched.

Triple Muse.
Tryst.
Vowel Imprint.
Walk on the Water.
Way a Child Might Believe, The.
With God.
Woman with Child.
Your Sacred Idiot with Me.

Brown, William Laird *See* **"Laird, William"**
Browning, Elizabeth Barrett (1806–61)
Adequacy.
Amy's Cruelty.
Apprehension, An.
August Voice, An.
Aurora Leigh.
Bereavement.
Bertha in the Lane.
Best Thing in the World, The.
Bianca Among the Nightingales.
Calls on the Heart.
Casa Guidi Windows.
Catarina to Camoens.
Change Upon Change.
Cheerfulness Taught by Reason.
Child Asleep, A.
Child's Grave at Florence, A.
Child's Thought of God, A.
Christmas Gifts.
Claim, The.
Comfort.
Confessions.
Consolation.
Court Lady, A.
Cowper's Grave.
Crowned and Buried.
Crowned and Wedded.
Cry of the Children, The.
Cry of the Human, The.
Dance, The.
De Profundis.
Dead Pan, The.
Dead Rose, A.
Denial, A.
Deserted Garden, The.
Died.
Discontent.
Drama of Exile, A.
Earth and Her Praisers.
Exaggeration.
Exile's Return, The.
False Step, A.
Felicia Hemans.
Finite and Infinite.
First News from Villafranca.
Flower in a Letter, A.
Flush or Faunus.
Forced Recruit, The.
Fourfold Aspect, The.
Futurity.
Garibaldi.
Grief.
Heaven and Earth.
Hector in the Garden.
Hiram Powers' "Greek Slave."
House of Clouds, The.
Hugh Stuart Boyd [His Blindness].
Hugh Stuart Boyd [His Death, 1848].
Hugh Stuart Boyd [Legacies].
Human Life's Mystery.
Insufficiency.
Irreparableness.
Island, An.
Isobel's Child.
Italy and the World.
King Victor Emanuel Entering Florence, April,
    1860.
King's Gift, The.
L.E.L.'s Last Question.
Lady Geraldine's Courtship.
Lady's "Yes," The.
Last Translation, The.
Lay of the Brown Rosary, The.
Lay of the Early Rose, A.
Lessons from the Gorse.
Life.
Life and Love.

Little Friend, The.
Little Mattie.
Look, The.
Lord Walter's Wife.
Lost Bower, The.
Love.
Loved Once.
Man and Nature.
Man's Requirements, A.
Marriage of Psyche and Cupid.
Mask, The.
May's Love.
Meaning of the Look, The.
Measure, The.
Mediator, The.
Memory and Hope.
Mercury Carries Psyche to Olympus.
Mother and Poet.
Mountaineer and Poet.
Mourning Mother, The.
Musical Instrument, A.
My Doves.
My Heart and I.
My Kate.
Napoleon III in Italy.
Nature's Remorses.
Night and the Merry Man.
Night and the Merry Man.
North and the South, The.
Ode to the Swallow.
On a Portrait of Wordsworth by B. R. Haydon.
Only a Curl.
Pain in Pleasure.
Parting Lovers.
Past and Future.
Patience Taught by Nature.
Perplexed Music.
Pet-Name, The.
Poet and the Bird, The.
Poet, The.
Poet's Vow, The.
Portrait, A.
Prisoner, The.
Proof and Disproof.
Prospect, The.
Psyche and Cerberus.
Psyche and Pan.
Psyche and Proserpine.
Psyche and Venus.
Psyche Gazing on Cupid.
Psyche Propitiating Ceres.
Psyche Wafted by Zephyrus.
Pyche and the Eagle.
Question and Answer.
Reed, A.
Rhapsody of Life's Progress, A.
Rhyme of the Duchess May.
Romance of the Ganges, A.
Romance of the Swan's Nest, The.
Romaunt of Margret, The.
Romaunt of the Page, The.
Runaway Slave at Pilgrim's Point, The.
Sabbath Morning at Sea, A.
Sea-Mew, The.
Sea-side walk, A.
Seraph and Poet, The.
Seraphim, The.
Since Without Thee We Do No Good.
Sleep, The.
Sleeping and Watching.
Song against Singing, A.
Song for the Ragged Schools of London, A.
Sonnets from the Portuguese.
Soul's Expression, The.
Soul's Travelling, The.
Sounds.
Stanzas: "I may sing; but minstrel's singing."
Student, The.
Substitution.
Summing Up in Italy.
Supplication for Love, A.
Sword of Castruccio Castracani, The.
Tale of Villafranca, A.
Tears.
That Day.
Thought for a Lonely Death-Bed, A.

To Bettine.
To Flush, My Dog.
To George Sand: A Desire.
To George Sand: A Recognition.
To Mary Russell Mitford.
Two Sayings, The.
Two Sketches.
Valediction, A: "God be with thee, my
    beloved,—God be with thee!."
Vanities.
Victoria's Tears.
View Across the Roman Campagna.
Virgin Mary to the Child Jesus, The.
Vision of Poets, A.
Void in Law.
Weakest Thing, The.
Weeping Saviour, The.
Where's Agnes?
Wine of Cyprus.
Wisdom Unapplied.
Woman's Shortcomings, A.
Work.
Work and Contemplation.
Year's Spinning, A.
Young Queen, The.

Browning, Robert (1812–89)
Abt Vogler.
Adam, Lilith, and Eve.
Aeschylus' Soliloquy.
After.
Amphibian.
Andrea del Sarto.
Another Way of Love.
Any Wife to Any Husband.
Apollo and the Fates.
Apparent Failure.
Appearances.
Arcades Ambo.
Aristophanes' Apology.
Artemis Prologizes.
At the "Mermaid."
Bad Dreams I.
Bad Dreams II.
Bad Dreams III.
Bad Dreams IV.
Balaustion's Adventure.
Bean-Feast, The.
Bean-Stripe: also, Apple-Eating, A.
Beatrice Signorini.
Before.
Ben Karshook's Wisdom.
Bifurcation.
Bishop Blougram's Apology.
Bishop Orders His Tomb at Saint Praxed's
    Church, The.
Blind man to the maiden said, The.
Boy and the Angel, The.
Burlesque for Palgrave on the Pronunciation of
    "Metamorphosis."
By the Fire-Side.
Caliban upon Setebos; or, Natural Theology in
    the Island.
Camel-Driver, A.
Cardinal and the Dog, The.
Cavalier Tunes.
Cenciaja.
Cherries.
Childe Roland to the Dark Tower Came.
Christmas-Eve.
Classicality Applied to Tea-Dealing: A Fancy
    Inspired by Westbourne Grove.
Cleon.
Clive.
Conclusion of a Compliment to the Captain.
Conclusion of a Sonnet on "Keely's
    Discovery."
Confessional, The.
Confessions.
Count Gismond.
Couplet for Furnivall on Two Publishers.
Cristina.
Cristina and Monaldeschi.
Dance of Death, The.
De Gustibus.
Deaf and Dumb.
Death in the Desert, A.

Delivery to the Secular Arm, The: A Scene
    During the Existence of the Spanish
    Inquisition at Antwerp, 1570.
Development.
Dialogue between Father and Daughter.
Dîs Aliter Visum; or, Le Byron de Nos Jours.
Doctor———.
Dogma Triumphant, The.
Donald.
Dubiety.
Eagle, The.
Earth's Immortalities.
Easter-Day.
Echetlos.
Englishman in Italy, The.
Epigram on School Days.
Epilogue: "At the midnight in the silence of
    the sleep-time."
Epilogue: "Oh, Love—no, Love! All the noise
    below, Love."
Epilogue: "On the first of the Feast of Feasts."
Epilogue: "Poets pour us wine, The."
Epistle Containing the Strange Medical
    Experience of Karshish, the Arab Physician,
    An.
Epps,
Eurydice to Orpheus.
Evelyn Hope.
Face, A.
Family, The.
Fears and Scruples.
Fifine at the Fair.
Filippo Baldinucci on the Privilege of Burial.
First-Born of Egypt, The.
Flight of the Duchess, The.
Flute-Music, with an Accompaniment.
Folkestone Limerick.
Forest Thought, A.
Forgiveness, A.
Founder of the Feast, The.
Fra Lippo Lippi.
Fust and His Friends.
Garden Fancies.
Gerousios Oinos.
Glove, The.
Gold Hair: A Story of Pornic.
Goldoni.
Good, to forgive.
Grammarian's Funeral, A.
Guardian-Angel, The.
Halbert and Hob.
Helen's Tower.
Herakles.
Heretic's Tragedy, The.
Hervé Riel.
Holy-Cross Day.
Home-Thoughts, from Abroad.
Home-Thoughts, from the Sea.
House.
Householder, The.
How It Strikes a Contemporary.
How They Brought the Good News from
    Ghent to Aix.
Humility.
Imperante Augusto Natus Est.
Impromptu Lines to Greet Marie Bancroft.
Impromptu on Hearing a Sermon by the Rev.
    T. R—Pronounced "Heavy."
Impromptu on Richard Wagner.
In a Balcony.
In a Gondola.
In a Year.
In Three Days.
Inapprehensiveness.
Incident of the French Camp.
Inn Album, The.
Inscription for a Sketch.
Instans Tyrannus.
Isle's Enchantress, The.
Italian in England, The.
Ivàn Ivànovitch.
Ixion.
James Lee's Wife.
Jochanan Hakkadosh.
Johannes Agricola in Meditation.
La Saisiaz.

Laboratory, The (Ancien Régime).
Lady and the Painter, The.
Last Poem.
Last Ride Together, The.
Life in a Love.
Light Woman, A.
Likeness, A.
Lines for a Gift.
Lines for a Painting by Leighton.
Lines for the Jubilee Window.
Lines for the Tomb of Levi Lincoln Thaxter.
Lines on Swinburne.
Lines to the Memory of James Dow.
Lost Leader, The.
Lost Mistress, The.
Love among the Ruins.
Love in a Life.
Lovers' Quarrel, A.
Magical Nature.
Martin Relph.
Mary Wollstonecraft and Fuseli.
Master Hugues of Saxe-Gotha.
May and Death.
Meeting at Night.
Melon-Seller, The.
Memorabilia
Mesmerism.
Mettle and Metal.
Mihrab Shah.
Misconceptions.
Mr Sludge, "The Medium."
"Moses" of Michael Angelo, The.
Muckle-Mouth Meg.
Muléykeh.
My Last Duchess.
My Star.
Names, The.
Nationality in Drinks.
Natural Magic.
Ned Bratts.
Never the Time and the Place.
Now.
Numpholeptos.
Of Pacchiarotto, and How He Worked in
    Distemper.
Oh Love, Love, thou that from the eyes
    diffusest.
Old Pictures in Florence.
On Benjamin Disraeli.
On Correggio.
On Ignaz Moscheles.
On Singers.
One Way of Love.
One Word More.
Pambo.
Pan and Luna.
Paracelsus.
Parting at Morning.
Patriot, The [An Old Story].
Pauline [or Pauline; A Fragment of a
    Confession].
Pearl, a Girl, A.
Pheidippides.
Pictor Ignotus.
Pied Piper of Hamelin, The.
Pietro of Abano.
Pillar at Sebzevar, A.
Pippa Passes.
Pisgah-Sights. I.
Pisgah-Sights. II.
Plot-Culture.
Poetics.
Ponte dell' Angelo, Venice.
Pope and the Net, The.
Popularity.
Porphyria's Lover.
Pretty Woman, A.
Prince Hohenstiel-Schwangau, Saviour of
    Society.
Prologue: "O the old wall here! How I could
    pass."
Prologue: "Poet's age is sad: for why?, The."
Prologue: "Pray, Reader, have you eaten
    ortolans."
Prospice.
Protus.

Rabbi Ben Ezra.
Rawdon Brown.
Red Cotton Night-Cap Country.
Reflections on Reading a Life of Dickens.
Rephan.
Replies to Challenges to Rhyme.
Respectability.
Response to a Translation by Longfellow.
Reverie.
Rhyme for a Child Viewing a Naked Venus in
   a Painting [of "The Judgement of Paris"].
Rhyme on Edward Burne-Jones.
Rhyming Exercises.
Rosny.
Round Robin, A.
Rudel to the Lady of Tripoli.
Saint Martin's Summer.
Saul.
Serenade at the Villa, A.
Shah Abbas.
She was fifteen—had great eyes.
Shop.
Sipping grog one day at sea.
Soliloquy of the Spanish Cloister.
Solomon and Balkis.
Song: "Nay but you, who do not love her."
Sonnet: "Eyes, calm beside thee, (Lady couldst
   thou know!)."
Sordello.
Speculative.
Spring Song.
Statue and the Bust, The.
Such a starved bank of moss.
Suggestion for a Telegraphic Birthday
   Greeting.
Summum Bonum.
Sun, The.
Terse Verse.
Through the Metidja to Abd-el-Kadr.
Thus I wrote in London, musing on my betters.
Time's Revenges.
To Edward FitzGerald.
To Miss Unger.
Toccata of Galuppi's, A.
Too Late.
Transcendentalism: A Poem in Twelve Books.
Transcriptions from the "Anacreontea."
Translation from Pindar's Seventh Olympian,
   Epode III.
Tray.
Twins, The.
Two Camels.
Two in the Campagna.
Two Poets of Croisic, The.
Up at a Villa—Down in the City.
Variation on Lines of Landor, A.
Very Original Poem, Written with Even a
   Greater Endeavour than Ordinary after
   Intelligibility, and Hitherto Only Published
   on the First Leaf of the Author's Son's
   Account-Book.
Wanting is—what?
Waring.
What a pretty tale you told me.
Which?
White Witchcraft.
Why I Am a Liberal.
With Bernard de Mandeville.
With Charles Avison.
With Christopher Smart.
With Daniel Bartoli.
With Francis Furini.
With George Bubb Dodington.
With Gerard de Lairesse.
Woman's Last Word, A.
Women and Roses.
Worst of It, The.
You are sick, that's sure—they say.
Youth and Art.

Buchanan, George (1506–82)
Pope from penance purgatorial, The.

Buchanan, George (1904–89)
Neaera when I'm there is adamant.
Rome conquered earth with arms, the sea with
   ships.

Bukowski, Charles (1920–94)
$$$$$$.
About Cranes.
About My Very Tortured Friend, Peter.
About Pain.
After the Reading.
Ah..
All I Know.
All the Casualties..
Almost Made Up Poem, An.
Alone with Everybody.
...American Express, Athens, Greece.
Another Bed.
Anthony.
Ants, The.
Art, An.
Artist.
Artists.
As Crazy As I Ever Was.
As I Lay Dying.
Ashes.
Ass But No Class.
Bad Action.
Beach Trip.
Beast, The.
Beauti-ful.
Beautiful Young Girl Walking Past the
   Graveyard—, The.
Bedpans.
Beds, Toilets, You and Me—.
Bee, The.
Beer.
Bee's 5th.
Beginning, A.
Best Way to Get Famous Is to Run Away, The.
Big Bastard with a Sword.
Big John of Echo Park.
Big Max.
Blackbirds Are Rough Today, The.
Blue Cheese and Chili Peppers.
Brave Bull.
Bravo.
Breakout.
Bring Down the Beams.
Buffalo Bill.
Change of Habit, A.
Chicago.
Chopin Bukowski.
Christmas Eve, Alone.
Clean Old Man.
Cockroach.
Cold Plums.
Communion.
Condition, The.
Conversation in a Cheap Room.
Conversation on Morality, Eternity and
   Copulation, A.
Counsel.
Countryside.
Coupons.
Cows in Art Class.
Crunch, The.
Dagwood and Blondie.
Dark Shades.
Darlings.
Day I Kicked Away a Bankroll, The.
Day the Epileptic Spoke, The.
Dead Now.
Dear Friend.
Dear Pa and Ma.
Death Wants More Death.
Defeat.
Destroying Beauty.
Dog.
Dogs.
Dogs of Egypt, The.
Dogs, The.
Don't Touch the Girls.
Doom and Siesta Time.
Dow Jones: Down.
Drill, The.
Eat.
Eat Your Heart Out.
Eaten by Butterflies.
Eating My Senior Citizen's Dinner at the
   Sizzler.

86'd.
Empire of Coins, An.
End of a Short Affair, The.
End, The.
Escape, The.
Eulogy to a Hell of a Dame—.
Everything.
Experience.
Face While Shaving.
Fall Out.
Famous Writer, The.
Farewell, Foolish Objects.
Farewell Thing While Breathing, A.
Fear.
56 Year Old Poem, A.
Fleg.
For Al—.
462-0614.
4:30 A.M.
Fragile!
Freedom: The Unmolested Eagle of Myself.
Friendly Advice to a Lot of Young Men.
Frozen Food Section.
Fuck.
Funny.
Genius of the Crowd, The.
Gentleman and the Bastard, The.
Gift, The.
Ginsberg?
Girl on the Bus Stop Bench, The.
Girls.
Girls at the Green Hotel, The.
Girls Coming Home.
Girls From Nowhere.
Girls in Pantyhose.
Gloomy Lady.
Gold Pocket Watch, A.
Goldfish.
Good Life, The.
Good Loser, The.
Good One, A.
Good Time Girl.
Goodbye.
Greek, The.
Green.
Guru.
Gypsies Near Del Mar, The.
Hangover and Sick Leave.
Hawley's Leaving Town.
Hello, Willie Shoemaker.
Here I Am.
Hey, Ezra, Listen to This.
High-Rise of the New World, The.
History of a Tough Motherfucker, The.
Hog.
Horse on Fire.
Horse With Greenblue Eyes, A.
Horsemeat.
How Come You're Not Unlisted?
How Do They Get Your Number?
How I Got Started.
How to Be a Great Writer.
Huge Ear Rings.
Hustle, The.
I Am Visited by an Editor and a Poet.
I Am with the Roots of Flowers.
I Cannot Stand Tears.
I Don't Need a Bedsheet with Slits for Eyes to
   Kill You In.
I Fall into It Without Trying.
I Have Lived in England.
I Have Shit Stains in My Underwear Too.
I Kneel.
I Made a Mistake.
I Wait in the White Rain.
I Was Born to Hustle Roses Down the Avenues
   of the Dead.
I Write This Upon the Last Drink's Hammer.
I'm Getting Back to Where I Was.
Imagination and Reality.
Imbecile Night.
In a Neighborhood of Murder.
Insane Always Loved Me, The.
Insomnia.
Interviewed by a Guggenheim Recipient.
Iron Mike.

Itch, Come and Gone.
It's Not Who Lived Here.
It's Nothing to Laugh About.
It's the Way You Play the Game.
I've Seen Too Many Glazed-Eyed Bums
    Sitting under a Bridge Drinking Cheap
    Wine.
Jack-Knife.
Japanese Wife, The.
John Dillinger Marches On.
Junkies.
Killer, A.
Kind of Lecture on a Dull Day When There
    Isn't Even a Fly Around to Kill, A.
Kings Are Gone, The.
Krutz.
Lady Poet, The.
Last Generation, The.
Layover.
Letter from the North.
Liberty.
Light Brown.
Like a Flower in the Rain.
Literary Life, The.
Little Girls, The.
Little Tigers Everywhere.
Longshot.
Look, The.
Loser, The.
Love.
Love Is a Dog from Hell.
Love Is a Piece of Paper Torn to Bits.
Love Poem, A.
Lovely Couple, A.
Luck.
Macho Man.
Madness.
Making It.
Man with the Hot Nose, The.
Me.
Meek Have Inherited, The.
Melancholia.
Mercy, Wherever You Are, Come Running in
    to Me and Grab Me in Your Good Arms—.
Mexican Girls, The.
Millionaire, The.
Minor Impulse to Complain, A.
Miracle is the Shortest Time, The.
Moaning and Groaning.
Monday Beach, Cold Day.
Most, The.
Mother and Son.
My Comrades.
My Friend.
My Groupie.
My Old Man.
Naked at 92 Degrees.
New Place, The.
Nice Place, A.
Nice Try.
Night I Fucked My Alarm Clock, The.
Night on a Visa Card.
Night They Took Whitey, The.
9 Rings.
99 to One.
Not All That Bad.
Not Quite So Soon.
Not To Worry.
Notations from a Muddled Indolence.
Note to the Boys in the Back Room, A.
Note Upon the Love Letters of Beethoven.
Nothing Subtle.
Now.
Now, If You Were Teaching Creative Writing,
    He Asked, What Would You Tell Them?
Numb Your Ass and Your Brain and Your
    Heart—.
O, We Are the Outcasts.
Object Lesson.
Oh, Yes.
Old Buddy, An.
Old Gang, The.
Old Man, Dead in a Room.
On a Night You Don't Sleep.
On and Off the Road.
On Being Recognized.

On Being 20.
On Going Back to the Street after Viewing an
    Art Show.
On Seeing an Old Civil War Painting with My
    Love.
On the Continent.
On the Failure of a Poet.
One for Old Snaggle-Tooth.
One for the Old Boy.
One for the Shoeshine Man.
One Hundred and Ninety-Nine Pounds of Clay
    Leaning Forward.
103 Degrees.
One Night Stand.
One of the Hottest.
One to the Breastplate.
Our Curious Position.
Out of the Blue.
Overhead Mirrors.
Pace is the Essence.
Pacific Telephone.
Pansies.
Parts of an Opera, Parts of a Guitar, Part of
    Nowhere.
Patriot of Life, A.
Photograph.
Place Didn't Look Bad, The.
Plate Glass Window, A.
Playing It Out.
Poem for Liz.
Poem for My 43rd Birthday.
Poem to a Most Affectionate Lady.
Practice ("I keep practicing death").
Practice ("Thinking more and more").
Prayer in Bad Weather.
Price, The.
Private First Class.
Problems About the Other Woman.
Professors, The.
Promenade.
Promise, The.
Puzzle, The.
Quiet Clean Girls in Gingham Dresses.
Rain or Shine.
Rat Rises, A.
Red Up and Down.
Regard Me.
Report Upon the Consumption of Myself, A.
Reprieve and Admixture.
Result.
Retreat, The.
Reunion.
Rose, Rose.
Sad-Eyed Mules of Men.
Sad Poem, A.
Sandra.
Sardines in Striped Dresses.
Saying Goodbye to Love.
Scarlet.
Seahorse.
2nd Novel, The.
Sex.
Sex and/or Love.
Sexpot.
She Came Out of the Bathroom With Her
    Flaming Red Hair and Said—.
She Said.
Shit Time.
Sickness, The.
Simplicity of Everything in Viet Nam, The.
Singing Is Fire.
Sitting in a Sandwich Joint.
6 A.M.
6 Foot Goddess, The.
60 Yard Pass.
Skaters, The.
Sky Sign.
Sleep.
Social.
Soirée.
Some of My Readers.
Some Picnic.
Somebody Always Breaking My Dainty
    Solitude..
Something.
Soul.

Space Creatures.
Spain Sits Like a Hidden Flower in My
    Coffeepot.
Sparks.
Spider, The.
Star, The.
Stethoscope Case, A.
Stolen.
Strange Moment, A.
Strangest Sight You Ever Did See—, The.
Suggestion for an Arrangement.
Suicide.
Sun Wields Mercy, The.
Sundays Kill More Men Than Bombs.
Swans Walk My Brain in April It Rains, The.
Sweater.
Sweaty Day in August, A.
Sweet Music.
Sword, The.
T.M.
Take It.
Talking to My Mailbox..
10 Lions and the End of the World.
Terminology.
Texan.
Thank God for Alleys.
There Once Was a Woman Who Put Her Head
    into an Oven.
Thermometer.
35 Seconds.
This.
This Poet.
This Then—.
3:30 A.M. Conversation.
Tonight.
Too Late.
Traffic Signals.
Training for Kid Aztec.
Transformation and Disfiguration.
Trapped.
Trapped.
Trench Warfare.
Trick to Dull Our Bleeding, A.
Troops, The.
Truce.
Trying to Get Even.
Turnabout.
12:18 A.M.
22,000 Dollars in 3 Months.
Twins.
225 Pounds.
2 Outside, As Bones Break in My Kitchen.
Unkind Poem, An.
Up Your Yellow River.
Upon First Reading the Immortal Literature of
    the World—.
Valentine Gift, A.
Very.
Walls, The.
Waving and Waving Goodbye.
We Will Taste the Islands and the Sea.
Weather Report.
What They Want.
What to Do with Contributor's Copies?
When I Think of Myself Dead.
When the Berry Bush Dies I'll Swim Down
    the Green River with My Hair on Fire.
Who in the Hell is Tom Jones?
Windy Night.
Winter.
Winter Comes to a Lot of Places in August.
With Vengeance Like a Tiger Crawls.
Word on the Quick and Modern Poem-Makers,
    A.
Worst and the Best, The.
Writing Is a State of Trance.
Wrong Number.
Yellow Cab.
You.
You Smoke a Cigarette.
Burns, Robert (1759–96)
Act Sederunt of the Session—A Scots Ballad.
Adam A———'s Prayer.
Address of Beelzebub.
Address to Edinburgh.
Address to General Dumourier.

Address to the Deil.
Address, to the Shade of Thomson, on Crowning His Bust, at *Ednam, Roxburgh-shire*, with Bays.
Address to the Tooth-Ache.
Address to the Unco Guid, or the Rigidly Righteous.
Address to the Woodlark.
Allan Water.
Altered from an Old English Song.
Amang the trees, where humming bees.
And I'll kiss thee yet, yet.
Anna.
Annotations in Verse.
Another [Epigram on Said Occasion].
Answer, The [To the Guidwife of Wauchope-House].
Answer to an Invitation.
Answer to the Foregoing—Extempore [Clarinda].
As I Cam[e] O'er [the] Cairney Mount.
As I was a wand'ring ae midsummer e'enin.
As I Went Out Ae May Morning.
At Brownhill Inn.
At Roslin Inn.
At Whigham's Inn, Sanquar.
Auld Farmer's New-Year-Morning Salutation to His Auld Mare, Maggie, on Giving Her the Accustomed Ripp of Corn to Hansel in the New-Year, The.
Auld Lang Syne.
Auld Man's Mare's Dead, The.
Auld Man's Winter Thought, The.
Auld Rob Morris.
Author's Earnest Cry and Prayer, to the Right Honorable and Honorable, the Scotch Representatives in the House of Commons, The.
Awa Whigs Awa.
Ballad, A: "There was a lass and she was fair."
Ballad, A: "While Prose-work and rhymes."
Banks o' Doon, The ("Ye banks and braes o' bonie [or bonnie] Doon").
Banks o' Doon, The ("Ye flowery banks o' bon[n]ie Doon").
Banks of Cree.
Banks of Nith, The.
Banks of the Devon, The.
Bannocks o' Bear-Meal.
Bard's Epitaph, A.
Battle of Sherra-Moor, The.
Bess[y] and Her Spinning-Wheel.
Beware o' Bonie Ann.
Birks of Aberfeldy, The [Composed on the Spot].
Birth-Day Ode. December 31st 1787, A.
Blue-Eyed Lassie, The.
Blythe Was She.
Bob o' Dumblane, The.
Bonie Bell.
Bonie Dundee.
Bonie Lad That's Far Awa, The.
Bonie Laddie, Highland Laddie.
Bonie Mary.
Bonnie Lesley.
Bonnie [or Bonny] Wee Thing, The.
Bonnie Peg.
Book-Worms, The.
Braes o' Ballochmyle, The.
Brigs of Ayr, a Poem. Inscribed to J. B*********, Esq; Ayr, The.
Broom Besoms ["I maun hae a wife, whatsoe'er she be"].
Broom Besoms ["Young and souple was I, when I lap the dyke"].
Brose and Butter.
Ca' the Ewes [or Yowes] [to the Knowes].
Ca' the Yowes [to the Knowes].
Caledonia.
Calf, The.
Campbells Are Comin, The.
Can Ye Labor Lea.
Can You Leave Me Thus, My Katy.
Captain's Lady, The.
Cardin o't, The.

Cares o' love are sweeter far, The.
Carl an the King Come.
Castle Gordon—*Intended to Be Sung to Morag*.
Cauld Frosty Morning.
Cauld Is the E'enin Blast.
Charlie He's My Darling.
Chloe.
Clarinda.
Cock up Your Beaver.
Comin[g] thro' [or through] the Rye.
Contented wi' Little.
Cotter's Saturday Night [nscribed to Robert Aiken [or R. A****], Esq.], The.
Country Lassie.
Craigieburn-Wood—A Song.
Dainty Davie.
Dean of Faculty—a New Ballad, The.
Death and Doctor Hornbook [A True Story].
Death and Dying Words of Poor Mailie, the Author's Only Pet Yowe, an Unco Mournfu' Tale, The.
Dedication to G**** H******* Esq, A.
De'il's [or Deil's] Awa wi' th' [or the] Exciseman, The.
Delia.
Despondency, an Ode.
Deuks Dang o'er My Daddie, The.
Down the Burn Davie.
Dream, A.
Dumfries Volunteers, The.
Dumfries Epigrams.
Duncan Davison.
Duncan Gray.
Duncan Gray ["Weary fa' you, Duncan Gray"].
Dusty Miller.
Elegy on Captain Matthew Henderson.
Elegy on Mister William Cruikshank A. M.
Elegy on Peg Nicholson.
Elegy on the Death of Robert Ruisseaux.
Elegy on the Year 1788.
English Song.
English Song.
Epigram on Capt. Francis Grose, the Celebrated Antiquary.
Epigram on Rough Roads.
Epigram on Said Occasion.
Epigram: "Whoe'er he be that sojourns here."
Epigrams on Lord Galloway.
Epistle to a Young Friend.
Epistle to Captn Willm Logan at Park.
Epistle to Davie, a Brother Poet.
Epistle to Hugh Parker.
Epistle to J. R******, Enclosing Some Poems.
Epistle to John Goldie in Kilmarnock, Author of, the Gospel Recovered.
Epistle to John Lapraik.
Epistle to Mr Tytler of Woodhouselee, Author of a Defence of Mary Queen of Scots.
Epistle to Robt. Graham Esq: of Fintry on the Election for the Dumfries String of Boroughs, Anno 1790.
Epitaph Extempore, on a Person Nicknamed the Marquis, Who Desired Burns to Write One on Him.
Epitaph for H——— L———, Esq., of L——.
Epitaph for J. H. Writer in Ayr.
Epitaph for William Nicol.
Epitaph. Here Lies Robert Fergusson, Poet.
Epitaph: "Lo worms enjoy the seat of bliss."
Epitaph on a Henpecked Country Squire.
Epitaph on a Schoolmaster.
Epitaph on a Wag in Mauchline.
Epitaph on D——— C———.
Epitaph on Holy Willie.
Epitaph on James Grieve, Laird of Boghead.
Epitaph on J-hn B-shby.
Epitaph on John Dove [Innkeeper, Mauchline].
Epitaph on Mr. Burton.
Epitaph on My Own Friend, and My Father's Friend, Wm Muir in Tarbolton Miln.
Epitaph on R. Muir.
Eppie McNab.
Extemporaneous Effusion on Being Appointed to the Excise, An.

Extempore.
Extempore Epistle to Mr. McAdam of Craigengillian, (Wrote in Nanse Tinnock's, Mauchline) in Answer to an Obliging Letter He Sent in the Commencement of My Poetic Career.
Extempore, in the Court of S———.
Extempore—On Being Shown a Beautiful County Seat Belonging to the Same [Maxwell of Cardoness].
Extempore—on Some Commemorations of Thomson.
Extempore [on the *Loyal Natives'* Verses].
Extempore Pinned to a Lady's Coach.
Extempore Reply to an Invitation.
Extempore—To Mr. Gavin Hamilton.
Extempore Verses on Dining with Lord Daer.
Fair Eliza.
Fair Jenny.
Farewell, The: "Farewell, old Scotia's bleak domains."
Farewell. To the Brethren of St. James' Lodge, Tarbolton, The.
Fête Champetre, The.
First Psalm, The.
First Six Verses of the Ninetieth Psalm, The.
Five Carlins—A Ballad—Tune, Chevy Chase, The.
Flow Gently, Sweet Afton.
For G. H. Esq.
For R. A. Esq.
For the Author's Father.
Fornicator. A New Song, The.
Frae the friends and Land I love.
Fragment, A: "One night as I did wander."
Fragment, A: "When first I came to Stewart Kyle."
Fragment, A: "When *Guilford* good our Pilot stood."
Fragment: "Altho' my bed were in yon muir."
Fragment—Epistle from Esopus to Maria.
Fragment: "Her flowing locks, the raven's wing."
Fragment: "Now health forsakes that angel face."
Fragment—on Glenriddel's Fox Breaking His Chain, A.
Fragment, Which Was Meant for the Beginning of an Elegy on the Late Miss Burnet of Monboddo, A.
Fragment: "Why, why tell thy lover."
Galla Water.
Gallant Weaver, The.
Galloway Tam.
Gardener wi' His Paddle—or, The Gardener's March, The.
German Lairdie, The.
Gie the Lass her Fairin'
Gloomy December.
Godly Girzie.
Grace after Meat.
Grace at Kirkudbright.
Grace before Dinner, Extempore, A.
Graces———at the Globe Tavern.
Green Grow the Rashes [A Fragment].
Green Grow[s] the Rashes.
Green Sleeves [and Tartan Ties].
Grim Grizzle.
Gude Wallace.
Gudeen to You Kimmer.
Guid Ale Keeps the Heart Aboon.
Had I the Wyte She Bade Me.
Halloween.
Henpeck'd Husband, The.
Here Awa' There Awa ["Here awa', there awa' wandering, Willie"].
Here's, a bottle and an honest friend.
Here's a Health to Ane I Lo'e Dear.
Here's a Health to Them That's Awa'
Here's His Health in Water.
Here's to Thy Health My Bonie Lass.
Heron Ballads, 1795, The, *sels*.
Hey Ca' thro'
Hey for a Lass wi' a Tocher.
Hey Tuti Tatey.
Highland Balou, The.

Highland Harry Back Again.
Highland Laddie.
Highland Lassie O.
Highland Mary.
Highland Widow's Lament, The.
Holy Fair, The.
Holy Tulzie, The.
Holy Willie's Prayer.
How lang and dreary is the night.
Hue and Cry of John Lewars, The.
Hughie Graham.
Humble Petition of Bruar Water to the Noble
    Duke of Athole, The.
Hunting Song.
I do confess thou art sae fair.
I dream'd I lay where flowers were springing.
I Hae a Wife o' My Ain.
I Look to the North.
I Love My Love in Secret.
I'll Ay[e] Ca' in by Yon Town.
Ill-fated Genius! Heaven-taught Fergusson.
I'll Mak You Be Fain to Follow Me.
I'm Owre [or O'er] Young to Marry Yet.
Impomptu, on Mrs. W. Riddell's Birthday, 4th
    Novr. 1793.
Inscription on a Goblet.
Interpolation.
Inventory, The.
It is na, Jean, thy bonie face.
It Was A' for Our Rightfu' King.
Jamie Come Try Me.
Jeremiah 15th Ch. 10 V.
Jessie—A New Scots Song.
Jockey Fou and Jenny Fain.
Jockey's Ta'en the Parting Kiss.
John Anderson, My Jo.
John Barleycorn [a Ballad].
John Come Kiss Me Now.
Johnie Blunt.
Johnie Cope.
Jolly Beggars, The.
Jolly Gauger, The.
Jumpin John.
Keekin' Glass, The.
Kellyburnbraes.
Ken ye ought o' Captain Grose?
Ken Ye What Meg o' the Mill Has Gotten.
Killiecrankie.
Kirk's Alarm, The.
Laddies by the banks o' Nith, The.
Lady Onlie.
Lament for James, Earl of Glencairn.
Lament. Occasioned by the Unfortunate Issue
    of a Friend's Amour, The.
Lament of Mary Queen of Scots on the
    Approach of Spring.
Lass of Ecclefechan, The.
Lass That Made the Bed for Me, The.
Lassie Lie near Me.
Lassie wi' the Lintwhite Locks.
Lazy Mist, The.
Lea-Rig, The.
Leezie Lindsay.
Let Me in This Ae Night.
Letter to J———s T———t, Gl—nc———r.
Libel Summons.
Lines Addressed to Mr. John Ranken.
Lines on Stirling.
Lines on the Author's Death.
Lines Sent to Sir John Whiteford, of
    Whiteford, Bart. with the Foregoing Poem.
Lines Written in the Kirk of Lamington.
Lines Written on a Bank-Note.
Lines *Written on a Window, at the King's Arms
    Tavern, Dumfries.*
Lines *Written on the Windows of the Globe
    Tavern, Dumfries.*
Lord Gregory.
Lord Ronald My Son.
Louis, What Reck I by Thee.
Lovely Davies.
Lovely Lass o' Inverness, The.
Lovely Polly Stewart.
Lover's Morning Salute to His Mistress, The.
Lying at a Reverend Friend's House One
    Night, the Author Left the Following *Verses*

in the Room Where He Slept.
Macpherson's Farewell.
Man Was Made to Mourn, a Dirge.
Mary Morison.
Mauchline Wedding, The.
Merry Hae I Been Teethin a Heckle.
Monody on Maria.
Mother's Lament for the Death of Her Son, A.
Muirland Meg.
Musing on the roaring ocean.
My Bonie Laddie's Young but He's Growin
    Yet.
My Collier Laddie.
My Eppie.
My Heart's in the Highlands.
My Lady's Gown There's Gairs upon't.
My Love She's But a Lassie Yet.
My Nannie's Awa'
My Peggy's Face.
My Tocher's the Jewel.
My Wife's a Wanton Wee Thing.
My Wife's a Winsome Wee Thing.
Nature's Law.
New Psalm for the Chapel of Kilmarnock, on
    the Thanksgiving-Day for His Majesty's
    Recovery, A.
Night was still, and o'er the hill, The.
Nine Inch Will Please a Lady.
Nithsdale's Welcome Hame.
Northern Lass, The.
O An Ye Were Dead Gudeman.
O Ay My Wife She Dang Me.
O Dear Minny What Shall I Do?
O, for Ane-and-Twenty Tam.
O ken ye what Meg o' the mill has gotten.
O Kenmure's on and awa, Willie.
O Lay Thy Loof in Mine Lass.
O leave novels, ye Mauchline belles.
O Mally's Meek, Mally's Sweet.
O May Thy Morn.
O [or Oh] Wert Thou in the Cauld Blast.
O raging Fortune's withering blast.
O Saw Ye My Maggie.
O Steer Her Up and Had Her Gaun.
O That I Had Ne'er Been Married.
O were I on Parnassus hill.
O Were My Love Yon Lilac[k] Fair.
Occasional Address, Spoken by Miss
    Fontenell, on Her Bnefit-Night, Decr. 4th.
    1793 —Written by Mr Burns
Ode [for General Washington's Birthday].
Ode, Sacred to the Memory of Mrs. ——— of
    ———.
Ode to Spring.
Ode to the Departed Regency-Bill—1789.
O'er the Water to Charlie.
Of A' the Airts [the Wind Can Blaw].
On a Bank of Flowers.
On a Celebrated Ruling Elder.
On a Dog of Lord Eglinton's.
On a Noisy Polemic.
On a Scotch Bard Gone to the West Indies.
On an Innkeeper in Tarbolton.
On Andrew Turner.
On Being Asked Why God Had Made Miss
    D——— So Little and Mrs A——— So
    Big.
On Captn. L———lles.
On Capt. W——— R-dd-ck of C-rb—ton.
On Chloris Requesting Me to Give Her a
    Spray of a Sloe-Thorn in Full Blossom.
On Commissary Goldie's Brains.
On Elphinston's Translation of Martial.
On Fergusson.
On Gabriel Richardson.
On Jessy Lewars.
On J-hn M-r-ne, Laird of L-gg-n.
On John McMurdo.
On Johnson's Opinion of Hampden.
On Marriage.
[On] Maxwell of Cardoness.
On Miss J. Scott, of Ayr.
On Mr. James Gracie.
On Mr. Pitt's [or Pit's] Hair-Powder Tax.
On Reading, in a Newspaper, the Death of J—
    —— McL———, Esq. Brother to a Young

Lady, a Particular Friend of the Author's.
On Robert Riddel.
On Scaring Some Waterfowl in Loch Turit, a
    Wild Scene among the Hills of Oughtertyre.
On Seeing a Wounded Hare Limp by Me,
    Which a Fellow Had Just Shot At.
On Seeing Miss Fontenelle in a Favourite
    Character.
On Seeing Mrs. Kemble in Yarico.
On the Birth of a Posthumous Child, Born in
    Peculiar Circumstances of Family Distress.
On the Death of Echo, a Lap-Dog.
On the Death of Sir J. Hunter Blair.
On the Death of the Late Lord President
    Dundas.
On the Duchess of Gordon's Reel Dancing.
On the Late Captain Grose's Peregrinations
    thro' Scotland, Collecting the Antiquities of
    That King.
On the Seas and Far Away.
On W. R———, Esq.
On Wee Johnie.
On William Graham [or W——— Gr-h-m],
    Esq., of Mossknowe [or M-sskn-w].
On Willie Chalmers.
Open the Door to Me, Oh!
Orananaoig, or, the Song of Death.
Ordination, The.
Parson's Looks, The.
Passion's Cry.
Patriarch, The.
Penitential Thought, in the Hour of Remorse—
    Intended for a Tragedy, A.
Phillis the Fair.
Ploughman, The.
Poem: "Friend o' the Poet, tired and leal."
Poem on Life.
Poetical Inscription, for an Altar to
    Independence at Kerrouchtry, the Seat of Mr.
    Heron, Written in Summer 1795.
Poet's Welcome to His Love-Begotten
    Daughter [the First Instance that Entitled
    Him to the Venerable Appellation of Father],
    A.
Poor Mailie's Elegy.
Posie, The.
Postscript [To W. S*****n, Ochiltree].
Prayer, in the Prospect of Death, A.
Prayer, under the Pressure of Violent Anguish,
    A.
Primrose, The.
Prologue: "No song nor dance I bring from
    yon great city."
Prologue: "When by a generous Public's kind
    acclaim."
Rantin' Dog, the Daddie o't, The.
Rantin Laddie, The.
Rantin, Rovin Robin.
Rattlin, Roarin Willie.
Raving winds around her blowing.
Red, Red Rose, A.
Reel o' Stumpie, The.
Remorse.
Reply to Robert Riddell.
Revision for Clarinda.
Rights of Woman—Spoken by Miss Fontenelle
    on Her Benefit Night, The.
Rigs o' Barley, The.
Robert Burns' Answer [to Epistle from a
    Taylor].
Robin Shure in Hairst.
Ronalds of the Bennals, The.
Rosebud, The.
Rowin 't in Her Apron, The.
Rusticity's ungainly form.
Sae Far Awa.
Sandy and Jockie.
Saw Ye My Phely (Quasi Dicat, Phillis).
Scotch Drink.
Scotch Song.
Scotish Ballad.
Scotish Song.
Scotish Song.
Scots Ballad.
Scots Prologue, *For Mrs. Sutherland's Benefit
    Night*, Spoken at the Theatre Dumfries.

Scots Wha Hae.
Scroggam.
Second Epistle to Davie.
Second Epistle to John Lapraik.
Seventh of November, The.
She Says She Lo'es Me Best of A'
Shepherd's Wife, The.
She's fair and fause that causes my smart.
Sic a Wife as Willie Had.
Silver Tassie, The.
Simmer's a Pleasant Time.
Sketch.
Sketch for an Elegy.
Sketch. Inscribed to the Rt. Hon. Ch. J. Fox Esq.
Sketch. New Year's Day. To Mrs. Dunlop.
Slave's Lament, The.
Solemn League and Covenant, The.
Somebody.
Song: "Adown winding Nith I did wander."
Song: "Again rejoicing Nature sees."
Song: "Anna, thy charms my bosom fire."
Song: "As I cam down by yon castle wa'."
Song: "As I stood by yon roofless tower."
Song: "Behind yon hills where Lugar flows."
Song: "Behold the hour, the boat arrive."
Song: "Blythe hae I been on yon hill."
Song, Composed in August.
Song: "Farewell, thou stream that winding flows."
Song: "From thee, ELIZA, I must go."
Song: "Full well thou knowest I love thee dear."
Song: "Gloomy night is gath'ring fast, The."
Song: "Had I a cave on some wild, distant shore."
Song: "I'll tell you a tale of a Wife."
Song: "In Mauchline there dwells six proper young Belles."
Song.—In the Character of a Ruined Farmer.
Song: "Let not Woman e'er complain."
Song: "Mark yonder pomp of costly fashion."
Song: "My father was a farmer upon the Carrick border O."
Song: "My girl she's airy, she's buxom and gay."
Song: "No Churchman am I for to rail and to write."
Song: "O, Logan, sweetly didst thou glide."
Song: "O once I loved [or lov'd] a bonnie lass."
Song: "O Philly, happy be that day."
Song: "O poortith cauld, and restless love."
Song: "O this is no my ain lassie."
Song: "O wat ye wha that lo'es me."
Song: "O wat ye wha's in yon town."
Song: "On Cessnock banks a lassie dwells."
Song—(On Chloris Being Ill).
Song. On Miss P——— K———, A.
Song. On Miss W. A.
Song: "Sensibility how charming."
Song: "Small birds rejoice in the green leaves returning, The."
Song: "Their groves o' sweet myrtle let Foreign Lands reckon."
Song: "Tho' women's minds, like winter winds."
Song: "Tibby I hae seen the day."
Song: "'Twas na her bonie blue e'e was my ruin."
Song: "Will ye go to the Indies, my Mary."
Sonnet—On Hearing a Thrush Sing on a Morning Walk in January.
Sonnet on the Death of Robert Riddel, Esq. of Glen Riddel, April 1794.
Sonnet upon Sonnets, A.
Sons of Old Killie, The.
Stanzas on the Same Occasion [in the Prospect of Death].
Stay, my Charmer, can you leave me.
Strathallan's Lament.
Such a Parcel of Rogues in a Nation.
Sutors o' Selkirk.
Sweet fa's the eve on Craigieburn.
Sweetest May.
Tale, A.

Tam Glen.
Tam o' Shanter; A Tale.
Tam Samson's Elegy.
Tam the Chapman.
Tarbolton Lasses, The.
Taylor fell thro' the bed, thimble an' a', The.
Taylor, The.
Then Guidwife Count the Lawin.
Theniel Menzies' Bony Mary.
There Grows a Bonie Brier-Bush.
There Was a Bonie Lass.
There was twa wives, and twa witty wives.
There'll Never Be Peace Till Jamie Comes Hame.
There's a youth in this city, it were a great pity.
There's News Lasses News.
Thine am I, my Chloris fair.
Third Epistle to J. Lapraik.
Thou hast left me ever, Jamie.
Thou Ling'ring Star.
Though fickle fortune has deceiv'd me.
Three Gude Fellows Ayont Yon Glen.
Tibbie Dunbar.
Tibbie Fowler.
To a Gentleman Who Had Sent Him a News-Paper, and Offered to Continue It Free of Expense.
To a Haggis.
To a Lady.
To a Louse [On Seeing One on a Lady's Bonnet at Church].
To a Mountain Daisy [On Turning One Down, with the Plough, in April—1786].
To a Mouse; On Turning Her up in Her Nest, with the Plough, November, 1785.
To a Young Lady, *Miss Jessy L———, Dumfries; with Books which the Bard Presented Her.*
To Alexander Cunningham.
To Alexander Findlater.
To an Artist.
To Captain G———, on Being Asked Why I Was Not to Be of the Party with Him and His Brother K-nm-re at Syme's.
To Captain Riddell.
To Chloris.
To Chloris.
To Clarinda.
To Daunton Me.
To Dr. Blacklock.
To Dr. John MacKenzie.
To Dr Maxwell, on Miss Jessy Staig's Recovery.
To James Smith.
To John Kennedy.
To John Syme.
To John Taylor.
To Maria.
To Miss C*********, a Very Young Lady.
To Miss Ferrier.
To Miss Graham of Fintray.
To Miss Isabella Macleod.
To Miₛₛ L———.
To Mr Gavin Hamilton, Mauchline.
To Mr. Graham of Fintry, On Being Appointed to My Excise Division.
To Mr. John Kennedy.
To Mr. McMurdo, with a Pound of Lundiefoot Snuff.
To Mr. S. McKenzie.
To Mrs. C———.
To Peter Stuart.
To Renton of Lamerton.
To R***** G***** of F*****, Esq.
To Robt. Graham of Fintry Esqr, with a Request for an Excise Division.
To Ruin.
To Symon Gray.
To Terraughty, on His Birth-Day.
To the Beautiful Miss Eliza J———n, on Her Principles of Liberty and Equality.
To the Honble Mr. R. M———, of P-nm-re, on His High Phaeton.
To the Memory of the Unfortunate Miss Burns 1791.

To the Rev. John McMath, Inclosing a Copy of *Holy Willie's Prayer*, Which He Had Requested.
To the Weaver's Gin Ye Go.
To William Creech.
To William Simpson, Ochiltree.
To William Stewart.
Toadeater, The.
Toast, A.
Tree of Liberty, The.
Trogger, The.
Twa Dogs, The.
Up and Warn A' Willie.
Up in the Morning Early.
Verse Composed and Repeated by *Burns*, to the Master of the House, on Taking Leave at a Place in the Highlands, Where He Had Been Hospitably Entertained, A.
Verses: "I am a keeper of the law."
Verses Intended to Be Written below a Noble Earl's Picture.
Verses Written on a Window of the Inn at Carron.
Versicles on Sign-Posts.
Vision, The.
Wae Is My Heart.
Waukrife Minnie, A.
Weary Pund o' Tow, The.
Wee Willie Gray.
We'll Hide the Couper behint the Door.
Wha Is That at My Bower-Door?
Wha'll M-w Me Now.
What can a young lassie, what shall a young lassie.
What Will I Do Gin My Hoggie Die.
When She Cam Ben She Bobbed.
When wild War's deadly blast was blawn.
Where braving angry Winter's storms.
Where Helen Lies.
Whistle. A Ballad, The.
Whistle, and I'll Come to You, My Lad.
Whistle o'er the Lave o't.
White Cockade, The.
Why Should Na Poor Folk Mowe.
Willie Brew'd [*or* Brewed] a Peck o' Maut.
Wilt thou be my Dearie.
Winter, a Dirge.
Winter It Is Past, The.
Winter Night, A.
Wren's Nest, The.
Written in Friar's Carse Hermitage on the Banks of Nith—June—1788.
Written under the Picture of the Celebrated Miss Burns.
Written with a Pencil over the Chimney-Piece, in the Parlour of the Inn at Kenmore, Taymouth.
Written with a Pencil, Standing by the Fall of Fyers, near Loch-Ness.
Wrote on the Blank Leaf of a Copy of My First Edition, Which I Sent to an Old Sweetheart, Then Married.
Ye Jacobites By Name.
Yon wild, mossy mountains sae lofty and wide.
Young Highland Rover, The.
Young Jockey was the blythest lad.
You're Welcome, Willie Stewart.

Byron, George Gordon Noel Byron, 6th Baron (1788–1824)
Address.
Address Intended to be Recited at the Caledonian Meeting.
Adieu, The.
Age of Bronze, The.
'All Is Vanity, Saith the Preacher.'
And Dost Thou Ask the Reason of My Sadness?
And Thou Art Dead, as Young and Fair.
And Wilt Thou Weep When I Am Low?
Another Simple Ballat.
Answer to a Beautiful Poem, Entitled "The Common Lot."
Answer to ———'s Professions of Affection.
Answer to Some Elegant Verses.
Answer to the Foregoing, Addressed to Miss———.

Aristomenes.

As the Liberty Lads o'er the Sea.

Away, Away, Ye Notes of Woe!

Ballad: "Of all the twice ten thousand bards."

Beppo; a Venetian Story.

Blues, The.

Bowles and Campbell.

Brave Champions! Go On with the Farce.

Braziers, It Seems, Are Preparing to Pass, The.

Bride of Abydos, The.

Bright Be the Place of Thy Soul!

By the Rivers of Babylon We Sat Down and Wept.

Cain: A Mystery.

Chain I Gave, The.

Childe Harold's Pilgrimage.

Childish Recollections.

Churchill's Grave.

Condolatory Address.

Conquest, The.

Cornelian, The.

Corsair, The.

Curse of Minerva, The.

Damaetas.

Darkness.

Dear Doctor, I Have Read Your Play.

Deformed Transformed, The.

Destruction of Sennacherib, The.

Devil's Drive, The.

Don Juan.

Dream, The.

Duel, The.

E Nihilo Nihil.

Egotism. A Letter to J.T. Becher.

Elegiac Stanzas on the Death of Sir Peter Parker, Bart.

Elegy: "Behold the blessings of a lucky lot!."

Elegy on Newstead Abbey.

Endorsement to the Deed of Separation, in the April of 1816.

English Bards and Scotch Reviewers.

Epigram on an Old Lady Who Had Some Curious Notions Respecting the Soul.

Epigrams: "Oh, Castlereagh! thou art a patriot now."

Epilogue: "There's something in a stupid ass."

Episode of Nisus and Euryalus, The.

Epistle to a Friend.

Epistle to Augusta.

Epitaph for Joseph Blacket.

Epitaph on a Friend.

Epitaph on John Adams, of Southwell.

Euthanasia.

Fare Thee Well.

Farewell! If Ever Fondest Prayer.

Farewell Petition to J.C.H., Esq.

Farewell to Malta.

Farewell to the Muse.

Fill the Goblet.

First Kiss of Love, The.

For Orford and for Waldegrave.

Fragment, A: "Could I remount the river of my years."

Fragment, A: "When, to their airy hall, my fathers' voice."

Fragment from the "Monk of Athos."

Fragment of an Epistle to Thomas Moore.

Fragment Written Shortly after the Marriage of Miss Chaworth.

From Anacreon.

From Anacreon.

From the French.

From the French.

From the Prometheus Vinctus of Aeschylus.

Giaour, The.

Girl of Cadiz, The.

God Maddens Him Whom 'T Is His Will to Lose.

Good Plays Are Scarce.

Granta—A Medley.

Harp the Monarch Minstrel Swept, The.

Heaven and Earth.

Here's a Happy New Year! But with Reason.

Here's to Her Who Long.

Herod's Lament for Mariamne.

Hints from Horace.

I Read the "Christabel."

I Saw Thee Weep.

I Would I Were a Careless Child.

Ich Dien.

If for Silver, or for Gold.

If Sometimes in the Haunts of Men.

If That High World.

Imitation of Tibullus.

Impromptu.

Impromptu, in Reply to a Friend.

In the Valley of Waters.

Inscription on the Monument of a Newfoundland Dog.

Irish Avatar, The.

Island, The.

Jephtha's Daughter.

Journal in Cephalonia.

Julian [A Fragment].

La Revanche.

Lachin y Gair.

Lament of Tasso, The.

L'Amitié Est L'Amour Sans Ailes.

Lara.

Last Words on Greece.

Lines Addressed to a Young Lady.

Lines: "Dear Becher, you tell me to mix with mankind."

Lines Inscribed upon a Cup Formed from a Skull.

Lines on Hearing That Lady Byron Was Ill.

Lines to a Lady Weeping.

Lines to Mr Hodgson.

Lines Written beneath a Picture.

Lines Written beneath an Elm in the Churchyard of Harrow.

Lines Written in an Album, at Malta.

Lines Written in the Travellers' Book at Orchomenus.

Lines Written on a Blank Leaf of the "Pleasures of Memory."

Love and Death.

Love and Gold.

Love's Last Adieu.

Lucietta. A Fragment.

Maid of Athens, Ere We Part.

Manfred.

Marino Faliero, Doge of Venice.

Martial, Lib. I. Epig. I.

Mazeppa.

Monody on the Death of the Right Hon. R. B. Sheridan.

My Dear Mr. Murray.

My Soul Is Dark.

Napoleon's Farewell.

Napoleon's Snuff-Box.

New Song to the Tune of "Whare Hae Ye Been a' Day, My Boy Tammy O? Courting O' a Young Thing, Just Come Frae Her Mammie O?"

New Vicar of Bray, The.

Newstead Abbey.

No Infant Sotheby, Whose Dauntless Head.

Occasional Prologue Delivered Previous to the Performance of "The Wheel of Fortune" at a Private Theatre, An.

Ode from the French.

Ode on Venice.

Ode to a Lady Whose Lover Was Killed by a Ball, Which at the Same Time Shivered a Portrait next His Heart.

Ode to Napoleon Buonaparte.

Ode to the Framers of the Frame Bill, An.

Oh factious viper! whose envenom'd tooth.

Oh How I Wish That an Embargo.

Oh! Snatch'd Away in Beauty's Bloom.

Oh! Weep for Those.

Oh You, Who in All Names Can Tickle the Town.

On a Change of Masters at a Great Public School.

On a Cornelian Heart Which Was Broken.

On a Distant View of the Village and School of Harrow on the Hill.

On a Royal Visit to the Vaults.

On Being Asked What Was the "Origin of Love."

On Finding a Fan.

On Jordan's Banks.

On Leaving Newstead Abbey.

On My Thirty-third Birthday.

On Parting.

On Revisiting Harrow.

On Sam Rogers.

On the Birth of John William Rizzo Hoppner.

On the Bust of Helen by Canova.

On the Day of the Destruction of Jerusalem by Titus.

On the Death of a Young Lady.

On the Eyes of Miss A——— H———.

On the Quotation "And My True Faith Can Alter Never, Though Thou Art Gone Perhaps Forever."

On the Star of "The Legion of Honour."

On This Day I Complete My Thirty-sixth Year.

Once Fairly Set Out on His Party of Pleasure.

One Struggle More, and I Am Free.

Oscar of Alva.

Ossian's Address to the Sun in "Carthon."

Parenthetical Address.

Parisina.

Pignus Amoris.

Prayer of Nature, The.

Prisoner of Chillon, The.

Prometheus.

Prophecy of Dante, The.

Queries to Casuists.

R. C. Dallas.

Remember Him Whom Passion's Power.

Remember Thee! Remember Thee!

Remembrance.

Remind Me Not, Remind Me Not.

Reply to Some Verses of J.M.B. Pigot, Esq., on the Cruelty of His Mistress.

Sardanapalus.

Saul.

She Walks In Beauty.

Siege of Corinth, The.

Sketch from Private Life, A.

So We'll Go No More A-Roving.

Soliloquy of a Bard in the Country.

Song: "Breeze of the night in gentler sighs."

Song of Saul before His Last Battle.

Song to the Suliotes.

Sonnet on the Nuptials of the Marquis Antonio Cavalli with the Countess Clelia Rasponi of Ravenna.

Sonnet, to Genevra.

Sonnet to Lake Leman.

Sonnet to the Prince Regent.

Sonnet, to the Same.

Spell Is Broke, the Charm is Flown, The.

Spirit Pass'd Before Me, A.

Stanzas: "Chill and mirk is the nightly blast."

Stanzas: "Could Love for ever."

Stanzas for Music.

Stanzas for Music.

Stanzas for Music.

Stanzas for Music.

Stanzas: "I heard thy fate without a tear."

Stanzas: "Oh!—my lonely—lonely—lonely Pillow!."

Stanzas: "Through cloudless skies, in silvery sheen."

Stanzas to a Lady on Leaving England.

Stanzas to a Lady, with the Poems of Camoëns.

Stanzas to Augusta.

Stanzas to Augusta.

Stanzas to Jessy.

Stanzas to the Po.

Stanzas Written on the Road between Florence and Pisa.

Substitute for an Epitaph.

Sun of the Sleepless!

Tear, The.

There Was a Time, I Need Not Name.

Thou Art Not False, But Thou Art Fickle.

Thoughts for a Speech of Lucifer, in the Tragedy of "Cain."

Thoughts Suggested by a College Examination.

Thy Days Are Done.

To a Beautiful Quaker.

To a Knot of Ungenerous Critics.
To a Lady ("This band which bound thy yellow hair").
To a Lady ("Oh! had my fate been joined with thine").
To a Lady ("When man, expell'd from Eden's bowers").
To a Lady Who Presented to the Author a Lock of Hair Braided with His Own, and Appointed a Night in December to Meet Him in the Garden.
To a Vain Lady.
To a Youthful Friend.
To an Oak at Newstead.
To Anne.
To Belshazzar.
To ———: "But once I dared to lift my eyes."
To Caroline ("Thinkst thou I saw thy beauteous eyes").
To Caroline ("You say you love, and yet your eye").
To Caroline ("When I hear you express an effection so warm").
To Caroline ("Oh when shall the grave hide for ever my sorrow?").
To D———.
To Dives (William Beckford). A Fragment.
To E———.
To Edward Noel Long, Esq.
To Eliza.
To Emma.
To Florence.
To George, Earl Delawarr.
To Harriet.
To Hook the Reader, You, John Murray.
To Lesbia.
To Lord Thurlow.
To M———.
To M.S.G.
To M.S.G.
To Marion.
To Mary on Receiving Her Picture.
To Mr. Murray.
To My Son.
To ———: "Oh! well I know your subtle Sex."
To Romance.
To the Author of a Sonnet Beginning " 'Sad Is My Verse,' You Say, 'And Yet No Tear'."
To the Countess of Blessington.
To the Duke of Dorset.
To the Earl of Clare.
To the Hon. Mrs. George Lamb.
To the Same.
To the Sighing Strephon.
To Thomas Moore.
To Thyrza.
To Time.
To Woman.
Translation from Anacreon.
Translation from Horace.
Translation from the Medea of Euripides.
Translation of the Epitaph on Virgil and Tibullus.
Translation of the Famoue Greek War Song *Deute Paides Tov Ellenon.*
Translation of the Romaic Song *Mpeno mes to periboli, Horaiotate Haide, k. t. l.*
Two Foscari, The.
Venice.
Verses Found in a Summer-House at Hales-Owen.
Version of Ossian's Address to the Sun, A.
Very Mournful Ballad, A.
Vision of Belshazzar, The.
Vision of Judgment, The.
Waltz, The.
Well! Thou Art Happy.
Were My Bosom As False As Thou Deem'st It to Be.
Werner; or, The Inheritance.
What Matter the Pangs of a Husband and Father.
What News, What News? Queen Orraca.
When Coldness Wraps This Suffering Clay.
When I Roved a Young Highlander.

When Thurlow This Damn'd Nonsense Sent.
When We Two Parted.
Who Kill'd John Keats?
Wild Gazelle, The.
Windsor Poetics.
World Is a Bundle of Hay, The.
Would You Go to the House by the True Gate.
Written After Swimming from Sestos to Abydos.
Written in "Letters to an Italian Nun and an English Gentleman: by J.J. Rousseau: Founded on Facts."
You Ask for a "Volume of Nonsense."
Youth, Nature, and Relenting Jove.

C

Calas, Nicolas
Agony Among the Crowd, The.
Narcissus in the Desert.
To Regain the Day Again.
Wrested from Mirrors.
Calderón de la Barca, Pedro (1600–81)
Cisma de Inglaterra, *sels.*
Magico Prodigioso, *sels.*
Callimachus (c.300–240 B.C.)
By Callimachus.
On Pallas Bathing.
Campion, Thomas (1567–1620)
Ad Amorem.
Ad ampliss. totius Angliae Cancellarium, Fr. Ba.
Ad Cambricum.
Ad Carolum Fitz Geofridum.
Ad Caspiam.
Ad Castricum.
Ad Chloen.
Ad Ed. Mychelburnum.
Ad Ed. Spencerum.
Ad Ge. Chapmannum.
Ad Graios.
Ad Guil. Camdenum.
Ad Io. Davisium.
Ad Io. Dolundum.
Ad Leam.
Ad Librum.
Ad Lucium.
Ad Melleam.
Ad Nashum.
Ad nobiliss. virum Gul. Percium.
Ad Rob. Caraeum Equitem Auratum Nobilissimum.
Ad Rusticum.
Ad Thamesin.
Ad Tho. Munsonium, equitem Auratum et Baronetum.
Advice to a Girl.
Are you what your faire lookes expresse?
As by the stream[e]s of Babylon [*or* Babilon].
As on a day Sabina fell asleepe.
Author of light, revive my dying spright.
Awake, Awake! [Thou Heavy Sprite].
Awake, thou spring of speaking grace, mute rest becomes not thee.
Ayres that Were Sung and Played, at *Brougham Castle* in *Westmerland*, in the Kings Entertainment, The.
Be thou then my beauty named.
Be Wise, and Fly Not.
Beautie Without Love Deformitie.
Beauty Is But a Painted Hell.
Beauty Is Not Bound.
Beauty, Since You So Much Desire.
Blame Not My Cheekes.
Bravely deckt, come forth, bright day.
Breake now my heart and dye! Oh no, she may relent.
Canto Quarto.
Come away, arm'd with loves delights.
Come, Cheerful Day!
Come Let Us Sound With Melodie.
Come, you pretty false-eyed wanton [*or* false-ey'd wanton].
Content.

Could my heart more tongues imploy.
Could my poore hart whole worlds of toungs employ.
De Catullo et Martiale.
De Epigrammate.
De Fran. Draco.
De horologio portabili.
De obitu Phil. Sydnaei equitis aurati generosissimi.
De Regis reditu e Scotia.
Dear If I with Guile.
Description of a Maske: Presented in the Banqueting Roome at *Whitehall*, on Saint Stephens Night Last, at the Marriage of the Right Honourable the Earle of *Somerset:* and the Right Noble the Lady FRANCES Howard.
Dolus.
Eiusdem ad Authorem.
Elegeia I (1595).
Elegia I (1619).
Elegie upon the Untimely Death of Prince *Henry*, An.
Ev'ry Dame affects good fame, what ere her doings be.
Fain Would I Wed.
Faine would I my love disclose.
Faire If You Expect Admiring.
Fire, fire, fire, fire!
Fire that must flame is with apt fuell fed.
First Love.
Follow Thy Fair Sun[ne] [Unhappy Shadow].
Follow your saint, follow with accents sweet.
Good men, shew, if you can tell.
Hark, All You Ladies [That Do Sleep].
Heart's Music.
Her fayre inflaming eyes.
Her rosie cheekes, her ever smiling eyes.
Hide not, sweetest Love, a sight so pleasing.
How eas'ly wert thou chained.
Hymn in Praise of Neptune, A.
I Care Not for These Ladies.
I must complain, yet doe enjoy my Love.
If any hath the heart to kill.
If Love loves truth, then women do[e] not love.
If thou longst so much to learne (sweet boy) what 'tis to love.
Illustrissimo, Potentissimoque Principi, *Frederico* Quinto, Rheni Comiti Palatino, Duci Bavariae, &c.
In Barnum ("In vinum solui cupis au filena quod hausit").
In Barnum ("Mortales decem tela inter Gallica Caesos").
In Bretonem.
In Cambrum.
In Crispinum.
In eosdem.
In Honour of the Author by *Tho: Campion* Doctor in Physicke. To the Reader.
In Laurentiam.
In Ligonem.
In Lycium et Clytham.
In Melleam ("Mellea mi si abeam promittit basea septem").
In Melleam ("Anxia dum natura nimis tibi, Mellea, fornam").
In Morachum.
In Nervam.
In obitum Gual. Devoreux fratris clariss. Comitus Essexiae.
In Obitum Hen. Mag. Brit. Principis.
In obitum Iacobi Huissii.
In Pandarum.
In Sannium.
In se.
Incipit Thomas Campianus Medicinae Doctor.
It Fell on a Summer's [*or* Sommers] Day [*or* Daie].
Jack and Joan.
Kind Are Her Answers.
Kisses.
Lamentation, A.
Leave prolonging thy distresse.
Lift up to heav'n, sad wretch, thy heavy

spright.
Lighten, heavy hart, thy spright.
Loe, when backe mine eye.
Lords Mask[e], The, *sels.*
Love Me or Not.
Maid's Complaint, A.
Man of Life Upright, The.
Maydes are simple, some men say.
Mistris [*or* Mistress] Since You So Much Desire.
Most sweet and pleasing are thy wayes, O God.
My Life's Delight.
Now let her change and spare not.
Now Winter Nights Enlarge.
O Come Quickly!
O deare, that I with thee might live.
O griefe, O spight, to see poore Vertue scorn'd.
O Love, where are thy Shafts, thy Quiver, and thy Bow?
O never to be moved.
O what unhop't for sweet supply!
Observations in the Art of English Poesie.
Of this Ensuing Discourse.
Oft have I sigh'd for him that heares me not.
Out of My Soul's Depth.
Peaceful Western Wind, The.
Peacefull westerne winde the wintrye stormes hath calmde, The.
Pin'd I am, and like to die.
Relation of the Late Royall Entertainment Given by the Right Honourable the Lord *Knowles*, at *Cawsome*-House neere *Redding*: to Our Most *Gracious Queene, Queene* ANNE, *in her* Progresse *toward the Bathe.*
Respect my faith, regard my service past.
Secret Love or Two I Must Confess[e], A.
See Where She Flies.
Seek the Lord.
Shadowes before the shining sunne do vanish.
Shall I come, if I swim? wide are the waves, you see.
Shall I Come, Sweet Love.
Shall I then hope when faith is fled?
Since she, ev'n shee, for whom I liv'd.
Sing a song of joy.
Sleep, Angry Beauty.
So many loves have I neglected.
So Quicke, So Hot, So Mad is Thy Fond Sute.
So sweet is thy discourse to me.
So Tir'd Are All My Thoughts.
Some can flatter, some can faine.
Song: "O sweet delight, O more than human[e] bliss[e]."
Spyres Curten, The.
Sweet, exclude me[e] not, nor be divided.
Tarry sweete love.
There is a garden in her face.
There Is None, O None but You.
Think'st thou to seduce me then.
Thou Art Not Fair[e].
Thou Joy'st, Fond Boy.
Though You Are Young [*or* Yoong].
Though your strangenesse frets my hart.
Thrice Toss[e] These Oaken Ashes in the Air [*or* Ayre].
Thus I Resolve.
To Campiani Epigramma de Instituto Authoris.
To his sweet Lute *Apollo* sung the motions of the Spheares.
To Music Bent Is My Retired Mind.
To My Honourable Friend, Sr. Thomas Mounson, *Knight and Baronet.*
To My Worthy Friend, Mr. John Mounson, Sonne and Heyre to Sir Thomas Mounson, Knight and Baronet.
To the Most Disconsolate Great Brittaine.
To the Most High and Mighty Prince Charles.
To the Most Illustrious and Mighty Fredericke the Fift, Count Palatine of the Rhein.
To the Most Princely and Vertuous the Lady Elizabeth.
To The Most Sacred King James.
To the Most Sacred Queen Anne.
To the Reader.
To the Right Honourable, Both in Birth and

Vertue, Francis, Earle of Cumberland.
To the Right, Noble, and Vertuous, Henry Lord Clifford, Sonne and Heyre to the Right Honourable, Francis, Earle of Cumberland.
To the World.
To the Worthy Author.
Turn Back, You Wanton Flyer.
Turne all thy thoughts to eyes.
Umbra.
Vaile, love, mine eyes, O hide from me.
Vain Men, Whose Follies.
Verba volant; verum: quid enim velocius illis?
View Mee, Lord.
Were My Heart as Some Men's Are.
What Fair[e] Pomp[e].
What Harvest Half So Sweet Is.
What If a Day [*or* a Month or a Year].
What is it that all men possesse, among themselves conversing.
What meanes this folly, now to brave it so.
What Then Is Love But Mourning?
When the God of Merrie Love.
When to Her Lute.
Where are all thy beauties now, all hearts enchaining? [*or* harts enchayning?].
Where shall I refuge seeke, if you refuse mee?
Where She Her Sacred Bower Adorns.
Whether away my sweetest deerest?
Why presumes thy pride on that, that must so private be.
Wise men patience never want.
Young and Simple though I Am.
Your Fair[e] Look[e]s Inflame [My Desire].

Campion, Thomas *and* **Philip Rosseter**
And would you faine the reason know.
And Would You See My Mistress' Face?
Aye me, that love should natures workes accuse!
If I hope, I pine; if I feare, I faint and die.
If I urge my kinde desires.
If she forsake me, I must die.
Kinde in unkindnesse, when will you relent.
Let him that will be free and keep his h[e]art from care.
Long have mine eies gaz'd with delight.
No grave for woe, yet earth my watrie teares devoures.
Reprove not love, though fondly thou hast lost.
Shall then a traiterous kis or a smile.
Sweete, come againe.
Though far from joy, my sorrowes are as far.
Unlesse there were consent twixt hell and heaven.
What harts content can he finde.
When Laura smiles her sight revives both night and day.

Capilupus, Hippolytus (*fl.* 16th cent.)
Christophori Columbi Tumulus.

Cardenal, Ernesto (b. 1925)
Drake in the Southern Sea.
Gethsemani, KY, *sels.*
Three Epigrams, *sels.*

Cardozo, Joaquim (b. 1897)
Cemetery of Childhood.
Elegy for Maria Alves.

Carew, Thomas (1594?–1640?)
Another [Epitaph on the Lady Mary Villiers].
Another [On the Duke of Buckingham].
Beautiful Mistress, A.
Boldness[e] in Love.
Carew's Masque.
Carver. To His Mistress, The.
Celia Bleeding, to the Surgeon.
Celia Singing ("You that think that love can convey").
Celia Singing ("Hark, how my Celia, with the choice").
Comparison, The.
Complement, The.
Conquest by Flight.
Cruel Mistress, A.
Dart, The.
Deposition from Love, A.
Disdain Returned.
Divine Love, A.

Divine Mistress, A.
Elegy on the La: Pen: Sent to My Mistress Out of France, An.
Elegy upon the Death of the Dean of [St.] Paul's, Dr. John Donne, An.
Epitaph on the Lady Mary Villiers ("The Lady Mary lies").
Epitaph on the Lady Mary Villiers ("This little vault, this narrow room").
Epitaph on the Lady S.: Wife of Sir W.S.
Eternity of Love Protested.
Fancy, A.
Fly That Flew into My Mistress'[s] Eye, A.
For a Picture Where a Queen Laments over the Tomb of a Slain Knight.
Four Songs, by Way of Chorus To a Play.
Good Counsel to a Young Maid.
Grief Engrossed.
Hymeneal Song, on the Nuptials of the Lady Ann Wentworth and the Lord Lovelace, An.
Hymeneal[l] Dialogue, An.
In Answer of an Elegiacal[l] Letter, Upon the Death of the King of Sweden [from Aurelian Townsend, Inviting Me to Write on That Subject].
In Praise of His Mistress.
In the Person of a Lady To Her Inconstant Servant.
Ingrateful[l] Beauty Threatened.
Lady, Rescued from Death by a Knight, Who in the Instant Leaves Her, Complains Thus, A.
Lips and Eyes.
Looking-Glass, A.
Lover, in the Disguise of an Amazon, Is Dearly Beloved of His Mistress, A.
Lover, upon an Accident Necessitating His Departure, Consults with Reason, A.
Love's Courtship.
Love's Force.
Maria Wentworth.
Married Woman, A.
Mediocrity in Love Rejected.
Mistake, The.
Mr. Carew to His Friend.
Murdering Beauty.
My Mistress Commanding Me to Return Her Letters.
New Year's Gift. To the King, A.
New Years Gift. To the Queen, A.
New Year's Sacrifice: To Lucinda, A.
Obsequies to the Lady Anne Hay.
On a Damask[e] Rose, Sticking upon a Lady's Breast.
On Mistress N.
On Sight of a Gentlewoman's Face in the Water.
On the Duke of Buckingham.
On the Marriage of T. K. and C. C.: The Morning Stormy.
Parting, Celia Weeps.
Pastoral[l] Dialogue, A.
Pastoral[l] Dialogue, A.
Persuasions to Enjoy.
Prayer to the Wind, A.
Protestation [A Sonnet], The.
Rapture, A.
Red and White Roses.
Second Rapture, The.
Secrecy [*or* Secresie] Protested.
Song[, A]: "Ask[e] me no more where Jove bestow[e]s."
Song: The Willing Prisoner to His Mistress.
Song: To Her Again[e], She Burning in a Fe[a]ver.
Spring, The.
Tinder, The.
To A.D., Unreasonable, Distrustful of Her Own Beauty.
To A. L.; Persuasions [*or* Perswasions] to Love.
To a Lady, Not Yet Enjoyed by Her Husband.
To a Lady That Desired I Would Love Her.
To Ben Jonson.
To Celia, upon Love's Ubiquity.
To Her in Absence; a Ship.

To His Jealous Mistress.
To His Mistress.
To His Mistress Retiring in Affection.
To Master W. Montague.
To Mistress Katherine Neville, on Her Green
    Sickness.
To My Cousin (C.R.) Marrying My Lady (A.).
To my Friend G.N. from Wrest.
To My Friend, Will. Davenant.
To My Honoured Friend, Master Thomas May,
    Upon His Comedy *The Heir*.
To My Inconstant Mistress [*or* Mistris].
To My Mistress [*or* Mistris], I Burning in
    Love.
To My Mistress Sitting by a River's Side; an
    Eddy.
To My Mistress[e] in My Absence.
To My Much Honoured Friend, Henry, Lord
    Carey of Leppington, Upon His Translation
    of Malvezzi.
To My Rival.
To My Worthy Friend, Master Davenant Upon
    His Excellent Play, *The Just Italian*.
To My Worthy Friend Master George Sands
    [*or* Sandys], on His Translation of the
    Psalms.
To One That Desired to Know My Mistress [*or*
    Mistris].
To One Who, When I Praised My Mistress'
    Beauty, Said I Was Blind.
To Saxham.
To T. H., a Lady Resembling My Mistress.
To the Countess of Anglesey.
To the King, at His Entrance into Saxham: By
    Master John Crofts.
To the New Year [For the Countess of
    Carlisle].
To the Painter.
To the Reader of Master William Davenant's
    Play [*The Wits*].
Tooth-Ache Cured by a Kiss, The.
Truce in Love Intreated.
Upon a Mole in Celia's Bosom.
Upon a Ribbon [*or* Ribband].
Upon Master Walter Montagu's Return from
    Travel.
Upon My Lord Chief Justice's Election of My
    Lady Anne Wentworth [*or* A.W.] for His
    Mistress.
Upon Some Alterations in My Mistress, after
    My Departure into France.
Upon the King's Sickness.
Upon the Sickness of E.S

Carpenter, Bogdana *See* **Carpenter, John**

Carrera Andrade, Jorge (d. 1903)
Cocoa Tree.
Man from Ecuador beneath the Eiffel Tower,
    A.
Mirror's Mission, The.
Notes of a Parachute Jumper.
Radicals.
Weathercock on the Cathedral of Quito, The.

Carruth, Hayden (b. 1921)
Abandoned Ranch, Big Bend.
Adolf Eichmann.
Æolian.
Algeria.
Alive.
All Things.
Almanach du Printemps Vivarois.
Anent Socrates, or Somebody.
Anima.
Anxious View of a Tree.
Apology for Using the Word "Heart" in Too
    Many Poems, An.
Assignment.
Asylum, The.
August.
August First.
August 14, 1961.
Backyard in California, A.
Baler, The.
Bearer, The.
Bears at Raspberry Time.
Billie Holiday.
Birds of Vietnam, The.

Birth of Venus, The.
Block.
Bloomingdale Papers, The, *sels*.
Bouquet in Dog Time.
Buddhist Painter Prepares to Paint, The.
Burning Dawn.
Cappadocian Song.
Capper Kaplinski at the North Side Cue Club.
Carnations.
Cave Painting.
Chase in Spring, The.
Chicory.
Clay Hill Anthology, The, *sels*.
Coming Down to the Desert at Lordsburg,
    N.M.
Comparative Iconography.
Concerning Necessity.
Continuo.
Contra Mortem.
Cows at Night, The.
Cowshed Blues, The.
Cross My Heart and Hope to Die, It Was the
    Very Same Song Exactly.
Crow's Mark.
Crucifixion.
Dedication in These Days.
Ekstase, Alptraum, Schlaf in einem Nest von
    Flammen.
Emergency Haying.
Essay.
Essay on Death.
Essay on Love.
Essay on Marriage.
Essay on Stone.
Eternal City.
Eternity Blues.
Études de Plusiers Paysages de l'Âme.
Event Itself, The.
Excursus of Reassurance in Begonia Time, An.
Existence Before Essence.
Existing Pool, The.
Expatiation on the Combining of Weathers at
    Thirty-Seventh and Indiana Where the
    Southern More or Less Crosses the Dog, An.
Fact of the Matter, The.
Family Reunion.
Far-removed Mountain Men, The.
Fat Lady, The.
For Papa.
Fourth.
Fragment: "Who can know more deeply than I
    your loneliness there?"
Freedom and Discipline.
French Hill.
Godhulivela.
Gods.
Green Mountain Idyl.
Ho-Hum Again.
Homage to John Lyly and Frankie Newton.
Homecoming.
Horologikos.
How Lewisburg, Pa., Escaped the Avenging
    Angel.
How To.
I Could Take.
I Know, I Remember, But How Can I Help
    You.
I Tell You For Several Years of My Madness I
    Heard the Voice of Lilith Singing in the
    Trees of Chicago.
If It Were Not for You.
Impossible Indispensability of the Ars Poetica,
    The.
In Memoriam.
In Russia.
In Tobey Woods.
Incident of May.
Incorrigible Dirigible, The.
Insomniac Sleeps Well for Once and, The.
"I've Never Seen Such a Real Hard Time
    Before": Three-Part Invention.
John Dryden.
Johnny Spain's White Heifer.
Journey to a Known Place.
Joy and Agony of Improvisation, The.
Lady.

Lana.
Language of Flowers, Etc, The.
Leaf from Mr. Dyer's Woods, A.
Letter to Maxine Sullivan.
Light in the Locust Tree.
Line, The.
Lines Written in an Asylum.
Listen.
Little Fire in the Woods, The.
Little Old Funky Homeric Blues for Herm, A.
Living Alone.
Loneliness[: An Outburst of Hexasyllables].
Loon on Forrester's Pond, The.
Lost.
Marge.
Marshall Washer.
Marvin McCabe.
Master, Grieved with Age, The.
Meadow House.
Meditation in the Presence of "Ostrich Walk."
Michigan Water: a Few Riffs before Dawn.
Mild Winter.
Missing the Bo in the Henhouse.
Mix the Ingredients.
Moonset.
Mother.
Mountain Cabin, The.
Mountain, The.
Mouse, The.
Museum Piece.
My Father's Face.
My Hut.
My Meadow.
Mythology of Dark and Light, The.
Names.
Naming for Love.
New Hartford.
New Orleans.
No Matter What, After All, and That Beautiful
    Word So.
No Supervening Thought of Grace.
None.
North Winter.
Not Transhistorical Death, or at Least Not
    Quite.
Notes from Robin Hill Cottage.
November: Indian Summer.
November Jeans Song.
Of Brook and Stone.
Of Distress Being Humiliated by the Classical
    Chinese Poets.
Oldest Killed Lake in North America, The.
On a Certain Engagement South of Seoul.
On Being Asked to Write a Poem Against the
    War in Vietnam.
On Canann Mountain Meadow.
Once and Again.
Once More.
Ontological Episode of the Asylum.
Opusthirteen.
Ovid, Old Buddy, I Would Discourse with You
    a While.
Pa McCabe.
Paragraphs.
Phone.
Poet, The.
Poetical Abstracts.
Point, The.
Post-Impressionist Susurration for the First of
    November, 1983, A.
Pray You Young Woman.
President's Speech, The.
Purana, Meaning Once Upon a Time.
Questions.
R.M.D.
Ravine, The.
Ray.
Re-Acquaintance.
Reflexive.
Regarding Chainsaws.
Renaissance.
Return to Love.
Rimrock, Where It Is.
Rummage.
Sam and Poll Go Back to the City.
Saving Way, The.

Septic Tanck.
Sex.
Shake, Well Before Using.
Silence.
Simple.
Sleeping Beauty, The.
Smallish Son, The.
Snow, The.
Sociology of Toyotas and Jade
    Chrysanthemums, The.
Sometimes When Lovers Lie Quietly Together,
    Unexpectedly One of Them Will Feel the
    Other's Pulse.
Song: Luxury.
Song of the Two Crows.
Song: So Often, So Long I Have Thought.
Song: So Why Does This Dead Carnation.
Song: "Summer burns on the edges of day."
Song: The Famous Vision of America.
Song: The Old, Old Man.
Song: The Young Man with the Guitar,
    Testing.
Songs About What Comes Down: The
    Complete Works of Mr. Septic Tanck, sels.
Sonnet: "Well, she told me I had an aura.
    "What?" I said."
Sonnet: "Whut do you spose thet thing is," Oi
    said. "Whut?"
Sonnets, sels.
Sorrow Song, The.
Sound of Snow, The.
Sparrows.
Speaking for Them.
Spring 1967.
Spring Notes from Robin Hill.
Stepping Backward.
Summer's Early End at Hudson's Bay.
"Sure," Said Benny Goodman.
Survival as Tao, Beginning at 5:00 A.M.
Tabula Rasa.
That I Had Had Courage When Young.
Thaw.
They Accuse Me of Not Talking.
This Decoration.
This Song.
Three Songs.
To Artemis.
To Know in Reverie the Only Phenomenology
    of the Absolute.
Too Tenuous.
Twilight Comes.
Two Romantic Pieces.
Underground the Darkness Is the Light.
Une Présence Absolue.
Unnatural Unselection.
Valentine.
Vermont.
Way of the Conventicle of the Trees, The.
What a Wonder Among the Instruments Is the
    Walloping Tramboone!
When Howitzers Began.
When I Wrote a Little.
Who Cares, Long as It's B-Flat.
Wild Swans at Norfolk, The.
Woodsmoke at 70.
Words in a Certain Appropriate Mode.
World as Will and Representation, The.
Wreck of the Circus Train, The.

Carus, Titus Lucretius See Lucretius
Carver, Dale R.
    Let's Roar, Your Honor.
Carver, Raymond (1939–90)
    Account, An.
    Adultery.
    Afghanistan.
    After Rainy Days.
    After Reading Two Towns in Provence.
    After the Fire.
    Afterglow.
    Afternoon, An.
    Alcohol.
    All Her Life.
    Anathema.
    Another Mystery.
    Artaud.
    Ashtray, The.

Asia.
Ask Him.
Aspens.
At Least.
At Night the Salmon Move.
At Noon.
At the Bird Market.
Attic, The.
Author of Her Misfortune, The.
Autopsy Room, The.
Autumn.
Away.
Bahia, Brazil.
Baker, The.
Balsa Wood.
Balzac.
Bankruptcy.
Beginnings.
Best Time of the Day, The.
Betrayal.
Blood.
Blue Stones, The.
Bobber.
Bonnard's Nudes.
Brass Ring, The.
Cadillacs and Poetry.
Car, The.
Catch, The.
Caucasus: A Romance, The.
Caution.
Cheers.
Cherish.
Child, The.
Circulation.
Cobweb, The.
Commerce.
Company.
Conspirators.
Contact, The.
Cougar, The.
Country Matters.
Cranes, The.
Current, The.
Cutlery.
Debate, The.
Deschutes River.
Distress Sale.
Don't Run.
Downstream.
Drinking While Driving.
Eagles.
Earwigs.
Egress.
Elk Camp.
Energy.
Eve of Battle, The.
Evening.
Extirpation.
Fear.
Fields, The.
Fishing Pole of the Drowned Man, The.
Five O'Clock in the Morning.
For Semra, with Martial Vigor.
For Tess.
For the Egyptian Coin Today, Arden, Thank
    You.
For the Record.
Foreboding.
Forever.
Forge, and a Scythe, A.
From the East, Light.
Garden, The.
Gift, The.
Grant, The.
Gravy.
Grief.
Haircut, A.
Hamid Ramouz (1818–1906).
Happiness.
Happiness in Cornwall.
Harley's Swans.
Hat, The.
Heels.
Highway 99E from Chico.
His Bathrobe Pockets Stuffed with Notes.
Hominy and Rain.

Hope.
House behind This One, The.
Hummingbird.
Hunter.
In a Greek Orthodox Church near Daphne.
In a Marine Light near Sequim, Washington.
In Switzerland.
In the Lobby of the Hotel del Mayo.
In the Trenches with Robert Graves.
In the Year 2020.
Interview.
Iowa Summer.
Its Course.
Jean's TV.
Juggler at Heaven's Gate, The.
Jungle, The.
Kafka's Watch.
Kitchen, The.
Late Afternoon, April 8, 1984.
Late Fragment.
Late Night with Fog and Horses.
Lemonade.
Letter.
Lightning Speed of the Past, The.
Limits.
Listening.
Little Room, The.
Loafing.
Locking Yourself Out, Then Trying to Get
    Back In.
Looking for Work 1.
Looking for Work 2.
Louise.
Luck.
Mail, The.
Mailman as Cancer Patient, The.
Man Outside, The.
March into Russia, The.
Margo.
Marriage.
Meadow, The.
Medicine.
Memory 1.
Memory 2.
Mesopotamia.
Migration.
Minuet, The.
Miracle.
Money.
Moon, the Train, The.
Morning, Thinking of Empire.
Mosque in Jaffa, The.
Mother.
Movement.
Music.
My Boat.
My Crow.
My Dad's Wallet.
My Daughter and Apple Pie.
My Death.
My Wife.
My Work.
Near Klamath.
Nearly.
Net, The.
News Carried to Macedonia, The.
Next Door.
Next Year.
Night Dampness.
No Heroics, Please.
No Need.
Not Far from Here.
NyQuil.
Offending Eel, The.
Old Days, The.
On an Old Photograph of My Son.
On the Pampas Tonight.
One More.
Other Life, The.
Our First House in Sacramento.
Out.
Oyntment to Alure Fish to the Bait.
Painter & the Fish, The.
Party, The.
Pen, The.
Phenomenon, The.

Phone Booth, The.
Photograph of My Father in His Twenty-
second Year.
Pipe, The.
Plus.
Poem for Dr Pratt, a Lady Pathologist.
Poem for Hemingway & W. C. Williams.
Poem for Karl Wallenda, Aerialist Supreme.
Poem I Didn't Write, The.
Poem Not against Songbirds, A.
Poem on My Birthday, July 2.
Poems.
Possible, The.
Powder-Monkey.
Prize, The.
Projectile, The.
Proposal.
Prosser.
Quiet Nights.
Radio Waves.
Rain.
Reaching.
Reading.
Reading Something in the Restaurant.
Rest, The.
Return.
Rhodes.
River, The.
Road, The.
Rogue River Jet-Boat Trip, Gold Beach,
Oregon, July 4, 1977.
Romanticism.
Scale.
Schooldesk, The.
Scratch, The.
Seeds.
Sensitive Girl, The.
September.
Shiftless.
Shooting.
Simple.
Sinew.
Sleeping.
Slippers.
Smoke and Deception.
Soda Crackers.
Some Prose on *Poetry*.
Something Is Happening.
Son.
Songs in the Distance.
Sorrel.
Sparrow Nights.
Spell.
Spring, 480 BC.
Squall, A.
Still Looking Out for Number One.
Stupid.
Sturgeon, The.
Such Diamonds.
Sudden Rain.
Summer Fog.
Summer in Sacramento, A.
Sunbather, to Herself, The.
Sunday Night.
Suspenders.
Sweet Light.
Tall Order, A.
Tel Aviv and *Life on the Mississippi*.
Thermopylae.
This Morning.
This Room.
This Word Love.
Those Days.
Threat.
Through the Boughs.
To Begin With.
To My Daughter.
Toes, The.
Tomorrow.
Torture.
Transformation.
Trestle, The.
Trying to Sleep Late on a Saturday Morning in
November.
Two Carriages.
Two Worlds.

Union Street: San Francisco, Summer 1975.
Venice.
Vigil.
Waiting.
Wake Up.
Walk, A.
Wenas Ridge.
Wes Hardin: From a Photograph.
What I Can Do.
What the Doctor Said.
What You Need for Painting.
What You Need to Know for Fishing.
Where the Groceries Went.
Where They'd Lived.
Where Water Comes Together with Other
Water.
White Field, The.
Wind.
Window, The.
Windows of the Summer Vacation Houses,
The.
Wine.
Winter Insomnia.
With a Telescope Rod on Cowiche Creek.
Woman Bathing.
Woolworth's, 1954.
Work.
World Book Salesman, The.
Yesterday.
Yesterday, Snow.
You Don't Know What Love Is.
Young Fire Eaters of Mexico City, The.
Young Girls, The.

Cary, Thomas (1597–1634)
Methodus Amandi.
On His Mistress[e] Going to Sea.

Cassian, Nina (b. 1924)
Tirade for the Next-to-Last Act.

**Castiglione, Baldassare, Count of Novilara
(1478–1529)**
On the Statue of *Cleopatra*, Made into a
Fountain by *Leo* the Tenth.

**Catullus (Gaius [*or* Caius] Valerius Catullus)
(87–c.54 B.C.)**
85: "I hate and love her. If you ask me why."
Carmina.
Let us live, my Lesbia, and let us love each
other.

Cavafy, Constantine P. (1863–1933)
Addition.
Afternoon Sun, The.
Aimilianos Monai, Alexandrian, 628–655 A.D.
Alexandrian Kings.
Alexandrian Merchant.
Alexandros Iannaios, and Alexandra.
Ancient Tragedy.
And I Reclined and Lay on Their Beds.
Anna Dalassini.
Anna Komnina.
Apollonios of Tyana in Rhodes.
Aristovoulos.
Artificial Flowers.
As Long as You Can.
At the Entrance to the Café.
At the Theater.
Athena's Vote.
Bacchic.
Bandaged Shoulder, The.
Bank of the Future, The.
Battle of Magnesia, The.
Becoming Stronger.
Before Antiochus Epiphanis.
Before the House.
Before the Statue of Endymion.
Before Time Could Change Them.
Beizades to His Beloved.
Blue Eyes.
Bouquets.
Builders.
By an Open Window.
Byzantine Gentleman, in Exile, Composing
Verses, A.
Candles.
Cat, The.
Chaldaic Image.

Chandelier.
Che Fece . . . Il Gran Rifiuto.
City, The.
Coins.
Come, O King of the Lacedaimonians.
Confusion.
Correspondence According to Baudelaire.
Craftsman of Winebowls.
Dangerous Remarks.
Dareios.
Days of 1896.
Days of 1908.
Days of 1909, '10 and '11.
Days of 1901.
Days of 1903.
Death of a General.
Death of the Emperor Tacitus, The.
December 1903.
Desires.
Desperation.
Dimaratos.
Displeased Viewer, A.
Displeasure of Selefkides, The.
Distinguishing Marks.
Dünya Güzeli.
Elegy of the Flowers.
End of Antony, The.
Enemies, The.
Envoys from Alexandria.
Epic in the Heart.
Epitaph of Antiochus, King of Kommagini.
Epitaph: "Stranger, beside the Ganges I lie, a
man."
Eternity.
Exiles.
Far Off.
Favor of Alexander Valas, The.
First Step, The.
Flowers White and Beautiful, as Were Most
Becoming.
Following the Formulas of Ancient Greco-
Syrian Magicians.
Footsteps of the Eumenides, The.
Footsteps, The.
For Ammonis, Who at Died at 29, in 610.
For the Shop.
Four Walls of My Room, The.
From the Drawer.
From the School of the Renowned Philosopher.
From the Ship.
Funeral of Sarpedon, The ("Heart of Zeus is
filled with grief, The").
Funeral of Sarpedon, The ("Zeus grieves
mightily. Patroklos").
Garments.
Glory of the Ptolemies, The.
God Forsakes Antony, The.
Good and Bad Weather.
Grand Procession of Priests and Laymen.
Gray.
Great Feast at the Home of Sosibios, A.
Greek from Ancient Times.
Half an Hour.
He Asked about the Quality.
He Came to Read.
He Swears.
Hereafter, The.
Herodis Attikos.
Hidden Things.
Horace in Athens.
Horses of Achilles, The.
Hospitality of Lagides, The.
House with a Garden.
I Went.
Ides of March, The.
If Actually Dead.
Illness of Kleitos, The.
Imenos.
In a Large Greek Colony, 200 B.C.
In a Town of Osroini.
In a Township of Asia Minor.
In an Old Book.
In Church.
In Sparta.
In the Cemetery.
In the Districts Surrounding Antioch.

In the Dull and Gloomy Village.
In the Evening.
In the House of the Soul.
In the Month of Athyr.
In the Port.
In the Same Space.
In the Street.
In the Wineshops.
In the Year 200 B.C.
Indian Image.
Inkwell, The.
Interruption.
Intervention of the Gods, The.
Ionian.
Ithaca.
I've Brought to Art.
I've Gazed So Long, So Much.
January 1904.
John Kantakuzinos Triumphs.
Julian and the Antiochians.
Julian at the Mysteries.
Julian in Nicomedia.
Julian, Seeing Contempt.
Kaisarion.
Kimon, Son of Learchos, Age 22, Student of
    Greek Literature (in Kyrini).
King Claudius.
King Dimitrios.
La Jeunesse Blanche.
Lohengrin.
Love, A.
Manuel Komninos.
Melancholy Hours.
Melancholy of Jason Kleander; Poet in
    Kommagini; 595 A.D.
Memory.
Mimiambi of Herodas, The.
Mirror in the Vestibule, The.
Monotony.
Morning Sea.
Myris: Alexandria, 340 A.D.
Naval Battle, The.
Nero's Term.
Next Table, The.
Nichori.
Nous N'osons Plus Chanter les Roses.
Ode and Elegy of the Roads.
Oedipus.
Of Colored Glass.
Of Dimitrios Sotir (162–150 B.C.).
Of the Jews (50 A.D.).
Old Man, An.
Old Men's Souls, The.
On an Italian Shore.
On Hearing of Love.
On the March to Sinopi.
On the Stairs.
One Night.
One of the dead woman's days, the ghost of a
    day.
One of Their Gods.
One Who Has Failed.
Orophernis.
Painted.
Passing Through.
Pawn, The.
Pelasgian Image.
Philhellene.
Picture of a Young Man, Twenty-three, Done
    by His Friend of the Same Age, an Amateur.
Pleasure in the Flesh.
Poet and the Muse, The.
Poseidonians.
Prayer: "To her depths the sea has taken a
    sailor."
Priam's Speeding Forth at Night.
Priest at the Serapeion.
Prince from Western Libya, A.
Procession of Dionysus.
Rain.
Regiment of Pleasure, The.
Remember, Body.
Rest I Will Tell to Those Below in Hades, The.
Return.
Return from Greece.
Salome.

Sam el Nesim.
Satrapy, The.
Second Odyssey, A.
September 1903.
Ships, The.
Simeon.
Since Nine O'Clock.
Singer.
So.
Sophist Departing from Syria.
Stephanos Skilitsis.
Suspicion.
Sweet Voices.
Taken.
Tarantians Divert Themselves, The.
Tears of the Sisters of Phaeton, The.
Temethos, Antiochian; 400 A.D.
Terror.
That They Might Appear.
That's the Man.
Theater of Sidon (400 A.D.).
Their Origin.
Theodotos.
Theophilos Palaiologos.
Thermopylae.
They Might Have Bothered.
Things Run Out.
31 B.C. in Alexandria.
Those Who Fought for the Achaian Alliance.
Timolaos the Syracusan.
To Abide.
To Jerusalem.
Tobacco Shop Window, The.
Tomb of Evrion.
Tomb of Iasis, The.
Tomb of Ignatios, The.
Tomb of Lanis, The.
Tomb of the Grammarian Lysias.
Trojans.
25th Year of His Life, The.
27 June 1906, 2 P.M.
Two Young Men, 23 to 24 Years Old.
Tyanan Sculptor.
Understanding.
Unfaithfulness.
Very Seldom.
Voice from the Sea.
Voices.
Vulnerant Omnes, Ultima Necat.
Waiting for the Barbarians.
Walls.
What Cannot Be.
When, My Friends, I Was in Love.
When the Watchman Saw the Light.
When They Surge, Excited.
Windows, The.
Wise Sense Imminent Events, The.
Word and Silence.
You Didn't Understand.
Young Man, a Writer—in His 24th Year, A.
Young Men of Sidon (400 A.D.).

Cavalcanti, Guido (1250–1301)
Alas, my spirits, when you see me.
Ballata: Concerning a Shepherd-maid.
Ballata: He perceives that his highest Love is
    gone from him.
Ballata: He reveals, in a Dialogue, his
    increasing Love for Mandetta.
Ballata: In Exile at Sarzana.
Ballata: Of a continual Death in Love.
Ballata: Of his Lady among other Ladies.
Beautiful Lady where Love shows himself,
    The.
Beauty of women and wise hearts.
Because I expect never to return.
Canzone: A Dispute with Death.
Canzone: A Song against Poverty.
Canzone: A Song of Fortune.
Canzone: He laments the Presumption and
    Incontinence of his Youth.
Check out the humpback, Manny.
Dante, a sighing messenger of the heart.
Each day I come to you an infinity of times.
Each fresh and sweet source.
Eyes of that gentle country girl, The.
Figure of my Lady, A.

Gianni, Guido greets.
I fear from my misfortune.
I found a shepherdess in a grove.
I have news to tell you, do you hear, Nerone.
I never used to think that my heart.
I pray you who speak of suffering.
I saw Love in eyes.
I see it in my Lady's eyes.
I was deep in thoughts of Love when I found.
If I ask Pity not to be.
If I were one worthy of Love.
If it were mine, you'd see every value.
If only Mercy befriended my desires.
If you see Love, Dante.
If you've forgotten me forever, Mercy.
In you flowers and greenery.
Love's amorous spiritual glance.
May I tell you the news of my eyes.
May you not drop your little jewel.
My foolish eyes, that first looked.
My latest cruel misfortune.
My soul is wildly terrified.
My young blossom.
O my Lady, didn't you see him.
Of foul matters I must speak.
Oh you, whose eyes carry.
Pity came to lonely me.
Since I must bear a sorrowing heart.
Since when must I draw life from death.
Sonnet: A Rapture concerning his Lady.
Sonnet: Guido answers the foregoing Sonnet,
    speaking with shame of his changed Love.
Sonnet: He compares all Things with his Lady,
    and finds them wanting.
Sonnet: He interprets Dante's Dream, related in
    the first Sonnet of the Vita Nuova.
Sonnet: He mistrusts the Love of Lapo Gianni.
Sonnet: He rebukes Dante for his way of Life,
    after the death of Beatrice.
Sonnet: He reports, in a feigned Vision, the
    successful Issue of Lapo Gianni's Love.
Sonnet: Of an ill-favoured Lady.
Sonnet: Of his Pain from a new Love.
Sonnet: Of the Eyes of a certain Mandetta, of
    Thoulouse, which resemble those of his
    Lady Joan, of Florence.
Sonnet: On the Detection of a false Friend.
Sonnet: To a Friend who does not pity his
    Love.
Sonnet: To a newly enriched Man; reminding
    him of the Wants of the Poor.
Sonnet: To his Lady Joan, of Florence.
Spirit deft wounds my eyes so.
Surely it wasn't your cultered mind.
Syllogism makes one from many, A.
To each captive and nobly gentle heart.
Wanting I send you certain poems.
We sad, despondent quills.
Who is this who came.
Why weren't my eyes blinded.
Woman asks me.
You could see when I met you.
You see me—one who goes crying.
You who've pierced my eyes to my heart.
Young Lady of Tolosa, A.
You've so filled my mind with pain.

Cavanagh, Clare See **Barańczak, Stanislaw**
Celan, Paul (1920–70)
Afternoon with Circus and Citadel.
All Your Seals Broken? Never.
Almonding one, you half-spoke only.
Argumentum e Silentio.
Ash-aureole behind.
Aspen Tree.
Assisi.
Because you found the trouble-shard.
Below a Painting.
Benedicta.
Black Flakes.
Black / like memory's wound.
Boomerang, on breath paths, A.
Bright / stones ride through the air, bright, The.
Broached year, The.
By Threes, By Fours.
By Twos.
Clearlit the seeds / I swam unto.

Coagula.
Cologne, at the Station.
Confidence.
Corona.
Count up the almonds.
Crocus, spotted from a.
Crowned out, / spit out into night.
Crystal.
Darkness.
Dead Man, The.
Deathfugue.
Dew. And I lay with you, you, in the trash.
Do not work ahead.
Don't write yourself.
Epitaph for François.
Etched away by the.
Eye, Open, An.
Flashlights, their / palaver.
Flower.
For Eric.
Frankfurt, September.
Havdalah.
Heat / counts us together, The.
Hollow homestead of life. In the venthole.
Homecoming.
I drink wine from two glasses.
I have cut bamboo.
I hear, the axe has flowered.
I Heard it Said.
I know you, you're the one bent over low.
Ice, Eden.
In-edger: Rembrandt.
In Egypt.
In Front of a Candle.
In Memoriam Paul Éluard.
In One.
In Prague.
In rivers north of the future.
In the air your root stays on, there.
In the reptile-car, past.
Industrious / mineral resources, domestic.
Inelligible this / world. Everything doubled.
Into the Distance.
Into the grooves.
Islandward.
It's all different from what you think, from
     what I think.
Just Think.
King's rage, stone-maned, out front.
King's way behind the false door, The.
Knock the / light-wedges away.
Landscape.
Landscape with urn beings.
Late and Deep.
Leaf, treeless, A.
Leap-centuries, leap- / seconds, leap-.
Lonely One, The.
Love Crown.
Mandorla.
Matière de Bretagne.
Mute autumn smells. The.
Near, in the aorta's arch.
Nearness of Graves.
No more sand art, no sand book, no masters.
Nocturnally Pursed.
Nocturne: "Sleep not. Be on your guard."
Nothingness, for our / names' sake.
Numbers, in league, The.
On a Journey.
Once, / I heard him.
Oozing, then / weedy stillness on the banks.
Paschal smoke, floating, with.
Poem-closed, poem-open.
Poles / are within us, The.
Pour the wasteland into your eye-sacks.
Praise of Distance.
Profuse announcement.
Psalm: "No one kneads us again out of earth
     and clay."
Radix, Matrix.
Remembrance.
Remnants of hearing, of seeing, in.
Rogues' and Gonifs' Ditty, A.
Rumbling: it is, A.
Sand from the Urns, The.
Scooped by the / great Eye- / less One.

Shibboleth.
Shofar place, The.
Show-fringes, sense-fringes.
Sketch of a Landscape.
Sleepscraps, wedges.
Sluice, The.
So you are turned—a Someone.
Solve.
Song in the Wilderness, A.
Speak You Too.
Speech-Grille.
Streak.
Stretto.
Syllable Pain, The.
Tabernacle Window.
Tankards, The.
Temple-pincers / eyed by your cheekbone.
Tenebrae.
That shining, yes, the one that.
There stood / a splinter of fig on your lip.
There was earth inside them, and.
There will be something, later.
Threadsuns / over the grayblack wasteness.
To night's order Over- / ridden, Over-.
To one who stood before the door, one.
To stand, in the shadow.
Todtnauberg.
Trace of a bite in Nowhere, The.
Travel Companion, The.
Tübingen, January.
Twelve Years.
Vinegrowers dig up.
Vintagers, The.
Voices, nicked into.
Wan-voiced, / flayed from the depths.
Wanderbush, you snare.
We lay / deep in the maquis as you.
Wellspring Rushes, The.
What happened? The stone stepped from the
     mountain.
What's written goes hollow, what's.
When I don't know, don't know.
Where? / At night in crumbling rockmass.
Where the word, that was undying, fell.
Whichever Stone You Lift.
Whitegray of a / steeply caved.
Winter.
With a Changing Key.
With all my thoughts I went.
With Letter and Clock.
With masts sung earthward.
With the persecuted in late, un- / silenced.
With wine and lostness, with.
Wolfsbean.
Word about going-to-the-depths, The.
World to be stuttered after.
You be like you, ever.
You lie amid a great listening.
You may safely.
You were my death.
Your / being over there tonight.
Zurich, at the Stork.

Chamfort, Nicolas-Sébastien Roch (1741–94)
Ask of all-healing, all consoling thought.
Better on your arse than on your feet.
Hope is a knave befools us evermore.
How hollow heart and full.
Live and clean forget from day to day.
Long after Chamfort.
Sleep till death.
Trouble with tragedy is the fuss it makes, The.

Char, René (b. 1907)
Allegiance.
At the Gates of Aerea.
Celebrating Giacometti.
Come Dance in Baronies.
Convergence of the Many.
Faction du Muet.
Fighters.
Septentrion.
To Friend-Tree of Counted Days.

Chaucer, Geoffrey (1340?–1400)
ABC, An.
Against Women Unconstant [*or* A Ballade
     against Woman Inconstant].
Anelida and Arcite.

Balade of Bon Conseill.
Balade of Complaint, A.
Book of the Duchesse, The.
Canterbury Tales, The.
Chaucer's Wordes unto Adam, his Owne
     Scriveyn.
Complaint of Annelida to False Arcite, The.
Complaint of Chaucer to His Empty Purse,
     The.
Complaint of Mars, The.
Complaint of Venus, The.
Complaint unto His Lady, A.
Complaint unto Pity, The.
Complaynt d'Amours.
Former Age, The.
Fortune.
Gentilesse.
House of Fame, The.
Lak of Stedfastnesse.
Legend of Good Women, The.
Lenvoy de Chaucer a Bukton.
Lenvoy de Chaucer a Scogan.
Merciles[s] Beaute [*or* Beautée *or* Beauty].
Parlement of Foules, The.
Proverbs: "What shul these clothes thus
     manyfold."
Queen Annelida and False Arcite.
To Rosamounde.
Troilus and Criseyde [*or* Criseide].
Womanly Noblesse.

Chesterton, G. K. (Gilbert Keith) (1874–1936)
Absent Friends.
Ad Amicos.
Adveniat Regnum Tuum.
Africa.
After Reading a Book of Modern Verse.
Afternoon Call, An.
Age of Reason, The.
Algernon Sydney.
Alone.
Ancient of Days, The.
Apocalypse ("First of the seals was opened;
     the gold of the dawn unsealed, The").
Apocalypse ("In seas and stones and painful
     lore of weeds").
Apology ("Alas, this Rembrandtesque
     design").
Apology, An.
Apology for a Letter Unposted, An.
Apology for Clowns, An.
Apology ("Forgive us you, whose pageant
     flames").
Apology of Bottom the Weaver, The.
Appeal of the Peers, The.
Arena, The.
Aristocrat, The.
Art Colours.
Artist, The.
As the Tree Falleth.
At Night.
Autumn.
Ave Maria.
Babe Unborn, The.
Ballad of Abbreviations, The.
Ballad of God-Makers, The.
Ballad of King Arthur, The.
Ballad of the Battle of Gibeon, The.
Barbara.
Battle.
Bay Combe.
Beaten Path, A.
Beatific Vision, The.
Beerbohm and Belloc.
Before a Statue of Cromwell.
Behind.
Bell, The.
Bellocose.
Benediction, A.
Black Virgin, The.
Blessed Are the Peacemakers.
Blessing, A ("I live in an age of varied powers
     and knowledge").
Blessing, A ("Sunlight in a child's hair").
Book of Wild Pictures, A.
Bootlaces.
Broad Minded Bishop Rebukes the Verminous
     St. Francis, A.

Buried City, The.
By a Reactionary.
By the Babe Unborn.
By the Sea.
Calvary, The.
Carpenter, The.
Child, The.
Chorus for a Play.
Chosen.
Christian Social Union, Nottingham, The.
Christmas Carol, A.
Christmas Carol, A: "God rest you merry gentlemen."
Christmas Rhyme, A.
Comfort for Communists.
Commercial Candour.
Comparisons.
Cosmic Factories, The.
Creation Day.
Creator, The.
Crooner, The.
Crown of Woman, The.
Crucified, The.
Crusader Returns from Captivity, The.
Crystal, The.
Curse in Free Verse, A.
Cyrano.
Daisy-Song.
Daisy, The.
Danton.
Darwinians at Play.
Dead Hero, The.
Deluge, The ("Though giant rains put out the sun").
Deluge, The ("When dark and deafening skies are bowed").
Desecraters, The.
Digby D'Avigdor.
Donkey, The.
Doubt.
E. C. B.
Earth's Champion.
Earth's Festival, The ("Let the wind be a whirl of trumpets").
Earth's Festival, The ("Walls and the dome of the evening, The").
Earth's Shame, The.
Earth's Vigil, The.
Easter Sunday.
Ecclesiastes.
Economics.
Education.
Ego.
Eheu Fugaces.
Election Echo, An.
Elegy in a Country Churchyard.
End of Fear, The.
English Graves, The.
Enid, An Invitation.
Epithalamium Argentum.
Escape, The.
Eskimo Song.
Eternal Heart, The.
Eternities.
Even unto the End of the World.
Evening.
Evolution.
Evolutionist to His Lady, The.
Fairy-Tale.
Fairy Tale, A.
Fanatic, The.
Femina Contra Mundum.
Fish, The.
For a War Memorial.
Fragment, A: "And the Woods, with gnarled and cruel."
Fragment from Dante.
Fragment in Correction of D. H. Lawrence.
Fragment: "Once more the man stood, saying 'A cottage-door.'"
Frances (A Fragment) ("'Twixt Bedford Park and Westminster").
Frances ("Dearest, whatever others see").
Frances ("God made thee mightily, my love").
Free Love: A Sonnet.
Friends.

Garden of the Virgin, The.
Gate of Everywhere, The.
Gentlemen Prefer Blondes.
Girl Guides.
Girls and Boys.
Gladstone.
Glencoe.
Gloria in Profundis.
God.
God of the Living, The.
Good Grocer, The (An Apology).
Good News.
Good Rich Man, The.
Grace, A.
Grass and Children.
Grave of Arthur, The.
Great Lord Archibald, The.
Green Leaves.
Happy Xmas, A.
Happy Xmas, A ("God rest you, merry gentlemen").
Happy Xmas, A ("Good King Wenceslas looked out").
Happy Xmas, A ("Observe the Convalescent Child").
Happy Xmas, A ("There came to Rhoda's Christmas feast").
Happy Xmas, A ("This Infant used to howl and yell").
Happy Xmas, A ("Upon me and my mackintosh").
Heirs of the Ages, The.
Henry Chard.
Heritage of Wonder, The.
Hero, The.
High Master and the Abbot of Fulham, The.
Higher Unity, The.
Holy of Holies, The.
Hope of the Year, The.
Horrible History of Jones, The.
House of Christmas, The.
Human Nature: or Marconi Memories.
Human Tree, The.
Humanity ("O'er the night-black city gazing, broken by the blaze and spark").
Humanity ("Poet, pallid and perverse, A").
Hunting of the Dragon, The.
Hymn, A.
Hymn for the Church Militant, A.
Hymn of the I.D.K., The.
Hymn of the Poor, The.
I Am.
Idolatry.
Idyll, An: "Tea is made; the red fogs shut round the house but the gas burns."
If I Could Sing.
Impermanence.
In Memoriam M. D.
In Memoriam P. D.
In October.
In the Balance.
In the Evening.
In the Lyme-Light.
Inscribed in a Copy of "Greybeards at Play."
Inscribed in a Copy of "The Ballad of the White Horse."
Inscribed in a Copy of "The Return of Don Quixote."
Inscription for Rhoda Bastable.
Inscription in "Poems and Ballads."
Interlude ("Here where the golden apples grow").
Interlude ("There sunken in deep woods they sang their song").
Invisible, The.
Invitation Declined, An.
It Is Not Well for Man to Be Alone.
J.D.C.: Chaunt of the Junior Debating Club.
J.D.C.: Ode; On the Second Annual Assembly of the Junior Debating Club, 1900.
J.D.C., The: A Celebration.
J.D.C., The: A Reunion.
J.D.C. Unhung, The.
Jazz, The.
Jealousy.

Joan.
Joseph.
Joys of Science, The.
Judgment of England, The.
Kingdom of Heaven, The.
King's Cross Station.
Kruger.
Lamp Post, The.
Last Hero, The.
Last Masquerade, The.
Laughter.
Lawrence [Solomon].
Legend of Good Women, The.
Legend of the Pessimist.
Lepanto.
Liberal Party, The.
Lilies of the Valley.
Lilies of the Valley (The Tragedy of an Idealist).
Limerick, A: "There was an old person of Lapland."
Lines by the Late Lord Tennyson (On Miss Spencer being transferred with her typewriter from the Study to the Dining Room).
Lines Inscribed for Mr. Thomas Hutchinson.
Lines on a Cricket Match.
Lines to a Young Lady Born Before April Fools' Day.
Lines to an Old Pro-Boer Who Asked for a Contribution to a Peace Periodical.
Lines to the Air of "Godolphin Horne."
Lines to the Statue of Ferdinand Foch.
Lines to Waterloo Station.
Lines Written in a Picture Book.
Lines Written in Dejection.
Lines Written in Oxford.
List, A.
Literal Land, The.
Little Litany, A.
Logic of Progress, The.
Logical Vegetarian, The.
London.
Lost.
Love: "Do I say no one has loved as I love?"
Love of God.
Love, We Have Looked on Many Shows.
Love's Trappist.
Lyme Regis Sed Sine Regina.
Macaroons.
Macaroons: An Ode.
Madge.
Madonna Mia.
Maid's Way, A.
Man, A.
Man and His Image, A.
Man Born on the Earth, A.
Man's Divine Equality.
Mariner, The.
Marriage Song, A.
Masterman and Chesterton.
Me Heart.
Mediaevalism.
Memory.
Men Like Gods.
Merger, The.
Midsummer Night's Dream, A.
Mildred.
Mirror of Madmen, The.
Mirth.
Mitre, The.
Modern Elfland.
Modern Magic, The.
Modern Manichee, The.
Monster, The.
Mortal Answers, The.
Mother of All.
Mr. Ford.
Mr Leonard Magnus.
Mrs. Baines.
Music.
Music.
Mystery, The.
Myth of Arthur, The.
Namesake.
Nativity by Botticelli, The.

Nativity, The.
Neglected Child, The.
New Fiction, The.
New Freethinker, The.
New Omar, The.
Nightmare.
Novelty, A.
Nursery Rhyme, A.
Nursery Rhymes No. 1: Property.
Nursery Rhymes No. 2: Education.
Nursery Rhymes No. 3.
Nurse's Song, The.
Old Gentleman in the Park, The.
Old Riddle, An.
Old Song, The.
On a Prohibitionist Poem.
On Being Forbidden to Feed the Dog.
On Being Thanked for a Favor.
On Himself.
On Lucian Oldershaw, Who Introduced Him to
    Frances.
On Professor Freud.
On Reading "God."
On Righteous Indignation.
On the Downs.
Orator of the Opposition, The.
Our Lady of Wain.
Our Ship Comes Home!
Outlaw, The.
Outline of History.
Pagans, The.
Parables ("Raven flapped o'er the rich man's
    roof, A").
Parables ("There was a man who dwelt in the
    east centuries ago").
Paradox, The.
Paraguay.
Pardon of Christmas, The.
Party Question, A.
Past and Present.
Patriotic Song, A.
Peace of Petrol, The.
Perfection.
Permanence.
Pessimist, The.
Philanthropist, The.
Pillar Box, The.
Pioneers, O Pioneers.
Plakkopytrixophylisperambulantiobatrix.
Player's Club, The.
Poland.
Poor Relations.
Port of London Authority, The.
Portrait, A ("Fair faces crowd on Christmas
    night").
Portrait, A ("Her hair is as a floating fire").
Post-Recessional.
Praise.
Praise of Dust, The.
Present Time, The.
Prologue to the Old Vic Pantomime.
Quotation, A.
Race-Memory.
Raid, A.
Rain, The.
Re-Born.
Real Anthem, The.
Red Cross Warrior, The.
Red Sea, The.
Refutation.
Regina Angelorum.
Reparation.
Resurrection.
Return of Eve, The.
Return to St. Paul's School, A.
Revolutionist, The: or Lines to a Statesman.
Rhyme for a Parlour Game.
Rhyme of Dust, A.
Riddle of the Conjurer, The.
Rival, A.
Road to Roundabout, The.
Rolling English Road, The.
Rotarians.
Saracen's Head, The.
Scorn of God, The.
Sea and Star.

Second Childhood, A.
Secrecy.
Secret People, The.
Shakespeare Memorial, The.
Silence.
Simon de Montfort.
Skeleton, The.
Snail, The.
Sociological Triolets.
Solitude Calls the Man.
Some Prophecies.
Some Revelations of Journalism.
Some Wishes at Xmas.
Song against Grocers, The.
Song Against Songs, The.
Song of Cosmopolitan Courage, A.
Song of Defeat, A.
Song of Labour, The.
Song of Right and Wrong, The.
Song of Self-Esteem, A.
Song of Songs, The.
Song of Swords, A.
Song of the Children, The.
Song of the Conspirators.
Song of the Cradle, The.
Song of the Dog Quoodle, The.
Song of the Great Sea Serpent, The.
Song of the Oak, The.
Song of the Sea-Wealth, The.
Song of the Strange Ascetic, The.
Song of the Wheel, The.
Song of the Wheels, The.
Song of Wild Fruit, A.
Song to an Old Tune.
Songs for the City.
Sonnet: "High on the wall that holds
    Jerusalem."
Sonnet: "If you have picked your lawn of
    leaves and snails."
Sonnet with the Compliments of the Season.
Sonnets in Summer Heat.
Speech Reported, A.
Spelling Lesson, A.
Spilth.
Spring Song, A.
St. Francis of Assisi.
St. Francis Xavier.
Standing Invitation, A.
Stilton and Milton; Or Literature in the 17th
    and 20th Centuries.
Strange Music, The.
Suddenly in the Midst.
Suffering.
Sunset and Dawn.
Sword of Surprise, The.
Tea Poet, The.
Temple of Earth, The.
Testament, A.
Thank God.
Thank-You.
'Thank-You' for Coming to Tea, A.
Theory.
There Is a Heart.
Thou Shalt Not Kill.
Thought and Reflections.
Three Conquistadors, The.
Three Realities, The.
Three Things.
To a Catherine Wheel.
To a Certain Nation.
To a Holy Roller.
To a Lady.
To a Poetess.
To a Tolerant Mother.
To a Turk.
To Captain Fryatt.
To Clare Nicholl.
To Dorothy Collins from G. K. Chesterton.
To Dorothy—on Her Birthday—with Love.
To E. H. and G. M.
To Edmund Clerihew Bentley.
To Enid the Huntress.
To Enid, Who Acted the Cat in Private
    Pantomime.
To Father O'Connor.
To Frances.

To Freda Spencer.
To Hilaire Belloc.
To His Love.
To His Wife, in Her Illness.
To J. L.
To L. K. C.
To L. K. C. from G. K. C.
To M. E. W.
To My Lady.
To Patricia Gilgert Who Acted.
To Punch.
To Rhoda.
To Rhoda, otherwise called Rohda.
To St. Michael, in Time of Peace.
To the Jesuits.
To the Unknown Warrior.
To Them That Mourn.
To Young Pessimists.
Together.
Towers of Time, The.
Trinity.
Trinkets, The.
Triolet: "I wish I were a jelly fish."
Triumph of Man, The ("I plod and peer amid
    mean sounds and shapes").
Triumph of Man, The ("Say: Who is this that
    cometh royally").
Truce of Christmas, The.
True Lovers.
True Sensibility.
True Sympathy; or, Prevention of Cruelty to
    Teachers.
Twilight.
Two Maidens, The.
Two Women, The.
Ubi Ecclesia.
Ultimate.
Uncreation.
Union, The.
Unpardonable Sin, The.
Unwritten.
Vanity.
Verdict, A.
Verses Made up in a Dream.
Vision.
Vision of Edens, A.
Voices.
Vulgarised.
Walk, A.
Walton-on-the-Naze.
Wedding in War-Time, A.
What Is a Buslus?
When I Came Back to Fleet Street.
White Witch, The.
Who Goes Home?
Wife of Flanders, The.
William of Orange.
Wine and Water.
Wise Men, The.
Wish, A.
Wood-Cutter, The.
Word, A.
World State, The.
World's Miser, The.
Worship.
Xmas Day.

Chiabrera, Gabriello (1552–1638)
Destined to war from very infancy.
Not without heavy grief of heart did He.
O flower of all that springs from gentle blood.
O Lelius, beauteous flower of gentleness.
O Thou who movest onward with a mind.
Pause, courteous Spirit!—Baldi supplicates.
Perhaps some needful service of the State.
There never breathed a man who, when his
    life.
Torquato Tasso rests within this tomb.
True it is that Ambrosio Salinero.
Weep not, belovèd Friends! nor let the air.

Cho Wen-chun (*fl.* 2nd cent.)
Lament of a Graying Woman.

Christov, Boris (b. 1945)
Body.
Spirit.

Chuang Tzu
Action and Non-Action.

Active Life.
Advising the Prince.
Apologies.
Autumn Floods.
Breath of Nature, The.
Confucius and the Madman.
Cracking the Safe.
Cutting up an Ox.
Duke Hwan and the Wheelwright.
Empty Boat, The.
Fighting Cock, The.
Five Enemies, The.
Flight of Lin Hui, The.
Good Fortune.
Great and Small.
Great Knowledge.
Hat Salesman and a Capable Ruler, A.
Importance of Being Toothless, The.
In My End Is My Beginning.
Inner Law, The.
Joy of Fishes, The.
Keng Sang Chu.
Keng's Disciple.
Kingly Man, The.
Lao Tzu's Wake.
Lost Pearl, The.
Man Is Born in Tao.
Man of Tao, The.
Man with One Foot and the Marsh Pheasant,
    The.
Metamorphosis.
Need to Win, The.
Owl and Phoenix.
P'eng That Was a K'un, The.
Perfect Joy.
Starlight and Non-Being.
Symphony for a Sea Bird.
Tao.
Three Friends.
Tower of the Spirit, The.
True Man, The.
Turtle, The.
Two Kings and No-Form.
Useless, The.
Useless Tree, The.
When a Hideous Man.
When Knowledge Went North.
When the Shoe Fits.
Where Is Tao?
Wholeness.
Woodcarver, The.

Chumacero, Alí
    Wanderings of the Tribe, The.
    Widower's Monologue.

Chung Yuan Liu (773–819)
    Birds have flown away from the mountains,
    The.

Ciardi, John (1916–86)
    A is for ANT.
    Abundance.
    Addio.
    Advertisement for a Reader.
    After Sunday Dinner We Uncles Snooze.
    Afternoon in the Park, An.
    Aging Lovers, The.
    Alec.
    Anatomy Lab.
    And Thy Mother.
    Annals.
    Another Comedy.
    Apartment with a View, An.
    Apology for a Lost Classicism, An.
    Apology for Not Invoking the Muse, An.
    Apprehendee Then Exited Vee-hicle.
    Aquarium.
    Are We Through Talking, I Hope?
    As I Would Wish You Birds.
    Aspect of the Air, An.
    At Cocktails.
    At First Flower of the Easy Day.
    At Least with Good Whiskey.
    At O'Hare.
    Audit at Key West.
    Aunt Mary.
    Autobiography of a Comedian.
    B is for BOMBERS, our national pride.

Baboon and the State, The.
Back.
Back Home in Pompeii.
Back through the Looking Glass to This Side.
Ballad of the Icondic.
Barmecide Feast.
Bashing the Babies.
Bedlam Revisited.
Bees and Morning Glories.
Being Called.
Benefits of an Education, The.
Between.
Bicentennial.
Biography.
Bird in Whatever Name, The.
Bird Watching.
Birds, like Thoughts.
Birthday.
Blue Movie.
Box Comes Home, A.
Boy.
Boy or Girl.
Bridal Photo, 1906.
C is for CAMEL, a very right beast.
Call It a Day.
Camptown.
Captain Nicholas Strong.
Cartographer of Meadows, The.
Carving the Turkey.
Catalpa, The.
Cathedral.
Censorship.
Censorship.
Cézanne.
Chelsea Naval Hospital.
Childe Horvald to the Dark Tower Came.
Christmas Alone in Key West.
Christmas Carol, A: "Stores wore Christmas
    perfectly, The."
Christmas Eve.
Clock in the Mirror, The.
Colossus in Quicksand, The.
Come Morning.
Conversation with Leonardo, A.
Coq au Vin.
Corpus Christi.
Counting on Flowers.
Cow, The.
Craft.
Crate of Sterling Loving Cups, A.
Credibility.
Credo ("I asked the doctor who had
    pronounced me dead").
Credo ("Today / Dr. William Carlos
    Williams").
Daemons.
Damn Her.
Damnation of Doves, A.
Darling.
Dawn of the Space Age.
Days.
Dead Pigeon on South Street.
Dear Sir.
Death of a Bomber.
Deaths about You when You Stir in Sleep, The.
December 13, 1979.
Dialogue.
Dialogue in the Shade, A.
Dialogue with Outer Space.
Diary Entry.
Differences.
Divorced, Husband Demolishes House.
Dogmatism.
Dolls, The.
Domestic Sonnet.
Done for the Doing.
Donne Ch'avete Intellètto d'Amore.
Down Narrow Stairs from a Thin Eye.
Dragons.
Dream, A.
Driving across the American Desert and
    Thinking of the Sahara.
East Sixty-seventh Street.
Echoes.
Eggs.
Elaine.
Elegy 1: "I fell from the bouncing tailgate to

roll in traffic."
Elegy 2: "I dream awake in the uptown
    morning."
Elegy for a Cave Full of Bones.
Elegy for a Sweet Sharpy.
Elegy for G. B. Shaw.
Elegy for Jog.
Elegy for Moral Self-Assurance and Country
    Virtue, An.
Elegy for Sam.
Elegy for the Face at Your Elbow.
Elegy: For You, Father.
Elegy Just in Case.
Elegy: "My father was born with a spade in his
    hand and traded it."
Elegy 3, Cavalcante.
Elegy: "Some gone like boys to school
    wearing their badges."
Elegy: "This is the body of my good gray
    practical dead."
11:02 A.M. The Bird Disappeared.
Emeritus Addresses the School, An.
Encounter.
English A.
Epitaph: "Here, time concurring (and it does)."
Epithalamium at St. Michael's Cemetary.
Evening of the Private Eye, An.
Evensong.
Every Time You Are Sleeping and I.
Everywhere That Universe.
Evil Eye, The.
Expendability.
Fable of Survival, A.
Faces.
Fast as You Can Count to Ten.
Feasts.
Figure Drawn in Wire, The.
Finally that Blue Receding Sphere.
Firsts.
Flowering Quince.
Food Notes.
Foolish Wing, The.
For Instance.
For Judith.
For Miller Williams.
For My Nephew Going to Bed.
For My Son John.
For Myra, John L., and Benn.
For Myra out of the Album.
Formalities, The.
4:00 A.M. on the Terrace.
Fragment of a Bas Relief.
Fragment: "To the laboratory then I went.
    What little."
Fragments [or Poems] from Italy.
Freshman Sonnet: Success.
Friends.
From Adam's Diary.
G, also inevitably, is for GNU.
Galileo and the Laws.
Generation Gap.
George Washington Brige.
Gift, The.
Glory, The.
God.
Going to the Dogs.
Goodmorning with Light.
Goodnight.
Gray Spring Morning, A.
Guide to Poetry, A.
Gulls Land and Cease to Be.
H is, reluctantly, for HUMAN, a word.
Happiness.
Hawk.
Health of Captains, The.
Heatwave.
High Tension Lines across a Landscape.
Homecoming—Massachusetts.
Hometown after a War.
I is, naturally enough, any author.
I Remember the House That Was.
I was Not Sleeping nor Awake.
I'm No Good for You.
Image of Man as a Gardener after Two World
    Wars.

Improvisation for a Southern Night.
In Paul's Room.
In Pity as We Kiss and Lie.
In Place of a Curse.
In Some Doubt but Willingly.
In the Audience.
In the Rich Farmer's Field.
In the Year of Many Conversions and the
    Private Soul.
Incident.
Inscription for Richard Eberhard, An.
Instances.
Interruption, An.
Invasion of Sleep Walkers, The.
Island Galaxy, An.
It Is for the Waking Man to Tell His Dreams.
It Is the Same Place Always Once Again.
It Took Four Flowerboats to Convoy My
    Father's Black.
J is, splendidly, for JOHN, my.
January 1, 1973.
January 2, 1978.
Joe with a Wooden Leg.
Joshua on Eighth Avenue.
Keeping.
Knothole in Spent Time, A.
Knowing Bitches.
Lamb, The.
Landscapes of My Name.
Last Rites.
Late Peaches.
Launcelot in Hell.
Leaving Longboat Key.
Letter for Those Who Grew Up Together.
Letter from a Death Bed.
Letter from a Metaphysical Countryside.
Letter from a Pander.
Letter from a Rubber Raft.
Letter from an Empty House.
Letter from an Island.
Letter Homeward.
Letter to Dante.
Letter to Mother.
Letter to Virginia Johnson.
Limits of Friendship, The.
Lines for Myra to Grow To.
Lines: "I did not have exactly a way of life."
Lines while Walking Home from a Party on
    Charles Street.
L'Inglese.
Little One, The.
Logician's Nocturne, The.
Love Poem, A: "I have labored for her love."
Love Sonnet: Believing Part of Almost All I
    Say.
Loving You Is Something to Do.
Lung Fish, The.
M is for MOTHERS, who are, above all.
Machine.
Magus, A.
Man and a Woman Might at This Moment, A.
Man Came Tuesday, A.
Manocalzata (Gloved Hand).
March Morning.
Massive Retaliation.
Matins.
Measurements.
Memo: Preliminary Draft of a Prayer to God
    the Father.
Memoir of a One-Armed Harp Teacher.
Memorial Day.
Memory of the Sad Chair, A.
Men marry what they need. I marry you.
Midnight.
Minus One.
Miss Olivia Branton.
Missouri Fable, A.
Mr. & Mrs.
Monday Morning: London.
Morning.
Morning: I Know Perfectly How in a Minute
    You Will Stretch and Smile.
Morning in the Park.
Mule.
Mutterings.
My Father Died Imperfect as a Man.

My Father's Watch.
My Tribe.
Mystic River.
N is for NANNYGOAT—the silly.
New Year's Eve.
Night Freight, Michigan.
Night Piece for My Twenty-seventh Birthday.
No White Birds Sings.
Notes.
Nothing Is Really Hard but to Be Real.
O is for OX, by which word we.
Obit.
Obsolescence.
Ode for School Convocation.
Oedipus Tyrannus.
Of Fish and Fishermen.
Old Man.
Old Man Confesses, An.
On a Photo of Sgt. Ciardi a Year Later.
On Being Sure and of What.
On Flunking a Nice Boy out of School.
On Looking East to the Sea with a Sunset
    behind Me.
On Meeting Miss B.
On Passion as a Literary Tradition.
On Sending Home My Civilian Clothes.
On the Orthodoxy and Creed of My Power
    Mower.
On the Patio.
On the Poet as a Damned Poor Thing.
One Dull Thing You Did Was to Die, Fletcher,
    The.
One Easter Not on the Calendar I Woke.
One Jay at a Time.
One Morning.
One Wet Iota.
Orders.
Overthrow, An.
Palaver's No Prayer.
Peaks.
Pencil Stub Journals.
Philosophical Poem.
Pilot in the Jungle, The.
Plea, A.
Poem for a Soldier's Girl.
Poem for Benn's Graduation from High
    School, A.
Poem for My Thirty-ninth Birthday.
Poem for My Twenty-ninth Birthday.
Poetry.
Poetry.
Poetry.
Poet's Words, The.
Port of Aerial Embarkation.
Possibilities.
Praise of Good Poets in a Bad Age, A.
Prayer to the Mountain, A.
Q may as well be for QUEEN.
Quirks.
R is for RAT, the noise in man's wall.
Reality and Willie Yeats.
Reply to S. K.
Requisitioning.
Returning Home.
Reverie during Briefing.
Rhetoric for Danny Keough to Recite at the
    Bar, A.
Rite, The.
Ritual for Singing Bat.
Roman Diary: 1951.
S.P.Q.R. A Letter from Rome.
Saipan.
Saturday.
Saturday, March 6.
Sea-Birds.
Sea Burial.
Sea Marshes in Winter.
Sea Shines, The.
Selectivity.
Serenade in a Drugstore.
Sermon Notes.
Shaft, The.
Shore Piece.
Size of Song, The.
Sleep (by Rousseau), A.
Small.

Small Elegy.
Snowy Heron.
Socializing with a Creature.
Some Figures for Who Must Speak.
Some Sort of Game.
Sometimes the Foundering Fury.
Song for an Allegorical Play.
Sorrow of Obedience, The.
Sounds.
Spring in Statue Square.
Spring Song ("Do you remember by morning
    when the sun").
Spring Song ("Wake early to the early robin").
Starlet.
Starry Heavens, the Moral Law, The.
Statement.
Stations.
Stills and Rapids of Your Nakedness, The.
Stone without Edges Has Not Been Mined,
    The.
Storm.
Styles.
Suburban.
Suburban Homecoming.
Successful Species, A.
Survival in Missouri.
T, the TURTLE, has been a long time coming.
Take-off over Kansas.
Talking Myself to Sleep at One More Hilton.
Temptation.
Ten Years Ago when I Played at Being Brave.
Tenzone.
Thanks to a Botanist, A.
Thinking about Girls.
This Morning.
This Moving Meaninglessness.
Thought about Sheik Bedreddin, A.
Thoughts on Looking into a Thicket.
Thousandth Poem for Dylan Thomas, A.
Three A.M. and Then Five.
Three Eggs Up.
Three Views of a Mother.
Thursday.
Time Is the Late Train into Albany.
To a Lovely Lady Gone to Theory.
To a Young American the Day after the Fall of
    Barcelona.
To Dudley Fitts.
To Judith Asleep.
To Lucasta, about That War.
To My Students.
To One "Investigated" by the Last Senate
    Committee, or the Next.
To W. T. Scott.
To Westward.
Tommy's Pond.
Traffic Victim Sends a Sonnet of Confused
    Thanks to God as the Sovereign Host, A.
Tragedy-Maker, The.
Tree, The.
Tree Trimming.
Trenta-Sei of the Pleasure We Take in the
    Early Death of Keats, A.
True or False.
Trying to Feel Something.
.22.
Twice, Away from Jack, I Thought of Him.
Two Dry Poems.
Two Egrets.
Two for Gertrude Kasle.
Two Hours.
Two Poems for Benn.
Two Songs for a Gunner.
Ugliness.
Useless Knowledge.
V-J Day.
Vale.
Verbal Generation, The.
Visit to Aunt Francesca, A.
Vodka.
Wafflebutt.
Was a Man.
Washing Your Feet.
Watching a Kettle Boil.
Week That Was, The.
What *Was* Her Name.

When a Man Dies.
When I Am Not Dead.
Why Don't You Write for Me?
Winter Music.
Yet Not to Listen to That Sung Nothing.

Cino da Pistoia (1270–1336)
Canzone: His Lament for Selvaggia.
Canzone: On the Death of Beatrice Portinari.
Madrigal: To his Lady Selvaggia Vergiolesi;
  likening his Love to a search for Gold.
Sonnet: A Trance of Love.
Sonnet: Death is not without but within him.
Sonnet: He answers Dante, confessing his
  unsteadfast Heart.
Sonnet: He answers the foregoing Sonnet, and
  prays Dante, in the name of Beatrice, to
  continue his great Poem.
Sonnet: He conceives of some Compensation
  in Death.
Sonnet: He impugns the verdicts of Dante's
  Commedia.
Sonnet: He interprets Dante's Dream, related in
  the first Sonnet of the Vita Nuova.
Sonnet: He owes nothing to Guido as a Poet.
Sonnet: Of the grave of Selvaggia, on the
  Monte della Sambuca.
Sonnet: To Love, in great Bitterness.

Clampitt, Amy (1920–94)
Alders.
Alice.
Amaranth and Moly.
Amherst.
Anatomy of Migraine, An.
Anniversary, The.
Ano Prinios.
Antiphonal.
Archaic Figure.
At a Rest Stop in Ohio.
At Easterly.
At Muker, Upper Swaledale.
Athena.
Atlas Immobilized.
August Darks, The.
Babel Aboard the Hellas International Express.
Balms.
Baroque Sunburst, A.
Bayou Afternoon.
Beach Glass.
Beach Pea, The.
Beethoven, Opus 111.
Berceuse.
Bertie Goes Hunting.
Birdham.
Black Buttercups.
Blueberrying in August.
Botanical Nomenclature.
Brought from Beyond.
Burial in Cypress Hills.
Burning Child, The.
Cadenza, A.
Camouflage.
Chichester.
Cloudberry Summer.
Coleorton.
Continental Drift.
Cooling Tower, The.
Cormorant in Its Element, The.
Cove, The.
Cure at Porlock, A.
Curfew, A.
Dahlia Gardens, The.
Dakota, The.
Dallas–Fort Worth: Redbud and Mistletoe.
Dancers Exercising.
Dejection: A Footnote.
Deleted Passage.
Discovery.
Dodona: Asked of the Oracle.
Easedale Tarn.
Easter Morning.
Edge of the Hurricane, The.
'Eighty-Nine.
Elgin Marbles, The.
Exmoor.
Field Pansy, The.
Fireweed.

Fog.
From a Clinic Waiting Room.
George Eliot Country.
Godfather Returns to Color TV, The.
Good Friday.
Gooseberry Fool.
Gradual Clearing.
Grasmere.
Grasses.
Green.
Hairline Fracture, A.
Halloween Parade, The.
Handed Down.
Having Lunch at Brasenose.
He Dreams of Being Warm.
Hedge of Rubber Trees. A.
Hermit Thrush, A.
Hickory Grove, The.
High Culture.
High Noon.
Highgate Cemetery.
Hippocrene.
Hispaniola.
Homeland.
Homer, A.D. 1982.
Horned Rampion, The.
Hurricane and Charlotte Mew, The.
Imago.
In Umbria: A Snapshot.
Iola, Kansas.
Isle of Wight, The.
John Donne in California.
Kingfisher, The.
Kudzu Dormant.
Leaving Yannina.
Let the Air Circulate.
Letters from Jerusalem.
Lindenbloom.
Local Genius, The.
London Inside and Outside.
Losing Track of Language.
Low Tide at Schoodic.
Man Feeding Pigeons.
Manhattan.
Margaret Fuller, 1847.
Margate.
Marginal Employment.
Marine Surface, Low Overcast.
Matoaka.
Matrix (Villa Serbelloni, Lake Como).
Meadowlark Country.
Medusa.
Medusa at Broadstairs.
Meridian.
Midsummer in the Blueberry Barrens.
Minor Tremor, A.
Mulciber at West Egg.
My Cousin Muriel.
Nereids of Seriphos, The.
New Life, A.
Nondescript.
Note from Leyden, A.
Notes on the State of Virginia.
Nothing Stays Put.
Odessa Steps, The.
Olive Groves of Thasos, The.
Olympia.
On the Disadvantages of Central Heating.
Or Consider Prometheus.
Outer Bar, The.
Palm Sunday.
Paumanok.
Perseus.
Perseus Airborne.
Portola Valley.
Prairie, The.
Procession at Candlemas, A.
Progress at Building Site With (Fewer)
  Pigeons.
Quarry, The.
Rain at Bellagio.
Real Estate.
Reedbeds of the Hackensack, The.
Remembering Greece.
Reservoirs of Mount Helicon, The.
Resumption, Or Possibly a Remission, A.

Ringing Doorbells.
Runes, Blurs, Sap Rising.
Rydal Mount.
Sacred Hearth Fire, The.
Saloniki.
Salvage.
Savannah.
Scaffold, A.
Sea Mouse.
Sed de Correr.
Seder Night.
Seed.
Seriphos Unvisited.
Shorebird-Watching.
Silence, A.
Slow Motion.
Smaller Orchid, The.
Spruce Has No Taproot, The.
Stacking the Straw.
Subway Singer, The.
Sun Underfoot Among the Sundews, The.
Sunday Music.
Syrinx.
Teignmouth.
Tempe in the Rain.
Tepoztlán.
Thermopylae.
Thinking Red.
Tidewater Winter.
Time.
Times Square Water Music.
Townhouse Interior with Cat.
Trasimene.
Urn-Burial and the Butterfly Migration.
Vacant Lot with Pokeweed.
Vacant Lot with Tumbleweed and Pigeons.
Venice Revisited.
Voyages.
War Memorial, The.
Waterfall, The.
Westward.
What the Light Was Like.
Whippoorwill in the Woods, A.
White.
Winchester: The Autumn Equinox.
Winter Burial, A.
Witness.
Woodlot, The.
Written in Water.

Clare, John (1793–1864)
Badger.
Badger, The, *sels.*
Bean Field, The.
Braggart.
Child Harold, *sels.*
Clown, The.
Don Juan, *sels.*
Dying Child, The.
Evening.
Evening.
Gipsies: "Gipsies seek wide sheltering woods
  again, The."
Gipsies: "Snow falls deep; the forest lies alone,
  The."
Grasshoppers.
Hedgehog, The.
I Am.
Impromptu on Winter.
Lout, The: "For Sunday's play he never makes
  excuse."
Lout, The: "No sort of learning ever hurts his
  head."
Love and Solitude.
Marten.
Merry Maid.
Mole-Catcher, The.
My Mary.
Old Man, The.
Scandal.
Shepherd's [*or* Shepheards] Calendar, The,
  sels.
Song: "I peeled bits of straw and I got switches
  too."
Sonnet: "I love to see the summer beaming
  forth."
Tramp, The.

Turkeys, *sels.*
Winter Evening.
Young Rabbits.

Claudian (Claudius Claudianus) (c.370–404)
Against Eutropius, *sels.*
From word to word th' ambiguous sense is
    played.
Obscure, unpriz'd, and dark, the magnet lies.

Claudianus, Claudius *See* **Claudian**
Clemens, Prudentius Aurelius *See* **Prudentius**
Clemens, Titus Flavius *See* **Clement of
    Alexandria**
**Clement of Alexandria (Titus Flavius Clemens)
    (c.150–c.220)**
Diatribe Against the Old Gods, *sels.*
Logos Our Teacher, The.
New Song, The.
Soldiers of Peace.

Clifton, Lucille (b. 1936)
Adam Thinking.
Alabama 9/15/63.
Album.
Amazons.
August.
Birth of Language, The.
Birthday 1999.
Blessing the Boats.
Coming of Fox, The.
Crabbing.
Dear Fox.
Death of Fred Clifton, The.
Death of Thelma Sayles.
Dialysis.
Donor.
Dream of Foxes, A.
Earth Is a Living Thing, The.
Eve Thinking.
Eve's version.
Far Memory.
Female.
Final Note to Clark.
Fox.
Further Note to Clark.
Garden of Delight, The.
Grief.
Hag Riding.
Heaven.
Here Yet Be Dragons.
If I Should.
Imagining Bear.
Jasper Texas 1998.
Lazarus.
Lazarus ("I am not the same man").
Lazarus ("On the third day i contemplate").
Leaving Fox.
Leda 1.
Leda 2.
Leda 3.
Libation.
Lives.
Lorena.
Lot's Wife 1988.
Lucifer Speaks in His Own Voice.
Lucifer Understanding at Last.
Lumpectomy Eve.
Memory.
Memphis.
Message of Thelma Sayles, The.
Moonchild.
My Dream About Being White.
My Dream About Falling.
My Dream About God.
My Dream About the Cows.
My Dream About the Poet.
My Dream About the Second Coming.
My Dream About Time.
1994.
Note, Passed to Superman.
Oh where have you fallen to.
One Year Later.
Peeping Tom.
Photograph.
Photograph, The: A Lynching.
Poem in Praise of Menstruation.
Poem to My Uterus.

Praise Song.
Quilting.
Remembering the Birth of Lucifer.
Report from the angel of eden.
Rust.
Shapeshifter Poems.
Signs.
Slaveship[s].
Sleeping Beauty.
Song at Midnight.
Sorrow Song.
Story Thus Far, The.
Study the Masters.
Telling Our Stories.
Times, The.
To My Last Period.
What Did She Know, When Did She Know It.
What I Think When I Ride the Train.
Whispered to Lucifer.
White Lady.
Why some people be mad at me sometimes.
Wild Blessings.
Wishes for Sons.
Women You Are Accustomed To, The.
Yeti Poet Returns to His Village to Tell His
    Story, The.

Clough, Arthur Hugh (1819–61)
About what sort of thing.
Adam and Eve.
Ah, what is love, our love, she said.
Alcaics.
Alteram Partem.
Amours de Voyage.
As one who shoots an arrow overhead.
Away, haunt not thou me.
Because a Lady chose to say.
Bethesda: A Sequel.
Blank Misgivings of a Creature Moving About
    in Worlds Not Realized.
Come Home, Come Home!
Come pleasant thoughts; sweet thoughts, at
    will.
Dance on, dance on, we see, we see.
Darkness.
Dipsychus [and the Spirit], *sels.*
Do duty feeling nought and truth believe.
Duty.
Easter Day II.
Easter Day. Naples, 1849.
Effusions of a School-Patriarch, The.
Enough, small Room,—though all too true.
Epi-strauss-ium.
From far and near / He drew the scattered
    ciphers.
From the contamination / Of laudation.
From thy far sources 'mid mountains airily
    climbing.
Go foolish thoughts, and join the throng.
He sate, no stiller stands a rock.
Here have I been these one and twenty years.
Homo Sum, Nihil Humani—.
How in all wonder Columbus got over.
Hymnos Aymnos.
I dreamed a dream: I dreamt that I espied.
If help there is not, but the Muse.
If to write, rewrite, and write again.
In controversial foul impureness.
In Stratis Viarum II.
In Stratis Viarum III.
In Stratis Viarum IV.
In the Great Metropolis.
Incident, An.
Irritability unnatural.
July's Farewell.
Latest Decalogue, The.
Light words they were, and lightly, falsely
    said.
Like one that in a dream would fain arise.
Look you, my simple friend, 'tis one of those.
Mari Magno, *sels.*
Mari Magno I.
My wind is turned to bitter north.
Natura Naturans.
Nay draw not yet the cork, my friend.
O happy they whose hearts receive.
O Heaven, and thou most loving family.

O Qui Me—!
O stream, descending to the sea.
O Theos Meta Sou.
O'Brien, most disconsolate of Men.
Oh, ask not what is love, she said.
Oh, I have done those things that my Soul
    fears.
Old things need not be therefore true.
Peschiera.
Pont-Y-Wern.
Qua Cursum Ventus.
Questioning Spirit, The.
Qui Laborat, Orat.
Resignation—to Faustus.
Sa Majestá Très Chrétienne.
Say Not the Struggle Nought Availeth.
Sectantem levia nervi deficiunt.
See! the faint green tinge from the western sky
    has.
Seven Sonnets.
Sic Itur.
Songs in Absence, *sels.*
Sweet streamlet bason! at thy side.
That out of sight is out of mind.
That there are powers above us I admit.
These vulgar ways that round me be.
Thesis and Antithesis.
Thou bidd'st me mark how swells with rage.
Thought may well be ever ranging.
Thoughts of Home.
To be, to be thine.
To spend unsolaced years of pain.
To the Great Metropolis.
To think that men of former days.
Truth is a golden thread seen here and there.
Upon the water in the boat.
Uranus.
Veni.
Were I with you or you with me.
What we, when face to face we see, *sels.*
What we, when face to face we see.
When Israel Came Out of Egypt.
When panting sighs the bosom fill.
Whence are ye, vague desires.
With Whom Is No Variableness, Neither
    Shadow of Turning.
Ye flags of Piccadilly, / Where I posted up and
    down.

"Clout, Colin" *See* **Spenser, Edmund**
Codrescu, Andrei (b. 1946)
À Face.
À Francis Ponge.
About Photography.
Against Meaning.
Alberta.
Alice's Brilliance.
All Wars Are Holy.
&.
And in her memory God knows.
& Power.
Architecture.
At Home.
Attempt to Spell, Incantate and Annoy.
Au Bout du Temps.
Ballad of the Typist.
Belligerence.
Best Side of Me, The.
Bi-lingual.
Biographical Notes.
Blues for Casanova.
Body Blues.
Books.
Breakfast Elegy.
Brief (Remembered) *Histoire* of Rejection, A.
Casino Pierre.
Casting.
Center Piece.
Christmas in New York.
Circle Jerk.
Cohere Britannia.
Comrade Past & Mister Present.
Cook in Hell, A.
Crossed Hands.
De Natura Rerum.
Dear Editors.
Dear Masoch.

Debts.
Demands of Exile.
Designs.
Differences, The.
Discovery of Prayer, The.
Dollar Air.
Dollar Dance.
Don't Wait for Me.
Dream (1).
Dream (2).
Dream Dogs.
Drizzle off the Ocean.
Drowning Another Peasant Inquisition.
Early Fix.
Election.
En Passant.
End Games.
Epitaph (1): "Julio hernadez does not lie here."
Epitaph (2): "He was a young guy with surrealist connections."
Ethnic Jammies.
Eugenio Montale in California.
Evening Particulier.
Every Tie.
Face Portrait.
Faith Relearned.
Fascination
Fear.
1st Avenue Basics.
First Icon with Gun, The.
5 Ways of Saying the Same Thing.
Food.
For Marg So She Could Fuck Again.
For Thom Gunn.
From a Trilogy of Birds.
Gambling Phoenix, The.
Game, A.
Getting There.
Ghouls of Candlemas, The.
Gifts of Percussion.
Gist.
Goldrush, The.
Good Morning.
Good Spirit, The.
Good Thing When I See One, A.
Grammar.
Grammar, A.
Here.
History.
History of the Growth of Heaven, The ("As a funny monk one is never sure where").
History of the Growth of Heaven, The ("*Tout ce qui existe est situé*" said max jacob and one day my situation").
Holy Grail, The.
Honesty can't be encouraged in individuals. It must.
Hop Scotch.
Horse Power.
Howdy.
Human Touch Misunderstood, A.
Hymn of Pan the Flower, The.
I Visit Brooklyn with a Queen in Mind.
Igni Natura Renovatur Integra (Nature Is Completely Renewed by Fire).
I'm careful with my dreams of death.
Imagination of Necessity, The.
Imported Days.
In Praise of the New Russian Writers.
In the Supermarket.
Indecent Assumption, the Slaughter Songs, The.
Inner Source, The.
Intention.
Introduction, The.
Invitation to a Molecular Feast.
Irony as Nursery.
It takes joy to listen and it is inspiring being listened to.
Jingling the Cookery.
Junk Dawn, NYC.
Junk Mail.
Lady Painter, The.
Late Night, San Francisco.
Leafy Angel, A.

Leaves of Nerves.
Les Fleurs du Cinéma.
Letter to Ezra Pound.
License to Carry a Gun, The.
Life on Film of St. Theresa, The.
Long Door.
Looks from Money.
Love & the Documents.
Love of a Coat, The.
Love Poem: "And while for the sake of sanity."
Mail.
"MAN" and "WOMAN," these are horrid words, they annoy me.
Manifesto.
3/6/81, Amtrack.
Marriage of Insult to Injury, The.
Matinée.
Memoria Voraciae Simplex.
Mnemogasoline.
Model Work.
Momentary Bafflement with Return Home at Dawn.
Monk, The.
More about Poems.
Moss.
Muffled by a Belt across the Mouth.
Music.
Music.
My Next Book.
Near Sonnet.
New Gazette, The.
New York.
Night of a Faun.
Not a Pot to Piss In.
Note.
November 6, 1984.
October 19.
October 17.
Ode to Curiosity.
Ode to Laryngitis.
Old Cities.
Old Photo.
On an Industrial Ruin.
On Organization.
On Translation.
Operations of Desire, The.
Opium for Archie Anderson.
Opium for Britt Wilkie.
Orbital Complexion.
Origin of Electricity, The.
Paper on Humor.
Park, The.
Partiti Sunt Vestimenta Mea Miserunt Sortem.
Pastoral: "Autumn blows a withered hand on."
Penal Cavalry, The.
Petite Histoire of Red Fascism, A.
Petite Madeleine.
Piano & Everything Nice.
Poem for Kyra.
Poem: "Supreme test of one's poem, The."
Poetry.
Poetry Paper.
Point, A.
Police, The.
Politics.
Port of Call.
Power.
Programme for the Double Barrel Life When It Hits, A.
Question of Personnel, The.
Rain.
Remembrance of My Forgotten Skinniness.
Reverse.
Reverse.
Roto: How the Bourgeoisie Dream.
Russia or The Weakness of Photography.
Sadness Unhinged.
San Francisco for Whomever.
Sarrasin's Wealth Song.
Saturnian Dilemma.
School Daze.
Sea Sickness.
Second Letter to Junk Jeannee of NYC.
Secret Training.
Seeing out of the Sub.

Selavie.
Serious Morning, A.
Shop.
Silence.
Sin of Wanting a New Refrigerator, The.
Slot-O-Topia.
Snail Sail.
Some Days.
Souls Looking for Bodies.
Space Soufflé.
Star Book.
Status of the Monk, The.
Staying with It.
Still, A.
Still Life.
Stock Report.
Stupor at the End of May.
Sunday Sermon.
Symmetry.
Talismanic Ceremony for Lucian, March 9, 1971, Intersection Church, San Francisco.
Telegram.
Telyric.
Testing. Testing.
Tête-à-Tête.
Tetrachlorine.
There is an orange rotting on the table.
Thieves, Seasons.
Thing, A.
Threat, The.
Three Types of Loss.
To My Heart.
To the Virgin as She Now Stands to the Monk after a Beatles Movie.
Toward the End of 1969.
Traffic.
Trains.
Travels of a Vigilante, The.
Urges, The.
Us.
Virgin Mule.
Volcanic Dirge & Co.
War & Peace.
West Is the Best and the Future Is Near, The.
When Lightning Struck, 1.
When Lightning Struck, 2.
Why Paint?
Why Write.
Winter in Istanbul.
Wishes.
"Woods" at Midnight, The.
Work.
Work & the Labor, The.
Working for Profit.
Worst Poems Make the Best "Poems," The.
Xerox the Spirit and Be Well.
Y Un Canción Por E.
Yes Log, The.
Your Country.
Zzzzzzzzzzzz.

Cold Mountain *See* **Han-shan (Cold Mountain)**

Coleridge, Samuel Taylor (1772–1834)
Absence.
Ad Lyram.
Ad Vilmum Axiologum.
Addressed to a Young Man of Fortune.
Alice Du Clos.
Alla Sua Amica.
Angel Visitant, An.
Answer to a Child's Question.
Anthem for the Children of Christ's Hospital.
Apologia pro Vita Sua.
Ballad of the Dark Ladié, The.
Barberry-Tree, The.
Bitter Reflection, A.
Blossoming of the Solitary Date-Tree, The.
Body Imaging Soul.
British Stripling's War-Song, The.
Catullian Hendecasyllables.
Character, A.
Charity in Thought.
Child's Evening Prayer, A.
Christabel.
Christmas Carol, A: "Shepherds went their hasty way, The."
Cologne.

Constancy to an Ideal Object.
Day-Dream, A.
Day-Dream, The.
Death of Wallenstein, The, *sels.*
Death Wish, A.
Dejection: An Ode.
Delinquent Travellers, The.
Desire.
Despair.
Destiny of Nations, The.
Destruction of the Bastile.
Devil's Thoughts, The.
Devonshire Road, A.
Drinking versus Thinking.
Dungeon, The.
Duty Surviving Self-Love.
Eagle and the Tortoise, The.
Effusions.
Elegy Imitated from One of Akenside's Blank-
  Verse Inscriptions.
Epitaph on an Infant.
Epitaph on an Infant.
Epitaph: "Stop, Christian passer-by!—Stop,
  child of God."
Epitaphium Testamentarium.
Eros aei lalethros hetairos.
Exchange, The.
Exile, An.
Faith, Hope, and Charity.
Fancy in Nubibus.
Farewell to Love.
Fears in Solitude [Written in April, 1798,
  during the Alarm of an Invasion].
Fire, Famine, and Slaughter.
First Advent of Love.
For a Market-Clock.
Forbearance.
Foster-Mother's Tale, The.
Fragment: "O'er the raised earth the gales of
  evening sigh."
France: An Ode.
Frost at Midnight.
Fruit Plucker, The.
Garden of Boccaccio, The.
Good Great Man, The.
Happy Home, The.
Happy Husband, The.
Her Thoughts.
Hexameters.
Home-Sick.
Homeless.
Homeric Hexameter, The.
Hope and Time.
Hope and Tranquillity.
Hour When We Shall Meet Again, The.
Human Life; on the Denial of Immortality.
Humility the Mother of Charity.
Hymn before Sunrise, in the Vale of
  Chamouni.
Hymn to the Earth.
If I Had but Two Little Wings.
Improvisatore, The.
Indifference of the Heavens, The.
Inscription for a Fountain on a Heath.
Inward Light.
Israel's Lament.
Keepsake, The.
Knight's Tomb, The.
Kubla Khan: or, A Vision in a Dream.
Letter to Sara Hutchinson.
Lewti.
Life.
Life in Death.
Limbo.
Lines Composed in a Concert-Room.
Lines on a Friend.
Lines on a Portrait of a Lady.
Lines Suggested by the Last Words of
  Berengarius.
Lines to a Beautiful Spring in a Village.
Lines to a Comic Author, on an Abusive
  Review.
Lines to Thomas Poole.
Lines Written at the King's Arms, Ross,
  Formerly the House of the "Man of Ross."
Lines Written in the Album at Elbingerode, in

the Har[t]z Forest.
Looking Seaward.
Loss.
Love.
Love and Friendship Opposite.
Love, Hope, and Patience in Education.
Lover's Complaint to His Mistress, A.
Love's Apparition and Evanishment.
Love's Burial-Place.
Love's Sanctuary.
Lunar Entrancement.
Mad Monk, The.
Mahomet.
Mathematical Problem, A.
Melancholy.
Metrical Feet.
Mighty Fountain, A.
Monody on the Death of Chatterton.
Moon and the Waves, The.
My Baptismal Birthday [*or* Birth-Day].
Names.
Ne Plus Ultra.
Netherlands, The.
Night-Mare Death in Life, The.
Night-Scene, The.
Nightingale, The.
Nose, The.
Not at Home.
Ode in the Manner of Anacreon, An.
Ode on the Departing Year.
Ode on the Ottery and Tiverton Church Music.
Ode to Georgiana, Duchess of Devonshire.
Ode to Sleep.
Ode to the Rain, An.
Ode to Tranquillity.
Old Man of the Alps, The.
On a Cataract.
On a Late Connubial Rupture in High Life.
On a Volunteer Singer.
On an Infant Which Died before Baptism.
On an Insignificant.
On Donne's First Poem.
On Donne's Poetry.
On My Joyful Departure from the City of
  Cologne.
On Observing a Blossom on the First of
  February 1796.
On Receiving an Account That His Only
  Sister's Death Was Inevitable.
On Revisiting the Sea-Shore, after Long
  Absence.
On Seeing a Youth Affectionately Welcomed
  by a Sister.
On the Christening of a Friend's Child.
On the Prospect of Establishing a Pantisocracy
  in America.
Ovidian Elegiac Metre, The.
Pains of Sleep, The.
Pang More Sharp Than All, The.
Pantisocracy.
Parliamentary Oscillators.
Perspiration: A Travelling Eclogue.
Phantom.
Phantom or Fact?
Philosophical Trinity, The.
Picture, The.
Poetical Epistles.
Presence of Love, The.
Psyche.
Raven, The.
Reason.
Reason for Love's Blindness.
Recantation.
Recollections of Love.
Reflections on Having Left a Place of
  Retirement.
Religious Musings.
Remorse, *sels.*
Reproof and Reply, The.
Rime of the Ancient Mariner, The.
Sancti Dominici Pallium.
Self-Knowledge.
Separation from Asra.
Silent City, A.
Snow-Drop, The.
Soliloquy on the Full Moon, She Being in a

Mad Passion, A.
Some Fragments, Mainly from Manuscripts of
  1797–8.
Song, ex improviso.
Song: "Though veiled in spires of myrtle
  wreath."
Songs of the Pixies.
Sonnet Composed on a Journey Homeward;
  the Author Having Received Intelligence of
  the Birth of a Son, 20 September 1796.
Sonnet on Quitting Christ's Hospital.
Sonnet on Receiving a Letter Informing Me of
  the Birth of a Son.
Sonnet to a Friend Who Asked How I Felt
  When the Nurse First Presented My Infant
  to Me.
Sonnet [to Charles Lloyd].
Sonnet to the River Otter.
Sonnet to William Linley.
Sonnets Attempted in the Manner of
  Contemporary Writers.
Stanger Minstrel, A.
Suicide's Argument, The.
Sunset, A.
Superstition.
Tell's Birth-Place.
This Lime-Tree Bower My Prison.
Thought, A.
Time, Real and Imaginary.
Timorous Hind, The.
To a Critic.
To a Friend [Charles Lamb] Who Had
  Declared His Intention of Writing No More
  Poetry.
To a Lady.
To a Lady.
To a Young Friend.
To a Young Lady.
To a Young Lady [Miss Lavinia Poole] on Her
  Recovery from a Fever.
To an Unfortunate Woman at the Theatre.
To an Unfortunate Woman Whom the Author
  Had Known in the Days of Her Innocence.
To Asra.
To Fortune.
To Mary Pridham.
To Matilda Betham from a Stranger.
To Mr. Pye.
To Nature.
To One Who Published in Print.
To Robert Southey.
To the Evening Star.
To the Rev. W. J. Hort.
To the Rev. George Coleridge.
To the Young Artist.
To Two Sisters.
To W. Wordsworth.
To William Godwin.
To William Wordsworth.
Tombless Epitaph, A.
Translation of a Greek Ode on Astronomy.
Translation of a Passage in Ottfried's Metrical
  Paraphrase of the Gospel.
Traveller through Infinity, The.
Tree of Mystery, The.
Tribute to Wordsworth.
Two Founts, The.
Two Round Spaces on the Tombstone, The.
Uncertainty in Love.
Unity with Nature.
Veil of Light, The.
Veil of Spirit, The.
Verses Addressed to J. Horne Tooke.
Verses Trivocular.
Virgin's Cradle-Hymn, The.
Visionary Hope, The.
Visit of the Gods, The.
W. H. *Eheu!*
Wanderings of Cain, The.
Water Ballad.
Wedded Love.
What Is Life?
Wills of the Wisp, The.
Wish, A.
Wish for Dreamful Sleep, A.
With Fielding's *Amelia.*

Work without Hope.
Youth and Age.
Zapolya, *sels.*

Collins, Billy (b. 1941)
Advice to Writers.
Afternoon with Irish Cows.
American Sonnet.
Another Reason Why I Don't Keep a Gun in
   the House.
Aristotle.
Bar Time.
Best Cigarette, The.
Blues, The.
Bonsai.
Books.
Brooklyn Museum of Art, The.
Budapest.
Butterfly Effect, The.
Canada.
Candle Hat.
Center.
Consolation.
Dancing toward Bethlehem.
Days.
Dead, The.
Death of Allegory, The.
Death of the Hat, The.
Design.
Dharma.
Directions.
Earthling.
First Reader.
Fishing on the Susquehanna in July.
Flight of the Reader, The.
Forgetfulness.
History of Weather, A.
History Teacher, The.
I Chop Some Parsley While Listening to Art
   Blakey's Version of "Three Blind Mice."
Idiomatic.
Insomnia ("Even though the house is deeply
   silent").
Insomnia ("After counting all the sheep in the
   world").
Introduction to Poetry.
Iron Bridge, The.
Japan.
Jealousy.
Lesson, The.
Lines Composed over Three Thousand Miles
   from Tintern Abbey.
Lines Lost among Trees.
Madmen.
Man in Space.
Man in the Moon, The.
Man Listening to Disc.
Marginalia.
Monday Morning.
Morning.
Movies, The.
My Heart.
My Number.
Night House, The.
Nightclub.
Nostalgia.
Not Touching.
November.
On Turning Ten.
Osso Buco.
Paradelle for Susan.
Passengers.
Pavilion.
Piano Lessons.
Picnic, Lightning.
Pinup.
Plight of the Troubadour.
Purity.
Questions about Angels.
Reading an Anthology of Chinese Poems.
Rival Poet, The.
Schoolsville.
Scotland.
Serenade: "Let the other boys from the
   village."
Shoveling Snow with Buddha.
Snow.

Snow Day.
Some Days.
Some Final Words.
Sonnet: "All we need is fourteen lines, well,
   thirteen now."
Splitting Wood.
Student of Clouds.
Sunday Morning with the Sensational
   Nightingales.
Taking Off Emily Dickinson's Clothes.
Three Wishes, The.
To a Stranger Born in Some Distant Country
   Hundreds of Years from Now.
Tomes.
Tuesday, June 4, 1991.
Vade Mecum.
Victoria's Secret.
Waitress, The.
Walking across the Atlantic.
Where I Live.
Winter Syntax.
Wires of the Night, The.
Workshop.

Cooper, Jane (b. 1924)
Acceptances.
After the Blackout (1965).
After the Bomb Tests.
All the Leaves Were Green.
All These Dreams.
Bedside Rune, A.
Being Southern.
Bermuda.
Blind Girl.
Bloodroot.
Blue Anchor, The.
Builder of Houses, The.
Calling, The.
Childhood in Jacksonville, Florida.
Children's Ward, The.
Circle, a Square, a Triangle and a Ripple of
   Water, A.
Class.
Clementene.
Conversation by the Body's Light.
Dispossessions.
Door, The.
Dream in Which the Routine Quality of My
   Imagination Is Fully Exposed.
Earthquake, The.
Estrangement.
Eve.
Evening Star (Georgia O'Keeffe).
Faithful, The.
Figure on the Far Side, The.
Flashboat, The.
For a Boy Born in Wartime.
For a Very Old Man, on the Death of His Wife.
For My Mother in Her First Illness, from a
   Window Overlooking Notre Dame.
For the Recorder of Suicides.
For Thomas Hardy.
From the Journal Concerning My Father.
Gaza.
Green Notebook, The.
Hobby Lobby, The.
Holding Out.
Hotel de Dream.
How Can I Speak for Her.
In a Room with Picassos.
In the House of the Dying.
In the Last Few Moments Came the Old
   German Cleaning Woman.
Infusion Room, The.
Iron.
Jittoku, Buddhist Mystic—15th Century.
Knowledge that Comes through Experience,
   The.
Leaving Water Hyacinths.
Letters.
Little Vesper, A.
Long, Disconsolate Lines.
Long View from the Suburbs, The.
March.
Mary Coldwell.
Messages.
Meteors.

Mission with the Night, A.
Morning on the St. John's.
Mourning Picture.
My Friend.
My Mother in Three Acts.
My Young Mother.
Nightmare of the Suburbs, A.
95°.
Nothing I Meant to Keep.
Obligations.
Olympic Rain Forest.
Ordinary Detail.
P.O.W.
Past, The.
Pencil Sketch of Self & Other.
Poem with Capital Letters, A.
Poetry as Continuity.
Practicing for Death.
Praise.
Rent.
River in All Lights, from an Upstairs Window,
   The.
Rock Climbing.
Roman Dream.
S. Eliason 66: *Double Portrait of Emily
   Dickinson and the Rev. Charles Wadsworth.*
Scattered Words for Emily Dickinson.
Seventeen Questions about KING KONG.
Snow in the City.
Song: "Here I am yours, and here, and here."
Starting with a Line from Roethke.
Suicide Note.
These High White Walls.
Threads: Rosa Luxemburg from Prison.
Twins.
Urge to Tell the Truth, The.
Vocation: A Life: *Suite Based on Four Words
   from Willa Cather.*
Wanda's Blues.
Weather of Six Mornings, The.
What the Seer Said.
Winter Road, The.

Corbett, William (b. 1942)
Above the cold.
Air and Light, The.
Alison's Letter Used as a Bookmark for
   Ungaretti's Poems.
Anthem: "Milton Avery Altmar."
At Charlesgate.
August.
Basil 1977-1993.
Between sets.
Bowl of Progresso Minestrone.
Bridgeport Station.
Bus Song.
Cold Lunch.
Collarbone.
Columbus Square Journal.
Crossing Borders.
Crossing the Footbridge over Storrow Drive.
Crossing the Public Garden.
D-Day 1989.
Dead of Winter.
Dear Joe.
Desert Storm.
Drive Home, The.
Driving Jazz.
Earrings of Madame de, The.
East Mauch Chunk - Jim Thorpe.
Ed.
Fall 1970.
Family.
February 29, 1988.
February 29th.
First of September.
For Joe Pernice.
For the Old Year.
Found in a Notebook.
Fred Astaire.
Haying.
Hero.
Homefires.
In out of this shower.
Joe Brainard.
Lake Road.
Last Words.

Late August.
Lines Written After Reading Frank O'Hara's
    "A Step Away from Them."
Listening for Jane.
Lockerbie.
Marga Barr.
Marie's irises / what with the furnace.
Marni's Birthday.
Melancholy.
Misremembered Edwin Denby Line.
My Father-in-Law's Coat.
Neighborhood.
Nine Lives.
1991.
O, July 1992.
Of Small Delights in Idleness.
Painters, The.
Pardon, a few towns over.
Passed on.
Poem: "Chalky swallow shit."
Poem for Me Mother.
Poem: "French blue morning."
"Poetry," John Wieners.
Poor. Old. China. Man.
Prayer.
Putting socks away.
Quartet.
Ray's letterpoem.
Reading.
Reading C. K. Williams's "The Critic."
Recipe for Contemplation.
Runaway Pond.
September Song.
Shoe, The.
Shower in June, A.
Thelonious Sphere Monk.
This Morning After.
To Kate Bluestein.
Tu Fu in English.
Under Ideal Conditions.
Vermont Apollinaire.
Walking Basil.
Way to Go, The.
When I Read John Wieners's Selected Poems.
Youth.

Corbière, Edouard Joachim *See* **Corbière,**
Tristan

Corbière, Tristan (Edouard Joachim Corbière)
(1845–75)
Letter from Mexico (Vera Cruz, 10 February,
    186–).
Old Roscoff.

Corkine, William
My Dearest Mistress.

Cortes, Alfonso
Aegeus in Prison.
Air.
Dirty Souls.
Flower of the Fruit, The.
Great Prayer.
Organ.
Space Song.
Sundown.
Three Sisters, The.
Truth, The.
When You Point Your Finger.

Cowley, Abraham (1618–67)
Mistress, The, *sels.*

Cowper, William (1731–1800)
Address to the Mob, An.
Against Interested Love.
Ah brother Poet! send me of your shade.
Alexander Selkirk.
Annus Memorabilis, 1789.
Another.
Another Version.
Answer to Stanzas Addressed to Lady Hesketh.
Anti-Thelyphthora.
Apology, An.
Attempt at the Manner of Waller, An.
Away goes Sussex William with his pack.
Beau's Reply.
Bee and the Pine-Apple, The.
Bid adieu, my sad heart, bid adieu to thy
    peace.

Boadicea: An Ode.
Card, A.
Castaway, The.
Catharina.
Catharina, the Second Part.
Charity.
Cock-Fighters Garland.
Colubriad, The.
Comparison, A.
Conversation.
Delia, th' unkindest girl on earth.
Distressed Travellers, The.
Dog and the Water-Lily, The.
Doves, The.
Epigram is but a feeble thing, An.
Epigram on the Refusal of the University of
    Oxford to Subscribe to His Translation of
    Homer.
Epigram: "To purify their wine some people
    bleed."
Epigrams on His Garden Shed.
Epistle to a Protestant Lady in France, An.
Epistle to Hill.
Epistle to Lady Austen.
Epistle to Robert Lloyd, Esq, An.
Epitaph, An: "Here lies one, who never drew."
Epitaph on a Free but Tame Redbreast.
Epitaph on a Hare.
Epitaph on Dr. Johnson.
Epitaph on Fop.
Epitaph on Mr. Chester.
Epitaph on Mrs. Higgins.
Epitaphium Alterum.
Expostulation.
Fable, A: "Raven, while with glossy breast,
    A."
Faithful Friend, The.
Flatting Mill, The.
Four Ages, The.
Fragment: "He came to him in the extasy of
    pray'r."
Friendship.
Gratitude.
Grief of an Heir, The.
Heroism.
Heu! Quam Remotus.
Hope.
Hope, like the short-liv'd ray that gleams
    awhile.
How blest the youth whom Fate ordains.
Human Frailty.
Hymn for the Sunday School at Olney.
Impromptu ["If John marries Mary, and Mary
    alone."].
Impromptu ["So I have seen the maids in
    vain."].
In a Letter to C.P.
In a Letter to the Same [C. P.].
In Memory of John Thorton.
In Seditionem Horrendum.
Inscription for a Bust of Homer.
Inscription for a Moss-House.
Inscription for a Stone.
Inscription for an Hermitage.
Inscription for the Tomb of Hamilton.
It is a maxim of much weight.
John Gilpin.
Judgment of the Poets, The.
Let Banister now lend his aid.
Letter in Verse.
Lily and the Rose, The.
Lines after the Manner of Homer.
Lines for a Memorial of Ashley Cowper.
Lines with Two Cockscombs.
Lines Written During a Period of Insanity.
Lines Written for Miss Patty More.
Lines Written in the Monthly Review.
Lines Written upon a Window-Shutter at
    Weston.
Longing To Be with Christ.
Love Abused.
Love of the World Reproved, The.
Methinks I see thee decently array'd.
Modern Patriot, The.
Moralizer Corrected, The.
Morning Dream, The.

Mortals around your destin'd heads.
Motto on the King's Clock.
Mutual Forbearance.
My pens are all spilt, and my ink-glass is dry.
Needless Alarm, The.
Negro's Complaint, The.
Nightingale and Glow-Worm, The.
Ode on *Sir Charles Grandison.*
Ode on the Marriage of a Friend.
Ode: Secundum Artem, An.
Ode to Apollo.
Ode to Peace.
Of Himself.
Olney Hymns.
On a Goldfinch Starved to Death in His Cage.
On a Letter of Miss Fanshawe.
On a Mischievous Bull.
On a Mistake in His Translation of Homer.
On a Plant of Virgin's Bower.
On a Review Condemning Thelyphthora.
On a Similar Occasion for the Year 1788.
On a Similar Occasion for the Year 1789.
On a Similar Occasion for the Year 1790.
On a Similar Occasion for the Year 1792.
On a Similar Occasion for the Year 1793.
On a Spaniel Called Beau Killing a Young
    Bird.
On Flaxman's Penelope.
On Hayley's Portrait.
On Her Endeavoring to Conceal Her Grief at
    Parting.
On His Approaching Visit to Hayley.
On His Majesty's Sea Bathing.
On His Portrait.
On Loyalty.
On Madan's Answer to Newton.
On Mrs. Montagu's Feather-Hangings.
On Observing Some Names of Little Note
    Recorded in the "Biographia Britannica."
On One Ignorant and Arrogant.
On Receiving Hayley's Picture.
On Receiving Heyne's Virgil.
On the Author of Letters on Literature.
On the Burning of Lord Mansfield's Library.
On the Death of Russell.
On the Engraver of His Pourtrait.
On the High Price of Fish.
On the Ice Islands Seen Floating in the
    German Ocean.
On the Lamented Death of Mrs.
    Throckmorton's Bullfinch.
On the Loss of the *Royal George.*
On the Promotion of Thurlow.
On the Queens's Visit to London.
On the Receipt of My Mother's Picture out of
    Norfolk [the Gift of My Cousin Ann
    Bodham].
On the Same.
On the Shortness of Life.
On Thurlow.
One parson, one poet, one belman, one crier.
Pairing Time Anticipated.
Philosopher and the King, The.
Pine-Apple and the Bee, The.
Pity for Poor Africans.
Poet, the Oyster, and Sensitive Plant, The.
Poet's New-Year's Gift, The.
Poplar Field, The.
Progress of Error, The.
R.S.S
R.S.S. Written in a Fit of Illness.
Reflection on the Foregoing Ode.
Report of an Adjudged Case.
Retaliation.
Retired Cat, The.
Retirement.
Riddle: "I am just two and two, I am warm, I
    am cold."
Rose, The.
Salad, The.
See Where the Thames, the Purest Stream.
Shrubbery, The.
Song, A: "On the green margin of the brook."
Song, A: "Sparkling eye, the mantling cheek,
    The."
Song: "No more shall hapless Celia's ears."

Song of Mercy and Judgment, A.
Song on Peace.
Song: "When all within is peace."
Sonnet Addressed to Mr. Phillips, A.
Sonnet to Henry Cowper.
Stanzas on Milton's Remains.
Stanzas Subjoined to the Yearly Bill of
    Mortality of the Parish of All Saints,
    Northampton; for the Year 1787.
Sunset and Sunrise.
Sweet Meat Has Sour Sauce.
Symptoms of Love, The.
Table Talk.
Tale, A: "In Scotland's realm, where trees are
    few."
Tale, Founded on a Fact, A.
Task, The.
Thanks for a Gift of Pheasants.
This ev'ning, Delia, you and I.
Thunder Storm, A.
Tirocinium; or, A Review of Schools.
To a Friend in Distress.
To a Lady ["Star that beams on Anna's breast,
    The"].
To a Young Friend.
To a Young Lady
To a Young Lady Who Stole a Pen.
To Anne Bodham.
To Delia.
To Dr. Austin.
To Dr. Darwin.
To George Romney, Esq.
To Gravina.
To Hayley.
To John Johnson.
To Lady Austen.
To Mary.
To Mary Unwin.
To Miss Creuzé.
To Miss Macartney.
To Mr. Newton.
To Mrs. King.
To Mrs. Newton.
To Mrs. Throckmorton.
To Mr. Newton [on His Return from
    Ramsgate].
To My Dearest Cousin, on Her Removal of us
    from Silver End, to Weston.
To Sir John Fenn.
To Sir Joshua Reynolds.
To the Immortal Memory of the Halibut on
    Which I Dined This Day, Monday, April 26,
    1784.
To the Nightingale.
To the Rev. Mr. Newton.
To the Rev. William Bull.
To Unwin.
To Warren Hastings.
To William Hayley, Esq.: In Reply to His
    Solicitation to Write with Him in a Literary
    Work.
To William Wilberforce, Esq.
Tom Raban.
Trail of Admiral Keppel, The.
Translation of Epitaph to Northcot.
Translation of Verses to Lloyd.
Truth.
Upon a Venerable Rival.
Valediction, The: "Farewell, false hearts!
    whose best affections fail."
Verses Written at Bath on Finding the Heel of
    a Shoe.
Votum.
When little more than boy in age.
Winter Nosegay, The.
Written after Leaving Her at New Burns.
Written in a Quarrel.
Yardley Oak.
Yearly Distress, The.

Crabbe, George (1754–1832)
Borough, The, *sels.*
On Receiving from a Lady a Present of a Ring.
Parish Register, The, *sels.*
Posthumous Tales, *sels.*
Sir Eustace Grey.
Tales, *sels.*

Tales of the Hall, *sels.*
Village, The, *sels.*
World of Dreams, The.

Crane, Hart (1899–1932)
After Jonah.
Air Plant, The.
Alert Pillow., The.
All This.
America's Plutonic Ecstasies.
And Bees of Paradise.
Annunciations.
At Melville's Tomb.
Bacardi Spreads the Eagle's Wing.
Bathers, The.
Black Tambourine.
Bridge of Estador, The.
Bridge, The.
Broken Tower, The.
By Nilus Once I Knew.
C33.
Carmen de Boheme.
Carrier Letter.
Chaplinesque.
Circumstance, The.
Dust Now Is.
Echoes.
Emblems of Conduct.
Enrich My Resignation.
Episode of Hands.
Eternity.
Euclid Avenue.
Fear.
Fernery, The.
For the Marriage of Faustus and Helen.
Forgetfulness.
Garden Abstract.
Great Western Plains, The.
Havana Rose.
Her Eyes Had.
Hieroglyphic.
Hive, The.
Hurricane, The.
I Have That Sure Enclitic.
I Rob My Breast.
Idiot, The.
Imperator Victus.
In a Court.
In Shadow.
Interior.
Interludium.
Island Quarry.
Key West.
Lachrymae Christi.
Legend.
Legende.
Mango Tree, The.
March.
Masters, The.
Meditation.
Medusa.
Mermen, The.
Modern Craft.
Moment Fugue.
Moth That Made God Blind, The.
My Grandmother's Love Letters.
Name for All, A.
North Labrador.
O Carib Isle!
O Moon, Thou Cool.
October-November.
Of an Evening Pulling Off a Little Experience
    (with the english language).
Old Song.
Paraphrase.
Passage.
Pastorale.
Persuasion, A.
Phantom Bark, The.
Pillar and the Post, The.
Porphyro in Akron.
Possessions.
Postscript.
Postscript, A.
Praise for an Urn.
Purgatorio.
Recitative.

Repose of Rivers.
Royal Palm.
Sad Indian, The.
Sea Raised Up, The.
Shall I Subsume.
Song for Happy Feast Days, A.
Sonnet: "Ere elfish Night shall sift another
    day."
Stark Major.
Sunday Morning Apples.
Supplication to the Muses on a Trying Day.
Tenderness and Resolution.
There Are the Local.
They Were There.
This Way Where November.
Thou Canst Read Nothing.
Three Locutions Des Pierrots.
Time Cannot Be Worn
To Conquer Variety.
To Earth.
To Emily Dickinson.
To Liberty.
To Portapovitch.
To Shakespeare.
To the Cloud Juggler.
To the Empress Josephine's Statue.
Traveller Born, A.
Visible the Untrue, The.
Voyages.
Well/Well/Not-At-All.
What Nots?
Wine Menagerie, The.
With a Photograph to Zell, Now Bound for
    Spain.
You Are That Frail.

Crane, Stephen (1871–1900)
Ah, God, the way your little finger moved.
Ah, haggard purse, why ope thy mouth.
All-feeling God, hear in the war-night.
And yet I have seen thee happy with me.
And you love me?
Aye, workman, make me a dream.
Behold, from the land of the farther suns.
Behold, the grave of a wicked man.
Black riders came from the sea.
Blustering god, / Stamping across the sky.
Bottles and bottles and bottles.
Chant you loud of punishments.
Charity, thou art a lie.
Chatter of a death-demon from a tree-top, The.
Do not weep, maiden, for war is kind.
Each small gleam was a voice.
Fast rode the knight.
Forth went the candid man.
Friend, your white beard sweeps the ground.
God came to a man, A.
God fashioned the ship of the world carefully.
God in wrath, A.
God lay dead in Heaven.
Grey and boiling street, A.
Have you ever made a just man?
I explain the silvered passing of a ship at night.
I have heard the sunset song of the birches.
I have seen thy face aflame.
I heard thee laugh.
I looked here; / I looked there.
I met a seer.
I saw a man pursuing the horizon.
I stood musing in a black world.
I stood upon a high place.
I stood upon a highway.
I walked in a desert.
I was in the darkness.
I wonder if sometimes in the dusk.
If I should cast off this tattered coat.
If there is a witness to my little life.
If you would seek a friend among men.
Impact of a dollar upon the heart, The.
In a lonely place.
In Heaven, / Some little blades of grass.
In the desert.
In the night.
Intermingled, / There come in wild revelling
    strains.
Intrigue.
"It was wrong to do this," said the angel.

Lad and a maid at a curve in the stream, A.
Learned man came to me once, A.
Legends.
Little birds of the night.
Little ink more or less!, A.
Livid lightnings flashed in the clouds, The.
Love forgive me if I wish you grief.
Love met me at noonday.
Love walked alone.
Man adrift on a slim spar, A.
Man feared that he might find an assassin, A.
Man said to the universe, A.
Man saw a ball of gold in the sky, A.
Man toiled on a burning road, A.
Man went before a strange god, A.
Many red devils ran from my heart.
Many workmen / Built a huge ball of masonry.
My cross! / Your cross?
Mystic shadow, bending near me.
Naked woman and a dead dwarf, A.
Newspaper is a collection of half-injustices, A.
Ocean said to me once, The.
Oh, a rare old wine ye brewed for me.
On the brown trail.
On the desert.
On the horizon the peaks assembled.
Once, a man, clambering to the house-tops.
Once, I knew a fine song.
Once I saw mountains angry.
Once I saw thee idly rocking.
Once there came a man.
Once there was a man.
One came from the skies.
Patent of a lord, The.
Places among the stars.
Row of thick pillars, A.
Rumbling, buzzing, turning, whirling Wheels.
Sage lectured brilliantly, The.
Should the wide world roll away.
Slant of sun on dull brown walls, A.
Soldier, young in years, young in ambitions, A.
Spirit sped, A.
Successful man has thrust himself, The.
Supposing that I should have the courage.
Tell brave deeds of war.
Tell me not in joyous numbers.
Tell me why, behind thee.
There came whisperings in the winds.
There exists the eternal fact of conflict.
There is a grey thing that lives in the tree-tops.
There was a great cathedral.
There was a man and a woman.
There was a man who lived a life of fire.
There was a man with tongue of wood.
There was, before me.
There was crimson clash of war.
There was One I met upon the road.
There was set before me a mighty hill.
There were many who went in huddled
   procession.
"Think as I think," said a man.
Three little birds in a row.
To the maiden.
Tradition, thou art for suckling children.
Trees in the garden rained flowers, The.
"Truth," said a traveller.
Two or three angels.
Unwind my riddle.
Upon the road of my life.
Walking in the sky.
Wayfarer / Perceiving the pathway to truth,
   The.
Well, then, I hate Thee, unrighteous picture.
What says the sea, little shell?
When a people reach the top of a hill.
When the prophet, a complacent fat man.
Why do you strive for greatness, fool?
With eye and with gesture.
Yes, I have a thousand tongues.
You say you are holy.
You tell me this is God?
Youth in apparel that glittered, A.

Crashaw, Richard (1613?–1649)
Acts 21; I Am Ready Not Onely To Be Bound
   but To Dye.
Adoro Te. The Hymn of Saint Thomas in

Adoration of the Blessed Sacrament.
Alexias.
Another on [Mr. Herrys].
Apology [or Apologie] for the Foregoing
   Hymn[e], An.
Authors Motto, The.
But Men loved Darkness[e] Rather Than [or
   Then] Light.
But Now They Have Seen, and Hated.
C[h]aritas Nimia; or, The Dear[e] Bargain.
Christs Victory.
Compline.
Death's Lecture.
Description of a Religious House and
   Condition of Life.
Easter Day.
Elegie on the Death of Doctor Porter, An.
Elegy upon the Death of Mr. Stanninow Fellow
   of Queenes Colledge.
Epitaph. Upon Doctor Brooke, An.
Epitaph Upon Husband and Wife Who Died
   and Were Buried Together, An.
Epitaph upon Mr. Ashton, a Conformable
   Citizen, An.
Epithalamium: "Come virgin Tapers of pure
   waxe."
Evensong.
Flaming Heart, The.
For the Hour of Prime.
Howres for the Hours of Matines, The.
Hymn for New Year's Day.
Hymn in the Assumption.
Hymn to the Name and Hono[u]r of the
   Admirable Saint[e] Teresa, A.
Hymne of the Nativity, Sung by the
   Shepheards, A.
I Am the Door [or Doore].
In Amorem Divinum.
In Cicatrices Domini Jesu.
In the Glorious Epiphanie of Our Lord God.
In the Holy Nativity of Our Lord God.
It Is Better To Go into Heaven with One Eye.
Lauda Sion Salvatorem.
Love's Horoscope.
[Mr. Herrys,] His Epitaph.
Music[k]'s Duel[l].
O Gloriosa Domina.
Ode on a Prayer-Book.
On a Foule Morning, Being Then to Take a
   Journey.
On Marriage.
On Mr. G. Herberts Booke, The Temple.
On Our Crucified Lord Naked, and Bloody.
On St. Peter Casting Away His Nets at Our
   Saviours Call.
On Saint Peter Cutting of Malchus His Eare.
On the Baptized Ethiopian.
On the Bleeding Wounds of Our Crucified
   Lord.
On the Blessed Virgins Bashfulnesse.
On the Frontispiece of Isaacsons Chronologie
   Explained.
On the Gunpowder-Treason.
On the Miracle of Loaves.
On the Miracle of Multiplied [or Multiplyed]
   Loaves.
On the Still Surviving Markes of Our Saviours
   Wounds.
On the Water of Our Lord's Baptism[e].
On the Wounds of Our Crucified Lord.
Our Lord in His Circumcision to His Father.
Out of Euphormio.
Out of Grotius his Tragedy of Christes
   Sufferinges.
Out of the Italian; a Song.
Prayer, A.
Psalmus 1.
Recommendation, The.
Samson to His Delilah.
Sancta Maria Dolorum.
Song: "Lord, when the sense of Thy sweet
   grace."
St. Peter's Shadow.
Tear[e], The.
Temperance or the Cheap Physitian upon the
   Translation of Lessius.

To a Young Gentle-Woman, Councel
   Concerning Her Choice.
To Our Blessed Lord upon the Choice of His
   Sepulchre.
To Our Lord, upon the Water Made Wine.
To Pontius Washing His Blood-Stained Hands.
To Pontius Washing His Hands.
To the Infant Martyrs.
To the Morning. Satisfaction for Sleepe.
To the Name above Every Name, the Name of
   Jesus, a Hymn.
To the Queen, an Apologie for the Length of
   the Following Panegyricke.
To the Queen's Majesty.
Two Went Up into the Temple To Pray.
Upon Bishop Andrewes's [or Andrewes His]
   Picture before His Sermons.
Upon Ford's Two Tragedies, "Loves Sacrifice"
   and "The Broken Heart."
Upon Lazarus His Teares.
Upon the Asse That Bore Our Saviour.
Upon the birth of the Princesse Elizabeth.
Upon the Death of a Freind.
Upon the Death of a Gentleman.
Upon the Death of Mister Herrys.
Upon the Death of the Most Desired Mister
   Herrys.
Upon the Duke of Yorke his Birth a
   Panegyricke.
Upon the Ensuing Treatises [of Mr. Shelford].
Upon the Faire Ethiopian Sent to a
   Gentlewoman.
Upon the Gunpowder Treason.
Upon the Gunpowder Treason.
Upon the Infant Martyrs.
Upon the Kings Coronation.
Upon the Kings Coronation.
Upon the Powder Day.
Upon the Sepulchre of our Lord.
Upon the Thornes Taken Downe from Our
   Lords Head Bloody.
Upon Two Greene Apricockes Sent to Cowley
   by Sir Crashaw.
Vexilla Regis.
Weeper, The.
Widow[e]'s Mites, The.
Wishes. To His (Supposed) Mistress[e].
With a Picture Sent to a Friend.
With Some Poems Sent to a Gentlewoman. I.
With Some Poems Sent to a Gentlewoman. II.

Creech, Thomas
To Mr Dryden, on Religio Laici.

Creeley, Robert (b. 1926)
A.
Act of Love, The.
After.
After Lorca.
After Mallarmé.
Again.
Again.
Age ("He is thinking of everyone").
Agh—man / thinks.
Air: "Cat Bird Singing."
Air: "The Love of a Woman."
Alba.
Alice.
All around / the town.
All That Is Lovely in Men.
All the fantasies that.
All the Way.
All this flesh, meat.
Ambition.
America.
American Love.
And.
Anger.
Animal, The.
Answer, The.
Anywhere.
Apocalypse Now.
Apology, The.
Apple Uppfle.
Arroyo.
The ("A's").
As Now It Would Be Snow.
As real as thinking.

As We Sit.
As You Come.
Awakening, The.
Away.
B———.
B.B.
Backwards.
Ball Game, The.
Ballad, A: "We have a song for the death in her body."
Ballad of the Despairing Husband.
Barcelona: February 13, 1977.
Be of Good Cheer.
Beach.
Bed, The.
Berlin: First Night & Early Morning.
Beside Her to Lie.
Beyond.
Billfold.
Bird, The.
Bird, the Bird, the Bird, The.
Birds, The.
Birthday, A.
Blesséd water, blesséd man.
Blue.
Blue Rabbit.
Blue Skies Motel.
Blues.
Bobbie ("Every one").
Bobbie ("Her voice").
"Bolinas and Me."
Box.
Box, The.
Boy, the.
Breaking Up Is Hard to Do.
Bresson's Movies.
Bringing you back here—.
Broken Back Blues.
Bruce & Linley's House.
Buffalo Evening.
Buildings.
Business, The.
But.
But.
But You.
Can feel it in the pushing.
Canada.
Cantos, The.
Canzone: "As would any sound make."
Car / moving / the hill / down, The.
Carnival, The.
Catching Cold.
Cebu.
Chance, The.
Change.
Changes, The.
Chanson.
Characteristically.
Charm, The.
Chasing the Bird.
Cheap Thrill.
Chicago.
Childish.
Children, The.
Christmas: May 10, 1970.
Ciano's.
Circle.
Circle, The.
Circles.
Citizen.
City, The.
Clock.
Colors.
Comfort.
Coming Home.
Conspiracy, The.
Continuing forward with a trembling.
Corn Close.
Could write of fucking—.
Counterpoint, A.
Country Western.
Crisis, The.
Crow, The.
Curse.
Damon & Pythias.
Dancing.

Davao Insular Hotel.
Day comes and goes, The.
Day was gathered on waking, The.
Days and Days.
Days in the train, a.
Days later—neither having.
Dead in the year—.
Dear.
Dear Dorothy.
Death.
Death of / one is, The.
Death of Venus, The.
Delight dances.
Desultory Days.
"Dicky the Stick"—.
Diction.
Dimensions.
Disappointment, The.
Dishonest Mailmen, The.
Distance.
Divisions.
"Do You Think."
Doggie Bags.
Don't Sign Anything.
Door, The ("It is hard going to the door").
Door, The ("Thump. Thump").
Down Home.
Dream, The ("What you think you").
Dream, The ("Lake in the head").
Dreams ("I was supposed to wake").
Dreams ("Tunneling through the earth").
Dreary, heavy / accumulation.
Drums, The.
Dying.
Ear, The.
Early Reading.
Easter.
Echo ("Broken heart, you / timeless wonder").
Echo ("Faint, persistent").
Echo ("I'm almost / done, the hour").
Echo ("Yes but your sweetness").
Echo Of.
Echoes ("Eight panes").
Echoes ("Step through the mirror").
Echoes ("Sudden / loss of hope, A").
Edge, The ("Long over whatever edge").
Edge, The ("Place it, / make the space").
Elements.
End.
End of the Day, The.
End, The.
Enough.
Entre Nous.
Envoi: "Particulars they want."
Epic.
Epic Expands, The.
Epigraph: "Lot's wife, / married to chance."
Eros.
Erotica.
Europeans, The.
Evening.
Every Day.
Eye o' the Storm.
Eye, The.
Eye, The.
Eyes.
Faces, The.
Fact, The.
Fall.
Falling.
Falling downhill—.
Family, The.
Fancy.
Fantasies / indulged, great.
Farm, The.
Festival, The.
Figures, The.
"Fine China."
Finger, The.
Fire.
Fire, The.
First Rain.
First / time is / the first, The.
First Time, The.
Flaubert's Early Prose.
Flesh.

Flesh's / signals.
Flower, The.
Flower, The.
Flowers.
Folk Song, A: "Hitch up honey for the / market race all."
"Follow the Drinking Gourd."
For a Bus on Its Side and the Man Inside It.
For a Friend.
For a Friend.
For a Screaming Lady.
For Allen.
For an Anniversary.
For Anybody.
For Arthur Okamura.
For Benny.
For Benny and Sabina.
For Betsy and Tom.
For Cheryl.
For Chuck Hinman.
For days neglected.
For Ebbe.
For Fear.
For Friendship.
For Helen.
For Irving.
For Joel.
For John Chamberlain.
For John Duff.
For Leslie.
For Lewis, to Say It.
For Love.
For Marisol.
For Martin.
For My Mother: Genevieve Jules Creeley.
For No Clear Reason.
For Pen ("Last day of year").
For Pen ("Reading, in the chair").
For Pen ("Thinking out / of the heart").
For Rainer Gerhardt.
For Rene Ricard.
"For Some Weeks."
For Somebody's Marriage.
For the Graduation ("Pretension has it").
For the Graduation ("Honor / of being").
For the Graduation: Bolinas, 1972.
For the New Year.
For Tom.
For W. C. W. ("Rhyme is after").
For W. C. W. ("Pleasure of the wit sustains").
For Walter Chappell.
For You.
Form of Adaptation, A.
Form of Women, A.
Forms' passage as.
Fort Collins Remembered.
Four.
Four Years Later.
Fragment, A: "On the street I am met with constant hostility."
Fragments: "Decorous, and forbearing further correction."
Friend.
Friend Says of Job.
Friend, The.
Friends, The.
From Pico & the Women: A Life.
Funny.
Gangster.
Gemini.
Gesture, The.
Get it anyway.
Gift of Great Value, A.
Gift, The.
Gifts.
Going.
Going Home.
Going to Bed.
Goodbye.
Greendoon's Song.
Greeting Card.
Guido, i' vorrei che tu e Lapo ed io.
Hamilton Hotel.
Hands, The.
Happy love, this.
Happy Man, The.

Harry.
Hart Crane.
Hart Crane 2.
Having to— / what do I think.
Heaven ("I don't want").
Heaven ("If life were easy").
Hélas.
Hello.
Help Heaven.
Herd, The.
Here Again ("After we / were all").
Here Again ("No sadness").
Here again, / shifting days.
Here ("Here is").
Here ("Little earth, water").
Here ("No one / else in the room").
Here ("Past time—those").
Here ("Since I can't").
Here ("Sounds like ball").
Here ("What / has happened").
Hero.
Hero, The.
Heroes.
Hey.
Hi There!
Hill, The.
Hole, The.
Home.
Hong Kong—Last Words.
Hong Kong Window.
Hotel Lobby.
Hotel Merlin.
House, The ("Mas-Soñer / Restaurat—Any").
House, The ("Mud put / upon mud").
How that fact of.
How wise age is—.
Human Song.
Hunger.
I.
I Am Held by My Fear of Death.
I cannot see you.
I can't / for this variance.
I don't hate you lately.
I Keep to Myself Such Measures.
I Know a Man.
I Love You.
I want to fuck you.
I was never so upset.
Ice Cream.
If.
If Happiness.
If I Had My Way.
If You.
If You're Going to Have One.
Illness, An.
Immoral Proposition, The.
In a Boat Shed.
In an Act of Pity.
In London.
In secret / the out's in—.
In the Fall.
In the house of.
In the / mouth—a.
Indians.
Inn / Kyoto.
Innocence, The.
Insistent / this yearning / toward.
Intervals.
Interview, The.
Invitation, The.
Invoice, The.
Irish.
Irishman's Lament on the Approaching Winter,
   An.
It Is at Times.
It is funny—strange—to see the young.
It's the scale.
Jack's Blues.
Jaws.
Je Vois dans le Hasard Tous les Biens Que
   J'espere.
Joke, The.
Joy.
Juggler's Thought.
July: Fargo Street.
June 6, 1970.

Just Friends.
Kate's.
Kick / of the foot against..., The.
Kid ("Kid left / out back waits, The").
Kid ("Smaller, no recall").
Kid, The.
Kids / Seoul.
Kids walking beach.
Kiki.
Kind of Act Of, The.
Kitchen.
Knokke.
Kore.
Korean slang.
Kyoto.
La Conca.
La Noche.
Lady Bird.
Lady in Black.
Language, The.
Last Mile, The.
Last sweet night, The.
Late Comer, The.
Later ("Drunks leaning on your arm").
Later ("If I could get").
Later ("It feels things").
Later ("Later than any time").
Later ("Shan't be winding").
Laughing.
Le Fou.
Learning.
Let something else be / the question—.
Letter, The.
Like a man committed to searching.
Like They Say.
Lion and the Dog, The.
Listless, / the heat rises—.
Little Time—and Place.
Littleton, N.H.
Loner.
Look.
Looking for a way.
Looking Out.
Loop, A.
Los Guitaristas.
Love Comes Quietly.
Love— / let it / Out, / open up.
Love ("Not enough. The question: what is").
Love: "There are words voluptuous."
Love ("Thing comes, The").
Love ("Tracking through this").
Love: "Will you be dust."
Lover, The.
Love's faint trace.
Lunch and After.
Man, The.
Manila.
Maria Speaks.
Marriage, A.
Mary's Fancy.
Massachusetts.
Master of All.
Maybe.
Measure, The.
Mechanic, The.
Medallion.
Memory ("Fresh, A").
Memory ("Nancy finally").
Memory, 1930.
Memory, The.
Men.
Men in my life were, The.
Menu, The.
Message, The.
Messengers, The.
Method, A.
Method of Actuality, The.
Midnight.
Milton Über Alles.
Mind's Heart.
Mirror, The.
Mobile Homes.
Moment.
Mommy.
Money.
Moon, The.

Morning ("Dam's broke").
Morning (8:10 AM).
Morning ("Light's bright glimmer").
Morning ("Shadows, on the far wall").
Mountains in the Desert, The.
Mouths Nuzz.
Movie Run Backward, The.
My Love.
Myself.
N. Truro Light—1946.
Name, The.
Names.
Names, The.
Nathaniel Hawthorne.
Nature.
Naughty Boy.
Neighbors.
Neither sadness nor desire.
New Moon.
New Year's.
News of the World.
News, The.
Night ("Born and bred / in Wellington").
Night in NYC.
Night ("Needs most / happily mutual").
Night Sky, A.
Night Time.
9:45 AM.
1971.
No.
No clouds out the window.
Not Again.
Not Now.
Note read re / letter of Lawrence's.
Now.
Now Then.
Now there is.
Numbers.
NYC—.
Obscene Poem, An.
Of Years.
Oh.
Oh, Love.
Oh Love ("My love is a boat").
Oh Mabel.
Oh Max.
Oh My Love.
Oh No.
Old Saying.
Old Song.
On a Theme by Lawrence, Hearing Purcell.
On Acid.
On Board.
On Phrase from Ginsberg's *Kaddish*.
On Vacation.
One.
One Day.
One / the Sun / Moon / one.
One thing / done, the.
One Way.
One World.
Operation, The.
Out.
Out Here.
Out of Sight.
Out Window: Taylor's Mistake.
Outside.
P—.
Pacing as with some consequent.
Paradox, The.
Park ("Like in the Brownie Books").
Park ("Why did that man").
Passage, The.
Pattern, The.
Pay.
Peace ("Waiting for a bus").
Peace ("You're looking at a chopper").
Pedigree, The.
Penitent, The.
People.
People, The.
People without their own scene.
Person.
Persons.
Phone.
Photo.

Picnic, The.
Picture, A.
Piece, A.
Pieces.
Pieces of cake crumbling.
Place, A.
Place ("Faded mind, / fading colors").
Place ("Let's take / any").
Place ("Long gone time").
Place, The ("Swoop of hawk").
Place, The ("What is the form is the gro- / tesquerie—the accident").
Place ("There was a path").
Place ("Thinking of you asleep on a").
Place ("This is an empty landscape").
Places ("All but / for me and Paul").
Places ("When I wake next").
Plan Is the Body, The.
Plan, The.
Please.
Pleasures of pain.
Poem, A: "If the water forms."
Poem for Beginners.
Poem for Bob Leed.
Poem for D. H. Lawrence.
Pool, The.
Poor.
Post Cards.
Prayer to Hermes.
Prejudice, The.
Pretension's.
Probable Truth.
Problem, The.
Prospect.
Province, The.
Provincetown.
Pryaer, A.
Puritan Ethos, The.
Question.
Question, The.
Quick-Step.
Quick talk / their speech—.
Rachel Had Said.
Rain.
Rain (2).
Rain, The.
Re C—.
Reason, A.
Reflections.
Remember.
Rescue, The.
Retrospect.
Return.
Revelation, The.
Rhyme, The.
Rhythm, The.
Riddle, The.
Riddle: "What'd you throw it on the floor for?"
Riding with Sal.
Rippling eyelids.
Rites, The.
River wandering down.
Roads.
Rocks, The.
Rose, The.
Sad Advice.
Saints, The.
Same.
Sanine to Leda.
Saturday Afternoon.
Say Something.
Sea ("Ever / to sleep").
Sea ("Salt and water").
Sea, The.
Self-Portrait.
Sentence, The.
Seoul Sounds.
Seventeenth Floor: Echoes of Singapore.
Shame, The.
She Is.
She Went to Stay.
She's Back!
Shot.
Sick.
Sight, A.

Sign Board, The.
Sign ("SIEMENS not").
Sign ("What you know of me").
Sing Song.
Sit Down.
Sitting Here.
Sitting up to fill pages.
Situation of feeling increasingly.
Skeleton, The.
Sleep.
Slow slowing—.
Smell of gum wrappers as of Saturday afternoon at movies.
Smell of stale air, The.
Smells, / sounds.
Smoke.
Snow, The.
So Big.
So-called poet of love, The.
So sweet / the body.
So There.
So tired.
Some Afternoon.
Some Echo.
Some Echoes.
Some nights, a fearful.
Some Place.
Somebody Died.
Something.
Something for Easter.
Somewhere.
Son: "What I took in my hand."
Song, A: "I had wanted a quiet testament."
Song: "God give you pardon from gratitude."
Song: "Grit / of things, The."
Song: "How simply / for another."
Song: "I woudn't / embarrass you."
Song: "Love has no other friends."
Song, The: "It still makes sense."
Song: "Those rivers run from that land."
Song: "Were I myself more blithe."
Song: "What do you / want, love. To be."
Song: "You look out and you see people."
Sopa.
Sound.
Sound, The.
Sounds.
Soup ("I know what you'd say").
Soup ("Trembling / with delight").
Souvenir, The.
Sparrows.
Speech.
Spring.
Spring in San Feliu.
Statue, The.
Step, A.
Step, A.
Still.
Still Dancers.
Still Life Or.
Still Too Young.
Stomping with Catullus.
Stone.
Story, The.
Such Flowers.
Such strangeness of mind I know.
Sufi Sam Christian.
Summa wancha.
Summer.
Sunset.
Surf: An Elegy, The.
Surgeons.
Sweet, sad / nostalgia—.
Swinging Down Central.
Table, The.
Talk ("One thing, strikes in").
Talk ("Talking Ginsbergian").
Talking.
Tally, A.
Teachings, The.
Tell Story.
Temper, The.
10:30 AM: Ralph Hotere's.
Testament, A.
Than I.
Thank You.

Thanks.
That day / in an oak tree—.
That's the way.
Then ("Don't go / to the mountains").
Then ("Put yourself where you'll be").
There.
There Is.
There is a space / of trees—.
There Is Water.
There ("Miles back").
There ("Place so, A").
There ("With all I know").
Theresa's Friends.
They ("I wondered what had").
They ("What could / they give me").
They Say.
They (2).
Things to Do in Tokyo.
Think.
Thinking ("I've thought of myself").
Thinking ("Had not thought of it").
Thinking of Walter Benjamin.
Thinking of Yeats.
This Day.
This wide, shallow bowl.
This World.
3 in 1.
Three Ladies, The.
Tiger, The.
Time ("Can't live / mindless").
"Time" is some sort of hindsight.
Time ("Moment to / moment the").
Time ("Out window roof's slope").
Time, The.
Time to go.
Time ("What happened to her").
Tiny Place, A.
To And.
To Bobbie.
To Say It.
To the One in the Gray Coat.
To Work Is to Contradict Contradications, to Do Violence to Natural Violence.
Token, A.
Total Parts of a World, The.
Touchstone.
Train Going By.
Trap, The.
Traveller, The.
Trees ("What shall I do with my friends").
Trees ("Thighs, trees").
Tunnel, The.
Turn, The.
Two ("Holding / for one").
Two (Light weights / light, to the hand").
Two Kids.
Two Times ("It takes so long to look down").
Two Times ("Image / docteur").
Two Ways of Looking in a Mirror.
Up Here.
Up in the Air.
Variation, A.
Variations.
Versions.
View, The.
Visit, The.
Wait for Me.
Waiting for a Bus "en Frente de la Iglesia."
Waiting ("He pushes behind the words").
Waiting ("Were you counting the days").
Walking.
Walking the Dog.
Wall, A.
Wall / one's up against, The.
Walls.
Wanting You.
War & Peace.
Warning, The.
Was.
Water.
Water Music.
Water (2).
The ("Water / waiting far, The").
Way.
Way, The.
We'll die / soon enough.

What / do you think it is.
What is love—.
What's for Dinner.
What's to be said.
When he and I.
Where we are there must.
Which Is to Say.
Which it / was, form, The.
Whip, The.
Why say to them.
Wicker Basket, A.
Wife, The.
Wind Lifts.
Wind, The.
Window.
Window, The ("Position is where you").
Window, The ("There will be no simple").
Winner, The.
Winter.
Wisdom.
Wish, A.
Wishes.
Woman, The ("I called her across the room").
Woman, The ("I have never / clearly given to you").
Women.
Women, The.
Words.
World, The.
Worry.
Xmas.
Xmas Poem: Bolinas.
Yah.
Yellow.
You ("Back and forth across").
You didn't think you.
You have nor face nor hands.
You haven't / fucked for months now.
You see the jerked.
You think in the circle.
You will never be here.
You ("You will remember little of yourself").
Young Woman.
"Your wish came true."
"You've Tried the World, Try Jesus."

Cuadra, Pablo Antonio
Birth of the Sun, The.
Cup with a Jaguar for the Drinking of Health.
Despairing Man Draws a Serpent, The.
Eye Is a Dog Howling in the Distance, The.
Faces of Girls Looking at Themselves in the River.
Jaguar Myth, The.
Lament of a Maiden for the Warrior's Death.
Meditation before an Ancient Poem.
Nahoa Urn, for a Woman.
Pain Is an Eagle Clinging to Your Name.
Secret of the Burning Stars, The.
Urn with a Political Profile.
World Is a Round Earthenware Plate, The.
Written Next to a Blue Flower.

Cullen, Countee (1903–46)
Advice to a Beauty.
After a Visit.
Any Human to Another.
Apostrophe to the Land.
At a Parting.
At the Wailing Wall in Jerusalem.
Atlantic City Waiter.
Ballad of the Brown Girl, The.
Black Christ, The.
Black Magdalens.
Black Majesty.
Bright Bindings.
Brown Boy to Brown Girl.
Brown Girl Dead, A.
Christus Natus Est.
Colored Blues Singer.
Colors.
Cor Cordium.
Counter Mood.
Dear Friends and Gentle Hearts.
Dictum.
Epilogue: "Lily, being white not red, The."
Epitaph: "She leans across a golden table."
Foolish Heart, The.

For a Mouthy Woman.
For a Pessimist.
For a Poet.
For an Anarchist.
For an Atheist.
For an Evolutionist and His Opponent.
For Daughters of Magdalen.
For Helen Keller.
For Joseph Conrad.
For Myself.
Four Epitaphs, *sels.*
From the Dark Tower.
Fruit of the Flower.
Ghosts.
Harsh World That Lashest Me.
Heritage.
Hunger.
I Have a Rendezvous with Life.
If You Should Go.
In Spite of Death.
Incident.
Judas Iscariot ("I think when Judas' mother heard").
Judas Iscariot ("Let's talk of Judas for a while").
Karenge Ya Marenge.
La Belle, La Douce, La Grande.
Lament: "Now let all lovely things embark."
Life's Rendezvous.
Lines for a Hospital.
Lines to My Father.
Litany of the Dark People, The.
Little Sonnet to Little Friends.
Love Tree, The.
Love's Way.
Magnets.
Medusa.
Minutely Hurt.
Mood.
More Than a Fool's Song.
Negro Mother's Lullaby, A.
Night Rain.
Not Sacco and Vanzetti.
Nothing Endures.
One Day We Played a Game.
Only the Polished Skeleton.
Pagan Prayer.
Pity the Deep in Love.
Poet, The.
Protest.
Proud Heart, The.
Requiescam.
Saturday's Child.
Scottsboro, Too, Is Worth Its Song.
Self Criticism.
She of the Dancing Feet Sings.
Shroud of Color, The.
Simon the Cyrenian Speaks.
Singing in the Rain.
Song in Spite of Myself.
Song of Praise.
Song of Praise, A.
Song of Sour Grapes, A.
Sonnet Dialogue.
Sonnet: "I have not loved you in the noblest way."
Sonnet: "I know now how a man whose blood is hot."
Sonnet: "Some for a little while do love, and some for long."
Sonnet: "These are no wind-blown rumors, soft say-sos."
Sonnet: "What I am saying now was said before."
Spring Reminiscence.
Street Called Crooked, The.
Tableau.
That Bright Chimeric Beast.
Therefore, Adieu.
Thorn Forever in the Breast, A.
Thoughts in a Zoo.
Threnody for a Brown Girl.
To a Brown Girl.
To an Unknown Poet.
To Certain Critics.
To Endymion.

To France.
To France.
To John Keats, Poet, at Springtime.
To One Not There.
To the Swimmer.
To the Three for Whom the Book.
Tribute.
Two Thoughts of Death.
Two Who Crossed a Line (She Crosses) (From where she stood the air she craved).
Two Who Crossed a Line (He rode across like a cavalier).
Ultimatum.
Uncle Jim.
Variations on a Theme.
Wind Bloweth Where It Listeth, The.
Wisdom Cometh with the Years.
Wise, The.
Yet Do I Marvel.
Youth Sings a Song of Rosebuds.

Cummings, E. E. (1894–1962)
A- / float on some.
A / mong crum / bling people(a).
Above a between-the-acts prattling of.
Adhuc sub Judice Lis.
After all white horses are in bed.
After five / times the poem.
After-Glow.
After screamgroa / ning.ish:ly.
After Seeing French Funeral.
After your poppied hair inaugurates.
Air, / be / comes / or.
All ignorance toboggans into know.
All in green went my love riding.
All nearness pauses,while a star can grow.
All stars are(and not one star only)love.
All which isn't singing is mere talking.
All worlds have halfsight,seeing either with.
Allbutnotquitemost.
Along the brittle treacherous bright streets.
Along the justexisting road to Roupy.
Always before your voice my soul.
Am was. Are Leaves Few this. Is these a or.
American critic ad 1935.
Amiable putrescence carpenters, An.
Among / these / red pieces of.
Ance)dance / -ing millions all.
A(ncient)a / weigh / tless.
&(all during the / dropsin).
And i imagine.
&-moon-He-be-hind-a-mills.
& sun & / sil / e / nce.
And this day it was Spring....us.
And what were roses. Perfume?for i do.
An(fragrance)Of / (Begins) / millions.
Annie died the other day.
Any man is wonderful.
Anyone Lived in a Pretty How Town.
Applaws) / "fell / ow."
"April" / this letter's dated.
Ardensteil-henarub-izabeth) / this noN.
As any(men's hells having wrestled with).
As freedom is a breakfastfood.
As if as / if a mys.
As is the sea marvelous.
As Joe Gould says in.
As one who(having written).
As that named Fred.
As usual i did not find him in cafes,the more dissolute atmosphere.
As / we lie side by side.
At dusk / just when.
At just 5 a / m i hear eng.
At the ferocious phenomenon of 5 o'clock i find myself gently decompos.
At the head of this street a gasping organ is waving moth-eaten.
Autumn is:that between there and here.
Awful darkness of the town, The.
B / eLl / s? / bE.
B / et / wee / n no / w dis.
Babylon slim / -ness of / evenslicing.
Ballad of an Intellectual.
Ballad of Love.
Ballad of the Scholar's Lament.
Ballade: "Does something lie who'd rather

stand."
Ballade of Soul.
Ballade: "White night roared with a huge north-wind, The."
Be of love(a little).
Be unto love as rain is unto colour^eate.
Beautiful / is the / unmea.
Because / an obstreperous grin minutely floats.
Because i love you)last night.
Because it's / Spring / thingS
Because / you go away i give roses who.
Because you take life in your stride(instead.
Bed is not very big, The.
Before the fragile gradual throne of night.
Being to timelessness as it's to time.
Being / twelve / who hast merely.
Being(just a little).
Belgium.
Between green / mountains.
Between nose-red gross.
Between the breasts / of bestial.
Beware beware beware / because because because.
Beyond the brittle towns asleep.
Beyond the stolid iron pond.
Bigness of cannon, The.
Birds(/ here,inven / ting air).
Birds meet above the new Moon.
!blac / k / agains / t.
Blossoming are people / nimbler than Really.
Blue the triangular why.
Blue woman with sticking out breasts hanging, A.
Both eaching come ghostlike.
Boy and the Man, The.
Boys i mean are not refined, The.
Breathe with me this fear.
BrIght / bRight s??? big / (soft).
Bud(spiggy nuvduh fienus).
Buncha hardboil guys frum duh A.C. fulla.
But also dying / (as well as).
But being not amazing:without love.
But granted that it's nothing paradoxically enough beyond mere personal.
"But / he" i / staring / into winter twi.
But if a living dance upon dead minds.
But if i should say.
But mr can you maybe listen there's.
But observe[though / once is never the beginning of.
But the other / day i was passing a certain.
But turning a corner ,i.
"but why should" / the / greatest.
Buy me an ounce and i'll sell you a pound.
By god i want above fourteenth.
By little accurate saints thickly which tread.
Cambridge ladies who live in furnished souls, The.
Candles and / Here Comes a glass box.
Chas sing does(who).
Chaucer.
Chérie / the very,picturesque,last Day.
Chilly,murky night, A.
Christ but they're few.
Ci-gît l Foetus(unborn to not die).
Cleopatra built / like a smooth arrow or.
Clown's smirk in the skull of a baboon, A.
Come a little further—why be afraid.
Come from his gal's.
Come,gaze win me upon this dome.
Come nothing to my comparable soul.
Come(all your mischief- / hatchers hatch).
Comedian stands on a corner,the sky is, The.
Coming of May, The.
Conceive a man,should he have anything.
Connotation of infinity, A.
Consider O / woman this / my body.
Cont)- / in / this / crazily.
Conversation with my friend is particularly.
"Could that"i marveled"be / you?"
Crazy jay blue) / demon laughshriek.
Cri / C / k / et / in.
Cruelly,love / walk the autumn long.
Curtains part) / the peacockappareled.
D-re-A-mi-N-gl-Y / leaves / (sEe).
Darling!because my blood can sing.

Dawn / and now.begins / feeling.
Dead every enormous piece.
Death(having lost)put on his universe.
Death's Chimney.
Dedicated to Dear Nana Clarke.
Dedication: "White rose my soul, The."
Denied night's face / have shadowless they?
Devil crept in eden wood.
Dick Mid's large bluish face without eyebrows.
Dim / i / nu / tiv / e this park is e.
Dirty colours of her kiss have just, The.
Dive for dreams / or a slogan may topple you.
Do. / omful / relaxing.
Do you remember when the fluttering dusk.
Does yesterday's perfection seem not quite.
Doll's boy's asleep / under a stile.
Dominic has / a doll wired.
Don't cries to please my.
Don't get me wrong oblivion.
Doveglion.
Dress was a suspicious madder,importing the cruelty of roses, The.
Dying is fine)but Death.
E / cco the uglies / t.
Eagle, The.
Early Summer Sketch.
Earth like a tipsy.
Ecco a letter starting "dearest we."
"Economic secu / rity" is a cu.
Emperor / sleeps in a palace of porphyry, The.
Emptied.hills.listen.
Enter no(silence is the blood whose flesh).
Enters give / whose lost is his found.
Epithalamion: "Thou aged unreluctant earth who dost."
Ev erythingex Cept: / that / 's what she's.
Even a pencil has fear to.
Even if all desires things moments be.
Every one of the red roses opened.
Everybody happy? / WE-WE-WE.
Except in your / honour.
Exit a kind of unkindness exit.
F / eeble a blu / r of cr.
F is for foetus(a).
Fabulous against ,a,fathoming jelly.
Fair ladies tall lovers / riding are through the.
Faithfully tinying at twilight voice.
Fame Speaks.
Fea / therr / ain / :dreamin.
Fearlessandbosomy / this / grand:gal.
Finis.
Fire stop thief help murder save the world.
First Jock he / was kilt a handsome.
First of All My Dreams, The.
First president to be loved by his, The.
First robin the; / you say something.
First she like a piece of ill-oiled.
Five Americans.
5 / derbies-with-men-in-them smoke Helmar.
Fl / a / tt / ene / d d.
Float / ing / ly) / i / (in Khoury's warm).
FloatfloaflofIf / lloloa.
Flotsam and jetsam / are gentlemen poeds.
Football with white eyebrows the, A.
For any ruffian of the sky.
For him alone life's worse than worst.
For prodigal read generous.
Four III.
Fragrant sag of fruit distinctly grouped, A.
From spiralling ecstatically this.
From the cognoscenti.
FULL SPEED ASTERN).
G / ra / D / ua / ILy &.
"Gay" is the captivating cognomen of a Young Woman of cambridge,mass.
Gee i like to think of dead it means nearer because deeper firmer.
Girl's Ring, A.
Glazed mind layed in a, A).
Glory is fallen out of, The.
God.
God gloats upon Her stunning flesh. Upon.
God pity me whom (god distinctly has).
God,Thine the hand that doth extend.
—GON splashes-sink.
Goo-dmore-ning(en / ter)nize-aday(most).

Goodby Betty,don't remember me.
Go(perpe)go / (tu)to(al).
Gr / eyhaire / d(m), A.
Granted the all / saving our young kiss only.
Great advantage of being alive, The.
Great Dante stands in Florence, looking down.
Great / man / is / gone, A.
Greedy the people, The.
GrEEn's d / an / cing on hollow was.
Grin without a / face(a look), A.
Guilt is the cause of more disauders.
Hair your a brook.
Handsome and clever and he went cruising.
Hanged / if n / y in a real hot spell.
Harder perhaps than a newengland bed.
Hate blows a bubble of despair into.
He as o / ld as who stag, A.
He does not have to feel because he thinks.
Helen.
Hello is what a mirror says.
Helves surling out of eakspeasies per(reel)hapsingly.
Her careful distinct sex whose sharp lips comb.
Her / flesh / Came / at.
Here is little Effie's Head.
Here is the ocean,this is moonlight:say.
Here pasture ends— / this girl and boy.
Here's s / omething round(& so).
Here's to opening and upward,to leaf and to sap.
Hills chime with thrush.
Hills / like poets put on, The.
Hips lOOsest OOping shoulders blonde& pastoral hair,strong.
Hist whist / little ghostthings.
Hokku.
Home means that / when the certainly.
Honour corruption villainy holiness.
!Hope / faith! / !life / love!
How dark and single,where he ends,the earth.
How generous is that himself the sun.
How many moments must(amazing each).
How / ses humble.
How this uncouth enchanted.
How / tinily / of / squir(two be).
Humanity i love you.
Humble one(gifted with / illimitable joy).
Hush) / noones / are coming.
I am a beggar always.
I am a little church(no great cathedral).
I am going to utter a tree,Noboby.
I am so glad and very.
I carry your heart with me(i carry it in).
I go to this window.
I have found what you are like.
I have looked upon thee—and I have loved thee.
I have loved,let us see if that's all.
I have seen her a stealthily frail.
I like my body when it is with your.
I like / to think that on.
I love you / for your little,startled,thoughtless ways.
I love you much(most beautiful darling).
I / (meet)t(touch).
I met a man under the moon.
I / never / guessed any / thing(even a).
I remark that this beach has been used too. much Too. originally.
I say no world.
I shall imagine life.
I Sing of Olaf Glad and Big.
I spoke to the.
I Thank You God.
"I think you like."
I walked the boulevard.
I was considering how.
I was sitting in mcsoreley's. outside it was New York and beauti- / fully snowing.
I will be / M o ving in the Street of her.
I will cultivate within.
I will wade out.
I'd think "wonder / if" if.
If.
If a cheerfulest Elephantangelchild should sit.
If being mortised with a dream.

If everything happens that can't be done.
If i believe / in death be sure.
If I Have Made, My Lady.
If i love You.
If i / or anybody don't.
If i should sleep with a lady called death.
If in beginning twilight of winter will stand.
If learned darkness from our searched world.
If night's mostness(and whom did merely day / close).
If seventy were young / and death uncommon.
If the / green / opens.
If the Lovestar grows most big.
If there are any heavens my mother will (all by herself) have.
If up's the wordd a world grows greener.
If within tonight's erect.
If you and i awakening.
If you can't eat you got to.
If you like my poems let them.
If(among / silent skies).
If(touched by love's own secret)we,like homing.
If(you are i why certainly).
IKEY(GOLDBERG)'S WORTH I'M.
I'll tell you a dream i had once i was away up in the sky Blue,everything.
I'm / asking / you dear to.
I'm very fond of.
(Im)c-a-t(mo).
Impossibly / motivated by midnight.
Impression.
In a middle of a room.
IN) all those who got.
In front of your house i.
In hammamet did camping queers et al).
In Healey's Palace I was sitting.
In heavenly realms of hellas dwelt.
In Just.
In making Marjorie god hurried.
In spite of everything.
In / Spring comes(no- / one).
In the rain- / darkness, the sunset.
In time of daffodils(who know.
In time's a noble mercy of proportion.
Infinite jukethrob smoke & swallow to dis.
Innerly / UningstrolL / (stamens & pistil).
Insu nli gh t / o / verand.
Inthe,exquisite; / morning sure lyHer eye s exactly sit,ata little roundtable.
Into a truly / curving form.
Into the smiting / sky tense.
Into the strenuous briefness.
Irreproachable ladies firmly lewd.
Is / it / because there struts a distinct silver lady.
Is there a flower(whom).
It Is At Moments After I Have Dreamed.
It is funny,you will be dead some day.
It is so long since my heart has been with yours.
It is winter a moon in the afternoon.
It may not always be so; and i say.
It really must / be Nice,never to.
It started when Bill's chip let on to.
It was a goodly co.
Item.
Item:is / Clumsily with of.
It)It will it.
It's jolly / odd what pops into.
It's just like a coffin's.
It's over a(see just).
It's / so damn sweet when Anybody.
I've come to ask you if there isn't a.
Ivory performing rose, The.
Jack's white horse(up).
Jake hates / all the girls(the).
Jehovah buried,Satan dead.
Jimmie's got a goil.
Joyful your complete fearless and pure love.
Joys faces friends / feet terrors fate.
Kike is the most dangerous, A.
Kind) / YM&WC / (of sort of).
"Kitty". sixteen,5'1",white,prostitute.
Kumrads die because they're told).
L(a / le / af / fa / ll / s).

Ladies and gentlemen this little girl.
Lady / i pray to what is unimaginable.
Lady,i will touch you with my mind.
Lady of Silence.
Lady,since your footstep.
Lady will you come with me into.
Lady you have written me a letter.
Laughing to find / Anyone's blind.
Lean candles hunger in.
Leastlessly / out / of this.
Let it go—the.
Let us lie here in the disturbing grass.
Let us suspect,chérie,this not very big.
(Let us tremble)a personal radiance sits.
Let's,from some loud unworld's most rightful wrong.
Let's live suddenly without thinking.
Let's start a magazine.
Life boosts herself rapidly at me.
Life hurl my.
Life is more true than reason will deceive.
Life / shuts &)opens the world.
Light cursed falling in a singular block.
Light Out), A.
Light's lives lurch / a once world quickly from rises.
Like a / grey / rock wanderin, A.
Like a little bear twilight.
Like most godhouses this particular house.
Lily has a rose.
Lis / -ten / you know what i mean when.
Listen / beloved / i dreamed.
Listen my children and you.
(Listen) / this a dog barks and.
Little horse is newlY, The.
Little joe gould has lost his teeth and doesn't know where.
Little ladies more / than dead exactly dance.
Little man / (in a hurry).
Little tree / little silent Christmas tree.
Lively and loathesome moe's respectably dead.
Logeorge / lo / wellifitisn't eddy how's the boy.
Long ago,between a dream and a dream.
Longing.
Look at this) / a 75 done.
Look / my fingers,which.
Lord John Unalive(having a fortune of fifteengrand).
Love is a guess / that deepens.
Love is a place.
Love is a spring at which.
Love is more thicker than forget.
Love is the every only god.
Love our so right.
Love was—entire excellently steep.
Love's absence is illusion,alias time.
Love's function is to fabricate unknownness.
Love's the i guess most only verb that lives.
Lucky means finding / Holes where.
Luminous tendril of celestial wish.
Maggie and Milly and Molly and May.
Maker of many mouths.
Man who had fallen among thieves, A.
Marianne Moore.
Mary green / cheerful & generous.
May i be gay.
May I Feel Said He.
May my heart always be open to little.
Maybe god / is a child.
Me Up at Does.
,Mean- / hum / a)now / (nit.
Meet mr universe(who clean).
Memorabilia.
Memory believes / fragrance of a town(whose).
Metamorphosis.
Mi(dreamlike)st / makes / big each dim.
Might these be thrushes climbing through almost(do they).
Mighty guest of merely me.
Mind is its own beautiful prisoner, The.
Mind's(/ I never you never), The.
Mist.
Mr. smith / is reading / his letter.
Mr U.
Mr youse needn't be so spry.

Mrs / and mr across the way are kind of.
Moan / (is) / ing / the she of the.
Moon falls through the autumn Behind prisons she grins, The.
Moon-in-the-Trees, / The old canoe awaits you.
Moon is hiding in, The.
Moon-lit snow is falling like strange candy into the big eyes of the, The.
Moon looked into my window, The.
Moon over gai.
MOOn Over tOwns mOOn.
Morsel miraculous and meaningless.
Mortals) / climbi / ng i / nto eachness begi.
Most(people / simply / can't).
Mouse)Won / derfully is.
Move / deeply,rain / (dream hugely)wish.
Much i cannot) / tear up the world:& toss.
Murderfully in midmost o.c.an.
Music.
Must being shall.
My darling since / you and.
My deathly body's deadly lady.
My eyes are fond of the east side.
My Father Moved Through Dooms Of Love.
My girl's tall with hard long eyes.
My humorous ghost precisely will.
My lady is an ivory garden.
My little heart is so wonderfully sorry.
My love is building a building.
My love / thy hair is one kingdom.
My mind is.
My naked lady framed.
My Prayer.
My smallheaded pearshaped.
My sonnet is A light goes on in.
My specialty is living said.
My strength becoming wistful in a glib.
My sweet old etcetera.
My uncle / Daniel fought in the civil.
My youthful lady will have other lovers.
My(his from daughter's mother's zero mind).
Myself,walking in Dragon st.
N / ot eth / eold almos.
N / OthI / n / g can / s / urPas / s.
N / Umb a / stree / t's wintr.
Nearer:breath of my breath:take not thy tingling.
Neither awake / (there's your general).
Neither could say / (it comes so slow).
Never could anyone / who simply lives to die.
Newly / cued / motif smites truly to beautifully.
Newlys of silence.
Next to of Course God America I.
Night.
Night shall eat these girls and boys.
The / nimble / heat / had.
Nine birds(rising / through a gold moment)climb.
Nite) / thatthis / crou / ched.
No man,if men are gods; but if gods must.
No time ago / or else a life.
Nobody could / in superhuman flights.
Nobody loses all the time.
Nobody loved this.
Nobody wears a yellow.
Nocturne: "When the lithe moonlight silently."
Noise.
Nonsun blob a / cold to.
Noone and a star stand,am to am.
Noone" autumnal this great lady's gaze.
Nor woman / (just as it be).
Noster, The.
Not time's how(anchored in what mountaining roots).
Nothing false and possible is love.
Nothing is more exactly terrible than.
"Nothing" the unjust man complained.
Nothing whichful about / thick big this.
Notice the convulsed orange inch of moon.
Nouns to nouns / wan / wan.
Now air is air and thing is thing:no bliss.
Now all the fingers of this tree(darling)have.
Now comes the good rain farmers pray for(and).

There are possibly 2 1/2 or impossibly 3.
There are 6 doors.
There are so many tictoc.
There is a here and.
There is a / moon sole.
These children singing in stone a.
These from my mother's greatgrandmother's
    rosebush white.
These people socalled were not given hearts.
These(whom'etends / blue nothing).
Thethe / the pink / Tartskids with.
They have hung the sky with arrows.
Theys sO alive.
Thing most new complete fragile intense, A.
Thing no is(of).
Think of it:not so long ago.
This cigarette is extremely long.
This evangelist / buttons with his big gollywog
    voice.
This fear is no longer dear. You are not going
    to America and.
This / forest pool / A so.
This is a rubbish of human rind.
This is the vase, Here.
This little bride & groom are.
This little huge / -eyed per-.
This little / pair had a little scare.
This man's heart / is true to his.
This mind made war.
This out of within itself moo.
This young question mark man.
This(a up green hugeness who and climbs).
This(let's remember)day died again and.
This(that / grey)white / (man)horse.
Thou / firsting a hugeness of twi / -light.
Thou in whose swordgreat story shine the
    deeds.
Though your sorrows not.
Three wealthy sisters swore they'd never part.
Through the tasteless minute efficient room.
Thrown a / -way It, A.
Thy face is a still white house of holy things.
Thy fingers make early flowers of.
Time,be kinderself and i.
Timeless / ly this / (merely and whose).
To stand(alone)in some.
To start,to hesitateø stop.
To William F. Bradbury.
Tonight the moon is round golden entire. It.
Total stranger one black day, A.
Touching you i say(it being Spring).
Trees / were in(give).
Trick of finding what you didn't lose, The.
True lovers in each happening of their hearts.
Tumbling-hair / picker of buttercups.
Tw / oo / ld / o / nce upo / n.
Twentyseven bums give a prostitute the once.
Twi- / is -Light bird.
2 little whos / (he and she).
2 shes / both not quite / young perfectly.
Two X.
Un / der fog / 's / touch.
Un(bee)mo / vi / n(in)g.
Unlove's the heavenless hell and homeless
    home.
Unnoticed woman from whose kind large flesh.
Until and i heard.
Unto thee i / burn incense.
Up into the silence the green.
Upon the room's / silence,i will sew.
Us if therefore must forget ourselves.
Utterly and amusingly I am pash.
Vision.
Voices to voices, lip to lip.
W.H.W., Jr.
Waddling / madam star, The.
Wanta / spendsix / dollars Kid.
Warped this perhapsy.
Water-Lilies.
Way to hump a cow is not, The.
We being not each other:without love.
We love each other very dearly.
We miss you,jack—tactfully you(with one
    cocked).
Weazened Irrefutable unastonished.
Wee people / dwelling / between serene.

Well)here's looking at ourselves.
We)under)over,the thing of floating Of.
What a proud dreamhorse
    pulling(smoothloomingly)through.
What does little Ernest croon.
What freedom's not some under's mere above.
What Got him was Noth.
What If a Much of a Which of a Wind.
What is / a / voyage / ?
What is strictly fiercely and wholly dies.
What is thy mouth to me?
What over and which under.
What time is it i wonder never mind.
What time is it?it is by every star.
Whatever's merely wilful, / and not
    miraculous.
When any mortal(even the most odd).
When citied day with the sonorous homes.
When / (day's amazing murder with).
When faces called flowers float out of the
    ground.
When / from a sidewalk.
When god decided to invent.
When God Lets My Body Be.
When hair falls off and eyes blur And.
When i am in boston,i do not speak.
When i have thought of you somewhat too.
When life is quite through with.
When muckers pimps and tratesmen.
When my love comes to see me it's.
When my sensational moments are no more.
When of your eyes one smile entirely brings
    down.
When parsing warmths of dusk construe.
When rain whom fear.
When serpents bargain for the right to squirm.
When the proficient poison of pure sleep.
When the spent day begins to frail.
When thou art dead,dead,and far from the
    splendid sin.
When thou hast taken thy last applause,and
    when.
When time delicately is sponging sum after.
When unto nights of autumn do complain.
When what hugs stopping earth than silent is.
When you are silent,shining host by guest.
When you rang at Dick Mid's Place.
When you went away it was morning.
When your honest redskin toma.
Whereas by dark really released,the modern.
Wherelings whenlings / (daughters of if but
    offspring of hopefear).
Where's Jack Was / General Was.
Where's Madge then / Madge and her men?
Which is the very.
While a once world slips from.
Whippoorwill this / moonday into.
White guardians of the universe of sleep.
Who are you,little i.
Who(at / her nons- / elf).
Who before dying demands not rebirth.
Who is this / dai / nty mademoiselle.
Who knows if the moon's.
Who sharpens every dull.
Who / threw the silver dollar up into the tree?
Who were so dark of heart they might not
    speak.
Who(is?are)who.
Who's most afraid of death?thou.
Whose are these(wraith a clinging with a
    wraith).
Why did you go.
Why / do the / fingers.
Why / don't / be / sil / ly.
Why from this her and him.
Why must itself up every of a park.
Why why / How many winds make wonderful.
Wild(at our first)beasts uttered human words.
Will i ever forget that precarious moment?
Will out of the kindness of their hearts a few
    philosophers tell me.
Will suddenly trees leap up from winter and
    will.
Will you teach a.
Willing pitifully to bewitch.
Wind has blown the rain away and blown, A.

Wind is a Lady with, The.
Windows go orange in the slowly.
Wing Wong,uninterred at twice.
The(/ Wistfully / dead seem generous)don't.
Without the mercy of / your eyes your.
Woman / of bronze / unhappy, A.
Workingman with hand so hairy-sturdy.
World is very big, and we, The.
Worshipping same / they squirm and they
    spawn.
Writhe and / gape of tortured.
Y is a WELL KNOWN ATHELETE'S BRIDE.
Yes but even / 4 or(&).
Yes is a pleasant country.
YgUDuh / ydoan / yunnuhstan.
Yonder deadfromtheneckup graduate of a.
You are like the snow only.
You are not going to,dear. You are not going to
    and.
You are tired, / (I think).
You asked me to come:it was raining a little.
You being in love.
You / in win / ter who sit.
You no / tice / nobod / y wants.
You said Is / there anything which.
You Shall Above All Things Be Glad and
    Young.
You shall sing my songs, O earth.
You which could grin three smiles into a dead.
Youful / larger / of smallish).
Young m / oon:be kind to olde.
Young / man sitting, The.
Your birthday comes to tell me this.
Your homecoming will be my homecoming.
Your little voice / Over the wires came leaping.
Yours is the music for no instrument.

Cunningham, James (Olumo) (b. 1936)
On a Letter.

Cunningham, James Vincent (1911–85)
Absence, my angel, presence at my side.
Acknowledgement.
Aged Lover Discourses in the Flat Style, The.
Agnosco Veteris Vestigia Flammae.
All Choice Is Error.
All in Due Time.
Another novel, and the prostitute.
Arms and the man I sing, and sing for joy.
Ars Amoris.
August Hail.
Autumn.
Beacon, The.
Bookplate.
Cantor's Theorem: In an Infinite Class the
    Whole Is No Greater Than Some of Its
    Parts.
Career was feminine, resourcesful, clever.
Chase, The.
Choice.
Coffee.
Consolatio Nova.
Convalescence.
Dear child whom I begot.
Distinctions at Dusk.
Distraction.
Dogdays.
Elders at their services begin, The.
Elegy for a Cricket.
Envoi: "Hear me, whom I betrayed."
Epigram: "And what is love?
    Misunderstanding, pain."
Epigram: "Good Fortune, when I hailed her
    recently."
Epigram: "Here lies my wife. Eternal peace."
Epigram: "Here lies New Critic who would fox
    us."
Epigram: "I had gone broke, and got set to
    come back."
Epigram: "You ask me how Contempt who
    claims to sleep."
Epigram: "You wonder why Drab sells her
    love for gold?"
Epigrams: A Journal.
Epigrams: "Old dissembler who lived out his
    lie, An."
Faint smile of distraction, moist response, A.
Fancy.

Fear.
Few Words, and Some His, In Memory of Clayton Stafford, A.
Five Epigrams, *sels.*
For a College Yearbook.
For a Woman with Child.
For My Contemporaries.
Friend, on This Scaffold Thomas More Lies Dead.
Gnothi Seauton.
Haecceity.
Half hour for coffee, and at night, A.
Helmsman, The; an Ode.
Horoscope.
Hymn in Adversity.
I drive Eastward. The ethics of return.
I grow old, but I know that Science some.
I married in my youth a wife.
I, Too, Have Been to the Huntington.
I write only to say this.
I write you in my need. Please write.
Identity, that spectator.
If one takes trouble to explain.
Illusion and delusion are that real.
In a few days now when two memories meet.
In Innocence.
In the thirtieth year of life.
Innocent to innocent.
Interview with Doctor Drink.
It Was in Vegas. Celibate and able.
Jack and Jill.
Lector Aere Perennior.
L'Esprit de Géométrie et L'Esprit de Finesse.
Life flows to death as rivers to the sea.
Lights of Love, The.
Passion.
Love, receive Lais' glass, the famous whore.
Love's Progress.
Man of Feeling, The.
Man who goes for Christian resignation, The.
Meditation on a Memoir.
Meditation on Statistical Method.
Memoir.
Metaphysical Amorist, The.
Mistress of scenes, good-by. Your maidenhead.
Modern Love.
Monday Morning.
Montana Fifty Years Ago.
Montana Pastoral.
Moral Poem, A.
My name is Ebenezer Brown.
New York: 5 March 1957.
Night-piece.
Noon.
Not for Charity.
Obsequies for a Poetess.
Oedipean Mom and Dad, An.
Old love is old resentment, novelty.
On a cold night I came through the cold rain.
On a Line from Bodenham's "Belvedere."
On Correggio's Leda.
On Doctor Drink.
On either side of the white line.
1 Corinthians 13: Commentary.
Original Sin.
Periphrastic Insult, Not a Banal, A.
Phoenix, The.
Portrait.
Predestined Space, The.
Prue loved her man: to clean, to mend.
Reader, it's time reality was faced.
Reason and Nature.
Ripeness Is All.
Solipsist, The.
Some twenty years of marital agreement.
Somnium Narrare, Vigilantis Est.
Statistics.
Summer Idyll.
Symposium, The.
There is a ghost town of abandoned love.
They.
Think.
This Tower of Sun.
Timor Dei.
To a Friend, on Her Examination for the Doctorate in English.

To My Daimon.
To My Wife.
To the Reader.
To Whom It May Concern.
Towards Tucson.
Traveller, the highway my guide, A.
True Religion, The.
Wandering Scholar's Prayer to St. Catherine of Egypt, The.
Who am I? I have pondered with my peers.
Who lives by wisdom and to others gives.
With every wife he can and you know why?
You have here no otherness.
Young Sensitive one summer on the Cape.
Your affair, my dear, need not be a mess.

D

da Bologna, Bernardo
    Inside that loving country girl.
Dante Alighieri (1265–1321)
    Ballata: He will gaze upon Beatrice.
    Canzone: He beseeches Death for the Life of Beatrice.
    Convito, *sels.*
    Dante's Vita Nuova.
    Divina Commedia, *sels.*
    First Canzone of the Convito, The.
    Guido, I would like that you and Lapo and I.
    La Nuvoletta.
    La Vita Nuova, *sels.*
    La Vita Nuova.
    Sestina: "I have reached, alas, the long shadow."
    Sestina: Of the Lady Pietra degli Scrovigni.
    Sonnet: He imagines a pleasant Voyage for Guido, Lapo Gianni, and himself, with their three Ladies.
    Sonnet: He rebukes Cino for Fickleness.
    Sonnet: Of Beatrice de' Portinari, on All Saints' Day.
    Sonnet: Of Beauty and Duty.
    Sonnet: On the 9th of June 1290.
    Sonnet: To certain Ladies; when Beatrice was lamenting her Father's Death.
    Sonnet: To the Lady Pietra degli Scrovigni.
    Sonnet: To the same Ladies; with their Answer.
    Sonnet: Written in Exile.
D'Arezzo, Fra Guittone (*fl.* 1250)
    Sonnet: To the Blessed Virgin Mary.
"Darío, Rubén" (Félix Rubén García Sarmiento) (1867–1916)
    Anagke.
    Autumn Poem, The.
    Autumn Verses.
    Ballad in Honor of the Muses of Flesh and Blood.
    Because of the Influence of Spring.
    Birds of the islands: in your gathering.
    Charterhouse, The.
    Cleopompus and Heliodemos.
    Colloquy of the Centaurs.
    Concerning the Cid.
    Divine Psyche, sweet invisible Butterfly.
    Dream's blue bird, The.
    Eheu!
    Exploit in the Bullring.
    First, a look.
    Flesh, a woman's heavenly flesh. Clay.
    For just a moment, O Swan, I will link my longings.
    Golden tortoise walks across the carpet, The.
    I am the one who just yesterday spoke.
    I love the faces pallid.
    I pursue a form that my style does not find.
    In Autumn.
    In Autumn ("I know that there are those who say, "Why don't you sing now'").
    In Spring.
    In Summer.
    In the Constellations.
    It was a gentle air, with leisurely turns.
    Ite, Missa Est.

Love your rhythm and give rhythm to your actions.
Metempsychosis.
My love, the night has come.
Nocturne: "I want to express my anguish in verses that tell."
Nocturne: "Silence of the night, a sorrowful silence."
Nocturne: "Those of you who auscultated the heart of the night."
Om.
Palimpsest: "Written in an old Aeolian dialect."
Poet put in his verses, The.
Prayer for the Dead (To Verlaine).
Reincarnations.
Salvador Díaz Mirón.
Singer goes all over the world, The.
Sonatina.
Song of Autumn in Springtime.
Spaniard.
Spes.
Sum.
Sweetness of the Angelus, divine in the morning, The.
To Phocas the Peasant.
To Roosevelt.
Towers of God! Poets!
Venus.
Walt Whitman.
What Gets You.
What sign do you give, O Swan, with your curving neck.
When the poor guy saw her pass.
White Page, The.
Davie, Donald (1922–95)
    Abbeyforde.
    Across the Bay.
    Admiral to His Lady, The.
    Advent.
    After a Change of Régime.
    After an Accident.
    After the Calamitous Convoy (July 1942).
    After the Match.
    Against Confidences.
    Agave in the West.
    Alzheimer's Disease.
    Amazonian.
    Among Artisans' Houses.
    And Our Eternal Home.
    Anglican Lady, An.
    Another Old Bolshevik.
    Apparition, An.
    Ars Poetica.
    Articulacy. Hints from the Koran.
    At Knaresborough.
    At the Café Parnasse.
    At the Cradle of Genius.
    At the Synod in St Patrick's.
    Attar of Roses.
    Aubade: "I wish for you that when you wake."
    August, 1968.
    Autumn Imagined.
    Back of Affluence.
    Balancing Acts.
    Barnsley and District.
    Barnsley, 1966.
    Battered Wife, The.
    Battlefield, A.
    Bedfordshire.
    Behind the North Wind.
    Being Angry with God.
    Belfast on a Sunday Afternoon.
    Bella & Rosa.
    Benedictus.
    Bent, The.
    Berkshire.
    Berryman.
    Bits and Pieces.
    Black Hoyden.
    Bolyai, the Geometer.
    Bougainville.
    Bowing the Head.
    Boyhood Misremembered.
    Brantôme.

Bride of Reason, The.
Buckinghamshire.
By the Road to Upper Midhope.
Cambridgeshire.
Cannibals.
Catullus on Friendship.
Chernobyl. A Disaster.
Cherry Ripe.
Cheshire.
Christening, A.
Christian Hero, A.
Christmas Syllabics for a Wife.
Christmas Week, 1948.
Chrysanthemums.
Church Militant.
Church of Ireland.
Cold Spring in Essex.
Comforter, The.
Commodore Barry.
Conditioned Air, A.
Condolence.
Cornwall.
Corrib. An Emblem.
County Durham.
Cowper's 'Yardley Oak': A Continuation.
Creature David, The.
Creon's Mouse.
Cumberland.
Curtains!
Cypress Avenue, The.
Dancing Measures.
David Dancing.
Death in the West, A.
Death of a Painter.
Demi-Exile. Howth.
Democrats.
Departed, The.
Depravity: Two Sermons.
Derbyshire.
Derbyshire Turf.
Devil on Ice.
Devonshire.
Dissentient Voice, A.
Dorset.
Dream Forest.
Dublin Georgian.
Dublin Georgian ("Thin brown orphan in his
    washed-out blue, A").
Dudwood.
Dule of a Dewsbury Matron.
Duplicity in Prayer.
Ecclesiastical Polity.
Eden.
Eight Years After.
Elders and Betters.
Elect, The.
Emigrant, to the Receding Shore.
Energies.
England.
England, for Ezra Pound.
English Revenant, An.
Epistle. To Enrique Caracciolo Trejo.
Equestrian Sestina.
Essex.
Evangelist, The.
Evening on the Boyne.
Except the Lord Build the House.
Expecting Silence.
Ezra Pound in Pisa.
Fairy Story.
Fare Thee Well.
Father, the Cavalier.
Fatherhood.
Feeders, The.
Felicity's Fourth Order.
For Doreen. A Voice from the Garden.
Forests of Lithuania, The.
Fountain of Arethusa, The.
Fountain of Cyanë, The.
Fountain, The.
From the New World.
Frontenac.
G. M. B.
Garden Party, The.
Gardens No Emblems.
Gardens of the Savoy, The.

Garland for Ivor Gurney, A.
Garland for Ronsard, A.
Gemona-del-Friuli, 1961–1976.
Glaphira 3.
Gloucestershire.
God Saves the King.
Going to Italy.
Grace in the Fore Street.
Grazia Deledda, Young.
Green River.
Gripping Serial.
Grudging Respect.
H. D.
Hampshire.
Hardness of Light, The.
Harrow, The.
Having No Ear.
Hawkshead and Dachau in a Christmas Glass.
Hearing Russian Spoken.
Heart Beats.
Heigh-ho on a Winter Afternoon.
Helena Morley.
Herefordshire.
Hermes and Mr Shaw.
Heroine of the Academy, A.
Hertfordshire.
Hill Field, The.
His Themes.
Homage to George Whitefield.
Homage to John L. Stephens.
Homage to William Cowper.
Horae Canonicae.
Hornet.
Hot Hands.
House-martin.
Housekeeping.
Humanly Speaking.
Huntingdonshire.
Hyphens.
Hypochondriac Logic.
I Have Said, Ye Are Gods.
If I Take the Wings of the Morning.
Immortal Longings. Before Surgery.
In California.
In Chopin's Garden.
In the Stopping Train.
Inditing a Good Matter.
Intervals in a Busy Life.
Iowa.
Ironist, The.
Jacob's Ladder.
January.
Jesuits in North America, The.
Jottings, not so Random.
July, 1964.
Just You Wait!
Kavyria.
Kent.
Killala.
Kingship.
Kites.
Knave of Hearts, The.
Lady Cochrane.
Lancashire.
Landfall among Friends.
Lasalle.
Late Anniversary, A.
Leicestershire.
Letter to Curtis Bradford, A.
Levity.
Life Encompassed.
Life of Service, The.
Lily at Noon, A.
Limited Achievement.
Lincolnshire.
Liverpool Epistle, A.
Livingshayes.
Lost Bride, The.
Love and the Times.
Love-Poems: for Mairi MacInnes.
Low Lands.
Machineries of Shame.
Magdalene.
Mamertinus on Rhetoric, A.D. 291.
Mandelstam in the Crimea.
Mandelstam, on Dante.

Mandelstam's Hope for the Best.
March.
Master & Man.
Measured Tread, A.
Meeting of Cultures, A.
Mens Sana in Corpore Sano.
Metals.
Meteorologist, September.
Method. For Ronald Gaskell.
Middlesex.
Midsummer's Eve.
Miracle, The.
Mr Sharp in Florence.
Monmouthshire.
Morning.
Mother.
Mustered into the Avant-Garde.
My Father's Honour.
Nashville Mornings.
New Year Wishes for the English.
1945.
Nineteen-Seventeen.
No Epitaph.
Nonconformist, The.
Norfolk.
North & South.
North Dublin.
North Sea, in a Snowstorm, The.
North Sea, The.
Northamptonshire.
Northern Metres.
Northumberland.
Nosegay, The.
Nottinghamshire.
Oak Openings.
Obiter Dicta.
On a Proposed Celebration of Ezra Pound.
On Bertrand Russell's 'Portraits from Memory'
On Edmund Spenser's House in Ireland.
On Generous Lines.
On Not Deserving.
On Sutton Strand.
On the Final Day.
Or, Solitude.
Ordinary God.
Oriental Visitor, An.
Orpheus.
Orvieto. The King of Clubs.
Our Father.
Our Lady.
Out of East Anglia.
Owl Minerva, The.
Ox-bow.
Oxfordshire.
Pacer in the Fresco, The. John the Baptist.
Pastor Errante.
Pelican.
Penelope.
Pietà.
Pilate.
Poem as Abstract.
Poet Redeemed & Dead.
Poet-Scholar, The.
Pontiac.
Poreč.
Preoccupation's Gift.
Priory of St Saviour, Glendalough, The.
Prolific Spell, The.
Protesilaus and Laodamia.
Pushkin. A Didactic Poem.
Put Not Your Trust in Princes.
Rain on South-East England.
Recollection of George Oppen in a Letter to an
    English Friend.
Red Rock of Utah.
Reflections on Deafness.
Rejoinder to a Critic.
Remembering the 'Thirties.
Reminded of Bougainville.
Replying to Reviewers.
Resolutions.
Reticence.
Revenge for Love.
Revulsion.
Right Lads, The.
Right Wing Sympathies.

Robinson Jeffers at Point Sur.
Rodez.
Rousseau in His Day.
Rutland.
Samuel Beckett's Dublin.
Savannah.
Saw I Never the Righteous Forsaken.
Screech-Owl.
'Sculpture' of Rhyme, The.
Sculptures in Hungary.
Scythian Charioteers, The.
Sea of Tiberias.
Seeing Her Leave.
Seeing through Me.
Selina, Countess of Huntingdon.
Seur, near Blois.
Short Run to Camborne.
Shropshire.
Siloam.
Sing unto the Lord a New Song.
Six Epistles to Eva Hesse.
Skelpick.
So Make Them Melt as the Dishousèd Snail.
Some Shires Revisited.
Somerset.
Song for These Crusaders, A.
Sonnet: "As massive and dispensable as
    sculpture."
Sorting Old Papers.
Sorting the Personae.
Sounds of a Devon Village.
Spring Song, A.
Staffordshire.
Standings.
Stratford on Avon.
Strathnaver.
Suffolk.
Summer Lightning.
Sunburst.
Sunday Morning.
Surrey.
Sussex.
Sylvae.
T. S. Eliot (1928).
Thanks to Industrial Essex.
Their Rectitude Their Beauty.
They, to Me.
Thirty-ninth Psalm, Adapted, The.
Thomas and Emma.
Thou Art Near at Hand, O Lord.
Though Dry, Not Dry.
Three Beyond.
Three Moral Discoveries.
Three Pastors in Berlin.
Through Bifocals.
Thyestes.
Tiger at the Movie-Show.
Time Passing, Beloved.
To a Bad Poet.
To a Brother in the Mystery.
To a Staffordshireman, from a Devon Villa.
To a Teacher of French.
To an American Classicist.
To C. T.
To Certain English Poets.
To Helen Keller.
To Londoners.
To Thom Gunn in Los Altos, California.
Toby to Aguecheek.
Townend, 1976.
Trevenen.
Treviso, the Pescheria.
Tunstall Forest.
Tuscan Brutus, The.
Tuscan Morning.
Twilight on the Waste Lands.
Two Dedications.
Two from Ireland.
Two Intercepted Letters.
Two Widows in Tashkent.
Under a Skylight.
Under St Paul's.
University of the South, The.
Utterings.
Vancouver.
Vengeance Is Mine, Saith the Lord.

Via Portello.
Vindication of Jovan Babič, The.
Viper-Man.
Vying.
War Criminal.
Warwickshire.
Waterfall at Powerscourt, The.
Wearing of the Green, The.
Well-found Poem.
West Virginia's Auburn.
Westmorland.
Where Depths Are Surfaces.
Widower.
Widowers.
Wild Boar Clough.
Wiltshire.
Wind at Penistone, The.
Winter Landscape near Ely, A.
Winter Landscapes.
Winter Talent, A.
Winter's Talents.
With the Grain.
Witness.
Woe unto Thee!
Wombwell on Strike.
Women and War.
Woodpigeons at Raheny.
Worcestershire.
Yorkshire.
Zion.
Zip!
Zodiac, The.

Davitt, Michael (b. 1950)
Mirror, The.

**De la Mare, Walter ("Walter Ramal") (1873–
1956)**
Abandoned Church, An.
Absalom.
Adieu.
Age.
Alexander.
All That's Past.
Alone ("Abode of the nightingale is bare,
    The").
Alone ("Very old woman / Lives in yon house,
    A").
Anatomy.
April.
April Moon.
Arabia.
Argument, The.
Ariel.
Assignation, The.
At Ease.
Autumn.
Awake!
Away.
Ballad of Christmas, A.
Banquo.
Be angry now no more!
Before Dawn.
Bells, The.
Beneath a motionless yew.
Betrayal.
Beware!
Bindweed, The.
Birthnight: To F, The.
Bitter Waters.
Blind Boy, The.
Bottle, The.
Break of Morning.
Breughel's Winter.
Bridge, The.
Bright Life.
Brother and Sister.
Cage, The ("Why did you flutter in vain hope,
    poor bird").
Cage, The ("Thou angel face—like a small
    exquisite cage").
Captive, The ("I twined a net").
Captive, The ("When gloaming droops").
Catechism, The.
Cherry Trees, The.
Child Asleep, A.
Children of Stare, The.
Clavichord.

Clear Eyes.
Comfort.
Corner Stone, The.
Courage.
Crazed.
Daisy, The.
Dark Château, The.
Dawn.
Death-Dream, The.
Decoy, The.
Defeat.
Disguise, The.
Dove, The.
Dream, A.
Dreamer, The ("O thou who givine helm and
    sword").
Dreamer, The ("Woods were still").
Dreams ("Be gentle, O hands of a child").
Dreams ("Ev'n one who has little travelled
    in").
Drugged.
Dry August Burned.
Dust to Dust.
Dwelling-Place, The.
Echo.
Empty House, The.
Encounter, The.
England.
English Downs.
Episodes.
Epitaph, An: "Here lies a most beautiful lady."
Epitaph, An: "Last, Stone, a little yet."
Estranged.
Euphrasy.
Even In The Grave.
Evening ("Little cirque, horizon-wide").
Evening ("When twilight darkens").
Exile.
Exile, The.
Eyes.
Faint Music.
Fairy in Winter, The.
Faithless.
Falstaff.
Familiar, The.
Fare Well.
Fat Woman, The.
Fear.
Feckless Dinner-Party, The.
Fleeting, The.
Flight, The.
Flotsam.
Flower, The.
Fog.
Fool's Song, The.
For All the Grief.
Foreboding ("Thou canst not see him standing
    by").
Foreboding ("Sycamore, by the heap of the
    dead").
Forests.
Forgiveness.
Futility.
Galliass, The.
Ghost, The ("Peace in thy hands").
Ghost, The ("Who knocks?").
Glance, The.
Glimpse, The.
Gloria Mundi.
Gold.
Goliath.
Good-bye.
Good Company.
Hamlet.
Happy Encounter, The.
Hare, A.
Haunted.
Hawthorn Hath a Deathly Smell, The.
Here Sleeps.
Heresy.
Homesick.
Horse in a Field.
Hospital.
Hour-Glass, The.
How Blind!
How Sleep the Brave.
Humanity.

Hunter, The.
I Sit Alone.
Iago.
Idleness.
Image, The.
Imagination's Pride, The.
Imogen.
Imp Within, The.
In a Library.
In Disgrace.
In the Dock.
In the Garden.
In Vain.
Incantation.
Interlude, An.
Invocation: "Burning fire shakes in the night,
    The."
Irrevocable, The.
Isaac Meek.
Jenny Wren.
Journey, The.
Juliet's Nurse.
Karma.
Keep Innocency.
Keys of Morning, The.
Last Arrow, The.
Last Chapter, The.
Last Coachload, The.
Life.
Linnet, The.
Listeners, The.
Little Salamander, The.
Looking Glass, The.
Lucy.
Macbeth.
Making a fire.
Marionettes, The.
Market-Place, The.
Martha.
Martins: September.
Massacre, The.
Memory ("When summer heat").
Memory ("Ah, memory").
Mercutio.
Mermaids, The.
Miracle, The.
Mirage.
Miss Loo.
Mist.
Mistress Fell.
Mrs. Grundy.
Moment, The.
Monologue, The.
Moonlight.
Moth, The.
Motley.
Mountains, The.
Mourn'st Thou Now?
Music ("When music sounds").
Music ("O restless fingers").
Music Unheard.
Myself.
Napoleon.
Never More, Sailor.
Never-To-Be.
News.
Night ("All from the light").
Night ("That shining moon").
Nocturne: "'Tis not my voice now speaks; but
    as a bird."
Nod.
Noon and Night Flower.
Not Only.
Not that way.
O Childish Mind!
Of a Son.
Oh, Why?
Old Angler, The.
Old Ben.
Old Men, The.
Old Summerhouse, The.
Old Susan.
Omen, The.
On the Esplanade.
One in the Public Gallery.

Ophelia.
Out Of Bounds.
Outskirts, The.
Owl, The ("What if to edge of dream").
Owl, The ("Doorbell jangled").
Peace.
Peeping Tom.
Phantom, The.
Pollie.
Polonius.
Portrait, A.
Pot Of Musk, A.
Prayer, A.
Quarry, The.
Queen Djenira.
Queen Wasp, A.
Quiet.
Quiet Enemy, The.
Rachel.
Railway Junction, The.
Reawakening, The.
Reconciliation.
Reflections.
Remembrance.
Remonstrance, The.
Reserved.
Revenant, The.
Reverie.
Riddle, A.
Riddlers, The.
Robin, A.
Rooks In October.
Rose.
Rose in Candlelight, A.
Rose in Water, A.
Round, The.
Sallie's Musical Box.
Satire, The.
Scarecrow, The.
Scribe, The.
Sea-Magic.
Self to self.
Shade, The.
Shadow ("Even the beauty").
Shadow ("Beware!").
Sign, A.
Silence.
Sleep.
Sleeper, The ("As Ann came in").
Sleeper, The ("Lovely, sleeping").
Slum Child, The.
Snow.
Snowdrop, The.
Snowflake, The.
Snowing.
Solitude.
Son of Melancholy, The.
Sorcery.
Sotto Voce.
Spark, The.
Spectre, The.
Speech.
Spirit of air, The.
Strange Spirit, The.
Stranger, The ("Half-hidden in a graveyard").
Stranger, The ("In the woods as I did walk").
Stratagem, The.
Suicide, The.
Sunday, A.
Sunk Lyonesse.
Sunken Garden, The.
Sunrise.
Swallows Flown.
Taciturn, The.
Tailor, The.
There Blooms No Bud in May.
They Told Me.
Thomas Hardy.
Thorn, The.
Three Cherry Trees, The.
Three Strangers, The.
Thule.
Thus Her Tale.
Time Passes.
Tired Cupid, The.
Titmouse.

TO E. T.: 1917.
To My Mother.
Tom's Angel.
Treachery.
Truce.
Tryst, The ("Flee into some forgotten night").
Tryst, The ("Faint now the colours").
Twice Lovely.
Twilight.
Unchanging, The.
Unfinished Dream, The.
Unforeseen.
Unheard Melodies.
Universe, The.
Unregarding.
Vacant Day, The.
Vain Finding.
Vain Questioning.
Veil, The.
Vigil.
Virtue.
Visionary, The.
Voice, The.
Voices.
Waiting.
Wanderers, The.
What?
When the rose is faded.
Where?
Where Is Thy Victory?
Which?
Which Way?
Who?
Who's that?
Widow, The.
Willow, The.
Window, The.
Winter ("Clouded with snow").
Winter ("Green mistletoe").
Winter Dusk.
Wreck, The.
Young Girl, A.

de Vries, Hendrik (1896–1989)
Fever.
My Brother.

Delany, Patrick (c.1685–1768)
Elegy on the Much Lamented Death of Mr.
    Demar, the Famous Rich Usurer [or Man],
    An.
From My Much Honored Friend at Heldelville.
To Thomas Sheridan.
Upon the Author.

Devecseri, Gábor (1917–71)
Women and Masks.

Dickey, James (b. 1923)
Adam in Winter.
Adultery.
Angel of the Maze, The.
Angina.
Antipolis.
Apollo.
Approaching Prayer.
Armor.
At Darien Bridge.
At the Home for Unwed Mothers.
Attempted Departure.
Autumn.
Awaiting the Swimmer.
Ax God:Sea Pursuit, The.
Baggage King, The.
Basics.
Bee, The.
Beholders, The.
Being, The.
Between Two Prisoners.
Birth, A.
Birthday Dream, The.
Blood.
Blowgun and Rattlesnake.
Bread.
Breath.
Buckdancer's Choice.
Bums, on Waking.
Cancer Match, The.
Celebration, The.
Change, The.

Chenille.
Cherrylog Road.
Circuit.
Coming Back to America.
Common Grave, The.
Courtship, The.
Craters.
Dark Ones.
Daughter.
Daybreak.
Deborah as Scion.
Deer among Cattle.
Diabetes.
Dog Sleeping on My Feet, A.
Doorstep, Lightning, Waif-Dreaming.
Dover: Believing in Kings.
Dream Flood, The.
Drifting.
Drinking from a Helmet.
Driver, The.
Drowning with Others.
Dusk of Horses, The.
Dust.
Eagles.
Eagle's Mile, The.
Enclosure, The.
Encounter in the Cage Country.
Escape, The.
Exchanges.
Expanses.
Eye-Beaters, The.
Faces Seen Once.
Facing Africa.
Falling.
False Youth: Autumn: Clothes of the Age.
False Youth: Two Seasons.
Farmers.
Fathers and Sons.
Fence Wire.
Fiend, The.
Firebombing, The.
Flash, The.
Fog Envelops the Animals.
Folk Singer of the Thirties, A.
For a Time and Place.
For Richard Wilbur.
For Robert Bhain Campbell.
For the Death of Vince Lombardi.
For the Last Wolverine.
For the Nightly Ascent of the Hunter Orion
    over a Forest Clearing.
For the Running of the New York City
    Marathon.
Form.
Fox Blood.
From Time.
Gamecock.
Gila Bend.
Goodbye to Serpents.
Head-Aim, The.
Heads.
Heaven of Animals, The.
Hedge Life.
Horses and Prisoners.
Hospital Window, The.
Hunting Civil War Relics at Nimblewill Creek.
Ice Skin, The.
Immortals.
In the Child's Night.
In the Lupanar at Pompeii.
In the Marble Quarry.
In the Mountain Tent.
In the Pocket.
In the Tree House at Night.
Inside the River.
Into the Stone.
Island, The.
Jewel, The.
Judas.
Knock.
Kudzu.
Lakes of Värmland.
Lazarus to the Assembled.
Leap, The.
Letter, A.
Liberator Explodes, The.

Lifeguard, The.
Listening to Foxhounds.
Little More, The.
Lord in the Air, the.
Low Voice, Out Loud.
Madness.
Magus, The.
Mangham.
Mary Sheffield.
Math.
May Day Sermon to the Women of Gilmer
    County, Georgia, by a Woman Preacher
    Leaving the Baptist Church.
Meadow Bridge.
Mercy.
Messages.
Mexican Valley.
Moon Flock.
Morning, A.
Movement of Fish, The.
Nameless.
Near Darien.
Night Bird.
Night Pool, The.
Obstructions.
Olympian, The.
On the Coosawattee.
On the Hill below the Lighthouse.
One, The.
Other, The.
Owl King, The.
Paestum.
Patience: In the Mill.
Performance, The.
Pine.
Place of the Skull, The.
Poem: "For having left the birds that left me."
Poem: "O death, so dear to me."
Poisoned Man, The.
Power and Light.
Purgation.
Purgation.
Pursuit from Under.
Rafters, The.
Rain Guitar, The.
Reading *Genesis* to a Blind Child.
Reincarnation (I) ["Still, passed through the
    spokes of an old wheel, on and around"].
Reincarnation (II).
Remnant Water.
Rib, The.
Root-light, or the Lawyer's Daughter.
Salt Marsh, The.
Saying of Farewell, A.
Scarred Girl, The.
Scratch, The.
Screened Porch in the Country, A.
Seeking the Chosen.
Shark's Parlor, The.
Sheep Child, The.
Six, The.
Slave Quarters.
Sled Burial, Dream Ceremony.
Sleepers.
Sleeping Out at Easter.
Small Song.
Snakebite.
Snow on a Southern State.
Snow Thickets.
Spring-Shock.
Springer Mountain.
Springhouse, Menses, Held Apple, House and
    Beyond.
Sprinter at Forty, The.
Strength of Fields, The.
String, The.
Summons, The.
Sun.
Sustainment.
Tapestry and Sail.
Them, Crying.
Three Poems with Yevtushenko.
Three, The.
To Be Done in Winter.
To His Children in Darkness.
To Landrum Guy, Beginning to Write at Sixty.

Tomb Stone.
Trees and Cattle.
Turning Away.
Twin Falls, The.
Two Poems of Flight Sleep.
Two Poems of Going Home.
Two Poems of the Military.
Two Women.
Underground Stream, The.
Undersea Fragment in Colons.
Veer-Voices: Two Sisters under Crows.
Vegetable King, The.
Venom.
Vessels.
Via appia.
Victory.
View of Fujiyama after the War, A.
Voyage of the Needle, The.
Walking on Water.
Walking the Fire Line.
Wall and Cloud.
Walter Armistead.
War Wound, The.
Wedding, The.
Weeds.
When.
Winter Trout.
Zodiac, The.

Dickey, William (b. 1928)
Afternoon Evening and Night in the Courtyard
    of the Museum of Modern Art.
Alligators and Paris and North America.
Androids.
Anniversary, The.
At Your Old House.
Avalanche.
Being Asked To Define Bourgeois
    Individuality.
Chickens in San Francisco.
Confidence.
Coyote's Song.
Die Älte Frau, Die Älte Marschallin.
Dog Under False Pretences.
Dolls Play at Hansel and Gretel, The.
Elegy Before the Time.
Ezekiel's Rabbit.
Face-Paintings of the Caduveo Indians.
For Every Last Batch When the Next One
    Comes Along.
Fred and the Holy Grail.
Gambling at Reno.
G.F. Died 1954, Aged 27.
Here There Are Three of Us Driving South in
    This Expensive Car.
Heroine, The.
His Death from Cancer.
History of the Moon, The.
In The Dreaming.
Joy.
Kindness, A.
Lady of Shalott, Her Mirror Broken, The.
Læstrygonians, The.
Life Moving More Rapidly Than Hands Can
    Manage.
Love among the Manichees.
Making Love.
Memoranda.
More Under Saturn.
Narcissus Unbound.
New Place, The.
One Incident of Many.
Part Song, With Concert of Recorders.
Performances.
Post-Therapy Room.
Pruned Roses, The.
Rainbow Grocery, The.
Sagittarius, Scorpio Rising.
Self Prepares for an Unwilling Journey, The.
Silver Creek Falls.
Stella Dallas.
Therefore.
Things Kept.
Virginia Woolf Gathers Mushrooms.
You White Cunning Devils.

Dickinson, Emily (1830–86)
Above Oblivion's Tide there is a Pier.

Abraham to kill him.
Absence disembodies—so does Death.
Absent Place—an April Day.
Abstinence from Melody.
Accept my timid happiness.
Acts of Light which beautified, The.
Admirations—and Contempts—of time, The.
Adrift! A little boat adrift!
Adulation is inexpensive.
Advance is Life's condition.
Affection is like bread.
Affection wants you to know it is here.
Afraid! Of whom am I afraid?
After a brief unconsciousness.
After a hundred years.
After all Birds have been investigated and laid
    aside.
After great pain a formal feeling comes.
After the great intrusion of Death.
After the Sun comes out.
Again—his voice is at the door.
Ah! dainty—dainty Death!
Ah, Moon—and Star!
Ah, Necromancy Sweet!
Ah, Teneriffe!
Air has no Residence, no Neighbor.
Air is soft as Italy, The.
All but Death can be Adjusted.
All Circumstances are the Frame.
All forgot for recollecting.
All I may, if small.
All men for Honor hardest work.
All overgrown by cunning moss.
All that I do.
All the letters I can write.
All these my banners be.
All things swept sole away.
All this and more, though is there more?
All we secure of Beauty.
Alone and in a Circumstance.
Alone, I cannot be.
Alter! When the Hills do—.
Altered look about the hills, An.
Although I put away his life.
Always begins.
Always Mine!
Am told that fasting gives to food.
Amalgams are abundant.
Amazing human [or Human] heart [or Heart].
Ambition cannot find him.
Amherst Heart is plain and whole, The.
Ample make this Bed.
Anatomical dishabille.
And I, consign myself to you.
And this of all my Hopes.
And with what body do they come?
Angel begins in the morning, The.
Angels, in the early morning.
Angle of a Landscape, The.
Anguish sometimes gives a cause.
Answer July.
Antiquated Grace, An.
Antiquated Tree, An.
Apology for Her.
Apparently with no surprise.
"Arcturus" is his other name.
Are Friends Delight or Pain?
Area— / no test of depth.
Arrows enamored of his Heart.
Art thou the thing I wanted?
Artists wrestled here!
As by the dead we love to sit.
As Children bid the Guest "Good Night."
As far from pity, as complaint.
As from the earth the light Balloon.
As Frost is best conceived.
As if I asked a common Alms.
As if some little Arctic flower.
As if the Sea should part.
As imperceptibly as grief.
As old as Woe.
As One does Sickness over.
As plan for Noon and plan for Night.
As Sleigh Bells seem in summer.
As subtle as tomorrow.
As Summer into Autumn slips.

As the Starved Maelstrom lap the Navies.
As Watchers hang upon the East.
As we pass Houses musing slow.
As we take nature, without permission.
As willing lid o'er weary eye.
Ascension has.
Ashes denote that Fire was.
Astounding subjects are the only ones, The.
At Half past Three, a single Bird.
At least—to pray—is left—is left.
At leisure is the Soul.
Atmospheric acquaintance, The.
Auctioneer of Parting, The.
Audacity of Bliss, said Jacob to the Angel.
Aurora.
Aurora is the effort.
Austin is a Poet, Austin writes a psalm.
Autumn is among us.
Autumn—overlooked my Knitting.
Away from Home are some and I.
Awful Tempest mashed the air, An.
Awkward as the homely are.
Baby's flight will embellish History.
Back from the cordial Grave I drag thee.
Baffled for just a day or two.
Banish Air from Air.
Bat, The.
Battle fought between the Soul, The.
Be gentle with it—Coax it.
Be Mine the Doom.
Beauty be not caused—It Is.
Beauty crowds me till I die.
Beauty is often timidity.
Because He loves Her.
Because I could not stop for Death.
Because my Brook is fluent.
Because that you are going.
Because the Bee may blameless hum.
Because 'twas Riches I could own.
Bee his burnished Carriage, A.
Bee is not afraid of me, The.
Bee, The.
Bees.
Before He comes we weigh the Time!
Before I got my eye put out.
Before the ice is in the pools.
Before you thought of Spring.
Beggar at the Door for Fame, The.
Beggar Lad—dies early, The.
Behind Me—dips Eternity.
Behold this little Bane.
Believing that we are to have no Face.
Belshazzar had a Letter.
Bereaved of all, I went abroad.
Bereavement in their death to feel.
Besides the autumn poets sing.
Besides this May.
Best Gains—must have the Losses' Test.
Best Things dwell out of Sight.
Best Witchcraft is Geometry.
Betrothed to Righteousness might be.
Better—than Music! For I—who heard it.
Between My Country—and the Others.
Between the form of Life and Life.
Bible is an antique Volume, The.
Bind me—I still can sing.
Biography first convinces us.
Bird came down the Walk, A.
Bird did prance—the Bee did play, The.
Bird her punctual music brings, The.
Bird must sing to earn the Crumb, The.
Bird would be a soundless thing, The.
Birds are very bold this Morning, The.
Birds begun at Four o'clock, The.
Birds reported from the South, The.
Birthday of but a single pang.
Black Berry—wears a Thorn in his side, The.
Blazing in Gold and quenching in Purple.
Bless God, he went as soldiers.
Bliss is the plaything of the child.
Blood is more showy (gaudy) than the Breath,
    The.
Bloom—is Result—to meet a Flower.
Bloom upon the Mountain—stated.
Blossom perhaps is an introduction, A.
Blossoms will run away.

Blunder is an estimate, The.
Bobolink is gone, The.
Body grows without, The.
Bone that has no Marrow, The.
Book is only the Heart's Portrait, A.
Bound—a trouble.
Brain—is wider than the Sky, The.
Brain, within its Groove, The.
Bring me the sunset in a cup.
Brother of Ingots—Ah Peru.
Brother of Ophir.
Brow is that of Deity, The.
Bulbs are in the sod, The.
Burdock—clawed my Gown, A.
Business enough indeed.
Bustle in a House, The.
Busy missing you.
But little Carmine hath her face.
Butterfly in honored Dust, The.
Butterfly obtains, The.
Butterfly upon the Sky, The.
Butterfly's Assumption Gown, The.
Butterfly's Numidian Gown, The.
By a departing light.
By a flower—By a letter.
By Chivalries as tiny.
By homely gift and hindered Words.
By my Window have I for Scenery.
By such and such an offering.
By the Sea.
Cages do not suit the Swiss.
Called Back.
Candor—my tepid friend.
Cap of Lead across the sky, A.
Career of flowers differs from ours, The.
Cat.
Caterpillar ("Fuzzy fellow, without feet").
Caterpillar ("How soft a caterpillar steps").
Cemetery, A.
Changelessness / is Nature's change.
Charm invests a face, A.
Chemical conviction, The.
Cherishing that is speechless, The.
Child's faith is new, The.
Chilly Peace infests the Grass, A.
Choice.
Choose Flowers that have no Fang, Dear.
Circumference thou Bride of Awe.
Civilization—spurns—the Leopard!
Climbing to reach the costly Hearts.
Clock stopped, A.
Clock strikes one that just struck two, The.
Cloud withdrew from the Sky, A.
Clouds their Backs together laid, The.
Clover's simple Flame, The.
Cocoon above! Cocoon below!
Coffin—is a small Domain, A.
Color, Caste, Denomination.
Color of the Grave is Green, The.
Come show thy Durham Breast.
Come slowly—Eden!
Competitions of the sky, The.
Complacency! My Father!
Conferring with myself.
Confirming All who analyze.
Conjecturing a Climate.
Conscious am I in my Chamber.
Consciousness is the only home.
Consulting summer's clock.
Consummation is the hurry of fools.
Contained in this short Life.
Cosmopolites without a plea.
Could Hope inspect her Basis.
Could I but ride indefinite.
Could—I do more—for Thee.
Could I—then—shut the door.
Could I visit the Beds.
Could live—did live.
Could mortal lip divine.
Could that sweet Darkness where they dwell.
Could you tell me how to grow.
Count not that far that can be had.
Counterfeit—a Plated Person, A.
Court is far away, The.
Crickets sang, The.
Crisis is a Hair.

Crisis is sweet and yet the Heart.
Crumbling elms and evergreens, The.
Crumbling is not an instant's Act.
Curious Cloud surprised the Sky, A.
Daisy follows soft the Sun, The.
Dandelion's pallid tube, The.
Danger is not at first.
Dare you see a Soul *at the White Heat?*
Darting fear, a pomp, a tear, A.
Dawn and Dew my Bearers be.
Day! A, Help! Help! Another Day!
Day came slow—till Five o'clock, The.
Day grew small, surrounded tight, The.
Day she goes, The.
Day that I was crowned, The.
Day undressed—Herself, The.
Days that we can spare, The.
Dear arrears of tenderness.
Dear friend, can you walk.
Dear March, Come in.
Dear Mr. Bowles found out too late.
Death blow is a Life blow to Some, A.
Death cannot plunder half so fast.
Death goes far around.
Death has only to touch a trifle.
Death is a Dialogue between.
Death is like the insect.
Death is perhaps an intimate friend.
Death is potential to that Man.
Death is the supple Suitor.
Death leaves Us homesick, who behind.
Death obtains the Rose.
Death sets a Thing significant.
Death warrants are supposed to be.
Death's Waylaying not the sharpest.
Declaiming Waters none may dread.
Deed knocks first at Thought, A.
Definition of Beauty is, The.
Defrauded I a Butterfly.
Delayed till she had ceased to know.
Delight—becomes pictorial.
Delight has no Competitor.
Delight is as the flight.
Delight's Despair at setting.
Denial—is the only fact.
Departed—to the Judgment.
Deprived of other Banquet.
Despair's advantage is achieved.
Devil, had he fidelity, The.
Devotion should always wear a fence.
Dew—is the Freshet in the Grass.
Dew suffices itself, A.
Diamond on the Hand, A.
Did life's penurious length.
Did Our Best Moment last.
Did she suffer—except to leave you?
Did the Harebell loose her girdle.
Did We abolish Frost.
Did we disobey Him?
Did you ever stand in a Cavern's Mouth.
Difference between Despair, The.
Dimple in the Tomb, A.
Distance—is not the Realm of Fox.
Distance that the dead have gone, The.
Distrustful of the Gentian.
Ditch is dear to the Drunken man, The.
Do People moulder equally.
Doctor calls it "revenge of the nerves," The.
Dominion lasts until obtained.
Don't put up my Thread and Needle.
Doom is the House without the Door.
Doom of Fruit without the Bloom, A.
Doomed—regard the Sunrise, The.
Door just opened on a street, A.
Doubt if it be Us, A.
Down Time's quaint stream.
Drab Habitation of Whom?
Drama's Vitallest Expression is the Common Day.
Dreams are the subtle Dower.
Dreams—are well—but Waking's better.
Drop fell on the Apple Tree, A.
Drop, that wrestles in the Sea, The.
Dropped into the Ether Acre.
Drowning is not so pitiful.
Drunkard cannot meet a Cork, A.

Dust behind I strove to join, The.
Dust is the only Secret.
Dust like the Mosquito, The.
Duties of the Wind are few, The.
Dying at my music!
Dying! Dying in the night!
Dying is a wild Night.
Dying need but little, Dear, The.
Dying Tiger—moaned for Drink, A.
Dying! To be afraid of thee.
Each Life Converges to some Centre.
Each Scar I'll keep for Him.
Each Second is the last.
Each that we lose takes part of us.
Earth has many keys, The.
Earth would not seem homelike without.
Eat the bit of cake in your garden.
Ecstasy to guess, The.
Eden is that Old-Fashioned House.
Element of Elegy, The.
Elijah's Wagon knew no thill.
Elizabeth told Essex.
Embarrassment of one another.
Emerson's intimacy with his "Bee."
Empty my Heart, of Thee.
Endanger it, and the Demand.
Ended, ere it begun.
Endow the Living—with the Tears.
Enough is so vast a sweetness.
Escape is such a thankful Word.
Escaping backward to perceive.
Essential oils—are wrung.
Estranged from Beauty, none can be.
Eternity.
Eternity may imitate.
Evening.
Event was directly behind Him, The.
Everywhere of Silver, An.
Except the Heaven had come so near.
Except the smaller size.
Except to Heaven, she is nought.
Exhiliration is the Breeze.
Exhiliration—is within.
Expanse cannot be lost.
Expectation—is Contentment.
Experience is the Angled Road.
Experiment escorts us last.
Experiment to me.
Expulsion from Eden grows indistinct.
Extol thee—could I? Then I will
Exultation is the going.
Face devoid of love or grace, A.
Face I carry with me—last, The.
Face in evanescence lain, The.
Face we choose to miss, The.
Fact that Earth is Heaven, The.
Facts by our side are never sudden.
Faded Boy—in sallow Clothes, A.
Fairer through Fading—as the Day.
Fairest Home I ever knew, The.
"Faith" is a fine invention.
Faith—is the Pierless Bridge.
Faithful "I am sorry", A.
"Faithful to the end" Amended.
"Faithful to the end" Amended.
"Faithful to the end" Amended.
Falsehood of Thee could I suppose.
Fame is a bee.
Fame is a fickle food.
Fame is the one that does not stay.
Fame is the tint that Scholars leave.
Fame of Myself, to justify.
Fame's Boys and Girls, who never die.
Far from Love the Heavenly Father.
Farthest Thunder that I heard, The.
Fascinating chill that music leaves, The.
Fate slew Him, but He did not drop.
Fear—like Dying, dilates trust.
Feather from the Whippoorwill, A.
Feet of people walking home, The.
Ferocious as a Bee without a wing.
Few, yet enough.
Fidelity never flickers.
Field of Stubble, lying sere, A.
Final Inch, The.
Finding is the first Act.

Fingers of the Light, The.
Finite life, little sister, A.
Finite—to fail, but infinite to Venture.
First Day that I was a Life, The.
First Day's Night had come, The.
First Mute Coming, A.
First We knew of Him was Death, The.
Fitter to see Him, I may be.
Flags Vex a Dying Face.
Flake the Wind exasperate, The.
Floss won't save you from an Abyss.
Flower keeps it's appointment.
Flower must not blame the Bee, The.
Flower will not trouble her, it has so small a Foot, A.
Flowers—Well—if anybody.
Follow wise Orion.
Footlights cannot improve the grave.
For Death—or rather.
For each ecstatic instant.
For every Bird a Nest.
For largest Woman's Heart I knew.
For the comprehension of Suffering.
For this—accepted Breath.
Forbidden Fruit a flavor has.
Forever at His side to walk.
Forever honored be the Tree.
Forever—is composed of Nows.
Forget! The lady with the Amulet.
Forgive me if I come too much.
Fortitude incarnate.
Four Trees—upon a solitary Acre.
Frequently the woods are pink.
Friend Anguish reveals is, The.
Friend is a / solemnity, A.
Friends are nations in themselves.
Frigid and sweet Her parting Face.
Fringed Gentian.
From all the Jails the Boys and Girls.
From Blank to Blank.
From Cocoon forth a Butterfly.
From his slim Palace in the Dust.
From Us She wandered now a Year.
Frost of Death was on the Pane, The.
Frost was never seen, The.
Full fed Rose on meals of Tint, A.
Funny—to be a Century.
Further in Summer than the Birds.
Future—never spoke, The.
Garlands for Queens, may be.
Gathered into the Earth.
Genius is the ignition of affection.
Gentian has a parched Corolla, The.
Gentian weaves her fringes, The.
Gethsemene and Cana.
Gift of neither Heaven nor Earth, The.
Give little Anguish.
Given in Marriage unto Thee.
Glass was the Street—in tinsel Peril.
Gleam of an heroic Act, The.
Glee—The great storm is over.
Glory is that bright tragic thing.
Glowing is her Bonnet.
Go not too near a House of Rose.
Go slow, my soul, to feed thyself.
"Go tell it." What a Message.
Go thy great way!
Go traveling with us!
God gave a Loaf to every Bird.
God is a distant—stately Lover.
God is indeed a jealous God.
God made no act without a cause.
God permits industrious Angels.
God seems much more friendly.
God's Residence.
Going from a world we know, The.
Going to Heaven!
Going—to—Her!
Going to Him! Happy letter!
Good Morning—Midnight.
Good night, because we must.
Good Night! Which put the Candle out?
Good times are always mutual.
Good to hide, and hear 'em hunt!
Good Will of a Flower, The.
Grace—Myself—might not obtain, The.

Grapes were big and fresh, The.
Grass, The.
Gratitude—is not the mention.
Gratitude is the timid wealth.
Grave my little cottage is, The.
Great Caesar! Condescend.
Great Hope fell, A.
Great Hungers feed themselves.
Great Streets of silence led away.
Grief is a Mouse.
Grief of wonder at her fate.
Growth of Man—like Growth of Nature.
Guest am I to have.
Guest is gold and crimson, The.
Had I a pleasure you had not.
Had I known that the first was the last.
Had I not seen the Sun.
Had I not This, or This, I said.
Had I presumed to hope.
Had this one Day not been.
Had we known the Ton she bore.
Had we less to say to those we love.
Had we our senses.
Had you an Hour unengrossed.
Hallowing of Pain, The.
"Happiness" without a cause, The.
Happy lip—breaks sudden, A.
Harm of Years is on him, The.
Has All.
Have any like Myself.
Have you got a Brook in your little heart.
He ate and drank the precious Words.
He forgo—and I—remembered.
He fought like those Who've nought to lose.
He found my Being—set it up.
He fumbles at your Soul.
He gave away his Life.
He has had his Future.
He is alive, this morning.
He lived the Life of Ambush.
He outstripped Time with but a Bout.
He parts Himself—like Leaves.
He preached upon "Breadth" till it argued him
   narrow.
He put the Belt around my life.
He scanned it—staggered.
He strained my faith.
He that is robbed and smiles.
He told a homely tale.
He touched me, so I live to know.
He was my host—he was my guest.
He was weak, and I was strong—then.
He went by sleep that drowsy route.
He who in Himself believes.
Healed Heart shows its shallow scar, The.
Heart asks Pleasure—first, The.
Heart has many Doors, The.
Heart has narrow Banks, The.
Heart is the Capital of the Mind, The.
Heart is the only workman, The.
Heart, not so heavy as mine.
Heart wants what it wants, The.
Heart! We [or Heart, we] will forget him!
Hearts in Amherst ache tonight, The.
Hearts that never lean, must fall, The.
"Heaven" has different Signs—to me.
Heaven is but a little way.
Heaven is so far of the Mind.
"Heaven"—is what I cannot reach!
Heaven vests for Each, The.
Heaven will not be as good as Earth.
"Heavenly Father"—take to thee.
Her breast is fit for pearls.
Her dying feels to me.
Her face was in a bed of hair.
Her final Summer was it.
Her Grace is all she has.
Her—'last Poems'
Her little Parasol to lift.
Her Losses make our Gains ashamed.
Her reluctances are sweeter.
Her smile was shaped like other smiles.
Her sovereign People.
Her spirit rose to such a height.
Her Sweet turn to leave the Homestead.
Her sweet Weight on my Heart at Night.

Her thot's tho' they are older.
Here, where the Daisies fit my Head.
Hereafter, I will pick no Rose.
Herein a Blossom lies.
High from the earth I heard a bird.
Hills erect their Purple Heads, The.
Hills in Purple syllables, The.
Himmaleh was known to stoop, The.
His Bill an Auger is.
His Bill is clasped—his Eye forsook.
His Cheek is his Biographer.
His Feet are shod with Gauze.
His Heart was darker then the starless night.
His Life was so shy and his tastes so unknown.
His little Hearse like Figure.
His Mansion in the Pool.
His Mind like Fabrics of the East.
His mind of man, a secret makes.
His oriental heresies.
His voice decrepit was with Joy.
Hollows round His eager Eyes, The.
Home is the riddle of the wise.
Home itself is far from home.
Honest Tear, An.
Honey you went so far to seek, The.
Hope is a strange invention.
Hope is a subtle Glutton.
"Hope" is the thing with feathers.
Hour for books, those enthralling friends, An.
Hour is a Sea, An.
Hours have Wings.
House upon the Height, A.
"Houses"—so the wise men tell me.
How brittle are the Piers.
How can we thank each other.
How dare the robins sing.
How destitute is he.
How far is it to Heaven?
How firm Eternity must look.
How fits his Umber Coat.
How fleet—how indiscreet an one.
How fortunate the Grave.
How good his Lava Bed.
How happy I was if I could forget.
How happy is the little Stone.
How Human Nature dotes.
How know it from a Summer's Day?
How lonesome the Wind must feel Nights.
How lonesome to be an Article!
How luscious is the dripping.
How many Flowers fail in Wood.
How many schemes may die.
How many times these low feet staggered.
How much of Source escapes with thee.
How much the present moment means.
How near this suffering Summer.
How News must feel when travelling.
How noteless Men, and Pleiads, stand.
How precious Thought and Speech are!
How ruthless are the gentle.
How sick—to wait—in any place—but thine.
How slow the Wind.
How small the furniture of bliss!
How soft this Prison is.
How spacious must be the Heart.
How still the Bells in Steeples stand.
How strange that Nature does not knock.
How sweet that he rose in the morning.
How sweet the "Life that now is."
How the old Mountains drip with Sunset.
How the Waters closed above Him.
How to repair my shattered ranks.
How vast is the chastisement of Beauty.
How well I knew Her not.
However you stem Nature.
Humming Birds and Orioles, The.
Hummingbird, A.
I always ran Home to Awe when a child.
I am afraid to own a Body.
I am alive—I guess.
I am ashamed—I hide.
I am bringing a still Granite Book.
I am glad you are in the open Air.
I am sorry you need Health.
I am speechlessly grateful for a friend.
I am studying music now with the jays.

I am sure I feel as Noah did.
I asked no other thing.
I bet with every Wind that blew.
I breathed enough to take the Trick.
I bring an unaccustomed wine.
I Came to buy a smile—today.
I Can Wade Grief.
I cannot be ashamed.
I cannot buy it—'tis not sold.
I cannot conjecture a form of space.
I cannot dance upon my Toes.
I cannot depict a friend to my mind.
I cannot live with You.
I cannot meet the Spring unmoved.
I cannot see my soul but know 'tis there.
I cannot tell how Eternity seems.
I cannot want it more.
I cant tell how it is.
I can't tell you—but you feel it.
I cautious, scanned my little life.
I confess that I love him.
I could bring You Jewels—had I a mind to.
I could die—to know.
I could not drink it, Sweet.
I could not prove the Years had feet.
I could not weigh myself, Myself.
I could suffice for Him, I knew.
I cried at Pity—not at Pain.
I cross till I am weary.
I did not reach Thee.
I died for Beauty—but was scarce.
I dreaded that first Robin, so.
I dream about father every night.
I dwell in Possibility.
I envy seas—whereon He rides.
I fear a Man of frugal Speech.
I fear we think too lightly of.
I fear you have much happiness.
I felt a Cleaving in my Mind.
I Felt a Funeral in My Brain.
I fit for them.
I found the words to every thought.
I gained it so.
I gave myself to Him—.
I got so I could take his name.
I groped for him before I knew.
I had a daily Bliss.
I had a guinea golden.
I had been hungry, all the Years.
I had hoped to express more.
I had no Cause to be awake.
I had no time to Hate.
I had not minded—Walls.
I had some things that I called mine.
I had the Glory—that will do.
I have a Bird in spring.
I have a King, who does not speak.
I have felt like a troubled Top.
I have long been a Lunatic on Bulbs.
I have never seen "Volcanoes."
I have no Life but this.
I have seen one Bird and part of another.
I have the friend who loves me.
I heard a Fly buzz—when I died.
I heard, as if I had no Ear.
I held a Jewel in my fingers.
I hesitate which word to take.
I hide myself within my flower.
I hope that you are well.
I hope you are joyful frequently.
I hope you may not go.
I hope you may sometime be.
I hope your rambles have been sweet.
I keep my pledge.
I knew a Bird that would sing as firm.
I knew that I had gained.
I know a place where Summer strives.
I know but little of Little Ones.
I know lives, I could miss.
I know not how to thank you.
I know of people in the Grave.
I know some lonely Houses off the Road.
I know Suspense, it steps so terse.
I know that He exists.
I know where Wells grow—Droughtless Wells.
I learned—at least—what Home could be.

I lift the lid to my box of Phantoms.
I like a look of Agony.
I like to see it lap the Miles.
I live with Him—I see His face.
I lived on Dread.
I lost a World—the other day!
I made slow Riches but my Gain.
I make His Crescent fill or lack.
I many times thought Peace had come.
I meant to find Her when I came.
I meant to have but modest needs.
I measure every Grief I meet.
I met a King this afternoon!
I never felt at Home—Below.
I never hear that one is dead.
I never hear the word "escape."
I never knew a broken Heart.
I never lost as much but twice.
I never saw a Moor.
I never told the buried gold.
I notice where Death has been introduced.
I noticed People disappeared.
I often passed the village.
I often wish I was a grass.
I often wonder how.
I pay—in Satin Cash.
I play at Riches—to appease.
I prayed, at first, a little Girl.
I raise only robins on my farm.
I read my sentence—steadily.
I reason, Earth is short.
I reckon—when I count at all.
I remember the leaves were falling.
I remember your coming as serious sweetness.
I robbed the Woods.
I rose—because He sank.
I saw no Way. The Heavens were stitched.
I saw that the Flake was on it.
I saw the Jays this Morning.
I saw the wind within her.
I see thee better—in the Dark.
I see thee clearer for the Grave.
I send Two Sunsets.
I send you a decrepit flower.
I shall keep singing!
I shall know why—when Time is over.
I shall not murmur if at last.
I shall watch your passage from Crutch to
   Cane.
I should have been too glad, I see.
I should not dare to be so sad.
I should not dare to leave my friend.
I showed her Heights she never saw.
I sing to use the Waiting.
I sometimes drop it, for a Quick.
I stepped from Plank to Plank.
I stole them from a Bee.
I sued the News—yet feared—the News.
I suppose the time will come.
I Taste a Liquor Never Brewed.
I tend my flowers for thee.
I think I was enchanted.
I think it sad to have a friend.
I think just how my shape will rise.
I think that the Root of the Wind is Water.
I think the Hemlock likes to stand.
I think the longest Hour of all.
I think to Live—may be a Bliss.
I thought that being a Poem one's self.
I thought that nature was enough.
I thought the Train would never come.
I thought to shun the Loneliness.
I thought your approbation Fame.
I tie my Hat—I crease my Shawl.
I took my Power in my Hand.
I Took My Power in My Hand.
I took one Draught of Life.
I tried to think a lonelier Thing.
I trust this sweet May Morning.
I trust you may have the dearest summer.
"I want"—it pleaded—All its life.
I was a Phoebe—nothing more.
I was the slightest in the House.
I was with you in all the loneliness.
I watched her face to see which way.
I watched the Moon around the House.

I weave for the Lamp of Evening.
I went to Heaven.
I went to thank Her.
I wish I might say one liquid word.
I wish one could be sure the suffering.
I work to drive the awe away.
I worked for chaff and earning Wheat.
I would distil a cup.
I would not paint—a picture.
I write in the midst of Sweet-Peas.
I Years had been from Home.
Icebergs italicize the Sea.
I'd rather recollect a setting.
Ideals are the Fairy Oil.
If all the griefs I am to have.
If any sink, assure that this, now standing.
If Anybody's Friend be Dead.
If Blame be my side   forfeit Mc.
If ever the lid gets off my head.
If He dissolve—then—there is nothing—more.
If He were living—dare I ask.
If I can stop one Heart from breaking.
If I could bribe them by a Rose.
If I could tell how glad I was.
If I may have it, when it's dead.
If I should cease to bring a Rose.
If I should die.
If I shouldn't be alive.
If I'm lost—now.
If it had no pencil.
If my Bark sink.
If Nature smiles—the Mother must.
If pain for peace prepares.
If recollecting were forgetting.
If roses had not faded.
If she had been the Mistletoe.
If the anguish of others helped one with one's
   own.
If the foolish, call them "flowers."
If the future is mighty as the past.
If this is "fading."
If those I loved were lost.
If What we could—were what we would.
If wrecked upon the Shoal of Thought.
If you were coming in the Fall.
If your Nerve, deny you.
Ignominy to receive, The.
Ignorance a Sunset, An.
I'll clutch—and clutch.
I'll send the feather from my Hat!
I'll tell you how the Sun rose.
I'm ceded—I've stopped being Theirs.
I'm Nobody! Who are you?
I'm saying every day.
I'm sorry for the Dead—Today.
I'm the little "Heart's Ease"!
I'm Wife . . . .
Image of Light, Adieu.
Immortal is an ample word.
Immortality of Flowers, The.
Immortality she gave, The.
Immured in Heaven!
Impossibility, like Wine.
In a World too full of Beauty for Peace.
In Ebon Box, when years have flown.
In falling Timbers buried.
In lands I never saw—they say.
In many and reportless places.
In rags mysterious as these.
In snow thou comest.
In this place of shafts, I hope.
In this short Life.
In thy long Paradise of Light.
In Winter in my Room.
Incarcerate me in yourself.
Incidents of love, The.
Inconceivably solemn!
Incredible never surprises us, The.
Incredible the Lodging.
Indian Summer.
Inferential Knowledge, The.
Infinite a sudden Guest, The.
"Infinite Beauty"—of which you speak, The.
Interview is acres.
Intrusiveness of flowers.
Inundation of the Spring, The.

Is Bliss then, such Abyss.
Is Heaven a Physician?
Is his sweet wife too faint to remember.
Is Immortality a bane.
Is is too late to touch you, Dear?
Is is true, dear Sue?
Is it a joyous expanse of Year.
Is it Intellect that the Patriot means.
Is not an absent friend as mysterious.
Is not the distinction of Affection.
Is this the Hope that opens and shuts.
It always felt to me—a wrong.
It bloomed and dropt, a Single Noon.
It came at last but prompter Death.
It came his turn to beg.
It can't be "Summer"!
It ceased to hurt me, though so slow.
It comforts the Criminal little to know.
It consoles the happy Sorrow of Autumn.
It did not surprise me.
It don't sound so terrible—quite—as it did.
It Dropped So Low in My Regard.
It feels a shame to be Alive.
It is a lonesome Glee.
It is a Suffering, to have a sea.
It is an honorable Thought.
It is Anguish I long conceal from you.
It is dead. Find it.
It is delicate that each Mind is itself.
It is easier to look behind at a pain.
It is easy to work when the soul is at play.
It is of Realms unratified.
It is solemn to remember.
It is still as distinct as Paradise.
It is the Meek that Valor wear.
It is very wrong that you were ill.
It knew no lapse, nor Diminution.
It knew no Medicine.
It makes no difference abroad.
It may have been she came to show you.
It might be lonelier.
It must have been as if he had come.
It perished with beautiful reluctance.
It rises—passes—on our South.
It stills, incites, infatuates.
It stole along so stealthy.
It struck me—every Day.
It tossed—and tossed.
It troubled me as once I was.
It was a Grave, yet bore no Stone.
It was a quiet seeming Day.
It was a quiet way—.
It was given to me by the Gods.
It was much—that far and ill.
It was not Death, for I stood up.
It was not Saint—it was too large.
It was so delicious to see you.
It was too late for Man.
It will be Summer—eventually.
It would have starved a Gnat.
It would never be Common—more—I said.
It would not know if it were spurned.
It's all I have to bring today.
It's coming—the postponeless Creature.
It's easy to invent a Life.
It's evening and the orchestra of winds.
It's fragrant news, to know they pine.
Its Hour with itself.
It's like the Light.
Its little Ether Hood.
It's thoughts—and just One Heart.
I've dropped my Brain—My Soul is numb.
I've got an arrow here.
I've heard an Organ talk, sometimes.
I've known a Heaven, like a Tent.
I've none to tell me to but Thee.
I've nothing else—to bring, You know.
I've seen a Dying Eye.
Jay his Castanet has struck, The.
Jennie—my Jennie Humphrey.
Jesus! thy Crucifix.
Joy that has no stem nor core, The.
Joy to have merited the Pain.
Joy we most revere, The.
Judge is like the Owl, The.
Judgment is justest.

Juggler's Hat her Country is, The.
Just as He spoke it from his Hands.
Just Once! Oh least Request!
Just so—Jesus—raps.
Kill your Balm—and its Odors bless you.
Knock with tremor.
Knows how to forget!
Labor might fatigue.
Lad of Athens, faithful be.
Lady feeds Her little Bird, The.
Lady red—amid the Hill, A.
Lain in Nature—so suffice us.
Lamp burns sure—within, The.
Landscapes reverence the Frost.
Lane of Yellow led the eye, A.
Largest Fire ever known, The.
Lassitudes of Contemplation, The.
Last Night that She Lived, The.
Last of Summer is Delight, The.
Lay this Laurel on the One.
Least Bee that brew.
Least Rivers—docile to some sea.
Left in immortal Youth.
Lest any doubt that we are glad that they were
   born Today.
Lest they should come—is all my fear.
Lest this be Heaven indeed.
Let down the Bars, Oh Death.
Let me not mar that perfect Dream.
Let me not thirst with this Hock at my Lip.
Let my first Knowing be of thee.
Let the phantom love that enrolls the sparrow.
Let Us play Yesterday.
"Lethe" in my flower.
Letter always seemed to me, A.
Letter is a joy of Earth, A.
Letter to Bee.
Life, and Death, and Giants.
Life is death we're lengthy at.
Life is so strong a vision.
Life is the finest secret.
Life—is what we make it.
Life that tied too tight escapes, The.
Life we have is very great, The.
Life's Trades.
Lifetime is for two.
Lift it—with the Feathers.
Light exists in Spring, A.
Light is sufficient to itself.
Lightly stepped a yellow star.
Lightning is a yellow Fork, The.
Lightning playeth—all the while, The.
Like a Memoir of the Sun.
Like Brooms of Steel.
Like Eyes that looked on Wastes.
Like Flowers, that heard the news of Dews.
Like her the Saints retire.
Like Men and Women Shadows walk.
Like Mighty Foot Lights—burned the Red.
Like Rain it sounded till it curved.
Like Some Old fashioned Miracle.
Like Time's insidious wrinkle.
Lilac is an ancient shrub, The.
Little bread, a crust, a crumb, A.
Little Dog that wags his tail, A.
Little East of Jordan, A.
Little garden within, The.
Little Madness in the Spring, A.
Little overflowing word, A.
Little package of Ceylon, The.
Little poem we will write unto our Cousin
   John, A.
Little Road—not made of Man, A.
Little sentences I began, The.
Little Snow was here and there, A.
Lives he in any other world.
Loneliness One dare not sound, The.
Lonesome for they know not What, The.
Long—long Sleep—a famous—Sleep, A.
Long sigh of the Frog, The.
Long Years apart can make no.
Longest day that God appoints, The.
Longing is like the Seed.
Look back on Time, with kindly eyes.
Look of thee, what is it like, The.
Loss of something ever felt I, A.

Love A Life Can Show, The.
Love can do all but raise the Dead.
Love—is anterior to Life.
Love is done when Love's begun.
Love Is That Later Thing.
Love is that one perfect labor.
Love of God may be taught, The.
Love reckons by itself—alone.
Love Thou Art High.
Love which comes without aspect, The.
Lovely Face to sit by, A.
Lovely flowers embarrass me, The.
Love's stricken "why."
Loving the Blest without Abode.
Low at my problem bending.
Low at the knee that bore her once.
Luck is not chance.
Luxury to apprehend, The.
Magic, as it electrifies.
Make me a picture of the sun.
Malay took the Pearl, The.
Mama never forgets her birds.
Man may make a Remark, A.
Manner of its Death, The.
Many a phrase has the English language.
Many an angel, with its needle.
Many can boast a hollyhock.
Many cross the Rhine.
March is the Month of Expectation.
Martyr Poets—did not tell, The.
Maturity only enhances mystery.
Me, change! Me, alter!
Me—come! My dazzled face.
Me from Myself—to banish.
Me prove it now—Whoever doubt.
Meeting by Accident.
Meeting is well worth parting.
Memory is a strange Bell.
Memory is the Sherry Flower.
Merchant of the Picturesque, The.
Midsummer, was it, when They died.
Mien to move a Queen, A.
Mighty dying of my Father, The.
Mind is so near itself, The.
Mind lives on the Heart, The.
Mine—by the Right of the White Election!
Mine Enemy is growing old.
Mine there is no Man would own, A.
Minor Toys of the Year are alike, The.
Missing All—prevented Me, The.
Mob within the heart, The.
Months have ends—the Years—a knot, The.
Moon is distant from the Sea, The.
Moon upon her fluent Route, The.
Moon was but a Chin of Gold, The.
More Life—went out—when He went.
More than the Grave is closed to me.
Morning.
Morning after Woe, The.
Morning is due to all.
Morning—is the place for Dew.
"Morning"—means "Milking"—to the Farmer.
Morning that comes but once.
Morning without you is a dwindled Dawn.
Morns are meeker than they were, The.
Morns like these—we parted.
Most important population, The.
Most of our Moments.
Most pathetic thing I do, The.
Most she touched me by her muteness.
Most triumphant Bird I ever knew or met, The.
Moth the hue of this, A.
"Mother," to me, is so sacred a Name.
Mother's dying almost stunned my spirit.
Mountain sat upon the Plain, The.
Mountains grow—unnoticed, The.
Mountains stood in Haze, The.
Much Madness is divinest Sense.
Mud is very deep, The.
Murmur in the Trees—to note, A.
Murmur of a Bee, The.
Murmuring of Bees, has ceased, The.
Mushroom is the Elf of Plants, The.
Musicians wrestle everywhere.
Must be a Woe.
Must I lose the Friend that saved my Life.

Mute thy Coronation.
My best Acquaintances are those.
My Cocoon tightens—Colors tease.
My Country, 'tis of thee.
My Eye is fuller than my vase.
My Faith is larger than the Hills.
My family of Apparitions.
My first well Day—since many ill.
My flowers are near and foreign.
My friend attacks my friend!
My friend must be a Bird.
My Garden—like the Beach.
My God—He sees thee.
My Heart ran so to thee.
My Heart upon a little Plate.
My life closed twice before its close.
My Life had stood—a Loaded Gun.
My life has been too simple and stern.
My little Balm might be o'erlooked.
My Maker—let me be.
My nosegays are for Captives.
My period had come for Prayer.
My Portion is Defeat—today.
My Reward for Being, was This.
My River runs to thee.
My Season's furthest Flower.
My Soul—accused me—And I quailed.
My Triumph lasted till the Drums.
My Wars are laid away in Books.
My wheel is in the dark!
My Worthiness is all my Doubt.
Myself can read the Telegrams.
Myself was formed—a Carpenter.
Mysteries of human nature, The.
Name—of it—is "Autumn," The.
Nature affects to be sedate.
Nature and God—I neither knew.
Nature Assigns the Sun.
Nature can do no more.
Nature gives her love.
Nature is a Haunted House.
Nature is our eldest mother.
"Nature" is what we see.
Nature must be too young to feel.
Nature rarer uses Yellow.
Nature, seems it to myself.
Nature—sometimes sears a Sapling.
Nature—the Gentlest Mother is.
Nature's faithful Blossoms.
Nearest Dream recedes—unrealized, The.
Nearness to Tremendousness, A.
Neither fearing Extinction.
Neither in Heaven nor Earth.
Never for Society.
New feet within my garden go.
Night is my favorite Day.
Night—there lay the Days between, A.
Night was wide, and furnished scant, The.
Night's capacity varies.
No Autumn's intercepting Chill.
No Bobolink—reverse His Singing.
No Brigadier throughout the Year.
No Crowd that has occurred.
No event of Wind or Bird.
No heart that broke but further went.
No ladder needs the bird but skies.
No Life can pompless pass away.
No Man can compass a Despair.
No man saw awe, nor to his house.
No matter—now—Sweet.
No matter where the Saints abide.
No Notice gave She, but a Change.
No Other can reduce.
No Passenger was known to flee.
No Prisoner be.
No Rack can torture me.
No Romance sold unto.
No Rose, yet felt myself a'bloom.
Nobody knows this little Rose.
None can experience stint.
None who saw it ever told it.
Noon—is the Hinge of Day.
Nor Mountain hinder Me.
Not a flake assaults my birds.
Not all die early, dying young.
Not all of life to live, is it.

Not any higher stands the Grave.
Not any more to be lacked.
Not any sunny tone.
Not in this World to see his face.
Not knowing when the Dawn will come.
Not One by Heaven defrauded stay.
Not probable—The barest Chance.
Not "Revelation" 'tis, that waits.
Not seeing, still we know.
Not Sickness stains the Brave.
Not so the infinite Relations—Below.
Not that he goes—we love him more.
Not to discover weakness is.
Not what the stars have done.
Not what We did, shall be the test.
Not with a Club, the Heart is broken.
Nothing in her Life became her.
Nothing inclusive of a human Heart.
Notice that is called the Spring, The.
November always seemed to me.
Now I knew I lost her.
Now I lay thee down to Sleep.
Now the Grass is Glass.
Obtaining but our own Extent.
Of Being is a Bird.
Of Brussels—it was not.
Of Consciousness, her awful Mate.
Of Course—I prayed.
Of Death I try to think like this.
Of Glory not a Beam is left.
Of God we ask one favor.
Of Life to own.
Of Nature I shall have enough.
Of nearness to her sundered Things.
Of Paradise' existence.
Of Paul and Silas it is said.
Of Silken Speech and Specious Shoe.
Of so divine a Loss.
Of the Heart that goes in, and closes the Door.
Of their peculiar light.
Of this is Day composed.
Of Tolling Bell I ask the cause?
Of Tribulation, these are They.
Of whom so dear.
Of Yellow was the outer Sky.
Oh Future! thou secreted peace.
Oh give it Motion—deck it sweet.
Oh, honey of an hour.
Oh Matchless Earth—We underrate.
Oh Shadow on the Grass.
Oh Sumptuous moment.
Oh there is much to speak of.
Oh what a Grace is this.
On a Columnar Self.
On my volcano grows the Grass.
On such a night, or such a night.
On that dear Frame the Years had worn.
On that specific Pillow.
On the World you colored.
On this long storm the Rainbow rose.
Once more, my now bewildered Dove.
One and One—are One.
One Anguish—in a Crowd.
One Blessing had I than the rest.
One crown that no one seeks.
One Crucifixion is recorded—only.
One Day is there of the Series.
One dignity delays for all.
One Joy of so much anguish.
One Life of so much Consequence!
One need not be a Chamber—to be Haunted.
One of the ones that Midas touched.
One Sister have I in our house.
One thing of it we borrow.
One who could repeat the Summer day, The.
One Year ago—jots what?
Ones that disappeared are back, The.
Only a Shrine, but Mine.
Only Balmless Wound, The.
Only Ghost I ever saw, The.
Only God—detect the Sorrow.
Only Love can wound.
Only News I know, The.
Open the Door, open the Door.
Opening and the Close, The.
Opinion is a flitting thing.

Organ is moaning, The.
Our journey had advanced.
Our little Kinsmen—after Rain.
Our little secrets slink away.
Our lives are Swiss.
Our man has mown today.
Our own possessions—though our own.
Our share of night to bear.
Ourselves we do inter with sweet derision.
Ourselves were wed one summer—dear.
Out of sight? What of that?
Outer—from the Inner, The.
Over and over, like a Tune.
Over the fence.
Over the fence.
Overtakelessness of those, The.
Pain—expands the Time.
Pain Has an Element of Blank.
Pain has but one Acquaintance.
Pang is more conspicuous in Spring, A.
Papa above!
Paradise is of the option.
Paradise is that old mansion.
Parasol is the umbrella's daughter, The.
Parents of Beauty, The.
Partake as doth the Bee.
Parting is one of the exactions.
Parting with Thee reluctantly.
Pass to thy Rendezvous of Light.
Past is not a package, The.
Past is such a curious Creature, The.
Patience—has a quiet Outer.
Pattern of the sun, The.
Peace is a fiction of our Faith.
Pedigree of Honey, The.
Pedigree of Honey, The.
Perception of an object costs.
Perhaps I asked too large.
Perhaps the dear, grieved Heart.
Perhaps they do not go so far.
Perhaps you smile at me.
Perhaps you think me stooping.
Perhaps you'd like to buy a flower.
Peril as a Possession.
Picture of the pretty Home, The.
Pigmy seraphs—gone astray.
Pile of Years is not so high, The.
Pink—small—and punctual.
Pit—but Heaven over it, A.
Plants went into camp last night, The.
Plated Life—diversified, A.
Please rest the Life so many own.
Poets light but Lamps, The.
Poor little Heart!
Poor torn heart, a tattered heart, A.
Popular Heart is a Cannon first, The.
Port of Peace has many Coves, The.
Portraits are to daily faces.
Power is a familiar growth.
Power to be true to You, The.
Power to fly is sweet, The.
Praise it—'tis dead.
Prank of the Heart at play on the Heart, The.
Prayer is the little implement.
Precious—moldering pleasure—'tis, A.
Precious to Me—She still shall be.
Presentiment—is that long Shadow—on the
    lawn.
Presumption has it's Affliction.
Pretty boarders are leaving the trees, The.
Pretty Rain from those sweet Eaves, The.
Prison gets to be a friend, A.
Products of my Farm are these, The.
Promise is firmer than a Hope, A.
Promise This, When You be Dying.
Prompt—executive Bird is the Jay, A.
Props assist the House, The.
Proud of my broken heart, since thou didst
    break it.
Province of the Saved, The.
Prudence is a tedious one.
Publication—is the Auction.
Pungent atom in the Air, The.
Purple—/ Color of a Queen, is this, The.
Purple—is fashionable twice.
Pursuing you in your transitions.

Put up my lute!
Quicker deceit dies, The.
Quite empty, quite at rest.
Rainbow never tells me, The.
Rat surrendered here, A.
Rat, The.
Rather arid delight.
Ravenousness of fondness, The.
Read—Sweet—how others—strove.
Rearrange a "Wife's" affection!
Recollect the Face of me.
Red—Blaze—is the Morning, The.
Red Leaves take the Green Leaves place, The.
"Red Sea," indeed! Talk not to me.
Rehearsal to Ourselves.
"Remember me" implored the Thief!
Remembrance has a Rear and Front.
Remorse—is Memory—awake.
Remove—from Accident of Loss.
Renunciation.
Renunciation—is a piercing Virtue.
Reportless Subjects, to the Quick.
Rests at Night.
Resurgam.
Reticent volcano keeps, The.
Reverse cannot befall.
Revolution is the Pod.
Ribbons of the Year.
Riddle we can guess, The.
Right to perish might be thought, The.
Risk is the Hair that holds the Tun.
Risks of Immortality, The.
Road to Paradise is plain, The.
Road was lit with Moon and star, The.
Robbed by Death—but that was easy.
Robin.
Robin for the Crumb, The.
Robin is the One, The.
Robin's my Criterion for Tune, The.
"Robins?" They are writing now, The.
Rose did caper on her cheek, The.
Saddest noise, the sweetest noise, The.
Safe Despair it is that raves.
Safe in their Alabaster Chambers.
Said Death to Passion.
Sailor cannot see the North, The.
Sang from the Heart, Sire.
Satisfaction—is the Agent.
Saucer holds a Cup, A.
Save me from the idolatry.
Savior! I've no one else to tell.
Savior must have been, The.
Savior's only signature, The.
Scatter a fragrant flower.
Science—so the Savants say, A.
Science will not trust us.
Sea said "Come" to the Brook, The.
Secret, The.
Secret told, A.
"Secrets" is a daily word.
Sepal, petal, and a thorn, A.
September's Baccalaureate.
Seraphic shame generosity causes, The.
Service without Hope, The.
Severer Service of myself.
Sexton! My Master's sleeping here.
Shade upon the mind there passes, A.
Shady friend—for Torrid days, A.
Shall I take thee, the Poet said.
Shame is the shawl of Pink.
She bore it till the simple veins.
She could not live upon the Past.
She dealt her pretty words like Blades.
She died at play, / Gambolled away.
She dwelleth in the Ground.
She hideth Her the last.
She is the Lane to the Indes.
She laid her docile Crescent down.
She lay as if at play.
She rose as high as His Occasion.
She Rose to His Requirement—Dropt.
She slept beneath a tree.
She sped as Petals of a Rose.
She staked her Feathers—Gained an Arc.
She talked of you before she went.
She went as quiet as the Dew.

Shells from the Coast mistaking.
She's happy, with a new Content.
Should you but fail at—Sea.
Show is not the Show, The.
Show me Eternity, and I will show you Memory.
Sic transit gloria mundi.
Sickness of this World it most occasions, A.
Silence is all we dread.
Silence' oblation to the Ear.
Single clover Plank, A.
Single Screw of Flesh, A.
Sister of Ophir.
Size circumscribes—it has no room.
Skies can't keep their secret!, The.
Sky is low—the Clouds are mean, The.
Slash of Blue, A.
Sleep is supposed to be.
Slips of the last rose of summer, The.
Sloop of Amber slips away, A.
Small weight is obnoxious, A.
Smiling back from Coronation.
Smouldering embers blush, The.
Snake, A.
Snake, The.
Snow beneath whose chilly softness.
Snow flakes / I counted till they danced so.
Snow that never drifts, The.
Snow, The.
So bashful when I spied her!
So delicate a diffidence.
So from the mould / Scarlet and Gold.
So gay a Flower.
So give me back to Death.
So glad we are—a Stranger'd deem.
So has a Daisy vanished.
So I pull my Stockings off.
So large my Will / The little that I may.
So much of Heaven has gone from Earth.
So much Summer.
So proud she was to die.
So set its Sun in Thee.
So the Eyes accost—and sunder.
So valiant is the intimacy.
So well that I can live without.
Society for me my misery.
Soft as the massacre of Suns.
Soft Sea washed around the House, A.
Soil of Flint, if steady tilled.
Solemn thing—it was—I said, A.
Solemn thing within the Soul, A.
Some Arrows slay but whom they strike.
Some Days retired from the rest.
Some keep the Sabbath going to Church.
Some one prepared this mighty show.
Some Rainbow—coming from the Fair!
Some say goodnight—at night.
Some such Butterfly be seen.
Some things that fly there be.
Some time is longer than the rest.
Some, too fragile for winter winds.
Some we see no more, Tenements of Wonder.
Some—Work for Immortality.
Some Wretched creature, savior take.
Somehow myself survived the Night.
Something in a summer's Day, A.
Sometimes with the Heart.
Somewhat, to hope for.
Somewhere upon the general Earth.
Sorrow almost resents love.
Sorrow, benighted with Fathoms.
Soto! Explore thyself!
Soul has Bandaged moments, The.
Soul must go by Death alone, The.
Soul selects her own Society, The.
Soul should always stand ajar, The.
Soul, take thy risk.
Soul that hath a Guest, The.
Soul unto itself, The.
Soul, Wilt thou toss again?
Soul's distinct connection, The.
Soul's Superior instants, The.
South Wind—has a pathos, A.
South Winds jostle them.
Sown in dishonor!
Sparrow took a Slice of Twig, A.

Speculate with all our might.
"Speech"—is a prank of Parliament.
Speech is one symptom of Affection.
Spell cannot be tattered, A.
Spider as an Artist, The.
Spider holds a Silver Ball, The.
Spider sewed at Night, A.
Spirit is the Conscious Ear, The.
Spirit lasts, but in what mode, The.
Split the Lark—and you'll find the Music.
Spring, and not a Blue Bird.
Spring comes on the World.
Spring is a happiness so beautiful.
Spring is the Period.
Spring's first conviction is a wealth.
Spry Arms of the Wind, The.
Spurn the temerity.
Stagnant pleasure like a Pool, A.
Stars are old, that stood for me, The.
Stem of a departed Flower, The.
Step lightly on this narrow spot.
Still as the Profile of a Tree.
Still own thee—still thou art.
Still—Volcano—Life, A.
Stimulus, beyond the Grave, The.
Stimulus of Loss, The.
Storm.
Strong Draughts of Their Refreshing Minds.
Struck, was I, not yet by Lightning.
Suburbs of a Secret, The.
Success is counted sweetest.
Success is dust, but an aim.
Such are the inlets of the mind.
Such is the Force of Happiness.
Summer begins to have the look.
Summer day on which you came, The.
Summer for thee, grant I may be.
Summer has been wide and deep, The.
Summer has two Beginnings.
Summer is shorter than any one.
Summer laid her simple Hat.
Summer that we did not prize, The.
Summer—we all have seen.
Summers of bloom—and months of frost.
Sun and Fog Contested, The.
Sun and Moon must make their haste, The.
Sun in reining to the West, The.
Sun is one—and on the Tare, The.
Sun—just touched the Morning, The.
Sun kept setting—setting—still, The.
Sun kept stooping—stooping—low!, The.
Sun retired to a cloud, The.
Sun went down—no Man looked on, The.
Sunrise runs for Both, The.
Sunset at Night—is natural.
Sunset stopped on Cottages, The.
Sunset that screens, reveals.
Superfluous were the Sun.
Superiority to Fate.
Surgeons must be very careful.
Surprise is like a thrilling—pungent.
Surrender.
Suspense.
Suspense—is Hostiler than Death.
Sweet Acclamation of Death divulges it, The.
Sweet and soft as summer, Darlings.
Sweet hours have perished here.
Sweet is it as Life.
Sweet Land of Liberty.
Sweet Mountains—Ye tell Me no lie.
Sweet Pirate of the heart.
Sweet—safe—Houses.
Sweet Skepticism of the Heart.
Sweet, to have had them lost.
Sweet toil for smitten hands.
Sweet—You forgot—but I remembered.
Sweetest Heresy received, The.
Sweetest way I think of you, The.
Sweets of Pillage, can be known, The.
Symptom of the Gale, The.
Take all away.
Take all away from me, but leave me Ecstasy.
Take Your Heaven further on.
Taken from men—this morning.
Taking up the fair Ideal.
Talk not to me of Summer Trees.

Talk with prudence to a Beggar.
Teach Him—When He makes the names.
Tell all the Truth but tell it slant.
Tell as a Marksman—were forgotten.
Tenderness has not a Date.
Test of Love—is Death, The.
Than Heaven more remote.
Thank God there is a world.
Thank her dear power for having come.
"Thank you" ebbs between us.
Thank you in my heart obstructs, The.
That a pansy is transitive.
That after horror that was us.
That Bareheaded life under the grass.
That bleeding beginning that every mourner knows.
That Distance was between Us.
That first Day, when you praised Me, Sweet.
That I did always love.
That is solemn we have ended.
That it is true, Master.
That it will never come again.
That Love is all there is.
That must be a silver bell.
That odd old man is dead a year.
That Possession fairest lies.
That sacred Closet when you sweep.
That she forgot me was the least.
That short—potential stir.
That Sorrow dare to touch the Loved.
That Such have died enable Us.
That sweet Physician, an approaching spring.
That the Divine has been human.
That this should feel the need of Death.
That we are permanent.
That you return to us alive.
That your loved Confederate and yourself.
Their Barricade against the Sky.
Their dappled importunity.
Their Height in Heaven comforts not.
Themself are all I have.
Then will I not repine.
There are Sweets of Pathos.
There are two Mays.
There are two Ripenings—one—of sight.
There came a Wind like a Bugle.
There comes a warning like a spy.
There comes an hour when begging stops.
There is a finished feeling.
There is a flower that Bees prefer.
There is a June when Corn is cut.
There is a Languor of the Life.
There is a morn by men unseen.
There is a pain—so utter.
There is a Shame of Nobleness.
There is a solitude of space.
There is a strength in proving that it can be borne.
There is a tall—pale snow storm.
There is a word / Which bears a sword.
There is a Zone whose even Years.
There is an arid Pleasure.
There is another Loneliness.
There is another sky.
There is no first, or last, in Forever.
There is no first, or last, in Forever.
There is no Frigate like a Book.
There is no Silence in the Earth—so silent.
There is not so much Life as talk of Life.
There is nothing sweeter than Honor, but Love.
There lurked a dread that you had gone.
There seems a spectral power.
There's a certain Slant of light.
There's been a Death, in the Opposite House.
There's something quieter than sleep.
There's the Battle of Burgoyne.
These are the days that Reindeer love.
These are the Nights that Beetles love.
These are the Signs to Nature's Inns.
These brief imperfect meetings.
These Fevered Days—to take them to the Forest.
These held their Wick above the West.
These Indian-Summer Days.
These—saw Visions.
These Strangers, In a Foreign World.

These tested Our Horizon.
They ask but our Delight.
They called me to the Window, for.
They dropped like Flakes.
They have a little Odor—that to me.
"They have not chosen me," he said.
They leave us with the Infinite.
They might not need me—yet they might.
They put Us far apart.
They say that absence conquers.
They Say That Time Assuages.
They shut me up in Prose.
They talk as slow as Legends grow.
They won't frown always—some sweet Day.
Things of which we want the proof, The.
Things that never can come back, are several, The.
Things we thought that we should do, The.
Think of that great courageous place.
Thirst.
This Bauble was preferred of Bees.
This Chasm, Sweet, upon my life.
This Consciousness that is aware.
This dirty—little—Heart.
This docile one inter.
This Dust, and its Feature.
This heart that broke so long.
This is a Blossom of the Brain.
This is a stern Winter.
This is but a fragment.
This Is My Letter to the World.
This—is the land—the Sunset washes.
This is the place they hoped before.
This Me—that walks and works—must die.
This Merit hath the worst.
This slow Day moved along.
"This tabernacle" is a blissful trial.
This that would greet—an hour ago.
This was a Poet—It is That.
This was in the White of the Year.
This World Is Not Conclusion.
Tho' I get home how late—how late.
Tho' my destiny be Fustian.
Those Cattle smaller than a Bee.
Those—dying then.
Those fair—fictitious People.
Those final Creatures—who they are.
Those not live yet.
Those that die seem near me.
Those who have been in the Grave the longest.
Though but a simple shelter.
Though the great Waters sleep.
Though thou walk through the Valley of the Shadow of Death.
Though we are each unknown to ourself.
Thought beneath so slight a film, The.
Thought went up my mind today, A.
Thousand questions rise to my lips, A.
Three times—we parted—Breath—and I.
Three Weeks passed since I had seen Her.
Thrill came slowly like a Boon for, The.
Throe upon the features, A.
Through lane it lay—through bramble.
Through the Dark Sod—as Education.
Through the strait pass of suffering.
Through those old Grounds of memory.
Through what transports of Patience.
Tie the Strings to my Life, My Lord.
Till Death—is narrow Loving.
Till it has loved—no man or woman.
Time does go on.
Time feels so vast that were it not.
Time is short and full.
Time's wily Chargers will not wait.
Tiniest ones are the mightiest, The.
Tint I cannot take—is best, The.
'Tis Anguish grander than Delight.
'Tis customary as we part.
'Tis easier to pity those when dead.
'Tis good—the looking back on Grief.
'Tis little I— could care for Pearls.
'Tis my first night beneath the Sun.
'Tis not that Dying hurts us so.
'Tis not the swaying frame we miss.
'Tis One by One—the Father counts.
'Tis Opposites—entice.

'Tis Seasons since the Dimpled War.
'Tis so appalling—it exhilirates.
'Tis so much joy! 'Tis so much joy!
'Tis Sunrise—Little Maid—Hast Thou.
'Tis true—They shut me in the Cold.
'Tis whiter than an Indian Pipe.
Title divine—is mine!
To all except anguish.
To an Emigrant, Country is idle.
To attempt to speak of what has been.
To be a Bell and Flower too.
To be alive—is Power.
To be certain we were to meet our Lost.
To be forgot by thee.
To be human is more than to be divine.
To be singular under plural circumstances.
To break so vast a Heart.
To come from Heaven is casual.
To come unto our own.
To congratulate the Redeemed is perhaps superfluous.
To di—without the Dying.
To die before it feared to die.
To die—takes just a little while.
To disappear enhances.
To divulge itself is Sorrow's Right.
To do a magnanimous thing.
To earn it by disdaining it.
To fight aloud, is very brave.
To fill a Gap.
To flee from memory.
To forget you would be impossible.
To fulfill the will of a powerless friend.
To hang our head, ostensibly.
To have been the missing Hero.
To have had such Daughters is sanctity.
To Hear an Oriole Sing.
To help our Bleaker Parts.
To her derided Home.
To him to whom Events and Omens.
To his simplicity.
To interrupt His Yellow Plan.
To know just how He suffered—would be dear.
To know that there is shelter.
To know you better as you flee.
To learn the Transport by the Pain.
To live lasts always, but to love.
To lose one's faith—surpass.
To lose thee—sweeter than to gain.
To love thee Year by Year.
To make a prairie it takes a clover and one bee.
To make even Heaven more heavenly.
To make One's Toilette—after Death.
To make Routine a Stimulus.
To mend each tattered Faith.
To multiply the Harbors.
To my quick ear the Leaves—conferred.
To my small Hearth His fire came.
To offer brave assistance.
To One denied to drink.
To own a Susan of my own.
To own the Art within the Soul.
To pile like Thunder to its close.
To put this World down, like a Bundle.
To see her is a Picture.
To see is perhaps never quite the sorcery.
To see the Summer Sky.
To tell the Beauty would decrease.
To the bright east she flies.
To the faithful Absence is condensed presence.
To the staunch Dust.
To their apartment deep.
To this World she returned.
To those who can estimate silence.
To try to speak, and miss the way.
To undertake is to achieve.
To venerate the simple days.
To wait an Hour—is long.
To which as to a Reservoir.
To Whom the Mornings stand for Nights.
Toad, can die of Light, A.
Today or this noon.
"Tomorrow"—whose location.
Tongue—to tell Him I am true!, A.
Too cold is this.

Too few the mornings be.
Too happy Time dissolves itself.
Too little way the House must lie.
Too peremptory a Courtship for Earth.
Too scanty 'twas to die for you.
Tooth upon Our Peace, A.
Touch lightly Nature's sweet Guitar.
Train went through a burial gate, A.
Transport one cannot contain, A.
Transport's mighty price is.
Travel why to Nature.
Treason of an accent, The.
Treason of an Accent, The.
Tree in Winter.
Trees like Tassels—hit—and swung, The.
Trespass of my rustic Love, The.
Trial as a Stimulus.
Tried always and Condemned by thee.
Triumph—may be of several kinds.
Tropic, indeed, a memory.
Trudging to Eden, looking backward.
Trust adjusts her "Peradventure."
Trust in the Unexpected.
Trusting the happy flower.
Trusty as the stars.
Truth—is as old as God.
Truth—is stirless, The.
'Twas a long Parting—but the time.
'Twas awkward, but it fitted me.
'Twas comfort in her Dying Room.
'Twas Crisis—All the length had passed.
'Twas fighting for his Life he was.
'Twas here my summer paused.
'Twas just this time, last year, I died.
'Twas later when the summer went.
'Twas Love—not me.
'Twas my one Glory.
'Twas such a little little boat.
'Twas the old—road—through pain.
'Twas warm—at first—like Us.
Twice had Summer her fair Verdure.
Two Butterflies went out at Noon.
Two Lengths has every Day.
Two swimmers wrestled on the spar.
Two Travellers perishing in Snow.
Two—were immortal twice.
'Twould ease—a Butterfly.
Unable are the Loved to die.
Uncertain lease—develops lustre.
Under the Light, yet under.
Undue Significance a starving man attaches.
Unfulfilled to Observation.
Union.
Unit, like Death, for Whom?
Unknown is the largest need, The.
Until the Desert knows.
Unto a broken heart.
Unto like Story—Trouble has incited me.
"Unto me?" I do not know you.
Unto my Books—so good to turn.
Unto the Whole—how add?
Unworthy of her Breast.
Up Life's Hill with my little Bundle.
Upon a Lilac Sea.
Upon Concluded Lives.
Upon his Saddle sprung a Bird.
Upon the gallows hung a wretch.
Valentine, A.
Valor in the dark.
Vanished.
Vastest earthly Day, The.
Veins of other Flowers, The.
Verily it snows.
Victory comes late.
Violets are by my side, The.
Vision of Immortal Life has been fulfilled, The.
Visitor in Marl, A.
Vivid in our immortal Group.
Voice that stands for Floods to me, The.
Volcanoes be in Sicily.
Voraciousness of that only gaze, The.
Wait till the Majesty of Death.
Warm in her Hand these accents lie.
"Was not" was all the Statement.
Water is deeper than the land, The.
Water, is taught by thirst.

Water makes many Beds.
Waters chased him as he fled, The.
Way Hope builds his House, The.
Way I read a Letter's—this, The.
Way to know the Bobolink, The.
We all have moments with the dust.
We are snatching our jewels from the frost.
We—Bee and I—live by the quaffing.
We can but follow to the Sun.
We cannot believe for each other.
We Cover Thee—Sweet Face.
We do not know the time we lose.
We do not play on Graves.
We don't cry—Tim and I.
We dream—it is good we are dreaming.
We go by detachments to the strange Home.
We grow accustomed to the Dark.
We have no statutes here.
We introduce ourselves.
We knew not that we were to live.
We learn in the Retreating.
We learned the Whole of Love.
We like a Hairbreadth 'scape.
We like March.
We like March—his shoes are Purple.
We lose—because we win.
We meet no Stranger.
We met as Sparks—Diverging Flints.
We miss a Kinsman more.
We miss Her, not because We see.
We must be careful what we say.
We must be less than Death.
We must bring no Twilight.
We never know how high we are.
We never know we go when we are going.
We outgrow love like other things.
We play at Paste.
We pray—to Heaven.
We read in a tremendous Book.
We read the words but know them not.
We remind her we love her.
We see—Comparatively.
We send the Wave to find the Wave.
We shall find the Cube of the Rainbow.
We should not mind so small a flower.
We shun because we prize her Face.
We shun it ere it comes.
We talked as Girls do.
We talked with each other about each other.
"We thank thee Oh Father" for these strange
    Minds.
We turn not older with years.
We wear our sober Dresses when we die.
We went to sleep as if it were a country.
We would'nt mind the sun, dear.
Weather is like Africa, The.
Weight with Needles on the pounds, A.
We'll pass without the parting.
Well upon the Brook, The.
Went up a year this evening!
Were it but Me that gained the Height.
Were it to be the last.
Were nature mortal lady.
Were the Velocity of Affection.
Wert Thou but ill—that I might show thee.
What a Hazard a Letter is!
What care the Dead, for Chanticleer.
What did They do since I saw Them?
What I can do—I will.
What I see not, I better see.
What if I say I shall not wait!
What indeed is Earth but a Nest.
What Inn is this.
What is—"Paradise."
What Miracles the News is!
What mystery pervades a well!
What shall I do now—it whimpers so.
What shall I do when the Summer troubles.
What Soft—Cherubic Creatures.
What sweeter Shelter than the Hearts.
What tenements of clover.
What Twigs We held by.
What we see we know somewhat.
What would I give to see his face?
Whatever awaits us of Doom or Home.
Whatever it is—she has tried it.

When a Lover is a Beggar.
When Bells stop ringing—Church—begins.
When Continents expire.
When Diamonds are a Legend.
When Etna basks and purrs.
When I count the seeds.
When I have seen the Sun emerge.
When I hoped I feared.
When I hoped, I recollect.
When I was small, a Woman died.
When Katie walks, this simple pair accompany
    her side.
When Memory is full.
When Night is almost done.
When One has given up One's life.
When overwhelmed to know.
When Roses cease to bloom, Sir.
When the Astronomer stops seeking.
When they come back—if Blossoms do.
When thou goest through the Waters.
When we have ceased to care.
When we stand on the tops of Things.
Where bells no more affright the morn.
Where every bird is bold to go.
Where I have lost, I softer tread.
Where Roses would not dare to go.
Where Ships of Purple—gently toss.
Where the Treasure is.
Where Thou art—that—is Home.
Where we owe so much it defies Money.
Whether my bark went down at sea.
Whether they have forgotten.
Which is best? Heaven.
Which is the best—the Moon or the Crescent?
Which misses most.
While Asters— / On the Hill.
While it is alive.
While others go to Church.
While we were fearing it, it came.
White as an Indian Pipe.
Who abdicated Ambush.
Who could be ill in March.
Who could be motherless.
Who Court obtain within Himself.
Who Giants know, with lesser Men.
Who goes to dine must take his Feast.
Who is it seeks my Pillow Nights.
Who knows how deep the Heart is.
Who knows where our hearts go.
Who loves you most.
Who "meddled" with the costly Hearts.
Who never lost, are unprepared.
Who never wanted—maddest Joy.
Who occupies this House?
Who saw no Sunrise cannot say.
Who were "the Father and the Son."
Whoever disenchants.
Whole Gulfs—of Red—and Fleets—of Red.
Whole of it came not at once, The.
Whose are the little beds, I asked.
Whose cheek is this?
Whose Pink career may have a close.
"Why do I love" You, Sir?
Why—do they shut Me out of Heaven?
Why is it Nobleness makes us ashamed.
Why make it doubt—it hurts it so.
Why should we hurry—why indeed?
Why the full heart is speechless.
Why the Thief ingredient accompanies all
    Sweetness.
Wife—at Daybreak I shall be, A.
Wild Blue sky abreast of Winds, A.
Wild Nights—Wild Nights!
Will is always near, dear, The.
Wind begun to knead the Grass, The.
Wind didn't come from the Orchard—today,
    The.
Wind drew off, The.
Wind that rose, A.
Wind, The.
Wind took up the Northern Things, The.
Wind's Visit, The.
Winged spark doth soar about, A.
Winter is good—his Hoar Delights.
Winter under cultivation.
Winters are so short, The.

Witchcraft has not a Pedigree.
Witchcraft was hung, in History.
With closer clutch for that which remains.
With Leopards for Playmates, the beautiful
    Child.
With Pinions of Disdain.
With sorrow that the Joy is past.
With sweetness unabated.
With thee—in the Desert.
Withdrawal of the Fuel of Rapture, The.
Within my Garden, rides a Bird.
Within my reach!
Within that little Hive.
Within thy Grave!
Without a smile—Without a Throe.
Without this—there is nought.
Wolfe demanded during dying.
Wonder—is not precisely Knowing.
Word dropped careless on a Page, A.
Word is dead, A.
Word made Flesh is seldom, A.
Words the happy say, The.
Work is a bleak redeemer.
Work of Her that went, The.
World made penniless by that departure.
World—stands—solemner—to me, The.
Worthlessness of Earthly things, The.
Would you like summer? Taste of ours.
Wounded Deer Leaps Highest, A.
Writing is brief and fleeting.
Yellow Man, Purple Man.
Yesterday is History.
Yesterday, Today, and Forever.
You are most illustrious.
You asked me if I wrote now?
You cannot make Remembrance grow.
You cannot put a Fire out.
You cannot take itself.
You constituted Time.
You have experienced Sanctity.
You know that Portrait in the Moon.
You left me—Sire—two Legacies.
You love me—you are sure.
You love the Lord—you cannot see.
You might not know I remembered you.
You said that I "was Great"—one Day.
You see I cannot see—your lifetime.
You see we keep a jealous Heart.
You spoke of "Hope" surpassing "Home."
You taught me Waiting with Myself.
You'll find—it when you try to die.
You'll know Her—by Her Foot.
You'll know it—as you know 'tis Noon.
Your coming is a symptom of Summer.
Your Gifts are from the Sky.
Your little mental gallantries.
Your relentless Music.
Your Riches—taught me—Poverty.
Your thoughts don't have words every day.
You're right—"the way is narrow."
Youth, like Indian Summer.
You've seen Balloons set—Haven't You?
Zeroes—taught us—Phosphorus, The.

Dickinson, Goldsworthy Lowes (1862–86)
Sun is gay or stark, The.

Diogenes Laertius (*fl.* A.D. 3d cent.)
Be gone ye blockheads, *Heraclitus* cries.

Dobyns, Stephen (b. 1941)
Connections.

Donne, John (1572–1631)
Air[e] and Angels.
Anatomy [*or* Anatomie] of the World, An: The
    First Anniversary.
Anniversary [*or* Anniversarie], The.
Antiquary.
Apparition, The.
Bait[e], The.
Blossom[e], The.
Break[e] of Day.
Broken Heart, The.
Burnt Ship, A.
Cales and Guiana.
Calm[e], The.
Canonization, The.
Community.
Computation, The.

Confined Love.
Cross, The.
Curse, The.
Damp[e], The.
Disinherited.
Dissolution, The.
Dream[e], The.
Ecstasy, The.
Elegies.
Elegy on Mistress Boulstred.
Elegy on the L. C.
Elegy on the Lady Markham.
Elegy upon the Death of Mistress Boulstred, An.
Elegy upon the Untimely Death of the Incomparable Prince Henry.
Epitaph on Himself.
Epithalamion at the Marriage of the Earl of Somerset.
Epithalamion Made at Lincoln's Inn [or Lincolnes Inne].
Epithalamion, or Marriage Song on the Lady Elizabeth and Count Palatine Being Married on St. Valentine's Day, An.
Expiration, The.
Fall of a Wall.
Farewell to Love.
Fever, A.
Flea, The.
Funeral[l], The.
Good Friday [or Goodfriday], 1613. Riding Westward.
Good-Morrow, The.
H. W. in Hibernia Belligeranti.
Hero and Leander.
Holy Sonnets.
Hymn to the Saints, and to Marquis Hamilton, An.
Hymn[e] to Christ, at the Author's Last Going into Germany, A.
Hymn[e] to God My God, In My Sickness[e], A.
Hymn[e] to God the Father, A.
Indifferent, The.
Jet Ring Sent, A.
Klockius.
Lame Beggar, A.
Lamentations of Jeremy, for the Most Part According to Tremellius.
Lecture upon the Shadow, A.
Legacy [or Legacie], The.
Letter to the Lady Carey, and Mistress Essex Rich, from Amiens, A.
Letter Written by Sir H. G. and J. D. alternis vicibus, A.
Liar, The.
Licentious Person, A.
Litany, A.
Lovers' Infiniteness[e].
Love's Alchemy [or Alchemie].
Love's Deity [or Deitie].
Love's Diet.
Love's Exchange.
Love's Growth.
Love's Usury.
Manliness.
Mercurius Gallo-Belgicus.
Message, The.
Negative Love.
Niobe.
Nocturnal[l] upon Saint Lucy's [or S. Lucy's or S. Lucies] Day, Being the Shortest Day, A.
Obscure Writer, An.
Obsequies to the Lord Harrington, Brother to the Lady Lucy, Countess of Bedford.
Of the Progress of the Soul: The Second Anniversary.
Paradox, The.
Phryne.
Primrose, The; Being at Montgomery Castle, upon the hill, on which it is situate.
Progress of the Soul, The.
Prohibition, The.
Pyramus and Thisbe.
Raderus.

Ralphius.
Relic, The.
Resurrection, Imperfect.
Satires.
Self Love.
Self[e] Accuser, A.
Sir John Wingfield.
Song: "Go and catch a falling star."
Song: "Sweetest love, I do not go[e]."
Sonnet. The Token.
Storm[e], The.
Sun Rising, The.
To E. of D. with Six Holy Sonnets.
To Mr B. B.
To Mr C. B.
To Mr E. G.
To Mr I. L ("Blessed [or Blesst] are your north parts, for all this long time").
To Mr I. L ("Of that short Roll of friends writ in my heart").
To Mr R. W ("If, as mine is, thy life a slumber be").
To Mr R. W ("Kindly I envy thy song's [or songs] perfection").
To Mr R. W ("Muse not that by thy mind thy body is led").
To Mr R. W ("Zealously my Muse doth salute all thee").
To Mr. Roland Woodward.
To Mr S. B.
To Mr T. W ("All hail, sweet poet, more full of more strong fire").
To Mr T. W ("At once, from hence, my lines and I depart").
To Mr T. W ("Haste thee harsh verse as fast as thy lame measure").
To Mr T. W ("Pregnant again with th' old twins hope, and fear").
To Mr Tilman after He Had Taken Orders.
To Mrs M. H.
To Mrs Magdalen Herbert: of St. Mary Magdalen.
To Sir Edward Herbert, at Juliers [or Julyers].
To Sir Henry Goodyer.
To Sir Henry Wotton, at His Going Ambassador to Venice.
To Sir Henry Wotton ("Here's no more news, than virtue, I may as well").
To Sir Henry Wotton ("Sir, more than kisses, letters mingle souls").
To the Countess of Bedford at New Year's Tide.
To the Countess of Bedford ("Honour is so sublime perfection").
To the Countess of Bedford ("Madam, / Reason is our soul's left hand, Faith her right").
To the Countess of Bedford ("Madam, / You have refined me, and to worthiest things").
To the Countess of Bedford ("Though I be dead, and buried, yet I have").
To the Countess of Bedford ("To have written then, when you writ, seemed to me").
To the Countess of Huntingdon ("Madam, / Man to God's image, Eve, to man's was made").
To the Countess of Huntingdon ("That unripe side of earth, that heavy clime").
To the Countess of Salisbury.
To the Lady Bedford.
Triple Fool, The.
Twickenham [or Twicknam] Garden.
Undertaking, The.
Upon the Annunciation and Passion Falling upon One Day. 1608.
Upon the Translation of the Psalms by Sir Philip Sidney, and the Countess of Pembroke His Sister.
Valediction, A: of My Name in the Window.
Valediction, A: of the Book.
Valediction, A: of Weeping.
Valediction: Forbidding Mourning, A.
Will, The.
Witchcraft by a Picture.
Woman's Constancy.

Doolittle, Hilda ("H. D.") (1886–1961)
Acon.
Adonis.
After Troy.
All Mountains.
Ancient Wisdom Speaks.
Antipater of Sidon.
Archer.
Ariadne.
At Baia.
At Croton.
At Eleusis.
At Ithaca.
Birds in Snow.
Body and Soul.
Calliope.
Calypso.
Cassandra.
Centaur Song.
Chance.
Chance Meeting.
Charioteer.
Child Poems.
Choros Sequence.
Christmas 1944.
Circe.
Cities.
Cliff Temple, The.
Contest, The.
Cuckoo Song.
Dancer, The.
Dead Priestess Speaks, A.
Delphi.
Demeter.
Dodona.
Ecce Sponsus.
Egypt.
Electra-Orestes, sels.
Epigram: "Golden one is gone from the banquets, The."
Epigrams.
Epitaph: "So I may say."
Erige Cor Tuum ad Me in Caelum.
Eros.
Eurydice.
Evadne.
Evening.
Flowering of the Rod, The.
Flute Song.
Fragment 36 [or Thirty-Six]: "I know not what to do."
Fragment 40: "Keep love and he wings."
Fragment 41: "Am I blind alas."
Fragment 68: "I envy you your chance of death."
Fragment 113: "Not honey, / not the plunder of the bee."
Garden.
Gift.
Gift, The.
God, The.
Halcyon.
Helen.
Heliodora.
Helios.
Helios and Athene.
Helmsman, The.
Hermes of the Ways.
Hermonax.
Hippolytus Temporizes.
Holy Satyr.
Huntress.
Hyacinth.
Hymen.
I Said.
If You Will Let Me Sing.
In Our Town.
In the Rain.
Islands, The.
Lais.
Late Spring.
Leda.
Let Zeus Record.
Lethe.
Look-out, The.
Loss.

Magician [Master].
Master, The.
May 1943.
Mid-day.
Moonrise.
Myrtle Bough.
Mysteries, The.
Night.
Nossis.
Orchard.
Oread.
Orestes Theme.
Orion Dead.
Other Sea-Cities.
Pear Tree.
Phaedra.
Poet, The.
Pool, The.
Prayer: "White, O white face."
Priest.
Prisoners.
Projector.
Projector II.
Psyche.
Pursuit.
Pygmalion.
R.A.F.
Red Roses for Bronze.
Scribe.
Sea Gods.
Sea Heroes.
Sea Iris.
Sea Lily.
Sea Poppies.
Sea Rose.
Sea Violet.
She Contrasts with Herself Hippolyta.
She Rebukes Hippolyta.
Sheltered Garden.
Shepherd, The.
Shrine, The.
Sigil.
Simaetha.
Sitalkas.
Song: "You are as gold."
Songs from Cyprus.
Storm.
Telesila.
Temple of the Sun, *sels.*
Thetis.
Thetis.
Toward the Piraeus.
Trance.
Tribute, The.
Tribute to the Angels.
Triplex.
Two Poems for Christmas, 1937.
Walls Do Not Fall, The.
Wash of cold river.
We Two.
When I Am a Cup.
White Rose.
White World.
Why Have You Sought?
Wind Sleepers, The.
Wine Bowl.

Dove, Rita (b. 1952)
Abduction, The.
Adolescence—I.
Adolescence—II.
Adolescence—III.
Agosta the Winged Man and Rasha the Black
   Dove.
Aircraft.
Anniversary.
Anti-Father.
Ants of Argos, The.
At the German Writers Conference in Munich.
Aurora Borealis.
Banneker.
Beauty and the Beast.
Belinda's Petition.
Bird Frau, The.
Boast, The.
Boccaccio: The Plague Years.
Catherine of Alexandria.

Catherine of Siena.
Centipede.
Champagne.
Charm, The.
Cholera.
Company.
Compendium.
Copper Beech, The.
Corduroy Road.
Courtship.
Courtship, Diligence.
David Walker (1785–1830).
Daystar.
Definition in the Face of Unnamed Fury.
Delft.
Dusting.
Early Morning on the Tel Aviv-Haifa Freeway.
Eastern European Eclogues.
Event, The.
Exeunt the Viols.
Father out Walking on the Lawn, A.
Fiammetta Breaks Her Peace.
First Kiss.
Fish in the Stone, The.
Five Elephants.
Flirtation.
For Kazuko.
Geometry.
Gospel.
Grape Sherbet.
Great Uncle Beefheart.
Happenstance.
Headdress.
Hill Has Something to Say, The.
Hill of Beans, A.
His Shirt.
House on Bishop Street, The.
House Slave, The.
Ike.
In the Bulrush.
In the Old Neighborhood.
Jiving.
Kadava Kumbis Devise a Way to Marry for
   Love, The.
Kentucky, 1833.
Left-Handed Cellist, The.
Lightnin' Blues.
Lines Muttered in Sleep.
Magic.
Motherhood.
My Father's Telescope.
Nestor's Bathtub.
Nexus.
Nigger Song: An Odyssey.
Night Watch.
Nightmare.
Notes from a Tunisian Journal.
Nothing Down.
November for Beginners.
Ö.
Obedience.
One Volume Missing.
Oriental Ballerina, The.
Pamela.
Parsley.
Pearls.
Pithos.
Pomade.
Primer for the Nuclear Age.
Promises.
Reading Hölderlin on the Patio with the Aid of
   a Dictionary.
Receiving the Stigmata.
Recovery.
Refrain.
Roast Possum.
Robert Schumann, Or: Musical Genius Begins
   with Affliction.
Roses.
Sahara Bus Trip, The.
Sailor in Africa, The.
Satisfaction Coal Company, The.
Secret Garden, The.
Shakespeare Say.
Sightseeing.
Slave's Critique of Practical Reason, The.

Small Town.
Snow King, The.
Someone's Blood.
Son, The.
Song. Summer.
Spy.
Straw Hat.
Stroke, The.
Suite for Augustus, A.
Sunday Greens.
Sunday Night at Grandfather's.
Taking in Wash.
Teach Us to Number Our Days.
Then Came Flowers.
This Life.
Thomas at the Wheel.
Three Days of Forest, a River, Free.
To Bed.
Tou Wan Speaks to Her Husband Liu Sheng.
Transport or Slaves From Maryland to
   Mississippi, The.
Under the Viaduct, 1932.
Upon Meeting Don L. Lee, in a Dream.
Variation on Gaining a Son.
Variation on Guilt.
Variation on Pain.
Weathering Out.
Why I Turned Vegetarian.
Wingfoot Lake.
Zeppelin Factory, The.

Drummond de Andrade, Carlos (1902–87)
Don't Kill Yourself.
Family Portrait.
In the Middle of the Road.
Infancy.
Irritated Office, The.
Memories of the Ancient World.
Seven-Sided Poem.
Song of Purification.
Table, The.
Travelling in the Family.

Dryden, John (1631–1700)
Absalom and Achitophel.
Absalom and Achitophel, Part 2.
Albion and Albanius, *sels.*
Alexander's Feast; or, The Power of Music [*or*
   Musique].
Annus Mirabilis, *sels.*
Aureng-Zebe.
Conquest of Granada, The, *sels.*
Don Sebastian, *sels.*
Duke of Guise, The, *sels.*
Epilogue Spoken by Mrs. Boutell.
Epilogue to the King and Queen.
Evening's Love, An, *sels.*
Hind and the Panther, The, *sels.*
Indian Emperor, The, *sels.*
King Arthur, *sels.*
Lady's Song, The.
Mac Flecknoe [or, A Satire upon the True-Blue
   Protestant Poet T. S.].
Medal [*or* Medall], The, *sels.*
Medal, The.
Milton.
New Song, A: "Sylvia the fair, in the bloom of
   fifteen."
Prologue to His Royal Highness.
Prologue to the Duchess.
Prologue to the King and Queen at the
   Opening of their Theatre.
Prologue to *The Tempest* [or *The Enchanted
   Island*].
Prologue to the University of Oxford, 1673.
Prologue to the University of Oxford, 1674.
Religio Laici.
Secret Love; or, The Maiden Queen, *sels.*
Secular Masque, The.
Song: "Fair, sweet and young, receive a prize."
Song: "Farewell fair Arminda, my joy and my
   grief."
Song for St Cecilia's Day, 1687, A.
Song: "Go tell Amynta, gentle swain."
Song: "High state and honours to others
   impart."
Song to a Fair Young Lady, Going Out of the

Town in the Spring.
Spanish Friar [or Fryar], The, *sels.*
Tears of Amynta for the Death of Damon, The.
Theodore and Honoria, From [Fables Ancient and Modern from] Boccace.
Threnodia Augustalis.
To Mr L. Maidwell on His New Method.
To My Dear Friend Mr Congreve [on His Comedy Called "The Double-Dealer"].
To My Friend Mr J. Northleigh.
To My Honoured [or Honour'd] Kinsman, John Driden [of Chesterton in the County of Huntingdon, Esquire].
To the Earl of Roscommon, on His Excellent *Essay on Translated Verse.*
To the Memory of Mr Oldham.
Translation of Dryden's Poem on Milton.
Troilus and Cressida, *sels.*
Tyrannic Love, *sels.*

Du Bellay, Joachim (1522–60)
Happy the Man.
Heureux Qui, comme Ulysse, A Fait un Beau Voyage.
Rome.
Roundel: "I come unto thee thru the hidden ways."
Ruins of Rome.
Sonnet from the Book of Regrets.
Visions of Bellay, The.

Dubie, Norman (b. 1945)
About Infinity.
Accident.
After Sky X.
After Spring Snow, What They Saw.
After Three Photographs of Brassaï.
Amen.
American Scene, An.
Amulet, The.
Anagram Born of Madness at Czernowitz, 23 November 1920.
Anima Poeta: A Christmas Entry for the Suicide, Mayakovsky.
Annual of the Dark Physics, An.
Apocrypha of Jacques Derrida, The.
Arkhangel'sk.
Ars Poetica.
At Midsummer.
At the Death of a Mongolian Peasant.
Audabe of the Singer and Saboteur, Marie Triste.
Baptismal.
Bellevue Exchange.
Bells in the Endtime of Gyurmey Tsultrim.
Blue Hog, A.
Buffalo Clouds over the Maestro Hoon.
Bus Stopped in Fields of Misdemeanor, The.
Caste Wife Speaks to the Enigmatic Parabolas, The.
Chemin de Fer.
Circus Ringmaster's Apology to God, The.
City of the Olesha Fruit, The.
Clouds of Magellan (Aphorisms of Mr. Canon Aspirin), The.
Coleridge Crossing the Plain of Jars [1833].
Comes Winter, the Sea Hunting.
Composer's Winter Dream, The.
Confession.
Coyote Creek.
Czar's Last Christmas Letter, The: A Barn in the Urals.
Danse Macabre.
Death of the Race Car Driver, The.
Depth of Field, A.
Descent into the Hours of the Peregrine.
Desert Deportation of 1915, The.
Diamond Persona, The.
Diatribe of the Kite, The.
Double Sphere, Cloven Sphere.
Dream.
Dream of Three Sisters, A.
Duchesse's Red Shoes, The.
Dun Cow and the Hag, The.
Elegies for the Ocher Deer on the Walls at Lascaux.
Elegy Asking that It Be the Last.
Elegy for Integral Domains, The.

Elegy for My Brother.
Elegy for Wright & Hugo.
Elegy to the Pulley of Superior Oblique.
Elegy to the Sioux.
Elizabeth's War with the Christmas Bear.
Elsinore in the Late Ancient Autumn.
Evening of the Pyramids, The.
Everlastings, The.
February: The Boy Breughel.
Fever.
Fifteenth-Century Zen Master, A.
Fish, The.
For Milarepa, In Ruse, on Rice Paper.
For Randall Jarrell, 1914–1965.
Fox Who Watched for the Midnight Sun, The.
Friary at Blossom, Prologue & Instructions, The.
Funeral, The.
Ganges, The.
Genesis Text for Larry Levis, Who Died Alone, A.
Gently Bent to Ease Us.
Ghost.
Ghosts on the Northern Land of Ur.
Grand Illusion.
Grandfather's Last Letter, A.
Grandmother.
Groom Falconer.
Her Monologue of Dark Crepe with Edges of Light.
Homage to Philip K. Dick.
Hour, The.
Hours, The.
Hummingbirds.
Huts at Esquimaux, The.
Ibis.
Immoralist, The.
In the Dead of the Night.
In the Time of False Messiahs.
Indian Summer.
Inside the City Walls.
Jeremiad.
La Pampa.
Lamentations.
Last Poem, Snow Tree.
Lion Grotto, The.
Looking up from Two Renaissance Paintings to the Massacre at Tiananmen Square.
Lord Myth.
Margaret's Speech.
Meister Eckhart.
Mercy Seat, The.
Monologue of Two Moons, Nudes with Crests. 1938.
Moths, The.
Near the Bridge of Saint-Cloud.
New Age at Airport Mesa.
New England, Autumn.
New England, Springtime.
Night before Thanksgiving, The.
Nine Black Poppies for Chac.
Nineteen Forty.
Northwind Escarpment.
Not the Cuckold's Dream.
November 23, 1989.
Obscure, The.
Ode to the Spectral Thief, Alpha.
Of Politics, & Art.
Old Night and Sleep.
Old Woman's Vision, An.
On the Chinese Abduction of Tibet's Child Panchen Lama.
Open Happens in the Midst of Beings, The.
Oration: Half-Moon in Vermont.
Parallax Monograph for Rodin, The.
Parish.
Pastoral: "It happened so fast. Fenya was in the straight."
Penelope.
Pennacesse Leper Colony for Women, Cape Cod, The: 1922.
Photographer's Annual, The.
Physical Moon beyond Paterson, A.
Pictures at an Exhibition.
Poem for My Friend, Clare. Or, With White Stupas We Remember Buddha.

Poem: "Mule kicked out in the trees, A. An Early."
Popham of the New Song.
Principia Mathematica: Einstein's Exile in an Old Dutch Winter.
Psalm 23.
Radio Sky.
Reader of the Sentences, The.
Renunciation of the Desert Primrose, A.
Revelation 20:11–15.
Revelations.
Safe Conduct.
Saints of Negativity, The.
Sanctuary.
Scrivener's Roses, The.
Seagull, The.
Several Measures for the Little Lost.
Shadows at Boxford, The.
Shipwreck.
Simple Philo of Alexandria.
Skeleton for Mr. Paul in Paradise, A.
Somebody'll Hav' to Shoot Ya Down.
Sun and Moon Flowers: Paul Klee, 1879–1940.
These Untitled Little Verses in Which, at Dawn, Two Obscure Dutch Peasants Struggled with an Auburn Horse.
Thomas Hardy.
Thomas Merton and the Winter Marsh.
Through a Glass Darkly.
To a Young Woman Dying at Weir.
Tomb Pond.
Train, The.
Trakl.
Trees of Madame Blavatsky, The.
Trolley from Xochimilco, The.
True Story of God, A.
Two Women on the Potomac Parkway.
Village Priest, A.
Wedding Party, The.
Widow of the Beast of Ingolstadt, The.
Widow Speaks to the Auroras of a December Night, A.
World Isn't a Wedding of the Artists of Yesterday, The.
You.

Dugan, Alan (b. 1923)
About the Pseudo St. Dionysius.
Absent Good Girl, Life of My Mind.
Accommodation to Detroit.
Actual Vision of Morning's Extrusion.
Address to a Bird on a Visit Home.
Admonitor: A Pearl for Arrogance.
Adultery.
Advertising in Paris.
After a Poem by Carlos Drummond de Andrade Translated by Elizabeth Bishop as *Don't Kill Yourself.*
Against a Sickness: To the Female Double Principle God.
Against France: On the Algerian Pleasures of Entity.
Against the Text "Art Is Immortal."
Against Veils on Exodus 33:23 and 34:33.
American against Solitude.
American Tourist to a Guatemalan Tarantula.
American Variation on How Rilke Loved a Princess and Got to Stay in Her Castle.
Another Cat Poem: A Cat Is Not a Dancer but a Hunter.
Another Cat Poem. To a Cat Person.
Answer to the Rilke Question.
Apollo.
Apology (to the Muse).
Argument to Love as a Person.
Attempted Rescue, The.
Autobiographical Libation to Erato Muse of Lyric Poetry.
Autumn at Baiae: For Cavafy.
Barefoot for a Scorpion.
Barefoot Homiletics, after Wittgenstein and Boswell.
Boast.
Boy and Education.
Branches of Water or Desire, The.
Brutalization under the Heart of Peace.

1. Business Jacob, the Angel Wrestler.
Butcher!, Borges, What a Shock!, The.
Carla Is a Horse Lover.
Closing Time at the Second Avenue Deli.
Coat of Arms.
2. Comment on "Business Jacob, the Angel
    Wrestler."
2. Comment on 1.
Confession of Heresy.
Conspiracy of Two against the World.
Conversation with a Dirty-Minded Little Girl.
Cooled Heels Lament against Frivolity, the
    Mask of Despair.
Cop-Shooting: On a Newspaper Photograph.
Courting Song: Attack! Attack! Attack!
Credo.
Crimes of Bernard, The.
Criticism of Bergson and Darwin.
Dark Tower, The.
Death's Chicken, Named Amelia.
Decimation before Phraäta, The.
Dedication for a Building.
Defendant.
Drunken Memories of Anne Sexton.
Dyng Seagull and the Great Whore of the
    World, The.
851.
Elegy for a Gifted Child.
Elegy for a Magician.
Elegy for a Puritan Conscience.
Elegy: "I know but will not tell."
Empirical Scene.
1. Enigma: Calm: Addressed to the Air.
Envy of Natural Formal Liberties, An.
Esthetics of Circumcision, The.
Expenses.
Fabrication of Ancestors.
Family Statements.
February Twelfth Birthday Statement.
Flower Grower in Aquarius.
For a Lost Girl.
For an Obligate Parasite.
For Euthanasia and Pain-Killing Drugs.
For Lisa.
For Masturbation.
Fragment on the British Museum.
Free Variation on a Translation from Greek.
From Heraclitus.
From Rome, for More Public Fountains in
    New York City.
From the Greek Anthology.
From the Theater Lobby.
Funeral Oration for a Mouse.
Gargoyle's Song for the Warming Trend.
General Prothalamion for Wartimes.
General Prothalamion in Populous Times.
Gifts Accompaniment, A.
Glad at the Cold (1955).
Grace for Thursday.
Hard-on Death.
Heart Attack in Bad Air.
His Hands Have Five Knives Each.
Holiday.
Homo Ludens: On an Argument with an Actor.
Hope against Pollution, A.
How We Heard the Name.
I Dreamed I Got a Letter from Ezra Pound.
I Have Met the Enemy and I Am Theirs.
Idyll of Ascension.
Imperial Song for Warmth.
Importation of Landscapes.
In Favor of a Free Public Library System.
In Memoriam: Aurelius Battaglia, and against
    His Tragic Sense of Life.
In Memoriam: Donald Mark Fall.
In Memoriam. Unfinished. For Robert Barlow.
    1950.
In the Forest.
Internal Migration: On Being on Tour.
Introduction to the Telephone.
Jack-Off of the Graveyard Shift, The.
Jewels of Indoor Glass.
Lament for Cellists and Jacqueline DuPré.
Landfall.
Last Statement for a Last Oracle.
Let Heroes Account to Love.

Letter to Donald Fall.
Letter to Eve.
Life and Death of the Cantata System, The.
Life Comparison.
Love and Money.
Love Song: Class Analysis.
Love Song: I and Thou.
Marxist Analysis of the Fifth Labor of
    Hercules.
Memorial Service for the Invasion Beach
    Where the Vacation in the Flesh Is Over.
Memories of a Boss in an Ad Agency.
Memories of 1936–7.
Memories of the Bowery.
Memories of Verdun.
Memory of Old Forms under Hell's Angels.
Mirror Perilous, The.
Mock Translation from the Greek.
Mockery Against the Irish Censorship.
Monologue for a Sixth Avenue Screamer.
Monologue of a Commercial Fisherman.
Moral Dream.
Morning at Speed Products.
Morning of the Dying Gigolo, The.
Morning Song.
Narcissus 2.
Natural Enemies of the Conch, The.
Night Scene before Combat.
Night Song for a Boy.
Nomenclature.
Noon's World.
Northern Statement for St. Cecilia.
Nostalgia for a Language.
Not to Choose.
Note.
Note of Quits.
Note: The Sea Grinds Things Up.
Notes Toward a Spring Offensive.
Oasis.
On a Baroque Clock.
On a Benign Bureaucratization of Death.
On a Desolation of the Animals at Night.
On a Dispossess Precept. 1.
On a Dispossess Precept. 2.
On a Fallen Statue Forbidden to the Women at
    Pompeii.
On a Hymn, Misprinted.
On a Myth. On a Conventional Wisdom.
On a Party.
On a Pocketknife. On Carrying.
On a Professional Couple in a Side-Show.
On a Seven-Day Diary.
On a Skunked Fox.
On a Snake.
On a Summer Goddess Who Should Be
    Nameless.
On a Travel Story from Wormwood Valley.
On Alexander and Aristotle, on a Black-on-
    Red Greek Plate.
On an Accident: On a Newspaper Story.
On an Architect.
On an East Wind from the Wars.
On an Old Advertisement and After a
    Photograph by Alfred Stieglitz.
On Being a Householder.
On Being Asked How Do You Feel after an
    Operation with Inadequate Anesthesia. This
    Is How I Feel.
On Being Easy in the Ritual of Separation.
On Being Out-Classed by Class.
On Being Unhappily in Love with Reason.
On Breeding, from Plutarch.
On Cabin Fever, On Boredom in the
    Countryside.
On Finding the Meaning of "Radiance."
On Finding the Tree of Life.
On Fingernails in Bloody Times.
On Fishing Being a Chancy Life.
On Flowers. On Negative Evolution.
On Gaining a Soul.
On Going Latent.
On Going up to Surgery in the Morning and in
    Favor of Pain-Killing Drugs.
On Halloween.
On Hat: On Vertical Mobility as a Concept.
On Herodotus.

On Hibernation in the Country.
On Hurricane Jackson.
On Inter-Relatedness in the Universe.
On Leaving Town.
On Lines 69–70, Book 4, of Virgil's Aeneid.
On Looking for Models.
On Naming a Baby Mimosa.
On Not Working and Then Working on
    Working and Then Not Working.
On Plumbing after an Air Raid.
On Rape Unattempted.
On Shields. Against World War 3.
On the Civil War on the East Coast of the
    United States of North America 1860–64.
On the Death of Norman Dukes.
On the Elk, Unwitnessed.
On the Liquidation of Zoology.
On the Long Island Railroad System.
On the Supposed Immorality of Orchids.
On Trading Time for Life by Work.
On Trees.
On Visiting a Veterans Hospital.
On Visiting Central Park Zoo.
On Voyage.
On Wearing Glasses.
On When McCarthy Was a Wolf among a
    Nation of Queer-Queers.
On Work.
On Zero.
One Waking in a Northern Fall.
Orpheus.
Oxymoronic Hospital Blues.
Passing through the Banford Tolls.
Perverse Explanation for Mutilated Statuary.
Philodendron.
Plague of Dead Sharks.
Poem: "After your first poetry reading."
Poem: "Always prudent but unprepared."
Poem: "Flowering balls!"
Poem for Elliot Carter on His 90th Birthday.
Poem: "In the old days either the plaintiff or
    the defendant won or lost."
Poem: "It is no wonder that new lovers run."
Poem: "Man applying gold leaf, A."
Poem: "Man with a box walked up to a woman
    with a boy, A."
Poem: "Oh that was not a scrap of flying Daily
    News."
Poem: "Person who can do, The."
Poem: "Pythagorean Silences, The."
Poem: "Tree was wet with the moon's, The."
Poem: "What was once an island with birds."
Poem: "Whatever was living is dead."
Poem: "What's the balm."
Portrait ("Captive flourished").
Portrait ("He wore the burnt-cork moustache").
Portrait ("What a beautiful young man").
Portrait from the Infantry.
Portrait in the Form of an Extended Conceit.
Portrait of a Lady.
Portrait of a Local Politician.
Prayer for One Leg.
Prayer: "God, I need a job because I need
    money."
Pretrial Hearing.
Prison Song.
Prose Poem.
Prothalamion of Quantum Mechanics.
Provincetown Totentanz.
Qualifications of Survivors.
Religious Question.
Remembering an Account Executive.
Repealer, The: "You're Too Wild."
Resolution of Hesitancies.
Retraction.
Riding Song for a Semi-Feudal Army, for
    Glubb Pasha, for Tortured Colonels.
Rising in Fall.
Romance of the Escaped Children.
Sailing to Jerusalem.
Saint Monday.
Sawyer's Rage against Trees Noble as Horses,
    A.
Scene (1946–7).
Self-Exhortation on Military Themes.
Sexist Lament: Ruin by Monitor.

Significance of Corn in American History, The.
Sixteen Lines on Marching.
So-Called Wild Horses of the Water, The.
Soliloquy: Ghost Dance for a Cripple.
"Space Is Not Merely a Background for
   Events, But Possesses an Autonomous
   Structure." —A. Einstein.
Speech for Aeneas.
Speech for Auden.
Speech to the Student Clowns at the Circus
   Clown School at Sarasota, Florida.
Spring Song for *Symplocarpus Fœtida* and Me.
Stability before Departure.
Stentor and Mourning.
Story for Actors.
Stutterer.
Suburban Exorcism.
Suffering Ophthalmologist, The.
Summer Gale.
Summer Heaven, Angels, Heaven.
Surviving the Hurricane.
Swing Shift Blues.
Takeoff on Armageddon —For Ronald Reagan.
Teacher's Lament.
Teacher's Vacation Lament in the Country.
There He Was.
Thesis, Antithesis and Nostalgia.
They Call It "Grumus Merdae."
This Morning Here.
Three as a Magic Number.
To a Colleague. From the Country.
To a Kid Who Believes in Astrology.
To a Red-Headed Do-Good Waitress.
To an Ex-Student.
To Paris: Fear of the Heights Reached.
Tourist Poem.
Touristic Note from the Gulf.
Transcribed Conversation in Praise of Cows.
Transformation.
Travel Advisory for a Night Shift.
Trial, A.
Tribute to Kafka for Someone Taken.
Triptych.
Two Comments on "Death's Chicken, Named
   Amelia."
Two Hatreds of Action.
Two Quits and a Drum, and Elegy for
   Drinkers.
Untitled Poem: "City is empty, like a
   dangerous area, The."
Untitled Poem: "Consternation in household!"
Untitled Poem: "Doctor and I have become
   intimate, The."
Untitled Poem: "I love the way the heel of my
   hand feels."
Untitled Poem: "I never saw any point."
Untitled Poem: "I used to enjoy the night-
   time."
Untitled Poem: "I'm in the house because."
Untitled Poem: "I'm waiting for you, but not
   purely."
Untitled Poem in Two Parts.
Untitled Poem: "I've promised that I will not
   care about things."
Untitled Poem: "Let them take to the air
   before."
Untitled Poem: "Monarchs, the butterflies, are
   commanded, The."
Untitled Poem: "Once on the beach at night I
   heard the waves."
Untitled Poem: "Once, one of my students read
   a book we had."
Untitled Poem: "One tries to be sober and
   respectable."
Untitled Poem: "One used to be able to say."
Untitled Poem: "Our German teacher used to
   say."
Untitled Poem: "Patients in the waiting room,
   The."
Untitled Poem: "Speciously individual."
Untitled Poem: "Two shots down and I'm
   exalted."
Untitled Poem: "What I remember most."
Untitled Poem: "When the window glass blows
   in."
Untitled Poem: "Who can abide whom or

what? That's."
Untitled Poem: "Why feel guilty because the
   death of a lover causes lust?."
Variation on a Theme by Stevens.
Variation on Themes by Roethke and Eliot.
Variation on "Winter's Onset from an
   Alienated Point of View."
Wall, Cave, and Pillar Statements, after Asôka.
War Duty.
Weeds as Partial Survivors.
What a Circus.
What Happened? What Do You Expect?
What It Really Means.
What the Hell, Rage, Give in to Natural
   Graces.
When I Was Drunk and Disorderly the Boston
   Policeman Told Me.
Why There Is No Class Solidarity in America I
   Read It In *The Times*. Aug. 2, 1987.
Winter for an Untenable Situation.
Winter Gale.
Winter's Onset from an Alienated Point of
   View.
Working World's Bloody Flux, The.

Dumas, Alexandre (1802–70)
   Lady of the Pearls, The. *sels*

Dunbar, Paul Laurence (1872–1906)
   Companion's Progress, A.
Absence.
Accountability.
Advice.
After a Visit.
After Many Days.
After the Quarrel.
After While.
Alexander Crummel—Dead.
Alice.
Anchored.
Angelina.
Ante-Bellum Sermon, An.
Appreciation.
At Candle-Lightin' Time.
At Cheshire Cheese.
At Loafing-Holt.
At Night.
At Sunset Time.
At the Tavern.
Awakening, The.
Back-Log Song, A.
Ballad: "I know my love is true."
Ballade: "By Mystic's banks I held my dream."
Banjo Song, A.
Barrier, The.
Behind the Arras.
Bein' Back Home.
Beyond the Years.
Black Samson of Brandywine.
Blue.
Bohemian, The.
Boogah Man, The.
Booker T. Washington.
Border Ballad, A.
Boy's Summer Song, A.
Breaking the Charm.
Bridal Measure, A.
By Rugged Ways.
By the Stream.
Cabin Tale, A.
Capture, The.
Career, A.
Change Has Come, The.
Change, The.
Changing Time.
Chappie, A.
Charity.
Chase, The.
Choice, A.
Chrismus Is A-Comin'
Chrismus on the Plantation.
Christmas.
Christmas Carol: "Ring out, ye bells!."
Christmas Folksong, A.
Christmas in the Heart.
"Chronic Kicker," The.
Circumstances Alter Cases.

Colored Band, The.
Colored Soldiers, The.
Columbian Ode.
Come and Kiss Me Sweet and Twenty.
Common Things.
Communion.
Comparison.
Compensation.
Comrade.
Concert, The.
Confessional.
Confidence, A.
Confirmation.
Conquerors, The.
Conscience and Remorse.
Content.
Coquette Conquered, A.
Corn-Song, A.
Corn-Stalk Fiddle, THe.
Crisis, The.
Critters' Dance, De.
Crumb, a Crumb, and a Little Seed, A.
Curiosity.
Curtain.
Dance, The.
Dat Ol' Mare o' Mine.
Dawn.
Day.
Deacon Jones' Grievance.
Dead.
Death.
Death of the First Born, The.
Death Song[, A].
Debt, The.
Delinquent, The.
Dely.
Deserted Plantation, The.
Despair.
Differences.
Dilettante, The: A Modern Type.
Dinah Kneading Dough.
Diplomacy.
Dirge for a Soldier.
Dirge: "Place this bunch of mignonette."
Disappointed.
Discovered.
Discovery, The.
Distinction.
Disturber, The.
Douglass.
Dove, The.
Dream Song I.
Dream Song II.
Dreamer, The.
Dreamin' Town.
Dreams.
Dreams.
Drizzle.
Drowsy Day, A.
Easter Ode, An.
Easy-Goin' Feller, An.
Emancipation.
Encouraged.
Encouragement.
End of the Chapter, The.
Equipment.
Ere Sleep Comes Down to Soothe the Weary
   Eyes.
Evening.
Expectation.
Faith.
Farewell Song.
Farewell to Arcady.
Farm Child's Lullaby, The.
Fisher Child's Lullaby, The.
Fishing.
Florida Night, A.
Foolin' wid de Seasons.
For the Man Who Fails.
For Theodore Roosevelt.
Forest Greeting, The.
Forever.
Fount of Tears, The.
Frederick Douglass.
Frolic, A.
From the Porch at Runnymede.

Fulfilment.
Garret, The.
Get Somebody Else.
God Reigns.
Goin' Back.
Goin' Home.
Golden Day, A.
Good-Night.
Gourd, The.
Grievance, A.
Growin' Gray.
Harriet Beecher Stowe.
Haunted Oak, The.
He Had His Dream.
Her Thought and His.
Home Longings.
Hope.
How Lucy Backslid.
How Shall I Woo Thee.
Howdy, Honey, Howdy!
Hunting Song.
Hymn, A: "Lead gently, Lord, and slow."
Hymn: "O li'l lamb out in de col'."
Hymn: "When storms arise."
If.
If I Could But Forget.
In a English Garden.
In August.
In May.
In Summer.
In Summer Time.
In the Morning.
In the Tents of Akbar.
Inspiration.
Invitation to Love.
Ione.
Itching Heels.
Jack Frost at Bedtime.
James Whitcomb Riley.
Jealous.
Jilted.
Joggin' Erlong.
John Boyle O'Reilly.
Johnny Speaks.
Just Whistle a Bit.
Justice.
Keep A-Pluggin' Away.
Keep a Song Up on de Way.
Kidnaped.
King is Dead, The.
Knight, The.
Lager Beer.
Land o' Used to Be, The.
Lapse, The.
Lawyers' Ways, The.
Lazy Day, A.
Lesson, The.
Letter, A.
Life.
Life's Tragedy.
Light, The.
Light was on the golden sands, The.
Li'l' Gal.
Lily of the Valley, The.
Limitations.
Lincoln.
Little Brown Baby.
Little Christmas Basket, A.
Little Lucy Landman.
Liza May.
Lonesome.
Long Ago.
'Long To'ds Night.
Longing.
Looking-Glass, The.
Lost Dream, A.
Love.
Love and Grief.
Love Despoiled.
Love Is a Star.
Love is the light of the world, my dear.
Love Letter, A.
Love Song, A: "Ah, love, my love is like a cry
   in the night."
Love-Song: "If Death should claim me for her
   own to-day."

Lover and the Moon, The.
Lover's Lane.
Love's Apotheosis.
Love's Castle.
Love's Chastening.
Love's Draft.
Love's Humility.
Love's Phases.
Love's Pictures.
Love's Seasons.
Lullaby: "Bedtime's come fu' little boys."
Lullaby: "Kiver up yo' haid, my little lady."
Lyric, A: "My lady love lives far away."
Made to Order Smile, The.
Madrigal, A: "Dream days of fond delight and
   hours."
Mare Rubrum.
Master-Player, The.
Masters, The.
Matter of Locality, A.
Meadow Lark, The.
Melancholia.
Memorial Day.
Memory of Martha, The.
Merry Autumn.
Misapprehension.
Misty Day, A.
Monk's Walk, The.
Morning.
Morning Song of Love.
Mortality.
Murdered Lover, The.
Musical, A.
My Best Girl.
My Corn-Cob Pipe.
My dear love died last night.
My Lady of Castle Grand.
My Little March Girl.
My Love Irene.
My Sort o' Man.
My Sweet Brown Gal.
Mystery, The.
Mystic Sea, The.
Nature and Art.
Negro Love Song, A.
News, The.
Night.
Night, Dim Night.
Night of Love.
Night on the Chesapeake.
Noddin' by de Fire.
Noon.
Nora: A Serenade.
Not They Who Soar!
Nutting Song.
October.
Ode for Memorial Day.
Ode to Ethiopia.
Oh little fledgling out of the nest.
Ol' Tunes, The.
Old.
Old Apple-Tree, The.
Old Cabin, The.
Old Front Gate, The.
Old High School and the New, The.
Old Homestead, The.
Old Memory, An.
Old Story, The.
On a Clean Book.
On the Death of W. C.
On the Dedication of Dorothy Hall.
On the River.
On the Road.
On the Sea Wall.
One Life.
Opportunity.
Our Martyred Soldiers.
Over the Hills.
Paradox, The.
Parted ("Breeze is blowin'").
Parted ("She wrapped her soul").
Parted ("Beyond the cornfields").
Party, The.
Passage, The.
Passion and Love.
Path, The.

Phantom Kiss, The.
Philosophy.
Photograph, The.
Phyllis.
Place Where the Rainbow Ends, The.
Plantation Child's Lullaby, The.
Plantation Melody, A.
Plantation Portrait, A.
Plea, A.
Poet and His Song, The.
Poet and the Baby, The.
Poet, The.
Pool, The.
Poor Withered Rose.
Possession.
Possum.
Possum Trot.
Prayer, A: "O Lord, the hard-won miles."
Precedent.
Preference, A.
Premonition.
Preparation.
Prometheus.
Promise.
Protest.
Puttin' the Baby Away.
Question, A.
Quilting, The.
Rain-Songs.
Real Question, The.
Religion.
Reluctance.
Remembered.
Resignation.
Response.
Retort.
Retrospection.
Riding to Town.
Right to Die, The.
Right's Security.
Rising of the Storm, The.
Rivals, The.
River of Ruin, The.
Roadway, A.
Robert Gould Shaw.
Roses.
Roses and Pearls.
Sailor's Song, A.
Sand-Man, The.
Scamp.
Sea speaks to me of you, The.
Secret, The.
Seedling, The.
She Gave Me a Rose.
She Told Her Beads.
Ships That Pass in the Night.
Signs of the Times.
Silence.
Sling Along.
Slow Through the Dark.
Snowin'
Soliloquy of a Turkey.
Song, A: "On a summer's day as I sat by a
   stream."
Song, A: "Thou art the soul of a summer's
   day."
Song: "Bee hit sip some honey f'om de
   matermony vine, De."
Song: "My heart to thy heart."
Song of Summer.
Song, The: "My soul, lost in the music's mist."
Song: "Wintah, summah, snow er shine."
Songs.
Sonnet: "Emblem of blasted hope and lost
   desire."
Sparrow, The.
Speakin' at de Cou't-House.
Speakin' o' Christmas.
Spellin'-Bee, The.
Spiritual, A.
Spring Fever.
Spring Song.
Spring Wooing, A.
Starry Night, A.
Stirrup Cup, The.

Suitor, The.
Sum, The.
Summer in the South.
Summer Night, A.
Summer Pastoral, A.
Summer's Night, A.
Sunset.
Suppose.
Sympathy ("I know what the caged bird feels").
Sympathy ("Tear another tear brings forth").
Temptation.
Thanksgiving Poem, A.
Then and Now.
Theology.
There are brilliant heights of sorrow.
Thou Art My Lute.
Till the Wind Gets Right.
Time to Tinker 'Roun'!
To a Captious Critic.
To a Dead Friend.
To a Lady Playing the Harp.
To a Poet and a Lady.
To a Violet Found on All Saints' Day.
To Alice Dunbar.
To an Ingrate.
To Booker T. Washington.
To Dan.
To Dr. James Newton Matthews, Mason, Ill.
To E. H. K.
To Her.
To J. Q.
To Kelly Miller, Jr.
To Louise.
To Mary Church Terrell.
To Miss Mary Britton.
To Pfrimmer.
To the Eastern Shore.
To the Memory of Mary Young.
To the Miami.
To the Road.
To the South.
Trouble in de Kitchen.
Tryst, The.
Turning of the Babies in the Bed, The.
Tuskegee Song.
Twell de Night Is Pas'
Twilight.
Two Little Boots.
Two Songs.
Unexpressed.
Unlucky Apple, The.
Unsung Heroes, The.
Vagrants.
Valse, The.
Vengeance is Sweet.
Veteran, The.
Virginia Reel, A.
Visitor, The.
Voice of the Banjo, The.
Wadin' in de Crick.
Waiting.
Warm Day in Winter, A.
Warrior's Prayer, The.
Way T'ings Come, De.
We Wear the Mask.
Welcome Address.
Weltschmertz.
W'en I Gits Home.
What's the Use.
When a Feller's Itchin' to be Spanked.
When All Is Done.
When de Co'n Pone's Hot.
When Dey 'Listed Colored Soldiers.
When Malindy Sings.
When Sam'l Sings.
When the Old Man Smokes.
When Winter Darkening All Around.
Whip-Poor-Will and Katy-Did.
with music.
Whittier.
Why Fades a Dream?
Wind and the Sea, The.
Winter-Song.
Winter's Approach.
Winter's Day, A.
With the Lark.

Wooing, The.
Worn Out.
Wraith, The.
Yesterday and Tomorrow.

Dunbar, William (c.1465–c.1530)
Amendis [*or* Amends] to the Telyouris [*or* Tailors] and Sowtaris [*or* Soutaris *or* Soutars *or* Shoemakers].
Ballat [*or* Ballad] of Our Lady, [Ane].
Ballat of the Abbot of Tungland, A.
Ballat of the Passioun, Ane.
Be diuers wyis and operatiounes.
Be mery, man, and tak nocht fer in mynd.
Be ye ane luvar, think ye nocht ye suld.
Complane I wald, wist I quhome till.
Done is a battell [*or* battle] on the dragon blak [*or* black].
Doverrit with dreme, devysing in my slummer.
Dremand me thocht that I did heir.
Dumbaris Dirige to the King.
Eftir geving I speik of taking.
Flyting of Dumbar [*or* Dunbar] and Kennedie [*or* Kennedy], The.
Four maner of folkis ar evill to pleis.
Fredome, honour and nobilnes.
Full oft I mvse and hes in thocht.
Gladethe, thoue queyne of Scottis regioun.
Goldyn [*or* Golden] Targe, The.
He that hes gold and grit riches.
How [*or* Followis How] Dumbar wes Desyrd to be ane Freir.
How sowld I rewill me or quhat wyis.
I seik [*or* seek] about[e] this warld onstable [*or* world unstable].
I thocht lang quhill sum lord come hame.
Illuster Lodouick, of France most cristin king.
In May as that Aurora did vpspring.
In Prais[e] of Women [*or* Wemen].
In secreit place this hyndir [*or* hindir] nycht [*or* nicht].
In to thir dirk and drublie day[i]s.
In vice most vicius he excellis.
Lament for the Makaris [*or* Makars or Makers].
Lang heff I maed of ladyes quhytt.
Lucina schyning in silence of the nycht.
Madam, your men said thai wald ryd.
Magryme, The.
Man, sen thy lyf is ay in weir.
Maner of Passyng to Confessioun, The.
Memento, homo, quod cinis es.
Murelandis man of vplandis mak, Ane.
Musing allone this hinder nicht.
My hartis tresure and swete assured fo.
My lordis of chalker, pleis yow to heir.
My prince in God, gif the guid grace.
Now cumis aige quhair yewth hes bene.
Now lythis off ane gentill knycht.
O gracious princes guid and fair.
O wreche [*or* wretch], be war [*or* beware], this warld [*or* world] will wend the[e] fro.
Off benefice, sir, at everie feist.
Off every asking followis nocht.
Off Februar the fyiftene nycht.
Of[f] Lentren in the first mornyng [*or* morning].
Petition of the Gray Horse, Auld Dunbar, [The].
Quha will behald of luve the chance.
Quhat is this lyfe bot ane straucht way to deid.
Quhen Merche wes with variand windis past.
Quho thinkis that he hes sufficence.
Quhom to sall I compleine my wo.
Renownit, ryall, right reuerend and serene.
Richt arely one Ask Wedinsday.
Rorate, celi, desuper!
Saluiour, suppois my sensualite.
Sanct saluatour, send siluer sorrow!
Schir, at this feist of benefice.
Schir, for your grace, bayth nicht and day.
Schir, I complane off iniuris.
Schir, ye haue [*or* have] mony seruitouris [*or* servitouris].
Schir, yit remember as befoir.
Sen that I am a presoneir.
Sir Ihon Sinclair begowthe to dance.

Tabill of Confessioun, The.
Testament of [Mr.] Andro Kennedy, The.
Thir ladeis fair that maks repair.
This hinder nycht, halff sleiping as I lay.
This hindir nycht in Dumfermeling.
This nycht in my sleip I wes agast.
This waverand warldis wretchidnes.
Thow that in hewin for our saluatioun.
To a Lady[e].
To Aberdein.
To dwell in court, my freind, gife that thow list.
To speik of gift or almous deidis.
To speik of science, craft or sapience.
To the Merchant[i]s of Edinburgh.
Tretis [*or* Book] of the Tua Mariit Wemen [*or* Two Married Women] and the Wedo[w] [*or* Widow], The.
Wardraipper of Wenus boure, The.

Duncan, Robert (1919–88)
Achilles' Song.
Adoration of the Virgin, The.
After a Long Illness.
After Reading H.D.'s *Hermetic Definitions*.
Albigenses, The.
Among My Friends.
Ballad of the Enamord Image, The.
Banners, The.
Beginning of Writing, The.
Bending the Bow.
Book of Resemblances, A.
Bring It Up from the Dark.
Circulations of the Song.
Dante Études, *sels.*
Descriptions of Imaginary Poetries.
Dreamers, The.
Festivals, The.
First Invention on the Theme of the Adam.
For a Muse Meant.
For a Song of the Languagers.
Four Songs the Night Nurse Sang.
Helmet of Goliath, The.
Human Communion. Traces, The.
Huon of Bordeaux.
I Am a Most Fleshly Man.
Illustrative Lines.
Imagining in Writing.
In Waking.
Kingdom of Jerusalem, The.
Maiden, The.
Mirror, The.
My Mother Would Be a Falconress.
Nel Mezzo del Cammin di Nostra Vita.
Often I Am Permitted to Return to a Meadow.
Passage Over Water.
Passages, *sels.*
Poem Beginning with a Line by Pindar, A.
Poem in Stretching, A.
Poetry, a Natural Thing.
Poetry Disarranged.
Reaper, The.
Roots and Branches.
Salvages: An Evening Place.
Sentinels, The.
Song of the Borderguard, The.
Source.
Structure of Rime, The, *sels.*
This Place Rumord to Have Been Sodom.
Upon Taking Hold.
Writing as Writing.
Years As Catches, The.

E

Eberhart, Nelle Richmond
New Entrepreneurial Plan.
Eberhart, Richard (b. 1904)
Adam Cast Forth.
Aesthetics after War.
Airman Considers His Power, An.
Am I My Neighbor's Keeper.
American Hakluyt.
Analogue of Unity in Multeity.
Angels, The.

Anima.
Anxiety I Felt in Guanajuato, The.
Apple Buds.
As If You Had Never Been.
Assassin, The.
At Night.
At The Canoe Club.
At the End of the War.
Attitudes.
Austere Poem.
Autumnal.
Ball Game.
Bells of a Chinese Temple, The.
Big Rock.
Birth and Death.
Birth of the Spirit, The.
Blessed Are the Angels in Heaven.
Bones of Coleridge, The.
Book of Nature, The.
Bower, The.
Breathless, The.
Broken Pen, The.
Broken Wing Theory.
Brotherhood of Men.
Burden.
Burr Oaks.
By the Stream.
Cage, The.
Cancer Cells, The.
Caravan of Silence.
Centennial For Whitman.
Ceremonial.
Ceremony By the Sea, A.
Child, The.
Christmas Tree.
Clam Diggers and Diggers of Sea Worms, The.
Clerihew for Alan Gaylord, A.
Coast of Maine.
Commas in Wintertime.
Commitment, A.
Concord Cats.
Configuration.
Cousin Florence.
Cover Me Over.
Critic With His Pained Eye, The.
Dam Neck, Virginia.
Day-Bed, The.
Dead Skunk.
Death in the Mines.
Deep Fishing.
Despair.
Difficulty of Ideas, The.
Dream, A.
Dream Journey of the Head and Heart.
Dream, The.
Dry Rot, The.
Edgar Lee Masters.
Emblem.
Emerson's Concord.
Emily Dickinson.
Enigma, The.
Equivalence of Gnats and Mice.
Evaluation Under a Pine Tree, Lying On Pine
    Needles, An.
Evening Bird Song.
Evil.
Examination of Psyche: Thoughts of Home.
Experience Evoked.
Explorer on Main Street, The.
Extremity.
Fables of the Moon.
Face, Ocean.
Fantasy of a Small Idea.
Fisher Cat, The.
Flag, The.
Flow of Thought.
Flux.
For a Lamb.
Forgotten Rock, The.
Formative Mastership.
Forms of the Human.
Fortune's Mist.
Four Exposures.
Four Lakes' Days.
Fragment of New York, 1929.
Froth.

Full of Joy Do Not Know; They Need Not,
    The.
Fury of Aerial Bombardment, The.
Garden God, The.
Gesture, The.
Giantess, The.
Gnat on My Paper.
Gnats.
Go to the Shine That's on a Tree.
Goal of Intellectual Man, The.
God and Man.
Gods of Washington, D.C, The.
Going.
Going Backward Going Forward.
Going to Maine.
Grave Piece.
Great Praises.
Great Principles Are Thrown Down by Time.
Groundhog Revisiting, The.
Groundhog, The.
Gulled.
Half-bent Man.
Hamlet Father, The.
Hand and the Shadow, The.
Hand, The.
Hard Structure of the World, The.
Hardening into Print.
Hardy Perennial.
Harvard Stadium.
Hatred of the Old River.
Haystack, The.
Height of Man, The.
Hill Dream of Youth, Thirty Years Later.
Homage to the North.
Hoot Owls.
Hop-Toad, The.
Hornets by the Sill.
Horse Chestnut Tree, The.
How It Is.
Human Being Is a Lonely Creature, The.
Humanist, The.
I Walked Out to the Graveyard to See the
    Dead.
I Walked over the Grave of Henry James.
I Went to See Irving Babbitt.
I Will Not Dare to Ask One Question.
Ichetucknee.
Ideal and the Real, The.
Ides of March, The.
'If I Could Only Live at the Pitch That Is near
    Madness'
Illusion of Eternity, The.
Imagining How It Would Be to Be Dead.
In a Hard Intellectual Light.
In after Time.
In Prisons of Established Craze.
In the Garden.
Inchiquin Lake, Penobscot Bay.
Incidence of Flight.
Incomparable Light, The.
Indian Pipe.
Ineffable, The.
Ives.
John Finley.
John Ledyard.
Kaire.
Key West.
Killer, The.
Kinaesthesia.
La Crosse at Ninety Miles an Hour.
Lament of a New England Mother, The.
Laocoön.
Largess, The.
Later or Sooner.
Learning from Nature.
Legend of Viable Women, A.
Let the Tight Lizard on the Wall.
Life and Death.
Life as Visionary Spirit.
Light From Above.
Light, Time, Dark.
Line of Verse of Yeats, A.
Lions Copulating.
Listing.
Long Swing, The.
Long Term Suffering.

Looking at the Stars.
Looking At The Stars.
Looking Head On.
Loon Call, A.
Lorca.
Loss.
Lost Children, The.
Lost, The.
Love among The Ruins.
Love Poem, A: "I am the lightness that I
    know."
Lucubration.
Lyric Absolute, The.
Maine Roustabout, A.
Mais L'Amour Infini Me Montera Dans
    L'Ame.
Man and Nature.
Man Who Was Blown Down by the Wind, A.
Man's Greed and Envy Are So Great.
Man's Type.
Marrakech.
Matador.
May Evening.
Maze.
Meaningless Poem.
Meditation, A.
Meditation Two.
Mediterranean Song.
Memory.
Memory.
Mind and Nature.
Mistaken Identity.
Moment of Equilibrium among the Islands.
Moment of Vision, The.
My Bones Flew Apart.
My Brains Are Slipping in the Fields of Eros.
My Golden and My Fierce Assays.
Mystery of the Abstract.
Mystical Beast in the Shadows, The.
Mysticism Has Not the Patience To Wait for
    God's Revelation.
Necessity.
New England Bachelor, A.
New Hampshire, February.
News.
Nexus.
1934.
Noble Man, The.
Nostalgia for Edith Sitwell.
Nothing But Change.
Now Is The Air Made of Chiming Balls.
O Wild Chaos!
Oak, The.
Ode to Silence.
Ode to the Chinese Paper Snake.
Oedipus.
Off Spectacle Island.
Old Dichotomy: Choosing Sides.
Old Fashioned American Business Man, An.
Old Question.
Old Tom.
Old Tree by the Penobscot.
On a Squirrel Crossing the Road in Autumn, in
    New England.
On Returning to a Lake in Spring.
On Seeing an Egyptian Mummy in Berlin,
    1932.
On Shooting Particles beyond the World.
On the Fragility of Mind.
On the Subtle Man.
Once More, O Ye.
Only in the Dream.
Opposition.
Opulence.
Orchard.
Ospreys in Cry.
Parker River, The.
Passage, The.
Perception as a Guided Missile.
Placation of Reality.
Place, The.
Play, The.
Poem as Trajectory, The.
Poet, The.
Poetry and Games.
Portrait of Rilke.

Project, The.
Prometheus.
Protagonists.
Quanta.
Quarrel with a Cloud.
Question Mark.
R. G. E.
Rape of the Cataract, The.
Reading Room, The New York Public Library.
Recapitulation, The.
Recognition.
Recollection of Childhood.
Redemption.
Refrains.
Request.
Request for Offering.
Retrospective Forelook.
Return of Odysseus, The.
Return, The.
Rifkin Movement.
River Water Music.
Ruby Daggett.
Rumination.
Sacrifice, The.
Sagacity.
Sailing to Buck's Harbor.
Sainte Anne De Beaupré.
Salem.
Sanders Theater.
Santa Claus in Oaxaca.
Scarf of June, The.
Scouring, The.
Sea Burial from the Cruiser *Reve*.
Sea-Hawk.
Sea-Ruck.
Sea Storm.
Seals, Terns, Time.
Seasons, The.
Secret Heart, The.
Seeing is Deceiving.
Sestina: "I die, no matter what I do I die."
Ship Burning and a Comet All in One Day, A.
Skier and the Mountain, The.
Slow Boat Ride.
Snow Cascades.
Snowfall, A.
Snowy Owl.
Solace.
Soldier Rejects His Times Addressing His
    Contemporaries, A.
Sometimes the Longing for Death.
Somewhere Else.
Soul.
Soul Longs to Return Whence It Came, The.
Sphinx.
Spider, The.
Spite Fence.
Spring Mountain Climb.
Standards, The.
Statue of Liberty.
Stealth and Subtleties of Growth.
Stopping a Kaleidoscope.
Suicide Note.
Suite in Prison.
Summer Landscape.
Sunday in October.
Supreme Authority of the Imagination, The.
Swallows Return, The.
Swinging Bridge, The.
Testament, A.
Testimony.
There Is an Evil in the Air.
This Fevers Me.
Three Kids.
Throwing the Apple.
Throwing Yourself Away.
Thrush Song at Dawn.
Time Passes.
To Auden on His Fiftieth.
To Evan.
To Harriet Monroe.
To Kenya Tribesmen, the Turkana.
To the Field Mice.
To the Mad Poets.
To William Carlos Williams.
Tobacconist of Eighth Street, The.

Track.
Transfer, The.
Transformation.
Tree Swallows.
Triptych.
Truncated Bird, The.
Truth, The.
Trying to Hold It All Together.
21st Century Man.
Two Loves.
Ultimate Song.
Undercliff Evening.
United 555.
Ur Burial.
Usurper.
Van Black, an Old Farmer in His Dell.
Vastness and Indifference of the World, The.
Velvet Rocks.
Verbalist of Summer, The.
Vermont Idyll.
Villanelle: "Christ is walking in your blood
    today."
Virgin, The.
Vision.
Vision through Timothy.
Voyage, The.
Waiting To Lean to the Master's Command.
Way Out, A.
Ways and Means.
Wedding on Cape Rosier, A.
Wedding, The.
What Gives.
When Doris Danced.
When Golden Flies Upon My Carcass Come.
Whenever I See Beauty I See Death.
Where Are Those High and Haunting Skies.
White Pines, Felled 1984.
Why.
Wild Life and Tamed Life.
Wild Swans of Inverane, The.
Winter Kill.
Wisdom of Insecurity, The.
Words.
World War.
Worldly Failure.
Yonder.
You Think They Are Permanent But They
    Pass.
Young and the Old, the.
Young Greek, Killed In The Wars, A.
Young Hunter, The.

Eichendorff, Joseph, Freiherr von (1788–1857)
Moonlight Night.

Eliot, T. S. (Thomas Stearns) (1888–1965)
Afternoon.
Agony in the Garret, An, *sels.*
Airs of Palestine, No. 2.
Animula.
Ash Wednesday [*or* Ash-Wednesday].
Aunt Helen.
Bacchus and Ariadne; 2nd Debate between the
    Body and Soul.
Ballade pour la grosse Lulu.
Boston Evening Transcript, The.
Burbank with a Baedeker: Bleistein with a
    Cigar.
Burnt Dancer, The.
Choruses from "The Rock."
Columbo and Bolo Verses.
Conversation Galante.
Convictions (Curtain Raiser).
Cooking Egg, A.
Coriolan.
Cousin Nancy.
Cultivation of Christmas Trees, The.
Dans le Restaurant.
Dedication to My Wife, A.
Defense of the Islands.
Do I know how I feel? Do I know what I
    think?
Easter: Sensations of April.
Engine, The.
Entretien dans un parc.
Eyes That Last I Saw in Tears.
First Caprice in North Cambridge.
First Debate between the Body and Soul.

Five-Finger Exercises.
Four Quartets.
Fourth Caprice in Montparnasse.
Fragments: "There was a jolly tinker came
    across the sea."
Gerontion.
Goldfish (Essence of Summer Magazines).
He said: this universe is very clever.
Hidden under the heron's wing.
Hippopotamus, The.
Hollow Men, The.
Humouresque.
Hysteria.
In silent corridors of death.
In the Department Store.
Inside the gloom / Of a garret room.
Interlude: in a Bar.
Interlude in London.
Introspection.
Journey of the Magi.
La Figlia Che Piange.
Landscapes.
Le Directeur.
Lines for an Old Man.
Love Song of J. Alfred Prufrock, The.
Love Song of St. Sebastian, The.
Lune de Miel.
Mandarins.
Marina.
Mélange Adultère de Tout.
Mr. Apollinax.
Mr. Eliot's Sunday Morning Service.
Morning at the Window.
Note on War Poetry, A.
O lord, have patience.
Ode on Independence Day, July 4th 1918.
Oh little voices of the throats of men.
Opera.
Paysage Triste.
Petit Epître.
Portrait of a Lady.
Preludes.
Rhapsody on a Windy Night.
Second Caprice in North Cambridge.
Silence.
Smoke that gathers blue and sinks, The.
Song for Simeon, A.
Suite Clownesque.
Suppressed Complex.
Sweeney Agonistes.
Sweeney among the Nightingales.
Sweeney Erect.
To the Indians Who Died in Africa.
To Walter de la Mare.
Tristan Corbière.
Triumph of Bullshit, The.
Waste Land, The.
While you were absent in the lavatory.
Whispers of Immortality.
Wind Sprang Up at Four o'Clock, The.

Éluard, Paul (Eugène Grindel) (1895–1952)
Confections.
Curfew.
From the Inside.
From the Outside.
Lady Love.
Out of Sight in the Direction of My Body.
Scarcely Disfigured.
Scene.
Second Nature.
Uncertain of the Crime.
Universe-Solitude.
Wolf, A.
Wolf, A.

**Elyas Yusof Nezami [*or* Nisami] Ganjavi] Elyas
Ysuof Nezami Ganjavi (c.1141–1217)**
While roses bloomed along the plain.

Emerson, Edward Bliss
Last Farewell, The.

Emerson, Ralph Waldo (1803–82)
Adirondacs, The.
Ah! not to me these dreams belong.
Ah strange strange strange.
All that thy virgin soul can ask be thine.
All the great & good.
All things rehearse.

Alone in Rome! Why Rome is lonely too.
Alphonso of Castile.
Always day & night.
Amulet, The.
Ancient drop of feudal blood, An.
Ancient lady who dwelt in Rome, An.
And as the light divided the dark.
And do I waste my time.
And Ellen, when the greybeard years.
And he like me is not too proud.
And hungry Debt beseiged my door.
And man of wit & mark.
And rival Coxcombs with enamored stare.
And the best gift of God.
And though he dearly prized the bards of fame.
And when I am entombed in my place.
Apology, The.
April.
Archangel Hope / Looks to the azure cope,
  The.
Around the man who seeks a noble end.
Art.
As I walked in the woods.
As the drop feeds its fated flower.
Ask not treasures from his store.
Asmodaean feat be mine, The.
Astræa.
At last the poet spoke.
At Plymouth in the friendly crowd.
At Sea, September 1833.
Atom displaces all atoms beside, The.
Atom from atom yawns as far.
Awed I behold once more.
Bacchus.
Bard or dunce is blest, but hard.
Be of good cheer, brave spirit; steadfastly.
Beauty.
Bended to fops who bent to him.
Berrying.
Best of life is presence of a muse, The.
Bird was gone the ghastly trees, The.
Blackbird's song the blackbird's song, The.
Blight.
Bluebeard. Let the gentle wife prepare.
Bohemian Hymn, The.
Borrow Urania's subtile wings.
Boston.
Boston Hymn.
Brahma.
Brave Empedocles defying fools, The.
Brother, no decrepitude.
Burn your literary verses.
But as this fugitive sunlight.
But God will keep his promise yet.
But if thou do thy best.
But Nature whistled with all her winds.
But never yet the man was found.
But O to see his solar eyes.
By art, by music, overthrilled.
By kinds I keep my kinds in check.
By the unacknowledged tie.
Character.
Chartist's Complaint, The.
Chladni strewed on glass the sand.
Circles.
Civil world will much forgive, The.
Cloud upon cloud / Clouds after rain.
Cloud upon cloud / The world is seeming.
Coil of space the cones of light, The.
Coin the daydawn into lines.
Comfort with a purring cat.
Compensation.
Compensation.
Comrade of the snow & wind.
Comrade or the book is good, The.
Concord Hymn.
Coral worm beneath the sea, The.
Crowning hour when bodies vie with souls,
  The.
Culture.
Cup of life is not so shallow, The.
Cupido.
Dangerous gift & grace is mine, A.
Dark Flower of Cheshire garden.
Days.
Days pass over me, The.

Day's Ration, The.
Dear are the pleasant memories.
Dear Brother, Would You Know the Life.
Dear Ellen, many a golden year.
Dervish whined to *Said*, The.
Dirge: "Knows he who tills this lonely field."
Discontented Poet: A Masque, The.
Divine Inviters! I accept.
Do that which you can do.
Dost thou not hear me Ellen.
Dull uncertain brain, A.
Dust unto dust! and shall no more be said.
Each and All.
Earth, The.
Easy to match what others do.
Elizabeth Hoar.
Enough is done highminded friend go sleep.
Eros.
Etienne de la Boéce.
Eve roved in Paradise, I've heard.
Ever the Rock of Ages melts.
Experience.
Fable: "Mountain and the squirrel, The."
Fame.
Far seen the river glides below.
Fate.
Fate.
Few are free / All might be.
Fine presentiments controlled him.
For deathless powers to verse belong.
For every god.
For fifteen winter days.
For Genius made his cabin wide.
For joy & beauty planted it.
For Lucifer, that old athlete.
For Lyra yet shall be the pole.
For Nature true & like in every place.
For that a man is a mark.
For what need I of book or priest.
Forbearance.
Forbore the ant hill, shunned to tread.
Forerunners.
Freedom.
Friends to me are frozen wine.
Friendship.
From a far mountain creeping down.
From Frodmer's Drama "The Friends."
From high to higher forces.
From Nature's beginning.
From the stores of eldest Matter.
Future, The.
Genial spark the poet felt, The.
Gentle Spring has charmed the earth.
Give All to Love.
Γνῶθι Σεαυτον.
Go boldly forth, and feast on being's banquet.
Go if thou wilt ambrosial Flower.
Go into the garden.
Go out into Nature and plant trees.
God only knew how Saadi dined.
God The Lord save Massachusetts.
Gods walk in the breath of the woods, The.
Good-bye.
Good Charles the springs adorer.
Grace.
Guy.
Hamatreya.
Hard is it to persuade the public mind of its
  plain duty & true interest.
Harp, The.
Have ye seen the caterpillar.
He could condense cerulean ether.
He lives not who can refuse me.
He loved to watch & wake.
He must have / Droll fancies sometimes cross
  his quiet thoughts.
He walked the streets of great New York.
He whom God had thus preferred.
Hearst thou, sweet spirit, thou hast heard
  before.
Heartily heartily / Nothing be false.
Heartily heartily sing.
Heavy blue chain, The.
Hermione.
Heroism.
His instant thought the Poet spoke.

History, *sels*.
History & prophecy are alike.
Hold of the Maker, not the made.
Holidays.
Honor bright o muse.
House, The.
How drearily in College hall.
Humble-Bee, The.
Husband has the nearest acres, The.
Hymn Sung at the Second Church, Boston, at
  the Ordination of Rev. Chandler Robbins.
I am alone. Sad is my solitude.
I am an exile from my home; heavily.
I am not black in my mind.
I call her beautiful;—she says.
I cannot find a place so lonely.
I care not whither I may go.
I grieve that better souls than mine.
I have an arrow that can find its mark.
I have found a nobler love.
I have no brothers & no peers.
I have supped with the gods tonight.
I know the appointed hour.
I leave the book, I leave the wine.
I left my dreamy page & sallied forth.
I live among ideal men.
I love thy music, mellow bell.
I must not borrow light.
I never knew but one.
I rake no coffined clay, nor publish wide.
I sat upon the ground.
I spread my gorgeous sail.
I to my garden went.
I use the knife.
I wear no badge; no tinsel star.
I will not hesitate to speak the word.
I will not live out of me.
Idealism.
If bright the sun, he tarries.
If curses be the wage of love.
If he go apart.
If thy body pine.
If wishes would carry me over the land.
Illusions.
Illusions like the tints of pearl.
In dreamy woods, what forms abound.
In Memoriam.
In My Garden.
In the deep heart of man a poet dwells.
In this sour world, o summerwind.
In Walden wood the chickadee.
Initial, Dæmonic, and Celestial Love.
Inscription on a Well in Memory of the
  Martyrs of the War.
Inspired we must forget our books.
Intellect.
Intellect.
Intellect / Gravely broods apart on joy.
Is Jove immortal / So is Cerberus at his portal.
Is the pace of nature slow?
It takes a philosopher or fool.
I've found the dainty malice out.
James Russell Lowell.
Kind & holy were the words.
King. If farmers make my land secure.
Know he who tills this lonely field.
Land was all electric, The.
Leave me, Fear! thy throbs are base.
Let not conceited sages laugh aloud.
Letters ("Every day brings a ship").
Letters ("My tongue is prone to lose the way").
Life.
Life is great / Men are small.
Like vaulters in the circus round.
Limits.
Lines on the Death of Miss M. B. Farnham.
Lobster-car, boat, or fishbasket.
Look danger in the eye it vanishes.
Loss and Gain.
Love and Thought.
Love / Asks nought his brother cannot give.
Lover's Petition.
Low December vault in June be up-lifted high.
Maia.
Maiden Speech of the Æolian Harp.
Manners.

Mask thy wisdom with delight.
May.
May-Day.
Merlin.
Merlin's Song.
Merops.
Miracle, The.
Mithridates.
Monadnoc.
More sweet than my refrain.
Motto to "Considerations by the Way."
Motto to "Fate."
Motto to "Gifts."
Motto to "New England Reformers."
Motto to "Power."
Motto to "The Poet."
Muse / Can at pleasure use, The.
Music.
Musketaquid.
My days roll by me like a train of dreams.
My Garden.
My Thoughts.
Nahant.
Nature.
Nature 1.
Nature 2.
Nature [1836].
Nature [1844].
Nature saith / I am not infinite.
Nature says, / These craggy hills that front the dawn.
Nature will not lose.
Natures web star broidered.
Nemesis.
New England Capitalist.
No fate, save by the victim's fault, is low.
No song so tuneful, quoth the fox.
Nominalist and Realist.
None spares another yet it pleases me.
No. 13 Hymn Written in Concord Sept. 1814.
Nun's Aspiration.
O Boston city lecture-hearing.
O sun! take off thy hood of clouds.
O what are heroes prophets men.
O What have I to do.
O what is Heaven but the fellowship.
October woods, wherein.
Ode, Inscribed to W.H. Channing.
Ode Sung in the Town Hall.
Ode to Beauty.
Oil & Wine, / Sparkling gems, & rich attire.
Old Age.
On a raisin stone.
On bravely through the sunshine & the showers.
On that night the poet went.
On the chamber, on the stairs.
On the Death of Mr. John Haskins.
On thee has God conferred.
Once the priest / Lived in an age.
One hand washes the other.
One night he dreamed of a palace fair.
Original—"Apropos."
Painting and Sculpture.
Pair of crystal eyes will lead me, A.
Pale Genius roves alone.
Panoply of Paradise is mine.
Papas Blondine / Grew tall & wise.
Park, The.
Parks & ponds are good by day.
Past, The.
Patch of meadow & upland, A.
Patient Pan / Drunken with nectar, The.
Pedants all / They would be original.
Perhaps thy lot in life is higher.
Philosophers are lined with eyes within.
Pilgrims, The.
Poem on Eloquence by R. W. Emerson.
Poem, Spoken Before the ΦBK Society, August, 1834.
Poet is at home, A.
Poet of poets / Is Time, the distiller.
Poets are colorpots.
Politics.
Pour the wine! pour the wine!
Problem, The.

Proteus.
Prudence.
Puff of air or dry or damp, A.
Put in, drive home the sightless wedges.
Quatrains.
Queen rejoices in her peers, A.
Quoth Saadi, when I stood before.
Rex.
Rhodora, The [On Being Asked Whence Is the Flower].
Romany Girl, The.
Roomy Eternity / Casts her schemes rarely.
Rubies.
Rules to men made evident, The.
S. R.
Saadi.
Saadi held the Muse in awe.
Saadi loved the new & old.
Samson stark at Dagon's knee.
Scholar is a ball thats spent.
Score of airy miles will smooth, A.
Sea reflects the rosy sky, The.
Sea-Shore.
Seashore.
Secret that should not be blown, The.
See how Romance adheres.
See yonder leafless trees against the sky.
Seemed, tho' the soft sheen all enchants.
Seemed to me—never maid.
Seyd planted when the deluge ploughed.
Shall the Muse sing for thousands & not sing.
She had wealth of mornings in her year.
She never comes to me.
She paints with white & red the moors.
She walked in flowers around my field.
Shout to the Sheperds, A.
Shun passion, fold the hands of thrift.
Silence.
Simple people each with basket or tool, The.
Since the devil hopping on.
Skeptic, The.
Snow-Storm [or Snowstorm], The.
Softens the air so cold & rude.
Solar insect on the wing.
Solution.
Song of Nature.
Song: "Shout for those whose course is done."
South Wind.
Sparrow is rich in her nest, THe.
Sphinx, The.
Spices in the plants that run.
Spirits of the wise, sit on the clouds, The.
Spiritual Laws.
Star seer Copernicus / Only could earn a curse.
Stout Sparta shrined the god of Laughter.
Such another peerless queen.
Sun athwart the cloud thought it no sin, The.
Sun is the sole inconsumable fire, The.
Sunshine was he.
Sursum Corda.
Suum Cuique.
Tact.
Teach me I am forgotten by the dead.
Teach me your mood, O patient stars!
Tell me maiden dost thou use.
Tell men what they knew before.
Terminus.
Terminus.
Test, The.
Thank the gods thy governors.
Thanks to those who go & come.
That each should in his house abide.
That wandering fire to me appears.
There are beggars in Iran and Araby.
There is in all the sons of men.
There is no evil but can speak.
Thermometer.
These trees like tho'ts that to visions congeal.
Thine Eyes Still Shined.
Things oft miscalling, as the hen-.
Think not the gods receive thy prayer.
This shining hour is an edifice.
This world is tedious.
Thou shalt make thy house.
Though her eye seek other forms.
Three Dimensions, The.

Threnody: "South-wind brings, The."
Titmouse, The.
To Ellen, at the South.
To Eva.
To every creature / Adam gave its name.
To J. W.
To Rhea.
To the Clock.
To the mizen, the main, & the fore.
To transmute crime to wisdom, & to stem.
Too late the anxious fire came.
Traitors tho' plumed & steel equipped.
Trimountain.
Try the might the Muse affords.
Turtle in swamp.
Two Rivers.
Una.
Unity.
Upon a rock yet uncreate.
Uriel.
Use will in man new grace reveal.
Vain against him were hostile blows.
Valedictory Poem.
Van Buren.
Visit, The.
Voluntaries.
Waldeinsamkeit.
Water.
We sauntered amidst miracles.
Wealth.
Webster.
What all the books of ages paint, I have.
What are all the flowers.
What avails it me.
What flowing central forces, say.
What from this barren being do we reap.
What is it to sail.
What never was no, & still will be.
When devils bite.
When Jane was absent Edgar's eye.
When success exalts thy lot.
When thou sittest moping.
When thy soul / Is filled with a just image fear not thou.
When wrath & terror changed Jove's regal port.
Where art thou / Thou beautiful dream.
Where is Skrymir? Giant Skrymir?
Where the fungus broad & red.
Who saw the hid beginnings
Whoso alas is young.
Why fear to die.
Why honor the new men.
Why should I live.
William does thy frigid soul.
William Rufus and the Jew.
Winds are cold, the days are dark, The.
Wisp & meteor nightly falling.
With the key of the secret he marches faster.
Woodnotes I ("For this present, hard").
Woodnotes II ("As sunbeams stream through liberal space").
Woods.
World-Soul, The.
Worship.
Would you know what joy is hid.
Written in a Volume of Goethe.
Written in Naples, March, 1833.
Written in Sickness.
Xenophanes.
Ye have Grace.
Yet sometimes to the sorrow stricken.
You shall not love me for what daily spends.

Enzensberger, Hans Magnus (b. 1929)
Apocalypse. Umbrian Master, about 1490.
Appearances.
Asphodels.
At Thirty-Three.
Bell Jar, The.
Bill of Fare.
Blank Sheet, The.
Camera Obscura.
Clothes.
Cold Comfort.
Comb, The.
Concert of Wishes.

Consistency.
Delete the Inapplicable.
Dept. of Philosophy.
Divorce, The.
Dream, A.
Employee, The.
End of Owls, The.
Fetish.
For the Grave of a Peace-Loving Man.
Force of Habit, The.
Frogs of Bikini, The.
Further Reasons Why Poets Do Not Tell the
   Truth.
Gillis van Conninxloo, Landscape. Panel, 65 x
   119 cm.
Hare in the Data Processing Centre, A.
Historical Process.
Holiday, The.
Homage to Gödel.
Identity Check.
Ironmonger's Shop, The.
Joy.
Karl Heinrich Marx.
Keeping Cool.
Lachesis Lapponica.
Language of the Country.
Last Supper. Venetian, Sixteenth Century.
Leeway.
Limbic System.
Middle Class Blues.
Midwives, The.
Model Towards a Theory of Cognition.
Notice of Loss.
Old Couples.
Old Revolution.
Other, The.
Poem about the Future.
Poison, The.
Portrait of a House Detective.
Precursors.
Purgatorio.
Remote House.
Reprieve, The.
Research Council.
Residual Light.
Rest of the Flight, The. Flemish, 1521.
Rondeau: "It's easy to talk."
Security Considerations.
Shadow Realm.
Shore.
Short History of the Bourgeoisie.
Sightseeing Tour.
Sleeping Pill.
Song for Those Who Know.
Staircase, A.
Strange Attractor.
Summer Poem.
Thoughts on the Run 1.
Thoughts on the Run 2.
Thoughts on the Run 3.
Thoughts on the Run 4.
Towards Eternal Peace.
Valse Triste et Sentimentale.
Vanished, The.
Vanished Work.
Vending Machine.
Visiting Ingres.

**Euenus (Euenus the Grammarian, Euenus of
   Askelon, Euenus of Paros)** (*fl.* **5th cent. B.C.**)
To the Swallow.

Euripides (485–406 B.C.)
Alcestis, *sels.*
Bacchae, *sels.*
Cyclops, The.
Hecuba, *sels.*
Hippolytus, *sels.*
Ion, *sels.*
Iphigenia [*or* Iphigeneia] in Aulis, *sels.*
Medea.
Phœnissae, *sels.*
Troades, *sels.*

F

Faiz, Faiz Ahmad (1911–84)
Bangla Desh: 1.
Bangla Desh: 3.
Bangla Desh: 2.
Elegy for Hassan Nasir.
If I Were Certain.

Farid-uddin Attar (1119–1202)
From "Bird Conversations."

Fayzi [*or* Faydi *or* Feisi *or* Feizi]
Eternal Watcher, who doth wake, The.
Wilt thou life's best elixir drain?

Fazio degli Uberti (1326–60)
Canzone: His Portrait of his Lady, Angiola of
   Verona.

Feldman, Ruth (b. 1911)
Airport.

Felltham, Owen *See* **Suckling, Sir John**

Feng-kan (Big Stick) (*fl.* c.8th cent.)
Actually there isn't a thing.
I have been to Tientai.
Sinking like a rock in the Sea.
Whenever Cold Mountain stops to visit.

Fenton, James (b. 1949)
Cambodia.
Children in Exile.
Chosun.
Dead Soldiers.
Exempla.
German Requiem, A.
God, A Poem.
In a Notebook.
Killer Snails, The.
Kingfisher's Boxing Gloves, The.
Letter to John Fuller.
Lines for Translation into Any Language.
Lollipops of the Pomeranian Baroque.
Lullaby for a Summer Recess.
Nest of Vampires.
Nothing.
Prison Island.
Skip, The.
Song That Sounds like This, The.
Staffordshire Murderer, A.
Tauler.
This Octopus Exploits Women.
Vacant Possession, A.
Vucceria.
Wild Life Studies, *sels.*
Wind.

Fergusson, Elizabeth Graeme (1737–1801)
Poem on the Death of Richard Stockton, A.

Ferlinghetti, Lawrence (b. 1919)
Adieu À Charlot.
And she "like a young year."
Ascending over Ohio.
Assassination Raga.
Astonished Heart, The.
At the *Gare Bruxelles-Midi.*
Autobiography.
Away above a harborful.
Baja Beatitudes.
Baja Revisited.
Baseball Canto.
Belated Palinode for Dylan Thomas.
Buddha in the Woodpile, A.
Café Notre Dame.
Canti Romani, *sels.*
Canticle of Jack Kerouac, The.
Carrara, Looking Seaward.
Cat, The.
Come lie with me and be my love.
Constantly Risking Absurdity.
Cro-Magnons.
Dark Portrait, A.
Deep Chess.
Deflowering.
Director of Alienation.
Dog.
Don't Let That Horse.
Dove sta amore / Where lies love.
Elegy on the Death of Kenneth Patchen, An.
Elegy to Dispel Gloom, An.

Endless Life.
Euphoria.
Expressionist History of German
   Expressionism.
Firenze, a Lifetime Later.
General Song of Humanity, The.
Goya & the Sleep of Reason.
Grottamare.
He with the Beating Wings.
Heap of Broken Images, A.
Hidden Door.
Hilarious God.
History of the World: a TV Docu-Drama.
Home Home Home.
I Genitori Perduti.
I have not lain with beauty all my life.
Imaginary Happening, London, An.
In Golden Gate Park that day.
In Goya's greatest scenes we seem to see.
In hintertime Praxiteles.
In Paris in a loud dark winter.
In woods where many rivers run.
It was a face which darkness could kill.
Jack of Hearts, The.
John Lennon in the Porto Santo Stefano.
Just as I used to say.
Ladakh Buddhess Biker.
Late Impressionist Dream.
Light, The.
Living Theatre, The.
L'Occupation Obsédée.
London / crossfigured / creeping with trams.
Lost Parents.
Love Nut, The.
Making Love in Poetry.
Man Who Rode Away, The.
Matisse at the Modern, Magritte at the Met.
Mock Confessional.
Morlaix: Into the Future with Neil Young.
Moscow in the Wilderness, Segovia in the
   Snow.
Mouth of truth, The.
New York—Albany.
Olbers' Paradox.
Old Italians Dying, The.
Old Sailors, The.
One of These Days.
Oral Messages, *sels.*
Overpopulation.
Painter's Dream, The.
Paris Transformations.
Pennycandystore beyond the El, The.
People Getting Divorced.
Photo of Emily, The.
Plan du Centre de Paris à Vol D'Oiseau.
Plough of Time, The.
Poem for Old Walt.
Poet as Fisherman.
Poet's eye obscenely seeing, The.
Populist Manifesto.
Pound at Spoleto.
Queens Cemetery, Setting Sun.
Reading Apollinaire by the Rogue River.
Rebels, The.
Report on a Happening in Washington Square
   San Francisco, A.
Retired Ballerinas, Central Park West.
Returning to Paris with Pissarro.
River Still To Be Found, A.
Roman Morn.
Rough Song of Animals Dying.
Sailing thru the straits of Demos.
San Jose Symphony Reception.
Sandinista Avioncitos.
Sarolla's women in their picture hats.
Sea and Ourselves at Cape Ann, The.
Sea Is Calm Tonight, The.
See / it was like this when.
Sherman's March Reglitterized.
Short Story on a Painting of Gustav Klimt.
Sometime During Eternity.
Spirit of the Crusades.
Sueño Real.
Sweet and various the woodlark.
That fellow on the boattrain who insisted.
They were putting up the statue.

Third World Calling.
Thoughts to a Concerto of Telemann.
Triste Corbiére.
Triumph of the Postmodern.
True Confessional.
Tunisian Nostalgia.
21.
25.
26.
Two Amsterdams.
Two Scavengers in a Truck, Two Beautiful
    People in a Mercedes.
Underwear.
Upon Reflection.
Uses of Poetry.
Vast Confusion, A.
Voix Glauque.
We squat upon the beach of love.
What could she say to the fantastic foolybear.
Wild Dreams of a New Beginning.
Wild Life Cameo, Early Morn.
With bells for hooves in sounding streets.
World is a beautiful place, The.

Figueredo, Alvaro
    Naked.
Flaccus, Quintus Horatius *See* **Horace**
Flaminius, Marc Antony (*fl.* **16th cent.**)
    Hymn 3.
Flaminius, Marc Antony (*fl.* **16th cent.**)
    Hymn 3.
Flavius Claudius Julianus; "Julian the Apostate"
    See **Julian, Emperor**
Foscolo, Ugo (**1778–1827**)
    Sonnet to Zante.
Francis Xavier, Saint (**1506–52**)
    Translation of a Hymn of St. Francis Xavier.
Frost, Robert (**1874–1963**)
    A-Wishing Well.
    Acceptance.
    Accidentally on Purpose.
    Acquainted with the Night.
    After Apple-Picking.
    Afterflakes.
    Aim Was Song, The.
    All Revelation.
    America Is Hard to See.
    Answer, An.
    Any Size We Please.
    Armful, The.
    Assurance.
    Astrometaphysical.
    At Woodward's Gardens.
    Atmosphere.
    Auspex.
    Away!
    Axe-Helve, The.
    Bad Island, The—Easter.
    Bear, The.
    Bearer of Evil Tidings, The.
    Beech.
    Bereft.
    Beyond Words.
    Birches.
    Birthplace, The.
    Black Cottage, The.
    Blue-Butterfly Day.
    Blue Ribbon at Amesbury, A.
    Blueberries.
    Boeotian.
    Bond and Free.
    Bonfire, The.
    Boundless Moment, A.
    Broken Drought, The.
    Brook in the City, A.
    Brown's Descent; or, The Willy-Nilly.
    Build Soil.
    Bursting Rapture.
    But outer Space.
    Cabin in the Clearing, A.
    Canis Major.
    Carpe Diem.
    Case for Jefferson, A.
    Census-Taker, A.
    Choose Something like a Star.
    Christmas Trees.
    Clear and Colder.
    Cliff Dwelling, A.

Closed for Good.
Cloud Shadow, A.
Cocoon, The.
Code, The.
Come In.
Concept Self-Conceived, A.
Considerable Speck, A.
Courage to Be New, The.
Cow in Apple Time, The.
Death of the Hired Man, The.
Demiurge's Laugh, The.
Departmental.
Desert Places.
Design.
Devotion.
Directive.
Discovery of the Madeiras, The.
Does No One at All Ever Feel This Way in the
    Least?
Door in the Dark, The.
Draft Horse, The.
Dream Pang, A.
Drumlin Woodchuck, A.
Dust in the Eyes.
Dust of Snow.
Egg and the Machine, The.
Empty Threat, An.
Encounter, An.
Ends.
Equalizer, An.
Escapist—Never.
Etherealizing.
Evening in a Sugar Orchard.
Exposed Nest, The.
Fear of God, The.
Fear of Man, The.
Fear, The.
Figure in the Doorway, The.
Fire and Ice.
Fireflies in the Garden.
Five Nocturnes.
Flood, The.
Flower Boat, The.
Flower-Gathering.
For John F. Kennedy; His Inauguration.
For Once, Then, Something.
Forgive, O Lord, my little jokes on Thee.
Fountain, a Bottle, a Donkey's Ears and Some
    Books, A.
Four-room shack aspiring high.
Fragmentary Blue.
Freedom of the Moon, The.
From a Milkweed Pod.
From Iron.
From Plane to Plane.
Gathering Leaves.
Generations of Men, The.
Ghost House.
Gift Outright, The.
Girl's Garden, A.
Going for Water.
Gold Hesperidee, The.
Good-by and Keep Cold.
Good Hours.
Grindstone, The.
Gum-Gatherer, The.
Haec Fabula Docet.
Hannibal.
Happiness Makes Up in Height for What It
    Lacks in Length.
Hill Wife, The.
Hillside Thaw, A.
Home Burial.
Housekeeper, The.
How Hard It Is to Keep from Being King
    When It's in You and in the Situation.
Hundred Collars, A.
Hyla Brook.
I Could Give All to Time.
I Will Sing You One-O.
Immigrants.
Importer, An.
In a Disused Graveyard.
In a Glass of Cider.
In a Poem.
In a Vale.

In Hardwood Groves.
In Neglect.
In the Home Stretch.
In Time of Cloudburst.
In winter in the woods alone.
Ingenuities of Debt, The.
Innate Helium.
Into My Own.
Investment, The.
Iota Subscript.
Iris by Night.
It Bids Pretty Fair.
It Is Almost the Year Two Thousand.
It takes all sorts of in- and outdoor schooling.
Kitchen Chimney, The.
Kitty Hawk.
Last Mowing, The.
Last Word of a Bluebird, The.
Late Walk, A.
Leaf-Treader, A.
Leaves Compared with Flowers.
Lesson for Today, The.
Line-Gang, The.
Line-Storm Song, A.
Lines Written in Dejection on the Eve of Great
    Success.
Literate Farmer and the Planet Venus, The.
Locked Out.
Lockless Door, The.
Lodged.
Lone Striker, A.
Looking for a Sunset Bird in Winter.
Loose Mountain, A.
Lost Follower, The.
Lost in Heaven.
Love and a Question.
Lovely Shall Be Choosers, The.
Lucretius versus the Lake Poets.
Maple.
Masque of Mercy, A.
Masque of Reason, A.
Master Speed, The.
Meeting and Passing.
Mending Wall.
Middleness of the Road, The.
Milky Way Is a Cowpath, The.
Minor Bird, A.
Misgiving.
Missive Missile, A.
Mood Apart, A.
Moon Compasses.
Most of It, The.
Mountain, The.
Mowing.
My Butterfly.
My November Guest.
Nature Note, A.
Need of Being Versed in Country Things, The.
Neither Out Far Nor In Deep.
Never Again Would Birds' Song Be The Same.
Never Naught Song, A.
New Hampshire.
No Holy Wars for Them.
Not of School Age.
Not Quite Social.
Not to Keep.
Nothing Gold Can Stay.
November.
Now Close the Windows.
Objection to Being Stepped On, The.
October.
Of the Stones of the Place.
Old Barn at the Bottom of the Fogs, The.
Old Man's Winter Night, An.
On a Bird Singing in its Sleep.
On a Tree Fallen across the Road.
On Being Chosen Poet of Vermont.
On Being Idolized.
On Going Unnoticed.
On Looking Up by Chance at the
    Constellations.
On Our Sympathy with the Under Dog.
On Taking from the Top to Broaden the Base.
On the Heart's Beginning to Cloud the Mind.
Once by the Pacific.
One More Brevity.

One Step Taken Backward.
Onset, The.
Our Doom to Bloom.
Our Hold on the Planet.
Our Singing Strength.
"Out, Out—."
Oven Bird, The.
Pan with Us.
Passing Glimpse, A.
Pasture, The.
Patch of Old Snow, A.
Paul's Wife.
Pea Brush.
Peaceful Shepherd, The.
Peck of Gold, A.
Peril of Hope.
Place for a Third.
Planners, The.
Plowmen.
Prayer in Spring, A.
Provide, Provide.
Putting in the Seed.
Quandary.
Quest of the Purple-Fringed, The.
Question, A.
Questioning Faces.
Rabbit Hunter, The.
Range-finding.
Record Stride, A.
Reflex, A.
Reluctance.
Revelation.
Riders.
Road Not Taken, The.
Roadside Stand, A.
Rogers Group, A.
Rose Family, The.
Rose Pogonias.
Runaway, The.
Sand Dunes.
Secret Sits, The.
Self-Seeker, The.
Semi-Revolution, A.
Serious Step Taken Lightly, A.
Servant to Servants, A.
Silken Tent, The.
Sitting by a Bush in Broad Sunlight.
Skeptic.
Snow.
Soldier, A.
Some Science Fiction.
Something for Hope.
Sound of Trees, The.
Spring Pools.
Star in a Stoneboat, A.
Stars.
Steeple on the House, A.
Stopping by Woods on a Snowy Evening.
Storm Fear.
Strong Are Saying Nothing, The.
Subverted Flower, The.
Sycamore.
Telephone, The.
Ten Mills.
Thatch, The.
There Are Roughly Zones.
They Were Welcome to Their Belief.
Time Out.
Time to Talk, A.
Times Table, The.
To a Moth Seen in Winter.
To a Thinker.
To a Young Wretch.
To an Ancient.
To Earthward.
To E.T.
To the Right Person.
To the Thawing Wind.
Too Anxious for Rivers.
Tree at My Window.
Trespass.
Trial by Existence, The.
Trial Run, A.
Triple Bronze.
Tuft of Flowers, The.
Two Leading Lights.

Two Look at Two.
Two Tramps in Mud Time.
Two Witches.
U. S. 1946 King's X.
Unharvested.
Unstamped Letter in Our Rural Letter Box, An.
Valley's Singing Day, The.
Vanishing Red, The.
Vantage Point, The.
Version.
Vindictives, The.
Voice Ways.
Waiting.
We vainly wrestle with the blind belief.
West-Running Brook.
What Fifty Said.
White-Tailed Hornet, The.
Why Wait for Science.
Wild Grapes.
Willful Homing.
Wind and the Rain, The.
Wind and Window Flower.
Winter Eden, A.
Wish to Comply, A.
Wood-Pile, The.
Young Birch, A.

G

Gaius Valerius Catullus *See* **Catullus**
Gallagher, Tess (b. 1943)
  Accomplishment.
  All Day the Light Is Clear.
  Amplitude.
  As If It Happened.
  Backdrop With Lovers, 1931.
  Ballad of Ballymote, The.
  Beginning to Say No.
  Bird-Window-Flying.
  Black Money.
  Black Silk.
  Boat Ride.
  Bonfire.
  Borrowed Ones, The.
  Breasts.
  Calm, The.
  Candle, Lamp & Firefly.
  Clearing.
  Coats, The.
  Coming Home.
  Conversation with a Fireman from Brooklyn.
  Corona.
  Cougar Meat.
  Cows, a Vision.
  Crêpes Flambeau.
  Croce e Delizia al Cor.
  Death of the Horses by Fire.
  Devotion: That It Flow; That There Be
    Concentration.
  Dim House, Bright Face.
  Disappearances in the Guarded Sector.
  Each Bird Walking.
  Even Now You Are Leaving.
  Ever After.
  Four Dancers at an Irish Wedding.
  From Dread in the Eyes of Horses.
  Gray Eyes.
  Hands of the Blindman, The.
  Harmless Streets.
  His Shining Helmet; Its Horsehair Crest.
  Horse in the Drugstore, The.
  Hug, The.
  I Save Your Coat, But You Lose It Later.
  If Blood Were Not as Powerful as It Is.
  If Poetry Were Not a Morality.
  In Maceio.
  Instructions to the Double.
  Into the Known.
  Kidnap[p]er.
  Linoleum.
  Love Poem to Be Read to an Illiterate Friend.
  Meeting, The.
  Message for the Sinecurist.
  My Mother Remembers That She Was

    Beautiful.
  Not There.
  On Your Own.
  Open Fire Near a Shed.
  Photograph of a Lighthouse Through Fog.
  Poem in Translation, A.
  Present.
  Reading Aloud.
  Redwing.
  Refusing Silence.
  Rhododendrons.
  Rijl.
  Ritual of Memories, The.
  Same Kiss After Many Years, The.
  Second Language.
  Simple Sonatina.
  Small Garden Near a Field.
  Snowheart.
  Some Painful Butterflies Pass Through.
  Some with Wings, Some with Manes.
  Stepping Outside.
  Still Moment at Dun Laoghaire.
  Story of a Citizen, The.
  Sudden Journey.
  Sugar.
  Survival of a Heart.
  Tableau Vivant.
  That Kind of Thing.
  Their Heads Bent Toward Each Other Like
    Flowers.
  3 A.M. Kitchen: My Father Talking.
  Time Lapse with Tulips.
  Under Stars.
  Unsteady Yellow.
  View from an Empty Chair.
  When You Speak to Me.
  Willingly.
  With Stars.
  Woman-Enough.
  Woman Who Raised Goats, The.
  Women's Tug of War at Lough Arrow.
  Woodcutting on Lost Mountain.
  Words Written Near a Candle.
  Zero.
Ganjavi, Elyas Ysuof Nezami *See* **Elyas Yusof
  Nezami** [*or* **Nisami**] **Ganjavi**
García Lorca, Federico (1895–1936)
  Abandoned.
  Abandoned Church.
  Adam.
  After a Walk.
  Afterwards ("I've pulled up to the doorway /
    of *Then*").
  Andalusian Songs, *sels.*
  At the Anonymous Tomb of Herrera y Reissig
    in the Cemetery of Montevideo.
  Autumn Song.
  Back of the World, *sels.*
  Backwaters, *sels.*
  Bad Heart.
  Ballad of Black Pain.
  Ballad of One Doomed to Die.
  Ballad of Our Lady of the Boat.
  Ballad of the Little Square.
  Ballad of the Marked Man.
  Ballad of the Moon Moon.
  Ballad of the Spanish Civil Guard.
  Ballad of the Three Rivers.
  Ballad of the Water of the Sea.
  Barrage of Firework Poems on the Occasion of
    the Poet's Birthday, *sels.*
  Beloved Sleeps on the Poet's Breast, The.
  Birth of Christ, The.
  Blacks Dancing to Cuban Rhythms.
  Blind Panorama of New York.
  Blue River, *sels.*
  Border.
  Candy Wrapper and Toy.
  Capriccios, *sels.*
  Captive.
  Caracols / Snails, *sels.*
  Casida of the Boy Wounded by the Water.
  Casida of the Branches.
  Casida of the Dark Doves.
  Casida of the Golden Girl.
  Casida of the Lament.

Casida of the Reclining Woman.
Cautiously the wind explores.
Childhood and Death.
Christmas on the Hudson.
Cicada!
Countries, *sels.*
Cow.
Cradle Song for Mercedes, in Death.
Cross, *sels.*
Crossroad.
Crucifixion.
Cry to Rome.
Cúckoo-Cuckoo-Cuckóo, *sels.*
Dance of Death.
Dance of the Moon in Santiago.
Dawn.
Dawn, The.
Day Poems.
Daydreams of a River.
Dead from Love.
Death.
Death of Antonito el Camborio, The.
Death of Little Tony Camborio, The.
Desire.
Desire of a Statue.
Dialogue of Amargo.
Diamond.
Double Poem of Lake Eden.
Dream.
Earth and Moon.
Elegy: "Like a censer filled with desire."
Elegy: To Silence.
Epitaph for a Bird, *sels.*
Epitaph for Isaac Albéniz.
Eros with a Cane, *sels.*
Evening ("It's now the hour / for being
  sincere").
Evening ("Rainy evening in exhausted gray").
Fable and Round of the Three Friends.
Fable of Three Friends to Be Sung in Rounds.
Fable: "Unicorns and cyclopses."
Fairs, *sels.*
Faithless Wife, The.
Fallen Weathervane, The.
Farewell: "If I die."
Feud, The.
Flamenco Vignettes.
Fly.
For Mercedes in Her Flight.
Four Ballads in Yellow.
From Out Here.
Gacela of Desperate Love.
Gacela of the Bitter Root.
Gacela of the Dark Death.
Gacela of the Dead Child.
Gacela of the Flight.
Gacela of the Morning Market.
Gacela of the Terrible Presence.
Gacela of Unforeseen Love.
Games, *sels.*
Garden in Umber; or The Garden of the
  Brownhaired Girls, *sels.*
Ghazal of the Market in the Morning.
Ghazals, *sels.*
Graphic of the Petenera.
Gypsy Nun, The.
Half Moon.
He Died at Dawn.
Herbals.
Hour of Stars.
In Another Mode.
In Malaga.
In Memoriam.
In the Forest of Clocks, *sels.*
In the Forest of the Lunar Grapefruits, *sels.*
In the Garden of the Lunar Grapefruits, *sels.*
In your eyes, the serpent.
Inquiry.
Interrupted Concert, The.
It Is True.
Jewish Cemetery.
Joke about Don Pedro on Horseback.
King of Harlem, The.
Knock, knock! / Who's there?
Lament for Ignacio Sánchez Mejías.
Landscape of a Pissing Multitude.

Landscape of a Vomiting Multitude.
Landscape with Two Graves and an Assyrian
  Dog.
Little Girl Drowned in the Well.
Little Infinite Poem.
Little Mad Boy, The.
Little Mute Boy, The.
Little Stanton.
Little Viennese Waltz.
Living Sky.
Lizard Is Crying, The.
Love, *sels.*
Lullaby in Death for Rosalía de Castro.
Madrigal for the City of Santiago.
Madrigal: "I looked into your eyes."
Madrigal: "My kiss was a pomegranate."
Madrigal to the City of Santiago.
Madrigals: "Like concentric waves / on the
  water."
Martyrdom of St. Eulalia.
Martyrdom of Saint Eulalia, The.
Meditations & Allegories of Water.
Minor Song.
Mirror Suite, *sels.*
Moments of Song, *sels.*
Moon and Panorama of the Insects.
Moon Rising, The.
Moon Songs, *sels.*
Morning.
Murder.
My Soul's Shadow.
Narcissus, *sels.*
New Heart.
New Songs.
New York.
Newton, *sels.*
Night of Sleepless Love.
Night Song of the Andalusian Sailors.
Night (Suite for Piano and Poet's Voice), *sels.*
1910.
Nocturne: "I am afraid / of dead leaves."
Nocturne of Emptied Space.
Nocturne of the Drowned Youth.
Nocturnes from the Window.
November.
Ocean.
Ode to Salvador Dalí.
Ode to the Most Holy Sacrament of the Altar.
Ode to Walt Whitman.
Oh secret voice of dark love!
Old Lizard, The.
Old Melancholy.
Omega.
On the Death of José de Ciria y Escalante.
Palimpsests, *sels.*
Palm Tree, The, *sels.*
Pause of the Clock.
Poem of the Gypsy *Siguiriya.*
Poem of the Saeta, *sels.*
Poem of the *Soleá.*
Poet Asks His Love about the "Enchanted
  City" of Cuenca, The.
Poet Asks His Love to Write Him, The.
Poet Prays to the Virgin for Help, The.
Poet Speaks with His Beloved on the
  Telephone, The.
Poet Tells the Truth, The.
Poplar and tower. / Living shade.
Preciosa and the Wind.
Prologue: "Here, my God, / is my heart."
Qasidas, *sels.*
Return, The, *sels.*
Rider's Song.
Road, The.
Ruin.
St. Gabriel.
St. Michael.
St. Raphael.
Saint Raphael (Córdoba).
Salutation, A.
Scene of the Lieutenant Colonel of the Civil
  Guard.
Schematic Nocturne.
Seaside Prints, *sels.*
Seawater Ballad.
Second Anniversary ("Dawn brings us the

smell").
Secrets, *sels.*
Shadow, *sels.*
Silly Song.
Siren and the Carabineer, The.
Six Capriccios.
Six Songs at Nightfall, *sels.*
Sketch for an Ode.
Sleepless City.
Sleepwalking Ballad.
Slow perfume, heart without a scale.
Solitude.
Some Souls.
Somnambule Ballad.
Song for the Moon.
Song of a Little Death.
Song of Despair.
Song of the Barren Orange Tree.
Song of the Rider (1860).
Song of the Shop Boy.
Songs for Children, *sels.*
Songs of Childhood, *sels.*
Songs to End With, *sels.*
Sonnet: "I know that my profile will be
  serene."
Sonnet in Homage to Manuel de Falla Offering
  Him Some Flowers.
Sonnet in the Manner of Góngora in Which the
  Poet Sends His Beloved a Dove.
Sonnet of the Garland of Roses.
Sonnet of the Sweet Complaint.
Spinster at Mass, The.
Spring Song.
Standards and Paradise of the Blacks.
Street of the Mutes, The.
Sublunar Cantos, *sels.*
Suicide.
Suite, *sels.*
Summer Hours, *sels.*
Summer Madrigal.
Sun Has Set, The.
Taking of Little Tony Camborio on the Seville
  Highway, The.
Thamar and Amnon.
Theories, *sels.*
Three Cities.
Three Crepuscular Poems.
3:00 p.m.
Three Portraits with Shading, *sels.*
Three Prints of the Sky.
To Carmela Condón, Thanking Her for Some
  Dolls.
Train Ride.
Tree, Tree.
Trees.
Trip to the Moon.
Two Girls.
Two Lovers Murdered by a Partridge.
Two Norms.
Two Sailors on the Beach.
Uncertain Solitude.
Unfaithful Wife, The.
Useless Song.
Variations.
Vignettes of the Wind.
Voices.
Waltz in the Branches.
Water Jets, *sels.*
Water Suite, *sels.*
Weathervane.
Wheels of Fortune, *sels.*
White Album, *sels.*
Word of wax. / Forget your word of wax.
Wounds of Love.
Your Childhood in Menton.

Gay, John (1685–1732)
  Avarus et Plutus.
  Lepus Multis Amicus.
  Papilio et Limax.
  Philosophus et Phasiani.

Gay, John and Alexander Pope
  Mary Gulliver to Capt. Lemuel Gulliver.

Ginsberg, Allen (1926–2000)
  Aether.
  After All, What Else Is There to Say?
  After Dead Souls.

After Lalon, *sels.*
After the Big Parade.
After Thoughts.
After Whitman & Reznikoff.
After Yeats.
Afternoon Seattle.
Airplane Blues.
America.
American Change.
American Sentences.
Angkor Wat.
Anti-Vietnam War Peace Mobilization.
Archetype Poem, The.
Arguments.
Asphodel, An.
At Apollinaire's Grave.
Atypical Affair, An.
Auto Poesy: On the Lam from Bloomington.
Autumn Gold: New England Fall.
Autumn Leaves.
Ayers Rock / Uluru Song.
'Back on Times Square, Dreaming of Times
    Square.'
Ballad of the Skeletons, The.
Ballade of Poisons.
Battleship Newsreel.
Bayonne Entering NYC.
Bayonne Turnpike to Tuscarora.
Beginning of a Long Poem of These States.
Beginning of a Poem of These States.
Big Beat.
Birdbrain!
Bixby Canyon.
Bixby Canyon Ocean Path Word Breeze.
Blame the Thought, Cling to the Bummer.
Blessed Be the Muses.
Blue Angel, The.
Bop Lyrics.
Bricklayer's Lunch Hour, The.
Broken Bone Blues.
Brooklyn College Brain.
Bus Ride Ballad Road to Suva.
Cabin in the Rockies.
Café in Warsaw.
Capitol Air.
Car Crash.
Carmel Valley.
Cézanne's Ports.
Chances "R."
Change, The: *Kyoto-Tokyo Express.*
Charnel Ground, The.
Chicago to Salt Lake by Air.
City Midnight Junk Strains.
Cleveland, the Flats.
C'mon Jack.
C'mon Pigs of Western Civilization Eat More
    Grease.
Come All Ye Brave Boys.
Come Back Christmas: Blues Stanza.
Complaint of the Skeleton to Time.
Consulting I Ching Smoking Pot Listening to
    the Fugs Sing Blake.
Contest of Bards.
Continuation of a Long Poem of These States.
Cosmopolitan Greetings.
Crash.
Crazy Spiritual, A.
Crossing Nation.
Dakar Doldrums.
Death News.
Death on All Fronts.
Death to Van Gogh's Ear!
December 31, 1978.
Defending the Faith.
Describe: The Rain on Dasaswamedh Ghat.
Desolation, A.
Do the Meditation Rock.
Do We Understand Each Other?
Don't Grow Old, *sels.*
Done, Finished with the Biggest Cock.
Dope Fiend Blues.
Dream, A.
Dream Record: June 8 1955.
"Drive All Blames into One."
Drowse Murmurs.
Easter Sunday.

Eastern Ballad, An.
Ecologue.
Ego Confession.
Elegy Che Guevara.
Elegy for Neal Cassady.
End, The.
Epigram on a Painting of Golgotha.
Eroica.
Europe! Europe!
Everybody Sing.
Eye Altering Alters All, The.
Falling Asleep in America.
Father Guru.
Fie My Fum.
First Party at Ken Kesey's with Hell's Angels.
Flash Back.
Flying Elegy.
Footnote to Howl.
For Creely's Ear.
4 AM Blues.
Four Haiku.
Fourth Floor, Dawn, Up All Night Writing
    Letters.
Fragment 1956.
Fragment: The Names II.
Friday the Thirteenth.
Funny Death.
Further Proposal, A.
Fyodor.
G.S. Reading Poesy at Princeton.
Galilee Shore.
Garden State.
Ghost May Come, A.
Going to Chicago.
Gospel Noble Truths.
Graffiti 12th Cubicle Men's Room Syracuse
    Airport.
Grant Park: August 28, 1968.
Green Automobile, The.
Green Valentine Blues.
Gregory Corso's Story.
Grim Skeleton.
Growing Old Again.
Guru.
Guru Blues.
Guru Om.
Hadda Be Playing on the Jukebox.
Hardon Blues.
Haunting Poe's Baltimore.
Havana 1953.
Have You Seen This Movie?
Heat.
Hiway Poesy: L.A.–Albuquerque–Texas–
    Witchita.
Holy Ghost on the Nod over the Body of Bliss.
Homage Vajracarya.
Homework.
Hospital Window.
How Come He Got Canned at the Ribbon
    Factory.
Howl.
Hum Bom!
Hymn: "No hyacinthine imagination can
    express this clock of meat bleakly pining."
I Am a Victim of Telephone.
I attempted to concentrate.
I Beg You Come Back & Be Cheerful.
I feel as if I am at a dead.
I Have Increased Power.
I Lay Love on My Knee.
I learned a world from each.
I made love to myself.
Ignu.
Imaginary Rose in a Book, An.
Imaginary Universes.
In a Moonlit Hermit's Cabin.
In Back of the Real.
In Death, Cannot Reach What Is Most Near.
In Memoriam: William Cannastra, 1922–1950.
In Society.
In the Baggage Room at Greyhound.
Independence Day.
Iron Horse.
Jaweh and Allah Battle.
Jimmy Berman Rag.
Journal Night Thoughts.

Junk Mail.
Kaddish.
Kansas City to Saint Louis.
Kiss Ass.
Kral Majales.
Lack Love.
Land O'Lakes, Wisc.
Land O'Lakes, Wisconsin: Vajrayana
    Seminary.
Las Vegas: Verses Improvised for El Dorado
    H.S. Newspaper.
Last Night in Calcutta.
Laughing Gas.
Lay Down Yr Mountain.
Lion for Real, The.
Long Live the Spiderweb.
Love Comes.
Love Forgiven.
Love Letter.
Love Poem on Theme by Whitman.
Love Replied.
Love Returned.
Lover's Garden, A.
Lysergic Acid.
Mad Gleam, A.
Magic Psalm.
Malest Cornifici Tuo Catullo.
Manhattan May Day Midnight.
Manhattan Thirties Flash.
Manifesto.
Man's Glory.
Many Loves.
Marijuana Notation.
Maturity.
May Days 1988.
Maybe Love.
Meaningless Institution, A.
Memory Gardens.
Mescaline.
Message.
Message II.
Metaphysics.
Methedrine Vision in Hollywood, A.
Milarepa Taste.
Mind Breaths.
Moments Return, The.
Morning.
Mugging.
My Alba.
My Sad Self.
Nagasaki Days.
Names, The.
Neruda's "Que dispierte el leñador."
New Stanzas for *Amazing Grace.*
New York Blues.
News Bulletin.
Night-Apple, The.
Night Gleam.
Northwest Passage.
Nov. 23, 1963: Alone.
NY Youth Call Annunciation.
Ode: My 24th Year.
Ode to Failure.
Ode to the Setting Sun.
Old Pond.
Old Village before I Die, The.
On Burroughs, Work.
On Illness.
On Neal's Ashes.
On Neruda's Death.
On Reading William Blake's "The Sick Rose."
136 Syllables at Rocky Mountain Dharma
    Center.
Open Window on Chicago, An.
Over Denver Again.
Over Kansas.
Over Laramie.
Past Silver Durango Over Mexic Sierra-
    Wrinkles.
Paterson.
Patna-Benares Express.
Pentagon Exorcism.
Personals Ad.
Pertussin.
Please Master.
Please Open the Window and Let Me In.

Plutonian Ode.
Poem on America, A.
Poem Rocket.
Portland Coliseum.
Prayer Blues.
Proclamation.
Prophecy, A.
Psalm I.
Psalm II: "Ah, still Lord, ah sweet Divinity."
Psalm III: "To God: to illuminate all men. Beginning with Skid Road."
Psalm IV.
Pull My Daisy.
Punk Rock Your My Big Crybaby.
Pussy Blues.
Put Down Your Cigarette Rag (Dont Smoke).
Rain-Wet Asphalt Heat, Garbage Curbed Cans Overflowing.
Reading Bai Juyi, *sels.*
Reading French Poetry.
Ready to Roll.
Reef Mantra.
Reflections at Lake Louise.
Reflections in Sleepy Eye.
Refrain.
Reply, The.
Return of Kral Majales.
Returning North of Vortex.
Returning to the Country for a Brief Visit.
Rising Over Night-Blackened Detroit Streets.
Rolling Thunder Stones.
Ruhr-Gebiet.
Sad Dust Glories.
Sakyamuni Coming Out from the Mountain.
Sather Gate Illumination.
Scribble.
Seabattle of Salamis Took Place off Perama.
September on Jessore Road.
Shrouded Stranger, The.
Shrouded Stranger, The.
Sickness Blues.
Siesta in Xbalba.
Slack Key Guitar.
Smoke Rolling Down Street.
Some Love.
Sometime Jailhouse Blues.
Song: "Weight of the world, The."
Sonora Desert-Edge.
Sphincter.
Spring Fashions.
Squeal.
Stanzas: Written at Night in Radio City.
Stay Away from the White House.
Stool Pigeon Blues.
Stotras to Kali Destroyer of Illusions.
Strange New Cottage in Berkeley, A.
Studying the Signs.
Sunflower Sutra.
Sunset.
Sunset S.S. Azemour.
Supermarket in California, A.
Sweet Boy, Gimme Yr Ass.
Sweet Levinsky.
Swirls of Black Dust on Avenue D.
Tears.
Television Was a Baby Crawling toward That Deathchamber.
Terms in Which I Think of Reality, The.
Tethnakin D'oligo Pideuis Fainom Alaia.
Teton Village.
These States: into L.A.
These States: to Miami Presidential Convention.
This Form of Life Needs Sex.
This Is about Death.
Those Two.
Thoughts on a Breath.
Thoughts Sitting Breathing.
345 W. 15th St.
To an Old Poet in Peru.
To Aunt Rose.
To Lindsay.
To P.O.
To Poe: Over the Planet, Air Albany– Baltimore.
To the Body.

To the Punks of Dawlish.
Today.
Tonite all is well . . . What a / terrible future. I am twenty-three.
Transcription of Organ Music.
Trembling of the Veil, The.
Tübingen–Hamburg Schlafwagen.
Two Boys Went Into a Dream Diner.
Two Dreams.
Two Sonnets.
Typical Affair, A.
Under the World There's a Lot of Ass, a Lot of Cunt.
Understand That This Is a Dream.
Uptown.
Verses Written for Student Antidraft Registration Rally 1980.
Very Dove, A.
Violence.
Vision 1948.
Voice of Rock, The.
Vomit Express.
Vow, A.
Voznesensky's "Silent Tingling."
Vulture Peak: Gridhakuta Hill.
Waking in New York.
Wales Visitation.
Walking Home at Night,
War Profit Litany.
We Rise on Sun Beams and Fall in the Night.
Western Ballad, A.
What I'd Like to Do.
What Would You Do If You Lost It.
What You Up To?
What's Dead?
White Shroud.
Who.
Who Be Kind To.
Who Runs America?
Who Will Take Over the Universe?
Why I Meditate.
Why Is God Love, Jack?
Wichita Vortex Sutra.
Wild Orphan.
Wings Lifted over the Black Pit.
Written in My Dream by W. C. Williams.
Written on Hotel Napkin: Chicago Futures.
Wrote This Last Night.
Xmas Gift.
Yes and It's Hopeless.
Yiddishe Kopf.
You Might Get in Trouble.

Gjuzel, Bogomil (b. 1939)
Flood at the International Writer's Workshop.
My Sister's Letter.
On the Way Back.
Prostitution.
When I Came Back.

Glück, Louise (b. 1943)
Abishag.
Adult Grief.
All Hallows.
Aphrodite.
Apple Trees, The.
Archipelago.
Aubade: "Today above the gull's call."
Autumnal.
Baskets.
Brennende Liebe.
Bridal Piece.
Brooding Likeness.
Cell, The.
Chicago Train, The.
Cottonmouth Country.
Cripple in the Subway, The.
Day Without Night.
Dedication to Hunger.
Departure.
Descending Figure.
Dream of Mourning, The.
Drowned Children, The.
Early December in Croton-on-Hudson.
Easter Season.
Edge, The.
Egg, The.
Elms.

Embrace, The.
End of the World, The.
Epithalamium: "There were others; their bodies."
Exile.
Fire, The.
Firstborn.
Flowering Plum.
For Jane Myers.
For My Mother.
Fortress, The.
From the Japanese.
Game, The.
Garden, The.
Gemini.
Gift, The.
Grandmother in the Garden.
Gratitude.
Gretel in Darkness.
Happiness.
Hawk's Shadow.
Here Are My Black Clothes.
Hesitate to Call.
Horse.
Hyacinth.
Illuminations.
Inlet, The.
Islander, The.
Japonica.
Jeanne d'Arc.
La Force.
Labor Day.
Lady in the Single, The.
Lamentations.
Late Snow.
Legend.
Letter from our Man in Blossomtime.
Letter from Provence.
Letters, The.
Liberation.
Love Poem.
Magi, The.
Marathon.
Memo from the Cave.
Meridian.
Messengers.
Metamorphosis.
Mirror, The.
Mock Orange.
Morning.
Mountain, The.
Murderess, The.
My Cousin in April.
My Life Before Dawn.
My Neighbor in the Mirror.
Mythic Fragment.
Nativity Poem.
Night Piece.
Northwood Path.
Nurse's Song.
Palais des Arts.
Parable, A.
Phenomenal Survivals of Death in Nantucket.
Pictures of the People in the War.
Pietà.
Poem: "In the early evening, as now, a man is bending."
Pomegranate.
Pond, The.
Porcelain Bowl.
Portland, 1968.
Portrait.
Portrait of the Queen in Tears.
Racer's Widow, The.
Reproach, The.
Return, The.
Returning a Lost Child.
Rosy.
Saturnalia.
School Children, The.
Scraps.
Seated Figure.
Shad-Blow Tree, The.
Silverpoint.
Slave Ship, The.

Solstice.
Still Life.
Swans.
Swimmer, The.
Tango.
Thanksgiving.
Thanksgiving.
To Autumn.
To Florida.
Tree House, The.
Triumph of Achilles, The.
12. 6. 71.
Under Taurus.
Undertaking, The.
Winter Morning.
World Breaking Apart.
Wound, The.

Goethe, Johann Wolfgang von (1749–1832)
Anacreon's Grave.
Arabian Ballad.
Confession.
Faust, *sels.*
Mignon's Song.
Song: "Joyful / And woful."

Goll, Iwan [*or* Yvan] (1891–1950)
Jean Sans Terre at the Final Port.
Jean Sans Terre Circles the Earth Seven Times.
Jean Sans Terre Discovers the West Pole.
Jean Sans Terre Leads the Caravan.
Jean Sans Terre Reviews the Fathers.

Gorenko, Anna Andreyevna *See* **Akhmatova, Anna Andreyevna**

Graves, Alfred Percival (1846–1931)
In the Name of Virtue.

Graves, Richard (1715–1804)
Single Fare.

Graves, Robert (1895–1985)
£. S. D.
Above the Edge of Doom.
Absent Crusader.
Accomplice, The.
Acrobats.
Advent of Summer.
Advice from a Mother.
Advocates.
After the Flood.
Against Witchcraft.
Age Gap.
Ageless Reason.
Ages of Oath, The.
Alice.
All Except Hannibal.
All I Tell You From My Heart.
Allie.
Always.
Ambience.
Ambrosia of Dionysus and Semele, The.
Ample Garden, The.
Ancestors.
Angry Samson.
Antorcha Y Corona, 1968.
Any Honest Housewife.
Apollo of the Physiologists.
Apple Island.
Apples and Water.
Ark, The.
Armistice Day, 1918.
Around the Mountain.
Arrears of Moonlight.
Arrow on the Vane.
Arrow Shots.
As a Less than Robber.
As All Must End.
As When the Mystic.
At Best, Poets.
At First Sight.
At the Gate.
At the Well.
Awakening, The.
Bank Account.
Bards, The.
Batxóca.
Beach, The.
Beatrice and Dante.
Beauty in Trouble.

Beds of Grainne and Diarmuid, The.
Beggar Maid and King Cophetua, The.
Between Hyssop and Axe.
Between Moon and Moon.
Between Trains.
Beware, Madam!
Bird of Paradise.
Birth of a Goddess.
Birth of Angels.
Bites and Kisses.
Black.
Black Goddess, The.
Blackening Sky.
Blanket Charge.
Blessed Sun.
Blind Arrow, A.
Blue-Fly, The.
Bower-Bird.
Bracelet, A.
Breakfast Table.
Brief Reunion.
Broken Compact.
Broken Girth, The.
Broken Neck.
Brother.
Call It a Good Marriage.
Carol of Patience.
Casse-Noisette.
Castle, The.
Cat-Goddesses.
Certain Mercies.
Change.
Charm for Sound Sleeping, A.
Child with Veteran.
Children of Darkness.
Chink, The.
Christmas Robin, The.
Circus Ring.
Cliff and Wave.
Cliff Edge, The.
Climate of Thought, The.
Cloak, The.
Cock in Pullet's Feathers.
Colophon.
Colours of Night, The.
Compact.
Complaint and Reply.
Confess, Marpessa.
Conjunction.
Consortium of Stones.
Cool Web, The.
Coronation Murder, The.
Coronet of Moonlight.
Counting the Beats.
Country Mansion, A.
Court of Love, A.
Crab-Tree, The.
Crane, The.
Crucibles of Love.
Cry Faugh!
Crystal, The.
Cuirassiers of the Frontier, The.
Cure, The.
Dance of Words.
Dancing Flame.
Dangerous Gift, The.
Dans un Seul Lit.
Darien.
Dawn Bombardment.
Dazzle of Darkness.
De Arte Poetica.
Dead Hand.
Death by Drums.
Death Grapple, The.
Death Room, The.
Deed of Gift.
Deliverance.
Depth of Love.
Descent into Hell.
Desert Fringe.
Despite and Still.
Devil's Advice to Story-Tellers, The.
Dialogue on the Headland.
Dilemma, The.
Discarded Love Poem, The.
Door, The.

Double Bass.
Down.
Down, Wanton, Down!
Dream of Frances Speedwell, A.
Dream of Hell, A.
Dream Recalled on Waking.
Dreaming Children.
Druid Love.
Earlier Lovers.
East Wind, An.
Ecstasy of Chaos.
1805.
Elsewhere.
Encounter, The.
End of Play.
Endless Pavement.
Envoi: "There is no now for us but always."
Eurydice.
Everywhere Is Here.
Expect Nothing.
Face in the Mirror, The.
Fact of the Act.
Falcon Woman, The.
Fallen Tower of Siloam, The.
Fast Bound Together.
Fetter, The.
Field-Postcard, The.
Finding of Love, The.
Fire Walker.
First Love.
Five.
Florist Rose, The.
Flowering Aloe, The.
Flying Crooked.
Food of the Dead.
Fools.
For Ever.
Forbidden Words.
Foreboding, The.
Former Attachment, A.
Fortunate Child.
Fragment: "Are you shaken, are you stirred."
Fragment of a Lost Poem.
Freehold.
Friday Night ("Love, the sole Goddess").
Friday Night ("On the brink of sleep").
Frightened Men.
Frog and the Golden Ball, The.
From the Embassy.
Front Door Soliloquy.
Frosty Night, A.
Full Moon.
Furious Voyage, The.
Garden, The.
Gardener.
Gateway, The.
Gentleman, The.
Gift of Sight.
Gold and Malachite.
Gold Cloud.
Golden Anchor.
Good Night to the Old Gods.
Gooseflesh Abbey.
Gorge, The.
Gorgon Mask.
Grace Notes.
Gratitude for a Nightmare.
Great-Grandmother, The.
Green Castle, The.
Green-Sailed Vessel, The.
Green Woods of Unrest, The.
Grotesques.
Growing Pains.
H.
Hag-Ridden.
Half-Finished Letter, The.
Halls of Bedlam, The.
Haunted House, The.
Hazel Grove, The.
Hearth, The.
Heaven.
Hell.
Henry and Mary.
Her Beauty.
Her Brief Withdrawal.
Hercules at Nemea.

Hero, The.
Hidden Garden, The.
Hills of May, The.
History of the Fall.
Home-Coming, The.
Hooded Flame.
Hoopoe Tells Us How, The.
Horizon.
How It Started.
Hung Wu Vase, The.
I Will Write.
Iago.
Ibycus of Samos.
I'd Die for You.
If No Cuckoo Sings.
Imminent Seventies, The.
Impossible Day, The.
Impossible, The.
In Broken Images.
In Disguise.
In Her Praise.
In No Direction.
In Perspective.
In Procession.
In the Vestry.
In the Wilderness.
In Time.
In Time of Absence.
In Trance At a Distance.
Injuries.
Inkidoo and the Queen of Babel.
Instructions to the Orphic Adept.
Interruption.
Invitation to Bristol.
Iron Palace.
Is Now the Time?
It Was All Very Tidy.
Jealous Man, A.
Joan and Darby.
Joseph and Mary.
Judgement of Paris.
Judges, The.
Jugum Improbum.
Jus Primae Noctis.
Knobs and Levers.
La Mejicana.
Lack.
Lament for Pasiphaë.
Lamia in Love.
Land of Whipperginny, The.
Language of the Seasons.
Last Fistful, The.
Last Poem, A.
Laugh, The.
Laureate, The.
Leap, The.
Leaving the Rest Unsaid.
Leda.
Legs, The.
Liadan and Curithir.
Like Owls.
Like Snow.
Lion-Gentle.
Lion Lover.
Logic.
Lollocks.
Lost Acres.
Lost Jewel, A.
Lost Love.
Lost World, A.
Love and Night.
Love as Lovelessness.
Love Charms.
Love Gifts.
Love in Barrenness.
Love Letter, The.
Love Story, A.
Love Without Hope.
Lovers in Winter.
Loving True, Flying Blind.
Lure of Murder.
Lyceia.
Man Does, Woman Is.
Man of Evil.
Mankind and Ocean.
Measure of Casualness, A.

Meeting, The.
Metaphor, The.
Mid-Winter Waking.
Midsummer Duet.
Miller's Man, The.
Mist.
Moon's Last Quarter, The.
Moon's Tear, The.
Mountain Lovers.
My Ghost.
My Name and I.
Myrrhina.
Naked and the Nude, The.
Name.
Name Day.
Narrow Sea, The.
Nature's Lineaments.
Near Eclipse, The.
Necklace, The.
Never Such Love.
New Eternity, The.
New Legends.
Next Time, The.
Nightmare of Senility.
No Letter.
No More Ghosts.
Nobody.
Non Cogunt Astra.
None the Wiser.
Not at Home.
Not to Sleep.
Nothing.
Nothing Now Astonishes.
O.
Oath, The.
Ogres and Pygmies.
Oldest Soldier, The.
Oleaster, The.
Olive-Yard, The.
On Dwelling.
On Giving.
On Portents.
On Rising Early.
One Hard Look.
Or To Perish Before Day.
Our Self.
Ours is No Wedlock.
Outlaws.
Ouzo Unclouded.
Pact, The.
Pandora.
Pardon, The.
Patience.
Pearl, The.
Penthesileia.
Perfectionists.
Persian Version, The.
Personal Packaging, Inc.
Philosopher, The.
Pier-Glass, The.
Pity.
Plea to Boys and Girls, A.
Poem: A Reminder.
Poem: A Reminder.
Poet's Curse, The.
Point of No Return.
Poisoned Day.
Poor Others.
Portrait, The.
Possessed.
Possibly.
Powers Unconfessed.
Prepared Statement, The.
Presence, The.
Pride of Love.
Pride of Progeny.
Primrose Bed, The.
Prison Walls.
Problems Of Gender.
Progress, The.
Prohibition, The.
Prometheus.
Promised Ballad, The.
Pure Death.
Purification.
Questions in a Wood.

Quiet Glades of Eden, The.
Quinque.
Raft, The.
Reader over My Shoulder, The.
Recognition.
Records.
Red Shower, The.
Reduced Sentence, A.
Reiteration, The.
Reproach.
Research and Development: Classified.
Restless Ghost, A.
Return.
Return of the Goddess [Artemis].
Rhea.
Richard Roe and John Doe.
Risk, The.
Robbers' Den.
Rocky Acres.
Rose, The.
Ruby and Amethyst.
Sail and Oar.
St Antony of Padua.
Scared Child, The.
Sea Horse, The.
Sea Side.
Second-Fated, The.
Secrecy.
Secret Land, The.
Secret Theatre.
Seldom Yet Now.
Semi-Detached.
Sentence, The.
September Landscape.
Septuagenarian, The.
Serpent's Tail.
Seven Years.
Sharp Ridge, The.
She Is No Liar.
She Tells Her Love While Half Asleep.
She to Him.
Shift of Scene, A.
Shot, The.
Should I Care.
Sick Love.
Silent Visit.
Sincèrement.
Singleness in Love.
Sirocco at Deyá.
Sit Mihi Terra Levis.
Slice of Wedding Cake, A.
Snap-Comb Wilderness, The.
Snapped Thread, The.
Solomon's Seal.
Something to Say.
Son Altesse.
Song: A Phoenix Flame.
Song: Basket of Blossom.
Song: Beyond Giving.
Song: Cherries or Lilies.
Song: Come, Enjoy Your Sunday!
Song: Crown of Stars.
Song: Dew-Drop and Diamond.
Song: Dream Warning.
Song: Fig Tree in Leaf.
Song: From Otherwhere or Nowhere.
Song: How Can I Care?
Song: Just Friends.
Song: Lift-Boy.
Song: Of Course.
Song: Olive Tree.
Song: Once More.
Song: Reconciliation.
Song: Seven Fresh Years.
Song: Sullen Moods.
Song: Sword and Rose.
Song: The Clocks of Time.
Song: The Far Side of Your Moon.
Song: The Palm Tree.
Song: The Promise.
Song: The Queen of Time.
Song: The Sigil.
Song: The Sundial's Lament.
Song: Though Once True Lovers.
Song: Three Rings for Her.
Song: To a Rose.

Song: To Become Each Other.
Song: Twinned Heart.
Song: Victims of Calumny.
Song: Wherever We May Be.
Song: Yesterday Only.
Song of Contrariety.
Spite of Mirrors.
Spoils.
Spring 1974.
Starred Coverlet, The.
Stolen Jewel.
Strangeness.
Strangling in Merrion Square, The.
Straw, The.
Strayed Message, The.
Succubus, The.
Suicide in The Copse, The.
Sun-Face and Moon-Face.
Superstition.
Surgical Ward: Men.
Survivor, The.
Sweet-Shop round the Corner, The.
Symptoms of Love.
Synthetic Such.
Terraced Valley, The.
Testament.
That Other World.
That Was the Night.
Theme of Death, The.
Theseus and Ariadne.
Thief.
Thieves, The.
This Holy Month.
Those Blind from Birth.
Those Who Came Short.
Three-Faced, The.
Three Locked Hoops.
Three Songs for the Lute.
Three Times in Love.
Three Words Only.
Three Years Waiting.
Through a Dark Wood.
Through Nightmare.
Tilth.
Time.
Time of Waiting, A.
Timeless Meeting.
Title of Poet, The.
To Be Called a Bear.
To Be in Love.
To Be Poets.
To Beguile and Betray.
To Bring the Dead to Life.
To Come of Age.
To Evoke Posterity.
To Juan at the Winter Solstice.
To Lucia at Birth.
To Myrto about Herself.
To Ogmian Hercules.
To Put It Simply.
To Sleep.
To Tell and Be Told.
To the Teumessian Vixen.
To Walk on Hills.
Toast to Death, A.
Tolling Bell.
Tomorrow's Envy of Today.
Torch and Crown, 1968.
Touch My Shut Lips.
Tousled Pillow.
Tower of Love, The.
Traditionalist, The.
Trial of Innocence.
Troll's Nosegay, The.
Troublesome Fame.
Troughs of Sea.
Trudge, Body!
True Evil.
True Joy.
True Magic.
Turn of the Moon.
Twice of The Same Fever.
Twin of Sleep, The.
Twins.
Two Crucial Generations.
Two Disciplines.

Two Witches, The.
Ugly Secret, The.
Ulysses.
Uncalendared Love.
Uncut Diamond, The.
Undead, The.
Under the Olives.
Under the Pot.
Unicorn and the White Doe.
Unnamed Spell, The.
Unpenned Poem, The.
Unposted Letter.
Until We Both.
Utter Rim, The.
Vain and Careless.
Vanity.
Variables of Green.
Villagers and Death, The.
Virgin Mirror.
Virus, The.
Visitation, The.
Vow, The.
Wall, The.
Wand, The.
Warning to Children.
Watch, The.
Weather of Olympus, The.
Wedding, The.
Welsh Incident.
What Can We Not Ask?
What Did I Dream?
What Did You Say?
What Is Love?
What Will Be, Is.
When and Why.
When Love Is Not.
White Goddess, The.
Whole Love.
Why of the Weather, The.
Wigs and Beards.
Wild Cyclamen.
Window Pane, The.
Window Sill, The.
Winged Heart, The.
With a Gift of Rings.
With Her Lips Only.
With the Gift of a Lion's Claw.
Within Reason.
Wm. Brazier.
Woman and Tree.
Woman of Greece.
Woman Poet and Man Poet.
Word, The.
Work Drafts.
Work-Room.
Wreath, The.
Yet Unsayable, The.
Young Cordwainer, The.
Young Sibyl, The.
Your Private Way.

Gray, Thomas (1716–71)
Agrippina.
Alliance of Education and Government, The.
Amatory Lines.
Bard, The [A Pindaric Ode].
Caradoc.
Conan.
Concluding Lines of Epitaph on Mrs Mason.
Death of Hoel, The.
Descent of Odin, The.
Elegy Written in a Country Churchyard.
Epitaph on a Child.
Epitaph on Mrs Jane Clarke.
Epitaph on Sir William Williams.
Fatal Sisters, The.
Fragment: "There pipes the woodlark, and the
    song[-]thrush there."
Hymn to Adversity.
Hymn to Ignorance.
Impromptu.
Long Story, A.
Ode for Music.
Ode on a Distant Prospect of Eton College.
Ode on the Death of a Favourite [or Favorite]
    Cat, Drowned in a Tub [or Bowl] of Gold
    Fishes.

Ode on the Pleasure Arising from Vicissitude.
Ode on the Spring.
Progress of Poesy, The.
Sketch of His Own Character.
Song: "Thyrsis, when we parted, swore."
Sonnet [on the Death of Mr. Richard West].
Stanzas to Mr. Bentley.
Tophet.
Triumphs of Owen, The.
William Shakespeare to Mrs Anne, Regular
    Servant to the Rev. Mr Precentor of York.

Gregory, Mrs. Horace *See* **Zaturenska, Marya**
    Alexandrovna

Grieve, Christopher Murray *See* **MacDiarmid,**
    Hugh

Grillparzer, Franz (1791–1872)
Field-Marshal Radetzky.

Grindel, Eugène *See* **Éluard, Paul**

Guérin, Charles (1873–1904)
Sorrow.

Guillaume de Lorris (c.1215–c.1278) *and* **Jean de**
    Meun (d. 1305)
Romance [*or* Romaunt] of the Rose, The.

Guillén, Jorge (1893–1984)
Death, from a Distance.
Horses, The.
I Want to Sleep.
Love Song to a Morning.
Nature Alive.

Guinicelli, Guido (*fl.* 13th cent.)
Canzone: Of the Gentle Heart.

Gunn, Thom (b. 1929)
Adolescence.
Adultery.
All Do Not All Things Well.
All Night, Legs Pointed East.
Allegory of the Wolf Boy, The.
Amorous Debate, An.
Annihilation of Nothing, The.
Another All-Night Party.
Apartment Cats.
Aqueduct.
As Expected.
At an Intersection.
At the Back of the North Wind.
At the Barriers.
At the Centre.
Autobiography.
Autumn Chapter in a Novel.
Back to Life.
Bally *Power Play*.
Barren Leaves.
Beach Head, The.
Beautician, The.
Bed, The.
Before the Carnival.
Behind the Mirror.
Being Born.
Berlin in Ruins.
Birthday Poem.
Black Jackets.
Blackie, the Electric Rembrandt.
Blank, A.
Bone.
Book of the Dead, The.
Breaking Ground.
Bringing to Light.
Bulletin from the Stadium, A.
Byrnies, The.
Cafeteria in Boston.
Captain in Time of Peace.
Carnal Knowledge.
Cat and the Wind, The.
Cherry Tree, The.
Claus von Stauffenberg.
Clock, The.
Colour Machine, The.
Confessions of the Life Artist.
Considering the Snail.
Conversation, The.
Conversation of Old Men, The.
Corporal, The.
Corridor, The.
Courage, a Tale.
Court Revolt, The.

Courtesies of the Interregnum.
Death's Door.
Diagrams.
Differences, The.
Discovery of the Pacific, The.
Dolly.
Donahue's Sister.
Drive to Los Alamos, A.
During an Absence.
Elegy: "I can almost see it."
Elvis Presley.
Exercise, The.
Expression.
Fair in the Woods, The.
Faustus Triumphant.
Feel of Hands, The.
Fennel.
Fever.
First Meeting with a Possible Mother-in-Law.
Flooded Meadows.
Flying above California.
For a Birthday.
For Signs.
From an Asian Tent.
From the Highest Camp.
From the Wave.
Garden of the Gods, The.
Geysers, The.
Girls Next Door, The.
Goddess, The.
Grasses.
Hampstead; the Horse Chestnut Trees.
Helen's Rape.
Her Pet.
Here Come the Saints.
Hide and Seek.
High Fidelity.
His Rooms in College.
Hotblood on Friday.
Hug, The.
Idea of Trust, The.
Improvisation.
In Praise of Cities.
In Santa Maria del Popolo.
In the Tank.
In Time of Plague.
Incident on a Journey.
Inherited Estate, The.
Innocence.
Inside-Outside Game, The.
Invitation, An.
Iron Landscapes (and the Statue of Liberty).
J Car, The.
Jack Straw's Castle.
Jamesian.
Jesus and His Mother.
Julian the Apostate.
June.
Justin.
JVC.
Keats at Highgate.
Kind of Ethics, A.
Kiss at Bayreuth, The.
La Prisonnière.
Lament: "Your dying was a difficult
enterprise."
Last Days at Teddington.
Lazarus Not Raised.
Legal Reform.
L'Epreuve.
Lerici.
Life of the Otter, The.
Lights among Redwood.
Lines for a Book.
Lines for My 55th Birthday.
Listening to Jefferson Airplane.
Lofty in the Palais de Danse.
Looking Glass.
Looks.
Loot.
Man with Night Sweats, The.
Mandrakes.
Map of the City, A.
Market at Turk.
Meat.
Memory Unsettled.

Menace, The.
Merlin in the Cave: He Speculates without a
Book.
Messenger, The.
Miracle, The.
Mirror for Poets, A.
Misanthropos.
Missing, The.
Modes of Pleasure ("I jump with terror seeing
him").
Modes of Pleasure ("New face, strange face,
for my unrest").
Moly.
Monster, The.
My Sad Captains.
Nasturtium.
Nature of an Action, The.
New York.
Night Piece, The.
Night Taxi.
1975.
No Speech from the Scaffold.
Odysseus on Hermes.
Old Meg.
Old Woman, The.
On the Move.
Outdoor Concert, The.
Outside the Diner.
Painkillers.
Patch Work.
Phaedra in the Farm House.
Philemon and Baucis.
Pierce Street.
Plan of Self-Subjection, A.
Plunge, The.
Punch Rubicundus.
Rastignac at 45.
Readings in French.
Reassurance, The.
Release, The.
Right Possessor, The.
Rites of Passage.
Road Map, The.
Rooftop, The.
Round and Round.
Sacred Heart.
St. Martin and the Beggar.
San Francisco Streets.
Sand Man, The.
Saturnalia.
Secret Sharer, The.
Seesaw.
Selves.
Separation, The.
Silver Age, The.
Skateboard.
Sketch of the Great Dejection, A.
Slow Waker.
Small Plane in Kansas.
Smoking Pot on the Bus.
Song of a Camera.
Stealer, The.
Still Life.
Street Song.
Sunlight.
Sweet Things.
Talbot Road.
Tamer and Hawk.
Taylor Street.
Tenderloin.
Terminal.
Thomas Bewick.
Thoughts on Unpacking.
Three.
Three for Children.
Three Songs, *sels.*
To a Dead Graduate Student.
To a Friend in Time of Trouble.
To His Cynical Mistress.
To Isherwood Dying.
To Natty Bumppo.
To the Dead Owner of a Gym.
To Yvor Winters, 1955.
Tom-Dobbin.
Touch.
Transients and Residents.

Trucker, A.
Unsettled Motorcyclist's Vision of His Death,
The.
Value of Gold, The.
Venetian Blind.
Victim, The.
Vigil of Corpus Christi, The.
Vox Humana.
Waitress.
Waking Dream, A.
Waking in a Newly Built House.
Well Dennis O'Grady.
Wheel of Fortune, The.
Wind in the Street.
Without a Counterpart.
Words.
Words for Some Ash.
Wound, The.
Wrestling.
Yellow Pitcher Plant.
Yoko.

Gurney, Diana
Possessions.
Riez Bailleul ("Riez Bailleul in blue tea-time").

Gurney, Ivor (1890–1937)
Above Ashleworth.
Advice.
After War.
Appeal for Death, An.
April—Dull Afternoon.
April Gale.
As They Draw to a Close.
Autumn.
Awakening, The.
Bach and the Sentry.
Ballad of the Three Spectres.
Bare Line of the Hill, The.
Battalion Is Now on Rest, The.
Behind the Line.
Between the Boughs.
Billet.
Bohemians, The.
Brimscombe.
Bronze Sounding, The.
Butchers and Tombs.
Canadians.
Change, The.
Clay.
Cloud, The.
Coin, The.
Companion—North-East Dug-Out.
Companions, The.
Compensations.
Coppice, The.
Cotswold Ways.
Daily—Old Tale.
Dancers, The.
Dark Tree, The.
Darkness Has Cheating Swiftness.
Depths, The.
Drachms and Scruples.
Dream, The.
Early Spring Dawn.
Escape, The.
February Dawn.
Felling a Tree.
First March.
First Poem.
First Time In.
For Mercy of Death.
Friendly Are Meadows.
Garden, The.
Generations.
George Chapman—The Iliad.
Glimmering Dusk.
Going Out at Dawn.
Had I a Song.
Hazlitt.
Hedger.
Hedges.
Hell's Prayer.
Here, If Forlorn.
High Hills, The.
Hoe Scrapes Earth, The.
I Would Not Rest.
In December.

In the Old Time.
Incense Bearers, The.
It Is near Toussaints.
It Is Winter.
Kettle Song.
La Gorgue.
Larches.
Last of the Book, The.
Laventie.
Lock Keeper, The.
London.
Longford Dawns.
Lovely Playthings.
Mangel-Bury, The.
March.
Memory.
Michaelmas.
Midnight.
Moments.
Musers Afar Will Say.
Near Spring.
New Year's Eve.
Not-Returning, The.
O Tree of Pride.
Of Cruelty.
Of Grandcourt.
Old Dreams.
Old Martinmas Eve.
Old Thought.
Old Times.
On Foscombe Hill.
On Somme.
On the Night.
Pain.
Pleasance Window, The.
Poet, The.
Portraits.
Possessions.
Quiet Fireshine.
Quiet Talk.
Regrets after Death.
Riez Bailleul ("Behind the line there mending
    reserve posts, looking").
Riez Bailleul ("Riez Bailleul in blue tea-time").
Robecq Again.
Sea-Marge.
Servitude.
Signallers.
Silent One, The, sels.
Silver Birch.
Smudgy Dawn.
Snow.
Soaking, The.
Soft Rain.
Song: "I had a girl's fancies."
Song: "O were there anything by half."
Song: "Only the wanderer."
Song: "Past my window dawn and down."
Song of Autumn.
Songs Come to the Mind.
Songs I Had, The.
Sonnet—September 1922.
Stars Sliding.
Strange Hells.
Swift and Slow.
That Centre of Old.
There Have Been Anguishes.
There Is a Man.
Time to Come.
To Crickley.
To God.
To His Love.
Touchstone—Watching Malvern, The.
Traffic in Sheets.
Turmut-Hoeing.
Two, The.
Varennes.
Walking Song.
War Poet.
Water Colours.
We Who Praise Poets.
What Evil Coil.
What Was Dear.
When from the Curve.
When I Am Covered.
When March Blows.

When the Body Might Free.
Where the Mire.
While I Write.
Wish, A.
Yesterday Lost.
Ypres—Minsterworth.

**Guyon, Jeanne Marie Bouvier de la Motte
(1648–1717)**
Acquiescence of Pure Love, The.
Aspirations of the Soul after God.
Child of God Longing to See Him Beloved, A.
Divine Justice Amiable.
Divine Love Endures No Rival.
Entire Surrender, The.
Figurative Description of the Procedure of
    Divine Love, A.
Glory to God Alone.
God Hides His People.
God Neither Known Nor Loved by the World.
Gratitude and Love to God.
Happy Solitude—Unhappy Men.
Joy in Martyrdom.
Joy of the Cross, The.
Living Water.
Love Faithful in the Absence of the Beloved.
Love Increased by Suffering.
Love of God the End of Life, The.
Love Pure and Fervent.
Nativity, The.
Necessity of Self-Abasement.
see also Watching unto God in the Night-
    Season.
Perfect Sacrifice, The.
Repose in God.
Scenes Favourable to Meditation.
Secrets of Divine Love Are to Be Kept, The.
Self-Diffidence.
Self-Love and Truth Incompatible.
Simple Trust.
Soul That Loves God Finds Him Every Where,
    The.
Swallow, The.
Testimony of Divine Adoption, The.
Triumph of Heavenly Love Desired, The.
Truth and Divine Love Rejected by the World.
Vicissitudes Experienced in the Christian Life,
    The.
Watching unto God in the Night-Season.

H

"H. D." See **Doolittle, Hilda**
Hacker, Marilyn (b. 1942)
Adult Entertainment.
After the Revolution.
Against Silence.
April Interval.
Art of a Novel, The.
Aube Provençale.
Autumn 1980.
Ballad of Ladies Lost and Found.
Before the War.
Callers, The.
Canzone: "Consider the three functions of the
    tongue."
Celles.
Chaplet for Judith Landry, A.
Christmas Crown, A.
Companion, The.
Country & Western.
Country & Western II.
Crépusule Provençale.
Days of 1959.
Days of 1944: Three Friends.
Dear Jool, I Miss You in Saint-Saturnin.
Elegy: "Crying from exile, I."
Elektra on Third Avenue.
Elevens.
Exiles.
Feeling and Form.
Fifteen to Eighteen.
For Elektra.
For Jean Migrenne.
For K.J., Leaving and Coming Back.

Forage Sestina.
Fourteen.
Geographer.
Gerda in the Aerie.
Going Back to the River.
Graffiti from the Gare Saint-Manqué.
Hang-Glider's Daughter, The.
Home, and I've.
Inheritances.
Iva's Birthday Poem.
Iva's Pantoum.
La Fontaine de Vaucluse, sels.
Languedocienne.
Last Time, The.
Late August.
Late August Letter.
Le Travail Rajeunit.
Letter from Goose Creek: April.
Lines Declining a Transatlantic Dinner
    Invitation.
Little Robber Girl Considers the Wide World,
    The.
Little Robber Girl Gets On in the Wide World,
    The.
Living in the Moment.
Mother.
Mother II.
Navigators, The, sels.
Nights of 1965: The Old Reliable.
Nights of 1962: The River Merchant's Wife.
1976.
1973.
Pantoum.
Part of a True Story.
Partial Analysis.
Peterborough.
Pornographic Poem.
Prayer for my Daughter.
Presentation Piece.
Regent's Park Sonnets, The.
Rhetoric.
Riposte.
Robber Woman, The.
Rooms in Bloomsbury.
Rune of the Finland Woman.
Sea Coming Indoors, The.
Separate Lives.
Separations, sels.
Sestina: "For a week now our bodies have
    whispered."
She Bitches about Boys.
Shirland Road.
Sisterhood.
Somewhere in a Turrent.
Sword.
Taking Notice, sels.
Third Snowfall.
Towards Autumn.
Two Cities.
Untoward Occurance at Embassy Poetry
    Reading.
Villanelle: "Every day our bodies separate."
Villanelle: Late Summer.
Why We Are Going Back to Paradise Island.

**Hadrian, Emperor (Publius Aelius Hadrianus)
(A.D. 76–138)**
Hadrian's Address to His Soul when Dying,
    sels.
My little soul, my vagrant charmer.

Hadrianus, Publius Aelius See **Hadrian, Emperor**
Hafiz [or Hafez] (1320–89)
Dearest, where thy shadow falls.
Epitaph: "Bethink, poor heart, what bitter kind
    of jest."
Friendship.
From the Persian of Hafiz.
Ghaselle.
Odes, sels.
On prince or bride no diamond stone.
They say, through patience, chalk.
To the Shah, from Hafiz.

Hall, Donald (b. 1928)
Abroad Thoughts from Home.
Acorns.
Adultery at Forty.
Airstrip in Essex, 1960, An.

Alligator Bride, The.
Apples.
At Delphi.
Baseball Players, The.
Beau of the Dead.
Between the Clock and the Bed.
Black Faced Sheep, The.
Blue Wing, The.
Body Politic, The.
Brief Lives.
By the Exeter River.
Carlotta's Confession.
Carol, A.
Child, The.
Child's Garden, A.
Christ Church Meadows, [Oxford].
Christmas Eve in Whitneyville, 1955.
Cider 5¢ a Glass.
Clown, The.
Coal Fire, The.
Coffee Cup, The.
Cold Water.
Columns of the Parthenon, The.
Conduct and Work.
Cops and Robbers.
Corner, The.
Couplet.
Dancers.
Day I Was Older, The.
Days, The.
Digging.
Dump, The.
Eating the Pig.
Edward's Anecdote.
Eleanor's Letters.
Elegy for Wesley Wells.
Exile.
Family, The.
Farm, The.
Fathers and Sons.
Fête.
Flies.
For an Exchange of Rings.
Foundations of American Industry, The.
Friend Revisited, A.
Gold.
Grace, A.
Granite and Grass.
Grave the Well, The.
Great Day in the Cows' House.
Green Shelf, The.
Grown-Ups, The.
Henyard Round, The.
High Pasture, The.
Hole, The.
Hut of the Man Alone, The.
Idea of Flying, The.
Illustration.
Impossible Marriage, The.
In the Old House.
Internal and External Forms.
Je Suis une Table.
Jealous Lovers, The.
Kicking the Leaves.
Kill, The.
King and Queen.
Kiss, The.
Letter to an English Poet.
Lone Ranger, The.
Long River, The.
Love Is Like Sounds.
Man in the Dead Machine, The.
Maple Syrup.
Marat's Death.
Match.
Material.
Maundy Thursday's Candles.
Merle Bascom's .22.
Milkers Broken Up.
Mr. and Mrs. Billings.
Mr. Wakeville on Interstate 90.
Moon Clock.
Moon, The.
Mount Kearsarge.
My Friend Felix.
My Son, My Executioner.

Mycenae.
Names of Horses.
New Animals.
New Hampshire.
1934.
No Color Man.
No Deposit.
Nose.
Notes For Nobody.
O Cheese.
O Flodden Field.
Old Home Week.
Old Houses.
Old Pilot, The.
Old Roses.
On a Horse Carved in Wood.
On Reaching the Age of Two Hundred.
Our Walk in Yorkshire.
Ox Cart Man.
Oysters and Hermits.
Passage to Worship.
Persistence of 1937.
Photographs of China.
Pictures of Philippa.
Poem, The: "It discovers by night."
Poem with One Foot.
Praise for Death.
President and Poet.
Presidentiad, The.
Raisin, The.
Reclining Figure.
Red Branch, The.
Religious Articles.
Repeated Shapes, The.
Revolution, The.
Rocker, The.
Scenic View.
Scream, The.
Sea, The.
Second Stanza, A.
Self-Portrait as a Bear.
September Ode.
Sestina: "Hang it all, Ezra Pound, there is only
    the one sestina."
Set of Seasons, A.
Sew.
Shudder[, The].
Sister by the Pond, A.
Sister on the Tracks, A.
Six Naps in One Day.
Sleeping.
Sleeping Giant, The.
Small Fig Tree, A.
Snow, The.
Some Oddities.
Southwest of Buffalo.
Speeches.
Stone Walls.
Stones.
Stories.
Stump.
Sums.
Sun, The.
Swan.
Table, The.
This Poem.
Three Movements, The.
To a Waterfowl.
To the Loud Wind.
Tomorrow.
Town of Hill, The.
Toy Bone, The.
Traffic.
Transcontinent.
Tree and the Cloud, The.
Tubes.
Twelve Seasons.
Umbrella, The.
Valley of Morning.
Village in East Anglia, A.
Waiting on the Corners.
Waters.
Wedding Party.
Wells.
Whip-Poor-Will.
White Apples.

Widows, The.
Wolf Knife.
Woolworth's.
Wreckage, The.
Young Watch Us, The.

**Halpern Moyshe Leyb [*or* Moishe-Leyb *or*
    Moishe-Leib] (1886–1932)**
Isaac Leybush Peretz.

Hamill, Sam (b. 1942)
Abstract.
Animus Mundi.
Another Duffer.
Arse Poetica.
At Rexroth's Grave.
Between You and Me.
Black Marsh Eclogue.
Blue Monody.
Body of Summer, The.
Cartographer's Wedding, The.
Classical Tragedy.
Cloistered.
Cold Fire, A.
Conscientious Objection.
Cooking.
Dead Letter.
Destination Zero.
Dragon in the Clouds, A.
Dresden Cattle.
Egg, the.
Elegy: "Always, the world we invent or build."
Elegy: "It is almost dawn."
End of the Road from Nantucket, The.
First Snow.
Friend.
From the Bunkers.
George Seferis in Sonora.
Getting It Wrong Again.
Gift of Tongues, The.
Gnostology.
Hellenic Triptych.
Hermes Rising.
Historical Romance.
Homage to Trakl.
Io No Piangeva.
Journey, The.
Jubilate Sutra.
Kah Tai Purgatorio.
Kali.
Kannon.
Leaf, A.
Letter to John Logan from La Push.
Letter to Robert Hedin.
Lifer.
Listen, Ianni.
Lover's Quarrel, A.
Malebolge: Prince William Sound.
Man in the Landscape.
Mountains and Rivers without End.
Naming the Beast.
Natural History.
Nihil Obstat.
October Frost.
Old Bones.
Organic Form.
Passport.
Pastoral.
Photograph of Kavafis, A.
Reading Seferis.
Requiem.
Rose for Solitude, A.
Saprophyte.
Scrutability.
Seated Figure.
September Sowing.
Sheep to Slaughter.
Sonnet.
Tammuz in the Garden.
Ten Thousand Sutras.
Treblinka Lights.
True Illumination Is Habitude.
Two Poems for Tanabata Matsuri.
Unforgiven.
Uta Mound, The.
Watching the Waves.
What the Water Knows.

With the Gift of a Nootka Rose.
Word for Spring, A.
Yellow Ribbons, Madness, Victory.

Hammon, Jupiter (1720?–1806?)
Address to Miss Phillis Wheatl[e]y, An.
Dialogue Entitled the Kind Master and Dutiful
    Servant, A.
Evening Thought, An. Salvation by Christ with
    Penetential Cries.
Poem for Children with Thoughts on Death, A.

Han-shan (Cold Mountain) (c.730–c.850)
Aboard this boat of rotten wood.
Above Cold Mountain the moon shines alone.
Again I see those who leave home.
All I see are fools.
All kinds of people exist under Heaven.
All my life too lazy to work.
All of you are priceless gems.
All the people I see / live awhile then die.
All the people I see / struggle over everything.
All you senseless buried heads.
Amid a thousand clouds and streams.
Among high cliffs.
Among the sages of the past.
Anger is a fire in the mind.
As humans we have needs.
As long as I stay in the village.
As long as we're bound by the Six Extremes.
At sunset I went down the western slope.
Beautiful Lady Lu, The.
Before the cliffs I sat alone.
Beneath high cliffs I live alone.
Birth and death are decreed.
Black-maned roan and coral whip, A.
Born thirty years ago.
Boys and grown-up men.
Bridegroom Liu is eighty-two.
Brothers share five districts.
Buddhist monks don't keep their precepts.
Building sky-high pavilions is useless.
Buy meat with blood still dripping.
Call friends over when you have wine.
Calligraphy unrestrained.
Chaos was happy.
Child who doesn't have a teacher, A.
Children I implore you.
Children of the Triple World.
Chuang-tzu said for his funeral.
Cinnabar Hills rise up to the clouds, The.
Clambering up the Cold Mountain path.
Cold Cliff's remoteness is what I like.
Cold Mountain has so many wonders.
Cold Mountain is a house.
Cold Mountain is a leakproof cliff.
Cold Mountain is nothing but clouds.
Cold Mountain is so cold.
Cold Mountain owns a house.
Cold Mountain Road is strange, The.
Cold Mountain speaks these words / as if he
    were a madman.
Cold Mountain speaks these words / these
    words no one believes.
Cold Mountain's remoteness.
Daily concerns are endless.
Deer live deep in the forest.
Disappointed impoverished scholars.
Don't stay poor my friend.
Down to the stream to watch the jade flow.
Dressed in sky-flower clothes.
Emperor Wu of the Han they say.
Exhaust your mind for profit and fame.
Farmer with acres of mulberry groves, A.
Fine young man on horseback, A.
Fire and smoke raged within.
Five Peaks turn to dust, The.
Floodplain river is wide, The.
For an image of life and death.
For the hundred years of human life.
Four or five dumb upstarts.
Frequent guest of hunger and cold, A.
From a lofty mountain peak.
Funny this den of Five Shades.
Gathering lotuses we called to each other.
Get your own clothes if you're cold.
Give me a hidden eddy.
Go ahead stockpile rhino horn.

Great Sea has no limit, The.
Greedy man who piles up wealth, A.
Group of girls play in fading light, A.
Haggling over fish and meat.
Hateful destinies cloud the eye.
Heaven is boundlessly high.
Here where I once stayed.
Here's a message for the faithful.
Here's a poem for you young lords.
Here's some advice for meat-eating people.
Hermit's heart is heavy, A.
Hey you followers of the Way.
Hey you people who leave home.
His two aspects are open and shut.
Homeless people I know, The.
How many ancient sages.
How many falls have I spent on Cold
    Mountain.
How many Tientai people.
Hundred-foot trees produced by Heaven.
I carried books and a hoe in my youth.
I chose a secluded place to live.
I close my overgrown door in vain.
I deplore this vulgar place.
I enjoy the simple path.
I have a coat.
I have a single cave.
I have heard on Mount Tientai.
I have six brothers.
I hiked yesterday to the summit.
I labored in vain reciting the Three Histories.
I live in the countryside.
I longed to visit the eastern cliff.
I love the joys of the mountains.
I met a brilliant scholar once.
I met a girl to the east.
I once knew a foolish man.
I reached Cold Mountain and all cares stopped.
I recall the days of my youth.
I recall the places I've been.
I recall twenty years ago.
I recently hiked to a temple in the clouds.
I retired to the edge of a forest.
I saw some trees by the river.
I see a bird of five colors.
I see hundreds of dogs.
I see people chanting sutras.
I see people everywhere.
I see someone deceiving others.
I see the Yellow River.
I see Tientai summit.
I sit on top of a boulder.
I spur my horse past ruins.
I usually live in seclusion.
I was so poor in the past.
Idle I called on an eminent monk.
If others are worthy accept them.
If pleasures come be happy.
If you were too dumb the life before.
If you would increase increase your essence.
If you're still and never speak.
I'll tell you a thing or two.
I'm poor alas and I'm sick.
Imagine a king-of-the-wheel.
In April when silkworms are small.
In Loyang so many girls.
In spring women flaunt their looks.
In this village is a house.
Inside Jade Hall is a curtain of pearls.
Is there a self or not.
I've always loved friends of the Way.
Last night I dreamt I went home.
Layered bloom of hills and streams, The.
Likeable excellent fellow, A.
Live without making visits.
Long ago during Liang times.
Look at the flower among the leaves.
Looking for refuge.
Man descended from Pride, A.
Man lives less than a hundred years, A.
Man who lives on rose-colored clouds, A.
Man with a good head and belly, A.
Mandarin ducks roost for the night.
Master of the brush and the sword, A.
Mister Shih had two sons.
Mistress Tsou of Tiyen.

Month when farmers escape the heat, The.
Moth-browed girl in town, A.
Mountain I live on, The.
Mountain man lives under thatch, A.
Mountains are so cold, The.
Multitude of stars is the late night's light, The.
My five-word poems number five hundred.
My home is below green cliffs.
My mind is like the autumn moon.
My parents stayed busy enough.
My path led through an old cemetery.
My scrolls are filled with the poems of
    immortals.
My writing and judgment aren't that bad.
New year ends a year of sorrow, The.
No matter how lofty your spirit.
No need to attack the faults of others.
Nothing to do I climbed Flower Peak.
Of very funny affairs.
Old and sick final years over a hundred.
Old Chung north of town.
Old lady who lives to the east, An.
On ancient rocks are ancient tracks.
On Cold Mountain Road.
On Cold Mountain there's a naked bug.
Once I reached Cold Mountain.
Once we're born we're confused.
One bottle is cast in gold.
One day I left the mountains.
Oriole on a flowering branch, An.
Our lives are circumscribed by dust.
Painted beams aren't for me.
Parrots live in western lands.
Peach would bloom through summer, The.
People can't explain.
People I see in this world, The.
People laugh about my poems.
People say cares never depart.
People search for cloud roads.
People think the body's their root.
People who meet Cold Mountain.
People who wander among clouds.
Pettiness really gets petty.
Pigs devour dead human flesh.
Pitiful hundred-year house, A.
Place where I've retired, The.
Poor donkey is short by a bushel, A.
Quick-thinking people I meet, The.
Raise girls but not too many.
Relaxing below Cold Cliff.
Resolute will can't be rolled up, A.
Rich have so many cares.
Rich men met in an elegant hall.
Rising beyond the sky.
Sad creatures of a transient existence.
Sage of Cold Mountain, The.
Seasonal round never stops, The.
Seng-yao I hear was a talented man.
Show me the person who doesn't die.
Since I came to Cold Mountain.
Since I escaped to Cold Mountain.
Sitting alone I keep slipping away.
So many kinds of people exist.
Some people fear a white head.
Some people flaunt their practice.
Some seek pleasure in love.
Someone points to a cedar.
Someone sighed *Cold Mountain sir*.
Spring water is pure in an emerald stream.
State relies on people, A.
Steam some sand for your dinner.
Stop right now I implore you.
Straining its eyes it scans the horizon.
Suffering of the Wheel is relentless, The.
Superior man's mind is terribly sharp, The.
Talking about food won't make you full.
Ten thousand miles from home.
There exists one kind of fool.
There exists one kind of person.
There exists one type of person / deserving of
    our laughter.
There exists one type of person / neither bad
    nor good.
There is no limit to changes.
There may be punctilious people.
There's a brilliant man somewhere.

There's a naked bug at Cold Mountain.
They act like drunks all day.
They don't walk the Noble Path.
They laugh at me hey farm boy.
They say when Shakyamuni.
They scrutinize worldly affairs.
Things all have their uses.
This maid is from Hantan.
This person is so uncertain.
This rare and heavenly creature.
This year's grain being still unripe.
Those days when I had money.
Three-spoked Wheel is relentless, The.
Three Worlds swarm with people, The.
Tientai Mountains are my home, The.
Today I sat before the cliffs.
Towering cliffs were the home I chose.
Trail to Cold Mountain is faint, The.
Tree grew here before the grove, A.
Trifle poor in the past, A.
Two turtles aboard an ox cart.
Unfortunate human disorder, The.
We don't see dew from this morning.
We hear about the ministers of state.
Wealth and position attract distant kin.
What is it about people that makes me sigh.
What is the saddest thing in the world.
What makes a young man grieve.
What's this crying for.
When an old man takes a young wife.
When birds sang this spring.
When hermits hide from society.
When I can't bear to watch birds play.
When Master Tung was young.
When stupid people read my poems.
When water is so clear it sparkles.
When will the treadmill of life and death stop.
Where clouds and mountains are piled to the
   sky.
Where Cold Mountain dwells in peace.
Where white clouds from high rugged crags.
White crane carries a bitter flower, A.
White whisk and sandalwood handle.
Who is this poor dreamer.
Who on earth is that.
Who takes the Cold Mountain Road.
Whoever has Cold Mountain's poems.
Whoever runs into a ghost or spirit.
Whose wine shop is this aglow.
Why am I so troubled.
Wife got tired of weaving, The.
Willows grow dark like mist, The.
Wise man isn't greedy, A.
Wise ones you ignore me.
World is full of busy people, The.
Yellow River is boundless, The.
Yesterday was so long ago.
Your rags are due to your past deeds.
You're not really hermits.
Zither and books are up to you.

HaNagid, Shmuel (993–1056)

Among My Friends.
Apple, The.
Ask the Dead and They'll Tell You.
Assistants Come to Judgment In Groups.
Be Glad, She Said.
Black of My Hair, The.
Cast Your Bread.
Child at One or Two, The.
Come Up and See the Court.
Commerce Has Markets.
Could Kings Right a People Gone Bad.
Critique, The.
Curse, The.
Day of Distress, A.
Delay Your Speech.
Did Your Father Leave You Glory.
Dream, The.
Earth to Man.
Earthquake, The.
Everything Hidden.
Fawn, The.
Fear Five to the Power of Five.
First War.
Flutter or Rest.
Foolish Enemy's Face Tells All, The.

Forgive the Man Who Sinned against You.
Friends, The.
Friends, a Fence Surrounds Us.
Gazelle, The.
Gazing through the Night.
Good Students Tend, The.
He Who Depends on the Princes.
He Who Lingers at the Court of the King.
He Whose Heart in His Heart.
Heart holds hidden knowledge, The.
He'll Bring You Trouble.
His Brother's Illness.
House of Prayer, The.
How Could You Loathe.
How I Helped the Wise.
I Quartered the Troops for the Night.
I'd Suck Bitter Poison from the Viper's Mouth.
If You Don't Have the Power to Pay.
If You Leave a Long-Loved Friend.
If You Shame a Man.
If You're Finding the Good at Fault.
I'll Show You a Fawn.
In Business Don't Get Involved.
In Fact I Love That Fawn.
Is There Any Frustration.
It's Heart That Discerns.
Jasmine.
King, The.
Know of the Limbs.
Lovers of Life.
Luxuries Ease.
Man's Wisdom Is in What He Writes.
Market, The.
Miracle at Sea, The.
Multiple Troubles of Man, The.
My Spirit.
On Fleeing His City.
On Lifting the Siege.
On the Death of Isaac, His Brother.
On Their Couches Stretched Out at the
   Treasury.
One Who Works and Buys Himself Books.
Pain, The.
Pass of Sand.
People Welcome the Rich.
Respect and Discretion.
Rich Are Small, The.
Rise Early.
Rouge in Appearance.
Sad Friend.
See the Fraud Flow By.
Send the Lord to the People.
Soar, Don't Settle.
Soul Opens inside You.
Stab Your Heart.
Suffer the World.
Take the Crystal.
They Stole My Sleep.
Three Things.
Time Defies and Betrays the Patricians.
To Yehosef, His Son.
Truth Is Hard.
Two Eclipses.
Tyrant Who Rules the Homeless and Poor,
   The.
Victory over Seville, The.
War with Yadir, The.
What Are These.
What's Familiar Is Sometimes Distanced.
When the Lord Is with You.
When You're Desperate.
Where's that Coy Gazelle.
Why Repeat the Sins.
Why Should the Hearts of You Purists.
Wise Understand, The.
You Felt the Fear of Death.
You Look through Open Eyes.
You Mock Me Now in Your Youth.
You Think There's No Hell That Will Hold
   You.
You Who'd Be Wise.
Your Loved Ones Depress You.
Your Manuscript Shines.
Your Years Are Sleep.
You're Trapped, My Tongue.
Youth Brings Us.

Hardy, Thomas (1840–1928)

A. H., 1855–1912.
Abbey Mason, The.
Aberdeen.
Absolute Explains, The.
According to the Mighty Working.
Aerolite, The.
After a Journey.
After a Romantic Day.
After Reading Psalms XXXIX, XL, etc.
After Schiller.
After the Burial.
After the Death of a Friend.
After the Last Breath.
After the Visit.
After the War.
Afternoon Service at Mellstock.
Afterwards.
Aged Newspaper Soliloquizes, The.
Ageing House, The.
Agnosto Theo [To an Unknown God].
Ah, Are You Digging on My Grave?
Alarm, The.
Alike and Unlike.
Amabel.
Ancient to Ancients, An.
And There Was a Great Calm
Anniversary, An.
Announcement, The.
Any Little Old Song.
Apostrophe to an Old Psalm Tune.
Appeal to America on Behalf of the Belgian
   Destitute, An.
Aquae Sulis.
Architectural Masks.
Aristodemus the Messenian.
As 'Twere To-night.
At a Bridal.
At a Country Fair.
At a Fashionable Dinner.
At a Hasty Wedding.
At a House in Hampstead.
At a Lunar Eclipse.
At a Pause in a Country Dance.
At a Rehearsal of One of J. M. B.'s Plays.
At a Seaside Town in 1869.
At an Inn.
At Casterbridge Fair.
At Castle Boterel.
At Day-Close in November.
At Lulworth Cove a Century Back.
At Madame Tussaud's in Victorian Years.
At Mayfair Lodgings.
At Middle-Field Gate in February.
At Moonrise and Onwards.
At Rushy-Pond.
At Shag's Heath.
At the Aquatic Sports.
At the Dinner-Table.
At the Entering of the New Year.
At the Mill.
At the Piano.
At the Railway Station, Upway.
At the Royal Academy.
At the War Office, London.
At the Wicket-Gate.
At the Word "Farewell."
At Waking.
At Wynard's Gap.
August Midnight, An.
Autumn in King's Hintock Park.
Autumn Rain-Scene, An.
Background and the Figure, The.
Backward Spring, A.
Bad Example, The.
Bags of Meat.
Ballad of Love's Skeleton, The.
Ballet, The.
Barthélémon at Vauxhall.
Beauty, The.
Beauty's Soliloquy during Her Honeymoon, A.
Bedridden Peasant, The.
Beeny Cliff.
Before and after Summer.
Before Knowledge.
Before Life and After.

Before Marching and After.
Before My Friend Arrived.
Bereft.
Bereft, She Thinks She Dreams.
Best She Could, The.
Best Times.
Between Us Now.
Beyond the Last Lamp.
Bird-Catcher's Boy, The.
Bird-Scene at a Rural Dwelling, A.
Birds at Winter Nightfall.
Blinded Bird, The.
Blow, The.
Boy's Dream, The.
Boys Then and Now.
Bride-Night Fire, The.
Bridge of Lodi, The.
Broken Appointment, A.
Brother, The.
Bullfinches, The.
Burghers, The.
Burning the Holly.
By Henstridge Cross at the Year's End.
By the Barrows.
By the Earth's Corpse.
By the Runic Stone.
Bygone Occasion, A.
Caged Goldfinch, The.
Caged Thrush Freed and Home Again, The.
Calf, The.
Call to National Service, A.
Cardinal Bembo's Epitaph on Raphael.
Caricature, The.
Carrier, The.
Casterbridge Captains, The.
Casual Acquaintance, The.
Catching Ballet of the Wedding Clothes, The.
Cathedral Façade at Midnight, A.
Change, The.
Channel Firing.
Chapel-Organist, The.
Cheval-Glass, The.
Child and the Sage, The.
Childhood among the Ferns.
Children and Sir Nameless, The.
Chimes Play "Life's a Bumper!" The.
Chimes, The.
Choirmaster's Burial, The.
Chosen, The.
Christening, The.
Christmas Ghost-Story, A.
Christmas in the Elgin Room.
Christmas: 1924.
Christmastide.
Church and the Wedding, The.
Church-Builder, The.
Church Romance, A.
Circular, A.
Circus-Rider to Ringmaster.
Clasped Skeleton, The.
Clock of the Years, The.
Clock-Winder, The.
Collector Cleans His Picture, The.
Colonel's Soliloquy, The.
Colour, The.
Come Not; Yet Come!
Comet at Yell'ham, The.
Coming of the End, The.
Coming up Oxford Street: Evening.
Commonplace Day, A.
Compassion.
Concerning Agnes.
Concerning His Old Home.
Confession to a Friend in Trouble, A.
Conformers, The.
Conjecture.
Contretemps, The.
Convergence of the Twain, The.
Conversation at Dawn, A.
Copying Architecture in an Old Minster.
Coquette, and After, The.
Coronation, The.
Could I but Will.
Countenance, A.
Country Wedding, The.
Cross-Currents.

Cry of the Homeless.
Curate's Kindness, The.
Curtains Now Are Drawn, The.
Cynic's Epitaph.
Dame of Athelhall, The.
Dance at the Phoenix, The.
Dark-Eyed Gentleman, The.
Darkling Thrush, The.
Daughter Returns, A.
Dawn after the Dance, The.
Days to Recollect.
Dead and the Living One, The.
Dead Bastard, The.
Dead Man Walking, The.
Dead Quire, The.
Dead "Wessex" the Dog to the Household.
Dear, The.
Death-Day Recalled, A.
Death of Regret, The.
Departure.
Destined Pair, The.
Difference, The.
Discouragement.
Discovery, The.
Dissemblers, The.
Ditty: "Beneath a knap where flown."
Division, The.
Dolls, The.
Domicilium.
Donaghadee.
Doom and She.
Drawing Details in an Old Church.
Dream-Follower, The.
Dream Is—Which?, The.
Dream of the City Shopwoman.
Dream or No, A.
Dream Question, A.
Drinking Song.
Drizzling Easter Morning, A.
Drummer Hodge.
Duel, The.
Duettist to Her Pianoforte, A.
During Wind and Rain.
Dynasts, The, *sels.*
East-End Curate, An.
Echo-Elf Answers, The.
Elopement, The.
Embarcation.
End of the Episode, The.
End of the Year 1912.
Enemy's Portrait, The.
England to Germany in 1914.
Epeisodia.
Epigraph to "The Woodlanders."
Epitaph for G. K. Chesterton.
Epitaph for George Moore.
Epitaph: "I never cared for Life: Life cared for me."
Epitaph on a Pessimist.
Eunice.
Evelyn G. of Christminster.
Evening in Galilee, An.
Evening Shadows.
Every Artemisia.
Everything Comes.
Exeunt Omnes.
Expectation and Experience.
Experience, An.
Expostulation, An.
Face at the Casement, The.
Faded Face, The.
Fading Rose, The.
Faintheart in a Railway Train.
Faithful Swallow, The.
Faithful Wilson.
Fallow Deer at the Lonely House, The.
Family Portraits.
Farm-Woman's Winter, The.
Farmer Dunman's Funeral.
Felled Elm and She, The.
Fetching Her.
Fiddler, The.
Fight on Durnover Moor, The.
Figure in the Scene, The.
First or Last.
First Sight of Her and After.

Five Students, The.
Flirt's Tragedy, The.
Flower's Tragedy, The.
For Life I Had Never Cared Greatly.
Forbidden Banns, The.
Forgotten Miniature, A.
Four Footprints.
Four in the Morning.
Fragment: "At last I entered a long dark gallery."
Freed the Fret of Thinking.
Friends Beyond.
From Her in the Country.
From Victor Hugo.
Frozen Greenhouse, The.
Gallant's Song.
Gap in the White, The.
Garden Seat, The.
Genitrix Laesa.
Genoa and the Mediterranean.
Gentleman's Epitaph on Himself and a Lady, Who Were Buried Together, A.
Gentleman's Second-Hand Suit, A.
Geographical Knowledge.
George Meredith (1828–1909).
Ghost of the Past, The.
Glimpse, The.
God-Forgotten.
God's Education.
God's Funeral.
Going and Staying.
Going of the Battery, The.
Going, The.
Graveyard of Dead Creeds, The.
Great Things.
Green Slates.
Growth in May.
Had You Wept.
Hap.
Harbour Bridge, The.
Harvest-Supper, The.
Hatband, The.
Haunter, The.
Haunting Fingers.
He Abjures Love.
He Did Not Know Me.
He Fears His Good Fortune.
He Follows Himself.
He Inadvertently Cures His Love-Pains.
He Never Expected Much.
He Prefers Her Earthly.
He Resolves to Say No More.
He Revisits His First School.
He Wonders about Himself.
Head above the Fog, The.
Heiress and Architect.
Henley Regatta.
Her Apotheosis.
Her Confession.
Her Death and After.
Her Definition.
Her Dilemma.
Her Father.
Her Haunting-Ground.
Her Immortality.
Her Initials.
Her Late Husband.
Her Love-Birds.
Her Reproach.
Her Second Husband Hears Her Story.
Her Secret.
Her Song.
Her Temple.
Heredity.
High-School Lawn, The.
His Country.
His Heart.
His Immortality.
His Visitor.
History of an Hour, The.
Homecoming, The.
Honeymoon Time at an Inn.
Horses Aboard.
House of Hospitalities, The.
House of Silence, The.
House with a History, A.

How Great My Grief.
How She Went to Ireland.
Hundred Years Since, A.
Hurried Meeting, A.
Husband's View, The.
I Am the One.
I Found Her out There.
I Have Lived with Shades.
I Knew a Lady.
I Look in Her Face.
I Look into My Glass.
I Looked Back.
I Looked Up from My Writing.
I Met a Man.
I Need Not Go.
I Rose and Went to Rou'tor Town.
I Rose Up as My Custom Is.
I Said and Sang Her Excellence.
I Said to Love.
I Say, "I'll Seek Her."
I Sometimes Think.
I Thought, My Heart.
I Travel as a Phantom Now.
I Was Not He.
I Was the Midmost.
I Watched a Blackbird.
I Worked No Wile to Meet You.
Ice on the Highway.
If It's Ever Spring Again.
If You Had Known.
Imaginings.
Impercipient, The.
In a Cathedral City.
In a Eweleaze near Weatherbury.
In a Former Resort after Many Years.
In a London Flat.
In a Museum.
In a Waiting-Room.
In a Whispering Gallery.
In a Wood.
In Childbed.
In Death Divided.
In Front of the Landscape.
In Her Precincts.
In St. Paul's a While Ago.
In Sherborne Abbey.
In Tenebris.
In the British Museum.
In the Days of Crinoline.
In the Evening.
In the Garden.
In the Marquee.
In the Mind's Eye.
In the Night She Came.
In the Old Theatre, Fiesole.
In the Servants' Quarters.
In the Seventies.
In the Small Hours.
In the Street.
In the Vaulted Way.
In Time of "The Breaking of Nations."
In Time of Wars and Tumults.
In Vision I Roamed.
In Weatherbury Stocks.
Inconsistent, The.
Inquiry, An.
Inscription, The.
Inscriptions for a Peal of Eight Bells.
Interloper, The.
Intra Sepulchrum.
It Never Looks Like Summer.
Ivy-Wife, The.
January Night, A.
Jezreel.
Jingle on the Times, A.
Jog-Trot Pair, A.
John and Jane.
Joys of Memory.
Jubilate.
Jubilee of a Magazine, The.
Julie-Jane.
June Leaves and Autumn.
Just the Same.
King's Experiment, The.
King's Soliloquy, A.
Kiss, A.

Known Had I.
Lacking Sense, The.
Lady in the Furs, The.
Lady of Forebodings, The.
Lady Vi.
Lament: "How she would have loved."
Lament of the Looking-Glass, The.
Last Chrysanthemum, The.
Last Journey, A.
Last Leaf, The.
Last Look round St. Martin's Fair.
Last Love-Word.
Last Performance, The.
Last Signal, The.
Last Time, The.
Last Week in October.
Last Words to a Dumb Friend.
Later Autumn, The.
Lausanne: In Gibbon's Old Garden: 11–12 P.M.
Leader of Fashion, A.
Leaving, A.
Leipzig.
Let Me Believe.
Let Me Enjoy.
Letter's Triumph, The.
Levelled Churchyard, The.
Liddell and Scott.
Life and Death at Sunrise.
Life Laughs Onward.
Light Snow-Fall after Frost, A.
Lines: "Before we part to alien thoughts and
    aims."
Lines to a Movement in Mozart's E-Flat
    Symphony.
Little Old Table, The.
Lizard, The.
Lodging-House Fuchsias, The.
Logs on the Hearth.
Lonely Days.
Long Plighted.
Looking Across.
Looking at a Picture on an Anniversary.
Looking Back.
Lorna the Second.
Lost Love.
Lost Pyx, The.
Louie.
Love-Letters, The.
Love the Monopolist.
Love Watches a Window.
Lover to Mistress.
Lying Awake.
Mad Judy.
Maid of Keinton Mandeville, The.
Maiden's Pledge, A.
Man, A.
Man He Killed, The.
Man Was Drawing near to Me, A.
Man Who Forgot, The.
Man with a Past, The.
Marble-Streeted Town, The.
Marble Tablet, The.
Masked Face, The.
Master and the Leaves, The.
Meditation on a Holiday.
Meeting with Despair, A.
Memorial Brass, The: 186–.
Memory and I.
Men Who March Away.
Merrymaking in Question, A.
Middle-Age Enthusiasms.
Midnight on Beechen, 187–.
Midnight on the Great Western.
Milestone by the Rabbit-Burrow, The.
Military Appointment, A.
Milkmaid, The.
Minute before Meeting, The.
Misconception.
Mismet.
Missed Train, The.
Mock Wife, The.
Molly Gone.
Moments of Vision.
Mongrel, The.
Month's Calendar, The.
Monument-Maker, The.

Moon Looks In, The.
Moth-Signal, The.
Mother Mourns, The.
Mound, The.
Murmurs in the Gloom.
Music in a Snowy Street.
Musical Box, The.
Musical Incident, A.
Musing Maiden, The.
Mute Opinion.
My Cicely.
My Spirit Will Not Haunt the Mound.
Nature's Questioning.
Near Lanivet, 1872.
Necessitarian's Epitaph, A.
Nettles, The.
Neutral Tones.
New Boots, The.
New Dawn's Business, The.
New Toy, The.
New Year's Eve.
New Year's Eve in War Time, A.
Newcomer's Wife, The.
News for Her Mother.
Night in November, A.
Night in the Old Home.
Night of Questionings, A.
Night of the Dance, The.
Night-Time in Mid-Fall.
Nightmare, and the Next Thing, A.
1967.
No Bell-Ringing.
No Buyers [or No Buyers: A Street Scene].
Noble Lady's Tale, The.
Nobody Comes.
Not Known.
Not Only I.
Nothing Matters Much.
O I Won't Lead a Homely Life.
Obliterate Tomb, The.
Occultation, The.
Often when Warring.
Old Excursions.
Old Furniture.
Old Gown, The.
Old Likeness, An.
Old Neighbour and the New, The.
Old Workman, The.
On a Discovered Curl of Hair.
On a Fine Morning.
On a Heath.
On a Midsummer Eve.
On an Invitation to the United States.
On Martock Moor.
On One Who Lived and Died Where He Was
    Born.
On Stinsford Hill at Midnight.
On Sturminster Foot-Bridge.
On the Belgian Expatriation.
On the Departure Platform.
On the Doorstep ("Rain imprinted the step's
    wet shine, The").
On the Doorstep ("She sits in her night-dress
    without the door").
On the Esplanade.
On the Portrait of a Woman About to Be
    Hanged.
On the Tune Called the Old-Hundred-and-
    Fourth.
On the Way.
Once at Swanage.
One Ralph Blossom Soliloquizes.
One We Knew.
One Who Married above Him.
Opportunity, The.
Orphaned Old Maid, The.
Our Old Friend Dualism.
Outside the Casement.
Overlooking the River Stour.
Oxen, The.
Pair He Saw Pass, The.
Panthera.
Paphian Ball, The.
Paradox.
Parting-Scene, A.
Passer-By, The.

Pat of Butter, The.
Paths of Former Time.
Paying Calls.
Peace-Offering, The.
Peace Peal, The.
Peasant's Confession, The.
Pedestrian, The.
Pedigree, The.
Penance.
Phantom Horsewoman, The.
Philosophical Fantasy, A.
Photograph, The.
Pine Planters, The.
Pink Frock, The.
Pity of It, The.
Place on the Map, The.
Places.
Placid Man's Epitaph, A.
Plaint to Man, A.
Plena Timoris.
Poet, A.
Poet's Thoughts, A.
Poor Man and a Lady, A.
Popular Personage at Home, A.
Postponement.
Practical Woman, A.
Premonitions.
Private Man on Public Men, A.
Problem, The.
Procession of Dead Days, A.
Prophetess, The.
Prospect, The.
Protean Maiden, The.
Proud Songsters.
Puzzled Game-Birds, The.
Queen Caroline to Her Guests.
Question of Marriage, A.
Quid Hic Agis?
Rain on a Grave.
Rake-hell Muses.
Rambler, The.
Rash Bride, The.
Re-Enactment, The.
Read by Moonlight.
Recalcitrants, The.
Refusal, A.
Regret Not Me.
Rejected Member's Wife, The.
Reluctant Confession.
Reminder, The.
Reminiscences of a Dancing Man.
Respectable Burgher, The.
Retty's Phases.
Revisitation, The.
Revulsion.
Riddle, The.
Rift, The.
Rival, The.
Robin, The.
Roman Gravemounds, The.
Roman Road, The.
Rome: At the Pyramid of Cestius near the
    Graves of Shelley and Keats.
Rome: Building a New Street in the Ancient
    Quarter.
Rome: On the Palatine.
Rome: The Vatican: Sala delle Muse.
Rose-Ann.
Rover Come Home, The.
Royal Sponsors.
Ruined Maid, The.
Sacred to the Memory.
Sacrilege, The.
Sailor's Mother, The.
St. Launce's Revisited.
San Sebastian.
Sapphic Fragment.
Satin Shoes, The.
Satires of Circumstance in Fifteen Glimpses.
Saying Good-bye.
Schreckhorn, The.
Sea Fight, The.
Seasons of Her Year, The.
Second Attempt, A.
Second Night, The.
Second Visit, The.

Seeing the Moon Rise.
Seen by the Waits.
Self-Glamourer, A.
Self-Unconscious.
Self-Unseeing, The.
Selfsame Song, The.
Sergeant's Song, The.
Seven Times, The.
Seventy-four and Twenty.
Sexton at Longpuddle, The.
Shadow on the Stone, The.
She at His Funeral.
She Charged Me.
She Did Not Turn.
She Hears the Storm.
She, I, and They.
She Opened the Door.
She Revisits Alone the Church of Her
    Marriage.
She Saw Him, She Said.
She, to Him.
She Who Saw Not.
She Would Welcome Old Tribulations.
Sheep-Boy, The.
Sheep Fair, A.
Shelley's Skylark.
Shiver, The.
Shortening Days at the Homestead.
Shut Out That Moon.
Sick Battle-God, The.
Side by Side.
Sigh, The.
Sign-Seeker, A.
Signs and Tokens.
Silences.
Sine Prole.
Singer Asleep, A.
Singing Lovers.
Singing Woman, The.
Single Witness, The.
Sitting on the Bridge.
Six Boards, The.
Sleep-Worker, The.
Slow Nature, The.
Snow in the Suburbs.
So, Time.
So Various.
Something Tapped.
Something That Saved Him, The.
Song from Heine.
Song of Hope.
Song of the Soldiers' Wives and Sweethearts.
Song to an Old Burden.
Song to Aurore.
Son's Portrait, The.
Souls of the Slain, The.
Sound in the Night, A.
Spectres That Grieve.
Spell of the Rose, The.
Spellbound Palace, A.
Spot, A.
Spring Call, The.
Squire Hooper.
Standing by the Mantlepiece.
Starlings on the Roof.
Statue of Liberty, The.
Strange House, The.
Stranger's Song, The.
Subalterns, The.
Summer Schemes.
Sun on the Bookcase, The.
Sun on the Letter, The.
Sunday Morning Tragedy, A.
Sundial on a Wet Day, The.
Sun's Last Look on the Country Girl, The.
Sunshade, The.
Superseded, The.
Supplanter, The.
Surview [or Surview: Cogitavi Vias Meas].
Suspense.
Sweet Hussy, The.
Tarrying Bridegroom, The.
Telegram, The.
Temporary the All, The.
Ten Years Since.
Tenant-for-Life, The.

Tess's Lament.
That Kiss in the Dark.
That Moment.
Then and Now.
There Seemed a Strangeness.
They Are Great Trees.
They Would Not Come.
Thing Unplanned, The.
Third Kissing-Gate, The.
This Summer and Last.
Thought in Two Moods, A.
Thoughts at Midnight.
Thoughts from Sophocles.
Thoughts of Phena.
Three Tall Men, The.
Throwing a Tree.
Thunderstorm in Town, A.
Timing Her.
To a Bridegroom.
To a Lady.
To a Lady Playing and Singing in the Morning.
To a Motherless Child.
To a Sea-Cliff.
To a Tree in London.
To a Well-Named Dwelling.
To an Actress.
To an Imposter of Rosalind.
To an Unborn Pauper Child.
To-Be-Forgotten, The.
To C. F. H.
To Carrey Clavel.
To Flowers from Italy in Winter.
To Life.
To Lizbie Browne.
To Louisa in the Lane.
To Meet, or Otherwise.
To My Father's Violin.
To Outer Nature.
To Shakespeare.
To Sincerity.
To the Moon.
Tolerance.
Torn Letter, The.
Tragedian to Tragedienne.
Trampwoman's Tragedy, A.
Transformations.
Tree and the Lady, The.
Tree, The.
Tresses, The.
Turnip-Hoer, The.
Two Houses, The.
Two Lips.
Two Men, The.
Two Rosalinds, The.
Two Serenades.
Two Soldiers, The.
Two Wives, The.
Two-Years' Idyll, A.
Unborn, The.
Under High-Stoy Hill.
Under the Waterfall.
Unkept Good Fridays.
Unkindly May, An.
Unknowing.
Unplanted Primrose, The.
Unrealized.
Upbraiding, An.
Upper Birch-Leaves, The.
Vagg Hollow.
Vagrant's Song.
Valenciennes.
Vampirine Fair, The.
Victorian Rehearsal, A.
Voice, The.
Voice of the Thorn, The.
Voice of Things, The.
Voices from Things Growing in a Churchyard.
V. R. 1819–1901.
Wagtail and Baby.
Waiting Both.
Walk, The.
Wanderer, The.
War-Wife of Catknoll, The.
Wasted Illness, A.
Watcher's Regret, A.
Watering-Place Lady Inventoried, A.

We Are Getting to the End.
We Field-Women.
We Sat at the Window.
We Say We Shall Not Meet.
Weary Walker, The.
Weathers [*or* Weather].
Wedding Morning, The.
Week, A.
Welcome Home.
Well-Beloved, The.
Wessex Heights.
West-of-Wessex Girl, The.
Wet August, A.
Wet Night, A.
Whaler's Wife, The.
What Did It mean?
What's There to Tell?
When Dead.
When I Set Out for Lyonnesse.
When Oats Were Reaped.
When Wearily We Shrink Away.
Where the Picnic Was.
Where They Lived.
Where Three Roads Joined.
While Drawing in a Churchyard.
Whipper-In, The.
Whispered at the Church-Opening.
Whitewashed Wall, The.
Who's in the Next Room?
Why Be at Pains?
Why Did I Sketch.
Why Do I?
Why She Moved House.
Widow Betrothed, The.
Wife and Another, A.
Wife Comes Back, A.
Wife in London, A.
Wind Blew Words, The.
Wind's Prophecy, The.
Winsome Woman, A.
Winter in Durnover Field.
Winter Night in Woodland.
Wish for Unconsciousness, A.
Wistful Lady, The.
Without Ceremony.
Without, Not within Her.
Wives in the Sere.
Woman Driving, A.
Woman I Met, The.
Woman in the Rye, The.
Woman Who Went East, The.
Woman's Fancy, A.
Woman's Trust, A.
Wood Fire, The.
Workbox, The.
Wound, The.
Xenophanes, the Monist of Colophon.
Year's Awakening, The.
Yell'ham-Wood's Story.
Yellow-Hammer, The.
You on the Tower.
You Were the Sort that Men Forget.
Young Churchwarden, The.
Young Glass-Stainer, The.
Young Man's Epigram on Existence, A.
Young Man's Exhortation, A.
Your Last Drive.
Youth Who Carried a Light, The.
Yuletide in a Younger World.
Zermatt: To the Matterhorn.

Harris, Lee O.
Ballad of Smiles and Tears, The.
Father William.

Harrison, Mary Field Stockton (1790–1866)
Poem on the Death of Mrs. Smith, A.

Hayden, Robert Earl (1913–80)
American Journal.
Approximations.
As My Blood Was Drawn.
Astronauts.
Aunt Jemima of the Ocean Waves.
Bahá'u'lláh in the Garden of Ridwan.
Ballad of Nat Turner, The.
Ballad of Remembrance, A.
Ballad of Sue Ellen Westerfield, The.
Beginnings.

Belsen, Day of Liberation.
Bone-Flower Elegy.
Broken Dark, The.
Burly Fading One, The.
Butterfly Piece.
Crispus Attucks.
Dance the Orange.
Dawnbreaker.
Diver, The.
Dogwood Trees, The.
Double Feature.
Dream, The.
El-Hajj Malik El-Shabazz.
Electrical Storm.
Elegies for Paradise Valley.
For a Young Artist.
Frederick Douglass.
Free Fantasia: Tiger Flowers.
From the Corpse Woodpiles, from the Ashes.
Full Moon.
Gulls.
Homage to Paul Robeson.
Homage to the Empress of the Blues.
Ice Storm.
Incense of the Lucky Virgin.
Inference of Mexico, An.
Islands, The.
John Brown.
Killing the Calves.
Kodachromes of the Island.
Lear Is Gay.
Letter.
Letter from Phillis Wheatley, A.
Lions, The.
Locus.
Middle Passage.
Mirages, The.
Monet's "Waterlilies."
Moose Wallow, The.
Mourning Poem for the Queen of Sunday.
'Mystery Boy' Looks for Kin in Nashville.
Names.
Night-Blooming Cereus, The.
Night, Death, Mississippi.
O Daedalus, Fly Away Home.
October.
On Lookout Mountain.
Paul Laurence Dunbar.
Peacock Room, The.
Performers, The.
Perseus.
Plague of Starlings, A.
Point, The.
Prisoners, The.
Rabbi, The.
Rag Man, The.
Return, The.
Richard Hunt's "Arachne."
Road in Kentucky, A.
Runagate Runagate.
Smelt Fishing.
Snow.
Snow Lamp, The, *sels.*
Soledad.
Sphinx.
Stars.
Summertime and the Living.
Tattooed Man, The.
Theme and Variation.
Theory of Evil.
Those Winter Sundays.
Tour 5.
Traveling through Fog.
Two Egyptian Portrait Masks.
Unidentified Flying Object.
Web, The.
Wheel, The.
Whipping, The.
Witch Doctor.
Words in the Mourning Time.
Year of the Child, The.
Zeus over Redeye.
Zinnias.

Heaney, Seamus (b. 1939)
Act of Union.
Afterwards, An.

Alphabets.
Anahorish.
Antaeus.
At Banagher.
At the Wellhead.
August Night, An.
Backward Look, The.
Badgers, The.
Bann Clay.
Barn, The.
Bat on the Road, A.
Birthplace, The.
Blackberry-Picking.
Bog Oak.
Bog Queen.
Bogland.
Bone Dreams.
Broagh.
Bye-Child.
Call, A.
Casualty.
Changes.
Chekhov on Sakhalin.
Churning Day.
Clearances.
Cloistered.
Damson.
Death of a Naturalist.
Digging.
Disappearing Island, The.
Diviner, The.
Dog Was Crying Tonight in Wicklow Also, A.
Dream of Jealousy, A.
Drink of Water, A.
England's Difficulty.
Errand, The.
Field of Vision.
Field Work.
Fireside.
Flight Path, The, *sels.*
Fodder.
Follower.
Forge, The.
Fosterling.
From the Canton of Expectation.
From the Frontier of Writing.
From the Republic of Conscience.
Funeral Rites.
Gifts of Rain.
Given Note, The.
Glanmore Revisited, *sels.*
Glanmore Sonnets.
Good-night.
Grauballe Man, The.
Gravel Walks, The.
Grotus and Coventina.
Guttural Muse, The.
Hailstones.
Harvest Bow, The.
Haw Lantern, The.
Hazel Stick for Catherine Ann, A.
Hercules and Antaeus.
In Memoriam Francis Ledwidge.
Incertus.
July.
Keeping Going.
King of the Ditchbacks, The.
Kinship.
Kite for Michael and Christopher, A.
Land.
Leavings.
Limbo.
Loaning, The, *sels.*
Lough Neagh Sequence, A.
Making Strange.
Man and Boy.
Markings.
Mid-Term Break.
Milk Factory, The.
Mint.
Mossbawn.
Mother of the Groom.
Mud Vision, The.
Mycenae Lookout.
Nerthus.
Nesting-Ground.

New Song, A.
Night Drive.
North.
Oracle.
Other Side, The.
Otter, The.
Outlaw, The.
Oysters.
Peninsula, The.
Personal Helicon.
Pillowed Head, A.
Pitchfork, The.
Plantation, The.
Poem: "Love, I shall perfect for you the child."
Poet's Chair.
Postscript.
Punishment.
Railway Children, The.
Rain Stick, The.
Relic of Memory.
Requiem for the Croppies.
Riddle, The.
Royal Prospect, A.
St Kevin and the Blackbird.
Sandstone Keepsake.
Seeing Things.
Serenades.
Servant Boy.
Settle Bed, The.
Sheelagh na Gig.
Shelf Life.
Shore Woman.
Singer's House, The.
Singing School.
Skunk, The.
Sloe Gin.
Sofa in the Forties, A.
Song: "Rowan like a lip-sticked girl, A."
Spoonbait, The.
Squarings, *sels.*
Station Island.
Stations of the West, The.
Stone Verdict, The.
Strand at Lough Beg, The.
Strand, The.
Strange Fruit.
Summer Home.
Sweeney in Flight.
Sweeney Redivivus, *sels.*
Swing, The.
Terminus.
Thatcher.
Tinder.
Tollund.
Tollund Man, The.
Toome.
Toome Road, The.
Transgression, A.
Trial Runs.
Triptych.
Two Lorries.
Two Stick Drawings.
Underground, The.
Undine.
Viking Dublin: Trial Pieces.
Villanelle for an Anniversary.
Visitant.
Walk, The.
Wanderer, The.
Wedding Day.
Weighing In.
Westering.
Whatever You Say Say Nothing, *sels.*
Wheels within Wheels.
Whinlands.
Whitby-sur-Moyola.
Widgeon.
Wife's Tale, The.
Wishing Tree, The.
Wolfe Tone.

Hegedüs, János
Owl, The.

Heine, Heinrich (1797–1856)
From Heine.
My Heart.

Translations from Heine.

Heliodorus (*fl.* c.220)
Beginning of Heliodorus, The.

Helsham, Richard (1682–1738)
Prologue to *Hippolytus*, Spoken by a Boy of
Six Years Old.

Herbert, George (1593–1633)
Aaron.
Affliction: "Kill me not every [*or* ev'ry] day."
Affliction (1).
Affliction (3).
Affliction (4).
Affliction (5).
Agony [*or* Agonie], The.
Altar, The.
Anagram.
Answer, The.
Antiphon: "Let all the world in ev'ry corner
sing / My God and King."
Antiphon (2): "Praised be the God of love."
Artillery [*or* Artillerie].
Assurance.
Avarice.
Bag, The.
Banquet, The.
Bitter-Sweet.
British Church, The.
Bunch of Grapes, The.
Business.
Call, The.
Charms and Knots.
Christmas.
Church-Floor[e], The.
Church-Lock and Key.
Church Militant, The.
Church Monuments.
Church-Music[k].
Church-Porch, The.
Church-Rents and Schisms.
Clasping of Hands.
Collar, The.
Complaining.
Confession.
Conscience.
Constancy.
Content.
Cross[e], The.
Dawning, The.
Death.
Decay.
Dedication, The: "Lord, my first fruits present
themselves to thee."
Denial[l].
Dialogue, A.
Dialogue-Anthem, A.
Discharge, The.
Discipline.
Divinity.
Doomsday.
Dotage.
Dulness[e].
Easter.
Easter Wings.
Elixir [*or* Elixer], The.
Employment: "He that is weary, let him sit."
Employment (1).
see also To the Lady Elizabeth Queen of
Bohemia.
Evensong [*or* Even-Song] ("Blest be the God
of love").
Evensong ("Day is spent, and hath his will on
me, The").
Faith.
Family [*or* Familie], The.
Flower, The.
Foil, The.
Forerunners, The.
Frailty.
Giddiness.
Glance, The.
Glimpse, The.
Good Friday.
Grace.
Gratefulness.
Grief.
Grieve Not the Holy Spirit, etc.

Heaven.
Holdfast, The.
Holy Baptism (1).
Holy Baptism (2).
Holy[*or* H.] Communion, The ("Not in rich
furniture, or fine array").
Holy Communion, The ("O gracious Lord,
how shall I know").
Holy Scriptures (1), The.
Holy Scriptures (2), The.
Home.
Hope.
Humility.
Invitation, The.
Jesu.
Jews, The.
Jordan (1).
Jordan (2).
Joseph's Coat.
Judgement.
Justice (1).
Justice (2).
Knell, The.
Lent.
L'Envoy.
Life.
Longing.
Love.
Love (1).
Love (2).
Love (3).
Love-Joy.
Love Unknown.
Man.
Man's Medley.
Mary [*or* Marie] Magdalene.
Mattens.
Method, The.
Misery [*or* Miserie].
Mortification.
Nature.
Obedience.
Odour, The (2 Corinthians: 2).
Offering, An.
Our Life Is Hid with Christ in God.
Paradise.
Parody [*or* Parodie], A.
Peace.
Pearl, The. Matth. 13:45.
Perirrhanterium.
Perseverance.
Posy [*or* Posie], The.
Praise (1).
Praise (2).
Praise (3).
Prayer (1): "Prayer the Church's banquet,
Angels' age."
Prayer (2).
Priesthood, The.
Providence.
Pulley, The.
Quidditie [*or* Quiddity], The.
Quip, The.
Redemption.
Repentance.
Reprisal[l], The.
Rose, The.
Sacrifice, The.
Search, The.
Self-Condemnation.
Sepulchre.
Sighs and Groans [*or* Grones].
Sin (1).
Sin (2): "O that I could a sin once see!"
Sinner, The.
Sin's Round.
Sion.
Size, The.
Son[ne], The.
Sonnet: "My God, where is that ancient heat
towards Thee."
Sonnet: "Sure Lord, there is enough in thee to
dry."
Star[re], The.
Storm, The.
Submission.

Sunday.
Superliminare.
Temper (1), The.
Temper (2), The.
Thanksgiving, The.
Time.
To All Angels and Saints.
To My Successor.
To the Lady Elizabeth Queen of Bohemia.
To the Right Hon. the Lord Chancellor (Bacon).
Trinity Sunday ("He that is one").
Trinity Sunday ("Lord, who hast formed me out of mud").
Twenty-third Psalm, The.
Ungratefulness.
Unkindness.
Vanity [or Vanitie] (1).
Vanity (2).
Virtue [or Vertue].
Water-Course, The.
Whitsunday.
Windows, The.
World, The.
Wreath, A.

Herbert, Zbigniew (b. 1924)
Achilles. Penthesilea.

Hernández, Miguel (1910–42)
Two Palm Trees, The.

Herrick, Robert (1591–1674)
Abels Bloud.
Abstinence.
Accusation.
Adversity ("Adversity hurts none, but onely such").
Adversity ("Love is maintain'd by wealth; when all is spent").
Advice the Best Actor.
Advice to a Maid.
Affliction.
After Autumne, Winter.
Again.
Againe.
Against Love.
Age Unfit for Love.
All Things Decay and Die.
All Things Run Well for the Righteous.
Almes ("Give, if thou canst, an Almes; if not, afford").
Almes ("Give unto all, lest he, whom thou deni'st").
Amber Bead, The.
Ambition ("In man, ambition is the common'st thing").
Ambition ("In wayes to greatnesse, think on this").
Anacreontic.
Anacreontic[k] Verse.
Anacreontike.
Angells.
Anger.
Another ("Art thou not destin'd? then, with hast, go on").
Another ("As Sun-beames pierce the glasse, and streaming in").
Another ("God is *Jehovah* cal'd; which name of His").
Another ("In the morning when ye rise").
Another ("Let the superstitious wife").
Another ("Love he that will; it best likes me").
Another ("Sin is an act so free, that if we shall").
Another ("Sin is the cause of death; and sin's alone").
Another ("That there's a God, we all do know").
Another ("The bloud of Abel was a thing").
Another ("The shame of mans face is no more").
Another ("Thou bidst me come; I cannot come; for why").
Another ("Thou had'st the wreath before, now take the Tree").
Another ("Wassaile the Trees, that they may beare").
Another ("Where love begins, there dead thy first desire").

Another Charme for Stables.
Another New-Yeeres Gift, or Song for the Circumcision.
Another of God.
Another on Her.
Another on Love.
Another on the Same.
Another to Bring in the Witch.
Another, to God ("Lord, do not beat me").
Another, to God ("Though thou beest all that Active Love").
Another, to His Saviour.
Another to Neptune.
Another to the Maids.
Another upon Her.
Another upon Her Weeping.
Anthea's Retractation.
Any Way for Wealth.
Apron of Flowers, The.
Argument of His Book, The.
Art above Nature, to Julia.
Ass[e], The.
Bacchanalian Verse, A.
Bachanalian Verse, A.
Bad May Be Better.
Bad Princes Pill Their People.
Bad Season Makes the Poet Sad, The.
Bad Wages for Good Service.
Bag of the Bee, The.
Baptisme.
Barley-Break; or, Last in Hell.
Bashfulnesse.
Bastards.
Beauty.
Bed-Man, or Grave-Maker, The.
Beggar to Mab, the Fairy [or Fairie] Queen, The.
Beggars.
Begger, The.
Beginning, Difficult.
Beginnings and Endings.
Being Once Blind, His Request to Biancha.
Bell-Man, The.
Bellman, The.
Best to Be Merry.
Beucolick, or Discourse of Neatherds, A.
Biting of Beggars.
Blame.
Blame the Reward of Princes.
Bleeding Hand, The: or, The Sprig of Eglantine Given to a Maid.
Body, The.
Bondman, The.
Bracelet of Pearle, The: To Silvia.
Bracelet to Julia, The.
Bribes and Gifts Get All.
Bride-Cake, The.
Broken Christall, The.
Bubble; a Song, The.
Bucolick betwixt Two, A: Lacon and Thyrsis.
Buriall.
By Use Comes Easinesse.
Calling, and Correcting.
Candor of Julias Teeth, The.
Canticle to Apollo, A.
Captived Bee, The; or, The Little Filcher.
Care a Good Keeper.
Carkanet, The.
Casualties.
Caution, A.
Caution in Councell.
Ceremonies for Candlemasse Day, The.
Ceremonies for Candlemas[se] Eve.
Ceremonies for Christmas[se].
Ceremony upon Candlemas Eve.
Change Common to All.
Change Gives Content.
Changes to Corinna, The.
Charm, A.
Charme, or an Allay for Love, A.
Charmes ("Bring the holy crust of bread").
Charmes ("This Ile tell ye by the way").
Charon and Phylomel, a Dialogue Sung.
Charroll Presented to Dr. Williams Bp. of Lincolne as a Newyears Guift, A.
Cheat of Cupid, The; or, The Ungentle Guest.

Cheerfulnesse in Charitie: or, The Sweet Sacrifice.
Cherrie-Ripe.
Cherry-Pit.
Chewing [of] the Cud, The.
Choose for the Best.
Chop-Cherry.
Christ.
Christian Militant.
Christmas Caroll Sung to the King in the Presence at White-Hall, A.
Christmasse-Eve, Another Ceremonie.
Christs Action.
Christs Birth.
Christs Incarnation.
Christs Part.
Christs Sadnesse.
Christs Suffering.
Christs Twofold Coming.
Christs Words on the Crosse, My God, My God.
Clemency.
Clemency in Kings.
Cloathes, Are Conspirators.
Cloaths for Continuance.
Clothes Do but Cheat and Cozen [or Cousen] Us.
Cloud, The.
Clouds.
Coblers Catch, The.
Cock-Crow.
Coheires.
Comfort in Calamity.
Comfort to a Lady upon the Death of Her Husband.
Comfort to a Youth That Had Lost His Love.
Comforts in Contentions.
Comforts in Crosses.
Coming of Good Luck, The.
Coming to Christ.
Confession.
Conformitie.
Conformity Is Comely.
Confusion of Face.
Conjuration, to Electra, A.
Connubii Flores, or the Well-Wishes at Weddings.
Consultation.
Content, Not Cates.
Contention.
Corinna's Going a-Maying.
Correction.
Counsell.
Country Life: To His Brother, M. Tho: Herrick.
Country Life, to the Honored Mr. Endymion Porter[, Groome of the Bed-Chamber to His Maj.], The.
Courage Cool'd.
Covetous Still Captives, The.
Credit of the Conquerer, The.
Cross-tree, The.
Crosse and Pile.
Crosses ("Our Crosses are no other then the rods").
Crosses ("Though good things answer many good intents").
Crowd and Company, The.
Cruell Maid, The.
Cruelties.
Cruelty.
Cruelty Base in Commanders.
Crutches.
Cunctation in Correction.
Curse, The. A Song.
Custard, The.
Dangers Wait on Kings.
Death Ends All Woe.
Defence for Women, A.
Definition of Beauty, The.
Delay.
Delaying Bride, The.
Delight in Disorder.
Deluge, The.
Deniall in Women No Disheartning to Men.
Departure of the Good Daemon, The.
Descripcion, The; of a Woman.

Devotion Makes the Deity.
Dew Sat on Julia's Hair.
Dialogue Betwixt Himselfe and Mistresse Eliza, A: Wheeler, Under the Name of Amarillis.
Diet.
Difference Betwixt King and Subjects, The.
Dirge of Jephthah's Daughter, The.
Dirge upon the Death of the Right Valiant Lord, Bernard Stuart, A.
Discontents in Devon.
Discord Not Disadvantageous.
Disswasions from Idlenesse.
Distance Betters Dignities.
Distrust ("To safeguard man from wrongs, there nothing must").
Distrust ("What ever men for Loyalty pretend").
Divination by a Daffadill [or Daffodil].
Doomes-Day.
Draw, and Drinke.
Draw Gloves.
Dream, The.
Dreame, The.
Dream[e]s.
Duty to Tyrants.
Eare-rings.
Ease.
Eclipse, The.
Eclogue, or Pastorall between Endimion Porter and Lycidas Herrick, An.
Elegy: "Since louely sweete, much like unto a Dewe."
Empires.
End Decreed, An.
End of His Work, The.
End, The ("Conquer we shall, but we must first contend").
End, The ("If well thou hast begun, goe on fore-right").
Entertainment, or Porch-Verse, at the Marriage of Mr. Henry Northleigh [or Hen. Northly] and the Most Witty Mrs. Lettice Yard, The.
Epitaph on a Man Who Had a Scold to His Wife.
Epitaph on the Tomb of Sir Edward Giles and His Wife in the South Aisle of Dean Prior Church.
Epitaph upon a Child, An.
Epitaph upon a Sober Matron, An.
Epitaph upon a Virgin, An.
Epithalamy to Sir Thomas Southwell and His Lady, An.
Eternity [or Eternitie].
Eucharist, The.
Evensong.
Event of Things Not in Our Power.
Evill.
Examples, or Like Prince, Like People.
Excesse.
Expenses Exhaust.
Eye, The ("Make me a heaven, and make me there").
Eye, The ("Wanton and lascivious eye, A").
Eyes, The.
Eyes before the Eares, The.
Factions.
Faire after Foule.
Fair[e] Days; or, Dawn[e]s Deceitful[l].
Faire Shewes Deceive.
Fairies, The.
Fairy Temple, The; or, Oberon's Chapel.
Faith.
Faith Four-square.
False Mourning.
Fame.
Fame Makes Us Forward.
Farewell Frost; or, Welcome the Spring.
Farewell, The: "Sweetest Loue since wee must part."
Fast, or Lent, The.
Feare.
Fear[e] Gets Force.
Felicitie Knowes No Fence.
Felicity, Quick of Flight.
Few Fortunate.

First Marrs or Makes, The.
First Work, and Then Wages.
Flatterie.
Foolishnesse.
Fortune.
Fortune Favours.
Four Sweet Months, The.
Four[e] Things Make Us Happy Here.
Frankincense, The.
Free Welcome.
Fresh Cheese and Cream.
Frolic[k], A.
Frozen Heart, The.
Frozen Zone, The; or, Julia Disdainful.
Funeral[l] Rites of the Rose, The.
Gain and Gettings.
Gentlenesse.
Glorie.
Glory.
God ("God (as the learned Damascen write)").
God ("God, in the *holy Tongue*, they call").
God ("God is more here, then in another place").
God ("In God there's nothing, but 'tis known to be").
God, and Lord.
God, and the King.
God Has a Twofold Part.
God Heares Us.
God Is One.
God Not to Be Comprehended.
God Sparing in Scourging.
God to Be First Served.
Gods Anger.
Gods Anger without Affection.
Gods Blessing.
Gods Bounty ("God, as He's potent, so He's likewise known").
Gods Bounty ("Gods Bounty, that ebbs lesse and lesse").
Gods Commands.
Gods Descent.
Gods Dwelling.
Gods Gifts Not Soon[e] Granted.
Gods Grace.
Gods Hands.
Gods Keyes.
Gods Mercy.
Gods Mirth, Mans Mourning.
Gods Pardon.
Gods Power.
Gods Presence ("God is all-present to what e'er we do").
Gods Presence ("God's evident, and may be said to be").
Gods Presence ("God's present ev'ry where; but most of all").
Gods Price, and Mans Price.
Gods Providence.
Gods Prt.
Gods Time Must End Our Trouble.
Gold and Frankincense.
Gold, before Goodnesse.
Good, and Bad.
Good Christians.
Good Death, A.
Good Friday: Rex Tragicus, or, Christ Going to His Cross[e].
Good Husband, A.
Good Luck Not Lasting.
Good Manners at Meat.
Good Men Afflicted Most.
Good-Night, or Blessing, The.
Good Precepts, or Counsell.
Goodnesse of His God, The.
Grace for a Child.
Grace for Children, A.
Great Boast, Small Rost.
Great Grief, Great Glory.
Great Maladies, Long Medicines.
Great Spirits Supervive.
Griefe ("Consider sorrowes, how they are aright").
Griefe ("Sorrowes divided amongst many, lesse").
Griefes.

Hag, The ("Hag is astride, The").
Hag, The ("Staff[e] is now greased [or greas'd], The").
Hand and Tongue, The.
Happinesse.
Happinesse to Hospitalitie, or a Hearty Wish to Good House-Keeping.
Hardning of Hearts.
Haste Hurtfull.
Head-Ake, The.
Health.
Heart, The.
Heaven ("Heaven is not given for our good works here").
Heaven ("Heav'n is most faire; but fairer He").
Hell ("Hell is no other, but a soundlesse pit").
Hell ("Hell is the place where whipping-cheer abounds").
Hell Fire ("One onely fire has Hell; but yet it shall").
Hell Fire ("Fire of Hell this strange condition hath, The").
Her Bed.
Her Legs.
His Age, Dedicated to His Peculiar Friend, Master John Wickes, under the Name of Posthumus.
His Almes.
His Answer to a Friend.
His Answer to a Question.
His Anthem, to Christ on the Crosse.
His Cavalier.
His Change.
His Charge to Julia at His Death.
His Comfort.
His Coming to the Sepulcher.
His Confession.
His Content in the Country.
His Covenant or Protestation to Julia.
His Creed.
His Desire.
His Dream[e].
His Ejaculation to God.
His Embalming to Julia.
His Farewell [or Fare-well] to Sack.
His Grange.
His Grange, or Private Wealth.
His Hope or Sheet-Anchor.
His Lachrimae or Mirth, Turn'd to Mourning.
His Last Request to Julia.
His Losse.
His Meditation upon Death.
His Misery in a Mistresse.
His Mistris to Him at His Farwell.
His Offering, with the Rest, at the Sepulcher.
His Own Epitaph.
His Parting from Mistress Dorothy Keneday.
His Petition.
His Poetry His Pillar.
His Power.
His Prayer for Absolution.
His Prayer to Ben Jonson.
His Protestation to Perilla.
His Recantation.
His Request to Julia.
His Return to London.
His Sailing from Julia.
His Saviour[']s Words, Going to the Cross[e].
His Tears to Thamesis [or Thamasis].
His Weaknesse in Woes.
His Winding-Sheet.
His Wish ("Fat be my Hinde; unlearned be my wife").
His Wish ("It is sufficient if we pray").
His Wish to God.
His Wish to Privacie.
His Words to Christ, Going to the Cross.
Hock-Cart, or Harvest Home, The.
Honours Are Hindrances.
Hony-Combe, The.
Hope Heartens.
Hope Well and Have Well: or, Faire after Foule Weather.
How He Would Drinke His Wine.
How His Soule Came Ensnared.
How Lillies Came White.

How Marigolds Came Yellow.
How Pansies or Hearts-Ease Came First.
How Primroses Came Green.
How Roses Came Red ("Roses at first were white").
How Roses Came Red ("'Tis said, as Cupid danced [or danc't] among").
How Springs Came First.
How the Wall-Flower Came First, and Why So Called.
How Violets Came Blue.
Humility.
Hunger.
Hymn[e] to Bacchus, A ("Daffadills g'en up to Thee").
Hymne to Bacchus, A ("I sing thy praise Iacchus").
Hymne to Cupid, An.
Hymne to Juno, An.
Hymne to Love, An.
Hymne to Sir Clipseby Crew, A.
Hymne to the Graces, A.
Hymne, to the Lares, A.
Hymne to the Muses, A.
Hymne to the Muses, An.
Hymne to Venus, and Cupid, A.
I Call and I Call.
Ill Government.
Impossibilities to His Friend.
In Praise of Women.
In the Dark None Dainty.
Invitation, The.
Jack and Jill.
Jehovah.
Jimmall Ring, or True-Love-Knot, The.
Judgement Day, The.
Judgment-Day, The.
Julia's Churching, or Purification.
Julia's Petticoat.
Just Man, A.
King and No King, A.
Kings.
Kings and Tyrants.
Kiss[e], A.
Kisse, The.
Kisses.
Kisses Loathesome.
Kissing and Bussing.
Kissing Usurie.
Labour.
Lamp, The.
Large Bounds Doe but Bury Us.
Larr's Portion, and the Poets Part.
Lasciviousnesse.
Last Stroke Strike Sure, The.
Laugh and Lie Downe.
Lawes ("When Lawes full power have to sway, we see").
Lawes ("Who violates the Customes, hurts the Health").
Lawne, The.
Laxare Fibulam.
Leanders Obsequies.
Lenitie.
Leprosie in Cloathes.
Leprosie in Houses.
Leven.
Liberty.
Life Is the Body's [or Bodies] Light.
Light Lightly Pleased.
Like Loves His Like.
Like Pattern, Like People.
Lilly in a Cristall, The.
Lines Have Their Linings, and Bookes Their Buckram.
Lip Labour.
Lips Tongueless[e].
Little and Loud.
Littlenesse No Cause of Leanesse.
Loading and Unloading.
Long and Lazy [or Lazie].
Long Life.
Long Lookt for Comes at Last.
Losse from the Heat.
Lots to Be Liked.
Love.

Love Dislikes Nothing.
Love Is a Sirrup.
Love Kill'd by Lack.
Love Me Little, Love Me Long.
Love Palpable.
Love Perfumes All Parts.
Love What It Is.
Lovers How They Come and Part.
Love's Play at Push-Pin.
Lyric to Mirth, A.
Lyric[k] for Legacies.
Mad Maid's Song, The.
Maiden-Blush, The.
Maids Nay's Are Nothing.
Manna.
Man's Dying-Place Uncertain.
Martha, Martha.
Matins [or Mattens], or Morning Prayer.
May-Pole, The.
Meane in Our Meanes, A.
Meane, The ("Imparitie doth ever discord bring").
Meane, The ("'Tis much among the filthy to be clean").
Meane Things Overcome Mighty.
Meat without Mirth.
Meddow Verse, The; or, Aniversary to Mistris Bridget Lowman.
Meditation for His Mistress[e], A.
Men Mind No State in Sicknesse.
Mercy.
Mercy and Love.
Merits Make the Man.
Mirth.
Miseries.
Mr. Hericke His Daughter's Dowrye.
Mr. Robert Hericke His Farwell unto Poetrie.
Mrs. Eliz. Wheeler, under the Name of the Lost Shepardesse.
Moderation ("In things a moderation keep[e]").
Moderation ("Let moderation on thy passions waite").
Money Gets the Mastery [or Masterie].
Money Makes the Mirth.
Montes Scripturarum, the Mounts of the Scriptures.
Mora Sponsi, the Stay of the Bridegroome.
More Mighty, the More Merciful, The.
More Modest, More Manly.
More Potent, Lesse Peccant.
Most Words, Lesse Workes.
Mount of the Muses, The.
Multitude.
Need.
Neglect.
Neutrality Loathsome.
Never Too Late to Dye.
New Charon, The.
New-Year's [or New-Yeares] Gift Sent to Sir Simeon Steward, A.
New-Yeeres Gift, or Circumcisions Song, Sung to the King in the Presence at White Hall, The.
New-Yeeres Gift, The.
Night-Piece, to Julia, The.
No Action Hard to Affection.
No Bashfulnesse in Begging.
No Coming to God without Christ.
No Danger to Men Desperate.
No Despight to the Dead.
No Difference in the Dark [or i'th'dark].
No Escaping the Scourging.
No Fault in Women.
No Loathsomnesse in Love.
No Lock against Lechery.
No Luck in Love.
No Man without Money.
No Paines, No Gaines.
No Shipwrack of Vertue. To a Friend.
No Spouse but a Sister.
No Time in Eternity.
No Want Where There's Little.
None Free from Fault.
None Truly Happy Here.
Nor Buying or Selling.
North and South.

Not Every Day Fit for Verse.
Not to Covet Much Where Little Is the Charge.
Not to Love.
Nothing Free-Cost.
Nothing New.
Number of Two, The.
Nuptiall Song, or Epithalamie, on Sir Clipseby Crew and His Lady, A.
Nuptiall Verse to Mistresse Elizabeth Lee, Now Lady Tracie.
Obedience.
Obedience in Subjects.
Oberon's Feast.
Oberon's Palace.
Observation ("Jewes, when they built Houses (I have read), The").
Observation ("Virgin-Mother stood at distance (there), The").
Observation ("Who to the North, or South, doth set").
Ode for Him [or Ben Jonson], An.
Ode on the Birth of Our Saviour, An.
Ode, or Psalme, to God, An.
Ode to Master Endymion Porter, upon His Brother's Death, An.
Ode to Sir Clipsebie Crew, An.
Of all the good things whatsoe're we do.
Of Love ("I do not love, nor can it be").
Of Love ("Ile get me hence").
Of Love ("Instruct me now, what love will do").
Of Love. A Sonnet.
Old Wives Prayer, The.
Olive Branch, The.
On a Perfum'd Lady.
On Fortune.
On Gelli-Flowers Begotten.
On Heaven.
On Himself ("A wearied Pilgrim, I have wandred here").
On Himselfe ("Aske me, why I do not sing").
On Himself[e] ("Born[e] I was to meet with age").
On Himself[e] ("Here down my wearied [or wearyed] limbs I'll [or Ile] lay").
On Himself[e] ("I fear[e] no Earthly Powers").
On Himself[e] ("(I will no longer kiss").
On Himselfe ("If that my Fate has now fulfill'd my yeere").
On Himselfe ("Ile sing no more, now will I longer write").
On Himselfe ("I'll [or Il'e] write no more of Love; but now repent").
On Himselfe ("Let me not live, if I not love").
On Himselfe ("Live by thy Muse thou shalt; when others die").
On Himself[e] ("Lost to the world; lost to my selfe [or myself]; alone").
On Himselfe ("Love-sick I am, and must endure").
On Himselfe ("One Eare tingles; some there be").
On Himselfe ("Some parts may perish; dye thou canst not all").
On Himselfe ("Weepe for the dead, for they have lost this light").
On Himselfe ("Work[e] is done: young men, and maidens set, The").
On Himselfe ("Young I was, but [or who] now am old").
On His Booke.
On Jone.
On Julia's Breath.
On Julias Lips.
On Julia's Picture.
On Love ("Love bade me aske a gift").
On Love ("Love is a kind of warre; Hence those who feare").
On Love ("That love 'twixt men do's ever longest last").
On Poet Prat.
On Tomasin Parsons.
Once Poore, Still Penurious.
Once Seen, and No More.
Orpheus.
Orpheus and Pluto.

Our Owne Sinnes Unseen.
Out of Time, Out of Tune.
Paine and Pleasure.
Pain[e] Ends in Pleasure.
Paines without Profit.
Painting Sometimes Permitted.
Panegyric to Sir Lewis Pemberton, A.
Paradise.
Paranæticall, or Advisive Verse, to His Friend,
    M. John Wicks.
Parasceve, or Preparation, The.
Parcæ, The; or, Three Dainty Destinies: The
    Armilet.
Parcell-gil't-Poetry.
Pardon.
Pardons.
Parkinsons Shade to the House of Mr.
    Pallauicine Taking His Death Ill.
Parliament of Roses to Julia, The.
Parting Verse, or Charge to His Supposed Wife
    when He Travelled, The.
Parting Verse, the Feast There Ended, The.
Passion.
Pastorall Sung to the King: Montano, Silvio,
    and Mirtillo, Shepards, A.
Pastorall upon the Birth of Prince Charles, A.
Patience in Princes.
Patience, or Comforts in Crosses.
Peace not Permanent.
Penitence ("Doctors, in the Talmud, say, The").
Penitence ("Who after his transgression doth
    repent").
Penitencie.
Perfume, The.
Persecutions Profitable.
Persecutions Purifie.
Perseverance.
Peter-penny, The.
Physitians.
Pillar of Fame, The.
Primitiæ to Parents, The.
Pitie to the Prostrate.
Pittie, and Punishment.
Plaudite, or End of Life, The.
Pleasures Pernicious.
Plots Not Still Prosperous.
Plunder, The.
Poet Hath Lost His Pipe, The.
Poet Loves a Mistress, but Not to Marry, The.
Poetry Perpetuates the Poet.
Poets.
Poets Good Wishes for the Most Hopefull and
    Handsome Prince, the Duke of Yorke, The.
Pollicie in Princes.
Pomander Bracelet, The.
Poore Mans Part, The.
Poores Portion, The.
Position in the Hebrew Divinity, A.
Possesions.
Posting to Printing.
Potentates.
Poverty and Riches.
Poverty the Greatest Pack.
Power and Peace.
Power in the People, The.
Pray and Prosper.
Prayer: "A prayer, that is said alone."
Prayers Must Have Poise.
Precepts.
Predestination.
Prescience.
Presence and Absence.
Present, The: or, The Bag of the Bee.
Present Government Grievous.
Present Time but Pleaseth, The.
Prevision, or Provision.
Pride Allowable in Poets.
Primrose, The.
Princes and Favourites.
Prognostick, A.
Proof to No Purpose.
Psalme or Hymne to the Graces, A.
Purgatory.
Purposes.
Putrefaction.
Quintell, The.

Raggs.
Rainbow, The.
Rainbow, The; or Curious Covenant.
Rapine Brings Ruine.
Readinesse.
Recompence.
Recompence, The.
Regression Spoiles Resolution.
Repletion.
Request to the Graces, An.
Rest.
Rest Refreshes.
Resurrection, The.
Resurrection, Possible, and Probable, The.
Revenge.
Reverence.
Reverence to Riches.
Rewards.
Rewards and Punishments.
Riches and Poverty.
Right Hand, The.
Ring Presented to Julia, A.
Roaring.
Rock of Rubies, The: and The Quarrie of
    Pearls.
Rod, The.
Rosarie, The.
Rose, The.
Rosemarie Branch, The.
Rules for Our Reach.
Sabbaths.
Sacrifice, by Way of Discourse betwixt
    Himselfe and Julia, The.
Sadness of Things for Sappho's Sickness, The.
Safety on the Shore.
Safety to Look to Ones Selfe.
Saint Distaffs Day, or the Morrow after
    Twelfth Day.
Salutation.
Satan.
Satisfaction for Sufferings.
Sauce for Sorrowes.
Scar[e]-Fire, The.
School or Perl of Putney, the Mistress of All
    Singular Manners, Mistresse Portman, The.
Science in God.
Seek[e] and Find[e].
Seest thou those diamonds which she wears.
Shame, No Statist.
Ship-Wrack.
Sho[o]e Tying, The.
Short and Long Both Likes.
Short Hymne to Larr, A.
Short Hymne to Venus, A.
Showre of Blossomes, The.
Showre of Roses, The.
Silence.
Silken Snake, The.
Sin ("Sin leads the way, but as it goes, it
    feels").
Sin ("Sin never slew a soule, unlesse there
    went").
Sin ("Sin no Existence; Nature none it hath").
Sin ("Since once reacht up to Gods eternall
    Sphere").
Sin ("There is no evill that we do commit").
Sin ("There's no constraint to do amisse").
Sin and Strife.
Sin Seen.
Sin Severely Punisht.
Sincerity.
Single Life Most Secure.
Sinners.
Sins Loathed, and Yet Loved.
Slavery.
Smart.
Smell of the Sacrifice, The.
Sobriety in Search.
Society.
Soft Musick.
Some Comfort in Calamity.
Song: "Burne, or drowne me, choose ye
    whether."
Song, A: "Loose no time nor youth but be."
Song to the Maskers, A.
Song upon Silvia, A.

Sonnet, A: "Ile dote noe more, nor shall mine
    eyes."
Sonnet of Perilla, A.
Sorrowes.
Sorrows Succeed.
Soul Is the Salt, The.
Soule, The.
Speake in Season.
Spell, The.
Staffe and Rod, The.
Star-Song, The; a Carol to the King; Sung at
    White-Hall.
Steam in Sacrifice.
Stool-Ball.
Strength to Support Soveraignty.
Studies to Be Supported.
Suffer Thou that Canst Not Shift.
Sufferance.
Sufferings.
Summe, and the Satisfaction, The.
Supreme Fortune Falls Soonest.
Surfeits.
Suspicion Makes Secure.
Suspition upon His Over-much Familiarity
    with a Gentlewoman, The.
Sweetnesse in Sacrifice.
Tapers.
Teare Sent to Her from Stanes, The.
Teares ("God from our eyes all teares hereafter
    wipes").
Teares ("Our present Teares here (not our
    present laughter)").
Teares ("Teares most prevaile; with teares too
    thou mayst move").
Teares ("Teares of Saints more sweet by farre,
    The").
Teares, and Laughter.
Teares are Tongues.
Temple, The.
Temporall Goods.
Temptations ("No man is tempted so, but may
    o'recome").
Temptations ("Temptations hurt not, though
    they have accesse").
Temptations ("Those Saints, which God loves
    best").
Ternarie of Littles, upon a Pipkin of Jellie [or
    Jelly] Sent to a Lady, A.
Thanksgiving.
Thanksgiving to God for His House, A.
Things Mortal Still Mutable.
Things of Choice, Long a Comming.
This, and the Next World.
Three Fatal[l] Sisters.
Tinkers Song, The.
Tithe [or Tythe], The: To the Bride.
To a Bed of Tulips.
To a Disdaynefull Fayre.
To a Friend.
To a Gentlewoman Objecting to Him His Grey
    Hairs.
To a Gentlewoman on Just Dealing.
To a Maid.
To a Mayd.
To All Young Men That Love.
To Anthea ("Ah my Anthea! must my heart
    still break?").
To Anthea ("Anthea I am going hence").
To Anthea ("Come Anthea, know thou this").
To Anthea ("If, deare Anthea, my hard fate it
    be").
To Anthea ("Let's call for Hymen if agreed
    thou art").
To Anthea ("Now is the time, when all the
    lights wax dim").
To Anthea ("Sick is Anthea, sickly is the
    spring").
To Anthea Lying in Bed.
To Anthea, Who May Command Him
    Anything.
To Apollo ("Phœbus! when that I a Verse").
To Apollo ("Thou mighty Lord and master of
    the Lyre").
To Bacchus, a Canticle.
To Be Merry.
To Biancha.

To Biancha, to Blesse Him.
To Blossoms.
To Carnations.
To Cedars.
To Cherry-Blossomes.
To Christ.
To Critic[k]s.
To Crown[e] It.
To Cupid.
To Daffodils [or Daffadills].
To Daisies, Not to Shut So Soon[e].
To Dean-bourn, a Rude River in Devon, by Which Sometimes He Lived.
To Death.
To Dewes. A Song.
To Dianeme ("Dear[e], though to part it be a hell").
To Dianeme ("Give me one kiss").
To Dianeme ("I co'd but see thee yesterday").
To Dianeme ("Show [or Shew] me thy feet; show [or shew] me thy legs, thy thighs").
To Dianeme ("Sweet, be not proud of those two eyes").
To Dianeme; a Ceremonie in Glocester.
To Doctor Alabaster.
To Electra ("I dare not ask a kiss[e]").
To Electra ("I'll [or Ile] come to thee in all those shapes").
To Electra ("Let not thy Tomb-stone er'e be laid by me").
To Electra ("More white than whitest Lillies far").
To Electra ("Shall I go to love and tell").
To Electra ("'Tis Ev'ning, my Sweet").
To Electra. Love Looks for Love.
To Enjoy the Time.
To Find[e] God.
To Flowers.
To Fortune.
To God ("Come to me God; but do not come").
To God ("Do with me, God! as Thou didst deal with John").
To God ("God gives not onely corne, for need").
To God ("God is all-sufferance here; here He doth show").
To God ("God! to my little meale and oyle").
To God ("God, who me gives a will for to repent").
To God ("God's undivided, One in Persons Three").
To God ("If any thing delight me for to print").
To God ("If I have plaid the Truant, or have here").
To God ("I'le come, I'le creep, (though Thou dost threat)").
To God ("Lord, I am like to mistletoe").
To God ("Make, make me Thine, my gracious God").
To God ("Pardon me God, (once more I Thee intreat)").
To God ("Thou hast promis'd, Lord, to be").
To God ("With golden Censers, and with Incense, here").
To God ("Work is done; now let my Lawrell be, The").
To God: An Anthem, Sung in the Chapel at White-Hall, before the King.
To God, His Gift.
To God, His Good Will.
To God, in Time of Plundering.
To God, on His Sickness[e].
To Groves.
To Heaven.
To His Angrie God.
To His Book ("Before the Press scarce one co'd see").
To His Book ("Go thou forth, my book, though late").
To His Booke ("Be bold my Booke, nor be abasht, or feare").
To His Booke ("Come thou not neere those men, who are like Bread").
To His Booke ("Goe thou forth my booke, though late").
To His Book[e] ("Have I not blessed [or blest]

thee? Then go forth; nor fear").
To His Book[e] ("If hap it must, that I must see thee lye").
To His Booke ("Like to a Bride, come forth my Book, at last").
To His Book[e] ("Make haste away, and let one be").
To His Booke ("While thou didst keep thy candor undefil'd").
To His Book[e] ("Who with thy leaves shall wipe (at need)").
To his Booke ("Take mine advise, and go not neere").
To His Booke ("Thou art a plant sprung up to wither never").
To His Brother in Law Master John Wingfield.
To His Brother Nicolas Herrick.
To His Closet-Gods.
To His Conscience.
To His Deare Valentine, Mistresse Margaret Falconbrige.
To His Deere God.
To His Dying Brother, Master William Herrick.
To His Ever-Loving God.
To His Faithfull Friend, Master John Crofts, Cup-bearer to the King.
To His False Mistris.
To His Friend, Master J. Jincks.
To His Friend, on the Untunable Times.
To His Friend to Avoid Contention of Words.
To His Girles.
To His Girles Who Would Have Him Sportfull.
To His Honour'd Friend, Sir Thomas Heale.
To His Honoured and Most Ingenious Friend Mr. Charles Cotton.
To His Honoured Friend, M. John Weare, Councellour.
To His Honoured Friend, Sir John Mynts.
To His Honoured Kinsman, Sir Richard Stone.
To His Honoured Kinsman Sir William Soame.
To His Household Gods.
To His Kinsman, Master Thomas Herrick, Who Desired to Be in His Book.
To His Kinsman, Sir Tho. Soame.
To His Kinswoman, Mrs. Penelope Wheeler.
To His Kinswoman, Mistresse Susanna Herrick.
To His Learned Friend M. Jo. Harmar, Phisitian to Colledge of Westminster.
To His Lovely Mistresses.
To His Maid Prew.
To His Mistress Objecting to Him Neither Toying or Talking.
To His Mistress[e] ("Choose me your Valentine").
To His Mistress[es] ("Help[e] me! help[e] me! now I call").
To His Mistresses ("Put on your silks, and piece by piece").
To His Muse ("Go wooe young Charles no more to looke").
To His Muse ("Were I to give thee Baptime, I wo'd chuse").
To His Muse ("Whither, mad maiden, wilt thou roame?").
To His Muse, Another to the Same.
To His Nephew, to Be Prosperous in His Art of Painting.
To His Paternall Countrey.
To His Peculiar Friend M. Jo: Wicks.
To His Peculiar Friend Master Thomas Shapcott, Lawyer.
To His Peculiar Friend Sir Edward Fish, Knight Baronet.
To His Savior [or Saviour]. The New Years [or yeers] Gift.
To His Saviour.
To His Saviour, a Child; a Present, by a Child.
To His Saviours Sepulcher: His Devotion.
To His Sister in Law, M. Susanna Herrick.
To His Sweet Saviour.
To His Tomb-Maker.
To His Valentine, on S. Valentines Day.
To His Verses.
To His Worthy Friend, M. Arthur Bartly.
To His Worthy Friend M. John Hall, Student of

Grayes-Inne.
To Worthy Friend, M. Tho. Falconbirge.
To His Worthy Kinsmen, Mr. Stephen Soame.
To Jealousie.
To Jos: Lo: Bishop of Exeter.
To Julia ("Help me, Julia, for to pray").
To Julia ("Holy waters hither bring").
To Julia ("How rich and pleasing thou, my Julia, art").
To Julia ("I am zeellesse, prethee pray").
To Julia ("Julia, when thy Herrick dies").
To Julia ("Offer thy gift; but first the Law commands").
To Julia ("Permit me, Julia, now to goe away").
To Julia ("Saints-bell calls; and, Julia, I must read, The").
To Julia, in Her Dawn, or Day-breake.
To Julia in the Temple.
To Julia, the Flaminica Dialis, or Queen-Priest.
To Keep a True Lent.
To Larr [or Lar].
To Laurels.
To Live Freely.
To Live Merrily, and to Trust to Good Verses.
To Love.
To Marygolds.
To M. Denham, on His Prospective Poem.
To M. Henry Lawes, the Excellent Composer[,] of His Lyrics.
To M. Kellam.
To M. Laurence Swetnaham.
To M. Leonard Willan His Peculiar Friend.
To Meadows [or Meddowes].
To Mistress Katherine Bradshaw, the Lovely, That Crowned Him with Laurel.
To Mistresse Amie Potter.
To Mistresse Dorothy Parsons.
To Mistresse Mary Willand.
To Momus.
To Music.
To Music: A Song.
To Music, to Becalm a Sweet-sick Youth.
To Music, to Becalm His Fever.
To My Dearest Sister M. Mercie Herrick.
To My Ill Reader.
To Myrrha Hard-Hearted.
To Oenone ("Sweet Oenone, doe but say").
To Oenone ("Thou saist [or sayest] Love['] s dart").
To Oenone ("What conscience, say, is it in thee").
To Pansies.
To Perenna ("How long, Perenna, wilt thou see").
To Perenna ("I a Dirge will pen for thee").
To Perenna ("Thou say'st I'm dull; if edge-lesse so I be").
To Perenna ("When I thy parts runne o're, I can't espie").
To Perenna, A Mistresse.
To Perilla.
To Phyllis to Love and Live with Him.
To Primroses Filled with Morning Dew.
To Prince Charles upon His coming to Exeter.
To Robin Redbreast.
To Rosemary and Baies.
To Roses in Julia's Bosome.
To Sapho ("Sapho, I will chuse to go").
To Sapho ("Thou saist thou lov'st me Sapho; I say no").
To Sappho.
To Silvia ("I am holy, while I stand").
To Silvia ("No more my Silvia, do I mean to pray").
To Silvia ("Pardon my trespasse (Silvia) I confesse").
To Silvia to Wed.
To Sir Clipsebie Crew.
To Sir Clipseby Crew.
To Sir George Parrie, Doctor of the Civill Law.
To Sir John Berkeley, Governour of Exeter.
To Springs and Fountains.
To Sycamores.
To the Detracter.
To the Earle of Westmerland.
To the Fever, Not To Trouble Julia.

To the Generous Reader.
To the Genius of His House.
To the Handsome Mistresse Grace Potter.
To the High and Noble Prince, George, Duke, Marquesse, and Earle of Buckingham.
To the Honoured, Master Endimion Porter.
To the King ("Give way, give way, now, now my Charles shines here").
To the King ("If when these Lyricks (Cesar) You shall heare").
To the King and Queen[e], upon Their Unhappy Distances.
To the King, to Cure the Evill.
To the King; Upon His Com[m]ing with His Army into the West.
To the King; Upon His Taking of Leicester.
To the King; Upon His Welcome to Hampton-Court.
To the Lady Crew, upon the Death of Her Child.
To the Lady Mary Villars, Governesse to the Princesse Henretta.
To the Ladyes.
To the Lark.
To the Little Spinners.
To the Lord Hopton, on His Fight in Cornwall.
To the Maids to Walke Abroad.
To the Most Accomplisht Gentleman, Master Edward Norgate, Clark of the Signet to His Majesty.
To the Most Accomplisht Gentleman Master Michael Oulsworth.
To the Most Comely and Proper M. Elizabeth Finch.
To the Most Fair and Lovely Mistress Anne Soame, Now Lady Abdie.
To the Most Illustrious and Most Hopefull[l] Prince, Charles, Prince of Wales.
To the Most Learned, Wise, and Arch-Antiquary, M. John Selden.
To the Most Virtuous Mistress Pot, Who Many Times Entertained Him.
To the Nightingale, and Robin-Red-Brest.
To the Painter, to Draw Him a Picture.
To the Passenger.
To the Patron of Poets, M. End: Porter.
To the Queene.
To the Reverend Shade of His Religious Father.
To the Right Gratious Prince, Lodwick, Duke of Richmond and Lenox.
To the Right Honourable Edward Earle of Dorset.
To the Right Honourable Mildmay, Earl of Westmorland.
To the Right Honourable, Philip, Earle of Pembroke, and Montgomerie.
To the Rose; a Song.
To the Sour[e] Reader.
To the Virgins, to Make Much of Time.
To the Water Nymphs, Drinking at the Fountain.
To the Western Wind.
To the Willow-Tree.
To the Yew and Cypress to Grace His Funeral.
To Violets.
To Virgins.
To Vulcan.
To Women, to Hide Their Teeth, if They Be Rotten or Rusty.
To Youth.
Transfiguration, The.
Treason.
True Friendship.
True Safety.
Truth.
Truth and Error.
Truth and Falsehood.
Twelfe Night, or King and Queene.
Twilight ("Twilight is no other thing (we say), The").
Twilight ("Twilight, no other thing is, Poets say").
Two Things Odious.
Ultimus Heroum: or, To the Most Learned, and to the Right Honourable, Henry, Marquesse

of Dorchester.
Up Tail[e]s All.
Upon a Black Twist, Rounding the Arm of the Countess of Carlisle.
Upon a Bleare-Ey'd Woman.
Upon a Cheap Laundresse: Epigram.
Upon a Cherrystone Sent to the Tip of the Lady Jemmonia Walgraves Eare.
Upon a Child.
Upon a Child. An Epitaph.
Upon a Child That Died [or Dyed].
Upon a Comely, and Curious Maide.
Upon a Crooked Maid.
Upon a Delaying Lady.
Upon a Flie.
Upon a Free Maid, with a Foule Breath.
Upon a Gentlewoman with a Sweet Voice.
Upon a Hoarse Singer.
Upon a Lady Faire, but Fruitlesse.
Upon a Lady That Dyed in Child-Bed, and Left a Daughter behind Her.
Upon a Maid ("Gone she is a long, long way").
Upon a Maide ("Hence a blessed soule is fled").
Upon a Maid[e] ("Here she lies [or lyes] (in Bed of Spice)").
Upon a Painted Gentlewoman.
Upon a Physitian.
Upon a Scarre in a Virgins Face.
Upon a Sowre-Breath Lady.
Upon a Virgin.
Upon a Virgin Kissing a Rose.
Upon a Wife That Dyed Mad with Jealousie.
Upon a Young Mother of Many Children.
Upon Adam Peapes.
Upon an Old Man a Residenciarie.
Upon an Old Woman.
Upon Batt.
Upon Ben Jo[h]nson.
Upon Bice.
Upon Blanch ("I have seen many Maidens to have haire").
Upon Blanch[e] ("Blanch[e] swears her Husband's lovely; when a scald").
Upon Blinks.
Upon Blisse.
Upon Boreman. Epig.
Upon Bran.
Upon Bridget.
Upon Brock.
Upon Buggins.
Upon Bunce: Epigram.
Upon Bungie.
Upon Burr.
Upon Candlemasse Day.
Upon Case.
Upon Center a Spectacle-Maker with a Flat Nose.
Upon Chub.
Upon Clunn.
Upon Cob.
Upon Cock.
Upon Comely a Good Speaker but an Ill Singer.
Upon Coone.
Upon Crab.
Upon Craw.
Upon Croot.
Upon Cuffe. Epig.
Upon Cupid ("As lately I a Garland bound").
Upon Cupid ("Love, like a Beggar, came to me").
Upon Cupid ("Love, like a Gypsie, lately came").
Upon Cupid ("Old wives have often told, how they").
Upon Cuts.
Upon Deb.
Upon Dol.
Upon Doll.
Upon Dundrige.
Upon Eeles.
Upon Electra.
Upon Electra's Teares.
Upon Faunus.
Upon Flimsey: Epigram.

Upon Flood, Or a Thankfull Man.
Upon Fone a School-master. Epigram.
Upon Franck ("Franck ne'r wore silk she sweares; but I reply").
Upon Franck ("Franck wo'd go scoure her teeth; and setting to't").
Upon Gander.
Upon Glasco. Epig.
Upon Glass: Epigram.
Upon God ("God is all fore-part; for, we never see").
Upon God ("God is ont only [or onely] said to be").
Upon God ("God when He takes my goods and chattels hence").
Upon Gorgonius.
Upon Greedy.
Upon Groynes.
Upon Grubs.
Upon Grudgings.
Upon Gryll.
Upon Gubbs.
Upon Guesse.
Upon Gut.
Upon Hanch a Schoolmaster.
Upon Her Almes.
Upon Her Blush.
Upon Her Eyes.
Upon Her Feet.
Upon Her Voice.
Upon Her Weeping.
Upon Himself ("Come, leave this loathed Country-life, and then").
Upon Himself ("I dislikt but even now").
Upon Himself ("Mop-eyed I am, as some have said").
Upon Himself ("Th'art hence removing, (like a Shepherds tent)").
Upon Himself ("Thou shalt not All die; for while Love's fire shines").
Upon Himselfe ("I am Sive-like, and can hold").
Upon Himselfe ("I co'd never love indeed").
Upon Himselfe ("I lately fri'd, but now behold").
Upon Himselfe Being Buried.
Upon His Departure Hence.
Upon His Eye-Sight Failing Him.
Upon His Gray Haires.
Upon His Julia.
Upon His Kinswoman Mrs. M. S.
Upon His Kinswoman Mistresse Bridget Herrick.
Upon His Kinswoman Mistris Elizabeth Herrick.
Upon His Sister-in-Law, Mistress Elizabeth Herrick.
Upon His Spaniel[l] Tracie [or Tracy].
Upon His Verses.
Upon Hog.
Upon Horne.
Upon Huncks: Epigram.
Upon Irene.
Upon Jack and Jill: Epigram.
Upon Jollies Wife.
Upon Jolly and Jilly.
Upon Jone and Jane.
Upon Judith.
Upon Julia's Breasts.
Upon Julia's Clothes.
Upon Julia's Fall.
Upon Julia's Haire, Bundled Up in a Golden Net.
Upon Julias Recovery.
Upon Julia's Ribband.
Upon Julia's Sweat.
Upon Julia's Unlacing Her Self.
Upon Julia's Voice.
Upon Julia['s] Washing Herself in the River.
Upon Kings.
Upon Leech.
Upon Letcher: Epigram.
Upon Linnit.
Upon Loach.
Upon Love ("Christall Violl Cupid brought, A").

Upon Love ("I held Love's head while it did ake").
Upon Love ("I plaid with Love, as with the fire").
Upon Love ("In a Dreame, Love bad me go").
Upon Love ("Love brought me to a silent Grove").
Upon Love ("Love, I have broke").
Upon Love ("Love is a circle, and an Endlesse Sphere").
Upon Love ("Love scorch'd my finger, but did spare").
Upon Love ("Love's a thing, (as I do heare)").
Upon Love ("Some salve to every sore, we may apply").
Upon Love, by Way of Question and Answer.
Upon Lucia.
Upon Lucia Dabled in the Deaw.
Upon Lucie.
Upon Luggs.
Upon Lulls.
Upon Lungs.
Upon Lupes.
Upon Luske.
Upon Madam Ursly.
Upon Magot a Frequenter of Ordinaries.
Upon Man.
Upon M. Ben Jo[h]nson: Epigram.
Upon Master Fletchers Incomparable Playes.
Upon M. William Lawes, the Rare Musitian.
Upon Mease.
Upon Megg.
Upon Mistress Elizabeth Wheeler under the Name of Amarillis.
Upon Mistresse Susanna Southwell, Her Cheeks.
Upon Much-More.
Upon Mudge.
Upon Nis.
Upon Nodes.
Upon One-Ey'd Broomsted.
Upon One Lillie, Who Marryed with a Maid Call'd Rose.
Upon One Who Said She Was Alwayes Young.
Upon Pagget.
Upon Parrat.
Upon Parson Beanes.
Upon Parting.
Upon Paske a Draper.
Upon Patrick a Footman.
Upon Paul.
Upon Pearch.
Upon Peason.
Upon Pennie.
Upon Pievish.
Upon Pimpe.
Upon Pink an Ill-Fac'd Painter.
Upon Prickles.
Upon Prig.
Upon Prigg.
Upon Prudence Baldwin Her Sickness[e].
Upon Prue [or Prew], His Maid.
Upon Punchin.
Upon Pusse and her Prentice.
Upon Ralph ("Curse not the mice, no grist of thine they eat").
Upon Ralph ("Ralph pares his nayles, his warts, his cornes, and Raph").
Upon Raspe.
Upon Reape.
Upon Rook: Epigram.
Upon Roots.
Upon Roses.
Upon Rumpe.
Upon Rush.
Upon Sapho.
Upon Sapho, Sweetly Playing, and Sweetly Singing.
Upon Scobble [Epigram].
Upon Shark.
Upon Shift.
Upon Shopter.
Upon Showbread [or Shewbread]: Epigram.
Upon Sibb.
Upon Sibilla.
Upon Silvia, a Mistresse.

Upon Skinns.
Upon Skoles.
Upon Skrew.
Upon Skurffe.
Upon Slouch.
Upon Smeaton.
Upon Snare, an Usurer.
Upon Sneape.
Upon Some Women.
Upon Spalt.
Upon Spenke.
Upon Spokes.
Upon Spunge.
Upon Spur.
Upon Strut.
Upon Sudds, a Laundress[e].
Upon Tap.
Upon Teage.
Upon Teares.
Upon the Bishop of Lincolne's Imprisonment.
Upon the Death of His Sparrow; an Elegie.
Upon the Lady Crew.
Upon the Losse of His Finger.
Upon the Loss[e] of His Mistresses.
Upon the Much Lamented, Mr. J. Warr.
Upon the Nipples of Julia's Breast.
Upon the Roses in Julias Bosome.
Upon the Same.
Upon the Troublesome Times.
Upon Time.
Upon Tooly.
Upon Trap.
Upon Trencherman.
Upon Trigg.
Upon Truggin.
Upon Tubbs.
Upon Tuck.
Upon Umber: Epigram.
Upon Urles.
Upon Ursley.
Upon Vinegar.
Upon Woman and Mary.
Upon Wrinkles.
Upon Zelot.
Verses.
Vertue.
Vertue Best United.
Vertue Is Sensible of Suffering.
Vine, The.
Virgin Mary, The ("To work a wonder, God would have her shown").
Virgin Mary, The ("Virgin Marie was (as I have read), The").
Vision, The ("Methought I saw (as I did dream[e] in bed)").
Vision, The ("Sitting alone (as one forsook)").
Vision to Electra, The.
Voice and Violl, The.
Vow to Mars, A.
Vow to Minerva, A.
Vow to Venus, A.
Wages.
Wake, The.
Want ("Need is no vice at all; though here it be").
Want ("Want is a softer Wax, that takes thereon").
Warre.
Wassaile, The.
Watch, The.
Way in a Crowd.
Way, The.
Weeping Cherry, The.
Welcome to Sack, The.
Welcome What Comes.
What God Is.
What Kind of Mistress[e] He Would Have.
When He Would Have His Verses Read.
Whips.
White Island.
Why Flowers Change Color.
Widow's Tears [or Widdowes Teares], The: or, Dirge of Dorcas.
Will Makes the Work, or Consent Makes the Cure, The.
Will the Cause of Woe, The.

Will to Be Working, A.
Willow Garland, The.
Wit Punisht, Prospers Most.
Women Uselesse.
Wounded Cupid, The.
Wounded Heart, The.
Writing.
Youth, and Age.
Zeal Required in Love.

Hesiod (fl. c.700 B.C.)
Theogony, sels.

Hill, Geoffrey (b. 1932)
After Cumae.
Annunciations.
Apology for the Revival of Christian Architecture in England, An.
Asmodai.
Assisi Fragments, The.
Bibliographers, The.
Bidden Guest, The.
Canaan.
Canticle for Good Friday.
Christmas Trees.
Churchill's Funeral.
Cowan Bridge; At the Site of 'Lowood School.'
Cycle.
De Jure Belli ac Pacis.
Distant Fury of Battle, The.
Doctor Faustus.
Elegiac Stanzas: On a Visit to Dove Cottage.
Fantasia on 'Horbury'; John Bacchus Dykes, 1859.
Florentines.
Four Poems Regarding the Endurance of Poets.
Funeral Music.
Genesis.
God's Little Mountain.
Guardians, The.
History as Poetry.
Holy Thursday.
Humanist, The.
Hymns to Our Lady of Chartres.
I Had Hope When Violence Was Ceas't.
Imaginative Life, The.
In Memory of Jane Fraser [or Frazer].
In Piam Memoriam.
Lachrimae; or Seven Tears Figured in Seven Passionate Pavans.
Little Apocalypse; Hölderlin: 1770–1843.
Locust Songs.
Mercian Hymns.
Merlin.
Metamorphoses.
Mystery of the Charity of Charles Péguy, The.
Of Coming-into-Being and Passing-Away.
Of Commerce and Society: Variations on a Theme.
Order of Service, An.
Orpheus and Eurydice.
Ovid in the Third Reich.
Pastoral, A: "Mobile, immaculate and austere."
Picture of a Nativity.
Pre-Raphaelite Notebook, A.
Psalms of Assize.
Requiem for the Plantagenet Kings.
Respublica.
Ritornelli.
Scenes with Harlequins.
September Song.
Sobieski's Shield.
Soliloquies.
Solomon's Mines.
Song Contest.
Songbook of Sebastian Arrurruz, The.
Sorrel.
Tenebrae.
Terribilis Est Locus Iste; Gaugin and the Pont-Aven School.
Three Baroque Meditations.
To the Nieuport Scout.
To the (Supposed) Patron.
Troublesome Reign, The.
Turtle Dove, The.
Two Chorale-Preludes: On Melodies by Paul

Celan.
Two Formal Elegies.
Veni Coronaberis.
White Ship, The.
Wreaths.

Ho Ch'e Ch'ang (659–744)
Returning after I left my home in childhood.

Hölderlin, Friedrich (1770–1843)
And you Diotima who walk humbly among the living.
Too long we lived for work and wages, we.

Homer (*fl.* **before 700 B.C.**)
Epigram of Homer, An.
Iliad, The, *sels.*
Odyssey, *sels.*

Hopkins, Gerard Manley (1844–89)
Ad Episcopum Salopiensem.
Ad Mariam.
Ad Matrem Virginem.
Ad Reverendum Patrem Fratrem Thomam Burke O.P. Collegium S. Beunonis Invisentem.
Alchemist in the City, The.
All as that moth call'd Underwing, alighted.
Andromeda.
Angelus ad Virginem.
As it fell upon a day.
As Kingfishers Catch Fire.
Ashboughs.
At a Welsh Waterfall.
At the Wedding March.
Barnfloor and Winepress.
Basket broad of woven white rods, A.
Beginning of the End, The.
Bellisle! that is a fabling name, but we.
Binsey Poplars (Felled 1879).
Blessed Virgin Compared to the Air We Breathe, The.
Boughs being pruned, birds preenèd, show more fair.
Brothers.
Bugler's First Communion, The.
But what indeed is ask'd of me?
By Mrs. Hopley.
Caged Skylark, The.
Candle Indoors, The.
Carrion Comfort.
Castara Victrix.
Cheery Beggar.
Cold whip-adder unespied, The.
Complaint, A.
Confirmed beauty will not bear a stress.
Continuation of R. Garnett's *Nix.*
Cuckoo, The.
Cywydd.
Daphne.
Dark-out Lucifer detesting this, The.
Dawn.
Denis, / Whose motionable, alert, most vaulting wit.
Did Helen steal my love from me?
Distance / Dappled with diminish'd trees.
Duns Scotus's Oxford.
During the eastering of untainted morns.
Earth and heaven, so little known, The.
Easter.
Easter Communion.
Ecquis Binas.
Elegiacs.
Elopement, The.
Epithalamion: "Hark, hearer, hear what I do; lend a thought now, make believe."
Escorial, The.
Felix Randal.
Floris in Italy.
For a Picture of Saint Dorothea.
Fragment of Anything You Like, A.
Fragments, *sels.*
Fragments on St. Winefred.
From any hedgerow, any copse.
Furl of fresh-leaved dogrose down, The.
Glimmer'd along the square-cut steep.
God's Grandeur.
Habit of Perfection, The.
Haec te jubent salvere, quod possunt, loca.
Hailstorm in May.

Half-way House, The.
Handsome Heart, The.
Harry Ploughman.
He hath abolished the old drouth.
He mightbe slow and something feckless first.
Heaven-Haven.
Henry Purcell.
Her prime of life—cut down too soon.
Hill / Heaven and every field, are still.
Hope holds to Christ.
How all is one way wrought!
Hurrahing in Harvest.
I am like a slip of comet.
I hear a noise of waters drawn away.
I must hunt down the prize.
I Wake and Feel the Fell of Dark, Not Day.
Il Mystico.
In Honour of St. Alphonsus Rodriguez.
In S. Winefridam.
In the staring darkness.
In the Valley of the Elwy.
In Themclam Virginem.
Inundatio Oxoniana.
Inversnaid.
Io.
Jesu Dulcis Memoria.
Lantern Out of Doors, The.
Late I fell in the ecstasy.
Leaden Echo and the Golden Echo, The.
Let me be to Thee as the circling bird.
Lines for a Picture of St. Dorothea.
Loss of the Eurydice, The.
Love me as I love thee. O double sweet!
Love Preparing to Fly.
Lover's Stars, The.
Margaret Clitheroe.
May Lines.
May Magnificat, The.
Miror surgentem per puram Oriona noctem.
Miss Story's character! too much you ask.
Moonless darkness stands between.
Moonrise.
Morning, Midday, and Evening Sacrifice.
Mothers are doubtless happier for their babes.
My Own Heart Let Me More Have Pity On.
My prayers must meet a brazen heaven.
Myself unholy, from myself unholy.
New Readings.
Nightingale, The.
No, they are come; their horn is lifted up.
No Worst, There Is None. Pitched Past Pitch of Grief.
Noise of falls I am possessèd by, A.
Nondum.
Not kind! to freeze me with forecast.
Now I am minded to take a pipe in hand.
O Death, Death, He is come.
O Deus, Ego Amo Te.
O what a silence is this wilderness!
O where is it, the wilderness.
Ochenaid Sant Francis Xavier, Apostol Yr Indiaid.
On St. Winefred.
On the Portrait of Two Beautiful Young People.
Or else their cooings came from bays of trees.
Oratio Patris Condren: O Jesu Vivens in Maria.
Oxford Bells.
Peace.
Peacock's Eye, The.
Penmaen Pool.
Pied Beauty.
Pilate.
Proved Etherege prudish, selfish, hypocrite, heartless.
Queen's Crowning, The.
Quique haec membra malis vis esse obnoxia multis.
Rainbow, The.
Ribblesdale.
Richard ("As void as clouds").
Richard ("He was a shepherd").
Rosa Mystica.
S. Thomae Aquinatis Rhythmus ad SS. Sacramentum.
St. Dorothea.

St. Winefred's Well.
Sea and the Skylark, The.
Sea Took Pity, The.
See how Spring opens with disabling cold.
Seven Epigrams.
Shakspere.
She Schools the Flighty Pupils of Her Eyes.
Shepherd's Brow, The.
Silver Jubilee, The.
Silver scarce-call-silver gloss, A.
Soldier, The.
Soliloquy of One of the Spies Left in the Wilderness, A.
Songs from Shakespeare, in Latin and Greek.
Sonnet: "Patience, hard thing! the hard thing but to pray."
Spelt from Sibyl's Leaves.
Spring.
Spring and Death.
Spring and Fall.
St. Thecla.
Starlight Night, The.
Stars were packed so close that night, The.
Stephen and Barberie.
Summa.
Summer Malison, The.
That Nature Is a Heraclitean Fire and of the Comfort of the Resurrection.
Thee, God, I come from, to Thee go.
Think of an opening page illuminèd.
Thou Art Indeed Just, Lord.
Times are nightfall, look, their light grows less, The.
To him who ever thought with love of me.
To His Watch.
To Oxford ("As Devonshire letters").
To Oxford ("New-dated from the terms").
To R. B.
To Seem the Stranger.
To What Serves Mortal Beauty?
Tomorrow meet you? O not tomorrow.
Tom's Garland: Upon the Unemployed.
Trees by their yield.
Trio of Triolets, A.
Vision of the Mermaids, A.
Voice from the World, A.
What being in rank-old nature should earlier have that breath been.
What Shall I Do for the Land that Bred Me.
When eyes that cast about the heights of heaven.
Where art thou friend, whom I shall never see.
Why if it be so, for the dismal morn.
Why should their foolish bands, their hopeless hearses.
Windhover, The.
Windy Day in Summer, A.
Winter with the Gulf Stream.
Woodlark, The.
Woods in Spring.
Wreck of the Deutschland, The.
Yes for a time they held as well.

Horace (Quintus Horatius Flaccus) (65–8 B.C.)
Epistles, *sels.*
Epodes, *sels.*
Horace, of the Art of Poetry.
Let *Caesar* spread his conquests far.
Odes, *sels.*
Satires, *sels.*
Three Odes of Horace.

Housman, A. E. (Alfred Edward) (1859–1936)
A. J. J.
Along the field as we came by.
As I gird on for fighting.
As through the Wild Green Hills of Wyre.
Ask me no more, for fear I should reply.
Astronomy.
Atys.
Be still, my soul, be still; the arms you bear are brittle.
Because I liked you better.
Bells in tower at evening toll.
Bredon Hill.
Bring, in this timeless grave to throw.
By shores and woods and steeples.
Carpenter's Son, The.

Chestnut casts his flambeaux, and the flowers, The.
Clunton and Clunbury.
Could man be drunk for ever.
Crossing Alone the Nighted Ferry.
Culprit, The.
Day of Battle, The.
Defeated, The.
Delight it is in youth and May.
Deserter, The.
Diffugere Nives.
Easter Hymn.
Eight o'Clock.
1887.
Epitaph: "Here dead lie we because we did not choose."
Epitaph, An: "Stay, if you list, O passer by the way."
Epitaph on an Army of Mercenaries.
Epithalamium: "He is here, Urania's son."
Fairies Break Their Dances, The.
Fancy's Knell.
Far in a western brookland.
Far known to sea and shore.
Farewell to a name and a number.
Farewell to barn and stack and tree.
Farms of home lie lost in even, The.
First of May, The.
For My Funeral.
For these of old the trader.
Friends.
From Far, from Eve and Morning.
From the wash the laundress sends.
Give me a land of boughs in leaf.
God's Acre.
Grenadier.
Half-way, for one commandment broken.
He looked at me with eyes I thought.
He, standing hushed, a pace or two apart.
He would not stay for me; and who can wonder?
Hell Gate.
Her Strong Enchantments Failing.
Here are the skies, the planets seven.
Ho, everyone that thirsteth.
How clear, how lovely bright.
Hughley Steeple.
I Counsel You Beware.
I did not lose my heart in summer's even.
I hoed and trenched and weeded.
I lay me down and slumber.
I promise nothing: friends will part.
I shall not die for you.
I to my perils.
I wake from dreams and turning.
If it chance your eye offend you.
If truth in hearts that perish.
Illic Jacet.
Immortal Part, The.
In midnights of November.
In My Own Shire.
In the morning, in the morning.
In valleys green and still.
Is my team plowing?
Isle of Portland, The.
It is no gift I tender.
It nods and curtseys and recovers.
Jar of Nations, The.
Lads in Their Hundreds, The.
Lancer.
Land of Biscay, The.
Laws of God, the laws of man, The.
Lent Lily, The.
Like mine, the veins of these that slumber.
Loitering with a vacant eye.
Look not in my eyes, for fear.
Loveliest of Trees, the Cherry Now.
March.
Merry Guide, The.
Mill-stream, now that noises cease, The.
My dreams are of a field afar.
New Mistress, The.
New Year's Eve.
Now dreary dawns the eastern light.
Now hollow fires burn out to black.
Now to her lap the incestuous earth.

Oh fair enough are sky and plain.
Oh on my breast in days hereafter.
Oh see how thick the goldcup flowers.
Oh stay at home, my lad, and plough.
Oh turn not in from marching.
Oh were he and I together.
Oh, when I Was in Love.
Oh who is that young sinner with the handcuffs on his wrists?
Olive, The.
On forelands high in heaven.
On moonlit heath and lonesome bank.
On the idle hill of summer.
On Wenlock Edge.
On your midnight pallet lying.
Oracles, The.
Others, I am not the first.
Parta Quies.
R. L. S.
Rain, it streams on stone and hillock, The.
Rainy Pleiads wester, The.
Recruit, The.
Reveille.
Revolution.
Sage to the Young Man, The.
Say, lad, have you things to do?
Shake hands, we shall never be friends, all's over.
Shot? so quick, so clean an ending?
Sigh that heaves the grasses, The.
Sinner's Rue.
Sloe was lost in flower, The.
Smooth between sea and land.
So Sound You Sleep.
Soldier from the wars returning.
Some can gaze and not be sick.
Spring Morning.
Stars Have Not Dealt Me, The.
Stars, I have seen them fall.
Stone, steel, dominions pass.
Street sounds to the soldiers' tread, The.
Tarry, delight, so seldom met.
Tell Me Not Here [It Needs Not Saying].
Terence, This Is Stupid Stuff.
There pass the careless people.
They say my verse is sad: no wonder.
They shall have breath that never were.
Think no more, lad; laugh, be jolly.
This time of year a twelvemonth past.
'Tis five years since, "An end," said I.
To an Athlete Dying Young.
To Stand Up Straight.
True Lover, The.
Twice a week the winter thorough.
Wake not for the world-heard thunder.
Weeping Pleiads wester, The.
We'll to the woods no more.
Welsh Marches, The.
Wenlock Edge.
West, The.
Westward on the high-hilled plains.
When Adam walked in Eden young.
When first my way to fair I took.
When green buds hang in the elm.
When I Was One-and-Twenty.
When I Watch the Living Meet.
When I would muse in boyhood.
When Israel out of Egypt came.
When smoke stood up from Ludlow.
When summer's end is nighing.
When the bells justle in the tower.
When the eye of day is shut.
When the lad for longing sighs.
White in the moon the long road lies.
Winds out of the west land blow, The.
Winter.
With Rue My Heart Is Laden.
With seed the sowers scatter.
World goes none the lamer, The.
Yon Far Country.
Yon flakes that fret the eastern sky.
Yonder see the morning blink.
You smile upon your friend to-day.
Young is the blood that yonder.

Howe, Fanny (b. 1940)
  Close Up.

Conclusively.
Goodbye, Post Office Square.
In the Spirit There Are No Accidents, *sels.*
Introduction to the World, *sels.*
Joy Had I Known, *sels.*
Lines Out to Silence, *sels.*
Nursery, The.
O'Clock, *sels.*
Poem from a Single Pallet, *sels.*
Q, *sels.*
Quietist, The, *sels.*
Robeson Street, *sels.*
Sea-Garden, The, *sels.*
Veteran.
Vineyard, The, *sels.*

Howe, Susan (b. 1937)
  Bride's Day.
  Cabbage Gardens.
  Chanting at the Crystal Sea.
  Fragments of a Liquidation.
  God's Spies.
  Her diary soared above her house.
  Hinge Picture.
  Pearl Harbor.
  Pythagorean Silence.
  Secret History of the Dividing Line.
  Some particular place fleeting.
  Speeches at the Barriers.
  THEIR / Book of Stella.
  Tuning the Sky.
  We that were wood / when that a wide wood was.
  WHITE FOOLSCAP / Book of Cordelia.
  (WHITE MARBLE) leaf frame shadow leaf.

Hsüeh T'ao (768–831)
  Spring-Gazing Songs.
  Weaving Love-Knots.

Hughes, Langston (1902–67)
  Abe Lincoln.
  Acceptance.
  Addition ("7 x 7 + love =").
  Addition ("Put 5 and 5 together").
  Advertisement for the Waldorf-Astoria.
  Advice.
  Aesthete [*or* Esthete] in Harlem.
  Afraid.
  Africa.
  Afro-American Fragment.
  After Many Springs.
  Air Raid: Barcelona.
  Air Raid over Harlem.
  Alabama Earth.
  Always the Same.
  America.
  American Heartbreak.
  America's Young Black Joe!
  Angels Wings.
  Angola Question Mark.
  Anne Spencer's Table.
  Announcement.
  April Rain Song.
  Ardella.
  Argument ("Now lookahere, gal").
  Argument ("White is right, / Yellow mellow").
  As Befits a Man.
  As I Grew Older.
  Ask Your Mama.
  Aspiration.
  August 19th.
  Aunt Sue's Stories.
  Autumn Note.
  Autumn Thought.
  Azikiwe in Jail.
  Baby.
  Backlash Blues, The.
  Bad Luck Card.
  Bad Man.
  Bad Morning.
  Ballad of Booker T.
  Ballad of Gin Mary.
  Ballad of Harry Moore.
  Ballad of Little Sallie.
  Ballad of Margie Polite, The.
  Ballad of Mary's Son.
  Ballad of Negro History, A.
  Ballad of Ozie Powell.

Ballad of Roosevelt.
Ballad of Sam Solomon.
Ballad of the Black Sheep.
Ballad of the Fool.
Ballad of the Fortune Teller.
Ballad of the Girl Whose Name Is Mud.
Ballad of the Gypsy.
Ballad of the Killer Boy.
Ballad of the Landlord.
Ballad of the Man Who's Gone.
Ballad of the Miser.
Ballad of the Pawnbroker.
Ballad of the Seven Songs.
Ballad of the Sinner.
Ballad of the Two Thieves.
Ballad of Walter White.
Ballads of Lenin.
Bar.
Barefoot Blues.
Battle Ground.
Be-Bop Boys.
Beale Street.
Beale Street Love.
Beaumont to Detroit: 1943.
Beauty.
Beggar Boy.
Being Old.
Bells Toll Kindly, The.
Better.
Bible Belt.
Big Buddy.
Big Sur.
Big-Timer, The.
Bird in Orbit.
Birmingham Sunday.
Birth.
Bitter Brew.
Bitter River, The.
Black Clown, The.
Black Dancers.
Black Gal.
Black Man Speaks, The.
Black Maria.
Black Panther.
Black Pierrot, A.
Black Seed.
Black Workers.
Blind.
Blue Bayou.
Blue Monday.
Blues at Dawn.
Blues Fantasy.
Blues in Stereo.
Blues on a Box.
Blues, The.
Boarding House.
Bombings in Dixie.
Bonds for All.
Bonds: In Memoriam.
Boogie: 1 A.M.
Border Line.
Bound No'th Blues.
Bouquet.
Brand New Clothes.
Brass Spittoons.
Breath of a Rose.
Brief Encounter.
Broadcast on Ethiopia.
Broadcast to the West Indies.
Broke.
Brotherly Love.
Brothers.
Buddy.
Bulwark.
Burden.
Cabaret.
Cabaret Girl Dies on Welfare Island.
Café: 3 A.M.
Call of Ethiopia.
Call to Creation.
Caribbean Sunset.
Carol of the Brown King.
Carolina Cabin.
Casual.
Casualty.
Cat and the Saxophone (2 A.M.), The.

Catch.
Change.
Chant for May Day.
Chant for Tom Mooney.
Chicago.
Chicago Blues.
Children's Rhymes ("By what sends").
Children's Rhymes ("When I was a chile we
    used to play").
Chippy.
Chord.
Christ in Alabama.
Christian Country, A.
Christmas Eve: Nearing Midnight in New
    York.
Christmas Story, The.
Circles.
City.
Closing Time.
College Formal: Renaissance Casino.
Color.
Colored Soldier, The.
Columbia.
Comment.
Comment against Lamp Post.
Comment on Stoop.
Comment on War.
Communion.
Communiqué.
Conservatory Student Struggles with Higher
    Instrumentation.
Consider Me.
Consumptive, The.
Convent.
Cora.
Corner Meeting.
Could Be.
Country.
Crap Game.
Croon.
Cross.
Crossing.
Crow Goes, Too.
Crowing Hen Blues.
Crowns and Garlands.
Cubes.
Cultural Exchange ("IN THE / IN THE QUARTER /
    IN THE QUARTER OF THE NEGROES").
Cultural Exchange ("In the Quarter of the
    Negroes / Where the doors are doors of
    paper").
Curious.
Dancer.
Dancers.
Danse Africaine.
Dare.
Dark Youth of the U.S.A.
Day.
Daybreak in Alabama.
Dead in There.
Dear Lovely Death.
Dear Mr. President.
Death in Africa.
Death in Harlem.
Death in Yorkville.
Death of an Old Seaman.
Death of Do Dirty: A Rounder's Song.
Deceased.
Declaration.
Deferred.
Delinquent.
Demand.
Demonstration.
Departure.
Desert.
Desire.
Dime.
Dimout in Harlem.
Dinner Guest: Me.
Disillusion.
Dive.
Dixie Man to Uncle Sam.
Dixie South Africa.
Do You Reckon?
Doorknobs.
Dove, The.

Down and Out.
Down Where I Am.
Draftees.
Drama for Winter Night (Fifth Avenue).
Dream.
Dream Boogie.
Dream Boogie: Variation.
Dream Dust.
Dream Keeper, The.
Dream of Freedom.
Dream Variation[s].
Dreamer.
Dreams.
Dressed Up.
Drum.
Drums.
Drunkard.
Dusk.
Dustbowl.
Dying Beast.
Early Evening Quarrel.
Earth Song.
Easy Boogie.
Elderly Leaders.
Elevator Boy.
Emperor Haile Selassie.
Empty House.
Encounter.
End.
Enemy.
English, The.
Ennui.
Envoy to Africa.
Epitaph: "Uncle Tom, / When he was alive."
Epitaph: "Within this grave lie."
Evenin' Air Blues.
Evening Song.
Evil.
Evil Morning.
Evil Woman.
Exits.
Expendable.
Explain It, Please.
Fact.
Fairies.
Faithful One.
Fantasy in Purple.
Farewell, A.
Fascination.
Feet o' Jesus.
50–50.
Figurette.
Figurine.
Final Call.
Final Curve.
Fire.
Fire-Caught.
Fired.
First of May.
Flatted Fifths.
Florida Road Workers.
Flotsam.
Fog.
For an Indian Screen.
For Dead Mimes.
For Russell and Rowena Jelliffe.
For Salome.
Formula.
Fortune Teller Blues.
403 Blues.
Fourth of July Thought.
Fragments: "Whispers / Of springtime."
Frederick Douglass: 1817–1895.
Free Man.
Freedom ("Freedom will not come").
Freedom ("Some folks think / By burning
    books").
Freedom ("Some folks think / By burning
    churches").
Freedom Seeker.
Freedom Train.
Freedom's Plow.
Friendly in a Friendly Way.
From Selma.
From Spain to Alabama.
Frosting.

Fulfillment.
Funeral.
Gal's Cry for a Dying Lover.
Gandhi Is Fasting.
Gangsters.
Garden.
Garment.
Gauge.
Genius Child.
Georgia Dusk.
Get Up off That Old Jive.
Ghosts of 1619.
Gifts.
Girl.
Give Us Our Peace.
Go Slow.
God.
God to Hungry Child.
Gods.
Gone Boy.
Good Bluffers.
Good Morning Revolution.
Good Morning, Stalingrad.
Goodbye Christ.
Gospel Cha-Cha.
Governor Fires Dean.
Graduation.
Grandpa's Stories.
Grant Park.
Grave Yard.
Green Memory.
Grief.
Grocery Store.
Gypsies.
Gypsy Man.
Gypsy Melodies.
Hard Daddy.
Hard Luck.
Harlem ("Here on the edge of hell").
Harlem Dance Hall.
Harlem Night.
Harlem Night Club.
Harlem Night Song.
Harlem Sweeties.
Havana Dreams.
Heart.
Heart of Harlem, The.
Heaven.
Helen Keller.
Hero—International Brigade.
Hey!
Hey! Hey!
Hey-Hey Blues.
High to Low.
History.
Homecoming.
Homesick Blues.
Honey Babe.
Hope ("He rose up on his dying bed").
Hope ("Sometimes when I'm lonely").
Hope for Harlem.
Horn of Plenty.
House in Taos, A.
House in the World.
How about It, Dixie.
How Thin a Blanket.
Hurt.
I Dream a World.
I Thought It Was Tangiers I Wanted.
I, Too.
If You Would.
If-ing.
Imagine.
Impasse.
In a Troubled Key.
In Explanation of Our Times.
In the Mist of the Moon.
In Time of Silver Rain.
Interne at Provident.
Irish Wake.
Is It True?
Island ("Wave of sorrow").
It Gives Me Pause.
Jaime.
Jam Session.
Jazz Band in a Parisian Cabaret.

Jazz Girl.
Jazzonia.
Jazztet Muted.
Jester, The.
Jesus, The.
Jim Crow Car.
Jim Crow's Last Stand.
Jitney.
Joe Louis ("Joe Louis is a man").
Joe Louis ("They worshipped Joe").
Johannesburg Mines.
Joy.
Judge William Hastie.
Judgment Day.
Juice Joint: Northern City.
Juke Box Love Song.
Juliet.
Junior Addict.
Just an Ordinary Guy.
Justice.
Kid in the Park.
Kid Sleepy.
Kids in School with Me, The.
Kids Who Die.
Ku Klux.
Labor Storm.
Lady in Cabaret.
Lady's Boogie.
Lament for Dark Peoples.
Lament of a Vanquished Beau, The.
Lament over Love.
Last Call.
Last Feast of Belshazzar, The.
Last Man Living, The.
Last Prince of the East.
Late Corner.
Late Last Night.
Laughers.
Lenin.
Lenox Avenue Bar.
Lenox Avenue: Midnight.
Lenox Avenue Mural, *sels.*
Let America Be America Again.
Letter from Spain.
Letter to Anne, A.
Letter to the Academy.
Liars.
Life Is Fine.
Likewise.
Lincoln Monument: Washington.
Lincoln Theatre.
Lincoln University: 1954.
Listen Here Blues.
Little Cats.
Little Green Tree.
Little Lyric (*Of Great Importance*).
Little Old Letter.
Little Song ("Carmencita loves Patrick").
Little Song ("Lonely people").
Little Song on Housing.
Live and Let Live.
Lonely Nocturne.
Lonesome Corner.
Lonesome Place.
Long Trip.
Long View: Negro.
Love.
Love Again Blues.
Love Song for Antonia.
Love Song for Lucinda.
Lover's Return.
Low to High.
Luck ("Sometimes a crumb falls").
Luck ("Sometimes a few scraps fall").
Lullaby (For a Black Mother).
Lumumba's Grave.
Ma Lord.
Ma Man.
Madam and Her Madam.
Madam and Her Might-Have-Been.
Madam and the Army.
Madam and the Census Man.
Madam and the Charity Child.
Madam and the Crime Wave.
Madam and the Fortune Teller.
Madam and the Insurance Man.

Madam and the Minister.
Madam and the Movies.
Madam and the Newsboy.
Madam and the Number Writer.
Madam and the Phone Bill.
Madam and the Rent Man.
Madam and the Wrong Visitor.
Madam's Calling Cards.
Madam's Christmas (or Merry Christmas
　　Everybody).
Madam's Past History.
Madrid [—1937].
Magnolia Flowers.
Mama and Daughter.
Mammy.
Man.
Man into Men.
March Moon.
Maybe.
Me and My Song.
Me and the Mule.
Mean Old Yesterday.
Mellow.
Memo to Non-White Peoples.
Merry Christmas.
Merry Go-Round.
Message to the President.
Metropolitan Museum.
Mexican Market Woman.
Midnight Chippie's Lament.
Midnight Dancer.
Midnight Raffle.
Midwinter Blues.
Migrant.
Migration.
Militant.
Minnie Sings Her Blues.
Minstrel Man.
Misery.
Miss Blues'es Child.
Mississippi.
Mississippi Levee.
Mister Sandman.
Mitchell Case, The.
Moan.
Monotony.
Monroe's Blues.
Montmartre.
Moonlight in Valencia: Civil War.
Moonlight Night: Carmel.
Morning After.
Moscow.
Mother in Wartime.
Mother to Son.
Motherland.
Motto.
Movies.
Mulatto.
My Beloved.
My Loves.
My People.
Mystery.
NAACP.
Natcha.
Naughty Child, The.
Necessity.
Negro.
Negro Dancers.
Negro Ghetto.
Negro Mother, The.
Negro Servant.
Negro Speaks of Rivers, The.
Neighbor.
Neon Signs.
New Cabaret Girl, The.
New Flowers.
New Moon.
New Song, A.
New Year.
New Yorkers.
Night: Four Songs.
Night Funeral in Harlem.
Night Song.
Nightmare Boogie.
No Regrets.
Nocturne for the Drums.

Nonette.
Northern Liberal.
Not a Movie.
Not Else—But.
Not Often.
Not What Was.
Note in Music.
Note on Commercial Theatre.
Note to All Nazis Fascists and Klansmen.
Nude Young Dancer.
Number.
Numbered.
Numbers.
October 16: The Raid.
Ode to Dinah.
Office Building: Evening.
Official Notice.
Old Age.
Old Dog Queenie.
Old Sailor.
Old Walt.
Old Youth.
On a Christmas Night.
On a Pallet of Straw.
One.
125th Street.
One More "S" in the U.S.A.
One-Way Ticket.
Only Woman Blues.
Open Letter to the South.
Oppression.
Our Land.
Out of Work.
Pair in One.
Pale Lady.
Parade.
Parisian Beggar Woman.
Park Bench.
Park Benching.
Passing.
Passing Love.
Pastoral: "Between the little clouds of heaven."
Pathological Puzzle.
Peace.
Peace Conference in an American Town.
Pennsylvania Station.
Personal.
Ph.D.
Pictures to the Wall.
Pierrot.
Piggy-back.
Plaint.
Po' Boy Blues.
Poem: "Ah, / My black one."
Poem: "All the tom-toms of the jungles beat in
    my blood."
Poem: "I loved my friend."
Poem: "When young spring comes."
Poem for an Intellectual on the Way Up to
    Submit to His Lady.
Poem for Youth.
Poem to a Dead Soldier.
Poem to Uncle Sam.
Poème d'Automne.
Poet to Bigot.
Poet to Patron.
Poor Girl's Ruination.
Poor Rover.
Poppy Flower.
Port Town.
Porter.
Postcard from Spain.
Prayer ("Gather up / In the arms of your pity").
Prayer ("I ask you this: / Which way to go?").
Prayer for a Winter Night.
Prayer Meeting.
Preference.
Prelude to Our Age.
Present.
Prime.
Prize Fighter.
Problems.
Projection.
Promised Land.
Puzzlement.

Question ("Said the lady, *Can you do*").
Question ("When the old junk man Death").
Question and Answer.
Raid.
Railroad Avenue.
Reasons Why.
Red Clay Blues.
Red Cross.
Red Roses.
Red Silk Stockings.
Refugee.
Refugee in America.
Relief.
Remembrance.
Rent-Party Shout: For a Lady Dancer.
Request.
Request for Requiems.
Restrictive Covenants.
Return to Sea.
Reverie on the Harlem River.
Revolution.
Ride, Red, Ride.
Ring, The.
Rising Waters.
Roar China!
Roland Hayes Beaten (Georgia: 1942).
Room.
Ruby Brown.
Ruined Gal, A.
S-sss-ss-sh!
Sailing Date.
Sailor.
Salute to Soviet Armies.
Saturday Night.
Scottsboro.
Sea Calm.
Sea Charm.
Search.
Seascape.
Seashore through Dark Glasses (Atlantic City).
Second Generation: New York.
Seven Moments of Love; An Un-Sonnet
    Sequence in Blues.
Shades of Pigmeat.
Shadows.
Shakespeare in Harlem.
Shall the Good Go Down?
Shame on You.
Share-Croppers.
Shearing Time.
Shepherd's Song at Christmas.
Shout.
Show Fare, Please.
Sick Room.
Signs of Spring.
Silence.
Silent One.
Silly Animals.
Sinner.
Sister.
Sister Johnson Marches.
Situation.
Six-Bits Blues.
Slave.
Slave Song.
Sleep.
Sliver.
Sliver of Sermon.
Slum Dreams.
Small Memory.
Snail.
Snake.
Snob.
So Long.
So Tired Blues.
Soledad.
Some Day.
Song: "Lovely, dark, and lonely one."
Song after Lynching.
Song for a Banjo Dance.
Song for a Dark Girl.
Song for Billie Holiday.
Song for Ourselves.
Song of Adoration.
Song of Spain.
Song of the Refugee Road.

Song of the Revolution.
Song to a Negro Wash-woman, A.
Songs.
Songs to the Dark Virgin.
South, The.
Southern Mammy Sings.
Southern Negro Speaks.
Speaking of Food.
Special Bulletin.
Spirituals.
Sport.
Spring for Lovers.
Stalingrad: 1942.
Star Seeker.
Stars.
Statement.
Steel Mills.
Still Here.
Stokely Malcolm Me.
Stony Lonesome.
Strange Hurt.
Stranger in Town.
Street Song.
Suburban Evening.
Subway Face.
Subway Rush Hour.
Success.
Suicide.
Suicide's Note.
Summer Evening (Calumet Avenue).
Summer Night.
Sun Song.
Sunday by the Combination.
Sunday Morning Prophecy.
Sunset—Coney Island.
Sunset in Dixie.
Sweet Words on Race.
Sylvester's Dying Bed.
Tag.
Tambourines.
Tapestry.
Teacher.
Tell Me.
Testament.
Testimonial.
Thanksgiving Time.
Theme for English B.
There.
There's Always Weather.
Third Degree.
This Puzzles Me.
Thorn, The.
Three Songs about Lynching, *sels*.
Tired.
To a Dead Friend.
To a Little Lover-Lass, Dead.
To Artina.
To Be Somebody.
To Beauty.
To Captain Mulzac.
To Certain "Brothers."
To Certain Intellectuals.
To Certain Negro Leaders.
To Dorothy Maynor.
To Make Words Sing.
To Midnight Nan at Leroy's.
To the Dark Mercedes of "El Palacio de
    Amor."
To the Little Fort of San Lazaro on the Ocean
    Front, Havana.
To You.
Today.
Tomorrow.
Tomorrow's Seed.
Too Blue.
Total War.
Tower.
Town of Scottsboro, The.
Trip: San Francisco.
Troubled Water.
Troubled Woman.
Trumpet Player.
Two Somewhat Different Epigrams.
Two Things.
Ultimatum.
Ultimatum: Kid to Kid.

Un-American Investigators.
Uncle Tom ("Uncle Tom is a legend and a dream").
Uncle Tom ("Within— / The beaten pride").
Underground, The.
Undertow.
Union.
Up-Beat.
Us: Colored.
Vagabonds.
Vari-Colored Song.
Visitors to the Black Belt.
Wait.
Wake.
Walkers with the Dawn.
Walls.
War.
Warning ("Daddy, / don't let your dog").
Warning: Augmented.
Watch Out, Papa.
Water-Front Streets.
Ways.
We, Too.
Wealth.
Weary Blues, The.
We're All in the Telephone Book.
West Texas.
What?
What I Think.
What? So Soon!
When Sue Wears Red.
When the Armies Passed.
Where Service Is Needed.
Where? When? Which?
White Man.
White Ones, The.
Who but the Lord?
Wide River.
Widow Woman.
Will V-Day Be Me-Day Too?
Wine-O.
Winter Moon.
Winter Sweetness.
Wisdom.
Wisdom and War.
Wise Men.
Without Benefit of Declaration.
Wonder.
Wooing, A.
Workin' Man.
World War II.
Worriation.
Year Round.
Yesterday and Today.
Young Bride.
Young Gal's Blues.
Young Negro Girl.
Young Prostitute.
Young Sailor.
Young Singer.
Youth.

Hughes, Ted (1930–98)
Anniversary.
Apple Dumps.
Apple Tragedy.
Astrological Conundrums.
At the bottom of the Arctic sea, they say.
Autumn Notes.
Bang—a burning, A.
Bawdry Embraced, *sels.*
Bayonet Charge.
Bear, The.
Bedtime Anecdote.
Being Christlike.
Birth of Rainbow.
Black Beast, The.
Black Coat.
Bones.
Boom, *sels.*
Bride and Groom Lie Hidden for Three Days.
Bringing in New Couples.
Bull Moses, The.
Cadenza.
Calves harshly parted from their mamas.
Canal's Drowning Black, The.
Casualty, The.

Cat and Mouse.
Chaucer.
Childish Prank, A.
Children.
Chinese History of Colden Water.
Cleopatra to the Asp.
Cock-Crows.
Collision with the earth has finally come.
Coming Down through Somerset.
Conjuring in Heaven.
Contender, The.
Cormorant, A.
Cranefly in September, A.
Crow, *sels.*
Crow and the Birds.
Crow Blacker than Ever.
Crow Hill.
Crow on the Beach.
Crow Tyrannosaurus.
Crow Wakes.
Crow's Account of the Battle.
Crow's Battle Fury.
Crow's Elephant Totem Song.
Crow's Fall.
Crow's First Lesson.
Crow's Last Stand.
Crow's Vanity.
Curlews [Llft].
Day He Died, The.
Deaf School.
Dehorning.
Descent.
Do Not Pick Up the Telephone.
Dogs Are Eating Your Mother, The.
Dove, A.
Dust As We Are.
Earth-Numb.
Earthenware Head, The.
Eclipse.
Eel, An.
Egg-Head.
Emily Brontë.
Error, The.
Esther's Tomcat.
Evening Thrush.
Examination at the Womb-Door.
Executioner, The.
Fallgrief's Girlfriends.
Famous Poet.
February.
February 17th.
Fern.
Fire-Eater.
Flayed Crow in the Hall of Judgement, A.
Folktale.
Football at Slack.
For Billy Holt.
For the Duration.
Fourth of July.
Fragment of an Ancient Tablet.
Full Moon and Little Frieda.
Ghost Crabs.
Gnat-Psalm.
Go Fishing.
God, A.
God, The.
Gog.
Grass-blade is not without, The.
Green Wolf, The.
Grosse Fuge.
Guide, The.
Gulkana, The.
Hare, The.
Harvest Moon, The.
Hawk Roosting.
Hen, The.
Heptonstall.
Heptonstall Old Church.
Her Husband.
Honey Bee, The.
Horrible Religious Error, A.
Horses, The.
How Water Began to Play.
Howling of Wolves, The.
I know well.
I see the oak's bride in the oak's grasp.

In Laughter.
In the Likeness of a Grasshopper.
In the M5 Restaurant.
Jaguar, The.
Japanese River Tales.
Kreutzer Sonata.
Lake, The.
Last of the 1st/5th Lancashire Fusiliers, The.
Leaf Mould.
Leaves.
Life Is Trying to Be Life.
Lineage.
Lines about Elias.
Little Whale Song.
Locket, the.
Long Tunnel Ceiling, The.
Lovepet, The.
Lovesong: "He loved her and she loved him."
Low Water.
Man Seeking Experience Enquires His Way of a Drop of Water, The.
March Calf, A.
Martyrdom of Bishop Farrar, The.
Match, A.
Mayday on Holderness.
Meeting.
Memory.
Memory, A.
Milesian Encounter on the Sligachan.
Moors.
Motorbike, A.
Mount Zion.
New Foal.
New Moon in January.
Night Arrival of Sea-Trout.
Notes for a Little Play.
November.
October Dawn.
October Salmon[, An].
Old Oats.
On the Reservations.
Once I said lightly.
Ophelia.
Opus 131.
Other, The.
Otter, An.
Out.
Owl's Song.
Performance.
Pibroch.
Pike.
Poets.
Primrose petal's edge, A.
Prometheus on His Crag, *sels.*
Prospero and Sycorax.
Rain.
Rain-charm for the Duchy.
Ravens.
Reckless Head.
Relic.
Remembering Teheran.
Retired Colonel, The.
Revenge Fable.
Rhododendrons.
Risen, The.
River.
River in March, The.
Robin Song.
Roe-Deer.
Sacrifice.
Salmon Eggs.
Scapegoats and Rabies.
Scream, The.
Second Glance at a Jaguar.
Seven Dungeon Songs, *sels.*
Sheep.
Shibboleth.
Six Young Men.
Sketching a Thatcher.
Skylarks.
Small Events.
Smile, The.
Snow.
Snowdrop.
Soliloquy: "Whenever I am got under my gravestone."

Sometimes it comes, a gloomy flap of
   lightning.
Song: "O lady, when the tipped cup of the
   moon blessed you."
Song of a Rat.
Speech Out of Shadow.
Stanbury Moor.
Stations.
Stealing Trout on a May Morning.
Still Life.
Stone, The.
Strangers.
Strawberry Hill.
Sunstroke.
Sunstruck.
Sunstruck Foxglove.
Swallow—rebuilding, The.
Swifts.
Telegraph Wires.
TV Off.
Tender Place, The.
Tern.
That Morning.
That Star.
Theology.
This is the maneater's skull.
Thistles.
Thought-Fox, The.
Thrushes.
Tiger-Psalm.
To Paint a Water Lily.
Tractor.
Tree.
Trees.
Two Tortoiseshell Butterflies.
Vampire.
View of a Pig.
Violet at Lough Aughresberg, A.
Walt.
Warriors of the North, The.
Water.
Waving goodbye, from your banked hospital
   bed.
When Men Got to the Summit.
Where I Sit Writing My Letter.
Widdop.
Wilfred Owen's Photographs.
Wind.
Witches.
Wodwo.
Woman Unconscious, A.
You Hated Spain.
Your tree—your oak.

Hyde, Lewis
Charisma.

I

Ibn I Yamin [*or* **Ibn Jemin** *or* **Amir Mahmud ibn
   Amir Yaminu 'd-Din Tughra'i] (d. 1368?)**
For two rewards, & nought beside.
From Ibn Jemin.
I read on the porch of a palace bold.
Whilst I disdain the populace.

Ignatow, David (1914–97)
About Money.
Above Everything.
Account in the Present Tense of How It all
   Happened, An.
Across the Room.
Adolescence.
Adonis.
Against the Evidence.
All Quiet.
And Rest.
And Step.
And That Night.
And the Same Words.
Apocrypha.
At Four o'Clock.
At This Moment.
Autumn 2.
Bagel, The.
Be like Me.

Behind His Eyes.
Between Shade and Sun.
Bird, The.
Birthday.
Blessing.
Blessing Myself.
Blood.
Blue.
Bothering Me at Last.
Bread Itself, The.
Brief Cases.
Brightness as a Poignant Light.
Business.
Buzz.
Cloud Creates, A.
Come!
Communion 1.
Communion 2.
Complex, The.
Concrete.
Consolation.
Content.
Coupling.
Crowding.
Death of a Lawn Mower.
Debate, The.
Despite the Plainness of the Day.
Dilemma.
Diner, The.
Discussion, A.
Dream, The.
Each Day.
Each of Us.
Each Stone.
Earth Hard.
East Bronx.
East Side West.
Ecology, An.
Envoi: "Strange judgment upon me."
Epilogue: "Trees are tall gods, The."
Epitaph: "There were no hidden motives to his
   life."
Errand Boy 1, The.
Europe and America.
Everyone.
Examine Me, I Am Continuous.
Father.
Father and Son.
Figures of the Human.
Finally.
First Coffin Poem.
First on TV, A.
Fish That Lives at the Bottom, The.
Fisherwoman, The.
Folk Singer, The.
For a Friend.
For All Friends.
For John Berryman.
For Medgar Evers.
For My Daughter.
For My Daughter in Reply to a Question.
For My Mother Ill.
For Now.
For One Moment.
For Yaedi.
For Your Fear.
Forever.
From a Dream.
From the Beginning.
From the Observatory.
Future, The.
Gentle Weight Lifter, The.
Get the Gasworks.
God's.
Going Down.
Hair.
Harold.
He Moves.
Hello.
Here I Am.
Here I Am with Mike.
Here in Bed.
His Name.
Hope, The.
How Come?
How Else.

I Am.
I Am Brother.
I Close My Eyes.
I Dream.
I Dream I Hurl a Spear.
I Have Spoken.
I Identify.
I Killed a Fly.
I Live Admiring the Sky.
I Live with My Contradictions.
I No Longer Want.
I Saw a Leaf.
I Shake My Fist at a Tree.
I Sink Back upon the Ground, Expecting to
   Die.
I Sleep.
I Want to Be Buried.
I Wish a God Were Possible.
I Write.
If We Could Be Brought.
Illusion, An.
I'm a Depressed Poem.
Image, The.
In a Dream 1.
In a Dream 2.
In Ancient Times.
In Dream.
In Limbo.
In Me.
In My Childhood.
In No Way.
In the Garden.
In the Woods.
In This Dream I Do Not Exist.
Information.
Inside Me Is the Peace of an Egg.
Interview 2, The.
Invocation: "Dirt and stone, if I may know you
   as you know yourselves."
It Is.
It's Not You I Miss.
I've Wanted to Write My Way into Paradise.
Journey, The.
Juggler, The.
Kaddish.
Knowledge.
Leaf, A.
Leaping from Ambush.
Life, The.
Life They Lead, The.
Lightly.
Longing.
Loose Gown, A.
Lost Childhood.
Love Poem for the Forty-Second Street
   Library.
Love We Had, The.
Meeting.
Melpomene in Manhattan.
Men You've Loved, The.
Metamorphosis, The.
Midnight.
Midnight 2.
Modern Fable, A.
Money and Grass.
Moral Tale, A.
Moving Picture.
Murderer, The.
My Enemies.
My Love for You.
My Own House.
My Place.
My Poetry Is for the Night.
Mystique.
Need, The.
Neighbors.
News Report.
Night.
1905.
No Theory.
Notes for a Lecture.
Now.
Now I Hear.
Nurse.
Oedipus Reformed.
Of That Fire.

Off to the Cemetery.
Old.
Omen, An.
On Freedom.
On the Death of Winston Churchill.
Once There Was a Woman Smiled at Me.
One Leaf.
Ontology, An.
Opening Paths.
Orgasm.
Outlaw, The.
Paint a Wall.
Peace.
Peace for Awhile.
Permanence.
Play Again.
Poem: "I am tired of you."
Premonitions.
Pricing.
Principle, The.
Prologue: "Mine was the life planned to go wrong."
Promenade.
Prose Poem in Six Parts.
Puzzle, The.
Question, The.
Reading at Night.
Reading the Headlines.
Refuse Man, The.
Reply, A.
Requiem, A: "My father, listening to music, that's me."
Rescue the Dead.
Reward, The.
Rightful One, The.
Ritual One.
Rockets, The.
Say Pardon.
Scenario.
Scissors.
Seasons, The.
Sediment.
See.
Self-Centered.
Self-Employed.
Semblance, A.
Separate Dead, The.
Separate Rooms.
Shadowing the Ground.
Shapely.
Ship, The.
Signal, The.
Simulacrum.
Simultaneously.
Sky.
Sky Is Blue, The.
Sometimes I Think I've Lived Too Long.
Song, The.
Stability.
Statement for the Times.
Stranger.
Subway.
Sunday at the State Hospital.
Sunlight, Piercing the Gloom of this House, The.
Talking to Myself.
Taste, The.
That's the Sum of It.
Their Mouths Full.
Thinking.
This Is Mortal.
This Is the Solution.
Three in Transition.
Thus Truly.
To an Apple.
To Oneself.
To Stay Alive.
Tomorrow.
Trough.
Two.
Two Friends.
Two Selves, The.
Vase, The.
Violence, The.
Wait.
Walk There.

Walt Whitman in the Civil War Hospitals.
Weather, The.
Whatever Contribution.
Where Nothing Is Hidden.
While I live.
Whistle or Hoot.
White Ceiling, The.
White-Haired, I Walk In on My Parents.
Who Could Have Believed It?
With Horace.
With My Back.
With Others.
With the Sun's Fire.
Without Recrimination.
Without Sexual Attraction.
Working Principle, A.
World, The.
Years of Loss, The.
You.

Isidorus (d. 450?)
On a Fowler.

Ivanov, Georgy [or Georgii] Vladimirovich (1894–1958)
Affair was badly flawed, The.
Losing yourself in thought, daydreaming.
Mirrors, reflecting each other.
Sleeping he saw Ophelia in his dream.
Thank god there is no Tsar.
That pointless happiness, was it worth it?

J

Cunningham, J. V.
I drive Westward. Tumble and loco weed.
Letter, A.
Nescit Vox Missa Reverti.
Night is still, The. The unfailing surf.
Soft lights, the companionship, the beers, The.
Sonnet on a Still Night.
With a Copy of Stevens' *Harmonium*.

Jackson, Laura Riding (1901–91)
Advertisement.
After Smiling.
After So Much Loss.
Afternoon.
Ageless Brow, An.
All Nothing, Nothing.
All the Time.
All Things.
And a Day.
And I.
And This Hard Jealousy.
As Many Questions as Answers.
As to a Frontispiece.
As Well as Any Other.
Auspice of Jewels.
Autobiography of the Present.
Back to the Mother Breast.
Be Grave, Woman.
Because I Sit Here So.
Because of Clothes.
Benedictory.
Beyond.
Biography of a Myth, The.
By Crude Rotation.
Care in Calling.
Celebration of Failure.
Chloe Or.
Christmas.
Christmas, 1937.
Chrysalis.
Come, Words, Away.
Concerning Food.
Courtesies of Authorship, The.
Cure of Ignorance.
Cycle of Industry, The.
Cycles of Strangeness.
Dear Possible.
Death as Death.
Decline of Prophecy.
Definition of Love, The.
Devil as Friend, The.
Dilemmist, The.
Ding-Donging.

Disclaimer of the Person.
Divestment of Beauty.
Doom in Bloom.
Druida.
Earth.
Echoes.
Elegy in a Spider's Web.
Enough.
Eventual Love.
Fact, The.
Faith upon the Waters.
Fates and the Mothers, The.
Finally.
Flowering Urn, The.
Footfalling.
For-ever Morning.
Forgiven Past, The.
Forgotten Girlhood.
Friendship on Visit.
From Later to Earlier.
Further Details.
Goat and Amalthea.
Grace.
Growth.
Helen's Burning.
Helen's Faces.
Hospitality to Words.
How Blind and Bright.
How Now We Talk.
I Am.
I Remember.
In Due Form.
In Nineteen Twenty-Seven.
In the Beginning.
Incarnations.
Intelligent Prayer.
It Has Been Read by All.
It Is Not Sad.
Jewels and After.
John and I.
Judgment, The.
Last Covenant, The.
Last Fellows.
Laura and Francisca.
Letter to Any Friend, A.
Letter to Man's Reasonable Soul.
Life of the Dead, The.
Life-Size Is Too Large.
Lucrece and Nara.
Lullaby, The.
Lying Spying.
Many Gentlemen.
Map of Places, The.
March, 1937.
Mask, The.
Meanwhile.
Memories of Mortalities.
Midsummer Duet.
Modern Superstition.
Mortal.
Nearly.
Need for Hell, A.
Need to Confide, The.
Nightmare, The.
No More Are Lovely Palaces.
No More than Is.
Nothing So Far.
Number, The.
O Vocables of Love.
Of All the World.
On a New Generation.
One Self.
Opening of Eyes.
Originally.
Plighted to Shame.
Poem Only.
Poet: A Lying Word.
Poets' Corner, The.
Postponement of Self.
Previous Night, A.
Pride of Head.
Prisms.
Quids, The.
Readers, The.
Reasons of Each, The.
Regret of War Ways.

Blind Sheep, The.
Boyg, Peer Gynt, the One Only One, The.
Breath of Night, The.
Bronze David of Donatello, The.
Burning the Letters.
Carnegie Library, Juvenile Division, The.
Charles Dodgson's Song.
Che Farò Senza Euridice.
Child, The.
Childhood.
Children Selecting Books in a Library.
Chipmunk's Day, The.
Christmas Roses, The.
Cinderella.
City, City!
Clock in the Tower of the Church, The.
Come to the Stone.
Conversation with the Devil, A.
Country Life, A.
Country Was, The.
Cow wandering in the bare field, The.
Dead in Melanesia, The.
Dead, The.
Dead Wingman, The.
Death.
Death of the Ball Turret Gunner, The.
Description of Some Confederate Soldiers, A.
Deutsch durch Freud
Dialogue between Soul and Body, A.
Difficult Resolution, The.
"Do such, wait so," you said; I waited. Did you wait?
Dream of Waking, The.
Dream, The.
Dreams.
Dummies.
Eighth Air Force.
Eine Kleine Nachtmusik.
Elementary Scene, The.
Emancipators, The.
End of the Rainbow, The.
English Garden in Austria, An.
Enormous Love, it's no good asking.
Essay on the Human Will, An.
Esthetic Theories: Art as Expression.
Evening.
Evening Star, The.
Face, The.
Faded.
Fairy Song.
Falling in love is never as simple.
Farewell Symphony, The.
Fat, aging, the child clinging to her hand.
Fear.
Field and Forest.
Field Hospital, A.
Fire at the Waxworks, The.
For the Madrid Road.
Front, A.
Game at Salzburg, A.
Germans Are Lunatics, The.
Ghost, a Real Ghost, A.
Ghost Story, A.
Girl Dreams that She Is Giselle, The.
Girl in a Library, A.
Gleaning.
Good-bye, Wendover; Good-bye, Mountain Home.
Great Night, The.
Grown-Up, The.
Gunner.
Hanged man on the gallows, The.
Happy Cat, The.
He.
Head of Wisdom, The.
Hohensalzburg: Fantastic Variations on a Theme of Romantic Character.
Hope ("To prefer the nest").
Hope ("Week is dealt out").
House in the Wood, The.
Hunt in the Black Forest, A.
I loved you, too. There was no use. I had no time.
Iceberg, The.
In a Hospital Garden.
In Galleries.

In Montecito.
In Nature There Is Neither Right nor Left nor Wrong.
In the Camp There Was One Alive.
In the Ward: The Sacred Wood.
In Those Days.
Indian Market in Mexico, An.
Indian, The.
Island, The.
Islands, The.
Jack.
Jamestown.
January 1938.
Jerome.
Jews at Haifa.
Jonah.
Kirilov on a Skyscraper.
Knight, Death, and the Devil, The.
La Belle au Bois Dormant.
Laboratory, The.
Lady Bates.
Lady on a Balcony, A.
Lament: "All is far."
Lament of the Children of Israel in Rome.
Le Poète Contumace.
Learners, The.
Leave.
Let's love each other for what we are.
Lines, The.
Little Poem, A.
London.
Lonely Man, The.
Loss.
Losses.
Lost Children, The.
Lost Love, The.
Lost World, The.
Lot is vacant still, The.
Love for One Orange, The.
Love, in its separate being.
Lullaby, A: "For wars his life and half a world away."
Machine-Gun, The.
Mail Call.
Man.
Man in Majesty.
Man Meets a Woman in the Street, A.
Man with the axe stands profound and termless, The.
Märchen, The.
Memoirs of Glückel of Hameln, The.
Metamorphoses, The.
Meteorite, The.
Miller, The.
Mockingbird, The.
Money.
Mother, Said the Child.
Moving.
My aunt kept turnips in a flock.
Nestus Gurley.
New Georgia.
News.
Next Day.
Night before the Night before Christmas, The.
1945: The Death of the Gods.
1914.
1938: Tales from the Vienna Woods.
1938: The Spring Dances.
90 North.
Nollekens.
Northern Snows, The.
November Ghosts, The.
Nursery Rhyme, A.
O My Name It Is Sam Hall.
O weary mariners, here shaded, fed.
Officers' Prison Camp Seen from a Troop-Train, An.
Old and the New Masters, The.
Old orchard in the middle of the forest, The.
Old Poems.
Old Song, An.
Olive Garden, The.
On the Railway Platform.
One Who Was Different, The.
Orestes at Tauris.
Orient Express, The.

Over the florid capitals.
Overture: The Hostages.
Owl's Bedtime Story, The.
Perfect Love Casteth Out Everything.
Perfectly Free Association, A.
Picture in the Paper, A.
Pilot from the Carrier, A.
Pilots, Man Your Planes.
Place of Death, The.
Player Piano, The.
Poem for Someone Killed in Spain, A.
Port of Embarkation.
Prayer at Morning, A.
Prince, The.
Princess Wakes in the Wood, The.
Prisoners.
Prologue to Wiley on November 17, 1941.
Protocols.
Quilt-Pattern, A.
Rabbit hurries to the brim of its wood, The.
Randall Jarrell, Office Hours 10–11.
Range in the Desert, The.
Reader, The.
Refugees, The.
Requiem for the Death of a Boy.
Rhapsody on Irish Themes, A.
Rising Sun, The.
Romance of Science, The.
Say Good-bye to Big Daddy.
Scherzo.
School of Summer, The.
Sears Roebuck.
Second Air Force.
Seductive Piece of Business, A.
See-er of Cities, The.
Seele im Raum.
1789–1939.
Sick Child, A.
Sick Nought, The.
Siegfried.
Sign, The.
Skaters, The.
Sleeping Beauty: Variation of the Prince, The.
Snow-Leopard, The.
Soldier [T. P.].
Soldier, The.
Soldier Walks under the Trees of the University, The.
Song: Not There.
Soul, A.
Sphinx's Riddle to Oedipus, The.
Stalag Luft.
State, The.
Story, A.
Street Has Changed, The.
Subway from New Britain to the Bronx, The.
Summer Night, A.
Survivor among Graves, The.
Terms.
There Was Glass and There Are Stars.
Thinking of the Lost World.
Three Bills.
Time and the Thing-in-Itself in a Textbook.
Times Worsen, The.
To Be Dead.
To the New World ("In that bad year and city of your birth").
To the New World ("Leaves are struck and dance, the bird is blown, The").
Today is almost over.
Tower, The.
Transient Barracks.
Traveler, The.
Tree, The.
Trees in Spring, The.
Truth, The.
Unicorn, The.
Up in the sky the star is waiting.
Utopian Journey, A.
Variation on "To Say to Go to Sleep," A.
Variations.
Venetian Blind, The.
War, A.
Ward in the States, A.
Washing.
Washing the Corpse.

Ways and the Peoples, The.
Well-to-Do Invalid, A.
Well Water.
What was longed for and, once, certain.
What's the Riddle.
When Achilles fought and fell.
When I Was Home Last Christmas.
When you and I were all.
Wide Prospect, The.
Widow's Song, The.
Wild Birds, The.
Windows.
Winter's Tale, The ("Guess what smells so ...
    You didn't guess").
Winter's Tale, The ("Storm rehearses through
    the bewildered fields, The").
Woman.
Woman at the Washington Zoo, The.
Women on a Bus.
X-Ray Waiting Room in the Hospital, The.
Zeno.

Jeffers, Robinson (1887–1962)
Advice to Pilgrims.
After Lake Leman.
Age in Prospect.
Air-Raid Rehearsals.
All night long the rush and trampling of water.
All the Little Hoof-Prints.
Animals.
Animula.
Answer, The.
Ante Mortem.
Antrim.
Apology for Bad Dreams.
Artist, An.
As the eye fails through age or disease.
Ascent to the Sierras.
At the Birth of an Age.
At the Fall of an Age.
At the near approach of a star...huge tides.
Autumn Evening.
Ave Caesar.
Be Angry at the Sun.
Beach, The.
Beaks of Eagles, The.
Beautiful Captive, The.
Beauty of Things, The.
Bed by the Window, The.
Bird with the Dark Plumes, The.
Birds.
Birds and Fishes.
Birth and Death.
Birth-Dues.
Birthday.
Birthday (Autobiography).
Bixby's Landing.
Blind Horses.
Blood-Guilt, The.
Bloody Sire, The.
Boats in a Fog.
Bowl of Blood, The.
Broadstone, The.
Broken Balance, The.
But I Am Growing Old and Indolent.
Calm and Full the Ocean.
Carmel.
Carmel Point.
Cassandra.
Cawdor.
Clouds of Evening.
Coast-Road, The.
Come Little Birds.
Consciousness.
Contemplation of the Sword.
Continent's End.
Contrast.
Credo.
Cremation.
Cretan Woman, The.
Cruel Falcon, The.
Crumbs or the Loaf.
Curb Science?
Cycle, The.
Dawn.
Day Is a Poem, The.
De Rerum Virtute.

Dead Men's Child, The.
Dead to Clemenceau: November 1929, The.
Dear Judas.
Decaying Lambskins.
Deer Lay Down Their Bones, The.
Delusion of Saints.
Diagram.
Distant Rainfall.
Divinely Superfluous Beauty.
Dog in the Sky, The.
Double Axe, The.
Drunken Charlie.
Eagle and hawk with their great claws and
    hooked heads.
Eagle Valor, Chicken Mind.
Edison.
End of the World.
Epic Stars, The.
Evening Ebb.
Excesses of God, The.
Explosion.
Extinct Vertebrate, An.
Eye, The.
Faith.
Fantasy.
Fawn's Foster-Mother.
Fire.
Fire on the Hills.
Flight of Swans.
Fog.
For Una.
Fourth Act.
Gale in April.
George Sterling.
George Sterling's Death.
Ghost.
Ghosts in England.
Giant's Ring, The.
Give Your Heart to the Hawks.
Give Your Wish Light.
Goethe, they say, was a great poet, Pindar,
    perhaps, was a great poet.
Going to Horse Flats.
Granddaughter.
Granite and Cypress.
Gray Weather.
Great Explosion, The.
Great Men.
Great Sunset, The.
Greater Grandeur.
Hand.
Hands.
Haunted Country.
Heavy and yellow with the clay wrack from
    the flooded valley.
Hellenistics.
Historical Choice.
Home.
Hooded Night.
Hope Is Not for the Wise.
House Dog's Grave, The.
Humanist's Tragedy, The.
Hungerfield.
Hurt Hawks.
I am seventy-four years old and suddenly all
    my strength.
I saw a regiment of soldiers shuffling and
    stumbling.
I Shall Laugh Purely.
I walk on my cliff above the Pacific Ocean and
    feel the tides.
In the Hill at Newgrange.
Ink-Sack.
Inquisitors, The.
Inscription for a Gravestone.
Intellectuals.
Invasion.
Iona: The Graves of the Kings.
Irish Headland, An.
It flows out of mystery into mystery: there is
    no beginning.
It is a pity the shock-waves.
It was good of my father, whom I hated at
    times.
Joy.
July Fourth by the Ocean.

King of Beasts, The.
Last Conservative, The.
Let Them Alone.
Life from the Lifeless.
Little Scraping, A.
Local Legend.
Love-Children.
Love the Wild Swan.
Loving Shepherdess, The.
Low Sky, The.
Machine, The.
Maid's Thought, The.
Mara.
Margrave.
Mathematicians and physics men, The.
May–June, 1940.
Medea.
Meditation on Saviors.
Memoir.
Metamorphosis.
Miching Mallecho.
Moments of Glory.
Monument.
Moon and Five Planets.
Morro Bay.
My Burial Place.
My Dear Love.
Natural Music.
Nerves.
Neutrals, The.
New Mexican Mountain.
New Year's Dawn, 1947.
New Year's Eve.
Night.
Night without Sleep.
Nightpiece.
No Resurrection.
Noon.
Northern Heather.
Not Our Good Luck.
Nova.
November Surf.
Now Returned Home.
Ocean ("Gray whales are going south").
Ocean ("It dreams in the deepest sleep").
Ocean's Tribute, The.
October Evening.
October Week-End.
Ode to Hengist and Horsa.
Oh, Lovely Rock.
Old age hath clawed me with his scaly clutch.
Old half blinded hawk—but how can he hunt
    with only one eye?, The.
Old Stone-Mason, The.
Old Wolf My Father, The.
On an Anthology of Chinese Poems.
On Building with Stone.
Orca.
Ordinary Newscaster, An.
Original Sin.
Ossian's Grave.
Our eyes by day are good enough: only the
    birds.
Oysters.
Passenger Pigeons.
Patronymic.
Pearl Harbor.
Pelicans.
People and a Heron.
Phenomena.
Place for No Story, The.
Pleasures.
Point Joe.
Point Pinos and Point Lobos.
Polar ice-caps are melting, the mountain
    glaciers, The.
Post Mortem.
Practical People.
Praise Life.
Prelude: "I drew solitude over me, on the lone
    shore."
Prescription of Painful Ends.
Purse-Seine, The.
Quia Absurdum.
Real and Half Real.
Rearmament.

Red Mountain.
Redeemer, A.
Resurrection.
Return.
Roan Stallion.
Rock and Hawk.
Salmon Fishing.
Salvage.
Science.
Second-Best.
Self-Criticism in February.
Seventieth Birthday.
Shakespeare's Grave.
Shane O'Neill's Cairn.
Shears, The.
Shine, Empire.
Shine, Perishing Republic.
Shine, Republic.
Shiva.
Shooting Season.
Sign-Post.
Silent Shepherds, The.
Sinverguenza.
Sirens, The.
Skunks.
So Many Blood-Lakes.
Soliloquy.
Solstice.
Soul's Desert, The.
Staggering Back toward Life.
Stars Go over the Lonely Ocean, The.
Steelhead, Wild Pig, the Fungus.
Still the Mind Smiles.
Stone Axe, The.
Storm blowing up, rain and dark weather and
    the roaring wind, The.
Subjected Earth.
Such Counsels You Gave to Me.
Summer Holiday.
Summit Redwood, The.
Tamar.
Teheran.
That Noble Flower.
Thebaid.
Their Beauty Has More Meaning.
Theory of Truth.
There is no God but God; he is all that exists.
There is this infinite energy, the power of God
    forever working.
Thurso's Landing.
Time of Disturbance.
To a Young Artist.
To Death.
To Kill in War Is Not Murder.
To the House.
To the Rock that Will Be a Cornerstone of the
    House.
To the Stone-Cutters.
To the Story-Tellers.
Tor House.
Torch-Bearers' Race, The.
Tower beyond Tragedy, The.
Trap, The.
Treasure, The.
Triad.
Two Christmas-Cards.
Unformed volcanic earth, a female thing, The.
Unnatural Powers.
Urchin, The.
Vices.
Vulture.
War-Guilt Trials.
Watch the Lights Fade.
We Are Those People.
What Are Cities For?
What Is Worthless?
What Odd Expedients.
What of It?
What's the best life for a man?
Where I?
Wilson in Hell.
Wind-Struck Music, The.
Winged Rock.
Wise Men in Their Bad Hours.
Women at Point Sur, The.
Woodrow Wilson.

World's Wonders, The.

Jiménez, Juan Ramón (1881–1958)
    Ten Short Poems.

Johnson, Esther ("Stella") (1681–1728)
    Elegy on the Much Lamented Death of Mr.
      Demar, the Famous Rich Usurer [*or* Man],
      An.

Johnson, Samuel (1709–84)
    Anacreon's Dove.
    Art thou too fall'n? ere anger could subside.
    Aurora Est Musis Amica.
    Ballad: "I put my hat upon my head."
    Ballad: "I therefore pray thee, Renny dear."
    Ballad: "Tender infant, meek and mild, The."
    Celestial pow'rs! that piety regard.
    Charade on Dr Thomas Barnard.
    Comets and Princes.
    Epigram on Colley Cibber.
    Epilogue to Horace's *Carmen Seculare*.
    Epilogue to *The Distrest Mother*, An.
    Epitaph on William Hogarth, An.
    Epitaph upon the Celebrated Claudy Phillips,
      Musician, Who Died Very Poor, An.
    Evening Ode, An.
    Extempore Elegy, An.
    Festina Lentè.
    French Distichs.
    Gnothi Seauton (Post Lexicon Anglicanum
      Auctum et Emendatum).
    Hermit Hoar.
    I Am Cassander Come Down from the Sky.
    In Rivum a Mola Stoana Lichfeldiæ
      Diffluentem.
    Irene, *sels.*
    Lines on Thomas Warton's Poems.
    London: A Poem.
    New Prologue Spoken at the Representation of
      Comus, A.
    Ode, An: "Stern winter now, by spring
      repress'd."
    Ode, De Skia Insula.
    Ode on a Lady Leaving Her Place of Abode,
      An; Almost Impromptu.
    Ode on Friendship, An.
    On a Daffodil, the First Flower the Author Had
      Seen That Year.
    On a Lady's Presenting a Sprig of Myrtle to a
      Gentleman.
    On Hearing Miss Thrale Deliberate about Her
      Hat.
    On Losing the Power of Speech.
    On Seeing a Portrait of Mrs Montagu.
    On the Death of Dr [*or* Mr] Robert Levet [a
      Practiser in Physic].
    Paraphrase.
    Parva qudem regio, sed relligione primorum.
    Prayer: "Summe Deus, cui cæca patent
      penetralia cordis."
    Prologue Spoken by Mr[.] Garrick at the
      Opening of the Theatre in Drury Lane, 1747.
    Prologue to Garrick's *Lethe*.
    Prologue to Goldsmith's *The Good Natur'd
      Man*.
    Prologue to Hugh Kelly's *A Word to the Wise*.
    Short Song of Congratulation [*or* To a Young
      Heir], A.
    Skia, an Ode on the Isle of Skye.
    Song, A: "Not the soft sighs of vernal gales."
    Song Composed for Fanny Burney, A.
    Soon fades the rose; once past the fragrant
      hour.
    Stella in Mourning.
    To a Young Lady on Her Birthday.
    To Eliza Plucking Laurel in Mr Pope's
      Gardens.
    To Lady Firebrace.
    To Lyce, an Elderly Lady.
    To Miss Hickman Playing on the Spinet.
    To Miss —: On Her Giving the Author a Gold
      and Silk Net-work Purse.
    To Miss —: On Her Playing upon the
      Harpsichord.
    To Mrs Thrale [on Her Thirty-fifth Birthday].
    To Posterity.
    Translation of Addison's
      Pugmaiogeranomachia; The Battle of the

      Pygmies and Cranes.
    Translation of Du Bellay's *Epigram on a Dog*.
    Translation of Lines in Baretti's *Easy
      Phraseology*.
    Translation of the Beginning of *Rio Verde*.
    Translation of the Latin Epitaph on Sir Thomas
      Hanmer, Written by Doctor Freind, A.
    Translations of Roy's Verses on Skaters.
    Turnip Vendor, The.
    Upon the Feast of St Simon and St Jude.
    Vanity of Human Wishes, The; The Tenth
      Satire of Juvenal Imitated.
    Vanity of Wealth, The.
    Verses in Baretti's Commonplace Book.
    Verses on the Death of His Mother.
    While Many a Merry Tale.
    Winter's Walk, The.
    Young Author, The.

Jonson, Ben (1572–1637)
    Against Jealousy [*or* Jealousie].
    And must I sing? What subject shall I choose?
    Another. In Defense of Their Inconstancy [*or*
      Inconstancie]. A Song.
    Another to Him.
    Author ad Librum.
    Bartholomew Fair, *sels.*
    Ben Jonson's Grace before King James.
    Celebration of Charis in Ten Lyric[k] Pieces
      [*or* Peeces], A.
    Charles Cavendish to His Posterity.
    Chloridia, *sels.*
    Christmas His Masque, *sels.*
    Cynthia's Revels, *sels.*
    Dedication of the King's New Cellar, The. To
      Bacchus.
    Dream[e], The.
    Elegy, An: "By those bright eyes, at whose
      immortal fires."
    Elegy, An: "Can beauty that did prompt me
      first to write."
    Elegy, An: "Since you must go, and I must bid
      farewell."
    Elegy, An: "That love's a bitter sweet, I ne'er
      conceive."
    Elegy, An: "Though beauty be the mark of
      praise."
    Elegy [*or* Elegie], An: "Let me be what I am,
      as Virgil cold."
    Elegy [*or* Elegie], An: "'Tis true, I'm broke!
      Vows, oaths, and all I had."
    Elegy [*or* Elegie] on the Lady Jane Pawlet [*or*
      Paulet], [Marchioness of Winton], An.
    Epicoene; or, The Silent Woman, *sels.*
    Epigram, An: "That you have seen the pride,
      beheld the sport."
    Epigram, An. To K[ing] Charles for a[n]
      Hundred Pounds He Sent Me in My
      Sickness. 1629.
    Epigram, An. To the Honoured———,
      Countess of———.
    Epigram, An. To the Household. 1630.
    Epigram, An. To the Small-Pox.
    Epigram, An. To Thomas Lo[rd] Ellsmere, the
      Last Term He Sat Chancellor.
    Epigram, An. To William, Earl of Newcastle
      ("They talk of fencing").
    Epigram, An. To William, Earl of Newcastle
      ("When first, my lord").
    Epigram on Sir Edward Coke, when He Was
      Lord Chief Justice of England, An.
    Epigram on the Court Pucell, An.
    Epigram on the Prince's Birth, An. 1630.
    Epigram on William, Lord Burl[eigh], Lo[rd]
      High Treasurer of England, An.
    Epigram. To a Friend and Son.
    Epigram to My Bookseller.
    Epigram to My Jovial Good Friend Mr Robert
      Dover, on His Great Instauration of His
      Hunting and Dancing at Cotswold, An.
    Epigram to My Muse, the Lady Digby, on Her
      Husband, Sir Kenelm Digby, An.
    Epigram. To our Great and Good K[ing]
      Charles on his Anniversary Day, An. 1629.
    Epigram to the Councillor That Pleaded and
      Carried the Cause, An.
    Epigram to the Queen, Then Lying In, An.
      1630.

Epigramma Martialis. Lib. VIII. lxxvii. The Same Translated.
Epistle Answering to One That Asked to Be Sealed of the Tribe of Ben, An.
Epistle to a Friend.
Epistle to a Friend, An ("Censure not sharply then, but me advise").
Epistle to a Friend, An ("Sir, I am thankful, first, to heaven, for you").
Epistle to a Friend, to Persuade [or Perswade] Him to the Wars [or Warres], An.
Epistle to Elizabeth, Countess of Rutland.
Epistle. To Katharine, Lady Aubigny.
Epistle to Master Arth[ur] Squib, An.
Epistle to Master John Selden, An.
Epistle to Mr Arthur Squib.
Epistle. To My Lady Covell.
Epistle to Sir Edward Sackville, Now Earl of Dorset, An.
Epitaph, An: "What beauty would have lovely styled."
Epitaph on Elizabeth, L. H.
Epitaph, on Henry L[ord] La-ware, An. To the Passer-By.
Epitaph on Master Philip Gray, An.
Epitaph on Master Vincent Corbet[t], An.
Epitaph on S. P. [or Salomon Pavy], a Child of Q[ueen] El[izabeth's] Chapel.
Epithalamion: or, a Song.
Epode: "Not to know vice at all, and keep[e] true state."
Eptiaph on Katherine, Lady Ogle.
Eupheme.
Execration upon Vulcan, An.
Expostulation with Inigo Jones, An.
Fair friend, 'tis true, your beauties move.
Fit of Rhyme [or Rime] against Rhyme [or Rime], A.
From The Touchstone of Truth.
Garland [or Ghyrlond] of the Blessèd Virgin Mary [or Marie], The.
Gypsies Metamorphosed, The, sels.
Haddington Masque, The, sels.
Here Follow Certain Other Verses, as Charms to Unlock the Mystery of the Crudities.
Hour-Glass [or Houre-Glasse], The.
Humble Petition of Poor Ben to the Best of Monarchs, Masters, Men, King Charles, The.
Hymn[e] on the Nativity [or Nativitie] of My Saviour, A.
Hymn[e] to God the Father, A.
In Authorem.
In the Person of Womankind [A Song Apologetic].
Inviting a Friend to Supper.
Irish Masque, The, sels.
Little Shrub Growing By, A.
Lord Bacon's Birthday.
Love Freed from Ignorance and Folly, sels.
Love Restored, sels.
Love's Triumph through Callipolis, sels.
Martial. Epigram XLVII, Book X.
Masque of Augurs, The, sels.
Masque of Beauty, The, sels.
Masque of Blackness, The, sels.
Masque of Hymen, sels.
Masque of Queens, The, sels.
Mercury Vindicated, sels.
Mind of the Frontispiece to a Book, The.
Musical Strife, The; in a Pastoral Dialogue.
My Picture Left in Scotland.
Neptune's Triumph, sels.
New Cry, The.
New Inn, The, sels.
New Year's Gift Sung to King Charles, A. 1635.
New years [or yeares], expect new gifts: sister, your harp[e].
News from the New World, sels.
Nymph's Passion, A.
Oberon, the Fairy Prince, sels.
Ode: "If men, and times were now."
Ode, An: "Helen, did Homer never see."
Ode, An: "High-spirited friend."

Ode Allegoric.
Ode Enthusiastic.
Ode, or Song, by All the Muses, An.
Ode to Himself, An.
Ode to Himself[e].
Ode to James, Earl of Desmond, An.
Ode. To Sir William Sydney, on His Birthday.
Of Death.
Of Life and Death.
Oh Do Not Wanton with Those Eyes.
On a Robbery.
On Bank the Usurer.
On Bawds and Usurers.
On Captain Hazard the Cheater.
On Cashiered Capt[ain] Surly.
On Cheveril [or Cheverel].
On Cheveril [or Cheverel] the Lawyer.
On Chuff, Banks the Usurer's Kinsman.
On Court-Parrot.
On Court-Worm[e].
On Don Surly.
On English Monsieur.
On Giles and Joan.
On Groin.
On Gut.
On Gypsy.
On Lieutenant Shift.
On Lip[pe] the Teacher.
On Lucy, Countess[e] of Bedford.
On Margaret Ratcliffe [or Radcliffe].
On Mill, My Lady's Woman.
On Mongrel Esquire.
On My First Daughter.
On My First Son[ne].
On Old Colt.
On Playwright ("Playwright, by chance, hearing some toys I had writ").
On Playwright ("Playwright convict of public wrongs to men").
On Poet-Ape.
On Reformed Gamester.
On Sir Cod the Perfumed.
On Sir John Roe ("In place of scutcheons, that should deck thy hearse").
On Sir John Roe ("What two brave perils of the private sword").
On Sir Voluptuous Beast.
On Something, that Walk[e]s Somewhere.
On Spies.
On the Author, Work, and Translator.
On the Famous Voyage.
On the Honoured Poems of His Honoured Friend, Sir John Beaumont, Baronet.
On the King's Birthday.
On the Magnetic Lady.
On the New Hot-House.
On the New Motion.
On the Right Honourable and Virtuous Lord Weston, L[ord] High Treasurer of England.
On the Same Beast.
On the Town's Honest Man.
On the Union.
Over the Door at the Entrance into the Apollo.
Panegyre, on the Happy Entrance of James, Our Sovreign, A.
Phoenix Analysed, The.
Pleasure Reconciled to Virtue, sels.
Poem Sent Me by Sir William Burlase, A.
Poetaster, The, sels.
Proludium.
Reverse on the Back Side, The.
Sad Shepherd, The, sels.
Satirical Shrub, A.
Sinner's Sacrifice, The.
Song, A: "Come, let us here enjoy the shade."
Song of the Moon, A.
Song of Welcome to King Charles, A.
Song. That Women Are but Men's Shadows.
Song. To Celia ("Drink to me only with thine eyes").
Sonnet to the Noble Lady, the Lady Mary Wroth, A.
Speech According to Horace, A.
Speech Presented unto King James at a Tilting, A.
Stay, view this stone: and, if thou beest not

such.
Those that in blood such violent pleasure have.
To a Friend.
To a Friend, an Epigram of Him.
To a Weak Gamester in Poetry.
To Alchemists.
To All, to Whom I Write.
To Alphonso [or Alfonso] Ferrabosco, on His Book.
To Benjamin Rudyerd.
To Brain-Hardy.
To Captain Hungry.
To Censorious Courtling.
To Clement Edmonds, on His Caesar's Commentaries Observed, and Translated.
To Courtling.
To Doctor Empiric[k].
To Edward Alleyn.
To Elizabeth, Countess of Rutland.
To Esmé, Lord Aubigny.
To Fine Grand.
To Fine Lady Would-Be.
To Fool or Knave.
To Francis Beaumont.
To Groom Idiot.
To Heaven.
To His Friend the Author upon His Richard.
To His Lady, Then Mrs Cary.
To His Much and Worthily Esteemed Friend the Author.
To Hornet.
To Inigo, Marquess Would Be, a Corollary.
To John Donne ("Donne, the delight of Phoebus, and each Muse").
To John Donne ("Who shall doubt, Donne, where [or whe'er] I a poet be[e]").
To K[ing] Charles and Q[ueen] Mary, for the Loss of Their First-Born. An Epigram Consolatory. 1629.
To King James ("How, best of kings, dost thou a scepter bear[e]").
To King James ("That we the [or thy] loss might know, and thou our love").
To King James ("Who would not be thy subject, James, t'obey").
To Lucy, Countess of Bedford.
To Lucy, Countess[e] of Bedford, with Mr. Donne's Satires [or Satyres].
To Mary, Lady Wroth ("How well, fair crown of your fair sex, might he").
To Mary, Lady Wroth ("Madam[e], had all antiquity [or antiquitie] been lost").
To Master John Burges.
To Mime.
To Mr Ben Jonson in His Journey, by Mr Craven.
To Mr John Burges.
To Mr Jonson upon These Verses.
To Mr Joshua Sylvester.
To Mrs Alice Sutcliffe, on Her Divine Meditations.
To Mrs Phillip Sidney.
To My Book.
To My Bookseller.
To My Chosen Friend the Learnèd Translator of Lucan, Thomas May, Esquire.
To My Dear Son, and Right-Learnèd Friend, Master Joseph Rutter.
To My Lord Ignorant.
To My L[ord] the King, on the Christening His Second Son James.
To My Mere English Censurer.
To My Muse.
To My Old Faithful Servant: And (by His Continued Virtue) My Loving Friend: The Author of this Work, Mr Rich[ard] Brome.
To My Truly-Beloved Friend, Mr Browne: On His Pastorals.
To My Worthy and Honoured Friend, Mr George Chapman, on His Translation of Hesiod's Works and Days.
To My Worthy Friend, Master Edward Filmer, on His Work Published.
To Old-End Gatherer.
To One That Desired Me Not to Name Him.
To Penshurst.

To Person Guilty ("Guilty, be wise; and though thou know'st the crimes").
To Person Guilty ("Guilty, because I bad[e] you late be wise").
To Pertinax Cob.
To Playwright.
To Prowl the Plagiary.
To Robert, Earl of Salisbury ("What need hast thou of me, or of my muse").
To Robert, Earl of Salisbury ("Who can consider thy right courses run").
To Sickness.
To Sir Annual Tilter.
To Sir Cod.
To Sir Edward Herbert.
To Sir Henry Cary.
To Sir Henry Goodyere.
To Sir Henry Nevil.
To Sir Henry [or Henrie] Savile [upon His Translation of Tacitus].
To Sir Horace Vere.
To Sir John Radcliffe.
To Sir Luckless Woo-All.
To Sir Ra[l]ph Shelton.
To Sir Robert Wroth.
To Sir Thomas Overbury.
To Sir Thomas Roe.
To Sir William Jephson.
To Sir William Uvedale.
To Susan, Countess of Montgomery.
To the Author.
To the Ghost of Martial.
To the Immortal[l] Memory [or Memorie] and Friendship of That Noble Pair[e], Sir Lucius Cary and Sir H. [or Henry] Morison.
To the King. On His Birthday. An Epigram Anniversary. Novem[ber] 19, 1632.
To the Learnèd Critic.
To the London Reader, on the Odcombian Writer, Polytopian Thomas the Traveller.
To the Memory of My Beloved, the Author Mr [or Master] William Shakespeare: And What He Hath Left Us.
To the Memory of That Most Honoured Lady Jane, Eldest Daughter to Cuthbert, Lord Ogle: and Countess of Shrewsbury.
To the Most Noble, and above His Titles, Robert, Earl of Somerset.
To the Parliament.
To the Reader ("Pray thee, take care, that tak'st my book[e] in hand").
To the Reader ("This figure, that thou here seest put").
To the Right Hon[oura]ble Hierome, L[ord] Weston. An Ode Gratulatory for His Return from His Embassy. 1632.
To the Right Honourable, the Lord High Treasurer of England. An Epistle Mendicant. 1631.
To the Right Honourable, the Lord Treasurer of England. An Epigram.
To the Right Noble Tom, Tell-Troth of His Travels, the Coriat of Odcombe, and His Book Now Going to Travel.
To the Same [Alphonso Ferrabosco].
To the Same [Benjamin Rudyerd] ("If I would wish, for truth, and not for show").
To the Same [Benjamin Rudyerd] ("Writing thyself, or judging others' writ").
To the Same; on the Same.
To the Same [Robert, Earl of Salisbury] [Upon the Accension of the Treasurership to Him].
To the Same Sir Cod.
To the Same Sir [Henry Goodyere].
To the Same [Sir John Roe].
To the Same [Sir Luckless Woo-All].
To the Same [Sir Thomas Roe].
To the World [A Farewell for a Gentlewoman, Virtuous and Noble].
To the Worthy Author M[r] John Fletcher.
To the Worthy Author on *The Husband*.
To Thomas, Earl of Suffolk.
To Thomas, Lord Chancellor.
To Thomas Palmer [on His Book *The Sprite of Trees and Herbs*].
To True Soldiers.

To William Camden.
To William, Earl[e] of Pembroke.
To William, Lord Mounteagle.
To William Roe ("Roe (and my joy to name) th'art now, to go").
To William Roe ("When Nature bids us leave to live, 'tis late").
Vision of Ben Jonson, on the Muses of His Friend M. Drayton, The.
Vision of Delight, The, *sels.*
Volpone, *sels.*
Why I Write Not of Love.

Jouve, Pierre Jean (1887–1976)
Kapuzinerberg (Salzburg).

Julian, Emperor (Flavius Claudius Julianus; "Julian the Apostate") (332–63)
From Julianus.

Justin Martyr, Saint (c.110–c.165)
Hortatory Address to the Greeks, *sels.*

Juvenal (c.50–c.130 A.D.)
Satires, *sels.*

K

Keats, John (1795–1821)
Acrostic.
Addressed to Haydon.
After Dark Vapours Have Oppressed Our Plains.
Ah! Ken Ye What I Met the Day.
All Gentle Folks Who Owe a Grudge.
And What Is Love? It Is a Doll Dressed Up.
Apollo to the Graces.
As from the Darkening Gloom a Silver Dove.
Blue! 'Tis the Life of Heaven, the Domain.
Bright Star.
Calidore. A Fragment.
Can Death Be Sleep, when Life Is But a Dream.
Cap and Bells, The; or, The Jealousies.
Dawlish Fair.
Day Is Gone and All Its Sweets Are Gone, The.
Endymion: A Poetic Romance.
Eve of St Agnes, The.
Eve of St. Mark, The.
Extracts from an Opera.
Faery Song.
Fairy Song.
Fall of Hyperion, The; A Dream.
Fancy.
Fill for Me a Brimming Bowl.
For There's Bishop's Teign.
Fragment of an Ode to Maia Written on May Day, 1818.
Fragment of the "Castle Builder."
Gif Ye Wol Stonden Hardie Wight.
Give Me Women, Wine, and Snuff.
God of the Meridian.
Great Spirits Now on Earth.
Gripus.
Happy Is England! I Could Be Content.
Hence Burgundy, Claret, and Port.
Hither, Hither, Love.
House of Mourning Written by Mr Scott, The.
How Many Bards Gild the Lapses of Time!
Human Seasons, The.
Hyperion.
I Cry Your Mercy, Pity, Love—Ay, Love!
I Stood Tip-Toe upon a Little Hill.
If by Dull Rhymes Our English Must Be Chained.
Imitation of Spenser.
In After-Time, a Sage of Mickle Lore.
In Drear-nighted December.
Isabella; or, The Pot of Basil.
Keen, Fitful Gusts Are Whispering Here and There.
King Stephen. A Fragment of a Tragedy.
La Belle Dame sans Merci [A Ballad].
Lamia.
Lines: "Unfelt, unheard, unseen."
Lines on the Mermaid Tavern.
Lines Written in the Highlands after a Visit to

Burns's Country.
Lines Written on 29 May / The Anniversary of the Restoration of Charles the 2nd.
Meg Merrilies [or Merrilees].
Nebuchadnezzar's Dream.
O Blush Not So! O Blush Not So!
O! How I Love, on a Fair Summer's Eve.
O Solitude! If I Must with Thee Dwell.
O Thou Whose Face Hath Felt the Winter's Wind.
Ode: "Bards of passion and of mirth."
Ode on a Grecian Urn.
Ode on Indolence.
Ode on Melancholy.
Ode to a Nightingale.
Ode to Apollo ("God of the golden bow").
Ode to Apollo ("In thy western halls").
Ode to Psyche.
Of Late Two Dainties Were before Me Placed.
On a Dream.
On a Leander Gem Which Miss Reynolds, My Kind Friend, Gave Me.
On First Looking into Chapman's Homer.
On Leaving Some Friends at an Early Hour.
On Oxford.
On Peace.
On Receiving a Curious Shell, and a Copy of Verses, from the Same Ladies.
On Receiving a Laurel Crown from Leigh Hunt.
On Seeing a Lock of Milton's Hair.
On Seeing the Elgin Marbles.
On Sitting Down to Read *King Lear* Once Again.
On the Grasshopper and [the] Cricket.
On the Sea.
On "The Story of Rimini."
On Visiting Staffa.
On Visiting the Tomb of Burns.
Otho the Great.
Pensive They Sit, and Roll Their Languid Eyes.
Poet, The.
Portrait, A.
Read Me a Lesson, Muse, and Speak It Loud.
Robin Hood.
See, the Ship in the Bay Is Riding.
Sleep and Poetry.
Song: "Hush, hush! tread softly! hush, hush my dear."
Song: "I had a dove and the sweet dove died."
Song: "Spirit here that reignest!."
Song: "Stay, ruby-breasted warbler, stay."
Song about Myself, A.
Song of Four Faeries.
Sonnet: "Where didst thou find, young Bard, thy sounding lyre?."
Specimen of an Induction to a Poem.
Spenser! A Jealous Honourer of Thine.
Stanzas: "You say you love; but with a voice."
Stanzas on Some Skulls in Beauly Abbey, near Inverness.
Sweet, Sweet Is the Greeting of Eyes.
Think Not of It, Sweet One, So.
This Living Hand, Now Warm and Capable.
This Mortal Body of a Thousand Days.
Three Undated Fragments.
'Tis the Witching Time [or Hour] of Night.
To a Cat.
To a Friend Who Sent Me Some Roses.
To a Young Lady Who Sent Me a Laurel Crown.
To Ailsa Rock.
To Autumn.
To B. R. Haydon, with a Sonnet Written on Seeing the Elgin Marbles.
To Charles Cowden Clarke.
To Chatterton.
To Emma.
To Fanny.
To George Felton Mathew.
To Georgiana Augusta Wylie.
To ———: "Had I a man's fair form, then might my sighs."
To Homer.
To Hope.

To J. H. Reynolds, Esq.
To James Rice.
To Kosciusko.
To Leigh Hunt, Esq.
To Lord Byron.
To [Mary Frogley].
To My Brother George ("Full many a dreary hour").
To My Brother George ("Many the wonders I this day").
To My Brothers.
To One Who Has Been Long in City Pent.
To Sleep.
To Some Ladies.
To the Ladies Who Saw Me Crowned.
To the Nile.
To ———: "Time's sea hath been five years at its slow ebb."
Two or Three Posies.
Two Sonnets on Fame, *sels.*
Upon My Life, Sir Nevis, I Am Piqued.
Welcome Joy, and Welcome Sorrow.
What Can I Do to Drive Away.
When I Have Fears [That I May Cease to Be].
When They Were Come unto the Faery's Court.
Where Be You [*or* Ye] Going, You [*or* Ye] Devon Maid?
Where's the Poet? Show Him! Show Him.
Why Did I Laugh Tonight?
Woman! When I Behold Thee Flippant, Vain.
Written in Disgust of Vulgar Superstition.
Written on a Blank Space at the End of Chaucer's Tale of "The Floure and the Lefe."
Written on the Day That Mr. Leigh Hunt Left Prison.

Kermani *See* **Khvaju of Kerman**

Khavarani, Awhad ad-Din 'Ali ibn Vahid ad-Din Muhammad *See* **"Anvari"**

Khayyám, Omar (d. 1123)
From Omar Chiam.
Make Friends.
On earth's wide thoroughfares below.
On two days it steads not to run from thy grave.
Unbar the door, since thou the Opener art.

Khvaju of Kerman (Kermani)
Exile, The.

Kinnell, Galway (b. 1927)
After Making Love We Hear Footsteps.
Another Night in the Ruins.
Avenue Bearing the Initial of Christ into the New World, The.
Bear, The.
Blackberry Eating.
Burn, The.
Cat, The.
Cellist, The.
Cemetary Angels.
Conception.
Daybreak.
Dead Shall Be Raised Incorruptible, The.
Fergus Falling.
52 Oswald Street.
Fire in Luna Park.
First Day of the Future.
First Song.
Flies.
Flower Herding on Mount Monadnock.
Fly, The.
For Robert Frost.
For William Carlos Williams.
Freedom, New Hampshire.
Frog Pond, The.
Fundamental Project of Technology, The.
Hen Flower, The.
How Many Nights.
Kissing the Toad.
Last Gods.
Lastness.
Little Sleep's-Head Sprouting Hair in the Moonlight.
Looking at Your Face.
Lost Loves.

Man in the Chair, The.
Middle of the Way.
My Mother's R & R.
Neverland.
Oatmeal.
Olive Wood Fire, The.
On the Tennis Court at Night.
Parkinson's Disease.
Perch, The.
Poem of Night.
Porcupine, The.
Prayer.
Rapture.
River That Is East, The.
Road between Here and There, The.
Ruins under the Stars.
Running on Silk.
Saint Francis and the Sow.
Sheffield Ghazal 4: Driving West.
Sheffield Ghazal 5: Passing the Cemetary.
Sow Piglet's Escapes, The.
Spindrift.
Supper after the Last, The.
That Silent Evening.
To a Child in Calcutta.
Tragedy of Bricks, The.
Under the Maud Moon.
Vapor Trail Reflected in the Frog Pond.
Wait.
Waking, The.
When One Has Lived a Long Time Alone.

Kinsella, Thomas (b. 1929)
Administrator.
All Is Emptiness, And I Must Spin.
Ancestor.
Ancient Ballet, An.
Anniversaries.
Another September.
Apostle of Hope.
Artists' Letters.
At the Crossroads.
At the Head Table.
At the Western Ocean's Edge.
Back Lane, The.
Baggot Street Deserta.
Ballydavid Pier.
Before Sleep.
Bell, The.
Beloved,.
Better is an handful with quietness.
Brothers.
Brothers in the Craft.
Butcher's Dozen.
C. G. Jung's 'First Years.'
Charlie.
Check.
Chrysalides.
Clarance Mangan.
Clearing, The.
Coda: "Nine are the enabling elements."
Country Walk, A.
Cover Her Face.
Crab Orchard Sanctuary, Late October.
Dance, The.
Death.
Death and the Professor.
Death Bed.
Departure Platforms.
Dick King.
Dispossessed, The.
Downstream ("We gave our craft to the slow-moving stream").
Dream.
Drowsing over *The Arabian Nights.*
Dura Mater.
Echoes.
Ely Place.
Endymion.
Entrance.
Exit.
Faith.
Fifth Sunday after Easter.
First Light.
Folk Wisdom.
Force of Eloquence, The.
Furnace, The.

Girl on a Swing.
Good Fight, The.
Good Night.
Hand of Solo, A.
Harmonies.
He carried me out of the lamplight.
Hen Woman.
Hesitate, cease to exist, glitter again.
High Road, The.
Household Spirits.
I have known the hissing assemblies.
I left the road where a stile entered the wood.
I wonder whether one expects.
In Memory.
In the Ringwood.
Interlude: Time's Mischief.
Intermezzo.
Invocation: "Sweet mother, sweet muscle."
Irwin Street.
Je t'adore.
King John's Castle.
Lady of Quality, A.
Land of Loss, The.
Landscape and Figure.
Last, The.
Laundress, The.
Lead.
Leaf-eater.
Liffey Hill, The.
Love.
Madonna.
Magnanimity.
Mask of Love.
Memory of W. H. Auden.
Messenger, The.
Midsummer.
Mirror in February.
Moment's Peace, A.
Monk, The.
Moralities.
Morning Coffee.
Museum.
Native Wisdom.
Navigators.
Night Conference, Wood Quay: 6 June 1979.
Night Songs.
Nightwalker.
Notes.
O Rome.
Office of the Dead.
Old Harry.
1.
One.
One Fond Embrace.
Open Court.
Our Mother.
Outdoor Gallery, An.
Overture.
Pause en Route.
Personal Places.
Phoenix Park.
Portrait of the Artist, A.
Portrait of the Engineer, A.
Remembering Old Wars.
Ritual of Departure ("Open the soft string that clasps in series").
Rituals of Departure.
Route of the Táin, The.
Sacrifice.
St. Catherine's Clock.
St Paul's Rocks: 16 February 1832.
Scylla and Charybdis.
Secret Garden, The.
Selected Life, A.
Settings.
Seven.
Shoals Returning, The.
Social Work.
Soft, to Your Places.
Soft Toy.
Song: "Engine screams and Murphy, isolate, The."
Song of the Night.
Songs of the Psyche.
Stable, The.
Stranger, The.

String Puppets.
Survivor.
Tao and Unfitness at Inistiogue on the River
   Nore.
Tara.
Tear.
Technical Supplement, A.
Test Case.
Tête à Tête.
Thinking of Mr D.
To Autumn.
Touching the River.
Traveller.
Travelling Companion, The.
Step forward and a lesser, A.
Tyrant Dying.
Vertical Man.
Visiting Hour.
We sat face to face at the kitchen table.
Wedding Morning.
Westland Row.
Worker in Mirror, at his Bench.
Wormwood.
Wyncote, Pennsylvania: A Gloss.

Kipling, Rudyard (1865–1936)
Absent-Minded Beggar, The.
Akbar's Bridge.
All the world over, nursing their scars.
American, An.
American Rebellion, The.
Anchor Song.
Answer, The.
Anvil, The.
Appeal, The.
Arithmetic on the Frontier.
Army Headquarters.
As the Bell Clinks.
Astrologer's Song, An.
At His Execution.
Ave Imperatrix!
Azrael's Count.
Back to the Army Again.
Ballad of Boh Da Thone, The.
Ballad of East and West, The.
Ballad of Fisher's Boardinghouse, The.
Ballad of Minepit Shaw, The.
Ballad of the "Bolivar," The.
Ballad of the *Clampherdown*, The.
Ballad of the King's Jest, The.
Ballad of the King's Mercy, The.
Ballad of the Red Earl, The.
Ballade of Burial, A.
Ballade of Jakko Hill, A.
Beasts Are Very Wise, The.
Bees and the Flies, The.
Before a Midnight Breaks in Storm.
Beginnings, The.
Bell Buoy, The.
Bells and Queen Victoria, The.
Belts.
Benfactors, The.
Betrothed, The.
Between the waving tufts of jungle-grass.
Big Steamers.
Bill 'Awkins.
"Birds of Prey" March.
Bobs.
Bonfires, The.
Boots.
Boy Scouts' Patrol Song, A.
Bridge-Guard in the Karroo.
Broken Men, The.
Brookland Road.
Brown Bess.
Buddha at Kamakura.
Burial, The.
Butterflies.
Cain and Abel.
Captive, The.
Carol, A: "Our Lord Who did the Ox
   command."
Cells.
Certain Maxims of Hafiz.
Chant-Pagan.
Charm, A.
Chartres Windows.

Children, The.
Choice, The.
Cholera Camp.
Christmas in India.
City of Brass, The.
City of Sleep, The.
Cleared.
Clerks and the Bells, The.
Coastwise Lights, The.
Code of Morals, A.
Coiner, The.
Cold Iron.
Columns.
Comforters, The.
Conundrum of the Workshops, The.
Covenant, The.
Craftsman, The.
Cruisers.
Cuckoo Song.
Curé, The.
Dane-Geld.
Danny Deever.
Dark children of the mere and marsh.
Dawn Wind, The.
Dead King, The [Edward VII; 1910].
Death-Bed, A.
Debits and Credits, *sels.*
Declaration of London, The.
Dedication, A: "And they were stronger hands
   than mine."
Dedication from "Barrack-Room Ballads."
Deep-Sea Cables, The.
Delilah.
Derelict, The.
Destroyers, The.
Dinah in Heaven.
Dirge of Dead Sisters.
Disciple, The.
Divided Destinies.
Doctors.
Dove of Dacca, The.
Dutch in the Medway, The.
Dykes, The.
'Eathen, The.
Eddi's Service.
Edgehill Fight.
Egg-Shell, The.
En-Dor.
England's Answer.
English Flag, The.
English Way, The.
Envoi: "There's a whisper down the field
   where the year has shot her yield."
Epitaphs of the War [1914–1918].
Et Dona Ferentes.
Evarra and His Gods.
Exiles' Line, The.
Expert, The.
Explanation, The.
Explorer, The.
Fabulists, The.
Fall of Jock Gillespie, The.
Farewell and adieu to you, Harwich Ladies.
Feet of the Young Men, The.
Female of the Species, The.
Files, The.
Fires, The.
First Chantey, The.
Flight, The.
Floods, The.
Flowers, The.
Follow Me 'Ome.
For All We Have and Are [1914].
For to Admire.
Ford o' Kabul River.
Four Angels, The.
Four-Feet.
Fox-Hunting.
France.
Frankie's Trade.
French Wars, The.
Friends, The.
Fuzzy-Wuzzy.
Galley-Slave, The.
Gallio's Song.
Gehazi.

General Joubert.
General Summary, A.
Gentlemen-Rankers.
Gertrude's Prayer.
Gethsemane.
Giffen's Debt.
Gift of the Sea, The.
Gipsy Trail, The.
Glories, The.
Glory of the Garden, The.
Gods of the Copybook Headings, The.
Grave of the Hundred Dead, The.
Great-Heart.
Gunga Din.
Half-Ballad of Waterval.
Helen All Alone.
Heritage, The.
His Apologies.
Holy War, The.
Houses, The.
Hyænas [*or* Hyenas], The.
Hymn before Action.
Hymn of Breaking Strain.
Hymn of the Triumphant Airman.
Hymn to Physical Pain.
If—.
Imperial Rescript, An.
In Springtime.
In the Matter of One Compass.
In the Neolithic Age.
Instructor, The.
Irish Guards, The.
Islanders, The.
Jacket, The.
James I.
Jester, The.
Jobson's Amen.
Jubal and Tubal Cain.
Jungle Book, The, *sels.*
Just-So Stories, *sels.*
Justice.
Kim, *sels.*
King and the Sea, The.
King Henry VII. And the Shipwrights.
King, The.
King's Job, The.
King's Pilgrimage, The.
King's Task, The.
Kitchener's School.
La Nuit Blanche.
Ladies, The.
Lament of the Border Cattle Thief, The.
Land and Sea Tales, *sels.*
Land, The.
Last Chantey, The.
Last Department, The.
Last of the Light Brigade, The.
Last Rhyme of True Thomas, The.
Last Suttee, The.
Legend of Mirth, The.
Legend of the Foreign Office, A.
Legends of Evil, The.
L'Envoi.
L'Envoi; Departmental Ditties.
'Less you want your toes trod off you'd better
   get back at once.
Lesson, The.
Lichtenberg.
Life's Handicap, *sels.*
Light That Failed, The, *sels.*
Liner She's a Lady, The.
Lollius.
London Stone.
Looking Glass, The.
Loot.
Lord Roberts.
Lost Legion, The.
Lovers' Litany, The.
Lowestoft Boat, The.
M. I.
MacDonough's Song.
Man Who Could Write, The.
Mandalay.
Mare's Nest, The.
Married Man, The.
Mary Gloster, The.

Mary, Pity Women!
Mary's Son.
Masque of Plenty, The.
McAndrew's Hymn.
Memories.
Men That Fought at Minden, The.
Merchantmen, The.
Mesopotamia.
Mine Sweepers.
Miracles, The.
Moon of Other Days, The.
Mother-Lodge, The.
Mother's Son, The.
Mulholland's Contract.
Municipal.
Muse among the Motors, The, *sels.*
My Boy Jack.
My Father's Chair.
My Rival.
Naaman's Song.
Native-Born, The.
Nativity, A.
Natural Theology.
Naulahka, The, *sels.*
Necessitarian, The.
Neighbours.
New Knighthood, The.
Non Nobis Domine!
Norman and Saxon.
North Sea Patrol, The.
Ode: "So long as memory, valour, and faith
    endure."
Ode to Liberty.
Old Issue, The.
Old Men, The.
Old Mother Laidinwool.
Old Song, An.
Oldest Song, The.
One Viceroy Resigns.
Only Son, The.
Oonts.
Open Door, The.
Our Fathers Also.
Our Fathers of Old.
Our Lady of the Sackcloth.
Our Lady of the Snows.
Outlaws, The.
Overland Mail, The.
Pageant of Elizabeth, A.
Pagett, M. P.
Palace, The.
Pan in Vermont.
Parting of the Columns, The.
Peace of Dives, The.
Penalty, The.
Pharaoh and the Sergeant.
Philadelphia.
Piet.
Pilgrim's Way, A.
Pink Dominoes.
Pirates in England, The.
Plain Tales from the Hills, *sels.*
Playmate, The.
Plea of the Simla Dancers, The.
Poison of Asps.
Poor Honest Men.
Poseidon's Law.
Possibilities.
Post That Fitted, The.
Power of the Dog, The.
Prairie, The.
Prayer of Miriam Cohen, The.
Prelude to "Departmental Ditties."
Press, The.
Pro-Consuls, The.
Public Waste.
Puck of Pook's Hill, *sels.*
Put forth to watch, unschooled, alone.
Puzzler, The.
Queen's Men, The.
Quest, The.
Question, The.
Rabbi's Song, The.
Rebirth.
Recall, The.
Recantation, A.

Recessional.
Rector's Memory, A.
Reeds of Runnymede, The.
Reformers, The.
Return of the Children, The.
Return, The.
Rhodes Memorial, Table Mountain.
Rhyme of the Three Captains, The.
Rhyme of the Three Sealers, The.
Rimmon.
River's Tale, The.
Roman Centurion's Song, The.
Romulus and Remus.
Route Marchin.'
Rowers, The.
Run of the Downs, The.
Runners, The.
Rupaiyat of Omar Kal'vin, The.
Russia to the Pacifists.
Sacrifice of Er-Heb, The.
St. Helena Lullaby, A.
Samuel Pepys.
Sappers.
Scholars, The.
School Song, A.
Screw-Guns.
Sea and the Hills, The.
Sea-Wife, The.
Second Jungle Book, The, *sels.*
Second Voyage, The.
Secret of the Machines, The.
Sergeant's Weddin', The.
Servant When He Reigneth, A.
Service Man, The.
Sestina of the Tramp-Royal.
Settler, The.
Seven Watchmen.
Shillin' a Day.
Shut-Eye Sentry, The.
Snarleyow.
Soldier an' Sailor Too.
Soldier, Soldier.
Song at Cock-Crow, A.
Song for the Women, The.
Song in Storm, A.
Song in the Desert, A.
Song of Bananas, A.
Song of Diego Valdez, The.
Song of French Roads, A.
Song of Seven Cities, The.
Song of Seventy Horses.
Song of the Banjo, The.
Song of the Cities, The.
Song of the Dead, The.
Song of the Dynamo.
Song of the English, A.
Song of the Galley-Slaves.
Song of the Lathes, The.
Song of the Men's Side.
Song of the Old Guard, The.
Song of the Red War-Boat.
Song of the Sons, The.
Song of the White Men, A.
Song of the Wise Children.
Song of Travel, A.
Sons of Martha, The.
South Africa.
Spies' March, The.
Stellenbosch.
Storm Cone, The.
Story of the Gadsbys, The, *sels.*
Story of Ung, The.
Story of Uriah, The.
Stranger, The.
Study of an Elevation, in Indian Ink.
Such As in Ships.
Supplication of the Black Aberdeen.
Sussex.
Tale of Two Cities, A.
That Day.
They killed a Child to please the Gods.
Things and the Man.
Thousandth Man, The.
Three-Decker, The.
Threshold, The.
Tin Fish.

To James Whitcomb Riley.
To the City of Bombay.
To the True Romance.
To the Unknown Goddess.
To Thomas Atkins.
Together.
Tomlinson.
Tommy.
Torn boughs trailing o'er the tusks aslant, The.
Totem, The.
Trade, The.
After Horace, *Book* 5, *Ode* 3.
Troopin.'
Truce of the Bear, The.
Truthful Song, The.
Two Kopjes.
Two Months.
Two Races.
Ubique.
Ulster.
Undertaker's Horse, The.
Vampire, The.
Verdicts, The.
Verses on Games.
Very Many People.
Veterans, The.
Virginity, The.
Voortrekker, The.
Wage-Slaves, The.
Waster, The.
Way through the Woods, The.
We now, held in captivity.
Wet Litany, The.
What Happened.
What the People Said.
When 'Omer Smote 'Is Bloomin' Lyre.
When the Great Ark.
White Horses.
White Man's Burden, The.
Widow at Windsor, The.
Widower, The.
Widow's Party, The.
Wilful-Missing.
With Drake in the Tropics.
With Scindia to Delhi.
Young British Soldier, The.
Young Queen, The.
Zion.

Kizer, Carolyn (b. 1925)
After Basho.
Afternoon Happiness.
Afterthoughts of Donna Elvira.
American Beauty, An.
Amusing Our Daughters.
Anniversaries: Claremont Avenue, from 1945.
Antique Father.
Arthur's Party.
Ashes, The.
Birthday Poem for a Childless Man.
Bitch.
Blessing, The.
By the Riverside.
Children.
Columns and Caryatids.
Complex Autumnal.
Copulating Gods, The.
Cultural Evolution.
Damnation, The.
Dangerous Games.
Days of 1986.
Death of a Public Servant, The.
Dixit Insipiens.
Dream of a Large Lady.
Dying Goddess, The.
Election Day, 1984.
Eleutheria.
Epithalamion: "You left me gasping on the
    shore."
Exodus.
Fearful Women.
Fin-de-Siècle Blues.
Final Meeting.
First of June Again, The.
Flower, The.
Food of Love.
For Jan as the End Draws Near.

For Jan, in Bar Maria.
For My Daughter.
For Sappho/After Sappho.
From an Artist's House.
Gerda.
Gift, The.
Glass, The.
Good Author, The.
Great Blue Heron, The.
Halation.
Heart's Limbo.
Heine Journal, A, *sels.*
Hera, Hung from the Sky.
Horseback.
How It Passes.
In Hell with Virg and Dan.
In the First Stanza.
In the Night.
Index, a Mountain.
Ingathering.
Intruder, The.
Italian Kittens, The.
Light, The.
Lines to Accompany Flowers for Eve.
Linked Verses.
Long Line of Doctors, A.
Lost in Translation.
Love Song: "Oh, to fall easily, easily; easily in
   Love."
Lovemusic.
Marriage Song: "We begin with the osprey
   who cries, 'Clang, clang!'"
Medicine ("Practice of medicine, The").
Medicine ("When the nurses, interns, doctors
   came running full tilt down the hall").
Month in Summer, A.
Mud Soup.
Muse, A.
Muse of Water, A.
My Good Father.
Night Sounds.
Not Writing Poems about Children.
October 1973.
On a Line from Julian.
On a Line from Sophocles.
On a Line from Valéry.
On Rising from the Dead.
One to Nothing.
Oration, The.
Parents' Pantoum.
Patient Lovers, The.
Pearl.
Persephone Pauses.
Plaint of the Poet in an Ignorant Age.
Poem for Your Birthday.
Poem, Small and Delible.
Poet's Household, A.
Postcards from Rotterdam.
Pro Femina, *sels.*
Promising Author.
Race Relations.
Reading Your Poems in Your House While
   You Are Away.
Running Away from Home.
Season of Lovers and Assassins.
Second Time Around.
Semele Recycled.
Shalimar Gardens.
Silent Man, The.
Singing Aloud.
Song for Muriel, A.
Streets of Pearl and Gold.
Suburbans, The.
Summer near the River.
Suppressing the Evidence.
Thrall.
Threatening Letter.
Through a Glass Eye, Lightly.
To a Visiting Poet in a College Dormitory.
To an Unknown Poet.
To My Friend, behind Walls.
To My Friend Who Rhymes with Peace.
Translation.
Trio.
Twelve o'Clock.
Two Poets by the Lake.

Ungrateful Garden, The.
Union of Women.
Valley of the Fallen, The.
Voyager.
Wars in Sweden, The.
Way We Write Letters, The.
What the Bones Know.
What Was in a Name.
Where I've Been All My Life.
Widow in Wintertime, A.
Winter Song.
Worms, The.

Knight, Fanny (1793–1882)
   To Anna Eliza Austen.
Knight, George (1795–1867)
   Bouts-Rimeés (Written at Chawton Cottage,
     1820).
   George Knight to His Dog Pincher.
Koch, Kenneth (1925–2002)
   Alive for an Instant.
   Art of Love, The.
   Art of Poetry, The.
   Artist, The.
   Aus Einer Kindheit.
   Boiling Water, The.
   Brassiere Factory, The.
   Bricks, The.
   Burning Mystery of Anna in 1951, The.
   Circus, The ("I remember when I wrote The
     Circus").
   Circus, The ("We will have to go away").
   Collected Poems.
   Days and Nights.
   Departure from Hydra, The.
   Desire for Spring.
   Down at the Docks.
   Fate.
   Fresh Air.
   Geography.
   Girl and Baby Florist Sidewalk Pram Nineteen
     Seventy Something.
   Hearing.
   In Bed.
   In Love with You.
   In the Morning.
   Locks.
   Lunch.
   Ma Provence.
   Magic of Numbers, The.
   On Beauty.
   On the Great Atlantic Rainway.
   Our Hearts.
   Permanently.
   Pleasures of Peace, The.
   Poem: "Thing / To do / Is organize / The sea,
     The."
   Railway Stationery, The.
   Simplicity of the Unknown Past, The.
   Sleeping with Women.
   Some General Instructions.
   Spring.
   Summery Weather.
   Taking a Walk with You.
   Thank You.
   Thanksgiving.
   To Marina.
   To You.
   Variations on a Theme by William Carlos
     Williams.
   West Wind.
   With Janice.
   You Were Wearing.
Komunyakaa, Yusef (b. 1947)
   Addendum.
   After Summer Fell Apart.
   After the Fall [of Saigon].
   After the Heart's Interrogation.
   Albino.
   Allegorical Seduction.
   Ambush.
   Annabelle.
   Anodyne.
   Apprenticeship.
   April Fools' Day.
   April's Anarchy.
   Articulation & Class.

At the Screen Door.
Audacity of the Lower Gods.
Back Then.
Banking Potatoes.
Beast & Burden, The: Seven Improvisations.
Beg Song.
Believing in Iron.
Bennelong's Blues.
Between Angels & Monsters.
Between Days.
Birds on a Powerline.
Birthday Song.
Black String of Days.
Blackberries.
Blasphemy.
Blessing the Animals.
Blue Light Lounge Sutra for the Performance
   Poets at Harold Park Hotel.
Blue Tonality.
Blues Chant Hoodoo Rival.
Boat People.
Borinken Blues.
Born Pretty in a Poor Country.
Boxing Day.
Boy Wearing a Dead Man's Clothes.
Boys in Dresses.
Brain to the Heart, The.
Break from the Bush, A.
Breaking Camp.
Breasts.
Bui Doi, Dust of Life.
Buried Light.
Butterfly-toed Shoes.
By Proxy.
Cage Walker, The.
Camouflaging the Chimera.
Captain Diable's Receptionist.
Cenotaph.
Chair Gallows.
Changes; or, Reveries at a Window
   Overlooking a Country Road, with Two
   Women Talking Blues in the Kitchen.
Charmed.
Child Stealer.
Child's Play.
Cinderella at Big Sur.
Combat Pay for Jody.
Communiqué.
Confessing My Ignorance.
Confluence.
Cooling Board, The.
Copacetic Mingus.
Cops Call Him Charlie, The.
Corners of Night.
Corrigenda.
Crack.
Cubism.
De Síntoma Profundo.
Dead at Quang Tri, The.
Death Threat Note.
Deck, The.
Delicate Conspiracy, A.
Different Story, A.
Dog Act, The.
Dog's Theology, The.
Dolphy's Aviary.
Donut Dollies.
Doppelgängers.
Double Limbo.
Dream Animal.
Dreambook Bestiary.
Eclogue at Daybreak.
Eclogue at Twilight.
Edge, The.
Eleemosynary.
Elegy for Thelonious.
(E)Motion.
Epilogue to the Opera of Dead on Arrival.
"Everybody's Reading Li Po" Silkscreened on
   a Purple T-Shirt.
Exchange Student Awaits the Arrival of an
   African Princess, An.
Eye Witness.
Eyeball Television.
Facing It.
Faith Healer.

Wokanmagulli.
Woman, I Got the Blues.
Work.
Yellow Dog Café.
Yellowjackets.
You and I Are Disappearing.

Korn, Rachel [*or* Rokhl] (1898–1982)
Generations.
Keep Hidden from Me.

Kumin, Maxine W. (b. 1925)
Accolade of the Animals, The.
Address to the Angels.
After Love.
After the Harvest.
Agnostic Speaks to Her Horse's Hoof, The.
Amanda Dreams She Has Died and Gone to the Elysian Fields.
Amanda Is Shod.
Apostrophe to a Dead Friend.
Appetite.
Appointment, The.
At a Private Showing in 1982.
Atlantic City 1939.
Bangkok Gang, The.
Beans.
Birthday Poem.
Body and Soul: A Meditation.
Bringing Back the Trumpeter Swan.
Calling, A.
Caring: A Dream.
Casablanca.
Catchment.
Chain, The.
Changing the Children.
Continuum: A Love Poem.
Creatures.
Custodian.
Deaths of the Uncles, The.
Distance.
Dreamer, the Dream, The.
Encounter in August.
Envelope, The.
Excrement Poem, The.
Eyes.
Family Reunion.
February.
Feeding Time.
Festung, Salzburg, The.
First Rain of Spring, The.
Food Chain, The.
For My Great-Grandfather: A Message Long Overdue.
400-Meter Freestyle.
Fräulein Reads Instructive Rhymes.
Game of Monopoly in Chavannes.
Getting Through.
Grandchild.
Grappling in the Central Blue.
Halfway.
Heaven as Anus.
Hello, Hello Henry.
Henry Manley Blues, The.
Henry Manley Looks Back.
Hermit Meets the Skunk, The.
Hermit Picks Berries, The.
Hermit Prays, The.
Hermit Wakes to Bird Sounds, The.
History Lesson.
Homage to Binsey Poplars.
How It Goes On.
How It Is.
How to Survive Nuclear War.
Hundred Nights, A.
In April, in Princeton.
In Memoriam P. W. Jr. 1921–1980.
In the Absence of Bliss.
In the Park.
In the Pea Patch.
In the Root Cellar.
In Warm Rooms, before a Blue Light.
Introducing the Fathers.
Itinerary of an Obsession.
Jesus Infection, The.
Joppa Diary, *sels.*
July, against Hunger.
Late Snow.

Leaving My Daughter's House.
Life's Work.
Living Alone with Jesus.
Long Approach, The.
Longing to Be Saved, The.
Making the Jam without You.
Marianne, My Mother, and Me.
Morning Swim.
Mud.
Mummies, The.
My Elusive Guest.
My Father's Neckties.
Night Launch.
Nightmare Factory, The.
Nurture.
On Being Asked to Write a Poem for the Centenary of the Civil War.
On Being Asked to Write a Poem in Memory of Anne Sexton.
On Reading an Old Baedeker in Schloss Leopoldskron.
Our Ground Time Here Will Be Brief.
Out in It.
Pawnbroker, The.
Photograph, U.S. Army Flying School, College Park, Maryland, 1909.
Photograph, Maryland Agricultural College Livestock Show, 1924.
Presence, The.
Progress Report.
Prothalamion.
Purgatory.
Quarry, Pigeon Cove.
Rejoicing with Henry.
Relearning the Language of April.
Repent.
Retrieval System, The.
Reviewing the Summer and Winter Calendar of the Next Life.
Seeing the Bones.
Selling of the Slaves, The.
Shelling Jacobs Cattle Beans.
Shopping in Ferney with Voltaire.
Sisyphus.
Sleeping with Animals.
Song for Seven Parts of the Body.
Sperm.
Splitting Wood at Six Above.
Stones.
Sunbathing on a Rooftop in Berkeley.
Survival Poem, The.
Territory.
Thinking of Death and Dogfood.
Thirties Revisited, The.
Thoughts on Saving the Manatee.
To Swim, to Believe.
Turning the Garden in Middle Age.
Vealers, The.
Video Cuisine.
Watering Trough.
We Are.
We Stood There Singing.
With the Caribou.
Woodchucks.
You Are in Bear Country.
Young Nun at Bread Loaf.

Kunitz, Stanley (b. 1905)
Abduction, The.
After the Last Dynasty.
Ambergris.
Among the Gods.
Approach of Autumn.
Approach to Thebes, The.
Around Pastor Bonhoeffer.
Artist, The.
As Flowers Are.
Benediction.
Between Me and the Rock.
Between the Acts.
Beyond Reason.
By Lamplight.
Careless Love.
Catch, The.
Change.
Chariot.
Class Will Come to Order, The.

Confidential Instructions.
Crystal Cage, The.
Customs Collector's Report, The.
Dark and the Fair, The.
Daughters of the Horseleech, The.
Day of Foreboding.
Deciduous Branch.
Dragonfly, The.
Eagle.
Economist's Song, The.
End of Summer.
Father and Son.
Firesticks.
First Love.
Fitting of the Mask, The.
Flight of Apollo, The.
Foreign Affairs.
Game, The.
Gladiators, The.
Goose Pond.
Grammar Lesson.
Green Ways.
Halley's Comet.
Harsh Judgment, The.
He.
Hemorrhage, The.
Hermetic Poem.
Hornworm: Autumn Lamentation.
Hornworm: Summer Reverie.
How Long Is the Night?
I Dreamed that I Was Old.
Illumination, The.
Image-Maker, The.
In a Strange House.
In the Dark House.
Indian Summer at Land's End.
Journal for My Daughter.
King of the River.
Knot, The.
Lamplighter: 1914.
Last Picnic, The.
Last Words.
Layers, The.
Lesson, The.
Lincoln Relics, The.
Long Boat, The.
Lovers Relentlessly.
Magic Curtain, The.
Master and Mistress.
Mound Builders, The.
Mulch, The.
My Mother's Pears.
My Sisters.
Night Letter.
Night-Piece.
Nocturne.
Old Clothes Man, The.
Old Cracked Tune, An.
Old Darned Man, The.
Open the Gates.
Organic Bloom.
Particular Lullaby.
Parting.
Passing Through.
Pivot, The.
Poem: "O Heart: this is a dream I had, or not a dream."
Portrait, The.
Promise Me.
Prophecy on Lethe.
Proteus.
Raccoon Journal.
Reckoning, The.
Reflection by a Mailbox.
Revolving Meditation.
River Road.
Robin Redbreast.
Round, The.
Route Six.
Science of the Night, The.
Scourge, The.
Sea, That Has No Ending, The.
She Wept, She Railed.
Signal from the House, The.
Signs and Portents.
Single Vision.

Snakes of September, The.
So Intricately Is This World Resolved.
Sotto Voce.
Spark of Laurel, A.
Strange Calendar.
Summing-up, The.
System, The.
Testing-Tree, The.
Thief, The.
Thing That Eats the Heart, The.
This Day This World.
Three Floors.
Three Small Parables for My Poet Friends.
Touch Me.
Transformations.
Tutored Child, The.
Unquiet Ones, The.
Unwithered Garland, The.
Very Tree.
Vita Nuova.
Waltzer in the House, The.
War against the Trees, The.
Way Down, The.
Welcome the Wrath.
Wellfleet Whale, The.
What of the Night?
When the Light Falls.
Words for the Unknown Makers.
Words of the Preacher, The.

Kuo Mo-jo (1892–1978)
Phoenix Undying, *sel.*

L

La Fontaine, Jean de (1621–95)
Grasshopper and the Ant, The.
Laberius, Decimus (c.115–43 B.C.)
Old Actor Addresses Julius Caesar, An.
Labrunie, Gérard *See* **Nerval, Gérard de**
"Laird, William" (William Laird Brown) (b. 1888)
Very Old Song, A.
Larkin, Philip (1922–85)
Absences.
Administration.
After-Dinner Remarks.
Afternoons.
Age.
All Catches Alight.
Ambulances.
And Now the Leaves Sudddenly Lose Strength.
And the Wave Sings because It Is Moving.
Annus Mirabilis.
Ape Experiment Room.
April Sunday Brings the Snow, An.
Arrival.
Arrivals, Departures.
Arundel Tomb, An.
As a War in Years of Peace.
As Bad as a Mile.
At Grass.
At the Chiming of Light upon Sleep.
At Thirty-One, when Some Are Rich.
Aubade: "I work all day, and get half-drunk at night."
Autobiography at an Air-Station.
Autumn.
Autumn Has Caught Us in Our Summer Wear.
Best Society.
Born Yesterday.
Bottle Is Drunk Out by One, The.
Breadfruit.
Bridge for the Living.
Broadcast.
Building, The.
By Day, a Lifted Study-Storehouse.
Card-Players, The.
Church Going.
Climbing the Hill within the Deafening Wind.
Come Then to Prayers.
Coming.
Coming at Last to Night's Most Thankful Springs.

Compline.
Conscript.
Continuing to Live.
Counting.
Cut Grass.
Daily Things We Do, The.
Dance, The.
Dancer, The.
Dawn.
Days.
Dear CHARLES, My Muse, Asleep or Dead.
Deceptions.
Dedicated, The.
Deep Analysis.
Disintegration.
Dockery and Son.
Dublinesque.
Essential Beauty.
Explosion, The.
Faith Healing.
Far Out.
Femmes Damnees.
Fiction and the Reading Public.
First Sight.
For Sidney Bechet.
Forget What Did.
Fragment from May.
Friday Night in the Royal Station.
Gathering Wood.
Going.
Going, Going.
Good for You, Gavin.
Having Grown Up in Shade of Church and State.
He Hears that His Beloved Has Become Engaged.
Heads in the Women's Ward.
Heaviest of Flowers, the Head.
Here.
High Windows.
Hills in Their Recumbent Postures, The.
Homage to a Government.
Home Is So Sad.
Horns of the Morning, The.
Hospital Visits.
House on the Edge of the Serious Wood, The.
How.
How Distant.
How to Sleep.
I Am Washed upon a Rock.
I Dreamed of an Out-Thrust Arm of Land.
I Have Started to Say.
I Put My Mouth.
I Remember, I Remember.
I See a Girl Dragged by the Wrists.
If Grief Could Burn Out.
If Hands Could Free You, Heart.
If My Darling.
Ignorance.
Importance of Elsewhere, The.
In Times When Nothing Stood.
Is It Now or for Always.
Kick Up the Fire, and Let the Flames Break Loose.
Large Cool Store, The.
Last Will and Testament.
Latest Face.
Letter to a Friend about Girls.
Life with a Hole in It, The.
Lift through the Breaking Day.
Like the Train's Beat.
Lines on a Young Lady's Photograph Album.
Literary World, The.
Little Lives of Earth and Form, The.
Livings.
Local Snivels through the Field, The.
Long Last.
Long Lion Days.
Long Roots Moor Summer to Our Side of Earth.
Long Sight in Age.
Love: "Difficult part of love, The."
Love Again.
Love Songs in Age.
Love, We Must Part Now.
Maiden Name.

Many Famous Feet Have Trod.
March Past, The.
Marriages.
Maturity.
May Weather.
Midsummer Night, 1940.
Midwinter Waking.
Modesties.
Money.
Moon Is Full Tonight, The.
Morning at Last: There in the Snow.
Morning Has Spread Again.
Mother, Summer, I.
Mower, The.
Mr Bleaney.
Mythological Introduction.
Myxomatosis.
Naturally the Foundation Will Bear Your Expenses.
Negative Indicative.
Neurotics.
New Eyes Each Year.
New Year.
Next, Please.
Night-Music.
MCMXIV.
No Road.
None of the Books Have Time.
North Ship, The.
Nothing Significant Was Really Said.
Nothing to Be Said.
Nursery Tale.
Observation.
Old Fools, The.
On Being Twenty-Six.
One Man Walking a Deserted Platform.
Out in the Lane I Pause.
Party Politics.
Past Days of Gales.
Pigeons.
Places, Loved Ones.
Plymouth.
Poem about Oxford.
Poetry of Departures.
Portrait.
Posterity.
Pour Away That Youth.
Reasons for Attendance.
Referred Back.
Sad Steps.
School in August, The.
Schoolmaster.
Scratch on the Scratch Pad.
Self's the Man.
Send No Money.
Show Saturday.
Since the Majority of Me.
Sinking Like Sediment through the Day.
Skin.
Slight Relax of Air Where Cold Was, A.
So through that unripe day you bore your head.
So You Have Been, Despite Parental Ban.
Solar.
Spirit Wooed, The.
Spring.
Spring Warning.
Stone Church Damaged by a Bomb, A.
Story.
Strangers.
Street Lamps.
Study of Reading Habits, A.
Success Story.
Summer Nocturne.
Sunny Prestatyn.
Sympathy in White Major.
Take One Home for the Kiddies.
Talking in Bed.
Thaw.
There Is No Language of Destruction.
This Be the Verse.
This Is the First Thing.
This Was Your Place of Birth, This Daytime Palace.
Time and Space Were Only Their Disguises.
To a Very Slow Air.
To Failure.

To My Wife.
To Put One Brick upon Another.
To the Sea.
To Write One Song, I Said.
Toads.
Toads Revisited.
Tops.
Traumerai.
Trees, The.
Triple Time.
Two Guitar Pieces.
Two Portraits of Sex.
Ugly Sister.
Ultimatum.
Under a Splendid Chestnut Tree.
Unfinished Poem.
View, The.
Waiting for Breakfast, while She Brushed Her
    Hair.
Wants.
Water.
We See the Spring Breaking across Rough
    Stone.
Wedding-Wind.
Whatever Happened?
When First We Faced, and Touching Showed.
When the Night Puts Twenty Veils.
When the Russian Tanks Roll Westward.
Whitsun Weddings, The.
Who Called Love Conquering.
Who Whistled for the Wind, That It Should
    Break.
Why Did I Dream of You Last Night?
Wild Oats.
Winter.
Winter Nocturne.
Winter Palace, The.
Wires.
Within the Dream You Said.
Writer, A.

Laughlin, James (b. 1914)
Above the City.
Admonition.
Advice to Aurelius.
After Martial.
After Rochester (or Somebody).
Alba.
America I Love You, *sels.*
Amo Amas Amat.
Among the Roses.
And Ole Ez said that the.
And Will That Magic World.
Anginal Equivalent, An.
Anti-Love Poem, An.
Antiphilus.
Apotropaic Decision, An.
Apsarases.
Arachne.
Ars Gratia Artis.
As in Music / A Reprise / Across Time.
Asmodeus.
At Benares.
At Eleusis.
At Our House.
At the Boule d'Or.
Atman of Sleep, The.
Atman, The.
Avalanche, The.
Ave Atque Vale.
Bad Night on Third Avenue, A.
Bavarian Gentian, The.
Beautiful Morning.
Beautiful One, The.
Before I Die.
Believer, The.
Berenice.
Bible Lady, The.
Bird of Endless Time, The.
Bit Different, A.
Bless You, Mr President.
Blowpipe Game, The.
Blue Flower, The.
Blue Footprints, The.
Box, The.
Bubble Bed, The.
Building 520, Bellevue.

Busy Day.
By the Numbers.
Can I Catch Up with the Future?
Can Language Be Taught with the Fingertips?
Can There Be a Female Bodhissatva?
Cardiac Autoscope, The.
Care and Feeding of a Poet, The.
Carmina Gemina.
Child, The.
Chimeras of Saint Helena, The.
Cincinnatus in Utah.
Cold, The.
Coming of Spring, The.
Confessio Amantis.
Confidential Report.
Cordelia.
Creatures of Prometheus, The.
Crucifixion in the Desert.
Crystal Palace Market.
Cultural Note.
Curious Romance, A.
Cynthia in California.
Da mi basia mille.
Dance of the Skin, The.
Danger / Road under Repair.
Dark Mutinous Shannon Waves, The,
De Contemptu Mundi.
Death Walkers, The.
Deathfear.
Deconstructed Man, The.
Deep Pool, the.
Delia Sequence, The.
Die Heimat.
Digging Down to China.
Doppelgaengers, The.
Down We Go.
Drawing Lesson, The.
Dream Not of Other Worlds.
Dropkick Me Jesus.
Dylan.
Easter in Pittsburgh.
Ein Kitzbuehler Tag (1947).
El camino de amor.
Elusive Time.
Empty Room, The.
Encounter at the Casino, Aix-les-Bains.
End of It All, The.
Endless Mirrors, The.
Enlacement, The.
Eraser, The.
Ermine, The.
Eros as Archaeologist.
Escape, The.
Ever So.
Experience of Blood.
Eyes Are the Guides of Love.
Failure of Communication in the Animal
    Kingdom, A.
Family Council of the Yakovlevs, The.
Family Portrait, The.
Fate of Actaeon, The.
Figlio Mio.
Firefly, The.
First Night, The.
Fisherwoman, The.
Flavius to Postumia.
Floating.
Floating Free.
Folk Wisdom.
For the First Time.
French, The.
Frightened Bird, The.
Full Life, The.
Garden of Delights, The.
Generations, The.
Getting Paid.
Girls as Windmills.
Go West Young Man.
God Bless America!
Goddess, The.
Graceful Exit, A.
Gracious Living.
Hand Trick, The.
Happy Poets, The.
Hard to Translate.
Having Failed.

He Did It to Please His Mother.
He Dreamed His Death.
He Lives in a Box.
Her Letters.
Her Reply.
Her Sweet Deceit.
Here I Am.
Herodotus Reports.
Highway 66.
Hitchhiker, The.
Holes.
Holy Rivers, The.
Hope Springs.
Hour Glass, The.
House of Light, The.
How Does It Look?
How Fortunate.
Hunting Dog, The.
I Am a Preposterous Beetle.
I Am Aware.
I am the Metoposcoper.
I Cannot Command You.
I Don't Know Where She Is Wandering
    Tonight.
I Float between the Spheres.
I Hate Love.
I Have Heard.
I Know How Every Poet.
I Like to Think of You.
I Like You.
I Live in Three Worlds.
I Love the Way.
I Love Therefore I Am I Suffer but I'm Alive.
I Love to See You.
I Saw Her First.
I Take a Certain Pride.
I Want to be Echopractic.
I Want to Breathe.
I'd Like to Be Putty.
If a Poet.
If You Are Only Flirting.
Il Pastor Fido.
I'm Fed Up with My Life.
I'm Not Lucky with Girls.
Importance of Dictionaries, The.
Importance of Silence, The.
In Another Country.
In Darmstadt.
In Egypt's Land.
In Hac Spe Vivo.
In Half Darkness.
In the Ballet.
In the Museum at Teheran.
In the Salzkammergut.
In the Snow.
In the Train.
Infantile Language, The.
Ingenium Nobis Ipsa Puella Facit.
Inn at Kirchstetten, The.
Inner Life of the Septic Tank, The.
Interdiction, The.
Into Each Life.
Inviolable Maiden, The.
Ipse Dixit.
Is It Written.
Is There a Danger.
It Can Happen.
It Does Me Good.
It Was the First Time.
It's Indelicate.
It's March.
It's Warm under Your Thumb.
James My Namesake.
Jealous Gods, The.
Job Description, A.
Judges of the Secret Court, The.
Junk Collector, The.
Junk Mail.
Kenners' Cat, The.
Kind-, The.
King's Bowman, The.
Kiss, The.
Kissing.
Knowledge.
La Tristesse.
L'Abécédérien de la Lubricité.

Lady Asks Me, A.
Lament of Professor Turbojet, The.
Large Opera Singer, The.
Last Caress, The.
Last Poem to Be Written, The.
Last Words.
Layers.
Leave-taking, A.
Les Amants.
Letter to Hitler, A.
Like Him I Need the Past.
Like the Octopus.
Limper, The.
Lines after Cummings.
Lines to Be Put into Latin.
Little Dog Laughs, The.
Little Heartsong, A.
Logistics.
Long-Distance Runner, The.
Long Night, The.
Lost Secrets, The.
Love Is a School.
Love Is Cumulative.
Love's Altar.
M & K.
Maker of Dreams, The.
Making a Love Poem.
Maledictus in Plebe Sit.
Market Discounts Love.
Martha Graham.
Mathematics of Chaos, The.
Maxima Dona Ferens.
Maze, The.
Mei Axis Mundi.
Merry Madness Hall.
Metropolitan Bard.
Mirror Girl, The.
Modest Proposal, A.
Moment on Earth, A.
Moon & Sun.
Moths, The.
Mountain Afterglow, The.
Mountain, The.
Munich Courier, The.
My Ambition.
My Granddaughter.
My Instructions.
My Muse.
My Old Gray Sweater.
My Secret.
Mysterious Disappearance, The.
Nameless Voyage, The.
Near Zermatt: The Drahtseilbahn.
Nereid, The.
Night at the Opera, A.
No Comparison.
No My Dear.
Non-World, The.
Nothing That's Lovely Can My Love Escape.
Now Love Speaks.
Now Strike the Golden Lyre Again.
Nowadays.
O Best of All Nights, Return and Return
    Again.
O Frères Humains.
O Hermes Trismegistus.
Obsession.
Occidit Brevis Lux.
Old Comedian, The.
Old Dr God.
On learning that he was about.
On the Gift of a Sapphire to My Wife Ann.
Orpheus.
Our Bicycles.
Our Meetings.
Out in the Pasture.
Owl of Minerva, The.
Paintings in the Museums of Munich and
    Vienna.
Parable, A.
Party on Olympus, The.
Patent Pending.
People Boxes, The.
Persephone Wears Bluejeans.
Person, The.
Piteous Sight, A.

Poem Factory, The.
Poem Seen as a Shell Game, The.
Poets.
Power of Poesy, The.
Preguntas sin Respuestas for Nicanor Parra.
Premula's Problem.
Prisoner of Childhood, The.
Prisoner's Song, The.
Problem Struck Me, The.
Prognosis.
Properate Tempus.
Questions, The.
Qui Nunquam Amavit.
Ravings of the Depraved Monk Benno of St.
    Gall Who Went Mad from Carnal Longing.
Reading the Obituary Page in The Times.
Real Bones.
Reclining Position, The.
Remembrance.
Return of Love, The.
Revenants, The.
Rhyme.
Rodent, The.
Rome: In the Café.
Sacks, The.
Saeta.
Saxo Cere.
Scribe, The.
Secret Words, The.
Secretary's Story, The.
Shameful Profession, The.
Shard of History, A.
She Asks Me.
She Is So Practical.
She Said in Apology.
She Says That I Put on Gloves.
She Seemed to Know.
She Walks No Longer in the Night.
Ship, The.
Sinking Stone, The.
Skaters, The.
Skiing without Skis.
Sleepless Night, A.
Small Group, A.
Smallest Blessing, The.
Snow in May.
So Much Depends.
So Slender.
Social Note.
Some Memories of E. P. (Drafts & Fragments).
Some of Us Come to Live.
Some People Think.
Somewhere in France.
Song: "O lovely lovely so lovely."
Song of the GIs & the MGs.
Songbird, The.
Sorrow.
Sorrows of Smindyrides, The.
Step on His Head.
Still Pond No More Moving.
Stranger in the House, The.
Stuttgart: In a Nightclub (Illegal).
Suggestion, A.
Summons, The.
Swarming Bees, The.
Sweet Kiss, A.
Take Off Your Socks!!
Tanka: "Winter has come."
Technical Notes.
Temporary Poems.
Ten Dollars Reward.
Tennesee.
Terror.
That Other World.
Then and Now.
This Is the Morte Saison.
This One Rhymes.
Three Skirmishes in the Endless Battle.
Through many nights of many years invincible.
Timor amoris conturbat me.
To My Lady in a Distant Land That She Forget
    Me Not.
To Smile or Not to Smile.
To that charming.
Touching.
Tragedy of Time, The.

Translation, A.
Trout, The.
Tuesday at 87 Rue de Rome.
Two Children.
Two Fragments from Pausanias.
Two Letters on Samos.
Two Parables from "The Ocean of Story."
Two Ships.
Two Spoons.
Unanswerable Question, The.
Under His Microscope.
Unenlightened Face, The.
Unsatisfactory Dream, The.
Upstate New York.
Vagrant, The.
Visitor, The.
Voices, The.
Waiters' Ballet, The.
Waiting for the Light.
We Met in a Dream.
Welcome, The.
Well All Right.
What Are You Smiling About.
What Is It Makes One Girl.
What Is the Need.
What Matters.
What the Animals Did.
What the Pencil Writes.
What touched me most.
When Does the Play Begin?
When I'm Missing You.
When you are far away.
When You Danced.
Who Is the Child.
Why.
Why Do You Never Enter My Dreams.
Why Not?
Why Shouldn't I.
Wild Anemone, The.
Will We Ever Go to the Lighthouse?
With My Third Eye.
Write on My Tomb.
You Are My Future.
You Came as a Thought.
You Invited Me.
You Know How a Cat.
You Were Asleep.
Your Early Life.
Your Error.
Your Eyes.
Your Love.
You've Set the Words.

Lawrence, D. H. (David Herbert) (1885–1930)
À la Maniere de D. H. Lawrence.
Absolute Reverence.
Abysmal Immortality.
After All Saints' Day.
After All the Tragedies Are Over.
After Dark.
After Many Days.
After School.
After the Opera.
Ah, Muriel!
Ah, with His Blessing Bright on Thy Mouth
    and Thy Brow.
All I Ask.
All-Knowing.
All of Roses.
All Sorts of Gods.
All Souls.
All Soul's Day.
All That We Have Is Life.
Almond Blossom.
Aloof in Gaiety.
Altercation.
Always This Paying.
American Eagle, The.
Amo Sacrum Vulgus.
Amour.
Anaxagoras.
And Jude the Obscure and His Beloved.
And Oh—That the Man I Am Might Cease to
    Be.
Andraitx—Pomegranate Flowers.
Another Ophelia.
Apostrophe to a Buddhist Monk.

Appeal, The.
Are You Pining?
Argonauts, The.
Aristocracy of the Sun.
As for Me, I'm a Patriot.
As Thyself!
Ass, The.
Assuming the Burden.
Astronomical Changes.
At a Loose End.
At Last.
At Midnight.
At the Bank in Spain.
At the Cearne.
At the Front.
At the Window.
Attack, The.
Attila.
August Holidays.
Auto-Da-Fé.
Autumn at Taos.
Autumn Rain.
Autumn Sunshine.
Aware.
Baby Asleep after Pain, A.
Baby-Movements.
Baby Running Barefoot.
Baby Songs Ten Months Old.
Baby Tortoise.
Bad Beginning, A.
Ballad of a Wilful Woman.
Ballad of Another Ophelia.
Bare Almond-Trees.
Bare Fig-trees.
Basta!
Bat.
Bathing Resort.
Battle of Life.
Bavarian Gentians.
Bawdy Can Be Sane.
Be a Demon!
Be It So.
Be Still!
Beautiful Old Age.
Behaviour.
Bei Hennef.
Being Alive.
Belief.
Bells.
Bereavement.
Best of School, The.
Beware, O My Dear Young Men.
Beware the Unhappy Dead!
Beyond the Rockies.
Bibbles.
Birdcage Walk.
Birth Night.
Birthday.
Bits.
Blank.
Blue Jay, The.
Blueness.
Bodiless God.
Body of God, The.
Bombardment.
Boredom, Ennui, Depression.
Both Sides of the Medal.
Boundary Stone, The.
Bourgeois and Bolshevist.
Bowls.
Bread upon the Waters.
Breath of Life, The ("Breath of life and the sharp winds of change").
Breath of Life, The ("Breath of life is in the sharp winds of change, The").
Bride, The.
British Sincerity.
British Workman and the Government, The.
Brittannia's Baby.
Broadcasting to the G.B.P.
Brooding Grief.
Brother and Sister.
But I Say unto You: Love One Another.
Butterfly.
Cabbage-Roses.
Call into Death.

Campions.
Can't Be Borne.
Canvassing for the Election.
Censors ("Censors are dead men").
Censors ("Trouble about those").
Cerebral Emotions.
Change.
Change of Government.
Change of Life.
Chastity.
Cherry Robbers.
Chief Mystery, The.
Children Singing in School.
Chimaera.
Choice.
Choice of Evils.
Church, The.
City-Life.
Classes.
Climb Down, O Lordly Mind.
Climbing Down.
Climbing Up.
Clydesider.
Cold Blood.
Coldness in Love.
Collier's Wife, The.
Combative Spirit, The.
Come Spring, Come Sorrow.
Coming Awake.
Coming of Quetzalcoatl, The.
Commandments.
Compari.
Conceit.
Conscience.
Conundrums.
Corot.
Correspondence in After Years.
Courage.
Cowardice and Impudence.
Cowards.
Craving for Spring.
Cross, The.
Cry of the Masses.
Cups.
Cypresses.
Daddy-Do-Nothing.
Dark Satanic Mills.
Dawn Verse, The.
Dead People.
Deadly Victorians, The.
Death.
Death of Our Era, The.
Death of the Baron, The.
December Night.
Decision, A.
Deeper Than Love ("And he was aware of life").
Deeper Than Love ("O love is a deep thing").
Deepest Sensuality, The.
Delight of Being Alone.
Demiurge.
Democracy.
Democracy is Service.
Demon Justice.
Departure.
Desire.
Desire Goes Down into the Sea.
Desire Is Dead.
Destiny.
Dies Illa.
Dies Irae.
Difference, The.
Difficult Death.
Disagreeable Advice.
Discipline.
Discord in Childhood.
Doe at Evening, A.
Dog-Tired.
Dolour of Autumn.
Dominant Woman.
Don Juan.
Don't Look at Me.
Don'ts.
Doors.
Drained Cup, The.
Drama, A.

Drawing-Room.
Dream-Confused.
Dreams Old and Nascent.
Dreams Old and Nascent: Nascent.
Dreams Old and Nascent: Old.
Drunk.
Eagle in New Mexico ("On a low cedar-bush").
Eagle in New Mexico ("Towards the sun").
Editorial Office.
Effort of Love, The.
Ego-Bound.
Ego-Bound Women.
Egoists, The.
Elderly Discontented Women.
Elegy: "Sun immense and rosy, The."
Elemental.
Elements, The.
Elephant.
Elephant Is Slow to Mate, The.
Elephants in the Circus.
Elephants Plodding.
Elixir.
Eloi, Eloi, Lama Sabachthani?
Elysium.
Emasculation.
Embankment at Night, before the War: Charity.
Embankment at Night, before the War: Outcasts.
Emotional Friend, The.
Emotional Lies.
En Masse.
End of Another Home Holiday.
End, The.
End, the Beginning, The.
Endless Anxiety.
Energetic Women.
England in 1929.
English Are So Nice!, The.
Enkindled Spring, The.
Erinnyes.
Erotic.
Escape.
Eve.
Evening Land, The.
Everlasting Flowers.
Evil Is Homeless.
Evil World-Soul, The.
Excursion Train.
Factory Cities, The.
Failure, A.
Fall of Day, The.
Fallen Leaves.
False Democracy and Real.
Fatality.
Fate and the Younger Generation.
Fatigue.
Fear of Society Is the Root of All Evil.
Fellow-Men.
Female Coercion.
Fidelity.
Fight! O My Young Men.
Figs.
Film Passion.
Finding Your Level.
Fire ("Fire is dearer to us").
Fire ("Wave them").
Fireflies in the Corn.
Firelight and Nightfall.
First Morning.
First Song of Huitzilopochtli.
Fish.
Flapper.
Flapper Vote.
Flat-Foot's Song.
Flat Suburbs, S.W., in the Morning.
Flowers.
Flowers and Men.
Food of the North.
For a Moment.
For All That.
For the Heroes Are Dipped in Scarlet.
Forecast.
Forget.
Forsaken and Forlorn.
Forte dei Marmi.
Four, The.

Free Will.
Fresh Water.
From a College Window.
Fronleichnam.
Frost Flowers.
Full Life.
Furniture.
Future Relationships.
Future Religion.
Future States.
Future War.
Gazelle Calf, The.
Gentleman, The.
Giorno dei Morti.
Gipsy.
Give Me a Sponge.
Give Us Gods.
Give Us the Thebaïd.
Gladness of Death.
Glimpses.
Gloire de Dijon.
Glory.
Glory of Darkness.
God.
God and the Holy Ghost.
God Is Born.
Gods.
Gods, The.
Gods! The Gods!, The.
Goethe and Pose.
Going Back.
Good Husbands Make Unhappy Wives.
Goodnight.
Grapes.
Grasshopper Is a Burden.
Great Newspaper Editor to His Subordinate,
    The.
Greeks Are Coming!, The.
Green.
Grey Evening.
Grief.
Gross, Coarse, Hideous.
Grudge of the Old, The.
Guards.
Guelder Roses.
Gulf, The.
Half-Blind, The.
Hands of God, The.
Hands of the Betrothed, The.
Hard-Boiled Conservatives.
Hark in the Dusk!
Have Done with It.
He-Goat.
Healing.
Heart of Man, The.
Henriette.
Hibiscus and Salvia Flowers.
Hills, The.
Him with His Tail in His Mouth.
History.
Hold Back!
Hostile Sun, The.
Houseless Dead, The.
How Beastly the Bourgeois Is.
Huitzilopochtli Gives the Black Blade of
    Death.
Huitzilopochtli's Watch.
Human Face, The.
Humanity Needs Pruning.
Humiliation.
Humility.
Humility Mongers.
Humming-Bird.
Hyde Park at Night, before the War.
Hymn to Nothingness.
Hymn to Priapus.
I Am in a Novel.
I Am like a Rose.
I Dare Do All.
I Heard Her Say.
I Wish I Knew a Woman.
If You Are a Man.
Ignoble Procession, The.
Image-Making Love.
Immoral Man.
Immorality ("It is only immoral").

Immorality ("Real immorality").
Impulse.
In a Boat.
In a Spanish Tram-Car.
In Church.
In Nottingham.
In the Cities.
In the Dark.
In Trouble and Shame.
Inheritance, The.
Initiation Degrees.
Innocent England.
Intimates.
Invocation to the Moon.
Irreverent Thoughts.
It's Either You Fight or You Die.
It's No Good!
Jealousy.
Jesus' Farewell.
Jeune Fille, The.
Kangaroo.
Keep It Up.
Kill Money.
Kiss, A.
Kisses in the Train.
Kissing and Horrid Strife.
Know-All.
Know Deeply, Know Thyself More Deeply.
Know Thyself.
Know Thyself, and That Thou Art Mortal.
Labour Battalion.
Lady Wife.
Last Hours.
Last Lesson of the Afternoon.
Last Words to Miriam.
Last Words to Muriel.
Late at Night.
Late War, The.
Latent Desire, The.
Latter-Day Sinners.
Laughter.
Leave Sex Alone.
Leaves of Grass, Flowers of Grass.
Leda.
Let the Dead Bury Their Dead.
Let There Be Light!
Let Us Be Men.
Let Us Talk, Let Us Laugh.
Letter from Town: On a Grey Morning in
    March.
Letter from Town: The Almond-Tree.
Liaison.
Liberty's Old Old Story.
Lies.
Lies about Love.
Life and the Human Consciousness.
Lightning.
Like the Green Candles of Malintzi.
Lilies in the Fire.
Listen to the Band!
Listening.
Little-Boy Brilliant.
Little Fish.
Little Town at Evening, The.
Little Wowser, The.
Living, A.
Living Quetzalcoatl, The.
Lizard.
Loggerheads.
London Mercury.
Loneliness.
Lonely, Lonesome, Loney—O!
Lord of the Morning Star.
Lord Tennyson and Lord Melchett.
Lords of Life Are the Masters of Death, The.
Lord's Prayer.
Loss.
Lotus and Frost.
Love: "One thing is certain, we've got to take
    hands off love."
Love as an Escape.
Love Comes Late.
Love Message.
Love On the Farm.
Love-Passage, A.
Love Song, A: "Reject me not if I should say

to you."
Love Storm.
Love Thy Neighbour.
Lucifer.
Lucky Little Britisher.
Lui et Elle.
Magnificent Democracy.
Malade.
Man, A.
Man and Bat.
Man and Machine.
Man at Play on the River, A.
Man in the Street, The.
Man Is More than *Homo Sapiens*.
Man of Tyre, The.
Man Reaches a Point.
Man Who Died, A.
Mana of the Sea.
Manifesto.
Man's Image.
Many Mansions.
Married in June.
Martyr à la Mode.
Masses and Classes.
Maximus.
Maybe.
Mediterranean in January.
Medlars and Sorb-Apples.
Meeting among the Mountains.
Men and Women.
Men Are Not Bad.
Men in New Mexico.
Men like Gods ("Men wanted to be like
    gods").
Men like Gods ("When men think they are like
    gods").
Mess of Love, The.
Metal for Resistance.
Michael Angelo.
Mid-Day Verse, The.
Middle-Class Children.
Middle Classes, The.
Middle of the World.
Mills of God, The.
Minorities in Danger.
Misery.
Modern Prayer.
Modern Problems.
Money.
Money-Madness.
Monologue of a Mother.
Moon Memory.
Moon New-Risen.
Moonrise.
Moral Clothing.
Morality.
Morning Work.
Mosquito, The.
Mosquito Knows, The.
Moth and Rust.
Mountain Lion.
Mournful Young Man.
Mowers, The.
Mr Squire.
Multitudes.
Murder.
Murderous Weapons.
Mutilation.
My Enemy.
My Little Critics.
My Name Is Jesus.
My Naughty Book.
My Way Is Not Thy Way.
Mystery.
Mystic.
Name the Gods!
Narcissus.
Natural Complexion.
Nemesis.
New Brooms.
New Heaven and Earth.
New Houses, New Clothes.
New Moon.
New Word, The.
New Year's Eve.
New Year's Night.

Next Morning.
Night.
Night Songs.
No Joy in Life.
No! Mr Lawrence!
No News.
Noble.
Noble Englishman, The.
Noise of Battle.
Noli Me Tangere.
Non-Existence.
Nonentity.
North Country, The.
Nostalgia.
Nothing to Save.
Nottingham's New University.
November by the Sea.
Now It's Happened.
Nullus.
O! Americans.
O! Start a Revolution.
Obscenity.
Obsequial Ode.
Oh Wonderful Machine!
Old Archangels.
Old Idea of Sacrifice, The.
Old Men.
Old Orchard, The.
Old People.
Old Song.
On and On and On.
On That Day.
On the Balcony.
On the Drum.
On the March.
On the Road.
One Woman to All Women.
Only Man.
Only the Best Matters.
Optimist, The.
Other Women Have Reared in Me.
Our Day Is Over.
Our Moral Age.
Oxford Voice, The.
Painter's Wife, The.
Paltry-Looking People.
Pang of Reminiscence, A.
Paradise Re-entered.
Parliament Hill in the Evening.
Passing-Bell, A.
Passing Visit to Helen.
Pax.
Peace.
Peace and War.
Peach.
Peacock.
Pear-Blossom.
People ("Great gold apples").
People ("I like people").
People, The.
People Who Care.
Phoenix.
Piano.
Piano, The.
Piccadilly Circus at Night.
Played-Out Game, A.
Poison.
Police Spies.
Pomegranate.
Poor Bit of a Wench!
Poor Young Things.
Portraits.
Poverty.
Prayer: "Give me the moon at my feet."
Prestige.
Primal Passions, The.
Proper Pride.
Property and No-Property.
Property Question, The.
Prophet.
Prophet in the Rose Garden, The.
Protestant Churches, The.
Punisher, The.
Purple Anemones.
Puss-Puss!
Question.

Quetzalcoatl Looks Down on Mexico.
Quite Forsaken.
Rabbit Snared in the Night.
Race and Battle.
Rainbow.
Rainbow, The.
Rallying-Point.
Reach Over.
Reading a Letter.
Reading in the Evening.
Real Democracy.
Reality of Peace, 1916.
Rebuked.
Red.
Red Geranium and Godly Mignonette.
Red-Herring.
Red Moon-Rise.
Red Wolf, The.
Refused Friendship.
Relativity.
Release.
Religion.
Reminder.
Renascence.
Repulsed.
Restlessness.
Resurrection.
Resurrection of the Flesh.
Retort to Jesus.
Retort to Whitman.
Return.
Return of Returns.
Revolutionary, The.
Revolutions as Such!
Riches.
Rise in the World, A.
Risen Lord, The.
River Roses.
Robot-Democracy.
Robot Feelings.
Rondeau of a Conscientious Objector.
Root of Our Evil, The.
Rose and Cabbage.
Rose Is Not a Cabbage, A.
Rose of All the World.
Rose of England, The.
Roses.
Roses on the Breakfast Table.
Ruination.
Saddest Day, The.
St John.
St Luke.
St Mark.
St Matthew.
Salt.
Salt of the Earth.
Salvation.
Sane and Insane.
Sane Revolution, A.
Sane Universe, The.
Satisfaction.
Scent of Irises.
School on the Outskirts.
Schoolmaster [A], The.
Schoolmaster [B], The.
Scientific Doctor, The.
Sea-Bathers.
Sea, The.
Sea, the Sea, The.
Sea-Weed.
Search for Love.
Search for Truth.
Second Song of Huitzilopochtli.
Secret Waters, The.
Seekers.
Self-Conscious People.
Self-Pity.
Self-Protection.
Self-Sacrifice ("Self-sacrifice, after all").
Self-Sacrifice ("Self-sacrifice is perhaps").
Sense of Truth.
Separated.
Service.
Seven Seals.
Sex and Trust.
Sex Isn't Sin.

Sex Won't Work.
Shades.
Shadow of Death, The.
Shadows.
She-Goat.
She Looks Back.
She Said as Well to Me.
She Was a Good Little Wife.
Shedding of Blood.
Ship of Death.
Ship of Death, The ("Have you built").
Ship of Death, The ("Now it is autumn").
Ships in Bottles.
Shows.
Sicilian Cyclamens.
Sick.
Sickness.
Side-Step, O Sons of Men!
Sigh No More.
Sight of God, The.
Signs of the Times.
Silence ("Come, holy Silence").
Silence ("Since I lost you").
Sinners.
Sleep.
Sleep and Waking.
Snake.
Snap-Dragon.
Snowy Day at School, A.
Snowy Day in School, A.
So Let Me Live.
So There!
Softly, Then, Softly.
Solomon's Baby.
Someone Will Enter between the Gates.
Son of the Morning Star.
Song: "Up in the high."
Song-Day in Autumn.
Song of a Man Who Has Come Through.
Song of a Man Who Is Loved.
Song of a Man Who Is Not Loved.
Song of Death.
Song of Don Ramon, The.
Song of the Dead.
Song of the Grey Dog, The.
Song to the Tune of La Cucaracha.
Songs I Learnt at School.
Sorrow.
Souls to Save.
Southern Night.
Space.
Spanish Privilege.
Spanish Wife, The.
Sphinx.
Spilling the Salt.
Spiral Flame.
Spirits Summoned West.
Spray.
Spring Morning.
St George and the Dragon.
Stand Up!
Stoic.
Stop It.
Storm in the Black Forest.
Street Lamps.
Strife.
Study.
Submergence.
Suburbs on a Hazy Day.
Sun in Me.
Sun-Men.
Sun-Women.
Sunday Afternoon in Italy.
Sunset.
Sunset Verse, The.
Suspense.
Swan.
Sympathy.
Tabernacle.
Tale Told by an Idiot, A.
Talk.
Talk of Faith.
Talk of Loyalty.
Tarantella.
Tarts.
Tease.

Temples.
Tender Reverence.
Terra Incognita.
There Are No Gods.
There Are Too Many People.
There Is No Way Out.
There Is Rain in Me.
There Was a Gay Bird Named Christine.
These Clever Women.
They Say the Sea Is Loveless.
Thief in the Night.
Things Made by Iron.
Things Men Have Made.
Think—!
Third Song of Huitzilopochtli.
Third Thing, The.
13 Pictures.
Thomas Earp.
Thought.
To a Certain Friend.
To Be Superior.
To Clarinda.
To Let Go or to Hold on—?
To Pino.
To Toss the Troubled Night Long.
To Women, as Far as I'm Concerned.
Today.
Tolerance.
Tommies in the Train.
Tortoise Family Connections.
Tortoise Gallantry.
Tortoise-Shell.
Tortoise Shout.
Touch.
Touch Comes.
Tourists.
Town in 1917.
Tragedy.
Train at Night, A.
Train, The.
Traitors.
Transformations.
Travel Is Over.
Trees in the Garden.
Triumph.
Triumph of the Machine, The.
Tropic.
Troth with the Dead.
True Democracy.
True Love at Last.
Trust.
Turkey-Cock.
Turned Down.
Twenty Years Ago.
Twilight ("Darkness comes out").
Twilight ("Twilight / thick underdusk").
Twilight ("Under the blue-grey twilight").
Two-Fold.
Two Fragments on Sleep.
Two Performing Elephants.
Two Ways of Living and Dying.
Two Wives.
Twofold.
Ultimate Reality.
Under the Oak.
Underneath.
Unhappy Souls.
Universe Flows, The.
Up He Goes!
Uprooted, The.
Valentine's Night.
Vengeance Is Mine.
Vibration of Justice.
Violets.
Violets for the Dead.
Virgin Mother, The.
Virgin Youth.
Vitality.
Volcanic Venus.
Wages.
Walk Warily.
Wandering Cosmos, The.
War-Baby.
Way Out, The.
We Are Transmitters.
We Can't Be Too Careful.

We Die Together.
We Have Gone Too Far.
Wealth.
Wedding Morn.
Wedlock.
Weeknight Service.
Welcome Death.
Welcome to Quetzalcoatl.
Wellsian Futures.
What Ails Thee?
What Are the Gods?
What Are the Wild Waves Saying?
What Do I Care?
What Does She Want?
What Have They Done to You?
What Is a Man to Do?
What Is He?
What Is Man without an Income.
What Matters.
What Quetzalcoatl Saw in Mexico.
What Then Is Evil?
What Would You Fight For?
Whatever Man Makes.
What's to Be Done.
What's Wrong.
When I Read Shakespeare.
When I Went to the Circus.
When I Went to the Film.
When Most Men Die.
When Satan Fell.
When the Ripe Fruit Falls.
When Wilt Thou Teach the People?
Whether or Not.
White Blossom, A.
White Horse, The.
Why—?
Why Does She Weep?
Wild Common, The.
Wild Things in Captivity.
Willy Wet-Leg.
Wind, the Rascal, The.
Winter Dawn.
Winter in the Boulevard.
Winter-Lull.
Winter's Tale, A.
Witch I, The.
Witch II, The.
Woe.
Women Want Fighters for Their Lovers.
Wonderful Spiritual Women.
Won't It Be Strange—?
Work.
Work of Creation, The.
Working Man, The.
Worm Either Way.
Worm Turns, The.
Worship.
Yew-Tree on the Downs, The.
You.
Young and Their Moral Guardians, The.
Young Are Not Greedy, The.
Young Are Not Mean in Material Things, The.
Young Fathers.
Young Soldier with Bloody Spurs, The.
Young Want to Be Just, The.
Young Wife, A.
Youth Mowing, A.

Le Roy, Jean
    Instant of Clearness.

Lee, Nathaniel (1653?–92)
    Constantine the Great, *sels.*
    Duke of Guise, The, *sels.*
    Princess of Cleves, The, *sels.*

Léger, Alexis Saint-Léger *See* **"Perse, St.-John"**

Lenau, Nikolaus (Nikolaus Franz Niembsch von Strehlenau) (1802–50)
    Postillion, The.
    Three Gipsies, The.

Leonidas of Alexandria (d. 450 B.C.)
    Upon Venus Putting on Mars His Armes.

Leopardi, Giacomo (1798–1837)
    Her Monument, the Image Cut Thereon.
    Leaf, The.

Levertov, Denise (1923–97)
    Abel's Bride.

About Marriage.
About Political Action in Which Each
    Individual Acts from the Heart.
Above the Cave.
Ache of Marriage, The.
Acolyte, The.
Action.
Advent 1966.
Age of Terror.
Air of November.
Alongside.
Altars in the Street, The.
Ancient Tree, An.
Annuals.
Annunciation.
Another Spring.
Antiphon, The: "And then once more."
April in Ohio.
Arrival (North Wales, 1897), An.
Art of the Octopus, The: Variations on a Found
    Theme.
Artist to Intellectual (Poet to Explainer).
As It Happens.
At David's Grave.
Autumnal.
Avowal, The.
Balance, The.
Bedtime.
Beginners.
Blake's Baptismal Font.
Blue Rim of Memory, The.
Braiding, The.
Breathing, The.
Bride, The.
Broken Sandal.
Bus.
Cabdriver's Smile, The.
Caedmon.
Cancion: "When I am the sky."
Candles in Babylon.
Cat as Cat, The.
Catpig, The.
Ce bruit da la mer.
Celebration.
Change, The.
Chant: Sunset, Somerville, Late Fall '75.
Chekhov on the West Heath.
Childhood's End.
Chill, The.
City Psalm.
Claritas.
Cloak, A.
Closed World, The.
Cloud Poems.
Clouds.
Cold Spring, The.
Come into Animal Presence.
Coming Fall, The.
Common Ground, A.
Concurrence.
Consulting the Oracle.
Continent.
Continuum.
Conversation in Moscow.
Conversion of Brother Lawrence.
Crack, The.
Craving.
Crosspurposes.
Crow Spring.
Cure of Souls, A.
Daughter (1), A.
Daughter (2), A.
Day Begins, A.
Dead, The.
Death in Mexico.
Death Psalm: O Lord of Mysteries.
Deaths.
Decipherings.
Depths, The.
Desolate Light.
Didactic Poem.
Disclosure, The.
Distance, The.
Divorcing.
Dogbrothers.
Don't You Hear that Whistle Blowin.'

Dragon of Revolutionary Love.
Dragonfly-Mother, The.
Dream Inscape.
During a Son's Dangerous Illness.
During the Eichmann Trial.
Dwellers at the Hermitage.
Earliest Spring.
Earth Psalm.
Earth Worm, The.
Earthwoman and the Waterwoman, The.
Effacement.
Else a great Prince in prison lies.
Elusive.
Elves, The.
Emblem (1).
Emblem (2).
Emissary, The.
Enduring Love.
English Field in the Nuclear Age, An.
Engraved.
Eros.
Eros at Temple Stream.
Evening Train.
Everything That Acts Is Actual.
Eyes and No-Eyes.
Face.
Face to Face.
Fellow Passengers.
Figure of Time, A.
Film, The.
First Love.
Five Poems from Mexico.
Flickering Mind.
Flowers of Sophia.
For a Child.
For Bet.
For Chile, 1977.
For Floss.
For Nikolai, Many Thousand Miles Away.
For the Blind.
For the New Year, 1981.
For Those Whom the Gods Love Less.
For X.
Fountain, The.
Fragment: "All one winter, in every crowded
    hall."
Fragrance of Life, Odor of Death.
Freedom.
Freeing of the Dust, The.
From a Plane.
From the Roof.
From the Train, Eastward.
Garden Wall, The.
Gone Away.
Goodbye to Tolerance.
Grace-Note, The.
Great Wave, The.
Greeting to the Vietnamese Delegates to the
    U.N.
Grey August.
Grey Sparrow Addresses the Mind's Ear.
Grief.
Ground-Mist, The.
Growth of a Poet.
Heights, Depths, Silence, Unceasing Sound of
    the Surf.
Her Delight.
Her Destiny.
Her Judgement.
Her Lament.
Her Nightmare.
Her Prayer.
Her Sadness.
Her Secret.
Her Sister.
Her Task.
Her Vision.
Hidden Monsters at the Mount Auburn
    Cemetery. A Found Poem.
Holiday.
Human Being.
Hunting the Phoenix.
Hymn to Eros.
Hypocrite Women.
I Learned that Her Name Was Proverb.
Ikon: The Harrowing of Hell.

Illustration [—a Footnote], The.
Illustrious Ancestors.
Improbable Truth.
In Abeyance.
In Memory of Boris Pasternak.
In Memory of Muriel Rukeyser.
In Mind.
In Question.
In Summer.
In Thai Binh (Peace) Province.
In Whom We Live and Move and Have Our
    Being.
Instant, The.
Intimation.
Into the Interior.
Isis Speaks.
Jacob's Ladder, The.
Journeyings.
Joy.
July 1968.
Kindness.
Kingdoms of Heaven.
Knowing the Unknown.
Lamentation, A.
Laying the Dust.
Le Motif.
Leaving Forever.
Letter.
Letter to Marek about a Photograph, A.
Letter to William Kinter of Muhlenberg, A.
Libation.
Life around Us, The.
Life at War.
Life in the Forest.
Life of Art, The.
Life of Others, The.
Listening to Distant Guns.
Living.
Living Alone (1).
Living Alone (2).
Living Alone (3).
Living for Two.
Living While It May.
Long Way Round, The.
Look at the Night (Temple, Early '60's), A.
Looking-glass.
Losing Track.
Love of Morning, The.
Love Poem: "Swimming through dark, slow."
Love Poem: "What you give me is."
Love Song.
Luxury.
Magic.
Making Peace.
Man, A.
Many Mansions, The.
Map of the Western Part of the County of
    Essex in England, A.
March, A.
Marriage 2, The.
Marriage, The.
Marta (Brazil, 1928).
Mass for the Day of St. Thomas Didymus.
Matins.
May Mornings, The.
May Our Right Hands Lose Their Cunning.
Melody Grundy.
Memories of John Keats.
Merritt Parkway.
Message.
Message, The.
Metamorphic Journal.
Métier of Blossoming, The.
Modes of Being.
Modulations for Solo Voice.
Mountain's Daily Speech is Silence, The.
Movement.
Music, A.
Mutes, The.
Mystery (Oaxaca, Mexico), A.
Mystery of Deep Candor, The.
Necessity, The.
News Items.
Night on Hatchet Cove.
Nightingale Road.
90th Year, The.

Note to Olga (1966), A.
Novel, The.
Novices, The.
O Taste and See.
Obsessions.
October.
Of Being.
Old Adam, The.
Old King, The.
Old People Dozing.
Olga Poems.
On a Theme from Julian's Chapter 20.
On the 32nd Anniversary of the Bombing of
    Hiroshima and Nagasaki.
On the Way.
Once Only.
Open Secret.
Our Bodies.
Overheard.
Overland to the Islands.
Part, The.
Partial Resemblance.
Passing Bell, The.
Pentimento.
Perspectives.
Photo Torn from The Times.
Pig-song.
Pilgrim Dreaming, A.
Pilots, The.
Place of Kindness, A.
Pleasures.
Poem at Christmas, 1972, during the Terror-
    Bombing of North Vietnam, A.
Poem Rising by Its Own Weight, The.
Poem: "Some are too much at home in the role
    of wanderer."
Poet and Person.
Poet Li Po Admiring a Waterfall, The.
Postcard.
Postcards: A Triptych, The.
Prayer for Revolutionary Love.
Prayer, The.
Presence.
Presence, The.
Primary Wonder.
Psalm Concerning the Castle.
Psalm: People Power at the Die-in.
Psalm Praising the Hair of Man's Body, A.
Pulse, The.
Puñal.
Quality of Genius, The.
Rain Spirit Passing.
Rainwalkers, The.
Re-Rooting.
Relearning the Alphabet.
Remembering.
Resolve, The.
Resting Figure.
Revivals.
Ripple, The.
Roast[ing] Potatoes.
Romance.
Room.
Runes, The.
St. Thomas Didymus.
Salvator Mundi: Via Crucis.
Sands of the Well.
Scornful Reprieve.
Second Didactic Poem.
Secret, The.
Seedtime.
September 1961.
Sequence, A.
Servant-Girl at Emmaus (A Painting by
    Velazquez), The.
Seth Thomas: A Love Poem.
Settling.
Shalom.
She and the Muse.
Showings, The: Lady Julian of Norwich, 1342-
    1416.
Six Variations.
Skew Lines.
Slowly.
Sojourns in the Parallel World.
Solitude, A.

Son, A.
Son, The.
Song for a Dark Voice.
Song for Ishtar.
Soothsayer, The.
Soul-Cake, A.
Sound of Fear, A.
Sound of the Axe.
Sparks.
Speech: For Antidraft Rally, D.C., March 22, 1980, A.
Spirits Appeased, The.
Split Mind, The.
Split Second.
St. Peter and the Angel.
Staying Alive, *sels.*
Stems.
Stepping Westward.
Stonecarver's Poem, The.
Strange Song.
Suspended.
Talk in the Dark.
Talking to Grief.
Talking to Oneself.
Tenebrae.
Terror.
That Passeth All Understanding.
Thirst Song.
Thread, The.
3 a.m., September 1, 1969.
Three Meditations.
Threshold.
Tide, The.
Time Past, A.
To Antonio Machado.
To Rilke.
To Speak.
To the Muse.
To the Reader.
To the Snake.
Too Easy: to Write of Miracles.
Too Much to Hope.
Traveler, A.
Travels.
Tree Telling of Orpheus, A.
Tropic Ritual.
Tulips, The.
Turn of the Head, A.
Two Artists.
Two Variations.
Unknown, The.
Unresolved.
Variation and Reflection on a Theme by Rilke.
Victors, The.
Vision, A.
Visit, A.
Visitant.
Volupté.
Voyage.
Vron Woods (North Wales), The.
Walk through the Notebooks, A.
Wanderer, A.
Wanderer, The.
Wanderer's Daysong.
Waving to the Devil.
Way It Is, The.
Ways of Conquest.
Wealth of the Destitute, The.
Web.
Wedding-Ring.
Weeping Woman.
Well, The.
What Harbinger?
What It Could Be.
What My House Would Be Like If It Were a Person.
What She Could Not Tell Him.
What Were They Like?
What Wild Dawns There Were.
Whisper, The.
Who Is at My Window.
Williams: An Essay.
Willows of Massachusetts, The.
Window, A.
Wings in the Pedlar's Pack.
Wings, The.

Winter Afternoons in the V & A, Pre-W.W. II.
Winterpig.
With Eyes at the Back of Our Heads.
Witness.
Woman Alone, A.
Woman Meets an Old Lover, A.
Woman, The.
Woodcut, A.
World Outside, The.
Writing in the Dark.
Writing to Aaron.
Young Man Travelling, A.

Levi, Primo (1919–87)
After R.M. Rilke.
Agave.
Almanac.
Annunciation.
Another Monday.
Arachne.
August.
Autobiography.
Avigliana.
Black Stars, The.
Bridge, A.
Buna.
Chess.
Chess 2.
Crescenzago.
Crow's Song, The.
Crow's Song 2, The.
Dark Band.
Decathlon Man.
Delilah.
Dromedary, The.
Dust.
Elephant, The.
11 February 1946.
Epitaph: "Oh you, passing by this hill—one."
First Atlas, The.
Flight.
Fly, The.
For Adolf Eichmann.
Gedale's Song.
Girl-Child of Pompei, The.
Give Us.
Glacier, The.
Gulls of Settimo, The.
Huayna Capac.
In the Beginning.
Laid Up.
Landing.
Leavetaking.
Lilith.
Memorandum Book.
Monday.
Mouse, A.
Nachtwache.
Old Mole.
On Trial.
Ostjuden.
Partisan.
Passover.
Pearl Oyster.
Pliny.
Profession, A.
Proxy.
Reveille.
Samson.
Shemà.
Sidereus Nuncius.
Singing.
Snail, The.
Song of Those Who Died in Vain.
Sunset at Fossoli.
Survivor, The.
Thaw, The.
There Were a Hundred.
Thieves.
To my Friends.
Toward the Valley.
12 July 1980.
25 February 1944.
2000.
Unfinished Business.
Unresolved Burdens.
Valley, A.

Via Cigna.
Voices.
Waiting.
Witch, The.
Wooden Heart.
Work, The.

Levine, Philip (b. 1928)
And the Trains Go On.
Angel Butcher.
Animals Are Passing from Our Lives.
Ashes.
Ask the Roses.
At the Fillmore.
Baby Villon.
Belief.
Belle Isle, 1949.
Blasting from Heaven.
Breath.
Buying and Selling.
Cemetery at Academy, California, The.
Children's Crusade, The.
Clouds.
Coming Home, *Detroit,* 1968.
Conductor of Nothing, The.
Detroit Grease Shop Poem.
Dog Poem.
Face, The.
Fist.
For Fran.
Fox, The.
Francisco, I'll Bring You Red Carnations.
Genius.
Gift for a Believer.
Goodbye.
Grandmother in Heaven.
Having Been Asked "What is a Man?" I Answer.
Hear Me.
Heaven.
Helmet, The.
Hold Me.
Holding On.
Horse, The.
How Much Can It Hurt?
How Much Earth.
I Could Believe.
I Was Born in Lucerne.
Jewish Graveyards, Italy.
Last Step, The.
Late Answer, A.
Late Moon.
Later Still.
Let Me Be.
Let Me Begin Again.
Letters for the Dead.
L'Homme et La Bête.
Lights I Have Seen Before.
Look.
Lost and Found.
Making It New.
Making Light of It.
Midget, The.
Milkweed.
Miracle, The.
My Poets.
My Son and I.
New Day, A.
New Season.
1933.
Nitrate.
No One Remembers.
Noon.
On a Drawing by Flavio.
On My Own.
On the Birth of Good & Evil During the Long Winter of '28.
On the Corner.
On the Edge.
On the Murder of Lieutenant José Del Castillo by the Falangist Bravo Martinez.
One for the Rose.
Ordinary Morning, An.
Pili's Wall.
Planting.
Poem Circling Hamtramck, Michigan, All Night in Search of You, The.

Poem of Flight, The.
Poem with No Ending, A, *sels.*
Rain Downriver.
Red Dust.
Renaming the Kings.
Roofs.
Salami.
Salts and Oils.
Saturday Sweeping.
7 Years from Somewhere.
Silent in America.
Sleepless Night, A.
Snow.
Sources.
Starlight.
Suit, The.
Sweet Will.
Theory of Prosody, A.
These Streets.
They Feed They Lion.
To a Child Trapped in a Barber Shop.
To a Fish Head Found on the Beach Near
    Málaga.
To Cipriano, in the Wind.
To My God in His Sickness.
To P.L., 1916–1937.
Told.
28.
Uncle.
Voice, The.
Waking an Angel.
Walk with Tom Jefferson, A.
Wednesday.
White Iris, The.
Winter Words.
Words.
You Can Have It.
Zaydee.

Li Po (701–62)
Drinking Together.
Exile's Letter.
In the Wineshop of Chinling.
Jewel Stairs' Grievance, The.
Knight, The.
Lament of the Frontier Guard.
Letter, A.
Long Banister Lane.
March, The.
Poem by the Bridge at Ten-shin.
Present for Tu Fu from Li Po, A.
River Song, The.
Solo.
Spotting the moonlight at my bedside.
Spring Song.
Summer Song.
Taking Leave of a Friend.
To Meng Hao-Jan.
Visitor, The.
Youth on Horseback, The.

Li Yü (937–78)
Bella Donna Iu.
Silently I ascend the western pavilion.

Lincoln, Abraham (1809–65)
Bear Hunt, The.
But Here's an Object.
My Childhood's Home.

Lindsay, Nicholas Vachel (1879–1931)
Above the Battle's Front.
Abraham Lincoln Walks at Midnight.
After Reading the Sad Story of the Fall of
    Babylon.
Aladdin and the Jinn.
Alexander Campbell.
Alone in the Wind, on the Prairie.
Amaranth, The.
Angel and the Clown, The.
Apology for the Bottle Volcanic, An.
Argument, An.
At Mass.
Babylon, Babylon, Babylon the Great.
Beggar Speaks, The.
Beggar's Valentine, The.
Being the Dedication of a Morning.
Beyond the Moon.
Billboards and Galleons.
Blacksmith's Serenade, The.

Booker Washington Trilogy, The.
Broncho That Would Not Be Broken, The.
Bryan, Bryan, Bryan, Bryan.
By the Spring at Sunset.
Caught in a Net.
Celestial Circus, The.
Censer-Moon, The.
Chinese Nightingale, The.
City That Will Not Repent, The.
Cold Sunbeams.
Comet of Prophecy, The.
Congo, The.
Cornfields, The.
Crickets on a Strike.
Curse for Kings, A.
Dancing for a Prize.
Dandelion, The.
Dangerous Little Boy Fairies, The.
Daniel.
Darling Daughter of Babylon.
Dirge for a Righteous Kitten, A.
Doctor Mohawk.
Doll's "Arabian Nights," A.
Dream of All the Springfield Writers, The.
Drunkard's Funeral, The.
Drunkards in the Street, The.
Drying Their Wings.
Eagle That Is Forgotten, The.
Eden in Winter.
Empty Boats, The.
Encyclopædia, The.
Epilogue to the Adventures While Preaching
    the Gospel of Beauty.
Epitaphs for Two Players.
Explanation of the Grasshopper, An.
Factory Windows Are Always Broken.
Fairy Bridal Hymn, The.
Fairy from the Apple-Seed, The.
Flower of Mending, The.
Flute of the Lonely, The.
Flying House, and the May Queen Eternal,
    The.
For All Who Ever Sent Lace Valentines.
Foreign Missions in Battle Array.
Galahad, Knight Who Perished.
Gamblers, The.
General William Booth Enters into Heaven.
Genesis.
Ghosts in Love.
Ghosts of the Buffaloes, The.
Golden Whales of California.
Gospel of Beauty, A.
Hail to the Sons of Roosevelt.
Hamlet.
Harps in Heaven.
Haughty Snail-King, The.
Heart of God.
Hearth Eternal, The.
Here's to the Spirit of Fire.
Honor Among Scamps.
How a Little Girl Danced.
How a Little Girl Sang.
How Dulcenia del Toboso Is Like the Left
    Wing of a Bird.
How Johnny Appleseed Walked Alone in the
    Jungles of Heaven.
How Samson Bore Away the Gates of Gaza.
I Heard Immanuel Singing.
I Know All This When Gipsy Fiddles Cry.
I Want to Go Wandering.
I Went Down into the Desert to Meet Elijah.
In Memory of a Child.
In Memory of My Friend, Joyce Kilmer, Poet
    and Soldier.
In Praise of Johnny Appleseed.
In Praise of Songs That Die.
In the Immaculate Conception Church.
In Which Roosevelt Is Compared to Saul.
Incense.
Indian Summer Day on the Prairie, An.
Invocation for "The Map of the Universe."
Jingo and the Minstrel, The.
John L. Sullivan, the Strong Boy of Boston.
Johnny Appleseed Speaks of Great Cities in
    the Future.
Johnny Appleseed Speaks of the Appleblossom

Amaranth That Will Come to This City.
Johnny Appleseed's Hymn to the Sun.
Johnny Appleseed's Ship Comes In.
Johnny Appleseed's Wife from the Palace of
    Eve.
Johnny Appleseed's Wife of the Mind.
Kalamazoo.
Kallyope Yell, The.
Kansas.
Kind of Scorn, A.
King Arthur's Men Have Come Again.
King of Yellow Butterflies, The.
Knight in Disguise, The.
Lame Boy and the Fairy, The.
Last Song of Lucifer, The.
Leaden-eyed, The.
Life Transcendent.
Lion, The.
Litany of the Heroes.
Little Turtle, The.
Look You, I'll Go Pray.
Love and Law.
Mae Marsh, Motion Picture Actress.
Master of the Dance, The.
Merciful Hand, The.
Moon Is a Painter, The.
Moon's the North Wind's Cooky, The.
Mouse That Gnawed the Oak-Tree Down, The.
My Lady in Her White Silk Shawl.
My Lady Is Compared to a Young Tree.
Mysterious Cat, The.
Net to Snare the Moonlight, A.
Niagara.
North Star Whispers to the Blacksmith's Son,
    The.
Old Horse in the City, The.
On Reading Omar Khayyam.
On the Garden Wall.
On the Road to Nowhere.
Our Guardian Angels and Their Children.
Our Mother Pocahontas.
Parvenu.
Path in the Sky, The.
Pearl of Biloxi, The.
Perfect Marriage, The.
Poems about the Moon, *sels.*
Poems Speaking of Buddha, Prince Siddartha.
Potatoes' Dance, The.
Prairie Battlements, The.
Prayer to All the Dead Among Mine Own
    People, A.
Preface to "Bob Taylor's Birthday."
Prologue to "Rhymes to be Traded for Bread."
Queen Mab in the Village.
Queen of Bubbles, The.
Rhyme About an Electrical Advertising Sign,
    A.
Rhyme for All Zionists, A.
Roosevelt.
Rose of Midnight, The.
Santa-Fé Trail (A Humoresque), The.
Scissors-Grinder, The.
Sea Serpent Chantey, The.
Sense of Humor, A.
Sew the Flags Together.
Shantung, [or The Empire of China is
    Crumbling Down].
Shield of Faith, The.
Song for Elizabeth, A.
Song in July, A.
Song of the Garden-Toad, The.
Song of the Sturdy Snails, The.
Sorceress!, The.
Soul of a Butterfly, The.
Soul of a Spider, The.
Soul of the City Receives the Gift of the Holy
    Spirit, The.
Spice-Tree, The.
Spider and the Ghost of the Fly, The.
Springfield Magical.
Springfield of the Far Future, The.
Star of My Heart.
Statue of Old Andrew Jackson, The.
Storm-Flower, The.
Strength of the Lonely, The.
Sun Says His Prayers, The.

Logan (continued)

Sunshine.
Sweet Briars of the Stairways.
Sweethearts of the Year.
Tale of the Tiger Tree, The.
This Section Is a Christmas Tree.
Three Poems About Mark Twain.
Tiger on Parade, The.
To a Golden-Haired Girl in a Louisiana Town.
To Eve, Man's Dream of Wifehood as
   Described by Milton.
To Gloriana.
To Jane Addams at the Hague.
To Lady Jane.
To Reformers in Despair.
Town of American Visions, The.
Tramp's Refusal, The.
Trap, The.
Traveller-Heart, The.
Tree of Laughing Bells or The Wings of the
   Morning, The.
Trial of the Dead Cleopatra in Her Beautiful
   and Wonderful Tomb, The.
Two Easter Stanzas.
Two Old Crows.
Unpardonable Sin, The.
Village Improvement Parade, The.
Visit to Mab, The.
Voice of St. Francis of Assisi, The.
Wedding of the Rose and the Lotus, The.
What Grandpa Mouse Said.
What Semiramis Said.
What the Clown Said.
What the Coal-Heaver Said.
What the Forester Said.
What the Ghost of the Gambler Said.
What the Gray-Winged Fairy Said.
What the Hyena Said.
What the Miner in the Desert Said.
What the Moon Saw.
What the Rattlesnake Said.
What the Scarecrow Said.
What the Sexton Said.
What the Snow Man Said.
When Peter Jackson Preached in the Old
   Church.
Where Is the Real Non-Resistant?
Who Knows?
Why I Voted the Socialist Ticket.
With a Rose, to Brunhilde.
Wizard in the Street, The.
Wizard Wind, The.
Would-Be Merman, The.
Written for a Musician.
Yankee Doodle.

Logan, John (1923–71?)

Abstract Love Poem.
Acapulco Canyon: Two Kodachromes.
Achilles and the King: A Verse Re-telling.
Assateague.
Assessment, The.
At Drumcliffe Churchyard, County Sligo.
Avocado.
Believe It.
Big Sur: Partington Cove.
Bridge of Change, The.
Brothers: Two Saltimbanques, The.
Byron at Shelley's Burning.
Cambridge Revery.
Cape Elizabeth: A Photograph.
Carmel: Point Lobos.
Century Piece for Poor Heine, A.
Chicago Scene.
Coming of Age.
Concert Scene.
Cycle for Mother Cabrini, A.
Dawn and a Woman.
Day in the Sun, A.
Dead Man's Room, The.
Death of Southwell, The.
Dialogue with La Mettrie, A.
Dream, The: A Reflection on Morris Graves's
   Paintings.
Dublin Suite: Homage to James Joyce.
Eight Poems on Portraits of the Foot.
Elegy for Dylan Thomas.
Elegy for the Rev. Mr. James B. Hodgson

(1892–1963).
Epilogue, Songs of the Spouses, Complaint of
   Love.
Experiment That Failed, The.
Feast of Friends, A.
February Awakening.
Five Preludes For Buffalo's Own Forest Lawn.
Gallery Walk: Fifteen Italian Drawings 1780–
   1890.
Gift, The.
Girl in the Fog, The.
Grace.
Grandfather's Railroad.
Grandmother Dead in the Aeroplane.
Heart to Heart Talk With My Liver.
Homage to Christina Rossetti.
Homage to Herman Melville.
Homage to John Muir.
Homage to John the Baptist.
Homage to Rainer Maria Rilke.
Honolulu and Back.
Lament for Misenus.
Lament in Spring.
Letter to a Young Father in Exile.
Letter to My Son.
Lines Against A Loved American Poet After
   Hearing An Irish One's Nickname.
Lines for a Friend Who Left.
Lines for a Young Man Who Talked.
Lines for a Young Wanderer in Mexico.
Lines for an Unknown Lover.
Lines for His Son in Satin.
Lines for Michael in the Picture.
Lines on His Birthday.
Lines on Locks (or Jail and the Erie Canal).
Lines to Catherine.
Lines to His Son on Reaching Adolescence.
Lives of the Poet, The.
Long Search, The.
Love Poem: "Last night you would not come."
Manhattan Movements.
March. The Museum. Buffalo. de Chirico.
Matinee.
Medicine Bow.
Middle-Aged Midwesterner at Waikiki Again.
Monologue for the Good Friday Christ.
Monologues of the Son of Saul.
Month of Saints, A.
Monument and the Shrine, The.
My Daughter's Wedding.
My Rebel Grandmother.
Narcisses: Vision and Retrospect.
New Poem.
New York Scene: May 1958.
Nighthawks: after Hopper's Painting.
Nude Kneeling in Sand.
On a Photograph by Aaron Siskind.
On a Prize Crucifix by a Student Sculptor.
On Reading Camus In Early March.
On the Death of Keats; Lines for Those Who
   Drown Twice.
On the Death of the Poet's Mother Thirty-
   Three Years Later.
On the House of a Friend.
Only the Dreamer Can Change the Dream.
Pagan Saturday.
Papa's House, Son's Room.
Paperboys, The.
Pass, The.
Pathological Case in Pliny, A.
Piano Scholar, The.
Picnic, The.
Poem for My Brother.
Poem for My Friend Peter at Pihana.
Poem for My Son.
Poem in Progress.
Poem, Slow to Come, On the Death of
   Cummings (1894-1962).
Poem: Tears, Spray, and Steam.
Poet Scratches His Head, The.
Present, The.
Prologue and Questions for St. Augustine On
   His Sixteenth Centenary.
Protest After a Dream.
Recollection on the Day of a First Book.
Rescue, The.

Return to the Island.
Returning Home.
Revisit to the Room of a Saint.
San Francisco Poem.
Saturday Afternoon at the Movies.
Search, The.
Sebastian in the Dream.
Shore Scene.
Short Life of the Hermit, A.
Song on the Dread of a Chill Spring.
Spirit of the Dead Watching: after Gaugin.
Spring of the Thief.
Spring Revelations.
Staying Awake.
Suite of Six Pieces for Siskind, A.
Suzanne.
Tale of a Later Leander.
Thirteen Preludes for Pioneer Square.
Thirty-Three Ring Circus, The.
Three Moves.
Three Poems on Aaron Siskind's Photographs.
Three Poems on Morris Graves' Paintings.
To a Young Poet Who Fled.
Transformation, The.
Traveling.
Trip to Four or Five Towns, A.
Twilight Land.
Two Poems for Women.
Two Poems of Greece.
Two Preludes for La Push.
Visit to Bill Merwin at His Hawaiian Home, A.
Weeping, The.
Whatnot, The.
Whistling Wings or White Turtle in the
   Watertree.
White Pass Ski Patrol.
Wooden Mirror, The.
Yellow Christ, The; after Gaugin.
Zoo, The.

Logue, Christopher (b. 1926)

Aardvark, The.
Air.
Air for the Witness of a Departure.
Ass's Song, The.
Cats are full of death.
Chinese England.
Come to the Edge.
Epitaph: "I am old."
For My Father.
Fragment.
Girls, The.
Good Taste.
His case is typical.
I Shall Vote Labour.
Isles of Jessamy, The.
I've worked here all my life.
Lily-White Boys, The, *sels.*
Loyal to the King.
Lullaby.
Madam / I have sold you.
Middle-aged man is approaching an all-night
   lavatory, A.
Nell's Circular Poem.
New Numbers.
O come all ye faithful.
Observe Details.
Professor Tucholsky's Facts.
Rat, O Rat.
September Song.
Singing Prayer, A.
Singles.
Song of Autobiography, The.
Song of the Dead Soldier, The.
Song of the Imperial Carrion, The.
Song of the Outsider, The.
Story of the Road, The.
Things.
To a Friend in Search of Rural Seclusion.
To My Fellow Artists.
Urbanal.
When I was serving my country.
Woke up this morning.

Longfellow, Henry Wadsworth (1807–82)

Aftermath.
Arsenal at Springfield, The.
Children's Hour, The.

Courtship of Miles Standish, The.
Cross of Snow, The.
Day Is Done, The.
Evangeline, a Tale of Acadie.
Fire of Drift-Wood, The.
Giles Corey of the Salem Farms.
Hawthorne.
Jewish Cemetery at Newport, The.
John Endicott.
Mezzo Cammin.
Morituri Salutamus.
My Lost Youth.
Nature.
Occultation of Orion, The.
Psalm of Life, A.
Ropewalk, The.
Seaweed.
Skeleton in Armor [or Armour], The.
Slave Singing at Midnight, The.
Snow-Flakes.
Song of Hiawatha, The, *sels.*
Tales of a Wayside Inn, *sels.*
Village Blacksmith, The.
Warning, The.
Wreck of the *Hesperus*, The.

Lope de Vega Carpio, Félix (1562–1635)
Pentecost Castle, The,
Song of the Virgin Mother, A.

Lorde, Audre (1934–92)
Afterimages.
American Cancer Society Or There Is More
  Than One Way to Skin a Coon.
And Don't Think I Won't Be Waiting.
And What About the Children.
As I Grew Up Again.
Ballad from Childhood.
Barren.
Bees, The.
Birthday Memorial to Seventh Street, A.
Black Mother Woman.
Blackstudies.
Bloodbirth.
Bridge Through My Window.
Brown Menace or Poem to the Survival of
  Roaches, The.
Cables To Rage Or I've Been Talking On This
  Street Corner.
Change of Season.
Coal.
Conclusion.
Conversations in Crisis.
Day They Eulogized Mahalia, The.
Dear Toni Instead of a Letter of
  Congratulation.
Dozens, The.
Dreams Bite.
Echo.
Equinox.
Evening News, The.
Family Resemblance, A.
Fantasy and Conversation.
Father Son and Holy Ghost.
Father, the Year Has Fallen.
For Each of You.
For My Singing Sister.
Gemini.
Generation.
Generation II.
Good Mirrors are Not Cheap.
Hard Love Rock.
Hard Love Rock II.
Keyfoods.
Love, Maybe.
Love Poem.
Maiden, The.
Martha.
Memorial I.
Memorial II.
Memorial III—from a Phone Booth on
  Broadway.
Mentor.
Monkeyman.
Movement Song.
Moving Out Or the End of Cooperative Living.
My Fifth Trip to Washington Ended in
  Northeast Delaware.

Need: A Chorale for Black Woman Voices.
Neighbors.
New Year's Day.
New York City 1970.
NOW.
Now That I Am Forever with Child.
Oaxaca.
October.
On a Night of the Full Moon.
Oya.
Pirouette.
Poem for a Poet, A.
Poem for Women in Rage, A.
Progress Report.
Release Time.
Relevant Is Different Points on the Circle.
Return.
Revolution Is One Form of Social Change.
Rites of Passage.
Rooming Houses are Old Women.
Sacrifice.
Separation.
Seventh Sign, The.
Sewerplant Grows In Harlem Or I'm a
  Stranger Here Myself.
Signs.
Sister, Morning Is a Time for Miracles.
Song for a Thin Sister.
Song: "Wild trees have bought me."
Sowing.
Spring People.
St. Louis Out of Time.
Story Books on a Kitchen Table, *sels.*
Suffer the Children.
Summer Oracle.
Suspension.
Teacher.
To a Girl Who Knew What Side Her Bread
  Was Buttered On.
To My Daughter the Junkie on a Train.
To the Girl Who Lives In a Tree.
Trip on the Staten Island Ferry, A.
Vietnam Addenda.
What My Child Learns of the Sea.
When the Saints Come Marching In.
Who Said It Was Simple.
Winds of Orisha, The.
Woman Thing, The.
Workers Rose on May Day or Postcript to Karl
  Marx, The.
Za Ki Tan Ke Parlay Lot.

Lowell, Robert (1917–77)
Abraham Lincoln.
After the Surprising Conversions.
Alexander.
Alfred Corning Clark.
Angling.
Anne Dick 1. 1936.
Anne Dick 2. 1936.
Artist's Model.
At the Indian Killer's Grave.
Attila, Hitler.
Beethoven.
Between the Porch and the Altar.
Beyond the Alps.
Bobby Delano.
Bosworth Field.
Bringing a Turtle Home.
Buenos Aires.
Careless Night.
Central Park.
Charles V by Titian.
Child's Song.
Christmas.
Christmas ("All too often now").
Christmas Tree.
Cicero, the Sacrificial Killing.
Coleridge.
Coleridge and Richard II.
Colloquy in Black Rock.
Commander Lowell.
Couple, The.
Dames du Temps Jadis.
Dante 3. Buonconte.
Das ewig Weibliche.
Death and the Bridge.

Death of Alexander.
Death of Anne Boleyn.
Death of Count Roland.
Death of the Sheriff, The.
Dolphin.
Double Vision.
Draw.
Drinker, The.
Drunken Fisherman, The.
Dunbarton.
During Fever.
Eight Months Later.
Elizabeth.
End of Camp Alamoosook.
Exile's Return, The.
Eye and Tooth.
Fall 1961.
Fall Weekend at *Milgate*.
Fat Man in the Mirror, The.
Father.
Father in a Dream.
Father's Bedroom.
First Love.
First Things.
Fishnet.
Flaw, The.
Flight.
Florence.
Flounder.
For Eugene McCarthy.
For George Santayana.
For Robert Kennedy Nineteen Twenty-Five to
  Sixty-Eight.
For Sale.
For the Union Dead.
Ford Madox Ford.
Fourth of July in Maine.
Foxfur.
Graduate, The.
Grandparents.
Growth (Harriet).
Hard Way, The.
Harriet ("Half a year").
Harriet ("Repeating fly").
Harriet ("Spring moved to summer").
Harriet's Dream.
Hawthorne.
Her Dead Brother.
History.
Holy Innocents, The.
Home After Three Months Away.
Ice.
In Memory of Arthur Winslow, *sels.*
In the Cage.
In the Mail.
Inauguration Day: January 1953.
It Did.
Ivana.
Joinville and Louis IX.
Jonathan Edwards in Western Massachusetts.
July in Washington.
Late Summer at *Milgate*.
Leaf-Lace Dress.
Left out of vacation.
Like Henry VIII, Mohammed got religion.
Long Summer.
Long Summers ("Months of it").
Long Summers ("Two in the afternoon").
Long Summers ("Up north here").
Lost Fish.
Lost Tune, The.
Mad Negro Soldier Confined at Munich, A.
Man And Wife.
Man and Woman.
March 1, The.
March 2, The.
Marcus Cato 95–42 B.C.
Marcus Cato 234–149 B.C.
Margaret Fuller Drowned.
Marlowe.
Mary Stuart.
Mary Winslow.
Memories of West Street and Lepke.
Mermaid.
Mermaid Emerging.
Mexico, *sels.*

Middle Age.
Mills of the Kavanaughs, The.
Mr. Edwards and the Spider.
Mother and Father 1.
Mother and Father 2.
Mother Marie Therese.
Mother, 1972.
Mouth of the Hudson, The.
My Heavenly Shiner (Elizabeth).
My Last Afternoon with Uncle Devereux
  Winslow.
Myopia: a Night.
Napoleon.
Near the Ocean.
Neo-Classical Urn, The.
New York 1962: Fragment.
Night Sweat.
Nihilist as Hero, The.
1930's ("After my marriage").
1930's ("Boys come").
1930's ("Circular moon").
1930's ("Humble in victory").
1930's ("My legs hinge").
1930's ("Shake of the electric fan").
1930's ("Vaporish closeness").
No Hearing ("Belief in God").
No Hearing ("Discovering").
No Messiah.
Nunc Est Bibendum, Cleopatra's Death.
Obit.
Old Flame, The.
Old snapshot from Venice 1952.
Opposite House, The.
Our Twentieth Wedding Anniversary
  (Elizabeth).
Outlivers (Harriet and Elizabeth).
Plane Ticket.
Plotted.
Public Garden, The.
Quaker Graveyard in Nantucket, The.
Randall Jarrell 1. October 1965.
Randall Jarrell 2.
Randall Jarrell 3.
Reading Myself.
Records.
Rembrandt.
Returning.
Returning Turtle.
Robert Frost.
Robespierre and Mozart as Stage.
Sailing Home from Rapallo.
Saint-Just 1767–93.
Seals.
Searching.
Serpent.
Serpent, The.
Sick.
Sir Thomas More.
Skunk Hour.
Sleepless.
Snake.
Soft Wood.
Stalin.
Sunrise.
Symptoms.
Tenth Muse.
Terminal Days at Beverly Farms.
Thanksgiving's Over.
These Winds.
To Daddy.
To Delmore Schwartz.
To Speak of Woe That Is in Marriage.
Two Walls.
Verdun.
Waking Early Sunday Morning.
Waking in the Blue.
Watchmaker God.
Water.
Waterloo.
We never see him now, except at dinner.
Where the Rainbow Ends.
Wildrose.
Will Not Come Back.
William Carlos Williams.
Window.
Words.

Words for Hart Crane.
Words for Muffin, a Guinea Pig.
Worst Sinner, Jonathan Edwards' God, The.
Lucan (Marcus Annaeus Lucanus) (A.D. 39–65)
  Ad Pisonem, *sels.*
  Civil War [Bellum Civile] *or* Pharsalia, *sels.*
  He's King of Mirth that slyly cheats our sense.
Lucanus, Marcus Annaeus *See* **Lucan**
Lucianus [*or* Lucian] (b. c.125, d. after 180)
  On an Infant.
Lucilius (d. c.102 B.C.)
  Miser and the Mouse, The.
  On an Old Woman.
Lucretius (Titus Lucretius Carus) (94–55 B.C.)
  De Rerum Natura (On the Nature of Things),
    sels.
Lux, Thomas (b. 1946)
  After a Few Whiffs of Another World.
  All the Slaves.
  Amiel's Leg.
  And Still It Comes.
  At Least Let Me Explain.
  At the Far End of a Long Wharf.
  Autobiographical.
  Backyard Swingset.
  Barn Fire.
  Beneath the Apple Branches Bent Dumbly.
  Big Picture, The.
  Bitterness of Children, The.
  Black Road Over Which Green Trees Grow.
  Boat in the Forest, A.
  Bodo.
  Cellar Stairs.
  Commercial Leech Farming Today.
  Creature Has a Purpose, The.
  Criss Cross Apple Sauce.
  Crows of Boston and New York, The.
  Dark Comes On In Blocks, In Cubes, The.
  Dawn Walk and Prayer.
  Deadhouse at the Workhouse, The.
  Ditto.
  Dr. Goebbel's Novels.
  Driver Ant, The.
  Early On, This Decade's Light Smelled.
  Edgar Allan Poe Meets Sarah Hale (Author of
    "Mary Had a Little Lamb").
  Elegy for Frank Stanford.
  Elegy for Robert Winner.
  Emily's Mom.
  Empty Pitchforks.
  Endive.
  Enemy the Wind, The.
  Falling Through the Leaves.
  Farmers.
  Floating Baby Paintings.
  Flying Noises.
  For My Daughter When She Can Read.
  Fourth Grade, The.
  Frankly, I Don't Care.
  Garden, The.
  Give It to the Wind.
  Glow Worm.
  Gold on Mule.
  Gorgeous Surfaces.
  Graveyard by the Sea.
  Great Advances in Vanity.
  Green, The.
  Grim Town in a Steep Valley.
  Haitian Cadavers.
  He Has Lived in Many Houses.
  Here's to Samuel Greenberg.
  His Job is Honest and Simple.
  His Spine Curved Just Enough.
  History Books.
  Horatian Notion, An.
  I Love You Sweatheart.
  If I Die Before I Wake.
  Impingement Sydrome.
  Institute of Defectology.
  Irreconcilabilia.
  It Must Be the Monk in Me.
  It's the Little Towns I Like.
  Job's Problems.
  Kalashnikov.
  Kwashiorkor; Marasmus.

Like a Wide Anvil From the Moon the Light.
Little Tooth, A.
Man Asleep in a Child's Bed.
Man Inside the Chipmunk Suit, The.
Man Takes His Daughter, Age Five, To a
  Public Execution by Guillotine, Paris, 1857,
  A.
Men With Small Heads.
Milkman and His Son, The.
Money.
Moon-Annoyed, Cognac's Ashen Thrill.
"Mr John Keats Five Feet Tall" Sails Away.
Mr. Pope.
Nazi at the Puppet Show, The.
Neighborhood of Make-Believe, The.
Night So Bright A Squirrel Reads, The.
Old Man Shoveling Snow.
Onomatopoeia.
Oxymoron Sisters, The.
Painfully Banal.
Pecked to Death by Swans.
Pedestrian.
People of the Other Village, The.
Perfect God, The.
Pismire Rising.
Poem in Thanks.
Portrait of the Man Who Drowned Wearing
  His Best Suit and Shoes.
Postcard to Baudelaire.
Princess Summer Fall Winter Spring.
Refrigerator, 1957.
Rilke and Lou.
River Between the Train and the Highway,
  The.
River Blindness (Onchocerciasis).
River That Scolds at All the Other Rivers, The.
Say Yes.
Sex in History.
Shaving the Graveyard.
Small Tin Parrot Pin, A.
Snake Lake.
So You Put the Dog to Sleep.
Solo Native.
Somebody's Aunt Out Swabbing Her Birdbath.
Spiders Wanting.
Streak of Blood That Once Was a Tiny Red
  Spider, A.
Sudd as Metaphor, The.
Swimming Pool, The.
Tarantulas on the Lifebuoy.
There Were Some Summers.
Thirst of Turtles, The.
This Space Available.
Time.
Torn Shades.
Towards.
Traveling Exhibit of Torture Instruments.
Triptych, Middle Panel Burning.
Ultima Thule.
Upon Seeing An Ultrasound Photo of an
  Unborn Child.
View From a Porch.
Virgule.
Voice You Hear When You Read Silently, The.
Walt Whitman's Brain Dropped on Laboratory
  Floor.
What I See When I Drive to Work.
What Montezuma Fed Cortés and His Men.
Wife Hits Moose.
Winter River.
You Go To School To Learn.
Lyndsay [*or* Lindsay], Sir David (c.1486–1555)
  Answer to the Kingis Flyting, The.
  Complaynt of Schir David Lindesay, The.
  Deploratioun of the Deith of Quene
    Magdalene, The.
  Dialog betwix Experience and ane Courteour,
    Ane, *sels.*
  Dreme, The.
  Justing Betwix James Watsoun and Jhone
    Barbour, The.
  Squyer Meldrum.
  Testament and Complaynt of our Soverane
    Lordis Papyngo, The.
  Testament of Squyer Meldrum, The.
  Tragedie of the Cardinall, The.

M

**MacDiarmid, Hugh (Christopher Murray
Grieve) (1892–1978)**
Another Epitaph on an Army of Mercenaries.
As Lovers Do.
At My Father's Grave.
At the Cenotaph.
Au Clair de la Lune.
Bagpipe Music.
Battle Continues, The, *sels.*
Bonnie Broukit Bairn, The.
Bracken Hills in Autumn.
Caledonian Antisyzygy, The.
Cheville.
Conception.
Cornish Heroic Song for Valda Trevlyn, *sels.*
Covenanters, The.
Credo.
Crowdieknowe.
Crystals like Blood.
Dead Liebknecht, The.
Direadh III.
Drunk Man Looks at the Thistle, A.
Dying Earth, The.
Dytiscus
Eemis-Stane, The.
Empty Vessel.
England Is Our Enemy, *sels.*
England's Double Knavery, *sels.*
Esplumeoir, *sels.*
Ex Vermibus.
Facing the Chair.
First Love.
Focherty.
Fool, The.
Frae Anither Window in Thrums, *sels.*
Further Passages from The Kind of Poetry I
    Want, *sels.*
Gairmscoile.
Glasgow, 1960.
Glass of Pure Water, The.
Glen of Silence, The.
Good-bye Twilight, *sels.*
Happy on Heimaey.
Harry Semen.
Hokum.
In Memoriam James Joyce, *sels.*
In the Children's Hospital.
In the Slums of Glasgow.
Innumerable Christ, The.
Island Funeral.
John Maclean (1879-1923).
Kind of Poetry I Want, The, *sels.*
Last Song, A.
Light and Shadow.
Little White Rose, The.
Lo! A Child Is Born.
Lourd on My Hert.
Love-sick Lass, The.
Milk-Wort and Bog Cotton.
Moment in Eternity, A.
My Love Is to the Light of Lights.
My Songs Are Kandym in the Waste Land.
O Ease My Spirit.
Ode to All Rebels, *sels.*
Of John Davidson.
Of My First Love.
Old Wife in High Spirits.
On a Raised Beach.
On the Ocean Floor.
One of the Principal Causes of War.
Perfect.
Plaited Like the Generations of Men, *sels.*
Poetry and Science.
Ross-shire Hills, The.
Sauchs in the Reuch Heuch Hauch, The.
Scotland.
Scotland Small?
Seamless Garment, The.
Second Hymn to Lenin, *sels.*
Servant Girl's Bed.
Skald's Death.
Skeleton of the Future, The.
Snares of Varuna, The, *sels.*

Stony Limits.
To a Friend and Fellow Poet.
To Hell wi' Happiness!
To My Friend the Late Beatrice Hastings.
Two Memories.
Two Parents, The.
Vision of Scotland, A.
War with England, The, *sels.*
Water Music, *sels.*
Water of Life.
Watergaw, The.
Weapon, The.
Well Hung.
Wheesht, Wheesht.
Why.
Wind-bags, The.
With the Herring Fishers.
World of Words, The, *sels.*
Wreck of the *Swan*, The.

MacFadden, Elizabeth
In Pity First to Human Kind.

MacGabhrain, Aodh *See* **MacGowran, Hugh**

**MacGowran, Hugh (Aodh MacGabhrain) (*fl.*
c.1720)**
Description of an Irish Feast, The.

MacLeish, Archibald (1892–1983)
Acknowledgement.
Actfive.
Aeterna Poetae Memoria.
Against Illuminations.
America Was Promises.
American Letter.
Ancestral.
& Forty-Second Street.
April in November.
Arrival and Departure.
Ars Poetica.
At the Lincoln Memorial.
Autobiography.
Autumn.
Baccalaureate.
Background with Revolutionaries.
Bahamas.
Ballad of the Corn-Cob and the Lie, The.
Bed, The.
Before March.
Black Day, The.
Black Humor.
Boatmen of Santorin, The.
Boy in the Roman Zoo.
Brave New World.
Broken Promise.
Brooks Atkinson.
Burial, The.
Burying Ground by the Ties.
Calypso's Island.
Captivity of the Fly.
Carrion Crow, The.
Cat in the Wood, The.
Chartres.
Cinema of a Man.
Colloquy for the States.
Companions.
Conquistador.
Contemporary Portrait.
Conversation in a Belfry.
Conway Burying Ground.
Cook County.
Corporate Entity.
Creator.
Critics on the Lawn.
Crossing.
Cummings.
Danger in the Air, The.
De Votre Bonheur Il ne Reste Que Vos Photos.
Definition of the Frontiers.
Definitions of Old Age.
Dr. Sigmund Freud Discovers the Sea Shell.
"Dover Beach"—a Note to That Poem.
Dozing on the Lawn.
Edwin Muir.
1892—19—.
Einstein.
Eleven.
Empire Builders.
End of the World, The.

Epistle to Be Left in the Earth.
Epistle to Léon-Paul Fargue.
Epitaph for John McCutcheon.
Eplenor.
Eternity, An.
Ever Since.
Excavation of Troy.
Ezry.
Family Group.
Farm, The.
For the Anniversary of My Mother's Death.
Galán.
Geography of this Time.
German Girls, The! The German Girls!
Good Man in a Bad Time, A.
Grazing Locomotives.
Great Contemporary Discoveries.
Hamlet of A. Macleish.
Hands.
Happy Marriage, The, *sels.*
Hearts' and Flowers'.
Hebrides.
Hemingway.
Hotel Breakfast.
How the River Ninfa Runs through the Ruined
    Town Beneath the Lime Quarry.
Hurricane.
Hypocrite Auteur.
Immortal Autumn.
Immortal Helix.
In and Come In.
Infinite Reason, The.
Interrogate the Stones.
Invocation to the Social Muse.
Journey Home.
La Foce.
L'An Trentiesme de Mon Eage.
Land's End.
Landscape as a Nude.
Late Abed.
Le Secret Humain.
Le Seul Malheur Est que Je ne Sais pas Lire.
Learned Men, The.
Liberty.
Linden Branch, The.
Linden Trees, The.
Lines for a Prologue.
Lines for an Interment.
Long Hot Summer.
Lost Speakers, The.
Man!
Man's Work, A.
March.
Mark Van Doren and the Brook.
Mark's Sheep.
Memorial Rain.
Memory Green.
Men.
Men of My Century Loved Mozart.
Midsummer Dawn.
Mistral Over the Graves.
Mother Goose's Garland.
Music and Drum.
My Naked Aunt.
Nat Bacon's Bones.
National Security.
New England Weather.
Night Dream, The.
Night Watch in the City of Boston.
No Lamp Has Ever Shown Us Where to Look.
Nocturne: "Earth, still heavy and warm with
    afternoon, The."
Not Marble nor the Gilded Monuments.
November.
Observations of P. Ovidus Naso on the
    Incidence of Sex in the Contemporary
    Novel.
Oil Painting of the Artist as the Artist.
Old Gray Couple (1), The.
Old Gray Couple (2), The.
Old Man to the Lizard, The.
Old Man's Journey.
Old Men in the Leaf Smoke, The.
Out of Sleep Awakened.
Pablo Casals.
Peepers in Our Meadow, The.

Pity's Sake.
Poem for the Time of Change.
Poem in Prose.
Poet.
Poetical Remains.
Poet's Laughter.
Pole Star for This Year.
Pony Rock.
Population Explosion.
Pot of Earth, The.
Psyche with the Candle.
Rainbow at Evening.
Rape of the Swan, The.
Reasons for Music.
Reef Fisher, The.
Renovated Temple, The.
Reply to Mr. Wordsworth.
Reproach to Dead Poets.
Return.
Revenant, The.
Revolution of the Children.
Rue Carpenter.
St. Philip's Church in Antigua.
Salute.
Seafarer.
Seeing.
Seeing.
Selene Afterwards.
Sentiments for a Dedication.
Sheep in the Ruins, The.
Ship in the Tomb.
Ship of Fools.
Ship's Log.
Signal, The.
Signature for Tempo.
Sketch for a Portrait of Mme. G———M———.
Snow Fall, The.
Snowflake Which Is Now and Hence Forever, The.
Some Aspects of Immortality.
Songs for Eve.
Spanish Lie, The.
Speech to a Crowd.
Speech to the Detractors.
Speech to Those Who Say Comrade.
Spring in These Hills.
Starved Lovers.
State Funeral: March 31, 1969.
Steamboat Whistle, The.
Sunset Piece, The.
Survivor.
Theory of Poetry.
They Come No More, Those Words, Those Finches.
Thrush in the Gaelic Islands, The.
Thunderhead.
Too-Late Born, The.
Tourist Death.
Treason Crime, The.
Tricked by Eternity the Heart.
Triumph of the Shell, The.
Two Poems from the War.
Two Priests, The.
Two Trees, The.
Two Women Talking.
Tyrant of Syracuse.
Unfinished History.
Verses for a Centennial.
Vicissitudes of the Creator.
Voyage.
Voyage en Provence.
Voyage to the Moon.
Voyage West.
Waking.
Way-Station.
What Any Lover Learns.
What Must.
What Riddle Asked the Sphinx.
What the Old Women Say.
Where a Poet's From.
Where the Hayfields Were.
White-Haired Girl.
Why the Face of a Clock is not Truly a Circle.
Wild Old Wicked Man, The.
Wildwest.
William Adams Delano.

Winter Is Another Country.
With Age Wisdom.
Woman on the Stair, The.
Wood Dove at Sandy Spring, The.
Words in Time.
Words to be Spoken.
Yacht for Sale.
Years of the Dog.
You Also, Gaius Valerius Catullus.
You, Andrew Marvell.
Young Dead Soldiers, The.

MacNeice, Louis (1907–63)
After the Crash.
Aftermath.
Alcohol.
All Over Again.
Among These Turf-Stacks.
Another Cold May.
Apple Blossom.
April Fool.
April Manifesto, An.
Areopagus.
As In Their Time.
Atlantic Tunnel, The.
Aubade for Infants.
Aubade: "Having bitten on life like a sharp apple."
August.
Autobiography.
Autolycus.
Autumn Journal.
Autumn Sequel.
Babel.
Bad Dream.
Bagpipe Music.
Bar-Room Matins.
Belfast.
Beni Hasan.
Birmingham.
Birthright.
Blasphemies, The.
Bluebells.
Bottleneck.
Brandy Glass, The.
Breaking Webs.
British Museum Reading Room, The.
Brother Fire.
Budgie.
Burnt Bridge, The.
Candles.
Carol: "To end all carols, darling."
Carrick Revisited.
Carrickfergus.
Casualty, The.
Charon.
Château Jackson.
Chess.
Children's Games.
Christmas Shopping.
Circe.
Circus.
Closing Album, The.
Cock o' the North.
Coda: "Maybe we knew each other better."
Conscript, The.
Constant.
Contact, A.
Conversation.
Convoy.
Corner Seat.
Country Week-End.
Cradle Song: "Clock's untiring fingers wind the wool of darkness, The."
Cradle Song: "Sleep, my darling, sleep."
Creditor, The.
Cromlech, The.
Cuckoo.
Cyclist, The.
Dark Age Glosses.
Day of Renewal.
Day of Returning.
Death of an Actress.
Death of an Old Lady.
Death-Wish, The.
Débâcle.
Déjà Vu.

Didymus.
Dogs in the Park.
Donegal Triptych.
Dowser, The.
Dreams in Middle Age.
Drunkard, The.
Ear, The.
Easter Returns.
Eclogue between the Motherless.
Eclogue by a Five-Barred Gate.
Eclogue for Christmas, An.
Eclogue from Iceland.
Elegy for Minor Poets.
Elephant Trunk.
Entered in the Minutes.
Entirely.
Epitaph for Liberal Poets.
Evening in Connecticut.
Evening Indoors.
Explorations.
Figure of Eight.
Flight of the Heart.
Flower Show.
Flowers in the Interval.
Genesis.
Glacier, The.
Glass Falling.
Godfather.
Good Dream.
Goodbye to London.
Grey Ones, The.
Greyness Is All.
Habits, The.
Half Truth from Cape Town.
Hand of Snapshots, A.
Hands and Eyes.
Happy Families.
Heated Minutes, The.
Hebrides, The.
Hiatus.
Hidden Ice.
Hold-up.
Homage to Clichés.
Homage to Wren.
House on a Cliff.
Icebergs.
Iceland.
Idle Talk.
Il Piccolo Rifiuto.
In Lieu.
Indian Village.
Individualist Speaks, The.
Indoor Sports.
Intimations of Mortality.
Introduction, The.
Invocation: "Dolphin plunge, fountain play."
Island, The.
Jehu.
Jericho.
Jigsaws.
June Thunder.
Jungle Clearance Ceylon.
Kingdom, The.
Lake in the Park, The.
Last before America.
Leaving Barra.
Letter from India.
Letter to Graham and Anna.
Libertine, The.
Littoral.
London Rain.
Lugubrious, Salubrious Seaside, The.
Mahabalipuram.
Mahavveray.
Mayfly.
Meeting Point.
Memoranda to Horace.
Messiah, The.
Mixer, The.
Morning Sun.
Museums.
Mutations.
National Gallery, The.
Nature Morte.
Nature Notes.
Neutrality.

New Jerusalem.
News-Reel, The.
No More Sea.
Nocturne: "Dark blood of night-time, The."
North Sea, The.
Nostalgia.
Notes for a Biography.
Novelettes.
Now That the Shapes of Mist.
Nuts in May.
October in Bloomsbury.
Ode: "To-night is so coarse with chocolate."
Off the Peg.
Old Masters Abroad.
Order to View.
Other Wing, The.
Our Sister Water.
Out of the Picture.
Pale Panther, The.
Park, The.
Passage Steamer.
Perdita.
Perseus.
Perspectives.
Pet Shop.
Place of a Skull.
Plain Speaking.
Plant and Phantom.
Plurality
Postcript to Iceland.
Poussin.
Prayer Before Birth.
Prayer in Mid-Passage.
Precursors.
Prognosis.
Prospect.
Ravenna.
Réchauffé.
Reflections.
Refugees.
Relics.
Rest House, The.
Restaurant Car.
Return, The.
Return to Lahore.
Revenant, The.
Riddle, The.
Rites of War.
River in Spate.
Round the Corner.
Sailing Orders.
Sand in the Air.
Satirist, The.
Schizophrene.
Selva Oscura.
Sleeping Winds.
Slow Movement.
Slow Starter, The.
Slum Song.
Snow.
Snow Man, The.
Soap Suds.
Solitary Travel.
Solstice.
Sports Page.
Spring Cleaning.
Spring Sunshine.
Spring Voices.
Springboard, The.
Star-Gazer.
Strand, The.
Street Scene.
Streets of Laredo, The.
Stygian Banks, The.
Stylite.
Suicide, The.
Suite for Recorders.
Sunday in the Park.
Sunday Morning.
Sunlight on the Garden, The.
Swing-Song.
Taken for Granted.
Tam Cari Capitis.
Taxis, The.
Thalassa.
This Is the Life.

This Way Out.
Thyestes.
Time for a Smoke.
To a Communist.
To Hedli ("Because the velvet image").
To Hedli ("Acting younger than I am and
    thinking older").
To Mary.
To Posterity.
To the Public.
Toast, A.
Train to Dublin.
Trains in the Distance.
Tree of Guilt, The.
Tree Party.
Trilogy for X.
Troll's Courtship.
Trolls, The.
Truisms, The.
Twelfth Night.
Under the Mountain.
Upon This Beach.
Valediction: "Their verdure dare not show . . .
    their verdure dare not show."
Variation on Heraclitus.
Visit to Rouen.
Visitations.
Vistas.
Wall, The.
Wessex Guidebook.
Western Landscape.
What is truth? says Pilate.
When We Were Children.
Whit Monday.
Window, The.
Windowscape.
Wiper, The.
Wolves.
Woods.
Yours Next.

Mahon, Derek (b. 1941)
Achill.
After the Titanic.
Afterlives.
Andean Flute, The.
Antarctica.
Antigone Riddle, The.
Apotheosis of Tins, The.
Aran.
As It Should Be.
Attic, The.
Autobiographies.
Banished Gods, The.
Beyond Howth Head.
Bird Sanctuary.
Birdlife.
Blackbird, The.
Brighton Beach.
Camus in Ulster.
Canadian Pacific.
Chinese Restaurant in Portrush, The.
Consolations of Philosophy.
Courtyards in Delft.
Craigvara House.
Dawn at Saint Patrick's.
Dawn Chorus, The.
Day Trip to Donegal.
De Quincey in Later Life.
Dejection [Ode].
Derry Morning.
Dirge, A.
Disused Shed in Co. Wexford, A.
Drawing Board, The.
Dream Play, The.
Dying Art, A.
Ecclesiastes.
Everything Is Going to Be All Right.
First Love.
Ford Manor.
Forger, The.
Garage in Co. Cork, A.
Ghosts.
Gipsies.
Girls on the Bridge.
Glengormley.
Globe in [North] Carolina, The.

Going Home.
Grandfather.
Greta.
Heraclitus on Rivers.
Homage to Malcolm Lowry.
Homecoming.
Hudson Letter, The.
Hunt by Night, The.
I Am Raftery.
Image from Beckett, An.
In Carrowdore Churchyard.
Jail Journal.
Katie at the Pool.
Kensington Notebook, A.
Kinsale.
Last of the Fire Kings, The.
Leaves.
Light Music.
Lives.
Mayo Tao, The.
Morning Radio.
Mt. Gabriel.
No Rest for the Wicked.
Noon at St. Michael's.
North Wind: Portrush.
Northern Star.
Nostalgias.
October in Hyde Park.
Old Snaps, The.
One of These Nights.
Ovid in Tomis.
Penshurst Place.
Portrait of the Artist, A.
Rage for Order.
Rathlin.
Refusal to Mourn, A.
Rock Music.
Roman Script.
Sea in Winter, The.
September in Gt. Yarmouth.
Shapes and Shadows.
Snow Party, The.
Songs of Praise.
Squince.
St. Patrick's Day.
Stanzas for Mary Stuart.
Stone Age Figure Far Below, A.
Studio, The.
Swim in Co. Wicklow, A.
Terminal Bar, The.
Thinking of Inis Oírr in Cambridge, Mass.
Tolerable Wisdom, A.
Tractatus.
Two Songs [for Doreen].
Unborn Child, An.
Woods, The.
Yaddo Letter, The.
Yellow Book, The.

Major, Clarence (b. 1936)
Aging Together.
Alone, I went into that special.
And as the memory of each.
And the single reality.
And who must remain.
Apple Core.
Apple-Maggot Fly, The.
Arriving Uninvited.
At Pointe de Rompe Talon.
At the Zoo in Spain.
Atelier Cézanne.
Balance and Beauty.
Ballroom Dark.
Being and Becoming.
Bernardston.
Beyond impasse.
Bill's.
Birds.
Bricks and Sleep.
Brief Visit to Venice.
Canal, this one, The.
Clay Bison in a Cave.
Coon Showman.
Cotton Club, The.
Dance Floor.
Dancing under the Stars at Nice.
Darwin's Dream.

Malherbe

Descendant of Solomon and the Queen of Sheba.
Dismal Moment Passing.
Dispute, The.
Divine Law: A Blue Beach Sermon.
Doll Believers, The.
Downwind.
Drawing from Life.
Dressed to Kill.
Eighteen-Dollar Taxi Trip to Tizapan and Back to Chapala.
En Promenade des Anglais.
Expanded Composition, The.
First.
Flowers for My Date.
Food for Thought; or, Death Is Physical.
Frenzy.
Gallup Swill-Hole, A; or, Cantina Blues.
Giant Red Woman.
Great Horned Owl, The.
Guy I Know on 47th and Cottage, A.
Harps.
Hazy Day in the Composition.
He gave the Fascisti salute.
Heartland Music.
Home on Rue du Bourg-Tibourg.
Honey Dripper.
In a blazing sunset.
In Absence of the Tree.
In Hollywood with the Zuni God of War.
In Salute again.
In the Armpit of the Hill.
In the hidden garden.
In Walked Bud with a Palette.
Jake Flower, The.
Kitchen Chair Poem #4.
Kitchen Chair Poem #5.
Life Story, A.
Little places. / Corte stella.
Little Rock.
Looking at Images Reflected in the Showcase Plate Glass.
Lost in the Desert.
Love Against Death.
Madman of the South Side.
Matthew.
Measure.
Montalban: Near the Ancient Fort.
Mother Junkie.
My Seasonal Body.
Nerve, The.
No Single Thing by Itself.
No Time for Self-Pity.
None of It Was.
Old woman comes, The.
On the Nature of Perspective.
On the Old Roman Road.
Other Side of the Wall, The.
Pencil Sketch.
Perfect Match, The.
Posing.
Pupa.
Rainy Season, The.
Read the Signs.
Revelation at Cap Ferrat.
Riders.
Round Midnight.
Sailing.
Sand Flesh and Sky.
Santa Maria Dei Frari.
Saving Just the Real.
See that stern castle?
Seine Split.
September Mendocino.
Sexual Conduct.
Sign Language.
Slave Trade, The: View from the Middle Passage.
Stillness and Vertigo.
String, The.
Study for a Geographical Trail.
Swallow the Lake.
Swine Who's Eclipsed Me, The.
Syncopated Cakewalk, The.
Tewa Victories.
Textures of Space, The.

Theme of Carnevale is a secret, The.
There he was, a boy, looking over.
They cut down the last tree.
Three Views of Horse.
Train Stop.
Un Poco Loco.
Unwanted Memory.
Venice dream of the mainland, A.
View from His Room.
Waiter in a California Vietnamese Restaurant.
Waiting in the Children's Hospital.
Way the Roundness Feels, The.
We climbed the hill to the carriages.
Words into Words Won't Go.
Wounded Bullfighter, The.
Wyoming.
You set out on a morning bright.
Young Woman.

Malherbe, François de (1555–1628)
Stanzas: "At length, my soul! thy fruitless hopes give o'er."

Mallarmé, Stéphane (1842–98)
Afternoon of a Faun.
Afternoon of a Faun, The.
Album Leaf.
Alms.
Anguish.
Another Fan; of Mademoiselle Mallarmé.
Apparition.
Autumn Lament.
Azure, The.
Beautiful suicide victoriously fled, The.
Bell-Ringer, The.
Clown Chastised, The.
Declaration at a Fair, The.
Demon of Analogy, The.
Does Pride at evening always fume.
Ecclesiastic, The.
Entire soul evoked, The.
Fan, A; of Madame Mallarmé.
Fan, A; of Méry Laurent.
Flight of Flaming Hair, The.
Flowers, The.
For the sake of voyaging—heedlessly.
Funereal Toast.
Futile Petition.
Gift of the Poem.
Glazier, The.
Glory.
Her pure nails on high displaying their onyx.
Hérodiade.
Homage: "Even a Dawn too numb."
Homage: "Silence already funereal spreads a pall, The."
Hushed to the crushing cloud.
Interrupted Performance, An.
Jinx, The.
Lace sweeps itself aside.
Little Air 1.
Little Air 2.
Little Air (Martial).
My old books closed upon Paphos's name.
Negress, A.
Newspaper Vendor, The.
Note to Whistler.
Old-Clothes Woman, The.
Phenomenon of the Future, A.
Pipe, The.
Poor Pale Child.
Prose.
Remembrance of Belgian Friends.
Reminiscence.
Renewal.
Roadmender, The.
Rondel: "Nothing you have when you awake."
Rondel: "We'll love each other if you choose."
Saint.
Salutation.
Sea Breeze.
Seller of Garlic and Onions, The.
Shoemaker, The.
Sigh.
Sonnet: "In the forgotten woods, when somber winter glowers."
Sonnet: "Lady / who burns without being burnt

or trying."
Sonnet: "So dear from far and near and white, and so."
Sprung from the croup and the flight.
Street Songs.
Summer Sadness.
Throw of the Dice, A.
To insert myself into your story.
Tomb.
Tomb of Charles Baudelaire, The.
Tomb of Edgar Poe, The.
Virginal, vibrant, and beautiful dawn, The.
Weary of Bitter Sleep.
What silk steeped in the balms of time.
When the shadow menaced with its fatal law.
White Water Lily, The.
Windows, The.
Winter Shiver.
Woman Selling Aromatic Herbs, The.
Workman's Wife, The.

Mandelstam [or Mandelshtam], Osip Emilevich (1892–1938)
Octets.
Summer Solstice.
Tristia.

Mao Tse-tung [or Mao Zedong] (1893–1976)
Spring in the Snow-Drenched Garden.

Marchenko, Nikolai Nikolaevich *See* **"Morshen, Nikolai Nikolaevich"**

Marino, Giambattista [or Giovanni Battista] (1569–1625)
Out of the Italain.
Strage degli innocenti, La, *sels.*

Maritain, Raissa
Autumn.
Chagall.
Cloud, The.
Eurydice.
Glass Orchard.
Glove, The.
Lake, The.
Mosaic: St. Praxed's.
Pillars.
Prisoner, The.
Recipe.
Restoration of the Pictures, The.

Marlowe, Christopher (1564–93)
Hero and Leander.
Passionate Shepherd To His Love, The.

Maro, Publius Vergilius *See* **Virgil [or Vergil]**

Martial (Marcus Valerius Martialis) (c.40–c.104)
1.32: "Sabinus, I don't like you. You know why?"
1.33: "In private she mourns not the late-lamented."
2.4: "Bert is beguiling with his mother."
2.5: "Believe me, sir, I'd like to spend whole days."
2.55: "You would be courted, dear, and I would love you."
2.68: "That I now call you by your name."
4.33: "You write, you tell me, for posterity."
4.69: "You serve the best wines always, my dear sir."
6.65: "'An epic epigram,' I heard you say."
Cinna, give me the man, when all is done.
Epigrams, *sels.*
He that would move another man to laughter.
Out of Martiall.
Some good, some middling, and some bad.

Martialis, Marcus Valerius *See* **Martial**
Martinengo, Luciano *See* **MacAfee, Norman**
Marvell, Andrew (1621–78)
Ad Regem Carolum Parodia [A Parody: To King Charles].
Ametas and Thestylis Making Hay-Ropes.
Bermudas.
Bludius et Corona [Blood and the Crown].
Character of Holland, The.
Clorinda and Damon.
Coronet, The.
Damon the Mower.
Daphnis and Chloe.
Definition of Love, The.
Dialogue Between The Resolved Soul and

Created Pleasure, A.
Dialogue between the Soul and [the] Body, A.
Dialogue between Thyrsis and Dorinda, A.
Dignissimo Suo Amico Doctori Witty.
Elegy upon the Death of My Lord Francis
    Villiers, An.
Epigramma in Duos Montes Amosclivium et
    Bilboreum: Farfacio [Epigram on Two
    Mountains, Almscliff and Bilbrough: To
    Fairfax].
Epitaph upon —, An.
Eyes and Tears.
Fair Singer, The.
First Anniversary of the Government under His
    Highness the Lord Protector, 1655, The.
Flecknoe, an English Priest at Rome.
Gallery, The.
Garden, The.
Horatian Ode upon Cromwell's Return from
    Ireland, An.
Hortus.
Illustrissimo Viro Domino Lanceloto Josepho
    de Maniban Grammatomanti.
In Eandem Reginae Sueciae Transmissam [To
    Christina, Queen of Sweden].
In Effigiem Oliveri Cromwell [On a Portrait of
    Oliver Cromwell].
In Legationem Domini Oliveri St John ad
    Provincias Foederatas.
Inscribenda Luparae [To Be Written on the
    Louvre].
Last Instructions to a Painter, The.
Letter to Doctor Ingelo, A.
Loyal Scot, The.
Match, The.
Mourning.
Mower Against Gardens, The.
Mower to the Glowworms [or Glow-Worms or
    Glo-Worms], The.
Mower's Song, The.
Music's Empire.
Nymph Complaining for the Death of Her
    Faun [or Fawn], The.
On a Drop of Dew.
On Mr Milton's "Paradise Lost."
On the Victory Obtained by Blake over the
    Spaniards, in the Bay of Santa [or Sancta]
    Cruz, in the Island of Tenerife, 1657.
Picture of Little T. C. in a Prospect of Flowers,
    The.
Poem upon the Death of Oliver Cromwell, A.
Pros Karolon ton Basilea [To King Charles].
Ros.
To His Coy Mistress.
To His Noble Friend, Mr Richard Lovelace,
    upon His Poems.
To His Worthy Friend Doctor Witty upon His
    Translation of the "Popular Errors."
Tom May's Death.
Two Songs at the Marriage of the Lord
    Fauconberg and the Lady Mary Cromwell.
Unfortunate Lover, The.
Upon an Eunuch: A Poet.
Upon Appleton House [To My Lord Fairfax].
Upon the Death of the Lord Hastings.
Upon the Hill and Grove at Bilbrough.
Young Love.

Matevski, Mateja
Equinox, *sels.*

Maunick, Edouard J. (b. 1931)
Seven Sides and Seven Syllables.

McGrath, Thomas (1916–90)
Afternoon of a McGrath.
Against the False Magicians.
Ah... to the Villages!
All the Dead Soldiers.
Anniversaries.
Another Season.
Ars Poetica: Or: Who Lives in the Ivory
    Tower?
Autumn Song.
Behold the Woman.
Beyond Seattle.
Beyond the Red River.
Black Train, The.
Blues for Jimmy.

Blues for the Old Revolutionary Woman.
Blues for Warren.
Bread of this World; Praises III, The.
Buffalo Coat, The.
Celebration.
Celebration for June 24.
Changeling, The.
Citizen Dreaming, The.
Coal Fire in Winter, A.
Columbus.
Dawn Song.
Death for the Dark Stranger.
Deep South.
Deprivation.
Don't Think You Know My Name!
Dream Range, The.
Dreams of Wild Horses, The.
Driving toward Boston I Run across One of
    Robert Bly's Old Poems.
Drowned Man: Death Between Two Rivers,
    The.
Edge of the River, The.
Emblems of Exile.
Encounter.
End of the Line, The.
End of the World, The.
Enemy, The.
Epitaph: "Again, traveller, you have come a
    long way led by that star."
Everything in Order.
Excursion: Or: O Columbus!, The.
Face of the Precipice is Black with Lovers,
    The.
Fatigue of Objects, The.
Flint and Steel.
For a Critic Who Tries to Write Poems.
Fresco: Departure for an Imperialist War.
From a Long Way Out of Pah-Gatzin-Kay.
Get Out of Town.
Go Ask the Dead.
Gone Away Blues.
Guiffre's Nightmusic.
Heroes of Childhood, The.
History.
In Dream Time.
In Early Autumn.
In Praise of Necessity.
In Sickness Like Sleep.
In the Sleep of Reason.
Incident in the Life of a Prophet, An.
Inheritance, The.
Lament for Pablo Neruda.
Legendary Progress.
Letter for Marian, A.
Little Odyssey of Jason Quint, of Science,
    Doctor, The.
Little Song about Charity, A.
Long Goodbye.
Long Way Outside Yellowstone, A.
Love in a Bus.
Mediterranean.
Memorial.
Migration of Cities, The.
Near Pah-Gotzin-Kay.
Need for Dictionaries II, The.
Need for Stoicism in the Stoa of Attalus, The.
News and the Weather, The.
Night Work.
Nocturne Militaire.
Note on the Late Elections, A.
Nuclear Winter.
Ode for the American Dead in Korea.
Offering.
Once We Meant It.
Ordonnance.
Orphan, The.
Parable.
Parable.
Passages.
People Are So Busy: Or: That's Life!
Perpetual Motion.
Poem: "Down the small and crooked road."
Poem: "How could I have come so far?"
Poem: "In the list of one thousand false
    addresses."
Poem: "Light flares from the tombstones.."

Poem: "Long wound of the summer—, The."
Poem: "My little son comes running with open
    arms!"
Poem: "My little son, laughing, singing.."
Poem: "Through the fog / The gulls."
Poem—Unfinished Poem.
Poem: "When I carry my little son in the
    cold."
Poem: "You out there, so secret."
Poet of the Prison Isle: Ritsos Against the
    Colonels, The.
Political Song for the Year's End.
Portents.
Praises.
Praises IV.
Progress of the Soul, The.
Proletarian in Abstract Light.
Proverbs of the Middle World.
Reading the Names of the Vietnam War Dead.
Rediscovery.
Remembering Loves and Deaths.
Remembering the Children of Auschwitz.
Repeated Journey, The.
Residencies.
Restless Night, The.
Return, The.
Return to Marsh Street.
Revisionist Poem: Machado.
Revisionist Poem—Octavio Paz.
Seekers, The.
Something Is Dying Here.
Sometimes.
Such Simple Love.
Theory, A.
Three Functions of Irony.
Topography of History, The.
Tourists at Ensenada.
Trinc: Praises II.
Triumphal March.
Trouble with the Times, The.
Two Songs from "The Hunted
    Revolutionaries."
Underground, The.
Up the Dark Valley.
Use of Books, The.
Used Up.
Uses of the Lost Poets.
Vision of Three Angels Viewing the Progress
    of Socialism.
War Resisters' Song.
Warrant for Pablo Neruda, A.
What We Think We Know.
When We Say Goodbye.
Winter Roads.
Woodcut.
World of the Perfect Tear, The.
World; The Lovers; Falling Stars, The.
You Can Start the Poetry Now, Or: News from
    Crazy Horse.
You Taught Me.

McHugh, Heather (b. 1948)
A.
Act, The.
Acts of God.
After Rilke.
Against a Dark Field.
Amenities, The.
Animal Song.
At a Loss.
Auto.
Bar and Grill.
Bear in English.
Better or Worse.
Big Ideas among Earthlings.
Blue Streak.
Breath.
Circus.
Coming.
Confessionist.
Connubial.
Constructive.
Curve.
Debtor's Prison Road.
Denomination.
Disappearee's Song.
Double Agent.

Dry Time.
Eastport.
Excerpt from an Argument with Enthusiasts, Concerning Inspiration.
Fable.
Faith.
Fall, The.
Fast.
Few Licks, A.
Field, The.
Five Threes (Fast Bike).
Fix.
For a Good Man.
For a Sad God.
Form.
Four Poems after Rilke.
From 20,000 Feet.
Ghost, The.
Gig at Big Al's.
Glimpse of Main Event.
Hag.
Hard.
High Jinx.
Hole Filler.
House, The.
Household.
Hurricane Can Cast, A.
I Knew I'd Sing.
ID.
Impressionist.
In a World of Taking, the Mistake.
In Praise of Pain.
Inflation.
Inside.
It Is 70 Degrees in Late November. Opening a Window, You Nearly Know.
Just Man.
Kind of Poor.
Labor.
Language Lesson 1976.
Lifelike.
Like.
Literal.
Live.
Lyricist's Lament, The.
Meaning Business.
Meantime.
Melted Money.
Message at Sunset for Bishop Berkeley.
Mind.
Most, The.
Mox Note.
My Shepherd.
Night in a World, A.
North Island Songs.
Not a Sin.
Numberless.
Nymph to Narcissus, The.
Or Else.
Orbit.
Ozone.
Patronage.
Place Where Things Got.
Point of Origin.
Politics.
Postcard from Provincetown.
Preferences.
Prothalamion.
Pupil.
Reservation.
Round Time.
Scenes from a Death.
Score, The.
Seal.
Sebastian's Mirror.
Shades.
Size of Spokane, The.
Solitary's Solace in the Natural Sciences.
Some Kind of Pine.
Song Calls the Star Little, The.
Spectacles.
Spilled.
Spot in Space and Time.
Stairwell.
Stall.
Stroke.

Syllables.
Take Care.
Tendencies.
32 Adults.
Thought of Night.
To a Christian.
To Go.
To God or Man.
To Have To.
To See the Light.
To the Quick.
Toward an Understanding.
Trouble with "In," The.
20–200 on 747.
Two Holidays.
Two-legged.
Two Loves.
Two St. Petersburgs.
Typewriter's the Kind, The.
Unguent.
Unspeakable.
Untitled.
Well.
What Could Hold Us.
What He Thought.
What Hell Is.
What Poems Are For.
When the Future Is Black.
Where.
White Mind and Roses.
Who Made Her.
Whoosh.
Window: Thing as Participle.
Woman Who Laughed on Calvary.

McMichael, James (b. 1939)
Compline.
Each in a Place Apart.
Four Good Things.
Great Garret, or 100 Wheels, The.
Inland Lighthouse, The.
Itinerary.
Its Time.
Lauds.
Matins.
Nones.
Pretty Blue Apron.
Prime.
Queen Anne Cottage, The.
Sext.
She.
Terce.
Vegetables, The.
Very Rich Hours, The.
Vespers.
World at Large, The.

Medici, Lorenzo de' (1449–92)
Beside a running brook my lady stands.
Leave, Cytherea, Your Enchanted Isle.

Meleager (fl. 1st cent. B.C.)
Upon a Maid That Died [or Dyed] the Day She Was Married [or Marryed].

Melo Neto, João Cabral de (b. 1920)
Cemetery in Pernambuco: Our Lady of Light.
Death and Life of a Severino, The, sels.

Melville, Herman (1819–91)
Aeolian Harp, The.
After the Pleasure Party.
Age of the Antonines, The.
America.
American Aloe on Exhibition, The.
Apathy and Enthusiasm.
Apparition, The.
Apparition, The—A Retrospect.
Archipelago, The.
Armies of the Wilderness, The.
Art.
At the Cannon's Mouth.
Ball's Bluff.
Battle of Stone River, Tennessee.
Bench of Boors, The.
Berg, The.
Billy Budd, Foretopman, sels.
Buddha.
Camoëns.
Canticle, A.

Clarel: A Poem and Pilgrimage in the Holy Land, sels.
Clover.
College Colonel, The.
Coming Storm, The.
Commemorative of a Naval Victory.
Conflict of Convictions, The.
Dupont's Round Fight.
Enthusiast, The.
Enviable Isles, The.
Far Off-Shore.
Field Asters.
Formerly a Slave.
Fortitude of the North, The.
Fragments of a Lost Gnostic Poem of the Twelfth [or 12th] Century.
Garden of Metrodorus, The.
Greek Architecture.
Greek Masonry.
Haglets, The.
Hearts-Of-Gold.
Herba Santa.
House-Top, The.
Immolated.
In a Bye-Canal.
In a Church of Padua.
In a Garret.
In the Desert.
In the Turret.
Inscription: "To them who crossed the flood."
Jack Roy.
John Marr.
Little Good Fellows, The.
Lone Founts.
Maldive Shark, The.
Malvern Hill.
March into Virginia, The.
March to the Sea, The.
Marchioness of Brinvilliers, The.
Margrave's Birthnight, The.
Martyr, The.
Milan Cathedral.
Misgivings.
Monody.
Montaigne and His Kitten.
Muster, The.
Night-March, The.
Off Cape Colona.
On Sherman's Men.
On the Grave.
On the Home Guards.
On the Photograph of Corps Commander.
On the Slain Collegians.
Parthenon, The.
Pebbles.
Pisa's Leaning Tower.
Pontoosuce.
Portent, The.
Ravaged Villa, The.
Reasonable Constitution, A.
Rebel Color-Bearers at Shiloh.
Rosary Beads.
Rusty Man, The.
Sheridan at Cedar Creek.
Shiloh [A Requiem].
Stonewall Jackson.
Temeraire, The.
Timoleon.
Tom Deadlight.
Trophies of Peace.
Tuft of Kelp, The.
Utilitarian View of the Monitor's Fight, A.
Venice.

Menander (342–290 B.C.)
From Menander.

Mencius (371?–288? B.C.)
Ox Mountain Parable, The.

Meng Hao Jan (689–740)
After the Party.
In spring you sleep and never know when the morn comes.
Late Spring.
Steering my little boat towards a misty islet.
To Wang Wei.

Meredith, George (1828–1909)
Adieu, adieu, my Friar, he cried.

Age of petty tit-for-tat, An.
Ah for that time when open daylight pours.
Ah! little Angel, child of bliss!
Aimée.
Alsace-Lorraine.
Alternation.
Ambition.
And tho' my friar's mandate is severe.
Aneurin's Harp.
Angel, be ye ne'er in doubt, An.
Angela Burdett-Coutts.
Angelic Love.
Antigone.
Appeasement of Demeter, The.
Appreciation.
Arabic Poems.
Archduchess Anne.
As from the fall of candlelight
As I turn'd into the market-place.
As often in a bun.
Ask, is Love divine.
Ass of Balaam, The.
At the Close.
At the first ball his wicket fell, and sins.
At the Funeral.
Atkins.
Atlas.
Au voleur, au voleur, au voleur!—.
Autumn Even-Song.
Ballad of Fair Ladies in Revolt, A.
Ballad of Past Meridian, A.
Ballad of the Lady Eglantine, The.
Beetle soars, the beetle spins, The.
Beggar's Soliloquy, The.
Believe me, I have studied men.
Bellerophon.
Beyond the meadow still where sweeps.
Black Richard.
Blame me not that I refuse.
Blest is the sword that leaps from sheath.
Blue Is the Sky.
Breath of the Briar.
Britain.
Brotherhood.
Bumble Bee—the Bumble Bee, The.
Burden of Strength, The.
But see what living glory floods the west.
By Morning Twilight.
By the Passeyr.
By the Rosanna.
C B M.
Cageing of Ares, The.
Call, The.
Camelus Saltat.
Camelus Saltat: Continued.
Candid Friend who strikes because he loves, The.
Capitalist, The.
Carol of Jack Frost, A.
Cassandra.
Centenary of Garibaldi, The.
Certain People, A.
Chambers of my heart are many, dear, The.
Change in Recurrence.
Child's Prayer, A.
Chillianwallah.
Chivalry.
Cleopatra.
Congress of Nations, The.
Cool you proceed at speed.
Could we know how kin we are.
Creation and the Prophet.
Creed.
Crisis, The.
Crown of Love, The.
Dalila.
Daphne.
Dark on the ridge of the cold salt wave.
Day is going, now 'tis noon, The.
Day of the Daughter of Hades, The.
Dear Heaven! for this sweet pledge of life.
Dear, my friend & honour'd madam! of hard facts I'm not a hoarder.
Dearest Dimpling, we believe.
Death of Winter, The.
Desert vulture / jealousy, The.

Desired as Summer rain.
Despots of Manchester, Oligarchs!
Dirge: "He has hid his face, and he's gone!"
Dirge in Woods.
Discipline of Wisdom, The.
Doe: A Fragment, The.
Dost thou behold some woeful soul.
Earth and a Wedded Woman.
Earth and Man.
Earth's Preference.
Earth's Secret.
Empedocles.
Emperor Frederick of Our Time, The.
Empty Purse: A Sermon to our Later Prodigal Son, The.
Empty Purse, The.
England before the Storm.
Epitaph on the Tombstone of James Christopher Wilson.
Events in a Rustic Mirror.
Fair Bedfellow, The.
Faith on Trial, A.
Falling of Sally, The.
Fall'n Is Lucifer.
Familiar Things.
Fireside.
Fireside Reverie.
First-Born, The.
Flower of the Ruins, The.
For any save a lover.
Force and His Master.
Foresight and Patience.
Forest History.
Fragments for "The Harvest Home" and "The Doe."
France.
Fresh Spring has come with flower and leaf to warn.
Friar uxorious!
Friend, when the thundercloud is low.
From labours through the night, outworn.
From lamplight and an aged leaf.
Fullness of love sleeps in us like a sea.
Fusion.
Garden Idyl, A.
Garden of Epicurus, The.
Gentleness of Death, The.
Glastonbury Thorn, The.
Glee.
Gordon, Jim, / Life and Limb.
Gordon of Khartoum.
Grace and Love.
Grandfather Bridgeman.
Hail, Common Sense! most rare of all!
Hard Weather.
Hatton's "God of War."
Hawarden.
He where the great sun looks his last.
Head of Bran the Blest, The.
Hear now the mission of good wine.
Hectate.
Her trousers are red; she wears a coatee.
Hernani.
Hilda's Morning and Evening Dose of Rhyme.
Holidays.
Hueless Love, The.
Hungarian Air.
Hymn to Colour.
I Chafe at Darkness.
I have a hope that's like a star.
I humm'd an air of sweet Mozart.
I look'd for my poet—he came not!
I looked from the book of the story of men.
I saw young Spring leap over the hills.
I say, that but for black Foakes'-day.
I seize in a central knot.
I wish'd the world a blindness.
I would I were with Jean.
Iconia.
If thou art sorrowful, hide thy face!
Il y a Cent Ans.
In all our daily war of words.
In Claremont woods we wandered once.
In the clear dark lake a lady dived.
In the Dry.
In the Sap.

In the time of early love.
In the Woods.
Infancy and Age.
Internal Harmony.
Invitation to the Country.
Ireland.
Irene ducks and runs amuck, The.
Islet the Dachs.
It is the young fresh rainy leaf.
Italy.
It's many a penny you'll pay to go.
J. C. M.
Jack & Harry.
John, John of Ottenhaw!
John Lackland.
Jolly Young Carpenter, The.
Josepha.
Joy is Fleet.
Juggling Jerry.
July.
Jump-to-Glory Jane.
Karl Onyx.
King Harald's Trance.
Kiss, and a clasp, and an eye to eye, A.
Labourer, The.
Lady C. M, The.
Lark Ascending, The.
Last Contention, The.
Later Alexandrian, A.
Lesson of Grief, The.
Lied von Castelli.
Like a blind child is the loving heart.
Line of eve o'er the moorland, A.
Lines to a Friend Visiting America.
Linnet-Hawker, The.
Little Foot-Page, The.
Lives there a man with such base mettle.
London by Lamplight.
Long was the conflict, but now 'tis done.
Longest Day, The.
Lord of old has dealt in blood, The.
Lords debate, the Commons brawl, The.
Love.
Love in the Valley.
Love is winged for two.
Love they alone the joyful heart.
Loyal Soldier, The.
Lucifer in Starlight.
M. M.
Madrigal: "Since Tuck is faithless found, no more."
Main Regret, The.
Manfred.
Margaret's Bridal-Eve.
Marian: "Clouds fly fast across the moon, The."
Marian: "She can be as wise as we."
Martin's Puzzle.
May Song.
Meditation under Stars.
Meeting.
Meeting, The.
Melampus.
Men and Man.
Mentor and Pupils.
Milton.
Miracle, The.
Miss Millicent Maxse was fond of her Ma.
Modern Love.
Monmouth.
Mortesto.
Mother to Babe.
Motley.
My jolly friar, / Now lift thy cowl.
My Lady has Diana's brows.
My Theme.
My Theme: Continued.
Napoléon.
Nature and Life.
Nature and Man.
New Era the Army of the Future the Egg of an Army, The.
New Year's Eve.
Night of Frost in May.
Night-Walk, The.
Night walks the earth with silver feet.

No boats oar slow, no barges pass.
Now dawns all waxen to your seal of life.
Nuptials of Attila, The.
O have you seen my Tuck? my bonny bonny Tuck!
O Mary Barrie, Mary Barrie.
O shrive me Friar, my ghostly Friar!
O 'tis my delight / In the dead of the night.
October 21, 1905.
Ode to H.I.M. Napoleon 3d.
Ode to the Spirit of Earth in Autumn.
Of Robin Redbreast's babes I told.
Old Chartist, The.
Olive Branch, The.
On Combe Bottom: Surrey.
On Como.
On Hearing the News from Venice.
On the Danger of War.
Once the fair Romance of story.
Open horizons round.
Or the single path— / Which the cool moon sheds.
Orchard and the Heath, The.
Orson of the Muse, An.
Outer and Inner.
Outside the Crowd.
Over the Hills.
Parody of Alfred Austin.
Pastorals.
Pasture Alp is webbed with shade, The.
Patriot Engineer, The.
Penetration and Trust.
Periander.
Phaéthôn.
Phantasy.
Philosopher! 'tis said you wail.
Phoebus with Admetus.
Pictures of the Rhine.
"Poems," says the title.
Poetry of Chaucer, The.
Poetry of Coleridge, The.
Poetry of Keats, The.
Poetry of Milton, The.
Poetry of Shakespeare, The.
Poetry of Shelley, The.
Poetry of Southey, The.
Poetry of Spenser, The.
Poetry of Wordsworth, The.
Point of Taste, The.
Preaching from a Spanish Ballad, A.
Prestige.
Progress.
Progression.
Promise in Disturbance, The.
Quake, quake, let us turn Quaker all!
Queen Zuleima.
Question Whither, The.
Rape of Aurora, The.
Reason.
Red Coats & the Blue, The.
Remember what a night of storm.
Reply of the County of Surrey to the Poet's Pathetic Address in Dispraise of Jean.
Requiem: "Where faces are hueless, where eyelids are dewless."
Revolution, The.
Rhine-Land.
Richard Lionheart.
Riddle for Men, The.
Roar through the Tall Twin Elm-Trees, A.
Rosalind.
Sage Enamoured and the Honest Lady, The.
St. Thérèse.
Schubert's "Farewell."
See the star yonder.
Seed-Time.
Sense and Spirit.
Shall I again have Lilac week?
She had a secret—bonny Bess!
She marries the knight she loves.
She rides in the park on a prancing bay.
She scarce has a word for Papa.
Shemselnihar.
Shipwreck of Idomeneus, The.
Sing aloud that she is mine.
Sleeping City, The.

Society.
Solon.
Song: Autumn.
Song: "Buy, buy, buy, / Is the Peace-markt cry."
Song: "Come to me in any shape!"
Song: "Daisy now is out upon the green, The."
Song: "Fair and false! No dawn will greet."
Song: "Flower unfolds its dawning cup, The."
Song: "Forever."
Song: "Full of thy glory am I."
Song: "God bless the little Island!"
Song: "I cannot lose thee for a day."
Song: "I would be the bounding deer."
Song: "I would I were the drop of rain."
Song in the Songless.
Song: "Love within the lover's breast."
Song: "Might I lie where leans her lute."
Song: "Moon is alone in the sky, The."
Song: "My chosen bride shall bless the plough."
Song: "My darling's love shall close me up."
Song: "No, no, the falling blossom is no sign."
Song: "O the wind, the wind, the wind doth blow."
Song: "O they canna' do without it."
Song of Courtesy, The.
Song of Drab, The.
Song of Ruark to Bhanavar the Beautiful.
Song of the New Zealander among the Ruins of Old London.
Song of Theodolinda, The.
Song: "Over the ferry, and over the ferry."
Song: "Pass we to another land."
Song: "Quick bird sings and pierces me, The."
Song: "Should thy love die; / O bury it not under ice-blue eyes!"
Song: Spring.
Song: The Wren.
Song: "Thou steppest from thy splendour."
Song: "Thou to me art such a spring."
Song: "Thou tremblest O my love! thy hand in mine."
Song: "Twelve arrows, and a bow, and spear."
Song: "Two wedded lovers watched the rising moon."
Song: "Under boughs of breathing May."
Song: "When on my faithful charger."
Song: "Who says, she is in danger."
Song: "Woo me now & you'll win me."
Sonnet: "Hateful are those false themes of speculation."
Sonnet to J.M.
Sorrows and Joys.
Soul, The.
South-West Wind in the Woodland.
South-Wester, The.
Spirit of Shakespeare: Continued, The.
Spirit of Shakespeare, The.
Squireless Kate.
Star Sirius, The.
State of Age, The.
Stave of Roving Tim, A.
Story of Sir Arnulph, The.
Sunrise.
Swallow came from over the sea, The.
Swathed round in mist and crown'd with cloud.
Sweet Justice of Norbiton, neighbour of Jones.
Sweet o' the Year, The.
Tardy Spring.
Teaching of the Blows of Fortune, The.
Teaching of the Nude, The.
Test of Manhood, The.
There fell a sudden rain.
There is for me no sweeter holiday.
There stood in her street a poor exile of Queen Je'n.
There was a fair footman of Torrington Square.
There was a young poet of Chelsea.
Think not, should your husband swear.
This love of nature, that allures to take.
Thou pirate nested over Alde!
Three Eagles and the Sleepy Lion, The.
Three Maidens, The.

Three Singers to Young Blood, The.
Thrush in February, The.
Time ("Heart may live a lifetime").
Time ("Sore never was heard so berhymed").
Time and Sentiment.
'Tis good to keep hinderward eyes.
'Tis I have seen the coming man.
'Tis midnight in the skies, my dear.
To a Friend Lost.
To A.M.
To a Nightingale ("O nightingale! how hast thou learnt").
To a Nightingale ("In the bowers of the rising moon").
To a Skylark.
To Alex. Smith, the "Glasgow Poet," on His Sonnet to "Fame."
To Cardinal Manning.
To Carlyle.
To Children.
To Colonel Charles.
To J.M.
To Lord Palmerston.
To-morrow I am going.
To P.A. Labouchère Esq.
To Plimmer, Verandah and Cello.
To R.H.H. with Daphne.
To Robin Redbreast.
To the Comic Spirit.
To the Merry Men of France.
Too cold for joy, too cold for woe.
Trafalgar Day.
Triad of British Evils, A.
Tuck, Demitroïa, / Ariadne, and Froyja.
Tuck, my treasure! Tuck, my pleasure!
Tuck, sweet charmer, tell me why.
Tuck, thou graceless sinner!—.
Tuck! Tuck! Once you would flatter me.
'Twas in a glimmering starlight.
'Twas yesterday such a black-dye-day.
Twilight Music.
Two Blackbirds, The.
Two Masks, The.
Union in Disseverance.
Unknown Fair Faces.
Violets.
Vital Choice, The.
Vittoria Concluding the Opera of "Camilla."
Vittoria's *Italia* Song.
Voyage of the "Ophir," The.
Wand of gold from the reaper's moon, A.
Wandering Willie.
War.
Warning, The.
Was it wise to count the ranks of teeth.
Wassail for the New Year, A.
Waves are pressing up with force, The.
We need some rallying point round which.
We sat beneath the humming pines.
We see the farther in the far.
We stood in the garden alone.
We violets white and blue.
Were men of such importance as they deem.
What makes it hard to understand.
When I Would Image.
When my little son leaps in my sight.
When stormy day is cold & gray.
When Will was at home in his palace of zinc.
While Janet eyes the Lanthorn's Magic.
While Nature mocks her truth with mimic shows.
Whimper of Sympathy.
Wild Rose and the Snowdrop, The.
Wild Rose, The.
Wilding little stubble flower, A.
Will o' the Wisp.
Will Whistle.
Wind & sea are as playmates.
Wind on the Lyre.
Windy Haymaking.
Winter Heavens.
Wisdom of Eld, The.
With the Huntress.
With the Persuader.
Woodland Peace.
Woodman and Echo.

Woods of Westermain, The.
Word from the Cannon's Mouth, A.
World is full of different fates, The.
World is young, the world is well, The.
World's Advance, The.
Ye noble Lords who bravely fight.
Years Had Worn Their Season's Belt, The.
Year's Sheddings, The.
Yes, we'll pic-nic in the woods.
Yet what is this? the spring returns.
You ask me what is Genius? 'tis that.
Young Princess, The.
Young Reynard.
Young Usurper, The.
Youth in Age.
Youth in Memory.
Youthful Quest, The.

Meredith, William (b. 1919)
About Opera.
About Poetry.
Accidents of Birth.
Account of a Visit to Hawaii, An.
Airman's Virtue.
American Living Room, The: A Tract.
Among Ourselves.
Assent to Wildflowers, An.
At the Confluence of the Colorado and the
    Little Colorado.
At the Natural History Museum.
At the Prado.
Ballet, The.
Battlewagon.
Birthday Exercise, A.
Carrier.
Cheer, The.
Chinese Banyan, The.
Consequences.
Country Stars.
Couple of Trees, A.
Couple Overhead, The.
Crossing Over.
Dalhousie Farm.
Do Not Embrace Your Mind's New Negro
    Friend.
Dreams of Suicide.
Dying Away.
Earth Walk.
Effort at Speech.
English Accounts.
Envoi: "Go, little book. If anybody asks."
Examples of Created Systems.
Fables about Error.
Fear of Beasts, The.
February 14.
Firescreen at Mount Vernon, A.
Fishvendor, The.
Five Accounts of a Monogamous Man.
Fledglings.
For Air Heroes.
For Guillaume Apollinaire.
For His Father.
For Two Lovers in the Year 2075 in the
    Canadian Woods.
Freezing.
Ghosts of the House, The.
Give and Take.
Godchildren.
Grace.
Grievances.
Hazard Faces a Sunday in the Decline.
Hazard's Optimism.
Here and There.
His Plans for Old Age.
His Students.
Homage to a Rake-Hell.
Homage to Paul Mellon, I. M. Pei, Their
    Gallery, and Washington City.
Housed (A Report on a Visiting Dog).
Hydraulics.
Ideogram.
Illiterate, The.
In a Copy of Yeats' Poems.
In Loving Memory of the Late Author of
    Dream Songs.
In Memoriam Stratton Christensen.
In Memory of Donald A. Stauffer.

In Memory of Robert Frost.
In the Middle of the Long Friendship.
In the Rif Mountains.
Jain Bird Hospital in Delhi, The.
John and Anne.
Journal Entry (April 1969, Villa Serbelloni).
Journal Entry (With the Udalls, June 1968).
June: Dutch Harbor.
Kodiak Poem, A.
Korean Woman Seated by a Wall, A.
Last Things.
Look at Me! Look at Me!
Major Work, A.
Memoirs.
Metaphysical Sonnet, A.
Mild-Spoken Citizen Finally Writes to the
    White House, A.
Miniature.
Music.
My Mother's Life.
Myself, Rousseau, a Few Others.
Nausea.
Navy Field.
Nixon's the One.
Not Both.
Notes for an Elegy.
Notre Dame de Chartres.
Of Kindness.
Of Possessions, in Winter.
Old Field Mowed for Appearances' Sake, An.
Old Photograph of Strangers, An.
On Falling Asleep by Firelight.
On Falling Asleep to Birdsong.
On Jenkins' Hill.
Open Sea, The.
Original Aversions.
Orpheus.
Parents.
Pastoral: "Girl lies down on the hill, The."
Perhaps the Best Time.
Poem about Morning.
Poem: "Swans on the river, a great, The."
Poem to Me.
Politics.
Preponderance, The.
Quarrel, The.
Quartet in F Major.
Recollection of Bellagio.
REM Sleep.
Remembering Robert Lowell.
Revenant, The.
Rhode Island.
Roots.
Rus in Urbe.
Seasons' Difference, The.
Sonnet on Rare Animals.
Squire Hazard Walks.
Starlight.
Sunrise with Crows.
Talking Back (To W. H. Auden).
Ten-Day Leave.
Thoughts on One's Head (In Plaster, with a
    Bronze Wash).
Three Sorts of Violence, The.
Transport.
Tree Marriage.
Two Japanese Poems.
Two Masks Unearthed in Bulgaria.
View of the Brooklyn Bridge, A.
Vision of Good Secrets, A.
Waking Dream about a Lost Child.
Walter Jenks' Bath.
What I Remember the Writers Telling Me
    When I Was Young.
Where He's Staying Now.
Wholesome.
Whorls.
Winter: He Shapes Up.
Winter on the River.
Winter Song.
Winter Verse for His Sister.
Wreck of the Thresher, The (Lost at Sea, April
    10, 1963).

Merrill, James (1926–95)
About the Phoenix.
After Greece.

After the ball.
After the Fire.
Amsterdam.
Angel.
Annie Hill's Grave.
Another August.
Banks of a Stream Where Creatures Bathe.
Black Mesa, The.
Black Swan, The.
Blue Eye, The.
Blue Grotto, The.
Book of Ephraim, The, sels.
Broken Bowl, The.
Broken Home, The.
Bronze.
Carpet Not Bought, A.
Channel 13.
Charioteer of Delphi, The.
Charles on Fire.
Childlessness.
Chimes for Yahya.
Clearing the Title.
Country of a Thousand Years of Peace, The.
Current, The.
David's Night in Veliès.
Days of 1941 and '44.
Days of 1971.
Days of 1964.
Days of 1935.
Dedication: "Hans, there are moments when
    the whole mind."
Domino.
Doodler, The.
Dream (Escape from the Sculpture Museum)
    and Waking.
Dreams About Clothes.
18 West 11th Street.
Five Old Favorites.
Flèche d'Or.
For Proust.
Friend of the Fourth Decade, The.
From a Notebook.
From the Cupola.
Grass.
Hotel de l'Univers et Portugal.
Hourglass.
House Fly, The.
House, The.
In Nine Sleep Valley.
In the Hall of Mirrors.
Island in the Works.
Kimono, The.
Komboloi.
Kostas Tympakianákis.
Last Mornings in California.
Last Words.
Little Fanfare for Felix Magowan.
Log.
Lorelei.
Mad Scene, The.
Maisie.
Manos Karastefanís.
Marsyas.
Matinees.
McKane's Falls.
Mirror.
Mornings in a New House.
Narrow Escape, A.
Nightgown.
Nike.
Octopus, The.
Olive Grove.
Orfeo.
Ouzo for Robin.
Page from the Koran.
Parrot Fish, The.
Peacock, The.
Peter.
Pier: Under Pisces, The.
Prism.
Radiometer.
Remora.
Renewal, A.
River Poem.
Roger Clay's Proposal.
Salome.

Santo.
Santorini: Stopping the Leak.
Scenes of Childhood.
School Play, The.
16. ix. 65.
Smile, The.
Strato in Plaster.
Summer People, The.
Swimming By Night.
Syrinx.
Tenancy, A.
Think Tank.
Thousand and Second Night, The.
Three Chores.
Time.
To a Butterfly.
To My Greek.
Topics.
Transfigured Bird.
Trees Listening to Bach.
Under Libra: Weights and Measures.
Up and Down.
Urban Convalescence, An.
Variations: The Air Is Sweetest That a Thistle
    Guards.
Verse for Urania.
Victor Dog, The.
Violent Pastoral.
Vision of the Garden, A.
Voices from the Other World.
Will, The.
Willow.
Willowware Cup.
Words for Maria.
World and the Child, The.
Yánnina.

Merton, Thomas (1915–68)
Advent.
Advice to a Young Prophet.
After the Night Office—Gethsemani Abbey.
All of the branches / None of the roots.
All the Way Down.
Anatomy of Melancholy, The.
And So Goodbye to Cities.
And the Children of Birmingham.
Annunciation, The.
Antipoem 1.
April.
April 4th 1968.
Argument: Of the Passion of Christ, An.
Ariadne.
Ariadne at the Labyrinth.
Ash Wednesday.
Atlas and the Fatman.
Aubade: Bermuda.
Aubade—Harlem.
Aubade: Lake Erie.
Aubade—the Annunciation.
Aubade—the City.
Baroque Gravure, A.
Be My Defender.
Bees love grass, The.
Ben's Last Fight.
Berceuse: to end the sorrow of mortals.
Betrayal, The.
Biography, The.
Birdcage Walk.
Blessed Virgin Mary Compared to a Window,
    The.
Bombarded City, The.
Bureaucrats: Diggers.
Cables to the Ace.
Calypso's Island.
Cana.
Candlemas Procession, The.
Canticle for the Blessed Virgin.
Captives—a Psalm, The.
Carol, A: "When Jesus got my broken back for
    Christmas, Juniors."
Carol: "Flocks feed by darkness with a noise
    of whispers."
Ceremony for Edward Dahlberg.
Chant to Be Used in Processions around a Site
    with Furnaces.
Chee$e.
Christina.

Christmas as to People.
Christmas Card, A.
Christopher Columbus.
City after Noon, The.
City's Spring, The.
Clairvaux.
Clairvaux Prison.
Comedy Card for a Serious Case.
Communion, The.
Conversations.
Crusoe.
Darjeeling.
Dark Encounter, The.
Dark Morning, The.
Death.
Dirge for a Town in France.
Dirge for the City of Miami.
Dirge for the Proud World.
Dirge for the World Joyce Died In.
Dirge: "Some one who hears the bugle neigh
    will know."
Dream at Arles on the Night of the Mistral, A.
Dry Places.
Duns Scotus.
Early Blizzard.
Early Legend, The.
Early Mass.
Earthquake.
Elegy for a Trappist.
Elegy for Ernest Hemingway, An.
Elegy for Five Old Ladies, An.
Elegy for James Thurber.
Elegy for the Monastery Barn.
Elias—Variations on a Theme.
Epitaph for a Public Servant.
Evening.
Evening of the Visitation, The.
Evening Prayer.
Evening: Zero Weather.
Exploits of a Machine Age.
Fable for a War.
Fall of Night, The.
Fall '66.
Fall, The.
Famous engines support type B network.
Figures for an Apocalypse.
First Lesson about Man.
Five breaths pray in me: sun moon.
Five Virgins, The.
Flight into Egypt, The.
For My Brother: Reported Missing In Action,
    1943.
For the Spanish Poet Miguel Hernandez.
Freedom as Experience.
From the Legend of St. Clement.
From the Second Chapter of a Verse History of
    the World.
Fugitive.
Geography of Lograire, The.
Gloss on the Sin of Ixion.
God Said "They Did Not Hear."
Grace's House.
Great Men of Former Times, The.
Greek Women, The.
Guns of Fort Knox, The.
Hagia Sophia.
Holy Child's Song, The.
Holy Communion: the City.
Holy Sacrament of the Altar, The.
Hopeless and Felons.
House of Caiphas, The.
How Long We Wait.
How to Enter a Big City.
Hrishikesa, destroyer of Titans, ogres and
    canailles.
Hymn for the Feast of Duns Scotus.
Hymn of Not Much Praise for New York City.
Hymn to Commerce.
I Have Called You.
Image of True Lovers' Death, The.
In Memory of the Spanish Poet Federico
    Garcia Lorca.
In Silence.
In the Rain and the Sun.
Invocation to St. Lucy, An.
Iphigenia: Politics.

It would be wrong to let one man.
Je Crois En L'Amour.
Kandy Express.
King Solomon: my master and the imbeciles.
La Comparsa en Oriente.
La Salette.
Lament for Javier Heraud.
Landfall, The.
Landscape.
Landscape: Wheatfields.
Le Secret.
Legacy of Herakleitos, The.
Lent.
Lent in a Year of War.
Les Cinq Vierges.
Letter to America, A.
Letter to My Friends, A.
Letter to Pablo Antonio Cuadra Concerning
    Giants, A.
Letters to Che: Canto Bilingue.
Like Ilium.
Lion, The.
Listen, Saints.
Litany: "All holy souls / pray for us fellows."
Litany: "It yawns at me the cavernous gulf."
Litany: "Sing miserere / For the men who must
    die."
Long Enough.
Lord Is Good, The.
Love Winter When the Plant Says Nothing.
Lubnan.
Macarius and the Pony.
Macarius the Younger.
Man in the Wind, The.
Man the Master.
Marks and numbers / Cut in skin.
Martin's Predicament or Atlas Watches Every
    Evening.
Merlin and the Deer.
Message to Be Inscribed on Mark Van Doren's
    Hamilton Medal.
Messenger from the Horizon, A.
Messenger, The.
Messias.
Moment of Truth, The.
Moon smiles like a queen, The.
Moslems' Angel of Death, The.
Mothers you have met before still need you.
Mysterious Song in the Spring of the Year, A.
Natural History.
Never Call a Babysitter in a Thunderstorm.
New Ribbon.
News from the School at Chartres.
Night-Flowering Cactus.
Night of Destiny, The.
Night Train, The.
Nocturne: "Night has a sea which quenches the
    machine."
Nombril Walketh on the Loam.
Note in Honor of Machiavelli, A.
Now the official nerve is analyzed.
Now you are all here you might as well know
    this is America we do what we like.
O cross, more splendid than all the stars.
O Sweet Irrational Worship.
Ode to the Present Century.
Ohio River—Louisville, The.
Ointment, The.
Old.
Old monk is turned loose / And can travel!,
    The.
On a Day in August.
On the Anniversary of My Baptism.
Oracle, The.
Origen.
Original Child Bomb.
Originators, The.
Paper Cranes.
Peril, The.
Philosophers, The.
Picture of a Black Child with a White Doll.
Picture of Lee Ying, A.
Pilgrims' Song.
Plessy vs Ferguson: Theme and Variations.
Poem: "Here is the man of the islands."
Poem in the Rain and the Sun.

Poem: "Light plays like a radio in the iron tree."
Poem: 1939.
Poem: "Watching, among the rifled branches, for the sun, our hero."
Poet, to His Book, The.
Practical Program for Monks, A.
Prayer of Thanksgiving Written for Victor Hammer, A.
Prelude: For the Feast of St. Agnes, A.
Pride of the Dead, The.
Prologo.
Prophet.
Proverbs.
Psalm, A: "When psalms surprise me with their music."
Psalm 132: A Modern Monastic Revision.
Public Affairs.
Quickening of St. John the Baptist, The.
Rahab's House.
Reader, The.
Reading Translated Poets, Feb. 1.
Readings from Ibn Abbad.
Reduced to This.
Regret, The.
Responsory, A.
Responsory, 1948, A.
Rievaulx: St. Ailred.
Rilke's Epitaph.
Rites for the Extrusion of a Leper.
Round and a Hope for Smithgirls, A.
Sacred Heart 2.
St. Agnes: A Responsory.
St. Alberic.
Saint Jason.
St. John Baptist.
St. John's Night.
St. Maedoc.
St. Malachy.
St. Paul.
St. Thomas Aquinas.
Secret, The.
Secular Signs.
Selection of Concrete Poems, A.
Seneca.
Senescente Mundo.
Seven Archaic Images.
Silver bird is E backward in cool pond water, The.
Sincerity.
Snare, The.
Solitary Life.
Some Bloody Mutiny.
Song, A: "When it was day, we heard the panes of windows."
Song: "Bottom of the sea has come, The."
Song: "Come where the grieving rivers of the night."
Song: Contemplation.
Song for Nobody.
Song for Our Lady of Cobre.
Song for the Blessed Sacrament.
Song for the Death of Averroës.
Song: If You Seek.
Song: In the Shows of the Round Ox.
Song of the Traveller, The.
Song: Sensation Time at the Home, A.
Song: "When rain, (sings light) rain has devoured my house."
Songs.
Songs of Experience; India, One.
Sowing of Meanings, The.
Special continuations: the Gethsemani racetrack.
Sponge Full of Vinegar, The.
Sports without Blood—a Letter to Dylan Thomas (1948).
Spring: Monastery Farm.
Spring Storm.
Storm at Night, The.
Stranger.
Strife between the Poet and Ambition, The.
Submerged Dragon.
Sundown.
Then from tomorrow.
Theory of Prayer.

There Has to Be a Jail for Ladies.
There is a little ceremony to be performed.
There Is a Way.
These Years a Winter.
Things and people goodbye / It is not that I prefer.
Three Postcards from the Monastery.
To a Severe Nun.
To Alfonso Cortes.
To the Immaculate Virgin, on a Winter Night.
Tonight There Is a Showing of Champion Lights.
Tower of Babel.
Tower of Babel—A Morality, The.
Transformation: For the Sacred Heart, The.
Trappist Abbey: Matins, The.
Trappist Cemetery—Gethsemani, The.
Trappists, Working.
Tropics.
Tune for Festive Dances in the Nineteen Sixties, A.
Twenty Three Point Prospectus for Small College in the Badlands.
Two British Airmen.
Two Desert Fathers.
Two States of Prayer.
Victory, The.
Vine, The.
Welcome.
Western Fellow Students Salute with Calypso Anthems the Movie Career of Robert Lax.
What are the marks of the enemy? / He has no wit.
What is beyond reproof / Is done in this building.
What to Think When It Rains Blood.
What Troubles I Have Seen in Birdlegged Spring.
When class was in the garden at Greylands.
When in the Soul of the Serene Disciple.
Whether There Is Enjoyment in Bitterness.
Whitsun Canticle, A.
Why Some Look up to Planets and Heroes.
Widow of Naim, The.
Winter Afternoon.
Winter's Night, The.
Wisdom.
With the World in My Blood Stream.
Word—a Responsory, The.

Meru, Adsched of *See* **Abu Nadhar 'Abdu'l 'Aziz**

Merwin, W. S. (William Stanley) (b. 1927)
Acclimatization.
After a Storm.
After the Harvests.
After the Solstice.
Age.
Air: "Naturally it is night."
Ali.
Animals from Mountains.
Animals, The.
Animula.
Another Year Come.
Apparition.
Apparitions.
Apples.
Approaches, The.
April.
Arrival, The.
As by Water.
As Though I Was Waiting for That.
Ascent.
Ash.
Asians Dying, The.
Assembly.
At the Same Time.
Autumn Evening.
Avoiding News by the River.
Ballade of Sayings.
Banishment in Winter.
Banquet, The.
Before That.
Beggars and Kings.
Beginning.
Beginning of the Plains.
Berryman.

Beyond You.
Birdie.
Birds on the Morning of Going, The.
Birthday, A.
Black Jewel, The.
Black Plateau, The.
Blessing, The.
Bread.
Bread and Butter.
Bread at Midnight.
Bridges, The.
Briefcase, The.
Burnt Child, The.
By Day and by Night.
By the Cloud Path.
By the Mango Trees.
Caesar.
Calling under the Breath, The.
Calm in April, A.
Cart, The.
Cat Ghosts.
Chaff, The.
Chase, The.
Child, The.
Church, The.
City.
Clear Skies, The.
Coin, The.
Cold before the Moonrise, The.
Come Back.
Coming Back in the Spring.
Contemporary, A.
Continuo, The.
Counting Houses, The.
Cow, The.
Crossing Place.
Crossroads of the World Etc., The.
Crows on the North Slope.
Cry, The.
Cuckoo Myth.
Current, The.
Day, The.
Daybreak.
Dead Hand.
Dead Hive, The.
Death of a Favorite Bird.
Debt, A.
December among the Vanished.
December Night.
Defeated, The.
Deluge, The.
Departure's Girl-Friend.
Different Stars, The.
Diggers, The.
Direction.
Distances, The.
Divinities.
Division.
Do Not Die.
Dogs.
Door, A ("Do you remember how I beat on the door").
Door, A ("This is a place where a door might be").
Door, A ("What is dying all over the world").
Door, A ("You walk on").
Dragonfly, The.
Dream Again, The.
Dreamers, The.
Drive Home, The.
Dry Stone Mason, The.
Dusk in Winter.
Early January.
Early One Summer.
Economy.
Edouard.
Elegy: "Who would I show it to."
Émigré.
Encampment at Morning, An.
Encounter.
End in Spring, An.
End of Summer.
Envoy from d'Aubigné.
Estuary, The.
Evening.
Exercise.

Eyes of Summer.
Falcons, The.
Family, A.
Fate.
Fear.
February.
Ferry Port.
Fields, The.
Fig Tree, The.
Finally.
Finding a Teacher.
Finding of Reasons, The.
Fireweed.
First Darkness, The.
Fishing.
Flea's Carrying Words, A.
Flies.
Flight, The.
Fly.
Folk Art.
Footprints on the Glacier.
For a Coming Extinction.
For Now.
For Saying That It Won't Matter.
For the Anniversary of My Death.
For the Grave of Posterity.
Forbears, The.
Foreword.
Fountain, The.
Fourth Psalm: The Cerements.
Free, The.
From a Series.
Full Moonlight in Spring.
Gardens of Zuñi, The.
Gift.
Glass.
Glimpse of the Ice.
Gods, The.
Going.
Going from the Green Window.
Grass Beginning July.
Green Water Tower.
Guardians.
Habits.
Hands, The.
Happens Every Day.
Hearing.
Heart, The.
Helmsmen, The.
Herds, The.
High Water.
History of Alchemy.
Hollow, A.
Home for Thanksgiving.
Homeland.
Horse, The.
Horses.
Hosts, The.
House to the West, A.
Houses, The.
How We Are Spared.
Huckleberry Woman.
Hulk, The.
Hydra, The.
I Live Up Here.
In a Clearing.
In Autumn.
In One of the Retreats of Morning.
In the Gorge.
In the Life of Dust.
In the Night Fields.
In the Pass.
In the Red Mountains.
In the Time of the Blossoms.
In the Winter of My Thirty-eighth Year.
Indigestion of the Vampire, The.
Initiate, The.
Inscription Facing Western Sea.
Inscription for a Burned Bridge.
Instructions to Four Walls.
Invocation: "Day hanging by its feet with a
  hole, The."
Is That What You Are.
Island.
Island City.
Island in the Harbor, An.

Islands.
It Is March.
James.
Judgment of Paris, The.
Junction.
June Rain.
Kin.
Kore.
Lackawanna.
Lake, The.
Lantern, The.
Lark.
Last One, The.
Last People.
Late Night in Autumn.
Late Snow.
Late Wonders.
Laughter.
Lemuel's Blessing.
Letter.
Letter from Gussie, A.
Letter to the Heart.
Line.
Line of Trees.
Little Horse.
Looking Back.
Looking East at Night.
Looking for Mushrooms at Sunrise.
Lost Month.
Love for October, The.
Man Who Writes Ants, The.
Man with One Leaf in October Night.
Marica Lart.
Meeting.
Memory of Spring.
Memory of Summer Facing West.
Memory of the Loss of Wings.
Middle of the Summer, The.
Midnight in Early Spring.
Migration.
Mist.
Morning, The.
Moths, The.
Mountain Days.
Mountain Town.
Mountains, The.
Mourner, The.
My Brothers the Silent.
My Friends.
Nails, The.
New Moon in November.
New Season, The.
News of the Assassin.
Next Moon, The.
Next, The.
Night of the Shirts, The.
Night Surf, The.
Night Wind.
Noah's Raven.
Nomad Songs.
North Wind.
Not These Hills.
November.
Now and Again.
Now It Is Clear.
Number, A.
Numbered Apartment.
Oars, The.
October.
Old Boast, The.
Old Flag.
Old Garden.
Old Room, The.
On Each Journey.
On the Mountain.
On the Silent Anniversary of a Reunion.
One Night.
One Time.
One Way.
Other Travelers to the River.
Owl, The.
Palace, The.
Palm.
Passage.
Pause by the Water.
Paw, The.

Peasant.
Pens, The.
Peril.
Photograph.
Pieces for Other Lives.
Pilate.
Piper, The.
Place of Backs, The.
Plane.
Plaster, The.
Plumbing, The.
Poem, The: "Coming late, as always."
Port, The.
Prayer of the Eyes, A.
Present, The.
Presidents.
Prints, The.
Provision.
Psalm: Our Fathers.
Purgatory, A.
Questions to Tourists Stopped by a Pineapple
  Field.
Quince.
Quoit, The.
Recognition.
Red House, The.
Remembering a Boatman.
Removal, The.
Resolution.
Reunion.
River of Bees, The.
Road.
Robin.
Rock, The.
Room, The.
Route with No Number.
Sadness, The.
Saint of the Uplands, The.
St. Vincent's.
Savonarola.
Scale in May, A.
School on the Roof, The.
Sea Cliffs at Kailua in December, The.
Search, The.
Second Psalm: The Signals.
Second Sight.
Second Time, The.
Separation.
September.
September Plowing.
Service.
Shaving without a mirror.
She Who Was Gone.
Sheep Clouds.
Sheridan.
Ship.
Ships Are Made Ready in Silence, The.
Shoe Repairs.
Shore.
Shore, The.
Shuttles, The.
Sibyl.
Sickness at the Equinox, A.
Signs.
Silence before Harvest, The.
Singer, The.
Sire.
Sleeping Mountain, The.
Snow, The.
Snowfall.
Snowline.
Some Last Questions.
Some of the Masts.
Something I've Not Done.
Son.
Song of Man Chipping an Arrowhead.
Sound of Rapids of Laramie River in Late
  August.
South.
Span.
Spring ("On the water the first wind").
Spring ("Glass stems of the clouds are
  breaking").
Spring Equinox Full Moon.
Standards.
Standing Nowhere.

Still Afternoon Light.
Strawberries.
Students of Justice, The.
Summer Canyon.
Summer Doorway.
Summer Night on the Stone Barrens.
Summits.
Sun.
Sun and Rain.
Sunset after Rain.
Sunset Water.
Surf-Casting.
Tale.
Talk of Fortune.
Talking.
Teachers.
Their Week.
Things.
Third Psalm: The September Vision.
This Day of This Month of This Year of This.
Thread, The.
Tidal Lagoon.
Time of Tree Cutting.
To Be Sung While Still Looking.
To My Brother Hanson.
To the Hand.
To the Rain.
To Where We Are.
Tool.
Track, The.
Trail into Kansas, The.
Traveling.
Trees.
Trestle, The.
Truth about Departures, The.
Twilight.
Under Black Leaves.
Under the Migrants.
Unfinished Book of Kings.
Unknown Forebear.
Unwritten, The.
Vineyard, The.
Vision.
Visitation.
Vocations.
Voice.
Walk-up.
Walking into Autumn.
Wanting a Soul in the South.
War, The.
Warm Pastures.
Watchers.
Water of the Suns, The.
Waters, The.
Wave, The.
Waving of a Hand, The.
Way Ahead, The.
Way to the River, The.
We Continue.
Web, The.
Well, The.
Western Country.
Wharf, The.
What Is Modern.
Wheels of the Trains, The.
When the Horizon Is Gone.
When the War Is Over.
When You Go Away.
Whenever I Go There.
White Summer Flower.
Who It Is.
Widow, The.
Windows, The.
Wine, The.
Wish.
Witnesses.
Woman from the River.
Wood, A.
Words.
Words from a Totem Animal.
Writing on a Fallen Leaf, The.
Yesterday.

Metastasio, Pietro (1698–1782)
Adriano in Syria, *sels.*
La Clemenza di Tito, *sels.*
To the grove, the meadow, the well.

Michelangelo Buonarroti (1474–1564)
Alas! Alas! for the way I've been betrayed.
Alas, Alas, that I am betrayed.
All rage, all misery, all show of strength.
All there's to say of him, no way of saying.
Already burdened with a heavy heart.
Although it's amply true your human face.
Although my heart had often been aflame.
Although time presses hard and prods us on.
Among the memory of all lovely things.
And sweet it is to see in summer time.
As by subtracting, my lady, one creates.
As I've carried in my heart this many a year.
As, working in hard stone to make the face.
Ashes to ashes, spirit to the sky.
Assured of death, of its timing, though, not so.
At times I project ahead.
Be sure, my eyes, you know.
Because age steals away.
Because there's half of me which, heaven-
    born.
Because there's never a time I'm not
    enchanted.
Blissful spirit, thanks to whom new passion.
Born, died. Now bedded by the churchyard
    wall.
Bracci born, A. From birth, born wailing, I'd.
Bracci, I, A, Alive because I'm dead.
Bracci once, A. The soul in me withdrew.
Braccio lies here. No less a tomb could show.
Braccio retrieves from earth the mortal scrim.
Bright in our minds, but in the dark earth
    stranded.
Bring back the day the reins hung slack and
    free.
Brow burning, in cool gloom, as sundown
    shears.
Burdened with years and crapulous with sin.
By a face of fiery cold, I'm set aflame.
By light more brilliant of a star more bright.
By merit of grace, the cross, and all we've
    suffered.
Cecchino here has laid his body low.
Certain of death, though not yet of the hour.
Chalices hammered into sword and helmet!
Closed now his shining eyes, that dazzled so
Cold stone, none knows but you, my gaol
    forever.
Confused, with itself at odds, soul fails to find.
Day and the Night speak, and what they say is,
    The.
Day in, day out, from childhood long ago.
Death didn't wish to lay Cecchino low.
Death shut those eyes, him too it shut below.
Death stretched an arm, stole fruit not ripened
    yet.
Drawn to each lovely thing, my doting eyes.
Earth lends us flesh, heaven lends the soul, the
    two.
Easily you confound.
Enclosed and hidden in a monstrous stone.
Every shut-in room or space, every covered
    one.
Eyelid, shadowing, doesn't interfere, The.
Fame keeps the epitaphs where they lie.
Fear of death! Who'd shove, The.
Fine lass or lady, they.
Flee from this Love, you lovers; flee the flame!
Flooded, the soul pours out.
For a reliable guide in my vocation.
For a safe haven, for escape at last.
For a wound from the searing arrows Love lets
    fly.
For the sugar, for the mule, those candles too.
From beneath two arching brows.
From clutch of clock and calendar now fled.
From eyes of my beloved one, come burning.
From grief I cherished to a rueful laugh.
From heaven it ventured forth, there must
    return.
From heaven my beauty, flawless and divine.
From ink, from pen in hand we see outflow.
From one all loveliness and all allure.
From the first whimper to the expiring sigh.
From what these eyes, my lady, see of you.
From where you triumphed in me, Love, right

here.
Give back to my eyes their flow, O spring, O
    river.
Goiter it seems I got from this backward
    craning, A.
Gone under now, the sun you loved to greet.
Grateful is Sleep, my life in stone bound fast.
Great beauty scattering its brilliant flame.
Great mercy, my lady, as likely as great pain.
Had I, when young, been leery of the glow.
Hating myself, the more I run away.
Having, my friend, your letter here in hand.
He who beguiles both time and death together.
He Who made all there is, made every part.
Her beauty's alive in heaven! I believe her.
Here I'm thought dead. Alive, I comforted.
His beautiful eyes! I hardly saw them, only.
His life gave yours rich reason for
    thanksgiving.
How can it be, as long experience shows.
How could I, since it's so.
How joyfully it shows, the garland there.
How much less torment to breathe out my
    soul.
How very sweet indeed the prayers I'd say.
Humbly I bow my shoulders, bear the yoke.
I do believe, if you were made of stone.
I fed on you, and with you, many a year.
I have your letter, thank you, as received.
I live for sinning, for the self that dies.
I made my eyes an entryway for poison.
I really believed, that first great day when,
    awed.
I think, indeed know well, some crushing sin.
I think it may be, so.
I was, for years and years now, wounded,
    killed.
I was happy, with fate favoring, to abide.
I weep, I burn—burn up!—my heart thereby.
I wish I'd want what I don't want, Lord, at all.
I wouldn't if I could, Love, check the urge.
I'd feel the more secure.
If a god, Love, can't you do.
If a joyous heart makes beautiful the face.
If any of those old proverbs, lord, make sense.
If Braccio's beauty, phoenix-like, could be.
If by its heaven-sent power the mind
    conceives.
If death has buried here, hardly in leaf.
If fire can melt down steel and shatter flint.
If fire, so quick to char.
If his bright eyes are closed and laid to rest.
If I'm more alive because love burns and chars
    me.
If I'm to believe my eyes now, your response.
If, in Your name, some image comes to mind.
If it could be, to revive my life once more.
If leaves aren't what you're wanting.
If longings for the immortal, which exalt.
If my rough hammer shapes the obdurate
    stone.
If nature now deferred to death, dejected.
If obligated by so great a favor.
If our very thirst for longer life bids fair.
If pure devotion, passion without stain.
If right desire takes wing.
If she rejoices in my tears, and you.
If sorrow makes one beautiful (it's said).
If the soul, in truth, from body once set free.
If the soul returns, that last.
If, through our eyes, the heart's seen in the
    face.
If, to rejoice, you crave our tears and woe.
If true (and it is) that with body's final breath.
If two hours' dying steals a hundred years.
If, vulnerable from early youth, a heart.
If we constrain the eyes' easy response.
If, when it caught my eye first, I'd been bolder.
If, while I lived, a someone, eyes on me.
I'll surely be thought a dullard in talent, art.
I'm dearer dead than ever I was, before.
I'm dearer to me, much more, than ever I was.
I'm death's forever, who, that one forlorn.
I'm here to say you've given earth your all.
I'm packaged in here like the pulp in fruit.
Impassioned as I am.

In everything I see, the meaning's plain.
In lovelier and crueller flesh than yours.
In me there's only death; my life's in you.
In such servility! and all so boring!
Inside, his soul could not be outside too.
It leaves me plunged in gloom and pain—yet dear.
It seems, Love, out you've flung.
It well may be, so vehement my sighing.
It's not enough, if it doesn't come from you.
Just as a flame, by wind and weather flailed.
Just as you cannot not be lovely here.
Just when I'm lost in adoration of you.
Kindly to others, to itself unkind.
Life's final hours: brought there by many a year.
Life's quick and brief; the more my days fly by.
Looks thrown away on others.
Love in your eyes? No; life and death are there.
Love long delayed comes kindly, by fortune's favor.
Love's Justification.
Man who's happy many a year, one hour, A.
Man within a woman—no, I'd say, A.
Maybe, so I'd look kindly on souls in need.
Mere mortal once. Divine, though, born to be.
More it seems I agonize, the more, The.
Mould's not alone in this, A.
My death is what I live on; seems to me.
My eyes are saddened by so much they see.
My fervent prayer, if any pity me.
My flesh turned earth, my bones turned naked shame.
My gaze saw no mere mortal on the day.
My infinite thoughts, so many gone awry.
My lady, how comes it about—what all can see.
My lady, if it's true.
My lady is so impetuous, devil-may-care.
My lady, these eyes see vividly—far, near.
My lady, you raise me so.
My lover stole my heart, just over there.
My name meant "Arms." But little help to me.
My reason, out of sorts with me, deplores.
My soul without a friend, without a guide.
Nature knows what it's doing: one cruel as you.
New and more commendable delight, A.
Night prevails where Phoebus—that's our sun, The.
No differently the guilty wretch hangs back.
No doubt much peril lies.
No mortal object did these eyes behold.
No need at all for your angel loveliness.
No other handsome face such power possessed.
No question but, when my desire's aflame.
No rest here for the wicked, as folk say.
No slightest chance on earth her heavenly eyes.
No way he who undid me can restore.
Not always so prized and cherished by us all.
Not death so much, but its terror rescues me.
Not even, in dreams sent soaring, can I imagine.
Not true that it's always grim with mortal sin.
Nothing the best of artists can conceive.
Now armed with biting ice, now tongues of fire.
Now on the left foot shuffling, now the right.
Now that I'm banned and routed from the fire.
O blessed souls, who high in heaven delight.
O cruel star, or say instead, cruel will.
O God, O God, O God, how can I be.
O lucky me, to look upon me dead!
O night, comforting night, dark though you are.
O noble soul, in whom, as mirrored, show.
Oh let me see You everywhere I go!
On earth, it's no unworthy soul that nurses.
Once born, death's our destination.
One of the Bracci, I. Now, as you see.
One way remains to loose me yet, dear Lord.
One Who made, and from utter nothing too, The.
Only with fire can men at forge and flue.

Peace, life—he found them in my open eyes.
Please tell me, Love, if that lady had a soul.
Power of a beautiful face lifts me to heaven, The.
Power of a lovely face impels me where?
Pray tell me, Love, if what my eyes can see.
Rancorous heart, cruel, pitiless, though showing.
Rid of a vexing and a heavy load.
Rid of this nagging nattering cadaver.
Say the face I'm speaking of now, hers I mean.
Seeing I'm yours, I rouse me from afar.
She's made her mind up, me.
Should the senses' rapturous burning override.
Since I'm too obligated.
So fond is fire of the frigid stone it waits.
So I can best endure.
So it wouldn't need to retrieve the total sum.
So, Love, it hasn't healed, not even the least.
So now it's over, my day's long voyage, through.
So tell me, Death, why not possess some face.
Sonnet of Michel Angelo Buonaroti.
Soul lives on, I know it, lying here, The.
Souls rise alive from the body's sad last bed.
Springtime, fresh and green, can never guess, The.
Straight down from heaven, and in the flesh, he came.
Such brightness, under earth now, put to shame.
Such wealth of promise lies.
Sun of Braccio's under earth, The. The sun.
Suppose a lady has no other graces.
Supposing the passionate fire your eyes enkindle.
Sweet, sweet, is sleep,—Ah! sweeter, to be stone.
Sweeter your face than grapes are, stewed to mush.
That whole way up to your brilliant diadem.
Then there's this giant—tall! So tall he can't.
There's nothing lower on earth, of less account.
There's pleasure in great favors done, but hidden.
This face, says art, alone.
Though always one and the same, the one same who.
Though bent with age, to me.
Though quite expensive, look, I've bought you this.
Though shouldered from the road I chose.
Though years and years in dour allurement lapped.
Though you with line and color excel, securing.
Through many a year and many a vain assay.
Through your fine eyes I see such mellow light.
Time now good-byes were said.
Time was my fire burned high, yes, even on ice.
To be less unworthy, my exalted lady.
To one of taste both flawless and robust.
To see that your famous beauty still endures.
To sleep, even more be made of stone: how these.
Too early fallen asleep here, I'm alive.
Too late for Love to set my heart aflame.
Too much! the way he flaunts himself around.
Uproot a plant—there's no way it can seal.
Well-nigh the voyage now is overpast.
Were it true that, besides my own, another's arms.
Were one allowed to kill himself right here.
What a chance I had! I should have, while I could.
What file's incessant bite.
What in your handsome face I see, my lord.
What wonder that—seeing how, beside your fire.
Whatever the eye finds lovely, in a flash.
What's to become of her, long years from now.
What's to become of me? What's this you're doing.

When blithely Love would lift me up to heaven.
When heaven confirmed your brilliance, most of all.
When the occasioner of my many a sigh.
When to that beauty that I saw before.
When with a clanking chain a master locks.
Whenever my past unrolls before these eyes.
Whenever remembrance of the one I love.
Where my love lives is nowhere in my heart.
Whether or not the light I long for, sent.
Who grieve now at my grave, in vain they pray.
Who rides by night on horseback, come the day.
Who's this that draws me forcibly to you?
Why ease the tension of this wild desire.
Why fallen so soon asleep? Not hard to tell.
Why only at long last, why next to never.
Wiles, guiles, smiles, gold and pearls, her gala ways.
With all my heart I love you; if not so.
With heart of sulphur, flesh of tinder too.
With much of time and life gone, all the more.
With no less joy than grief and consternation.
Within this tomb our handsome Braccio's laid.
Wo is me woe's me when I think.
Woman's beauty, new, A.
World and all its fables long ago, The.
You give me only what you're glutted with.
You know, my Lord, that I too know you know.
You revel in my torments, only you.
Young Braccio's buried here. To mend a lack.
Your beauty an angel's, Lady, you were meant.
Your beauty, Love, stuns mortal reckonings.
Your kindness to me, and the ways of fate.
Your lovely eyes, now bent.
Your merciful, sweet care.

Mickiewicz, Adam (1798–1855)
  Mushroom Gatherers, The.

Millay, Edna St. Vincent ("Nancy Boyd") (1892–1950)
  Above These Cares.
  Admetus, from my marrow's core I do.
  Afternoon on a Hill.
  Agnostic, The.
  Alms.
  Amorphous is the mind; its quality.
  Ancient Gesture, An.
  And if I die, because that part of me.
  And is indeed truth beauty?—at the cost.
  And must I then, indeed, Pain, live with you.
  And you as well must die, belovèd dust.
  Anguish, The.
  Animal Ball, The.
  Apostrophe to Man.
  Apple-trees bud, but I do not, The.
  Armenonville.
  As men have loved their lovers in times past.
  As sharp as in my childhood, still.
  As to some lovely temple, tenantless.
  Ashes of Life.
  Assault.
  At least, my dear.
  Aubade: "Cool and beautiful as the blossom of the wild carrot."
  Autumn.
  Autumn Chant.
  Autumn Daybreak.
  Baccalaureate Hymn.
  Ballad of Chaldon Down, The.
  Ballad of the Harp-Weaver, The.
  Be sure my coming was a sharp offense.
  Bean-Stalk, The.
  Being Young and Green.
  Believe, if ever the bridges of this town.
  Betrothal, The.
  Black hair you'd say she had, or rather.
  Blight.
  Blue-Flag in the Bog, The.
  Bluebeard.
  Bobolink, The.
  Buck in the Snow, The.
  Burial.
  By goodness and by evil so surrounded, how

can the heart.
Cairn, The.
Cameo, The.
Cap D'Antibes.
Cave Canem.
Cherish you then the hope I shall forget.
Childhood Is the Kingdom Where Nobody
　Dies.
Christmas Canticle.
City Trees.
Clearly my ruined garden as it stood.
Come home, victorious wounded!—let the
　dead.
Concert, The.
Conscientious Objector.
Count them unclean, these tears that turn no
　mill.
Counting-out Rhyme.
Courage that my mother had, The.
Curse, The.
Czecho-Slovakia.
Daphne.
Dawn.
Death of Autumn, The.
Deep in the muck of unregarded doom.
Departure.
Desolation Dreamed Of.
Dirge Without Music.
Doubt No More that Oberon.
Dragonfly, The.
Dream of Saba.
Dream, The.
Ebb.
Eel-Grass.
Elaine.
Elegy before Death.
English Sparrows.
Enormous moon, that rise behind these hills.
Epitaph for the Race of Man.
Epitaph: "Grieve not for happy Claudius, he is
　dead."
Establishment is shocked. Stir no adventure.
Euclid Alone Has Looked on Beauty Bare.
Even in the moment of our earliest kiss.
Evening on Lesbos.
Exiled.
Fatal Interview.
Fawn, The.
Feast.
Felicity of Grief!—even Death being kind.
Few come this way; not that the darkness.
First Fig.
Fitting, The.
Fledgling, The.
Fontaine, Je Ne Boirai Pas De Ton Eau!
For Pao-Chin, a Boatman on the Yellow Sea.
For Warmth Alone, for Shelter Only.
From a Train Window.
From a Very Little Sphinx.
Gardener in Haying-Time, The.
God's World.
Gone in good sooth you are: not even in
　dream.
Goose-Girl, The.
Grief that is grief and properly so hight.
Grow not too high, grow not too far from
　home.
Grown-up.
Hangman's Oak.
Hardy Garden, The.
Hawkweed, The.
Hearing Your Words, and Not a Word Among
　Them.
Heart, have no pity on this house of bone.
Heart once broken is a heart no more, The.
Hedge of Hemlocks, The.
Here in a Rocky Cup.
Here is a wound that never will heal, I know.
His stalk the dark delphinium.
How did I bear it—how could I possibly as a
　child.
How healthily their feet upon the floor.
How innocent of me and my dark pain.
How innocent we lie among.
How Naked, How Without a Wall.
Humoresque.

Huntsman, What Quarry?
Hyacinth.
I, Being Born A Woman.
I do but ask that you be always fair.
I Dreamed I Moved among the Elysian Fields.
I, in disgust with the living, having read.
I know I am but summer to your heart.
I know my mind and I have made my choice.
I know the face of Falsehood and her tongue.
I must not die of pity; I must live.
I pray you if you love me, bear my joy.
I said in the beginning, did I not?
I said, seeing how the winter gale increased.
I see so clearly now my similar years.
I shall forget you presently, my dear.
I shall go back.
I think I should have loved you presently.
I will put Chaos into fourteen lines.
I woke in the night and heard the wind, and it
　blowing half a gale.
If I die solvent—die, that is to say.
If I should learn, in some quite casual way.
If, in the Foggy Aleutians.
If in the years to come you should recall.
If it should rain—(the sneezy moon).
If Still Your Orchards Bear.
If to be left were to be left alone.
Impression: Fog Off the Coast of Dorset.
In the Grave No Flower.
Indifference.
Inert Perfection.
Inland.
Intense and terrible, I think, must be the
　loneliness.
Intention to Escape from Him.
Interim.
Into the golden vessel of great song.
Invocation to the Muses.
It is the fashion now to wave aside.
Jesus to His Disciples.
Journal.
Journey.
Justice Denied in Massachusetts.
Keen.
Kin to Sorrow.
Lament: "Listen, children: / Your father is
　dead."
Leaf and the Tree, The.
Let you not say of me when I am old.
Lethe.
Life, were thy pains as are the pains of hell.
Light comes back with Columbine.
Lines for a Grave-Stone.
Lines Written in Recapitulation.
Little Ghost, The.
Little Hill, The.
Look how the bittersweet with lazy muscle
　moves aside.
Lord Archer, Death, whom sent you in your
　stead?
Love is not all: it is not meat nor drink.
Love is not blind. I see with single eye.
Love me no more, now let the god depart.
Love, though for this you riddle me with darts.
Loving you less than life, a little less.
Low-Tide.
Macdougal Street.
Mariposa.
Memorial to D. C.
Memory of Cape Cod.
Memory of Cassis.
Memory of England.
Men Working.
Menses.
Merry Maid, The.
Midnight Oil.
Mindful of you the sodden earth in spring.
Mist in the Valley.
Modern Declaration.
Moon, that against the lintel of the west.
Moriturus.
Mortal Flesh, Is Not Your Place in the
　Ground?
Most wicked words!-forbear to speak them out.
My earnestness, which might at first offend.
My Heart, Being Hungry.

My most distinguished guest and learnèd
　friend.
My Spirit, Sore from Marching.
My words that once were virtuous and
　expressed.
My worship from this hour the Sparrow-
　Drawn.
Nay, learnèd doctor, these fine leeches fresh.
Never May the Fruit Be Plucked.
New England Spring, 1942.
Night is my sister, and how deep in love.
No Earthly Enterprise.
No further from me than my hand.
No lack of counsel from the shrewd and wise.
No rose that in a garden ever grew.
Northern April.
Not for a Nation.
Not in a silver casket cool with pearls.
Not in this chamber only at my birth.
Not only love plus awful grief.
Not So Far as the Forest.
Not that it matters, not that my heart's cry.
Not, to me, less lavish—though my dreams
　have been splendid.
Not with libations, but with shouts and
　laughter.
Now by the path I climbed, I journey back.
Now by this moon, before this moon shall
　wane.
Now let the mouth of wailing for a time.
Now that the west is washed of clouds and
　clear.
Nuit Blanche.
O ailing Love, compose your struggling wing!
Oak-Leaves, The.
October—An Etching.
Ode to Silence.
Of all that ever in extreme disease.
Of what importance, O my lovely girls, my
　dancers, O my lovely boys.
Oh, Oh, you will be sorry for that word!
Oh, sleep forever in the Latmian cave.
Oh, think not I am faithful to a vow!
Olympian gods, mark now my bedside lamp.
On First Having Heard the Skylark.
On Hearing a Symphony of Beethoven.
On the Wide Heath.
On Thought in Harness.
Once more into my arid days like dew,
Only until this cigarette is ended.
Parsi Woman, The.
Passer Mortuus Est.
Pastoral: "If it were only still!"
Pear Tree, The.
Penitent, The.
Peril upon the paths of this desire.
Philosopher, The.
Pigeons, The.
Pity me not because the light of day.
Plaid Dress, The.
Plum Gatherer, The.
Poem and Prayer for an Invading Army.
Poet and His Book, The.
Pond, The.
Portrait.
Portrait by a Neighbour.
Pretty Love, I Must Outlive You.
Princess Recalls Her One Adventure, The.
Pueblo Pot.
Rabbit, The.
Ragged Island.
Read history: so learn your place in Time.
Read history: thus learn how small a space.
Recuerdo.
Renascence.
Rendezvous.
Return from Town, The.
Return, The.
Road to Avrillé, The.
Road to the Past, The.
Rosemary.
Sappho Crosses the Dark River into Hades.
Say that We Saw Spain Die.
Say what you will, and scratch my heart to
　find.
Scrub.

Sea at sunset can reflect, The.
Second Fig.
See how these masses mill and swarm.
Shall I be prisoner till my pulses stop.
She Is Overheard Singing.
Short Story.
Shroud, The.
Siege.
Since I cannot persuade you from this mood.
Since of no creature living the last breath.
Singing-Woman from the Wood's Edge, The.
Sky-coloured bird, blue wings with no more
    spots of spotless white.
Small Hands, Relinquish All.
Snow Storm, The.
Solid Sprite Who Stands Alone, The.
Some Things Are Dark.
Sometimes, oh, often, indeed, in the midst of
    ugly adversity, beautiful.
Sometimes when I am wearied suddenly.
Song: "Beautiful Dove, come back to us in
    April."
Song for Young Lovers in a City.
Song: "Gone, gone again is Summer the
    lovely."
Song of a Second April.
Sonnet: "Oh, my belovèd, have you thought of
    this."
Sonnet: "Time, that renews the tissues of this
    frame."
Sonnet to Gath.
Sonnet: "What lips my lips have kissed, and
    where, and why."
Sonnets from an Ungrafted Tree.
Sorrow.
Sorrowful dreams remembered after waking.
Souvenir.
Spring.
Spring and the Fall, The.
Spring in the Garden.
Spring Song.
Steepletop.
Still will I harvest beauty where it grows.
Strange thing that I, by nature nothing prone.
Strawberry Shrub, The.
Suicide, The.
Summer, be seen no more within this wood.
Sweet love, sweet thorn, when lightly to my
    heart.
Tavern.
Thanksgiving Dinner.
That Love at length should find me out and
    bring.
Theme and Variations.
There at Dusk I Found You.
There is a well into whose bottomless eye.
Think not, nor for a moment let your mind.
This beast that rends me in the sight of all.
This Dusky Faith.
This / Is mine, and I can hold it.
This should be simple; if one's power were
    great.
Those hours when happy hours were my estate.
Thou art not lovelier than lilacs,—no.
Thou famished grave, I will not fill thee yet.
Three Songs from "The Lamp and the Bell."
Three Songs of Shattering.
Through the Green Forest.
Thursday.
Time does not bring relief; you all have lied.
Time, that is pleased to lengthen out the day.
To a Calvinist in Bali.
To a Friend Estranged from Me.
To a Musician.
To a Poet that Died Young.
To a Snake.
To a Young Girl.
To a Young Poet.
To Elinor Wylie.
To hold secure the province of Pure Art.
To Inez Milholland.
To Jesus on His Birthday.
To Kathleen.
To One Who Might Have Borne a Message.
To S. M.
To S. V. B.—June 15, 1940.

To the Maid of Orleans.
To the Not Impossible Him.
To the Wife of a Sick Friend.
To Those Without Pity.
To whom the house of Montagu.
Tranquility at length, when autumn comes.
Travel.
Tree Ceremonies.
Tristan.
Truce for a Moment.
Truck-Garden Market-Day.
True Encounter, The.
Two Voices.
Underground System.
Unexplorer, The.
Upon this age, that never speaks its mind.
Valentine.
Visit to the Asylum, A.
We have gone too far; we do not know how to
    stop: impetus.
We talk of taxes, and I call you friend.
Weeds.
Well, I have lost you; and I lost you fairly.
West Country Song.
What chores these churls do put upon the
    great.
What rider spurs him from the darkening east.
What Savage Blossom.
What's this of death, from you who never will
    die?
When Caesar Fell.
When did I ever deny, though this was fleeting.
When I too long have looked upon your face.
When It Is Over.
When the tree-sparrows with no sound through
    the pearl-pale air.
When the Year Grows Old.
When we are old and these rejoicing veins.
When we that wore the myrtle wear the dust.
When you are dead, and your disturbing eyes.
When you, that at this moment are to me.
Where can the heart be hidden in the ground.
Whereas at morning in a jeweled crown.
Who hurt you so.
Wild-cat, gnat and I.
Wild Swans.
Wine from These Grapes.
Winter Night.
Witch-Wife.
Women have loved before as I love now.
Wood Road, The.
Wraith.
Yet in an hour to come, disdainful dust.
You loved me not at all, but let it go.
You say: "Since life is cruel enough at best."
Your face is like a chamber where a king.

Miller, Jane (b. 1925)
    Black Holes, Black Stockings, *sels.*
Milosz, Czeslaw (b. 1911)
    Abode.
    Account.
    Adam and Eve.
    After.
    After Enduring.
    After Paradise.
    After Traveling.
    Against the Poetry of Philip Larkin.
    Album of Dreams.
    Alcoholic Enters the Gates of Heaven, An.
    Aleksander Wat's Tie.
    All Hallows' Eve.
    Amazement.
    America.
    And the City Stood in Its Brightness.
    And Yet.
    And Yet the Books.
    Anka.
    Annalena.
    Appeal, An.
    Ars Poetica?
    Artificer.
    At a Certain Age.
    At Dawn.
    At Noon.
    At Yale.
    Autumn.

Awakened.
Ball, A.
Ballad of Levallois.
Before Majesty.
Beinecke Library.
Biography of an Artist.
Birth.
Blacksmith Shop.
Bobo's Metamorphosis.
Body.
Book in the Ruins, A.
Boy, A.
By a Stream.
Bypassing Rue Descartes.
Caesarea.
Caffé Greco.
Calling to Order.
Campo dei Fiori.
Capri.
Child of Europe.
Christoper Robin.
City of My Youth.
City, The.
City without a Name.
Confession, A.
Consciousness.
Counsels.
Craftsman.
Creating the World.
Dante.
Dawns.
Day of Generation.
December 1.
Dedication: "You whom I could not save."
Distance.
Dithyramb.
Early Morning.
Earth.
Either-Or.
Elegy for N. N.
Elegy for Y. Z.
Encounter.
Esse.
Evening.
Example.
Fall, The.
Family, A.
Far Away.
Far West.
Farewell: "I speak to you, my son."
Father Ch., Many Years Later.
Fear-Dream (1918).
Felicitous Life, A.
Filina.
Flight.
For Jan Lebenstein.
For My Eighty-eighth Birthday.
Forget.
Frivolous Conversation, A.
From My Dentist's Window.
From the Chronicles of the Town of Pornic.
From the Rising of the Sun.
Garden of Earthly Delights, The.
Garden of Earthly Delights, The: Hell.
Gardener.
Gates of the Arsenal, The.
Gathering Apricots.
Gift.
Good Night.
Greek Portrait.
Hall, A.
Happenings Elsewhere.
Happiness.
Head, The.
Helene.
Helene's Religion.
Heraclitus.
Higher Arguments in Favor of Discipline.
Honest Description of Myself with a Glass of
    Whiskey at an Airport.
Hooks of a Corset, The.
Hour, An.
How It Should Be in Heaven.
How It Was.
How Ugly.
Human Fly, A.

Hymn: "There is no one between you and me."
I Do Not Understand.
I Sleep a Lot.
Idea.
If.
In a Buggy at Dusk.
In a City.
In a Jar.
In a Parish.
In Black Despair.
In Common.
In Milan.
In Music.
In Salem.
In Szetejnie.
In Warsaw.
Incantation.
Incarnated.
Inheritor.
Initiation.
Into the Tree.
Island.
It Was Winter.
Journey, The.
Kazia.
King Popiel.
La Belle Époque.
L'Accélération de l'Histoire.
Lake.
Large finger-like leaves of an Hawaiian fern.
Lastingness.
Late Ripeness.
Lecture, A.
Legend, A.
Lessons.
Linnaeus.
Lithuania, After Fifty-two Years.
Magic Mountain, A.
Magpiety.
Mary Magdalen and I.
Master, The.
Meadow, A.
Meaning.
Meditation.
Mid-Twentieth-Century Portrait.
Mistake, A.
Mister Hanusevich.
Mittelbergheim.
My Faithful Mother Tongue.
My Grandfather Sigismund Kunat.
My-ness.
My Secrets.
Nation, A.
New Province, A.
1945.
1913.
No More.
Not This Way.
Notes.
O! ("O happiness! To see an iris").
O! ("O lips half opened, eyes half closed, the rosy nipple of your unveiled nakedness, Judith!").
O! ("O the quiet of water under the rocks, and the yellow silence of the afternoon").
O! ("O what sadness unaware that it's sadness!").
Obviously.
Ocean.
Ode for the Eightieth Birthday of Pope John Paul II.
Ode to a Bird.
Oeconomia Divina.
Old Women.
On a Beach.
On Angels.
On Parting with My Wife, Janina.
On Pilgrimage.
On Poetry, upon the Occasion of Many Telephone Calls after Zbigniew Herbert's Death.
On Prayer.
On the Death of a Poet.
On the Inequality of Men.
On the Other Side.

On the Road.
One and Many.
One More Contradiction.
One More Day.
Opposed to Each Other.
Pastels by Degas.
Pelicans.
Persons.
Philology.
Philosopher's Home, A.
Photograph, A.
Pierson College.
Plato's Dialogues.
Poet at Seventy.
Poetic State, A.
Polka-dot Dress, A.
Portal, A.
Portrait with a Cat, A.
Powers.
Prayer: "Approaching ninety, and still with a hope."
Preparation.
Prescription.
Proof.
Rays of Dazzling Light.
Reading the Japanese Poet Issa (1762–1826).
Reading the Notebook of Anna Kamienska.
Readings.
Realism.
Reconciliation.
Report.
Retired.
Return.
Return to Kraków in 1880.
Rite, The.
Rivers Grow Small.
Rivers ("'So lasting they are, the rivers!' Only think. Sources somewhere in the mountains").
Rivers ("Under various names, I have praised only you, rivers!").
Road-side Dog.
Rozewicz.
Run, A.
Sarajevo.
Seasons.
Secretaries.
Selecting Iwaszkiewicz's Poems.
Sentences.
Separate Notebooks, The.
Should, Should Not.
Six Lectures in Verse.
Skull, A.
Slow River.
So-called Life.
So Little.
Song on Porcelain.
Song, The: "Earth flows away from the shore where I stand."
Songs of Adrian Zieliński.
Specimens.
Spider.
Spirit of the Laws, The.
Statue of a Couple.
Story, A.
Study of Loneliness.
Submerged.
Table 1.
Table 2.
Task, A.
Temptation.
Texas.
Thankfulness.
Theodicy.
Thesis and Counter-Thesis.
They Will Place There Telescreens.
This.
This Only.
This World.
Thistle, the Nettle, The.
Those Corridors.
Three Talks on Civilization.
Throughout Our Lands.
Tidings.
To a Hazel Tree.
To Allen Ginsberg.

To find my home in one sentence, concise, as if hammered in metal.
To Mrs. Professor in Defense of My Cat's Honor and Not Only.
To My Daimonion.
To Raja Rao.
To Robert Lowell.
To Robinson Jeffers.
Translating Anna Swir on an Island of the Caribbean.
Treatise on Poetry, A.
Two Poems, sels.
Unde Malum.
Undressing Justine.
Veni Creator.
View, The.
Vipera Berus.
Voices of Poor People.
Voyeur.
Wall of a Museum, The.
Wanda.
Watering Can.
What Does It Mean.
What I Learned from Jeanne Hersch.
What Once Was Great.
When After a Long Life.
When the Moon.
Wherever.
Whiteness.
Why.
Window.
Winter.
With Her.
With not-quite truth.
With Trumpets and Zithers.
Woe!
World, The.
Year 1900, The.
Year, The.
Yellow Bicycle.
Yokimura.
You, Vanquished.
You Who Wronged.
You Whose Name.
Youth.
Zdziechowski.
Zone of Silence.

Milton, John (1608–74)
Another on the Same.
Arcades.
At a Solemn Music[k].
At a Vacation Exercise [in the Col[l]e[d]ge [, Part Latin, Part English]].
Canzone: "Scoffing, amorous maidens and young men."
Comus; a Masque Presented at Ludlow Castle.
Damon's Epitaph.
Elegiac Verses.
Elegy 1: To Charles Diodati.
Elegy 2: On the Death of the Beadle of Cambrdige University.
Elegy 3: On the Death of the Bishop of Winchester.
Elegy 4: To Thomas Young.
Elegy 6: To Charles Deodati.
Elegy 7: "Not yet did I know your laws, enticing Amathusia."
Elegy 5: On the Coming of Spring.
Epitaph on the Marchioness of Winchester, An.
Fable of the Peasant and the Overlord, The.
Hobsons Epitaph.
I with foolish mind and heedless zeal formerly.
Il Penseroso.
L'Allegro.
Lycidas.
Manso.
Nature Does Not Suffer Decay.
On His Deceased Wife.
On Shakespear[e].
On the Death of a Fair Infant Dying of a Cough.
On the Death of the Bishop of Ely.
On the Death of the Vice-Chancellor, a Physician.
On the Detraction Which Followed upon My Writing Certain Treatises.

On the Engraver of His Likeness.
On the Fifth of November.
On the Gunpowder Plot.
On the Inventor of Gunpowder.
On the Morning of Christ's Nativity.
On the Platonic Idea as Aristotle Understood It.
On the Same ["James derided the Purgatorial fire of the soul"].
On the Same ["Thus did you strive to vouchsafe James to Heaven"].
On the Same ["Whom impious Rome had just marked out for her curses"].
On the University Carrier Who Sick'n'd.
On Time.
Paradise Lost.
Paradise Regained [or Regain'd].
Paraphrase on Psalm 114, A.
Passion, The.
Philosopher on His Way to His Death.
Psalm 114.
Psalm 136.
Samson Agonistes.
Slothful Sleep.
Song: on [or of] May Morning.
Sonnet 1: "O Nightingale, that on yon bloomy Spray."
Sonnet 2: "Charming lady, she whose beautiful name honors."
Sonnet 3: "As on a rugged mountain at the darkening of evening."
Sonnet 4: "Diodati, and I will say it to you with wonder."
Sonnet 5: "In truth your fair eyes, my lady."
Sonnet 6: "Young, gentle, and candid lover that I am."
Sonnet 9: "Ladie [or Lady], that in the prime of earliest youth."
Sonnet: On the Religious Memorie of Mrs. Catherine Thomason.
To Charles Diodati.
To Christina.
To Cyriack Skinner.
To John Rouse.
To Leonora Singing in Rome.
To Mr. Lawrence.
To Mr. Cyriack Skinner upon His Blindness.
To Mr. H. Lawes On His Airs.
To My Father.
To Salzilli, a Roman Poet, Being Ill.
To Sir Henry Vane the Younger.
To the Lady Margaret Ley.
To the Lord General Cromwell.
To the Same ["Another Leonora captured the poet Torquato"].
To the Same ["Why, credulous Naples, do you vaunt your clear-voiced Siren"].
Translation of a Simile in Paradise Lost.
Upon the Circumcision.
Verse from Defensio Secunda.
Verse from Pro Populo Anglicano Defensio.
When the Assault Was Intended to the City.

Mir, M. Safdar
Elegy: "In the May breeze."

Mistral, Frédéric (1830–1914)
Mirèio, sels.
Obsession, The.

Mistral, Gabriela (Lucila Godoy Alcayaga) (1889–1957)
Air Flower, The.
Air, The.
Alpaca, The.
Argentine Round.
Artist's Decalogue, The.
Ballad: "He passed by with another woman."
Body, The.
Bones of the Dead, The.
Bread.
California Poppy.
Caribbean Sea.
Catalonian Woman.
Chilean Earth.
Christmas Star, The.
Close to Me.
Clover Patch.
Coconut Palms, The.

Concepción.
Confession.
Dawn.
Drops of Gall.
Dusk.
Escape, The.
Fig, The.
Flour.
For Noel.
Foreign Woman, The.
Fruit.
Future, The.
Giraffe, The.
God Wills It.
Grace.
Guardian Angel.
Heaven's Carriage.
Hollow Walnut, The.
In Praise of Gold.
In Praise of Salt.
In Praise of Small Towns.
In Praise of Stones.
Lady Spring.
Lark, The.
Little Box from Olinalá, The.
Little New Moon, The.
Mayten, The.
Morning.
Mother Pomegranate.
My Mother.
Night.
Other, The.
Owl, An.
Paradise.
Parrot, The.
Peacock, The.
Pine Forest.
Poplar Trees, The.
Prison Sentence, The.
Quechuan Song.
Rat, The.
Refreshment.
Request for Blanca, A.
Riches.
Rocking.
Rose, The.
Round of Aromas.
Round of Colors.
Round of the Rainbow.
Sad Mother, The.
Sea, The.
Slow Rain, The.
Song of the Dead Girls.
Sonnets of Death 5.
Summit.
Talcahuano.
Things.
Those Who Do Not Dance.
To See Him Again.
To the Clouds.
Useless Vigil, The.
Valparaíso.
Vigilant Woman, The.
Wall.
What Do You Feel Underground?
Wild Strawberry, The.
You Had Me.

Molière (Jean Baptiste Poquelin) (1622–73)
Tartuffe.

Molodovsky [or Molodowsky], Kadya (1894–1975)
There Are Such Springlike Nights.
White Night.

Montale, Eugenio (1896–1981)
Above the scribbled wall.
Agave on the Reef, The.
Anniversary.
Another Moon Effect.
Argyll Tour.
Ark, The.
Arsenio.
At first light, when.
Autumn Quarries.
Bagni di Lucca.
Balcony, The.
Ballad Written in a Hospital.

Bangs, The.
Bibe a Ponte all'Asse.
Black Trout, The.
Boats on the Marne.
Bring me the sunflower, let me plant it.
Buffalo.
Canebrake sends its little shoots, The.
Capercaillie, The.
Chrysalis.
Correspondences.
Costa San Giorgio.
Day and Night.
Dead, The.
Delta.
Distant, I was with you when your father.
Don't ask us for the word to frame.
Don't escape into the shade.
Dora Markus.
Earrings, The.
Eastbourne.
Eclogue: "It was good getting lost."
Eel, The.
Encounter.
End of Childhood.
English Horn.
Ezekiel Saw the Wheel.
Falsetto.
Fan, The.
Farewells, whistling in the dark, waves, coughs.
Feeble sistrum in the wind.
Fiesole Window.
Florentine Madrigals.
Flower that repeats, The.
Flux.
For an Album.
For an "Homage to Rimbaud."
Frog, first to strike his chord, The.
From a Swiss Lake.
From a Tower.
From the Train.
Frost on the windowpanes; the sick.
Garden, The.
Gerti's Carnival.
Glory of expanded noon.
Gondola that glides, The.
Green lizard, if it darts, The.
Happiness achieved, for you.
Haul your paper ships on the seared.
Hitler Spring, The.
Hoopoe, happy bird maligned.
Hope of even seeing you again, The.
House by the Sea.
House of the Customs Men, The.
I free your forehead of the ice.
I know a ray of sun (of God?) can still.
I know the moment when a raw grimace.
I think back on your smile, and for me it's a clear pool.
If They've Compared You.
In Sleep.
In the Greenhouse.
In the Park.
In the Park at Caserta.
In the Rain.
In the Style of Filippo De Pisis, on Sending Him This Book.
Incantation.
Indian Serenade.
Iris.
Is it salt that strafes or hail? It slays.
Keepsake.
Leaving a Dove.
Lemons, The.
Like a Fantasia.
Lindau.
Line of dancing children on the shore, The.
Little Testament.
Local Train.
Low Tide.
Magenta-colored clouds were gathering.
Magnolia's Shadow, The.
Many years, and one still harder.
Maybe one morning, walking in dry, glassy air.
Mediterranean.
Metropolitan Christmas, A.

Minstrels.
Moiré.
My life, I ask of you no stable.
Near Capua.
Near Finistère.
Near Siena.
Near Vienna.
New Stanzas.
News from Mount Amiata.
Often I've encountered evil.
Old Lines.
On an Unwritten Letter.
On the Greve.
On the Highest Column.
On the Llobregat.
On the Threshhold.
Other Lines.
Palio.
Parades of 1949, The.
Personae Separatae.
Pico Farnese Elegy.
Poems for Camillo Sbarbaro.
Pool.
Prisoner's Dream, The.
Promenade.
Punta del Mesco.
Red Lily, The.
Reed that softly, The
Return, The.
Sarcophagi.
Seacoasts, / a few blades of sword grass are
    enough.
See the sign; it flares.
Shears, don't cut away that face.
Shore of Versilia.
Sit the noon out, pale and lost in thought.
Slope.
So be it. Blare of a cornet.
Spirit that dispenses, The.
Stanzas: "I'm searching vainly for the point the
    blood."
Storm, The.
Summer.
Syria.
There the Tritone surges.
Times at Bellosguardo.
To Liuba, Leaving.
To My Mother.
Two in Twilight.
Valmorbia, flowering clouds of plants.
Visit to Fadin.
Voice That Came with the Coots.
Well's pulley creaks, The.
What you knew of me.
Where the tennis court once was.
White-and-black sine, The.
Why wait? The squirrel beats his torch-tail.
Wind on the Crescent.
Winter Light.
You know: I'm going to lose you again.
Your Flight.
Your hand was trying the keyboard.
You've named a tree for me? It isn't nothing.

Monti, Vincenzo (1754–1823)
Coward thought has struck me.

Moore, Marianne Craig (1887–1972)
Apparition of Splendor.
Arctic Ox, The.
Armor's Undermining Modesty.
Arthur Mitchell.
Avec Ardeur.
Baseball and Writing.
Bird-witted.
Blessed Is the Man.
Blue Bug.
Bowls.
Buffalo, The.
By Disposition of Angels.
Camellia Sabina.
Camperdown Elm, The.
Carnegie Hall: Rescued.
Carriage from Sweden, A.
Charity Overcoming Envy.
Combat Cultural.
Critics and Connoisseurs.
Dream.

Efforts of Affection.
Egyptian Pulled Glass Bottle in the Shape of a
    Fish, An.
Elephants.
England.
Enough ("Am I a fanatic? The opposite").
Enough ("Some in the Godspeed").
Expedient, An—Leonardo da Vinci's—and a
    Query.
Fables of La Fontaine, *sels.*
Face, A.
Fish, The.
For February 14th.
Four Quartz Crystal Clocks.
Frigate Pelican, The.
Granite and Steel.
Grave, A.
He "Digesteth Harde Yron."
He Wrote the History Book.
His Shield.
Hometown Piece for Messrs. Alston and
    Reese.
I May, I Might, I Must.
Icosasphere, The.
In Distrust of Merits.
In Lieu of the Lyre.
In the Days of Prismatic Color.
In the Public Garden.
In This Age of Hard Trying, Nonchalance Is
    Good and.
Injudicious Gardening.
Jellyfish, A.
Jerboa, The.
Keeping Their World Large.
Labors of Hercules, The.
Leonardo Da Vinci's.
Light is Speech.
Like a Bulwark.
Logic and The Magic Flute.
Love in America.
Magician's Retreat, The.
Marriage.
Melchior Vulpius.
Mercifully.
Mind, Intractable Thing, The.
Mind Is an Enchanting Thing, The.
Monkey Puzzle, The.
Monkeys, The.
Nevertheless.
New York.
Nine Nectarines.
No Better Than a "Withered Daffodil."
No Swan So Fine.
Nothing Will Cure the Sick Lion But To Eat an
    Ape.
Novices.
O To Be A Dragon.
Octopus, An.
Old Amusement Park.
Pangolin, The.
Paper Nautilus, The.
Part of a Novel, Part of a Poem, Part of a Play,
    sels.
Past Is the Present, The.
Pedantic Literalist.
People's Surroundings.
Peter.
Picking and Choosing.
Plumet Basilisk, The.
Poetry: "I, too, dislike it: there are things that
    are important beyond all this fiddle."
Prevalent At One Time.
Propriety.
Reminiscent of a Wave At the Curl.
Rescue With Yul Brynner.
Rigorists.
Rosemary.
Saint Nicholas.
Sea Unicorns and Land Unicorns.
Silence.
Smooth Gnarled Crape Myrtle.
Snakes, Mongooses, Snake-Charmers, and the
    Like.
Sojourn in the Whale.
Spenser's Ireland.
St. Valentine.

Staff of Aesculapius, The.
Student, The.
Style.
Sun.
Sycamore, The.
Tell Me, Tell Me.
Then the Ermine.
Those Various Scalpels.
Tippoo's Tiger.
To a Chameleon.
To a Giraffe.
To a Prize Bird.
To a Snail.
To a Steam Roller.
To Military Progress.
To Statecraft Embalmed.
To the Peacock of France.
To Victor Hugo of My Crow Pluto.
Tom Fool at Jamaica.
Values in Use.
Virginia Britannia.
Voracities and Verities Sometimes Are
    Interacting.
W. S. Landor.
Web One Weaves of Italy, The.
What Are Years?
When I Buy Pictures.
Wood Weasel, The.

Moraes, Vinícius de (b. 1913)
Song: "Never take her away."
Sonnet of Intimacy.

More, Saint Thomas *See* **More, Sir Thomas**

**More, Sir Thomas (Saint Thomas More) (1478–
1535)**
Astrologer, The.

**Mörike [*or* Möricke], Eduard Friedrich (1804–
75)**
Beauty Rohtraut.
Forest Murmurs.
Forsaken Girl, The.

**"Morshen, Nikolai Nikolaevich" (Nikolai
Nikolaevich Marchenko) (b. 1917)**
Two Poems.

Moschus (*fl.* 3d cent. B.C.)
By Moschus.
Fragment of the Elegy on the Death of Bion.
Out of the Greeke Cupid's Cryer.
Pan, Echo, and the Satyr.

Muldoon, Paul (b. 1951)
Aftermath.
Aisling.
Anseo.
Apple Slump.
Armageddon, Armageddon.
Asra.
At Martha's Deli.
At Master McGrath's Grave.
Avenue, The.
Bang.
Bangle (Slight Return), The.
Bangle, The.
Bearded Woman, by Ribera, The.
Beaver.
Bechbretha.
Behold the Lamb.
Between Takes.
Big Foot.
Big House, The.
Big Liz.
Birth, The.
Bishop, The.
Black Cat.
Blemish.
Blewits.
Blissom.
Blowing Eggs.
Boon.
Boundary Commission, The.
Bran.
Brazil.
Briefcase, The.
Brock.
Burma.
Capercaillies.
Cass and Me.

Cauliflowers.
Centaurs, The.
Cheesecake.
Cherish the Ladies.
Chinook.
Christo's.
Cider.
Clonfeacle.
Come into My Parlour.
Coney, The.
Country Club, The.
Cows.
Crossing the Line.
Cuba.
Cuckoo Corn.
Cure for Warts, The.
Dancers at the Moy.
De Secretis Mulierum.
Destroying Angel, The.
Ducking Stool, The.
Duffy's Circus.
Early Warning.
Earthquake, The.
Easter Island.
Edward Kienholz: *The State Hospital.*
Electric Orchard, The.
Elizabeth.
Epona.
Errata.
February.
Field Hospital, The.
Footling.
Fox, The.
Fridge, The.
Frog, The.
From Strength to Strength.
Gathering Mushrooms.
Geography Lesson, The.
Girls in the Poolroom, The.
Glanders.
Gold.
Gone.
Good Friday, 1971. Driving Westward.
Grass Widow.
Green Gown.
Grief.
Hay.
Hedgehog.
Hedges in Winter.
History.
Holy Thursday.
Hopewell Haiku.
Horses.
How to Play Championship Tennis.
Hug, The.
I Remember Sir Alfred.
Identities.
Immram.
Immrama.
Incantata.
Indians on Alcatraz, The.
Ireland.
Journey to Cracow, A.
Kate Whiskey.
Key, The.
Kissing and Telling.
Kissing Seat, The.
Lag.
Largesse.
Lass of Aughrim, The.
Last Poems, *sels.*
Leaving an Island.
Little Black Book, The.
Lives of the Saints.
Long Finish.
Longbones.
Lost Tribe, The.
Lull.
Lunch with Pancho Villa.
Ma.
Macha.
Madoc: A Mystery.
Making the Move.
Marriage of Strongbow and Aoife, The.
Mary Farl Powers: *Pink Spotted Torso.*
Meeting the British.

Merman, The.
Milkweed and Monarch.
Mink.
Mist-Net, The.
Mixed Marriage, The.
More a Man Has the More a Man Wants, The.
Mudroom, The.
Mules.
My Father and I and Billy Two Rivers.
My Grandfather's Wake.
Narrow Road to the Deep North, The.
Ned Skinner.
Nightingales.
Now, Now.
October 1950.
One Desire, The.
Ontario.
Oscar.
Our Lady of Ardboe.
Palm Sunday.
Panther, The.
Paris.
Party Piece.
Paul Klee: *They're Biting.*
Paunch.
Plot, The.
Plovers.
Point, The.
Princess and the Pea, The.
Profumo.
Promises, Promises.
Quoof.
Radio Horse, The.
Right Arm, The.
Rucksack, The.
Rune.
Salmon of Knowledge, The.
Seanchas.
7, Middagh Street.
Sightseers, The.
Skeffington's Daughter.
Sky-Woman.
Sleeve Notes.
Soap-Pig, The.
Something Else.
Something of a Departure.
Sonogram, The.
Sushi.
Symposium.
Tea.
They That Wash on Thursday.
Thinking of the Goldfish.
Three Deer, Mount Rose, August 1995.
Throwback, The.
Thrush.
Toe-Tag, The.
Tract.
Train, The.
Trance.
Trifle, A.
Truce.
Twice.
Unicorn Defends Himself, The.
Upriver Incident, The.
Vampire.
Vaquero.
Vespers.
Waking Father, The.
Weepies, The.
Whim.
White.
White Shoulders.
Why Brownlee Left.
Wind and Tree.
Wire.
Wishbone, The.
Wood, The.
Yarrow.
Year of the Sloes, for Ishi, The.
Yggdrasill.

Murray, Peter
    Receipt to Frighten away the Dean, A.
Muslih-Din [*or* Musliud-Din] *See* **Sadi [*or* Saadi**
    or **Sa'di],**

N

Nash, Dorothy (b. 1898)
    Do Sphinxes Think?
    Old Is for Books.
Nash, Ogden (1902–71)
    Absence Makes the Heart Grow Heart Trouble.
    Absentees, The.
    Advice outside a Church.
    After the Christening.
    All, All Are Gone, the Old Familiar
        Quotations.
    Allow Me, Madam, But It Won't Help.
    All's Brillig in Tin Pan Alley.
    Always Marry an April Girl.
    And How Keen Was the Vision of Sir Launfal?
    And Three Hundred and Sixty-Six in Leap
        Year.
    Anniversary, The.
    Ant, The.
    Any Millenniums Today, Lady?
    Anybody Else Hate Nickynames?
    Anybody for Money? or, Just Bring Your Own
        Basket.
    April Yule, Daddy!
    Are You a Snodgrass?
    Arthur.
    Aside to Husbands.
    Ask Daddy, He Won't Know.
    Asp, The.
    Assorted Chocolates.
    Astigmatic Naturalist, The.
    Away from It All.
    Bankers Are Just Like Anybody Else, Except
        Richer.
    Banquet, The.
    Barmaids Are Diviner Than Mermaids.
    Bas Ben Adhem, A.
    Bat, The.
    Beginner's Guide to the Ocean, A.
    Big Tent Under the Roof, The.
    Biological Reflection.
    Birdies, Don't Make Me Laugh.
    Birds, The.
    Birth Comes to the Archbishop.
    Birthday on the Beach.
    Boop-Boop-Adieup, Little Group!
    Brief Guide to New York, A.
    Brief Guide to Rhyming, or, How Be the Little
        Busy Doth?, A.
    Bugs.
    Bulletin Has Just Come In, A.
    Buses Headed for Scranton, The.
    Caesar Knifed Again, or, Culture Biz Gets
        Hep, Boffs Profs.
    Calendar-Watchers, or, What's So Wonderful
        about Being a Patriarch, The.
    Calf, The.
    Calling Spring VII-MMMC.
    Camel, The.
    Can I Get You a Glass of Water? or, Please
        Close the Glottis after You.
    Canary, The.
    Cantaloupe, The.
    Captain John Smith.
    Caraway Seed, The.
    Caribou, The.
    Carol for Children, A.
    Cat Naps Are Too Good for Cats.
    Caution to Everybody, A.
    Celery.
    Centipede, The.
    Chacun à Son Berlitz.
    Change Here for Wichita Falls, or, Has
        Anybody Seen My Wanderlust?
    Cherub, The.
    Child Is Father to the Man, But with More
        Authority, The.
    Children's Party.
    Child's Guide to Parents, A.
    Chipmunk, The.
    City, The.
    Clean Conscience Never Relaxes, A.
    Clean Platter, The.
    Club Car, The.

Mules, The.
"My Child Is Phlegmatic..."—Anxious Parent.
My Daddy.
My Dear, How Ever Did You Think Up This Delicious Salad?
My My.
My Trip Daorba.
Name Is Too Familiar, The.
Nature Knows Best.
Nature-Walks, or, Not to Mention a Dopping of Sheldrakes.
Necessary Dirge, A.
Never Mind the Overcoat, Button Up That Lip.
Nevertheless.
Next!
Nine Miles to the Railroad.
No Doctors Today, Thank You.
No Woe Is Gossamer to Mr. Bessemer.
No Wonder Our Fathers Died.
Not Even for Brunch.
Not George Washington's, Not Abraham Lincoln's, but Mine.
Nothing but Nature.
Now Tell Me About Yourself.
Now You See It, Now I Don't.
Nymph and the Shepherd, or She Went That-a-Way, The.
Oafishness Sells Good, Like an Advertisement Should.
Octopus, The.
Oh, Please Don't Get Up!
Oh, Shucks, Ma'am, I Mean Excuse Me.
Oh, Stop Being Thankful All over the Place.
Oh to Be Odd!
Old Men.
On Waking to the Third Rainy Morning of a Long Week End.
One Man's Meed Is Another Man's Overemphasis.
One Night in Oz.
One Third of a Calendar.
Our Child Doesn't Know Anything.
Out Is Out.
Outcome of Mr. Buck's Superstition, The.
Oyster, The.
Panther, The.
Pappy Wants a Poppy.
Parable for Sports Writers, Society Columnists, Bond Salesmen, and Poets.
Parent, The.
Parsley for Vice-President!
Parsnip, The.
Party Next Door, The.
Party, The.
Passionate Pagan and the Dispassionate Public, The.
Pediatric Reflection.
Peekaboo, I Almost See You.
People.
People upstairs, The.
Perfect Husband, The.
Period Period.
Phœnix, The.
Piano Tuner, Untune Me That Tune.
Pig, The.
Pipe Dreams.
Platitudinous Reflection.
Plea for a League of Sleep, A.
Please Keep on Forwarding.
Please Leave Father Alone.
Please Pass the Biscuit.
Political Reflection.
Polterguest, My Polterguest.
Poor Mr. Strawbridge.
Porcupine, The.
Porpoise, The.
Portrait of the Artist as a Prematurely Old Man.
Posies from a Second Childhood, or, Hark How Gaffer Do Chaffer.
Possessions Are Nine Points of Conversation.
Prayer at the End of a Rope.
Preface to the Past.
Pretty Halcyon Days.
Pride Goeth Before a Raise or Ah, There, Mrs. Cadwallader-Smith.

Private Dining Room, The.
Procrastination Is All of the Time.
Purist, The.
Put Back Those Whiskers, I Know You.
Queen Is in the Parlor, The.
Quick, Hammacher, My Stomacher!
Rabbits, The.
Rapunzel, Rapunzel, Let's Let Down Our Hair.
Raven, Don't Stay Away from My Door—A Chant for April First.
Reflection of the Fallibility of Nemesis.
Reflection On a Wicked World.
Reflection on Babies.
Reflection on Caution.
Reflection on Ingenuity.
Reflection on the Passage of Time, Its Inevitability and Its Quirks.
Reflections on Ice-breaking.
Reflections on the Vernacular.
Reminiscent Reflection.
Requiem: "There was a young belle of old Natchez."
Rhinoceros, The.
Riding on a Railroad Train.
Ring out the Old, Ring in the New, but Don't Get Caught in Between.
Roll On, Thou Deep and Dark Blue Copy Writer—Roll!
Rooster, The.
Sage of Darien, The.
Samson Agonistes.
Scram, Lion!
Screen with the Face with the Voice, The.
Sea-Gull, The.
Seaside Serenade.
Second Limick.
Second Month It's Not Itemized, The.
Sedative Reflection.
Seeing Eye to Eye Is Believing.
Self-Effacement of Electra Thorne, The.
September Is Summer, Too.
September Morn.
Seven Spiritual Ages of Mrs. Marmaduke Moore, The.
Shark, The.
Shinking Song.
Sic Semper Mr. Sherman's Temper, or Kindly Place Your Order in English.
Skink, The.
Slow Down, Mr. Ganderdonk, You're Late.
Smelt, The.
Snark Was a Boojum Was a Prawn, The.
Sniffle, The.
So Does Everybody Else, Only Not So Much.
So I resigned from the Chu Chin Chowder and Marching Club.
So Penseroso.
So That's Who I Remind Me Of.
Soliloquy in Circles.
Solitude of Mr. Powers, The.
Some of My Best Friends Are Children.
Song Before Breakfast.
Song for a Temperature of a Hundred and One.
Song for Ditherers.
Song for Pier Something or Other.
Song of the Open Road.
Song to Be Sung by the Father of Infant Female Children.
Splash!
Spring Comes to Murray Hill.
Spring Song.
Squirrel, The.
Stitch Too Late Is My Fate, A.
Strange Case of Mr. Ballantine's Valentine, The.
Strange Case of Mr. Fortague's Disappointment, The.
Strange Case of Mr. Niobob's Transmogrification, The.
Strange Case of Mr. O'Banion's Come-Uppance, The.
Strange Case of Mr. Palliser's Palate, The.
Strange Case of Mr. Pauncefoot's Broad Mind, The.
Strange Case of Mr. Wood's Frustration, The.
Strange Case of Mr. Donnybrooks's Boredom,

The.
Strange Case of the Ambitious Caddy, The.
Strange Case of the Blackmailing Dove, The.
Strange Case of the Cautious Motorist, The.
Strange Case of the Dead Divorcee, The.
Strange Case of the Entomologist's Heart, The.
Strange Case of the Girl o' Mr. Sponsoon's Dreams, The.
Strange Case of the Irksome Prude, The.
Strange Case of the Lovelorn Letter Writer, The.
Strange Case of the Lucrative Compromise, The.
Strange Case of the Pleasing Taxi-Driver, The.
Strange Case of the Renegade Lyric Writer, The.
Summer Serenade.
Summergreen for President.
Suppose He Threw It in Your Face.
Suppose I Darken Your Door.
Swan, The.
Table Talk.
Tableau at Twilight.
Taboo to Boot.
Tale of Custard the Dragon, The.
Tarkington, Thou Should'st Be Living in This Hour.
Tell It to the Eskimos or Tell it to the Esquimaux.
Termite, The.
Terrible People, The.
That Reminds Me.
That's Funny, Wasn't It? No, It Won't Be.
Theatrical Reflection.
There Are More Ways to Roast a Pig than Burning the House Down.
There Were Giants in Those Days or Maybe There Weren't.
There'll Always Be a War between the Sexes.
There's Always an Ubblebub.
There's Nothing Like Instinct, Fortunately.
They Won't Believe, on New Year's Eve, that New Year's Day Will Come What May.
Third Limick.
This Is My Own, My Native Tongue.
This Was Told Me in Confidence.
Thoughts Thought after a Bridge Party.
Thoughts Thought on an Avenue.
Thoughts Thought While Waiting for a Pronouncement from a Doctor.
Thunder over the Nursery.
Time Marches On.
Tin Wedding Whistle.
To a Lady Passing Time Better Left Unpassed.
To Ee Is Human.
Tomorrow, Partly Cloudy.
Tortoise, The.
Traveler's Rest.
Trouble with Women Is Men, The.
Try It Suns. and Hols.; It's Closed Then.
Tune for an Ill-Tempered Clavichord.
Turkey, The.
Turns in a Worm's Lane.
Turtle, The.
Tweedledee and Tweedledoom.
Two and One Are a Problem.
Two Dogs Have I.
Two Goes into Two Once, If You Can Get It There.
Two Songs for a Boss Named Mr. Longwell.
Unanswered by Request.
Under the Floor.
Unselfish Husband, The.
Unwinged Ones, The.
Up from the Egg; the Confessions of a Nuthatch Avoider.
Up from the Wheelbarrow.
Very Funny, Very Funny.
Very Unclubbable Man, The.
Visit From Dr. Fell, A.
Visit, The.
Visitors Laugh at Locksmiths.
Voluble Wheel Chair, The.
Wapiti, The.
Warning to Wives, A.
Wasp, The.

Watched Example Never Boils, A.
Watchman, What of the First First Lady?
We Don't Need to Leave Yet, Do We? Or, Yes We Do.
We Would Refer You to Our Service Department, If We Had One.
Wednesday Matinee.
Wendigo, The.
What Almost Every Woman Knows Sooner or Later.
What I Know About Life.
What Is Bibbidi-Bobbidi-Boo in Sanskrit?
What, No Oysters?
What, No Sheep?
What the Well-Read Patient Is Talking About, or, Look, Ma, What I Got!
What to Do until the Doctor Goes or It's Tomorrow Than You Think.
What's in a Name? Here's What's in a Name.
What's in a Name? Some Letter I Always Forget.
What's the Matter, Haven't You Got Any Sense of Humor?
What's the Use.
When the Devil Was Sick Could He Prove It?
When You Say That, Smile! or All Right Then, Don't Smile.
Where There's a Will, There's Velleity.
Who Called That Robin a Piccolo Player?
Who Did Which? or Who Indeed?
Who Taught Caddies to Count? or A Burnt Golfer Fears the Child.
Who Understands Who Anyhow?
Why the Postman Has to Ring Twice, or, Yellow Envelope, Where Have You Gone?
Wild Jackass, The.
Will Consider Situation.
Will You Have Your Tedium Rare or Medium?
Woman Pulls the Wires.
Wombat, The.
Word about Winter, A.
Word on Wind, A.
Yes and No.
You and Me and P.B. Shelley.
You Bet Travel Is Broadening.
You Can Be a Republican, I'm a Genocrat.
You Have More Freedom in a House.
Your Lead, Partner, I Hope We've Read the Same Book.

Naso, Publius Ovidius *See* **Ovid**

Nemerov, Howard (b. 1920)
Above.
According to His Seasons.
Advice from the Holy Tomb.
After Commencement.
Aftermath.
Again.
Ahasuerus.
Amnesty.
Analogue.
And Is Silent.
Angel and Stone.
Anniversary.
Antigone.
Armistice.
Ars Poetica.
Art Song.
At a Country Hotel.
At the Airport.
August, 1945.
Autumnal.
Backward Look, The.
Bacterial War, The.
Baron Baedeker Blew His Nose and, Sighing, Departed, The.
Beautiful Lawn Sprinkler, The.
Beekeeper Speaks, The.
Beginner's Guide.
Behavior.
Being of Three Minds.
Between the Window and the Screen.
Beyond the Pleasure Principle.
Blue Suburban.
Blue Swallows, The.
Book of Kells, The.
Boom!

Boy with Book of Knowledge.
Brainstorm.
Breaking of Rainbows, The.
Brief Journey West, The.
Brueghel: The Triumph of Time.
Burning the Leaves.
Cabinet of Seeds Displayed, A.
Cain.
Canossa.
Capitals.
Carol: "Now is the world withdrawn all."
Casting.
Celestial Globe.
Central Park.
Cherry Tree, The.
Christmas Morning.
Chromium-Plated Hat. Inlaid with Scenes from Siegfried, A.
Clock With No Hands, A.
Cloud Seeding.
Common Saw, A.
Common Wisdom, The.
Companions, The.
Consent, The.
Conversing with Paradise.
Cosmic Comics.
Creation Myth on a Moebius Band.
Creation of Anguish.
Critic.
Crocodile at the Ancient Tombs.
Crossing, The.
Cuckoo King, The.
Cybernetics.
Daily Globe, The.
Dancer's Reply, The.
Dandelions.
Day on the Big Branch, A.
De Anima.
Dead River.
Death and the Maiden.
Death of God, The.
Debate with the Rabbi.
Decorated Skull in a University Museum.
Deep Woods.
Departure of the Ships.
Dependencies, The.
Deposition, The.
Dial Tone, The.
Dialectical Songs.
Dialogue.
Distances They Keep, The.
Distraction.
Don Juan to the Statue.
Doomsday Books, The.
Dragonfly, The.
Drama.
Drawing Lessons.
Dream of Flying Comes of Age, The.
Druidic Rimes.
Du rêve, de la mathématique, et de la mort.
Earthquake in the West, The.
Ecstasies of Dialectic, The.
Einstein & Freud & Jack.
Elegy for a Nature Poet.
Elegy of Last Resort.
End of Summer School, The.
Endegeeste.
Ending, An.
Endor.
Enthusiasm for Hats.
Epigrams.
Epitaph: "Crazy, girls, crazy. Don is gone."
Epitaph: "Of the Great World he knew not much."
Epitaph on a Philosopher the Reports of Whose Death Have Been Grossly Minimized.
Equations of a Villanelle.
Europe.
Eve.
Exasperations of a Novelist.
Extract from Memoirs.
Fable of the War, A.
Fables of the Moscow Subway.
Fall Again, The.
Fall Song.

False Solomon's Seal.
Fiction.
Figures of Thought.
First Day, The.
First Leaf, The.
First Point of Aries, The.
First Snow.
Flame of a Candle, The.
Flower Arrangements.
Fontenelle.
For Robert Frost, in the Autumn, in Vermont.
For the Squadron.
For W———, Who Commanded Well.
Fortune Teller, The.
Four Ages, The.
Four Sonnets.
Fourth of July, The.
Fragment from Correspondence.
From a Record of Disappointment.
From the Desk of the Laureate: For Immediate Release.
Frozen City, The.
Fugue.
Full Professor, A.
Ginkgoes in Fall.
Glass Dialectic.
Gnomes.
God of This World, The.
Going Away.
Goldfish.
Goose Fish, The.
Grace to Be Said at the Supermarket.
Grace to Be Said before Committee Meetings.
Grand Central, with Soldiers, in Early Morning.
Great Society, Mark X, The.
Growing a Ghost.
Guide to the Ruins.
Gulls, The.
Gyroscope.
Harvest Home, A.
He.
Hero Comes Home in His Hamper, and Is Exhibited at the World's Fair, The.
Hero with Girl and Gorgon.
Hide & Seek.
History of a Literary Movement.
History of Hair from World War II to the Present.
Holding the Mirror Up to Nature.
Home for the Holidays.
Hope.
Human Condition, The.
Human Things.
I Only Am Escaped Alone to Tell Thee.
Icehouse in Summer, The.
Idea.
In the Black Museum.
In the Commercial Gardens.
In the Glass of Fashion.
Instructions for Use of This Toy.
Interiors.
Interview, An.
Iron Characters, The.
Issue of Life, An.
Journey of the Snowmen.
Junction, on a Warm Afternoon, The.
Keeping Informed in D.C.
Kicks.
Knowledge.
Landscape with Figures.
Late Butterflies.
Late Late Show.
Late Summer.
Lean and Hungry Look, A.
Learning by Doing.
Learning the Trees.
Life, A.
Life Cycle of Common Man.
Lightning Storm on Fuji.
Limits.
Lines & Circularities.
Lion & Honeycomb.
Lives of Gulls and Children, The.
Lobsters.
Loon's Cry, The.

Lore.
Lot Later.
Lot's Wife.
Madrigal: "She is the darkness where I
    wander."
Maestria.
Maia.
Maiden with Orb and Planets.
Make Big Money at Home! Write Poems in
    Spare Time!
Make Love Not War.
Mapmaker on His Art, The.
Market-Place, The.
Marriage of Heaven and Earth, The.
Mars.
Master at a Mediterranean Port, The.
May Day Dancing, The.
Measure of Poetry, The.
Memory of My Friend, A.
Memory of the War, A.
Metamorphoses.
Metaphysical Automobile, The.
Metropolitan Sunday.
Midsummer's Day.
Mirror, The.
Mrs. Mandrill.
Modern Poet, A.
Moment.
Money.
Moonshine.
Morality, A.
Morning Sun.
Moses.
Most Expensive Picture in the World, The.
Mousemeal.
Mud Turtle, The.
Murder of William Remington, The.
Mystery Story.
Myth & Ritual.
Nature Morte.
Near the Old People's Home.
Nebuchadnezzar, Solus.
Negro Cemetery Next to a White One, A.
New Weapons in the Old War.
Nicodemus.
Night before Christmas, The.
Nightmare.
Nothing Will Yield.
Novelists.
Observation of October.
Of Experience.
Old Colonial Imperialist, An.
Old Country, The.
Old Days, The.
Old Photograph, An.
Old Picture, An.
Old Soldiers' Home, The.
Old Warplane, An.
On a Text: Jonah IV, xi.
On Being a Member of the Jury for a Poetry
    Prize.
On Being Asked for a Peace Poem.
On Certain Wits.
On Getting Out Of Vietnam.
On Reading "The Love and Death of Cornet
    Christopher Rilke."
On the Platform.
On the Threshold of His Greatness, the Poet
    Comes Down With a Sore Throat.
One Forever Alien.
One Moment in Eternity.
One Way.
Origin.
Orphic Scenario.
Ozymandias II.
Painter Dreaming in the Scholar's House, The.
Painting a Mountain Stream.
Paraphrase from Notebooks.
Peace in Our Time.
Philosophy.
Phoenix, The.
Photograph of a Girl, The.
Picture, A.
Place of Value, The.
Plane.
Playing Skittles.

Playing the Inventions.
Pockets.
Poem of Margery Kempe, A.
Poet as Eagle Scout, The.
Poet at Forty, The.
Polonius Passing Through a Stage.
Pond, The.
Portrait of Three Conspirators.
Poverty Programs, The.
Power to the People.
Praising the Poets of That Country.
Predecessor of Perseus, A.
Presidential Address to a Party of Exiles.
Priest's Curse on Dancing, The.
Primer of the Daily Round, A.
Prism.
Private Eye, The.
Projection.
Puzzle, The.
Quaerendo Invenietis.
Quarry, The.
Questions.
Race, The.
Realities.
Redeployment.
Reflexion of a Novelist.
Reflexions on the Seizure of the Suez.
Refusal of a Kindness Offered.
Relation of Art and Life, A.
Remorse for Time, The.
Rent in the Screen, The.
Returning to Europe.
Riddle the Sphinx Forgot, A.
Rope's End, The.
Route Two.
Runes.
Salt Garden, The.
Sanctuary, The.
Sandpipers.
Santa Claus.
Sarabande.
Sarajevo.
Scales of the Eyes, The.
Second-Best Bed, The.
Seeing Things.
September Shooting.
September, the First Day of School.
Sestina 1: "Thickness of paint or flesh cannot
    deface."
Sestina 2: "No waste is trackless: all terrain the
    lost."
Seven Macabre Songs.
Shells.
Sightseers.
Singular Metamorphosis, A.
Situation Does Not Change, The.
Sleeping Beauty.
Small Moment.
Small Moon.
Snow Globe, The.
Snowflakes.
Soldier Who Lived Through the War, The.
Solipsism & Solecism.
Somewhere.
Song of Degrees, A.
Song: "Provide your friend with almanacs."
Sonnet at Easter.
Sonnet: "Form of Christ cut from dark wood,
    the pale, A."
Sonnet: "It seems to be the trouble, everyone."
Speculation.
Spell before Winter, A.
Spy, The.
Stare of the Man from the Provinces, The.
Statues in the Public Gardens, The.
Steps for a Dancer.
Still Life I.
Still Life II.
Still Life III.
Storm Windows.
Strange Metamorphosis of Poets.
Student Dies in 100 Yard Dash.
Style.
Suburban Prophecy.
Succession.
Summer's Elegy.

Sunday.
Sunday at the End of Summer.
Sunderland.
Sunglasses, The.
Sweeper of Ways, The.
Tale.
Tapestry, The.
There.
These Words Also.
Thirtieth Anniversary Report of the Class of
    '41.
This, That, & the Other.
Thought.
Thought of Trees, The.
Threshold.
To a Friend.
To a Scholar in the Stacks.
To Clio, Muse of History.
To D———, Dead by Her Own Hand.
To David, about His Education.
To H. M.
To Lu Chi.
To My Least Favorite Reviewer.
To the Babylonians.
To the Bleeding Hearts Association of
    American Novelists.
To the Governor & Legislature of
    Massachusetts.
To the Mannequins.
To the Memory of John Wheelwright.
To the Poets.
To the Rulers.
Town Dump, The.
Translation.
Trees.
Trial and Death, a Double Feature.
Triumph of Education, The.
Truth.
Truth of the Matter, The.
TV.
Two Girls.
Two Pair.
Two Poems.
Two Sides to an Outside: Meditation from
    Empson.
Two Views of a Philosopher.
Under the Bell Jar.
Unscientific Postscript.
Vacuum, The.
Vermeer.
View from an Attic Window, The.
View from Pisgah, The.
View, The.
Virgin and Martyr.
Waiting Rooms.
Walking Down Westgate in the Fall.
Warning: Children at Play.
Watching Football on TV.
Way of Life, A.
Weather of the World, The.
Western Approaches, The.
What Kind of a Guy Was He?
Wheel King, The.
Who Did Not Die in Vain.
Winter Exercise.
Winter Lightning, The.
Wolves in the Zoo.
World as Brueghel Imagined It, The.
Writing.
Young Woman.
Zalmoxis.
Zander on God.

**Neruda, Pablo (Neftalí Ricardo Reyes Basualto)
(1904–73)**
All Seated.
Ambassador, The.
Another.
Another One.
Bell-Ringer, The.
Bell Tower of Authenay, The.
Bird.
Bomb (II).
Century Dying, A.
Cherries.
Child of the Moon.
Cold.

Coming Back.
Conditions.
Danger, The.
Dead Dog.
Different Ship, A.
Dying.
Earth.
Egoist.
Final.
First Winter.
Gift, The.
Heavy Surf, A.
Heights of Macchu Picchu, III, The.
Herbalist's Rose, The.
Homecomings.
I Come Back from a Journey.
I Went.
Initial.
Inside.
Let's Wait.
Little Devils.
Midday Construction.
Negative Hands.
XIX, The.
Ode to Laziness.
Oliverio Girondo.
One Comes Back.
Pardon Me.
Pedro Is When.
Physics.
Possessions.
Question Book, *sels.*
Red Bird, *sels.*
Runaway Sun.
Same Story.
Search.
Separate Rose, The, *sels.*
Sick Man in the Sun.
Sitting Down.
Skystones, *sels.*
Some Beasts.
Some Creature.
Star.
Successions.
This Broken Bell.
This Is Simple.
To Puente Curvo on the Maldonado Spit in
    Uruguay.
Today How Many Hours.
Today Isn't Everything.
2 8 3 2 5 6 7 4 5 4 9.
Untenable Situation, An.
Wars, The.
Winter.

Nerval, Gérard de (Gérard Labrunie) (1808–55)
Antéros.
Mute Phenomena, The.

Ní Chonaill, Eibhlín
Keen.

Ni Dhomhnaill, Nuala (b. 1952)
Orphan at the Door, An.
Race, The.

Niedecker, Lorine (b. 1903)
Adirondack Summer.
Ah your face.
Alcoholic dream.
Alliance.
Allied Convoy / Reaches Russia.
Alone / a still state hard.
Along the river / wild sunflowers.
Am I real way out in space.
And what you liked.
Art Center.
As I paint the street.
As I shook the dust.
As praiseworthy / The power of breathing.
Asa Gray wrote Increase Lapham.
Ash woods, willow, close to shore.
Audubon.
Automobile Accident.
Autumn.
Autumn Night.
Badlands, The.
Ballad of Basil, The.
Bashō.
Beautiful girl.

Beyond What.
Bird singing.
Birds' mating-fight.
Black Hawk held: In reason.
Bombings.
Bonpland.
Boy tossed the news, The.
Broad-leaved Arrow-head, The.
Brought the enemy down.
Brown muskrat, noiseless, The.
Cabin door flew open, The.
Can knowledge be conveyed that isn't felt?
Canvass.
Chicory Flower / on Campus.
Chimney Sweep.
Churchill's Death.
City Talk.
Cleaned all surfaces.
Clothesline post is set, The.
Club 26.
Come In.
Coming out of Sleep.
Consider.
Consider at the outset.
Coopered at Fish Creek.
Could You Be Right.
Country's economics sick, A.
Cricket-song.
Darwin.
Dead / she now lay deaf to death.
Dear Mona, Mary and all.
Dear Paul: / the sheets of your father's book of
    poetry.
Death of my poor father, The.
Depression Years.
Domestic and Unavoidable.
Don't shoot the rail!
Don't tell me property is sacred!
Du Bay.
Dusk— / He's spearing from a boat.
Easter.
Easter Greeting.
Elegant office girl, The.
Element Mother, The, *sels.*
Eleventh of progressional, The.
Energy glows at the lips.
European Travel / (Nazi New Order).
Fall.
Fancy Another Day Gone.
February almost March bites the cold.
Florida.
Fog-thick morning.
For best work.
For Exhibition.
For sun and moon and radio.
Foreclosure.
Frog noise / suddenly stops.
From my bed I see.
Gen. Rodimstev's Story / (Stalingrad).
Get a load.
Government men said Don't plant wheat, The.
Grampa's got his old age pension.
Hand Crocheted Rug.
Happy New Year.
He built four houses.
He lived—childhood summers.
He moved in light.
Hear / where her snow-grave is.
Here it gives the laws for fishing thru the ice.
Hi, Hot-and-Humid.
High, lovely, light.
His Carpets Flowered.
Hop press.
Horse, hello.
Hospital Kitchen.
How bright you'll find young people.
How white the gulls.
I am sick with the Time's buying sickness.
I doubt I'll get silk stockings out.
I fear this war.
I hear the weather.
I Heard.
I knew a clean man.
I lost you to water, summer.
I married.
I rose from marsh mud.

I said to my head, Write somethng.
I sit in my own house.
I spent my money.
I Visit / the Graves.
I walked / from Chicago to Big Bull Falls
    (Wausau).
If he is of constant depth.
If I Were a Bird.
If only my friend.
I'm a sharecropper.
In Europe they grow a new bean while here.
In Leonardo's light.
In moonlight lies.
In the great snowfall before the bomb.
In the transcendence.
I've been away from poetry.
Jefferson and Adams.
Jesse James and his brother Frank.
Jim Poor's his name.
July, waxwings.
Just before she died.
Katharine Anne.
Keen and lovely man moved as in a dance.
L. Z ("Acre of music, An").
Lady in the Leopard Coat,
Lake Superior.
Land of four o'clocks is here, The.
Last night the trash barrel.
Laundromat.
Laval, Pomeret, Pétain.
Lawnmower's one of the babies I'd have, A.
Let's play a game.
Letter from Ian.
Letter from Paul.
Lights, lifts.
Linnaeus in Lapland.
Look close.
Look, the woods, the sky, our home.
Lugubre for a child.
LZ ("He walked—loped—the bridge").
LZ's.
Man of law, The.
March.
Margaret Fuller.
Memorial Day.
Men leave the car, The.
Missus Dora.
Mr. Van Ess bought 14 washcloths?
Monster owl, A.
Motor cars / like china.
Mourning Dove.
Museum man!, The.
Music, lady, The.
Musical Toys.
My coat threadbare.
My father said "I remember."
My friend the black and white collie.
My friend tree.
My Life by Water.
My life is hung up.
My man says the wind blows from the south.
My mother saw the green tree toad.
Nearly landless and on the way to water.
New! / Reason explodes. Atomic split.
New-sawed.
News.
Next Year or I Fly My Rounds Tempestuous.
1937.
No matter where you are.
No retiring summer stroke.
Not all harsh sounds displease.
Not all that's heard is music. We leave.
Not feeling well, my wood uncut.
Nothing nourishing.
Nothing to speak of.
Now go to the party.
Now in one year.
Number of Britons killed, The.
Nursery Rhyme.
O late fall.
O let's glee glow as we go.
O Tannenbaum.
Obliteration, The.
Oh ivy green.
Old Hamilton hailed the man from the grocery
    store.

Old man who seined.
Old Mother turns blue and from us.
On a Row of Cabins / Next My Home.
On Columbus Day he set out for the north.
On Hearing / the Wood Pewee.
Otherwise.
Paean to Place.
Park / "a Darling Walk / for the Mind," The.
Paul, hello / what do you know.
Paul / now six years old.
Paul / when the leaves.
Peace.
People, people.
Petrou his name was sorrow.
Pioneers.
Poems at the Porthole.
Poet Percival said: I struck a lode.
Poet's Work.
Popcorn-can cover.
President of the Holding Company, The.
Progression.
Property is poverty.
Regards to Mr. Glover.
River-marsh-drowse.
Santayana's.
Scuttle up the workshop.
Scythe.
See the girls in shorts on their bicycles.
Seven years a charming woman wore.
She grew where every spring.
She had tumult of the brain.
She was a mourner too. Now she's gone.
Shut up in woods.
Sky / in my favor.
Slip of a girl-announcer, The.
So He Said / on Radio.
So this was I.
So you're married, young man.
Some float off on chocolate bars.
Some have chimes.
Something in the water.
Sorrow moves in wide waves.
Spirals.
Spring / stood there.
Springtime's wide.
Stage Directions.
Student, A.
Subliminal.
Summer's away, I traded my chicks for trees.
Sunday's motor-cars.
Swedenborg.
Swept snow, Li Po.
Synamism.
T. E. Lawrence.
Tea.
Tell me a story about the war.
Ten o'clock.
Terrible things coming up.
That woman!—eyeing houses.
Their apples fall down.
There was a bridge once that said I'm going.
There's a better shine.
They came at a pace.
They live a cool distance.
They've lost their leaves.
Thomas Jefferson.
Thomas Jefferson Inside.
Three Americans.
Thure Kumlien.
To a Maryland Editor, 1943.
To Aeneas who closed his piano.
To foreclose.
To My Pres- / sure Pump.
To My Small / Electric Pump.
To Paul now old enough to read.
To see the man who took care of our stock.
To war they kept.
To whom / can I leave.
Traces of Living Things.
Tradition.
Transition.
Trees over the roof.
Troubles to win.
Truth / gives heat.
Two old men.
Understand me, dead is nothing.

Van Gogh.
Van Gogh could see.
Violin Debut.
Voyageurs / sang, rowed.
War.
Wartime.
Watching Dan- / cers on Skates.
We know him—Law and Order League.
We physicians watch the juices rise.
What a woman!—hooks men like rugs.
What bird would light.
What horror to awake at night.
When brown folk lived a distance.
When do we live again Ann.
When Johnny (Chapman) Appleseed.
White / among the green pads.
Who was Mary Shelley?
Why can't I be happy.
Wild and wavy event, The.
Wild strawberries.
Wilderness.
Will You Write Me a Christmas Poem?
Wintergreen Ridge.
Woman in middle life.
Woman with Umbrella.
Working man appeared in the street, A.
You are my friend.
You know, he said, they used to make.
You see here.
Young girl to marry.
Young in Fall I said: the birds.
Young ones go away to school, The.
Your erudition.
Your father to me in your eighth summer.

Nijhoff, Martinus
    Song of the Foolish Bees.
Nimatullah [or Ni'matu'llah], Seid [or Sayyid] (d. 1431)
    Song of Seyd [or Seid] Nimetollah of Kuhistan.
Nonnus (fl. 5th cent.)
    Dionysiaca, sels.
Norton, John (1651–1716)
    Funeral Elegy Upon that Pattern and Patron of Virtue, A.

O

Ocampo, Silvina
    Infinite Horses, The.
O'Hara, Frank (1926–66)
    Adieu to Norman, Bon Jour to Joan and Jean-Paul.
    Alma.
    Animals.
    Ann Arbor Variations.
    Answer to Voznesensky and Evtushenko.
    Anxiety.
    Argonauts, The.
    Ashes on a Saturday Afternoon.
    Aus Einem April.
    Autobiographia Literaria.
    Ave Maria.
    Avenue A.
    Biotherm [for Bill Berkson].
    Blocks.
    Captain Bada.
    Chez Jane.
    Colloque Sentimental.
    Commercial Variations.
    Cornkind.
    Critic, The.
    Day and Night in 1952.
    Day Lady Died, The.
    Easter.
    Essay on Style.
    F. (Missive & Walk) I. #53.
    Fantasy.
    First Dances.
    For Grace, after a Party.
    For James Dean.
    For the Chinese New Year and for Bill Berkson.
    Getting Up Ahead of Someone (Sun).

Hatred.
Having a Coke with You.
Heroic Sculpture.
Hôtel Transylvanie.
Hunter, The.
Image of Leda, An.
Image of the Buddha Preaching.
In Favor of One's Time.
In Memory of My Feelings.
Interior (With Jane).
Invincibility.
Jane Awake.
Joe's Jacket.
John Button Birthday.
July Is Over and There's Very Little Trace.
Kitville.
Les Étiquettes Jaunes.
Les Luths.
Lover, The.
Mary Desti's Ass.
Mayakovsky.
Meditations in an Emergency.
Memorial Day 1950.
Mexican Guitar, A.
Mozart Chemisier.
Muse Considered As a Demon Lover, The.
Music.
My Heart.
My Heat.
Naphtha.
1951.
Now That I Am in Madrid and Can Think.
Ode: "Idea of justice may be precious, An."
Ode on Causality.
Ode on Necrophilia.
Ode: Salute to the French Negro Poets.
Ode (To Joseph Lesueur) on the Arrow That Flieth by Day.
Ode to Michael Goldberg ('s Birth and Other Births).
Ode to Tanaquil Leclercq: "Smiling through my own memories of painful excitement your wide eyes."
On Looking at La Grande Jatte, the Czar Wept Anew.
On Rachmaninoff's Birthday ("You'll never be mentally sober").
On Rachmaninoff's Birthday ("Tenderly upon your cold, tired eyes").
On Seeing Larry Rivers' Washington Crossing the Delaware at the Museum of Modern Art.
Pastoral Dialogue, A.
Personal Poem.
Petit Poème en Prose.
Pleasant Thought from Whitehead, A.
Poem: "And tomorrow morning at 8 o'clock in Springfield, Massachusetts."
Poem: "At night Chinamen jump."
Poem: "Eager note on my door said "Call me," The."
Poem: "Hate is only one of many responses."
Poem: "I don't know as I get what D.H. Lawrence is driving at."
Poem: "I ran through the snow like a young Czarevitch!"
Poem: "I watched an armory combing its bronze bricks."
Poem in Envy of Cavalcanti, A.
Poem In January.
Poem: "Instant coffeee with slightly sour cream."
Poem: "Ivy is trembling in the hammock, The."
Poem: "Khrushchev is coming on the right day!"
Poem: "Let's take a walk, you."
Poem: "Light clarity avocado salad in the morning."
Poem: "Now it is the 27th."
Poem: "Now the violets are all gone, the rhinoceroses, the cymbals."
Poem: "O solo mio, hot diggety, nix 'I wather think I can'."
Poem Read at Joan Mitchell's.
Poem: "So many echoes in my head."
Poem: "That's not a cross look it's a sign of

life."
Poem: "There I could never be a boy."
Poem: "To be idiomatic in a vacuum."
Poem: "Twin spheres full of fur and noise."
Poem V (F) W.
Poem: "When I am feeling depressed and
    anxious sullen."
Poetry.
Post the Lake Poets Ballad.
Postcard from John Ashbery, A.
Radio.
Rant, A.
Rhapsody.
Romanze, or the Music Students.
Saint.
St. Paul and All That.
Savoy.
Second Avenue.
Sleeping on the Wing.
Song: "Is it dirty."
Sonnet for Jane Freilicher, A.
Spirit Ink, The.
Spleen.
Step Away from Them, A.
Steps.
Summer Breezes.
Tarquin.
Terrestrial Cuckoo, A.
Three-Penny Opera, The.
To a Poet.
To Gottfried Benn.
To Hell with It.
To Jane; and in Imitation of Coleridge.
To the Film Industry in Crisis.
To the Harbormaster.
Today.
True Account of Talking to the Sun at Fire
    Island, A.
"Unfinished," The.
Variations on Pasternak's "Mein Liebchen, Was
    Willst Du Noch Mehr?"
Walking to Work.
What Appears to Be Yours.
Why I Am Not a Painter.
You Are Gorgeous and I'm Coming.
Young Poet, A.

Oliver, Mary (b. 1935)
Acid.
Alex.
Alligator Poem.
Anne.
Answers.
At Blackwater Pond.
August.
Aunt Elsie's Night Music.
Aunt Leaf.
Bailing the Boat.
Being Country Bred.
Beyond the Snow Belt.
Bitterness, A.
Black Snake, The.
Black Walnut Tree, The.
Blossom.
Bone Poem.
Buck Moon—From the Field Guide to Insects.
Buddha's Last Instruction, The.
Certain Sharpness in the Morning Air, A.
Clam Man.
Creeks.
Crossing the Swamp.
Crows.
Dogfish.
Dream of Trees, A.
Dreams.
Egret, The.
Egrets.
Encounter.
Entering the Kingdom.
Esquimos Have No Word for "War," The.
Family, The.
Farm Country.
Field near Linden, Alabama.
First Snow.
Fish, The.
Five A.M. in the Pinewoods.
Gannets.

Ghosts.
Going to Walden.
Goldenrod.
Goldfinches.
Happiness.
Hattie Bloom.
Hawk.
Her Grave.
Hermit Crab, The.
House, The.
Hummingbird Pauses at the Trumpet Vine.
Humpbacks.
Hunter's Moon—Eating the Bear.
Ice.
In Blackwater Woods.
Indonesia.
Journey, The.
Kookaburras, The.
Lamps, The.
Landscape.
Last Days.
Learning About the Indians.
Letter from Home, A.
Lightning.
Lilies.
Lilies Break Open Over the Dark Water, The.
Little Owl Who Lives in the Orchard.
Lonely, White Fields.
Magellan.
Marengo.
Maybe.
Meeting, A.
Moccasin Flowers.
Morning.
Morning at Great Pond.
Morning in a New Land.
Morning Poem.
Moths, The.
Murderer's House, The.
Mushrooms.
Mussels.
Nature.
Night Flight.
Night Traveler, The.
1945—1985: Poem for the Anniversary.
No Voyage.
October.
On Winter's Margin.
One or Two Things.
Peonies.
Picking Blueberries, Austerlitz, New York,
    1957.
Ponds, The.
Poppies.
Rabbit, The.
Rage.
Rain.
Rain in Ohio.
Return, The.
Rice.
River Styx, Ohio, The.
Robert Schumann.
Roses.
Roses, Late Summer.
Sea, The.
Singapore.
Skunk Cabbage.
Sleeping in the Forest.
Snowshoe Hare, The.
Some Herons.
Some Questions You Might Ask.
Spring ("In April the Morgan was bred. I was
    chased away").
Spring ("Somewhere").
Spring Azures.
Spring in the Classroom.
Stanley Kunitz.
Starfish.
Strawberry Moon.
Summer Day, The.
Sun, The.
Sunflowers, The.
Sunrise.
Swan, The.
Swans on the River Ayr.
Swimming Lesson, The.

Tecumseh.
This Morning Again It Was in the Dusty Pines.
Three Poems for James Wright.
Truro Bear, The.
Turtle, The.
Two Kinds of Deliverance.
University Hospital, Boston.
Visitor, A.
Vultures.
Water Snake.
Waterfall, The.
Whelks.
When Death Comes.
White Flowers.
White Night.
White Owl Flies Into and Out of the Field.
Wild Geese.
Winter.
Winter in the Country.
Wolf Moon.

Olson, Charles (1910–70)
A B Cs.
A B Cs (2).
A B Cs (3—for Rimbaud).
À Constance, This Day.
Absolutely Vernal.
Abstract #1, Yucatan.
Abt the dead he sd.
Across Space and Time.
Adamo Me.
Advantage, The.
Afica.
Afternoon.
Alba, The.
All Havens Astern.
All Pink from the Bath She Slept.
All things stand out against the sky.
All You Can Do.
Allegory of Wealth, The.
Americans, The ("Cosmologist says, The").
Americans, The ("What the cosmologist meant
    by what constitutes").
Anecdotes of the Late War.
Anniversary.
Anubis will stare.
Applause.
As I went in and out I heard pieces.
As if Hallam Movius had placed a grid over it,
    and plumb-
As snow lies on the hill love's blackness lies.
As the Dead Prey upon Us.
As the shield goddess, Mycenae.
As though there were no flowing.
Assuming the Soul Is a Bitch.
Asymptotes.
At midnight, after hours of love, I ate.
At Yorktown.
Atalanta.
Babe, The.
Bagatto.
Ballad for Americans.
Barley or rye / blue and white green.
Beauty / is to lay hold of Love.
Being Altogether Literal, & Specific.
Big Fat Fly, A.
Bigmans.
Bigmans II.
Binnacle, The.
Birth's Obituary.
Black Mt. College Has a Few Words for a
    Visitor.
Boat, The.
Borne down by the inability to lift the
    heaviness.
Bride, The.
Buffalo Ode.
Burial Ground.
Business, The.
By Cure of—Sulfa.
Canto One Hundred and One.
Carrying water to the Youth in Honor of
    Sappho Jane Harrison & Miss Duncan.
Cause, the Cause, The.
Chain of memory is resurrection I am a vain
    man, The.
Christmas.

She.
She-Bear, The.
She-Bear (II), The.
She, Thus.
She Who Hits at Will.
Shenandoah.
Shut in kept off.
Siena.
Signs.
Sin is inferiority. The mother's cooperation in the birth of her daughter.
Sing, Mister, Sing.
Sit by the Window and Refuse.
Six Inch Chapter—in Verse, A.
Small Birds, to Agree with the Leaves, Come in the Fall.
Snow, The.
Snow White was always waiting for The Prince.
So the Norse / were neurotic.
Some partial cloudiness will flow locally, mostly.
Song, The: "More than the sennet of the solstice pipe."
Soul, The.
Spring Song for Cagli, A.
Stone and Flower Series.
Story, A.
Story of an Olson, and Bad Thing, The.
Sut Lovingood.
Tanto e Amara.
Tenement twilightish landscape.
There Are Sounds.
There Is No River Which Is Called Lethe.
There they were.
There Was a Youth Whose Name Was Thomas Granger.
These Days.
Thing Was Moving, The.
This.
This Man's Weakness Is Straw.
This Year.
Thoughts of the Time.
Thy Gleeman Who Flattered Thee.
To a Poet Who Read in Gloucester.
To Empty the Mind.
To Gerhardt, There, among Europe's Things of Which He Has Written Us.
To the Algae.
To the She-Bear: The 1st Song.
To Try to Get Down One Citizen as Against Another.
Tomorrow.
Toss, for John Cage, A.
Town, The.
Translation, A.
Treatment, The.
Trinacria.
Troilus.
True Numbers.
Turn now and rise.
2 Propositions and 3 Proof.
Undazzled, keen, / love sits.
Under every green tree, sex.
Unfinished (raw) hero—un-, The.
Variations Done for Gerald Van De Wiele.
War on the Mind in a Time of Love.
Well.
West.
What Had to Go.
What's Wrong with Pindar.
When One Age Goes with It Suddenly Its Errors Evaporate.
White Horse.
Who.
Who slays the Spanish sun.
Whole World, The.
Will: termite mothers.
Will: the rat.
Will To, The.
Willie Francis and the Electric Chair.
Winds / which blew my daughter, The.
Winter After, The.
Winter Solstice.
With what I got out.
Without the Season of Structure, Modes Lie

Like Gods Thrown Down.
Woman's Nipples Is the Rose of the World, A.
Writ, The.
X to the Nth.
Year Is a Great Circle or the Year Is a Great Mistake, The.
Yellow of the Mask, The.
You, Hart Crane.
You know, verse.
Your Eyes.

Olumo *See* **Cunningham, James**

Oppen, George (b. 1908)
Acapulco.
All This Strangeness.
Alpine.
Amalgamated, The.
Animula.
Antique.
Any Way But Back.
Armies of the Plain.
Artist.
As I lift the glass to drink.
As I saw.
Astray over earth.
Bad times: / The cars pass.
Bahamas.
Ballad: "Astrolabes and lexicons."
Barbarity, A.
Beautiful as the sea.
Belvedere.
Biblical Tree, The.
Bicycles and the Apex, The.
Bill before his death.
Birthplace: New Rochelle.
Blood from the Stone.
Bolt / In the frame.
Book of Job and a Draft of a Poem to Praise the Paths of the Living, The.
Boy's Room.
Brain / All / Nuclei.
Bronx Zoo.
Building of the Skyscraper, The.
California.
Carpenter's Boat.
Chartres.
Church Interior.
City of Keansburg, The.
Civil war photo.
Closed car—closed in glass.
Coastal Strip.
Comforters, The.
Confession.
Crowded Countries of the Bomb, The.
Cultural Triumph, A.
Daedalus: The Dirge.
Deaths everywhere.
Debt.
Disasters.
Drawing.
Dream of Politics, A.
Dream, The.
Eagles and Alone.
Eclogue: "Men talking, The."
Edge of the ocean, The.
Epigram: "I have been insulted in St Peter's."
Eros.
Evening, water in a glass, The.
Exodus.
Five Poems about Poetry.
Flight.
Flight 162.
Forms of Love, The.
Founder, The.
Fragonard, / Your spiral women.
From a Photograph.
From a Phrase of Simone Weil's and Some Words of Hegel's.
From Disaster.
From the Friendly Local Press.
From this distance thinking toward you.
From Up-State.
Generation of Drivers.
Gift: The Gifted.
Giovanni's *Rape of the Sabine Women* at Wildenstein's.
Gold on Oak Leaves.

Guest Room.
He de dark.
Her ankles are watches.
Hills, The.
Historic Pun.
If It All Went Up in Smoke.
Image.
Image of the Engine.
In Memoriam Charles Reznikoff.
Inlet.
It brightens up into the branches.
Kind of Garden, A: A Poem for My Sister.
Knowledge not of sorrow, you were, The.
Laced gaiter, A.
Language of New York, A.
Latitude, Longitude.
Law of Poetry, The.
Leviathan.
Light of Day.
Lighthouses, The.
Lights, paving—, The.
Little Pin, The: Fragment.
Mary.
Mast / Inaudibly soars; bole-like, tapering, The.
Maudit.
Mayan Ground, The.
Memory at 'The Modern.'
Memory of Oars.
Men of Sheepshead, The.
Modern Incident, A.
Monument ("To exist, to be among things").
Monument ("Public silence indeed is nothing").
Mother and Child.
Mount Desert Island.
Myself I Sing.
Myth of the Blaze.
Narrative.
Narrative, A.
Nation.
Natural, The.
Near the Beginning.
Near your eyes.
Neighbors.
New People, The.
Niece.
Night Scene.
No interval of manner.
11/22/63.
O city ladies.
O Western Wind.
Occurrences, The ("Limited air drafts").
Occurrences, The ("Simplest / Words say the grass blade, The").
Of Being Numerous.
Of Hours.
Of This All Things.
Old man, The.
On the water, solid.
Orpheus.
Ozymandias.
Parkway.
Part of the Forest.
Party on Shipboard.
Pedestrian.
Penobscot.
People, the People, The.
Philai Te Kou Philai.
Phonemes, The.
Pigeons fly from the dark bough, The.
Poem about the Garden, A.
Poem, The ("How shall I light").
Poem, The ("Never / the chess game").
Poem, The ("Poetry of the meaning of words, A").
Political Poem, A.
Population.
Populist.
Power, the Enchanted World.
Powers, The.
Preceded by mounted police.
Preface, A: "If he goes rowing in the park tho he may row so well that."
Presses were busy enough.
Primitive.
Pro Nobis.

Probity.
Product.
Psalm: "In the small beauty of the forest."
Quotations.
Rationality.
Red Hook: December.
Rembrandt's Old Woman Cutting Her Nails.
Resistance, The.
Resolve, The.
Resort.
Return.
Route.
Sara in Her Father's Arms.
Say.
Seated Man.
Semantic.
Semaphoring chorus.
Semite.
She lies, hip high.
She Steals Birds.
Shore, The.
Solution.
Some San Francisco Poems.
Song, The.
Song, the Winds of Downhill.
Source, The.
Space, The.
Speech at Soli, The.
Squall.
Squirrel's Stance, The.
Steamer at the pier.
Story.
Strange Are the Products.
Stranger's Child.
Street.
Students Gather, The.
Sunnyside Child.
Survival: Infantry.
Sympathy co incidence: that the.
Technologies.
Theological Definition, A.
Theological Question, The.
This land: / The hills, round under straw.
This room, / the circled wind.
Three wide / Funnels raked aft, and the masts
    slanted, The.
Thus / Hides the.
Till Other Voices Wake Us.
Time of the Missile.
To C. T.
To Find a Way.
To Make Much.
To the Muse.
To the Poets: To Make Much of Life.
Tongues, The.
Tourist Eye.
Town, a town.
Travelogue.
Tug against the river.
Tugs of Hull, The.
Two Romance Poems.
Undertaking in New Jersey, The.
Us.
Valentine.
Visit (1).
Visit (2).
Volkswagen.
Voyage.
Vulcan.
Waking Who Knows.
West.
What Will Happen.
Wheelers and Dealers: The Theory of Games.
When, having entered.
Whirl Wind Must, The.
White. From the / Under arm of T.
Who comes is occupied.
Who Shall Doubt.
Wind Makes Up, A.
Without self-mutilation there can be no
    withdrawing from our fellows.
Woman, said Diane, speaking wisely, A.
Workman.
World, World—.
Written structure.
Zulu Girl, The.

**O'Rahilly [or O'Reilly or Ó Rathaille], Egan [or
    Aodhagán] (1670–1726)**
Poet Egan O'Rahilly, Homesick in Old Age,
    The.
Orlandi, Guido
("Friend, I well know that you know how to
    polish").
If, my friend, you would have said of Mary so.
Prolonged Sonnet: He finds fault with the
    Conceits of the foregoing Sonnet.
To the sound of trumpets rather than horns.
Orléans, Charles, Duc d' (1391–1465)
Dieu Qu'il la Fait.
Rondeau: "Year has cast its cloak away, The."
Orr, Gregory (b. 1947)
A la Mystérieuse.
Adolescence.
After a Death.
After Botticelli's *Birth of Venus*.
After Piero di Cosimo's *Venus, Mars, and
    Amor.*
After the Guest.
Available Now: Archaic Torsos of Both Sexes.
Be–all.
Beggar's Song.
Beginning.
Best.
Bolt from the Blue.
Brave Child, The.
Bridge, The.
Builders, The.
Cage, The.
Caged Owl, The.
Celestial Desolations.
Chateaubriand on the Niagara Frontier, 1791.
City of Salt, The.
Cliff, The.
Daffodil Poem.
Dark Night, A.
Demonstration, The.
Dinner, The.
Ditch, The.
Doll, The.
Domestic Life.
Dream of Fifty, A.
Driving Home after a Funeral.
Elegy: "Here are consoling pieties."
Elegy: "Not only doesn't the Ohio."
Entrance to the Underworld, The.
Everything.
Excavation, The.
Fall.
Far below, plowed fields vibrated.
Fast, The.
Father's Song.
Field in New England, A.
Fields took on their final.
Fifth Month, The.
Friday Lunchbreak.
Gathering the Bones Together.
Getting Dressed.
Ghosts Listen to Orpheus Sing, The.
Gift, The.
Girl with Eighteen Nightgowns, The.
Glukupikron.
Going Out.
Gray Fox, The.
Half-Dead Black Cherry Tree across the Road
    from My Childhood House, A.
Hand, The: "Brightness Falls from the Air."
Hats, The.
Heart.
Here.
His Dream: The Black Tree / Thirst.
His Grief.
His Lament.
Horses.
Hotel St. Louis, New York City, Fall 1969.
I was moving down the bank.
If There's a God.
If your gaze takes in.
In Haiti [or Haitian Suite].
In the cave mouth I stopped.
In the shadows at the clearing's.
Indian Summer.
Investigation.

Journey, The.
King of the Earthworms, The.
Lament: "I thought of you."
Large White Rock Called "The Sleeping
    Angel," A.
Leaving the Asylum.
Life, A.
Like Any Other Man.
Lines Written in Dejection, Oklahoma.
Litany, A: "I remember him falling beside me."
Lost Children, The.
Love Poem: "Black biplane crashes through
    [or into] the window, A [or The]."
Lucky.
Making Beasts.
Manhattan Island Poem.
Memorial Day.
Migrant Camps, The.
Moment, A.
Morning Song.
Muse of Midnight.
My body was never married.
My Father's Voice.
Nantucket Morning / This World.
Neighbors.
Nothing and the Incident in the Streets.
November.
October.
On a Highway East of Selma, Alabama.
On the Lawn at Ira's.
Once the two of us.
Origin of the Marble Forest.
Overtaken by Fog While Climbing.
Parable, A.
Paradise.
Paradise Lightning Dazzle.
Poem in New York.
Poem: "This life like no other."
Poem to the Mother.
Poem: "Truth's in myth not fact, The."
Pond, The.
Reading Late in the Cottage.
Reverie.
River, The.
Room, The.
Screaming Out Loud.
Self-Portrait at Twenty.
Shaky Spectrum.
Shelf Is a Ledge, A.
Singing the Pain Back into the Wound.
Sleeping Alone in a Small Room.
Snail, The.
Snake no bigger, A.
Solitary Confinement.
Some Notes on Shadows.
Some Part of the Lyric.
Song, A: "Other world's not for me, The."
Song: Early Death of the Mother.
Song of the Invisible Corpse in the Field.
Spring Floods.
Story Sassetta Paints, A.
Sunday School Picnic: What Endures.
Swamp Songs.
Tableau Vivant.
Talk, The.
Teachers, The.
There.
Three Songs.
Tin Cup.
To My Father, Dying.
Transients Welcome.
(Trauma) Storm.
Tree, The.
Trick, The.
Tristan and Iseult.
Trying to Sleep.
Two Lines from the Brothers Grimm.
Two Poems about Nothing.
Vase, The.
Virginia Backyard: July.
Visit to the Island of Lost Souls.
Voyages, The.
Walking Home after the First Encounter.
Washing My Face.
We Must Make a Kingdom of It.

Wedge, The.
Weeds, The.
Western Invention of Lyrical Nature, The.
What I'm Saying.
When Eurydice saw him.
When I first saw her.
When I was alive—only glimpses.
When they said I must leave hell.
Who'd Want to Be a Man?
Wild Heart.
Work Gloves.

Ovid (Publius Ovidius Naso) (43 B.C.–A.D. 17)
Amores, *sels.*
Art of Love, The, *sels.*
Elegies, *sels.*
Galatea.
Heroides, *sels.*
Metamorphoses, *sels.*
Remediae Amoris, *sels.*
Tristium, *sels.*

Owen, Goronwy (1723–69)
Prudent Simplicity.

Owen, Wilfred (1893–1918)
A Terre.
All Sounds Have Been As Music.
Antaeus: A Fragment.
Anthem for Doomed Youth.
Apologia Pro Poemate Meo.
Arms and the Boy.
Asleep.
At a Calvary near the Ancre.
Beauty.
Bold Horatius.
Bugles Sang.
Calls, The.
Chances, The.
Conscious.
Dead-Beat, The.
Disabled.
Dulce et Decorum Est.
Elegy in April and September.
End, The.
Exposure.
Fates, The.
Fragment: "As bronze may be much
    beautified."
Fragment: "Cramped in that funnelled hole,
    they watched the dawn."
Fragment: "I saw his round mouth's crimson
    deepen as it fell."
Fragment: "Not one corner of a foreign field."
From My Diary, July 1914.
Futility.
Greater Love.
Happiness.
Has Your Soul Sipped?
Hospital Barge at Cérisy.
Imbecile, The.
Insensibility.
Inspection.
Kind Ghosts, The.
Last Laugh, The.
Le Christianisme.
Letter, The.
Long Ages Past.
Maundy Thursday.
Mental Cases.
Miners.
Music.
My Shy Hand.
Next War, The.
1914.
O World of Many Worlds.
On My Songs.
One Remains, The.
Parable of the Old Men and the Young, The.
Promisers, The.
Purple.
Roads Also, The.
S.I.W.
Send-Off, The.
Sentry, The.
Shadwell Stair.
Show, The.
Six o'clock in Princes Street.
Sleeping Beauty, The.

Smile, Smile, Smile.
Soldier's Dream.
Song of Songs.
Sonnet Autumnal.
Sonnet: "Be slowly lifted up, thou long black
    arm."
Sonnet, to a Child.
Spells and Incantation (a Fragment).
Spring Offensive.
Storm.
Strange Meeting.
This is the Track.
To a Comrade in Flanders.
To Eros.
To My Friend (With an Identity Disc).
To the Bitter Sweet-heart: a Dream.
To ———: "Three rompers run together, hand
    in hand."
Training.
Unreturning, The.
Winter Song.

Owens, Samuel
Poem, A: "Ye Sons of Levi, Church Divines."

P

Pagis, Dan (b. 1930)
Acrobatics.
Already.
Ancient Complaint, An.
April.
Art of Contraction, The.
Autobiography.
Beginning, The.
Bestiary.
Bisection.
Brain.
Bridgehead Photograph.
Brothers.
Caveman Is Not about to Talk, The.
Central Park, Twilight.
Come.
Conversation.
Cycle, The.
Deceased Writer, The: Photograph in the Rain.
Devotion.
Draft of a Reparations Agreement.
Early Winter, Long Island.
Ein Leben.
Encounters.
End of the Questionnaire.
End of Winter, The.
Epilogue to Robinson Crusoe.
Europe, Late.
Exposure.
Failure.
Final Examination.
Final Report.
Footprints.
For a Literary Survey.
For How Long.
Fragments of an Elegy.
Freedom Machine, The.
Grand Duke of New York, The.
Harvests.
He'll Come Out for Sure.
Homily.
How To.
In the Laboratory.
Information.
Instructions for Crossing the Border.
Jason's Grave in Jerusalem.
Lament for a Master of Style.
Last Ones, The.
Lesson in Observation, A.
Limits of Physics, The.
Memorial Evening.
Modest Sum, A.
Moment at the Louvre, A.
Moments of Old Age.
New Lover, A.
Opening to Satan, An.
Out of Line.
Outside an Air Base, California.

Pages in an Album.
Picture Postcard from Our Youth.
Point of Departure.
Portrait, The.
Readiness, The.
Ready for Parting.
Real-Life Story.
Recognition.
Runner Artist, The.
Scarabs.
Seashell.
Shot, The.
Siege.
Silent Movie.
Small Poetics, A.
Snake.
Sominex.
Souvenir, The.
Spaceship.
Sport.
Story, The.
Sudden Heart.
Sugarduke.
Testimony.
Tidings.
Tortoise, The.
Toward Home.
Tower, The.
Tropical Greenhouse.
Twelve Faces of the Emerald.
Twenty Years in the Valley.
Visit to a Physicist.
Wall Calender.
Wind From Variable Directions.
Writers.
Written in Pencil in the Sealed Railway-Car.

Palés Matos, Luis (1898–1959)
Prelude in Boricua.

Paley, Grace (b. 1922)
Age.
Ant! / lugging half an ounce, An.
Arboreal Mystery, An.
At the Battery.
Autumn.
Bee! / drowning in, A.
Beef.
Bob Visits Friends.
Boy His Mother, The.
Bridges.
Choir Singing, The.
Connections: Vermont Vietnam (I).
Connections: Vermont Vietnam (II).
Dance in Jinotega, The.
Definition.
Desert Wasn't Loved Enough said Reich, The.
Drowning (I).
Drowning (II).
Faces.
False strawberry is.
Families.
Family.
Fear.
Five-Day Week, The.
For Danny.
For George (I).
For George (II).
For Jan.
For Mike and Jeannie: Resisters Fifteen Years
    Later.
For My Daughter.
For My Friend Who Planted a Tree for His
    Daughter Jane.
Four Short Pieces.
Fund Appeal.
Hand-Me-Downs.
Having Arrived by Bike at Battery Park.
He Wanders.
Here.
House: Some Instructions.
Housing.
How to Tell a Story (My Method) (Most of the
    Time).
I Gave Away That Kid.
I See My Friend Everywhere.
Illegal Aliens.
Immigrant Story, The.

Counselor, The.
Danger of Writing Defiant Verse, The.
Dark Girl's Rhyme, The.
Day-Dreams.
Daylight Savings.
De Profundis.
Dilemma.
Directions for Finding the Bard.
Distance.
Drama, The; A Hymn of Hate.
Dramatists, The.
Dream Lies Dead, A.
Epitaph: "First time I died, I walked my ways, The."
Epitaph for a Darling Lady.
Evening Primrose, The.
Excursion Into Assonance.
Experience.
Fable: "Oh, there once was a lady, and so I've been told."
Fair Weather.
Fairly Sad Tale, A.
False Friends, The.
Fantasy.
Far-Sighted Muse, The.
Faut de Mieux.
Fighting Words.
Figures in Popular Literature.
Finis.
Flaw in Paganism, The.
Folk Song.
Folk Tune.
For a Favorite Grand-Daughter.
For a Lady Who Must Write Verse.
For a Sad Lady.
For an Unknown Lady.
For R.C.B.
Fragment: "Why should we set these hearts of ours above."
From a Letter from Lesbia.
Frustration.
Fulfillment.
Garden-Spot.
General Review of the Sex Situation.
Gentlest Lady, The.
Godmother.
Godspeed.
Grande Passion.
Grandfather Said It.
Guinevere at Her Fireside.
Gunman and the Débutante, The.
Healed.
Hearthside.
Homebody, The.
How Bold It Is.
Husbands; A Hymn of Hate.
I Know I Have Been Happiest.
I Shall Come Back.
Idyl.
Immortals, The.
In the Meadow.
Incurable.
Indian Summer.
Inscription for the Ceiling of a Bedroom.
Interior.
Interview.
Inventory.
Invictus.
Iseult of Brittany.
Lady in Back, The.
Lady's Reward, The.
Landscape.
Last Question, The.
Leal, The.
Letter to Ogden Nash.
Letter to Robert Benchley; Roughing It in the Country at the Birches, Maine.
Liebestod.
Life's Valentines.
Light of Love.
Lines on Reading Too Many Poets.
Little Old Lady in Lavender Silk, The.
Little Words.
Love Song: "My own dear love, he is strong and bold."
Love Song: "Suppose we two were cast away."
Lullaby: "Sleep, pretty lady, the night is enfolding you."
Lynn Fontanne.
Lyric.
Maid-Servant at the Inn, The.
Marilyn Marilyn.
Meeting-Place.
Memories.
Men.
Men; A Hate Song.
Men I'm Not Married To.
Midnight.
Monody.
Mood.
Moral Tales for the Young ("Little Gormley stole a purse").
Moral Tales for the Young ("Maude, the brightest of the sex").
Mortal Enemy.
Movies; A Hymn of Hate.
Musical Comedy Thought, A.
My Own.
Neither Blood Nor Bowed.
New Love, The.
News Item.
Ninon De L'Enclos, On Her Last Birthday.
Nocturne: "Always I knew that it could not last."
Now at Liberty.
Observation.
Of a Woman, Dead Young.
Oh Look—I Can Do It Too.
On Being a Woman.
On Cheating the Fiddler.
One Perfect Rose.
Ornithology for Beginners.
Our Cousins.
Our Office; An Intimate Glimpse of Vanity Fair—En Famille A Hate Song.
Our Own Home Talent.
Paean.
Paging Saint Patrick.
Parable for a Certain Virgin.
Partial Comfort.
Parties; A Hymn of Hate.
Passionate Freudian to His Love, The.
Passionate Screen Writer to His Love, The.
Paths.
Pattern.
Penelope.
Philosophy.
Pictures in the Smoke.
Pig's-Eye View of Literature, A.
Plea.
Poem in the American Manner.
Portrait, A.
Portrait of the Artist.
Post-Graduate.
Pour Prendre Congé.
Prayer for a New Mother.
Prayer for a Prayer.
Prisoner.
Prologue to a Saga.
Promise.
Prophetic Soul.
Purposely Ungrammatical Love Song.
Rainy Night.
Recurrence.
Red Dress, The.
Relatives; A Hate Song.
Renunciation.
Requiescat.
Résumé.
Reuben's Children.
Rhyme Against Living.
Rhyme of an Involuntary Violet.
Rondeau: "Give me a rose, cool-petaled, virgin white."
Rondeau: "It isn't fair, to me, when you're away."
Rondeau Redoublé.
Rosemary ("Ah, no, I dare not lose myself in dreams").
Rosemary ("I wear your fragrant memory, like a spray of mignonette").
Roundel: "She's passing fair; but so demure is she."
Salome's Dancing-Lesson.
Sanctuary.
Satin Dress, The.
Sea, The.
Searched Soul, The.
Second Love.
Second Oldest Story, The.
Sight.
Slackers; A Hate Song.
Small Hours, The.
Social Note.
Solace.
Somebody's Song.
Somewhat Delayed Spring Song.
Song: "And shall we build a little nest."
Song: "Clarabelle has golden hair."
Song for an April Dusk.
Song for the First of the Month.
Song in a Minor Key.
Song in the Worst Possible Taste.
Song of a Contented Heart.
Song of a Hopeful Heart.
Song of Americans Resident in France.
Song of One of the Girls.
Song of Perfect Propriety.
Song of Social Life in Hollywood.
Song of the Conventions.
Song of the Open Country.
Song of the Wildnerness.
Song: "When all the world was younger."
Song: "When summer used to linger."
Sonnet for the End of a Sequence.
Sonnet: "In seemly burial, love may not rest."
Sonnet On An Alpine Night.
Sonnet: "Sweeter your laugh than trill of lark at dawn."
Spring Song.
Star Light, Star Bright.
Story.
Story of Mrs. W———.
Summary.
Summer Resorts; A Hymn of Hate.
Superfluous Advice.
Surprise.
Swan Song.
Sweet Violets.
Symptom Recital.
Temps Perdu.
Temptress, The.
Testament.
Theory.
There Was One.
They Part.
Thin Edge, The.
Thought for a Sunshiny Morning.
Thoughts.
Threat to a Fickle Lady.
Threnody: "Lilacs blossom just as sweet."
To a Lady.
To a Much Too Unfortunate Lady.
To Elspeth.
To Marjorie Rambeau; In "Daddy's Gone A-Hunting."
To My Dog.
To Myrtilla, On Easter Day.
Tombstones in the Starlight.
Transition.
Trifler, The.
Triolet, A: "You'll be returning, one day."
Triolet: "Give back the heart that I gave."
Triolet: "It is never the cost of the gift."
Triolets: "Herewith I send you my heart."
Trusting Heart, The.
Two-Volume Novel.
Ultimatum.
Unfortunate Coincidence.
Vers Démodé.
Verse for a Certain Dog.
Verse Reporting Late Arrival at a Conclusion.
Verses in the Night.
Very Short Song, A.
Veteran, The.
Victoria.
Wail.

Wanderlust.
War Song.
Well-Worn Story, A.
When We Were Very Sore; Lines on
    Discovering that You Have Been Advertised
    as America's A.A. Milne.
Whistling Girl, The.
White Lady, The.
Willow, The.
Wisdom.
With Best Wishes.
Wives; A Hymn of Hate.
Women; A Hate Song.
Woodland Song.
Words of Comfort to Be Scratched on a
    Mirror.
Younger Set, The; A Hymn of Hate.

**Paros, Euenus the Grammarian, Euenus of
Askelon, Euenus of** *See* **Euenus**

Parra, Nicanor (b. 1914)
Butterfly.
Imperfect Lover, The.
Mummies.
Paradise of Squares.
Piano Solo.
Poetry Ends with Me.
Soda Fountains.
What the Deceased Had to Say about Himself.

Pasolini, Pier Paolo (1922–75)
Appendix to the "Religion': A Light.
Ashes of Gramsci, The.
Beautiful Banners, The.
Civil Song.
Desperate Vitality, A.
Gramsci's Ashes, *sels.*
Lines from the Testament.
One of the Many Epilogs.
Plan of Future Works.
Poetry of the Tradition, The.
Prayer to My Mother.
Reality.
Religion of My Time, The.
Southern Dawn.
Tears of the Excavator, The.

Pasternak, Boris Leonidovich (1890–1960)
Breakup, The.
Death of a Voice.
Earth, The.
God of Details, The.
Illness, *sels.*
Inside the Storm.
New York in August.
Oh had we known it turns out so.
Orford.
Portland.
Some Future Moon.
To Anna Akhmátova.
White Night.

Patchen, Kenneth (1911–72)
After an Old Song.
Age of Pericles, The.
Ah, God, dear Brother, the mild and frowning
    rose.
All Is Safe.
All That Night Lights Were Seen Moving in
    Every Direction.
All the Bright Foam of Talk.
All the Day.
All the Flowery.
All the Roses of the World.
Always Another Viewpoint.
Among Ourselves and with All Nations.
And a Man Went Out Alone.
And He Had Wilder Moments.
And her look touching the air between us like
    a hand alive to the.
And I, Too, Am Something of a Stranger Here,
    My Friend.
And in Another Place Uses the Same Phrase.
And What with the Blunders.
And When Freedom Is Achieved.
Animal I wanted, The.
Anna Karenina and the Love-sick River.
Appian Way, The.
Ark: Angelus: Anvil.

As Frothing Wounds of Roses.
As in the green sky.
As She Was Thus Alone in the Clear
    Moonlight.
As we are so wonderfully done with each
    other.
At Grandmother's Wake.
At the Entrance to the Other World.
Attila.
Authority of Krajova, The.
Autobiographical Note.
Autumn Is the Crows' Time.
Avarice and Ambition Only Were the First
    Builders of Towns and Founders of Empire.
Backcountry Blues.
Battle of Unameit, The.
Be music, night, / That her sleep may go.
Beautiful You Are.
Behold, One of Several Little Christs.
Being so hideous that the air weeps blood.
Beyond the Dark Cedars.
Billion Freedoms, The.
Biography of Southern Rain.
Bird-Queen, The.
Black Panther and the Little Boy, The.
Blind Maidens of Our Homelessness, The.
Blind'd be the last of men.
Blood of the Sun.
Body Beside the Ties, The.
Boxers Hit Harder When Women Are Around.
Breathe on the living.
Builders, The.
But of Life?
But the Images of His Former Dreams Still
    Haunted Him.
Can the Harp Shoot Through Its Propellers?
Career for a Child of Five.
Carts of the wee blind lass, The.
Catfish River Lullaby.
Character of Love Seen as a Search for the
    Lost, The.
Childhood of the Hero.
Christ! Christ! Christ! that the world.
Class of 1934.
Cleveland, Oh?
Climate of War, The.
Cloth of the Tempest, The.
Colony of the Sun, The.
Constant Bridegrooms, The.
Continual Ministry of Thy Anger, The:
Continuation of the Landscape.
Country Excursion.
Court of First Appeal.
Creation.
Crossing on Staten Island Ferry.
Crowded Net, The.
Cruelkind Swans, The.
Cruelties of the Sportive Power.
Curly Blue Buppo, The.
Daft Little Shoe Clerk Decided It Would Be
    Fun to Go Up.
Day of Rabblement.
Dazzling Burden, The.
Death Will Amuse Them.
Deathsong for a Maiden.
Deer and the Snake, The.
Delighted with Bluepink.
Demonstration.
Destruction of Carthage, The.
Devotion, A.
Do me that love.
Do the Dead Know What Time It Is?
Don't Wash Your Hair in the Streetcar, Nora
    Dear.
Dostoyevsky.
Down in Ol' Dontcaradama.
Down in the Lone Valley.
Each Is Alone, Each Is Everything.
Early in the Morning.
Easy Decision, An.
Easy Rider.
Ecstasy of the Pure.
Egypt.
Eight Early Poems.
Elegy for the Silent Voices and the Joiners of
    Everything.

Empire of Persia, The.
Encounter at Nightfall.
Eve of St. Agony, or the Middle Class Was
    Sitting on Its Fat.
Event at Konna, The.
Everlasting Contenders, The.
Evidence? What Evidence...?
Examination into Life and Death, An.
Executions in Moscow, The.
Expectant Shelters, The.
Fall of the Evening Star.
Family Portrait.
Farewell to the Bluewoman.
Fellow Soul, Sound Hunting to Thy
    Immeasurable Heart.
Fields of Earth.
Fifth Dimension.
Figure Motioned with Its Mangled Hand
    Toward the Wall Behind It, The.
Firing, The.
First came the Lion-Rider, across the green
    fields of the morning.
First Crusades, The!
Flowers to the House.
Fog.
Fog Over the Sea and the Sun Going Down.
Folly of Clowns.
For losing her love all would I profane.
For Miriam ("As beautiful as the hands").
For Miriam ("Do I not deal with angels").
For Miriam ("Little birds sit on your
    shoulders").
For Miriam ("O my dearest").
For Miriam ("Sea is awash with roses O they
    blow, The").
For the Mother of My Mother's Mother.
For whose adornment the mouths.
Forms of Knowledge, The.
Fox, The.
From My High Love.
Gautama in the Deer Park at Benares.
"Gentle and Giving" and Other Sayings.
Give you a lantern.
Grand Palace of Versailles, The.
Great Birds, The.
Great Sadnesses, The.
Great-Sledmakers, The.
Green Fires, The.
Hangman's Great Hands, The.
Harrowed by These Apprehensions He
    Resolved to Commit Himself.
Have You Killed Your Man for Today?
Having Been Near.
He Is an.
He Is Guarded by Crowds and Shackled with
    Formalities.
He Thought of Mad Ellen's Ravings and of the
    Wretched Skeleton on the Rock.
He Was Alone (As in Reality) Upon His
    Humble Bed.
Heaven and Earth.
Heine, Too, Lived in Germany.
Her Talents...Of.
Here might have been the thinking of
    mountains.
History in a Minor Key.
History Is a Throne and a Gate.
Hold thy tongue, death!
House, and a Dead Man In It.
Hovenweep.
How God Was Made.
How Jimsey O'Roon and Peter Stack, Coal
    Miners, Came to Be Put in the Ferbettville
    (Pa.) Jail Early One Saturday Night.
How Old the World Is!
How silent are the things of heaven.
Hunted City, The.
Hunter, The.
Hymn to a Trench Gun.
I always return to this place.
I Can't Understand! I Can't Understand!
I Care What Happens.
I Don't Want to Startle You but They Are
    Going to Kill Most of Us.
I Feel Drunk All the Time.
I Got the Fat Poet into a Corner.

I have lighted the candles, Mary.
I Have No Place to Take Thee.
I Never Had Any Other Desire So Strong.
I Sent a Mental to My Love.
I Suddenly Became Conscious That This Thing Was Looking at Me Intently.
I suggest that this day be made holy.
I'd want her eyes to fill with wonder.
If a Poem Can Be Headed into Its Proper Current.
If We Are to Know Where We Live.
In a Crumbling.
In horror the God-thrown lie.
In Judgment of the Leaf.
In Memory of Kathleen.
In Order to.
In shadings of an obscure punishment.
In the Courtyard of Secret Life.
In the footsteps of the walking air.
In Your Body All Bodies Lie.
Instructions for Angels.
Intimate Guest, The.
Into another mission.
Investigation of Certain Interesting Questions.
Irate Songster, The.
Irkalla's White Caves,
It Depends on Whose Science.
It Is Big Inside a Man.
It Is for Us the Living.
It Takes Few Kinds.
It Was a Bomby Evening.
It Was Being.
It's a Smallworld.
It's Because Your Heart Is Pure, Honey.
It's My Town!
Joe Hill Listens to the Praying.
Just outside Tombstone.
Kibali-Ituri.
Knowledge of Old Towns, The.
Known Soldier, The.
Ladder, The.
Lament for the Makers of Songs.
Lao Tsze.
Last Full Measure of Devotion, The.
Lasting Seasons, The.
Latesummer Blues.
Leaflet (One).
Leaflet (Two).
Legend for a Little Child.
Lenada.
Let Me In!
Let Us Have Madness Openly.
Letter on Liberty, A.
Letter on the Use of Machine Guns at Weddings, A.
Letter to a Policemen in Kansas City, A.
Letter to the Inventors of a Tradition, A.
Letter to the Liberals, A.
Letter to the Old Men.
Letter to the Young Men, A.
Letter to Those Who Are About to Die.
Like a Mourningless Child.
Limpidity of Silences.
Lions of fire, The.
Little Black Train, The.
Little Cannibal's Bedtimesong.
Lives of the Swan.
Lonesome Boy Blues.
Lost Poem, A.
Lowellville Cemetery: Twilight.
Loyalty Is the Life You Are.
Lunch Wagon on Highway 57.
Lute in the Attic, The.
Magic Car, The.
Magical Mouse, The.
Man Is to Man a Beast.
Man Lives Here, A.
Man with the Golden Adam's Apple, The.
Manifold Fusions, The.
Matchstick-Viewed-without-Regard-to-Its-Outer-Surface, A.
May I Ask You a Question, Mr. Youngstown Sheet & Tube?
Meaning of Life, The.
Meben.
Mechanical Heart, The.

Meditation of My Lady of Sorrows.
Message from the Assistant Chief of the Fly People, A.
Midnight Special.
Mirru.
Mohammed.
Moon came out full, you could see the white breathing of the.
Moon "Continued."
Morning, My Prince—the Eye That Walks.
Mule of water, The.
Murder of Two Men by a Young Kid Wearing Lemon-colored Gloves, The.
My Coat Is Dirty.
My Generation Reading the Newspapers.
My Pretty Animals.
Naked Land, The.
Nervousness of Memory, The.
New Being, The.
Nice Day for a Lynching.
Night Has Been as Beautiful as Virginia.
1935.
Niobe.
No one ever works alone.
Nocturne for the Heirs of Light.
Not If He Has Any Sense, He Won't Be Back.
Not Many Kingdoms Left.
Note for a Diary.
November in Ohio.
Now I Went Down to the Ringside and Little Henry Armstrong Was There.
Now If You.
O All Down within the Pretty Meadow.
O Everliving Queen!
O fiery river / Flow out over the land.
O Fill Your Sack with Tiger Cubs.
O Howling Cells.
O kind watchers came.
O my darling troubles heaven.
O my love / The pretty towns.
'O Now the Drenched Land Wakes.'
O She Is as Lovely-Often as Every Day.
O sleeping falls the maiden snow.
O terrible is the highest thing.
O the sledbirds rides over the willow.
O What a Revolution!
O when I take my love out walking.
Of the same beauty were stars made.
Often Was It.
Ohio River Blues.
Old Lean Over the Tombstones, The.
Old lean over the tombstones, the, The.
Old Man.
Old Pair of Shoes, An.
Oldest Conversation, The.
On My Side.
On the South-West Coast of Erehwemos Stands a Romantic Little Village.
Opening the Window.
Orange Bears, The.
Origin of Baseball, The.
Other Side: The Green Home, The.
Outlaw of the Lowest Planet, The.
Overworld, The.
Palms for a Catholic Child.
Pastoral: "Dove walks with sticky feet, The."
Pathway, The.
Paxdominisit Sem Pervobiscum Etcumspiri Tutuo.
Peace in this green field.
Permanent Migrations, The.
Peter's Diary in Goodentown.
Pick Up the Evening Paper.
Plate of Steaming Fish, A.
Pleasures of This Gentle Day.
Plow Horses.
Poem: "Feeling chilled in that cold country."
Poem in the Form of a Letter: to Lauro de Bosis.
Poem Written after Reading Certain Poets.
Poems which are written by the soul.
Polly—An Almost-True Story.
Poor Child with the Hooked Hands, The.
Poor Gorrel.
Portrait of the Artist as an Interior Decorator.
Portrait on an American Theme.

Prayer Not To Go to Paradise with the Asses.
Preparation for the Highest Being.
Pretty glow on the water.
Progress to a View of Life.
Put the rest away, O put the rest away!
Quantity of Mercy, The.
Queer Client and the Forest-Inn, The.
Question Is, Who Is Afraid of What, The?
Radiance in a Dark Wood, The.
Reason for Skylarks, The.
Red Wine and Yellow Hair.
Religion Is That I Love You.
Rest, heart of the tired world.
Rising a Little.
Rites of Darkness, The.
Roses of Life, The.
Saturday Night in the Parthenon.
Second People, The.
Shadows and Spring Flowers.
Shapes.
Shapes and Intensities of This Man, This Confucius, The.
She Had Concealed Him in a Deep Dark Cave.
She is the prettiest of creatures.
Should Be Sufficient.
Slums, The.
Small but Brilliant Fire Blazed in the Grate, A.
Snow is deep on the ground, The.
So Be It.
So It Ends.
So Near—And Yet.
Soldier and the Star, The.
Soon It Will.
Sovereign of the wilderness!
Spirit of Noplace, The.
Stars go to sleep so peacefully, The.
State of the Nation, The.
Stayed No Longer in the Place Than to Hire a Guide for the Next Stage.
Strange, Moving Lights of People Handle Holinesses Unknown, The.
Strange thing I said to Sam is the way they die, The.
Stranger, The.
Street Corner College.
Sturdy Legs, That.
Sure There Is Food.
Temple, A.
That We Here Highly Resolve.
Theory of Nato-geography as Advanced by the Tiaphidian Man.
There are no losses.
There Are Two.
There Is Nothing False in Thee.
There Is One Who Watches.
There is the hand that has nothing attached to it, no arm no chest.
There's a Train Leaving Soon.
These are my great ones.
These Have Gone with Silent Hands, Seeking.
These Unreturning Destinies.
Thinking Rock.
This Early Day.
This Man Was Your Brother.
This Summer Day.
This summer earth.
Those Upon Whom God Has Labored.
Though I Had Much More To Say.
Thus Far So Nobly Advanced.
Time to Believe!, A.
To Be Charmed.
To Be Holy, Be Wholly Your Own.
To Say If You Love Someone.
To the Jewish People.
To the Tune of an Ancient Song.
To Whom It May Concern.
Tomorrow.
Tribes of Rakala, The.
Trueblue Gentleman, A.
Turner.
23rd Street Runs into Heaven.
Two for History.
Two Ghosts Together.
Unanswering Correspondences, The.
Under a Tree.
Under the green ledge.

Unfulfilling Brightnesses, The.
Unnatural History of Peru, The.
Unreturning Hosts, The.
Valley-sleeper, the Children, the Snakes, and
   the Giant, The.
Vanishing Institution, A.
Village Tudda, The.
Vines with Their.
Virtue.
Waiting Can Be Pretty Lousy.
Waking into Sleep.
Wanderers of the Pale Wood.
Watcher, The.
Watching Neighbors' Children.
Way men live is a lie, The.
We Are Not Worthy, Lord.
We Go Out Together.
We Hold These Truths to Be Self-Evident.
We Leave You Pleasure.
We Must Be Slow.
We Mutually Pledge to Each Other.
Weekend Bathers.
What Happened in the Camps.
What I'd like to know is.
What Is the Beautiful?
What Splendid Birthdays.
What the Grecian Earns.
What There Is.
When in the Course of Human Events.
When the stones burst into flame.
When We Were Here Together.
Where Every Prospect.
Where my stag-antlered love moves.
Where Two O'clock Came From.
White lions are roaring on the water.
Who Walks There?
Who'll that be.
Wide, wide in the rose's side.
Winter at the Inn.
Winter Poem.
Wolf of winter, The.
World Whose Sun Retreats Before the Brave,
   A.
World Will Little Note, The.
Worn on the.
Wouldn't You Be after a Jaunt of
   964,000,000,000,000 Million Miles?
Written after Reading an Item in the Paper
   about a Young Lady Who Went Mad.
Yellow Stones—Sea of Majestic Doves.
Yesterday They Tried.
You May All Go Home Now.
You Must Have Some Idea Where They've
   Gone.

Paul the Deacon (c.720–800)
Ut Queant.

Pavlovski, Radovan
Climate and Lyre.

Paz, Octavio (b. 1914)
Along Galeana Street.
Grove, The.
Hymn Among the Ruins.
January First.
Key of Water, The.
Landscape.
Objects & Apparitions.

Peiyu, Gong See **"Shu Ting"**

Penn, Robert E.
Dream.

Percival, William
Description in Answer to *The Journal*, A, *sels.*

Perrot, James Leigh (1735–1817)
On Capt. Foote's Marriage with Miss Patton.
Riddles: "Two brothers wisely kept apart,
   together are employ'd."

**"Perse, St.-John" (Alexis Saint-Léger Léger)
   (1887–1975)**
Blank of the Wall, The.

Pessoa, Fernando (1888–1935)
Absurd Hour, *sels.*
Advice.
Analysis.
At the wheel of the Chevrolet on the road to
   Sintra.
Audible smile of the leaves.

Autopsychography.
Beyond God.
Cat, you tumble down the street.
Christmas.
Circle, The.
Gods grant us this one, The.
He came by, wanting to speak with me on a
   downtown street.
I ask the gods only to forget me.
I don't want the sincere gifts.
I have a terrible cold.
I heard it told that once when Persia.
I only ask the gods to grant me.
I sleep. If I dream, I do not know on waking.
I the roses love in the gardens of Adonis.
If, after I die, they want to write my biography.
If you want to kill yourself, how come you
   don't want to kill yourself.
I'm a Runaway.
I'm beginning to know myself. I don't exist.
I'm so full of feeling.
Inscriptions, *sels.*
Interval.
It's raining. There is silence, since the rain
   itself.
Keeper of Sheep, The, *sels.*
Liberty.
Lightly, listlessly, my thoughts.
Lightly, quickly, soft.
Lisbon Revisited (1926).
Lisbon Revisited (1923).
Live, you say, in the present.
Loophole.
Lydia, we know nothing. We are strangers.
Lydia, when our Autumn comes.
Maritime Ode.
Master, my dear master!
Message.
My gesture that destroys.
No, don't say a word!
No one, in the vast and virgin jungle.
Not just those who hate and those who envy
   us.
Note.
Nothing comes of nothing. We are nothing.
Now ashen gray tinges the balding brow.
Oblique Rain, *sels.*
Ode, *sels.*
One after another, hard-pressed waves.
Opium Eater.
Poem in a Straight Line.
Poem: "Sky, the blueness of quiet light."
Psyche-type (Psychotype).
Recalling who I was, I see somebody else.
Salutation to Walt Whitman.
Sensationist Poem, A.
Sleep that comes over me, The.
Snow threw a silent towel over everything,
   The.
Some mysterious phantom's sudden hand.
Sonnet: "Could I say what I think, could I
   express."
Startling reality of things, The.
Story of Salomon Waste, The.
There are sicknesses worse than sicknesses.
35 Sonnets, *sels.*
This.
To be great, be whole; exclude.
To travel! Leave countries behind!
Tobacco Shop.
Twelve Poems from *The Keeper of the Flocks*.
We Took the Town After a Heavy Bombing.
Whatever stops is death, and is our death.
Written in a Book Abandoned on the Trip.

Petrarca, Francesco See **Petrarch**
Petrarch (Francesco Petrarca) (1304–74)
After I fled the place where many years.
Air weighed down, and the oppressive cloud,
   The.
Alas her sweet expression, pleasure-filled.
Alas how unprepared I was at first.
Alas, I burn, and no one will believe it.
Alas, that time has now passed over when.
Alas, the last of days when I was glad.
Alexander, before the sepulchre.
Already you have done, remorseless Death.

Although another's fault takes from me what.
Angels and the souls of the elect, The.
Anger reduced Alexander the Great.
Any lady desiring fame and honour.
Apollo—if you nourish still desires.
As life eternal is the sight of God.
At every step, I find I must look back.
Be it, Sennuccio, clearly understood.
Because our life is short.
Because she bore upon her face Love's banner.
Because the road to mercy is shut off.
Birds, singing and lamenting once again.
Blazing knot which twenty-one whole years,
   The.
Blest soul, so often coming back to me.
Breath, the fragrance, and the cooling shade,
   The.
Breeze blowing those blond locks and curling
   them.
But—now her pleasant gentle modest mien.
By now there is no way I could break loose.
By then I knew my flourishing green age.
Charming pallor clothing her sweet smile, The.
Clear, fresh, and pleasant water.
Closer that I come to that last day, The.
Clothing of green, deep crimson, black, or
   purple.
Column and the Laurel-tree are broken, The.
Column of glory, strong stay and support.
Could a more dreadful vision ever be?
Could I but pour out into powerful rhyme.
Could I but take revenge upon that one.
Cruel the star (if stars are powerful).
Death has no power to make that sweet face
   bitter.
Death has put out the sun which dazed my
   eyes.
Death, you have left this world, without its
   sun.
Descending from the sky I see Aurora.
Diana did not more delight her lover.
Each time I call to mind the hour, the place.
Ever mine [*or* myn] hap[pe] is slack and
   slo[w] in coming [*or* commyng].
Every day seems to me a thousand years.
Exhilarated flowers, and lucky grasses.
Father of heaven, for all the days now lost.
For every living creature on this earth.
Foul Babylon has overstepped the mark.
Fountain of sorrow, dwelling-place of wrath.
Fresh, flowery hill, so full of shade, so green.
From loveliest eyes, and from the visage
   which.
From lovely clear and polished living ice.
From Spain to the Hydaspes in the East.
From the new Babylon where shame is dead.
From thought to thought, along each mountain
   top.
From what circle of heaven, from what idea.
Full of that indescribable delight.
Full of that strong desire which sunders me.
Gentle breeze that, through fresh greenery,
   The.
Glancing by chance at my unusual pallor.
Gluttony, sleep, swans-down of idleness.
Go, my sad rhymes, until you reach the stone.
Go, my warm sighs, and melt her frozen heart.
Gold and pearls, and blossoms, white and red,
   The.
Good luck is slow to reach me, always late.
Graces denied to almost everyone.
Had but the light come just a little nearer.
Had I believed those words would turn out
   dear.
Hannibal won indeed, yet failed to take.
Happy and sad, together and yet sole.
Happy in sleep, content to lie around.
Happy season of my early prime, The.
He, who in Thessaly was all too keen.
He who is adamant to live his life.
He Who reveals His providence and art.
Heavenly breeze that breathes throughout the
   green, The.
Her golden hair was blowing in the breeze.
Her hard heart and her will to cruelty.
Hills on which I left myself behind, The.

How fortunate that instant when there came.
How many times already Love has said.
How much I envy you, gluttonous ground.
How oft have I, my dear [or dere] and cruel[l] foe.
How often do I come to this retreat.
How strangely this world wags! Now what distressed.
I am so weary and so heavy laden.
I cannot keep silent, and I fear my tongue.
I do not know, alas, where I should turn.
I feed my mind on such a noble food.
I feel the ancient breeze, see with delight.
I feel the bitter rain of tears distilled.
I find no peace, yet have no war in hand.
I fly on wings of fancy up to heaven.
I go in mourning for those years of mine.
I go on listening, but I cannot hear.
I have a thousand times, dear enemy.
I have been nowhere else where I could see.
I have been shown a myriad slopes and more.
I have by now my sixteenth year of sighs.
I have loved always, and I do love still.
I have not seen you lay your veil apart.
I have prayed Love, and yet again I pray.
I knew already, Love, our human ploys.
I knew—so much heaven opened up my eyes.
I know that nover with a tranquil mind.
I must direct these lines so full of sorrow.
I raised myself in thought to where I found.
I ran beneath the shade of shining leaves.
I really did believe I would go on.
I sang once: now I weep; and I take pleasure.
I saw a lady; on each side a lover.
I saw a lady underneath green laurel.
I saw angelic qualities on earth.
I saw twelve ladies sailing at their ease.
I see, my noble lady.
I see, spread out and waving in the breeze.
I seem to hear that messenger once more.
I sensed my spirits flagging day by day.
I think and think, and in my thoughts I feel.
I thought my wings were fledged for such a flight.
I used to stray far from the fountainhead.
I used to take the blame, but now excuse.
I walk, alone and troubled, desert places.
I was so blest by sheer good luck and Love.
I weep all day; and in the night-time, when.
I wept, but now I sing: my living sun.
I wish to sing no more as once I did.
I would write poems of love of such a kind.
If an unfeigning heart, and amorous faith.
If but that honoured branch which turns away.
If but these thoughts that hurt.
If I could hope by dying to be rid.
If I had lingered longer in the cave.
If I said it, may I be held to scorn.
If, in this fourteenth year of all my sighs.
If Love does not bring better thoughts to bear.
If neither Love nor Death blights this endeavour.
If Polyclitus studied earnestly.
If that attractive look of hers can kill.
If the mountain by which this valley's closed.
If Virgil and Homer had but seen that sun.
If virtuous love can merit a reward.
If, when Simone laboured to depict.
If you, by showing signs of your unease.
If you want me again under your yoke.
I'm caught by Love within a harsh embrace.
In doubtful state I weep, at times I sing.
In her, two enemies were brought together.
In sheer amazement, Love and I together.
In the best season of our earthly span.
Is this the nest in which my phoenix put.
It makes me weary when I realise.
It was my love and grief which drove my tongue.
It was the day Apollo's rays turned pale.
I've never seen the sun rise in such glory.
Jove and Caesar were never so moved—the one.
Julius Caesar, when false Ptolemy.
Just as a moth, enamoured of the light.
Kindly fortune that made me once so happy.

Lady much more radiant than the sun, A.
Lady, who now with our Original.
L'aura, my breeze, so often breathes upon.
L'aura, the gentle breeze that clears the hills.
Leave me, unhappy thoughts, leave me in peace!
Let us pause, Love, to see her and her worth.
Life flies from us, and does not pause one hour.
Life is most dear; and then, it seems to me.
Lightning-flashes of her lovely glance, The.
Little white-haired man moves off from where, The.
Long for the evening, loathe the coming dawn.
Long waiting has by now so worn me out.
Look at that hill, my sad heart, where we stood.
Looking upon the light of those clear eyes.
Lord Love, to whom all hearts and minds are known.
Lord Love, who holds the chief place in my mind.
Lord Love, you see this lady full of scorn.
Love, Fortune, and my mind (hardly aware).
Love had revealed to me a tranquil harbour.
Love, I have sinned, and recognise my sin.
Love kept me burning one-and-twenty years.
Love, kindling in our hearts an ardent fire.
Love, lend a hand to my afflicted mind.
Love makes me go where I had rather not.
Love, Nature, and this lovely gentle soul.
Love set me up to be his arrows' mark.
Love spurs and at the same time reins me in.
Love used to weep, and sometimes I did too.
Love was perhaps a happy thing onetime.
Love, who can promise so beguilingly.
Love, who in good times kept me company.
Love with his right hand opened my left side.
Lust goads, and Love goes with me as a guide.
May heaven's anger blaze down on your head!
Merely to look upon your sacred City.
More happily than I no ship has ever.
More I spread wings of desire to fly, The.
Most glorious Virgin, you are clothed in glory.
My days have gone by swifter than a deer.
My enemy, who often lets you gaze.
My eyes, that sun of ours is shut away.
My face and hair are changing; I grow old.
My faithful glass has very often told.
My heavy life is hanging on a thread.
My ills oppress me, and I fear the worst.
My love for you has never wearied me.
My mad desire has strayed so far, and strays.
My noble lord, all that I have in mind.
My soul, prophetic of your coming loss.
My soul, who see, hear, read, think, speak, and write.
My thoughts talked with each other pleasantly.
My vessel laden with oblivion.
My wish has always been to live alone.
Nightingale, that so harmoniously, The.
Nine times Latona's son had turned his gaze.
Nine Variations on Themes from Petrarch.
No loving mother doting on her son.
No weary weather-beaten mariner.
Noble lineage with calm humility.
Noble spirit, the ruler of that body.
Noble tree, which I loved well and long, The.
Not only that one hand when it is bare.
Not seldom, when her semblance has been kind.
Not stars that wander through the open sky.
Not the Ticino, Arno, Varo, Tiber.
Now blessed be the day, the month, the year.
Now could I but describe with what sweet breath.
Now earth and sky are still, winds blow no more.
Now if not love, what is it that I feel?
Now should my life endure to this extent.
Now that your soul is loosened from that knot.
Now Zephirus brings back the better weather.
O day, O hour, O instant at the last.
O dearest glances, O persuasive breath.
O Envy, enemy to all that's good.
O happy spirit that so charmingly.

O Italy, my land, words cannot heal.
O long expected up in Heaven, O blest.
O lovely hand, clutched tightly round my heart.
O noble soul, glowing with worthiness.
O precious liberty, how you reveal.
O time, O turning sky, speeding away.
O wasted steps, O wanderings in the mind.
O you, my one inestimable gem.
On the greensward there was a milk-white deer.
On the left shore of the Tyrrhenian Sea.
Once I had hopes (so fervent was my rhyme).
Once more Love sends to me that pleasing thought.
One day when I was looking from my window.
Orso, there never was a lake or river.
Orso, upon your charger you may put.
Out of a thousand ladies I saw one.
Over the course of time I think your smile.
Over the grasses Love had spread his net.
Place me where flowers and grass scorch in the sun.
Pleasant obduracy, and calm rejection.
Po, you are quick to take my outer shell.
Poor little bird, singing as you flit by.
Quickening Sun, that bough I love alone.
Royal nature, and a most refined, A.
Rushing river, forcing your rapid way.
Sea has not such creatures in its waves, The.
Seed of Charlemagne, his noble head, The.
Sennuccio, I'm half here. Oh, were I all.
Sennuccio, though you leave your friend alone.
Seventeen years since first I felt the full.
She comes to mind—no, is already there.
She, much more beautiful than others are.
She used to come and comfort me in sleep.
She was alive in me upon a time.
Sight of her, angelic and serene, The.
Since fire is not extinguished by more fire.
Since Love was driving me to my old haunts.
Since through my destiny.
Since what I hope for's taking far too long.
Since you and I so many times have seen.
So feeble is the thread that doth the burden stay.
Sometimes I am ashamed that I have never.
Sonnet: "If grief dismiss me not to them that rest."
Sonnets to Laura, sels.
Soon as madonna comes into my heart.
Sparrow on house-top never was alone.
Star of love was blazing in the east, The.
Stars, the sky, the elements have put, The.
Such is the fear those eyes strike into me.
Sweet anger, sweet disdain, sweet times of peace.
That always bitter, always honoured day.
That bravery, which came to flower in you.
That cheek of yours that has been tired with weeping.
That fire I liked to think had been extinguished.
That lady whom I always have in mind.
That lovely lady who possessed your heart.
That miracle—which in these days of ours.
That other sun by whom the path was shown.
That powerful lord from whom we cannot hide.
That time of day the rapid sky inclines.
That which in colour and in scent outdid.
That window has my everlasting hate.
That window where one sun is visible.
There are some creatures in the world with eyes.
These kindly rhymes by which you have made known.
Thinking of what today adorns the sky.
This breeze, stirring green laurel and my lady's.
This creature with a bear's or tiger's heart.
This is on earth the happiest bit of land.
This noble soul, starting to move away.
This phoenix, so extravagantly plumed.
This short-lived and this fragile happiness.
Those eyes of which so warmly I would speak.

Those eyes that wounded me in such a way.
Though I have tried to keep you from all
　blame.
Thought is rapid, and so short the time, The.
Three days before, my soul reached such a
　place.
Through her I swapped the Arno for the
　Sorgue.
Till both my temples are completely white.
Time had come for me to establish peace, The.
To some it may well seem I pitch my style.
To wreak what sweet revenge is his to wreak.
Towards the dawn, when *l'aura* (the mild
　breeze).
Translation from Petrarch.
Two blushing roses, gathered recently.
Under a lucky star I saw those eyes.
Under the very hills where at the first.
Under the wrath of my dear enemy.
Unexpected angel glided down, An.
Unless, through blind desire which breaks the
　heart.
Upon that face for which I sigh and pine.
Valley re-echoing with woes of mine.
Very instant he has loosed his shot, The.
Victorious and triumphal laurel-tree.
Visions of Petrarch, The.
Walking these woods and these unfriendly
　ways.
We are to be his victim after all.
Weep, ladies; as you weep, let Love weep too.
Weep now, my eyes; accompany my heart.
What do you think, my soul? Will there be
　peace?
What fate of mine, what trickery, what force.
What fear is mine when I recall that day.
What is the matter? And why do you turn.
What pitying messenger, what angel was.
What should I do? Love, what do you advise?
Whatever wonder is found.
When hope was flourishing.
When I begin to send out sighs and call.
When I have stared for some time fixedly.
When I hear you attractively speak out.
When I look back and see how the swift years.
When little birds complaining, or green leaves.
When Lord Love makes her cast her glances
　down.
When my passion—that with two glowing
　spurs.
When out of all the ladies in her sphere.
When she arrives where greatest beauty is.
When that planet which divides the hours.
When that tree moves from where it ought to
　be.
When the first tree was level with the ground.
When the sun sinks his golden chariot.
Whenever her white foot moves through the
　green.
Whenever Love makes his assaults on me.
Whenever my gentle faithful comforter.
Where did Love ever get the gold, to give.
Where is the forehead that with one slight
　shake.
Wherever I turn my eyes or let them rest.
While I still keep you turned, though tired, my
　eyes.
While my poor heart was being eaten still.
Who wants to see what can be done by Nature.
With food in which Lord Love seems to
　abound.
With my deep sighs I fill the ambient air.
With my long-honoured, dear, and cruel lord.
With no regret, not envying anyone.
Yearning yet chaste eyes she held upon, The.
You were a haven once, my little room.
You who can hear in scattered rhymes the
　sound.
You've made the loveliest face, O Death, turn
　pale.

**Petronius Arbiter (Caius Petronius Arbiter) (d.
66 A.D.)**
　Doing, a filthy pleasure is, and short.
　Jokes, repartees, and laugh, and pun polite.
　Out of Petronius.
　Satyricon, *sels.*

Phaedrus (*fl.* c.8 A.D.)
　Fabulae, *sels.*
Philemon (361–263 B.C.)
　By Philemon.
Piccolo, Lucio (1903–69)
　Unstill Universe.
　Veneris Venefica Agrestis.
Pickup *See* **Shih-te (Pickup)**
Pico della Mirandola, Giovanni (1463–94)
　Golden Sestina, The.
Piercy, Marge (b. 1936)
　Ache's End.
　All Clear.
　Apologies.
　At the Core.
　Athena in the Front Lines.
　Attack of the Squash People.
　Barbie Doll.
　Beauty I Would Suffer For.
　Best Defense is Offensive, The.
　Breaking Camp.
　Bridging.
　Bronchitis on the 14th Floor.
　Bumpity Road to Mutual Devotion, The.
　Burying Blues for Janis.
　Butt of Winter, The.
　Cast Off, The.
　Cats Like Angels.
　Cats of Greece, The.
　Cod Summer.
　Community.
　Concerning the Mathematician.
　Consumer, The.
　Councils.
　Crabs.
　Crescent Moon Like a Canoe.
　Crippling, The.
　Crows.
　Curse of the Earth Magician on a Metal Land.
　Cyclist, The.
　Daily Life of the Worker Bee, The.
　Death of the Small Commune, The.
　Digging In.
　Doing It Differently.
　Doors in the Wind and the Water.
　Erasure.
　Excursions, Incursions.
　Few Ashes for Sunday Morning, A.
　For Jeriann's Hands.
　For Shoshana Rihn—Pat Swinton.
　For Strong Women.
　For the Young Who Want To.
　Friend, The.
　Gasman Invites the Skyscrapers to Dance.
　Gift of Light, A.
　Girl in White.
　Going In.
　Gracious Goodness.
　Greater Grand Rapids Lover, The.
　Half Past Home.
　Hallow Eve with Spaces for Ghosts.
　Hand Games.
　Hello Up There.
　High Frequency.
　Homely War, The.
　Homesick.
　I Am A Light You Could Read By.
　I Awoke with the Room Cold.
　I Will Not Be Your Sickness.
　Icon.
　If They Come in the Night.
　In the Men's Room(s).
　In the Wet.
　Inside Chance, The.
　Intruding.
　It Breaks.
　Juan's Twilight Dance.
　Just Anger, A.
　Kneeling at the Pipes.
　Landed Fish.
　Lansing Bad Penny Come Again Blues, The.
　Laocoön is the Name of the Figure.
　Laying Down the Tower.
　Learning Experience.
　Let Us Gather at the River.

　Letter to be Disguised as a Gas Bill.
　Living in the Open.
　Long Death, The.
　Longest Night, The.
　Looking at Quilts.
　Love of Lettuce, The.
　Market Economy, The.
　Married Walk in a Hot Place, A.
　Martha as the Angel Gabriel.
　Meetings Like Hungry Beaks.
　Morning Athletes.
　Morning Half-Life Blues, The.
　Neighbor, The.
　Never-Never.
　Night Flight.
　Night Letter.
　Noon of the Sunbather.
　Nuisance, The.
　On Castle Hill.
　Peaceable Kingdom, The.
　Perpetual Migration, The.
　Phyllis Wounded.
　Poet Dreams of a Nice Warm Motel, The.
　Postcard from the Garden.
　Proposal for Recycling Wastes, A.
　Provocation of the Dream, The.
　Rainy 4th.
　Rape Poem.
　Right Thinking Man.
　Right to Life.
　Root Canal, The.
　Rough Times.
　S. Dead.
　Sabbath of Mutual Respect, The.
　Sand Roads, *sels.*
　Secretary Chant, The.
　Seedlings in the Mail.
　September Afternoon at Four O'Clock.
　Shadow Play For Guilt, A.
　Shadows of the Burning.
　Sign.
　Simple-Song.
　Skimpy Day at the Solstice.
　Skyscrapers of the Financial District Dance
　　with Gasman, The.
　Smalley Bar.
　Snow in May.
　Snow, Snow.
　Sojourners.
　Some Collisions Bring Luck.
　Somehow.
　Song of the Fucked Duck.
　Spring Offensive of the Snail, The.
　Thrifty Lover, The.
　To Be of Use.
　To the Pay Toilet.
　Track of the Master Builder, The.
　Trajectory of the Traveling Susan.
　Twelve-Spoked Wheel Flashing, The.
　Unclench Yourself.
　Under the Grind.
　Unlearning to Not Speak.
　Valley Where I Don't Belong, A.
　Visiting a Dead Man on a Summer Day.
　Walking into Love.
　We Become New.
　What the Owl Sees.
　What You Waited For.
　What's That Smell in the Kitchen?
　Why the Soup Tastes Like the *Daily News.*
　Wind is the Wall of the Year.
　Window of the Woman Burning, The.
　Woman in the Ordinary, The.
　Women's Laughter.
　Work of Artifice, A.
　You Ask Why Sometimes I Say Stop.
Pindar (c.518–c.438 B.C.)
　Pythian Odes, *sels.*
"Ping Hsin" (Hsieh Wang-ying) (b. 1900)
　Old Man and the Child, The.
Pinkerton, Helen
　Alike and Yet Unlike: General Richard Taylor
　　Writes to Henry Adams.
　Autumn Drought.
　Celebration.
　Coast Hillside.

Crossing the Pedregal.
Degrees of Shade.
Elegy at Beaverhead County, Montana.
Epigrams: "*Phony* now has good fortune and a wife."
Error Pursued.
For an End.
For Edgar Bowers.
Gift, The.
Good Friday.
Holy Sonnets.
Indecision.
Lemuel Shaw's Meditation.
Literary Theorist.
Melville's Letter to William Clark Russell.
Melvilliana.
Nature Note: The California Poison Oak.
On a Painting by Todd Price of the 16th Michigan Infantry.
On an Early Cycladic Harpist (2500 B.C.) in the Archaeological Museum in Athens.
On an Early Cycladic Harpist (2600-2500 B.C.) in the J. Paul Getty Museum.
On Blakelock's *Moonlit Landscape* in the de Young Museum.
On Breughel the Elder's *The Harvesters* (1565) in the Metropolitan Museum.
On Caravaggio's *Conversion of St. Paul* (1600) in Santa Maria del Popolo, Rome.
On Dieric Bouts's *Virgin and Child* (1460) in the California Palace of the Legion of Honor.
On Dürer's *Etching of Pilate Washing His Hands* (1512).
On Emily Dickinson.
On Erastus Salisbury Field's *The Israelites Crossing the Red Sea* (1863?).
On Fitz Hugh Lane's *Approaching Storm, Owl's Head, 1860*.
On G.B. Tiepolo's Etching *Adoration of the Magi* (1753) in the Stanford Museum.
On Gari Melchers's *Writing* (1905) in the Los Angeles County Museum of Art.
On Goya's *Duel with Cudgels* (ca. 1820), a "Black Painting" in the Prado.
On Jan van Huysum's *Vase of Flowers* (1722) in the J. Paul Getty Museum.
On Leonard Baskin's Etching *Benevolent Angel*.
On Rembrandt's *Etching of Joseph Telling His Dream* (1636).
On Rembrandt's *Self-Portrait* (1658) in the Frick Museum.
On an Attic Red-Figured Amphora (490 B.C.) by the "Berlin Painter" in the Metropolitan Museum.
On the Jamb-Statues of the Portail Royal (1150) on Chartres Cathedral.
On the Southworth and Hawes Daguerreotype of Massachusetts Supreme Court Chief Justice Lemuel Shaw (1851).
On the Two Marys in a Fresco of the Crucifixion.
On the Virgin and Child Carved in Oak (Auvergne, 1150-1200) in the Metropolitan Museum.
On Vermeer's *Young Woman with a Water Jug* (1658) in the Metropolitan Museum.
On Watteau's *Pilgrimage to Cythera* (1717) in the Louvre.
On Winslow Homer's *Moonlight on Water* (1895) in the Los Angeles County Museum of Art.
Original Sin.
Point Lobos, 1950.
Pool, The.
Red-Tailed Hawk.
Return, The.
Romantic Eros, The.
Sierra Nevada Hike.
Subjectivity.
Three Poems from Michelangelo.
Visible and Invisible.

Pinsky, Robert (b. 1940)
At Pleasure Bay.
Avenue.

Ceremony for Any Beginning.
Changes, The.
City Dark, The.
City Elegies.
Cold, The.
Creation According to Ovid.
Daughter.
December Blues.
Desecration of the Gravestone of Rose P.
Discretions of Alcibiades.
Doctor Frolic.
Dreamer, The.
Dying.
Essay on Psychiatrists.
Exile.
Explanation of America, An.
Faeryland.
Falling Asleep.
Figured Wheel, The.
First Early Mornings Together.
Flowers.
From the Childhood of Jesus.
Garden, The.
Generation Before, The.
Ghost Hammer, The.
Ginza Samba.
Heartmoss, The.
Hearts, The.
History of My Heart.
Hut.
Ice-Storm, The.
Icicles.
If You Could Write One Great Poem, What Would You Want It to Be About?
Immortal Longings.
Impossible to Tell.
In Berkeley.
Jesus and Isolt.
Lair.
Lament for the Makers.
Library Scene.
Long Branch, New Jersey.
Long Branch Song, A.
Memoir.
Memorial.
New Saddhus, The.
Night Game, The.
Old Man, An.
Old Woman.
Personal Devil, The.
Picture.
Pilgrimage.
Pleasure Pier.
Poem about People.
Poem with Refrains.
Questions, The.
Ralegh's Prizes.
Refinery, The.
Rhyme of Reb Nachman, The.
Round.
Sadness and Happiness.
Saving, The.
Sentences, The.
Shirt.
Shiva and Parvati Hiding in the Rain.
Song of Reasons.
Sonnet: "Afternoon sun on her back."
Spelunker.
Street of Furthest Memory, The.
Street, The.
Tennis.
Three on Luck.
Time of Year, the Time of Day, The.
To My Father.
Uncreation, The.
Unseen, The.
Visions of Daniel.
Volume, The.
Voyage to the Moon.
Waiting.
Waking Up.
Want Bone, The.
What Why When How Who.
Window.
Woman, A.

Plath, Sylvia (1932–63)
Above the Oxbow.
Admonitions.
Aerialist.
Aftermath.
Alicante Lullaby.
All the Dead Dears.
Amnesiac.
Among the Narcissi.
Appearance, An.
Apprehensions.
April Aubade.
April 18.
Aquatic Nocturne.
Ariel.
Arrival of the Bee Box, The.
Babysitters, The.
Balloons.
Barren Woman.
Battle-Scene.
Bee Meeting, The.
Beekeeper's Daughter, The.
Beggars, The.
Berck-Plage.
Birthday Present, A.
Bitter Strawberries.
Black Pine Tree in an Orange Light.
Black Rook in Rainy Weather.
Blackberrying.
Blue Moles.
Bluebeard.
Brasilia.
Bucolics.
Bull of Bendylaw, The.
Burning the Letters.
Burnt-out Spa, The.
By Candlelight.
Candles.
Channel Crossing.
Child.
Childless Woman.
Child's Park Stones.
Cinderella.
Circus in Three Rings.
Colossus, The.
Companionable Ills, The.
Contusion.
Conversation among the Ruins.
Courage of Shutting-Up, The.
Couriers, The.
Crossing the Water.
Crystal Gazer.
Cut.
Daddy.
Danse Macabre.
Dark Wood, Dark Water.
Dead, The.
Death and Co.
Death of Myth-making, The.
Denouement.
Departure.
Detective, The.
Dialogue between Ghost and Priest.
Dialogue *En Route*.
Dirge for a Joker.
Dispossessed, The.
Disquieting Muses, The.
Doom of Exiles.
Doomsday.
Dream, The.
Dream with Clam-Diggers.
Eavesdropper.
Edge.
Electra on Azalea Path.
Ella Mason and Her Eleven Cats.
Elm.
Epitaph for Fire and Flower.
Epitaph in Three Parts.
Event.
Everlasting Monday, The.
Eye-Mote, The.
Fable of the Rhododendron Stealers.
Face Lift.
Family Reunion.
Faun.

Fearful, The.
Female Author.
Fever 103°.
Fiesta Melons.
Finisterre.
Firesong.
For a Fatherless Son.
Frog Autumn.
Full Fathom Five.
Getting There.
Ghost's Leavetaking, The.
Gigolo.
Glutton, The.
Go Get the Goodly Squab.
Goatsucker.
Gold Mouths Cry.
Goring, The.
Great Carbuncle, The.
Green Rock, Winthrop Bay.
Gulliver.
Hanging Man, The.
Hardcastle Crags.
Heavy Women.
Hermit at Outermost House, The.
I Am Vertical.
I Want, I Want.
In Midas' Country.
In Plaster.
Incommunicado.
Insolent Storm Strikes at the Skull.
Insomniac.
Jailer, The.
Jilted.
Kindness.
Lady and the Earthenware Head, The.
Lady Lazarus.
Lament: "Sting of bees took away my father,
   The."
Landowners.
Last Words.
Leaving Early.
Lesbos.
Lesson in Vengeance, A.
Letter in November.
Letter to a Purist.
Life, A.
Little Fugue.
Lorelei.
Love Is a Parallax.
Love Letter.
Lyonnesse.
Magi.
Magnolia Shoals.
Man in Black.
Manor Garden, The.
Mary's Song.
Maudlin.
Mayflower.
Medallion.
Medusa.
Memoirs of a Spinach-Picker.
Metamorphoses of the Moon.
Metaphors.
Midsummer Mobile.
Mirror.
Miss Drake Proceeds to Supper.
Monologue at 3 A.M.
Moon and the Yew Tree, The.
Moonrise.
Moonsong at Morning.
Morning in the Hospital Solarium.
Morning Song.
Munich Mannequins, The.
Mushrooms.
Mussel Hunter at Rock Harbor.
Mystic.
Natural History.
Net-Menders, The.
Never Try to Trick Me with a Kiss.
New Year on Dartmoor.
Nick and the Candlestick.
Night Dances, The.
Night Shift.
Notes to a Neophyte.
November Graveyard.
Ode for Ted.

Old Ladies' Home.
On Deck.
On Looking into the Eyes of a Demon Lover.
On the Decline of Oracles.
On the Difficulty of Conjuring Up a Dryad.
On the Plethora of Dryads.
Other, The.
Other Two, The.
Ouija.
Owl.
Paralytic.
Parliament Hill Fields.
Perseus.
Pheasant.
Poem for a Birthday.
Poems, Potatoes.
Point Shirley.
Polly's Tree.
Poppies in July.
Poppies in October.
Princess and the Goblins, The.
Private Ground.
Prologue to Spring.
Prospect.
Purdah.
Pursuit.
Queen's Complaint, The.
Rabbit Catcher, The.
Ravaged Face, The.
Recantation.
Resolve.
Rhyme.
Rival, The.
Sculptor.
Secret, A.
Sheep in Fog.
Shrike, The.
Sleep in the Mojave Desert.
Sleepers, The.
Snakecharmer.
Snowman on the Moor, The.
Soliloquy of the Solipsist.
Song for a Revolutionary Love.
Song for a Summer's Day.
Sonnet: To Eva.
Sonnet to Satan.
Sonnet: To Time.
Sorcerer Bids Farewell to Seem, A.
Southern Sunrise.
Sow.
Spider.
Spinster.
Stars over the Dordogne.
Stillborn.
Stings.
Stopped Dead.
Street Song.
Strumpet Song.
Suicide off Egg Rock.
Surgeon at 2 A.M., The.
Swarm, The.
Tale of a Tub.
Temper of Time.
Terminal.
Thalidomide.
Thin People, The.
Three Women.
Times Are Tidy, The.
Tinker Jack and the Tidy Wives.
To a Jilted Lover.
To Eva Descending the Stair.
Totem.
Touch-and-Go.
Tour, The.
Trial of Man, The.
Trio of Love Songs.
Tulips.
Two Campers in Cloud Country.
Two Lovers and a Beachcomber by the Real
   Sea.
Two Sisters of Persephone.
Two Views of a Cadaver Room.
Two Views of Withens.
Vanity Fair.
Virgin in a Tree.
Waking in Winter.

Watercolor of Grantchester Meadows.
Whiteness I Remember.
Whitsun.
Widow.
Winter Landscape, with Rooks.
Winter Ship, A.
Winter Trees.
Wintering.
Winter's Tale, A.
Words.
Words for a Nursery.
Words Heard, by Accident, over the Phone.
Wreath for a Bridal.
Wuthering Heights.
Yaddo: The Grand Manor.
Yadwigha, on a Red Couch, among Lilies.
Years.
You're.
Zoo Keeper's Wife.

Plato (*fl.* 492–347 B.C.)
   Kissing Helena.
   On a Bath.
   They said the Muses were but nine, and then.
   To Stella.

Poe, Edgar Allan (1809–49)
   Al Aaraaf.
   Annabel Lee.
   Bells, The.
   Bridal Ballad.
   City in the Sea, The.
   Coliseum, The.
   Conqueror Worm, The.
   Dream, A.
   Dream-Land [*or* Dreamland].
   Dream within a Dream, A.
   Dreams.
   Eldorado.
   Enigma, An.
   Eulalie—A Song.
   Evening Star.
   Fairyland [*or* Fairy-Land].
   For Annie.
   Happiest Day, the Happiest Hour, The.
   Haunted Palace, The.
   Hymn: "At morn—at noon—at twilight dim."
   Israfel.
   Lake: To———, The.
   Lenore.
   Raven, The.
   Romance.
   Scenes from Politian.
   Sleeper, The.
   Sonnet—Silence.
   Sonnet—To Science.
   Spirits of the Dead.
   Stanzas: "How often we forget all time, when
      lone."
   Tamerlane.
   To ———: "Bowers whereat, in dreams, I see,
      The."
   To F———.
   To F—S S. O—D.
   To Helen ("Helen, thy beauty is to me").
   To Helen ("I saw thee once").
   To ———: "I heed not that my earthly lot."
   To ———: "I saw thee on thy bridal day."
   To M. L. S———.
   To My Mother.
   To ———: "Not long ago, the writer of these
      lines."
   To One in Paradise.
   To the River ———.
   Ulalume [*or* Ulalume—a Ballad].
   Valentine, A.
   Valley of Unrest, The.

Pope, Alexander (1688–1744)
   Alley, The.
   Another [Epigram].
   Answer to the Following Question of Mrs.
      Howe.
   Argus.
   Artemisia.
   Balance of Europe, The.
   Bounce to Fop.
   Challenge: A Court Ballad, The.
   Dialogue, A.

Dunciad, The.

Elegy to the Memory of an Unfortunate Lady.

Eloisa to Abelard.

Epigram from the French: "Sir, I admit your general [or gen'ral] Rule."

Epigram in a Maid of Honour's Prayer-Book.

Epigram: "My Lord complains, that Pope, stark mad with gardens."

Epigram on the Toasts of the Kit-Cat Club, Anno 1716.

Epigram: "Peter complains, that God has given."

Epigram: "When other Ladies to the Groves go down."

Epigrams Occasion'd by an Invitation to Court.

Epigrams Occasioned by Cibber's Verses in Praise of Nash.

Epilogue to Mr Rowe's Jane Shore.

Epilogue to the Satires, in Two Dialogues.

Epistle V, to Mr. Addison.

Epistle IV, to Richard Boyle, Earl of Burlington.

Epistle I, to Sir Richard Temple, Lord Cobham.

Epistle III, to Allen Lord Bathurst.

Epistle to Dr. Arbuthnot.

Epistle to James Craggs, Esq., Secretary of State.

Epistle to Miss Blount, with the Works of Voiture.

Epistle to Miss [or Miss Teresa] Blount, on Her Leaving the Town after the Coronation.

Epistle to Mr. Jervas, with Dryden's Translation of Fresnoy's Art of Painting.

Epistle to Robert Earl of Oxford and Earl Mortimer.

Epistle [II,] to a Lady[: Of the Characters of Women].

Epistle [II,] to a Lady[: Of the Characters of Women].

Epitaph for One Who Would Not Be Buried in Westminster Abbey.

Epitaph for One Who Would Not Be Buried in Westminster Abbey.

Epitaph Intended for Mr. Rowe, in Westminster Abbey.

Epitaph (of By-Words).

Epitaph on Charles Earl of Dorset.

see also Epitaph on the Count of Mirandula.

Epitaph on Dr. Francis Atterbury, Bishop of Rochester, Who Died in Exile at Paris, 1732; a Dialogue.

Epitaph on Edmund Duke of Buckingham, Who Died in the Nineteenth Year of His Age, 1735.

Epitaph on General Henry Withers, in Westminster-Abbey, 1729.

Epitaph on James Craggs, Esq., in Westminster Abbey.

Epitaph on John Knight, Who Died Oct. 2, 1733.

Epitaph on Mr. Elijah Fenton, at Easthamstead in Berks, 1730.

Epitaph on Mrs. Corbet, Who Died of a Cancer in Her Breast.

Epitaph on Sir Godfrey Kneller, in Westminster-Abbey, 1723.

Epitaph on Sir William Trumbal.

Epitaph on the Count of Mirandula.

Epitaph on the Hon. Simon Harcourt.

Epitaph on the Monument of the Honourable Robert Digby, and of his Sister Mary, erected by their Father the Lord Digby, in the Church of Sherborne in Dorsetshire, 1727.

Epitaph: "Well then, poor G——— lies under ground!"

Essay on Criticism, An.

Essay on Man, An.

Farewell to London in the Year 1715, A.

First Epistle of the First Book of Horace Imitated, The.

First Epistle of the Second Book of Horace Imitated, The.

First Ode of the Fourth Book of Horace Imitated, The.

First Satire of the Second Book of Horace [Imitated], The.

For Sir W. Trumbull.

Fragment of Brutus, an Epic.

Garden, The.

Happy Life of a Country Parson, The.

Imitation of Chaucer.

Impromptu to Lady Winchelsea.

Intended for Sir Isaac Newton.

Lamentation of Glumdalclitch for the Loss of Grildrig, The.

Lines on a Drawing of a Monument to Swift's Grandfather.

Macer: A Character.

Messiah [a Sacred Eclogue, in Imitation of Virgil's Pollio].

Occasioned by Some Verses of his Grace the Duke of Buckingham.

Ode for Music on St. Cecilia's Day.

Ode on Solitude.

Ode on Solitude.

Ode: The Dying Christian to His Soul.

Of a Lady Singing to Her Lute.

Of Her Picture.

Of Her Sickness.

Of Her Sighing.

Of Her Walking in a Garden after a Shower.

Of the Lady Who Could Not Sleep in a Stormy Night.

On a Certain Lady at Court.

On a Fan of the Author's Design, in Which Was Painted the Story of CEPHALUS and PROCRIS, with the Motto, AURA VENI.

On a Lady Who P-ssed [or P———st] at the Tragedy of Cato.

On His Grotto at Twickenham.

On Lady Mary Wortley Montagu's Portrait.

On Mr. Gay, in Westminster Abbey, 1732.

On Receiving from the Right Hon. the Lady Frances Shirley a Standish and Two Pens.

On Silence.

On the Countess of Burlington Cutting Paper.

Paraphrase on Thomas à Kempis, A.

Part of the Ninth Ode of Horace Imitated.

Pastorals.

Phryne.

Presentation Verses to Nathaniel Pigott.

Presenting a Lark.

Prologue Design'd for Mr. Durfy's Last Play.

Prologue to a Play for Mr. Dennis's Benefit, in 1733, when He Was Old, Blind, and in Great Distress, a Little before His Death, A.

Prologue to Mr. Addison's Tragedy of Cato.

Prologue to the Three Hours after Marriage.

Rape of the Lock, The; An Heroi-Comical Poem.

River, The.

Sandys's Ghost, or a Proper New Ballad on the New Ovid's Metamorphosis as it Was Intended to Be.

Sappho to Phaon.

Satire IV of Dr. John Donne, Versified.

Satire II of Dr. John Donne, Versified.

Second Epistle of the Second Book of Horace Imitated, The.

Second Satire of the First Book of Horace Imitated, The.

Second Satire of the Second Book of Horace Imitated, The.

Seventh Epistle of the First Book of Horace Imitated, The.

Six Maidens, The.

Sixth Epistle of the First Book of Horace Imitated, The.

Sixth Satire of the Second Book of Horace Imitated, The.

Temple of Fame, The.

Three Gentle Shepherds, The.

To a Lady with the Temple of Fame.

To Belinda on the Rape of the Lock.

To Eustace Budgell, Esq., on His Translation of the Characters of Theophrastus.

To Mr. Gay, Congratulating Pope on Finishing His House and Gardens.

To Mr. John Moore, Author of the Celebrated Worm-Powder.

To Mr. Thomas Southern, on His Birth-Day, 1742.

To Mrs. M. B. on Her Birth-Day.

To Quinbus Flestrin the Man-Mountain, a Lilliputian Ode.

To Sir Godfrey Kneller, on His Painting for Me the Statues of Apollo, Venus and Hercules.

To the Earl of Burlington Asking Who Writ the Libels against Him.

Translator, The.

Two Chorus's to the Tragedy of Brutus.

Two or Three, or a Receipt to Make a Cuckold.

Umbra.

Universal Prayer [Deo Opt. Max.], The.

Verbatim from Boileau.

Verses Left by Mr. Pope, on His Lying in the Same Bed which Wilmot, the Celebrated Earl of Rochester, Slept in, at Adderbury, then Belonging to the Duke of Argyle, July 9th, 1739.

Verses Occasioned by an & c. at the End of Mr. D'Urfy's Name in the Title to One of His Plays.

Verses to Be Placed under the Picture of England's Arch-Poet: Containing a Compleat Catalogue of His Works.

Verses to be Prefix'd before Bernard Lintot's New Miscellany.

Version of the First Psalm, for the Use of a Young Lady, A.

Weeping.

Windsor-Forest [or Windsor Forest].

Pope, Alexander See **Gay, John**

Popovski, Anté

  Samuel, sels.

Poquelin, Jean Baptiste See **Molière**

Pound, Ezra (1885–1972)

  Aegupton.

  Alba.

  Alba Belingalis.

  Alchemist, The.

  Alma Sol Veneziae.

  Amitites.

  And Thus in Nineveh.

  Anima Sola.

  Another Man's Wife.

  Apparuit.

  April.

  Aria.

  Arides.

  At the Heart o' Me.

  Aube of the West Dawn. Venetian June.

  Autumnus.

  Aux Belles de Londres.

  Ballad for Gloom.

  Ballad of the Goodly Fere.

  Ballad of the Sun's Hunting.

  Ballad of Wine Skins.

  Ballad Rosalind.

  Ballata, Fragment.

  Ballatetta.

  Battle Dawn.

  Beautiful Toilet, The.

  Beddoesque.

  Blandula, Tenulla [or Tenella], Vagula.

  Blazed.

  Cantos.

  Canzon: "Heart mine, art mine, whose embraces."

  Canzon: The Spear.

  Canzon: The Vision.

  Canzon: The Yearly Slain.

  Canzone: Of Angels.

  Canzone: Of Incense.

  Capilupus Sends Greeting to Grotus.

  Choice, The.

  Chommoda.

  Cino.

  Coda: "O My songs."

  Coitus.

  Coming of War, The; Actaeon.

  Comraderie.

  Contemporania, sels.

  Cry of the Eyes, The.

  Dance Figure.

  Das Babenzorn.

Dawn Song, A.
Decadence, The.
Donzella Beata.
Δωρια.
Echoes.
Effects of Music upon a Company of People.
Encounter, The.
Envoi: "Well have I loved ye, / little songs of mine."
Epigrams: "O ivory, delicate hands!"
Epilogue: "I bring you the spoils, my nation."
Epitaphs: "Fu I loved the high cloud and the hill."
Era Mea.
Erat Hora.
Et Faim Sallir les Loups des Boys.
Ezra on the Strike.
"Fair Helena" by Rackham.
Famam Librosque Cano.
Fault of It, The.
Fifine Answers.
Fistulae.
For a Berry Voice.
For a Play.
For E. McC ("Gone ere the tang of earth").
For E. McC ("Gone while your tastes were keen to you").
For Italico Brass.
For the Triumph of the Arts.
For Ysolt. The Triad of Dawn.
Fortunatus.
Fragmenti.
Francesca.
Fratello Mio, Zephyrus.
From Chebar.
From the Saddle.
Garden, The.
Garret, The.
Girl, A.
Gnomic Verses.
Grace before Song.
Greek Epigram.
Guido Invites You Thus.
Guillaume de Lorris Belated.
Hills Whence, The.
Histrion.
Homage to Sextus Propertius.
Homage to Wilfrid Scawen Blunt.
Hugh Selwyn Mauberley (Life and Contacts).
I have felt the lithe wind.
I Wait.
Idyl for Glaucus, An.
Immorality, An.
In a Station of the Metro.
In Durance.
In Epitaphium.
In Epitaphium Eius.
In Exitum Cuiusdam.
In Morte De.
In Tempore Senectutis ("For we are old / And the earth passion dyeth").
In Tempore Senectutis ("When I am old / I will not have you look apart").
In That Country.
In the Old Age of the Soul.
Invern.
"It Is a Shame"—with Apologies to the Modern Celtic School.
Ité.
La Fraisne.
La Regina Avrillouse.
Lake Isle, The.
Langue d'Oc, *sels.*
L'Art.
Laudantes Decem Pulchritudinis Johannae Templi.
Legend of the Chippewa Spring and Minnehaha, the Indian Maiden.
Les Millwin.
Leviora.
Li Bel Chasteus.
L'Invitation.
Logical Conclusion, The.
Lotus-Bloom.
Love-Song to Eunoë.
Lucifer Caditurus.

Lustra, *sels.*
Madrigale: "Clear is my love but shadowed."
Maestro di Tocar.
Malrin.
Marvoil.
Masks.
Meditatio.
Mesmerism.
Motif.
N. Y.
Na Audiart.
Narcotic Alcohol.
Near Perigord.
Needle, The.
Nel Biancheggiar.
Nicotine.
Night Litany.
Nils Lykke.
O Atthis.
Object, An.
Occidit.
Octave.
Of Jacopo del Sellaio.
Oltre la Torre: Rolando.
On His Own Face in a Glass.
Our Respectful Homages to M. Laurent Tailhade.
Pact, A.
Pagani's, November 8.
Pan is Dead.
Paracelsus in Excelsis.
Partenza di Venezia.
Pastoral: "Young lady opposite, The."
Pax Saturni.
Phasellus Ille.
Piazza San Marco.
Piccadilly.
Picture, The.
Piere Vidal Old.
Planh.
Plotinus.
Plunge.
Poem: Abbreviated from the Conversation of Mr. T. E. H.
Portrait.
Portrait d'une Femme.
Praise of Ysolt.
Prelude: Over the Ognisanti.
Prologue, A: "What light hath passed us in the silent ways?"
Prometheus.
Purveyors General.
Quia Amore Langueo.
Quies.
Redivivus.
Redondillas, or Something of That Sort.
Reflection.
Return, The.
Revolt.
Rosa Sempiterna.
Roundel for Arms.
Rouse, A.
Rune, The.
Salutation.
Salvationists.
Salve O Pontifex!
San Vio. June.
Sandalphon.
Scriptor Ignotus.
Sestina: Altaforte.
Sestina for Ysolt.
Shalott.
She is a thing too frail to know.
Silet.
Song in the Manner of Housman.
Song: "Love thou thy dream."
Song of the Bowmen of Shu.
Song of the Degrees, A.
Sonnet: Chi È Questa?
Sonnet: "If on the tally-board of wasted days."
Sonnet in Tenzone.
Sonnet of the August Calm.
Speech for Psyche in the Golden Book of Apuleius.
Spring, The.
Statement of Being.

Sub Mare.
Summons, The.
Swinburne: A Critique.
Tally-Ho.
Tame Cat.
Tea Shop, The.
That Pass between the False Dawn and the True.
Thersites: On the Surviving Zeus.
Thoughts moving / in her eyes.
Threnos.
To a City Sending Him Advertisements.
To E. B. B.
To Guido Cavalcanti.
To Hulme (T. E.) and Fitzgerald (A Certain).
To La Contessa Bianzafior (Cent. XIV).
To Our Lady of Vicarious Atonement.
To T. H. The Amphora.
To the Dawn: Defiance.
To the Raphaelite Latinists.
To Ysolt. For Pardon.
Tomb at [*or of*] Akr Çaar, The.
Tree, The.
Und Drang.
Vana.
Victorian Eclogues.
Villanelle: The Psychological Hour.
Villonaud for This Yule.
Villonauld, A. Ballad of the Gibbet.
Virginal, A.
White Stag, The.
Xenia ("And / Unto thine eyes my heart").
Xenia ("Come let us play with our own toys").
Xenia ("Out of the overhanging gray mist").

Prime, Benjamin Young (1733–91)
Poetical Correspondence between Palemon and Æmilia, A.

Prince, Lucy Terry *See* **Terry, Lucy**

Prior, Matthew (1664–1721)
Translation of Prior's Chloe and Euphelia.

Propertius (Sextus Propertius) (c.54 B.C.–A.D. c.2)
Ghost, The.
Prayer for His Lady's Life.
When Thou Must Home.

Propertius, Sextus *See* **Propertius**

Prudentius (Prudentius Aurelius Clemens) (348–c.410)
Fortune and Hope! I've made my port.

Prunty, Wyatt
Actuarial Wife, The.
Annals of Jack.
Baseball.
Baseball Team of Unknown Navy Pilots, Pacific Theater, 1944, A.
Black Water.
Blood.
Books, The.
Box of Leaves, A.
Breaking Child, The.
Caligula in Blue.
Child's Christmas in Georgia, A.
Coach.
Cold.
Cousins, Brothers, Sisters.
Covined Bird, The.
Crosswords.
Crows, The.
Depression, the War, and Gypsy Rose Lee, The.
Distance into Place, The.
Domestic of the Outer Banks.
Downtown Bus, The.
Dr. Williams' Garden.
Effervescent Mrs. G, The.
Elderly Lady Crossing on Green.
Extravagant Love.
Eyeing the World.
Falling Through the Ice.
Family Act, The.
Family Portrait for Our Daughter, A.
Ferris Wheel, The.
Flying at Night.
Foliage Tour, The.
Forest Fire.
Four Winter Flies.

Funerals, The.
Gnostic at the Zoo, The.
Good-bye.
Great Thoughts and Noble Feelings.
Grown Men at Touch.
Hand-me-down, The.
Haying.
Husband.
Insomnia.
Intermittent Light, An.
Kite, The.
Lake House, The.
Late Days.
Late Fall, Late Light.
Learning the Bicycle.
Letter.
Letter for the End.
March.
Memorial Day.
Miss Lucy.
Monument, The.
Name, The.
Namesake, The.
New Territory.
Nineteenth Hole, The.
Note of Thanks, A.
Oh General, Oh Spy, Oh Bureaucrat!
Old Cadets, The
Old Declaratives.
Our Tree of Opposites.
Player Piano, The.
Playing by Ear.
Poem, The: "Gnarled avenues the years have
    mapped."
Pyromaniac, The.
Razed House, The.
Reading Before We Read, Horoscope and
    Weather.
Recovery.
Retirement Catalogue, A.
Rio.
Rooms Without Walls.
Saying it Back.
Seasons.
Sequence.
Since the Noon Mail Stopped.
Sisters.
Sneeze, The.
Sorrows of Lester Buster, The.
Stick Builder.
Stillness.
Taking Down, The.
Tent, The.
Thaumatrope.
This.
Times Between, The.
To be Sung on the Fourth of July.
Towards a Relative Ending.
Two Kinds of Cause.
Vegetable Garden, The.
Wallace Stevens Remembers Halloween.
Water.
Water Slide Along the Beach.
Wedding Stop, The.
Widow's Halloween, The.
Wild Horses, The.
Window Washer, The.
Winter's Tale, A.
Yes.
Zamboni's Law.

Pugliesi, Giacomino (*fl.* 13th cent.)
Canzone: Of his Dead Lady.

Pulci, Luigi (1432–84)
Morgante Maggiore, The.

Q

Quasimodo, Salvatore (1901–68)
Agrigentum Road, The.

R

Raine, Kathleen Jessie (b. 1908)
Acacia Tree.
After Fifty-five Years.
Afternoon sunlight plays.
Ah, many, many are the dead.
All that is: / The unbroken surface of the sea.
All things new / But I: no shadow.
Amo Ergo Sum.
And that was all his life.
Angelus.
April's new apple buds on an old lichened tree.
Bad Dream, A.
Banked winter cloud.
Behind the lids of sleep.
Bheinn Naomh.
Binah.
Blue butterflies' eyed wings.
Bright cloud, / Bringer of rain to far fields.
By the River Eden.
Campanula.
Canna's Basalt Crags.
Chartres Annunciation, The.
Childhood.
Childhood Memory.
Cloud,
Columbines.
Crossing the sound I summoned you in
    thought.
Daisies of Florence.
Dead, The.
Dear ones in the house of the dead.
Descent Into Hades.
Dream.
Dream-flowers.
Dream of Roses, A.
Dreams.
Eider afloat in the bay.
Eileann Chanaidh.
Elementals, The.
Eternal Child, The.
Eudaimon.
Falling Leaves.
Fateless Ones, The.
Flower, memory—.
For the Visitors' Book.
Forest is multitude.
From vague regions of sleep I come again.
Frost-rime edges blades of grass.
Golden Leaf, The.
Halt, The.
Harvest of learning I have reaped.
Heirloom.
Her Room.
Hieros Gamos.
High Summer.
Hollow Hill, The.
Holy Isles, The.
House of Music, A.
Hyacinth, The.
I breathe the air you have breathed.
I could have told much by the way.
I felt, under my old breasts, this April day.
I went out in the naked light.
If I choose remorse.
If, into this evening as the grass receives the
    dew.
If you have ceased.
Images.
In the Beck.
Into what pattern, into what music have the
    spheres whirled us.
It is in us they burn.
I've read all the books but one.
Journey, The.
Kore.
Lachesis.
Last night I seemed in your embrace.
Leaf, The.
Letter to Pierre Emmanuel.
Lifelong ago such days.
London air dims.
Long ago I thought you young, bright daimon.
Marriage of Psyche, The.

Medea.
Message.
Message from Home.
Moment, The.
Moment, The.
Monessie Gorge.
Moon golden towards the full.
My day's plan to write.
My Father's Birthday.
My feet in the ever-moving sea.
My Mother's Birthday.
My sight with the clouds.'
Natura Naturans.
Night in Martindale.
Night Sky.
Night Thought.
Nocturn: "Night comes, an angel stands."
Old Paintings on Italian Walls.
On a Shell-strewn Beach.
On an Ancient Isle.
On its way I see.
On Leaving Ullswater.
Once I heard your voice.
Oracles.
Oval Portrait: Jessie Wilkie, The.
Oval the golden moon.
Painting by Winifred Nicholson, A.
Path, The.
Peace of Mind.
Petal of white rose.
Poet Answers the Accuser, The.
Poet is of those, The.
Polluted tide, / Desecrated earth destroyed.
Quenching the Red.
Rainbow, beautiful and clear light, A.
Return, The.
Returning from Church.
Rock.
Rose.
Scala Coeli.
Self.
Seventh Day.
Shells.
Silver Stag, The.
Six calices yellow gold.
Soliloquy Upon Love.
Spell Against Sorrow.
Spell of Sleep.
Spell to Bring Lost Creatures Home.
Sphere, The.
Star of Bethlehem.
Star, The.
Statues.
Still skies, still seas.
Testimony.
There Shall Be No More Sea.
These watery diamond spheres.
This little house / No smaller than the world.
Three Poems of Incarnation.
Three Poems on Illusion.
To the Sun.
Today as I / Looked up at the sky's great face.
Today: / This leafy apple-tree, gray.
Traveller, The.
Triad.
Turner's Seas.
Two Invocations of Death.
Under these hills too high and bare.
Unloved, The.
Vegetation.
Water.
Whales.
What does this day bestow?
What have I to regret.
What message from imagined Paradise.
When I woke up to the snow.
Who listens, when in the concert-hall.
Wilderness, The.
Wind.
Winds.
Winter Paradise.
Winter Solstice.
With a Wave of Her Old Hand.
Word Made Flesh.
World: / Image on water, waves.
World, The.

Ralegh

Young or old / What was I but a story told.
Your gift of life was idleness.

Ralegh, Sir Walter (1552?–1618)

Advice, The.
Ah wretched they that worship vanities.
Ancients called me Chaos: my great yeares.
Arcadians the earth inhabited, The.
Arte of English Poesie, The.
Authours Epitaph, Made by Himself, The.
Because that stealing immortalitie.
Calybes plough not their barren soile, The.
Commendatory Verses to Edmund Spenser's
    Fairy Queen, sels.
Conjectural First Draft of the Petition to Queen
    Anne.
Cretians ever lyars were, they care not what
    they say, The.
Description of Love, A.
Diseases, famine, enemies, in us no change
    have wrought.
Epitaph on Sir Philip Sidney.
Epitaph on the Earl of Leicester [or Leceister].
Even they that have no murdrous will.
Excuse, The.
Farewell to False Love, A.
Farewell to the Court.
Fayne Would I But I Dare Not.
First of all is God, and the same last is he, The.
From the Diary of John Manningham of the
    Middle Temple.
From the Earth, and from thy bloud, O heaven,
    they came.
From wisedome Fortune differs farre.
Giants did advance their wicked hand, The.
Have speciall care, that valiant povertie.
Heaven and Earth one forme did beare.
Homage to Diana.
I have no wine of Gaza, nor Falerna wine.
I sacrifice to God the Beefe, which you adore.
If a Phoenincian born I am, what then?
If Croesus over Halys goe.
If Cynthia Be a Queen.
In Commendation of George Gascoigne's Steel
    Glass.
In the Grace of Wit, of Tongue and Face.
Lie, The.
Like to a Hermit[e] Poor[e].
My Body in the Walls Captived.
Nine furlongs strecht lies Tityus, who for his
    wicked deedes.
No Pleasure, Without Some Payne.
Nymph's [or Nimphs] Reply to the Shepherd
    [or Sheepheard], The.
Ocean's Love to Cynthia, The, sels.
On the Card[e]s, and Dice.
On the Snuff of a Candle.
One fire than other burnes more forcibly.
Passionate Man[']s Pilgrimage, The.
Poem of Sir Walter Rawleighs, A.
Poem Put into My Lady Laiton's Pocket, A.
Poesie to Prove Affection is Not Love, A.
Saturne to be the fatter is not knowne.
Shall I, Like an Hermit, Dwell.
Sir Walter Ralegh to the Queene.
Sir Walter Ralegh's [or S.W. Raghlies] Petition
    to the Queene 1618.
Sir Walter Ra[u]le[i]gh to His Son[ne].
Things thus agreed: Titan made Saturne
    sweare.
To the Translator of Lucan [or Lucan's
    Pharsalia, 1614].
What Is Our Life?
Yet though thou fetch thy pedegree so farre.

"Ramal, Walter" See **De la Mare, Walter**

Ramanujan, A. K. (b. 1929)

Alien.
Anxiety.
Any Cow's Horn Can Do It.
Army Ants.
As Eichmann Said, My Brother Said.
Astronomer.
At Forty.
At Zero.
August.
Birthdays.
Black Hen, The.

Blind Spots.
Bosnia.
Breaded Fish.
Bulls.
Butcher's Tao.
Case History.
Certain Democrat, A.
Chess under Trees.
Chicago Zen.
Christmas.
Compensations.
Connect!
Contraries.
Conventions of Despair.
Copper Vat, A.
Dancers in a Hospital.
Day Went Dark, The.
Death and the Good Citizen.
Death in Search of a Comfortable Metaphor.
Devotee's Complaint, A.
Difference, The.
Difficulty.
Drafts.
Dream in an Old Language.
Ecology.
Elegy: "Grown son's tears in a restaurant mix
    their salt, A."
Elements of Composition.
Engagement.
Entries for a Catalogue of Fears.
Epitaph on a Street Dog.
Excerpts from a Father's Wisdom.
Extended Family.
Eyes, Ears, Noses, and a Thing about Touch.
Fall, The.
Fear.
Fear No Fall.
Fire.
Fizzle.
Fog.
Foundlings in the Yukon.
From Where?
Guru, The.
He Too Was a Light Sleeper Once.
Highway Stripper.
Hindoo, The: He Doesn't Hurt a Fly or a
    Spider Either.
Hindoo, The: He Reads His Gita and Is Calm
    at All Events.
Hindoo, The: The Only Risk.
Hindu to His Body, A.
History.
I Could Have Rested.
If Eyes Can See.
Image for Politics, An.
Images ("I will pass from his mind").
Images ("Mothers smear bitter neem").
In March.
In the Zoo.
Instead of a Farewell.
It.
It Does Not Follow, but When in the Street.
KMnO$_4$ in Grandfather's Shaving Class.
Lac into Seal.
Lapse of Memory, A.
Last of the Princes, The.
Leaky Tap after a Sister's Wedding, A.
Lines to a Granny.
Lines: "Who's this out there."
Looking and Finding.
Looking for a Cousin on a Swing.
Looking for the Centre.
Love 1: What She Said.
Love 2: What He Said, Groping.
Love 3: What He Said, Remembering.
Love 4: What He Said, to His Daughter.
Love 5.
Love 6: Winter.
Love Poem for a Wife, 1.
Love Poem for a Wife, 2.
Love Poem for a Wife and Her Trees.
Man and Woman in Camera and Out.
Meditation, A.
Middle Age.
Minor Sacrifice, A.
Moulting.

Museum.
Mythologies 1.
Mythologies 2.
Mythologies 3.
No Amnesiac King.
No Fifth Man.
No Man Is an Island.
Not Knowing.
Obituary.
Of Mothers.
Old Indian Belief.
On a Delhi Sundial.
On Memory.
On Not Learning from Animals.
On the Death of a Poem.
On the Very Possible Jaundice of an Unborn
    Daughter.
One More after Reading Homer.
One More on a Deathless Theme.
One Reads.
One, Two, Maybe Three, Arguments against
    Suicide.
Opposable Thumb, The.
Pain.
Pain: Trying to Find a Metaphor.
Pleasure.
Poem on Particulars, A.
Poetry and Our City.
Poona Train Window.
Poor Man's Riches 1, A.
Poor Man's Riches 2, A.
Poverty.
Prayers to Lord Murugan.
Questions.
Rather Foolish Sentiment, A.
Real Estate.
Report, A.
Rickshaw-Wallah, The.
River, A.
Routine Day Sonnet.
Ruler, A.
Salamanders.
Saturdays.
Second Sight.
Self-Portrait.
Shadows.
Small-scale Reflections on a Great House.
Smalltown, South India.
Snakes.
Snakes and Ladders.
Some Indian Uses of History on a Rainy Day.
Some Monarchs and a Wish.
Some People.
Some Relations.
Sometimes.
Son to Father to Son.
Sonnet: "Time moves in and out of me."
Still Another for Mother.
Still Another View of Grace.
Still Life.
Striders, The.
Take Care.
That Tree.
This Pair.
Three Dreams.
Time and Time Again.
Time to Stop.
To a Friend Far Away.
Towards Simplicity.
Traces.
Turning Around.
Two Styles in Love.
Watchers, The.
Waterfalls in a Bank.
When It Happens.
Which Reminds Me.
Wobbly Top, A.
Zoo Gardens Revisited.

Ransom, John Crowe (1888–1974)

Address to the Scholars of New England.
Amphibious Crocodile.
Antique Harvesters.
April Treason.
Armageddon.
Bells for John Whiteside's Daughter.
Blackberry Winter.

Blue Girls.
Captain Carpenter.
Dead Boy.
Dog.
Eclogue: "Jane Sneed Began it: My poor John, alas."
Emily Hardcastle, Spinster.
Equilibrists, The.
First Travels of Max.
Good Ships.
Her Eyes.
Hilda.
Jack's Letter.
Janet Waking.
Judith of Bethulia.
Lady Lost.
Man without Sense of Direction.
Miriam Tazewell.
Moments of Minnie.
Morning.
Necrological.
Nocturne: "Where now has our young Adam."
Old Man Playing with Children.
Old Mansion.
On the Road to Wockensutter.
Our Two Worthies.
Painted Head.
Parting at Dawn.
Parting, without a Sequel.
Persistent Explorer.
Philomela.
Piazza Piece.
Prometheus in Straits.
Puncture.
Romance of a Youngest Daughter.
Rose, The.
Sixteen Poems in Eight Pairings.
Somewhere Is Such a Kingdom.
Spectral Lovers.
Spiel of [the] Three Mountebanks.
Survey of Literature.
Tall Girl, The.
Two Gentlemen in Bonds.
Two in August.
Vaunting Oak.
Vision by Sweetwater.
What Ducks Require.
Winter Remembered.

Rashid, N. M.
Izhab-O-Rasai (Expression and Reach).

Rexroth, Kenneth (1905–82)
Adonis in Summer.
Adonis in Winter.
Advantages of Learning, The.
Advent.
After the Anthology.
Again at Waldheim.
Air and Angels.
Aix-en-Provence.
American Century, The.
Among the Cypresses at the End of the Way of the Cross.
Andrée Rexroth ("Now once more gray mottled buckeye branches").
Andrée Rexroth ("Purple and green, blue and white").
Andrée Rexroth ("Years have gone, The. It is spring").
Andromeda Chained to Her Rock the Great Nebula in Her Heart.
Another Early Morning Exercise.
Another One.
Another Spring.
Apple Garths of Avalon, The.
At Lake Desolation.
Ausonius, Epistle 7.
Bad Old Days, The.
Bei Wannsee.
Bestiary, A.
Blood and Sand.
Blue Sunday.
Blues.
Bonapartisme.
Bread and Butter Letter, A.
Camargue.
Chicago Cabaret.

Christmas Note for Geraldine Udell, A.
Cinque Terre.
City of the Moon, The.
Climbing Milestone Mountain, August 22, 1937.
Codicil.
Confusion.
Confusion of the Senses.
Crisis, The.
Dative Haruspices.
De Fera Dormita.
Death, Judgment, Heaven, Hell.
Delia Rexroth ("California rolls into").
Delia Rexroth ("Under your illkempt yellow roses").
Dialogue of Watching, A.
Discrimination.
Doubled Mirrors.
Dragon and the Unicorn, The.
Earth Sky Sea Trees Birds House Beasts Flowers.
Easy Lessons in Geophagy.
Education.
Empty Mirror.
Entrance.
Equation for Marie, An.
Et pour Eux Seuls, les Paradis Chantent Encore.
Fact ("Chirotherium tracks occur").
Fact ("In the encyclopedia").
Falling Leaves and Early Snow.
Family, The.
Fifty.
Fish Peddler and Cobbler.
Floating.
Flower Sutra, The.
Flute Overheard, A.
For Eli Jacobson.
For the Chinese Actress, Gardenia Chang.
Fragrance of the teapot, The.
From the Paris Commune to the Kronstadt Rebellion.
From the Persian (2).
Fundamental Disagreement with Two Contemporaries.
Further Advantages of Learning.
Gambling.
Gas or Novocain.
Gentlemen, I Address You Publicly.
Giant Weapon, The.
Gic to Har.
Golden Section.
Gradualism.
Growing.
Habeas Corpus.
Hanged Man, The.
Hapax.
Harmodius and Aristogeiton.
Heart Unbroken and the Courage Free, The.
Heart's Garden, the Garden's Heart, The.
High Provence.
Hiking on the Coast Range.
Hojoki.
Homer in Basic.
Homestead Called Damascus, The.
Horny Dilemma.
Human, Avian, Vegetable, Blood.
Ice Shall Cover Nineveh.
Illusion.
Imitations of the Chinese.
In the Memory of Andrée Rexroth.
Incarnation.
Incense.
Into the Shandy Westerness.
Inversely, as the Square of Their Distances Apart.
It Is a German Honeymoon.
It Rolls On.
It Turns Over.
January Night.
La Vie en Rose.
Lantern and a Shadow, A.
Last Visit to the Swimming Pool Soviets.
Late Half Moon.
Leaving L'Atelier—Aix-en-Provence.
Leda Hidden.

Lesson in Geography, A.
Letter to Wystan Hugh Auden, A.
Letter to Yvor Winters, A.
Light on the Pewter Dish, The.
Lights in the Sky are Stars, The.
Living Pearl, A.
Loneliness.
Lost Etc.
Love Poems of Marichiko, The.
Lucretius, 3, 1053–1076.
Lute Music.
Lyell's Hypothesis Again.
Martial—12, 52.
Mary and the Seasons.
Maximian, Elegy 5.
Me.
Me Again.
Memorandum.
Metempsychosis.
Mirror.
Mirror in the Woods, The.
Mississippi River.
Mocking Birds.
Monads.
Mother Goose.
Motto on the Sundial, The.
My Heart's as Gay as a Young Sunflower.
Neatness Is All.
Neoclassicist, A.
New Objectives, New Cadres.
New Year, The.
Night below Zero.
No!
No Word.
Noretorp-Noretsyh.
North Palisade, the End of September, 1939.
Northampton, 1922–San Francisco, 1939.
November has hung the locust.
Oaxaca 1925.
Observations in a Cornish Teashop.
Ōkeanos and the Golden Sickle.
Old Song and Dance, The.
Old Street.
On a Beautiful Bar Butterfly in the Black Cat.
On a Flyleaf of Rime—Gaspara Stampa.
On Flower Wreath Hill.
On the Post Office.
On What Planet.
140 Syllables.
Only Years.
Open the Blind.
Organization Men in Affluent Society.
Organon.
Orphic Soul, The.
Ottffssente.
Our Home Is in the Rocks.
Parity.
Park in the Public's or in the Public, Parks.
Past and Future Turn About.
Phaedo.
Phoenix and the Tortoise, The.
Phronesis.
Place, The.
Pliny—9, 36—Lampridius—29.
Portrait of a Lady.
Portrait of the Author as a Young Anarchist.
Precession of the Equinoxes.
Privacy.
Prolegomenon to a Theodicy, A.
Proust's Madeleine.
Prufrock in Wonderland.
Red Maple Leaves.
Reflecting Trees of Being and Not Being, The.
Requiem for the Spanish Dead.
Requiem: "Thousand leaves slant down across the rain, A."
Revolt.
Rosa Mundi.
Rose Colored Glasses.
Runaway.
Saint John.
Schatten Küsse, Schatten Liebe.
Sense of Proportion.
Sharp in My Heart.
She Is Away [or Marthe Away (She Is Away)].
Signature of All Things, The.

Silver Swan, The.
Singing Voice, A.
Song at the Winepresses, A.
Song for a Dancer.
Songs for Marie's Lutebook.
Sottoportico San Zaccaria.
Speak not, let no word break.
Star and Crescent.
Still on Water.
Stone and Flower.
Strength through Joy.
Such Was Our Garden.
Suchness.
Sufficient The.
Survival of the Fittest.
Theory of Numbers.
There shall come faint light.
They Say This Isn't a Poem.
Thin Edge of Your Pride, The.
Thou Shalt Not Kill.
Time Is an Inclusion Series Said McTaggart.
Time Is the Mercy of Eternity.
Time Spirals.
To Another.
Took.
Toward an Organic Philosophy.
Travelers in Erewhon.
Un Bel di Vedremo.
Under Soracte.
Unpeopled, Conventional Rose-Garden, The.
Untitled: "I am fifty-two years old."
Untitled, 6 September 1969.
Value in Mountains.
Value Neuter.
Valuta.
Venice.
Very Early Morning Exercise, A.
Vicenza.
Vitamins and Roughage.
Void Only.
We Come Back.
Wednesday of Holy Week, 1940.
Wheel Revolves, The.
When You Asked for It.
Working Day, The.
Written to Music.
Xmas Coming.
Yin and Yang.
You did not know she was eternal? There.
Your Birthday in the California Mountains.
Yugao.

Rich, Adrienne (b. 1929)
Abnegation.
Absent-Minded Are Always to Blame, The.
After a Sentence in "Malte Laurids Brigge."
After Dark.
After Twenty Years.
Afterwake, The.
Afterward.
Air without Incense.
Always the Same.
Amnesia.
Annotation for an Epitaph.
Antinoüs: The Diaries.
Any Husband to Any Wife.
Apology.
Apology.
Artificial Intelligence.
At a Bach Concert.
At a Deathbed in the Year Two Thousand.
At Hertford House.
At Majority.
At the Jewish New Year.
Atlas of the Difficult World, An.
Attention.
August.
Aunt Jennifer's Tigers.
Autumn Equinox.
Autumn Sequence.
Bears.
Blood-Sister.
Blue Ghazals, The.
Book, The.
Boundary.
Break, The.
Breakfast in a Bowling Alley in Utica, New

York.
Burning of Paper instead of Children, The.
Burning Oneself In.
Burning Oneself Out.
By No Means Native.
Capital, The.
Cartographies of Silence.
Celebration in the Plaza, The.
Change of World, A.
Charleston in the Eighteen-Sixties.
Classmate, The.
Clock in the Square, A.
Colophon.
Concord River.
Continuum.
Contradictions: Tracking Poems, *sels.*
Corpse-Plant, The.
Culture and Anarchy.
Darklight, *sels.*
Days: Spring, The.
Delta.
Demon Lover, The.
Desert as Garden of Paradise, The.
Design in Living Colors.
Dialogue.
Diamond Cutters, The.
Dien Bien Phu.
Diving into the Wreck.
Double Monologue.
Dreamwood.
Eastern War Time, *sels.*
Eastport to Block Island.
Education of a Novelist.
Epilogue for a Masque of Purcell.
Essential Resources.
Euryclea's Tale.
Explorers, The.
Face.
Face to Face.
Fact of a Doorframe, The.
Final Notations.
First Things.
Five O'Clock, Beacon Hill.
5:30 A.M.
Flesh and Blood.
Focus.
For a Russian Poet.
For a Sister.
For Ethel Rosenberg.
For Julia in Nebraska.
For L.G.: Unseen for Twenty Years.
For Memory.
For the Conjunction of Two Planets.
For the Dead.
For the Felling of an Elm in the Harvard Yard.
For the Record.
Frame.
From a Chapter on Literature.
From a Survivor.
From an Old House in America.
From Morning-Glory to Petersburg.
From the Prison House.
Gabriel.
Ghazal.
Ghazals: Homage to Ghalib.
Ghost of a Chance.
Grandmothers.
Halfway.
He Remembereth That We Are Dust.
Heroines.
Holding Out.
Holiday.
House at the Cascades, The.
Hunger.
I Am in Danger—Sir.
I Dream I'm the Death of Orpheus.
I Heard a Hermit Speak.
Ideal Landscape.
Images for Godard.
Implosions.
In the Evening.
In the North.
In the Wake of Home.
In the Woods.
In Time of Carnival.
Incipience.

Innocents, The.
Insomniacs, The.
Insusceptibles, The.
Integrity.
Itinerary.
Jerusalem.
Juvenilia.
Key, The.
Knight, The.
Knot, The.
Kursaal at Interlaken, The.
Lag, The.
Landscape of the Star.
Last Song.
Leaflets.
Letter from the Land of Sinners.
Letters: March 1969.
Life and Letters.
Like This Together.
Likeness.
Living in Sin.
Living Memory.
Loser, The.
Love in the Museum.
Lovers Are like Children.
Lucifer in the Train.
Marriage in the 'Sixties, A.
Marriage Portion, The.
Mathilde in Normandy.
Meditations for a Savage Child.
Merely to Know.
Middle-Aged, The.
Mirror in Which Two Are Seen as One, The.
Missing the Point.
Moth Hour.
Mother-in-Law.
Mother-Right.
Mourning Picture.
Moving in Winter.
Natural Resources.
Necessities of Life.
New Year Morning.
Night.
Night in the Kitchen.
Night-Pieces: For a Child.
Night Watch.
Nightbreak.
Ninth Symphony of Beethoven Understood at
    Last as a Sexual Message, The.
Noon.
North American Time.
Not Like That.
Novella.
November 1968.
Observer, The.
On Edges.
Open-Air Museum.
Orient Wheat.
Orion.
Our Whole Life.
Parting: I, The.
Parting: II, The.
Passing On.
Paula Becker to Clara Westhoff.
Peace.
Peeling Onions.
Perennial Answer, The.
Phantasia for Elvira Shatayev.
Phenomenology of Anger, The.
Photograph of the Unmade Bed, The.
Picnic.
Pictures by Vuillard.
Pieces.
Pierrot Le Fou.
Planetarium.
Platform, The.
Poetry: I.
Poetry: III.
Postcard.
Power.
Prisoners, The.
Prospect, The.
Prospective Immigrants Please Note.
Purely Local.
Rafts, The.
Rain of Blood, The.

Rape.
Raven, The.
Re-forming the Crystal.
Readings of History.
Recorders in Italy.
Reliquary.
Return of the Evening Grosbeaks, The.
Revivalist in Boston, A.
Roadway, The.
Roofwalker, The.
Roots.
Rural Reflections.
Rustication.
Sapling springs, the milkweed blooms, The:
   obsolete Nature.
September 21.
Shooting Script.
Side by Side.
Sisters.
6/21.
Snapshots of a Daughter-in-Law.
Snow.
Snow Queen, The.
So many minds in search of bodies.
Solfeggietto.
Song: "You're wondering if I'm lonely."
Sources.
Spirit of Place, The.
Splittings.
Spring Thunder.
Springboard, The.
Stand Up.
Stelae, The.
Stepping Backward.
Storm Warnings.
Stranger, The.
Stranger, The.
Strayed Village, The.
Study of History.
Sunday Evening.
Tattered Kaddish.
Tear Gas.
This Beast, This Angel.
To Frantz Fanon.
To Judith, Taking Leave.
To the Airport.
Tourist and the Town, The.
Transcendental Etude.
Transit.
Translations.
Tree, The.
Trees, The.
Trying to Talk with a Man.
Turning, sels.
Turning the Wheel.
Twenty-one Love Poems.
Two Poems.
Two Songs.
Ultimate Act, The.
Uncle Speaks in the Drawing Room, The.
Unsaid Word, An.
Unsounded.
Upcountry.
Upper Broadway.
Valediction Forbidding Mourning, A.
Versailles.
Vertigo.
View of Merton College, A.
View of the Terrace, A.
Villa Adriana.
Violence.
Waking in the Dark.
Walden 1950.
Walk by the Charles, A.
Wave, The.
Well, The.
What Ghosts Can Say.
When/Then.
When This Clangor in the Brain.
When We Dead Awaken.
When your sperm enters me, it is altered.
White Night.
Why Else but to Forestall This Hour.
Wild Sky, The.
Will to Change, The.
Winter.

Woman Dead in Her Forties, A.
Woman Mourned by Daughters, A.
Women.
Yom Kippur 1984.
Your Letter.

Riley, James Whitcomb (1849–1916)
Abe Martin.
Absence of Little Wesley, The.
Adjustable Lunatic, An, sels.
After Death.
After the Frost.
Afterwhiles.
Albumania.
All-Golden, The.
All-kind Mother, The.
Almost beyond Endurance.
America.
America's Thanksgiving.
Ancient Printerman, The.
Another Ride from Ghent to Aix.
Anselmo.
Apart.
Armazindy.
Art and Love.
Art and Poetry.
Artemus of Michigan, The.
As Created.
As I Sit in the Silence.
As My Uncle Ust to Say.
As We Read Burns.
Assassin, An.
Assassin, The.
At Aunty's House.
At Bay.
At Broad Ripple.
At Crown Hill.
At Dusk.
At His Wintry Tent.
At Last.
At Madame Manicure's.
At Ninety in the Shade.
At Noon—and Midnight.
At Sea.
At "The Literary."
At Utter Loaf.
August.
August.
Autographic.
Autumn.
Autumnal Extravaganza, An.
Autumnal Tonic, An.
Away.
Babe Herrick.
Babyhood.
Baby's Dying.
Back from a Two-Years' Sentence.
Back from Town.
Backward Look, A.
Ballad, A: "Crowd about me, little children."
Ballad from April, A.
Ballad of Smiles and Tears, The.
Ballade of the Coming Rain, The.
Ban, The.
Barefoot Boy, A.
Bat, The.
Be Our Fortunes as They May.
Bear Family, A.
Beautiful City, The.
Becalmed.
Because.
Bed, The.
Bedouin.
Bee-Bag, The.
Being His Mother.
Bells Jangled.
Benjamin Harrison.
Bereaved.
Best Is Good Enough, The.
Best of All.
Best Times, The.
Billy and His Drum.
Billy Could Ride.
Billy Goodin.'
Billy Miller's Circus-Show.
Billy's Alphabetical Animal Show.
Bin a-Fishin.'

Blind.
Blind Girl, The.
Blooms of May.
Blossoms on the Trees, The.
"Blue-Monday" at the Shoe Shop.
Book of Joyous Children, The.
Boy-Friend, The.
Boy Lives on Our Farm, The.
Boy Patriot, The.
Boy's Candidate, The.
Boy's Mother, A.
Boys of the Old Glee Club, The.
Boys, The.
Brave Refrain, A.
Bride, A.
Brook-Song, The.
Brudder Sims.
Bryant.
Bub Says.
Bumblebee, The.
Busch and Tommy.
By Any Other Name.
By Her White Bed.
Canary at the Farm, A.
Case in P'int, A.
Cassander.
Chairley Burke's in Town.
Chant of the Cross-bearing Child, The.
Charles H. Philips.
Charms.
Child-World, A, sels.
Children of the Childless, The.
Child's Christmas Carol.
Child's Home—Long Ago, A.
Christ, The.
Christine.
Christine's Song.
Christmas Afterthought.
Christmas along the Wires.
Christmas Glee, A.
Christmas Greeting.
Christmas Long Ago, The.
Christmas Memory, A.
Christmas Season.
Christmas-Time Jingle, A.
Circus-Day Parade, The.
Circus Parade, The.
Claude Matthews.
Climatic Sorcery.
Close the Book.
Clover, The.
Company Manners.
Conqueror, The.
Coon-Dog Wess.
Country Editor, The.
Country Pathway, A.
Craqueodoom.
Cuored o' Skeerin.
Cup of Tea, A.
Curly Locks.
Curse of the Wandering Foot, The.
Cyclone, The.
Dan O'Sullivan.
Dan Paine.
Das Krist Kindel.
Dave Field.
Dawn, Noon and Dewfall.
Days Gone By, The.
Dead in Sight of Fame.
Dead Joke and the Funny Man, The.
Dead Leaves.
Dead Lover, The.
Dead, My Lords.
Dead Selves.
Dead Wife, The.
Dear Hands.
Dearth.
Death.
Death Is Dead.
Decoration Day on the Place.
Defective Santa Claus, A.
Deformed.
Discouraging Model, A.
Ditty of No Tone, A.
Diverted Tragedy, A.
Doc Sifers.

Doctor, The.
Dolores.
Donn Piatt of Mac-o-chee.
Doodle-Bug's Charm, The.
Dos't o' Blues, A.
Dot Leedle Boy.
Down around the River.
Down on Wriggle Crick.
Down to the Capital.
Dream.
Dream, A.
Dream-March.
Dream of Autumn, A.
Dream of Inspiration, A.
Dream of Long Ago, A.
Dream of the Little Princess, The.
Dream Unfinished, A.
Dreamer, Say.
Drum, The.
Dubious "Old Kriss," A.
Dusk Song—The Beetle.
Earthquake, The.
Edgar Wilson Nye.
Edge of the Wind, The.
Elizabeth.
Elmer Brown.
Emerson.
Empty Glove, An.
Empty Nest, An.
Empty Song, The.
End, An.
Enduring, The.
Equity—?
Erasmus Wilson.
Ere I Went Mad.
Eros.
Eternity.
Eugene Field.
Evagene Baker.
Even as a Child.
Evensong.
Exceeding All.
Extremes.
Ezra House.
Faith.
Fall-Crick View of the Earthquake, A.
False and True.
Fame.
Fantasy, A.
Farmer Whipple—Bachelor.
Father William.
Feel in the Chris'mas-Air, A.
Fessler's Bees.
Few of the Bird-Family, A.
Find the Favorite.
Fire at Night.
First Bluebird, The.
Fishing Party, The.
Flying Islands of the Night, The.
Folks at Lonesomeville.
Fool-Youngens.
For This Christmas.
For You.
Friday Afternoon.
Friend of a Wayward Hour.
Frog, The.
From a Balloon.
From Below.
From Delphi to Camden.
From the Headboard of a Grave in Paraguay.
Fruit-Piece, A.
Full Harvest, A.
Funniest Thing in the World, The.
Funny Little Fellow, The.
General Lew Wallace.
George A. Carr.
George Mullen's Confession.
Ginoine Ar-tickle, The.
Give Me the Baby.
Gladness.
Glamour.
Glimpse of Pan, A.
Go Read Your Book!
Go, Winter!
God's Mercy.
Goin' to the Fair.

Golden Wedding, A.
Goldie Goodwin.
Good-By, A.
Good-by er Howdy-do.
Good-by, Old Year.
Good Man, A.
Good, Old-fashioned People, The.
Grampa's Choice.
Grandfather Squeers.
Granny.
Grant.
Great Explorer, The.
Great God Pan, The.
Green Fields and Running Brooks.
Green Grass of Old Ireland, The.
Griggsby's Station.
Gudewife, The.
Guide, The.
Guinevere.
Guiney-Pigs.
Gustatory Achievement, A.
Happy Little Cripple, The.
Harlie.
Harp of the Minstrel, The.
Harper, The.
Has She Forgotten?
He and I.
He Called Her In.
He Cometh in Sweet Sense.
Henry Irving.
Henry W. Grady.
Her Beautiful Eyes.
Her Beautiful Hands.
Her Choice.
Her Hair.
Her Light Guitar.
Her Lonesomeness.
Her Poet-Brother.
Her Smile of Cheer and Voice of Song.
Her Valentine.
Her Waiting Face.
Hereafter, The.
Herr Weiser.
Highest Good, The.
Hik-Tee-Dik.
Hint of Spring, A.
Hired Man's Dog-Story, The.
Hired Man's Faith in Children, The.
His Christmas Sled.
His Heart of Constant Youth.
His Last Picture.
His Love of Home.
His Mother.
His Mother's Way.
His Pa's Romance.
His Room.
His Vigil.
Hobo Voluntary, A.
Home Again.
Home Ag'in.
Home at Night.
Home-Folks.
Home-Made Fairy Tale, A.
Home-made Riddles.
Home-Voyage, The.
Honey Dripping from the Comb.
Hoodoo, The.
Hoosier Calendar, A.
Hoosier Folk-Child, The.
Hoosier in Exile, The.
Hoosier Spring-Poetry.
Hope.
Hoss, The.
Hour before the Dawn, The.
How Did You Rest, Last Night?
How It Happened.
How John Quit the Farm.
Humble Singer, A.
Hunter Boy, The.
Hymb of Faith, A.
Hymn Exultant.
I' Got to Face Mother To-Day!
I Smoke My Pipe.
Idiot, An.
If I Knew What Poets Know.
Ike Walton's Prayer.

Illileo.
Impetuous Resolve, An.
Impromptu Fairy-Tale, An.
Impromptu on Roller Skates, An.
In a Box.
In Bohemia.
In Days to Come.
In Fervent Praise of Picnics.
In State.
In Swimming-Time.
In the Afternoon.
In the Corridor.
In the Dark.
In the Evening.
In the Heart of June.
In the Night.
In the South.
Indiana.
Intellectual Limitations.
Invocation, An.
Iron Horse, The.
Iry and Billy and Jo.
It's *Got* to Be.
Jack-in-the-Box.
Jack the Giant-Killer.
Jap Miller.
Jargon-Jingle.
Jaybird, The.
Jim.
Job Work.
John Alden and Percilly.
John Boyle O'Reilly.
John Brown.
John McKeen.
John Tarkington Jameson.
John Walsh.
Johnson's Boy.
Jolly Miller, The.
Joney.
Josh Billings.
Judith.
June.
June at Woodruff.
Just as of Old.
Just to Be Good.
Kathleen Mavourneen.
Katydids, The.
Kind Old Man, The.
King of Oo-Rinktum-Jing, The.
King, The.
Kingry's Mill.
Kissing the Rod.
Knee-deep in June.
Kneeling with Herrick.
Land of Thus-and-So, The.
Land of Used-to-Be, The.
Larry Noolan's New Year.
Last Christmas Was a Year Ago.
Last Night—and This.
Last Words.
Laughing Song.
Laughter.
Laughter Holding Both His Sides.
Laughter of the Rain, The.
Law of the Perverse, The.
Lawyer and Child.
Leave-Taking, A.
Lee O. Harris.
Leedle Dutch Baby.
Legend Glorified, The.
Lelloine.
Leonainie.
Let Something Good Be Said.
Let Us Forget.
Letter to a Friend, A.
Lewis D. Hayes.
Liberty.
Life at the Lake.
Life-Lesson, A.
Life Term, A.
Light of Love, The.
Like His Mother Used to Make.
Lincoln.
Lincoln—The Boy.
Lines fer Isaac Bradwell, of Indanoplis, Ind.,
    County-Seat of Marion.

Lines for an Album.
Lines: "Portentous sound! mysteriously vast."
Lines: "Thou little naked statuette."
Lines to an Onsettled Young Man.
Lines to Perfesser John Clark Ridpath.
Lisper, The.
Lisping in Numbers.
Little Coat, The.
Little Cousin Jasper.
Little David.
Little Dead Man, The.
Little Dick and the Clock.
Little Dog-Woggy, The.
Little Fat Doctor, The.
Little-Girl-Two-Little-Girls.
Little Girly-Girl.
Little Johnts's Chris'mus.
Little Lady, The.
Little Lame Boy's Views, A.
Little Maid-o'-Dreams.
Little Man in the Tin-Shop, The.
Little Mandy's Christmas Tree.
Little Marjorie.
Little Mock-Man, The.
Little Old Poem That Nobody Reads, The.
Little Orphant Annie.
Little-Red-Apple Tree, The.
Little Tiny Kickshaw, The.
Little Town o' Tailholt, The.
Little White Hearse, The.
Little Woman, The.
Liz-Town Humorist, A.
'Lizabuth-Ann on Bakin'-Day.
Local Politician from Away Back, A.
Lockerbie Fair.
Lockerbie Street.
Longfellow ("O gentlest Kinsman of
  Humanity!").
Longfellow ("Words have talked with him").
Longfellow's Love for the Children.
Lord Bacon.
Lost Kiss, The.
Lost Love, A.
Lost Path, The.
Lost Thrill, The.
Louella Wainie.
Lounger, A.
Loveliness, The.
Lovely Child, The.
Lovely Husband, The.
Love's as Broad as Long.
Loving Cup, The.
Lugubrious Whing-Whang, The.
Lullaby: "Maple strews the embers of its
  leaves, The."
Luther A. Todd.
Luther Benson.
Mabel.
Mad Lover, The.
Man by the Name of Bolus, A.
Man in the Moon, The.
Man of Many Parts, A.
Man's Devotion.
Marthy Ellen.
Masque of the Seasons, A.
Max and Jim.
McFeeters' Fourth.
Me and Mary.
Meredith Nicholson.
Merman, The.
Michael Flynn and the Baby.
Mr. Foley's Christmas.
Mister Hop-Toad.
Mr. What's-His-Name.
Mona Machree.
'Mongst the Hills o' Somerset.
Monsieur le Secretaire.
Monument for the Soldiers, A.
Moon-drowned.
Moonshiner's Serenade.
Morning.
Morton.
Mortul Prayer, A.
Mother.
Mother Goose.
Mother Sainted, The.

Mother-Song, A.
Motto, A.
Mr. Silberberg.
Mrs. Benjamin Harrison.
Mulberry Tree, The.
Muskingum Valley, The.
Mute Singer, The.
My Bachelor Chum.
My Boy.
My Bride That Is to Be.
My Conscience.
My Dancin'-Days Is Over.
My Father's Halls.
My First Spectacles.
My First Womern.
My Foe.
My Friend.
My Henry.
My Jolly Friend's Secret.
My Laddie wi' the Bashfu' Grace.
My Mary.
My Night.
My Old Friend.
My Philosofy.
My Ruthers.
My White Bread.
Mylo Jones's Wife.
Name of Old Glory, The.
Name Us No Names No More.
Natural Perversities.
Naturalist, The.
Naughty Claude.
Nessmuk.
Never Talk Back.
New Year's Nursery Jingle.
New Year's Plaint, A.
New Year's Time at Willards's, A.
Nicholas Oberting.
Nine Little Goblins, The.
No Boy Knows.
Noble Old Elm, The.
Noblest Service, The.
Nonsense Rhyme, A.
Noon Interval, A.
Noon Lull, A.
North and South.
Nothin' to Say.
O. Henry.
O Life! O Beyond!
Oh, Her Beauty.
Old Band, The.
Old Bob White.
Old Chums.
Old Days, The.
Old-fashioned Bible, The.
Old-Fashioned Roses.
Old Friend, An.
Old Granny Dusk.
Old Guitar, The.
Old Hand-Organ, The.
Old Haymow, The.
Old Hec's Idolatry.
Old Home by the Mill, The.
Old Indiany.
Old John Clevenger on Buckeyes.
Old John Henry.
Old Man and Jim, The.
Old Man, The.
Old Man Whiskery-Whee-Kum-Wheeze.
Old Man's Memory, An.
Old Man's Nursery Rhyme.
Old October.
Old, Old Wish, The.
Old Played-out Song, A.
Old Retired Sea-Captain, The.
Old School-Chum, The.
Old Sweetheart of Mine, An.
Old Swimmin'-Hole, The.
Old-Timer, An.
Old Times Were the Best, The.
Old Tramp, The.
Old Trundle-Bed, The.
Old Winters on the Farm.
Old Year and the New, The.
Old Year's Address, An.
Ole Bull.

On a Fly-Leaf.
On a Splendud Match.
On a Youthful Portrait of Stevenson.
On Any Ordenary Man in a High State of
  Laughture and Delight.
On Reading Dr. Henry van Dyke's Volume of
  Poems—Music.
On the Banks o' Deer Crick.
On the Death of Little Mahala Ashcraft.
On the Sunny Side.
One Afternoon.
One Angel.
One with a Song.
Only a Dream.
Onward Trail, The.
Orchard Lands of Long Ago, The.
Order for A Song, An.
Orlie Wilde.
Oscar C. McCulloch.
Our Boyhood Haunts.
Our Hired Girl.
Our Kind of a Man.
Our Little Girl.
Our Old Friend Neverfail.
Our Own.
Our Queer Old World.
Ours.
Out of Nazareth.
Out of Reach.
Out of the Dark and the Dearth.
Out of the Hitherwhere.
Out to Old Aunt Mary's.
Out-worn Sappho, An.
Over the Eyes of Gladness.
Pan.
Pansies.
Pap's Old Sayin.'
Parent Reprimanded, A.
Parting Guest, A.
Passing Hail, A.
Passing of a Heart, The.
Paths of Peace, The.
Peace-Hymn of the Republic, A.
Pen-Pictur' of a Cert'in Frivvolus Old Man, A.
Penalty of Genius, The.
Perversity.
Pet Coon, The.
Phantom, A.
Philiper Flash.
Piper's Son, The.
Pipes of Pan, The.
Pixy People, The.
Plain Sermons.
Plaint Human, The.
Plantation Hymn.
Poems Here at Home, The.
Poet of the Future, The.
Poet's Wooing, A.
Ponchus Pilut.
Poor Man's Wealth, A.
Poor Student, The.
Prayer Perfect, The.
Preacher's Boy, The.
Prior to Miss Belle's Appearance.
Private Theatricals.
Proem to "Home-Folks."
Proem: "We found him in that Far-away that
  yet to us seems near."
Prose or Verse?
Prospective Glimpse, A.
Puck.
Quarrel, The.
Quest of the Fathers, The.
Quest, The.
Quiet Lodger, The.
Rabbit.
Rabbit in the Cross-Ties.
Raggedy Man on Children, The.
Raggedy Man, The.
Rain, The.
Rainy Morning, The.
Rambo-Tree, The.
Reach Your Hand to Me.
Red Riding-Hood.
Regardin' Terry Hut.
Requiescat.

Rest, The.
Rhymes of Ironquill, The.
Rider of the Knee, The.
Right Here at Home.
Ringworm Frank.
Ripest Peach, The.
Rival, The.
Rivals, The; or the Showman's Ruse.
Robert Burns Wilson.
Robins' Other Name, The.
Romancin.'
Romaunt of King Mordameer, The.
Rosamond C. Bailey.
Rose in October, A.
Rose-Lady, The.
Rose, The.
Rossville Lectur' Course, The.
Rough Sketch, A.
Rubáiyát of Doc Sifers.
Runaway Boy, The.
Sad Perversity.
Same Old Story, The.
Say Something to Me.
Schoolboy's Favorite, The.
Scotty.
Scraps.
Scrawl, A.
Sea-Song from the Shore, A.
September Dark.
Serenade, The: "Midnight is not more
    bewildering, The."
Serenade—To Nora.
Sermon of the Rose, The.
Session with Uncle Sidney, A.
Shadow and Shine.
She "Displains" It.
Shoemaker, The.
Short'nin' Bread Song—Pieced Out, A.
Shower, The.
Silence.
Silent Singer, The.
Silent Victors, The.
Simple Recipe, A.
Since My Mother Died.
Singer, The.
Sis Rapalye.
Sister Jones's Confession.
Sleep ("Thou drowsy god").
Sleep ("Ophaned, I cry to thee").
Sleeping Beauty, A.
Slumber-Song.
Smitten Purist, The.
Snow in the Air.
Soldier, The.
Soldiers Here To-Day.
Some Christmas Youngsters.
Some Imitations.
Some Scattering Remarks of Bub's.
Some Songs after Master-Singers.
Someday.
Somep'n Common-like.
Something.
Song Discordant.
Song for Christmas, A.
Song—for November.
Song o' Cheer, A.
Song: "O I would I had a lover!"
Song of Parting.
Song of Singing, A.
Song of the Bullet.
Song of the Cruise, A.
Song of the New Year.
Song of the Road, A.
Song of Yesterday, The.
Songs of a Life-Time.
Songs Tuneless.
South Wind and the Sun, The.
Southern Singer, A.
Speeding of the King's Spite, The.
Sphinx, The.
Spirits at Home.
Spoiled Child, The.
Spring Song and a Later, A.
Squire Hawkins's Story.
Squirt-Gun Uncle Maked Me, The.
Stanzas for a New Song.

Stepmother, The.
Strange Young Man, The.
Sudden Shower, A.
Summer Afternoon, A.
Summer Sunrise, A.
Summer-Time and Winter-Time.
Summer-Time, The.
Summer's Day, A.
Sun and Rain.
Suspense.
Sutter's Claim.
Symptoms.
T. C. Philips.
Tale of the Airly Days, A.
Tennyson.
Test, A.
Test of Love, A.
Text, The.
Thanksgiving.
Thanksgiving Day at Hunchley's.
That-air Young-un.
That Night.
That Other Maud Miller.
Their Sweet Sorrow.
Them Flowers.
Them Old Cheery Words.
There Is a Need.
Thinkin' Back.
This Dear Child-Hearted Woman That Is Dead.
This Man Jones.
Thomas the Pretender.
Thoughts fer the Discuraged Farmer.
Thoughts of Youth, The.
Thoughts on a Pore Joke.
Thoughts on the Late War.
Three Dead Friends.
Three Jolly Hunters, The.
Three Several Birds.
Three Singing Friends.
Through Sleepy-Land.
Time.
Time of Clearer Twitterings.
Tinkle of Bells, A.
Tired Out.
To a Boy Whistling.
To a Jilted Swain.
To a Poet-Critic.
To a Poet on His Marriage.
To a Skull.
To Almon Keefer.
To an Importunate Ghost.
To Annie.
To Benj. S. Parker.
To Bliss Carman.
To Edgar Wilson Nye.
To Edmund Clarence Stedman.
To Elizabeth.
To Hattie—on Her Birthday.
To Hear Her Sing.
To James Newton Matthews.
To Joel Chandler Harris.
To Leonainie.
To Lesley.
To My Good Master.
To My Old Friend, William Leachman.
To My Sister.
To Robert Burns.
To Robert Louis Stevenson.
To Rudyard Kipling.
To Santa Claus.
To the Boy with a Country.
To the Cricket.
To—"The J. W. R. Literary Club."
To the Judge.
To the Mother.
To the Quiet Observer.
To the Serenader.
To the Wine-God Merlus.
To "Uncle Remus."
Toil.
Tom Johnson's Quit.
Tom Van Arden.
Tommy Smith.
Touch of Loving Hands, The.
Town and Country.
Town Karnteel, The.

Toy-Balloon, The.
Toy Penny-Dog, The.
Tradin' Joe.
Train-Misser, The.
Traveling Man, The.
Treasure of the Wise Man, The.
Tree-Toad, The.
Tress of Hair, A.
Trestle and the Buck-Saw, The.
Tribute of His Home, The.
Truly Marvelous, The.
Tugg Martin.
Twilight Stories.
Twins, The ("One's the pictur' of his Pa").
Twins, The ("We're the Twins").
Twintorette, A.
Two Sonnets to the June-Bug.
Uncle Dan'l in Town over Sunday.
Uncle Sidney.
Uncle Sidney's Logic.
Uncle Sidney's Rhymes.
Uncle Sidney's Views.
Uncle William's Picture.
Uncomforted.
Unheard, The.
Uninterpreted.
Unknown Friends.
Unless.
Unspoken.
Up and Down Old Brandywine.
Us Farmers in the Country.
Used-to-Be, The.
Variation, A.
Very Tall Boy, A.
Vision of Rabbi Ben Issac, The.
Vision of Summer, A.
Voice from the Farm, A.
Voice of Peace, The.
Voices, The.
Wait.
Wait for the Morning.
Waitin' fer the Cat to Die.
Wandering Jew, The.
Want to Be Whur Mother Is.
Wash Lowry's Reminiscence.
Watches of the Night, The.
Water-Color, A.
Way It Wuz, The.
Way the Baby Came, The.
Way the Baby Woke, The.
We Are Not Always Glad When We Smile.
We Defer Things.
We Must Believe.
We Must Get Home.
We to Sigh Instead of Sing.
Werewife, The.
Wet-Weather Talk.
What a Dead Man Said.
What Chris'mas Fetched the Wigginses.
What Little Saul Got, Christmas.
What "Old Santa" Overheard.
What Redress.
What Smith Knew about Farming.
What the Wind Said.
What They Said.
What Title?
Whatever the Weather May Be.
When Age Comes On.
When Baby Played.
When Baby Slept.
When Baby Woke.
When Bessie Died.
When de Folks Is Gone.
When Early March Seems Middle May.
When Evening Shadows Fall.
When I Do Mock.
When It Rains.
When June Is Here.
When Lide Married *Him*.
When Maimie Married.
When Mother Combed My Hair.
When My Dreams Come True.
When Old Jack Died.
When Our Baby Died.
When She Comes Home.
When the Frost Is on the Punkin.

When the Green Gits Back in the Trees.
When the Hearse Comes Back.
When the World Bu'sts Through.
When Uncle Doc Was Young.
When We First Played "Show."
When We Three Meet.
Where-Away.
Where Shall We Land?
Where the Children Used to Play.
Which Ane.
While Cigarettes to Ashes Turn.
While the Musician Played.
Whitheraways, The.
Whittier—at Newburyport.
Who Bides His Time.
Who Santy Claus Wuz.
Wholly Unscholastic Opinion, A.
Why.
Wife-Blessed, The.
William Brown.
William McKinley.
William Pinkney Fishback.
Windy Day, A.
Winter Fancies.
Witch of Erkmurden, The.
With a Child-Book.
With Her Face.
With the Current.
Worn out Pencil, A.
Wortermelon Time.
Wraith of Summer-Time, A.
Wrangdillion, A.
Writin' Back to the Home Folks.
Written in Bunner's "Airs from Arcady."
Ye Scholar.
Yellowbird, The.
Ylladmar.
You May Not Remember.
Young Old Man, The.
Your Height Is Ours.
Your Violin.
Youth and Age.
Youthful Patriot, The.
Youthful Press, The.

Rilke, Rainer Maria (1875–1926)
Affectionate Taxes to France, *sels.*
After-Flight.
Angels' Surprise.
Ardent Country.
Autumn Day.
Autumn Fire.
Autumn Hammer.
Ball, The.
Bella.
Bitter Pleasure.
Blank Joy.
Breasts.
But It Is Purer to Die.
Butterfly.
Calm of Animals, The.
Cat.
Cemetary.
Cemetary in Flaach.
Cemetary in Ragaz.
Child at the Mirror, The.
Child at the Window Sill.
Child, The.
Child in Red.
Childhood.
Clouds.
Comfort Me.
Cruel Song.
Cuckoo.
Cursed Child.
Dance on the Staircase, The.
Das Kleine Weinjahr.
Dead, The.
Departure.
Distant Movement.
Divine Disgrace.
Double in the Mirror, The.
Doubt.
Dream Movement.
Evening Love Song.
Faded Offering.
Fall.

Few Easter Eggs, A.
Fire's Reflection.
For Monique.
Fragments, *sels.*
From Father to Son.
Fugitives, The.
Funeral.
Future, The.
Geranium.
Gestures.
Gong.
Goodbyes, Still More Goodbyes.
Graves.
Great Indulgent Heart.
Great Pardon, The.
Grisaille.
Growing Old.
Happy Men and Women.
He Can Find No Rest.
Heart's Noise.
Heavy Dead, The.
Holy Ghost.
In This Life of Neglect.
Its Summer Night.
Judgments.
Lemon and Laburnum.
Lesson, The.
Let's Leave.
Lies 1.
Lies 2.
Lies 3.
Loss.
Lost Nights.
Lost Things.
Lying to a Child.
Magician, The.
Mask, The.
Masks Offer Themselves.
Melon.
Memories of Muzot.
Menace.
Migration of Powers, The.
Moment Between Masks.
Morning Melancholy.
Motherhood.
Music.
Narcissus.
Night Drive.
Night Has Come.
No One Speaks of Them.
Nostalgia.
Nothing's Left.
Notre Dame.
Orchard.
Orchards, *sels.*
Orphan Song.
Orphan, The.
Orphan Wind.
Ossuary.
Our Tears.
Pensive Flower.
Poet, The.
Prisoners.
Prose Poem.
Reading Flowers.
Resurrected Christ, The.
Rose.
Rose on Sunday.
Roses, The, *sels.*
Sacred Place.
Saint Catherine.
Saint Sulpice.
Saltimbanques.
Scale.
Shade.
Silent Whole, The.
Sketch.
Sleep.
Small Notebook.
Soap Bubbles.
Solitude.
Soloist.
Some Perfume.
Song: "Let's pretend we are shepherds."
Song: "You, to whom I don't confide."
Spring.

Springtime.
Stubborn Man.
Summer Day.
Survival.
Telling You All.
These Are the Days.
Three Carriers, The.
To Betsy Steiger.
To Isabelle Trumpy.
To Jean-Louis Vandoyer.
To M.
To Madame Jeanne-Renée Dubost.
To Madame the Baronness Renée De Brimont.
To Marie Laurencin.
To Marina Zwetajewa-Efron.
To Mimi Romanelli.
To Miss Nicola B.
To Miss Sophy Giauque.
To Monique and Blaise Briod.
To Natalie Clifford Barney.
To Nigrovorine Who is Leaving.
To Odilon-Jean Périer.
To Pia Di Valmarana.
To Serve as an Epitaph for the Beautiful
    Madame B.
To Speak a Flower.
To the Moon.
Toys.
Trumpets.
Tuck a Child.
Two Poems.
Unicorn, The.
Unknown Woman's Afternoon.
Valaisian Quatrains, The, *sels.*
"Victories," The.
Victory Asleep.
Wait, The.
Walnut Tree.
Water Lily.
What Survives.
White Lily.
Wind, The.
Windows, The, *sels.*
Winged Seed.
Winter.
Wise and Foolish Virgins, The.
Woman at Her Mirror.

Rimbaud, Arthur (1854–91)
After the Flood.
Anguish.
Antique.
At the Green Inn, Five P.M.
Bad Blood.
Barbaric.
Being Beauteous.
Blackcurrant River.
Blacksmith, The.
Bottom.
Bridges, The.
Broom, The.
Caesars' Rage.
Centre: the Emperor, apotheosis.
Child who picked up bullets, Pubescent Lad,
    The.
Childhood.
Cities ("Official acropolis surpasses the most
    colossal conceptions of modern barbarity,
    The").
Cities ("These are cities! This is a people for
    whom these dream Alleghenies and these
    Lebanons have risen into being!").
City.
Comedy of Thirst.
Crows.
Cunning.
Customs Men, The.
Damned Cherub.
Dead of '92 and '93, The.
Democracy.
Departure.
Deserts of Love, The.
Devotions.
Does she dance? . . . in the first blue hours.
Dresser, The.
Drunken Boat.
Drunken Boat [*or* Barge], The, *sels.*

Evening Prayers.
Evil.
Exiles.
Fairy.
Farewell.
Faun's Head.
Festivals of Hunger.
Festivals of Patience.
Fête Galante.
First Communions.
First Delirium. The Foolish Virgin. The Infernal Bridegroom.
First Night.
Flowerbeds of amaranth as far as.
Flowers.
Fragments According to the Gospel.
Genie.
H.
Hands of Jeanne-Marie, The.
Hanged Men Dance.
Hear the bellow.
Historic Evening.
I was sitting in a Third-Class carriage; an old priest.
Idol, The. Arsehole Sonnet.
Impossible, The.
In Spring, no doubt I prefer the drinking-place.
Just Man, The.
Lightning.
Lilies.
Lives.
Lovely Morning Thought.
Memory.
Mess-room by Night.
Metropolitan.
Michael and Christine.
Morning.
Morning of Drunkenness.
Movement.
My Bohemia (Fantasy).
My Little Lovebirds.
Mystical.
Night in Hell.
Nina Answers Back.
O seasons, o châteaux.
O the ashen face, the horsehair escutcheon.
Old Lady's Old Men!
On summer nights, under the shopfront's piercing eyes.
Once, animals spewed sperm as they charged.
Once, if I remember well, my life was a banquet where all hearts opened.
Ophelia.
Orphans' New Year Gifts.
Our buttocks aren't like theirs. Many times I've seen.
Parade.
Paris War-Cry.
Parisian Orgy, or Paris Filling Up Again.
Phrases ("Overcast morning in July, An. A Taste of ashes wafts throught the air").
Phrases ("When the world has been reduced to a single dark wood for our four astonished eyes").
Poor People in Church.
Progress, big baby, wore shoes by Humanity.
Promontory.
Recollection.
Remembrances of Senility.
Romance.
Royalty.
Ruts.
Sales.
Saturnian Hypotyposes, Ex-Belmontet.
Scenes.
Sealed Lips. Seen in Rome.
Seascape.
Seated.
Second Delirium. Alchemy of the Word.
Sensation.
Seven-year-old Poets.
Shame.
Sisters of Charity.
Squatting Down.
Star's wept pink deep inside your ears, The.
State of Siege?

Stupidities.
Stupidities—Second Series.
Sun and Skin.
Tale.
Tartufe's Punishment.
Tear.
To a Reason.
To Music.
To my bedside reading, books of sublime artistry.
Tortured Heart.
Tramps.
Venus Emerging.
Vigils.
Vowels.
Vulgar Nocturne.
War.
What do they mean to us, my heart, the sheets of blood.
What the Poet is Told on the Subject of Flowers.
Wide-eyed.
Winter Dream.
Winter Festival.
Workers.
Young Couple.
Youth.

Ritsos, Yannis (b. 1909)
Absence.
Abstracted Painter.
Accented Colors.
Achilles after Death.
Acrobat, An.
Acrobatics.
Actual Cause, The.
Adolescent.
After a Settlement of Debts.
After Death.
After the Breakdown of the Treaty between the Lacedaemonians and the Athenians.
After the Ceremony.
After the Defeat.
After the Fire.
Afternoon ("Afternoon is full").
Afternoon ("When I am old").
Agamemnon.
Alcméne.
Almost a Conjuror.
Almost Complete.
Alterations.
Always So.
Ancient Amphitheater.
Apples of the Hesperides 1, The.
Apples of the Hesperides 2, The.
Ascent.
Assistance.
At Nausicä's House.
At the Harbor's Edge.
Audible and the Inaudible, The.
Beauty.
Belfry.
Biased Man, The.
Bitter Knowledge.
Black Boat, The.
Blood.
Bloodletting.
Bodies.
Bridge, The; An Uncalled-for Apology.
Builders.
Calculated Behavior.
Calm.
Cardplayers.
Carnal Word.
Center, The.
Charioteer 1970.
Choice.
Coincidentally.
Common Miracles.
Compromises.
Condensation.
Conformity.
Conjunction "Or," The.
Conqueror, The.
Contradictions.
Corridor.
Country Woman.

Courage or Ignorance.
Craftsman, The.
Danger Outstripped.
Dangers.
Deadly Victory.
Departures 1.
Departures 2.
Departures 3.
Descent.
Deterioration.
Displacement.
Distant, The.
Distinct Motion.
Double Condemnation.
Doubtful Encounters.
Doxology.
Earth's Attraction, The.
Encounter.
Encounters.
End of a Day, The.
Episode.
Esteem.
Etesian Winds.
Ethography.
Evaluation.
Evening Procession.
Exhibits.
Exile's Journals 1, *sels.*
Exile's Journals 2, *sels.*
Exile's Journals 3, *sels.*
Exonerated.
Experiences.
Extinction.
Exultation.
Eyes of the Statue, The.
Eyewitness.
Face or Mask?
Farmer.
Fate of the Observer, The.
Final Agreement.
Final Hour.
Final Obol, The.
First Sensual Delight, The.
First Series, *sels.*
Flute-Player, The.
For Greater Accuracy.
Forbidden Ground.
Forged Passport.
Fulfillment.
Fundamentals, The.
Generalization of Distrust.
Golden Fleece, The.
Gradations.
Gradually Stripped Bare.
Graves of Our Ancestors, The.
Greek Cart-Drivers.
Hands.
Harvest of the Void.
Hearing.
Helen.
Helen's House.
Hill, The.
Hints.
His Glasses.
His Lamp.
His Lamp toward Daybreak.
Honest Confrontation.
Honesty.
Hour of Song.
Hues of a Cloud.
Hunters.
Idiot, The.
Imitation of an Imitation.
Immobilizing the Boundless.
Imponderous Night, The.
In the Old Garden.
In the Rain.
Incense.
Indications.
Indiscriminately.
Inertia.
Inevitables.
Inevitably.
Interchanges.
Invalid's Day, An.
Invention of the Center.

Field of Glory, The.
Firelight.
Flammonde.
Fleming Helphenstine.
Flying Dutchman, The.
For a Dead Lady.
For Arvia.
Fragment: "Faint white pillars that seem to fade."
Garden, The.
George Crabbe.
Gift of God, The.
Growth of "Lorraine," The.
Her Eyes.
Hillcrest.
Horace to Leuconoë.
House on the Hill, The.
How Annandale Went Out.
Inferential.
Isaac and Archibald.
Island, An.
Job the Rejected.
John Brown.
John Evereldown.
John Gorham.
Klondike, The.
Lancelot.
Late Summer.
Lazarus.
Leffingwell.
L'Envoi.
Leonora.
Lingard and the Stars.
Lisette and Eileen.
Llewellyn and the Tree.
London Bridge.
Long Race, The.
Lost Anchors.
Luke Havergal.
Man against the Sky, The.
Many Are Called.
Master, The.
Merlin.
Mill, The.
Miniver Cheevy.
Mr Flood's Party.
Modernities.
Momus.
Monadnock through the Trees.
Neighbors.
New Tenants, The.
Nimmo.
Octaves.
Old King Cole.
Old King's New Jester, The.
Old Story, An.
Old Trails.
On the Night of a Friend's Wedding.
On the Way.
Partnership.
Pasa Thalassa Thalassa.
Peace on Earth.
Pilot, The.
Pity of the Leaves, The.
Poor Relation, The.
Rahel to Varnhagen.
Rat, The.
Recalled.
Rembrandt to Rembrandt.
Return of Morgan and Fingal, The.
Reuben Bright.
Revealer, The.
Richard Cory.
Sage, The.
Sainte-Nitouche.
Shadrach O'Leary.
Siege Perilous.
Song at Shannon's, A.
Sonnet: "Master and the slave go hand in hand, The."
Sonnet: "Oh for a poet—for a beacon bright."
Sonnet: "When we can all so excellently give."
Souvenir.
Stafford's Cabin.
Story of the Ashes and the Flame, The.

Sunken Crown, The.
Supremacy.
Tact.
Tasker Norcross.
Tavern, The.
Theophilus.
Thomas Hood.
Three Quatrains.
Three Taverns, The.
Torrent, The.
Town Down the River, The.
Tree in Pamela's Garden, The.
Twilight Song.
Two Gardens in Linndale.
Two Men.
Two Quatrains.
Two Sonnets.
Uncle Ananias.
Unforgiven, The.
Vain Gratuities.
Valley of the Shadow, The.
Verlaine.
Veteran Sirens.
Vickery's Mountain.
Villanelle of Change.
Voice of Age, The.
Wandering Jew, The.
Whip, The.
White Lights, The.
Wilderness, The.
Wise Brothers, The.
Woman and the Wife, The.
Zola.

Rochfort, George (c.1682–1730)
Answer.
With Music and Poetry Equally Blessed.

Roethke, Theodore (1908–63)
Abyss, The.
Academic.
Adamant, The.
Against Disaster.
All Morning.
All the Earth, All the Air.
Apparition, The.
Auction, The.
Ballad of the Clairvoyant Widow.
Bat, The.
Beast, The.
Big Wind.
Boy and the Bush, The.
Bring the Day!
Carnations.
Ceiling, The.
Chair, The.
Changeling, The.
Child on Top of a Greenhouse.
Chums, The.
Coming of the Cold, The.
Cow, The.
Cuttings ("Sticks-in-a-drowse").
Cuttings ("This urge, wrestle resurrection of dry sticks").
Cycle, The.
Death Piece.
Decision, The.
Dinky.
Dolor.
Donkey, The.
Double Feature.
Dream, The.
Duet.
Dying Man, The.
Elegy for Jane.
Elegy: "Her face like a rain-beaten stone on the day she rolled off."
Elegy: "Should every creature be as I have been."
Epidermal Macabre.
Favorite, The.
Feud.
Field of Light, A.
Flower Dump.
Follies of Adam, The.
For An Amorous Lady.
Forcing House.
Four for Sir John Davies.

Frau Bauman, Frau Schmidt, and Frau Schwartze.
Genesis.
Gentle, The.
Geranium, The.
Give Way, Ye Gates.
Gnu, The.
Gob Music.
Goo Girl.
Happy Three, The.
Harsh Country, The.
Heard in a Violent Ward.
Her Longing.
Her Reticence.
Her Time.
Her Words.
Her Wrath.
Heron, The.
Highway: Michigan.
Hippo, The.
His Foreboding.
I Cry, Love! Love!
I Knew A Woman.
I Need, I Need.
I Waited.
Idyll: "Now as from maple to elm the flittermice skitter and twirl."
In a Dark Time.
In Evening Air.
In Praise of Prairie.
Infirmity.
Interlude.
Judge Not.
Kitty-Cat Bird, The.
Lady and the Bear, The.
Lamb, The.
Last Words.
Light Breather, A.
Light Comes Brighter, The.
Light Listened.
Light Poem.
Lines upon Leaving a Sanitarium.
Lizard, The ("He too has eaten well").
Lizard, The ("Time to Tickle a Lizard, The").
Long Alley, The.
Long Live the Weeds.
Lost Son, The.
Love's Progress.
Lull.
Manifestation, The.
Marrow, The.
Meadow Mouse, The.
Meditation in Hydrotherapy.
Meditations of an Old Woman.
Memory.
Mid-Country Blow.
Minimal, The.
Moment, The.
Monotony Song, The.
Moss-Gathering.
Motion, The.
My Dim-Wit Cousin.
My Papa's Waltz.
Myrtle.
Myrtle's Cousin.
Night Crow.
Night Journey.
No Bird.
North American Sequence.
O Lull Me, Lull Me.
O, Thou Opening, O.
Old Florist.
On the Quay.
On the Road to Woodlawn.
Once More, the Round.
Open House.
Orchids.
Orders for the Day.
Other, The.
Otto.
Our Lady's Winter Words.
Philander.
Pickle Belt.
Pike, The.
Plaint.
Poetaster.

Praise to the End!
Prayer before Study.
Prayer: "If I must of my Senses lose."
Premonition, The.
Prognosis.
Pure Fury, The.
Reckoning, The.
Reminder, The.
Renewal, The.
Reply, The.
Reply to a Lady Editor.
Reply to Censure.
Restored, The.
Return, The.
Right Thing, The.
River Incident.
Root Cellar.
Rouse for Stevens, A.
Saginaw Song, The.
Sale.
Sensibility! O La!
Sensualists, The.
Sententious Man, The.
Sequel, The.
Serpent, The.
Shape of the Fire, The.
She.
Shimmer of Evil, The.
Shy Man, The.
Signals, The.
Silence.
Siskins, The.
Sloth, The.
Slow Season.
Slug.
Small, The.
Snake.
Song for the Squeeze-Box.
Song: "From whence cometh song?"
Song: "My wrath, where's the edge."
Song, The: "I met a ragged man."
Song: "This fair parcel of summer's."
Storm, The.
Supper with Lindsay.
Surly One, The.
Swan, The.
Thing, The.
Three Epigrams.
To My Sister.
Tranced, The.
Transplanting.
Tree, the Bird, The.
Unextinguished, The.
Unfold! Unfold!
Vernal Sentiment.
Verse with Allusions.
Visitant, The.
Voice, The.
Wagtail, The.
Waking, The.
Waking, The.
Walk in Late Summer, A.
Weed Puller.
Whale, The.
Where Knock Is Open Wide.
Wish for a Young Wife.
Words for the Wind.
Yak, The.
Young Girl, The.

Rogers, John (1630–84)
Upon Mrs. Anne Bradstreet, Her Poems, Etc.

Rolfe, Edwin (1909–54)
Eyes of a Blind Man.

Ronsard, Pierre de (1524–85)
When You Are Old.

Roscommon, Wentworth Dillon, 4th Earl of (1637–85)
On Mr Dryden's *Religio Laici*.

Rosseter, Philip *See* **Campion, Thomas**

Rossetti, Christina Georgina (1830–94)
Acme.
Advent ("'Come,' thou dost say to Angels").
Advent ("Earth grown old").
Advent ("This Advent moon shines cold and clear").

Advent Sunday.
After Communion.
After Death.
After This the Judgement.
Afterthought, An.
Afterward He Repented, and Went.
Agnellina orfanellina.
Ah Lord, Lord, if my heart were right with Thine.
Ah welladay and wherefore am I here?
Ahi culla vuota! ed ahi sepolcro pieno.
Alas, alas! for the self-destroyed / Vanish as images from a glass.
Alas my Lord, / How should I wrestle all the livelong night.
All beneath the sun hasteth, / All that hath begun wasteth.
All Flesh Is Grass.
All heaven is blazing yet / With the meridian sun.
All night I dream you love me well.
All Saints ("As grains of sand").
All Saints ("They are flocking").
All Saints ("They have brought gold").
All Saints: Martyrs.
All the bells were ringing / And all the birds were singing.
All Things Wait upon Thee.
"All Thy Works Praise Thee, O Lord": A Processional of Creation.
Alleluia! or Alas! my heart is crying.
Alone Lord God, in Whom our trust and peace.
Along the highroad the way is too long.
Alphabet, An.
Amami, t'amo / Figliolin mio.
Amen.
Amico pesce, poiver vorrà.
Amor Mundi.
Amore E Dispetto.
Amore E Dovere.
And is this August weather? nay not so.
And Now Why Tarriest Thou?
And There Was No More Sea.
Angeli al capo, al piede.
Angels at the foot, / And Angels at the head.
Animuccia, vagantuccia, morbiduccia.
Annie ("It is not for earthly").
Annie ("Annie is fairer than her kith").
Another Spring.
Answer, An.
Antipas.
Apple Gathering, An.
Are They Not All Ministering Spirits?
Are Ye Not Much Better Than They?
Ariadne To Theseus.
Arrossisce la rosa: e perchè mai?
As a King, ...Unto the King.
As Cold Water to a Thirsty Soul, So Is Good News from a Far Country.
As dying, and behold we live!
As froth on the face of the deep, / As foam on the crest of the sea.
As the Apple Tree among the Trees of the Wood.
As the dove which found no rest / For the sole of her foot, flew back.
As the Doves to Their Windows.
As the Sparks Fly Upwards.
As Thy Days, So Shall Thy Strength Be.
Ascension Day.
Ascension Eve.
Ash Wednesday ("My God, my God").
Ash Wednesday ("Jesus, do I love Thee?").
At Home.
At Last.
Aura dolcissima, ma donde siete?
Autumn ("Fade tender lily").
Autumn ("I dwell alone—; I dwell alone, alone").
Autumn Violets.
Awake, Thou That Sleepest.
Baby cry— / Oh fie!
Baby lies so fast asleep.
Babylon the Great.
Baby's cradle with no baby in it, A.
Ballad of Boding, A.

Ballad: "Soft white lamb in the daisy meadow."
Balm in Gilead.
Basta una notte a maturare il fungo.
Beautiful For Situation.
Beauty Is Vain.
Because He First Loved Us.
Because Thy Love hath sought me, / All mine is Thine and Thine is mine.
Bed of Forget-Me-Nots, A.
Before the Beginning.
Before the Paling of the Stars.
Before the Throne, and Before the Lamb.
Behold a Shaking.
Behold, I stand at the door and knock.
Behold, It Was Very Good.
Behold the Man!
"Beloved, let us love one another," says St. John.
Beloved, yield thy time to God, for He / Will make eternity thy recompense.
Better Resurrection, A.
Better So.
Birchington Churchyard.
Bird or Beast?
Bird Raptures.
Bird Song, A.
Bird's-Eye View, A.
Birthday, A.
Bitter for Sweet.
Blind from my birth, / Where flowers are springing.
Books In the Running Brooks.
Bourne, The.
Boy Johnny.
Brandons Both.
Bread and Milk for Breakfast.
Bride Song.
Bride Song, A.
Brother Bruin.
Brownie, Brownie, let down your milk.
Bruised Reed Shall He Not Break, A.
Buds and Babies.
Bundle of Myrrh Is My Well-Beloved unto Me, A.
Burial Anthem.
Buried.
Bury Hope out of sight, / No book for it and no bell.
But Thy Commandment Is Exceeding Broad.
By the Sea.
By the Waters of Babylon.
By the Waters of Babylon. B.C. 570.
By Way of Remembrance.
Called To Be Saints.
Can I know it?—Nay.— / Shall I know it?— Yea.
Candlemas Dialogue, A.
Cannot Sweeten.
Capo che chinasi, / Occhi che chiudonsi.
Cardinal Newman.
Care flieth, / Hope and fear together.
Cast down but not destroyed, chastened not slain.
Castle-Builder's World, A.
Caterpillar, The.
Cavalli marittimi / Urtansi in guerra.
Changing Chimes.
Charade.
Charades.
Charity.
Charity Never Faileth.
Charon.
Chiefest among Ten Thousand, The.
Chiesa E Signore.
Child's Talk in April.
Chill, A.
Chill blank world. Yet over the utmost sea, A.
Chilly Night, A.
Chinaman, The.
Christian and Jew. A Dialogue.
Christmas Carol, A: "In the bleak mid-winter."
Christmas Carol, A: "Thank God, thank God, we do believe."
Christmas Carols.
Christmas Day.

Christmas Eve.
Christmastide.
Churchyard Song of Patient Hope, A.
City Mouse and the Garden Mouse, The.
City plum is not a plum, A.
Clever little Willie wee, / Bright eyed, blue
  eyed little fellow.
Coast-Nightmare, A.
Cobwebs.
Come cheer up, my lads, 'tis to glory we steer!
Come Unto Me.
Comparisons.
Confluents.
Consider.
Consider the Lilies of the Field ("Flowers
  preach to us").
Consider the Lilies of the Field ("Solomon
  most glorious in array").
Convent Threshold, The.
Conversion of St. Paul.
Cor Mio.
Cor mio, cor mio / Più non ti veggo, ma mi
  rammento.
Corydon's Lament and Resolution.
Counsel, A.
Counterblast on Penny Trumpet.
Cousin Kate.
Cried Out with Tears.
Crimson curtains round my mother's bed.
Crown of Windflowers, A.
Crying, my little one, footsore and weary?
Cuccurucù! Cuccurucù! / All'alba il gallo
  canta.
Currants on a bush, / And figs upon a stem.
Dancing on the hill-tops, / Singing in the
  valleys.
Darkness and light are both alike to Thee.
Daughter of Eve, A.
Day and night the Accuser makes no pause.
Day Is At Hand, The.
Days are clear, / Day after day, The.
Days of Vanity.
De Profundis.
Dead before Death.
Dead Bride, The.
Dead City, The.
Dead Hope.
Dear Angels and dear disembodied Saints.
Dear old woman in the lane, The.
Death.
Death Is Swallowed Up in Victory.
Death of a First-Born, A.
Death-Watches.
Death's Chill Between.
Descent from the Cross, The.
Despair.
Despised and Rejected.
Diamond or a coal? / A diamond, if you
  please, A.
"Ding a ding," / The sweet bells sing.
Dirge, A.
Dirge, A: "Why were you born when the snow
  was falling?"
Discovery, A.
Divine and Human Pleading.
Do This, and He Doeth It.
Doeth Well...Doeth Better.
Dog lies in his kennel, The.
Dost Thou Not Care?
Dream, A.
Dream Land.
Dream-Love.
Dream, The.
Dumb Friend, A.
D'un sonno profondissimo.
Dying Man to His Betrothed, The.
E babbo e mamma ha il nostro figliolino.
Earth and Heaven.
Earth has clear call of daily bells, / A chancel-
  vault of gloom and star.
Earth Shall Tremble at the Look of Him, The.
Easter Carol, An.
Easter Day.
Easter Even ("Tempest over and gone").
Easter Even ("There is nothing more that they
  can do").

Easter Monday.
Easter Morning.
Easter Tuesday.
Echo.
Echo from Willowwood, An.
1885. St. Valentine's Day.
1884.
1886, St. Valentine's Day.
1878.
1879.
Eleanor.
Eleventh Hour, The.
Ellen Middleton.
Embertide.
End, An.
End Is Not Yet, The.
End of Time, The.
Endure Hardness.
Enrica, 1865.
Epiphany.
Epiphanytide.
Epitaph: "Slave yet wearing on my head a
  crown, A."
Escape to the Mountain.
Eva.
Eve.
Every One That Is Perfect Shall Be as His
  Master.
Everything that is born must die.
Exceeding Bitter Cry, An.
Experience bows a sweet contented face.
Exultate Deo.
Eye Hath Not Seen.
Faint, Yet Pursuing.
Fair Margaret.
Fair World Tho' a Fallen, A.
Faith and Hope are wings to Love.
Faithless Shepherdess, The.
Fata Morgana.
Feast of the Annunciation.
Feast of the Presentation.
February 14. 1883.
Ferry Me across the Water.
First Spring Day, The.
Fisher-Wife, A.
Flint.
Floral Teaching.
Flowers Appear on the Earth, The.
Fluttered Wings.
Fly Away, Fly Away.
For a Mercy Received.
For Advent.
For All.
For Each.
For H.P.
For One Sake.
For Rosaline's Album.
For Thine Own Sake, O My God.
Forget Me Not.
Foss'io regina / Tu re saresti.
4th May Morning.
Freaks of Fashion.
Frisky Lamb, A.
Frog's Fate, A.
From early dawn until the flush of noon.
From House to Home.
From Mestastasio.
From Sunset to Star Rise.
From the Antique ("It's a weary life, it is").
From the Antique ("Wind shall lull us yet").
General Assembly and Church of the Firstborn,
  The.
German-French Campaign, 1870–1871, The.
Ghost's Petition, The.
Go In Peace.
Goal in sight! Look up and sing, / Set faces
  full against the light, The.
Goblin Market.
God Is Our Hope and Strength.
God's Acre.
Gold of that Land is Good, The.
Golden Glories.
Golden Holly.
Golden Silences.
Gone Before.
Gone for Ever.

Gone to his rest / Bright little Bouby!
Good Friday ("Am I a stone").
Good Friday ("Easter and the resurrection").
Good Friday Evening.
Good Friday Morning.
Good Lord, today / I scarce find breath to say.
Good Shepherd, The.
Goodbye in fear, goodbye in sorrow.
Gran freddo è infuori, e dentro è freddo un
  poco.
Grant us such grace that we may work Thy
  Will.
Greatest of These Is Charity, The.
Green Cornfield, A.
Growing in the vale / By the uplands hilly.
Grown and Flown.
Grown Cold.
Guesses.
Had Fortune parted us / Fortune is blind.
Hail, noble face of noble friend!
Half Dead.
Half Moon Shows a Face of Plaintive
  Sweetness, The.
Handy Mole who plied no shovel, A.
Hark! the Alleluias of the great salvation.
Have I not striven, my God, and watched and
  prayed?
Have Patience.
Have You Forgotten?
He and She.
He Cannot Deny Himself.
He Shall Go No More Out.
Hear what the mournful linnets say.
Heart Knoweth Its Own Bitterness, The
  ("Weep yet awhile").
Heart Knoweth Its Own Bitterness, The
  ("When all the overwork of life").
Heart's Chill Between.
Heartsease in my garden bed, / With
  sweetwilliam white and red.
Heaven.
Heaven Is Heaven.
Heaven Is Not Far.
Heaven Overarches Earth and Sea.
Heaven's chimes are slow, but sure to strike at
  last.
Heaviness May Endure for a Night, But Joy
  Cometh in the Morning.
Heavy heart, if ever heart was heavy, A.
Helen Grey.
Helpmeet For Him, A.
Henry Hardiman.
Her Seed; It Shall Bruise Thy Head.
Herself a Rose Who Bore the Rose.
Hills are tipped with sunshine, while I walk /
  In shadows dim and cold.
His Banner over Me Was Love.
Hollow-Sounding and Mysterious.
Holy City, New Jerusalem, The.
Holy Innocents.
Holy Innocents.
Hop-o'-my-thumb and little Jack Horner.
Hope and Joy.
Hope Carol, A.
Hope in Grief.
Hope is the counterpoise of fear / While night
  enthrals us here.
Hopeless Case, A.
Hoping Against Hope.
Hopping frog, hop here and be seen.
Horses of the Sea, The.
Hour and the Ghost, The.
House of cards / Is neat and small, A.
How great is little man! / Sun, moon, and stars
  respond to him.
How many authors are my first!
How Many Seconds in a Minute?
How One Chose.
Hurt No Living Thing.
Husband and Wife.
Hymn for Christmas Day, A.
Hymn: "O the bitter shame and sorrow."
Hymn: "To the God Who reigns on high."
I am a King, / Or an Emperor rather.
I Am Small and of No Reputation.
I caught a little ladybird.

I Do Not Look for Love That Is a Dream.
I Do Set My Bow in the Cloud.
I dreamt I caught a little owl.
I dug and dug amongst the snow.
I fancy the good fairies dressed in white.
I followed Thee, my God, I followed Thee / To see the end.
I Gave a Sweet Smell.
I have a little husband / And he is gone to sea.
I Have a Message unto Thee.
I have a Poll parrot, / And Poll is my doll.
I have but one rose in the world.
I have done with hope.
I Have Fought a Good Fight.
I know a baby, such a baby,— / Round blue eyes and cheeks of pink.
I Know You Not.
I lift mine eyes to see: earth vanisheth.
I Look for the Lord.
I, Lord, Thy foolish sinner low and small.
I love you and you know it—this at least.
I planted a hand / And there came up a palm.
I said "All's over"—& I made my.
I said within myself: I am a fool.
I See That All Things Come to an End.
I seek among the living & I seek.
I sit a queen, and am no widow, and shall see no sorrow.
I sit among the green shady valleys oft.
I toiled on, but thou.
I Will Arise.
I Will Come and Heal Him.
I Will Lift Up Mine Eyes unto the Hills ("I am pale with sick desire").
I Will Lift Up Mine Eyes unto the Hills ("When sick of life").
I wish I were a little bird.
If a mouse could fly, / Or if a crow could swim.
If a pig wore a wig.
If all were rain and never sun.
If I Had Words.
If I should ever say "my heart is in my home."
If I Were a Queen.
If love is not worth loving, then life is not worth living.
If not with hope of life, / Begin with fear of death.
If Only.
If stars dropped out of heaven, / And if flowers took their place.
If the moon came from heaven, / Talking all the way.
If the sun could tell us half / That he hears and sees.
If thou be dead, forgive and thou shalt live.
If Thou Sayest, Behold, We Knew It Not.
Il Rosseggiar Dell'Oriente Canzoniere.
Imitated From the Arpa Evangelica: Page 121.
Immalee.
"Immurata" Sister, An.
In a Certain Place.
In An Artist's Studio.
In July / No goodbye.
In Patience.
In Progress.
In resurrection is it awfuller.
In tema e in pena addio.
In the Day of His Espousals.
In the Lane.
In the meadow—what in the meadow?
In the Round Tower at Jhansi, June 8, 1857.
In the Willow Shade.
In weariness and painfulness St. Paul.
Iniquity of the Fathers upon the Children, The.
Introspective.
Is It Well with The Child?
Is the Moon Tired?
Isidora.
It Is Finished.
It is not death, O Christ, to die for Thee: / Nor is that silence of a silent land.
Italia, Io Ti Saluto!
Jerusalem of fire / And gold and pearl and gem.
Jessie Cameron.

Jesus alone:—if thus it were to me.
Johnny.
Joy is but sorrow, / While we know.
Joy of Saints, like incense turned to fire, The.
Judge Not According to the Appearance.
Judge Nothing before the Time.
Key-Note, The.
King of Kings and Lord of Lords.
"Kookoorookoo! kookoorookoo!" / Crows the cock before the morn.
La rosa china il volto rosseggiato.
Lady Isabella.
Lady Isabella.
Lambs at Play.
Lambs of Grasmere, 1860, The.
Last Answer, The.
Last *Complaint*, The.
Last Look, The.
Last Night.
Last Rites.
Last Words of St. Telemachus, The.
Later Life: A Double Sonnet of Sonnets.
Laughing Life cries at the feast.
Lay Up for Yourselves Treasures in Heaven.
Leaf from leaf Christ knows; / Himself the Lily and the Rose.
L. E. L.
Lent.
Let Everything That Hath Breath Praise the Lord.
Let Patience Have Her Perfect Work ("Can man rejoice").
Let Patience Have Her Perfect Work ("I saw a bird alone").
Let Them Rejoice in Their Beds ("Crimson as the rubies").
Let Them Rejoice in Their Beds ("Winds sing to us").
Let's Be Merry.
Lie a-bed, / Sleepy head, / Shut up eyes, bo-peep.
Life and Death.
Life Hidden.
Life Out of Death.
Life that was born today / Must make no stay.
Life's Parallels, A.
Lift up thine eyes to seek the invisible.
Light Love.
Light of Light.
Like As the Hart Desireth the Water Brooks.
Lily has a smooth stalk, / Will never hurt your hand, The.
Lily has an air, / And the snowdrop a grace, The.
L'Incognita.
Lines Given with a Penwiper.
Lines to My Grandfather.
Linnet in a gilded cage,— / A linnet on a bough, A.
Lisetta all' Amante.
Listen, and I will tell you of a face.
Listening.
Long Barren.
Long Looked For.
Look on This Picture and on This.
Looking back along life's trodden way.
Looking Forward.
Lord, by what inconceivable dim road / Thou leadest man on footsore pilgrimage!
Lord, carry me.—Nay, but I grant thee strength.
Lord, comest Thou to me?
Lord, dost Thou look on me, and will not I.
Lord, give me love that I may love Thee much.
Lord God of Hosts, most Holy and most High.
Lord, grant me grace to love Thee in my pain.
Lord, Grant Us Calm.
Lord, grant us eyes to see and ears to hear, / And souls to love and minds to understand.
Lord, grant us grace to rest upon Thy word.
Lord, hast Thou so loved us, and will not we.
Lord, I am feeble and of mean account.
Lord, I am here.—But, child, I look for thee.
Lord, It Is Good for Us to Be Here.
Lord Jesu, Thou art sweetness to my soul.
Lord Jesus, who would think that I am Thine?

Lord, make me one with Thine own faithful ones.
Lord, make me pure: / Only the pure shall see Thee as Thou art.
Lord, make us all love all: that when we meet / Even myriads of earth's myriads at Thy Bar.
Lord, Save Us, We Perish.
Lord Thomas and Fair Margaret.
Lord, Thou art fulness, I am emptiness.
Lord, we are rivers running to Thy sea.
Lord, what have I that I may offer Thee?
Lord, what have I to offer? sickening fear.
Lotus-Eaters: Ulysses to Penelope, The.
Love and Death.
Love and Hope.
Love Attacked.
Love builds a nest on earth and waits for rest.
Love Defended.
Love Ephemeral.
Love from The North.
Love hath a name of Death.
Love is all happiness, love is all beauty.
Love Is Strong as Death.
Love Is Stronger than Death.
Love Lies Bleeding.
Love loveth Thee, and wisdom loveth Thee.
Love of Christ Which Passeth Knowledge, The.
Love, to be love, must walk Thy way / And work Thy Will.
Lowest Place, The.
Lowest Room, The.
Lugubre e vagabondo in terra e in mare.
Lullaby: "Love me,—I love you / Love me, my baby."
Lullaby, oh lullaby! / Flowers are closed and lambs are sleeping.
Luscious and Sorrowful.
Maggie a Lady.
Maiden May.
Maiden-Song.
Man's life is but a working day / Whose tasks are set aright.
Margaret has a milking-pail, / And she rises early.
Margery.
Mariana.
Martyr, A ("Inner not outer").
Martyr, A ("It is over the horrible pain").
Martyr, The.
Martyrs' Song.
Marvel of Marvels.
Mary Magdalene and the Other Mary.
Massacre of Perugia, The.
Master Is Come, and Calleth for Thee, The.
Maude Clare.
Maundy Thursday.
May ("I cannot tell you").
May ("Sweet life is dead— / Not so").
May-Time.
Me and my gift: kind Lord, behold.
Me you often meet / In London's crowded street.
Meeting.
Memento Mori.
Memory.
Methinks the ills of life I fain would shun.
Michael F. M. Rossetti.
Mid-Lent.
Milking-Maid, The.
Minnie and Mattie.
Minnie bakes oaten cakes, / Minnie brews ale.
Mirage.
Mirrors of Life and Death.
Mr. and Mrs. Scott, and I.
Mix a Pancake.
Monday in Holy Week.
Monna Innominata.
Months: A Pageant, The.
Months, The.
Moonshine.
Mother and Child.
Mother Country.
Motherless baby and babyless mother.
Motherless soft lambkin / Alone upon a hill.
My baby has a father and a mother.

My baby has a mottled fist.
My Dream.
My Friend.
My God, wilt Thou accept, and will not we / Give aught to Thee?
My Mouse.
My old admiration before I was twenty.
My Old Friends.
Name of Jesus, The.
Ne' sogni ti veggo.
Nel verno accanto al fuoco.
New creatures; the Creator still the Same.
New Enigmas.
Next of Kin.
Night and Death.
Ninna nanna, ninna nanna!
No, Thank You, John.
Noble Sisters.
None other Lamb, none other Name.
None With Him.
Not Yours But You.
Novice, The.
Now They Desire.
Now They Desire a Better Country.
O Christ my God Who seest the unseen.
O Christ our All in each, our All in all!
O ciliegia infiorita.
O Death Where Is Thy Sting?
O foolish Soul! to make thy count / For languid falls and much forgiven.
O glorious sea that in each climbing wave.
O Lady Moon.
O Lord, I am ashamed to seek Thy Face / As tho' I loved Thee as Thy saints love Thee.
O Lord, I cannot plead my love of Thee.
O Lord, on Whom we gaze and dare not gaze, / Increase our faith that gazing we may see.
O Lord, when Thou didst call me, didst Thou know.
O Lucifer, Son of the Morning!
O marinaro che mi apporti tu?
O mine enemy / Rejoice not over me!
O Sailor, Come Ashore.
O thou who tell'st me that all hope is over.
O uommibatto / Agil, giocondo.
O wind, where have you been.
O wind, why do you never rest.
O ye, who are not dead and fit.
O ye who love today, / Turn away / From Patience with her silver ray.
October Garden, An.
Of each sad word which is more sorrowful.
Of Him That Was Ready to Perish.
Of My Life.
Offering of the New Law, the One Oblation Once Offered, The.
Oh, Fair To See.
Oh fair to see / Bloom-laden cherry tree.
Oh knell of a passing time, / Will it never cease to chime?
Oibò, piccina / Tutto atterrita.
Old and New Year Ditties.
Old-World Thicket, An.
On Albina.
On Keats, 18 January, 1948 (Eve of St Agnes).
On the Death of a Cat.
On the note you do not send me.
On the Wing.
Once.
Once for All. (Margaret).
1 and 1 are 2— / That's for me and you.
One Certainty, The.
One Day.
One Foot on Sea, and One on Shore.
One of the Dead.
One of the Soldiers with a Spear Pierced His Side.
One Sea-Side Grave.
One Swallow Does Not Make a Summer.
One woe is past. Come what come will.
Only Believe.
Otto ore suonano: / Picchia il postino.
Our Church Palms are Budding Willow Twigs.
Our heaven must be within ourselves / Our home and heaven the work of faith.
Our life is long. Not so, wise Angels say.

Our little baby fell asleep.
Our Mothers, lovely women pitiful; / Our sisters, gracious in their life and death.
Our Widowed Queen.
Out of the Deep.
P.R.B, The.
Palm Sunday.
Paradise.
Paradise: in a Symbol.
Parting after parting, / Sore loss and gnawing pain.
Passing and Glassing.
Passing away the bliss, / The anguish passing away.
Passion Flower hath sprung up tall, The.
Passiontide.
Pastime.
Patience must dwell with Love, for Love and Sorrow.
Patience of Hope.
Pause, A.
Peace I Leave wth You.
Peach tree on the southern wall, The.
Peacock has a score of eyes, The.
Peal of Bells, A.
Perfect Love Casteth Out Fear.
Pesano rena e pena.
Peter Grump.
Pin Has a Head, A.
Piteous my rhyme is / What while I muse of love and pain.
Pitia a Damone.
Plague, The.
Playing at bob cherry / Tom and Nell and Hugh.
Pocket handkerchief to hem, A.
Poor Ghost, The.
Porco la zucca / Fitta in parrucca!
Portrait, A.
Portraits.
Postman, The.
Praise of Love.
Praying Always.
Present and Future.
Prince's Progress, The.
Prodigal Son, A.
Promises like Pie-Crust.
Purification of St. Mary the Virgin, The.
Purpurea rosa / Dolce, odorosa.
Pussy has a whiskered face, / Kitty has such pretty ways.
Quanto a Lei grata io sono.
Queen of Hearts, The.
Queen Rose.
Quinquagesima.
Rainbow, The.
Ransomed of the Lord, The.
Redeeming the Time.
Reflection.
Rejoice with Me.
Remember [Me].
Repining.
Rest.
Resurgam.
Resurrection Eve.
Riddle, A: "There is one that has a head without an eye."
Ring Posy, A.
Ring upon her finger, / Walks the bride, A.
Rivals.
River Thames (?).
Rogationtide.
Rosalind.
Rose has thorns as well as honey, A.
Rose Plant in Jericho, A.
Rose that blushes rosy red, The.
Rose, The ("Gentle, gentle river").
Rose, The ("O Rose").
Rose with such a bonny blush, The.
Roses blushing red and white, / For delight.
Roses on a brier, / Pearls from out the bitter sea.
Rosy maiden Winifred, / With a milkpail on her head.
Roundel seems to fit a round of days, A.
Royal Princess, A.

Ruin.
Ruined Cross, The.
S'addormentò la nostra figliolina.
Safe where I cannot lie yet, / Safe where I hope to lie too.
St. Andrew's Church.
St. Barnabas.
St. Bartholomew.
St. Elizabeth of Hungary.
St. Mark.
St. Michael and all Angels.
St. Peter ("Launch out into").
St. Peter ("St. Peter once").
St. Valentine's Day 1881.
Saints and Angels.
Salta, ranocchio, e mostrati.
Sappho.
Scarce tolerable life, which all life long.
Scavai la neve,—sì che scavai!
Seasons ("Crocuses and snowdrops wither").
Seasons ("In springtime").
Seasons ("Oh the cheerful budding time").
Seeking Rest.
Seldom Can't.
Septuagesima.
Serenade.
Seven vials hold Thy wrath: but what can hold.
Sexagesima.
Shadows Today.
Shall I Forget?
Shall not the Judge of all the earth do right?
She Came from The Uttermost Part of the Earth.
She Shall Be Brought unto the King.
Short is time, and only time is bleak.
Shut Out.
Sì che il fratello s'ha falconcello.
Sick Child's Meditation, A.
Sing me a song— / What shall I sing?
Sing-Song.
Sinner's own fault? So it was, The.
Sir Eustace Grey.
Sir Winter.
Sister Maude.
Sit Down in the Lowest Room.
Sketch, A.
Slain from the Foundation of the World.
Slain in their high places: fallen on rest.
Sleep at Sea.
Sleep, Sleep Happy Child; All Creation Slept and Smiled.
Sleeping at Last.
Smile and a Sigh, A.
So Great a Cloud of Witnesses.
So I began my walk of life; no stop.
So I grew half delirious and quite sick.
Soeur Louise De La Miséricorde.
Solitary Rose, The.
Some ladies dress in muslin full and white.
Somewhere Or Other.
Son, Remember.
Song for the Least of All Saints, A.
Song: "I have loved you for long long years Ellen."
Song: "I saw her; she was lovely."
Song: "It is not for her even brow."
Song of Flight, A.
Song of the Star, The.
Song: "Oh roses for the flush of youth."
Song: "Oh what comes over the sea."
Song: "She sat and sang alway."
Song: "Stream moaneth as it floweth, The."
Song: "Two doves upon the selfsame branch."
Song: "We buried her among the flowers."
Song: "When I am dead, my dearest."
Songs in a Cornfield.
Sonnet from the Psalms.
Sonnet: "Some say that love and joy are one: and so."
Sooner or later: yet at last / The Jordan must be past.
Sorrow hath a double voice, / Sharp today but sweet tomorrow.
Soul rudderless, unbraced.
Sound Sleep.
Sposa velata, / Innanellata.

Spring.
Spring Fancies.
Spring is come again not as at first.
Spunta la margherita.
St. John, Apostle.
Standing Afar Off for the Fear of Her Torment.
Strange voices sing among the planets which.
Stroke a flint, and there is nothing to admire.
Study (A Soul), A.
Subject To Like Passions as We Are.
Succession of Kings, The.
Summer ("Winter is cold-hearted").
Summer ("Come, cuckoo, come").
Summer ("Hark to the song").
Summer ("Rushes in a watery place").
Summer Is Ended.
Summer Is Ended, The.
Summer nights are short, / Where northern
     days are long, The.
Summer Wish, A.
Sunday Before Advent.
Sunshine.
Surely He Hath Borne Our Griefs.
Surely there is an aching void within.
Sursum Corda.
Sweet Death.
Sweetness of rest when Thou sheddest rest.
Swift and sure the swallow.
Symbols.
Take Care Of Him.
Take No Thought for The Morrow.
Tasso and Leonora.
Tempus Fugit.
Testimony, A.
That Eden of earth's sunrise cannot vie.
That No Man Take Thy Crown.
That Where I Am, There Ye May Be Also.
That Which Hath Been Is Named Already, and
     It Is Known That It Is Man.
Then I Commended Mirth.
Then Shall Ye Shout.
Then They That Feared the Lord Spake Often
     One to Another.
Then Whose Shall Those Things Be?
There Is a Budding Morrow in Midnight.
There Remaineth Therefore a Rest.
There Remaineth Therefore a Rest for the
     People of God ("Come blessed sleep").
There Remaineth Therefore a Rest to the
     People of God ("Come blessed sleep, most
     full, most perfect, come").
There's Snow on the Fields.
They Desire a Better Country.
They lie at rest, our blessed dead.
They Put Their Trust in Thee, and Were Not
     Confounded.
They Shall Be as White as Snow.
They Toil Not, Neither Do They Spin.
This near-at-hand land breeds pain by measure.
Thou Art Fairer Than the Children of Men.
Thou, God, Seest Me.
Thou Knewest...Thou Oughtest Therefore.
Thread of Life, The.
Three Enemies, The.
Three little children / On the wide wide earth.
Three Moments.
Three Nuns.
Three Plum Buns.
Three Seasons.
Three Stages.
Thro' burden and heat of the day.
Thy fainting spouse, yet still Thy spouse.
Thy Friend and Thy Father's Friend Forget
     Not.
Thy lilies drink the dew, / Thy lambs the rill,
     and I will drink them too.
Thy Name, O Christ, as incense streaming
     forth.
Thy Servant Will Go and Fight with This
     Philistine.
Till Tomorrow.
Time lengthening, in the lengthening seemeth
     long.
Time of Waiting, The.
Time passeth away with its pleasure and pain.
Time seems not short: / If so I call to mind.

Tirsi, A.
To Every Seed His Own Body.
To Lalla, Reading My Verses Topsy-Turvy.
To Mary Rossetti.
To My Fior-Di-Lisa.
To My First Love, My Mother.
To My Friend Elizabeth.
To My Mother on Her Birthday.
To the End.
To What Purpose Is This Waste?
Toadstool comes up in a night, A.
Today's Burden.
Toll, bell, toll. For hope is flying / Sighing
     from the earthbound soul.
Touching "Never."
Trees' Counselling, The.
Triad, A.
Trinity Sunday.
True Story, A.
Truly the Light Is Sweet.
Tu scendi dalle stelle, O Re del Cielo.
Tuesday in Holy Week.
Tune Me, O Lord, into One Harmony.
Twice.
Twilight Calm.
Twilight Night.
Two Parted.
Two Pursuits.
Two Rossettis (Brothers They), The.
Two Thoughts of Death.
Udite, si dolgono mesti fringuelli.
Under the ivy bush / One sits sighing.
Under Willows.
Undine.
Unforgotten.
Unspotted lambs to follow the one Lamb.
Until the Day Break.
Uphill.
Vain Shadow, A.
Valentine, 1877, A.
Valentine to My Mother, A.
Valentines From C.G.R.
Valentines to My Mother, 1880.
Vanity of Vanities ("Of all the downfalls").
Vanity of Vanities ("Ah woe is me for pleasure
     that is vain").
Venus's Looking-Glass.
Versi.
Vigil of all Saints.
Vigil of St. Bartholomew.
Vigil of St. Peter.
Vigil of the Annunciation.
Vigil of the Presentation.
Was Thy Wrath against the Sea?
Watchers, The.
Water Spirit's Song, The.
Way of the World, The.
We are of those who tremble at Thy word.
We know not when, we know not where.
Weary in Well-Doing.
Wednesday in Holy Week.
Wee wee husband, / Give me some money.
Weigh all my faults and follies righteously.
What?
What Are Heavy?
What are these lovely ones, yea, what are
     these?
What do the stars do / Up in the sky.
What Does the Bee Do?
What does the donkey bray about?
What Good Shall My Life Do Me? ("Have
     dead men").
What Good Shall My Life Do Me? ("No hope
     in life, yet there is hope").
What Hath God Wrought!
What is it Jesus saith unto the soul?
What Is Pink?
What Is That to Thee? Follow Thou Me.
What is the beginning? Love. What the course?
     Love still.
What is this above thy head, / O Man?
What Sappho Would Have Said Had Her Leap
     Cured Instead of Killing Her.
What to Do?
What will it be, O my soul, what will it be.
What will you give me for my pound?

What Would I Give?
What's in a Name?
When fishes set umbrellas up.
When I Was in Trouble I Called upon the
     Lord.
When My Heart Is Vexed, I Will Complain
     ("Fields are white to harvest").
When My Heart Is Vexed I Will Complain ("O
     Lord, how canst Thou say Thou lovest
     me?").
When the cows come home the milk is
     coming.
When wickedness is broken as a tree / Paradise
     comes to light, ah holy land!
Where Innocent Bright-Eyed Daisies Are.
Where love is, there comes sorrow / Today or
     else tomorrow.
Where Neither Rust Nor Moth Doth Corrupt.
Where never tempest heaveth, / Nor sorrow
     grieveth.
Where shall I find a white rose blowing?
Where Their Worm Dieth Not, and the Fire Is
     Not Quenched.
White hen sitting / On white eggs three, A.
Whither the Tribes Go Up, Even the Tribes of
     the Lord.
Whitsun Day.
Whitsun Eve ("As many as I love").
Whitsun Eve ("White dove cooeth in her
     downy nest, The").
Whitsun Monday.
Whitsun Tuesday.
Who cares for earthly bread tho' white?
Who Has Seen the Wind?
Who Hath Despised the Day of Small Things?
Who Have a Form of Godliness.
Who Shall Deliver Me?
Who shall my wandering thoughts steady &
     fix.
Who sits with the King in His Throne? Not a
     slave but a Bride.
Who would wish back the Saints upon our
     rough.
Whole Head Is Sick, and the Whole Heart
     Faint, The.
Whom the Lord Loveth He Chasteneth.
Why?
Why did baby die.
Wife to Husband.
Will of the Lord Be Done, The.
Will These Hands Ne'er Be Clean?
Will you be there? my yearning heart has
     cried.
Wind Has Such a Rainy Sound, The.
Winter: My Secret.
Winter Rain.
Wintry Sonnet, A.
Wisdom.
Wishes: Sonnet.
Within the Veil.
Word for the Dumb, A.
World, The.
World's Harmonies, The.
Worship God.
Would that I were a turnip white.
Wouldst thou give me a heavy jewelled crown.
Wrens and robins in the hedge.
Yawn, A.
Ye Are Come unto Mount Sion.
Ye Have Forgotten the Exhortation.
Ye That Fear Him, Both Small and Great.
Yea, blessed and holy is he that hath part in the
     First / Resurrection!
Yea, I Have a Goodly Heritage.
Yea, if Thou wilt, Thou canst put up Thy
     sword.
Year Afterwards, A.
Year's Windfalls, A.
Yes, I too could face death and never shrink.
Yet A Little While.
Yet a Little While.
You who looked on passed ages as a glass.
Young Death.
Young Men Aye Were Fickle Found Since
     Summer Trees Were Leafy.
Your brother has a falcon.

Zara ("I dreamed that loving me").
Zara ("Now the pain beginneth").
Zara ("Pale sad face of her").
Zion Said.

Rossetti, Dante Gabriel (1828–82)
Adieu.
After the French Liberation of Italy.
After the German Subjugation of France, 1871.
Alas, So Long!
Ant-sting's prickly at first, An.
As balmly as the breath of her you love.
As much as in a hundred years, she's dead.
Aspecta Medusa.
Astarte Syriaca.
At her step the water-hen.
At the Sun-Rise in 1848.
Autumn Song.
Ave.
Beauty and the Bird.
Blessed Damozel, The.
Bride's Prelude, The.
Burden of Nineveh, The.
Card-Dealer, The.
Carillon, The.
Cassandra.
Chimes.
Church Porch 1, The.
Church Porch 2, The.
Cloud Confines, The.
Czar Alexander the Second.
Dante at Verona.
Dantis Tenebræ (In Memory of my Father).
Dawn on the Night-Journey.
Day-Dream, The.
Death-Parting, A.
Dennis Shand.
Down Stream.
During Music.
Eden Bower.
English May.
Even So.
Fiammetta.
Fin di Maggio.
First Love Remembered.
Five English Poets, sels.
For "An Allegorical Dance of Women" by
    Andrea Mantegna.
For An Annunciation, Early German.
For "Our Lady of the Rocks" by Leonardo da
    Vinci.
For "Ruggiero and Angelica" by Ingres.
For Spring, by Sandro Botticelli, in the
    Accademia of Florence.
For The Holy Family, by Michelangelo, in the
    National Gallery.
For 'The Wine of Circe' by Edward Burne
    Jones.
Found.
From the Cliffs: Noon.
Golden robe, yet will she wear, A.
Honeysuckle, The.
House of Life, The, sels.
I shut myself in with my soul.
Insomnia.
Jenny.
King's Tragedy, The.
La Bella Mano.
Lady's Lament, The.
Last Confession, A.
Last Three from Trafalgar, The.
Little While, A.
Love-Lily.
Love's Nocturn.
Marriage of St Katharine, by the same, A; in
    the Hospital of St John at Bruges.
Mary Magdalene at the Door of Simon the
    Pharisee.
Mary's Girlhood.
Match with the Moon, A.
Memory.
Mnemosyne.
My Sister's Sleep.
Near Brussels—A Half-way Pause.
New Year's Burden, A.
O thou whose name, being alone, aloud.
Old Song Ended, An.

On Burns.
On Certain Elizabethan Revivals.
On Refusal of Aid between Nations.
On the Site of a Mulberry-Tree; Planted by
    Wm. Shakespeare; felled by the Rev. F.
    Gastrell.
On the 'Vita Nuova' of Dante.
Orchard-Pit, The.
Pandora.
Parted Presence.
Passover in the Holy Family, The.
Pax Vobis.
Penumbra.
Place de la Bastille, Paris.
Plighted Promise.
Portrait, The.
Possession.
Proserpina.
Question, The.
Raleigh's Cell in the Tower.
Rose Mary.
Sea-Limits, The.
Sea-Spell, A.
Seed of David, The.
She bound her green sleeve on my helm.
Sister Helen.
Song and Music.
Song of the Bower, The.
Soothsay.
Spheral Change.
Spring.
Staff and Scrip, The.
Staircase of Notre Dame, Paris, The.
Stratton Water.
Stream's Secret, The.
Sunset Wings.
Three Shadows.
Tiber, Nile, and Thames.
To Art.
To Philip Bourke Marston, inciting me to
    Poetic Work.
To Thomas Woolner.
Troy Town.
Untimely Lost: Oliver Madox Brown. Born
    1855; Died 1874.
Venetian Pastoral, by Giorgone, in the Louvre,
    A ("Water for anguish of the solstice—
    nay").
Venetian Pastoral, by Giorgone, in the Louvre,
    A ("Water for anguish of the solstice—
    yea").
Venus Verticordia.
Virgin and Child, by Hans Memmeling, A; in
    the Academy of Bruges.
Vox Ecclesiae, Vox Christi.
Was it a friend or foe that spread these lies?
Wellington's Funeral.
White Ship, The.
Who shall say what is said in me.
Winter.
With golden mantle, rings, and necklace fair.
Woodspurge, The.
Words on the Window-Pane.
World's Worth.
Would God I knew there were a God to thank.
Young Fir-Wood, A.

Rukeyser, Muriel (1913–80)
Absalom.
After Melville.
After Their Quarrel.
Afterwards.
Air.
Ajanta.
Akiba.
All Souls.
All the Little Animals.
All the way through the forest, a sound of
    birdsong.
Alloy.
Along History.
Among Grass.
And a girl singing in the symbol air.
Anemone.
Ann Burlak.
Another Day. A Game of Toys. Paul, Telling
    the Game.
Another Day (And then the cow).
Another Day (Child among his powers).

Another Day (Day Lilies, Yellow Daisies).
Another Day. For a Moment Slipping Back,
    Again the Unreal King.
Another Day (I will now sing).
Another Day. In a Field of Peace the Child,
    Playing. The Child Preparing for Daytime
    Sleep.
Another Day (Miss Lorence).
Another Day. Paul in the Mountains of
    Fantasy. Paul Tells His Adventure.
Another Day. The Children Are All Eating.
Another Day (You can't come).
Another Day (You sit there).
Are You Born? / I.
Are You Born? / II.
Arthur Peyton.
Artifact.
As he stood near the plane, they heard him
    say.
Asleep and Awake.
Asylum Song.
Back Tooth.
Backside of the Academy, The.
Ballad of Orange and Grape.
Ballad Theme, A.
Beast in View.
Before Danger.
Believing in Those Inexorable Laws.
Bill, The.
Birth, A.
Birth of Venus, The.
Blood is Justified, The.
Blue Flower, The.
Blue Spruce.
Book of the Dead, The.
Born in December.
Boy with His Hair Cut Short.
Boys in the Branches.
Boys of These Men Full Speed.
Breaking Open.
Breaking the nets of the world, in glimpses
    going.
Breathing Landscape.
Brilliant, the full-bodied, the real of the world
    in their powers, The.
Bringing.
Bubble of Air.
Bunk Johnson Blowing.
Burlesque.
Burning Bush.
Burnishing, Oakland.
But in these years, what is free, what is strong?
Campaign.
Canal.
Cannibal Bratuscha.
Cats and a Cock.
Certain Music, A.
Chapman.
Chapultepec Park / I.
Chapultepec Park / II.
Charm for Cantinflas, A.
Child and Mother.
Child in the Great Wood.
Child of the root, among your apples and
    forests.
Child wakes in the morning to enter a country,
    The.
Children, the Sandbar, That Summer.
Children's Orchard, The.
Christmas Eve.
Citation for Horace Gregory.
City of Monuments.
Clouds, Airs, Carried me Away.
Clues.
Conjugation of the Paramecium, The.
Cornfield, The.
Correspondences.
Course.
Crayon House.
Cries From Chiapas.
Cruise, The.
Dam, The.
Darkness Music.
Deep in the Century of Opposites.
Delta Poems.
Desdichada.

Despisals.
Destruction of Grief.
Disease, The.
Disease: After-Effects, The.
Divining Water.
Do you know Hitler? Does he like you?
Do you know what I play to be, in bed at
   night?
Doctors, The.
Don Baty, the Draft Resister.
Double Dialogue: *Homage to Robert Frost.*
Double Ode.
Down from Chicago Bryan came.
Down the stairs flying, looks at the surfaces.
Dream-Drumming.
Dreaming we were awake, we heard the rivers.
Driveway.
Drowning Young Man, The.
Drunken Girl.
During the journey there come moments of
   waking.
Easter Eve 1945.
Eccentric Motion.
Eel.
Effort at Speech between Two People.
Eighth Elegy. Children's Elegy.
Endless.
Evening Plaza, San Miguel.
Everything here is real and of our joy.
Exile of Music.
Eyes of Night-Time.
F.O.M.
Fable: "Yes it was the prince's kiss."
Face of the Dam: Vivian Jones.
Facing Sentencing.
Father dreams that he was hid in a tree, The.
Fields where we slept.
Fifth Elegy. A Turning Wind.
Fighting for Roses.
Filament carrying morning through the waves,
   A.
First Elegy. Rotten Lake.
Flashing Cliff, A.
Flying Red Horse, The.
Flying to Hanoi.
Foghorn in Horror.
For a Mexican Painter.
For Fun.
For Kayle Boyle.
For Memory.
For My Son.
Forerunners.
Formosa.
Four in a Family.
Fourth Elegy. The Refugees.
From a Play: Publisher's Song.
From the Duck-Pond to the Carousel.
From the throat he can rally strength.
   Remembering.
Game of Ball, A.
Game of Darts at the Chesterfield Arms, A.
Gates, The.
Gauley Bridge.
George Robinson: Blues.
Gibbs.
Gift.
Gift-Poem ("December steel done").
Gift-Poem ("Year in its cold beginning, The").
Girl at the Play.
Gold Leaf.
Gradus ad Parnassum.
Grand Central Station.
Green Limits.
Gullies as deep as halls held these surveyors.
Gyroscope, The.
Handclap.
Haying Before Storm.
He Had a Quality of Growth.
He is breaking the nets in his wildness for the
   real.
He starts awake in the city. Orion believing.
He turned cruel. Absorbed in his own cruelty.
He turns through the lucid stars of a lit city.
He would do as he had done in other states.
Hero Speech.
His Dream of Flood: And Eden.

His father is lost and away.
His gay words, words of delight.
His Head is Full of Faces.
Holy Family.
Homage to Literature.
How was he first aware he would never walk
   again?
How We Did It.
I have tried to show the atom as a source.
I used to press tools in the Texas oil fields.
Ice from the wings, a rattle against metal. All
   right, come down.
Ice-gate over the land, a shock of closure.
If you look at your succession of desires.
In a Dark House.
In a summer forest, when the profuse season.
In Hades, Orpheus.
In Her Burning.
In Our Time.
In the last hour of night, a zebra racing dawn.
In the Night the Sound Woke Us.
In the Underworld.
In your time, there have been those who spoke
   clearly.
Into the the air far. Into the opposites.
Iris.
Iris-Eaters, The.
Islands.
It is the sixth year of the war in China.
It Is There.
Ives.
Jetty. Dover, The.
Juanita Tinsley.
Judith.
Junk-Heap at Murano.
Käthe Kollwitz.
Key, The.
King's Mountain.
Knowledge my nakedness.
Landscape with Wave Approaching.
Lat. 10 Degrees North, Long. 45 Degrees
   West.
Leaving New York, I looked back fourteen
   times.
Leg in a Plaster Cast, A.
Letter to the Front.
Letter, Unposted.
Light falling on that filled will drives.
Lilienthal said: I heard him saying words like
   these.
Little Stone in the Middle of the Road, in
   Florida, A.
Loan, The.
Long Enough. Long Enough.
Long Past Moncada.
Looking.
Looking at Each Other.
Lost Romans, The.
Louis Sonnet, A.
Love and its Doors and Windows.
Lover as Fox.
Lynchings of Jesus, The.
M-Day's Child is Fair of Face.
Madboy's Song.
Make and be eaten, the poet says.
Man in a plane looks at the surface of land, A.
Man sits in the rocking bedroom, claws, The.
Martin Luther King, Malcolm X.
Mary Sleeth.
Mearl Blankenship.
Mediterranean.
Meeting, The.
Mendings.
Metaphor to Action.
Minotaur, The.
Miss Lorence, you are a tree with leaves on.
More Clues.
More of a Corpse Than a Woman.
Mortal Girl.
Mother Garden's Round.
Motive of All of It, The.
Mountain: One from Bryant.
Movie.
Mrs. Walpurga.
Ms. Lot.
My name is Timmy Torin.

My toes feel like nothing they are so cold.
Myth.
Neruda, the Wine.
Network that emerges. At the ocean, A.
Nevertheless the Moon.
Night Feeding.
Night-Music.
Nine Poems for the Unborn Child.
Ninth Elegy. The Antagonists.
Niobe Now.
Noguchi.
Not leaves, not lightning, not the greatness of
   rivers.
Not to Be Printed, Not to Be Said, Not to Be
   Thought.
Not Yet.
Notes for a Poem.
Now he plays with the other children.
Now that the river has changed, my dear.
Nuns in the Wind.
Of Money. And the Past.
Oh, he *is* sweet. I do love him sometimes.
On the Death of Her Mother.
One Month.
One Soldier.
Orgy.
Orpheus.
Otherworld.
Outer Banks, The.
Outpost.
Overthrow of One o'Clock at Night, The.
Painters.
Palos Verdes Cliffs.
Panacea.
Paper Anniversary.
Parades. Rattle of palm trees. The silver
   planes.
Parallel Invention.
Peace the great meaning has not been defined.
Phaneron.
Place at Albert Bay, The.
Place-Rituals.
Poem as Mask, The.
Poem: "Green going through the jungle of
   those years."
Poem: "I lived in the first century of world
   wars."
Poem Out of Childhood.
Poem White Page White Page Poem.
Portrait of a Man, with a Background of
   Holdings.
Pouring Milk Away.
Power.
Power never domminion. / Some other power.
Power of Suicide, The.
Power of war leads to a plan of lives, The.
Praise of the Committee.
Preamble.
Private Life of the Sphinx.
Professionals see the signs in the dice, the
   signs in the cards and clouds, The.
Question, The.
Radio silence of aircraft over the dense ocean.
Rang and rang, rang in a small boy's head.
Reading Time: 1 Minute 26 Seconds.
Recovering.
Red bridge fastening this city to the forest, A.
Resurrection of the Right Side.
Return, The.
Ringling.
Risen Image Shines, The.
Rite.
Road, The.
Rock Flow, River Mix.
Rondel: "Now that I am fifty-six."
Rune.
Running of the Grunion, The.
Ryder.
Sacred Lake.
St. Roach.
Salamander.
Sand-Quarry with Moving Figures.
Say it depends on the interpretation.
Sea has opened, the limit of his dream, The.
Sea Mercy.
Searching / Not Searching.

Second Elegy. Age of Magicians.
Secrets of American Civilization.
Seeming, The.
Segre Song.
Seventh Avenue.
Seventh Elegy. Dream-Singing Elegy.
Shooting Gallery.
Shortest Way Home, The.
Silence of Volcanoes.
Simple Experiment, A.
Six Canons, The.
Sixth Elegy. River Elegy.
Sixth Night: Waking, The.
Slow Death of the Dragon.
Slow Dialogue between Pain and Roosevelt.
Song for Dead Children.
Song, from "Mr. Amazeen on the River."
Song from *Puck Fair*.
Song: Love in Whose Rich Honor.
Song: Lying in Daylight.
Song of Another Tribe, A.
Song: Remembering Movies.
Song, the Brain-Coral.
Song: The Star in the Nets of Heaven.
Song: "Voice flew out of the river as morning
    flew, A."
Song: "World is full of loss; bring, wind, my
    love, The."
Sonnet: "My thoughts through yours refracted
    into speech."
Soul and Body of John Brown, The.
Sound of screaming for thirteen centuries, A.
Sounds of night in the country of the
    opposites.
Speaking Tree, The.
Speech for the Assistant, from Houdini.
Speech of the Mother, from "The Middle of
    the Air."
Speed, We Say.
Spirals and Fugues.
Statement by Willkie after Returning from
    England.
Statement: Philippa Allen.
Story, A.
Street corner to corner he will talk all day.
Structure is rising. It takes on shape, it takes on
    meaning, A.
Structure of the Plane, The.
Study in a Late Subway.
Suicide Blues.
Suite for Lord Timothy Dexter.
Summer, the Sacramento.
Sun-Artist, The.
Sun on the faces. On the knotted rocks.
Sundays, They Sleep Late.
Surrounded, The.
Target Practice.
Tarpaper shack and the red rose bush, The.
Tenth Elegy. Elegy in Joy.
Then.
Then I Saw What the Calling Was.
Theory of Flight.
There is a knotless line westward, past terraces.
There they slept. They left the train.
They dug up the grave, while a banjo and two
    guitars.
They pray. Security against oldness.
They rule out of our justice and our despair.
They talk to each other, and he holds her hand.
Third Elegy. The Fear of Form.
This House, This Country.
This is going to be about smoke.
This is what lit the hunters of smoke and the
    paths of the forest.
This Morning.
This Place in the Ways.
Thousands of Days.
Three Black Women.
Three Sides of a Coin.
Time Hinder Not Me; His Arms Reach Here
    and There.
Time of finks and nobles, A.
To Enter That Rhythm Where the Self Is Lost.
To follow the hard sunlight on the northern
    harbor.
To keep the weakness secret. To deny it and

break through.
Track cuts west. Slant roof, sun-catcher, The.
Traditional Tune.
Transgress, The.
Tree.
Tree of rivers flowing through our lives, A.
Tree of rivers seen and forgotten, The.
Trinity Churchyard.
Trophies.
Tunnel, The.
Two Illuminations, The.
Two Years.
Unborn Song.
Until I stand on the January platform.
Up past the burnt hills. Distance and the
    crowd.
Victims, a Play for the Home, The.
Voices.
Voices of Waking.
Waiting for Icarus.
War Comes into my Room, The.
Wards, The.
Watchers, The.
Water-hammer, the history of ice, The.
Water Night.
Waterlily Fire.
Wedding Presents.
Welcome from War.
West Virginia.
What Do I Give You?
What Do We See?
What do you know of America? I asked a little
    Russian schoolgirl.
What do you write?
What Have You Brought Home from the
    Wars?
What I See.
What They Said.
Whatever roams the air is traveling.
Wheels and galleries of the control of tears.
When he began to witness, it was not to a
    journey.
When the true things meet us at the place we
    reach, they are all.
When the young man reaches his full height.
Where will you be tonight? Past Lisbon, flying.
Wherever.
Who in One Lifetime.
Willkie in the *Gulliver*.
Willkie—Stopless Falling through Air.
Willkie: Words from Russia.
Wind arrow, wind rose, the wind currents in
    air.
Woman and Emblems.
Woman as Market.
Wooden Spring.
Word of Mouth.
Work, for the Day Is Coming.
Work in the loss of mass, The.
Wreath of Women.
Writer, The.
Young Girl of the Mississippi Valley, The.
Young Men, The.

Rukeyser, Muriel *and* Leif Sjoberg
Night Flight: New York.
Speed of Darkness, The.

Rumi, Jelaluddin [*or* Jalal al-Din] (1207–73)
Acts of Helplessness.
After the Meditation.
Ali in Battle.
All day and night, music.
All our lives we've looked.
All Rivers at Once.
Are you jealous of the ocean's generosity.
Awkward Comparison, An.
Ayaz and the King's Pearl.
Babbling Child, A.
Basket of Fresh Bread, A.
Be Melting Snow.
Bird delegation came to Solomon complaining,
    A.
Birdsong brings relief.
Birdsong from Inside the Egg.
Birdwings.
Bismillah.
Blocked Road, The.

Body Intelligence.
Bonfire at Midnight.
Bowl, A.
Breadmaking.
Breeze at dawn has secrets to tell you, The.
Buoyancy.
Burnt Kabob.
Cat and the Meat, The.
Center of the Fire, The.
Checkmate.
Chickpea to Cook.
Childhood Friends.
Children's Game, A.
Chinese Art and Greek Art.
Christ is the population of the world.
Come to the orchard in Spring.
Community of the Spirit, A.
Constant Conversation.
Core of Masculinity, The.
Craftsman pulled a reed from the reedbed, A.
Craftsmanship and Emptiness.
Cry Out in Your Weakness.
Dalqak's Message.
Dance, when you're broken open.
Daylight, full of small dancing particles.
Debtor Sheikh, The.
Deliberation.
Dervish at the Door.
Dissolver of Sugar.
Diver's Clothes Lying Empty, The.
Do you think I know what I'm doing?
Does sunset sometimes look like the sun's
    coming up?
Dog in the Doorway, The.
Don't let your throat tighten.
Dove in the Eaves, A.
Dream That Must Be Interpreted, The.
Drumsound rises on the air.
Drunks fear the police.
Dying, Laughing.
Each Note.
Egypt That Doesn't Exist, An.
Elephant in the Dark.
Emptiness.
Empty Garlic, An.
Enough Words?
Far Mosque, The.
Fasting.
Father Reason.
Flute, The.
Flutes for Dancing.
Food Sack, The.
Force of Friendship, The.
Fragile Vial, The.
Freshness, The.
Friend comes into my body, The.
Friend, our closeness is this.
Gamble everything for love.
Gift of Water, The.
Gnats inside the Wind.
Gone, inner and outer.
Granary Floor, The.
Granite and Wineglass.
Grasses, The.
Great Wagon, A.
Green Ears.
Ground Cries Out, The.
Guest House, The.
Hallaj.
Held like this, to draw in milk.
Human Honesty.
Humble living does not diminish. It fills.
I am filled with you.
I am so small I can barely be seen.
I called through your door.
I circle your nest tonight.
I Come Before Dawn.
I Have Five Things to Say.
I have lived on the lip.
I have phrases and whole pages memorized.
I Have Such a Teacher.
I honor those who try.
I reach for a piece of wood. It turns into a lute.
I saw you last night in the gathering.
I stand up, and this one of me.
I used to be shy.

I want to hold you close like a lute.
I would love to kiss you.
If the beloved is everywhere.
If you want what visible reality.
I'm Not Saying This Right.
Importance of Gourdcrafting, The.
Imra'u 'l-Qays.
In a boat down a fast-running creek.
In Baghdad, Dreaming of Cairo: In Cairo,
  Dreaming of Baghdad.
In Between Stories.
In the Arc of Your Mallet.
In the slaughterhouse of love, they kill.
In your light I learn how to love.
Inside water, a waterwheel turns.
Jesus on the Lean Donkey.
Joy at Sudden Disappointment.
Judge a Moth by the Beauty of Its Candle.
Just-Finishing Candle, A.
Keep walking, though there's no place to get
  to.
King and the Handmaiden and the Doctor, The.
Lame Goat, The.
Late, by myself, in the boat of myself.
Least Figure, The.
Let your throat-song.
Light You Give Off, The.
Like This.
Listen to presences inside poems.
Long String, The.
Love Dogs.
Man and a Woman Arguing, A.
Many Wines, The.
Meadowsounds.
Milk of Millennia, The.
Minute I heard my first love story, The.
Morning wind spreads its fresh smell, The.
Moses and the Shepherd.
Mouse and a Frog, A.
Mouse and the Camel, The.
Muhammad and the Huge Eater.
Music Master.
Music, The.
My Worst Habit.
Mystery does not get clearer by repeating the
  question, The.
Nasuh.
New Moon, Hilal.
New Rule, The.
Night Air, The.
No better love than love with no object.
No Flag.
No Room for Form.
Not a Day on Any Calendar.
Of Being Woven.
Omar and the Old Poet.
On Resurrection Day.
One Who Wraps Himself.
Only Breath.
Out beyond ideas of wrongdoing and
  rightdoing.
Pale sunlight.
Phrasing Must Change, The.
Pickaxe, The.
Polishing the Mirror.
Private Banquet, The.
Put This Design in Your Carpet.
Question, The.
Quietness.
Real value comes with madness.
Reed Flute's Song, The.
Rough Metaphors.
Saladin's Begging Bowl.
Sanai.
Say I Am You.
Secret turning in us, A.
Seed Market, The.
Send the Chaperones Away.
Servant Who Loved His Prayers, The.
Sexual Urgency, What a Woman's Laughter
  Can Do, and the Nature of True Virility.
Shape of My Tongue, The.
Sheba's Gifts to Solomon.
Sheba's Hesitation.
Sheba's Throne.
Sheikh Kharraqani and His Wretched Wife.

Sheikh Who Played with Children, The.
Shreds of Steam.
Slave, be aware that the Lord.
Snake-Catcher and the Frozen Snake, The.
Solomon to Sheba.
Solomon's Crooked Crown.
Some nights stay up till dawn.
Someone Digging in the Ground.
Someone who goes with half a loaf of bread.
Something opens our wings. Something.
Sometimes I Forget Completely.
Song about a Donkey, A.
Soul, The.
Special Plates.
Spring.
Spring Is Christ.
Steambath, The.
Story Water.
Sublime Generosity.
Sun is love, The. The lover.
Sunrise Ruby, The.
Talking in the Night.
Talking through the Door.
Tattooing in Qazwin.
Tending Two Shops.
Tent, The.
There is a light seed grain inside.
There is a way between voice and presence.
There's a strange frenzy in my head.
There's Nothing Ahead.
These gifts from the Friend, a robe.
They try to say what you are, spiritual or
  sexual?
Think that you're gliding out from the face of
  a cliff.
Thirsty Fish, A.
This moment this love comes to rest in me.
This piece of food cannot be eaten.
This that is tormented and very tired.
This We Have Now.
This World Which Is Made of Our Love for
  Emptiness.
Three Brothers and the Chinese Princess, The.
Three Fish, The.
Three Quatrains, sels.
Today, like every other day, we wake up
  empty.
Two Friends.
Two Kinds of Intelligence.
Two Ways of Running.
Unfold Your Own Myth.
Unmarked Boxes.
Vigil, The.
Visions of Daquqi, The.
Walk to the well.
Water from Your Spring.
Waterwheel, The.
Wax.
Way of love is not, The.
We are the mirror as well as the face in it.
We are the night ocean filled.
We have a huge barrel of wine, but no cups.
We have this way of talking, and we have
  another.
We Three.
Wean Yourself.
What Jesus Runs Away From.
When I am with you, we stay up all night.
When I remember your love.
When We Pray Alone.
When you are with everyone but me.
When you feel your lips becoming infinite.
Where Are We?
Where Everything Is Music.
Which is worth more, a crowd of thousands.
Who Makes These Changes?
Who Says Words with My Mouth.
Who sees inside from outside?
Why Wine Is Forbidden.
Wine we really drink is our own blood, The.
Wished-For Song, A.
Witness, the Darling, The.
Worm's Waking, The.
You have said what you are.
You Sweep the Floor.
You that come to birth and bring the mysteries.

You've so distracted me.
Zikr.

S

Saba, Umberto (1883–1957)
Siren, A.
Sacchetti, Franco (1335–1400?)
On a Fine Day.
On a Wet Day.
Sadi [or Saadi or Sa'di] (1184–1291)
Had I the world for my enemy.
I said, "I do not fear the."
In Senahar, my first born sleeps.
Pain of love's a better fate, The.
Salve Senescentem.
Who loves his friend with his heart of hearts.
Salinas, Pedro (1892–1951)
Not in Marble Palaces.
Sandburg, Carl (1878–1967)
A. E. F.
Abracadabra Boys, The.
Accomplished Facts.
Acquaintance with Death, Sir.
Adelaide Crapsey.
Again?
Air Circus.
Alice Corbin Is Gone.
Alix.
All Day Long.
Alley Rats.
Almanac.
Alone and Not Alone.
Aloof.
Altgeld.
Always the Mob.
Ambassadors of Grief.
Among the Red Guns.
And So Today.
And They Obey.
And This Will Be All?
Anecdote of Hemlock for Two Athenians.
Anna Imroth.
Answer, The.
Anywhere and Everywhere People.
Aprons of Silence.
Arithmetic.
Ashurnatsirpal III.
At a Window.
At the Gates of Tombs.
Atlas, How Have You Been?
Auburn.
Auctioneer.
Autumn Movement.
Aztec.
Aztec Mask.
Baby Face.
Baby Song of the Four Winds.
Baby Toes.
Baby Vamps.
Back Yard.
Balloon Faces.
Baltic Fog Notes.
Band Concert.
Bars.
Bas-Relief.
Basket.
Bath.
Be Ready.
Beat, Old Heart.
Bee Song.
Between Two Hills.
Between Worlds.
Bilbea.
Biography.
Bird Footprint.
Bird Talk.
Bitter Summer Thoughts.
Bitter Summer Thoughts—No. 3.
Bitter Summer Thoughts—No. XXII.
Black Horizons.
Blacklisted.
Blizzard Notes.
Blossom Themes.

Blue Island Intersection.
Blue Maroons.
Blue Ridge.
Bluebird, What Do You Feed On?
'Boes.
Bones.
Books Men Die For.
Boxes and Bags.
Boy and Father.
Brainwashing.
Branches.
Brancusi.
Brass Keys.
Bricklayer Love.
Bright Conversation with Saint-Ex.
Brim.
Bringers.
Broadway.
Broken-Face Gargoyles.
Broken Hearted Soprano.
Broken Sky.
Broken Sonnet.
Broken Tabernacles.
Bronzes ("Bronze General Grant").
Bronzes ("They ask me to handle bronzes").
Brown Gold.
Bubbles.
Buckwheat.
Buffalo Bill.
Buffalo Dusk.
Bug Spots.
Bundles.
Butter Colors.
Buttons.
Buyers and Sellers.
Caboose Thoughts.
Cadenza.
Cahokia.
Cahoots.
Caligari.
Call the Next Witness.
Calls.
Canadians and Pottawatomies.
Carlovingian Dreams.
Cartoon.
Chamfort.
Changing Light Winds.
Chasers.
Cheap Blue.
Cheap Rent.
Chicago Boy Baby.
Chicago Poet.
Chicks.
Child.
Child Face.
Child Margaret.
Child Moon.
Child of the Romans.
Chillicothe.
Choices.
Choose.
Chords.
Chromo.
Circle of Doors.
City Number.
Clark Street Bridge.
Clean Curtains.
Clean Hands.
Clefs.
Clinton South of Polk.
Clocks.
Coin, A.
Consolation Sonata.
Cool Tombs.
Corn and Beans.
Corn Hut Talk.
Corn Prattlings.
Cornfield Ridge and Stream.
Cornucopia.
Counting.
Couple, A.
Couples.
Crabapple Blossoms.
Crabapples.
Crapshooters.
Cricket Match.

Crimson.
Crimson Changes People.
Crimson Rambler.
Cripple.
Crisscross.
Crossed Numbers.
Crossing the Ohio When Poppies Bloom in
    Ashtabula.
Crossing the Paces.
Crucible.
Cumulatives.
Cups of Coffee.
Curse of a Rich Polish Peasant on His Sister
    Who Ran Away with a Wild Man.
Dan.
Dancer.
Daybreak.
Death Snips Proud Men.
Deep Sea Wandering.
Destroyers.
Dialogue.
Different Kinds of Good-by.
Dinosaur Bones, The.
Do You Want Affidavits?
Docks.
Dogheads.
Doors.
Dragoons, I tell you the white hydrangeas turn
    rust and go soon.
Dream Girl.
Dreaming Fool.
Dreams in the Dusk.
Drowsy.
Drumnotes.
Dunes.
Dust.
Dusty Doors.
Dynamiter.
Early Copper.
Early Hours.
Early Lynching.
Early Moon.
Electric Sign Goes Dark, An.
Elephants Are Different to Different People.
Eleventh Avenue Racket.
Elm Buds.
Enemy Number One.
Epistle: "Jesus loved the sunsets on Galilee."
Even Numbers.
Evening Questions.
Evening Sea Wind.
Evening Sunsets Witness and Pass On, The.
Evening Waterfall.
Ever a Seeker.
Explanations of Love.
Face.
Falltime.
Fame If Not Fortune.
Far Rockaway Night Till Morning.
Fate.
Feather Lights.
Fellow Citizens.
Fence, A.
Field People.
Fifty-Fifty.
Fight.
Films.
Finish.
Fins.
Fire Dreams.
Fire-Logs.
Fire Pages.
Fireborn Are at Home in Fire, The.
First Sonata for Karlen Paula.
Fish Crier.
Five Cent Balloons.
Five Towns on the B. and O.
Flanders.
Flash Crimson.
Flat Lands.
Flat Waters of the West in Kansas.
Flowers Tell Months.
Flux.
Flying Fish.
Fog.
Fog Numbers.

Fog Portrait.
Follies.
Foolish About Windows.
For You.
Forgotten Wars.
Four Brothers, The.
Four Preludes on Playthings of the Wind.
Four Steichen Prints.
Fourth of July Night.
Foxgloves.
François Villon Forgotten.
Freedom is a Habit.
Frog Songs.
From the Shore.
Galoots.
Garden Wireless.
Gargoyle.
Girl in a Cage.
Glass House Canticle.
Glimmer.
God Is No Gentleman.
Gold Mud.
Goldwing Moth.
Gone.
Gong of Time, The.
Good Morning, America.
Good Night.
Government.
Graceland.
Grass.
Grassroots.
Graves.
Great Hunt, The.
Great Proud Wagon Wheels Go On, The.
Grieg Being Dead.
Guaranteed Antique.
Gypsy.
Gypsy Mother.
Half Moon In a High Wind.
Half Way.
Halsted Street Car.
Hammer, The.
Hammers Pounding.
Handfuls.
Hangman at Home, The.
Happiness.
Harbor, The.
Harmonica Humdrums.
Harrison Street Court.
Harsk, Harsk.
Harvest.
Harvest Sunset.
Has-Been, The.
Hate.
Hats.
Haunts.
Have Me.
Hazardous Occupations.
Haze.
Haze Gold.
Head.
Heavy and Light.
Helga.
Hell on the Wabash.
Hells and Heavens.
Hemlock and Cedar.
High Moments.
His Own Face Hidden.
Hits and Runs.
Hogh Conspiratorial Persons.
Home Fires.
Home Thoughts.
Honey and Salt.
Honky Tonk in Cleveland, Ohio.
Hoodlums.
Hoof Dusk.
Horse Fiddle.
Horses and Men in the Rain.
House.
How Much?
How Yesterday Looked.
Humdrum.
Hummingbird Woman.
Hunger and Cold.
Hungry and Laughing Men.
I Am the People, the Mob.

I Sang.
Ice Handler.
If So Hap May Be.
Iglits and His Wife.
Illinois Farmer.
Impasse.
Implications.
Impossible Iambics.
Improved Farm Land.
In a Back Alley.
In a Breath.
In Tall Grass.
In the Shadow of the Palace.
Instructions.
Interior.
Iron.
Is There Any Easy Road to Freedom?
Is Wisdom a Lot of Language?
Isle of Patmos.
It Is Much.
Jabberers.
Jack.
Jack London and O. Henry.
Jan Kubelik.
Jan, the Son of Thomas.
Jaws.
Jazz Fantasia.
John Ericsson Day Memorial, 1918.
Joke Gold.
Joliet.
Joy.
Jug.
June.
Jungheimer's.
Junk Man, The.
Just Before April Came.
Kansas Lessons.
Keepsake Boxes.
Killers ("I am put high").
Killers ("I am singing to you").
Kin.
Kisses, Can You Come Back Like Ghosts?
Kisses Forgotten.
Knucks.
Kreisler.
Lackawanna Twilight.
Lake Michigan Morning.
Landscape ("On a mountain-side").
Landscape ("See the trees").
Landscape Including Three States of the
   Union.
Languages.
Last Answers.
Laughing Blue Steel.
Laughing Corn.
Lavender Lilies.
Lawyer.
Lawyers Know Too Much, The.
Leather Leggings.
Legends.
Lesson.
Let Love Go On.
Let Them Ask Your Pardon.
Letter S.
Letters to Dead Imagists.
Liars, The.
Lief the Lucky.
Light and Moonbells.
Limited.
Lines Written for Gene Kelly to Dance To.
Little Candle.
Little Girl, Be Careful What You Say.
Little Sketch.
Little Word, Little White Bird.
Loam.
Localities.
Loin Cloth.
Long Guns.
Long Shadow of Lincoln: A Litany, The.
Losers.
Losses.
Lost.
Lovable Babblers.
Love Beyond Keeping.
Love in Labrador.
Love Is a Deep and a Dark and a Lonely.

Love Letter to Hans Christian Andersen.
Lumber Yard Pools at Sunset.
Madison and 42nd.
Mag.
Mamie.
Mammy Hums.
Man and Dog on an Early Winter Morning.
Man, the Man-Hunter.
Man the Moon Shooter.
Man with the Broken Fingers, The.
Manitoba Childe Roland.
Manual System.
Manufactured Gods.
Many Handles.
Many Hats.
March of the Hungry Mountains.
Margaret.
Maroon with Silver Frost.
Mascots.
Mask ("Fling your red scarf").
Mask ("To have your face left overnight").
Masses.
Maybe.
Mayor of Gary, The.
Meadow in Summer.
Medallion.
Medley.
Memoir.
Memoir of a Proud Boy.
Memoranda.
Metamorphosis.
Methusaleh Saw Many Repeaters.
Milk-White Moon, Put the Cows to Sleep.
Mill-Doors.
Million Young Workmen, 1915, A.
Mist Forms.
Mist Marches Across the Valley.
Mist, The.
Mr. Attila.
Mr. Longfellow and His Boy.
M'Liss and Louie.
Mockers Go to Kansas in Spring.
Mohammed Bek Hadjetlache.
Moist Moon People.
Moments of Dawn Riders.
Momus.
Money, Politics, Love, and Glory.
Monkey of Stars.
Monosyllabic.
Monotone.
Moon Hammock.
Moon Path.
Moon Riders.
Moon Rondeau.
Moonlight and Maggots.
Moonset.
More Country People.
Morning Glory Blue.
Muckers.
Mummy.
Murmurings in a Field Hospital.
My People.
Mysterious Biography.
Name Us a King.
Near Keokuk.
Neighbors.
Never Born.
Never Two Songs the Same.
New Farm Tractor.
New Feet.
New Hampshire Again.
New Song for Indiana Ophelias.
New Weather.
Nigger.
Night Bells.
Night Movement—New York.
Night Stuff.
Night's Nothings Again.
Nightsong.
Nocturn 4: "Claims of the sea, of the tide,
   move out, The."
Nocturn Cabbage.
Nocturne in a Deserted Brickyard.
Noon Hour.
North Atlantic.
Now They Bury Her Again.

Number Man.
Oak Arms.
October Paint.
Offering and Rebuff.
Old Deep Sing-Song.
Old-Fashioned Requited Love.
Old Flagman, The.
Old Hokusai Print.
Old Music for Quiet Hearts.
Old Osawatomie.
Old Timers.
Old Woman.
Omaha.
On a Flimmering Floom You Shall Ride.
On a Railroad Right of Way.
On the Breakwater.
On the Way.
One Modern Poet.
One Parting.
Onion Days.
Oomba.
Open Letter to the Poet Archibald MacLeish
   Who Has Forsaken His Massachusetts Farm
   to Make Propaganda for Freedom.
Osawatomie.
Our Hells.
Our Prayer of Thanks.
Out of the Rainbow End.
Out of White Lips.
Palladiums.
Pals.
Panels.
Paper I.
Paper II.
Pass, Friend.
Passers-by.
Paula.
Peace Between Wars.
Peace, Night, Sleep.
Peach Blossoms.
Pearl Fog.
Pearl Horizons.
Pencils.
Pennsylvania.
People of the Eaves, I Wish You Good
   Morning.
People Who Must.
People with Proud Chins.
People, Yes, The.
Personalia.
Personality.
Phizzog.
Pick-Offs.
Picnic Boat.
Pigeon.
Places.
Plaster.
Plowboy.
Plunger.
Pods.
Poems Done on a Late Night Car.
Pool.
Pool of Bethesda.
Poplar and Elm.
Poppies.
Population Drifts.
Portrait.
Portrait of a Child Settling Down for an
   Afternoon Nap.
Portrait of a Motorcar.
Potato Blossom Songs and Jigs.
Potomac River Mist.
Potomac Town in February.
Prairie.
Prairie Waters by Night.
Prairie Woodland.
Prayer after World War.
Prayers of Steel.
Precious Moments.
Press is Peculiar, The.
Primer Lesson.
Props.
Proud and Beautiful.
Proud of Their Rags.
Proud Torsos.
Psalm of the Bloodbank.

Psalm of Those Who Go Forth before
   Daylight.
Public Letter to Emily Dickinson.
Purple Martins.
Put Off the Wedding Five Times and Nobody
   Comes to It.
Questionnaire.
Quotations.
Rain Winds Blow Doors Open.
Rakeoff and the Getaway, The.
Rat Riddles.
Ready to Kill.
Real Avenue News.
Red and White.
Red-Headed Restaurant Cashier.
Red Son, The.
Redhaw Rain.
Remembered Women.
Remorse.
Repetitions.
Riddles and Whims.
Right to Grief, The.
Ripe Corn.
River Moon.
River Moons.
River Roads.
Road and the End, The.
Rose Bawn.
Runaway Colors.
Rusty Crimson.
Salvage.
Sand Scribblings.
Sandhill People.
Sandpipers.
Santa Fe Sketches.
Sarah's Letter to Peter.
Savoir Faire.
Sayings of Henry Stephens.
Scriptsmith.
Scripture.
Scroll.
Sea Chest.
Sea Hold, The.
Sea Slant.
Sea-Wash.
Sea Wisdom.
Seven Eleven.
Seventeen Months.
Shadows Fall Blue on the Mountains.
Shag-Bark Hickory.
She Opens the Barn Door Every Morning.
Sheep.
Shenandoah.
Shenandoah Journey.
Shirt ("Remember once").
Shirt ("My shirt is a token and symbol").
Shoes of Travel.
Shovel Man, The.
Silver Nails.
Silver Point.
Silver Wind.
Singing Nigger.
Sins of Kalamazoo, The.
Sixteen Months.
Sketch.
Sketch of a Poet.
Sky Pieces.
Sky Talk.
Skyscraper.
Skyscraper Loves Night, The.
Skyscrapers Stand Proud.
Slabs of the Sunburnt West.
Slants at Buffalo, New York.
Sleep Impression.
Sleep Song.
Sleepyheads.
Slippery.
Slow Program.
Small Homes.
Smoke.
Smoke and Steel.
Smoke Blue.
Smoke Rose Gold.
Smoke Shapes.
Snatch of Sliphorn Jazz.
Snow.

So to Speak.
Soiled Dove.
Solo for Saturday Night Guitar.
Soup.
South Wind Says So, The.
Southern Pacific.
Spanish.
Special Starlight.
Speech.
Sphinx, A.
Splinter.
Spray.
Spring Carries Surprises.
Spring Cries.
Spring Grass.
Spring Wind.
Star Silver.
Stars.
Stars, Songs, Faces.
Statistics.
Still Life.
Storms Begin Far Back.
Street Window.
Streets Too Old.
Striped Cats, Old Men and Proud Stockings.
Stripes.
Style.
Suburban Sicilian Sketches.
Subway.
Sumach and Birds.
Summer Grass.
Summer Shirt Sale.
Summer Stars.
Sun Dancer.
Sunset from Omaha Hotel Window.
Sunsets.
Sweeping Wendy: Study in Fugue.
Swell People.
Swirl.
Tall Man, A.
Tall Timber.
Tangibles.
Tawny.
Teamster's Farewell, A.
Telegram.
Tentative (First Model) Definitions of Poetry.
Testament.
Testimony Regarding a Ghost.
Theme in Yellow.
Themes in Contrast.
Theorem.
There Are Different Gardens.
They All Want to Play Hamlet.
They Ask Each Other Where They Came
   From.
They Ask: Is God, Too, Lonely?
They Buy with an Eye to Looks.
They Met Young.
They Will Say.
Thimble Islands.
Thin Strips.
This—For the Moon—Yes?
This Street Never Sleeps.
Thou Art Like a Flower.
Three Balls.
Three Fragments for Fishers of Destiny.
Three Ghosts.
Three Hills Look Different in the Moonshine.
Three Pieces on the Smoke of Autumn.
Three Shrines.
Three Slants at New York.
Three Spring Notations on Bipeds.
Three Violins.
Threes.
Throw Roses.
Throwbacks.
Timber Moon.
Timber Wings.
Timesweep.
To a Contemporary Bunkshooter.
To a Dead Man.
To Beachey, 1912.
To Certain Journeymen.
To Know Silence Perfectly.
To the Ghost of John Milton.
Trafficker.

Trinity Place.
Troths.
Turn of the Wheel.
Two.
Two Fish.
Two Humpties.
Two Items.
Two Moon Fantasies.
Two Neighbors.
Two Nocturns.
Two Strangers Breakfast.
Two Women.
Two Women and Their Fathers.
Under.
Under a Hat Rim.
Under a Telephone Pole.
Under the Capitol Dome.
Under the Harvest Moon.
Understandings in Blue.
Unintentional Paint.
Unknown War, The.
Uplands in May.
Upstairs.
Upstream.
Useless Words.
Valley Song ("Sunset swept").
Valley Song ("Your eyes and the valley are
   memories").
Variations on a Theme.
Vaudeville Dancer.
Very Very Important.
Village in Late Summer.
Waiting.
Waiting for the Chariot.
Walking Man of Rodin, The.
Wall Shadows.
Wanting the Impossible.
Wars.
Was Ever a Dream a Drum?
Washerwoman.
Washington Monument by Night.
Way of the World, The.
We Have Gone Through Great Rooms
   Together.
We Must Be Polite.
Webs.
Wedding Postponed.
Weeds.
When Death Came April Twelve 1945.
Whiffletree.
Whiffs of the Ohio River at Cinncinnati.
Whirls.
White Ash.
White Hands.
White Shoulders.
Whitelight.
Who Am I?
Wilderness.
Wind Horses.
Wind on the Way, The.
Wind Sings Welcome in Early Spring, The.
Wind Song.
Windflower Leaf.
Window.
Windy City, The.
Wingtip.
Winter Gold.
Winter Milk.
Winter Weather.
Wistful.
Without Notice Beforehand.
Without the Cane and the Derby.
Woman with a Past.
Women Washing Their Hair.
Work Gangs.
Working Girls.
Worms and the Wind.
Year, The.
Yellow Evening Star.
Yes, the Dead Speak to Us.
You Shall Have Homes.
Young Bullfrogs.
Young Sea.

Sannazarius, Actius Sincerus *See* **Sannazaro,
Jacopo**

Sannazaro, Jacopo (Actius Sincerus Sannazarius) (1458–1530)
Like to these unme[a]surable montains [*or* mountayns].

Sappho (*fl.* c.612 B.C.)
Bright-throned, undying Aphrodite.
Deduke Men A Selanna.
Farewell to Anactoria.
He is, I should say, on a level.
I loved you, Leslie, long ago.
Love strikes me again, that makes the legs give way.
One Girl.
Sappho.
Someone I tell you will remember us.
Song of the Rose.

Sarmiento, Félix Rubén García *See* **"Dario, Rubén"**

Sarton, May (1914–95)
Action of Therapy, The.
All Souls.
Annunciation.
Apple Tree in May.
Approach—Calcutta, The.
At Delphi.
At Lindos.
At Muzot,
Autumn Sonnets, The, *sels.*
Ballad of Johnny, The.
Ballad of the Sixties.
Baroque Image.
Bears and Waterfalls.
Because What I Want Most Is Permanence.
Behind What Little Mirror.
Binding the Dragon.
Birthday on the Acropolis.
Burial.
Caged Bird, The.
Celebration for George Sarton, A.
Charleston Plantations.
Child's Japan, A.
Christmas Letter to a Psychiatrist.
Clavichord, The.
Composition.
Death and the Lovers.
Der Abschied.
Divorce of Lovers, A, *sels.*
Dutch Interior.
Easter Morning.
Easter, 1968.
Eine Kleine Snailmusik.
Evening Music.
Evening Walk in France.
Exchange of Gifts, An.
Fear of Angels, The.
Fig, The.
First Autumn, The.
First Snow.
Flower-Arranging Summer, A.
Franz, a Goose.
Frog, that Naked Creature, The.
Furies, The.
Garden of Childhood, The.
Gestalt at Sixty.
Giant in the Garden.
Girl with 'Cello.
Glass of Water, A.
Godhead as Lynx, The.
Greeting.
Guest, A.
Hard Death, A.
House in Winter, The.
Humpty Dumpty.
In Time Like Air.
Intruder, An.
Invocation: "Come out of the dark earth."
Invocation to Kali, The.
Italian Garden.
Japanese Prints.
Jonah.
Journey toward Poetry.
Lady and the Unicorn, The.
Lady with a Falcon.
Lament for Toby, a French Poodle.
Letter from Chicago.
Letter to James Stephens, A.

Light Left On, A.
Lion and the Rose, The.
March-Mad.
Mediterranean.
Memory of Swans.
Metamorphosis.
Metaphysical Garden, The.
Monticello.
Moth in the Schoolroom.
Mud Season.
Muse as Medusa, The.
My Father's Death.
My Sisters, O My Sisters.
Myself to Me.
Myth.
Narcissus.
Nativity.
Night Watch.
Nostalgia for India.
Notes from India.
Now I Become Myself.
Nursery Rhyme.
Of Grief.
Of the Seasons.
Olive Grove, The.
On a Winter Night.
On Being Given Time.
Parrot, A.
Phoenix, The.
Portrait by Holbein.
Prayer before Work.
Prisoner at a Desk.
Proteus.
Prothalamion.
Puritan, The.
Recognition, A.
Return.
Return of Aphrodite, The.
Snow Light, The.
Song: "No, I will never forget you and your great eyes."
Song: "Now let us honor with violin and flute."
Stone Walls.
Storm of Angels, A.
Strangers.
Sun Boat.
Swans, The.
These Images Remain.
These Pure Arches.
These Were Her Nightly Journeys.
To the Living, *sels.*
To the North.
Tortured, The.
Village Tale, A.
We Sat Smoking at a Table.
We'll to the Woods No More, the Laurels Are Cut Down.
Where Dream Begins.
Who Wakes.
Winter Carol.
Work of Happiness, The.

Schiller, Johann Christoph Friedrich von (1759–1805)
Evening, after a Picture.
Piccolomini, The, *sels.*

Scholasticus, Agathias *See* **Agathias**

Schuyler, James (1923–91)
Advent.
Adverts.
After Joe Was at the Island.
Afterward ("Is as much as before").
Afterward ("Then it snowed").
Ajaccio Violets.
Alice Faye at Ruby Foo's.
Almanac, An.
Amy Lowell Thoughts.
Andrew Lord Poems.
April and Its Forsythia.
Arches.
At Darragh's I.
At the Beach.
August First, 1974.
August Night.
Autumn Leaves.
Await.
Awoke.

Back.
Beaded Balustrade.
Beautiful Funerals.
Belated Birthday Poem, A.
Below the Stairs.
Birds.
Bleeding Gums.
Blizzard.
Blossoming Oakwood.
Blue.
Blue towel, A.
Bluet, The.
Boer War Bread Strike.
Buildings.
Buried at Springs.
Buttered Greens.
Cardinal, A.
Cenotaph, The.
Chapel, A.
Closed Gentian Distances.
Cornflowers.
Crocus Night.
Crystal Lithium, The.
Day, The ("Because of a coolness").
Day, The ("Day is gray, The").
Daylight.
Dear Joe.
December.
Dec. 28, 1974.
Deep Winter.
Dining Out with Doug and Frank.
Dog Wants His Dinner, The.
Dorabella's Naples Watercolor.
Dreams.
Earth's Holocaust.
East Window on Elizabeth Street, An.
8/12/70.
Elizabethans Called It Dying, The.
Empathy and New Year.
En Route to Southampton.
Evening.
Evening Wind.
Evenings in Vermont.
Eyes.
Eyes at the Window.
Fabergé.
Fauré Ballade, The.
Fauré's Second Piano Quartet.
February.
February 13, 1975.
Few Days, A.
Flashes.
Footnote.
For Bob Dash.
Four Poems.
Freely Espousing.
Frock.
"From the next."
Going.
Good Morning.
Grand Duo.
Grave, A.
Gray Day.
Gray, Intermittently Blue, Eyed Hero.
Green Door, The.
Greenwich Avenue.
Greetings from the Chateau.
Growing Dark.
Gulls.
Hats.
Haze.
Head, A.
Heather and Calendulas.
Held Breath, A.
Horse-Chestnut Trees and Roses.
Hudson Ferry.
Hymn to Life.
I Sit Down to Type.
I Think.
Ilford Rose Book.
In a Churchyard.
In Earliest Morning.
In January.
In the Round.
In Wiry Winter.
Industrial Archaeology.

Janis Joplin's Dead: Long Live Pearl.
Jelly Jelly.
Joint.
June.
June 30, 1974.
Just before Fall.
Korean Mums.
Labor Day.
Let's All Hear It for Mildred Bailey!
Letter Poem #3.
Letter Poem #2.
Letter to a Friend: Who Is Nancy Daum?
Light Blue Above.
Light from Canada.
Light Within, The.
Like Lorraine Ellison.
Lilacs.
Linen.
Looking Forward to See Jane Real Soon.
Man in Blue, A.
March Here.
Mark.
Master of the Golden Glow, The.
May, 1972.
May 24th or So.
Mike.
Milk.
Money Musk.
Mood Indigo.
Moon.
Morning of the Poem, The.
Morning, The.
Name Day, A.
New Yorker, A.
Night, The.
Noon Office.
November.
Now and Then.
O Sleepless Night.
October.
October 5, 1981.
On the Dresser.
Oriane.
Our Father.
Over the Hills.
Overcast, Hot.
Pastime.
Penobscot.
People Who See Bubbles Rise.
Perhaps.
Photograph, A.
Picnic Cantata, A.
Poem, A: "Tags of songs, like salvaged
    buttons."
Poem: "How about an oak leaf."
Poem: "I do not always understand what you
    say."
Poem: "I got my hair cut."
Poem: "This beauty that I see."
Poem: "Wind tears up the sun, The."
Poem: "Your enchantment / enchains me,
    stretched."
Princess Di.
Procession.
Quick, Henry, the Flit!
Rachmaninoff's Third.
Rain.
Red Brick and Brown Stone.
Reunion, A.
Roof Garden.
Rose of Marion, The.
Roxy.
Royals.
Running Footsteps.
Salute.
Saturday Night.
Scarlet Tanager.
Seeking.
Self-Pity Is a Kind of Lying, Too.
September.
Shadowy Room.
Shaker.
Shimmer.
Simone Signoret.
Six Something.
Sky Eats Up the Trees, The.

Sleep ("Friends who come").
Sleep ("With its burden").
Sleep-Gummed Eyes.
Snow, The.
Snowdrop, The.
So Good.
Sometimes.
Song: "I'm about to go shopping."
Song: "Light lies layered in the leaves, The."
Sonnet: "August, tasting of ripe grapes and
    afternoon sleep."
Sorting, Wrapping, Packing, Stuffing.
Sparks.
Spring.
Standing and Watching.
Steaming Ties.
Stone Knife, A.
Stun.
Suddenly.
Sun Cab, A.
Sunday ("Mint bed is in").
Sunday ("Pears hang on the trees by stems").
Sunset.
Table of Green Fields, A.
Things to Do.
Thinness.
This Dark Apartment.
This Notebook.
This Soft October.
Three Gardens.
3/23/66.
Thursday.
To Frank O'Hara.
Today.
Tom.
Tomorrow.
Tom's Attempt to Seduce Big Brother Steve.
Tom's Dream.
Trash Book, The.
Trip.
Two.
Under the Hanger.
Unlike Joubert.
Up.
"Used Handkerchiefs 5¢."
Velvet Roses.
Vermont Diary, A.
View, A.
Virginia Woolf.
Voyage Autour de Mes Cartes Postales.
Walk, The.
Walter Scott.
Was It.
Watching You.
We Are Leaves.
We Walk.
What.
What Ails My Fern?
White.
White Boat, Blue Boat.
White City, A.
Wild Eggs.
With Frank and George at Lexington.
Witley Court.
Wonderful World.
Wystan Auden.
Yellow Flowers.
You're.

Scott, Sir Walter (1771–1832)
Bridal of Trierman, The, *sels.*
Gray Brother, The.
Hellvellyn.
Hunting Song.
Ivanhoe, *sels.*
Jock of Hazeldean.
Lady of the Lake, The, *sels.*
Lay of the Last Minstrel, The, *sels.*
Lord of the Isles, The, *sels.*
Marmion, *sels.*
On the Massacre of Glencoe, 1692.
Palmer, The.
Pibroch of Donuil Dhu.
Quentin Durward, *sels.*
Rokeby, *sels.*
Spindle Song, The.

Sedulius (*fl.* c.435)
Solis Ortus Cardine, A.
Seidl, Johann Gabriel (1804–75)
Hans Euler.
To the High-Flyers.
Seifert, Jaroslav (1901–86)
And Now Goodbye.
Apple Tree with Cobweb Strings.
At one of his readings a long time ago.
At the Tomb of the Czech Kings.
Autobiography.
Bach Concerto, A.
Berthe Soucaret.
Birds' Voices in the Tree Tops.
Bombing of the Town of Kralupy, The.
Canal Gardens.
Chaplet of Sage, A.
Cry of the Spectres, The.
Dance of the Girls' Chemises.
Dead of Lidice, The.
Demolition Report.
Dialogue.
Dome of the Observatory, The.
Fan, The.
Fingerprints.
Four Small Windows.
Fragment of a Letter.
Funeral under My Window.
Garland on the Wrist, A.
Grave of Signor Casanova, The.
Halley's Comet.
Hands of Venus, The.
Head of the Virgin Mary, The.
Honeymoon.
How painful I would find it.
Hundred Times Nothing, A.
Hunt for the Kingfisher, The.
If one could tell one's heart.
If you call poetry a song.
In an Empty Room.
Lines for the Painter Ota Janeček.
Lost Paradise.
Lovers, those evening pilgrims.
Lunar Ironmongery.
Merry-Go-Round with White Swan.
Mistress of Poets, The.
Model, The.
Moscow.
Mr Krösing's Top Hat.
Nocturnal Darkness.
Nocturnal Divertimento.
November 1918.
November Rain.
Once only did I see / the sun so blood-red.
Opening Poem.
Our Lady of Žižkov.
Panorama.
Parting.
Philosophy.
Place of Pilgrimage.
Plague Column, The.
Prague.
Prologue: "To be a poet is no easy task."
Prospect of Prague, A.
Red-Hot Fruit.
Relay Tower, The.
Reluctant whispers of kissed lips.
Robed in Light, *sels.*
Royal Pavilion, The.
St George's Basilica.
Salute to the Madrid Barricades.
Silence Full of Sleighbells.
Sinful City.
Smoke of Marijuana, The.
Sometimes we are tied down by memories.
Song about Girls, A.
Song at the End, A.
Song from an Intermezzo.
Song of the Native Land.
Song of the Nightingale, The.
Song of the Sweepings.
Song: "We wave a handkerchief."
Spanish Vineyards.
Striking of the Tower Clock, The.
Struggle with the Angel.
To Be a Poet.

To Prague.
Transformations.
Umbrella from Piccadilly, An.
Verses from an Old Tapestry.
View from Charles Bridge.
Visit to the Painter Vladimír Komárek, A.
Wax Candle, The.
Wet Picture.
When in the history books.
Window on Birds' Wings.
Year 1934, The.
You have skin pale like a snowdrop.

Sendak, Maurice (b. 1928)
Navajo Blanket, The.

Seneca (4 B.C.–A.D. 65)
Hercules Furens, *sels.*
Hippolytus, *sels.*
Thyestes, *sels.*
Troades, *sels.*

Sexton, Anne (1928–74)
Abortion, The.
Addict, The.
Admonitions to a Special Person.
After Auschwitz.
Again and Again and Again.
All My Pretty Ones.
Ambition Bird, The.
And One for My Dame.
Angel Food Dogs, The.
Angels of the Love Affair.
Anna Who Was Mad.
As It Was Written.
Assassin, The.
August 8th.
August 17th.
Author of the Jesus Papers Speaks, The.
Baby Picture.
Balance Wheel, The.
Ballad of the Lonely Masturbator, The.
Barefoot.
Bat.
Bayonet.
Bells, The.
Big Boots of Pain, The.
Big Heart, The.
Black Art, The.
Break Away, The.
Break, The.
Breast, The.
Briar Rose (Sleeping Beauty).
Buying the Whore.
Child Bearers, The.
Children, The.
Christmas Eve.
Cigarettes and Whiskey and Wild, Wild
  Women.
Cinderella.
Civil War, The.
Clothes.
Cockroach.
Consecrating Mother, The.
Consorting with Angels.
Courage.
Cripples and Other Stories.
Crossing the Atlantic.
Curse against Elegies, A.
"Daddy" Warbucks.
Dead Heart, The.
Death Baby, The.
Death King, The.
Death of the Fathers, The.
Demon.
Despair.
Division of Parts, The.
Divorce.
Divorce, Thy Name Is Woman.
Doctor of the Heart, The.
Doctors.
Doors, Doors, Doors.
Double Image, The.
Dreaming the Breasts.
Earth, The.
Earth Falls Down, The.
Earthworm.
Eighteen Days without You.
Elegy in the Classroom.

Elizabeth Gone.
End, Middle, Beginning.
Errand, The.
Evil Eye, The.
Evil Seekers, The.
Exorcists, The.
Expatriates, The.
Fallen Angels, The.
Falling Dolls, The.
Farmer's Wife, The.
Faustus and I.
February 11th.
February 4th.
February 17th.
February 3rd.
February 20th.
February 21st.
Fierceness of Female, The.
Fire Thief, The.
Firebombers, The.
Fish That Walked, The.
Flee on Your Donkey.
Flight.
Food.
For Eleanor Boylan Talking with God.
For God While Sleeping.
For John, Who Begs Me Not to Enquire
  Further.
For Johnny Pole on the Forgotten Beach.
For Mr. Death Who Stands with His Door
  Open.
For My Lover, Returning to His Wife.
For the Year of the Insane.
Fortress, The.
45 Mercy Street.
Frenzy.
Frog Prince, The.
From the Garden.
Funnel.
Furies, The.
Ghosts.
God-Monger, The.
Godfather Death.
Gods.
God's Backside.
Going Gone.
Gold Key, The.
Grandfather, Your Wound.
Gull.
Hangman, The.
Hansel and Gretel.
Her Kind.
Hex, The.
Hoarder, The.
Hog.
Hornet.
Horse.
House, The.
Housewife.
Hurry Up Please It's Time.
Hutch.
I Remember.
Imitations of Drowning.
In Celebration of My Uterus.
In Excelsis.
In the Beach House.
In the Deep Museum.
Interrogation of the Man of Many Hearts, The.
Inventory of Goodbyes, The.
Iron Hans.
Is It True?
It is a Spring Afternooon.
January 1st.
January 19th.
January 24th.
Jesus Asleep.
Jesus Awake.
Jesus Cooks.
Jesus Dies.
Jesus Raises Up the Harlot.
Jesus Suckles.
Jesus Summons Forth.
Jesus, the Actor, Plays the Holy ghost.
Jesus Unborn.
Jesus Walking.
June Bug.

Just Once.
KE 6-8018.
Keeping the City.
Killing the Love.
Killing the Spring.
Kind Sir: These Woods.
Kiss, The.
Kite, The.
Knee Song.
Lament: "Someone is dead."
Landscape Winter.
Leaves That Talk.
Legend of the One-Eyed Man, The.
Lessons in Hunger.
Letter Written During a January Northeaster.
Letter Written on a Ferry While Crossing Long
  Island Sound.
Letters to Dr. Y.
Little Girl, My String Bean, My Lovely
  Woman.
Little Peasant, The.
Little Uncomplicated Hymn, A.
Live.
Lobster.
Locked Doors.
Lost Ingredient, The.
Lost Lie, The.
Love Letter Written in a Burning Building.
Love Plant, The.
Love Song for K. Owyne.
Love Song: "I was / the girl of the chain
  letter."
Loving the Killer.
Lullaby: "It is a summer evening."
Madame Arrives in the Mail.
Maiden without Hands, The.
Making a Living.
Man and Wife.
March 4th.
March 7th.
Mary's Song.
May 30th.
Menstruation at Forty.
Mr. Mine.
Money Swing, The.
Moon Song, Woman Song.
Moose.
Moss of His Skin, The.
Mother and Daughter.
Mother and Jack and the Rain.
Mothers.
Music Swims Back to Me.
My Friend, My Friend.
Not So. Not So.
Noon Walk on the Asylum Lawn.
Now.
Nude Swim, The.
O Ye Tongues.
Obsessive Combination of Ontological Inscape,
  Trickery and Love, An.
Oh.
Old.
Old Dwarf Heart.
One-Eye, Two-Eyes, Three-Eyes.
One-Legged Man, The.
Operation, The.
Other, The.
Pain for a Daughter.
Papa and Mama Dance, The.
Passion of the Mad Rabbit, The.
Play, The.
Poet of Ignorance, The.
Porcupine.
Portrait of an Old Woman on the College
  Tavern Wall.
Praying on a 707.
Praying to Big Jack.
Protestant Easter.
Raccoon.
Rapunzel.
Rats Live on No Evil Star.
Red Dance, The.
Red-Riding Hood.
Red Roses.
Red Shoes, The.
Riding the Elevator into the Sky.

Ringing the Bells.
Risk, The.
Road Back, The.
Room of My Life, The.
Rowing.
Rowing Endeth, The.
Rumpelstiltskin.
Said the Poet to the Analyst.
Saints Come Marching In, The.
Sea Corpse, The.
Seal.
Self in 1958.
Sermon of the Twelve Acknowledgements,
    The.
Sheep.
Shout, The.
Sickness unto Death, The.
Silence, The.
Small Wire.
Snail.
Snake.
Snow.
Snow White and the Seven Dwarfs.
Some Foreign Letters.
Somewhere in Africa.
Song for a Lady.
Song for a Red Nightgown.
Speaking Bitterness.
Stand-Ins, The.
Star-Nosed Mole.
Starry Night, The.
Story for Rose on the Midnight Flight to
    Boston, A.
Suicide Note.
Sun, The.
Surgeon, The.
Sweeney.
Sylvia's Death.
Taker, The.
Talking to Sheep.
Telephone.
That Day.
There You Were.
Those Times.
Three Green Windows.
To a Friend Whose Work Has Come to
    Triumph.
To Like, to Love.
To Lose the Earth.
Torn Down from Glory Daily.
Touch, The.
Truth the Dead Know, The.
Twelve Dancing Princesses, The.
Twelve-Thousand-Day Honeymoon, The.
Two Hands.
Two Sons.
Unknown Girl in the Maternity Ward.
Us.
Uses.
Venus and the Ark.
Waiting Head, The.
Waking Alone.
Walking in Paris.
Wall, The.
Wallflower.
Wanting to Die.
Water.
Wedding Night, The.
Wedding Ring Dance, The.
Wedlock, The.
Welcome Morning.
Whale.
What the Bird with the Human Head Knew.
What's That.
When Man Enters Woman.
When the Glass of My Body Broke.
Where I Live in This Honorable House of the
    Laurel Tree.
Where It Was at Back Then.
White Snake, The.
Wifebeater, The.
Witch's Life, The.
With Mercy for the Greedy.
Woman with Girdle.
Wonderful Musician, The.
Words.

Yellow.
You All Know the Story of the Other Woman.
You, Doctor Martin.
Young.
Your Face on the Dog's Neck.

Shapiro, Karl (1913–2000)
Adam and Eve.
Adult Bookstore.
Alphabet, The.
And Now, the Weather.
At Auden's Grave.
Auto Wreck.
Back, The.
Boy-Man.
Buick.
Calder, A.
California Petrarchan.
Cathedral Bells, The.
Conscientious Objector, The.
Crucifix in the Filing Cabinet, The.
Cut Flower, A.
Dirty Word, The.
Dome of Sunday, The [or A].
Drug Store.
Essay on Chess.
Figurehead, The.
First Time, The.
Fly, The.
Girls Fighting, Broadway.
Glass Poem.
Grant's Tomb Revisited.
Haircut.
Homewreck.
Hospital.
Humanities Building, The.
I Am an Atheist Who Says His Prayers.
Impact.
Intellectual, The.
Interlude, The.
Israel.
Leg, The.
Love for a Hand.
Manhole Covers.
Messias.
Mongolian Idiot.
My Grandmother.
Nebraska.
Necropolis.
New Ring, The.
Nigger.
Office Love.
Olive Tree, The.
Pigeons, The.
Poet.
Poet in Residence.
Premises.
Progress of Faust, The.
Retirement.
Room in Rome, A.
Scyros.
Solipsism.
Spider Mums, The.
Statue of Liberty.
Synagogue, The.
Tingling Back, The.
Tornado Warning.
Travelogue for Exiles.
Twins, The.
University.
V-Letter.
Vietnam Memorial.
Waitress.
Washington Cathedral.
White Negress, The.

Shelley, Percy Bysshe (1792–1822)
Adonais; An Elegy on the Death of John
    Keats.
Alastor; or, The Spirit of Solitude.
Allegory, An.
Another Fragment to Music.
Another Version of the Same.
Arethusa.
Autumn: A Dirge.
Aziola, The.
Bigotry's Victim.
Birth of Pleasure, The.

Boat on the Serchio, The.
Bridal Song, A: "Golden gates of Sleep unbar,
    The."
Buona Notte.
Cancelled Passage.
Cancelled Stanza.
Cenci, The.
Charles the First.
Cloud, The.
Daemon of the World, The; A Fragment.
Death ("Death is here").
Death ("They die").
Death knell is ringing, The.
Devil's Walk, The.
Dialogue, A.
Dirge, A: "Rough wind, that moanest loud."
Dirge for the Year.
England in 1819.
Epipsychidion.
Epitaph: "These are two friends whose lives
    were undivided."
Epitaphium.
Epithalamium: "Night, with all thine eyes look
    down!"
Evening: Ponte al Mare, Pisa.
Evening: To Harriet.
Exhortation, An.
Eyes: A Fragment.
Feelings of a Republican on the Fall of
    Bonaparte.
Fiordispina.
Fragment: A Roman's Chamber.
Fragment: A Serpent-Face.
Fragment: A Tale Untold.
Fragment: A Wanderer.
Fragment: "Alas! this is not what I thought life
    was."
Fragment: Amor Aeternus.
Fragment: "And that I walk thus proudly
    crowned withal."
Fragment: Apostrophe to Silence.
Fragment: Beauty's Halo.
Fragment: Death in Life.
Fragment: "Follow to the deep wood's weeds."
Fragment from the Wandering Jew.
Fragment: "Gentle story of two lovers young,
    A."
Fragment: "Great Spirit whom the sea of
    boundless thought."
Fragment: Home.
Fragment: "I faint, I perish with my love! I
    grow."
Fragment: "I stood upon a heaven-cleaving
    turret."
Fragment: "I would not be a king—enough."
Fragment: Igniculus Desiderii.
Fragment: "Is it that in some brighter sphere."
Fragment: Life Rounded with Sleep.
Fragment: Love the Universe To-day.
Fragment: Love's Tender Atmosphere.
Fragment: May the Limner.
Fragment: "Methought I was a billow in the
    crowd."
Fragment: Milton's Spirit.
Fragment: Music and Sweet Poetry.
Fragment: "My head is wild with weeping for
    a grief."
Fragment: "O thou immortal deity."
Fragment of a Ghost Story.
Fragment of a Satire on Satire.
Fragment of a Sonnet: Farewell to North
    Devon.
Fragment of a Sonnet: To Harriet.
Fragment: Omens.
Fragment on Keats.
Fragment: Pater Omnipotens.
Fragment: Rain.
Fragment: Rain.
Fragment: Rome and Nature.
Fragment: "Rude wind is singing, The."
Fragment: Satan Broken Loose.
Fragment: "Such hope, as is the sick despair of
    good."
Fragment: Sufficient Unto the Day.
Fragment: The Deserts of Dim Sleep.

Fragment: The False Laurel and the True.
Fragment: The Lady of the South.
Fragment: The Lake's Margin.
Fragment: The Sepulchre of Memory.
Fragment: The Vine-Shroud.
Fragment: Thoughts Come and Go in Solitude.
Fragment: To a Friend Released from Prison.
Fragment: To Byron.
Fragment: To Italy.
Fragment: To Music, A.
Fragment: To One Singing.
Fragment: To the Mind of Man.
Fragment: To the Moon.
Fragment: To the People of England.
Fragment: "Unrisen splendour of the brightest sun."
Fragment: "Viewless and invisible Consequence, The."
Fragment: "Wake the serpent not—lest he."
Fragment: Wedded Souls.
Fragment: "What men gain fairly —that they should possess."
Fragment: "When a lover clasps his fairest."
Fragment: "When soft winds and sunny skies."
Fragment: Wine of the Fairies.
Fragment: "Ye gentle visitations of calm thought."
Fragment: Zephyrus the Awakener.
Fragments of an Unfinished Drama.
Fragments Supposed to Be Parts of Otho.
Fragments Written for Hellas.
From the Arabic: An Imitation.
From the Original Draft of the Poem to William Shelley.
Fugitives, The.
Ginevra.
Good-Night.
Hate-Song, A.
Hellas.
Hymn of Pan.
Hymn to Intellectual Beauty.
In Horologium.
Indian Serenade, The.
Invocation to Misery.
Isle, The.
Julian and Maddalo; A Conversation.
Lament, A: "O world! O life! O time!"
Letter to Maria Gisborne.
Liberty.
Lines: "Cold earth slept below, The."
Lines: "Far, far away, O ye."
Lines: "That time is dead for ever, child!"
Lines to a Critic.
Lines to a Reviewer.
Lines: "We meet not as we parted."
Lines: "When the lamp is shattered [or shatter'd]."
Lines Written among the Euganean Hills.
Lines Written During the Castlereagh Administration.
Lines Written in the Bay of Lerici.
Lines Written on Hearing the News of the Death of Napoleon.
Love.
Love, Hope, Desire and Fear.
Love's Philosophy.
Love's Rose.
Magnetic Lady to Her Patient, The.
Marenghi.
Marianne's Dream.
Mask [or Masque] of Anarchy, The.
Mighty Eagle.
Mont Blanc.
Music.
Mutability ("Flower that smiles").
Mutability ("We are as clouds").
New National Anthem, A.
O that a chariot of cloud were mine!
Ode to Heaven.
Ode to Liberty.
Ode to Naples.
Ode to the West Wind.
Ode Written October, 1819, An.
Oedipus Tyrannus; or, Swellfoot the Tyrant.
On a Faded Violet.

On a Fête at Carlton House: Fragment.
On an Icicle That Clung to the Grass of a Grave.
On Death.
On Fanny Godwin.
On Leaving London for Wales.
On Robert Emmet's Grave.
On the Medusa of Leonardo da Vinci in the Florentine Gallery.
Original Poetry by Victor and Cazire.
Orpheus.
Otho.
Ozymandias.
Passage of the Apennines.
Past, The.
Peter Bell the Third.
Pine Forest of the Cascine Near Pisa, The.
Poems from St. Irvyne, or, The Rosicrucian.
Posthumous Fragments of Margaret Nicholson.
Prince Athanase; a Fragment.
Prometheus Unbound [A Lyrical Drama in Four Acts].
Queen Mab.
Question, The.
Remembrance.
Retrospect, The: CWM Elan, 1812.
Revolt of Islam, The.
Rosalind and Helen; A Modern Eclogue.
Scene from "Tasso."
Sensitive Plant, The.
Similes for Two Political Characters of 1819.
Solitary, The.
Song from the Wandering Jew.
Song of Proserpine.
Song: "Rarely, rarely, comest thou."
Song to the Men of England.
Sonnet: Lift Not the Painted Veil: "Lift not the painted veil which those who live."
Sonnet: On Launching Some Bottles Filled with Knowledge into the Bristol Channel.
Sonnet: Political Greatness.
Sonnet: To a Balloon Laden with Knowledge.
Sonnet to Byron.
Sonnet: "Ye hasten to the grave! What seek ye there."
Stanza from a Translation of the Marseillaise Hymn.
Stanza: "If I walk in Autumn's even."
Stanza, Written at Bracknell.
Stanzas—April, 1814.
Stanzas Written in Dejection, near Naples [or —December 1818, near Naples].
Summer and Winter.
Summer Evening Churchyard, A.
Sunset, The.
Tale of Society As It Is, A: From Facts, 1811.
Time.
Time Long Past.
To a Skylark.
To a Star.
To Constantia.
To Constantia, Singing.
To Death.
To Edward Williams.
To Emilia Viviani.
To Harriet ("It is not blasphemy").
To Harriet ("Thy look of love").
To ———: "I fear thy kisses, gentle maiden."
To Ianthe.
To Ireland.
To Jane: The Invitation.
To Jane: The keen stars were twinkling.
To Jane: The Recollection.
To Mary———.
To Mary Shelley ("World is dreary").
To Mary Shelley ("My dearest Mary").
To Mary, Who Died in This Opinion.
To Mary Wollstonecraft Godwin.
To-Morrow.
To ———: "Music, when soft voices die."
To Night.
To ———: "Oh! there are spirits of the air."
To ———: "One word is too often profaned."
To Sophia [Miss Stacey].
To the Lord Chancellor.
To the Moon.

To the Moonbeam.
To the Nile.
To the Queen of My Heart.
To the Republicans of North America.
To ———: "When passion's trance is overpast."
To William Shelley ("Billows on the beach").
To William Shelley ("My lost William").
To William Shelley ("Thy little footsteps").
To Wordsworth.
To ———: "Yet look on me—take not thine eyes away."
Tower of Famine, The.
Triumph of Life, The.
Two Spirits[: An Allegory], The.
Verses on a Cat.
Vision of the Sea, A.
Wandering Jew's Soliloquy, The.
Waning Moon, The.
Witch of Atlas, The.
With a Guitar, to Jane.
Woodman and the Nightingale, The.
World's Wanderers, The.
Zucca, The.

Sheridan, Thomas (1687–1738)
Ad Te, Doctissime Delany.
Another Picture of Dan.
Answer.
Ballyspellin.
Be Still, Thou Busy Foolish Thing.
Birthday Poem on the Anniversary of the Birth of the Rev. Dr. Swift, D. S. P. D. Nov. 30, 1737, A.
Copy of a Copy of Verses from Thomas Sheridan, Clerk, to George Nim-Dan-Dean, Esq., A.
Cur Me Bespateras, Blaterans Furiosè Poeta.
Description of Doctor Delany's Villa, A.
Drapier's Ballad, The.
Elegy on the Much Lamented Death of Mr. Demar, the Famous Rich Usurer [or Man], An.
Epilogue, The: "Now all is done, learned spectators, tell."
Epilogue to Julius Caesar, The.
Figures of Speech.
Five Ladies' Answer to the Beau, with the Wig and Wings at His Head, The.
Grouse Pouts.
Grouse Pouts Are Come In.
Highlander Once Fought a Frenchman at Margate, A.
His Modest Apology for Knocking Out a News-Boy's Teeth, Who Told Him His Works Would Not Sell.
How Can I Finish What You Have Begun?
Humble Petition of Stella's Friends, The.
I Can't but Wonder, Mr. Dean.
I Like Your Collyrium.
I Ritu a Verse o Na Molli o Mi Ne.
I Send This at Nine.
I Wish Your Reverence Were Here to Hear the Trumpets.
If These Can't Keep Your Ladies Quiet.
I'll Write While I Have Half an Eye in My Head.
Invitation, The.
Invitation to Dinner, from Doctor Sheridan to Doctor Swift, An.
Joshua Battus's Sepeech to the Paparliament.
Last Speech and Dying Words of Daniel Jackson, The.
Letter from a Cobbler in Patrick's Street to Jet Black, A.
Letter from Dr. Sheridan to Dr. Swift, A.
Letter of Advice to the Right Hon. John Earl of Orrery, A.
Mr. Sheridan's Prologue to the Greek Play of Phaedra and Hippolytus; Designed to Have Been Spoke by a Boy of Six Years Old.
My Hens Are Hatching.
My Pedagogue Dear, I Read with Surprise.
My Walk It Is Finished.
New Simile for the Ladies, A.
New Year's Gift for the Dean of St. Patrick's Given Him at Quilca, 1723/24, A.

Now to Lampoon Myself for My Presumption.
O Would that Enemy I Dread, My Fate.
Ode, An: "Early Queen of Light arise."
Of Epigram.
Of Figures Peculiar to Prosody.
Of Knowing the Gender of Nouns by
    Termination, *sels.*
Of Prosody, *sels.*
Of Quantity Which Depends upon the
    Authority of the Poets.
Of the Genders of Nouns.
On the Same.
Original of Punning, The.
Our River Is Dry.
Palinodia.
Pedagogue's Answer, The.
Perlegi Versus Versos, Jonathan Bone, Tersos.
Poem Delivered to the Reverend Doctor Swift,
    Dean of St. Patrick's, Dublin, by a Young
    Nobleman, November 30, 1725, Being the
    Dean's Birthday, A.
Prologue Designed for the Play of *Oedipus*,
    Written in Greek, and Performed by Mr.
    Sheridan's Scholars, at the King's Inn Hall,
    on Tuesday the 10th of December, 1723, A.
Prologue Spoke by Mr. Elrington at the
    Theatre-Royal on Saturday the First of April,
    A.
Prologue Spoken at Mr. Sheridan's School.
Prologue Spoken before a Greek Play, at the
    Reverend Dr. Sheridan's School, at the
    Breaking-Up of His Scholars for Christmas,
    1728.
Prologue to a Play Performed at Mr. Sheridan's
    School Spoke by One of His Scholars, A.
Prologue to *Julius Caesar*, as It Was Acted at
    Madam Violante's Booth, Dec. the 15th,
    1732, by Some of the Young Gentlemen in
    Dr. Sheridan's School, A.
Prologue to the Farce of *Punch Turned
    Schoolmaster.*
Riddle, A: "Because I am by nature blind."
Scribbler from the Northern Bear, A.
Sheridan to Dan Jackson.
Sick Lion and the Ass, The.
So on the Stream the Silver Swan.
Some Nymphs May Boast External Grace.
Song, The: "My time, O ye Grattans, was
    happily spent."
Tale of the T——d, The.
Tanti Vi Sed I Tanti Vi.
Thus Cacus-like, His Calves He Backwards
    Pulls.
Thus Did Great Socrates Improve the Mind.
Thus Puppies that Adore the Dark.
To Dean Swift.
To George Nim-Dan-Dean, Esq. upon His
    Incomparable Verses, &c. of August 2d,
    1721.
To His Excellency Our Lord Carteret, Lord
    Lieutenant of Ireland: The Humble Petition
    of Lord Viscount Mont-Cashel, and the Rest
    of His School-Fellows.
To the Author of "Tom Pun-Sibi
    Metamorphosed."
To the Dean.
To the Dean of St. Patrick's ("Dear Dean, I'm
    in a sad condition").
To the Dean of St. Patrick's ("Dear Sir, since
    you in humble wise").
To the Dean of St. Patrick's ("Since your
    poetic prancer is turned into Cancer").
To the Dean of St. Patrick's ("Sir, your
    Billingsgate Muse methinks does begin").
To the Dean, when in England, in 1726.
To the Honorable Mr. D. T.
To the Rev. Doctor Swift, Dean of St.
    Patrick's. A Birthday Poem. Nov. 30, 1736.
To the Right Honorable the Lord Viscount
    Mont-Cassel.
To the Same.
Tom Punsibi's Letter to Dean Swift.
Upon a Certain Bookseller, or Printer, in
    Utopia, *sels.*
Upon Stealing a Crown when the Dean Was
    Asleep.

Upon William Tisdall, D. D.
Vivitur Parvo Malè, Sed Canebat.
When G——le Has Her Mind at Ease.
While Footman-like He Waits in Every Hall.
You Made Me in Your Last a Goose.
You Shall Want Nothing Fit for Mortal Man.
You That Would Read the Bible.

Shih-te (Pickup) *(fl. c.8th cent.)*
Behold the glow of the moon.
Black Dragon Pearl in his left hand, The.
Buddha forsook the joys of rank, The.
Buddhas care for mortal beings.
Buddhas leave behind sutras.
By and large the monks I meet.
Cold Mountain is a cold mountain.
Committing crimes behind closed doors.
Doesn't anyone see.
Drunk on delusion greed and anger.
Flock of timid sheep, A.
For a mud ball dropped in water.
I advise the monks I meet.
I have millions of gathas.
I live in a place without limits.
I see someone short on sense.
I sigh when I see learned men.
I sigh when I see worldly people.
I was Pickup from the first.
If you wonder who stays happy.
Keeping your mind wide-open.
My poems are poems alright.
No waxing or waning essentially still.
Old buddha road is deserted, The.
Partial to pine cliffs and lonely trails.
Past thousands of layers of mountains and
    clouds.
People crowd by in the dust.
People who leave home want to be free.
Pine moon looks so cold, The.
Silver stars dot the beam.
Since I came to Tientai Temple.
Since monkeys can be taught.
Son demands a wife, A.
Take these mortal incarnations.
There exists one type of person.
Those who leave home leave to be free.
Those who leave home nowadays.
Triple World is a turning wheel, The.
Up high the trail turns steep.
We all possess the buddha of buddhas.
We slip into Tientai caves.
When men and women marry.
Who knows how to catch rats.
Wine of wisdom is so cold, The.
Woods and springs make me smile.
World has billions of people, The.
World has its know-it-alls, The.
Worldly people make me sigh.
Young man studied letters and arms, A.

Shirley, James (1596–1666)
Love's Hue and Cry.
To His Mistress [*or* Mistris] Confined.
Would you know what's soft? I dare.

Shtoltsenberg, Aba (1905–41)
Bolsheviks.

"Shu Ting" (Gong Peiyu) (b. 1952)
?.!
Bits of Reminiscence.
Brother, I Am Here.
Missing You.
Perhaps . . .
Returning Home.
Singing Flower, The.
To——.
To the Oak.
When You Come Past My Window.

Sidney, Sir Philip (1554–86)
Arcadia, *sels.*
Astrophil and Stella.
Lady of May, The, *sels.*
Leave Me O Love.
Like as the Dove.
Oft Have I Mused.
Scourge of life, and death's extreme disgrace,
    The.
Since, shunning pain, I ease can never find.

Thou Blind Man's Mark.
Thou Pain, the only guest of loathed constraint.
When Love, puffed up with rage of high
    disdain.
You better sure shall live, not evermore.

Silkin, Jon *See* **McDuff, David**

Silliman, Ron (b. 1946)
Engines.

Simic, Charles (b. 1938)
Amazing Potato Peeler, The.
Animal Acts.
Animals and Birds.
Aunt Lettuce, I want to peek under your skirt.
Austerities.
Autumn Air ("Many centuries ago").
Autumn Air ("Many years ago in China").
Ax.
Baby Pictures of Famous Dictators.
Ballad of the Wheel, The.
Ballad: "What's that approaching like dusk like
    poverty."
Bedtime Story.
Begotten of the Spleen.
Bestiary for the Fingers of My Right Hand.
Bird, The.
Black Days.
Body and Soul.
Breasts.
Brooms.
Butcher Shop.
Chairs.
Charles Simic.
Charon's Cosmology.
Chicken Without a Head, The.
Childhood of Parmenides, The.
Chorus for One Voice.
Classic Ballroom Dances.
Closed House.
Cockroach.
Cold Blue Tinge.
Cold, The.
Concerning My Neighbors, the Hittites.
Crows.
Day Marked with a Small White Stone, A.
December Trees ("Bare Woods").
December Trees ("Dark Woods").
Description.
Devotions.
Dismantling the Silence.
Drawing the Triangle.
Drawn to Perspective.
East[ern] European Cooking.
Elegy: "Note / as it gets darker."
Elementary Cosmology.
Empire of Dreams.
Eraser.
Errata.
Euclid Avenue.
Evening.
Evening with the Master, An ("With a stick").
Evening with the Master, An ("With a tiny bid
    whistle").
Explorers.
Eyes Fastened with Pins.
Fable: "In my favorite one."
Fall Day, A.
Fear.
February.
Figuring.
Fool's Paradise.
Forest Birds.
Fork.
Furniture Mover.
Further Adventures of Charles Simic.
Gallows Etiquette.
Game, The.
Gospel Hour.
Gravity.
Great Horned Owl, The.
Great Infirmities.
Grocery.
Guest, The.
Happy End.
Harsh Climate.
Healer, The.
Help Wanted.

History.
History Book.
Homeless, The.
Hurricane Season.
Immortal Prankster.
In Midsummer Quiet.
Inheritance.
Inner Man, The.
Interlude.
Invention of Nothing.
Knife.
Landscape with Crutches, A.
Lesson, The.
Little Tear Gland That Says, The.
Madonnas Touched Up with Goatees [or a goatee].
Man, The.
Marching.
Midpoint.
Misfortune Is on the Way.
My Beloved.
My Shoes.
My Weariness of Epic Proportions.
Navigator ("I summoned Christopher Columbus").
Navigator ("I thought of Christopher Columbus").
Needle.
Northern Exposure.
Note.
Note Slipped Under a Door.
Nursery Rhyme.
Old Couple.
Old Mountain Road.
Overcoat, The.
Partial Explanation, The.
Pastoral: "I came to a meadow."
Peaceful Kingdom.
Peaceful Trees.
Piety.
Pillow, The.
Place, The.
Poem: "Every morning I forget how it is."
Poem: "My father writes all day, all night."
Poem without a Title.
Point, The.
Position without a Magnitude.
Primer.
Prison.
Prisoner, The.
Prodigy.
Psalm: "Old ones to the side."
Punch Minus Judy.
Quiet Talk with Oneself, A.
Rosalia.
Rough Outline.
Rural Delivery.
School for Dark Thoughts.
Sewing Machine.
Shaving at Night.
Shirt.
Shortcut.
Sleep.
Small Wonders.
Solitude.
Solving the Riddle ("Cloud's a clue").
Solving the Riddle ("Shadow is a clue").
Soup, The ("Take the lump").
Soup, The ("Together in the pot").
Spoon.
Spoons with Realistic Dead Flies on Them.
Stone.
Stream, The.
Strictly Bucolic.
Suitcase Strapped with a Rope, A.
Summer Morning.
Summons, The.
Tapestry.
Terms, The.
There They Stand Unaware of Their Wretchedness.
Thus.
Tomb of Stéphane Mallarmé, The.
Toy Factory.
Travel[l]ing.
Travel[l]ing Slaughterhouse.

Trees at Night.
Tub, A.
Two Riddles.
Unknown One, The.
Variant, The.
Venus.
Wall, A.
Watch Repair.
Watermelons.
Way It Is, The.
What the White Had to Say ("Because I am").
What the White Had to Say ("Because I'm nothing").
Whispers.
Whispers in the Next Room.
White.
Window Washer.
Winter Night.
Writings of the Mystics, The.

Simonides (c.556–468 B.C.)
On a Military Graveyard.
Sisson, Charles Hubert (b. 1914)
Carmen Saeculare.
Sjoberg, Leif *See* **Rukeyser, Muriel**
Smart, Christopher (1722–71)
Apollo and Daphne.
Author Apologizes to a Lady, for His Being a Little Man, The.
Care and Generosity.
Country Squire and the Mandrake, The.
Epistle to Dr. Nares.
Epistle to John Sherratt, Esq, An.
Epitaph on Henry Fielding, Esq.
Hail Energeia! hail, my native tongue.
Hymn to the Supreme Being.
Hymns and Spiritual Songs for the Fasts and Festivals of the Church of England.
Hymns for the Amusement of Children.
Inscriptions on an Aeolian Harp.
Jubilate Agno.
Lines with a Pocket Book.
Munificence and Modesty.
Ode to Admiral Sir George Pocock.
Ode to General Draper.
Ode to Lady Harriot.
On a Bed of Guernsey Lilies.
On an Eagle Confined in a College-Court.
On Gratitude.
On Taking a Batchelor's Degree.
On the Eternity of the Supreme Being.
On the Goodness of the Supreme Being.
On the Immensity of the Supreme Being.
On the Omniscience of the Supreme Being.
On the Power of the Supreme Being.
Reason and Imagination.
Song to David, A.
Story of a Cock and a Bull, A.
Sweets of Evening, The.
To Ethelinda.
To Miss H—— with Some Music.
To Mrs. Dacosta.
To My Worthy Friend, Mr. T.B. One of the People Called Quakers.
To the Rev. Mr. Powell.
Smedley, Jonathan (1671–1729)
Satyr, A, *sels.*
Smith, Stevie (1902–71)
Abominable Lake, The.
Actress, The.
Adelaide Abner.
Admire Cranmer!
Advice to Young Children.
After-Thought, The.
Agnostic, An.
Ah, Will the Saviour...?
Airy Christ, The.
Alfred the Great.
All Things Pass.
Alone in the Woods.
Ambassador, The.
Analysand.
And the Clouds Return after the Rain.
Angel Boley.
Angel Face.
Angel of Grace.

Anger's Freeing Power.
Animula, Vagula, Blandula.
Appetite.
Après la Politique, la Haine des Bourbons.
Arabella.
Archie and Tina.
Ass, The.
At School.
Aubade: "My dove, my doe."
Avondale.
Avondall.
Away, Melancholy.
Bag-Snatching in Dublin.
Bandol (Var).
Barlow.
Be Off!
Behind the Knight.
Bereaved Swan, The.
Bereavement.
Best Beast of the Fat-Stock Show at Earls Court, The.
Beware the Man.
Bishops of the Church of England, The.
Black March.
Blood Flows Back, The.
Blue from Heaven, The.
Boat, The.
Bog-Face.
Bottle of Aspirins, The.
Breughel.
Brickenden, Hertfordshire.
British Song, A.
Broken Friendship, The.
Broken Heart, The.
But Murderous.
Bye Baby Bother.
Can It Be?
Castle, The.
Cat Asks Mouse Out.
Ceci est digne de gens sans dieu.
Celtic Fringe, The.
Celts, The.
Ceux Qui Luttent.
Childe Rolandine.
Children of the Cross, The.
Choosers, The.
Christmas.
Cock-a-Doo.
Cock and the Hen, The.
Coeur Simple.
Come.
Come, Death (1).
Come, Death (2).
Come On, Come Back.
Commuted Sentence, The.
Company.
Conventionalist, The.
Conviction (i).
Conviction (ii).
Conviction (iii).
Conviction IV.
Cool and Plain.
Cool as a Cucumber.
Correspondence between Mr. Harrison in Newcastle and Mr. Sholto Peach Harrison in Hull.
Cousin, The.
Croft.
Crown of Bays, The.
Crown of Gold, The.
Darling Daughters.
Days of Yore, The.
Dear Child of God.
Dear Female Heart.
Dear Karl.
Dear Muse.
Death-Bed of a Financier.
Death Bereaves Our Common Mother Nature Grieves for My Dead Brother.
Death Came to Me.
Death in the Rose Garden.
Death of Mr. Mounsel.
Death of the Dog Belvoir.
Death Sentence, The.
Deathly Child, The.
Death's Ostracism.

Dedicated Dancing Bull and the Water Maid, The.
Deeply Morbid.
Deserter, The.
Devil-My-Wife, The.
Dido's Farewell to Aeneas.
Die Lorelei.
Dirge: "From a friend's friend I taste friendship."
Distractions and the Human Crowd.
Do Not!
Do Take Muriel Out.
Doctor, The.
Does No Love Last?
Donkey, The.
Dream.
Dream of Comparison, A.
Dream of Nourishment, A.
Drugs Made Pauline Vague.
Duty Was His Lodestar.
Easy.
Edmonton, Thy Cemetery.
Egocentric.
Emily Writes Such a Good Letter.
Eng.
Engine Drain, The.
English, The.
English Visitor, The.
Es War Einmal.
Eulenspiegelei.
Evangelie, or, The Figure of Literary Corruption, Seeking Glory Not Truth.
Every Lovely Limb's a Desolation.
Everything Is Swimming.
Exeat.
Face, The.
Fafnir and the Knights.
Failed Spirit, The.
Fairy Bell, The.
Fairy Story.
Fallen, Fallen.
Farewell: "Farewell dear friends."
Father for a Fool, A.
Feminine Charm.
Film Star, The.
Fish, Fish.
Flow, Flow, Flow.
Fool, The.
Forgive Me, Forgive Me.
Forgot!
Forlorn Sea, The.
Francesca in Winter.
Freddy.
Friend, The.
Friends of the River Trent.
Friskers, or, Gods and Men.
Frog Prince, The.
From My Notes for a Series of Lectures on Murder.
From the Coptic.
From the County Lunatic Asylum.
From the French (1).
From the French (2).
From the Greek.
From the Italian.
Frozen Lake, The.
Fugitive's Ride, The.
Fuite d'Enfance.
Full Well I Know.
Galloping Cat, The.
Ghost of Ware, The.
Girls!
Gnädiges Fräulein.
God and Man.
God and the Devil.
God Speaks.
God the Drinker.
God the Eater.
Goodnight.
Governess, The.
Grange, The.
Grave by a Holm-Oak.
Great Unaffected Vampires and the Moon.
Happiness.
Harold's Leap.
Hast Du Dich Verirrt?

Hat, The.
He Told His Life Story to Mrs. Courtly.
Heavenly City, The.
Heber.
Hendecasyllables.
Her-zie.
Hippy-Mo.
Homage to John Cowper Powys.
Hostage, The.
Hound of Ulster, The.
House of Mercy, A.
House of Over-Dew, The.
How Cruel Is the Story of Eve.
How Do You See?
How Far Can You Press a Poet?
How Slowly Time Lengthens.
Human Affection.
Humane Materialist at the Burning of a Heretic, A.
Hymn to the Seal.
I Am.
I Am a Girl Who Loves to Shoot.
I Could Let Tom Go—But What about the Children.
I Do Not Speak.
I Had a Dream.
I Hate This Girl.
I Like to Play with Him.
I Love.
I Remember.
I Rode With My Darling.
I Was So Full.
I Wish.
If I Lie Down.
I'll Have Your Heart.
In Canaan's Happy Land.
In My Dreams.
In Protocreation.
In the Night.
In the Park.
Infant.
Infelice.
Intimation of Immortality.
Is It Happy?
Is It Wise?
It Filled My Heart with Love.
Jew Is Angry with His Friend Who Does Not Believe in Circumcision, A.
Jumbo.
Jungle Husband, The.
King Hamlet's Ghost.
King in Funeral Procession, A.
La Gretchen de Nos Jours (I).
La Gretchen de Nos Jours (II).
La Speakerine de Putney.
Lads of the Village, The.
Lady of the Well-Spring, The.
Lady "Rogue" Singleton.
Lament of a Slug-a-Bed's Wife.
Last Turn of the Screw, The.
Le Désert de l'Amour.
Le Majeur Ydow.
Le Revenant.
Le Singe qui swing.
Leader, The.
Light of Life, The.
Lightly Bound.
Listener, The.
Little Boy Lost.
Little Boy Sick.
Little Child of Brightest Face.
Little Daughters of America, The.
Loin de l'Être.
Longing for Death because of Feebleness.
Look!
Look, Look.
Lord Barrenstock.
Lord Mope.
Lord Say-and-Seal.
Lot's Wife.
Louise.
Love Me!
Magic Morning, The.
Magna Est Veritas.
Magnificent Words.
Major Macroo.

Man I Am, A.
Man Is a Spirit.
Man Saul, The.
Maximilian Esterhazy.
Mrs. Arbuthnot.
Mrs. Blow and her Animals.
Mistress Osmosis.
Monsieur Pussy-Cat, Blackmailer.
Mother.
Mother, among the Dustbins.
Mother's Hearse, A.
Mr. Over.
Mrs Simpkins.
Murder.
Murderer, The.
Mutchmore and Not-So.
My Cat Major.
My Cats.
My Hat.
My Heart Goes Out.
My Heart Was Full.
My Muse.
My Soul.
Nature and Free Animals.
N'est-ce pas assez de ne me point haïr?
Never Again.
New Age, The.
Night Thoughts.
Night-Time in the Cemetery.
Nipping Pussy's Feet in Fun.
No Categories!
No More People.
No Respect.
Noble and Ethereal.
Nodding.
Nor We of Her to Him.
Northumberland House.
Not Waving But Drowning.
Nourish Me on an Egg.
November.
Now Pine-Needles.
Numbers.
O Happy Dogs of England.
O Pug!
Oblivion.
Occasional Yarrow, The.
Oh Christianity, Christianity.
Oh Grateful Colours, Bright Looks!
Oh, If Only.
Oh Stubborn Race of Cadmus' Seed.
Oh What Is the Thing He Done?
Old Ghosts.
Old Sweet Dove of Wiveton, The.
On the Death of a German Philosopher.
On Walking Slowly after an Accident.
One of Many.
Orphan Reformed, The.
Our Bog is Dood.
Our Office Cat.
Out of Time.
Pad, Pad.
Papa Love Baby.
Parents.
Parklands, The.
Parrot.
Passing Cloud, The.
Past, The.
Pearl.
Persephone.
Persian, The.
Phèdre.
Photograph, The.
Piggy to Joey.
Pleasures of Friendship, The.
Poet!
Poet Hin, The.
Poets Are Silent, The.
Poor Soul, Poor Girl!
Portrait (I).
Portrait (II).
Pretty.
Private Means Is Dead.
Progression.
Proud Death with Swelling Port.
Quand on n'a pas ce que l'on aime, il faut aimer ce que l'on a—.

Queen and the Young Princess, The.
Reason, The.
Recluse, The.
Recognition Not Enough.
Rehearsal, The.
Religious Man, A.
Rencontres Funestes.
Repentance of Lady T, The.
Reversionary.
Ride, The.
River Deben, The.
River God, The.
River Humber, The.
Road Up.
Roman Road, The.
Rothebât.
Sad Heart, The.
Sad Mother, The.
Saffron.
Saint Anthony and the Rose of Life.
Sallow Bird, The.
Satin-Clad.
Scorpion.
Sea-Widow, The.
Seymour and Chantelle or Un Peu de Vice.
She Said.
Shooting Incident, The.
Si Peu Séduisante.
Siesta.
Silence and Tears.
Singing Cat, The.
Sliding Mountain, The.
Small Lady, The.
Smile, The.
So Can Anger.
So to Fatness Come.
Soldier Dear to Us, A.
Some Are Born.
Songe d'Athalie.
Songster, The.
Sorrowful Girl, The.
Souvenir de Monsieur Poop.
Spanish School.
Starling, The.
Story I Have Told, The.
Stroke, The.
Study to Deserve Death.
Suburb.
Suburban Classes, The.
Suicide's Epitaph.
Sunt Leones.
Tableau de l'Inconstance des Mauvais Anges.
Tender Only to One.
Tenuous and Precarious.
Thank You.
This Englishwoman.
This Is Disgraceful and Abominable.
Thought Is Superior.
Thoughts about the Christian Doctrine of
    Eternal Hell.
Thoughts about the Person from Porlock.
To a Dead Vole.
To a Lady in a Train.
To an American Publisher.
To Carry the Child.
To Dean Inge Lecturing on Origen.
To School!
To the Dog Belvoir.
To the Tune of The Coventry Carol.
Toll of the Roads, The.
Torquemada.
Touch and Go.
True Tyrant or the Spirit of Duty Rebuked,
    The.
Under Wrong Trees... or Freeing the Colonial
    Peoples.
Unpopular, Lonely and Loving.
Unser Vater.
Up and Down.
Upon a Grave.
V.
Valuable.
Venus When Young Choosing Death.
Villains.
Violent Hand, The.
Virtuoso, The.

Voice from the Tomb (1).
Voice from the Tomb (2).
Voice from the Tomb (3).
Voice from the Tomb (4).
Voice from the Tomb (5).
Voices about the Princess Anemone.
Voices against England in the Night.
Votaries of Both Sexes Cry First to Venus.
Wanderer, The.
Warden, The.
Was He Married?
Was It Not Curious?
Watchful.
Weak Monk, The.
Wedding Photograph, The.
What Is She Writing? Perhaps It Will Be
    Good.
What Is the Time?; or, St. Hugh of Lincoln.
When the Sparrow Flies.
When the Wind.
When Walking.
Where Are You Going?
White Thought, The.
Who Is This Who Howls and Mutters?
Who Killed Lawless Lean?
Who Shot Eugenie?
Why Are the Clergy...?
Why Do I.
Why Do You Rage?
Widowhood or The Home-Coming of Lady
    Ross.
Wild Dog, The.
Will Ever?
Will Man Ever Face Fact and Not Feel Flat?
Word, The.
Wretched Woman.
Yes, I Know.
Zoo, The.

Snyder, Gary (b. 1930)
Above Pate Valley.
Across Lamarck Col.
After Work.
Aged Tamba Temple Plum Tree Song.
Alabaster.
All through the Rains.
Anasazi.
Arktos.
Arts Council Meets in Eureka, The.
As for Poets.
At Tower Peak.
At White River Roadhouse in the Yukon.
August on Sourdough, a Visit from Dick
    Brewer.
Axe Handles.
Bath, The.
Bed in the Sky, The.
Beneath My Hand and Eye the Distant Hills,
    Your Body.
Berry Feast, A.
Berry Territory.
Blue Sky, The.
Bomb Test.
Bubbs Creek Haircut.
Building.
Burning Island.
Burning the Small Dead.
By Frazier Creek Falls.
Call of the Wild, The.
Canyon Wren, The.
Cartagena.
Changing Diapers.
Circumambulating Arunachala.
Control Burn.
Cool around the Fire, The.
Could She See the Whole Real World with Her
    Ghost Breast Eyes Shut under a Blouse Lid?
Crash.
Dead by the Side of the Road, The.
Dillingham, Alaska, the Willow Tree Bar.
Dogs, Sheep, Cows, Goats.
Dullness in February: Japan.
Egg, The.
Elk Trails.
Engine Room, S.S. Sappa Creek, The.
Ethnobotany.
Everybody Lying on Their Stomachs, Head

toward the Candle, Reading, Sleeping,
    Drawing.
Fear Not.
Feathered Robe, The.
Fence Posts.
Fire in the Hole.
Firing, The.
For a Stone Girl at Sanchi.
For All.
For Example.
For/From Lew.
For John Chappell.
For Lew Welch in a Snowfall.
For Nothing.
For the Boy Who Was Dodger Point Lookout
    Fifteen Years Ago.
For the Children.
For the West.
Four Poems for Robin.
Foxtail Pine.
Front Lines.
Gen.
Getting in the Wood.
Go Round.
Goofing Again.
Hay for the Horses.
He Shot Arrows, but Not at Birds Perching.
High Quality Information.
Hop, Skip, and Jump.
How Poetry Comes to Me.
I can't stand these bird-songs.
I have lived at Cold Mountain.
I settled at Cold Mountain long ago.
I Went Into the Maverick Bar.
In a tangle of cliffs I chose a place.
In my first thirty years of life.
In the House of the Rising Sun.
In the mountains it's cold.
It.
It Pleases.
I've lived at Cold Mountain—how many
    autumns.
Kai, Today.
Kisiabaton.
Kušiwoqqób.
Kyoto Born in Spring Song.
Kyoto: March.
L M F B R.
Late October Camping in the Sawtooths.
Late Snow & Lumber Strike of the Summer of
    Fifty-four, The.
Lines on a Carp.
Little Songs for Gaia.
Long Hair.
Longitude 170° West, Latitude 35° North.
Look Back.
Love.
Magpie's Song.
Makings.
Manichaeans, The.
Manzanita.
Marin-An.
Meeting the Mountains.
Men ask the way to Cold Mountain.
Message from Outside.
Mid-August at Sourdough Mountain Lookout.
Migration of Birds.
Milton by Firelight.
Mother Earth: Her Whales.
Mother of the Buddhas, Queen of Heaven,
    Mother of the Sun; Marici, Goddess of the
    Dawn.
My home was at Cold Mountain from the start.
Myths and Texts, *sels.*
Nanao Knows.
Nansen.
Night.
Night Herons.
No Matter, Never Mind.
No Shoes No Shirt No Service.
Nooksack Valley.
North Beach Alba.
North Coast, The.
Not Leaving the House.
O Mother Gaia.
Off the Trail.

Oil.
Old Dutch Woman, The.
Old Rotting Tree Trunk Down.
Old Woman Nature.
On Climbing the Sierra Matterhorn Again after
    Thirty-One Years.
On Our Way to Khajuraho.
On Vulture Peak.
Once at Cold Mountain, troubles cease.
Once Only.
"One Should Not Talk to a Skilled Hunter
    about What Is Forbidden by the Buddha."
One Year.
Painting the North San Juan School.
Path to Han-shan's place is laughable, The.
Persimmons, The.
Pine River.
Pine Tree Tops.
Piute Creek.
Poem Left in Sourdough Mountain Lookout.
Point Reyes.
Prayer for the Great Family.
Public Bath, The.
Rainbow Body.
Real Work, The.
Regarding Wave.
Removing the Plate of the Pump on the
    Hydraulic System of the Backhoe.
Revolution in the Revolution in the
    Revolution.
Right in the Trail.
Ripples on the Surface.
Riprap.
River in the Valley.
Roots.
Running Water Music.
Running Water Music II.
Sappa Creek, The.
Saying Farewell at the Monastery After
    Hearing the Old Master Lecture on "Return
    to the Source."
Seaman's Ditty.
7.IV.64.
7:VII.
Shark Meat.
Sinecure for P. Whalen, A.
Six Years.
Sixth-Month Song in the Foothills.
Some critic tried to put me down.
Song of the Slip.
Song of the Tangle.
Song of the Taste.
Sours of the Hills.
Soy Sauce.
Spel Against Demons.
Spring, The.
Spring water in the green creek is clear.
Straight-Creek—Great Burn.
Straits of Malacca 24 Oct 1957.
Surrounded by Wild Turkeys.
Sweat, The.
Talking Late with the Governor about the
    Budget.
Target Practice.
Thin Ice.
This Tokyo.
Thoughts on Looking at a Samuel Palmer
    Etching at the Tate.
Three Deer One Coyote Running in the Snow.
Three Poems for Joanne.
Through the Smoke Hole.
Tiny Energies.
To Fire.
Tōji.
Tomorrow's Song.
Toward Climax.
Trade, The.
Travelling to the Capital.
True Night.
Truth Like the Belly of a Woman Turning,
    The.
Twelve Hours Out of New York After Twenty-
    Five Days at Sea.
Two Fawns That Didn't See the Light This
    Spring.
Two Immortals.

Uluru Wild Fig Song.
Under the Skin of It.
Vapor Trails.
Volcano in Kyushu, A.
Walk, A.
Water.
Wave.
Way West, Underground, The.
We Make Our Vows Together with All Beings.
What Happened Here Before.
What Have I Learned.
What You Should Know to Be a Poet.
When men see Han-Shan.
Why Log Truck Drivers Rise Earlier Than
    Students of Zen.
Wild Edge, The.
Without.
Word Basket Woman.
Work to Do Toward Town.
Working on the '58 Willys Pickup.
Yase: September.
Years, The.

Sophocles (c.495–c.406 B.C.)
Antigone, *sels.*
Oedipus at Colonus, *sels.*
Oedipus the King [*or* Oedipus Rex], *sels.*
Philoctetes, *sels.*
Reverie.
Women of Trachis, *sels.*

Southerne, Thomas (1660–1746)
Disappointment, The, *sels.*
Loyal Brother, The, *sels.*

Spender, Stephen (1909–95)
Absence.
Acts Passed Beyond.
Adam.
Air Raid Across the Bay at Plymouth.
Art Student.
Auden at Milwaukee.
Auden's Funeral.
Awaking.
Barn, The.
Beethoven's Death Mask.
Boy, Cat, Canary.
Conscript, The.
Cornet Cornelius Rilke.
Coward, The.
Cyril Connolly.
Double Shame, The.
Dream, The.
Driving through Snow.
Dusk.
Elegy for Margaret.
Elementary School Classroom in a Slum, An.
Empty House.
Epilogue to a Human Drama.
Exiles, The.
Express, The.
Footnote, A.
From My Diary.
Furies, The.
Generous Days, The.
Girl Who Has Drowned Herself Speaks, A.
Grandparents.
Hamburg, 1929.
Helmut.
I Think Continually of Those Who Were Truly
    Great.
Icarus.
Ice.
In Attica.
In 1929.
In Railway Halls.
Landscape near an Aerodrome, The.
Late Stravinsky Listening to Late Beethoven.
Little Coat, The.
Lost Days.
Louis MacNeice.
Man-Made World, A.
Marston.
My Brother Luis.
My Parents.
Never Being.
Nocturne: "Their six-weeks-old daughter lies."
Not to You.
One.

One More New Botched Beginning.
Perhaps.
Photograph, The.
Polar Exploration.
Port Bou.
Prisoners, The.
Public Son of a Public Man, The.
Pylons, The.
Question of Identity, A.
Rejoice in the Abyss.
Remembering Cincinnatti, 1953.
Room above the Square, The.
Seascape.
Shadow of War.
Sign *Faehre nach Wilm*, The.
Sleepless.
Solipsist.
Song: "Stranger, you who hide my love."
Spiritual Explorations.
Stopwatch and an Ordnance Map, A.
Subject, Object, Sentence.
Thoughts During an Air Raid.
To Manuel Altolaguirre.
To My Daughter.
Tom's a-Cold.
Trance, The.
Trigorin.
Uncreating Chaos (Double Portrait in a
    Mirror), The.
Unemployed.
Us.
Van der Lubbe.
War God, The.
What I Expected.
Word.

Spenser, Edmund (1552?–99)
Amoretti.
Astrophel.
Colin Clouts Come Home Againe.
Commendatory Sonnets.
Daphnaïda.
Epithalamion: "Ye learned sisters which have
    oftentimes."
Faerie Queene, The.
Fowre Hymnes.
Muiopotmos: or The Fate of the Butterflie.
Prosopopoia: or Mother Hubberds Tale.
Prothalamion.
Ruines of Time, The.
Shepheardes [*or* Shepeards *or* Shepherd's]
    Calender, The.
Teares of the Muses, The.
Virgils Gnat.
Visions of the World's Vanity [*or* Vanitie].

Stafford, Wendell Phillips (1861–1954)
Little Gift, A.
Roll Call.

Stafford, William (1914–93)
Story That Could Be True, A.
Accountability.
Across Kansas.
Address to the Senior Class.
Adults Only.
After Arguing against the Contention That Art
    Must Come from Discontent.
Afternoon in the Stacks, An.
Afterwards.
Allegiances.
American Gothic.
Animal That Drank up Sound, The.
Annals of *Tai Chi*: "Push Hands."
Any Time.
Archival Print, An.
Are you Mr. William Stafford?
Around You, Your House.
Arrival.
Artist, Come Home.
As Pippa Lilted.
Ask Me.
Assuming Control.
Assurance.
At Cove on the Crooked River.
At Fort Worden: Calling Names.
At Fourth and Main in Liberal, Kansas, 1932.
At Lascaux.
At Liberty School.

At noon comes the lift—sunlight.
At Our House.
At the Bomb Testing Site.
At the Chairman's Housewarming.
At the Fair.
At the Grave of My Brother.
At the Grave of My Brother: Bomber Pilot.
At the Klamath Berry Festival.
At the Old Place.
At the Playground.
At the Un-National Monument along the
    Canadian Border.
At This Point on the Page.
Atavism.
Atwater Kent.
Aunt Mabel.
B.C.
Back Home.
Before It Burned over: A Sioux Grass Chant.
Before the Big Storm.
Being an American.
Believer.
Bess.
Bi-Focal.
Big Bang.
Big House, The.
Biography.
Bird inside a Box, A.
Boom Town.
Bridge Begins in the Trees, A.
Bring the North.
Burning a Book.
By a River in the Osage Country.
By the Deschutes Shore.
Catechism, A.
Cave Painting.
Ceremony.
Ceremony, A: Doing the Needful.
Charades.
Choosing a Dog.
Circle of Breath.
Clash.
Climbing along the River.
Concealment, The: Ishi, the Last Wild Indian.
Connections.
Consolations.
Cottonwood.
Course in Creative Writing, A.
Coyote.
Coyote in the Zoo, The.
Cro-Magnon.
Crossing Our Campground.
Day Millicent Found the World, The.
Dedication, A: "We stood by the library. It was
    an August night."
Dedications / Pledges / Commitments.
Deer Stolen.
Different Things.
Distractions.
Dream of Now, The.
Dropout.
Earth Dweller.
Easter Morning.
Elegy: "Responsible sound of the lawnmower,
    The."
Emily, this Place, and You.
Entering History.
Epitaph Ending in And, The.
Evidence.
Existences.
Explaining the Big One.
Fall Journey.
Fall Wind.
Family Turn, A.
Farewell, Age Ten, A.
Farm on the Great Plains, The.
Father and Son.
Father's Voice.
Few Snorts from a Wild One, A.
Fiction.
Fifteen.
Final Exam: American Renaissance.
First Grade.
Fish Counter at Bonneville, The.
Five AM.
Fixers.

For a Daughter Gone Away.
For a Lost Child.
For My Young Friends Who Are Afraid.
For Our Party Last Night.
For the Unknown Enemy.
Found in a Storm.
Freedom.
Freedom of Expression.
Friends.
Friends, Farewell.
Gesture toward an Unfound Renaissance, A.
Ghalib Decides to Be Reticent.
Gift, The.
Glances.
Glass Face in the Rain, A.
Godiva County, Montana.
Grace Abounding.
Ground Zero [December 1982].
Ground Zero [June 1982].
Growing Up.
Gutters of Jackson: Cache Street North.
Haycutters.
History Display.
Holcomb, Kansas.
Home State.
Homecoming.
Honeysuckle.
How It Began.
How It Is.
How It Is with Family.
How the Real Bible Is Written.
How These Words Happened.
How to Regain Your Soul.
Hunger.
Ice-Fishing.
Identities.
If I Could Be Like Wallace Stevens.
In a Corner.
In Camp.
In Dear Detail, by Ideal Light.
In Fear and Valor.
In Fur.
In Hurricane Canyon.
In Medias Res.
In Response to a Question.
In the All-Verbs Navaho World.
In the Book.
In the Deep Channel.
In the Night Desert.
In the Oregon Country.
In the White Sky.
Incident.
Indian Cave Jerry Ramsey Found, The.
Indian Caves in the Dry Country.
Influential Writers.
Inheriting the Earth: Quail.
Inscribed on a Prayer Wheel and Spun.
Introduction to Some Poems, An.
Is This Feeling about the West Real?
It Still Happens Now.
It's heavy to drag, this big sack of what.
Jermiah at Miminagish.
Joe's Corner.
Journey, A.
Judgments.
Juncos.
Just Thinking.
Keeping a Journal.
Keepsakes.
Key of C— an interlude for Marvin.
Lake Chelan.
Last Class, The.
Late at Night ("Falling separate into the dark").
Learning.
Learning, Any Time.
Letting You Go.
Level Light.
Life, a Ritual, A.
Life Work.
Light by the Barn, The.
Listening.
Lit Instructor.
Little Girl by the Fence at School, The.
Little Rooms.
Little Ways that Encourage Good Fortune, The.
Living on the Plains.

Living on the Plains ("Carefully, sending
    leaves always toward the sun").
Living Statues.
Long Distance.
Looking across the River.
Looking for Gold.
Looking for Someone.
Looking for You.
Lyf so short, The.
Magic Mountain, The.
Malheur before Dawn.
Many Things are Hidden by the Light.
Maybe.
Meditation.
Meditation in the Waiting Room.
Mein Kampf.
Memorial for My Mother, A.
Memorial: Son Bret, A.
Men.
Merci Beaucoup.
Messae from the Wanderer, A.
Message from Space, A.
Midwest.
Mr. or Mrs. Nobody.
Moment Again.
Mother's Day.
Move to California, The.
My Father: October 1942.
My Hands.
My Life.
My Mother Was a Soldier.
My Name Is William Tell.
Near.
Network.
New Every Day.
New Letters from Thomas Jefferson.
Next Time.
1940.
1932.
No Praise, No Blame.
Not in the Headlines.
Not Very Loud.
Note.
Notes for the Program.
Notice What This Poem Is Not Doing.
November.
Objector.
Ode to Garlic.
Old Blue.
Old Glory.
Old Hamer Place.
Old Prof.
On a Church Lawn.
On Quitting a Little College.
Once in the 40s.
One Evening.
One Home.
108 East 19th.
One Man.
One Night.
One Time.
Oregon Message, An.
Our Cave.
Our City Is Guarded by Automatic Rockets.
Our Kind.
Our People.
Our Story.
Our Way Those days before These Days.
Outside.
Over in Montana.
Over the Mountains.
Over the North Jetty.
Parentage.
Paso por Aquí.
Passing Remark.
Peace Walk.
Peleg Lookout.
People of the South Wind.
People Who Went By in Winter.
Places with Meaning.
Poetry.
Prairie Town.
Purifying the Language of the Tribe.
Put These in Your Pipe.
Putting the Sonnet to Work.
Quo Vadis.

Reaching Out to Turn on a Light.
Reading with Little Sister: A Recollection.
Real People.
Recoil.
Religion Back Home.
Remarks on My Character.
Remembering.
Remembering Brother Bob.
Report from a Far Place.
Report to Crazy Horse.
Reporting Back.
Representing Far Places.
Rescued Year, The.
Research Team in the Mountains, The.
Retirement.
Returned to Say.
Right to Die.
Ritual to Read to Each Other, A.
Ruby Was Her Name.
Run before Dawn.
RX Creative Writing: Identity.
Saint Matthew and All.
Salvaged Parts.
Sayings from the Northern Ice.
Sayings of the Blind.
School Days.
School Play.
Security.
Serving with Gideon.
Sioux Haiku.
Size of a Fist, The.
Sky.
Slow News from Our Place.
Smoke.
So Long.
Some Remarks When Richard Hugo Came.
Some Shadows.
Something That Happens Right Now.
Something to Declare.
Song in the Manner of Flannery O'Connor, A.
Sound from the Earth, A.
Sparkle Depends on Flaws in the Diamond,
    The.
Spirit of Place: Great Blue Heron.
Star in the Hills, The.
Stared Story, A.
Starting with Little Things.
Stereopticon.
Stillborn.
Stories from Kansas.
Stories to Live in the World With.
Storm Warnings.
Story Time.
Style.
Sure You Do.
Surrounded by Mountains.
Survival.
Swerve, The.
Thanksgiving for My Father, A.
That Year.
They Carved an Animal.
Things I Learned Last Week.
Things in the Wild Need Salt.
Things That Happen.
Things That Hurt Me.
Thinking about Being Called Simple by a
    Critic.
Thinking for Berky.
Third Street.
Thirteenth and Pennsylvania.
.38.
Through the Junipers.
Tillamook Burn, The.
Time Capsule.
Together Again.
Toward the End.
Traveling Through the Dark.
Trip, The.
Trouble with Reading, The.
Troubleshooting.
Trying to Tell It.
Tuned in Late One Night.
Turn Over Your Hand.
Ultimate Problems.
Universe is One Place.
Vacation.

Vacation Trip.
Visit Home, A.
Vita.
Vocation.
Vocatus atque Non Vocatus.
Waiting in Line.
Waking at 3 A.M.
Walk in the Country, A.
Walking the Borders.
Walking West.
Wanderer Awaiting Preferment, The.
Watching Sandhill Cranes.
Watching the Jet Planes Dive.
Way I Write, The.
Way It Is, The.
Ways to Live.
We Interrupt to Bring You.
Weather Report.
Well Rising, The.
West of Here.
What Gets Away.
What's in My Journal.
When I Met My Muse.
When You Go Anywhere.
Where We Are.
Whispered in Winter.
Whispered into the Ground.
Why I Am a Poet.
Why I Am Happy.
Why the Sun Comes Up.
Widow.
Wild Horse Love.
Wind from a Wing, A.
Wind World.
With Kit, Age 7, at the Beach.
With My Crowbar Key.
With Neighbors One Afternoon.
Witness.
Wovoka's Witness.
Writing It Down.
Yellow Cars.
Yes.
You and Art.
You Don't Know the End.
You Reading This, Be Ready.
Young.
Your Life.

Stampa, Gaspara (c.1523–54)
Portrait of Her Lover.
With Deep Repentance for My Wasted Days.

Statius, Publius Papinius (A.D. c.61–96)
Sylvae [or Sìlvae], sels.
Thebais [or Thebaid], sels.

Stein, Gertrude (1874–1946)
Birthday Book, A.
Brim Beauvais.
Comedy like That, A.
Dates.
Emp Lace.
Go in Green.
Hotel François Ier.
Lifting Belly.
Little Novel, A.
Mark Twain Centenary.
Marry Nettie.
Men.
More Grammar for a Sentence.
New.
One or Two. I've Finished.
Painted Lace.
Patriarchal Poetry.
Practice of Oratory.
Prudence Caution and Foresight: A Story of
    Avignon.
Sonatina Followed by Another, A.
Stanzas in Meditation.
Study Nature.
Subject-Cases: The Background of a Detective
    Story.
Tillie.
What Does She See When She Shuts Her Eyes.
With a Wife.
Yet Dish.

"Stella" See **Johnson, Esther**

Stevens, Wallace (1879–1955)
Academic Discourse at Havana.
Adagio.
Add This to Rhetoric.
Adult Epigram.
Afield.
After Music.
Agenda.
All things imagined are of earth compact.
American Sublime, The.
Americana.
Analysis of a Theme.
Anatomy of Monotony.
And even as I passed beside the booth.
Anecdote of Canna.
Anecdote of Men by the Thousand.
Anecdote of the Abnormal.
Anecdote of the Jar.
Anecdote of the Prince of Peacocks ("In the
    land of the peacocks, the prince thereof").
Anecdote of the Prince of Peacocks ("In the
    moonlight / I met Berserk").
Angel Surrounded by Paysans.
Anglais Mort à Florence.
Annual Gaiety.
Another Weeping Woman.
Anything Is Beautiful If You Say It Is.
Apostrophe to Vincentine, The.
Arcades of Philadelphia the Past.
Architecture.
Arrival at the Waldorf.
Artificial Populations.
As at a Theatre.
As You Leave the Room.
Asides on the Oboe.
Attempt to Discover Life.
Auroras of Autumn, The.
Autumn.
Autumn Refrain.
Bagatelles the Madrigals, The.
Ballade of the Pink Parasol.
Banal Sojourn.
Banjo Boomer.
Bantams in Pine-Woods.
Bed of Old John Zeller, The.
Beginning, The.
Bird with the Coppery, Keen Claws, The.
Blanche McCarthy.
Blue Buildings in the Summer Air, The.
Botanist on Alp (No. 1).
Botanist on Alp (No. 2).
Bouquet of Belle Scavoir.
Bouquet of Roses in Sunlight.
Bouquet, The.
Bowl.
Brave Man, The.
Burghers of Petty Death.
Candle a Saint, The.
Carnet de Voyage.
Cathedrals are not built along the sea.
Celle Qui Fût Héaulmiette.
Certain Phenomena of Sound.
Chaos in Motion and Not in Motion.
Chiaroscuro.
Child Asleep in Its Own Life, A.
Chocorua to Its Neighbor.
Clear Day and No Memories, A.
Colloquy with a Polish Aunt.
Colors.
Come, said the world, thy youth is not all play.
Comedian as the Letter C, The.
Common Life, The.
Communications of Meaning.
Completely New Set of Objects, A.
Concert of Fishes, A.
Connoisseur of Chaos.
Continual Conversation with a Silent Man.
Contrary Theses (I).
Contrary Theses (II).
Conversation with Three Women of New
    England.
Cortège for Rosenbloom.
Country Words.
Countryman, The.
Course of a Particular, The.
Creations of Sound, The.

Credences of Summer.
Crude Foyer.
Cuban Doctor, The.
Cuisine Bourgeoise.
Curtains in the House of the Metaphysician, The.
Cy Est Pourtraicte, Madame Ste Ursule, et Les Unze Mille Vierges.
Damask.
Dance of the Macabre Mice.
Death of a Soldier, The.
Debris of Life and Mind.
Delightful Evening.
Depression before Spring.
Description without Place.
Desire & the Object.
Desire to Make Love in a Pagoda, The.
Dezembrum.
Dinner Bell in the Woods.
Discovery of Thought, A.
Dish of Peaches in Russia, A.
Disillusionment of Ten O'Clock.
Doctor of Geneva, The.
Dolls.
Domination of Black.
Dove in Spring, The.
Dove in the Belly, The.
Drum-Majors in the Labor Day Parade, The.
Dry Loaf.
Dutch Graves in Bucks County.
Dwarf, The.
Earthy Anecdote.
Eclogue: "Lying in the mint."
Elsie's mirror only shows.
Emperor of Ice-Cream, The.
Esthétique du Mal.
Evening without Angels.
Examination of the Hero in a Time of War.
Exercise for Professor X, An.
Explanation.
Exposition of the Contents of a Cab.
Extracts from Addresses to the Academy of Fine Ideas.
Extraordinary References.
Fabliau of Florida.
Fading of the Sun, A.
Farewell to Florida.
Farewell without a Guitar.
Final Soliloquy of the Interior Paramour.
First Warmth.
Fish-Scale Sunrise, A.
Floral Decorations for Bananas.
Florists Wears Knee-Breeches, The.
Flyer's Fall.
For an Old Woman in a Wig.
Forces, the Will & the Weather.
Frogs Eat Butterflies. Snakes Eat Frogs. Hogs Eat Snakes. Men Eat Hogs.
From a Junk.
From a Vagabond.
From the Misery of Don Joost.
From the Packet of Anacharsis.
Gallant Chateau.
Ghosts as Cocoons.
Gigantomachia.
Girl in a Nightgown.
Glass of Water, The.
God is Good. It Is a Beautiful Night.
Golden Woman in a Silver Mirror, A.
Good Man, Bad Woman.
Good Man Has No Shape, The.
Gray Room.
Gray Stones and Gray Pigeons.
Green Plant, The.
Gubbinal.
Hand as a Being, The.
Hang up brave tapestries.
He sang, and, in her heart, the sound.
Headache.
Hermitage at the Center, The.
Hibiscus on the Sleeping Shores.
Hieroglyphica.
High-Toned Old Christian Woman, A.
Holiday in Reality.
Home Again.
Homunculus et La Belle Etoile.

House Was Quiet and the World Was Calm, The.
How Now, O, Brightener.
How sweet it is to find an asphodel.
How to Live. What to Do.
Human Arrangement.
Hymn from a Watermelon Pavilion.
I am weary of the plum and of the cherry.
I found it flaming in the scarlet rose.
I have lived so long with the rhetoricians.
I sang an idle song of happy youth.
I strode along my beaches like a sea.
Idea of Order at Key West, The.
Idiom of the Hero.
If I love thee, I am thine.
If only birds of sudden white.
If we are leaves that fall upon the ground.
Imago.
Imitation of Sidney: To Stella. (Miss B?).
In a Bad Time.
In a Crowd.
In a Garden.
In April.
In the Carolinas.
In the Clear Season of Grapes.
In the Element of Antagonisms.
In the Sun.
In Town.
Indian River.
Indigo Glass in the Grass, The.
Infanta Marina.
Infernale.
Inscription for a Monument.
Invective against Swans.
Irish Cliffs of Moher, The.
Jack-Rabbit, The.
Jasmine's Beautiful Thoughts Underneath the Willow.
Jouga.
July Mountain.
Jumbo.
Lack of Repose, The.
Landscape with Boat.
Large Red Man Reading.
Last Looks at the Lilacs.
Late Hymn from the Myrrh-Mountain.
Latest Freed Man, The.
Le Monocle de Mon Oncle.
Lebensweisheitspielerei.
Les Plus Belles Pages.
Less and Less Human, O Savage Spirit.
L'Essor Saccadé.
Lettres d'un Soldat.
Life is long in the desert.
Life Is Motion.
Life on a Battleship.
Like Decorations in a Nigger Cemetery.
Lions in Sweden.
Load of Sugar-Cane, The.
Local Objects.
Loneliness in Jersey City.
Long and Sluggish Lines.
Looking across the Fields and Watching the Birds Fly.
Lot of People Bathing in a Stream, A.
Lulu Gay.
Lulu Morose.
Lunar Paraphrase.
Lytton Strachey, Also, Enters into Heaven.
Madame La Fleurie.
Man and Bottle.
Man Carrying Thing.
Man from the waste evolved.
Man on the Dump, The.
Man Whose Pharynx Was Bad, The.
Man with the Blue Guitar, The.
Mandolin and Liqueurs.
Martial Cadenza.
Meditation ("How long have I meditated").
Meditation ("There were feet").
Meditation Celestial & Terrestrial.
Memorandum.
Men Made out of Words.
Men That Are Falling, The.
Metamorphosis.
Metaphor as Degeneration.

Metaphors of a Magnifico.
Metropolitan Melancholy.
Mrs. Alfred Uruguay.
Montrachet-le-Jardin.
Morning Song.
Motive for Metaphor, The.
Mountains Covered with Cats.
Mozart, 1935.
Mud Master.
Mythology reflects its region, A. Here.
Naked Eye of the Aunt, The.
Negation.
New England Verses.
New Life.
News and the Weather, The.
Night-Song.
Night-wind of August, The.
No Possum, No Sop, No Taters.
Nomad Exquisite.
Noon-Clearing.
Not Ideas about the Thing but the Thing Itself.
Note on Moonlight.
Notes toward a Supreme Fiction.
Novel, The.
Nuances of a Theme by Williams.
Nudity at the Capital.
Nudity in the Colonies.
Nuns Painting Water-Lilies.
O Florida, Venereal Soil.
Oak Leaves Are Hands.
Ode: "Night in May!, A."
Odorous bush I seek, An.
Of Bright & Blue Birds & the Gala Sun.
Of Hartford in a Purple Light.
Of Heaven Considered as a Tomb.
Of Mere Being.
Of Modern Poetry.
Of the Surface of Things.
Old Lutheran Bells at Home, The.
Old Man Asleep, An.
On an Old Horn.
On the Adequacy of Landscape.
On the Ferry.
On [or Of] the Manner of Addressing Clouds.
On the Road Home.
On the Way to the Bus.
One day more.
One of the Inhabitants of the West.
One of Those Hibiscuses of Damozels.
Only to name again.
Ordinary Evening in New Haven, An.
Ordinary Women, The.
Our Stars Come from Ireland.
Outside of Wedlock.
Outside the Hospital.
Owl in the Sarcophagus, The.
Owl's Clover.
Page from a Tale.
Paisant Chronicle.
Palace of the Babies.
Paltry Nude Starts on a Spring Voyage, The.
Parochial Theme.
Pastor Caballero, The.
Pastoral Nun, A.
Pediment of Appearance, The.
Peter Parasol.
Peter Quince at the Clavier.
Phases.
Phosphor Reading by His Own Light.
Piano Practice at the Academy of the Holy Angels.
Pieces.
Pierrot.
Place of the Solitaires, The.
Plain Sense of Things, The.
Planet on the Table, The.
Pleasures of Merely Circulating, The.
Plot Against the Giant, The.
Ploughing on Sunday.
Poem That Took the Place of a Mountain, The.
Poem with Rhythms.
Poem Written at Morning.
Poems of Our Climate, The.
Poesie Abrutie.
Poetry Is a Destructive Force.
Polo Ponies Practicing.

Postcard from the Volcano, A.
Prejudice against the Past, The.
Prelude to Objects.
Presence of an External Master of Knowledge.
Primitive like an Orb, A.
Primordia.
Prologues to What Is Possible.
Public Square, The.
Puella Parvula.
Pure Good of Theory, The.
Quatrain: "Go not, young cloud, too boldly through the sky."
Quatrain: "He sought the music of the distant spheres."
Questions Are Remarks.
Quiet Normal Life, A.
Rabbit as King of the Ghosts, A.
Re-statement of Romance.
Reader, The.
Reality Is an Activity of the Most August Imagination.
Red Fern, The.
Red Loves Kit.
Region November, The.
Repetitions of a Young Captain.
Reply to Papini.
Rest.
Revolutionists Stop for Orangeade, The.
River of Rivers in Connecticut, The.
Rivers flow on idly in their light, The.
Rock, The.
Role of the Idea in Poetry, The.
Romance for a Demoiselle Lying in the Grass.
Room on a Garden, A.
Sad Strains of a Gay Waltz.
Sail of Ulysses, The.
Sailing after Lunch.
St. Armorer's Church from the Outside.
Saint John and the Back-Ache.
Saturday Night at the Chiropodist's.
Sea Surface Full of Clouds.
Search for Sound Free from Motion, The.
Secret Man.
Self-Respect.
Sense of the Sleight-of-Hand Man, The.
Shape of the Coroner, The.
She that winked her sandal fan.
Shower.
Sick Man, The.
Silver Plough-Boy, The.
Six Significant Landscapes.
Sketch of the Ultimate Politician.
Snow and Stars.
Snow Man, The.
So-and-So Reclining on Her Couch.
Solitaire under the Oaks.
Some Friends from Pascagoula.
Somnambulisma.
Sonatina to Hans Christian.
Song: "Ah yes! beyond these barren walls."
Song: "Month—a year—of idle work, A."
Song of Fixed Accord.
Song: "She loves me or loves me not."
Song: "There are great things doing."
Song: "This is the house of her."
Sonnet: "Build up the walls about me; close each door."
Sonnet: "Explain my spirit—adding word to word."
Soul of happy youth is never lost, The.
Souls of Women at Night, The.
Stars at Tallapoosa.
Street Songs.
Study of Images 1.
Study of Images 2.
Study of Two Pears.
Sun This March, The.
Sunday Morning.
Surprises of the Superhuman, The.
Table Talk.
Tattoo.
Tea.
Tea at the Palaz of Hoon.
Testamentum.
Theory.
There, a rocket in the Wain.

There is my spectre.
There shines the morning star! Through the forlorn.
Things of August.
Thinking of a Relation between the Images of Metaphors.
Thirteen Ways of Looking at a Blackbird.
This as Including That.
This is the lilac-bush.
This Solitude of Cataracts.
This Vast Inelegance.
Though Valentine brings love.
Thought Revolved, A.
Through dreary winter had my soul endured.
Thunder by the Musician.
Tides.
To an Old Philosopher in Rome.
To Madame Alda, Singing a Song, in a White Gown.
To Miss Gage.
To the Morn.
To the One of Fictive Music.
To the Roaring Wind.
Tradition.
Twilight.
Two at Norfolk.
Two Figures in Dense Violet Night.
Two Illustrations That the World Is What You Make of It.
Two Letters.
Two Tales of Liadoff.
Two Versions of the Same Poem.
Ultimate Poem Is Abstract, The.
United Dames of America.
Vacancy in the Park.
Valentine, A.
Valley Candle.
Variations on a Summer Day.
Vignette.
Virgin Carrying a Lantern, The.
Vita Mea.
Waving Adieu, Adieu, Adieu.
Weak Mind in the Mountains, A.
Weeping Burgher, The.
Well Dressed Man with a Beard, The.
What have I to do with Arras.
What They Call Red Cherry Pie.
What We See Is What We Think.
When I think of all the centuries long dead.
Who Lies Dead?
Widow, The.
Wild Ducks, People and Distances.
Wind Shifts, The.
Window in the Slums, A.
Winter Bells.
Winter Melody.
Woman in Sunshine, The.
Woman Looking at a Vase of Flowers.
Woman Sings a Song for a Soldier Come Home, A.
Woman That Had More Babies than That, The.
Woman Who Blamed Life on a Spaniard, The.
Word with José Rodríguez-Feo, A.
World as Meditation, The.
World without Peculiarity.
Worms at Heaven's Gate, The.
Yellow Afternoon.
Yet mystery is better than the light.
You say this is the iris?

Stock, Robert (1923–81)
Academy of Sincerity.
Adam in Extremis.
Adam Lay Ibounden.
Aeneas Underground.
Again I'm Torched and Wonder What We've Wrought.
All I Wanted to Say.
Ambassador From India.
Anacreontic for a Chinese Scholar.
And You, Too, Brutus.
Anonymous Secrets.
Antaeus.
Ashes Ashes All Fall Down.
At an Abandoned Shrine of Saint Mary Aegyptian.
Azazel.

Ballade to be Read in the Medici Gardens.
Banquet, The.
Barrier Snow.
Battle Scene.
Battleground.
Beacon, The.
Bellerophon and the Portable Universe.
Buried Talents, The.
Calentures.
Camellia, The.
Cathedral, The.
Cenotaph for Two Butterflies.
Certain Paralipomena to an Unbegun Epic.
Certain Pretexts.
Circe.
Costa Rican Pastoral.
Curriculum Vitae.
Cushing.
Dance, The.
Dear Mr. Worldly Wiseman.
Doctor Will Be Back Too Late, The.
Dollmaker, The.
Double Ballade of Newfangled Ladies, A.
Drunkenness.
Elemental Trust.
Enigma of a Final Scene.
Epistle to Prescott S. Liddell.
Epistle to Simon Perchik.
Epistle to Spencer Holst.
Epistle to Suzanne Joslyn Fosberg.
Errant Mole and the Loveliest of Hawks, The.
Evangelists, The.
Extra-Terrestrial Function of Spokes.
Farewell to Baedeker.
First Last Will & Testament.
First Row, The.
Flabbergasting of the True & False Basilisk, The.
For Sharon, As Soon As She Wants It.
Form of Pity, A.
Four Inscriptions for the Sundial of a Lost Race of Polyphemus.
From Wherever I Am.
Game of the Thunderbolt Goddesses, The.
Giorgione's *Tempest*.
Go As Played in the Best Circles; Or Rotten Axe-Handle.
God Victimized.
Going Too Far.
Grate, The.
Great High Feasts on the Birthdays of Little Men.
Grief.
Grunion Run.
Haiku: "You are the bright bird."
Hand.
Hard Facts.
Henry Hudson.
Hostage, The.
Houynhnm's Holiday.
How They Hunt the Quck Red Fox.
Hymn Directed Somewhere Toward the Pantheon.
"I'd Understand Yer Poemes Better," Writes the Lady Editor from San Francisco, "If I Knowed What the Words Mean."
Imitation of Horace; Carmina 1.6.
Impromptu with a Breeze.
In Transformation of an Imago.
Incredible Activities in the Eyrie.
Inquest.
Inscription for a Temple of Cloacina.
Instructions to Any Painter for a "Coronation of Inés de Castro."
Interpretation of High Finance.
Inversion Factor.
Invisible Golden Sections.
J.
Jacob Agonistes.
Just Another Apotheosis.
Koan for Two Minutes of Intensive Meditation.
Laying-Out of Lazarus.
Lifeline Train to Puerto Limón.
Lines to a White Persian Sleeping.
Lines Upon Delia And to the Chevaliers of the Cordon Bleu.

Lock, The.
Logos.
Louis XI.
Lullaby for Now.
Man-Giraffe.
Man Who Was Pregnant with Envy, The.
Mary on the Death of Joachim.
May Morning Admonition.
Metamorphosis.
Millais Loquacious.
Miracle of the Roses, The.
Mithridates 5.
Model for an Object in X Space.
Model for an Object in Y Space.
Model for an Object in Z Space.
Monkey's Address to Others of His Kind, A.
Moses on Pisgah.
Motives of a Two-Headed Turtle.
National Anthem; Imitation of Carlos
    Drummond de Andrade's "*Hino Nacional.*"
Night Crawlers.
Nightmare Song.
Now Are We Remembered.
On a Gift of Leaves From Dove Cottage Close,
    Grasmere.
151st Psalm, The.
One of the Old Ones.
Pantoum on Some Lines From Camões.
Part of a Tarot Fortune.
Patio.
Paul Klee.
Pietà.
Pinch, The.
Plant Called Yarrow, The.
Poem on Holy Saturday.
Poem to Be Printed on a Very White Page.
Poem Written on the Typewriter.
Poet Mário Faustino Descends Into Hades and
    Rises to the Empyrean.
Poet's Bestiary.
Poet's Prescription of Shamelessness, The.
Portrait of Gertrude Stein.
Primeval Landscape with Politician and Dodo
    Bird.
Prometheus Passes the Toast.
Prophets, The.
Prose for the Children of Aborted Revolution.
Prose Parables.
Queen Anne's Lace.
Rachel and Leah.
Reconstruction.
Red Clay Speech.
Rescuers, The.
Revelation According to the Beloved.
Reverse Metamorphosis.
Rococo Birdbath with Figurine of Daphne as
    Warning to Virgins.
Rose in Ice.
Roseapples and Nudes.
Saxifrage.
Scene From Life.
Seasons in a Landscape of Woman, The.
Selected Poems of Mañuel Bandeira, The.
Separation, *sels.*
Several Large Rocks in a Swiftly Rushing
    Stream.
Shakespeare in Vietnam.
Sharing It With Angels.
Shield Against the Trampling Foe, A.
Sigismundo Malatesta Brings His Favorite
    Philosopher's Bones to Italy.
Signing the Poem.
Silenus' Epitaph.
Singing, The.
Sir John Mandeville and I Sat Up Talking.
Sitting for a Self-Portrait.
Sixth Station, The.
Slaughtering the Cow.
Small Rain, The.
Solo for Four.
Space Between Two Blades of Grass Meets an
    Intractable Ego, The.
Star-Apple.
Storm.
Study of a House with Garden Attached.
Swift Completion of Their Appointed Rounds,

The.
Synapse, The.
Taking Stock of Lot.
That the Sestina is What it is Despite What it
    is Not.
This Book is for Harriette.
Tight-Rope Construction Surrounded by a
    Thousand Sonnets.
To My Inebriety.
To Peg.
To The Discreet Reader: An Induction to
    Indiscretions.
To Tui: Not to Hie Herself Off To Only God
    Knows How Dire & Pestilential A South Sea
    Island, But to Come With Us To Found Her
    Community in Brazil; Together With Some
    Preposterous Notes Toward an
    Ornithomancy of Lovingkindness.
Trajectory of a Scream.
Transfiguration: Natura Naturans.
Translated from Silence.
Triadic Node for Tim Reynold's Digestion.
Twelth Night, Gift Horses, and of Certain
    Reversals.
Ultimate Poem, The.
Unmapped Road.
Variations Within Instances
Verses After Which the Mourning Statue is
    Presumed to Speak.
Visitation.
Voyager Takes Pause, A.
Walking with Angels.
Wandering Jew and the Heavenly Hosts, The.
Wherein the Maker's Right Hand Moralizes
    the Way to a Familiar but Rare Felicity,
    Whatwhile the Left Hand Seemingly
    Knoweth Not Its Brother's Ambages and So
    Falleth in the Way of an Undiscerning
    Subtraction.
Wind in the Mirror.
With a Machet Across My Knees.
Word with Norman Rosten.
Wrestling with Angels.
Young Grimshaw.

Stockton, Annis Boudinot (1736–1801)
Acrostic for Abby Stockton.
Acrostic for Georgeana Cuthbert.
Addressed to a Student of Divinity.
Addressed to General Washington, in the Year
    1777, after the Battles of Trenton and
    Princeton.
After a Night of Perplexing Dreams.
Almira to Celadon, Founded on a Story in a
    Magazine.
Anniversary Elegy on the Death of Mr
    Stockton the 28th of Feb 1783.
Birth Day Ode, A.
Bridal Wish Adressed to Mr S. Stockton and
    His Lady the Morning after Their Maraige,
    The.
By a Lady in America to Her Husband in
    England.
Caprice, a Fragment.
Compos'd in a Dancing Room, December 69.
Disappointment, an Ode 1756 to Mr Stockton,
    The.
Doubt, a Pastoral Ballad—1762.
Dream, an Ode, 1756, The.
Elegiack Ode on the 28th Day of February
    1782, An. The Anniversary of Mr.
    Stockton's Death.
Elegy: "For thee I drop the tender tear."
Elegy in the Extreme Illness of a Friend
    Whose Disorder Was the Bursting of a
    Blood Vesel in His Breast, An.
Elegy Inscribed to Richard J Stockton Esqr
    [Feb. 28, 1787].
Elegy on the Death of a Young Lady, An.
Elegy on the Death of Miss Chandler, as if
    Written in Her Fathers Church Yard.
Elegy on the Death of Mrs Dickinson. The
    Event Was Communicated at the Sea Shore.
Elegy on the Death of Mrs Wilson, April the
    19, 1786, An.
Elegy on the Destruction of the Trees by the
    Isicles Sunday and Monday of Feb, the 17th

and 18th, 1788.
Epigram Addressed to Two Clergymen Who
    Had Been Trying in Jest to Put Some
    Constructions on the Conversation That Was
    Not Meant, An.
Epigram to Fidelia.
Epistle to a Friend Who Urg'd to Have Some
    Poetry Sent Her in the Year 1759, in the
    Winter, An.
Epistle to General Washington [May 26, 1787].
Epistle—To Lucius.
Epitaph by a Young Lady, Design'd by
    Herself, An.
Epithalamium, The: "Ye woodland choirs come
    consecrate the lay."
Extemporal Ode in a Sleepless Night, An. By a
    Lady, (Mrs. S. of New-Jersey) while
    Attending on Her Husband in a Long and
    Painful Illness.
Fragment, Janu'ry 1786.
Fragment on Hearing the Account of Mrs
    Ramseys Death.
Fragment on the Death of a Minester.
How blest the soul to whom indulgent heaven.
Hymn Written in the Year 1753, A.
Ill Penserosa, an Ode.
Impromptu Epigram upon Being Asked to
    Accompany Three or Four Very Fine Girls
    with Some Gentleman in a Rural Walk.
Impromptu Epitaph on the Grave Digger of
    Princeton—1769.
Impromptu Ode before Day on the 24th of
    Dec, Christmas Morning, An.
Impromptu on Hearing that a Print of the
    Guliteene with Our Beloved Presidents
    Figure under It Was Executed in Mr Genets
    Family—under His Sanction.
Impromptu on Reading the Several Motions
    Made against Mr. Hamilton.
Impromptu on Seeing a Very Agreeable
    Gentleman and Lady, Particular Friends
    Conversing Together.
Impromptu on the Morning of my Sons
    Weding Day Which Was Ushered in by a
    Fall of Snow and Soon after Cleared by a
    Very Bright Sun.
Impromptu Written with a Pencil in a Chinese
    Temple in the Garden of Mr Elisha
    Boudinot.
Invitation Ode to a Young Lady in New York
    from Her Friend in the Country—New
    Brunswick May the 22d 1753, An.
Lavinia and Amanda, a Pastoral.
Lines Impromptu on Miss Morgans Birth Day.
Lines on a Young Gentleman Who Died of the
    Yellow Fever at Princeton a Day or Two
    after He Fled from the City for Fear of It.
Lines on Hearing of the Death of Doctor
    Franklin.
Lines on Seeing Mrs Elizabeth Witherspoon
    Put in the Grave.
Lines on the Death of Mrs Hill Suppos'd to Be
    Spoken by Her Sister Mrs Clymer.
Lines on the Death of Mrs Petit of
    Philadelphia.
Lines to My Brother from a Pavillion in His
    Garden.
Lucinda and Aminta, a Pastoral, on the
    Capture of Lord Cornwallis and the British
    Army, by General Washington.
Lyric Ode, A.—Feb. 28.
Meditation on the 3d Verse of the 28th Chapter
    of Mathew.
Ode, An: "Yes tis an easy thing to view."
Ode for Christmas Day, An.
Ode on the Birth Day of the Illustrious George
    Washington President of the United States,
    An.
Ode, to Amanda, An.
Ode to Constantius.
Ode to Doctor Smith on His Birth Day March
    the 16th, 1791, An.
Ode to Solitude Inscribed to Mrs Boudinot,
    An.
Ode—Written 1756, An.
On a Little Boy Going to Play on a Place from

Whence He Had Just Fallen.
On an Enclosure of Roses in Which Is the Grave of Miss Mary Morgan a Young Lady of 13 Years of Age Daughter of Col Morgan.
On Doctor Rushes Birth Day the 5th of January—after Ten Days Thick Fog.
On Exodus 30.18.
On Hearing of the News of the Capture of Lord Cornwallis and the British Army, by Gen. Washington.
On Hearing of the Out Powering of the Divine Spirit in Nassau Hall, Feb 24 1757.
On Hearing that General Warren Was Killed on Bunker-Hill, on the 17th of June 1775.
On Hearing the Cooing of a Dove, a Song.
On Reading Dr Beaties Hermit.
On Seeing Mrs Macauly Graham.
On the Birth Day of the Revd Doctor Witherspoon, 1788.
On the Celebration of the Birth of the Dauphin of France.
On the Death of General Montgomery.
On the Return of Col Laurens from His Confinement in the Tower of London.
On the Suns Setting Clear after a Three Days Storm.
Peace, a Pastoral Dialogue.—Part the Second.
Poetical Correspondence between Palemon and Æmilia, A.
Poetical Epistle, Addressed by a Lady of New-Jersey, to Her Niece, upon Her Marriage, in This City, A.
Prospect, The. By a Lady in Princeton.
Question, upon Being Told in Jest by Mr Stockton that He Was Not Loved Much, The.
Resignation, an Elegiac Ode, February the 28th, 1788.
Restoration of a Stolen Fan, The. To ———.
Sarcasm against the Ladies in a Newspaper, A; An Impromptu Answer.
Satire on the Fashionable Pompoons Worn by the Ladies in the Year 1753. by a Gentleman, A; Answered by a Young Lady of Sixteen.
Sensibility, an Ode.
Short Elegy to the Memory of Her Husband, A.
Soliliguy in a Sleepless Night.
Some Traits of the Character of Mrs. Powel as a Model for a Young Lady Who Said She Admired Her More than Any Other Woman.
Sudden Production of Mrs. Stockton's in One of Those Many Anxious Nights in Which She Watched with Mr. Stockton in His Last Illness, A.
Sweet Mariana gentle maid adieu.
Tears of Friendship. Elegy the Third.—To a Friend Just Married, and Who Had Promised to Write, on Parting, but Had Neglected It.
Tears of Friendship, The. Elegy the 4th.
Thoughts on the Pythagorian System.
To a Friend Going to Sea.
To a Friend Who Had Persuaded Emelia to Marry, an Ode.
To a Little Miss a Year Older than the One to Whom the Glass Was Promised, with a Toy Looking Glass.
To a Little Miss, with a Toy Looking glass.
To Amanda—Who Was Obliging Enough to Delight Her Friend with Singing Every Evening Two Songs Which She Was Very Fond Off.
To Aspasio.
To Doctor Rush Enclosing the Foregoing Ode of 1782.
To Doctor Smith on His Birth Day March 16th, 92.
To Doctor Smith on His Birth Day March the 16th, 1790.
To General Washington, An Epistle.
To General Washington [Aug. 26, 1783].
To Laura.
To Laura—a Card.
To Miss Mary Stockton, an Epistle the 10th of

Janu 78.
To Miss Mary Stockton, an Epistle upon Some Gentleman Refusing to Admit Ladies of Their Circle into the Parlour till Supper Where They Met for Conversation and Business Once a Week.
To Mr Lewis Pintard on His Retirement at New Rochelle.
To Mr Stockton on His Departure from America to England, 1769.
To Mrs Powel, an Ode.
To Mrs Rush, on Her Birth Day.
To My Burrissa.
To Richard John Stockton Esqr, Inclosing the Preceding Elegy [Feb. 28, 1787].
To the Honourable Col. Peter Schuyler.
To the President of the United States.
To the Visitant, from a Circle of Ladies, on Reading His Paper. No. 3, in the Pennsylvania Chronicle.
Vision, The.
Why wanders my friend in this grove?
Wise nature here has done her kindest part.
Wish on a Wedding Day Morning, The.
Wish to Miss Hannah Stockton, The.

Strehlenau, Nikolaus Franz Niembsch von *See* **Lenau, Nikolaus**

Suckling, Sir John (1609–42)
Against Absence.
Against Fruition ("Fie upon hearts").
Against Fruition ("Stay here, fond youth, and ask no more").
Aglaura.
Answer to Some Verses Made in His Praise, An.
Ballad[e] [upon a Wedding], A.
Barber, A.
Barley-Break , A.
Brennoralt.
Candle, A.
Cantilena Politica-Jocunda Facta Post Principis Discessum In Hispaniam.
Careless Lover, The.
Deformed Mistress, The.
Desdain.
Detraction Execrated.
Ei Men Een Mathein.
Expostulation, The.
Farewell to Love.
Goblins, The.
Guiltless Inconstant, The.
His Dream.
Invocation, The: "Ye juster Powers of Love and Fate."
Love and Debt Alike Troublesome.
Love Turned to Hatred.
Love's Burning-Glass.
Love's Clock.
Love's Offence.
Love's Representation.
Love's Siege.
Love's World.
Loving and Beloved.
Lutea Allison.
Metamorphosis, The.
Miracle, The.
My dearest rival, lest [*or* least] our love.
Non Est Mortale Quod Opto.
On New-Year's Day 1640, to the King.
Pedlar of Small-Wares, A.
Perjury Excused.
Poem with the Answer, A.
Proffered Love Rejected.
Prologue of the Author's to a Masque at Witten, A.
Sad One, The.
Sir John Suckling's Answer.
Soldier, A.
Song: "Crafty boy that had full oft assay'd, The."
Song: "Honest lover whosoever."
Song: "I prithee send me back my heart."
Song: "I prithee spare me, gentle boy."
Song: "If you refuse me once and think again."
Song: "Unjust decrees, that do at once exact."

Sonnet: "Dost see how unregarded now."
Sonnet: "Of thee, kind boy, I ask no red and white."
Sonnet: "O[h]! for some honest lover's ghost."
Summons to Town, A.
Supplement of an Imperfect Copy of Verses of Mr. William Shakespeare's, By the Author, A.
To a Lady That Forbade to Love before Company.
To B.C.
To His Much Honoured the Lord Lepington upon His Translation of Malvezzi, His "Romulus" and "Tarquin."
To His Rival.
To Master Davenant for Absence.
To My Friend Will. Davenant, on His Other Poems.
To My Friend Will. Davenant, upon His Poem of "Madagascar."
To My Lady E.C. at Her Going Out of England.
Upon A.M.
Upon L.M. Weeping.
Upon My Lady Carlisle's Walking in Hampton Court Garden.
Upon My Lord Brohall's Wedding.
Upon Sir John Lawrence's Bringing Water over the Hills [to My L. Middlesex His House at Witten].
Upon T.C. Having the Pox.
Upon the Black Spots Worn, by My Lady D.E.
Upon the First Sight of My Lady Seymour.
Upon Two Sisters.
Verses: "I am confirm'd a woman can."
Wits, The; A Session[s] of the Poets.
Woman's Constancy.

Suckling, Sir John (1609–42) *and* **Owen Felltham (c.1602–68)**
Song: "When, dearest, I but think on [*or of*] thee."

Swenson, May (b. 1919)
Above Bear Lake.
Above the Arno.
After the Flight of Ranger 7.
All That Time.
Almanac.
Alternate Hosts.
Alyscamps at Arles, The.
Angels at "Unsubdued."
Another Spring Uncovered.
Any Object.
April Light.
As Long Ago As Far Away.
At First, at Last.
At Truro.
Beast.
Beauty of the Head, The.
Beginning to Squall.
Big-Hipped Nature.
Birthday.
Bison Crossing Near Mt. Rushmore.
Bleeding.
Blue.
Blue Bottle, The.
Cabala.
Camoufleur.
Camping in Madera Canyon.
Captain Holm.
Catbird in Redbud.
Centaur, The.
City Garden in April, A.
Cloud-Mobile, The.
Come in Go Out.
Comet Watch on Indian Key—Night of April 10, 1986.
Couple, A.
Crossing, The.
Cumuli.
Daffodildo.
Day Is Laid By, A.
Day Like Rousseau's *Dream*, A.
Day Moon, The.
Dear Elizabeth.
Death, Great Smoothener.
Death Invited.

Deciding.
Digging in the Garden of Age I Uncover a Live Root.
Downward.
Dream, A.
Dream after Nanook.
Each like a Leaf.
Early Morning: Cape Cod.
Earth Your Dancing Place.
Engagement, The.
Even Sea, The.
Evolution.
Exchange, The.
Fable for When There's No Way Out.
Feel like a Bird.
Feel Me.
Flag of Summer.
Fluffy Stuff, The.
Flying Home from Utah.
Forest.
Fountain Piece.
Fountains of Aix.
From Sea Cliff, March.
Garden at St. John's, The.
Gods | Children.
Goodbye, Goldeneye.
Goodnight.
Green Red Brown and White.
Haymaking.
Hearing the Wind at Night.
Her Management.
Horse.
How Everything Happens (Based on a Study of the Wave).
How to Be Old.
Hurricane at Sea, A.
I Look at My Hand.
I will be earth you be the flower.
I Will Lie Down.
If I Had Children.
In the Bodies of Words.
In the Yard.
Incantation.
Lake Scene, A.
Landing on the Moon.
Laocoön Dream Recorded in Diary Dated 1943.
Last Day.
Lightning, The.
Little Rapids, The.
Living Tenderly.
Loaf of Time, A.
Look Closer.
Love Sleeping.
Lying and Looking.
Manyone Flying.
Mornings Innocent.
Motherhood.
My Farm.
Naked in Borneo.
Nature.
New Pair, A.
News from the Cabin.
North Rim, The.
November Night.
Ocean, Whale-Shaped.
October.
October Textures.
Of Rounds.
Old No. 1.
On Addy Road.
On Its Way.
On the Edge.
Once There Were Glaciers.
One Morning in New Hampshire.
One of the Strangest.
Orbiter 5 Shows How Earth Looks from the Moon.
Order of Diet.
Out of the Sea, Early.
Overboard.
Pair, A.
Picasso: "Dream." Oil 1932.
Pigeon Woman.
Playhouse, The.
Poplar's Shadow, The.

Process, The.
Promontory Moment, The.
Question.
Rain at Wildwood.
Red Bird Tapestry, The.
Running on the Shore.
Rusty Autumn.
St. Augustine-by-the-Sea.
Scroppo's Dog.
Sea, The.
Secure.
Seeing Jupiter.
Shu Swamp, Spring.
Sketch for a Landscape.
Skopus.
Sleeping Overnight on the Shore.
Snow Geese at Jamaica Bay, The.
Snowy, The.
Solar Corona.
Speed.
Spring by Robert Lowell / (Photograph by Trudi Fuller).
Spring Uncovered.
Staring at the Sea on the Day of the Death of Another.
Stick, The.
Still Turning.
Stone Gullets.
Stripping and Putting On.
Subconscious Sea.
Subject of the Waves, A.
Summer's Bounty.
Sunday in the Country.
Surface, The.
Survey of the Whole.
Swimmers.
Thickening Mat, The.
This Morning.
Tide at Long Point, The.
Tree in Spring, A.
Trinity Churchyard, Spring 1961.
Truth is Forced, The.
View to the North.
Waking from a Nap on the Beach.
Water Picture.
Waterbird.
Wave and the Dune, The.
Weather.
Wednesday at the Waldorf.
What I Did on a Rainy Day.
Willets, The.
Woods at Night, The.
Yes, the Mystery.
Zambesi and Ranee.
Zero in the Cove.

Swift, Jonathan (1667–1745)
Ad Amicum Eruditum Thomam Sheridan [To My Learned Friend, Thomas Sheridan].
Addenda Quaedam.
Advice to a Parson.
Advice to the Grub Street Verse-Writers.
Anglo-Latin Verses.
Another Reply by the Dean.
Answer to a Scandalous Poem, An.
Answer to Delany's Riddle, The.
Answer to Dr. Delany, The.
Answer to Dr. Delany's Fable of the Pheasant and the Lark, An.
Answer to "Paulus," The.
Answer to the Ballyspellin Ballad, An.
Answer to Vanessa's Rebus, The.
Apollo.
Apollo Outwitted.
Apollo to the Dean.
Apollo's Edict.
Apology to the Lady Carteret, An.
Atlas.
Author upon Himself, The.
Author's Manner of Living, The.
Aye and No.
Aye and No: A Fable.
Ballad on the Game of Traffic, A.
Ballad to the Tune of the Cutpurse [*or* "The Cut-Purse"], A.
Bank Thrown Down, The.
Baucis and Philemon.

Beasts' Confession to the Priest, The.
Beau's Reply to the Five Ladies' Answer, The.
Beautiful Young Nymph Going to Bed, A.
Bec's Birthday.
Behold! a proof of Irish sense!
Billet to the Company of Players.
Cadenus and Vanessa.
Can you match with me.
Cantata, A.
Cassinus and Peter.
Character of Sir Robert Walpole, The.
Character, Panegyric, and Description of the Legion Club, A.
Clad All in Brown.
Clever Tom Clinch Going to Be Hanged.
Copy of Verses upon Two Celebrated Modern Poets, A.
Corinna.
Dan Jackson's Reply.
Daphne.
Day of Judgement, The.
Dean and the Duke, The.
Dean of St. Patrick's to Thomas Sheridan, The.
Dean Smedley Gone to Seek His Fortune.
Dean Swift's Answer to the Reverend Dr. Sheridan.
Dean to Himself on St. Cecilia's Day, The.
Dean to Thomas Sheridan, The.
Dean's Answer to "Upon Stealing a Crown," The.
Dean's Reasons for Not Building at Drapier's Hill, The.
Death and Daphne.
Description of a City Shower, A.
Description of a Salamander, The.
Description of an Irish Feast, The.
Description of Mother Ludwell's Cave, A.
Description of the Morning, A.
Desire and Possession.
Dialogue between an Eminent Lawyer and Dr. Swift, Dean of St. Patrick's.
Dialogue between Captain Tom and Sir Henry Dutton Colt, A.
Dick, a Maggot.
Dick's Variety.
Dingley and Brent.
Directions for a Birthday Song.
Discovery, The.
Dr. Swift to Mr. Pope.
Dr. Swift's Answer to Dr. Sheridan.
Dog and the Thief, The.
Dorinda dreams of dress abed.
Drapier's Hill.
Dunkirk to be Let, *sels.*
Elegy on Dicky and Dolly, An.
Elegy on the Much Lamented Death of Mr. Demar, the Famous Rich Usurer [*or* Man], An.
Elegy On the Supposed Death of Mr. Partridge, the Almanac Maker.
Elephant, The.
Epigram, An: "Friend Rundle fell with grievous bump."
Epigram, An: "In your indignation what mercy appears."
Epigram: "Lord Pam in the church (could [*or* cou'd] you think it) kneeled [*or* kneel'd] down."
Epigram on Fasting.
Epigram on Scolding, An.
Epigram on the Hermitage at Richmond.
Epigram on Wood's Brass Money, An.
Epilogue to a Play for the Benefit of the Weavers in Ireland, An.
Epistle upon an Epistle, An.
Excellent New Ballad, An.
Excellent New Song, An.
Excellent New Song on a Seditious Pamphlet, An.
Excellent New Song upon His Grace Our Good Lord Archbishop of Dublin, An.
Fable of Midas, The.
Fable of the Bitches, The.
Fable of the Widow and Her Cat, A.
Faggot, The.
Famous Prediction of Merlin, A, *sels.*

First Ode of the Second Book of Horace Paraphrased and Addressed to Richard Steele, Esq, The.
First of April, The.
From Dr. Swift to Dr. Sheridan.
Furniture of a Woman's Mind, The.
George Nim-Dan-Dean, Esq. to Mr. Sheridan.
George Nim-Dan-Dean's Invitation to Mr. Thomas Sheridan.
Grand Question Debated, The.
Hardship Put upon Ladies, The.
Helter Skelter.
His Grace's Answer to Jonathan.
History of Vanbrug's House, The.
Holyhead. September 25, 1727.
Horace, Book I, Ode XIV.
Horace, Epistle VII, Book I: Imitated and Addressed to the Earl of Oxford.
Horace, Lib. 2, Sat. 6.
In pity to the emptying town.
In Sickness.
Ireland.
Journal of a Modern Lady, The.
Judas.
Lady Acheson Weary of the Dean.
Lady's Dressing Room, The.
Left-Handed Letter to Dr. Sheridan, A.
Letter from Dean Swift to Dean Smedley, A.
Letter to the Reverend Dr. Sheridan, A.
Libel on the Reverend Dr. Delany and His Excellency John, Lord Carteret.
Life and Genuine Character of Dr Swift, The.
Lines from Cadenus to Vanessa.
Lines to Pope.
Love Song in the Modern Taste, A.
Mad Mullinix and Timothy.
Mary the Cook-Maid's Letter to Dr. Sheridan.
Mr. Jason Hassard, a Woolen Draper in Dublin.
Mrs. Harris's Petition.
My Lady's Lamentation and Complaint against the Dean.
New Year's Gift for Bec, A.
Occasioned by Sir William Temple's Late Illness and Recovery.
Ode to Dr. William Sancroft.
Ode to the Athenian Society.
Ode to the Honourable Sir William Temple.
Ode to the King.
On a Printer's Being Sent to Newgate.
On a Very Old Glass.
On Burning a Dull Poem.
On Censure.
On Cutting Down the Old Thorn at Market Hill.
On Dan Jackson's Picture.
On Dr. Rundle.
On Dreams.
On His Own Deafness.
On Lord Carteret's Arms.
On Mr. Pulteney Being Put Out of the Council.
On Mrs. Biddy Floyd.
On Noisy Tom.
On Paddy's Character of "The Intelligencer."
On Poetry: a Rhapsody.
On Psyche.
On Reading Dr. Young's Satires.
On Seeing Verses Written upon Windows in Inns.
On Stephen Duck, the Thresher, and Favourite Poet.
On the Archbishop of Cashel and Bettesworth.
On the Burning of Whitehall in 1698.
On the Collar of Mrs. Dingley's Lap-Dog.
On the Five Ladies at Sot's Hole, with the Doctor at Their Head.
On the Irish Bishops.
On the Irish Club.
On the Little House by the Churchyard of Castleknock.
On the Words "Brother Protestants and Fellow Christians."
On Wisdom's Defeat in a Learned Debate.
On Wood the Ironmonger.
Panegyric on the Dean, A.
Panegyric on the Reverend Dean Swift, A.
Paper book is sent by Boyle, A.

Parson's Case, The.
Part of a Summer, The.
Part of the Ninth Ode of the Fourth Book of Horace.
Pastoral Dialogue, A.
Pastoral Dialogue between Richmond Lodge and Marble Hill, A.
Peace and Dunkirk.
Pethox the Great.
Phyllis [or Phillis] [or Progress of Love, The].
Place of the Damned [or Damn'd], The.
Poetical Epistle to Dr. Sheridan, A.
Portrait from the Life, A.
Power of Time, The.
Probatur Aliter.
Problem, The.
Progress of Beauty, The.
Progress of Marriage, The.
Progress of Poetry, The.
Prometheus.
Quibbling Elegy on the Worshipful Judge Boat, A.
Quiet Life and a Good Name, A.
Receipt to Restore Stella's Youth, A.
Revolution at Market Hill, The.
Riddles.
Riddling Letter, A.
Robin and Harry.
Run upon the Bankers, The.
Satire on an Inconstant Lover, A.
Satirical Elegy on the Death of a Late Famous General, A.
Scriblerian Verses.
Serious Poem upon William Wood, A.
Sheridan, a Goose.
Sheridan's Submission.
Simile, A.
Stella at Woodpark.
Stella's Birthday, 1725.
Stella's Birthday ([March 13,] 1727).
Stella's Birthday (1723).
Stella's Birthday; Written in the Year 1718[/9].
Storm, The.
Strephon and Chloe.
Swift to Sheridan.
Three Epigrams.
Tim and the Fables.
To a Friend Who Had Been Much Abused in Many Inveterate Libels.
To a Lady.
To Betty the Grisette.
To Charles Ford, Esq. on His Birthday.
To Dean Swift.
To Dr. Delany, on the Libels Writ against Him.
To Dr. Helsham.
To Dr. Sheridan.
To His Grace the Archbishop of Dublin.
To Janus.
To Lord Harley, since Earl of Oxford, on His Marriage.
To Mr. Congreve.
To Mr. Delany.
To Mr. Gay.
To Mr. Harley's Surgeon.
To Mr. Sheridan, upon His Verse, Written in Circles.
To Mrs. Houghton of Bormount.
To Quilca.
To Stella.
To Stella on Her Birthday, Written AD 1721–2.
To Stella, Visiting Me in My Sickness.
To Stella, Who Collected and Transcribed His Poems.
To the Earl of Oxford, Late Lord Treasurer.
To the Earl of Peterborough.
To Thomas Sheridan.
Toland's Invitation to Dismal to Dine with the Calves' Head Club.
Tom Mullinex and Dick.
Town Eclogue, A.
Traulus.
True and Faithful Inventory of the Goods Belonging to Dr. Swift, Vicar of Laracor; upon Lending His House to the Bishop of Meath, until His Own Was Built [or till His Palace Was Rebuilt], A.

Twelve Articles.
Upon Four Dismal Stories in the Doctor's Letter.
Upon the Horrid Plot Discovered by Harlequin the Bishop of Rochester's French Dog.
Upon the South Sea Project.
Vanbrug's House.
Verses from Quilca.
Verses Left in a Window of Dublin Castle.
Verses Made for the Women Who Cry Apples, etc.
Verses Made in Swift's Sleep.
Verses Occasioned by the Sudden Drying Up of St. Patrick's Well near Trinity College, Dublin.
Verses on I Know Not What.
Verses on the Death of Dr. Swift, D.S.P.D.
Verses on the Revival of the Order of the Bath.
Verses on the Upright Judge.
Verses Said to Be Written on the Union.
Verses Spoken Extempore by Dean Swift on His Curate's Complaint of Hard Duty.
Verses Wrote in a Lady's Ivory Table-Book.
Virtues of Sid Hamet the Magician's Rod, The.
When Mrs. Welch's chimney smokes.
Whitshed's Motto on His Coach.
Windsor Prophecy, The.
Wood, an Insect.
Yahoo's Overthrow, The.

Swinburne, Algernon Charles (1837–1909)
After Death.
Anactoria.
At Eleusis.
Atalanta in Calydon, sels.
August.
Ballad of Burdens, A.
Ballad of Death, A.
Ballad of Life, A.
Before Parting.
Christmas Carol, A: "Three damsels in the queen's chamber."
Hendecasyllabics.
In The Orchard.
Interlude, An.
Itylus.
Kissing Her Hair.
Laus Veneris.
Leave-taking, A.
Leper, The.
Les Noyades.
Lyke-Wake Song, A.
Masque of Queen Bersabe, The.
May Janet.
Old Saying, An.
Phaedra.
Sapphics.
Sundew, The.
Triumph of Time, The.

Sze, Arthur (b. 1950)
Alba.
Ansel Adams Card, The.
Antares.
Apache Plume.
Aphrodisiac, The.
Archipelago.
Axis, The.
Axolotl.
Before Completion.
Black Java Pepper.
Black Lightning.
Brueghel.
Cedar Fires.
Chance, The.
Cloud Chamber, The.
Cornucopia, The.
Corona, The.
Day Can Become a Zen Garden of Raked Sand, The.
Dazzled.
Diamond Point, The.
Do Not Speak Keresan to a Mescalero Apache.
Early Autumn.
Edna Bay.
Empty Words.
Every Where and Every When.
Evil Grigri.

Execution of Maximilian, The.
Fauve.
Fern, Coal, Diamond.
Flower Path, The.
Forget Fez.
From the Rooftop.
Frost.
Great Square Has No Corners, A.
Great White Shark, The.
Halibut, The.
He Will Come to My Funeral with a White
   Flower.
Here.
Horse Face.
Ice Floe.
Impressions of the New Mexico Legislature.
In Your Honor.
June Ghazal.
Juniper Fires.
Kaiseki.
Kayaking at Night on Tomales Bay.
Keokea.
Knife at the Jugular.
Lament: "Let me pick / olives in the
   moonlight."
Leaves of a Dream Are the Leaves of an
   Onion, The.
Li Po.
Listening to a Broken Radio.
Los Alamos Museum, The.
Lupine.
Magnetized.
Metastasis.
Miracles.
Mistaking Water Hemlock for Parsley.
Moenkopi.
Moment of Creation, The.
Moon Is a Diamond, The.
Morning Shutters.
Murmur, The.
Mushroom Hunting in the Jemez Mountains.
Negative, The.
Network, The.
New Wave.
Noah's / Dove.
North to Taos.
Nothing Can Heal the Severed Nerves of a
   Hand?
Olive Grove, The.
Olive Night.
Oolong.
Opal, The.
Original Memory.
Owl, The.
Parallax.
Pentimento.
Piranhas.
Pouilly-Fuissé.
Pulse, The.
Rattlesnake Glyph.
Red Octopus.
Redshifting Web, The.
Rehearsal, The.
Renga: "We hunger for the iridescent shine of
   an abalone shell."
Shapes of Leaves, The.
Shooting Star.
Shuttle.
Silence, The.
Silk Road, The.
Silver Trade, The.
Singer with Eyes of Sand, A.
Six Persimmons.
Slanting Light.
Sliding Away.
Solderer, The.
Sound Lag.
Splash, Flow.
Spring Snow.
Standing on an Alder Bridge over a Creek.
Strawberries in Wooden Bowls.
Streamers.
String Diamond, The.
Taoist Painter, The.
Ten Thousand to One.
Three A.M., in Winter.

Throwing Salt on a Path.
To a Composer.
Tsankawi.
Unnamable River, The.
Viewing Photographs of China.
Waking, The.
Wang Wei.
Wasabi.
Weather Shifts, The.
Whiteout.
Wood Whittler, The.
Written the Day I Was to Begin a Residency at
   the State Penitentiary.
X Ray.

Szymborska, Wisława (b. 1923)
Acrobat, The.
Advertisement.
Allegro Ma Non Troppo.
Archeology.
Atlantis.
Autotomy.
Beheading.
Birds Returning.
Birthday.
Bodybuilders' Contest.
Born.
Brueghel's Two Monkeys.
Byzantine Mosaic, A.
Cat in an Empty Apartment.
Cave, The.
Century's Decline, The.
Children of Our Age.
Children of Our Era.
Circus Animals.
Classic, The.
Clochard.
Clothes.
Clouds.
Coloratura.
Commemoration.
Conversation with a Rock.
Conversation with a Stone.
Could Have.
Dinosaur Skeleton.
Discovery.
Dream, A.
Dream of the Old Tortoise, The.
Drinking Wine.
Elegiac Calculation.
End and Beginning.
End and the Beginning, The.
Evaluation of an Unwritten Poem.
Experiment.
Family Album.
Frozen Motion.
Funeral.
Going Home.
Great Man's House, A.
Hatred.
Hermitage.
Hitler's First Photograph.
I am too close for him to dream about me.
In Abundance.
In Broad Daylight.
In Heraclitus' River.
In Praise of Dreams.
In Praise of Feeling Bad about Yourself.
In Praise of My Sister.
Interview with a Child.
Into the Ark.
Joy of Writing, The.
Landscape.
Large Number, A.
Leaving the Cinema.
Letters of the Dead, The.
Lot's Wife.
Love at First Sight.
Man's Household, A.
May 16, 1973.
Maybe All This.
Medieval Miniature, A.
Miracle Fair.
Moment in Troy, A.
Museum.
Negative.
No End of Fun.

No Title Required.
Note, A.
Notes from a Nonexistent Himalayan
   Expedition.
Nothing nothinged itself for me as well.
Nothing Twice.
Nothing's a Gift.
On Death, without Exaggeration.
On the Banks of the Styx.
One Version of Events.
Onion, The.
Openness.
Opinion on the Question of Pornography, An.
Our Ancestors' Short Lives.
Palaeolithic Fertility Fetish, A.
Parting with a View.
People on the Bridge.
People on the Bridge, The.
Pi.
Pietà.
Plotting with the Dead.
Poem in Honor Of, A.
Poetry Reading.
Psalm: "How leaky are the borders of man-
   made states!"
Psalm: "Oh, the leaky boundaries of man-made
   states!"
Pursuit.
Railroad Station, The.
Reality Demands.
Returning Birds.
Rubens' Women.
Séance.
Seen from Above.
Silence of Plants, The.
Sky.
Slapstick.
Smiles.
Soliloquy for Cassandra.
Some Like Poetry.
Some People.
Speech at the Lost and Found, A.
Stage Fright.
Starvation Camp at Jasło.
Still.
Suicide's Room, The.
Surplus.
Tale Begun, A.
Tarsier.
Terrorist, He's Watching, The.
Thank-You Note, A.
Theatre Impressions.
Thomas Mann.
Torture.
Tortures.
Tower of Babel, The.
Travel Elegy.
True Love.
Turn of the Century, The.
Under a Certain Little Star.
Under One Small Star.
Unexpected Meeting, An.
Utopia.
View with a Grain of Sand.
Vocabulary.
Voices.
Warning.
Water.
We knew the world backwards and forwards.
We're Extremely Fortunate.
Word on Statistics, A.
Writing a Résumé.

T

Taliesin (*fl.* c.550)
Song of Taliesin.
Tasso, Torquato (1544–95)
Amore Fuggitivo.
Camoëns, he the accomplished and the good.
White moon, star-strewn sky.
Tate, Allen (1899–1979)
Aeneas at New York.
Aeneas at Washington.

Anabasis, The.
Ancestors, The.
Art.
Battle of Murfreesboro.
Bizarre.
Bored to Choresis.
Brief Message.
Buried Lake, The.
Calidus Juventa?
Causerie.
Cold Pastoral.
Credo in Intellectum Videntem.
Cross, The.
Cul-de-Sac.
Day.
Death of Little Boys.
Debt.
Ditty: "Moon will run all consciences to cover,
   The."
Dusk.
Eager Youths to a Dead Girl.
Eagle, The.
Eclogue of the Liberal and the Poet.
Edges.
Elegy for Eugenesis.
Elegy: "No more the white refulgent streets."
Emblems.
Euthanasia.
Eye, The.
Fair Cuirass Shattered.
Farewell Rehearsed.
Flapper, The.
For a Dead Citizen.
Fragment of a Meditation.
Historical Epitaphs.
Hitch Your Wagon to a Star.
Homily.
Horatian Epode to the Duchess of Malfi.
Idiot.
Idyl: "In a valley late bees with whining gold."
Inside and Outside.
Intellectual Detachment.
Ivory Tower, The.
John Milton.
Jubilo.
Last Days of Alice.
Light.
Lityerses.
Long Fingers.
Lycambes Talks to John.
Madness.
Maimed Man, The.
Mary McDonald.
Meaning of Death, The.
Meaning of Life, The.
Mediterranean, The.
Message from Abroad.
Mr. Pope.
More Sonnets at Christmas.
Mother and Son.
Non Omnis Moriar.
Nuptials.
Oath, The.
Ode to Fear.
Ode to Our Young Pro-consuls of the Air.
Ode to the Confederate Dead.
Paradigm, The.
Parthenia.
Pastoral: "Enquiring fields, courtesies, The."
Pauper, A.
Perimeters.
Procession.
Progress of Œnia, The.
Quality of Mercy.
Records.
Red Stains.
Reflections in an Old House.
Resurgam.
Retroduction to American History.
Robber Bridegroom, The.
Seasons of the Soul.
Shadow and Shade.
Sinbad.
Sonnet: "Could I be sure that I shall see the
   day."

Sonnet to Beauty.
Sonnets at Christmas.
Sonnets of the Blood.
Stranger.
Subway, The.
Suicide.
Swimmers, The.
Tercets of the Triad.
These Deathy Leaves.
To a Prodigal Old Maid.
To a Romantic.
To a Romantic Novelist.
To the Lacedemonians.
To the Romantic Traditionists.
Traveller, The.
Trout Map, The.
True Believer.
Twelve, The.
Two Conceits.
Unnatural Love.
Vision Beatific.
William Blake.
Winter Mask.
Wolves, The.

Tate, James (b. 1943)
Absences.
Alfonso Lacklustre.
Alternatives.
Amherst to Easthampton.
Amnesia People.
Ash Manor.
Aunt Edna.
Autumn.
Awkward Silence.
Blue Booby, The.
Blue Spill.
Bluebird Houses.
Book of Lies, The.
Breathing.
Brother of the Unknown Ancient Man.
Bug Sleep.
Chaste Stranger, The.
Coda: "Love is not worth so much."
Coming Down Cleveland Avenue.
Conjuring Roethke.
Constant Defender.
Consumed.
Contagion.
Cycle of Dust.
Deadlines.
Deaf Girl Playing.
Dear Reader.
Delicate Riders, The.
Dime Found in the Snow, A.
Dreamy Cars Graze on the Dewy Boulevard.
Dry Cup.
Eagle Exterminating Company, The.
Earthworks.
End of the Line, The.
Epithalamion for Tyler.
Failed Tribute to the Stonemason of Tor
   House, Robinson Jeffers.
First Lesson.
Five Years Old.
Flight.
For Mother on Father's Day.
Frivolous Blind Death Child.
From the Hole.
Fuck the Astronauts.
Glassy Harbor, The.
Goodtime Jesus.
Grace.
Graveside.
Guide to the Stone Age, The.
Heatstroke.
Horseshoe, The.
Hostile Philharmonic Orchestra, The.
How the Friends Met.
I Take Back All My Kisses.
If It Would All Please Hurry.
If You Would Disappear at Sea.
Images of Little Compton, Rhode Island.
Immortals, The.
In a Motel on Lake Erie.
In a Town for Which I Know No Name.
In the Realm of the Ignition.

Indian Undertaker, The.
Initiation, The.
Interruptions.
Intimidations of an Autobiography.
It's Not the Heat So Much as the Humidity.
Jangling Yarn, A.
Jelka Revisited.
Jo Jo's Fireworks—Next Exit.
Land of Little Sticks, 1945.
Last Days of April, The.
Late Harvest.
Leaping Woman.
Lewis and Clark Overheard in Conversation.
Life of Poetry, The.
List of Famous Hats, The.
Lost Pilot, The.
Man with Wooden Leg Escape Prison.
Manna.
Marfa.
Memo to the Dark Angel.
Mirror, The.
Motorcyclists, The.
Move, The.
My Girl.
My Great Great Etc. Uncle Patrick Henry.
Mystic Moment.
Nature Poem: Demanding Stiff Sentences.
Nausea, Coincidence.
Neighbors.
No Rest for the Gambler.
Nobody's Business.
On the Subject of Doctors.
On the World's Birthday.
Paint 'Til You Faint.
Pet Deer, The.
Pity Ascending with the Fog.
Poem for the Sandman.
Poem: "High in Hollywood Hills a door
   opens."
Poem (I Can't Speak for the Wind).
Poem: "Language was almost impossible in
   those days."
Poem: "Silence that tunnels forever, A."
Poem to Some of my Recent Poems.
President Slumming, The.
Pride's Crossing.
Private Intrigue of Melancholy, The.
Prose Poem.
Radical Departure, A.
Rape in the Engineering Building.
Read the Great Poets.
Reapers of the Water.
Recipe for Sleep.
Rescue.
Responsible Romance, The.
Riven Doggeries.
River's Story.
Rooster.
Sadness of My Neighbors, The.
Saint John of the Cross in Prison.
Same Tits.
Sensitive Ears.
Shadowboxing.
Shy One, The.
Sloops in the Bay.
Smart and Final Iris.
Soup of Venus, The.
South End.
Spring Was Begging to Be Born.
Stella Maris.
Storm.
Success Comes to Cow Creek.
Summer Night.
Tabernacle, The.
Teaching the Ape to Write Poems.
Tell Them Was Here.
Thoughts While Reading *The Sand Reckoner*.
Time X.
To Fuzzy.
Today I Am Falling.
Toward Saint Looey.
Tragedy Comes to the Bad Lands.
Tragedy's Greatest Hits.
Trap, The.
Tryst, The.
Twilight Sustenance Hiatus.

Uncle.
Up Here.
Vagabond, A.
Village 104.
Voyage from Stockholm to Take Advantage of Lower Prices on the Finnish Island of Åland.
Wait for Me.
Waking.
Wedding, A.
Wheelchair Butterfly, The.
When the Nomads Come Over the Hill.
Why I Will Not Get Out of Bed.
Wild Cheese, The.
With a Child All Day.
Yellow Newspaper and a Wooden Leg.
Yonder.

Tate, Nahum (1652–1715)
Absalom and Achitophel, Part 2.
Upon the Author of the following Poem.

Tennyson, Alfred Tennyson, 1st Baron (1809–92)
Audley Court.
Break, Break, Break.
Character, A.
Charge of the Light Brigade, The.
Crossing the Bar.
Daisy, The.
Dead Prophet, The.
Dream of Fair Women, A.
Dying Swan, The.
Eagle, The.
Edwin Morris.
Enoch Arden.
Far-Far-Away.
Farewell, A: "Flow down, cold rivulet, to the sea."
Fatima.
Flower in the Crannied Wall.
Frater Ave Atque Vale.
Golden Year, The.
Hendecasyllabics.
Idylls of the King.
In Memoriam A. H. H.
In the Garden at Swainston.
In the Valley of Cauteretz.
June Bracken and Heather.
Kraken, The.
Lady of Shalott, The.
Locksley Hall.
Locksley Hall Sixty Years After.
Lotus-Eaters, The.
Mariana.
Mariana in the South.
Maud [A Monodrama].
Morte d'Arthur.
Move Eastward, Happy Earth, and Leave.
Northern Farmer: New Style.
Ode on the Death of the Duke of Wellington.
Œnone.
On a Mourner.
Palace of Art, The.
Parnassus.
Prefatory Poem to My Brother's Sonnets.
Princess, The.
Roses on the Terrace, The.
St. Simeon Stylites.
Sir Galahad [or The Purple Heart].
Sir Launcelot and Queen Guinevere.
Spirit Haunts the Year's Last Hours, A.
Supposed Confessions of a Second-rate Sensitive Mind.
Tithonus.
To Alfred Tennyson, My Grandson.
To E. Fitzgerald.
To E.L., on His Travels in Greece.
To J. S. [James Spedding].
To Mary Boyle.
To the Marquis of Dufferin and Ava.
To the Queen.
To the Rev. F. D. Maurice.
To Ulysses.
To Virgil [or Vergil].
To —. With the Following Poem.
Two Voices, The.
Ulysses.
Vision of Sin, The.
Will.

Terry, Lucy (c.1730–1821)
Bars Fight [August 28, 1746].

Theocritus (c.310–c.250 B.C.)
Cyclops, The.
Idylls, sels.

Thomas, Dylan (1914–53)
After the Funeral.
All All and All the Dry Worlds Lever.
Altarwise by Owl-Light.
Among Those Killed in the Dawn Raid Was a Man Aged a Hundred.
And Death Shall Have No Dominion.
Author's Prologue.
Ballad of the Long-legged Bait.
Because the Pleasure-Bird Whistles.
Before I Knocked.
Ceremony after a Fire Raid.
Conversation of Prayer, The.
Deaths and Entrances.
Do Not Go Gentle into That Good Night.
Do You Not Father Me.
Ears in the Turrets Hear.
Elegy: "Too proud to die; broken and blind he died."
Especially When the October Wind.
Fern Hill.
Find Meat on Bones.
Force That Through the Green Fuse Drives the Flower, The.
Foster the Light.
From Love's First Fever to Her Plague.
Grief Ago, A.
Grief Thief of Time.
Hand That Signed the Paper, The.
Here in This Spring.
Hold Hard, These Ancient Minutes in the Cuckoo's Month.
Holy Spring.
How Shall My Animal.
How Soon the Servant Sun.
Hunchback in the Park, The.
I Dreamed My Genesis.
I Fellowed Sleep.
I Have Longed to Move Away.
I, in My Intricate Image.
I Make This in a Warring Absence.
I See the Boys of Summer.
If I Were Tickled by the Rub of Love.
If My Head Hurt a Hair's Foot.
In Country Sleep.
In My Craft or Sullen Art.
In the Beginning.
In the White Giant's Thigh.
Incarnate Devil.
Into Her Lying Down Head.
It Is the Sinner's Dust-Tongued Bell.
Lament: "When I was a windy boy and a bit."
Lie Still, Sleep Becalmed.
Light Breaks Where No Sun Shines.
Love in the Asylum.
My Hero Bares His Nerves.
My World Is Pyramid.
Not from This Anger.
Now.
O Make Me a Mask.
On a Wedding Anniversary.
On No Work of Words.
On the Marriage of a Virgin.
Once below a Time.
Once It Was the Colour of Saying.
Our Eunuch Dreams.
Out of the Sighs.
Over Sir John's Hill.
Poem in October.
Poem on His Birthday.
Process in the Weather of the Heart, A.
Refusal to Mourn the Death, by Fire, of a Child in London, A.
Saint About to Fall, A.
Seed-at-Zero, The.
Shall Gods Be Said to Thump The Clouds.
Should Lanterns Shine.
Spire Cranes, The.
Then Was My Neophyte.
There Was a Saviour.
This Bread I Break.

This Side of the Truth.
To-day, This Insect.
To Others than You.
Tombstone Told When She Died, The.
Twenty-four Years.
Unluckily for a Death.
Vision and Prayer.
Was There a Time.
We Lying by Seasand.
When All My Five and Country Senses See.
When I woke.
When, Like a Running Grave.
When Once the Twilight Locks No Longer.
Where Once the Waters of Your Face.
Why East Wind Chills.
Winter's Tale, A.

Thomas of Celano (1200?–55?)
Dies Irae.

Thomson, James (1700–48)
Complaint on the Miseries of Life, A.
Upon Happiness.

Thoreau, Henry David (1817–62)
Ah, 'tis in vain the peaceful din.
All things are current found.
All things decay.
Among the worst of men that ever lived.
And once again.
Any fool can make a rule.
Assabet, The.
At midnight's hour I raised my head.
Atlantides, The.
Away! away! away! away!
Behold these flowers.
Better wait.
Between the traveller and the setting sun.
Bluebirds, The.
"Book of Gems," The.
Breeze's Invitation, The.
Brother where dost thou dwell?
But now "no war nor battle's sound."
Chicadee, The.
Cliffs.
Cock-crowing.
Conscience is instinct bred in the house.
Coward ever sings no song, The.
Death cannot come too soon.
Deeds of king and meanest hedger, The.
Delay.
Delay in Friendship.
Departure, The.
Die and be buried who will.
Each more melodious note I hear.
Each summer sound.
Earth, The.
Ep on a Good Man.
Epitaph: "Here lies an honest man."
Epitaph on an Engraver.
Epitaph on Pursy.
Ep[itaph] on the World.
Evening Wind, The.
Except, returning, by the Marlboro.
Fair Haven ("When little hills like lambs did skip").
Fair Haven ("When Winter fringes every bough").
Fall of the Leaf, The ("Grown tired of this rank summer's wealth").
Far oer The bow.
Farewell.
Fisher's Son, The.
Fog.
For though the eaves [or Caves] were rabitted [or rabbeted or rabbited].
Forever in my dream & in my morning thought.
Freshet, The.
Friend, The.
Friends— / They cannot help.
Friendship ("I think awhile of Love").
Friendship ("Let such pure hate").
Friendship ("Now we are partners").
Funeral Bell, The.
Godfrey of Boulogne.
Good how can we trust?, The.
Great Friend.
Great God I ask thee for no meaner pelf.

Greater is the depth of sadness.
Greece.
Guido's Aurora.
Have ye no work for a man to do.
He knows no change who knows the true.
Hero, The.
How little curious is man.
I am bound, I am bound, for a distant shore.
I am the Autumnal sun.
I am the little Irish boy.
I arose before light.
I do not fear my thoughts will die.
I have rolled near some other spirits path.
I have seen some frozenfaced connecticut.
I knew a man by sight.
I love a careless streamlet.
I mark the summer's swift decline.
I sailed up a river with a pleasant wind.
I saw a delicate flower had grown up two feet
 high.
I seek the Present Time.
I was born upon thy bank, river.
I was made erect and lone.
I will obey the strictest law of love.
If from your price ye will not swerve.
I'm contented you should stay.
I'm guided in the darkest night.
I'm not alone.
I'm thankful that my life doth not deceive.
In Adams fall.
In days of yore, tis said, the swimming alder.
In the busy streets, domains of trade.
In the East fames are won.
Independence.
Inspiration ("If thou wilt but stand").
Inspiration ("Whate'er we leave to God").
Inward Morning, The.
It is a real place.
I've heard my neighbor's pump at night.
I've searched my faculties around.
I've seen ye, sisters, on the mountain-side.
Just Made Perfect, The.
Last night as I lay gazing with shut eyes.
Life.
Life is a summer's day.
Love.
Loves Farewell.
Low in the eastern sky.
Man Man is the Devil.
Manhood.
May Morning.
Men say they know many things.
Methinks that by a strict behavior.
Moon moves up her smooth and sheeny path,
 The.
Moon now rises to her absolute rule, The.
Moon, The.
Morning.
Mountains in the Horizon, The.
Music.
My Boots.
My friends, my noble friends, know ye.
My friends, why should we live?
My ground is high.
My life has been the poem I would have writ.
My love must be as free.
Nature.
Needles of the pine, The.
Noon.
Not unconcerned Wachusett rears his head.
Offer, The.
Old Marlborough Road, The.
Old meeting-house bell.
On fields oer which the reaper's hand has
 passed.
On Ponkawtasset, since, we took our way.
On shoulders whirled in some eccentric orbit.
On the Sun Coming Out in the Afternoon.
Only the slave knows of the slave.
Our Country.
Peal of the Bells, The.
Pens to mend, and hands to guide.
Poet's Delay, The.
Poverty.
Pray to what earth does this sweet cold belong.
Rabbit leaps, The.

Respectable folks, The.
Rosa Sanguinea, The.
Rumors from an Aeolian Harp.
Salmon Brook.
Shrike, The.
Sic Vita.
Sluggish smoke curls up from some deep dell,
 The.
Sometimes I hear the veery's clarion.
Soul's Season, The.
Stanzas: "Nature doth have her dawn each
 day."
Strange that so many fickle gods, as fickle as
 the weather.
Such near aspects had we.
Such water do the gods distill.
Sympathy.
'T will soon appear if we but look.
Tall Ambrosia.
Tell me ye wise ones if ye can.
That Phaeton of our day.
Thaw, The.
Then spend an age in whetting thy desire.
They who prepare my evening meal below.
Thou dusky spirit of the wood.
'Tis very fit the ambrosia of the gods.
To a Marsh Hawk in Spring.
To a Stray Fowl.
To day I climbed a handsome rounded hill.
To Edith.
To the Comet.
To the Mountains.
Travelling.
True kindness is a pure divine affinity.
Truth—Goodness—Beauty—those celestial
 thrins.
'Twas thirty years ago.
Until at length the north winds blow.
Vireo, The.
Voyagers Song.
Wait not till I invite thee, but observe.
Wait not till slaves pronounce the word.
Walden.
We see the *planet* fall.
We should not mind if on our ear there fell.
What's the railroad to me?
When breathless noon hath paused on hill and
 vale.
When in some cove I lie.
When the toads begin to ring.
When with pale cheek and sunken eye I sang.
Where I have been.
Where'er thou sail'st who sailed with me.
Who equallest the coward's haste.
Who hears the parson.
Who sleeps by day and walks by night.
Why toll the bell today.
Within the circuit of this plodding life.
Ye do command me to all virtue ever.
Yet let us Thank the purblind race.
You Boston folks & Roxbury people.
You must not only aim aright.

Tibullus (Albius Tibullus) (c.59–c.19 B.C.)
Elegies, *sels.*
Sulpicia to Cerinthus.

Tibullus, Albius *See* **Tibullus**
Tisdall, William (1669–1735)
Tom Pun-Sibi Metamorphosed: Or, The Giber
 Gibed.
Tollas, Tibor (b. 1920)
Prison Poem.
They've Blocked Every Window.
Tomlinson, Charles (b. 1927)
Abiquiu.
Above Carrara.
Above Manhattan.
Above the Rio Grande.
Adam.
Aesthetic.
After a Death.
After the Storm.
Against Extremity.
Against Portraits.
Against Travel.
Albuquerque.

All Afternoon.
Anecdote.
Annunciation.
Antecedents.
Apparition, The.
Appearance.
Aqueduct.
Ararat.
Arch, The.
Archer, The.
Ariadne and the Minotaur.
Arizona Desert.
Arizona Highway.
Arrival, The.
Arroyo Hondo.
Arroyo Seco.
Ars Poetica.
Art of Poetry, The.
Assassin.
At a Glance.
At Barstow.
At Dawn.
At Delft.
At Holwell Farm.
At Saint Mary's Church.
At Sant' Antimo.
At Stoke.
At the Autumn Equinox.
At the Edge.
At the Hill Fort.
At the Trade Center.
At Trotsky's House.
At Wells: Polyphony.
Atlantic, The.
Autumn.
Autumn Piece.
Awakening, The.
Backward Glance, A.
Barometer, The.
Barque Nornen.
Bead, The.
Beautiful Aeroplane, The.
Beech, The ("Blizzards have brought down").
Beech, The ("Nakedly muscular").
Beethoven Attends the C Minor Seminar.
Before the Concert.
Before the Dance.
Below Tintern.
Biography of the Author: A Cento, A.
Black Brook.
Black Nude.
Blade, The.
Blaubeuren.
Bone.
Bootblack, The.
Bridges.
Brilliant Silence.
Butterflies, The.
Byzantium.
Canal.
Carrara Revisited.
Carscape.
Casarola.
Castle, The.
Catacomb.
Cavern, The.
Ceci n'est pas une Pipe.
Cézanne at Aix.
Chaconne for Unaccompanied Violin.
Chance.
Chances of Rhyme, The.
Charlotte Corday.
Château de Muzot.
Chestnut Avenue: at Alton House, The.
Chief Standing Water.
Churchyard Wall, The.
Civilities of Lamplight.
Class.
Cloud Change.
Clouds.
Cochiti.
Comedy.
Compact, The: at Volterra.
Composition.
Confluence.
Consolations for Double Bass.

Conspiracy, The.
Constitution Day.
Couplet.
Cradock Newton: From an Epitaph.
Crane, The.
Cronkhite Beach.
Crossing Brooklyn Ferry.
Crow.
Curtain Call.
Da Capo.
Daisies, The.
Dates: Penkhull New Road.
De Sole.
Death in the Desert, A.
Death in Venice.
Death of Elizabeth Grieve, The.
Death of the Infanta, The.
Death of Will, The.
Departure.
Descartes and the Stove.
Desert Autumn.
Dialectic.
Dialogue.
Discrepancies.
Distinctions.
Doggerel for My Seventieth Birthday. A
Door in the Wall, The.
Door, The.
Double Rainbow, The.
Down From Colonnata.
Dream, A.
Dream, The.
Drive.
During Rain.
Eden.
Eight Observations on the Nature of Eternity.
Elegy for Henry Street.
Elemental.
Embassy.
Encounter.
End, The.
Epilogue, The: "It was a dream delivered the
   epilogue."
Epitaph: "Enamoured by / Brevity in method."
Etruria Vale.
Event.
Face and Image.
Far Point.
Farewell to Van Gogh.
Faring, The.
Farmer's Wife: at Fostons Ash, The.
Fiascherino.
Fire in a Dark Landscape.
Fireflies.
Flame.
Flight, The.
Flood, The.
Flute Music.
For a Godchild.
For A Granddaughter, sels.
For Danton.
For Miriam.
Fountain.
Four Kantian Lyrics.
Fox Gallery, The.
Fox, The.
Foxes' Moon.
From the Motorway.
Frondes Agrestes.
Frost.
Fruit, for sculpture.
Gap, The.
Garland for Thomas Eakins, A.
Gate, The.
Geese Going South.
Geneva Restored.
Giovanni Diodati.
Given Grace, A.
Glacier, The.
Gladstone Street.
Glass Grain.
Gli Scafari.
Gorge, The.
Gossamers, The.
Green Quinces.
Greeting, The.

Gull.
Hacienda.
Hand at Callow Hill Farm, The.
Harvest.
Harvest Festival: at Ozleworth.
Hawks.
Hawthorn in Trent Vale, The.
Hay.
Head Hewn with an Axe.
Headland, The.
Hedgerows.
Hero Sandwiches.
Hesitation, The.
High Summer.
Hill, The.
Hill Walk.
History.
History of a Malady.
Hokusai on the Trent.
House in the Quarry, The.
How Far.
How Still the Hawk.
Hyphens.
Ice Cream at Blauenberg.
Icos.
Idrigill.
Idyll: "Door: / PER L'UNIVERSO / is what it
   says, A."
Images of Perfection.
Impalpabilities, The.
In a Brooklyn Park.
In April.
In Arden.
In Connecticut.
In December ("Cattle are crowding").
In December ("Fog, as it enters").
In Defence of Metaphysics.
In Longfellow's Library.
In March.
In Memoriam Thomas Hardy.
In Memory of George Oppen.
In Michoacán.
In October.
In the Balance.
In the Borghese Gardens.
In the Estuary.
In the Fullness of Time.
In the Intensity of Final Light.
In the Studio.
In the Ward.
In Verdi Square.
In Winter Woods.
Insistence of Things, The.
Instance, The.
Instead of an Essay.
Into Distance.
Jam Trap, The.
Jemez.
John Maydew or The Allotment.
Journey, The.
Jubilación.
Juliet's Garden.
Lacoste.
Lament for Doormen.
Landing, The.
Las Trampas U. S. A.
Last Days of the Miser.
Last Judgement.
Last of Night, The.
Le Musée Imaginaire.
Legend ("Hill-top schloss, The").
Legend ("Midas eyes").
Lesson, The.
Letter from Costa Brava.
Letter to Uehata.
Letters from Amherst.
Lighthouse, The.
Lines.
Lines Written in the Euganean Hills.
Little Night Music, A.
Littleton Whale, The.
Logic.
Los Pobrecitos.
Macduff.
Machiavelli in Exile.
Mackinnon's Boat.

Maillol.
Maine Winter.
Maintenant.
Marat Dead.
Marine.
Marl Pits, The.
Matachines, The.
Mausoleum, The.
Meditation on John Constable, A.
Mediterranean, The.
Mélisande.
Melody.
Metamorphosis, The.
Mictlantecuhtli.
Midlands.
Miracle of the Bottle and the Fishes, The.
Mirror in the Roadway, The.
Misprint.
Mr. Brodsky.
Mistlines.
Moment, The.
Montage.
More Foreign Cities.
Morwenna's Cliff.
Movements.
Mushrooms.
Music's Trinity.
Nature Poem.
Near and the Far, The.
Near Ceibwr.
Near Corinium.
Near Hartland.
Near York.
Night at the Opera, A.
Night Fishers.
Night-Piece: The Near and the Far.
Night Ride.
Night-Train, The.
Night Transfigured.
Nine Variations in a Chinese Winter Setting.
Northern Spring.
Oaxaca Bus, The.
Object in a Setting.
Observation of Facts.
October.
Ode to Arnold Schoenberg.
Of Beginning Light.
Of Lady Grange.
Of the Winter Ball Game.
Old Man at Valdez.
Old Man's Beard.
On a Landscape by Li Ch'eng.
On a May Night.
On a Mexican Straw Christ.
On a Pig's Head.
On Eleventh Street.
On Madison.
On the Hall at Stowey.
On the Mountain.
On the Principle of Blowclocks.
On the Tlacolula Bus.
On Water.
One Day of Autumn.
One World.
Operation, The.
Oppositions.
Or Traveller's Joy.
Order of Saying, The.
Orion over Farne.
Over Brooklyn Bridge.
Over Elizabeth Bridge: a Circumvention.
Oxen: Ploughing at Fiesole.
Palm of the Hand.
Paring the Apple.
Paris in Sixty-Nine.
Parsnips.
Perfection, The.
Picking Mushrooms by Moonlight.
Picture of J. T. in a Prospect of Stone, The.
Plaza, The.
Poem for My Father.
Poem: "It falls onto my page like rain."
Poem: "Muscles which move the eyeballs,
   The."
Poem: "Space / window / that looks into
   itself."

Poem: "Upended, it crouches on broken limbs."
Poem: "Wakening with the window over fields."
Ponte Veneziano.
Poolville, N.Y.
Portobello Carnival 1973.
Portrait in Stone.
Portrait of Mrs. Spaxton.
Portrait of the Artist I.
Portrait of the Artist II.
Portugeuse Pieces, *sels.*
Prelude, A.
Process, A.
Programme Note.
Prometheus.
Promise, The.
Prose Poem.
Providence.
Quarai.
Quarry, The.
Question, The ("Having misread the house, What").
Question, The ("Curve of lamps").
Race, The.
Recompense, The.
Reeds.
Reflections.
Remembering Williams.
Request, The.
Response to Hopkins.
Retrospect, A: 1951-91.
Return, The.
Return to Hinton.
Revolution Piazza Di Spagna.
Rhenish Winter.
Rhymes.
Rich, The.
Ritornello.
Roe Deer, The.
Rose for Janet, A.
Rose-hips.
Rower.
Rubh An' Dunain.
Ruin, The.
Rumour.
San Fruttuoso.
Santa Maria delle Nevi.
Saving the Appearances.
Scar, The.
Sconset.
Scream, The.
Sea Change.
Sea is Open to the Light, The.
Sea Poem.
Second Song.
Self-Portrait: David, A.
Sense of Distance, A.
Severnside.
Shadow, The.
Shaft, The.
Shell, The.
Ship's Waiters.
Shout, The.
Siena in Sixty-Eight.
Sight and Flight.
Skullshapes.
Sky Writing.
Small Action Poem.
Snapshot.
Snow Fences, The.
Snow Signs.
Song: "To enter the real."
Sound of Time, The.
Spring Symphony, The.
Square, The.
Stair, The.
Steel.
Stone Speech.
Stone Walls: at Chew Magna.
Suggestions for the Improvement of a Sunset.
Swimming Chenango Lake.
Tarquinia.
Tax Inspector, The.
Teotihuacán.
Terminal Tramps.

Their Voices Rang.
Theory of Regress.
Thief's Journal, The.
Three Wagnerian Lyrics.
Through Binoculars.
Through Closed Eyes.
Thunder in Tuscany.
Tiger Skull.
To Be Engraved on the Skull of a Cormorant.
To Ivor Gurney.
To See the Heron.
To Vasko Popa In Rome.
Tout Entouré de Mon Regard.
Track of the Deer, The.
Tramontana at Lerici.
Translating the Birds.
Tree.
Tree, The ("I had seen a tree before").
Tree, The ("This child, shovelling away").
Two Poems on titles proposed by Octavio and Marie José Paz.
Two Views of Two Ghost Towns.
Under the Bridge.
Under the Moon's Reign.
Up at La Serra.
Urlicht.
Ute Mountain.
Valestrieri.
Valle de Oaxaca.
Van Gogh.
Variant on a Scrap of Conversation.
Variation on Paz.
Venice.
View, The.
Walking to Bells.
Walks.
Way In, The.
Way of a World, The.
Weathercocks, The.
Weatherman.
Weeper in Jalisco.
Well, The ("Leaning on").
Well, The ("We loosen the coping-stone").
What Virginia Said.
Whip, The.
White Van, The.
Wind.
Windshield, The.
Winter.
Winter Encounters.
Winter Journey, *sels.*
Winter-Piece.
Witnesses, The.
Word in Edgeways, A.
Words for the Madrigalist.
Wrestlers on the Vase, The.
Writing on Sand.
Zipangu.

Tommaseo, Niccolò (1802–74)
Farewell, A.
Young Girl, The.

Tracey, Michael
Critical Minute, The, *sels.*

Trakl, Georg (1887–1914)
De Profundis.
Helian.
Rats, The.
Sleep.
Trumpets.
Winter Night, A.

Tranströmer, Tomas (b. 1931)
Name, The.

Tsang, K'o Chia (b. 1905)
Three Generations.

Ts'un Hsu Li (*fl.* 10th cent.)
In Dream's Wake.

Tsvetayeva [*or* Tsvetaeva], Marina Ivanovna (1892–1941)
I will win you away from every earth, from every sky.
Seeing off the beloved ones, I.

Tu Fu (712–76)
Adviser to the Court.
Banishment.
Déjeuner sur l'herbe.

For the Prince in Exile.
Lo Yu Park.
Meandering River Poems, The.
My Home Town.
Profile of a Lady.
Testament.
Thwarted.
To Li Po.
Tu Fu to Li Po.
Visit.
Visit in Winter to the Temple of His Mystical Majesty, A.

U

Uhland, Johann Ludwig *See* **Uhland, Ludwig**
Uhland, Ludwig (Johann Ludwig Uhland) (1787–1862)
Boy's Death, The.
Good Comrade, The.
Landlady's Daughter, The.

Ungaretti, Giuseppe (1888–1970)
Meditations on Death.

Unknown
Alba Innominata.
Anagram, An.
Another.
Another ["Art thou some individual of a kind"].
Another ["At three-score winters' end I died"].
Another ["Miser, traversing his house, A"].
Another of the Same Nature, Made Since.
Another ["Painter, this likeness is too strong"].
Another ["Take to thy bosom, gentle earth, a swain"].
Another to Mrs. Anne Bradstreet, Author of this Poem.
Answer, The [By the Gentleman of the Navy].
Art Thou That She.
Ballade de Marguerite.
Ballata: Of True and False Singing.
Battle of Brunanburh.
By Heraclides.
Circumstance.
Dies Iræ (The Day of Wrath).
Do Not, Oh, Do Not Prize.
Dole of the King's Daughter, The.
Elegy on the Deplorable Death of Mr. Thomas Sheridan, Author of *Alexander's Overthrow, or, The Downfall of Babylon*, Who Departed This Mortal Life on Thursday the 8th of March, 1721/22, An.
Epistle in Behalf of Our Irish Poets to the Right Hon. Lady C——t, An, *sels.*
For pearls, plunge in the sea.
Four Sambas.
From the Persian (1).
Geordie [An Old Ballad].
Homeric Hymns, *sels.*
I cannot wonder at Apollo now.
I have come home. Fortune and Hope, goodbye!
Imitation of Anacreon's Grasshopper, Applied to Mr. T. S., Commonly Known by the Name of Skeleton, An.
In Praise of the Author, Mistress Anne Bradstreet, Virtue's True and Lively Pattern.
John of Tours.
Jubilemus omnes una Deo nostro qui creavit omnia.
Letter to Tom Punsibi, Occasioned by Reading His Excellent Farce, Called *Alexander's Overthrow, or, The Downfall of Babylon*, A.
Maid, The.
My Father's Close.
Myself and Pangur.
Names of the Hare, The.
New Jingle on Tom Dingle, A.
On a Battered Beauty.
On a Good Man.
On a Thief.
On a True Friend.
On an Ugly Fellow.
On Envy.

On Female Inconstancy.
On Flatterers.
On Hermocratia.
On Invalids.
On Late-acquired Wealth *or* Riches.
On Miltiades.
On Niobe.
On Pedigree.
On the Astrologers.
On the Grasshopper.
On the Reed.
Only three things lengthen life.
Pere Bouhours' Fountain Made Muddy by the
     Translator.
Poem on Tom Pun——bi on Occasion of His
     Late Death, and in Vindication of Some
     Verses Written, Entitled "Sheridan's
     Resurrection," A.
Prose in Advent Time.
Punegyric upon Tom Pun-sibi's *Ars Pun-ica*,
     A.
Puppet-Show, The, *sels.*
Rivals, The.
Seafarer, The.
Simile Latinised, A.
Song of Blodeuwedd, The.
Spirit of Plato.
Tam Lin.
Teach your child to earn his meal.
To Demosthenis.
To Health.
To Mr Dryden, on his Poem called *Religio
     Laici.*
To My Dear Sister, the Author of these Poems.
To My Worthy Friend T S——, D. D. On His
     Incomparable Translation of and Notes on
     Persius.
Tom Pun-Sibi's Resurrection Disproved.
Tom Punsibi's Farewell to the Muses.
Tomb Cover of Imam Riza.
Two Spring Charms.
Upon Mr. Sheridan's Turning Author, 1716.
Upon the Author.
Vigil of Venus, The.
Westphalian Song.
Youth and Lordship.
Unknown, fr. Sumerian cuneiform
     Slave, Come to My Service!
Unknown, sometimes at. to **Thomas Sheridan**
     Answer to the Christmas-Box, An.
     Assist Me, My Muse, Whilst I Labor to Limn
         Him.
     Blunder of All Blunders, on the Wonder of All
         Wonders, The.
     Directions for Laughing.
     Enigma.
     Enigma in the Last *Mercury* Explained, The.
     Epilogue Designed to Be Spoken by Alonzo, at
         the Acting of *The Revenge* by Some
         Schoolboys.
     Fable of the Lion and Other Beasts, A.
     Faithful Inventory of the Furniture Belonging
         to ——— Room in T. C. D., A.
     He That Imposes an Oath.
     How Are They Bandied Up and Down by Fate.
     Hunting Song, A.
     Impromptu on Parting from Elizabeth
         MacFadden, An.
     Letter of Advice to the Reverend Dr. D-la-y,
         Humbly Proposed to the Consideration of a
         Certain Great Lord, A.
     Lines Written on a Window in the Episcopal
         Palace at Kilmore.
     Linnet and the Jay, The.
     Love, the Most Gen'rous Passion of the Mind.
     Now in This Thankless World the Givers.
     Ode, An, *sels.*
     On Fabricius.
     On Paddy's Character of "The Intelligencer."
     On Potatoes.
     On the Revd. Dr. Swift, D. S. P. D. Leaving
         His Fortune to Build an Hospital for Idiots
         and Lunatics.
     On the Same.
     Paddy's Choice.
     Peg Ratcliff the Hostess's Invitation to Dean

Swift.
     Punch's Petition to the Ladies.
     Riddle by T-m Pun——i, Addressed to D——
         h, A.
     Sheridan's Masterpiece; or, Tom Pun-Sibi's
         Folly Complete, *Alexander's Overthrow, or
         The Downfall of Babylon,* as It Was Acted at
         Mr. Lyddal's in Dame Street, December
         11th, 1721.
     To That Most Splendid and Learned
         Gentleman, Sir Richard Bulstrode, on
         Account of the Sacred Poems Recently
         Written by Him.
     To the Editor of *The Dublin Journal.*
     Trip to Temple-Oge, Stephen's Green and the
         Bason, A: or, An Election of Dublin
         Beauties.
     Verses on a Wooden Leg.
     Verses Written on One of the Windows at
         Delville.
     While Fame Is Young, Too Weak to Fly Away.
     Wonderful Man, Part the Third.
Unknown, sometimes at. to **Sir Walter Ralegh**
     As You Came from the Holy Land [of
         Walsingham],
     Epitaph on the Earl of Salisbury.
     Shall I, Like an Hermit, Dwell.
     Songe Made by Sir Walter Rawley, A.
     To his Singular Friend, William Lithgow.
     Vertue the Best Monument.
Updike, John (b. 1932)
     À l'École Berlitz.
     Academy.
     Accumulation.
     Aerie.
     Agatha Christie and Beatrix Potter.
     Air Show.
     Airport.
     Amish, The.
     Amoeba.
     Angels, The.
     Another Dog's Death.
     Antigua.
     Apologies to Harvard.
     At the End of the Rainbow.
     Authors' Residences.
     Average Egyptian Faces Death, The.
     Azores.
     B.W.I.
     Back Bay.
     Back from Vacation.
     Bath after Sailing.
     Beautiful Bowel Movement, The.
     Bendix.
     Bicycle Chain, A.
     Bindweed.
     Bitter Life, A.
     Blessing, The.
     Blked.
     Boil.
     Brazil.
     Burning Trash.
     Business Acquaintances.
     Calder's Hands.
     Calendar.
     Caligula's Dream.
     Camera.
     Capacity.
     Cars in Caracas, The.
     Celery.
     Charleston.
     Chloë's Poem.
     Clan, The.
     Classical Optical.
     Cloud Shadows.
     Code, The.
     Commencement, Pingree School.
     Comp. Religion.
     Condo Moon.
     Conversation.
     Cosmic Gall.
     Courtesy Call.
     Crab Crack.
     Cunts.
     Daughter.
     Dea ex Machina.

Décor.
Deities and Beasts.
Déjà, Indeed.
Descent of Mr. Aldez, The.
Die Neuen Heiligen.
Dilemma in the Delta.
Dog's Death.
Dream and Reality.
Dream Objects.
Due Respect.
Duet, with Muffled Brake Drums.
Dutch Cleanser.
Each Summer's Swallows.
Earthworm.
East Hampton—Boston by Air.
Elderly Sex.
Elm.
Enemies of a House.
Energy: A Villanelle.
English Train Compartment.
Erotic Epigrams.
Eurydice.
Even Egrets Err.
Ex-Basketball Player.
Exposé,
Exposure.
Fall.
Farewell to the Shopping District of Antibes.
Fargo.
February 22.
Fellatio.
Fever.
Fireworks.
Fleckings, The.
Flirt.
Flurry.
Fly.
Food.
Fritillary, The.
From Above.
Frost.
Furniture, The.
Generic College.
Glasses.
Golfers.
Goodbye, Göteborg.
Gradations of Black.
Granite.
Great Scarf of Birds, The.
Grief of Cafeterias, The.
Handkerchiefs of Khaibar Khan, The.
Heading for Nandi.
High-Hearts, The.
Hoeing.
Home Movies.
Hot Water.
House Growing, The.
How to Be Uncle Sam.
Humanities Course.
Hymn to These Newly Abbreviated States.
I Missed His Book, but I Read His Name.
Imaginable Conference, An.
In Extremis.
In Memoriam.
In Memoriam Felis Felis.
In Praise of $(C_{10}H_9O_5)x$.
Indianapolis.
Insomnia the Gem of the Ocean.
Iowa.
Island Sun.
Jolly Greene Giant, The.
July.
Kenneths.
Klimt and Schiele Confront the Cunt.
L.A.
Lament, for Cocoa.
Lamplight.
Landing in the Rain at La Guardia.
Late January.
Leaving Church Early.
Les Saints Nouveaux.
Light Switches.
Literary Dublin.
Little Poems.
Living with a Wife.
Long Shadow.

Maples in a Spruce Forest.
March: A Birthday Poem.
Marching through a Novel.
Marriage Counsel.
Meditation on a News Item.
Melancholy of Storm Windows, The.
Melting.
Menagerie at Versailles in 1775, The.
Miami.
Midpoint.
Milady Reflects.
Millipede, The.
Mime.
Minority Report.
Miss Moore at Assembly.
Mr. High-Mind.
Mites.
Mobile of Birds.
Moderate, The.
Modest Mound of Bones, A.
Modigliani's Death Mask.
Moons of Jupiter, The.
Mosquito.
Mountain Impasse.
Mouse Sex.
Movie House.
Munich.
My Children at the Dump.
Naked Ape, The.
Natural Question.
Nature.
Neotony.
Newlyweds, The.
News from the Underworld.
Night Flight, over Ocean.
Note to the Previous Tenants.
November.
Nuda Natens.
Oddly Lovely Day Alone, An.
Ode, An: "I'm going to write a novel, hey."
Ohio.
Old-Fashioned Lightning Rod.
Omega.
On an Island.
On the Inclusion of Miniature Dinosaurs in
    Breakfast Cereal Boxes.
On the Recently Minted Hundred-Cent Piece.
On the Way to Delphi.
One-Year-Old, The.
Open Letter to Voyager II, An.
Origin of Laughter, The.
Orthodontia.
Oxford, Thirty Years After.
Pain.
Painted Wives.
Pale Bliss.
Party Knee.
Pear like a Potato, A.
Penumbrae.
Perfection Wasted.
Phenomena.
Philological.
Pillow.
Planting a Mailbox.
Planting Trees.
Player Piano.
Plow Cemetery.
Poem for a Far Land.
Poisoned in Nassau.
Pompeii.
Pooem.
Pop Smash, Out of Echo Chamber.
Popular Revivals 1956.
Postcards from Soviet Cities.
Publius Vergilius Maro, the Madison Avenue
    Hick.
Query.
Rack of Paperbacks, A.
Raining in Magens Bay.
Rats.
Recital.
Reel.
Relatives.
Report of Health.
Returning Native.
Revelation.

Richmond.
Rio de Janeiro.
Rockettes, The.
Roman Portrait Busts.
Room 28.
Sails on All Saints' Day.
Sand Dollar.
São Paulo.
Scenic.
Sea Knell.
Seagulls.
Seal in Nature.
Seattle Uplift.
Self-Service.
Sensualist, The.
Seven New Ways of Looking at the Moon.
Seven Odes to Seven Natural Processes.
Seven Stanzas at Easter.
Shaving Mirror.
Shillington.
Shipbored.
Short Days, The.
Shuttle, The.
Sin City, D.C.
Skyey Developments.
Sleeping with You.
Sleepless in Scarsdale.
Small-City People.
Snapshots.
Snowdrops 1987.
Solitaire.
Solitary Pond, The.
Some Frenchmen.
Sometime Sportsman Greets the Spring, The.
Somewhere.
Song of Paternal Care, A.
Song of the Open Fireplace.
Sonic Boom.
Sonnet to Man-Made Grandeur.
South of the Alps.
Spanish Sonnets.
Spring Song.
Squirrels Mating.
Story of My Life, The.
Stunt Flier, The.
Styles of Bloom.
Suburban Madrigal.
Summer: West Side.
Sunday.
Sunday in Boston.
Sunday Rain.
Sunflower.
Sunglasses.
Sunshine on Sandstone.
Superman.
Switzerland.
Tao in the Yankee Stadium Bleachers.
Taste.
Tax-Free Encounter.
Telephone Poles.
Thin Air.
Thoughts While Driving Home.
3 A.M.
Time's Fool.
To a Box Turtle.
To a Dead Flame.
To a Waterbed.
To an Usherette.
To Ed Sissman.
Tome-Thoughts, from the *Times*.
Toothache Man.
Topsfield Fair.
Tossing and Turning.
Touch of Spring.
Trees Eat Sunshine.
Tropical Beetles.
Tsokadze O Altitudo.
Tulsa.
Tune, in American Type.
Two Hoppers.
Two Sonnets Whose Titles Came to Me
    Simultaneously.
Typical Optical.
Upon Learning That a Bird Exists Called the
    Turnstone.
Upon Learning That a Town Exists in Virginia

Called Upperville.
Upon Looking into Sylvia Plath's *Letters
    Home.*
Upon Shaving Off One's Beard.
Upon the Last Day of His Forty-Ninth Year.
V. B. Nimble, V. B. Quick.
Vermont.
Vibration.
Vision, A.
Visions of Mackenzie King, The.
Vow.
Waiting Rooms.
Wash.
Washington.
Washington: Tourist View.
White Dwarf.
Why the Telephone Wires Dip and the Poles
    Are Cracked and Crooked.
Widener Library, Reading Room.
Wind.
Winter Ocean.
Within a Quad.
Wooden Darning Egg, A.
Working Outdoors in Winter.
You Who Swim.
Young Matrons Dancing.
Youth's Progress.
Zoo Bats.
Zulus Live in Land without a Square.

V

Valéry, Paul (1871–1945)
    Helen.
Vallejo, César (1892–1938)
    Anger.
    Big People, The.
    Black Stone on Top of a White Stone.
    Divine Falling of Leaves, A.
    Down to the Dregs.
    Estais Muertos.
    Eternal Dice, The.
    I am Freed.
    Our Daily Bread.
    Peace, the Wasp.
    Testimony.
    White Rose.
Van Duyn, Mona (b. 1921)
    Advice to a God.
    After midnight, and my sister Lizzie.
    Along the Road.
    Annual and Perennial Problem, An.
    At Père Lachaise.
    Ballad of Blossom, The.
    Bedtime Stories.
    Billings and Cooings from "The Berkeley
        Barb."
    Birthday Card for a Psychiatrist.
    Caring for Surfaces.
    Case of The, The.
    Causes.
    Challenger, The.
    Christmas Card, After the Assassinations, A.
    Cinderella's Story.
    Cities of the Plain, The.
    Colorado.
    Creation, The.
    Day in Late October, A.
    Death By Aesthetics.
    Dwarf in the Woods.
    Earth Tremors Felt in Missouri.
    Economics.
    Elementary Attitudes.
    End of May.
    Eros to Howard Nemerov.
    Essay on Criticism, An.
    Evening Stroll in the Suburbs.
    Fall.
    Fear of Flying, The.
    First Flight.
    Folks built that barn, your great grandfather,
        and them, The.
    Footnotes to "The Autobiography of Bertrand
        Russell."

From Yellow Lake: An Interval.
Gardener to His God, The.
Garland for Christopher Smart, A.
Gentle Snorer, The.
Good Man, The.
Good Resolution, The.
Goodbye, A.
Goya's "Two Old People Eating Soup."
Gray's Apocrypha.
Growing Up Askew.
Hermit of Hudson Pond, The.
Homework.
In the Cold Kingdom.
In the Hospital for Tests.
In the Missouri Ozarks.
In the Old Country, then, two ladies and two
    boys.
Insight.
Into Mexico.
Ja, we had it hard.
Just full of springs the world was in Illinois.
Kind of Music, A.
Learners, The.
Leda.
Leda Reconsidered.
Letters from a Father.
Lives of the Poets.
Madrid, May, 1977.
Madrid, 1974.
Marriage, with Beasts.
Midas and Wife.
Miser, The.
Moose in the Morning, Northern Maine.
Nap.
New Land.
Notes from a Suburban Heart.
Oh well, they had such a big garden.
Old widow lady, and went out to do her chore,
    An.
Open Letter from a Constant Reader.
Open Letter, Personal.
Outlandish Agon.
Paratrooper.
Peony Stalks.
Photographs.
Pietà, Rhenish, 14th C., the Cloisters, The.
Placet Experiri.
Postcards from Cape Split.
Pot-au-feu.
Quebec Suite.
Quiet Afternoon at Home, A.
Reading of Rex Stout, A.
Recovery.
Relationships.
Relative and an Absolute, A.
Remedies, Maladies, Reasons.
Ringling Brothers, Barnum and Bailey.
Saleswomen in Bakery Shops.
Sentimental Delusion, A.
Serious Case, A.
Sestina for Warm Seasons.
Since You Asked Me.
Small Excursion, A.
Speak, Memory!
Spell of Conjunctivitis, A.
Stream, The.
Such things there are, we don't know.
Talker, The.
That was in 1875, and we come through.
That was in 1875, then we moved here.
That was my grandfather, nearly went to
    prison.
3 A.M. in a War Year.
Three Valentines to the Wide World.
Time of Bees, A.
To My Godson, on His Christening.
To Poets' Worksheets in the Air-Conditioned
    Vault of a Library.
To Record One Must Be Unwary.
Toward a Definition of Marriage.
Twins, The.
Two Poems for Sub-Zero Times.
Two Poems, with Birds.
View, A.
Vision Test, The.
Voyeur, The.

Walking the Dog: A Diatribe.
We alwus had to herd cattle.
Well, that old big fat man.
Well, that was Saturday, day before Easter.
West Branch Ponds, Kokadjo, Maine.
What I Want to Say.
What the Motorcycle Said.
Winter's Tale, by a Wife, A.
Wish to Be Believed, The.
With Warm Regards to Miss Moore and Mr.
    Ransom.
Woman Waiting.

Van Geel, Christian J.
Homecoming.
Sleepwalking.

Various authors
Complimentary Pieces to Milton.
Four Medieval Latin Poems.
Variations of Greek Themes.

Verlaine, Paul (1844–96)
Asleep in the Valley.

Very, Jones (1831–80)
Abdolonymus—The Sidonian.
Abolition of Serfdom in Russia, The.
Absent, The.
Acorn, The.
African's First Sight of the Ocean, The.
Age Changeful and Worldly, The.
"Agriculture the Source of Individual and of
    National Prosperity."—Anne Pratt.
Altar, The.
Ambitione inani pectus caret.
Ancient Burial Places in Peabody, The.
And a little child shall lead them. Isaiah 11.6.
Apostle, The.
Apostles, The.
Appeal.
April Snow, The.
Arab Steed, The.
Arabella Johnson.
"Are there Few that be Saved?" Luke 13:23.
Arethusa Meadow.
Ark, The.
Arrival, The.
As ye sow, so shall ye reap.
At Sea ("Day follows day, and week succeeds
    to week").
At Sea ("Frail woman there and childhood's
    tender years").
Autumn Days.
Autumn Flowers.
Autumn Flowers, The.
Autumn Leaf, The.
Autumn Leaves.
Azalea Swamp.
Baker's Island Light, The.
Barberry Bush, The.
Barberry-Pickers, The.
Barque Aurelia of Boston, The.
Be Not Many Teachers.
Be of Good Courage.
Beauty.
Bee Hive, The.
Beginning and the End, The.
Behold He Is at Hand That Doth Betray Me.
Behold, I Make All Things New.
Bible Does Not Sanction Polygamy, The.
Bible, The.
Birds of Passage, The.
Birds, The.
Birth-Day of the Soul, The.
Birthright Church, The.
Bitter-Sweet Rocks.
Blessed Are They That Mourn.
Blessed are they that mourn: for they shall be
    comforted.
"Blessed are they that mourn: for they shall be
    comforted." Math. 5:4.
Blessing of Rain, The.
Blueberry Blossoms, The.
Book of Life, The.
Boy's Dream, The: A Ballad.
Branch, The.
Bread from Heaven, The.
Brethren, The.
Bride, The.

Bridge of Time, The.
Broken Bowl, The.
Builders, The.
Bunch of Flowers, The.
Cadmus.
Call, The ("Come thou and labor with me I
    will give").
Call, The ("Why art thou not awake my
    son?").
Calling, The.
Camphene Lamp, The.
Capt. Samuel Cook.
Cause, The.
Cemetery of Harmony Grove, The.
Change.
Change in the Seasons.
Charge, The.
Charity.
Cherry Birds, The.
Childhood's Songs.
Children, The.
Child's Answer, The.
Child's Dream of Reaching the Horizon, The.
Christ Abiding Forever.
Christ, The.
Christian Commonwealth, A.
Christian Influence.
Christmas.
Christ's Capture in the Garden: A Paraphrase.
Christ's Compassion.
Christ's Final Victory.
Church, The.
City of God, The.
City, The.
Clay, The.
Clock, The.
Clouded Morning, The ("Morning comes, and
    thickening clouds prevail, The").
Clouded Morning, The ("Morning comes; and
    thickening fogs prevail, The").
Coasters, The.
Cold cold thy lips my gentle boy.
Cold Spring in North Salem, The.
Columbine, The.
Columbines and Anemones.
Come Unto Me.
Comet, The.
Comfort.
Coming, The.
Common School, The.
Communion, The.
Compassion.
Complaint, The.
Conclusion: "Descendants of the Puritans!
    whose fame."
Congregational Singing.
Congress of Peace at Brussels, The.
Conspiracy, The.
Corner Stone, The.
Corrupt Tree, The.
Cottage, The.
Cows Waiting at the Pasture Gate, The.
Creation, The.
Crisis, The.
Crocus, The.
Cross, The ("I must go on, till in my tearful
    line").
Cross, The ("Raised on high, above the city").
Cup, The.
Daily News, The.
Dark Day, The.
Day.
Day Begins to Dawn, The.
Day Calling Us to a New Life, The.
Day Lily, The.
Day, not for Gain, The.
Day of Denial, The.
Day, The.
Day Unto Day Uttereth Speech.
Dead Elm, The.
Dead, The.
Death.
Death Decay and Change.
Death of Lafayette.
Death of Man, The.
Decay.
Departure, The.

Desert, The.
Destruction of Public Property by Mobs, The.
Disciple, The.
Discontent.
Distant, The.
Do Nations Ever Become Insane?
Dwellings of the Just, The.
Dying Leaf, The.
Dying Words of John Foster: "I Can Pray, and
    That's a Glorious Thing."
E Pluribus Unum.
Each Day a Prophecy.
Eagles, The.
Early Companions.
Earth is parched with heat, flowers droop and
    die, The.
Earth, The.
East India Marine Museum, The.
Eden.
Education.
Effort.
Eheu! fugaces, Posthume, Posthume, Labuntur
    anni.
Elm Seed, The.
Endecott.
Ends for Which a Nation Exists, The.
English Sparrows.
Enoch.
Eternal Life.
Evening Choir, The.
Evening Walk, An.
Evergreen, The.
Every Day a Day of Freedom.
Evolution.
Eye and Ear, The.
Fair Morning, The.
Faith and Light.
Faith ("Hast thou but faith thou shalt the
    mountain bid").
Faith in the Resurrection Confirmed.
Faith in Time of War.
Faith of the First Christians, The.
Faith ("There is no faith; the mountain stands
    within").
Falling Leaf, The.
Farewell: "Farewell dear England, and thy
    Church farewell!"
Father, The.
Fear not: for they that are with us are more
    than they that are with them. 2 Kings 6:16.
Feast, The.
Field and Wood, The.
Fig Tree, The.
Finishing the Work.
Fireflies, The.
First Atlantic Telegraph, The.
First of May, The.
First Shall Be Last, The.
First Telegraphic Message, The.
Flee to the Mountains.
Flesh, The.
Flight, The.
Flood, The.
Foe, The.
For the Sailors' Fair.
For We Walk by Faith, Not by Sight.
Forbearance.
Forevermore.
Forgive Me My Trespasses.
Forgiveness.
Forsaken Harvest Field, The.
Fossil Flower, The.
Fox and the Bird, The.
Fragments, The.
Freedmen of the Mississippi Valley, The.
Freedom and Union.
Freedom National, Slavery Sectional.
Friendship.
Friendship: To J. M. S.
Frost, The.
Frozen Ship, The.
Fruit, The.
Fugitive Slaves, The.
Fulness of the Gentiles, The.
Funerals, The.
Future State of the Wicked and Its Duration,

The.
Garden, The.
Ghost, The.
Giants, The.
Gift, The.
Gifts of God, The.
Give and it shall be given unto you. Spiritual
    Debtors.
Give me an eye, that manly deeds.
Glacial Marks on Our Hills, The.
Glutton, The.
God Not Afar Off.
God's Host.
Goliath.
Good Gift, The.
Good Ground, The.
Good Samaritan, The.
Good, The.
Gospel the Reconciling Power, The.
Great Facts of Christ's History, The.
Grief.
Guest, The.
Guido's Aurora.
Hacker School House, The.
Hallowed be thy Name.
Hand and Foot, The [or Hand and the Foot,
    The].
Harvest, The ("Plant it springs it rears its
    drooping head, The").
Harvest, The ("They love me not, who at my
    table eat").
Hast thou ever heard the voice of nature.
Hath the Rain a Father? Or Who Hath
    Begotten the Drops of Dew? Job 38:28.
Haunts of my youth farewell! A while I leave.
He Was Acquainted with Grief.
Health of Body Dependent on the Soul.
Heart, The.
Heavenly Rest, The.
Help.
Help of the Spirit, The.
Hepatica in Winter, The.
Heralds of the Spring, The.
Here let the Church her holy mission prove.
Hindoo Converts: On the Domestic Trials of
    Hindoo Converts. Report of Unitarian
    Mission in India.
History.
Holy Land, The.
Holy of Holies, The.
Home and Heaven.
Home of my youth! Where first my lot was
    cast.
Home, The ("Love builds for us a bower").
Home, The ("See! from yon low-roofed
    cottage shines a light").
Home, The ("Supper o'er, with books, or
    converse sweet, The").
Homeless Wind, The.
Hope.
Horsemen on the Sands, The.
Hour Before the Dawn, The.
Hour, The.
Hours, The.
House Not Made with Hands, Eternal in the
    Heavens, The.
House, The.
Houstonia, The.
How Come the Dead?
How Faith Comes.
Humanity Mourning for Her Children Slain in
    War.
Humble, The.
Humility.
Humming Bird, The.
Husbandman, The.
Hymn: "Amidst the pastures green."
Hymn: "As by the quickening breath of
    Spring."
Hymn: Christ's Invitation in the Apocalypse.
Hymn: "From out its large estate."
Hymn: "He loveth not! he knows not God!"
Hymn: Home.
Hymn: I Am the Way.
Hymn in Drought.
Hymn: "In the shock of mighty armies."

Hymn: Nature's Sympathy with Freedom.
Hymn: Nevertheless, when the Son of Man
    cometh, shall he find faith on the earth?
    Luke 18:8.
Hymn: "Not tears alone for natural grief."
Hymn on the Logos: The Light Still Shining in
    the Darkness.
Hymn: Our Country's Dead.
Hymn: "Our voices with our hearts we lift."
Hymn: Prayer for the Gift of the Holy Spirit.
Hymn: Reflections at the Close of the Year.
Hymn: So also will God, through Jesus, bring
    with him them who sleep.
Hymn: Sung at the Celebration of the Fourth
    of July, in Salem, 1854.
Hymn: Sung at the Dedication of Plummer
    Hall, Salem, Oct. 6, 1857.
Hymn, Sung at the Dedication of the New
    Stone Church of the North Society in Salem
    June 22d, 1836.
Hymn: Sung at the Dedication of the Peabody
    Academy of Science, Aug. 18, 1869.
Hymn: Sung at the Eulogy on Abraham
    Lincoln June 1st 1865.
Hymn, Sung at the Fiftieth Anniversary of the
    Essex Historical Society, Salem. April 21,
    1871.
Hymn, Sung at the Thompson Jubilee, at
    Barre, Jan. 12, 1854.
Hymn: Sung at the Unitarian Festival, in
    Faneuil Hall, May 26th 1863.
Hymn: The Cause of Peace.
Hymn: The Dew.
Hymn: The Efficacy of a Mother's Prayer.
Hymn: The Forms of Nature, and the Unity of
    Their Origin.
Hymn: The Good Fight.
Hymn: The Light of Life.
Hymn: The New Life of Humanity.
Hymn: The Promise of the Spirit.
Hymn: The Rest of the Righteous.
Hymn: The Spirit Itself Maketh Intercession
    for Us.
Hymn: The Spiritual Body.
Hymn: The Way of the Righteous Easy.
Hymn: The Word Before All Things.
Hymn: "Thou who keepst us each together."
Hymn: "Though few, with noble purpose
    came."
Hymn to the Living.
Hymn: Waiting for Christ.
I Am the Bread of Life.
I Am the Light of the World.
I Am the Way.
I murmur not though hard the lot.
I Prayed, Thy Kingdom Come.
I saw a child, whose eyes had never drank.
I Was Sick and in Prison.
Idler, The.
Immortal, The.
Impatience.
Incarnation, The.
Indian Relics.
Indian Remains.
Indians' Belief in a Future State, The.
Indian's Petition, The.
Indian's Retort, The.
Influence of Channing, The.
Influence of Puritanism.
Influence of the Night on Faith and
    Imagination, The.
International Exhibition at Philadelphia, The.
Interpreting God's Ways.
Interpreting Nature.
Intuitions of the Soul, The.
Invitation, The ("Stay where thou art, thou
    need'st not further go").
Invitation, The ("There is no sound but thou
    dost hear my voice").
Invitation to the Robin.
Inward Direction.
Inward Phenomena.
"It is vain to say, that this is the country of the
    'white man.' It is the country of man."
    Charles Sumner.
Jacob Wrestling with the Angel.

Jacob's Well.
Jew, The.
John.
John Woolman.
Jonathan Huntington Bright.
Journey, The.
Joy ("Joy Thou giv'st no man can take away, The").
Joy ("Thou hast a moon for every cloudy night").
Jupiter as the Evening Star.
Just Shall Live by Faith, The.
Just, The.
Justification by Faith.
Kind Words.
King Philip.
Kingdom of God Is Within You, The.
Kingdom of Heaven: In Its Growth and Coming a Mystery, The.
Kingdom of the Truth, The.
King's Arm Chair, The.
Know Thyself: Suggested by Hearing Dr. A. E. Miller's Lectures on the Human Body.
Knowledge and Truth.
Kossuth.
Labor and Rest.
Laborer, The.
Laborers, The.
Lament of the Flowers, The.
Land.
Landing, The.
Last, The.
Latter Rain, The ("Latter rain,—it falls in anxious haste, The").
Lead Me to the Rock That Is Higher Than I.
Lessons of History Unlearned, The.
Life.
Life and Death.
Life of the Flower, The.
Light from Within, The.
Light of Freedom Necessary to National Progress, The.
Lines on Mount Auburn.
Lines on Reading the Death of Rev. Henry Ware, Jr.
Lines on the Old Danvers Burying Ground.
Lines Suggested by Hearing the Beach, at F. Peabody's Mills, South Salem. December 21. 1833.
Lines Suggested by Seeing a Butterfly Sculptured Upon a Tomb.
Lines To ——— On the Death of His Friend.
Lines, Written on Reading Stuart's Account of the Treatment of Slaves in Charleston.
Living God, The.
Location.
Longing.
Longing for the Spring, A.
Looking Before and After.
Lost Sheep, The ("Beneath the wild thorn").
Lost Sheep, The ("Though many, many sheep I have").
Lost, The ("Fairest day that ever yet has shone, The").
Lost, The ("They wander, straggling sheep without a fold").
Love.
Love Needing a Visible Object.
Man of Science, The.
Man's Accountability.
Man's First Experience of Winter.
Man's Heart Prophesieth of Peace.
Man's Need of a Spiritual Birth.
May Flower, The.
McLean Asylum, Somerville.
Meek, The.
Memory ("Soon the silver chord is broken").
Memory ("Soon the waves, so lightly bounding").
Message, The ("On the bare alder bough").
Message, The ("There is no voice but it is born of Me").
Meteorologists, The.
Midas.
Military surprises and the capture of capitals, are the events of a by-gone age. D'Israeli.

Mind the Greatest Mystery, The.
Miser, The.
Mission of the Friends to the Emperor Nicholas, The.
Moon was shining on the deck, The.
Morn may lend its golden smile, The.
Morning.
Morning Hymn for a Little Child.
Morning Watch, The.
Moses as Leader of Israel.
Moses at the Bush.
Moses in Infancy.
Moss and Its Teachings, The.
Motive.
Mound Builders, The.
Mountain, The.
Mourner, The.
Mt. Shasta: A Painting, by H. O. Young.
Mustard Seed, The.
My Church.
My Dear Brother Washington.
My Father's House.
My Garden.
My Meat and Drink.
My Mother's Voice.
My People are destroyed for lack of Knowledge. Hosea 4:6.
My Sheep.
Narrow Way, The.
National Thanksgiving, The.
National Unity ("Nobler unity, than that which came, A").
National Unity ("Unity complete, assured, and high, A").
Nation's Life of Slow Growth, A.
Nature a Living Teacher.
Nature ("Bubbling brook doth leap when I come by, The").
Nature ("I love to sit on the green hill's side").
Nature Intelligible.
Nature ("Nature, my love for thee is deeper far").
Nature ("Nature would speak through her first master man").
Nature Repeats Her Lessons.
Nature Teaches Only Love.
Nature Teaches Us of Time and Its Duration.
Nature's Help for the Soul.
Nature's Invitation.
Naumkeck River.
New Aqueduct, The.
New Birth, The.
New Body, The.
New Jerusalem, The ("I saw the city, 'twas not built by hands").
New Jerusalem, The ("There are towers; where they are").
New Man, The.
New Sea, The.
New World, The.
New Year, The.
Newspaper, The.
Night.
Night Blooming Cereus, The.
Nine O'Clock Bell, The.
Nodding Meadow Lily, The.
Norman's Rocks.
North River.
Not as the World giveth.
O, cleave not to the things of earth.
O heaven born muse! inspire my humble lay.
"O Lord, How Long?"
Oak and the Poplar, The.
Obedience.
Ocean's Treasures.
October ("All day, amidst the forests' splendor bright").
October ("How beautiful the sight of woods still fair").
Ode to Freedom.
Old Age.
Old Houses of Salem: Illustrated by George M. White.
Old Organ of the East Society Salem, The.
Old Planters, The.
Old Road, The.

Old Things Are Passed Away.
Oliver C. Felton, Esq., of Brookfield.
On a Hyacinth from Georgia.
On a Lichen from North Cape.
On an Ear of Wheat Brought, By My Brother.
On Finding the Truth.
On Hearing the Clock Strike.
On reading the Memorial of John White Browne.
On Receiving a Flower from the Rev. C. H. A. Dall, in India.
On Seeing the Portrait of Helen Ruthven Waterston.
On Seeing the Victoria Regia in Bloom.
On Seeing the White Mountains.
On Some Beautiful Crocuses.
On Some Blue and Golden Columbines.
On Some Eternals from a Friend's Garden.
On the Beautiful Roses.
On the Bunyan Tableau.
On the Completion of the Pacific Telegraph.
On the First Church Built by the Puritans in 1634.
On the Great Divisions of the Christian Church, the Catholic, the Protestant, and the Greek.
On the Great Earthquake in New Grenada.
On the Increase in Crime Since the Late Civil War.
On the late Disgraceful Scene in Congress.
On the Late Mild Winter.
On the Late Tornado, at Wallingford, Conn.
On the Mountain Ash Tree.
On the Nebraska Bill.
On the Neglect of Public Worship.
On the Neglect of the Study of History.
On the Sudden Snow.
On the Three Hundredth Anniversary of Shakespeare's Birthday.
On the Wild Flowers of the Art Exhibition.
On Viewing the Falls of Niagara, as Photographed by George Barker.
On visiting the beautiful estate of H. H. Hunnewell, Esq., at Wellesley.
One generation passeth away, and another generation cometh: but the earth abideth for ever. Ecclesiastes 1:4.
Origin of Man, The.
Original Hymn ("Not unto men alone has come").
Original Hymn ("We welcome, with the opening year").
Our Dear Mother.
Our Lighthouses.
Our Native Sparrows.
Our Soldiers' Graves.
Outward Conquests Not Enough.
Painted Columbine, The.
Paradise.
Parting Hymn.
Passage Bird, The.
Past, The.
Path of Peace, The.
Peace Congress the Promise of a Higher Civilization, The.
Perfect Love that Casts Out Fear, The.
Petrels, The.
Philanthropy Before Nationality.
Philosophy and Religion.
Physician, The.
Pilgrim, The.
Plagues of Egypt, The.
Plant, The.
Pleasure ("Goddess of pleasure, where thy golden car?").
Pleasure ("With business haste, or with a worldly mind").
Poet, The.
Poet's Plea, The.
Political Ambition.
Pompeii.
Poor Clergyman, The.
Poor, The.
Portrait, The.
Potato Blight, The.
Praise.

Prayer for Rain.
Prayer of Jabez, The.
Prayer, The ("Father! help them who walk in their own light").
Prayer, The ("Wilt Thou not visit me?").
Preacher, The.
Preparation for Life's Voyage.
Presence, The.
Priest, The.
Primitive Worship.
Prison.
Prisoner, The.
Prodigal, The.
Promise, The ("I come the rushing wind that shook the place").
Promise, The ("Words I give thee they are not thine own, The").
Prophet, The.
Pure in Heart, The.
Purification of the Temple, The.
Puritan Church and State 1, The.
Puritan Church and State 2, The.
Puritan Church and State 3, The.
Rachel.
Rail Road, The.
Rain Clouds.
Rain, The ("Rain descends; each drop some drooping flower, The").
Ramble, The.
Reaper, The.
Reapers Are the Angels, The.
Reconciling Power, The.
Redeemed, The.
Redeeming the Time.
Reflections on the History of Nations.
Relief.
Religion.
Removal, The.
Repent for the kingdom of Heaven is at hand.
Resurrection, The.
Return of the Columbine, The.
Return of the Savior, The.
Revelation.
Revelation of the Spirit Through the Material World, The.
Reverence.
Reward, The.
Rights of Man, The.
River, The.
Robe, The.
Robin, The.
Robin's Song, The.
Rock, The.
Rose, The.
Sabbath, The ("Bright is the morn, and hushed is every sound").
Sabbath, The ("Thy rest has come thy long expected rest").
Sabbatia, The.
Sacrifice.
Sailing on Cakes of Ice in the North River.
Salem ("Boast not, my native spot, thy sons were first").
Salem ("They reach a harbor spacious and secure").
Salvation Is of the Lord: The Book of Jonah 2.9.
Same, The.
Sayings.
Scepticism with Regard to the Gospels.
Scholar Dreaming, The.
Search for the Truth Not Vain, The.
Seasons, The.
Seed, The.
Sensibility to the Beauty and Fragrance of Flowers.
Sepulchre of the Books, The.
Serpent, The.
Servant, The.
Serving-Man, The.
Set Times, and the Boundaries of Nations, Appointed by God, The.
Settler, The.
Shelter, The.
Shepherd's Life, The.
Ship Rock.

Sick, The.
Sickness.
Sight of the Ocean, The.
Sign, The.
Signs in the Natural World.
Silent, The.
Simmons Mobile Alabama.
Slave, The.
Slavery.
Sleigh Ride.
Sliding Rock, The.
Slowness of Belief in a Spiritual World, The.
Snare, The.
Snow Bird, The.
Snow Drop, The.
So is every one who is born of the spirit.
Soldier and the Statesman, The.
Soldier of the Cross, The.
Solitary Gentian, The.
Solitary Worshipper, The.
Son of Man, The.
Son, The.
Song Composed by Mr. J. Very, A.
Song: I Love the Light.
Song: "I sought the flowers, but o'er them lay."
Song: "No more around the social board."
Song of the Early Spring.
Song, The.
Song: The Summer Day.
Song: "They sing of Zion, city built of old."
Song: We Have No Ship at Sea.
Song: Words of Love to a Parent.
Sonnet, A: "Thy beauty fades and with it too my love."
Sonnet: "I gazed upon the silent burial-ground."
Sonnet, To the Rev. James Flint, D. D., On reading his Collection of Poems.
Soul in Dreams, The.
Soul-Sickness.
Soul's Freedom, The.
Soul's Invitation, The.
Soul's Opportunities, The.
Soul's Preparation for Adversity, The.
Soul's Questioning of the Universe, and Its Beginning, The.
Soul's Rest, The.
South River at Sunset, The.
Sower, The.
Sparrows and the Crop of Weeds, The.
Spheres, The.
Spirit Land, The ("Father! Thy wonders do not singly stand").
Spirit Land, The ("Open our eyes that we the world may see").
Spirit, The.
Spiritual Birth, The.
Spiritual Intercourse.
Spring and Summer Flowers.
Spring ("I have not lived the flesh has hedged me in").
Spring in the Soul.
Spring ("Look! Winter now in trembling haste").
Spring ("Spring returns, and, with fresh ardor filled, The").
Spring ("Stem that long has borne the wintry blast, The").
Standley's Grove.
Star, The.
Stars, The.
State Rights.
Statue of Flora, The.
Still a Day to Live.
Still-Born, The.
Still Small Voice, The.
Stock-Gilly Flowers, The.
Stony Desert of Life, The.
Stranger's Gift, The.
Strangers, The.
Strong Man, The.
Struggle, The.
Succory, The.
Sumach Leaves, The.
Sun, The.

Sunset after a Clouded Day in April.
Sunset in Derby's Woods.
Sunset in Haverhill, A.
Sunset, The.
Superfluities.
Swift, The.
Take ye heed, watch and pray: for ye know not when the time is. Mark 13:33.
Task, The.
Teaching of History Confirmed, The.
Teachings of the Spirit, The.
Telephone, The.
Temple, The.
Temptation, The.
Tenant, The.
Tent, The.
Terror.
Thanksgiving Flowers.
Then shall all the tribes of the earth mourn.
There shall be one Flock, one Shepherd.
They Who Hunger.
Thieves, The.
Things Before, The.
Things Unseen.
This Morn.
This Mortal Shall put on Immortality.
Thorns, The.
Thou know'st not what thy Lord will say.
Thoughts and Desires.
Thy Better Self.
Thy Brother's Blood.
Thy Father's House.
Thy Name.
Tide, The.
Time.
Time's House.
'Tis a Great Thing to Live.
'Tis Finished.
To a Cloud.
To All.
To an Ancient Locust-Tree.
To Charles W. Felt Esq. On His New Type-Setting Machine.
To Him That Hath Shall Be Given.
To him who overcometh.
To notice other days were pages given.
To the Fishermen.
To the Memory of Alpheus Crosby.
To the Memory of the Rev. James Chisholm.
To the Memory of the Rev. James Flint, D. D.
To the Misses Williams, On Seeing Their Beautiful Paintings of Wild Flowers.
To the Pure All Things Are Pure.
To the Salem Gazette, on the Completion of Its First Century.
Today.
Torn Flower, The.
Traveller at the Depot, The.
Tree of Liberty, The.
Tree, The ("I love thee when thy swelling buds appear").
Tree, The ("I too will wait with thee returning spring").
Trees of Life, The.
Triennial, The.
Triumphs of Science, and of Faith, The.
True Knowledge Necessary for the Voyage of Life.
True Light, The.
True Worshipers, The.
"Tuesday night, the schooner Weaver, of Glen Creek, N.J., went to pieces near Sandy Hook, and her entire crew were lost."— Transcript, March 22d.
Unfaithful Servants, The.
Unrevealed, The.
Unripe Fruit, The.
Untimely Arguments.
Unto you is born a Saviour.
Vagrant at the Church Door, The.
Veil of the Temple, The.
Veil Upon the Heart, The.
Violet, The.
Voice in the Poplars, The.
Voice of God, The.
Voice of Nature in Youth and Age, The.

Voting in the Old North Church.
Walk in Harmony Grove, A.
Walk in the Pastures, A.
War, The.
Warrior, The.
Washington.
Watcher, The.
Watchman, The.
Way, The.
Weary and Heavy Laden, The.
Welcome Written for the Essex Institute Fair.
What Is a Word?
What Is the Word?
What more delightful than to wander forth.
What of Our Country?
What of the Night?
White Dove and the Snow, The.
White Horse, The.
Whiteweed, The.
Whither Shall I Go from Thy Spirit.
Who Hath Ears to Hear Let Him Hear!
Widow, The.
Wild Rose of Plymouth, The.
Will, The.
William Cullen Bryant.
Wind-Flower, The.
Winter Bird, The.
Winter Night, The.
Winter ("Perils of the ocean safely o'er, The").
Winter ("There is a winter in the godless
     heart").
Winter Rain, The.
Winthrop's Fleet.
Withered Leaf—seen on a Poet's Table, A.
Withered Tree, The.
Wolf and the Lamb Shall Feed Together, The.
Woodwax in Bloom, The.
Woodwax, The.
Word, A.
Word, The ("Voice that speaks when thou art
     in thy tomb, The").
Word, The ("Word! it cannot fail; it ever
     speaks, The").
Word, The ("Word where is it? hath it voice,
     The").
World, The ("End of all thou seest is near,
     The").
World, The ("'Tis all a great show").
Worm, The.
Worship ("But, still preserved by pious care
     behold").
Worship ("There is no worship now—the idol
     stands").
Wounded Pigeon, The.
Ye Gave Me No Meat.
Ye have hoarded up treasure in the last days.—
     James 5:3.
Yellow Violets, The.
Yet Once More.
Yoke, The.
Young Drummer Boy of Libby Prison, The.
Yourself.
Youth and the Stream, The.
Zodiacal Light, The.

Villon, François (1431–65)
Ballad[e] of Dead Ladies, The.
Ballade in Old French.
Ballade of Forgiveness.
Ballade of the Ladies of Time Past.
Ballade to End With, A.
Caption for a Photograph of Four Organized
     Criminals.
Complaint of the Fair Armoress [or
     Armouress], The.
Epitaph in Form of a Ballad, The.
Gone Ladies.
His Mother's Service to Our Lady.
To Death, of His Lady.

**Virgil [or Vergil] (Publius Vergilius Maro) (70–19
     B.C.)**
Aeneid (Dryden translation), sels.
Aeneid [or Eneados or Aeneis], The, sels.
Eclogues, sels.
Georgics, sels.
Pastorals, sels.

Vogl, Johann N. (1802–66)
Love of the Woods.
Recognition, The.
Sweetheart of the Csikos, The.
To an Old Gipsy.

Voltaire (François Marie Arouet) (1694–1778)
To Madame du Châtelet.

**Voznesensky [or Voznesenskii], Andrey [or
     Andrei] Andreievich (b. 1933)**
Antiworlds.
Arrow in the Wall, An.
Dead Still.
Foggy Street.
Phone Booth.

Vroman, Leo (b. 1915)
Our Family.

W

Walcott, Derek (b. 1930)
Adam's Song.
Air.
Another Life.
As John to Patmos.
Banyan Tree, Old Year's Night, The.
Beachhead.
Bleecker Street, Summer.
Blues.
Brise Marine.
Castaway, The.
Che.
City's Death by Fire, A.
Codicil.
Cold Spring Harbor.
Coral.
Crusoe's Island.
Crusoe's Journal.
Dark August.
Early Pompeian.
Easter.
Egypt, Tobago.
Elegy: "Our hammock swung between
     Americas."
Endings.
Europa.
Exile.
Far Cry from Africa, A.
Fist, The.
Flock, The.
Forest of Europe.
Fortunate Traveller, The.
From This Far.
Glory Trumpeter, The.
Goats and Monkeys.
God Rest Ye Merry, Gentlemen.
Gulf, The.
Guyana.
Harbour, The.
Homage to Edward Thomas.
Homecoming: Anse La Raye.
Hotel Normandie Pool, The.
Hurucan.
In a Green Night.
Islands.
Jean Rhys.
Koenig of the River.
Lampfall.
Landfall, Grenada.
Laventille.
Lesson for This Sunday, A.
Letter from Brooklyn, A.
Liberator, The.
Love after Love.
Love in the Valley.
Man Who Loved Islands, The.
Map of Europe, A.
Map of the New World.
Mass Man.
Midsummer, sels.
Midsummer, Tobago.
Missing the Sea.
Morning Moon, The.
Names.
Nearing Forty.

Negatives.
New World.
Nights in the Gardens of Port of Spain.
North and South.
Oddjob, a Bull Terrier.
Old New England.
Orient and Immortal Wheat.
Origins.
Parang.
Piano Practice.
Pocomania.
Polish Rider, The.
Prelude: "I, with legs crossed along the
     daylight, watch."
Preparing for Exile.
Return to D'Ennery; Rain.
Ruins of a Great House.
Sabbaths, W.I.
Saddhu of Couva, The.
Sainte Lucie.
Schooner Flight, The.
Sea Canes.
Sea-Chantey, A.
Sea Grapes.
Sea is History, The.
Season of Phantasmal Peace, The.
Spoiler's Return, The.
Star.
Star-Apple Kingdom, The.
Sunday Lemons.
Swamp, The.
Tales of the Islands.
Tarpon.
To Return to the Trees.
Two Poems on the Passing of an Empire.
Upstate.
Verandah.
Village Life, A.
Volcano.
Wales.
Walk, The.
Winding Up.

Walker, Alice (b. 1944)
Abduction of Saints, The.
African Images, Glimpses from a Tiger's Back.
After the Shrink.
Armah: October 12, 1990.
At First.
Attentiveness.
Awakening, The.
Ballad of the Brown Girl.
Baptism.
Be Nobody's Darling.
Beast.
Beyond What.
Black Mail.
Black Prince, The.
Burial.
Chic Freedom's Reflection.
Clutter-up People.
Compulsory Chapel.
Confession.
Democratic Order, The: Such Things in
     Twenty Years I Understood.
Diamonds on Liz's Bosom, The.
Did This Happen to Your Mother? Did Your
     Sister Throw Up a Lot?
Each One, Pull One.
Eagle Rock.
Early Losses: a Requiem.
Ending.
Enemy, The.
Even as I Hold You.
Every Morning.
Excuse.
Exercises on Themes from Life.
Expect Nothing.
Facing the Way.
Family Of.
Few Sirens, A.
First, They Said.
For My Sister Molly Who in the Fifties.
For Two Who Slipped Away Almost Entirely.
Forbidden Things.
Forgive Me If My Praises.
Forgiveness.

Gift ("He said: Here is my soul").
Gift ("You intend no doubt").
Girl Who Died #1, The.
Girl Who Died #2, The.
Good Night, Willie Lee, I'll See You in the
    Morning.
Gray.
Having Eaten Two Pillows.
He Said.
He Said Come.
How Poems Are Made: A Discredited View.
Hymn: "I well remember / A time when."
I Said to Poetry.
If There Was Any Justice.
If "Those People" Like You.
I'm Really Very Fond.
In Answer to Your Silly Question.
In These Dissenting Times.
In Uganda an Early King.
Instant of Our Parting, The.
J, My Good Friend (Another Foolish Innocent).
Janie Crawford.
January 10, 1973.
Johann.
Judge Every One with Perfect Calm.
Karamojongs.
Killers.
Kiss, The.
Last Time, The.
Light Baggage.
Listen.
Lonely Particular.
Lost My Voice? Of Course.
Love Is Not Concerned.
Malcolm.
Medicine.
Mississippi Winter I.
Mississippi Winter II.
Mississippi Winter III.
Mississippi Winter IV.
Moody.
More Love to His Life.
Mornings / of an impossible love.
My Daughter Is Coming!
My Heart Has Reopened to You.
My Husband Says.
Mysteries.
Natural Star.
Nature of This Flower Is to Bloom, The.
Ndebele.
Never Offer Your Heart to Someone Who Eats
    Hearts.
New Face.
1971.
No Fixed Place.
No One Can Watch the Wasichu.
Nothing Is Right.
Now That the Book Is Finished.
Old Warrior Terror, The.
On Being Asked to Leave a Place of Honor for
    One of Comfort, Preferably in the Northern
    Suburbs.
On Sight.
On Stripping Bark from Myself.
Once.
Once, Again.
Overnights.
Pagan.
Perfection.
Poem at Thirty-nine.
QPP, The.
Rage.
Reassurance.
Remember?
Representing the Universe.
Revolutionary Petunias.
Right to Life, The: What Can the White Man
    Say to the Black Woman?
S M.
She Said.
Smell of Lebanon, The.
So We've Come at Last to Freud.
Some Things I Like about My Triple Bloods.
Song: "World is full of colored, The."
Songless.
South: The Name of Home.

Storm.
Streaking (A Phenomenon Following the
    Sixties).
Suicide.
Talking to My Grandmother Who Died Poor.
Telling.
There are no tigers.
There were palm trees.
These Days.
These Mornings of Rain.
They Who Feel Death.
Thief.
Thing Itself, The.
Threatened.
To Die before One Wakes Must Be Glad.
To the Man in the Yellow Terry.
Torture.
View from Rosehill Cemetery: Vicksburg.
Walker.
Warning.
We Alone.
We Have a Beautiful Mother.
We Have a Map of the World.
Well.
What Ovid Taught Me.
What the Finger Writes.
When Golda Meir Was in Africa.
While Love Is Unfashionable.
Who?
Will.
Winnie Mandela We Love You.
Without Commercials.
Woman Is Not a Potted Plant, A.
"Women of Color" Have Rarely Had the
    Opportunity to Write about Their Love
    Affairs.
Your Soul Shines.

Wang Ch'ang-ling (698–757)
    Chant of the Frontiersman.

Wang Chien (768?–833?)
    Newlywed's Cuisine, The.

Wang-ying, Hsieh *See* **"Ping Hsin"**

Ward, Nathaniel (1578–1652)
    Mercury shew'd Apollo, Bartas Book.

Warren, Robert Penn (1905–89)
    Acquaintance with Time in Early Autumn.
    Admonition to the Dead.
    Admonition to Those Who Mourn.
    After Restless Night.
    After Teacups.
    After the Dinner Party.
    Afterward.
    Aged Man Surveys the Past.
    Aging Man at Noon in Timeless Noon of
        Summer.
    Aging Painter Sits Where the Great Tower
        Heaves Down Midnight.
    Ah, Anima!
    Alf Burt, Tenant Farmer.
    Amazing Grace in the Back Country.
    American Portrait: Old Style.
    Another Dimension.
    Answer to Prayer.
    Antinomy: Time and Identity.
    Apologia for Grief.
    Arizona Midnight.
    Aspen Leaf in Windless World.
    Athenian Death.
    Aubade for Hope.
    Audubon: A Vision.
    August Moon.
    August Revival: Crosby Junction.
    Auto-da-fé.
    Autumn Twilight Piece.
    Autumnal Equinox on Mediterranean Beach.
    Ballad: Between the Boxcars [1923].
    Ballad of Billie Potts, The.
    Ballad of Mister Dutcher and the Last
        Lynching in Gupton.
    Ballad of Your Puzzlement.
    Basic Syllogism.
    Bearded Oaks.
    Better Than Counting Sheep.
    Bicentennial.
    Birth of Love.

Blessèd Accident.
Blow, West Wind.
Boy Wandering in Simms' Valley.
Boyhood in Tobacco Country.
Breaking the Code.
Brotherhood in Pain.
Calendar.
Caribou.
Chain Saw at Dawn in Vermont in Time of
    Drouth.
Chief Joseph of the Nez Perce.
Cocktail Party.
Code Book Lost.
Cold Colloquy.
Commuter's Entry in a Connecticut Diary.
Composition in Gold and Red-Gold.
Convergences.
Corner of the Eye, The.
Covered Bridge.
Crime.
Croesus in Autumn.
Cross, The.
Crusade.
Cycle.
Dawn.
Day Dr. Knox Did It, The.
Dead Horse in Field.
Death Mask of a Young Man.
Deep—Deeper Down.
Delight.
Delusion?—No!
Departure.
Distance Between, The: Picnic of Old Friends.
Diver.
Doubleness in Time.
Dragon-Tree.
Dream, Dump-Heap, and Civilization.
Dream of a Dream.
Dreaming in Daylight.
Eagle Descending.
Easter Morning: Crosby Junction.
Eidolon.
Empire.
Empty White Blotch on Map of Universe: A
    Possible View.
End of Season.
English Cocker: Old and Blind.
Evening Hawk.
Evening Hour.
Fall Comes in Back-Country Vermont.
Far West Once.
Fatal Interview: Penthesilea and Achilles.
Fear and Trembling.
Few Axioms for a Young Man, A.
Fierce Horsemen, The.
Filling Night with the Name: Funeral as Local
    Color.
First Dawn Light.
First Moment of Autumn Recognized.
First Time, The.
Flaubert in Egypt.
Folly on Royal Street before the Raw Face of
    God.
For a Friend Who Thinks Himself Urbane.
For a Self-Possessed Friend.
Forever O'Clock.
Function of Blizzard.
Garden, The.
Garden Waters.
Garland for You.
Genealogy.
Glimpses of Seasons.
Globe of Gneiss.
Going West.
Golden Hills of Hell, The.
Goodbye.
Goodbye.
Grackles, Goodbye.
Have You Ever Eaten Stars?
Heart of Autumn.
Heart of the Backlog.
Heat Lightning.
Heat Wave Breaks.
History.
History during Nocturnal Snowfall.
Holy Writ.

Homage to Emerson, On Night Flight to New
    York.
Homage to Theodore Dreiser.
Hope.
How to Tell a Love Story.
I Am Dreaming of a White Christmas: The
    Natural History of a Vision.
Identity and Argument for Prayer.
If.
If Ever.
If Snakes Were Blue.
Images on the Tomb.
Immanence.
Immortality Over the Dakotas.
In the Mountains.
Inevitable Frontier.
Instant on Crowded Street.
Institute of the Impossible.
Interjection #1: The Need For Re-evaluation.
Interjection #2: Caveat.
Interjection #3: I Know a Place Where All Is
    Real.
Interjection #4: Bad Year, Bad War: A New
    Year's Card, 1969.
Interjection #5: Solipsism and Theology.
Interjection #6: What You Sometimes Feel on
    Your Face at Night.
Interjection #8: Or, Sometimes, Night.
Internal Injuries.
Island of Summer.
It Is Not Dead.
John's Birches.
Kentucky Mountain Farm.
Language Barrier.
Last Laugh.
Last Meeting.
Last Metaphor, The.
Last Night Train.
Last Walk of Season.
Late Subterfuge.
Lesson in History.
Letter from a Coward to a Hero.
Letter of a Mother.
Letter to a Friend.
Limited, The.
Literal Dream.
Little Black Heart of the Telephone.
Little Boy and Lost Shoe.
Little Girl Wakes Early.
Loose Shutter, The.
Lord Jesus, I Wonder.
Loss, of Perhaps Love, in Our World of
    Contingency.
Love Recognized.
Love's Parable.
Love's Voice.
Man Coming of Age.
Mediterranean Basin.
Memory Forgotten.
Mexico is a Foreign Country: Five Studies in
    Naturalism.
Midnight.
Midnight Outcry.
Millpond Lost.
Milton: A Sonnet.
Minneapolis Story.
Minnesota Recollection.
Mirror, The.
Mission, The.
Monologue at Midnight.
Moonlight's Dream, The.
Mortal Limit.
Mortmain.
Mountain Mystery.
Mountain Plateau.
Mr. Dodd's Son.
Muted Music.
Myth of Mountain Sunrise.
Nameless Thing.
Natural History.
Nature of a Mirror, The.
New Dawn.
News Photo.
Night Walking.
No Bird Does Call.
Nocturne: Traveling Salesman in Hotel

Bedroom.
Not Quite Like a Top.
Nursery Rhymes.
October Picnic Long Ago.
Old Dog Dead.
Old Flame.
Old Love.
Old Nigger on One-Mule Cart Encountered
    Late at Night When Driving Home from
    Party in the Back Country.
Old Photograph of the Future.
Old-Time Childhood in Kentucky.
On Into the Night.
Only Poem, The.
Original Sin: A Short Story.
Orphanage Boy.
Owl, The.
Pacific Gazer.
Paradigm of Seasons.
Paradox.
Paradox of Time.
Part of What Might Have Been a Short Story,
    Almost Forgotten.
Passers-By on Snowy Night.
Patriotic Tour and Postulate of Joy.
Penological Study: Southern Exposure.
Picnic Remembered.
Place, The.
Platonic Drowse.
Platonic Lassitude.
Pondy Woods.
Portraits of Three Ladies.
Prairie Harvest.
Praise.
Praises for Mrs. Dodd.
Preternaturally Early Snowfall in Mating
    Season.
Pro Sua Vita.
Problem in Spatial Composition, A.
Problem of Autobiography / Vague
    Recollection or Dream?
Problem of Knowledge.
Prognosis: A Short Story, the End of Which
    You Will Know Soon Enough.
Promises.
Prophecy.
Pursuit.
Question and Answer.
Question at Cliff-Thrust.
Questions You Must Learn to Live Past.
Ransom.
Rather Like a Dream.
Rattlesnake Country.
Re-interment: Recollection of a Grandfather.
Reading Late at Night, Thermometer Falling.
Recollection in Upper Ontario, from Long
    Before.
Red-Tail Hawk and Pyre of Youth.
Remark for Historians.
Resolution.
Return, The: An Elegy.
Revelation.
Rumor at Twilight.
Rumor Verified.
Safe in Shade.
Sea Hates the Land, The.
Season Opens on Wild Boar in Chianti.
Seasons.
Shoes In Rain Jungle.
Short Thoughts for Long Nights.
Sila.
Sister Water.
Sitting on Farm Lawn on Sunday Afternoon.
Sky.
Small Eternity.
Small White House.
Smile, The.
Snowfall.
Snowshoeing Back to Camp in Gloaming.
So Frost Astounds.
So You Agree with What I Say? Well, What
    Did I Say?
Some Quiet, Plain Poems.
Somewhere.
Sonnets of Two Summers.
Speleology.

Star-Fall.
Summer Afternoon and Hypnosis.
Summer Rain in Mountains.
Sunset.
Sunset Scrupulously Observed.
Sunset Walk in Thaw-Time in Vermont.
Swimming in the Pacific.
Synonyms.
Tale of Time.
Terror.
There's a Grandfather's Clock in the Hall.
Three Darknesses.
Three Poems.
Time as Hypnosis.
Timeless, Twinned.
Tires on Wet Asphalt at Night.
To a Face in the Crowd.
To a Friend Parting.
To a Little Girl, One Year Old, in a Ruined
    Fortress.
To Certain Old Masters.
To One Awake.
Toward Rationality.
Trips to California.
True Love.
True Nature of Time, The.
Truth.
Trying to Tell You Something.
Tryst on Vinegar Hill.
Twice Born.
Two Pieces after Suetonius.
Two Studies in Idealism: Short Survey of
    American and Human History.
Uncertain Season in High Country.
Unless.
Upwardness.
Variation: Ode to Fear.
Vermont Ballad: Change of Season.
Vermont Thaw.
Vision ("I shall build me a house").
Vision ("Vision will come").
Vision under the October Mountain: A Love
    Poem.
Waiting.
Waking to Tap of Hammer.
Was It One of the Long Hunters of Kentucky
    who Discovered Boone at Sunset?
Way to Love God, A.
Ways of Day.
Weather Report.
What is the Voice that Speaks?
What Voice at Moth-Hour.
What Was the Throught.
Whatever You Now Are.
When Life Begins.
When the Tooth Cracks—Zing!
Whistle of the 3 A.M.
Whole Question, The.
Why Boy Came to Lonely Place.
Why Have I Wandered the Asphalt of
    Midnight?
Why You Climbed Up.
Wild Oats.
Wind and Gibbon.
Winter Dreams.
Winter Wheat: Oklahoma.
Wrestling Match, The.
You Sort Old Letters.
Youth Stares at Minoan Sunset.
Youthful Picnic Long Ago: Sad Ballad on Box.
Youthful Truth-Seeker, Half-Naked, at Night,
    Running down Beach South of San
    Francisco.

Warton, Thomas, the Younger (1728–90)
    Come, gentle sleep, death's image though thou
    art.

Weiss, Theodore (b. 1916)
    After Five Years.
    Another and Another and.
    As You Like It.
    Autobiographia Illiteraria.
    Barracks Apt. 14.
    Before the Night.
    Blithewood.
    Building, A.
    Caliban Remembers.

Camel in the Snow.
Certain Village, A.
Charm Against the Toothache, A.
Clothes Maketh the Man.
Commonplace, A.
Cure, The.
Dance Called David, The.
Death of Fathers, The.
Earthrise.
Egyptian Passage, An.
Far Out, Far In.
Fire at Alexandria, The.
Fresh Paint.
Giant Yea, The.
Gothic Tale, A.
Gunsight.
Heir Apparent, The.
Here and Now, The.
Hook, The.
Hostage, The.
House of Fire.
In the Round.
Into Summer.
Last Day and the First, The.
Last Letters, The.
Late Train, The.
Letter from the Pygmies, A.
Library Revisited, The.
Life of, The.
Living Room, A.
Local Matter, A.
Making It.
Malady.
Medium, The.
November Late.
Off to Patagonia.
On Stuffing a Goose.
Pair of Shoes, A.
Place of Laughter, The.
Pleasure, Pleasure.
Poem Recalled, A.
Polish Question, The.
Preface.
Quarrel, The.
Rapture The.
Recoveries.
Russian Lesson.
Slow Fuse, A.
Sonata Pathétique.
Storeroom, The.
Studying French.
Sultry Dawn.
Sum of Destructions, A.
Summer Thunderstorm, A.
Ten Little Rembrandts.
Things of the Past.
This Gray Age.
Trip through Yucatán, A.
Views and Spectacles.
Working Day, A.
World to Do, A.
"Yes, But . . . ."
Youngest Son, The.

Whalen, Philip (1923–2002)
Address to the Boobus.
All of it went on the wrong page.
Allegorical Painting: Capitalistic Society
    Destroyed by the Contradiction Within
    Itself. (Second Five-Year Plan).
Alleyway.
America!
America Inside & Outside Bill Brown's House
    in Bolinas.
April Showers Bring Rain?
Bay Trees Were About to Bloom, The.
Bead.
Behind the Door.
Birthday Poem.
Bleakness, Farewell.
Boobus Hierophante.
California Is Odious but Indispensable.
Chanson d'Outre Tombe.
Chariot, The.
Complaint: To the Muse.
Composition.
Compulsive Obligatory Paranoia Flashes.

Conditions That Prevail, The.
Confession and Penance.
Congress of Vienna, The.
Crowded.
Daydream, The.
Dear Mr President.
Defective Circles.
Detachment, Wisdom and Compassion.
Dharma Youth League, The.
Dharmakaya.
Discriminations.
Distraction Fit, A.
Dream.
Dream & Excursus, Arlington Massachusetts.
Dream Poems.
Duerden's Garage, Stinson Beach.
Dying Tooth Song.
EAMD.
Early Autumn in Upper Noe Valley.
Early Spring.
Epigrams & Imitations.
Failing.
5th Position.
For Albert Saijo.
For Allen, on His 60th Birthday.
For Brother Antoninus.
For Clark Coolidge.
For My Father.
Fourth of October, 1963, The.
Friendship Greetings.
Further Notice.
Garden, The.
Giant Sequoias.
Ginkakuji Michi.
Goddess.
Good News and Gospel.
Grand Design, The.
Growing and Changing.
Haiku, for Gary Snyder.
Haiku for Mike.
High-tension on Low-pressure Non-
    accomplishment Blues.
Historical Disquisitions.
Homage to Hart Crane.
Homage to Lucretius.
Homage to Rodin.
Homage to St. Patrick, García Lorca, & the
    Itinerant Grocer.
Homage to William Seward Burroughs.
"Horrible Incredible Lies": Keith Lampe
    Spontaneously.
Hot Springs Infernal in the Human Beast.
How to Be Successful & Happy Without
    Anybody Else Finding Out About It.
Hymnus Ad Patrem Sinensis.
"I Told Myself": Bobbie Spontaneously.
I wrote 2 letters & a postcard.
If You're So Smart, Why Ain't You Rich?
Imaginary Splendors.
Imagination of the Taj Mahal.
In the Night.
Inside Stuff.
International Date Line, Monday/Monday
    27:XI:67.
Irregular Ode, An.
Japanese Tea Garden Golden Gate Park in
    Spring.
Labor Day.
Lemon Trees.
L'Enfant Prodigue.
Letter to Thomas Clark 22:VII:71 from Bolinas
    where He Sat beside Me to Help to Write it,
    The.
Life and Death and a Letter to My Mother
    Beyond Them Both.
Life at Bolinas. The Last of California.
Life in the City: In Memoriam Edward
    Gibbon.
Life of Literature, The.
Literary Life in the Golden West.
Look Look Look.
Lotus Sutra, Naturalized, The.
Love Love Love Again.
Luxury in August.
M.
Mahayana.

Many Colored Squares.
Many Pages Must Be Thrown Away.
Mask.
Message.
Metaphysical Insomnia Jazz. Mumonkan
    XXIX.
Metaphysical Town Hall and Bookshop, The.
Money Is the Roost of All Eagles.
Monument Rescue Dim.
Morning Walk, A.
Murals Not Yet Dreamed.
Native Speech.
"NEFAS" / the Roman said.
Obsolete Models.
Occasional Dilemmas.
October First.
Ode for You.
Ode to Music, The.
Old Age Echoes.
One of My Favorite Songs Is Stormy Weather.
Palimpsest.
Past Ruin'd Ilion.
Penny for the Old Guy, A.
Plums, Metaphysics, an Investigation, a Visit,
    and a Short Funeral Ode.
Plus Ça Change.
Preface, The: "Continous fabric (nerve movie?)
    exactly as wide as these lines, A."
Prose Take-Out, Portland, 13:ix:58.
Public Opinions.
Radio Again, The.
Raging Desire & c.
Revolution, A.
Rich Interior, After Thomas Mann.
Road-Runner, The.
Romantic & Beautiful Poem Inspired by the
    Recollection of William Butler Yeats, His
    Life & Work, A.
Sad Song.
Sanjusangendo.
Scenes of Life at the Capital, *sels.*
Self-Portrait Sad, 22:ix:58.
Since You Ask Me.
Slop Barrel, The.
Some of These Days.
Somebody Else's Problem Bothers Me.
Something Nice About Myself.
Song for 2 Balalaikas on the Corner of 3rd &
    Market.
Song to Begin *Rohatsu.*
Soufflé.
Sourdough Mountain Lookout.
Spring Musick.
Stolen and Abandoned.
Success Is Failure.
"Sun Rises and Sets in That Child," So My
    Grandmother Used to Say, The.
T / O.
Take, 25:iii:59.
Talking Picture, The.
Tassajara.
Tears and Recriminations.
10:X:57, 45 Years Since the Fall of the Ch'ing
    Dynasty.
That Eyes! Those Nose!
That One.
3 Days Ago.
Three Mornings.
To a Poet.
To the Memory Of.
To the Moon.
To the Revolutionary Cadres of Balboa,
    Malibu & Santa Barbara.
Treading More Water.
Treading Water.
True Confessions.
Turn, The.
20:vii:58, On Which I Renounce the Notion of
    Social Responsiblity.
Universal & Susquehanna Mercy Co. Dayton,
    O., The.
Up in Michigan.
Vector Analysis.
Violins in Chaos?
Vision of Delight, The.
Vision of the Bodhisattvas, A.

Walking.
Walking beside the Kamogawa, Remembering Nansen and Fudo and Gary's Poem.
War Poem for Diane di Prima.
What About It?
What Are You Studying, These Days?
What? Writing in the Dining Room?
What's New?
White River Ode.
Winter, The ("Wheelbarrow's tire is flat, muddy ground now sets").
Winter, The ("Why do I fear the true winter death to come").

Wheatley, Phillis (c.1753–84)
Address to the Atheist, by P. Wheatley at the Age of 14 Years—1767, An.
Address to the Deist—1767, An.
America.
Answer to the *Rebus*, by the Author of These Poems, An.
Atheism.
Deism.
Elegy on Leaving, An.
Elegy, Sacred to the Memory of that Great Divine, the Reverend and Learned Dr. Samuel Cooper, An.
Elegy Sacred to the Memory of the Rev'd Samuel Cooper, D.D., An.
Elegy, To Miss. Mary Moorhead, on the Death of Her Father, The Rev. Mr. John Moorhead, An.
Farewell[l] to America, A. To Mrs. S. W.
Funeral Poem on the Death of C. E. an Infant of Twelve Months, A.
Goliath of Gath.
Hymn to Humanity, An.
Hymn to the Evening, An.
Hymn to the Morning, An.
Isaiah 63. 1–8.
Liberty and Peace, a Poem.
Niobe in Distress for Her Children Slain by Apollo.
Ocean.
Ode to Neptune.
On Being Brought from Africa to America.
On Friendship.
On Imagination.
On Messrs Hussey and Coffin.
On Recollection.
On the Capture of General Lee.
On the Death of a Young Gentleman.
On the Death of a Young Lady of Five Years of Age.
On the Death of Dr. Samuel Marshall. 1771.
On the Death of General Wooster.
On the Death of J. C. an Infant.
On the Death of Mr. Snider Murder'd by Richardson.
On the Death of the Rev. Dr. Sewell. 1769.
On the Death of the Rev. Mr. George Whitefield [1770].
On Virtue.
Philis's Reply to the Answer in Our Last by the Gentleman in the Navy.
Prayer: "Oh my Gracious Preserver!"
Thoughts on the Works of Providence.
To a Clergyman on the Death of His Lady.
To a Gentleman and Lady on the Death of the Lady's Brother and Sister, and a Child of the Name Avis, Aged One Year.
To a Gentleman of the Navy.
To a Gentleman on His Voyage to *Great-Britain* for the Recovery of His Health.
To a Lady and Her Children, on the Death of Her Son and Their Brother.
To a Lady on Her Coming to North-America with Her Son, for the Recovery of Her Health.
To a Lady on Her Remarkable Preservation in an Hurricane in *North-Carolina*.
To a Lady on the Death of Her Husband.
To a Lady on the Death of Three Relations.
To Captain H—D, of the 65th Regiment.
To His Excellency General Washington.
To His Honour the Lieutenant-Governor, on the Death of His Lady. *March* 24, 1773.

To Maecenas.
To Mr. and Mrs.—, on the Death of Their Infant Son.
To S. M., a Young African Painter.
To the Hon.ble Commodore Hood on His Pardoning a Deserter.
To the Honourable T. H. Esq; on the Death of His Daughter.
To the King's Most Excellent Majesty. 1768.
To the Rev. Dr. Thomas Amory on Reading His Sermons on Daily Devotion.
To the Right Honourable William, Earl of Dartmouth.
To the University of Cambridge, in New-England.
Voice of Freedom, The.

Whitman, Walt (1819–92)
Aboard at a Ship's Helm.
Abraham Lincoln, Born Feb. 12, 1809.
Adieu to a Soldier.
After an Interval.
After the Argument.
After the Dazzle of Day.
After the Sea-Ship.
After the Supper and Talk.
Ages and Ages Returning at Intervals.
Ah Poverties, Wincings, and Sulky Retreats.
All Is Truth.
Ambition.
America.
Among the Multitude.
Apostroph.
Apparitions.
Are You the New Person Drawn toward Me?
Army Corps on the March, An.
Artilleryman's Vision, The.
As Adam Early in the Morning.
As at Thy Portals Also Death.
As Consequent, Etc.
As I Ebb'd with the Ocean of Life.
As I Lay with My Head in Your Lap Camerado.
As I Ponder'd [or Pondered] in Silence.
As I Sit Writing Here.
As I Walk These Broad Majestic Days.
As I Watch'd the Ploughman Ploughing.
As If a Phantom Caress'd Me.
As in a Swoon.
As the Greek's Signal Flame.
As the Time Draws Nigh.
As They Draw to a Close.
As Toilsome I Wander'd Virginia's Woods.
Ashes of Soldiers.
Ashes of Soldiers: Epigraph.
Assurances.
Base of All Metaphysics, The.
Bathed in War's Perfume.
Beat! Beat! Drums!
Beautiful Women.
Beauty of the Ship, The.
Beginners.
Beginning My Studies.
Behold This Swarthy Face.
Bivouac on a Mountain Side.
Blood-Money.
Boston Ballad [1854], A.
Bravest Soldiers, The.
Bravo, Paris Exposition!
Broadway.
Broadway Pageant, A.
By Blue Ontario's Shore.
By Broad Potomac's Shore.
By the Bivouac's Fitful Flame.
Calming Thought of All, The.
Camps of Green.
Carol Closing Sixty-Nine.
Cavalry Crossing a Ford.
Centenarian's Story, The.
Chanting the Square Deific.
Child's Amaze, A.
Christmas Greeting, A.
City Dead-House, The.
City of Orgies.
City of Ships.
Clear Midnight, A.
Columbian's Song, The.

Come, Said My Soul.
Come Up from the Fields Father.
Commonplace, The.
Continuities.
Crossing Brooklyn Ferry.
Dalliance of the Eagles, The.
Darest Thou Now O Soul.
Dead Emperor, The.
Dead Tenor, The.
Death and Burial of McDonald Clarke, a Parody, The.
Death of General Grant.
Death of the Nature-Lover, The.
Death's Valley.
Debris.
Delicate Cluster.
Dirge for Two Veterans.
Dismantled Ship, The.
Dying Veteran, The.
Earth, My Likeness.
Eidolons.
Eighteen Sixty-One.
Election Day, November, 1884.
End of All, The.
Ended Day, An.
Ethiopia Saluting the Colors.
Europe, the 72d and 73d Year of These States.
Evening Lull, An.
Excelsior.
Faces.
Facing West from California's Shores.
Fame's Vanity.
Fancies at Navesink.
Farm Picture, A.
Fast-Anchor'd Eternal O Love!
Few Drops Known, The.
First Dandelion, The.
First O Songs for a Prelude.
Font of Type, A.
For Him I Sing.
For Queen Victoria's Birthday.
For Us Two, Reader Dear.
For You O Democracy.
France, The 18th Year of These States.
From Far Dakota's Cañons (June 25, 1876).
From Montauk Point.
From My Last Years.
From Paumanok Starting I Fly Like a Bird.
From Pent-up Aching Rivers.
Full of Life Now.
Germs.
Give Me the Splendid Silent Sun.
Gliding o'er All.
Glimpse, A.
Gods.
Going Somewhere.
Good-Bye, My Fancy!
Grand is the Seen.
Great Are the Myths.
Halcyon Days.
Hand-Mirror, A.
Hast Never Come to Thee an Hour.
Here the Frailest Leaves of Me.
Hours Continuing Long.
House of Friends, The.
How Solemn as One by One.
I Am He That Aches with Love.
I Dream'd in a Dream.
I Hear America Singing.
I Hear It Was Charged against Me.
I Heard You Solemn-Sweet Pipes of the Organ.
I Saw in Louisiana a Live-Oak Growing.
I Saw Old General at Bay.
I Sing the Body Electric.
I Sit and Look Out.
I Thought That Knowledge Alone Would Suffice.
I Was Looking a Long While.
In Cabin'd Ships at Sea.
In Former Songs.
In Paths Untrodden.
In the New Garden.
Inca's Daughter, The.
Interpolation Sounds.
Italian Music in Dakota.
Joy, Shipmate, Joy!

Kiss to the Bride, A.
Kosmos.
L of G.
L. of G.'s Purport.
Last Droplets.
Last Invocation, The.
Laws for Creations.
Leaf for Hand in Hand, A.
Leaflets.
Lessons.
Life.
Life and Death.
Lingering Last Drops.
Lo, Victress on the Peaks.
Locations and Times.
Long, Long Hence.
Long, Too Long America.
Look Down Fair Moon.
Love That Is Hereafter, The.
Mannahatta ("I was asking for something").
Mannahatta ("My city's fit and noble").
March in the Ranks Hard-Prest, and the Road
    Unknown, A.
Me Imperturbe.
Mediums.
Memories.
Memories of President Lincoln.
Miracles.
Mirages.
Mississippi at Midnight, The.
Mother and Babe.
My Canary Bird.
My Departure.
My Legacy.
My Picture-Gallery.
My 71st Year.
Myself and Mine.
Mystic Trumpeter, The.
Native Moments.
Nay, Tell Me Not To-day the Publish'd Shame.
New Year's Day, 1848.
Night on the Prairies.
No Labor-Saving Machine.
Noiseless Patient Spider, A.
Not Heat Flames Up and Consumes.
Not Heaving from My Ribb'd Breast Only.
Not Meagre, Latent Boughs Alone.
Not My Enemies Ever Invade Me.
Not the Pilot.
Not Youth Pertains to Me.
Now Finalè to the Shore.
Now Lift Me Close.
Now Precedent Songs, Farewell.
O Hymen! O Hymenee!
O Living Always, Always Dying.
O Magnet-South.
O Me! O Life!
O Star of France (1870–71).
O Sun of Real Peace.
O Tan-Faced Prairie-Boy.
O You Whom I Often and Silently Come.
Ode: "O, God of Columbia! O, Shield of the
    Free!"
Of Him I Love Day and Night.
Of Many a Smutch'd Deed Reminiscent.
Of That Blithe Throat of Thine.
Of the Terrible Doubt of Appearances.
Offerings.
Old Age's Lambent Peaks.
Old Age's Ship & Crafty Death's.
Old Chants.
Old Ireland.
Old Man's Thought of School, An.
Old Salt Kossabone.
Old War-Dreams.
On Journeys through the States.
On, on the Same, Ye Jocund Twain!
On the Beach at Night.
On the Beach at Night Alone.
On the Same Picture.
Once I Pass'd through a Populous City.
One Hour to Madness and Joy.
One Song, America, Before I Go.
One Thought Ever at the Fore.
One's-Self I Sing.
Or, from That Sea of Time.

Orange Buds by Mail from Florida.
Osceola.
Others May Praise What They Like.
Our Future Lot.
Our Old Feuillage.
Out from Behind This Mask.
Out of May's Shows Selected.
Out of the Cradle Endlessly Rocking.
Out of the Rolling Ocean the Crowd.
Outlines for a Tomb.
Over the Carnage Rose Prophetic a Voice.
Ox-Tamer, The.
Pallid Wreath, The.
Passage to India.
Patrolling Barnegat.
Paumanok.
Paumanok Picture, A.
Pensive and Faltering.
Pensive on Her Dead Gazing.
Perfections.
Persian Lesson, A.
Pioneers! O Pioneers!
Play-Ground, The.
Poem of Remembrances for a Girl or a Boy of
    These States.
Poets to Come.
Portals.
Prairie-Grass Dividing, The.
Prairie States, The.
Prairie Sunset, A.
Prayer of Columbus.
Promise to California, A.
Proud Music of the Storm.
Punishment of Pride, The.
Queries to My Seventieth Year.
Quicksand Years.
Race of Veterans.
Reconciliation.
Recorders Ages Hence.
Red Jacket (from Aloft).
Respondez!
Resurgemus.
Return of the Heroes, The.
Reversals.
Riddle Song, A.
Rise O Days from Your Fathomless Deeps.
Roaming in Thought.
Roots and Leaves Themselves Alone.
Rounded Catalogue Divine Complete, The.
Runner, The.
Sail Out for Good, Eidólon Yacht!
Salut au Monde!
Savantism.
Says.
Scented Herbage of My Breast.
Shakspeare-Bacon's Cipher.
Ship Ahoy!
Ship Starting, The.
Shut Not Your Doors.
Sight in Camp [in the Daybreak Gray and
    Dim], A.
Singer in the Prison, The.
Sleepers, The.
Small the Theme of My Chant.
So Far, and So Far, and On toward the End.
So Long!
Sobbing of the Bells, The.
Solid, Ironical, Rolling Orb.
Sometimes with One I Love.
Song at Sunset.
Song for All Seas, All Ships.
Song for Certain Congressmen.
Song for Occupations, A.
Song of Joys, A.
Song of Myself.
Song of Prudence.
Song of the Answerer.
Song of the Banner at Daybreak.
Song of the Broad-Axe [or Broad-Ax].
Song of the Exposition.
Song of the Open Road.
Song of the Redwood-Tree.
Song of the Rolling Earth, A.
Song of the Universal.
Soon Shall the Winter's Foil Be Here.
Sounds of the Winter.

Souvenirs of Democracy.
Spain, 1873–74.
Spanish Lady, The.
Sparkles from the Wheel.
Spirit That Form'd This Scene.
Spirit Whose Work Is Done.
Spontaneous Me.
Starting from Paumanok.
States!
Still Though the One I Sing.
Stronger Lessons.
Supplement Hours.
Tears.
Tests.
Thanks in Old Age.
That Music Always Round Me.
That Shadow My Likeness.
Then Shall Perceive.
There Was a Child Went Forth.
These Carols.
These I Singing in Spring.
Thick-Sprinkled Bunting.
Think of the Soul.
This Compost.
This Day, O Soul.
This Moment Yearning and Thoughtful.
Thou Mother with Thy Equal Brood.
Thou Orb Aloft Full-Dazzling.
Thou Reader.
Thought.
Thought ("Of obedience, faith, adhesiveness").
Thought ("Of Justice—as if Justice could be
    any thing but the same ample law,
    expounded by natural judges and saviors").
Thought ("Of persons arrived at high positions,
    ceremonies, wealth, scholarships, and the
    like").
Thought ("As I sit with others at a great feast,
    suddenly while the music is playing").
Thought of Columbus, A.
Thoughts.
Thoughts ("Of public opinion").
Thoughts ("Of these years I sing").
Thoughts—I: Visages.
Thoughts—6: "Of What I Write."
Time to Come.
To a Certain Cantatrice.
To a Certain Civilian.
To a Common Prostitute.
To a Foil'd European Revolutionaire.
To a Historian.
To a Locomotive in Winter.
To a President.
To a Pupil.
To a Stranger.
To a Western Boy.
To Be at All.
To-day and Thee.
To Foreign Lands.
To Get the Final Lilt of Songs.
To Him That Was Crucified.
To Old Age.
To One Shortly to Die.
To Rich Givers.
To Soar in Freedom and in Fullness of Power.
To the East and to the West.
To the Garden the World.
To the Leaven'd Soil They Trod.
To the Man-of-War Bird.
To the Pending Year.
To the Reader at Parting.
To the States.
To the States, To Identify the 16th, 17th, or
    18th Presidentiad.
To the Sun-set Breeze.
To Thee Old Cause.
To Think of Time.
To Those Who've Fail'd.
To You.
To You ("Let us twain walk aside from the
    rest").
To You ("Stranger, if you passing meet me and
    desire to speak to me, why should you not
    speak to me?").
Torch, The.
Transpositions.

Trickle Drops.
True Conquerors.
Turn O Libertad.
Twenty Years.
Twilight.
Twilight Song, A.
Two Rivulets.
Unexpress'd, The.
Unfolded Out of the Folds.
United States to Old World Critics, The.
Unnamed Lands.
Unseen Buds.
Untold Want, The.
Vigil Strange I Kept on the Field One Night.
Virginia—the West.
Visor'd.
Vocalism.
Voice from Death, A.
Voice of the Rain, The.
Wallabout Martyrs, The.
Wandering at Morn.
Warble for Lilac-Time.
Washington's Monument, February, 1885.
We All Shall Rest at Last.
We Two Boys Together Clinging.
We Two, How Long We Were Fool'd.
Weave In, My Hardy Life.
What Am I After All.
What Best I See in Thee.
What Place Is Besieged?
What Ship Puzzled at Sea.
What Think You I Take My Pen in Hand?
When I Heard At The Close Of The Day.
When I Heard the Learn'd Astronomer.
When I Peruse the Conquer'd Fame.
When I Read the Book.
When the Full-Grown Poet Came.
While behind All, Firm and Erect.
While Not the Past Forgetting.
Whispers of Heavenly Death.
Who Is Now Reading This?
Who Learns My Lesson Complete.
Whoever You Are Holding Me Now in Hand.
With All Thy Gifts.
With Antecedents.
With Husky-Haughty Lips, O Sea!
Woman Waits for Me, A.
World below the Brine, The.
World Take Good Notice.
Wound-Dresser, The.
Year of Meteors (1859–60).
Year That Trembled and Reel'd beneath Me.
Years of the Modern.
Yet, Yet Ye Downcast Hours.
Yonnondio.
You Felons on Trial in Courts.
You Lingering Sparse Leaves of Me.
Young Grimes.
Youth, Day, Old Age and Night.

Whittier, John Greenleaf (1807–92)
Abraham Davenport.
Abram Morrison.
Adjustment.
After Election.
Album Verses.
All's Well.
Among the Hills.
Amy Wentworth.
Andrew Rykman's Prayer.
Angel of Patience, The.
Angels of Buena Vista, The.
Anniversary Poem.
Answer, The.
April.
Arisen at Last.
Artist of the Beautiful, An.
Astræa.
Astræa at the Capitol.
At Eventide.
At Last.
At Port Royal.
At School-Close.
At Washington.
Autograph, An ("I write my name as one").
Autograph, An ("Years that since we met").
Autumn Thoughts.

Banished from Massachusetts.
Barbara Frietchie.
Barclay of Ury.
Barefoot Boy, The.
Bartholdi Statue, The.
Battle Autumn of 1862, The.
Bay of Seven Islands, The.
Bayard Taylor.
Benedicite.
Benevolence.
Between the Gates.
Birchbrook Mill.
Birthday Wreath, The.
Bolivar.
Book, The.
Branded Hand, The.
Brewing of Soma, The.
Bridal of Pennacook, The.
Brother of Mercy, The.
Brown Dwarf of Rügen, The.
Brown of Ossawatomie.
Bryant on His Birthday.
Burial of Barber.
Burning Drift-Wood.
Burns.
By Their Works.
Cable Hymn, The.
Calef in Boston.
Call of the Christian, The.
Captain's Well, The.
Cassandra Southwick.
Centennial Hymn.
Chalkley Hall.
Changeling, The.
Channing.
Chapel of the Hermits, The.
Chicago.
Child-Songs.
Christian Slave, The.
Christian Tourists, The.
Christmas Carmen, A.
Christmas of 1888, The.
Cities of the Plain, The.
Clear Vision, The.
Clerical Oppressors.
Cobbler Keezar's Vision.
Common Question, The.
Conductor Bradley.
Conquest of Finland, The.
Countess, The.
Crisis, The.
Cross, The.
Crucifixion, The.
Cry of a Lost Soul, The.
Curse of the Charter-Breakers, The.
Cypress-Tree of Ceylon, The.
Daniel Neall.
Daniel Wheeler.
Day, A.
Day's Journey, A.
Dead Feast of the Kol-Folk, The.
Dead Ship of Harpswell, The.
Dedication: "I would the gift I offer here."
Deity, The.
Democracy.
Demon of the Study, The.
Derne.
Disarmament.
Disenthralled, The.
Divine Compassion.
Dole of Jarl Thorkell, The.
Double-Headed Snake of Newbury, The.
Dream of Pio Nono, The.
Dream of Summer, A.
Drovers, The.
Drunkard to His Bottle, The.
Earthquake, The.
Easter Flower Gift, An.
Ego.
Ein Feste Burg Ist Unser Gott.
Elliott.
Emancipation Group, The.
Eternal Goodness, The.
Eva.
Eve of Election, The.
Evening in Burmah.

Exile's Departure, The.
Exiles, The.
Expostulation.
Extract from "A New England Legend."
Ezekiel.
Fair Quakeress, The.
Familist's Hymn, The.
Farewell, A: "What shall I say, dear friends, to whom I owe."
Farewell, The: "Gone, gone,—sold and gone."
Female Martyr, The.
First-Day Thoughts.
First Flowers, The.
Fishermen, The.
Fitz-Greene Halleck.
Flowers in Winter.
Follen.
For an Autumn Festival.
For Righteousness' Sake.
Forgiveness.
Fountain, The.
Fragment, A: "Dreadful burden of our sins we feel, The."
Fratricide, The.
Freed Islands, The.
Freedom in Brazil.
Frémont Campaign Song, A.
Friend's Burial, The.
From Perugia.
Frost Spirit, The.
Fruit-Gift, The.
Funeral Tree of the Sokokis.
Gallows, The.
Garden.
Garibaldi.
Garrison.
Garrison of Cape Ann, The.
George L. Stearns.
Gift of Tritemius, The.
Giving and Taking.
Godspeed.
Golden Wedding of Longwood, The.
Gone.
Grave by the Lake, The.
Greeting.
Greeting, A.
Hampton Beach.
Haschish, The.
Haverhill.
Hazel Blossoms.
Healer, The.
Help.
Henchman, The.
Hermit of the Thebaid, The.
Hero, The.
Hill-Top, The.
Hive at Gettysburg, The.
Holy Land, The.
Home-Coming of the Bride, The.
Homestead, The.
How Mary Grew.
How the Robin Came.
How the Women Went from Dover.
Howard at Atlanta.
Human Sacrifice, The.
Hunters of Men, The.
Huskers, The.
Hymn for the Celebration of Emancipation at Newburyport.
Hymn for the House of Worship at Georgetown.
Hymn for the Opening of Plymouth Church.
Hymn for the Opening of Thomas Starr King's House of Worship.
Hymn: "O Holy Father! just and true."
Hymn: "O Thou, whose presence went before."
Hymn of the Children.
Hymn of the Dunkers.
Hymn Sung at Christmas by the Scholars of St. Helena's Island, S.C.
Hymns from the French of Lamartine.
Hymns of the Brahmo Somaj.
I Was a Stranger and Ye Took Me in.
Ichabod[!].
In Memory.

In Peace.
In Quest.
In Remembrance of Joseph Sturge.
In School-Days.
In the Evil Days.
In the "Old South."
Inscription: "Eagle, stooping from yon snow-blown peaks, The."
Inscriptions.
Invocation: "Through Thy clear spaces, Lord, of old."
Isabel.
Isabella of Austria.
Italy.
James Russell Lowell.
John Underhill.
Jubilee Singers, The.
Judith at the Tent of Holofernes.
June on the Merrimac.
Kallundborg Church.
Kansas Emigrants, The.
Kathleen.
Kenoza Lake.
Khan's Devil, The.
King Solomon and the Ants.
King Volmer and Elsie.
King's Missive, The.
Kinsman.
Knight of St. John, The.
Kossuth.
Lakeside, The.
Lament, A: "Circle is broken, one seat is forsaken, The."
Landmarks, The.
Last Eve of Summer, The.
Last Walk in Autumn, The.
Laurels, The.
Laus Deo!
Lay of Old Time, A.
Le Marais du Cygne.
Legacy, A.
Legend of St. Mark, The.
Legend of the Lake, A.
Leggett's Monument.
Letter, A.
Letter from a Missionary of the Methodist Episcopal Church South, in Kansas, to a Distiguished Politician.
Letter to Lucy Larcom.
Lexington.
Library, The.
Light That Is Felt, The.
Lines from a Letter to a Young Clerical Friend.
Lines on a Fly-Leaf.
Lines on Leaving Appledore.
Lines on the Death of S. Oliver Torrey.
Lines on the Portrait of a Celebrated Publisher.
Lines Written in an Album.
Lost Occasion, The.
Lost Statesman, The.
Lucy Hooper.
Lumbermen, The.
Lydia H. Sigourney.
Mabel Martin.
Maids of Attitash, The.
Mantle of St. John de Matha, The.
Marguerite.
Mary Garvin.
Massachusetts.
Massachusetts to Virginia.
Maud Muller.
Mayflowers, The.
Meeting, The.
Memorial, A.
Memories.
Memory, A.
Memory of Burns, The.
Men of Old, The.
Merrimac, The.
Metacom.
Milton.
Minister's Daughter, The.
Miriam.
Missionary, The.
Mrs. Choate's House-Warming.
Mithridates at Chios.

Mogg Megone.
Moloch in State Street.
Moral Warfare, The.
Mount Agiochook.
Mountain Pictures.
Mulford.
My Birthday.
My Dream.
My Namesake.
My Playmate.
My Psalm.
My Soul and I.
My Thanks.
My Triumph.
Mystery, A.
Mystic's Christmas, The.
Name, A.
Naples.
Nauhaught, the Deacon.
New Exodus, The.
New Hampshire.
New Wife and the Old, The.
New Year, The.
Norembega.
Norsemen, The.
Norumbega Hall.
O. W. Holmes on His Eightieth Birthday.
Ocean.
Official Piety.
Old Burying-Ground, The.
On a Fly-Leaf of Longfellow's Poems.
On a Prayer-Book.
On Receiving an Eagle's Quill from Lake Superior.
On the Big Horn.
One of the Signers.
Oriental Maxims.
Our Autocrat.
Our Country.
Our Master.
Our River.
Our State.
Outdoor Reception, An.
Over-Heart, The.
Overruled.
Pæan.
Pageant, The.
Palatine, The.
Palestine.
Palm-Tree, The.
Panorama, The.
Pass of the Sierra, The.
Past and Coming Year, The.
Pastoral Letter, The.
Peace Autumn, The.
Peace Convention at Brussels, The.
Peace of Europe, The.
Pennsylvania Hall.
Pennsylvania Pilgrim, The.
Pentucket.
Pictures.
Pine-Tree, The.
Pipes at Lucknow, The.
Poet and the Children, The.
Poor Voter on Election Day, The.
Prayer of Agassiz, The.
Prayer-Seeker, The.
Preacher, The.
Pressed Gentian, The.
Prisoner for Debt, The.
Prisoners of Naples, The.
Problem, The.
Proclamation, The.
Proem: "I love the old melodious lays."
Prophecy of Samuel Sewall, The.
Pumpkin, The.
Quaker Alumni, The.
Quaker of the Olden Time, The.
Quakers Are Out, The.
Questions of Life.
R. S. S., at Deer Island on the Merrimac.
Rabbi Ishmael.
Randolph of Roanoke.
Ranger, The.
Rantoul.
Raphael.

Red Riding-Hood.
Red River Voyageur, The.
Reformer, The.
Relic, The.
Remembrance.
Rendition, The.
Requirement.
Requital.
Response.
Reunion, The.
Revelation.
Revisited.
Reward, The.
Ritner.
River Path, The.
Robin, The.
"Rock" in El Ghor, The.
Rock-Tomb of Bradore, The.
Sabbath Scene, A.
Saint Gregory's Guest.
St. John.
St. Martin's Summer.
Samuel E. Sewall.
Samuel J. Tilden.
Sea Dream, A.
Seed-Time and Harvest.
Seeking of the Waterfall, The.
Sentence of John L. Brown, The.
Shadow and the Light, The.
Ship-Builders, The.
Shoemakers, The.
Sicilian Vespers, The.
Singer, The.
Sisters, The.
Sisters, The: A Picture by Barry, The.
Skipper Ireson's Ride.
Slave-Ships, The.
Slaves of Martinique, The.
Snow-Bound [or Snow-Bound; a Winter Idyl].
Song, A: "Beneath thy skies, November!"
Song for the Time, A.
Song of Harvest, A.
Song of Slaves in the Desert.
Song of the Vermonters, 1779, The.
Spirit of the North, The.
Spiritual Manifestation, A.
Stanzas: "Bind up thy tresses, thou beautiful one."
Stanzas for the Times.
Star of Bethlehem, The.
Storm on Lake Asquam.
Story of Ida, The.
Summer by the Lakeside.
Summer Pilgrimage, A.
Summons, A.
Summons, The.
Sumner.
Sunset on the Bearcamp.
Swan Song of Parson Avery, The.
Sweet Fern.
Sycamores, The.
Tauler.
Telling the Bees.
Tent on the Beach, The.
Texas.
Thiers.
Thomas Starr King.
Three Bells, The.
Thy Will Be Done.
To a Cape Ann Schooner.
To a Friend.
To a Poetical Trio in the City of Gotham.
To a Southern Statesman.
To Avis Keene.
To Charles Sumner.
To Delaware.
To E. C. S
To Englishmen.
To ———: "Fair Nature's priestesses! to whom."
To Faneuil Hall.
To Fredrika Bremer.
To G. G.
To George B. Cheever.
To J. P.
To James T. Fields.

To John C. Frémont.
To Lucy Larcom.
To Lydia Maria Child.
To ———: "Maiden! with the fair brown tresses."
To Massachusetts.
To My Friend on the Death of His Sister.
To My Old Schoolmaster.
To My Sister.
To Oliver Wendell Holmes.
To Pennsylvania.
To Pius IX.
To Ronge.
To Samuel E. Sewall and Harriet W. Sewall.
To the Memory of Charles B. Storrs.
To the Memory of Thomas Shipley.
To the Reformers of England.
To the Thirty-Ninth Congress.
To William H. Seward.
To William Lloyd Garrison.
Toussaint L'Ouverture.
Trailing Arbutus, The.
Trinitas.
Truce of Piscataqua, The.
Trust.
Two Angels, The.
Two Elizabeths, The.
Two Loves, The.
Two Rabbins, The.
Utterance.
Vale of the Merrimac, The.
Valuation.
Vanishers, The.
Vaudois Teacher, The.
Vesta.
Vision of Echard, The.
Voices, The.
Vow of Washington, The.
Voyage of the Jettie.
Waiting, The.
Watchers, The.
Welcome to Lowell, A.
Well of Loch Maree, The.
What of the Day?
What State Street Said to South Carolina, and What South Carolina Said to State Street.
What the Birds Said.
What the Traveller Said at Sunset.
What the Voice Said.
Wife of Manoah to Her Husband, The.
William Forster.
William Francis Bartlett.
Wilson.
Wind of March, The.
Winter Roses.
Wish of To-day, The.
Wishing Bridge, The.
Witch of Wenham, The.
Within the Gate.
Woman, A.
Wood Giant, The.
Word for the Hour, A.
Word, The.
Wordsworth.
World's Convention, The.
Worship.
Worship of Nature, The.
Wreck of Rivermouth, The.
Yankee Girl, The.
Yorktown.

Whyte, Laurence
Some Critical Annotations, on Various Subjects Which Have Been Handled by Several Authors, *sels.*

Wilbur, Richard (b. 1921)
Advice from the Muse.
Advice to a Prophet.
After the Last Bulletins.
Agent, The.
Alatus.
All That Is.
All These Birds.
Altitudes.
&.
Another Voice.
Apology.

April 5, 1974.
Aspen and the Stream, The.
Attention Makes Infinity.
Avowal, The.
Ballade for the Duke of Orléans.
Baroque Wall-Fountain in the Villa Sciarra, A.
Beacon, The.
Beasts.
Beautiful Changes, The.
Bell Speech.
Beowulf.
Black Birch in Winter, A.
Black November Turkey, A.
Boy at the Window.
C Minor.
Caserta Garden.
Castles and Distances.
Catch, The.
Ceremony.
Children of Darkness.
Christmas Hymn, A.
Chronic Condition, A.
Cicadas.
Clearness.
Complaint.
Conjuration.
Cottage Street, 1953.
Courtyard Thaw, A.
Death of a Toad, The.
Digging for China.
Driftwood.
Dubious Night, A.
Dutch Courtyard, A.
Eight Riddles from Symphosius.
Epistemology.
Event, An.
Exeunt.
Eye, The.
Fable, A.
Fall in Corrales.
Fern-Beds in Hampshire County.
Finished Man, A.
Fire-Truck, A.
First Snow in Alsace.
Five Women Bathing in Moonlight.
Flippancies.
Flumen Tenebrarum.
Folk Tune.
For Dudley.
For Ellen.
For K. R. on Her Sixtieth Birthday.
For the New Railway Station in Rome.
For the Student Strikers.
For W. H. Auden.
Fourth of July, The.
From the Lookout Rock.
Games One.
Games Two.
Gemini.
Giacometti.
Giaour and the Pacha, The.
Gifts, The.
Glance from the Bridge, A.
Gnomons.
Good Servant, The.
Grace.
Grasse: The Olive Trees.
Grasshopper, A.
Hamlen Brook.
He Was.
Hole in the Floor, A.
Icarium Mare.
In a Bird Sanctuary.
In a Churchyard.
In Limbo.
In the Elegy Season.
In the Field.
In the Smoking-Car.
John Chapman.
John Chrysostom.
Juggler.
June Light.
Junk.
La Rose des Vents.
Lamarck Elaborated.
Lament: "Nashe's old queens who bartered

young and fair."
Late Aubade, A.
Leaving.
L'Etoile.
Lightness.
Lilacs, The.
Looking into History.
Love Calls Us to the Things of This World.
Loves of the Puppets.
Lying.
March.
Marché aux Oiseaux.
Marginalia.
Matthew VIII, 28 ff.
Mechanist, The.
Melongène.
Merlin Enthralled.
Mill, The.
Miltonic Sonnet for Mr. Johnson on His Refusal of Peter Hurd's Official Portrait, A.
Mind.
Mind-Reader, The.
Mined Country.
Museum Piece.
My Father Paints the Summer.
Next Door.
Objects.
October Maples, Portland.
Ode to Pleasure.
On Freedom's Ground.
On Having Mis-identified a Wild Flower.
On the Eyes of an SS Officer.
On the Marginal Way.
Orchard Trees, January.
Pangloss's Song: A Comic-Opera Lyric.
Parable.
Pardon, The.
Part of a Letter.
Peace of Cities, The.
Pelican, The.
Peter.
Piazza di Spagna, Early Morning.
Piccola Commedia.
Pity.
Place Pigalle.
Plain Song for Comadre, A.
Playboy.
Poplar, Sycamore.
Potato.
Praise in Summer.
Prisoner of Zenda, The.
Problem from Milton, A.
Proof, The.
Puritans, The.
Regatta, The.
Riddle, A.
Ride, The.
Rillons, Rillettes.
Rule, The.
Running.
Seed Leaves.
Shad-Time.
Shallot, A.
Shame.
She.
Simile for Her Smile, A.
Simplification, A.
Sirens, The.
Sketch, A.
Sleepless at Crown Point.
Some Riddles from Symphosius.
Someone Talking to Himself.
Song, A: "As at the bottom of a seething well."
Sonnet: "Winter deepening, the hay all in, The."
Speech for the Repeal of the McCarran Act.
Statues.
Still, Citizen Sparrow.
Stop.
Storm in April, A.
Summer Morning, A.
Sun and Air.
Sunlight Is Imagination.
Superiorities.
Teresa.

Terrace, The.
Then.
Thyme Flowering among Rocks.
To an American Poet Just Dead.
To His Skeleton.
To Ishtar.
To the Etruscan Poets.
Transit.
Trolling for Blues.
Two Quatrains for First Frost.
Two Riddles from Aldhelm.
Two Songs in a Stanza of Beddoes'.
Two Voices in a Meadow.
Tywater.
Undead, The.
Under a Tree.
Under Cygnus.
Up, Jack.
Violet and Jasper.
Voice from under the Table, A.
Walgh-Vogel, The.
Walking to Sleep.
Water Walker.
Waters, The.
Wedding Toast, A.
Wellfleet: The House.
Winter Spring.
Wood, A.
"World Without Objects Is a Sensible
    Emptiness, A."
Worlds.
Writer, The.
Wyeth's Mild Cans.
Year's End.

Wilde, Oscar (1854–1900)
Amor Intellectualis.
Apologia.
At Verona.
Athanasia.
Ave Imperatrix.
Ave Maria Gratia Plena.
Ballad of Reading Gaol, The.
Burden of Itys, The.
By the Arno.
Camma.
Canzonet.
Chanson.
Charmides.
E Tenebris.
Easter Day.
Endymion.
Fabien dei Franchi.
Fantaisies Décoratives.
From Spring Days to Winter.
Garden of Eros, The.
Grave of Keats, The.
Grave of Shelley, The.
Harlot's House, The.
Hélas!
Her Voice.
Humanitad.
Impression de Voyage.
Impression du Matin.
Impression: Le Réveillon.
Impressions ("Lily's withered chalice falls,
    The").
Impressions ("Sea is flecked with bars of grey,
    The").
In the Forest.
In the Gold Room: A Harmony.
Italia.
La Bella Donna della Mia Mente.
Le Jardin des Tuileries.
Libertatis Sacra Fames.
Lotus Leaves.
Louis Napoleon.
Madonna Mia.
My Voice.
New Helen, The.
New Remorse, The.
Pan: Double Villanelle.
Panthea.
Phèdre.
Portia.
Quantum Mutata.

Queen Henrietta Maria.
Quia Multum Amavi.
Ravenna.
Requiescat.
Rome Unvisited.
Roses and Rue.
San Miniato.
Santa Decca.
Sen Artysty; or, The Artist's Dream.
Serenade: "Western wind is blowing fair, The."
Silentium Amoris.
Sonnet on Approaching Italy.
Sonnet on Hearing the *Dies Iræ* Sung in the
    Sistine Chapel.
Sonnet on the Massacre of the Christians in
    Bulgaria.
Sonnet on the Sale by Auction of Keats' Love
    Letters.
Sonnet to Liberty.
Sonnet Written in Holy Week at Genoa.
Sphinx, The.
Sweet I blame you not for mine the fault was,
    had I not been made of common clay.
Symphony in Yellow.
Tædium Vitæ.
Theatre at Argos, The.
Theocritus: A Villanelle.
Theoretikos.
To Milton.
To My Wife: With a Copy of My Poems.
True Knowledge, The.
Under the Balcony.
Urbs Sacra Æterna.
Vision, A.
Vita Nuova.
Wasted Days.
With a Copy of 'A House of Pomegranates.'

Williams, C. K. (Charles Kenneth) (b. 1936)
Acids.
Admiral Fan, The.
After That.
Allies: According to Herodotus.
Alzheimer's: The Husband.
Alzheimer's: The Wife.
Another Dollar.
Ashes Ashes We All Fall Down.
Baby, I don't want.
Bad Mouth.
Becoming Somebody Else.
Before This.
Beginning of April, The.
Being Alone.
Beyond.
Bishop Tutu's Visit to the White House: 1984.
Blades.
Blame.
Bob.
Body, The.
Bread.
Bringing It Home.
Call, The.
Cautionary, The.
Cave, The.
Cellophane.
Child Psychology.
Clay out of Silence.
Color of Time, The.
Combat.
Conscience.
Covenant, The.
Cracks.
Crawl.
Creams.
Crime.
Crime, The.
Critic, The.
Dawn.
Day for Anne Frank, A.
Did I write this.
Dimensions.
Dirty Talker: D Line, Boston, The.
Dog, The.
Dominion: Depression.
Don't.
Downwards.

Dream of Mind: The Gap, A.
Dream, The.
Drought.
Easter.
Elms.
End of Drought.
Ethics.
Even If I Could.
Experience.
Failure.
Faint Praise.
Fast Food.
Fat.
Fifteen.
Fire.
First Desires.
Flat.
Fleas, too, / have fled, The.
Flight.
Floor.
For Children When They Grow Up.
For Gail, When I Was Five.
Friends.
From My Window.
From Now On.
Game, The.
Gas Station, The.
Gift, The.
Giving It Up.
Good Mother: Out.
Greed.
Guatemala: 1964.
Hail goes / dancing, The.
Halves.
Hard Part, The.
Harm.
Helen.
Herakles.
Hercules, Deianira, Nessus.
History.
Hog Heaven.
Holiday: / every / yard or, A.
Hood.
Hooks.
Hounding Mercy.
How Humble We Were before This.
I Am the Bitter Name.
I know / nothing anymore.
I sit in my room.
I'd forgotten and / how could I ever.
Image, The.
In the Heart of the Beast.
In the middle / of a bite of.
In the next life.
In There.
Inches.
Innings.
Instinct.
Insult, The.
Interrogation II.
It Is Teeming.
It Is This Way with Men.
It's over now. I watch.
Jetsam.
Junior High School Concert: Salle Rossini.
Just Right.
Keep It.
Kin.
Kingdom of Stinking Wishes, The.
Knot, The.
Last Deaths, The.
Last, The.
Le Petit Salvié.
Like Little Birds.
Listen carefully. / I'm meditating.
Little Shirt, The.
Long Bells, The.
Long Naked Walk of the Dead, The.
Loss.
Love: Beginnnings.
Love: Wrath.
Love: Youth.
Madder.
Man Who Owns Sleep, The.
Matter, The.
Medusa.

Men.
Mirror, The.
Modern, The.
Mornings: Catherine.
Most excruciating / thing, The.
My Book, My Book.
My Fly.
My Mother's Lips.
Near the Haunted Castle.
Neglect.
New Car.
Next to the Last Poem about God, The.
Nickname of Hell, The.
Nostalgia.
Nut, The.
Of What Is Past.
On Learning of a Friend's Illness.
On the Other Hand.
On the Roof.
One of the Muses.
Or.
Orchid, The.
Other Side, The.
Park, The.
Past, The.
Patience Is When You Stop Waiting.
Peace.
Penance.
Philadelphia. 1978.
Poem for the Governments, A.
Politics.
Poor Hope.
Portions of Manslayer.
Prodigy, The.
Question, The.
Rabbit Fights for His Life the Leopard Eats
     Lunch, The.
Race of the Flood, The.
Racists.
Rampage, The.
Reading: Early Sorrow.
Reading: Winter.
Refuge, Serpent-Riders.
Regulars, The.
Repression.
Resentment.
Ribbons.
Room.
Rungs.
Saint Sex.
Sanctity, The.
Saturday.
Scar.
Secrets.
Shade, The.
Shadows.
Shame.
Shells ("It's horrible").
Shells ("Shells of fearful insensitivity").
Signs.
Silence, The.
Sky, Water.
Sleeping Over.
Snow: I.
Snow: II.
So / mucked up with.
Solid, The.
Soliliquies.
Soon.
Sorrow, The.
Souls.
Spider Psyche.
Spirit the Triumph, The.
Spit.
Spring: another / joke. / This run-down.
Still Life.
Sting, The.
Storm, The.
Suicide: Anne.
Tails.
Tar.
Ten Below.
That night, / winter, / rain.
That the world / is going.
Then the Brother of the Wind.
They Warned Him Then They Threw Him

Away.
They wash you / when.
Thinking Thought.
Thirst.
This Day.
This Is a Sin.
This is what, / at last, it is.
Three Seasons and a Gorilla.
Time: 1978.
Time: 1976.
To Listen.
To Market.
Toil.
Trappers.
Trash.
Travelers.
Twice More.
Undead, The.
Vehicle: Absence.
Vehicle: Conscience.
Vehicle: Violence.
Villanelle of the Suicide's Mother.
Waking Jed.
War.
What a sound his.
What Did the Man Do with the Clouds?
What Is and Is Not.
What Must I Do To Be Lost?
What we are / given.
When.
When / you were small, I.
Winter, / damn, / again.
With Ignorance.
Work.
World's Greatest Tricycle-Rider, The.
You're two, that's great.
Yours.

Williams, Francis (c.1700–70)
     Ode, An: "At length revolving fates th'
         expected year."

Williams, Miller (b. 1930)
     Accident: A Short Story.
     Adjusting to the Light.
     Aesthetic Distance.
     Affair, The.
     After a Brubeck Concert.
     After the Revolution for Jesus a Secular Man
         [or the Associate Professor] Prepares His
         Final Remarks.
     After You Die You Don't Give a Piddling
         Damn.
     Aging Actress Sees Herself a Starlet on the
         Late Show, The.
     Agreeing.
     And Then.
     And Then I Headed on Back Home.
     And When in Scenes of Glory.
     Animals.
     Architecture of the American Mind.
     Art Photographer Puts His Model at Ease, The.
     As You Both Shall Live.
     Associate Professor Delivers an Exhortation to
         His Failing Students, The.
     Associate Professor (Mad Scientist) to (His
         Love) His Student in Physics 100 Lab.
     At the Children's Hospital in Little Rock.
     At the Christening of an Infant the Mind of the
         Young Preacher Wanders Again.
     At Three Every Thursday Afternoon.
     August Evening Outside of Nashville, An.
     Autopsy.
     Ballad of a Little Delta Town.
     Before.
     Being Here.
     Believing.
     Believing in Symbols.
     Beside an Open Grave the Mind of the Young
         Preacher Comes Almost to Terms.
     Book, The.
     Buying and Selling.
     Catch with Reuben.
     Caterpillar, The.
     Caution.
     Children's Games.
     Christmas Poem, A.
     Closing the House.

Clutter of Silence: Invention for Two Voices.
Coming Out.
Compassion.
Coping.
Curator, The.
Day in the Death, A.
Deadsong for a Neighbor Child Who Ran
     Away to the Woods.
Death of Chet Baker, The.
Despairing of Understanding We Fall Into
     Decadence.
Divorce.
Documenting It.
During a Funeral Service the Mind of the
     Young Preacher Wanders Again.
During the Hymn Before the Christmas
     Sermon the Mind of the Young Preacher
     Wanders Again.
Dust.
E-mail.
Entropy.
Euglena.
Evening: A Studio in Rome.
Everyone Dies in a Light Rain.
Everything Is Fine Here. How Are You?
Excuse Me.
Fifty.
Firebreathers at the Café Deux Magots, The.
First Date.
Fly Me to the Moon.
Folding His *USA Today* He Makes His Point in
     the Blue Star Café.
Footnote on the Invention of Small Pleasures.
For a Girl I Know about to Be a Woman.
For All Our Great-Grandchildren.
For Fred Carpenter Who Died in His Sleep.
For J. William Fulbright on the Day of His
     Death.
For Jordan With Love the Eighth Year of the
     Slaughter: A Minuet for Army Boots and
     Orchestra.
For Lucinda, Robert, and Karyn.
For Lucy, on the Twelfth Month.
For Rebecca, for Whom Nothing Has Been
     Written Page after Page.
For Reuben, at Twelve Months.
For Robert, Son of Man.
For Victor Jara.
Form and Theory of Poetry.
Fred.
Friend, The.
Funeral.
Geography of Time, The.
Getting the Message.
Ghost of His Wife Comes to Tell Him How It
     Is, The.
Ghosts.
Gift of Prophecy Lost, The.
Glass Darkly, A.
God.
Going.
Going Deaf.
Good Son, A.
Green Mansions.
Groom Kisses the Bride and the Mind of the
     Young Preacher Wanders Again, The.
He Glimpses a Nobler Vision.
He Shuts His Eyes for the Layman's Long
     Prayer about Lust and the Mind of the
     Young Preacher Wanders Again.
He Speaks to His Arguing Friends and to
     Himself.
Hello.
Hello. I'll Bet You Don't Know Who This Is.
Her, Though.
Holiday Inn: Surrounded by Someone Else's
     Reunion He Comes to Terms.
House in the Vacant Lot, The.
How Did You Ever Live Without It? A
     Peppermill with a Light.
How It's Born in Us to Understand That There
     Are Two Sides to Every Question.
How the Elephant Got His Hump.
How to Stop Smoking.
How We May By Chance Pronounce the
     Unsuspected Residence of a Ghost.

Husband.
I Can Only Stay for Fifteen Minutes.
I Go Out of the House for the First Time.
ICU: Space/Time in the Waiting Room.
If Ever There Was One.
If Every Person There Is But One.
In a Gradually Moving Car Somewhere in
  Calcutta.
In Another Town.
In Extremis *in Hardy, Arkansas*.
In Nashville, Standing in the Wooden Circle
  Sawed Out from the Old Ryman Stage, the
  Picker has a vision.
In the Beginning.
In Your Own Words Without Lying Tell
  Something of Your Background With
  Particular Attention to Anything Relating to
  the Position For Which You Are Applying.
  Press Down.
Inference.
It Came to Pass on a Planet Third from a
  Minor Sun in a Solar System Out on the
  Edge of One of the Galaxies.
It Is Not That It Came to Nothing, Emiliano.
It's Hard to Think the Brain.
Jonah on His Deathbed.
Jonathan Aging.
Jonathan at Last.
Jonathan Confronts the Question.
Jonathan Entertaining.
Jonathan Happy.
Jonathan in Awe.
Jonathan in Mourning.
Jonathan Losing.
Jonathan Seduced.
Jonathan's Secret.
Journalist Buys a Pig Farm, The.
June Twenty, *Three Days After*.
La Ultima Carta: A Young Wife Writes to Her
  Husband in the Mountains.
Last Person to Speak His Language is Dying,
  The.
Late Show.
Lay of the Badde Wyf.
Learning.
Learning Russian.
Learning to Read.
Lesson on the Twentieth Century, A.
Let Me Tell You.
Liberal Imagination, The.
Light in the Eyes, The.
Listen.
Little Poem, A.
Living on the Surface.
Logos.
Longing, The.
Lost in Ladispoli.
Love and How It Becomes Important in Our
  Day to Day Lives.
Love Poem: "Six o'clock and / the sun rises."
Love Poem with Toast.
Main Street.
Man in the Bar Says He Has Something to
  Say, A.
Man Who Believes in Five, The.
Man Who Stays Up Late, The.
Manifold Usefulness of an Education, The.
Mecanic on Duty at All Times.
Memory.
Memphis, 2 P.M. [*or* 2:00 P.M.].
Mise-en-Scène.
Missing Persons.
Money.
Morning at the Zagorsk Monastery Outside
  Moscow.
Muse of the Evening.
Muse, The.
My Wife Reads the Paper at Breakfast on the
  Birthday of the Scottish Poet.
Neighbor, The.
Newspaper Picture of Spectators at a Hotel
  Fire, A.
Normandy Beach.
Note to God Concerning a Point from an
  Earlier Communication, A.
Notes from the Agent on Earth: How to be

Human.
Of History and Hope.
Office Party, The.
Old Detective Begins His Last Interrogation
  Looking for the Truth as Always, The.
Old Man Leaves His Church for the Last Time,
  An.
On a Photograph of My Mother at Seventeen.
On a Trailways Bus a Man Who Holds His
  Head Strangely Speaks to the Seat Behind
  Him.
On Hearing About the Death of Mitzi Mayfair.
On Not Writing a Love Poem.
On Seeing a Photograph by Mathew Brady.
On Seeing Projected Figures for War Dead in
  the Twentieth Century.
On the Death of a Middle-Aged Man.
On the Sacrifice of a Siamese Twin at Birth.
On the Symbolic Consideration of Hands and
  the Significance of Death.
On the Way Home From Nowhere, New Year's
  Eve.
On Word That the Old Children's Stories Have
  Been Brought Up to Date.
One Day a Woman.
One of the Crowd on the Shore Tells How It
  Was.
One of Those Rare Occurrences on a City Bus.
Ones that Are Thrown Out, The.
Origami.
Original Sin.
Out of a Clear Sky.
Paying Some Slight Attention to His Birthday
  the Associate Professor goes about His
  Business Considering What He Sees and a
  Kind of Praise.
People.
Personals.
Picker.
Pity and Fear.
Plain.
Poem for Emily, A.
Politics.
Potter, Vidalia.
Prison.
Professor.
Promotion, The.
Pulling Back.
Quantum Theory Made Simple.
Question of Time, A.
Reading the Newspaper on Microfilm.
Rebecca at Play.
Remembering the Man.
Remembering Walter.
Rituals.
Rock.
Rodin: The Cathedral.
Romance.
Rubaiyat for Sue Ella Tucker.
Ruby Tells All.
Running into Things.
Sale.
Schumann Adds Trombones to His Second
  Symphony After Mendelssohn Conducts the
  First Performance.
Self-Control.
Senator Explains a Vote, The.
Serial Murderer Says Something to the Priest,
  The.
71 South.
She Prays for Her Husband, the Good Pastor,
  Lying on His Deathbed at Last.
She Talks to Her Sister, Briefly By on the Way
  to West Memphis.
Showing Late Symptoms She First Tries to Fix
  Herself in the Minds of Her Children.
Shrinking Lonesome Sestina, The.
Sir.
Sissy, The.
Sitting Alone at Sunrise: Problems in the
  Space-Time Continuum.
Six Moral Virtues, The: Grace, Style, Class,
  Kindness, and Wisdom.
Sleeping With Friends.
Some Lines Finished Just Before Dawn at the
  Bedside of a Dying Student It has Snowed

All Night.
Something to Believe In.
Standing Close to Greatness.
Stopping to Look at a Crèche in a Jewelry
  Store Window.
Story, A.
Story, The.
Stripper, The.
Style.
Summer Afternoon an Old Man Gives Some
  Thought to the Central Questions, A.
Sunset: The Canary Islands.
Survivor, The.
Talking to Himself He Gets a Few Things
  Settled in His Mind.
Tearing Down the Hotel.
10,000-Year-Old Tree Discovered Shades Two
  and Half Acres.
Tenth Anniversary Photograph, 1952, A.
Thanatopsis.
Things.
Think Also of Horseshoes.
Think of Judas That He Did Love Jesus.
Thinking about Bill, Dead of AIDS
Thinking Friday Night with a Gothic Storm
  Going About Final Causes and Logos and
  Mitzi Mayfair.
Thought as It Turns, A.
To a Friend, an Unhappy Poet.
To One Who Went Too Far.
Toast to Floyd Collins, A.
Today is Wednesday.
True Story of What Happened, The.
Truth and Truthfulness.
Trying.
Trying to Remember.
Unknown Sailor, The.
Unto One of the Least of These.
Vanishing Point, The.
Vision and Prayer.
Visitor's Guide to the Blue Planet, The.
Voice of America.
Waiting for the Paper to be Delivered.
Waking from a Dream.
Walking After Supper.
War and Peace.
We.
Weatherman.
Well-Ordered Life, The.
When I Am Dead, My Dearest.
Where to Turn When Sorrow Comes like a
  Black Bull in Your Dreams.
Why God Permits Evil: For Answers to This
  Question of Interest to Many Write Bible
  Answers, Dept. E-7.
Wide Place in the Road.
Widow, The.
Wiedersehen.
Woman in the Room, The.
Woman with Dog.
Words.
WWI.
Year They Outlawed Baseball, The.
You Wouldn't Say They Didn't Get Along
  Exactly.
Young Instructor Talks to Himself Winding Up
  the Semester, The.

**Williams, Tennessee (Thomas Lanier Williams)
  (1914–83)**
Across the Space.
After a Visit.
Androgyne, Mon Amour.
Angels of Fructification, The.
Apparition.
As I stood in my room tonight, drinking a
  solitary toast.
Ave Atque Vale.
Beanstalk Country, The.
Blond Mediterraneans, The.
Brain's Dissection, The.
Cabin.
Cacti.
Can I forget.
Case of the Crushed Petunias, The: A Lyrical
  Fantasy, *sels.*
Challenge to Poets, A.

Complexity, The.
Composition.
Con Brio.
Confidence, A.
Conquest.
Construction.
Contemporania.
Controversy, The.
Conventional Ballad.
Convivio.
Coronal, A.
Counter, The.
Crimson Cyclamen, The.
Crude Lament.
Crystal Maze, A.
Cuchulain.
Cure, The.
Daisy.
Dance, The ("In Brueghel's great picture").
Dance, The ("When the snow falls the flakes").
Danse Russe.
Dark Day, The.
Dawn.
Daybreak.
Dead Baby, The.
Death ("He's dead").
Death ("So this is death that I").
Death by Radio.
Death of Franco of Cologne, The: His
    Prophecy of Beethoven.
Death of See, The.
Death the Barber.
Decenber.
Deceptrices, The.
Dedication for a Plot of Ground.
Deep Religious Faith.
Defective Record, The.
Defense.
Defiance to Cupid.
Delicacies, The.
Della Primavera Transportata al Morale.
Descent.
Descent, The.
Descent of Winter, The.
Desert Music, The.
Design for November.
Desolate Field, The.
Detail ("Doc, I bin lookin' for you").
Detail ("Her milk don't seem to").
Detail ("Hey!").
Detail ("I had a misfortune in September").
Details for Paterson.
Dish of Fruit, The.
Disputants, The.
Divertimiento.
Drink.
Drugstore Library.
Drunk and the Sailor, The.
Drunkard, The.
Early Martyr, An.
East Coocoo.
Education a Failure.
El Hombre.
Election Day.
Elegy for D.H. Lawrence, An.
End of the Parade, The.
End of the Rope, The.
Entity, The.
Epigramme: "Hast ever seen a man."
Epitaph: "Old willow with hollow branches,
    An."
Eternity.
Eternity, An.
Eve.
Every Day.
Exercise.
Exercise, An.
Exercise No. 2.
Exultation, An.
Eyeglasses, The.
Farmer, The.
Fertile.
15 Years Later.
Fight, The.
Figueras Castle.
Fine Work with Pitch and Copper.

Fire Spirit.
First Praise.
Fish.
Flattery.
Flight to the City.
Flower, The ("Petal, colorless and without
    form, A").
Flower, The ("This too I love").
Flowers Alone, The.
Flowers by the Sea.
Flowing River, A.
Folded Skyscraper, A, *sels.*
Fond Farewell, A.
Fool's Song, The.
Foot-Note, A.
For a Low Voice.
For Eleanor and Bill Monahan.
For G.B.S., Old.
For Viola: De Gustibus.
Foreign.
Formal Design, A.
4th of July.
Fragment: "As for him who."
Fragment: "My God, Bill, what have you
    done?"
Fragment to W. C. W.'s Romance.
Franklin Square.
From a Book.
From a Play.
From a Window.
From "The Birth of Venus," Song.
Fruit, The.
Full Moon.
Gayest of Bright Flowers, The.
Genesis.
Genius, The.
Gentle Man, The.
Gentle Negress, The ("No other such
    luxuriace: the").
Gentle Negress, The ("Wandering among the
    chimneys").
Gentle Rejoinder, The.
Girl, The ("Wall, as I watched, came neck-
    high, The").
Girl, The ("With big breasts").
Goat, The.
Good Night.
Goodnight, A.
Gossips, The.
Gothic Candor.
Graceful Bastion, The.
Graph.
Graph for Action.
Great Figure, The.
Great Mullen.
Green Eyes.
Greeting for Old Age.
Grotesque.
Gulls.
Halfworld, The.
Hard Core of Beauty, The.
Hard Listener, The.
Hard Times.
He Has Beaten about the Bush Long Enough.
Healall.
Heel & Toe to the End.
Hermaphroditic Telephones, The.
Hero.
Hey Red!
Hic Jacet.
High Bridge above the Tagus River at Toledo,
    The.
His Daughter.
History.
History of Love, A.
Homage.
Horned Purple.
Horse Show, The.
Horse, The.
Host, The.
Hounded Lovers, The.
House, The.
How Bad It Is to Say.
How Has the Way Been Found?
Hula-Hula.
Hunter, The.

Hurricane, The.
Hymn to Love Ended.
I Will Sing a Joyous Song.
I Would Not Change For Thine.
Idyl: "They say to me, "There is."
Idyl: "Wine of the grey sky."
Illegitimate Things.
Immortal.
Impromptu: The Suckers.
In Chains.
In Harbor.
In San Marco, Venezia.
In Sisterly Fashion.
In the 'Sconset Bus.
Incognito.
Informative Object, An.
Injury, The.
Intelligent Sheepman and the New Cars, The.
Interests of 1926.
Invitation ("We live in this flat blue basin").
Invitation ("You who had the sense").
Invocation and Conclusion.
Io Baccho!
It Is a Living Coral.
It Is a Small Plant.
Italian Garden, The.
Item.
Ivy Crown, The.
January.
Jersey Lyric.
Jingle.
June 9.
Jungle, The.
K. McB.
Keller Gegen Dom.
King!, The.
La Belle Dame de Tous les Jours.
La Flor.
La Lune, A.
Labrador.
Lady speaks, The.
Lament: "What face, in the water."
Last Turn, The.
Last Words of My English Grandmother, The.
Last Words of My Grandmother.
Late for Summer Weather.
Late Singer, The.
Le Médecin Malgré Lui.
Lear.
Lesson, The.
Libertad! Igualdad! Fraternidad!
Light Becomes Darkness.
Light Hearted William.
Light Shall Not Enter.
Lily, The.
Lines: "Leaves are greygreen."
Lines on Receiving *The Dial's* Award: 1927.
Lion, The.
Locust Tree in Flower, The.
Lonely Street, The.
Look, there goes the young lady across the
    street.
Love.
Love Charm, The.
Love Poem, A: "Basic hatred / sometimes has
    a flower."
Love Song: "Daisies are broken."
Love Song: First Version, 1915, A.
Love Song: "I lie here thinking of you."
Love Song: "Sweep the house clean."
Love Song: "You have come between me and
    the terrifying presence."
Lovely Ad.
Loving Dexterity, The.
Lustspiel.
M.B.
Mama.
Man and Nature.
Man in a Room.
Man to a Woman, A.
Maneuver [*or* Manoeuvre], The.
March.
March Is a Light.
Marianne Moore.
Marriage.
Marriage of Souls, The.

Marriage Ritual, A.
Martin and Katherine.
May 1st Tomorrow.
Memory of April.
Men, The.
Mental Hospital Garden, The.
Metric Figure ("There is a bird in the poplars").
Metric Figure ("Gotta hold your nose").
Metric Figure ("Veils of clarity").
Mezzo Forte.
Middle.
Midwinter.
Min Schleppner.
Mind Hesitant, The.
Mind's Games, The.
Mirrors, The.
Misericordia.
Mistrust of the Beloved.
Mists Over the River.
Modest Achievement, The.
Monstrous Marriage, The.
Moon and Stars.
Moon, The.
Moral, The.
Morning.
Motor-Barge, The.
Mounted as an Amazon.
Mujer.
My Luv.
Naked.
Nantucket.
Navajo.
Negro Woman, A.
New Cathedral Overlooking the Park, The.
New Clouds, The.
New England.
New Mexico.
Night.
Night Rider, The.
Nightingales, The.
No Good Too.
Non-Entity, The.
Note, A.
Note to Music: Brahms 1st Piano Concerto.
Nun's Song.
Observer, The.
Offering.
Ogre, The.
Ol' Bunk's Band.
Old-Fashioned German Christmas Card, An.
Old House, The.
Old Men, The.
Old Worshipper, The.
On a Proposed Trip South.
On First Opening the Lyric Year.
On Gay Wallpaper.
On St. Valentine's Day.
Orchard, The.
Orchestra, The.
Ordeal, The.
Our (American) Ragcademicians.
Overture to a Dance of Locomotives.
Painting, The.
Passaic, N.J.
Passer Domesticus.
Pastoral 1: "Old man who goes about, The."
Pastoral 2: "If I talk to things."
Pastoral: "If I say I have heard voices."
Pastoral: "Little sparrows, The."
Pastoral: "When I was younger."
Paterson, *sels.*
Paterson.
Paterson, Book V: The River of Heaven.
Paterson: The Falls.
Paul.
Pause, The.
Peace.
Peace on Earth.
Perfection.
Period Piece: 1834.
Perpetuum Mobile: The City.
Petunia, The.
Philomena Andronico.
Phoenix and the Tortoise, The.
Picture of a Nude in a Machine Shop.
Picture Showing.

Pictures from Brueghel.
Pigheaded Poet.
Pink Locust, The.
Place (Any Place) to Transcend All Places, A.
Play.
Plea for Mercy, A.
Poem: "As the cat."
Poem: "Daniel Boone, the father of Kentucky."
Poem for Norman Macleod, A.
Poem: "Looking up, of a sudden."
Poem: "On getting a card."
Poem: "Plastic surgeon who has, The."
Poem: "Rose fades, The."
Poem, The: "It's all in / the sound. A song."
Poet and His Poems, The.
Polar Bear, The.
Poor, The ("By constantly tormenting them").
Poor, The ("It's the anarchy of poverty").
Porous.
Portent.
Portrait in Greys, A.
Portrait of a Lady.
Portrait of a Woman at Her Bath.
Portrait of a Woman in Bed.
Portrait of a Young Man with a Bad Heart.
Portrait of the Author.
Portrait of the Times, A.
Postlude.
Pot of Flowers, The.
Predicter of Famine, The.
Prelude, A: "I know only the bare rocks of today."
Prelude to Winter.
Primrose.
Problem, The.
Proletarian Portrait.
Promenade.
Province, The.
Quality of Heaven, The.
Queen-Anne's-Lace.
Question and Answer.
Quietness.
R R Bums, The.
Rain.
Raindrops on a Briar.
Raleigh Was Right.
Raper from Passenack, The.
Rapid Transit.
Rare Gist, The.
Rat, The.
Readie Pome.
Red Lily, The.
Red Wheelbarrow, The.
Red-Wing Blackbird, The.
Rendezvous.
Resemblance, The.
Return to Work, The.
Revelation, The.
Reverie and Invocation.
Rewaking, The.
Rhymed Address: The Lobster.
Rigamarole.
Right of Way, The.
Riposte.
Ritualists, The.
River Rhyme.
River Rhyme II.
Rock-Old Dogma, The.
Rocking Woman, The.
Rogation Sunday.
Romance Moderne.
Rose, The.
Rose, The ("Rose is obsolete, The").
Rose, The ("Stillness of the rose, The").
Rosebush in an Unlikely Garden, A.
Rumba! Rumba!
Russia.
Sadness of the Sea, The.
Sale, The.
Sappho, Be Comforted.
Savage Beast, The.
Sea-Elephant, The.
Sea, The.
Sea-Trout and Butterfish.
Seafarer.

Self-Portrait 1.
Self-Portrait 2.
Self, The.
Semblables, The.
Seraph.
Shadow, The.
Shadows.
She Who Turns Her Head.
Shoot It Jimmy!
Short Poem.
Sicilian Emigrant's Song.
Sick African.
Silence.
Simplex Sigilum Veri: A Catalogue.
Sketch for a Portrait of Henry Ford.
Sleeping Brute, The.
Slow Movement.
Sluggishly.
Smell.
Smiling Dane, A.
Snow Begins, The.
Solstice.
Some Simple Measures in the American Idiom and the Variable Foot.
Sometimes It Turns Dry and the Leaves Fall before They Are Beautiful.
Song: "Beauty is a shell."
Song: "Black-winged gull, The."
Song: "I'd rather read an account."
Song: "If I / could count the silence."
Song: "Pluck the florets from."
Song: "Russia! Russia! you might say."
Song: "You are forever April."
Sonnet in Search of an Author.
Sort of a Song, A.
Soughing Wind, The.
Sound of Waves, The.
Source, The.
Sparrow, The.
Sparrows among Dry Leaves.
Spirit of '76.
Spouts.
Spring.
Spring and All.
Spring is Here Again, Sir.
Spring Song.
Spring Storm.
Spring Strains.
St. Francis Einstein of the Daffodils ("In March's black boat").
St. Francis Einstein of the Daffodils ("Sweet land").
St. Valentine.
Still Life.
Still Lifes.
Stillness.
Stone Crock, The.
Storm, The.
Stormy.
Stroller.
Struggle of Wings.
Stylist, The.
Sub Terra.
Summer Song.
Sun Bathers, The.
Sun, The.
Sunday.
Sunflowers.
Suzanne.
Suzy.
Swaggering Gait, The.
Sympathetic Portrait of a Child.
Tailpiece.
Tapiola.
10/14.
Term, The.
Testament of Perpetual Change, The.
These.
These Purists.
Thing, The.
Thinker, The.
Thinking Back Toward Christmas: A Statement for the Virgin.
This Florida: 1924.
This Is Just to Say.
This Is Pioneer Weather.

Thistle.
Thoughtful Lover, The.
3 A.M. The Girl with the Honey Colored Hair.
Three Graces, The.
Three Nahuatl Poems.
Three Sonnets.
3 Stances.
Threnody: "Christian coin, The."
Thursday.
Time the Hangman.
Title, The.
To.
To a Chinese Woman.
To a Dead Journalist.
To a Dog Injured in the Street.
To a Friend.
To a Friend Concerning Several Ladies.
To a Lovely Old Bitch.
To a Man Dying on His Feet.
To a Mexican Pig-Bank.
To a Poor Old Woman.
To a Solitary Disciple.
To a Sparrow.
To a Woman Seen Once.
To a Wood Thrush.
To a Woodpecker.
To All Gentleness.
To an Elder Poet.
To an Old Jaundiced Woman.
To Be Closely Written on a Small Piece of
    Paper Which Folded into a Tight Lozenge
    Will Fit Any Girl's Locket.
To Be Hungry Is to Be Great.
To Be Recited to Flossie on Her Birthday.
To Close.
To Daphne and Virginia.
To Elsie.
To Flossie.
To Ford Madox Ford in Heaven.
To Greet a Letter-Carrier.
To Have Done Nothing.
To Mark Anthony in Heaven.
To My Friend Ezra Pound.
To the Dean.
To the Ghost of Marjorie Kinnan Rawlings.
To the Outer World.
To the Shade of Po Chü-I.
To Waken an Old Lady.
To Wish Myself Courage.
Tolstoy.
Tract.
Tragic Detail.
Trala Trala Trala La-le-la.
Transitional.
Translation.
Translations from the Spanish.
Tree.
Tree and Sky.
Trees.
Trees, The.
Tribute to Neruda the Poet Collector of
    Seashells.
Tribute to the Painters.
Tulip Bed, The.
Turkey in the Straw.
Turtle, The.
Twelve Line Poem.
Two Aspects of April.
Two Deliberate Exercises.
Two Pendants: For the Ears.
Unfrocked Priest, The.
Unison, A.
United Front, The.
United States, The.
Unknown, The.
Uses of Poetry, The.
Usurers of Heaven, The.
Venus Over the Desert.
View.
View by Color Photography on a Commercial
    Calendar.
View of a Lake.
Virtue.
Virtuous Agent, The.
Visit, The.
Vision of Labor, A: 1931.

Waiting.
Wanderer, The: A Rococo Study.
War, the Destroyer.
Weasel Snout.
Well Disciplined Bargeman, The.
When Fresh, It Was Sweet.
When Structure Fails Rhyme Attempts to
    Come to the Rescue.
Wide Awake, Full of Love.
Widow's Lament in Springtime, The.
Wild Orchard.
Wildflower, The.
Willow Poem.
Wind Increases, The.
Wind of the Village.
Winter.
Winter Quiet.
Winter Sunset.
Winter Trees.
Woman in Front of a Bank, A.
Woman Walking.
Woodpecker, The.
Woodthrush, The.
Words Lying Idle, The.
Words, the Words, the Words, The.
World Contracted to a Recognizable Image,
    The.
World Narrowed to a Point, The.
Writer's Prologue to a Play in Verse.
Wrong Door, The.
Yachts, The.
Yellow Chimney, The.
Yellow Flower, The.
Yellow Season, The.
Yellow Tree Peony, The.
You Have Pissed Your Life.
Young Cat and the Chrysanthemums, The.
Young Housewife, The.
Young Laundryman, The.
Young Love.
Young Sycamore.
Young Woman at a Window ("She sits with").
Young Woman at a Window ("While she sits").
Youth and Beauty.

Wilner, Eleanor (b. 1931)
Abstraction.
Admonition.
All the Wide Grin of Him.
Ambition.
Amelia.
American Painting, with Rain.
American Sublime, The: Robert Penn Warren.
Ars Poetica.
As Far as It Goes, and Back.
As Soft and as Pink as a Nursery.
Atget's Gardens.
Bailing Out—A Poem for the 1970s.
Bat Cave.
Beauty and the Beast.
Being as I Was, How Could I Help.
Beyond the Second Landing.
Bird in the Laurel's Song, The.
Blessing.
Bridge Passage: Variations on Two Scales.
Candied.
Changing the Imperatives.
Classical Proportions of the Heart.
Closing Ceremonies for the Bicentennial.
Coda, Overture.
Comment on the Relevance of Modern Science
    to the Everyday Lives of the Larger
    Animals, A.
Concerto.
Conditional Riff.
Continuous Is Broken, and Resumes, The.
Conversation with a Japanese Student.
Desert Parable.
Dinner Party.
East of the Sun, West of the Moon.
Elegy for a Writer.
Eleusis.
Emigration.
End of the Line, The.
Epitaph: "Young then, / we were bored
    already."
Ex Libris.

Facing into It.
Filling in the Blanks.
Fourth David, The.
Freed from Another Context.
Generic Vision, 1991.
Green Connection, The.
Having Eaten of the Tree of Knowledge.
Her Body Is Private.
High Noon at Los Alamos.
How to Get in the Best Magazines.
Hunting Manual.
Illuminator, The.
Instructions to Painters by Wang Wei, Eighth
    Century.
Iphigenia, Setting the Record Straight.
It's Not Cold Here.
Job's Wife, a Twentieth-Century Casting
    Script.
Judgment.
Kazuko's Vision.
Killing the Grubs.
Knowing the Enemy.
Labyrinth.
Lament: "All morning I have been reading
    poems."
Lament of the Valkyrie, The.
Landing.
Last Man, The.
Laurels.
Leda's Handmaiden.
Literal = The Abstract, The: A
    Demonstration.
Love of What Is Not, The.
Love Uncommanded.
Made by Hand.
Maya.
Meditation on the *Wen-Fu*.
Messenger, The.
Metamorphoses at a College for Women.
Middle-Class Vantage.
Midway the Journey of This Life.
Minor Epic.
Miriam's Song.
Moonsnails.
Mt. Fuji and the Martial Arts.
Mulch, The.
Muse, The.
My Mother's Portrait.
Nandin's Tail.
Natural History.
Never Apologize for Poetry.
Night Fishing in the Sound.
Now I Can Go On and On.
Ode to Innocence.
Of a Sun She Can Remember.
Off the Hook.
Oldest Desire, The.
On Ethnic Definitions.
On the Road to Larry Robin's Bookstore.
Operations: Desert Shield, Desert Storm.
Pillar, The.
Poem of Exile, A.
Postscript.
Private Space, A.
Reading the Bible Backwards.
Recovery.
Renegade.
Round Fish, The.
Salute to Donald Davie.
Sarah's Choice.
Secret Garden, The.
See-Saw.
Short History of Philosophy, A.
So Quietly the World.
Sunflowers, Repossessed.
Those Who Come After.
Thoughts of a Retired Diamond Cutter.
Towers of Silence, The.
Trümmerfrauen.
Tucson Gardens.
Two Pairs of Eyes.
Ume: *Plum*.
Unstrung.
Up against It.
Water Lace and White Eyes.
What Was Going On.

What Was Left Over.
When Asked to Lie Down on the Altar.
Winged Victory.
Winter Garden.
Without Regret.
Women Talking.
Working the Block.
World Is Not a Meditation, The.
You, Failed Pronoun.
Zero at the Bone.

Woodbridge, Benjamin (1622–84)
Upon the Author. By a Known Friend.

Wordsworth, Dorothy (1771–1855)
Cottager to Her Infant, (By My Sister), The.

Wordsworth, William (1770–1850)
1811.
Address to Kilchurn Castle, upon Loch Awe.
Address to My Infant Daughter, Dora on Being
Reminded That She Was a Month Old That
Day, September 16.
Address to Silence.
Address to the Ocean.
Address to the Scholars of the Village School
of—1798.
Address to the Sons of Burns, after Visiting
Their Father's Grave (August 14th, 1803).
Admonition.
Advance—come forth from the Tyrolean
ground.
Aërial Rock—Whose Solitary Brow.
Affliction of Margaret, The.
Airey-Force Valley.
Alas! what boots the long laborious quest.
Alcaeus to Sappho.
Alice Fell; or, Poverty.
Along the mazes of this song I go.
Among all lovely things my Love had been.
Anacreon.
And is it among rude untutored Dales.
Andrew Jones.
Anecdote for Fathers.
Animal Tranquillity and Decay.
Anticipation. October, 1803.
Apology.
Are souls then nothing? Must at length the die.
Argument for Suicide.
Armenian Lady's Love, The.
Artegal and Eldure.
As when, upon the smooth pacific deep.
At Applethwaite, near Keswick.
At Bologna, in Remembrance of the Late
Insurrections, 1837.
At Bologna, in Remembrance of the Late
Insurrections, 1837, Continued: "As leaves
are to the tree wheron they grow."
At Bologna, in Remembrance of the Late
Insurrections, 1837, Continued: "Hard task!
exclaim the undisciplined, to lean."
At Furness Abbey ("Here, where, of havoc
tired and rash undoing").
At Furness Abbey ("Well have yon Railway
Labourers to this ground").
At the Grave of Burns (1803, Seven Years
After His Death).
At the Isle of Wight. 1793.
Author's Voyage down the Rhine (Thirty Years
Ago).
Avaunt all specious pliancy of mind.
Avon, The.
Away, away, it is the air.
Ballad, A: "And will you leave me thus alone."
Beauty and Moonlight.
Beggars.
"Beloved Vale!" I said, "when I shall con."
Birth of Love, The.
Blest Statesman He, Whose Mind's Unselfish
Will.
Blind Highland Boy, The; A Tale Told by the
Fire-side, After Returning to the Vale of
Grasmere.
Borderers, The. A Tragedy.
Bothwell Castle.
Brave Schill! by death delivered, take thy
flight.
Brook, that hast been my solace days and

weeks.
Brook! whose society the Poet seeks.
Brothers, The.
Brownie, The.
Brownie's Cell, The.
By a Blest Husband Guided, Mary Came.
By Moscow Self-Devoted to a Blaze.
By the Sea-Side.
By the Side of Rydal Mere.
Calais, August, 1802.
Calais, August 15, 1802.
Call not the royal Swede unfortunate.
Calm is the Fragrant air, and loth to lose.
Cantata, from Metastasio.
Captivity.—Mary Queen of Scots.
Carved, Matthew, with a master's skill.
Cenotaph.
Cento Made By Wordsworth, A.
Character, A.
Character of the Happy Warrior.
Characteristics of a Child Three Years Old.
Childless Father, The.
Come ye that are disturbed, this steady voice.
Companion to the Foregoing [Love Lies
Bleeding].
Complaint, A.
Complaint of a Forsaken Indian Woman, The.
Composed after a Journey across the
Hambleton [or Hamilton] Hills, Yorkshire.
Composed after Reading a Newspaper of the
Day.
Composed among the Ruins of a Castle in
North Wales.
Composed at Cora Linn in Sight of Wallace's
Tower.
Composed at Neidpath Castle, the Property of
Lord Queensberry,1803.
Composed by the Sea-Shore.
Composed by the Sea-Side, near Calais,
August, 1802.
Composed by the Side of Grasmere Lake.
Composed During a Storm.
Composed in One of the Valleys of
Westmoreland, on Easter Sunday.
Composed in Roslin Chapel, During a Storm.
Composed in the Glen of Loch Etive.
Composed in the Valley near Dover, on the
Day of Landing.
Composed near Calais, on the Road Leading to
Ardres, August 7, 1802.
Composed on a May Morning.
Composed on the Banks of a Rocky Stream.
Composed on the Eve of the Marriage of a
Friend in the Vale of Grasmere, 1812.
Composed upon an Evening of Extraordinary
Splendour and Beauty.
Composed upon Westminster Bridge,
September 3, 1802.
Composed When a Probability Existed of Our
Being Obliged to Quit Rydal Mount as a
Residence.
Composed While the Author Was Engaged in
Writing a Tract, Occasioned by the
Convention of Cintra.
Contrast; the Parrot and the Wren, The.
Convict, The.
Could I the priest's consent have gained.
Countess' Pillar.
Crescent-Moon, the Star of Love, The.
Cuckoo and the Nightingale, The.
Cuckoo-Clock, The.
Danish Boy; A Fragment, The.
Dear native brooks, your ways I have pursued.
Decay of Piety.
Departure from the Vale of Grasmere. August,
1803.
Descriptive Sketches Taken During a
Pedestrian Tour among the Alps.
Desponding Father! Mark This Altered Bough.
Devotional Incitements.
Dion.
Dirge: "I bring ye little noisy crew!"
Dirge Sung by a Minstrel.
Discharged Soldier, The.
Distressful gift! this Book receives.
Dog—An Idyllium, The.

Eagle and the Dove, The.
Eagles.
Earl of Breadalbane's Ruined Mansion, and
Family Burial-Place, near Killin, The.
Ecclesiastical Sonnets.
Effusion in the Pleasure-Ground on the Banks
of the Bran, Near Dunkeld.
Egyptian Maid; or, The Romance of the Water
Lilly, The.
1811.
1801.
1810 ("Ah! where is Palafox? Nor tongue nor
pen").
1810 ("O'erweening statesmen have full long
relied").
1830.
Elegiac Musings in the Grounds of Coleorton
Hall, thc Seat of the Late Sir G.H.
Beaumont, BART.
Elegiac Stanzas (Addressed to Sir G.H.B. upon
the Death of His Sister-in-Law).
Elegiac Stanzas Composed in the Churchyard
of Grasmere.
Elegiac Stanzas Suggested by a Picture of
Peele Castle, in a Storm, Painted by Sir
George Beaumont.
Elegiac Verses in Memory of My Brother, John
Wordsworth.
Elegy Written in the Same Place upon the
Same Occasion.
Ellen Irwin; or, The Braes of Kirtle.
Emigrant Mother, The.
Emperors and Kings, How Oft Have Temples
Rung.
Epigram on an Event in Col. Evans's
Redoubted Performances in Spain.
Epistle to Sir George Howland Beaumont,
BART.
Epitaph in Grasmere Church.
Epitaph in the Chapel Yard of Langdale,
Westmoreland.
Epitaph: "Six months to six years added he
remained."
Ere with Cold Beads of Midnight Dew.
Even as a dragon's eye that feels the stress.
Evening Walk, An; Addressed to a Young
Lady.
Excursion, The.
Expostulation and Reply.
Extempore Effusion upon the Death of James
Hogg.
Extract from the Conclusion of a Poem,
Composed in Anticipation of Leaving
School.
Fact, and an Imagination or, Canute and
Alfred, on the Sea-Shore, A.
Fair Prime of Life! Were It Enough to Gild.
Fairest, brightest, hues of ether fade, The.
Fancy and Tradition.
Farewell, A: "Farewell thou little Nook of
mountain-ground."
Farewell Lines.
Farmer of Tilsbury Vale, The.
Feel for the Wrongs of Universal Ken.
Feelings of a French Royalist, on the
Disinterment of the Remains of the Duke
D'Enghien.
Feelings of a Noble Biscayan at One of Those
Funerals 1810.
Feelings of the Tyrolese.
Fidelity.
Filial Piety.
Flower Garden at Coleorton Hall,
Leicestershire, A.
Fly, some kind Harbinger, to Grasmere-dale.
For a Seat in the Groves of Coleorton.
For the Spot Where the Hermitage Stood on St
Herbert's Island, Derwent-Water.
Force of Prayer, The; or, The Founding of
Bolton Priory; A Tradition.
Foregoing Subject Resumed, The.
Foresight.
Forsaken, The.
Forth from a Jutting Ridge, Around Whose
Base.

Fountain, The.
Four Fiery Steed Impatient of the Rein.
Fragment: A Somersetshire Tragedy.
Fragment: "For let the impediment be what it may."
Fragment from Dove Cottage Manuscript 44 (I).
Fragment: "In vain did Time and Nature."
Fragment of a "Gothic" Tale.
Fragment of an Intended Poem on Milton, Written in the Copy of *Paradise Lost* Which Belonged to Wordsworth at Cambridge.
Fragment: Redundance.
Fragment: The Baker's Cart.
Fragment: "Witness thou / The dear companion of my lonely walk."
Fragments: Drafts, Mostly or All for a Poem on a Heroic Theme.
Fragments from the Alfoxden Note-Book (I).
Fragments from the Alfoxden Note-Book (II).
Fragments from the Alfoxden Notebook (III).
Fragments from the "Christabel" Note-book.
French and the Spanish Guerrillas, The.
French Army in Russia 1812–1813, The.
French Revolution as It Appeared to Enthusiasts at Its Commencement. Reprinted from "The Friend."
From the Dark Chambers of Dejection Freed.
Germans on the Heights of Hochheim, The.
Glad Sight Wherever New with Old.
Gleaner (Suggested By a Picture), The.
Glen-Almain; or, the Narrow Glen.
Go Back to Antique Ages, If Thine Eyes.
Gold and Silver Fishes in a Vase.
Goody Blake and Harry Gill.
Gordale.
Grace Darling.
Gravestone upon the Floor in the Cloisters of Worcester Cathedral, A.
Great men have been among us; hands that penned.
Green Linnet, The.
Grief, thou hast lost an ever ready friend.
Guilt and Sorrow; or Incidents upon Salisbury Plain.
Gypsies.
Hail, Twilight, sovereign of one peaceful hour!
Hail, Zaragoza! If with unwet eye.
Hark! 'Tis the Thrush, Undaunted, Undeprest.
Hart-Leap Well.
Hart's-Horn Tree, near Penrith.
Haunted Tree; To———, The.
Help for the Memory of the Grand Independent; A New Song, A.
Her Eyes Are Wild.
Her Only Pilot the Soft Breeze, the Boat.
Highland Broach, The.
Highland Hut.
Hint from the Mountains for Certain Political Pretenders.
Hofer.
Home at Grasmere.
Horn of Egremont Castle, The.
Horse, The.
Hour-bell sounds, and I must go, The.
How Beautiful the Queen of Night, on High.
How Rich That Forehead's Calm Expanse!
How sweet it is, when mother Fancy rocks.
Humanity.
I find it written of SIMONIDES.
I Heard (Alas! 'Twas Only in a Dream).
I know an aged Man constrained to dwell.
I love upon a stormy night.
I only looked for pain and grief.
I Wandered Lonely As a Cloud.
I watch, and long have watched, with calm regret.
Idiot Boy, The.
Idle Shepherd-Boys, The; or, Dungeon-Ghyll Force. A Pastoral.
If This Great World of Joy and Pain.
If thou indeed derive thy light from Heaven.
Illustrated Books and Newspapers.
Imitation of Juvenal — Satire VIII.
In Allusion to Various Recent Histories and Notices of the French Revolution.

In Allusion to Various Recent Histories and Notices of the French Revolution, Concluded.
In Allusion to Various Recent Histories and Notices of the French Revolution, Continued.
In due observance of an ancient rite.
In My Mind's Eye a Temple, Like a Cloud.
In Part from Moschus's Lament for Bion.
In the First Page of an Album by One Whose Handwriting Is Wretchedly Bad.
In the Sound of Mull.
In the Woods of Rydal.
In These Fair Vales Hath Many a Tree.
Incident Characteristic of a Favourite Dog.
Incipient Madness.
Indignation of a High-Minded Spaniard 1810.
Infant M— M—, The.
Inscription for a Monument in Crossthwaite Church, in the Vale of Keswick.
Inscription for a Seat by a Roadside, Half Way up a Steep Hill, Facing the South.
Inscription for a Seat by the Pathway Side Ascending to Windy Brow.
Inscription for the Moss-Hut at Dove Cottage.
see also Inscription in the Grounds of Coleorton, the Seat of Sir George Beaumont, BART., Leicestershire *and* Written at the Request of Sir George Beaumont, BART., and in His Name, for an Urn, Placed by Him at the T.
see also Written at the Request of Sir George Beaumont, BART., and in His Name, for an Urn, Placed by Him at the Termination of a Newly-Planted Avenue, in the Same Grounds *and* Inscription in a Garden of the Same.
Inscription on a Rock at Rydal Mount.
Inscriptions Supposed to Be Found in and near a Hermit's Cell; 1818.
Intent on Gathering Wool from Hedge and Brake.
Invocation to the Earth; February, 1816.
Is there a power that can sustain and cheer.
It is a beauteous evening, calm and free.
It is no spirit who from heaven hath flown.
It is not to be thought of that the Flood.
It was an April morning: fresh and clear.
Jewish Family (in a Small Valley Opposite St Goar, upon the Rhine), A.
June, 1820.
Just Vengeance Claims Thy Soul for Rights Invaded?
King of Sweden, The.
Kitten and [the] Falling Leaves, The.
Labourer's Noon-Day Hymn, The.
Lady Whom You Here Behold, The.
Lament of Mary Queen of Scots on the Eve of a New Year.
Laodamia.
Last of the Flock, The.
Leaves That Rustled on This Oak-Crowned Hill, The.
Let More Ambitious Poets Take the Heart.
Lines Composed a Few Miles above Tintern Abbey on Revisiting the Banks of the Wye During a Tour, July 13, 1798.
Lines Inscribed in a Copy of His Poems Sent to the Queen for the Royal Library at Windsor.
Lines: "Loud is the Vale! the Voice is up."
Lines: "Nay, Traveller."
Lines on the Expected Invasion 1803.
Lines Suggested By a Portrait from the Pencil of F. Stone.
Lines Written as a School Exercise at Hawkshead, Anno Aetatis 14.
Lines Written in Early Spring.
Lines Written in the Album of the Countess of Lonsdale.
Lines Written on a Blank Leaf in a Copy of the Author's Poem "The Excursion," upon Hearing of the Death of the Late Vicar of Kendal.
Lines Written While Sailing in a Boat at

Evening.
Little Onward Lend Thy Guiding Hand, A.
Lo! Where She Stands Fixed in a Saint-like Trance.
London 1802.
Longest Day; Addressed to My Daughter, The.
Look now on that Adventurer who hath paid.
Louisa [After Accompanying Her on a Mountain Excursion].
Love Lies Bleeding.
Lucy.
Lucy Gray; or, Solitude.
Lyre! Though Such Power Do in Thy Magic Live.
Malham Cove.
Mark the concentrated hazels that enclose.
Martial courage of a day is vain, The.
Massy Ways Carried across These Heights, The.
Maternal Grief.
Matron of Jedborough and Her Husband, The.
Matthew.
Memorials of a Tour in Italy, 1837.
Memorials of a Tour of the Continent; 1820.
Memory.
Men of the Western World! In Fate's Dark Book.
Methought I saw the footsteps of a throne.
Michael [A Pastoral Poem].
Modern Athens, The.
More May not Be by Human Art Exprest.
Morning Exercise, A.
Most Alluring Clouds That Mount the Sky, The.
Motto Intended for Poems on the Naming of Places.
My heart leaps up when I behold.
Narrow girdle of rough stones and crags, A.
Near Dover, September 1802.
Night in June, A.
Night-Piece, A.
Night Thought, A.
No spade for leagues had won a rood of earth.
Norman Boy, The.
Not in the Lucid Intervals of Life.
Not Love, not War, nor the Tumultuous Swell.
November, 1806.
November, 1813.
November 1 [1815].
November, 1836.
Nun's Well, Brigham.
Nutting.
O Nightingale! thou surely art.
Oak and the Broom, The; A Pastoral.
Oak of Guernica! Tree of holier power.
Occasioned by the Battle of Waterloo February, 1816.
Occasioned by the Battle of Waterloo (the Last Six Lines Intended for an Inscription) February, 1816.
October, 1803.
October, 1803 ("One might believe that natural miseries").
October, 1803 ("When, looking on the present face of things").
Ode Composed on May Morning.
Ode: 1814.
Ode: 1815.
Ode: Intimations of Immortality from Recollections of Early Childhood.
Ode on the Installation of His Royal Highness Prince Albert as Chancellor of the University of Cambridge, July, 1847.
Ode: The Morning of the Day Appointed for a General Thanksgiving. January 18, 1816.
Ode to Apollo.
Ode to Duty.
Ode to Lycoris.
Ode to Lycoris; May, 1817.
Ode: "Who rises on the banks of Seine."
O'er the wide earth, on mountain and on plain.
Oh What a Wreck! How Changed in Mien and Speech!
Old Cumberland Beggar, The.
Old Man Travelling [Animal Tranquillity and Decay, a Sketch].

On a High Part of the Coast in Cumberland.

On a Portrait of the Duke of Wellington upon the Field of Waterloo, by Haydon.

On Seeing a Needlecase in the Form of a Harp; the Work of E.M.S

On Seeing Some Tourists of the Lakes Pass by Reading; a Practice Very Common.

On the Banks of a Rocky Stream.

On the Death of an Unfortunate Lady.

On the Death of His Majesty (George the Third).

On the Departure of Sir Walter Scott from Abbotsford, for Naples.

On the Detraction Which Followed the Publication of a Certain Poem.

On the Extinction of the Venetian Republic.

On the Final Submission of the Tyrolese.

On the Power of Sound.

On the Projected Kendal and Windermere Railway.

On the Same Occasion.

On the Same Occasion [on Seeing the Foundation Preparing for the Erection of Rydal Chapel].

On the Sight of a Manse in the South of Scotland.

Once I could hail (howe'er serene the sky).

Orchard Pathway, The.

Oxford, May 30, 1820.

Oxford, May Thirtieth, Eighteen Twenty.

Parsonage in Oxfordshire, A.

Pass of Kirkstone, The.

Passage from John Wilson's The Angler's Tent.

Passage from Mary Barker's Lines Addressed to a Noble Lord (His Lordship Will Know Why).

Pelayo.

Pelion and Ossa flourish side by side.

Personal Talk.

Pet Lamb, The; A Pastoral.

Peter Bell; a Tale.

Pibroch's note, discountenanced or mute.

Picture of Daniel in the Lions' Den, at Hamilton Palace.

Pilgrim's Dream; or, The Star and the Glow-Worm, The.

Placard for a Poll Bearing an Old Shirt.

Place of Burial in the South of Scotland, A.

Plea for Authors, May, 1838, A.

Poems Composed or Suggested During a Tour, in the Summer of 1833.

Poet and the Caged Turtledove, The.

Poet!—He Hath Put His Heart to School, A.

Poet to His Grandchild; Sequel to "A Plea for Authors."

Poet's Dream, The.

Poet's Epitaph, A.

Poor Robin.

Power of Music.

Prelude, Prefixed to the Volume Entitled "Poems Chiefly of Early and Late Years."

Prelude, The; Growth of a Poet's Mind [1805 vers.].

Prelude, The; Growth of a Poet's Mind [1850 vers.].

Presentiments.

Primrose of the Rock, The.

Prithee, Gentle Lady, List.

Prophecy February, 1807, A.

Protest against the Ballot.

Proud Were Ye, Mountains, When, in Times of Old.

Rains at length have ceased, the winds are stilled, The.

Recluse, The, sels.

Recollection of the Portrait of King Henry Eighth, Trinity Lodge, Cambridge.

Redbreast Chasing the Butterfly, The.

Redbreast, The [Suggested in a Westmoreland Cottage].

Remembrance of Collins, Composed upon the Thames near Richmond.

Repentance; A Pastoral Ballad.

Resolution and Independence.

Rest and Be Thankful!

Retirement.

Reverie of Poor Susan, The.

River Duddon [A Series of Sonnets], The.

Road extended o'er a heath, The.

Rob Roy's Grave.

Roman Antiquities.

Roman Antiquities Discovered at Bishopstone, Herefordshire.

Ruined Cottage, The.

Rural Architecture.

Rural Illusions.

Russian Fugitive, The.

Ruth [or, The Influences of Nature].

Said Secrecy to Cowardice and Fraud.

Sailor's Mother, The.

St Catherine of Ledbury.

Salisbury Plain.

Say, what is Honour?—"'Tis the finest sense."

Scorn not the Sonnet; Critic, you have frowned.

September 1, 1802.

September, 1815.

September, 1819 ("Departing summer hath assumed").

September, 1819 ("Sylvan slopes with corn-clad fields, The").

Septimi Gades.

Sequel to Beggars Composed Many Years After.

Seven Sisters, or, the Solitude of Binnorie, The.

She was a Phantom of delight.

Shepherd, looking eastward softly said, The.

Siege of Vienna Raised by John Sobieski February, 1816.

Simon Lee, the Old Huntsman; with an incident in which he was concerned.

Simplon Pass, The.

Small Celandine, The.

So Fair, So Sweet, Withal So Sensitive.

Soft As a Cloud Is Yon Blue Ridge.

Solitary Reaper, The.

Song at the Feast of Brougham Castle upon the Restoration of Lord Clifford, the Shepherd, to the Estates and Honours of His Ancestors.

Song for the Spinning Wheel (Founded upon a Belief Prevalent among the Pastoral Vales of Westmoreland).

Song for the Wandering Jew.

Sonnet: Composed While the Author Was Engaged in Writing a Tract Occasioned by the Convention of Cintra.

Sonnet: "England! the time is come when thou shouldst wean."

Sonnet in the Pass of Killicranky.

Sonnet: "Nuns fret not at their convent's narrow room."

Sonnet on Milton.

Sonnet on Seeing Miss Helen Maria Williams Weep at a Tale of Distress.

Sonnet: To———.

Sonnet to a Picture by Lucca Giordano in the Mureo Borbonico at Naples.

Sonnet (To an Octogenarian).

Sonnet Translated from the Italian of Milton.

Sonnet: "Why should we weep or mourn, Angelic boy."

Sonnet Written by Mr — Immediately after the Death of His Wife.

Sonnets upon the Punishment of Death.

Spanish Guerillas 1811.

Sparrow's Nest, The.

Squib on Colonel Evans, A.

St Paul's.

Stanzas Written in My Pocket-Copy of Thomson's "Castle of Indolence."

Star-Gazers.

Stars Are Mansions Built by Nature's Hand, The.

Steamboats, Viaducts, and Railways.

Stepping Westward.

Stray Pleasures.

Suggested at Tyndrum in a Storm.

Suggested by a Picture of the Bird of Paradise.

Suggested by a View from an Eminence in Inglewood Forest.

Suggested by Mr W. Westall's Views of the Caves, etc., in Yorkshire.

Surprised by joy—impatient as the Wind.

Sweet was the walk along the narrow lane.

Tables Turned, The.

There is a bondage worse, far worse, to bear.

There is a little unpretending Rill.

There Is a Pleasure in Poetic Pains.

There is an Eminence—of these our hills.

There was a spot.

These Chairs they have no words to utter.

This Lawn, a Carpet All Alive.

Thorn, The.

Those [or These] words were uttered as in [or in a] pensive mood.

Though narrow be that old Man's cares, and near.

Though Pulpits and the Desk May Fail.

Though the Bold Wings of Poesy Affect.

Thought[s] of a Briton on the Subjugation of Switzerland.

Thoughts on the Seasons.

Thoughts Suggested the Day Following, on the Banks of Nith, near the Poet's Residence.

Three Graves, The.

Through Cumbrian wilds, in many a mountain cove.

Tinker, The.

'Tis He Whose Yester-Evening's High Disdain.

'Tis said that some have died for love.

To a Butterfly ("I've watched you now a full half-hour").

To a Butterfly ("Stay near me—do not take thy flight!").

To a Child [Written in Her Album].

To a Friend, Composed near Calais, on the Road Leading to Ardres, August 7, 1802.

To a Lady.

To a Painter ("All praise the likeness by the skill portrayed").

To a Painter ("Though I beheld at first with blank surprise").

To a Sexton.

To a Sky-Lark.

To a Skylark.

To a Snow-Drop.

To a Young Lady Who Had Been Reproached for Taking Long Walks in the Country.

To B. R. Haydon.

To B.R. Haydon, On Seeing His Picture of Napoleon Buonaparte on the Island of St Helena.

To Enterprise.

To H. C., Six Years Old.

To I.F.

To ———: "If these brief Records, by the Muses' art."

To —, in Her Seventieth Year.

To Joanna.

To Lady Beaumont.

To ———: "Let other bards of angels sing."

To ———: "Look at the fate of summer flowers."

To Lucca Giordano.

To M. H.

To May.

To Melpomene.

To My Sister.

To ———: "O dearer far than light and life are dear."

To—, on Her First Ascent to the Summit of Helvellyn.

To Rotha Q—.

To S.H.

To Sleep ("Fond words have oft been spoken").

To Sleep ("Flock of sheep that leisurely pass by, A").

To Sleep ("O gentle sleep! do they belong to thee").

To the Author's Portrait.

To the Clouds.

To the Cuckoo ("Not the whole warbling grove").

To the Cuckoo ("O blithe New-comer! I have heard").

To the Daisy ("Bright Flower! whose home is everywhere").

To the Daisy ("In youth from rock to rock I went").
To the Daisy ("Sweet Flower! belike one day to have").
To the Daisy ("With little here to do or see").
To the Evening Star over Grasmere Water.
To the Highland Girl of Inversneyde.
To the Lady E.B. and the Hon. Miss P.
To the Lady Fleming on Seeing the Foundation Preparing for the Erection of Rydal Chapel, Westmoreland.
To the Lady Mary Lowther.
To the Memory of Raisley Calvert.
To the Men of Kent (October, 1803).
To the Moon (Composed by the Seaside,—on the Coast of Cumberland).
To the Moon (Rydal).
To the Pennsylvanians.
To the Planet Venus.
To the Planet Venus, an Evening Star.
To the Poet, John Dyer.
To the Rev. Christopher Wordsworth, D.D., Master of Harrow School.
To the Same Flower [The Small Celandine].
To the Small Celandine.
To the Sons of Burns, after Visiting the Grave of Their Father.
To the Spade of a Friend (An Agriculturist).
To the Torrent at the Devil's Bridge, North Wales, 1824.
To the Utilitarians.
To Thomas Clarkson, on the Final Passing of the Bill for the Abolition of the Slave Trade. March, 1807.
To Toussaint L'Ouverture.
To — Upon the Birth of Her First-Born Child, March, 1833.
To ———: " 'Wait, prithee, wait!' this answer Lesbia threw."
Tradition of Oker Hill in Darley Dale, Derbyshire, A.
Translation of a Celebrated Greek Song.
Travelling.
Triad, The.
Tribute to the Memory of the Same Dog.
Troilus and Cresida.
Trosachs, The.
Tuft of Primroses, The.
Two April Mornings, The.
Two Epigrams on Byron's *Cain*.
Two Thieves, The; or, the Last Stage of Avarice.
Unremitting Voice of Nightly Streams, The.
Upon a Portrait.
Upon Perusing the "Epistle [To Sir George Howland Beaumont]" Thirty Years after Its Composition.
Upon seeing a Coloured Drawing of the Bird of Paradise in an Album.
Upon the Late General Fast. March, 1832. *see also* On a Celebrated Event in Ancient History.
Upon the Sight of a Beautiful Picture.
Upon the Sight of the Portrait of a Female Friend.
Vale of Esthwaite, The.
Valedictory Sonnet.
Vaudracour and Julia.
Vernal Ode.
View from the Top of Black Comb.
Voice of the Derwent, The.
Volant Tribe of Bards on Earth Are Found, A.
Waggoner, The.
Wansfell! This Household Has a Favoured Lot.
Water Fowl.
Waterfall and the Eglantine, The.
We Are Seven.
Weak is the will of Man, his judgement blind.
Western clouds a deepening gloom display, The.
Westmoreland Girl, The.
What Heavenly Smiles! O Lady Mine.
What if our numbers barely could defy.
What is it that tells my soul the Sun is setting?
When first I journeyed hither, to a home.

When Haughty Expectations Prostrate Lie.
When I have borne in memory what has tamed.
When Philoctetes in the Lemnian Isle.
When Severn's Sweeping Flood Had Overthrown.
When slow from pensive twilight's latest gleams.
When, to the attractions of the busy world.
Where lies the Land to which yon Ship must go?
Where Lies the Truth? Has Man in Wisdom's Creed.
While Anna's Peers and Early Playmates Tread.
While Beams of Orient Light Shoot Wide and High.
Whirl-blast from behind the hill, A.
White Doe of Rylstone, The; or, The Fate of the Nortons.
Who but Is Pleased to Watch the Moon on High.
Who fancied what a pretty sight.
Why Art Thou Silent [Is Thy Love a Plant].
Why, Minstrel, These Untuneful Murmurings.
Widow on Windmere Side, The.
Wild Duck's Nest, The.
Winter's Evening, A.
Wishing-Gate, The.
Wishing-Gate Destroyed, The.
With a Small Present.
With Ships the sea was sprinkled far and nigh.
World is too much with us; late and soon, The.
Wren's Nest, A.
Written after the Death of Charles Lamb. *see also* Inscription in the Grounds of Coleorton, the Seat of Sir George Beaumont, BART., Leicestershire *and* Inscription in a Garden of the Same.
Written in a Grotto.
Written in Germany on One of the Coldest Days of the Century.
Written in London, September, 1802.
Written in March [While Resting on the Bridge at the Foot of Brother's Water].
Written in Mrs Field's Album opposite a Pen-and-Ink Sketch in the Manner of a Rembrandt Etching Done by Edmund Field.
Written in the Strangers' Book at "The Station," Opposite Bowness.
Written in Very Early Youth.
Written upon a Blank Leaf in "The Compleat Angler."
Written with a Pencil upon a Stone in the Wall of the House (an Out-House), on the Island at Grasmere.
Written with a Slate Pencil on a Stone, on the Side of the Mountain of Black Comb.
Written with a Slate Pencil upon a Stone, the Largest of a Heap Lying near a Deserted Quarry, upon One of the Islands at Rydal.
Yarrow Revisited.
Yarrow Unvisited [1803].
Yarrow Visited [September, 1814].
Yes, it was the mountain Echo.
Yes! Thou Art Fair, Yet Be Not Moved.
Yew-Trees.
Young England—What Is Then Become of Old.

Wright, Charles (b. 1935)

Absence Inside an Absence.
After Reading T'ao Ch'ing, I Wander Untethered through the Short Grass.
After Reading Tu Fu, I Go Outside to the Dwarf Orchard.
After Reading Wang Wei, I Go Outside to the Full Moon.
After Rereading Robert Graves, I Go Outside to Get My Head Together.
All Landscape Is Abstract, and Tends to Repeat Itself.
American Twilight.
Apologia Pro Vita Sua.
Appalachian Book of the Dead, The.
Appalachian Book of the Dead 2, The.

Appalachian Book of the Dead 3, The.
Appalachian Book of the Dead 4, The.
Appalachian Book of the Dead 5, The.
Appalachian Book of the Dead 6, The.
Arkansas Traveller.
Ars Poetica.
Ars Poetica 2.
As Our Bodies Rise, Our Names Turn into Light.
Autumn's Sidereal, November's a Ball and Chain.
Back Yard Boogie Woogie.
Bad Memory Makes You a Metaphysician, a Good One Makes You a Saint, A.
Bar Giamaica, 1959-60.
Basic Dialogue.
Bicoastal Journal.
Black Zodiac.
Blaise Pascal Lip-syncs the Void.
Body Language.
Broken English.
California Dreaming.
California Spring.
Called Back.
Chickamauga.
Childhood's Body.
China Journal.
China Mail.
Chinese Journal.
Christmas East of the Blue Ridge.
Cicada.
Cicada Blue.
Composition in Grey and Pink.
Cryopexy.
Dead Color.
December Journal.
Deep Measure.
Disjecta Membra.
Dog Day Vespers.
Dog Yoga.
Driving through Tennessee.
Driving to Passalacqua, 1960.
Drone and Ostinato.
Early Saturday Afternoon, Early Evening.
East of the Blue Ridge, Our Tombs Are in the Dove's Throat.
Easter 1989.
Freezing Rain.
Gate City Breakdown.
George Trakl Journal.
Giorgio Morandi and the Talking Eternity Blues.
Half February.
Hawaii Dantesca.
Holy Ghost Asketh for Us with Mourning and Weeping Unspeakable, The.
Holy Thursday.
Homage to Cesare Pavese.
Homage to Claude Lorrain.
Homage to Paul Cézanne.
If You Talk the Talk, You Better Walk the Walk.
In the Kingdom of the Past, the Brown-Eyed Man is King.
In the Valley of the Magra.
Indian Summer 2.
Italian Days.
It's Turtles All the Way Down.
Jesuit Graves.
Journal of English Days, A.
Journal of One Significant Landscape, A.
Journal of Southern Rivers, A.
Journal of the Year of the Ox, A.
Journal of Three Questions, A.
Journal of True Confessions, A.
Laguna Blues.
Laguna Dantesca.
Landscape as Metaphor, Landscape as Fate and a Happy Life.
Landscape with Seated Figure and Olive Trees.
Language Journal.
Last Journal.
Light Journal.
Lives of the Artists.
Lives of the Saints.
Local Journal.

Lonesome Pine Special.
Looking across Laguna Canyon at Dusk, West-by-Northwest.
Looking Again at What I Looked at for Seventeen Years.
Looking at Pictures.
Looking Outside the Cabin Window, I Remember a Line by Li Po.
Looking West from Laguna Beach at Night.
Lost Bodies.
Lost Souls.
Mantova.
Maple on the Hill.
March Journal.
May Journal.
Meditation on Form and Measure.
Meditation on Song and Structure.
Meditation on Summer and Shapelessness.
Mid-winter Snowfall in the Piazza Dante.
Miles Davis and Elizabeth Bishop Fake the Break.
Monastery at Vršac, The.
Mondo Angelico.
Mondo Henbane.
Mount Caribou at Night.
Negatives 2.
New Year's Eve, 1979.
Night Journal.
Night Journal II.
North American Bear.
Not everyone can see the truth, but he can be it.
October.
October 2.
Opus Posthumous.
Opus Posthumous 2.
Opus Posthumous 3.
Ordinary Afternoon in Charlottesville, An.
Ostinato and Drone.
Other Side of the River, The.
Paesaggio Notturno.
Passing the Morning under the Serenissima.
Peccatology.
Poem Almost Wholly in My Own Manner.
Poem Half in the Manner of Li Ho.
Portrait of the Artist with Hart Crane.
Portrait of the Artist with Li Po.
Primitive Journal.
Primitive Journal II.
Quotations.
Reading Lao Tzu Again in the New Year.
Reading Rorty and Paul Celan One Morning in Early June.
Remembering Spello, Sitting Outside in Prampolini's Garden.
Reply to Wang Wei.
Returned to the Yaak Cabin, I Overhear an Old Greek Song.
Roma I.
Roma II.
St. Augustine and the Arctic Bear.
Saturday Morning Journal.
Self-Portait ("In Murray, Kentucky I lay once").
Self-Portait ("Someday they'll find me out, and my lavish hands").
Self-Portait ("Charles on the Trevisan, right bridge").
Self-Portait ("Marostica, Val di Ser. Bassano del Grappa").
Self-Portait ("Pictures in the air have few visitors, The").
Silent Generation, The.
Silent Journal.
Sitting at Dusk in the Back Yard after the Mondrian Retrospective.
Sitting Outside at the End of Autumn.
Sky Diving.
Southern Cross, The.
Spring Abstract.
Spring Storm.
Sprung Narratives.
Star Turn.
Star Turn 2.
Step-Children of Paradise.
Still Life on a Matchbox Lid.
Still Life with Spring and Time to Burn.

Still Life with Stick and Word.
Stray Paragraphs in April, Year of the Rat.
Stray Paragraphs in February, Year of the Rat.
Summer Storm.
T'ang Notebook.
Tennessee Line.
There Is No Shelter.
Thinking About the Night Sky, I Remember a Poem by Tu Fu.
Thinking about the Poet Larry Levis One Afternoon in Late May.
Thinking of David Summers at the Beginning of Winter.
Thinking of Winter at the Beginning of Summer.
Three Poems for the New Year, *sels.*
Three Poems of Departure.
To Giacomo Leopardi in the Sky.
To the Egyptian Mummy in the Etruscan Museum at Cortona.
Two Stories.
Umbrian Dreams.
Under the Nine Trees in January.
Venetian Dog.
Venexia 1.
Venexia 2.
Vesper Journal.
Virginia Reel.
Waiting for Tu Fu.
Watching the Equinox Arrive in Charlottesville, September 1992.
When You're Lost in Juarez, in the Rain, and It's Eastertime Too.
Winter-Worship.
With Eddie and Nancy in Arezzo at the Caffè Grande.
With Simic and Marinetti at the Giubbe Rosse.
Writing Life, The.
Yard Journal.
Yard Work.

Wright, James (1643–1713)
Girl Walking into a Shadow, A.
Wright, James (1927–80)
Accusation, The.
Alarm, The.
All the Beautiful are Blameless.
American Twilights, 1957.
American Wedding.
Angel, The.
Arrangements with Earth for Three Dead Friends.
Arriving in the Country Again.
As I Step over a Puddle at the End of Winter, I Think of an Ancient Chinese Governor.
Assignation, The.
At the Executed Murderer's Grave.
At the Slackening of the Tide.
At Thomas Hardy's Birthplace, 1953.
Autumn Begins in Martins Ferry, Ohio.
Autumnal.
Before a Cashier's Window in a Department Store.
Beginning.
Blessing, A.
Blue Teal's Mother.
Breath of Air, A.
Brush Fire.
But Only Mine.
By a Lake in Minnesota.
Centenary Note: Inscribed to Little Crow, Leader of the Sioux Rebellion in Minnesota, 1862, A.
Christmas Greeting, A.
Cold Divinities, The.
Come Forth.
Complaint.
Confession to J. Edgar Hoover.
Depressed by a Book of Bad Poetry, I Walk toward an Unused Pasture and Invite the Insects to Join Me.
Devotions.
Dog in a Cornfield.
Dream of Burial, A.
Echo for the Promise of Georg Trakl's Life.
Eclogue at Nash's Grove.
Eisenhower's Visit to Franco, 1959.

Elegy for the Poet Morgan Blum, An.
Elegy in a Firelit Room.
Eleutheria.
Erinna to Sappho.
Evening.
Father.
Fear Is What Quickens Me.
Fishermen, The.
Fit against the Country, A.
For the Marsh's Birthday.
From a Bus Window in Central Ohio, Just before a Thunder Shower.
Frontier, The.
Gambling in Stateline, Nevada.
Gesture by a Lady with an Assumed Name, A.
Ghost, The.
Girl in a Window, A.
Goodbye to the Poetry of Calcium.
Having Lost My Sons, I Confront the Wreckage of the Moon: Christmas, 1960.
Horse, The.
How My Fever Left.
Humming a Tune for an Old Lady in West Virginia.
I Am a Sioux Brave, He Said in Minneapolis.
I Was Afraid of Dying.
Idea of the Good, The.
In a Viennese Cemetery.
In Fear of Harvests.
In Memory of a Spanish Poet.
In Memory of Leopardi.
In Memory of the Horse David, Who Ate One of my Poems.
In Ohio.
In Response to a Rumor that the Oldest Whorehouse in Wheeling, West Virginia, Has Been Condemned.
In Shame and Humiliation.
In Terror of Hospital Bills.
In the Cold House.
In the Face of Hatred.
Inscription for the Tank.
Jewel, The.
Katy Did.
Lament for My Brother on a Hayrake.
Larry.
Late November in a Field.
Life, The.
Lifting Illegal Nets by Flashlight.
Lights in the Hallway, The.
Listening to the Mourners.
Little Girl on Her Way to School, A.
Living by the Red River.
Lying in a Hammock at William Duffy's Farm in Pine Island, Minnesota.
Mad Fight Song for William S. Carpenter, 1966, A.
Many of Our Waters: Variations on a Poem by a Black Child.
March.
Mary Bly.
Message Hidden in an Empty Wine Bottle that I Threw into a Gully of Maple Trees One Night at an Indecent Hour, A.
Milkweed.
Miners.
Minneapolis Poem, The.
Moon.
Moral Poem Freely Accepted from Sappho, A.
Morality of Poetry, The.
Morning Hymn to a Dark Girl.
Mutterings Over the Crib of a Deaf Child.
My Grandmother's Ghost.
Northern Pike.
Note Left in Jimmy Leonard's Shack, A.
Offense, The.
Offering for Mr. Bluehart, An.
Old Age Compensation.
Old Man Drunk.
On Minding One's Own Business.
On the Skeleton of a Hound.
Outside Fargo, North Dakota.
Paul.
Poem Written under an Archway in a Discontinued Railroad Station, Fargo, North Dakota, A.

Poem about Breasts, A.
Poem about George Doty in the Death House,
    A.
Poem by Garnie Braxton, A.
Poem for Kathleen Ferrier.
Poems to a Brown Cricket.
Poor Washed Up by Chicago Winter, The.
Prayer in My Sickness, A.
Prayer to Escape from the Market Place, A.
Prayer to the Lord Ramakrishna, A.
Presentation of Two Birds to My Son, A.
Quail, The.
Quest, The.
Rain.
Red Jacket's Grave.
Refusal, The.
Revelation, The.
RIP.
River Down Home, The.
Saint Judas.
Sappho.
Seasonless, The.
Secret Gratitude, A.
Shadow and the Real, The.
She Hid in the Trees from the Nurses.
Sitting in a Small Screenhouse on a Summer
    Morning.
Small Blue Heron, The.
Small Frogs Killed on the Highway.
Snowstorms in the Midwest.
So She Said.
Song for the Middle of the Night, A.
Sparrows in a Hillside Drift.
Speak.
Spring Images.
Stages on a Journey Westward.
Summer Memory in the Crowded City, A.
Sun Tan at Dusk.
Three Sentences for a Dead Swan.
Three Stanzas From Goethe.
Three Steps to the Graveyard.
To a Dead Drunk.
To a Defeated Savior.
To a Friendly Dun.
To a Fugitive.
To a Hostess Saying Goodnight.
To a Troubled Friend.
To Flood Stage Again.
To Harvey, Who Traced the Circulation.
To the August Fallen.
To the Evening Star: Central Minnesota.
To the Muse.
To the Poets in New York.
Today I Was So Happy, So I Made this Poem.
Trouble.
Trying to Pray.
Twilights.
Two Hangovers.
Two Horses Playing in the Orchard.
Two Poems about President Harding.
Two Postures beside a Fire.
Undermining of the Defense Economy, The.
Way to Make a Living, A.
What the Earth Asked Me.
Willy Lyons.
Winter Day in Ohio, A.
Witches Waken the Natural World in Spring.
Written in a Copy of Swift's Poems, for Wayne
    Burns.
Youth.

Wright, Jay (b. 1935)
Abstract of Knowledge, The / The First Test.
Albuquerque Graveyard, The.
Baptism in the Lead Avenue Ditch.
Beginning Again.
Benjamin Banneker Helps to Build a City.
Benjamin Banneker Sends His *Almanac* to
    Thomas Jefferson.
Birthday, The.
Chapultepec Castle.
Crispus Attucks.
Death of an Unfamiliar Sister, The.
Destination: Accomplished.
End of an Ethnic Dream, The.
Eye of God, the Soul's First Vision, The.
Family Reunion.

First Principles.
Homecoming.
Homecoming Singer, The.
Idiotic and Politic.
Inscrutability.
Inside Chapultepec Castle.
Invention of a Garden, The.
Invitation to Madison County, An.
Jason Visits His Gypsy.
Logbook of Judgments.
Love's Dozen.
Meeting Her in Chapultepec.
Morning: Leaving Calle Gigantes.
Museums in Chapultepec, The.
Night Ride.
Non-Birthday Poem for My Father, A.
Origins.
Preparing to Leave Home.
Regeneration, The.
Rhythm, Charts and Changes.
Sense of Comedy, The: 1.
Sketch for an Aesthetic Project.
Twenty-Two Tremblings of the Postulant.
W. E. B. DuBois at Harvard.
Walking Chapultepec.
Wednesday Night Prayer Meeting.

Wroth [*or* Wroath], Mary Sidney, Countess of
Montgomery (1587?–1651?)
Love's Victorie.
Pamphilia to Amphilanthus.
Urania.

Wu of Han, Emperor (156–87 B.C.)
Hiding Our Love.
Skein, The.

Wyatt, Sir Thomas (1503?–42)
Absence! Absenting causeth me to complain.
Absence, alas, / Causeth me pass.
Accused though I be without desert.
After great storms the calm returns.
Against the rock I climb, both high and hard.
Ah, my heart, ah, what aileth thee.
Ah, Robin, / Jolly Robin.
Alas, dear heart! what hap [*or* hope] had I.
Alas, Fortune, what aileth thee.
Alas, madam[e], for stealing [*or* stelying] of a
    kiss [*or* kysse].
Alas! my dear, the word thou spakest.
Alas, poor man, what hap have I.
Alas, the grief and deadly wo[e]ful smart[!].
All heavy minds.
All in thy sight my life doth whole depend.
All ye that know of care and heaviness.
Alone musing, / Remembering.
And if an eye may save or slay.
Answer that ye made to me, my dear, The [*or*
    Th'].
Answer, The.
Argument, Th.'
As power and wit will me assist.
At last withdraw your cruelty.
At mo[o]st mischief.
Avising the bright beams of these fair eyes.
Ballad of Will, The.
Because I have thee still kept from lies and
    blame.
Behold, love, thy power how she despiseth!
Being as none is, I do complain.
Betrayal.
Blame Not My Lute.
But sithens you it assay to kill.
By bolstered words I am borne in hand.
Caesar, when that the traitor of Egypt.
Comfort at hand! Pluck up thy heart.
Comfort thyself, my wo[e]ful heart.
Comparison of Love to a Streame Falling from
    the Alpes.
Complaining, alas, without redress.
Courtier's Life, The.
Deem as ye list. Upon good cause.
Defamed guiltiness by silence unkempt.
Desire, alas, my master and my foe.
Desire to sorrow doth me constrain.
Dido am I, the founder first of Carthage.
Disdain.
Disdain me not without desert.
Disdain not, madam, on him to look.

Divers[e] [*or* Dyvers] doth[e] use, as I have
    heard and kno[w].
Do way, do way, ye little wily prat!
Double, diverse, sullen, and strange.
Driven by desire, I did this deed.
Driven by desire to set affection.
Driving to desire, adread also to dare.
Duress of pains and grievous smart.
Enemy [*or* en'my] of life, decayer of all kind,
    The [*or* Th'].
Epitaph of Sir Thomas Gravener, [Knight], An.
Face that should content me wonders [*or*
    wondrous] well, A.
Farewell, all my welfare.
Farewell, the reign of cruelty!
Flaming sighs that boil within my breast, The.
For shamefast harm of great and hateful need.
For to love her for her looks lovely.
For want of [*or* I] will in woe I plain.
Fortune doth frown.
Fortune, what aileth thee.
From thought to thought, from hill to hill love
    doth me lead.
Fruit of all the service that I serve, The.
Full well it may be seen.
Furious gun in his raging ire, The.
Give place all ye that doth rejoice.
Go, burning sighs, unto the frozen heart.
Greeting to you both in hearty wise.
Grudge on who list, this is my lot.
Had I wist that now I wot.
Hap happeth oft unlooked for.
Hate whom ye list for I care not.
He is not de[a]d that sometime [*or* somtyme]
    hath a fall.
Heart and service to you proffered, The.
Heart oppressed [*or* oppress'd] with desperate
    thought.
Help[e] me to seek [*or* seke] for I lost it there.
His Reward.
Honesty.
Horrible of hue, hideous to behold.
I abide and better abide.
I am as I am and so will I be.
I am ready and ever will be.
I have been a lover.
I have sought long with steadfastness.
I know not where my heavy sighs to hide.
I lead a life unpleasant, nothing glad.
I love, loved, and so doth she.
I might by no means surmise.
I must go walk the woods so wild.
I see my plaint with open ears.
I see that chance hath chosen me.
I see the change from that that was.
If amorous faith in heart unfeigned.
If chance assigned [*or* assign'd].
If ever man might him avaunt.
If fancy [*or* fansy] would favour.
If I might have at mine own will.
If it be so that I forsake thee.
If thou wilt mighty be, flee from the rage.
If waker care, if sudden [*or* sodayne] pale
    colo[u]r.
If with complaint the pain might be expressed.
In aeternum I was once determed.
In doubtful breast whilst motherly Pity.
In faith I not [well] what to say.
In mourning wise since daily I increase.
In Spayn.
In wilful riches I have found poverty.
Iopas's Song.
It burneth yet, alas, my heart's desire.
It may be good like it who list.
It was my choice, it was no chance.
Joy so short alas, the pain so near, The.
Knot which first my heart did strain, The.
Lady gave me a gift she had not, A.
Lament my loss[e], my labo[u]r, and my pain
    [*or* payne].
Liberty.
Like as the bird in the cage enclosed.
Like as the swan towards her death.
Like as the wind with raging blast.
Live thou gladly if so thou may.
Lively sparks that issue from those eyes, The.

Lo, how I seek and sue to have.
Lo, what it is to love!
Long love that in my thought doth harbo[u]r, The.
Longer to muse.
Longer to trow ye.
Loss is small to lose such one, The.
Love and Fortune and my mind, rememb'rer.
Love hath again.
Love whom ye list and spare not.
Lover Showeth How He Is Forsaken of Such as He Sometime Enjoyed, The.
Lover's Appeal, The.
Lucks, my fair falcon, and your fellows all.
Madam, I you require.
Madam, Withouten Many Words.
Marvel No More.
May Time.
Me list no more to sing.
Might I as well within my song belay.
Mistrustful minds be moved.
Most wretched heart, most miserable.
Mourning my heart doth sore oppress.
My heart I gave thee not to do it pain.
My hope, alas, hath me abused.
My love is like unto th'eternal fire.
My love took scorn my service to retain.
My Lute, Awake!
My Pen.
My sweet, alas, forget me not.
Nature that gave the bee so feat a grace.
No! Indeed.
Now all of change.
Now must I learn to feign.
Now must I le[a]rn[e] to live [or lyve] at rest.
O, cruel heart, where is thy faith?
O goodly hand.
O miserable sorrow withouten cure!
O, what undeserved cruelty.
Of Carthage he, that worthy warrior.
Of purpose Love chose first for to be blind.
Once in your grace I know I was.
Pain of all pain, the most grievous pain.
Pass forth, my wonted cries.
Patience.
Patience, for I have wrong.
Patience for my device.
Patience of all my smart.
Penitential Psalms, sels.
Perdy [or Perdie or Perdye], I said[e] it [or yt] not.
Pillar [or Piller] perished [or pearisht] is whe[a]rto I le[a]nt, The.
Plain ye, mine eyes. Accompany my heart.
Process of time worketh such wonder.
Promise, A.
Protest, A.
Prove whether I do change, my dear.
Quondam was I in my lady's grace.
'Resound my voice, ye woods.'
Restful place, reviver of my smart, The.
Right true it is and said full yore ago.
Satires, sels.
Shall she never out of my mind.
She sat and sewed that hath done me the wrong.
She that should most, perceiveth least.
Sighs are my food, drink are my tears.
Since love is such that, as ye wot.
Since Love will needs that I shall love.
Since so ye please to hear me plain.
Since that my language without eloquence.
Since ye delight to know.
Since you will needs that I shall sing.
Sith I myself displease thee.
Sith it is so that I am thus refused.
So unwarely was never no man caught [or cawght].
Sometime I fled the fire that me brent.
Sometime I sigh, sometime I sing.
Sonnet: 'Each man me telleth.'
Speak thou and speed, where will or power ought [or aught] help'th.
Spite hath no power to make me sad.
Spite of their spite which they in vain.
Stand Whoso List.

Steadfastness.
Such hap as I am happed in.
Such is the course that nature's kind hath wrought.
Such vain thought as wonted to mislead me.
Suffering in sorrow, in hope to attain.
Sufficed not, madame, that you did tear.
Take heed betime, lest ye be spied.
That time that mirth did steer my ship.
There was never file half so well filed.
There was never nothing more me pained [or payned].
Thou hast no faith of him that hath none.
Thou sleepest fast and I with woeful heart.
Though I cannot your cruelty constrain.
Though I myself be bridled of my mind.
Though of the sort there be that feign.
Though some do grudge to see me joy.
Though this the [or thy] port and I thy servant true.
Thy promise was to love me best.
To cause accord or to ag[g]re[e].
To make an end of all this strife.
To my mishap, alas, I find.
To rail or jest, ye know I use it not.
To seek each where where man doth live.
To wet your eye withouten tear.
To whom should I sue to ease my pain?
To wish and want and not obtain.
Unstable dream[e] [or dreme], according [or accordyng] to the place.
Varium et Mutabile.
Venomous thorns that are so sharp and keen.
Venus, in sport, to please therewith her dear.
Vulcan begat me. Minerva me taught.
Wandering gadling in the summer tide, The.
Was I never yet of your love grieved.
What death is worse than this?
What Does This Mean?
What needeth these threnning words and wasted wind?
What rage is this? What furo[u]r of what kind [or kynd]?
What should I say.
What thing is that that I both have and lack.
What vaileth [or 'vaileth] truth [or trouth]? or by it to take pain [or payn]?
What word is that that changeth not.
What would ye more of me, your slave, require.
When first mine eyes did view and mark.
When that I call unto my mind.
Where shall I have at mine own will.
Who hath he[a]rd of such[e] cruelty before.
Who list his wealth and ease retain.
Who would have ever thought.
Whoso List to Hunt.
Will ye see what wonders love hath wrought?
Within my breast I never thought it gain.
Ye know my heart, my lady dear.
Ye old mule, that thin[c]k your self so fair [or fayre].
Your looks so often cast.

Y

Yeats, William Butler (1865–1939)
Acre of Grass, An.
Adam's Curse.
After Long Silence.
Against Unworthy Praise.
All Things Can Tempt Me.
Alternative Song for the Severed Head in "The King of the Great Clock Tower."
Among School Children.
Anashuya and Vijaya.
Another Song of a Fool.
Apparitions, The.
Appointment, An.
Are You Content.
Arrow, The.
At Algeciras—a Meditation upon Death.
At Galway Races.
At The Abbey Theatre.
Baile and Aillinn.

Ballad of Father Gilligan, The.
Ballad of Father O'Hart, The.
Ballad of Moll Magee, The.
Ballad of the Foxhunter, The.
Balloon of the Mind, The.
Beautiful Lofty Things.
Before the World Was Made.
Beggar to Beggar Cried.
Black Tower, The.
Blessed, The.
Blood and the Moon.
Broken Dreams.
Bronze Head, A.
Brown Penny.
Byzantium.
Cap and Bells, The.
Cat and the Moon, The.
Chambermaid's First Song, The.
Chambermaid's Second Song, The.
Choice, The.
Chosen.
Church and State.
Circus Animals' Desertion, The.
Cloak, the Boat, and the Shoes, The.
Coat, A.
Cold Heaven, The.
Collarbone [or Collar-Bone] of a Hare, The.
Colonel Martin.
Come Gather Round Me Parnellites.
Coming of Wisdom with Time, The.
Conjunctions.
Consolation.
Coole Park and Ballylee, 1931.
Coole Park, 1929.
Countess Cathleen in Paradise, The.
Cradle Song, A: "Angels are stooping, The."
Crazed Girl, A.
Crazed Moon, The.
Crazy Jane and Jack the Journeyman.
Crazy Jane and the Bishop.
Crazy Jane Grown Old Looks at the Dancers.
Crazy Jane on God.
Crazy Jane on the Day of Judgment.
Crazy Jane Reproved.
Crazy Jane Talks with the Bishop.
Cuchulain Comforted.
Curse of Cromwell, The.
Dancer at Cruachan and Cro-Patrick, The.
Dawn, The.
Death.
Death of Cuchulain, The.
Dedication to a Book of Stories Selected from the Irish Novelists.
Deep-sworn Vow, A.
Delphic Oracle upon Plotinus, The.
Demon and Beast.
Dialogue of Self and Soul, A.
Dolls, The.
Double Vision of Michael Robartes, The.
Down by the Salley Gardens.
Dream of Death, A.
Drinking Song, A.
Drunken Man's Praise of Sobriety, A.
Easter 1916.
Ego Dominus Tuus.
Ephemera.
Everlasting Voices, The.
Faery Song, A.
Fallen Majesty.
Falling of the Leaves, The.
Fascination of What's Difficult, The.
Father and Child.
Fergus and the Druid.
Fiddler of Dooney, The.
First Confession, A.
Fish, The.
Fisherman, The.
Folly of Being Comforted, The.
Fool by the Roadside, The.
For Anne Gregory.
Four Ages of Man, The.
Fragments: "Locke sank into a swoon."
Friends.
Friend's Illness, A.
Ghost of Roger Casement, The.
Gift of Harun Al-Rashid, The.

Girl's Song.
Gratitude to the Unknown Instructors.
Great Day, The.
Grey Rock, The.
Gyres, The.
Happy Townland, The.
Harp of Aengus, The.
Hawk, The.
He and She.
He Gives His Beloved Certain Rhymes.
He Hears the Cry of the Sedge.
He Remembers Forgotten Beauty.
He Reproves the Curlew.
He Tells a Valley Full of Lovers.
He Tells of the Perfect Beauty.
He Thinks of His Past Greatness When a Part
    of the Constellations of Heaven.
He Thinks of Those Who Have Spoken Evil of
    His Beloved.
He Wishes for the Cloths of Heaven.
He Wishes His Beloved Were Dead.
Heart of the Woman, The.
Her Anxiety.
Her Dream.
Her Praise.
Her Triumph.
Her Vision in the Wood.
High Talk.
His Bargain.
His Confidence.
His Dream.
His Phoenix.
Host of the Air, The.
Hosting of the Sidhe, The.
Hound Voice.
Hour before Dawn, The.
I Am of Ireland.
I walked among the seven woods of Coole.
Image from a Past Life, An.
Imitated from the Japanese.
In Memory of Alfred Pollexfen.
In Memory of Eva Gore-Booth and Con
    Markievicz.
In Memory of Major Robert Gregory.
In Tara's Halls.
In the Seven Woods.
Indian to His Love, The.
Indian upon God, The [or An].
Into the Twilight.
Irish Airman Foresees His Death, An.
John Kinsella's Lament for Mrs. Mary Moore.
King and No King.
Lady's First Song, The.
Lady's Second Song, The.
Lady's Third Song, The.
Lake-Isle of Innisfree, The.
Lamentation of the Old Pensioner, The.
Lapis Lazuli.
Last Confession, A.
Leaders of the Crowd, The.
Leda and the Swan.
Lines Written in Dejection.
Living Beauty, The.
Long-Legged Fly.
Lover Asks Forgiveness because of His Many
    Moods.
Lover Mourns for the Loss of Love, The.
Lover Pleads with His Friend for Old Friends,
    The.
Lover Speaks to the Hearers of His Songs in
    Coming Days, The.
Lover Tells of the Rose in His Heart, The.
Lover's Song, The.
Love's Loneliness.
Lullaby: "Beloved, may your sleep be sound."
Mad as the Mist and Snow.
Madness of King Goll, The.
Magi, The.
Maid Quiet.
Man and the Echo.
Man Who Dreamed of Faeryland, The.
Man Young and Old, A.
Mask, The.
Meditation in Time of War, A.
Meditation of the Old Fisherman, The.
Meditations in Time of Civil War.

Meeting.
Memory.
Memory of Youth, A.
Men Improve with the Years.
Meru.
Michael Robartes and the Dancer.
Michael Robartes Bids His Beloved Be at
    Peace.
Model for the Laureate, A.
Mohini Chatterjee.
Mongan Laments the Change That Has Come
    upon Him and His Beloved.
Moods, The.
Mother of God, The.
Mountain Tomb, The.
Municipal Gallery Revisited, The.
Nativity, A.
Needle's Eye, A.
Never Give All the Heart.
New Faces, The.
News for the Delphic Oracle.
Nineteen Hundred and Nineteen.
Nineteenth Century and After, The.
No Second Troy.
O Do Not Love Too Long.
Oil and Blood.
Old Age of Queen Maeve, The.
Old Memory.
Old Men Admiring Themselves in the Water,
    The.
Old Stone Cross, The.
Old Tom Again.
On a Picture of a Black Centaur by Edmund
    Dulac.
On a Political Prisoner.
On Being Asked for a War Poem.
On Those That Hated "The Playboy of the
    Western World" 1907.
On Woman.
O'Rahilly, The.
Owen Aherne and His Dancers.
Parnell.
Parnell's Funeral.
Parting.
Paudeen.
Peace.
Peacock, The.
People, The.
Phases of the Moon, The.
Pilgrim, The.
Pity of Love, The.
Players Ask for a Blessing on the Psalteries
    and on Themselves, The.
Poet Pleads with the Elemental Powers, The.
Poet to His Beloved, A.
Politics.
Prayer for My Daughter, A.
Prayer for My Son, A.
Prayer for Old Age, A.
Prayer on Going into My House.
Presences.
Prologue to Responsibilities.
Quarrel in Old Age.
Ragged Wood, The.
Realists, The.
Reconciliation.
Red Hanrahan's Song about Ireland.
Remorse for Intemperate Speech.
Results of Thought, The.
Resurrection, The, *sels.*
Ribh at the Tomb of Baile and Aillinn.
Ribh Considers Christian Love Insufficient.
Ribh Denounces Patrick.
Ribh in Ecstasy.
Roger Casement.
Rose of Battle, The.
Rose of Peace, The.
Rose of the World, The.
Rose Tree, The.
Running to Paradise.
Sad Shepherd, The.
Sailing to Byzantium.
Saint and the Hunchback, The.
Scholars, The.
Second Coming, The.
Secret Rose, The.

September 1913.
Seven Sages, The.
Shadowy Waters, The.
Shepherd and Goatherd.
Sixteen Dead Men.
Solomon and the Witch.
Solomon to Sheba.
Song, A: "I thought no more was needed."
Song from "The Player Queen,"A.
Song of the Happy Shepherd, The.
Song of the Old Mother, The.
Song Of Wandering Aengus, The.
Sorrow of Love, The.
Spilt Milk.
Spirit Medium, The.
Spur, The.
Statistics.
Statues, The.
Stick of Incense, A.
Stolen Child, The.
Stream and Sun at Glendalough.
Sweet Dancer.
Swift's Epitaph.
Symbols.
That the Night Come.
There.
These Are the Clouds.
Those Dancing Days Are Gone.
Those Images.
Thought from Propertius, A.
Three Beggars, The.
Three Bushes, The.
Three Hermits, The.
Three Marching Songs.
Three Monuments, The.
Three Movements.
Three Songs to the One Burden.
Three Things.
To a Child Dancing in the Wind.
To a Friend Whose Work Has Come to
    Nothing.
To a Poet, Who Would Have Me Praise Certain
    Bad Poets, Imitators of His and Mine.
To a Shade.
To a Squirrel at Kyle-Na-No.
To a Wealthy Man Who Promised a Second
    Subscription to the Dublin Municipal
    Gallery if It Were Proved the People Wanted
    Pictures.
To a Young Beauty.
To a Young Girl.
To an Isle in the Water.
To Be Carved on a Stone at Thoor Ballylee.
To Dorothy Wellesley.
To His Heart, Bidding It Have No Fear.
To Ireland in the Coming Times.
To Some I Have Talked with by the Fire.
To the Rose upon the Rood of Time.
Tom at Cruachan.
Tom O'Roughley.
Tom the Lunatic.
Towards Break of Day.
Tower, The.
Travail of Passion, The.
Two Kings, The.
Two Songs of a Fool.
Two Songs Rewritten for the Tune's Sake.
Two Trees, The.
Two Years Later.
Unappeasable Host, The.
Under Ben Bulben.
Under Saturn.
Under the Moon.
Under the Round Tower.
Upon a Dying Lady.
Upon a House Shaken by the Land Agitation.
Vacillation.
Valley of the Black Pig, The.
Veronica's Napkin.
Vision, A, *sels.*
Wanderings of Oisin, The.
What Magic Drum?
What Then?
What Was Lost.
Wheel, The.
When Helen Lived.

When You Are Old.
Whence Had They Come?
While I, from that reed-throated whisperer.
White Birds, The.
Who Goes with Fergus?
Wild Old Wicked Man, The.
Wild Swans at Coole, The.
Wisdom.
Witch, The.
Withering of the Boughs, The.
Woman Homer Sung, A.
Words.
Young Man's Song.
Youth and Age.

Z

Zagajewski, Adam (b. 1945)
Airport in Amsterdam.
Albi.
Ancient History.
Anecdote of Rain.
Anton Bruckner.
Apartment for Scholars.
Apes.
At Daybreak.
At Midnight.
Autumn.
Bakery.
Barbarians.
Bells, The.
Blackbird.
Blackened River, The.
Burgundy's Grasslands.
Canvas.
Castle.
Cello.
Chinese Poem.
Churches of France, The.
Circus.
City Unknown.
City Where I Want to Live, The.
Close of Summer, The.
Covenant.
Creation of the World, The.
Cruel.
Dark God, the Light God, The.
Dead Sparrow.
Death of a Pianist.
December.
December Wind.
Degas: *The Milliner's Shop*.
Don't Allow the Lucid Moment to Dissolve.
Dutch Painters.
Early Hours, The.
Electric Elegy.
Elegy for the Living.
Elegy: "It was a gray landscape, houses small."
Epicure From My Staircase, The.
Escalator.
Esprit D'Escalier.
Europe Goes to Sleep.
Europe in Winter.
Farewell for Zbigniew Herbert.
Fence. Chestnut Trees, A.
Fever.
Fire.
Fire, Fire.
Flame, A.
For Gabriela Münter.
For M.
For You.
Franz Schubert: A Press Conference.
From Memory.
From the Lives of Things.
Fruit.
Generation, The.
Georges Seurat: Factory.
Good Friday in the Tunnels of the Métro.
Gothic, The.
Greenhouse, The.
He Acts.
History of Solitude, A.
Holy Saturday in Paris.

House, The.
Houston, 6 P.M.
How Clowns Go.
How Does the Man Look Who's Right.
How High the Moon.
I Walked Through the Medieval Town.
I Wasn't In This Poem.
Immortality.
In May.
In Strange Cities.
In the Beauty Created by Others.
In the Encyclopedias, No Room for Osip
    Mandelstam.
In the Past.
In the Trees.
Incorporeal Ruler.
Iron.
Islands and Towers.
It Comes to a Standstill.
Just Children.
Kierkegaard on Hegel.
King, A.
Late Beethoven.
Late Feast.
Lava.
Letter from a Reader.
Life Sentence.
Light of Lamps, The.
Lightning.
Lindens.
Line Four.
Little Waltz.
Long Afternoons.
Lullaby.
Matches.
Moment ("Clear moments are so short").
Moment ("In the Romanesque church round
    stones").
Morandi.
Morning in Vicenza, A.
Moses.
Moths.
My Aunts.
My Masters.
Mysticism for Beginners.
Name Edmund, The.
New World.
Night ("Because you're only dead").
Night ("Dances beautifully").
1969.
Ode to Plurality.
Ode to Softness.
On Swimming.
Opus Posthumous.
Out Walking.
Over America.
Palm Sunday.
Password.
Persephone.
Philosophers.
Planetarium.
Poems on Poland.
Polish Biographical Dictionary in a Library in
    Houston, The.
Postcards.
Presence.
Quick Poem, A.
R. Says.
Reading Books.
Referendum.
Refugees.
River, A.
Room I Work In, The.
Russia Comes Into Poland.
Sad, Tired.
Sails.
Schopenhauer's Crying.
Self-Portrait.
Self, The.
Sénanque.
Senza Flash.
Separation.
September.
September Afternoon in the Abandoned
    Barracks.
Seventeen.

She Wrote in Darkness.
Shell.
Simone Weil Watches the Rhône Valley.
Sisters of Mercy.
Smoke.
Song of an Emigré.
Soul, The.
Speak Softly.
Square D'Orléans.
Stary Sacz.
Summer.
Summer's Fullness.
Sunrise Over Cassis.
Talk with Friedrich Nietzsche, A.
Tarbes.
That Force.
That's Sicily.
There Will Be a Future.
Thirties, The.
This.
Three Angels.
Three Kings, The.
Three Voices.
Tierra Del Fuego.
To.
To Go to Lvov.
To My Older Brother.
To Myself, In an Album.
To See.
Tongue.
Transformation.
Traveler.
Treatise on Emptiness.
Trial, The.
Truth.
Try to Praise the Mutilated World.
Twenty-Five Years.
Twenty-Year-Old Soldiers.
Vacation.
Van Gogh's Face.
Vaporetto.
Vermeer's Little Girl.
View of Delft, A.
View of Krakow, A.
Wanderer, A.
Watching Shoah in a Hotel Room in America.
We Know Everything.
Where the Breath Is.
Wild Cherries.
Wind at Night.
Without End.
Without Form.
World's Prose, The.
You Are My Silent Brethren.
Your Telephone Call.

**Zaturenska, Marya Alexandrovna (Mrs. Horace
    Gregory) (1902–82)**
Affliction of William Cowper, The.
Afternoon of a Doll.
All Is Well with the Child.
Another Snowstorm.
Background with Harpsichord.
Bird and the Muse.
Blue Flower, The.
Cascades and Fountains.
Casket of Pandora, The.
Castaways, The.
Child in the Crystal.
Chorale for Autumn.
Chorale for the Seasons.
Cold Morning Sky.
Daisy, The.
Daphne.
Dark Year, The.
Death Is the Serpent.
Dialogue.
Dream, The.
Dream Message.
Elegy and Nocturne for Lora Baxter.
Émigrés, The.
Empress Marie Louise, The.
Epitaph for a Careless Beauty.
Familiar, The.
Flowing of the River, The.
For a Child.
For the Seasons.

Forest of Arden.
Fountains of Rome, The, *sels.*
Four Ghosts.
Friend's Song, A.
From a Winter Journal.
Fulfillment.
Future in Miniature.
Garden at Cliveden, The.
Girl and Scarecrow.
Girl in a Library.
Girl Takes Her Place Among the Mothers, The.
Golden Mirror, The.
Head of Medusa.
Homage to Christina Rossetti.
Hymn to Artemis, the Destroyer.
I Know an Island.
Image of a Friend.
Imperfect, The.
Interpreter of Silence, The.
Interview in Midsummer.
Invaders, The.
Island, The.
Lament of Catherine Howard, Fifth Queen of
    Henry VIII.
Late Arrival.
Leaves from the Book of Dorothy Wordsworth.
Listening Landscape, The.
Lullaby: "Ruin falls on blackening skies."
Luna and Leopardi.
Lunar Tides, The.
Madness of Jean-Jacques Rousseau, The, *sels.*
May Morning: Hudson Pastoral.
Metaphysics of the Night.
Mirrored Room, The.
Narrow Hemisphere, The.
O Like a Young Tree.
O Lyric March.
Old House, The.
Old Tale, An.
Once in an Ancient Book.
Pilgrimage.
Places.
Question, The.
Quiet Countries: The World of Hans Christian
    Andersen.
Quiet House, The.
Reflections On a Centaur.
Runaway, The.
Séance, The.
Shakespearean Cycle, A.
Silence and the Wayfarer.
Siren Music.
Snowstorm in January.
Snowy Woods, The.
Song for a Season.
Song: "Life with her weary eyes."
Song of the Forsaken Lilac Tree.
Soul's Haven.
Spellbound.
Spinners.
Spring Morning.
Strange Captivity.
Terraces of Light.
Theme from Louise Labé, A.
They Pass.
Twisted Tree, The.
Uninvited Guest, The.
Unsepulchred, 1914–1918, The.
Variation on a Polish Folk Song.
Variations on a Theme by George Herbert.
Virgin, the Doe, and the Leper, The.
Virgin with a Lamp.
Voices in Air.
Voyage.
Water Lilies: A Nocturne.
White Dress, The.
Winter Rose, The.
Woman at the Piano.
World of the Salamanders, The.
Young Dancers, The.
Young Girl Singing, A.

Zukofsky, Louis (1904–78)
African Violet.
After Charles Sedley.
After reading.
Ah spring, when with a thaw of blue.

Air.
Alba (1952).
All of December Toward New Year's.
All Wise.
Aloe.
Alpine Rosy Bells.
And so till we have died.
And Without.
Anew, sun, to fire summer.
Another Ashtray.
Artemisia.
As to How Much.
Ashtray.
Aster.
Atque in Perpetuum A.W.
Azalea.
Barely and *widely.*
Bayberry.
Bearded Iris.
Belly Locks Shnooks Oakie.
Bird that cries like a baby, The.
Butter-and-Eggs.
Can a mote of sunlight defeat its purpose.
Catullus viii.
Celia's Birthday Poem.
Charlock per Winkle.
Che Di Lor Suona Su Nella Tua Vita.
Chicory.
Chloride of Lime and Charcoal.
Chokecherry.
Chrysanthemum.
Cinquefoil.
Claims.
Clover.
Cockle.
Coleus.
Crocus.
Dahlia.
Daisy.
Dandelion.
Daruma.
Deutzia.
Dogwood.
Drive, fast kisses.
Dutch White Iris.
1892-1941.
Even if love convey.
Finally a Valentine.
For Selma Gubin's Umbrellas.
For you I have emptied the meaning.
For Zadkine.
Forsythia.
Four-o'clock.
4 Other Countries.
"Further than."
Gamut.
George Washington.
Glad they were there.
Grape-Hyacinth.
Grassflower.
Grecian Windflower.
Green leaf that will outlast the winter.
Green plant grows, The.
Guests, The.
Guillaume de Machault (1300-1377) Ballade:
    Ploures, dames.
Gulls over a rotting hull.
H.T.
Has the sum.
Head Lines.
Heart us invisibly thyme time.
Heart's Ease.
Heights, The.
Her face the Book of—Love Delights in—
    Praises.
Hill.
Homage.
Honesty.
Honeysuckle.
Hyacinth.
I Sent Thee Late.
I Walk in the Old Street.
Impatiens.
In the midst of things.
Incident, An.
I's (Pronounced *Eyes*).

It's hard to see but think of a sea.
Jade.
Jaunt.
Judge and the Bird, The.
Last cigarette / a companion, A.
Lavender Cotton.
Laws Can Say, The.
Letter of Poor Birds, The.
Light.
Lilac.
Lilies.
Lily-of-the-Valley.
Lily-of-the-Valley Fortunei.
Lines of this new song are nothing, The.
Liveforever.
Madrigal for 3 Voices, A.
Mantis.
"Mantis," An Interpretation.
Marigold.
Marriage Song for Florence and Harry, A.
Men in the kitchens, The.
Michtam.
Motet.
Mountain Laurel.
My nephew / And my new.
Narcissus.
1959 Valentine.
Non Ti Fidar.
Not it was no dream of coming death.
Old.
Old Poet Moves to a New Aprtment 14 Times,
    The.
On Valentine's Day to Friends.
One friend.
One lutenist played *look*; your through was
    drink.
"One oak fool box";—the pun.
Or a Valentine.
Oxalis.
Pachysandra.
Pamphylian.
Perch Less.
Peri Poietikes.
Petunia.
Phlox.
Poem Beginning "The."
Poppy Anemone.
Pretty.
Privet.
Pussy Willow.
Que J'ay Dit Devant.
Queen Anne's Lace.
Rains, the rains, The.
Raspberry.
Reading and Talking.
Record, The.
Rose-of-Sharon.
Roses.
Ryokan's scroll.
Send regards to Ida the bitch.
Sequence 1944-6.
Shang Cup.
Slipperwort.
Snow-Wreath.
Snowdrop.
Snowflake.
So sounds grass, and if it is sun or no sun.
So That Even a Lover.
Some time has gone.
Song for the Year's End, A.
Songs of Degrees.
Spearmint.
Spider or Ribbon Plant.
Spirea.
Spook's Sabbath, Five Bowings.
Sprengeri.
Starglow.
Strange / To reach that age.
Stratford-on-Avon.
Telephus Sedum.
The.
This Is After All Vacation.
This year / that Valentine is / late.
Thyme.
To Friends, for Good Health.
To My Baby Paul.

SUBJECT INDEX

*Poems under each subject heading are listed alphabetically by author. Subjects range from specific (*Dublin, Ireland *or* Mandela, Nelson*) to the general (*Faith *or* Imagination*).*

    Some subject headings show cross-references to related subjects. The subject category Love *is so broad that it appears here only to refer the user to related subjects.*

A

Aardvarks
Logue, C. Aardvark, The.
Aaron (Bible)
Herbert, G. Aaron.
Abandonment
Ai. Detective, The.
Amichai [*or* Amikhai]. Elegy on an Abandoned Village.
Atwood. Four Small Elegies.
Blake, W. Love's Secret.
Campion, T. Maid's Complaint, A.
Carew, T. Lady, Rescued from Death by a Knight, Who in the Instant Leaves Her, Complains Thus, A.
To His Mistress Retiring in Affection.
To Master W. Montague.
Carruth, H. Abandoned Ranch, Big Bend.
De la Mare. Abandoned Church, An.
Dickey, W. Dog Under False Pretences.
Donne. To Mr I. L. ("Blessed [*or* Blesst] are your north parts, for all this long time").
Dove, R. Adolescence—III.
Dubie. Near the Bridge of Saint-Cloud.
Frost, R. Hill Wife, The.
Hacker, M. Celles.
Hayden, R. Incense of the Lucky Virgin.
Hughes, L. Lament over Love.
Mama and Daughter.
Midwinter Blues.
Jacobsen, J. They Never Were Found.
Three Children, The.
Komunyakaa. Bul Doi, Dust of Life.
My Father's Love Letters [*or* Loveletters].
Levertov. Passing Bell, The.
Lorde. And Don't Think I Won't Be Waiting.
MacNeice. Valediction: "Their verdure dare not show . . . their verdure dare not show."
Merwin. Letter from Gussie, A.
Nash, O. Exit, Pursued by a Bear.
Maybe You Can't Take It with You, but Look What Happens When You Leave It Behind.
Neruda. This Broken Bell.
Owen, W. To Eros.
Piercy. It Breaks.
Prunty. Old Declaratives.
Stillness.
Ransom, J. Lady Lost.
Rich, A. In the Wake of Home.
Riley, J. Little Dog-Woggy, The.
Rilke. Soloist.
Rimbaud, A. Memory.
Rossetti, C. Margery.
Spender, S. Song: "Stranger, you who hide my love."
Szymborska, W. Cat in an Empty Apartment.
Tomlinson, C. Idrigill.
Three Wagnerian Lyrics.
Two Views of Two Ghost Towns.
Whalen, P. Alleyway.
Williams, C. K. Neglect.
Wordsworth, W. Thorn, The.
Wyatt, S. Lover Showeth How He Is Forsaken of Such as He Sometime Enjoyed, The.
Lover's Appeal, The.

Yeats. John Kinsella's Lament for Mrs. Mary Moore.
Zagajewski. September Afternoon in the Abandoned Barracks.
Abbey Theatre, Dublin
Yeats. At The Abbey Theatre.
Abbeys
See **Monasteries**
Abel
See **Cain and Abel**
Abelard and Heloise
Pope, A. Eloisa to Abelard.
Villon. Ballade of the Ladies of Time Past.
Aberdeen, Scotland
Dunbar, W. To Aberdein.
Hardy, T. Aberdeen.
Whittier. Barclay of Ury.
Abishag
Glück, L. Abishag.
Abolitionists
Cullen, C. Negro Mother's Lullaby, A.
Dove, R. David Walker (1785–1830).
Dunbar, P. Douglass.
Hayden, R. Runagate Runagate.
Rukeyser, M. Soul and Body of John Brown, The.
Thoreau. Wait not till slaves pronounce the word.
Very. Abolition of Serfdom in Russia, The.
Freedom National, Slavery Sectional.
John Woolman.
On the Nebraska Bill.
Whittier. Brown of Ossawatomie.
Burial of Barber.
Cross, The.
Daniel Neall.
Daniel Wheeler.
Emancipation Group, The.
Follen.
For Righteousness' Sake.
George L. Stearns.
How Mary Grew.
James Russell Lowell.
Leggett's Monument.
Lines from a Letter to a Young Clerical Friend.
Massachusetts.
New Year, The.
Panorama, The.
Randolph of Roanoke.
Song, A: "Beneath thy skies, November!"
Song for the Time, A.
Sumner.
To Charles Sumner.
To George B. Cheever.
To Lydia Maria Child.
To the Memory of Charles B. Storrs.
To the Memory of Thomas Shipley.
To William Lloyd Garrison.
William Forster.
World's Convention, The.
Wordsworth, W. To Thomas Clarkson, on the Final Passing of the Bill for the Abolition of the Slave Trade. March, 1807.
Aborigines
Clifton, L. Yeti Poet Returns to His Village to Tell His Story, The.

Komunyakaa. Bennelong's Blues.
Protection of Moveable Cultural Heritage.
Visitation.
Snyder, G. Uluru Wild Fig Song.
Williams, M. Green Mansions.
Abortion
Ai. Abortion.
Atwood. Christmas Carols.
Clifton, L. Donor.
Glück, L. Egg, The.
Hardy, T. Reluctant Confession.
Jonson, B. To Fine Lady Would-Be.
Milosz, C. Yokimura.
Piercy. Provocation of the Dream, The.
Right to Life.
Sabbath of Mutual Respect, The.
Ramanujan. When It Happens.
Sexton. Abortion, The.
Walker, A. Ballad of the Brown Girl.
Williams, W. Cold Front, A.
Wilner, E. Love of What Is Not, The.
Abraham
Amichai [*or* Amikhai]. Real Hero of the Sacrifice of Isaac, The.
Real Hero, The.
Dickinson, E. Abraham to kill him.
Milton. Paraphrase on Psalm 114, A.
Nemerov. Nicodemus.
Orr, G. Three Songs.
Owen, W. Parable of the Old Men and the Young, The.
Wilner, E. Sarah's Choice.
Absence
Angelou. After.
Arnold, M. Summer Night, A.
Beckett, S. Vieil aller / vieux arrêts.
Berry, W. Praise.
Brodsky, J. At a Lecture.
Song, A: "I wish you were here, dear."
Brontë, E. From our evening fireside now.
Browning, R. Never the Time and the Place.
Byron, G. To Thyrza.
Carew, T. Mr. Carew to His Friend.
To Her in Absence; a Ship.
Upon Some Alterations in My Mistress, after My Departure into France.
Carver, R. Forge, and a Scythe, A.
No Need.
Cavafy. What Cannot Be.
Chuang Tzu. Starlight and Non-Being.
Coleridge, S. Day-Dream, The.
Hour When We Shall Meet Again, The.
If I Had but Two Little Wings.
Stanger Minstrel, A.
Cooper, J. For My Mother in Her First Illness, from a Window Overlooking Notre Dame.
Crane, H. Carrier Letter.
Old Song.
Creeley. Away.
Berlin: First Night & Early Morning.
Knokke.
Little Time—and Place.
Passage, The.
Place ("Thinking of you asleep on a").
Sight, A.
Sign Board, The.
Smoke.

Song: "Those rivers run from that land."
Turn, The.
Cunningham, J. Absence, my angel, presence at my side.
Davie, D. Robinson Jeffers at Point Sur.
Thou Art Near at Hand, O Lord.
De la Mare. Alone.
Spectre, The.
Voice, The.
Dickinson, E. Absence disembodies—so does Death.
Is not an absent friend as mysterious.
It was not Death, for I stood up.
My life closed twice before its close.
They say that absence conquers.
To the faithful Absence is condensed presence.
You love me—you are sure.
Donne. To Mr I. L ("Blessed [or Blesst] are your north parts, for all this long time").
To Mr T. W ("At once, from hence, my lines and I depart").
Dunbar, P. Absence.
Waiting.
Duncan, R. Passage Over Water.
Gallagher, T. Kidnap[p]er.
Ginsberg, A. Dakar Doldrums.
Love Letter.
Gunn, T. Annihilation of Nothing, The.
Colour Machine, The.
During an Absence.
Hardy, T. Voice, The.
Herrick. Presence and Absence.
Hughes, L. Better.
Homecoming.
Ignatow, D. It's Not You I Miss.
Laughlin, J. Empty Room, The.
Mysterious Disappearance, The.
Lawrence, D. H. Quite Forsaken.
Return.
Levertov. Crow Spring.
Soul-Cake, A.
Lowell, R. Home After Three Months Away.
MacDiarmid, H. Empty Vessel.
Meredith, W. Give and Take.
In Memoriam Stratton Christensen.
Merwin. December among the Vanished.
Little Horse.
Provision.
Separation.
Unfinished Book of Kings.
Millay, E. Oh, Oh, you will be sorry for that word!
Milosz, C. How It Was.
View, The.
Montale. Canebrake sends its little shoots, The.
Earrings, The.
Muldoon, P. Why Brownlee Left.
Nemerov. Small Moon.
Neruda. Dying.
Parker, D. Absence.
Petrarch. Happy and sad, together and yet sole.
Piercy. All Clear.
Breaking Camp.
Raine, K. All that is: / The unbroken surface of the sea.
Angelus.
Wilderness, The.
Ransom, J. Jack's Letter.
Winter Remembered.
Rich, A. Splittings.
Rilke. Lost Things.
Ritsos. Absence.
Distant, The.
Rossetti, C. Fisher-Wife, A.
Smith, S. When the Sparrow Flies.
Spender, S. Absence.
Stevens, W. Gallant Chateau.
Suckling, S. Against Absence.
To Master Davenant for Absence.
Szymborska, W. Parting with a View.
Tennyson, A. Daisy, The.
Thomas, D. I Make This in a Warring Absence.
Tomlinson, C. Track of the Deer, The.
Wilbur, R. "World without Objects Is a Sensible Emptiness, A."
Williams, C. K. Hard Part, The.

Williams, M. Missing Persons.
Wordsworth, W. Why Art Thou Silent [Is Thy Love a Plant].
Wright, C. Absence Inside an Absence.
Wyatt, S. Absence, alas, / Causeth me pass.
Zukofsky, L. Guests, The.
See also **Isolation; Loneliness; Separation**

Abundance
Berry, W. Arrival, The.
Song (1).
Bukowski. Sexpot.
Ciardi, J. Abundance.
Barmecide Feast.
Creeley. Manila.
Emerson, R. Nature.
Jeffers, R. Trap, The.
Mistral, G. Flour.
Swenson, M. Summer's Bounty.
Sze. Cornucopia, The.

Acacia
Montale. Shears, don't cut away that face.
Raine, K. Acacia Tree.
Wilbur, R. Part of a Letter.

Academia
Berryman. Farewell to Miles.
Professor's Song, A.
Burns, R. Dean of Faculty—a New Ballad, The.
Ciardi, J. Guide to Poetry, A.
Ode for School Convocation.
Vale.
Clampitt. Homer, A.D. 1982.
Cummings, E. E. Yonder deadfromtheneckup graduate of a.
Cunningham, J. To a Friend, on Her Examination for the Doctorate in English.
Davie, D. Heroine of the Academy, A.
Liverpool Epistle, A.
Enzensberger, H. Dept. of Philosophy.
Hall, D. Brief Lives.
Hopkins, G. By Mrs. Hopley.
Jarrell, R. Esthetic Theories: Art as Expression.
Time and the Thing-in-Itself in a Textbook.
Kinnell. For William Carlos Williams.
Larkin, P. Posterity.
Logue, C. Professor Tucholsky's Facts.
Nemerov. Decorated Skull in a University Museum.
Full Professor, A.
Relation of Art and Life, A.
Olson, C. I'm With You.
Ransom, J. Prometheus in Straits.
Rich, A. Autumn Equinox.
Roethke. Academic.
Rossetti, C. P.R.B, The.
Rukeyser, M. Gibbs.
Updike. Academy.
Generic College.
Humanities Course.
Story of My Life, The.
Whitman, W. When I Heard the Learn'd Astronomer.
Williams, W. He Has Beaten about the Bush Long Enough.
Our (American) Ragcademicians.
Wright, J. W. E. B. DuBois at Harvard.

Acadia and Acadians
Longfellow, H. Evangeline, a Tale of Acadie.

Accent
Ciardi, J. Firsts.
Davie, D. At Knaresborough.
Lawrence, D. H. Oxford Voice, The.
Nash, O. Chacun à Son Berlitz.
Everybody's Mind to Me a Kingdom Is, or, A Great Big Wonderful World It's.
This Is My Own, My Native Tongue.

Acceptance
Angelou. John J.
Berry, W. September 2, 1969.
Borges. Simplicity.
Bradstreet, A. Here Follows Some Verses upon the Burning of Our House [July 10th, 1666. Copied Out of a Loose Paper].
Broumas, O. Prayer with Martial Stance.
Burns, R. Contented wi' Little.
Orananaoig, or, the Song of Death.

Though fickle fortune has deceiv'd me.
Written in Friar's Carse Hermitage on the Banks of Nith—June—1788.
Ye Jacobites by Name.
Chuang Tzu. Metamorphosis.
Clifton, L. Praise Song.
Collins, B. November.
Creeley. "Bolinas and Me."
Days and Days.
For Martin.
Cummings, E. E. Gee i like to think of dead it means nearer because deeper firmer.
It may not always be so; and i say.
Let it go—the.
Dickinson, E. It ceased to hurt me, though so slow.
"Why do I love" You, Sir?
Eberhart, R. Life and Death.
Emerson, R. Terminus.
Ferlinghetti, L. Elegy to Dispel Gloom, An.
Frost, R. Acceptance.
Glück, L. My Cousin in April.
Hardy, T. Looking Back.
New Dawn's Business, The.
Herrick. To Vulcan.
Ignatow, D. Principle, The.
Without Recrimination.
Kinnell. Prayer.
Kunitz, S. Knot, The.
Levine, P. On My Own.
MacNeice. Selva Oscura.
To Mary.
Meredith, G. Faith on Trial, A.
Outer and Inner.
Philosopher! 'tis said you wail.
Merwin. On the Silent Anniversary of a Reunion.
Olson, C. Kingfishers, The.
Piercy. I Will Not Be Your Sickness.
Rich, A. Letter from the Land of Sinners.
Loser, The.
Rossetti, C. Advent.
Cried Out with Tears.
Death's Chill Between.
Had Fortune parted us / Fortune is blind.
Heart's Chill Between.
Lord, what have I to offer? sickening fear.
My God, wilt Thou accept, and will not we / Give aught to Thee?
Of Him That Was Ready to Perish.
When I Was in Trouble I Called upon the Lord.
Rukeyser, M. Desdichada.
Shelley, P. To———: "One word is too often profaned."
Stafford, W. Afterwards.
With Neighbors One Afternoon.
Whitman, W. Me Imperturbe.
To a Common Prostitute.
Whittier. Woman, A.
Williams, M. Summer Afternoon an Old Man Gives Some Thought to the Central Questions, A.
Wright, J. Eye of God, the Soul's First Vision, The.
Zukofsky, L. Catullus viii.

Accidents
Atwood. This is a mistake, / these arms and legs.
Beck, K. Hungarian Horse-Herd, The.
Berryman. Damn You, Jim D., You Woke Me Up.
Bierce. Californian Summer Pictures.
Bishop, E. Trouvée.
Bukowski. Jack-Knife.
Carruth, H. Wreck of the Circus Train, The.
Corbett, W. At Charlesgate.
Creeley. Place, The ("What is the form is the gro- / tesquerie—the accident").
Cuadra, P. Cup with a Jaguar for the Drinking of Health.
Davie, D. After an Accident.
Dickey, J. Falling.
Sustainment.
Dubie. Accident.
Train, The.
Dugan, A. Jewels of Indoor Glass.

Frost, R.　Door in the Dark, The.
Objection to Being Stepped On, The.
"Out, Out—."
Hardy, T.　I Worked No Wile to Meet You.
Herrick.　Bracelet of Pearle: To Silvia, The.
Broken Christall, The.
Casualties.
Kipling, R.　Dove of Dacca, The.
Komunyakaa.　Story, A.
Larkin, P.　Whatever Happened?
Lawrence, D. H.　Collier's Wife, The.
Levertov.　Concurrence.
MacNeice.　After the Crash.
Meredith, G.　Gordon, Jim, / Life and Limb.
Merrill, J.　Broken Bowl, The.
Nash, O.　Lather as You Go.
Orr, G.　Moment, A.
Paley, G.　For Mike and Jeannie: Resisters
Fifteen Years Later.
Piercy.　S. Dead.
Plath.　Cut.
Prunty.　Sneeze, The.
Two Kinds of Cause.
Rimbaud, A.　Stupidities—Second Series.
Roethke.　Elegy for Jane.
Sexton.　Break, The.
Snyder, G.　Crash.
Stafford, W.　Fifteen.
Life Work.
Van Duyn.　Reading of Rex Stout, A.
Warren, R.　Ballad: Between the Boxcars
[1923].
Recollection in Upper Ontario, from Long
Before.
Williams, C. K.　Child Psychology.
Williams, W.　Detail.
See also **Airplane Crashes; Automobile
Accidents; Disasters; Nuclear Accidents;
Railroad Wrecks; Shipwrecks**
Accordions
Blok.　Accordeon.
Hall, D.　Wedding Party.
Accounting and Accountants
Ritsos.　Striding Over.
Achebe, Chinua
Komunyakaa.　Keeper of the Vigil.
Achilles
Auden.　Shield of Achilles, The.
Campion, T.　Breake now my heart and dye! Oh
no, she may relent.
Cavafy.　Horses of Achilles, The.
Unfaithfulness.
Cullen, C.　Sonnet: "I have not loved you in the
noblest way."
Duncan, R.　Achilles' Song.
Glück, L.　Triumph of Achilles, The.
Graves, R.　Penthesileia.
Herbert, Z.　Achilles. Penthesilea.
Logan, J.　Achilles and the King: A Verse Re-
telling.
Pagis.　Tortoise, The.
Ritsos.　Achilles after Death.
Agamemnon.
First Sensual Delight, The.
Simic.　My Weariness of Epic Proportions.
Stock, R.　Rescuers, The.
Warren, R.　Fatal Interview: Penthesilea and
Achilles.
Acorns
Dickey, J.　Seeking the Chosen.
Hall, D.　Acorns.
Hughes, T.　I see the oak's bride in the oak's
grasp.
Acquiescence
Carruth, H.　Smallish Son, The.
Guyon.　Acquiescence of Pure Love, The.
Entire Surrender, The.
Figurative Description of the Procedure of
Divine Love, A.
Nativity, The.
see also Watching unto God in the Night-
Season.
Self-Diffidence.
Herrick.　Event of Things Not in Our Power.
No Luck in Love.

To Fortune.
Hughes, T.　Tree.
MacLeish.　What Any Lover Learns.
Stafford, W.　Parentage.
Acrobatics and Acrobats
Carver, R.　Poem for Karl Wallenda, Aerialist
Supreme.
Dugan, A.　What a Circus.
Graves, R.　Acrobats.
Gunn, T.　Before the Carnival.
Logan, J.　Thirty-Three Ring Circus, The.
Pagis.　Acrobatics.
Ramanujan.　Alien.
Rilke.　Saltimbanques.
Ritsos.　Acrobat, An.
Acrobatics.
Rukeyser, M.　Ringling.
Smith, S.　Look, Look.
Stock, R.　Inversion Factor.
Szymborska, W.　Acrobat, The.
See also **Circus; Tightropes and Tightrope
Walkers; Trapezes and Trapeze Artists**
Acrostic (form)
Stockton, A.　Acrostic for Abby Stockton.
Acrostic for Georgeana Cuthbert.
Actaeon
Laughlin, J.　Fate of Actaeon, The.
Acting and Actors
Ai.　James Dean.
Ashbery, J.　Popular Songs.
Berryman.　Meeting.
Borges.　Everything and Nothing.
Burns, R.　On Seeing Miss Fontenelle in a
Favourite Character.
Prologue: "When by a generous Public's kind
acclaim."
Campion, T.　In Ligonem.
Cavafy.　Young Men of Sidon (400 A.D.).
Ciardi, J.　Starlet.
Clampitt.　Godfather Returns to Color TV, The.
Dugan, A.　Homo Ludens: On an Argument
with an Actor.
Story for Actors.
Eberhart, R.　Man's Greed and Envy Are So
Great.
Ginsberg, A.　Blue Angel, The.
Gunn, T.　Looks.
Hardy, T.　Noble Lady's Tale, The.
To an Actress.
Tragedian to Tragedienne.
Herrick.　Upon Comely a Good Speaker but an
Ill Singer.
Jacobsen, J.　Variations on Variety.
Jonson, B.　To Edward Alleyn.
Kumin, M.　Casablanca.
Laughlin, J.　Goddess, The.
On learning that he was about.
Lindsay, N.　Epitaphs for Two Players.
Knight in Disguise, The.
Mae Marsh, Motion Picture Actress.
Tramp's Refusal, The.
Lux.　Man Inside the Chipmunk Suit, The.
Melville, H.　Coming Storm, The.
Merrill, J.　School Play, The.
Nash, O.　Boop-Boop-Adieup, Little Group!
Queen Is in the Parlor, The.
Self-Effacement of Electra Thorne, The.
O'Hara, F.　Mexican Guitar, A.
To the Film Industry in Crisis.
Parker, D.　Actors; A Hate Song.
Actresses; A Hate Song.
Certain Lady, A.
Lynn Fontanne.
Marilyn Marilyn.
Song of Social Life in Hollywood.
To Marjorie Rambeau; In "Daddy's Gone A-
Hunting."
Pinsky.　Picture.
Rexroth, K.　Christmas Note for Geraldine
Udell, A.
For the Chinese Actress, Gardenia Chang.
Riley, J.　Henry Irving.
Private Theatricals.
Sandburg, C.　They All Want to Play Hamlet.
Schuyler, J.　Two.

Sexton.　Play, The.
Sheridan, T.　Prologue Designed for the Play of
Oedipus, Written in Greek, and Performed by
Mr. Sheridan's Scholars, at the King's Inn Hall,
on Tuesday the 10th of December, 1723, A.
Prologue to Julius Caesar, as It Was Acted at
Madam Violante's Booth, Dec. the 15th,
1732, by Some of the Young Gentlemen in
Dr. Sheridan's School, A.
Prologue to the Farce of Punch Turned
Schoolmaster.
Smith, S.　Actress, The.
Wilbur, R.　Prisoner of Zenda, The.
Wilde, O.　Camma.
Fabien dei Franchi.
Phèdre.
Portia.
Queen Henrietta Maria.
Williams, M.　Aging Actress Sees Herself a
Starlet on the Late Show, The.
On Hearing About the Death of Mitzi Mayfair.
Williams, W.　15 Years Later.
Yeats.　Players Ask for a Blessing on the
Psalteries and on Themselves, The.
Adam and Eve
Amichai [or Amikhai].　I was weaned from the
curse of Adam.
I've Already Been Weaned.
Angelou.　Couple, The.
Bierce.　Infralapsarian.
Blake, W.　Ghost of Abel, The.
Borges.　Adam Cast Forth.
Adam Is Your Ashes.
Browning, E.　Drama of Exile, A.
Poet's Vow, The.
Byron, G.　Impromptu.
Carruth, H.　Museum Piece.
Chaucer.　Chaucer's Wordes unto Adam, his
Owne Scriveyn.
Ciardi, J.　From Adam's Diary.
Clifton, L.　Adam Thinking.
Birth of Language, The.
Grief.
Report from the angel of eden.
Story Thus Far, The.
Clough.　Adam and Eve.
Crane, H.　Garden Abstract.
Cullen, C.　One Day We Played a Game.
Cunningham, J.　Original Sin.
Davie, D.　Eden.
De la Mare.　Dream, A.
Exile, The.
Dickey, J.　Eagle's Mile, The.
Poisoned Man, The.
Dugan, A.　Letter to Eve.
Eberhart, R.　Ineffable, The.
Throwing the Apple.
Emerson, R.　But never yet the man was found.
Eve roved in Paradise, I've heard.
García Lorca.　Adam.
Graves, R.　Apple Island.
History of the Fall.
Quiet Glades of Eden, The.
Hill, G.　Assisi Fragments, The.
Hughes, T.　Apple Tragedy.
Childish Prank, A.
Theology.
Lawrence, D. H.　Birth Night.
Renascence.
Levertov.　Blake's Baptismal Font.
Lindsay, N.　Eden in Winter.
Genesis.
To Eve, Man's Dream of Wifehood as
Described by Milton.
Meredith, W.　Original Aversions.
Milosz, C.　Adam and Eve.
Gardener.
Happenings Elsewhere.
Into the Tree.
Olson, C.　Anubis will stare.
Orr, G.　Fall.
Patchen.　Man with the Golden Adam's Apple,
The.
Plath.　Dialogue En Route.
Roethke.　Follies of Adam, The.
Rossetti, C.　Bird or Beast?

That Eden of earth's sunrise cannot vie.
Rossetti, D.   Eden Bower.
Sexton.   Rats Live on No Evil Star.
Shapiro, K.   Adam and Eve.
Snyder, G.   Milton by Firelight.
Stock, R.   Adam in Extremis.
   Adam Lay Ibounden.
   Invisible Golden Sections.
   Metamorphosis.
Thomas, D.   Ceremony after a Fire Raid.
Thoreau.   In Adams fall.
Tomlinson, C.   Adam.
   Fountain.
   In Arden.
Very.   Serpent, The.
Walcott.   Adam's Song.
   New World.
Weiss, T.   Charm Against the Toothache, A.
Whitman, W.   As Adam Early in the Morning.
   To the Garden the World.
Williams, M.   Footnote on the Invention of
   Small Pleasures.
Williams, W.   Adam.
   Eve.
Wilner, E.   Candied.
   Continuous Is Broken, and Resumes, The.
Yeats.   Adam's Curse.
See also **Eve**

Adams, Abigail
Niedecker.   Three Americans.
   Wild and wavy event, The.

Adams, John
Niedecker.   Jefferson and Adams.
   Three Americans.

Admiration
Ammons.   Still.
Angelou.   Just for a Time.
Bishop, E.   To a Tree.
Bukowski.   Eulogy to a Hell of a Dame—.
   Mother and Son.
Burns, R.   Address, to the Shade of Thomson,
   on Crowning His Bust, at *Ednam, Roxburgh-
   shire*, with Bays.
   Answer, The [To the Guidwife of Wauchope-
   House].
   Epistle to Mr Tytler of Woodhouselee, Author
   of a Defence of Mary Queen of Scots.
   Extempore Epistle to Mr. McAdam of
   Craigengillian, (Wrote in Nanse Tinnock's,
   Mauchline) in Answer to an Obliging Letter
   He Sent in the Commencement of My Poetic
   Career.
   Extempore—on Some Commemorations of
   Thomson.
   Of A' the Airts [the Wind Can Blaw].
   Second Epistle to John Lapraik.
   To Renton of Lamerton.
   Verses Intended to Be Written below a Noble
   Earl's Picture.
Byron, G.   She Walks In Beauty.
Campion, T.   To the Worthy Author.
Carew, T.   Comparison, The.
   Complement, The.
   Divine Love, A.
   Good Counsel to a Young Maid.
   Lips and Eyes.
   Mistake, The.
   New Years Gift. To the Queen, A.
   On a Damask[e] Rose, Sticking upon a Lady's
   Breast.
   To A. L.; Persuasions [*or* Perswasions] to Love.
   To My Worthy Friend Master George Sands [*or*
   Sandys], on His Translation of the Psalms.
Cavalcanti.   Beautiful Lady where Love shows
   himself, The.
   Beauty of women and wise hearts.
   In you flowers and greenery.
   May I tell you the news of my eyes.
   My young blossom.
   Sonnet: A Rapture concerning his Lady.
   Sonnet: He compares all Things with his Lady,
   and finds them wanting.
   Sonnet: To his Lady Joan, of Florence.
   Who is this who came.
Char.   Allegiance.
Clare, J.   Love and Solitude.

Coleridge, S.   To Matilda Betham from a
   Stranger.
Cortes.   When You Point Your Finger.
Creeley.   Birds, The.
   Dear Dorothy.
   Flower, The.
   For a Friend.
   Wind, The.
Cuadra, P.   Nahoa Urn, for a Woman.
Cullen, C.   To John Keats, Poet, at Springtime.
Cummings, E. E.   Because you take life in your
   stride(instead.
   Spirit colossal / (& daunted by always).
Dante Alighieri.   Sestina: "I have reached, alas,
   the long shadow."
Davie, D.   Glaphira 3.
Dickey, W.   Narcissus Unbound.
Dickinson, E.   Adulation is inexpensive.
   I always ran Home to Awe when a child.
Enzensberger, H.   Comb, The.
Fergusson, E.   Poem on the Death of Richard
   Stockton, A.
Ferlinghetti, L.   Pound at Spoleto.
Gallagher, T.   Horse in the Drugstore, The.
Graves, R.   Your Private Way.
Gunn, T.   Bone.
   Selves.
   Thomas Bewick.
Gurney, I.   Lock Keeper, The.
Hacker, M.   Elektra on Third Avenue.
Herrick.   On Tomasin Parsons.
   School or Perl of Putney, the Mistress of All
   Singular Manners, Mistresse Portman, The.
   To the Most Accomplist Gentleman, Master
   Edward Norgate, Clark of the Signet to His
   Majesty.
   Upon the Nipples of Julia's Breast.
   Weeping Cherry, The.
Hughes, T.   Fallgrief's Girlfriends.
   Song: "O lady, when the tipped cup of the moon
   blessed you."
Keats.   Addressed to Haydon.
   Extracts from an Opera.
   Great Spirits Now on Earth.
   To Charles Cowden Clarke.
Koch, K.   Burning Mystery of Anna in 1951,
   The.
   In Love with You.
   On Beauty.
   Summery Weather.
   To Marina.
Lindsay, N.   Being the Dedication of a Morning.
   Life Transcendent.
   My Lady in Her White Silk Shawl.
   My Lady Is Compared to a Young Tree.
   Roosevelt.
   To a Golden-Haired Girl in a Louisiana Town.
   To Gloriana.
   To Lady Jane.
   Town of American Visions, The.
Lorde.   Dear Toni Instead of a Letter of
   Congratulation.
   Hard Love Rock.
   Mentor.
   Poem for a Poet, A.
   To a Girl Who Knew What Side Her Bread Was
   Buttered On.
Lowell, R.   Alfred Corning Clark.
MacNeice.   Solstice.
   Under the Mountain.
Mahon.   Aran.
Melville, H.   College Colonel, The.
   Jack Roy.
   Marchioness of Brinvilliers, The.
   On the Photograph of Corps Commander.
   Sheridan at Cedar Creek.
Meredith, G.   To a Friend Lost.
   When I Would Image.
Michelangelo Buonarroti.   How joyfully it
   shows, the garland there.
   Just as you cannot not be lovely here.
   My lady, if it's true.
   To be less unworthy, my exalted lady.
Olson, C.   For Sappho, Back.
Orlandi, G.   To the sound of trumpets rather
   than horns.

Orléans, C.   Dieu Qu'il la Fait.
Owen, W.   Long Ages Past.
Parker, D.   Interview.
Petrarch.   Alas her sweet expression, pleasure-
   filled.
   Alexander, before the sepulchre.
   Any lady desiring fame and honour.
   Graces denied to almost everyone.
   Her golden hair was blowing in the breeze.
   I cannot keep silent, and I fear my tongue.
   I feed my mind on such a noble food.
   I saw twelve ladies sailing at their ease.
   If Virgil and Homer had but seen that sun.
   In sheer amazement, Love and I together.
   Love, lend a hand to my afflicted mind.
   Noble lineage with calm humility.
   O noble soul, glowing with worthiness.
   Pleasant obduracy, and calm rejection.
   Royal nature, and a most refined, A.
   This short-lived and this fragile happiness.
   Through her I swapped the Arno for the Sorgue.
   Victorious and triumphal laurel-tree.
   When I begin to send out sighs and call.
   When out of all the ladies in her sphere.
Pound, E.   Na Audiart.
Prunty.   Letter for the End.
Raine, K.   Old Paintings on Italian Walls.
Ralegh, S.   If Cynthia Be a Queen.
Rexroth, K.   Dialogue of Watching, A.
   Education.
Rolfe, E.   Eyes of a Blind Man.
Rossetti, C.   My old admiration before I was
   twenty.
   Roundel seems to fit a round of days, A.
   Two Rossettis (Brothers They), The.
Sarton, M.   Recognition, A.
Schuyler, J.   Belated Birthday Poem, A.
Shirley, J.   Would you know what's soft? I dare.
Smart, C.   Ode to Lady Harriot.
   To Miss H—— with Some Music.
Stafford, W.   Passing Remark.
Stockton, A.   Acrostic for Georgeana Cuthbert.
   Fragment on the Death of a Minester.
   Impromptu on Seeing a Very Agreeable
   Gentleman and Lady, Particular Friends
   Conversing Together.
   Ode to Constantius.
   Ode to Doctor Smith on His Birth Day March
   the 16th, 1791, An.
   On Seeing Mrs Macauly Graham.
   Some Traits of the Character of Mrs. Powel as a
   Model for a Young Lady Who Said She
   Admired Her More than Any Other Woman.
   To Doctor Smith on His Birth Day March the
   16th, 1790.
   To Mrs Powel, an Ode.
   To My Burrissa.
Swift, J.   Ode to Dr. William Sancroft.
   Ode to the Athenian Society.
   Ode to the Honourable Sir William Temple.
Warren, R.   Birth of Love.
   For a Self-Possessed Friend.
   Praise.
Wilbur, R.   Piazza di Spagna, Early Morning.
   Praise in Summer.
Wilde, O.   La Bella Donna della Mia Mente.
   Madonna Mia.
   Portia.
Williams, C. K.   Just Right.
   New Car.
   Silence, The.
Williams, M.   And Then I Headed on Back
   Home.
Zukofsky, L.   Celia's Birthday Poem.
   Chloride of Lime and Charcoal.
   Her face the Book of—Love Delights in—
   Praises.

Adolescence
Ai.   Journalist, The.
Auden.   Adolescence.
Berryman.   Freshman Blues.
Carver, R.   Luck.
   Woolworth's, 1954.
Ciardi, J.   Encounter.
Cooper, J.   Pencil Sketch of Self & Other.
Davie, D.   Grazia Deledda, Young.

Nosegay, The.
Dickey, J. Sheep Child, The.
Dove, R. Adolescence—I.
  Adolescence—II.
Dubie. Monologue of Two Moons, Nudes with
  Crests. 1938.
Dugan, A. Scene (1946–7).
  Teacher's Lament.
Graves, R. Dream of Frances Speedwell, A.
  Growing Pains.
Gunn, T. Adolescence.
  Slow Waker.
Ignatow, D. Adolescence.
Jeffers, R. October Week-End.
Komunyakaa. Sex, Magnolias, & Speed.
Kunitz, S. Game, The.
Logan, J. Lines to His Son on Reaching
  Adolescence.
Lowell, R. Ivana.
Lux. Little Tooth, A.
McHugh, H. Meantime.
Merrill, J. Matinees.
Muldoon, P. Boon.
  Geography Lesson, The.
  Profumo.
Nash, O. Tarkington, Thou Should'st Be Living
  in This Hour.
Olson, C. Gloss, A.
Oppen. Speech at Soli, The.
Orr, G. Adolescence.
  Walking Home after the First Encounter.
Riley, J. Thoughts of Youth, The.
Rilke. Breasts.
Roethke. Pickle Belt.
Rukeyser, M. Question, The.
Sexton. Little Girl, My String Bean, My Lovely
  Woman.
  Love Song: "I was / the girl of the chain letter."
  Young.
Shapiro, K. Drug Store.
Smith, S. Conventionalist, The.
  What Is She Writing? Perhaps It Will Be Good.
Stafford, W. Adults Only.
  Fifteen.
Updike. Orthodontia.
Williams, C. K. Child Psychology.
  Fifteen.
  Hood.
Williams, M. For a Girl I Know about to Be a
  Woman.
  In Your Own Words Without Lying Tell
  Something of Your Background With
  Particular Attention to Anything Relating to
  the Position For Which You Are Applying.
  Press Down.
  Original Sin.
Williams, W. Horned Purple.
  Suzy.

Adonis
Bion. Fragment of the Elegy on the Death of
  Adonis.
  Lament for Adonis.
"H. D." Adonis.
Pessoa. I the roses love in the gardens of
  Adonis.
Rexroth, K. Adonis in Winter.

Adoption and the Adopted
Brontë, E. Two Children, The.
Gunn, T. Blank, A.
Hughes, L. Madam and the Charity Child.
Laughlin, J. Kind-, The.
Rossetti, C. Motherless baby and babyless
  mother.

Adultery and Adulterers
Angelou. They Went Home.
Berry, W. Marriage.
Bierce. Oneiromancy.
Burns, R. Epitaph on a Wag in Mauchline.
Byron, G. Parisina.
Campion, T. In Crispinum.
Carew, T. Secrecy [or Secresie] Protested.
  To His Mistress Retiring in Affection.
Carver, R. Kitchen, The.
Creeley. Anger.
Cunningham, J. Faint smile of distraction, moist
  response, A.

Modern Love.
  Portrait.
  Your affair, my dear, need not be a mess.
"Dario." First, a look.
Dickey, J. Adultery.
Dugan, A. Adultery.
García Lorca. Unfaithful Wife, The.
Gunn, T. Adultery.
Hall, D. Adultery At Forty.
  Edward's Anecdote.
Hardy, T. On Martock Moor.
  War-Wife of Catknoll, The.
Heaney, S. Punishment.
Herrick. Upon Letcher: Epigram.
  Upon Scobble [Epigram].
Hughes, L. Sister.
Jonson, B. On Old Colt.
  On Sir Voluptuous Beast.
  On the Same Beast.
Laughlin, J. Fisherwoman, The.
  French, The.
  Parable, A.
Lawrence, D. H. Two Wives.
Logan, J. Homage to Herman Melville.
Lowell, R. Death of Anne Boleyn.
Meredith, G. Preaching from a Spanish Ballad,
  A.
Mistral, G. Sonnets of Death 5.
More, S. Astrologer, The.
Muldoon, P. Country Club, The.
Parker, D. Guinevere at Her Fireside.
Pinsky. Discretions of Alcibiades.
  Street, The.
Plath. Other, The.
Poe. Scenes from Politian.
Prunty. Sorrows of Lester Buster, The.
Rexroth, K. Adonis in Winter.
Sandburg, C. Couples.
Sexton. For My Lover, Returning to His Wife.
  Little Peasant, The.
Stock, R. Millais Loquacious.
Walcott. Adam's Song.
Williams, M. Ballad of a Little Delta Town.
  Question of Time, A.
Williams, W. Great Mullen.
Zaturenska. Lament of Catherine Howard, Fifth
  Queen of Henry VIII.

Advent
Auden. Flight into Egypt, The.
  For the Time Being; a Christmas Oratorio.
Herrick. Christs Twofold Coming.
Merton. Advent.
Rossetti, C. Advent.
  Advent Sunday.
  Sooner or later: yet at last / The Jordan must be
  past.
  Sunday Before Advent.
Schuyler, J. Advent.

Adventure and Adventurers
Apollinaire. Pretty Redhead, The.
Auden. History of Science, The.
Berryman. Captain's Song, The.
Brooks, G. Old Mary.
Bukowski. On Being 20.
Cavafy. Ithaca.
Eberhart, R. American Hakluyt.
  Height of Man, The.
  Sea Storm.
  Stealth and Subtleties of Growth.
Merrill, J. Narrow Escape, A.
  Thousand and Second Night, The.
Merton. Ben's Last Fight.
  Crusoe.
Parker, D. Song of Perfect Propriety.
Rossetti, C. Lotus-Eaters: Ulysses to Penelope,
  The.
Sandburg, C. Moments of Dawn Riders.
  Red Son, The.
Thoreau. In days of yore, tis said, the
  swimming alder.

Advertising
Burns, R. Versicles on Sign-Posts.
Codrescu. Junk Mail.
Collins, B. Victoria's.
Cummings, E. E. Poem, or Beauty Hurts Mr.
  Vinal.

Dickinson, E. I'm Nobody! Who are you?
Dugan, A. Advertising in Paris.
  Monologue for a Sixth Avenue Screamer.
  Poem: "Man applying gold leaf, A."
  Remembering an Account Executive.
Ginsberg, A. Junk Mail.
Hardy, T. Circular, A.
Laughlin, J. Cardiac Autoscope, The.
Lux. This Space Available.
Merton. Proverbs.
Nash, O. Roll On, Thou Deep and Dark Blue
  Copy Writer—Roll!
  Song of the Open Road.
  Strange Case of the Lucrative Compromise,
  The.
  What, No Sheep?
Schuyler, J. Adverts.
Szymborska, W. Advertisement.
Tate, J. Same Tits.
Updike. Publius Vergilius Maro, the Madison
  Avenue Hick.
Williams, M. How Did You Ever Live Without
  It? A Peppermill with a Light.
  Personals.
Williams, W. Lovely Ad.
Zagajewski. Van Gogh's Face.
See also Billboards

Advice
Amichai [or Amikhai]. Advice for Good Love.
  Advice of good love: do not love.
  My friend, what you're doing now.
Atwood. After all you are quite.
Berry, W. Manifesto: the Mad Farmer
  Liberation Front.
Blake, W. Song 3rd By an Old Shepherd.
Bogan, L. Young Mage, The.
Browning, E. Wisdom Unapplied.
Bukowski. Counsel.
  Friendly Advice to a Lot of Young Men.
  How to Be a Great Writer.
  Now, If You Were Teaching Creative Writing,
  He Asked, What Would You Tell Them?
Burns, R. Country Lassie.
  Epistle to a Young Friend.
  Prologue: "No song nor dance I bring from yon
  great city."
  Written in Friar's Carse Hermitage on the Banks
  of Nith—June—1788.
Campion, T. Advice to a Girl.
Carew, T. Conquest by Flight.
Chaucer. Balade of Bon Conseill.
  Proverbs: "What shul these clothes thus
  manyfold."
Ciardi, J. To My Students.
Coleridge, S. On Revisiting the Sea-Shore, after
  Long Absence.
Collins, B. Advice to Writers.
Creeley. Sad Advice.
  Way, The.
Cunningham, J. Who lives by wisdom and to
  others gives.
Delany, P. To Thomas Sheridan.
Dickey, W. Being Asked To Define Bourgeois
  Individuality.
  Life Moving More Rapidly Than Hands Can
  Manage.
Donne. To E. of D. with Six Holy Sonnets.
Emerson, R. Discontented Poet: A Masque,
  The.
  Do that which you can do.
  Kind & holy were the words.
  To Rhea.
Graves, R. Advice from a Mother.
Gurney, I. Advice.
Han-shan. Whoever has Cold Mountain's
  poems.
Hardy, T. Young Man's Exhortation, A.
Herbert, G. Perirrhanterium.
Herrick. Advice the Best Actor.
  Caution in Councell.
  Consultation.
  Counsell.
  Good Precepts, or Counsell.
  Paranæticall, or Advisive Verse, to His Friend,
  M. John Wicks.
  To his Booke.

Housman. Carpenter's Son, The.
Sage to the Young Man, The.
When I Was One-and-Twenty.
Jarrell, R. Hanged man on the gallows, The.
Jonson, B. Martial. Epigram XLVII, Book X.
Kipling, R. If—.
One Viceroy Resigns.
Koch, K. Art of Love, The.
Art of Poetry, The.
On Beauty.
Some General Instructions.
Korn. Generations.
Kumin, M. Henry Manley Looks Back.
Laughlin, J. Advice to Aurelius.
Cultural Note.
Logan, J. Lines to His Son on Reaching
Adolescence.
Lorde. For Each of You.
For My Singing Sister.
MacLeish. Seafarer.
Millay, E. If in the years to come you should
recall.
Niedecker. Poet's Work.
Olson, C. Rufus Woodpecker visited the
President.
Parker, D. Counselor, The.
For a Favorite Grand-Daughter.
For an Unknown Lady.
Grandfather Said It.
Ralegh, S. Sir Walter Ra[u]le[i]gh to His
Son[ne].
Ramanujan. Excerpts from a Father's Wisdom.
Rexroth, K. Letter to Wystan Hugh Auden, A.
Rich, A. I Heard a Hermit Speak.
Riley, J. As My Uncle Ust to Say.
Uncle Sidney's Logic.
Robinson, E. Old King's New Jester, The.
Voice of Age, The.
Rossetti, C. Versi.
Rumi. Empty Garlic, An.
Sandburg, C. Snatch of Sliphorn Jazz.
Three Fragments for Fishers of Destiny.
Sexton. Sermon of the Twelve
Acknowledgements, The.
Sheridan, T. Letter of Advice to the Right Hon.
John Earl of Orrery, A.
Stock, R. For Sharon, As Soon As She Wants
It.
Millais Loquacious.
Stockton, A. Poetical Epistle, Addressed by a
Lady of New-Jersey, to Her Niece, upon Her
Marriage, in This City, A.
Tate, J. Recipe for Sleep.
Warren, R. Few Axioms for a Young Man, A.
Williams, M. For a Girl I Know about to Be a
Woman.
For All Our Great-Grandchildren.
For Reuben, at Twelve Months.
Six Moral Virtues, The: Grace, Style, Class,
Kindness, and Wisdom.
Story, A.
Stripper, The.
Williams, T. Counsel.
Look Both Ways Crossing Streets.
Zagajewski. Letter from a Reader.

Aegean Sea
Clampitt. Remembering Greece.

Aeneas
Dugan, A. Speech for Aeneas.
Merton. Like Ilium.
Niedecker. As I shook the dust.
To Aeneas who closed his piano.
Stock, R. Aeneas Underground.
Beacon, The.
Tate, A. Aeneas at New York.
Aeneas at Washington.
Virgil [or Vergil]. All breathed in silence, and
intensely gazed.
Amazons with Crescent-formed shield, The.
Anchises to Aeneas.
Arms, and the Man I sing, the first who bore.
Ev'n yet his voice from Hell's dread shades we
hear.
For healthful indigence in vain they pray.
Golden Bough, The.
Hesperia the Gr[a]ecians call the place.

In the main[e] sea the i[s]le of Cre[e]te doth lie.
Now when the Gods had crushed the Asian
State.
Of mortal Justice if thou scorn the rod.
Queene anone commands the waightie bowle,
The.
Saturne descending from the heavens high.
She who to lift her heavy eyes had tried.
Some old Auruncans, I remember well.
There is a Land which Greekes Hesperia name.
This scarcely uttered they advance, and straight.
Thus was Italy mov'd—nor did the chief.

Aeneid, The (Virgil)
Dugan, A. On Lines 69–70, Book 4, of Virgil's
Aeneid.
Logan, J. Lament for Misenus.

Aengus
Yeats. Harp of Aengus, The.
Song Of Wandering Aengus, The.

Aeschylus
Wilde, O. Vision, A.

Aesop
Crane, H. Black Tambourine.

Affection
Amichai [or Amikhai]. Gifts of Love.
I Sat in the Happiness.
In the Middle of This Century.
Letter, A.
Mutual Lullaby, A.
My Mother Baked the Whole World for Me.
Placenta of Love, A.
Poems for a Woman.
Six Poems for Tamar.
What a man on a bald mountain in Jerusalem!
Begley, T. Your Sacred Idiot with Me.
Berryman. He Resigns.
Bierce. Rosalie.
To Maude.
To Thee, My Darling.
Bishop, E. Casabianca.
One Art.
Blake, W. How Sweet I Roamed [or Roam'd]
from Field to Field.
Bly, R. Good Silence, The.
In the Month of May.
Indigo Bunting, The.
Borges. Anticipation of Love.
Causes, The.
My Last Tiger.
Unending Rose, The.
Bradstreet, A. Another.
Before the Birth of One of Her Children.
Letter to Her Husband, Absent upon Public[k]
Employment, A.
To Her Father, with Some Verses.
Broumas, O. Contemplation, The.
Your Sacred Idiot with Me.
Browning, E. L.E.L.'s Last Question.
My Kate.
Parting Lovers.
Proof and Disproof.
Question and Answer.
Void in Law.
Browning, R. Lost Mistress, The.
Meeting at Night.
Porphyria's Lover.
Two in the Campagna.
Burns, R. Extempore Epistle to Mr. McAdam of
Craigengillian, (Wrote in Nanse Tinnock's,
Mauchline) in Answer to an Obliging Letter
He Sent in the Commencement of My Poetic
Career.
Highland Mary.
It is na, Jean, thy bonie face.
My Eppie.
My Wife's a Winsome Wee Thing.
O May Thy Morn.
O [or Oh] Wert Thou in the Cauld Blast.
Red, Red Rose, A.
Reply to Robert Riddell.
Scotish Song.
She Says She Lo'es Me Best of A'.
Song: "'Twas na her bonie blue e'e was my
ruin."
To Chloris.

To Mr. McMurdo, with a Pound of Lundiefoot
Snuff.
Young Jockey was the blythest lad.
Byron, G. She Walks In Beauty.
Stanzas: "Could Love for ever."
Stanzas to Jessy.
To Thyrza.
Campion, T. Follow Thy Fair Sun[ne]
[Unhappy Shadow].
Carew, T. Fly That Flew into My Mistress'[s]
Eye, A.
In Praise of His Mistress.
Song[, A]: "Ask[e] me no more where Jove
bestow[e]s."
To my Friend G.N. from Wrest.
To My Rival.
Tooth-Ache Cured by a Kiss, The.
Carver, R. All Her Life.
Hummingbird.
In a Marine Light near Sequim, Washington.
No Need.
Cavafy. Craftsman of Winebowls.
Epic in the Heart.
On Hearing of Love.
Temethos, Antiochian; 400 A.D.
When, My Friends, I Was in Love.
Chuang Tzu. Flight of Lin Hui, The.
Ciardi, J. Returning Home.
Clampitt. Hermit Thrush, A.
London Inside and Outside.
Coleridge, S. Her Thoughts.
Lines on a Portrait of a Lady.
To the Rev. George Coleridge.
Crabbe, G. On Receiving from a Lady a Present
of a Ring.
Creeley. Act of Love, The.
Air: "Cat Bird Singing."
Boy, the.
Fall.
For Walter Chappell.
Greeting Card.
I Love You.
If I Had My Way.
Love Comes Quietly.
Night ("Needs most / happily mutual").
Oh Mabel.
Song, A: "I had wanted a quiet testament."
To Bobbie.
Cullen, C. To One Not There.
Cummings, E. E. But if a living dance upon
dead minds.
Clown's smirk in the skull of a baboon, A.
Great advantage of being alive, The.
Hate blows a bubble of despair into.
If everything happens that can't be done.
If i love You.
If(touched by love's own secret)we,like homing.
In spite of everything.
Love is more thicker than forget.
Love is the every only god.
Love's function is to fabricate unknownness.
Now all the fingers of this tree(darling)have.
O by the by / has anybody seen.
Somewhere i have never travelled, gladly
beyond.
Yes is a pleasant country.
Cunningham, J. In Innocence.
Letter, A.
Davie, D. Bits and Pieces.
Love-Poems: for Mairi MacInnes.
Time Passing, Beloved.
De la Mare. Ghost, The.
Dickinson, E. Affection is like bread.
Affection wants you to know it is here.
Genius is the ignition of affection.
If I may have it, when it's dead.
Is not the distinction of Affection.
It stills, incites, infatuates.
Love A Life Can Show, The.
Love Is That Later Thing.
Love Thou Art High.
Ravenousness of fondness, The.
Soul selects her own Society, The.
Were the Velocity of Affection.
Donne. Canonization, The.
Ecstasy, The.

Funeral[l], The.
Good-Morrow, The.
Nocturnal[l] upon Saint Lucy's [or S. Lucy's or S. Lucies] Day, Being the Shortest Day, A.
Relic, The.
Song: "Sweetest love, I do not go[e]."
Valediction, A: of the Book.
Valediction, A: of Weeping.
Valediction: Forbidding Mourning, A.
Dunbar, P.   Negro Love Song, A.
Emerson, R.   Kind & holy were the words.
Fenton, J.   Nothing.
Gallagher, T.   Hug, The.
Ginsberg, A.   To Aunt Rose.
Glück, L.   Hawk's Shadow.
Graves, R.   Circus Ring.
   Colophon.
   Compact.
   Depth of Love.
   Five.
   Friday Night.
   Gorge, The.
   Her Brief Withdrawal.
   Iago.
   In Perspective.
   Lost Love.
   Love Charms.
   Necklace, The.
   None the Wiser.
   On Giving.
   Pity.
   Poet's Curse, The.
   Pride of Progeny.
   Pure Death.
   Quinque.
   Records.
   Reiteration, The.
   Risk, The.
   Seven Years.
   She Tells Her Love While Half Asleep.
   Sincèrement.
   Song: Cherries or Lilies.
   Song: Dew-Drop and Diamond.
   Song: Victims of Calumny.
   Strangeness.
   Strangling in Merrion Square, The.
   Three Locked Hoops.
   Three Words Only.
   Timeless Meeting.
   To Be in Love.
   Touch My Shut Lips.
   When Love Is Not.
Guillaume de Lorris et al.   Romance [or Romaunt] of the Rose, The.
Gunn, T.   High Fidelity.
   Tamer and Hawk.
Hall, D.   Gold.
Hamill, S.   Cooking.
   True Illumination Is Habitude.
Hardy, T.   After a Journey.
   Church Romance, A.
   Going, The.
   She Hears The Storm.
Heaney, S.   Call, A.
   Grotus and Coventina.
   Royal Prospect, A.
Herbert, G.   Affliction (1).
   Bitter-Sweet.
Herrick.   Another.
   Eclipse, The.
   His Mistris to Him at His Farwell.
   How His Soule Came Ensnared.
   Martha, Martha.
   No Action Hard to Affection.
   On Julias Lips.
   On Love.
   Parliament of Roses to Julia, The.
   To Anthea.
   To Electra.
   To Julia.
   To Mistresse Dorothy Parsons.
   To My Dearest Sister M. Mercie Herrick.
   To Sapho.
   Upon Love.
   Upon Lucia Dabled in the Deaw.
Hopkins, G.   Love me as I love thee. O double

sweet!
Housman.   Because I liked you better.
   So Sound You Sleep.
Hughes, L.   Gal's Cry for a Dying Lover.
   My Loves.
Hughes, T.   Fragment of an Ancient Tablet.
   Leaf Mould.
   Memory, A.
Jacobsen, J.   Brother Peter Considers Mulroy Drunk under the Rosebush.
Jonson, B.   Elegy, An: "Though beauty be the mark of praise."
   My Picture Left in Scotland.
   Song. To Celia ("Drink to me only with thine eyes").
   Sonnet to the Noble Lady, the Lady Mary Wroth, A.
Keats.   La Belle Dame sans Merci [A Ballad].
   To Emma.
   To Georgiana Augusta Wylie.
   To ———: "Had I a man's fair form, then might my sighs."
   To Some Ladies.
   Upon My Life, Sir Nevis, I Am Piqued.
Kinnell.   Parkinson's Disease.
Kinsella, T.   Girl on a Swing.
Koch, K.   Permanently.
Kumin, M.   Continuum: a Love Poem.
Larkin, P.   Why Did I Dream of You Last Night?
Laughlin, J.   Graceful Exit, A.
   I Like You.
   Last Poem to Be Written, The.
   Lines to Be Put into Latin.
   Vagrant, The.
   When you are far away.
   Who Is the Child.
   You Were Asleep.
Levertov.   Love Poem: "What you give me is."
   Time Past, A.
   Woman Meets an Old Lover, A.
Logan, J.   Gift, The.
Longfellow, H.   Children's Hour, The.
Lorde.   Dozens, The.
   Poem for a Poet, A.
   Progress Report.
Lowell, R.   Dunbarton.
   Grandparents.
Lux.   Amiel's Leg.
   I Love You Sweatheart.
   Towards.
MacLeish.   Old Gray Couple (2), The.
   Poem in Prose.
Mahon.   Noon at St. Michael's.
Mallarmé.   Another Fan; of Mademoiselle Mallarmé.
   Fan, A; of Madame Mallarmé.
Marvell.   Definition of Love, The.
   Fair Singer, The.
   Gallery, The.
   Mower to the Glowworms [or Glow-Worms or Glo-Worms], The.
Meredith, W.   Assent to Wildflowers, An.
   Pastoral: "Girl lies down on the hill, The."
   Perhaps the Best Time.
Millay, E.   At least, my dear.
   I shall go back.
   Modern Declaration.
Mistral, G.   You Had Me.
Montale.   Anniversary.
Nash, O.   Love Me but Leave My Dog Alone.
   Reflection on Caution.
Nemerov.   New Weapons in the Old War.
Neruda.   Dead Dog.
Niedecker.   Can knowledge be conveyed that isn't felt?
O'Hara, F.   Kitville.
   Poem: "So many echoes in my head."
   To Jane; and in Imitation of Coleridge.
Olson, C.   À Constance, This Day.
   Heart is a clock, The.
   She.
Orléans, C.   Dieu Qu'il la Fait.
Owen, W.   Song of Songs.
Pagis.   Real-Life Story.
Parker, D.   One Perfect Rose.

Pasolini.   Appendix to the "Religion": A Light. Prayer to My Mother.
Pessoa.   Now ashen gray tinges the balding brow.
Petrarch.   Because she bore upon her face Love's banner.
   Graces denied to almost everyone.
   If Virgil and Homer had but seen that sun.
   If you, by showing signs of your unease.
   Love used to weep, and sometimes I did too.
   Love with his right hand opened my left side.
   Noble tree, which I loved well and long, The.
   Now could I but describe with what sweet breath.
   Quickening Sun, that bough I love alone.
   Since Love was driving me to my old haunts.
   Thought is rapid, and so short the time, The.
   When I hear you attractively speak out.
   When little birds complaining, or green leaves.
   Where is the forehead that with one slight shake.
   You've made the loveliest face, O Death, turn pale.
Poe.   To One in Paradise.
   Valentine, A.
Pope, A.   Rape of the Lock, The; an Heroi-Comical Poem.
Prime, B.   Poetical Correspondence between Palemon and Æmilia, A.
Prunty.   Our Tree of Opposites.
Raine, K.   Hieros Gamos.
   Soliloquy Upon Love.
Ralegh, S.   Arte of English Poesie, The.
   Excuse, The.
   Poesie to Prove Affection is Not Love, A.
Ramanujan.   LOVE 4: What He Said, to His Daughter.
Riley, J.   Judith.
   Little Woman, The.
   One Afternoon.
   One Angel.
   Quest, The.
   Scrawl, A.
   Test of Love, A.
   Touch of Loving Hands, The.
   Tress of Hair, A.
   Twintorette, A.
   Where Shall We Land?
   With Her Face.
Rilke.   Lesson, The.
   Night Has Come.
   To Isabelle Trumpy.
   To Pia Di Valmarana.
Roethke.   For An Amorous Lady.
   I Knew A Woman.
Rossetti, C.   Death's Chill Between.
   Dog lies in his kennel, The.
   Heart's Chill Between.
L. E. L.
   My Mouse.
   Piteous my rhyme is / What while I muse of love and pain.
   So I grew half delirious and quite sick.
   Somewhere Or Other.
   To My First Love, My Mother.
   To My Friend Elizabeth.
Rukeyser, M.   Among Grass.
   Orpheus.
   Song, the Brain-Coral.
Rumi.   All our lives we've looked.
   I have phrases and whole pages memorized.
Sarton, M.   Letter to James Stephens, A.
Schuyler, J.   Letter Poem #2.
   Letter Poem #3.
   Oriane.
   Watching You.
   You're.
Seifert.   Birds' Voices in the Tree Tops.
Shapiro, K.   Twins, The.
Shelley, P.   To Jane: The keen stars were twinkling.
   To ———: "Music, when soft voices die."
Sheridan, T.   I Ritu a Verse o Na Molli o Mi Ne.
Simic.   My Beloved.
   Old Couple.
Smith, S.   Freddy.

Human Affection.
Spender, S. One.
Spenser, E. Epithalamion: "Ye learned sisters which have oftentimes."
Stein, G. Sonatina Followed by Another, A.
Stock, R. Lines Upon Delia And to the Chevaliers of the Cordon Bleu.
Seasons in a Landscape of Woman, The.
Stockton, A. Acrostic for Georgeana Cuthbert.
Almira to Celadon, Founded on a Story in a Magazine.
Caprice, a Fragment.
Disappointment, an Ode 1756 to Mr Stockton, The.
Doubt, a Pastoral Ballad—1762.
Dream, an Ode, 1756, The.
Epistle—To Lucius.
Fragment on Hearing the Account of Mrs Ramseys Death.
Lavinia and Amanda, a Pastoral.
Ode, An: "Yes tis an easy thing to view."
Ode to Constantius.
Poetical Correspondence between Palemon and Æmilia, A.
Question, upon Being Told in Jest by Mr Stockton that He Was Not Loved Much, The.
To Mrs Powel, an Ode.
Wise nature here has done her kindest part.
Suckling, S. Desdain.
Swift, J. Stella's Birthday ([March 13,] 1727).
Szymborska, W. Love at First Sight.
Openness.
Tate, J. If You Would Disappear at Sea.
Marfa.
Tomlinson, C. Backward Glance, A.
Letter to Uehata.
Unknown, sometimes at. to Sir Walter Ralegh. As You Came from the Holy Land [of Walsingham].
Van Duyn. Garland for Christopher Smart, A.
Notes from a Suburban Heart.
Walker, A. Love Is Not Concerned.
Warren, R. Answer to Prayer.
Mountain Mystery.
Paradox.
So Frost Astounds.
Whalen, P. Distraction Fit, A.
Something Nice About Myself.
Whitman, W. Base of All Metaphysics, The.
Sometimes with One I Love.
When I Heard At The Close Of The Day.
Woman Waits for Me, A.
Wilbur, R. June Light.
Williams, C. K. Being Alone.
Dog, The.
Snow: II.
Williams, M. Despairing of Understanding We Fall Into Decadence.
Poem for Emily, A.
Sir.
Williams, T. Shadow Wood.
Williams, W. Love Song: "Sweep the house clean."
Wordsworth, W. Louisa [After Accompanying Her on a Mountain Excursion].
Wright, C. Still Life with Spring and Time to Burn.
Wyatt, S. Long love that in my thought doth harbo[u]r, The.
Lover Showeth How He Is Forsaken of Such as He Sometime Enjoyed, The.
My Lute, Awake!
Yeats. Down by the Salley Gardens.
Drinking Song, A.
Folly of Being Comforted, The.
Lullaby: "Beloved, may your sleep be sound."
Solomon to Sheba.
When You Are Old.
Zagajewski. At Midnight.
For M.
For You.
Wind at Night.
Zaturenska. For a Child.
Spellbound.
Zukofsky, L. *Barely* and *widely.*
Celia's Birthday Poem.

Finally a Valentine.
On Valentine's Day to Friends.
Record, The.

Affliction
Amichai [*or* Amikhai]. Ibn Gabirol.
Cooper, J. Dispossessions.
Cowper, W. To a Friend in Distress.
Dugan, A. Night Song for a Boy.
Guyon. Vicissitudes Experienced in the Christian Life, The.
Herbert, G. Affliction (1).
Herrick. Affliction.
Comforts in Crosses.
Good Men Afflicted Most.
Pain[e] Ends in Pleasure.
Persecutions Profitable.
Kipling, R. Natural Theology.
Komunyakaa. Floor Plans.
Kunitz, S. Harsh Judgment, The.
Scourge, The.
Orr, G. Investigation.
Self-Portrait at Twenty.
Who'd Want to Be a Man?
Riley, J. Chant of the Cross-bearing Child, The.
Luther Benson.
Someday.
Wait for the Morning.

Afghanistan
Carver, R. Afghanistan.
Kipling, R. Ballad of the King's Jest, The.
Ballad of the King's Mercy, The.

Afghanistan War (1979–1989)
Brodsky, J. Lines on the Winter Campaign, 1980.

Africa and Africans
Angelou. Africa.
For Us, Who Dare Not Dare.
Berrigan, T. Certain Slant of Sunlight, A.
Bierce. Strained Relations.
Browning, R. Home-Thoughts, from the Sea.
Through the Metidja to Abd-el-Kadr.
Carruth, H. Algeria.
Cooper, J. Seventeen Questions about KING KONG.
Cullen, C. Brown Boy to Brown Girl.
Heritage.
Dunbar, P. Ode to Ethiopia.
Eberhart, R. Lions Copulating.
Eliot, T. S. To the Indians Who Died in Africa.
Hardy, T. Drummer Hodge.
Hughes, L. Africa.
Afro-American Fragment.
Angola Question Mark.
Ballad of Negro History, A.
Call of Ethiopia.
Cubes.
Danse Africaine.
Death in Africa.
Drums.
Emperor Haile Selassie.
Envoy to Africa.
Fog.
Johannesburg Mines.
Me and My Song.
Motherland.
Negro.
Poem: "All the tom-toms of the jungles beat in my blood."
We, Too.
Jacobsen, J. My Small Aunt.
Short Views in Africa.
Kizer, C. Race Relations.
Koch, K. Geography.
Komunyakaa. Exchange Student Awaits the Arrival of an African Princess, An.
Keeper of the Vigil.
Lost Wax.
Lawrence, D. H. Tropic.
Lindsay, N. Congo, The.
Meredith, G. Gordon of Khartoum.
Moore, M. Jerboa, The.
Nemerov. Two Poems.
Walcott. Far Cry from Africa, A.
Walker, A. African Images, Glimpses from a Tiger's Back.
Karamojongs.

There are no tigers.
There were palm trees.
Wheatley, P. Philis's Reply to the Answer in Our Last by the Gentleman in the Navy.
Williams, W. Gentle Negress, The.

African-American Power
Angelou. No No No No.
Pusher, The.
Hughes, L. I, Too.
Roland Hayes Beaten (Georgia: 1942).
Lorde. NOW.

African Americans
Ai. Chance.
Passing Through.
Riot Act, April 29, 1992.
Angelou. Ain't That Bad.
Amoebaean for Daddy.
Black Ode.
Calling of Names, The.
Family Affairs.
On Working White Liberals.
Passing Time.
Sepia Fashion Show.
Song for the Old Ones.
Still I Rise.
Thank You, Lord.
Through the Inner City to the Suburbs.
To a Husband.
To a Suitor.
Weekend Glory.
Bishop, E. Cootchie.
Songs for a Colored Singer.
Brooks, G. Ballad of Rudolph Reed, The.
Gay Chaps at the Bar.
We Real Cool.
Browning, E. Runaway Slave at Pilgrim's Point, The.
Carruth, H. Mountain, The.
Sam and Poll Go Back to the City.
Crane, H. Black Tambourine.
Cullen, C. Black Christ, The.
Black Majesty.
Brown Girl Dead, A.
Colored Blues Singer.
From the Dark Tower.
Heritage.
Litany of the Dark People, The.
Pagan Prayer.
Shroud of Color, The.
Song of Praise, A.
Yet Do I Marvel.
Cummings, E. E. Theys sO alive.
Dove, R. Wingfoot Lake.
Dunbar, P. Black Samson of Brandywine.
Colored Band, The.
Colored Soldiers, The.
Negro Love Song, A.
Unsung Heroes, The.
We Wear the Mask.
When Dey 'Listed Colored Soldiers.
Emerson, R. I am not black in my mind.
García Lorca. King of Harlem, The.
Standards and Paradise of the Blacks.
Hayden, R. Beginnings.
Frederick Douglass.
O Daedalus, Fly Away Home.
Hughes, L. Afraid.
Afro-American Fragment.
Air Raid over Harlem.
America.
American Heartbreak.
America's Young Black Joe!
As I Grew Older.
Aunt Sue's Stories.
Ballad of Harry Moore.
Ballad of Margie Polite, The.
Ballad of Negro History, A.
Ballad of Sam Solomon.
Ballad of the Seven Songs.
Ballad of Walter White.
Be-Bop Boys.
Beale Street.
Beaumont to Detroit: 1943.
Bible Belt.
Birmingham Sunday.
Bitter River, The.

Black Clown, The.
Black Dancers.
Black Gal.
Black Man Speaks, The.
Black Panther.
Black Seed.
Black Workers.
Blue Bayou.
Boogie: 1 a.m.
Brass Spittoons.
Brotherly Love.
Brothers.
Children's Rhymes ("When I was a chile we
    used to play").
Christ in Alabama.
Colored Soldier, The.
Consider Me.
Cross.
Crowns and Garlands.
Dark Youth of the U.S.A.
Dear Mr. President.
Death in Yorkville.
Deferred.
Dinner Guest: Me.
Dixie Man to Uncle Sam.
Do You Reckon?
Dream Boogie.
Dream Boogie: Variation.
Drums,
Final Call.
Flatted Fifths.
For Russell and Rowena Jelliffe.
Freedom Train.
Freedom's Plow.
Get Up Off That Old Jive.
Ghosts of 1619.
Graduation.
Harlem ("Here on the edge of hell").
Harlem Sweeties.
High to Low.
I, Too.
Imagine.
Jim Crow Car.
Jim Crow's Last Stand.
Joe Louis ("Joe Louis is a man").
Juice Joint: Northern City.
Laughers.
Letter from Spain.
Likewise.
Lincoln Theatre.
Lincoln University: 1954.
Little Song on Housing.
Long View: Negro.
Low to High.
Man into Men.
Me and My Song.
Mellow.
Merry-Go-Round.
Message to the President.
Midnight Dancer.
Migrant.
Migration.
Mississippi.
Mitchell Case, The.
Mulatto.
My People.
Mystery.
NAACP.
Negro.
Negro Dancers.
Negro Ghetto.
Negro Mother, The.
Negro Servant.
Negro Speaks of Rivers, The.
Neighbor.
New Song, A.
Not a Movie.
Note on Commercial Theatre.
October 16: The Raid.
One-Way Ticket.
Parade.
Porter.
Postcard from Spain.
Prayer Meeting.
Prelude to Our Age.
Projection.

Red Silk Stockings.
Restrictive Covenants.
Roland Hayes Beaten (Georgia: 1942).
Ruby Brown.
Share-Croppers.
Song for a Dark Girl.
Song to a Negro Wash-woman, A.
South, The.
Southern Mammy Sings.
Southern Negro Speaks.
Stokely Malcolm Me.
Summer Evening (Calumet Avenue).
Sun Song.
Theme for English B.
To Captain Mulzac.
To Certain Negro Leaders.
Trumpet Player.
Uncle Tom ("Uncle Tom is a legend and a
    dream").
Us: Colored.
Vari-Colored Song.
Visitors to the Black Belt.
We, Too.
Weary Blues, The.
West Texas.
What? So Soon!
When Sue Wears Red
Where Service Is Needed.
Will V-Day Be Me-Day Too?
Young Negro Girl.
Jarrell, R.   Lady Bates.
Kinnell.   Avenue Bearing the Initial of Christ
    into the New World, The.
Komunyakaa.   Addendum.
Changes; or, Reveries at a Window Overlooking
    a Country Road, with Two Women Talking
    Blues in the Kitchen.
Doppelgängers.
Family Tree.
Gift Horse.
Mismatched Shoes.
Sex, Magnolias, & Speed.
Lindsay, N.   Booker Washington Trilogy, The.
Congo, The.
Logan, J.   Grandfather's Railroad.
Lorde.   Coal.
Generation II.
Lowell, R.   For the Union Dead.
Mad Negro Soldier Confined at Munich, A.
Melville, H.   Formerly a Slave.
Merton.   Plessy vs Ferguson: Theme and
    Variations.
Nemerov.   Negro Cemetery Next to a White
    One, A.
Parker, D.   Dark Girl's Rhyme, The.
Rukeyser, M.   George Robinson: Blues.
Three Black Women.
Sandburg, C.   Nigger.
Singing Nigger.
Shapiro, K.   Nigger.
Walcott.   Swamp, The.
Warren, R.   Tryst on Vinegar Hill.
Wheatley, P.   On Being Brought from Africa to
    America.
Whitman, W.   Ethiopia Saluting the Colors.
Williams, W.   Sick African.
Time the Hangman.
Wordsworth, W.   September 1, 1802.
Wright, J.   Albuquerque Graveyard, The.
Confession to J. Edgar Hoover.
End of an Ethnic Dream, The.
Homecoming Singer, The.
W. E. B. DuBois at Harvard.

Afterlife
Ai.   General George Armstrong Custer: My Life
    in the Theater.
Amichai [or Amikhai].   From All the Spaces.
In the Garden, at the White Table.
Baudelaire.   Posthumous Remorse.
Berrigan, T.   Wrong Train.
Bierce.   Contentment.
Finis Æternitatis.
Borges.   His End and His Beginning.
Brontë, E.   Lines: "I die; but when the grave
    shall press."

Wide cathedral aisles are lone, The.
Cavafy.   Hereafter, The.
Rest I Will Tell to Those Below in Hades, The.
Clifton, L.   Heaven.
Codrescu.   Crossed Hands.
Cowper, W.   Translation of Epitaph to Northcot.
Crane, H.   Circumstance, The.
Creeley.   Beyond.
Cullen, C.   Poet, The.
Cummings, E. E.   If there are any heavens my
    mother will (all by herself) have.
Dickinson, E.   Of nearness to her sundered
    Things.
Dubie.   Dream of Three Sisters, A.
Eberhart, R.   Ides of March, The.
Emerson, R.   Spirits of the wise, sit on the
    clouds, The.
Fenton, J.   Kingfisher's Boxing Gloves, The.
Gurney, I.   It Is Near Toussaints.
Regrets After Death.
Guyon.   Acquiescence of Pure Love, The.
Child of God Longing To See Him Beloved, A.
Han-shan.   Chuang-tzu said for his funeral.
HaNagid.   Know of the Limbs.
Heancy, S.   Afterwards, An.
Herrick.   His Charge to Julia at His Death.
Plaudite, or End of Life, The.
Housman.   They shall have breath that never
    were.
Hughes, L.   Judgment Day.
Hughes, T.   Crow's Elephant Totem Song.
Risen, The.
Jackson, L.   Then Follows.
Jacobsen, J.   Mourner Betrayed.
Jeffers, R.   Inscription for a Gravestone.
Kumin, M.   In the Park.
Shopping in Ferney with Voltaire.
Kunitz, S.   Way Down, The.
Laughlin, J.   Leave-taking, A.
Lawrence, D. H.   Like the Green Candles of
    Malintzi.
My Way Is Not Thy Way.
Song of the Dead.
Levi, P.   Epitaph: "Oh you, passing by this
    hill—one."
Levine, P.   Breath.
Logue, C.   Ass's Song, The.
MacNeice.   This Is the Life.
Mahon.   Consolations of Philosophy.
Leaves,
Marvell.   Dialogue between Thyrsis and
    Dorinda, A.
Tom May's Death.
Merrill, J.   Voices from the Other World.
Michelangelo Buonarroti.   As I've carried in my
    heart this many a year.
Bracci, I, A. Alive because I'm dead.
If the soul returns, that last.
If true (and it is) that with body's final breath.
In lovelier and crueller flesh than yours.
Mere mortal once. Divine, though, born to be.
Milton.   On the Death of the Bishop of Ely.
Montale.   To My Mother.
Oliver, M.   Roses, Late Summer.
Orr, G.   November.
Song, A: "Other world's not for me, The."
Pagis.   Sominex.
Parker, D.   I Shall Come Back.
Patchen.   At the Entrance to the Other World.
Rexroth, K.   Martial—12, 52.
Riley, J.   Afterwhiles.
Beautiful City, The.
Hereafter, The.
O Life! O Beyond!
Paths of Peace, The.
Rilke.   To Serve as an Epitaph for the Beautiful
    Madame B.
What Survives.
Rimbaud, A.   Night in Hell.
Rukeyser, M.   My name is Timmy Torin.
Sandburg, C.   To a Dead Man.
Szymborska, W.   On the Banks of the Styx.
Thoreau.   Deeds of king and meanest hedger,
    The.
Very.   Indians' Belief in a Future State, The.
Whitman, W.   Unnamed Lands.

Williams, C. K.   Giving It Up.
Williams, M.   After You Die You Don't Give a Piddling Damn.
   Ghost of His Wife Comes to Tell Him How It Is, The.
   Serial Murderer Says Something to the Priest, The.
   She Prays for Her Husband, the Good Pastor, Lying on His Deathbed at Last.
Wright, J.   Willy Lyons.
Zagajewski.   In May.
   Without End.

Afternoon
Ammons.   Three.
Borges.   Afternoon, The.
Carruth, H.   Backyard in California, A.
De la Mare.   In the Garden.
Jackson, L.   Afternoon.
Millay, E.   Afternoon on a Hill.
Mistral, G.   Summit.
Nemerov.   Harvest Home, A.
O'Hara, F.   Tarquin.
Olson, C.   Afternoon.
Riley, J.   One Afternoon.
Ritsos.   Afternoon.
Tomlinson, C.   All Afternoon.
   Carscape.
   Eight Observations on the Nature of Eternity.
   Hokusai on the Trent.
Vallejo.   Down to the Dregs.
Wright, C.   Sitting Outside at the End of Autumn.
Zagajewski.   Long Afternoons.

Afton River, Scotland
Burns, R.   Flow Gently, Sweet Afton.

Agamemnon
Cavafy.   When the Watchman Saw the Light.
Heaney, S.   Mycenae Lookout.
Jeffers, R.   Tower beyond Tragedy, The.
Merton.   Greek Women, The.
Ritsos.   Agamemnon.

Agassiz, Louis
Whittier.   Prayer of Agassiz, The.

Aggression
Bukowski.   Transformation and Disfiguration.
Clare, J.   Turkeys.
Creeley.   Riddle: "What'd you throw it on the floor for?"
Lawrence, D. H.   Attila.
Levertov.   May Our Right Hands Lose Their Cunning.
Lindsay, N.   Lion, The.
Nash, O.   Tweedledee and Tweedledoom.
Thomas, D.   If My Head Hurt a Hair's Foot.

Aging
Amichai [or Amikhai].   1924.
   Akhziv.
   All These Make a Dance Rhythm.
   Autobiography, 1952.
   Autobiography in the Year 1952.
   Bedouin Goes North, A.
   For My Birthday.
   Hamadiya.
   Haydn, Opus 76, Number 5.
   How did a banner begin? Let's assume there was something whole.
   Last Word is the Captain, The.
   Late Marriage.
   Life.
   My former student is in the traffic police.
   My friend, what you're doing now.
   On My Birthday.
   Pace Like That, A.
   There Are Candles That Remember.
   When I was young, the country was young too. My father.
Angelou.   On Reaching Forty.
Armantrout.   Generation.
Arnold, M.   Growing Old.
Ashbery, J.   Tone Poem, A.
Atwood.   After all you are quite.
   Aging Female Poet on Laundry Day.
   Aging Female Poet Sits on the Balcony.
   Girl and Horse, 1928.
   Keep.

Auden.   Doggerel by a Senior Citizen.
   Old People's Home.
Price, The.
   Prologue at Sixty.
Baudelaire.   Black Bile ("No writing-desk crammed full of music, twine").
   Rara Avis.
Beckett, S.   Saint-Lô.
Berry, W.   Ripening.
Berryman.   At Chinese Checkers.
   Damned.
   Point of Age, A.
Bierce.   Study in Gray, A.
Bishop, E.   Mountain, The.
Bly, R.   Defeated.
   Dream of Retarded Children, A.
   For My Son Noah, Ten Years Old.
   Night Frogs.
   Visiting the Farallones.
   Watcher, The.
Borges.   Elegy: "Oh destiny of Borges."
   That Man.
   To One No Longer Young.
   Two Forms of Insomnia.
Bradstreet, A.   Of the Four Ages of Man.
Brodsky, J.   1972.
   Elegy: "Sweetheart, losing your looks, go to live in a village."
   Porta San Pancrazio.
   Song of Welcome.
Brontë, E.   Love and Friendship.
   O evening, why is thy light so sad?
   Why do I hate that lone green dell?
Brooks, G.   Old Mary.
   Sunset of the City, A.
Broumas, O.   Between Two Seas.
   Sometimes, as a Child.
Browning, R.   By the Fire-Side.
   Prologue: "Poet's age is sad: for why?, The."
   Rabbi Ben Ezra.
   Youth and Art.
Bukowski.   American Express, Athens, Greece.
   Clean Old Man.
   Doom and Siesta Time.
   For Al—.
   One of the Hottest.
   Poem for My 43rd Birthday.
   This Then—.
Burns, R.   Broom Besoms ["Young and souple was I, when I lap the dyke"].
   Deuks Dang o'er My Daddie, The.
   John Anderson, My Jo.
   Lazy Mist, The.
   Sketch. New Year's Day. To Mrs. Dunlop.
Byron, G.   Fill the Goblet.
   L'Amitié Est L'Amour Sans Ailes.
   On This Day I Complete My Thirty-sixth Year.
   Stanzas for Music.
   To Edward Noel Long, Esq.
   To the Countess of Blessington.
   To Time.
Campion, T.   First Love.
Carew, T.   Disdain Returned.
Carruth, H.   Capper Kaplinski at the North Side Cue Club.
   Essay on Love.
   Excursus of Reassurance in Begonia Time, An.
   Insomniac Sleeps Well for Once and, The.
   Living Alone.
   Marge.
   New Hartford.
   No Supervening Thought of Grace.
   Opusthirteen.
   Rummage.
   Sex.
   Silence.
   Song: Luxury.
   Song: The Old, Old Man.
   That I Had Had Courage When Young.
   Twilight Comes.
   Valentine.
Cavafy.   Before Time Could Change Them.
   Elegy of the Flowers.
   Melancholy of Jason Kleander; Poet in Kommagini; 595 A.D.
   Since Nine O'Clock.

Cho Wen-chun.   Lament of a Graying Woman.
Ciardi, J.   At O'Hare.
   Audit at Key West.
   Elegy for the Face at Your Elbow.
   Emeritus Addresses the School, An.
   Generation Gap.
   Obsolescence.
   Old Man Confesses, An.
   Poem for My Thirty-ninth Birthday.
   Washing Your Feet.
Clampitt.   Seder Night.
   Winter Burial, A.
   Written in Water.
Clifton, L.   1994.
   Rust.
Clough.   Dance on, dance on, we see, we see.
   July's Farewell.
Coleridge, S.   Improvisatore, The.
   This Lime-Tree Bower My Prison.
Collins, B.   On Turning Ten.
   Scotland.
Cooper, J.   Bloodroot.
   Childhood in Jacksonville, Florida.
   Nothing I Meant to Keep.
Corbett, W.   For the Old Year.
   September Song.
Corkine.   My Dearest Mistress.
Cowper, W.   Inscription for a Stone.
   Lines for a Memorial of Ashley Cowper.
   Moralizer Corrected, The.
   Song: "No more shall hapless Celia's ears."
   To Mary.
   To William Hayley, Esq.: In Reply to His Solicitation to Write with Him in a Literary Work.
Creeley.   After.
   Age ("He is thinking of everyone").
   Box.
   Chanson.
   Children, The.
   Faces, The.
   For Irving.
   For Pen ("Reading, in the chair").
   For the Graduation.
   Going Home.
   Lunch and After.
   Milton Über Alles.
   Myself.
   Out Here.
   Prayer to Hermes.
   Still Too Young.
   Testament, A.
   Then ("Put yourself where you'll be").
   There ("With all I know").
Cummings, E. E.   Harder perhaps than a newengland bed.
   My uncle / Daniel fought in the civil.
   Nobody wears a yellow.
   Noone" autumnal this great lady's gaze.
   oDE: "O / the sweet & aged people."
   Somebody knew Lincoln somebody Xerxes.
   Time,be kind;herself and i.
   Tw / oo / ld / o / nce upo / n.
   Whatever's merely wilful, / and not miraculous.
   When hair falls off and eyes blur And.
   When time delicately is sponging sum after.
Cunningham, J.   Epigram: "You wonder why Drab sells her love for gold?"
   I grow old, but I know that Science some.
   Moral Poem, A.
   To My Wife.
"Dario."   Eheu!
   I am the one who just yesterday spoke.
   Song of Autumn in Springtime.
Davie, D.   And Our Eternal Home.
   Artifex in Extremis.
   Autumn Imagined.
   Heigh-ho on a Winter Afternoon.
   Liverpool Epistle, A.
   Mens Sana in Corpore Sano.
   Penelope.
   So Make Them Melt as the Dishousèd Snail.
   Toby to Aguecheek.
De la Mare.   Brother and Sister.
   Karma.
   News.

On the Esplanade.
Time Passes.
Dickey, W. At Your Old House.
Do they remember me?
Fretful and sick, you ask.
Fretful and sick, you long.
Nevertheless, sleep / And as your eyes close.
No, the night has gone.
Yes, they remember you.
Dickinson, E. Little Snow was here and there, A.
My Wars are laid away in Books.
We outgrow love like other things.
We turn not older with years.
Donne. Canonization, The.
Dugan, A. American against Solitude.
Boast.
Letter to Donald Fall.
Poem: "After your first poetry reading."
Summer Heaven, Angels, Heaven.
Untitled Poem: "Two shots down and I'm exalted."
Dunbar, P. At Sunset Time.
Lost Dream, A.
Vengeance is Sweet.
Eberhart, R. Edgar Lee Masters.
Experience Evoked.
God and Man.
Half-bent Man.
Hardy Perennial.
Haystack, The.
Emerson, R. Brother, no decrepitude.
I know the appointed hour.
Terminus.
Thanks to those who go & come.
Valedictory Poem.
Woods.
Frost, R. In the Home Stretch.
To Earthward.
What Fifty Said.
Gallagher, T. Borrowed Ones, The.
My Mother Remembers That She Was Beautiful.
Some with Wings, Some with Manes.
Ginsberg, A. Aether.
Autumn Leaves.
Don't Grow Old.
Growing Old Again.
Old Village before I Die, The.
Some Love.
Sphincter.
Glück, L. End of the World, The.
For My Mother.
Portrait of the Queen in Tears.
To Autumn.
Graves, R. Change.
Dazzle of Darkness.
Imminent Seventies, The.
Suicide in The Copse, The.
Gunn, T. For a Birthday.
Gurney, I. Bronze Sounding, The.
When the Body Might Free.
Hacker, M. Mother II.
Hall, D. *Couplet.*
Dancers.
Days, The.
Friend Revisited, A.
Grown-Ups, The.
Hole, The.
In the Old House.
Mr. Wakeville on Interstate 90.
My Son, My Executioner.
Hamill, S. Leaf, A.
Letter to Robert Hedin.
Passport.
Han-shan. All the people I see.
Inside Jade Hall is a curtain of pearls.
Where clouds and mountains are piled to the sky.
HaNagid. Among My Friends.
Black of My Hair, The.
Child at One or Two, The.
Fear Five to the Power of Five.
My Spirit.
You Mock Me Now in Your Youth.
Youth Brings Us.

Hardy, T. Ageing House, The.
At Madame Tussaud's in Victorian Years.
At the Dinner-Table.
Church Romance, A.
Circus-Rider to Ringmaster.
Colonel's Soliloquy, The.
Ghost of the Past, The.
God's Education.
Her Apotheosis.
In a Eweleaze near Weatherbury.
In the Night She Came.
Lament of the Looking-Glass, The.
Revisitation, The.
Seeing the Moon Rise.
She, to Him.
Ten Years Since.
Under High-Stoy Hill.
Voice of Things, The.
Woman Who Went East, The.
Hayden, R. Lear Is Gay.
Heaney, S. Fosterling.
Herbert, G. Answer, The.
Mortification.
Herrick. Changes to Corinna, The.
Courage Cool'd.
His Age, Dedicated to His Peculiar Friend, Master John Wickes, under the Name of Posthumus.
On Himselfe.
To a Bed of Tulips.
To a Gentlewoman Objecting to Him His Grey Hairs.
To His Friend, on the Untunable Times.
To His Mistress[es].
Upon Silvia, a Mistresse.
Upon Wrinkles.
Housman. Loveliest of Trees, the Cherry Now.
Say, lad, have you things to do?
When first my way to fair I took.
When summer's end is nighing.
Hughes, L. After Many Springs.
Change.
Pictures to the Wall.
Watch Out, Papa.
Hughes, T. Sketching a Thatcher.
Ignatow, D. In a Dream 2.
Old.
Two Friends.
Jacobsen, J. Survivor's Ballad.
Jarrell, R. Aging.
All or None.
Bad Music, The.
Face, The.
Faded.
Island, The.
Next Day.
Old Song, An.
Player Piano, The.
Jeffers, R. Age in Prospect.
Birthday.
But I Am Growing Old and Indolent.
For Una.
Jonson, B. My Picture Left in Scotland.
To the World [A Farewell for a Gentlewoman, Virtuous and Noble].
Keats. In Drear-nighted December.
Kinnell. Frog Pond, The.
Kinsella, T. In Memory.
Kipling, R. His Apologies.
Kizer, C. For Jan as the End Draws Near.
On a Line from Sophocles.
Koch, K. Magic of Numbers, The.
Komunyakaa. Bennelong's Blues.
Corners of Night.
Poet Whose Photo Never Grows Old, A.
Sagittarius Approaching Thirty-Five.
Way the Cards Fall, The.
Kumin, M. Casablanca.
Distance.
Kunitz, S. Goose Pond.
Passing Through.
Summing-up, The.
Transformations.
Larkin, P. Age.
Breadfruit.
Dockery and Son.

I Have Started to Say.
Long Last.
Long Sight in Age.
Love Songs in Age.
Nothing to Be Said.
Old Fools, The.
On Being Twenty-Six.
Referred Back.
Triple Time.
View, The.
Winter Palace, The.
Laughlin, J. Confessio Amantis.
Layers.
My Old Gray Sweater.
Lawrence, D. H. Beware, O My Dear Young Men.
Monologue of a Mother.
So There!
Young Are Not Mean in Material Things, The.
Levertov. Man, A.
What Wild Dawns There Were.
Woman Alone, A.
Levi, P. Partisan.
Levine, P. 28.
Breath.
For Fran.
Late Moon.
Look.
My Son and I.
New Day, A.
Red Dust.
Salts and Oils.
Logan, J. Assessment, The.
Medicine Bow.
Transformation, The.
Logue, C. Fragment.
Nell's Circular Poem.
Longfellow, H. Morituri Salutamus.
Nature.
Lorde. As I Grew Up Again.
Generation II.
Lux. Little Tooth, A.
MacLeish. Bed, The.
Conway Burying Ground.
Definitions of Old Age.
Dozing on the Lawn.
Hebrides.
Old Gray Couple (2), The.
Old Man's Journey.
Old Men in the Leaf Smoke, The.
Ship's Log.
They Come No More, Those Words, Those Finches.
With Age Wisdom.
Mahon. Brighton Beach.
St. Patrick's Day.
Major, C. Aging Together.
Matthew.
Marvell. To His Coy Mistress.
McGrath, T. Changeling, The.
Dream Range, The.
Orphan, The.
Progress of the Soul, The.
Uses of the Lost Poets.
McHugh, H. To the Quick.
Meredith, G. Atlas.
But see what living glory floods the west.
Fresh Spring has come with flower and leaf to warn.
I have a hope that's like a star.
Motley.
Time.
Time and Sentiment.
Wisdom of Eld, The.
Youth in Age.
Youth in Memory.
Meredith, W. Birthday Exercise, A.
His Plans for Old Age.
Last Things.
Sunrise with Crows.
Winter Verse for His Sister.
Merrill, J. After the Fire.
Black Mesa, The.
Hourglass.
Kimono, The.
Lorelei.

Mirror.
Prism.
Tenancy, A.
Time.
Verse for Urania.
Will, The.
Merwin. Another Year Come.
From a Series.
In the Winter of My Thirty-eighth Year.
Late Night in Autumn.
Numbered Apartment.
Passage.
Resolution.
River of Bees, The.
Sibyl.
Michelangelo Buonarroti. Gone under now, the
sun you loved to greet.
Rancorous heart, cruel, pitiless, though showing.
What's to become of her, long years from now.
Wo is me woe's me when I think.
Millay, E. Grown-up.
Sonnet: "Oh, my belovèd, have you thought of
this."
Milosz, C. Caffé Greco.
Dawns.
Rivers Grow Small.
When After a Long Life.
Montale. End of Childhood.
Line of dancing children on the shore, The.
Muldoon, P. February.
Nash, D. Old Is for Books.
Nash, O. Birthday on the Beach.
Calendar-Watchers, or, What's So Wonderful
about Being a Patriarch, The.
Crossing the Border.
Eheu! Fugaces, or, What a Difference a Lot of
Days Make.
For a Good Dog.
Good Parent's Garden of Vision, A.
Lines on Facing Forty.
Lines to Be Scribbled on Somebody Else's
Thirtieth Milestone.
Preface to the Past.
Nemerov. Boy with Book of Knowledge.
First Leaf, The.
Landscape with Figures.
Old Soldiers' Home, The.
Poet at Forty, The.
Thirtieth Anniversary Report of the Class of
'41.
Young Woman.
Neruda. Ambassador, The.
Niedecker. Not feeling well, my wood uncut.
Regards to Mr. Glover.
There's a better shine.
Young in Fall I said: the birds.
O'Hara, F. Hatred.
Oppen. Birthplace: New Rochelle.
Resort.
Orr, G. Life, A.
Owen, W. Sonnet, to a Child.
Pagis. Moments of Old Age.
Pages in an Album.
Portrait, The.
Paley, G. Age.
Choir Singing, The.
For My Daughter.
On the Deck.
One Day I Decided.
One of the Softer Sorrows of Age.
Sad Children's Song, The.
Parker, D. Afternoon.
Ballade at Thirty-Five.
Braggart.
Indian Summer.
Ninon De L'Enclos, On Her Last Birthday.
Swan Song.
Pasolini. Lines from the Testament.
Pasternak, B. Oh had we known it turns out so.
Patchen. Street Corner College.
Pessoa. Now ashen gray tinges the balding
brow.
Petrarch. My face and hair are changing; I grow
old.
Now should my life endure to this extent.
Once more Love sends to me that pleasing

thought.
Seventeen years since first I felt the full.
Piercy. Sign.
Plath. Mirror.
Old Ladies' Home.
Tinker Jack and the Tidy Wives.
Poe. Eldorado.
Happiest Day, the Happiest Hour, The.
Pope, A. Prologue Design'd for Mr. Durfy's
Last Play.
Prologue to a Play for Mr. Dennis's Benefit, in
1733, when He Was Old, Blind, and in Great
Distress, a Little before His Death, A.
To Mrs. M. B. on Her Birth-Day.
Pound, E. Beautiful Toilet, The.
Tea Shop, The.
Prunty. Recovery.
Since the Noon Mail Stopped.
Yes.
Raine, K. Winter Paradise.
Young or old / What was I but a story told.
Ralegh, S. Nymph's [or Nimphs] Reply to the
Shepherd [or Sheepheard], The.
Ramanujan. Entries for a Catalogue of Fears.
He Too Was a Light Sleeper Once.
LOVE 3: What He Said, Remembering.
Sonnet: "Time moves in and out of me."
Ransom, J. Blue Girls.
Rexroth, K. Andrée Rexroth ("Purple and
green, blue and white").
Christmas Note for Geraldine Udell, A.
Fifty.
Fish Peddler and Cobbler.
Gic to Har.
Illusion.
Me.
Only Years.
Sense of Proportion.
Songs for Marie's Lutebook.
Your Birthday in the California Mountains.
Rich, A. Autumn Equinox.
Halfway.
Life and Letters.
Middle-Aged, The.
Necessities of Life.
Transcendental Etude.
Upper Broadway.
When This Clangor in the Brain.
Riley, J. Dead Selves.
Feel in the Chris'mas-Air, A.
It's Got to Be.
Letter to a Friend, A.
Little Fat Doctor, The.
Loveliness, The.
My Boy.
My Dancin'-Days Is Over.
My First Spectacles.
Our Queer Old World.
Sad Perversity.
Spring Song and a Later, A.
Thinkin' Back.
To Annie.
When Age Comes On.
Youth and Age.
Rilke. Growing Old.
Lost Nights.
Rimbaud, A. War.
Youth.
Ritsos. Experiences.
Marpessa's Selection.
What's the Use?
Robinson, E. Amaryllis.
Isaac and Archibald.
Veteran Sirens.
Roethke. Feud.
Other, The.
Our Lady's Winter Words.
Sententious Man, The.
Rossetti, C. Dumb Friend, A.
Lowest Room, The.
Rukeyser, M. In Her Burning.
Letter, Unposted.
Sadi [or Saadi or Sa'di]. Salve Senescentem.
Sandburg, C. Ever a Seeker.
Glimmer.
Junk Man, The.

Let Them Ask Your Pardon.
Streets Too Old.
Trafficker.
Working Girls.
Schuyler, J. Few Days, A.
Tomorrow.
Seifert. Autobiography.
Fan, The.
Transformations.
Sexton. Two Sons.
Shapiro, K. Retirement.
"Shu Ting." Returning Home.
Simic. Whispers.
Smith, S. Pad, Pad.
Progression.
Snyder, G. Sweat, The.
Spender, S. From My Diary.
What I Expected.
Stafford, W. Evidence.
Growing Up.
How the Real Bible Is Written.
Retirement.
Size of a Fist, The.
Sure You Do.
Waiting in Line.
Stockton, A. Ode, An: "Yes tis an easy thing to
view."
Swenson, M. How to Be Old.
This Morning.
View to the North.
Swift, J. Receipt to Restore Stella's Youth, A.
Stella's Birthday, 1725.
Stella's Birthday; Written in the Year 1718[/9].
Tate, A. Last Days of Alice.
Meaning of Life, The.
To a Prodigal Old Maid.
Tennyson, A. June Bracken and Heather.
Thomas, D. I See the Boys of Summer.
Lament: "When I was a windy boy and a bit."
Process in the Weather of the Heart, A.
When Once the Twilight Locks No Longer.
Thoreau. Die and be buried who will.
Music.
Tomlinson, C. Doggerel for My Seventieth
Birthday, A.
On the Hall at Stowey.
Trakl. Helian.
Tu Fu. My Home Town.
Testament.
Unknown. Only three things lengthen life.
Updike. Dutch Cleanser.
Golfers.
Melancholy of Storm Windows, The.
Shillington.
To a Dead Flame.
Upon the Last Day of His Forty-Ninth Year.
Van Duyn. Challenger, The.
Colorado.
Sestina for Warm Seasons.
Stream, The.
Very. Autumn Flowers.
Walcott. Codicil.
Nearing Forty.
Parang.
Walker, A. Mississippi Winter III.
Warren, R. Acquaintance with Time in Early
Autumn.
American Portrait: Old Style.
Grackles, Goodbye.
No Bird Does Call.
Questions You Must Learn to Live Past.
Rather Like a Dream.
Swimming in the Pacific.
Uncertain Season in High Country.
Vermont Ballad: Change of Season.
Waiting.
When Life Begins.
Weiss, T. This Gray Age.
Whalen, P. For Allen, on His 60th Birthday.
High-tension on Low-pressure Non-
accomplishment Blues.
Labor Day.
Obsolete Models.
Old Age Echoes.
Whitman, W. Apparitions.
My 71st Year.

Queries to My Seventieth Year.
Whittier.   At Eventide.
   Greeting.
   My Birthday.
   O. W. Holmes on His Eightieth Birthday.
   Reunion, The.
   Sea Dream, A.
   To My Old Schoolmaster.
   To Oliver Wendell Holmes.
   Voyage of the Jettie.
Wilbur, R.   Black Birch in Winter, A.
   For K. R. on Her Sixtieth Birthday.
   Next Door.
Wilde, O.   Sweet I blame you not for mine the
   fault was, had I not been made of common
   clay.
Williams, C. K.   Alzheimer's: The Wife.
   Fifteen.
   Tails.
   World's Greatest Tricycle-Rider, The.
Williams, M.   And Then.
   Documenting It.
   Fifty.
   In Nashville, Standing in the Wooden Circle
   Sawed Out from the Old Ryman Stage, the
   Picker has a vision.
   Jonathan Aging.
   Jonathan Entertaining.
   Love Poem with Toast.
   Shrinking Lonesome Sestina, The.
   Talking to Himself He Gets a Few Things
   Settled in His Mind.
   Vanishing Point, The.
   Visitor's Guide to the Blue Planet, The.
Williams, T.   Ave Atque Vale.
Williams, W.   Another Old Woman.
   Death of Franco of Cologne, The: His Prophecy
   of Beethoven.
   Descent, The.
   For G.B.S., Old.
   Old Worshipper, The.
   Poem: "Looking up, of a sudden."
   Rocking Woman, The.
   Three Graces, The.
   To a Man Dying on His Feet.
   To Wish Myself Courage.
   Wide Awake, Full of Love.
Wordsworth, W.   September, 1819.
   Sequel to Beggars Composed Many Years After.
   To ———: "Look at the fate of summer
   flowers."
Wright, C.   After Reading Tu Fu, I Go Outside
   to the Dwarf Orchard.
   China Mail.
   Hawaii Dantesca.
   Journal of Southern Rivers, A.
Wright, J.   Fishermen, The.
   In the Cold House.
   Many of Our Waters: Variations on a Poem by a
   Black Child.
   Message Hidden in an Empty Wine Bottle that I
   Threw into a Gully of Maple Trees One Night
   at an Indecent Hour, A.
   Old Age Compensation.
   Old Man Drunk.
   Three Steps to the Graveyard.
   Youth.
Wyatt, S.   There was never file half so well
   filed.
   Ye old mule, that thin[c]k your self so fair [or
   fayre].
Yeats.   Broken Dreams.
   Coming of Wisdom with Time, The.
   Crazy Jane Grown Old Looks at the Dancers.
   Crazy Jane Talks with the Bishop.
   Fallen Majesty.
   Folly of Being Comforted, The.
   Her Vision in the Wood.
   Lines Written in Dejection.
   Living Beauty, The.
   Man Young and Old, A.
   Memory of Youth, A.
   Men Improve with the Years.
   New Faces, The.
   Song, A: "I thought no more was needed."
   Sweet Dancer.

   Wild Swans at Coole, The.
   Young Man's Song.
   Youth and Age.
Zaturenska.   Cascades and Fountains.
   Girl Takes Her Place Among the Mothers, The.
   Narrow Hemisphere, The.
   Reflections On a Centaur.
Zukofsky, L.   Strange / To reach that age.
   Valentine, A.
See also Middle Age; Old Age
Agnosticism and Agnostics
Hardy, T.   Impercipient, The.
Kumin, M.   Agnostic Speaks to Her Horse's
   Hoof, The.
Meredith, G.   Thou pirate nested over Alde!
Millay, E.   Agnostic, The.
Pessoa.   Poem: "Sky, the blueness of quiet
   light."
Smith, S.   Agnostic, An.
See also Doubt
Agoraphobia
Nash, O.   On Waking to the Third Rainy
   Morning of a Long Week End.
Agriculture
Rexroth, K.   Motto on the Sundial. The
   Very.   "Agriculture the Source of Individual and
   of National Prosperity."—Anne Pratt.
See also Farming and Farmers
Aguirre, Lope de
   Ai.   Gilded Man, The.
Agustini, Delmira
   Olson, C.   Grinning monster out side the system.
AIDS
   Ai.   Visitation.
   Gunn, T.   Courtesies of the Interregnum.
   J Car, The.
   Lament: "Your dying was a difficult enterprise."
   Man with Night Sweats, The.
   Memory Unsettled.
   Missing, The.
   Reassurance, The.
   Sacred Heart.
   Still Life.
   Terminal.
   To the Dead Owner of a Gym.
   Words for Some Ash.
   Hacker, M.   Nights of 1965: the Old Reliable.
   Williams, M.   Thinking about Bill, Dead of
   AIDS.
Air
   Atwood.   Variation on the Word Sleep.
   Berrigan, T.   Red Shift.
   Bishop, E.   Colder the Air, The.
   Clampitt.   Let the Air Circulate.
   Cooper, J.   Starting with a Line from Roethke.
   Creeley.   For Allen.
   De la Mare.   Spirit of air, The.
   Dickey, J.   Immortals.
   Night Bird.
   Dickinson, E.   Air has no Residence, no
   Neighbor.
   'Tis whiter than an Indian Pipe.
   Dugan, A.   1. Enigma: Calm: Addressed to the
   Air.
   2. Comment on 1.
   Eberhart, R.   Imagining How It Would Be to Be
   Dead.
   Now Is the Air Made of Chiming Balls.
   Emerson, R.   Score of airy miles will smooth, A.
   Hardy, T.   Garden Seat, The.
   Hopkins, G.   Blessed Virgin Compared to the
   Air We Breathe, The.
   Larkin, P.   To a Very Slow Air.
   Lawrence, D. H.   Four, The.
   Lux.   Poem in Thanks.
   Millay, E.   Above These Cares.
   Mistral, G.   Air, The.
   Raine, K.   Lifelong ago such days.
   Rukeyser, M.   Air.
   Sarton, M.   Composition.
   Schuyler, J.   Deep Winter.
   In Wiry Winter.
   Light Blue Above.
   Simic.   Autumn Air.
   Wilbur, R.   Attention Makes Infinity.

   Sun and Air.
   Wright, J.   Breath of Air, A.
Air Conditioning
   Davie, D.   Conditioned Air, A.
Air Plants
   Crane, H.   Air Plant, The.
   Emerson, R.   See yonder leafless trees against
   the sky.
Air Travel
   Carver, R.   Miracle.
   Ciardi, J.   Back through the Looking Glass to
   This Side.
   Port of Aerial Embarkation.
   Take-off over Kansas.
   Collins, B.   Passengers.
   Creeley.   9:45 AM.
   On Board.
   Davie, D.   England.
   Eberhart, R.   United 555.
   Ginsberg, A.   Airplane Blues.
   Over Laramie.
   Wings Lifted over the Black Pit.
   Kumin, M.   Our Ground Time Here Will Be
   Brief.
   Larkin, P.   Naturally the Foundation Will Bear
   Your Expenses.
   McHugh, H.   20–200 on 747.
   Point of Origin.
   Size of Spokane, The.
   Nash, O.   Unwinged Ones, The.
   Oppen.   Flight 162.
   Pinsky.   Immortal Longings.
   Prunty.   Flying at Night.
   Sexton.   Flight.
   Story for Rose on the Midnight Flight to
   Boston, A.
   Swenson, M.   Flying Home from Utah.
   Tomlinson, C.   Landing, The.
   Updike.   Airport.
   East Hampton—Boston by Air.
   From Above.
   Landing in the Rain at La Guardia.
   Night Flight, over Ocean.
   Shuttle, The.
   Van Duyn.   Elementary Attitudes.
   Fear of Flying, The.
   First Flight.
   Warren, R.   Homage to Emerson, On Night
   Flight to New York.
   Immortality Over the Dakotas.
   Zagajewski.   Over America.
See also Airports
Air Warfare
   Ciardi, J.   Massive Retaliation.
   Dickey, J.   Firebombing, The.
   Eberhart, R.   Dam Neck, Virginia.
   Fury of Aerial Bombardment, The.
   "H. D."   Erige Cor Tuum ad Me in Caelum.
   R.A.F.
   Hall, D.   Airstrip in Essex, 1960, An.
   Hill, G.   To the Nieuport Scout.
   Jarrell, R.   Dead Wingman, The.
   Death of the Ball Turret Gunner, The.
   Eighth Air Force.
   Field Hospital, A.
   Front, A.
   Gunner.
   Losses.
   Perfectly Free Association, A.
   Pilot from the Carrier, A.
   Pilots, Man Your Planes.
   Range in the Desert, The.
   Second Air Force.
   Siegfried.
   Jeffers, R.   Air-Raid Rehearsals.
   Fantasy.
   Great Sunset, The.
   Two Christmas-Cards.
   Lawrence, D. H.   Bombardment.
   MacNeice.   Brother Fire.
   Meredith, W.   Nausea.
   Merton.   Long Enough.
   Nemerov.   Old Warplane, An.
   Rukeyser, M.   Radio silence of aircraft over the
   dense ocean.

Structure of the Plane, The.
Spender, S.   Air Raid Across the Bay at
  Plymouth.
  Thoughts During an Air Raid.
Tate, A.   Ode to Our Young Pro-consuls of the
  Air.
Thomas, D.   Ceremony after a Fire Raid.
  Refusal to Mourn the Death, by Fire, of a Child
  in London, A.
Williams, M.   We.
Yeats.   Irish Airman Foresees His Death, An.
Airline Stewardesses
Carver, R.   Jungle, The.
Dickey, J.   Falling.
Ferlinghetti, L.   Ascending over Ohio.
Airplane Crashes
Ammons.   Elegy for a Jet Pilot.
Ciardi, J.   Pilot in the Jungle, The.
Corbett, W.   Lockerbie.
Davie, D.   Cannibals.
Dickey, J.   Liberator Explodes, The.
  Patience: In the Mill.
Dubie.   Bells in the Endtime of Gyurmey
  Tsultrim.
Ginsberg, A.   Crash.
Hall, D.   Man in the Dead Machine, The.
Hughes, T.   Casualty, The.
Jarrell, R.   Front, A.
  Pilot from the Carrier, A.
Laughlin, J.   Above the City.
Meredith, W.   At the Confluence of the
  Colorado and the Little Colorado.
  Notes for an Elegy.
Prunty.   Old Cadets, The.
Updike.   On an Island.
Airplanes
Ammons.   Sitting Down, Looking Up.
Ciardi, J.   Letter Homeward.
Clampitt.   Perseus Airborne.
Dickey, J.   Liberator Explodes, The.
  Two Poems of Flight Sleep.
Feldman, R.   Airport.
Gunn, T.   Small Plane in Kansas.
Hall, D.   Grave the Well, The.
  Old Pilot, The.
  Persistence of 1937.
Hill, G.   To the Nieuport Scout.
Jeffers, R.   Machine, The.
Kipling, R.   Hymn of the Triumphant Airman.
Kumin, M.   Address to the Angels.
  Photograph, U.S. Army Flying School, College
  Park, Maryland, 1909.
Laughlin, J.   Lament of Professor Turbojet, The.
  That Other World.
Levertov.   From a Plane.
Logan, J.   Grandmother Dead in the Aeroplane.
Meredith, W.   For Air Heroes.
  Navy Field.
Merwin.   Plane.
Oppen.   Flight.
Piercy.   Night Flight.
Pinsky.   Immortal Longings.
Prunty.   Flying at Night.
Rukeyser, M.   Structure of the Plane, The.
Sandburg, C.   Air Circus.
  Bas-Relief.
Tomlinson, C.   Beautiful Aeroplane, The.
  Sky Writing.
Updike.   Air Show.
Warren, R.   Immortality Over the Dakotas.
  Sunset Scrupulously Observed.
Williams, M.   Remembering the Man.
  True Story of What Happened, The.
Wilner, E.   Winter Garden.
Zagajewski.   Over America.
Zukofsky, L.   Jaunt.
See also **Aviation and Aviators**
Airports
Amichai [*or* Amikhai].   Human Bodies.
Ciardi, J.   At O'Hare.
Creeley.   Apocalypse Now.
  Manila.
  Out Here.
Feldman, R.   Airport.
Laughlin, J.   Lament of Professor Turbojet, The.

Milosz, C.   Honest Description of Myself with a
  Glass of Whiskey at an Airport, Let Us Say, in
  Minneapolis, An.
Nemerov.   At the Airport.
Paley, G.   Illegal Aliens.
Zagajewski.   Airport in Amsterdam.
See also **Air Travel**
Ajanta, India
Rukeyser, M.   Ajanta.
Akhmatova, Anna
Gallagher, T.   Stepping Outside.
Pasternak, B.   To Anna Akhmátova.
Alabama (state)
Clifton, L.   Alabama 9/15/63.
Hughes, L.   Alabama Earth.
  Ballad of Ozie Powell.
  Croon.
  Daybreak in Alabama.
  Scottsboro.
  Town of Scottsboro, The.
Williams, M.   Plain.
Alaska
Hughes, T.   Gulkana, The.
Kumin, M.   With the Caribou.
Sze.   Edna Bay.
Albatrosses
Baudelaire.   Albatross, The.
Coleridge, S.   Rime of the Ancient Mariner,
  The.
Albinos
Komunyakaa.   Albino.
Alcatraz
Blue Cloud.   Alcatraz.
  When's the Last Boat to Alcatraz?
Muldoon, P.   Indians on Alcatraz, The.
Alcestis
Robinson, E.   As a World Would Have It.
Alchemy and Alchemists
Baudelaire.   Alchemist of Sorrows, The.
Bogan, L.   Alchemist, The.
Borges.   Alchemist, The.
Browning, R.   Paracelsus.
Clifton, L.   Quilting.
Donne.   Love's Alchemy [*or* Alchemie].
Han-shan.   Emperor Wu of the Han they say.
Hopkins, G.   Alchemist in the City, The.
Jonson, B.   To Alchemists.
Merwin.   History of Alchemy.
Olson, C.   Bagatto.
  Double, double, root and branch.
Plath.   Recantation.
Pound, E.   Alchemist, The.
Simic.   Poem without a Title.
Alcibiades
Pinsky.   Discretions of Alcibiades.
Warren, R.   Athenian Death.
Alcoholism and Alcoholics
Ai.   I Can't Get Started.
Baudelaire.   Murderer's Wine.
Bukowski.   Beer.
  Spider, The.
Carruth, H.   Incorrigible Dirigible, The.
  Marge.
Carver, R.   Alcohol.
  Anathema.
  Cheers.
  From the East, Light.
  Hope.
  Iowa Summer.
  Jean's TV.
  Luck.
  Miracle.
  Next Year.
  NyQuil.
  Phenomenon, The.
  Photograph of My Father in His Twenty-second
  Year.
  Possible, The.
  Reading.
  Rogue River Jet-Boat Trip, Gold Beach,
  Oregon, July 4, 1977.
  To My Daughter.
  Union Street: San Francisco, Summer 1975.
  Yesterday, Snow.

Cunningham, J.   Interview with Doctor Drink.
Glück, L.   Seconds.
Heaney, S.   Casualty.
Herrick.   To M. Kellam.
  Upon Blinks.
  Upon Guesse.
  Upon Punchin.
  Upon Tap.
Hughes, L.   Ballad of Gin Mary.
  Christian Country, A.
Logan, J.   Heart to Heart Talk with My Liver.
Lowell, R.   Drinker, The.
Meredith, W.   John and Anne.
Milosz, C.   Alcoholic Enters the Gates of
  Heaven, An.
Nash, O.   Reflections on Ice-breaking.
Niedecker.   Alcoholic dream.
Pound, E.   Epitaphs: "Fu I loved the high cloud
  and the hill."
Rexroth, K.   Proust's Madeleine.
Roethke.   My Papa's Waltz.
Schuyler, J.   Over the Hills.
Stock, R.   To My Inebriety.
Updike.   To Ed Sissman.
Van Duyn.   Fall.
  Recovery.
Williams, W.   Aigeltinger.
  Io Baccho!
See also **Drunkards**
Alder Trees
Carruth, H.   Once More.
Clampitt.   Alders.
Levertov.   Victors, The.
Ale
Burns, R.   Guid Ale Keeps the Heart Aboon.
  Lady Onlie.
Alexander Jannaeus, King of Judah
Cavafy.   Alexandros Iannaios, and Alexandra.
Alexander the Great, King of Macedon
Carver, R.   Wine.
Cavafy.   In the Year 200 B.C.
De la Mare.   Alexander.
Dryden, J.   Alexander's Feast; or, The Power of
  Music [*or* Musique].
Dugan, A.   How We Heard the Name.
  On Alexander and Aristotle, on a Black-on-Red
  Greek Plate.
Gunn, T.   From an Asian Tent.
Lowell, R.   Alexander.
  Death of Alexander.
Riley, J.   Lawyer and Child.
Rukeyser, M.   Speaking Tree, The.
Wilbur, R.   Worlds.
Alexandria, Egypt
Borges.   Alexandria, A.D. 641.
Cavafy.   31 B.C. in Alexandria.
  Alexandrian Kings.
  Exiles.
  Glory of the Ptolemies, The.
Alfonso X, King of Castile and León
Emerson, R.   Alphonso of Castile.
Algeria
Dugan, A.   Against France: On the Algerian
  Pleasures of Entity.
Ali, Muhammad
Komunyakaa.   Once the Dream Begins.
Alice in Wonderland
Clampitt.   Alice.
Graves, R.   Alice.
Tate, A.   Last Days of Alice.
Wilbur, R.   Fourth of July, The.
Alienation
Amichai [*or* Amikhai].   Someplace.
Angelou.   Chicken-Licken.
  Detached, The.
  Faces.
Arnold, M.   Buried Life, The.
Ashbery, J.   Errors.
  Wet Casements.
Berryman.   Traveller, The.
Blok.   Hard to Be Moving among Them.
Bly, R.   Snowbanks North of the House.
  Winter Poem.
Borges.   Stranger, The.
Brontë, E.   Deep, deep down in the silent grave.

It is not pride, it is not shame.
Lonely at her window sitting.
Weaned from life and torn away.
Woods, you need not frown on me.
Brooks, G.   Bronzeville Man with a Belt in the Back.
Carver, R.   Energy.
Celan.   Mute autumn smells. The.
Shibboleth.
Clare, J.   I Am.
Codrescu.   *Petite Histoire* of Red Fascism, A.
Creeley.   Form of Women, A.
Moon, The.
Dickey, W.   Here There Are Three of Us Driving South in This Expensive Car.
Dickinson, E.   Much Madness is divinest Sense.
Duncan, R.   Passage Over Water.
Eliot, T. S.   Do I know how I feel? Do I know what I think?
Gerontion.
Journey of the Magi.
Love Song of J. Alfred Prufrock, The.
Love Song of J. Alfred Prufrock, The (Prufrock among the Women).
Love Song of J. Alfred Prufrock, Resumed, The.
Portrait of a Lady.
Prufrock's Pervigilium.
Rhapsody on a Windy Night.
Emerson, R.   Blight.
Intellect.
Enzensberger, H.   Language of the Country.
Ferlinghetti, L.   Director of Alienation.
Frost, R.   In Neglect.
Gallagher, T.   Boat Ride.
Ginsberg, A.   America.
Paterson.
Hacker, M.   Sisterhood.
Hall, D.   Exile.
Umbrella, The.
Hayden, R.   Soledad.
Heaney, S.   Guttural Muse, The.
Herrick.   Once Seen, and No More.
Hopkins, G.   To Seem the Stranger.
Housman.   There pass the careless people.
Komunyakaa.   Crack.
Larkin, P.   Importance of Elsewhere, The.
Laughlin, J.   Stranger in the House, The.
Levertov.   Wanderer, A.
Logue, C.   Song of the Outsider, The.
Lorde.   Dozens, The.
Meredith, G.   London by Lamplight.
Merton.   Cables to the Ace.
Merwin.   Acclimatization.
Fields, The.
Mistral, G.   Foreign Woman, The.
Montale.   Line of dancing children on the shore, The.
Nash, O.   Very Unclubbable Man, The.
Neruda.   Century Dying, A.
Oppen.   Return.
Pasolini.   Reality.
Pessoa.   Lydia, we know nothing. We are strangers.
Pinsky.   Poem about People.
Pound, E.   In a Station of the Metro.
Raine, K.   Unloved, The.
Rich, A.   After Dark.
Stranger, The.
Robinson, E.   Mr Flood's Party.
Rukeyser, M.   Effort at Speech between Two People.
Sandburg, C.   Useless Words.
Shapiro, K.   My Grandmother.
Retirement.
Solipsism.
Travelogue for Exiles.
Washington Cathedral.
Stafford, W.   Not in the Headlines.
Stevens, W.   Anglais Mort à Florence.
Tate, J.   Contagion.
Tomlinson, C.   Aqueduct.
Mr. Brodsky.
Winter.
Williams, C. K.   Park, The.
Shame.
Solid, The.

Williams, M.   Divorce.
I Go Out of the House for the First Time.
Sissy, The.
Well-Ordered Life, The.
Williams, W.   Pigheaded Poet.
Wordsworth, W.   World is too much with us; late and soon, The.
Wyatt, S.   Fortune, what aileth thee.
I must go walk the woods so wild.
Zaturenska.   Castaways, The.
Virgin, the Doe, and the Leper, The.
Zukofsky, L.   "Further than."

Aliens
Ai.   Jimmy Hoffa's Odyssey.
Dubie.   Accident.
Stafford, W.   Tuned in Late One Night.
Williams, M.   He Glimpses a Nobler Vision.
It Came to Pass on a Planet Third from a Minor Sun in a Solar System Out on the Edge of One of the Galaxies.
Longing, The.
Wilner, E.   Love of What Is Not, The.

All Souls' Day
Hardy, T.   I Rose Up as My Custom Is.
Lawrence, D. H.   All Soul's Day.
Rukeyser, M.   All Souls.

All Souls' Night
Glück, L.   All Hallows.

Alligators
Dickey, W.   Alligators and Paris and North America.
Hall, D.   Alligator Bride, The.
Nash, O.   Purist, The.
Oliver, M.   Alligator Poem.
See also **Crocodiles**

Alliteration
Berrigan, T.   Epithalamion: "Pussy put her paw into the pail of paint."

Almanacs
Bishop, E.   Sestina: "September rain falls on the house."

Almond Trees and Almonds
Herrick.   Upon His Kinswoman Mistresse Bridget Herrick.
Upon Sibilla.
Lawrence, D. H.   Bare Almond-Trees.
Flowers.
Letter from Town: The Almond-Tree.

Alpaca
Mistral, G.   Alpaca, The.

Alphabet
Beckett, S.   Home Olga.
Burns, R.   Tale, A.
Ciardi, J.   B is for BOMBERS, our national pride.
Coleridge, S.   Indifference of the Heavens, The.
Dubie.   After Sky X.
Graves, R.   H.
Heaney, S.   Alphabets.
Riley, J.   Billy's Alphabetical Animal Show.
Rimbaud, A.   Vowels.
Rossetti, C.   Alphabet, An.
Shapiro, K.   Alphabet, The.
Whalen, P.   M.

Alphabet Poems
Nemerov.   Primer of the Daily Round, A.

Alpheus
Levertov.   Well, The.
Shelley, P.   Arethusa.

Alps
Byron, G.   Manfred.
Ciardi, J.   L'Inglese.
Coleridge, S.   Hymn before Sunrise, in the Vale of Chamouni.
Dickinson, E.   Our lives are Swiss.
Hardy, T.   Schreckhorn, The.
Laughlin, J.   Ein Kitzbuehler Tag (1947).
Meredith, G.   By the Rosanna.
Oppen.   Alpine.
Stevens, W.   Botanist on Alp (No. 1).
Botanist on Alp (No. 2).
Wordsworth, W.   Advance—come forth from the Tyrolean ground.
Descriptive Sketches Taken During a Pedestrian Tour among the Alps.

Alsace, France
Wilbur, R.   First Snow in Alsace.
Altars
Ginsberg, A.   Voice of Rock, The.
Heaney, S.   Grotus and Coventina.
Westering.
Herbert, G.   Altar, The.
Rilke.   Holy Ghost.
Robinson, E.   Altar, The.
Tomlinson, C.   In Michoacán.
Very.   Altar, The.
Zaturenska.   Virgin with a Lamp.
Altgeld, John Peter
Lindsay, N.   Bryan, Bryan, Bryan, Bryan.
Eagle That Is Forgotten, The.
Sandburg, C.   Altgeld.
Altolaguirre, Manuel
Spender, S.   To Manuel Altolaguirre.
Alumni
Eberhart, R.   I Went to See Irving Babbitt.
Merton.   Western Fellow Students Salute with Calypso Anthems the Movie Career of Robert Lax.
Nemerov.   Thirtieth Anniversary Report of the Class of '41.
Whittier.   Reunion, The.
Amaryllis (mythology)
Campion, T.   I Care Not for These Ladies.
Amazon Rain Forest
Ammons.   Jungle Knot.
Levertov.   Marta (Brazil, 1928).
Williams, M.   Green Mansions.
Amazons
Clifton, L.   Amazons.
Herbert, Z.   Achilles. Penthesilea.
Warren, R.   Fatal Interview: Penthesilea and Achilles.
Amber
Cavafy.   Tears of the Sisters of Phaeton, The.
Ambition
Amichai [or Amikhai].   I am like a leaf that knows its limits.
Ammons.   Play.
Atwood.   Eating Fire.
Bly, R.   Watering the Horse.
Borges.   Boast of Quietness.
My Whole Life.
Browning, E.   Night and the Merry Man.
Bukowski.   Talking to My Mailbox..
Burns, R.   On J-hn M-r-ne, Laird of L-gg-n.
Campion, T.   Ad Rob. Caraeum Equitem Auratum Nobilissimum.
In Cambrum.
Carruth, H.   Rummage.
Cavafy.   They Might Have Bothered.
Ciardi, J.   Crate of Sterling Loving Cups, A.
Darling.
Done for the Doing.
Freshman Sonnet: Success.
One Easter Not on the Calendar I Woke.
Clampitt.   Cormorant in Its Element, The.
Creeley.   Ambition.
Cunningham, J.   For My Contemporaries.
Davie, D.   Vying.
De la Mare.   Miracle, The.
Drummond de Andrade.   Irritated Office, The.
Dugan, A.   February Twelfth Birthday Statement.
Portrait.
Enzensberger, H.   Visiting Ingres.
Gurney, I.   I Would Not Rest.
Old Dreams.
Hafiz [or Hafez].   On prince or bride no diamond stone.
HaNagid.   On Fleeing His City.
Soar, Don't Settle.
Herrick.   Ambition.
Hughes, T.   Other, The.
Jackson, L.   Plighted to Shame.
Jeffers, R.   Margrave.
Such Counsels You Gave to Me.
What's the best life for a man?
Johnson, S.   Vanity of Human Wishes, The; The Tenth Satire of Juvenal Imitated.
Longfellow, H.   Mezzo Cammin.

Lux.   Man Inside the Chipmunk Suit, The.
Major, C.   Life Story, A.
Meredith, G.   Ambition.
 Internal Harmony.
Merton.   Strife between the Poet and Ambition,
 The.
Nash, O.   Strange Case of the Irksome Prude,
 The.
 There'll Always Be a War between the Sexes,
 or, A Woman Can Be Sometimes Pleased, but
 Never Satisfied.
Parker, D.   Ballade of Understandable
 Ambitions.
 Fulfillment.
 Philosophy.
 Red Dress, The.
Pessoa.   Story of Salomon Waste, The.
Pope, A.   Macer: A Character.
Rexroth, K.   Horny Dilemma.
 New Objectives, New Cadres.
 Untitled: "I am fifty-two years old."
Riley, J.   Singer, The.
Rilke.   To Speak a Flower.
Rukeyser, M.   Citation for Horace Gregory.
 Hero Speech.
 Metaphor to Action.
 What do you know of America? I asked a little
 Russian schoolgirl.
Rumi.   No Flag.
Sexton.   Ambition Bird, The.
Spender, S.   Public Son of a Public Man, The.
Very.   Ambitione inani pectus caret.
Whalen, P.   Homage to St. Patrick, García
 Lorca, & the Itinerant Grocer.
 How to Be Successful & Happy Without
 Anybody Else Finding Out About It.
Wilde, O.   Sen Artysty; or, The Artist's Dream.
Williams, C. K.   Refuge, Serpent-Riders.
Wordsworth, W.   To Enterprise.
Wyatt, S.   Against the rock I climb, both high
 and hard.
 Speak thou and speed, where will or power
 ought [or aught] help'th.

Ambulances
Larkin, P.   Ambulances.
Nash, O.   Hi-Ho the Ambulance-O.

America
Ai.   Blue Suede Shoes.
 More.
Angelou.   America.
 Request.
Ashbery, J.   Pyrography.
Atwood.   Two-Headed Poems.
Berrigan, T.   Lady.
Berry, W.   We Who Prayed and Wept.
Berryman.   American Lights, Seen from Off
 Abroad.
 Have a Genuine American Horror-&-Mist on
 the Rocks.
 Lightning, The.
Bierce.   Crime of 1903, The.
 Invocation.
 Rational Anthem, A.
Blake, W.   Visions of the Daughters of Albion.
Brodsky, J.   Exeter Revisited.
 Lullaby of Cape Cod.
Burns, R.   Slave's Lament, The.
Carruth, H.   Song: The Famous Vision of
 America.
Ciardi, J.   Box Comes Home, A.
 Letter to Mother.
Clampitt.   Local Genius, The.
 Prairie, The.
Clifton, L.   Grief.
Codrescu.   Ethnic Jammies.
 School Daze.
Coleridge, S.   On the Prospect of Establishing a
 Pantisocracy in America.
Corbett, W.   Painters, The.
Creeley.   America.
Cummings, E. E.   He does not have to feel
 because he thinks.
 I Sing of Olaf Glad and Big.
 Next to of Course God America I.
 O pr / gress verily thou art m.
 O to be in finland.

Opening of the chambers close.
Poem, or Beauty Hurts Mr. Vinal.
Remarked Robinson Jefferson.
Season 'tis,my lovely lambs, The.
Woman / of bronze / unhappy, A.
"Dario."   To Roosevelt.
Davie, D.   Agave in the West.
 From the New World.
 Iowa.
 Letter to Curtis Bradford, A.
 Pastor Errante.
 T. S. Eliot (1928).
Dickey, J.   Coming Back to America.
Dickinson, E.   Sweet Land of Liberty.
 Union.
Donne.   Cales and Guiana.
Dugan, A.   Love and Money.
 Significance of Corn in American History, The.
Eberhart, R.   Inchiquin Lake, Penobscot Bay.
 Yonder.
Emerson, R.   Ode Sung in the Town Hall.
 Poem, Spoken Before the ΦBK Society, August,
 1834.
Ferlinghetti, L.   Autobiography.
 Poet's eye obscenely seeing, The.
 Sailing thru the straits of Demos.
Frost, R.   America Is Hard to See.
 Gift Outright, The.
 Serious Step Taken Lightly, A.
Ginsberg, A.   After Dead Souls.
 America.
 And ninety-nine soldiers piled on the train at
 Amarillo.
 Autumn again, you wouldn't know in the city.
 Autumn Gold: New England Fall.
 Bayonne Turnpike to Tuscarora.
 Beginning of a Long Poem of These States.
 Beginning of a Poem of These States.
 Crazy Spiritual, A.
 Crossing Nation.
 Ecologue.
 Either we blow ourselves up now and die, like
 the old tribe of man, arguing among neutrons.
 Funky barn, black hills approaching Fulton.
 Have You Seen This Movie?
 Hiway Poesy: L.A.–Albuquerque–Texas–
 Witchita.
 In the Baggage Room at Greyhound.
 Independence Day.
 Iron Horse.
 Kansas City to Saint Louis.
 Kansas! Kansas! Shuddering at last!
 Over Kansas.
 Overpopulation, overpopulation / Give me 3
 acres of land.
 Poem on America, A.
 Reflections in Sleepy Eye.
 Stotras to Kali Destroyer of Illusions.
 Supermarket in California, A.
 Television Was a Baby Crawling toward That
 Deathchamber.
 These States: into L.A.
 Who Runs America?
 Who Will Take Over the Universe?
 Wichita Vortex Sutra.
 Wings Lifted over the Black Pit.
Hall, D.   Grave the Well, The.
Hardy, T.   On an Invitation to the United States.
Hayden, R.   [American Journal].
Hill, G.   Locust Songs.
Howe, S.   Chanting at the Crystal Sea.
 Secret History of the Dividing Line.
Hughes, L.   America.
 American Heartbreak.
 Columbia.
 Freedom's Plow.
 I, Too.
 Let America Be America Again.
 One More "S" in the U.S.A.
 Poem: "All the tom-toms of the jungles beat in
 my blood."
 We're All in the Telephone Book.
Ignatow, D.   Get the Gasworks.
Jarrell, R.   Jamestown.
 To the New World.
Jeffers, R.   Eagle Valor, Chicken Mind.

Historical Choice.
 Invasion.
 July Fourth by the Ocean.
 Shine, Empire.
 Shine, Perishing Republic.
 Shine, Republic.
 Teheran.
Kipling, R.   American, An.
 Choice, The.
 Deep-Sea Cables, The.
 Question, The.
 White Man's Burden, The.
Kizer, C.   Anniversaries: Claremont Avenue,
 from 1945.
 Ashes, The.
Larkin, P.   Faith Healing.
Laughlin, J.   God Bless America!
 Judges of the Secret Court, The.
Lawrence, D. H.   American Eagle, The.
 Evening Land, The.
 O! Americans.
Levertov.   Continent.
 Fragrance of Life, Odor of Death.
 In Thai Binh (Peace) Province.
 Weeping Woman.
Levine, P.   One for the Rose.
 Silent in America.
 Sources.
Lindsay, N.   Bryan, Bryan, Bryan, Bryan.
 Gospel of Beauty, A.
Lorde.   Vietnam Addenda.
Lux.   Backyard Swingset.
 Triptych, Middle Panel Burning.
MacLeish.   America Was Promises.
 American Letter.
 At the Lincoln Memorial.
 Background with Revolutionaries.
 Ballad of the Corn-Cob and the Lie, The.
 Colloquy for the States.
 Conversation in a Belfry.
 Empire Builders.
 Invocation to the Social Muse.
 Men.
 Oil Painting of the Artist as the Artist.
Major, C.   Looking at Images Reflected in the
 Showcase Plate Glass.
McGrath, T.   Topography of History, The.
 Two Songs from "The Hunted Revolutionaries."
Melville, H.   America.
Meredith, G.   Lines to a Friend Visiting
 America.
Meredith, W.   Nixon's the One.
Merton.   1. Now you are all here you might as
 well know this is America we do what we like.
 Christopher Columbus.
 Letter to America, A.
Milosz, C.   America.
Moore, M.   Love in America.
Muldoon, P.   Immram.
 Madoc: A Mystery.
Nash, O.   Columbus.
 Look What You Did, Christopher!
Nemerov.   Boy with Book of Knowledge.
 One Forever Alien.
O'Hara, F.   Ave Maria.
 Hatred.
 Mozart Chemisier.
Olson, C.   17th century men / who founded this
 land.
 Abt the dead he sd.
 Across Space and Time.
 Ballad for Americans.
 Being Altogether Literal, & Specific, and
 Seeking at the Same Time to be Successfully
 Explicit.
 "Enthusiasm", An.
 Hustings, The.
 Nerves Are Staves, and When the Tears Come
 There Is Voice, The.
 Of the United States.
 Rufus Woodpecker visited the President.
Paley, G.   Leaflet.
Parker, D.   Poem in the American Manner.
Patchen.   Joe Hill Listens to the Praying.
 Lenada.
 Letter to Those Who Are About to Die.

O fiery river / Flow out over the land.
When in the Course of Human Events.
Piercy.   Peaceable Kingdom, The.
Visiting a Dead Man on a Summer Day.
Pinsky.   Explanation of America, An.
Prunty.   To be Sung on the Fourth of July.
Rexroth, K.   American Century, The.
Rich, A.   Open-Air Museum.
Sources.
Riley, J.   America's Thanksgiving.
Child's Home—Long Ago, A.
Roethke.   Night Journey.
Rukeyser, M.   Blood is Justified, The.
Book of the Dead, The.
Campaign.
Juanita Tinsley.
Movie.
Road, The.
This House, This Country.
West Virginia.
What do you know of America? I asked a little
Russian schoolgirl.
Sandburg, C.   And So Today.
Ever a Seeker.
Good Morning, America.
Out of White Lips.
Smoke and Steel.
Threes.
Schuyler, J.   Industrial Archaeology.
Sexton.   Firebombers, The.
Shout, The.
Shapiro, K.   And Now, the Weather..
I Am an Atheist Who Says His Prayers.
Manhole Covers.
Statue of Liberty.
Snyder, G.   Dullness in February: Japan.
For the West.
I Went Into the Maverick Bar.
Two Immortals.
What Happened Here Before.
Stafford, W.   Final Exam: American
Renaissance.
Stevens, W.   Anecdote of the Jar.
Stock, R.   National Anthem; Imitation of Carlos
Drummond de Andrade's "Hino Nacional."
Stockton, A.   On the Celebration of the Birth of
the Dauphin of France.
Sze.   Listening to a Broken Radio.
Tate, A.   Historical Epitaphs.
Ode to the Confederate Dead.
Tomlinson, C.   Word in Edgeways, A.
Updike.   Air Show.
Fargo.
Minority Report.
Very.   Finishing the Work.
"It is vain to say, that this is the country of the
'white man.' It is the country of man."
Charles Sumner.
Light of Freedom Necessary to National
Progress, The.
National Unity ("Nobler unity, than that which
came, A").
State Rights.
What of Our Country?
Walcott.   Blues.
Elegy: "Our hammock swung between
Americas."
Glory Trumpeter, The.
Gulf, The.
Upstate.
Warren, R.   Bicentennial.
Whalen, P.   America!
Wheatley, P.   America.
Whitman, W.   Ages and Ages Returning at
Intervals.
America.
Apostroph.
As Consequent, Etc.
Bravo, Paris Exposition!
By Blue Ontario's Shore.
Carol Closing Sixty-Nine.
Columbian's Song, The.
Election Day, November, 1884.
For You O Democracy.
From Paumanok Starting I Fly like a Bird.
Full of Life Now.

House of Friends, The.
I Hear America Singing.
O Magnet-South.
Ode: "O, God of Columbia! O, Shield of the
Free!"
On Journeys through the States.
One Song, America, Before I Go.
Or, from That Sea of Time.
Orange Buds by Mail from Florida.
Our Old Feuillage.
Passage to India.
Poem of Remembrances for a Girl or a Boy of
These States.
Prairie-Grass Dividing, The.
Prairie States, The.
Respondez!
Return of the Heroes, The.
Small the Theme of My Chant.
Song of Myself.
Song of the Banner at Daybreak.
Starting from Paumanok.
States!
Thou Mother with Thy Equal Brood.
Thou Orb Aloft Full-Dazzling.
Thoughts.
To-day and Thee.
To Foreign Lands.
To the East and to the West.
To the Leaven'd Soil They Trod
To the States, To Identify the 16th, 17th, or 18th
Presidentiad.
Twilight Song, A.
United States to Old World Critics, The.
Virginia—the West.
Wandering at Morn.
Washington's Monument, February, 1885.
With All Thy Gifts.
With Antecedents.
Wound-Dresser, The.
Years of the Modern.
Yonnondio.
Whittier.   On Receiving an Eagle's Quill from
Lake Superior.
Our Country.
Vow of Washington, The.
Wilbur, R.   On Freedom's Ground.
Williams, C. K.   Admiral Fan, The.
In the Heart of the Beast.
Williams, M.   Architecture of the American
Mind.
Of History and Hope.
Williams, W.   Song: "Russia! Russia! you might
say."
To Elsie.
Wright, C.   Lonesome Pine Special.
Wright, J.   American Twilights, 1957.
Eclogue at Nash's Grove.
Frontier, The.
In Memory of a Spanish Poet.
Stages on a Journey Westward.
Zagajewski.   Europe Goes to Sleep.
Houston, 6 P.M.
Zukofsky, L.   Jaunt.
See also **United States**

American Indians
See **Native Americans**

**American Military Government in Germany
(post–WW II)**
Laughlin, J.   Hard to Translate.
Logistics.
Song of the GIs & the MGs.
Why Not?

American Revolution
Burns, R.   Fragment, A: "When *Guilford* good
our Pilot stood."
Cowper, W.   Modern Patriot, The.
Dunbar, P.   Black Samson of Brandywine.
Emerson, R.   Concord Hymn.
Song: "Shout for those whose course is done."
Kipling, R.   American Rebellion, The.
MacNeice.   Jehu.
Niedecker.   Wild and wavy event, The.
Olson, C.   King's Mountain.
To Empty the Mind.
Stockton, A.   Addressed to General Washington,
in the Year 1777, after the Battles of Trenton

and Princeton.
Lucinda and Aminta, a Pastoral, on the Capture
of Lord Cornwallis and the British Army, by
General Washington.
On Hearing of the News of the Capture of Lord
Cornwallis and the British Army, by Gen.
Washington.
On Hearing that General Warren Was Killed on
Bunker-Hill, on the 17th of June 1775.
On the Death of General Montgomery.
On the Return of Col Laurens from His
Confinement in the Tower of London.
Peace, a Pastoral Dialogue.—Part the Second.
Vision, The.
Thoreau.   Ah, 'tis in vain the peaceful din.
Wheatley, P.   Voice of Freedom, The.
Whitman, W.   Centenarian's Story, The.
Wallabout Martyrs, The.
Whittier.   Lexington.
Yorktown.
Wilbur, R.   On Freedom's Ground.
Zaturenska.   Garden at Cliveden, The.

Americans
Auden.   On the Circuit.
Chesterton.   Ballad of Abbreviations, A.
Crane, H.   America's Plutonic Ecstasies.
Pillar and the Post, The.
Creeley.   Korean slang.
Davie, D.   Letter to Curtis Bradford, A.
Dugan, A.   Qualifications of Survivors.
Speech for Auden.
Eberhart, R.   Statue of Liberty.
Emerson, R.   Ancient drop of feudal blood, An.
At Sea, September 1833.
Ferlinghetti, L.   Baseball Canto.
Buddha in the Woodpile, A.
Home Home Home.
Two Scavengers in a Truck, Two Beautiful
People in a Mercedes.
Frost, R.   Gift Outright, The.
Gurney, I.   Portraits.
Hughes, L.   Just an Ordinary Guy.
Madam's Calling Cards.
Ignatow, D.   Notes for a Lecture.
Jeffers, R.   Ave Caesar.
July Fourth by the Ocean.
Kipling, R.   American, An.
American Rebellion, The.
Choice, The.
Koch, K.   You Were Wearing.
Laughlin, J.   Kind-, The.
Lawrence, D. H.   English Are So Nice!, The.
O! Americans.
McHugh, H.   Language Lesson 1976.
Nash, O.   Ms. Found under a Serviette in a
Lovely Home.
Scram, Lion!
Olson, C.   17th century men / who founded this
land.
Americans, The.
I, Mencius, Pupil of the Master.
Oppen.   Generation of Drivers.
Myself I Sing.
Parker, D.   Song of Americans Resident in
France.
Shapiro, K.   Boy-Man.
Shelley, P.   To the Republicans of North
America.
Stafford, W.   Being an American.
Stock, R.   National Anthem; Imitation of Carlos
Drummond de Andrade's "Hino Nacional."
Very.   Indian's Retort, The.
Warren, R.   Bicentennial.
Weiss, T.   Things of the Past.
Whalen, P.   Bleakness, Farewell.
Whitman, W.   For You O Democracy.
I Hear America Singing.
Mediums.
Nay, Tell Me Not To-day the Publish'd Shame.
Our Old Feuillage.
Prairie-Grass Dividing, The.
Race of Veterans.
Starting from Paumanok.
Williams, W.   Impromptu: The Suckers.
Poem: "Daniel Boone, the father of Kentucky."
Question and Answer.

Wilner, E.　Amelia.
　American Painting, with Rain.

Amherst, Massachusetts
Clampitt.　Amherst.
Wilbur, R.　Altitudes.

Amish, The
Updike.　Amish, The.

Amnesia
Carver, R.　Alcohol.
Plath.　Amnesiac.
Ramanujan.　Lapse of Memory, A.
　No Amnesiac King.
Tranströmer.　Name, The.

Amputees
Ai.　Back in the World.
Ammons.　Run-Through, The.
Ciardi, J.　Joe with a Wooden Leg.
Herrick.　Upon the Losse of His Finger.
Jarrell, R.　Terms.
Komunyakaa.　John Says.
　Phantom Limbs.
MacDiarmid, H.　In the Children's Hospital.
Owen, W.　Disabled.
Shapiro, K.　Leg, The.

Amsterdam, Netherlands
Broumas, O.　Home Movies.
Ferlinghetti, L.　Two Amsterdams.
Merrill, J.　Amsterdam.
Schuyler, J.　Sometimes.
Zagajewski.　Airport in Amsterdam.

Amusement Parks
Dugan, A.　Scene (1946–7).
Moore, M.　Old Amusement Park.
Pinsky.　Ralegh's Prizes.
Prunty.　Ferris Wheel, The.

Anacreon
Goethe.　Anacreon's Grave.

Analysis
Creeley.　Pedigree, The.
MacNeice.　Cromlech, The.
Zukofsky, L.　"Mantis," An Interpretation.

Anarchism and Anarchists
Bukowski.　This.
Cullen, C.　For an Anarchist.
Frost, R.　Case for Jefferson, A.
Merrill, J.　18 West 11th Street.
Rexroth, K.　Portrait of the Author as a Young
　Anarchist.
Rimbaud, A.　What do they mean to us, my
　heart, the sheets of blood.
Shelley, P.　Mask [or Masque] of Anarchy, The.

Ancestry and Ancestors
Amichai [or Amikhai].　All the Generations
　before Me.
　Family.
　God's Hand in the World.
　I Feel Just Fine in My Pants.
　Jews in the Land of Israel.
　Luxury.
　Luxury, A.
　My Mother Comes From the Days.
　Since Then.
Angelou.　Family Affairs.
Atwood.　Book of Ancestors.
Berryman.　Ancestor.
Borges.　1972.
　Borges, The.
　Embarking on the Study of Anglo-Saxon
　　Grammer.
　Page to Commemorate Colonel Suárez, Victor at
　　Junín, A.
　Search, The.
　Sepulchral Inscription.
　To the Son.
　Yesterdays.
Brooks, G.　Sundays of Satin-Legs Smith, The.
Broumas, O.　Easter.
Clampitt.　Prairie, The.
Cooper, J.　How Can I Speak for Her.
Crane, S.　Once I saw mountains angry.
Creeley.　And.
Cullen, C.　Heritage.
Davie, D.　Seeing through Me.
Eberhart, R.　Statue of Liberty.
Emerson, R.　Forerunners.

Thank the gods thy governors.
Thou shalt make thy house.
Why honor the new men.
Fenton, J.　Chosun.
Graves, R.　Ancestors.
　Flowering Aloe, The.
　Front Door Soliloquy.
　Song: The Queen of Time.
Hardy, T.　Pedigree, The.
　She, I, and They.
　Sine Prole.
Hayden, R.　Beginnings.
Heaney, S.　Digging.
　Kinship.
Herrick.　Upon Clunn.
Howe, S.　Chanting at the Crystal Sea.
　Hinge Picture.
Hughes, T.　Lineage.
　Shibboleth.
Jackson, L.　Mortal.
　That Ancient Line.
Jeffers, R.　Patronymic.
Kinsella, T.　Ancestor.
Kipling, R.　Heritage, The.
Komunyakaa.　Genealogy.
　Little Man around the House.
　Mismatched Shoes.
　Salt.
Kumin, M.　On Being Asked to Write a Poem
　for the Centenary of the Civil War.
Laughlin, J.　Family Portrait, The.
　Take Off Your Socks!!
Levertov.　Illustrious Ancestors.
MacDiarmid, H.　Direadh III.
Merwin.　Forbears, The.
　Sire.
　Track, The.
　Unknown Forebear.
　Wood, A.
Olson, C.　Chain of memory is resurrection I am
　a vain man, The.
　So the Norse / were neurotic.
　To Gerhardt, There, among Europe's Things of
　　Which He Has Written Us in His "Brief an
　　Creely und Olson."
　Winds / which blew my daughter, The.
Patchen.　We Leave You Pleasure.
Prunty.　Winter's Tale, A.
Ralegh, S.　Yet though thou fetch thy pedegree
　so farre.
Ramanujan.　Hindoo, The: He Doesn't Hurt a
　Fly or a Spider Either.
Ritsos.　Graves of Our Ancestors, The.
Rukeyser, M.　Bubble of Air.
　Bunk Johnson Blowing.
　For My Son.
Sandburg, C.　Turn of the Wheel.
Shapiro, K.　Messias.
　Nigger.
Simic.　Closed House.
Stafford, W.　People Who Went By in Winter.
Stock, R.　Drunkenness.
Szymborska, W.　Our Ancestors' Short Lives.
Tate, A.　Ancestors, The.
　Emblems.
Tate, J.　My Great Great Etc. Uncle Patrick
　Henry.
　Tell Them Was Here.
Unknown.　On Pedigree.
Updike.　Toothache Man.
Walker, A.　In These Dissenting Times.
Warren, R.　Genealogy.
Weiss, T.　Things of the Past.
Williams, M.　After a Brubeck Concert.
Wordsworth, W.　Song at the Feast of Brougham
　Castle upon the Restoration of Lord Clifford,
　the Shepherd, to the Estates and Honours of
　His Ancestors.
Wright, C.　Arkansas Traveller.
Yeats.　Dedication to a Book of Stories Selected
　from the Irish Novelists.
　Three Marching Songs.

Anchors
Herrick.　End of His Work, The.
　His Hope or Sheet-Anchor.
Kipling, R.　Anchor Song.

Andalusia, Spain
García Lorca.　Ballad of Black Pain.
　Ballad of the Marked Man.
　Ballad of the Moon Moon.
　Ballad of the Spanish Civil Guard.
　Ballad of the Three Rivers.
　Dead from Love.
　Death of Little Tony Camborio, The.
　Dialogue of Amargo.
　Elegy: "Like a censer filled with desire."
　Feud, The.
　Flamenco Vignettes.
　Graphic of the Petenera.
　Gypsy Nun, The.
　Martyrdom of St. Eulalia.
　Poem of the Gypsy *Siguiriya.*
　Poem of the *Soleá.*
　Preciosa and the Wind.
　Sleepwalking Ballad.
　St. Gabriel.
　St. Michael.
　St. Raphael.
　Summer Madrigal.
　Taking of Little Tony Camborio on the Seville
　　Highway, The.
　Three Cities.
　Unfaithful Wife, The.

Andersen, Hans Christian
Sandburg, C.　Love Letter to Hans Christian
　Andersen.
Stevens, W.　Sonatina to Hans Christian.
Zaturenska.　Quiet Countries: The World of
　Hans Christian Andersen.

Anderson, Sherwood
Carver, R.　Harley's Swans.

Andrea del Sarto
See **Sarto, Andrea del**

Andromeda
Hopkins, G.　Andromeda.
Rexroth, K.　Andromeda Chained to Her Rock
　the Great Nebula in Her Heart.

Anemones
Lawrence, D. H.　Purple Anemones.
MacLeish.　Hearts' and Flowers'.
Very.　Columbines and Anemones.

Anesthesia
Dugan, A.　On Being Asked How Do You Feel
　after an Operation with Inadequate Anesthesia.
　This Is How I Feel.

Angels
Amichai [or Amikhai].　Jacob and the Angel.
Ammons.　Crippled Angel, A.
Baudelaire.　Rebel, The.
Bierce.　Finis Æternitatis.
Brodsky, J.　Angel.
Broumas, O.　Landscape with Angels.
Browning, E.　Heaven and Earth.
　Seraphim, The.
Browning, R.　Guardian-Angel, The.
Burns, R.　To an Artist.
Cavafy.　Indian Image.
Ciardi, J.　Dialogue in the Shade, A.
　Finally that Blue Receding Sphere.
　Glory, The.
Clampitt.　'Eighty-Nine.
Clifton, L.　Lucifer Understanding at Last.
　Report from the angel of eden.
Codrescu.　Souls Looking for Bodies.
Collins, B.　Questions about Angels.
Crane, S.　Two or three angels.
Crashaw.　Flaming Heart, The.
De la Mare.　Tom's Angel.
Dickinson, E.　Again—his voice is at the door.
　Angel begins in the morning, The.
　Angels, in the early morning.
　Cloud withdrew from the Sky, A.
　Forever honored be the Tree.
　God permits industrious Angels.
　God's Residence.
　Little East of Jordan, A.
　Many an angel, with its needle.
　What did They do since I saw Them?
Donne.　Air[e] and Angels.
Drummond de Andrade.　Song of Purification.
Dubie.　Mercy Seat, The.

Dugan, A. 1. Business Jacob, the Angel Wrestler.
Dunbar, P. Jack Frost at Bedtime.
Eberhart, R. Angels, The.
Incomparable Light, The.
Portrait of Rilke.
Vision.
Emerson, R. Around the man who seeks a noble end.
Bended to fops who bent to him.
Discontented Poet: A Masque, The.
Dull uncertain brain, A.
He whom God had thus preferred.
Shall the Muse sing for thousands & not sing.
Graves, R. Birth of Angels.
Gardener.
True Joy.
HaNagid. Day Of Distress, A.
Herrick. Angells.
Upon Teares.
Hopkins, G. Shepherd's Brow, The.
Hughes, L. Angels Wings.
Jacobsen, J. Tree Angel.
Jarrell, R. Archangel's Song, The.
Kinnell. Cemetary Angels.
Kipling, R. Azrael's Count.
Legend of Mirth, The.
Komunyakaa. In the Labor Camp of Good Intentions.
Kumin, M. Address to the Angels.
Laughlin, J. After Rochester (or somebody).
Lawrence, D. H. Hymn to Nothingness.
Lucifer.
Old Archangels.
Walk Warily.
Levertov. Jacob's Ladder, The.
Vision, A.
Levi, P. Annunciation.
Levine, P. Angel Butcher.
Waking an Angel.
Lindsay, N. Our Guardian Angels and Their Children.
Lux. Floating Baby Paintings.
Mallarmé. Saint.
Maritain. Restoration of the Pictures, The.
McGrath, T. Two Songs from "The Hunted Revolutionaries."
Meredith, G. Story of Sir Arnulph, The.
Merrill, J. Angel.
Dedication: "Hans, there are moments when the whole mind."
Merton. Moslems' Angel of Death, The.
Merwin Is That What You Are.
Milosz, C. On Angels.
Mistral, G. Guardian Angel.
Montale. I free your forehead of the ice.
Magenta-colored clouds were gathering.
Nash, O. Cherub, The.
O'Hara, F. In Favor of One's Time.
Muse Considered As a Demon Lover, The.
Olson, C. Hear my prayer my father.
I met my Angel last night on Cinvat Bridge.
Orr, G. Large White Rock Called "The Sleeping Angel," A.
Patchen. Instructions for Angels.
Pinkerton, H. On Leonard Baskin's Etching Benevolent Angel.
Poe. Israfel.
Pound, E. Sandalphon.
Prunty. Cousins, Brothers, Sisters.
Raine, K. Chartres Annunciation, The.
Nocturn: "Night comes, an angel stands."
Rexroth, K. Suchness.
Rich, A. Gabriel.
This Beast, This Angel.
Riley, J. Funny Little Fellow, The.
Tommy Smith.
Rilke. Fall.
He Can Find No Rest.
Our Tears.
To Odilon-Jean Périer.
Rimbaud, A. Damned Cherub.
Ritsos. Common Miracles.
Rossetti, C. Advent.
Angels at the foot, / And Angels at the head.
Are They Not All Ministering Spirits?

Baby lies so fast asleep.
Dear Angels and dear disembodied Saints.
Divine and Human Pleading.
From House to Home.
Holy Innocents.
If stars dropped out of heaven, / And if flowers took their place.
Our life is long. Not so, wise Angels say.
This near-at-hand land breeds pain by measure.
Three little children / On the wide wide earth.
Watchers, The.
Ye Have Forgotten the Exhortation.
Sandburg, C. Isle of Patmos.
Sarton, M. Annunciation.
Fear of Angels, The.
Nativity.
Song: "No, I will never forget you and your great eyes."
Storm of Angels, A.
Schuyler, J. Head, A.
Sexton. Angels of the Love Affair.
Consorting with Angels.
Fallen Angels, The.
Locked Doors.
Smith, S. Angel Face.
Angel of Grace.
Crown of Bays, The.
Fallen, Fallen.
From the Coptic.
Galloping Cat, The.
I Rode with My Darling.
No Categories!
No More People.
Tableau de l'Inconstance des Mauvais Anges.
Violent Hand, The.
Stevens, W. Angel Surrounded by Paysans.
Stock, R. Jacob Agonistes.
Walking with Angels.
Wrestling with Angels.
Stockton, A. Meditation on the 3d Verse of the 28th Chapter of Mathew.
Swenson, M. Angels at "Unsubdued."
Szymborska, W. Slapstick.
Thomas Mann.
Tomlinson, C. Annunciation.
Trakl. De Profundis.
Whitman, W. Play-Ground, The.
Whittier. Two Angels, The.
Williams, C. K. Saint Sex.
Williams, T. Stonecutter's Angels, The.
Williams, W. Incognito.
Wordsworth, W. She was a Phantom of delight.
Wright, J. Alarm, The.
Angel, The.
Larry.
Secret Gratitude, A.
Zagajewski. Three Angels.
Zukofsky, L. Lilac.

Anger

Ammons. Making Waves.
Baudelaire. Black Bile ("When heavy, threatening skies weigh like a lid").
Berry, W. Anger against Beasts.
Berryman. Cloud and Flame.
Blake, W. Was I angry with Hayley who used me so ill.
Blue Cloud. Backward Dancer.
Broumas, O. Maenad.
Mosaic.
Browning, R. Halbert and Hob.
Bukowski. Love Is a Piece of Paper Torn to Bits.
Report Upon the Consumption of Myself, A.
Byron, G. And Dost Thou Ask the Reason of My Sadness?
Campion, T. See Where She Flies.
Carver, R. Earwigs.
Ciardi, J. Improvisation for a Southern Night.
Creeley. Anger.
Crisis, The.
Dream, The.
Friends, The.
Goodbye.
Hands, The.
Out of Sight.
Temper, The.

Visit, The.
Cunningham, J. Envoi: "Hear me, whom I betrayed."
Davie, D. Being Angry with God.
Depravity: Two Sermons.
Devil on Ice.
De la Mare. Be angry now no more!
How Blind!
Making a fire.
Dugan, A. Internal Migration: On Being on Tour.
On Being Unhappily in Love with Reason.
Eberhart, R. Hatred of the Old River.
Throwing the Apple.
Glück, L. Labor Day.
Graves, R. No Letter.
Gunn, T. At an Intersection.
"H. D." Ariadne.
Chance Meeting.
Hacker, M. 1976.
Fifteen to Eighteen.
Iva's Pantoum.
Hall, D. "Between the Clock and the Bed."
Edward's Anecdote.
Han-shan. Anger is a fire in the mind.
HaNagid. Fear Five to the Power of Five.
Herrick. Anger.
Gods Anger.
Gods Anger without Affection.
To His Angrie God.
To the Rose; a Song.
Upon Irene.
Hughes, L. Hard Daddy.
Rent-Party Shout: For a Lady Dancer.
Jackson, L. And I.
Rugged Black of Anger, The.
Keats. Lines Written on 29 May / The Anniversary of the Restoration of Charles the 2nd.
Kipling, R. Et Dona Ferentes.
Komunyakaa. Woebegone.
Kumin, M. Changing the Children.
Hundred Nights, A.
Lawrence, D. H. What Ails Thee?
Working Man, The.
Levine, P. Fist.
Fox, The.
Horse, The.
Letters for the Dead.
Logan, J. My Rebel Grandmother.
Meredith, G. Black Richard.
Merwin. Savonarola.
Nash, O. Don't Be Cross, Amanda.
There'll Always Be a War between the Sexes, or, A Woman Can Be Sometimes Pleased, but Never Satisfied.
O'Hara, F. Rant, A.
Oliver, M. Acid.
Rage.
Orr, G. My Father's Voice.
Patchen. Hangman's Great Hands, The.
Irate Songster, The.
Petrarch. Anger reduced Alexander the Great.
Piercy. Just Anger, A.
Neighbor, The.
Plath. Courage of Shutting-Up, The.
Purdah.
Rich, A. Nightbreak.
Phenomenology of Anger, The.
Riley, J. Variation, A.
Roethke. Song: "My wrath, where's the edge."
Rossetti, C. Seven vials hold Thy wrath: but what can hold.
Rukeyser, M. Gift-Poem.
Rumi. Light You Give Off, The.
Sandburg, C. Choose.
Sarton, M. Stone Walls.
Sexton. Again and Again and Again.
Assassin, The.
Bayonet.
Telephone.
Smith, S. Anger's Freeing Power.
Dear Child of God.
So Can Anger.
Spender, S. Prisoners, The.
Thomas, D. Do Not Go Gentle into That Good

Night.
Not from This Anger.
Vallejo. Anger.
Whalen, P. One of My Favorite Songs Is
  Stormy Weather.
Williams, C. K. Blame.
Reading: Early Sorrow.
Williams, W. Fond Farewell, A.
Wordsworth, W. Indignation of a High-Minded
  Spaniard 1810.
Wright, J. Revelation, The.

See also **Quarrels**

Anglo-Saxons
Borges. Embarking on the Study of Anglo-
  Saxon Grammer.
Saxon (A.D. 449), A.
To a Saxon Poet.

Angola
Hughes, L. Angola Question Mark.

Animal Migration
Carver, R. Migration.
Merwin. In a Clearing.
Rexroth, K. It Rolls On.

Animals
Atwood. Animals in That Country, The.
Cyclops.
Dreams of the Animals.
Auden. Address to the Beasts.
Our Hunting Fathers.
Berry, W. To the Unseeable Animal.
Berryman. Animal Trainer, The.
Bishop, E. Armadillo, The.
Word with You, A.
Blue Cloud. Walking thru twisted hollow
  pathways.
Bogan, L. Variation on a Sentence.
Browning, E. Island, An.
Browning, R. White Witchcraft.
Bukowski. Seahorse.
Byron, G. Wild Gazelle, The.
Carruth, H. Essay.
Cavafy. House with a Garden.
Ciardi, J. Domestic Sonnet.
G, also inevitably, is for GNU.
Sounds.
Clampitt. Good Friday.
Sea Mouse.
Slow Motion.
Clifton, L. Earth Is a Living Thing, The.
Creeley. Animal, The.
Blue Rabbit.
Herd, The.
Cullen, C. Thoughts in a Zoo.
Cummings, E. E. O the sun comes up-up-up in
  the opening.
Dickey, J. Deer among Cattle.
For the Last Wolverine.
Heaven of Animals, The.
Hedge Life.
Dickey, W. Love among the Manichees.
Dickinson, E. Little Dog that wags his tail, A.
Most important population, The.
Pretty boarders are leaving the trees, The.
Dugan, A. Letter to Eve.
Dunbar, P. Critters' Dance, De.
Eberhart, R. Illusion of Eternity, The.
Mystical Beast in the Shadows, The.
Vastness and Indifference of the World, The.
Emerson, R. On the chamber, on the stairs.
Enzensberger, H. End of Owls, The.
Gallagher, T. Cows, a Vision.
García Lorca. Poet Prays to the Virgin for Help,
  The.
Graves, R. Allie.
"H. D." Scribe.
Hacker, M. Exiles.
Hall, D. Child's Garden, A.
New Animals.
HaNagid. Market, The.
Hughes, L. Comment.
Silly Animals.
Hughes, T. Astrological Conundrums.
Bull Moses, The.
Crow Hill.
Ignatow, D. In the Woods.

Jacobsen, J. Animals, The.
First Woman.
Foreign Lands, The.
Presences.
Jeffers, R. Animals.
Hurt Hawks.
Kipling, R. Eddi's Service.
Komunyakaa. Blessing the Animals.
Dreambook Bestiary.
Kumin, M. Accolade of the Animals, The.
Catchment.
Creatures.
Feeding Time.
Presence, The.
Retrieval System, The.
Reviewing the Summer and Winter Calender of
  the Next Life.
Larkin, P. Little Lives of Earth and Form, The.
Laughlin, J. Ever So.
Failure of Communication in the Animal
  Kingdom, A.
Lawrence, D. H. Glory.
Him with His Tail in His Mouth.
Morality.
Self-Pity.
St Matthew.
Levertov. Come into Animal Presence.
Else a great Prince in prison lies.
Levine, P. Animals Are Passing from Our
  Lives.
Logan, J. Thirty-Three Ring Circus, The.
Lux. Night So Bright a Squirrel Reads, The.
MacNeice. Pet Shop.
Major, C. Darwin's Dream.
McHugh, H. Animal Song.
Just Man.
Politics.
Meredith, W. On Falling Asleep by Firelight.
Merrill, J. Channel 13.
Merwin. Visitation.
Millay, E. Animal Ball, The.
Milosz, C. To Mrs. Professor in Defense of My
  Cat's Honor and Not Only.
Moore, M. Jerboa, The.
Monkeys, The.
Pangolin, The.
Nash, O. Bulletin Has Just Come In, A.
Caribou, The.
Exit, Pursued by a Bear.
I Happen to Know.
Mr. Burgess, Meet Mr. Barmecide.
Nemerov. Tale.
Neruda. Some Beasts.
O'Hara, F. Heroic Sculpture.
Olson, C. Lower Field—Enniscorthy.
Obit.
Only the Red Fox, Only the Crow.
Oppen. Myth of the Blaze.
Pagis. Bestiary.
Patchen. Animal I wanted, The.
My Pretty Animals.
Plath. Go Get the Goodly Squab.
Wuthering Heights.
Zoo Keeper's Wife.
Ramanujan. On Not Learning from Animals.
Ransom, J. Spiel of [the] Three Mountebanks.
Rexroth, K. Bestiary, A.
Riley, J. Billy's Alphabetical Animal Show.
Guiney-Pigs.
Noon Lull, A.
Rilke. Calm of Animals, The.
Ritsos. Therapy.
Roethke. For An Amorous Lady.
Rossetti, C. 1885. St. Valentine's Day.
Hurt No Living Thing.
If a mouse could fly, / Or if a crow could swim.
Mirrors of Life and Death.
Peacock has a score of eyes, The.
What does the donkey bray about?
When the cows come home the milk is coming.
Rukeyser, M. Afterwards.
All the Little Animals.
Sandburg, C. Sky Talk.
Sarton, M. Godhead as Lynx, The.
Schuyler, J. Dog Wants His Dinner, The.
Sexton. White Snake, The.

Simic. Animal Acts.
Animals and Birds.
Smith, S. Best Beast of the Fat-Stock Show at
  Earls Court, The.
Can It Be?
I Am a Girl Who Loves to Shoot.
It Filled My Heart with Love.
Listener, The.
Mrs. Blow and her Animals.
Nature and Free Animals.
Photograph, The.
Shooting Incident, The.
Snyder, G. Berry Territory.
Dogs, Sheep, Cows, Goats.
Thoughts on Looking at a Samuel Palmer
  Etching at the Tate.
Three Deer One Coyote Running in the Snow.
Stafford, W. Roll Call.
Stock, R. Monkey's Address to Others of His
  Kind, A.
Swenson, M. Beast.
News from the Cabin.
Swift, J. Beasts' Confession to the Priest, The.
Szymborska, W. Circus Animals.
In Praise of Feeling Bad about Yourself.
Tarsier.
Thomas, D. How Shall My Animal.
Thoreau. Rabbit leaps, The.
Updike. Deities and Beasts.
High-Hearts, The.
Menagerie at Versailles in 1775, The.
Philological.
Popular Revivals 1956.
Topsfield Fair.
Van Duyn. Good Man, The.
Goodbye, A.
Kind of Music, A.
Marriage, with Beasts.
Whitman, W. Ox-Tamer, The.
World below the Brine, The.
Whittier. Red Riding-Hood.
Wilbur, R. Beasts.
Walgh-Vogel, The.
Williams, C. K. Ribbons.
Sky, Water.
Williams, T. Comforter and the Betrayer, The.
Wright, J. Brush Fire.
In Shame and Humiliation.
To the Evening Star: Central Minnesota.

See also **Death of Animals**

Animism
De la Mare. Spirit of air, The.
Strange Spirit, The.
Wanderers, The.
Rich, A. Trees, The.
Warren, R. Ah, Anima!
Wright, C. Journal of One Significant
  Landscape, A.

Ann Arbor, Michigan
Brodsky, J. Autumn evening in the modest
  square, An.

Anniversaries
Berry, W. Anniversary, An.
Burns, R. Seventh of November, The.
Dickey, W. Anniversary, The.
Donne. Anniversary [or Anniversarie], The.
Hardy, T. Looking at a Picture on an
  Anniversary.
Hopkins, G. Silver Jubilee, The.
Kinsella, T. Anniversaries.
McGrath, T. Anniversaries.
Merwin. For the Anniversary of My Death.
On the Silent Anniversary of a Reunion.
Nash, O. Anniversary, The.
Nemerov. Anniversary.
Riley, J. Golden Wedding, A.
Robinson, E. Woman and the Wife, The.
Thomas, D. On a Wedding Anniversary.

Annunciation of the Virgin
Donne. Upon the Annunciation and Passion
  Falling upon One Day. 1608.
García Lorca. St. Gabriel.
Gunn, T. Jesus and His Mother.
Levertov. Annunciation.
Levi, P. Annunciation.

Merton. Annunciation, The.
Aubade—the Annunciation.
Messenger, The.
Rossetti, C. Feast of the Annunciation.
Vigil of the Annunciation.
Tomlinson, C. Annunciation.

Antaeus
Heaney, S. Antaeus.
Hercules and Antaeus.
Owen, W. Antaeus: A Fragment.
Stock, R. Antaeus.
Wilner, E. Recovery.

Antarctica
Kumin, M. In Warm Rooms, Before a Blue
Light.
Mahon. Antarctica.
McHugh, H. Preferences.

Anteaters
Moore, M. Pangolin, The.

Antelopes
Kumin, M. Catchment.
Wright, J. Spring Images.
See also **Elands**

Anthropology and Anthropologists
Davie, D. Thyestes.
Dugan, A. In Memoriam. Unfinished. For
Robert Barlow. 1930.
Jacobsen, J. Pitch Lake.
Mahon. Stone Age Figure Far Below, A.
Williams, M. Tearing Down the Hotel.

Anti-Semitism
Ammons. In Strasbourg in 1349.
Ignatow, D. Harold.
Kumin, M. In the Absence of Bliss.

Anticipation
Ammons. Tooling Up.
Ashbery, J. At North Farm.
Berryman. Night and the City.
Browning, R. In Three Days.
Burns, R. Carl an the King Come.
Extempore Reply to an Invitation.
Song, Composed in August.
Campion, T. Come away, arm'd with loves
delights.
Coleridge, S. Ballad of the Dark Ladié, The.
Blossoming of the Solitary Date-Tree, The.
Crane, H. Persuasion, A.
Creeley. Waiting ("Were you counting the
days").
Dickinson, E. Consummation is the hurry of
fools.
Presentiment—is that long Shadow—on the
lawn.
Dugan, A. Untitled Poem: "I'm waiting for you,
but not purely."
Dunbar, P. Expectation.
Waiting.
Ferlinghetti, L. Heap of Broken Images, A.
Graves, R. Expect Nothing.
No Letter.
Not to Sleep.
Gurney, I. First Poem.
"H. D." At Ithaca.
Hardy, T. On the Way.
Riddle, The.
Timing Her.
Hayden, R. Night-Blooming Cereus, The.
Heaney, S. From the Canton of Expectation.
Jacobsen, J. Coming, The.
Koch, K. Bricks, The.
Larkin, P. Next, Please.
Lawrence, D. H. Craving for Spring.
Endless Anxiety.
No News.
Suspense.
Turned Down.
Levi, P. Waiting.
Lorde. Father, the Year Has Fallen.
Memorial III—from a Phone Booth on
Broadway.
Rooming Houses are Old Women.
McGrath, T. Fatigue of Objects, The.
Meredith, G. Appreciation.
Lords debate, the Commons brawl, The.
Marian: "Clouds fly fast across the moon, The."

Shall I again have Lilac week?
Tuck, my treasure! Tuck, my pleasure!
Wand of gold from the reaper's moon, A.
Niedecker. Young girl to marry.
O'Hara, F. Lover, The.
St. Paul and All That.
What Appears to Be Yours.
Rexroth, K. La Vie en Rose.
Roethke. Song: "My wrath, where's the edge."
Schuyler, J. Await.
Tennyson, A. Move Eastward, Happy Earth,
and Leave.
Williams, C. K. Past, The.
Zukofsky, L. Valentine, A.

Antigone
Davie, D. Creon's Mouse.
Meredith, G. Antigone.
Nemerov. Antigone.
Palmer, M. So with his daughter Antigone.
Smith, S. Oh Stubborn Race of Cadmus' Seed.
Wilner, E. Operations: Desert Shield, Desert
Storm.
Zagajewski. Soul, The.

Antioch (capital of Seleucid Syria)
Cavafy. Grand Procession of Priests and
Laymen.
Greek from Ancient Times.
Julian and the Antiochians.
They Might Have Bothered.

Antiques
Bukowski. 56 Year Old Poem, A.
Burns, R. Ken ye ought o' Captain Grose?
On the Late Captain Grose's Peregrinations
thro' Scotland, Collecting the Antiquities of
That King.
Dickinson, E. We outgrow love like other
things.
Dugan, A. 851.
Graves, R. Hung Wu Vase, The.
Oppen. Antique.
Schuyler, J. "Used Handkerchiefs 5¢."
Zukofsky, L. Shang Cup.

Antony (Marc Antony)
Cavafy. 31 B.C. in Alexandria.
End of Antony, The.
God Forsakes Antony, The.
In a Township of Asia Minor.
Love, A.
Dickinson, E. I never knew a broken Heart.
Lawrence, D. H. Universe Flows, The.
Williams, W. To Mark Anthony in Heaven.

Antrim
See **County Antrim, Northern Ireland**

Ants
Bly, R. Ant Mansion, The.
Ants.
Bukowski. Ants, The.
Ciardi, J. A is for ANT.
Emerson, R. Forbore the ant hill, shunned to
tread.
Frost, R. Departmental.
Johnson, S. Paraphrase.
La Fontaine. Grasshopper and the Ant, The.
Levi, P. Dark Band.
Lux. Driver Ant, The.
Merwin. Man Who Writes Ants, The.
Moore, M. Critics and Connoisseurs.
Nash, O. Ant, The.
Nemerov. Between the Window and the Screen.
Paley, G. Ant! / lugging half an ounce, An.
Then.
Pessoa. My gesture that destroys.
Ramanujan. Army Ants.
Old Indian Belief.
Simic. Solitude.
Wright, C. Journal of Three Questions, A.

Anxiety
Amichai [*or* Amikhai]. Haydn, Opus 76,
Number 5.
I'm in Great Trouble.
Ammons. Anxiety.
Berry, W. Peace of Wild Things, The.
Berryman. How Do You Do, Dr Berryman, Sir?
Bukowski. Big Bastard with a Sword.
Burns, R. Song: "Blythe hae I been on yon

hill."
Campion, T. Ad Melleam.
Dolus.
Pin'd I am, and like to die.
Campion, T. *et al.* If she forsake me, I must die.
What harts content can he finde.
Carruth, H. Living Alone.
Carver, R. Fear.
Seeds.
Chuang Tzu. Owl and Phoenix.
Collins, B. Flight of the Reader, The.
Creeley. Going to Bed.
Kid ("Kid left / out back waits, The").
Names.
NYC—.
Rites, The.
Something.
Waiting ("He pushes behind the words").
Window, The.
Dickinson, E. Crisis is a Hair.
You love me—you are sure.
Dugan, A. Untitled Poem: "I used to enjoy the
night-time."
Eberhart, R. Anxiety I Felt in Guanajuato, The.
Enzensberger, H. Employee, The.
Frost, R. Armful, The.
Hall, D. Fathers and Sons.
Shudder [, The].
HaNagid. Day Of Distress, A.
Hardy, T. Homecoming, The.
Suspense.
Hayden, R. Ice Storm.
Herbert, G. Conscience.
Herrick. Sorrows Succeed.
Hopkins, G. She Schools the Flighty Pupils of
Her Eyes.
Kunitz, S. Game, The.
Lawrence, D. H. Endless Anxiety.
Levertov. Looking-glass.
Lorde. Memorial III—from a Phone Booth on
Broadway.
MacNeice. Prognosis.
McGrath, T. Enemy, The.
Heroes of Childhood, The.
In Dream Time.
Legendary Progress.
Letter for Marian, A.
Parable.
Poem: "Light flares from the tombstones...."
Restless Night, The.
Meredith, G. Call, The.
Il y a Cent Ans.
In all our daily war of words.
Waves are pressing up with force, The.
Merrill, J. Komboloi.
Merton. First Lesson about Man.
Merwin. Mountains, The.
Michelangelo Buonarroti. Man who's happy
many a year, one hour, A.
Montale. Gerti's Carnival.
White-and-black sine, The.
Nash, O. "My Child Is Phlegmatic..."—Anxious
Parent.
Strange Case of Mr. Fortague's Disappointment,
The.
Under the Floor.
We Don't Need to Leave Yet, Do We? Or, Yes
We Do.
When the Devil Was Sick Could He Prove It?
O'Hara, F. Anxiety.
Orr, G. Voyages, The.
Pessoa. There are sicknesses worse than
sicknesses.
Piercy. Under the Grind.
Ramanujan. Anxiety.
Middle Age.
Snakes.
Rich, A. Picnic.
Sunday Evening.
Rilke. Calm of Animals, The.
Roethke. Silence.
Sarton, M. Gestalt at Sixty.
Stockton, A. Soliliguy in a Sleepless Night.
Sudden Production of Mrs. Stockton's in One of
Those Many Anxious Nights in Which She
Watched with Mr. Stockton in His Last

Illness, A.
Warren, R.   Internal Injuries.
Williams, C. K.   Fire.
Williams, T.   Covenant.
Wright, C.   Laguna Blues.
Zukofsky, L.   And so till we have died.
   You three:—my wife.

Apartments
Brodsky, J.   Blues.
Clampitt.   Dakota, The.
   Real Estate.
   Townhouse Interior with Cat.
Cooper, J.   Rent.
Gunn, T.   Apartment Cats.
Hall, D.   Old Houses.
Hughes, L.   Madam and the Rent Man.
Jarrell, R.   Hope.
Koch, K.   In the Morning.
Levertov.   From the Roof.
Lorde.   Moving Out Or the End of Cooperative
   Living.
Major, C.   Kitchen Chair Poem #5.
Merrill, J.   Tenancy, A.
Merwin.   Walk-up.
Oppen.   Tourist Eye.
Paley, G.   On the Fourth Floor.
Rich, A.   Living in Sin.
Ritsos.   Corridor.
Szymborska, W.   Cat in an Empty Apartment.
Tate, J.   Flight.
Tomlinson, C.   Lament for Doormen.
Updike.   Note to the Previous Tenants.
Williams, C. K.   Flight.
Williams, T.   Problem.
Zagajewski.   Apartment for Scholars.

Apathy
Amichai [or Amikhai].   Someplace.
Atwood.   Notes towards a Poem That Can
   Never Be Written.
Auden.   Musée des Beaux Arts.
Bukowski.   Winter.
Clough.   Here have I been these one and twenty
   years.
Cummings, E. E.   Lis / -ten / you know what i
   mean when.
   Most(people / simply / can't).
   Of all the blessings which to man.
Emerson, R.   He walked the streets of great
   New York.
Enzensberger, H.   At Thirty-Three.
   Holiday, The.
   Song for Those Who Know.
Glück, L.   Returning a Lost Child.
Kipling, R.   Russia to the Pacifists.
Lindsay, N.   Leaden-eyed, The.
MacNeice.   Easter Returns.
Shapiro, K.   Hospital.
Stafford, W.   Ritual to Read to Each Other, A.
Williams, C. K.   Ethics.
   Ten Below.
Williams, T.   Wine-Drinkers, The.

Apes
Ciardi, J.   After Sunday Dinner We Uncles
   Snooze.
   Dialogue in the Shade, A.
Larkin, P.   Ape Experiment Room.
Smith, S.   Le Singe qui swing.
Tate, J.   Teaching the Ape to Write Poems.
Zagajewski.   Apes.

Aphrodite
Baudelaire.   Voyage to Cythera, A.
Broumas, O.   Aphrodite.
Browning, R.   Oh Love, Love, thou that from
   the eyes diffusest.
Ciardi, J.   Interruption, An.
Glück, L.   Aphrodite.
"H. D."   Simaetha.
Lawrence, D. H.   Man of Tyre, The.
Medici.   Leave, Cytherea, Your Enchanted Isle.
Meredith, G.   Vital Choice, The.
   With the Persuader.
Olson, C.   Ring of, The.
Rimbaud, A.   Sun and Skin.
Sappho.   Bright-throned, undying Aphrodite.

See also **Venus (goddess)**

Apocalypse
Amichai [or Amikhai].   Sort of an Apocalypse.
Blok.   Voice from the Chorus, A.
Broumas, O.   Eros.
Clampitt.   New Life, A.
Enzensberger, H.   Apocalypse. Umbrian Master,
   about 1490.
Graves, R.   Interruption.
Kinsella, T.   Wormwood.
Kunitz, S.   Halley's Comet.
Lawrence, D. H.   Dies Illa.
   Stoic.
Lowell, R.   Harriet.
MacLeish.   Long Hot Summer.
McGrath, T.   End of the World, The.
Merton.   Figures for an Apocalypse.
Montale.   Ezekiel Saw the Wheel.
   Frog, first to strike his chord, The.
Olson, C.   End of the World / is the Turn-About,
   The.
Rukeyser, M.   Third Elegy. The Fear of Form.
Stock, R.   Elemental Trust.
Very.   Hymn: Christ's Invitation in the
   Apocalypse.
Wilbur, R.   Advice to a Prophet.
Williams, M.   Quantum Theory Made Simple.

See also **End of the World; Judgment Day**

Apollinaire, Guillaume
Ferlinghetti, L.   Reading Apollinaire by the
   Rogue River.
Ginsberg, A.   At Apollinaire's Grave.
Meredith, W.   For Guillaume Apollinaire.
Seifert.   November 1918.

Apollo
Borges.   Poet of the Thirteenth Century, A.
Browning, R.   Apollo and the Fates.
Burns, R.   To John Taylor.
Campion, T.   To his sweet Lute *Apollo* sung the
   motions of the Spheares.
Carruth, H.   Little Old Funky Homeric Blues for
   Herm, A.
Cavafy.   Unfaithfulness.
Cowper, W.   Ode to Apollo.
Dugan, A.   Apollo.
   Mock Translation from the Greek.
Emerson, R.   Comrade or the book is good, The.
Graves, R.   Apollo of the Physiologists.
"H. D."   Evadne.
Herrick.   Canticle to Apollo, A.
   To Apollo.
Keats.   Apollo to the Graces.
   Ode to Apollo.
Kunitz, S.   Flight of Apollo, The.
Levertov.   Prayer, The.
Melville, H.   Ravaged Villa, The.
Meredith, G.   Phoebus with Admetus.
   Rape of Aurora, The.
Millay, E.   Daphne.
Petrarch.   Apollo—if you nourish still desires.
   Nine times Latona's son had turned his gaze.
Ritsos.   Actual Cause, The.
   Marpessa's Selection.
Robinson, E.   Many Are Called.
Schiller.   Evening, after a Picture.
Sexton.   Where I Live in This Honorable House
   of the Laurel Tree.
Smart, C.   Apollo and Daphne.
Swift, J.   Apollo.
   Apollo Outwitted.
   Apollo to the Dean.
   Apollo's Edict.
   First of April, The.
Williams, W.   After Song, An.

Apoplexy
See **Strokes**

Apostles
Browning, R.   Death in the Desert, A.
Dickinson, E.   Of Paul and Silas it is said.
Herrick.   Salutation.
Pound, E.   Ballad of the Goodly Fere.
Robinson, E.   Three Taverns, The.
Rossetti, C.   Ascension Day.
Tate, A.   Twelve, The.
Wilbur, R.   Peter.

Appalachia
Amichai [or Amikhai].   Poems of Spring in the
   Appalachian Mountains.

Apple Blossoms
Sandburg, C.   Crabapple Blossoms.
   June.

Apple Trees and Apples
Amichai [or Amikhai].   Inside the Apple.
   With Her in an Apple.
Armantrout.   As We're Told.
Bogan, L.   Crossed Apple, The.
Bose, B.   Still Life.
Clifton, L.   My Dream About Falling.
Crane, H.   Sunday Morning Apples.
Crane, S.   God came to a man, A.
Creeley.   Juggler's Thought.
   Surgeons.
Cummings, E. E.   It's over a(see just).
Dunbar, P.   Old Apple-Tree, The.
   Unlucky Apple, The.
Eberhart, R.   Apple Buds.
Emerson, R.   Always day & night.
Frost, R.   After Apple-Picking.
   Gold Hesperidee, The.
   Unharvested.
   Wood-Pile, The.
Gurney, I.   Ypres—Minsterworth.
Hall, D.   Apples.
HaNagid.   Apple, The.
Hughes, T.   Apple Dumps.
   Apple Tragedy.
Ignatow, D.   To an Apple.
Keats.   O Blush Not So! O Blush Not So!
Larkin, P.   As Bad as a Mile.
Lawrence, D. H.   Medlars and Sorb-Apples.
   Mystic.
   Old Orchard, The.
Lindsay, N.   Fairy from the Apple-Seed, The.
   In Praise of Johnny Appleseed.
Lux.   Beneath the Apple Branches Bent
   Dumbly.
Major, C.   Apple Core.
   Apple-Maggot Fly, The.
Meredith, G.   Breath of the Briar.
Milosz, C.   Window.
Muldoon, P.   Apple Slump.
Nemerov.   Primer of the Daily Round, A.
Niedecker.   Their apples fall down.
Olson, C.   My apple branch dressed.
Paley, G.   For My Friend Who Planted a Tree
   for His Daughter Jane.
   Leaves Apples.
Parker, D.   Apple Tree, The.
Patchen.   Carts of the wee blind lass, The.
Ramanujan.   If Eyes Can See.
Riley, J.   Little-Red-Apple-Tree, The.
Ritsos.   Apples of the Hesperides 1, The.
   Apples of the Hesperides 2, The.
Rossetti, C.   Apple Gathering, An.
Rossetti, D.   Orchard-Pit, The.
Rukeyser, M.   Tree.
Sappho.   One Girl.
Seifert.   Apple Tree with Cobweb Strings.
Simic.   History.
   Interlude.
Thoreau.   'Twas thirty years ago.
Tomlinson, C.   Paring the Apple.
Warren, R.   Composition in Gold and Red-Gold.
Wilbur, R.   John Chapman.
Williams, C. K.   I'd forgotten and / how could I
   ever.
Williams, W.   Perfection.
   Wild Orchard.
Wright, J.   Two Horses Playing in the Orchard.
Yeats.   Song Of Wandering Aengus, The.

Apprentices
Jonson, B.   To My Old Faithful Servant: And
   (by His Continued Virtue) My Loving Friend:
   The Author of this Work, M[r] Rich[ard]
   Brome.
Muldoon, P.   Sushi.

Approval
Bukowski.   Twins.
Davie, D.   At Knaresborough.
Dickinson, E.   I thought your approbation Fame.
Merton.   King Solomon: my master and the

imbeciles.
Piercy. I Will Not Be Your Sickness.

Apricot Trees and Apricots
Milosz, C. Gathering Apricots.

April
Bourne, V. Silk Worm, The.
Browning, R. Home-Thoughts, from Abroad.
Clampitt. He Dreams of Being Warm.
Cummings, E. E. "but why should" / the / greatest.
If(among / silent skies).
When faces called flowers float out of the ground.
De la Mare. April.
Cherry Trees, The.
Eberhart, R. This Fevers Me.
Emerson, R. April.
Gentle Spring has charmed the earth.
More sweet than my refrain.
García Lorca. Spring Song.
Glück, L. My Cousin in April.
Gurney, I. April—Dull Afternoon.
April Gale.
Jeffers, R. Gale in April.
Komunyakaa. April's Anarchy.
Kumin, M. Relearning the Language of April.
Levertov. April in Ohio.
Talking to Oneself.
Levine, P. Sleepless Night, A.
Told.
McHugh, H. Fix.
Merton. April.
Millay, E. Northern April.
Road to Avrillé, The.
Song of a Second April.
Spring.
Nash, O. Always Marry an April Girl.
Oliver, M. Blossom.
Pagis. April.
Parker, D. Well-Worn Story, A.
Sandburg, C. Branches.
Just Before April Came.
Plowboy.
Three Spring Notations on Bipeds.
Shelley, P. Fragment: May the Limner.
Swenson, M. April Light.
On the Edge.
Tomlinson, C. In April.
Very. April Snow, The.
Whittier. April.
Wilbur, R. Gnomons.
Storm in April, A.
Williams, W. Della Primavera Transportata al Morale.
Two Aspects of April.

April Fool's Day
MacNeice. April Fool.
Swift, J. First of April, The.

Aquariums
Ciardi, J. Aquarium.
Kumin, M. Repent.
Lowell, R. For the Union Dead.
Rexroth, K. Monads.
Stock, R. One of the Old Ones.

Aquinas, St. Thomas
See **Thomas Aquinas, Saint**

Arab-Israeli Wars
Amichai [*or* Amikhai]. 1978 Reunion of Palmach Veterans at Ma-ayan Harod.
And I am always like this fleeing from hurt and pain.
And in spite of all that, I must.
Anniversaries of War.
Blood that stands the member erect, The.
City where I was born was destroyed by cannons, The.
Dicky was hurt.
Even my loves are measured by the wars.
I found an old book on animals.
I have nothing to say about the war.
I left the Evening Land by the will of the night.
In the summer, nations come to one another.
Let Memory Mountain remember instead of me.
Like the Streams in the Negev.
Mark Them with Signs.

Mister Beringer, whose son.
New homeland was built, The.
On the lot that was a short-cut for lovers.
"Rustle of History's Wings," as They Used to Say Then, The.
Since Then.
Sometimes I think of my fathers.
Temporary Poem of My Time.
Travels of Benjamin the Last, of Tudela, The.
U.N. Headquarters in the High Commissioner's House in Jerusalem, The.
War broke out in autumn, in the no-man's land.
We Did What We Had To.
What was the message of the burned man?
"Where was he wounded?" You don't know.
Wild Peace.
Wildpeace.
Bloch, C. We Did What We Had To.
Celan. Just Think.
Dugan, A. Riding Song for a Semi-Feudal Army, for Glubb Pasha, for Tortured Colonels.
Ginsberg, A. Jaweh and Allah Battle.

Arabia
De la Mare. Arabia.
Lindsay, N. Doll's "Arabian Nights," A.

Arabs
Amichai [*or* Amikhai]. Arab Shepherd Is Searching for His Goat on Mount Zion, An.
Arab Shepherd Seeks a Kid on Mount Zion, A.
Browning, R. Through the Metidja to Abd-el-Kadr.
Gallagher, T. Rijl.
Goethe. Arabian Ballad.

Arachne
Hayden, R. Richard Hunt's "Arachne."
Levi, P. Arachne.

Aran Islands, Ireland
Mahon. Aran.

Arbor Day
Amichai [*or* Amikhai]. Poem for Arbor Day.

Arbus, Diane
Nemerov. To D———, Dead by Her Own Hand.

Arbutus
Dickinson, E. Pink—small—and punctual.
Whitman, W. For Queen Victoria's Birthday.
Whittier. Mayflowers, The.
Trailing Arbutus, The.

Arcadia
Dunbar, P. Ballade: "By Mystic's banks I held my dream."
Farewell to Arcady.
Ralegh, S. Arcadians the earth inhabited, The.

Archaeology and Archaeologists
Amichai [*or* Amikhai]. End of the Archaeological Season in Eyn Gedi.
Evidence.
Museum at Akhziv.
Auden. Archaeology.
Brodsky, J. Letter to an Archaeologist.
Eberhart, R. Dry Rot, The.
Hardy, T. Clasped Skeleton, The.
Heaney, S. Bog Queen.
Kinship.
Punishment.
Strange Fruit.
Jacobsen, J. Daughter to Archeologist.
In the Crevice of Time.
Komunyakaa. Glass Ark, The.
Milosz, C. Ball, A.
Rukeyser, M. Artifact.
Schuyler, J. Industrial Archaeology.
Szymborska, W. Archeology.
Updike. Toothache Man.
Williams, W. Smiling Dane, A.

Archery
Chuang Tzu. Need to Win, The.
Frost, R. Version.
Graves, R. Blind Arrow, A.
Michelangelo Buonarroti. I think it may be, so.
Tomlinson, C. Archer, The.
Voznesensky [*or* Voznesenskii]. Arrow in the Wall, An.

Architecture and Architects
Atwood. City Planners, The.

Carruth, H. Meadow House.
Davie, D. Dublin Georgian ("Thin brown orphan in his washed-out blue, A").
Emerson, R. Problem, The.
Hardy, T. Abbey Mason, The.
Heiress and Architect.
Hopkins, G. Boughs being pruned, birds preenèd, show more fair.
Jonson, B. Expostulation with Inigo Jones, An.
To Inigo, Marquess Would Be, a Corollary.
Melville, H. Greek Architecture.
Greek Masonry.
Meredith, W. Homage to Paul Mellon, I. M. Pei, Their Gallery, and Washington City.
Milosz, C. For Jan Lebenstein.
Palmer, M. I am an architect in Vienna.
Piercy. Track of the Master Builder, The.
Stevens, W. Architecture.
Tomlinson, C. Albuquerque.
Dates: Penkhull New Road.

Arctic
Brodsky, J. Polar Explorer, A.
Davie, D. After the Calamitous Convoy (July 1942).
Behind the North Wind
Gunn, T. From the Highest Camp.
Hall, D. Wolf Knife.
Niedecker. Linnaeus in Lapland.
Spender, S. Polar Exploration.
Whitman, W. Of That Blithe Throat of Thine.
Whittier. Spirit of the North, The.

Arethusa
Shelley, P. Arethusa.
Very. Arethusa Meadow.

Argentina
Borges. 1972.
Deathwatch on the Southside.
Ode Written in 1966.
Streets, The.
Susana Bombal.
Carver, R. On the Pampas Tonight.
"Dario." Spaniard.
Komunyakaa. Let's Say.
Lowell, R. Buenos Aires.
Mistral, G. Argentine Round.

Arguments
Amichai [*or* Amikhai]. On Some Other Planet You May Be Right.
Bierce. Controversy.
Cavalcanti. Surely it wasn't your cultered mind.
Creeley. Then ("Don't go / to the mountains").
Dugan, A. Crimes of Bernard, The.
Ginsberg, A. Arguments.
Hughes, L. Argument ("Now lookahere, gal").
Ignatow, D. Debate, The.
White Ceiling, The.
Kinsella, T. At the Head Table.
Portrait of the Artist, A.
Meredith, W. Quarrel, The.
Riley, J. Jap Miller.
Never Talk Back.
Quarrel, The.
Thanksgiving Day at Hunchley's.
Ritsos. Summer.
Rumi. Man and a Woman Arguing, A.
Warren, R. Revelation.
Williams, M. He Speaks to His Arguing Friends and to Himself.
In Another Town.
Words.

See also **Quarrels**

Ariadne
Merton. Ariadne.
Ariadne at the Labyrinth.
Simic. In Midsummer Quiet.
Tomlinson, C. Ariadne and the Minotaur.

Aristocracy
Berry, W. Aristocracy, The.
Burns, R. Address of Beelzebub.
Extempore Verses on Dining with Lord Daer.
Verses Intended to Be Written below a Noble Earl's Picture.
Dickey, W. Dog Under False Pretences.
Graves, R. Cloak, The.
Hill, G. Funeral Music.

Aristotle
Lawrence, D. H.   Aristocracy of the Sun.
Magnificent Democracy.
Rise in the World, A.
Meredith, G.   Miss Millicent Maxse was fond of
her Ma.
Rich, A.   Uncle Speaks in the Drawing Room,
The.
Tu Fu.   Lo Yu Park.
Wilbur, R.   Complaint.
Williams, W.   Impromptu: The Suckers.
Aristotle
Dugan, A.   On Alexander and Aristotle, on a
Black-on-Red Greek Plate.
Eberhart, R.   Commitment, A.
Great Principles Are Thrown Down by Time.
Kaire.
Milton.   On the Platonic Idea as Aristotle
Understood It.
Arithmetic
Cavafy.   Addition.
Sandburg, C.   Arithmetic.
Arizona (state)
Ai.   Hitchhiker, The.
Carruth, H.   Rimrock, Where It Is.
Cunningham, J.   Towards Tucson.
Hacker, M.   Country & Western II.
Sze.   Moenkopi.
Tomlinson, C.   Arizona Desert.
Warren, R.   Arizona Midnight.
Wilner, E.   Tucson Gardens.
Ark, The
Gjuzel.   Flood at the International Writer's
Workshop.
Graves, R.   Ark, The.
Jacobsen, J.   Trial Run.
Levertov.   Ache of Marriage, The.
Montale.   Ark, The.
Nemerov.   Fall Again, The.
Riley, J.   Song of the Cruise, A.
Szymborska, W.   Into the Ark.
Thomas, D.   Author's Prologue.
Tomlinson, C.   Ararat.
Weiss, T.   Charm Against the Toothache, A.
See also **Noah**
Arkansas (state)
Angelou.   My Arkansas.
Ciardi, J.   For Miller Williams.
Davie, D.   Siloam.
Wright, C.   Arkansas Traveller.
Armada
See **Spanish Armada**
Armenia and Armenians
Davie, D.   Mandelstam's Hope for the Best.
Dubie.   Desert Deportation of 1915, The.
Armies
Crane, S.   Black riders came from the sea.
When a people reach the top of a hill.
Davie, D.   In Chopin's Garden.
Northumberland.
Dugan, A.   Decimation before Phraäta, The.
García Lorca.   Ballad of the Spanish Civil
Guard.
Hughes, L.   Salute to Soviet Armies.
When the Armies Passed.
Jeffers, R.   Ghosts in England.
Melville, H.   Armies of the Wilderness, The.
Night-March, The.
Patchen.   Knowledge of Old Towns, The.
Stafford, W.   Learning.
Tate, J.   Bluebird Houses.
Whalen, P.   Homage to William Seward
Burroughs.
Armistice
Frost, R.   November.
Graves, R.   Armistice Day, 1918.
Hardy, T.   And There Was a Great Calm.
Peace Peal, The.
Kipling, R.   London Stone.
Nemerov.   Armistice.
See also **Peace**
Armstrong, Louis
Schuyler, J.   Beautiful Funerals.
Army Life
Amichai [*or* Amikhai].   In the long nights our

room was closed off and.
Lips of dead men whisper where they lie, The.
My father spent four years inside their war.
Preface first: the two of them, the brittle, A.
Dugan, A.   Riding Song for a Semi-Feudal
Army, for Glubb Pasha, for Tortured Colonels.
Gurney, I.   Bohemians, The.
First March.
Laventie.
Of Grandcourt.
Varennes.
Housman.   Grenadier.
New Mistress, The.
Jarrell, R.   Absent with Official Leave.
Good-bye, Wendover; Good-bye, Mountain
Home.
Lines, The.
Mail Call.
Second Air Force.
Soldier [T. P.].
Transient Barracks.
Kipling, R.   Back to the Army Again.
Boots.
Cholera Camp.
Danny Deever.
'Eathen, The.
Gentlemen-Rankers.
Gunga Din.
Jacket, The.
Loot.
Mandalay.
Men That Fought at Minden, The.
Oonts.
Roman Centurion's Song, The.
Route Marchin'
Shut-Eye Sentry, The.
Snarleyow.
Troopin'.
Young British Soldier, The.
Lawrence, D. H.   Young Soldier with Bloody
Spurs, The.
Warren, R.   Prophecy.
Whitman, W.   Adieu to a Soldier.
Bivouac on a Mountain Side.
By the Bivouac's Fitful Flame.
Camps of Green.
Cavalry Crossing a Ford.
Wright, C.   Italian Days.
See also **Soldiers**
Arnold, Matthew
Ferlinghetti, L.   Sea Is Calm Tonight, The.
Arranged Marriage
See **Marriage, Arranged**
Arrows
Brodsky, J.   Persian Arrow.
Cavalcanti.   Oh you, whose eyes carry.
De la Mare.   Hunter, The.
Dickinson, E.   I've got an arrow here.
Emerson, R.   I have an arrow that can find its
mark.
Ye have Grace.
Merwin.   Song of Man Chipping an Arrowhead.
Michelangelo Buonarroti.   For a wound from the
searing arrows Love lets fly.
Voznesensky [*or* Voznesenskii].   Arrow in the
Wall, An.
Wilner, E.   Meditation on the *Wen-Fu.*
Art and Artists
Ai.   Back in the World.
Momento Mori.
Atwood.   Later in Belleville: Career.
Auden.   Composer, The.
Baudelaire.   Bad Luck.
Death of Artists, The.
Guiding Lights, The.
On a Portrait of Honoré Daumier.
Ransom, The.
Berryman.   Ecce Homo.
Bishop, E.   Monument, The.
One Art.
Blake, W.   All Pictures thats Panted with sense
& with Thought.
Blakes apology for His Catalogue.
Now Art has lost its mental Charms.
O dear Mother outline of knowledge most sage.

On Sir Joshua Reynolds.
On the Great Encouragement Given By English
Nobility & Gentry to Correggio Rubens
Rembrandt Reynolds Gainsborough Catalani
Ducrowe & Dilbury Doodle.
On the Venetian Painter.
Orator Prigg.
Pretty Epigram for [Those] the Entertainment of
Those Who [Pay] Have Paid Great Sums in
the Venetian & Flemish Ooze, A.
Rafael Sublime Majestic Graceful Wise.
To Venetian Artists.
Venetian; all thy Colouring is no more.
When I see a Rubens Rembrandt [or] Correggio.
You say their Pictures well Painted be.
Blok.   Artist, The.
Blue Cloud.   For Ace.
Bogan, L.   To an Artist, to Take Heart.
Bourne, V.   Denner's Old Woman.
Tears of a Painter, The.
Brodsky, J.   At Carol Willink's Exhibition.
Browning, E.   Hiram Powers' "Greek Slave."
Browning, R.   At the "Mermaid."
Beatrice Signorini.
Cleon.
Deaf and Dumb.
Dîs Aliter Visum; or, Le Byron de Nos Jours.
Fra Lippo Lippi.
How It Strikes a Contemporary.
Lady and the Painter, The.
One Word More.
Youth and Art.
Bukowski.   Bring Down the Beams.
Experience.
On Going Back to the Street after Viewing an
Art Show.
Burns, R.   To an Artist.
Byron, G.   Condolatory Address.
Carruth, H.   Buddhist Painter Prepares to Paint,
The.
Lana.
Museum Piece.
Post-Impressionist Susurration for the First of
November, 1983, A.
This Decoration.
Cavafy.   Half an Hour.
I've Brought to Art.
Their Origin.
Ciardi, J.   Annals.
Conversation with Leonardo, A.
Lines while Walking Home from a Party on
Charles Street.
Two for Gertrude Kasle.
Verbal Generation, The.
Clampitt.   Balms.
Marginal Employment.
Coleridge, S.   Apologia pro Vita Sua.
To a Critic.
To Matilda Betham from a Stranger.
To Mr. Pye.
To the Young Artist.
With Fielding's *Amelia.*
Collins, B.   Madmen.
Cooper, J.   In a Room with Picassos.
Olympic Rain Forest.
Corbett, W.   Above the cold.
Joe Brainard.
Poem: "French blue morning."
Creeley.   Figures, The.
For John Chamberlain.
Cummings, E. E.   Conversation with my friend
is particularly.
If I Have Made, My Lady.
If you like my poems let them.
Mr youse needn't be so spry.
My naked lady framed.
Picasso / you give us Things.
Pity his how illimitable plight.
S.T.
Some ask praise of their fellows.
This mind made war.
To start, to hesitate; to stop.
Davie, D.   Cherry Ripe.
Dublin Georgian.
Feeders, The.
Hill Field, The.

July, 1964.
Limited Achievement.
Nonconformist, The.
Resolutions.
Tiger at the Movie-Show.
To a Brother in the Mystery.
Tuscan Brutus, The.
With the Grain.
Dickinson, E. Artists wrestled here!
I work to drive the awe away.
Nature is a Haunted House.
Donne. To Mr B. B.
Dugan, A. Against the Text "Art Is Immortal."
Retraction.
Speech to the Student Clowns at the Circus
Clown School at Sarasota, Florida.
Dunbar, P. Nature and Art.
Duncan, R. Nel Mezzo del Cammin di Nostra
Vita.
Eberhart, R. Cancer Cells, The.
Commitment, A.
Fortune's Mist.
Looking Head On.
On the Fragility of Mind.
Eliot, T. S. Afternoon.
Emerson, R. Art.
By art, by music, overthrilled.
Enough is done highminded friend go sleep.
Loss and Gain.
My Garden.
Try the might the Muse affords.
Enzensberger, H. Apocalypse. Umbrian Master,
about 1490.
Summer Poem.
Ferlinghetti, L. London / crossfigured / creeping
with trams.
Plan du Centre de Paris à Vol D'Oiseau.
Triumph of the Postmodern.
Ginsberg, A. Cézanne's Ports.
This Is about Death.
Gray, T. Ode for Music.
Gunn, T. Confessions of the Life Artist.
Expression.
Selves.
"H. D." Red Roses for Bronze.
Hacker, M. Ballad of Ladies Lost and Found.
Hall, D. This Poem.
Hardy, T. Figure in the Scene, The.
Herrick. Art above Nature, to Julia.
Painting Sometimes Permitted.
Upon Man.
Hill, G. Pre-Raphaelite Notebook, A.
Hughes, L. Metropolitan Museum.
Plaint.
Jacobsen, J. Interrupted, The.
Jarrell, R. Head of Wisdom, The.
In Galleries.
Old and the New Masters, The.
Jeffers, R. Artist, An.
To a Young Artist.
Vices.
Keats. On Seeing the Elgin Marbles.
Kinsella, T. Portrait of the Artist, A.
Kipling, R. Conundrum of the Workshops, The.
Evarra and His Gods.
Jubal and Tubal Cain.
L'Envoi.
Story of Ung, The.
Kizer, C. From an Artist's House.
Streets of Pearl and Gold.
Koch, K. Artist, The.
Our Hearts.
Komunyakaa. Blasphemy.
Kunitz, S. Artist, The.
Chariot.
Crystal Cage, The.
Laughlin, J. Blowpipe Game, The.
Merry Madness Hall.
Levertov. Artist to Intellectual (Poet to
Explainer).
Life of Art, The.
Pentimento.
Two Artists.
Lindsay, N. Mae Marsh, Motion Picture
Actress.
Logan, J. Gallery Walk: Fifteen Italian

Drawings 1780–1890.
Manhattan Movements.
Logue, C. To My Fellow Artists.
Lowell, R. Beethoven.
Lost Tune, The.
Lux. Horatian Notion, An.
MacLeish. Corporate Entity.
Mahon. Dying Art, A.
Girls on the Bridge.
Major, C. Expanded Composition, The.
In Salute again.
Montalban: Near the Ancient Fort.
Mallarmé. Homage: "Even a Dawn too numb."
Note to Whistler.
Weary of Bitter Sleep.
Maritain. Mosaic: St. Praxed's.
Melville, H. Art.
Meredith, W. Wholesome.
Merrill, J. Dreams About Clothes.
Merton. Originators, The.
Michelangelo Buonarroti. For a reliable guide
in my vocation.
My soul without a friend, without a guide.
With heart of sulphur, flesh of tinder too.
Millay, E. And if I die, because that part of me.
To hold secure the province of Pure Art.
Milosz, C. At Yale.
Biography of an Artist.
For Jan Lebenstein.
In a Buggy at Dusk.
Wanda.
Mistral, G. Artist's Decalogue, The.
Montale. In the Style of Filippo De Pisis, on
Sending Him This Book.
Moore, M. When I Buy Pictures.
Muldoon, P. Christo's.
Nash, O. Everybody Makes Poets.
Nemerov. To Clio, Muse of History.
Niedecker. They live a cool distance.
O'Hara, F. Memorial Day 1950.
Why I Am Not a Painter.
Oliver, M. Dream of Trees, A.
Olson, C. "Enthusiasm," An.
For Cy Twombly Faced with His First Chicago
& N.Y. Shows.
Knowing All Ways, Including the Transposition
of Continents.
So the Norse / were neurotic.
Oppen. Drawing.
Fragonard, / Your spiral women.
Giovanni's Rape of the Sabine Women at
Wildenstein's.
Narrative
Pagis. Art of Contraction, The.
Palmer, M. Dearest Reader.
Parker, D. Our Own Home Talent.
Portrait of the Artist.
Parra, N. Paradise of Squares.
Patchen. Continual Ministry of Thy Anger, The.
Portrait of the Artist as an Interior Decorator.
Paz. Objects & Apparitions.
Pinkerton, H. On an Attic Red-Figured
Amphora (490 B.C.) by the "Berlin Painter" in
the Metropolitan Museum.
On an Early Cycladic Harpist (2500 B.C.) in the
Archaeological Museum in Athens.
On Dieric Bouts's Virgin and Child (1460) in
the California Palace of the Legion of Honor.
On G.B. Tiepolo's Etching Adoration of the
Magi (1753) in the Stanford Museum.
On Leonard Baskin's Etching Benevolent Angel.
On Vermeer's Young Woman with a Water Jug
(1658) in the Metropolitan Museum.
Pope, A. Epitaph on Sir Godfrey Kneller, in
Westminster-Abbey, 1723.
To Sir Godfrey Kneller, on His Painting for Me
the Statues of Apollo, Venus and Hercules.
Pound, E. "Fair Helena" by Rackham.
Of Jacopo del Sellaio.
Picture, The.
Ramanujan. Black Hen, The.
Time to Stop.
Ransom, J. Painted Head.
Rashid, N. Izhab-O-Rasai (Expression and
Reach).
Rexroth, K. Last Visit to the Swimming Pool

Soviets.
Rich, A. 7/12/68.
7/13/68.
7/14/68: i.
7/16/68: i.
7/16/68: ii.
7/26/68: i.
7/26/68: II.
8/1/68.
8/8/68: i.
8/8/68: ii.
At a Bach Concert.
August fourth nineteen sixty eight.
Aunt Jennifer's Tigers.
Burning Oneself Out.
Diamond Cutters, The.
Ghazals: Homage to Ghalib.
July seventeenth nineteen sixty eight.
Pierrot Le Fou.
Rural Reflections.
Riley, J. Art and Love.
Art and Poetry.
His Last Picture.
In Bohemia.
Orlie Wilde,
Wait.
Water-Color, A.
Ritsos. Meaning of Art, The.
Usefulness of Art, The.
Robinson, E. Caput Mortuum.
Rossetti, C. In An Artist's Studio.
Rossetti, D. For "Our Lady of the Rocks" by
Leonardo da Vinci.
Rukeyser, M. Homage to Literature.
Käthe Kollwitz.
Painters.
Sun-Artist, The.
Rumi. Chinese Art and Greek Art.
In your light I learn how to love.
Schuyler, J. After Joe Was at the Island.
Back.
Dear Joe.
Fauré Ballade, The.
Morning of the Poem, The.
Red Brick and Brown Stone.
Trash Book, The.
Seifert. Lines for the Painter Ota Janeček.
Model, The.
Visit to the Painter Vladimír Komárek, A.
Shapiro, K. Poet.
Poet in Residence.
Room in Rome, A.
White Negress, The.
Simic. Travel[l]ing Slaughterhouse.
Smith, S. Choosers, The.
Full Well I Know.
New Age, The.
Snyder, G. Thoughts on Looking at a Samuel
Palmer Etching at the Tate.
Spender, S. Art Student.
Grandparents.
Stafford, W. After Arguing against the
Contention That Art Must Come from
Discontent.
For Our Party Last Night.
You and Art.
Stevens, W. Anecdote of the Jar.
Man with the Blue Guitar, The.
Prelude to Objects.
So-and-So Reclining on Her Couch.
Sze. Taoist Painter, The.
Wood Whittler, The.
Tate, A. Art.
Intellectual Detachment.
Tate, J. Read the Great Poets.
Tennyson, A. Palace of Art, The.
Thomas, D. In My Craft or Sullen Art.
Tomlinson, C. Chances of Rhyme, The.
Distinctions.
Fountain.
Revolution Piazza Di Spagna.
Tu Fu. Visit in Winter to the Temple of His
Mystical Majesty, A.
Updike. Angels, The.
Calder's Hands.
Fleckings, The.

Gradations of Black.
Les Saints Nouveaux.
Modigliani's Death Mask.
Two Hoppers.
Van Duyn. Homework.
Learners, The.
Very. On the Wild Flowers of the Art
    Exhibition.
Walcott. Map of Europe, A.
Walker, A. Songless.
Weiss, T. Library Revisited, The.
Whalen, P. Murals Not Yet Dreamed.
Whitman, W. Eidolons.
Whittier. Artist of the Beautiful, An.
Flowers in Winter.
On a Prayer-Book.
Wilbur, R. Museum Piece.
Ode to Pleasure.
Williams, C. K. Refuge, Serpent-Riders.
Williams, M. Art Photographer Puts His Model
    at Ease, The.
Before.
Curator, The.
Williams, W. All the Fancy Things.
Art, The.
Artist, The.
Painting, The.
Title, The.
Two Deliberate Exercises.
Wilner, E. Conversation with a Japanese
    Student.
Illuminator, The.
Meditation on the *Wen-Fu.*
Mt. Fuji and the Martial Arts.
Wordsworth, W. Foregoing Subject Resumed,
    The.
Gleaner (Suggested By a Picture), The.
How Rich That Forehead's Calm Expanse!
Lyre! Though Such Power Do in Thy Magic
    Live.
On Seeing a Needlecase in the Form of a Harp;
    the Work of E.M.S.
Poet!—He Hath Put His Heart to School, A.
To Lucca Giordano.
Upon the Sight of a Beautiful Picture.
Vale of Esthwaite, The.
Written in Mrs Field's Album opposite a Pen-
    and-Ink Sketch in the Manner of a Rembrandt
    Etching Done by Edmund Field.
Wright, C. Lives of the Artists.
Quotations.
Sitting at Dusk in the Back Yard after the
    Mondrian Retrospective.
Summer Storm.
Yeats. Curse of Cromwell, The.
Lapis Lazuli.
Nativity, A.
Zagajewski. In the Beauty Created by Others.
King, A.
River, A.
Zukofsky, L. Even if love convey.
Shang Cup.
Spook's Sabbath, Five Bowings.
You three:—my wife.
See also **Artists' Colonies**

Artaud, Antonin
Carver, R. Artaud.
Kumin, M. At a Private Showing in 1982.
In April, in Princeton.

Artemis
Broumas, O. Artemis.
Browning, R. Artemis Prologizes.
Meredith, G. Vital Choice, The.
Rexroth, K. After the Anthology.
Zaturenska. Hymn to Artemis, the Destroyer.

Arthurian Legend
Chesterton. Myth of Arthur, The.
Ciardi, J. Launcelot in Hell.
Hill, G. Merlin.
Laughlin, J. Inviolable Maiden, The.
Parker, D. Guinevere at Her Fireside.
Robinson, E. Lancelot.
Merlin.
Smith, S. Blue from Heaven, The.
Tennyson, A. Lady of Shalott, The.
Morte d'Arthur.

Wilner, E. Minor Epic.
Wordsworth, W. Egyptian Maid; or, The
    Romance of the Water Lilly, The.

Artifacts
Amichai [*or* Amikhai]. At the Maritime
    Museum.
Evidence.
Open Internalized.
Brodsky, J. Persian Arrow.
Burns, R. On the Late Captain Grose's
    Peregrinations thro' Scotland, Collecting the
    Antiquities of That King.
Hughes, T. Relic.
Mahon. Dying Art, A.
Orr, G. Excavation, The.
Ramanujan. Copper Vat, A.
Rich, A. Open-Air Museum.
Ritsos. Perhaps.

Artists' Colonies
Robinson, E. Hillcrest.

Ascension Day
Auden. Ascension Day, 1964.
Beckett, S. Ascension.
Herrick. Clouds.
Rossetti, C. Ascension Day.
Ascension Eve.

Ash Trees
Hopkins, G. Ashboughs.
Merwin. In the Time of the Blossoms.
Very. On the Mountain Ash Tree: In front of
    the house of the late Capt. Robert W. Gould.

Ashbery, John
Koch, K. Circus, The.
Fate.
O'Hara, F. Postcard from John Ashbery, A.
"Unfinished," The.
Schuyler, J. Dining Out with Doug and Frank.
Fauré Ballade, The.

Ashes
Bukowski. Ashes.
Clampitt. Urn-Burial and the Butterfly
    Migration.
Ginsberg, A. On Neal's Ashes.
Hall, D. Coal Fire, The.
Kizer, C. Ashes, The.
Levine, P. Ashes.
Merwin. Ash.
Sandburg, C. Pool.
White Ash.
Simic. Primer.
Stafford, W. Burning a Book.

Asia
Blok. Scythians, The.
Brodsky, J. Admonition, An.
Eberhart, R. Rape of the Cataract, The.
Ginsberg, A. Angkor Wat.
Jarrell, R. Wide Prospect, The.
Lowell, R. Father's Bedroom.
Merrill, J. Willowware Cup.
Nash, O. So I resigned from the Chu Chin
    Chowder and Marching Club.

Asian-Americans
Carruth, H. Eternity Blues.

Asians
Creeley. If You're Going to Have One.
See also **Chinese, The; Japanese, The**

Aspen Trees
Hopkins, G. Binsey Poplars (Felled 1879).
Komunyakaa. Initials on Aspens.
Wilbur, R. Aspen and the Stream, The.
See also **Poplar Trees**

Asphodels
Enzensberger, H. Asphodels.
Williams, W. Asphodel, That Greeny Flower.
Paterson, Book 5: The River of Heaven.

Aspirations
Ammons. Alternatives.
Dove, R. Magic.
Duncan, R. Nel Mezzo del Cammin di Nostra
    Vita.
Hughes, L. Aspiration.
Deferred.
To Be Somebody.
Lindsay, N. On the Road to Nowhere.

Lorde. Seventh Sign, The.
MacDiarmid, H. Dytiscus.
Meredith, G. Open horizons round.
Nash, O. Eheu! Fugaces, or, What a Difference
    a Lot of Days Make.
Petrarch. I see, my noble lady.
To some it may well seem I pitch my style.
When out of all the ladies in her sphere.
Riley, J. Highest Good, The.
Impetuous Resolve, An.

Assassinations and Assassins
Ai. Jack Ruby on Ice.
Jimmy Hoffa's Odyssey.
Oswald Incognito & Astral Travels.
Berryman. Formal Elegy.
Borges. Conjectural Poem.
General Quiroga Rides to His Death in a
    Carriage.
Davie, D. After a Change of Régime.
Chernobyl. A Disaster.
Dickinson, E. Apparently with no surprise.
Ferlinghetti, L. Assassination Raga.
Elegy to Dispel Gloom, An.
Gunn, T. Claus von Stauffenberg.
Julian the Apostate.
Hall, D. "Marat's Death."
Kipling, R. Ave Imperatrix!
Lorde. Equinox.
MacLeish. State Funeral: March 31, 1969.
Melville, H. Martyr, The.
Merton. April 4th 1968.
Merwin. News of the Assassin.
Oppen. 11/22/63.
Armies of the Plain.
Riley, J. Assassin, An.
Assassin, The.
Rimbaud, A. Morning of Drunkenness.
Rossetti, D. Czar Alexander the Second.
Rukeyser, M. Martin Luther King, Malcolm X.
Tomlinson, C. Assassin.
At Trotsky's House.
Charlotte Corday.
Marat Dead.
Whitman, W. Spanish Lady, The.

Asses
Logue, C. Ass's Song, The.
Muldoon, P. Epona.
See also **Donkeys**

Assisi, Italy
Celan. Assisi.

Assistance
Cowper, W. Human Frailty.
Lindsay, N. Flower of Mending, The.
Piercy. Gracious Goodness.
Williams, C. K. When.

Assurance
Bukowski. Out of the Blue.
Creeley. Window, The.
Dickey, W. Confidence.
Rossetti, C. Until the Day Break.
Tomlinson, C. Request, The.

Assyria and Assyrians
Bishop, E. Wading at Wellfleet.
Byron, G. Destruction of Sennacherib, The.
Rossetti, D. Burden of Nineveh, The.

Astaire, Fred
Corbett, W. Fred Astaire.

Asteroids
Laughlin, J. Bless You, Mr President.

Astrology and Astrologers
Crashaw. Love's Horoscope.
Cunningham, J. Horoscope.
Dickey, J. Zodiac, The.
Dickey, W. Sagittarius, Scorpio Rising.
Dickinson, E. Nature Assigns the Sun.
Dugan, A. To a Kid Who Believes in
    Astrology.
Graves, R. Non Cogunt Astra.
Kipling, R. Astrologer's Song, An.
Laughlin, J. Is It Written.
More, S. Astrologer, The.
Pagis. Come.
Ramanujan. Astronomer.
Rich, A. For the Conjunction of Two Planets.
Schuyler, J. Picnic Cantata, A.

Sexton. Madame Arrives in the Mail.
Unknown. On the Astrologers.
Wilbur, R. Flumen Tenebrarum.

Astronauts
Hayden, R. Astronauts.
Williams, W. Heel & Toe to the End.

Astronomy and Astronomers
Ciardi, J. Galileo and the Laws.
  My Father's Watch.
  Some Sort of Game.
Clough. Uranus.
Coleridge, S. Translation of a Greek Ode on
  Astronomy.
Dickinson, E. Nature Assigns the Sun.
Donne. Good Friday [*or* Goodfriday], 1613.
  Riding Westward.
Emerson, R. Star seer Copernicus / Only could
  earn a curse.
Ferlinghetti, L. Olbers' Paradox.
Jeffers, R. Great Explosion, The.
Lawrence, D. H. Astronomical Changes.
Levi, P. Sidereus Nuncius.
McHugh, H. Spot in Space and Time.
Nimatullah [*or* Ni'matu'llah]. Song of Seyd [*or*
  Seid] Nimetollah of Kuhistan.
Ramanujan. Astronomer.
Rexroth, K. Late Half Moon.
Rich, A. For the Conjunction of Two Planets.
  Planetarium.
Rukeyser, M. Sacred Lake.
Stafford, W. Message from Space, A.
Swenson, M. As Long Ago As Far Away.
  Comet Watch on Indian Key—Night of April
    10, 1986.
  If I Had Children.
  Of Rounds.
  Seeing Jupiter.
  Solar Corona.
Very. Slowness of Belief in a Spiritual World,
  The.
Whitman, W. When I Heard the Learn'd
  Astronomer.

Atalanta
Olson, C. Atalanta.
Swinburne. Before the Beginning of Years.
  Not as with Sundering of the Earth.
  O That I Now.
  We Have Seen Thee, O Love.
  When the Hounds of Spring.
  Who Hath Given Man Speech?

Atheism
Chesterton. On Reading "God."
Cullen, C. For an Atheist.
HaNagid. Ask the Dead and They'll Tell You.
Hardy, T. Impercipient, The.
Lawrence, D. H. There Are No Gods.
Lowell, R. For George Santayana.
Nemerov. Memory of My Friend, A.
Schuyler, J. I Sit Down to Type.
Sexton. Play, The.
Swift, J. Lines to Pope.
Wheatley, P. Address to the Atheist, by P.
  Wheatley at the Age of 14 Years—1767, An.
  Atheism.
Wright, C. Composition in Grey and Pink.

Athena
Callimachus. On Pallas Bathing.
Cavafy. Athena's Vote.
Clampitt. Athena.
"H. D." Helios and Athene.
Piercy. Athena in the Front Lines.
Wilde, O. Charmides.

See also **Minerva**

Athens, Greece
Browning, R. Pheidippides.
Byron, G. Maid of Athens, Ere We Part.
Meredith, G. Solon.
Muldoon, P. Dancers at the Moy.
Nemerov. On Getting Out Of Vietnam.
Patchen. Age of Pericles, The.
Sandburg, C. Anecdote of Hemlock for Two
  Athenians.
Swift, J. Ode to the Athenian Society.
Wordsworth, W. Modern Athens, The.
  Translation of a Celebrated Greek Song.

Athletics and Athletes
Davie, D. After the Match.
Dickey, J. Olympian, The.
Gunn, T. Courtesies of the Interregnum.
Housman. To an Athlete Dying Young.
Hughes, L. America's Young Black Joe!
Levi, P. Decathlon Man.
Olson, C. I Mean, No.
Piercy. Morning Athletes.
Rexroth, K. Vitamins and Roughage.
Updike. Ex-Basketball Player.
Whitman, W. Runner, The.

Atlanta, Georgia
Whittier. Howard at Atlanta.

Atlantic Charter
Hughes, L. Envoy to Africa.

Atlantic City, New Jersey
Hughes, L. Seashore through Dark Glasses
  (Atlantic City).
Kumin, M. Atlantic City 1939.

Atlantic Ocean
Clampitt. Remembering Greece.
Collins, B. Walking across the Atlantic.
Cowper, W. Castaway, The.
Eberhart, R. Child, The.
Glück, L. Lady in the Single, The.
Kipling, R. Deep-Sea Cables, The.
Longfellow, H. Seaweed.
Sandburg, C. North Atlantic.
Sexton. Crossing the Atlantic.
Tomlinson, C. Atlantic, The.

Atlantis
Lindsay, N. Song in July, A.
Szymborska, W. Atlantis.

Atomic Bomb
Ai. Chance.
  Testimony of J. Robert Oppenheimer, The.
Ciardi, J. V-J Day.
Cooper, J. After the Bomb Tests.
Davie, D. Rejoinder to a Critic.
Dubie. Renunciation of the Desert Primrose, A.
Dugan, A. Actual Vision of Morning's
  Extrusion.
Eberhart, R. On Shooting Particles beyond the
  World.
Frost, R. U. S. 1946 King's X.
Ginsberg, A. Plutonian Ode.
Komunyakaa. 1984.
  For You, Sweetheart, I'll Sell Plutonium
    Reactors.
Levertov. On the 32nd Anniversary of the
  Bombing of Hiroshima and Nagasaki.
Merton. La Salette.
  Original Child Bomb.
Niedecker. Could You Be Right.
  New! / Reason explodes. Atomic split.
  O Tannenbaum.
Stafford, W. At the Bomb Testing Site.
Stock, R. Elemental Trust.
Sze. Los Alamos Museum, The.
Warren, R. New Dawn.
Williams, C. K. Dream, The.
Wilner, E. High Noon at Los Alamos.
See also **Hiroshima, Japan; Nuclear War**

Atoms
Brodsky, J. At a Lecture.
Dickinson, E. Choice.
Emerson, R. Atom displaces all atoms beside,
  The.
  Atom from atom yawns as far.
Meredith, W. Walter Jenks' Bath.
Raine, K. Scala Coeli.
Rukeyser, M. I have tried to show the atom as a
  source.

Atonement
Arnold, M. Sick King in Bokhara, The.
Byron, G. Lines Addressed to a Young Lady.
Herrick. Abels Bloud.
  Recompence, The.
Jeffers, R. Fire.
Pinsky. Avenue.
Smart, C. Hymn to the Supreme Being.

Attics
Mahon. Attic, The.
Nemerov. View from an Attic Window, The.

Sandburg, C. Upstairs.

Attucks, Crispus
Hayden, R. Crispus Attucks.
Wright, J. Crispus Attucks.

Auctions
Hardy, T. Bags of Meat.
Kumin, M. Selling of the Slaves, The.
Levine, P. Buying and Selling.
McHugh, H. At a Loss.
Roethke. Auction, The.
Sandburg, C. Auctioneer.
Wilde, O. Sonnet on the Sale by Auction of
  Keats' Love Letters.

Auden, W. H. (Wystan Hugh)
Berryman. Shirley & Auden.
Corbett, W. Reading C. K. Williams's "The
  Critic."
Davie, D. Cheshire.
Dugan, A. Speech for Auden.
Eberhart, R. To Auden on His Fiftieth.
  Trying to Hold It All Together.
Kinsella, T. Memory of W.H. Auden.
Meredith, W. Talking Back (To W. H. Auden).
Rexroth, K. Letter to Wystan Hugh Auden, A.
Schuyler, J. Wystan Auden.
Shapiro, K. At Auden's Grave.
Spender, S. Auden at Milwaukee.
  Auden's Funeral.
Weiss, T. As You Like It.
Wilbur, R. For W. H. Auden.

Audubon, John James
Clampitt. Winchester: The Autumn Equinox.
Eberhart, R. Key West.
Niedecker. Audubon.
  To whom / can I leave.
Warren, R. Audubon: A Vision.

August
Ammons. Mid-August.
Atwood. Late August.
Bly, R. August Rain.
Clampitt. August Darks, The.
Corbett, W. August.
  Late August.
Dunbar, P. In August.
Eberhart, R. Loon Call, A.
Hardy, T. August Midnight, An.
  Wet August, A.
Lawrence, D. H. August Holidays.
Levi, P. August.
Merton. On a Day in August.
Merwin. Sound of Rapids of Laramie River in
  Late August.
Millay, E. If Still Your Orchards Bear.
Nemerov. Ending, An.
Oliver, M. August.
Plath. In Midas' Country.
Rich, A. August.
Riley, J. August.
Rossetti, C. And is this August weather? nay
  not so.
Schuyler, J. Sonnet: "August, tasting of ripe
  grapes and afternoon sleep."
Sexton. I Remember.
Snyder, G. Mid-August at Sourdough Mountain
  Lookout.
Swinburne. August.
Walcott. Dark August.
Williams, M. August Evening Outside of
  Nashville, An.

Augustine, Saint
Herrick. Confession.
Logan, J. Prologue and Questions for St.
  Augustine On His Sixteenth Centenary.
Nemerov. Frozen City, The.
Whittier. Shadow and the Light, The.

Augustus (Octavian)
Cavafy. In a Township of Asia Minor.

Aunt Jemima
Hayden, R. Aunt Jemima of the Ocean Waves.

Aunts
Amichai [*or* Amikhai]. Throw Pillows.
Blue Cloud. To-ta Ti-om.
Ciardi, J. Aunt Mary.
  Visit to Aunt Francesca, A.
Clifton, L. Praise Song.

Cooper, J. In the House of the Dying.
Creeley. I Love You.
Davie, D. Abbeyforde.
De la Mare. Mrs. Grundy.
Dunbar, P. Appreciation.
Eliot, T. S. Aunt Helen.
Ferlinghetti, L. Photo of Emily, The.
Ginsberg, A. To Aunt Rose.
Jacobsen, J. My Small Aunt.
Lawrence, D. H. Change of Government.
Paley, G. My Father Said.
Plath. Tour, The.
Prunty. Distance into Place, The.
Ramanujan. History.
Rich, A. Aunt Jennifer's Tigers.
Robinson, E. Aunt Imogen.
Roethke. Elegy: "Her face like a rain-beaten stone on the day she rolled off."
Sexton. Some Foreign Letters.
  Walking in Paris.
Stafford, W. Aunt Mabel.
  Family Turn, A.
Tate, J. Aunt Edna.
Zagajewski. My Aunts.

Aurora Borealis (Northern Lights)
Dubie. Widow Speaks to the Auroras of a December Night, A.

Auschwitz, Poland
Levi, P. Buna.
McGrath, T. Remembering the Children of Auschwitz.
Rukeyser, M. Breaking Open.
Sexton. After Auschwitz.
Zagajewski. Blackened River, The.

Australia
Ginsberg, A. Ayers Rock / Uluru Song.
Heaney, S. Requiem for the Croppies.
Kipling, R. Lichtenberg.
  Ode: "So long as memory, valour, and faith endure."
  Young Queen, The.
Komunyakaa. Bennelong's Blues.
  Corners of Night.
  Frank's Poem.
  Gerry's Jazz.
  Heroes of Waterloo.
  In the Mirror.
  Meditations on a Dingo.
  New Gold Mountain.
  Protection of Moveable Cultural Heritage.
  Report from the Lucky Country.
  Under the Harbour Bridge.
  Visitation.
  Waratah.
  White Lady.
Muldoon, P. Bangle, The.
Very. Stony Desert of Life, The.

Austria
Kumin, M. On Reading an Old Baedeker in Schloss Leopoldskron.
Laughlin, J. In the Salzkammergut.
  Inn at Kirchstetten, The.
  Remembrance.
Zagajewski. Anton Bruckner.

Authorship and Authors
Bradstreet, A. Author to Her Book, The.
Browning, E. Vision of Poets, A.
Hardy, T. At a Rehearsal of One of J.M.B.'s Plays.
Herrick. Argument of His Book, The.
  On His Booke.
  Poetry Perpetuates the Poet.
  To His Book[e].
  To His Booke.
  To His Learned Friend M. Jo. Harmar, Phisitian to to Colledge of Westminster.
  To Sir George Parrie, Doctor of the Civill Law.
Johnson, S. Young Author, The.
Jonson, B. To His Much and Worthily Esteemed Friend the Author.
  To the Worthy Author on *The Husband*.
Nash, O. So That's Who I Remind Me Of.
Piercy. For the Young Who Want To.
Pope, A. Prologue to the *Three Hours after Marriage*.

Pound, E. Lake Isle, The.
Rich, A. Frame.
Robinson, E. Book of Annandale, The.
  George Crabbe.
  Verlaine.
Updike. Agatha Christie and Beatrix Potter.
  Authors' Residences.
  Clan, The.
  Die Neuen Heiligen.
  I Missed His Book, but I Read His Name.
  Jolly Greene Giant, The.
  Tome-Thoughts, from the *Times*.
Wordsworth, W. Plea for Authors, May, 1838, A.
  Poet to His Grandchild; Sequel to "A Plea for Authors."

Automation
Moore, M. Four Quartz Crystal Clocks.
Prunty. Player Piano, The.

Automobile Accidents
Ai. James Dean.
Amichai [*or* Amikhai]. First Rain on a Burned Car, The.
Ciardi, J. Traffic Victim Sends a Sonnet of Confused Thanks to God as the Sovereign Host, A.
Clampitt. 'Eighty-Nine.
Cooper, J. All the Leaves Were Green.
Dugan, A. On an Accident: On a Newspaper Story.
Glück, L. Racer's Widow, The.
Jackson, L. It Has Been Read by All.
Lux. Wife Hits Moose.
Meredith, W. Earth Walk.
Muldoon, P. Good Friday, 1971. Driving Westward.
Nash, O. Strange Case of the Cautious Motorist, The.
Ramanujan. Dancers in a Hospital.
Roethke. Highway: Michigan.
Schuyler, J. Stun.
Shapiro, K. Auto Wreck.
Stafford, W. My Father: October 1942.
Sze. Ice Floe.
Warren, R. Going West.
  Minneapolis Story.
  Old Nigger on One-Mule Cart Encountered Late at Night When Driving Home from Party in the Back Country.
Williams, C. K. Travelers.
Williams, M. Accident: A Short Story.
Williams, W. Man and Nature.
  Romance Moderne.

Automobile Racing
Dubie. Death of the Race Car Driver, The.
Glück, L. Racer's Widow, The.

Automobiles
Ammons. Auto Mobile.
Bishop, E. Filling Station.
Bly, R. Driving toward the Lac Qui Parle River.
Bukowski. Dogs.
  Stolen.
Carruth, H. Eternity Blues.
  Sociology of Toyotas and Jade Chrysanthemums, The.
  Song: Luxury.
Ciardi, J. Craft.
Cummings, E. E. She being Brand.
Davie, D. Pontiac.
Dickey, J. Cherrylog Road.
Dickey, W. Things Kept.
Ginsberg, A. Green Automobile, The.
  Wrote This Last Night.
Gunn, T. All Do Not All Things Well.
McHugh, H. Auto.
Nash, O. Poor Mr. Strawbridge.
  Strange Case of Mr. Niobob's Transmogrification, The.
  Strange Case of the Cautious Motorist, The.
Nemerov. Fugue.
Parker, D. One Perfect Rose.
Patchen. Magic Car, The.
Sandburg, C. Portrait of a Motorcar.
Shapiro, K. Buick.
Stafford, W. Old Blue.
  Traveling Through the Dark.

Trip, The.
  Yellow Cars.
Tate, J. In the Realm of the Ignition.
Tomlinson, C. Arch, The.
Updike. Cars in Caracas, The.
  Duet, with Muffled Brake Drums.
  Self-Service.
  Short Days, The.
  Thin Air.
Williams, C. K. New Car.
Williams, M. Lesson on the Twentieth Century, A.
Williams, W. Ballad of Faith.
  Intelligent Sheepman and the New Cars, The.
Zukofsky, L. Pretty.
See also **Driving and Drivers**

Autumn
Amichai [*or* Amikhai]. Autumn Is Near and Memory of My Parents.
  Autumn is Near and the Memory of My Parents.
  Beginning of Autumn in the Hills of Ephraim.
  Fall in Connecticut.
Ammons. Autumn Song.
  Equinox.
  Grass Miracles, The.
  Here & Now.
Angelou. Late October.
Apollinaire. Autumn.
  Autumn Crocuses.
Baudelaire. Autumn Sonnet.
  Song of Autumn.
Berry, W. October 10.
  Snake, The.
Blake, W. To Autumn.
Blok. Autumn Freedom.
Blue Cloud. Autumn Morning.
  Sweet Corn.
Bly, R. Fire of Despair Has Been Our Savior, The.
  In Rainy September.
  Silence.
Bogan, L. Simple Autumnal.
Brodsky, J. Autumn in Norenskaia.
Brontë, E. O come with me, thus ran the song.
  Old church tower and garden wall, The.
  Song.
Brooks, G. Sunset of the City, A.
Browning, R. By the Fire-Side.
Burns, R. Song, Composed in August.
Carruth, H. Emergency Haying.
  November: Indian Summer.
  Once More.
  This Song.
Cavafy. By an Open Window.
Clampitt. Winchester: The Autumn Equinox.
Corbett, W. September Song.
  Vermont Apollinaire.
Crane, H. October-November.
  Pastorale.
  Sunday Morning Apples.
Creeley. Knokke.
  This Day.
Cummings, E. E. Allbutnotquitemost.
  Always before your voice my soul.
  Autumn is:that between there and here.
  !blac / k / agains / t.
  Cruelly,love / walk the autumn long.
  Dim / i / nu / tiv / e this park is e.
  It's over a(see just).
  O purple finch / please tell me why.
  Timeless / ly this / (merely and whose).
  To stand(alone)in some.
  Wind has blown the rain away and blown, A.
Cunningham, J. Autumn.
"Dario." In Autumn ("I know that there are those who say, "Why don't you sing now'").
Dickey, J. Autumn.
Dickinson, E. As Summer into Autumn slips.
  Autumn is among us.
  Autumn—overlooked my Knitting.
  I remember the leaves were falling.
  It consoles the happy Sorrow of Autumn.
  Morns are meeker than they were, The.
  Name—of it—is "Autumn," The.
  Red Leaves take the Green Leaves place, The.
  Summer has been wide and deep, The.

Dugan, A.   Variation on a Theme by Stevens.
Dunbar, P.   Merry Autumn.
  Signs of the Times.
Eberhart, R.   Autumnal.
  Book of Nature, The.
  Hornets by the Sill.
  In the Garden.
  Loon Call, A.
  Spider, The.
  Vermont Idyll.
Ferlinghetti, L.   New York—Albany.
Frost, R.   Clear and Colder.
  My November Guest.
  Quest of the Purple-Fringed, The.
García Lorca.   Sun Has Set, The.
Ginsberg, A.   Autumn again, you wouldn't
    know in the city.
  Autumn Gold: New England Fall.
Glück, L.   All Hallows.
  Thanksgiving.
Graves, R.   September Landscape.
Gunn, T.   Autumn Chapter in a Novel.
Gurney, I.   Autumn.
  Bronze Sounding, The.
  Michaelmas.
  O Tree of Pride.
  Old Thought.
  Song of Autumn.
  Ypres—Minsterworth.
Hacker, M.   Late August.
Hall, D.   Kicking the Leaves.
  Stone Walls.
Hamill, S.   Friend.
  Saprophyte.
Hardy, T.   Autumn in King's Hintock Park.
  Autumn Rain-Scene, An.
  Best She Could, The.
  Days to Recollect.
  Last Chrysanthemum, The.
  Last Week in October.
  Later Autumn, The.
  News for Her Mother.
  Night in November, A.
  Shortening Days at the Homestead.
  Upper Birch-Leaves, The.
Hopkins, G.   Hurrahing in Harvest.
  Now I am minded to take a pipe in hand.
  Spring and Fall.
Housman.   Tell Me Not Here [It Needs Not
    Saying].
Hughes, L.   Autumn Note.
  Autumn Thought.
  Poème d'Automne.
Hughes, T.   Autumn Notes.
  October Dawn.
Ignatow, D.   Autumn 2.
Jacobsen, J.   It Is the Season.
Jeffers, R.   Autumn Evening.
Keats.   To Autumn.
Kinsella, T.   Another September.
  To Autumn.
Kipling, R.   Two Months.
Kizer, C.   Complex Autumnal.
Kumin, M.   Mummies, The.
Kunitz, S.   Approach of Autumn.
  End of Summer.
Larkin, P.   Afternoons.
  Autumn.
  Autumn Has Caught Us in Our Summer Wear.
  Mother, Summer, I.
  Past Days of Gales.
Lawrence, D. H.   At the Window.
  Autumn at Taos.
  Autumn Sunshine.
  Butterfly.
  Dolour of Autumn.
  Guelder Roses.
  Ship of Death, The.
  Song-Day in Autumn.
Levertov.   Air of November.
  Autumnal.
  Coming Fall, The.
  Settling.
Levine, P.   Zaydee.
Longfellow, H.   Aftermath.
Lorde.   What My Child Learns of the Sea.

MacLeish.   Autumn.
  Immortal Autumn.
  Old Men in the Leaf Smoke, The.
  Survivor.
  Tourist Death.
  Winter Is Another Country.
Mallarmé.   Sigh.
Maritain.   Autumn.
McGrath, T.   Another Season.
  Autumn Song.
  Beyond the Red River.
  Black Train, The.
  In Early Autumn.
Melville, H.   Pontoosuce.
Meredith, G.   Autumn Even-Song.
  Ode to the Spirit of Earth in Autumn.
  Seed-Time.
  Song: Autumn.
Merwin.   Autumn Evening.
  Late Night in Autumn.
  Love for October, The.
  Man with One Leaf in October Night.
  New Season, The.
  Now and Again.
  September Plowing.
  Sickness at the Equinox, A.
  Under Black Leaves.
  Walking into Autumn.
  Writing on a Fallen Leaf, The.
Millay, E.   Autumn.
  Autumn Chant.
  Autumn Daybreak.
  Death of Autumn, The.
  God's World.
  Now that the west is washed of clouds and
    clear.
  Song: "Gone, gone again is Summer the lovely."
  Spring and the Fall, The.
Milosz, C.   Mittelbergheim.
Nemerov.   Again.
  Autumnal.
  Burning the Leaves.
  Consent, The.
  Elegy of Last Resort.
  First Leaf, The.
  For Robert Frost, in the Autumn, in Vermont.
  Late Butterflies.
  Walking Down Westgate in the Fall.
Niedecker.   Autumn.
  Autumn Night.
  Fall.
  O late fall.
  They've lost their leaves.
  Transition.
O'Hara, F.   Poem: "Eager note on my door said
    'Call me,' The."
Owen, W.   Sonnet Autumnal.
Paley, G.   Autumn.
  Leaves Apples.
  When I Was Asked How I Could Leave
    Vermont in the Middle of October.
Pasternak, B.   God of Details, The.
Patchen.   Autumn Is the Crows' Time.
Pessoa.   Lydia, when our Autumn comes.
Piercy.   Some Collisions Bring Luck.
Plath.   Gold Mouths Cry.
  Letter in November.
Prunty.   Foliage Tour, The.
  Late Fall, Late Light.
Riley, J.   Autumn.
  Autumnal Extravaganza, An.
  Dream of Autumn, A.
  King, The.
  Rambo-Tree, The.
  When the Frost Is on the Punkin.
Rilke.   Autumn Day.
  Autumn Fire.
Roethke.   Slow Season.
Rossetti, C.   Autumn.
  Bitter for Sweet.
  Can I know it?—Nay.— / Shall I know it?—
    Yea.
  Death-Watches.
  October Garden, An.
Rukeyser, M.   Salamander.
Sandburg, C.   Auburn.

  Autumn Movement.
  Buckwheat.
  Corn Prattlings.
  Cornucopia.
  Falltime.
  First Sonata for Karlen Paula.
  Lake Michigan Morning.
  On a Railroad Right of Way.
  Poplar and Elm.
  Sleep Impression.
  Tawny.
  Theme in Yellow.
  Three Pieces on the Smoke of Autumn.
  Timber Moon.
  Under the Harvest Moon.
Sarton, M.   First Autumn, The.
Schuyler, J.   Autumn Leaves.
  Held Breath, A.
  Master of the Golden Glow, The.
  People Who See Bubbles Rise.
Shelley, P.   Autumn: A Dirge.
  Ode to the West Wind.
Simic.   Fall Day, A.
Stafford, W.   Fall Wind.
Stevens, W.   Autumn.
Swenson, M.   October Textures.
  On Its Way.
  Rusty Autumn.
  View to the North.
Swinburne.   Hendecasyllabics.
Sze.   Strawberries in Wooden Bowls.
Tate, A.   Seasons of the Soul.
Thomas, D.   Poem in October.
Thoreau.   Fall of the Leaf, The ("Grown tired of
    this rank summer's wealth").
  I am the Autumnal sun.
  I mark the summer's swift decline.
  Soul's Season, The.
  Tall Ambrosia.
Tomlinson, C.   At Holwell Farm.
  At the Autumn Equinox.
  Autumn.
  Autumn Piece.
  Blaubeuren.
  Gossamers, The.
  One Day of Autumn.
  Valestrieri.
  White Van, The.
Trakl.   Rats, The.
Tu Fu.   Déjeuner sur l'herbe.
Updike.   Great Scarf of Birds, The.
  November.
Van Duyn.   Day in Late October, A.
Very.   Autumn Days.
  Autumn Flowers.
  Autumn Flowers, The.
  Autumn Leaves.
  Dying Leaf, The.
  Sumach Leaves, The.
Warren, R.   Acquaintance with Time in Early
    Autumn.
  Autumn Twilight Piece.
  Composition in Gold and Red-Gold.
  Croesus in Autumn.
  First Moment of Autumn Recognized.
  Heart of Autumn.
Whittier.   Autumn Thoughts.
  Battle Autumn of 1862, The.
  Day, A.
  Fruit-Gift, The.
  Last Eve of Summer, The.
  Last Walk in Autumn, The.
  Song of Harvest, A.
  St. Martin's Summer.
Wilbur, R.   Alatus.
  Fall in Corrales.
  October Maples, Portland.
Williams, C. K.   Listen carefully. / I'm
    meditating.
Williams, T.   In Jack-O'-Lantern's Weather.
Williams, W.   10/14.
  Autumn.
  Pause, The.
  Prelude to Winter.
  Sometimes It Turns Dry and the Leaves Fall
    before They Are Beautiful.

Yellow Season, The.
Wilner, E.　Facing into It.
Mulch, The.
Wordsworth, W.　Let More Ambitious Poets
　Take the Heart.
Longest Day; Addressed to My Daughter, The.
September, 1815.
September, 1819.
Wright, C.　Appalachian Book of the Dead, The.
Autumn's Sidereal, November's a Ball and
　Chain.
Maple on the Hill.
Miles Davis and Elizabeth Bishop Fake the
　Break.
October 2.
Waiting for Tu Fu.
Watching the Equinox Arrive in Charlottesville,
　September 1992.
Wright, J.　Autumn Begins in Martins Ferry,
　Ohio.
Autumnal.
Lament for My Brother on a Hayrake.
Yeats.　Falling of the Leaves, The.
Zagajewski.　Autumn.
Chinese Poem.
Zaturenska.　Chorale for Autumn.
Zukofsky, L.　World autumn, The.

Avalanches
Frost, R.　On Taking from the Top to Broaden
　the Base.
Laughlin, J.　Avalanche, The.
Montale.　Slope.

Aviation and Aviators
Cooper, J.　Meteors.
Hall, D.　Airstrip in Essex, 1960, An.
Old Pilot, The.
Jarrell, R.　Dead Wingman, The.
Death of the Ball Turret Gunner, The.
Learners, The.
Losses.
Siegfried.
Levine, P.　Poem of Flight, The.
Nemerov.　Dream of Flying Comes of Age, The.
Sandburg, C.　To Beachey, 1912.
Snyder, G.　Vapor Trails.
Spender, S.　Landscape near an Aerodrome,
　The.
Updike.　Sonic Boom.
See also **Air Travel; Air Warfare; Airports**

Avignon, France
Glück, L.　Letter from Provence.
Stein, G.　Prudence Caution and Foresight: A
　Story of Avignon.

Avocados
Logan, J.　Avocado.

Axes
Collins, B.　Splitting Wood.
Frost, R.　Axe-Helve, The.
Levertov.　Sound of the Axe.
Plath.　Words.
Rumi.　Pickaxe, The.
Simic.　Ax.
Snyder, G.　Axe Handles.
Stock, R.　Go As Played in the Best Circles; Or
　Rotten Axe-Handle.

Ayr, Scotland
Burns, R.　Braes o' Ballochmyle, The.
Brigs of Ayr, a Poem. Inscribed to J.
　B*********, Esq; Ayr, The.
Flow Gently, Sweet Afton.
Song: "Gloomy night is gath'ring fast, The."
Thou Ling'ring Star.

Azaleas
Very.　Azalea Swamp.
Zukofsky, L.　Azalea.

Aztecs
Clampitt.　Tepoztlán.
Ferlinghetti, L.　Baja Beatitudes.
Lux.　What Montezuma Fed Cortés and His
　Men.
Sandburg, C.　Aztec Mask.
Dusty Doors.
Stafford, W.　Ultimate Problems.
Tomlinson, C.　In Michoacán.
　Mictlantecuhtli.

Williams, W.　Three Nahuatl Poems.

B

Babel, Tower of
Merton.　Tower of Babel.
Tower of Babel—A Morality, The.
Szymborska, W.　Tower of Babel, The.

Babies
Auden.　Mundus et Infans.
Blake, W.　Cradle Song, A: "Sleep, sleep, beauty
　bright."
Broumas, O.　Memory Piece / for Baby Jane.
Browning, E.　Sleeping and Watching.
Burns, R.　Bonie Dundee.
Rowin 't in Her Apron, The.
Ciardi, J.　For Myra out of the Album.
Clampitt.　At a Rest Stop in Ohio.
Coleridge, S.　Frost at Midnight.
Sonnet to a Friend Who Asked How I Felt
　When the Nurse First Presented My Infant to
　Me.
Cooper, J.　For a Boy Born in Wartime.
Creeley.　Human Song.
Cummings, E. E.　Youful / larger / of smallish).
Davie, D.　Christening, A.
Dickey, J.　Magus, The.
Dickey, W.　For Every Last Batch When the
　Next One Comes Along.
Dugan, A.　On a Dispossess Precept. 2.
Dunbar, P.　Little Brown Baby.
Poet and the Baby, The.
Puttin' the Baby Away.
Turning of the Babies in the Bed, The.
Two Little Boots.
Glück, L.　Egg, The.
My Cousin in April.
Graves, R.　Call It a Good Marriage.
To Lucia at Birth.
Hacker, M.　Country & Western II.
Hardy, T.　New Toy, The.
Herrick.　Upon a child.
Howe, F.　Nursery, The.
Hughes, L.　Lullaby (For a Black Mother).
Jarrell, R.　Bats.
Johnson, S.　Ballad: "Tender infant, meek and
　mild, The."
Kinnell.　Olive Wood Fire, The.
Koch, K.　Girl and Baby Florist Sidewalk Pram
　Nineteen Seventy Something.
Komunyakaa.　Wet Nurse.
Kumin, M.　Grandchild.
Larkin, P.　Born Yesterday.
Lawrence, D. H.　Baby Asleep after Pain, A.
Baby-Movements.
Baby Running Barefoot.
Baby Songs Ten Months Old.
War-Baby.
Lorde.　Now That I Am Forever with Child.
Lux.　Upon Seeing An Ultrasound Photo of an
　Unborn Child.
MacNeice.　Aubade for Infants.
Mahon.　Unborn Child, An.
McHugh, H.　Size of Spokane, The.
Who Made Her.
Merrill, J.　Little Fanfare for Felix Magowan.
Merton.　Never Call a Babysitter in a
　Thunderstorm.
Merwin.　Marica Lart.
Nash, O.　After the Christening.
Come On In, the Senility Is Fine.
It Must Be the Milk.
Our Child Doesn't Know Anything.
Pediatric Reflection.
Reflection on Babies.
Song to Be Sung by the Father of Infant Female
　Children.
Thunder over the Nursery.
Niedecker.　Katharine Anne.
Wartime.
Oppen.　Sara in Her Father's Arms.
Orr, G.　Hand, The: "Brightness Falls from the
　Air."
Pagis.　Pages in an Album.

Plath.　By Candlelight.
Candles.
Death and Co.
Event.
For a Fatherless Son.
Gulliver.
I Want, I Want.
Magi.
Morning Song.
New Year on Dartmoor.
Nick and the Candlestick.
Night Dances, The.
You're.
Ramanujan.　Alien.
Riley, J.　Babe Herrick.
Babyhood.
Baby's Dying.
Give Me the Baby.
John Tarkington Jameson.
King of Oo-Rinktum-Jing, The.
Leedle Dutch Baby.
Lullaby: "Maple strews the embers of its leaves,
　The."
Michael Flynn and the Baby.
Phantom, The.
Way the Baby Came, The.
Way the Baby Woke, The.
When Baby Played.
When Baby Slept.
When Baby Woke.
Rossetti, C.　Angels at the foot, / And Angels at
　the head.
Baby cry— / Oh fie!
Baby lies so fast asleep.
Baby's cradle with no baby in it, A.
Ballad: "Soft white lamb in the daisy meadow."
Christmas Day.
Crimson curtains round my mother's bed.
Crying, my little one, footsore and weary?
Dog lies in his kennel, The.
Holy Innocents.
Husband and Wife.
I know a baby, such a baby,— / Round blue
　eyes and cheeks of pink.
Lie a-bed, / Sleepy head, / Shut up eyes, bo-
　peep.
Light Love.
Lullaby: "Love me,—I love you / Love me, my
　baby."
Lullaby, oh lullaby! / Flowers are closed and
　lambs are sleeping.
Motherless baby and babyless mother.
My baby has a father and a mother.
My baby has a mottled fist.
Our little baby fell asleep.
Why did baby die.
Your brother has a falcon.
Rukeyser, M.　Do you know what I play to be,
　in bed at night?
Night Feeding.
Sandburg, C.　Baby Vamps.
Chicago Boy Baby.
Portrait of a Child Settling Down for an
　Afternoon Nap.
Sixteen Months.
Slippery.
Sexton.　Falling Dolls, The.
Hangman, The.
Unknown Girl in the Maternity Ward.
Smith, S.　But Murderous.
Bye Baby Bother.
Dream of Nourishment, A.
Infant.
Sad Mother, The.
She Said..
Valuable.
Snyder, G.　Changing Diapers.
Kyoto Born in Spring Song.
Stafford, W.　Stillborn.
Updike.　Stunt Flier, The.
Whalen, P.　Alleyway.
Whitman, W.　From Pent-up Aching Rivers.
Williams, C. K.　Creams.
Kingdom of Stinking Wishes, The.
Rampage, The.
You're two, that's great.

Williams, M.   For Reuben, at Twelve Months.
   Ones that Are Thrown Out, The.
   Poem for Emily, A.
Williams, W.   Struggle of Wings.
Wordsworth, D.   Cottager to Her Infant, (By My
   Sister), The.
Wordsworth, W.   Emigrant Mother, The.
   Her Eyes Are Wild.
   Infant M— M—, The.
Wright, J.   Mary Bly.
   Song for the Middle of the Night, A.
Yeats.   Dolls, The.
   Song from "The Player Queen,"A.
See also **Infant Death**

Baby-Sitting and Baby-Sitters
Amichai [*or* Amikhai].   Parents Left the Child,
   The.
Kunitz, S.   Magic Curtain, The.
Merton.   Never Call a Babysitter in a
   Thunderstorm.
Plath.   Babysitters, The.

Babylon
Ammons.   Coming to Sumer.
   Sumerian.
Bishop, E.   Burglar of Babylon, The.
De la Mare.   Bitter Waters.
Levertov.   Candles in Babylon.
Lindsay, N.   Babylon, Babylon, Babylon the
   Great.
   Darling Daughter of Babylon.
Merton.   Captives—a Psalm, The.
Nemerov.   To the Babylonians.
Rossetti, C.   Babylon the Great.
   By the Waters of Babylon.
   By the Waters of Babylon. B.C. 570.
Sandburg, C.   Ashurnatsirpal III.
   Bilbea.

Bacchus
Emerson, R.   Bacchus.
Herrick.   Bacchanalian Verse, A.
   Hymn[e] to Bacchus, A.
   Hymne to Bacchus, A.
   To Bacchus, a Canticle.
Jonson, B.   Dedication of the King's New
   Cellar. To Bacchus, The.
Ransom, J.   Nocturne: "Where now has our
   young Adam."

Bach, Johann Sebastian
Bly, R.   Six Winter Privacy Poems.
Cooper, J.   My Friend.
Gurney, I.   Bach and the Sentry.
Merrill, J.   Trees Listening to Bach.
Moore, M.   Dream.
Niedecker.   Slip of a girl-announcer, The.
Sandburg, C.   Number Man.
Whalen, P.   Spring Musick.
Williams, W.   Divertimiento.
Zagajewski.   Good Friday in the Tunnels of the
   Métro.

Bachelors
Eberhart, R.   New England Bachelor, A.
Herrick.   Single Life Most Secure.
   To His Tomb-Maker.
   Upon the Loss[e] of His Mistresses.
Nash, O.   Tune for an Ill-Tempered Clavichord.
Riley, J.   Farmer Whipple—Bachelor.
   My Bachelor Chum.
   My Jolly Friend's.

Backs
Lorde.   Monkeyman.
Lux.   His Spine Curved Just Enough.
Shapiro, K.   Back, The.

Bacon, Sir Francis
Bierce.   Novum Organum.
Campion, T.   Ad ampliss. totius Angliae
   Cancellarium, Fr. Ba.
De la Mare.   Polonius.
Herbert, G.   To the Right Hon. the Lord
   Chancellor (Bacon).
Jonson, B.   Lord Bacon's Birthday.
Riley, J.   Lord Bacon.
Whitman, W.   Shakspeare-Bacon's Cipher.

Bacteria
Nemerov.   Bacterial War, The.

Badgers
Clare, J.   Badger.
   Untitled.
Heaney, S.   Badgers, The.
Hughes, T.   Coming Down through Somerset.
Muldoon, P.   Brock.
Stafford, W.   You Don't Know the End.
Tomlinson, C.   Scream, The.

Bagels
Ignatow, D.   Bagel, The.

Baggage
Dickey, J.   Baggage King, The.
Ginsberg, A.   In the Baggage Room at
   Greyhound.

Bagpipes
Logue, C.   Air.
MacDiarmid, H.   Bagpipe Music.
MacNeice.   Bagpipe Music.
Tomlinson, C.   Mr. Brodsky.
Whittier.   Pipes at Lucknow, The.

Bahamas
Eberhart, R.   Scouring, The.
MacLeish.   Bahamas.
Oppen.   Bahamas.

Baker, Chet
Williams, M.   Death of Chet Baker, The.

Baking and Bakers
Amichai [*or* Amikhai].   My Mother Baked the
   Whole World for Me.
Mistral, G.   Bread.
Rumi.   Breadmaking.
Zagajewski.   Bakery.

Balaam
Meredith, G.   Ass of Balaam, The.

Baldness
Donne.   Licentious Person, A.
Herrick.   On Jone.
   Upon Blanch.

Ballet
Brodsky, J.   Classical ballet, let's say, is beauty's
   keep, The.
Crane, H.   To Portapovitch.
Dickinson, E.   I cannot dance upon my Toes.
Graves, R.   Casse-Noisette.
   Two Disciplines.
Hardy, T.   Ballet, The.
Meredith, W.   Ballet, The.
O'Hara, F.   Ode to Tanaquil Leclerq.
Wilbur, R.   L'Etoile.

Balloons
Bishop, E.   Armadillo, The.
Dickinson, E.   You've seen Balloons set—
   Haven't You?
Pagis.   Bestiary.
Plath.   Balloons.
   Morning Song.
Riley, J.   From a Balloon.
   Toy-Balloon, The.
Sandburg, C.   Balloon Faces.
   Five Cent Balloons.

Ballrooms
Komunyakaa.   Tuesday Night at the Savoy
   Ballroom.
Major, C.   Ballroom Dark.

Balls
Berryman.   Ball Poem, The.
Milosz, C.   Ball, A.
Rilke.   Ball, The.
Wilbur, R.   Juggler.
Williams, M.   Catch with Reuben.

Ballylee, Ireland
Yeats.   Coole Park and Ballylee, 1931.
   To Be Carved on a Stone at Thoor Ballylee.

Baltimore, Maryland
Cullen, C.   Incident.
Dubie.   Jeremiad.
Ginsberg, A.   Haunting Poe's Baltimore.
Sarton, M.   Night Watch.

Balzac, Honoré de
Carver, R.   Balzac.

Bamboo
Sze.   Wang Wei.

Bananas
Kipling, R.   Song of Bananas, A.
Sandburg, C.   Unintentional Paint.

Stevens, W.   Floral Decorations for Bananas.

Bandits
Borges.   1891.

Bands
Dunbar, P.   Colored Band, The.
Riley, J.   Old Band, The.

Bangkok, Thailand
Eberhart, R.   Rape of the Cataract, The.
Williams, T.   Separate Poem, A.

Bangladesh
Faiz.   Bangla Desh: 1.
   Bangla Desh: 2.
   Bangla Desh: 3.

Banjos
Dunbar, P.   Banjo Song, A.
   Voice of the Banjo, The.
Hughes, L.   Song for a Banjo Dance.
Kipling, R.   Song of the Banjo, The.

Banking and Bankers
Ai.   Greed.
Amichai [*or* Amikhai].   Box, The.
Bukowski.   Sweater.
Cavafy.   Bank of the Future, The.
Delany, P.   Elegy on the Much Lamented Death
   of Mr. Demar, the Famous Rich Usurer [*or*
   Man], An.
Graves, R.   Bank Account.
Hughes, L.   To the Little Fort of San Lazaro on
   the Ocean Front, Havana.
Johnson, E.   Elegy on the Much Lamented
   Death of Mr. Demar, the Famous Rich Usurer
   [*or* Man], An.
Nash, O.   Anybody for Money? or, Just Bring
   Your Own Basket.
   Bankers Are Just Like Anybody Else, Except
   Richer.
   Ma, What's a Banker? or, Hush, My Child.
Olson, C.   Friend, The.
Sheridan, T.   Elegy on the Much Lamented
   Death of Mr. Demar, the Famous Rich Usurer
   [*or* Man], An.
Swift, J.   Bank Thrown Down, The.
   Elegy on the Much Lamented Death of Mr.
   Demar, the Famous Rich Usurer [*or* Man],
   An.
   Run upon the Bankers, The.
Williams, W.   Simplex Sigilum Veri. A
   Catalogue.
   To a Mexican Pig-Bank.
   Woman in Front of a Bank, A.
See also **Financiers**

Banneker, Benjamin
Wright, J.   Benjamin Banneker Helps to Build a
   City.
   Benjamin Banneker Sends His *Almanac* to
   Thomas Jefferson.

Baptism
Ciardi, J.   Evil Eye, The.
Coleridge, S.   My Baptismal Birthday [*or* Birth-
   Day].
Crashaw.   On the Baptized Ethiopian.
   On the Water of Our Lord's Baptism[e].
Hardy, T.   Christening, The.
   Royal Sponsors.
Herbert, G.   Love.
Herrick.   Baptisme.
   To Julia.
Logan, J.   Homage to John the Baptist.
Merton.   On the Anniversary of My Baptism.
Walcott.   City's Death by Fire, A.
Walker, A.   Baptism.
Williams, C. K.   Acids.
Wordsworth, W.   To Rotha Q—.
Wright, J.   Baptism in the Lead Avenue Ditch.
See also **Christenings**

Bar Mitzvah
Amichai [*or* Amikhai].   My son, the softness of
   your face already shows.

Barbarians
Cavafy.   Waiting for the Barbarians.
Zagajewski.   Barbarians.

Barbecues
See **Picnics and Barbecues**

Barberries
Very. Barberry-Pickers, The.

Barbers and Barbershops
Laughlin, J. Amo Amas Amat.
  Ars Gratia Artis.
Levine, P. To a Child Trapped in a Barber
  Shop.
Nash, O. I'll Get One Tomorrow.
Simic. Whispers.
Suckling, S. Barber, A.
Updike. Aerie.

Barcelona, Spain
Ciardi, J. Reply to S. K.
Creeley. Barcelona: February 13, 1977.
Hughes, L. Air Raid: Barcelona.
Levine, P. Francisco, I'll Bring You Red
  Carnations.
  Hear Me.
Paley, G. On the Ramblas A Tree A Girl.

Bards
Burns, R. Epistle to John Lapraik.
  Lament for James, Earl of Glencairn.
Byron, G. Ballad: "Of all the twice ten
  thousand bards."
  Lines Written in the Travellers' Book at
  Orchomenus.
  Soliloquy of a Bard in the Country.
Emerson, R. And though he dearly prized the
  bards of fame.
  Bard or dunce is blest, but hard.
  Divine Inviters! I accept.
  Genial spark the poet felt, The.
  James Russell Lowell.
  On that night the poet went.
Graves, R. Bards, The.
Gray, T. Bard, The [A Pindaric Ode].
  Long Story, A.
  Progress of Poesy, The.
Keats. 'How Many Bards Gild the Lapses of
  Time!'
  Sonnet: "Where didst thou find, young Bard, thy
  sounding lyre?"
Kipling, R. In the Neolithic Age.
  Last Rhyme of True Thomas, The.
Meredith, G. Aneurin's Harp.
Taliesin. Song of Taliesin.
Whitman, W. As I Ponder'd [*or* Pondered] in
  Silence.
  By Blue Ontario's Shore.
Wordsworth, W. Idle Shepherd-Boys, The; or,
  Dungeon-Ghyll Force. A Pastoral.

Barges
Dubie. Somebody'll Hav' to Shoot Ya Down.
Levertov. Music, A.
Oppen. On the water, solid.
Williams, W. Motor-Barge, The.
  Well Disciplined Bargeman, The.

Barley
Burns, R. John Barleycorn [a Ballad].

Barns
Bly, R. Opening the Door of a Barn I Thought
  Was Empty on New Year's Eve.
Frost, R. Old Barn at the Bottom of the Fogs,
  The.
Hall, D. Great Day in the Cows' House.
Heaney, S. Barn, The.
Lux. Barn Fire.
  His Spine Curved Just Enough.
McHugh, H. Stall.
Merton. Elegy for the Monastery Barn.
Nemerov. Human Things.
Spender, S. Barn, The.
Wright, J. Summer Memory in the Crowded
  City, A.

Baroque
Bogan, L. Baroque Comment.
Fenton, J. Lollipops of the Pomeranian
  Baroque.
Milosz, C. For Jan Lebenstein.
Szymborska, W. Rubens' Women.

Barrel Organs
Riley, J. Old Hand-Organ, The.
See also **Hurdy-Gurdies**

Bars and Bartenders
Ai. Sweet, The.
Blok. I Am Nailed to a Bar with Liquor.
Bukowski. Don't Touch the Girls.
  My Friend.
  Training for Kid Aztec.
  Yellow Cab.
Carver, R. Extirpation.
Ciardi, J. Rhetoric for Danny Keough to Recite
  at the Bar, A.
Collins, B. Bar Time.
Corbett, W. Crossing the Public Garden.
  In out of this shower.
Creeley. Billfold.
  Ciano's.
Cummings, E. E. Dick Mid's large bluish face
  without eyebrows.
  I was sitting in mcsoreley's. outside it was New
  York and beauti- / fully snowing.
  In Healey's Palace I was sitting.
  Infinite jukethrob smoke & swallow to dis.
  Oil tel duh woil doi sez.
  She sits dropping on a caret of clenched arms.
  Them which despair.
  Waddling / madam star, The.
Cunningham, J. New York: 5 March 1957.
Dickey, W. Confidence.
Dugan, A. Memories of the Bowery.
  Swing Shift Blues.
Eliot, T. S. Interlude: in a Bar.
Gallagher, T. Instructions to the Double.
Ginsberg, A. Uptown.
Gunn, T. Fever.
Gurney, I. It Is Winter.
Hall, D. Repeated Shapes, The.
Hughes, L. Bar.
  Juice Joint: Northern City.
  Lenox Avenue Bar.
Jacobsen, J. Notes from a Lenten Bar.
Kinsella, T. Open Court.
Laughlin, J. Bad Night on Third Avenue, A.
Lawrence, D. H. Ships in Bottles.
Levine, P. Midget, The.
  Poem Circling Hamtramck, Michigan, All Night
  in Search of You, The.
Logan, J. Chicago Scene.
Mahon. Terminal Bar, The.
Major, C. Alone, I went into that special.
McHugh, H. Bar and Grill.
Nash, O. How Do You Say Ha-Ha in French.
Niedecker. Club 26.
Patchen. State of the Nation, The.
Rimbaud, A. In Spring, no doubt I prefer the
  drinking-place.
Ritsos. Uncompromising, The.
Sandburg, C. Jungheimer's.
Snyder, G. I Went Into the Maverick Bar.
Tate, J. Failed Tribute to the Stonemason of Tor
  House, Robinson Jeffers.
Tomlinson, C. Far Point.
Updike. Décor.
Whitman, W. Glimpse, A.
Wilbur, R. Violet and Jasper.
Williams, C. K. Bob.
  Medusa.
Williams, M. Christmas Poem, A.
  Glass Darkly, A.
  Man in the Bar Says He Has Something to Say,
  A.
Williams, W. At the Bar.
Wright, J. Old Man Drunk.

Barters
Moore, M. New York.

Baseball
Creeley. Ball Game, The.
Eberhart, R. Ball Game.
Ferlinghetti, L. Baseball Canto.
Hall, D. Baseball Players, The.
  Couplet.
  Old Home Week.
Jacobsen, J. Deaf-Mutes at the Ballgame.
Kizer, C. One to Nothing.
Komunyakaa. Glory.
Logan, J. Brothers: Two Saltimbanques, The.
Moore, M. Baseball and Writing.
  Hometown Piece for Messrs. Alston and Reese.

Nash, O. Hand Me Down My Old School
  Sliding Pads, or, There's a Hint of Strawberry
  Leaves in the Air.
Olson, C. Pitcher, how / exactly is.
Patchen. Origin of Baseball, The.
Pinsky. Night Game, The.
Prunty. Baseball.
  Baseball Team of Unknown Navy Pilots, Pacific
  Theater, 1944, A.
Sandburg, C. Hits and Runs.
Updike. Tao in the Yankee Stadium Bleachers.
Williams, M. Wiedersehen.
  Year They Outlawed Baseball, The.
Williams, W. At the Ball Game.

Basho (Matsuo Basho)
Mahon. Snow Party, The.
Niedecker. Alliance.
  Bashō.
  In the transcendence.
Pinsky. Impossible to Tell.

Basketball
Komunyakaa. Slam, Dunk, & Hook.
Updike. Ex-Basketball Player.

Bathrooms
Ignatow, D. Here I Am.
Logue, C. Middle-aged man is approaching an
  all-night lavatory, A.

Baths and Bathing
Ammons. Foot-Washing, The.
Berryman. Young Woman's Song.
Callimachus. On Pallas Bathing.
Carver, R. Woman Bathing.
Crane, H. Bathers, The.
Davie, D. After the Match.
Dubie. Bellevue Exchange.
Hardy, T. Aquae Sulis.
Jacobsen, J. Country Bath.
Jonson, B. On the New Hot-House.
Kipling, R. Naaman's Song.
Kumin, M. Watering Trough.
Laughlin, J. Fate of Actaeon, The.
Lawrence, D. H. Bathing Resort.
  Forte Dei Marmi.
  Gloire de Dijon.
  Gods! The Gods!, The.
  Sea-Bathers.
Meredith, W. Walter Jenks' Bath.
Nash, O. And Three Hundred and Sixty-Six in
  Leap Year.
  Samson Agonistes.
  Splash!
Olson, C. All Pink from the Bath She Slept.
  Carrying water to the Youth in Honor of Sappho
  Jane Harrison & Miss Duncan if She Had.
Patchen. Saturday Night in the Parthenon.
  Weekend Bathers.
Petrarch. Diana did not more delight her lover.
Plath. Battle-Scene.
  Tale of a Tub.
Plato. On a Bath.
Roethke. Meditation in Hydrotherapy.
Rukeyser, M. From a Play: Publisher's Song.
Rumi. Nasuh.
Sandburg, C. Slippery.
Schuyler, J. March Here.
Simic. Tub, A.
Snyder, G. Bath, The.
  Public Bath, The.
Stock, R. Roseapples and Nudes.
Tate, J. Waking.
Wilbur, R. Five Women Bathing in Moonlight.
Williams, W. Portrait of a Woman at Her Bath.
Zukofsky, L. "Further than."

Bats
Cummings, E. E. I'd think "wonder / if" if.
Dickinson, E. Bat, The.
Heaney, S. Bat on the Road, A.
Jarrell, R. Bats.
Kinsella, T. I left the road where a stile entered
  the wood.
Kizer, C. Intruder, The.
Kumin, M. Hundred Nights, A.
Lawrence, D. H. Bat.
  Man and Bat.
Nash, O. Bat, The.

Roethke. Bat, The.
Sexton. Bat.
Updike. Zoo Bats.
Warren, R. Rumor at Twilight.
Wilbur, R. Mind.
Wilner, E. Bat Cave.

Battlefields
Achillini, C. Wars and of arms some sing, but I.
Amichai [or Amikhai]. Ruhama.
Ammons. At Dawn in 1098.
Blok. On the Field of Kulikovo.
Borges. Sepulchral Inscription.
Brodsky, J. Cappadocia.
Brontë, E. There swept adown that dreary glen.
Burns, R. Battle of Sherra-Moor, The.
  Bonie Laddie, Highland Laddie.
  Killiecrankie.
Cavafy. Battle of Magnesia, The.
Clampitt. Thermopylae.
Cummings, E. E. Earth like a tipsy.
Davie, D. Battlefield, A.
Dugan, A. Notes Toward a Spring Offensive.
  Takeoff on Armageddon —For Ronald Reagan.
Emerson, R. Concord Hymn.
  I am not black in my mind.
  In Memoriam.
Fenton, J. Wind.
Graves, R. Dawn Bombardment.
Gunn, T. Beach Head, The.
Gurney, I. On Somme.
Hall, D. "O Flodden Field."
HaNagid. Victory Over Seville, The.
Hardy, T. In Time of Wars and Tumults.
  San Sebastian.
  Valenciennes.
Hill, G. Distant Fury of Battle, The.
  Pastoral, A: "Mobile, immaculate and austere."
Hughes, T. Crow's Account of the Battle.
  Crow's Fall.
Keats. King Stephen. A Fragment of a Tragedy.
Li Po. March, The.
Melville, H. Inscription: "To them who crossed the flood."
  Shiloh [A Requiem].
Pagis. Siege.
Sandburg, C. Grass.
  New Feet.
Stock, R. Battle Scene.
Szymborska, W. Reality Demands.
Tennyson, A. Morte d'Arthur.
Thoreau. Ah, 'tis in vain the peaceful din.
  But now "no war nor battle's sound."
Whitman, W. Vigil Strange I Kept on the Field One Night.
Whittier. Watchers, The.
Zaturenska. Unsepulchred, 1914–1918, The.

Baucis and Philemon
Gunn, T. Philemon and Baucis.
Swift, J. Baucis and Philemon.

Baudelaire, Charles
Cavafy. Correspondence According to Baudelaire.
Clampitt. Scaffold, A.
Ginsberg, A. Marijuana Notation.
Gunn, T. Readings in French.
Lux. Postcard to Baudelaire.
Mallarmé. Tomb of Charles Baudelaire, The.

Bavaria
Carruth, H. To Know in Reverie the Only Phenomenology of the Absolute.
Updike. Munich.

Bay Trees
See **Laurels**

Bayous
Clampitt. Bayou Afternoon.

Beaches
Amichai [or Amikhai]. Akhziv.
  At the Beach.
  Poems of Akhziv.
Ammons. Constant, The.
  Expressions of Sea Level.
  February Beach.
Arnold, M. Dover Beach.
Berryman. Traveller, The.
Bishop, E. End of March, The.

Bukowski. On a Night You Don't Sleep.
Ciardi, J. Shore Piece.
Clampitt. Beach Glass.
  Beach Pea, The.
Creeley. Beach.
  La Conca.
  Obscene Poem, An.
  Sea ("Ever / to sleep").
  This World.
Cummings, E. E. Because i love you)last night.
  How many moments must(amazing each).
  I remark that this beach has been used too.
    much Too. originally.
  Maggie and Milly and Molly and May.
Cunningham, J. Night is still, The. The unfailing surf.
Davie, D. Across the Bay.
  Poreč.
Dickey, J. Circuit.
  Immortals.
  Two Women.
Dickinson, E. By the Sea.
Dugan, A. Memorial Service for the Invasion Beach Where the Vacation in the Flesh Is Over.
Eberhart, R. Ceremony By the Sea, A.
Emerson, R. Lobster-car, boat, or fishbasket.
Glück, L. Lady in the Single, The.
  Silverpoint.
Graves, R. Beach, The.
Gunn, T. Beach Head, The.
  Three.
Gurney, I. Sea-Marge.
Hardy, T. At the Aquatic Sports.
Heaney, S. Sandstone Keepsake.
  Strand at Lough Beg, The.
Housman. Smooth between sea and land.
Hughes, T. Crow on the Beach.
Jacobsen, J. Class, The.
  Reading on the Beach.
Jeffers, R. Beach, The.
Komunyakaa. Break from the Bush, A.
  Newport Beach, 1979.
Kumin, M. Night Launch.
Kunitz, S. Prophecy on Lethe.
Laughlin, J. Full Life, The.
Lawrence, D. H. Restlessness.
Levertov. For Nikolai, Many Thousand Miles Away.
  Tropic Ritual.
Logan, J. Two Preludes for La Push.
Lux. Dawn Walk and Prayer.
MacNeice. Lugubrious, Salubrious Seaside, The.
  Strand, The.
  Upon This Beach.
Mahon. Brighton Beach.
Meredith, W. Rhode Island.
Millay, E. Eel-Grass.
  Low-Tide.
Milosz, C. On a Beach.
Mistral, G. In Praise of Salt.
Nash, O. Don't Look Now.
  Pretty Halcyon Days.
  Seaside Serenade.
Nemerov. Salt Garden, The.
Olson, C. Lordly and Isolate Satyrs, The.
Oppen. Acapulco.
Pagis. Information.
Patchen. Fifth Dimension.
Plath. Point Shirley.
  Two Lovers and a Beachcomber by the Real Sea.
Prunty. Water Slide Along the Beach.
Raine, K. On a Shell-strewn Beach.
Rexroth, K. Cinque Terre.
Rich, A. Parting: I, The.
Riley, J. Faith.
Rilke. Let's Leave.
  To Marina Zwetajewa-Efron.
Ritsos. Small Invitation, A.
Rukeyser, M. Children, the Sandbar, That Summer.
Sandburg, C. Sandhill People.
Schuyler, J. You're.
Sexton. Kite, The.

Sea Corpse, The.
  There You Were.
Shelley, P. Fragment: The Lake's Margin.
Snyder, G. North Coast, The.
  Point Reyes.
  Running Water Music.
Stafford, W. With Kit, Age 7, at the Beach.
Stevens, W. Fabliau of Florida.
Stock, R. Grunion Run.
Swenson, M. Flag of Summer.
  Goodbye, Goldeneye.
  Waking from a Nap on the Beach.
Tomlinson, C. Stone Speech.
  Writing on Sand.
Updike. Antigua.
  Raining in Magens Bay.
  Rio de Janeiro.
  Sunglasses.
Walcott. Beachhead.
Warren, R. Autumnal Equinox on Mediterranean Beach.
  Cross, The.
  End of Season.
  Paradox.
  Youthful Truth-Seeker, Half-Naked, at Night, Running down Beach South of San Francisco.
Whitman, W. As If a Phantom Caress'd Me.
  On the Beach at Night.
  On the Beach at Night Alone.
Whittier. Tent on the Beach, The.
Wilbur, R. On the Marginal Way.
  Waters, The.
Williams, M. Woman with Dog.
Wright, C. Looking West from Laguna Beach at Night.
Wright, J. At the Slackening of the Tide.
Yeats. To a Child Dancing in the Wind.
See also **Shores**

Beads
Dunbar, P. She Told Her Beads.
Merrill, J. Komboloi.
Tomlinson, C. Bead, The.

Beans
Browning, R. Bean-Feast, The.
Clare, J. Bean Field, The.
Herrick. Littlenesse No Cause of Leanesse.
Jarrell, R. Gleaning.
Kumin, M. Beans.
  Shelling Jacobs Cattle Beans.
Sandburg, C. Corn and Beans.

Beards
Creeley. Boy, the.
Dove, R. This Life.
Ignatow, D. In the Woods.
Updike. Upon Shaving Off One's Beard.

Bears
Atwood. Dream 3: Night Bear Which Frightened Cattle.
Blue Cloud. Bear: A Totem Dance As Seen by Raven.
Bly, R. Schoolcraft's Diary Written on the Missouri: 1830.
Carruth, H. Bears at Raspberry Time.
Carver, R. Hat, The.
Clampitt. Hispaniola.
Corbett, W. Driving Jazz.
Cummings, E. E. Like a little bear twilight.
Dubie. Elizabeth's War with the Christmas Bear.
Dunbar, P. Cabin Tale, A.
Eberhart, R. Winter Kill.
Frost, R. Bear, The.
Graves, R. To Be Called A Bear.
Hall, D. Self-Portrait as a Bear.
Hughes, T. Bear, The.
  That Morning.
Kinnell. Bear, The.
  Lastness.
Kipling, R. Truce of the Bear, The.
Kumin, M. Encounter in August.
  In the Park.
  You Are in Bear Country.
Levertov. To the Reader.
Lincoln, A. Bear Hunt, The.
McHugh, H. Bear in English.

Milosz, C.   Story, A.
Nemerov.   Goose Fish, The.
Oliver, M.   Happiness.
  Spring.
  Truro Bear, The.
Rich, A.   Bears.
Riley, J.   Bear Family, A.
Roethke.   Lady and the Bear, The.
Rossetti, C.   Brother Bruin.
Sarton, M.   Bears and Waterfalls.
Snyder, G.   Right in the Trail.
  Way West, Underground, The.
Warren, R.   Mission, The.
  Winter Dreams.
Wilner, E.   Comment on the Relevance of
  Modern Science to the Everyday Lives of the
  Larger Animals, A.
  East of the Sun, West of the Moon.
Wright, J.   March.

Beatings
Angelou.   Kind of Love, Some Say, A.
Blue Cloud.   For Ace.
Hughes, L.   Third Degree.
  Who but the Lord?
Laughlin, J.   Piteous Sight, A.

Beatniks
Berrigan, T.   Pandora's Box, An Ode.
Creeley.   Peace ("You're looking at a chopper").
Ginsberg, A.   America.
  'Back on Times Square, Dreaming of Times
   Square.'
  Bop Lyrics.
  Dream Record: June 8 1955.
  Fragment 1956.
  Fragment: The Names II.
  Howl.
Komunyakaa.   Letter to Bob Kaufman.

Beatrice Portinari
Cino da Pistoia.   Canzone: On the Death of
  Beatrice Portinari.
Dante Alighieri.   Ballata: He will gaze upon
  Beatrice.
  Canzone: He beseeches Death for the Life of
   Beatrice.
  Dante's Vita Nuova.
  La Vita Nuova.
  Sonnet: Of Beatrice de' Portinari, on All Saints'
   Day.
  Sonnet: To certain Ladies; when Beatrice was
   lamenting her Father's Death.
  Sonnet: To the same Ladies; with their Answer.
Graves, R.   Beatrice and Dante.

Beaumont, Francis
Jonson, B.   To Francis Beaumont.
Wordsworth, W.   At Applethwaite, near
  Keswick.
  For a Seat in the Groves of Coleorton.

Beauty
Alcman.   Astymelusa.
Amichai [or Amikhai].   In the Middle of This
  Century.
Angelou.   Black Ode.
  Phenomenal Woman.
Apollinaire.   Pretty Redhead, The.
Arnold, M.   Growing Old.
Ashbery, J.   Le Livre Est sur la Table.
Auden.   Dichtung und Wahrheit.
Baudelaire.   Beauty.
  Dancing Death.
  Hymn to Beauty.
  Ideal, The.
  Love of Artifice, The.
  Merciless Madrigal.
  Passing Glance, A.
  Proud Ship, The.
  To a Red-headed Beggar.
  Total Harmony.
  What will you say, hermetic soul? Resigned.
Berry, W.   River Bridged and Forgot, The.
Berryman.   Canto Amor.
  Meeting.
Bierce.   Basilica.
Bogan, L.   Juan's Song.
  Question in a Field.
Brontë, E.   I've been wandering in the

greenwoods.
Broumas, O.   Buenos Días.
  P.S.
Browning, E.   Best Thing in the World, The.
  Hiram Powers' "Greek Slave."
  May's Love.
  Where's Agnes?
Browning, R.   Guardian-Angel, The.
  Magical Nature.
  Pretty Woman, A.
  Song: "Nay but you, who do not love her."
  Women and Roses.
Bukowski.   Girls at the Green Hotel, The.
  Huge Ear Rings.
Burns, R.   Answer to the Foregoing—
  Extempore [Clarinda].
  Beware o' Bonie Ann.
  Blythe Was She.
  Bonnie Lesley.
  Bonnie [or Bonny] Wee Thing, The.
  Bonnie Peg.
  Chloe.
  Delia.
  Fragment: "Her flowing locks, the raven's
   wing."
  Fragment, Which Was Meant for the Beginning
   of an Elegy on the Late Miss Burnet of
   Monboddo, A.
  Hey for a Lass wi' a Tocher.
  Humble Petition of Bruar Water to the Noble
   Duke of Athole, The.
  I do confess thou art sae fair.
  Jessie—A New Scots Song.
  Lovely Davies.
  Lovely Polly Stewart.
  Lover's Morning Salute to His Mistress, The.
  My Lady's Gown There's Gairs upon't.
  My Peggy's Face.
  O Mally's Meek, Mally's Sweet.
  She Says She Lo'es Me Best of A'.
  Song: "Adown winding Nith I did wander."
  Song. On Miss P——— K———, A.
  Theniel Menzies' Bony Mary.
  To Maria.
  To Miss C*********, a Very Young Lady.
  To Miss Ferrier.
  Where braving angry Winter's storms.
  Yon wild, mossy mountains sae lofty and wide.
Byron, G.   Girl of Cadiz, The.
  Oh! Snatch'd Away in Beauty's Bloom.
  On the Eyes of Miss A——— H———.
  She Walks In Beauty.
  Sonnet, to Genevra.
  Sonnet, to the Same.
  Stanzas for Music.
  To M———.
  To Mary on Receiving Her Picture.
Callimachus.   On Pallas Bathing.
Campion, T.   Ad Cambricum.
  Are you what your faire lookes expresse?
  Beautie Without Love Deformitie.
  Beauty Is But a Painted Hell.
  Beauty Is Not Bound.
  Her rosie cheekes, her ever smiling eyes.
  I must complain, yet doe enjoy my Love.
  In Melleam.
  So sweet is thy discourse to me.
  There is a garden in her face.
  There Is None, O None but You.
  Thou Art Not Fair[e].
  Thou Joy'st, Fond Boy.
  Though You Are Young [or Yoong].
  Vain Men, Whose Follies.
  Where She Her Sacred Bower Adorns.
  Why presumes thy pride on that, that must so
   private be.
Campion, T. et al.   When Laura smiles her sight
  revives both night and day.
Carew, T.   Beautiful Mistress, A.
Carver.   To His Mistress, The.
  Comparison, The.
  Complement, The.
  Disdain Returned.
  Divine Mistress, A.
  Fancy, A.
  Ingrateful[l] Beauty Threatened.

Lover, in the Disguise of an Amazon, Is Dearly
  Beloved of His Mistress, A.
  Murdering Beauty.
  My Mistress Commanding Me to Return Her
   Letters.
  Obsequies to the Lady Anne Hay.
  On Mistress N.
  On Sight of a Gentlewoman's Face in the Water.
  On the Marriage of T. K. and C. C.: The
   Morning Stormy.
  Pastoral[l] Dialogue, A.
  Song[, A]: "Ask[e] me no more where Jove
   bestow[e]s."
  Tinder, The.
  To A.D., Unreasonable, Distrustful of Her Own
   Beauty.
  To A. L.; Persuasions [or Perswasions] to Love.
  To a Lady That Desired I Would Love Her.
  To my Friend G.N. from Wrest.
  To One Who, When I Praised My Mistress'
   Beauty, Said I Was Blind.
  To the Painter.
Carruth, H.   Birth of Venus, The.
Cavafy.   At the Entrance to the Café.
  Days of 1901.
  Dünya Güzeli.
  In a Town of Osroini.
  I've Gazed So Long, So Much.
  Mirror in the Vestibule, The.
Cavalcanti.   Beauty of women and wise hearts.
  Check out the humpback, Manny.
  Each fresh and sweet source.
  I see it in my Lady's eyes.
  My young blossom.
  Sonnet: A Rapture concerning his Lady.
  Sonnet: He compares all Things with his Lady,
   and finds them wanting.
  Sonnet: To his Lady Joan, of Florence.
  Who is this who came.
Chaucer.   Book of the Duchesse, The.
  Merciles[s] Beaute [or Beautée or Beauty].
  To Rosamounde.
  Womanly Noblesse.
Ciardi, J.   Bees and Morning Glories.
  Catalpa, The.
Clampitt.   Written in Water.
Clifton, L.   Song at Midnight.
  To My Last Period.
Coleridge, S.   Song, ex improviso.
Collins, B.   Nightclub.
Cowper, W.   Song, A: "Sparkling eye, the
  mantling cheek, The."
  Song: "No more shall hapless Celia's ears."
Crane, H.   Bathers, The.
Crashaw.   Upon the Faire Ethiopian Sent to a
  Gentlewoman.
  [With Some Poems Sent to a Gentlewoman. I].
Creeley.   Birthday, A.
  Chance, The.
  She's Back!
  Was.
  Water Music.
  Women, The.
Cullen, C.   Advice to a Beauty.
  Bright Bindings.
  Life's Rendezvous.
  Medusa.
  Song of Praise, A.
  To John Keats, Poet, at Springtime.
Cummings, E. E.   Christ but they're few.
  Cleopatra built / like a smooth arrow or.
  Every one of the red roses opened.
  Except in your / honour.
  Helen.
  Here's s / omething round(& so).
  I love you / for your little,startled,thoughtless
   ways.
  I shall imagine life.
  "I think you like."
  If i love You.
  Is there a flower(whom).
  Let's,from some loud unworld's most rightful
   wrong.
  Life is more true than reason will deceive.
  Moon-lit snow is falling like strange candy into
   the big eyes of the, The.

Morsel miraculous and meaningless.
Mr youse needn't be so spry.
My love / thy hair is one kingdom.
My naked lady framed.
Nothing whichful about / thick big this.
O purple finch / please tell me why.
Open green those / (dear).
Perhaps it is to feel strike.
Poem, or Beauty Hurts Mr. Vinal.
Pretty a day, A.
Puella Mea.
River of Mist, The.
These from my mother's greatgrandmother's
   rosebush white.
This young question mark man.
Thy face is a still white house of holy things.
Time,be kind;herself and i.
To start,to hesitate;to stop.
Until and i heard.
Whatever's merely wilful, / and not miraculous.
When my love comes to see me it's.
Where's Madge then / Madge and her men?
White guardians of the universe of sleep.
Who are you,little i.
Why / do the / fingers.
Without the mercy of / your eyes your.
You are like the snow only.
You said Is / there anything which.
Cunningham, J. Epigram: "You wonder why
   Drab sells her love for gold?"
Dante Alighieri. Sestina; Of the Lady Pietra
   degli Scrovigni.
Sonnet: Of Beauty and Duty.
De la Mare. Age.
Epitaph, An: "Here lies a most beautiful lady."
Looking Glass, The.
Ophelia.
Phantom, The.
Shadow.
Sleeper, The.
Three Cherry Trees, The.
Treachery.
Unchanging, The.
Vain Finding.
Veil, The.
When the rose is faded.
Dickinson, E. Acts of Light which beautified,
   The.
All we secure of Beauty.
Awkward as the homely are.
Beauty be not caused—It Is.
Beauty crowds me till I die.
Beauty is often timidity.
Charm invests a face, A.
Definition of Beauty is, The.
Estranged from Beauty, none can be.
How vast is the chastisement of Beauty.
I died for Beauty—but was scarce.
In a World too full of Beauty for Peace.
"Infinite Beauty"—of which you speak, The.
Neither in Heaven nor Earth.
Parents of Beauty, The.
So gay a Flower.
Donne. Letter to the Lady Carey, and Mistress
   Essex Rich, from Amiens, A.
Undertaking, The.
Dunbar, P. Alice.
Love's Pictures.
Song, A: "On a summer's day as I sat by a
   stream."
Duncan, R. Poetry, a Natural Thing.
Salvages: An Evening Place.
Eberhart, R. Opulence.
Prometheus.
Transformation.
Whenever I See Beauty I See Death.
White Pines, Felled 1984.
Éluard, P. Scarcely Disfigured.
Emerson, R. And do I waste my time.
Beauty.
Chladni strewed on glass the sand.
Dear Ellen, many a golden year.
Each and All.
For joy & beauty planted it.
Harp, The.
I call her beautiful;—she says.

Illusions like the tints of pearl.
In the deep heart of man a poet dwells.
O what are heroes prophets men.
Ode to Beauty.
Rhodora, The [On Being Asked Whence Is the
   Flower].
She had wealth of mornings in her year.
Tell me maiden dost thou use.
To Eva.
Would you know what joy is hid.
Ferlinghetti, L. Carrara, Looking Seaward.
I have not lain with beauty all my life.
Light, The.
Gallagher, T. Present.
Glück, L. Letter from our Man in Blossomtime.
Mirror, The.
Graves, R. Blessed Sun.
Dangerous Gift, The.
Down, Wanton, Down!
Green Woods of Unrest, The.
Her Beauty.
Love in Barrenness.
Necklace, The.
September Landscape.
Tousled Pillow.
"H. D." Ancient Wisdom Speaks.
I Said.
Song: "You are as gold."
Hafiz [or Hafez]. Dearest, where thy shadow
   falls.
Han-shan. Inside Jade Hall is a curtain of
   pearls.
Hardy, T. Aberdeen.
Background and the Figure, The.
Beauty, The.
Beauty's Soliloquy during Her Honeymoon, A.
Best She Could, The.
Concerning Agnes.
Eunice.
Faithful Wilson.
To an Imposter of Rosalind.
To Outer Nature.
Heaney, S. Nerthus.
Herbert, G. Sonnet: "Sure Lord, there is enough
   in thee to dry."
Herrick. Another Upon Her.
Apron of Flowers, The.
Art above Nature, to Julia.
Beauty.
Candor of Julias Teeth, The.
Cloud, The.
Definition of Beauty, The.
Delight in Disorder.
Descripcion; of a Woman, The.
Dew Sat on Julia's Hair.
Eclipse, The.
Elegy: "Since louely sweete, much like unto a
   Dewe."
Epitaph upon a Virgin, An.
Mrs. Eliz. Wheeler, Under the Name of the Lost
   Shepardesse.
Neglect.
On Tomasin Parsons.
Request to the Graces, An.
Rosarie, The.
To a Mayd.
To Anthea Lying in Bed.
To Electra.
To Mistresse Mary Willand.
To Perenna.
To the Handsome Mistresse Grace Potter.
To the Most Comely and Proper M. Elizabeth
   Finch.
Upon a Comely, and Curious Maide.
Upon a Painted Gentlewoman.
Upon Her Blush.
Upon Her Feet.
Upon His Julia.
Upon Julia's Clothes.
Upon Julia's Haire, Bundled up in a Golden
   Net.
Upon Silvia, a Mistresse.
Upon the Nipples of Julia's Breast.
Upon the Roses in Julias Bosome.
Upon Wrinkles.
Weeping Cherry, The.

Hölderlin. Too long we lived for work and
   wages, we.
Hopkins, G. As it fell upon a day.
Boughs being pruned, birds preenèd, show more
   fair.
Confirmed beauty will not bear a stress.
Daphne.
Floris in Italy.
Pied Beauty.
To What Serves Mortal Beauty?
Hughes, L. Beauty.
Harlem Sweeties.
In the Mist of the Moon.
My People.
To Beauty.
When Sue Wears Red.
Hughes, T. Fallgrief's Girlfriends.
I know well.
Jackson, L. Divestment of Beauty.
Helen's Burning.
Mask, The.
There Is Much At Work.
Jacobsen, J. Fish Tank Room, The.
Landscape Finally with Human Figure.
Jarrell, R. Head of Wisdom, The.
Jeffers, R. At the Fall of an Age.
Beauty of Things, The.
Birds and Fishes.
Divinely Superfluous Beauty.
Give Your Heart to the Hawks.
Hope is Not for the Wise.
Invasion.
Irish Headland, An.
It was good of my father, whom I hated at
   times.
Life from the Lifeless.
New Year's Eve.
Ocean's Tribute, The.
Rearmament.
Red Mountain.
Such Counsels You Gave to Me.
Their Beauty Has More Meaning.
Johnson, S. To Lady Firebrace.
Jonson, B. Elegy, An: "By those bright eyes, at
   whose immortal fires."
Elegy [or Elegie], An: "Let me be what I am, as
   Virgil cold."
Elegy [or Elegie] on the Lady Jane Pawlet [or
   Paulet], [Marchioness of Winton], An.
Fair friend, 'tis true, your beauties move.
Ode, An: "Helen, did Homer never see."
Ode Enthusiastic.
To Mary, Lady Wroth ("Madam[e], had all
   antiquity [or antiquitie] been lost").
Keats. Ode on a Grecian Urn.
To Georgiana Augusta Wylie.
To the Ladies Who Saw Me Crowned.
To ———: "Time's sea hath been five years at
   its slow ebb."
Khayyám, O. From Omar Chiam.
Kinnell. Saint Francis and the Sow.
Kinsella, T. Portrait of the Artist, A.
Kizer, C. Pearl.
Koch, K. On Beauty.
Kunitz, S. Particular Lullaby.
Larkin, P. Latest Face.
Like the Train's Beat.
Laughlin, J. In Half Darkness.
Love Is Cumulative.
You Invited Me.
Lawrence, D. H. Amour.
Bodiless God.
Fronleichnam.
One Woman to All Women.
Pomegranate.
Roses on the Breakfast Table.
Shows.
So Let Me Live.
Levertov. Human Being.
Love Song.
March, A.
Lindsay, N. Alone in the Wind, on the Prairie.
My Lady in Her White Silk Shawl.
My Lady Is Compared to a Young Tree.
To Gloriana.
To Lady Jane.

Logan, J. Carmel: Point Lobos.
  Lines for His Son in Satin.
Lux. Gorgeous Surfaces.
  Great Advances in Vanity.
MacDiarmid, H. Milk-Wort and Bog Cotton.
MacLeish. Excavation of Troy.
  Landscape as a Nude.
  Not Marble nor the Gilded Monuments.
  Two Poems from the War.
  Years of the Dog.
MacNeice. Circe.
Mallarmé. Hérodiade.
Meredith, G. Angel, be ye ne'er in doubt, An.
  Ballad of the Lady Eglantine, The.
  Grace and Love.
  Hectate.
  She rides in the park on a prancing bay.
  To A.M.
  When I Would Image.
  Years Had Worn Their Season's Belt, The.
Merrill, J. Peacock, The.
Merton. Philosophers, The.
Michelangelo Buonarroti. Although it's amply
    true your human face.
  Among the memory of all lovely things.
  As I've carried in my heart this many a year.
  Bracci once, A. The soul in me withdrew.
  By a face of fiery cold, I'm set aflame.
  By light more brilliant of a star more bright.
  Closed now his shining eyes, that dazzled so.
  Drawn to each lovely thing, my doting eyes.
  Earth lends us flesh, heaven lends the soul, the
    two.
  For a reliable guide in my vocation.
  From grief I cherished to a rueful laugh.
  From heaven it ventured forth, there must
    return.
  From heaven my beauty, flawless and divine.
  From what these eyes, my lady, see of you.
  He Who made all there is, made every part.
  Her beauty's alive in heaven! I believe her.
  His beautiful eyes! I hardly saw them, only.
  I really believed, that first great day when,
    awed.
  If a joyous heart makes beautiful the face.
  If Braccio's beauty, phoenix-like, could be.
  If I'm to believe my eyes now, your response.
  If nature now deferred to death, dejected.
  If we constrain the eyes' easy response.
  I'm death's forever, who, that one forlorn.
  Inside, his soul could not be outside too.
  Just as you cannot not be lovely here.
  Man within a woman—no, I'd say, A.
  More it seems I agonize, the more, The.
  My lady, these eyes see vividly—far, near.
  Nature knows what it's doing: one cruel as you.
  No other handsome face such power possessed.
  No slightest chance on earth her heavenly eyes.
  No way he who undid me can restore.
  O noble soul, in whom, as mirrored, show.
  Power of a beautiful face lifts me to heaven,
    The.
  Pray tell me, Love, if what my eyes can see.
  So it wouldn't need to retrieve the total sum.
  Such brightness, under earth now, put to shame.
  Suppose a lady has no other graces.
  Supposing the passionate fire your eyes
    enkindle.
  Sweeter your face than grapes are, stewed to
    mush.
  To see that your famous beauty still endures.
  Too much! the way he flaunts himself around.
  What in your handsome face I see, my lord.
  When heaven confirmed your brilliance, most of
    all.
  Why fallen so soon asleep? Not hard to tell.
  Wiles, guiles, smiles, gold and pearls, her gala
    ways.
  Young Braccio's buried here. To mend a lack.
  Your beauty, Love, stuns mortal reckonings.
Millay, E. And is indeed truth beauty?—at the
    cost.
  And you as well must die, belovèd dust.
  "Euclid Alone Has Looked on Beauty Bare."
  How did I bear it—how could I possibly as a
    child.

Love is not blind. I see with single eye.
  Portrait.
  Spring.
  Still will I harvest beauty where it grows.
  To Kathleen.
  What's this of death, from you who never will
    die?
  When I too long have looked upon your face.
Milosz, C. No More.
  One More Day.
Milton. Sonnet 2: "Charming lady, she whose
    beautiful name honors."
Mistral, G. Artist's Decalogue, The.
Muldoon, P. De Secretis Mulierum.
Nash, O. Aside to Husbands.
  Biological Reflection.
Nemerov. Dandelions.
  Young Woman.
O'Hara, F. Having a Coke with You.
  Poem: "O solo mio, hot diggety, nix 'I wather
    think I can'."
Olson, C. Beauty / is to lay hold of Love.
  Epigon.
  For a Lady of Whom I Speak.
  For Sappho, Back.
  Kingfishers, The.
  La Chute.
  Lordly and Isolate Satyrs, The.
  Red Mallows.
  Thing Was Moving, The.
  Your Eyes.
Orléans, C. Dieu Qu'il la Fait.
Orr, G. Best.
Owen, W. Beauty.
  Imbecile, The.
  Purple.
Paley, G. No Love.
Parker, D. Epitaph for a Darling Lady.
  Grande Passion.
  Lullaby: "Sleep, pretty lady, the night is
    enfolding you."
  Ninon De L'Enclos, On Her Last Birthday.
  Prophetic Soul.
  Renunciation.
Roundel: "She's passing fair; but so demure is
    she."
  Sonnet On An Alpine Night.
  Sonnet: "Sweeter your laugh than trill of lark at
    dawn."
  To a Lady.
  To Myrtilla, On Easter Day.
Patchen. Beautiful You Are.
  Demonstration.
  Hold thy tongue, death!
  Hovenweep.
  O my love / The pretty towns.
  O She Is as Lovely-Often as Every Day.
  Of the same beauty were stars made.
  She is the prettiest of creatures.
  What Is the Beautiful?
Petrarch. Already you have done, remorseless
    Death.
  Any lady desiring fame and honour.
  As life eternal is the sight of God.
  Breeze blowing those blond locks and curling
    them.
  But—now her pleasant gentle modest mien.
  Charming pallor clothing her sweet smile, The.
  From loveliest eyes, and from the visage which.
  From what circle of heaven, from what idea.
  Full of that indescribable delight.
  Her golden hair was blowing in the breeze.
  If Polyclitus studied earnestly.
  In her, two enemies were brought together.
  I've never seen the sun rise in such glory.
  Let us pause, Love, to see her and her worth.
  My days have gone by swifter than a deer.
  Not only that one hand when it is bare.
  Sometimes I am ashamed that I have never.
  Stars, the sky, the elements have put, The.
  That always bitter, always honoured day.
  This noble soul, starting to move away.
  This phoenix, so extravagantly plumed.
  This short-lived and this fragile happiness.
  Under a lucky star I saw those eyes.
  Upon that face for which I sigh and pine.

Victorious and triumphal laurel-tree.
  When she arrives where greatest beauty is.
  Where did Love ever get the gold, to give.
  Wherever I turn my eyes or let them rest.
  Who wants to see what can be done by Nature.
Piercy. Barbie Doll.
  Beauty I Would Suffer For.
Poe. Al Aaraaf.
  Eulalie—A Song.
  Israfel.
  Lake: To———, The.
  Sleeper, The.
  Stanzas: "How often we forget all time, when
    lone."
  To Helen.
  To ———: "Not long ago, the writer of these
    lines."
  To the River ———.
  Valley of Unrest, The.
Pope, A. Of Her Picture.
  Of Her Walking in a Garden after a Shower.
  Presenting a *Lark*.
Pound, E. Dance Figure.
  Na Audiart.
Raine, K. Amo Ergo Sum.
  Cloud.
  Turner's Seas.
Ralegh, S. In the Grace of Wit, of Tongue and
    Face.
  Poem of Sir Walter Rawleighs, A.
Ransom, J. Hilda.
  Judith of Bethulia.
Rexroth, K. Dialogue of Watching, A.
  Song for a Dancer.
Riley, J. Discouraging Model, A.
  Her Beautiful Eyes.
  In the South.
  Little Lady, The.
  Loveliness, The.
  Lovely Child, The.
  Oh, Her Beauty.
Rilke. Bella.
  To Miss Nicola B.
  To Serve as an Epitaph for the Beautiful
    Madame B.
Rimbaud, A. Being Beauteous.
  Second Delirium. Alchemy of the Word.
Ritsos. Beauty.
  Invisible Glory.
  Probabilities.
  Summer Sorrow.
Roethke. I Knew A Woman.
Rossetti, C. Annie.
  Beauty Is Vain.
  Behold, It Was Very Good.
  Books In the Running Brooks.
  Buds and Babies.
  Cousin Kate.
  De Profundis.
  Earth and Heaven.
  Easter Morning.
  Eleanor.
  Exultate Deo.
  Floral Teaching.
  Fluttered Wings.
  For Advent.
  From early dawn until the flush of noon.
  Growing in the vale / By the uplands hilly.
  Helen Grey.
  His Banner over Me Was Love.
  Holy City, New Jerusalme, The.
  If stars dropped out of heaven, / And if flowers
    took their place.
  Immalee.
  Lady Isabella.
  Last Look, The.
  Lily has a smooth stalk, / Will never hurt your
    hand, The.
  Lily has an air, / And the snowdrop a grace,
    The.
  Listen, and I will tell you of a face.
  Lord, make me one with Thine own faithful
    ones.
  Love is all happiness, love is all beauty.
  Luscious and Sorrowful.
  On Albina.

Once.
Peter Grump.
Praise of Love.
Queen Rose.
Rose, The.
Rose with such a bonny blush, The.
Seasons.
Serenade.
Song: "I saw her; she was lovely."
Summer.
There Is a Budding Morrow in Midnight.
To What Purpose Is This Waste?
Valentines From C.G.R.
Versi.
What Is Pink?
What is this above thy head, / O Man?
Who Hath Despised the Day of Small Things?
Within the Veil.
World's Harmonies, The.
Rukeyser, M.   Woman and Emblems.
Rumi.   Gift of Water, The.
Today, like every other day, we wake up empty.
You Sweep the Floor.
Sandburg, C.   Autumn Movement.
Baby Face.
Flash Crimson.
Foxgloves.
Monotone.
Murmurings in a Field Hospital.
My People.
Personalia.
Proud and Beautiful.
Sumach and Birds.
They Buy with an Eye to Looks.
Two.
Sappho.   One Girl.
Song of the Rose.
Sarton, M.   Memory of Swans.
Portrait by Holbein.
Swans, The.
Schuyler, J.   Poem: "This beauty that I see."
Seifert.   Apple Tree with Cobweb Strings.
Berthe Soucaret.
Hands of Venus, The.
Lines for the Painter Ota Janeček.
Wet Picture.
Sexton.   Snow White and the Seven Dwarfs.
Shapiro, K.   Cut Flower, A.
Shelley, P.   Fragment: Beauty's Halo.
Hymn to Intellectual Beauty.
To Sophia [Miss Stacey].
Sheridan, T.   I Ritu a Verse o Na Molli o Mi Ne.
Prologue Spoken before a Greek Play, at the
    Reverend Dr. Sheridan's School, at the
    Breaking-Up of His Scholars for Christmas,
    1728.
Shirley, J.   Love's Hue and Cry.
Would you know what's soft? I dare.
Smart, C.   Ode to Lady Harriot.
Smith, S.   Lady of the Well-Spring, The.
Pretty.
Rehearsal, The.
Sorrowful Girl, The.
Spender, S.   From My Diary.
Stevens, W.   Peter Quince at the Clavier.
Suckling, S.   Non Est Mortale Quod Opto.
Sonnet: "Dost see how unregarded now."
To B.C.
Upon the First Sight of My Lady Seymour.
Upon Two Sisters.
Suckling, S. *et al.*   Song: "When, dearest, I but
    think on [*or* of] thee."
Swenson, M.   Mornings Innocent.
Swift, J.   Lady's Dressing Room, The.
Progress of Beauty, The.
Stella's Birthday; Written in the Year 1718[/9].
Swinburne.   Ballad of Death, A.
Ballad of Life, A.
Sapphics.
Szymborska, W.   Drinking Wine.
Tate, A.   Sonnet to Beauty.
Tennyson, A.   To —. With the Following Poem.
Unknown.   Art Thou That She.
Do Not, Oh, Do Not Prize.
Unknown, sometimes at. to Sir Walter Ralegh.
As You Came from the Holy Land [of

Walsingham].
Updike.   Eurydice.
Penumbrae.
South of the Alps.
Sunshine on Sandstone.
Youth's Progress.
Van Duyn.   Midas and Wife.
Villon.   Complaint of the Fair Armoress [*or*
    Armouress], The.
Gone Ladies.
Walcott.   As John to Patmos.
Warren, R.   Arizona Midnight.
Auto-da-fé.
Interjection #8: Or, Sometimes, Night.
Whalen, P.   Irregular Ode, An.
Whitman, W.   Beautiful Women.
Love That Is Hereafter, The.
My Canary Bird.
Song of the Answerer.
Song of the Rolling Earth, A.
Then Shall Perceive.
Whittier.   Artist of the Beautiful, An.
Clear Vision, The.
Fair Quakeress, The.
Hazel Blossoms.
Pictures.
Sea Dream, A.
Stanzas: "Bind up thy tresses, thou beautiful
    one."
Sunset on the Bearcamp.
To ———: "Maiden! with the fair brown
    tresses."
Wilbur, R.   Beautiful Changes, The.
Caserta Garden.
Piazza di Spagna, Early Morning.
Potato.
Still, Citizen Sparrow.
Thyme Flowering among Rocks.
Transit.
Wilde, O.   Apologia.
La Bella Donna della Mia Mente.
Madonna Mia.
Williams, C. K.   Hooks.
Love: Wrath.
Williams, M.   Book, The.
Williams, W.   At Dawn.
Ce-Lia The Immortal Beauty.
Green Eyes.
Hard Core of Beauty, The.
Homage.
La Belle Dame de Tous les Jours.
Red Lily, The.
Song: "Beauty is a shell."
Wordsworth, W.   Anacreon.
Composed upon an Evening of Extraordinary
    Splendour and Beauty.
Composed upon Westminster Bridge, September
    3, 1802.
Contrast; the Parrot and the Wren, The.
Glad Sight Wherever New with Old.
Gleaner (Suggested By a Picture), The.
Gold and Silver Fishes in a Vase.
How Rich That Forehead's Calm Expanse!
I Heard (Alas! 'Twas Only in a Dream).
I Wandered Lonely As a Cloud.
Jewish Family in a Small Valley Opposite St
    Goar, upon the Rhine), A.
Lady Whom You here Behold, The.
Lyre! Though Such Power Do in Thy Magic
    Live.
November 1 [1815].
Prithee, Gentle Lady, List.
So Fair, So Sweet, Withal So Sensitive.
Suggested by a Picture of the Bird of Paradise.
To a Skylark.
To —, in Her Seventieth Year.
To ———: "Let other bards of angels sing."
To—, on Her First Ascent to the Summit of
    Helvellyn.
To the Highland Girl of Inversneyde.
Vernal Ode.
While Beams of Orient Light Shoot Wide and
    High.
Wild Duck's Nest, The.
Written in the Strangers' Book at "The Station,"
    Opposite Bowness.

Yes! Thou Art Fair, Yet Be Not Moved.
Wright, C.   Night Journal.
Spring Abstract.
Wright, J.   All the Beautiful are Blameless.
Eleutheria.
Logbook of Judgments.
Shadow and the Real, The.
To a Hostess Saying Goodnight.
Wyatt, S.   Nature that gave the bee so feat a
    grace.
Yeats.   Arrow, The.
Beautiful Lofty Things.
Before the World Was Made.
Broken Dreams.
Crazed Girl, A.
Crazy Jane Talks with the Bishop.
Dream of Death, A.
Folly of Being Comforted, The.
He Remembers Forgotten Beauty.
He Tells of the Perfect Beauty.
His Phoenix.
Living Beauty, The.
Memory.
Michael Robartes and the Dancer.
No Second Troy.
Old Men Admiring Themselves in the Water,
    The.
Secret Rose, The.
Symbols.
Thought from Propertius, A.
To a Young Beauty.
Zagajewski.   In the Beauty Created by Others.
King, A.
Zaturenska.   Epitaph for a Careless Beauty.
Old Tale, An.
Zukofsky, L.   H.T.
World autumn, The.

Beauty and the Beast
Duncan, R.   Four Songs the Night Nurse Sang.

Beauty Parlors
Jacobsen, J.   Moon Will Restore the Virginity of
    My Sister, The.

Beavers
Schuyler, J.   Awoke.

Bedouins
Amichai [*or* Amikhai].   Bedouin Goes North, A.
Bedouin in Love.
Riley, J.   Bedouin.
Out of Nazareth.

Bedrooms
Cavafy.   Afternoon Sun, The.
Ignatow, D.   Separate Rooms.
Komunyakaa.   Between Days.
Lowell, R.   Father's Bedroom.
Mahon.   Studio, The.
Montale.   Metropolitan Christmas, A.
Oppen.   Theological Definition, A.
Rexroth, K.   Incense.
Riley, J.   His Room.
Sexton.   February 4th.
Now.
Smith, S.   Goodnight.

Beds
Amichai [*or* Amikhai].   I Want to Die in My
    Own Bed.
Benserade, I.   Translation of Lines by
    Benserade.
Bukowski.   Beds, Toilets, You and Me—.
Burns, R.   Lass That Made the Bed for Me, The.
Cummings, E. E.   Bed is not very big, The.
Eberhart, R.   Day-Bed, The.
Graves, R.   Window Pane, The.
Gunn, T.   Bed, The.
Heaney, S.   Settle Bed, The.
Herrick.   Her Bed.
Koch, K.   In Bed.
Larkin, P.   Sad Steps.
Talking In Bed.
Laughlin, J.   Bubble Bed, The.
Lowell, R.   Man And Wife.
Parker, D.   Inscription for the Ceiling of a
    Bedroom.
Riley, J.   Old Trundle-Bed, The.
Ritsos.   Fulfillment.
Rossetti, C.   Crimson curtains round my

mother's bed.
Sexton.   Song for a Red Nightgown.
Simic.   Inheritance.
Walker, A.   Overnights.

Beech Trees and Beechnuts
Clampitt.   Runes, Blurs, Sap Rising.
Dove, R.   Copper Beech, The.
Frost, R.   Beech.
  Boundless Moment, A.
Spender, S.   Barn, The.
Tomlinson, C.   Beech, The.
  Near Hartland.

Beef
Nash, O.   Calf, The.
Paley, G.   Beef.

Beer
Bukowski.   Beer.
Carruth, H.   Marvin McCabe.
Dunbar, P.   Lager Beer.
Eberhart, R.   Clerihew for Alan Gaylord, A.
Herrick.   Coblers Catch, The.
  Tinkers Song, The.
  Upon Prig.
  Upon Spunge.
Housman.   Terence, This Is Stupid Stuff.
Logan, J.   Spring Revelations.
McGrath, T.   Mediterranean.
  Trinc: Praises II.
Meredith, G.   O have you seen my Tuck? my
  bonny bonny Tuck!
Rimbaud, A.   Evening Prayers.
Schuyler, J.   Trash Book, The.
Williams, M.   Glass Darkly, A.

Bees and Beekeeping
Ammons.   Drought.
  Lonesome Valley.
  Mechanics.
  Second Carolina Said-Song.
  Transfer.
Bogan, L.   Animal, Vegetable and Mineral.
Bourne, V.   Innocent Thief, The.
Bukowski.   Pansies.
Carew, T.   Upon a Mole in Celia's Bosom.
Carver, R.   Nearly.
Ciardi, J.   Bees and Morning Glories.
Cowper, W.   Bee and the Pine-Apple, The.
  Pine-Apple and the Bee, The.
De la Mare.   Quiet Enemy, The.
Dickinson, E.   Bee his burnished Carriage, A.
  Bee, The.
  Bees.
  Come slowly—Eden!
  Could I but ride indefinite.
  Did the Harebell loose her girdle.
  His Feet are shod with Gauze.
  His oriental heresies.
  Letter to Bee.
  Of Silken Speech and Specious Shoe.
  Single clover Plank, A.
  We—Bee and I—live by the quaffing.
  What tenements of clover.
Duncan, R.   After Reading H.D.'s *Hermetic
  Definitions*.
Eberhart, R.   In the Garden.
  Sunday in October.
Emerson, R.   Humble-Bee, The.
  Sparrow is rich in her nest, THe.
Frost, R.   White-Tailed Hornet, The.
Hamill, S.   Nihil Obstat.
Herrick.   Captived Bee; or, The Little Filcher,
  The.
  Dream, The.
  Present: or, The Bag of the Bee, The.
Hughes, L.   Black Workers.
Hughes, T.   Honey Bee, The.
Kinnell.   Fly, The.
Komunyakaa.   Two.
Laughlin, J.   Swarming Bees, The.
Lawrence, D. H.   Coming Awake.
Lorde.   Bees, The.
McHugh, H.   To Go.
Meredith, G.   Bumble Bee—the Bumble Bee,
  The.
  Fullness of love sleeps in us like a sea.
Merton.   Bees love grass, The.
Merwin.   Dead Hive, The.

Muldoon, P.   Bechbretha.
Nemerov.   And Is Silent.
  Beekeeper Speaks., The.
Nijhoff.   Song of the Foolish Bees.
Oppen.   Latitude, Longitude.
Paley, G.   Bee! / drowning in, A.
Palmer, M.   I killed a bee on the Street of
  Scissors.
Piercy.   Daily Life of the Worker Bee, The.
Plath.   Arrival of the Bee Box, The.
  Beekeeper's Daughter, The.
  Stings.
  Swarm, The.
  Wintering.
Riley, J.   Bumblebee, The.
  Fessler's Bees.
Rossetti, C.   When the cows come home the
  milk is coming.
Sandburg, C.   Bee Song.
  In Tall Grass.
Swenson, M.   Couple, A.
Van Duyn.   Time of Bees, A.
Very.   Bee Hive, The.
Wright, C.   Journal of Three Questions, A.

Beethoven, Ludwig van
Berryman.   Beethoven Triumphant.
Bukowski.   Bee's 5th.
  Note Upon the Love Letters of Beethoven.
  Sardines in Striped Dresses.
Clampitt.   Beethoven, Opus 111.
Collins, B.   Another Reason Why I Don't Keep
  a Gun in the House.
Dubie.   Composer's Winter Dream, The.
Eberhart, R.   Kinaesthesia.
Ginsberg, A.   Eroica.
Hughes, T.   Opus 131.
Jarrell, R.   Head of Wisdom, The.
Lowell, R.   Beethoven.
MacLeish.   Pablo Casals.
Meredith, W.   Quartet in F Major.
Millay, E.   On Hearing a Symphony of
  Beethoven.
Milosz, C.   Master, The.
Rich, A.   Ninth Symphony of Beethoven
  Understood at Last as a Sexual Message, The.
Ritsos.   Moonlight Sonata.
Spender, S.   Beethoven's Death Mask.
  Late Stravinsky Listening to Late Beethoven.
Tomlinson, C.   Beethoven Attends the C Minor
  Seminar.
Zagajewski.   Late Beethoven.
Zukofsky, L.   This Is After All Vacation.

Beetles
Ammons.   Motion for Motion.
Dickinson, E.   These are the Nights that Beetles
  love.
Dove, R.   Roses.
Levertov.   Continuum.
Olson, C.   I had had / a beetle.
Ramanujan.   Lac into Seal.
Riley, J.   Dusk Song—The Beetle.
Szymborska, W.   Seen from Above.
Updike.   Tropical Beetles.

Beets
Nash, O.   Parsnip, The.

Begging and Beggars
Baudelaire.   To a Red-headed Beggar.
Berry, W.   Guest, The.
  Music, A.
Bishop, E.   Pink Dog.
Browning, R.   Twins, The.
Burns, R.   Jolly Gauger, The.
Ciardi, J.   Coq au Vin.
  Matins.
  Roman Diary: 1951.
Cooper, J.   Mission with the Night, A.
Corbett, W.   Pardon, a few towns over.
Cummings, E. E.   But mr can you maybe listen
  there's.
  Right here the other night something.
Davie, D.   Grudging Respect.
De la Mare.   Owl, The.
Dickinson, E.   Beggar Lad—dies early, The.
  I never lost as much but twice.
  It came his turn to beg.
  Let me not thirst with this Hock at my Lip.

Most she touched me by her muteness.
There comes an hour when begging stops.
When a Lover is a Beggar.
Donne.   Lame Beggar, A.
  To Mr T. W. ("Pregnant again with th' old twins
  hope, and fear").
Dugan, A.   Variation on "Winter's Onset from
  an Alienated Point of View."
Emerson, R.   There are beggars in Iran and
  Araby.
Gunn, T.   Improvisation.
  St. Martin and the Beggar.
Herrick.   Beggar to Mab, the Fairy [*or* Fairie]
  Queen, The.
  Beggars.
  Begger, The.
  Biting of Beggars.
  His Petition.
  No Bashfulnesse in Begging.
  Upon Guesse.
  Upon Her Almes.
Housman.   He looked at me with eyes I thought.
Hughes, L.   Beggar Boy.
  Parisian Beggar Woman.
Komunyakaa.   Eleemosynary.
  Soliloquy: Man Talking to a Mirror.
Lawrence, D. H.   From a College Window.
Lindsay, N.   Honor Among Scamps.
  Prologue to "Rhymes to be Traded for Bread."
Mallarmé.   Alms.
McGrath, T.   Emblems of Exile.
Meredith, G.   Beggar's Soliloquy, The.
  Bellerophon.
Merwin.   Beggars and Kings.
Oliver, M.   Acid.
Orr, G.   Beggar's Song.
  Tin Cup.
Pessoa.   He came by, wanting to speak with me
  on a downtown street.
Plath.   Applicant, The.
  Beggars, The.
Ramanujan.   One Reads.
  Poverty.
Riley, J.   Old Hand-Organ, The.
Suckling, S.   Song: "I prithee send me back my
  heart."
Tate, J.   Voyage from Stockholm to Take
  Advantage of Lower Prices on the Finnish
  Island of Åland.
Thomas, D.   Hunchback in the Park, The.
Whalen, P.   Song for 2 Balalaikas on the Corner
  of 3rd & Market.
Williams, T.   Mendicant Order, A.
Wordsworth, W.   Beggars.
  Old Cumberland Beggar, The.
Yeats.   Beggar to Beggar Cried.
  Hour before Dawn, The.
  Three Beggars, The.
  Under the Round Tower.
See also **Homeless, The; Vagabonds**

Belfast, Northern Ireland
Brodsky, J.   Belfast Tune.
Davie, D.   Belfast on a Sunday Afternoon.
MacNeice.   Belfast.
Mahon.   Afterlives.
  Brighton Beach.
  Northern Star.
Muldoon, P.   Aisling.
  Trifle, A.

Belgium
Auden.   Brussels in Winter.
Cummings, E. E.   Belgium.
Davie, D.   Hyphens.
Hardy, T.   Appeal to America on Behalf of the
  Belgian Destitute, An.
  Cry of the Homeless.
  On the Belgian Expatriation.
Mallarmé.   Remembrance of Belgian Friends.
Rossetti, D.   Carillon, The.

Belief
Amichai [*or* Amikhai].   At the Seashore.
Berry, W.   Below.
Borges.   I Am Not Even Dust.
Clough.   O happy they whose hearts receive.
Crane, S.   I saw a man pursuing the horizon.
Creeley.   Mirror, The.

Dickinson, E.   Incredible never surprises us, The.
Neither fearing Extinction.
Spirit lasts, but in what mode, The.
We cannot believe for each other.
Duncan, R.   Song of the Borderguard, The.
Eberhart, R.   Height of Man, The.
Emerson, R.   I have found a nobler love.
Frost, R.   They Were Welcome to Their Belief.
We vainly wrestle with the blind belief.
Hardy, T.   Graveyard of Dead Creeds, The.
Herrick.   To Silvia.
Hill, G.   Bidden Guest, The.
Howe, F.   Veteran.
Kizer, C.   Dixit Insipiens.
Laughlin, J.   Believer, The.
Lawrence, D. H.   Belief.
Levertov.   Suspended.
Levine, P.   Belief.
I Could Believe.
Logan, J.   Believe It.
MacLeish.   America Was Promises.
Major, C.   No Single Thing by Itself.
Melville, H.   Margrave's Birthnight, The.
Merton.   Je Crois En L'Amour.
Nash, O.   Seeing Eye to Eye Is Believing.
Neruda.   Dead Dog.
Olson, C.   I hang on by,
Quatrain: "Do not, at this high time, desert."
Patchen.   Court of First Appeal.
Time to Believe!, A.
Pessoa.   Christmas.
Rossetti, C.   Have I not striven, my God, and watched and prayed?
Lord, carry me.—Nay, but I grant thee strength.
Rukeyser, M.   Lilienthal said : I heard him saying words like these.
This Place in the Ways.
Willkie—Stopless Falling through Air.
Sandburg, C.   Manufactured Gods.
Smith, S.   God the Eater.
Stafford, W.   Believer.
Weiss, T.   Last Day and the First, The.
Whittier.   Cypress-Tree of Ceylon, The.
Williams, M.   Man Who Believes in Five, The.
Williams, T.   Mornings on Bourbon Street.
Wright, C.   Ars Poetica 2.
See also **Faith**

Bellevue Hospital, New York City
Codrescu.   Music.
Dubie.   Bellevue Exchange.
Dugan, A.   Dedication for a Building.
Laughlin, J.   Building 520, Bellevue.

Bells
Baudelaire.   Cracked Bell, The.
Blok.   They Do Not Trade, Sleep, or Remember.
Chesterton.   Bell, The.
Clough.   See! the faint green tinge from the western sky has.
Collins, B.   Japan.
Crane, H.   Broken Tower, The.
Cummings, E. E.   Anyone Lived in a Pretty How Town.
B / eLl / s? / bE.
"Dario."   Sweetness of the Angelus, divine in the morning, The.
Davie, D.   Oriental Visitor, An.
De la Mare.   Bells, The.
Dickinson, E.   How still the Bells in Steeples stand.
When Bells stop ringing—Church—begins.
Dubie.   Hours, The.
Emerson, R.   I love thy music, mellow bell.
Hardy, T.   Chimes, The.
Christmas in the Elgin Room.
Drawing Details in an Old Church.
Peace Peal, The.
Herrick.   Bellman, The.
Housman.   Bredon Hill.
When the bells justle in the tower.
Hughes, L.   Bells Toll Kindly, The.
Jackson, L.   Ding-Donging.
Kinsella, T.   Bell, The.
Kipling, R.   Bell Buoy, The.
Bells and Queen Victoria, The.
Clerks and the Bells, The.

Lawrence, D. H.   Bells.
Passing-Bell, A.
Levertov.   Magic.
Lindsay, N.   In Memory of My Friend, Joyce Kilmer, Poet and Soldier.
MacLeish.   Signal, The.
Mallarmé.   Bell-Ringer, The.
Merrill, J.   Chimes for Yahya.
Neruda.   This Broken Bell.
Olson, C.   Mind's Notice, The.
Owen, W.   Anthem for Doomed Youth.
Poe.   Bells, The.
Riley, J.   Tinkle of Bells, A.
Rossetti, C.   All the bells were ringing / And all the birds were singing.
"Ding a ding," / The sweet bells sing.
Peal of Bells, A.
Toll, bell, toll. For hope is flying / Sighing from the earthbound soul.
Sandburg, C.   Light and Moonbells.
Night Bells.
When Death Came April Twelve 1945.
Sexton.   Ringing the Bells.
Smith, S.   Fairy Bell, The.
Stevens, W.   Old Lutheran Bells at Home, The.
Swift, J.   On His Own Deafness.
Thoreau.   Old meeting-house bell.
Peal of the Bells, The.
Why toll the bell today.
Tomlinson, C.   Walking to Bells.
Very.   Nine O'Clock Bell, The.
Whittier.   Red River Voyageur, The.
Skipper Ireson's Ride.
Wilbur, R.   Bell Speech.
Dubious Night, A.
Williams, T.   Lyric: "Glad morning, coming, The."
Williams, W.   Catholic Bells, The.
Zagajewski.   Bells, The.

Belshazzar
Byron, G.   Vision of Belshazzar, The.
Hughes, L.   Last Feast of Belshazzar, The.
Stevens, W.   Country Words.

Ben Bulben, Ireland
Yeats.   Under Ben Bulben.

Benches
Hughes, L.   Park Benching.

Bengal
Ginsberg, A.   September on Jessore Road.

Benjamin, Walter
Creeley.   Thinking of Walter Benjamin.

Beowulf
Borges.   Poem Written in a Copy of *Beowulf*.
Wilbur, R.   Beowulf.

Bergman, Ingmar
Dubie.   Through a Glass Darkly.

Berkeley, California
Clampitt.   Minor Tremor, A.
Ginsberg, A.   Strange New Cottage in Berkeley, A.
Kumin, M.   Sunbathing on a Rooftop in Berkeley.
Pinsky.   In Berkeley.
Whalen, P.   Many Pages Must Be Thrown Away.

Berkeley, George
Borges.   Things ("Fallen volume, hidden by the others, The").
Davie, D.   Fountain, The.
McHugh, H.   Message at Sunset for Bishop Berkeley.

Berlin, Germany
Brodsky, J.   Berlin Wall Tune, The.
Carruth, H.   August 14, 1961.
Clampitt.   Archaic Figure.
Davie, D.   Three Pastors in Berlin.

Bermuda
Cooper, J.   Bermuda.
Marvell.   Bermudas.
Merton.   Aubade: Bermuda.

Bernhardt, Sarah
Wilde, O.   Phèdre.

Berrigan, Daniel
Rich, A.   Burning of Paper instead of Children,

The.

Berrigan, Ted
Komunyakaa.   Insufficient Blue.

Berryman, John
Bishop, E.   Thank-You Note.
Broumas, O.   Landscape with Poets.
Ciardi, J.   Trying to Feel Something.
Cooper, J.   Mourning Picture.
Poem with Capital Letters, A.
Davie, D.   Berryman.
Dugan, A.   Answer to the Rilke Question.
Ignatow, D.   For John Berryman.
Meredith, W.   In Loving Memory of the Late Author of *Dream Songs*.
John and Anne.
Merwin.   Berryman.
Stock, R.   Nightmare Song.

Bertrand de Born
Pound, E.   Na Audiart.
Near Perigord.
Sestina: Altaforte.

Bestiality
Cummings, E. E.   In hammamet did camping queers et al).
Dickey, J.   Sheep Child, The.
Rumi.   Importance of Gourdcrafting, The.

Bethlehem
Browning, E.   Virgin Mary to the Child Jesus, The.
Parker, D.   Maid-Servant at the Inn, The.
Raine, K.   Star of Bethlehem.
Sandburg, C.   Star Silver.
Yeats.   Second Coming, The.

Betrayal
Angelou.   Communication I.
Baudelaire.   My Beatrice.
Blok.   Commander's Footsteps, The.
Bly, R.   In Mourning for Betrayal.
Brontë, E.   But the hearts that once adored me.
His land may burst the galling chain.
I'm standing in the forest now.
To A.G.A.
Written in the Gaaldine Prison Caves to A.G.A.
Browning, E.   Romance of the Ganges, A.
Burns, R.   As I was a wand'ring ae midsummer e'enin.
Awa Whigs Awa.
Can You Leave Me Thus, My Katy.
Hughie Graham.
Laddies by the banks o' Nith, The.
Lord Gregory.
Robin Shure in Hairst.
Saw Ye My Phely (Quasi Dicat, Phillis).
Song: "Had I a cave on some wild, distant shore."
Thou hast left me ever, Jamie.
Byron, G.   Endorsement to the Deed of Separation, in the April of 1816.
Carruth, H.   Event Itself, The.
Carver, R.   Betrayal.
Mosque in Jaffa, The.
Cavafy.   Dimaratos.
Coleridge, S.   Eros aei lalethros hetairos.
To One Who Published in Print.
Creeley.   Anger.
Places ("When I wake next").
Cullen, C.   Judas Iscariot.
Cummings, E. E.   It started when Bill's chip let on to.
Cunningham, J.   Agnosco Veteris Vestigia Flammae.
da Bologna, B.   Inside that loving country girl.
Davie, D.   Black Hoyden.
Catullus on Friendship.
Dickinson, E.   That she forgot me was the least.
Emerson, R.   Traitors tho' plumed & steel equipped.
Webster.
Graves, R.   Above the Edge of Doom.
Golden Anchor.
Horizon.
Impossible, The.
Lamia in Love.
Lost Jewel, A.
Not at Home.

Pardon, The.
Wreath, The.
HaNagid. Fawn, The.
Hardy, T. At Shag's Heath.
Broken Appointment, A.
Mongrel, The.
Rose-Ann.
Herrick. Cock-Crow.
Gods Price, and Mans Price.
His Words to Christ, Going to the Cross.
Hopkins, G. Did Helen steal my love from me?
Housman. Is my team plowing?
Hughes, L. Could Be.
Ignatow, D. Each Day.
Kipling, R. Declaration of London, The.
Disciple, The.
Memories.
Song at Cock-Crow, A.
Ulster.
Lawrence, D. H. Traitors.
Two Wives.
MacLeish. Woman on the Stair, The.
Meredith, G. Once the fair Romance of story.
Merton. Betrayal, The.
House of Caiphas, The.
Michelangelo Buonarroti. There's pleasure in
great favors done, but hidden.
Millay, E. Bluebeard.
My Spirit, Sore from Marching.
Raine, K. And that was all his life.
Ralegh, S. Farewell to False Love, A.
Ransom, J. Winter Remembered.
Rossetti, C. Dying Man to His Betrothed, The.
Easter Even.
Two Parted.
Rukeyser, M. Handclap.
Sixth Elegy. River Elegy.
Sexton. Legend of the One-Eyed Man, The.
Shelley, P. Love's Rose.
Swift, J. Judas.
Unknown. Dole of the King's Daughter, The.
Very. Behold He Is at Hand That Doth Betray
Me.
Whitman, W. Blood-Money.
Whittier. Ichabod[!].
Williams, C. K. Soliliquies.
Williams, T. Comforter and the Betrayer, The.
Wyatt, S. And if an eye may save or slay.
Behold, love, thy power how she despiseth!
Betrayal.
But sithens you it assay to kill.
Defamed guiltiness by silence unkempt.
Longer to trow ye.
Lover Showeth How He Is Forsaken of Such as
He Sometime Enjoyed, The.
O, cruel heart, where is thy faith?
Once in your grace I know I was.
Who would have ever thought.

Betrothal
Browning, E. Crowned and Wedded.
Rhyme of the Duchess May.
Romance of the Ganges, A.
Cavafy. Che Fece . . . Il Gran Rifiuto.
Coleridge, S. Keepsake, The.
Riley, J. John Alden and Percilly.
Stein, G. Marry Nettie.

Bible
Akhmatova, A. Lot's Wife.
Amichai [*or* Amikhai]. Biblical Meditations.
Children's Procession.
From the Book of Esther I Filtered the
Sediment.
From the Scroll of Esther, I filtered out the
sediment.
I Want to Confuse the Bible.
Summer Evening at the Window with Psalms.
Berryman. Search, The.
Bishop, E. Over 2000 Illustrations and a
Complete Concordance.
Borges. Fragments from an Apocryphal Gospal.
Celan. In Egypt.
Cowper, W. To Mary Unwin.
Cunningham, J. 1 Corinthians 13: Commentary.
Dickinson, E. Bible is an antique Volume, The.
Donne. Upon the Translation of the Psalms by
Sir Philip Sidney, and the Countess of

Pembroke His Sister.
Emerson, R. But never yet the man was found.
We sauntered amidst miracles.
Graves, R. After the Flood.
Hall, D. Maundy Thursday's Candles.
Hardy, T. After Reading Psalms XXXIX, XL,
etc.
Respectable Burgher, The.
Heaney, S. Other Side, The.
Herbert, G. Holy Scriptures (1), The.
Holy Scriptures (2), The.
Thanksgiving, The.
Herrick. His Wish to God.
Lip Labour.
Montes Scripturarum, the Mounts of the
Scriptures.
Jackson, L. Readers, The.
Laughlin, J. Bible Lady, The.
Logan, J. Homage to John the Baptist.
Lux. Floating Baby Paintings.
Merrill, J. Salome.
Milosz, C. Readings.
With Her.
Nemerov. Book of Kells, The.
Olson, C. In the Hills South of Capernaum,
Port.
Raine, K. My day's plan to write.
Riley, J. Brudder Sims.
Old-fashioned Bible, The.
Sandburg, C. Methusaleh Saw Many Repeaters.
Scripture.
Sarton, M. Jonah.
Seifert. Lost Paradise.
Sheridan, T. You That Would Read the Bible.
Simic. Begotten of the Spleen.
Smart, C. Jubilate Agno.
Song to David, A.
Smith, S. Magnificent Words.
Stafford, W. How the Real Bible Is Written.
In the Book.
Saint Matthew and All.
Very. Bible, The.
Scepticism with Regard to the Gospels.
Weiss, T. Working Day, A.
Wilbur, R. Matthew VIII, 28 ff.
Peter.
Simplification, A.
Wilner, E. Reading the Bible Backwards.

Bicentennial, U.S.
Warren, R. Bicentennial.
Wilner, E. Closing Ceremonies for the
Bicentennial.

Bicycles and Bicycling
Blue Cloud. Expedition.
Broumas, O. Way a Child Might Believe, The.
Collins, B. Scotland.
Heaney, S. Wheels within Wheels.
Komunyakaa. Ten Speeds.
Laughlin, J. Our Bicycles.
MacNeice. Cyclist, The.
Milosz, C. Day of Generation.
Yellow Bicycle.
Montale. Buffalo.
Oppen. Bicycles and the Apex, The.
Piercy. Cyclist, The.
Prunty. Learning the Bicycle.
Ritsos. Myopic Child, A.
Williams, C. K. World's Greatest Tricycle-
Rider, The.

Bigamy and Bigamists
Hardy, T. Wife and Another, A.

Billboards
Larkin, P. Sunny Prestatyn.
Lux. This Space Available.
Nash, O. Song of the Open Road.

Billiards
Cummings, E. E. Newly / cued / motif smites
truly to beautifully.
Surely / Cued / motif smites truly to Beautifully,
The.
Robinson, E. Doctor of Billiards.

Biography
Amichai [*or* Amikhai]. Autobiography, 1952.
Auden. Change of Air, A.
Carver, R. Hamid Ramouz (1818–1906).

Ciardi, J. Autobiography of a Comedian.
Codrescu. Biographical Notes.
Cooper, J. Long View from the Suburbs.
Creeley. I.
Cunningham, J. Meditation on a Memoir.
Memoir.
Dickinson, E. Biography first convinces us.
Like a Memoir of the Sun.
Kizer, C. My Good Father.
Kumin, M. Marianne, My Mother, and Me.
Larkin, P. Posterity.
Laughlin, J. Scribe, The.
Levi, P. Autobiography.
Logue, C. Song of Autobiography, The.
Lux. Mr. Pope.
Major, C. Life Story, A.
Pessoa. If, after I die, they want to write my
biography.
Rimbaud, A. Lives.
Sandburg, C. Biography.
Tate, J. Intimidations of an Autobiography.
Warren, R. Problem of Autobiography / Vague
Recollection or Dream?
Weiss, T. Autobiographia Illiteraria.
Whitman, W. When I Read the Book.
Williams, W. Visit, The.
Zagajewski. Polish Biographical Dictionary in a
Library in Houston, The.

Birch Trees
Carruth, H. Meadow House.
Frost, R. Birches.
Pea Brush.
Young Birch, A.
Gurney, I. Silver Birch.
Hardy, T. Upper Birch-Leaves, The.
Niedecker. For best work.
Schuyler, J. 8/12/70.
Warren, R. John's Birches.
Wilbur, R. Black Birch in Winter, A.
Williams, W. Portrait of the Author.

Bird Migration
Dugan, A. Envy of Natural Formal Liberties,
An.
Gurney, I. Here, If Forlorn.
Hughes, T. Swifts.
Merwin. Migration.
Sexton. Balance Wheel, The.
Tomlinson, C. Geese Going South.
Warren, R. Heart of Autumn.
See also **Animal Migration**

Bird-watching
Carver, R. With a Telescope Rod on Cowiche
Creek.
Ciardi, J. Bird Watching.
Clampitt. Shorebird-Watching.
Eberhart, R. Snowy Owl.
Nash, O. Up from the Egg; the Confessions of a
Nuthatch Avoider.
Schuyler, J. In Wiry Winter.
Van Duyn. Letters from a Father.

Birds
Ammons. Center.
City Limits, The.
Contingency.
Doubling the Nerve.
Mirrorment.
September Drift.
Auden. Bird-Language.
Decoys, The.
Their Lonely Betters.
Berry, W. Architecture, An.
Bird Killer, The.
For the Future.
Hidden Singer, The.
Wild, The.
Bierce. Nanine.
Bishop, E. Five Flights Up.
Some Dreams They Forgot.
Blake, W. Birds, The.
How Sweet I Roamed [*or* Roam'd] from Field
to Field.
Blue Cloud. Hobo Bird.
Bly, R. Loon's Cry, The.
Bogan, L. Statue and Birds.
Brontë, E. Redbreast, Early in the morning.

Browning, E. Deserted Garden, The.
Island, An.
Man and Nature.
Bukowski. Singing Is Fire.
Burns, R. Hunting Song.
On Scaring Some Waterfowl in Loch Turit, a
Wild Scene among the Hills of Oughtertyre.
Phillis the Fair.
Carruth, H. Birds of Vietnam, The.
Wild Swans at Norfolk, The.
Carver, R. At the Bird Market.
Poem Not against Songbirds, A.
Through the Boughs.
Chuang Tzu. P'eng That Was a K'un, The.
Symphony for a Sea Bird.
Ciardi, J. As I Would Wish You Birds.
Bird in Whatever Name, The.
Bird Watching.
Birds, like Thoughts.
No White Birds Sings.
Sea-Birds.
Size of Song, The.
Small Elegy.
Snowy Heron.
Clampitt. Bayou Afternoon.
Brought from Beyond.
Camouflage.
Meadowlark Country.
Shorebird-Watching.
Syrinx.
Whippoorwill in the Woods, A.
Clifton, L. Signs.
Codrescu. From a Trilogy of Birds.
Coleridge, S. Answer to a Child's Question.
Cooper, J. Morning on the St. John's.
Cowper, W. Faithful Friend, The.
On Mrs. Montagu's Feather-Hangings.
Pairing Time Anticipated.
Tale, A: "In Scotland's realm, where trees are
few."
Crane, H. Carrier Letter.
Crane, S. Little birds of the night.
Once, I knew a fine song.
Three little birds in a row.
Creeley. 3 in 1.
Bird, The.
Birds, The.
Chanson.
Cummings, E. E. At just 5 a / m i hear eng.
Birds(/ here,inven / ting air).
Birds meet above the new Moon.
For any ruffian of the sky.
Hills chime with thrush.
If everything happens that can't be done.
May my heart always be open to little.
Nine birds(rising / through a gold
moment)climb.
Now(more near ourselves than we).
SNOW / cru / is / ingw Hi.
Swi(/ across!gold's / rouNdly.
Until and i heard.
Without the mercy of / your eyes your.
"Dario." Birds of the islands: in your gathering.
Davie, D. Screech-Owl.
De la Mare. Dawn.
Estranged.
Martins: September.
Riddlers, The.
Rooks In October.
Speech.
Thomas Hardy.
Titmouse.
Who?
Dickey, J. Owl King, The.
Reincarnation (II).
Three, The.
Dickinson, E. Before you thought of Spring.
Bird came down the Walk, A.
Bird her punctual music brings, The.
Bird must sing to earn the Crumb, The.
Birds are very bold this Morning, The.
Birds begun at Four o'clock, The.
Birds reported from the South, The.
Cat.
For every Bird a Nest.
High from the earth I heard a bird.

His Bill an Auger is.
His Bill is clasped—his Eye forsook.
"Hope" is the thing with feathers.
I have a Bird in spring.
I have seen one Bird and part of another.
Lady feeds Her little Bird, The.
Mama never forgets her birds.
Most triumphant Bird I ever knew or met, The.
No ladder needs the bird but skies.
Of Being is a Bird.
Ones that disappeared are back, The.
Out of sight? What of that?
Saddest noise, the sweetest noise, The.
Upon his Saddle sprung a Bird.
Dove, R. In the Old Neighborhood.
Dugan, A. Address to a Bird on a Visit Home.
Apology (to the Muse).
Branches of Water or Desire, The.
Dunbar, P. Crumb, a Crumb, and a Little Seed,
A.
Oh little fledgling out of the nest.
Preparation.
Sympathy.
Two Songs.
Eberhart, R. By the Stream.
Evening Bird Song
Go to the Shine That's on a Tree.
I Walked Out to the Graveyard to See the Dead.
Incidence of Flight.
Learning from Nature.
Now Is the Air Made of Chiming Balls.
Old Tom.
Opulence.
Thrush Song at Dawn.
Truncated Bird, The.
Ultimate Song.
Young Hunter, The.
Emerson, R. As I walked in the woods.
If bright the sun, he tarries.
May.
Miracle, The.
Farid-uddin Attar. From "Bird Conversations."
Ferlinghetti, L. General Song of Humanity, The.
He with the Beating Wings.
L'Occupation Obsédée.
Frost, R. Exposed Nest, The.
Hill Wife, The.
Last Word of a Bluebird, The.
Looking for a Sunset Bird in Winter.
Minor Bird, A.
Never Again Would Birds' Song Be The Same.
On a Bird Singing in its Sleep.
Oven Bird, The.
Gallagher, T. Bird-Window-Flying.
Candle, Lamp & Firefly.
Some Painful Butterflies Pass Through.
Unsteady Yellow.
Ginsberg, A. Very Dove, A.
Graves, R. Ambience.
Gray, T. Fragment: "There pipes the woodlark,
and the song[-]thrush there."
Gunn, T. On the Move.
Gurney, I. Here, If Forlorn.
"H. D." Birds in Snow.
Hall, D. "Internal and External Forms."
Hamill, S. George Seferis in Sonora.
Han-shan. I see a bird of five colors.
Oriole on a flowering branch, An.
Parrots live in western lands.
Hardy, T. Bird-Catcher's Boy, The.
Bird-Scene at a Rural Dwelling, A.
Blinded Bird, The.
Boy's Dream, The.
Puzzled Game-Birds, The.
Selfsame Song, The.
Weathers [or Weather].
Yellow-Hammer, The.
Heaney, S. Oracle.
Serenades.
Herrick. To His Maid Prew.
Hopkins, G. As Kingfishers Catch Fire.
Windhover, The.
Hughes, T. Cormorant, A.
Crow and the Birds.
Curlews [Lift].
Heptonstall Old Church.

Last of the 1st/5th Lancashire Fusiliers, The.
Skylarks.
Swifts.
Ignatow, D. Bird, The.
Omen, An.
Peace.
Whistle or Hoot.
Jackson, L. Of All the World.
Jacobsen, J. Birds,The.
Insomniac's Bird.
Noon.
Of Pairs.
Jarrell, R. Country Life, A.
Loss.
Mockingbird, The.
Jeffers, R. Birds.
Birds and Fishes.
Winged Rock.
Keats. 'How Many Bards Gild the Lapses of
Time!'
Komunyakaa. Birds on a Powerline.
Charmed.
Song Thief, The.
Kumin, M. Hermit Wakes to Bird Sounds, The.
In Warm Rooms, Before a Blue Light,
Laughlin, J. Alba.
Bird of Endless Time, The.
Frightened Bird, The.
Lawrence, D. H. Blue Jay, The.
Living, A.
Many Mansions.
Sigh No More.
Levertov. Alongside.
Claritas.
Stems.
Levine, P. Red Dust.
Logan, J. Three Poems on Morris Graves'
Paintings.
Logue, C. Song of the Imperial Carrion, The.
Lorde. Ballad from Childhood.
Trip on the Staten Island Ferry, A.
MacDiarmid, H. Caledonian Antisyzygy, The.
Ex Vermibus.
Glen of Silence, The.
Perfect.
MacLeish. Critics on the Lawn.
Voyage en Provence.
Mahon. Bird Sanctuary.
Major, C. Apple Core.
Birds.
Frenzy.
No Time for Self-Pity.
Mallarmé. Little Air 2.
Maritain. Autumn.
McGrath, T. Face of the Precipice is Black with
Lovers, The.
Inheritance, The.
Meredith, G. July.
Night of Frost in May.
Song: "Quick bird sings and pierces me, The."
Song: The Wren.
South-Wester, The.
Two Blackbirds, The.
Meredith, W. Jain Bird Hospital in Delhi, The.
On Falling Asleep to Birdsong.
Merton. Silver bird is E backward in cool pond
water, The.
Merwin. Birds on the Morning of Going, The.
Death of a Favorite Bird.
Lark.
Millay, E. Black hair you'd say she had, or
rather.
Bobolink, The.
Pigeons, The.
Sky-coloured bird, blue wings with no more
spots of spotless white.
Milosz, C. Ode to a Bird.
Mistral, G. Grace.
Montale. Capercaillie, The.
Hoopoe, happy bird maligned.
Moore, M. Bird-witted.
Smooth Gnarled Crape Myrtle.
To a Prize Bird.
To the Peacock of France.
Muldoon, P. Bangle, The.
Elizabeth.

Mist-Net, The.
Nightingales.
Plovers.
Nash, O.   Birdies, Don't Make Me Laugh.
Birds, The.
Grackle, The.
Up from the Egg; the Confessions of a Nuthatch Avoider.
Nemerov.   Distances They Keep, The.
Neruda.   Bird.
Niedecker.   Bird singing.
Birds' mating-fight.
July, waxwings.
Lights, lifts.
Thure Kumlien.
O'Hara, F.   Easter.
Oliver, M.   Rabbit, The.
Olson, C.   Grinning monster out side the system.
Round & a Canon, A.
Small Birds, to Agree with the Leaves, Come in the Fall.
Variations Done for Gerald Van De Wiele.
Oppen.   Cultural Triumph, A.
She Steals Birds.
Space, The.
Workman.
Orr, G.   On the Lawn at Ira's.
Paley, G.   For George (II).
Parker, D.   Ornithology for Beginners.
Patchen.   Bird-Queen, The.
Great Birds, The.
O the sledbirds rides over the willow.
Poor Gorrel.
Petrarch.   Poor little bird, singing as you flit by.
Piercy.   Crippling, The.
Pinsky.   First Early Mornings Together.
Plath.   Goatsucker.
Poe.   Romance.
Prunty.   Cold.
Raine, K.   London air dims.
My day's plan to write.
Ramanujan.   In the Zoo.
Ransom, J.   Lady Lost.
Somewhere Is Such a Kingdom.
Rexroth, K.   It Is a German Honeymoon.
Rich, A.   Return of the Evening Grosbeaks, The.
Riley, J.   Few of the Bird-Family, A.
Song o' Cheer, A.
Yellowbird, The.
Ritsos.   Courage or Ignorance.
Relation of the Unrelated, The.
Tree, A.
Roethke.   All Morning.
Kitty-Cat Bird, The.
Reply, The.
Siskins, The.
Tree, the Bird, The.
Young Girl, The.
Rossetti, C.   1885. St. Valentine's Day.
All the bells were ringing / And all the birds were singing.
Another Spring.
Bird Song, A.
Birthday, A.
Child's Talk in April.
Fly Away, Fly Away.
Freaks of Fashion.
Gone for Ever.
Green Cornfield, A.
Heaven Is Heaven.
If the sun could tell us half / That he hears and sees.
Mirrors of Life and Death.
Paradise: in a Symbol.
Summer.
Summer nights are short, / Where northern days are long, The.
White hen sitting / On white eggs three, A.
Rumi.   Birdsong brings relief.
Imra'u 'l-Qays.
Think that you're gliding out from the face of a cliff.
Three Fish, The.
Way of love is not, The.
Sandburg, C.   Bird Footprint.
Bird Talk.

Cheap Rent.
Little Word, Little White Bird.
Margaret.
River Roads.
Sandhill People.
Santa Fe Sketches.
Spring Cries.
Three Spring Notations on Bipeds.
Wingtip.
Sarton, M.   Caged Bird, The.
Franz, a Goose.
Parrot, A.
Phoenix, The.
Swans, The.
Schuyler, J.   In Wiry Winter.
Seifert.   Birds' Voices in the Tree Tops.
In an Empty Room.
Sexton.   Balance Wheel, The.
Torn Down from Glory Daily.
What the Bird with the Human Head Knew.
Shelley, P.   Fragment: Omens.
Simic.   Animals and Birds.
Bird, The.
Forest Birds.
Smith, S.   Avondall.
British Song, A.
Hippy-Mo.
Sallow Bird, The.
Spender, S.   Boy, Cat, Canary.
Stafford, W.   Bird inside a Box, A.
Juncos.
New Every Day.
Over the North Jetty.
Troubleshooting.
Stevens, W.   Not Ideas about the Thing but the Thing Itself.
Of Mere Being.
On an Old Horn.
Somnambulisma.
Stock, R.   Poem to Be Printed on a Very White Page.
To Tui: Not to Hie Herself Off To Only God Knows How Dire & Pestilential A South Sea Island.
Swenson, M.   Angels at "Unsubdued."
Camoufleur.
Dear Elizabeth.
Fable for When There's No Way Out.
Feel like a Bird.
Fountain Piece.
Manyone Flying.
New Pair, A.
On Addy Road.
Pair, A.
Red Bird Tapestry, The.
Waterbird.
Willets, The.
Woods at Night, The.
Szymborska, W.   Birds Returning.
Returning Birds.
Tate, J.   Blue Booby, The.
Eagle Exterminating Company, The.
Thomas, D.   Because the Pleasure-Bird Whistles.
Over Sir John's Hill.
Spire Cranes, The.
Thoreau.   Shrike, The.
Sometimes I hear the veery's clarion.
Thou dusky spirit of the wood.
To a Stray Fowl.
Vireo, The.
Tomlinson, C.   Encounter.
In the Estuary.
Translating the Birds.
Updike.   Each Summer's Swallows.
Great Scarf of Birds, The.
Mobile of Birds.
Upon Learning That a Bird Exists Called the Turnstone.
Van Duyn.   Letters from a Father.
Very.   Birds of Passage, The.
Birds, The.
Cherry Birds, The.
Fox and the Bird, The.
Our Native Sparrows.
Passage Bird, The.

Petrels, The.
Robin, The.
Robin's Song, The.
Snow Bird, The.
Sparrows and the Crop of Weeds, The.
Swift, The.
Winter Bird, The.
Walcott.   Flock, The.
Season of Phantasmal Peace, The.
Warren, R.   Heart of Autumn.
Patriotic Tour and Postulate of Joy.
Whalen, P.   Plus Ça Change.
Road-Runner, The.
Whitman, W.   Of That Blithe Throat of Thine.
Out of the Cradle Endlessly Rocking.
To the Man-of-War Bird.
Wilbur, R.   All These Birds.
Event, An.
From the Lookout Rock.
Games Two.
In a Bird Sanctuary.
Marché aux Oiseaux.
Sketch, A.
Still, Citizen Sparrow.
Wilde, O.   From Spring Days to Winter.
Williams, C. K.   That the world / is going.
Williams, M.   Folding His *USA Today* He Makes His Point in the Blue Star Café.
Williams, W.   Bird.
Bird's Companion, The.
Birdsong, The.
Breakfast.
Passer Domesticus.
Struggle of Wings.
To Waken an Old Lady.
Unknown, The.
Wilner, E.   Bird in the Laurel's Song, The.
Freed from Another Context.
Literal = The Abstract, The: A Demonstration.
Wordsworth, W.   Contrast; the Parrot and the Wren, The.
In the Woods of Rydal.
Incipient Madness.
June, 1820.
Morning Exercise, A.
Redbreast, The [Suggested in a Westmoreland Cottage].
Reverie of Poor Susan, The.
Sailor's Mother, The.
Suggested by a Picture of the Bird of Paradise.
Upon seeing a Coloured Drawing of the Bird of Paradise in an Album.
Water Fowl.
Wren's Nest, A.
Wright, C.   Meditation on Song and Structure.
Wright, J.   Invention of a Garden, The.
Little Girl on Her Way to School, A.
Presentation of Two Birds to My Son, A.
RIP.
Summer Memory in the Crowded City, A.
Yeats.   White Birds, The.
Zukofsky, L.   For Zadkine.
Gulls over a rotting hull.
Perch Less.
See also **Waterfowl**

Birds' Nests
Cummings, E. E.   I / never / guessed any / thing(even a).
Heaney, S.   Nesting-Ground.
Wilbur, R.   Lightness.
Williams, C. K.   That the world / is going.
Wordsworth, W.   Wren's Nest, A.

Birds of Paradise
Graves, R.   Bird of Paradise.
Wordsworth, W.   Suggested by a Picture of the Bird of Paradise.

Birmingham, Alabama
Hughes, L.   Birmingham Sunday.
Bombings in Dixie.
Merton.   And the Children of Birmingham.
Picture of a Black Child with a White Doll.

Birmingham, England
MacNeice.   Birmingham.

Birth
Ai.   Country Midwife, The: A Day.

Amichai [or Amikhai]. On the Day My Daughter Was Born No One Died.
Poem: "As at the beginning of birth."
Armantrout. Fiction ("When the woman's face contorted and she clutched the railing for support, we knew she would die").
Arnold, M. In Utrumque Paratus.
Beckett, S. Chaque jour envie.
Sanies I.
Berry, W. Birth (Near Port William), The.
Her First Calf.
Blue Cloud. We sit balanced.
Bly, R. December 23, 1926.
Bradstreet, A. Before the Birth of One of Her Children.
Broumas, O. Little Red Riding Hood.
No Harm Shall Come.
Pealing, The.
Woman with Child.
Byron, G. On the Birth of John William Rizzo Hoppner.
Chesterton. Donkey, The.
Clifton, L. Remembering the Birth of Lucifer.
Cooper, J. For a Boy Born in Wartime.
Crashaw. Upon the birth of the Princesse Elizabeth.
Cummings, E. E. And i imagine.
Little horse is newlY, The.
Pity his how illimitable plight.
De la Mare. Birthnight: To F, The.
Of a Son.
Dickey, J. Daughter.
For a Time and Place.
Dove, R. Variation on Guilt.
Drummond de Andrade. Seven-Sided Poem.
Dugan, A. Let Heroes Account to Love.
Eberhart, R. Return of Odysseus, The.
Emerson, R. What from this barren being do we reap.
Enzensberger, H. Midwives, The.
Ferlinghetti, L. True Confessional.
Glück, L. Garden, The.
Graves, R. Name.
Woman of Greece.
Gunn, T. Being Born.
Hacker, M. Christmas Crown, A.
Hardy, T. Life and Death at Sunrise.
To an Unborn Pauper Child.
Unborn, The.
Heaney, S. Pillowed Head, A.
Herrick. Epitaph upon a Sober Matron, An.
Upon a Lady That Dyed in Child-Bed, and Left a Daughter behind Her.
Upon Batt.
Hughes, T. Birth of Rainbow.
Examination at the Womb-Door.
February 17th.
New Foal.
Salmon Eggs.
Ignatow, D. Coupling.
Jackson, L. Room.
Jeffers, R. Birthday (Autobiography).
Jonson, B. Epigram on the Prince's Birth. 1630, An.
Epigram to the Queen, Then Lying In. 1630, An.
Kinnell. Under the Maud Moon.
Kizer, C. Birthday Poem for a Childless Man.
Kumin, M. Birthday Poem.
History Lesson.
Sleeping with Animals.
Larkin, P. This Was Your Place of Birth, This Daytime Palace.
Lawrence, D. H. Demiurge.
God Is Born.
Levertov. Map of the Western Part of the County of Essex in England, A.
Levine, P. Let Me Be.
Lindsay, N. Star of My Heart.
Lorde. And What About the Children.
Now That I Am Forever with Child.
Lux. For My Daughter When She Can Read.
MacDiarmid, H. Lo! A Child Is Born.
Major, C. Frenzy.
Mallarmé. Gift of the Poem.
McMichael. Pretty Blue Apron.

Molodovsky [or Molodowsky]. There Are Such Springlike Nights.
Muldoon, P. Mules.
October 1950.
Oliver, M. Meeting, A.
Olson, C. Epigon.
Ferrini—I.
La Chute III.
Ode on Nativity, An.
Ring of, The.
Sin is inferiority. The mother's cooperation in the birth of her daughter.
Translation, A.
Pagis. He'll Come Out for Sure.
Parker, D. Maid-Servant at the Inn, The.
Patchen. After an Old Song.
Piercy. Provocation of the Dream, The.
Plath. Morning Song.
Prunty. Namesake, The.
Winter's Tale, A.
Ramanujan. Birthdays.
Engagement.
Questions.
Riley, J. At Last.
Rimbaud, A. Old Lady's Old Men!
Rossetti, C. Before the Paling of the Stars.
Blind from my birth, / Where flowers are springing.
Death.
Everything that is born must die.
Hymn for Christmas Day, A.
Purification of St. Mary the Virgin, The.
To Mary Rossetti.
Rukeyser, M. Are You Born? / I.
Are You Born? / II.
Ballad Theme, A.
Birth, A.
Unborn Song.
Woman and Emblems.
Sandburg, C. Between Worlds.
Chicks.
Ever a Seeker.
Fog Numbers.
Harsk, Harsk.
Jan Kubelik.
Special Starlight.
Striped Cats, Old Men and Proud Stockings.
Shelley, P. Fragment: Life Rounded with Sleep.
Spender, S. Grandparents.
Stockton, A. On the Celebration of the Birth of the Dauphin of France.
Swenson, M. Nature.
Sze. Murmur, The.
Szymborska, W. Born.
Thomas, D. In the Beginning.
Vision and Prayer.
Unknown. On Hermocratia.
Song of Blodeuwedd, The.
Updike. Amoeba.
Van Duyn. Paratrooper.
To My Godson, on His Christening.
Whitman, W. Out of the Cradle Endlessly Rocking.
Woman Waits for Me, A.
Wilde, O. Ave Maria Gratia Plena.
Williams, C. K. They wash you / when.
Williams, M. People.
Williams, T. Speech from the Stairs.
Williams, W. Birth, The.
Catastrophic Birth.
Yeats. Consolation.
Stick of Incense, A.

Birth Control
Jonson, B. To Fine Lady Would-Be.
See also **Abortion**

Birth Defects
Muldoon, P. Blemish.
Williams, M. Ones That Are Thrown Out, The.

Birthdays
Amichai [or Amikhai]. 1924.
Birthday.
For My Birthday.
On My Birthday.
Angelou. On Reaching Forty.
Auden. Many Happy Returns.
Berrigan, T. 44th Birthday Evening, at Harris's.

Something Amazing Just Happened.
Bukowski. Poem for My 43rd Birthday.
Burns, R. Impromptu, on Mrs. W. Riddell's Birthday, 4th Novr. 1793.
To Terraughty, on His Birth-Day.
Byron, G. On My Thirty-third Birthday.
On This Day I Complete My Thirty-sixth Year.
Carver, R. Poem on My Birthday, July 2.
Ciardi, J. Birthday.
Obsolescence.
Poem for My Thirty-ninth Birthday.
Clifton, L. Birthday 1999.
Corbett, W. Marni's Birthday.
Cowper, W. To Miss Creuzé.
Creeley. Loner.
Cummings, E. E. Your birthday comes to tell me this.
De la Mare. Lucy.
Dickinson, E. Birthday of but a single pang.
One Year ago—jots what?
Dugan, A. February Twelfth Birthday Statement.
Eberhart, R. To Auden on His Fiftieth.
Ginsberg, A. To P.O.
Gunn, T. Lines for My 55th Birthday.
Hacker, M. Iva's Birthday Poem.
Hall, D. On Reaching the Age of Two Hundred.
Hopkins, G. Complaint, A.
Ignatow, D. Birthday.
Jacobsen, J. Birthday Party, The.
Jeffers, R. Birthday.
Johnson, S. Short Song of Congratulation [or To a Young Heir], A.
To Mrs Thrale [on Her Thirty-fifth Birthday].
Jonson, B. Ode, or Song, by All the Muses, An.
Ode. To Sir William Sydney, on His Birthday.
Kizer, C. Birthday Poem for a Childless Man.
For My Daughter.
Poem for Your Birthday.
Komunyakaa. Gift Horse.
Kumin, M. Birthday Poem.
Distance.
Kunitz, S. Passing Through.
Larkin, P. Dear CHARLES, My Muse, Asleep or Dead.
Lawrence, D. H. Birthday.
Levi, P. 12 July 1980.
Logan, J. Coming of Age.
Lines on His Birthday.
Lorde. Birthday Memorial to Seventh Street, A.
Merrill, J. Ouzo for Robin.
Merwin. Birthday, A.
Nash, O. Birthday on the Beach.
Lady Thinks She Is Thirty, A.
Lines to Be Scribbled on Somebody Else's Thirtieth Milestone.
Not George Washington's, Not Abraham Lincoln's, but Mine.
Party, The.
Niedecker. Regards to Mr. Glover.
O'Hara, F. John Button Birthday.
Poem: "Now it is the 27th."
Orr, G. Dream of Fifty, A.
Patchen. What Splendid Birthdays.
Plath. Birthday Present, A.
Pope, A. To Mr. Thomas Southern, on His Birth-Day, 1742.
To Mrs. M. B. on Her Birth-Day.
Ramanujan. Birthdays.
Rexroth, K. Your Birthday in the California Mountains.
Riley, J. To Hattie—on Her Birthday.
To My Sister.
Rossetti, C. Birthday, A.
To My Mother on Her Birthday.
Rukeyser, M. Rondel: "Now that I am fifty-six."
Voices of Waking.
Schuyler, J. November.
Sheridan, T. Poem Delivered to the Reverend Doctor Swift, Dean of St. Patrick's, Dublin, by a Young Nobleman, November 30, 1725, Being the Dean's Birthday, A.
Stafford, W. Biography.
Stein, G. Birthday Book, A.
Stockton, A. Birth Day Ode, A.

Lines Impromptu on Miss Morgans Birth Day.
Ode on the Birth Day of the Illustrious George
  Washington President of the United States,
  An.
Ode to Doctor Smith on His Birth Day March
  the 16th, 1791, An.
On Doctor Rushes Birth Day the 5th of
  January—after Ten Days Thick Fog.
On the Birth Day of the Revd Doctor
  Witherspoon, 1788.
To Doctor Smith on His Birth Day March 16th,
  92.
To Doctor Smith on His Birth Day March the
  16th, 1790.
To Mrs Rush, on Her Birth Day.
Swenson, M.   Birthday.
Swift, J.   Bec's Birthday.
  Stella's Birthday (1723).
  Stella's Birthday, 1725.
  Stella's Birthday ([March 13,] 1727).
  Stella's Birthday; Written in the Year 1718[/9].
  To Stella on Her Birthday, Written AD 1721–2.
Thomas, D.   Poem in October.
  Poem on His Birthday.
Van Duyn.   Birthday Card for a Psychiatrist.
  Sestina for Warm Seasons.
Whalen, P.   Birthday Poem.
  Literary Life in the Golden West.
Whitman, W.   For Queen Victoria's Birthday.
Whittier.   My Birthday.
  To Oliver Wendell Holmes.
Wilbur, R.   For K. R. on Her Sixtieth Birthday.
Williams, C. K.   Saturday.
Williams, M.   Paying Some Slight Attention to
  His Birthday the Associate Professor Goes
  about His Business.
Williams, W.   Trala Trala Trala La-le-la.
  Turkey in the Straw.
Wright, J.   Birthday, The.
Zukofsky, L.   In the midst of things.

Birthmarks

Armantrout.   Birthmark: The Pretext.
Wright, J.   Accusation, The.

Birthplaces

Coleridge, S.   Tell's Birth-Place.
Davie, D.   Conditioned Air, A.
Frost, R.   Birthplace, The.
Hardy, T.   Domicilium.
Heaney, S.   Birthplace, The.
Hughes, L.   New Yorkers.
Jonson, B.   To Penshurst.
Levine, P.   I Was Born in Lucerne.
Milosz, C.   In Szetejnie.
Petrarch.   He Who reveals His providence and
  art.
Stafford, W.   Across Kansas.
Williams, C. K.   Most excruciating / thing, The.

Bishop, Elizabeth

Swenson, M.   Dear Elizabeth.
  In the Bodies of Words.

Bison

Major, C.   Clay Bison in a Cave.
See also **Buffaloes**

Bitterness

Amichai [*or* Amikhai].   People in the Dark
  Always See.
Auden.   Stark bewölkt.
  We Too Had Known Golden Hours.
Baudelaire.   Obsession.
Broumas, O.   Bitterness.
Browning, R.   Dîs Aliter Visum; or, Le Byron
  de Nos Jours.
Bukowski.   Blackbirds Are Rough Today, The.
  Day I Kicked Away a Bankroll, The.
  Empire of Coins, An.
  I Am with the Roots of Flowers.
  I Wait in the White Rain.
  Man with the Hot Nose, The.
  Mercy, Wherever You Are, Come Running in to
    Me and Grab Me in Your Good Arms—.
  Minor Impulse to Complain, A.
  O, We Are the Outcasts.
  One Hundred and Ninety-Nine Pounds of Clay
    Leaning Forward.
  Practice.

Regard Me.
Carew, T.   In the Person of a Lady To Her
  Inconstant Servant.
  Lover, in the Disguise of an Amazon, Is Dearly
    Beloved of His Mistress, A.
  Song: To Her Again[e], She Burning in a
    Fe[a]ver.
  To Celia, upon Love's Ubiquity.
  To My Inconstant Mistress [*or* Mistris].
Cavalcanti.   My latest cruel misfortune.
Crane, S.   In the desert.
Davie, D.   Artifex in Extremis.
De la Mare.   They Told Me.
Dove, R.   Definition in the Face of Unnamed
  Fury.
Dunbar, P.   Then and Now.
Eberhart, R.   Hill Dream of Youth, Thirty Years
  Later.
Eliot, T. S.   Lines for an Old Man.
García Lorca.   Dialogue of Amargo.
  Gacela of the Bitter Root.
Graves, R.   Laureate, The.
"H. D."   Eros.
  Red Roses for Bronze.
Han-shan.   Aboard this boat of rotten wood.
Hardy, T.   He Abjures Love.
  Old Excursions.
  Torn Letter, The.
Herrick.   Another on Love.
  To M. Laurence Swetnaham.
Hughes, T.   Her Husband.
Keats.   All Gentle Folks Who Owe a Grudge.
Lawrence, D. H.   Grudge of the Old, The.
  Monologue of a Mother.
Lorde.   American Cancer Society Or There Is
  More Than One Way to Skin a Coon.
  And Don't Think I Won't Be Waiting.
  Cables To Rage Or I've Been Talking On This
    Street Corner.
  Conversations in Crisis.
  New York City 1970.
  Spring People.
  Who Said It Was Simple.
Lux.   Bitterness of Children, The.
MacNeice.   Il Piccolo Rifiuto.
Merton.   Whether There Is Enjoyment in
  Bitterness.
Millay, E.   Scrub.
Mistral, G.   Slow Rain, The.
Oliver, M.   Bitterness, A.
  Certain Sharpness in the Morning Air, A.
Parker, D.   Burned Child, The.
  Convalescent.
  Distance.
  False Friends, The.
  Godspeed.
  Iseult of Brittany.
  Landscape.
  Monody.
  Purposely Ungrammatical Love Song.
  Sonnet: "In seemly burial, love may not rest."
  Summary.
  Swan Song.
  Wail.
  Well-Worn Story, A.
  When We Were Very Sore; Lines on
    Discovering that You Have Been Advertised
    as America's A.A. Milne.
  Wisdom.
  With Best Wishes.
Patchen.   Letter to the Old Men.
Petrarch.   Happy season of my early prime, The.
Piercy.   Crippling, The.
  Letter to be Disguised as a Gas Bill.
Poe.   To ———: "I heed not that my earthly
  lot."
Prunty.   Actuarial Wife, The.
Raine, K.   Columbines.
Rilke.   Bitter Pleasure.
Ritsos.   Toward What?
Rossetti, C.   So I began my walk of life; no
  stop.
  Spring is come again not as at first.
Smith, S.   I'll Have Your Heart.
  In the Night.
  Lightly Bound.

Mother.
Night Thoughts.
Smile, The.
Williams, C. K.   Flat.
  Herakles.
  Kin.
  Philadelphia: 1978.
Yeats.   Her Vision in the Wood.

Black (color)

Coleridge, S.   Ne Plus Ultra.
Creeley.   Lady in Black.
García Lorca.   Song of the Rider (1860).
Graves, R.   Black.
Laughlin, J.   Box, The.
Levertov.   Wings, The.
Ritsos.   Marine.
Sandburg, C.   Sweeping Wendy: Study in
  Fugue.
Walcott.   Goats and Monkeys.

Black Power

Hughes, L.   Black Panther.
See also **African-American Power**

Blackberries

Heaney, S.   Blackberry-Picking.
Kinnell.   Blackberry Eating.
Komunyakaa.   Blackberries.
Oliver, M.   August.
Plath.   Blackberrying.

Blackbirds

Ammons.   Bay Bank.
  Script.
Blue Cloud.   Red-winged Blackbird.
Emerson, R.   Blackbird's song the blackbird's
  song, The.
Hardy, T.   I Watched a Blackbird.
Heaney, S.   St Kevin and the Blackbird.
Mahon.   Blackbird, The.
Raine, K.   Frost-rime edges blades of grass.
Stevens, W.   Thirteen Ways of Looking at a
  Blackbird.
Williams, C. K.   Greed.
Williams, W.   Birds, The.
  Red-Wing Blackbird, The.
Zagajewski.   Blackbird.

Blackouts

Cooper, J.   After the Blackout (1965).
Dickey, J.   Ice Skin, The.
Hughes, L.   Dimout in Harlem.

Blacks

Ai.   Hoover Trismegistus.
  Riot Act, April 29, 1992.
Cullen, C.   From the Dark Tower.
Hayden, R.   Beginnings.
Hughes, L.   Always the Same.
  Angola Question Mark.
  Argument ("White is right, / Yellow mellow").
  Ballad of Negro History, A.
  Black Clown, The.
  Black Gal.
  Black Man Speaks, The.
  Black Pierrot, A.
  Black Seed.
  Broadcast to the West Indies.
  Brothers.
  Carol of the Brown King.
  Color.
  Cubes.
  Dream Variation[s].
  Emperor Haile Selassie.
  Lament for Dark Peoples.
  Letter from Spain.
  Lullaby (For a Black Mother).
  Me and My Song.
  Me and the Mule.
  Negro.
  Negro Mother, The.
  Negro Speaks of Rivers, The.
  Nightmare Boogie.
  Poem: "Ah, / My black one."
  Prelude to Our Age.
  Question and Answer.
  Song: "Lovely, dark, and lonely one."
  Visitors to the Black Belt.
  We, Too.
  When Sue Wears Red.

Who but the Lord?
Komunyakaa. Let's Say.
Laughlin, J. Bit Different, A.
Lowell, R. For the Union Dead.
Mallarmé. Negress, A.
Walker, A. Remember?
Wheatley, P. On Being Brought from Africa to
   America.
Williams, F. Ode, An: "At length revolving
   fates th' expected year."
Williams, T. Dark Arm, Hanging over the Edge
   of Infinity.

See also **African Americans**

Blacksmiths
Burns, R. To John Taylor.
Dickinson, E. Dare you see a Soul *at the White
   Heat?*
Graves, R. Red Shower, The.
Hopkins, G. Felix Randal.
Lindsay, N. North Star Whispers to the
   Blacksmith's Son, The.
Longfellow, H. Village Blacksmith, The.
Milosz, C. Blacksmith Shop.
Rimbaud, A. Blacksmith, The.

Blake, William
Ginsberg, A. Psalm 4.
Lawrence, D. H. Dark Satanic Mills.
Levertov. Blake's Baptismal Font.
Levine, P. My Poets.
Nemerov. Frozen City, The.
Oliver, M. Spring Azures.
Roethke. Supper with Lindsay.
Rukeyser, M. Homage to Literature.
Tate, A. William Blake.

Blasphemy
Chaucer. Lenvoy de Chaucer a Scogan.
Herrick. Upon Brock.
Komunyakaa. Blasphemy.
MacNeice. Blasphemies, The.
Wilbur, R. Simplification, A.

Blessings
Amichai [*or* Amikhai]. Psalm: "Psalm on the
   day, A."
Berry, W. Woods.
Burns, R. At Roslin Inn.
   On John McMurdo.
   Phillis the Fair.
   To a Young Lady, *Miss Jessy L———,
   Dumfries; with Books which the Bard
   Presented Her.*
   To Miss C*********, a Very Young Lady.
   To Terraughty, on His Birth-Day.
Campion, T. Ad Graios.
Celan. Benedicta.
Clifton, L. Blessing the Boats.
   Wild Blessings.
De la Mare. Prayer, A.
Dickinson, E. One Blessing had I than the rest.
Dugan, A. Letter to Donald Fall.
Frost, R. Answer, An.
HaNagid. I'll Show You a Fawn.
Herrick. Crutches.
   Gods Blessing.
   Gods Bounty.
   Good-Night, or Blessing, The.
   Grace for a Child.
   Grace for Children, A.
   Loading and Unloading.
   None Truly Happy Here.
   Poores Portion, The.
   Riches and Poverty.
   To Biancha, to Blesse Him.
   To Dianeme.
   To Dianeme; a Ceremonie in Glocester.
   To God.
   Wassaile, The.
   Welcome What Comes.
Ignatow, D. Blessing.
Jackson, L. Benedictory.
Jarrell, R. Blind Sheep, The.
Jonson, B. Ben Jonson's Grace before King
   James.
Lorde. Relevant Is Different Points on the
   Circle.
MacNeice. Ode: "To-night is so coarse with

chocolate."
Merton. Secular Signs.
Merwin. Blessing, The.
   Hosts, The.
   Lemuel's Blessing.
Riley, J. Anselmo.
   Friend of a Wayward Hour.
   Lines for an Album.
   On Any Ordenary Man in a High State of
   Laughture and Delight.
Rossetti, C. Gold of that Land is Good, The.
   Hail, noble face of noble friend!
   Heavy heart, if ever heart was heavy, A.
   Love builds a nest on earth and waits for rest.
   Perfect Love Casteth Out Fear.
Rukeyser, M. Voices of Waking.
Rumi. Burnt Kabob.
   Unmarked Boxes.
Whittier. Barefoot Boy, The.
   Benedicite.
   Godspeed.
Yeats. Blessed, The.
   Players Ask for a Blessing on the Psalteries and
   on Themselves, The.
   Prayer on Going into My House.

Blindness
Baudelaire. Blind, The.
Berry, W. Music, A.
   To Know the Dark.
Blake, W. How to Know Love from Deceit.
Borges. Blind Man, A.
   Blind Man, The.
   June, 1968.
   Maker, The ("He had never dwelled on the
   pleasures of memory").
   On Acquiring an Encyclopedia.
   Poem of the Gifts.
   Saturday, A.
   Talismans.
   Unending Rose, The.
Browning, E. Hugh Stuart Boyd [His
   Blindness].
Browning, R. Blind man to the maiden said,
   The.
Campion, T. In Morachum.
Carew, T. To One Who, When I Praised My
   Mistress' Beauty, Said I Was Blind.
Cavalcanti. Why weren't my eyes blinded.
Collins, B. I Chop Some Parsley While
   Listening to Art Blakey's Version of "Three
   Blind Mice."
Cooper, J. Blind Girl.
   Door, The.
Crashaw. Samson to His Delilah.
De la Mare. Euphrasy.
Dickey, J. Reading *Genesis* to a Blind Child.
Dickinson, E. Before I got my eye put out.
   Who saw no Sunrise cannot say.
Eberhart, R. Going.
   Oedipus.
Ferlinghetti, L. Just as I used to say.
   That fellow on the boattrain who insisted.
Frost, R. Haec Fabula Docet.
Gallagher, T. Reading Aloud.
Graves, R. Those Blind from Birth.
Hardy, T. At a Country Fair.
   Blinded Bird, The.
Heaney, S. At the Wellhead.
Herrick. Being Once Blind, His Request to
   Biancha.
   Upon His Eye-Sight Failing Him.
   Upon Reape.
Hughes, L. Blind.
Jarrell, R. Blind Man's Song, The.
   Blind Sheep, The.
   Sphinx's Riddle to Oedipus, The.
Jeffers, R. I saw a regiment of soldiers shuffling
   and stumbling.
Kipling, R. Put forth to watch, unschooled,
   alone.
Komunyakaa. Sitting in a Rocking Chair, Going
   Blind.
Levertov. Consulting the Oracle.
   For the Blind.
   Solitude, A.
Lux. River Blindness (Onchocerciasis).

McGrath, T. Parable.
Milton. On His Deceased Wife.
   To Mr. Cyriack Skinner upon His Blindness.
Niedecker. Musical Toys.
Orr, G. Snail, The.
Paley, G. Fund Appeal.
Ramanujan. LOVE 6: Winter.
Riley, J. Blind.
   Blind Girl, The.
Ritsos. Mutual Concessions.
   Scrutiny.
   Stages of Ignorance.
Rolfe, E. Eyes of a Blind Man.
Rossetti, C. Blind from my birth, / Where
   flowers are springing.
   Sketch, A.
Stafford, W. One Time.
   Sayings of the Blind.
Sze. Black Lightning.
Warren, R. Milton: A Sonnet.
Weiss, T. Before the Night.
Williams, M. Some Lines Finished Just Before
   Dawn at the Bedside of a Dying Student It has
   Snowed All Night.

Blizzards
Blok. Caught by the Blizzard.
   O What is the Setting Sun's Radiance to Me.
Frost, R. Willful Homing.
Hacker, M. Third Snowfall.
Merton. Early Blizzard.
Oliver, M. Beyond the Snow Belt.
Schuyler, J. Blizzard.
Spender, S. Remembering Cincinnatti, 1953.
Warren, R. Function of Blizzard.
Weiss, T. Malady.
Williams, W. Blizzard.

See also **Storms**

Blood
Baudelaire. Fountain of Blood.
Carew, T. Celia Bleeding, to the Surgeon.
Carver, R. Blood.
Cavafy. Bandaged Shoulder, The.
Coleridge, S. Loss.
Cooper, J. Iron.
Dickey, J. Poisoned Man, The.
   Scratch, The.
Dickey, W. Performances.
Dickinson, E. Name—of it—is "Autumn," The.
Donne. Flea, The.
Duncan, R. My Mother Would Be a Falconress.
Emerson, R. Ancient drop of feudal blood, An.
Faiz. Bangla Desh: 1.
   Bangla Desh: 2.
Frost, R. Flood, The.
Gunn, T. Book of the Dead, The.
   Faustus Triumphant.
Heaney, S. Damson.
Herrick. Upon a Child That Died [*or* Dyed].
Hughes, T. Vampire.
Jarrell, R. Islands, The.
   That Noble Flower.
Jeffers, R. So Many Blood-Lakes.
Laughlin, J. Experience of Blood.
Lawrence, D. H. Cold Blood.
   Mosquito Knows, The.
   Red.
   Shedding of Blood.
Logan, J. Experiment That Failed, The.
Lorde. Need: A Chorale for Black Woman
   Voices.
   Separation.
Lux. Streak of Blood That Once Was a Tiny
   Red Spider, A.
MacDiarmid, H. One of the Principal Causes of
   War.
Merton. What to Think When It Rains Blood.
Montale. Stanzas: "I'm searching vainly for the
   point the blood."
Neruda. Danger, The.
O'Hara, F. Poem: "Eager note on my door said
   'Call me,' The."
Prunty. Blood.
Ramanujan. Fizzle.
Rich, A. Rain of Blood, The.
Ritsos. Blood.
   Bloodletting.

Rossetti, C.   Babylon the Great.
 Cannot Sweeten.
 I Have Fought a Good Fight.
 Whitsun Eve.
Rumi.   Center of the Fire, The.
Sandburg, C.   Crimson Changes People.
 Fight.
 Psalm of the Bloodbank.
 Smoke and Steel.
Simic.   Butcher Shop.
Stafford, W.   Ceremony.
Swenson, M.   Bleeding.
Tate, A.   Red Stains.
 Sonnets of the Blood.
Vallejo.   Our Daily Bread.
Walker, A.   Suicide.
Whitman, W.   Trickle Drops.
Williams, T.   Siege, The.
Wright, J.   Living by the Red River.
 To Harvey, Who Traced the Circulation.

Blue (color)
Bogan, L.   Variation on a Sentence.
Emerson, R.   Heavy blue chain, The.
Frost, R.   Fragmentary Blue.
Ignatow, D.   Blue.
Keats.   Blue! 'Tis the Life of Heaven, the
 Domain.
Lawrence, D. H.   Blueness.
Merrill, J.   Blue Eye, The.
Patchen.   Curly Blue Buppo, The.
Ritsos.   Month of Cleansing.
Sandburg, C.   Bluebird, What Do You Feed On?
 Cheap Blue.
 Morning Glory Blue.
 Understandings in Blue.
Schuyler, J.   Footnote.
Snyder, G.   Blue Sky, The.
Swenson, M.   Early Morning: Cape Cod.
Tate, J.   Blue Booby, The.
 Blue Spill.
Wright, C.   Cicada Blue.
Zaturenska.   Blue Flower, The.

Blue Jays
Ammons.   Winter Scene.
Ciardi, J.   One Jay at a Time.
 Socializing with a Creature.
Cummings, E. E.   Crazy jay blue) / demon
 laughshriek.
Dickinson, E.   Jay his Castanet has struck, The.
Riley, J.   Jaybird, The.

Bluebells
Brontë, E.   To the Bluebell.
Tomlinson, C.   Metamorphosis, The.

Blueberries
Clampitt.   Blueberrying in August.
Kumin, M.   Hermit Picks Berries, The.

Bluebirds
Dickinson, E.   After all Birds have been
 investigated and laid aside.
Eberhart, R.   Now Is the Air Made of Chiming
 Balls.
Frost, R.   Last Word of a Bluebird, The.
Riley, J.   First Bluebird, The.
Sandburg, C.   Bluebird, What Do You Feed On?
Thoreau.   Bluebirds, The.

Bluefish
Wilbur, R.   Trolling for Blues.

Blues (mood)
Angelou.   Good Woman Feeling Bad, A.
 My Life Has Turned to Blue.
Carruth, H.   Cowshed Blues, The.
Creeley.   Blues.
Dunbar, P.   Blue.
Hughes, L.   Blue Monday.
 Blues, The.
 Blues at Dawn.
 Bound No'th Blues.
 Evenin' Air Blues.
 Hard Daddy.
 Hey!
 Hey! Hey!
 Hey-Hey Blues.
 Homesick Blues.
 Love Again Blues.
 Minnie Sings Her Blues.

Misery.
 Miss Blues'es Child.
 Monroe's Blues.
 Po' Boy Blues.
 Red Clay Blues.
 Too Blue.
 Weary Blues, The.
Komunyakaa.   Changes; or, Reveries at a
 Window Overlooking a Country Road.
 No-Good Blues.
 Woman, I Got the Blues.
Rexroth, K.   Blue Sunday.
 Written to Music.
Riley, J.   Dos't o' Blues, A.
Schuyler, J.   Roxy.
Williams, T.   Kitchen Door Blues.
See also **Melancholy**

Blues (music)
Ai.   Passing Through.
Carruth, H.   Billie Holiday.
 Expatiation on the Combining of Weathers at
 Thirty-Seventh and Indiana, An.
Collins, B.   Blues, The.
Cullen, C.   Colored Blues Singer.
Cummings, E. E.   One slipslouch twi /
 tterstamp.
Dove, R.   Shakespeare Say.
Hayden, R.   Homage to the Empress of the
 Blues.
Hughes, L.   Blues Fantasy.
 Blues on a Box.
 Misery.
 Monroe's Blues.
 Weary Blues, The.
Komunyakaa.   Blue Tonality.
 Mississippi John Hurt.
 Villon/Leadbelly.
Rexroth, K.   Written to Music.
Schuyler, J.   Beautiful Funerals.
 Let's All Hear It for Mildred Bailey!
 Roxy.
Walcott.   Blues.
Williams, T.   Heavenly Grass.
 Sugar in the Cane.

Bly, Robert
Laughlin, J.   After Martial.

Board Games
Jacobsen, J.   Dream of Games, A.
Kumin, M.   Game of Monopoly in Chavannes.

Boarding Houses
Atwood.   Roominghouse, Winter.
Carver, R.   To Begin With.
Kipling, R.   Ballad of Fisher's Boardinghouse,
 The.
Larkin, P.   Mr Bleaney.
Orr, G.   Transients Welcome.
Riley, J.   Quiet Lodger, The.

Boars
Davie, D.   Wild Boar Clough.
Tomlinson, C.   At the Autumn Equinox.

Boasting
Ammons.   Emplacement.
Angelou.   Little Girl Speakings.
Cavafy.   Aimilianos Monai, Alexandrian, 628–
 655 A.D.
Ciardi, J.   Poetry.
Cummings, E. E.   Buncha hardboil guys frum
 duh A.C. fulla.
Dunbar, P.   Career, A.
HaNagid.   How I Helped the Wise.
Hardy, T.   Epitaph for George Moore.
Herrick.   Great Boast, Small Rost.
 Upon Mease.
 Upon One Who Said She Was Alwayes Young.
 Upon Pievish.
 Upon Spunge.
Merwin.   Old Boast, The.
Nash, O.   Oh, Stop Being Thankful All over the
 Place.
 People.
Sandburg, C.   Primer Lesson.

Boats and Boating
Ammons.   Raft.
Atwood.   Boat, A.
Berry, W.   Plan, The.

Bishop, E.   Arrival at Santos.
 Fish, The.
Browning, E.   Romance of the Ganges, A.
Carver, R.   Downstream.
 My Boat.
 Quiet Nights.
 Scale.
Clifton, L.   Blessing the Boats.
Coleridge, S.   Water Ballad.
Dickey, J.   Drifting.
 Facing Africa.
 Lifeguard, The.
Dunbar, P.   On the River.
 Passage, The.
Eberhart, R.   Angels, The.
 Ship Burning and a Comet All in One Day, A.
 Slow Boat Ride.
 Waiting To Lean to the Master's Command.
Frost, R.   Flower Boat, The.
Gallagher, T.   Boat Ride.
 Woman-Enough.
 Words Written Near a Candle.
Gurney, I.   Dream, The.
 March.
Hall, D.   Long River, The.
Hamill, S.   Kah Tai Purgatorio.
Han-shan.   Aboard this boat of rotten wood.
Heaney, S.   Seeing Things.
 Shore Woman.
Hopkins, G.   As it fell upon a day.
Hughes, L.   Fog.
Jeffers, R.   Boats in a Fog.
Kipling, R.   Lowestoft Boat, The.
Koch, K.   Poem: "Thing / To do / Is organize /
 The sea, The."
Komunyakaa.   Boat People.
 Reed Boat, A.
Kunitz, S.   Long Boat, The.
Lawrence, D. H.   In a Boat.
Levertov.   To Rilke.
 What Harbinger?
Lindsay, N.   Empty Boats, The.
 Path in the Sky, The.
Logan, J.   Pass, The.
Lux.   Boat in the Forest, A.
MacLeish.   Boatmen of Santorin, The.
Marvell.   Bermudas.
Meredith, G.   Song: "Over the ferry, and over
 the ferry."
 There is for me no sweeter holiday.
Merrill, J.   Blue Grotto, The.
 Parrot Fish, The.
Merwin.   After a Storm.
 Remembering a Boatman.
 Some of the Masts.
Montale.   Boats on the Marne.
 Moiré.
Niedecker.   He built four houses.
Oliver, M.   Bailing the Boat.
Olson, C.   Boat, The.
 Measure.
Oppen.   Mast / Inaudibly soars; bole-like,
 tapering, The.
 Product.
Plath.   Crossing the Water.
Rilke.   Sketch.
Rimbaud, A.   Drunken Boat.
Ritsos.   Black Boat, The.
 Exonerated.
 Probabilities.
Rossetti, C.   Charon.
 O glorious sea that in each climbing wave.
 Rainbow, The.
 River Thames (?).
Rumi.   In a boat down a fast-running creek.
Sandburg, C.   Docks.
 Lost.
 Picnic Boat.
Sarton, M.   Sun Boat.
Smith, S.   Magic Morning, The.
Stevens, W.   Sailing after Lunch.
Swenson, M.   Beauty of the Head, The.
 Beginning to Squall.
 Old No. 1.
Sze.   Kayaking at Night on Tomales Bay.
 Li Po.

Tate, J.   Reapers of the Water.
Tomlinson, C.   Venice.
Tu Fu.   Déjeuner sur l'herbe.
Very.   Barque Aurelia of Boston, The.
Whittier.   Voyage of the Jettie.
Wilbur, R.   Regatta, The.
Wilner, E.   Poem of Exile, A.
Zukofsky, L.   Ways, The.
See also **Ferry Boats; Freighters; Ships and Shipbuilding; Tugboats; Yachts**

Bobolinks
Dickinson, E.   Bobolink is gone, The.
No Bobolink—reverse His Singing.
Way to know the Bobolink, The.

Bobwhites
Merton.   O Sweet Irrational Worship.
Riley, J.   Old Bob White.
Song o' Cheer, A.

Bodies
Amichai [*or* Amikhai].   And I am always like this fleeing from hurt and pain.
Body Is the Cause of Love, The.
Bride Without a Dowry, A.
Here.
Human Bodies.
Hymn to a Masseuse.
Ammons.   Body Politic.
Plexus.
Song: "Merging into place against a slope of trees."
Touching Down.
Armantrout.   My Associates.
Plan, The.
Atwood.   Deaths of the Other Children, The.
Fortification, A.
We are hard on each other.
Baudelaire.   Posthumous Work.
Proud Ship, The.
Beckett, S.   D'abord / à plat sur du dur.
Berryman.   Freshman Blues.
Huddle of Need, A.
Bly, R.   Horse of Desire, The.
Origin of the Praise of God, The.
We Love This Body.
Bogan, L.   Cartography.
Bradstreet, A.   Of the Four Humors in Man's Constitution.
Brooks, G.   Still Do I Keep My Look, My Identity.
Broumas, O.   Body.
Masseuse, The.
Memory Piece / for Baby Jane.
Sweeping the Garden.
Carruth, H.   Assignment.
Cavafy.   Remember, Body.
Chuang Tzu.   Metamorphosis.
Ciardi, J.   Anatomy Lab.
Tenzone.
Clifton, L.   Poem to My Uterus.
Codrescu.   Body Blues.
Books.
Crossed Hands.
For Marg So She Could Fuck Again.
Tête-à-Tête.
War & Peace.
Coleridge, S.   Body Imaging Soul.
Life in Death.
Veil of Spirit, The.
Collins, B.   Night House, The.
Cooper, J.   Conversation by the Body's Light.
Creeley.   Alba.
American Love.
Box.
Circle.
Enough.
Eye, The.
Flesh.
For a Screaming Lady.
Let something else be / the question—.
Looking Out.
Now.
Places ("When I wake next").
Plan Is the Body, The.
Trees.
Wall, A.
Cummings, E. E.   But turning a corner ,i.

In making Marjorie god hurried.
Look / my fingers,which.
Perhaps it was Myself sits down in this chair. There were two chairs,in fact.
Sometimes i am alive because with.
You said Is / there anything which.
Davie, D.   Attar of Roses.
Dickey, W.   Narcissus Unbound.
Dickinson, E.   Body grows without, The.
I am afraid to own a Body.
Prison gets to be a friend, A.
These—saw Visions.
Donne.   Ecstasy, The.
Resurrection, Imperfect.
Dubie.   American Scene, An.
Dugan, A.   Actual Vision of Morning's Extrusion.
Branches of Water or Desire, The.
Let Heroes Account to Love.
One Waking in a Northern Fall.
Poem. "Pythagorean Silences, The."
Prayer for One Leg.
Duncan, R.   I Am a Most Fleshly Man.
Eberhart, R.   Ball Game.
Face, Ocean.
Giantess, The.
Nothing But Change.
Refrains.
Wedding, The.
Eliot, T. S.   Dedication to My Wife, A.
Éluard, P.   Out of Sight in the Direction of My Body.
Emerson, R.   Crowning hour when bodies vie with souls, The.
If thy body pine.
Poets are colorpots.
Fayzi [*or* Faydi *or* Feisi *or* Feizi].   Eternal Watcher, who doth wake, The.
Gallagher, T.   Each Bird Walking.
Ginsberg, A.   Broken Bone Blues.
Change, The: *Kyoto-Tokyo Express.*
On Neal's Ashes.
Sphincter.
Under the World There's a Lot of Ass, a Lot of Cunt.
Graves, R.   Cock in Pullet's Feathers.
Thieves, The.
Trudge, Body!
Gunn, T.   Man With Night Sweats, The.
Stealer, The.
"H. D."   Contest, The.
Hacker, M.   Mother II.
Presentation Piece.
Hamill, S.   Ten Thousand Sutras.
Heaney, S.   Bog Queen.
Herrick.   Body, The.
Great Spirits Supervive.
Life Is the Body's [*or* Bodies] Light.
Hughes, L.   Red Silk Stockings.
Hughes, T.   Fragment of an Ancient Tablet.
Speech Out of Shadow.
Ignatow, D.   At This Moment.
I Dream I Hurl a Spear.
Jacobsen, J.   Greek Wind, The.
Kizer, C.   Food of Love.
Komunyakaa.   Anodyne.
Slam, Dunk, & Hook.
Kumin, M.   Body and Soul: A Meditation.
Song for Seven Parts of the Body.
Larkin, P.   Mr Bleaney.
Laughlin, J.   Maze, The.
Real Bones.
Rhyme.
When you are far away.
Lawrence, D. H.   Bodiless God.
Body of God, The.
Demiurge.
Eloi, Eloi, Lama Sabachthani?
She Said as Well to Me.
Levertov.   Gone Away.
Our Bodies.
Logan, J.   Dialogue with La Mettrie, A.
Heart to Heart Talk with My Liver.
Lux.   Swimming Pool, The.
Marvell.   Dialogue between the Soul and [the] Body, A.

McGrath, T.   Behold the Woman.
Rediscovery.
McHugh, H.   Tendencies.
Woman Who Laughed on Calvary.
Meredith, W.   Where He's Staying Now.
Merwin.   Deluge, The.
Some Last Questions.
When the Horizon Is Gone.
Michelangelo Buonarroti.   Cecchino here has laid his body low.
From heaven my beauty, flawless and divine.
Man within a woman—no, I'd say, A.
My flesh turned earth, my bones turned naked shame.
Milosz, C.   Body.
Mistral, G.   Body, The.
Montale.   Stanzas: "I'm searching vainly for the point the blood."
Nash, O.   Don't Look Now.
Niedecker.   News.
O'Hara, F.   Poem: "When I am feeling depressed and anxious sullen."
Olson, C.   Cross-Legged, the Spider and the Web.
Elements of clothes, an arm and hand the head of a cock.
Gate Is Prouti, The.
It is a nation of nothing but poetry.
Lalage!
Moebius Strip, The.
My poor dumb body.
Woman's Nipples Is the Rose of the World, A.
Orr, G.   Getting Dressed.
Paley, G.   My Father Said.
When this old body.
Palmer, M.   τροπη.
Piercy.   Cats Like Angels.
Friend, The.
Prunty.   Recovery.
Ralegh, S.   Lie, The.
Ramanujan.   Elements of Composition.
Hindu to His Body, A.
Saturdays.
Towards Simplicity.
Rexroth, K.   Habeas Corpus.
Vitamins and Roughage.
Rich, A.   Splittings.
Rilke.   Resurrected Christ, The.
To Marie Laurencin.
Rimbaud, A.   Idol, The. Arsehole Sonnet.
Our buttocks aren't like theirs. Many times I've seen.
Ritsos.   Bodies.
Inevitables.
Roethke.   Epidermal Macabre.
Orders for the Day.
Rossetti, C.   Soul rudderless, unbraced.
Rukeyser, M.   Endless.
Handclap.
Rumi.   Body Intelligence.
On Resurrection Day.
Pickaxe, The.
Story Water.
Sandburg, C.   Cadenza.
Walking Man of Rodin, The.
Sexton.   August 17th.
Earth, The.
In Celebration of My Uterus.
Mother and Daughter.
Mr. Mine.
Simic.   Ax.
Body and Soul.
Smart, C.   Author Apologizes to a Lady, for His Being a Little Man, The.
Smith, S.   Man Is a Spirit.
This Englishwoman.
Snyder, G.   Alabaster.
Bath, The.
Egg, The.
Swenson, M.   Lying and Looking.
Manyone Flying.
Question.
Sketch for a Landscape.
Szymborska, W.   Rubens' Women.
Tortures.
Updike.   In Extremis.

Van Duyn. Gray's Apocrypha.

Warren, R. Auto-da-fé.

Whalen, P. Allegorical Painting: Capitalistic Society Destroyed by the Contradiction Within Itself. (Second Five-Year Plan).

Whitman, W. Come, Said My Soul.

I Sing the Body Electric.

Wilbur, R. Shallot, A.

Williams, C. K. Fat.

For Gail, When I Was Five.

I know / nothing anymore.

To Market.

Williams, M. I Go Out of the House for the First Time.

Sale.

Williams, W. United States, The.

Wilner, E. Muse, The.

Wright, C. Body Language.

Lost Bodies.

Wright, J. Dog in a Cornfield.

Girl in a Window, A.

Inscrutability.

Jewel, The.

Offense, The.

Twenty-Two Tremblings of the Postulant.

Yeats. Crazy Jane Talks with the Bishop.

Lady's Second Song, The.

Lady's Third Song, The.

Michael Robartes and the Dancer.

Oil and Blood.

Zukofsky, L. So That Even a Lover.

See also **Nudity and Nudists**

Bodybuilding

Szymborska, W. Bodybuilders' Contest.

Boer War

Hardy, T. At the War Office, London.

Christmas Ghost-Story, A.

Colonel's Soliloquy, The.

Departure.

Drummer Hodge.

Embarcation.

Going of the Battery, The.

Song of the Soldiers' Wives and Sweethearts.

Souls of the Slain, The.

Wife in London, A.

Kipling, R. Absent-Minded Beggar, The.

Bridge-Guard in the Karroo.

Chant-Pagan.

Columns.

Dirge of Dead Sisters.

General Joubert.

Islanders, The.

Lesson, The.

Lichtenberg.

M. I.

Old Issue, The.

Parting of the Columns, The.

Piet.

Return, The.

Rimmon.

Settler, The.

Stellenbosch.

Two Kopjes.

Meredith, G. At the Close.

Schuyler, J. Boer War Bread Strike.

Bogart, Humphrey

Kumin, M. Casablanca.

Bogs

Blok. Little Priest of the Fen, The.

Heaney, S. Bog Queen.

Bogland.

Kinship.

Tollund Man, The.

Smith, S. Our Bog is Dood.

Bohemian Life

Clampitt. Cadenza, A.

Hedge of Rubber Trees. A.

My Cousin Muriel.

Gurney, I. Bohemians, The.

Laughlin, J. Merry Madness Hall.

Parker, D. Bohemia.

Bohemians; A Hate Song.

Rexroth, K. Last Visit to the Swimming Pool Soviets.

Riley, J. In Bohemia.

Rimbaud, A. My Bohemia (Fantasy).

Boleyn, Anne

Lowell, R. Death of Anne Boleyn.

Wyatt, S. Whoso List to Hunt.

Bolsheviks

Davie, D. Another Old Bolshevik.

Lawrence, D. H. Bourgeois and Bolshevist.

Choice of Evils.

Cowardice and Impudence.

Half-Blind, The.

Hard-Boiled Conservatives.

Property and No-Property.

Property Question, The.

Shtoltsenberg. Bolsheviks.

Bombs and Bombing

Amichai [*or* Amikhai]. Diameter of the Bomb, The.

Radius of the bomb was twelve inches, The.

Bierce. After Portsmouth.

Ciardi, J. B is for BOMBERS, our national pride.

Death of a Bomber.

Fable of Survival, A.

Massive Retaliation.

Poem for My Twenty-ninth Birthday.

Clampitt. Perseus Airborne.

Clifton, L. Alabama 9/15/63.

Davie, D. Two from Ireland.

Dubie. Psalm 23.

Dugan, A. On Plumbing after an Air Raid.

Ginsberg, A. Hum Bom!

Hughes, L. Air Raid: Barcelona.

Ballad of Harry Moore.

Birmingham Sunday.

Bombings in Dixie.

Moonlight in Valencia: Civil War.

Hughes, T. Woman Unconscious, A.

Ignatow, D. All Quiet.

Birthday.

Taste, The.

Jarrell, R. Angels at Hamburg, The.

Siegfried.

Truth, The.

Jeffers, R. Great Explosion, The.

Laughlin, J. Logistics.

Levertov. Fragrance of Life, Odor of Death.

MacNeice. Swing-Song.

Merrill, J. 18 West 11th Street.

Merton. Bombarded City, The.

Sports without Blood—a Letter to Dylan Thomas (1948).

Milosz, C. City, The.

Montale. Frost on the windowpanes; the sick.

Muldoon, P. Trifle, A.

Niedecker. Bombings.

Rexroth, K. Venice.

Sexton. Firebombers, The.

Smith, S. No More People.

Spender, S. Epilogue to a Human Drama.

Rejoice in the Abyss.

Stafford, W. Ground Zero [December 1982].

Some Remarks When Richard Hugo Came.

Szymborska, W. Terrorist, He's Watching, The.

Warren, R. New Dawn.

Wilbur, R. Mined Country.

Wilner, E. Bat Cave.

See also **Air Warfare**

Bonds

Hughes, L. Bonds for All.

Bonds: In Memoriam.

Bones

Baudelaire. Dancing Death.

Bly, R. Counting Small-Boned Bodies.

Broumas, O. Oh Earth.

Ciardi, J. Elegy for a Cave Full of Bones.

Corbett, W. Collarbone.

De la Mare. Thus Her Tale.

Dickey, J. Rib, The.

Donne. Relic, The.

Dugan, A. On a Travel Story from Wormwood Valley.

Graves, R. Broken Neck.

Hall, D. Columns of the Parthenon, The.

Heaney, S. Bone Dreams.

Herrick. Proof to No Purpose.

Hughes, T. Relic.

Kumin, M. Seeing the Bones.

Turning the Garden in Middle Age.

Laughlin, J. Crucifixion in the Desert.

Real Bones.

Levi, P. Elephant, The.

MacLeish. Immortal Helix.

Merwin. For Saying That It Won't Matter.

Milton. On Shakespear[e].

Oliver, M. Bone Poem.

Olson, C. Marry the Marrow.

Orr, G. Fast, The.

Pagis. Exposure.

Pinsky. Want Bone, The.

Roethke. I Cry, Love! Love!

Sandburg, C. Dinosaur Bones, The.

Sexton. Loving the Killer.

Stock, R. Sigismundo Malatesta Brings His Favorite Philosopher's Bones to Italy.

Updike. Dream and Reality.

Modest Mound of Bones, A.

Williams, T. This Cryptic Bone.

See also **Skeletons**

Bonhoeffer, Dietrich

Dubie. Widow of the Beast of Ingolstadt, The.

Kunitz, S. Around Pastor Bonhoeffer.

Bonnard, Pierre

Carver, R. Bonnard's Nudes.

Ramanujan. LOVE 4: What He Said, to His Daughter.

Bonsai

Collins, B. Bonsai.

Piercy. Work of Artifice, A.

Boobies

Tate, J. Blue Booby, The.

Books

Armantrout. Book, The.

Bogan, L. Man Alone.

Borges. For a Version of *I Ching*.

Guardian of the Books, The.

Inferno 5, 129.

June, 1968.

On Acquiring an Encyclopedia.

Things ("Fallen volume, hidden by the others, The").

Bradstreet, A. Author to Her Book, The.

Browning, E. Hugh Stuart Boyd [Legacies].

Little Friend, The.

Burns, R. Book-Worms, The.

O leave novels, ye Mauchline belles.

To a Young Lady, *Miss Jessy L———, Dumfries; with Books which the Bard Presented Her.*

To Miss L———.

Byron, G. You Ask for a "Volume of Nonsense."

Campion, T. Ad Librum.

To the Reader.

Carew, T. Fancy, A.

Chuang Tzu. Duke Hwan and the Wheelwright.

Clampitt. Balms.

Codrescu. Books.

Indecent Assumption, the Slaughter Songs, The.

Star Book.

Collins, B. Books.

Marginalia.

Tomes.

Cowper, W. On Madan's Answer to Newton.

Crane, S. I met a seer.

Cummings, E. E. If everything happens that can't be done.

Cunningham, J. On Doctor Drink.

Dickinson, E. Book is only the Heart's Portrait, A.

He ate and drank the precious Words.

Hour for books, those enthralling friends, An.

It is still as distinct as Paradise.

It stills, incites, infatuates.

Precious—moldering pleasure—'tis, A.

There is no Frigate like a Book.

Unto my Books—so good to turn.

Donne. Valediction, A: of the Book.

Dove, R. One Volume Missing.

Dunbar, P. On a Clean Book.

Sonnet: "Emblem of blasted hope and lost desire."

Eberhart, R.　Request.
Ruby Daggett.
Emerson, R.　Ancient lady who dwelt in Rome,
　An.
Inspired we must forget our books.
What all the books of ages paint, I have.
Written in a Volume of Goethe.
Graves, R.　Colophon.
Gunn, T.　To a Dead Graduate Student.
Gurney, I.　First Poem.
Hall, D.　Illustration.
Three Movements, The.
Han-shan.　Four or five dumb upstarts.
HaNagid.　One Who Works and Buys Himself
　Books.
Herrick.　Argument of His Book, The.
Lines Have Their Linings, and Bookes Their
　Buckram.
On His Booke.
To God.
To His Book[e].
To His Booke.
To His Closet-Gods.
To Momus.
To My Ill Reader.
To Sir George Parrie, Doctor of the Civill Law.
To the High and Noble Prince, George, Duke,
　Marquesse, and Earle of Buckingham.
To the Lady Mary Villars, Governesse to the
　Princesse Henretta.
To the Most Illustrious and Most Hopeful[l]
　Prince, Charles, Prince of Wales.
To the Most Learned, Wise, and Arch-
　Antiquary, M. John Selden.
To the Right Honourable, Philip, Earle of
　Pembroke, and Montgomerie.
Ignatow, D.　1905.
Against the Evidence.
Jackson, L.　Readers, The.
Troubles of a Book, The.
Unread Pages.
Jarrell, R.　Author to the Reader, The.
Carnegie Library, Juvenile Division, The.
Children Selecting Books in a Library.
Reader, The.
Jonson, B.　Author ad Librum.
On the Honoured Poems of His Honoured
　Friend, Sir John Beaumont, Baronet.
To Mrs Alice Sutcliffe, on Her Divine
　Meditations.
To My Bookseller.
To the Reader ("This figure, that thou here seest
　put").
To the Same [Sir Henry Goodyere].
Vision of Ben Jonson, on the Muses of His
　Friend M. Drayton, The.
Keats.　Keen, Fitful Gusts Are Whispering Here
　and There.
Kinsella, T.　Drowsing over *The Arabian Nights*.
Larkin, P.　New Eyes Each Year.
Study of Reading Habits, A.
Laughlin, J.　Bavarian Gentian, The.
Box, The.
Inn at Kirchstetten, The.
Letter to Hitler, A.
Prognosis.
Lawrence, D. H.　My Naughty Book.
To Pino.
Logan, J.　Recollection on the Day of a First
　Book.
Lowell, R.　Father's Bedroom.
Lux.　Streak of Blood That Once Was a Tiny
　Red Spider, A.
McGrath, T.　Use of Books, The.
Meredith, G.　I looked from the book of the
　story of men.
"Poems," says the title.
Merton.　Poet, to His Book, The.
Merwin.　Envoy from d'Aubigné.
Milosz, C.　And Yet the Books.
Book in the Ruins, A.
Woe!
Milton.　On the Detraction Which Followed
　upon My Writing Certain Treatises.
To John Rouse.
Moore, M.　He Wrote the History Book.

Mörike [*or* Möricke].　Forest Murmurs.
Muldoon, P.　Making the Move.
Nash, O.　Lecturer in Bookstore.
Nemerov.　Du rêve, de la mathématique, et de la
　mort.
Paley, G.　Traveler.
Palmer, M.　Dear M ("Look this figure half-
　hidden is not a book").
Secret remains in the book, The.
τροπη.
Parker, D.　Books; A Hymn of Hate.
Pessoa.　Liberty.
Pound, E.　Rosa Sempiterna.
Prunty.　Books, The.
Raine, K.　I've read all the books but one.
Rich, A.　Burning of Paper instead of Children,
　The.
Riley, J.　Go Read Your Book!
Lines fer Isaac Bradwell, of Indanoplis, Ind.,
　County-Seat of Marion.
Sandburg, C.　Books Men Die For.
Medley.
This—For the Moon—Yes?
Schuyler, J.　This Notebook.
Sexton.　February 20th.
Sheridan, T.　Mr. Sheridan's Prologue to the
　Greek Play of Phaedra and Hippolytus.
Simic.　History Book.
Writings of the Mystics, The.
Smart, C.　Lines with a Pocket Book.
Stafford, W.　Afternoon in the Stacks, An.
Burning a Book.
Magic Mountain, The.
Stock, R.　Millais Loquacious.
Selected Poems of Mañuel Bandeira, The.
Wherein the Maker's Right Hand Moralizes the
　Way to a Familiar but Rare Felicity.
Stockton, A.　Sarcasm against the Ladies in a
　Newspaper, A; An Impromptu Answer.
Tomlinson, C.　Chief Standing Water.
Updike.　Ode, An: "I'm going to write a novel,
　hey."
Rack of Paperbacks, A.
Tome-Thoughts, from the *Times*.
Van Duyn.　Day in Late October, A.
Very.　Sepulchre of the Books, The.
Walcott.　Volcano.
Warren, R.　Literal Dream.
Weiss, T.　Caliban Remembers.
Fire at Alexandria, The.
Life of, The.
Whitman, W.　As the Time Draws Nigh.
By Broad Potomac's Shore.
In Cabin'd Ships at Sea.
L of G.
L. of G.'s Purport.
Shut Not Your Doors.
Whoever You Are Holding Me Now in Hand.
Wilde, O.　With a Copy of 'A House of
　Pomegranates'
Williams, C. K.　Critic, The.
My Book, My Book.
Williams, M.　Book, The.
Williams, W.　Coronal, A.
Wilner, E.　Ex Libris.
Wordsworth, W.　Distressful gift! this Book
　receives.
Expostulation and Reply.
On the Detraction Which Followed the
　Publication of a Certain Poem.
Prelude, Prefixed to the Volume Entitled "Poems
　Chiefly of Early and Late Years."
Tables Turned, The.
To the Rev. Christopher Wordsworth, D.D.,
　Master of Harrow School.
Written upon a Blank Leaf in "The Compleat
　Angler."
Yeats.　Realists, The.
Ribh at the Tomb of Baile and Aillinn.
When You Are Old.
Zagajewski.　Reading Books.

Bookstores
Simic.　Writings of the Mystics, The.
Wilner, E.　On the Road to Larry Robin's
　Bookstore.
Zagajewski.　Treatise on Emptiness.

Bookworms
Burns, R.　Book-Worms, The.
Stock, R.　Selected Poems of Mañuel Bandeira,
　The.
Boone, Daniel
Warren, R.　Was It One of the Long Hunters of
　Kentucky who Discovered Boone at Sunset?
Booth, Edwin
Melville, H.　Coming Storm, The.
Booth, William
Lindsay, N.　General William Booth Enters into
　Heaven.
Bootlegging and Bootleggers
Muldoon, P.　Kate Whiskey.
Boots
Dunbar, P.　Two Little Boots.
Hardy, T.　New Boots, The.
Thoreau.　My Boots.
Borden, Lizzie
Gallagher, T.　Instructions to the Double.
Boredom
Ashbery, J.　Darlene's Hospital.
Atwood.　Letter from Persephone.
Baudelaire.　Black Bile ("Worthless and wealthy,
　decrepit and young").
To the Reader.
Bierce.　King of Bores, The.
Brodsky, J.　MCMXCIV.
Bukowski.　Not Quite So Soon.
Training for Kid Aztec.
Ciardi, J.　Obit.
This Morning.
Clampitt.　Meridian.
Cummings, E. E.　Ballad of the Scholar's
　Lament.
Davie, D.　Though Dry, Not Dry.
Dugan, A.　On Cabin Fever, On Boredom in the
　Countryside.
HaNagid.　Pain, The.
Lawrence, D. H.　Boredom, Ennui, Depression.
Last Lesson of the Afternoon.
To a Certain Friend.
Mallarmé.　Renewal.
Nash, O.　Our Child Doesn't Know Anything.
Spring Comes to Murray Hill.
Strange Case of Mr. Donnybrooks's Boredom,
　The.
Orr, G.　Vase, The.
Parker, D.　Song for an April Dusk.
Sandburg, C.　Humdrum.
Williams, C. K.　End of Drought.
Bores
Nash, O.　So Does Everybody Else, Only Not
　So Much.
There Were Giants in Those Days or Maybe
　There Weren't.
Will You Have Your Tedium Rare or Medium?
Parker, D.　Bores; A Hymn of Hate.
Borges, Jorge Luis
Borges.　Borges and I.
Dream of Pedro Henríquez Ureña, The.
Elegy: "Oh destiny of Borges."
That Man.
Borgia, Lucretia
Carver, R.　For the Record.
Smith, S.　Yes, I Know.
Borneo
Swenson, M.　Naked in Borneo.
Boston, Massachusetts
Brodsky, J.　Elegy: For Robert Lowell.
Ciardi, J.　Bedlam Revisited.
Benefits of an Education, The.
Feasts.
Knothole in Spent Time, A.
Shaft, The.
Corbett, W.　February 29th.
Poor. Old. China. Man.
Cummings, E. E.　My humorous ghost precisely
　will.
When i am in boston,i do not speak.
Emerson, E.　Last Farewell, The.
Emerson, R.　Boston.
O Boston city lecture-hearing.
Trimountain.

Hall, D. Woolworth's.
Lowell, R. At the Indian Killer's Grave.
Death from Cancer.
For the Union Dead.
Mary Winslow.
Public Garden, The.
Where the Rainbow Ends.
MacLeish. Night Watch in the City of Boston.
McGrath, T. Driving toward Boston I Run
across One of Robert Bly's Old Poems.
Moore, M. In the Public Garden.
Plath. Winter's Tale, A.
Robinson, E. Boston.
Sexton. Just Once.
Updike. Back Bay.
Sunday in Boston.
Whitman, W. Boston Ballad [1854], A.
Whittier. Calef in Boston.
In the "Old South."
King's Missive, The.
Landmarks, The.
Moloch in State Street.
To Faneuil Hall.

Boston Tea Party
Emerson, R. Boston.

Bosworth Field, Battle of (1485)
Lowell, R. Bosworth Field.

Botany and Botanists
Ammons. Photosynthesis.
Clampitt. Botanical Nomenclature.
Milosz, C. Linnaeus.
Niedecker. Bonpland.
Wintergreen Ridge.
Stevens, W. Botanist on Alp (No. 1).

Botany Bay, Australia
Komunyakaa. Wokanmagulli.

Botticelli, Sandro
Logan, J. Prologue and Questions for St.
Augustine On His Sixteenth Centenary.
Orr, G. After Botticelli's *Birth of Venus*.
Rossetti, D. For Spring, by Sandro Botticelli, in
the Accademia of Florence.

Bottles
Han-shan. One bottle is cast in gold.
Lawrence, D. H. Ships in Bottles.
Swenson, M. Blue Bottle, The.

Boundaries
Borges. Limit, The.
Limits.
Creeley. Arroyo.
Edge, The ("Long over whatever edge").
Davie, D. To Thom Gunn in Los Altos,
California.
Howe, S. Secret History of the Dividing Line.
Szymborska, W. Psalm: "How leaky are the
borders of man-made states!"

Bourgeoisie
Angelou. Sepia Fashion Show.
Auden. Unknown Citizen, The.
Brooks, G. Man of the Middle Class, A.
Bukowski. Day I Kicked Away a Bankroll, The.
Carruth, H. World as Will and Representation,
The.
Cummings, E. E. Cambridge ladies who live in
furnished souls, The.
I say no world.
Dickey, W. Being Asked To Define Bourgeois
Individuality.
Enzensberger, H. At Thirty-Three.
Middle Class Blues.
Short History of the Bourgeoisie.
Hardy, T. Lady in the Furs, The.
Larkin, P. Toads.
Lawrence, D. H. Bourgeois and Bolshevist.
Choice of Evils.
Climbing Up.
Cowardice and Impudence.
Half-Blind, The.
How Beastly the Bourgeois Is.
Ignoble Procession, The.
Middle Classes, The.
Prestige.
Property and No-Property.
Property Question, The.
Red-Herring.

Worm Either Way.
Levertov. Tenebrae.
Nash, O. What the Well-Read Patient Is Talking
About, or, Look, Ma, What I Got!
Nemerov. Life Cycle of Common Man.
Rimbaud, A. To Music.
Williams, M. Romance.
See also **Proletariat**

Bowery, The, New York City
Dugan, A. Memories of the Bowery.

Bowlers
See **Bowling and Bowlers**

Bowling and Bowlers
Jacobsen, J. Lawn Bowlers, The.
Moore, M. Bowls.

Bowls
Jacobsen, J. Fish Tank Room, The.
Rumi. Bowl, A.

Boxing and Boxers
Bukowski. Art, An.
Empire of Coins, An.
Loser, The.
Dugan, A. On Hurricane Jackson.
Hayden, R. Free Fantasia: Tiger Flowers.
Hughes, L. Joe Louis ("Joe Louis is a man").
Prize Fighter.
Komunyakaa. Boxing Day.
Punchdrunk.
McHugh, H. Glimpse of Main Event.
Patchen. Now I Went Down to the Ringside and
Little Henry Armstrong Was There.
Sandburg, C. Boxes and Bags.
Tate, J. Shadowboxing.
Williams, C. K. Vehicle: Violence.

Boy Scouts
Kipling, R. Boy Scouts' Patrol Song, A.

Boys
Bishop, E. Casabianca.
Burns, R. My Bonie Laddie's Young but He's
Growin Yet.
Carew, T. Dart, The.
Carver, R. Happiness.
Ciardi, J. Boy.
Clifton, L. Peeping Tom.
Dickey, J. Little More, The.
Dubie. Train, The.
Dunbar, P. Boy's Summer Song, A.
Eberhart, R. Horse Chestnut Tree, The.
Gunn, T. Allegory of the Wolf Boy, The.
Blackie, The Electric Rembrandt.
Hall, D. Young Watch Us, The.
Hardy, T. Boy's Dream, The.
Boys Then and Now.
Kinnell. First Song.
Kipling, R. If—.
Komunyakaa. Boys in Dresses.
Life & Times of Billy Boy, The.
Kumin, M. Fräulein Reads Instructive Rhymes.
Photograph, Maryland Agricultural College
Livestock Show, 1924.
Laughlin, J. Digging Down to China.
Lawrence, D. H. Discipline.
Little-Boy Brilliant.
Logan, J. Acapulco Canyon: Two
Kodachromes.
Brothers: Two Saltimbanques, The.
Only the Dreamer Can Change the Dream.
Paperboys, The.
Sebastian in the Dream.
Longfellow, H. My Lost Youth.
Lorde. Bees, The.
Lux. Fourth Grade, The.
Milosz, C. Boy, A.
Olson, C. Anniversary.
Spring Song for Cagli, A.
Pagis. He'll Come Out for Sure.
Limits of Physics, The.
Patchen. Street Corner College.
Prunty. Wild Horses, The.
Riley, J. Barefoot Boy, A.
Extremes.
Iry and Billy and Jo.
My Boy.
No Boy Knows.
Ritsos. Hues of a Cloud.

Yard, The.
Schuyler, J. Head, A.
Thoreau. I am the little Irish boy.
Very. Boy's Dream, The: A Ballad.
Warren, R. Boy Wandering in Simms' Valley.
Somewhere.
When Life Begins.
Whitman, W. We Two Boys Together Clinging.
Williams, M. Sissy, The.
Williams, T. Winter Smoke Is Blue and Bitter.
Williams, W. Hard Times.
Horned Purple.
Wilner, E. Facing into It.
Wordsworth, W. Rural Architecture.
Zaturenska. Child in the Crystal.
See also **Childhood and Children; Youth**

Bradstreet, Anne
Norton, J. Funeral Elegy Upon that Pattern and
Patron of Virtue, A.
Rogers, J. Upon Mrs. Anne Bradstreet, Her
Poems, Etc.
Unknown. Anagram, An.
Another.
Another to Mrs. Anne Bradstreet, Author of this
Poem.
I cannot wonder at Apollo now.
In Praise of the Author, Mistress Anne
Bradstreet, Virtue's True and Lively Pattern.
To My Dear Sister, the Author of these Poems.
Upon the Author.
Woodbridge. Upon the Author. By a Known
Friend.

Brahma
Emerson, R. Brahma.
Proteus.

Brahms, Johannes
Borges. To Johannes Brahms.
Logan, J. Concert Scene.
Stevens, W. Anglais Mort à Florence.

Brains
Auden. Ode to the Diencephalon.
Campion, T. In Nervam.
Clampitt. Anatomy of Migraine, An.
Codrescu. Dream (1).
Dickinson, E. Brain—is wider than the Sky,
The.
Brain, within its Groove, The.
Where the Treasure is.
Enzensberger, H. Limbic System.
Gunn, T. Listening to Jefferson Airplane.
Komunyakaa. Brain to the Heart, The.
Raw Data for an Unfinished Questionnaire.
Kunitz, S. Organic Bloom.
Lux. Walt Whitman's Brain Dropped on
Laboratory Floor.
Nemerov. Cybernetics.
Pagis. Brain.
Sandburg, C. Brainwashing.
Simic. Harsh Climate.
Williams, M. It's Hard to Think the Brain.
Williams, W. Play.
Wilner, E. Laurels.

Brancusi, Constantin
Shapiro, K. White Negress, The.

Brandy
MacNeice. Brandy Glass, The.

Braque, Georges
Tomlinson, C. Miracle of the Bottle and the
Fishes, The.

Brazil
Bierce. False Prophecy, A.
Brodsky, J. Rio Samba.
Carver, R. Bahia, Brazil.
Davie, D. Helena Morley.
Mistral, G. Fruit.
Prunty. Rio.
Stock, R. Poet Mário Faustino Descends Into
Hades and Rises to the Empyrean.
Voyager Takes Pause, A.
Unknown. Four Sambas.
Updike. Brazil.
Rio de Janeiro.
São Paulo.
Whittier. Freedom in Brazil.

Bread
Atwood. All Bread.
Brooks, G. My Dreams, My Works Must Wait Till after Hell.
Burns, R. Bannocks o' Bear-Meal.
Crashaw. On the Miracle of Multiplied [or Multiplyed] Loaves.
Dickinson, E. Indian Summer.
Dunbar, P. Dinah Kneading Dough.
Hall, D. Valley of Morning.
Herrick. Larr's Portion, and the Poets Part.
Upon Pennie.
Ignatow, D. Bread Itself, The.
Levertov. Acolyte, The.
McGrath, T. Bread of this World; Praises III, The.
Merwin. Bread.
Chaff, The.
Mistral, G. Bread.
Riley, J. My White Bread.
Short'nin' Bread Song—Pieced Out, A.
Rimbaud, A. Wide-eyed.
Rumi. Basket of Fresh Bread, A.
Schuyler, J. Boer War Bread Strike.
Simic. Austerities.
Swenson, M. Loaf of Time, A.
Thomas, D. This Bread I Break.

Breakfast
Eberhart, R. Angels, The.
Graves, R. Breakfast Table.
Kinnell. Oatmeal.
Laughlin, J. Here I Am.
Lawrence, D. H. Roses on the Breakfast Table.
MacLeish. Hotel Breakfast.
Nash, O. Eight O'Clock Peril, The.
Rich, A. Breakfast in a Bowling Alley in Utica, New York.
Rossetti, C. Bread and Milk for Breakfast.
Sandburg, C. Two Strangers Breakfast.
Vallejo. Our Daily Bread.
Williams, W. Promenade.

Breasts
Carew, T. On a Damask[e] Rose, Sticking upon a Lady's Breast.
Upon a Mole in Celia's Bosom.
Clifton, L. 1994.
Lumpectomy Eve.
Cummings, E. E. Life boosts herself rapidly at me.
Wing Wong,uninterred at twice.
Gallagher, T. Breasts.
Herrick. Fresh Cheese and Cream.
How Roses Came Red.
To Roses in Julia's Bosome.
Upon Julia's Breasts.
Upon the Nipples of Julia's Breast.
Komunyakaa. Breasts.
Wet Nurse.
Lawrence, D. H. Song of a Man Who Is Loved.
McGrath, T. Rediscovery.
Oppen. Zulu Girl, The.
Orr, G. Girl with Eighteen Nightgowns, The.
Rilke. Breasts.
Sexton. Breast, The.
Dreaming the Breasts.
Mr. Mine.
Simic. Breasts.
Smart, C. To Ethelinda.
Smith, S. Dream of Nourishment, A.
This Englishwoman.
Williams, W. Still Life.
Wright, J. Poem about Breasts, A.

Breath
Amichai [or Amikhai]. Support for My Breathing.
Berry, W. Cold Pane, The.
Byron, G. Song: "Breeze of the night in gentler sighs."
Creeley. "Do You Think."
Le Fou.
Dickey, J. Basics.
Breath.
Dickinson, E. I breathed enough to take the Trick.
Duncan, R. For a Muse Meant.

Ginsberg, A. Mind Breaths.
Herrick. On Julia's Breath.
To Julia.
Upon a Free Maid, with a Foule Breath.
Upon a Sowre-Breath Lady.
Upon Jone and Jane.
Upon Linnit.
Upon Lungs.
Ignatow, D. Business.
Jacobsen, J. Wind in the Sunporch, The.
Komunyakaa. One-Breath Song.
Laughlin, J. Atman of Sleep, The.
I Want to Breathe.
Levertov. In Whom We Live and Move and Have Our Being.
Levine, P. Breath.
McHugh, H. Excerpt from an Argument with Enthusiasts, Concerning Inspiration.
Ritsos. For Greater Accuracy.
Rumi. Don't let your throat tighten.
Only Breath.
Sheridan, T. Upon William Tisdall, D. D.
Stafford, W. Moment Again.
People of the South Wind.
Tate, J. Breathing.
Zagajewski. Where the Breath Is.

Brecht, Bertolt
Celan. Leaf, treeless, A.

Bricks and Bricklayers
Ginsberg, A. Bricklayer's Lunch Hour, The.
Heaney, S. Damson.
Koch, K. Bricks, The.
Major, C. Bricks and Sleep.
Merwin. Dry Stone Mason, The.
Sandburg, C. Bricklayer Love.

Brides
Amichai [or Amikhai]. Bride Without a Dowry, A.
Broumas, O. Betrothal / the Bride's Lament.
Browning, E. Lay of the Brown Rosary, The.
Rhyme of the Duchess May.
Byron, G. Sonnet on the Nuptials of the Marquis Antonio Cavalli with the Countess Clelia Rasponi of Ravenna.
Carew, T. Hymeneal Song, on the Nuptials of the Lady Ann Wentworth and the Lord Lovelace, An.
Married Woman, A.
To Mistress Katherine Neville, on Her Green Sickness.
Coleridge, S. To Mary Pridham.
De la Mare. Episodes.
Donne. Epithalamion at the Marriage of the Earl of Somerset.
Eberhart, R. Wedding, The.
"H. D." Hymen.
Hall, D. Alligator Bride, The.
Herrick. Delaying Bride, The.
Tithe [or Tythe]: To the Bride, The.
Jacobsen, J. Instances of Communication.
Meleager. Upon a Maid That Died [or Dyed] the Day She Was Married [or Marryed].
Meredith, G. Margaret's Bridal-Eve.
Olson, C. Bride, The.
Poe. Bridal Ballad.
To ———: "I saw thee on thy bridal day."
Riley, J. Bride, A.
My Bride That Is to Be.
Rossetti, C. Advent Sunday.
Boy Johnny.
Bride Song, A.
Ring upon her finger, / Walks the bride, A.
Who sits with the King in His Throne? Not a slave but a Bride.
Simic. Rough Outline.
Smith, S. I Remember.
Spenser, E. Epithalamion: "Ye learned sisters which have oftentimes."
Stockton, A. Bridal Wish Adressed to Mr S. Stockton and His Lady the Morning after Their Maraige, The.
Whitman, W. Kiss to the Bride, A.
Whittier. Home-Coming of the Bride, The.

See also **Weddings**

Bridges
Armantrout. Getting Warm.
Burns, R. Brigs of Ayr, a Poem. Inscribed to J. B*********, Esq; Ayr, The.
Ciardi, J. George Washington Brige.
Collins, B. Iron Bridge, The.
Crane, H. Bridge of Estador, The.
De la Mare. Bridge, The.
Dickey, J. At Darien Bridge.
Meadow Bridge.
Dickinson, E. How brittle are the Piers.
Dugan, A. Advertising in Paris.
Hardy, T. On Sturminster Foot-Bridge.
Hughes, L. Trip: San Francisco.
Hughes, T. Long Tunnel Ceiling, The.
Kipling, R. Akbar's Bridge.
Levi, P. Bridge, A.
Levine, P. 7 Years from Somewhere.
Logan, J. Bridge of Change, The.
Pass, The.
Merwin. Bridges, The.
Inscription for a Burned Bridge.
Trestle, The.
Nash, O. Poor Mr. Strawbridge.
Neruda. To Puente Curvo on the Maldonado Spit in Uruguay.
Paley, G. Bridges.
Piercy. Bridging.
Rimbaud, A. Bridges, The.
Ritsos. Bridge, The; An Uncalled-for Apology.
Rossetti, C. Rainbow, The.
Rukeyser, M. Network that emerges. At the ocean, A.
Red bridge fastening this city to the forest, A.
Sandburg, C. Clark Street Bridge.
Stock, R. Night Crawlers.
Tomlinson, C. Aqueduct.
Bridges.
Over Elizabeth Bridge: a Circumvention.
Ponte Veneziano.
Warren, R. Covered Bridge.
Wilbur, R. Glance from the Bridge, A.
Simile for Her Smile, A.
Williams, M. In Another Town.
Williams, W. Spirit of '76.
Wilner, E. Bridge Passage: Variations on Two Scales.
Wordsworth, W. Composed upon Westminster Bridge, September 3, 1802.

Bridges, Robert
Hopkins, G. To R. B.

Briefcases
Ignatow, D. Brief Cases.

Brighton, England
Mahon. Brighton Beach.

Bristol, England
Graves, R. Invitation to Bristol.

British Columbia, Canada
Tomlinson, C. Far Point.

British Empire
Davie, D. Demi-Exile. Howth.
English Revenant, An.
Shropshire.
Emerson, R. Song: "Shout for those whose course is done."
Graves, R. Single Fare.
Hardy, T. Coronation, The.
Hughes, L. Azikiwe in Jail.
English, The.
Explain It, Please.
Gandhi Is Fasting.
Kipling, R. Arithmetic on the Frontier.
Army Headquarters.
Ballad of Boh Da Thone, The.
Ballad of East and West, The.
"Birds of Prey" March.
Boots.
Burial, The.
Cholera Camp.
Christmas in India.
Dedication from "Barrack-Room Ballads."
Delilah.
England's Answer.
Flowers, The.
Ford o' Kabul River.

Grave of the Hundred Dead, The.
Gunga Din.
Houses, The.
Irish Guards, The.
Jobson's Amen.
Kitchener's School.
Legend of the Foreign Office, A.
Lesson, The.
Lichtenberg.
Lost Legion, The.
Man Who Could Write, The.
Mandalay.
Masque of Plenty, The.
Moon of Other Days, The.
Native-Born, The.
New Knighthood, The.
One Viceroy Resigns.
Oonts.
Our Lady of the Snows.
Overland Mail, The.
Pagett, M. P.
Pharaoh and the Sergeant.
Plea of the Simla Dancers, The.
Post That Fitted, The.
Pro-Consuls, The.
Public Waste.
Recessional.
Rhodes Memorial, Table Mountain.
Route Marchin'.
Screw-Guns.
Settler, The.
Song for the Women, The.
Song of the Banjo, The.
Song of the Cities, The.
Song of the Sons, The.
Study of an Elevation, in Indian Ink.
Tale of Two Cities, A.
Things and the Man.
To the City of Bombay.
To Thomas Atkins.
What the People Said.
Widow at Windsor, The.
Widow's Party, The.
Young Queen, The.
Logue, C.   Song of the Dead Soldier, The.
   Song of the Imperial Carrion, The.
Muldoon, P.   Meeting the British.
Smart, C.   Ode to Admiral Sir George Pocock.
   Ode to General Draper.
   Story of a Cock and a Bull, A.
Wilde, O.   Ave Imperatrix.

British Museum, London
Eliot, T. S.   Afternoon.
Hardy, T.   In the British Museum.
MacNeice.   British Museum Reading Room,
   The.
Rossetti, D.   Burden of Nineveh, The.
Wordsworth, W.   Ode on the Installation of His
   Royal Highness Prince Albert.

Brittany, France
Browning, R.   Hervé Riel.
Logan, J.   Yellow Christ, The; after Gaugin.

Broadway, New York City
Rich, A.   Upper Broadway.
Robinson, E.   White Lights, The.
Sandburg, C.   Broadway.
   Electric Sign Goes Dark, An.
Whitman, W.   Broadway.
   Broadway Pageant, A.

Brodsky, Joseph
Muldoon, P.   Hug, The.
Walcott.   Forest of Europe.
Zagajewski.   Morning in Vicenza, A.

Brontë, Charlotte
Dickinson, E.   All overgrown by cunning moss.

Brontë, Emily
Hughes, T.   Emily Brontë.

Bronx, The, New York City
Ignatow, D.   East Bronx.
Levine, P.   Walk with Tom Jefferson, A.
Updike.   Tao in the Yankee Stadium Bleachers.

Brooklyn Bridge
Crane, H.   Bridge, The.
Dugan, A.   Boast.
Meredith, W.   View of the Brooklyn Bridge, A.

Moore, M.   Granite and Steel.
Tomlinson, C.   Over Brooklyn Bridge.

Brooklyn, New York City
Clampitt.   Burial in Cypress Hills.
Codrescu.   I Visit Brooklyn with a Queen in
   Mind.
Collins, B.   Brooklyn Museum of Art, The.
Crane, H.   With a Photograph to Zell, Now
   Bound for Spain.
Davie, D.   For Doreen. A Voice from the
   Garden.
Dugan, A.   Elegy for a Magician.
Gallagher, T.   Conversation with a Fireman from
   Brooklyn.
Oppen.   Men of Sheepshead, The.
   Red Hook: December.
   Visit (2).
Pagis.   Bridgehead Photograph.
Tomlinson, C.   Crossing Brooklyn Ferry.
   In a Brooklyn Park.
   Over Brooklyn Bridge.
Whitman, W.   Centenarian's Story, The.
   Crossing Brooklyn Ferry.

Brooks and Streams
Ammons.   Brooks & Other Notions.
   If Anything Will Level with You Water Will.
   Peracute Lucidity.
   Runoff.
Burns, R.   Birks of Aberfeldy, The [Composed
   on the Spot].
   Down the Burn Davie.
   Humble Petition of Bruar Water to the Noble
   Duke of Athole, The.
Carruth, H.   Of Brook and Stone.
Carver, R.   With a Telescope Rod on Cowiche
   Creek.
Clough.   Sweet streamlet bason! at thy side.
Coleridge, S.   Lines to a Beautiful Spring in a
   Village.
   Water Ballad.
   Wish, A.
Crane, S.   Lad and a maid at a curve in the
   stream, A.
De la Mare.   Who?
Dickinson, E.   Have you got a Brook in your
   little heart.
Dunbar, P.   Wadin' in de Crick.
Emerson, R.   Old Age.
Frost, R.   Brook in the City, A.
   Going for Water.
   Hyla Brook.
   West-Running Brook.
García Lorca.   Ballad of the Little Square.
Gurney, I.   On Foscombe Hill.
Hall, D.   Cold Water.
Hopkins, G.   Inversnaid.
   Winter with the Gulf Stream.
Kinsella, T.   Downstream ("We gave our craft to
   the slow-moving stream").
Levertov.   Resolve, The.
Merrill, J.   Banks of a Stream Where Creatures
   Bathe.
Merwin.   Crossing Place.
Milosz, C.   By a Stream.
Montale.   Delta.
Olson, C.   Afica.
   Day Song.
Riley, J.   At Broad Ripple.
   Brook-Song, The.
   Green Fields and Running Brooks.
   On the Banks o' Deer Crick.
   Up and Down Old Brandywine.
Roethke.   Lady and the Bear, The.
Smith, S.   Brickenden, Hertfordshire.
   Occasional Yarrow, The.
Snyder, G.   Water.
Swenson, M.   Little Rapids, The.
Tennyson, A.   Farewell, A: "Flow down, cold
   rivulet, to the sea."
Thoreau.   I love a careless streamlet.
   Salmon Brook.
   When in some cove I lie.
Tomlinson, C.   Black Brook.
   Confluence.
Warren, R.   Dream of a Dream.
   Garden Waters.

Wilbur, R.   Hamlen Brook.
Wordsworth, W.   Brook! whose society the Poet
   seeks.
   Fragment from Dove Cottage Manuscript 44 (I).
   It was an April morning: fresh and clear.
   On the Banks of a Rocky Stream.
   There is a little unpretending Rill.
See also **Rivers**

Brooms
Lawrence, D. H.   New Brooms.
Levine, P.   Saturday Sweeping.
Rimbaud, A.   Broom, The.
Simic.   Brooms.
Wordsworth, W.   Oak and the Broom, The; A
   Pastoral.

Brotherhood
Berry, W.   Gathering, The.
   Horses.
Burns, R.   On Fergusson.
   Sons of Old Killie, The.
Emerson, R.   Rex.
Frost, R.   Tuft of Flowers, The.
Hardy, T.   Wind Blew Words, The.
Hopkins, G.   Epithalamion: "Hark, hearer, hear
   what I do; lend a thought now, make believe."
Hughes, L.   America.
   Brotherly Love.
   Brothers.
   I Dream a World.
   Open Letter to the South.
   Projection.
   To Captain Mulzac.
Kipling, R.   Ballad of East and West, The.
   Mother-Lodge, The.
   Pilgrim's Way, A.
   Two Races.
Levertov.   Catpig, The.
   Dogbrothers.
MacLeish.   Speech to Those Who Say Comrade.
Meredith, G.   Creed.
Moore, M.   In Distrust of Merits.
Niedecker.   Happy New Year.
Ransom, J.   Armageddon.
Sandburg, C.   Long Shadow of Lincoln: A
   Litany, The.
Thoreau.   Friendship ("I think awhile of Love,
   and while I think").
   In the busy streets, domains of trade.
Whitman, W.   Full of Life Now.
   I Dream'd in a Dream.
   I Hear It Was Charged against Me.
   One Thought Ever at the Fore.
   Salut au Monde!
   Starting from Paumanok.
   To Him That Was Crucified.
   To the East and to the West.
Williams, W.   Convivio.
Wordsworth, W.   Feel for the Wrongs of
   Universal Ken.

Brothers
Ai.   Blue Suede Shoes.
   One Man Down.
Angelou.   Kin.
Bembo, P.   You, too, my brother in your hour of
   Spring.
Berryman.   Letter to His Brother.
   Travelling South.
Bly, R.   Dream of a Brother, A.
Browning, E.   Court Lady, A.
Campion, T.   To the Most High and Mighty
   Prince Charles.
Carver, R.   Cranes, The.
Clampitt.   Chichester.
   Curfew, A.
   Urn-Burial and the Butterfly Migration.
Clifton, L.   August.
   Heaven.
Cooper, J.   Figure on the Far Side, The.
Corbett, W.   Ed.
Creeley.   World, The.
De la Mare.   Brother and Sister.
Dickey, J.   In the Tree House at Night.
   String, The.
   Vessels.
Dickinson, E.   Vivid in our immortal Group.
Dove, R.   Song. Summer.

Dubie. Elegy for My Brother.
Dunbar, P. Ione.
Emerson, R. In Memoriam.
Frost, R. To E.T.
Gunn, T. Invitation, An.
Han-shan. I have six brothers.
HaNagid. His Brother's Illness.
  On the Death of Isaac, His Brother.
Heaney, S. Mid-Term Break.
Herrick. To His Brother in Law Master John
  Wingfield.
  To His Dying Brother, Master William Herrick.
Hopkins, G. Brothers.
Hughes, T. Sacrifice.
Jonson, B. Speech Presented unto King James
  at a Tilting.
Keats. To My Brother George.
  To My Brothers.
Kinnell. Another Night in the Ruins.
  My Mother's R & R.
Kizer, C. Amusing Our Daughters.
Kumin, M. In Memoriam P. W. Jr. 1921–1980.
Levine, P. You Can Have It.
Logan, J. Brothers: Two Saltimbanques, The.
  Grace.
  Pass, The.
  Poem for My Brother.
Lowell, R. Her Dead Brother.
MacLeish. Family Group.
Melville, H. Timoleon.
Merton. For My Brother: Reported Missing In
  Action, 1943.
Orr, G. After the Guest.
  Gathering the Bones Together.
  Litany, A: "I remember him falling beside me."
  Moment, A.
  Spring Floods.
Pagis. Brothers.
Patchen. Moon came out full, you could see the
  white breathing of the.
Ransom, J. Two Gentlemen in Bonds.
Riley, J. Busch and Tommy.
  Max and Jim.
  Prior to Miss Belle's Appearance.
Robinson, E. Two Gardens in Linndale.
Rossetti, C. Portraits.
Sexton. For Johnny Pole on the Forgotten
  Beach.
  Papa and Mama Dance, The.
"Shu Ting." Brother, I Am Here.
Smith, S. Death Bereaves Our Common Mother
  Nature Grieves for My Dead Brother.
Spender, S. My Brother Luis.
Stafford, W. At the Grave of My Brother.
  At the Grave of My Brother: Bomber Pilot.
  Remembering Brother Bob.
Stock, R. Dear Mr. Worldly Wiseman.
Tate, A. Sonnets of the Blood.
Tennyson, A. Prefatory Poem to My Brother's
  Sonnets.
Thoreau. Brother where dost thou dwell?
Van Duyn. Twins, The.
Williams, T. Tuesday's Child.
Williams, W. Portrait of the Author.
Wordsworth, W. Brothers, The.
  Elegiac Verses in Memory of My Brother, John
  Wordsworth.
  Tradition of Oker Hill in Darley Dale,
  Derbyshire, A.
  When, to the attractions of the busy world.
Wright, J. Lament for My Brother on a
  Hayrake.
Zagajewski. To My Older Brother.
Brown, Clifford
Brodsky, J. In Memory of Clifford Brown.
Brown, Jerry (Edmund Gerald Brown, Jr.)
Snyder, G. He Shot Arrows, but Not at Birds
  Perching.
  Talking Late with the Governor about the
  Budget.
Brown, John
Cullen, C. Negro Mother's Lullaby, A.
Hayden, R. John Brown.
Hughes, L. October 16: The Raid.
Melville, H. Portent, The.
Riley, J. John Brown.

Robinson, E. John Brown.
Rukeyser, M. Soul and Body of John Brown,
  The.
Sandburg, C. Osawatomie.
Whittier. Brown of Ossawatomie.
Browning, Elizabeth Barrett
Browning, R. Flight of the Duchess, The.
  Lost Mistress, The.
Dickinson, E. Her—'last Poems.'
McGrath, T. Near Pah-Gotzin-Kay.
Nash, D. Old Is for Books.
Pound, E. To E. B. B.
Browning, Robert
Borges. Browning Resolves to Be a Poet.
Browning, R. Inscription for a Sketch.
Meredith, G. On Hearing the News from
  Venice.
Nash, D. Old Is for Books.
Sandburg, C. Manitoba Childe Roland.
Bruce, Lenny
Ai. Boys and Girls, Lenny Bruce, or Back from
  the Dead.
Bruckner, Anton
Zagajewski. Anton Bruckner.
Brueghel, Pieter
Auden. Musée des Beaux Arts.
De la Mare. Breughel's Winter.
Dubie. February: The Boy Breughel.
Nemerov. Brueghel: The Triumph of Time.
  Hope.
  World as Brueghel Imagined It, The.
Pinkerton, H. On Breughel the Elder's *The
  Harvesters* (1565) in the Metropolitan
  Museum.
Plath. Two Views of a Cadaver Room.
Sze. Brueghel.
Williams, W. Dance, The.
  Parable of the Blind, The.
  Pictures from Brueghel.
Brussels, Belgium
Auden. Brussels in Winter.
Whittier. Peace Convention at Brussels, The.
Brutus (Marcus Junius Brutus)
Davie, D. Dream Forest.
Pope, A. Two Chorus's to the Tragedy of
  Brutus.
Bryan, William Jennings
Lindsay, N. Bryan, Bryan, Bryan, Bryan.
Bryant, William Cullen
Rukeyser, M. Mountain: One from Bryant.
Very. William Cullen Bryant.
Whittier. Bryant on His Birthday.
Bubbles
Herrick. Bubble; a Song, The.
Rilke. Soap Bubbles.
Sandburg, C. Bubbles.
Schuyler, J. People Who See Bubbles Rise.
Budapest, Hungary
Enzensberger, H. Sightseeing Tour.
Tomlinson, C. Over Elizabeth Bridge: a
  Circumvention.
Buddha and Buddhism
Carruth, H. Buddhist Painter Prepares to Paint,
  The.
Collins, B. Shoveling Snow with Buddha.
Cooper, J. Jittoku, Buddhist Mystic—15th
  Century.
Dubie. Ghosts on the Northern Land of Ur.
  On the Chinese Abduction of Tibet's Child
  Panchen Lama.
  Poem for My Friend, Clare. Or, With White
  Stupas We Remember Buddha.
Eberhart, R. Way Out, A.
Feng-kan. I have been to Tientai.
Ferlinghetti, L. Buddha in the Woodpile, A.
Ginsberg, A. Do the Meditation Rock.
  For Creely's Ear.
  Guru Om.
  Homage Vajracarya.
  Mind Breaths.
  Reflections at Lake Louise.
  Sakyamuni Coming Out from the Mountain.
  What Would You Do If You Lost It.
Hamill, S. Ten Thousand Sutras.

Han-shan. Again I see those who leave home.
  All my life too lazy to work.
  Among the sages of the past.
  Boys and grown-up men.
  Buddhist monks don't keep their precepts.
  Cold Mountain is a leakproof cliff.
  Daily concerns are endless.
  Five Peaks turn to dust, The.
  For the hundred years of human life.
  Here's a message for the faithful.
  Hey you people who leave home.
  Homeless people I know, The.
  How many ancient sages.
  I have a single cave.
  I have six brothers.
  I see people chanting sutras.
  I see people everywhere.
  I was so poor in the past.
  Imagine a king-of-the-wheel.
  I've always loved friends of the Way.
  Long ago during Liang times.
  On Cold Mountain Road.
  One bottle is cast in gold.
  People can't explain.
  People think the body's their root.
  Quick-thinking people I meet, The.
  Steam some sand for your dinner.
  Stop right now I implore you.
  Talking about food won't make you full.
  They say when Shakyamuni.
  World is full of busy people, The.
Ignatow, D. I Am.
Jeffers, R. Meditation on Saviors.
  Theory of Truth.
Kipling, R. Buddha at Kamakura.
Komunyakaa. 2527th Birthday of the Buddha.
Laughlin, J. Can There Be a Female
  Bodhissatva?
  Unenlightened Face, The.
  What Are You Smiling About.
  With My Third Eye.
Lindsay, N. Poems Speaking of Buddha, Prince
  Siddartha.
Melville, H. Buddha.
Meredith, G. 'Tis good to keep hinderward
  eyes.
Merton. Five breaths pray in me: sun moon.
Oliver, M. Buddha's Last Instruction, The.
Pinsky. Hearts, The.
Rexroth, K. Empty Mirror.
  Further Advantages of Learning.
  Heart's Garden, the Garden's Heart, The.
  It Is a German Honeymoon.
Shih-te. Black Dragon Pearl in his left hand,
  The.
  Buddha forsook the joys of rank, The.
  Buddhas care for mortal beings.
  Buddhas leave behind sutras.
  Cold Mountain is a cold mountain.
  I have millions of gathas.
  Old buddha road is deserted, The.
  Triple World is a turning wheel, The.
  We all possess the buddha of buddhas.
  Who knows how to catch rats.
  Worldly people make me sigh.
Snyder, G. Circumambulating Arunachala.
  Regarding Wave.
Whalen, P. Detachment, Wisdom and
  Compassion.
  Dharma Youth League, The.
  Dharmakaya.
  Lotus Sutra, Naturalized, The.
  Mahayana.
  Metaphysical Insomnia Jazz. Mumonkan XXIX.
  Sanjusangendo.
  Tassajara.
  Vision of the Bodhisattvas, A.
  Walking beside the Kamogawa, Remembering
  Nansen and Fudo and Gary's Poem.
Wilner, E. Blessing.
See also **Zen Buddhism**
Buenos Aires, Argentina
Amichai [*or* Amikhai]. Ballad in the Streets of
  Buenos Aires.
Borges. Adrogué.
  Cyclical Night, The.

Elegy: "Oh destiny of Borges."
Epilogue: "Now that the number of steps you were given."
Mythical Founding of Buenos Aires, The.
New England, 1967.
Streets, The.
García Lorca. Song of the Shop Boy.

"Buffalo Bill" (William Frederick Cody)
Cummings, E. E. Portrait.
Sandburg, C. Buffalo Bill.

Buffaloes
Atwood. Buffalo in Compound: Alberta.
Blue Cloud. Death Chant.
Kipling, R. Dark children of the mere and marsh.
Lindsay, N. Ghosts of the Buffaloes, The.
Moore, M. Buffalo, The.
Oliver, M. Ghosts.
Sandburg, C. Buffalo Dusk.
Stafford, W. Paso por Aquí.
Swenson, M. Bison Crossing Near Mt. Rushmore.

Bugles and Buglers
Merwin. Second Psalm: The Signals.
Nash, O. Edouard.
Owen, W. Bugles Sang.
Whitman, W. Beat! Beat! Drums!

Buildings and Builders
Amichai [or Amikhai]. Poem about Repairs to My House.
Berry, W. For the Rebuilding of a House.
Browning, R. Apparent Failure.
Cavafy. Builders.
Clampitt. Progress at Building Site With (Fewer) Pigeons.
Codrescu. Architecture.
Cooper, J. Builder of Houses, The.
Cowper, W. Epigrams on His Garden Shed.
Inscription for an Hermitage.
Crane, S. Many workmen / Built a huge ball of masonry.
Creeley. For John Duff.
Invitation, The.
Dove, R. Corduroy Road.
Dugan, A. Love Song: I and Thou.
Duncan, R. Nel Mezzo del Cammin di Nostra Vita.
Emerson, R. One night he dreamed of a palace fair.
Graves, R. Fallen Tower of Siloam, The.
Gunn, T. Diagrams.
Hacker, M. Forage Sestina.
Hall, D. Traffic.
Jonson, B. To Penshurst.
Keats. Fragment of the "Castle Builder."
Kipling, R. Hymn of Breaking Strain.
Palace, The.
Romulus and Remus.
Truthful Song, The.
Komunyakaa. Instructions for Building Straw Huts.
Laughlin, J. House of Light, The.
Levine, P. Making It New.
Lorde. Workers Rose on May Day or Postcript to Karl Marx, The.
MacLeish. Burying Ground by the Ties.
Marvell. Inscribenda Luparae [To Be Written on the Louvre].
Upon Appleton House [To My Lord Fairfax].
Muldoon, P. One Desire, The.
Neruda. Midday Construction.
Oppen. Tourist Eye.
Orr, G. Builders, The.
Piercy. Gasman Invites the Skyscrapers to Dance.
Prunty. Stick Builder.
Ramanujan. Real Estate.
Ritsos. Builders.
Sandburg, C. Shovel Man, The.
Schuyler, J. Buildings.
East Window on Elizabeth Street, An.
Green Door, The.
Greenwich Avenue.
Witley Court.
Snyder, G. Building.
Stevens, W. Architecture.

Sze. Ice Floe.
Opal, The.
Tomlinson, C. Above Manhattan.
Crane, The.
Tu Fu. Visit in Winter to the Temple of His Mystical Majesty, A.
Updike. Sonnet to Man-Made Grandeur.
Very. Corner Stone, The.
Weiss, T. Building, A.
Whittier. Norumbega Hall.
Wilbur, R. For the New Railway Station in Rome.
Williams, C. K. Sanctity, The.
Williams, M. Believing.
Tearing Down the Hotel.
Williams, W. Defective Record, The.
Vsion of Labor, A: 1931.
Wordsworth, W. Written with a Pencil upon a Stone.

Bukowski, Charles
Carver, R. You Don't Know What Love Is.

Bulgaria
Meredith, W. Two Masks Unearthed in Bulgaria.

Bull Run, Battles of (1861, 1862)
Lowell, R. March 1, The.
Melville, H. Fortitude of the North, The.
March into Virginia, The.

Bullets
Dove, R. Teach Us to Number Our Days.
Riley, J. Song of the Bullet.
Ritsos. Unjust, The.
Simic. Poem without a Title.

Bullfights and Bullfighters
Amichai [or Amikhai]. Bull Returns, The.
Bukowski. Brave Bull.
"Dario." Exploit in the Bullring.
Eberhart, R. Lorca.
Matador.
García Lorca. Lament for Ignacio Sánchez Mejías.
Jacobsen, J. Matadors, The.
Major, C. Wounded Bullfighter, The.
Olson, C. This.
Plath. Goring, The.
Swenson, M. Death Invited.
Tomlinson, C. Theory of Regress.
Wilner, E. Ode to Innocence.

Bullfinches
Cowper, W. On the Lamented Death of Mrs. Throckmorton's Bullfinch.
Hardy, T. Bullfinches, The.

Bulls
Amichai [or Amikhai]. Bull Returns, The.
Cowper, W. On a Mischievous Bull.
Eberhart, R. Matador.
Glück, L. Brooding Likeness.
Heaney, S. Outlaw, The.
Hughes, T. Bull Moses, The.
Dehorning.
Lawrence, D. H. St Luke.
Olson, C. He / in the dark stall, no day now for him, to paw.
Riley, J. Nicholas Oberting.
Smart, C. Story of a Cock and a Bull, A.
Smith, S. Dedicated Dancing Bull and the Water Maid, The.
Swenson, M. Death Invited.
Williams, W. Bull, The.
Wilner, E. Nandin's Tail.
Ode to Innocence.

Bullying and Bullies
Angelou. Thirteens (Black), The.
Thirteens (White), The.
Bukowski. Bee, The.
Big Max.
Hughes, T. Dehorning.
Lindsay, N. Dangerous Little Boy Fairies, The.
Nash, O. Introduction, The.
Spender, S. My Parents.
Stafford, W. Dropout.
Williams, C. K. Hood.
Love: Wrath.

Bunker Hill, Battle of (1775)
Stockton, A. On Hearing that General Warren

Was Killed on Bunker-Hill.

Bunting, Basil
Niedecker. Ballad of Basil, The.

Bunyan, John
Browning, R. Ned Bratts.
Kipling, R. Holy War, The.
Very. On the Bunyan Tableau.

Bureaucracy and Bureaucrats
Auden. Unknown Citizen, The.
Brodsky, J. Anno Domini.
Cavafy. Satrapy, The.
Davie, D. Pilate.
Thanks to Industrial Essex.
Frost, R. Departmental.
Hughes, L. Madam and the Census Man.
Kinsella, T. Administrator.
Kipling, R. Army Headquarters.
General Summary, A.
Last Department, The.
Man Who Could Write, The.
Masque of Plenty, The.
Pagett, M. P.
Plea of the Simla Dancers, The.
Public Waste.
Rupaiyat of Omar Kal'vin, The.
Study of an Elevation, in Indian Ink.
Prunty. Oh General, Oh Spy, Oh Bureaucrat!
Smith, S. Choosers, The.

Burglars
Ciardi, J. Missouri Fable, A.
Dugan, A. They Call It "Grumus Merdae."
Riley, J. Piper's Son, The.
Ritsos. Eyewitness.
Williams, M. Romance.

Burgundy, France
Zagajewski. Burgundy's Grasslands.

Burial
Amichai [or Amikhai]. My Mother Died on Shavuot.
Ammons. First Carolina Said-Song.
Baudelaire. Burial, A.
Beckett, S. Malacoda.
Berryman. Poet's Final Instructions, The.
Callimachus. By Callimachus.
Carruth, H. French Hill.
My Father's Face.
Carver, R. Another Mystery.
My Dad's Wallet.
Cavafy. Flowers White and Beautiful, as Were Most Becoming.
Ciardi, J. Box Comes Home, A.
Elegy for a Sweet Sharpy.
Elegy: "This is the body of my good gray practical dead."
Sea Burial.
Clampitt. Burial in Cypress Hills.
Cowper, W. Another.
Inscription for a Stone.
De la Mare. Never More, Sailor.
Dickey, J. Sled Burial, Dream Ceremony.
Sleepers.
Eberhart, R. Dead Skunk.
Gesture, The.
Sea Burial from the Cruiser Reve.
Frost, R. Home Burial.
Gurney, I. When I Am Covered.
Hardy, T. Her Late Husband.
I Found Her Out There.
Herrick. Bed-Man, or Grave-Maker, The.
Buriall.
Rosemarie Branch, The.
To Anthea.
To the Passenger.
Upon a Child That Died [or Dyed].
Upon Himselfe Being Buried.
Upon Prue [or Prew], His Maid.
Hughes, L. Death of an Old Seaman.
Red Roses.
Stony Lonesome.
Ignatow, D. Going Down.
I Want to Be Buried.
Reading the Headlines.
Sky.
Jeffers, R. Delusion of Saints.
In the Hill at Newgrange.

My Burial Place.
Shane O'Neill's Cairn.
Kipling, R.   Ballade of Burial, A.
Lawrence, D. H.   Let the Dead Bury Their
  Dead.
MacLeish.   Burial, The.
  Conway Burying Ground.
Mahon.   Stone Age Figure Far Below, A.
Meredith, W.   REM Sleep.
Merwin.   Dry Stone Mason, The.
Millay, E.   Burial.
Mistral, G.   What Do You Feel Underground?
Nash, O.   Tweedledee and Tweedledoom.
Niedecker.   Dead / she now lay deaf to death.
  She was a mourner too. Now she's gone.
Pagis.   Siege.
Riley, J.   John Boyle O'Reilly.
Ritsos.   Hill, The.
Robinson, E.   Leonora.
Rossetti, C.   Ye Have Forgotten the Exhortation.
Stevens, W.   Testamentum.
Stockton, A.   Lines on Seeing Mrs Elizabeth
  Witherspoon Put in the Grave.
Tomlinson, C.   Tax Inspector, The.
Very.   Ancient Burial Places in Peabody, The.
Warren, R.   Cross, The.
Whitman, W.   Of Him I Love Day and Night.
  Vigil Strange I Kept on the Field One Night.
Williams, T.   With Military Honors.
Wright, J.   Alarm, The.
  Dream of Burial, A.
  Regeneration, The.
See also **Cemeteries; Funerals; Graves;**
  Mausoleums; Tombs

Burial Mounds
Ammons.   Treeful of Cleavage Flared
  Branching, A.
Very.   Mound Builders, The.

Burke, Edmund
Wilbur, R.   Marché aux Oiseaux.

Burlesque
See **Striptease**

Burma
Kipling, R.   Ballad of Boh Da Thone, The.
  Grave of the Hundred Dead, The.
  Mandalay.
Muldoon, P.   Burma.
Whittier.   Evening in Burmah.

Burne-Jones, Edward
Rossetti, D.   For 'The Wine of Circe' by
  Edward Burne Jones.

Burns, Robert
Burns, R.   Rantin, Rovin Robin.
Crane, H.   Song for Happy Feast Days, A.
Keats.   On Visiting the Tomb of Burns.
  This Mortal Body of a Thousand Days.
Nash, O.   Everything's Haggis in Hoboken, or,
  Scots Wha Hae Hae.
Riley, J.   As We Read Burns.
  Robert Burns Wilson.
  To Robert Burns.
Rossetti, D.   On Burns.
Whittier.   Burns.
  Memory of Burns, The.
Williams, W.   Address.
Wordsworth, W.   Address to the Sons of Burns,
  after Visiting Their Father's Grave (August
  14th, 1803).
  At the Grave of Burns (1803, Seven Years After
  His Death).
  Thoughts Suggested the Day Following, on the
  Banks of Nith, near the Poet's Residence.
  To the Sons of Burns, after Visiting the Grave of
  Their Father.

Burr, Aaron
Robinson, E.   On the Way.
Schuyler, J.   Eyes at the Window.

Burr, Theodosia
Schuyler, J.   Eyes at the Window.

Burros
See **Donkeys**

Burroughs, William
Ginsberg, A.   Funky barn, black hills
  approaching Fulton.
  Kansas City to Saint Louis.

On Burroughs, Work.

Bus Terminals
Amichai [*or* Amikhai].   Hour of Grace, An.
Ginsberg, A.   In the Baggage Room at
  Greyhound.
Komunyakaa.   Child's Play.

Buses
Atwood.   Bus to Alliston, Ontario, The.
Bishop, E.   Moose, The.
Clampitt.   At a Rest Stop in Ohio.
  Iola, Kansas.
  Witness.
Creeley.   Peace ("Waiting for a bus").
Gunn, T.   Smoking Pot on the Bus.
Levertov.   Bus.
Levine, P.   Ordinary Morning, An.
McGrath, T.   Love in a Bus.
Nash, O.   Buses Headed for Scranton, The.
Paley, G.   In the Bus.
Prunty.   Downtown Bus, The.
Rimbaud, A.   State of Siege?
Tomlinson, C.   Oaxaca Bus, The.
Williams, M.   On a Trailways Bus a Man Who
  Holds His Head Strangely Speaks to the Seat
  Behind Him.
  One of Those Rare Occurrences on a City Bus.
Williams, W.   In the 'Sconset Bus.
Wright, J.   Destination: Accomplished.

Business and Businessmen
Bukowski.   Dow Jones: Down.
Chuang Tzu.   Hat Salesman and a Capable
  Ruler, A.
Ciardi, J.   Back through the Looking Glass to
  This Side.
Codrescu.   Poetry Paper.
Cummings, E. E.   Exit a kind of unkindness
  exit.
De la Mare.   Isaac Meek.
Dickinson, E.   I asked no other thing.
Dugan, A.   1. Business Jacob, the Angel
  Wrestler.
  On Hat: On Vertical Mobility as a Concept.
  On Trading Time for Life by Work.
  Sexist Lament: Ruin by Monitor.
Eberhart, R.   Emerson's Concord.
  Old Fashioned American Business Man, An.
Ginsberg, A.   Birdbrain!
  Who Runs America?
HaNagid.   In Business Don't Get Involved.
Hughes, L.   Madam's Past History.
Laughlin, J.   Confidential Report.
  Market Discounts Love.
  Small Group, A.
  What the Animals Did.
MacLeish.   Corporate Entity.
Merton.   Gloss on the Sin of Ixion.
Merwin.   Briefcase, The.
Nash, O.   Snark Was a Boojum Was a Prawn,
  The.
Olson, C.   Business, The.
  Dramatis Personae.
Rukeyser, M.   Dam, The.
  Time of finks and nobles, A.
Sheridan, T.   To the Same.
Smith, S.   Villains.
Updike.   Business Acquaintances.
  Imaginable Conference, An.
  Tax-Free Encounter.
Williams, M.   Promotion, The.
See also **Accounting and Accountants;**
  Advertising; Banking and Bankers;
  Capitalism; Commerce; Financiers; Insurance

Butchering and Butchers
Chuang Tzu.   Cutting up an Ox.
Hardy, T.   Bags of Meat.
Levine, P.   Angel Butcher.
  Animals Are Passing from Our Lives.
McGrath, T.   Another Season.
Nash, O.   Calf, The.
Paley, G.   Psalm: "Their shoes are stuccoed with
  sawdust and blood."
Ramanujan.   Butcher's Tao.
Robinson, E.   Reuben Bright.
Simic.   Butcher Shop.
Tomlinson, C.   On a Pig's Head.

Updike.   Modest Mound of Bones, A.
Williams, C. K.   Racists.

Butter
Hardy, T.   Pat of Butter, The.
Heaney, S.   Churning Day.
Nash, O.   Arthur.

Buttercups
Parker, D.   In the Meadow.

Butterflies
Ammons.   Butterflyweed.
  Trap.
Brodsky, J.   Butterfly, The.
Browning, R.   Amphibian.
Carruth, H.   Chase in Spring, The.
Ciardi, J.   Quirks.
Clampitt.   Urn-Burial and the Butterfly
  Migration.
Collins, B.   Butterfly Effect, The.
Cooper, J.   Practicing for Death.
Crane, H.   Moth That Made God Blind, The.
"Dario."   Divine Psyche, sweet invisible
  Butterfly.
Dickinson, E.   Butterfly in honored Dust, The.
  Butterfly obtains, The.
  Butterfly upon the Sky, The.
  Butterfly's Assumption Gown, The.
  Butterfly's Numidian Gown, The.
  Caterpillar.
  Cocoon above! Cocoon below!
  Defrauded I a Butterfly.
  From Cocoon forth a Butterfly.
  His oriental heresies.
  My Cocoon tightens—Colors tease.
  Some such Butterfly be seen.
  Two Butterflies went out at Noon.
  What tenements of clover.
Dugan, A.   On Inter-Relatedness in the
  Universe.
  Untitled Poem: "Monarchs, the butterflies, are
  commanded, The."
Duncan, R.   Roots and Branches.
Eberhart, R.   Undercliff Evening.
Emerson, R.   Have ye seen the caterpillar.
Frost, R.   Blue-Butterfly Day.
  My Butterfly.
  Tuft of Flowers, The.
Graves, R.   Flying Crooked.
Hayden, R.   Butterfly Piece.
Hughes, T.   Two Tortoiseshell Butterflies.
Jackson, L.   Chrysalis.
Kipling, R.   Butterflies.
Lawrence, D. H.   Butterfly.
Lindsay, N.   King of Yellow Butterflies, The.
  Song for Elizabeth, A.
  Soul of a Butterfly, The.
Meredith, W.   Nausea.
Merrill, J.   To a Butterfly.
Milosz, C.   Specimens.
Moore, M.   To a Steam Roller.
Muldoon, P.   Milkweed and Monarch.
Nemerov.   Crossing, The.
  Late Butterflies.
Oliver, M.   One or Two Things.
Parra, N.   Butterfly.
Raine, K.   Blue butterflies' eyed wings.
Ramanujan.   Some Monarchs and a Wish.
Rexroth, K.   Orphic Soul, The.
Rilke.   Butterfly.
Stock, R.   Cenotaph for Two Butterflies.
Tomlinson, C.   Butterflies, The.
Van Duyn.   Speak, Memory!
Very.   Lines Suggested by Seeing a Butterfly
  Sculptured Upon a Tomb.
Walcott.   Lesson for This Sunday, A.
Wilde, O.   Symphony in Yellow.
Williams, C. K.   Friends.
  In the next life.
Williams, W.   Graceful Bastion, The.
  Informative Object, An.
Wordsworth, W.   To a Butterfly ("I've watched
  you now a full half-hour").
Wright, J.   Spring Images.
Zukofsky, L.   Daruma.

Buzzards
Hughes, L.   Dying Beast.
Rossetti, C.   Sketch, A.

Stevens, W.   Jack-Rabbit, The.
Stock, R.   Evangelists, The.
Tomlinson, C.   High Summer.
  Translating the Birds.
Warren, R.   Pondy Woods.
See also **Vultures**

Byron, George Gordon Noel Byron, 6th Baron
Arnold, M.   Memorial Verses.
Byron, G.   On This Day I Complete My Thirty-
  sixth Year.
Davie, D.   Two Intercepted Letters.
Dugan, A.   Dark Tower, The.
Gunn, T.   Lerici.
Keats.   To Lord Byron.
Koch, K.   Art of Poetry, The.
Logan, J.   Byron at Shelley's Burning.
Meredith, G.   Manfred.
Pasternak, B.   Oh had we known it turns out so.
Shelley, P.   Fragment: To Byron.
  Sonnet to Byron.
Wordsworth, W.   Passage from Mary Barker's
  Lines Addressed to a Noble Lord (His Lordship
  Will Know Why).
  Two Epigrams on Byron's *Cain*.

Byzantium
Cavafy.   Anna Dalassini.
  Anna Komnina.
  In Church.
  John Kantakuzinos Triumphs.
  Of Colored Glass.
  Theophilos Palaiologos.
Gunn, T.   Punch Rubicundus.
Szymborska, W.   Byzantine Mosaic, A.
Yeats.   Byzantium.
  Sailing to Byzantium.

C

Cabala
Swenson, M.   Cabala.
Cabbages
Gurney, I.   Garden, The.
Lawrence, D. H.   Rose Is Not a Cabbage, A.
Oliver, M.   Skunk Cabbage.
Sandburg, C.   Nocturn Cabbage.
Swenson, M.   Shu Swamp, Spring.
Cactus
Williams, T.   Cacti.
Cadavers
Carver, R.   Autopsy Room, The.
Ciardi, J.   Anatomy Lab.
Dubie.   After Three Photographs of Brassaï.
Lux.   Haitian Cadavers.
Ramanujan.   Death and the Good Citizen.
See also **Corpses**
Cadiz, Spain, Battle of (1596)
Donne.   Cales and Guiana.
  Sir John Wingfield.
Cads
Herrick.   Upon Dundrige.
  Upon Rumpe.
  Upon Urles.
Kipling, R.   Delilah.
Caedmon
Heaney, S.   Whitby-sur-Moyola.
Levertov.   Caedmon.
Caesar, Julius
Auden.   Fall of Rome, The.
Bukowski.   Anthony.
Cavafy.   Ides of March, The.
  Theodotos.
Jonson, B.   To Clement Edmonds, on His
  Caesar's Commentaries Observed, and
  Translated.
Laberius, D.   Old Actor Addresses Julius
  Caesar, An.
Lindsay, N.   Trial of the Dead Cleopatra in Her
  Beautiful and Wonderful Tomb, The.
Millay, E.   When Caesar Fell.
Sheridan, T.   Prologue to *Julius Caesar*, as It
  Was Acted at Madam Violante's Booth.
Stock, R.   Ambassador from India.

Cafés
Amichai [*or* Amikhai].   Caffè Dante in New
  York—3.
  Like the Streams in the Negev.
Brodsky, J.   Café Trieste: San Francisco.
Cummings, E. E.   5 / derbies-with-men-in-them
  smoke Helmar.
Davie, D.   At the Café Parnasse.
Eliot, T. S.   Sweeney among the Nightingales.
Kizer, C.   Italian Kittens, The.
Komunyakaa.   Ghost Video.
  Yellow Dog Café.
Laughlin, J.   Rome: In the Café.
Logan, J.   Nighthawks: after Hopper's Painting.
Milosz, C.   Caffé Greco.
  Lastingness.
Montale.   Bibe a Ponte all'Asse.
Updike.   Grief of Cafeterias, The.
Wright, C.   Bar Giamaica, 1959-60.
  Mid-winter Snowfall in the Piazza Dante.
  With Eddie and Nancy in Arezzo at the Caffè
  Grande.
  With Simic and Marinetti at the Giubbe Rosse.
Zagajewski.   World's Prose, The.
Cain and Abel
Baudelaire.   Abel and Cain.
Blake, W.   Ghost of Abel, The.
Clough.   Adam and Eve.
Coleridge, S.   Wanderings of Cain, The.
Herrick.   Abels Bloud.
  Another.
Kipling, R.   Cain and Abel.
Nemerov.   Cain.
Orr, G.   Three Songs.
Pagis.   Autobiography.
  Brothers.
  Written in Pencil in the Sealed Railway-Car.
Stock, R.   First Row, The.
Very.   Thy Brother's Blood.
Cakes
Amichai [*or* Amikhai].   Wonderful Baker, The.
Bishop, E.   Going to the Bakery.
Cummings, E. E.   This little bride & groom are.
Calcutta, India
Ginsberg, A.   Heat.
Kinnell.   To a Child in Calcutta.
Williams, M.   In a Gradually Moving Car
  Somewhere in Calcutta.
Calder, Alexander
Shapiro, K.   Calder, A.
Updike.   Calder's Hands.
Caliban
Browning, R.   Caliban upon Setebos; or, Natural
  Theology in the Island.
Levertov.   Freeing of the Dust, The.
Weiss, T.   Caliban Remembers.
California (state)
Amichai [*or* Amikhai].   North of San Francisco.
Angelou.   California Prodigal.
Bierce.   Californian Summer Pictures.
  Judex Judicatus.
Carruth, H.   Backyard in California, A.
Clampitt.   John Donne in California.
  Portola Valley.
Codrescu.   Eugenio Montale in California.
  West Is the Best and the Future Is Near, The.
Davie, D.   Across the Bay.
  In California.
  Robinson Jeffers at Point Sur.
  To Thom Gunn in Los Altos, California.
Gunn, T.   Flying Above California.
  Geysers, The.
  Lights among Redwood.
Hughes, L.   Big Sur.
Jarrell, R.   In Montecito.
Jeffers, R.   Carmel.
  Carmel Point.
  Clouds of Evening.
  Loving Shepherdess, The.
  Morro Bay.
  Return.
  Thurso's Landing.
  Women at Point Sur, The.
Kizer, C.   Afternoon Happiness.
  For Jan as the End Draws Near.

Laughlin, J.   Highway 66.
Lindsay, N.   Golden Whales of California.
Major, C.   September Mendocino.
Milosz, C.   It Was Winter.
  To Robinson Jeffers.
Mistral, G.   California Poppy.
Oppen.   Belvedere.
  California.
  Guest Room.
Plath.   Sleep in the Mojave Desert.
Rexroth, K.   Vitamins and Roughage.
Rukeyser, M.   Burnishing, Oakland.
Shapiro, K.   California Petrarchan.
Snyder, G.   Burning the Small Dead.
  Hay for the Horses.
  Marin-An.
Stafford, W.   Star in the Hills, The.
Warren, R.   Trips to California.
Whalen, P.   California Is Odious but
  Indispensable.
Whitman, W.   Facing West from California's
  Shores.
  Promise to California, A.
  Song of the Redwood-Tree.
Whittier.   Pass of the Sierra, The.
Wright, C.   California Dreaming.
  Looking across Laguna Canyon at Dusk, West-
  by-Northwest.
  Looking West from Laguna Beach at Night.
  Sprung Narratives.
Caligula
Updike.   Caligula's Dream.
Calligraphy
Wilner, E.   Poem of Exile, A.
Zukofsky, L.   (Ryokan's scroll).
Calling Cards
Hughes, L.   Madam's Calling Cards.
Calliope (muse)
Lindsay, N.   Kallyope Yell, The.
Calm
Amichai [*or* Amikhai].   Great Calm: Questions
  and Answers.
Atwood.   Boat, A.
Beckett, S.   Bon bon il est un pays.
  Sitôt sorti de l'ermitage.
Berry, W.   Envoy: "Love, all day there has been
  at the edge of my mind."
  Grace.
Broumas, O.   Contemplation, The.
  Imaginary Sufi Garden.
Bukowski.   Not Quite So Soon.
Clare, J.   Evening.
Cowper, W.   R.S.S. Written in a Fit of Illness.
Cummings, E. E.   Love is a guess / that
  deepens.
  N / OthI / n / g can / s / urPas / s.
Donne.   Calm[e], The.
Eberhart, R.   Sea Storm.
Graves, R.   Poisoned Day.
Gurney, I.   Quiet Fireshine.
Hamill, S.   Kah Tai Purgatorio.
Hardy, T.   Epigraph to "The Woodlanders."
Hayden, R.   Islands, The.
Herrick.   To Music, to Becalm a Sweet-sick
  Youth.
Hughes, T.   Horses, The.
Jackson, L.   Ageless Brow, An.
Jeffers, R.   Now Returned Home.
MacNeice.   Evening Indoors.
Merwin.   Calm in April, A.
Orr, G.   Fields took on their final.
Parker, D.   Thin Edge, The.
Ramanujan.   Hindoo, The: He Reads His GITA
  and Is Calm at All Events.
  Hindoo, The: The Only Risk.
Rilke.   Calm of Animals, The.
Rossetti, C.   Grant us such grace that we may
  work Thy Will.
  In Progress.
  There Remaineth Therefore a Rest for the
  People of God.
  What Sappho Would Have Said Had Her Leap
  Cured Instead of Killing Her.
Shelley, P.   Fragment: "Ye gentle visitations of
  calm thought."

Wordsworth, W.   Composed by the Side of Grasmere Lake.
It is a beauteous evening, calm and free.
Rains at length have ceased, the winds are stilled, The.
Stars Are Mansions Built by Nature's Hand, The.

Calvary
Dickinson, E.   That I did always love.
McHugh, H.   Woman Who Laughed on Calvary.
Robinson, E.   Calvary.
See also **Crucifixion, The**

Calves
Berry, W.   Her First Calf.
Hall, D.   Great Day in the Cows' House.
Hardy, T.   Calf, The.
Hughes, T.   Birth of Rainbow.
Calves harshly parted from their mamas.
March Calf, A.
Kumin, M.   Vealers, The.
Muldoon, P.   From Strength to Strength.
Nash, O.   Calf, The.
Orr, G.   Friday Lunchbreak.
Tomlinson, C.   Macduff.

Calvinism
Clough.   Latest Decalogue, The.
Hall, D.   Impossible Marriage, The.
Kipling, R.   McAndrew's Hymn.
Lowell, R.   Mr. Edwards and the Spider.
Millay, E.   To a Calvinist in Bali.

Calypso (mythology)
Broumas, O.   Calypso.
MacLeish.   Calypso's Island.
Merton.   Calypso's Island.

Camaraderie
McGrath, T.   Blues for Jimmy.
Restless Night, The.
Triumphal March.
Owen, W.   Apologia Pro Poemate Meo.
Riley, J.   Liz-Town Humorist, A.
To Edgar Wilson Nye.
See also **Friendship**

Cambodia and Cambodians
Ai.   Detective, The.
Fenton, J.   Cambodia.
Dead Soldiers.

Cambridge, England
Coleridge, S.   Absence.
Wilbur, R.   Violet and Jasper.

Cambridge, Massachusetts
Borges.   Cambridge.
Corbett, W.   Crossing the Footbridge over Storrow Drive.
Cummings, E. E.   Awful darkness of the town, The.
Eberhart, R.   How It Is.
Eliot, T. S.   First Caprice in North Cambridge.
Second Caprice in North Cambridge.
Schuyler, J.   Four Poems.
See also **Harvard University**

Cambridge University
Berryman.   London.
Message.
Other Cambridge, The.
Transit.
Bourne, V.   Sparrows Self-Domesticated.
Davie, D.   On Bertrand Russell's 'Portraits from Memory.'
Kipling, R.   Scholars, The.
Milton.   Elegy 1: To Charles Diodati.

Cambridgeshire, England
Davie, D.   Low Lands.

Camden, William
Campion, T.   Ad Guil. Camdenum.
Jonson, B.   To William Camden.

Camellias
Moore, M.   Camellia Sabina.
Schuyler, J.   Chapel, A.
Stock, R.   Camellia, The.

Camelot
Riley, J.   Guinevere.
Robinson, E.   Lancelot.
Merlin.
Tennyson, A.   Lady of Shalott, The.

Morte d'Arthur.

Camels
Ciardi, J.   C is for CAMEL, a very right beast.
Kipling, R.   Oonts.
Levi, P.   Dromedary, The.
Nash, O.   Camel, The.
Rumi.   Ground Cries Out, The.
Mouse and the Camel, The.
Weiss, T.   Camel in the Snow.

Cameras
Ciardi, J.   On a Photo of Sgt. Ciardi a Year Later.
Thanks to a Botanist, A.
Gunn, T.   Song of a Camera.
Ramanujan.   Man and Woman in Camera and Out.
Tomlinson, C.   Snapshot.
See also **Photography and Photographers**

Campaigns, Political
Clampitt.   Ringing Doorbells.
Lindsay, N.   Bryan, Bryan, Bryan, Bryan.
Rukeyser, M.   Professionals see the signs in the dice, the signs in the cards and clouds, The.
They pray. Security against oldness.
See also **Voting and Voters**

Campanula
Raine, K.   Campanula.

Campbell, Roy
MacDiarmid, H.   Major Road Ahead.
One loves the temporal, some unique manifestation.

Camping
Blue Cloud.   Camp.
Broumas, O.   Banner.
Carver, R.   Elk Camp.
Dickey, J.   Place of the Skull, The.
Sleeping Out at Easter.
Emerson, R.   Adirondacs, The.
Jeffers, R.   Oh, Lovely Rock.
Kinnell.   Middle of the Way.
Kinsella, T.   Song of the Night.
Logan, J.   Acapulco Canyon: Two Kodachromes.
Lux.   Poem in Thanks.
Major, C.   Riders.
Meredith, W.   Journal Entry (With the Udalls, June 1968).
Pinsky.   Saving, The.
Plath.   Two Campers in Cloud Country.
Rexroth, K.   Fish Peddler and Cobbler.
Floating.
Snyder, G.   August on Sourdough, a Visit from Dick Brewer.
Bubbs Creek Haircut.
Cool around the Fire, The.
For the Boy Who Was Dodger Point Lookout Fifteen Years Ago.
Late October Camping in the Sawtooths.
Stafford, W.   At Cove on the Crooked River.
Swenson, M.   Camping in Madera Canyon.
North Rim, The.
Warren, R.   First Time, The.
Wilner, E.   Middle-Class Vantage.
Wright, C.   Other Side of the River, The.

Campuses
Niedecker.   Chicory Flower / on Campus.
See also **Colleges and Universities**

Camus, Albert
Logan, J.   On Reading Camus In Early March.
Mahon.   Camus in Ulster.

Canaan
Merwin.   Approaches, The.
Milton.   Paraphrase on Psalm 114, A.
Smith, S.   In Canaan's Happy Land.

Canada
Atwood.   At the Tourist Centre in Boston.
Thoughts from Underground.
Two-Headed Poems.
Collins, B.   Canada.
Creeley.   Canada.
Davie, D.   Jesuits in North America, The.
Letter to Curtis Bradford, A.
Gurney, I.   Canadians.
Kipling, R.   Our Lady of the Snows.

Prairie, The.
Kumin, M.   With the Caribou.
Levertov.   Continent.
Mahon.   Canadian Pacific.
Whittier.   St. John.

Canals
Gurney, I.   Lock Keeper, The.
Hughes, T.   Canal's Drowning Black, The.
Long Tunnel Ceiling, The.
Major, C.   Canal, this one, The.
There he was, a boy, looking over.
Melville, H.   In a Bye-Canal.
Tomlinson, C.   Canal.

Canaries
Nash, O.   Canary, The.
Riley, J.   Canary at the Farm, A.
Whitman, W.   My Canary Bird.
Wilbur, R.   Pity.

Cancer (disease)
Ai.   Chance.
More.
Auden.   Miss Gee.
Carver, R.   Mailman as Cancer Patient, The.
Something Is Happening.
What the Doctor Said.
Clifton, L.   Amazons.
Dialysis.
Lumpectomy Eve.
Cooper, J.   Twins.
Dickey, J.   Cancer Match, The.
For the Death of Vince Lombardi.
Dickey, W.   Elegy Before the Time.
Dubie.   Funeral, The.
Dugan, A.   For Euthanasia and Pain-Killing Drugs.
In Memoriam: Aurelius Battaglia, and against His Tragic Sense of Life.
On the Death of Norman Dukes.
Portrait.
Eberhart, R.   Cancer Cells, The.
García Lorca.   Little Stanton.
Jacobsen, J.   Rock-Plant Wife, The.
Jarrell, R.   Christmas Roses, The.
Kizer, C.   American Beauty, An.
Lorde.   American Cancer Society Or There Is More Than One Way to Skin a Coon.
Orr, G.   Talk, The.
Pinsky.   Ice-Storm, The.
Memorial.
Ramanujan.   Bosnia.
Elegy: "Grown son's tears in a restaurant mix their salt, A."
Rich, A.   Woman Dead in Her Forties, A.
Sexton.   Operation, The.
Spender, S.   Elegy for Margaret.
Stafford, W.   Bess.

Candlemas
Clampitt.   Procession at Candlemas, A.
Codrescu.   Ghouls of Candlemas, The.
Herrick.   Ceremonies for Candlemasse Day, The.
Ceremonies for Candlemas[se] Eve.
Ceremony upon Candlemas Eve.
To Perenna.
Upon Candlemasse Day.
Merton.   Candlemas Procession, The.

Candles
Amichai [*or* Amikhai].   There Are Candles That Remember.
Cavafy.   Candles.
That They Might Appear.
Creeley.   Of Years.
Warning, The.
De la Mare.   Reverie.
Rose in Candlelight, A.
Dunbar, P.   At Candle-Lightin' Time.
Herrick.   Tapers.
To Mistresse Mary Willand.
Lawrence, D. H.   All Souls.
MacDiarmid, H.   Servant Girl's Bed.
Millay, E.   First Fig.
Second Fig.
Nemerov.   Flame of a Candle, The.
Piercy.   I Am A Light You Could Read By.
Plath.   By Candlelight.

Candles.
Rumi.   Just-Finishing Candle, A.
Seifert.   Wax Candle, The.
Stevens, W.   Valley Candle.
Suckling, S.   Candle, A.
Wilbur, R.   For K. R. on Her Sixtieth Birthday.

Candy
Broumas, O.   Sugar.
Ferlinghetti, L.   Pennycandystore beyond the El,
   The.
Nash, O.   Reflections on Ice-breaking.

Candy Stores
Ferlinghetti, L.   Pennycandystore beyond the El,
   The.

Cannibalism and Cannibals
Davie, D.   Cannibals.
Eberhart, R.   Explorer on Main Street, The.
MacNeice.   Thyestes.
Patchen.   Little Cannibal's Bedtimesong.
Rukeyser, M.   Cannibal Bratuscha.

Canning
Van Duyn.   Homework.

Canoes and Canoeing
Crane, S.   Lad and a maid at a curve in the
   stream, A.
O'Hara, F.   Terrestrial Cuckoo, A.
Oppen.   Travelogue.
Rexroth, K.   Floating.
Snyder, G.   Canyon Wren, The.
Warren, R.   Antinomy: Time and Identity.

Canonical Hours
Davie, D.   Horae Canonicae.

Canova, Antonio
Byron, G.   On the Bust of Helen by Canova.

Canyons
Logan, J.   Acapulco Canyon: Two
   Kodachromes.
Meredith, W.   Journal Entry (With the Udalls,
   June 1968).
Rexroth, K.   Mirror.

Cape Breton Island, Nova Scotia
Bishop, E.   Cape Breton.

Cape Cod, Massachusetts
Brodsky, J.   Lullaby of Cape Cod.
Creeley.   Provincetown.
Millay, E.   Memory of Cape Cod.
Schuyler, J.   Rose of Marion, The.
Swenson, M.   Early Morning: Cape Cod.

Capital Punishment
Jeffers, R.   Margrave.
Logue, C.   His case is typical.
   Lullaby.
MacDiarmid, H.   Facing the Chair.
Olson, C.   Willie Francis and the Electric Chair.
Plath.   Trial of Man, The.
Whittier.   Gallows, The.
   Human Sacrifice, The.
Williams, M.   Thanatopsis.
Wordsworth, W.   Sonnets upon the Punishment
   of Death.
See also **Executions and Executioners**

Capitalism
Bierce.   Political Economy.
Clampitt.   Hispaniola.
Codrescu.   Circle Jerk.
Cummings, E. E.   Memorabilia.
Emerson, R.   New England Capitalist.
   Since the devil hopping on.
Enzensberger, H.   Language of the Country.
Ginsberg, A.   Kral Majales.
Hughes, L.   God to Hungry Child.
   Goodbye Christ.
   To the Little Fort of San Lazaro on the Ocean
      Front, Havana.
   Wait.
   White Man.
Komunyakaa.   For You, Sweetheart, I'll Sell
   Plutonium Reactors.
Kunitz, S.   Economist's Song, The.
Larkin, P.   Homage to a Government.
Laughlin, J.   God Bless America!
   Market Discounts Love.
   Small Group, A.
Lawrence, D. H.   Always This Paying.

But I Say unto You: Love One Another.
   Cry of the Masses.
   For All That.
   Latent Desire, The.
   Love as an Escape.
   Money.
   Money-Madness.
   Mosquito Knows, The.
   Why—?
   Young Are Not Greedy, The.
Lux.   Haitian Cadavers.
   You Go To School To Learn.
MacDiarmid, H.   My Songs Are Kandym in the
   Waste Land.
MacLeish.   Empire Builders.
McGrath, T.   Vision of Three Angels Viewing
   the Progress of Socialism.
Meredith, G.   Capitalist, The.
   Song: "Buy, buy, buy, / Is the Peace-markt cry."
Merrill, J.   Clearing the Title.
Merton.   Proverbs.
   Songs of Experience; India, One.
Niedecker.   Van Gogh could see.
Olson, C.   Being Altogether Literal, & Specific.
Paley, G.   NOW.
Shapiro, K.   Drug Store.
   Humanities Building, The.
Simic.   Grocery.
Snyder, G.   Trade, The.
Williams, W.   Libertad! Igualdad! Fraternidad!
See also **Banking and Bankers; Business and
   Businessmen; Financiers**

Cappadocia
Brodsky, J.   Cappadocia.
Cavafy.   Dareios.
   Orophernis.
   Tyanan Sculptor.

Captivity
Cowper, W.   On a Goldfinch Starved to Death in
   His Cage.
De la Mare.   Bitter Waters.
   Captive, The.
Dickinson, E.   Prison gets to be a friend, A.
Dugan, A.   Prison Song.
Dunbar, P.   Sympathy.
Graves, R.   Moon's Tear, The.
Kipling, R.   Captive, The.
   Half-Ballad of Waterval.
Komunyakaa.   Under House Arrest.
Lawrence, D. H.   There Is No Way Out.
   Wild Things in Captivity.
Logan, J.   Pathological Case in Pliny, A.
MacLeish.   Captivity of the Fly.
Meredith, G.   Two Blackbirds, The.
Merwin.   Midnight in Early Spring.
   Passage.
Orr, G.   Cage, The.
Rich, A.   For a Sister.
Rukeyser, M.   Woman and Emblems.
Sidney, S.   Like as the Dove.
Smart, C.   On an Eagle Confined in a College-
   Court.
Stock, R.   Rose in Ice.
Very.   I Was Sick and in Prison.
Williams, C. K.   Souls.
Williams, T.   Sanctuary.
Wordsworth, W.   Gold and Silver Fishes in a
   Vase.
Zaturenska.   Strange Captivity.

Caravaggio, Michelangelo Merisi da
Gunn, T.   In Santa Maria del Popolo.
Pinkerton, H.   On Caravaggio's *Conversion of
   St. Paul* (1600) in Santa Maria del Popolo,
   Rome.

Card Games
Borges.   Truco.
Codrescu.   Partiti Sunt Vestimenta Mea Miserunt
   Sortem Contra Me ad Incarte Cla a Filii a
   Eniol Liebee Braya Braguesca et Belzebuth.
Davie, D.   Orvieto. The King of Clubs.
Dickey, W.   Face-Paintings of the Caduveo
   Indians.
Dove, R.   Sailor in Africa, The.
Duncan, R.   Poem in Stretching, A.
Graves, R.   Song: Sword and Rose.

Kinsella, T.   Hand of Solo, A.
Larkin, P.   Card-Players, The.
Nash, O.   Your Lead, Partner, I Hope We've
   Read the Same Book.
Parker, D.   Bridge Fiend, The.
Prunty.   Late Days.
Ritsos.   Cardplayers.
Rossetti, C.   House of cards / Is neat and small,
   A.
   Queen of Hearts, The.
Updike.   Solitaire.
Williams, M.   Caution.

Cardiff, Wales
Wordsworth, W.   When Severn's Sweeping
   Flood Had Overthrown.

Cardinals (ornithology)
Carruth, H.   Meditation in the Presence of
   "Ostrich Walk."
   Song: The Old, Old Man.
Schuyler, J.   Cardinal, A.

Cargoes
See **Freighters**

Caribbean Islands
Baudelaire.   To a Creole Lady.
See also **West Indies**

Caribbean Sea
Crane, H.   To the Empress Josephine's Statue.
Hughes, L.   Caribbean Sunset.
Jacobsen, J.   Reading on the Beach.
   Waking.
Merton.   Poem: "Here is the man of the
   islands."
Millay, E.   Dream of Saba.
Mistral, G.   Caribbean Sea.
Walcott.   Sea-Chantey, A.
See also **West Indies**

Caribou
Kumin, M.   With the Caribou.

Caring
De la Mare.   Mrs. Grundy.
Glück, L.   Portrait.
Graves, R.   Crucibles of Love.
   Should I Care.
   Song: How Can I Care?
   Virgin Mirror.
MacNeice.   Flight of the Heart.
Piercy.   Hand Games.
   In the Wet.
Rossetti, C.   Because He First Loved Us.
   Lord, carry me.—Nay, but I grant thee strength.
Stafford, W.   Remembering Brother Bob.
Wright, J.   Arrangements with Earth for Three
   Dead Friends.
   Mutterings Over the Crib of a Deaf Child.

Carlotta (empress of Mexico)
Wright, J.   Chapultepec Castle.

Carlyle, Thomas
Graves, R.   Something to Say.
Meredith, G.   To Carlyle.

Carmel, California
Hughes, L.   Moonlight Night: Carmel.
Jeffers, R.   Carmel.
   Carmel Point.
   Tor House.
Logan, J.   Carmel: Point Lobos.
Tate, J.   Failed Tribute to the Stonemason of Tor
   House, Robinson Jeffers.

Carnivals
Bishop, E.   Pink Dog.
Ginsberg, A.   Big Beat.
Gunn, T.   Before the Carnival.
Jacobsen, J.   Carney Elegy.
Major, C.   Theme of Carnevale is a secret, The.
Merrill, J.   Think Tank.
Montale.   Gerti's Carnival.
Nash, O.   Lecturer in Bookstore.
Prunty.   Rio.
Rich, A.   In Time of Carnival.
Tomlinson, C.   Portobello Carnival 1973.

Caroline of Ansbach
Sheridan, T.   Ode, An: "Early Queen of Light
   arise."

Carousels
Carver, R.   Brass Ring, The.

Swenson, M.   Still Turning.

See also **Merry-Go-Rounds**

Carp
Wright, J.   Lifting Illegal Nets by Flashlight.

Carpe Diem
Angelou.   Come, And Be My Baby.
Baudelaire.   Games of Chance.
Berrigan, T.   I Heard Brew Moore Say, One Day.
Browning, R.   Youth and Art.
Burns, R.   Here's, a bottle and an honest friend.
Hey Ca' thro'.
Sketch. New Year's Day. To Mrs. Dunlop.
Song: "My father was a farmer upon the Carrick border O."
Byron, G.   To Caroline.
Carew, T.   To A. L.; Persuasions [*or* Perswasions] to Love.
Corkine.   My Dearest Mistress.
Cowper, W.   Written in a Quarrel.
Creeley.   So There.
Cullen, C.   I Have a Rendezvous with Life.
Cummings, E. E.   For him alone life's worse than worst.
Granted the all / saving our young kiss only.
My Father Moved Through Dooms Of Love.
One's not half two. It's two are halves of one.
Ponder, darling, these busted statues.
Song: "But we've the may / (for you are in love)."
What freedom's not some under's mere above.
What If a Much of a Which of a Wind.
"Dario."   Autumn Poem, The.
Emerson, R.   Fame.
Fine presentiments controlled him.
Go boldly forth, and feast on being's banquet.
How drearily in College hall.
Frost, R.   Carpe Diem.
Hardy, T.   Best She Could, The.
Queen Caroline to Her Guests.
Herrick.   Anacreontic.
Best To Be Merry.
Corinna's Going a-Maying.
End Decreed, An.
Paranæticall, or Advisive Verse, to His Friend, M. John Wicks.
To Electra.
To Enjoy the Time.
To Live Freely.
To Sappho.
To Silvia to Wed.
To the Virgins, to Make Much of Time.
To Youth.
Hughes, L.   Song for a Banjo Dance.
Keats.   Fancy.
Lindsay, N.   Tiger on Parade, The.
MacLeish.   Speech to a Crowd.
Marlowe.   Passionate Shepherd to His Love, The.
Marvell.   To His Coy Mistress.
Young Love.
Melville, H.   Rosary Beads.
Merwin.   This Day of This Month of This Year of This.
Way to the River, The.
Millay, E.   I shall forget you presently, my dear.
Oliver, M.   Peonies.
Parker, D.   On Cheating the Fiddler.
Pessoa.   I the roses love in the gardens of Adonis.
Ralegh, S.   Nymph's [*or* Nimphs] Reply to the Shepherd [*or* Sheepheard], The.
Ransom, J.   Blue Girls.
Morning.
Old Man Playing with Children.
Rilke.   Dead, The.
Robinson, E.   Horace to Leuconoë.
Rossetti, C.   Maiden May.
Sandburg, C.   If So Hap May Be.
Moments of Dawn Riders.
Two Neighbors.
Tate, J.   South End.
Thoreau.   I seek the Present Time.
Williams, W.   Song: "Pluck the florets from."
Zaturenska.   Runaway, The.

Carpentry and Carpenters
Carver, R.   Powder-Monkey.
Chesterton.   Carpenter, The.
Davie, D.   With the Grain.
Dickinson, E.   Myself was formed—a Carpenter.
Props assist the House, The.
Jacobsen, J.   Trial Run.
Komunyakaa.   Apprenticeship.
Deck, The.
Oppen.   Carpenter's Boat.
Workman.
Szymborska, W.   Man's Household, A.
Wilbur, R.   Hole in the Floor, A.

Carpets
Rumi.   Put This Design in Your Carpet.

See also **Rugs and Carpets**

Carriages
Blok.   I Am Nailed to a Bar with Liquor.
Borges.   General Quiroga Rides to His Death in a Carriage.
Burns, R.   To the Honble Mr. R. M———, of P-nm-re, on His High Phaeton.
De la Mare.   Last Coachload, The.
McMichael.   Great Garret, or 100 Wheels, The.
Montale.   Near Capua.
Moore, M.   Carriage from Sweden, A.
Tomlinson, C.   Poem; "Wakening with the window over fields."

Cars
Amichai [*or* Amikhai].   First Rain on a Burned Car.
Carver, R.   Car, The.
Summer in Sacramento, A.
Clampitt.   Salvage.
Corbett, W.   February 29th.
Ignatow, D.   That's the Sum of It.
Major, C.   Being and Becoming.
Meredith, W.   Nixon's the One.
Oppen.   Closed car—closed in glass.
Evening, water in a glass, The.
Volkswagen.
Paley, G.   For Mike and Jeannie: Resisters Fifteen Years Later.
Warren, R.   Tires on Wet Asphalt at Night.
Williams, M.   Memphis, 2 P.M. [*or* 2:00 P.M.].

See also **Automobiles**

Cartoons
Riley, J.   Abe Martin.

Carts
Merwin.   Cart, The.
Ritsos.   Greek Cart-Drivers.

Carving and Carvers
Atwood.   Some Objects of Wood and Stone.
Chuang Tzu.   Woodcarver, The.
Davie, D.   On Generous Lines.
Priory of St Saviour, Glendalough, The.
Komunyakaa.   Lost Wax.
Pinkerton, H.   On the Virgin and Child Carved in Oak (Auvergne, 1150-1200) in the Metropolitan Museum.
Stafford, W.   They Carved an Animal.
Stock, R.   Dollmaker, The.
Sze.   Wood Whittler, The.

Cary, Sir Lucius
Jonson, B.   To the Immortal[l] Memory [*or* Memorie] and Friendship of That Noble Pair[e], Sir Lucius Cary and Sir H. [*or* Henry] Morison.

Casanova, Giovanni
Seifert.   Grave of Signor Casanova, The.

Casement, Roger David
Yeats.   Ghost of Roger Casement, The.
Roger Casement.

Cassady, Neal
Ginsberg, A.   Elegy for Neal Cassady.
Green Automobile, The.
Many Loves.
On Neal's Ashes.

Cassandra
Bogan, L.   Cassandra.
Heaney, S.   Mycenae Lookout.
Jeffers, R.   Cassandra.
Tower beyond Tragedy, The.
Meredith, G.   Cassandra.

Ritsos.   Actual Cause, The.
Robinson, E.   Cassandra.
Rossetti, D.   Cassandra.
Szymborska, W.   Soliloquy for Cassandra.

Caste Systems, Indian
Dubie.   Caste Wife Speaks to the Enigmatic Parabolas, The.

Castile
See **Spain**

Castlereagh, Robert Stewart, 2d Viscount
Byron, G.   Epigrams: "Oh, Castlereagh! thou art a patriot now."
Shelley, P.   Similes for Two Political Characters of 1819.

Castles
Borges.   Palace, The.
Parable of the Palace.
Brontë, E.   Written in Aspin Castle.
Burns, R.   Castle Gordon—*Intended to Be Sung to Morag*.
Lines on Stirling.
Cummings, E. E.   My love is building a building.
Graves, R.   Castle, The.
Hacker, M.   Celles.
Hopkins, G.   Escorial, The.
Jackson, L.   No More Are Lovely Palaces.
Kinsella, T.   King John's Castle.
Levertov.   Psalm Concerning the Castle.
Major, C.   See that stern castle?
Merwin.   Service.
Poe.   Haunted Palace, The.
Smith, S.   Castle, The.
Tomlinson, C.   Château de Muzot.
Legend.
Wilbur, R.   Castles and Distances.
Wordsworth, W.   Address to Kilchurn Castle, upon Loch Awe.
Bothwell Castle.
Composed among the Ruins of a Castle in North Wales.
Elegiac Stanzas Suggested by a Picture of Peele Castle, in a Storm, Painted by Sir George Beaumont.
Fragment of a "Gothic" Tale.
Horn of Egremont Castle, The.
Vale of Esthwaite, The.
Wright, J.   Chapultepec Castle.
Inside Chapultepec Castle.
Yeats.   Blood and the Moon.
Zagajewski.   Castle.
Zaturenska.   Terraces of Light.

Castration
Jeffers, R.   Oysters.

Castriot, George
See **Savonarola, Girolamo**

Castro, Fidel
Updike.   Meditation on a News Item.

Catalpa Trees
Ciardi, J.   Catalpa, The.

Catbirds
Creeley.   Air: "Cat Bird Singing."
Swenson, M.   Catbird in Redbud.

Catechism
Emerson, R.   We sauntered amidst miracles.
Stafford, W.   Catechism, A.

Caterpillars
Bly, R.   Caterpillar, A.
Dickinson, E.   Caterpillar.
Emerson, R.   Have ye seen the caterpillar.
Hughes, T.   In the Likeness of a Grasshopper.
Kunitz, S.   Hornworm: Autumn Lamentation.
Hornworm: Summer Reverie.
Ritsos.   Deterioration.
Rossetti, C.   Caterpillar, The.
Very.   Worm, The.
Williams, M.   Caterpillar, The.

Cathedrals
Borges.   Two Cathedrals, The.
Carrera Andrade.   Weathercock on the Cathedral of Quito, The.
Ciardi, J.   Cathedral.
Crane, S.   There was a great cathedral.
Davie, D.   At the Synod in St Patrick's.

Hardy, T.   Abbey Mason, The.
   Cathedral Façade at Midnight, A.
   In a Cathedral City.
Major, C.   In Salute again.
Melville, H.   Milan Cathedral.
Montale.   Leaving a Dove.
Oppen.   Chartres.
Rukeyser, M.   Evening Plaza, San Miguel.
Seifert.   Place of Pilgrimage.
Shapiro, K.   Cathedral Bells, The.
Stock, R.   Cathedral, The.
Williams, W.   New Cathedral Overlooking the
   Park, The.
Zagajewski.   Gothic, The.

Cather, Willa
Cooper, J.   Vocation: A Life: *Suite Based on
   Four Words from Willa Cather*.
Rich, A.   For Julia in Nebraska.

Catherine of Siena, Saint
Cunningham, J.   Wandering Scholar's Prayer to
   St. Catherine of Egypt, The.
Dove, R.   Catherine of Siena.
Logan, J.   Lines to Catherine.
Rilke.   Saint Catherine.

Catholicism and Catholics
Apollinaire.   Zone.
Browning, R.   Holy-Cross Day.
Ciardi, J.   Apartment with a View, An.
   Evil Eye, The.
Coleridge, S.   Sancti Dominici Pallium.
Cummings, E. E.   Candles and / Here Comes a
   glass box.
Dryden, J.   Swallow, privileged above the rest,
   The.
Eliot, T. S.   Hippopotamus, The.
García Lorca.   Cry to Rome.
   Ode to the Most Holy Sacrament of the Altar.
   Spinster at Mass, The.
Graves, R.   Cuirassiers of the Frontier, The.
Herbert, G.   To the Lady Elizabeth Queen of
   Bohemia.
Hughes, T.   Martyrdom of Bishop Farrar, The.
Jacobsen, J.   Chosen, The.
   Non Sum Dignus.
Kinnell.   Avenue Bearing the Initial of Christ
   into the New World, The.
Lawrence, D. H.   Church, The.
Levertov.   Conversion of Brother Lawrence.
Logan, J.   Cycle for Mother Cabrini, A.
   Middle-Aged Midwesterner at Waikiki Again.
   Month of Saints, A.
   Spring of the Thief.
   Wooden Mirror, The.
Lowell, R.   Beyond the Alps.
   For George Santayana.
   Thanksgiving's Over.
Lux.   Sex in History.
Milosz, C.   Helene's Religion.
Patchen.   Palms for a Catholic Child.
Robinson, E.   Erasmus.
Schuyler, J.   I Sit Down to Type.
   Mark.
Stock, R.   Dollmaker, The.
Tomlinson, C.   On a Mexican Straw Christ.
Whittier.   Pastoral Letter, The.
Wilde, O.   Sonnet on Hearing the *Dies Iræ* Sung
   in the Sistine Chapel.
Williams, M.   Note to God Concerning a Point
   from an Earlier Communication, A.
Williams, W.   Catholic Bells, The.
   Light Becomes Darkness.

Cats
Baudelaire.   Cat.
   Cat, The.
   Cats.
Bierce.   In Memoriam.
Bishop, E.   Lullaby for the Cat.
Borges.   Beppo.
   To a Cat.
Bourne, V.   Familiarity Dangerous.
Bukowski.   History of a Tough Motherfucker,
   The.
   I Was Born to Hustle Roses Down the Avenues
   of the Dead.
   Little Tigers Everywhere.
   One for the Old Boy.

Terminology.
Cavafy.   Cat, The.
Celan.   By Threes, By Fours.
Ciardi, J.   Damn Her.
   On Being Sure and of What.
Clampitt.   Spruce Has No Taproot, The.
   Townhouse Interior with Cat.
Codrescu.   Howdy.
Cowper, W.   Colubriad, The.
   Retired Cat, The.
Crane, H.   Chaplinesque.
Creeley.   Love ("Thing comes, The").
Cummings, E. E.   Float / ing / ly) / i / (in
   Khoury's warm).
   (Im)c-a-t(mo).
   Why did you go.
De la Mare.   Comfort.
   Maerchen.
Dickey, W.   Lady of Shalott, Her Mirror Broken,
   The.
Dickinson, E.   Cat.
Dubie.   In the Dead of the Night.
Dugan, A.   Another Cat Poem: A Cat Is Not a
   Dancer but a Hunter.
   Another Cat Poem. To a Cat Person.
   Note.
   On a Desolation of the Animals at Night.
   Why There Is No Class Solidarity in America I
   Read It In *The Times*. Aug. 2, 1987.
Eberhart, R.   Concord Cats.
   Key West.
   Old Tom.
   Vastness and Indifference of the World, The.
Emerson, R.   Comfort with a purring cat.
Ferlinghetti, L.   Cat, The.
Graves, R.   Frightened Men.
Gray, T.   Ode on the Death of a Favourite [*or*
   Favorite] Cat, Drowned in a Tub [*or* Bowl] of
   Gold Fishes.
Gunn, T.   Apartment Cats.
   Cat and the Wind, The.
Hall, D.   Alligator Bride, The.
Hardy, T.   Last Words To a Dumb Friend.
   Roman Gravemounds, The.
Herrick.   Upon Pusse and her Prentice.
Hughes, L.   Little Cats.
Hughes, T.   Cat and Mouse.
   Esther's Tomcat.
Jackson, L.   Further Details.
Jacobsen, J.   Reading Aloud at Dusk.
Jarrell, R.   Happy Cat, The.
   Lonely Man, The.
Keats.   To a Cat.
Kinnell.   Cat, The.
Kizer, C.   Italian Kittens, The.
   Widow in Wintertime, A.
Komunyakaa.   Charmed.
Laughlin, J.   Kenners' Cat, The.
   Through many nights of many years invincible.
Levertov.   Cat as Cat, The.
   Catpig, The.
Levine, P.   Theory of Prosody, A.
Lindsay, N.   Dirge for a Righteous Kitten, A.
   Mysterious Cat, The.
MacLeish.   Cat in the Wood, The.
Major, C.   Old woman comes, The.
McHugh, H.   Place Where Things Got.
Merrill, J.   Maisie.
Merwin.   Cat Ghosts.
Milosz, C.   Portrait with a Cat, A.
   To Mrs. Professor in Defense of My Cat's
   Honor and Not Only.
Moore, M.   Peter.
Nash, O.   Cat Naps Are Too Good for Cats.
   Kitten, The.
Oliver, M.   Morning.
Olson, C.   Not a rat-hole, a cat-hole: the knife of
   time; on the ledge, overlooking.
Pessoa.   Cat, you tumble down the street.
Piercy.   Cats of Greece, The.
   I Awoke with the Room Cold.
Plath.   Ella Mason and Her Eleven Cats.
Prunty.   Eyeing the World.
Riley, J.   Find the Favorite.
Rilke.   Cat.
Rossetti, C.   On the Death of a Cat.

Pussy has a whiskered face, / Kitty has such
   pretty ways.
Sandburg, C.   Three Slants at New York.
Shelley, P.   Verses on a Cat.
Smart, C.   Jubilate Agno.
Smith, S.   Cat Asks Mouse Out.
   Celtic Fringe, The.
   Conviction (iii).
   Friskers, or, Gods and Men.
   Galloping Cat, The.
   Monsieur Pussy-Cat, Blackmailer.
   My Cat Major.
   My Cats.
   Nipping Pussy's Feet in Fun.
   Nodding.
   Our Office Cat.
   Singing Cat, The.
Stock, R.   May Morning Admonition.
Swenson, M.   Beast.
Swift, J.   Fable of the Widow and Her Cat, A.
Szymborska, W.   Cat in an Empty Apartment.
Tomlinson, C.   Annunciation.
Unknown.   Myself and Pangur.
Updike.   Daughter.
Van Duyn.   At Père Lachaise.
Warren, R.   What Was the Throught.
Weiss, T.   Making It.
Whalen, P.   Congress of Vienna, The.
   Walking beside the Kamogawa, Remembering
   Nansen and Fudo and Gary's Poem.
Williams, W.   Cats' Month, The.
   Complete Destruction.
   Mujer.
   Poem: "As the cat."
   Young Cat and the Chrysanthemums, The.
Yeats.   Cat and the Moon, The.
   Two Songs of a Fool.
See also **Kittens**

Cattle
Glück, L.   Thanksgiving.
Han-shan.   Don't stay poor my friend.
Hardy, T.   Bags of Meat.
Herrick.   Bucolick betwixt Two: Lacon and
   Thyrsis, A.
Hughes, T.   Birth of Rainbow.
   March Calf, A.
Jeffers, R.   Wind-Struck Music, The.
Kipling, R.   Lament of the Border Cattle Thief,
   The.
   Mulholland's Contract.
McHugh, H.   Just Man.
Merwin.   In a Clearing.
Muldoon, P.   Cherish the Ladies.
See also **Bulls; Cowboys; Cows; Meat**

Catullus
Campion, T.   De Catullo et Martiale.
   In Cambrum.
Davie, D.   Catullus on Friendship.
Laughlin, J.   Can Language Be Taught with the
   Fingertips?
   Technical Notes.
MacLeish.   You Also, Gaius Valerius Catullus.
Millay, E.   Passer Mortuus Est.
Parker, D.   From a Letter from Lesbia.
Tennyson, A.   Frater Ave Atque Vale.
Zukofsky, L.   Catullus viii.
   In the midst of things.

Caution
Browning, E.   Wisdom Unapplied.
Bukowski.   Counsel.
Creeley.   First Time, The.
   For Benny and Sabina.
   I Know a Man.
Cullen, C.   Advice to a Beauty.
   To a Brown Girl.
Eberhart, R.   Scouring, The.
Hacker, M.   Adult Entertainment.
Herrick.   Safety on the Shore.
   Safety to Look to Ones Selfe.
Jacobsen, J.   Lines to a Poet.
Kumin, M.   You Are in Bear Country.
Kunitz, S.   So Intricately Is This World
   Resolved.
Meredith, G.   England before the Storm.
   'Tis good to keep hinderward eyes.

Nash, O.   Strange Case of the Cautious
   Motorist, The.
Piercy.   Girl in White.
Roethke.   Monotony Song, The.
Stock, R.   Certain Pretexts.
Williams, M.   Caution.
Williams, T.   Look Both Ways Crossing Streets.
Yeats.   Never Give All the Heart.

Cavafy, Constantine P.
Hamill, S.   Photograph of Kavafis, A.
Ritsos.   After Death.
   Evaluation.
   Final Hour.
   His Glasses.
   His Lamp toward Daybreak.
   Misunderstandings.
   On Form.
   Places of Refuge.
   Poet's Space, The.
   Putting out the Lamp.

Cavalcanti, Guido
Cino da Pistoia.   Sonnet: He owes nothing to
   Guido as a Poet.
Dante Alighieri.   Guido, I would like that you
   and Lapo and I.
O'Hara, F.   Poem in Envy of Cavalcanti, A.
Pound, E.   To Guido Cavalcanti.

Cavaliers
Browning, R.   Cavalier Tunes.
Herrick.   His Cavalier.

Cavalry
Brooks, G.   Riders to the Blood-Red Wrath.
Housman.   Lancer.
   Soldier from the wars returning.
Riley, J.   King, The.
Tennyson, A.   Charge of the Light Brigade, The.
Whitman, W.   Cavalry Crossing a Ford.

Cavemen
Kipling, R.   King, The.
   Story of Ung, The.
Mahon.   Hunt by Night, The.
Pagis.   Caveman Is Not about to Talk, The.
Rukeyser, M.   Painters.
Stafford, W.   At Lascaux.
   They Carved an Animal.
Szymborska, W.   Cave, The.
See also **Man, Primitive**

Caves
Coleridge, S.   Catullian Hendecasyllables.
Gunn, T.   Merlin in the Cave: He Speculates
   without a Book.
Hall, D.   Child, The.
Jeffers, R.   Hands.
Kinsella, T.   Survivor.
Komunyakaa.   Memory Cave.
Logan, J.   Big Sur: Partington Cove.
Major, C.   Clay Bison in a Cave.
Merwin.   Bread.
   Son.
Olson, C.   On All Sides.
Patchen.   Irkalla's White Caves.
Pinsky.   Spelunker.
Pope, A.   On His Grotto at Twickenham.
Rukeyser, M.   Ajanta.
Stafford, W.   At Lascaux.
   Cave Painting.
   Indian Cave Jerry Ramsey Found, The.
   Indian Caves in the Dry Country.
   Our Cave.
   They Carved an Animal.
Szymborska, W.   Cave, The.
Tomlinson, C.   Cavern, The.
Warren, R.   Speleology.
Williams, W.   Avenue of Poplars, The.
Wilner, E.   Bat Cave.
Wordsworth, W.   Suggested by Mr W. Westall's
   Views of the Caves, etc., in Yorkshire.
   To the Lady Mary Lowther.

Caviar
Williams, W.   For Viola: De Gustibus.

Cecilia, Saint
Auden.   Anthem for St. Cecilia's Day.
Crane, H.   Sonnet: "Ere elfish Night shall sift
   another day."
Davie, D.   Nashville Mornings.

Dryden, J.   Alexander's Feast; or, The Power of
   Music [*or* Musique].
   Song for St Cecilia's Day, 1687, A.
Dugan, A.   Northern Statement for St. Cecilia.
Pope, A.   Ode for Music on St. Cecilia's Day.

Celan, Paul
Dubie.   Anagram Born of Madness at
   Czernowitz, 23 November 1920.
Zagajewski.   Good Friday in the Tunnels of the
   Métro.

Celandine
Wordsworth, W.   Small Celandine, The.
   To the Same Flower [The Small Celandine].
   To the Small Celandine.

Celery
Nash, O.   Celery.
Updike.   Celery.

Celibacy
Bukowski.   Almost Made Up Poem, An.
Ciardi, J.   Censorship.
Graves, R.   Starred Coverlet, The.
Lowell, R.   Like Henry VIII, Mohammed got
   religion.
Nash, O.   Tune for an Ill-Tempered Clavichord.
Ramanujan.   Pleasure.
See also **Bachelors; Virginity and Virgins**

Cellars
Gunn, T.   Bringing to Light.
Kumin, M.   In the Root Cellar.
Lux.   Cellar Stairs.
Roethke.   Root Cellar.

Cellos
Dugan, A.   Lament for Cellists and Jacqueline
   DuPré.
Kinnell.   Cellist, The.
Zagajewski.   Cello.

Celts
MacDiarmid, H.   Wreck of the *Swan*, The.
Smith, S.   Celts, The.

Cemeteries
Auden.   Island Cemetery, An.
Beckett, S.   Ne manquez pas à Tanger.
Berry, W.   Meadow, The.
Bierce.   Presentiment.
Borges.   Recoleta Cemetary.
Cardozo.   Cemetery of Childhood.
Carver, R.   Ask Him.
   In Switzerland.
Cavafy.   In the Cemetery.
Clampitt.   Highgate Cemetery.
Creeley.   I.
Cummings, E. E.   Allbutnotquitemost.
   One / t / hi / s / snowflake.
Dickinson, E.   Cemetery, A.
   Chilly Peace infests the Grass, A.
   Where every bird is bold to go.
Dubie.   Baptismal.
Eberhart, R.   Soul Longs to Return Whence It
   Came, The.
Frost, R.   Home Burial.
García Lorca.   Jewish Cemetery.
Gray, T.   Elegy Written in a Country
   Churchyard.
Hardy, T.   Friends Beyond.
   Levelled Churchyard, The.
   Merrymaking in Question, A.
   Paying Calls.
   Sexton at Longpuddle, The.
   Supplanter, The.
   Voices from Things Growing in a Churchyard.
   While Drawing in a Churchyard.
Hill, G.   Distant Fury of Battle, The.
Housman.   God's Acre.
   Hughley Steeple.
Ignatow, D.   Here I Am.
Keats.   On Visiting the Tomb of Burns.
Kipling, R.   King's Pilgrimage, The.
Lawrence, D. H.   Giorno dei Morti.
Levertov.   Hidden Monsters at the Mount
   Auburn Cemetery. A Found Poem.
Levine, P.   Cemetery at Academy, California,
   The.
Longfellow, H.   Jewish Cemetery at Newport,
   The.
Lowell, R.   Dunbarton.

Quaker Graveyard in Nantucket, The.
Lux.   Graveyard by the Sea.
McGrath, T.   Poem: "Light flares from the
   tombstones...."
McHugh, H.   Kind of Poor.
Melo Neto.   Cemetery in Pernambuco: Our Lady
   of Light.
Meredith, W.   English Accounts.
Merton.   Trappist Cemetery—Gethsemani, The.
Milosz, C.   Abode.
   Powers.
Montale.   Voice That Came with the Coots.
Nemerov.   Negro Cemetery Next to a White
   One, A.
Oppen.   Eros.
Piercy.   Visiting a Dead Man on a Summer Day.
Rexroth, K.   Again at Waldheim.
Riley, J.   At Crown Hill.
Rilke.   Cemetary in Flaach.
   Cemetary in Ragaz.
Ritsos.   Statues in the Cemeteries, The.
Rossetti, C.   Birchington Churchyard.
Rukeyser, M.   Trinity Churchyard.
Sandburg, C.   Cool Tombs.
   Trinity Place.
Schuyler, J.   In a Churchyard.
Seifert.   Lost Paradise.
Simonides.   On a Military Graveyard.
Smith, S.   Edmonton, Thy Cemetery.
   English Visitor, The.
   Great Unaffected Vampires and the Moon.
   Night-Time in the Cemetery.
   Out of Time.
Swenson, M.   Trinity Churchyard, Spring 1961.
Tate, A.   Ode to the Confederate Dead.
Tomlinson, C.   After a Death.
   Ice Cream at Blauenberg.
Updike.   Plow Cemetery.
Vallejo.   Our Daily Bread.
Van Duyn.   At Père Lachaise.
Very.   Cemetery of Harmony Grove, The.
   Lines on the Old Danvers Burying Ground.
Warren, R.   Evening Hour.
Whitman, W.   Camps of Green.
   Ode: "O, God of Columbia! O, Shield of the
     Free!"
Whittier.   Hive at Gettysburg, The.
   Old Burying-Ground, The.
Wilbur, R.   In a Churchyard.
Williams, W.   Children, The.
   For a Low Voice.
   On First Opening the Lyric Year.
Wilner, E.   On Ethnic Definitions.
Wordsworth, W.   Elegiac Stanzas Composed in
   the Churchyard of Grasmere.
   Place of Burial in the South of Scotland, A.
Wright, J.   Albuquerque Graveyard, The.
   Three Steps to the Graveyard.
   Way to Make a Living, A.
See also **Burial; Graves; Mausoleums; Tombs**

Censorship
Bishop, E.   Word with You, A.
Donne.   Raderus.
Dugan, A.   Mockery Against the Irish
   Censorship.
Laughlin, J.   Somewhere in France.
Lawrence, D. H.   13 Pictures.
   Auto-Da-Fé.
   Broadcasting to the G.B.P.
   Censors.
   Innocent England.
Major, C.   Gallup Swill-Hole, A; or, Cantina
   Blues.
Nash, O.   Invocation: "Senator Smoot
   (Republican, Ut.)."
   Legal Reflection.
Ritsos.   They.
   Transposition.
Swift, J.   On Censure.

Centaurs
"Dario."   Colloquy of the Centaurs.
Palimpsest: "Written in an old Aeolian dialect."
Muldoon, P.   Centaurs, The.
Swenson, M.   Centaur, The.
Williams, C. K.   Hercules, Deianira, Nessus.
Wilner, E.   Having Eaten of the Tree of

Knowledge.
Yeats. On a Picture of a Black Centaur by Edmund Dulac.
Zaturenska. Reflections On a Centaur.

Centipedes
Dove, R. Centipede.
Nash, O. Centipede, The.

Central America
Dubie. Nine Black Poppies for Chac.
See also **Latin America and Latin Americans**

Central Park, New York City
Ferlinghetti, L. Sherman's March Reglitterized.
Lowell, R. Central Park.
Nemerov. Central Park.
Pagis. Central Park, Twilight.
Rukeyser, M. From the Duck-Pond to the Carousel.
Schuyler, J. Dining Out with Doug and Frank.
Tomlinson, C. In Verdi Square.

Ceremonial Songs (genre)
See **Wedding Songs**

Ceres
See **Demeter**

Cereus, Night-blooming
Hayden, R. Night-Blooming Cereus, The.
Merton. Night-Flowering Cactus.

Certainty
Creeley. Down Home.
For a Friend.
For Somebody's Marriage.
Je Vois dans le Hasard Tous les Biens Que J'espere.
Kate's.
Persons.
Cullen, C. Brown Boy to Brown Girl.
Jeffers, R. Nova.
Kinsella, T. Land of Loss, The.
Korn. Keep Hidden from Me.
Laughlin, J. Interdiction, The.
MacNeice. Greyness Is All.
Williams, T. Old Men Are Fond.

Cervantes Saavedra, Miguel de
Borges. Parable of Cervantes and Don Quixote.
Readers.
Soldier of Urbina, A.

Ceylon
See **Sri Lanka**

Cézanne, Paul
Ciardi, J. Cézanne.
Komunyakaa. Cubism.
Major, C. Atelier Cézanne.
In Walked Bud with a Palette.
Rexroth, K. Aix-en-Provence.
Tomlinson, C. Cézanne at Aix.
Williams, W. Cézanne.
Delicacies, The.

Chagall, Marc
Ferlinghetti, L. Don't Let That Horse.
Maritain. Chagall.

Chainmail
Corbett, W. Lines Written After Reading Frank O'Hara's "A Step Away from Them."
Dickey, J. Lakes of Värmland.

Chairs
Hardy, T. Garden Seat, The.
Heaney, S. Poet's Chair.
Kipling, R. My Father's Chair.
Neruda. All Seated.
Sitting Down.
Pagis. Bestiary.
Rimbaud, A. Seated.
Roethke. Chair, The.
Simic. Chairs.
Tate, J. Trap, The.
Whittier. Legend of the Lake, A.

Chameleons
Levertov. Wanderer, The.
Moore, M. To a Chameleon.

Champions
Dickey, J. Olympian, The.

Chance
Amichai [*or* Amikhai]. Almost a Love Poem.
Let the Coin Decide.
Same Embroidery, the Same Pattern, The.

Ammons. Raft.
Beckett, S. À l'instant de s'entendre dire.
Blake, W. If you play a Game of Chance know before you begin.
Borges. For a Version of *I Ching*.
Things That Might Have Been.
Carew, T. Dart, The.
Carver, R. Don't Run.
Codrescu. Secret Training.
Creeley. Business, The.
Conspiracy, The.
Epigraph: "Lot's wife, / married to chance."
Happy love, this.
Place, The ("What is the form is the gro- / tesquerie—the accident").
Song: "Those rivers run from that land."
Davie, D. Prolific Spell, The.
Graves, R. Pandora.
Hardy, T. Philosophical Fantasy, A.
Herrick. Casualties.
Large Bounds Doe but Bury Us.
Jeffers, R. Stone Axe, The.
Levine, P. Theory of Prosody, A.
Lindsay, N. Tiger on Parade, The.
Mallarmé. Throw of the Dice, A.
Meredith, W. Accidents of Birth.
Nash, O. Don't Look for the Silver Lining, Just Wait for It.
Nemerov. Sonnet: "It seems to be the trouble, everyone."
Orr, G. Paradise.
River, The.
Palmer, M. Fractal Song.
Pinsky. Ginza Samba.
Rukeyser, M. Willkie—Stopless Falling through Air.
Sandburg, C. If So Hap May Be.
Sarton, M. Strangers.
Shapiro, K. Pigeons, The.
Simic. Elementary Cosmogony.
Tomb of Stéphane Mallarmé, The.
Szymborska, W. In Abundance.
Love at First Sight.
Séance.
Tomlinson, C. Chance.
Unknown. Circumstance.
Warren, R. Blessèd Accident.
Williams, M. Believing in Symbols.
Wyatt, S. He is not de[a]d that sometime [*or* somtyme] hath a fall.
Varium et Mutabile.
See also **Fate; Fortune**

Change
Amichai [*or* Amikhai]. Caffè Dante in New York—3.
Evening hours of the soul.
Ammons. Equinox.
Angelou. Changes.
In Retrospect.
To a Man.
Atwood. Eventual Proteus.
She Considers Evading Him.
Wereman, The.
Auden. As I Walked Out One Evening.
Change of Air, A.
Dark Years, The.
Forty Years On.
Prologue at Sixty.
Shock, A.
Berry, W. Awake at Night.
Dance, The.
Goods.
Meeting, The.
Old Elm Tree by the River, The.
Recognition, The.
Traveling at Home.
Borges. Clouds ("There cannot be a single thing which is").
Northern Suburb.
Brodsky, J. So Forth.
Broumas, O. Sea Change.
Browning, E. Change Upon Change.
Island, An.
Browning, R. Prologue: "Poet's age is sad: for why?, The."
Bukowski. On Being 20.

Reunion.
Sardines in Striped Dresses.
Take It.
Burns, R. Extempore.
Song: "Let not Woman e'er complain."
Carew, T. Persuasions to Enjoy.
Upon Some Alterations in My Mistress, after My Departure into France.
Char. At the Gates of Aerea.
Chuang Tzu. Active Life.
Autumn Floods.
Clampitt. Nothing Stays Put.
Clough. July's Farewell.
Coleridge, S. Constancy to an Ideal Object.
Duty Surviving Self-Love.
Pang More Sharp Than All, The.
Cowper, W. On the Shortness of Life.
To a Friend in Distress.
Yardley Oak.
Creeley. Change.
Diction.
For Love.
Littleton, N.H.
Rain (2).
Surgeons.
Cummings, E. E. As freedom is a breakfastfood.
As is the sea marvelous.
If seventy were young / and death uncommon.
Metamorphosis.
My mind is.
Think of it:not so long ago.
You are like the snow only.
You are not going to,dear. You are not going to and.
Cunningham, J. Haecceity.
Davie, D. Mustered into the Avant-Garde.
De la Mare. Looking Glass, The.
Dickinson, E. At Half past Three, a single Bird.
Changelessness / is Nature's change.
He touched me, so I live to know.
Sic transit gloria mundi.
We outgrow love like other things.
Dove, R. Jiving.
Ö.
Straw Hat.
Sunday Greens.
Wingfoot Lake.
Dugan, A. From Heraclitus.
Poem: "Whatever was living is dead."
Dunbar, P. Change Has Come, The.
Eberhart, R. Haystack, The.
Inchiquin Lake, Penobscot Bay.
Nothing But Change.
Redemption.
Stopping a Kaleidoscope.
Tobacconist of Eighth Street, The.
Emerson, R. Amulet, The.
Holidays.
Once the priest / Lived in an age.
Proteus.
To Ellen, at the South.
Frost, R. Directive.
Nothing Gold Can Stay.
Ginsberg, A. Brooklyn College Brain.
Complaint of the Skeleton to Time.
Understand That This Is a Dream.
Glück, L. Cottonmouth Country.
Here Are My Black Clothes.
Graves, R. Change.
Finding of Love, The.
Freehold.
Good Night to the Old Gods.
If No Cuckoo Sings.
Gunn, T. Rites of Passage.
Words.
Gurney, I. Autumn.
Change, The.
Hacker, M. Letter from Goose Creek: April.
Rooms in Bloomsbury.
Hall, D. Exile.
"King and Queen."
Love Is Like Sounds.
September Ode.
Tree and the Cloud, The.
Wedding Party.

Han-shan. Seasonal round never stops, The.
There is no limit to changes.
Hardy, T. According to the Mighty Working.
Ancient to Ancients, An.
Chimes, The.
Going and Staying.
His Visitor.
In a Former Resort after Many Years.
Jubilee of a Magazine, The.
Man Who Forgot, The.
Night of Questionings, A.
Places.
Second Visit, The.
Starlings on the Roof.
Temporary the All, The.
There Seemed a Strangeness.
Voice of Things, The.
Where They Lived.
Hayden, R. Full Moon.
Theme and Variation.
Herrick. Change Common to All.
Change Gives Content.
Fair[e] Days; or, Dawn[e]s Deceitful[l].
Hope Well and Have Well: or, Faire after Foule
Weather.
Impossibilities to His Friend.
Speake in Season.
Upon Judith.
Upon Shift.
Upon Skrew.
Upon Trap.
Housman. Oh, When I Was In Love.
Hughes, L. Dear Lovely Death.
Jacobsen, J. Fire Will Not Change.
Jarrell, R. In Montecito.
Old orchard in the middle of the forest, The.
Street Has Changed, The.
Jeffers, R. Beaks of Eagles, The.
Diagram.
Summer Holiday.
Jonson, B. Epistle. To Katharine, Lady
Aubigny.
Keats. After Dark Vapours Have Oppressed Our
Plains.
Bright Star.
Kinnell. Lost Loves.
Kipling, R. Our Fathers Also.
Three-Decker, The.
Truthful Song, The.
Very Many People.
Lawrence, D. H. Breath of Life, The.
Change.
For All That.
Phoenix.
Stop It.
Levine, P. Later Still.
New Season.
Lindsay, N. To Reformers in Despair.
Logan, J. Bridge of Change, The.
Logue, C. O come all ye faithful.
Lux. Beneath the Apple Branches Bent
Dumbly.
Postcard to Baudelaire.
MacNeice. Breaking Webs.
Figure of Eight.
Half Truth from Cape Town.
Hiatus.
Mutations.
Perdita.
Precursors.
Snow.
Trains in the Distance.
Mahon. Heraclitus on Rivers.
Merton. Ode to the Present Century.
Merwin. Whenever I Go There.
Milosz, C. Rivers Grow Small.
Montale. Green lizard, if it darts, The.
Nash, O. That's Funny, Wasn't It? No, It Won't
Be.
To Ee Is Human.
Two Goes into Two Once, If You Can Get It
There.
Nemerov. Dependencies, The.
First Leaf, The.
Midsummer's Day.
Paraphrase from Notebooks.

Situation Does Not Change, The.
Western Approaches, The.
Oliver, M. Snowshoe Hare, The.
Olson, C. In Cold Hell, in Thicket.
Kingfishers, The.
Other Than.
Pagis. Encounters.
Parker, D. Nocturne: "Always I knew that it
could not last."
Transition.
Patchen. My Generation Reading the
Newspapers.
That We Here Highly Resolve.
When the stones burst into flame.
Pessoa. Christmas.
Piercy. Sign.
Twelve-Spoked Wheel Flashing, The.
Valley Where I Don't Belong, A.
Wind is the Wall of the Year.
Pope, A. Epistle [II,] to a Lady[: Of the
Characters of Women].
Prunty. March.
Razed House, The.
Raine, K. Cloud.
High Summer.
Sphere, The.
Rexroth, K. Motto on the Sundial, The.
Rich, A. 7/12/68.
7/13/68.
7/14/68: i.
7/16/68: i.
7/16/68: ii.
7/26/68: i.
7/26/68: II.
8/1/68.
8/8/68: i.
8/8/68: ii.
August fourth nineteen sixty eight.
Change of World, A.
For Julia in Nebraska.
Ghazals: Homage to Ghalib.
In the Evening.
July seventeenth nineteen sixty eight.
Marriage in the 'Sixties, A.
Necessities of Life.
Phenomenology of Anger, The.
Prospective Immigrants Please Note.
Walk by the Charles, A.
Ritsos. Alterations.
Robinson, E. Ballade of Broken Flutes.
Villanelle of Change.
Rossetti, C. Along the highroad the way is too
long.
From Mestastasio.
Half Moon Shows a Face of Plaintive
Sweetness, The.
In Progress.
Rukeyser, M. Everything here is real and of our
joy.
Jetty. Dover, The.
Not leaves, not lightning, not the greatness of
rivers.
Now that the river has changed, my dear.
Sandburg, C. Blacklisted.
Eleventh Avenue Racket.
First Sonata for Karlen Paula.
Languages.
Lesson.
Man the Moon Shooter.
Moon Hammock.
New Weather.
Sarton, M. Ballad of the Sixties.
First Autumn, The.
On a Winter Night.
Shelley, P. Lament, A: "O world! O life! O
time!"
Lines: "When the lamp is shattered [or
shatter'd]."
Mutability.
Smith, S. Grange, The.
Snyder, G. Pine River.
Stafford, W. Looking for Someone.
Szymborska, W. Reality Demands.
Thoreau. He knows no change who knows the
true.
Tomlinson, C. Letter from Costa Brava.

Northern Spring.
One World.
Process, A.
Question, The.
Sea Change.
Two Poems on titles proposed by Octavio and
Marie José Paz.
Way of a World, The.
Updike. Back Bay.
In Memoriam Felis Felis.
Late January.
Shillington.
Whalen, P. Plus Ça Change.
Whitman, W. As Consequent, Etc.
In the New Garden.
O Me! O Life!
Old Ireland.
Reversals.
So Long!
To a Foil'd European Revolutionaire.
Whittier. Home-Coming of the Bride, The.
My Playmate.
Reunion, The.
Sea Dream, A.
To Ronge.
Wilbur, R. Beautiful Changes, The.
For the New Railway Station in Rome.
Speech for the Repeal of the McCarran Act.
Williams, C. K. Bread.
Experience.
Gift, The.
Of What Is Past.
Shame.
Soon.
When / you were small, I.
Williams, M. Animals.
Talking to Himself He Gets a Few Things
Settled in His Mind.
Williams, T. Island Is Memorable to Us, The.
Little Town, The.
Williams, W. Approaching Hour, The.
Catastrophic Birth.
United Front, The.
Wordsworth, W. Wishing-Gate Destroyed, The.
Wright, J. Cold Divinities, The.
Wyatt, S. Divers[e] [or Dyvers] doth[e] use, as
I have heard and kno[w].
Once in your grace I know I was.
Prove whether I do change, my dear.
Thou hast no faith of him that hath none.
Yeats. Lamentation of the Old Pensioner, The.
Mongan Laments the Change That Has Come
upon Him and His Beloved.
Old Men Admiring Themselves in the Water,
The.
Zagajewski. Lava.
Zaturenska. Daphne.
Émigrés, The.
See also **Transience**

Changelings
Roethke. Changeling, The.
Smith, S. Eulenspiegelei.
Unknown. Tam Lin.
Williams, T. Changeling.

Channing, William Henry
Emerson, R. Ode, Inscribed to W.H. Channing.
Whittier. Channing.

Chanteys
See **Sea Chanteys**

Chanukah
See **Hanukkah**

Chaos
Ammons. Chaos Staggered Up the Hill.
Misfit, The.
Bukowski. Simplicity of Everything in Viet
Nam, The.
Burns, R. Ode to the Departed Regency-Bill—
1789.
Byron, G. Darkness.
Collins, B. Butterfly Effect, The.
Duncan, R. Years As Catches, The.
Eberhart, R. Extremity.
O Wild Chaos!
Emerson, R. Who saw the hid beginnings.
Ginsberg, A. Angkor Wat.

Friday the Thirteenth.
I Beg You Come Back & Be Cheerful.
Reply, The.
Graves, R.　Ecstasy of Chaos.
Han-shan.　Chaos was happy.
Hardy, T.　What's There to Tell?
Laughlin, J.　Mathematics of Chaos, The.
Lawrence, D. H.　Think—!
Lowell, R.　For the Union Dead.
MacNeice.　Aftermath.
Millay, E.　I will put Chaos into fourteen lines.
Palmer, M.　Fractal Song.
Ralegh, S.　Ancients called me Chaos: my great
　yeares.
Riley, J.　Silence.
Rukeyser, M.　Nuns in the Wind.
Sarton, M.　Action of Therapy, The.
Stevens, W.　Idiom of the Hero.
Williams, C. K.　Crime, The.
Williams, W.　Descent.
Yeats.　Second Coming, The.

Chaplin, Charlie
Crane, H.　Chaplinesque.
Sandburg, C.　Without the Cane and the Derby.

Chapman, George
Gurney, I.　George Chapman—The Iliad.
Jonson, B.　To My Worthy and Honoured
　Friend, Mr George Chapman, on His
　Translation of Hesiod's *Works and Days*.
Keats.　On First Looking into Chapman's
　Homer.

Chapman, John ("Johnny Appleseed")
Lindsay, N.　In Praise of Johnny Appleseed.
　Johnny Appleseed Speaks of the Appleblossom
　　Amaranth That Will Come to This City.
　Johnny Appleseed's Ship Comes In.
　Johnny Appleseed's Wife from the Palace of
　　Eve.
　Johnny Appleseed's Wife of the Mind.
Niedecker.　When Johnny (Chapman)
　Appleseed.
Wilbur, R.　John Chapman.

Chariots
Davie, D.　Scythian Charioteers, The.
Whalen, P.　Chariot, The.

Charity
Ammons.　Civics.
Bandeira.　Brazilian Tragedy.
Berry, W.　Guest, The.
Bishop, E.　Miracle for Breakfast, A.
Browning, R.　Twins, The.
Coleridge, S.　Faith, Hope, and Charity.
Cowper, W.　Charity.
Crane, S.　Charity, thou art a lie.
Crashaw.　C[h]aritas Nimia; or, The Dear[e]
　Bargain.
Dickinson, E.　If I can stop one Heart from
　breaking.
Emerson, R.　Motto to "Considerations by the
　Way."
Euenus.　To the Swallow.
Graves, R.　Certain Mercies.
Herbert, G.　To My Successor.
Herrick.　Almes.
　Biting of Beggars.
　Cheerfulnesse in Charitie: or, The Sweet
　　Sacrifice.
　His Almes.
　Upon Grudgings.
　Upon Her Almes.
　Upon Sibilla.
　Upon Urles.
Hopkins, G.　To him who ever thought with love
　of me.
Jarrell, R.　Money.
Kipling, R.　Song for the Women, The.
Komunyakaa.　Eleemosynary.
　Speaking of Luck.
Lawrence, D. H.　Embankment at Night, before
　the War: Charity.
Lindsay, N.　Net to Snare the Moonlight, A.
　Prologue to "Rhymes to be Traded for Bread."
Meredith, G.　Burden of Strength, The.
　Main Regret, The.
Moore, M.　Charity Overcoming Envy.

Paley, G.　Fund Appeal.
Riley, J.　Little Johnts's Chris'mus.
Rimbaud, A.　Sisters of Charity.
Rossetti, C.　Behold, I stand at the door and
　knock.
　Charity.
　Charity Never Faileth.
　Despised and Rejected.
Rumi.　Debtor Sheikh, The.
Very.　Charity.
Whitman, W.　To Rich Givers.
Whittier.　Captain's Well, The.
　Giving and Taking.
　Hymn of the Children.
　"I Was a Stranger and Ye Took Me in."
　In the Evil Days.
　Red Riding-Hood.
　Saint Gregory's Guest.
　Trust.
　Valuation.
　Voices, The.
Wordsworth, W.　Narrow girdle of rough stones
　and crags, A.
　To the Lady Fleming on Seeing the Foundation
　　Preparing for the Erection of Rydal Chapel,
　　Westmoreland.
See also **Philanthropy and Philanthropists**

Charles I, King of England
Borges.　Morning of 1649, A.
Herrick.　Bad Season Makes the Poet Sad, The.
　To the King.
　To the King and Queen[e], upon Their Unhappy
　　Distances.
　To the King, upon His Com[m]ing with His
　　Army into the West.
　To the King, upon His Taking of Leicester.
　To the King, upon His Welcome to Hampton-
　　Court.
Jonson, B.　Epigram on the Prince's Birth. 1630,
　An.
　Epigram. To K[ing] Charles for a[n] Hundred
　　Pounds He Sent Me in My Sickness. 1629,
　　An.
　Epigram. To our Great and Good K[ing] Charles
　　on his Anniversary Day. 1629, An.
　Epigram. To the Household. 1630, An.
　Humble Petition of Poor Ben to the Best of
　　Monarchs, Masters, Men, King Charles, The.
　New Year's Gift Sung to King Charles. 1635, A.
　New years [*or* yeares], expect new gifts: sister,
　　your harp[e].
　On the King's Birthday.
　Song of Welcome to King Charles, A.
　To K[ing] Charles and Q[ueen] Mary, for the
　　Loss of Their First-Born.
　To My L[ord] the King, on the Christening His
　　Second Son James.
　To the King. On His Birthday. An Epigram
　　Anniversary. Novem[ber] 19, 1632.
Shelley, P.　Charles the First.

Charles II, King of England
Dryden, J.　Absalom and Achitophel.
Herrick.　Pastorall Upon the Birth of Prince
　Charles, A.
　To His Muse.
　To Prince Charles upon his coming to Exeter.
　To the Most Illustrious and Most Hopeful[l]
　　Prince, Charles, Prince of Wales.
Keats.　Lines Written on 29 May / The
　Anniversary of the Restoration of Charles the
　2nd.
Marvell.　Ad Regem Carolum Parodia [A
　Parody: To King Charles].
　Last Instructions to a Painter, The.
　Pros Karolon ton Basilea [To King Charles].

Charles, Prince of Wales
Schuyler, J.　Overcast, Hot.

Charles River, Massachusetts
Corbett, W.　Crossing the Footbridge over
　Storrow Drive.
Rich, A.　Walk by the Charles, A.

Charleston, South Carolina
Rich, A.　Charleston in the Eighteen-Sixties.
Updike.　Charleston.

Charm
Burns, R.　Blue-Eyed Lassie, The.
Coleridge, S.　Snow-Drop, The.
Herrick.　Charm, A.
　Charme, or an Allay for Love, A.
　Charmes.
Ransom, J.　Vision by Sweetwater.
Rossetti, C.　Helpmeet For Him, A.
Tomlinson, C.　Request, The.
Yeats.　Memory.

Charms (genre)
Campion, T.　Thrice Toss[e] These Oaken Ashes
　in the Air [*or* Ayre].
Herrick.　Another.
　Another Charme for Stables.
　Another to Bring in the Witch.
　Charmes.
　Spell, The.
Kipling, R.　Charm, A.
Rukeyser, M.　Charm for Cantinflas, A.

Charon
Eberhart, R.　Enigma, The.
Herrick.　Charon and Phylomel, a Dialogue
　Sung.
　New Charon, The.
MacNeice.　Charon.
Millay, E.　Sappho Crosses the Dark River into
　Hades.
Orr, G.　I was moving down the bank.
Simic.　Charon's Cosmology.
Unknown.　On Niobe.

Chartres, France
Eberhart, R.　Retrospective Forelook.
Kipling, R.　Chartres Windows.
MacLeish.　Chartres.
Meredith, W.　Notre Dame de Chartres.
Merton.　News from the School at Chartres.
Oppen.　Chartres.

Chastity
Atwood.　Women's Issue, A.
Bogan, L.　Ad Castitatem.
Campion, T.　Ad Cambricum.
　Ad Leam.
Crashaw.　To a Young Gentle-Woman, Councel
　Concerning Her Choice.
Cunningham, J.　Reader, it's time reality was
　faced.
"H. D."　She Rebukes Hippolyta.
Herrick.　Another.
　His Recantation.
　Like Loves His Like.
　No Spouse but a Sister.
　To His Tomb-Maker.
　To Love.
　To the Little Spinners.
　Upon Himselfe.
　Upon Love.
Lawrence, D. H.　Chastity.
　Virgin Youth.
Meredith, G.　Vital Choice, The.
　With the Huntress.
Petrarch.　By then I knew my flourishing green
　age.
　If virtuous love can merit a reward.
　In her, two enemies were brought together.
　Life is most dear; and then, it seems to me.
　Victorious and triumphal laurel-tree.
Ralegh, S.　Shall I, Like an Hermit, Dwell.
Suckling, S.　Lutea Allison.
Unknown, sometimes at. to Sir Walter Ralegh.
　Shall I, Like an Hermit, Dwell.
Yeats.　Three Bushes, The.

Chatterton, Thomas
Coleridge, S.　Monody on the Death of
　Chatterton.
　O Spirit blest! / Whether th' eternal Throne
　around.
Keats.　To Chatterton.

Chaucer, Geoffrey
Campion, T.　Elegeia I (1595).
Cummings, E. E.　Chaucer.
Hughes, T.　Chaucer.
Keats.　Written on a Blank Space at the End of
　Chaucer's Tale of "The Floure and the Lefe."
Meredith, G.　Poetry of Chaucer, The.

Cheerfulness
Browning, E.   Cheerfulness Taught by Reason.
Creeley.   Be of Good Cheer.
Cummings, E. E.   Jack's white horse(up).
Graves, R.   Song: Come, Enjoy Your Sunday!
Herrick.   Cheerfulnesse in Charitie: or, The
    Sweet Sacrifice.
Kipling, R.   English Way, The.
Meredith, W.   Cheer, The.
Riley, J.   On the Sunny Side.
Ritsos.   Small Confession.
Rossetti, C.   Gone to his rest / Bright little
    Bouby!
    Rosy maiden Winifred, / With a milkpail on her
    head.
Rumi.   I used to be shy.
Wordsworth, W.   From the Dark Chambers of
    Dejection Freed.
    I Wandered Lonely As a Cloud.

Cheese
Hall, D.   O Cheese.
Herrick.   Fresh Cheese and Cream.
Merton.   Chee$e.
Patchen.   Rising a Little.
Tate, J.   Wild Cheese, The.

Chekhov, Anton
Brodsky, J.   Homage to Chekhov.
Clampitt.   Prairie, The.
Dubie.   Seagull, The.
Heaney, S.   Chekhov on Sakhalin.
Levertov.   Chekhov on the West Heath.

Chemical Warfare
Auden.   James Honeyman.
Cummings, E. E.   Lis / -ten / you know what i
    mean when.
Kipling, R.   Gethsemane.
Merwin.   Asians Dying, The.
Owen, W.   Dulce et Decorum Est.

Chemistry and Chemists
Graves, R.   Research and Development:
    Classified.
Ramanujan. $KMnO_4$ in Grandfather's Shaving
    Class.

Chernobyl
Paley, G.   In Aix.

Cherry Trees and Cherries
Ammons.   Winter Scene.
Berry, W.   Fall.
Blue Cloud.   Chokecherries.
Campion, T.   There is a garden in her face.
Davie, D.   Cherry Ripe.
De la Mare.   Cherry Trees, The.
Gunn, T.   Cherry Tree, The.
Herrick.   Cherrie-Ripe.
    Cherry-Pit.
    To Cherry-Blossoms.
    Upon Mistresse Susanna Southwell, Her
    Cheeks.
Housman.   Loveliest of Trees, the Cherry Now.
Lawrence, D. H.   Cherry Robbers.
    Song: "Up in the high."
Logan, J.   February Awakening.
Lux.   Refrigerator, 1957.
Nemerov.   Cherry Tree, The.
Neruda.   Cherries.
Niedecker.   Happy New Year.
Orr, G.   Half-Dead Black Cherry Tree across the
    Road from My Childhood House, A.
Parker, D.   Cherry White.
Rossetti, C.   Let's Be Merry.
    Oh fair to see / Bloom-laden cherry tree.
    Playing at bob cherry / Tom and Nell and Hugh.
Whalen, P.   Japanese Tea Garden Golden Gate
    Park in Spring.
Williams, W.   Bare Tree, The.
    Cherry Blossoms at Evening.
    Orchard, The.
Zagajewski.   Wild Cherries.

Chesapeake Bay
Dunbar, P.   Night on the Chesapeake.
    To the Eastern Shore.
Sandburg, C.   Sea Hold, The.

Chess
Amichai [or Amikhai].   Great Fatigue.
Borges.   Chess.

Cavafy.   Pawn, The.
Cooper, J.   Figure on the Far Side, The.
Ferlinghetti, L.   Deep Chess.
Levi, P.   Chess.
    Chess 2.
MacNeice.   Chess.
Montale.   New Stanzas.
Pessoa.   I heard it told that once when Persia.
Ramanujan.   Chess under Trees.
Robinson, E.   Atherton's Gambit.
Rumi.   Drunks fear the police.
Shapiro, K.   Essay on Chess.
Simic.   Prodigy.
Wright, C.   Mid-winter Snowfall in the Piazza
    Dante.

Chesterton, Gilbert Keith
Hardy, T.   Epitaph for G. K. Chesterton.

Chestnut Trees and Chestnuts
Eberhart, R.   Horse Chestnut Tree, The.
Longfellow, H.   Village Blacksmith, The.
Tomlinson, C.   Chestnut Avenue: at Alton
    House, The.

Chicago, Illinois
Berrigan, T.   Chicago Morning.
Carruth, H.   Michigan Water: a Few Riffs before
    Dawn.
    Snow, The.
Ginsberg, A.   Open Window on Chicago, An.
    Written on Hotel Napkin: Chicago Futures.
Hughes, L.   Chicago.
    Chicago Blues.
    Migrant.
    Summer Evening (Calumet Avenue).
    Visitors to the Black Belt.
Levine, P.   New Day, A.
Logan, J.   Chicago Scene.
    Zoo, The.
McGrath, T.   Migration of Cities, The.
Ramanujan.   Chicago Zen.
    Take Care.
Rexroth, K.   Bad Old Days, The.
Rukeyser, M.   Third Elegy. The Fear of Form.
Sandburg, C.   Chicago Boy Baby.
    Clinton South of Polk.
    Mamie.
    Real Avenue News.
    Windy City, The.
Whittier.   Chicago.
Wright, J.   Poor Washed Up by Chicago Winter,
    The.

Chickadees
Emerson, R.   In Walden wood the chickadee.
    Titmouse, The.
Thoreau.   Chicadee, The.
See also **Titmice**

Chickens
Burns, R.   To Alexander Findlater.
Carruth, H.   Missing the Bo in the Henhouse.
Dickey, W.   Chickens in San Francisco.
Dugan, A.   Death's Chicken, Named Amelia.
Emerson, R.   No song so tuneful, quoth the fox.
Frost, R.   Blue Ribbon at Amesbury, A.
Hall, D.   Henyard Round, The.
Herrick.   Upon Cock.
Ignatow, D.   No Theory.
Lawrence, D. H.   Flat-Foot's Song.
Patchen.   'In the footsteps of the walking air.'
Rossetti, C.   White hen sitting / On white eggs
    three, A.
Sandburg, C.   Chicks.
Simic.   Chicken Without a Head, The.
Smith, S.   Cock and the Hen, The.
Williams, W.   Red Wheelbarrow, The.
Wright, J.   Presentation of Two Birds to My
    Son, A.

Child Abuse
Ai.   Child Beater.
    False Witness.
Angelou.   To Beat the Child Was Bad Enough.
Bly, R.   Snow Geese.
Broumas, O.   Eye of Heart.
    Offertory.
Clifton, L.   What Did She Know, When Did She
    Know It.
Davie, D.   Grazia Deledda, Young.

Dove, R.   Taking in Wash.
Hayden, R.   Whipping, The.
Heaney, S.   Bye-Child.
Komunyakaa.   Stepfather: A Girl's Song.
    Stepmother: A Boy's Song.
Lawrence, D. H.   Discord in Childhood.
Prunty.   Rooms Without Walls.
Sexton.   Wifebeater, The.
Smith, S.   Lord Barrenstock.
    Papa Love Baby.

Child Labor
Hughes, L.   Old Youth.
Sandburg, C.   They Will Say.

Childhood and Children
Ai.   Good Shepherd, The: Atlanta, 1981.
Amichai [or Amikhai].   Child is Something Else
    Again, A.
    Children's Procession.
    Closing the Jaffa Port.
    God Takes Pity on Kindergarten Children.
    Half-Sized Violin.
    I Guard the Children.
    I Was the Moon.
    In My Childhood.
    My Child Wafts Peace.
    My Children.
    My Son.
    Parents Left the Child, The.
    Summer Evening in the Jerusalem Mountains.
    What is it? An airplane at dawn. No.
    When I Was a Child.
Angelou.   Elegy: "I lay down in my grave."
    John J.
    Kin.
    Little Girl Speakings.
Armantrout.   Book, The.
Ashbery, J.   Young Son, The.
Auden.   Price, The.
    Schoolchildren.
Bassani, G.   Looking Out from Ferrara.
Berry, W.   Our Children, Coming of Age.
    To Tanya at Christmas.
Berryman.   At Chinese Checkers.
    Ball Poem, The.
    Hello.
Bishop, E.   In the Waiting Room.
    Squatter's Children.
Bogan, L.   Kept.
Bourne, V.   On the Picture of a Sleeping Child.
Bradstreet, A.   Author to Her Book, The.
    In Reference to Her Children, 23 June, 1659 [or
    1659].
Brontë, E.   I.M. to I.G.
    I saw thee, child, one summer's day.
    Mild the mist upon the hill.
    Song to A.A.
    Two Children, The.
    Upon her soothing breast.
Brooks, G.   Bronzeville Woman in a Red Hat.
    Notes from the Childhood and the Girlhood.
    Womanhood, The.
Broumas, O.   Demeter.
    Stars in Your Name.
    Woman with Child.
Browning, E.   Child Asleep, A.
    Cry of the Children, The.
    Deserted Garden, The.
    Fourfold Aspect, The.
    Hector in the Garden.
    Isobel's Child.
    Life.
    Lost Bower, The.
    Pet-Name, The.
    Romance of the Ganges, A.
    Song against Singing, A.
    Tale of Villafranca, A.
    To Bettine.
    Void in Law.
Browning, R.   Epigram on School Days.
Bukowski.   Bee, The.
    Seahorse.
    Upon First Reading the Immortal Literature of
    the World—.
Burns, R.   O That I Had Ne'er Been Married.
    On the Birth of a Posthumous Child.
    To Miss C*********, a Very Young Lady.

Byron, G. Childish Recollections.
On a Distant View of the Village and School of
Harrow on the Hill.
Cardozo. Cemetery of Childhood.
Carruth, H. Sound of Snow, The.
World as Will and Representation, The.
Carver, R. Child, The.
Louise.
Chesterton. Blessing, A ("Sunlight in a child's
hair").
Ciardi, J. Dream, A.
Echoes.
For My Nephew Going to Bed.
Letter for Those Who Grew Up Together.
One Morning.
Thursday.
Clampitt. Imago.
In Umbria: A Snapshot.
Clifton, L. Lot's Wife 1988.
Sorrow Song.
Clough. Incident, An.
Thou bidd'st me mark how swells with rage.
Thoughts of Home.
Coleridge, S. Anthem for the Children of
Christ's Hospital.
Fruit Plucker, The.
On the Christening of a Friend's Child.
Youth and Age.
Collins, B. First Reader.
On Turning Ten.
Cooper, J. Builder of Houses, The.
Children's Ward, The.
Leaving Water Hyacinths.
My Young Mother.
Past, The.
Practicing for Death.
Cowper, W. Hymn for the Sunday School at
Olney.
Crane, H. Idiot, The.
Crane, S. Trees in the garden rained flowers,
The.
Creeley. Cantos, The.
Charm, The.
Children, The.
Fragment, A: "On the street I am met with
constant hostility."
Hey.
Kid ("Smaller, no recall").
Kids / Seoul.
Method of Actuality, The.
Mommy.
On Board.
People.
Sitting Here.
Time ("Out window roof's slope").
Cullen, C. Incident.
Saturday's Child.
Cummings, E. E. Being / twelve / who hast
merely.
Here pasture ends— / this girl and boy.
Hist whist / little ghostthings.
I walked the boulevard.
I'd think "wonder / if" if.
In Just.
Little man / (in a hurry).
Little tree / little silent Christmas tree.
One nonsufficiently inundershood.
Sitting in a tree-.
So little he is.
Sonnet entitled how to run the world).
These children singing in stone a.
Who are you,little i.
Davie, D. Boyhood Misremembered.
Prolific Spell, The.
Shropshire.
De la Mare. Children of Stare, The.
Dry August Burned.
Incantation.
Irrevocable, The.
Keys of Morning, The.
Massacre, The.
Myself.
O Childish Mind!
Pollie.
Reserved.
Reverie.

Slum Child, The.
Sunday, A.
Sunken Garden, The.
To My Mother.
Unheard Melodies.
Universe, The.
Winter Dusk.
Young Girl, A.
Dickey, J. Form.
Rafters, The.
Voyage of the Needle, The.
Dickey, W. Dolls Play at Hansel and Gretel,
The.
For Every Last Batch When the Next One
Comes Along.
Memoranda.
Dickinson, E. Bliss is the plaything of the child.
Child's faith is new, The.
From all the Jails the Boys and Girls.
God permits industrious Angels.
It troubled me as once I was.
Let Us play Yesterday.
Little Dog that wags his tail, A.
New feet within my garden go.
One Sister have I in our house.
Ravenousness of fondness, The.
They won't frown always—some sweet Day.
Trudging to Eden, looking backward.
With Leopards for Playmates, the beautiful
Child.
Drummond de Andrade. Infancy.
Dubie. Descent into the Hours of the Peregrine.
Diatribe of the Kite, The.
Elegy for My Brother.
Grandfather's Last Letter, A.
Inside the City Walls.
Lion Grotto, The.
Of Politics, & Art.
Pictures at an Exhibition.
Poem: "Mule kicked out in the trees, A. An
Early."
Revelation 20:11–15.
Dugan, A. Autobiographical Libation to Erato
Muse of Lyric Poetry.
Expenses.
On a Party.
On Going Latent.
On the Long Island Railroad System.
Romance of the Escaped Children.
Thesis, Antithesis and Nostalgia.
Variation on Themes by Roethke and Eliot.
Dunbar, P. Boy's Summer Song, A.
Charity.
Little Brown Baby.
Liza May.
Lullaby: "Bedtime's come fu' little boys."
Scamp.
Wadin' in de Crick.
When a Feller's Itchin' to be Spanked.
Eberhart, R. Book of Nature, The.
Child, The.
'If I Could Only Live at the Pitch That Is near
Madness.'
Incomparable Light, The.
Lost Children, The.
Old Tree by the Penobscot.
Orchard.
Recollection of Childhood.
Three Kids.
Eliot, T. S. Animula.
Cultivation of Christmas Trees, The.
Emerson, R. Awed I behold once more.
Dirge: "Knows he who tills this lonely field."
Motto to "The Poet."
Fenton, J. Nest of Vampires.
Ferlinghetti, L. In woods where many rivers
run.
Pennycandystore beyond the El, The.
Frost, R. Birches.
Home Burial.
Maple.
Gallagher, T. Amplitude.
Disappearances in the Guarded Sector.
View from an Empty Chair.
García Lorca. 1910.
Ballad of the Little Square.

Ballad of the Moon Moon.
Childhood and Death.
Little Mute Boy, The.
Little Stanton.
Your Childhood in Menton.
Ginsberg, A. Gregory Corso's Story.
Two Boys Went Into a Dream Diner.
Glück, L. Apple Trees, The.
Descending Figure.
Drowned Children, The.
End of the World, The.
Firstborn.
Gift, The.
Grandmother in the Garden.
Illuminations.
Portrait.
Returning a Lost Child.
School Children, The.
Scraps.
Tree House, The.
Graves, R. Alice.
Child with Veteran.
Dreaming Children.
Hero, The.
Sweet-Shop Round The Corner, The.
Warning to Children.
Wm. Brazier.
Gray, T. Ode on a Distant Prospect of Eton
College.
Gunn, T. Blank, A.
Courage, a Tale.
Hide and Seek.
Three.
Gurney, I. Hedges.
Wish, A.
"H. D." At Eleusis.
Hacker, M. 1976.
Geographer.
Iva's Pantoum.
Little Robber Girl Considers the Wide World,
The.
Sword.
Third Snowfall.
Hall, D. Child, The.
Exile.
Illustration.
Sleeping Giant, The.
Toy Bone, The.
Hammon. Poem for Children with Thoughts on
Death, A.
Han-shan. Fire and smoke raged within.
Hardy, T. Childhood among the Ferns.
Children and Sir Nameless, The.
Her Death and After.
In a Waiting-Room.
Oxen, The.
Hayden, R. Rabbi, The.
Those Winter Sundays.
Whipping, The.
Year of the Child, The.
Heaney, S. Alphabets.
Bye-Child.
Clearances.
Death of a Naturalist.
England's Difficulty.
Follower.
Hazel Stick for Catherine Ann, A.
Personal Helicon.
Railway Children, The.
Sofa in the Forties, A.
Transgression, A.
Wheels within Wheels.
Herbert, G. Holy Baptism (2).
Herrick. Grace for a Child.
Upon Gubbs.
Upon Jolly and Jilly.
Upon Ralph.
Hill, G. Cowan Bridge; At the Site of 'Lowood
School.'
Hopkins, G. At the Wedding March.
By Mrs. Hopley.
Handsome Heart, The.
Spring and Fall.
Howe, S. Pearl Harbor.
Hughes, L. Children's Rhymes ("By what
sends").

Genius Child.
Kid in the Park.
Madam and the Charity Child.
Migration.
Naughty Child, The.
Old Youth.
To Be Somebody.
Hughes, T. Children.
Deaf School.
Memory.
Ignatow, D. In Limbo.
In My Childhood.
Journey, The.
Lost Childhood.
Jackson, L. Fates and the Mothers, The.
Laura and Francisca.
Jacobsen, J. Allhallows Party.
Birthday Party, The.
Class, The.
Coming, The.
Eyes of the Children at the Brink of the Sea's
  Grasp, The.
Innocents, The.
Loss of Sounds.
My Uncle a Child.
Primer, The.
Spring, Says the Child.
Three Children, The.
Tiger.
Jarrell, R. Carnegie Library, Juvenile Division,
  The.
Childhood.
Children Selecting Books in a Library.
Cinderella.
Elementary Scene, The.
Gleaning.
Head of Wisdom, The.
Hope.
Lady Bates.
Lost Children, The.
Lost World, The.
Moving.
Quilt-Pattern, A.
Sick Child, A.
Thinking of the Lost World.
Truth, The.
Jeffers, R. Solstice.
Johnson, S. In Rivum a Mola Stoana Lichfeldiæ
  Diffluentem.
Keats. 'Tis the Witching Time [or Hour] of
  Night.
Kinnell. First Song.
Freedom, New Hampshire.
To a Child in Calcutta.
Kinsella, T. Hand of Solo, A.
High Road, The.
Irwin Street.
Liffey Hill, The.
Settings.
Kipling, R. Butterflies.
Kizer, C. By the Riverside.
Children.
Gerda.
Not Writing Poems about Children.
Pearl.
Worms, The.
Koch, K. Aus Einer Kindheit.
You Were Wearing.
Komunyakaa. Albino.
Believing in Iron.
Gloria's Clues.
Halloween, the Late Fifties.
Happiness.
Looking for Choctaw.
Mumble Peg.
Seasons between Yes & No.
Sunday Afternoons.
Touch.
Toys in a Field.
Venus's-flytraps.
Kumin, M. Atlantic City 1939.
Changing the Children.
First Rain of Spring, The.
Game of Monopoly in Chavannes.
Grandchild.
Halfway.

History Lesson.
Hundred Nights, A.
Thirties Revisited, The.
Kunitz, S. Testing-Tree, The.
Larkin, P. I Remember, I Remember.
This Be The Verse.
Laughlin, J. Child, The.
It's March.
James My Namesake.
My Granddaughter.
Our Bicycles.
Parable, A.
Step on His Head.
Sweet Kiss, A.
Two Children.
When Does the Play Begin?
Who Is the Child.
Your Early Life.
Lawrence, D. H. After School.
I Heard Her Say.
Piano.
Piano, The.
Punisher, The.
Snowy Day in School, A.
White Horse, The.
Young Fathers.
Levertov. Childhood's End.
Earliest Spring.
Evening Train.
For a Child.
Levi, P. Girl-Child of Pompei, The.
Levine, P. Belle Isle, 1949.
Children's Crusade, The.
Hold Me.
Lost and Found.
Milkweed.
On My Own.
Pili's Wall.
To a Child Trapped in a Barber Shop.
Lindsay, N. How Dulcenia del Toboso Is Like
  the Left Wing of a Bird.
Master of the Dance, The.
Logan, J. On Reading Camus In Early March.
Picnic, The.
Poem for My Son.
Present, The.
Shore Scene.
Longfellow, H. Children's Hour, The.
My Lost Youth.
Lorde. And What About the Children.
As I Grew Up Again.
Ballad from Childhood.
Blackstudies.
Bloodbirth.
Conclusion.
Equinox.
Release Time.
Relevant Is Different Points on the Circle.
Rites of Passage.
Sacrifice.
Seventh Sign, The.
Signs.
Song for a Thin Sister.
Teacher.
To My Daughter the Junkie on a Train.
What My Child Learns of the Sea.
Woman Thing, The.
Lowell, R. Child's Song.
Harriet.
My Last Afternoon with Uncle Devereux
  Winslow.
Returning.
Lux. Amiel's Leg.
At the Far End of a Long Wharf.
Bitterness of Children, The.
Cellar Stairs.
Falling Through the Leaves.
Man Inside the Chipmunk Suit, The.
Men With Small Heads.
Nazi at the Puppet Show, The.
Princess Summer Fall Winter Spring.
Refrigerator, 1957.
There Were Some Summers.
Triptych, Middle Panel Burning.
MacDiarmid, H. First Love.
Of John Davidson.

MacLeish. Ancestral.
Eleven.
Hebrides.
Revolution of the Children.
MacNeice. Carrick Revisited.
Children's Games.
Soap Suds.
Taken for Granted.
Major, C. Doll Believers, The.
Sexual Conduct.
Marvell. Picture of Little T. C. in a Prospect of
  Flowers, The.
McGrath, T. Heroes of Childhood, The.
Remembering the Children of Auschwitz.
Uses of the Lost Poets.
McHugh, H. Better or Worse.
Circus.
Melted Money.
Mind.
Meredith, G. Ah! little Angel, child of bliss!
Child's Prayer, A.
Fair Bedfellow, The.
First-Born, The.
Holidays.
Infancy and Age.
Mother to Babe.
Motley.
Orchard and the Heath, The.
Philosopher! 'tis said you wail.
World is young, the world is well, The.
Meredith, W. Country Stars.
Dalhousie Farm.
Godchildren.
Look at Me! Look at Me!
Music.
Waking Dream about a Lost Child.
Merrill, J. Broken Home, The.
Chimes for Yahya.
Days of 1935.
Days of 1941 and '44.
Salome.
Scenes of Childhood.
School Play, The.
Up and Down.
Verse for Urania.
Vision of the Garden, A.
World and the Child, The.
Merton. Birdcage Walk.
Landscape.
Winter's Night, The.
Merwin. Animals from Mountains.
Birdie.
Child, The.
Lake, The.
Span.
Windows, The.
Millay, E. As sharp as in my childhood, still.
Cairn, The.
Childhood Is the Kingdom Where Nobody Dies.
From a Very Little Sphinx.
Milosz, C. Capri.
Portrait with a Cat, A.
Powers.
Mistral, G. Fruit.
Guardian Angel.
Refreshment.
Sad Mother, The.
You Had Me.
Montale. End of Childhood.
Poems for Camillo Sbarbaro.
Punta del Mesco.
Shore of Versilia.
Muldoon, P. Cass and Me.
Early Warning.
Right Arm, The.
Nash, O. Birdies, Don't Make Me Laugh.
Child Is Father to the Man, But with More
  Authority, The.
Children's Party.
Come On In, the Senility Is Fine.
Crossing the Border.
Don't Cry, Darling, It's Blood All Right.
Father, Dear Father, Go Jump in the Lake, or,
  You're Costlier than You Think.
Fee Fi Ho Hum, No Wonder Baby Sucks Her
  Thumb.

Guppy, The.
I Want a Drink of Water, but Not from the
  Thermos.
I'll Take the High Road Commission.
Little Feet.
One Third of a Calendar.
Parent, The.
Piano Tuner, Untune Me That Tune.
Preface to the Past.
Queen Is in the Parlor, The.
Some of My Best Friends Are Children.
Nemerov. Central Park.
Home for the Holidays.
Icehouse in Summer, The.
Lives of Gulls and Children, The.
Mars.
Puzzle, The.
Remorse for Time, The.
Sleeping Beauty.
Snow Globe, The.
Triumph of Education, The.
Warning: Children at Play.
Niedecker. Coming out of Sleep.
Dear Paul: / the sheets of your father's book of
  poetry.
High, lovely, light.
If he is of constant depth.
Paul / now six years old.
Tell me a story about the war.
Understand me, dead is nothing.
O'Hara, F. Autobiographia Literaria.
Blocks.
Cornkind.
Ode on Causality.
Ode to Michael Goldberg ('s Birth and Other
  Births).
Poem: "There I could never be a boy."
Olson, C. Fable for Slumber.
Ferrini—I.
One Night Ma / Lay with Pa.
Oppen. Any Way But Back.
Birthplace: New Rochelle.
Exodus.
Pedestrian.
Street.
Sunnyside Child.
West.
Orr, G. Brave Child, The.
Caged Owl, The.
Ditch, The.
Father's Song.
Lost Children, The.
Making Beasts.
My Father's Voice.
Origin of the Marble Forest.
Sunday School Picnic: What Endures.
Teachers, The.
Owen, W. Happiness.
To ———: "Three rompers run together, hand
  in hand."
Pagis. Ein Leben.
Souvenir, The.
Paley, G. For Danny.
In the Bus.
It's True.
My Mother: 33 Years Later.
Note to Grandparents.
Question.
Sad Children's Song, The.
Parker, D. Moral Tales for the Young ("Maude,
  the brightest of the sex").
Patchen. Black Panther and the Little Boy, The.
Career for a Child of Five.
Childhood of the Hero.
Event at Konna, The.
Mirru.
Reason for Skylarks, The.
Watching Neighbors' Children.
Pinsky. Daughter.
From the Childhood of Jesus.
Icicles.
Saving, The.
Song of Reasons.
Street, The.
Woman, A.
Plath. Brasilia.

Child.
Childless Woman.
Getting There.
Prunty. Child's Christmas in Georgia, A.
Cousins, Brothers, Sisters.
Good-bye.
Rooms Without Walls.
Since the Noon Mail Stopped.
Wallace Stevens Remembers Halloween.
Water Slide Along the Beach.
Winter's Tale, A.
Yes.
Raine, K. Childhood.
Childhood Memory.
Eternal Child, The.
Message.
My Father's Birthday.
Spell to Bring Lost Creatures Home.
Three Poems of Incarnation.
Ramanujan. Lines to a Granny.
Love Poem for a Wife, 1.
Minor Sacrifice, A.
Rexroth, K. Homer in Basic.
Homestead Called Damascus, The.
Letter to Wystan Hugh Auden, A.
Rich, A. Afterwake, The.
Bears.
Classmate, The.
In the Wake of Home.
Innocents, The.
Night-Pieces: For a Child.
Not Like That.
Riley, J. Backward Look, A.
Barefoot Boy, A.
Boys, The.
Children of the Childless, The.
Days Gone By, The.
Extremes.
Grampa's Choice.
Harlie.
Hired Man's Faith in Children, The.
In the Night.
Land of Thus-and-So, The.
Land of Used-to-Be, The.
Life-Lesson, A.
Little Orphant Annie.
Little-Red-Apple Tree, The.
Longfellow's Love for the Children.
Lovely Child, The.
Mr. Silberberg.
Mulberry Tree, The.
Old Sweetheart of Mine, An.
Our Boyhood Haunts.
Our Little Girl.
Raggedy Man on Children, The.
Rider of the Knee, The.
Runaway Boy, The.
She "Displains" It.
Spoiled Child, The.
Summer's Day, A.
Uncle Sidney.
Uncle Sidney's Logic.
Want to Be Whur Mother Is.
When We First Played "Show."
Where-Away.
Where the Children Used to Play.
Rilke. Child at the Mirror, The.
Child at the Window Sill.
Child, The.
Childhood.
Cursed Child.
Great Indulgent Heart.
Lemon and Laburnum.
Lying to a Child.
Sleep.
Tuck a Child.
Rimbaud, A. First Communions.
Seven-year-old Poets.
War.
Wide-eyed.
Ritsos. Myopic Child, A.
Robinson, E. For Arvia.
Roethke. Child on Top of a Greenhouse.
My Papa's Waltz.
Where Knock Is Open Wide.
Rossetti, C. Charade.

Child's Talk in April.
Clever little Willie wee, / Bright eyed, blue eyed
  little fellow.
Frisky Lamb, A.
Isidora.
Mother and Child.
Three little children / On the wide wide earth.
Rukeyser, M. Another Day. A Game of Toys.
Paul, Telling the Game.
Another Day (And then the cow).
Another Day (Child among his powers).
Another Day (Day Lilies, Yellow Daisies).
Another Day (I will now sing).
Another Day (Miss Lorence).
Another Day. The Children Are All Eating.
Another Day (You can't come).
Another Day (You sit there).
Are You Born? / II.
Boy with His Hair Cut Short.
Child and Mother.
Child wakes in the morning to enter a country,
  The.
Children, the Sandbar, That Summer.
Crayon House.
Destruction of Grief.
Do you know Hitler? Does he like you?
Eighth Elegy. Children's Elegy.
Father dreams that he was hid in a tree, The.
Fourth Elegy. The Refugees.
From the Duck-Pond to the Carousel.
Gift.
He turned cruel. Absorbed in his own cruelty.
His father is lost and away.
In the last hour of night, a zebra racing dawn.
My toes feel like nothing they are so cold.
Not Yet.
Now he plays with the other children.
Poem Out of Childhood.
Sea has opened, the limit of his dream, The.
Victims, a Play for the Home, The.
When he began to witness, it was not to a
  journey.
Rumi. Babbling Child, A.
Sheikh Who Played with Children, The.
Sandburg, C. Baby Face.
Buffalo Bill.
Child.
Child Face.
Child Margaret.
Child Moon.
Chillicothe.
Clinton South of Polk.
Five Cent Balloons.
Helga.
House.
Margaret.
Never Born.
People with Proud Chins.
Seventeen Months.
Spring Wind.
Three Spring Notations on Bipeds.
Winter Milk.
Sarton, M. Ballad of Johnny, The.
Garden of Childhood, The.
Giant in the Garden.
Seifert. Dome of the Observatory, The.
Halley's Comet.
Prologue: "To be a poet is no easy task."
Year 1934, The.
Sexton. Baby Picture.
Children, The.
Double Image, The.
Fortress, The.
January 1st.
Little Uncomplicated Hymn, A.
Praying to Big Jack.
Red Roses.
Shout, The.
Those Times.
Shapiro, K. Solipsism.
Shelley, P. To William Shelley.
Simic. Austerities.
Childhood of Parmenides, The.
Cold Blue Tinge.
Figuring.
Game, The.

Primer.
Prodigy.
Smith, S.   Advice to Young Children.
Archie and Tina.
Bog-Face.
Children of the Cross, The.
Cousin, The.
Deathly Child, The.
Governess, The.
Last Turn of the Screw, The.
Little Child of Brightest Face.
Louise.
Maximilian Esterhazy.
Mother's Hearse, A.
My Heart Was Full.
Northumberland House.
One of Many.
Our Bog is Dood.
Parklands, The.
Queen and the Young Princess, The.
Soldier Dear to Us, A.
To Carry the Child.
Unser Vater.
Spender, S.   Elementary School Classroom in a
    Slum, An.
Empty House.
Footnote, A.
My Parents
To My Daughter.
Stafford, W.   At Liberty School.
First Grade.
Living on the Plains.
Mother's Day.
Over the Mountains.
Remembering Brother Bob.
School Days.
School Play.
Third Street.
Stock, R.   J.
Star-Apple.
Trajectory of a Scream.
Stockton, A.   To a Little Miss a Year Older than
    the One to Whom the Glass Was Promised.
To a Little Miss, with a Toy Lookingglass.
Swenson, M.   Centaur, The.
If I Had Children.
Playhouse, The.
Swift, J.   Corinna.
Szymborska, W.   Hitler's First Photograph.
Interview with a Child.
Moment in Troy, A.
Tale Begun, A.
Tate, A.   Eye, The.
Tate, J.   Five Years Old.
Frivolous Blind Death Child.
Poem for the Sandman.
With a Child All Day.
Yellow Newspaper and a Wooden Leg.
Thomas, D.   Conversation of Prayer, The.
Fern Hill.
This Side of the Truth.
Tomlinson, C.   For a Godchild.
Picture of J. T. in a Prospect of Stone, The.
Trakl.   Trumpets.
Unknown.   Teach your child to earn his meal.
Updike.   Conversation.
July.
One-Year-Old, The.
Vallejo.   Big People, The.
Van Duyn.   Bedtime Stories.
Three Valentines to the Wide World.
Very.   Boy's Dream, The: A Ballad.
Childhood's Songs.
Child's Dream of Reaching the Horizon, The.
Sliding Rock, The.
Walcott.   Cold Spring Harbor.
Lesson for This Sunday, A.
Walker, A.   Enemy, The.
Warren, R.   American Portrait: Old Style.
Boyhood in Tobacco Country.
Little Boy and Lost Shoe.
Little Girl Wakes Early.
Moonlight's Dream, The.
October Picnic Long Ago.
Old Dog Dead.
Old Flame.

Old-Time Childhood in Kentucky.
Safe in Shade.
Speleology.
What Voice at Moth-Hour.
Weiss, T.   Charm Against the Toothache, A.
World to Do, A.
Whitman, W.   After the Argument.
Play-Ground, The.
There Was a Child Went Forth.
Whittier.   Autograph, An.
Barefoot Boy, The.
Child-Songs.
Hymn of the Children.
In School-Days.
Light That Is Felt, The.
Lines Written in an Album.
My Namesake.
My Playmate.
Name, A.
Poet and the Children, The.
Wilbur, R.   Boy at the Window.
Digging for China.
Pardon, The.
Statues.
Wilde, O.   Le Jardin des Tuileries.
Williams, C. K.   Before This.
Blades.
Body, The.
Color of Time, The.
For Gail, When I Was Five.
Gift, The.
Good Mother: Out.
I Am the Bitter Name.
I'd forgotten and / how could I ever.
My Mother's Lips.
Of What Is Past.
Park, The.
Reading: Early Sorrow.
Scar.
Sorrow, The.
Still Life.
Tails.
Ten Below.
Waking Jed.
When / you were small, I.
Williams, M.   At the Children's Hospital in
    Little Rock.
Deadsong for a Neighbor Child Who Ran Away
    to the Woods.
For Lucinda, Robert, and Karyn.
Of History and Hope.
Rebecca at Play.
Showing Late Symptoms She First Tries to Fix
    Herself in the Minds of Her Children.
Vanishing Point, The.
Williams, T.   In Jack-O'-Lantern's Weather.
Look Both Ways Crossing Streets.
My Little One.
Which Is My Little Boy.
Williams, W.   Child and Vegetables.
Death of Franco of Cologne, The: His Prophecy
    of Beethoven.
Hic Jacet.
Portent.
Sympathetic Portrait of a Child.
To.
Waiting.
Wilner, E.   Amelia.
As Soft and as Pink as a Nursery.
Made by Hand.
Wordsworth, W.   Anecdote for Fathers.
"Beloved Vale!" I said, "when I shall con."
Characteristics of a Child Three Years Old.
Infant M— M—, The.
Intent on Gathering Wool from Hedge and
    Brake.
Little Onward Lend Thy Guiding Hand, A.
My heart leaps up when I behold.
Ode: Intimations of Immortality from
    Recollections of Early Childhood.
Ruth [or, The Influences of Nature].
To a Child [Written in Her Album].
To H. C., Six Years Old.
We Are Seven.
While Anna's Peers and Early Playmates Tread.
Wright, J.   Evening.

Little Girl on Her Way to School, A.
Mutterings Over the Crib of a Deaf Child.
Note Left in Jimmy Leonard's Shack, A.
Poem by Garnie Braxton, A.
Sappho.
Song for the Middle of the Night, A.
Twilights.
Yeats.   Among School Children.
Cradle Song, A: "Angels are stooping, The."
Prayer for My Daughter, A.
To a Child Dancing in the Wind.
Zagajewski.   How High the Moon.
Just Children.
Sisters of Mercy.
Zaturenska.   All Is Well with the Child.
For a Child.
Future in Miniature.
Interpreter of Silence, The.
Invaders, The.

See also **Adolescence; Boys; Death in Childhood;
Girls; Youth**

Chile
Kizer, C.   October 1973.
Laughlin, J.   People Boxes, The.
Preguntas sin respuestas for Nicanor Parra.
Levertov.   For Chile, 1977.
Mistral, G.   Chilean Earth.
Clover Patch.
Concepción.
Mayten, The.
Talcahuano.
Valparaíso.
Williams, M.   For Victor Jara.

Chimney Sweepers
Graves, R.   Wm. Brazier.
Niedecker.   Chimney Sweep.

Chimneys
Cummings, E. E.   Death's Chimney.
Frost, R.   Kitchen Chimney, The.
Graves, R.   Under the Pot.
Williams, W.   Yellow Chimney, The.

China
Bierce.   Voice from Pekin, A.
Brodsky, J.   Letters from the Ming Dynasty.
Corbett, W.   D-Day 1989.
Dubie.   Elegies for the Ocher Deer on the Walls
    at Lascaux.
Looking up from Two Renaissance Paintings to
    the Massacre at Tiananmen Square.
Eberhart, R.   Ode to the Chinese Paper Snake.
Ultimate Song.
Hall, D.   Photographs of China.
Hughes, L.   Roar China!
Kizer, C.   Ashes, The.
Where I've Been All My Life.
Laughlin, J.   Digging Down to China.
Li Po.   Summer Song.
Lindsay, N.   Chinese Nightingale, The.
Incense.
Shantung, or The Empire of China is Crumbling
    Down.
Mao Tse-tung [or Mao Zedong].   Spring in the
    Snow-Drenched Garden.
Merton.   Picture of Lee Ying, A.
O'Hara, F.   Poem: "At night Chinamen jump."
Rexroth, K.   Another Early Morning Exercise.
Imitations of the Chinese.
Rukeyser, M.   It is the sixth year of the war in
    China.
Simic.   Autumn Air.
Sze.   Red Octopus.
Viewing Photographs of China.
Tomlinson, C.   Nine Variations in a Chinese
    Winter Setting.
Tu Fu.   Testament.
Wilbur, R.   Digging for China.
Wright, C.   China Journal.

Chinatowns
Komunyakaa.   New Gold Mountain.
Sze.   Shuttle.

Chinaware
Merrill, J.   Willowware Cup.
Milosz, C.   Song on Porcelain.
Moore, M.   No Swan So Fine.

Chinese Poetry
Zagajewski. Chinese Poem.
Chinese, The
Carruth, H. Of Distress Being Humiliated by
the Classical Chinese Poets.
Collins, B. Reading an Anthology of Chinese
Poems of the Sung Dynasty.
Dubie. Shipwreck.
Eberhart, R. Bells of a Chinese Temple, The.
Gallagher, T. Rijl.
Some Painful Butterflies Pass Through.
Jeffers, R. On an Anthology of Chinese Poems.
Kizer, C. Anniversaries: Claremont Avenue,
from 1945.
Lost in Translation.
Komunyakaa. New Gold Mountain.
Rendezvous.
Mahon. Chinese Restaurant in Portrush, The.
Nemerov. To Lu Chi.
Rexroth, K. To Another.
Very Early Morning Exercise, A.
Rossetti, C. Chinaman, The.
Rumi. Chinese Art and Greek Art.
Sandburg, C. Bronzes.
Whalen, P. Hymnus Ad Patrem Sinensis.
Chipmunks
Ciardi, J. Useless Knowledge.
Cummings, E. E. & sun & / sil / e / nce.
Eberhart, R. Vastness and Indifference of the
World, The.
Jarrell, R. Chipmunk's Day, The.
Nash, O. Chipmunk, The.
Chirico, Giorgio de
Logan, J. March. The Museum. Buffalo. de
Chirico.
Pagis. Devotion.
Chivalry
De la Mare. Keep Innocency.
Graves, R. Absent Crusader.
Hardy, T. Then and Now.
Keats. Calidore. A Fragment.
Specimen of an Induction to a Poem.
To [Mary Frogley].
Melville, H. Rusty Man, The.
Meredith, G. Archduchess Anne.
Ballad of the Lady Eglantine, The.
Lives there a man with such base mettle.
Nash, O. How Now, Sirrah? Oh, Anyhow.
Chocolates
Creeley. Song: "Were I myself more blithe."
Levertov. Her Delight.
Nash, O. Assorted Chocolates.
Choctaw, The
Ai. Ice.
Choices
Bierce. Lacking Factor, A.
Bukowski. 35 Seconds.
Byron, G. God Maddens Him Whom 'T Is His
Will to Lose.
Campion, T. Could my poore hart whole worlds
of toungs employ.
What meanes this folly, now to brave it so.
Carew, T. Married Woman, A.
Carruth, H. Lost.
Carver, R. Bahia, Brazil.
Cunningham, J. All Choice Is Error.
Choice.
Dickey, W. Coyote's Song.
Dickinson, E. I'm ceded—I've stopped being
Theirs.
Donne. To Mr B. B.
Dugan, A. Not to Choose.
Frost, R. Lovely Shall Be Choosers, The.
Graves, R. Dans un Seul Lit.
Down, Wanton, Down!
Sharp Ridge, The.
Whole Love.
Hardy, T. Private Man on Public Men, A.
Herrick. Choose for the Best.
Will the Cause of Woe, The.
Ignatow, D. Forever.
Jackson, L. Dilemmist, The.
Nightmare, A.
Jacobsen, J. Margins of Choice.
Jarrell, R. Conversation with the Devil, A.

Jonson, B. Epode: "Not to know vice at all, and
keep[e] true state."
Kunitz, S. Beyond Reason.
Larkin, P. After-Dinner Remarks.
Dockery and Son.
How Distant.
Places, Loved Ones.
Lawrence, D. H. Free Will.
Impulse.
Levertov. Freedom.
Meredith, W. Consequences.
Myself, Rousseau, a Few Others.
Merwin. Air: "Naturally it is night."
I Live Up Here.
Route with No Number.
Nash, O. Strange Case of the Lucrative
Compromise, The.
Olson, C. In Cold Hell, in Thicket.
Paley, G. Life.
Parker, D. Choice, The.
Folk Tune.
Ultimatum.
Piercy. Right to Life.
Ransom, J. Romance of a Youngest Daughter.
Rich, A. Roofwalker, The.
Riley, J. Her Choice.
My Ruthers.
Ritsos. Choice.
Rossetti, C. All heaven is blazing yet / With the
meridian sun.
Ballad of Boding, A.
Brandons Both.
If a mouse could fly, / Or if a crow could swim.
Rumi. Many Wines, The.
Sandburg, C. Choices.
Choose.
Stock, R. Motives of a Two-Headed Turtle.
Szymborska, W. One Version of Events.
Wilbur, R. Sirens, The.
Williams, C. K. Halves.
What we are / given.
Wright, C. Lost Souls.
Wyatt, S. Like as the bird in the cage enclosed.
Yeats. Choice, The.
Choking
Creeley. End, The.
Pinsky. Saving, The.
Cholera
Dove, R. Cholera.
Kipling, R. Cholera Camp.
Chopin, Frédéric François
Clampitt. Berceuse.
Davie, D. In Chopin's Garden.
Niedecker. To Aeneas who closed his piano.
Zagajewski. Square D'Orléans.
Zaturenska. Imperfect, The.
Christchurch, New Zealand
Creeley. Catching Cold.
Christenings
Coleridge, S. On the Christening of a Friend's
Child.
Hardy, T. To C.F.H.
Parker, D. Godmother.
Ritsos. Country Woman.
Van Duyn. To My Godson, on His Christening.
Williams, M. At the Christening of an Infant
the Mind of the Young Preacher Wanders
Again.
See also **Baptism**
Christianity and Christians
Ai. Charisma.
Mother's Tale, The.
Amichai [*or* Amikhai]. Straight from Prejudice.
Angelou. Lord, in My Heart.
Bierce. Christian.
Bishop, E. Brazil, January 1, 1502.
Bly, R. Empty Place, An.
Bradstreet, A. Occasional Meditations: "By
night, when others soundly slept."
Brodsky, J. Nunc Dimittis.
Browning, E. Earth and Her Praisers.
View Across the Roman Campagna.
Work and Contemplation.
Browning, R. Death in the Desert, A.
Easter-Day.

Gold Hair: A Story of Pornic.
Holy-Cross Day.
Buchanan, G. Pope from penance purgatorial,
The.
Campion, T. Come Let Us Sound With
Melodie.
To the World.
Cavafy. Dangerous Remarks.
Dünya Güzeli.
Grand Procession of Priests and Laymen.
Hereafter, The.
Illness of Kleitos, The.
In Church.
In the Cemetery.
In the Districts Surrounding Antioch.
Julian at the Mysteries.
Julian in Nicomedia.
Manuel Komninos.
Myris: Alexandria, 340 A.D.
Priest at the Serapeion.
Tomb of Ignatios, The.
Vulnerant Omnes, Ultima Necat.
Word and Silence.
You Didn't Understand.
Chesterton. Blessing, A ("I live in an age of
varied powers and knowledge").
Clement of Alexandria. New Song, The.
Clifton, L. Far Memory.
Clough. Sa Majestá Très Chrétienne.
Coleridge, S. Religious Musings.
Collins, B. Sunday Morning with the
Sensational Nightingales.
Cowper, W. Hymn for the Sunday School at
Olney.
Progress of Error, The.
Reflection on the Foregoing Ode.
Song of Mercy and Judgment, A.
Truth.
Crashaw. Howres for the Hours of Matines,
The.
Cullen, C. Mood.
Sonnet: "I know now how a man whose blood
is hot."
Cunningham, J. Man who goes for Christian
resignation, The.
"Dario." Sweetness of the Angelus, divine in
the morning, The.
Davie, D. Advent.
Anglican Lady, An.
Christian Hero, A.
Church Militant.
Dissentient Voice, A.
Ecclesiastical Polity.
Elect, The.
Helena Morley.
Livingshayes.
Priory of St Saviour, Glendalough, The.
Dickinson, E. I'm ceded—I've stopped being
Theirs.
Is it a joyous expanse of Year.
Dubie. Meister Eckhart.
Dunbar, P. Light, The.
Religion.
Dunbar, W. Ballat of the Passioun, Ane.
Eberhart, R. Once More, O Ye.
United 555.
Eliot, T. S. Ballade pour la grosse Lulu.
Easter: Sensations of April.
Mr. Eliot's Sunday Morning Service.
Emerson, R. We sauntered amidst miracles.
Fergusson, E. Poem on the Death of Richard
Stockton, A.
Ferlinghetti, L. Sometime During Eternity.
García Lorca. Abandoned Church.
Ballad of Our Lady of the Boat.
Birth of Christ, The.
Martyrdom of St. Eulalia.
Ode to the Most Holy Sacrament of the Altar.
Poem of the *Saeta*.
St. Gabriel.
St. Michael.
Graves, R. Awakening, The.
Hammon. Dialogue Entitled the Kind Master
and Dutiful Servant, A.
Poem for Children with Thoughts on Death, A.
Herbert, G. British Church, The.

Church Militant, The.
Church-Rents and Schisms.
Cross[e], The.
Priesthood, The.
Herrick.   Christian Militant.
Crosses.
Good Christians.
On Himself[e].
Hopkins, G.   On the Portrait of Two Beautiful
    Young People.
Housman.   New Year's Eve.
Hughes, L.   Christian Country, A.
Madam and the Minister.
Merry Christmas.
Prayer Meeting.
Spirituals.
Sunday Morning Prophecy.
Jacobsen, J.   We Pray Most Earnestly.
Kinnell.   Avenue Bearing the Initial of Christ
    into the New World, The.
Komunyakaa.   Cooling Board, The.
Faith Healer.
Kumin, M.   Living Alone with Jesus.
Laughlin, J.   Easter in Pittsburgh.
Lawrence, D. H.   Cross, The.
Jesus' Farewell.
Retort to Jesus.
Song of Don Ramon, The.
Levertov.   Showings, The: Lady Julian of
    Norwich, 1342-1416.
Wings in the Pedlar's Pack.
Logan, J.   Prologue and Questions for St.
    Augustine On His Sixteenth Centenary.
MacNeice.   Belfast.
McHugh, H.   To a Christian.
Meredith, G.   Garden of Epicurus, The.
Song of Theodolinda, The.
Merton.   Letter to Pablo Antonio Cuadra
    Concerning Giants, A.
Two Desert Fathers.
Michelangelo Buonarroti.   Assured of death, of
    its timing, though, not so.
Milosz, C.   Either-Or.
Father Ch., Many Years Later.
Ode for the Eightieth Birthday of Pope John
    Paul II.
Old Women.
Zdziechowski.
Montale.   Iris.
News from Mount Amiata.
There the Tritone surges.
Muldoon, P.   Our Lady of Ardboe.
Nemerov.   Frozen City, The.
Sonnet: "Form of Christ cut from dark wood,
    the pale, A."
Olson, C.   Easter.
Obit.
Owen, W.   Maundy Thursday.
Paley, G.   Choir Singing, The.
Pasolini.   Religion of My Time, The.
Petrarch.   I am so weary and so heavy laden.
It was my love and grief which drove my
    tongue.
Little white-haired man moves off from where,
    The.
Most glorious Virgin, you are clothed in glory.
Seed of Charlemagne, his noble head, The.
Since you and I so many times have seen.
That lovely lady who possessed your heart.
Pinkerton, H.   Indecision.
Plath.   Medusa.
Raine, K.   Harvest of learning I have reaped.
Rexroth, K.   Wednesday of Holy Week, 1940.
Riley, J.   Luther Benson.
Vision of Rabbi Ben Issac, The.
Rimbaud, A.   Bad Blood.
First Communions.
Fragments According to the Gospel.
Impossible, The.
Poor People in Church.
Robinson, E.   Three Taverns, The.
Rossetti, C.   Christian and Jew. A Dialogue.
I Know You Not.
Testimony, A.
Sandburg, C.   Washerwoman.
Scott, S.   Gray Brother, The.

Seifert.   Place of Pilgrimage.
Shapiro, K.   Synagogue, The.
Smart, C.   Epistle to John Sherratt, Esq, An.
Hymns and Spiritual Songs for the Fasts and
    Festivals of the Church of England.
Hymns for the Amusement of Children.
Jubilate Agno.
Song to David, A.
Smith, S.   House of Over-Dew, The.
How Do You See?
Noble and Ethereal.
Oh Christianity, Christianity.
Sunt Leones.
Thoughts about the Christian Doctrine of
    Eternal Hell.
Why Do You Rage?
Stafford, W.   108 East 19th.
Stevens, W.   Blue Buildings in the Summer Air,
    The.
High-Toned Old Christian Woman, A.
Old Lutheran Bells at Home, The.
Sunday Morning.
Stock, R.   Poem on Holy Saturday.
Stockton, A.   Fragment, Janu'ry 1786.
How blest the soul to whom indulgent heaven.
Hymn Written in the Year 1753, A.
Meditation on the 3d Verse of the 28th Chapter
    of Mathew.
Ode for Christmas Day, An.
Ode to Solitude Inscribed to Mrs Boudinot, An.
On Hearing of the Out Powering of the Divine
    Spirit in Nassau Hall, Feb 24 1757.
Swift, J.   Lines to Pope.
On the Words "Brother Protestants and Fellow
    Christians."
Tate, J.   Reapers of the Water.
Tabernacle, The.
Thomas, D.   Altarwise by Owl-Light.
Before I Knocked.
Vision and Prayer.
Thoreau.   Just Made Perfect, The.
Who hears the parson.
Van Duyn.   Old widow lady, and went out to do
    her chore, An.
Pietà, Rhenish, 14th C., the Cloisters, The.
Relative and an Absolute, A.
Very.   Congregational Singing.
Faith of the First Christians, The.
Justification by Faith.
On the Great Divisions of the Christian Church.
To the Memory of the Rev. James Flint, D. D.
Wheatley, P.   Address to the Atheist, An.
Address to the Deist—1767, An.
Atheism.
Deism.
Elegy, To Miss. Mary Moorhead, on the Death
    of Her Father.
On Being Brought from Africa to America.
On Messrs Hussey and Coffin.
On the Death of a Young Gentleman.
On the Death of a Young Lady of Five Years of
    Age.
On the Death of the Rev. Dr. Sewell. 1769.
Prayer: "Oh my Gracious Preserver!"
Thoughts on the Works of Providence.
Whitman, W.   To Him That Was Crucified.
Whittier.   Brown Dwarf of Rügen, The.
By Their Works.
Call of the Christian, The.
Christian Tourists, The.
Holy Land, The.
How Mary Grew.
Nauhaught, the Deacon.
Red River Voyageur, The.
Wilbur, R.   Rule, The.
Wilde, O.   Sonnet on the Massacre of the
    Christians in Bulgaria.
Williams, M.   And When in Scenes of Glory.
In the Beginning.
In Your Own Words Without Lying Tell
    Something of Your Background.
Old Man Leaves His Church for the Last Time,
    An.
Wordsworth, W.   Composed in Roslin Chapel,
    During a Storm.
Decay of Piety.

Eagle and the Dove, The.
Inscription for a Monument in Crossthwaite
    Church, in the Vale of Keswick.
On the Same Occasion [on Seeing the
    Foundation Preparing for the Erection of
    Rydal Chapel].
Wright, C.   Lost Bodies.
October 2.
Wright, J.   Family Reunion.
Yeats.   Ribh Considers Christian Love
    Insufficient.
Veronica's Napkin.

Christmas
Ammons.   Christmas Eve.
Auden.   Blessed Event.
Berrigan, T.   For You.
Berry, W.   To Tanya at Christmas.
Brodsky, J.   Anno Domini.
Lagoon.
Second Christmas by the shore, A.
Browning, E.   Christmas Gifts.
Virgin Mary to the Child Jesus, The.
Carruth, H.   Essay on Death.
Song: The Young Man with the Guitar, Testing.
Chesterton.   House of Christmas, The.
Ciardi, J.   Christmas Alone in Key West.
Christmas Carol, A: "Stores wore Christmas
    perfectly, The."
Coleridge, S.   Homeless.
Corbett, W.   Bus Song.
Crashaw.   Hymne of the Nativity, Sung by the
    Shepheards, A.
In the Holy Nativity of Our Lord God.
To the Queen's Majesty.
Creeley.   Christmas: May 10, 1970.
Xmas.
Cullen, C.   Christus Natus Est.
Cummings, E. E.   And i imagine.
Little tree / little silent Christmas tree.
Davie, D.   Christmas Week, 1948.
Hawkshead and Dachau in a Christmas Glass.
De la Mare.   Before Dawn.
Dunbar, P.   Back-Log Song, A.
Chrismus Is A-Comin'
Christmas.
Christmas Carol: "Ring out, ye bells!"
Christmas Folksong, A.
Christmas in the Heart.
Little Christmas Basket, A.
Speakin' o' Christmas.
Eberhart, R.   Christmas Tree.
Eliot, T. S.   Cultivation of Christmas Trees, The.
Frost, R.   To a Young Wretch.
García Lorca.   Christmas on the Hudson.
Ginsberg, A.   Overpopulation, overpopulation /
    Give me 3 acres of land.
These States: into L.A.
Glück, L.   Nativity Poem.
Graves, R.   Carol of Patience.
Christmas Robin, The.
"H. D."   Christmas 1944.
Hacker, M.   Christmas Crown, A.
Hall, D.   Family, The.
Waiting on the Corners.
Hardy, T.   Burning the Holly.
Christmastide.
House of Hospitalities, The.
Nightmare, and the Next Thing, A.
Oxen, The.
Reminder, The.
Yuletide in a Younger World.
Herbert, G.   Christmas.
Herrick.   Ceremonies for Christmas[se].
Christs Birth.
Ode on the Birth of Our Saviour, An.
Saint Distaffs Day, or the Morrow after Twelfth
    Day.
Upon Candlemasse Day.
Upon Tuck.
Hopkins, G.   Moonless darkness stands between.
Hughes, L.   Christmas Story, The.
Madam's Christmas (or Merry Christmas
    Everybody).
Merry Christmas.
On a Christmas Night.
Jackson, L.   Christmas.

Weeknight Service.
Lindsay, N.   In the Immaculate Conception Church.
Logan, J.   Long Search, The.
  Month of Saints, A.
MacLeish.   St. Philip's Church in Antigua.
Mahon.   Songs of Praise.
Major, C.   Harps.
  Santa Maria Dei Frari.
Melville, H.   In a Church of Padua.
Meredith, W.   Notre Dame de Chartres.
Merwin.   Ash.
  Church, The.
Neruda.   Bell Tower of Authenay, The.
Oppen.   Church Interior.
Owen, W.   Le Christianisme.
Paley, G.   Choir Singing, The.
Raine, K.   Returning from Church.
Rimbaud, A.   Poor People in Church.
Rossetti, C.   St. Andrew's Church.
Schuyler, J.   Mark.
Seifert.   Our Lady of Žižkov.
  St George's Basilica.
Simic.   Gravity.
  Winter Night.
Stevens, W.   Gray Stones and Gray Pigeons.
Swift, J.   On His Own Deafness.
  Verses on the Upright Judge.
Tate, A.   Sonnets at Christmas.
Thomas, D.   It Is the Sinner's Dust-Tongued Bell.
Thoreau.   Who hears the parson.
Tomlinson, C.   Arroyo Seco.
  At Saint Mary's Church.
  In Michoacán.
  Las Trampas U. S. A.
  Santa Maria delle Nevi.
  Tax Inspector, The.
Very.   Evening Choir, The.
  Hymn, Sung at the Dedication of the New Stone Church of the North Society in Salem June 22d, 1836.
  My Church.
  On the First Church Built by the Puritans in 1634.
  Voting in the Old North Church.
Whitman, W.   March in the Ranks Hard-Prest, and the Road Unknown, A.
Whittier.   Book, The.
  Hymn for the House of Worship at Georgetown.
  Hymn for the Opening of Plymouth Church.
  Hymn for the Opening of Thomas Starr King's House of Worship.
  In the "Old South."
  Kallundborg Church.
  Landmarks, The.
Wilbur, R.   Dubious Night, A.
  Plain Song for Comadre, A.
Williams, M.   Old Man Leaves His Church for the Last Time, An.
Williams, W.   Problem, The.
Wordsworth, W.   Composed in Roslin Chapel, During a Storm.
  For a Seat in the Groves of Coleorton.
  Inscription for a Monument in Crossthwaite Church, in the Vale of Keswick.
  On the Same Occasion [on Seeing the Foundation Preparing for the Erection of Rydal Chapel].
  When Severn's Sweeping Flood Had Overthrown.
Wright, J.   Morning: Leaving Calle Gigantes.
  Wednesday Night Prayer Meeting.
Zagajewski.   Albi.
  Churches of France, The.

Churchill, Winston Leonard Spencer
Ignatow, D.   On the Death of Winston Churchill.
Niedecker.   Churchill's Death.

Churchyards
Browning, R.   Spring Song.
Clampitt.   Palm Sunday.
Gray, T.   Elegy Written in a Country Churchyard.
Mahon.   In Carrowdore Churchyard.
Rossetti, C.   Birchington Churchyard.
Swenson, M.   Trinity Churchyard, Spring 1961.

Cibber, Colley
Johnson, S.   Epigram on Colley Cibber.

Cicadas
Eberhart, R.   Largess, The.
García Lorca.   Cicada!
Laughlin, J.   Long Night, The.
McGrath, T.   Poem: "Long wound of the summer—, The."
Montale.   Shears, don't cut away that face.
Ritsos.   School Holidays.
Van Duyn.   Walking the Dog: A Diatribe.
Wilbur, R.   Cicadas.
Wright, C.   Cicada.

Cid (Rodrigo or Ruy Díaz de Vivar)
"Darío."   Concerning the Cid.

Cigarettes
Amichai [or Amikhai].   Support for My Breathing.
Collins, B.   Best Cigarette, The.
Cummings, E. E.   This cigarette is extremely long.
Enzensberger, H.   Vending Machine.
Ginsberg, A.   Put Down Your Cigarette Rag (Dont Smoke).
Hughes, T.   Memory, A.
Lorde.   American Cancer Society Or There Is More Than One Way to Skin a Coon.
Nash, O.   There Are More Ways to Roast a Pig than Burning the House Down or You Can Always Stick Your Head in a Volcano.
  Thoughts Thought after a Bridge Party.
Niedecker.   Energy glows at the lips.
Zukofsky, L.   Incident, An.
  Last cigarette / a companion, A.
See also **Smoking and Smokers**

Cigars
Kipling, R.   Betrothed, The.
Mallarmé.   Entire soul evoked, The.
Sandburg, C.   Crimson.
  Noon Hour.

Cinderella
Broumas, O.   Cinderella.
Jarrell, R.   Cinderella.
Plath.   Cinderella.
Sexton.   Cinderella.
Van Duyn.   Cinderella's Story.

Circe
Atwood.   Circe / Mud Poems.
Auden.   Circe.
Broumas, O.   Circe.
Gunn, T.   Moly.
"H. D."   Circe.
MacNeice.   Circe.
Rossetti, D.   For 'The Wine of Circe' by Edward Burne Jones.
Stock, R.   Circe.

Circumcision
Amichai [or Amikhai].   State of Affairs.
Crashaw.   Our Lord in His Circumcision to His Father.
Dugan, A.   Esthetics of Circumcision, The.
Herrick.   Another New-Yeeres Gift, or Song for the Circumcision.
  New-Yeeres Gift, or Circumcisions Song, The.
  To His Savior [or Saviour]. The New Years [or yeers] Gift.
  Upon Zelot.
Milton.   Upon the Circumcision.
Smith, S.   Jew Is Angry with His Friend Who Does Not Believe in Circumcision, A.

Circus
Berryman.   Animal Trainer, The.
Bishop, E.   Cirque d'Hiver.
Brodsky, J.   MCMXCV.
Carruth, H.   Wreck of the Circus Train, The.
Dickinson, E.   I've known a Heaven, like a Tent.
Dove, R.   Hill of Beans, A.
Emerson, R.   Like vaulters in the circus round.
Ferlinghetti, L.   Constantly Risking Absurdity.
Heaney, S.   Wheels within Wheels.
Koch, K.   Circus, The.
Komunyakaa.   Between Angels & Monsters.
Larkin, P.   For Sidney Bechet.
Lawrence, D. H.   On the Drum.

Two Performing Elephants.
  When I Went to the Circus.
Logan, J.   Thirty-Three Ring Circus, The.
MacNeice.   Circus.
McHugh, H.   Bear in English.
  Circus.
  Unspeakable.
Muldoon, P.   Duffy's Circus.
Nash, O.   Big Tent Under the Roof, The.
Olson, C.   Her Dream, Half Remembered.
Plath.   Circus in Three Rings.
  Denouement.
Prunty.   Family Act, The.
Riley, J.   Billy Miller's Circus-Show.
  Circus-Day Parade, The.
  Circus Parade, The.
  This Man Jones.
Rukeyser, M.   Destruction of Grief.
  Ringling.
Sandburg, C.   Air Circus.
  Hazardous Occupations.
Sexton.   Bells, The.
Smith, S.   This Is Disgraceful and Abominable.
Stafford, W.   Little Gift, A.
Szymborska, W.   Circus Animals.
Van Duyn.   Ringling Brothers, Barnum and Bailey.
Williams, T.   Les Etoiles d'un Cirque.
Williams, W.   Artist, The.
  Phoenix and the Tortoise, The.
Zagajewski.   Circus.

Cities
Ammons.   City Limits, The.
Angelou.   Through the Inner City to the Suburbs.
Armantrout.   View.
Arnold, M.   In Utrumque Paratus.
Ashbery, J.   Rivers and Mountains.
  Unctuous Platitudes.
Atwood.   City Planners, The.
Auden.   Paysage Moralisé.
Baudelaire.   Last Light.
Berry, W.   Mad Farmer in the City, The.
Bierce.   Passing Show, The.
  Vision of Doom, A.
Bishop, E.   From the Country to the City.
  Night City.
  One Art.
Blok.   Red Glow in the Sky, A.
Borges.   Benares.
  Web, The.
Brodsky, J.   Plato Elaborated.
Broumas, O.   Lying In.
  Next to the *Café Chaos*.
Browning, E.   My Doves.
  Soul's Travelling, The.
Browning, R.   Up at a Villa—Down in the City.
Bukowski.   Night on a Visa Card.
Carruth, H.   Snow, The.
  Thaw.
Cavafy.   City, The.
Clampitt.   Saloniki.
  Vacant Lot with Tumbleweed and Pigeons.
Clough.   Sic Itur.
  To the Great Metropolis.
Coleridge, S.   Hope and Time.
  Silent City, A.
Crane, H.   Euclid Avenue.
  Porphyro in Akron.
Creeley.   City, The.
  Night in NYC.
Cummings, E. E.   As usual i did not find him in cafes,the more dissolute atmosphere.
  At the head of this street a gasping organ is waving moth-eaten.
  Because / an obstreperous grin minutely floats.
  Blue woman with sticking out breasts hanging, A.
  Even if all desires things moments be.
  —GON splashes-sink.
  He as o / ld as who stag, A.
  Helves surling out of eakspeasies per(reel)hapsingly.
  I walked the boulevard.
  My sonnet is A light goes on in.
  (One!) / the wisti-twisti barber.

One winter afternoon / (at the magical hour).
Only as what(out of a flophouse)floats.
Paris,thou art not.
Phonograph's voice like a keen spider skipping, The.
Spring(side / walks are)is.
Taxis toot whirl people moving perhaps laugh into the slowly.
Twentyseven bums give a prostitute the once.
What a proud dreamhorse pulling(smoothloomingly)through.
When / from a sidewalk.
Davie, D.   Agave in the West.
Zion.
Donne.   To Sir Henry Wotton ("Sir, more than kisses, letters mingle souls").
Dove, R.   Spy.
Straw Hat.
Under the Viaduct, 1932.
Dugan, A.   On Leaving Town.
Eberhart, R.   To Harriet Monroe.
Eliot, T. S.   *Boston Evening Transcript*, The.
Morning at the Window.
Preludes.
Rhapsody on a Windy Night.
Silence.
Éluard, P.   Scene.
Fenton, J.   Doctor Gliedschirm, skin specialist, surgeries 14–16 hours or by appointment.
German Requiem, A.
Ginsberg, A.   Two Sonnets.
Gunn, T.   Bringing to Light.
In Praise of Cities.
Map of the City, A.
Night Taxi.
Tenderloin.
Gurney, I.   Time to Come.
"H. D."   Cities.
Other Sea-Cities.
Tribute, The.
Hacker, M.   Two Cities.
Hall, D.   Poem With One Fact.
Transcontinent.
Hardy, T.   From Her in the Country.
Nightmare, and the Next Thing, A.
Herrick.   Peace not Permanent.
To His Muse.
Upon Hinmself.
Hopkins, G.   Alchemist in the City, The.
Housman.   In My Own Shire.
Ignatow, D.   Come!
Question, The.
Where Nothing is Hidden.
Jacobsen, J.   Softly.
Tiger.
Jarrell, R.   City, City!
Jeffers, R.   What are Cities For?
Kipling, R.   Song of Seven Cities, The.
Song of the Cities, The.
To the City of Bombay.
Larkin, P.   Arrival.
Bridge for the Living.
Lawrence, D. H.   City-Life.
In the Cities.
North Country, The.
Levertov.   City Psalm.
Living Alone (1).
Obsessions.
Whisper, The.
Window, A.
World Outside, The.
Levi, P.   August.
Levine, P.   These Streets.
Lindsay, N.   Springfield Magical.
Logan, J.   Trip to Four or Five Towns, A.
MacNeice.   Birmingham.
Morning Sun.
Street Scene.
Major, C.   Arriving Uninvited.
McGrath, T.   Dawn Song.
Migration of Cities, The.
Return to Marsh Street.
Underground, The.
Meredith, G.   Linnet-Hawker, The.
Sleeping City, The.
Tardy Spring.

Meredith, W.   Fishvendor, The.
Rus in Urbe.
Merton.   And So Goodbye to Cities.
Aubade—the City.
City's Spring, The.
Holy Communion: the City.
How to Enter a Big City.
Merwin.   Acclimatization.
Before That.
City.
Coming Back in the Spring.
Counting Houses, The.
Island City.
Rock, The.
Milosz, C.   City, The.
In a City.
Legend, A.
Temptation.
Whiteness.
Montale.   Day and Night.
Nash, O.   City, The.
Nemerov.   From a Record of Disappointment.
Frozen City, The.
Sestina 2: "No waste is trackless: all terrain the lost."
Situation Does Not Change, The.
Stare of the Man from the Provinces, The.
O'Hara, F.   Poem: "Now the violets are all gone, the rhinoceroses, the cymbals."
Song: "Is it dirty."
Olson, C.   Part of the Series on the Paths, A.
To Try to Get Down One Citizen as Against Another.
Oppen.   Bicycles and the Apex, The.
Nation.
Pedestrian.
Source, The.
Paley, G.   Fear.
Parker, D.   Song of the Open Country.
Song of the Wildnerness.
Patchen.   23rd Street Runs into Heaven.
All That Night Lights Were Seen Moving in Every Direction.
He Was Alone (As in Reality) Upon His Humble Bed.
Piercy.   Learning Experience.
Pinsky.   Avenue.
City Dark, The.
City Elegies.
Poe.   City in the Sea, The.
Pope, A.   Epistle to Miss [*or* Miss Teresa] Blount, on Her Leaving the Town after the Coronation.
Ramanujan.   Poetry and Our City.
Riley, J.   Artemus of Michigan, The.
Rilke.   To Marie Laurencin.
Trumpets.
Rimbaud, A.   Cities ("Official acropolis surpasses the most colossal conceptions of modern barbarity, The").
City.
Metropolitan.
Rossetti, C.   Dead City, The.
Mr. and Mrs. Scott, and I.
True Story, A.
Rukeyser, M.   Eel.
Sixth Elegy. River Elegy.
Wooden Spring.
Sandburg, C.   Blue Island Intersection.
Cahoots.
City Number.
Fellow Citizens.
Flat Lands.
Good Morning, America.
Hats.
Osawatomie.
Passers-by.
People Who Must.
Prayers of Steel.
Santa Fe Sketches.
Skyscraper.
Slants at Buffalo, New York.
Smoke Blue.
Streets Too Old.
They Will Say.
Windy City, The.

Schuyler, J.   Morning, The.
Sexton.   Keeping the City.
Mr. Mine.
Snyder, G.   7:VII.
Cartagena.
Spender, S.   Hamburg, 1929.
Stock, R.   Curriculum Vitae.
Swenson, M.   City Garden in April, A.
Garden at St. John's, The.
Swift, J.   Description of a City Shower, A.
Description of the Morning, A.
Tomlinson, C.   Geneva Restored.
More Foreign Cities.
Updike.   São Paulo.
Small-City People.
Walcott.   City's Death by Fire, A.
Whalen, P.   Life in the City: In Memoriam Edward Gibbon.
Whitman, W.   Once I Pass'd through a Populous City.
Sparkles from the Wheel.
Wilbur, R.   After the Last Bulletins.
For the New Railway Station in Rome.
Peace of Cities, The.
Shame.
Williams, C. K.   Snow: I.
Williams, T.   Soft City, The.
Williams, W.   Approach to a City.
Bastard Peace, A.
Bitter World of Spring, The.
Construction.
Flower, The.
Grotesque.
Metric Figure.
Perpetuum Mobile: The City.
Predicter of Famine, The.
Wilner, E.   What Was Going On.
Wordsworth, W.   Composed upon Westminster Bridge, September 3, 1802.
Wright, J.   Destination: Accomplished.
River Down Home, The.
Yeats.   Coole Park, 1929.
Zagajewski.   Ancient History.
At Daybreak.
City Unknown.
City Where I Want to Live, The.
In Strange Cities.
Late Feast.
Lindens.
To See.
See also **Towns; Villages**
Civil Defense
Williams, M.   We.
Civil Rights Movement
Hughes, L.   Ballad of Walter White.
Brotherly Love.
Demonstration.
Northern Liberal.
Undertow.
Kizer, C.   Poem, Small and Delible.
Oppen.   Book of Job and a Draft of a Poem to Praise the Paths of the Living, The.
Orr, G.   Demonstration, The.
On a Highway East of Selma, Alabama.
Solitary Confinement.
See also **Protest, Social**
Civil Service
Han-shan.   My writing and judgment aren't that bad.
Who is this poor dreamer.
Kizer, C.   Death of a Public Servant, The.
Tu Fu.   Thwarted.
Civil War, Spain
Hughes, L.   Air Raid: Barcelona.
Hero—International Brigade.
Letter from Spain.
Madrid [—1937].
Moonlight in Valencia: Civil War.
Postcard from Spain.
Song of Spain.
Tomorrow's Seed.
Jarrell, R.   For the Madrid Road.
Kizer, C.   October 1973.
Valley of the Fallen, The.
Levine, P.   Francisco, I'll Bring You Red

Carnations.
Hear Me.
MacDiarmid, H. Major Road Ahead.
One loves the temporal, some unique
  manifestation.
Merton. In Memory of the Spanish Poet
  Federico Garcia Lorca.
Niedecker. 1937.
Rukeyser, M. Mediterranean.
Seifert. Salute to the Madrid Barricades.
Spanish Vineyards.
Spender, S. Port Bou.
To Manuel Altolaguirre.
Williams, W. Figueras Castle.
See also **Spain**

Civil War, United States
Berryman. Ancestor.
Bierce. At a "National Encampment."
Confederate Flags, The.
Death of Grant, The.
Hesitating Veteran, The.
To E. S. Salomon.
Bishop, E. From Trollope's Journal.
Borges. Note for a Fantastic Story.
Ciardi, J. Memorial Day.
Dickey, J. Hunting Civil War Relics at
  Nimblewill Creek.
Dubie. Her Monologue of Dark Crepe with
  Edges of Light.
Huts at Esquimaux, The.
Dugan, A. Fabrication of Ancestors.
On the Civil War on the East Coast of the
  United States of North America 1860–64.
Dunbar, P. Colored Soldiers, The.
News, The.
Robert Gould Shaw.
Unsung Heroes, The.
When Dey 'Listed Colored Soldiers.
Emerson, R. Boston Hymn.
Voluntaries.
Frost, R. Black Cottage, The.
Hayden, R. Dream, The.
Ignatow, D. Walt Whitman in the Civil War
  Hospitals.
Jarrell, R. Description of Some Confederate
  Soldiers, A.
Kumin, M. On Being Asked to Write a Poem
  for the Centenary of the Civil War.
Kunitz, S. Lincoln Relics, The.
Lowell, R. For the Union Dead.
Melville, H. Apparition, The—A Retrospect.
Armies of the Wilderness, The.
At the Cannon's Mouth.
Ball's Bluff.
Battle of Stone River, Tennessee.
Canticle, A.
College Colonel, The.
Fortitude of the North, The.
House-Top, The.
Malvern Hill.
March into Virginia, The.
March to the Sea, The.
On Sherman's Men.
On the Grave.
On the Home Guards.
On the Slain Collegians.
Portent, The.
Rebel Color-Bearers at Shiloh.
Sheridan at Cedar Creek.
Shiloh [A Requiem].
Stonewall Jackson.
Utilitarian View of the Monitor's Fight, A.
Olson, C. Anecdotes of the Late War.
As if Hallam Movius had placed a grid over it,
  and plumb-.
Civil War, The.
Connection, The.
Oppen. Civil war photo.
Pinkerton, H. Alike and Yet Unlike: General
  Richard Taylor Writes to Henry Adams.
Crossing the Pedregal.
Lemuel Shaw's Meditation.
Melville's Letter to William Clark Russell.
Rich, A. Charleston in the Eighteen-Sixties.
Riley, J. Ezra House.
Gladness.

Peace-Hymn of the Republic, A.
Thoughts on the Late War.
Rukeyser, M. City of Monuments.
Sandburg, C. Hammers Pounding.
Shenandoah.
Tate, A. Battle of Murfreesboro.
Ode to the Confederate Dead.
Updike. Richmond.
Very. Crisis, The.
Faith in Time of War.
Hymn: Our Country's Dead.
Ode to Freedom.
On the Completion of the Pacific Telegraph.
On the Increase in Crime Since the Late Civil
  War.
Our Soldiers' Graves.
Warren, R. Two Studies in Idealism: Short
  Survey of American and Human History.
Whitman, W. Adieu to a Soldier.
Army Corps on the March, An.
Artilleryman's Vision, The.
As I Lay with My Head in Your Lap Camerado.
As Toilsome I Wander'd Virginia's Woods.
Ashes of Soldiers: Epigraph.
Bathed in War's Perfume.
Beat! Beat! Drums!
Bivouac on a Mountain Side.
By the Bivouac's Fitful Flame.
Cavalry Crossing a Ford.
City of Ships.
Come Up from the Fields Father.
Death of General Grant.
Delicate Cluster.
Dirge for Two Veterans.
Eighteen Sixty-One.
Ethiopia Saluting the Colors.
First O Songs for a Prelude.
From Paumanok Starting I Fly Like a Bird.
Give Me the Splendid Silent Sun.
How Solemn as One by One.
I Saw Old General at Bay.
Lo, Victress on the Peaks.
March in the Ranks Hard-Prest, and the Road
  Unknown, A.
O Sun of Real Peace.
Over the Carnage Rose Prophetic a Voice.
Race of Veterans.
Reconciliation.
Sight in Camp [in the Daybreak Gray and Dim],
  A.
Song of the Banner at Daybreak.
Spirit Whose Work Is Done.
To a Certain Civilian.
Turn O Libertad.
Twilight Song, A.
Vigil Strange I Kept on the Field One Night.
Virginia—the West.
While Not the Past Forgetting.
World Take Good Notice.
Wound-Dresser, The.
Year That Trembled and Reel'd beneath Me.
Whittier. Anniversary Poem.
At Port Royal.
Barbara Frietchie.
Battle Autumn of 1862, The.
Ein Feste Burg Ist Unser Gott.
Hymn for the Celebration of Emancipation at
  Newburyport.
Hymn Sung at Christmas by the Scholars of St.
  Helena's Island, S.C.
Laus Deo!
Lost Occasion, The.
Peace Autumn, The.
Thy Will Be Done.
To Englishmen.
To John C. Frémont.
To Samuel E. Sewall and Harriet W. Sewall.
Watchers, The.
What the Birds Said.
Word for the Hour, A.

Civil Wars, England
Browning, R. Cavalier Tunes.
Herrick. Bad Season Makes the Poet Sad, The.
Obedience.
Upon the Troublesome Times.
Kipling, R. Edgehill Fight.

Marvell. Elegy upon the Death of My Lord
  Francis Villiers, An.
Milton. To the Lord General Cromwell.
When the Assault Was Intended to the City.

Civilization
Blok. Scythians, The.
Bourne, V. Thracian, The.
Brodsky, J. After Us.
Letter to an Archaeologist.
MCMXCIV.
Plato Elaborated.
Cavafy. Waiting for the Barbarians.
Ciardi, J. Measurements.
Davie, D. Among Artisans' Houses.
Eliot, T. S. Choruses from "The Rock."
Waste Land, The.
Emerson, R. Adirondacs, The.
Enough is done highminded friend go sleep.
Water.
World-Soul, The.
Ferlinghetti, L. Vast Confusion, A.
Ginsberg, A. C'mon Pigs of Western
  Civilization Eat More Grease.
Hall, D. New Hampshire.
Hill, G. After Cumae.
Elegiac Stanzas: On a Visit to Dove Cottage.
Of Commerce and Society: Variations on a
  Theme.
Howe, S. Cabbage Gardens.
Chanting at the Crystal Sea.
Hinge Picture.
Secret History of the Dividing Line.
Hughes, L. Broadcast on Ethiopia.
Lament for Dark Peoples.
Letter to the Academy.
Poem: "All the tom-toms of the jungles beat in
  my blood."
Hughes, T. Fourth of July.
Jeffers, R. Decaying Lambskins.
Hellenistics.
New Mexican Mountain.
Sign-Post.
Still the Mind Smiles.
What is Worthless?
Kipling, R. Benefactors, The.
City of Brass, The.
For All We Have and Are [1914].
White Man's Burden, The.
Koch, K. Our Hearts.
Lawrence, D. H. Man, A.
Lindsay, N. Gospel of Beauty, A.
MacLeish. Sheep in the Ruins, The.
Mahon. Image from Beckett, An.
Merton. Martin's Predicament or Atlas Watches
  Every Evening.
Milosz, C. Three Talks on Civilization.
Tidings.
Nash, O. Tell It to the Eskimos or Tell it to the
  Esquimaux.
We Would Refer You to Our Service
  Department, If We Had One.
Neruda. Danger, The.
Patchen. Man Is to Man a Beast.
Pinsky. Figured Wheel, The.
Rich, A. Meditations for a Savage Child.
Rimbaud, A. After the Flood.
Rukeyser, M. Lost Romans, The.
Outpost.
Sandburg, C. At the Gates of Tombs.
Chillicothe.
Good Morning, America.
Stafford, W. At Cove on the Crooked River.
Stevens, W. Anecdote of the Jar.
Botanist on Alp (No. 1).
Tomlinson, C. Theory of Regress.
Warren, R. Dream, Dump-Heap, and
  Civilization.
Wright, J. Horse, The.
Yeats. Long-Legged Fly.
Meru.

Clams and Clamming
Creeley. Provincetown.
Eberhart, R. Clam Diggers and Diggers of Sea
  Worms, The.
Oliver, M. Clam Man.
See also **Oysters; Shells**

Clans
Blue Cloud.   Wolf.
Burns, R.   Campbells Are Comin, The.
Wordsworth, W.   Brownie, The.
See also **Culloden, Battle of (1746)**

Clare
Davie, D.   Midsummer's Eve.

Class
HaNagid.   People Welcome the Rich.
Komunyakaa.   Salt.
Martial.   2.68: "That I now call you by your name."
Meredith, W.   American Living Room, The: A Tract.
Tu Fu.   Testament.
Whalen, P.   Historical Disquisitions.
See also **Social Class**

Classicism
Borges.   To a Minor Poet of the Greek Anthology.
Ciardi, J.   Apology for a Lost Classicism, An.
Clough.   Resignation—to Faustus.
Coleridge, S.   Garden of Boccaccio, The.
Tombless Epitaph, A.
Cummings, E. E.   Ballad of the Scholar's Lament.
When i am in boston,i do not speak.
Davie, D.   Scythian Charioteers, The.
Thyestes.
To an American Classicist.
Emerson, R.   I rake no coffined clay, nor publish wide.
"H. D."   I Said.
Nossis.
Hardy, T.   Liddell and Scott.
Jarrell, R.   English Garden in Austria, An.
Jonson, B.   Fit of Rhyme [*or* Rime] against Rhyme [*or* Rime], A.
Laughlin, J.   And Ole Ez said that the.
Merrill, J.   To My Greek.
Olson, C.   At midnight, after hours of love, I ate.
Poe.   To Helen.
Pound, E.   Return, The.
Rexroth, K.   Gas or Novocain.
Horny Dilemma.
Phoenix and the Tortoise, The.
Pliny—9, 36—Lampridius—29.
Sandburg, C.   Child of the Romans.
Southern Pacific.
Tate, A.   Aeneas at Washington.
Mediterranean, The.
Walcott.   Sea Grapes.
Williams, W.   After Song, An.
Yeats.   Bronze Head, A.
Zagajewski.   Ancient History.

Cleanliness
Collins, B.   Advice to Writers.
Graves, R.   It Was All Very Tidy.
Herrick.   Meane, The.
Upon Brock.
Housman.   Oh, When I Was In Love.
Jacobsen, J.   Dishwasher as Absolution.
Lux.   His Job is Honest and Simple.
Nash, O.   Child Is Father to the Man, But with More Authority, The.
O'Hara, F.   Song: "Is it dirty."
Wilbur, R.   Plain Song for Comadre, A.

Cleopatra
Akhmatova, A.   Cleopatra.
Berryman.   Song from "Cleopatra."
Castiglione.   On the Statue of *Cleopatra*.
Cavafy.   Alexandrian Kings.
Cummings, E. E.   Cleopatra built / like a smooth arrow or.
"Dario."   Metempsychosis.
Eberhart, R.   Dry Rot, The.
Hughes, T.   Cleopatra to the Asp.
Lawrence, D. H.   Universe Flows, The.
Lindsay, N.   Trial of the Dead Cleopatra in Her Beautiful and Wonderful Tomb, The.
Lowell, R.   Nunc Est Bibendum, Cleopatra's Death.
Meredith, G.   Cleopatra.
Nash, O.   Asp, The.

Rossetti, C.   Study (A Soul), A.
Updike.   Dilemma in the Delta.

Clergy
Arnold, M.   In Harmony with Nature.
Berryman.   Song of the Demented Priest, The.
Browning, R.   Bishop Blougram's Apology.
Bishop Orders His Tomb at Saint Praxed's Church, The.
Soliloquy of the Spanish Cloister.
Burns, R.   Calf, The.
Elegy on Peg Nicholson.
Holy Tulzie, The.
Kirk's Alarm, The.
Lines *Written on a Window, at the King's Arms Tavern, Dumfries.*
On a Celebrated Ruling Elder.
To the Rev. John McMath, Inclosing a Copy of *Holy Willie's Prayer,* Which He Had Requested.
Byron, G.   Bowles and Campbell.
New Vicar of Bray, The.
Cowper, W.   Yearly Distress, The.
Crashaw.   Upon Bishop Andrewes's [*or* Andrewes His] Picture before His Sermons.
Donne.   To Mr Tilman after He Had Taken Orders.
Dubie.   Revelation 20:11–15.
Emerson, R.   Hymn Sung at the Second Church, Boston.
Once the priest / Lived in an age.
Fenton, J.   Staffordshire Murderer, A.
Herbert, G.   Aaron.
Collar, The.
Priesthood, The.
Windows, The.
Herrick.   To Jos: Lo: Bishop of Exeter.
Upon Glass: Epigram.
Upon Trap.
Hill, G.   Fantasia on 'Horbury'; John Bacchus Dykes, 1859.
Hopkins, G.   Habit of Perfection, The.
Jonson, B.   Epigram, An: "That you have seen the pride, beheld the sport."
On Lip[pe] the Teacher.
Kipling, R.   Curé, The.
Eddi's Service.
Our Lady of the Sackcloth.
Lawrence, D. H.   At the Bank in Spain.
Death of the Baron, The.
Logan, J.   Experiment That Failed, The.
MacLeish.   Acknowledgement.
Marvell.   Flecknoe, an English Priest at Rome.
Milton.   Elegy 2: On the Death of the Beadle of Cambrdige University.
Lycidas.
Owens, S.   Poem, A: "Ye Sons of Levi, Church Divines."
Rimbaud, A.   Squatting Down.
Tartufe's Punishment.
Robinson, E.   Sainte-Nitouche.
Stevens, W.   Gray Stones and Gray Pigeons.
Stockton, A.   Epigram Addressed to Two Clergymen, An.
Swift, J.   Ode to Dr. William Sancroft.
On the Irish Bishops.
Tate, J.   Vagabond, A.
Tennyson, A.   To the Rev. F. D. Maurice.
Unknown, sometimes at. to Sir Walter Ralegh.
Epitaph on the Earl of Salisbury.
Wheatley, P.   Elegy, Sacred to the Memory of that Great Divine, the Reverend and Learned Dr. Samuel Cooper, An.
To the Rev. Dr. Thomas Amory on Reading His Sermons on Daily Devotion.
Whittier.   Clerical Oppressors.
Gallows, The.
Inscriptions.
Letter from a Missionary of the Methodist Episcopal Church South.
Lines from a Letter to a Young Clerical Friend.
Minister's Daughter, The.
Official Piety.
Pastoral Letter, The.
Sabbath Scene, A.
Yeats.   Ballad of Father Gilligan, The.
See also **Rabbis**

Clerks
Robinson, E.   Clerks, The.
Roethke.   Dolor.
See also **Office Workers**

Cleveland, Ohio
Ginsberg, A.   Cleveland, the Flats.
Koch, K.   Artist, The.
Patchen.   Cleveland, Oh?
Sandburg, C.   Honky Tonk in Cleveland, Ohio.

Clichés
Clough.   That out of sight is out of mind.
Merton.   Anatomy of Melancholy, The.
Muldoon, P.   Symposium.
Nash, O.   Oh, Stop Being Thankful All over the Place.
Sandburg, C.   Put Off the Wedding Five Times and Nobody Comes to It.

Cliff Dwellers
Williams, W.   Testament of Perpetual Change, The.

Cliffs
"H. D."   Cliff Temple, The.
Hardy, T.   Beeny Cliff.
To a Sea-Cliff.
Merwin.   Sea Cliffs at Kailua in December, The.
Millay, E.   Ragged Island.
Niedecker.   Wintergreen Ridge.
Orr, G.   Cliff, The.
Paz.   Landscape.
Plath.   Finisterre.
Raine, K.   Canna's Basalt Crags.
Swenson, M.   From Sea Cliff, March.
Tomlinson, C.   Morwenna's Cliff.
Near Ceibwr.
Warren, R.   Question at Cliff-Thrust.
Wordsworth, W.   Gordale.

Climbing
Ammons.   Cougar.
Reward.
Cooper, J.   Rock Climbing.
Hughes, T.   When Men Got to the Summit.
Jacobsen, J.   Leaf with Berry.
Logan, J.   Medicine Bow.
Merwin.   Ascent.
Michelangelo Buonarroti.   That whole way up to your brilliant diadem.
Ritsos.   Ascent.
Stafford, W.   After Arguing against the Contention That Art Must Come from Discontent.
Warren, R.   Delusion?—No!
Dreaming in Daylight.
Why You Climbed Up.
Wilner, E.   Beyond the Second Landing.

Clinton, Bill (William Jefferson Clinton)
Ai.   Blood in the Water.

Clocks
Baudelaire.   Clock, The.
Bishop, E.   Paris, 7 A.M.
Browning, E.   Hugh Stuart Boyd [Legacies].
Campion, T.   De horologio portabili.
Cavafy.   Vulnerant Omnes, Ultima Necat.
Ciardi, J.   Clock in the Mirror, The.
Coleridge, S.   For a Market-Clock.
Cowper, W.   Motto on the King's Clock.
Cummings, E. E.   There are so many tictoc.
Dickinson, E.   Clock stopped, A.
Dugan, A.   On a Baroque Clock.
Emerson, R.   To the Clock.
García Lorca.   Pause of the Clock.
Graves, R.   Counting the Beats.
Gunn, T.   Clock, The.
Hall, D.   Alligator Bride, The.
"Between the Clock and the Bed."
Hardy, T.   Clock-Winder, The.
Copying Architecture in an Old Minster.
Hughes, L.   Bells Toll Kindly, The.
Jackson, L.   Wind, the Clock, the We, The.
Jacobsen, J.   Clock, The.
Levertov.   Seth Thomas: A Love Poem.
Lowell, R.   Fall 1961.
MacLeish.   Why the Face of a Clock is not Truly a Circle.
MacNeice.   Slow Starter, The.
Moore, M.   Four Quartz Crystal Clocks.

Nemerov. Clock With No Hands, A.
Niedecker. There's a better shine.
Ramanujan. At Zero.
On a Delhi Sundial.
Time and Time Again.
Rich, A. Clock in the Square, A.
Riley, J. Little Dick and the Clock.
Sandburg, C. Clocks.
Solo for Saturday Night Guitar.
Tate, J. Time X.
Tomlinson, C. At Delft.
Very. Clock, The.
Warren, R. Forever O'Clock.
There's a Grandfather's Clock in the Hall.
Whalen, P. Defective Circles.
Wilbur, R. Bell Speech.
Wordsworth, W. Cuckoo-Clock, The.
See also **Watches**

Cloisters, The, New York City
Borges. Cloisters, The.

Clothing
Amichai [or Amikhai]. Sheepskin Coat.
Burns, R. Wee Willie Gray.
Carruth, H. November Jeans Song.
Cavafy. Garments.
Ciardi, J. On Sending Home My Civilian
Clothes.
Codrescu. Casting.
Love of a Coat, The.
Collins, B. Taking Off Emily Dickinson's
Clothes.
Cowper, W. Methinks I see thee decently
array'd.
Crane, S. Youth in apparel that glittered, A.
Dickinson, E. We outgrow love like other
things.
Dugan, A. 851.
Dunbar, P. Bohemian, The.
Enzensberger, H. Clothes.
Ferlinghetti, L. Underwear.
Gallagher, T. Black Silk.
Coats, The.
I Save Your Coat, But You Lose It Later.
Gjuzel. When I Came Back.
Hacker, M. Part of a True Story.
Hall, D. Pictures of Philippa.
Han-shan. Get your own clothes if you're cold.
I have a coat.
Hardy, T. Gentleman's Second-Hand Suit, A.
Old Gown, The.
Pink Frock, The.
Thunderstorm in Town, A.
Herrick. Art above Nature, to Julia.
Cloathes, Are Conspirators.
Cloaths for Continuance.
Clothes Do But Cheat and Cozen [or Cousen]
Us.
Delight in Disorder.
Julia's Petticoat.
Leprosie in Cloathes.
Lilly in a Christal, The.
Raggs.
Upon Cuts.
Upon Electra.
Upon Julia's Clothes.
Upon Julia's Ribband.
Upon Julia's Unlacing Her Self.
Upon Lupes.
Upon Shift.
Upon Skrew.
Hughes, L. Brand New Clothes.
Dressed Up.
What?
When Sue Wears Red.
Jackson, L. Because of Clothes.
One Self.
Komunyakaa. Boy Wearing a Dead Man's
Clothes.
Kunitz, S. Old Clothes Man, The.
Larkin, P. Large Cool Store, The.
Laughlin, J. My Old Gray Sweater.
Take Off Your Socks!!
Lawrence, D. H. Moral Clothing.
Levine, P. Suit, The.
Merrill, J. Dreams About Clothes.
Michelangelo Buonarroti. How joyfully it

shows, the garland there.
Kindly to others, to itself unkind.
Milosz, C. Aleksander Wat's Tie.
Nash, O. Man With Two New Suits, The.
Requiem: "There was a young belle of old
Natchez."
Nemerov. Pockets.
Niedecker. Hand Crocheted Rug.
See the girls in shorts on their bicycles.
Seven years a charming woman wore.
Olson, C. Elements of clothes, an arm and hand
the head of a cock.
Paley, G. In Hanoi 1969.
Parker, D. Satin Dress, The.
Patchen. My Coat Is Dirty.
Pinsky. Shirt.
Prunty. Hand-me-down, The.
Riley, J. Little Coat, The.
Ritsos. After Death.
Remembrance.
Under Oblivion.
Undressing of the Hanged Man, The.
Rossetti, C. Bread and Milk for Breakfast.
Sandburg, C. Films.
Summer Shirt Sale.
Schuyler, J. Frock.
Velvet Roses.
Seifert. Dance of the Girls' Chemises.
Sexton. Clothes.
Song for a Red Nightgown.
Sheridan, T. Prologue Spoke by Mr. Elrington,
A.
Simic. Overcoat, The.
Piety.
Smith, S. Si Peu Séduisante.
Snyder, G. No Shoes No Shirt No Service.
Spender, S. Little Coat, The.
Swenson, M. Question.
Szymborska, W. Clothes.
Updike. Courtesy Call.
Weiss, T. Clothes Maketh the Man.
Wilbur, R. Catch, The.
Love Calls Us to the Things of This World.
Williams, C. K. Vehicle: Absence.
See also **Jewelry**

Clouds
Bogan, L. Train Tune.
Borges. Clouds ("High in the air these placid
mountains or").
Brodsky, J. Clouds ("High in the air these
placid mountains or").
Brontë, E. Still as she looked the iron clouds.
Browning, E. House of Clouds, The.
Man and Nature.
Coleridge, S. Fancy in Nubibus.
Collins, B. Student of Clouds.
Crane, H. To the Cloud Juggler.
Cunningham, J. Distinctions at Dusk.
Dickey, J. Wall and Cloud.
Dickinson, E. Curious Cloud surprised the Sky,
A.
Dubie. You.
Frost, R. Lost in Heaven.
Gurney, I. Cloud, The.
Hall, D. Tree and the Cloud, The.
Hardy, T. Sheep-Boy, The.
Herrick. Her Bed.
Hughes, L. Garment.
Ignatow, D. Cloud Creates, A.
Jacobsen, J. Presences.
Levertov. Clouds.
Levine, P. Roofs.
Maritain. Cloud, The.
Meredith, G. On Como.
South-Wester, The.
Merwin. By the Cloud Path.
Clear Skies, The.
Mistral, G. To the Clouds.
Nash, O. Cherub, The.
Olson, C. Clouds, The.
Raine, K. Bright cloud, / Bringer of rain to far
fields.
Cloud.
Lifelong ago such days.
My sight with the clouds'.
Rilke. Clouds.

Evening Love Song.
Rossetti, C. Rainbow, The.
Sandburg, C. Broken Sky.
Evening Sea Wind.
Sky Talk.
Schuyler, J. Gray Day.
Shelley, P. Cloud, The.
Sheridan, T. New Simile for the Ladies, A.
Stafford, W. No Praise, No Blame.
Stevens, W. On [or Of] the Manner of
Addressing Clouds.
Sea Surface Full of Clouds.
Swenson, M. Cloud-Mobile, The.
Cumuli.
Swift, J. Answer to a Scandalous Poem, An.
Szymborska, W. Clouds.
Tomlinson, C. Above the Rio Grande.
Clouds.
Into Distance.
Updike. Cloud Shadows.
Descent of Mr. Aldez, The.
Very. Clouded Morning, The ("Morning comes,
and thickening clouds prevail, The").
To a Cloud.
Warren, R. Timeless, Twinned.
Williams, W. Clouds, The.
Idyl: "Wine of the grey sky."
Wordsworth, W. I Wandered Lonely As a
Cloud.
Most Alluring Clouds That Mount the Sky, The.
To the Clouds.
Yeats. These Are the Clouds.
Zaturenska. Terraces of Light.

Clough, Arthur Hugh
Arnold, M. Thyrsis.

"Clout, Colin"
See **Spenser, Edmund ("Colin Clout")**

Clover
Ammons. Mechanics.
Berry, W. February 2, 1968.
Dickinson, E. His oriental heresies.
Eberhart, R. Cover Me Over.
Melville, H. Clover.
Mistral, G. Clover Patch.
Riley, J. Clover, The.
Williams, T. Clover.
Zukofsky, L. Clover.

Clowns
Clare, J. Clown, The.
Creeley. Out of Sight.
Cummings, E. E. One winter afternoon / (at the
magical hour).
Dugan, A. Speech to the Student Clowns at the
Circus Clown School at Sarasota, Florida.
Hall, D. Clown, The.
Hughes, L. Black Clown, The.
Jacobsen, J. Suite for All Clown's Day.
Logan, J. Thirty-Three Ring Circus, The.
Mallarmé. Clown Chastised, The.
Patchen. Folly of Clowns.
Zagajewski. How Clowns Go.
See also **Circus**

Clumsiness
Dunbar, P. My Best Girl.
Olson, C. Day Song, the Day After.
Siena.

Coal Mining and Coal Miners
Davie, D. Barnsley, 1966.
County Durham.
Dugan, A. Portrait in the Form of an Extended
Conceit.
Hughes, T. Her Husband.
Lawrence, D. H. Collier's Wife, The.
Lorde. Coal.
Mahon. Portrait of the Artist, A.
Merwin. Quoit, The.
Owen, W. Miners.
Rossetti, C. Diamond or a coal? / A diamond, if
you please, A.

Cobblers
Sheridan, T. Letter from a Cobbler in Patrick's
Street to Jet Black, A.
See also **Shoes**

Coca Cola
O'Hara, F. Having a Coke with You.

Olson, C.   Being Altogether Literal, & Specific.

Cocaine
Clifton, L.   White Lady.
Gunn, T.   Smoking Pot on the Bus.
Komunyakaa.   Cinderella at Big Sur.
Crack.
Sandburg, C.   Snow.

Cockfighting
Ai.   Cockfighter's Daughter, The.
Chuang Tzu.   Fighting Cock, The.
Cowper, W.   Cock-Fighters Garland.
Tale, Founded on a Fact, A.
Merwin.   Folk Art.
See also **Roosters**

Cockroaches
Bukowski.   Cockroach.
Ginsberg, A.   Come Back Christmas: Blues
Stanza.
Jacobsen, J.   Fittest, The.
Piercy.   Kneeling at the Pipes.
Rukeyser, M.   St. Roach.
Sexton.   Cockroach.
Simic.   Cockroach.
Stock, R.   Swift Completion of Their Appointed
Rounds, The.
Williams, C. K.   What a sound his.

Cocks
See **Roosters**

Cocoa
Carrera Andrade.   Cocoa Tree.

Coconuts
Mistral, G.   Coconut Palms, The.

Coercion
Lindsay, N.   Harps in Heaven.
Williams, C. K.   Interrogation II.

Coffee
Bukowski.   Luck.
Cunningham, J.   Coffee.
Hall, D.   Je Suis une Table.
Nash, O.   Coffee with the Meal.
O'Hara, F.   Poem: "Instant coffee with slightly
sour cream."
Riley, J.   Like His Mother Used to Make.
Walcott.   Gulf, The.

Coffins
Byron, G.   On a Royal Visit to the Vaults.
Windsor Poetics.
Ciardi, J.   Box Comes Home, A.
Dickinson, E.   Coffin—is a small Domain, A.
Hardy, T.   Not Only I.
Six Boards, The.
Three Tall Men, The.
Ignatow, D.   First Coffin Poem.
Merwin.   Fourth Psalm: The Cerements.
Pagis.   Memorial Evening.
Robinson, E.   Leonora.

Coins
Amichai [*or* Amikhai].   Let the Coin Decide.
Borges.   Iron Coin, The.
To a Coin.
Carver, R.   For the Egyptian Coin Today, Arden,
Thank You.
Cavafy.   Coins.
Philhellene.
Davie, D.   Tuscan Brutus, The.
Duncan, R.   Salvages: An Evening Place.
Gurney, I.   Coin, The.
Hughes, L.   Fact.
Midnight Raffle.
Meredith, G.   Cleopatra.
Nemerov.   Money.
Pagis.   New Lover, A.
Ritsos.   Final Obol, The.
Inevitables.
Reverse Side.
Sandburg, C.   Coin, A.
In a Back Alley.
Updike.   On the Recently Minted Hundred-Cent
Piece.

Cold
Atwood.   Midwinter, Presolstice.
You Are Happy.
Berry, W.   Cold, The.
Snake, The.

Bishop, E.   Colder the Air, The.
Blok.   Earth's Heart Is Growing Cold Again.
Brodsky, J.   In Memory of Clifford Brown.
Burns, R.   Cauld Frosty Morning.
Cauld Is the E'enin Blast.
Lines Written in the Kirk of Lamington.
O [*or* Oh] Wert Thou in the Cauld Blast.
Carew, T.   Song: To Her Again[e], She Burning
in a Fe[a]ver.
To My Mistress [*or* Mistris], I Burning in Love.
Carver, R.   Deschutes River.
Corbett, W.   For Joe Pernice.
Creeley.   As Now It Would Be Snow.
Blue.
Davie, D.   Samuel Beckett's Dublin.
Dickey, J.   Form.
Ice Skin, The.
Dickinson, E.   'Twas warm—at first—like Us.
Dugan, A.   Glad at the Cold (1955).
Dunbar, P.   Misty Day, A.
Eberhart, R.   Commas in Wintertime.
Lost Children, The.
Emerson, R.   Winds are cold, the days are dark,
The.
Frost, R.   There Are Roughly Zones.
Hall, D.   Table, The.
Waiting on the Corners.
Han-shan.   Frequent guest of hunger and cold,
A.
Herrick.   Health.
Upon Himselfe.
Hughes, T.   November.
Jacobsen, J.   "It's a Cold Night," Said Coney to
Coney.
Kipling, R.   Open Door, The.
Laughlin, J.   Cold, The.
Lawrence, D. H.   Coldness in Love.
Levertov.   For the Blind.
Lux.   Winter River.
MacNeice.   Another Cold May.
Mahon.   Tolerable Wisdom, A.
Meredith, G.   Carol of Jack Frost, A.
Night of Frost in May.
Or the single path— / Which the cool moon
sheds.
Tardy Spring.
Merrill, J.   David's Night in Veliès.
Nightgown.
Merwin.   Cold before the Moonrise, The.
Forbears, The.
Sunset after Rain.
Millay, E.   When the Year Grows Old.
Muldoon, P.   Vespers.
Nash, O.   Samson Agonistes.
Nemerov.   Winter Lightning, The.
Neruda.   Cold.
Niedecker.   Popcorn-can cover.
O'Hara, F.   Poem In January.
Prunty.   Cold.
Roethke.   Coming of the Cold, The.
Rossetti, C.   Chill, A.
Crying, my little one, footsore and weary?
There's Snow on the Fields.
Rukeyser, M.   Speech for the Assistant, from
Houdini.
Sandburg, C.   Hunger and Cold.
Sarton, M.   To the North.
Seifert.   Model, The.
Sexton.   God's Backside.
Simic.   Cold, The.
Harsh Climate.
Winter Night.
Snyder, G.   Late October Camping in the
Sawtooths.
Swenson, M.   View to the North.
Tate, J.   Poem (I Can't Speak for the Wind).
Tomlinson, C.   In the Balance.
Object in a Setting.
Tramontana at Lerici.
Wilbur, R.   Wyeth's Mild Cans.
Williams, C. K.   Snow: II.
Williams, W.   Cold Night, The.
Wright, J.   In the Cold House.
Zaturenska.   Mirrored Room, The.

Cold War
Davie, D.   After a Change of Régime.

Chernobyl. A Disaster.
Three Pastors in Berlin.
Ginsberg, A.   America.
Hughes, L.   Relief.
Hughes, T.   Woman Unconscious, A.
Zagajewski.   1969.

Colds (illness)
Creeley.   Catching Cold.
Nash, O.   Fahrenheit *Gesundheit*.
Sniffle, The.
Pessoa.   I have a terrible cold.
Roethke.   Ceiling, The.
Williams, C. K.   Shade, The.

Coleridge, Samuel Taylor
Clampitt.   Coleorton.
Cure at Porlock, A.
Dejection: A Footnote.
Rydal Mount.
Dubie.   Coleridge Crossing the Plain of Jars
[1833].
Dream of Three Sisters, A.
Eberhart, R.   Bones of Coleridge, The.
Frost, R.   Most of It, The.
Gunn, T.   Keats at Highgate.
Lowell, R.   Coleridge.
Coleridge and Richard II.
Meredith, G.   Poetry of Coleridge, The.
Muldoon, P.   Madoc: A Mystery.
Nash, O.   I Can Hardly Wait for the Sandman.
Smith, S.   Thoughts about the Person from
Porlock.
Zaturenska.   Leaves from the Book of Dorothy
Wordsworth.

Colleges and Universities
Amichai [*or* Amikhai].   At the University of
New Orleans.
NYU.
Berryman.   Crisis.
In & Out.
Nowhere.
Two Organs.
Burns, R.   Dean of Faculty—a New Ballad, The.
Clampitt.   Homer, A.D. 1982.
Collins, B.   Monday Morning.
Cunningham, J.   For a College Yearbook.
Davie, D.   University of the South, The.
Dugan, A.   Internal Migration: On Being on
Tour.
Emerson, R.   Valedictory Poem.
Frost, R.   Lucretius versus the Lake Poets.
Gunn, T.   His Rooms in College.
Heaney, S.   Cloistered.
Herrick.   To His Kinsman, Master Thomas
Herrick, Who Desired to Be in His Book.
Hughes, L.   Governor Fires Dean.
Lincoln University: 1954.
Theme for English B.
Jarrell, R.   Randall Jarrell, Office Hours 10-11.
Soldier Walks under the Trees of the University,
The.
Kipling, R.   Clerks and the Bells, The.
Kizer, C.   To a Visiting Poet in a College
Dormitory.
Twelve O'Clock.
Laughlin, J.   And Ole Ez said that the.
Lawrence, D. H.   From a College Window.
In Nottingham.
Nottingham's New University.
Merton.   Twenty Three Point Prospectus for
Small College in the Badlands.
Moore, M.   Student, The.
Nash, O.   Caesar Knifed Again, or, Culture Biz
Gets Hep, Boffs Profs.
One Man's Meed Is Another Man's
Overemphasis.
Olson, C.   It is a nation of nothing but poetry.
Parker, D.   College Boys; A Hymn of Hate.
Plath.   Resolve.
Shapiro, K.   Humanities Building, The.
University.
Smart, C.   On an Eagle Confined in a College-
Court.
Spender, S.   One More New Botched Beginning.
Stafford, W.   On Quitting a Little College.
Stockton, A.   Prospect, The. By a Lady in
Princeton.

Updike. Generic College.
Very. Song: "No more around the social board."
Wheatley, P. To the University of Cambridge, in New-England.
Whittier. Norumbega Hall.
  Spiritual Manifestation, A.
Wilbur, R. Finished Man, A.
Wilner, E. Metamorphoses at a College for Women.
Wordsworth, W. Oxford, May 30, 1820.
See also **Students**

Collies
Niedecker. My friend the black and white collie.

Cologne, Germany
Celan. Cologne, at the Station.
Coleridge, S. Cologne.
  On My Joyful Departure from the City of Cologne.

Colonialism
Bradstreet, A. Dialogue between Old England and New, A.
Cavafy. In a Large Greek Colony, 200 B.C.
  Tarantians Divert Themselves, The.
Cowper, W. Charity.
Creeley. America.
Dubie. Indian Summer.
Dugan, A. Against France: On the Algerian Pleasures of Entity.
Dunbar, P. Conquerors, The.
Hill, G. Locust Songs.
Hughes, L. Azikiwe in Jail.
  Envoy to Africa.
  Explain It, Please.
  Merry Christmas.
Kipling, R. Song of the White Men, A.
  South Africa.
  White Man's Burden, The.
Maunick. Seven Sides and Seven Syllables.
Rimbaud, A. Bad Blood.
Rukeyser, M. Suite for Lord Timothy Dexter.
Unknown. Answer, The [By the Gentleman of the Navy].
Updike. B.W.I.
Walcott. Far Cry from Africa, A.
  North and South.
See also **British Empire; Imperialism**

Colorado River
Meredith, W. At the Confluence of the Colorado and the Little Colorado.
Sandburg, C. Many Hats.

Colorado (state)
Berrigan, T. Certain Slant of Sunlight, A.
Komunyakaa. Returning the Borrowed Road.
Very. On Some Blue and Golden Columbines from Pike's Peak, Colorado.
Whitman, W. Spirit That Form'd This Scene.

Colors
Bishop, E. Pleasure Seas.
Borges. Blind Man, The.
Bukowski. It's Nothing to Laugh About.
Clampitt. Thinking Red.
Codrescu. Alice's Brilliance.
Creeley. Greendoon's Song.
Cullen, C. Colors.
Cummings, E. E. Come a little further—why be afraid.
Davie, D. Iowa.
De la Mare. Window, The.
Dickinson, E. Yellow Man, Purple Man.
Dubie. February: The Boy Breughel.
Eberhart, R. Vermont Idyll.
Gunn, T. Colour Machine, The.
Gurney, I. Water Colours.
Hall, D. No Color Man.
  Pictures of Philippa.
Hardy, T. Colour, The.
Hughes, T. Crow's Fall.
Levertov. For the Blind.
Mistral, G. Round of Colors.
Olson, C. Color is image.
Pound, E. Song of the Degrees, A.
Rich, A. Design in Living Colors.
Ritsos. Accented Colors.
  Experiences.

Untamed.
Rossetti, C. Freaks of Fashion.
  What Is Pink?
Sandburg, C. Brown Gold.
  Butter Colors.
  Haze Gold.
  Lake Michigan Morning.
  Maroon with Silver Frost.
  My People.
  Never Two Songs the Same.
  October Paint.
  Runaway Colors.
  Small Homes.
  Themes in Contrast.
  Two Fish.
  Wind Sings Welcome in Early Spring, The.
  Winter Gold.
Schuyler, J. Standing and Watching.
Smith, S. Oh Grateful Colours, Bright Looks!
Stevens, W. Colors.
  Domination of Black.
Swenson, M. Blue.
  Green Red Brown and White.
Tomlinson, C. Distinctions.
  Suggestions for the Improvement of a Sunset.
Whalen, P. Homage to Hart Crane.
Williams, W. Portrait in Greys, A.
Wright, C. Cryopexy.
Zukofsky, L. For Selma Gubin's Umbrellas.

Colosseum, Rome
Poe. Coliseum, The.

Colts
Frost, R. Runaway, The.
Lindsay, N. Broncho That Would Not Be Broken, The.
See also **Horses**

Columbia University
Merton. Western Fellow Students Salute with Calypso Anthems the Movie Career of Robert Lax.

Columbus, Christopher
Clough. How in all wonder Columbus got over.
Dunbar, P. Columbian Ode.
Emerson, R. Poem, Spoken Before the ΦBK Society, August, 1834.
  Valedictory Poem.
Frost, R. America Is Hard to See.
Hughes, T. Fourth of July.
Logan, J. Experiment That Failed, The.
McGrath, T. Columbus.
Merton. Christopher Columbus.
Nash, O. Columbus.
  Look What You Did, Christopher!
Sandburg, C. Destroyers.
  Mysterious Biography.
Simic. Navigator.
Whitman, W. Passage to India.
  Prayer of Columbus.
  Thought of Columbus, A.

Comas
Ai. Sleeping Beauty.
Kizer, C. Lines to Accompany Flowers for Eve.
Meredith, G. King Harald's Trance.

Combs
Enzensberger, H. Comb, The.
Riley, J. When Mother Combed My Hair.

Comedians
Ai. Boys and Girls, Lenny Bruce, or Back from the Dead.
Ciardi, J. Autobiography of a Comedian.
Jacobsen, J. Suite for All Clown's Day.
Laughlin, J. Old Comedian, The.
Lindsay, N. Knight in Disguise, The.
Meredith, G. As often in a bun.
Plath. Dirge for a Joker.
Szymborska, W. Slapstick.

Comets
Ammons. Dominion.
Blok. Caught by the Blizzard.
Eberhart, R. Ship Burning and a Comet All in One Day, A.
Hardy, T. Comet at Yell'ham, The.
Hopkins, G. —I am like a slip of comet.
Johnson, S. Comets and Princes.
Kunitz, S. Halley's Comet.

Lindsay, N. Comet of Prophecy, The.
Marvell. Mower to the Glowworms [*or* Glow-Worms *or* Glo-Worms], The.
Seifert. Halley's Comet.
Swenson, M. Comet Watch on Indian Key—Night of April 10, 1986.
Thoreau. To the Comet.
Tomlinson, C. Recompense, The.
Very. Comet, The.

Comfort
Amichai [*or* Amikhai]. Such as Sorrow.
  Summer Begins.
Beckett, S. Mots survivants.
Berry, W. Envoy: "Love, all day there has been at the edge of my mind."
  In Rain.
  Thought of Something Else, The.
  Wild Geese, The.
Broumas, O. To Draw the Warmth of Flesh from Subtle Graphite.
Browning, E. Comfort.
  Thought for a Lonely Death-Bed, A.
Creeley. Comfort.
  Phone.
Cullen, C. To France.
Emerson, R. Comfort with a purring cat.
  Maiden Speech of the Æolian Harp.
  Nature saith / I am not infinite.
  Sunshine was he.
Enzensberger, H. Short History of the Bourgeoisie.
Gurney, I. Glimmering Dusk.
  Kettle Song.
  Snow.
Hall, D. Edward's Anecdote.
Hardy, T. At the Railway Station, Upway.
  Problem, The.
  To a Lady Playing and Singing in the Morning.
Herrick. Comfort In Calamity.
  Comfort to a Youth That Had Lost His Love.
  His Comfort.
  On Fortune.
Hopkins, G. No Worst, There Is None. Pitched Past Pitch of Grief.
Housman. In My Own Shire.
Jackson, L. Back to the Mother Breast.
Keats. Why Did I Laugh Tonight?
Melville, H. Herba Santa.
Mistral, G. Sad Mother, The.
Nash, O. Eheu! Fugaces, or, What a Difference a Lot of Days Make.
  Have You Tried Staying Awake? or, They'll Find a Way to Stop That, Too.
Parker, D. Condolence.
  Lyric.
  Solace.
  Words of Comfort to Be Scratched on a Mirror.
Raine, K. Binah.
Rilke. Comfort Me.
  Orphan Song.
Rossetti, C. Balm in Gilead.
  Charity Never Faileth.
  Fair World Tho' a Fallen, A.
  Methinks the ills of life I fain would shun.
  Standing Afar Off for the Fear of Her Torment.
  There's Snow on the Fields.
  Thou Knewest...Thou Oughtest Therefore.
  What Is That to Thee? Follow Thou Me.
  Zion Said.
Sandburg, C. At a Window.
  Haunts.
Walker, A. Facing the Way.
Williams, M. When I Am Dead, My Dearest.
Williams, T. Comforter and the Betrayer, The.

Comic Strips
Ashbery, J. Farm Implements and Rutabagas in a Landscape.
Clifton, L. Final Note to Clark.
Sandburg, C. Cartoon.

Commandments
Bierce. New Decalogue, The.
Borges. Fragments from an Apocryphal Gospal.
See also **Ten Commandments**

Commencement Day
Emerson, R. Valedictory Poem.

Nemerov. After Commencement.
Smart, C. On Taking a Batchelor's Degree.
Stafford, W. Address to the Senior Class.

Commerce
Dugan, A. Retraction.
Emerson, R. Poets are colorpots.
Ginsberg, A. Studying the Signs.
HaNagid. Commerce Has Markets.
Herrick. Society.
Jarrell, R. Soldier, The.
Kipling, R. Big Steamers.
  Merchantmen, The.
  Peace of Dives, The.
  Such As in Ships.
Koch, K. You Were Wearing.
Meredith, G. Olive Branch, The.
Merton. Hymn to Commerce.
Nemerov. Guide to the Ruins.
Olson, C. Being Altogether Literal, & Specific.
Zukofsky, L. Song for the Year's End, A.

See also **Barters; Business and Businessmen**

Communes
Amichai [*or* Amikhai]. Kibbutz Gvar-'Am.
  Sweet Voice from the Kibbutz, The.
Piercy. Death of the Small Commune, The.

Communication
Angelou. Communication I.
  Communication II.
Armantrout. Theories.
Ashbery, J. Train Rising Out of the Sea.
Atwood. Against Still Life.
  Their Attitudes Differ.
  We hear nothing these days.
Beckett, S. Tailpiece.
Bly, R. Hawk, The.
Bukowski. Out of the Blue.
Carruth, H. Marvin McCabe.
  Names.
  Renaissance.
  Sonnet: "Well, she told me I had an aura.
    "What?" I said."
  They Accuse Me of Not Talking.
Ciardi, J. Encounter.
  Requisitioning.
  Some Figures for Who Must Speak.
  Sorrow of Obedience, The.
  Week That Was, The.
Collins, B. Winter Syntax.
Creeley. Act of Love, The.
  Answer, The.
  Conspiracy, The.
  Rain.
  Than I.
Cuadra, P. Nahoa Urn, for a Woman.
Cummings, E. E. If you and i awakening.
  Lady,i will touch you with my mind.
  May I Feel Said He.
  O / sure)but / nobody unders(no).
Dickinson, E. Speech is one symptom of
    Affection.
Duncan, R. Human Communion. Traces, The.
  Upon Taking Hold.
Ferlinghetti, L. At the *Gare Bruxelles-Midi*.
  Come lie with me and be my love.
Frost, R. Missive Missile, A.
Gallagher, T. Refusing Silence.
Glück, L. Seated Figure.
Graves, R. Starred Coverlet, The.
  What Did You Say?
Hardy, T. Last Signal, The.
Herrick. His Answer to a Friend.
  Upon Love, by Way of Question and Answer.
Jackson, L. World and I, The.
Jacobsen, J. Calling Collect.
  Instances of Communication.
Kipling, R. Code of Morals, A.
  Dove of Dacca, The.
  Fabulists, The.
  Puzzler, The.
Levertov. Letter.
MacNeice. Babel.
  Idle Talk.
  To Posterity.
McGrath, T. Letter for Marian, A.
Merton. Conversations.
Merwin. Door, A ("Do you remember how I

beat on the door").
Millay, E. Hearing Your Words, and Not a
    Word Among Them.
Olson, C. There Are Sounds.
Paley, G. Poem about Storytelling, A.
Palmer, M. Voice and Address.
Piercy. Councils.
  Hand Games.
  Simple-Song.
Ransom, J. Two in August.
Rich, A. Cartographies of Silence.
  Implosions.
  In the Evening.
  Nightbreak.
  Our Whole Life.
  Valediction Forbidding Mourning, A.
Riley, J. Say Something to Me.
Robinson, E. Tact.
Rukeyser, M. Effort at Speech between Two
    People.
  Sonnet: "My thoughts through yours refracted
    into speech."
  War Comes into my Room, The.
  Watchers, The.
Rumi. Thirsty Fish, A.
Sexton. From the Garden.
Stafford, W. How It Is with Family.
  Ritual to Read to Each Other, A.
  Tuned in Late One Night.
Sze. Black Lightning.
  Empty Words.
Updike. À l'École Berlitz.
  Bicycle Chain, A.
  Lamplight.
Van Duyn. Quiet Afternoon at Home, A.
  Toward a Definition of Marriage.
  Wish to Be Believed, The.
Voznesensky [*or* Voznesenskii]. Phone Booth.
Warren, R. Code Book Lost.
  Trying to Tell You Something.
Williams, C. K. To Listen.
Williams, W. Love Song: "You have come
    between me and the terrifying presence."
Zukofsky, L. Rains, the rains, The.

Communion
García Lorca. Ode to the Most Holy Sacrament
    of the Altar.
Jacobsen, J. Instances of Communication.
Milosz, C. City of My Youth.
Montale. In the Park.
Rimbaud, A. First Communions.

See also **Eucharist**

Communism
Aragon. Red Front, The.
Berryman. Communist.
Bishop, E. Lullaby for the Cat.
Bukowski. 22,000 Dollars in 3 Months.
Carrera Andrade. Radicals.
Codrescu. *Petite Histoire* of Red Fascism, A.
Cummings, E. E. Kumrads die because they're
    told).
  Red-rag and pink-flag.
  Thanksgiving (1956).
Dove, R. Eastern European Eclogues.
Ginsberg, A. America.
  Kral Majales.
Hughes, L. Goodbye Christ.
MacDiarmid, H. Seamless Garment, The.
MacNeice. To a Communist.
Rexroth, K. Another Early Morning Exercise.
Rich, A. For Ethel Rosenberg.
Tomlinson, C. Prometheus.
  Siena in Sixty-Eight.
  Up at La Serra.
Williams, W. Choral: The Pink Church.
  Foot-Note, A.
  Jingle.
  Rogation Sunday.

Commuting and Commuters
Dubie. Two Women on the Potomac Parkway.
Ferlinghetti, L. Home Home Home.
Komunyakaa. NJ Transit.
Levertov. Evening Train.
Levi, P. Another Monday.
Lux. What I See When I Drive to Work.
Warren, R. Commuter's Entry in a Connecticut

Diary.
  Last Night Train.

See also **Suburbs and Suburban Life**

Companionship and Companions
Ai. Why Can't I Leave You?
Amichai [*or* Amikhai]. Advice of good love: do
    not love.
  And as Far as Abu Ghosh.
  Ballad in the Streets of Buenos Aires.
  Between.
  Both Together and Each Apart.
  Door of the house opened by mistake, The.
  Forecast.
  I Told You It Would Be So—And You Didn't
    Believe.
  In My Worst Dreams.
  In the Middle of This Century.
  Instead of a Love Poem.
  Love Poem: "People use each other."
  Now in the Din.
  Now to Break.
  Outing with a Woman.
  Pinecones on the Tree Above.
  Placenta of Love, A.
  Poems for a Woman.
  To Hurl Haunting Memories.
  With Her in an Apple.
Ammons. Spinejacking.
Angelou. Alone.
  Conceit, A.
Armantrout. Overhearing.
Ashbery, J. Love Poem, A.
Atwood. After the agony in the guest /
    bedroom, you lying by the.
  Circle Game, The.
  Eventual Proteus.
  Hesitations Outside the Door.
  Is/Not / Not.
  Lying here, everything in me.
  Their Attitudes Differ.
  They Are Hostile Nations.
  They were all inaccurate.
  This is a mistake, / these arms and legs.
  What is it, it does not.
  You are the sun / in reverse, all energy.
  You take my hand and.
Auden. Lullaby: "Lay your sleeping head, my
    love."
  Two Climbs.
Beckett, S. Mots survivants.
Berrigan, T. Coda: Song.
  She.
Berry, W. Except.
  To Tanya at Christmas.
Bly, R. Man and a Woman Sit Near Each Other.
Borges. Nostalgia for the Present.
Broumas, O. Amazon Twins.
  By Whose Hand.
  Contemplation, The.
  Field.
  Joinery.
  Lullaby: "I see you, centered."
  Mitosis.
  Pastoral Jazz.
  Plunging into the Improbable.
  Rumpelstiltskin.
  Way a Child Might Believe, The.
Browning, R. Dîs Aliter Visum; or, Le Byron
    de Nos Jours.
Bukowski. Another Bed.
  Blue Cheese and Chili Peppers.
  Lady Poet, The.
  Miracle is the Shortest Time, The.
  Night on a Visa Card.
Burns, R. Dainty Davie.
  O May Thy Morn.
  O [*or* Oh] Wert Thou in the Cauld Blast.
  Red, Red Rose, A.
Carver, R. Ashtray, The.
  Fishing Pole of the Drowned Man, The.
  For Tess.
  Haircut, A.
  Happiness in Cornwall.
  Margo.
  Morning, Thinking of Empire.
  My Work.

Road, The.
Slippers.
Cavafy. Favor of Alexander Valas, The.
Kimon, Son of Learchos, Age 22, Student of
    Greek Literature (in Kyrini).
Myris: Alexandria, 340 A.D.
Two Young Men, 23 to 24 Years Old.
Char. Convergence of the Many.
Ciardi, J. Aging Lovers, The.
For Instance.
I'm No Good for You.
Mr. & Mrs.
Plea, A.
Poem for a Soldier's Girl.
Shore Piece.
Clifton, L. Leaving Fox.
Coleridge, S. Day-Dream, A.
To Two Sisters.
Cooper, J. Door, The.
Earthquake, The.
Faithful, The.
Rent.
Creeley. Bobbie ("Her voice").
For Love.
For Pen ("Reading, in the chair").
If I Had My Way.
Love: "Will you be dust."
Of Years.
Rose, The.
Say Something.
She Is.
Spring in San Feliu.
Then ("Don't go / to the mountains").
Cullen, C. Ghosts.
Cummings, E. E. Love's function is to fabricate
    unknownness.
Cunningham, J. Aged Lover Discourses in the
    Flat Style, The.
Old love is old resentment, novelty.
Davie, D. Love and the Times.
Time Passing, Beloved.
Treviso, the Pescheria.
De la Mare. Comfort.
Disguise, The.
Flower, The.
Good Company.
Remonstrance, The.
Dickinson, E. He was my host—he was my
    guest.
I hope you may not go.
I learned—at least—what Home could be.
I was with you in all the loneliness.
Lifetime is for two.
When thou goest through the Waters.
Wild Nights—Wild Nights!
Donne. Canonization, The.
Dubie. Circus Ringmaster's Apology to God,
    The.
Immoralist, The.
Dugan, A. Conspiracy of Two against the
    World.
Glad at the Cold (1955).
Note of Quits.
Prothalamion of Quantum Mechanics and
    Astrophysics.
Dunbar, P. To Her.
Enzensberger, H. Old Couples.
Frost, R. Pasture, The.
Ginsberg, A. Green Automobile, The.
Graves, R. Narrow Sea, The.
Song: Once More.
Terraced Valley, The.
Gunn, T. Thoughts on Unpacking.
Touch.
Gurney, I. Companion—North-East Dug-Out.
Companions, The.
Hacker, M. Companion, The.
Dear Jool, I Miss You in Saint-Saturnin.
Little Robber Girl Gets On in the Wide World,
    The.
Hamill, S. Cold Fire, A.
Jubilate Sutra.
With the Gift of a Nootka Rose.
Hayden, R. Dogwood Trees, The.
Heaney, S. Dream of Jealousy, A.
Field Work.

Royal Prospect, A.
Herrick. Not To Love.
To Phyllis to Love and Live with Him.
To the Maids to Walke Abroad.
Wounded Heart, The.
Hughes, L. Numbered.
Hughes, T. Bride and Groom Lie Hidden for
    Three Days.
Fallgrief's Girlfriends.
Folktale.
Lovepet, The.
Other, The.
Jackson, L. Benedictory.
I Am.
John And I.
Kinnell. 52 Oswald Street.
Rapture.
Waking, The.
Kinsella, T. Echoes.
Kizer, C. For Jan as the End Draws Near.
Month in Summer, A.
Komunyakaa. Dolphy's Aviary.
Glass Ark, The.
Uncertainty in Blue.
Kumin, M. Continuum: a Love Poem.
Kunitz, S. Ambergris.
Lovers Relentlessly.
Night-Piece.
Promise Me.
Science of the Night, The.
Lawrence, D. H. Compari.
Levertov. Bedtime.
Don't You Hear that Whistle Blowin'.
Enduring Love.
Engraved.
Everything That Acts Is Actual.
From the Roof.
Holiday.
Libation.
Losing Track.
Luxury.
Marriage, The.
Sequence, A.
Levi, P. 12 July 1980.
Levine, P. To a Fish Head Found on the Beach
    Near Málaga.
Lindsay, N. For All Who Ever Sent Lace
    Valentines.
Genesis.
Johnny Appleseed's Wife from the Palace of
    Eve.
Spice-Tree, The.
Logan, J. Traveling.
Lorde. Memorial I.
To the Girl Who Lives In a Tree.
Lowell, R. Man and Woman.
Lux. Rilke and Lou.
Towards.
MacLeish. Old Gray Couple (1), The.
MacNeice. All Over Again.
Coda: "Maybe we knew each other better."
Mahon. Two Songs [for Doreen].
Major, C. Aging Together.
Harps.
Perfect Match, The.
McGrath, T. Celebration.
Perpetual Motion.
McHugh, H. Connubial.
Dry Time.
Household.
Score, The.
Solitary's Solace in the Natural Sciences.
Toward an Understanding.
Trouble with "In," The.
Meredith, G. Appreciation.
Dost thou behold some woeful soul.
Hueless Love, The.
In Claremont woods we wandered once.
Jack & Harry.
Love is winged for two.
Marian: "Clouds fly fast across the moon, The."
Song: "I cannot lose thee for a day."
Time and Sentiment.
Meredith, W. Accidents of Birth.
Merrill, J. Bronze.
Merwin. Birthday, A.

Kore.
Morning, The.
Twilight.
Michelangelo Buonarroti. I'm dearer dead than
    ever I was, before.
Your beauty an angel's, Lady, you were meant.
Montale. Other Lines.
Two in Twilight.
Nash, O. You Can Be a Republican, I'm a
    Genocrat.
Nemerov. Blue Suburban.
Day on the Big Branch, A.
Realities.
Neruda. Successions.
Niedecker. Cabin door flew open, The.
Club 26.
I knew a clean man.
In Leonardo's light.
My man says the wind blows from the south.
Watching Dan- / cers on Skates.
Wilderness.
Orr, G. Builders, The.
Daffodil Poem.
Wild Heart.
Owen, W. Apologia Pro Poemate Meo.
Palmer, M. Notes for Echo Lake 8.
Parker, D. Ballade at Thirty-Five.
Cassandra Drops into Verse.
Danger of Writing Defiant Verse, The.
Day-Dreams.
Fighting Words.
General Review of the Sex Situation.
Grande Passion.
Idyl.
Incurable.
Prophetic Soul.
Second Love.
Song of a Contented Heart.
Pasolini. One of the Many Epilogs.
Pasternak, B. White Night.
Pessoa. Lydia, we know nothing. We are
    strangers.
Petrarch. Happy and sad, together and yet sole.
Soon as *madonna* comes into my heart,
Two blushing roses, gathered recently.
Piercy. It Breaks.
Prunty. Late Days.
Our Tree of Opposites.
Ramanujan. Still Life.
Rexroth, K. Entrance.
Growing.
Oaxaca 1925.
Rich, A. After Twenty Years.
Autumn Equinox.
Blood-Sister.
Five O'Clock, Beacon Hill.
Flesh and Blood.
Holding Out.
In the Evening.
Living in Sin.
Marriage in the 'Sixties, A.
Paula Becker to Clara Westhoff.
Photograph of the Unmade Bed, The.
Pieces.
Pierrot Le Fou.
Prisoners, The.
Roots.
Side by Side.
Stepping Backward.
To Judith, Taking Leave.
When/Then.
When We Dead Awaken.
Woman Dead in Her Forties, A.
Riley, J. Art and Love.
Because.
From Below.
He and I.
His Vigil.
In Days to Come.
In the Afternoon.
In the Heart of June.
Life at the Lake.
Light of Love, The.
Little Woman, The.
Lost Path, The.
One Afternoon.

Same Old Story, The.
Song of the Road, A.
Variation, A.
Voice from the Farm, A.
When My Dreams Come True.
Why.
Rimbaud, A.   Festivals of Hunger.
First Delirium. The Foolish Virgin. The Infernal
   Bridegroom.
My Little Lovebirds.
Young Couple.
Ritsos.   Miniature.
Robinson, E.   Captain Craig.
Companion, The.
Firelight.
Tasker Norcross.
Vain Gratuities.
Rossetti, C.   Portraits.
Rukeyser, M.   Back Tooth.
They talk to each other, and he holds her hand.
Rumi.   Of Being Woven.
Sometimes I Forget Completely.
We are the night ocean filled.
Sexton.   Balance Wheel, The.
Shelley, P.   From the Arabic: An Imitation.
Letter to Maria Gisborne.
Simic.   Old Couple.
Stafford, W.   Our Story.
Stockton, A.   Impromptu on Seeing a Very
   Agreeable Gentleman and Lady.
Swenson, M.   I will be earth you be the flower.
In the Yard.
Mornings Innocent.
Pair, A.
Swift, J.   Stella's Birthday, 1725.
To Stella.
To Stella, Visiting Me in My Sickness.
Twelve Articles.
Szymborska, W.   Nothing nothinged itself for
   me as well.
Tate, A.   Perimeters.
Red Stains.
Tate, J.   Blue Booby, The.
End of the Line, The.
Flight.
Motorcyclists, The.
Soup of Venus, The.
Wait for Me.
Thoreau.   Low in the eastern sky.
My love must be as free.
Stanzas: "Nature doth have her dawn each day."
Tomlinson, C.   Doggerel for My Seventieth
   Birthday, A.
Uhland.   Good Comrade, The.
Walcott.   Lampfall.
Village Life, A.
Walker, A.   Forgive Me If My Praises.
Gift.
Warren, R.   After the Dinner Party.
August Moon.
Smile, The.
Tryst on Vinegar Hill.
Weiss, T.   Camel in the Snow.
Wilbur, R.   Gifts, The.
Williams, C. K.   Covenant, The.
Friends.
Hard Part, The.
In There.
One of the Muses.
Ribbons.
Sting, The.
To Market.
Toil.
Williams, M.   As You Both Shall Live.
Despairing of Understanding We Fall Into
   Decadence.
Fly Me to the Moon.
Her, Though.
Love Poem with Toast.
Toast to Floyd Collins, A.
Words.
Williams, T.   Ave Atque Vale.
Cabin.
Couple, The.
Covenant.
Death Is High.

Her Head on the Pillow.
One and Two.
Separate Poem, A.
You and I.
Williams, W.   My Luv.
Sub Terra.
Wright, C.   Self-Portait.
Wright, J.   Night Ride.
Wyatt, S.   If it be so that I forsake thee.
Zagajewski.   In the Beauty Created by Others.
Zaturenska.   Another Snowstorm.
Zukofsky, L.   One friend.
Reading and Talking.
See also **Friendship**

Compassion
Amichai [*or* Amikhai].   Arab Shepherd Is
   Searching for His Goat on Mount Zion, An.
Angelou.   I Almost Remember.
Bukowski.   One for Old Snaggle-Tooth.
Byron, G.   Sonnet to the Prince Regent.
Tear, The.
Coleridge, S.   Inward Light.
Crane, H.   Chaplinesque.
Creeley.   Ballad, A: "We have a song for the
   death in her body."
Phone.
Token, A.
World, The.
Cullen, C.   Magnets.
Dickinson, E.   I wish I might say one liquid
   word.
Tenderness has not a Date.
This Is My Letter to the World.
Donne.   Ralphius.
Eberhart, R.   Question Mark.
Hamill, S.   Animus Mundi.
Jeffers, R.   Crumbs or the Loaf.
Lawrence, D. H.   Tender Reverence.
Levertov.   Skew Lines.
Levi, P.   Decathlon Man.
Levine, P.   Coming Home, *Detroit*, 1968.
Milosz, C.   On a Beach.
Parker, D.   After a Spanish Proverb.
Ransom, J.   Puncture.
Rich, A.   Knight, The.
Riley, J.   Text, The.
Ritsos.   Understanding.
Rossetti, C.   Lines Given with a Penwiper.
Rumi.   Solomon's Crooked Crown.
Smith, S.   Full Well I Know.
Whittier.   Healer, The.
Minister's Daughter, The.
Wilbur, R.   Gifts, The.
Williams, C. K.   Color of Time, The.
Day for Anne Frank, A.
Neglect.
Williams, M.   Compassion.
Williams, W.   Seraph.
Wordsworth, W.   Fragment: The Baker's Cart.
Sonnet on Seeing Miss Helen Maria Williams
   Weep at a Tale of Distress.
Wright, J.   Saint Judas.
Zukofsky, L.   Reading and Talking.
Song for the Year's End, A.

Competition
Bourne, V.   Strada's Nightingale.
Bukowski.   Ants, The.
Creeley.   So There.
Emerson, R.   Fable: "Mountain and the squirrel,
   The."
Ferlinghetti, L.   Deep Chess.
Graves, R.   Woman Poet and Man Poet.
"H. D."   Toward the Piraeus.
Housman.   This time of year a twelvemonth
   past.
Kumin, M.   400-Meter Freestyle.
Laughlin, J.   Inner Life of the Septic Tank, The.
Levi, P.   Decathlon Man.
Lux.   River That Scolds at All the Other Rivers,
   The.
Merrill, J.   Marsyas.
Nash, O.   Malice Domestic.
O'Hara, F.   Hôtel Transylvanie.
Petrarch.   Orso, upon your charger you may put.
Ramanujan.   At Forty.
Ransom, J.   Two Gentlemen in Bonds.

Riley, J.   Speeding of the King's Spite, The.
Rukeyser, M.   Trophies.
Suckling, S.   Wits, The; A Session[s] of the
   Poets.
Swift, J.   Tom Mullinex and Dick.
Williams, C. K.   Love: Youth.
See also **Rivalry**

Complacency
Browning, E.   Loved Once.
Collins, B.   Monday Morning.
Creeley.   End of the Day, The.
Same.
Warning, The.
Cummings, E. E.   Of all the blessings which to
   man.
Dickinson, E.   Complacency! My Father!
Dugan, A.   Confession of Heresy.
Meredith, G.   Familiar Things.
Rumi.   Childhood Friends.
Shapiro, K.   Buick.
Smith, S.   Eng.
Leader, The.
Williams, C. K.   Experience.
What we are / given.

Computers
Pagis.   Writers.
Rich, A.   Artificial Intelligence.
Williams, M.   E-mail.

Comraderie
Herrick.   Jack and Jill.
Williams, C. K.   Sanctity, The.

Concentration
Chuang Tzu.   Woodcarver, The.
Parra, N.   Butterfly.
Tate, J.   First Lesson.

Concentration Camps
Amichai [*or* Amikhai].   Little Ruth.
Ciardi, J.   Gift, The.
Clampitt.   Burning Child, The.
Davie, D.   Hawkshead and Dachau in a
   Christmas Glass.
Dubie.   Aubade of the Singer and Saboteur,
   Marie Triste.
Fenton, J.   Doctor Gliedschirm, skin specialist,
   surgeries 14–16 hours or by appointment.
German Requiem, A.
Hamill, S.   Treblinka Lights.
Hayden, R.   Belsen, Day of Liberation.
Hughes, T.   Lines about Elias.
Jarrell, R.   Camp in the Prussian Forest, A.
In the Camp There Was One Alive.
Protocols.
Levi, P.   Buna.
Gedale's Song.
Proxy.
Sunset at Fossoli.
Merton.   Chant to Be Used in Processions
   around a Site with Furnaces.
Pinsky.   Unseen, The.
Ritsos.   1 December 1948.
24 November 1948.
26 November 1948.
27 November 1948.
30 November 1948.
7 December 1948.
23 January 1949.
26 January 1949.
30 January 1949.
Simic.   Begotten of the Spleen.
Szymborska, W.   Starvation Camp at Jasło.
Williams, C. K.   Day for Anne Frank, A.
Zagajewski.   Summer's Fullness.
See also **Auschwitz, Poland; Holocaust;
Internment**

Conception
Dickinson, E.   Solemn thing—it was—I said, A.
Heaney, S.   Act of Union.
Herrick.   Observation.
Tithe [*or* Tythe]: To the Bride, The.
Upon a Lady Faire, but Fruitlesse.
Jeffers, R.   Dead Men's Child, The.
Kinnell.   Conception.
Kumin, M.   Sperm.
Laughlin, J.   On learning that he was about.
MacDiarmid, H.   Harry Semen.

Rukeyser, M.   Running of the Grunion, The.
Williams, M.   Voice of America.

Concerts
Coleridge, S.   Lines Composed in a Concert-
  Room.
Dunbar, P.   Concert, The.
Gunn, T.   Outdoor Concert, The.
Sandburg, C.   Band Concert.
Williams, C. K.   Junior High School Concert:
  Salle Rossini.
Prodigy, The.
Williams, M.   Schumann Adds Trombones to
  His Second Symphony After Mendelssohn
  Conducts the First Performance.

Concord, Massachusetts
Emerson, R.   At Plymouth in the friendly crowd.
Concord Hymn.
Musketaquid.
Rich, A.   Concord River.
Walden 1950.
Thoreau.   But now "no war nor battle's sound."
  Yet let us Thank the purblind race.

Concrete Poetry
See **Shaped Poetry**

Coney Island, New York City
García Lorca.   Landscape of a Vomiting
  Multitude.
Hughes, L.   Sunset—Coney Island.

Confederacy
Bierce.   Confederate Flags, The.
Tate, A.   Battle of Murfreesboro.
Ode to the Confederate Dead.
See also **Civil War, United States**

Confessions
Ai.   Priest's Confession, The.
Amichai [*or* Amikhai].   Now in the Din.
Baudelaire.   Confession.
Berry, W.   Purification, A.
Browning, E.   Confessions.
Browning, R.   Confessional, The.
Forgiveness, A.
Carver, R.   Transformation.
Creeley.   Europeans, The.
Hill, The.
Song: "I woudn't / embarrass you."
Davie, D.   Three Pastors in Berlin.
Donne.   To the Countess of Bedford ("Though I
  be dead, and buried, yet I have").
Gunn, T.   Confessions of the Life Artist.
Hall, D.   Carlotta's Confession.
Herbert, G.   Trinity Sunday.
Herrick.   Confession.
His Confession.
To God.
Hughes, L.   Third Degree.
Jackson, L.   Need to Confide, The.
Logan, J.   Lines for a Young Man Who Talked.
Wooden Mirror, The.
Lowell, R.   Between the Porch and the Altar.
McHugh, H.   Confessionist.
Melville, H.   In a Church of Padua.
Meredith, G.   O shrive me Friar, my ghostly
  Friar!
Tuck, Demitroïa, / Ariadne, and Froyja.
Milosz, C.   At a Certain Age.
Prescription.
Task, A.
Vipera Berus.
Mistral, G.   Confession.
Muldoon, P.   Cuba.
Pessoa.   Sonnet: "Could I say what I think,
  could I express."
Riley, J.   Sister Jones's Confession.
Sexton.   Talking to Sheep.
Smith, S.   Hostage, The.
Man I Am, A.
Swift, J.   Beasts' Confession to the Priest, The.
Walker, A.   Confession.
Whitman, W.   As I Lay with My Head in Your
  Lap Camerado.
Trickle Drops.
Wilbur, R.   Mind-Reader, The.
Williams, M.   Coming Out.
Williams, W.   Keller Gegen Dom.
Wright, J.   Confession to J. Edgar Hoover.

Confidence
Browning, E.   Apprehension, An.
Fenton, J.   Tauler.
Herrick.   First Marrs or Makes, The.
Larkin, P.   He Hears That His Beloved Has
  Become Engaged.
Nash, O.   There's Nothing Like Instinct,
  Fortunately.
Piercy.   Unlearning to Not Speak.
Sandburg, C.   Fireborn Are at Home in Fire,
  The.
Striped Cats, Old Men and Proud Stockings.
Tate, J.   Shy One, The.
Williams, W.   Swaggering Gait, The.
Yeats.   His Confidence.

Conflict
Amichai [*or* Amikhai].   Half the People in the
  World.
Hour of Grace, An
Wildpeace.
Atwood.   They Are Hostile Nations.
Yes at first you / go down smooth as.
Carew, T.   To Master W. Montague.
To My Friend, Will. Davenant.
To One That Desired to Know My Mistress [*or*
  Mistris].
Chuang Tzu   Advising the Prince.
Creeley.   Eros.
Fancy
Friends, The.
Question, The.
Sopa.
Whip, The.
Wife, The.
Cunningham, J.   Jack and Jill.
Davie, D.   Gripping Serial.
Eberhart, R.   Laocoön.
Graves, R.   Pearl, The.
To Lucia at Birth.
Larkin, P.   If My Darling.
Laughlin, J.   Three Skirmishes in the Endless
  Battle.
Voices, The.
Lawrence, D. H.   Woe.
Lorde.   Love, Maybe.
MacGowran.   Description of an Irish Feast, The.
Major, C.   Seine Split.
Melville, H.   After the Pleasure Party.
America.
Armies of the Wilderness, The.
Meredith, G.   Sonnet to J.M.
Nash, O.   What's the Matter, Haven't You Got
  Any Sense of Humor?
Nemerov.   Deposition, The.
On Getting Out Of Vietnam.
Rexroth, K.   Memorandum.
Rukeyser, M.   Ninth Elegy. The Antagonists.
Sarton, M.   Jonah.
Walcott.   North and South.
Wyatt, S.   To make an end of all this strife.
Will ye see what wonders love hath wrought?
Yeats.   Meeting.

Conformity
Auden.   Unknown Citizen, The.
Bly, R.   Executive's Death, The.
Brodsky, J.   Postcard, A.
Carruth, H.   Spring 1967.
Crane, S.   "Think as I think," said a man.
Cummings, E. E.   Everybody happy? / WE-WE-
  WE.
IN) all those who got.
Most(people / simply / can't).
My specialty is living said.
Of Ever-Ever Land i speak.
Peopleshaped toomany-ness far too, A.
There are possibly 2 1/2 or impossibly 3.
Davie, D.   Nonconformist, The.
Dickinson, E.   Much Madness is divinest Sense.
Emerson, R.   Easy to match what others do.
Graves, R.   It Was All Very Tidy.
Hall, D.   Mr. Wakeville on Interstate 90.
Herrick.   Conformitie.
Conformity Is Comely.
Hughes, L.   Wise Men.
Jeffers, R.   Intellectuals.
Lindsay, N.   Congo, The.

MacNeice.   Habits, The.
Hidden Ice.
McGrath, T.   Ode for the American Dead in
  Korea.
Melville, H.   Enthusiast, The.
Olson, C.   Conqueror.
Sarton, M.   Frog, that Naked Creature, The.
Prisoner at a Desk.
Shapiro, K.   University.
Stevens, W.   Disillusionment of Ten O'Clock.
Thomas, D.   I Fellowed Sleep.
Williams, C. K.   Flat.

Confucius and Confucianism
Kizer, C.   Cultural Evolution.

Confusion
Amichai [*or* Amikhai].   I Want to Confuse the
  Bible.
What a Complicated Mess.
Beckett, S.   Saint-Lô.
Burns, R.   O Dear Minny What Shall I Do?
Carew, T.   Lover, upon an Accident
  Necessitating His Departure, Consults with
  Reason, A.
To His Mistress Retiring in Affection.
To Mistress Katherine Neville, on Her Green
  Sickness.
Carver, R.   Stupid.
Cary, T.   Methodus Amandi.
Cavafy.   Confusion.
Cowper, W.   See Where the Thames, the Purest
  Stream.
Creeley.   Chasing the Bird.
Fancy.
Mind's Heart.
Plan, The.
Please.
Sign ("SIEMENS" not").
Snow, The.
That day / in an oak tree—.
Thinking.
Dickey, W.   History of the Moon, The.
Ferlinghetti, L.   Overpopulation.
Vast Confusion, A.
Frost, R.   Cabin in the Clearing, A.
Gallagher, T.   3 A.M. Kitchen: My Father
  Talking.
Graves, R.   In Broken Images.
Sincèrement.
Sweet-Shop Round The Corner, The.
Han-shan.   When will the treadmill of life and
  death stop.
Hardy, T.   I Was the Midmost.
Herrick.   Confusion of Face.
Jacobsen, J.   Mr. Mahoney.
Jarrell, R.   Story, A.
Jeffers, R.   Triad.
Lawrence, D. H.   Embankment at Night, before
  the War: Charity.
Lorde.   Bloodbirth.
New Year's Day.
October.
Pirouette.
Merton.   1. Now you are all here you might as
  well know this is America we do what we like.
Mothers you have met before still need you.
Michelangelo Buonarroti.   Now on the left foot
  shuffling, now the right.
Nash, D.   Do Sphinxes Think?
Nash, O.   Calling Spring VII-MMMC.
Song for Ditherers.
Strange Case of Mr. Pauncefoot's Broad Mind,
  The.
Unanswered by Request.
What's in a Name? Some Letter I Always
  Forget.
Who Did Which? or Who Indeed?
Piercy.   Song of the Fucked Duck.
Plath.   Appearance, An.
Riley, J.   Ballad from April, A.
Rumi.   Does sunset sometimes look like the
  sun's coming up?
Sandburg, C.   Under the Capitol Dome.
Tate, J.   Prose Poem.
Williams, C. K.   Dirty Talker: D Line, Boston,
  The.
History.

I sit in my room.
Shadows.
Williams, M.   Listen.

Congo River
Angelou.   For Us, Who Dare Not Dare.

Congreve, William
Dryden, J.   To My Dear Friend Mr Congreve
[on His Comedy Called "The Double-Dealer"].

Connecticut (state)
Amichai [or Amikhai].   Fall in Connecticut.
Carruth, H.   Sound of Snow, The.
Eberhart, R.   Project, The.
River Water Music.
Scouring, The.
Hall, D.   Days, The.
Sleeping Giant, The.
Tomorrow.
Wreckage, The.
Meredith, W.   Here and There.
Stevens, W.   River of Rivers in Connecticut,
The.
Tate, J.   Chaste Stranger, The.
Tomlinson, C.   In Connecticut.

Conquistadors
Ai.   Gilded Man, The.
Crane, H.   Imperator Victus.
Frost, R.   Vindictives, The.
Levi, P.   Huayna Capac.
Lux.   What Montezuma Fed Cortés and His
Men.
MacLeish.   Conquistador.

Conrad, Joseph
Borges.   Manuscript Found in a Book of Joseph
Conrad.
Carruth, H.   Eternity Blues.
Cullen, C.   For Joseph Conrad.
Milosz, C.   Pierson College.
Walcott.   Volcano.

Conscience
Baudelaire.   Examination of Conscience, The.
Bly, R.   Getting Up Late.
Byron, G.   Answer to ———'s Professions of
Affection.
Celan.   For Eric.
De la Mare.   Memory.
Dickinson, E.   Who is it seeks my Pillow
Nights.
Dunbar, P.   Conscience and Remorse.
Fenton, J.   Vacant Possession, A.
Graves, R.   With Her Lips Only.
Hardy, T.   He Follows Himself.
Heaney, S.   From the Republic of Conscience.
Herrick.   Sabbaths.
To His Conscience.
To Oenone.
Hopkins, G.   Candle Indoors, The.
Jeffers, R.   New Year's Dawn, 1947.
Lawrence, D. H.   Conscience.
Young Want to Be Just, The.
Lowell, R.   Symptoms.
Nash, O.   Clean Conscience Never Relaxes, A.
Inter-Office Memorandum.
Reflection of the Fallibility of Nemesis.
Parra, N.   Soda Fountains.
Riley, J.   My Conscience.
Sandburg, C.   Clean Hands.
Cups of Coffee.
Stafford, W.   Not in the Headlines.
Szymborska, W.   In Praise of Feeling Bad about
Yourself.
Thoreau.   Conscience is instinct bred in the
house.
Tu Fu.   Testament.
Wilbur, R.   Mind-Reader, The.
Peter.
Williams, C. K.   Conscience.
How Humble We Were before This.
Wilner, E.   Judgment.

Conscientious Objectors
Hamill, S.   Conscientious Objection.
Lawrence, D. H.   Rondeau of a Conscientious
Objector.
Lowell, R.   After the Surprising Conversions.
Memories of West Street and Lepke.
Shapiro, K.   Conscientious Objector, The.

Stafford, W.   Objector.
Wind from a Wing, A.
See also **Pacifism and Pacifists**

Consciousness
Ammons.   Attention.
Bridge.
Coming To.
Peak.
Watch, The.
Atwood.   Out.
Berry, W.   Observance.
Thought of Something Else, The.
Clampitt.   Anatomy of Migraine, An.
Creeley.   Divisions.
Lion and the Dog, The.
Little Time—and Place.
Measure, The.
Numbers.
On Acid.
Poem for D. H. Lawrence.
Cummings, E. E.   Take for example this.
Cunningham, J.   Convalescence.
De la Mare.   Riddle, A.
Snowdrop, The.
Dickinson, E.   Consciousness is the only home.
My Cocoon tightens—Colors tease.
Of Consciousness, her awful Mate.
Too little way the House must lie.
We learned the Whole of Love.
Dugan, A.   Trial, A.
Frost, R.   Silken Tent, The.
Ginsberg, A.   Do We Understand Each Other?
Eastern Ballad, An.
Eye Altering Alters All, The.
Manifesto.
Mind Breaths.
Refrain.
Hardy, T.   Aerolite, The.
I Travel as a Phantom Now.
New Year's Eve.
Jeffers, R.   Consciousness.
Kunitz, S.   Firesticks.
Lawrence, D. H.   Climbing Down.
Nemesis.
Nullus.
Terra Incognita.
Levertov.   Life around Us, The.
MacNeice.   Good Dream.
Mallarmé.   Prose.
Weary of Bitter Sleep.
Merwin.   Apparition.
Child, The.
Looking for Mushrooms at Sunrise.
Milosz, C.   Powers.
To Mrs. Professor in Defense of My Cat's
Honor and Not Only.
Niedecker.   Sorrow moves in wide waves.
Oliver, M.   Spring.
Oppen.   Who Shall Doubt.
Pessoa.   Analysis.
Master, my dear master!
Rexroth, K.   Equation for Marie, An.
Prufrock in Wonderland.
Rukeyser, M.   Sea has opened, the limit of his
dream, The.
Tree of rivers seen and forgotten, The.
Rumi.   No Room for Form.
Sandburg, C.   Fireborn Are at Home in Fire,
The.
Stafford, W.   Ritual to Read to Each Other, A.
Swenson, M.   Evolution.
Subconscious Sea.
Tomlinson, C.   Bootblack, The.
Movements.
Tout Entouré de Mon Regard.
Van Duyn.   Kind of Music, A.
Three Valentines to the Wide World.
Two Poems, with Birds.
Warren, R.   Antinomy: Time and Identity.
Williams, C. K.   Waking Jed.
Zukofsky, L.   "Mantis," An Interpretation.
Or a Valentine.
You three:—my wife.

Conservation
Broumas, O.   Eros.
Dubie.   Coyote Creek.

Dugan, A.   On Flowers. On Negative Evolution.
Enzensberger, H.   End of Owls, The.
Poison, The.
Levertov.   3 a.m., September 1, 1969.
Rexroth, K.   Gic to Har.
See also **Ecology and Ecologists**

Consolation
Amichai [or Amikhai].   Summer Evening at the
Window with Psalms.
Atwood.   What is it, it does not.
Brontë, E.   To Imagination.
Browning, E.   Consolation.
Carver, R.   All Her Life.
Cavafy.   What Cannot Be.
Cavalcanti.   I fear from my misfortune.
Collins, B.   Consolation.
Cowper, W.   Epistle to a Protestant Lady in
France, An.
Davie, D.   Winter Landscape near Ely, A.
Dove, R.   Five Elephants.
Emerson, R.   Patch of meadow & upland, A.
Komunyakaa.   Safe Subjects.
Mahon.   Consolations of Philosophy.
Michelangelo Buonarroti.   If his bright eyes are
closed and laid to rest.
O night, comforting night, dark though you are.
To sleep, even more be made of stone: how
these.
Milosz, C.   Awakened.
Counsels.
Orr, G.   Dream of Fifty, A.
In the shadows at the clearing's.
Petrarch.   Blest soul, so often coming back to
me.
From loveliest eyes, and from the visage which.
It was my love and grief which drove my
tongue.
No loving mother doting on her son.
Sennuccio, though you leave your friend alone.
Thinking of what today adorns the sky.
Thought is rapid, and so short the time, The.
What pitying messenger, what angel was.
With food in which Lord Love seems to abound.
Rich, A.   Fact of a Doorframe, The.
Riley, J.   Kissing the Rod.
Life-Lesson, A.
Little Old Poem That Nobody Reads, The.
Order for A Song, An.
Out of Reach.
Shadow and Shine.
What a Dead Man Said.
Rossetti, C.   Death of a First-Born, A.
Stafford, W.   Consolations.
Van Duyn.   Open Letter from a Constant
Reader.
Wheatley, P.   Funeral Poem on the Death of C.
E. an Infant of Twelve Months, A.
On the Death of a Young Lady of Five Years of
Age.
To a Clergyman on the Death of His Lady.
To a Lady on the Death of Three Relations.
To His Honour the Lieutenant-Governor, on the
Death of His Lady. *March* 24, 1773.
To the Honourable T. H. Esq; on the Death of
His Daughter.
Williams, C. K.   Call, The.
Williams, T.   Strangers pass me on the street.
Wyatt, S.   Comfort at hand! Pluck up thy heart.

Conspiracy
Byron, G.   Marino Faliero, Doge of Venice.
Cavafy.   Aristovoulos.
Great Feast at the Home of Sosibios, A.
Ginsberg, A.   Hadda Be Playing on the Jukebox.
Gunn, T.   Court Revolt, The.
Kipling, R.   Cleared.
Komunyakaa.   Fragging.
Good Joe.
Nemerov.   Portrait of Three Conspirators.
Ritsos.   Recognition.
Tomlinson, C.   Conspiracy, The.

Constable, John
Collins, B.   Student of Clouds.
Tomlinson, C.   Meditation on John Constable,
A.

Constancy
Stockton, A.   Almira to Celadon, Founded on a Story in a Magazine.

See also **Fidelity**

Constantinople, Turkey
Cavafy.   Taken.

Constellations
Borges.   South, The.
Cummings, E. E.   What time is it i wonder never mind.
"Dario."   In the Constellations.
Eliot, T. S.   Sweeney among the Nightingales.
Emerson, R.   For Lyra yet shall be the pole.
Frost, R.   Canis Major.
On Looking Up by Chance at the Constellations.
Gurney, I.   Stars Sliding.
Levertov.   Look at the Night (Temple, Early '60's), A.
Mallarmé.   Her pure nails on high displaying their onyx.
Throw of the Dice, A.
Merton.   Lion, The.
Muldoon, P.   Armageddon, Armageddon.
Pagis.   Come.
Rexroth, K.   Lesson in Geography, A.
Letter to Yvor Winters, A.
Lights in the Sky are Stars, The.
Rich, A.   Orion.
Planetarium.
Ritsos.   To Orpheus.
Tomlinson, C.   Orion over Farne.
Wilbur, R.   In the Field.
Under Cygnus.
Wyatt, S.   Iopas's Song.

See also **Sky; Stars**

Construction Workers
Clampitt.   Progress at Building Site With (Fewer) Pigeons.
Komunyakaa.   Sandhog.
Laughlin, J.   Danger / Road under Repair.

See also **Buildings and Builders**

Consumerism
Bierce.   Political Economy.
Cummings, E. E.   Jehovah buried,Satan dead.
Poem, or Beauty Hurts Mr. Vinal.
Emerson, R.   Since the devil hopping on.
Jeffers, R.   Trap, The.
Laughlin, J.   Market Discounts Love.
Meredith, G.   Song: "Buy, buy, buy, / Is the Peace-markt cry."
Merton.   Proverbs.
Merwin.   Things.
Nash, O.   I Remember Yule.
Nemerov.   Life Cycle of Common Man.
Niedecker.   So you're married, young man.
Olson, C.   War on the Mind in a Time of Love.
Sandburg, C.   Name Us a King.

Contempt
Bukowski.   Man with the Hot Nose, The.
Thank God for Alleys.
Burns, R.   Extempore [on the *Loyal Natives'* Verses].
Cavafy.   Hospitality of Lagides, The.
Creeley.   Ballad, A: "We have a song for the death in her body."
Cullen, C.   Song of Sour Grapes, A.
Emerson, R.   I've found the dainty malice out.
Hughes, L.   Ballad of the Girl Whose Name Is Mud.
Keats.   All Gentle Folks Who Owe a Grudge.
Levertov.   Grace-Note, The.
McGrath, T.   Proletarian in Abstract Light.
Millay, E.   Oh, Oh, you will be sorry for that word!
Rossetti, C.   Frog's Fate, A.
Some ladies dress in muslin full and white.
Sarton, M.   Of Grief.
Warren, R.   Sea Hates the Land, The.

Contentment
Amichai [*or* Amikhai].   I Feel Just Fine in My Pants.
Bly, R.   In the Month of May.
Love Poem in Twos and Threes.
Man and a Woman Sit Near Each Other.
Brodsky, J.   Six Years Later.

Browning, E.   Past and Future.
Bukowski.   Hello, Willie Shoemaker.
One for the Shoeshine Man.
Plate Glass Window, A.
Poem for My 43rd Birthday.
We Will Taste the Islands and the Sea.
Burns, R.   Anna.
Bess[y] and Her Spinning-Wheel.
Birks of Aberfeldy, The [Composed on the Spot].
Contented wi' Little.
Country Lassie.
Fragment: "Altho' my bed were in yon muir."
Galla Water.
Lea-Rig, The.
Louis, What Reck I by Thee.
My Collier Laddie.
Ronalds of the Bennals, The.
Song: "Behind yon hills where Lugar flows."
Sonnet—On Hearing a Thrush Sing on a Morning Walk in January.
Written in Friar's Carse Hermitage on the Banks of Nith—June—1788.
Campion, T.   Ad Lucium.
Content.
In eosdem.
O what unhop't for sweet supply!
Campion, T. *et al.*   Though far from joy, my sorrowes are as far.
Carruth, H.   Renaissance.
Twilight Comes.
Carver, R.   Bankruptcy.
Ciardi, J.   Three A.M. and Then Five.
Clare, J.   Sonnet: "I love to see the summer beaming forth."
Collins, B.   Osso Buco.
Cowper, W.   How blest the youth whom Fate ordains.
To Lady Austen.
Crane, S.   Youth in apparel that glittered, A.
Creeley.   Innocence, The.
Rain, The.
So There.
Song: "How simply / for another."
Thank You.
This wide, shallow bowl.
Two Ways of Looking in a Mirror.
Cullen, C.   To France.
Davie, D.   Cold Spring in Essex.
Felicity's Fourth Order.
Dickey, W.   Joy.
Dickinson, E.   I'm sorry for the Dead—Today.
Their Height in Heaven comforts not.
Dunbar, P.   Content.
Foolin' wid de Seasons.
Limitations.
Emerson, R.   Day's Ration, The.
Enzensberger, H.   Bell Jar, The.
Graves, R.   Everywhere Is Here.
Nothing Now Astonishes.
Strangeness.
What Will Be, Is.
Gurney, I.   In the Old Time.
Hacker, M.   April Interval.
Herbert, G.   Family [*or* Familie], The.
Jesu.
Herrick.   Content, Not Cates.
His Content in the Country.
His Grange.
His Grange, or Private Wealth.
His Wish.
Lots to Be Liked.
Repletion.
Short and Long Both Likes.
To His Deere God.
Welcome What Comes.
Housman.   Here are the skies, the planets seven.
Ignatow, D.   Content.
Keats.   For There's Bishop's Teign.
Kumin, M.   Amanda Dreams She Has Died and Gone to the Elysian Fields.
Laughlin, J.   Believer, The.
Lawrence, D. H.   Beautiful Old Age.
Lonely, Lonesome, Loney—O!
Song of a Man Who Is Loved.
Levine, P.   Suit, The.

Words.
Longfellow, H.   Day Is Done, The.
MacNeice.   Now That the Shapes of Mist.
Marvell.   Garden, The.
McGrath, T.   Celebration for June 24.
Poem: "Down the small and crooked road."
Progress of the Soul, The.
Meredith, G.   Beyond the meadow still where sweeps.
Could we know how kin we are.
Desert vulture / jealousy, The.
Desired as Summer rain.
Fullness of love sleeps in us like a sea.
Love they alone the joyful heart.
Song: "I cannot lose thee for a day."
There is for me no sweeter holiday.
Woodland Peace.
World is full of different fates, The.
Michelangelo Buonarroti.   And sweet it is to see in summer time.
Millay, E.   Above These Cares.
Milosz, C.   Gift.
O'Hara, F.   Saint.
Parker, D.   Song of a Contented Heart.
Pessoa.   Startling reality of things, The.
Piercy.   If They Come in the Night.
Poe.   Eulalie—A Song.
Prunty.   Wedding Stop, The.
Riley, J.   At Broad Ripple.
In Swimming-Time.
Kneeling with Herrick.
My Philosofy.
Robinson, E.   Burning Book [*or* the Contented Metaphysician], The.
Firelight.
Rossetti, C.   And There Was No More Sea.
Do This, and He Doeth It.
Sandburg, C.   Anywhere and Everywhere People.
Honey and Salt.
Sarton, M.   Work of Happiness, The.
Schuyler, J.   Blue towel, A.
Letter Poem #3.
Seidl.   To the High-Flyers.
Sexton.   I Remember.
Smith, S.   Ass, The.
Deeply Morbid.
My Heart Was Full.
Stafford, W.   Why I Am Happy.
Thomas, D.   Once below a Time.
Updike.   Upon Learning That a Town Exists in Virginia Called Upperville.
Whitman, W.   Glimpse, A.
Wilbur, R.   Ballade for the Duke of Orléans.
Williams, M.   Tenth Anniversary Photograph, 1952, A.
Williams, W.   Idyl: "They say to me, 'There is'."
Wordsworth, W.   Danish Boy; A Fragment, The.
Farmer of Tilsbury Vale, The.
Ode to Apollo.
Sonnet: "Nuns fret not at their convent's narrow room."
Stray Pleasures.
Yeats.   Are You Content.
Lake-Isle of Innisfree, The.
Peacock, The.
Zukofsky, L.   Pretty.

See also **Happiness**

Continuity
Amichai [*or* Amikhai].   Deganya.
Evening hours of the soul.
Kibbutz Gvar-'Am.
Songs of Continuity.
Ammons.   Eternal City, The.
Hymn 5: "Assure us you side with order: throw."
Motion for Motion.
Saliences.
Atwood.   Circle Game, The.
Borges.   Adam Is Your Ashes.
Two Forms of Insomnia.
Carruth, H.   Song: "Summer burns on the edges of day."
Chuang Tzu.   In My End Is My Beginning.
Ciardi, J.   Afternoon in the Park, An.

Collins, B.   To a Stranger Born in Some Distant Country Hundreds of Years from Now.
Creeley.   Again.
  For the Graduation.
  Milton Über Alles.
  Night in NYC.
  Sentence, The.
  Testament, A.
Dugan, A.   Untitled Poem: "Once, one of my students read a book we had."
Duncan, R.   Beginning of Writing, The.
Eberhart, R.   Big Rock.
  Parker River, The.
Emerson, R.   Brother, no decrepitude.
Hardy, T.   Heredity.
  In a Museum.
  In the British Museum.
  Life Laughs Onward.
Hill, G.   Cycle.
Jeffers, R.   Hope is Not for the Wise.
  Point Pinos and Point Lobos.
  Torch-Bearers' Race, The.
Kipling, R.   Truthful Song, The.
Kumin, M.   Excrement Poem, The.
Levertov.   Continuum.
Levine, P.   Milkweed.
Lindsay, N.   Preface to "Bob Taylor's Birthday."
McGrath, T.   Drowned Man: Death Between Two Rivers, The.
  Mediterranean.
  Political Song for the Year's End.
Milosz, C.   Return to Kraków in 1880.
Nemerov.   Dependencies, The.
  Rope's End, The.
Neruda.   Initial.
Oliver, M.   Bone Poem.
  In Blackwater Woods.
Olson, C.   Other Than.
  Toss, for John Cage, A.
Piercy.   Martha as the Angel Gabriel.
  On Castle Hill.
Prunty.   Namesake, The.
Raine, K.   In the Beck.
  Shells.
  Water.
Rexroth, K.   It Rolls On.
  Lute Music.
  We Come Back.
Rich, A.   Readings of History.
Ritsos.   Same as Always.
Snyder, G.   Makings.
Szymborska, W.   Reality Demands.
Warren, R.   Interjection #2: Caveat.
  Platonic Lassitude.
Whittier.   Sunset on the Bearcamp.
Wilner, E.   Continuous Is Broken, and Resumes, The.
Zagajewski.   Chinese Poem.

Contrariness
Baudelaire.   Serpent's Tooth, The.
Berry, W.   Contrariness of the Mad Farmer, The.
Donne.   Cross, The.
Herrick.   Contention.
Melville, H.   Parthenon, The.

Contrition
Creeley.   Letter, The.
Davie, D.   G. M. B.
Milosz, C.   Three Talks on Civilization.
Parker, D.   Little Old Lady in Lavender Silk, The.
Petrarch.   More happily than I no ship has ever.

Convalescence
Coleridge, S.   To a Young Lady [Miss Lavinia Poole] on Her Recovery from a Fever.
Cunningham, J.   Convalescence.
Dickinson, E.   I shall watch your passage from Crutch to Cane.
  My first well Day—since many ill.
Emerson, R.   Give All to Love.
Glück, L.   To Florida.
Plath.   Among the Narcissi.
Schuyler, J.   Afterward.

Conventionality
Beckett, S.   À peine à bien mené.
  Ainsi a-t-on beau.
Hall, D.   Mr. Wakeville on Interstate 90.

Hardy, T.   Christening, The.
  Recalcitrants, The.
Ransom, J.   Nocturne: "Where now has our young Adam."

Convents
Clifton, L.   Far Memory.
García Lorca.   Gypsy Nun, The.
Hughes, L.   Convent.

See also **Nuns**

Conversation
Atwood.   Conversation, A.
Berry, W.   In Memory: Stuart Egnal.
Berryman.   Poem for Bhain, A.
  Tea.
Bishop, E.   Wit, The.
Bukowski.   She Came Out of the Bathroom With Her Flaming Red Hair and Said—.
  She Said.
Campion, T.   Awake, thou spring of speaking grace, mute rest becomes not thee.
Carruth, H.   Sam and Poll Go Back to the City.
  Septic Tanck.
Carver, R.   Extirpation.
  Mesopotamia.
Cary, T.   Methodus Amandi.
Cavafy.   Rest I Will Tell to Those Below in Hades, The.
Celan.   Leaf, treeless, A.
  Zurich, at the Stork.
Cowper, W.   Conversation.
Crane, H.   Praise for an Urn.
Creeley.   Interview, The.
  Rites, The.
Cummings, E. E.   Logeorge / lo / wellifitisn't eddy how's the boy.
  Now two old ladies sit peacefully knitting.
  Oil tel duh woil doi sez.
Davie, D.   Berkshire.
De la Mare.   In the Garden.
Dickinson, E.   Writing is brief and fleeting.
Dunbar, P.   Drizzle.
Eberhart, R.   At The Canoe Club.
Eliot, T. S.   Conversation Galante.
Frost, R.   Meeting and Passing.
Gallagher, T.   When You Speak to Me.
García Lorca.   Murder.
Gunn, T.   Conversation of Old Men, The.
  Conversation, The.
  Jamesian.
  Keats at Highgate.
Hacker, M.   Villanelle: Late Summer.
Hall, D.   Speeches.
Ignatow, D.   Opening Paths.
Jackson, L.   Talking World, The.
Kinsella, T.   Open Court.
Kizer, C.   Arthur's Party.
Komunyakaa.   Insinuations.
Larkin, P.   Talking In Bed.
Laughlin, J.   Bible Lady, The.
Lawrence, D. H.   Drawing-Room.
  Talk.
Levertov.   Conversation in Moscow.
Longfellow, H.   Fire of Drift-Wood, The.
Lorde.   Conversations in Crisis.
  Fantasy and Conversation.
Merrill, J.   Charles on Fire.
  Narrow Escape, A.
Merton.   Conversations.
Millay, E.   I, Being Born A Woman.
Milosz, C.   In Milan.
  Plato's Dialogues.
Nash, O.   Is This Seat Taken? Yes, or, My Neck Is Sticking In.
  Let's Not Play Lotto, Let's Just Talk.
  Mr. Barcalow's Breakdown.
Olson, C.   As I went in and out I heard pieces.
Pagis.   Conversation.
Paley, G.   On the Bank Street Pier.
  Street Corner Dialogue.
Palmer, M.   At the table we say.
Patchen.   There's a Train Leaving Soon.
Rich, A.   Dialogue.
Roethke.   Supper with Lindsay.
Rumi.   Constant Conversation.
  Talking in the Night.
  Talking through the Door.

Schuyler, J.   Master of the Golden Glow, The.
Stein, G.   Sonatina Followed by Another, A.
Stevens, W.   Conversation with Three Women of New England.
  On the Road Home.
Thomas, D.   Conversation of Prayer, The.
Tomlinson, C.   Rhenish Winter.
  Word in Edgeways, A.
Updike.   Thoughts While Driving Home.
Van Duyn.   Footnotes to "The Autobiography of Bertrand Russell."
  Talker, The.
Williams, C. K.   Politics.
Williams, M.   Man in the Bar Says He Has Something to Say, A.
  On a Trailways Bus a Man Who Holds His Head Strangely Speaks to the Seat Behind Him.
  Unto One of the Least of These.
Yeats.   To Some I Have Talked with by the Fire.
Zagajewski.   At Midnight.
Zukofsky, L.   Reading and Talking.

Conversion
Amichai [*or* Amikhai].   To a Convert.
Cavafy.   Tomb of Ignatios, The.
Davie, D.   Church Militant.
Emerson, R.   William Rufus and the Jew.
Merton.   St. Paul.
Muldoon, P.   Clonfeacle.
Ransom, J.   Persistent Explorer.
Riley, J.   Vision of Rabbi Ben Issac, The.
Wheatley, P.   On Being Brought from Africa to America.
Whittier.   Call of the Christian, The.

Conviction
Ciardi, J.   On Being Sure and of What.
Creeley.   As Now It Would Be Snow.
  Way, The.
Davie, D.   August, 1968.

Convoys
MacNeice.   Convoy.

Cook, Captain James
Atwood.   Reincarnation of Captain Cook, The.
Davie, D.   I Have Said, Ye Are Gods.
  Trevenen.

Cooking and Cooks
Berry, W.   Grandmother, The.
Bishop, E.   Lines Written in the Fannie Farmer Cookbook.
Brodsky, J.   Cabbage and Carrot.
Carver, R.   After the Fire.
Ciardi, J.   Food Notes.
Clampitt.   Gooseberry Fool.
Codrescu.   Dream (2).
Cowper, W.   Salad, The.
Dunbar, P.   Capture, The.
  Curiosity.
Graves, R.   Under the Pot.
Gunn, T.   Meat.
Hamill, S.   Cooking.
Herrick.   Upon Dol.
  Upon Hog.
Jacobsen, J.   Chanterelles, The.
  Emperor's Cook, The.
Kizer, C.   Mud Soup.
Levine, P.   Grandmother in Heaven.
McGrath, T.   Bread of this World; Praises III, The.
Muldoon, P.   Sushi.
Nash, O.   Malice Domestic.
  Second Limick.
  Strange Case of Mr. Palliser's Palate, The.
Nemerov.   Lobsters.
Piercy.   What's That Smell in the Kitchen?
Riley, J.   'Lizabuth-Ann on Bakin'-Day.
Rossetti, C.   Minnie bakes oaten cakes, / Minnie brews ale.
  Mix a Pancake.
Rumi.   Chickpea to Cook.
Schuyler, J.   Joint.
Sexton.   Jesus Cooks.
Sheridan, T.   Tale of the T——d, The.
Sze.   Shuttle.
Tate, J.   Soup of Venus, The.
Van Duyn.   Reading of Rex Stout, A.

Saleswomen in Bakery Shops.
Wang Chien. Newlywed's Cuisine, The.
Williams, C. K. So / mucked up with.

Coole, Ireland
Yeats. Coole Park, 1929.
Coole Park and Ballylee, 1931.
I walked among the seven woods of Coole.
In the Seven Woods.
Wild Swans at Coole, The.

Copernicus, Nicholas
Emerson, R. Star seer Copernicus / Only could earn a curse.
Wilbur, R. Fourth of July, The.

Coral
Emerson, R. Coral worm beneath the sea, The.
Walcott. Coral.

Cordelia
Howe, S. God's Spies.
WHITE FOOLSCAP / Book of Cordelia.
Laughlin, J. Cordelia.

Córdoba, Spain
García Lorca. St. Raphael.

Corinth, Greece
Byron, G. Siege of Corinth, The.
"H. D." Antipater of Sidon.

Coriolanus
Laughlin, J. He Did It to Please His Mother.

Cormorants
Clampitt. Cormorant in Its Element, The.
Tomlinson, C. To Be Engraved on the Skull of a Cormorant.

Corn
Blue Cloud. Sweet Corn.
Bly, R. Snowfall in the Afternoon.
Dugan, A. Significance of Corn in American History, The.
Dunbar, P. Corn-Stalk Fiddle, THe.
Lawrence, D. H. Fireflies in the Corn.
Lindsay, N. Cornfields, The.
Life Transcendent.
Melville, H. Trophies of Peace.
Muldoon, P. Cuckoo Corn.
Rukeyser, M. Cornfield, The.
Sandburg, C. Bitter Summer Thoughts—No. 3.
Corn and Beans.
Corn Prattlings.
Cornfield Ridge and Stream.
Cricket Match.
Early Copper.
Harvest.
Laughing Corn.
Ripe Corn.
Whittier. Huskers, The.

Cornell, Joseph
Kunitz, S. Crystal Cage, The.
Paz. Objects & Apparitions.

Cornwall, England
Davie, D. Cornwall.
Short Run to Camborne.

Corpses
Amichai [or Amikhai]. In the garden, at the white table.
Ammons. Whaleboat Sturck,The.
Baudelaire. Carefree Corpse, The.
Carrion.
Carrion, A.
Martyr, A.
Bly, R. Counting Small-Boned Bodies.
Bukowski. On Seeing an Old Civil War Painting with My Love.
Ciardi, J. Addio.
Overthrow, An.
Dickinson, E. Do People moulder equally.
Dubie. Village Priest, A.
Eberhart, R. When Golden Flies Upon My Carcass Come.
Gunn, T. Lazarus Not Raised.
Heaney, S. Grauballe Man, The.
Strange Fruit.
Housman. Some can gaze and not be sick.
Hughes, T. View of a Pig.
Jarrell, R. To Be Dead.
Washing the Corpse.
Komunyakaa. Touch-up Man.

Laughlin, J. How Does It Look?
MacDiarmid, H. Dead Liebknecht, The.
Mahon. Stone Age Figure Far Below, A.
Michelangelo Buonarroti. My flesh turned earth, my bones turned naked shame.
Plath. Two Views of a Cadaver Room.
Prunty. Crows, The.
Rexroth, K. Our Home Is in the Rocks.
Riley, J. After Death.
In State.
Little Dead Man, The.
What a Dead Man Said.
Rossetti, C. In a Certain Place.
Rumi. Babbling Child, A.
No Room for Form.
Swinburne. After Death.
Sze. Execution of Maximilian, The.
Williams, M. Autopsy.
Wilner, E. Closing Ceremonies for the Bicentennial.
Yeats. Oil and Blood.
See also **Necrophilia**

Corruption
Ai. Greed.
Auden. We Too Had Known Golden Hours.
Berry, W. River Bridged and Forgot, The.
Bly, R. Executive's Death, The.
Browning, E. View Across the Roman Campagna.
Byron, G. Answer to ——'s Professions of Affection.
Carver, R. For the Record.
Wenas Ridge.
Cavafy. They Might Have Bothered.
Chaucer. Former Age, The.
Coleridge, S. To an Unfortunate Woman Whom the Author Had Known in the Days of Her Innocence.
Creeley. News of the World.
Davie, D. Depravity: Two Sermons.
Graves, R. Accomplice, The.
Man of Evil.
Questions in a Wood.
Wigs and Beards.
Han-shan. Again I see those who leave home.
Herrick. Bad Princes Pill Their People.
Hughes, L. Bad Man.
Goodbye Christ.
Prime.
Un-American Investigators.
Jeffers, R. Be Angry at the Sun.
Delusion of Saints.
Going to Horse Flats.
Ink-Sack.
Ordinary Newscaster, An.
Sinverguenza.
Skunks.
Stars Go Over the Lonely Ocean, The.
Jonson, B. On English Monsieur.
Kipling, R. Bees and the Flies, The.
Legend of the Foreign Office, A.
What Happened.
Komunyakaa. Gloria's Clues.
Kunitz, S. System, The.
Tutored Child, The.
Lawrence, D. H. Nottingham's New University.
Riches.
Lindsay, N. What the Moon Saw.
MacLeish. Black Day, The.
Conversation in a Belfry.
Good Man in a Bad Time, A.
Tricked by Eternity the Heart.
Michelangelo Buonarroti. Chalices hammered into sword and helmet!
New and more commendable delight, A.
Milosz, C. Counsels.
Nation, A.
You Who Wronged.
Milton. Lycidas.
Nemerov. Poverty Programs, The.
Olson, C. What Had to Go.
Plath. Firesong.
Rimbaud, A. Customs Men, The.
Roethke. Prognosis.
Rossetti, C. Babylon the Great.
Thy Friend and Thy Father's Friend Forget Not.

Sandburg, C. Hogh Conspiratorial Persons.
Soiled Dove.
Shapiro, K. Washington Cathedral.
Shelley, P. Fragment: "Gentle story of two lovers young, A."
Lines Written During the Castlereagh Administration.
Shih-te. World has its know-it-alls, The.
Smith, S. Evangelie, or, The Figure of Literary Corruption, Seeking Glory Not Truth.
Spenser, E. Faerie Queene, The.
Book 2, Canto 6.
Book 2, Canto 8.
Book 2, Canto 12.
Book 3.
Book 3, Canto 9.
Book 4.
Book 4, Canto 1.
Book 4, Canto 9.
Book 4, Canto 11.
Book 4, Canto 12.
Book 5.
Book 5, Canto 2.
Book 6.
Book 7.
Swift, J. On the Burning of Whitehall in 1698.
On the Five Ladies at Sot's Hole.
Unknown, sometimes at. to Sir Walter Ralegh.
Epitaph on the Earl of Salisbury.
Williams, M. Senator Explains a Vote, The.

Corso, Gregory
Laughlin, J. Power of Poesy, The.

Cortés, Hernán
Lux. What Montezuma Fed Cortés and His Men.
Wilner, E. Winged Victory.

Coruña, La, Spain
García Lorca. Ballad of Our Lady of the Boat.

Cosmetics
Donne. Phryne.
Herrick. Neglect.
Upon Judith.
Upon Sibilla.
Kizer, C. Pearl.
Swift, J. Progress of Beauty, The.
Unknown. On a Battered Beauty.

Cosmology
Ciardi, J. Some Sort of Game.
Cummings, E. E. Kind) / YM&WC / (of sort of).
McHugh, H. Spot in Space and Time.

Cosmos
Brodsky, J. Via Funari.
Browning, R. Reverie.
Ciardi, J. Starry Heavens, the Moral Law, The.
Cortes. Space Song.
Dugan, A. About the Pseudo St. Dionysius.
Laughlin, J. Mathematics of Chaos, The.
Levi, P. Black Stars, The.
Mallarmé. When the shadow menaced with its fatal law.
Ramanujan. Traces.
Rexroth, K. Hapax.
Sandburg, C. Scriptsmith.
Seifert. Dome of the Observatory, The.
Shelley, P. Daemon of the World, The; A Fragment.
Sze. Kaiseki.
Szymborska, W. Warning.
Wilner, E. See-Saw.
See also **Creation**

Costa Rica
Stock, R. Costa Rican Pastoral.

Cotswold Hills, England
Davie, D. Gloucestershire.
Gurney, I. Coppice, The.
February Dawn.
Felling a Tree.
Friendly Are Meadows.
Hell's Prayer.
High Hills, The.
Larches.
Old Thought.
Song: "Past my window dawn and down."

While I Write.
Tomlinson, C. To Ivor Gurney.

Cotton
Angelou. Miss Scarlet, Mr. Rhett and other
   Latter-Day Saints.
Levine, P. Ashes.
Whittier. Haschish, The.

Counterfeiting and Counterfeiters
Lawrence, D. H. Aloof in Gaiety.

Counting
Dickinson, E. 'Tis One by One—the Father
   counts.
Eberhart, R. Soldier Rejects His Times
   Addressing His Contemporaries, A.
Ignatow, D. Information.
Olson, C. Kin.
Rossetti, C. 1 and 1 are 2— / That's for me and
   you.
Schuyler, J. Six Something.

Country Clubs
Hughes, L. Undertow.
Laughlin, J. Gracious Living.

Country Life
Ammons. Hardweed Path Going.
   Medicine for Tight Spots.
Berry, W. At a Country Funeral.
   Dream, The.
Berryman. Long Home, The.
Bishop, E. From the Country to the City.
Bogan, L. Old Countryside.
Browning, E. Soul's Travelling, The.
Bukowski. Countryside.
Burns, R. As I Went Out Ae May Morning.
   Ballad, A: "There was a lass and she was fair."
   Bess[y] and Her Spinning-Wheel.
   Bob o' Dumblane, The.
   Brose and Butter.
   Cotter's Saturday Night, The.
   Country Lassie.
   Epistle to Hugh Parker.
   Grim Grizzle.
   To the Weaver's Gin Ye Go.
   Waukrife Minnie, A.
Ciardi, J. Elegy for Moral Self-Assurance and
   Country Virtue, An.
   Letter from a Metaphysical Countryside.
Clare, J. Mole-Catcher, The.
Coleridge, S. Reflections on Having Left a
   Place of Retirement.
Cowper, W. Salad, The.
   Task, The.
Creeley. City, The.
   Farm, The.
Cunningham, J. Montana Fifty Years Ago.
   Montana Pastoral.
Davie, D. Sounds of a Devon Village.
Donne. To Sir Henry Wotton ("Sir, more than
   kisses, letters mingle souls").
Dryden, J. To My Honoured [or Honour'd]
   Kinsman, John Driden.
Dugan, A. On Cabin Fever, On Boredom in the
   Countryside.
   On Hibernation in the Country.
   To a Colleague. From the Country.
Dunbar, P. At Loafing-Holt.
   Diplomacy.
   Land o' Used to Be, The.
Frost, R. Case for Jefferson, A.
   Directive.
   Need of Being Versed in Country Things, The.
   Roadside Stand, A.
Graves, R. On Dwelling.
Gurney, I. Bare Line of the Hill, The.
   Where the Mire.
Hall, D. Merle Bascom's .22.
   Names of Horses.
   Ox Cart Man.
   Twelve Seasons.
Hardy, T. Bird-Scene at a Rural Dwelling, A.
   In Time of "The Breaking of Nations."
Herrick. Bucolick betwixt Two: Lacon and
   Thyrsis, A.
   Country Life: To His Brother, M. Tho: Herrick.
   Country Life, to the Honored Mr. Endymion
   Porter, The.

Eclogue, or Pastorall between Endimion Porter
   and Lycidas Herrick, An.
His Content in the Country.
His Grange.
His Grange, or Private Wealth.
Larr's Portion, and the Poets Part.
Saint Distaffs Day, or the Morrow after Twelfth
   Day.
To His Muse.
To Phyllis to Love and Live with Him.
Upon Himnself.
Jacobsen, J. Country Bath.
   Country Drive-In.
Jarrell, R. Country Life, A.
Jonson, B. To Penshurst.
Keats. Dawlish Fair.
   For There's Bishop's Teign.
   To One Who Has Been Long in City Pent.
   Where Be You [or Ye] Going, You [or Ye]
   Devon Maid?
Kinnell. Ruins under the Stars.
   When One Has Lived a Long Time Alone.
Komunyakaa. Changes; or, Reveries at a
   Window Overlooking a Country Road.
Langston Hughes.
   When Men Can't Trust Hands with Wood.
Kumin, M. Henry Manley Blues, The.
   Henry Manley Looks Back.
   How It Goes On.
   Rejoicing with Henry.
Lawrence, D. H. Letter from Town: The
   Almond-Tree.
   Love On the Farm.
   Whether or Not.
Levine, P. These Streets.
Longfellow, H. Fire of Drift-Wood, The.
Lux. There Were Some Summers.
   View From a Porch.
Mahon. Woods, The.
Major, C. Heartland Music.
   Pencil Sketch.
Marvell. Garden, The.
McGrath, T. Ah... to the Villages!
Melville, H. Immolated.
Meredith, G. Beyond the meadow still where
   sweeps.
   Grandfather Bridgeman.
   Invitation to the Country.
   Or the single path— / Which the cool moon
   sheds.
Merwin. By the Mango Trees.
Michelangelo Buonarroti. New and more
   commendable delight, A.
Millay, E. Return, The.
Muldoon, P. Lull.
   Wood, The.
Nash, O. Nine Miles to the Railroad.
Nemerov. At a Country Hotel.
Niedecker. On Columbus Day he set out for the
   north.
   To see the man who took care of our stock.
Oliver, M. Being Country Bred.
   Farm Country.
   Winter in the Country.
Parker, D. Cassandra Drops into Verse.
   Letter to Robert Benchley; Roughing It in the
   Country at the Birches, Maine.
   Song of the Open Country.
Patchen. Backcountry Blues.
   We Must Be Slow.
Plath. Song for a Summer's Day.
Pope, A. Epistle to Miss [or Miss Teresa]
   Blount, on Her Leaving the Town after the
   Coronation.
   Happy Life of a Country Parson, The.
Rexroth, K. There shall come faint light.
Rich, A. Rural Reflections.
Riley, J. At Aunty's House.
   At "The Literary."
   Country Editor, The.
   Country Pathway, A.
   Good, Old-fashioned People, The.
   Griggsby's Station.
   My Ruthers.
   Summer's Day, A.
   Town and Country.

Uncle Dan'l in Town over Sunday.
Us Farmers in the Country.
Voice from the Farm, A.
When the Frost Is on the Punkin.
Rilke. Ardent Country.
   From Father to Son.
Rimbaud, A. Nina Answers Back.
Rossetti, C. Milking-Maid, The.
Sandburg, C. Flanders.
   More Country People.
   Potato Blossom Songs and Jigs.
Sarton, M. Apple Tree in May.
   Charleston Plantations.
   Puritan, The.
Schuyler, J. Evenings in Vermont.
   Korean Mums.
   Vermont Diary, A.
   Walk, The.
Seidl. To the High-Flyers.
Sheridan, T. My Hens Are Hatching.
Simic. Rural Delivery.
Smart, C. To My Worthy Friend, Mr. T.B. One
   of the People Called Quakers.
Smith, S. I Love.
Snyder, G. After Work.
Stafford, W. Light by the Barn, The.
   Song in the Manner of Flannery O'Connor, A.
   Universe is One Place.
Stockton, A. Invitation Ode to a Young Lady in
   New York from Her Friend in the Country, An.
   To Miss Mary Stockton, an Epistle the 10th of
   Janu 78.
   To Mr Lewis Pintard on His Retirement at New
   Rochelle.
Swenson, M. Sunday in the Country.
Swift, J. To Quilca.
   Verses from Quilca.
Sze. Brueghel.
Tate, J. Land of Little Sticks, 1945.
Thomas, D. In Country Sleep.
Tomlinson, C. Casarola.
   Portrait of Mrs. Spaxton.
Van Duyn. Postcards from Cape Split.
Walcott. Upstate.
Warren, R. Boyhood in Tobacco Country.
   Sitting on Farm Lawn on Sunday Afternoon.
Whitman, W. Farm Picture, A.
Williams, C. K. It Is Teeming.
   Sleeping Over.
Williams, W. Aftermath, The.
   Raleigh Was Right.
   Woman Walking.
Wordsworth, W. 1830.
   Inscription for the Moss-Hut at Dove Cottage.
Wright, C. December Journal.
   Three Poems of Departure.
   Two Stories.
Wright, J. Arriving in the Country Again.
   Summer Memory in the Crowded City, A.
Yeats. Lake-Isle of Innisfree, The.
Zukofsky, L. Che Di Lor Suona Su Nella Tua
   Vita.

County Antrim, Northern Ireland
MacNeice. Carrickfergus.
Mahon. North Wind: Portrush.
   Rathlin.

County Cork, Ireland
Mahon. Garage in Co. Cork, A.
   Kinsale.
   Penshurst Place.

County Donegal, Ireland
Muldoon, P. Good Friday, 1971. Driving
   Westward.

County Galway, Ireland
Davie, D. Corrib. An Emblem.

County Meath, Ireland
Davie, D. Wearing of the Green, The.
Muldoon, P. My Grandfather's Wake.

County Sligo, Ireland
Yeats. Lake-Isle of Innisfree, The.

Courage
Atwood. Notes towards a Poem That Can
   Never Be Written.
Baudelaire. Sisina.
Berryman. Dangerous Year, The.

To a Woman.
Bierce. Two Types.
Borges. Milonga of Don Nicanor Paredes.
Brodsky, J. North of Delphi.
Brontë, E. No Coward Soul is Mine.
Brooks, G. "Strong Men, Riding Horses."
Browning, R. Arcades Ambo.
Burns, R. Macpherson's Farewell.
  O Kenmure's on and awa, Willie.
Byron, G. On the Star of "The Legion of
  Honour."
Cavafy. Come, O King of the Lacedaimonians.
Char. Fighters.
Clough. Say Not the Struggle Nought Availeth.
Crane, S. Tell brave deeds of war.
Creeley. Dishonest Mailmen, The.
Cummings, E. E. You which could grin three
  smiles into a dead.
De la Mare. Courage.
Dickinson, E. Bless God, he went as soldiers.
  I think to Live—may be a Bliss.
  I Took My Power in My Hand.
  I took my Power in my Hand.
  If your Nerve, deny you.
Dunbar, P. To Dr. James Newton Matthews,
  Mason. III
Eliot, T. S. Defense of the Islands.
Emerson, R. Look danger in the eye it vanishes.
  Titmouse, The.
Frost, R. Courage to Be New, The.
Glück, L. From the Japanese.
Graves, R. Until We Both.
Gurney, I. On Somme.
HaNagid. If You Don't Have The Power To
  Pay.
Herrick. More Mighty, the More Merciful, The.
  More Modest, More Manly.
  On Love.
  To His Muse, Another to the Same.
  To the Lord Hopton, on His Fight in Cornwall.
Housman. Loitering with a vacant eye.
  Sage to the Young Man, The.
Hughes, L. Song: "Lovely, dark, and lonely
  one."
  Walkers with the Dawn.
Jonson, B. On Playwright ("Playwright convict
  of public wrongs to men").
Lawrence, D. H. Courage.
Logan, J. Tale of a Later Leander.
Lowell, R. Marcus Cato 95–42 B.C.
  Sir Thomas More.
MacLeish. Pablo Casals.
McGrath, T. Poem: "Down the small and
  crooked road."
Melville, H. At the Cannon's Mouth.
  Rebel Color-Bearers at Shiloh.
Meredith, G. Crown of Love, The.
  Song of Drab, The.
  Squireless Kate.
  To Cardinal Manning.
  To J.M.
Millay, E. Courage that my mother had, The.
Milosz, C. Story, A.
Nash, O. How Now, Sirrah? Oh, Anyhow.
  It's Snug to Be Smug.
Oppen. Kind of Garden, A: A Poem for My
  Sister.
Orr, G. Brave Child, The.
Owen, W. Spring Offensive.
Paley, G. Learning from Barbara Deming.
Parker, D. Penelope.
Ralegh, S. On the Snuff of a Candle.
Rich, A. Trying to Talk with a Man.
Ritsos. Courage or Ignorance.
Roethke. Reply to Censure.
Rossetti, C. For a Mercy Received.
  I Do Not Look for Love That Is a Dream.
  I Have Fought a Good Fight.
  Yes, I too could face death and never shrink.
Rukeyser, M. To keep the weakness secret. To
  deny it and break through.
Rumi. Core of Masculinity, The.
Sexton. Courage.
Smith, S. Can It Be?
  Harold's Leap.
Tennyson, A. Charge of the Light Brigade, The.

Thoreau. In days of yore, tis said, the
  swimming alder.
Unknown. On Miltiades.
Whitman, W. Bravest Soldiers, The.
Whittier. Barbara Frietchie.
  Conductor Bradley.
  Three Bells, The.
Wordsworth, W. Martial courage of a day is
  vain, The.
  Occasioned by the Battle of Waterloo (the Last
  Six Lines Intended for an Inscription)
  February, 1816.
  Ode: The Morning of the Day Appointed for a
  General Thanksgiving. January 18, 1816.
  Westmoreland Girl, The.
Wright, J. Mad Fight Song for William S.
  Carpenter, 1966, A.

Courtesy
Hall, D. Grave The Well, The.
Meredith, G. Song of Courtesy, The.
Robinson, E. Flammonde.
Whittier. To ———: "Fair Nature's priestesses!
  to whom."

Courtiers
Browning, E. Romaunt of Margret, The.
Browning, R. In a Balcony.
De la Mare. Heresy.
Donne. To Sir Henry Wotton ("Here's no more
  news, than virtue, I may as well").
  To the Countess of Bedford ("Madam, / You
  have refined me, and to worthiest things").
Graves, R. Son Altesse.
Hardy, T. Royal Sponsors.
Herrick. Dialogue Betwixt Himselfe and
  Mistresse Eliza, A.
  Eclogue, or Pastorall between Endimion Porter
  and Lycidas Herrick, An.
Jonson, B. Epigram, An: "That you have seen
  the pride, beheld the sport."
  On Court-Parrot.
  On Court-Worm[e].
  To Courtling.
Keats. Cap and Bells; or, The Jealousies, The.
Ransom, J. Vaunting Oak.
Rossetti, C. I am a King, / Or an Emperor
  rather.
Tu Fu. Lo Yu Park.
  Thwarted.

Courtship
Amichai [or Amikhai]. As It Was.
Angelou. To a Suitor.
  Where We Belong, A Duet.
Ashbery, J. Long Novel, A.
  More Pleasant Adventures.
Auden. As I Walked Out One Evening.
Bierce. Serenade: "Listen, maiden, to my
  strain."
Blake, W. How Sweet I Roamed [or Roam'd]
  from Field to Field.
  Love's.
  Some look. to see the sweet Outlines.
Brooks, G. Lovely Love, A.
Browning, E. Amy's Cruelty.
  Lady Geraldine's Courtship.
  Lord Walter's Wife.
  Man's Requirements, A.
  Question and Answer.
  Year's Spinning, A.
Browning, R. In a Balcony.
  Light Woman, A.
  Serenade at the Villa, A.
Burns, R. Allan Water.
  Ballad, A: "There was a lass and she was fair."
  Ca' the Ewes [or Yowes] [to the Knowes].
  Ca' the Yowes [to the Knowes].
  Comin[g] thro' [or through] the Rye.
  Dainty Davie.
  Down the Burn Davie.
  Duncan Davison.
  Duncan Gray.
  Halloween.
  I Love My Love in Secret.
  I'll Mak You Be Fain to Follow Me.
  John Come Kiss Me Now.
  Lassie wi' the Lintwhite Locks.
  Lea-Rig, The.

Leezie Lindsay.
  Mary Morison.
  O Lay Thy Loof in Mine Lass.
  O Steer Her Up and Had Her Gaun.
  On Willie Chalmers.
  Rigs o' Barley, The.
  Scotish Ballad.
  She Says She Lo'es Me Best of A'
  Song: "Behind yon hills where Lugar flows."
  Song, Composed in August.
  There Grows a Bonie Brier-Bush.
  Tibbie Dunbar.
  Tibbie Fowler.
  Waukrife Minnie, A.
  Whistle, and I'll Come to You, My Lad.
Byron, G. Reply to Some Verses of J.M.B.
  Pigot, Esq., on the Cruelty of His Mistress.
  Stanzas to a Lady, with the Poems of Camoëns.
  To a Vain Lady.
  To Romance.
Campion, T. Ad Caspiam.
  Advice to a Girl.
  As on a day Sabina fell asleepe.
  Be Wise, and Fly Not.
  Come, you pretty false-eyed wanton [or false-
  ey'd wanton].
  Dear If I with Guile.
  Dolus.
  Hide not, sweetest Love, a sight so pleasing.
  I Care Not for These Ladies.
  If any hath the heart to kill.
  If thou longst so much to learne (sweet boy)
  what 'tis to love.
  In Laurentiam.
  In Melleam.
  Love Me or Not.
  Maydes are simple, some men say.
  Now Winter Nights Enlarge.
  Shall I Come, Sweet Love.
  So many loves have I neglected.
  So Quicke, So Hot, So Mad is Thy Fond Sute.
  Tarry sweete love.
  Think'st thou to seduce me then.
  Though your strangenesse frets my hart.
  Thus I Resolve.
  What Fair[e] Pomp[e].
  What meanes this folly, now to brave it so.
  Whether away my sweetest deerest?
Campion, T. *et al.* Aye me, that love should
  natures workes accuse!
  If I urge my kinde desires.
  Kinde in unkindnesse, when will you relent.
  Sweete, come againe.
Carew, T. Boldness[e] in Love.
  Good Counsel to a Young Maid.
  Love's Courtship.
  Pastoral[l] Dialogue, A.
  To A. L.; Persuasions [or Perswasions] to Love.
  To a Lady That Desired I Would Love Her.
Cary, T. Methodus Amandi.
Chaucer. Anelida and Arcite.
  Complaint unto His Lady, A.
  Complaynt d'Amours.
  Parlement of Foules, The.
  To Rosamounde.
  Troilus and Criseyde [or Criseide].
  Womanly Noblesse.
Ciardi, J. Letter from a Pander.
Coleridge, S. Night-Scene, The.
  To an Unfortunate Woman at the Theatre.
  To the Evening Star.
Collins, B. Plight of the Troubadour.
  Serenade: "Let the other boys from the village."
Crashaw. Out of the Italian; a Song.
  [With Some Poems Sent to a Gentlewoman. I].
  [With Some Poems Sent to a Gentlewoman. II].
Cummings, E. E. As freedom is a
  breakfastfood.
  Except in your / honour.
  If i love You.
  Let it go—the.
  Who knows if the moon's.
  Yes is a pleasant country.
Cunningham, J. Ars Amoris.
"Dario." In Spring.
Davie, D. Late Anniversary, A.

Dickinson, E.   Death is the supple Suitor.
   God is a distant—stately Lover.
   Her Sweet turn to leave the Homestead.
Donne.   Letter Written by Sir H. G. and J. D.
   alternis vicibus, A.
   Prohibition, The.
   To the Countess of Huntingdon ("That unripe
   side of earth, that heavy clime").
Dove, R.   Adolescence—III.
   Courtship.
   Courtship, Diligence.
Dryden, J.   Song: "Fair, sweet and young,
   receive a prize."
Dugan, A.   Courting Song: Attack! Attack!
   Attack!
Dunbar, P.   Circumstances Alter Cases.
   Confidence, A.
   Coquette Conquered, A.
   Discovered.
   How Shall I Woo Thee.
   Howdy, Honey, Howdy!
   Li'l' Gal.
   My Best Girl.
   On the Road.
   Sling Along.
   Spring Wooing, A.
   Suitor, The.
   Wooing, The.
Eberhart, R.   When Doris Danced.
Frost, R.   Line-Storm Song, A.
García Lorca.   Street of the Mutes, The.
   Tree, Tree.
Glück, L.   Swans.
Graves, R.   Arrow Shots.
   Bites and Kisses.
   Bower-Bird.
   Coronet of Moonlight.
   Five.
   For Ever.
   Green-Sailed Vessel, The.
   Hazel Grove, The.
   Hills of May, The.
   Hoopoe Tells Us How, The.
   Inkidoo and the Queen of Babel.
   Love and Night.
   Love Gifts.
   Perfectionists.
   Possibly.
   Promised Ballad, The.
   Quinque.
   She to Him.
   Song: The Promise.
   Song: To Become Each Other.
   Uncut Diamond, The.
   Unnamed Spell, The.
Guillaume de Lorris *et al.*   Romance [*or*
   Romaunt] of the Rose, The.
Hardy, T.   Catching Ballet of the Wedding
   Clothes, The.
   Epitaph on a Pessimist.
   Flirt's Tragedy, The.
   Gallant's Song.
   I Was Not He.
   I Worked No Wile to Meet You.
   Letter's Triumph, The.
   Why Be at Pains?
Heine, H.   My Heart.
Herrick.   Chop-Cherry.
   Conjuration, to Electra, A.
   Corinna's Going a-Maying.
   Hymne to the Graces, A.
   Leven.
   On Love.
   To Electra. Love Looks for Love.
   To His Valentine, on S. Valentines Day.
   To Mistresse Amie Potter.
   To Rosemary and Baies.
   To Silvia.
   To the Lark.
   To the Virgins, to Make Much of Time.
   Up Tail[e]s All.
   Upon a Cherrystone Sent to the Tip of the Lady
   Jemmonia Walgraves Eare.
   Upon a Delaying Lady.
   Zeal Required in Love.
Hopkins, G.   Castara Victrix.

Continuation of R. Garnett's *Nix*.
   Daphne.
   Lover's Stars, The.
   Tomorrow meet you? O not tomorrow.
Housman.   Along the field as we came by.
   Delight it is in youth and May.
   Oh see how thick the goldcup flowers.
   Sloe was lost in flower, The.
   This time of year a twelvemonth past.
Hughes, L.   Ballad of Little Sallie.
   Cat and the Saxophone (2 a.m.), The.
   Wooing, A.
Hughes, T.   Two Tortoiseshell Butterflies.
Jonson, B.   Song. To Celia ("Drink to me only
   with thine eyes").
   To the Same [Sir Luckless Woo-All].
Keats.   Stanzas: "You say you love; but with a
   voice."
   To Fanny.
   To ———: "Had I a man's fair form, then
   might my sighs."
   To [Mary Frogley].
   Where Be You [*or* Ye] Going, You [*or* Ye]
   Devon Maid?
Laughlin, J.   Translation, A.
   You Invited Me.
Lawrence, D. H.   Cherry Robbers.
   Drained Cup, The.
   Hands of the Betrothed, The.
   I Wish I Knew a Woman.
   Liaison.
   Sunday Afternoon in Italy.
   Tortoise Gallantry.
   Turned Down.
Levertov.   Young Man Travelling, A.
Lindsay, N.   Blacksmith's Serenade, The.
   For All Who Ever Sent Lace Valentines.
Logan, J.   Bride's Song, The.
   Bridegroom's Song, The.
   Complaint, The.
   Epilogue.
   Epilogue, Songs of the Spouses, Complaint of
   Love.
   Matinee.
   Picnic, The.
   Tale of Courtship.
Mahon.   Penshurst Place.
Major, C.   Flowers for My Date.
Marlowe.   Passionate Shepherd To His Love,
   The.
Martial.   2.55: "You would be courted, dear, and
   I would love you."
Marvell.   To His Coy Mistress.
McHugh, H.   Whoosh.
Meredith, G.   Crown of Love, The.
   Iconia.
   Love in the Valley.
   O shrive me Friar, my ghostly Friar!
   Sing aloud that she is mine.
   Song: Spring.
   Song: "Under boughs of breathing May."
   Vital Choice, The.
Merrill, J.   From the Cupola.
Muldoon, P.   Boon.
Nash, O.   Advice outside a Church.
   Emancipation of Mr. Poplin, or, Skoal to the
   Skimmerless.
   Sedative Reflection.
   Strange Case of Mr. Ballantine's Valentine, The.
   Strange Case of the Girl o' Mr. Sponsoon's
   Dreams, The.
   Strange Case of the Lovelorn Letter Writer, The.
   That Reminds Me.
   To a Lady Passing Time Better Left Unpassed.
O'Hara, F.   Lover, The.
Olson, C.   Day Song, the Day After.
   Soul, The.
Parker, D.   Folk Song.
   For an Unknown Lady.
   Indian Summer.
   One Perfect Rose.
   Rhyme of an Involuntary Violet.
   Social Note.
   Unfortunate Coincidence.
Patchen.   Figure Motioned with Its Mangled
   Hand Toward the Wall Behind It, The.

Great Birds, The.
   Not If He Has Any Sense, He Won't Be Back.
   O when I take my love out walking.
   On the South-West Coast of Erehwemos Stands
   a Romantic Little Village.
   Polly—An Almost-True Story.
   We Go Out Together.
   Who'll that be.
Ralegh, S.   Arte of English Poesie, The.
   Description of Love, A.
   Excuse, The.
   Fayne Would I But I Dare Not.
   In the Grace of Wit, of Tongue and Face.
   Nymph's [*or* Nimphs] Reply to the Shepherd
   [*or* Sheepheard], The.
   Sir Walter Ralegh to the Queen.
Ramanujan.   Rather Foolish Sentiment, A.
Ransom, J.   Piazza Piece.
Riley, J.   In the South.
   Poet's Wooing, A.
Rimbaud, A.   Nina Answers Back.
Roethke.   For An Amorous Lady.
Rossetti, C.   Amor Mundi.
   Cousin Kate.
   Jessie Cameron.
   Maiden-Song.
   No, Thank You, John.
   Noble Sisters.
   Prince's Progress, The.
   Triad, A.
Seifert.   Smoke of Marijuana, The.
Sexton.   White Snake, The.
Shirley, J.   To His Mistress [*or* Mistris]
   Confined.
Smith, S.   Barlow.
   I Like to Play with Him.
   Le Désert de l'Amour.
   Magic Morning, The.
Spender, S.   Acts Passed Beyond.
Stafford, W.   Glances.
Suckling, S.   Barley-Break , A.
   Detraction Execrated.
   Love's Siege.
   Love's World.
   Loving and Beloved.
   Song: "Honest lover whosoever."
   Sonnet: "Of thee, kind boy, I ask no red and
   white."
Swinburne.   Ballad of Burdens, A.
   May Janet.
   Old Saying, An.
Tate, J.   Hostile Philharmonic Orchestra, The.
Walker, A.   Did This Happen to Your Mother?
   Did Your Sister Throw Up a Lot?
Warren, R.   Old Flame.
Whalen, P.   Palimpsest.
   Slop Barrel, The.
Whitman, W.   Dalliance of the Eagles, The.
Williams, W.   First Praise.
   Portrait of a Young Man with a Bad Heart.
Wordsworth, W.   Ellen Irwin; or, The Braes of
   Kirtle.
Wroth [*or* Wroath].   Urania.
Wyatt, S.   For to love her for her looks lovely.
   I have sought long with steadfastness.
   If waker care, if sudden [*or* sodayne] pale
   colo[u]r.
   Long love that in my thought doth harbo[u]r,
   The.
   Madam, Withouten Many Words.
   Since Love will needs that I shall love.
   What needeth these threnning words and wasted
   wind?
   When first mine eyes did view and mark.
Yeats.   Cap and Bells, The.
   Her Triumph.
See also **Dating**
Cousins
Browning, E.   Aurora Leigh.
Ciardi, J.   Ugliness.
Clampitt.   My Cousin Muriel.
Eliot, T. S.   Cousin Nancy.
Jacobsen, J.   Poems for My Cousin.
Kumin, M.   Sperm.
Major, C.   Sexual Conduct.
Parker, D.   Our Cousins.
Ramanujan.   Looking for a Cousin on a Swing.

Real Estate.
Riley, J. Little Cousin Jasper.
Roethke. My Dim-Wit Cousin.
Rossetti, C. Maggie a Lady.

Coventry, England
Larkin, P. I Remember, I Remember.

Cowardice and Cowards
Browning, R. Martin Relph.
Burns, R. Johnie Cope.
  Laddies by the banks o' Nith, The.
  On Capt. W——— R-dd-ck of C-rb—ton.
Dugan, A. Memories of Verdun.
  Two Hatreds of Action.
Eliot, T. S. Gerontion.
  Love Song of J. Alfred Prufrock, Resumed, The.
  Love Song of J. Alfred Prufrock, The.
  Love Song of J. Alfred Prufrock, The (Prufrock among the Women).
  Prufrock's Pervigilium.
Emerson, R. This world is tedious.
Herrick. Fear[e] Gets Force.
  No Despight to the Dead.
Housman. Day of Battle, The.
  My dreams are of a field afar.
Jonson, B. On Mongrel Esquire.
  To Brain-Hardy
Lawrence, D. H. Cowardice and Impudence.
  Cowards.
  Laughter.
  Willy Wet-Leg.
Levine, P. Heaven.
Oliver, M. Kookaburras, The.
Rexroth, K. Hanged Man, The.
Ritsos. Spinelessly.
Roethke. Prognosis.
Smith, S. No Respect.
Thoreau. Coward ever sings no song, The.

Cowboys
Atwood. Backdrop Addresses Cowboy.
Hall, D. Lone Ranger, The.
Muldoon, P. Vaquero.
Tomlinson, C. At Barstow.
Warren, R. Rattlesnake Country.
Williams, M. Pity and Fear.

Cowper, William
Blake, W. William Cowper Esqre.
Browning, E. Cowper's Grave.
Davie, D. Homage to William Cowper.
  Huntingdonshire.
Zaturenska. Affliction of William Cowper, The.

Cows
Berry, W. Her First Calf.
Bly, R. Opening the Door of a Barn I Thought Was Empty on New Year's Eve.
Burns, R. Calf, The.
  Grim Grizzle.
Carruth, H. Cows at Night, The.
  Cowshed Blues, The.
  Godhulivela.
  Johnny Spain's White Heifer.
Ciardi, J. Cow, The.
Clampitt. Woodlot, The.
Clifton, L. My Dream About the Cows.
Collins, B. Afternoon with Irish Cows.
Creeley. Don't Sign Anything.
Dickey, J. Trees and Cattle.
Dugan, A. Transcribed Conversation in Praise of Cows.
Frost, R. Cow in Apple Time, The.
Gallagher, T. Cows, a Vision.
García Lorca. Cow.
Hall, D. Great Day in the Cows' House.
Hardy, T. Calf, The.
Herrick. Supreme Fortune Falls Soonest.
Hughes, T. Chaucer.
  Dehorning.
Kinnell. Freedom, New Hampshire.
Levertov. Her Sister.
Merwin. Cow, The.
Muldoon, P. Cows.
Nash, O. Cow, The.
Paley, G. Beef.
Riley, J. Lines: "Portentous sound! mysteriously vast."
Ritsos. Orestes.

Roethke. Cow, The.
Rossetti, C. Brownie, Brownie, let down your milk.
  When the cows come home the milk is coming.
Rukeyser, M. Another Day (And then the cow).
Sandburg, C. Milk-White Moon, Put the Cows to Sleep.
Stock, R. Slaughtering the Cow.
Tate, J. Intimidations of an Autobiography.
Tomlinson, C. Macduff.
Van Duyn. Ballad of Blossom, The.
  Just full of springs the world was in Illinois.
Very. Cows Waiting at the Pasture Gate, The.
Warren, R. Uncertain Season in High Country.
Williams, M. Paying Some Slight Attention to His Birthday the Associate Professor Goes about His Business.

Coyote (mythology)
Blue Cloud. At Bald Rock with Old John.
  Old Tom would tell us.

Coyotes
Hamill, S. Man in the Landscape.
Stafford, W. Coyote.
  Coyote in the Zoo, The.
  Outside.
Tomlinson, C. Anecdote.
Warren, R. Arizona Midnight.

Crab Apple Trees and Crab Apples
Muldoon, P. Early Warning.
Sandburg, C. Crabapples.

Crabbe, George
Davie, D. Trevenen.
Robinson, E. George Crabbe.

Crabs and Crabbing
Ammons. Help.
Atwood. Landcrab I.
  Landcrab II.
Clifton, L. Crabbing.
Dugan, A. Life Comparison.
Graves, R. With the Gift of a Lion's Claw.
Hughes, T. Ghost Crabs.
Jacobsen, J. Fiddler Crab.
Plath. Mussel Hunter at Rock Harbor.
Updike. Crab Crack.

See also **Hermit Crabs; Horseshoe Crabs**

Cracow, Poland
See **Krakow [*or* Cracow], Poland**

Craftsmanship
Cavafy. Craftsman of Winebowls.
  Procession of Dionysus.
Cowper, W. Flatting Mill, The.
Kunitz, S. Words for the Unknown Makers.
Ritsos. Craftsman, The.
Rumi. Craftsman pulled a reed from the reedbed, A.
  Craftsmanship and Emptiness.
Snyder, G. Axe Handles.
Stock, R. Dollmaker, The.
Sze. Wood Whittler, The.

Crane, Hart
Clampitt. Voyages.
Creeley. Hart Crane.
Logan, J. Lines Against A Loved American Poet After Hearing An Irish One's Nickman.
Lowell, R. Words for Hart Crane.
Lux. Here's to Samuel Greenberg.
Olson, C. Birth's Obituary.
  You, Hart Crane.
Williams, T. As I stood in my room tonight, drinking a solitary toast.
Wright, C. Portrait of the Artist with Hart Crane.

Cranes (ornithology)
Blok. Autumn Day.
Bukowski. About Cranes.
Carruth, H. Too Tenuous.
Carver, R. Cranes, The.
Han-shan. White crane carries a bitter flower, A.
Niedecker. Churchill's Death.
Olson, C. Landscape, Without Color.
Stafford, W. Watching Sandhill Cranes.

Cranmer, Thomas
Davie, D. Widower.
Smith, S. Admire Cranmer!

Crazy Horse (Oglala Sioux Chief)
Blue Cloud. Crazy Horse Monument.
MacLeish. Wildwest.
Stafford, W. Cottonwood.
  Report to Crazy Horse.
  Sioux Haiku.
  Sound from the Earth, A.

Creation
Ashbery, J. Other Cindy, The.
Auden. Anthem: "Let us praise our Maker, with true passion extol Him."
Bierce. Creation.
Blue Cloud. Earth and Creation.
  Sandhills That None May Visit.
  We sit balanced.
  White Corn Sister.
Bogan, L. Homunculus.
Borges. James Joyce.
  Maker, The ("He had never dwelled on the pleasures of memory").
  Mythical Founding of Buenos Aires, The.
Brodsky, J. Axiom.
Browning, E. Measure, The.
Browning, R. Johannes Agricola in Meditation.
Cavafy. Chaldaic Image.
Celan. Psalm: "No one kneads us again out of earth and clay."
Chesterton. Donkey, The.
Chuang Tzu. Perfect Joy.
Ciardi, J. One Wet Iota.
  Styles.
Crane, S. God fashioned the ship of the world carefully.
Cuadra, P. Secret of the Burning Stars, The.
Cummings, E. E. As if as / if a mys.
  Here's to opening and upward,to leaf and to sap.
  Love is the every only god.
  Pity his how illimitable plight.
  Swim so now million many worlds in each.
  Take for example this.
  This is the vase, Here.
  We love each other very dearly.
  When god decided to invent.
De la Mare. Glance, The.
  Riddle, A.
  Scribe, The.
  Snowdrop, The.
Dickey, J. Reading *Genesis* to a Blind Child.
Dickinson, E. It's easy to invent a Life.
  Just as He spoke it from his Hands.
Eberhart, R. Goal of Intellectual Man, The.
  Maze.
  Spring Mountain Climb.
  Wisdom of Insecurity, The.
Emerson, R. From the stores of eldest Matter.
  Hold of the Maker, not the made.
  Rhodora, The [On Being Asked Whence Is the Flower].
  Upon a rock yet uncreate.
Frost, R. Sitting by a Bush in Broad Sunlight.
Glück, L. Lamentations.
Graves, R. Five.
  Hell.
  Quinque.
Herbert, G. Man.
  Pulley, The.
Herrick. Eye, The.
Hill, G. Genesis.
Housman. 'Tis five years since, "An end," said I.
Hughes, T. Crow Blacker than Ever.
  Poets.
  Widdop.
Jackson, L. In the Beginning.
Jarrell, R. Birth of Venus, The.
  In the Ward: The Sacred Wood.
  Man in Majesty.
  Unicorn, The.
Jeffers, R. De Rerum Virtute.
  There is this infinite energy, the power of God forever working.
Kipling, R. Dedication, A: "And they were stronger hands than mine."
  Hymn of Breaking Strain.
Komunyakaa. Two Cranial Murals.
Laughlin, J. Mathematics of Chaos, The.

Lawrence, D. H.   End, The Beginning, The.
 God Is Born.
 Him with His Tail in His Mouth.
 Let There Be Light!
 Michael Angelo.
 Work of Creation, The.
Levi, P.   In the Beginning.
Levine, P.   Children's Crusade, The.
 Pili's Wall.
 Rain Downriver.
Lindsay, N.   Sunshine.
MacDiarmid, H.   My Love Is to the Light of
 Lights.
MacLeish.   Creator.
 Vicissitudes of the Creator.
Mallarmé.   Gift of the Poem.
Melville, H.   Venice.
Meredith, G.   You ask me what is Genius? 'tis
 that.
Meredith, W.   Examples of Created Systems.
Merwin.   Beginning.
 Division.
 First Darkness, The.
 Flies.
 Robin.
Michelangelo Buonarroti.   He Who made all
 there is, made every part.
 One Who made, and from utter nothing too,
 The.
Millay, E.   This should be simple; if one's
 power were great.
Milosz, C.   Creating the World.
Nemerov.   Creation Myth on a Moebius Band.
 First Day, The.
Neruda.   Gift, The.
 Midday Construction.
 Sitting Down.
Olson, C.   Lamp, The.
 Liturgical / eighth day, The.
Pagis.   Beginning, The.
Patchen.   How God Was Made.
 Theory of Nato-geography as Advanced by the
 Tiaphidian Man, A.
Piercy.   Athena in the Front Lines.
Pinsky.   Creation According to Ovid.
Ralegh, S.   From the Earth, and from thy bloud,
 O heaven, they came.
 Heaven and Earth one forme did beare.
Ramanujan.   No Fifth Man.
Rashid, N.   Izhab-O-Rasai (Expression and
 Reach).
Rossetti, C.   "All Thy Works Praise Thee, O
 Lord": A Processional of Creation.
Rukeyser, M.   All the way through the forest, a
 sound of birdsong.
 Child of the root, among your apples and
 forests.
 During the journey there come moments of
 waking.
 Gyroscope, The.
 He Had a Quality of Growth.
 Power of war leads to a plan of lives, The.
 Sixth Night: Waking, The.
 Structure is rising. It takes on shape, it takes on
 meaning, a.
Sandburg, C.   Glass House Canticle.
 Special Starlight.
Smith, S.   God and the Devil.
 God Speaks.
 Nature and Free Animals.
 Passing Cloud, The.
Snyder, G.   No Matter, Never Mind.
Spender, S.   Adam.
Stafford, W.   Big Bang.
 Vocatus atque Non Vocatus.
Swenson, M.   Once There Were Glaciers.
Thomas, D.   In the Beginning.
Thomson, J.   Upon Happiness.
Tomlinson, C.   Maillol.
 Portrait in Stone.
 Small Action Poem.
Unknown.   Prose in Advent Time.
Very.   Man has forgot his Origin; in vain.
 Not suffering for their sins in former state.
 Origin of Man, The.
Warren, R.   It Is Not Dead.

Wheatley, P.   Ocean.
Whitman, W.   Laws for Creations.
 Love That Is Hereafter, The.
Whittier.   Clear Vision, The.
 Invocation: "Through Thy clear spaces, Lord, of
 old."
 Last Walk in Autumn, The.
 Revelation.
 Summer by the Lakeside.
Wilbur, R.   Games Two.
 On the Marginal Way.
 Praise in Summer.
 Two Voices in a Meadow.
Williams, C. K.   Nut, The.
Williams, M.   In the Beginning.
 Out of a Clear Sky.
 Waking from a Dream.
Wilner, E.   See-Saw.
Wright, C.   Night Journal.
Yeats.   Before the World Was Made.
 Rose of the World, The.
Zagajewski.   Creation of the World, The.
See also **Cosmology**
Creativity
 Ammons.   Muse.
 Blok.   I Want to Live.
 Bly, R.   Meditation on Philosophy, A.
 Cavafy.   For the Shop.
 Ships, The.
 Cortes.   Three Sisters, The.
 Creeley.   Figures, The.
 Moment.
 Pryaer, A.
 Cummings, E. E.   Move / deeply,rain / (dream
 hugely)wish.
 No man,if men are gods;but if gods must.
 To start,to hesitate;to stop.
 Duncan, R.   Illustrative Lines.
 Ferlinghetti, L.   Adieu À Charlot.
 Populist Manifesto.
 Ginsberg, A.   Aether.
 Mescaline.
 Hall, D.   This Poem.
 Hardy, T.   Plaint to Man, A.
 Jarrell, R.   Cow wandering in the bare field,
 The.
 Man in Majesty.
 Jonson, B.   Epistle to Elizabeth, Countess of
 Rutland.
 Ode to James, Earl of Desmond, An.
 To a Weak Gamester in Poetry.
 Lawrence, D. H.   Absolute Reverence.
 Things Men Have Made.
 Whatever Man Makes.
 Levertov.   For Those Whom the Gods Love
 Less.
 To the Muse.
 Marvell.   Upon an Eunuch: A Poet.
 Michelangelo Buonarroti.   From ink, from pen
 in hand we see outflow.
 Mörike [*or* Möricke].   Forest Murmurs.
 Piercy.   For Jeriann's Hands.
 Rich, A.   Diamond Cutters, The.
 Schuyler, J.   For Bob Dash.
 Stafford, W.   Course in Creative Writing, A.
 Stevens, W.   Man with the Blue Guitar, The.
 Walker, A.   Beast.
 Wright, C.   Journal of True Confessions, A.
Creatures
 De la Mare.   Ariel.
 Fog.
 Forests.
 Idleness.
 Eberhart, R.   Mystical Beast in the Shadows,
 The.
 Herrick.   Like Loves His Like.
 Hughes, T.   Canal's Drowning Black, The.
 Neruda.   Some Creature.
 Orr, G.   Making Beasts.
 Raine, K.   Spell to Bring Lost Creatures Home.
 Riley, J.   Wrangdillion, A.
 Rossetti, C.   So I grew half delirious and quite
 sick.
 Yeats.   High Talk.
See also **Animals**

Cremation
 Dubie.   Baptismal.
 Eberhart, N.   New Entrepreneurial Plan.
 Jeffers, R.   Cremation.
 Milosz, C.   On Parting with My Wife, Janina.
 Ramanujan.   Obituary.
 Tate, J.   Yellow Newspaper and a Wooden Leg.
 Williams, W.   Complete Destruction.
Cressida
See **Troilus and Cressida**
Crete
 "H. D."   Phaedra.
 Ralegh, S.   Cretians ever lyars were, they care
 not what they say, The.
 Robinson, E.   Chorus of Old Men in "Ægeus",
 The.
**Crèvecoeur, J. Hector St. John (Michel
 Guillaume Jean de Crèvecoeur)**
 Niedecker.   To Paul now old enough to read.
Cricket (game)
 Hughes, T.   Sunstruck.
 Meredith, G.   At the first ball his wicket fell,
 and sins.
 Merton.   Sports without Blood—a Letter to
 Dylan Thomas (1948).
Crickets
 Bishop, E.   Behind Stowe.
 Bourne, V.   Cricket, The.
 Browning, R.   What a pretty tale you told me.
 Cummings, E. E.   Cri / C / k / et / in.
 García Lorca.   Little Mute Boy, The.
 Hamill, S.   October Frost.
 Keats.   On the Grasshopper and [the] Cricket.
 Lindsay, N.   Crickets on a Strike.
 Merwin.   Black Jewel, The.
 Riley, J.   To the Cricket.
 Sandburg, C.   Buckwheat.
 Cricket Match.
 Splinter.
 Stafford, W.   Animal That Drank up Sound, The.
 Wright, J.   Poems to a Brown Cricket.
 Zukofsky, L.   When the crickets.
Crime and Criminals
 Ai.   Greed.
 Atwood.   Marrying the Hangman.
 Bierce.   To a Censor.
 Bishop, E.   Burglar of Babylon, The.
 Borges.   1891.
 Brodsky, J.   Homage to Yalta.
 Bukowski.   Cold Plums.
 Chaucer.   Former Age, The.
 Chuang Tzu.   Cracking the Safe.
 Cummings, E. E.   Dick Mid's large bluish face
 without eyebrows.
 It started when Bill's chip let on to.
 Davie, D.   War Criminal.
 Dickinson, E.   I know some lonely Houses off
 the Road.
 It comforts the Criminal little to know.
 Dugan, A.   Adultery.
 Jack-Off of the Graveyard Shift, The.
 Éluard, P.   Uncertain of the Crime.
 Ginsberg, A.   Mugging.
 Tonite I walked out of my red apartment door
 on East tenth street's dusk.
 Hall, D.   Cops and Robbers.
 Hardy, T.   In the Servants' Quarters.
 Herrick.   Rules for Our Reach.
 Upon Boreman. Epig.
 Upon Letcher: Epigram.
 Housman.   Oh who is that young sinner with the
 handcuffs on his wrists?
 Hughes, L.   Ballad of the Killer Boy.
 Big-Timer, The.
 Death of Do Dirty: A Rounder's Song.
 Madam and the Crime Wave.
 Ignatow, D.   Father and Son.
 Jonson, B.   On a Robbery.
 Kipling, R.   Outlaws, The.
 Laughlin, J.   Busy Day.
 Shard of History, A.
 Lux.   Autobiographical.
 Major, C.   Swine Who's Eclipsed Me, The.
 Marvell.   Bludius et Corona [Blood and the
 Crown].

Meredith, W.   Effort at Speech.
Milton.   On the Gunpowder Plot.
Muldoon, P.   Immram.
   More a Man Has the More a Man Wants, The.
Niedecker.   Jesse James and his brother Frank.
Olson, C.   Gonfalon Raised Tonight, The.
Pope, A.   Rape of the Lock, The; an Heroi-
   Comical Poem.
Riley, J.   His Mother.
Rimbaud, A.   Bad Blood.
Ritsos.   Suspect, The.
Sandburg, C.   Alley Rats.
   Cahoots.
   Rakeoff and the Getaway, The.
Sze.   Ansel Adams Card, The.
Tate, J.   I Take Back All My Kisses.
Unknown.   Geordie [An Old Ballad].
Very.   On the Increase in Crime Since the Late
   Civil War.
Villon.   Caption for a Photograph of Four
   Organized Criminals.
Warren, R.   Crime.
Whitman, W.   You Felons on Trial in Courts.
Whittier.   Curse of the Charter-Breakers, The.
   Slave Ships, The.
Williams, C. K.   Crime.
   Crime, The.
Williams, M.   In Extremis In Hardy, Arkansas.
Wordsworth, W.   Borderers, The. A Tragedy.
   Peter Bell; a Tale.
Wright, J.   To a Fugitive.
See also Prisons and Prisoners
Crimean War
Kipling, R.   Last of the Light Brigade, The.
Meredith, G.   Loyal Soldier, The.
   Red Coats & the Blue, The.
Tennyson, A.   Charge of the Light Brigade, The.
Very.   Mission of the Friends to the Emperor
   Nicholas, The.
Cripples
Angelou.   Willie.
Gunn, T.   Dolly.
HaNagid.   One Who Works and Buys Himself
   Books.
Jacobsen, J.   Reading Aloud at Dusk.
Kumin, M.   In Memoriam P. W. Jr. 1921–1980.
Oppen.   Vulcan.
Owen, W.   Disabled.
Riley, J.   Deformed.
   Happy Little Cripple, The.
Sandburg, C.   Cripple.
Sexton.   Cripples and Other Stories.
   One-Eye, Two-Eyes, Three-Eyes.
   One-Legged Man, The.
Smith, S.   Bereavement.
See also Handicaps and the Handicapped
Criticism and Critics
Baudelaire.   Debut of the Dancer, A. B., The.
Berryman.   Crisis.
   Olympus.
Bierce.   Cynic perforce from studying mankind.
   Rational Anthem, A.
   Substance or Shadow.
   To a Censor.
Browning, E.   Summing Up in Italy.
Browning, R.   Dialogue between Father and
   Daughter.
Bukowski.   Dear Pa and Ma.
   She Said.
Burns, R.   Robert Burns' Answer [to Epistle
   from a Taylor].
   To Captain Riddell.
Byron, G.   Answer to Some Elegant Verses.
   Dear Doctor, I Have Read Your Play.
   Parenthetical Address.
   To a Knot of Ungenerous Critics.
   To Lord Thurlow.
   To the Author of a Sonnet Beginning " 'Sad Is
   My Verse,' You Say, 'And Yet No Tear' ."
Campion, T.   Ad Nashum.
Ciardi, J.   Guide to Poetry, A.
Coleridge, S.   Lines to a Comic Author, on an
   Abusive Review.
   To a Critic.
Collins, B.   Workshop.

Corbett, W.   Reading C. K. Williams's "The
   Critic."
Cowper, W.   Lines Written in the Monthly
   Review.
   On a Review Condemning Thelyphthora.
Cullen, C.   To Certain Critics.
Cummings, E. E.   American critic ad 1935.
Cunningham, J.   Epigram: "Here lies New Critic
   who would fox us."
"Dario."   To Roosevelt.
Davie, D.   July, 1964.
   Rejoinder to a Critic.
   Replying to Reviewers.
Dickinson, E.   Your relentless Music.
Dugan, A.   February Twelfth Birthday
   Statement.
   Untitled Poem: "When the window glass blows
   in."
Dunbar, P.   To a Captious Critic.
Eberhart, R.   Critic With His Pained Eye, The.
HaNagid.   Critique, The.
Herrick.   Hymne to Sir Clipseby Crew, A.
   To Critic[k]s.
   To His Muse.
   To the Detracter.
   Upon Nis.
   Upon the Same.
Hopkins, G.   Proved Etherege prudish, selfish,
   hypocrite, heartless.
Johnson, S.   Prologue to Hugh Kelly's A Word
   to the Wise.
Jonson, B.   Epigram to My Bookseller.
   Epistle to a Friend, An ("Censure not sharply
   then, but me advise").
   Ode to Himself[e].
   On Cheveril [or Cheverel].
   On the Magnetic Lady.
   To Censorious Courtling.
   To Courtling.
   To Fool or Knave.
   To John Donne ("Who shall doubt, Donne,
   where [or whe'er] I a poet be[e]").
   To Mr Jonson upon these Verses.
   To My Mere English Censurer.
   To Playwright.
   To the Learnèd Critic.
   To the Same [Alphonso Ferrabosco].
   To the Worthy Author Mr John Fletcher.
Keats.   House of Mourning Written by Mr Scott,
   The.
Koch, K.   Pleasures of Peace, The.
Laughlin, J.   Maledictus In Plebe Sit.
Lawrence, D. H.   Editorial Office.
   Mr Squire.
   My Little Critics.
   Thomas Earp.
MacLeish.   Brooks Atkinson.
MacNeice.   Prayer in Mid-Passage.
Marvell.   To His Noble Friend, Mr Richard
   Lovelace, upon His Poems.
McGrath, T.   For a Critic Who Tries to Write
   Poems.
Meredith, G.   Camelus Saltat.
   Camelus Saltat: Continued.
   Point of Taste, The.
Nash, O.   If He Scholars, Let Him Go.
Nemerov.   Critic.
   On Certain Wits.
   Refusal of a Kindness Offered.
   To My Least Favorite Reviewer.
O'Hara, F.   Answer to Voznesensky and
   Evtushenko.
   Critic, The.
Olson, C.   Issues from the Hand of God.
Parker, D.   Song in the Worst Possible Taste.
   When We Were Very Sore; Lines on
   Discovering that You Have Been Advertised
   as America's A.A. Milne.
Petrarch.   To some it may well seem I pitch my
   style.
Piercy.   Letter to be Disguised as a Gas Bill.
Pinkerton, H.   Literary Theorist.
Pope, A.   Essay on Criticism, An.
   Prologue to the Three Hours after Marriage.
Riley, J.   To a Poet-Critic.
   Wholly Unscholastic Opinion, A.

Shelley, P.   Lines to a Critic.
   Lines to a Reviewer.
Snyder, G.   Some critic tried to put me down.
Stafford, W.   Freedom of Expression.
   Thinking about Being Called Simple by a Critic.
Swift, J.   Epigram on Scolding, An.
Tennyson, A.   Hendecasyllabics.
Updike.   Moderate, The.
   Vision, A.
Whalen, P.   Chanson d'Outre Tombe.
Whittier.   To Charles Sumner.
Williams, C. K.   Critic, The.
Wordsworth, W.   On the Detraction Which
   Followed the Publication of a Certain Poem.
   Scorn not the Sonnet; Critic, you have frowned.
Yeats.   On Those That Hated "The Playboy of
   the Western World" 1907.
   To a Poet, Who Would Have Me Praise Certain
   Bad Poets, Imitators of His and Mine.
Zagajewski.   Barbarians.
Crocodiles
Nash, O.   Purist, The.
Rossetti, C.   My Dream.
See also Alligators
Crocuses
Berry, W.   Planting Crocuses.
Schuyler, J.   Spring.
Very.   Crocus, The.
   On Some Beautiful Crocuses: In Front of the
   House of B. H. Silsbee, Esq.
Croesus
Warren, R.   Croesus in Autumn.
Cromwell, Oliver
Chesterton.   Before a Statue of Cromwell.
Emerson, R.   Fate.
Marvell.   First Anniversary of the Government
   under His Highness the Lord Protector, 1655,
   The.
   Horatian Ode upon Cromwell's Return from
   Ireland, An.
   In Effigiem Oliveri Cromwell [On a Portrait of
   Oliver Cromwell].
   Poem upon the Death of Oliver Cromwell, A.
Milton.   To the Lord General Cromwell.
Wilde, O.   Quantum Mutata.
Yeats.   Curse of Cromwell, The.
Croquet
MacNeice.   Soap Suds.
Cross, The
Cavafy.   Grand Procession of Priests and
   Laymen.
Crane, H.   Mermen, The.
Crane, S.   My cross! / Your cross?
Donne.   Cross, The.
Guyon.   Joy of the Cross, The.
Hardy, T.   Wood Fire, The.
Herrick.   Christs Words on the Crosse, My God,
   My God.
   Crosses.
Hughes, L.   Late Corner.
Lawrence, D. H.   Cross, The.
Merton.   O cross, more splendid than all the
   stars.
Riley, J.   Chant of the Cross-bearing Child, The.
Rilke.   Sacred Place.
Rossetti, C.   Behold the Man!
   Lord, what have I to offer? sickening fear.
   Ruined Cross, The.
   Watchers, The.
   What is it Jesus saith unto the soul?
Sandburg, C.   Loin Cloth.
Sexton.   With Mercy for the Greedy.
Shapiro, K.   Crucifix in the Filing Cabinet, The.
Smith, S.   Children of the Cross, The.
Stevens, W.   Botanist on Alp (No. 2).
Tate, A.   Cross, The.
Very.   Soldier of the Cross, The.
Warren, R.   Cross, The.
Whittier.   Mantle of St. John de Matha, The.
See also Crucifixion, The
Crowds
Cummings, E. E.   People who, The.
Emerson, R.   And he like me is not too proud.
   Look danger in the eye it vanishes.
Herrick.   Crowd and Company, The.

Way in a Crowd.
Ignatow, D. Be Like Me.
Lawrence, D. H. Submergence.
Petrarch. You were a haven once, my little
  room.
Pound, E. In a Station of the Metro.
Ramanujan. Some People.
Sandburg, C. Always the Mob.
  I Am the People, the Mob.
Tomlinson, C. What Virginia Said.
Warren, R. Mountain Plateau.
  To a Face in the Crowd.
Williams, M. Newspaper Picture of Spectators
  at a Hotel Fire, A.
Williams, T. Problem.
  Strangers pass me on the street.
Williams, W. At the Ball Game.
Zagajewski. Covenant.

Crowns
Browning, E. Crowned and Wedded.
Cavafy. Of Colored Glass.
Herrick. To his deare Valentine, Mistresse
  Margaret Falconbrige.
Marvell. Coronet, The.
Robinson, E. Sunken Crown, The.
Rossetti, C. Crown of Windflowers, A.
Smith, S. Crown of Gold, The.

Crows
Blue Cloud. Crow.
  Crow's Flight.
  Road 37C.
Carver, R. My Crow.
Creeley. Crow, The.
Dickey, J. Veer-Voices: Two Sisters under
  Crows.
Dickinson, E. Spring, and not a Blue Bird.
Dugan, A. Admonitor: A Pearl for Arrogance.
Ferlinghetti, L. Triste Corbiére.
Frost, R. Dust of Snow.
Hughes, T. Black Beast, The.
  Childish Prank, A.
  Crow and the Birds.
  Crow Blacker than Ever.
  Crow on the Beach.
  Crow Tyrannosaurus.
  Crow's Account of the Battle.
  Crow's Battle Fury.
  Crow's Fall.
  Crow's First Lesson.
  Crow's Last Stand.
  Crow's Vanity.
  Examination at the Womb-Door.
  Flayed Crow in the Hall of Judgement, A.
  Horrible Religious Error, A.
  Lineage.
Jacobsen, J. Thing about Crows, The.
Levertov. Crow Spring.
Levi, P. Crow's Song, The.
Lindsay, N. Two Old Crows.
Lux. Crows of Boston and New York, The.
MacLeish. Black Humor.
Mahon. Birdlife.
Meredith, W. Sunrise with Crows.
Merwin. Crows on the North Slope.
  New Moon in November.
Nash, O. Chacun à Son Berlitz.
Oliver, M. Crows.
Patchen. Autumn Is the Crows' Time.
Piercy. Crows.
Prunty. Crows, The.
Rimbaud, A. Blackcurrant River.
  Crows.
Roethke. Night Crow.
Simic. Crows.
  Fable: "In my favorite one."
Tomlinson, C. Crow.
  In March.
  Maine Winter.
Updike. Why the Telephone Wires Dip and the
  Poles Are Cracked and Crooked.

Crucifixion, The
Auden. Shield of Achilles, The.
Berryman. Disciple, The.
Blake, W. Nail his neck to the cross nail it with
  a nail.
Borges. Christ on the Cross.

Luke 23.
Browning, E. Seraphim, The.
Carruth, H. Crucifixion.
  Emergency Haying.
Celan. Tenebrae.
Crashaw. In Cicatrices Domini Jesu.
  On Our Crucified Lord Naked, and Bloody.
  On the Bleeding Wounds of Our Crucified Lord.
  On the Still Surviving Markes of Our Saviours
    Wounds.
  To Our Blessed Lord upon the Choice of His
    Sepulchre.
  To Pontius Washing His Blood-Stained Hands.
  To Pontius Washing His Hands.
  Upon the Thornes Taken Downe from Our
    Lords Head Bloody.
Cullen, C. Simon the Cyrenian Speaks.
Dickinson, E. I should have been too glad, I
  see.
  Must be a Woe.
  One Crucifixion is recorded—only.
  "Remember me" implored the Thief!
  To put this World down, like a Bundle.
Donne. Good Friday [or Goodfriday], 1613.
  Riding Westward.
Dunbar, W. Ballat of the Passioun, Ane.
García Lorca. Crucifixion.
Hall, D. Maundy Thursday's Candles.
Hardy, T. Wood Fire, The.
Herbert, G. Home.
  Sacrifice, The.
Herrick. Cross-tree, The.
  Gods Price, and Mans Price.
  His Anthem, to Christ on the Crosse.
  His Saviour[']s Words, Going to the Cross[e].
  His Words to Christ, Going to the Cross.
  Observation.
  Summe, and the Satisfaction, The.
Hill, G. Canticle for Good Friday.
Hopkins, G. Pilate.
Hughes, L. Ballad of Mary's Son.
  Ballad of the Two Thieves.
  Encounter.
Hughes, T. God, A.
  What is Worthless?
Jeffers, R. Dear Judas.
Levertov. Ikon: The Harrowing of Hell.
  On a Theme from Julian's Chapter 20.
Logan, J. On a Prize Crucifix by a Student
  Sculptor.
  Sebastian in the Dream.
Meredith, G. Song of Theodolinda, The.
Merton. Biography, The.
  Sponge Full of Vinegar, The.
Merwin. Folk Art.
Patchen. Pastoral: "Dove walks with sticky feet,
  The."
Petrarch. It was the day Apollo's rays turned
  pale.
Pinkerton, H. On the Two Marys in a Fresco of
  the Crucifixion.
Pound, E. Ballad of the Goodly Fere.
Riley, J. Christ, The.
Ritsos. Nails, The.
Robinson, E. Calvary.
Rossetti, C. Behold the Man!
  Bundle of Myrrh Is My Well-Beloved unto Me,
    A.
  Good Friday.
  Good Friday Evening.
  Good Friday Morning.
  It Is Finished.
  Mary Magdalene and the Other Mary.
  One of the Soldiers with a Spear Pierced His
    Side.
Rukeyser, M. Gates, The.
Sandburg, C. Early Lynching.
  Silver Nails.
Sexton. In the Deep Museum.
Shapiro, K. New Ring, The.
Stock, R. Sixth Station, The.
Van Duyn. Pietà, Rhenish, 14th C., the
  Cloisters, The.
Very. Cross, The ("I must go on, till in my
  tearful line").
Whittier. Crucifixion, The.

Wilde, O. Sonnet Written in Holy Week at
  Genoa.
See also **Calvary; Cross, The**
Cruelty
Baudelaire. Living Dead, The.
  Merciless Madrigal.
Campion, T. Her fayre inflaming eyes.
Carew, T. Cruel Mistress, A.
  Elegy on the La: Pen: Sent to My Mistress Out
    of France, An.
  Looking-Glass, A.
  To His Mistress.
  To My Mistress [or Mistris], I Burning in Love.
Carver, R. Louise.
Ciardi, J. Faces.
Creeley. Dream, The.
  Hill, The.
  Operation, The.
Dickey, W. Memoranda.
Dickinson, E. She dealt her pretty words like
  Blades.
Gurney, I. Of Cruelty.
"H. D." Ariadne.
Hacker, M. Why We Are Going Back to
  Paradise Island.
Hall, D. September Ode.
Hardy, T. Face at the Casement, The.
  God's Education.
  Son's Portrait, The.
Herrick. Biting of Beggars.
  Cruelties.
  Cruelty.
  Cruelty Base in Commanders.
  To Dianeme.
  Upon Grubs.
  Upon Grudgings.
Jarrell, R. Snow-Leopard, The.
Jeffers, R. Orca.
Lawrence, D. H. Cherry Robbers.
Levertov. Place of Kindness, A.
Lowell, R. Attila, Hitler.
Lux. Swimming Pool, The.
Meredith, G. Society.
Millay, E. To Those Without Pity.
O'Hara, F. Invincibility.
Olson, C. Allegory of Wealth, The.
Petrarch. Cruel the star (if stars are powerful).
Piercy. Friend, The.
Prunty. Two Kinds of Cause.
Rich, A. Burning Oneself In.
  Photograph of the Unmade Bed, The.
Rilke. Saint Catherine.
Ritsos. Roots of the World, The.
Rossetti, C. Amore E Dovere.
  Ariadne To Theseus.
  Behold, I stand at the door and knock.
  Tirsi, A.
Shelley, P. Bigotry's Victim.
Smith, S. Adelaide Abner.
  How Cruel Is the Story of Eve.
Williams, C. K. Conscience.
  Dirty Talker: D Line, Boston, The.
  Love: Wrath.
Wordsworth, W. When Philoctetes in the
  Lemnian Isle.
Wyatt, S. Alas! my dear, the word thou spakest.
  Alone musing, / Remembering.
  At last withdraw your cruelty.
  Disdain not, madam, on him to look.
  Heart oppressed [or oppress'd] with desperate
    thought.
  If with complaint the pain might be expressed.
  Longer to muse.
  Love hath again.
  Since ye delight to know.
  Thou sleepest fast and I with woeful heart.
  Though I cannot your cruelty constrain.
  Who hath he[a]rd of such[e] cruelty before.
Zagajewski. Cruel.
Cruelty to Animals
Bukowski. Brave Bull.
  I Cannot Stand Tears.
  Love Is a Piece of Paper Torn to Bits.
  Object Lesson.
Burns, R. Elegy on Peg Nicholson.
  On Seeing a Wounded Hare Limp by Me,

Which a Fellow Had Just Shot At.
Carver, R.   Hat, The.
Clare, J.   Badger.
Dunbar, P.   Forest Greeting, The.
Hardy, T.   Blinded Bird, The.
  Compassion.
Jeffers, R.   Memoir.
Kinnell.   Bear, The.
  Porcupine, The.
Kipling, R.   Beasts Are Very Wise, The.
Kumin, M.   Heaven as Anus.
  Repent.
  Vealers, The.
Merwin.   Fly.
Muldoon, P.   Epona.
Nemerov.   Kicks.
Ramanujan.   Zoo Gardens Revisited.
Rossetti, C.   Brother Bruin.
Sarton, M.   Village Tale, A.
Smith, S.   Es War Einmal.
  This Is Disgraceful and Abominable.
Walcott.   Lesson for This Sunday, A.
Williams, C. K.   Ten Below.

Crusades
Ammons.   At Dawn in 1098.
Borges.   Ariosto and the Arabs.
Cavafy.   To Jerusalem.
Chesterton.   Lepanto.
Davie, D.   Song for These Crusaders, A.
Ferlinghetti, L.   Spirit of the Crusades.
Graves, R.   Absent Crusader.
Kumin, M.   In the Absence of Bliss.
Lowell, R.   Joinville and Louis IX.
Patchen.   First Crusades, The!
Petrarch.   O long expected up in Heaven, O
  blest.
  Seed of Charlemagne, his noble head, The.
Rimbaud, A.   Hanged Men Dance.
Thoreau.   Godfrey of Boulogne.

Crystals
Emerson, R.   Put in, drive home the sightless
  wedges.
Lawrence, D. H.   Why Does She Weep?
MacDiarmid, H.   Crystals like Blood.
Zaturenska.   Child in the Crystal.

Cuba
Ai.   Cuba, 1962.
García Lorca.   Blacks Dancing to Cuban
  Rhythms.
Lowell, R.   Fall 1961.
Patchen.   Leaflet (One).

Cuchulain (Irish legendary hero)
Hughes, T.   Skylarks.
Smith, S.   Hound of Ulster, The.
Williams, W.   Cuchulain.
Yeats.   Cuchulain Comforted.
  Death of Cuchulain, The.

Cuckoldry and Cuckolds
Burns, R.   O An Ye Were Dead Gudeman.
  We'll Hide the Couper behint the Door.
Jonson, B.   To Hornet.
MacDiarmid, H.   Focherty.
Pope, A.   Two or Three, or a Receipt to Make a
  Cuckold.
See also **Adultery and Adulterers**

Cuckoos
Auden.   Short Ode to the Cuckoo.
"H. D."   Cuckoo Song.
Hopkins, G.   Cuckoo, The.
Kipling, R.   Cuckoo Song.
MacNeice.   Cuckoo.
Merwin.   Cuckoo Myth.
Montale.   On the Llobregat.
Nash, O.   Cuckoo, The.
Nemerov.   Cuckoo King, The.
Rilke.   Cuckoo.
Simic.   Immortal Prankster.
  Way It Is, The.
Wordsworth, W.   Cuckoo and the Nightingale,
  The.
  Cuckoo-Clock, The.
  To the Cuckoo.

Culloden, Battle of (1746)
Burns, R.   Lovely Lass o' Inverness, The.

Cults
Ai.   Charisma.
Komunyakaa.   Jonestown: More eyes for
  Jadwiga's Dream.

Cultural Revolution (China)
Kizer, C.   Cultural Evolution.

Culture
Atwood.   Charivari.
Burns, R.   Scots Prologue, *For Mrs.
  Sutherland's Benefit Night,* Spoken at the
  Theatre Dumfries.
Cavafy.   Distinguishing Marks.
Codrescu.   On Translation.
Davie, D.   Tiger at the Movie-Show.
Emerson, R.   Culture.
Fenton, J.   Lollipops of the Pomeranian
  Baroque.
  This Octopus Exploits Women.
Ginsberg, A.   Studying the Signs.
Koch, K.   You Were Wearing.
Levine, P.   Sources.
Lindsay, N.   For All Who Ever Sent Lace
  Valentines.
Merton.   Letter to Pablo Antonio Cuadra
  Concerning Giants, A.
Nash, O.   Caesar Knifed Again, or, Culture Biz
  Gets Hep, Boffs Profs.
  Exit, Pursued by a Bear.
Oliver, M.   Esquimos Have No Word for "War,"
  The.
Olson, C.   Kingfishers, The.
Pinsky.   Figured Wheel, The.
Shapiro, K.   Drug Store.
Snyder, G.   Axe Handles.
Tomlinson, C.   Le Musée Imaginaire.
Tu Fu.   Visit in Winter to the Temple of His
  Mystical Majesty, A.
Williams, W.   All the Fancy Things.

Cumberland, England
Davie, D.   Cumberland.

Cummings, E. E. (Edward Estlin)
Logan, J.   Poem, Slow to Come, On the Death
  of Cummings (1894-1962).

Cunningham, Merce
Olson, C.   Merce of Egypt.

Cupid
Ammianus Marcellinus.   Out of the Italian.
Blake, W.   To Chloes breast young Cupid slily
  stole.
  Why was Cupid a Boy.
Browning, E.   Marriage of Psyche and Cupid.
  Psyche Gazing on Cupid.
Byron, G.   From Anacreon.
Campion, T.   Ad Amorem.
  Mistris [*or* Mistress] Since You So Much
  Desire.
  O Love, where are thy Shafts, thy Quiver, and
  thy Bow?
  Umbra.
  When the God of Merrie Love.
Carew, T.   Love's Courtship.
  Song: The Willing Prisoner to His Mistress.
De la Mare.   Encounter, The.
  Last Arrow, The.
  Tired Cupid, The.
Emerson, R.   Cupido.
  Initial, Dæmonic, and Celestial Love.
Glück, L.   Reproach, The.
Guillaume de Lorris *et al.*   Romance [*or*
  Romaunt] of the Rose, The.
Herrick.   Bag of the Bee, The.
  Cheat of Cupid; or, The Ungentle Guest, The.
  How Lillies Came White.
  How Roses Came Red.
  Hymne to Cupid, An.
  Hymne to Love, An.
  Hymne to Venus, and Cupid, A.
  Showre of Blossomes, The.
  To Cupid.
  To Oenone.
  Upon Cupid.
  Upon Love.
  Wounded Cupid, The.
Jonson, B.   Why I Write Not of Love.
Milton.   Elegy 7: "Not yet did I know your

laws, enticing Amathusia."
Moschus.   By Moschus.
  Out of the Greeke Cupid's Cryer.
Petrarch.   Very instant he has loosed his shot,
  The.
Riley, J.   Same Old Story, The.
Suckling, S.   Metamorphosis, The.
  To B.C.
Wroth [*or* Wroath].   Love's Victorie.

Cupidity
Herrick.   Any Way for Wealth.

Cups
Dickey, W.   Fred and the Holy Grail.
"H. D."   When I Am a Cup.
Herrick.   Sincerity.
Lawrence, D. H.   Cups.
Levertov.   Magic.
Palmer, M.   Painted Cup, The.
Riley, J.   Loving Cup, The.
Ritsos.   Audible and the Inaudible, The.
  Departures 3.
Schuyler, J.   Shimmer.
Tomlinson, C.   Given Grace, A.
Zukofsky, L.   Shang Cup.

Curic, Marie
Rich, A.   Power.

Curiosity
Codrescu.   Ode to Curiosity.
Crane, H.   Shall I Subsume.
Creeley.   Time ("What happened to her").
Dickinson, E.   Unknown is the largest need,
  The.
Duncan, R.   Helmet of Goliath, The.
Hacker, M.   Nights of 1962: The River
  Merchant's Wife.
Jackson, L.   Further Details.
Komunyakaa.   "Everybody's Reading Li Po"
  Silkscreened on a Purple T-Shirt.
Laughlin, J.   Your Early Life.
Lawrence, D. H.   Tease.
Lorde.   Ballad from Childhood.
Nash, D.   Do Sphinxes Think?
Nash, O.   I Spy, or, The Depravity of Privacy.
  Never Mind the Overcoat, Button Up That Lip.
Schuyler, J.   East Window on Elizabeth Street,
  An.
Szymborska, W.   Conversation with a Rock.
Williams, C. K.   For Gail, When I Was Five.
  Knot, The.

Curses
Burns, R.   Epitaph on Mr. Burton.
Cavafy.   When the Watchman Saw the Light.
Coleridge, S.   Devonshire Road, A.
  Rime of the Ancient Mariner, The.
Donne.   Curse, The.
Emerson, R.   Burn your literary verses.
  If curses be the wage of love.
Graves, R.   Return.
HaNagid.   Curse, A.
Hardy, T.   No Bell-Ringing.
Herrick.   Curse. A Song, The.
  To His Book[e].
  To the Sour[e] Reader.
Lindsay, N.   Curse for Kings, A.
Nash, O.   Lines To Be Mumbled At Ovington's.
  Oh, Shucks, Ma'am, I Mean Excuse Me.
Nemerov.   Priest's Curse on Dancing, The.
Rilke.   Cursed Child.
Rukeyser, M.   Transgress, The.
Sandburg, C.   Curse of a Rich Polish Peasant on
  His Sister Who Ran Away with a Wild Man,
  Whiffletree.
Smith, S.   Cool as a Cucumber.
  Thoughts about the Person from Porlock.
Swinburne.   After Death.
Wordsworth, W.   Three Graves, The.
Wright, J.   Song for the Middle of the Night, A.
Yeats.   Crazy Jane and the Bishop.

Custer, George Armstrong
Ai.   General George Armstrong Custer: My Life
  in the Theater.
MacLeish.   Wildwest.
Whitman, W.   From Far Dakota's Cañons (June
  25, 1876).

D

Custom
  Herrick. Lawes.
  MacNeice. Off the Peg.
  Riley, J. Law of the Perverse, The.

Cyclamen
  Lawrence, D. H. Sicilian Cyclamens.

Cyclops
  García Lorca. Fable: "Unicorns and cyclopses."
  Theocritus. Cyclops, The.

Cynicism and Cynics
  Bierce. Cynic perforce from studying mankind.
  Bukowski. 60 Yard Pass.
    Freedom: The Unmolested Eagle of Myself.
    Kind of Lecture on a Dull Day When There Isn't Even a Fly Around to Kill, A.
    Report Upon the Consumption of Myself, A.
    Soul.
    Swans Walk My Brain in April It Rains, The.
    With Vengeance Like a Tiger Crawls.
  Creeley. Citizen.
    Stomping with Catullus.
  Cummings, E. E. Crazy jay blue) / demon laughshriek.
  Dickinson, E. Hereafter, I will pick no Rose.
  Dunbar, P. Vengeance is Sweet.
  Eberhart, R. Old Fashioned American Business Man, An.
  Frost, R. Demiurge's Laugh, The.
  Gunn, T. To His Cynical Mistress.
  Hardy, T. Christmas: 1924.
    Cynic's Epitaph.
    He Never Expected Much.
  Laughlin, J. Antiphilus.
  Lawrence, D. H. Little-Boy Brilliant.
  Logan, J. Protest After a Dream.
  Melville, H. Apparition, The.
  Nash, O. Strange Case of Mr. O'Banion's Come-Uppance, The.
  Parker, D. Certain Lady, A.
    Comment.
    Far-Sighted Muse, The.
    Inscription for the Ceiling of a Bedroom.
    Lady's Reward, The.
    Love Song: "Suppose we two were cast away."
    Song: "And shall we build a little nest."
    Symptom Recital.
    Unfortunate Coincidence.
  Piercy. Poet Dreams of a Nice Warm Motel, The.
  Smith, S. Infant.
  Stafford, W. Meditation.
  Wilbur, R. Matthew VIII, 28 ff.
  Williams, C. K. Hog Heaven.
    You're two, that's great.
  Williams, M. Note to God Concerning a Point from an Earlier Communication, A.

Cypress Trees
  Borges. Leaves of the Cypress, The.
  Davie, D. Cypress Avenue, The.
  Herrick. To the Yew and Cypress to Grace His Funeral.
  Jeffers, R. Granite and Cypress.
  Lawrence, D. H. Cypresses.
  Snyder, G. Kisiabaton.
  Tomlinson, C. At Sant' Antimo.

Cyprus
  Broumas, O. Knife & the Bread, The.
  Rossetti, C. St. Barnanbas.

Czars
  Bierce. After Portsmouth.
    Saith the Czar.
  Dubie. Czar's Last Christmas Letter, The: A Barn in the Urals.
  Rossetti, D. Czar Alexander the Second.
  Zaturenska. Four Ghosts.

Czech Republic [formerly Czechoslovakia]
  Auden. Forty Years On.
  Hughes, L. Song for Ourselves.
  Millay, E. Czecho-Slovakia.
  Seifert. Birds' Voices in the Tree Tops.
    Bombing of the Town of Kralupy, The.
  Walker, A. Kiss, The.

Da Vinci, Leonardo
  Niedecker. In Leonardo's light.
  See also **Leonardo da Vinci**

Dachau, Germany
  Davie, D. Hawkshead and Dachau in a Christmas Glass.
  Dubie. Aubade of the Singer and Saboteur, Marie Triste.

Dachshunds
  Meredith, G. Islet the Dachs.

Daedalus
  Brodsky, J. Daedalus in Sicily.
  Oppen. Daedalus: The Dirge.

Daffodils
  Beckett, S. Thither.
  Clampitt. Kudzu Dormant.
  Eliot, T. S. Easter: Sensations of April.
  Herrick. Divination by a Daffadill [or Daffodil].
    To Daffodils [or Daffadills].
  Johnson, S. On a Daffodil, the First Flower the Author Had Seen That Year.
  Levertov. Intimation.
  MacLeish. Companions.
  McGrath, T. Black Train, The.
  Rossetti, C. Growing in the vale / By the uplands hilly.
  Schuyler, J. In a Churchyard.
  Swenson, M. Daffodildo.
  Wordsworth, W. I Wandered Lonely As a Cloud.

Daggers
  Borges. 1891.
    Blade in the Northside, A.
    Dagger, The.

Dahlias
  Zukofsky, L. Dahlia.

Daisies
  Ammons. Loss.
  Burns, R. To a Mountain Daisy.
  Ciardi, J. Counting on Flowers.
  Coleridge, S. Fragment: "O'er the raised earth the gales of evening sigh."
  Herrick. To Daisies, Not to Shut So Soon[e].
  Rossetti, C. Where Innocent Bright-Eyed Daisies Are.
    Who Hath Despised the Day of Small Things?
  Sexton. Break Away, The.
  Tennyson, A. Daisy, The.
  Tomlinson, C. Daisies, The.
  Wilbur, R. Mechanist, The.
  Williams, W. Chicory and Daisies.
  Wordsworth, W. To a Child [Written in Her Album].
    To the Daisy ("Bright Flower! whose home is everywhere").
  Zaturenska. Daisy, The.
  Zukofsky, L. Daisy.

Dali, Salvador
  García Lorca. Ode to Salvador Dalí.

Damascus, Syria
  Montale. On the Highest Column.

Damnation and the Damned
  Baudelaire. Damned Women ("Half-hidden in the dying light's caress").
  Bierce. Vision of Doom, A.
  Burns, R. Epitaph on D——— C———.
    Epitaph on Holy Willie.
  Graves, R. Descent into Hell.
    Red Shower, The.
    Song: Lift-Boy.
  Hill, G. Ovid in the Third Reich.
  Hughes, L. Fire.
  Kizer, C. Damnation, The.
  Rexroth, K. Mother Goose.
  Rimbaud, A. Damned Cherub.
    Just Man, The.
    Night in Hell.
    Once, if I remember well, my life was a banquet where all hearts opened.
  Rossetti, C. I Know You Not.
    Toll, bell, toll. For hope is flying / Sighing from the earthbound soul.

Da Vinci, Leonardo (column 3)
  Shelley, P. To the Lord Chancellor.
  Swift, J. Place of the Damned [or Damn'd], The.
  Walcott. Orient and Immortal Wheat.
  Whittier. Cry of a Lost Soul, The.

Dams
  Hall, D. Town of Hill, The.
  Kipling, R. Giffen's Debt.
  Rukeyser, M. Dam, The.
    Face of the Dam: Vivian Jones.
    Statement: Philippa Allen.
  Stafford, W. Fish Counter at Bonneville, The.

Danae
  Bogan, L. Stanza: "No longer burn the hands that seized."
  Duncan, R. Mirror, The.
  Yeats. Unappeasable Host, The.

Dancing and Dancers
  Baudelaire. Debut of the Dancer, A. B., The.
    In glistening shot-silk she seems to wind.
  Berry, W. Dance, A.
    Dance, The.
    Our Children, Coming of Age.
    Song (3).
    Wheel, The.
  Berryman. King David Dances.
  Blok. Accordeon.
  Blue Cloud. Backward Dancer.
    Bear: A Totem Dance As Seen by Raven.
    For Ace.
    Tomorrow.
    Wolf.
  Bly, R. Praise for All Dancers.
  Brodsky, J. Classical ballet, let's say, is beauty's keep, The.
  Browning, E. Dance, The.
  Bukowski. Don't Touch the Girls.
  Burns, R. On the Duchess of Gordon's Reel Dancing.
    Reel o' Stumpie, The.
  Carver, R. Letter.
    Minuet, The.
  Ciardi, J. Camptown.
    Dream, A.
  Clampitt. Dancers Exercising.
  Clifton, L. My Dream About Being White.
  Codrescu. Sea Sickness.
    Worst Poems Make the Best "Poems," The.
  Collins, B. Dancing toward Bethlehem.
  Crane, H. To Portapovitch.
  Creeley. Dancing.
    Fragments: "Decorous, and forbearing further correction."
    Los Guitaristas.
    Quick-Step.
    Still Dancers.
  Cullen, C. She of the Dancing Feet Sings.
  Cummings, E. E. Floatfloaflofff / lloloa.
    Jimmie's got a goil.
    Ladies and gentlemen this little girl.
    Six / are in a room's dark around).
    Ta / ppin / g / toe / hip.
  Davie, D. Dancing Measures.
    Lost Bride, The.
  Dickinson, E. I cannot dance upon my Toes.
  Dunbar, P. Angelina.
    Critters' Dance, De.
    Dance, The.
    Frolic, A.
    Valse, The.
    Virginia Reel, A.
  Eberhart, R. When Doris Danced.
  Eliot, T. S. Burnt Dancer, The.
  Ferlinghetti, L. Retired Ballerinas, Central Park West.
  Gallagher, T. Four Dancers at an Irish Wedding.
  García Lorca. Graphic of the Petenera.
  Glück, L. Tango.
  Graves, R. How It Started.
  Gunn, T. 1975.
    Lofty in the Palais de Danse.
  Gurney, I. Dancers, The.
  Hall, D. Dancers.
  Hardy, T. At a Pause in a Country Dance.
    Ballet, The.
    Dance at the Phoenix, The.

Dawn after the Dance, The.
Fiddler, The.
In the Marquee.
Night of the Dance, The.
Reminiscences of a Dancing Man.
Herrick. Song to the Maskers, A.
Housman. Fancy's Knell.
Hughes, L. College Formal: Renaissance Casino.
Dancer.
Dancers.
Danse Africaine.
Dream Boogie.
Dream Variation[s].
Jazzonia.
Juice Joint: Northern City.
Ma Man.
Midnight Dancer.
Negro Dancers.
Nude Young Dancer.
Rent-Party Shout: For a Lady Dancer.
Song for a Banjo Dance.
Sunday by the Combination.
Ignatow, D. From the Beginning.
Jacobsen, J. Limbo Dancer, The.
Tango.
Jarrell, R. Girl Dreams That She Is Giselle, The.
Jeffers, R. New Mexican Mountain.
Kipling, R. Plea of the Simla Dancers, The.
Koch, K. Our Hearts.
Komunyakaa. Butterfly-toed Shoes.
Tuesday Night at the Savoy Ballroom.
Larkin, P. Dancer, The.
Laughlin, J. In the Ballet.
Martha Graham.
So Slender.
When You Danced.
Lawrence, D. H. Fronleichnam.
Tarantella.
Levertov. For Bet.
Lindsay, N. Dancing for a Prize.
How a Little Girl Danced.
Logan, J. Lines for a Young Wanderer in Mexico.
Mahon. Andean Flute, The.
Major, C. Dance Floor.
Dancing under the Stars at Nice.
Revelation at Cap Ferrat.
Tewa Victories.
Mallarmé. Note to Whistler.
Meredith, G. I would I were with Jean.
Meredith, W. Ballet, The.
Millay, E. Of what importance, O my lovely girls, my dancers, O my lovely boys.
Mistral, G. Chilean Earth.
Those Who Do Not Dance.
Moore, M. Arthur Mitchell.
Nemerov. Dancer's Reply, The.
May Day Dancing, The.
Priest's Curse on Dancing, The.
Steps for a Dancer.
Niedecker. Watching Dan- / cers on Skates.
O'Hara, F. Alma.
First Dances.
Ode to Tanaquil Leclercq.
Olson, C. Merce of Egypt.
Moebius Strip, The.
Sing, Mister, Sing.
Paley, G. Dance in Jinotega, The.
Parker, D. Marilyn Marilyn.
Salome's Dancing-Lesson.
Pound, E. Dance Figure.
Rexroth, K. Song for a Dancer.
Riley, J. My Dancin'-Days Is Over.
Rilke. Cruel Song.
Ritsos. New Dance, The.
Roethke. Once More, the Round.
Rossetti, C. Brother Bruin.
Rukeyser, M. Rock Flow, River Mix.
Three Black Women.
Rumi. Dance, when you're broken open.
Daylight, full of small dancing particles.
Music Master.
Sandburg, C. Cadenza.
Couples.

Dancer.
Lines Written for Gene Kelly to Dance To.
Mask.
Vaudeville Dancer.
Schuyler, J. Alice Faye at Ruby Foo's.
Sexton. Red Dance, The.
Twelve Dancing Princesses, The.
Wedding Ring Dance, The.
Smith, S. Dedicated Dancing Bull and the Water Maid, The.
Stafford, W. At the Klamath Berry Festival.
Stevens, W. Dance of the Macabre Mice.
Life Is Motion.
Silver Plough-Boy, The.
Stock, R. Game of the Thunderbolt Goddesses, The.
Stockton, A. Compos'd in a Dancing Room, December 69.
Szymborska, W. Frozen Motion.
Tomlinson, C. Before the Dance.
Cochiti.
Tu Fu. Lo Yu Park.
Updike. Rockettes, The.
Young Matrons Dancing.
Wilbur, R. Grace.
Williams, W. Artist, The.
Canthara.
Dance, The.
Danse Russe.
Heel & Toe to the End.
Hula-Hula.
Overture to a Dance of Locomotives.
Philomena Andronico.
Rumba! Rumba!
When Fresh, It Was Sweet.
Wordsworth, W. I Wandered Lonely As a Cloud.
Yeats. Double Vision of Michael Robartes, The.
Fiddler of Dooney, The.
Sweet Dancer.
Zaturenska. Young Dancers, The.
See also **Ballet; Waltzes and Waltzing**

Dandelions
Blue Cloud. Red-winged Blackbird.
Dickinson, E. Dandelion's pallid tube, The.
Its little Ether Hood.
We should not mind so small a flower.
Hamill, S. Sonnet.
Lindsay, N. Dandelion, The.
Nemerov. Dandelions.
Orr, G. Fifth Month, The.
Stafford, W. On a Church Lawn.
Whitman, W. First Dandelion, The.
Zukofsky, L. Dandelion.

Danger
Amichai [*or* Amikhai]. Dangerous Country.
Auden. Legend.
Carver, R. Late Afternoon, April 8, 1984.
Jackson, L. Jewels and After.
Merwin. Peril.
Montale. Return, The.
Niedecker. No matter where you are.
Petrarch. Because she bore upon her face Love's banner.
Rilke. Fugitives, The.

Daniel (Bible)
Emerson, R. Γνῶθι Σεαυτόν.
Glück, L. Gretel in Darkness.
Lindsay, N. Daniel.
Pinsky. Visions of Daniel.

Dante Alighieri
Akhmatova, A. Dante.
Berryman. Dante's Tomb.
Borges. Inferno 5, 129.
Byron, G. Prophecy of Dante, The.
Carruth, H. Excursus of Reassurance in Begonia Time, An.
Cavalcanti. Dante, a sighing messenger of the heart.
Each day I come to you an infinity of times.
If you see Love, Dante.
Sonnet: He interprets Dante's Dream, related in the first Sonnet of the Vita Nuova.
Sonnet: He rebukes Dante for his way of Life, after the death of Beatrice.

Chaucer. House of Fame, The.
Ciardi, J. Another Comedy.
Letter to Dante.
Cino da Pistoia. Canzone: On the Death of Beatrice Portinari.
Sonnet: He conceives of some Compensation in Death.
Sonnet: He impugns the verdicts of Dante's Commedia.
Sonnet: He interprets Dante's Dream, related in the first Sonnet of the Vita Nuova.
Creeley. Guido, i' vorrei che tu e Lapo ed io.
Cummings, E. E. Great Dante stands in Florence, looking down.
Davie, D. Mandelstam, on Dante.
Emerson, R. Solution.
Enzensberger, H. Identity Check.
Graves, R. Beatrice and Dante.
Hamill, S. Malebolge: Prince William Sound.
Keats. On a Dream.
Kizer, C. In Hell with Virg and Dan.
Kunitz, S. Illumination, The.
Lowell, R. Dante 3. Buonconte.
McGrath, T. Migration of Cities, The.
Michelangelo Buonarroti Straight down from heaven, and in the flesh, he came.
Milosz, C. Dante.
Pound, E. Rosa Sempiterna.
Roethke. Her Wrath.
Rossetti, D. Dante at Verona.
On the 'Vita Nuova' of Dante.
Sandburg, C. Our Hells.
Tomlinson, C. Idyll: "Door: / *PER L'UNIVERSO* / is what it says, A."
Wilde, O. At Verona.
Wright, C. Southern Cross, The.

Daphne
Glück, L. Mythic Fragment.
Undertaking, The.
"H. D." If You Will Let Me Sing.
Meredith, G. Daphne.
Millay, E. Daphne.
Petrarch. Nine times Latona's son had turned his gaze.
Pound, E. Tree, The.
Smart, C. Apollo and Daphne.
Stock, R. Rococo Birdbath with Figurine of Daphne as Warning to Virgins.
Swift, J. Death and Daphne.
Zaturenska. Daphne.
Zukofsky, L. For Zadkine.

Daredevils
Cowper, W. Card, A.
Sandburg, C. Hazardous Occupations.

Darkness
Amichai [*or* Amikhai]. People in the Dark Always See.
What is it? An old shed for tools.
Ammons. Two Motions.
Armantrout. Light.
Atwood. Interlunar.
Projected Slide of an Unknown Soldier.
Solstice Poem.
Beckett, S. Noire soeur.
Berry, W. Bird Killer, The.
Breaking.
Creation Myth.
Current, The.
Farmer and the Sea, The.
Fear of Darkness, The.
Returning.
Seventeen Years.
Song in a Year of Catastrophe.
To Know the Dark.
Bly, R. Snowfall in the Afternoon.
Borges. Talismans.
Brodsky, J. I Sit by the Window.
Brontë, E. Spellbound.
Byron, G. Darkness.
Carew, T. Beautiful Mistress, A.
Carruth, H. Mountain Cabin, The.
Clampitt. August Darks, The.
Crane, S. I was in the darkness.
Creeley. Anger.
For Leslie.
Hero, The.

I Know a Man.
Persons.
Rhythm, The.
Shame, The.
Somewhere.
You ("Back and forth across").
Cummings, E. E.   I was considering how.
When citied day with the sonorous homes.
De la Mare.   Disguise, The.
Juliet's Nurse.
Unforeseen.
Dickey, J.   Rafters, The.
Spring-Shock.
Dickinson, E.   Lightning is a yellow Fork, The.
Presentiment—is that long Shadow—on the
lawn.
We grow accustomed to the Dark.
Dunbar, P.   Love is the light of the world, my
dear.
Slow Through the Dark.
Duncan, R.   Albigenses, The.
Bring It Up from the Dark.
Huon of Bordeaux.
Eberhart, R.   Light, Time, Dark.
Parker River, The.
Poet, The.
Emerson, R.   And as the light divided the dark.
Good Charles the springs adorer.
Winds are cold, the days are dark, The.
Gallagher, T.   Reading Aloud.
Graves, R.   Children of Darkness.
Jealous Man, A.
Gunn, T.   Annihilation of Nothing, The.
Feel of Hands, The.
Vigil of Corpus Christi, The.
Gurney, I.   Darkness Has Cheating Swiftness.
Guyon.   Scenes Favourable to Meditation.
Hamill, S.   Elegy: "Always, the world we invent
or build."
Herrick.   In the Dark None Dainty.
Hill, G.   Of Coming-into-Being and Passing-
Away.
Hopkins, G.   In the staring darkness.
Hughes, L.   As I Grew Older.
Ignatow, D.   Hope, The.
Jarrell, R.   90 North.
Afterwards.
Komunyakaa.   Cage Walker, The.
Praising Dark Places.
Sitting in a Rocking Chair, Going Blind.
Lawrence, D. H.   After Dark.
At Midnight.
Blueness.
Firelight and Nightfall.
Glory of Darkness.
Hark in the Dusk!
In the Dark.
Reach Over.
Young Wife, A.
Levertov.   Closed World, The.
For a Child.
Writing in the Dark.
Levine, P.   Late Moon.
Longfellow, H.   Children's Hour, The.
Lux.   Dark Comes On In Blocks, In Cubes, The.
McGrath, T.   In Sickness Like Sleep.
Remembering the Children of Auschwitz.
Merton.   Dark Encounter, The.
Responsory, A.
Merwin.   First Darkness, The.
Michelangelo Buonarroti.   Every shut-in room
or space, every covered one.
Milton.   Il Penseroso.
Nemerov.   Advice from the Holy Tomb.
Madrigal: "She is the darkness where I wander."
Oliver, M.   Lamps, The.
Olson, C.   Sans Name.
Orr, G.   Dark Night, A.
Patchen.   Rites of Darkness, The.
Pinsky.   City Dark, The.
Raine, K.   Quenching the Red.
Riley, J.   Last Night—and This.
Out of the Dark and the Dearth.
Robinson, E.   Valley of the Shadow, The.
Roethke.   In a Dark Time.
Shimmer of Evil, The.

Rossetti, C.   O Lucifer, Son of the Morning!
Remember [Me].
Shadows Today.
Strange voices sing among the planets which.
Sarton, M.   Girl with 'Cello.
Simic.   Elegy: "Note / as it gets darker."
Snyder, G.   How Poetry Comes to Me.
Stafford, W.   Many Things are Hidden by the
Light.
One Night.
Traveling Through the Dark.
Swenson, M.   Cabala.
Tollas, T.   They've Blocked Every Window.
Tomlinson, C.   Civilities of Lamplight.
Fire in a Dark Landscape.
Fireflies.
Unknown.   From the Persian (1).
Vallejo.   Big People, The.
Warren, R.   Speleology.
Three Darknesses.
Wilbur, R.   Beacon, The.
Williams, M.   On the Way Home From
Nowhere, New Year's Eve.
Wright, J.   Beginning.
Lights in the Hallway, The.
On Minding One's Own Business.
Revelation, The.
Zagajewski.   She Wrote in Darkness.
Zukofsky, L.   Can a mote of sunlight defeat its
purpose.

Darling, Grace Horsley
Wordsworth, W.   Grace Darling.

Darwin, Charles
Clampitt.   Good Friday.
Dickinson, E.   Why the Thief ingredient
accompanies all Sweetness.
Major, C.   Darwin's Dream.
Niedecker.   Darwin.
Orr, G.   Shelf Is a Ledge, A.
See also **Evolution**

Dating
Amichai [*or* Amikhai].   Gifts of Love.
Angelou.   Country Lover.
Brodsky, J.   Centaurs 2.
Bukowski.   Parts of an Opera, Parts of a Guitar,
Part of Nowhere.
Dunbar, P.   Lover's Lane.
Negro Love Song, A.
Gunn, T.   Lofty in the Palais de Danse.
Komunyakaa.   Rendezvous.
Laughlin, J.   At the Boule d'Or.
Lux.   Painfully Banal.
Niedecker.   Fancy Another Day Gone.
Parker, D.   News Item.
Riley, J.   Boy-Friend, The.
Updike.   To an Usherette.
Williams, M.   First Date.
Personals.
See also **Courtship**

Daughters
Ai.   Cockfighter's Daughter, The.
Amichai [*or* Amikhai].   On the Day My
Daughter Was Born No One Died.
There Are Candles That Remember.
Atwood.   Red Shirt, A.
Berrigan, T.   In the 51st State.
Bierce.   Rosalie.
Blue Cloud.   Girl Child.
Little Fawn.
Brooks, G.   Jessie Mitchell's Mother.
Browning, E.   Romaunt of Margret, The.
Bukowski.   Sitting in a Sandwich Joint.
Burns, R.   Poet's Welcome to His Love-
Begotten Daughter, A.
Written under the Picture of the Celebrated Miss
Burns.
Byron, G.   Jephtha's Daughter.
Campion, T.   Ad Cambricum.
Carruth, H.   Essay on Death.
Carver, R.   Energy.
My Daughter and Apple Pie.
Seeds.
To My Daughter.
Ciardi, J.   Lines for Myra to Grow To.
Clifton, L.   Album.
Quilting.

Coleridge, S.   Old Man of the Alps, The.
Cooper, J.   For My Mother in Her First Illness,
from a Window Overlooking Notre Dame.
Creeley.   Fire, The.
Sitting Here.
De la Mare.   Glance, The.
On the Esplanade.
Owl, The.
Dickey, J.   Root-light, or the Lawyer's Daughter.
Dove, R.   Variation on Guilt.
Dubie.   Bus Stopped in Fields of Misdemeanor,
The.
Comes Winter, the Sea Hunting.
Eberhart, R.   Vastness and Indifference of the
World, The.
Eliot, T. S.   Marina.
Emerson, R.   What from this barren being do we
reap.
Gallagher, T.   Borrowed Ones, The.
Glück, L.   Morning.
Graves, R.   Frosty Night, A.
Hacker, M.   Iva's Birthday Poem.
Mother.
Prayer for my Daughter.
Robber Woman, The.
Towards Autumn.
Hamill, S.   Natural History.
Han-shan.   Raise girls but not too many.
Hardy, T.   Lorna the Second.
Statue of Liberty, The.
Sunday Morning Tragedy, A.
Herrick.   Mr. Hericke his Daughter's Dowrye.
To the Lady Mary Villars, Governesse to the
Princesse Henretta.
Hughes, L.   Mama and Daughter.
Ignatow, D.   For My Daughter.
For My Daughter in Reply to a Question.
Future, The.
His Name.
Jacobsen, J.   Daughter to Archeologist.
Jarrell, R.   Lost Children, The.
Jonson, B.   On My First Daughter.
To Elizabeth, Countess of Rutland.
Kinnell.   Little Sleep's-Head Sprouting Hair in
the Moonlight.
Parkinson's Disease.
Under the Maud Moon.
Kizer, C.   Amusing Our Daughters.
Blessing, The.
For My Daughter.
Thrall.
Korn.   Generations.
Kumin, M.   Envelope, The.
Leaving My Daughter's House.
Making the Jam without You.
Seeing the Bones.
Sunbathing on a Rooftop in Berkeley.
We Stood There Singing.
Kunitz, S.   Journal for My Daughter.
Levertov.   Daughter (1), A.
Daughter (2), A.
Logan, J.   My Daughter's Wedding.
Two Poems for Women.
Longfellow, H.   Wreck of the *Hesperus*, The.
Lorde.   Dear Toni Instead of a Letter of
Congratulation.
Lowell, R.   Home After Three Months Away.
Lux.   Criss Cross Apple Sauce.
For My Daughter When She Can Read.
Little Tooth, A.
Man Takes His Daughter, Age Five, To a Public
Execution by Guillotine, Paris, 1857, A.
MacLeish.   White-Haired Girl.
Mahon.   Katie at the Pool.
Mallarmé.   Another Fan; of Mademoiselle
Mallarmé.
Gift of the Poem.
Meredith, G.   Doe: A Fragment, The.
She scarce has a word for Papa.
Moraes, V.   Song: "Never take her away."
Muldoon, P.   Skeffington's Daughter.
Nash, O.   Good Parent's Garden of Vision, A.
In Which the Poet Is Ashamed but Pleased.
Niedecker.   Depression Years.
Olson, C.   Winds / which blew my daughter,
The.

Oppen. Exodus.
  From a Photograph.
Orr, G. Gift, The.
Paley, G. For My Daughter.
Pinsky. Daughter.
Prunty. Family Portrait for Our Daughter, A.
  Learning the Bicycle.
Ransom, J. Bells for John Whiteside's
  Daughter.
Rexroth, K. American Century, The.
  Family, The.
  Living Pearl, A.
  Mary and the Seasons.
  Metempsychosis.
  Proust's Madeleine.
  Wheel Revolves, The.
Rich, A. Woman Mourned by Daughters, A.
Riley, J. Nothin' to Say.
  To Lesley.
Ritsos. Country Woman.
  Unexpectedly.
Rossetti, C. There Is a Budding Morrow in
  Midnight.
  Versi.
Sexton. Little Girl, My String Bean, My Lovely
  Woman.
  Mother and Daughter.
  Pain for a Daughter.
Smith, S. Bereavement.
  Darling Daughters.
  Feminine Charm.
  Human Affection.
Spender, S. To My Daughter.
Stafford, W. For a Daughter Gone Away.
Stock, R. For Sharon, As Soon As She Wants
  It.
Stockton, A. Acrostic for Abby Stockton.
  To Mrs Rush, on Her Birth Day.
  Wise nature here has done her kindest part.
Updike. Commencement, Pingree School.
  Daughter.
  Song of Paternal Care, A.
Walcott. Early Pompeian.
Walker, A. Forgiveness.
  My Daughter Is Coming!
  Poem at Thirty-nine.
Whittier. Farewell, The: "Gone, gone,—sold
  and gone."
Wilbur, R. Writer, The.
Williams, C. K. Fifteen.
  Gift, The.
  Last Deaths, The.
  Nickname of Hell, The.
Williams, M. Caterpillar, The.
  For Rebecca, for Whom Nothing Has Been
    Written Page after Page.
  Poem for Emily, A.
Williams, W. Ogre, The.
  Youth and Beauty.
Wordsworth, W. Address to My Infant
  Daughter, Dora on Being Reminded That She
  Was a Month Old That Day, September 16.
  Three Graves, The.
Wright, J. Origins.
Yeats. Father and Child.
  Prayer for My Daughter, A.

David (Bible)
Berryman. King David Dances.
Bradstreet, A. David's Lamentation for Saul
  and Jonathan.
Browning, R. Saul.
Byron, G. Harp the Monarch Minstrel Swept,
  The.
Davie, D. Creature David, The.
  David Dancing.
  God Saves the King.
De la Mare. Goliath.
Glück, L. Abishag.
  Parable, A.
Jarrell, R. Bronze David of Donatello, The.
Lindsay, N. In Which Roosevelt Is Compared to
  Saul.
Logan, J. Ah, so our first load of honey heavy
  Christmas trees.
  Far off the road on the left on a slight rolling
  hill.

I did but taste a little of the honey with the.
If the half moon stamp of a sacred hoof showed
  Cadmus.
In my dream I know I see my father Saul a
  king.
  Monologues of the Son of Saul.
Rossetti, C. Thy Servant Will Go and Fight
  with This Philistine.
Smart, C. Song to David, A.
Swinburne. Masque of Queen Bersabe, The.
Very. Goliath.
Wheatley, P. Goliath of Gath.
Wilner, E. Salute to Donald Davie.

David (statue)
Cunningham, J. I, Too, Have Been to the
  Huntington.
Wilner, E. Fourth David, The.

Davies, Sir John
Campion, T. Ad Io. Davisium.
Roethke. Four for Sir John Davies.

Davis, Miles
Corbett, W. Hero.

Dawn
Ammons. Making.
  Rectitude.
Angelou. Brief Innocence.
Baudelaire. First Light.
  Spiritual Dawn.
Beckett, S. Alba.
Blue Cloud. Autumn Morning.
  Dawn.
Bly, R. Dawn in Threshing Time.
Borges. Break of Day.
Browning, E. Sabbath Morning at Sea, A.
Burns, R. Chloe.
Carruth, H. Michigan Water: a Few Riffs before
  Dawn.
  Stepping Backward.
Ciardi, J. In Some Doubt but Willingly.
Cooper, J. Morning on the St. John's.
Creeley. That's the way.
Cummings, E. E. Dawn / and now.begins /
  feeling.
  Lady of Silence.
"Dario." In Autumn.
De la Mare. Before Dawn.
  Break of Morning.
  Dawn.
  Forests.
  Glimpse, The.
  Stranger, The.
Dickinson, E. It was a quiet way—.
  Not knowing when the Dawn will come.
Dunbar, P. Dawn.
Eberhart, R. Four Lakes' Days.
  Hoot Owls.
  Line of Verse of Yeats, A.
  Parker River, The.
  Thrush Song at Dawn.
Emerson, R. Coin the daydawn into lines.
Ferlinghetti, L. Upon Reflection.
García Lorca. Dawn, The.
Ginsberg, A. Fourth Floor, Dawn, Up All Night
  Writing Letters.
Glück, L. Aubade: "Today above the gull's
  call."
Graves, R. Return of the Goddess [Artemis].
Gurney, I. Early Spring Dawn.
  February Dawn.
  Going Out at Dawn.
  Longford Dawns.
  Lovely Playthings.
  Smudgy Dawn.
  Song: "Past my window dawn and down."
  Two, The.
Hardy, T. Dawn after the Dance, The.
Heliodorus. Beginning of Heliodorus, The.
Herrick. To Anthea Lying in Bed.
  To Julia, in Her Dawn, or Day-breake.
Housman. Fairies Break Their Dances, The.
  Reveille.
Hughes, L. Daybreak in Alabama.
  Lonely Nocturne.
Hughes, T. Cock-Crows.
  Roe-Deer.
  Strangers.

Jeffers, R. Dawn.
Johnson, S. Aurora Est Musis Amica.
Keats. Imitation of Spenser.
Kinnell. First Day of the Future.
Kinsella, T. First Light.
Kipling, R. Hymn of the Triumphant Airman.
Larkin, P. Dawn.
Lawrence, D. H. Quite Forsaken.
  Winter Dawn.
Levertov. In Summer.
  What Wild Dawns There Were.
Levine, P. Making Light of It.
  New Day, A.
  Words.
Logan, J. Dawn and a Woman.
Longfellow, H. Children's Hour, The.
Lux. Dawn Walk and Prayer.
MacLeish. Midsummer Dawn.
Mahon. Dawn Chorus, The.
McGrath, T. Dawn Song.
Melville, H. Clover.
Meredith, G. By Morning Twilight.
  Sunrise.
Meredith, W. Ideogram.
Merwin. Black Plateau, The.
  Daybreak.
  How We Are Spared.
Millay, E. Autumn Daybreak.
  Dawn.
  Recuerdo.
Milosz, C. At Dawn.
  Dawns.
  Early Morning.
Mistral, G. Dawn.
Montale. Like a Fantasia.
Owen, W. Fragment: "Cramped in that
  funnelled hole, they watched the dawn."
Petrarch. Birds, singing and lamenting once
  again.
Riley, J. Hour before the Dawn, The.
  Out of the Dark and the Dearth.
  Requiescat.
Ritsos. Putting out the Lamp.
Rossetti, C. "Kookoorookoo! kookoorookoo!" /
  Crows the cock before the morn.
Rossetti, D. Dawn on the Night-Journey.
Rukeyser, M. Chapultepec Park / I.
  During the journey there come moments of
  waking.
Sandburg, C. Alone and Not Alone.
  Daybreak.
  First Sonata for Karlen Paula.
  Nightsong.
  Sarah's Letter to Peter.
  She Opens the Barn Door Every Morning.
  Themes in Contrast.
Smith, S. Aubade: "My dove, my doe."
Stafford, W. At the Old Place.
  Malheur before Dawn.
Stevens, W. Brave Man, The.
Swenson, M. Out of the Sea, Early.
Thomas, D. Light Breaks Where No Sun
  Shines.
Thoreau. Cock-crowing.
  Guido's Aurora.
  Stanzas: "Nature doth have her dawn each day."
Tomlinson, C. At Dawn.
  Cloud Change.
  Last of Night, The.
  Of Beginning Light.
Very. Day Begins to Dawn, The.
  Fair Morning, The.
Warren, R. Dawn.
  First Dawn Light.
  Myth of Mountain Sunrise.
Weiss, T. Sultry Dawn.
Wilde, O. By the Arno.
  Lotus Leaves.
Williams, C. K. Dawn.
Williams, T. Daybreak Thought for Maria, A.
Williams, W. Chinese Nightingale.
  Dawn.
  Daybreak.
Wordsworth, W. Ode Composed on May
  Morning.
  While Beams of Orient Light Shoot Wide and

High.
Wright, J. Little Girl on Her Way to School, A.
Yeats. Dawn, The.
Zagajewski. At Daybreak.
Zaturenska. Spring Morning.
Zukofsky, L. Alba (1952).
See also **Morning; Sunrise**

Day
Ammons. Day.
  Quince Bush, The.
Angelou. Plagued Journey, A.
Berrigan, T. Peace.
Berryman. Meditation.
Browning, E. Island, An.
Collins, B. Days.
Creeley. Every Day.
  For Benny and Sabina.
  Hi There!
  Wind Lifts.
Cummings, E. E. Impression.
  Out of midsummer's blazing most not night.
  Put off your faces,Death:for day is over.
Cunningham, J. Dogdays.
De la Mare. Disguise, The.
Dickinson, E. Day came slow—till Five
  o'clock, The.
  First Day's Night had come, The.
  Some say goodnight—at night.
Dunbar, P. Day.
  Drowsy Day, A.
  Warm Day in Winter, A.
Eberhart, R. Autumnal.
  Bells of a Chinese Temple, The.
  By the Stream.
  Clam Diggers and Diggers of Sea Worms, The.
  Commitment, A.
  Four Exposures.
  Four Lakes' Days.
  Off Spectacle Island.
  Soldier Rejects His Times Addressing His
    Contemporaries, A.
Emerson, R. Always day & night.
  Days.
  Days pass over me, The.
  If bright the sun, he tarries.
  My days roll by me like a train of dreams.
  What flowing central forces, say.
Graves, R. Children of Darkness.
"H. D." Mid-day.
Herrick. Dream[e]s.
Hopkins, G. Windy Day in Summer, A.
Jackson, L. And a Day.
Keats. To My Brother George.
Kinnell. Middle of the Way.
Kipling, R. Hymn of the Triumphant Airman.
Larkin, P. Days.
  Lift through the Breaking Day.
  Long Lion Days.
Lawrence, D. H. Fall of Day, The.
Levertov. Celebration.
McHugh, H. Song Calls the Star Little, The.
Merton. Song, A: "When it was day, we heard
  the panes of windows."
Merwin. Day, The.
Nash, O. Midsummer's Daymare.
Neruda. First Winter.
  Inside.
Oliver, M. Morning at Great Pond.
Olson, C. Dragon-Fly, The.
  Going from Battle to Battle.
  Seven Songs, The.
Petrarch. For every living creature on this earth.
Rexroth, K. Working Day, The.
Rossetti, C. Awake, Thou That Sleepest.
  Day Is At Hand, The.
  Days are clear, / Day after day, The.
  Easter Even.
  Is the Moon Tired?
  "Kookoorookoo! kookoorookoo!" / Crows the
    cock before the morn.
  Let Them Rejoice in Their Beds.
  Oh knell of a passing time, / Will it never cease
    to chime?
  Praying Always.
  Smile and a Sigh, A.
  Summer nights are short, / Where northern days

are long, The.
Sandburg, C. Clark Street Bridge.
  Daybreak.
  Harmonica Humdrums.
Schuyler, J. White Boat, Blue Boat.
Smith, S. Aubade: "My dove, my doe."
Thoreau. Guido's Aurora.
Very. Day.
Walcott. Star.
Warren, R. Ways of Day.
Whittier. Day's Journey, A.
Wilbur, R. Death of a Toad, The.
  Sun and Air.
  Sunlight Is Imagination.
Williams, M. Coping.
Williams, W. Advent of Today.
  Full Moon.
Wordsworth, W. Composed on a May Morning.
Zukofsky, L. Que J'ay Dit Devant.

Daydreams
Ashbery, J. Instruction Manual, The.
  Mixed Feelings.
Berry, W. Thought of Something Else, The.
Bishop, E. End of March, The.
Brontë, E. Little while, a little while, A.
Bukowski. Eaten by Butterflies.
  Interviewed by a Guggenheim Recipient.
  Parts of an Opera, Parts of a Guitar, Part of
    Nowhere.
  Thermometer.
Clough. Come pleasant thoughts; sweet
    thoughts, at will.
Coleridge, S. Day-Dream, A.
  Day-Dream, The.
Dunbar, P. By the Stream.
Hall, D. Days, The.
  In the Old House.
Ivanov, G. Losing yourself in thought,
    daydreaming.
Komunyakaa. Ghost Chant, et alii.
Lux. It Must Be the Monk in Me.
MacDiarmid, H. Harry Semen.
Nash, O. Spring Comes to Murray Hill.
Parker, D. Day-Dreams.
Rexroth, K. Thin Edge of Your Pride, The.
Robinson, E. Miniver Cheevy.
Sarton, M. Nostalgia for India.
  We Sat Smoking at a Table..
"Shu Ting." Bits of Reminiscence.
Very. Scholar Dreaming, The.
Whalen, P. Daydream, The.
Zaturenska. Future in Miniature.
See also **Dreams and Dreaming**

De Hooch, Pieter
Sarton, M. Dutch Interior.
Tomlinson, C. Paring the Apple.
Wilbur, R. Objects.

De la Mare, Walter
Eliot, T. S. To Walter de la Mare.

Deafness
Davie, D. Reflections on Deafness.
Hughes, T. Deaf School.
Jacobsen, J. Deaf-Mutes at the Ballgame.
Lowell, R. Marcus Cato 234–149 B.C.
Ritsos. At the Harbor's Edge.
Swift, J. On His Own Deafness.
Sze. Empty Words.
Tate, J. Deaf Girl Playing.
Williams, M. Going Deaf.
Wright, J. Mutterings Over the Crib of a Deaf
    Child.

Dean, James
Ai. James Dean.
O'Hara, F. For James Dean.

Death and the Dead
Ai. Conversation.
  Ice.
  Nothing but Color.
  One Man Down.
  Ravine, The.
  She Didn't Even Wave.
Amichai [*or* Amikhai]. All These Make a
    Dance Rhythm.
  Anniversary of My Father's Death, The.
  Death of Assia G., The.

Diameter of the Bomb, The.
Farewell.
First Rain on a Burned Car, The.
From the Book of Esther I Filtered the
    Sediment.
"He left two sons," they say.
Huleikat—The Third Poem about Dicky.
I Want to Die in My Own Bed.
In the Garden, at the White Table.
Luxury, A.
My Father in a White Space Suit.
My Father's Death.
My Mother Comes From the Days.
My Mother Died on Shavuot.
My Mother's Death and the Lost Battles for the
    Future of Her Children.
Now She's Breathing.
On Mount Muhraka.
Songs of Continuity.
Too Many.
Wonderful Baker, The.
Yom Kippur.
Your Life and Death, Father.
Ammons. Account, The.
  Consignee.
  Dying in a Mirthful Place.
  Hymn 3: "In the hour of extreme."
  Play.
  Run-Through, The.
  Satyr Formalist.
Angelou. Elegy: "I lay down in my grave."
  Gamut, The.
  Lesson, The.
  Mourning Grace.
Armantrout. Precedence.
Arnold, M. Memorial Verses.
  Requiescat.
  Thyrsis.
Ashbery, J. Flowering Death.
  How Much Longer Will I Be Able to Inhabit the
    Divine Sepulcher.
  Saying It to Keep It from Happening.
Atwood. Another Elegy.
  Deaths of the Other Children, The.
  Four Small Elegies.
  Machine. Gun. Nest.
  Settlers, The.
  This Is a Photograph of Me.
Auden. As I Walked Out One Evening.
  Clocks cannot tell our time of day.
  Death's Echo.
  Friday's Child.
  In Memory of W. B. Yeats.
  O What Is That Sound [Which So Thrills the
    Ear].
  Old People's Home.
Baudelaire. Carrion, A.
  Curious Man's Dream, A.
  Death of Artists, The.
  Death of Lovers, The.
  Death of the Poor, The.
  Posthumous Remorse.
  Sisters of Mercy.
Beckett, S. Alba.
  Je voudrais que mon amour meure.
  Jusque dans la caverne ciel et sol.
  La nuit venue où l'âme allait.
  Mort de A.D.
  Morte parmi.
  Plus loin un autre commémore.
  Poem: "I would like my love to die."
Bembo, P. You, too, my brother in your hour of
    Spring.
Berrigan, T. I Heard Brew Moore Say, One
    Day.
  Last Poem.
  People Who Died.
Berry, W. Boone.
  Canticle.
  Clear Days, The.
  Cold Pane, The.
  Dark with power.
  Discipline, A.
  Elegy: "All day our eyes could find no resting
    place."
  Farmer Among the Tombs, The.

For the Hog Killing.
Grandmother, The.
In Memory: Stuart Egnal.
Man Walking and Singing, A.
Marriage, an Elegy, A.
Meadow, The.
Meeting, A.
Morning's News, The.
Necessity of Faith, The.
Poem for J.
Poem: "Willing to die, / you give up."
Praise, A.
Requiem: "We will see no more."
Ripening.
Slip, The.
Snake, The.
Sparrow.
Sycamore, The.
Three Elegiac Poems.
Wheel, The.
Wish to Be Generous, The.
Berryman. Dante's Tomb.
Epilogue: "He died in December. He must
    descend."
Handshake, the Entrance, The.
Message.
Poet's Final Instructions, The.
Possessed, The.
Sanctuary.
Scots Poem.
Whether There Is Sorrow in the Demons.
Bertrans [or Bertran or Bertrand] de Born.
Planh for the Young English King.
Bierce. Another Way.
Finis Æternitatis.
Guest, A.
Here Salomon's body reposes.
Here Stanford lies, who thought it odd.
J.F.B.
T. A. H.
Trencher-Knight, A.
William F. Smith.
Year's "Casualties", A.
Bion. Lament for Adonis.
Bishop, E. Cootchie.
First Death in Nova Scotia.
Man-Moth, The.
Blake, W. And his legs carried it like a long
    fork.
Another [Epitaph]: "Here lies John Trot, the
    Friend of all mankind."
Epitaph, An: "Come knock your heads against
    this stone."
Blok. Dances of Death.
Blue Cloud. Backward Dancer.
Grandma Marie Potts.
Bly, R. Ant Mansion, The.
Christmas Eve Service at Midnight at St.
    Michael's.
Hawk, The.
In Mourning for Betrayal.
Bogan, L. Exhortation.
My Voice Not Being Proud.
Sonnet: "Dark, underground, is furnished with
    the bone."
Borges. 1964.
Alhambra.
Camden, 1892.
Deathwatch on the Southside.
Dream of Pedro Henríquez Ureña, The.
Elegy: "Three very ancient faces stay with me."
Enigmas, The.
Epilogue: "Now that the number of steps you
    were given."
For Leopoldo Lugones.
Inscription on Any Tomb.
Limits.
Maker, The ("He had never dwelled on the
    pleasures of memory").
Milonga of Albornoz.
Milonga of Don Nicanor Paredes.
Milonga of Manuel Flores.
Recoleta Cemetary.
Remorse for Any Death.
Someone.
To My Father.

Two Versions of "Knight, Death and the Devil."
Web, The.
Where Can They Have Gone?
Yellow Rose, A.
Bourne, V. Ode on the Death of a Lady.
Bradstreet, A. Before the Birth of One of Her
    Children.
Epitaph on my Dear and Ever Honored Mother
    Mrs. Dorothy Dudley.
In Memory of My Dear Grandchild Anne
    Bradstreet.
Of the Four Ages of Man.
To My Dear and Loving Husband.
To the Memory of My Dear and Ever Honored
    Father Thomas Dudley Esq.
To the Memory of My Dear Daughter in Law,
    Mrs. Mercy Bradstreet.
Upon a Fit of Sickness, Anno 1632.
Brodsky, J. Elegy: For Robert Lowell.
Epitaph for a Centaur.
Funeral of Bobò, The.
In Memoriam.
On the Death of Zhukov.
Törnfallet.
Transatlantic.
Brontë, E. A.S. to G.S.
At such a time, in such a spot.
Aye there it is! It wakes tonight.
Battle had passed from the height, The.
Come, walk with me.
Death.
Death Of A.G.A., The.
Death Scene, A.
Deep, deep down in the silent grave.
E.W. to A.G.A.
Far, far away is mirth withdrawn.
H.A. and A.S.
Heaven's glory shone where he was laid.
Here, with my knee upon thy stone.
How Clear She Shines!
I gazed within thine earnest eyes.
I.M. to I.G.
I saw thee, child, one summer's day.
I see around me tombstones grey.
It is too late to call thee now.
Lines by Claudia.
Long Neglect Has Worn Away.
Methinks this heart should rest awhile.
Night of storms has passed, The.
Night was dark, yet winter breathed, The.
Night Wind, The.
No Coward Soul is Mine.
None but one beheld him dying.
Not many years but long enough to see.
O come again; what chains withhold.
O mother, I am not regretting.
O wander not so far away!
Philosopher, The.
Remembrance.
Rosina.
Shed no tears o'er that tomb.
Sleep brings no joy to me.
Song: "King Julius left the south country."
Stanzas: "I'll not weep that thou art going to
    leave me."
Stanzas to———.
Start not! upon the minister wall.
There shines the moon, at noon of night.
There swept adown that dreary glen.
Thousand sounds of happiness, A.
'Tis moonlight, summer moonlight.
To A.S., 1830.
Warning and Reply.
Why ask to know the date—the clime?
Wind was rough which tore, The.
Yes, holy be thy resting place.
Brooks, G. In Honor of David Anderson
    Brooks, My Father.
Last Quatrain of the Ballad of Emmett Till, The.
Mentors.
We Real Cool.
White Troops Had Their Orders but the Negroes
    Looked Like Men.
Broumas, O. Choir, The.
Elegy: "Somebody left the world last night, I
    felt it."

Eros.
Host.
Mercy.
On Earth.
Périsprit.
Stars in Your Name.
Walk on the Water.
Browning, E. Dead Rose, A.
Died..
Felicia Hemans.
Fourfold Aspect, The.
Grief.
Hugh Stuart Boyd [His Death, 1848].
L.E.L.'s Last Question.
Life and Love.
Mother and Poet.
Sleep, The.
Sounds.
Thought for a Lonely Death-Bed, A.
Browning, R. After.
Arcades Ambo.
Bishop Orders His Tomb at Saint Praxed's
    Church, The.
Dance of Death, The.
Doctor———.
Evelyn Hope.
Gold Hair: A Story of Pornic.
Lines on Swinburne.
Lines to the Memory of James Dow.
Lost Leader, The.
May and Death.
Prospice.
Bukowski. Bedpans.
Beds, Toilets, You and Me—.
Conversation in a Cheap Room.
Conversation on Morality, Eternity and
    Copulation, A.
Death Wants More Death.
Doom and Siesta Time.
Eat.
Eulogy to a Hell of a Dame—.
Everything.
Farewell Thing While Breathing, A.
Freedom: The Unmolested Eagle of Myself.
Gift, The.
Goodbye.
I Wait in the White Rain.
I Write This Upon the Last Drink's Hammer.
Japanese Wife, The.
Kind of Lecture on a Dull Day When There
    Isn't Even a Fly Around to Kill, A.
Meek Have Inherited, The.
Naked at 92 Degrees.
Nothing Subtle.
Old Man, Dead in a Room.
On Seeing an Old Civil War Painting with My
    Love.
One for the Old Boy.
Our Curious Position.
Poem for Liz.
Practice.
Result.
Rose, Rose.
Sky Sign.
Sleep.
Suggestion for an Arrangement.
There Once Was a Woman Who Put Her Head
    into an Oven.
Truce.
Up Your Yellow River.
What They Want.
When I Think of Myself Dead.
Worst and the Best, The.
You Smoke a Cigarette.
Burns, R. Address, to the Shade of Thomson,
    on Crowning His Bust.
Another [Epigram on Said Occasion].
Bard's Epitaph, A.
Death and Doctor Hornbook [A True Story].
Elegy on Captain Matthew Henderson [or Capt.
    M——— H———].
Elegy on Mister William Cruikshank A. M.
Elegy on the Death of Robert Ruisseaux.
Epigram on Said Occasion.
Epitaph Extempore, on a Person Nicknamed the
    Marquis.

Epitaph for H——— L———, Esq., of L——
 —.
Epitaph for J. H. Writer in Ayr.
Epitaph for William Nicol.
Epitaph. Here Lies Robert Fergusson, Poet.
Epitaph: "Lo worms enjoy the seat of bliss."
Epitaph on a Schoolmaster.
Epitaph on D——— C———.
Epitaph on Holy Willie.
Epitaph on J-hn B-shby.
Epitaph on James Grieve, Laird of Boghead.
Epitaph on John Dove [Innkeeper, Mauchline].
Epitaph on Mr. Burton.
Epitaph on My Own Friend, and My Father's
 Friend, Wm Muir in Tarbolton Miln.
Epitaph on R. Muir.
Extempore—on Some Commemorations of
 Thomson.
For G. H. Esq.
For R. A. Esq.
For the Author's Father.
Fragment, Which Was Meant for the Beginning
 of an Elegy on the Late Miss Burnet of
 Monboddo, A.
Highland Mary.
Ill-fated Genius! Heaven-taught Fergusson.
Lament for James, Earl of Glencairn.
Lines Addressed to Mr. John Ranken.
Lines on the Author's Death.
Lines Sent to Sir John Whiteford.
Macpherson's Farewell.
Man Was Made to Mourn, a Dirge.
Merry Hae I Been Teethin a Heckle.
Monody on Maria.
On a Celebrated Ruling Elder.
On a Noisy Polemic.
On an Innkeeper in Tarbolton.
On Captn. L———lles.
On Fergusson.
On Gabriel Richardson.
On J-hn M-r-ne, Laird of L-gg-n.
On Reading, in a Newspaper, the Death of J—
 —— McL———, Esq.
On Robert Riddel.
On the Death of Sir J. Hunter Blair.
On the Death of the Late Lord President
 Dundas.
On W. R———, Esq.
On Wee Johnie.
On William Graham [or W——— Gr-h-m],
 Esq., of Mossknowe [or M-sskn-w].
Orananaoig, or, the Song of Death.
Prayer, in the Prospect of Death, A.
Sketch for an Elegy.
Sonnet on the Death of Robert Riddel, Esq.
Stanzas on the Same Occasion [in the Prospect
 of Death].
Tam Samson's Elegy.
Tam the Chapman.
Thou Ling'ring Star.
Where Helen Lies.
Byron, G. Adieu, The.
And Thou Art Dead, as Young and Fair.
Answer to a Beautiful Poem, Entitled "The
 Common Lot."
Aristomenes.
Bright Be the Place of Thy Soul!
Churchill's Grave.
Destruction of Sennacherib, The.
Duel, The.
Elegiac Stanzas on the Death of Sir Peter
 Parker, Bart.
Epigram on an Old Lady Who Had Some
 Curious Notions Respecting the Soul.
Epitaph for Joseph Blacket.
Epitaph on John Adams, of Southwell.
Euthanasia.
Fragment, A: "Could I remount the river of my
 years."
If Sometimes in the Haunts of Men.
If That High World.
Inscription on the Monument of a
 Newfoundland Dog.
Last Words on Greece.
Lines Written beneath an Elm in the Churchyard
 of Harrow.

Love and Death.
Manfred.
Monody on the Death of the Right Hon. R. B.
 Sheridan.
Ode from the French.
Ode to a Lady Whose Lover Was Killed by a
 Ball.
Oh factious viper! whose envenom'd tooth.
Oh! Snatch'd Away in Beauty's Bloom.
On the Death of a Young Lady.
One Struggle More, and I Am Free.
Stanzas: "I heard thy fate without a tear."
Thoughts for a Speech of Lucifer, in the
 Tragedy of "Cain."
To Caroline.
To Thyrza.
Youth, Nature, and Relenting Jove.
Campion, T. De obitu Phil. Sydnaei equitis
 aurati generosissimi.
Elegie upon the Untimely Death of Prince
 Henry, An.
In Morachum.
In obitum Gual. Devoreux fratris clariss.
 Comitus Essexiae.
In Obitum Hen. Mag. Brit. Principis.
In obitum Iacobi Huissii.
Lamentation, A.
Leave prolonging thy distresse.
To the Most High and Mighty Prince Charles.
To the Most Illustrious and Mighty Fredericke
 the Fift, Count Palatine of the Rhein.
To the Most Princely and Vertuous the Lady
 Elizabeth.
To The Most Sacred King James.
Umbra.
Carew, T. Another [On the Duke of
 Buckingham].
Elegy on the La: Pen: Sent to My Mistress Out
 of France, An.
Elegy upon the Death of the Dean of [St.]
 Paul's, Dr. John Donne, An.
Epitaph on the Lady Mary Villiers, An.
For a Picture Where a Queen Laments over the
 Tomb of a Slain Knight.
Grief Engrossed.
Maria Wentworth.
On the Duke of Buckingham.
To the Countess of Anglesey.
Upon the Sickness of E.S.
Carruth, H. Algeria.
Anent Socrates, or Somebody.
Bearer, The.
Crucifixion.
Essay on Death.
Essay on Marriage.
Études de Plusiers Paysages de l'Âme.
Fat Lady, The.
Fragment: "Who can know more deeply than I
 your loneliness there?"
French Hill.
Ho-Hum Again.
Homecoming.
Mother.
No Supervening Thought of Grace.
None.
Not Transhistorical Death, or at Least Not
 Quite.
Questions.
Ravine, The.
Song: So Often, So Long I Have Thought.
Song: So Why Does This Dead Carnation.
Carver, R. Account, An.
Another Mystery.
Egress.
House behind This One, The.
Letter.
Meadow, The.
My Death.
Powder-Monkey.
Rest, The.
Sleeping.
Cavafy. Afternoon Sun, The.
Death of a General.
In the Port.
Stephanos Skilitsis.
Sweet Voices.

Voice from the Sea.
Voices.
Cavalcanti. Canzone: A Dispute with Death.
My latest cruel misfortune.
Celan. Aspen Tree.
By Twos.
Darkness.
Dead Man, The.
Deathfugue.
In Front of a Candle.
In Memoriam Paul Éluard.
In Prague.
Nearness of Graves.
Nocturnally Pursed.
Profuse announcement.
Sluice, The.
Song in the Wilderness, A.
Stretto.
Travel Companion, The.
Voices, nicked into.
Winter.
You were my death.
Chamfort. Sleep till death.
Trouble with tragedy is the fuss it makes, The.
Chesterton. Last Hero, The.
Chiabrera. Destined to war from very infancy.
Not without heavy grief of heart did He.
O flower of all that springs from gentle blood.
O Lelius, beauteous flower of gentleness.
O Thou who movest onward with a mind.
Pause, courteous Spirit!—Baldi supplicates.
Perhaps some needful service of the State.
There never breathed a man who, when his life.
Torquato Tasso rests within this tomb.
True it is that Ambrosio Salinero.
Weep not, belovèd Friends! nor let the air.
Chuang Tzu. Lao Tzu's Wake.
Three Friends.
Ciardi, J. Apartment with a View, An.
Aunt Mary.
Credo ("I asked the doctor who had pronounced
 me dead").
Elegy 1: "I fell from the bouncing tailgate to
 roll in traffic."
Elegy for a Sweet Sharpy.
Elegy for Sam.
Elegy: For You, Father.
Epithalamium at St. Michael's Cemetary.
Expendability.
Finally that Blue Receding Sphere.
In Paul's Room.
Invasion of Sleep Walkers, The.
It Took Four Flowerboats to Convoy My
 Father's Black.
Letter from a Death Bed.
Limits of Friendship, The.
Loving You Is Something to Do.
Minus One.
Mystic River.
One Dull Thing You Did Was to Die, Fletcher,
 The.
Poetry.
Sea Burial.
Thousandth Poem for Dylan Thomas, A.
Was a Man.
What Was Her Name.
When a Man Dies.
When I Am Not Dead.
Cino da Pistoia. Canzone: His Lament for
 Selvaggia.
Canzone: On the Death of Beatrice Portinari.
Sonnet: Death is not without but within him.
Sonnet: He conceives of some Compensation in
 Death.
Sonnet: Of the grave of Selvaggia, on the Monte
 della Sambuca.
Clampitt. Anatomy of Migraine, An.
Chichester.
Curfew, A.
'Eighty-Nine.
My Cousin Muriel.
Procession at Candlemas, A.
Urn-Burial and the Butterfly Migration.
What the Light Was Like.
Winter Burial, A.
Clare, J. I Am.

Clifton, L.   August.
Death of Fred Clifton, The.
Death of Thelma Sayles.
Lot's Wife 1988.
Sorrow Song.
Clough.   Epi-strauss-ium.
Codrescu.   All Wars Are Holy.
I'm careful with my dreams of death.
Worst Poems Make the Best "Poems," The.
Coleridge, S.   Death Wish, A.
Elegy Imitated from One of Akenside's Blank-
Verse Inscriptions.
Epitaph: "Stop, Christian passer-by!—Stop,
child of God."
Epitaphium Testamentarium.
Israel's Lament.
Life in Death.
Lines on a Friend.
Monody on the Death of Chatterton.
Ne Plus Ultra.
O Spirit blest! / Whether th' eternal Throne
around.
Old Man of the Alps, The.
On an Insignificant.
On Receiving an Account That His Only
Sister's Death Was Inevitable.
On Seeing a Youth Affectionately Welcomed by
a Sister.
Separation from Asra.
W. H. *Eheu!*
Collins, B.   Dead, The.
My Number.
Picnic, Lightning.
Purity.
Tomes.
Where I Live.
Wires of the Night, The.
Cooper, J.   Faithful, The.
Hotel de Dream.
In the House of the Dying.
Long, Disconsolate Lines.
Mourning Picture.
Roman Dream.
Corbett, W.   At Charlesgate.
First of September.
Joe Brainard.
Last Words.
Lines Written After Reading Frank O'Hara's "A
Step Away from Them."
My Father-in-Law's Coat.
Cowper, W.   Epitaph on a Hare.
Epitaph on Dr. Johnson.
Epitaphium Alterum.
Inscription for a Stone.
Inscription for the Tomb of Hamilton.
On the Death of Russell.
On the Shortness of Life.
Crane, H.   Broken Tower, The.
Circumstance, The.
Her Eyes Had..
Paraphrase.
Possessions.
Praise for an Urn.
Crane, S.   Behold, the grave of a wicked man.
Chatter of a death-demon from a tree-top, The.
If I should cast off this tattered coat.
Ocean said to me once, The.
There is a grey thing that lives in the tree-tops.
Crashaw.   Another on [Mr. Herrys].
Death's Lecture.
Elegie on the Death of Doctor Porter, An.
Elegy upon the Death of Mr. Stanninow Fellow
of Queenes Colledge.
Epitaph Upon Husband and Wife Who Died and
Were Buried Together, An.
[Mr. Herrys,] His Epitaph.
Recommendation, The.
Upon the Death of a Freind.
Upon the Death of a Gentleman.
Upon the Death of Mister Herrys.
Upon the Death of the Most Desired Mister
Herrys.
Creeley.   After Lorca.
And.
Days and Days.
Death.

Death of Venus, The.
Dying.
Festival, The.
Flaubert's Early Prose.
For My Mother: Genevieve Jules Creeley.
Heroes.
Last Mile, The.
Memory, 1930.
Message, The.
Moment.
N. Truro Light—1946.
Probable Truth.
Rhythm, The.
Swinging Down Central.
That day / in an oak tree—.
World, The.
Cuadra, P.   Faces of Girls Looking at
Themselves in the River.
Lament of a Maiden for the Warrior's Death.
Cullen, C.   Brown Girl Dead, A.
Epilogue: "Lily, being white not red, The."
Foolish Heart, The.
For an Anarchist.
For an Evolutionist and His Opponent.
In Spite of Death.
Only the Polished Skeleton.
Poet, The.
Protest.
Proud Heart, The.
Requiescam.
Sonnet Dialogue.
Threnody for a Brown Girl.
Two Thoughts of Death.
Wise, The.
Cummings, E. E.   After Seeing French Funeral.
Am was. Are Leaves Few this. Is these a or.
Annie died the other day.
But the other / day i was passing a certain.
Come nothing to my comparable soul.
Connotation of infinity, A.
Death(having lost)put on his universe.
Death's Chimney.
Dedicated to Dear Nana Clarke.
Don't get me wrong oblivion.
Dying is fine)but Death.
First president to be loved by his, The.
Gee i like to think of dead it means nearer
because deeper firmer.
Glory is fallen out of, The.
Great / man / is / gone, A.
Handsome and clever and he went cruising.
Hate blows a bubble of despair into.
Here is little Effie's Head.
Hips lOOsest OOping shoulders blonde&
pastoral hair,strong.
How dark and single,where he ends,the earth.
I am going to utter a tree,Noboby.
I like / to think that on.
If i should sleep with a lady called death.
It is funny,you will be dead some day.
It)It will it.
It's just like a coffin's.
Let us suspect,chérie,this not very big.
Lively and loathesome moe's respectably dead.
Memory believes / fragrance of a town(whose).
My love is building a building.
Nobody loses all the time.
Nor woman / (just as it be).
Now that fierce few.
Now two old ladies sit peacefully knitting.
Of all things under our.
One Fine Day.
One X.
Only as what(out of a flophouse)floats.
Portrait.
Put off your faces,Death:for day is over.
Quick i the death of thing.
Rain or hail / sam done.
S.F.D.
Since feeling is first.
Softly from its still lair in Plympton Street.
Somebody knew Lincoln somebody Xerxes.
Sonnet IV.
Suppose / Life is an old man carrying flowers
on his head.
That which we who're alive in spite of mirrors.

This is a rubbish of human rind.
Whatever's merely wilful, / and not miraculous.
When God Lets My Body Be.
When life is quite through with.
When thou art dead,dead,and far from the
splendid sin.
When unto nights of autumn do complain.
Who before dying demands not rebirth.
Who's most afraid of death?thou.
The(/ Wistfully / dead seem generous)don't.
You no / tice / nobod / y wants.
Young / man sitting, The.
Cunningham, J.   Epigram: "Here lies my wife.
Eternal peace."
Life flows to death as rivers to the sea.
My name is Ebenezer Brown.
Dante Alighieri.   Canzone: He beseeches Death
for the Life of Beatrice.
Dante's Vita Nuova.
La Vita Nuova.
"Dario."   Nocturne: "Silence of the night, a
sorrowful silence."
Davie, D.   After an Accident.
Death in the West, A.
Departed, The.
Harrow, The.
Intervals in a Busy Life.
Mother.
Nineteen-Seventeen.
Penelope.
Three Beyond.
Davitt.   Mirror, The.
De la Mare.   Age.
Anatomy.
Assignation, The.
Autumn.
Away.
Betrayal.
Bottle, The.
Bridge, The.
Bright Life.
Cage, The.
Death-Dream, The.
Defeat.
Epitaph, An: "Here lies a most beautiful lady."
Even In The Grave.
Faithless.
Familiar, The.
Fare Well.
Flotsam.
Goliath.
Good Company.
Here Sleeps.
Hospital.
How Sleep the Brave.
Imogen.
Isaac Meek.
Juliet's Nurse.
Keep Innocency.
Keys of Morning, The.
Life.
Marionettes, The.
Mistress Fell.
Motley.
Music Unheard.
Peace.
Reconciliation.
Remembrance.
Revenant, The.
Sallie's Musical Box.
Satire, The.
Shadow.
Snowflake, The.
Sorcery.
Taciturn, The.
Thorn, The.
TO E. T.: 1917.
Truce.
Virtue.
Waiting.
What?
Where?
Where Is Thy Victory?
Delany, P.   Elegy on the Much Lamented Death
of Mr. Demar, the Famous Rich Usurer [or
Man], An.

Dickey, J.   Attempted Departure.
Breath.
Deborah as Scion.
Eagle's Mile, The.
Farmers.
For Robert Bhain Campbell.
Gila Bend.
Hospital Window, The.
Island, The.
Poem: "For having left the birds that left me."
Sled Burial, Dream Ceremony.
Sleepers.
String, The.
To Be Done in Winter.
Tomb Stone.
Vessels.
Via appia.
Dickey, W.   And he lies dead—.
And I, who lay so warm and quiet there—.
At Maganosc / in the stone bedroom.
Come, Doctor, we must fly someotherwhere.
Doctor, I did not see that you were there.
Elegy Before the Time.
For we have gone a curious way from there.
G.F. Died 1954, Aged 27.
Here, in the summer city.
His Death from Cancer.
I did not know you when you came in there.
If forgiveness comes / it will be gradual.
In The Dreaming.
In the dreaming / we walk throug the streets of
   Oxford.
Part Song, With Concert of Recorders.
Thinking of me / think of what was.
We meet, eating, smoking.
Who made you come and find the door to there?
Dickinson, E.   Absence disembodies—so does
   Death.
Admirations—and Contempts—of time, The.
Advance is Life's condition.
Afraid! Of whom am I afraid?
After a brief unconsciousness.
After a hundred years.
After the great intrusion of Death.
Ah! dainty—dainty Death!
All but Death can be Adjusted.
As by the dead we love to sit.
As from the earth the light Balloon.
Back from the cordial Grave I drag thee.
Because I could not stop for Death.
Believing that we are to have no Face.
Bereavement in their death to feel.
Brain—is wider than the Sky, The.
Brain, within its Groove, The.
Bustle in a House, The.
By a departing light.
Choice.
Color, Caste, Denomination.
Could I visit the Beds.
Dear friend, can you walk.
Death blow is a Life blow to Some, A.
Death cannot plunder half so fast.
Death goes far around.
Death has only to touch a trifle.
Death is a Dialogue between.
Death is like the insect.
Death is perhaps an intimate friend.
Death is potential to that Man.
Death is the supple Suitor.
Death leaves Us homesick, who behind.
Death obtains the Rose.
Death sets a Thing significant.
Death warrants are supposed to be.
Did she suffer—except to leave you?
Distance that the dead have gone, The.
Do People moulder equally.
Doom is the House without the Door.
Doomed—regard the Sunrise, The.
Dreams are the subtle Dower.
Dropped into the Ether Acre.
Dust is the only Secret.
Dust like the Mosquito, The.
Dying! Dying in the night!
Dying is a wild Night.
Dying need but little, Dear, The.
Dying! To be afraid of thee.

Each Second is the last.
Endow the Living—with the Tears.
Except to Heaven, she is nought.
Face I carry with me—last, The.
Fear—like Dying, dilates trust.
Finite life, little sister, A.
First We knew of Him was Death, The.
Flags Vex a Dying Face.
Footlights cannot improve the grave.
For Death—or rather.
Frost of Death was on the Pane, The.
Great Hope fell, A.
Grief of wonder at her fate.
Had I presumed to hope.
He fought like those Who've nought to lose.
He fumbles at your Soul.
Heart asks Pleasure—first, The.
Her dying feels to me.
Her final Summer was it.
His Life was so shy and his tastes so unknown.
Home itself is far from home.
How fortunate the Grave.
How many times these low feet staggered.
How sweet that he rose in the morning.
How sweet the "Life that now is."
How to repair my shattered ranks.
I died for Beauty—but was scarce.
I Felt a Funeral in My Brain.
I heard a Fly buzz—when I died.
I keep my pledge.
I know of people in the Grave.
I know that He exists.
I like a look of Agony.
I meant to find Her when I came.
I never hear that one is dead.
I never lost as much but twice.
I notice where Death has been introduced.
I read my sentence—steadily.
I see thee clearer for the Grave.
I should not dare to leave my friend.
If any sink, assure that this, now standing.
If Anybody's Friend be Dead.
If He were living—dare I ask.
If I may have it, when it's dead.
If I should cease to bring a Rose.
If I should die.
If I shouldn't be alive.
If this is "fading."
In falling Timbers buried.
It came at last but prompter Death.
It don't sound so terrible—quite—as it did.
It perished with beautiful reluctance.
It was not Death, for I stood up.
It's coming—the postponeless Creature.
I've seen a Dying Eye.
Last Night that She Lived, The.
Let down the Bars, Oh Death.
Life is death we're lengthy at.
Long—long Sleep—a famous—Sleep, A.
Love Is That Later Thing.
Manner of its Death, The.
Me prove it now—Whoever doubt.
Meeting is well worth parting.
Midsummer, was it, when They died.
Mighty dying of my Father, The.
More Life—went out—when He went.
More than the Grave is closed to me.
Mother's dying almost stunned my spirit.
My life closed twice before its close.
My Life had stood—a Loaded Gun.
My Triumph lasted till the Drums.
Not all of life to live, is it.
Nothing in her Life became her.
Of Death I try to think like this.
Of nearness to her sundered Things.
Oh give it Motion—deck it sweet.
On this long storm the Rainbow rose.
One dignity delays for all.
Only Balmless Wound, The.
Overtakelessness of those, The.
Pain has but one Acquaintance.
Praise it—'tis dead.
Promise This, When You be Dying.
Right to perish might be thought, The.
Robbed by Death—but that was easy.
Safe in their Alabaster Chambers.

Said Death to Passion.
Secret, The.
Shade upon the mind there passes, A.
She bore it till the simple roots.
She died at play, / Gambolled away.
She lay as if at play.
Sickness of this World it most occasions, A.
So give me back to Death.
So proud she was to die.
Some things that fly there be.
Some Wretched creature, savior take.
Somehow myself survived the Night.
Soul must go by Death alone, The.
Soul should always stand ajar, The.
Soul, take thy risk.
Stem of a departed Flower, The.
Still own thee—still thou art.
Summer has two Beginnings.
Sun kept setting—setting—still, The.
Suspense—is Hostiler than Death.
Sweet Acclamation of Death divulges it, The.
Sweet hours have perished here.
Sweet is it as Life.
Sweet—safe—Houses.
Sweet, to have had them lost.
Test of Love—is Death, The.
That after horror that was us.
That Bareheaded life under the grass.
That odd old man is dead a year.
That short—potential stir.
That the Divine has been human.
That this should feel the need of Death.
That we are permanent.
There comes an hour when begging stops.
There is a finished feeling.
There is a word / Which bears a sword.
There's a certain Slant of light.
There's been a Death, in the Opposite House.
There's something quieter than sleep.
They put Us far apart.
This Consciousness that is aware.
This docile one inter.
This heart that broke so long.
This Me—that walks and works—must die.
Those not live yet.
Those that die seem near me.
Those who have been in the Grave the longest.
Three times—we parted—Breath—and I.
Throe upon the features, A.
Tie the Strings to my Life, My Lord.
'Tis easier to pity those when dead.
'Tis so appalling—it exhilirates.
'Tis Sunrise—Little Maid—Hast Thou.
To die before it feared to die.
To die—takes just a little while.
To forget you would be impossible.
To him to whom Events and Omens.
To know just how He suffered—would be dear.
Toad, can die of Light, A.
Too scanty 'twas to die for you.
Train went through a burial gate, A.
Tried always and Condemned by thee.
'Twas comfort in her Dying Room.
'Twas fighting for his Life he was.
'Twas just this time, last year, I died.
'Twas warm—at first—like Us.
Two swimmers wrestled on the spar.
Two Travellers perishing in Snow.
Under the Light, yet under.
Unit, like Death, for Whom?
Upon Concluded Lives.
Vanished.
Vision of Immortal Life has been fulfilled, The.
Visitor in Marl, A.
Vivid in our immortal Group.
Wait till the Majesty of Death.
We all have moments with the dust.
We can but follow to the Sun.
We don't cry—Tim and I.
We go by detachments to the strange Home.
We must be less than Death.
We never know we go when we are going.
We wear our sober Dresses when we die.
What care the Dead, for Chanticleer.
What if I say I shall not wait!
What Inn is this.

Whatever it is—she has tried it.
When One has given up One's life.
While it is alive.
Who knows where our hearts go.
Whole of it came not at once, The.
With closer clutch for that which remains.
With sorrow that the Joy is past.
Word is dead, A.
You'll find—it when you try to die.
Your little mental gallantries.
You're right—"the way is narrow."
Donne. Blossom[e], The.
Computation, The.
Dissolution, The.
Elegy on Mistress Boulstred.
Elegy on the L. C.
Elegy on the Lady Markham.
Elegy upon the Death of Mistress Boulstred, An.
Elegy upon the Untimely Death of the Incomparable Prince Henry.
Epitaph on Himself.
Expiration, The.
Funeral[l], The.
Hero and Leander.
Hymn to the Saints, and to Marquis Hamilton, An.
Hymn[e] to God My God, In My Sickness[e], A.
Obsequies to the Lord Harrington.
Paradox, The.
Pyramus and Thisbe.
Song: "Sweetest love, I do not go[e]."
To the Lady Bedford.
Valediction, A: of Weeping.
Valediction: Forbidding Mourning, A.
Dove, R. Company.
Event, The.
Oriental Ballerina, The.
Teach Us to Number Our Days.
Thomas at the Wheel.
Tou Wan Speaks to Her Husband Liu Sheng.
Zeppelin Factory, The.
Drummond de Andrade. Table, The.
Dryden, J. To the Memory of Mr Oldham.
Dubie. Confession.
Death of the Race Car Driver, The.
Elegy for Integral Domains, The.
Elegy for My Brother.
Elegy to the Pulley of Superior Oblique.
Genesis Text for Larry Levis, Who Died Alone, A.
Grandfather's Last Letter, A.
Mercy Seat, The.
Pastoral: "It happened so fast. Fenya was in the straight."
Sanctuary.
Dugan, A. 851.
Death's Chicken, Named Amelia.
Hard-on Death.
In Memoriam: Aurelius Battaglia, and against His Tragic Sense of Life.
Memorial Service for the Invasion Beach Where the Vacation in the Flesh Is Over.
Two Comments on "Death's Chicken, Named Amelia."
Untitled Poem: "Once on the beach at night I heard the waves."
Dunbar, P. Alexander Crummel—Dead.
Behind the Arras.
Border Ballad, A.
"Chronic Kicker," The.
Communion.
Compensation.
Dead.
Death.
Death of the First Born, The.
Death Song[, A].
Dirge: "Place this bunch of mignonette."
Frederick Douglass.
Goin' Home.
In the Tents of Akbar.
Love-Song: "If Death should claim me for her own to-day."
Masters, The.
My dear love died last night.

News, The.
On the Death of W. C.
Paradox, The.
Premonition.
Puttin' the Baby Away.
Remembered.
Right to Die, The.
To a Dead Friend.
To Alice Dunbar.
To the Memory of Mary Young.
Two Little Boots.
W'en I Gits Home.
When All Is Done.
Dunbar, W. Lament for the Makaris [or Makars or Makers].
Duncan, R. After a Long Illness.
Huon of Bordeaux.
Reaper, The.
Eberhart, N. New Entrepreneurial Plan.
Eberhart, R. Apple Buds.
At Night.
Cage, The.
Ceremony By the Sea, A.
Death in the Mines.
Edgar Lee Masters.
Emily Dickinson.
Examination of Psyche: Thoughts of Home.
Flux.
Forgotten Rock, The.
Gesture, The.
Grave Piece.
Hardy Perennial.
Horse Chestnut Tree, The.
I Walked over the Grave of Henry James.
I Will Not Dare to Ask One Question.
Ides of March, The.
Imagining How It Would Be to Be Dead.
John Finley.
John Ledyard.
Largess, The.
Life and Death.
Loss.
Man Who Was Blown Down by the Wind, A.
Meditation, A.
Nexus.
Nostalgia for Edith Sitwell.
Old Tom.
On Seeing an Egyptian Mummy in Berlin, 1932.
Once More, O Ye.
Passage, The.
Perception as a Guided Missile.
Poet, The.
Rumination.
Scouring, The.
Sestina: "I die, no matter what I do I die."
Sometimes the Longing for Death.
Suite in Prison.
Swallows Return, The.
There Is an Evil in the Air.
To Kenya Tribesmen, the Turkana.
Track.
Truncated Bird, The.
Trying to Hold It All Together.
Two Loves.
Ur Burial.
Virgin, The.
Ways and Means.
When Golden Flies Upon My Carcass Come.
Whenever I See Beauty I See Death.
Young Greek, Killed In The Wars, A.
Young Hunter, The.
Eliot, T. S. Aunt Helen.
Hollow Men, The.
In silent corridors of death.
Marina.
Song for Simeon, A.
Wind Sprang Up at Four o'Clock, The.
Emerson, R. All the great & good.
Dirge: "Knows he who tills this lonely field."
Dust unto dust! and shall no more be said.
Good-bye.
Hearst thou, sweet spirit, thou hast heard before.
I am alone. Sad is my solitude.
I love thy music, mellow bell.
In Memoriam.
Leave me, Fear! thy throbs are base.

Lines on the Death of Miss M. B. Farnham.
My days roll by me like a train of dreams.
Nun's Aspiration.
On the Death of Mr. John Haskins.
Original—"Apropos."
Shall the Muse sing for thousands & not sing.
She never comes to me.
Spirits of the wise, sit on the clouds, The.
Teach me I am forgotten by the dead.
Teach me your mood, O patient stars!
Terminus.
To J. W.
Visit, The.
What avails it me.
Why fear to die.
Why should I live.
Enzensberger, H. For the Grave of a Peace-Loving Man.
Fenton, J. Cambodia.
Dead Soldiers.
God, A Poem.
Letter to John Fuller.
Prison Island.
Fergusson, E. Poem on the Death of Richard Stockton, A.
Ferlinghetti, L. Elegy on the Death of Kenneth Patchen, An.
Man Who Rode Away, The.
Old Italians Dying, The.
Queens Cemetery, Setting Sun.
Sometime During Eternity.
Frost, R. Away!
Death of the Hired Man, The.
Departmental.
Fire and Ice.
Hill Wife, The.
Home Burial.
In a Disused Graveyard.
"Out, Out—."
Place for a Third.
Stopping by Woods on a Snowy Evening.
Times Table, The.
To E.T.
Wind and the Rain, The.
Gallagher, T. Accomplishment.
Candle, Lamp & Firefly.
Coats, The.
Dim House, Bright Face.
Small Garden Near a Field.
Sugar.
Survival of a Heart.
Tableau Vivant.
Their Heads Bent Toward Each Other Like Flowers.
With Stars.
García Lorca. Abandoned Church.
Autumn Song.
Ballad of One Doomed to Die.
Ballad of the Marked Man.
Ballad of the Moon Moon.
Childhood and Death.
Dance of the Moon in Santiago.
Dead from Love.
Death.
Death of Little Tony Camborio, The.
Dialogue of Amargo.
Farewell: "If I die."
Feud, The.
Flamenco Vignettes.
Gacela of the Dark Death.
Graphic of the Petenera.
Lament for Ignacio Sánchez Mejías.
Lullaby in Death for Rosalía de Castro.
Nocturne of the Drowned Youth.
Omega.
Poem of the *Soleá*.
Sleepless City.
Sleepwalking Ballad.
Song of a Little Death.
Three Cities.
Ginsberg, A. At Apollinaire's Grave.
Atypical Affair, An.
Death News.
Death on All Fronts.
Don't Grow Old.
Dream Record: June 8 1955.

Elegy for Neal Cassady.
Epigram on a Painting of Golgotha.
Fragment: The Names II.
Hymn: "No hyacinthine imagination can express this clock of meat bleakly pining."
In Memoriam: William Cannastra, 1922–1950.
Kaddish.
Memory Gardens.
Names, The.
On Neal's Ashes.
On Neruda's Death.
On Reading William Blake's "The Sick Rose."
Reply, The.
Sad Dust Glories.
Teacher / bring me to heaven.
Under the World There's a Lot of Ass, a Lot of Cunt.
What's Dead?
White Shroud.
Glück, L.   Adult Grief.
Apple Trees, The.
Chicago Train, The.
Descending Figure.
Dream of Mourning, The.
Drowned Children, The.
Fire, The.
Firstborn.
Garden, The.
Hyacinth.
Japonica.
La Force.
Late Snow.
Metamorphosis.
Phenomenal Survivals of Death in Nantucket.
Racer's Widow, The.
Swimmer, The.
Goethe.   Arabian Ballad.
Graves, R.   Dead Hand.
Down.
Dreaming Children.
Iago.
It Was All Very Tidy.
Leaving the Rest Unsaid.
Narrow Sea, The.
Presence, The.
Pure Death.
Reiteration, The.
Sharp Ridge, The.
Sit Mihi Terra Levis.
Song: Cherries or Lilies.
Song: To Become Each Other.
Suicide in The Copse, The.
Sweet-Shop Round The Corner, The.
Theme of Death, The.
Title of Poet, The.
To Be Poets.
To Bring the Dead to Life.
Toast to Death, A.
True Evil.
Twice Of The Same Fever.
Twin of Sleep, The.
Undead, The.
Villagers and Death, The.
Virus, The.
Gray, T.   Concluding Lines of Epitaph on Mrs Mason.
Descent of Odin, The.
Elegy Written in a Country Churchyard.
Epitaph on Mrs Jane Clarke.
Epitaph on Sir William Williams.
Ode on the Death of a Favourite [or Favorite] Cat, Drowned in a Tub [or Bowl] of Gold Fishes.
Sonnet [on the Death of Mr. Richard West].
Guillén, J.   Death, from a Distance.
Gunn, T.   Beautician, The.
Book of the Dead, The.
Corporal, The.
Death's Door.
Elegy: "I can almost see it."
From an Asian Tent.
Garden of the Gods, The.
In Time of Plague.
Inherited Estate, The.
J Car, The.
Lament: "Your dying was a difficult enterprise."

Lerici.
My Sad Captains.
Old Woman, The.
Reassurance, The.
Sacred Heart.
Sketch of the Great Dejection, A.
To a Dead Graduate Student.
To Isherwood Dying.
To the Dead Owner of a Gym.
Unsettled Motorcyclist's Vision of His Death, The.
Victim, The.
Words for Some Ash.
Gurney, I.   Above Ashleworth.
Appeal for Death, An.
Drachms and Scruples.
For Mercy of Death.
It Is Near Toussaints.
Regrets After Death.
Swift and Slow.
When I Am Covered.
"H. D."   Body and Soul.
Charioteer.
Choros Sequence.
Dead Priestess Speaks, A.
Epigram: "Golden one is gone from the banquets, The."
Epitaph: "So I may say."
Fragment 68: "I envy you your chance of death."
Helen.
Loss.
Priest.
Prisoners.
Wine Bowl.
Hacker, M.   Autumn 1980.
Ballad of Ladies Lost and Found.
Elegy: "Crying from exile, I."
Elevens.
For Elektra.
Geographer.
Mother.
Nights of 1965: the Old Reliable.
Presentation Piece.
Sword.
Hafiz [or Hafez].   Epitaph: "Bethink, poor heart, what bitter kind of jest."
From the Persian of Hafiz.
Hall, D.   Beau of the Dead.
Body Politic, The.
Carlotta's Confession.
Child's Garden, A.
Christmas Eve in Whitneyville, 1955.
Coffee Cup, The.
Eleanor's Letters.
Elegy for Wesley Wells.
Exile.
Flies.
Hole, The.
Hut of the man alone, The.
Idea of Flying, The.
In the Old House.
Man in the Dead Machine, The.
Mr. and Mrs. Billings.
My Friend Felix.
My Son, My Executioner.
No Deposit.
Praise for Death.
Raisin, The.
Red Branch, The.
Religious Articles.
Shudder [, The].
Sleeping.
Small Fig Tree, A.
Snow, The.
Traffic.
White Apples.
Halpern, M.   Isaac Leybush Peretz.
Hamill, S.   Treblinka Lights.
Han-shan.   All the people I see.
Fine young man on horseback, A.
I close my overgrown door in vain.
Old Chung north of town.
Show me the person who doesn't die.
Stop right now I implore you.
HaNagid.   Ask the Dead and They'll Tell You.

On the Death of Isaac, His Brother.
You Felt the Fear of Death.
Hardy, T.   A.H., 1855–1912.
After the Death of a Friend.
After the Last Breath.
Afterwards.
Amabel.
Announcement, The.
At Castle Boterel.
At Mayfair Lodgings.
At the Mill.
Beeny Cliff.
Casual Acquaintance, The.
Channel Firing.
Choirmaster's Burial, The.
Concerning Agnes.
Conversation at Dawn, A.
Dead Quire, The.
Death-Day Recalled, A.
Death of Regret, The.
Drummer Hodge.
Duel, The.
During Wind and Rain.
Epitaph: "I never cared for Life: Life cared for me."
Evening Shadows.
Every Artemisia.
Fading Rose, The.
Fallow Deer at the Lonely House, The.
Felled Elm and She, The.
Fragment: "At last I entered a long dark gallery."
Friends Beyond.
Going, The.
Harvest-Supper, The.
Her Death and After.
Her Secret.
I Found Her Out There.
I Met a Man.
If You Had Known.
In the Evening.
Inquiry, An.
Intra Sepulchrum.
Julie-Jane.
King's Soliloquy, A.
Lament: "How she would have loved."
Last Journey, A.
Last Performance, The.
Last Words To a Dumb Friend.
Life and Death at Sunrise.
Lodging-House Fuchsias, The.
Looking Across.
Nettles, The.
Neutral Tones.
New Dawn's Business, The.
Night of Questionings, A.
Not Only I.
Nothing Matters Much.
Old Likeness, An.
On One Who Lived and Died Where He Was Born.
One Ralph Blossom Soliloquizes.
Paradox.
Rash Bride, The.
Regret Not Me.
Seen by the Waits.
Sexton at Longpuddle, The.
She Hears The Storm.
Slow Nature, The.
Squire Hooper.
Subalterns, The.
Sun's Last Look on the Country Girl, The.
Thoughts of Phena.
Three Tall Men, The.
To-Be-Forgotten, The.
To Louisa in the Lane.
Transformations.
Upbraiding, An.
Voice, The.
When Dead.
Where the Picnic Was.
While Drawing in a Churchyard.
Whipper-In, The.
Who's in the Next Room?
Why She Moved House.
Wife in London, A.

Woman's Fancy, A.
Your Last Drive.
Harrison, M.   Poem on the Death of Mrs. Smith, A.
Hayden, R.   Approximations.
Broken Dark, The.
Burly Fading One, The.
Mourning Poem for the Queen of Sunday.
Paul Laurence Dunbar.
Heaney, S.   Badgers, The.
Call, A.
Casualty.
Clearances.
Funeral Rites.
Grauballe Man, The.
In Memoriam Francis Ledwidge.
King of the Ditchbacks, The.
Mid-Term Break.
Triptych.
Wishing Tree, The.
Heine, H.   From Heine.
Herbert, G.   Death.
Dialogue-Anthem, A.
Doomsday.
Life.
Mortification.
Redemption.
Virtue [or Vertue].
Herrick.   After Autumne, Winter.
Age Unfit for Love.
Bed-Man, or Grave Maker, The.
Comfort to a Youth That Had Lost His Love.
Death Ends All Woe.
Dirge of Jephthah's Daughter, The.
Elegy: "Since louely sweete, much like unto a Dewe."
Funeral[l] Rites of the Rose, The.
Gods Keyes.
Good Death, A.
Grace for a Child.
His Answer to a Friend.
His Last Request to Julia.
His Meditation upon Death.
His Winding-Sheet.
No Despight to the Dead.
Ode to Master Endymion Porter, upon His Brother's Death, An.
On Himselfe.
Parkinsons Shade to the House of Mr. Pallauicine Taking His Death Ill.
Posting to Printing.
Putrefaction.
Teares, and Laughter.
To Anthea.
To Biancha.
To Death.
To Electra.
To God, on His Sickness[e].
To His Kinswoman, Mistresse Susanna Herrick.
To His Lovely Mistresses.
To His Paternall Countrey.
To Julia.
To Perilla.
To the Nightingale, and Robin-Red-Brest.
To the Passenger.
To the Reverend Shade of His Religious Father.
Transfiguration, The.
Upon a child.
Upon a Maide.
Upon a Wife That Dyed Mad with Jealousie.
Upon an Old Man a Residenciarie.
Upon Ben Jo[h]nson.
Upon Hanch a Schoolmaster.
Upon Prue [or Prew], His Maid.
Upon the Losse of His Finger.
Widow's Tears [or Widdowes Teares]: or, Dirge of Dorcas, The.
Hill, G.   Funeral Music.
Guardians, The.
In Memory of Jane Fraser [or Frazer].
Merlin.
Two Formal Elegies.
White Ship, The.
Hopkins, G.   Felix Randal.
Glimmer'd along the square-cut steep.
Her prime of life—cut down too soon.

No Worst, There Is None. Pitched Past Pitch of Grief.
O Death, Death, He is come.
Spring and Death.
Why should their foolish bands, their hopeless hearses.
Housman.   A. J. J.
Along the field as we came by.
Ask me no more, for fear I should reply.
Because I liked you better.
Bredon Hill.
Crossing Alone the Nighted Ferry.
Epitaph.
Farms of home lie lost in even, The.
For My Funeral.
Friends.
Hughley Steeple.
I shall not die for you.
If truth in hearts that perish.
Illic Jacet.
Is my team plowing?
Isle of Portland, The.
Like mine, the veins of these that slumber.
Now to her lap the incestuous earth.
Oh on my breast in days hereafter.
On your midnight pallet lying.
Rain, it streams on stone and hillock, The.
Say, lad, have you things to do?
Shot? so quick, so clean an ending?
So Sound You Sleep.
Some can gaze and not be sick.
Stone, steel, dominions pass.
This time of year a twelvemonth past.
To an Athlete Dying Young.
Wake not for the world-heard thunder.
When I Watch the Living Meet.
When smoke stood up from Ludlow.
When the eye of day is shut.
Winter.
With Rue My Heart Is Laden.
Yon flakes that fret the eastern sky.
Hughes, L.   As Befits a Man.
Birmingham Sunday.
Boarding House.
Casual.
Dead in There.
Dear Lovely Death.
Death in Africa.
Deceased.
Departure.
Drum.
Exits.
Fantasy in Purple.
For Dead Mimes.
Gal's Cry for a Dying Lover.
Girl.
Irish Wake.
Judgment Day.
Kids Who Die.
Madam and the Wrong Visitor.
Mammy.
Peace.
Poem to a Dead Soldier.
Prayer for a Winter Night.
Question ("When the old junk man Death").
Red Roses.
Slave.
Sport.
Stony Lonesome.
Sylvester's Dying Bed.
Teacher.
There.
To a Little Lover-Lass, Dead.
Tower.
Wake.
Ways.
Widow Woman.
Young Bride.
Young Gal's Blues.
Hughes, T.   Anniversary.
Bayonet Charge.
Black Coat.
Casualty, The.
Day He Died, The.
Examination at the Womb-Door.
Executioner, The.

Heptonstall.
Leaves.
Life Is Trying to Be Life.
New Moon in January.
Old Oats.
Ravens.
Risen, The.
Small Events.
Soliloquy: "Whenever I am got under my gravestone."
TV Off.
View of a Pig.
Waving goodbye, from your banked hospital bed.
Woman Unconscious, A.
Ignatow, D.   And Rest.
Bothering Me at Last.
For My Daughter.
For My Daughter in Reply to a Question.
For Now.
In Dream.
Interview 2, The.
Invocation: "Dirt and stone, if I may know you as you know yourselves."
Pricing.
Prose Poem In Six Parts.
Reading the Headlines.
Refuse Man, The.
Their Mouths Full.
Walt Whitman in the Civil War Hospitals.
Without Recrimination.
Jackson, L.   Cycles of Strangeness.
Death as Death.
Elegy in a Spider's Web.
Lying Spying.
Respect for the Dead.
Room.
Second-Death.
Then Wherefore Death.
Time Beneath, The.
Jacobsen, J.   Arrivals, The.
Autopsy, The.
Colloquy.
Emperor's Cook, The.
Gathering, The.
How We Learn.
Limbo Dancer, The.
Margins of Choice.
Mourner Betrayed.
Poems for My Cousin.
Pondicherry Blues.
They Never Were Found.
Jammes.   Prayer to Go to Paradise with the Donkeys, A.
Jarrell, R.   Afterwards.
Automaton, The.
Black Swan, The.
Boyg, Peer Gynt, the One Only One, The.
Che Farò Senza Euridice.
Dead, The.
Death of the Ball Turret Gunner, The.
Difficult Resolution, The.
Dream of Waking, The.
Essay on the Human Will, An.
Hanged man on the gallows, The.
Iceberg, The.
In the Camp There Was One Alive.
In the Ward: The Sacred Wood.
Islands, The.
January 1938.
Knight, Death, and the Devil, The.
La Belle au Bois Dormant.
Laboratory, The.
Losses.
Mother, Said the Child.
One Who Was Different, The.
Place of Death, The.
Poem for Someone Killed in Spain, A.
Prince, The.
Say Good-bye to Big Daddy.
Scherzo.
Seele im Raum.
Sleeping Beauty: Variation of the Prince, The.
To Be Dead.
Truth, The.
Utopian Journey, A.

Washing the Corpse.
Well-to-Do Invalid, A.
What was longed for and, once, certain.
When I Was Home Last Christmas.
Women on a Bus.
Jeffers, R.   Antrim.
Bed by the Window, The.
Birth and Death.
Cawdor.
Coast-Road, The.
Come Little Birds.
Cremation.
Deer Lay Down Their Bones, The.
Drunken Charlie.
Eagle and hawk with their great claws and hooked heads.
Ghosts in England.
Give Your Wish Light.
Greater Grandeur.
Hungerfield.
I am seventy-four years old and suddenly all my strength.
In the Hill at Newgrange.
Iona: the Graves of the Kings.
Loving Shepherdess, The.
Low Sky, The.
May-June, 1940.
Medea.
Monument.
My Burial Place.
No Resurrection.
Ode to Hengist and Horsa.
Old age hath clawed me with his scaly clutch.
Original Sin.
Ossian's Grave.
Purse-Seine, The.
Seventieth Birthday.
Shears, The.
Shooting Season.
Sirens, The.
To Death.
Vulture.
Where I?
Johnson, E.   Elegy on the Much Lamented Death of Mr. Demar, An.
Johnson, S.   On the Death of Dr [or Mr] Robert Levet [a Practiser in Physic].
Translation of the Latin Epitaph on Sir Thomas Hanmer, A.
Verses on the Death of His Mother.
Jonson, B.   Charles Cavendish to His Posterity.
Elegy [or Elegie] on the Lady Jane Pawlet [or Paulet], An.
Epitaph, An: "What beauty would have lovely styled."
Epitaph on Elizabeth, L. H.
Epitaph, on Henry L[ord] La-ware. To the Passer-By, An.
Epitaph on Master Philip Gray, An.
Epitaph on Master Vincent Corbet[t], An.
Eptiaph on Katherine, Lady Ogle.
Little Shrub Growing By, A.
Ode to Himself, An.
Of Death.
Of Life and Death.
On Margaret Ratcliffe [or Radcliffe].
On Sir John Roe ("In place of scutcheons, that should deck thy hearse").
Stay, view this stone: and, if thou beest not such.
To the Memory of That Most Honoured Lady Jane.
To the World [A Farewell for a Gentlewoman, Virtuous and Noble].
Keats.   Ah! Ken Ye What I Met the Day.
As from the Darkening Gloom a Silver Dove.
Bright Star.
Can Death Be Sleep, When Life Is But a Dream.
Song: "I had a dove and the sweet dove died."
To Chatterton.
When I Have Fears [That I May Cease to Be].
Written in Disgust of Vulgar Superstition.
Khayyám, O.   From Omar Chiam.
On two days it steads not to run from thy grave.
Kinnell.   Dead Shall Be Raised Incorruptible,

The.
Fire in Luna Park.
Freedom, New Hampshire.
Looking at Your Face.
Neverland.
Sheffield Ghazal 5: Passing the Cemetary.
Sow Piglet's Escapes, The.
Spindrift.
Kinsella, T.   Ballydavid Pier.
Butcher's Dozen.
Death.
Death and the Professor.
Death Bed.
Dick King.
Dura Mater.
Good Fight, The.
Land of Loss, The.
Messenger, The.
Pause en Route.
Stable, The.
Tear.
Tyrant Dying.
Vertical Man.
Kipling, R.   Answer, The.
Appeal, The.
Azrael's Count.
Ballade of Burial, A.
Burial, The.
Dead King, The [Edward VII; 1910].
Dedication from "Barrack-Room Ballads."
Doctors.
En-Dor.
Explanation, The.
Follow Me 'Ome.
Gift of the Sea, The.
Last Department, The.
Last Suttee, The.
L'Envoi; Departmental Ditties.
Mary Gloster, The.
My Boy Jack.
Neighbours.
Old Mother Laidinwool.
Possibilities.
Queen's Men, The.
Snarleyow.
Song of the Dead, The.
Things and the Man.
Tomlinson.
Undertaker's Horse, The.
Widower, The.
Kizer, C.   Food of Love.
On a Line from Valéry.
Koch, K.   Circus, The.
Komunyakaa.   1938.
April Fools' Day.
Between Days.
Boy Wearing a Dead Man's Clothes.
Landscape for the Disappeared.
Sitting in a Rocking Chair, Going Blind.
Steel Plate, The.
Waiting for a Tree through a Window.
Wall, The.
You and I Are Disappearing.
Kumin, M.   Apostrophe to a Dead Friend.
Atlantic City 1939.
February.
How It Is.
In Memoriam P. W. Jr. 1921–1980.
Introducing the Fathers.
Itinerary of an Obsession.
Retrieval System, The.
Reviewing the Summer and Winter Calender of the Next Life.
Splitting Wood at Six Above.
Thinking of Death and Dogfood.
Kunitz, S.   Dragonfly, The.
Last Words.
Larkin, P.   Ambulances.
April Sunday Brings the Snow, An.
At the Chiming of Light upon Sleep.
Aubade: "I work all day, and get half-drunk at night."
Church Going.
Compline.
Dublinesque.
Hospital Visits.

I Have Started to Say.
Local Snivels through the Field, The.
Mower, The.
Next, Please.
Sympathy in White Major.
Unfinished Poem.
Laughlin, J.   Atman, The.
Ave Atque Vale.
Before I Die.
Building 520, Bellevue.
Dark Mutinous Shannon Waves, The.
Deathfear.
Dylan.
He Dreamed His Death.
Last Poem to Be Written, The.
Leave-taking, A.
My Old Gray Sweater.
Reading the Obituary Page in *The Times*.
Sleepless Night, A.
Sorrow.
Summons, The.
Tennesee.
Welcome, The.
Lawrence, D. H.   All Souls.
All Soul's Day.
At Last.
Beware the Unhappy Dead!
Birthday.
Bride, The.
Brother and Sister.
Call into Death.
Cherry Robbers.
Dead People.
Death.
Death of Our Era, The.
Death of the Baron, The.
Difficult Death.
Drama, A.
Endless Anxiety.
Erinnyes.
Everlasting Flowers.
Fatality.
Full Life.
Giorno dei Morti.
Gladness of Death.
Grief.
Houseless Dead, The.
Huitzilopochtli Gives the Black Blade of Death.
Huitzilopochtli's Watch.
Hymn to Priapus.
Initiation Degrees.
Let the Dead Bury Their Dead.
Like the Green Candles of Malintzi.
Man Who Died, A.
My Way Is Not Thy Way.
New Heaven and Earth.
New Word, The.
New Year's Night.
No News.
Obsequial Ode.
On That Day.
Pear-Blossom.
People Who Care.
Rabbit Snared in the Night.
Resurrection.
Revolutionary, The.
Shadow of Death, The.
Shadows.
Ship of Death, The.
Sleep.
So Let Me Live.
Song of Death.
Song of the Dead.
Spirits Summoned West.
Sympathy.
Troth with the Dead.
Two Wives.
Violets.
Violets for the Dead.
We Have Gone Too Far.
Welcome Death.
What Quetzalcoatl Saw in Mexico.
When Most Men Die.
When the Ripe Fruit Falls.
Levertov.   Another Spring.
At David's Grave.

Change, The.
Clouds.
Daughter (2), A.
Dead, The.
Death in Mexico.
Death Psalm: O Lord of Mysteries.
Didactic Poem.
Emissary, The.
Living for Two.
Note to Olga (1966), A.
Olga Poems.
Three Meditations.
Visitant.
What Were They Like?
Levi, P.   25 February 1944.
Crow's Song, The.
Epitaph: "Oh you, passing by this hill—one."
Levine, P.   1933.
And the Trains Go On.
Angel Butcher.
Baby Villon.
Belief.
Cemetery at Academy, California, The.
Children's Crusade, The.
Face, The.
Francisco, I'll Bring You Red Carnations.
Having Been Asked "What is a Man?" I
     Answer.
Hear Me.
Horse, The.
How Much Can It Hurt?
I Could Believe.
Jewish Graveyards, Italy.
Late Answer, A.
Let Me Be.
Letters for the Dead.
L'Homme et La Bête.
Lost and Found.
Miracle, The.
No One Remembers.
On a Drawing by Flavio.
On the Birth of Good & Evil During the Long
     Winter of '28.
On the Murder of Lieutenant José Del Castillo
     by the Falangist Bravo Martinez, July 12,
     1936.
Red Dust.
To a Fish Head Found on the Beach Near
     Málaga.
To Cipriano, in the Wind.
To My God in His Sickness.
To P.L., 1916–1937.
Uncle.
Voice, The.
Waking an Angel.
Lindsay, N.   Drunkard's Funeral, The.
Hearth Eternal, The.
I Want to Go Wandering.
Prairie Battlements, The.
Prayer to All the Dead Among Mine Own
     People, A.
What the Sexton Said.
Logan, J.   Byron at Shelley's Burning.
Dead Man's Room, The.
Elegy for the Rev. Mr. James B. Hodgson
     (1892–1963).
Grandmother Dead in the Aeroplane.
Lines on His Birthday.
Poem, Slow to Come, On the Death of
     Cummings (1894-1962).
Weeping, The.
Logue, C.   Air.
For My Father.
Song of the Imperial Carrion, The.
Woke up this morning.
Longfellow, H.   Cross of Snow, The.
Hawthorne.
Jewish Cemetery at Newport, The.
Lorde.   Day They Eulogized Mahalia, The.
Equinox.
Father Son and Holy Ghost.
Martha.
Memorial I.
Memorial II.
Suffer the Children.
Lowell, R.   Alfred Corning Clark.

Dante 3. Buonconte.
Death and the Bridge.
Death of Alexander.
For Robert Kennedy Nineteen Twenty-Five to
     Sixty-Eight.
For Sale.
Harriet.
Her Dead Brother.
History.
Ice.
Mary Winslow.
Mills of the Kavanaughs, The.
Mother Marie Therese.
Mr. Edwards and the Spider.
Nunc Est Bibendum, Cleopatra's Death.
Quaker Graveyard in Nantucket, The.
Sailing Home from Rapallo.
Two Walls.
Where the Rainbow Ends.
Lux.   Deadhouse at the Workhouse, The.
Elegy for Robert Winner.
Frankly, I Don't Care.
Here's to Samuel Greenberg.
If I Die Before I Wake.
Pecked to Death by Swans.
MacDiarmid, H.   At My Father's Grave.
Dead Liebknecht, The.
Empty Vessel.
Island Funeral.
John Maclean (1879-1923).
Of John Davidson.
Skald's Death.
Stony Limits.
Watergaw, The.
Wreck of the *Swan*, The.
MacLeish.   1892—19—.
Boatmen of Santorin, The.
Burial, The.
Burying Ground by the Ties.
Conway Burying Ground.
Cummings.
Dozing on the Lawn.
Epistle to Be Left in the Earth.
Eternity, An.
For the Anniversary of my Mother's Death.
Great Contemporary Discoveries.
Hemingway.
Immortal Helix.
Interrogate the Stones.
Man!
Mark Van Doren and the Brook.
Mother Goose's Garland.
My Naked Aunt.
Nat Bacon's Bones.
Old Gray Couple (1), The.
Old Gray Couple (2), The.
William Adams Delano.
Words to be Spoken.
MacNeice.   After the Crash.
Bar-Room Matins.
Beni Hasan.
Burnt Bridge, The.
Casualty, The.
Charon.
Death of an Actress.
Death-Wish, The.
Eclogue between the Motherless.
Epitaph for Liberal Poets.
Place of a Skull.
Revenant, The.
Rites of War.
Sunlight on the Garden, The.
This Is the Life.
Wall, The.
Mahon.   In Carrowdore Churchyard.
Major, C.   Downwind.
Love Against Death.
Saving Just the Real.
Swallow the Lake.
Mallarmé.   Funereal Toast.
Her pure nails on high displaying their onyx.
Homage: "Even a Dawn too numb."
Sonnet: "In the forgotten woods, when somber
     winter glowers."
Tomb.
Tomb of Charles Baudelaire, The.

Tomb of Edgar Poe, The.
Maritain.   Prisoner, The.
Marvell.   Damon the Mower.
Dialogue between Thyrsis and Dorinda, A.
Elegy upon the Death of My Lord Francis
     Villiers, An.
Epitaph upon —, An.
Poem upon the Death of Oliver Cromwell, A.
To His Coy Mistress.
Tom May's Death.
Upon the Death of the Lord Hastings.
McGrath, T.   Blues for Jimmy.
Blues for Warren.
Death for the Dark Stranger.
Drowned Man: Death Between Two Rivers,
     The.
Epitaph: "Again, traveller, you have come a
     long way led by that star."
Go Ask the Dead.
Memorial.
Passages.
People Are So Busy: Or: That's Life!
Poem: "Down the small and crooked road."
McHugh, H.   Or Else.
Scenes from a Death.
Stairwell.
Take Care.
Unspeakable.
Meleager.   Upon a Maid That Died [*or* Dyed]
     the Day She Was Married [*or* Marryed].
Melo Neto.   Cemetery in Pernambuco: Our Lady
     of Light.
Melville, H.   Ball's Bluff.
Haglets, The.
Monody.
On the Grave.
On the Home Guards.
On the Slain Collegians.
Meredith, G.   Angela Burdett-Coutts.
Ballad of Past Meridian, A.
C B M.
Cassandra.
Dirge: "He has hid his face, and he's gone!"
Dirge in Woods.
Emperor Frederick of Our Time, The.
Epitaph on the Tombstone of James Christopher
     Wilson.
Force and His Master.
Gentleness of Death, The.
Gordon of Khartoum.
Hawarden.
Hear now the mission of good wine.
Hueless Love, The.
J. C. M.
Lady C. M, The.
Love.
Love they alone the joyful heart.
M. M.
Margaret's Bridal-Eve.
On Hearing the News from Venice.
Requiem: "Where faces are hueless, where
     eyelids are dewless."
State of Age, The.
To a Friend Lost.
Vittoria Concluding the Opera of "Camilla."
Year's Sheddings, The.
Meredith, W.   Dying Away.
English Accounts.
February 14.
For His Father.
Give and Take.
In Memory of Donald A. Stauffer.
Metaphysical Sonnet, A.
Revenant, The.
Wreck of the Thresher, The (Lost at Sea, April
     10, 1963).
Merrill, J.   Annie Hill's Grave.
Broken Home, The.
Country of a Thousand Years of Peace, The.
Flèche d'Or.
Friend of the Fourth Decade, The.
Hotel de l'Univers et Portugal.
Salome.
Smile, The.
Yánnina.
Merton.   Death.

Dirge: "Some one who hears the bugle neigh will know."
Elegy for Ernest Hemingway, An.
Elegy for Five Old Ladies, An.
Elegy for James Thurber.
Great Men of Former Times, The.
Guns of Fort Knox, The.
Lament for Javier Heraud.
Litany: "Sing miserere / For the men who must die."
Moslems' Angel of Death, The.
Mysterious Song in the Spring of the Year, A.
Picture of a Black Child with a White Doll.
Poem: 1939.
Pride of the Dead, The.
Prologo.
Responsory, 1948, A.
Rilke's Epitaph.
Songs.
Sponge Full of Vinegar, The.
Two British Airmen.
Merwin. For the Anniversary of My Death.
Glimpse of the Ice.
Hydra, The.
James.
Looking East at Night.
Next, The.
Scale in May, A.
Son.
Strawberries.
Unfinished Book of Kings.
Waving of a Hand, The.
Michelangelo Buonarroti. All there's to say of him, no way of saying.
Although my heart had often been aflame.
Assured of death, of its timing, though, not so.
Born, died. Now bedded by the churchyard wall.
Bracci born, A. From birth, born wailing, I'd.
Bracci once, A. The soul in me withdrew.
Braccio retrieves from earth the mortal scrim.
Cecchino here has laid his body low.
Closed now his shining eyes, that dazzled so.
Cold stone, none knows but you, my gaol forever.
Day and the Night speak, and what they say is, The.
Death didn't wish to lay Cecchino low.
From clutch of clock and calendar now fled.
From where you triumphed in me, Love, right here.
Gone under now, the sun you loved to greet.
Her beauty's alive in heaven! I believe her.
Here I'm thought dead. Alive, I comforted.
If Braccio's beauty, phoenix-like, could be.
If his bright eyes are closed and laid to rest.
If it could be, to revive my life once more.
If nature now deferred to death, dejected.
If, to rejoice, you crave our tears and woe.
If true (and it is) that with body's final breath.
If two hours' dying steals a hundred years.
I'm dearer dead than ever I was, before.
I'm death's forever, who, that one forlorn.
Inside, his soul could not be outside too.
Mere mortal once. Divine, though, born to be.
My name meant "Arms." But little help to me.
No doubt much peril lies.
No way he who undid me can restore.
Not death so much, but its terror rescues me.
One of the Bracci, I. Now, as you see.
So tell me, Death, why not possess some face.
Soul lives on, I know it, lying here, The.
Souls rise alive from the body's sad last bed.
Such brightness, under earth now, put to shame.
Sun of Braccio's under earth, The. The sun.
Sweet, sweet, is sleep,—Ah! sweeter, to be stone.
Well-nigh the voyage now is overpast.
When the occasioner of my many a sigh.
Whenever remembrance of the one I love.
Millay, E. And you as well must die, belovèd dust.
Buck in the Snow, The.
Childhood Is the Kingdom Where Nobody Dies.
Conscientious Objector.
Elegy before Death.
Epitaph: "Grieve not for happy Claudius, he is dead."
I Dreamed I Moved among the Elysian Fields.
If I die solvent—die, that is to say.
Keen.
Lines for a Grave-Stone.
Moriturus.
Passer Mortuus Est.
Shroud, The.
To S. V. B.—June 15, 1940.
Valentine.
Wine from These Grapes.
Milosz, C. Anka.
Beinecke Library.
Caffé Greco.
Campo dei Fiori.
Dedication: "You whom I could not save."
Elegy for Y. Z.
Fall, The.
Flight.
Gathering Apricots.
Hall, A.
Magic Mountain, A.
Mister Hanusevich.
On Poetry, upon the Occasion of Many Telephone Calls after Zbigniew Herbert's Death.
On the Death of a Poet.
Polka-dot Dress, A.
With Her.
You Whose Name.
Milton. Another on the Same.
Damon's Epitaph.
Epitaph on the Marchioness of Winchester, An.
Hobsons Epitaph.
Lycidas.
On His Deceased Wife.
On Shakespear[e].
On the Death of the Vice-Chancellor, a Physician.
On the Same ["Thus did you strive to vouchsafe James to Heaven"].
On the University Carrier Who Sick'n'd [or Sickened] in the Time of His Vacancy.
On Time.
Sonnet: On the Religious Memorie of Mrs. Catherine Thomason.
Mistral, G. Bones of the Dead, The.
Foreign Woman, The.
My Mother.
Song of the Dead Girls.
Sonnets of Death 5.
What Do You Feel Underground?
Montale. Dead, The.
From a Tower.
Shore of Versilia.
Visit to Fadin.
Moore, M. Grave, A.
What Are Years?
Muldoon, P. Fox, The.
Now, Now.
Soap-Pig, The.
Nash, O. Crossing the Border.
Old Men.
People.
Tweedledee and Tweedledoom.
Nemerov. According to His Seasons.
Anniversary.
August, 1945.
Baron Baedeker Blew His Nose and, Sighing, Departed, The.
Between the Window and the Screen.
Elegy for a Nature Poet.
Epitaph: "Crazy, girls, crazy. Don is gone."
For W———, Who Commanded Well.
Grace to Be Said at the Supermarket.
In the Glass of Fashion.
On Reading "The Love and Death of Cornet Christopher Rilke."
One Moment in Eternity.
Photograph of a Girl, The.
Place of Value, The.
Sestina 1: "Thickness of paint or flesh cannot deface."
Situation Does Not Change, The.
Small Moment.
Speculation.
Student Dies in 100 Yard Dash.
To a Friend.
To the Memory of John Wheelright.
Under the Bell Jar.
Virgin and Martyr.
Who Did Not Die in Vain.
Neruda. Bell-Ringer, The.
Coming Back.
Different Ship, A.
Final.
Heights of Macchu Picchu, III, The.
Herbalist's Rose, The.
Initial.
Midday Construction.
Oliverio Girondo.
Search.
Sick Man in the Sun.
Today How Many Hours.
Untenable Situation, An.
Niedecker. Along the river / wild sunflowers.
Dead / she now lay deaf to death.
Old Mother turns blue and from us.
O'Hara, F. Alma.
Ashes on a Saturday Afternoon.
Day Lady Died, The.
Hatred.
Hôtel Transylvanie.
Poem: "And tomorrow morning at 8 o'clock in Springfield, Massachusetts."
"Unfinished," The.
Oliver, M. Black Snake, The.
Ghosts.
Marengo.
Rain.
Visitor, A.
When Death Comes.
White Flowers.
White Owl Flies Into and Out of the Field.
Olson, C. Abt the dead he sd.
Anubis will stare.
As snow lies on the hill love's blackness lies.
As the Dead Prey upon Us.
At Yorktown.
Birth's Obituary.
Burial Ground.
Conqueror.
Death of Europe, The.
Diaries of Death.
He / in the dark stall, no day now for him, to paw.
Just Inside the Vigil of Christmas.
La Chute.
La Chute II.
La Préface.
Marry the Marrow.
Newly Discovered "Homeric" Hymn, A.
Part of the Series on the Paths, A.
Sans Name.
Story of an Olson, and Bad Thing, The.
Tanto e Amara.
There Was a Youth Whose Name Was Thomas Granger.
Thing Was Moving, The.
Town, The.
Variations Done for Gerald Van De Wiele.
Oppen. Survival: Infantry.
Orr, G. City of Salt, The.
Driving Home after a Funeral.
Everything.
Gathering the Bones Together.
Gray Fox, The.
Origin of the Marble Forest.
Song of the Invisible Corpse in the Field.
Spring Floods.
To My Father, Dying.
Owen, W. Asleep.
End, The.
Futility.
Last Laugh, The.
Miners.
Next War, The.
Strange Meeting.
To My Friend (With an Identity Disc).
Unreturning, The.
Pagis. Autobiography.
Draft of a Reparations Agreement.

Fragments of an Elegy.
How To.
Ready for Parting.
Twenty Years in the Valley.
Paley, G. Drowning (I).
For George (I).
For George (II).
For Jan.
For Mike and Jeannie: Resisters Fifteen Years Later.
I See My Friend Everywhere.
Sometimes.
Palmer, M. Notes for Echo Lake 3.
Said the Speaker.
Parker, D. Braggart.
Condolence.
Epitaph: "First time I died, I walked my ways, The."
Epitaph for a Darling Lady.
Garden-Spot.
Homebody, The.
Liebestod.
My Own.
Rainy Night.
Requiescat.
Résumé.
Testament.
Thought for a Sunshiny Morning.
Threat to a Fickle Lady.
Tombstones in the Starlight.
Trifler, The.
White Lady, The.
Willow, The.
Parra, N. What the Deceased Had to Say about Himself.
Pasolini. Ashes of Gramsci, The.
Desperate Vitality, A.
Pasternak, B. Death of a Voice.
Patchen. Ah, God, dear Brother, the mild and frowning rose.
All That Night Lights Were Seen Moving in Every Direction.
All the Bright Foam of Talk.
And a Man Went Out Alone.
At Grandmother's Wake.
Battle of Unameit, The.
Body Beside the Ties, The.
Breathe on the living.
Creation.
Crossing on Staten Island Ferry.
Death Will Amuse Them.
Deathsong for a Maiden.
Destruction of Carthage, The.
Devotion, A.
Do the Dead Know What Time It Is?
Early in the Morning.
Encounter at Nightfall.
Everlasting Contenders, The.
Examination into Life and Death, An.
Executions in Moscow, The.
Fox, The.
From My High Love.
Have You Killed Your Man for Today?
Hold thy tongue, death!
House, and a Dead Man In It.
I Feel Drunk All the Time.
I Have No Place to Take Thee.
In a Crumbling.
In Memory of Kathleen.
In shadings of an obscure punishment.
In the Courtyard of Secret Life.
Irkalla's White Caves.
It Is for Us the Living.
Lament for the Makers of Songs.
Last Full Measure of Devotion, The.
Lasting Seasons, The.
Lowellville Cemetery: Twilight.
Matchstick-Viewed-without-Regard-to-Its-Outer-Surface, A.
Now If You.
O All Down within the Pretty Meadow.
O Everliving Queen!
O Howling Cells.
O terrible is the highest thing.
Old Man.
Oldest Conversation, The.

Pathway, The.
Permanent Migrations, The.
Portrait on an American Theme.
Prayer Not To Go to Paradise with the Asses.
Radiance in a Dark Wood, The.
Religion Is That I Love You.
So It Ends.
There Is One Who Watches.
These are my great ones.
These Have Gone with Silent Hands, Seeking.
These Unreturning Destinies.
This Early Day.
Those Upon Whom God Has Labored.
To the Tune of an Ancient Song.
Tomorrow.
Unreturning Hosts, The.
We Hold These Truths to Be Self-Evident.
We Leave You Pleasure.
White lions are roaring on the water.
You May All Go Home Now.
Petrarch. Alas her sweet expression, pleasure-filled.
Alas, the last of days when I was glad.
Already you have done, remorseless Death.
Breath, the fragrance, and the cooling shade, The.
By then I knew my flourishing green age.
Could a more dreadful vision ever be?
Death has no power to make that sweet face bitter.
Every day seems to me a thousand years.
How much I envy you, gluttonous ground.
I feel the ancient breeze, see with delight.
I go on listening, but I cannot hear.
I have been nowhere else where I could see.
I raised myself in thought to where I found.
I seem to hear that messenger once more.
If I could hope by dying to be rid.
If you want me again under your yoke.
In her, two enemies were brought together.
It was my love and grief which drove my tongue.
Kindly fortune that made me once so happy.
L'aura, my breeze, so often breathes upon.
Love had revealed to me a tranquil harbour.
Love, Nature, and this lovely gentle soul.
My days have gone by swifter than a deer.
My soul, prophetic of your coming loss.
My thoughts talked with each other pleasantly.
One day when I was looking from my window.
She comes to mind—no, is already there.
That which in colour and in scent outdid.
That window has my everlasting hate.
This short-lived and this fragile happiness.
Thought is rapid, and so short the time, The.
Time had come for me to establish peace, The.
What pitying messenger, what angel was.
When hope was flourishing.
When I look back and see how the swift years.
When little birds complaining, or green leaves.
When she arrives where greatest beauty is.
When the first tree was level with the ground.
While my poor heart was being eaten still.
Yearning yet chaste eyes she held upon, The.
You've made the loveliest face, O Death, turn pale.
Piercy. Barbie Doll.
Hallow Eve with Spaces for Ghosts.
Landed Fish.
Long Death, The.
Married Walk in a Hot Place, A.
On Castle Hill.
Proposal for Recycling Wastes, A.
S. Dead.
What You Waited For.
Pinkerton, H. Original Sin.
Pinsky. At Pleasure Bay.
Dying.
Ice-Storm, The.
Impossible to Tell.
Memorial.
Plath. All the Dead Dears.
April 18.
Bee Meeting, The.
Berck-Plage.
Birthday Present, A.

Daddy.
Dead, The.
Death and Co.
Detective, The.
Dirge for a Joker.
Edge.
Electra on Azalea Path.
Epitaph in Three Parts.
Getting There.
Lady Lazarus.
Lament: "Sting of bees took away my father, The."
Last Words.
Point Shirley.
Stings.
Totem.
Poe. Annabel Lee.
City in the Sea, The.
Conqueror Worm, The.
For Annie.
Lenore.
Raven, The.
Sleeper, The.
Spirits of the Dead.
To My Mother.
To One in Paradise.
Ulalume [or Ulalume—a Ballad].
Pope, A. Epitaph for One Who Would Not Be Buried in Westminster Abbey.
Epitaph Intended for Mr. Rowe, in Westminster Abbey.
Epitaph (of By-Words).
Epitaph on Charles Earl of Dorset.
Epitaph on Dr. Francis Atterbury, Bishop of Rochester.
Epitaph on Edmund Duke of Buckingham.
Epitaph on General Henry Withers.
Epitaph on James Craggs, Esq.
Epitaph on John Knight.
Epitaph on Mr. Elijah Fenton.
Epitaph on Mrs. Corbet, Who Died of a Cancer in Her Breast.
Epitaph on Sir Godfrey Kneller.
Epitaph on Sir William Trumbal.
Epitaph on the Hon. Simon Harcourt.
Epitaph on the Monument of the Honourable Robert Digby, and of his Sister Mary.
Epitaph: "Well then, poor G——— lies under ground!"
Ode: The Dying Christian to His Soul.
On Mr. Gay, in Westminster Abbey, 1732.
Pound, E. And Thus in Nineveh.
Coda: "O My songs."
For E. McC ("Gone while your tastes were keen to you").
Sandalphon.
Threnos.
Tomb at [or of] Akr Çaar, The.
Villonaud for This Yule.
Propertius. When Thou Must Home.
Prunty. Two Kinds of Cause.
Pugliesi. Canzone: Of his Dead Lady.
Raine, K. After Fifty-five Years.
Ah, many, many are the dead.
All that is: / The unbroken surface of the sea.
And that was all his life.
Crossing the sound I summoned you in thought.
Dead, The.
Dear ones in the house of the dead.
Descent Into Hades.
Dream.
Eider afloat in the bay.
From vague regions of sleep I come again.
If, into this evening as the grass receives the dew.
If you have ceased.
Journey, The.
Kore.
Last night I seemed in your embrace.
These watery diamond spheres.
Two Invocations of Death.
With a Wave of Her Old Hand.
Ralegh, S. Authours Epitaph, Made by Himself, The.
Epitaph on Sir Philip Sidney.
On the Snuff of a Candle.

Passionate Man[']s Pilgrimage, The.
Sir Walter Ra[u]le[i]gh to His Son[ne].
Ramanujan. Birthdays.
  Breaded Fish.
  Death and the Good Citizen.
  Death in Search of a Comfortable Metaphor.
  Hindu to His Body, A.
  History.
  Some People.
Ransom, J. Piazza Piece.
Rexroth, K. Andrée Rexroth ("Now once more
  gray mottled buckeye branches").
  Delia Rexroth ("California rolls into").
  Growing.
  Martial—12, 52.
  Neoclassicist, A.
  Our Home Is in the Rocks.
Rich, A. At a Deathbed in the Year Two
  Thousand.
  Corpse-Plant, The.
  Final Notations.
  For the Dead.
  From a Survivor.
  I Dream I'm the Death of Orpheus.
  Moth Hour.
  Mourning Picture.
  Paula Becker to Clara Westhoff.
  Phantasia for Elvira Shatayev.
  Readings of History.
  Stelae, The.
  Tattered Kaddish.
  To Frantz Fanon.
  Why Else but to Forestall This Hour.
  Woman Dead in Her Forties, A.
  Woman Mourned by Daughters, A.
Riley, J. At His Wintry Tent.
  Away.
  Bryant.
  Claude Matthews.
  Dead Lover, The.
  Dead, My Lords.
  Dead Selves.
  Death.
  Death Is Dead.
  Edgar Wilson Nye.
  Eugene Field.
  Harlie.
  Henry W. Grady.
  Her Smile of Cheer and Voice of Song.
  Idiot, An.
  John Walsh.
  Josh Billings.
  Lee O. Harris.
  Lewis D. Hayes.
  Mother Sainted, The.
  Old Chums.
  Onward Trail, The.
  Out of Reach.
  Over the Eyes of Gladness.
  Rest, The.
  Rival, The.
  Silent Singer, The.
  This Dear Child-Hearted Woman That Is Dead.
  Three Dead Friends.
  To Benj. S. Parker.
  To Elizabeth.
Rilke. Bella.
  But It Is Purer to Die.
  Dead, The.
  Double in the Mirror, The.
  Few Easter Eggs, A.
  Graves.
  Heavy Dead, The.
  No One Speaks of Them.
  Ossuary.
  Summer Day.
Rimbaud, A. Sisters of Charity.
Ritsos. Accented Colors.
  After Death.
  Afternoon.
  Almost Complete.
  Beauty.
  Biased Man, The.
  Condensation.
  Country Woman.
  Dangers.

Forged Passport.
Indiscriminately.
Morning in Salerno 4.
Only.
Ready Man, The.
Secret Pain of the Decor, The.
Without a Mirror Now.
Robinson, E. Amaryllis.
  Chorus of Old Men in "Ægeus", The.
  Cortège.
  Exit.
  For a Dead Lady.
  Fragment: "Faint white pillars that seem to
    fade."
  Inferential.
  Lisette and Eileen.
  Luke Havergal.
  Many Are Called.
  Old Story, An.
  Recalled.
  Whip, The.
Roethke. Death Piece.
  Dying Man, The.
  Elegy for Jane.
  Elegy: "Her face like a rain-beaten stone on the
    day she rolled off."
  Frau Bauman, Frau Schmidt, and Frau
    Schwartze.
  Judge Not.
  No Bird.
  Plaint.
  Sale.
  Slug.
  Tranced, The.
  Unfold! Unfold!
Rossetti, C. After Death.
  Afterward He Repented, and Went.
  All Flesh Is Grass.
  All heaven is blazing yet / With the meridian
    sun.
  All Saints.
  Alleluia! or Alas! my heart is crying.
  Amen.
  Answer, An.
  Are They Not All Ministering Spirits?
  As dying, and behold we live!
  As Thy Days, So Shall Thy Strength Be.
  At Home.
  Autumn.
  Awake, Thou That Sleepest.
  Ballad: "Soft white lamb in the daisy meadow."
  Before the Beginning.
  Behold a Shaking.
  Beloved, yeild thy time to God, for He / Will
    make eternity thy recompense.
  Better So.
  Bird's-Eye View, A.
  Bourne, The.
  Burial Anthem.
  Buried.
  Bury Hope out of sight, / No book for it and no
    bell.
  But Thy Commandment Is Exceeding Broad.
  Can I know it?—Nay.— / Shall I know it?—
    Yea.
  Cardinal Newman.
  Charon.
  Chill blank world. Yet over the utmost sea, A.
  Chilly Night, A.
  Chruchyard Song of Patient Hope, A.
  Convent Threshold, The.
  Counsel, A.
  Day and night the Accuser makes no pause.
  Days of Vanity.
  Dead before Death.
  Dead Bride, The.
  Dead City, The.
  Death.
  Death Is Swallowed Up in Victory.
  Death-Watches.
  Death's Chill Between.
  Despair.
  Dirge, A.
  Doeth Well...Doeth Better.
  Dream Land.
  Dying Man to His Betrothed, The.

Easter Monday.
Easter Tuesday.
Eleventh Hour, The.
Ellen Middleton.
End, An.
End Is Not Yet, The.
Eve.
Everything that is born must die.
Faint, Yet Pursuing.
Fair World Tho' a Fallen, A.
Floral Teaching.
Flowers Appear on the Earth, The.
For Advent.
For All.
For Each.
For Rosaline's Album.
From the Antique.
General Assembly and Church of the Firstborn,
  The.
Goal in sight! Look up and sing, / Set faces full
  against the light, The.
Golden Silences.
Gone Before.
Gone to his rest / Bright little Bouby!
Guesses.
Half Dead.
He Shall Go No More Out.
Heart Knoweth Its Own Bitterness, The.
Heaven's chimes are slow, but sure to strike at
  last.
Heaviness May Endure for a Night, But Joy
  Cometh in the Morning.
Henry Hardiman.
Husband and Wife.
I Have a Message unto Thee.
I have but one rose in the world.
I lift mine eyes to see: earth vanisheth.
I love you and you know it—this at least.
I See That All Things Come to an End.
If not with hope of life, / Begin with fear of
  death.
If thou be dead, forgive and thou shalt live.
"Immurata" Sister, An.
In a Certain Place.
In resurrection is it awfuller.
Iniquity of the Fathers upon the Children, The.
Isidora.
It is not death, O Christ, to die for Thee: / Nor
  is that silence of a silent land.
Judge Nothing before the Time.
Lady Isabella.
Last Answer, The.
Last *Complaint*, The.
Last Look, The.
Last Words of St. Telemachus, The.
Laughing Life cries at the feast.
Lent.
Let Them Rejoice in Their Beds.
Life and Death.
Life Hidden.
Life Out of Death.
Long Looked For.
Looking back along life's trodden way.
Looking Forward.
Lord, make me one with Thine own faithful
  ones.
Lord, make us all love all: that when we meet /
  Even myriads of earth's myriads at Thy Bar.
Lord Thomas and Fair Margaret.
Love and Death.
Love hath a name of Death.
Love Is Strong as Death.
Love Is Stronger than Death.
Martyr, A.
May.
Mirrors of Life and Death.
Mother Country.
My Friend.
My Old Friends.
Next of Kin.
Night and Death.
None With Him.
Now They Desire.
O Death Where Is Thy Sting?
O Lucifer, Son of the Morning!
Of My Life.

On the Death of a Cat.
One Day.
One of the Dead.
One Sea-Side Grave.
One woe is past. Come what come will.
Only Believe.
Our Church Palms are Budding Willow Twigs.
Our heaven must be within ourselves / Our home and heaven the work of faith.
Our Mothers, lovely women pitiful; / Our sisters, gracious in their life and death.
Parting after parting, / Sore loss and gnawing pain.
Passing and Glassing.
Pause, A.
Peal of Bells, A.
Peter Grump.
Pitia a Damone.
Plague, The.
Poor Ghost, The.
Portrait, A.
Prince's Progress, The.
Remember [Me].
Repining.
Rest.
Resurrection Eve.
Rosalind.
Ruined Cross, The
Safe where I cannot lie yet, / Safe where I hope to lie too.
Sappho.
Scarce tolerable life, which all life long.
Septuagesima.
Shall I Forget?
Sir Eustace Grey.
Slain in their high places: fallen on rest.
Sleep at Sea.
Sleeping at Last.
Son, Remember.
Song: "Oh roses for the flush of youth."
Songs in a Cornfield.
Summer Is Ended, The.
Sweet Death.
Take Care Of Him.
Then They That Feared the Lord Spake Often One to Another.
Then Whose Shall Those Things Be?
There Remaineth Therefore a Rest.
There Remaineth Therefore a Rest for the People of God.
There Remaineth Therefore a Rest to the People of God.
They lie at rest, our blessed dead.
Three Moments.
Three Nuns.
Thy Servant Will Go and Fight with This Philistine.
Toll, bell, toll. For hope is flying / Sighing from the earthbound soul.
Triad, A.
Two Thoughts of Death.
Under Willows.
Uphill.
Watchers, The.
We are of those who tremble at Thy word.
Wednesday in Holy Week.
What Good Shall My Life Do Me?
What to Do?
When My Heart Is Vexed I Will Complain.
When wickedness is broken as a tree / Paradise comes to light, ah holy land!
Where never tempest heaveth, / Nor sorrow grieveth.
Where Their Worm Dieth Not, and the Fire Is Not Quenched.
Whither the Tribes Go Up, Even the Tribes of the Lord.
Who cares for earthly bread tho' white?
Who shall my wandering thoughts steady & fix.
Who would wish back the Saints upon our rough.
Why?
Ye Have Forgotten the Exhortation.
Year Afterwards, A.
You who looked on passed ages as a glass.
Young Death.

Young Men Aye Were Fickle Found Since Summer Trees Were Leafy.
Zara.
Rossetti, D.   Ardour and Memory.
Autumn Idleness.
Barren Spring.
Beauty's Pageant.
Birth-Bond, The.
Blessed Damozel, The.
Body's Beauty.
Bridal Birth.
Broken Music.
Choice, The ("Eat thou and drink; to-morrow thou shalt die").
Choice, The ("Think thou and act; to-morrow thou shalt die").
Choice, The ("Watch thou and fear; to-morrow thou shalt die").
Cloud and Wind.
Dark Day, A.
Dark Glass, The.
Day of Love, A.
Death-in-Love.
Death's Songsters.
Equal Troth.
Farewell to the Glen.
From Dawn to Noon.
Genius in Beauty.
Gracious Moonlight.
He and I.
Heart of the Night, The.
Heart's Compass.
Heart's Haven.
Heart's Hope.
Her Gifts.
Hero's Lamp.
Hill Summit, The.
Hoarded Joy.
Hope Overtaken.
Inclusiveness.
Kiss, The.
Known in Vain.
Lamp's Shrine, The.
Landmark, The.
Last Fire.
Life-in-Love.
Life the Beloved.
Lost Days.
Lost on Both Sides.
Love and Hope.
Love Enthroned.
Love-Letter, The.
Love-Moon, The.
Love-Sweetness.
Lovers' Walk, The.
Love's Baubles.
Love's Fatality.
Love's Last Gift.
Love's Lovers.
Love's Testament.
Lovesight.
Memorial Thresholds.
Michelangelo's Kiss.
Mid-Rapture.
Monochord, The.
Moonstar, The.
Morrow's Message, The.
My Sister's Sleep.
Newborn Death ("And thou, O Life, the lady of all bliss").
Newborn Death ("To-day Death seems to me an infant child").
Nuptial Sleep.
Old and New Art (Not as These).
Old and New Art (St Luke the Painter).
Old and New Art (The Husbandmen).
One Hope, The.
Orchard-Pit, The.
Parted Love.
Passion and Worship.
Portrait, The.
Pride of Youth.
Retro me, Sathana!
Secret Parting.
Severed Selves.
Silent Noon.

Sleepless Dreams.
Song-Throe, The.
Sonnet, A: "Sonnet is a moment's monument, A."
Soul-Light.
Soul's Beauty.
Soul's Sphere, The.
Stillborn Love.
Sun's Shame, The ("As some true chief of men, bowed down with stress").
Sun's Shame, The ("Beholding youth and hope in mockery caught").
Superscription, A.
Supreme Surrender.
Through Death to Love.
Transfigured Life.
Trees of the Garden, The.
True Woman (Her Heaven).
True Woman (Her Love).
True Woman (Herself).
Vain Virtues.
Vase of Life, The.
Venus Victrix.
Willowwood ("And now Love sang: but his was such a song").
Willowwood ("I sat with Love upon a woodside well").
Willowwood ("O ye, all ye that walk in Willowwood").
Willowwood ("So sang he: and as meeting rose and rose").
Winged Hours.
Without Her.
Youth's Antiphony.
Youth's Spring-Tribute.
Rukeyser, M.   Arthur Peyton.
Book of the Dead, The.
Course.
Delta Poems.
Doctors, The.
Dreaming we were awake, we heard the rivers.
Driveway.
For Memory.
Gibbs.
In the Night the Sound Woke Us.
Iris.
Madboy's Song.
Mary Sleeth.
Mearl Blankenship.
Mother Garden's Round.
On the Death of Her Mother.
Outer Banks, The.
Power.
Power of Suicide, The.
Sea Mercy.
Shooting Gallery.
Slow Death of the Dragon.
Sun on the faces. On the knotted rocks.
Then.
What They Said.
Rumi.   Dying, Laughing.
Sanai.
Unmarked Boxes.
Sandburg, C.   Acquaintance with Death, Sir.
And So Today.
Anecdote of Hemlock for Two Athenians.
Anna Imroth.
Black Horizons.
Bones.
Books Men Die For.
Brancusi.
Chamfort.
Cool Tombs.
Death Snips Proud Men.
Drumnotes.
Dunes.
Dusty Doors.
Electric Sign Goes Dark, An.
Fence, A.
Finish.
Fog Numbers.
Four Brothers, The.
Grass.
Graves.
Grieg Being Dead.
Guaranteed Antique.

Have Me.
Haze.
Illinois Farmer.
In a Breath.
Instructions.
Iron.
Jaws.
Junk Man, The.
Killers.
Lavender Lilies.
Liars, The.
Losers.
Losses.
Man, the Man-Hunter.
Man with the Broken Fingers, The.
Memoir of a Proud Boy.
Million Young Workmen, 1915, A.
Mist Forms.
Mummy.
Murmurings in a Field Hospital.
Never Born.
Now They Bury Her Again.
Old Osawatomie.
Pals.
Places.
Ready to Kill.
Repetitions.
Right to Grief, The.
Sandhill People.
Slabs of the Sunburnt West.
Smoke.
Southern Pacific.
Swirl.
Testament.
Themes in Contrast.
Throw Roses.
To a Dead Man.
To Certain Journeymen.
Troths.
Under the Harvest Moon.
Waiting for the Chariot.
When Death Came April Twelve 1945.
Woman with a Past.
Yes, the Dead Speak to Us.
Sarton, M. All Souls.
Burial.
Celebration for George Sarton, A.
Death and the Lovers.
Letter from Chicago.
Moth in the Schoolroom.
My Father's Death.
Of Grief.
Schuyler, J. "From the next."
Grave, A.
Heather and Calendulas.
Mike.
Scott, S. Palmer, The.
Seifert. At one of his readings a long time ago.
Cry of the Spectres, The.
Dead of Lidice, The.
If one could tell one's heart.
Lunar Ironmongery.
Mistress of Poets, The.
Moscow.
Nocturnal Divertimento.
November 1918.
November Rain.
Salute to the Madrid Barricades.
Song of the Nightingale, The.
Song of the Sweepings.
Struggle with the Angel.
Umbrella from Piccadilly, An.
Wax Candle, The.
Sexton. All My Pretty Ones.
Assassin, The.
Clothes.
Curse against Elegies, A.
Death Baby, The.
Death King, The.
Elizabeth Gone.
For Johnny Pole on the Forgotten Beach.
For Mr. Death Who Stands with His Door Open.
Godfather Death.
Hex, The.
Hurry Up Please It's Time.
I called him *Comfort*.

I'm dreaming the My Lai soldier again.
It's music you've never heard.
Jesus Dies.
KE 6-8018.
Lament: "Someone is dead."
Leaves That Talk.
Letters to Dr. Y.
Live.
Making a Living.
May 30th.
Moss of His Skin, The.
Oh.
Sea Corpse, The.
Somewhere in Africa.
Starry Night, The.
Sweeney.
Taker, The.
Truth the Dead Know, The.
Waiting Head, The.
Wanting to Die.
What has it come to, Dr. Y.
Shapiro, K. Auto Wreck.
Cut Flower, A.
Hospital.
Interlude, The.
My Grandmother.
Necropolis.
Scyros.
Vietnam Memorial.
Shelley, P. Adonais; An Elegy on the Death of
John Keats.
Daemon of the World, The; A Fragment.
Death.
Death knell is ringing, The.
Dialogue, A.
Fragment: Death in Life.
Fragment: Life Rounded with Sleep.
Fragment: Omens.
Lament, A: "O world! O life! O time!"
Mask [*or* Masque] of Anarchy, The.
On a Faded Violet.
On Death.
see also Scene from "Tasso."
Sonnet: "Ye hasten to the grave! What seek ye
there."
Summer Evening Churchyard, A.
To Death.
To Night.
Sheridan, T. Elegy on the Much Lamented
Death of Mr. Demar.
Sidney, S. Leave Me O Love.
Oft Have I Mused.
Simic. Closed House.
Eyes Fastened with Pins.
Marching.
Navigator.
Needle.
Soup, The.
Smart, C. Epitaph on Henry Fielding, Esq.
Smith, S. Ambassador, The.
Angel Boley.
Après la Politique, la Haine des Bourbons.
Arabella.
Ass, The.
Bereavement.
Black March.
Boat, The.
Come, Death (1).
Come, Death (2).
Company.
Crown of Bays, The.
Death-Bed of a Financier.
Death Bereaves Our Common Mother Nature
Grieves for My Dead Brother.
Death Came to Me.
Death of Mr. Mounsel.
Death of the Dog Belvoir.
Death Sentence, The.
Death's Ostracism.
Die Lorelei.
Do Take Muriel Out.
Edmonton, Thy Cemetery..
Exeat.
Farewell: "Farewell dear friends."
Flow, Flow, Flow.
From the Coptic.

Fuite d'Enfance.
God the Drinker.
Grave by a Holm-Oak.
Harold's Leap.
How Far Can You Press a Poet?
If I Lie Down.
Le Revenant.
Longing for Death because of Feebleness.
Mr. Over.
Mrs. Arbuthnot.
Mrs Simpkins.
Murder.
My Heart Goes Out.
Night-Time in the Cemetery.
Not Waving But Drowning.
Parklands, The.
Poet!
Poor Soul, Poor Girl!
Private Means Is Dead.
Progression.
Proud Death with Swelling Port.
Quand on n'a pas ce que l'on aime, il faut aimer
ce que l'on a—.
Reversionary.
River Deben, The.
Siesta.
Silence and Tears.
Study to Deserve Death.
Tender Only to One.
To a Lady in a Train.
To the Dog Belvoir.
Toll of the Roads, The.
Upon a Grave.
Venus When Young Choosing Death.
Voice from the Tomb (1).
Who Killed Lawless Lean?
Who Shot Eugenie?
Why Do I.
Zoo, The.
Snyder, G. For/From Lew.
For John Chappell.
For Lew Welch in a Snowfall.
I have lived at Cold Mountain.
Word Basket Woman.
Spender, S. Beethoven's Death Mask.
Boy, Cat, Canary.
Coward, The.
Cyril Connolly.
Elegy for Margaret.
Furies, The.
Girl Who Has Drowned Herself Speaks, A.
In Attica.
My Brother Luis.
Never Being.
Perhaps.
Spiritual Explorations.
Stopwatch and an Ordnance Map, A.
Trigorin.
Stafford, W. 108 East 19th.
At the Grave of My Brother.
Aunt Mabel.
Bess.
Circle of Breath.
Dedication, A: "We stood by the library. It was
an August night."
Fall Journey.
Ground Zero [December 1982].
In Fear and Valor.
Memorial for My Mother, A.
My Father: October 1942.
Right to Die.
Swerve, The.
Traveling Through the Dark.
Weather Report.
You Don't Know the End.
Stampa. Portrait of Her Lover.
Stevens, W. Botanist on Alp (No. 2).
Burghers of Petty Death.
Cortège for Rosenbloom.
Death of a Soldier, The.
Dutch Graves in Bucks County.
Emperor of Ice-Cream, The.
Flyer's Fall.
Metaphor as Degeneration.
Of Heaven Considered as a Tomb.
Owl in the Sarcophagus, The.

Postcard from the Volcano, A.
Somnambulisma.
Sunday Morning.
Worms at Heaven's Gate, The.
Stock, R.   Mary on the Death of Joachim.
Pantoum on Some Lines From Camões.
Stockton, A.   After a Night of Perplexing
    Dreams.
Anniversary Elegy on the Death of Mr Stockton
    the 28th of Feb 1783.
Elegy on the Death of a Young Lady, An.
Elegy on the Death of Miss Chandler, as if
    Written in Her Fathers Church Yard.
Elegy on the Death of Mrs Dickinson. The
    Event Was Communicated at the Sea Shore.
Elegy on the Death of Mrs Wilson, April the 19,
    1786, An.
Fragment on Hearing the Account of Mrs
    Ramseys Death.
Fragment on the Death of a Minester.
Impromptu Epitaph on the Grave Digger of
    Princeton—1769.
Lines on a Young Gentleman Who Died of the
    Yellow Fever.
Lines on Hearing of the Death of Doctor
    Franklin.
Lines on Seeing Mrs Elizabeth Witherspoon Put
    in the Grave.
Lines on the Death of Mrs Petit of Philadelphia.
Meditation on the 3d Verse of the 28th Chapter
    of Mathew.
On an Enclosure of Roses in Which Is the
    Grave of Miss Mary Morgan.
Short Elegy to the Memory of Her Husband, A.
Suckling, S.   Song: "I prithee spare me, gentle
    boy."
Swenson, M.   Death, Great Smoothener.
Feel Me.
I Will Lie Down.
In the Bodies of Words.
Question.
Staring at the Sea on the Day of the Death of
    Another.
Swift, J.   Death and Daphne.
Elegy on Dicky and Dolly, An.
Elegy on the Much Lamented Death of Mr.
    Demar, An.
Elegy On the Supposed Death of Mr. Partridge,
    the Almanac Maker.
In Sickness.
Paper book is sent by Boyle, A.
Quibbling Elegy on the Worshipful Judge Boat,
    A.
Satirical Elegy on the Death of a Late Famous
    General, A.
Swinburne.   After Death.
Ballad of Death, A.
Kissing Her Hair.
Les Noyades.
Lyke-Wake Song, A.
Triumph of Time, The.
Sze.   Execution of Maximilian, The.
Kayaking at Night on Tomales Bay.
Silk Road, The.
Slanting Light.
Sliding Away.
Szymborska, W.   Cat in an Empty Apartment.
Elegiac Calculation.
In Broad Daylight.
Letters of the Dead, The.
On Death, without Exaggeration.
On the Banks of the Styx.
Plotting with the Dead.
Tate, A.   Anabasis, The.
Calidus Juventa?
Cross, The.
Eager Youths to a Dead Girl.
Elegy for Eugenesis.
Emblems.
For a Dead Citizen.
Intellectual Detachment.
Light.
Non Omnis Moriar.
Nuptials.
Oath, The.
Procession.

Reflections in an Old House.
Stranger.
Tennyson, A.   Crossing the Bar.
Dead Prophet, The.
Dying Swan, The.
Far-Far-Away.
In the Garden at Swainston.
In the Valley of Cauteretz.
Lady of Shalott, The.
Morte d'Arthur.
Prefatory Poem to My Brother's Sonnets.
Spirit Haunts the Year's Last Hours, A.
St. Simeon Stylites.
Tithonus.
To J. S. [James Spedding].
Terry, L.   Bars Fight [August 28, 1746].
Thomas, D.   After the Funeral.
Among Those Killed in the Dawn Raid Was a
    Man Aged a Hundred.
And Death Shall Have No Dominion.
Conversation of Prayer, The.
Deaths and Entrances.
Do Not Go Gentle into That Good Night.
Elegy: "Too proud to die; broken and blind he
    died."
Force That Through the Green Fuse Drives the
    Flower, The.
Hand That Signed the Paper, The.
Lament; "When I was a windy boy and a bit."
Now.
Poem on His Birthday.
Then Was My Neophyte.
To-day, This Insect.
Tombstone Told When She Died, The.
Unluckily for a Death.
When, Like a Running Grave.
Thoreau.   Death cannot come too soon.
Epitaph on an Engraver.
Tomlinson, C.   After a Death.
Catacomb.
Cradock Newton: From an Epitaph.
Curtain Call.
De Sole.
Death in the Desert, A.
Death of Elizabeth Grieve, The.
For Miriam.
In Memoriam Thomas Hardy.
In Memory of George Oppen.
Mausoleum, The.
Remembering Williams.
Return, The.
To Vasko Popa In Rome.
Tree, The.
Trakl.   De Profundis.
Uhland.   Good Comrade, The.
Landlady's Daughter, The.
Ungaretti.   Meditations on Death.
Unknown.   Elegy on the Deplorable Death of
    Mr. Thomas Sheridan, An.
On a Good Man.
On Invalids.
Tom Pun-Sibi's Resurrection Disproved.
Unknown, sometimes at. to Sir Walter Ralegh.
    Songe Made by Sir Walter Rawley, A.
Vertue the Best Monument.
Updike.   Bath after Sailing.
Fall.
Millipede, The.
Perfection Wasted.
To Ed Sissman.
Vallejo.   Black Stone on Top of a White Stone.
Estais Muertos.
Eternal Dice, The.
Our Daily Bread.
Testimony.
White Rose.
Van Duyn.   Creation, The.
Reading of Rex Stout, A.
Stream, The.
Van Geel.   Sleepwalking.
Verlaine.   Asleep in the Valley.
Very.   Cup, The.
Dead Elm, The.
Dead, The.
Death.
Death Decay and Change.

Death of Man, The.
Dying Words of John Foster: "I Can Pray, and
    That's a Glorious Thing."
How Come the Dead?
Indian Remains.
Lines on Reading the Death of Rev. Henry
    Ware, Jr.
Lines To ——— On the Death of His Friend.
Oliver C. Felton, Esq., of Brookfield.
On reading the Memorial of John White
    Browne.
Our Dear Mother.
To the Memory of Alpheus Crosby.
To the Memory of the Rev. James Chisholm.
To the Memory of the Rev. James Flint, D. D.
Yourself.
Villon.   Ballade in Old French.
Ballad[e] of Dead Ladies, The.
Ballade to End With, A.
Vroman.   Our Family.
Walcott.   Landfall, Grenada.
Letter from Brooklyn, A.
Sea Canes.
Verandah.
Village Life, A.
Walker, A.   Burial.
Girl Who Died #1, The.
Girl Who Died #2, The.
Good Night, Willie Lee, I'll See You in the
    Morning.
To Die before One Wakes Must Be Glad.
Warren, R.   Admonition to the Dead.
Admonition to Those Who Mourn.
After the Dinner Party.
Apologia for Grief.
Athenian Death.
Better Than Counting Sheep.
Boy Wandering in Simms' Valley.
Calendar.
Chain Saw at Dawn in Vermont in Time of
    Drouth.
Death Mask of a Young Man.
Doubleness in Time.
Fall Comes in Back-Country Vermont.
I Am Dreaming of a White Christmas: The
    Natural History of a Vision.
Minnesota Recollection.
Mortmain.
Old Love.
Old Nigger on One-Mule Cart Encountered Late
    at Night.
Praises for Mrs. Dodd.
Reading Late at Night, Thermometer Falling.
So You Agree with What I Say? Well, What Did
    I Say?
Tale of Time.
There's a Grandfather's Clock in the Hall.
Weiss, T.   Last Letters, The.
Local Matter, A.
Whalen, P.   Walking beside the Kamogawa,
    Remembering Nansen and Fudo and Gary's
    Poem.
Wheatley, P.   On the Death of a Young
    Gentleman.
On the Death of the Rev. Mr. George Whitefield
    [1770].
To a Gentleman and Lady on the Death of the
    Lady's Brother and Sister.
To a Lady on the Death of Three Relations.
Whitman, W.   As at Thy Portals Also Death.
As I Watch'd the Ploughman Ploughing.
As If a Phantom Caress'd Me.
As They Draw to a Close.
As Toilsome I Wander'd Virginia's Woods.
Ashes of Soldiers.
Assurances.
City Dead-House, The.
Come Up from the Fields Father.
Dead Tenor, The.
Death and Burial of McDonald Clarke, a
    Parody, The.
Death of the Nature-Lover, The.
Death's Valley.
Dying Veteran, The.
End of All, The.
Gliding o'er All.

Great Are the Myths.
In Former Songs.
Joy, Shipmate, Joy!
Last Invocation, The.
My Departure.
Now Finalè to the Shore.
O Living Always, Always Dying.
Of Him I Love Day and Night.
Old Age's Ship & Crafty Death's.
Old Salt Kossabone.
On the Same Picture.
Or, from That Sea of Time.
Osceola.
Out of the Cradle Endlessly Rocking.
Outlines for a Tomb.
Pallid Wreath, The.
Pensive and Faltering.
Portals.
Sight in Camp [in the Daybreak Gray and Dim],
    A.
Sobbing of the Bells, The.
This Compost.
Thought.
Time to Come.
To One Shortly to Die.
To Think of Time.
Two Rivulets.
Vigil Strange I Kept on the Field One Night.
We All Shall Rest at Last.
Whispers of Heavenly Death.
Yet, Yet Ye Downcast Hours.
Whittier.   Andrew Rykman's Prayer.
At Last.
Autumn Thoughts.
Between the Gates.
Bolivar.
Dead Feast of the Kol-Folk, The.
Dead Ship of Harpswell, The.
Eva.
Female Martyr, The.
Friend's Burial, The.
Gone.
In Memory.
In Peace.
In Remembrance of Joseph Sturge.
Isabella of Austria.
Kinsman.
Lament, A: "Circle is broken, one seat is
    forsaken, The."
Lines on the Death of S. Oliver Torrey.
Lucy Hooper.
Marguerite.
Memorial, A.
Missionary, The.
Mulford.
Naples.
New Wife and the Old, The.
Old Burying-Ground, The.
Palatine, The.
Poet and the Children, The.
R. S. S., at Deer Island on the Merrimac.
Rantoul.
Samuel J. Tilden.
Sisters, The: A Picture by Barry, The.
Telling the Bees.
Thomas Starr King.
To the Memory of Charles B. Storrs.
To the Memory of Thomas Shipley.
William Forster.
Wilbur, R.   Another Voice.
Bell Speech.
Beowulf.
Castles and Distances.
Finished Man, A.
For Dudley.
For W. H. Auden.
In a Churchyard.
Lightness.
Lilacs, The.
Merlin Enthralled.
Mill, The.
Pardon, The.
Pity.
Puritans, The.
To an American Poet Just Dead.
To His Skeleton.

Tywater.
Up, Jack.
Voice from under the Table, A.
Year's End.
Wilde, O.   Chanson.
Requiescat.
Williams, C. K.   Becoming Somebody Else.
Clay out of Silence.
Covenant, The.
Dream, The.
Even If I Could.
Faint Praise.
Friends.
From Now On.
Giving It Up.
Hail goes / dancing, The.
Helen.
Inches.
Le Petit Salvié.
Little Shirt, The.
Long Naked Walk of the Dead, The.
They wash you / when.
This Day.
To Listen.
Villanelle of the Suicide's Mother.
Williams, M.   And Then.
Autopsy.
Closing the House.
Day in the Death, A.
Death of Chet Baker, The.
Everyone Dies in a Light Rain.
For Fred Carpenter Who Died in His Sleep.
For Victor Jara.
Ghosts.
In Nashville, Standing in the Wooden Circle
    Sawed Out from the Old Ryman Stage.
Jonathan at Last.
Last Person to Speak His Language is Dying,
    The.
Learning.
On Hearing About the Death of Mitzi Mayfair.
On the Death of a Middle-Aged Man.
On the Symbolic Consideration of Hands and
    the Significance of Death.
People.
Rituals.
She Prays for Her Husband, the Good Pastor,
    Lying on His Deathbed at Last.
Some Lines Finished Just Before Dawn at the
    Bedside of a Dying Student It has Snowed
    All Night.
Story, The.
Survivor, The.
Thanatopsis.
Things.
When I Am Dead, My Dearest.
Where to Turn When Sorrow Comes like a
    Black Bull in Your Dreams.
Widow, The.
Williams, T.   Death Is High.
Odyssey.
Problem.
Williams, W.   Complete Destruction.
Death.
Death of Franco of Cologne, The: His Prophecy
    of Beethoven.
Death the Barber.
End of the Rope, The.
Eternity, An.
Last Words of My English Grandmother, The.
Last Words of My Grandmother.
Note, A.
Observer, The.
Picture Showing.
Rapid Transit.
Smiling Dane, A.
Spring Song.
Stone Crock, The.
To a Dead Journalist.
To a Dog Injured in the Street.
To the Ghost of Marjorie Kinnan Rawlings.
Tragic Detail.
Two Pendants: For the Ears.
Widow's Lament in Springtime, The.
Wilner, E.   Elegy for a Writer.
Towers of Silence, The.

Wordsworth, W.   Address to the Scholars of the
    Village School of—1798.
Argument for Suicide.
Ballad, A: "And will you leave me thus alone."
By a Blest Husband Guided, Mary Came.
Cenotaph.
Could I the priest's consent have gained.
Dirge Sung by a Minstrel.
Elegiac Stanzas (Addressed to Sir G.H.B. upon
    the Death of His Sister-in-Law).
Elegiac Verses in Memory of My Brother, John
    Wordsworth.
Elegy Written in the Same Place upon the Same
    Occasion.
Ellen Irwin; or, The Braes of Kirtle.
Epitaph in Grasmere Church.
Epitaph in the Chapel Yard of Langdale,
    Westmoreland.
Forth from a Jutting Ridge, Around Whose
    Base.
Glen-Almain; or, the Narrow Glen.
Hour-bell sounds, and I must go, The.
Laodamia.
Lines: "Loud is the Vale! the Voice is up."
Lines Written on a Blank Leaf in a Copy of the
    Author's Poem "The Excursion."
Matthew.
Methought I saw the footsteps of a throne.
November, 1836.
On the Death of an Unfortunate Lady.
On the Death of His Majesty (George the
    Third).
Seven Sisters, or, the Solitude of Binnorie, The.
She was a Phantom of delight.
Sonnet Written by Mr — Immediately after the
    Death of His Wife.
Sonnets upon the Punishment of Death.
Surprised by joy—impatient as the Wind.
Thoughts Suggested the Day Following, on the
    Banks of Nith.
To a Sexton.
To ———: "O dearer far than light and life are
    dear."
To the Memory of Raisley Calvert.
Two April Mornings, The.
Upon Perusing the "Epistle [To Sir George
    Howland Beaumont"] Thirty Years after Its
    Composition.
Upon the Sight of the Portrait of a Female
    Friend.
Wright, C.   All Landscape Is Abstract, and
    Tends to Repeat Itself.
Appalachian Book of the Dead, The.
Appalachian Book of the Dead 2, The.
Arkansas Traveller.
Ars Poetica 2.
Called Back.
China Mail.
Early Saturday Afternoon, Early Evening.
Hawaii Dantesca.
Homage to Cesare Pavese.
Homage to Paul Cézanne.
Indian Summer 2.
Jesuit Graves.
Lives of the Artists.
Lives of the Saints.
Lost Bodies.
Maple on the Hill.
Meditation on Form and Measure.
Opus Posthumous.
Portrait of the Artist with Li Po.
Quotations.
Southern Cross, The.
Thinking about the Poet Larry Levis One
    Afternoon in Late May.
To Giacomo Leopardi in the Sky.
Wright, J.   Abstract of Knowledge, The / The
    First Test.
Alarm, The.
All the Beautiful are Blameless.
Angel, The.
Arrangements with Earth for Three Dead
    Friends.
Assignation, The.
At the Executed Murderer's Grave.
At the Slackening of the Tide.

At Thomas Hardy's Birthplace, 1953.
Before a Cashier's Window in a Department
    Store.
But Only Mine.
Centenary Note: Inscribed to Little Crow,
    Leader of the Sioux Rebellion in Minnesota,
    1862, A.
Christmas Greeting, A.
Death of an Unfamiliar Sister, The.
Devotions.
Dream of Burial, A.
Echo for the Promise of Georg Trakl's Life.
Eclogue at Nash's Grove.
Elegy for the Poet Morgan Blum, An.
Erinna to Sappho.
First Principles.
Frontier, The.
Gesture by a Lady with an Assumed Name, A.
Girl Walking into a Shadow, A.
Humming a Tune for an Old Lady in West
    Virginia.
I Am a Sioux Brave, He Said in Minneapolis.
I Was Afraid of Dying.
Idea of the Good, The.
In a Viennese Cemetery.
Inscription for the Tank.
Katy Did.
Lament for My Brother on a Hayrake.
Life, The.
Many of Our Waters: Variations on a Poem by a
    Black Child.
Message Hidden in an Empty Wine Bottle that I
    Threw into a Gully of Maple Trees One Night
    at an Indecent Hour, A.
Miners.
Minneapolis Poem, The.
Northern Pike.
Note Left in Jimmy Leonard's Shack, A.
Offense, The.
Offering for Mr. Bluehart, An.
Old Age Compensation.
Old Man Drunk.
On the Skeleton of a Hound.
Origins.
Paul.
Poem about George Doty in the Death House,
    A.
Refusal, The.
Regeneration, The.
Saint Judas.
Small Blue Heron, The.
Small Frogs Killed on the Highway.
Speak.
Three Sentences for a Dead Swan.
To a Dead Drunk.
To a Defeated Savior.
To a Friendly Dun.
To Harvey, Who Traced the Circulation.
To the Muse.
Today I Was So Happy, So I Made this Poem.
Two Poems about President Harding.
Way to Make a Living, A.
Willy Lyons.
Winter Day in Ohio, A.
Wyatt, S.   Enemy [or en'my] of life, decayer of
    all kind, The [or Th'].
In mourning wise since daily I increase.
Plain ye, mine eyes. Accompany my heart.
Stand Whoso List.
To make an end of all this strife.
Yeats.   Baile and Aillinn.
Ballad of Father O'Hart, The.
Ballad of the Foxhunter, The.
Byzantium.
Circus Animals' Desertion, The.
Cold Heaven, The.
Countess Cathleen in Paradise, The.
Crazy Jane and the Bishop.
Death.
Double Vision of Michael Robartes, The.
Dream of Death, A.
Fool by the Roadside, The.
He Thinks of His Past Greatness When a Part of
    the Constellations of Heaven.
He Wishes His Beloved Were Dead.
His Dream.

In Memory of Alfred Pollexfen.
In Tara's Halls.
Irish Airman Foresees His Death, An.
Last Confession, A.
Man and the Echo.
Man Who Dreamed of Faeryland, The.
Mountain Tomb, The.
Sailing to Byzantium.
Shepherd and Goatherd.
That the Night Come.
Three Bushes, The.
Three Things.
To a Shade.
Tom O'Roughley.
Upon a Dying Lady.
Vacillation.
Zagajewski.   Airport in Amsterdam.
Albi.
Ancient History.
Blackbird.
Generation, The.
In May.
King, A.
Life Sentence.
Light of Lamps, The.
Morning in Vicenza, A.
My Aunts.
Name Edmund, The.
New World.
Night.
Over America.
Postcards.
Seventeen.
Smoke.
To.
Twenty-Five Years.
You Are My Silent Brethren.
Zaturenska.   Death Is the Serpent.
Elegy and Nocturne for Lora Baxter.
Old Tale, An.
Séance, The.
Soul's Haven.
Twisted Tree, The.
Variation on a Polish Folk Song.
Zukofsky, L.   Air.
H.T.

See also **Mortality**

Death in Childhood
Amichai [or Amikhai].   Elegy on the Lost Child,
    The.
Angelou.   Child Dead in Old Seas.
To Beat the Child Was Bad Enough.
Atwood.   Death of a Young Son by Drowning.
Bishop, E.   First Death in Nova Scotia.
Bradstreet, A.   In Memory of My Dear
    Grandchild Anne Bradstreet.
In Memory of My Dear Grandchild Elizabeth
    Bradstreet.
On My Dear Grandchild Simon Bradstreet.
Brontë, E.   Farewell To Alexandria, A.
To the Bluebell.
Browning, E.   Child's Grave at Florence, A.
Isobel's Child.
Little Mattie.
Burns, R.   To the Memory of the Unfortunate
    Miss Burns 1791.
Carew, T.   Another [Epitaph on the Lady Mary
    Villiers].
Epitaph on the Lady Mary Villiers.
Carver, R.   Lemonade.
Cavafy.   Aristovoulos.
Ciardi, J.   Little One, The.
Clare, J.   Dying Child, The.
Clifton, L.   Sorrow Song.
Times, The.
Coleridge, S.   Epitaph on an Infant.
On an Infant Which Died before Baptism.
Corbett, W.   Alison's Letter Used as a
    Bookmark for Ungaretti's Poems.
Dickinson, E.   How the Waters closed above
    Him.
Is his sweet wife too faint to remember.
Not all die early, dying young.
Some, too fragile for winter winds.
Taken from men—this morning.
Vision of Immortal Life has been fulfilled, The.

Who "meddled" with the costly Hearts.
Donne.   Niobe.
Dubie.   Annual of the Dark Physics, An.
Blue Hog, A.
Revelation 20:11–15.
Dugan, A.   Elegy for a Gifted Child.
Dunbar, P.   Death of the First Born, The.
Eberhart, R.   Lost Children, The.
Emerson, R.   Threnody: "South-wind brings,
    The."
What from this barren being do we reap.
Frost, R.   Home Burial.
"Out, Out—."
García Lorca.   Gacela of the Dead Child.
Little Girl Drowned in the Well.
Gray, T.   Epitaph on a Child.
Hall, D.   Baseball Players, The.
Child's Garden, A.
Hardy, T.   Dead Bastard, The.
Heaney, S.   Limbo.
Mid-Term Break.
Herrick.   Epitaph upon a Child, An.
To the Lady Crew, Upon the Death of her Child.
Upon a Child. An Epitaph.
Upon a Child That Died [or Dyed].
Hughes, L.   Birmingham Sunday.
Naughty Child, The.
Ignatow, D.   Play Again.
Jackson, L.   It Has Been Read by All.
Jarrell, R.   Come to the Stone.
Lady Bates.
Lost Children, The.
Protocols.
Requiem for the Death of a Boy.
Jonson, B.   Epitaph on S. P. [or Salomon Pavy].
On My First Daughter.
On My First Son[ne].
Why I Write Not of Love.
Kinnell.   Olive Wood Fire, The.
Kipling, R.   Gift of the Sea, The.
Return of the Children, The.
Levertov.   During a Son's Dangerous Illness.
Levine, P.   Goodbye.
Lindsay, N.   In Memory of a Child.
Lorde.   Rites of Passage.
Lucianus [or Lucian].   On an Infant.
Major, C.   Honey Dripper.
Kitchen Chair Poem #4.
Waiting in the Children's Hospital.
Michelangelo Buonarroti.   Born, died. Now
    bedded by the churchyard wall.
Death shut those eyes, him too it shut below.
Death stretched an arm, stole fruit not ripened
    yet.
Earth lends us flesh, heaven lends the soul, the
    two.
Gone under now, the sun you loved to greet.
His beautiful eyes! I hardly saw them, only.
If death has buried here, hardly in leaf.
No other handsome face such power possessed.
O lucky me, to look upon me dead!
Why fallen so soon asleep? Not hard to tell.
Young Braccio's buried here. To mend a lack.
Milton.   On the Death of a Fair Infant Dying of
    a Cough.
Montale.   Summer.
Orr, G.   After the Guest.
Doll, The.
Elegy: "Here are consoling pieties."
Litany, A: "I remember him falling beside me."
Moment, A.
Pessoa.   We Took the Town After a Heavy
    Bombing.
Pope, A.   Epigram: "*Peter* complains, that God
    has given."
Prunty.   Covined Bird, The.
Falling Through the Ice.
Letter.
Ramanujan.   Minor Sacrifice, A.
Ransom, J.   Bells for John Whiteside's
    Daughter.
Dead Boy.
Riley, J.   Absence of Little Wesley, The.
Baby's Dying.
Bereaved.
Dot Leedle Boy.

Give Me the Baby.
Little Coat, The.
Little David.
Little Mandy's Christmas Tree.
Little Marjorie.
Mabel.
On the Death of Little Mahala Ashcraft.
Prior to Miss Belle's Appearance.
Sis Rapalye.
That-air Young-un.
To Leonainie.
Uncomforted.
When Bessie Died.
When Our Baby Died.
Rossetti, C. Baby lies so fast asleep.
Baby's cradle with no baby in it, A.
Death.
Death of a First-Born, A.
Is It Well with The Child?
Michael F. M. Rossetti.
Sleep, Sleep Happy Child; All Creation Slept and Smiled.
Why did baby die.
Rukeyser, M. Song for Dead Children.
Sadi [or Saadi or Sa'di]. In Senahar, my first born sleeps.
Schuyler, J. Head, A.
Stafford, W. Consolations.
Crossing Our Campground.
For a Lost Child.
Memorial: Son Bret, A.
Stillborn.
Third Street.
Tate, A. Death of Little Boys.
Thomas, D. Refusal to Mourn the Death, by Fire, of a Child in London, A.
Very. Cold cold thy lips my gentle boy.
Wheatley, P. Funeral Poem on the Death of C. E. an Infant of Twelve Months, A.
On the Death of a Young Lady of Five Years of Age.
On the Death of J. C. an Infant.
To Mr. and Mrs.—, on the Death of Their Infant Son.
Whittier. Legend of the Lake, A.
Vesta.
Wilde, O. Requiescat.
Williams, C. K. Vehicle: Absence.
Williams, M. Deadsong for a Neighbor Child Who Ran Away to the Woods.
On the Sacrifice of a Siamese Twin at Birth.
Remembering Walter.
Wordsworth, W. By a Blest Husband Guided, Mary Came.
Childless Father, The.
Epitaph: "Six months to six years added he remained."
In due observance of an ancient rite.
Lucy Gray; or, Solitude.
Maternal Grief.
Sonnet: "Why should we weep or mourn, Angelic boy."
Surprised by joy—impatient as the Wind.
We Are Seven.

Death in War
Brodsky, J. Bosnia Tune.
Carver, R. Eve of Battle, The.
In the Trenches with Robert Graves.
Thermopylae.
Cavafy. Horses of Achilles, The.
Thermopylae.
Those Who Fought for the Achaian Alliance.
Corbière. Letter from Mexico (Vera Cruz, 10 February, 186–).
HaNagid. Victory Over Seville, The.
Heaney, S. Requiem for the Croppies.
Hughes, L. Bonds: In Memoriam.
Colored Soldier, The.
Expendable.
Hero—International Brigade.
Moonlight in Valencia: Civil War.
Official Notice.
Poem to a Dead Soldier.
Tomorrow's Seed.
When the Armies Passed.
Kipling, R. Nativity, A.

Laughlin, J. Summons, The.
Levertov. Dragon of Revolutionary Love.
Talk in the Dark.
Logue, C. Song of the Dead Soldier, The.
Meredith, W. Notes for an Elegy.
Merwin. Asians Dying, The.
Sheridan.
Pessoa. We Took the Town After a Heavy Bombing.
Prunty. Child's Chistmas in Georgia, A.
Nineteenth Hole, The.
Riley, J. Silent Victors, The.
Stafford, W. At the Grave of My Brother: Bomber Pilot.
Stevens, W. Death of a Soldier, The.
Stockton, A. On Hearing that General Warren Was Killed on Bunker-Hill.
On the Death of General Montgomery.
Very. Humanity Mourning for Her Children Slain in War.
Hymn: Our Country's Dead.
Our Soldiers' Graves.
Wheatley, P. On the Death of General Wooster.
Wilde, O. Louis Napoleon.

See also **War Dead**
Death of Animals
Ai. Antihero, The.
I Have Got to Stop Loving You. So I Have Killed My Black Goat.
Ammons. Mule Song.
Armantrout. Traveling Through the Yard.
Baudelaire. Carrion, A.
Berry, W. Snake, The.
Bierce. In Memoriam.
Blue Cloud. Death Chant.
For a Dog-killed Doe.
Bly, R. Dead Seal [near McClure's Beach], The.
Dried Sturgeon, The.
Hollow Tree, A.
Browning, E. Sea-Mew, The.
Bukowski. Coupons.
Dogs.
One for the Old Boy.
Singing Is Fire.
Winter.
Burns, R. Auld Man's Mare's Dead, The.
Death and Dying Words of Poor Mailie, the Author's Only Pet Yowe, The.
Elegy on Peg Nicholson.
On the Death of Echo, a Lap-Dog.
Poor Mailie's Elegy.
What Will I Do Gin My Hoggie Die.
Carruth, H. Bears at Raspberry Time.
Cave Painting.
Essay.
Ciardi, J. Dead Pigeon on South Street.
Elegy for Jog.
Island Galaxy, An.
Small Elegy.
Corbett, W. Basil 1977-1993.
Cowper, W. Epitaph on a Hare.
Cummings, E. E. Me Up at Does.
Dickey, J. Heaven of Animals, The.
Dickinson, E. His Bill is clasped—his Eye forsook.
Dubie. Amen.
Blue Hog, A.
Danse Macabre.
Jeremiad.
Obscure, The.
Psalm 23.
Dugan, A. Dying Seagull and the Great Whore of the World, The.
Funeral Oration for a Mouse.
Plague of Dead Sharks.
What Happened? What Do You Expect?
Eberhart, R. Dead Skunk.
For a Lamb.
Ferlinghetti, L. Rough Song of Animals Dying.
Frost, R. Draft Horse, The.
García Lorca. Cow.
Gray, T. Ode on the Death of a Favourite [or Favorite] Cat, Drowned in a Tub [or Bowl] of Gold Fishes.
Hamill, S. Man in the Landscape.
Sheep to Slaughter.

Hardy, T. Last Words To a Dumb Friend.
Robin, The.
Hayden, R. Gulls.
Killing the Calves.
Plague of Starlings, A.
Herrick. Upon His Spaniel[l] Tracie [or Tracy].
Hughes, L. Dying Beast.
Hughes, T. Coming Down through Somerset.
February 17th.
Sheep.
Small Events.
Song of a Rat.
Strawberry Hill.
View of a Pig.
What is it this time the dark barn again.
Jacobsen, J. Cul de Sac.
Death and the Turtle.
Good Fortune of Pigeons, The.
On My Island.
Starfish, The.
Jarrell, R. Laboratory, The.
Jeffers, R. House Dog's Grave, The.
Hurt Hawks.
Kinnell. Hen Flower, The.
Kipling, R. Power of the Dog, The.
Kizer, C. Italian Kittens, The.
Komunyakaa. April's Anarchy.
Charmed.
Eclogue at Twilight.
Happiness.
Immolatus.
Magpies.
Kumin, M. How It Goes On.
Thinking of Death and Dogfood.
Kunitz, S. Robin Redbreast.
Wellfleet Whale, The.
Laughlin, J. Through many nights of many years invincible.
Levertov. Day Begins, A.
Lindsay, N. Dirge for a Righteous Kitten, A.
Eagle That Is Forgotten, The.
Tiger on Parade, The.
Lux. So You Put the Dog to Sleep.
Major, C. None of It Was.
Marvell. Nymph Complaining for the Death of Her Faun [or Fawn], The.
McGrath, T. Used Up.
Meredith, G. Islet the Dachs.
No boats oar slow, no barges pass.
Young Reynard.
Merwin. Ali.
Cow, The.
Death of a Favorite Bird.
Millay, E. Buck in the Snow, The.
Milosz, C. Spider.
Montale. Capercaillie, The.
Muldoon, P. Behold the Lamb.
Ned Skinner.
Panther, The.
Nash, O. For a Good Dog.
Neruda. Dead Dog.
Oliver, M. Encounter.
Ghosts.
Her Grave.
Olson, C. Round & a Canon, A.
Pagis. In the Laboratory.
Petrarch. Under the very hills where at the first.
Prunty. Coach.
Raine, K. Silver Stag, The.
Whales.
Ransom, J. Janet Waking.
Riley, J. When Old Jack Died.
Ritsos. Extinction.
Rossetti, C. Last Rites.
On the Death of a Cat.
Sandburg, C. Half Way.
Sarton, M. Lament for Toby, a French Poodle.
Shapiro, K. Impact.
Snyder, G. Dead by the Side of the Road, The.
Stafford, W. By the Deschutes Shore.
Meditation.
Traveling Through the Dark.
Stock, R. Slaughtering the Cow.
Swenson, M. On Addy Road.
Szymborska, W. Birds Returning.
Seen from Above.

Updike. Another Dog's Death.
Dog's Death.
Mouse Sex.
Warren, R. Cross, The.
Dead Horse in Field.
Going West.
Old Dog Dead.
Orphanage Boy.
Season Opens on Wild Boar in Chianti.
Sila.
Wilbur, R. Death of a Toad, The.
Pardon, The.
Williams, C. K. Shells.
Williams, M. 71 South.
Animals.
Jonathan in Mourning.
Summer Afternoon an Old Man Gives Some
    Thought to the Central Questions, A.
Williams, T. Miss Puma, Miss Who?
Wordsworth, W. Dog—An Idyllium, The.
Last of the Flock, The.
Wright, J. Brush Fire.
Small Frogs Killed on the Highway.
Sparrows in a Hillside Drift.
Zagajewski. Dead Sparrow.

Debauchery
Baudelaire. Allegory.
Sisters of Mercy.
Beckett, S. Dortmunder.
Byron, G. Damaetas.
Carver, R. Union Street: San Francisco,
    Summer 1975.
Cavafy. Days of 1901.
Tomb of Iasis, The.
Graves, R. Blue-Fly, The.
Hafiz [or Hafez]. Ghaselle.
Johnson, S. Short Song of Congratulation [or
    To a Young Heir], A.
Jonson, B. On Gut.
Keats. Give Me Women, Wine, and Snuff.
Kizer, C. Days of 1986.
Whitman, W. Hand-Mirror, A.
Wyatt, S. Courtier's Life, The.

Debt
Carver, R. Bankruptcy.
Cavafy. Days of 1908.
Ciardi, J. Man Came Tuesday, A.
Dickinson, E. I gave myself to Him—.
Where we owe so much it defies Money.
Donne. Ralphius.
Dugan, A. Not to Choose.
Dunbar, P. Debt, The.
Emerson, R. And hungry Debt beseiged my
    door.
Nature will not lose.
Frost, R. Closed for Good.
Ingenuities of Debt, The.
Graves, R. Bank Account.
Herrick. Bell-Man, The.
Long Lookt for Comes at Last.
Summe, and the Satisfaction, The.
To God.
Upon Bunce: Epigram.
Upon Paske a Draper.
Hughes, L. Madam and the Insurance Man.
Jonson, B. Epistle to a Friend.
Epistle to Mr Arthur Squib.
Kipling, R. Rowers, The.
Levi, P. Unresolved Burdens.
Lux. Deadhouse at the Workhouse, The.
Meredith, G. Sweet Justice of Norbiton,
    neighbour of Jones.
Merwin. Debt, A.
Nash, O. First Payment Deferred.
Friendly Touch, The.
Second Month It's Not Itemized, The.
Parker, D. Song of a Contented Heart.
Plath. Dispossessed, The.
Ritsos. Other Man, The.
Rumi. Debtor Sheikh, The.
Stock, R. Interpretation of High Finance.
Suckling, S. Love and Debt Alike Troublesome.
Szymborska, W. Nothing's a Gift.
Tate, A. Debt.
Whittier. Prisoner for Debt, The.
Williams, W. Detail.

Wright, J. Before a Cashier's Window in a
    Department Store.
Decadence
Cummings, E. E. Come,gaze with me upon this
    dome.
Jehovah buried,Satan dead.
Of Ever-Ever Land i speak.
Proud of his scientific attitude.
Space being(don't forget to remember)Curved.
Worshipping same / they squirm and they
    spawn.
Eliot, T. S. Burbank with a Baedeker: Bleistein
    with a Cigar.
Choruses from "The Rock."
Interlude in London.
Mr. Apollinax.
Mr. Eliot's Sunday Morning Service.
Portrait of a Lady.
Sweeney among the Nightingales.
Sweeney Erect.
Waste Land, The.
Whispers of Immortality.
Herrick. Leprosie in Houses.
Jonson, B. Ode: "If men, and times were now."
On the Magnetic Lady.
Kipling, R. City of Brass, The
Islanders, The.
Laughlin, J. Owl of Minerva, The.
Lindsay, N. Beggar Speaks, The.
Trap, The.
MacNeice. Belfast.
Goodbye to London.
Individualist Speaks, The.
Thyestes.
To Posterity.
Nemerov. Baron Baedeker Blew His Nose and,
    Sighing, Departed, The.
Olson, C. Who.
Pound, E. Portrait d'une Femme.
Rossetti, C. Babylon the Great.
P.R.B, The.
Stevens, W. Academic Discourse at Havana.
Updike. Taste.
Warren, R. Bearded Oaks.
Wilde, O. Theoretikos.
Williams, C. K. Ethics.
Wordsworth, W. Illustrated Books and
    Newspapers.
Wyatt, S. Like as the wind with raging blast.
Decalogue
Bierce. New Decalogue, The.
Mistral, G. Artist's Decalogue, The.
See also **Ten Commandments**
Decay
Atwood. Another Elegy.
Sunday Drive, A.
Auden. Dark Years, The.
Paysage Moralisé.
Baudelaire. Carrion, A.
Blue Cloud. Deeper Than a Dream.
Sandhills That None May Visit.
Browning, E. Irreparableness.
Browning, R. Protus.
Saint Martin's Summer.
Carruth, H. Speaking for Them.
Thaw.
Coleridge, S. Song: "Though veiled in spires of
    myrtle wreath."
Corbett, W. Dead of Winter.
Cullen, C. Apostrophe to the Land.
Cummings, E. E. ,Mean- / hum / a)now / (nit.
Of this wilting wall the colour drub.
Dickinson, E. Crumbling is not an instant's Act.
Eberhart, R. Groundhog, The.
Scarf of June, The.
Virgin, The.
When Golden Flies Upon My Carcass Come.
Eliot, T. S. Choruses from "The Rock."
Gerontion.
Hollow Men, The.
Waste Land, The.
Frost, R. Range-finding.
Wood-Pile, The.
Ginsberg, A. Ecologue.
Sunflower Sutra.
Hall, D. At Delphi.

Columns of the Parthenon, The.
Elegy for Wesley Wells.
"King and Queen."
Old Pilot, The.
Red Branch, The.
Village in East Anglia, A.
Han-shan. All of you are priceless gems.
Pitiful hundred-year house, A.
Hardy, T. Flower's Tragedy, The.
Jingle on the Times, A.
Herbert, G. Decay.
Herrick. All Things Decay and Die.
Putrefaction.
Upon the Roses in Julias Bosome.
Hughes, T. Heptonstall Old Church.
Jeffers, R. For Una.
Last Conservative, The.
Polar ice-caps are melting, the mountain
    glaciers, The.
Prescription of Painful Ends.
Skunks.
Kizer, C. Streets of Pearl and Gold.
Kunitz, S. Approach of Autumn.
Old Clothes Man, The.
Larkin, P. Heaviest of Flowers, the Head.
Levi, P. Laid Up.
Lindsay, N. What the Hyena Said.
McGrath, T. Need for Stoicism in the Stoa of
    Attalus, The.
Merton. Now the official nerve is analyzed.
Nash, O. Exit, Pursued by a Bear.
Nemerov. Baron Baedeker Blew His Nose and,
    Sighing, Departed, The.
Clock With No Hands, A.
First Leaf, The.
Midsummer's Day.
Quarry, The.
Neruda. This Broken Bell.
Olson, C. Kingfishers, The.
Piercy. Death of the Small Commune, The.
Why the Soup Tastes Like the *Daily News*.
Plath. Burnt-out Spa, The.
Pope, A. Epistle V, to Mr. Addison.
Raine, K. What message from imagined
    Paradise.
Ramanujan. Elements of Composition.
Rich, A. Diving into the Wreck.
House at the Cascades, The.
Moth Hour.
Orient Wheat.
Roadway, The.
When This Clangor in the Brain.
Ritsos. Why the Question?
Robinson, E. Ballade of Broken Flutes.
Dead Village, The.
House on the Hill, The.
Rossetti, C. Ruin.
Shelley, P. Fragment: "Rude wind is singing,
    The."
Fragment: The Vine-Shroud.
Lines Written During the Castlereagh
    Administration.
Ozymandias.
Stevens, W. Worms at Heaven's Gate, The.
Swift, J. To Quilca.
Thomas, D. I See the Boys of Summer.
Thoreau. All things decay.
Tomlinson, C. Desert Autumn.
Updike. Enemies of a House.
Very. Death Decay and Change.
Walcott. Banyan Tree, Old Year's Night, The.
Wilbur, R. Junk.
Williams, C. K. Admiral Fan, The.
Flight.
Williams, W. Raleigh Was Right.
Wordsworth, W. I watch, and long have
    watched, with calm regret.
Pibroch's note, discountenanced or mute.
There is a bondage worse, far worse, to bear.
Wright, C. Local Journal.
Wright, J. On the Skeleton of a Hound.
Wyatt, S. Like as the wind with raging blast.
December
Burns, R. Gloomy December.
Eberhart, R. Homage to the North.
Emerson, R. Low December vault in June be

Department Stores
  Eliot, T. S.   In the Department Store.
  Kizer, C.   Poem, Small and Delible.
  McHugh, H.   What Could Hold Us.

Depression (economic)
  Cooper, J.   Wanda's Blues.
  Dugan, A.   Elegy for a Magician.
    On the Long Island Railroad System.
  Komunyakaa.   1931.
  Kumin, M.   Introducing the Fathers.
  Kunitz, S.   Old Darned Man, The.
  Lux.   Somebody's Aunt Out Swabbing Her
    Birdbath.
  Niedecker.   Depression Years.
    To see the man who took care of our stock.
  Oppen.   Bad times: / The cars pass.
  Prunty.   Depression, the War, and Gypsy Rose
    Lee, The.

See also **Great Depression**

Depression (psychological)
  Baudelaire.   Black Bile ("Worthless and wealthy,
    decrepit and young").
  Berryman.   Lightning, The.
  Brontë, E.   And first an hour of mournful
    musing.
    I'll come when thou art saddest.
    O God of heaven! the dream of horror.
    That dreary lake, that midnight sky.
    Wind, sink to rest in the heather.
  Bukowski.   Beer.
    For Al—.
    Something.
    Weather Report.
  Campion, T. *et al.*   No grave for woe, yet earth
    my watrie teares devoures.
  Carver, R.   Simple.
  Clampitt.   Hippocrene.
  Collins, B.   Scotland.
  HaNagid.   Your Loved Ones Depress You.
  Hayden, R.   Ice Storm.
  Hughes, T.   Locket, the.
  Ignatow, D.   I'm a Depressed Poem.
  Keats.   To J. H. Reynolds, Esq.
  Lawrence, D. H.   Boredom, Ennui, Depression.
  Lux.   Emily's Mom.
  Major, C.   Jake Flower, The.
  Meredith, G.   Long was the conflict, but now
    'tis done.
  Meredith, W.   Dreams of Suicide.
  Nash, O.   So Penseroso.
  Parker, D.   Rhyme Against Living.
    Sight.
    Story of Mrs. W———.
    Symptom Recital.
  Patchen.   Crowded Net, The.
    Ohio River Blues.
  Rossetti, C.   When My Heart Is Vexed I Will
    Complain.
  "Shu Ting."   Brother, I Am Here.
  Smith, S.   My Muse.
  Warren, R.   Pursuit.
  Wordsworth, W.   I Wandered Lonely As a
    Cloud.
  Wright, C.   Dog Yoga.
  Wright, J.   Beginning Again.

See also **Melancholy; Mental Illness**

Dereliction
  Carver, R.   Return.
  Komunyakaa.   Cops Call Him Charlie, The.
  Warren, R.   Somewhere.
  Wordsworth, W.   Decay of Piety.

Descartes, René
  Beckett, S.   Whoroscope.
  Borges.   Descartes.
  Eberhart, R.   Retrospective Forelook.
  Nemerov.   Endegeeste.
  Tomlinson, C.   Descartes and the Stove.
  Zagajewski.   Fire, Fire.

Deserts
  Ammons.   Driving Through.
    When Rahman Rides.
  Brodsky, J.   Lullaby: "Birth I gave you in a
    desert."
  Broumas, O.   Away from Water.
  Carruth, H.   Abandoned Ranch, Big Bend.

  Coming Down to the Desert at Lordsburg, N.M.
    Rimrock, Where It Is.
  Ciardi, J.   Driving across the American Desert
    and Thinking of the Sahara.
  Crane, S.   I walked in a desert.
    In the desert.
    On the desert.
  Creeley.   Night Sky, A.
  De la Mare.   Image, The.
  Dickey, J.   Gila Bend.
  Dove, R.   Sahara Bus Trip, The.
  Drummond de Andrade.   Travelling in the
    Family.
  Dubie.   Desert Deportation of 1915, The.
    Evening of the Pyramids, The.
    Renunciation of the Desert Primrose, A.
  Dugan, A.   Against the Text "Art Is Immortal."
  Ginsberg, A.   Ayers Rock / Uluru Song.
  Hughes, L.   Desert.
  Ignatow, D.   Ship, The.
  Jarrell, R.   Range in the Desert, The.
  Kinnell.   Supper after the Last, The.
  Kinsella, T.   Dream.
  Kipling, R.   Song in the Desert, A.
  Kizer, C.   Food of Love.
  Komunyakaa.   Man Who Carries the Desert
    Around Inside Himself, The: For Wally.
  Kunitz, S.   Old Cracked Tune, An.
  Laughlin, J.   Creatures of Prometheus, The.
    Crucifixion in the Desert.
  Levi, P.   Flight.
  Lindsay, N.   I Went Down into the Desert to
    Meet Elijah.
  Major, C.   Lost in the Desert.
  Melville, H.   In the Desert.
  Meredith, G.   Song: "Thou to me art such a
    spring."
  Merton.   Dry Places.
  Muldoon, P.   Vaquero.
  Pagis.   Snake.
  Paley, G.   Desert Wasn't Loved Enough said
    Reich, The.
  Plath.   Sleep in the Mojave Desert.
  Raine, K.   Moment, The.
  Rich, A.   Turning the Wheel.
  Rossetti, C.   I dug and dug amongst the snow.
  Rumi.   Tent, The.
  Shelley, P.   Ozymandias.
  Stafford, W.   At the Bomb Testing Site.
    In the Night Desert.
  Stock, R.   Azazel.
    Dance, The.
  Sze.   Moenkopi.
    Singer with Eyes of Sand, A.
    Three A.M., in Winter.
  Tomlinson, C.   Arizona Desert.
    Death in the Desert, A.
    Near and the Far, The.
  Very.   Desert, The.
    Stony Desert of Life, The.
  Walker, A.   On Sight.
  Warren, R.   Unless.
  Whittier.   Song of Slaves in the Desert.
  Williams, W.   New Mexico.

Desire
  Ai.   Blood in the Water.
  Amichai [*or* Amikhai].   Caffè Dante in New
    York—1.
    Greatest Desire of All, The.
    Look, Thoughts, and Dreams.
    Straight from Prejudice.
    You Carry the Weight of Heavy Buttocks.
  Ammons.   Love Song: "Like the hills under
    dusk you."
  Angelou.   Black Ode.
    Here's to Adhering.
    On Diverse Deviations.
    Prescience.
    Zorro Man, A.
  Ashbery, J.   Blessing in Disguise, A.
    Lament Upon the Waters, The.
  Atwood.   Against Still Life.
    I look up, you are standing.
    Spring again, can I stand it.
    There Is Only One of Everything.
    Variation on the Word *Sleep.*

  Woman Who Could Not Live With Her Faulty
    Heart, The.
  Baudelaire.   Damned Women ("Like ruminating
    cattle on the sand").
    Death of Lovers, The.
    Giantess, The.
    I love you as I love the night itself.
    Meditation.
    Ruin.
  Beckett, S.   Cascando.
    Être là sans mâchoires sans dents.
    Sanies I.
  Berry, W.   Design of a House, The.
    Marriage.
  Berryman.   Desire Is a World by Night.
    Desires of Men and Women.
    Down & Back.
    Song of the Young Hawaiian, The.
  Bierce.   One Morning.
  Blake, W.   Beneath the white thorn lovely May.
  Blok.   She Came in from the Frost.
  Bly, R.   At Midocean.
    Cry Going Out over Pastures, The.
  Bogan, L.   Dream, The.
  Borges.   Parting.
  Brodsky, J.   Homage to Chekhov.
  Broumas, O.   Absence of Noise Presence of
    Sound.
    Circe.
    Fast.
    Four Beginnings / for Kyra.
    Heart Believes with Blows.
    Home Movies.
    Io.
    Jewel Lotus Harp.
    Leda and Her Swan.
    Moon Conjunct Ace of Cups.
    Namaste.
    Ode: "Ask me no more."
    P.S.
    Perennial.
    She Loves.
    Sleeping Beauty.
    Still Life.
    Sugar.
  Browning, E.   Man's Requirements, A.
  Browning, R.   In a Gondola.
    Pretty Woman, A.
    Song: "Nay but you, who do not love her."
  Burns, R.   Allan Water.
    Anna.
    Bonnie [*or* Bonny] Wee Thing, The.
    Cardin o't, The.
    Cauld Frosty Morning.
    Delia.
    Duncan Davison.
    Dusty Miller.
    Gallant Weaver, The.
    Green Sleeves [and Tartan Ties].
    I'll Ay[e] Ca' in by Yon Town.
    It is na, Jean, thy bonie face.
    Jamie Come Try Me.
    Lass That Made the Bed for Me, The.
    Let Me in This Ae Night.
    Mary Morison.
    O Lay Thy Loof in Mine Lass.
    O Saw Ye My Maggie.
    O Were My Love Yon Lilac[k] Fair.
    Passion's Cry.
    Revision for Clarinda.
    Scotish Song.
    Song: "As I cam down by yon castle wa'."
    Tam Glen.
    There's News Lasses News.
    Thine am I, my Chloris fair.
    Tibbie Dunbar.
    To Chloris.
    To Miss Isabella Macleod.
    To the Weaver's Gin Ye Go.
    Wilt thou be my Dearie.
    Young Jockey was the blythest lad.
  Byron, G.   Lucietta. A Fragment.
    To a Beautiful Quaker.
    To M.S.G.
  Campion, T.   Ad Melleam.
    Be thou then my beauty named.

Be Wise, and Fly Not.
Beauty, Since You So Much Desire.
Dear If I with Guile.
Fain Would I Wed.
Faine would I my love disclose.
Fire, fire, fire, fire!
First Love.
Hide not, sweetest Love, a sight so pleasing.
How eas'ly wert thou chained.
In eosdem.
In Lycium et Clytham.
In Pandarum.
Leave prolonging thy distresse.
Love Me or Not.
My Life's Delight.
O deare, that I with thee might live.
O Love, where are thy Shafts, thy Quiver, and
   thy Bow?
Oft have I sigh'd for him that heares me not.
Respect my faith, regard my service past.
Shall I come, if I swim? wide are the waves,
   you see.
Sleep, Angry Beauty.
So Quicke, So Hot, So Mad is Thy Fond Sute.
Song: "O sweet delight, O more than human[e]
   bliss[e]."
Tarry sweete love.
There Is None, O None but You.
Vaile, love, mine eyes, O hide from me.
What meanes this folly, now to brave it so.
Where She Her Sacred Bower Adorns.
Whether away my sweetest deerest?
Young and Simple though I Am.
Your Fair[e] Look[e]s Inflame [My Desire].
Campion, T. *et al.*   And would you faine the
   reason know.
And Would You See My Mistress' Face?
Kinde in unkindnesse, when will you relent.
Sweete, come againe.
Unlesse there were consent twixt hell and
   heaven.
Carew, T.   Love's Courtship.
Mediocrity in Love Rejected.
New Years Gift. To the Queen, A.
Second Rapture, The.
To My Worthy Friend Master George Sands [*or*
   Sandys], on His Translation of the Psalms.
To One That Desired to Know My Mistress [*or*
   Mistris].
Carruth, H.   Almanach du Printemps Vivarois.
August.
Concerning Necessity.
Ekstase, Alptraum, Schlaf in einem Nest von
   Flammen.
Fourth.
Green Mountain Idyl.
If It Were Not for You.
Incident of May.
Purana, Meaning Once Upon a Time.
Three Songs.
Carver, R.   Blue Stones, The.
Hunter.
Catullus.   Let us live, my Lesbia, and let us love
   each other.
Cavafy.   At the Entrance to the Café.
At the Theater.
Blue Eyes.
Desires.
Far Off.
Half an Hour.
He Asked about the Quality.
He Came to Read.
In the Dull and Gloomy Village.
I've Gazed So Long, So Much.
On the Stairs.
Regiment of Pleasure, The.
Remember, Body.
Return.
So.
Tobacco Shop Window, The.
When They Surge, Excited.
Cavalcanti.   Check out the humpback, Manny.
Eyes of that gentle country girl, The.
Gianni, Guido greets.
I found a shepherdess in a grove.
Sonnet: Of the Eyes of a certain Mandetta, of

Thoulouse, which resemble those of his Lady
   Joan, of Florence.
Chesterton.   Joseph.
Chuang Tzu.   Five Enemies, The.
Ciardi, J.   On the Poet as a Damned Poor Thing.
Clampitt.   Chichester.
Clifton, L.   Report from the angel of eden.
Clough.   Come pleasant thoughts; sweet
   thoughts, at will.
Whence are ye, vague desires.
Codrescu.   Alberta.
Architecture.
Operations of Desire, The.
Coleridge, S.   Desire.
Collins, B.   Not Touching.
Cowper, W.   Delia, th' unkindest girl on earth.
Of Himself.
Symptoms of Love, The.
Crane, H.   Legend.
Possessions.
Thou Canst Read Nothing..
Crane, S.   And yet I have seen thee happy with
   me.
Love forgive me if I wish you grief.
Once I saw thee idly rocking.
Creeley.   Ballad of the Despairing Husband.
"Bolinas and Me."
Ciano's.
Comfort.
Eyes.
Flesh.
For W.C.W.
Kid, The.
Menu, The.
Night ("Needs most / happily mutual").
Now Then.
Old Song.
Smell of gum wrappers as of Saturday afternoon
   at movies.
Snow, The.
Song: "What do you / want, love. To be."
To Bobbie.
Two Times.
Women.
Cummings, E. E.   After your poppied hair
   inaugurates.
Ballade: "White night roared with a huge north-
   wind, The."
Because i love you)last night.
Before the fragile gradual throne of night.
Except in your / honour.
First of All My Dreams, The.
Goodby Betty,don't remember me.
How / tinily / of / squir(two be).
I have looked upon thee—and I have loved thee.
I have loved,let us see if that's all.
I spoke to thee.
If learned darkness from our searched world.
In front of your house i.
In the rain- / darkness, the sunset.
It Is At Moments After I Have Dreamed.
Item.
I've come to ask you if there isn't a.
Lady will you come with me into.
Lean candles hunger in.
Love is a guess / that deepens.
Mind is its own beautiful prisoner, The.
My eyes are fond of the east side.
My humorous ghost precisely will.
My lady is an ivory garden.
My sweet old etcetera.
Notice the convulsed orange inch of moon.
O Thou to whom the musical white spring.
On the Madam's best april the.
Open your heart: / i'll give you a treasure.
Puella Mea.
Silently if,out of not knowable.
Skies may be blue;yes.
So isn't small one littlest why.
Somewhere i have never travelled, gladly
   beyond.
Speaking of love(of).
Spring has been exquisite and the, The.
Sweet spring is your.
Thee will i praise between those rivers whose.
Thing most new complete fragile intense, A.

This cigarette is extremely long.
Thy fingers make early flowers of.
Unto thee i / burn incense.
We love each other very dearly.
When my love comes to see me it's.
When my sensational moments are no more.
When of your eyes one smile entirely brings
   down.
Which is the very.
Willing pitifully to bewitch.
"Dario."   First, a look.
I love the faces pallid.
Ite, Missa Est.
My love, the night has come.
Palimpsest: "Written in an old Aeolian dialect."
Davie, D.   Dule of a Dewsbury Matron.
Hot Hands.
Master & Man.
De la Mare.   Homesick.
Invocation: "Burning fire shakes in the night,
   The."
Out Of Bounds.
Dickey, W.   Læestrygonians, The.
Dickinson, E.   Heart wants what it wants, The.
I cannot live with You.
To see her is a Picture.
When we have ceased to care.
Wild Nights—Wild Nights!
Donne.   Canonization, The.
Lovers' Infiniteness[e].
Love's Diet.
Dove, R.   Happenstance.
His Shirt.
Secret Garden, The.
Sunday Greens.
Dugan, A.   Untitled Poem: "What I remember
   most."
Dunbar, P.   Change, The.
If I Could But Forget.
In a English Garden.
Night, Dim Night.
Retort.
Eberhart, R.   On Seeing an Egyptian Mummy in
   Berlin, 1932.
On the Fragility of Mind.
Passage, The.
Request.
Request for Offering.
Supreme Authority of the Imagination, The.
Transfer, The.
Eliot, T. S.   Burnt Dancer, The.
Dedication to My Wife, A.
In the Department Store.
Love Song of J. Alfred Prufrock, Resumed, The.
Love Song of J. Alfred Prufrock, The.
Love Song of J. Alfred Prufrock, The (Prufrock
   among the Women).
Paysage Triste.
Prufrock's Pervigilium.
Emerson, R.   Ode to Beauty.
To Rhea.
Ferlinghetti, L.   Astonished Heart, The.
Love Nut, The.
Short Story on a Painting of Gustav Klimt.
Frost, R.   Discovery of the Madeiras, The.
Fire and Ice.
Gallagher, T.   Photograph of a Lighthouse
   Through Fog.
García Lorca.   Casida of the Reclining Woman.
Desire.
Madrigal: "I looked into your eyes."
Preciosa and the Wind.
Summer Madrigal.
Two Girls.
Ginsberg, A.   Done, Finished with the Biggest
   Cock.
Fie My Fum.
Green Automobile, The.
Malest Cornifici Tuo Catullo.
Why Is God Love, Jack?
Written in My Dream by W. C. Williams.
Glück, L.   Aubade: "Today above the gull's
   call."
Early December in Croton-on-Hudson.
Elms.
Embrace, The.

Mirror, The.
Northwood Path.
Portrait of the Queen in Tears.
Graves, R.   Ample Garden, The.
Arrears of Moonlight.
Beds of Grainne and Diarmuid, The.
Between Trains.
Black Goddess, The.
Cure, The.
Endless Pavement.
Fire Walker.
Fragment: "Are you shaken, are you stirred."
Hoopoe Tells Us How, The.
Judgement of Paris.
La Mejicana.
Lamia in Love.
Last Poem, A.
Leap, The.
Lure of Murder.
Name Day.
Patience.
Possessed.
Quiet Glades of Eden, The.
Snap-Comb Wilderness, The.
Snapped Thread, The.
Song: The Far Side of Your Moon.
Stolen Jewel.
Symptoms Of Love.
To Myrto About Herself.
To the Teumessian Vixen.
Troughs of Sea.
True Joy.
Under the Olives.
Unnamed Spell, The.
Watch, The.
Wild Cyclamen.
Young Cordwainer, The.
Guinicelli.   Canzone: Of the Gentle Heart.
Gurney, I.   Song: "I had a girl's fancies."
"H. D."   Cassandra.
Helmsman, The.
She Contrasts with Herself Hippolyta.
Simaetha.
Hall, D.   Exile.
"Kiss, The."
Love Is Like Sounds.
Passage to Worship.
"Reclining Figure."
Wells.
Han-shan.   One day I left the mountains.
HaNagid.   In Fact I Love That Fawn.
Where's that Coy Gazelle.
Hardy, T.   Chosen, The.
From Victor Hugo.
In the Street.
Love Watches a Window.
Lover to Mistress.
Maiden's Pledge, A.
Seven Times, The.
To Meet, or Otherwise.
Hernández, M.   Two Palm Trees, The.
Herrick.   Against Love.
Another.
Begger, The.
Change Gives Content.
Charme, or an Allay for Love, A.
Frozen Zone; or, Julia Disdainful, The.
His Misery in a Mistresse.
Hymne to Love, An.
Julia's Petticoat.
Love Kill'd by Lack.
Night-Piece, to Julia, The.
Of Love.
On Himselfe.
On Love.
Pastorall Sung to the King: Montano, Silvio, and
    Mirtillo, Shepards, A.
Things of Choice, Long a Comming.
To All Young Men That Love.
To Anthea.
To Bacchus, a Canticle.
To Cupid.
To Dewes. A Song.
To Electra.
To His Mistress[es].
To Perenna.

To Springs and Fountains.
To the Little Spinners.
Upon Cupid.
Upon Irene.
Upon Julia's Clothes.
Upon Julia['s] Washing Herself in the River.
Upon Love.
Upon Love, by Way of Question and Answer.
Want.
What Kind of Mistress[e] He Would Have.
Hughes, L.   Desire.
Fascination.
In the Mist of the Moon.
Midnight Dancer.
Preference.
Red Silk Stockings.
Songs to the Dark Virgin.
Spring for Lovers.
When Sue Wears Red.
Wide River.
Hughes, T.   Folktale.
Guide, The.
Japanese River Tales.
Sunstruck Foxglove.
Ignatow, D.   Now.
Once There Was a Woman Smiled at Me.
Jackson, L.   Be Grave, Woman.
Jacobsen, J.   Mexican Peacock, The.
Travelers, The.
Jarrell, R.   Over the florid capitals.
Jeffers, R.   Cawdor.
Divinely Superfluous Beauty.
Maid's Thought, The.
Thurso's Landing.
Johnson, S.   Song, A: "Not the soft sighs of
    vernal gales."
Jonson, B.   Elegy, An: "By those bright eyes, at
    whose immortal fires."
Song, A: "Come, let us here enjoy the shade."
Keats.   Extracts from an Opera.
Fill for Me a Brimming Bowl.
Hither, Hither, Love.
Lines: "Unfelt, unheard, unseen."
Of Late Two Dainties Were before Me Placed.
Stanzas: "You say you love; but with a voice."
To Emma.
Woman! When I Behold Thee Flippant, Vain.
Kinsella, T.   Drowsing over *The Arabian Nights*.
String Puppets.
Kipling, R.   Oldest Song, The.
Komunyakaa.   Apprenticeship.
Delicate Conspiracy, A.
Hard Up.
Night Muse & Mortar Round.
Sunbather.
Kunitz, S.   Sotto Voce.
Touch Me.
Larkin, P.   Wants.
Laughlin, J.   Apotropaic Decision, An.
Arachne.
As in Music / A Reprise / Across Time.
Confessio Amantis.
Fate of Actaeon, The.
Girls as Windmills.
If You Are Only Flirting.
Inviolable Maiden, The.
Is It Written.
It's Warm Under Your Thumb.
Nothing That's Lovely Can My Love Escape.
Occidit brevis lux.
Rome: In the Café.
Song: "O lovely lovely so lovely."
That Other World.
This Is the Morte Saison.
Touching.
Visitor, The.
Voices, The.
Lawrence, D. H.   After Many Days.
And Jude the Obscure and His Beloved.
Appeal, The.
Bad Beginning, A.
Basta!
Come Spring, Come Sorrow.
December Night.
Deeper Than Love.
Desire.

Desire Goes Down into the Sea.
Desire Is Dead.
Dog-Tired.
Elixir.
Failure, A.
Forecast.
Frost Flowers.
Grasshopper Is a Burden.
Hands of the Betrothed, The.
In Trouble and Shame.
Latent Desire, The.
Lotus and Frost.
Love Message.
Man Reaches a Point.
Manifesto.
Mess of Love, The.
Narcissus.
On the Balcony.
Other Women Have Reared in Me.
Paradise Re-entered.
Primal Passions, The.
Red.
Restlessness.
Rose of All the World.
She Was a Good Little Wife.
Snap-Dragon.
Sunday Afternoon in Italy.
Temples.
These Clever Women.
To Toss the Troubled Night Long.
Virgin Youth.
Wedding Morn.
What Does She Want?
Witch I, The.
Witch II, The.
Women Want Fighters for Their Lovers.
Levertov.   July 1968.
Unknown, The.
Variation and Reflection on a Theme by Rilke.
What She Could Not Tell Him.
Levine, P.   Poem Circling Hamtramck,
    Michigan, All Night in Search of You, The.
Logan, J.   Lines for an Unknown Lover.
Suzanne.
Lope de Vega.   Pentecost Castle, The.
Lorde.   Conversations in Crisis.
Lux.   Say Yes.
Time.
MacLeish.   Thunderhead.
MacNeice.   Troll's Courtship.
Major, C.   En Promenade des Anglais.
Mallarmé.   Afternoon of a Faun.
Flight of Flaming Hair, The.
Futile Petition.
Negress, A.
Summer Sadness.
Marvell.   Ametas and Thestylis Making Hay-
    Ropes.
Match, The.
Mower's Song, The.
McGrath, T.   Celebration for June 24.
Sometimes.
War Resisters' Song.
McHugh, H.   To Go.
McMichael.   She.
Melville, H.   After the Pleasure Party.
In a Bye-Canal.
Meredith, G.   Adieu, adieu, my Friar, he cried.
Ask, is Love divine.
Breath of the Briar.
Love is winged for two.
O Mary Barrie, Mary Barrie.
See the star yonder.
Was it wise to count the ranks of teeth.
Meredith, W.   Illiterate, The.
Perhaps the Best Time.
Politics.
Winter Song.
Merrill, J.   Kimono, The.
Lorelei.
Octopus, The.
Variations: The Air Is Sweetest That a Thistle
    Guards.
Merwin.   Islands.
Michelangelo Buonarroti.   If a god, Love, can't
    you do.

If, vulnerable from early youth, a heart.
Love's Justification.
No need at all for your angel loveliness.
Not death so much, but its terror rescues me.
Say the face I'm speaking of now, hers I mean.
She's made her mind up, the.
So fond is fire of the frigid stone it waits.
Who's this that draws me forcibly to you?
Why ease the tension of this wild desire.
Woman's beauty, new, A.
Millay, E. Fatal Interview.
Philosopher, The.
To a Musician.
Milosz, C. Account.
Honest Description of Myself with a Glass of
   Whiskey at an Airport, An.
Mister Hanusevich.
When the Moon.
Milton. Sonnet 2: "Charming lady, she whose
   beautiful name honors."
Montale. From a Swiss Lake.
I know a ray of sun (of God?) can still.
Magenta-colored clouds were gathering.
Muldoon, P. Boon.
Something of a Departure.
Nash, O. Emancipation of Mr. Poplin, or, Skoal
   to the Skimmerless.
Song for Pier Something or Other.
Strange Case of the Girl o' Mr. Sponsoon's
   Dreams, The.
Strange Case of the Lovelorn Letter Writer, The.
To a Lady Passing Time Better Left Unpassed.
Nemerov. Sestina 1: "Thickness of paint or
   flesh cannot deface."
Niedecker. Truth / gives heat.
O'Hara, F. Poem: "I don't know as I get what
   D.H. Lawrence is driving at."
St. Paul and All That.
Variations on Pasternak's "Mein Liebchen, Was
   Willst Du Noch Mehr?"
Oliver, M. Blossom.
Hattie Bloom.
Olson, C. À Constance, This Day.
Of Mathilde.
Troilus.
War on the Mind in a Time of Love.
White Horse.
Oppen. Forms of Love, The.
Orlandi, G. ("Friend, I well know that you
   know how to polish").
Orr, G. Fifth Month, The.
November.
We Must Make a Kingdom of It.
Owen, W. Fates, The.
Long Ages Past.
Music.
Song of Songs.
To the Bitter Sweet-heart: a Dream.
Paley, G. Here.
On the Deck.
Palmer, M. Idem 1.
Pasolini. Reality.
Patchen. I Never Had Any Other Desire So
   Strong.
I'd want her eyes to fill with wonder.
Pessoa. Interval.
Petrarch. Apollo—if you nourish still desires.
Because our life is short.
Diana did not more delight her lover.
Happy season of my early prime, The.
How strangely this world wags! Now what
   distressed.
I have not seen you lay your veil apart.
I have prayed Love, and yet again I pray.
I sensed my spirits flagging day by day.
Just as a moth, enamoured of the light.
Love, kindling in our hearts an ardent fire.
Love set me up to be his arrows' mark.
My mad desire has strayed so far, and strays.
No weary weather-beaten mariner.
Now should my life endure to this extent.
Once more Love sends to me that pleasing
   thought.
Sennuccio, I'm half here. Oh, were I all.
She, much more beautiful than others are.
Since fire is not extinguished by more fire.

So feeble is the thread that doth the burden stay.
That powerful lord from whom we cannot hide.
That time of day the rapid sky inclines.
When I have stared for some time fixedly.
When out of all the ladies in her sphere.
Piercy. Nuisance, The.
Pinsky. History of My Heart.
Poe. Dream within a Dream, A.
To F——.
To F——S S. O—D.
To Helen.
To ——: "Not long ago, the writer of these
   lines."
Pope, A. Presenting a *Lark*.
Prunty. Pyromaniac, The.
Ralegh, S. Poesie to Prove Affection is Not
   Love, A.
Ramanujan. I Could Have Rested.
Looking for a Cousin on a Swing.
Mythologies 3.
Rexroth, K. Chicago Cabaret.
From the Persian (2).
Rich, A. Re-forming the Crystal.
Two Songs.
Riley, J. Dolores.
Sister Jones's Confession.
Ylladmar.
Rilke. Narcissus.
Ritsos. Alcméne.
Robinson, E. John Evereldown.
Tavern, The.
Roethke. Favorite, The.
Four for Sir John Davies.
Her Longing.
I Knew A Woman.
Love's Progress.
Marrow, The.
Memory.
Other, The.
Pure Fury, The.
Renewal, The.
Sententious Man, The.
Sequel, The.
She.
Swan, The.
Verse with Allusions.
Voice, The.
Rossetti, C. Hope Carol, A.
Like As the Hart Desireth the Water Brooks.
Margery.
Ransomed of the Lord, The.
Roses on a brier, / Pearls from out the bitter sea.
Soeur Louise De La Miséricorde.
Subject To Like Passions as We Are.
Till Tomorrow.
What Would I Give?
Rukeyser, M. Cries From Chiapas.
Eyes of Night-Time.
If you look at your succession of desires.
Looking at Each Other.
Meeting, The.
Song of Another Tribe, A.
Two Illuminations, The.
What I See.
Rumi. Center of the Fire, The.
Great Wagon, A.
Someone who goes with half a loaf of bread.
Sandburg, C. Adelaide Crapsey.
At a Window.
Aztec.
Bricklayer Love.
Broken Hearted Soprano.
Calls.
Circle of Doors.
Dream Girl.
Evening Questions.
Evening Waterfall.
Gone.
Great Hunt, The.
Have Me.
Horse Fiddle.
Jan Kubelik.
Joy.
Love Beyond Keeping.
Manitoba Childe Roland.
M'Liss and Louie.

Moon Rondeau.
Offering and Rebuff.
Old-Fashioned Requited Love.
On the Breakwater.
One Parting.
Paula.
Poems Done on a Late Night Car.
Red-Headed Resstaurant Cashier.
Red Son, The.
Sarah's Letter to Peter.
Shirt.
Spanish.
They Met Young.
Thou Art Like a Flower.
Two Moon Fantasies.
Variations on a Theme.
White Ash.
Sappho. Sappho.
Sarton, M. Death and the Lovers.
Prothalamion.
Schuyler, J. Sleep.
Table of Green Fields, A.
Tom.
Seifert. Apple Tree with Cobweb Strings.
Berthe Soucaret.
Dance of the Girls' Chemises.
Dialogue.
Fingerprints.
Four Small Windows.
Fragment of a Letter.
Hunt for the Kingfisher, The.
In an Empty Room.
Lines for the Painter Ota Janeček.
Merry-Go-Round with White Swan.
Place of Pilgrimage.
Smoke of Marijuana, The.
Song about Girls, A.
Song of the Sweepings.
Striking of the Tower Clock, The.
To Be a Poet.
Wet Picture.
Sexton. Ambition Bird, The.
Farmer's Wife, The.
Jesus Asleep.
To Like, to Love.
Where I Live in This Honorable House of the
   Laurel Tree.
Shapiro, K. Back, The.
Glass Poem.
Haircut.
Shelley, P. Love, Hope, Desire and Fear.
To the Queen of My Heart.
Sidney, S. Thou Blind Man's Mark.
Smith, S. Appetite.
Fool, The.
I Could Let Tom Go—But What about the
   Children.
La Gretchen de Nos Jours (II).
Longing for Death because of Feebleness.
Love Me!
Shooting Incident, The.
Tender Only to One.
Snyder, G. Beneath My Hand and Eye the
   Distant Hills, Your Body.
Four Poems for Robin.
Manichaeans, The.
Three Poems for Joanne.
Stein, G. Lifting Belly.
Stevens, W. Peter Quince at the Clavier.
Poems of Our Climate, The.
Stock, R. All I Wanted to Say.
Study of a House with Garden Attached.
Suckling, S. Against Absence.
Guiltless Inconstant, The.
Love's Burning-Glass.
Miracle, The.
Song: "Crafty boy that had full oft assay'd,
   The."
Sonnet: "Dost see how unregarded now."
Swenson, M. Laocoön Dream Recorded in
   Diary Dated 1943.
Swift, J. Desire and Possession.
Swinburne. Sapphics.
Sze. Fern, Coal, Diamond.
Great White Shark, The.
Tate, J. Mirror, The.

My Girl.
Pride's Crossing.
Thomas, D.   If I Were Tickled by the Rub of
   Love.
Into Her Lying Down Head.
Tibullus.   Sulpicia to Cerinthus.
Tomlinson, C.   Death of Will, The.
Tu Fu.   Lo Yu Park.
Unknown.   Art Thou That She.
Vallejo.   I am Freed.
Van Duyn.   Billings and Cooings from "The
   Berkeley Barb."
Voltaire.   To Madame du Châtelet.
Warren, R.   Birth of Love.
Whalen, P.   Raging Desire & c.
Whitman, W.   As Adam Early in the Morning.
Fast-Anchor'd Eternal O Love!
From Pent-up Aching Rivers.
I Heard You Solemn-Sweet Pipes of the Organ.
Not Heat Flames Up and Consumes.
O You Whom I Often and Silently Come.
Out of the Rolling Ocean the Crowd.
To the Garden the World.
When I Heard At The Close Of The Day.
Whittier.   Henchman, The.
Wilbur, R.   Apology.
Complaint.
L'Etoile.
Piccola Commedia.
Playboy.
She.
Voice from under the Table, A.
Wilde, O.   In the Gold Room: A Harmony.
Williams, C. K.   Game, The.
Love: Beginnnings.
Love: Youth.
On the Other Hand.
Orchid, The.
Sting, The.
With Ignorance.
Williams, M.   Associate Professor (Mad
   Scientist) to (His Love) His Student in Physics
   100 Lab.
How to Stop Smoking.
If Ever There Was One.
Professor.
Williams, T.   Legend, The.
Shallow Pool, The.
Swimmer and Fish Group.
Williams, W.   Appeal.
Attic Which Is Desire, The.
Chanson.
Design for November.
Song: "You are forever April."
Spring Song.
Venus Over the Desert.
Woman Walking.
Wordsworth, W.   To ————: " 'Wait, prithee,
   wait!' this answer Lesbia threw."
Wright, C.   Laguna Dantesca.
Thinking of David Summers at the Beginning of
   Winter.
Wright, J.   Abstract of Knowledge, The / The
   First Test.
Accusation, The.
Angel, The.
Assignation, The.
Before a Cashier's Window in a Department
   Store.
Erinna to Sappho.
Girl in a Window, A.
Girl Walking into a Shadow, A.
In a Viennese Cemetery.
Lights in the Hallway, The.
Offense, The.
Poem about Breasts, A.
Sappho.
Shadow and the Real, The.
Wyatt, S.   Comparison of Love to a Streame
   Falling from the Alpes.
Desire, alas, my master and my foe.
Desire to sorrow doth me constrain.
Divers[e] [*or* Dyvers] doth[e] use, as I have
   heard and kno[w].
Driven by desire, I did this deed.
For want of [*or* I] will in woe I plain.

Furious gun in his raging ire, The.
Grudge on who list, this is my lot.
If amorous faith in heart unfeigned.
If fancy [*or* fansy] would favour.
If thou wilt mighty be, flee from the rage.
It burneth yet, alas, my heart's desire.
Lively sparks that issue from those eyes, The.
Long love that in my thought doth harbo[u]r,
   The.
Lover Showeth How He Is Forsaken of Such,
   The.
So unwarely was never no man caught [*or*
   cawght].
Sometime I fled the fire that me brent.
Such vain thought as wonted to mislead me.
Though I myself be bridled of my mind.
Yeats.   Arrow, The.
First Confession, A.
Love's Loneliness.
Politics.
What Magic Drum?
What Then?
Zagajewski.   That Force.
Zukofsky, L.   1959 Valentine.
One lutenist played *look*; your through was
   drink.
The.
See also **Erotic Love; Lust**

Desolation
Berry, W.   Desolation.
Brontë, E.   Coldly, bleakly, drearily.
It was night, and on the mountains.
Old Hall of Elbë, ruined, lonely now.
Remembrance.
Byron, G.   Darkness.
Carruth, H.   Cappadocian Song.
Celan.   Assisi.
Ice, Eden.
Stretto.
There was earth inside them, and.
Crane, S.   Behold, from the land of the farther
   suns.
Creeley.   Enough.
Marriage, A.
Night Sky, A.
Cullen, C.   Black Magdalens.
De la Mare.   Bitter Waters.
Defeat.
Gallagher, T.   Bonfire.
Ginsberg, A.   In Back of the Real.
Vulture Peak: Gridhakuta Hill.
"H. D."   Tribute, The.
Hsüeh T'ao.   Weaving Love-Knots.
Hughes, L.   Desert.
Troubled Woman.
Ignatow, D.   In Ancient Times.
Jeffers, R.   Place for No Story, The.
Kizer, C.   Night Sounds.
Winter Song.
Kunitz, S.   How Long Is the Night?
Sea, That Has No Ending, The.
Levertov.   Desolate Light.
Lux.   Grim Town in a Steep Valley.
MacNeice.   Order to View.
Windowscape.
Mallarmé.   Azure, The.
Jinx, The.
Sea Breeze.
Michelangelo Buonarroti.   Give back to my eyes
   their flow, O spring, O river.
In me there's only death; my life's in you.
Millay, E.   Desolation Dreamed Of.
Feast.
Milosz, C.   Nation, A.
Oeconomia Divina.
Sarajevo.
Temptation.
Why.
Oliver, M.   River Styx, Ohio, The.
Oppen.   Myth of the Blaze.
Return.
Orr, G.   Celestial Desolations.
Ransom, J.   Emily Hardcastle, Spinster.
Riley, J.   Absence of Little Wesley, The.
Christine.
Mother-Song, A.

My Mary.
Our Own.
Shadow and Shine.
Ritsos.   Small Dialogue.
Rossetti, C.   Castle-Builder's World, A.
I Look for the Lord.
Rukeyser, M.   Certain Music, A.
Rumi.   When I remember your love.
Seifert.   Window on Birds' Wings.
Shelley, P.   Tower of Famine, The.
Simic.   Fall Day, A.
Smith, S.   Every Lovely Limb's a Desolation.
Stevens, W.   Dry Loaf.
Thomas, D.   Hand That Signed the Paper, The.
Very.   Lament of the Flowers, The.
Williams, C. K.   Neglect.
Wu of Han [*or* Wu Ti *or* Ou-ty *or* Liu Ch'e *or*
   Liu Ch'u].   Skein, The.
Yeats.   Meru.

Despair
Ammons.   Hope's Okay.
Arnold, M.   Self-Dependence.
Baudelaire.   Out of the Depths I Called to Thee.
Beckett, S.   Cascando.
Berry, W.   Desolation.
Berryman.   Despair.
Form, The.
No.
Song of the Bridegroom, The.
Blake, W.   Song: "My silks and fine array."
Blok.   Florence.
Yes. This Is the Call of Inspiration.
Bly, R.   Fire of Despair Has Been Our Savior,
   The.
Snowbanks North of the House.
When the Dumb Speak.
Brontë, E.   Castle Wood.
Darkness was overtraced on every face.
F. de Samara to A. G. A.
I know not how it falls on me.
I would have touched the heavenly key.
In dungeons dark I cannot sing.
It will not shine again.
Sleep brings no joy to me.
Sympathy.
What use is it to slumber here.
Wind, I hear it sighing, The.
Written on Returning to the P. of I. on the 10th
   of January, 1827.
Browning, E.   Loved Once.
Mask, The.
Nature's Remorses.
Proof and Disproof.
Bukowski.   Blackbirds Are Rough Today, The.
One Hundred and Ninety-Nine Pounds of Clay
   Leaning Forward.
Rat Rises, A.
When the Berry Bush Dies I'll Swim Down the
   Green River with My Hair on Fire.
Wrong Number.
Burns, R.   Despondency, an Ode.
Fragment: "Now health forsakes that angel
   face."
Raving winds around her blowing.
Thou hast left me ever, Jamie.
To Ruin.
Byron, G.   And Wilt Thou Weep When I Am
   Low?
Epistle to a Friend.
Herod's Lament for Mariamne.
Julian [A Fragment].
La Revanche.
Lament of Tasso, The.
Lines Written beneath a Picture.
One Struggle More, and I Am Free.
Remembrance.
Reply to Some Verses of J.M.B. Pigot, Esq., on
   the Cruelty of His Mistress.
Stanzas: "Chill and mirk is the nightly blast."
Campion, T.   Breake now my heart and dye! Oh
   no, she may relent.
O never to be moved.
Spyres Curten, The.
Carruth, H.   Eternal City.
Spring 1967.
Carver, R.   Attic, The.

Cavafy. City, The.
Windows, The.
Cavalcanti. Alas, my spirits, when you see me.
Ballata: In Exile at Sarzana.
I never used to think that my heart.
My foolish eyes, that first looked.
O my Lady, didn't you see him.
Clough. My wind is turned to bitter north.
Coleridge, S. Despair.
Visionary Hope, The.
Work without Hope.
Cowper, W. Castaway, The.
Lines Written During a Period of Insanity.
Crane, S. Oh, a rare old wine ye brewed for
me.
Creeley. Ballad of the Despairing Husband.
Dream, The.
For Love.
Woman, The.
Cuadra, P. Despairing Man Draws a Serpent,
The.
Cullen, C. At a Parting.
Therefore, Adieu.
De la Mare. Euphrasy.
Futility.
Macbeth.
Mirage.
Dickinson, E. Despair's advantage is achieved.
Doubt if it be Us, A.
I cannot live with You.
It might be lonelier.
It was not Death, for I stood up.
I've dropped my Brain—My Soul is numb.
No Man can compass a Despair.
One Joy of so much anguish.
Safe Despair it is that raves.
Somewhat, to hope for.
There's a certain Slant of light.
This Chasm, Sweet, upon my life.
Dove, R. Aurora Borealis.
Dugan, A. American Variation on How Rilke
Loved a Princess and Got to Stay in Her
Castle.
Dunbar, P. Blue.
Despair.
One Life.
River of Ruin, The.
Ships That Pass in the Night.
There are brilliant heights of sorrow.
Worn Out.
Wraith, The.
Duncan, R. Bring It Up from the Dark.
Eberhart, R. Despair.
Lost, The.
Necessity.
Sestina: "I die, no matter what I do I die."
Suicide Note.
Éluard, P. Scarcely Disfigured.
Enzensberger, H. Rondeau: "It's easy to talk."
Ferlinghetti, L. In Golden Gate Park that day.
Rough Song of Animals Dying.
Gallagher, T. Ballad of Ballymote, The.
García Lorca. Gacela of the Terrible Presence.
Suicide.
Useless Song.
Ginsberg, A. Yes and It's Hopeless.
Glück, L. Memo from the Cave.
World Breaking Apart.
Graves, R. Raft, The.
"H. D." Cassandra.
Fragment 40: "Keep love and he wings."
Fragment 68: "I envy you your chance of
death."
Hacker, M. 1976.
Hall, D. Praise for Death.
Hardy, T. Coming Up Oxford Street: Evening.
Darkling Thrush, The.
Her Love-Birds.
Meeting with Despair, A.
Murmurs in the Gloom.
Herbert, G. Affliction (4).
Assurance.
Collar, The.
Decay.
Denial[l].
Glimpse, The.

Home.
Longing.
Herrick. Fear[e] Gets Force.
No Danger to Men Desperate.
Hopkins, G. Alchemist in the City, The.
Carrion Comfort.
Fragment of Anything You Like, A.
I Wake and Feel the Fell of Dark, Not Day.
Leaden Echo and the Golden Echo, The.
My prayers must meet a brazen heaven.
No Worst, There Is None. Pitched Past Pitch of
Grief.
Pilate.
Stephen and Barberie.
Thou Art Indeed Just, Lord.
Trees by their yield.
Voice from the World, A.
Why if it be so, for the dismal morn.
Housman. I promise nothing: friends will part.
Shot? so quick, so clean an ending?
Spring Morning.
Twice a week the winter thorough.
World goes none the lamer, The.
Hughes, L. Bad Luck Card.
How Thin a Blanket.
Ruined Gal, A.
Jeffers, R. Air-Raid Rehearsals.
Johnson, S. Winter's Walk, The.
Keats. Day Is Gone and All Its Sweets Are
Gone, The.
La Belle Dame sans Merci [A Ballad].
To Hope.
Larkin, P. Life with a Hole in It, The.
There Is No Language of Destruction.
Lawrence, D. H. And Oh—That the Man I Am
Might Cease to Be.
Ballad of Another Ophelia.
Erotic.
Forsaken and Forlorn.
Impulse.
Labour Battalion.
Loggerheads.
Misery.
Next Morning.
Stoic.
Under the Oak.
What Do I Care?
What Is a Man to Do?
Levertov. In Memory of Muriel Rukeyser.
Levi, P. Black Stars, The.
Lorde. Generation.
McGrath, T. Citizen Dreaming, The.
Don't Think You Know My Name!
End of the Line, The.
Everything in Order.
Nuclear Winter.
Meredith, G. Blame me not that I refuse.
I Chafe at Darkness.
Love they alone the joyful heart.
Song: "Forever."
Too cold for joy, too cold for woe.
Merrill, J. Time.
Merton. Litany: "It yawns at me the cavernous
gulf."
Merwin. Mountains, The.
Wave, The.
Michelangelo Buonarroti. Brow burning, in
cool gloom, as sundown shears.
Millay, E. Above These Cares.
No Earthly Enterprise.
Milosz, C. In Black Despair.
Obviously.
Mörike [or Möricke]. Forsaken Girl, The.
Nemerov. Redeployment.
Niedecker. I married.
O'Hara, F. Meditations in an Emergency.
Olson, C. As snow lies on the hill love's
blackness lies.
Cry pain, & the dogs of yrself devour.
February 10, One Year Too Late.
Jas Jargon.
Return, The.
She, Thus.
Tanto e Amara.
Oppen. People, the People, The.
Paley, G. What If (This Week).

Parker, D. Coda: "There's little in taking or
giving."
Patchen. Blind Maidens of Our Homelessness,
The.
Christ! Christ! Christ! that the world.
Eve of St. Agony, or the Middle Class Was
Sitting on Its Fat.
Lost Poem, A.
Morning, My Prince—the Eye That Walks.
O Fill Your Sack with Tiger Cubs.
Stars go to sleep so peacefully, The.
Pessoa. Loophole.
Opium Eater.
There are sicknesses worse than sicknesses.
Petrarch. I walk, alone and troubled, desert
places.
If Love does not bring better thoughts to bear.
Love, Fortune, and my mind (hardly aware).
My vessel laden with oblivion.
Not stars that wander through the open sky.
She was alive in me upon a time.
Sight of her, angelic and serene, The.
Plath. Event.
Moon and the Yew Tree, The.
Purdah.
Ravaged Face, The.
Sonnet: To Eva.
Street Song.
Winter Landscape, with Rooks.
Raine, K. Medea.
Ralegh, S. If Cynthia Be a Queen.
My Body in the Walls Captived.
Ramanujan. Conventions of Despair.
Looking and Finding.
Rexroth, K. Requiem for the Spanish Dead.
Rich, A. Antinoüs: The Diaries.
Riley, J. Sleep.
Time.
When I Do Mock.
Rilke. Cruel Song.
Ritsos. Inevitably.
Roethke. Against Disaster.
Feud.
In a Dark Time.
Surly One, The.
Rossetti, C. Better Resurrection, A.
Dead Hope.
Fair Margaret.
If Only.
Old-World Thicket, An.
What Would I Give?
When My Heart Is Vexed, I Will Complain.
Rossetti, D. Woodspurge, The.
Rukeyser, M. Down from Chicago Bryan came.
Rumi. Burnt Kabob.
Tent, The.
Sarton, M. Christmas Letter to a Psychiatrist.
My Father's Death.
Prisoner at a Desk.
Where Dream Begins.
Seifert. Smoke of Marijuana, The.
Sexton. 45 Mercy Street.
Big Boots of Pain, The.
December 2nd.
December 11th.
December 18th.
Despair.
Eighteen Days without You.
End, Middle, Beginning.
February 17th.
Flight.
Her Kind.
Sickness unto Death, The.
Shelley, P. England in 1819.
Fragment: "Such hope, as is the sick despair of
good."
Invocation to Misery.
Lament, A: "O world! O life! O time!"
Lines Written among the Euganean Hills.
see also Scene from "Tasso."
Stanza, Written at Bracknell.
Stanzas Written in Dejection, near Naples [or —
December 1818, near Naples].
Simic. Black Days.
Smith, S. Appetite.

Bereaved Swan, The.
Blood Flows Back, The.
Bog-Face.
Do Take Muriel Out.
Does No Love Last?
Forgot!
Friend, The.
I Am.
I Rode With My Darling.
Poor Soul, Poor Girl!
Rothebât.
Sad Heart, The.
Sea-Widow, The.
Spender, S. Trigorin.
Swift, J. Phyllis [or Phillis] [or Progress of
 Love, The].
Tate, J. Lost Pilot, The.
Tennyson, A. Mariana.
Mariana in the South.
Œnone.
Supposed Confessions of a Second-rate
 Sensitive Mind.
Two Voices, The.
Thomas, D. Saint About to Fall, A.
Where Once the Waters of Your Face.
Unknown. Circumstance.
Very. Forevermore.
Walcott. Laventille.
Wilde, O. San Miniato.
Vita Nuova.
Williams, C. K. Bread.
Dimensions.
Loss.
Portions of Manslayer.
Williams, W. Drunkard, The.
Portrait of the Author.
These.
Wordsworth, W. Away, away, it is the air.
Ballad, A: "And will you leave me thus alone."
Complaint of a Forsaken Indian Woman, The.
Composed near Calais, on the Road Leading to
 Ardres, August 7, 1802.
In Part from Moschus's Lament for Bion.
Lament of Mary Queen of Scots on the Eve of a
 New Year.
Reverie of Poor Susan, The.
Sonnet Written by Mr — Immediately after the
 Death of His Wife.
'Tis said that some have died for love.
Written in London, September, 1802.
Wright, C. Primitive Journal.
Wright, J. Lying in a Hammock at William
 Duffy's Farm in Pine Island, Minnesota.
Wyatt, S. Absence! Absenting causeth me to
 complain.
After great storms the calm returns.
Alas, poor man, what hap have I.
All heavy minds.
All in thy sight my life doth whole depend.
Because I have thee still kept from lies and
 blame.
Comfort thyself, my wo[e]ful heart.
Enemy [or en'my] of life, decayer of all kind,
 The [or Th'].
For shamefast harm of great and hateful need.
Fruit of all the service that I serve, The.
Heart oppressed [or oppress'd] with desperate
 thought.
I lead a life unpleasant, nothing glad.
I see that chance hath chosen me.
Joy so short alas, the pain so near, The.
Like as the swan towards her death.
Love and Fortune and my mind, rememb'rer.
Most wretched heart, most miserable.
My hope, alas, hath me abused.
O, what undeserved cruelty.
Pillar [or Piller] perished [or pearisht] is
 whe[a]rto I le[a]nt, The.
Plain ye, mine eyes. Accompany my heart.
Restful place, reviver of my smart, The.
She sat and sewed that hath done me the wrong.
Since you will needs that I shall sing.
Suffering in sorrow, in hope to attain.
There was never nothing more me pained [or
 payned].
To wish and want and not obtain.

What death is worse than this?
Yeats. Mongan Laments the Change That Has
 Come upon Him and His Beloved.
Reconciliation.
Two Songs Rewritten for the Tune's Sake.
Destiny
Amichai [or Amikhai]. Hadera.
Borges. Chess.
Elegy: "Oh destiny of Borges."
Iron Coin, The.
Limits.
To a Coin.
Carver, R. Garden, The.
Cavafy. Nero's Term.
Ciardi, J. Man and a Woman Might at This
 Moment, A.
Frost, R. Gift Outright, The.
Hughes, T. That Star.
Laughlin, J. Is It Written.
She Seemed to Know.
With My Third Eye.
Levertov. Annunciation.
Her Destiny.
Her Vision.
Isis Speaks.
Mahon. Last of the Fire Kings, The.
Michelangelo Buonarroti. One Who made, and
 from utter nothing too, The.
Montale. Chrysalis.
Mediterranean.
Orr, G. River, The.
Pasternak, B. Oh had we known it turns out so.
Pessoa. Maritime Ode.
Petrarch. I knew already, Love, our human
 ploys.
Pinsky. Hearts, The.
Riley, J. Best Is Good Enough, The.
Seifert. Hands of Venus, The.
Tate, J. Consumed.
Zaturenska. Uninvited Guest, The.
See also **Fate**
Destruction
Ai. Testimony of J. Robert Oppenheimer, The.
Amichai [or Amikhai]. Elegy on an Abandoned
 Village.
Ammons. Makers, The.
Atwood. Four Small Elegies.
It Is Dangerous to Read Newspapers.
Newsreel: Man and Firing Squad.
Berry, W. Against the War in Vietnam.
Dark with power.
In This World.
Supplanting, The.
Want of Peace, The.
Berryman. Long Home, The.
Blue Cloud. Gentle Earthquake, A.
Hurricane Andrew.
Borges. Alexandria, A.D. 641.
Bukowski. Change of Habit, A.
Destroying Beauty.
Dogs.
I've Seen Too Many Glazed-Eyed Bums Sitting
 under a Bridge Drinking Cheap Wine.
Byron, G. On the Day of the Destruction of
 Jerusalem by Titus.
Ciardi, J. Divorced, Husband Demolishes
 House.
Clampitt. Scaffold, A.
Crane, H. Eternity.
Creeley. Answer, The.
"Oh My Love."
Some Afternoon.
Dickey, W. Afternoon Evening and Night in the
 Courtyard of the Museum of Modern Art.
Donne. Broken Heart, The.
Duncan, R. Passage Over Water.
Eberhart, R. Dream, A.
Fantasy of a Small Idea.
Groundhog Revisiting, The.
Laocoön.
Necessity.
Protagonists.
Swinging Bridge, The.
Testimony.
Truncated Bird, The.
United 555.

White Pines, Felled 1984.
Words.
World War.
Emerson, R. Water.
Fenton, J. Wind.
Frost, R. Bursting Rapture.
Gallagher, T. Death of the Horses by Fire.
Unsteady Yellow.
Goll, I. Jean Sans Terre Reviews the Fathers.
Graves, R. Mist.
Twins.
Gray, T. Impromptu.
Gunn, T. Lofty in the Palais de Danse.
Hall, D. Corner, The.
HaNagid. Earthquake, The.
Hughes, L. Shall the Good Go Down?
Hughes, T. Executioner, The.
Lovepet, The.
Stone, The.
Ignatow, D. Come!
Jarrell, R. Traveler, The.
Jeffers, R. Beautiful Captive, The.
Decaying Lambskins.
End of the World.
Little Scraping, A.
Summer Holiday.
What of It?
Jonson, B. Execration upon Vulcan, An.
Kinnell. Ruins under the Stars.
Kipling, R. Song of Seven Cities, The.
Kizer, C. Index, a Mountain.
Komunyakaa. Crack.
Urban Renewal.
Kunitz, S. Last Picnic, The.
Laughlin, J. Avalanche, The.
Lawrence, D. H. At Last.
Breath of Life, The.
Dies Illa.
Levi, P. Give Us.
Lindsay, N. Soul of a Spider, The.
Lux. Barn Fire.
MacDiarmid, H. Glen of Silence, The.
MacLeish. Night Watch in the City of Boston.
Population Explosion.
MacNeice. Débâcle.
Jungle Clearance Ceylon.
McGrath, T. Citizen Dreaming, The.
Melville, H. Pisa's Leaning Tower.
Ravaged Villa, The.
Mencius. Ox Mountain Parable, The.
Meredith, W. Three Sorts of Violence, The.
Merrill, J. Nike.
Urban Convalescence, An.
Merton. Letter to Pablo Antonio Cuadra
 Concerning Giants, A.
Merwin. Chase, The.
Savonarola.
Milosz, C. Farewell: "I speak to you, my son."
Flight.
Song on Porcelain.
Olson, C. La Torre.
Mathematical Secret, and the Apron, The.
Scream to the Editor, A.
Town, The.
Oppen. Survival: Infantry.
Owen, W. To Eros.
Pagis. Lesson in Observation, A.
Patchen. Destruction of Carthage, The.
Piercy. Kneeling at the Pipes.
Long Death, The.
Poe. Sonnet—To Science.
Raine, K. It is in us they burn.
Polluted tide, / Desecrated earth destroyed.
Rich, A. For the Record.
Rossetti, C. Alas, alas! for the self-destroyed /
 Vanish as images from a glass.
God Is Our Hope and Strength.
Hear what the mournful linnets say.
Rukeyser, M. For Fun.
Sand-Quarry with Moving Figures.
Sandburg, C. At the Gates of Tombs.
Prayers of Steel.
Seifert. Demolition Report.
Sinful City.
Shapiro, K. Tornado Warning.
Shelley, P. Lines Written During the

Castlereagh Administration.
Tower of Famine, The.
Spender, S.   Nocturne: "Their six-weeks-old
    daughter lies."
Perhaps.
Stafford, W.   Big House, The.
Swift, J.   On the Burning of Whitehall in 1698.
Szymborska, W.   End and Beginning.
End and the Beginning, The.
Williams, C. K.   Don't.
Downwards.
Williams, T.   Cabin.
Wilner, E.   Abstraction.
Wordsworth, W.   Composed at Neidpath Castle,
    the Property of Lord Queensberry,1803.
Rural Architecture.
Wyatt, S.   Like as the wind with raging blast.
Will ye see what wonders love hath wrought?
Zagajewski.   December.

Detectives
Nash, O.   Don't Guess, Let Me Tell You.
Plath.   Detective, The.
Williams, M.   Old Detective Begins His Last
    Interrogation Looking for the Truth as Always,
    The.

Determination
Angelou.   Still I Rise.
Atwood.   Planters, The.
Eberhart, R.   Old Question.
Hardy, T.   In the Seventies,
Lindsay, N   Mouse That Gnawed the Oak-Tree
    Down, The.
Moore, M.   I May, I Might, I Must.
Oliver, M.   Journey, The.
Piercy.   For the Young Who Want To.
Woman in the Ordinary, The.
Rich, A.   Power.
Sarton, M.   Humpty Dumpty.
Williams, W.   Dedication for a Plot of Ground.
To an Old Jaundiced Woman.
Wyatt, S.   Lo, how I seek and sue to have.
No! Indeed.
Though some do grudge to see me joy.

Detroit, Michigan
Davie, D.   Pontiac.
Dugan, A.   Accommodation to Detroit.
Levine, P.   Belle Isle, 1949.
Coming Home, *Detroit*, 1968.
Detroit Grease Shop Poem.
Ordinary Morning, An.
Saturday Sweeping.
Snow.
You Can Have It.
O'Hara, F.   Alma.

Developing Countries
Van Duyn.   Economics.

Development
Amichai [or Amikhai].   Poems of continuity,
    mines and graves.
Creeley.   Cebu.
Davie, D.   Through Bifocals.
Dugan, A.   On the Liquidation of Zoology.
Rilke.   Child, The.
Swenson, M.   Goodbye, Goldeneye.
Szymborska, W.   On the Banks of the Styx.

Devil
Baudelaire.   Point of No Return, The.
Ruin.
Borges.   Two Versions of "Knight, Death and
    the Devil."
Ciardi, J.   Nothing Is Really Hard but to Be
    Real.
Clifton, L.   Eve's version.
Lucifer Speaks in His Own Voice.
Lucifer Understanding at Last.
Oh where have you fallen to.
Remembering the Birth of Lucifer.
Whispered to Lucifer.
Dugan, A.   Crimes of Bernard, The.
Tourist Poem.
Jackson, L.   Devil As Friend, The.
Levertov.   Waving to the Devil.
Milosz, C.   Gardener.
Thoreau.   Who hears the parson.

See also **Satan**

Devonshire, England
Davie, D.   Devonshire.
Livingshayes.
Some Shires Revisited.
Sounds of a Devon Village.
Herrick.   Discontents in Devon.
To His Household Gods.

Dew
Ammons.   Right On.
Creeley.   My Love.
Graves, R.   Song: Dew-Drop and Diamond.
Herrick.   Dew Sat on Julia's Hair.
To Dewes. A Song.
To Primroses Filled with Morning Dew.
Marvell.   On a Drop of Dew.
Ros.
Very.   Hymn: The Dew.

Diabetes
Hacker, M.   Fifteen to Eighteen
Fourteen.

Dialects
Ciardi, J.   Firsts.

Diana
See **Artemis**

Diana (mythology)
Cullen, C.   To Endymion.
"Dario."   Palimpsest: "Written in an old Aeolian
    dialect."
Gallagher, T.   Instructions to the Double.
Meredith, G.   My Lady has Diana's brows.
Ralegh, S.   Homage to Diana.
Zaturenska.   Theme from Louise Labé, A.

Diaries
Bishop, E.   From Trollope's Journal.
Creeley.   End.
Koch, K.   Artist, The.
Larkin, P.   Forget What Did.
Lorde.   Martha.
Patchen.   Note for a Diary.
Stafford, W.   Keeping a Journal.
What's in My Journal.
Swift, J.   Verses Wrote in a Lady's Ivory Table-
    Book.
Walcott.   Islands.
Whalen, P.   April Showers Bring Rain?

Dice
Ammons.   My Dice Are Crystal.
Orr, G.   Paradise.

Dickens, Charles
Browning, R.   Reflections on Reading a Life of
    Dickens.
Major, C.   He gave the Fascisti salute.

Dickinson, Emily
Berryman.   Your Birthday in Wisconsin You Are
    140.
Ciardi, J.   Instances.
Clampitt.   Amherst.
Collins, B.   Taking Off Emily Dickinson's
    Clothes.
Cooper, J.   Scattered Words for Emily
    Dickinson.
Crane, H.   To Emily Dickinson.
Eberhart, R.   Wedding on Cape Rosier, A.
Lux.   Emily's Mom.
MacLeish.   In and Come In.
Nash, O.   Chipmunk, The.
Pinkerton, H.   On Emily Dickinson.
Rich, A.   I Am in Danger—Sir.
Sandburg, C.   Letters to Dead Imagists.
Public Letter to Emily Dickinson.
Swenson, M.   Daffodildo.
Tomlinson, C.   Letters from Amherst.
Wilbur, R.   Altitudes.

Dictionaries
Hardy, T.   Liddell and Scott.
Johnson, S.   Gnothi Seauton (Post Lexicon
    Anglicanum Auctum et Emendatum).
Laughlin, J.   Importance of Dictionaries, The.
McGrath, T.   Need for Dictionaries II, The.
Zagajewski.   Polish Biographical Dictionary in a
    Library in Houston, The.

Dido
Ausonius.   I am that Dido which thou here do'st
    see.
Dugan, A.   Speech for Aeneas.

Smith, S.   Dido's Farewell to Aeneas.
Stock, R.   Beacon, The.
Wyatt, S.   Dido am I, the founder first of
    Carthage.

Dieting
Herrick.   Diet.
Nash, O.   I Can't Have a Martini, Dear, but You
    Take One.
Parker, D.   Paean.

Digby, Lady Venetia
Jonson, B.   Epigram to My Muse, the Lady
    Digby, An.
Eupheme.

Digging and Diggers
Atwood.   Digging.
Celan.   There was earth inside them, and.
Hall, D.   Digging.
Laughlin, J.   Digging Down to China.
Levertov.   Re-Rooting.
Merwin.   Diggers, The.
Rumi.   Someone Digging in the Ground.
Sandburg, C.   Muckers.
Simic.   Game, The.
Stockton, A.   Impromptu Epitaph on the Grave
    Digger of Princeton—1769.
Wilbur, R.   Digging for China.

Dikes
Kipling, R.   Dykes, The.

Dillinger, John
Bukowski.   John Dillinger Marches On.

Diners
Atwood.   They Eat Out.
Eberhart, R.   Hand, The.
Gunn, T.   Cafeteria in Boston.
Ignatow, D.   Diner, The.
Logan, J.   Nighthawks: after Hopper's Painting.
Williams, C. K.   Regulars, The.

Dinosaurs
Sandburg, C.   Dinosaur Bones, The.
Szymborska, W.   Dinosaur Skeleton.
Updike.   On the Inclusion of Miniature
    Dinosaurs in Breakfast Cereal Boxes.

Diogenes
Melville, H.   Apparition, The.

Dionysus
Broumas, O.   Maenad.
Carruth, H.   Gods.
Cavafy.   Procession of Dionysus.
Crane, H.   Lachrymae Christi.
Euripides.   Choros Translations.
Graves, R.   Ambrosia of Dionysus and Semele,
    The.

Diplomacy and Diplomats
Amichai [or Amikhai].   UN Headquarters in the
    High Commissioner's Residence in Jerusalem.
Cavafy.   Envoys from Alexandria.
Davie, D.   From the New World.
Donne.   To Sir Henry Wotton, at His Going
    Ambassador to Venice.
Emerson, R.   Tact.
Jonson, B.   To the Right Hon[oura]ble Hierome,
    L[ord] Weston.
Marvell.   In Legationem Domini Oliveri St John
    ad Provincias Foederatas [On the Embassy of
    Lord Oliver St John to the United Provinces].
Letter to Doctor Ingelo, A.
Meredith, G.   While Nature mocks her truth
    with mimic shows.
Paley, G.   In Hanoi 1969.
Smith, S.   Ambassador, The.
Williams, M.   For J. William Fulbright on the
    Day of His Death.

Dirigibles
Carruth, H.   Incorrigible Dirigible, The.

Dirt
Carver, R.   Fields, The.
Ignatow, D.   Invocation: "Dirt and stone, if I
    may know you as you know yourselves."
Kinnell.   Supper after the Last, The.
Komunyakaa.   Praising Dark Places.
Swenson, M.   This Morning.

Disabilities
Ciardi, J.   Joe with a Wooden Leg.
Dickinson, E.   Anatomical dishabille.

Dugan, A.   Prayer for One Leg.
Soliloquy: Ghost Dance for a Cripple.
Ginsberg, A.   Crazy Spiritual, A.
Glück, L.   Cripple in the Subway, The.
Late Snow.
Kumin, M.   Sisyphus.
Laughlin, J.   Limper, The.
Lindsay, N.   Lame Boy and the Fairy, The.
Mistral, G.   Those Who Do Not Dance.
Owen, W.   Disabled.
Imbecile, The.
Rich, A.   Transit.
Ritsos.   Yard, The.
Rukeyser, M.   Slow Dialogue between Pain and Roosevelt.

Disappointment
Auden.   We Too Had Known Golden Hours.
Bukowski.   Trapped.
Burns, R.   Here's a Health to Ane I Lo'e Dear.
I dream'd I lay where flowers were springing.
Carruth, H.   Incident of May.
Cowper, W.   Hope, like the short-liv'd ray that gleams awhile.
Love Abused.
Creeley.   Echo ("Broken heart, you / timeless wonder").
Love ("Not enough. The question: what is").
Thinking.
Dickinson, E.   I showed her Heights she never saw.
It would never be Common—more—I said.
This is the place they hoped before.
Whoever disenchants.
Dove, R.   Lightnin' Blues.
Ginsberg, A.   Long Live the Spiderweb.
Graves, R.   Timeless Meeting.
Hardy, T.   Broken Appointment, A.
Expectation and Experience.
Homecoming, The.
I Said and Sang Her Excellence.
John and Jane.
No Buyers [or No Buyers: A Street Scene].
O I Won't Lead a Homely Life.
Herrick.   Invitation, The.
Housman.   Yonder see the morning blink.
Jeffers, R.   Local Legend.
Self-Criticism in February.
Levine, P.   Blasting from Heaven.
Lorde.   My Fifth Trip to Washington Ended in Northeast Delaware.
Sewerplant Grows In Harlem Or I'm a Stranger Here Myself.
MacLeish.   Against Illuminations.
White-Haired Girl.
Meredith, G.   I look'd for my poet—he came not!
Madrigal: "Since Tuck is faithless found, no more."
Once the fair Romance of story.
Reply of the County of Surrey to the Poet's Pathetic Address in Dispraise of Jean.
'Twas yesterday such a black-dye-day.
Was it wise to count the ranks of teeth.
Waves are pressing up with force, The.
We stood in the garden alone.
While Nature mocks her truth with mimic shows.
Nash, O.   Have a Seat behind the Potted Palm, Sir.
Strange Case of Mr. Fortague's Disappointment, The.
Strange Case of Mr. Wood's Frustration, The.
Try It Suns. and Hols.; It's Closed Then.
Oppen.   People, the People, The.
Parker, D.   One Perfect Rose.
Ralegh, S.   Farewell to False Love, A.
Rich, A.   Prospect, The.
Snapshots of a Daughter-in-Law.
Rossetti, C.   Of each sad word which is more sorrowful.
Rumi.   Joy at Sudden Disappointment.
Schuyler, J.   August Night.
Shelley, P.   Fragment: "Alas! this is not what I thought life was."
Stockton, A.   Disappointment, an Ode 1756 to Mr Stockton, The.

Tate, J.   My Great Great Etc. Uncle Patrick Henry.
Tragedy's Greatest Hits.
Wordsworth, W.   Star-Gazers.
Yarrow Visited [September, 1814].
Wyatt, S.   Answer that ye made to me, my dear, The [or Th'].
Give place all ye that doth rejoice.
If ever man might him avaunt.
In wilful riches I have found poverty.
Sith it is so that I am thus refused.
Thou hast no faith of him that hath none.

Disarmament
See **Militarism; Pacifism and Pacifists**

Disasters
Amichai [or Amikhai].   Try to Remember Some Details.
Ammons.   Eternal City, The.
Beckett, S.   Imagine si ceci.
Berryman.   Tampa Stomp.
Bierce.   Something in the Papers.
Ciardi, J.   Diary Entry.
Creeley.   News of the World.
Dickinson, E.   It was a quiet seeming Day.
Eberhart, R.   Three Kids.
Graves, R.   Fallen Tower of Siloam, The.
Hamill, S.   Malebolge: Prince William Sound.
Herrick.   Comfort In Calamity.
Hughes, T.   In Laughter.
Long Tunnel Ceiling, The.
Jeffers, R.   Night Without Sleep.
Kipling, R.   Dove of Dacca, The.
Giffen's Debt.
Kizer, C.   Suppressing the Evidence.
Larkin, P.   Explosion, The.
Laughlin, J.   People Boxes, The.
Levertov.   News Items.
Levi, P.   Girl-Child of Pompei, The.
Logue, C.   Singing Prayer, A.
Meredith, G.   Phaëthôn.
Merwin.   Late Wonders.
Oppen.   From Disaster.
Petrarch.   One day when I was looking from my window.
Plath.   Doomsday.
Ramanujan.   Report, A.
Rexroth, K.   Prolegomenon to a Theodicy, A.
Rossetti, C.   Repining.
Whitman, W.   Voice from Death, A.
Whittier.   Chicago.
Williams, M.   Survivor, The.

Discipline
Berry, W.   Discipline, A.
Broumas, O.   Prayer with Martial Stance.
Ciardi, J.   Boy.
Dugan, A.   Decimation before Phraäta, The.
Graves, R.   Two Disciplines.
Hamill, S.   Old Bones.
Han-shan.   Raise girls but not too many.
Herbert, G.   Discipline.
Kipling, R.   That Day.
Lawrence, D. H.   Discipline.
How can I teach you when your blue.
Schoolmaster [A], The.
Meredith, G.   To Children.
Merton.   When in the Soul of the Serene Disciple.
Milosz, C.   Higher Arguments in Favor of Discipline.
Riley, J.   Pap's Old Sayin'
Rossetti, C.   Seldom Can't.
Williams, C. K.   Good Mother: Out.

Discontent
Atwood.   They were all inaccurate.
Browning, E.   Adequacy.
Discontent.
Exaggeration.
Bukowski.   9 Rings.
I Have Lived in England.
I Write This Upon the Last Drink's Hammer.
Literary Life, The.
Look, The.
With Vengeance Like a Tiger Crawls.
Burns, R.   O Ay My Wife She Dang Me.
O That I Had Ne'er Been Married.
Byron, G.   I Would I Were a Careless Child.

Carruth, H.   Ho-Hum Again.
Codrescu.   Sea Sickness.
Creeley.   Chicago.
For an Anniversary.
For the New Year.
Gift, The.
Irish.
Roads.
Sick.
Something for Easter.
There Is.
Tunnel, The.
Yellow.
Emerson, R.   Discontented Poet: A Masque, The.
Enzensberger, H.   Middle Class Blues.
Song for Those Who Know.
Gay, J. *et al.*   Mary Gulliver to Capt. Lemuel Gulliver.
Ginsberg, A.   Paterson.
Graves, R.   Lovers in Winter.
Gunn, T.   Autumn Chapter in a Novel.
HaNagid.   How Could You Loathe.
Hardy, T.   Rift, The.
Herbert, G.   Affliction (1).
Herrick.   Adversity.
Discontents in Devon.
Not To Love.
Kipling, R.   Four Angels, The.
Larkin, P.   Sinking Like Sediment through the Day.
Who Called Love Conquering.
Lawrence, D. H.   Beware the Unhappy Dead!
Courage.
Elderly Discontented Women.
Lindsay, N.   Song of the Garden-Toad, The.
Springfield Magical.
MacNeice.   Corner Seat.
Nature Morte.
To Hedli.
Wolves.
McGrath, T.   Ah... to the Villages!
Meredith, G.   Promise in Disturbance, The.
Millay, E.   Hearing Your Words, and Not a Word Among Them.
Rendezvous.
O'Hara, F.   Ode (To Joseph Lesueur) on the Arrow That Flieth by Day.
Philemon.   By Philemon.
Plath.   Lesbos.
Spinster.
Riley, J.   Lines to an Onsettled Young Man.
Plaint Human, The.
Smith, S.   Actress, The.
Easy.
Repentance of Lady T, The.
Warden, The.
Stafford, W.   After Arguing against the Contention That Art Must Come from Discontent.
Thomas, D.   I Have Longed to Move Away.
Tomlinson, C.   Way In, The.
Updike.   Academy.
Williams, C. K.   Fat.
I sit in my room.
Rampage, The.
What Did the Man Do with the Clouds?
Williams, W.   Raleigh Was Right.
Wordsworth, W.   Fragment: A Somersetshire Tragedy.
Song for the Wandering Jew.
Yeats.   He Hears the Cry of the Sedge.
Zukofsky, L.   Even if love convey.

Discothèques
Ginsberg, A.   Chances "R."

Discovery
Amichai [or Amikhai].   Poem of Spring.
Auden.   Legend.
Bly, R.   Finding the Father.
Borges.   Iceland.
Limit, The.
Browning, R.   Reverie.
Bukowski.   Greek, The.
One Night Stand.
Carew, T.   Ingrateful[l] Beauty Threatened.
Creeley.   They.

Cummings, E. E.   Here's s / omething round(& so).
Davie, D.   Bolyai, the Geometer.
Dugan, A.   On Finding the Meaning of "Radiance."
Eberhart, R.   Nostalgia for Edith Sitwell.
Ferlinghetti, L.   Plough of Time, The.
Gunn, T.   Discovery of the Pacific, The.
To Natty Bumppo.
Gurney, I.   Cotswold Ways.
Hall, D.   Poem, The: "It discovers by night."
Three Movements, The.
Hughes, T.   Chinese History of Colden Water.
Jackson, L.   Fact, The.
Kipling, R.   Explorer, The.
Laughlin, J.   Deep Pool, the.
Levertov.   Garden Wall, The.
Overland to the Islands.
Pleasures.
Secret, The.
Lorde.   Ballad from Childhood.
MacLeish.   Voyage West.
MacNeice.   All Over Again.
Truisms, The.
Vistas.
Millay, E.   "Euclid Alone Has Looked on Beauty Bare."
Milosz, C.   Inheritor.
Owen, W.   Music.
Piercy.   Erasure.
Raine, K.   Winds.
Robinson, E.   Discovery.
Rukeyser, M.   West Virginia.
Sandburg, C.   Child Moon.
Leather Leggings.
Schuyler, J.   Bluet, The.
Sexton.   Kiss, The.
Shapiro, K.   Leg, The.
Stafford, W.   Security.
Szymborska, W.   Discovery.
Warren, R.   History.
Whitman, W.   Thought of Columbus, A.

Disdain
Campion, T.   Fire that must flame is with apt fuell fed.
Follow Thy Fair Sun[ne] [Unhappy Shadow].
Chesterton.   World State, The.
Creeley.   Gift, The.
Memory, The.
Davie, D.   Revulsion.
Donne.   To the Countess of Bedford ("Honour is so sublime perfection").
Glück, L.   My Neighbor in the Mirror.
Lorde.   Suffer the Children.
McGrath, T.   Proletarian in Abstract Light.
Michelangelo Buonarroti.   Nature knows what it's doing: one cruel as you.
Petrarch.   He, who in Thessaly was all too keen.
I'm caught by Love within a harsh embrace.
Plath.   Daddy.
Pope, A.   Epigram: "My Lord complains, that Pope, stark mad with gardens."
Ralegh, S.   If Cynthia Be a Queen.
Wilbur, R.   Simplification, A.
Williams, C. K.   Kin.
Williams, W.   Unfrocked Priest, The.
Wyatt, S.   Behold, love, thy power how she despiseth!
My Lute, Awake!

Disease
Beckett, S.   Ooftish.
Carruth, H.   Marge.
New Hartford.
Carver, R.   Migration.
Cummings, E. E.   Come,gaze with me upon this dome.
Davie, D.   Alzheimer's Disease.
Hypochondriac Logic.
Iowa.
Recollection of George Oppen in a Letter to an English Friend.
Eberhart, R.   Virgin, The.
Emerson, R.   For fifteen winter days.
Written in Sickness.
Glück, L.   Fortress, The.
Hayden, R.   As My Blood Was Drawn.

Herrick.   Leprosie in Houses.
Physitians.
Prognostick, A.
Upon Urles.
Hughes, L.   Pathological Puzzle.
Kinnell.   Parkinson's Disease.
McHugh, H.   Unspeakable.
Muldoon, P.   Aisling.
Nash, O.   Bulletin Has Just Come In, A.
Paley, G.   For Jan.
Piercy.   Crabs.
Ramanujan.   Fizzle.
Rossetti, C.   Henry Hardiman.
Rukeyser, M.   Bill, The.
Cornfield, The.
Disease: After-Effects, The.
Disease, The.
Sandburg, C.   Cripple.
Schuyler, J.   What Ails My Fern?
Stockton, A.   Lines on a Young Gentleman Who Died of the Yellow Fever.
Wilbur, R.   Pangloss's Song: A Comic-Opera Lyric.
Williams, C. K.   Alzheimer's: The Husband.
Alzheimer's: The Wife.
Williams, M.   Thinking about Bill, Dead of AIDS.
Williams, T.   Summer Belvedere, The.

Disgrace
Carver, R.   Distress Sale.
Cavafy.   Displeasure of Selefkides, The.
Char.   Faction du Muet.
Creeley.   Penitent, The.
Davie, D.   Elders and Betters.
De la Mare.   In Disgrace.
Hughes, L.   Ballad of the Girl Whose Name Is Mud.
Michelangelo Buonarroti.   I live for sinning, for the self that dies.
Were it true that, besides my own, another's arms.
Petrarch.   Foul Babylon has overstepped the mark.
Fountain of sorrow, dwelling-place of wrath.
May heaven's anger blaze down on your head!
Rich, A.   Book, The.
Wilde, O.   Italia.
To Milton.

Dishonesty
Bly, R.   Letter to Her.
Dove, R.   Compendium.
HaNagid.   King, The.
Hardy, T.   To a Sea-Cliff.
Herrick.   Upon Eeles.
Jonson, B.   On Bawds and Usurers.
On Cheveril [or Cheverel] the Lawyer.
Nemerov.   Sonnet: "It seems to be the trouble, everyone."
Pessoa.   Autopsychography.
Poem in a Straight Line.
Piercy.   Song of the Fucked Duck.
Wordsworth, W.   To the Pennsylvanians.

Dishonor
Brontë, E.   Sleep Not, Dream Not.
Jonson, B.   On Mongrel Esquire.
To Captain Hungry.
Kipling, R.   Last of the Light Brigade, The.
Melville, H.   Stonewall Jackson.

Disillusion
Angelou.   Accident.
Bly, R.   Aban Kavost and Ivar Oakeson.
Woman Bewildered, The.
Browning, R.   James Lee's Wife.
Patriot, The [An Old Story].
Saint Martin's Summer.
Carew, T.   Ingrateful[l] Beauty Threatened.
Carver, R.   Offending Eel, The.
Creeley.   Changes, The.
Hunger.
Roads.
Same.
There ("Place so, A").
Cullen, C.   Bright Bindings.
La Belle, La Douce, La Grande.
Dickinson, E.   Loss of something ever felt I, A.
Split the Lark—and you'll find the Music.

Ferlinghetti, L.   Poet's eye obscenely seeing, The.
See / it was like this when.
We squat upon the beach of love.
Gallagher, T.   In Maceio.
Ginsberg, A.   America.
Goll, I.   Jean Sans Terre Discovers the West Pole.
HaNagid.   First War.
Hughes, L.   Bulwark.
Disillusion.
Pictures to the Wall.
Koch, K.   Thanksgiving.
Levertov.   Remembering.
MacNeice.   Refugees.
Meredith, G.   Aimée.
It is the young fresh rainy leaf.
Merton.   Whether There Is Enjoyment in Bitterness.
Milosz, C.   Caesarea.
Montale.   Magnolia's Shadow, The.
Oliver, M.   House, The.
Olson, C.   Knowing All Ways, Including the Transposition of Continents.
Owen, W.   Dulce et Decorum Est.
Sleeping Beauty, The.
Sonnet Autumnal
Sonnet, to a Child.
To ———: "Three rompers run together, hand in hand."
Patchen.   1935.
Among Ourselves and with All Nations.
I Care What Happens.
Lament for the Makers of Songs.
Let Us Have Madness Openly.
So Be It.
Watcher, The.
World Will Little Note, The.
Piercy.   Curse of the Earth Magician on a Metal Land.
Raine, K.   Star, The.
Rich, A.   Afterward.
Snow Queen, The.
Robinson, E.   Another Dark Lady.
Rossetti, C.   Whole Head Is Sick, and the Whole Heart Faint, The.
Schuyler, J.   Labor Day.
Poem: "How about an oak leaf."
Shelley, P.   Alastor; or, The Spirit of Solitude.
Prince Athanase; a Fragment.
Stevens, W.   Disillusionment of Ten O'Clock.
Plain Sense of Things, The.
Swift, J.   Cassinus and Peter.
Tomlinson, C.   Jam Trap, The.
Wilbur, R.   Someone Talking to Himself.
Williams, C. K.   In the Heart of the Beast.
Most excruciating / thing, The.
Then the Brother of the Wind.
Yeats.   Old Stone Cross, The.

Disorder
Ammons.   Identity.
Atwood.   Solstice Poem.
Berry, W.   February 2, 1968.
Bishop, E.   Filling Station.
Dickinson, E.   I have felt like a troubled Top.
Eberhart, R.   Passage, The.
Ferlinghetti, L.   Rebels, The.
San Jose Symphony Reception.
Gunn, T.   Wheel of Fortune, The.
Herrick.   Delight in Disorder.
His Change.
Ignatow, D.   Discussion, A.
Meredith, G.   Age of petty tit-for-tat, An.
Triad of British Evils, A.
Merrill, J.   Broken Bowl, The.
Nash, O.   Mules, The.
Rumi.   Acts of Helpessness.
Stevens, W.   Bed of Old John Zeller, The.
Connoisseur of Chaos.
Whitman, W.   Beat! Beat! Drums!

Displacement
Brodsky, J.   Lagoon.
Carver, R.   Heels.
Creeley.   Evening.
Maybe.
Davie, D.   To Thom Gunn in Los Altos,

California.

Disraeli, Benjamin
Browning, R.   On Benjamin Disraeli.
Major, C.   He gave the Fascisti salute.

Distrust
Byron, G.   On Sam Rogers.
Carew, T.   To His Jealous Mistress.
Cavalcanti.   Sonnet: He mistrusts the Love of
  Lapo Gianni.
Creeley.   Of Years.
  Place, A.
  Stomping with Catullus.
Davie, D.   Put Not Your Trust in Princes.
  Where Depths Are Surfaces.
Graves, R.   Love Letter, The.
Herrick.   Anacreontike.
  Distrust.
  Suspicion Makes Secure.
Hughes, L.   Madam and Her Might-Have-Been.
Ransom, J.   Her Eyes.
Rich, A.   Like This Together.
Ritsos.   Generalization of Distrust.
Suckling, S.   Guiltless Inconstant, The.
Williams, C. K.   Mirror, The.
  Question, The.

Diversity
Cavafy.   In a Town of Osroini.
Clampitt.   Babel Aboard the Hellas International
  Express.
Dunbar, P.   Accountability.
Emerson, R.   Once the priest / Lived in an age.
Hardy, T.   So Various.
Kipling, R.   Two Races.
MacLeish.   Colloquy for the States.
Ralegh, S.   I sacrifice to God the Beefe, which
  you adore.
Rossetti, C.   To My Fior-Di-Lisa.

Dives (Bible)
Kipling, R.   Peace of Dives, The.

Diving and Divers
Atwood.   Younger Sister, Going Swimming.
Broumas, O.   Sometimes, as a Child.
Gunn, T.   Plunge, The.
Hayden, R.   Diver, The.
Housman.   Oh fair enough are sky and plain.
Kumin, M.   Quarry, Pigeon Cove.
McHugh, H.   Few Licks, A.
Meredith, G.   In the clear dark lake a lady
  dived.
Montale.   Falsetto.
Orr, G.   River, The.
Rich, A.   Diving into the Wreck.
  Springboard, The.
Rumi.   Diver's Clothes Lying Empty, The.
Tomlinson, C.   San Fruttuoso.
Warren, R.   Diver.
Williams, T.   Diving Bell, The.

Divining and Diviners
Heaney, S.   Diviner, The.
Herrick.   Divination by a Daffadill [or Daffodil].
Kunitz, S.   Day of Foreboding.
Rexroth, K.   Dative Haruspices.
Rukeyser, M.   Divining Water.
Swift, J.   Virtues of Sid Hamet the Magician's
  Rod, The.

Divorce
Bly, R.   Woman Bewildered, The.
Bukowski.   Drill, The.
  Imagination and Reality.
  Sundays Kill More Men Than Bombs.
Byron, G.   To Eliza.
Ciardi, J.   Divorced, Husband Demolishes
  House.
Cooper, J.   Holding Out.
  Urge to Tell the Truth, The.
Dunbar, P.   Chappie, A.
Enzensberger, H.   Divorce, The.
Ferlinghetti, L.   People Getting Divorced.
Graves, R.   In the Vestry.
Kunitz, S.   River Road.
Levertov.   Divorcing.
  Wedding-Ring.
Lux.   Criss Cross Apple Sauce.
Mahon.   Yaddo Letter, The.
Merrill, J.   Broken Home, The.

Nash, O.   Strange Case of the Dead Divorcee,
  The.
Piercy.   Laocoön is the Name of the Figure.
Sandburg, C.   Fifty-Fifty.
Sexton.   Break Away, The.
  Divorce.
  February 21st.
Updike.   My Children at the Dump.
Williams, M.   Divorce.
Williams, W.   Genesis.

Doctors
Auden.   Art of Healing, The.
Browning, R.   Artemis Prologizes.
  Classicality Applied to Tea-Dealing: A Fancy
    Inspired by Westbourne Grove.
  Doctor————.
  Epistle Containing the Strange Medical
    Experience of Karshish, the Arab Physician,
    An.
  You are sick, that's sure—they say.
Bukowski.   Stethoscope Case, A.
Burns, R.   Death and Doctor Hornbook [A True
  Story].
  To Dr Maxwell, on Miss Jessy Staig's Recovery.
Crane, H.   Havana Rose.
Crashaw.   Temperance or the Cheap Physitian
  upon the Translation of Lessius.
De la Mare.   Of a Son.
Dunbar, P.   To Dan.
Herrick.   Physitians.
  Upon a Physitian.
Hughes, L.   Interne at Provident.
Johnson, S.   On the Death of Dr [or Mr] Robert
  Levet [a Practiser in Physic].
Jonson, B.   To Doctor Empiric[k].
Kipling, R.   Doctors.
Kizer, C.   Medicine ("Practice of medicine,
  The").
Lawrence, D. H.   Scientific Doctor, The.
Meredith, W.   Grace.
Milosz, C.   I Sleep a Lot.
Nash, O.   Cousin Euphemia Knows Best, or,
  Physician, Heal Somebody Else.
Niedecker.   We physicians watch the juices rise.
Orr, G.   Migrant Camps, The.
Pinsky.   Doctor Frolic.
Plath.   Surgeon at 2 A.M, The.
Ramanujan.   Pain.
Riley, J.   Busch and Tommy.
  Doc Sifers.
  Doctor, The.
  Noblest Service, The.
Robinson, E.   How Annandale Went Out.
Rukeyser, M.   Arthur Peyton.
Rumi.   King and the Handmaiden and the
  Doctor, The.
Sexton.   Doctor of the Heart, The.
  Doctors.
  Surgeon, The.
Smith, S.   Doctor, The.
Stockton, A.   On Doctor Rushes Birth Day.
Swift, J.   To Dr. Helsham.
  To Dr. Sheridan.
Sze.   Murmur, The.
Tate, J.   On the Subject of Doctors.
Wheatley, P.   On the Death of Dr. Samuel
  Marshall. 1771.
Whittier.   Healer, The.
Williams, W.   Cold Front, A.
  Complaint.
  Le Médecin Malgré Lui.
  Poor, The.
  To Close.
  Young Love.
See also **Hospitals; Medicine; Nurses**

Dodo Birds
Wilbur, R.   Walgh-Vogel, The.

Dogs
Amichai [or Amikhai].   Dog After Love, A.
Auden.   Talking to Dogs.
Bishop, E.   Five Flights Up.
  Pink Dog.
Bose, B.   Dog, The.
Browning, E.   Flush or Faunus.
  To Flush, My Dog.
Browning, R.   Tray.

Bukowski.   Dog.
  Dogs, The.
  Monday Beach, Cold Day.
Burns, R.   On a Dog of Lord Eglinton's.
  On the Death of Echo, a Lap-Dog.
  Twa Dogs, The.
Byron, G.   Inscription on the Monument of a
  Newfoundland Dog.
Carruth, H.   Underground the Darkness Is the
  Light.
Ciardi, J.   Between.
  Elegy for Jog.
  Going to the Dogs.
  Knowing Bitches.
  Midnight.
  One Easter Not on the Calendar I Woke.
  Suburban.
Clampitt.   Bertie Goes Hunting.
Codrescu.   Dream Dogs.
Collins, B.   Another Reason Why I Don't Keep
  a Gun in the House.
  Dharma.
  To a Stranger Born in Some Distant Country
    Hundreds of Years from Now.
Corbett, W.   Basil 1977-1993.
  Lake Road.
  Misremembered Edwin Denby Line.
  September Song.
Cowper, W.   Beau's Reply.
  Dog and the Water-Lily, The.
  Epitaph on Fop.
  On a Spaniel Called Beau Killing a Young Bird.
Crane, H.   Great Western Plains, The.
Creeley.   For Allen.
  Lion and the Dog, The.
  Messengers, The.
  Walking the Dog.
Dickey, J.   Madness.
Dickey, W.   Dog Under False Pretences.
Dubie.   Dream of Three Sisters, A.
  Jeremiad.
Dugan, A.   Memorial Service for the Invasion
  Beach Where the Vacation in the Flesh Is
  Over.
Eberhart, R.   Key West.
Emerson, R.   I have an arrow that can find its
  mark.
Ferlinghetti, L.   Dog.
Frost, R.   Canis Major.
  On Our Sympathy with the Under Dog.
  One More Brevity.
Gallagher, T.   Story of a Citizen, The.
Ginsberg, A.   Defending the Faith.
Gunn, T.   Her Pet.
  Vigil of Corpus Christi, The.
  Yoko.
Hall, D.   Kill, The.
Han-shan.   I see hundreds of dogs.
Hardy, T.   Ah, Are You Digging on My Grave?
  Dead "Wessex" the Dog to the Household.
  Mongrel, The.
  Popular Personage at Home, A.
  Why She Moved House.
Heaney, S.   Dog Was Crying Tonight in
  Wicklow Also, A.
Hughes, L.   Old Dog Queenie.
  Poor Rover.
Hughes, T.   Dogs Are Eating Your Mother, The.
Jackson, L.   Cure of Ignorance.
Jacobsen, J.   Dogs, The.
  Mr. Tantripp's Day.
  Night Patrol.
  Tiger.
Jeffers, R.   House Dog's Grave, The.
Johnson, S.   Translation of Du Bellay's *Epigram
  on a Dog.*
Kinsella, T.   Brothers.
Kipling, R.   Dinah in Heaven.
  Four-Feet.
  His Apologies.
  Power of the Dog, The.
  Supplication of the Black Aberdeen.
Komunyakaa.   Dog's Theology, The.
  Double Limbo.
  Meditations on a Dingo.
Kumin, M.   Custodian.

Hermit Meets the Skunk, The.
Laughlin, J. Hunting Dog, The.
Lawrence, D. H. As Thyself!
Bibbles.
Lords of Life Are the Masters of Death, The.
Song of the Grey Dog, The.
Levertov. Dogbrothers.
Grey August.
Kindness.
Overland to the Islands.
Strange Song.
Levine, P. Dog Poem.
Lux. So You Put the Dog to Sleep.
MacNeice. Dogs in the Park.
McHugh, H. My Shepherd.
Spot in Space and Time.
Meredith, G. As I turn'd into the market-place.
Over the Hills.
To Children.
Meredith, W. Housed (A Report on a Visiting Dog).
Merrill, J. Victor Dog, The.
Merwin. Ali.
Dogs.
New Season, The.
Milosz, C. Road-side Dog.
Montale. Near Vienna.
Muldoon, P. Bran.
Oscar.
Nash, O. Dog's Best Friend Is His Illiteracy, A.
For a Good Dog.
Love Me but Leave My Dog Alone.
Please Pass the Biscuit.
Two Dogs Have I.
Neruda. Dead Dog.
Niedecker. My friend the black and white collie.
Oliver, M. Her Grave.
Olson, C. She Who Hits at Will.
Paley, G. Old Dog's Song, The.
Parker, D. Balto; The Lead Dog of the Team that Brough Antitoxin to Nome.
To My Dog.
Verse for a Certain Dog.
Patchen. He Is an.
Pope, A. Argus.
Bounce to Fop.
Prunty. Coach.
Ramanujan. Epitaph on a Street Dog.
Riley, J. Coon-Dog Wess.
Hired Man's Dog-Story, The.
Iry and Billy and Jo.
Little Dog-Woggy, The.
Rossetti, C. Hop-o'-my-thumb and little Jack Horner.
Pussy has a whiskered face, / Kitty has such pretty ways.
Rumi. Dog in the Doorway, The.
Love Dogs.
Sandburg, C. Dan.
Dogheads.
Sarton, M. Lament for Toby, a French Poodle.
Village Tale, A.
Schuyler, J. Oriane.
Sexton. Your Face on the Dog's Neck.
Simic. Variant, The.
Smith, S. Après la Politique, la Haine des Bourbons.
Death of the Dog Belvoir.
Goodnight.
Hound of Ulster, The.
Jumbo.
O Happy Dogs of England.
O Pug!
To the Dog Belvoir.
Wild Dog, The.
Stafford, W. Choosing a Dog.
Swenson, M. Scroppo's Dog.
Swift, J. On the Collar of Mrs. Dingley's Lap-Dog.
Tate, J. Riven Doggeries.
Updike. Dog's Death.
Van Duyn. Ballad of Blossom, The.
Footnotes to "The Autobiography of Bertrand Russell."
Goodbye, A.

We alwus had to herd cattle.
Warren, R. English Cocker: Old and Blind.
Old Dog Dead.
Sila.
Whalen, P. Early Spring.
Treading Water.
Turn, The.
Wilbur, R. Pardon, The.
Williams, C. K. Dog, The.
Williams, M. Listen.
Politics.
Woman with Dog.
Williams, T. Ole 'Sephus (Monologue to a Coon Dog).
Williams, W. April is the Saddest Month.
Banner Bearer, The.
Complexity, The.
In the 'Sconset Bus.
Savage Beast, The.
To a Dog Injured in the Street.
Wilner, E. Water Lace and White Eyes.
Wordsworth, W. Dog—An Idyllium, The.
Fidelity.
Incident Characteristic of a Favourite Dog.
Tribute to the Memory of the Same Dog.
Wright, C. Venetian Dog.
Wright, J. Dog in a Cornfield.
On the Skeleton of a Hound.
See also **Puppies**
Dolls
Atwood. Five Poems for Dolls.
Ciardi, J. Dolls, The.
Collins, B. Some Days.
Cummings, E. E. Dominic has / a doll wired.
Dubie. Poem: "Mule kicked out in the trees, A. An Early."
Gunn, T. Dolly.
Hardy, T. Dolls, The.
Kinsella, T. Soft Toy.
Komunyakaa. Nazi Doll, The.
Levertov. Partial Resemblance.
Major, C. Doll Believers, The.
Palmer, M. Of This Cloth Doll Which.
Ramanujan. Difference, The.
Riley, J. Christine's Song.
Diverted Tragedy, A.
Rossetti, C. All the bells were ringing / And all the birds were singing.
I have a Poll parrot, / And Poll is my doll.
Sexton. Falling Dolls, The.
Self in 1958.
Stock, R. Dollmaker, The.
Weiss, T. Autobiographia Illiteraria.
Wilner, E. Of a Sun She Can Remember.
Yeats. Dolls, The.
Zaturenska. Afternoon of a Doll.
Dolphins
Bishop, E. Riverman, The.
Heaney, S. Shore Woman.
Lawrence, D. H. They Say the Sea Is Loveless.
Lowell, R. Dolphin.
Nash, O. Porpoise, The.
Williams, M. Living on the Surface.
Domestic Abuse
Ai. Finished.
Mother's Tale, The.
Broumas, O. Landscape with Driver.
Carver, R. My Daughter and Apple Pie.
Possible, The.
Davie, D. Battered Wife, The.
Dugan, A. What Happened? What Do You Expect?
Hamill, S. Naming the Beast.
Hughes, L. Beale Street Love.
Evil Woman.
Komunyakaa. Born Pretty in a Poor Country.
Major, C. Kitchen Chair Poem #5.
Ramanujan. Opposable Thumb, The.
Williams, M. Fred.
Dominican Republic
Dove, R. Parsley.
Don Juan
Baudelaire. Don Juan in the Underworld.
Blok. Commander's Footsteps, The.
Byron, G. Canto the Ninth.

Canto the Tenth.
Don Juan.
Lawrence, D. H. Don Juan.
Nemerov. Don Juan to the Statue.
Stock, R. Enigma of a Final Scene.
Don Quixote
Borges. Parable of Cervantes and Don Quixote.
Readers.
Soldier of Urbina, A.
Melville, H. Rusty Man, The.
Wilbur, R. Parable.
Donegal
Mahon. Chinese Restaurant in Portrush, The.
Day Trip to Donegal.
See also **County Donegal, Ireland**
Donkeys
Chesterton. Donkey, The.
Crane, S. Man toiled on a burning road, A.
Dubie. Elegy for Wright & Hugo.
Hall, D. At Delphi.
Jammes. Prayer to Go to Paradise with the Donkeys, A.
Kipling, R. Legends of Evil, The.
Meredith, G. Ass of Balaam, The.
Nash, O. Wild Jackass, The.
Roethke. Donkey, The.
Monotony Song, The.
Rumi. After the Meditation.
Song about a Donkey, A.
Smith, S. Donkey, The.
Thomas, D. After the Funeral.
Williams, M. Stopping to Look at a Crèche in a Jewelry Store Window.
Donne, John
Carew, T. Elegy upon the Death of the Dean of [St.] Paul's, Dr. John Donne, An.
Clampitt. John Donne in California.
Coleridge, S. On Donne's Poetry.
Jonson, B. To John Donne ("Donne, the delight of Phoebus, and each Muse").
Rukeyser, M. Homage to Literature.
Dons
Eberhart, R. To Auden on His Fiftieth.
See also **Teaching and Teachers**
Doorbells
Whalen, P. Occasional Dilemmas.
Doors
Carver, R. Egress.
Cooper, J. Door, The.
Creeley. Box, The.
Chicago.
Door, The.
Return.
Cummings, E. E. There are 6 doors.
Eberhart, R. Perception as a Guided Missile.
Emerson, R. Tell men what they knew before.
Frost, R. Lockless Door, The.
Graves, R. Door, The.
Hardy, T. She Opened the Door.
Herrick. No Lock against Lechery.
Khayyám, O. Unbar the door, since thou the Opener art.
Kipling, R. Open Door, The.
Larkin, P. Mr Bleaney.
Lawrence, D. H. Doors.
Merwin. Door, A ("Do you remember how I beat on the door").
Piercy. Doors in the Wind and the Water.
Ralegh, S. My Body in the Walls Captived.
Ritsos. Knocking.
Rumi. Talking through the Door.
Sandburg, C. Circle of Doors.
Doors.
Stafford, W. Journey, A.
Tomlinson, C. Door in the Wall, The.
Door, The.
Small Action Poem.
Whalen, P. Behind the Door.
Whitman, W. Portals.
Dorset, England
Davie, D. Dorset.
Hardy, T. Domicilium.
Once at Swanage.
Overlooking the River Stour.
Roman Road, The.

Dostoyevsky, Feodor
Ginsberg, A. Fyodor.
Lawrence, D. H. Reading in the Evening.
Orr, G. Trick, The.
Patchen. Dostoyevsky.
Doubt
Arnold, M. Dover Beach.
Berryman. Nones.
  Vespers.
Brooks, G. Love Note I: Surely.
Bukowski. Fuck.
Burns, R. Primrose, The.
Cavafy. Suspicion.
Creeley. Happy Man, The.
  Mechanic, The.
  They (2).
  Token, A.
"Dario." Dream's blue bird, The.
Dickinson, E. Split the Lark—and you'll find
  the Music.
  Surrender.
  Sweet Skepticism of the Heart.
  This World Is Not Conclusion.
  Those—dying then.
Emerson, R. We sauntered amidst miracles.
Gallagher, T. Into the Known.
  On Your Own.
  Time Lapse with Tulips.
Guyon. Vicissitudes Experienced in the
  Christian Life, The.
Hacker, M. Last Time, The.
HaNagid. Good Students Tend, The.
Herbert, G. Affliction (1).
Herrick. Seek[e] and Find[e].
Kipling, R. As the Bell Clinks.
Lawrence, D. H. Can't Be Borne.
Lowell, R. Tenth Muse.
Mallarmé. When the shadow menaced with its
  fatal law.
Merrill, J. Carpet Not Bought, A.
O'Hara, F. Ode: "Idea of justice may be
  precious, An."
  To the Harbormaster.
Petrarch. In doubtful state I weep, at times I
  sing.
Ransom, J. Somewhere Is Such a Kingdom.
Rexroth, K. Memorandum.
Rilke. Doubt.
Rossetti, C. After Communion.
  Until the Day Break.
Sandburg, C. Impossible Iambics.
  Maybe.
Schuyler, J. Daylight.
Simic. Old Mountain Road.
Smith, S. Why Do You Rage?
Stockton, A. Doubt, a Pastoral Ballad—1762.
Tennyson, A. Supposed Confessions of a
  Second-rate Sensitive Mind.
Tomlinson, C. Descartes and the Stove.
Weiss, T. "Yes, But . . ."
Wilbur, R. Agent, The.
  Dubious Night, A.
Williams, C. K. Mirror, The.
  Politics.
  Question, The.
Williams, M. He Speaks to His Arguing Friends
  and to Himself.
See also **Agnosticism and Agnostics**
Douglass, Frederick
Dunbar, P. Douglass.
  Frederick Douglass.
Hayden, R. Frederick Douglass.
Hughes, L. Frederick Douglass: 1817–1895.
Dover, England
Arnold, M. Dover Beach.
Auden. Dover.
Dickey, J. Dover: Believing in Kings.
Ferlinghetti, L. Sea Is Calm Tonight, The.
Rukeyser, M. Jetty. Dover, The.
Doves
Armantrout. Traveling Through the Yard.
Browning, E. My Doves.
Campion, T. What Harvest Half So Sweet Is.
Ciardi, J. Damnation of Doves, A.
"Dario." Anagke.

Davie, D. Woodpigeons at Raheny.
De la Mare. Dove, The.
Dickinson, E. Once more, my now bewildered
  Dove.
Dugan, A. Poem: "Tree was wet with the
  moon's, The."
Dunbar, P. Dove, The.
Eberhart, R. Child, The.
Gallagher, T. Zero.
Hughes, L. Dove, The.
Hughes, T. Dove, A.
Keats. Song: "I had a dove and the sweet dove
  died."
Kipling, R. Dove of Dacca, The.
MacLeish. Wood Dove at Sandy Spring, The.
Millay, E. Song: "Beautiful Dove, come back to
  us in April."
Montale. Leaving a Dove.
Nash, O. Strange Case of the Blackmailing
  Dove, The.
Niedecker. Hear / where her snow-grave is.
  Mourning Dove.
Paley, G. In Aix.
Rossetti, C. As the dove which found no rest /
  For the sole of her foot, flew back.
  As the Doves to Their Windows.
  Look on This Picture and on This.
  Thy fainting spouse, yet still Thy spouse.
Sidney, S. Like as the Dove.
Smith, S. Old Sweet Dove of Wiveton, The.
Stafford, W. Epitaph Ending in And, The.
Stevens, W. Dove in Spring, The.
  Song of Fixed Accord.
  Thinking of a Relation between the Images of
    Metaphors.
Stockton, A. On Hearing the Cooing of a Dove,
  a Song.
Williams, T. Morgenlied.
Wordsworth, W. Poet and the Caged
  Turtledove, The.
To ———: " 'Wait, prithee, wait!' this answer
  Lesbia threw."
Zukofsky, L. Wire.
See also **Turtle Doves**
Down's Syndrome
See **Mental Retardation**
Dowries
Burns, R. My Tocher's the Jewel.
Herrick. Mr. Hericke his Daughter's Dowrye.
  Single Life Most Secure.
Laughlin, J. Family Council of the Yakovlevs,
  The.
Dragonflies
Bogan, L. Dragonfly, The.
Hughes, T. To Paint a Water Lily.
Kunitz, S. Dragonfly, The.
Levertov. Dragonfly-Mother, The.
Millay, E. Dragonfly, The.
Nemerov. Dragonfly, The.
Olson, C. Dragon-Fly, The.
Dragons
Ciardi, J. Dragons.
Davie, D. Fairy Story.
Hall, D. Some Oddities.
Major, C. You set out on a morning bright.
Meredith, G. Forest History.
Merton. Submerged Dragon.
Moore, M. O To Be A Dragon.
  Plumet Basilisk, The.
Nash, O. Dragons Are Too Seldom.
  Tale of Custard the Dragon, The.
Patchen. Where Two O'clock Came From.
Rukeyser, M. Slow Death of the Dragon.
Rumi. Snake-Catcher and the Frozen Snake,
  The.
Sarton, M. Binding the Dragon.
Smith, S. Fafnir and the Knights.
Drake, Sir Francis
Campion, T. De Fran. Draco.
  Incipit Thomas Campianus Medicinae Doctor. In
  Peragrantissimi, Itinerosissimi,
  Montiscandentissimique Peditis, Thomae
  Coryati, viginti-hebdomadarium *Diarium, sex*
  pedibus gradiens, partim vero claudicans,
  Encomiasticon.

Cardenal. Drake in the Southern Sea.
Davie, D. Devonshire.
Kipling, R. Frankie's Trade.
  With Drake in the Tropics.
Drawing
Broumas, O. To Draw the Warmth of Flesh
  from Subtle Graphite.
Bukowski. Bring Down the Beams.
Clough. Upon the water in the boat.
Cowper, W. To George Romney, Esq.
Graves, R. Wild Cyclamen.
Hall, D. Illustration.
Hardy, T. Why Did I Sketch.
Laughlin, J. Drawing Lesson, The.
Levine, P. On a Drawing by Flavio.
Logan, J. Gallery Walk: Fifteen Italian
  Drawings 1780–1890.
  Present, The.
Major, C. Drawing from Life.
  Expanded Composition, The.
Merrill, J. Doodler, The.
  Vision of the Garden, A.
Milton. On the Engraver of His Likeness.
Nemerov. Drawing Lessons.
Oppen. Drawing.
Orr, G. Room, The.
Pagis. Portrait, The.
Rilke. To Miss Nicola B.
Ritsos. Need of Proof.
  Roughly Square.
Rukeyser, M. Crayon House.
Simic. Drawing the Triangle.
Swenson, M. My Farm.
Sze. Pentimento.
Drayton, Michael
Jonson, B. Vision of Ben Jonson, on the Muses
  of His Friend M. Drayton, The.
Dreams and Dreaming
Ai. More.
Amichai [*or* Amikhai]. And as Far as Abu
  Ghosh.
  I Dreamed.
  In My Worst Dreams.
  Look: Thoughts and Dreams.
Angelou. To a Freedom Fighter.
Armantrout. Overhearing.
Ashbery, J. Hop o' My Thumb.
  Landscape (After Baudelaire).
Atwood. Dream 1: the Bush Garden.
  Dream 3: Night Bear Which Frightened Cattle.
  Dreams of the Animals.
  Flying Inside Your Own Body.
  Nightshade on the Way to School.
  Variation on the Word *Sleep*.
Auden. Lesson, The.
  Misunderstanding, A.
Baudelaire. Parisian Dream.
Beckett, S. Rêve / sans fin.
  Serena II.
Berrigan, T. Crystal.
Berry, W. Dream, The.
  Meeting, A.
Berryman. Desire Is a World by Night.
  Search, The.
Bierce. Another Way.
  Christian.
  Oneiromancy.
Bishop, E. Sleeping Standing Up.
  Summer's Dream, A.
Blake, W. Land of Dreams, The.
Blok. Illusion.
  Russia.
Blue Cloud. Deeper Than a Dream.
  First Light.
  Storm Mountain Face.
  Sweetgrass.
Bly, R. Cornpicker Poem.
  Dream of a Brother, A.
  Dream of Retarded Children, A.
  Dream of What Is Missing, A.
  Dream on the Night of First Snow, A.
  Four Ways of Knowledge.
  Orchard Keeper, The.
Bogan, L. Come, Sleep.
  Dream, The.
  Meeting, The.

Borges.   Break of Day.
Descartes.
Dream.
Dream of Pedro Henríquez Ureña, The.
Dream, The.
Dreamtigers.
For Leopoldo Lugones.
Happiness.
His End and His Beginning.
I Am Not Even Dust.
Mirrors.
New England, 1967.
Nightmare.
Ragnarök.
Soldier of Urbina, A.
Brodsky, J.   On Love.
Brontë, E.   Day Dream, A.
'High waving heather'
How Clear She Shines!
Night of storms has passed, The.
Stars.
Brooks, G.   My Dreams, My Works Must Wait
    Till after Hell.
Broumas, O.   Absence of Noise Presence of
    Sound.
After *The Little Mariner*.
Host.
Landscape Without Touch.
Browning, E.   Isobel's Child.
Memory and Hope.
Romaunt of Margret, The.
Browning, R.   Bad Dreams I.
Bad Dreams II.
Bad Dreams III.
Bad Dreams IV.
Statue and the Bust, The.
Women and Roses.
Bukowski.   Nice Try.
On the Continent.
Burns, R.   I dream'd I lay where flowers were
    springing.
Byron, G.   Away, Away, Ye Notes of Woe!
Darkness.
Dream, The.
To ———: "But once I dared to lift my eyes."
To M.S.G.
Carruth, H.   Sleeping Beauty, The.
Carver, R.   Current, The.
Looking for Work 1.
Looking for Work 2.
Road, The.
Cavalcanti.   Sonnet: He interprets Dante's
    Dream, related in the first Sonnet of the Vita
    Nuova.
Chaucer.   Book of the Duchesse, The.
House of Fame, The.
Ciardi, J.   Colossus in Quicksand, The.
Dream, A.
I was Not Sleeping nor Awake.
Cino da Pistoia.   Sonnet: A Trance of Love.
Sonnet: He interprets Dante's Dream, related in
    the first Sonnet of the Vita Nuova.
Clampitt.   Burning Child, The.
Deleted Passage.
Clifton, L.   Birthday 1999.
Dream of Foxes, A.
My Dream About Being White.
My Dream About Falling.
My Dream About God.
My Dream About the Poet.
My Dream About the Second Coming.
My Dream About Time.
Women You Are Accustomed To, The.
Clough.   I dreamed a dream: I dreamt that I
    espied.
Codrescu.   Dream (1).
Dream (2).
Dream Dogs.
I'm careful with my dreams of death.
Moss.
Coleridge, S.   If I Had but Two Little Wings.
Kubla Khan: or, A Vision in a Dream.
Two Founts.
Wish for Dreamful Sleep, A.
Cooper, J.   Estrangement.
Corbett, W.   Ed.

O, July 1992.
Cortes.   Great Prayer.
Cowper, W.   Morning Dream, The.
Crabbe, G.   World of Dreams, The.
Crane, H.   Echoes.
Creeley.   Death of Venus, The.
Dream, The.
Dreams.
For No Clear Reason.
Saints, The.
Sleep.
That day / in an oak tree—.
Three Ladies, The.
Woman, The.
Cullen, C.   For a Poet.
Hunger.
Cummings, E. E.   2 little whos / (he and she).
And what were roses. Perfume?for i do.
An(fragrance)Of / (Begins) / millions.
Be unto love as rain is unto colour^eate.
Blue the triangular why.
Dive for dreams / or a slogan may topple you.
Doll's boy's asleep / under a stile.
Fair ladies tall lovers / riding are through the.
Fea / therr / ain / :dreamin.
First of All My Dreams, The.
Here pasture ends— / this girl and boy.
If a cheerfuleet Elephantangelchild should sit.
If being mortised with a dream.
If the Lovestar grows most big.
I'll tell you a dream i had once i was away up
    in the sky Blue,everything.
It Is At Moments After I Have Dreamed.
Leastlessly / out / of this.
Listen / beloved / i dreamed.
Long ago,between a dream and a dream.
My darling since / you and.
My eyes are fond of the cast side.
My sweet old etcetera.
Now i lay(with everywhere around).
Out of the mountain of his soul comes.
Perfectly a year,we watched Together les enfants
    jumping and.
Perished have safe small.
Poets yeggs and thirsties.
Precisely as unbig a why as i'm.
Sonnet entitled how to run the world).
Sonnet: "I dreamed I was among the
    conquerors."
Supposing i dreamed this).
Thethe / the pink / Tartskids with.
Tw / oo / ld / i / nce upo / n.
What a proud dreamhorse
    pulling(smoothloomingly)through.
When you are silent,shining host by guest.
White guardians of the universe of sleep.
Why why / How many winds make wonderful.
You are tired, / (I think).
Cunningham, J.   Somnium Narrare, Vigilantis
    Est.
Davie, D.   David Dancing.
Hermes and Mr Shaw.
De la Mare.   Anatomy.
Assignation, The.
Dark Château, The.
Death-Dream, The.
Dream, A.
Dreamer, The.
Dreams.
Epitaph, An: "Last, Stone, a little yet."
Flotsam.
Glimpse, The.
Massacre, The.
Miss Loo.
Nocturne: "'Tis not my voice now speaks; but
    as a bird."
Remembrance.
Reverie.
Shade, The.
Stranger, The.
Three Strangers, The.
Unfinished Dream, The.
Universe, The.
Unregarding.
Voices.
Where Is Thy Victory?

Dickey, J.   Birthday Dream, The.
Sled Burial, Dream Ceremony.
Dickey, W.   Avalanche.
Dickinson, E.   Dreams—are well—but Waking's
    better.
I dream about father every night.
I have a King, who does not speak.
In Winter in my Room.
Night's capacity varies.
We dream—it is good we are dreaming.
Within that little Hive.
Donne.   Dream[e], The.
Dove, R.   Oriental Ballerina, The.
This Life.
Upon Meeting Don L. Lee, in a Dream.
Dubie.   Amulet, The.
Dream of Three Sisters, A.
New England, Autumn.
Sanctuary.
Skeleton for Mr. Paul in Paradise, A.
Dugan, A.   In Memoriam: Donald Mark Fall.
Dunbar, P.   Dream Song I.
Dream Song II.
Dreamer, The.
Dreamin' Town.
Dreams.
Ere Sleep Comes Down to Soothe the Weary
    Eyes.
He Had His Dream.
If.
Lost Dream, A.
Over the Hills.
Pool, The.
Why Fades a Dream?
Duncan, R.   Dreamers, The.
Festivals, The.
Often I Am Permitted to Return to a Meadow.
Sentinels, The.
Eberhart, R.   Book of Nature, The.
Caravan of Silence.
Dream, A.
Dream Journey of the Head and Heart.
Dream, The.
In after Time.
Love Poem, A: "I am the lightness that I know."
Only in the Dream.
Passage, The.
Verbalist of Summer, The.
When Doris Danced.
Eliot, T. S.   Wind Sprang Up at Four o'Clock,
    The.
Emerson, R.   Ah! not to me these dreams
    belong.
Terminus.
Enzensberger, H.   Dream, A.
Ferlinghetti, L.   Late Impressionist Dream.
Painter's Dream, The.
Sueño Real.
Frost, R.   After Apple-Picking.
Hill Wife, The.
Gallagher, T.   As If It Happened.
Candle, Lamp & Firefly.
Disappearances in the Guarded Sector.
Meeting, The.
Tableau Vivant.
Ginsberg, A.   Dream, A.
Dream Record: June 8 1955.
Drowse Murmurs.
Meaningless Institution, A.
Understand That This Is a Dream.
Vision 1948.
White Shroud.
Glück, L.   12. 6. 71.
Dream of Mourning, The.
Graves, R.   Arrears of Moonlight.
Dawn Bombardment.
Dream of Frances Speedwell, A.
Dream Recalled on Waking.
Friday Night.
Garden, The.
Hag-Ridden.
In Procession.
In Trance At A Distance.
Promised Ballad, The.
Secret Land, The.
Song: Dream Warning.

Song: Once More.
Theseus and Ariadne.
Through Nightmare.
To Sleep.
What Did I Dream?
Window Sill, The.
Gunn, T.   Barren Leaves.
Small Plane in Kansas.
Waking Dream, A.
Wheel of Fortune, The.
Without a Counterpart.
"H. D."   At Baia.
Hall, D.   Milkers Broken Up.
New Animals.
Six Naps in One Day.
Town of Hill, The.
White Apples.
Woolworth's.
Hamill, S.   Abstract.
HaNagid.   Dream, The.
He'll Bring You Trouble.
Hardy, T.   Bereft, She Thinks She Dreams.
Dream-Follower, The.
Dream Is—Which? The.
Dream or No, A.
In the Marquee.
In the Small Hours.
Last Journey, A.
Self-Unseeing, The.
Shadow on the Stone, The.
Hayden, R.   Bone-Flower Elegy.
Heaney, S.   Dream of Jealousy, A.
Herrick.   Dreame, The.
Dream[e]s.
His Dream[e].
Upon Love.
Vine, The.
Vision, The.
Vision to Electra, The.
Hughes, L.   As I Grew Older.
Beale Street.
Dream.
Dream Boogie.
Dream Dust.
Dream Keeper, The.
Dream of Freedom.
Dream Variation[s].
Dreamer.
Dreams.
Havana Dreams.
I Dream a World.
Lincoln University: 1954.
Little Song ("Lonely people").
Mister Sandman.
Morning After.
Nightmare Boogie.
Oppression.
Pictures to the Wall.
Slum Dreams.
To You.
Water-Front Streets.
Hughes, T.   Astrological Conundrums.
Ignatow, D.   Dream, The.
From a Dream.
I Dream.
In a Dream 1.
In a Dream 2.
In Dream.
In This Dream I Do Not Exist.
Ontology, An.
Ivanov, G.   Sleeping he saw Ophelia in his
dream.
Jackson, L.   Nightmare, The.
Jacobsen, J.   Dream Habitués, The.
Dream of Games, A.
Gathering, The.
Jarrell, R.   Afterwards.
Dead Wingman, The.
Dream of Waking, The.
Dream, The.
Dreams.
Girl Dreams That She Is Giselle, The.
Girl in a Library, A.
House in the Wood, The.
Lost Love, The.
Night before the Night before Christmas, The.

Jonson, B.   Dream[e], The.
Keats.   Fall of Hyperion, The; A Dream.
Nebuchadnezzar's Dream.
On a Dream.
To J. H. Reynolds, Esq.
Kinsella, T.   C. G. Jung's 'First Years.'
Dream.
Night Songs.
Wormwood.
Kipling, R.   Divided Destinies.
If—.
Kizer, C.   Flower, The.
October 1973.
Komunyakaa.   Dream Animal.
Kumin, M.   Caring: A Dream.
Dreamer, the Dream, The.
Longing to Be Saved, The.
Making the Jam without You.
Nightmare Factory, The.
Kunitz, S.   Poem: "O Heart: this is a dream I
had, or not a dream."
Larkin, P.   Morning Has Spread Again.
Traumerai.
Why Did I Dream of You Last Night?
Laughlin, J.   Frightened Bird, The.
He Dreamed His Death.
I Cannot Command You.
Large Opera Singer, The.
Maker of Dreams, The.
Mountain, The.
Skiing without Skis.
Unsatisfactory Dream, The.
Visitor, The.
We Met in a Dream.
Why Do You Never Enter My Dreams.
Lawrence, D. H.   At a Loose End.
Dream-Confused.
Dreams Old and Nascent.
Dreams Old and Nascent: Nascent.
Dreams Old and Nascent: Old.
Martyr à la Mode.
Thief in the Night.
To Toss the Troubled Night Long.
Levertov.   Broken Sandal.
Don't You Hear that Whistle Blowin'
Dream Inscape.
Emblem (1).
Runes, The.
To Rilke.
Levi, P.   Reveille.
Levine, P.   Ask the Roses.
Lindsay, N.   Alone in the Wind, on the Prairie.
Last Song of Lucifer, The.
Logan, J.   Only the Dreamer Can Change the
Dream.
Protest After a Dream.
Sebastian in the Dream.
Lorde.   Barren.
Dreams Bite.
Rites of Passage.
Song: "Wild trees have bought me."
Sowing.
St. Louis Out of Time.
Lowell, R.   Couple, The.
Harriet's Dream.
Lux.   Elegy for Robert Winner.
Man Asleep in a Child's Bed.
MacLeish.   Lines for a Prologue.
Night Dream, The.
Two Women Talking.
MacNeice.   Bad Dream.
Dreams in Middle Age.
Good Dream.
Mahon.   Dawn Chorus, The.
Day Trip to Donegal.
Dream Play, The.
Major, C.   Beyond impasse.
Darwin's Dream.
Descendant of Solomon and the Queen of
Sheba.
Venice dream of the mainland, A.
Mallarmé.   Afternoon of a Faun, The.
Renewal.
Rondel: "Nothing you have when you awake."
Maritain.   Restoration of the Pictures, The.
McGrath, T.   Dream Range, The.

In Dream Time.
In the Sleep of Reason.
McHugh, H.   Double Agent.
Stairwell.
Meredith, G.   Phantasy.
Meredith, W.   Birthday Exercise, A.
Fear of Beasts, The.
My Mother's Life.
REM Sleep.
Waking Dream about a Lost Child.
Merrill, J.   Dream (Escape from the Sculpture
Museum) and Waking.
Dreams About Clothes.
Mad Scene, The.
Olive Grove.
Merton.   Dream at Arles on the Night of the
Mistral, A.
Lent in a Year of War.
Secret, The.
Merwin.   Dream Again, The.
Dreamers, The.
One Night.
To the Hand.
War, The.
Millay, E.   Dream of Saba.
Dream, The.
Milosz, C.   Album of Dreams.
Hall, A.
Milton.   On His Deceased Wife.
Mistral, G.   Escape, The.
Montale.   In the Greenhouse.
Muldoon, P.   Horses.
Nash, O.   Cat Naps Are Too Good for Cats.
I Can Hardly Wait for the Sandman.
It Figures.
Nemerov.   Frozen City, The.
Poet as Eagle Scout, The.
Rent in the Screen, The.
Returning to Europe.
Sleeping Beauty.
Winter Exercise.
Niedecker.   Subliminal.
O'Hara, F.   Fantasy.
Sleeping on the Wing.
Oliver, M.   Dreams.
Rage.
Olson, C.   As though there were no flowing.
Conversation Galante.
Her Dream, Half Remembered.
Translation, A.
Oppen.   Alpine.
Barbarity, A.
Dream, The.
Resort.
Orr, G.   Life, A.
Washing My Face.
Owen, W.   Soldier's Dream.
Strange Meeting.
To the Bitter Sweet-heart: a Dream.
Paley, G.   In This Dream.
NOW.
One Day.
Palmer, M.   Dream Called "The House of Jews,"
A.
Notes for Echo Lake 11.
Portrait Now Before Then.
View from an Apartment.
Parker, D.   Dream Lies Dead, A.
Pasolini.   Beautiful Banners, The.
One of the Many Epilogs.
Patchen.   Irkalla's White Caves.
Penn, R.E.   Dream.
Pessoa.   I sleep. If I dream, I do not know on
waking.
Petrarch.   L'aura, my breeze, so often breathes
upon.
Whenever my gentle faithful comforter.
Pinsky.   Dreamer, The.
Plath.   Dream, The.
Dream with Clam-Diggers.
Ghost's Leavetaking, The.
Sleepers, The.
Terminal.
Waking in Winter.
Poe.   Dream, A.
Dream-Land [or Dreamland].

Dream within a Dream, A.
Dreams.
Fairyland [or Fairy-Land].
To ———: "Bowers whereat, in dreams, I see, The."
To One in Paradise.
Raine, K. Behind the lids of sleep.
Dream.
Dream-flowers.
Dream of Roses, A.
Dreams.
Elementals, The.
Hieros Gamos.
Last night I seemed in your embrace.
Still skies, still seas.
Ramanujan. One More on a Deathless Theme.
Three Dreams.
Rexroth, K. Adonis in Summer.
Equation for Marie, An.
Neoclassicist, A.
Prolegomenon to a Theodicy, A.
Rich, A. Incipience.
Jerusalem.
Lag, The.
Night Watch.
Riley, J. Bells Jangled.
Dream-March.
Dream of Inspiration, A.
Dream of Long Ago, A.
Dream of the Little Princess, The.
Fantasy, A.
Glamour.
Little Maid-o'-Dreams.
Romaunt of King Mordameer, The.
Through Sleepy-Land.
When My Dreams Come True.
While the Musician Played.
Rilke. Dream Movement.
Rimbaud, A. Winter Dream.
Robinson, E. Altar, The.
Miniver Cheevy.
Roethke. Dream, The.
Memory.
Rossetti, C. All night I dream you love me well.
Ballad of Boding, A.
Coast-Nightmare, A.
Echo.
Fata Morgana.
For One Sake.
Hopeless Case, A.
I dreamt I caught a little owl.
Mirage.
My Dream.
Old-World Thicket, An.
On the Wing.
Reflection.
Sound Sleep.
Tasso and Leonora.
Two Parted.
What?
Yet A Little While.
Rossetti, D. Orchard-Pit, The.
Rukeyser, M. Cannibal Bratuscha.
Child in the Great Wood.
Clues.
Dream-Drumming.
His Dream of Flood: And Eden.
In a Dark House.
Nevertheless the Moon.
Phaneron.
Recovering.
Seventh Elegy. Dream-Singing Elegy.
Three Black Women.
Water Night.
Whatever roams the air is traveling.
Rumi. Dream That Must Be Interpreted, The.
In Baghdad, Dreaming of Cairo: In Cairo, Dreaming of Baghdad.
Sandburg, C. Among the Red Guns.
Between Two Hills.
Bringers.
Buffalo Bill.
Carlovingian Dreams.
Consolation Sonata.
Dream Girl.
Dreaming Fool.

Dreams in the Dusk.
Dusty Doors.
Fire-Logs.
Gone.
Mamie.
Monkey of Stars.
Moonlight and Maggots.
Murmurings in a Field Hospital.
Pick-Offs.
Portrait of a Motorcar.
Prayers of Steel.
Rain Winds Blow Doors Open.
Sixteen Months.
Smoke and Steel.
Tangibles.
Waiting.
Was Ever a Dream a Drum?
Sarton, M. Nursery Rhyme.
These Were Her Nightly Journeys.
Where Dream Begins.
Schuyler, J. Dreams.
Sleep.
Tom's Dream.
Velvet Roses.
Seifert. Nocturnal Divertimento.
November Rain.
Sexton. 45 Mercy Street.
Author of the Jesus Papers Speaks, The.
Old.
Stand-Ins, The.
Three Green Windows.
Where It Was at Back Then.
Shapiro, K. Love for a Hand.
Shelley, P. Indian Serenade, The.
Marianne's Dream.
"Shu Ting." Singing Flower, The.
Simic. Empire of Dreams.
Smith, S. Avondall.
Be Off!
Death's Ostracism.
Dream.
Dream of Nourishment, A.
I Had a Dream.
In My Dreams.
My Hat.
Songe d'Athalie.
Voice from the Tomb (2).
Snyder, G. For a Stone Girl at Sanchi.
Spender, S. Dream, The.
Dusk.
Trance, The.
Stafford, W. Dream of Now, The.
Inscribed on a Prayer Wheel and Spun.
Living on the Plains.
Meditation in the Waiting Room.
Vocation.
Stevens, W. Disillusionment of Ten O'Clock.
Hibiscus on the Sleeping Shores.
Stock, R. Hand.
Stockton, A. After a Night of Perplexing Dreams.
Dream, an Ode, 1756, The.
Suckling, S. His Dream.
Swenson, M. Dream, A.
Dream after Nanook.
Laocoön Dream Recorded in Diary Dated 1943.
Love Sleeping.
Picasso: "Dream." Oil 1932.
Subconscious Sea.
Swift, J. On Dreams.
Sze. Silk Road, The.
Szymborska, W. Dream, A.
Dream of the Old Tortoise, The.
In Praise of Dreams.
Plotting with the Dead.
Thomas, D. I Fellowed Sleep.
Our Eunuch Dreams.
When Once the Twilight Locks No Longer.
Thoreau. Forever in my dream & in my morning thought.
Tomlinson, C. Dream, A.
Dream, The.
Epilogue, The: "It was a dream delivered the epilogue."
Scream, The.
Variation on Paz.

Ts'un Hsu Li. In Dream's Wake.
Updike. Caligula's Dream.
Dream and Reality.
Dream Objects.
Visions of Mackenzie King, The.
Van Duyn. Nap.
Voznesensky [or Voznesenskii]. Antiworlds.
Warren, R. Dream, Dump-Heap, and Civilization.
Dream of a Dream.
Garden Waters.
I Am Dreaming of a White Christmas: The Natural History of a Vision.
Language Barrier.
Literal Dream.
Mission, The.
Recollection in Upper Ontario, from Long Before.
Waking to Tap of Hammer.
Whatever You Now Are.
Winter Dreams.
Weiss, T. Medium, The.
Dream.
Dream Poems.
Whitman, W. Old War-Dreams.
Ship Ahoy!
Whittier. Dream of Pio Nono, The.
My Dream.
Mystery, A.
Pageant, The.
Sabbath Scene, A.
Wilbur, R. Beasts.
Folk Tune.
In Limbo.
In the Smoking-Car.
Merlin Enthralled.
Walking to Sleep.
Wilde, O. Sen Artysty; or, The Artist's Dream.
Williams, C. K. Covenant, The.
Crime, The.
Dream of Mind: The Gap, A.
History.
Knot, The.
Last, The.
Long Bells, The.
Room.
Shadows.
Shells.
To Listen.
Williams, M. Man Who Stays Up Late, The.
Waking from a Dream.
Williams, W. Libertad! Igualdad! Fraternidad!
Revelation, The.
Thursday.
Two Pendants: For the Ears.
Wilner, E. Being as I Was, How Could I Help.
Wordsworth, W. Expostulation and Reply.
Fragments from the Alfoxden Note-Book (II).
I Heard (Alas! 'Twas Only in a Dream).
Pilgrim's Dream; or, The Star and the Glow-Worm, The.
Wright, C. Mantova.
Umbrian Dreams.
Wright, J. American Twilights, 1957.
But Only Mine.
Dream of Burial, A.
Moral Poem Freely Accepted from Sappho, A.
Poem about Breasts, A.
To a Defeated Savior.
To a Fugitive.
Wyatt, S. Lover Showeth How He Is Forsaken, The.
Yeats. Dream of Death, A.
He Wishes for the Cloths of Heaven.
Her Dream.
His Dream.
Host of the Air, The.
Lover Tells of the Rose in His Heart, The.
Poet to His Beloved, A.
Presences.
Rose of the World, The.
To the Rose upon the Rood of Time.
Towards Break of Day.
Under the Moon.
Under the Round Tower.

White Birds, The.
Withering of the Boughs, The.
Zaturenska. Dream Message.
Dream, The.
Voyage.
Zukofsky, L. Not it was no dream of coming death.

Dreiser, Theodore
Warren, R. Homage to Theodore Dreiser.

Dress
Collins, B. Taking Off Emily Dickinson's Clothes.
Parker, D. Red Dress, The.
Satin Dress, The.
Rilke. Child in Red.
See also **Clothing**

Driftwood
Kinnell. Spindrift.
Logan, J. Two Preludes for La Push.
Swenson, M. Stick, The.
Wilbur, R. Driftwood.

Drinking Water
Bishop, E. Under the Window: Ouro Prêto.

Drinks and Drinking
Ai. I Can't Get Started.
Apollinaire. Rhenish Night.
Atwood. After the agony in the guest / bedroom, you lying by the.
Beckett, S. Bois seul.
Brooks, G. We Real Cool.
Browning, E. Wine of Cyprus.
Bukowski. 3:30 A.M. Conversation.
American Express, Athens, Greece.
I Am Visited by an Editor and a Poet.
I Am with the Roots of Flowers.
Nice Place, A.
Practice.
Soirée.
Somebody Always Breaking My Dainty Solitude.
Suicide.
Thank God for Alleys.
Burns, R. Auld Lang Syne.
Epistle to J. R******, Enclosing Some Poems.
Epitaph on John Dove [Innkeeper, Mauchline].
Gudeen to You Kimmer.
Here's, a bottle and an honest friend.
Hey Tuti Tatey.
Inscription on a Goblet.
Lady Onlie.
My Love She's But a Lassie Yet.
On Gabriel Richardson.
Scotch Drink.
Song: "No Churchman am I for to rail and to write."
Tam o' Shanter; A Tale.
Then Guidwife Count the Lawin.
Theniel Menzies' Bony Mary.
There was twa wives, and twa witty wives.
To Clarinda.
To Mr. John Kennedy.
To Mr. S. McKenzie.
To William Stewart.
Weary Pund o' Tow, The.
Whistle. A Ballad, The.
Willie Brew'd [*or* Brewed] a Peck o' Maut.
Byron, G. Fill the Goblet.
Lines Inscribed upon a Cup Formed from a Skull.
Carruth, H. Notes from Robin Hill Cottage.
Carver, R. Drinking While Driving.
Miracle.
Suspenders.
Cavafy. Bacchic.
Celan. Tankards, The.
Chesterton. Logical Vegetarian, The.
Ciardi, J. Apartment with a View, An.
Clifton, L. Libation.
Coleridge, S. Drinking versus Thinking.
Ode in the Manner of Anacreon, An.
Crane, H. Wine Menagerie, The.
Creeley. She's Back!
Thanks.
Cunningham, J. Interview with Doctor Drink.
Towards Tucson.

Davie, D. To an American Classicist.
Dickey, W. G.F. Died 1954, Aged 27.
Dickinson, E. I Taste a Liquor Never Brewed.
I would distil a cup.
Strong Draughts of Their Refreshing Minds.
We—Bee and I—live by the quaffing.
Drummond de Andrade. Seven-Sided Poem.
Table, The.
Dugan, A. Drunken Memories of Anne Sexton.
Untitled Poem: "Two shots down and I'm exalted."
Dunbar, P. At the Tavern.
Preference, A.
Stirrup Cup, The.
Eberhart, R. Ship Burning and a Comet All in One Day, A.
Frost, R. In a Glass of Cider.
Graves, R. Ouzo Unclouded.
Gunn, T. Another All-Night Party.
Donahue's Sister.
Hall, D. Cider 5¢ A Glass.
Han-shan. Month when farmers escape the heat, The.
Hardy, T. Great Things.
Heaney, S. Drink of Water, A.
Sloe Gin.
Herrick. Anacreontic[k] Verse.
Bacchanalian Verse, A.
Coblers Catch, The.
Frolic[k], A.
Hymn[e] to Bacchus, A.
Hymne, to the Lares, A.
To Live Merrily, and To Trust to Good Verses.
Upon Sponge.
Wassaile, The.
Welcome to Sack, The.
Housman. Terence, This Is Stupid Stuff.
Hughes, L. Bar.
Cat and the Saxophone (2 a.m.), The.
Christian Country, A.
Deceased.
Flatted Fifths.
Hey-Hey Blues.
Juice Joint: Northern City.
Listen Here Blues.
Morning After.
Neighbor.
Wine-O.
Hughes, T. Apple Tragedy.
Jonson, B. Song. To Celia ("Drink to me only with thine eyes").
Keats. Hence Burgundy, Claret, and Port.
Kipling, R. Jacket, The.
Komunyakaa. White Lady.
Larkin, P. Aubade: "I work all day, and get half-drunk at night."
Laughlin, J. Bad Night on Third Avenue, A.
Lawrence, D. H. Cups.
Drunk.
Song to the Tune of *La Cucaracha*.
Logan, J. Heart to Heart Talk With My Liver.
MacDiarmid, H. Old Wife in High Spirits.
MacNeice. Alcohol.
Brandy Glass, The.
Toast, A.
Yours Next.
Mahon. Terminal Bar, The.
Mallarmé. Salutation.
Meredith, G. Her trousers are red; she wears a coatee.
Yes, we'll pic-nic in the woods.
Merrill, J. Ouzo for Robin.
Montale. Bibe a Ponte all'Asse.
Muldoon, P. Cider.
Green Gown.
Nash, O. Club Car, The.
Drink with Something in It, A.
It Must Be the Milk.
Nevertheless.
Reflections on Ice-breaking.
Sic Semper Mr. Sherman's Temper, or Kindly Place Your Order in English.
Nemerov. Day on the Big Branch, A.
Fourth of July, The.
Moonshine.
O'Hara, F. Anxiety.

Joe's Jacket.
Mozart Chemisier.
Patchen. Great-Sledmakers, The.
Riley, J. Guide, The.
To the Wine-God Merlus.
Rimbaud, A. Evening Prayers.
Tear.
Robinson, E. Miniver Cheevy.
Mr Flood's Party.
Roethke. Gob Music.
My Papa's Waltz.
Song for the Squeeze-Box.
Rossetti, C. Better Resurrection, A.
Rumi. Gone, inner and outer.
Sheridan, T. Perlegi Versus Versos, Jonathan Bone, Tersos.
Song, The: "My time, O ye Grattans, was happily spent."
Snyder, G. I Went Into the Maverick Bar.
Stock, R. Anacreontic for a Chinese Scholar.
Drunkenness.
Prometheus Passes the Toast.
Swift, J. Poetical Epistle to Dr. Sheridan, A.
Tate, J. Contagion.
Last Days of April, The.
Stella Maris.
Tu Fu. Lo Yu Park.
Thwarted.
Van Duyn. Fall.
Walcott. God Rest Ye Merry, Gentlemen.
Warren, R. Cocktail Party.
Whalen, P. Prose Take-Out, Portland, 13:ix:58.
Wilbur, R. Voice from under the Table, A.
Williams, C. K. Friends.
Williams, M. For Jordan With Love the Eighth Year of the Slaughter.
Friend, The.
Glass Darkly, A.
How the Elephant Got His Hump.
Toast to Floyd Collins, A.
Williams, W. Drink.
Lines on Receiving *The Dial's* Award: 1927.
World Narrowed to a Point, The.
Yeats. Drinking Song, A.
See also **Alcoholism and Alcoholics; Drunkards**

Driving and Drivers
Bly, R. Driving toward the Lac Qui Parle River.
Three Kinds of Pleasures.
Broumas, O. Roadside.
Carver, R. Highway 99E from Chico.
Corbett, W. Drive Home, The.
Driving Jazz.
Creeley. "Follow the Drinking Gourd."
I Know a Man.
Mobile Homes.
Cummings, E. E. She being Brand.
Cunningham, J. I drive Eastward. The ethics of return.
I drive Westward. Tumble and loco weed.
On either side of the white line.
Dove, R. Nigger Song: An Odyssey.
Ginsberg, A. Bayonne Turnpike to Tuscarora.
Crazy Spiritual, A.
Funky barn, black hills approaching Fulton.
Green Automobile, The.
Kansas City to Saint Louis.
Overpopulation, overpopulation / Give me 3 acres of land.
These States: into L.A.
Hall, D. My Friend Felix.
Heaney, S. From the Frontier of Writing.
Night Drive.
Peninsula, The.
Postscript.
Hughes, T. Rain-charm for the Duchy.
Ignatow, D. Simulacrum.
Kinnell. Sheffield Ghazal 4: Driving West.
Kinsella, T. Traveller.
Kipling, R. Fox-Hunting.
Kumin, M. Jesus Infection, The.
Long Approach, The.
Lux. Black Road Over Which Green Trees Grow.
What I See When I Drive to Work.
Wife Hits Moose.
MacNeice. Wiper, The.

McHugh, H.   Auto.
  Eastport.
Meredith, W.   Earth Walk.
Merwin.   Drive Home, The.
Muldoon, P.   Good Friday, 1971. Driving
  Westward.
Ni Dhomhnaill.   Race, The.
Olson, C.   De Los Cantares.
Oppen.   Generation of Drivers.
Orr, G.   Lament: "I thought of you."
Pasolini.   One of the Many Epilogs.
Pessoa.   At the wheel of the Chevrolet on the
  road to Sintra.
Prunty.   Elderly Lady Crossing on Green.
Ramanujan.   Highway Stripper.
Ritsos.   Greek Cart-Drivers.
Rukeyser, M.   Sand-Quarry with Moving
  Figures.
Sexton.   Road Back, The.
Spender, S.   Driving through Snow.
Stevens, W.   Reality Is an Activity of the Most
  August Imagination.
Swenson, M.   Speed.
Sze.   Chance, The.
  Listening to a Broken Radio.
Tate, J.   In the Realm of the Ignition.
  Jo Jo's Fireworks—Next Exit.
Tomlinson, C.   Arch, The.
  Arroyo Hondo.
  Carscape.
  Drive.
  Night Ride.
  Way In, The.
Van Duyn.   Vision Test, The.
Warren, R.   Going West.
  Old Nigger on One-Mule Cart Encountered Late
  at Night.
  Tires on Wet Asphalt at Night.
Williams, M.   71 South.
  Funeral.
  Pulling Back.
Williams, W.   Right of Way, The.
Zagajewski.   Quick Poem, A.
Zukofsky, L.   Jaunt.
See also **Automobiles**

Drought
Ai.   Tenant Farmer, The.
Amichai [*or* Amikhai].   Bedouin Goes North, A.
Ammons.   Return.
  Sorting.
Ciardi, J.   Two Dry Poems.
Frost, R.   Broken Drought, The.
Hughes, T.   Rain-charm for the Duchy.
Montale.   Glory of expanded noon.
Rumi.   Green Ears.
Very.   Hymn in Drought.
  Rain Clouds.
Williams, C. K.   Drought.
Williams, W.   Words Lying Idle, The.

Drowning
Ai.   Go.
  Talking to His Reflection in a Shallow Pond.
Ammons.   Turning a Moment to Say So Long.
Atwood.   Death of a Young Son by Drowning.
  This Is a Photograph of Me.
Broumas, O.   Heart Believes with Blows.
Carver, R.   Downstream.
  Fishing Pole of the Drowned Man, The.
  Lemonade.
Cavafy.   Prayer: "To her depths the sea has
  taken a sailor."
Clampitt.   Handed Down.
  What the Light Was Like.
Cowper, W.   Castaway, The.
Crane, S.   Man adrift on a slim spar, A.
Dickinson, E.   Drowning is not so pitiful.
Donne.   Burnt Ship, A.
  Hero and Leander.
Dubie.   Margaret's Speech.
García Lorca.   Casida of the Boy Wounded by
  the Water.
  Little Girl Drowned in the Well.
  Nocturne of the Drowned Youth.
Glück, L.   Drowned Children, The.
Graves, R.   Miller's Man, The.
Gray, T.   Ode on the Death of a Favourite [*or*

Favorite] Cat, Drowned in a Tub [*or* Bowl] of
  Gold Fishes.
Gunn, T.   Behind the Mirror.
  Lerici.
"H. D."   Loss.
Hardy, T.   Mongrel, The.
Heaney, S.   Limbo.
  Seeing Things.
Herrick.   Deluge, The.
  Faire Shewes Deceive.
  Leanders Obsequies.
Hill, G.   White Ship, The.
Hopkins, G.   Wreck of the Deutschland, The.
Hughes, L.   Naughty Child, The.
Hughes, T.   Ophelia.
Jeffers, R.   Beach, The.
Kinsella, T.   Shoals Returning, The.
Komunyakaa.   Let's Say.
Logan, J.   Rescue, The.
Lowell, R.   Margaret Fuller Drowned.
  Mother Marie Therese.
Lux.   Portrait of the Man Who Drowned
  Wearing His Best Suit and Shoes.
MacNeice.   Death of an Old Lady.
Meredith, W.   Wreck of the Thresher, The (Lost
  at Sea, April 10, 1963).
Milton.   Lycidas.
Muldoon, P.   Upriver Incident, The.
Olson, C.   Pacific Lament.
Orr, G.   Dark Night, A.
Pagis.   Sport.
Paley, G.   Drowning (I).
  Drowning (II).
Palmer, M.   False Portrait of Hanna H.
Parker, D.   Résumé.
Plath.   Epitaph in Three Parts.
Prunty.   Falling Through the Ice.
  Letter.
Ramanujan.   Breaded Fish.
Riley, J.   That-air Young-un.
  William Brown.
Rimbaud, A.   Ophelia.
Rossetti, C.   Love and Death.
Rukeyser, M.   Drowning Young Man, The.
  Exile of Music.
Schuyler, J.   Grave, A.
Sexton.   Imitations of Drowning.
Smith, S.   Boat, The.
  Not Waving But Drowning.
Stock, R.   Nightmare Song.
Updike.   Pop Smash, Out of Echo Chamber.
Warren, R.   Mr. Dodd's Son.
Wilbur, R.   Marginalia.
Williams, M.   Remembering Walter.
Wright, J.   All the Beautiful are Blameless.
  In Response to a Rumor that the Oldest
  Whorehouse in Wheeling, West Virginia, Has
  Been Condemned.
  Note Left in Jimmy Leonard's Shack, A.
  River Down Home, The.
  To a Defeated Savior.
  To the Muse.

Drowsiness
Dunbar, P.   Drowsy Day, A.
Riley, J.   Serenade, The: "Midnight is not more
  bewildering, The."
  Summer Afternoon, A.
Rossetti, C.   Lotus-Eaters: Ulysses to Penelope,
  The.

Drug Addiction
Ai.   Boys and Girls, Lenny Bruce, or Back from
  the Dead.
Angelou.   Junkie Monkey Reel.
  Letter to an Aspiring Junkie.
Bukowski.   Girls.
  Junkies.
Clifton, L.   White Lady.
Creeley.   Chasing the Bird.
Ginsberg, A.   Dope Fiend Blues.
Gunn, T.   Street Song.
Hughes, L.   Junior Addict.
Jarrell, R.   Say Good-bye to Big Daddy.
Kinnell.   Burn, The.
Komunyakaa.   Crack.
Lorde.   To My Daughter the Junkie on a Train.
Mahon.   De Quincey in Later Life.

Major, C.   Mother Junkie.
Orr, G.   If There's a God.
Schuyler, J.   Mike.
Sexton.   Addict, The.
Smith, S.   Drugs Made Pauline Vague.
Williams, T.   Night Visit.

Drugs
Angelou.   Pusher, The.
Berrigan, T.   Things To Do in Providence.
Berryman.   Drugs Alcohol Little Sister.
Bukowski.   Big John of Echo Park.
  Girls.
  Old Gang, The.
  Overhead Mirrors.
Clampitt.   Cure at Porlock, A.
Codrescu.   Junk Dawn, NYC.
Creeley.   Chasing the Bird.
  Jack's Blues.
  Xmas Poem: Bolinas.
Enzensberger, H.   Sleeping Pill.
Ginsberg, A.   Aether.
  Auto Poesy: On the Lam from Bloomington.
  Laughing Gas.
  Mescaline.
  Methedrine Vision in Hollywood, A.
  News Bulletin.
  Pertussin.
Gunn, T.   Another All-Night Party.
  In Time of Plague.
  Painkillers.
  Victim, The.
Komunyakaa.   Doppelgängers.
  John Says.
Lorde.   For My Singing Sister.
MacNeice.   Messiah, The.
Muldoon, P.   Gathering Mushrooms.
  Unicorn Defends Himself, The.
Nemerov.   Frozen City, The.
Orr, G.   If There's a God.
Stafford, W.   RX Creative Writing: Identity.
Whittier.   Brewing of Soma, The.

Drugstores
Ciardi, J.   Serenade in a Drugstore.
Simic.   Venus.

Druids
Graves, R.   Druid Love.
Yeats.   Fergus and the Druid.

Drums
Bogan, L.   Drum, The.
Graves, R.   Death by Drums.
Hardy, T.   Drummer Hodge.
Heaney, S.   July.
Hughes, L.   Danse Africaine.
  Drum.
  Drums.
Komunyakaa.   Back Then.
  Ode to a Drum.
MacLeish.   End of the World, The.
  Music and Drum.
Olson, C.   Drum World, The.
  For My Friend.
  La Chute.
Riley, J.   Billy and His Drum.
  Drum, The.
Rukeyser, M.   Dream-Drumming.
Rumi.   Drumsound rises on the air.
Sandburg, C.   Was Ever a Dream a Drum?
Whitman, W.   Beat! Beat! Drums!

Drunkards
Baudelaire.   Ragpickers' Wine.
Blok.   I Am Nailed to a Bar with Liquor.
  Stranger, The.
Bukowski.   4:30 A.M.
  As Crazy As I Ever Was.
  Dear Friend.
  Farewell, Foolish Objects.
  Night They Took Whitey, The.
  Not All That Bad.
  On and Off the Road.
  Overhead Mirrors.
  Shit Time.
  Some Picnic.
  Star, The.
  Training for Kid Aztec.
  Twins.

Burns, R.   Gudeen to You Kimmer.
Johnie Blunt.
O ken ye what Meg o' the mill has gotten.
Song: "No Churchman am I for to rail and to write.
Then Guidwife Count the Lawin.
Byron, G.   Epitaph on John Adams, of Southwell.
Carver, R.   Cougar, The.
For Semra, with Martial Vigor.
Kitchen, The.
Wine.
Chesterton.   Rolling English Road, The.
Ciardi, J.   Joshua on Eighth Avenue.
Clampitt.   Hedge of Rubber Trees. A.
Creeley.   Later ("Drunks leaning on your arm").
Thanks.
Cummings, E. E.   Glazed mind layed in a, A).
Gr / eyhaire / d(m), A.
He as o / ld as who stag, A.
In Healey's Palace I was sitting.
The / nimble / heat / had.
Softly from its still lair in Plympton Street.
Cunningham, J.   Interview with Doctor Drink.
De la Mare.   Drugged.
Dickinson, E.   Ditch is dear to the Drunken man, The.
Drunkard cannot meet a Cork, A.
I Taste a Liquor Never Brewed.
Dugan, A.   Memories of the Bowery.
On Hibernation in the Country.
Two Quits and a Drum, and Elegy for Drinkers.
Variation on "Winter's Onset from an Alienated Point of View."
When I Was Drunk and Disorderly the Boston Policeman Told Me.
Dunbar, P.   Delinquent, The.
Lager Beer.
Fenton, J.   Skip, The.
Graves, R.   Point of No Return.
Gunn, T.   Outside the Diner.
Hafiz [or Hafez].   Ghaselle.
Hamill, S.   Letter to John Logan from La Push.
Herrick.   Upon Blisse.
Upon Buggins.
Upon Huncks: Epigram.
Upon One-Ey'd Broomsted.
Upon Parrat.
Vision, The.
Housman.   Could man be drunk for ever.
Terence, This Is Stupid Stuff.
Hughes, L.   Ballad of Gin Mary.
Drunkard.
Wine-O.
Ignatow, D.   At Four O'Clock.
Subway.
Jacobsen, J.   Brother Peter Considers Mulroy Drunk under the Rosebush.
Jeffers, R.   Drunken Charlie.
Jonson, B.   On Captain Hazard the Cheater.
Kipling, R.   Cells.
Giffen's Debt.
Shut-Eye Sentry, The.
Laughlin, J.   Dylan.
What Matters.
Levine, P.   Sweet Will.
Li Po.   Drinking Together.
Lindsay, N.   Drunkard's Funeral, The.
Drunkards in the Street, The.
Lux.   Portrait of the Man Who Drowned Wearing His Best Suit and Shoes.
MacNeice.   Drunkard, The.
Meng Hao Jan.   Late Spring.
Meredith, W.   Couple Overhead, The.
Niedecker.   Mr. Van Ess bought 14 washcloths?
Oliver, M.   Alex.
Oppen.   Night Scene.
Riley, J.   Case in P'int, A.
Man by the Name of Bolus, A.
Rimbaud, A.   Morning of Drunkenness.
Stupidities—Second Series.
Ritsos.   Striding Over.
Robinson, E.   Miniver Cheevy.
Mr Flood's Party.
Roethke.   Surly One, The.
Rumi.   Children's Game, A.

Drunks fear the police.
Who Says Words with My Mouth.
Sandburg, C.   Jack London and O. Henry.
Schuyler, J.   Ajaccio Violets.
Sexton.   Cigarettes and Whiskey and Wild, Wild Women.
Stock, R.   Drunkenness.
To My Inebriety.
Tomlinson, C.   Terminal Tramps.
Van Duyn.   Fall.
Warren, R.   Folly on Royal Street before the Raw Face of God.
Whalen, P.   Lotus Sutra, Naturalized, The.
Wilbur, R.   Voice from under the Table, A.
Williams, C. K.   Bob.
Toil.
Williams, M.   Christmas Poem, A.
Williams, T.   Wine-Drinkers, The.
Williams, W.   Drunkard, The.
Wright, J.   Christmas Greeting, A.
I Am a Sioux Brave, He Said in Minneapolis.
Inscription for the Tank.
Larry.
Morning: Leaving Calle Gigantes.
Non-Birthday Poem for My Father, A.
Note Left in Jimmy Leonard's Shack, A.
To a Dead Drunk.
Yeats.   Drunken Man's Praise of Sobriety, A.
Hour before Dawn, The.
See also **Alcoholism and Alcoholics**

Dryads
"H. D."   Acon.

Dryden, John
Byron, G.   Verses Found in a Summer-House at Hales-Owen.
Pope, A.   Epitaph Intended for Mr. Rowe, in Westminster Abbey.

Du Bois, W. E. B. (William Edward Burghardt)
Walker, A.   "Women of Color" Have Rarely Had the Opportunity to Write about Their Love Affairs.
Wright, J.   W. E. B. DuBois at Harvard.

Dublin, Ireland
Davie, D.   North Dublin.
On Sutton Strand.
Samuel Beckett's Dublin.
Heaney, S.   Viking Dublin: Trial Pieces.
Kinsella, T.   Open Court.
Larkin, P.   Dublinesque.
Logan, J.   Dublin Suite: Homage to James Joyce.
Mahon, D.   Dawn at Saint Patrick's.
Updike.   Literary Dublin.
Wright, C.   Jesuit Graves.

Ducks
Campion, T.   De Fran. Draco.
Carver, R.   Sorrel.
Coleridge, S.   Parliamentary Oscillators.
Dunbar, P.   Capture, The.
Han-shan.   Mandarin ducks roost for the night.
Heaney, S.   Widgeon.
Logan, J.   Three Moves.
Major, C.   In a blazing sunset.
Nash, O.   Duck, The.
Patchen.   Trueblue Gentleman, A.
Ransom, J.   What Ducks Require.
Rossetti, C.   When the cows come home the milk is coming.
Wordsworth, W.   Wild Duck's Nest, The.

Duels
Browning, R.   After.
Before.
Count Gismond.
Byron, G.   Duel, The.
Hardy, T.   Duel, The.
Pinkerton, H.   On Goya's *Duel with Cudgels* (ca. 1820), a "Black Painting" in the Prado.

Dullness
Bukowski.   Good Loser, The.
Unkind Poem, An.
Davie, D.   Limited Achievement.
Dryden, J.   Mac Flecknoe [or, A Satire upon the True-Blue Protestant Poet T. S.].
Hall, D.   No Color Man.
Hughes, L.   Lady in Cabaret.

Lawrence, D. H.   No! Mr Lawrence!
Worm Turns, The.
Mallarmé.   Renewal.
Pound, E.   Les Millwin.

Dumps
Brodsky, J.   At the City Dump in Nantucket.
McHugh, H.   What Could Hold Us.
Nemerov.   Town Dump, The.
Rich, A.   Open-Air Museum.
Stevens, W.   Man on the Dump, The.
Tomlinson, C.   From the Motorway.
Updike.   My Children at the Dump.

Dunbar, Paul Laurence
Hayden, R.   Paul Laurence Dunbar.

Duncan, Robert
Zukofsky, L.   Her face the Book of—Love Delights in—Praises.

Dunes
Ammons.   Corsons Inlet.
Dunes.
February Beach.
Saliences.
So I Said I Am Ezra.
Frost, R.   Sand Dunes.
Sandburg, C.   Dunes.
Swenson, M.   Wave and the Dune, The.

Dunkirk, France
Swift, J.   Old Lewis thus the terms of peace to burnish.
Peace and Dunkirk.

Duns Scotus
Hopkins, G.   Duns Scotus's Oxford.
Merton.   Duns Scotus.
Hymn for the Feast of Duns Scotus.

Dürer, Albrecht
Jarrell, R.   Knight, Death, and the Devil, The.
Pinkerton, H.   On Dürer's Etching of Pilate Washing His Hands (1512).
Simic.   Travel[l]ing Slaughterhouse.
Wilner, E.   Postscript.

Dusk
Amichai [or Amikhai].   Now the Lifeguards Have All Gone Home.
Ammons.   Celestial.
Left.
Baudelaire.   End of the Day, The.
Borges.   Patio.
Unknown Street.
Carver, R.   Afterglow.
Cunningham, J.   Distinctions at Dusk.
Obsequies for a Poetess.
Dubie.   Hour, The.
Gurney, I.   Glimmering Dusk.
Han-shan.   At sunset I went down the western slope.
Hughes, L.   Magnolia Flowers.
Jacobsen, J.   Fish Tank Room, The.
Levertov.   In Question.
Merwin.   Black Plateau, The.
Dusk in Winter.
Mistral, G.   Dusk.
Montale.   Frog, first to strike his chord, The.
Prunty.   Intermittent Light, An.
Riley, J.   At Dusk.
Old Granny Dusk.
Simic.   Elegy: "Note / as it gets darker."
Unknown One, The.
Stafford, W.   By the Deschutes Shore.
Warren, R.   Hope.
What Voice at Moth-Hour.
Whitman, W.   Hours Continuing Long.
Wright, C.   Blaise Pascal Lip-syncs the Void.
Looking across Laguna Canyon at Dusk, West-by-Northwest.
Zagajewski.   Three Voices.
See also **Twilight**

Dust
Burns, R.   Dusty Miller.
Chesterton.   Praise of Dust, The.
Dickinson, E.   Death is a Dialogue between.
Eberhart, R.   Imagining How It Would Be to Be Dead.
Frost, R.   Meeting and Passing.
Peck of Gold, A.
Gunn, T.   Words for Some Ash.

Jacobsen, J. Softly.
Terrestrial.
Komunyakaa. *Bui Doi*, Dust of Life.
Levertov. Freeing of the Dust, The.
Laying the Dust.
Levi, P. Dust.
Merwin. In the Life of Dust.
Rich, A. He Remembereth That We Are Dust.
Rukeyser, M. George Robinson: Blues.
Sandburg, C. Dust.
Mummy.
Shih-te. People crowd by in the dust.
Warren, R. Forever O'Clock.

Dutch, The
Brodsky, J. Dutch Mistress.
Riley, J. Leedle Dutch Baby.
Robinson, E. Rembrandt to Rembrandt.
Zagajewski. Dutch Painters.

Dutch Wars
Kipling, R. Dutch in the Medway, The.
Marvell. Character of Holland, The.
Last Instructions to a Painter, The.
Loyal Scot, The.

Duty
Amichai [or Amikhai]. We Have Done Our
Duty.
Brontë, E. M. Douglas to E.R. Gleneden.
Carver, R. One More.
Clough. Do duty feeling nought and truth
believe.
Duty.
Cowper, W. Hope.
Crane, S. Soldier, young in years, young in
ambitions, A.
Dante Alighieri. Sonnet: Of Beauty and Duty.
Davie, D. His Themes.
De la Mare. How Sleep the Brave.
Eberhart, R. Burden.
Emerson, R. Voluntaries.
Frost, R. Stopping by Woods on a Snowy
Evening.
Graves, R. Her Brief Withdrawal.
Lion-Gentle.
Pride of Love.
Guyon. Love of God the End of Life, The.
Herrick. Duty to Tyrants.
Jeffers, R. Historical Choice.
Thurso's Landing.
Kipling, R. Eddi's Service.
King's Job, The.
King's Task, The.
Pro-Consuls, The.
Reformers, The.
Song in Storm, A.
Melville, H. In the Turret.
Merton. Mysterious Song in the Spring of the
Year, A.
Merwin. Letter from Gussie, A.
Nash, O. Kind of an Ode to Duty.
Ralegh, S. Sir Walter Ralegh to the Queen.
Roethke. Last Words.
Rossetti, C. Praise of Love.
Sandburg, C. And They Obey.
Smith, S. Duty Was His Lodestar.
I Could Let Tom Go—But What about the
Children.
Queen and the Young Princess, The.
True Tyrant or the Spirit of Duty Rebuked, The.
Stafford, W. Traveling Through the Dark.
Tennyson, A. Charge of the Light Brigade, The.
Whittier. Abraham Davenport.
Anniversary Poem.
Samuel E. Sewall.
Wordsworth, W. Fragment: "For let the
impediment be what it may."
Occasioned by the Battle of Waterloo.
Ode to Duty.

Dwarfs
Blok. Illusion.
Coleridge, S. Two Founts, The.
Dubie. Pictures at an Exhibition.
Patchen. I Suddenly Became Conscious That
This Thing Was Looking at Me Intently.
Sexton. Rumpelstiltskin.
Smart, C. Author Apologizes to a Lady, for His
Being a Little Man, The.

E

E-mail (electronic mail)
Williams, M. E-mail.

Eagles
Blue Cloud. Searching for Eagles.
Browning, R. Eagle, The.
Carver, R. Eagles.
Coleridge, S. Eagle and the Tortoise, The.
Cummings, E. E. Eagle, The.
Dickey, J. Eagles.
Eagle's Mile, The.
Frost, R. Auspex.
Jeffers, R. Beaks of Eagles, The.
Fire on the Hills.
Kunitz, S. Eagle.
Lawrence, D. H. American Eagle, The.
Eagle in New Mexico.
St John.
Lindsay, N. Eagle That Is Forgotten, The.
Merrill, J. Violent Pastoral.
Nash, O. Strange Case of Mr. O'Banion's
Come-Uppance, The.
Rossetti, C. "Beloved, let us love one another,"
says St. John.
Shelley, P. Mighty Eagle.
Smart, C. On an Eagle Confined in a College-
Court.
Stock, R. Incredible Activities in the Eyrie.
Tate, A. Eagle, The.
Tate, J. Eagle Exterminating Company, The.
Tennyson, A. Eagle, The.
Thoreau. My love must be as free.
Tomlinson, C. Cochiti.
Very. Eagles, The.
Warren, R. Eagle Descending.
Whitman, W. Dalliance of the Eagles, The.
Whittier. On Receiving an Eagle's Quill from
Lake Superior.
Wilner, E. American Sublime, The: Robert
Penn Warren.
Wordsworth, W. Eagles.

Earhart, Amelia
Wilner, E. Amelia.

Ears
Emerson, R. Dost thou not hear me Ellen.
Rumi. Send the Chaperones Away.

Earth
Ammons. Dunes.
Atwood. You Begin.
Auden. Bucolics.
Et in Arcadia Ego.
Ode to Gaea.
Beckett, S. Serena II.
Berry, W. Awake at Night.
Below.
Broken Ground, The.
Current, The.
Earth and Fire.
Enriching the Earth.
Mad Farmer's Love Song, The.
Marriage, an Elegy, A.
On the Hill Late at Night.
Satisfactions of the Mad Farmer, The.
Silence, The.
Stones, The.
Want of Peace, The.
Bierce. Geotheos.
Blue Cloud. Earth and Creation.
Browning, E. Earth and Her Praisers.
Heaven and Earth.
Man and Nature.
Browning, R. Reverie.
Bukowski. Sun Wields Mercy, The.
Byron, G. When Coldness Wraps This
Suffering Clay.
Wild Gazelle, The.
Cardozo. Elegy for Maria Alves.
Clifton, L. Earth Is a Living Thing, The.
Codrescu. Mail.
Coleridge, S. Delinquent Travellers, The.
Faith, Hope, and Charity.
Hymn to the Earth.
Ode on the Departing Year.
Cooper, J. Praise.

Cortes. Space Song.
Crane, H. Interior.
Shall I Subsume.
To Earth.
Creeley. Envoi: "Particulars they want."
For a Friend.
For the Graduation.
Here ("What / has happened").
June 6, 1970.
Kiki.
Province, The.
Sunset.
Cummings, E. E. All worlds have
halfsight,seeing either with.
As if as / if a mys.
Bigness of cannon, The.
I say no world.
Maker of many mouths.
O Sweet Spontaneous.
Old mr ly / fresh from a fu.
Silent unday by silently not night.
De la Mare. Bright Life.
Futility.
Gloria Mundi.
Music.
Sleep.
Snow.
Dickey, J. For a Time and Place.
Immortals.
Moon Flock.
Dickinson, E. If roses had not faded.
Oh Matchless Earth—We underrate.
What indeed is Earth but a Nest.
Donne. To Mr Tilman after He Had Taken
Orders.
Valediction, A: of Weeping.
Duncan, R. Ballad of the Enamord Image, The.
Eberhart, R. Cover Me Over.
Fantasy of a Small Idea.
Forms of the Human.
Go to the Shine That's on a Tree.
Hard Structure of the World, The.
Ideal and the Real, The.
Maze.
Memory.
Soul Longs to Return Whence It Came, The.
Spring Mountain Climb.
Stopping a Kaleidoscope.
Emerson, R. Atom from atom yawns as far.
Hamatreya.
In this sour world, o summerwind.
None spares another yet it pleases me.
Patch of meadow & upland, A.
Patient Pan / Drunken with nectar, The.
Softens the air so cold & rude.
That each should in his house abide.
This world is tedious.
Frost, R. No Holy Wars for Them.
Goll, I. Jean Sans Terre Circles the Earth Seven
Times.
Gunn, T. Aqueduct.
Hamill, S. Lover's Quarrel, A.
HaNagid. Earth to Man.
Heaney, S. Nerthus.
Herrick. Another.
To His Paternall Countrey.
White Island.
Hill, G. Genesis.
In Piam Memoriam.
Hopkins, G. God's Grandeur.
Ribblesdale.
Housman. Here are the skies, the planets seven.
Hughes, L. Earth Song.
Hughes, T. River.
Ignatow, D. Kaddish.
Jackson, L. Earth.
Jacobsen, J. Planet, The.
Jarrell, R. Archangel's Song, The.
Blind Sheep, The.
Jeffers, R. Autumn Evening.
Beautiful Captive, The.
Broken Balance, The.
Eye, The.
Flight of Swans.
Hope is Not for the Wise.
Irish Headland, An.

It flows out of mystery into mystery: there is no
   beginning—.
Life from the Lifeless.
Metamorphosis.
Shine, Perishing Republic.
Subjected Earth.
Unformed volcanic earth, a female thing, The.
Kipling, R.   Sestina of the Tramp-Royal.
Koch, K.   Geography.
Lawrence, D. H.   Fidelity.
Four, The.
Mediterranean in January.
There Are Too Many People.
Transformations.
Travel Is Over.
Levertov.   Earth Psalm.
Earthwoman and the Waterwoman, The.
O Taste and See.
What It Could Be.
Levine, P.   Clouds.
How Much Earth.
On a Drawing by Flavio.
Rain Downriver.
Snow.
They Feed They Lion.
To My God in His Sickness.
To P.L., 1916–1937.
Walk with Tom Jefferson, A.
Lindsay, N.   Comet of Prophecy, The.
Sew the Flags Together.
Lorde.   Dreams Bite.
Sowing.
MacDiarmid, H.   Bonnie Broukit Bairn, The.
Little White Rose, The.
O Ease My Spirit.
MacLeish.   Hands.
Seafarer.
Speech to a Crowd.
Sunset Piece, The.
Meredith, W.   Earth Walk.
Merrill, J.   Childlessness.
Millay, E.   God's World.
Milosz, C.   Song, The: "Earth flows away from
   the shore where I stand."
Nash, O.   Any Millenniums Today, Lady?
Nemerov.   Celestial Globe.
Knowledge.
Loon's Cry, The.
O'Hara, F.   Invincibility.
Oliver, M.   Night Flight.
Olson, C.   Binnacle, The.
Canto One Hundred and One.
Drum World, The.
Flower grows, The.
King of the Wood / King of the Dead.
May 31, 1961.
Sing, Mister, Sing.
Whole World, The.
Patchen.   Early in the Morning.
Eve of St. Agony, or the Middle Class Was
   Sitting on Its Fat.
Great Birds, The.
How Old the World Is!
In Your Body All Bodies Lie.
Instructions for Angels.
Lao Tsze.
Lenada.
Letter to the Old Men.
Message from the Assistant Chief of the Fly
   People, A.
My Coat Is Dirty.
My Generation Reading the Newspapers.
O kind watchers came.
O my love / The pretty towns.
Other Side: The Green Home, The.
Overworld, The.
Pick Up the Evening Paper.
Preparation for the Highest Being.
Red Wine and Yellow Hair.
Rest, heart of the tired world.
Snow is deep on the ground, The.
Sure There Is Food.
Temple, A.
Valley-sleeper, the Children, the Snakes, and the
   Giant, The.
What the Grecian Earns.

What There Is.
World Whose Sun Retreats Before the Brave, A.
World Will Little Note, The.
Raine, K.   Into what pattern, into what music
   have the spheres whirled us.
This little house / No smaller than the world.
Word Made Flesh.
World: / Image on water, waves.
World, The.
Rich, A.   Atlas of the Difficult World, An.
Rilke.   Heavy Dead, The.
To Speak a Flower.
Rossetti, C.   Advent.
Buried.
De Profundis.
Earth and Heaven.
Earth has clear call of daily bells, / A chancel-
   vault of gloom and star.
Heaven Is Heaven.
Heaven Overarches Earth and Sea.
Heaven's chimes are slow, but sure to strike at
   last.
His Banner over Me Was Love.
Horses of the Sea, The.
I Look for the Lord.
If stars dropped out of heaven, / And if flowers
   took their place.
Look on This Picture and on This.
Present and Future.
Roses on a brier, / Pearls from out the bitter sea.
Sexagesima.
Strange voices sing among the planets which.
This near-at-hand land breeds pain by measure.
To What Purpose Is This Waste?
Vain Shadow, A.
What is this above thy head, / O Man?
Who cares for earthly bread tho' white?
Rukeyser, M.   He Had a Quality of Growth.
Sadi [or Saadi or Sa'di].   Had I the world for
   my enemy.
Sandburg, C.   Atlas, How Have You Been?
Be Ready.
Early Copper.
Leather Leggings.
Loam.
Sarton, M.   At Muzot.
Composition.
Invocation: "Come out of the dark earth."
Prothalamion.
Puritan, The.
Stone Walls.
Schuyler, J.   Earth's Holocaust.
Sexton.   As It Was Written.
Earth, The.
Smart, C.   On the Immensity of the Supreme
   Being.
Smith, S.   In Protocreation.
Snyder, G.   For Nothing.
Little Songs for Gaia.
O Mother Gaia.
Stafford, W.   Earth Dweller.
In Response to a Question.
Things in the Wild Need Salt.
Suckling, S.   Love's World.
Swenson, M.   Earth Your Dancing Place.
Once There Were Glaciers.
Orbiter 5 Shows How Earth Looks from the
   Moon.
Sze.   Before Completion.
Every Where and Every When.
Fern, Coal, Diamond.
Thomas, D.   This Bread I Break.
Thoreau.   Earth, The.
Ep[itaph] on the World.
Tomlinson, C.   Ararat.
Dialogue.
Updike.   Vibration.
Vallejo.   Eternal Dice, The.
Voznesensky [or Voznesenskii].   Antiworlds.
Walker, A.   We Have a Beautiful Mother.
Warren, R.   Not Quite Like a Top.
Weiss, T.   Earthrise.
Whitman, W.   Earth, My Likeness.
Love That Is Hereafter, The.
Song of the Rolling Earth, A.
This Compost.

Wilbur, R.   Attention Makes Infinity.
Caserta Garden.
On Having Mis-identified a Wild Flower.
Worlds.
Williams, C. K.   Clay out of Silence.
Don't.
Williams, W.   At Kenneth Burke's Place.
Wordsworth, W.   Composed upon Westminster
   Bridge, September 3, 1802.
Wright, J.   Alarm, The.
Arrangements with Earth for Three Dead
   Friends.
At Thomas Hardy's Birthplace, 1953.
Eye of God, the Soul's First Vision, The.
Fit against the Country, A.
Ghost, The.
Goodbye to the Poetry of Calcium.
Horse, The.
Poem for Kathleen Ferrier.
What the Earth Asked Me.
Yeats.   Before the World Was Made.
Zagajewski.   Incorporeal Ruler.
Sails.
Zukofsky, L.   Gamut.
World autumn, The.

Earthquakes
Blue Cloud.   Gentle Earthquake, A.
Clampitt.   Minor Tremor, A.
Cooper, J.   Earthquake, The.
Davie, D.   Gemona-del-Friuli, 1961–1976.
Dickinson, E.   Still—Volcano—Life, A.
HaNagid.   Earthquake, The.
Laughlin, J.   People Boxes, The.
Merton.   Atlas and the Fatman.
Earthquake.
Riley, J.   Earthquake, The.
Fall-Crick View of the Earthquake, A.
When the World Bu'sts Through.
Schuyler, J.   Shadowy Room.
Van Duyn.   Earth Tremors Felt in Missouri.
Very.   On the Great Earthquake in New
   Grenada.
Whittier.   Earthquake, The.

"Eastaway, Edward"
See **Thomas, Edward ("Edward Eastaway")**
Easter
Berryman.   Heaven.
Blok.   They Do Not Trade, Sleep, or Remember.
Browning, R.   Easter-Day.
Carruth, H.   Æolian.
Chesterton.   Easter Sunday.
Ciardi, J.   Lamb, The.
Two Egrets.
Clampitt.   Easter Morning.
Clough.   Easter Day II.
Easter Day. Naples, 1849.
Crashaw.   Easter Day.
Dunbar, P.   Easter Ode, An.
Eliot, T. S.   Easter: Sensations of April.
Glück, L.   Easter Season.
Hardy, T.   Drizzling Easter Morning, A.
Herbert, G.   Easter.
Easter Wings.
Hopkins, G.   Easter.
Easter Communion.
That Nature Is a Heraclitean Fire and of the
   Comfort of the Resurrection.
Housman.   Easter Hymn.
Loveliest of Trees, the Cherry Now.
Laughlin, J.   Easter in Pittsburgh.
MacNeice.   Easter Returns.
Nemerov.   Sonnet at Easter.
Niedecker.   Easter Greeting.
High, lovely, light.
Olson, C.   Easter.
Parker, D.   To Myrtilla, On Easter Day.
Rexroth, K.   Ausonius, Epistle 7.
Riley, J.   Hymn Exultant.
Rilke.   Few Easter Eggs, A.
Rossetti, C.   Easter Carol, An.
Easter Day.
Easter Even.
Easter Monday.
Easter Morning.
Our Church Palms are Budding Willow Twigs.
Rukeyser, M.   Easter Eve 1945.

Sarton, M.   Easter Morning.
Sexton.   Passion of the Mad Rabbit, The.
　Protestant Easter.
Smith, S.   Conviction (ii).
Stafford, W.   Easter Morning.
Stock, R.   Prose Parables.
Updike.   Seven Stanzas at Easter.
Van Duyn.   Well, that was Saturday, day before
　Easter.
Walcott.   Easter.
Warren, R.   Easter Morning: Crosby Junction.
Whittier.   Easter Flower Gift, An.
Wilde, O.   Easter Day.
Williams, C. K.   Easter.
Wordsworth, W.   Composed in One of the
　Valleys of Westmoreland, on Easter Sunday.
Yeats.   Easter 1916.

Easter Island
Muldoon, P.   Easter Island.

Easter Rebellion (1916)
Yeats.   Easter 1916
　Rose Tree, The.
　Sixteen Dead Men.
　Three Songs to the One Burden.

Eating
Atwood.   Carrying Food Home in Winter.
　Eating Snake.
Berry, W.   Prayer after Eating.
Bierce, Trencher-Knight, A.
Brooks, G.   Bean Eaters, The.
Bukowski.   Eat.
Codrescu.   Dream (2).
　Love Poem: "And while for the sake of sanity."
Collins, B.   Osso Buco.
Cowper, W.   To the Immortal Memory of the
　Halibut.
Crane, S.   In the desert.
Creeley.   Apple Uppfle.
Dickey, J.   Bread.
Dickinson, E.   Deprived of other Banquet.
Donne.   Liar, The.
　To Mr T. W ("Pregnant again with th' old twins
　hope, and fear").
Drummond de Andrade.   Table, The.
Dunbar, P.   Possum.
Emerson, R.   God only knew how Saadi dined.
Ginsberg, A.   C'mon Pigs of Western
　Civilization Eat More Grease.
Gunn, T.   J Car, The.
　Waitress.
Hall, D.   Moon, The.
　Self-Portrait as a Bear.
Han-shan.   Pigs devour dead human flesh.
Herbert, G.   Love (3).
Herrick.   Content, Not Cates.
　Custard, The.
　Hymne, to the Lares, A.
　Littlenesse No Cause of Leanesse.
　Meat without Mirth.
　Panegyric to Sir Lewis Pemberton, A.
　To Sir Clipseby Crew.
　Upon Grubs.
　Upon Gryll.
　Upon Jack and Jill: Epigram.
　Upon Lungs.
　Upon Magot a Frequenter of Ordinaries.
　Upon Mease.
　Upon Showbread [or Shewbread]: Epigram.
　Upon Skinns.
　Upon Skurffe.
　Upon Tooly.
Hughes, T.   Crow Tyrannosaurus.
Jonson, B.   Inviting a Friend to Supper.
　On Gut.
Kizer, C.   Food of Love.
Lawrence, D. H.   Bowls.
MacNeice.   Brandy Glass, The.
Meredith, G.   Tuck, thou graceless sinner!—.
Nash, O.   Bugs.
　Celery.
　Everybody Eats Too Much Anyhow.
　Isn't That a Dainty Dish? No!
　Termite, The.
O'Hara, F.   Blocks.
　Essay on Style.
Ramanujan.   Questions.

Riley, J.   Billy Goodin.'
Rukeyser, M.   Night Feeding.
Simic.   East[ern] European Cooking.
Swenson, M.   Order of Diet.
Updike.   Trees Eat Sunshine.
Williams, C. K.   For Gail, When I Was Five.
　Greed.
　Modern, The.
Williams, W.   This Is Just to Say.
　To a Poor Old Woman.
See also **Food; Gluttony and Gluttons**

Eating Disorders
Nash, O.   Curl Up and Diet.

Echo (mythology)
Campion, T.   Elegia I (1619).
McHugh, H.   Nymph to Narcissus, The.
Rossetti, C.   Echo.
Spenser, E.   Epithalamion: "Ye learned sisters
　which have oftentimes."
See also **Narcissus (mythology)**

Echoes
Amichai [or Amikhai].   "He left two sons," they
　say.
Ashbery, J.   Late Echo.
Bishop, E.   Chemin de Fer.
Clough.   See! the faint green tinge from the
　western sky has.
Creeley.   Characteristically
　Echo ("I'm almost / done, the hour").
　Some Echoes.
　Variations.
De la Mare.   Echo.
Hardy, T.   Echo-Elf Answers, The.
Palmer, M.   Echo.
Ritsos.   Ancient Amphitheater.
Tomlinson, C.   Walking to Bells.
Wordsworth, W.   Yes, it was the mountain Echo.

Eckhart, Meister
Dubie.   Meister Eckhart.
　Reader of the Sentences, The.

Eclipses
Baudelaire.   Possessed.
Graves, R.   Near Eclipse, The.
HaNagid.   Two Eclipses.
Hardy, T.   At a Lunar Eclipse.
Schuyler, J.   Moon.

Ecology and Ecologists
Blue Cloud.   Dogwood Blossoms.
Carruth, H.   Cave Painting.
　Names.
　Oldest Killed Lake in North America, The.
　Too Tenuous.
Ciardi, J.   Mystic River.
Cowper, W.   Poplar Field, The.
Dugan, A.   Untitled Poem: "One used to be able
　to say."
Frost, R.   To a Young Wretch.
Hamill, S.   Io no piangeva.
　Malebolge: Prince William Sound.
Hopkins, G.   Binsey Poplars (Felled 1879).
　Inversnaid.
Kinsella, T.   St Paul's Rocks: 16 February 1832.
Kunitz, S.   War against the Trees, The.
Laughlin, J.   End of It All, The.
MacDiarmid, H.   My Songs Are Kandym in the
　Waste Land.
Piercy.   Why the Soup Tastes Like the *Daily
　News*.
Ramanujan.   Ecology.
Roethke.   Moss-Gathering.
Snyder, G.   Call of the Wild, The.
　Dillingham, Alaska, the Willow Tree Bar.
　For All.
　Front Lines.
　Mother Earth: Her Whales.
　Tomorrow's Song.
　Toward Climax.
Spender, S.   I Think Continually of Those Who
　Were Truly Great.
See also **Conservation; Pollution**

Economics and Economists
Ai.   Riot Act, April 29, 1992.
Ammons.   Tight.
Kunitz, S.   Economist's Song, The.
Laughlin, J.   God Bless America!

Niedecker.   Their apples fall down.
Smart, C.   Care and Generosity.
Van Duyn.   Economics.
Wright, J.   Undermining of the Defense
　Economy, The.

Ecstasy
Berryman.   Mysteries, The.
Browning, R.   Now.
Cavafy.   One Night.
Cortes.   Air.
Cummings, E. E.   Her careful distinct sex whose
　sharp lips comb.
　(Let us tremble)a personal radiance sits.
Dickinson, E.   I hope that you are well.
　Take all away from me, but leave me Ecstasy.
　Transport one cannot contain, A.
Donne.   Ecstasy, The.
Dove, R.   Catherine of Alexandria.
Dugan, A.   On Cabin Fever, On Boredom in the
　Countryside.
Duncan, R.   Years As Catches, The.
Eberhart, R.   On Seeing an Egyptian Mummy in
　Berlin, 1932.
Ferlinghetti, L.   Euphoria.
　Making Love in Poetry.
Goethe.   Song: "Joyful / And woful."
Graves, R.   Ecstasy of Chaos.
"H. D."   Psyche.
Hall, D.   Fête.
Hardy, T.   On Stinsford Hill at Midnight.
Hopkins, G.   Late I fell in the ecstasy.
Jarrell, R.   Man in Majesty.
Millay, E.   As sharp as in my childhood, still.
Rexroth, K.   Love Poems of Marichiko, The.
Rimbaud, A.   Morning of Drunkenness.
　Sun and Skin.
Rumi.   Breadmaking.
　Many Wines, The.
Schuyler, J.   Photograph, A.
Whitman, W.   One Hour to Madness and Joy.
Yeats.   Ribh in Ecstasy.

Eden
Amichai [or Amikhai].   I've Already Been
　Weaned.
Armantrout.   Plan, The.
Borges.   Adam Cast Forth.
Browning, E.   Drama of Exile, A.
Clifton, L.   Eve Thinking.
　Garden of Delight, The.
　Lucifer Understanding at Last.
　Report from the angel of eden.
　Story Thus Far, The.
Crane, H.   Garden Abstract.
Cummings, E. E.   Devil crept in eden wood.
Davie, D.   Eden.
De la Mare.   Exile, The.
Dickey, J.   Poisoned Man, The.
Dickinson, E.   Did the Harebell loose her girdle.
　Eden is that Old-Fashioned House.
　Expulsion from Eden grows indistinct.
　Not seeing, still we know.
　Wild Nights—Wild Nights!
Dugan, A.   Letter to Eve.
Dunbar, P.   Unlucky Apple, The.
Eberhart, R.   Adam Cast Forth.
　Throwing the Apple.
Emerson, R.   Eve roved in Paradise, I've heard.
Frost, R.   Winter Eden, A.
Graves, R.   Conjunction.
　History of the Fall.
Hopkins, G.   Spring.
Housman.   When Adam walked in Eden young.
Hughes, T.   Horrible Religious Error, A.
　Theology.
Jacobsen, J.   For Those Who Have Not Eaten
　the Apple.
Kipling, R.   L'Envoi.
Larkin, P.   At the Chiming of Light upon Sleep.
　High Windows.
Lawrence, D. H.   Eve.
　Paradise Re-entered.
Lindsay, N.   Eden in Winter.
MacNeice.   Apple Blossom.
Merton.   Lent in a Year of War.
Orr, G.   Fall.
Pagis.   Tropical Greenhouse.

Plath. Snakecharmer.
Raine, K. On its way I see.
  Under these hills too high and bare.
Rossetti, C. Sexagesima.
  That Eden of earth's sunrise cannot vie.
Rossetti, D. Eden Bower.
Spender, S. Adam.
Stock, R. Metamorphosis.
Thomas, D. Incarnate Devil.
Tomlinson, C. Adam.
  Eden.
  In Arden.
  To Ivor Gurney.
Very. Eden.
  Garden, The.
Walcott. Crusoe's Island.
  New World.
Weiss, T. Working Day, A.
Whitman, W. To the Garden the World.
Whittier. Garden.
  Lay of Old Time, A.
Wilbur, R. Problem from Milton, A.
See also **Adam and Eve**

Edinburgh, Scotland
Burns, R. Address to Edinburgh.
Dunbar, W. To the Merchant[i]s of Edinburgh.
Niedecker. Letter from Ian.

Edison, Thomas Alva
Jeffers, R. Edison.

Editors
Bierce. J.F.B.
Byron, G. To Mr. Murray.
Cummings, E. E. Mr U.
Eliot, T. S. Airs of Palestine, No. 2.
Lawrence, D. H. Great Newspaper Editor to His
  Subordinate, The.
Riley, J. Country Editor, The.
Roethke. Reply to a Lady Editor.

Education
Cavafy. Apollonios of Tyana in Rhodes.
Coleridge, S. Love, Hope, and Patience in
  Education.
Collins, B. First Reader.
Cowper, W. Tirocinium; or, A Review of
  Schools.
Cummings, E. E. As Joe Gould says in.
  Bud(spiggy nuvduh fienus).
Dickinson, E. Through the Dark Sod—as
  Education.
  Water, is taught by thirst.
Dugan, A. Boy and Education.
Eberhart, R. Killer, The.
Emerson, R. Easy to match what others do.
  He must have / Droll fancies sometimes cross
  his quiet thoughts.
Ginsberg, A. Sather Gate Illumination.
Gray, T. Alliance of Education and
  Government, The.
Hardy, T. Young Man's Epigram on Existence,
  A.
Heaney, S. Alphabets.
Keats. In After-Time, a Sage of Mickle Lore.
Lux. You Go To School To Learn.
Meredith, G. Discipline of Wisdom, The.
  Empty Purse: A Sermon to our Later Prodigal
  Son, The.
Millay, E. Intention to Escape from Him.
Milton. To Cyriack Skinner.
Nemerov. Sweeper of Ways, The.
  To David, about His Education.
  Triumph of Education, The.
Oliver, M. Answers.
Rexroth, K. Lucretius, 3, 1053–1076.
Spender, S. Elementary School Classroom in a
  Slum, An.
Stockton, A. To the Visitant, from a Circle of
  Ladies.
Updike. À l'École Berlitz.
Very. Education.
Whitman, W. To a Pupil.
  When I Heard the Learn'd Astronomer.
Williams, M. Manifold Usefulness of an
  Education, The.
Wordsworth, W. Lines Written as a School
  Exercise at Hawkshead, Anno Aetatis 14.

See also **Colleges and Universities; Scholarship
  and Scholars; Students; Teaching and Teachers**

Edward III, King of England
Blake, W. King Edward the Third.

Edward IV, King of England
Blake, W. Prologue, Intended for a Dramatic
  Piece of King Edward the Fourth.

Edward VII, King of England
Kipling, R. Dead King, The [Edward VII;
  1910].

Edwards, Jonathan
Borges. Jonathan Edwards.
Lowell, R. After the Surprising Conversions.
  Jonathan Edwards in Western Massachusetts.
  Mr. Edwards and the Spider.
  Worst Sinner, Jonathan Edwards' God, The.

Eels
Hughes, T. Eel, An.
Lux. At the Far End of a Long Wharf.
Montale. Eel, The.
Muldoon, P. Briefcase, The.
Nash, O. Eel, The.

Eggs
Brodsky, J. Ab Ovo.
Ciardi, J. Eggs.
  Three Eggs Up.
  Tommy's Pond.
Clampitt. Camouflage.
Corbett, W. Shower in June, A.
Hamill, S. Egg, the.
Herrick. Her Legs.
  Upon Tooly.
Hughes, L. Bar.
Hughes, T. Salmon Eggs.
Ignatow, D. Debate, The.
Kumin, M. In Warm Rooms, Before a Blue
  Light.
MacLeish. Vicissitudes of the Creator.
Merrill, J. Transfigured Bird.
Muldoon, P. Blowing Eggs.
Ritsos. Nocturnal.
Rossetti, C. Hear what the mournful linnets say.
  White hen sitting / On white eggs three, A.
Rumi. Birdsong from Inside the Egg.
Sandburg, C. Chicks.
  Smoke Shapes.
  Two Humpties.
Schuyler, J. Wild Eggs.
Smith, S. Nourish Me on an Egg.
Swenson, M. Fable for When There's No Way
  Out.

Egotism and Egotists
Ammons. Reversal.
Bierce. Word to the Unwise, A.
Bukowski. 56 Year Old Poem, A.
  Macho Man.
Carew, T. Ingrateful[l] Beauty Threatened.
Clare, J. Braggart.
Creeley. Immoral Proposition, The.
Davie, D. In the Stopping Train.
Eberhart, R. 'If I Could Only Live at the Pitch
  That Is near Madness'
  My Brains Are Slipping in the Fields of Eros.
  Scouring, The.
  Usurper.
Ginsberg, A. Ego Confession.
Lawrence, D. H. Be It So.
  Ego-Bound.
  Ego-Bound Women.
  Egoists, The.
  Escape.
  Gulf, The.
  Jealousy.
  Self-Conscious People.
  Self-Sacrifice.
  Strife.
Lindsay, N. What the Scarecrow Said.
MacNeice. Budgie.
  To the Public.
Meredith, G. Lucifer in Starlight.
Meredith, W. Look at Me! Look at Me!
Nash, O. Self-Effacement of Electra Thorne,
  The.
Nemerov. Hero Comes Home in His Hamper,
  and Is Exhibited at the World's Fair, The.

Olson, C. Fable for Slumber.
Rukeyser, M. Chapman.
Smith, S. Dear Karl.
  Egocentric.
Spender, S. Subject, Object, Sentence.
  Trigorin.
Stock, R. Space Between Two Blades of Grass
  Meets an Intractable Ego, The.
Van Duyn. Talker, The.
Warren, R. Interjection #5: Solipsism and
  Theology.
Williams, C. K. Alzheimer's: The Husband.
See also **Individualism and Individualists**

Egrets
Ciardi, J. Two Egrets.
Oliver, M. Egret, The.
  Egrets.
Updike. Even Egrets Err.

Egypt
Amichai [*or* Amikhai]. Sharm A-Sheikh.
Browning, R. First-Born of Egypt, The.
Carruth, H. Fact of the Matter, The.
Castiglione. On the Statue of *Cleopatra*, Made
  into a Fountain by *Leo* the Tenth.
Cavafy. Mimiambi of Herodas, The.
  Sam el Nesim.
Celan. In Egypt.
Clough. When Israel Came Out of Egypt.
Crane, H. By Nilus Once I Knew.
Cummings, E. E. Cleopatra built / like a smooth
  arrow or.
Eberhart, R. Dry Rot, The.
  Sphinx.
  Ultimate Song.
"H. D." Egypt.
Hopkins, G. Soliloquy of One of the Spies Left
  in the Wilderness, A.
Kipling, R. Naaman's Song.
  Pharaoh and the Sergeant.
Lindsay, N. Trial of the Dead Cleopatra in Her
  Beautiful and Wonderful Tomb, The.
MacNeice. Réchauffé.
Meredith, G. Foresight and Patience.
Patchen. Egypt.
Pound, E. Spring, The.
Shelley, P. Ozymandias.
Updike. Average Egyptian Faces Death, The.
  Dilemma in the Delta.
Very. Plagues of Egypt, The.
Walcott. Egypt, Tobago.
Warren, R. Flaubert in Egypt.
Whittier. New Exodus, The.
Zagajewski. Covenant.
Zukofsky, L. So sounds grass, and if it is sun or
  no sun.

Eichmann, Adolf
Carruth, H. Adolf Eichmann.
Levertov. During the Eichmann Trial.
  When We Look Up.
Levi, P. For Adolf Eichmann.
Merton. Epitaph for a Public Servant.
Ramanujan. As Eichmann Said, My Brother
  Said.

Einstein, Albert
Dubie. *Principia Mathematica:* Einstein's Exile
  in an Old Dutch Winter.
Ginsberg, A. Xmas Gift.
Kizer, C. Twelve O'Clock.
Komunyakaa. Raw Data for an Unfinished
  Questionnaire.
MacLeish. Einstein.
Niedecker. How bright you'll find young
  people.
Williams, W. St. Francis Einstein of the
  Daffodils.

Eisenhower, Dwight David
Dickey, J. Two Poems of the Military.
Lowell, R. Inauguration Day: January 1953.
Wright, J. Eisenhower's Visit to Franco, 1959.

El Dorado
Montale. Costa San Giorgio.
Poe. Eldorado.

El Salvador
Paley, G. In San Salvador (I).
  In San Salvador (II).

Women's Prison, The: El Salvador / The Ballad of Visiting Day.

Elands
Jarrell, R.   Seele im Raum.

Electric Appliances
Logue, C.   Madam / I have sold you.
Nash, O.   What, No Sheep?
Niedecker.   To My Small / Electric Pump.

Electricity
Ciardi, J.   High Tension Lines across a Landscape.
Dickey, J.   Power and Light.
Hughes, T.   Tender Place, The.
Kipling, R.   Song of the Dynamo.
Lawrence, D. H.   Storm in the Black Forest.
Lindsay, N.   Rhyme About an Electrical Advertising Sign, A.
Prunty.   Two Kinds of Cause.
Simic.   Unknown One, The.

Elephants
Cummings, E. E.   Silently little blue elephant shyly(he was terri), The.
Hughes, T.   Crow's Elephant Totem Song.
Jacobsen, J.   Short Views in Africa.
Kipling, R.   'Less you want your toes trod off you'd better get back at once.
Municipal.
Torn boughs trailing o'er the tusks aslant, The.
Lawrence, D. H.   Elephant.
Elephant Is Slow to Mate, The.
Elephants in the Circus.
Elephants Plodding.
On the Drum.
Two Performing Elephants.
Levi, P.   Elephant, The.
MacNeice.   Elephant Trunk.
McHugh, H.   Unspeakable.
Moore, M.   Elephants.
Muldoon, P.   Burma.
Pagis.   Bestiary.
Parker, D.   Ballade of Unfortunate Mammals.
Rumi.   Elephant in the Dark.
Sandburg, C.   Elephants Are Different to Different People.
Swift, J.   Elephant, The.
Wilner, E.   Short History of Philosophy, A.
What Was Left Over.

Elevators
Dugan, A.   On Hat: On Vertical Mobility as a Concept.
Hughes, L.   Elevator Boy.
Nemerov.   Fiction.
Rilke.   Dream Movement.
Sexton.   Riding the Elevator into the Sky.

Elgin Marbles
Hardy, T.   Christmas in the Elgin Room.
Keats.   On Seeing the Elgin Marbles.

Elijah (Bible)
Dickinson, E.   Elijah's Wagon knew no thill.
Levi, P.   Passover.

"Eliot, George" (Mary Ann [or Marian] Evans Lewes Cross)
Clampitt.   George Eliot Country.
Highgate Cemetery.
Medusa at Broadstairs.
Dickinson, E.   She is the Lane to the Indes.

Eliot, T. S. (Thomas Stearns)
Cummings, E. E.   Out of the pants which cover me.
Ferlinghetti, L.   Sea and Ourselves at Cape Ann, The.
Rukeyser, M.   Citation for Horace Gregory.

Elizabeth I, Queen of England
Bishop, E.   Britannia Rules the Waves.
Bradstreet, A.   In Honour of that High and Mighty Princess Queen Elizabeth.
Burns, R.   Lament of Mary Queen of Scots on the Approach of Spring.
Campion, T.   Ad Thamesin.
Shadowes before the shining sunne do vanish.
Dickinson, E.   Elizabeth told Essex.
Dubie.   Elizabeth's War with the Christmas Bear.
Kipling, R.   Looking Glass, The.
Pageant of Elizabeth, A.

Together.
Spenser, E.   Colin Clouts Come Home Againe.
Tomlinson, C.   At Saint Mary's Church.

Elizabeth II, Queen of England
Seifert.   Umbrella from Piccadilly, An.

Elk
Carver, R.   Elk Camp.
Ciardi, J.   Some Figures for Who Must Speak.
Dugan, A.   On the Elk, Unwitnessed.
Kumin, M.   On Being Asked to Write a Poem in Memory of Anne Sexton.
Nash, O.   Wapiti, The.
Warren, R.   First Time, The.

Ellington, Edward Kennedy (Duke)
Major, C.   Cotton Club, The.

Elliot, Ebenezer
Whittier.   Elliott.

Elm Trees
Berry, W.   Old Elm Tree by the River, The.
Byron, G.   Lines Written beneath an Elm in the Churchyard of Harrow.
Davie, D.   Iowa.
Hardy, T.   Felled Elm and She, The.
Levertov.   Living While It May.
MacLeish.   Long Hot Summer.
Two Trees, The.
Melville, H.   Malvern Hill.
Moore, M.   Camperdown Elm, The.
Plath.   Elm.
Riley, J.   Noble Old Elm, The.
Sandburg, C.   Elm Buds.
Poplar and Elm.
Tomlinson, C.   Tree.
Updike.   Elm.
Very.   Dead Elm, The.
Elm Seed, The.
Williams, C. K.   Elms.

Elopement
Hardy, T.   In Sherborne Abbey.
Hopkins, G.   Elopement, The.
Keats.   Eve of St Agnes, The.
Longfellow, H.   Skeleton in Armor [or Armour], The.
Riley, J.   I' Got to Face Mother To-Day!
Last Christmas Was a Year Ago.
Marthy Ellen.
Sandburg, C.   Curse of a Rich Polish Peasant on His Sister Who Ran Away with a Wild Man.
Scott, S.   Jock of Hazeldean.

Elves
Bishop, E.   Behind Stowe.
De la Mare.   Unfinished Dream, The.
Dunbar, P.   Discovery, The.
Keats.   La Belle Dame sans Merci [A Ballad].
Levertov.   Elves, The.
Riley, J.   Das Krist Kindel.
Unknown.   Tam Lin.
See also **Fairies**

Ely, England
Eberhart, R.   Slow Boat Ride.
Milton.   On the Death of the Bishop of Ely.

Emancipation (1863–1865)
Dunbar, P.   Deserted Plantation, The.
Emancipation.
To the South.
Hughes, L.   Long View: Negro.
Whittier.   Astræa at the Capitol.
At Port Royal.
Hymn for the Celebration of Emancipation at Newburyport.
Jubilee Singers, The.
Laus Deo!
Proclamation, The.

Embryos
Rukeyser, M.   For a Mexican Painter.
Rumi.   Wean Yourself.

Emeralds
Pagis.   Twelve Faces of the Emerald.

Emerson, Ralph Waldo
Borges.   Emerson.
Leaves of the Cypress, The.
Dickinson, E.   Emerson's intimacy with his "Bee."
Eberhart, R.   Emerson's Concord.

Riley, J.   Emerson.

Emigration and Emigrants
Baudelaire.   Invitation to a Voyage.
Burns, R.   Address of Beelzebub.
Lines Written on a Bank-Note.
On a Scotch Bard Gone to the West Indies.
Davie, D.   Emigrant, to the Receding Shore.
Middlesex.
Sussex.
Dickinson, E.   Away from Home are some and I.
To an Emigrant, Country is idle.
Fenton, J.   Children in Exile.
Hall, D.   Sister on the Tracks, A.
Jarrell, R.   To the New World.
Milosz, C.   Bypassing Rue Descartes.
To Robert Lowell.
Wilner, E.   Emigration.
Zaturenska.   Émigrés, The.
See also **Immigration and Immigrants**

Emmet, Robert
Shelley, P.   On Robert Emmet's Grave.

Empedocles
Emerson, R.   Brave Empedocles defying fools, The.
Meredith, G.   Empedocles.

Emperors and Empresses
Bierce.   False Prophecy, A.
Voice from Pekin, A.
Borges.   Parable of the Palace.
Cavafy.   Death of the Emperor Tacitus, The.
John Kantakuzinos Triumphs.
Manuel Komninos.
Of Colored Glass.
Theophilos Palaiologos.
Dugan, A.   Autumn at Baiae: For Cavafy.
Jacobsen, J.   Emperor's Cook, The.
Laughlin, J.   It Does Me Good.
Warren, R.   Empire.
Wright, J.   Chapultepec Castle.
Zaturenska.   Empress Marie Louise, The.

Empire State Building, New York City
Berrigan, T.   Bean Spasms.
Schuyler, J.   Six Something.

Emptiness
Amichai [or Amikhai].   Statistics.
You Are So Small and Slight in the Rain.
Ammons.   Unsaid.
Angelou.   After.
Ashbery, J.   As You Came from the Holy Land.
Atwood.   I am sitting on the / edge of the impartial.
Paper Bag, A.
Berry, W.   Wild, The.
Borges.   Everything and Nothing.
Bukowski.   Girls From Nowhere.
Carruth, H.   Words in a Certain Appropriate Mode.
Cavafy.   September 1903.
Chuang Tzu.   Action and Non-Action.
Empty Boat, The.
Useless Tree, The.
Where Is Tao?
Cowper, W.   My pens are all spilt, and my ink-glass is dry.
Creeley.   Beyond.
Dishonest Mailmen, The.
Envoi: "Particulars they want."
Flesh.
Hole, The.
Ice Cream.
Joy.
Language, The.
Men.
On Vacation.
Rain (2).
Sign Board, The.
Cullen, C.   After a Visit.
Hunger.
Cummings, E. E.   Emptied.hills.listen.
Cunningham, J.   Monday Morning.
De la Mare.   Empty House, The.
Eberhart, R.   Waiting To Lean to the Master's Command.
Eliot, T. S.   Conversation Galante.

Gerontion.
Hollow Men, The.
Waste Land, The.
Gallagher, T. Coming Home.
García Lorca. Nocturne of Emptied Space.
Ginsberg, A. Land O'Lakes, Wisc.
Glück, L. Solstice.
Graves, R. Florist Rose, The.
Not at Home.
Recognition.
Thief.
Guillén, J. I Want to Sleep.
Hacker, M. Last Time, The.
Han-shan. All my life too lazy to work.
Hardy, T. Exeunt Omnes.
Herbert, G. Dotage.
Hughes, L. Empty House.
Summer Night.
Hughes, T. Black Beast, The.
Kipling, R. Derelict, The.
Laughlin, J. Empty Room, The.
Lawrence, D. H. Tarantella.
Winter Dawn.
Lindsay, N. Leaden-eyed, The.
McGrath, T. Encounter.
McHugh, H. Where.
Meredith, G. Song: "Fair and false! No dawn will greet."
Merwin. As Though I Was Waiting for That.
Millay, E. Bluebeard.
Montale. Balcony, The.
Neruda. Sick Man in the Sun.
Oppen. Population.
Patchen. I always return to this place.
Piercy. Gasman Invites the Skyscrapers to Dance.
Morning Half-Life Blues, The.
Prunty. Old Declaratives.
Raine, K. Her Room.
Unloved, The.
Ramanujan. At Zero.
Rexroth, K. Void Only.
Rich, A. Blue Ghazals, The.
Demon Lover, The.
Riley, J. Empty Nest, An.
Ritsos. Departures 1.
Exultation.
Rossetti, C. Castle-Builder's World, A.
Rumi. Buoyancy.
Craftsmanship and Emptiness.
Emptiness.
This World Which Is Made of Our Love for Emptiness.
When you are with everyone but me.
Salinas, P. Not in Marble Palaces.
Shapiro, K. Nebraska.
Williams, C. K. Admiral Fan, The.
For Children When They Grow Up.
Hounding Mercy.
Madder.
Rabbit Fights for His Life the Leopard Eats Lunch, The.
Spring: another / joke. / This run-down.
Undead, The.
Williams, W. These.
Wright, C. Cicada.
Dog Yoga.
Zagajewski. Square D'Orléans.
Treatise on Emptiness.
Zukofsky, L. Lines of this new song are nothing, The.

Emus
Muldoon, P. Bangle, The.

Enchantment
Blok. Stranger, The.
Brontë, E. Spellbound.
Browning, R. Isle's Enchantress, The.
Burns, R. Answer to the Foregoing— Extempore [Clarinda].
Carew, T. In Praise of His Mistress.
Tinder, The.
To One Who, When I Praised My Mistress' Beauty, Said I Was Blind.
Cavafy. Nichori.
When, My Friends, I Was in Love.
Creeley. Still Dancers.

Cummings, E. E. Emperor / sleeps in a palace of porphyry, The.
To stand(alone)in some.
Ferlinghetti, L. Café Notre Dame.
Graves, R. Or To Perish Before Day.
Hardy, T. As 'Twere To-night.
First Sight of Her and After.
In a Whispering Gallery.
Paphian Ball, The.
Shiver, The.
Herrick. To Music: A Song.
Keats. La Belle Dame sans Merci [A Ballad].
Lawrence, D. H. Witch I, The.
Lindsay, N. Master of the Dance, The.
Michelangelo Buonarroti. I'm dearer to me, much more, than ever I was.
Mickiewicz. Mushroom Gatherers, The.
Petrarch. Graces denied to almost everyone.
Pope, A. Of Her Picture.
Raine, K. Your gift of life was idleness.
Riley, J. Dream.
Lelloine.
Moon-drowned.
Serenade, The: "Midnight is not more bewildering, The."
Southern Singer, A.
Shelley, P. Fragments of an Unfinished Drama.
Szymborska, W. Drinking Wine.
Williams, T. Lyric: "Her footsteps were a season's coming."

End of the World
Angelou. On a Bright Day, Next Week.
Beckett, S. Imagine si ceci.
Browning, R. Childe Roland to the Dark Tower Came.
Bukowski. 10 Lions and the End of the World.
End, The.
On the Failure of a Poet.
Worst and the Best, The.
Byron, G. Darkness.
Crane, S. God lay dead in Heaven.
Should the wide world roll away.
Creeley. Elements.
Cummings, E. E. If in beginning twilight of winter will stand.
Now does our world descend.
What If a Much of a Which of a Wind.
When god decided to invent.
While a once world slips from.
De la Mare. Sign, A.
Dugan, A. Takeoff on Armageddon —For Ronald Reagan.
Eberhart, R. Ides of March, The.
Enzensberger, H. End of Owls, The.
Ferlinghetti, L. Reading Apollinaire by the Rogue River.
Frost, R. Fire and Ice.
Once by the Pacific.
Glück, L. End of the World, The.
Graves, R. Warning to Children.
Hughes, T. Woman Unconscious, A.
Jackson, L. World's End.
Jarrell, R. Dialogue between Soul and Body, A.
Jeffers, R. End of the World.
I Shall Laugh Purely.
Kinnell. Fundamental Project of Technology, The.
Levertov. Sound of the Axe.
MacLeish. End of the World, The.
Mahon. Morning Radio.
McGrath, T. End of the World, The.
Meredith, G. Creation and the Prophet.
Merton. Martin's Predicament or Atlas Watches Every Evening.
Senescente Mundo.
Milosz, C. L'Accélération de l'Histoire.
Niedecker. Obliteration, The.
Pagis. Lesson in Observation, A.
Pinsky. Uncreation, The.
Raine, K. It is in us they burn.
Rexroth, K. Venice.
Rukeyser, M. Noguchi.
Shapiro, K. Scyros.
Simic. Hurricane Season.
Smart, C. Hail wonrous being who in power supreme.

On the Eternity of the Supreme Being.
Snyder, G. L M F B R.
Stafford, W. We Interrupt to Bring You.
Tomlinson, C. Epilogue, The: "It was a dream delivered the epilogue."
Van Duyn. Relative and an Absolute, A.
Weiss, T. Last Day and the First, The.
Wilbur, R. Advice to a Prophet.
Williams, C. K. Clay out of Silence.
Downwards.
That the world / is going.
Williams, M. Entropy.
He Glimpses a Nobler Vision.
Wilner, E. Zero at the Bone.
Wright, C. October.
See also **Apocalypse; Judgment Day**

Endangered Species
Atwood. Elegy for the Giant Tortoises.
Hughes, T. February.
Komunyakaa. Dream Animal.
Kumin, M. Bringing Back the Trumpeter Swan.
Homage to Binsey Poplars.
Thoughts on Saving the Manatee.
With the Caribou.
Merwin. For a Coming Extinction.
Shore, The.
Oliver, M. Ghosts.
Stafford, W. Roll Call.

Endecott, John
Very. Endecott.

Endurance
Amichai [*or* Amikhai]. Half the People of the World.
To Die, to Be Torn.
Beckett, S. Pas à pas.
Berryman. Sanctuary.
Bishop, E. Night City.
Borges. Things.
Bourne, V. Ode on the Death of a Lady.
Burns, R. O, for Ane-and-Twenty Tam.
Byron, G. Love and Death.
To a Lady.
To the Earl of Clare.
Carver, R. Soda Crackers.
Chuang Tzu. Autumn Floods.
Coleridge, S. Forbearance.
Cullen, C. Harsh World That Lashest Me.
De la Mare. Courage.
Dugan, A. Advertising in Paris.
Emerson, R. Character.
Ferlinghetti, L. Thoughts to a Concerto of Telemann.
Gunn, T. Rastignac at 45.
"H. D." Ancient Wisdom Speaks.
Hardy, T. Coming of the End, The.
Jacobsen, J. Figure.
Jeffers, R. All the Little Hoof-Prints.
Granite and Cypress.
It is a pity the shock-waves.
Old Stone-Mason, The.
Kinsella, T. Beloved.
Kipling, R. Old Men, The.
Kunitz, S. Welcome the Wrath.
Larkin, P. I See a Girl Dragged by the Wrists.
Lawrence, D. H. Race and Battle.
MacLeish. Actfive.
Chartres.
Snowflake Which Is Now and Hence Forever, The.
McHugh, H. Form.
Merrill, J. After Greece.
Merwin. We Continue.
Michelangelo Buonarroti. Humbly I bow my shoulders, bear the yoke.
Milton. Nature Does Not Suffer Decay.
O'Hara, F. Poem: "Light clarity avocado salad in the morning."
Olson, C. He treads on edges of being where the drop.
I hang on by.
Piercy. Ache's End.
Plath. Firesong.
Smith, S. Study to Deserve Death.
Stafford, W. Consolations.
Whittier. Within the Gate.
Yeats. Travail of Passion, The.

See also **Fortitude**

Endymion
Cavafy. Before the Statue of Endymion.
Cullen, C. To Endymion.
Emerson, R. Manners.
Keats. Endymion: A Poetic Romance.
Kinsella, T. Endymion.
Millay, E. "Oh, sleep forever in the Latmian cave."
Wilde, O. Endymion.

Enemies
Baudelaire. Enemy, The.
Borges. Leaves of the Cypress, The.
Byron, G. Imitation of Tibullus.
Carew, T. Truce in Love Intreated.
Cavafy. Enemies, The.
De la Mare. Hare, A.
Dickinson, E. Rat, The.
Emerson, R. Bended to fops who bent to him.
Skeptic, The.
Hafiz [*or* Hafez]. To the Shah, from Hafiz.
HaNagid. Foolish Enemy's Face Tells All, The.
Hardy, T. Enemy's Portrait, The.
Man He Killed, The.
Herrick. Discord Not Disadvantageous.
Pitie to the Prostrate.
Hughes, L. Enemy.
Ibn-i-Yamin [*or* Ibn Jemin *or* Amir Mahmud ibn Amir Yaminu'd-Din Tughra'i]. For two rewards, & nought beside.
Ignatow, D. My Enemies.
Kipling, R. France.
Piet.
Laughlin, J. Cynthia in California.
Lawrence, D. H. My Enemy.
Levi, P. Partisan.
Merton. What are the marks of the enemy? / He has no wit.
Millay, E. First Fig.
Parker, D. Ballade of a Great Weariness.
Leal, The.
Riley, J. My Foe.
Robinson, E. New Tenants, The.
Sadi [*or* Saadi *or* Sa'di]. Had I the world for my enemy.
Stafford, W. For the Unknown Enemy.
Whitman, W. Reconciliation.
Wyatt, S. Right true it is and said full yore ago.

Energy
Cowper, W. Inscription for a Stone.
Moralizer Corrected, The.
Creeley. Massachusetts.
Gunn, T. My Sad Captains.
Lawrence, D. H. We Are Transmitters.
Rossetti, C. I Will Arise.
Rukeyser, M. I have tried to show the atom as a source.
Not leaves, not lightning, not the greatness of rivers.
Tree of rivers flowing through our lives, A.
Updike. Energy: A Villanelle.

Engineers
Kinsella, T. Portrait of the Engineer, A.
Kipling, R. Hymn of Breaking Strain.
McAndrew's Hymn.
Sappers.
Study of an Elevation, in Indian Ink.
Moore, M. Icosasphere, The.
Tomlinson, C. On the Principle of Blowclocks.
Williams, W. Aigeltinger.

England
Auden. On This Island.
Berryman. Shirley & Auden.
Bierce. Strained Relations.
Blake, W. When Klopstock England Defied.
Borges. Saxon (A.D. 449), A.
Bradstreet, A. Dialogue between Old England and New, A.
Brodsky, J. In England.
Browning, R. Home-Thoughts, from Abroad.
Home-Thoughts, from the Sea.
Nationality in Drinks.
Burns, R. Dumfries Volunteers, The.
Scots Ballad.
Such a Parcel of Rogues in a Nation.

Byron, G. Irish Avatar, The.
Oh factious viper! whose envenom'd tooth.
Campion, T. Ad Guil. Camdenum.
Elegeia I (1595).
Carruth, H. Once and Again.
Chesterton. Elegy in a Country Churchyard.
Rolling English Road, The.
World State, The.
Clampitt. Dejection: A Footnote.
Easedale Tarn.
Grasmere.
Hurricane and Charlotte Mew, The.
Sacred Hearth Fire, The.
Teignmouth.
Cowper, W. Address to the Mob, An.
Boadicea: An Ode.
Expostulation.
Lily and the Rose, The.
On the Promotion of Thurlow.
Table Talk.
To Sir Joshua Reynolds.
Crashaw. Upon the Duke of *Yorke* his Birth a Panegyricke.
Davie, D. Bedfordshire.
Buckinghamshire.
Cambridgeshire.
County Durham.
Derbyshire.
Derbyshire Turf.
Dudwood.
England.
England, for Ezra Pound.
English Revenant, An.
Hampshire. .
Herefordshire.
Hertfordshire.
Huntingdonshire.
Out of East Anglia.
Rain on South-East England.
Rutland.
Some Shires Revisited.
Stratford on Avon.
Westmorland.
Wild Boar Clough.
Winter's Talents.
De la Mare. England.
How Sleep the Brave.
Dickinson, E. Robin's my Criterion for Tune, The.
Dryden, J. Mac Flecknoe [or, A Satire upon the True-Blue Protestant Poet T. S.].
Eberhart, R. Ultimate Song.
Ginsberg, A. Night Gleam.
Gurney, I. Above Ashleworth.
Battalion Is Now On Rest, The.
Behind the Line.
Brimscombe.
Musers Afar Will Say.
Riez Bailleul ("Riez Bailleul in blue tea-time").
Servitude.
That Centre of Old.
To Crickley.
Touchstone—Watching Malvern, The.
Where the Mire.
Hall, D. Village in East Anglia, A.
Hardy, T. Call to National Service, A.
On an Invitation to the United States.
Heaney, S. Leavings.
Herbert, G. British Church, The.
Hill, G. Funeral Music.
Mercian Hymns.
Hopkins, G. To Seem the Stranger.
What Shall I Do for the Land that Bred Me.
Housman. 1887.
Clunton and Clunbury.
New Mistress, The.
On Wenlock Edge.
Hughes, T. Emily Brontë.
Mayday on Holderness.
Motorbike, A.
Rain-charm for the Duchy.
Widdop.
Jeffers, R. Ghosts in England.
Subjected Earth.
Two Christmas-Cards.
Jonson, B. Epigram to the Queen, Then Lying

In. 1630, An.
New Year's Gift Sung to King Charles. 1635, A.
On the Union.
To My L[ord] the King, on the Christening His Second Son James.
To Penshurst.
To the King. On His Birthday. An Epigram Anniversary. Novem[ber] 19, 1632.
To the Right Hon[oura]ble Hierome, L[ord] Weston. An Ode Gratulatory for His Return from His Embassy. 1632.
Keats. Happy Is England! I Could Be Content.
Lines Written on 29 May / The Anniversary of the Restoration of Charles the 2nd.
On Peace.
Kipling, R. Absent-Minded Beggar, The.
American Rebellion, The.
Anvil, The.
Bells and Queen Victoria, The.
Big Steamers.
Broken Men, The.
Brown Bess.
Chant-Pagan.
Charm, A.
Coastwise Lights, The.
Dane-Geld.
Dawn Wind, The.
Deep-Sea Cables, The.
Dutch in the Medway, The.
Edgehill Fight.
England's Answer.
English Flag, The.
Et Dona Ferentes.
Flowers, The.
France.
French Wars, The.
Glory of the Garden, The.
In Springtime.
Islanders, The.
James I.
King Henry VII. And the Shipwrights.
King's Job, The.
King's Task, The.
Land, The.
Last of the Light Brigade, The.
Memories.
My Father's Chair.
Norman and Saxon.
Open Door, The.
Pirates in England, The.
Reeds of Runnymede, The.
Return, The.
River's Tale, The.
Roman Centurion's Song, The.
Secret of the Machines, The.
Together.
Ulster.
With Drake in the Tropics.
Kizer, C. Silent Man, The.
Larkin, P. Having Grown Up in Shade of Church and State.
MCMXIV.·
Naturally the Foundation Will Bear Your Expenses.
Lawrence, D. H. As for Me, I'm a Patriot.
Clydesider.
England in 1929.
English Are So Nice!, The.
Flapper Vote.
Innocent England.
Rose and Cabbage.
Rose Is Not a Cabbage, A.
Rose of England, The.
Spirits Summoned West.
MacNeice. October in Bloomsbury.
Marvell. First Anniversary of the Government, The.
Last Instructions to a Painter, The.
On the Victory Obtained by Blake over the Spaniards.
Poem upon the Death of Oliver Cromwell, A.
Upon Appleton House [To My Lord Fairfax].
Meredith, G. Aneurin's Harp.
Atkins.
Britain.
Call, The.

Congress of Nations, The.
England before the Storm.
Head of Bran the Blest, The.
Ireland.
John Lackland.
Labourer, The.
Lines to a Friend Visiting America.
Loyal Soldier, The.
New Era the Army of the Future the Egg of an Army, The.
Old Chartist, The.
Outside the Crowd.
Patriot Engineer, The.
Poetry of Chaucer, The.
Poetry of Shakespeare, The.
Red Coats & the Blue, The.
Song: "God bless the little Island!"
Song of the New Zealander among the Ruins of Old London.
Three Eagles and the Sleepy Lion, The.
To Colonel Charles.
To Lord Palmerston.
To the Merry Men of France.
Voyage of the "Ophir," The.
Warning, The.
Wassail for the New Year, A.
Ye noble Lords who bravely fight.
Merton.   When class was in the garden at Greylands.
Millay, E.   Memory of England.
Niedecker.   Bombings.
Oppen.   Tugs of Hull, The.
Pope, A.   Epitaph on Dr. Francis Atterbury, Bishop of Rochester.
Fragment of *Brutus*, an Epic.
Windsor-Forest [*or* Windsor Forest].
Ralegh, S.   Sir Walter Ralegh's [*or* S.W. Raghlies] Petition to the Queene 1618.
Rossetti, C.   Succession of Kings, The.
Rukeyser, M.   Otherworld.
Shelley, P.   England in 1819.
Fragment: To the People of England.
New National Anthem, A.
Song to the Men of England.
Smith, S.   I Love.
O Happy Dogs of England.
Suburban Classes, The.
Voices against England in the Night.
Spenser, E.   Ruines of Time, The.
Suckling, S.   Cantilena Politica-Jocunda Facta Post Principis Discessum In Hispaniam.
Tennyson, A.   To the Marquis of Dufferin and Ava.
Tomlinson, C.   Bridges.
Dates: Penkhull New Road.
John Maydew or The Allotment.
Midlands.
Response to Hopkins.
Return to Hinton.
To Ivor Gurney.
Unknown.   Answer, The [By the Gentleman of the Navy].
Updike.   English Train Compartment.
Walcott.   Exile.
Far Cry from Africa, A.
Wheatley, P.   Farewel[l] to America, A. To Mrs. S. W.
Philis's Reply to the Answer in Our Last by the Gentleman in the Navy.
Whittier.   Freed Islands, The.
Hymn: "O Holy Father! just and true."
To the Reformers of England.
Wilde, O.   Ave Imperatrix.
Theoretikos.
To Milton.
Williams, W.   Exultation, An.
Wilner, E.   Salute to Donald Davie.
Wordsworth, W.   Artegal and Elidure.
Composed by the Sea-Side, near Calais, August, 1802.
Composed in the Valley near Dover, on the Day of Landing.
It is not to be thought of that the Flood.
Lines on the Expected Invasion 1803.
Lines Written as a School Exercise at Hawkshead, Anno Aetatis 14.

London 1802.
Ode: The Morning of the Day Appointed for a General Thanksgiving. January 18, 1816.
Sonnet: "England! the time is come when thou shouldst wean."
Sonnet in the Pass of Killicranky.
View from the Top of Black Comb.
When I have borne in memory what has tamed.
Young England—What Is Then Become of Old.
Wright, C.   Journal of English Days, A.
Yeats.   Ghost of Roger Casement, The.
On a Political Prisoner.
Zukofsky, L.   Stratford-on-Avon.
See also **Civil Wars, England**

England, Church of
See **Church of England**

English Channel
Kipling, R.   French Wars, The.
Wet Litany, The.

English, The
Blake, W.   Why Should I Care for the Men of Thames?
Byron, G.   Girl of Cadiz, The.
World Is a Bundle of Hay, The.
Campion, T.   Bravely deckt, come forth, bright day.
To the Most Disconsolate Great Brittaine.
Chesterton.   Secret People, The.
Ciardi, J.   L'Inglese.
Coleridge, S.   Fears in Solitude [Written in April, 1798, during the Alarm of an Invasion].
Cummings, E. E.   Flotsam and jetsam / are gentlemen poeds.
It was a goodly co.
Q:dwo / we know of anything which can.
Davie, D.   Helena Morley.
Middlesex.
New Year Wishes for the English.
Dunbar, P.   Letter, A.
Hughes, L.   English, The.
Kipling, R.   Absent-Minded Beggar, The.
Anvil, The.
Beginnings, The.
Belts.
English Way, The.
Et Dona Ferentes.
Flowers, The.
Fuzzy-Wuzzy.
General Joubert.
Gentlemen-Rankers.
Islanders, The.
Jacket, The.
Jobson's Amen.
Kitchener's School.
Ladies, The.
Loot.
Lost Legion, The.
Native-Born, The.
Norman and Saxon.
Puzzler, The.
Song of the Dead, The.
Song of the English, A.
To Thomas Atkins.
Waster, The.
Young British Soldier, The.
Koch, K.   Departure from Hydra, The.
Lawrence, D. H.   British Sincerity.
Brittannia's Baby.
Broadcasting to the G.B.P.
Emasculation.
English Are So Nice!, The.
Gentleman, The.
How Beastly the Bourgeois Is.
Little-Boy Brilliant.
Lucky Little Britisher.
Man in the Street, The.
Middle-Class Children.
Noble Englishman, The.
Rose and Cabbage.
We Can't Be Too Careful.
MacNeice.   Solitary Travel.
Milton.   To the Lord General Cromwell.
Nash, O.   Ms. Found under a Serviette in a Lovely Home.
Oafishness Sells Good, Like an Advertisement Should.

Scram, Lion!
Rexroth, K.   Observations in a Cornish Teashop.
Schuyler, J.   Witley Court.
Shelley, P.   Song to the Men of England.
Smart, C.   Ode to General Draper.
Smith, S.   Celts, The.
Eng.
English, The.
Oh, If Only.
This Englishwoman.
Tomlinson, C.   Class.
Whittier.   To Englishmen.
Wordsworth, W.   Decay of Piety.
Protest against the Ballot.

Engraving and Engravers
Baudelaire.   Fantastic Engraving, A.
Bierce.   On Stone.
Donne.   Valediction, A: of My Name in the Window.
Levertov.   Engraved.
Thoreau.   Epitaph: "Here lies an honest man."
Epitaph on an Engraver.
Tomlinson, C.   To Be Engraved on the Skull of a Cormorant.

Envy
Ausonius.   On Nanus Mounted on an Ant.
Bukowski.   Millionaire, The.
Byron, G.   To D———.
Campion, T.   Ad Lucium.
Catullus.   Let us live, my Lesbia, and let us love each other.
Creeley.   Europeans, The.
Dickinson, E.   I envy seas—whereon He rides.
Donne.   Song: "Go and catch a falling star."
Eberhart, R.   Man's Greed and Envy Are So Great.
Emerson, R.   I have found a nobler love.
Fenton, J.   Skip, The.
Gallagher, T.   Same Kiss After Many Years, The.
HaNagid.   When You're Desperate.
Hardy, T.   Singing Lovers.
Herrick.   Not to Covet Much Where Little is the Charge.
Jonson, B.   On the Right Honourable and Virtuous Lord Weston.
Kipling, R.   Divided Destinies.
My Rival.
Meredith, G.   Brotherhood.
Moore, M.   Charity Overcoming Envy.
Nash, O.   Possessions Are Nine Points of Conversation.
Parker, D.   To a Lady.
To Myrtilla, On Easter Day.
Petrarch.   How much I envy you, gluttonous ground.
O Envy, enemy to all that's good.
Riley, J.   Penalty of Genius, The.
Plain Sermons.
To a Boy Whistling.
Smith, S.   Barlow.
Night Thoughts.
Stock, R.   Man Who Was Pregnant with Envy, The.
Tomlinson, C.   Green Quinces.
Unknown.   On Envy.
Wilbur, R.   All These Birds.
Williams, W.   Drunkard, The.
See also **Jealousy**

Epic Poetry
Byron, G.   From Anacreon.
Koch, K.   Art of Poetry, The.
Pope, A.   To Belinda on the Rape of the Lock.
Tennyson, A.   Morte d'Arthur.

Epictetus
Arnold, M.   To a Friend.

Epicureanism
Zagajewski.   Epicure From My Staircase, The.

Epigrams
Byron, G.   Martial, Lib. I. Epig. I.
Campion, T.   Ad Castricum.
De Epigrammate.
De Fran. Draco.
In Bretonem.
In Nervam.

Cardenal. Shots were heard last night / Out by the burial ground.
Suddenly in the night the sirens.
We wake up with guns going off.
Cavafy. Young Men of Sidon (400 A.D.).
Cowper, W. Epigram is but a feeble thing, An.
Cunningham, J. Epigrams: A Journal.
Epigrams: "Old dissembler who lived out his lie, An."
Herrick. Upon Pusse and her Prentice.
Jonson, B. To All, to Whom I Write.
To My Book.
To My Mere English Censurer.
To the Ghost of Martial.
Martial. 6.65: "'An epic epigram,' I heard you say."
Sheridan, T. Of Epigram.

Epiphany
Ammons. Epiphany.
Borges. Yellow Rose, A.
Montale. Garden, The.
Rexroth, K. Gic to Har.
Rumi. Worm's Waking, The.
Stafford, W. Day Millicent Found the World, The.
Toward the End.
Stock, R. Sir John Mandeville and I Sat Up Talking,
Warren, R. When the Tooth Cracks—Zing!
See also **Twelfth Night**

Epitaphs
Bradstreet, A. Epitaph on my Dear and Ever Honored Mother Mrs. Dorothy Dudley.
Byron, G. Here's a Happy New Year! But with Reason.
Substitute for an Epitaph.
Cavafy. Epitaph of Antiochus, King of Kommagini.
Epitaph: "Stranger, beside the Ganges I lie, a man."
For Ammonis, Who Died at 29, in 610.
In the Month of Athyr.
Kimon, Son of Learchos, Age 22, Student of Greek Literature (in Kyrini).
Ciardi, J. Epitaph: "Here, time concurring (and it does)."
Crashaw. Epitaph. Upon Doctor Brooke, An.
Epitaph upon Mr. Ashton, a Conformable Citizen, An.
[Mr. Herrys,] His Epitaph.
Davie, D. No Epitaph.
Obiter Dicta,
Two Intercepted Letters.
De la Mare. Epitaph, An: "Last, Stone, a little yet."
Gray, T. Elegy Written in a Country Churchyard.
Hardy, T. Epitaph: "I never cared for Life: Life cared for me."
Gentleman's Epitaph on Himself and a Lady, Who Were Buried Together, A.
Herrick. Epitaph on the Tomb of Sir Edward Giles and His Wife.
To His Tomb-Maker.
Jeffers, R. George Sterling's Death.
Merton. Rilke's Epitaph.
Michelangelo Buonarroti. Bright in our minds, but in the dark earth stranded.
Fame keeps the epitaphs where they lie.
Parker, D. Epitaph for a Darling Lady.
Ralegh, S. Authours Epitaph, Made by Himself, The.
Epitaph on the Earl of Leicester [*or* Leceister].
Rich, A. Annotation for an Epitaph.
Riley, J. From the Headboard of a Grave in Paraguay.
Worn-out Pencil, A.
Stockton, A. Epitaph by a Young Lady, Design'd by Herself, An.
Thoreau. Ep on a Good Man.
Epitaph: "Here lies an honest man."
Epitaph on Pursy.
Tomlinson, C. Cradock Newton: From an Epitaph.
Epitaph: "Enamoured by / Brevity in method."
Unknown. Tomb Cover of Imam Riza.

Unknown, sometimes at. to Sir Walter Ralegh. Songe Made by Sir Walter Rawley, A.
Whitman, W. As Toilsome I Wander'd Virginia's Woods.
Williams, W. Address, An.
Wordsworth, W. Could I the priest's consent have gained.
Epitaph in Grasmere Church.
Epitaph in the Chapel Yard of Langdale, Westmoreland.
Gravestone upon the Floor in the Cloisters of Worcester Cathedral, A.

Equality
Burns, R. Extempore Verses on Dining with Lord Daer.
To the Beautiful Miss Eliza J———n, on Her Principles of Liberty and Equality.
Carew, T. Rapture, A.
Cowper, W. Negro's Complaint, The.
Creeley. Eye, The.
Fact, The.
Night ("Needs most / happily mutual").
Dickey, J. Basics.
Dickinson, E. Color, Caste, Denomination.
Emerson, R. Boston.
Herrick. Conformity Is Comely
Levertov. Prayer for Revolutionary Love.
Merton. All of the branches / None of the roots.
Plessy vs Ferguson: Theme and Variations.
Rossetti, C. There Remaineth Therefore a Rest.
Sandburg, C. Graceland.
Psalm of the Bloodbank.
Ward, N. Mercury shew'd Apollo, Bartas Book.
Whitman, W. America.
Song for Occupations, A.
Thought.
Thoughts—I: Visages.
Whittier. Our Country.
Poor Voter on Election Day, The.
Williams, F. Ode, An: "At length revolving fates th' expected year."
Wordsworth, W. What if our numbers barely could defy.
Yeats. Paudeen.
See also **Social Class**

Erie Canal
Logan, J. Lines on Locks (or Jail and the Erie Canal).

Erne (river), Ireland
Muldoon, P. Yggdrasill.

Eros
Cavafy. At the Entrance to the Café.
Before the House.
Laughlin, J. Da mi basia mille.
Timor amoris conturbat me.
See also **Cupid**

Erosion
Berry, W. Dance, A.
Davie, D. Twilight on the Waste Lands.
Dugan, A. Against the Text "Art Is Immortal."
Fragment on the British Museum.
MacDiarmid, H. My Songs Are Kandym in the Waste Land.
McHugh, H. Hard.
Montale. Lindau.
Sandburg, C. Handfuls.
Tomlinson, C. Compact, The: at Volterra.
Poem: "Upended, it crouches on broken limbs."
Sea Poem.
Wilbur, R. On the Marginal Way.

Erotic Love
Achillini, C. Wars and of arms some sing, but I.
Ai. Nothing but Color.
Reunions with a Ghost.
Amichai [*or* Amikhai]. Aching bones of lovers, The.
Advice for Good Love.
Anniversaries of Love.
Balled in the Streets of Buenos Aires.
Bedouin in Love.
Body Is the Cause of Love, The.
Changes, Mistakes, Loves.
Hamadiya.
In a Foreign Country.
In the Middle of This Century.

Instead of Words.
Love Song: "This is how it started: suddenly it felt."
Memory of Love—Opening the Will.
Memory of Love—Terms and Conditions.
On Some Other Planet You May Be Right.
On the Day I Left.
Pinecones on the Tree Above.
Pity, A. We Were Such a Good Invention.
Poems for a Woman.
Poems of Akhziv.
Precise Woman, A.
Six Poems for Tamar.
Summer or Its End, A.
Threading.
To My Love, Combing Her Hair.
Tourist.
Ammons. Guitar Recitativos.
Love Song: "Like the hills under dusk you."
Angelou. Remembrance.
Shaker, Why Don't You Sing?
Zorro Man, A.
Ariosto. Night and Day.
Armantrout. Language of Love.
Plan, The.
Ashbery, J. My Erotic Double.
Atwood. I look up, you are standing.
Auden. As I Walked Out One Evening.
Legend.
Uncle Henry.
Baudelaire. Balcony, The.
Damned Women ("Half-hidden in the dying light's caress").
Death of Lovers, The.
Girandole, The.
Her Hair.
Jewels.
Lover's Wine.
Song for an Afternoon.
World Away, A.
Begley, T. Vowel Imprint.
Berry, W. Dance, The.
Earth and Fire.
Fear of Love, The.
Song: "I tell my love in rhyme."
To Tanya at Christmas.
Bierce. Possibility, A.
To Nanine.
Bishop, E. Late Air.
Three Valentines.
Blake, W. Visions of the Daughters of Albion.
Bly, R. At Midocean.
At the Time of Peony Blossoming.
Ferns.
Horse of Desire, The.
Listening to the Köln Concert.
Bogan, L. Frightened Man, The.
Juan's Song.
Rhyme.
Borges. Anticipation of Love.
Inferno 5, 129.
Parting.
Brodsky, J. Love Song: "If you were drowning, I'd come to the rescue."
On Love.
Seven Strophes.
Twenty Sonnets to Mary Queen of Scots.
Broumas, O. Betrothal / the Bride's Lament.
Caritas.
Days of Argument and Blossom.
Fast.
Four Beginnings / for Kyra.
Love Lines.
Mornings Remembering Last Nights.
Ode: "Ask me no more."
P.S.
Vowel Imprint.
Browning, E. Psyche Gazing on Cupid.
Romance of the Swan's Nest, The.
Browning, R. Confessions.
Last Ride Together, The.
Meeting at Night.
Burns, R. Had I the Wyte She Bade Me.
Lass That Made the Bed for Me, The.
Muirland Meg.
O May Thy Morn.

O Saw Ye My Maggie.
Ode to Spring.
Patriarch, The.
Red, Red Rose, A.
Rigs o' Barley, The.
Song: "My girl she's airy, she's buxom and gay."
Trogger, The.
Byron, G.   Cornelian, The.
Last Words on Greece.
On This Day I Complete My Thirty-sixth Year.
One Struggle More, and I Am Free.
So We'll Go No More A-Roving.
Stanzas to the Po.
To a Lady Who Presented to the Author a Lock of Hair Braided with His Own.
To Thyrza.
Campion, T.   Ad Amorem.
I Care Not for These Ladies.
It Fell on a Summer's [or Sommers] Day [or Daie].
Secret Love or Two I Must Confess[e], A.
Thou Art Not Fair[e].
Carew, T.   On the Marriage of T. K. and C. C.: The Morning Stormy.
Rapture, A.
Second Rapture, The.
Song[, A]: "Ask[e] me no more where Jove bestow[e]s."
Carver, R.   Afghanistan.
Cherish.
Gift, The.
Hummingbird.
Sensitive Girl, The.
This Word Love.
Waiting.
Woman Bathing.
Catullus.   Let us live, my Lesbia, and let us love each other.
Cavafy.   Bandaged Shoulder, The.
Beizades to His Beloved.
December 1903.
Two Young Men, 23 to 24 Years Old.
Young Man, a Writer—in His 24th Year, A.
Cavalcanti.   Alas, my spirits, when you see me.
Ballata: Concerning a Shepherd-maid.
Ballata: He perceives that his highest Love is gone from him.
Ballata: He reveals, in a Dialogue, his increasing Love for Mandetta.
Ballata: Of a continual Death in Love.
Ballata: Of his Lady among other Ladies.
Dante, a sighing messenger of the heart.
Each fresh and sweet source.
I found a shepherdess in a grove.
I never used to think that my heart.
I saw Love in eyes.
I see it in my Lady's eyes.
I was deep in thoughts of Love when I found.
If I were one worthy of Love.
If you see Love, Dante.
If you've forgotten me forever, Mercy.
Love's amorous spiritual glance.
Of foul matters I must speak.
Oh you, whose eyes carry.
Since when must I draw life from death.
Sonnet: A Rapture concerning his Lady.
Sonnet: Guido answers the foregoing Sonnet.
Sonnet: He mistrusts the Love of Lapo Gianni.
Sonnet: He reports, in a feigned Vision, the successful Issue of Lapo Gianni's Love.
Sonnet: Of his Pain from a new Love.
Sonnet: To a Friend who does not pity his Love.
Surely it wasn't your cultered mind.
To each captive and nobly gentle heart.
Wanting I send you certain poems.
Woman asks me.
You who've pierced my eyes to my heart.
Celan.   Corona.
Love Crown.
Ciardi, J.   Cézanne.
Credibility.
Deaths about You when You Stir in Sleep, The.
For Judith.
In Pity as We Kiss and Lie.
Logician's Nocturne, The.

Love Poem, A: "I have labored for her love."
Loving You Is Something to Do.
Sometimes the Foundering Fury.
To Judith Asleep.
Cino da Pistoia.   Madrigal: To his Lady Selvaggia Vergiolesi.
Sonnet: A Trance of Love.
Sonnet: He interprets Dante's Dream, related in the first Sonnet of the Vita Nuova.
Sonnet: Of the grave of Selvaggia, on the Monte della Sambuca.
Clampitt.   Having Lunch at Brasenose.
Smaller Orchid, The.
Clough.   Ah, what is love, our love, she said.
Do duty feeling nought and truth believe.
Homo Sum, Nihil Humani—.
Natura Naturans.
O Theos Meta Sou.
Oh, ask not what is love, she said.
Thought may well be ever ranging.
To be, be thine.
Codrescu.   Love Poem: "And while for the sake of sanity."
Coleridge, S.   First Advent of Love.
Love and Friendship Opposite.
Ode in the Manner of Anacreon, An.
To an Unfortunate Woman Whom the Author Had Known in the Days of Her Innocence.
Cooper, J.   Acceptances.
March.
Obligations.
Pencil Sketch of Self & Other.
Song: "Here I am yours, and here, and here."
Corkine.   My Dearest Mistress.
Crane, S.   And you love me?
I heard thee laugh.
Intrigue.
Love forgive me if I wish you grief.
Love met me at noonday.
Love walked alone.
Once I saw thee idly rocking.
Should the wide world roll away.
Tell me why, behind thee.
Crashaw.   Out of the Italian; a Song.
Creeley.   Places ("When I wake next").
Question, The.
Sight, A.
Two Times.
Woman, The.
Cullen, C.   At a Parting.
Bright Bindings.
Brown Boy to Brown Girl.
If You Should Go.
Love Tree, The.
Love's Way.
One Day We Played a Game.
Pity the Deep in Love.
Song of Praise.
Song of Praise, A.
Sonnet: "I have not loved you in the noblest way."
Street Called Crooked, The.
To a Brown Girl.
Variations on a Theme.
Wind Bloweth Where It Listeth, The.
Cummings, E. E.   After your poppied hair inaugurates.
Amiable putrescence carpenters, An.
And this day it was Spring....us.
As / we lie side by side.
Because i love you)last night.
Bed is not very big, The.
Before the fragile gradual throne of night.
Dirty colours of her kiss have just, The.
Five Americans.
Her careful distinct sex whose sharp lips comb.
Her / flesh / Came / at.
I like my body when it is with your.
I will be / M o ving in the Street of her.
If i believe / in death be sure.
I'll tell you a dream i had once i was away up in the sky Blue,everything.
Light cursed falling in a singular block.
Luminous tendril of celestial wish.
May I Feel Said He.
Moon is hiding in, The.

My deathly body's deadly lady.
My lady is an ivory garden.
My love / thy hair is one kingdom.
My strength becoming wistful in a glib.
My sweet old etcetera.
O It's Nice To Get Up In,the slipshod mucous kiss.
Reason let others give and realness bring.
Sapphics.
Sh estiffl / ystrut sal.
She,straddling my lap.
Sunlight was over.
Thee will i praise between those rivers whose.
There is a / moon sole.
Upon the room's / silence,i will sew.
Voices to voices, lip to lip.
What is thy mouth to me?
When i have thought of you somewhat too.
When the spent day begins to frail.
When you went away it was morning.
You asked me to come:it was raining a little.
Cunningham, J.   All Choice Is Error.
Epigram: "And what is love? Misunderstanding, pain."
Dante Alighieri.   Dante's Vita Nuova.
Guido, I would like that you and Lapo and I.
La Vita Nuova.
Sestina: Of the Lady Pietra degli Scrovigni.
Sonnet: On the 9th of June 1290.
Sonnet: To certain Ladies; when Beatrice was lamenting her Father's Death.
Sonnet: To the Lady Pietra degli Scrovigni.
"Dario."   Autumn Poem, The.
Autumn Verses.
Dream's blue bird, The.
Flesh, a woman's heavenly flesh. Clay.
In Spring.
Song of Autumn in Springtime.
Davie, D.   Admiral to His Lady, The.
Dickey, J.   Cherrylog Road.
On the Hill below the Lighthouse.
Dickey, W.   Making Love.
Dickinson, E.   Rose did caper on her cheek, The.
Surrender.
We went to sleep as if it were a country.
Wild Nights—Wild Nights!
You love me—you are sure.
Donne.   Air[e] and Angels.
Anniversary [or Anniversarie], The.
Bait[e], The.
Canonization, The.
Confined Love.
Dissolution, The.
Dream[e], The.
Ecstasy, The.
Farewell to Love.
Flea, The.
Good-Morrow, The.
Indifferent, The.
Love's Alchemy [or Alchemie].
Love's Deity [or Deitie].
Love's Growth.
Love's Usury.
Sun Rising, The.
To Mr C. B.
To the Countess of Huntingdon ("That unripe side of earth, that heavy clime").
Dove, R.   For Kazuko.
Dryden, J.   New Song, A: "Sylvia the fair, in the bloom of fifteen."
Dubie.   After Spring Snow, What They Saw.
At Midsummer.
Circus Ringmaster's Apology to God, The.
Dream.
Fever.
Dugan, A.   Poem: "Person who can do, The."
Dunbar, P.   Negro Love Song, A.
Eberhart, R.   My Brains Are Slipping in the Fields of Eros.
Eliot, T. S.   Love Song of St. Sebastian, The.
Éluard, P.   Curfew.
Lady Love.
Out of Sight in the Direction of My Body.
Scarcely Disfigured.
Universe-Solitude.

Emerson, R.   Eros.
 Give All to Love.
 Love and Thought.
 Ode to Beauty.
Faiz.   If I Were Certain.
Fazio degli Uberti.   Canzone: His Portrait of his
  Lady, Angiola of Verona.
Ferlinghetti, L.   Come lie with me and be my
  love.
 Tunisian Nostalgia.
García Lorca.   Autumn Song.
 Elegy: "Like a censer filled with desire."
 It Is True.
 Little Viennese Waltz.
 Madrigal: "I looked into your eyes."
 Minor Song.
 New Heart.
 Nocturne: "I am afraid / of dead leaves."
 Nocturne of Emptied Space.
 Summer Madrigal.
 Two Girls.
 Your Childhood in Menton.
Ginsberg, A.   I Lay Love on My Knee.
 Love Comes.
 Love Forgiven.
 Love Poem on Theme by Whitman.
 Love Replied.
 Love Returned.
 Malest Cornifici Tuo Catullo.
 Many Loves.
 Message.
 Song: "Weight of the world, The."
 Tethnakin D'oligo Pideuis Fainom Alaia.
Glück, L.   Aubade: "Today above the gull's
  call."
 Garden, The.
 Happiness.
 Lady in the Single, The.
 Mirror, The.
 Northwood Path.
 Reproach, The.
Graves, R.   Age Gap.
 Bites and Kisses.
 Conjunction.
 Crystal, The.
 Dancing Flame.
 Discarded Love Poem, The.
 Down, Wanton, Down!
 Dream of Hell, A.
 Druid Love.
 Earlier Lovers.
 Elsewhere.
 Envoi: "There is no now for us but always."
 Jus Primae Noctis.
 Loving True, Flying Blind.
 Moon's Tear, The.
 Mountain Lovers.
 Not at Home.
 Ours is No Wedlock.
 Poet's Curse, The.
 Prohibition, The.
 She Tells Her Love While Half Asleep.
 Song: Seven Fresh Years.
 Song: The Queen of Time.
 Testament.
 To Come of Age.
 Two Crucial Generations.
Guinicelli.   Canzone: Of the Gentle Heart.
Gunn, T.   Bed, The.
 For a Birthday.
 Hug, The.
 Lines for My 55th Birthday.
 Monster, The.
Gurney, I.   March.
"H. D."   Epigrams.
Hacker, M.   Aube Provençale.
 Ballad of Ladies Lost and Found.
 Elektra on Third Avenue.
 For K.J., Leaving and Coming Back.
 Pantoum.
 Presentation Piece.
 Separate Lives.
 Sestina: "For a week now our bodies have
  whispered."
 Villanelle: "Every day our bodies separate."
 Villanelle: Late Summer.

Hamill, S.   Body of Summer, The.
 Cartographer's Wedding, The.
 Journey, The.
 Jubilate Sutra.
 Kannon.
 Sonnet.
Han-shan.   Oriole on a flowering branch, An.
Hardy, T.   Beeny Cliff.
 Neutral Tones.
Heaney, S.   Field Work.
 Poem: "Love, I shall perfect for you the child."
 Undine.
 Walk, The.
Herbert, G.   Love (3).
Herrick.   Bride-Cake, The.
 Her Bed.
 Her Legs.
 Lawne, The.
 Love Dislikes Nothing.
 Love Perfumes All Parts.
 No Loathsomnesse in Love.
 To Anthea.
 To Anthea, Who May Command Him Anything.
 To Dianeme.
 To Electra.
 To Julia, in Her Dawn, or Day-breake.
 Upon Julia's Breasts.
 Upon Julia's Clothes.
 Upon Loach.
 Vine, The.
 Vision to Electra, The.
Hill, G.   Troublesome Reign, The.
Housman.   Because I liked you better.
 He would not stay for me; and who can
  wonder?
 If truth in hearts that perish.
 Look not in my eyes, for fear.
 Shake hands, we shall never be friends, all's
  over.
 When I Was One-and-Twenty.
Hughes, L.   Beale Street Love.
 Black Pierrot, A.
 Breath of a Rose.
 Cora.
 Could Be.
 Fascination.
 Fired.
 Harlem Night Song.
 Juke Box Love Song.
 Lament over Love.
 Love.
 Love Again Blues.
 Love Song for Antonia.
 Love Song for Lucinda.
 Lover's Return.
 Ma Man.
 Midwinter Blues.
 Minnie Sings Her Blues.
 My Beloved.
 My Loves.
 Pale Lady.
 Passing Love.
 Poem: "Ah, / My black one."
 Poem for an Intellectual on the Way Up to
  Submit to His Lady.
 Reasons Why.
 Ring, The.
 To Artina.
 Troubled Water.
 Wooing, A.
Hughes, T.   Bride and Groom Lie Hidden for
  Three Days.
 Lovepet, The.
 Lovesong: "He loved her and she loved him."
Ignatow, D.   Each Day.
 Each of Us.
 For Your Fear.
 I Dream I Hurl a Spear.
 Love We Had, The.
 Men You've Loved, The.
 My Love for You.
 Principle, The.
Jackson, L.   Be Grave, Woman.
 Biography of a Myth, The.
 Definition of Love, The.
 Druida.

Eventual Love.
In Due Form.
It Is Not Sad.
Meanwhile.
O Vocables of Love.
Readers, The.
Rhythms of Love.
Several Love-Stories.
Take Hands.
To a Loveless Lover.
When Love Becomes Words.
Wishing More Dear.
You or You.
Jacobsen, J.   Autopsy, The.
 Carney Elegy.
 Lovers, The.
 There Is Good News.
Jacopo da Lentino.   Sonnet: Of [or To] his Lady
  in Heaven.
Jeffers, R.   For Una.
 Hungerfield.
 Resurrection.
Keats.   Bright Star.
 Dawlish Fair.
 Eve of St Agnes, The.
Kinnell.   52 Oswald Street.
 Perch, The.
 Rapture.
 Running on Silk.
 That Silent Evening.
 Waking, The.
Kinsella, T.   Beloved,.
 Echoes.
 Madonna.
 Phoenix Park.
 Tête à Tête.
Kizer, C.   Copulating Gods, The.
 Food of Love.
 Gift, The.
 Glass, The.
 Light, The.
 Love Song: "Oh, to fall easily, easily, easily in
  Love."
 Lovemusic.
 Patient Lovers, The.
 Summer near the River.
Koch, K.   Art of Love, The.
 In Bed.
 Sleeping with Women.
Komunyakaa.   Allegorical Seduction.
 Breasts.
 Insufficient Blue.
 Lover.
 Piccolo, The.
 Providence.
 Sandhog.
 Whispering Gallery, The.
Kumin, M.   After Love.
 We Are.
Kunitz, S.   First Love.
 Touch Me.
Laughlin, J.   Alba.
 Amo Amas Amat.
 Anti-Love Poem, An.
 Bird of Endless Time, The.
 Can Language Be Taught with the Fingertips?
 Can There Be a Female Bodhissatva?
 Confessio Amantis.
 Deconstructed Man, The.
 Delia Sequence, The.
 El camino de amor.
 Elusive Time.
 Eros as Archaeologist.
 Escape, The.
 Eyes Are the Guides of Love.
 First Night, The.
 Flavius to Postumia.
 Her Letters.
 Her Reply.
 Her Sweet Deceit.
 Hunting Dog, The.
 I Am Aware.
 I Hate Love.
 I Love to See You.
 Il Pastor Fido.
 In Another Country.

In Half Darkness.
In the Ballet.
In the Museum at Teheran.
Inn at Kirchstetten, The.
It Can Happen.
It's Indelicate.
Jealous Gods, The.
Kiss, The.
La Tristesse.
Les Amants.
Like the Octopus.
Limper, The.
Lines after Cummings.
Love Is a School.
Love's Altar.
Market Discounts Love.
Near Zermatt: The Drahtseilbahn.
Now Love Speaks.
Nowadays.
O Best of All Nights, Return and Return Again.
Our Meetings.
Qui Nunquam Amavit.
Return of Love, The.
Revenants, The.
Rhyme.
Sinking Stone, The.
Snow in May.
Summons, The.
This Is the Morte Saison.
Three Skirmishes in the Endless Battle.
Timor amoris conturbat me.
To My Lady in a Distant Land That She Forget
    Me Not.
Translation, A.
Two Letters on Samos.
Two Spoons.
Voices, The.
What Is It Makes One Girl.
When you are far away.
Wild Anemone, The.
You Are My Future.
You Know How a Cat.
You've Set the Words.
Lawrence, D. H.   All of Roses.
  Gloire de Dijon.
  New Year's Eve.
  Paradise Re-entered.
  True Love at Last.
  Young Wife, A.
Levertov.   Eros at Temple Stream.
  Face to Face.
  Hymn to Eros.
  Love Poem.
Logan, J.   Assateague.
  Gift, The.
  Love Poem: "Last night you would not come."
  Suzanne.
Logue, C.   Air for the Witness of a Departure.
  Nell's Circular Poem.
  O come all ye faithful.
  Woke up this morning.
Lorde.   Bridge Through My Window.
  Echo.
  Love Poem.
  On a Night of the Full Moon.
  Progress Report.
Lowell, R.   Man And Wife.
MacDiarmid, H.   Water of Life.
MacFadden, E.   In Pity First to Human Kind.
MacLeish.   What Must.
  Woman on the Stair, The.
Mahon.   First Love.
  Two Songs [for Doreen].
Major, C.   Love Against Death.
  Nerve, The.
  Pupa.
  Way the Roundness Feels, The.
Mallarmé.   Afternoon of a Faun, The.
  Apparition.
  Fan, A; of Méry Laurent.
  Futile Petition.
  Rondel: "We'll love each other if you choose."
  Sonnet: "Lady / who burns without being burnt
    or trying."
  Summer Sadness.
Marino.   Out of the Italain.

Marlowe.   Passionate Shepherd To His Love,
    The.
Marvell.   To His Coy Mistress.
McHugh, H.   Reservation.
Meredith, W.   Crossing Over.
  For Two Lovers in the Year 2075 in the
    Canadian Woods.
  Poem: "Swans on the river, a great, The."
Merrill, J.   From the Cupola.
Merwin.   Kore.
Michelangelo Buonarroti.   Although it's amply
    true your human face.
  Although my heart had often been aflame.
  Although time presses hard and prods us on.
  Because there's half of me which, heaven-born.
  Because there's never a time I'm not enchanted.
  Drawn to each lovely thing, my doting eyes.
  Easily you confound.
  Fine lass or lady, they.
  Flee from this Love, you lovers; flee the flame!
  Flooded, the soul pours out.
  For a safe haven, for escape at last.
  From beneath two arching brows.
  From eyes of my beloved one, come burning.
  From ink, from pen in hand we see outflow.
  From one all loveliness and all allure.
  From where you triumphed in me, Love, right
    here.
  Great beauty scattering its brilliant flame.
  Had I, when young, been leery of the glow.
  Hating myself, the more I run away.
  How could I, since it's so.
  How much less torment to breathe out my soul.
  Humbly I bow my shoulders, bear the yoke.
  I do believe, if you were made of stone.
  I made my eyes an entryway for poison.
  I think it may be, so.
  I was, for years and years now, wounded, killed.
  I was happy, with fate favoring, to abide.
  I'd feel the more secure.
  If fire can melt down steel and shatter flint.
  If fire, so quick to char.
  If I'm more alive because love burns and chars
    me.
  If obligated by so great a favor.
  If pure devotion, passion without stain.
  If she rejoices in my tears, and you.
  If the soul, in truth, from body once set free.
  If the soul returns, that last.
  If, to rejoice, you crave our tears and woe.
  If, when it caught my eye first, I'd been bolder.
  I'll surely be thought a dullard in talent, art.
  I'm dearer to me, much more, than ever I was.
  In everything I see, the meaning's plain.
  In lovelier and crueller flesh than yours.
  It seems, Love, out you've flung.
  It well may be, so vehement my sighing.
  Just when I'm lost in adoration of you.
  Love in your eyes? No; life and death are there.
  Mould's not alone in this, A.
  My death is what I live on; seems to me.
  My lady, you raise me so.
  My lover stole my heart, just over there.
  My reason, out of sorts with me, deplores.
  No differently the guilty wretch hangs back.
  No question but, when my desire's aflame.
  No rest here for the wicked, as folk say.
  No slightest chance on earth her heavenly eyes.
  Not even, in dreams sent soaring, can I imagine.
  Not true that it's always grim with mortal sin.
  Nothing the best of artists can conceive.
  Now on the left foot shuffling, now the right.
  O blessed souls, who high in heaven delight.
  O cruel star, or say instead, cruel will.
  O God, O God, O God, how can I be.
  O noble soul, in whom, as mirrored, show.
  Please tell me, Love, if that lady had a soul.
  Seeing I'm yours, I rouse me from afar.
  Should the senses' rapturous burning override.
  So I can best endure.
  Suppose a lady has no other graces.
  That whole way up to your brilliant diadem.
  Though bent with age, to me.
  Through many a year and many a vain assay.
  Through your fine eyes I see such mellow light.
  Uproot a plant—there's no way it can seal.

What in your handsome face I see, my lord.
What's to become of me? What's this you're
    doing.
When blithely Love would lift me up to heaven.
When to that beauty that I saw before.
Whenever remembrance of the one I love.
With all my heart I love you; if not so.
With much of time and life gone, all the more.
You know, my Lord, that I too know you know.
Your beauty, Love, stuns mortal reckonings.
Your kindness to me, and the ways of fate.
Your lovely eyes, now bent.
Your merciful, sweet care.
Millay, E.   I think I should have loved you
    presently.
  Night is my sister, and how deep in love.
  She Is Overheard Singing.
Milosz, C.   After Paradise.
  Annalena.
  Initiation.
  Photograph, A.
Mistral, G.   Ballad: "He passed by with another
    woman."
  God Wills It.
  Useless Vigil, The.
Montale.   You've named a tree for me? It isn't
    nothing.
Neruda.   Physics.
Olson, C.   It's Not / the Erotic.
Oppen.   Of This All Things.
Orlandi, G.   Prolonged Sonnet: He finds fault
    with the Conceits of the foregoing Sonnet.
Orr, G.   Like Any Other Man.
  Nantucket Morning / This World.
  Once the two of us.
  Swamp Songs.
  We Must Make a Kingdom of It.
  When I first saw her.
Ovid.   Galatea.
Owen, W.   Music.
  To Eros.
Pagis.   New Lover, A.
Parker, D.   After a Spanish Proverb.
  Anecdote.
  Ballade of Unfortunate Mammals.
  Burned Child, The.
  But Not Forgotten.
  Choice, The.
  Christmas, 1921.
  Dark Girl's Rhyme, The.
  Distance.
  Fair Weather.
  Fairly Sad Tale, A.
  Fantasy.
  Folk Tune.
  For a Favorite Grand-Daughter.
  Fragment: "Why should we set these hearts of
    ours above."
  How Bold It Is.
  I Know I Have Been Happiest.
  Immortals, The.
  Last Question, The.
  Liebestod.
  Love Song: "My own dear love, he is strong
    and bold."
  Mood.
  New Love, The.
  Now at Liberty.
  Passionate Freudian to His Love, The.
  Paths.
  Pattern.
  Pictures in the Smoke.
  Plea.
  Portrait, A.
  Post-Graduate.
  Pour Prendre Congé.
  Promise.
  Purposely Ungrammatical Love Song.
  Recurrence.
  Renunciation.
  Requiescat.
  Rondeau Redoublé.
  Searched Soul, The.
  Second Love.
  Somebody's Song.
  Somewhat Delayed Spring Song.

Song: "And shall we build a little nest."
Song in a Minor Key.
Sonnet: "In seemly burial, love may not rest."
Summary.
Theory.
There Was One.
Thin Edge, The.
Thoughts.
To a Much Too Unfortunate Lady.
Trifler, The.
Triolets: "Herewith I send you my heart."
Trusting Heart, The.
Two-Volume Novel.
Ultimatum.
Unfortunate Coincidence.
Verse Reporting Late Arrival at a Conclusion.
Very Short Song, A.
War Song.
Well-Worn Story, A.
Wisdom.
Pasolini. One of the Many Epilogs.
Reality.
Southern Dawn.
Pasternak, B. Portland.
Patchen. All That Night Lights Were Seen
    Moving in Every Direction.
And her look touching the air between us like a
    hand alive to the.
And What with the Blunders.
As Frothing Wounds of Roses.
As She Was Thus Alone in the Clear Moonlight.
As we are so wonderfully done with each other.
Be music, night, / That her sleep may go.
Beautiful You Are.
Builders, The.
Character of Love Seen as a Search for the Lost,
    The.
Colony of the Sun, The.
Do me that love.
Early in the Morning.
Fall of the Evening Star.
Farewell to the Bluewoman.
First came the Lion-Rider, across the green
    fields of the morning.
For losing her love all would I profane.
For Miriam.
Give you a lantern.
Harrowed by These Apprehensions He Resolved
    to Commit Himself to the Mercy of the
    Storm.
Having Been Near.
He Thought of Mad Ellen's Ravings.
Heaven and Earth.
Her Talents...Of.
I Sent a Mental to My Love.
In Judgment of the Leaf.
In Memory of Kathleen.
It's Because Your Heart Is Pure, Honey.
Lute in the Attic, The.
Meditation of My Lady of Sorrows.
Not Many Kingdoms Left.
O my darling troubles heaven.
O my love / The pretty towns.
O sleeping falls the maiden snow.
Pretty glow on the water.
Put the rest away, O put the rest away!
Religion Is That I Love You.
She Had Concealed Him in a Deep Dark Cave.
She is the prettiest of creatures.
Stayed No Longer in the Place Than to Hire a
    Guide for the Next Stage.
There's a Train Leaving Soon.
Thinking Rock.
To Say If You Love Someone.
Waiting Can Be Pretty Lousy.
When We Were Here Together.
Where my stag-antlered love moves.
Written after Reading an Item in the Paper about
    a Young Lady Who Went Mad upon
    Forsaking Her Lover.
Yellow Stones—Sea of Majestic Doves.
Petrarch. After I fled the place where many
    years.
Alas how unprepared I was at first.
Alas, that time has now passed over when.
Already you have done, remorseless Death.

At every step, I find I must look back.
Be it, Sennuccio, clearly understood.
By then I knew my flourishing green age.
Charming pallor clothing her sweet smile, The.
Clear, fresh, and pleasant water.
Could I but pour out into powerful rhyme.
Cruel the star (if stars are powerful).
Diana did not more delight her lover.
Exhilarated flowers, and lucky grasses.
From lovely clear and polished living ice. .
From what circle of heaven, from what idea.
Full of that indescribable delight.
Heavenly breeze that breathes throughout the
    green, The.
Her golden hair was blowing in the breeze.
How many times already Love has said.
I cannot keep silent, and I fear my tongue.
I feed my mind on such a noble food.
I feel the ancient breeze, see with delight.
I find no peace, yet have no war in hand.
I have been nowhere else where I could see.
I have been shown a myriad slopes and more.
I have loved always, and I do love still.
I knew already, Love, our human ploys.
I knew—so much heaven opened up my eyes.
I must direct these lines so full of sorrow.
I raised myself in thought to where I found.
I really did believe I would go on.
I sang once: now I weep; and I take pleasure.
I saw a lady; on each side a lover.
I see, my noble lady.
I thought my wings were fledged for such a
    flight.
I used to stray far from the fountainhead.
I walk, alone and troubled, desert places.
I would write poems of love of such a kind.
If I said it, may I be held to scorn.
If, in this fourteenth year of all my sighs.
If Love does not bring better thoughts to bear.
If virtuous love can merit a reward.
If you want me again under your yoke.
In sheer amazement, Love and I together.
Is this the nest in which my phoenix put.
It makes me weary when I realise.
It was my love and grief which drove my
    tongue.
It was the day Apollo's rays turned pale.
I've never seen the sun rise in such glory.
Jove and Caesar were never so moved—the one.
L'aura, the gentle breeze that clears the hills.
Leave me, unhappy thoughts, leave me in
    peace!
Long for the evening, loathe the coming dawn.
Lord Love, to whom all hearts and minds are
    known.
Lord Love, who holds the chief place in my
    mind.
Love, Fortune, and my mind (hardly aware).
Love had revealed to me a tranquil harbour.
Love kept me burning one-and-twenty years.
Love, Nature, and this lovely gentle soul.
Love, who can promise so beguilingly.
Lust goads, and Love goes with me as a guide.
More happily than I no ship has ever.
My days have gone by swifter than a deer.
My ills oppress me, and I fear the worst.
My love for you has never wearied me.
My soul, prophetic of your coming loss.
No weary weather-beaten mariner.
Noble lineage with calm humility.
Not stars that wander through the open sky.
Now if not love, what is it that I feel?
O Envy, enemy to all that's good.
O precious liberty, how you reveal.
On the greensward there was a milk-white deer.
Over the grasses Love had spread his net.
Rushing river, forcing your rapid way.
Sennuccio, I'm half here. Oh, were I all.
She comes to mind—no, is already there.
Since Love was driving me to my old haunts.
Since through my destiny.
Soon as *madonna* comes into my heart.
That cheek of yours that has been tired with
    weeping.
That lady whom I always have in mind.
That miracle—which in these days of ours.

That other sun by whom the path was shown.
That powerful lord from whom we cannot hide.
That which in colour and in scent outdid.
This breeze, stirring green laurel and my lady's.
This is on earth the happiest bit of land.
Those eyes that wounded me in such a way.
Till both my temples are completely white.
Time had come for me to establish peace, The.
To wreak what sweet revenge is his to wreak.
Towards the dawn, when *l'aura* (the mild
    breeze).
Unexpected angel glided down, An.
Valley re-echoing with woes of mine.
Weep now, my eyes; accompany my heart.
When she arrives where greatest beauty is.
Whenever Love makes his assaults on me.
With my long-honoured, dear, and cruel lord.
You who can hear in scattered rhymes the
    sound.
Petronius Arbiter. Doing, a filthy pleasure is,
    and short.
Piercy. You Ask Why Sometimes I Say Stop.
Pinkerton, H. Coast Hillside.
For an End.
Pinsky. Shiva and Parvati Hiding in the Rain.
Pound, E. In Epitaphium Eius.
Marvoil.
Na Audiart.
Piere Vidal Old.
Speech for Psyche in the Golden Book of
    Apuleius.
Villonaud for This Yule.
Virginal, A.
Prunty. Caligula in Blue.
Ralegh, S. Nymph's [or Nimphs] Reply to the
    Shepherd [or Sheepheard], The.
Ramanujan. LOVE 2: What He Said, Groping.
Two Styles in Love.
Ransom, J. Equilibrists, The.
Rexroth, K. Dialogue of Watching, A.
Hanged Man, The.
High Provence.
Incarnation.
Inversely, as the Square of Their Distances
    Apart.
Lantern and a Shadow, A.
Lute Music.
My Heart's as Gay as a Young Sunflower.
Old Song and Dance, The.
Open the Blind.
Rosa Mundi.
Runaway.
She Is Away [or Marthe Away (She Is Away)].
Rich, A. Night Watch.
Riley, J. Bedouin.
Rilke. Blank Joy.
Happy Men and Women.
Nothing's Left.
Song: "You, to whom I don't confide."
To Jean-Louis Vandoyer.
Rimbaud, A. Romance.
Ritsos. Carnal Word.
Roethke. I Knew A Woman.
Rossetti, C. All night I dream you love me well.
Amore E Dispetto.
Amore E Dovere.
Annie.
Ariadne To Theseus.
At Last.
Bed of Forget-Me-Nots, A.
Birthday, A.
Brandons Both.
Cor Mio.
Corydon's Lament and Resolution.
Despair.
Dream, A.
Dream, The.
Echo from Willowwood, An.
Fair Margaret.
Faithless Shepherdess, The.
From Mestastasio.
Grown Cold.
Have You Forgotten?
If I Were a Queen.
Il Rosseggiar Dell'Oriente Canzoniere.
In the Lane.

Isidora.
Lisetta all' Amante.
Listening.
Long Looked For.
Look on This Picture and on This.
Lord Thomas and Fair Margaret.
Love and Death.
Love Attacked.
Love Defended.
Mariana.
Moonshine.
Novice, The.
O thou who tell'st me that all hope is over.
One Foot on Sea, and One on Shore.
Pitia a Damone.
Rosalind.
Song: "I have loved you for long long years Ellen."
Till Tomorrow.
Tirsi, A.
To My Fior-Di-Lisa.
To the End.
Touching "Never."
Two Parted.
Undine.
Versi.
Year Afterwards, A.
Young Men Aye Were Fickle Found Since Summer Trees Were Leafy.
Zara.
Zion Said.
Rossetti, D.   Ardour and Memory.
Autumn Idleness.
Barren Spring.
Beauty's Pageant.
Birth-Bond, The.
Blessed Damozel, The.
Body's Beauty.
Bridal Birth.
Broken Music.
Choice, The ("Eat thou and drink; to-morrow thou shalt die").
Choice, The ("Think thou and act; to-morrow thou shalt die").
Choice, The ("Watch thou and fear; to-morrow thou shalt die").
Cloud and Wind.
Dark Day, A.
Dark Glass, The.
Day of Love, A.
Death-in-Love.
Death's Songsters.
Equal Troth.
Farewell to the Glen.
From Dawn to Noon.
Genius in Beauty.
Gracious Moonlight.
He and I.
Heart of the Night, The.
Heart's Compass.
Heart's Haven.
Heart's Hope.
Her Gifts.
Hero's Lamp.
Hill Summit, The.
Hoarded Joy.
Hope Overtaken.
Inclusiveness.
Insomnia.
Kiss, The.
Known in Vain.
Lamp's Shrine, The.
Landmark, The.
Last Fire.
Life-in-Love.
Life the Beloved.
Lost Days.
Lost on Both Sides.
Love and Hope.
Love Enthroned.
Love-Letter, The.
Love-Moon, The.
Love-Sweetness.
Lovers' Walk, The.
Love's Baubles.
Love's Fatality.

Love's Last Gift.
Love's Lovers.
Love's Testament.
Lovesight.
Memorial Thresholds.
Michelangelo's Kiss.
Mid-Rapture.
Monochord, The.
Moonstar, The.
Morrow's Message, The.
Newborn Death ("And thou, O Life, the lady of all bliss").
Newborn Death ("To-day Death seems to me an infant child").
Nuptial Sleep.
Old and New Art (Not as These).
Old and New Art (St Luke the Painter).
Old and New Art (The Husbandmen).
One Hope, The.
Parted Love.
Passion and Worship.
Portrait, The.
Pride of Youth.
Retro me, Sathana!
Secret Parting.
Severed Selves.
Silent Noon.
Sleepless Dreams.
Song-Throe, The.
Sonnet, A: "Sonnet is a moment's monument, A."
Soul-Light.
Soul's Beauty.
Soul's Sphere, The.
Stillborn Love.
Sun's Shame, The ("As some true chief of men, bowed down with stress").
Sun's Shame, The ("Beholding youth and hope in mockery caught").
Superscription, A.
Supreme Surrender.
Through Death to Love.
Transfigured Life.
Trees of the Garden, The.
True Woman (Her Heaven).
True Woman (Her Love).
True Woman (Herself).
Vain Virtues.
Vase of Life, The.
Venus Victrix.
Willowwood ("And now Love sang: but his was such a song").
Willowwood ("I sat with Love upon a woodside well").
Willowwood ("O ye, all ye that walk in Willowwood").
Willowwood ("So sang he: and as meeting rose and rose").
Winged Hours.
Without Her.
Youth's Antiphony.
Youth's Spring-Tribute.
Rukeyser, M.   Anemone.
Drunken Girl.
Nevertheless the Moon.
Parallel Invention.
Song: Lying in Daylight.
Song: Remembering Movies.
Three Sides of a Coin.
Tunnel, The.
What I See.
Rumi.   I want to hold you close like a lute.
Like This.
Minute I heard my first love story, The.
Sandburg, C.   Explanations of Love.
Let Love Go On.
Love Is a Deep and a Dark and a Lonely.
Moon Rondeau.
Offering and Rebuff.
Sappho.   I loved you, Leslie, long ago.
Love strikes me again, that makes the legs give way.
Schuyler, J.   Await.
Blue towel, A.
Daylight.
Perhaps.

Photograph, A.
Poem: "Your enchantment / enchains me, stretched."
Sleep.
Steaming Ties.
Up.
Was It.
Watching You.
We Are Leaves.
Seifert.   Berthe Soucaret.
Canal Gardens.
Dance of the Girls' Chemises.
Fingerprints.
Fragment of a Letter.
Grave of Signor Casanova, The.
Honeymoon.
Hunt for the Kingfisher, The.
If one could tell one's heart.
Lovers, those evening pilgrims.
Merry-Go-Round with White Swan.
November Rain.
Our Lady of Žižkov.
Plague Column, The.
Prospect of Prague, A.
Relay Tower, The.
Silence Full of Sleighbells.
Song from an Intermezzo.
Song of the Nightingale, The.
Striking of the Tower Clock, The.
Struggle with the Angel.
When in the history books.
You have skin pale like a snowdrop.
Sexton.   Song for a Lady.
That Day.
Us.
Shapiro, K.   Girls Fighting, Broadway.
Shelley, P.   Indian Serenade, The.
"Shu Ting."   "?!"
To ———.
To the Oak.
When You Come Past My Window.
Simic.   Breasts.
Elegy: "Note / as it gets darker."
Hurricane Season.
My Beloved.
Snyder, G.   After Work.
Spenser, E.   Epithalamion: "Ye learned sisters which have oftentimes."
Stafford, W.   Glances.
Stampa.   Portrait of Her Lover.
Stein, G.   Lifting Belly.
Stock, R.   All I Wanted to Say.
Cenotaph for Two Butterflies.
Instructions to Any Painter for a "Coronation of Inés de Castro."
Now Are We Remembered.
Reconstruction.
Revelation According to the Beloved.
Sharing It With Angels.
This Book is for Harriette.
Suckling, S.   Against Fruition.
Careless Lover, The.
Desdain.
Expostulation, The.
Farewell to Love.
Love Turned to Hatred.
Love's Clock.
Love's Representation.
Love's Siege.
Miracle, The.
My dearest rival, lest [or least] our love.
Perjury Excused.
Song: "If you refuse me once and think again."
Sonnet: "O[h]! for some honest lover's ghost."
To a Lady That Forbade to Love before Company.
Upon A.M.
Upon My Lady Carlisle's Walking in Hampton Court Garden.
Verses: "I am confirm'd a woman can."
Swenson, M.   Love Sleeping.
Swinburne.   In The Orchard.
Interlude, An.
Laus Veneris.
Sze.   Alba.
Apache Plume.

Kaiseki.
Morning Shutters.
Six Persimmons.
Szymborska, W. Commemoration.
  Love at First Sight.
  True Love.
Tate, J. Coda: "Love is not worth so much."
  End of the Line, The.
  Last Days of April, The.
  Stella Maris.
Thomas, D. In My Craft or Sullen Art.
Thoreau. I'm guided in the darkest night.
  Love.
Tomlinson, C. Backward Glance, A.
Unknown. From the Persian (1).
Updike. Blessing, The.
  Chloë's Poem.
  Erotic Epigrams.
  Nuda Natens.
  Sleeping with You.
  You Who Swim.
Van Duyn. 3 A. M. in a War Year.
  Footnotes to "The Autobiography of Bertrand
    Russell."
  Leda.
  Leda Reconsidered.
  Sentimental Delusion, A.
Voznesensky [*or* Voznesenskii]. Dead Still.
Walker, A. I'm Really Very Fond.
  Smell of Lebanon, The.
Warren, R. Aging Painter Sits Where the Great
  Tower Heaves Down Midnight.
  Cold Colloquy.
  Goodbye.
  Love's Voice.
  Vision under the October Mountain: A Love
    Poem.
Weiss, T. Hook, The.
Whalen, P. Irregular Ode, An.
  Money Is the Roost of All Eagles.
Whitman, W. Among the Multitude.
  As Adam Early in the Morning.
  From Pent-up Aching Rivers.
  Spontaneous Me.
  When I Heard At The Close Of The Day.
  Whoever You Are Holding Me Now in Hand.
Wilbur, R. Apology.
  Late Aubade, A.
  Loves of the Puppets.
  Pangloss's Song: A Comic-Opera Lyric.
  Someone Talking to Himself.
Wilde, O. Apologia.
  Garden of Eros, The.
  Her Voice.
  Quia Multum Amavi.
  Roses and Rue.
  Silentium Amoris.
  Sweet I blame you not for mine the fault was,
    had I not been made of common clay.
  Under the Balcony.
  Vita Nuova.
Williams, C. K. Game, The.
  Orchid, The.
Williams, M. August Evening Outside of
  Nashville, An.
  Before.
  Clutter of Silence: Invention for Two Voices.
  Fly Me to the Moon.
  How to Stop Smoking.
  Love Poem with Toast.
  On Not Writing a Love Poem.
  Something to Believe In.
  You Wouldn't Say They Didn't Get Along
    Exactly.
  Young Instructor Talks to Himself Winding Up
    the Semester, The.
Williams, T. Faint as Leaf Shadow.
  Lyric: "Can it be again."
Williams, W. Jungle, The.
  Queen-Anne's-Lace.
  Rewaking, The.
  St. Valentine.
Wright, J. Eleutheria.
  Gesture by a Lady with an Assumed Name, A.
  Lights in the Hallway, The.
  Love's Dozen.

Meeting Her in Chapultepec.
Rhythm, Charts and Changes.
Sappho.
So She Said.
Twenty-Two Tremblings of the Postulant.
Wyatt, S. Ah, my heart, ah, what aileth thee.
  His Reward.
  I have been a lover.
  Lover Showeth How He Is Forsaken of Such as
    He Sometime Enjoyed, The.
  My love is like unto th'eternal fire.
  Varium et Mutabile.
Yeats. Brown Penny.
  Father and Child.
  Last Confession, A.
  Lullaby: "Beloved, may your sleep be sound."
  Ragged Wood, The.
  Ribh in Ecstasy.
Zagajewski. For M.
Zaturenska. For the Seasons.
  Garden at Cliveden, The.
  Late Arrival.
  Places.
Zukofsky, L. Catullus viii.
  Drive, fast kisses.
See also **Sex**

Error
Amichai [*or* Amikhai]. Changes, Mistakes,
  Loves.
Beckett, S. De pied ferme.
Cowper, W. Four Ages, The.
  Progress of Error, The.
Creeley. Eye, The.
  Sight, A.
  Water.
Dugan, A. On a Hymn, Misprinted.
Herrick. Truth and Error.
Komunyakaa. Corrigenda.
  Please.
Ransom, J. Parting, without a Sequel.
Simic. Errata.

Escalators
Zagajewski. Escalator.

Escape
Ai. Kid, The.
Amichai [*or* Amikhai]. Great Calm: Questions
  and Answers.
Auden. Half Way.
Browning, R. Flight of the Duchess, The.
Bukowski. Hangover and Sick Leave.
Carver, R. Prize, The.
Cooper, J. All These Dreams.
Cummings, E. E. Notice the convulsed orange
  inch of moon.
  You are tired, / (I think).
Dickey, J. Attempted Departure.
Dickey, W. Rainbow Grocery, The.
Dickinson, E. Escape is such a thankful Word.
  I never hear the word "escape."
Dove, R. Pamela.
  Three Days of Forest, a River, Free.
Eberhart, R. Grave Piece.
Enzensberger, H. Security Considerations.
  Thoughts on the Run 1.
  Thoughts on the Run 2.
Frost, R. Escapist—Never.
  How Hard It Is to Keep from Being King When
    It's in You and in the Situation.
"H. D." Calliope.
Hardy, T. Wish for Unconsciousness, A.
Hayden, R. O Daedalus, Fly Away Home.
  Runagate Runagate.
Housman. Shot? so quick, so clean an ending?
Hughes, L. Freedom Seeker.
  West Texas.
Kinnell. Sow Piglet's Escapes, The.
Kipling, R. Ballad of Minepit Shaw, The.
  Wilful-Missing.
Koch, K. Brassiere Factory, The.
Kunitz, S. Route Six.
Laughlin, J. Escape, The.
Lawrence, D. H. Love as an Escape.
Levine, P. And the Trains Go On.
  Walk with Tom Jefferson, A.
MacNeice. Cradle Song: "Sleep, my darling,
  sleep."

Flight of the Heart.
Spring Sunshine.
Woods.
Mallarmé. Clown Chastised, The.
  Sea Breeze.
  Windows, The.
McGrath, T. Get Out of Town.
Milosz, C. Flight.
Olson, C. All Havens Astern.
Orr, G. Two Lines from the Brothers Grimm.
Pagis. Footprints.
  Instructions for Crossing the Border.
  Last Ones, The.
  Tidings.
Parker, D. Dark Girl's Rhyme, The.
Pessoa. Loophole.
Ransom, J. Morning.
Rich, A. Mother-Right.
  Prospect, The.
Riley, J. Runaway Boy, The.
  Sleep.
Rimbaud, A. Impossible, The.
Rukeyser, M. Target Practice.
Shelley, P. Fugitives, The.
Simic. Suitcase Strapped with a Rope, A.
Smith, S. Come On, Come Back.
  Fugitive's Ride, The.
  I Wish.
  Who Shot Eugenie?
Tate, A. Light.
Tate, J. Flight.
  Man with Wooden Leg Escape Prison.
  Rape in the Engineering Building.
Whitman, W. We Two, How Long We Were
  Fool'd.
Williams, C. K. History.
Williams, M. Deadsong for a Neighbor Child
  Who Ran Away to the Woods.
Wilner, E. Renegade.
Wright, J. In the Face of Hatred.
  Prayer to Escape from the Market Place, A.
  Small Blue Heron, The.
  Snowstorms in the Midwest.
  To a Fugitive.
Wyatt, S. Double, diverse, sullen, and strange.
  Farewell, the reign of cruelty!
  If I might have at mine own will.
  Liberty.
  Longer to muse.
  Now all of change.
  Now must I le[a]rn[e] to live [*or* lyve] at rest.
  Sith I myself displease thee.
  To make an end of all this strife.

Eschatology
See **End of the World**

Eskimos
Ai. Sweet, The.
Jacobsen, J. Food.
Koch, K. Geography.
Meredith, W. Kodiak Poem, A.
Oliver, M. Esquimos Have No Word for "War,"
  The.
Rexroth, K. Park in the Public's or in the
  Public, Parks.
Warren, R. Sila.

Essex, England
Davie, D. Essex.
  Thanks to Industrial Essex.
Levertov. Map of the Western Part of the
  County of Essex in England, A.

Esther, Book of (Bible)
Lindsay, N. Rhyme for All Zionists, A.

Estrangement
Atwood. I can't tell you my name.
Berryman. Her & It.
Bly, R. In Rainy September.
Browning, R. In a Year.
  Rephan.
  Worst of It, The.
Byron, G. Lines on Hearing That Lady Byron
  Was Ill.
  Remind Me Not, Remind Me Not.
  To George, Earl Delawarr.
  To Lesbia.
  To the Same.

Carver, R.   Balsa Wood.
  This Room.
Cooper, J.   Estrangement.
Crane, H.   Stark Major.
Creeley.   Place ("Thinking of you asleep on a").
Dickey, J.   Turning Away.
Dunbar, P.   Parted.
  Song, A: "Thou art the soul of a summer's day."
Eliot, T. S.   Love Song of J. Alfred Prufrock,
    Resumed, The.
  Love Song of J. Alfred Prufrock, The.
  Love Song of J. Alfred Prufrock, The (Prufrock
    among the Women).
  Prufrock's Pervigilium.
Faiz.   Bangla Desh: 3.
Gallagher, T.   Photograph of a Lighthouse
    Through Fog.
Graves, R.   Iago.
  Moon's Last Quarter, The.
  Semi-Detached.
  This Holy Month.
  Unposted Letter.
  Wall, The.
  Wand, The.
  Winged Heart, The.
  Woman Poet and Man Poet.
"H. D."   In the Rain.
Hardy, T.   Side by Side.
  What Did It mean?
Hopkins, G.   Beginning of the End, The.
  Lover's Stars, The.
  Voice from the World, A.
Hughes, L.   Lament for Dark Peoples.
Jeffers, R.   Birth-Dues.
Lowell, R.   Man And Wife.
  To Speak of Woe That Is in Marriage.
MacNeice.   Bluebells.
  Selva Oscura.
Merrill, J.   Renewal, A.
Merwin.   Psalm: Our Fathers.
Montale.   Two in Twilight.
Muldoon, P.   Vespers.
Olson, C.   Distances, The.
Plath.   Conversation among the Ruins.
Ransom, J.   Parting at Dawn.
  Two in August.
Rich, A.   After Dark.
  In the Evening.
  Like This Together.
  Mother-in-Law.
Sexton.   Love Letter Written in a Burning
    Building.
Smith, S.   Adelaide Abner.
  Broken Friendship, The.
  La Gretchen de Nos Jours (I).
  Rothebât.
  Sea-Widow, The.
Voznesensky [or Voznesenskii].   Arrow in the
    Wall, An.
Williams, C. K.   Crawl.
  Trash.
  Twice More.
Williams, W.   Postlude.
Wright, J.   Death of an Unfamiliar Sister, The.
Wyatt, S.   I must go walk the woods so wild.
Yeats.   Ephemera.
  Memory of Youth, A.
  O Do Not Love Too Long.

Eternity
Ammons.   Eternal City, The.
  Whose Timeless Reach.
Blake, W.   Each Man is in His Spectres power.
Bogan, L.   I Saw Eternity.
Borges.   Afternoon, The.
Brontë, E.   I'm happiest when most away.
  Lines: "I die; but when the grave shall press."
  No Coward Soul is Mine.
  Was it with the fields of green.
Browning, R.   Last Ride Together, The.
  Rephan.
Bukowski.   Our Curious Position.
Byron, G.   If That High World.
  When Coldness Wraps This Suffering Clay.
Cavafy.   Eternity.
Celan.   Tankards, The.
Ciardi, J.   Dialogue with Outer Space.

Cummings, E. E.   Connotation of infinity, A.
  I was considering how.
  If i believe / in death be sure.
  Noone and a star stand,am to am.
  One Fine Day.
  Out of the mountain of his soul comes.
  Stand with your lover on the ending earth.
  True lovers in each happening of their hearts.
De la Mare.   Moment, The.
  Snowing.
Dickinson, E.   Always begins.
  As if the Sea should part.
  Because I could not stop for Death.
  Blunder is an estimate, The.
  Eternity may imitate.
  How firm Eternity must look.
  I cannot tell how Eternity seems.
  Is it a joyous expanse of Year.
  It was a quiet way—.
  Only News I know, The.
  Our journey had advanced.
  Show me Eternity, and I will show you
    Memory.
  There is no first, or last, in Forever.
  Time feels so vast that were it not.
  Writing is brief and fleeting.
Donne.   Anniversary [or Anniversarie], The.
Dunbar, P.   Forever.
Eberhart, R.   Emily Dickinson.
  Illusion of Eternity, The.
  Once More, O Ye.
Emerson, R.   Days.
  Dear Ellen, many a golden year.
  Roomy Eternity / Casts her schemes rarely.
  Spiritual Laws.
Fayzi [or Faydi or Feisi or Feizi].   Eternal
    Watcher, who doth wake, The.
Ferlinghetti, L.   Cro-Magnons.
  River Still To Be Found, A.
Graves, R.   Always.
  Envoi: "There is no now for us but always."
  Fast Bound Together.
  For Ever.
  Half-Finished Letter, The.
  Hazel Grove, The.
  Impossible Day, The.
  New Eternity, The.
  Song: Yesterday Only.
  Tomorrow's Envy of Today.
Guyon.   Living Water.
  Simple Trust.
Hall, D.   Shudder [, The].
Herrick.   Eternity [or Eternitie].
  Love What It Is.
  No Time in Eternity.
  Penitence.
  Sabbaths.
  Sin and Strife.
  To His Honoured Kinsman, Sir Richard Stone.
  Wages.
  White Island.
Housman.   Bring, in this timeless grave to
    throw.
  If truth in hearts that perish.
  Immortal Part, The.
Hughes, T.   Pibroch.
Jarrell, R.   Venetian Blind, The.
Jeffers, R.   It flows out of mystery into mystery:
    there is no beginning—.
Keats.   Bright Star.
Kunitz, S.   Change.
Larkin, P.   Is It Now Or For Always.
Lawrence, D. H.   Fatality.
  Non-Existence.
  Sickness.
Lindsay, N.   In Memory of a Child.
MacLeish.   Eternity, An.
  Pole Star for This Year.
Mallarmé.   Windows, The.
Melville, H.   Montaigne and His Kitten.
Merwin.   Animula.
Milosz, C.   How It Should Be in Heaven.
Nemerov.   Somewhere.
Olson, C.   Day Song.
  Drum World, The.
  For My Friend.

Raine, K.   Banked winter cloud.
  Hyacinth, The.
  If you have ceased.
  Rock.
Rexroth, K.   Et pour Eux Seuls, les Paradis
    Chantent Encore.
Riley, J.   Eternity.
Ritsos.   Thanksgiving.
Robinson, E.   Sage, The.
Roethke.   I Knew A Woman.
Rossetti, C.   As the Doves to Their Windows.
  Bed of Forget-Me-Nots, A.
  Beloved, yield thy time to God, for He / Will
    make eternity thy recompense.
  Birchington Churchyard.
  Earth Shall Tremble at the Look of Him, The.
  End of Time, The.
  For Each.
  From the Antique.
  Goodbye in fear, goodbye in sorrow.
  Let Patience Have Her Perfect Work.
  Life's Parallels, A.
  New creatures; the Creator still the Same.
  Parting after parting, / Sore loss and gnawing
    pain.
  Patience of Hope.
  Rest.
  Short is time, and only time is bleak.
  There Remaineth Therefore a Rest to the People
    of God.
  Time lengthening, in the lengthening seemeth
    long.
  Time passeth away with its pleasure and pain.
  Time seems not short: / If so I call to mind.
  Trinity Sunday.
  Unforgotten.
Sandburg, C.   Sea-Wash.
Schuyler, J.   Daylight.
Smart, C.   Hail wonrous being who in power
    supreme.
  On the Eternity of the Supreme Being.
Smith, S.   Intimation of Immortality.
Szymborska, W.   Pi.
Thomas, D.   All All and All the Dry Worlds
    Lever.
Tomlinson, C.   Eight Observations on the Nature
    of Eternity.
Very.   Eternal Life.
  Forevermore.
Warren, R.   Small Eternity.
Wilde, O.   Athanasia.
Wordsworth, W.   Lines Written While Sailing in
    a Boat at Evening.
Wright, C.   Composition in Grey and Pink.
  Giorgio Morandi and the Talking Eternity Blues.
  To Giacomo Leopardi in the Sky.
Yeats.   Ephemera.
  Needle's Eye, A.
  Tom at Cruachan.
  Whence Had They Come?
See also **Immortality**

Ethiopia
Crashaw.   On the Baptized Ethiopian.
Dunbar, P.   Ode to Ethiopia.
Hughes, L.   Broadcast on Ethiopia.
  Call of Ethiopia.
  Emperor Haile Selassie.

Etiquette
Beckett, S.   À peine à bien mené.
Bishop, E.   Manners.
Browning, R.   Respectability.
Byron, G.   To Marion.
Chuang Tzu.   Apologies.
Creeley.   Way, The.
Herrick.   Good Manners at Meat.
  Panegyric to Sir Lewis Pemberton, A.
  To a Gentlewoman on Just Dealing.
  Upon Showbread [or Shewbread]: Epigram.
Ignatow, D.   Say Pardon.
Ramanujan.   Chess under Trees.
Sandburg, C.   We Must Be Polite.
Simic.   Gallows Etiquette.
Williams, M.   Truth and Truthfulness.
Williams, W.   Raper from Passenack, The.

Eton College
Gray, T.   Ode on a Distant Prospect of Eton

College.

Etruscan Civilization
Lawrence, D. H. Cypresses.
Tomlinson, C. Tarquinia.
Wilbur, R. To the Etruscan Poets.

Eucharist
Herbert, G. Agony [or Agonie], The.
Banquet, The.
H[oly] Communion, The.
Holy Communion, The.
Love (3).
Superliminare.
Herrick. Eucharist, The.
Hopkins, G. Bugler's First Communion, The.
Merton. Communion, The.
Holy Sacrament of the Altar, The.
Thomas, D. This Bread I Break.

See also **Last Supper**

Euclid
Cunningham, J. Cantor's Theorem: In an Infinite Class the Whole Is No Greater Than Some of Its Parts.
Millay, E. "Euclid Alone Has Looked on Beauty Bare."

Eulalia, Saint
García Lorca. Martyrdom of St. Eulalia.

Euripides
Wilde, O. Vision, A.

Europa
Walcott. Europa.

Europe
Apollinaire. Zone.
Blake, W. Europe; A Prophecy.
Blok. Scythians, The.
Browning, E. North and the South, The.
Clampitt. Imago.
Cummings, E. E. Hanged / if n / y in a real hot spell.
Davie, D. Bella & Rosa.
Cold Spring in Essex.
Tiger at the Movie-Show.
Dove, R. Eastern European Eclogues.
Eberhart, R. Yonder.
Emerson, R. At Sea, September 1833.
Ginsberg, A. Europe! Europe!
Hill, G. Of Commerce and Society: Variations on a Theme.
Ignatow, D. Europe and America.
Jeffers, R. Bowl of Blood, The.
Laughlin, J. Bit Different, A.
Logan, J. Traveling.
Lowell, R. Beyond the Alps.
MacLeish. Cinema of a Man
Memory Green.
Oil Painting of the Artist as the Artist.
Meredith, G. To Lord Palmerston.
Wassail for the New Year, A.
Meredith, W. Memoirs.
Merton. Night Train, The.
Milosz, C. Child of Europe.
Earth.
La Belle Époque.
Rivers ("'So lasting they are, the rivers!' Only think. Sources somewhere in the mountains").
Sarajevo.
Nash, O. My Trip Daorba.
Nemerov. Europe.
Returning to Europe.
Olson, C. To Gerhardt, There, among Europe's Things of Which He Has Written Us in His "Brief an Creely und Olson."
Plath. Stopped Dead.
Pope, A. Balance of Europe, The.
Rossetti, C. Massacre of Perugia, The.
Simic. East[ern] European Cooking.
Tomlinson, C. Mediterranean, The.
Whitman, W. Europe, the 72d and 73d Year of These States.
Wordsworth, W. Bruges ("Bruges I saw attired with golden light").
Incident at Bruges.
Memorials of a Tour of the Continent; 1820.
Zagajewski. Europe Goes to Sleep.
Europe in Winter.
Houston, 6 P.M.

Summer's Fullness.

Eurydice
Atwood. Eurydice.
Browning, R. Eurydice to Orpheus.
Graves, R. Eurydice.
"H. D." Eurydice.
Hill, G. Orpheus and Eurydice.
Jarrell, R. Che Farò Senza Euridice.
Maritain. Eurydice.
Orr, G. Entrance to the Underworld, The.
Far below, plowed fields vibrated.
His Dream: The Black Tree / Thirst.
If your gaze takes in.
In the cave mouth I stopped.
Snake no bigger, A.
Wedge, The.
When Eurydice saw him.
When I first saw her.
When I was alive—only glimpses.
When they said I must leave hell.
Ritsos. Descent.

Euthanasia
Dugan, A. For Euthanasia and Pain-Killing Drugs.
Jeffers, R. Hurt Hawks.
Tate, A. Euthanasia.
Williams, C. K. When.
Williams, M. Her, Though.

Evangelism and Evangelists
Cummings, E. E. Skinny voice / of the leatherfaced, The.
This evangelist / buttons with his big gollywog voice.
Davie, D. Evangelist, The.
Hayden, R. Witch Doctor.
Merwin. Saint of the Uplands, The.
Rich, A. Revivalist in Boston, A.
Robinson, E. Evangelist's Wife, An.
Rossetti, C. St. Bartholomew.
Vigil of St. Bartholomew.
Sandburg, C. To a Contemporary Bunkshooter.
Warren, R. Amazing Grace in the Back Country.

Eve
Berryman. Gislebertus' Eve.
Carruth, H. I Tell You For Several Years of My Madness I Heard the Voice of Lilith Singing in the Trees of Chicago.
Ciardi, J. Ten Years Ago when I Played at Being Brave.
Clifton, L. Eve Thinking.
Eve's version.
Cooper, J. Eve.
Eberhart, R. Throwing the Apple.
Frost, R. Never Again Would Birds' Song Be The Same.
Graves, R. History of the Fall.
Hughes, T. Theology.
Lawrence, D. H. Eve.
Pagis. Written in Pencil in the Sealed Railway-Car.
Rossetti, C. Afterthought, An.
Eve.
Smith, S. Dream of Comparison, A.
How Cruel Is the Story of Eve.
Wilbur, R. She.
Yeats. Adam's Curse.

Evening
Amichai [or Amikhai]. Beginning of Autumn in the Hills of Ephraim.
Auden. As I Walked Out One Evening.
Baudelaire. Evening Harmony.
Meditation.
Bishop, E. Going to the Bakery.
Blake, W. To the Evening Star.
Bly, R. Surprised by Evening.
Borges. Patio.
Tankas.
Bukowski. I Kneel.
Imbecile Night.
Burns, R. Lea-Rig, The.
Carruth, H. Tabula Rasa.
Carver, R. Evening.
Ciardi, J. Evensong.
Clare, J. Evening.

Winter Evening.
Creeley. Buffalo Evening.
Cummings, E. E. At the ferocious phenomenon of 5 o'clock i find myself gently decompos.
Fragrant sag of fruit distinctly grouped, A.
Sometime,perhaps in Paris we will.
Windows go orange in the slowly.
Davie, D. Evening on the Boyne.
De la Mare. Evening.
Myself.
Spark, The.
Tailor, The.
Thomas Hardy.
Dickinson, E. As willing lid o'er weary eye.
Crickets sang, The.
It's evening and the orchestra of winds.
Lightly stepped a yellow star.
Dove, R. Reading Hölderlin on the Patio with the Aid of a Dictionary.
Eberhart, R. Evening Bird Song.
Memory.
Frost, R. Stopping by Woods on a Snowy Evening.
García Lorca. Evening ("Rainy evening in exhausted gray").
Gray, T. Elegy Written in a Country Churchyard.
Gurney, I. Quiet Fireshine.
"H. D." Evening.
Heaney, S. Good-night.
Herrick. Evensong.
Hughes, L. Wonder.
Hughes, T. Full Moon and Little Frieda.
Jarrell, R. Evening.
Jeffers, R. Autumn Evening.
Johnson, S. Evening Ode, An.
Kinsella, T. Before Sleep.
Larkin, P. Coming.
Going.
Longfellow, H. Fire of Drift-Wood, The.
Meng Hao Jan. Steering my little boat towards a misty islet.
Merton. Evening.
Song, A: "When it was day, we heard the panes of windows."
Merwin. Autumn Evening.
Evening.
Middle of the Summer, The.
Witnesses.
Montale. Low Tide.
Petrarch. Long for the evening, loathe the coming dawn.
Rexroth, K. Silver Swan, The.
Star and Crescent.
Riley, J. When Evening Shadows Fall.
Ritsos. Inevitables.
Roethke. In Evening Air.
Sandburg, C. Evening Questions.
Evening Sea Wind.
Evening Waterfall.
How Yesterday Looked.
Moon Path.
Sarton, M. Evening Music.
Light Left On, A.
Schuyler, J. Poem: "How about an oak leaf."
Shelley, P. Evening: Ponte al Mare, Pisa.
Evening: To Harriet.
Simic. Evening.
Smart, C. Sweets of Evening, The.
Snyder, G. Work to Do Toward Town.
Tate, J. Glassy Harbor, The.
Trakl. De Profundis.
Very. Evening Walk, An.
Warren, R. Evening Hawk.
Wheatley, P. Hymn to the Evening, An.
Williams, T. Evening.
Towns Become Jewels.
Wordsworth, W. Composed upon an Evening of Extraordinary Splendour and Beauty.
Crescent-Moon, the Star of Love, The.
It is a beauteous evening, calm and free.
Wright, J. Brush Fire.
Zagajewski. Late Feast.
Moses.

See also **Twilight**

Evening Star
Blake, W. To the Evening Star.
Bogan, L. Evening-Star.
Carruth, H. Anima.
  Tabula Rasa.
Coleridge, S. To the Evening Star.
Cummings, E. E. Thou / firsting a hugeness of
  twi / -light.
Ivanov, G. That pointless happiness, was it
  worth it?
Jeffers, R. Evening Ebb.
Millay, E. Now that the west is washed of
  clouds and clear.
Stevens, W. Homunculus et La Belle Etoile.
  Martial Cadenza.
Very. Jupiter as the Evening Star.
See also **Venus (planet)**

Evers, Medgar
Ignatow, D. For Medgar Evers.

Evictions
Davie, D. Sunday Morning.
Wordsworth, W. Composed When a Probability
  Existed of Our Being Obliged to Quit Rydal
  Mount as a Residence.

Evil
Auden. Danse Macabre.
Berryman. Amos.
  Opus Dei.
Blake, W. Marriage of Heaven and Hell, The.
Bogan, L. At a Party.
Bukowski. In a Neighborhood of Murder.
Byron, G. Sketch from Private Life, A.
  Thoughts for a Speech of Lucifer, in the
  Tragedy of "Cain."
  To Dives (William Beckford). A Fragment.
Coleridge, S. Christabel.
Cowper, W. Cock-Fighters Garland.
Davie, D. Eight Years After.
  Ironist, The.
Dugan, A. Takeoff on Armageddon —For
  Ronald Reagan.
Duncan, R. Albigenses, The.
Eberhart, R. Evil.
  Fantasy of a Small Idea.
  Formative Mastership.
  Ineffable, The.
  Laocoön.
  Meditation Two.
Emerson, R. I will not live out of me.
  O Boston city lecture-hearing.
  There is no evil but can speak.
Frost, R. Bearer of Evil Tidings, The.
  Design.
  Quandary.
Graves, R. Man of Evil.
  Succubus, The.
  True Evil.
Gray, T. Tophet.
Hayden, R. As My Blood Was Drawn.
  Theory of Evil.
Herrick. Another.
  Evill.
  His Confession.
  Neutrality Loathsome.
  Spell, The.
Housman. Delight it is in youth and May.
  Epitaph, An: "Stay, if you list, O passer by the
  way."
Jarrell, R. Blind Sheep, The.
Jeffers, R. Orca.
Kunitz, S. Between the Acts.
Lawrence, D. H. Dark Satanic Mills.
  Departure.
  Doors.
  Evil Is Homeless.
  Evil World-Soul, The.
  First Song of Huitzilopochtli.
  Immorality.
  Men Are Not Bad.
  Murder.
  Murderous Weapons.
  Our Moral Age.
  Root of Our Evil, The.
  Second Song of Huitzilopochtli.
  Snake.
  Song of the Grey Dog, The.

Strife.
  Third Song of Huitzilopochtli.
  What Then Is Evil?
Lindsay, N. Above the Battle's Front.
MacLeish. Black Humor.
Mahon. No Rest for the Wicked.
McGrath, T. Death for the Dark Stranger.
Meredith, G. Black Richard.
  We see the farther in the far.
Milosz, C. One More Day.
  Theodicy.
  Unde Malum.
Montale. Often I've encountered evil.
Nemerov. August, 1945.
Olson, C. Evil.
Patchen. Where Every Prospect.
Pinkerton, H. Romantic Eros, The.
Plath. Lesson in Vengeance, A.
Poe. Sonnet—Silence.
Riley, J. Rough Sketch, A.
Rossetti, C. True Story, A.
  Who shall my wandering thoughts steady & fix.
Sarton, M. Intruder, An.
Sexton. After Auschwitz.
  Dead Heart, The.
  Evil Eye, The.
  Evil Seekers, The.
  Is It True?
Smith, S. Angel Boley.
  Lord Barrenstock.
  To the Tune of The Coventry Carol.
Thoreau. Man Man is the Devil.
Walcott. God Rest Ye Merry, Gentlemen.
Whitman, W. I Sit and Look Out.
  Roaming in Thought.
Williams, C. K. Bishop Tutu's Visit to the
  White House: 1984.
  How Humble We Were before This.
Williams, M. Why God Permits Evil: For
  Answers to This Question of Interest to Many
  Write Bible Answers, Dept. E-7.
Williams, W. Mirrors, The.
Wyatt, S. Nature that gave the bee so feat a
  grace.

Evolution
Auden. Progress?
Ciardi, J. Possibilities.
Cullen, C. For an Evolutionist and His
  Opponent.
Dugan, A. Criticism of Bergson and Darwin.
  On Flowers. On Negative Evolution.
Emerson, R. Nature [1836].
  Three Dimensions, The.
Frost, R. Accidentally on Purpose.
Ginsberg, A. Falling Asleep in America.
Graves, R. Hearth, The.
Lawrence, D. H. Self-Protection.
Merwin. Water of the Suns, The.
Milosz, C. Either-Or.
Nemerov. Tale.
Orr, G. Visit to the Island of Lost Souls.
Pagis. Readiness, The.
Sandburg, C. Man the Moon Shooter.
  Wilderness.
Smith, S. Religious Man, A.
Swenson, M. Evolution.
Szymborska, W. Note, A.
  Speech at the Lost and Found, A.
  Thomas Mann.
Updike. Naked Ape, The.
Very. Evolution.
  Man has forgot his Origin; in vain.
  Not suffering for their sins in former state.
  Origin of Man, The.
Wilbur, R. Lamarck Elaborated.
Zagajewski. Apes.
See also **Darwin, Charles; Extinction; Genetics
and Geneticists**

Ex-lovers
Ai. Momento Mori.
Amichai [*or* Amikhai]. Again, a Love Is
  Finished.
  Ballad in the Streets of Buenos Aires.
  Dog After Love, A.
  Farewell: "Fare thee well, it was your face, and
  now the face of memory."

Hamadiya, Memory of Bliss.
  "History's Wings Beating," They Used to Say.
  I Will Have to Begin.
  In the Morning It Was Still Night.
  In this valley, where many waters.
  Open Closets Are Sad.
  Release Her.
  "Rustle of History's Wings," as They Used to
  Say Then, The.
  Same Embroidery, the Same Pattern, The.
  You Carry the Weight of Heavy Buttocks.
Baudelaire. Perfume-flask, The.
Blok. Chivalry.
Broumas, O. Bitterness.
  Blues / for J.C.
  Landscape with Driver.
  Mosaic.
Carver, R. Interview.
  Jean's TV.
  Phone Booth, The.
  Reading Something in the Restaurant.
  Where They'd Lived.
  Windows of the Summer Vacation Houses, The.
Cavafy. Before Time Could Change Them.
  Desperation.
  Flowers White and Beautiful, as Were Most
  Becoming.
  Following the Formulas of Ancient Greco-
  Syrian Magicians.
  From the Drawer.
  Gray.
  In the Wineshops.
  Kimon, Son of Learchos, Age 22, Student of
  Greek Literature (in Kyrini).
  Love, A.
Cooper, J. Long View from the Suburbs.
Crane, S. And yet I have seen thee happy with
  me.
  I have seen thy face aflame.
  I wonder if sometimes in the dusk.
Creeley. Breaking Up Is Hard to Do.
Cunningham, J. I write only to say this.
  Love's Progress.
  Original Sin.
Davie, D. Lost Bride, The.
  Revenge for Love.
Dugan, A. Apollo.
  To an Ex-Student.
García Lorca. Fable of Three Friends to Be
  Sung in Rounds.
Ginsberg, A. Rain-Wet Asphalt Heat, Garbage
  Curbed Cans Overflowing.
Hughes, L. Cora.
  Madam and Her Might-Have-Been.
  No Regrets.
Ignatow, D. Each Day.
Jackson, L. Druida.
  To a Loveless Lover.
Kizer, C. Halation.
  Month in Summer, A.
  Winter Song.
Komunyakaa. Strands.
  Translating Footsteps.
Kunitz, S. After the Last Dynasty.
  Dark and the Fair, The.
Laughlin, J. Apotropaic Decision, An.
  Crystal Palace Market.
  Eros as Archaeologist.
  In the Salzkammergut.
  It's Indelicate.
  Mysterious Disappearance, The.
  Sinking Stone, The.
  Snow in May.
Medici. Beside a running brook my lady stands.
Mistral, G. To See Him Again.
Parker, D. Absence.
  Accursed, The.
  Ballade of a Great Weariness.
  Burned Child, The.
  Convalescent.
  Dramatists, The.
  Fable: "Oh, there once was a lady, and so I've
  been told."
  False Friends, The.
  Fantasy.
  Finis.

Godspeed.
Healed.
I Know I Have Been Happiest.
I Shall Come Back.
Light of Love.
Lyric.
Memories.
Monody.
Mortal Enemy.
Nocturne: "Always I knew that it could not last."
Plea.
Rosemary ("Ah, no, I dare not lose myself in dreams").
Second Love.
Song of a Hopeful Heart.
Sonnet for the End of a Sequence.
Surprise.
There Was One.
They Part.
Threnody: "Lilacs blossom just as sweet."
Very Short Song, A
Well-Worn Story, A.
Pasternak, B.   Breakup, The.
Rexroth, K.   Gambling.
Northampton, 1922–San Francisco, 1939.
Schatten Küsse, Schatten Liebe.
Sharp in My Heart.
Survival of the Fittest.
Yugao.
Riley, J.   End, An.
Her Beautiful Hands.
In State.
Leave-Taking, A.
Leonainie.
Let Us Forget.
Mad Lover, The.
My Mary.
Passing of a Heart, The.
Rival, The.
Same Old Story, The.
That Night.
Tinkle of Bells, A.
What They Said.
You May Not Remember.
Ritsos.   Moonlight Sonata.
Rossetti, D.   Even So.
Seifert.   Grave of Signor Casanova, The.
Stock, R.   Synapse, The.
Sze.   Miracles.
Tate, J.   Why I Will Not Get Out of Bed.
Warren, R.   Goodbye.
Old Love.
Snowfall.
You Sort Old Letters.
Wilde, O.   My Voice.
Williams, M.   E-mail.
Williams, T.   Blond Mediterraneans, The.
Lady, Anemone.
October Song.
Rented Room, The.
Song: "Girls that have loved me."
Wright, J.   Idiotic and Politic.
Wu of Han [or Wu Ti or Ou-ty or Liu Ch'e or Liu Ch'u].   Skein, The.
Zaturenska.   Theme from Louise Labé, A.

Examinations
Han-shan.   My writing and judgment aren't that bad.
Who is this poor dreamer.
Laughlin, J.   Cardiac Autoscope, The.
Riley, J.   Test, A.
Szymborska, W.   Brueghel's Two Monkeys.

Excavations
Brecht, B.   Legend of the Dead Soldier, The.
Cavafy.   Mimiambi of Herodas, The.
Gurney, I.   Coin, The.
Hill, G.   Solomon's Mines.
MacNeice.   Dowser, The.
Tomlinson, C.   Near Corinium.

Excrement
Ciardi, J.   Suburban.
Creeley.   Echo ("Faint, persistent").
Kumin, M.   Excrement Poem, The.
Logue, C.   Loyal to the King.
McHugh, H.   Unspeakable.

Niedecker.   Energy glows at the lips.
Rumi.   Muhammad and the Huge Eater.
Sheridan, T.   Tale of the T——d, The.
Updike.   Beautiful Bowel Movement, The.

Executions and Executioners
Ai.   Hangman.
Atwood.   Newsreel: Man and Firing Squad.
Borges.   Morning of 1649, A.
Browning, R.   Martin Relph.
Muckle-Mouth Meg.
Bukowski.   Big Bastard with a Sword.
Burns, R.   Hughie Graham.
Cullen, C.   Not Sacco and Vanzetti.
Cunningham, J.   Friend, on This Scaffold Thomas More Lies Dead.
Dickinson, E.   Upon the gallows hung a wretch.
Gunn, T.   No Speech from the Scaffold.
Hall, D.   Sums.
Han-shan.   Here's a poem for you young lords.
Superior man's mind is terribly sharp, The.
Hardy, T.   Stranger's Song, The.
Heaney, S.   Strange Fruit.
Housman.   Carpenter's Son, The.
Eight O'Clock.
On moonlit heath and lonesome bank.
Hughes, L.   August 19th.
Hughes, T.   Executioner, The.
Kipling, R.   Ballad of the King's Mercy, The.
Danny Deever.
Komunyakaa.   Feet Nailed to the Floor.
Ogoni.
Logan, J.   Pathological Case in Pliny, A.
Logue, C.   Lullaby.
Lowell, R.   Death of Anne Boleyn.
Saint-Just 1767–93.
Sir Thomas More.
Lux.   Man Takes His Daughter, Age Five, To a Public Execution by Guillotine, Paris, 1857, A.
MacLeish.   Galán.
Meredith, G.   Josepha.
Milton.   Philosopher on His Way to His Death, A.
Pagis.   Opening to Satan, An.
Patchen.   Executions in Moscow, The.
Joe Hill Listens to the Praying.
Ralegh, S.   Sir Walter Ra[u]le[i]gh to His Son[ne].
Ritsos.   Under Oblivion.
Sandburg, C.   Hangman at Home, The.
Simic.   Toy Factory.
Smith, S.   Death Sentence, The.
Humane Materialist at the Burning of a Heretic, A.
One of Many.
Stock, R.   Miracle of the Roses, The.
Swift, J.   Clever Tom Clinch Going to Be Hanged.
Sze.   Execution of Maximilian, The.
Szymborska, W.   Beheading.
Pietà.
Villon.   Epitaph in Form of a Ballad, The.
Warren, R.   Auto-da-fé.
Wilde, O.   Ballad of Reading Gaol, The.
Wilner, E.   Up against It.
Wyatt, S.   In mourning wise since daily I increase.

See also **Capital Punishment; Hanging**

Exercise
Broumas, O.   Away from Water.
Gunn, T.   Exercise, The.
Hardy, T.   Pedestrian, The.
Kumin, M.   Body and Soul: A Meditation.
Meredith, G.   Beetle soars, the beetle spins, The.
Walker, A.   Every Morning.

Exhilaration
Browning, R.   Now.
Prologue: "O the old wall here! How I could pass."
Dickinson, E.   Exhiliration is the Breeze.
Exhiliration—is within.
How small the furniture of bliss!
Impossibility, like Wine.
No Rose, yet felt myself a'bloom.
'Tis Anguish grander than Delight.
Transport's mighty price is.
Why the full heart is speechless.

Withdrawal of the Fuel of Rapture, The.
Eberhart, R.   Hardening into Print.
Ichetucknee.
Levertov.   City Psalm.
Letter to William Kinter of Muhlenberg, A.
Sparks.
Lorde.   NOW.
Nash, O.   No Doctors Today, Thank You.
Nemerov.   First Point of Aries, The.
Frozen City, The.
Rich, A.   Night in the Kitchen.
Shelley, P.   O that a chariot of cloud were mine!
Stock, R.   Just Another Apotheosis.

Exile
Amichai [or Amikhai].   Half the People of the World.
Jews in the Land of Israel.
Auden.   Exiles, The.
Bly, R.   Dream of Retarded Children, A.
Borges.   Exile (1977), The.
Brodsky, J.   Classical ballet, let's say, is beauty's keep, The.
In the Lake District.
Infinitive.
Letters to a Roman Friend.
Lullaby of Cape Cod.
May 24, 1980.
Brontë, E.   Lines by Claudia.
Loud without the wind was roaring.
Visionary, The.
Browning, E.   Exile's Return, The.
Burns, R.   Birth-Day Ode. December 31st 1787, A.
Frae the friends and Land I love.
Highland Harry Back Again.
My Heart's in the Highlands.
Byron, G.   Prophecy of Dante, The.
Campion, T.   As by the stream[e]s of Babylon [or Babilon].
Cardenal.   Dog barks far out, A.
Every evening the L & N.
I do not know who is out in the snow.
I turned out the light to see the snow.
Like Empty Beer Cans.
Like the flights of ducks.
Long freight train / Wakes me in my cell, The.
Sound of passing cars, (if a car comes), The.
Spring has come with its smell of Nicaragua.
That auto horn sounds familiar.
When the first signs go on.
Zinc roofs in the moonlight, The.
Carruth, H.   Ovid, Old Buddy, I Would Discourse with You a While.
Cavafy.   Byzantine Gentleman, in Exile, Composing Verses, A.
Epitaph: "Stranger, beside the Ganges I lie, a man."
Exiles.
Cavalcanti.   Ballata: In Exile at Sarzana.
Celan.   Cologne, at the Station.
In One.
Mute autumn smells. The.
Clampitt.   Black Buttercups.
Codrescu.   Demands of Exile.
Crane, H.   Purgatorio.
Dante Alighieri.   Sonnet: Written in Exile.
De la Mare.   Exile.
Exile, The.
Emerson, R.   I am an exile from my home; heavily.
Gunn, T.   First Meeting with a Possible Mother-in-Law.
Right Possessor, The.
Guyon.   Soul That Loves God Finds Him Every Where, The.
Hacker, M.   Exiles.
Hall, D.   Exile.
Herbert, G.   see also To the Lady Elizabeth Queen of Bohemia.
Hughes, L.   Black Seed.
Hughes, T.   Descent.
Khvaju of Kerman.   Exile, The.
Kipling, R.   Broken Men, The.
St. Helena Lullaby, A.
Kizer, C.   Ingathering.
Silent Man, The.

Laughlin, J.   La Tristesse.
MacNeice.   Eclogue from Iceland.
Mahon.   Banished Gods, The.
  Ovid in Tomis.
Maritain.   Pillars.
Maunick.   Seven Sides and Seven Syllables.
Meredith, G.   Song: "Forever."
Merwin.   Banishment in Winter.
  Western Country.
Michelangelo Buonarroti.   Your beauty an
  angel's, Lady, you were meant.
Millay, E.   Exiled.
Milosz, C.   In a City.
  My Faithful Mother Tongue.
Montale.   Dora Markus.
Nemerov.   Presidential Address to a Party of
  Exiles.
  To the Babylonians.
Pagis.   Instructions for Crossing the Border.
Petrarch.   Merely to look upon your sacred City.
Pinsky.   Exile.
Plath.   Doom of Exiles.
Pope, A.   Epitaph on Dr. Francis Atterbury,
  Bishop of Rochester.
Ralegh, S.   Farewell to the Court.
Rich, A.   Book, The.
  By No Means Native.
Riley, J.   Hoosier in Exile, The.
Robinson, E.   Aaron Stark.
  Island, An.
Rukeyser, M.   Another Day. Paul in the
  Mountains of Fantasy.
  Fourth Elegy. The Refugees.
  Judith.
  Mediterranean.
  Song: "World is full of loss; bring, wind, my
  love, The."
Shapiro, K.   Synagogue, The.
  Travelogue for Exiles.
Spender, S.   Exiles, The.
Stafford, W.   1932.
Tomlinson, C.   Of Lady Grange.
Tu Fu.   For the Prince in Exile.
Walcott.   Banyan Tree, Old Year's Night, The.
  Exile.
  Hotel Normandie Pool, The.
  North and South.
  Preparing for Exile.
  Return to D'Ennery; Rain.
Walker, A.   Be Nobody's Darling.
Whittier.   Exile's Departure, The.
Wilde, O.   At Verona.
Wilner, E.   Poem of Exile, A.
Wyatt, S.   I must go walk the woods so wild.
Zagajewski.   Refugees.
Zaturenska.   Castaways, The.

Existentialism and Existentialists
Beckett, S.   Flux cause.
Crane, S.   Man said to the universe, A.
Davie, D.   Samuel Beckett's Dublin.
Dickey, W.   Therefore.
Ignatow, D.   Diner, The.
Roethke.   Duet.
Rossetti, C.   Ah welladay and wherefore am I
  here?
Sandburg, C.   Cumulatives.
Spender, S.   Solipsist.
Tomlinson, C.   Juliet's Garden.
Williams, C. K.   Gas Station, The.
Wright, J.   As I Step over a Puddle at the End of
  Winter, I Think of an Ancient Chinese
  Governor.

Exodus
Dugan, A.   Against Veils on Exodus 33:23 and
  34:33.
Dunbar, P.   Ante-Bellum Sermon, An.
Kizer, C.   Exodus.
Nemerov.   Moses.
Oppen.   Exodus.
Tomlinson, C.   Flight, The.

Experience
Amichai [or Amikhai].   Like the Inner Wall of a
  House.
Angelou.   Wonder.
Apollinaire.   Pretty Redhead, The.
Ashbery, J.   As You Came from the Holy Land.

Atwood.   Yes at first you / go down smooth as.
Berrigan, T.   Ann Arbor Song.
  Around the Fire.
  Last Poem.
  Wrong Train.
Borges.   My Whole Life.
Brontë, E.   Old Stoic, The.
  Why do I hate that lone green dell?
Browning, E.   Fourfold Aspect, The.
  Perplexed Music.
Bukowski.   Friendly Advice to a Lot of Young
  Men.
Coleridge, S.   Christabel.
Cowper, W.   Upon a Venerable Rival.
Crane, S.   Little birds of the night.
Creeley.   Lover, The.
  That day / in an oak tree—.
  Wisdom.
Cummings, E. E.   All ignorance toboggans into
  know.
  But if a living dance upon dead minds.
  Conceive a man,should he have anything.
  Here's to opening and upward,to leaf and to sap.
  If everything happens that can't be done.
  May my heart always be open to little.
  Of Ever-Ever Land i speak.
  One's not half two. It's two are halves of one..
  Since feeling is first.
  Sonnet entitled how to run the world).
  This mind made war.
  Voices to voices, lip to lip.
  What a proud dreamhorse
  pulling(smoothloomingly)through.
Cunningham, J.   On a Line from Bodenham's
  "Belvedere."
Dickinson, E.   Experience is the Angled Road.
  Far from Love the Heavenly Father.
  I stepped from Plank to Plank.
Eberhart, R.   Experience Evoked.
  Rumination.
Emerson, R.   Experience.
Ferlinghetti, L.   Autobiography.
Ginsberg, A.   Howl.
Graves, R.   Those Who Came Short.
Hacker, M.   Hang-Glider's Daughter, The.
Han-shan.   Child who doesn't have a teacher, A.
Hardy, T.   Two Houses, The.
Heaney, S.   Wanderer, The.
Hill, G.   God's Little Mountain.
Hughes, L.   Aesthete [or Esthete] in Harlem.
  Disillusion.
  Old Age.
Jeffers, R.   To a Young Artist.
Kipling, R.   Bonfires, The.
  Craftsman, The.
  Men That Fought at Minden, The.
  Sestina of the Tramp-Royal.
  Tomlinson.
  When 'Omer Smote 'Is Bloomin' Lyre.
Lawrence, D. H.   Courage.
  Wealth.
  When the Ripe Fruit Falls.
Levertov.   In Mind.
Levine, P.   28.
  One for the Rose.
  Salts and Oils.
MacLeish.   L'An Trentiesme de Mon Eage.
Merton.   All the Way Down.
  Marks and numbers / Cut in skin.
Milosz, C.   For Jan Lebenstein.
Nash, O.   Experience to Let.
Nemerov.   Of Experience.
Neruda.   Bell-Ringer, The.
Owen, W.   All Sounds Have Been As Music.
  Sonnet Autumnal.
Parker, D.   Summary.
Pasolini.   Tears of the Excavator, The.
Piercy.   Married Walk in a Hot Place, A.
  Perpetual Migration, The.
"Ping Hsin."   Old Man and the Child, The.
Pope, A.   Epistle I, to Sir Richard Temple, Lord
  Cobham.
Raine, K.   High Summer.
  I breathe the air you have breathed.
Ransom, J.   Blue Girls.
Rich, A.   Diving into the Wreck.

Rimbaud, A.   Departure.
  O seasons, o châteaux.
Robinson, E.   Isaac and Archibald.
  Twilight Song.
Rossetti, C.   Experience bows a sweet contented
  face.
  If the moon came from heaven, / Talking all the
  way.
Sandburg, C.   Almanac.
  Anywhere and Everywhere People.
  Explanations of Love.
  Localities.
  Love Is a Deep and a Dark and a Lonely.
  Methusaleh Saw Many Repeaters.
  Sketch of a Poet.
  We Have Gone Through Great Rooms Together.
  Worms and the Wind.
Seifert.   If you call poetry a song.
Szymborska, W.   View with a Grain of Sand.
Thoreau.   Manhood.
Van Duyn.   Insight.
  Moose in the Morning, Northern Maine.
  New Land.
  Paratrooper.
  To My Godson, on His Christening.
Weiss, T.   Trip through Yucatán, A.
Whitman, W.   Beautiful Women.
  Myself and Mine.
  Song of Joys, A.
  Stronger Lessons.
  When I Heard the Learn'd Astronomer.
Williams, C. K.   This is what, / at last, it is.
  Undead, The.
Williams, M.   Before.
  In Nashville, Standing in the Wooden Circle
  Sawed Out from the Old Ryman Stage.
  Ruby Tells All.
Wordsworth, W.   World is too much with us;
  late and soon, The.
Wright, C.   Mid-winter Snowfall in the Piazza
  Dante.
Zaturenska.   Narrow Hemisphere, The.

Exploring and Explorers
Atwood.   Explorers, The.
  Further Arrivals.
  Reincarnation of Captain Cook, The.
Berry, W.   July, 1773.
Blue Cloud.   Expedition.
Borges.   Gunnar Thorgilsson (1816-1879).
  Mythical Founding of Buenos Aires, The.
Brodsky, J.   Polar Explorer, A.
Bukowski.   Best Way to Get Famous Is to Run
  Away, The.
Cardenal.   Drake in the Southern Sea.
Carver, R.   News Carried to Macedonia, The.
Clampitt.   Brought from Beyond.
  Quarry, The.
Clough.   As one who shoots an arrow overhead.
  How in all wonder Columbus got over.
Davie, D.   Bougainville.
  Christian Hero, A.
  Homage to John L. Stephens.
  Killala.
  Lasalle.
Donne.   Cales and Guiana.
  Calm[e], The.
  Storm[e], The.
  To Mr R. W ("If, as mine is, thy life a slumber
  be").
Eberhart, R.   Cage, The.
Frost, R.   America Is Hard to See.
Hardy, T.   Rover Come Home, The.
Jacobsen, J.   Explorer.
Kipling, R.   Explorer, The.
  Lost Legion, The.
  Merchantmen, The.
  Song of Travel, A.
  Voortrekker, The.
  With Drake in the Tropics.
Levertov.   Into the Interior.
Levine, P.   7 Years from Somewhere.
  New Day, A.
Lux.   Ultima Thule.
MacLeish.   Voyage West.
Mallarmé.   For the sake of voyaging—
  heedlessly.

Marvell. Bermudas.
McGrath, T. Poem—Unfinished Poem.
Merton. Christopher Columbus.
Merwin. Gardens of Zuñi, The.
Milosz, C. Caesarea.
Nash, O. Look What You Did, Christopher!
Oliver, M. Magellan.
Orr, G. Chateaubriand on the Niagara Frontier, 1791.
Pessoa. Message.
Pinsky. Spelunker.
Rich, A. Explorers, The.
Unsounded.
Riley, J. Great Explorer, The.
Sandburg, C. Lief the Lucky.
Shapiro, K. Waitress.
Simic. Explorers.
Walcott. Liberator, The.
Warren, R. Empire.
History.
Speleology.
Whitman, W. Of That Blithe Throat of Thine.
Passage to India.
Thought of Columbus, A.
Whittier. Seeking of the Waterfall, The.

Explosions
Amichai [or Amikhai]. What is it? An airplane at dawn. No.
Emerson, R. Put in, drive home the sightless wedges.
Komunyakaa. Fragging.
Larkin, P. Explosion, The.
Milosz, C. Artificer.
Stafford, W. Big Bang.
Wyatt, S. Furious gun in his raging ire, The.

Exposure
Hughes, L. Strange Hurt.

Exterminating and Exterminators
Browning, R. Pied Piper of Hamelin, The.
Bukowski. Terminology.
Carver, R. Nearly.
Dubie. Revelations.
Jacobsen, J. Blue-Eyed Exterminator, The.
Lorde. Vietnam Addenda.
Tate, J. Eagle Exterminating Company, The.
Wilner, E. Killing the Grubs.

Extinction
Amichai [or Amikhai]. Of a Vanished Kingdom.
Carver, R. Extirpation.
Cavafy. Things Run Out.
Clifton, L. Here Yet Be Dragons.
Dickey, J. For the Last Wolverine.
Dugan, A. Untitled Poem: "One used to be able to say."
Enzensberger, H. End of Owls, The.
Vanished Work.
Jeffers, R. Extinct Vertebrate, An.
Passenger Pigeons.
Komunyakaa. Dream Animal.
Levertov. Vron Woods (North Wales), The.
Meredith, W. At the Natural History Museum.
Merwin. End in Spring, An.
For a Coming Extinction.
In Autumn.
Last People.
Plumbing, The.
Port, The.
Shoe Repairs.
Nash, O. Caution to Everybody, A.
Next!
Niedecker. Could You Be Right.
Oliver, M. Ghosts.
Piercy. Homesick.
Sandburg, C. Buffalo Dusk.
Stafford, W. Roll Call.
Updike. Popular Revivals 1956.
Wilbur, R. Walgh-Vogel, The.
Williams, M. Folding His *USA Today* He Makes His Point in the Blue Star Café.
Last Person to Speak His Language is Dying, The.

Extrasensory Perception
Dubie. Open Happens in the Midst of Beings, The.

Graves, R. Foreboding, The.
Wilbur, R. Mind-Reader, The.

Extraterrestrial Intelligence
Stafford, W. Message from Space, A.

Extreme Unction
Wilbur, R. Rule, The.

Eyeglasses
Dugan, A. On Wearing Glasses.
Herrick. Upon Center a Spectacle-Maker with a Flat Nose.
Nash, O. And How Keen Was the Vision of Sir Launfal?
Parker, D. News Item.
Rexroth, K. Revolt.
Riley, J. My First Spectacles.
Ritsos. His Glasses.
Myopic Child, A.
Updike. Glasses.
Typical Optical.
Williams, W. Eyeglasses, The.

Eyes
Amichai [or Amikhai]. I Sat in the Happiness.
Atwood. You Fit into Me.
Baudelaire. Berthe's Eyes.
Uncertain Skies.
Bishop, E. Britannia Rules the Waves.
Three Sonnets for the Eyes.
Bogan, L. Medusa.
Brontë, E. God of Visions.
Burns, R. Blue-Eyed Lassie, The.
Song: "O this is no my ain lassie."
Byron, G. On the Eyes of Miss A——— H———.
Cavafy. Blue Eyes.
Far Off.
Cavalcanti. Sonnet: Of the Eyes of a certain Mandetta, of Thoulouse.
Ciardi, J. Evil Eye, The.
Cooper, J. Blind Girl.
Crashaw. Weeper, The.
Creeley. Alice.
As real as thinking.
Disappointment, The.
Eye, The.
Eyes.
For Leslie.
Friend, The.
Hello.
Some Echoes.
Cuadra, P. Eye Is a Dog Howling in the Distance, The.
Cummings, E. E. Life hurl my.
Open green those / (dear).
So isn't small one littlest why.
The(oo)is / lOOk / (aliv / e)e / yes.
De la Mare. Clear Eyes.
Euphrasy.
Eyes.
Happy Encounter, The.
Treachery.
Twilight.
Vain Finding.
Window, The.
Dickey, J. Daughter.
Dickinson, E. I like a look of Agony.
Like Eyes that looked on Wastes.
Donne. Message, The.
Witchcraft by a Picture.
Eberhart, R. Mystical Beast in the Shadows, The.
Eliot, T. S. Eyes That Last I Saw in Tears.
Emerson, R. Dost thou not hear me Ellen.
Far seen the river glides below.
Illusions like the tints of pearl.
Pair of crystal eyes will lead me, A.
What are all the flowers.
When Jane was absent Edgar's eye.
Gallagher, T. Accomplishment.
Ritual of Memories, The.
Graves, R. Everywhere Is Here.
Gunn, T. Kiss at Bayreuth, The.
Looks.
To Natty Bumppo.
Herrick. Bashfulnesse.
Eye, The.
Eyes, The.

Upon Franck.
Upon Her Eyes.
Upon His Julia.
Hopkins, G. She Schools the Flighty Pupils of Her Eyes.
Jacobsen, J. At Night.
Jonson, B. Oh Do Not Wanton with Those Eyes.
Song. To Celia ("Drink to me only with thine eyes").
Kizer, C. Through a Glass Eye, Lightly.
Kumin, M. Eyes.
Laughlin, J. Eyes Are the Guides of Love.
Your Eyes.
Logan, J. Narcisses: Vision and Retrospect.
Lowell, R. Eye and Tooth.
MacDiarmid, H. Milk-Wort and Bog Cotton.
MacNeice. Grey Ones, The.
Marvell. Eyes and Tears.
McHugh, H. Orbit.
Pupil.
Merwin. Deluge, The.
Michelangelo Buonarroti. Because there's never a time I'm not enchanted,
Closed now his shining eyes, that dazzled so.
Eyelid, shadowing, doesn't interfere, The.
From eyes of my beloved one, come burning.
Your lovely eyes, now bent.
Millay, E. Tavern.
Muldoon, P. Blemish.
Olson, C. Babe, The.
Dura.
Your Eyes.
Owen, W. Fates, The.
Parker, D. Sight.
Patchen. I always return to this place.
I Suddenly Became Conscious That This Thing Was Looking at Me Intently.
Petrarch. By now there is no way I could break loose.
How fortunate that instant when there came.
Those eyes that wounded me in such a way.
Weep now, my eyes; accompany my heart.
Yearning yet chaste eyes she held upon, The.
Plath. Eye-Mote, The.
On Looking into the Eyes of a Demon Lover.
Raine, K. Seventh Day.
Ransom, J. Her Eyes.
Riley, J. Her Beautiful Eyes.
Ritsos. Exhibits.
Eyes of the Statue, The.
Rukeyser, M. Eyes of Night-Time.
Rumi. I am so small I can barely be seen.
Sandburg, C. Brim.
Pick-Offs.
Shag-Bark Hickory.
Spanish.
Sweeping Wendy: Study in Fugue.
Under a Hat Rim.
Valley Song.
Schuyler, J. Eyes.
Shelley, P. Eyes: A Fragment.
Sheridan, T. I Like Your Collyrium.
Perlegi Versus Versos, Jonathan Bone, Tersos.
Stevens, W. Tattoo.
Tomlinson, C. Poem: "Muscles which move the eyeballs, The."
Through Closed Eyes.
Updike. Typical Optical.
Very. Give me an eye, that manly deeds.
Wilbur, R. On the Eyes of an SS Officer.
Williams, M. Light in the Eyes, The.
Williams, T. Eyes, The.
Williams, W. Weasel Snout.
Wilner, E. Two Pairs of Eyes.
Yeats. Cat and the Moon, The.
Drinking Song, A.
Zukofsky, L. World autumn, The.

Ezra
Ammons. So I Said I Am Ezra.
Berryman. Prayer of the Middle-Aged Man, The.

F

Faces

Amichai [*or* Amikhai]. I am like a leaf that knows its limits.
Atwood. Head against White.
Bogan, L. Song for the Last Act.
Borges. Mirror, The.
  Paradiso 31, 108.
Burns, R. Fragment: "Her flowing locks, the raven's wing."
Campion, T. There is a garden in her face.
Carew, T. Lips and Eyes.
Codrescu. Face Portrait.
Creeley. Eye o' the Storm.
  Faces, The.
  Just Friends.
  Sign Board, The.
  Soup ("Trembling / with delight").
  To Bobbie.
Cummings, E. E. Babylon slim / -ness of / evenslicing.
De la Mare. Anatomy.
  Cage, The.
  Veil, The.
  Widow, The.
Dickey, J. Faces Seen Once.
Dickinson, E. Face devoid of love or grace, A.
  Lovely Face to sit by, A.
  These—saw Visions.
Eberhart, R. Face, Ocean.
Gallagher, T. Even Now You Are Leaving.
  Not There.
Graves, R. Face in the Mirror, The.
Gunn, T. Rastignac at 45.
Hall, D. Raisin, The.
Herrick. Upon a Scarre in a Virgins Face.
  Upon Crab.
  Upon His Julia.
  Upon Mistresse Susanna Southwell, Her Cheeks.
  Upon Spalt.
Hopkins, G. Think of an opening page illuminèd.
Hughes, L. 125th Street.
  Subway Face.
Jacopo da Lentino. Sonnet: Of his Lady's Face.
Kinnell. Looking at Your Face.
Kunitz, S. Fitting of the Mask, The.
Lawrence, D. H. Human Face, The.
  Portraits.
Levertov. Face.
  Looking-glass.
  Photo Torn from The Times.
Lux. Shaving the Graveyard.
Merwin. Economy.
Michelangelo Buonarroti. Sweeter your face than grapes are, stewed to mush.
Milosz, C. Esse.
Moore, M. Face, A.
Nemerov. Sestina 1: "Thickness of paint or flesh cannot deface."
Niedecker. Ah your face.
Olson, C. True Numbers.
Pagis. Bisection.
  How To.
Paley, G. Faces.
Pound, E. In a Station of the Metro.
Ramanujan. On Memory.
Rich, A. Face.
Riley, J. Her Waiting Face.
  Rough Sketch, A.
  With Her Face.
Rochfort, G. Answer.
Rossetti, C. Descent from the Cross, The.
  I know a baby, such a baby,— / Round blue eyes and cheeks of pink.
Rumi. All our lives we've looked.
Sandburg, C. Aztec Mask.
  Child Face.
  Face.
  Halsted Street Car.
  Mask.
  Momus.
  Monotone.

  Passers-by.
  Phizzog.
  Under a Hat Rim.
Shelley, P. Fragment: A Serpent-Face.
Sheridan, T. Answer.
Smith, S. Face, The.
  Repentance of Lady T, The.
Stafford, W. Evidence.
  Glass Face in the Rain, A.
  Looking for You.
  When You Go Anywhere.
Stock, R. Wind in the Mirror.
Swenson, M. Sketch for a Landscape.
Swift, J. Progress of Beauty, The.
Szymborska, W. Smiles.
Tomlinson, C. Face and Image.
Updike. Shaving Mirror.
Whitman, W. Faces.
Williams, C. K. In There.
  Waking Jed.
  With Ignorance.
Wright, J. Accusation, The.
Wyatt, S. Face that should content me wonders [*or* wondrous] well, A.
Zagajewski. Van Gogh's Face.

Factories

Ammons. North Jersey.
  Nucleus.
Bishop, E. Varick Street.
Blok. Factory, The.
Bukowski. Sparks.
Dickey, W. Life Moving More Rapidly Than Hands Can Manage.
Hall, D. Traffic.
Heaney, S. Milk Factory, The.
Hughes, L. Steel Mills.
Ignatow, D. Get the Gasworks.
Kipling, R. Song of the Lathes, The.
Koch, K. Brassiere Factory, The.
Lawrence, D. H. Factory Cities, The.
Levi, P. Crescenzago.
Lindsay, N. Factory Windows Are Always Broken.
Longfellow, H. Ropewalk, The.
Oppen. Debt.
Plath. Night Shift.
Sandburg, C. Anna Imroth.
  Mill-Doors.
Simic. Toy Factory.
Tomlinson, C. Dates: Penkhull New Road.
  Etruria Vale.
Williams, C. K. To Market.
Williams, W. Classic Scene.
Zagajewski. Georges Seurat: Factory.

Faerie Queene, The

Koch, K. Art of Poetry, The.
Wordsworth, W. White Doe of Rylstone, The; or, The Fate of the Nortons.

Failure

Berryman. Nones.
Bly, R. August Rain.
Browning, E. Romance of the Ganges, A.
  Romaunt of Margret, The.
Bukowski. Word on the Quick and Modern Poem-Makers, A.
Ciardi, J. On Flunking a Nice Boy out of School.
Cowper, W. Distressed Travellers, The.
Creeley. For Lewis, to Say It.
  For the New Year.
  Pay.
Cummings, E. E. Nobody loses all the time.
Dickinson, E. Success is counted sweetest.
Dunbar, P. For the Man Who Fails.
Emerson, R. Cloud upon cloud / Clouds after rain.
Ginsberg, A. How Come He Got Canned at the Ribbon Factory.
  I feel as if I am at a dead.
  Last Night in Calcutta.
  Ode to Failure.
  Walking Home at Night.
Glück, L. Legend.
Han-shan. Disappointed impoverished scholars.
  Whose wine shop is this aglow.
Hardy, T. He Did Not Know Me.

  Her Confession.
Herrick. Paines without Profit.
  Plots Not Still Prosperous.
Housman. Shake hands, we shall never be friends, all's over.
Hughes, T. Crow's First Lesson.
Jackson, L. Celebration of Failure.
  Plighted to Shame.
Jacobsen, J. Birdsong of the Lesser Poet.
Jonson, B. Ode: "If men, and times were now."
  Ode to Himself, An.
  Ode to Himself[e].
Kinsella, T. Beloved,.
Kipling, R. That Day.
Kizer, C. Mud Soup.
Larkin, P. Success Story.
  To Failure.
Lux. Pedestrian.
MacLeish. Hands.
Merwin. Gods, The.
  Savonarola.
Oppen. Comforters, The.
Pagis. Failure.
Parker, D. Ballade of a Complete Flop.
Pessoa. Story of Salomon Waste, The.
Piercy. Death of the Small Commune, The.
Prunty. Sequence.
Robinson, E. Bewick Finzer.
  Clavering.
  Old Trails.
  Shadrach O'Leary.
  Wise Brothers, The.
Rossetti, C. Septuagesima.
  Swift and sure the swallow.
  Symbols.
Rukeyser, M. Paper Anniversary.
Szymborska, W. Returning Birds.
Updike. Player Piano.
Weiss, T. Youngest Son, The.
Whalen, P. Dharma Youth League, The.
  Failing.
Whitman, W. To Those Who've Fail'd.
Wilbur, R. In the Smoking-Car.
Williams, C. K. Failure.
Yeats. To a Friend Whose Work Has Come to Nothing.

Fairies

Coleridge, S. Songs of the Pixies.
"Dario." In Autumn.
De la Mare. Fairy in Winter, The.
Dunbar, P. Discovery, The.
Graves, R. Lollocks.
Hardy, T. On a Midsummer Eve.
Herrick. Beggar to Mab, the Fairy [*or* Fairie] Queen, The.
  Fairies, The.
  Fairy Temple; or, Oberon's Chapel, The.
  Oberon's Feast.
  Oberon's Palace.
  Temple, The.
Housman. Fairies Break Their Dances, The.
Hughes, L. Fairies.
Keats. Cap and Bells; or, The Jealousies, The.
  Faery Song.
  Fairy Song.
  La Belle Dame sans Merci [A Ballad].
  Song of Four Faeries.
  When They Were Come unto the Faery's Court.
Kipling, R. Ballad of Minepit Shaw, The.
Lindsay, N. Cold Sunbeams.
  Dancing for a Prize.
  Dangerous Little Boy Fairies, The.
  Fairy from the Apple-Seed, The.
  Lame Boy and the Fairy, The.
  What the Gray-Winged Fairy Said.
Poe. Fairyland [*or* Fairy-Land].
Rexroth, K. Valuta.
Riley, J. Bee-Bag, The.
  Little Orphant Annie.
  Pixy People, The.
  Puck.
Rimbaud, A. Fairy.
Rossetti, C. I fancy the good fairies dressed in white.
Shelley, P. Fragment: Wine of the Fairies.
Smith, S. Cool as a Cucumber.

Wright, J. Evening.
Yeats. Faery Song, A.
Stolen Child, The.
See also **Elves; Goblins**

Fairs
Auden. Fairground.
Berryman. World's Fair.
Burns, R. Rattlin, Roarin Willie.
Gunn, T. At the Barriers.
Fair in the Woods, The.
Hardy, T. At a Country Fair.
At Casterbridge Fair.
Expectation and Experience.
Last Look round St. Martin's Fair.
Sheep Fair, A.
Kumin, M. Photograph, Maryland Agricultural
College Livestock Show, 1924.
Larkin, P. Show Saturday.
Merwin. Coin, The.
Riley, J. Goin' to the Fair.
Little Lame Boy's Views, A.
Lockerbie Fair.
Sandburg, C. Honky Tonk in Cleveland, Ohio.
Stafford, W. Adults Only.
At the Fair.
Updike. Topsfield Fair.
Very. Welcome Written for the Essex Institute
Fair.
Whitman, W. Bravo, Paris Exposition!
Williams, W. Dance, The.

Fairy Tales
Ashbery, J. Märchenbilder.
Collins, B. Three Wishes, The.
Davie, D. Fairy Story.
Dickey, W. Dolls Play at Hansel and Gretel,
The.
Glück, L. Gretel in Darkness.
Graves, R. To Juan at the Winter Solstice.
Jacobsen, J. Primer, The.
Jarrell, R. House in the Wood, The.
Märchen, The.
Mörike [*or* Möricke]. Forest Murmurs.
Muldoon, P. Princess and the Pea, The.
Nash, O. Fee Fi Ho Hum, No Wonder Baby
Sucks Her Thumb.
Olson, C. Snow White was always waiting for
The Prince.
Plath. Battle-Scene.
Prunty. Annals of Jack.
Riley, J. Home-Made Fairy Tale, A.
Truly Marvelous, The.
Rukeyser, M. Fable: "Yes it was the prince's
kiss."
Sandburg, C. Love Letter to Hans Christian
Andersen.
Sexton. Briar Rose (Sleeping Beauty).
Frog Prince, The.
Rapunzel.
Smith, S. Fairy Story.
Frog Prince, The.
Spenser, E. Prosopopoia: or Mother Hubberds
Tale.
Van Duyn. Cinderella's Story.
Williams, C. K. Near the Haunted Castle.
Williams, M. On Word That the Old Children's
Stories Have Been Brought Up to Date.
Zaturenska. Quiet Countries: The World of
Hans Christian Andersen.

Fairyland
Graves, R. Land of Whipperginny, The.

Faith
Ambrose. Aeterne Rerum Conditor.
Splendor Paternae Gloriae.
Amichai [*or* Amikhai]. I Told You It Would Be
So—And You Didn't Believe.
Ammons. Tossup.
Angelou. Just Like Job.
Arnold, M. Dover Beach.
Berry, W. Homecoming, A.
Necessity of Faith, The.
Berryman. Facts & Issues, The.
Pacifist's Song, The.
Blake, W. Hes a Blockhead who wants a proof
of what he Cant Percieve.
Mock On, Mock On, Voltaire, Rousseau.

You dont believe I wont attempt to make ye.
Bly, R. Conversation with a Holy Woman Not
Seen for Many Years.
Brontë, E. No Coward Soul is Mine.
Visionary, The.
Brooks, G. Firstly Inclined to Take What It Is
Told.
Broumas, O. With God.
Browning, E. Drama of Exile, A.
Romance of the Ganges, A.
Browning, R. Bad Dreams I.
Byron, G. Stanzas to Augusta.
Were My Bosom As False As Thou Deem'st It
to Be.
Campion, T. Out of My Soul's Depth.
Carruth, H. Names.
Once and Again.
Carver, R. Transformation.
Cavafy. Lohengrin.
Manuel Komninos.
Cavalcanti. If you've forgotten me forever,
Mercy.
Chiabrera. O Thou who movest onward with a
mind.
Ciardi, J. Fable of Survival, A.
Clifton, L. Far Memory.
Clough. In controversial foul impureness.
O happy they whose hearts receive.
Codrescu. Faith Relearned.
Coleridge, S. Faith, Hope, and Charity.
Cowper, W. Hope.
Lively Hope, and Gracious Fear.
Lord Will Happiness Divine, The.
My former hopes are fled.
O Lord, my best desire fulfil.
Olney Hymns.
True Pleasures.
Crane, H. Recitative.
Crashaw. Adoro Te. The Hymn of Saint
Thomas in Adoration of the Blessed
Sacrament.
Creeley. Circle.
Mechanic, The.
Poem, A: "If the water forms."
Sufi Sam Christian.
Cullen, C. Counter Mood.
Lines to My Father.
Sonnet: "These are no wind-blown rumors, soft
say-sos."
Cummings, E. E. Here is little Effie's Head.
I Thank You God.
Jehovah buried Satan dead.
No time ago / or else a life.
That melancholy / fellow'll play / his
handorgan.
Cunningham, J. 1 Corinthians 13: Commentary.
Hymn in Adversity.
"Dario." Charterhouse, The.
Sum.
Davie, D. Articulacy. Hints from the Koran.
De la Mare. Catechism, The.
Dickinson, E. Child's faith is new, The.
Dust like the Mosquito, The.
"Faith" is a fine invention.
Faith—is the Pierless Bridge.
"Faithful to the end" Amended.
He strained my faith.
How brittle are the Piers.
I know that He exists.
I never lost as much but twice.
I never saw a Moor.
I think to Live—may be a Bliss.
My Faith is larger than the Hills.
Nearest Dream recedes—unrealized, The.
On a Columnar Self.
Read—Sweet—how others—strove.
This is a Blossom of the Brain.
This World Is Not Conclusion.
Those—dying then.
To lose one's faith—surpass.
To mend each tattered Faith.
To pile like Thunder to its close.
What I see not, I better see.
Donne. Elegy upon the Untimely Death of the
Incomparable Prince Henry.
To Mr. Roland Woodward.

Dugan, A. On When McCarthy Was a Wolf
among a Nation of Queer-Queers.
Dunbar, P. After Many Days.
After While.
By Rugged Ways.
Faith.
Mare Rubrum.
Resignation.
Slow Through the Dark.
Eberhart, R. On the Fragility of Mind.
Emerson, R. Character.
Honor bright o muse.
Problem, The.
Worship.
Fenton, J. God, A Poem.
Frost, R. Innate Helium.
Glück, L. Jeanne d'Arc.
Graves, R. Ample Garden, The.
Dancing Flame.
Poet's Curse, The.
Possessed.
Woman and Tree.
Guyon. Aspirations of the Soul after God.
Divine Love Endures No Rival.
Glory to God Alone.
Love Faithful in the Absence of the Beloved.
Love of God the End of Life, The.
Necessity of Self-Abasement.
Perfect Sacrifice, The.
Secrets of Divine Love Are To Be Kept, The.
Self-Diffidence.
Truth and Divine Love Rejected by the World.
Han-shan. Here's a message for the faithful.
HaNagid. Day Of Distress, A.
Dream, The.
Friends, A Fence Surrounds Us.
Send the Lord to the People.
War with Yadir, The.
When the Lord Is With You.
Hardy, T. Between Us Now.
Impercipient, The.
Herbert, G. Affliction (5).
Affliction (1).
Affliction: "Kill me not every [*or* ev'ry] day."
Artillery [*or* Artillerie].
Assurance.
Bag, The.
Banquet, The.
Bitter-Sweet.
Charms and Knots.
Church-Floor[e], The.
Collar, The.
Complaining.
Content.
Discharge, The.
Discipline.
Divinity.
Elixir [*or* Elixer], The.
Employment (1).
Faith.
Flower, The.
Forerunners, The.
Glance, The.
Grace.
Holy Baptism (2).
Justice (1).
Knell, The.
Love.
Love (1).
Love Unknown.
Method, The.
Nature.
Peace.
Pearl, The. Matth. 13:45.
Perseverance.
Praise (1).
Quidditie [*or* Quiddity], The.
Repentance.
Search, The.
see also To the Lady Elizabeth Queen of
Bohemia.
Sepulchre.
Sin (1).
Sonnet: "My God, where is that ancient heat
towards Thee."
Submission.

Superliminare.
Temper (1), The.
Temper (2), The.
Thanksgiving, The.
Trinity Sunday.
Twenty-third Psalm, The.
Windows, The.
Herrick. Faith.
Faith Four-square.
His Creed.
His Words to Christ, Going to the Cross.
Lamp, The.
Parasceve, or Preparation, The.
To God.
Upon Spenke.
Upon Woman and Mary.
Hopkins, G. Carrion Comfort.
God's Grandeur.
He hath abolished the old drouth.
Nondum.
O Deus, Ego Amo Te.
Trees by their yield.
Housman. If it chance your eye offend you.
Jackson, L. In Due Form.
Jacobsen, J. First Woman.
Notes from a Lenten Bar.
Jacopo da Lentino. Sonnet: Of [*or* To] his Lady
in Heaven.
Jeffers, R. Credo.
No Resurrection.
Quia Absurdum.
Thebaid.
Keats. O Thou Whose Face Hath Felt the
Winter's Wind.
Khayyám, O. Unbar the door, since thou the
Opener art.
Kinnell. Wait.
Kinsella, T. Faith.
Kipling, R. Old Song, An.
Recessional.
Song of the English, A.
To the True Romance.
Kizer, C. To My Friend Who Rhymes with
Peace.
Komunyakaa. Instructions for Building Straw
Huts.
Lawrence, D. H. Talk of Faith.
Levertov. Flickering Mind.
St. Thomas Didymus.
Levine, P. 28.
Lindsay, N. Heart of God.
In the Immaculate Conception Church.
Johnny Appleseed Speaks of the Appleblossom
Amaranth That Will Come to This City.
Shield of Faith, The.
Sun Says His Prayers, The.
Where Is the Real Non-Resistant?
Lux. Wife Hits Moose.
MacLeish. Actfive.
MacNeice. Carol: "To end all carols, darling."
Creditor, The.
Major, C. Arriving Uninvited.
Mallarmé. When the shadow menaced with its
fatal law.
McGrath, T. Against the False Magicians.
McHugh, H. Faith.
Melville, H. Conflict of Convictions, The.
Meredith, G. Ass of Balaam, The.
Faith on Trial, A.
Lord of old has dealt in blood, The.
Sense and Spirit.
Song of Theodolinda, The.
Test of Manhood, The.
To J.M.
Merton. Death.
Michelangelo Buonarroti. I wish I'd want what
I don't want, Lord, at all.
In me there's only death; my life's in you.
Millay, E. Oh, think not I am faithful to a vow!
This Dusky Faith.
Milosz, C. Ode for the Eightieth Birthday of
Pope John Paul II.
Prayer: "Approaching ninety, and still with a
hope."
Veni Creator.
Milton. On Time.

Mistral, F. Obsession, The.
Montale. Little Testament.
Nemerov. Sonnet: "Form of Christ cut from
dark wood, the pale, A."
O'Hara, F. Poem: "When I am feeling
depressed and anxious sullen."
Olson, C. Babe, The.
In one age or other, if not in this.
Quatrain: "Do not, at this high time, desert."
Willie Francis and the Electric Chair.
Owen, W. Has Your Soul Sipped?
Last Laugh, The.
Pessoa. My gesture that destroys.
Petrarch. Lady, who now with our Original.
Piercy. Seedlings in the Mail.
Pinkerton, H. Holy Sonnets.
Ransom, J. Eclogue: "JANE SNEED BEGAN IT:
My poor John, alas."
Riley, J. Brudder Sims.
Faith.
Hymb of Faith, A.
Legend Glorified, The.
Out of Nazareth.
Thoughts fer the Discuraged Farmer.
Vision of Rabbi Ben Issac, The.
Robinson, E. Credo.
Siege Perilous.
Rossetti, C. All beneath the sun hasteth, / All
that hath begun wasteth.
Behold, I stand at the door and knock.
Charades.
Charity.
Come Unto Me.
Comparisons.
Divine and Human Pleading.
Fair Margaret.
Faith and Hope are wings to Love.
For a Mercy Received.
Greatest of These Is Charity, The.
I followed Thee, my God, I followed Thee / To
see the end.
I Know You Not.
I lift mine eyes to see: earth vanisheth.
In weariness and painfulness St. Paul.
Leaf from leaf Christ knows; / Himself the Lily
and the Rose.
Lord God of Hosts, most Holy and most High.
Lord, It Is Good for Us to Be Here.
Lord Jesu, Thou art sweetness to my soul.
Lord Jesus, who would think that I am Thine?
Lowest Room, The.
Moonshine.
O Lord, on Whom we gaze and dare not gaze, /
Increase our faith that gazing we may see.
O Lord, when Thou didst call me, didst Thou
know.
Offering of the New Law, The.
Our heaven must be within ourselves / Our
home and heaven the work of faith.
Ransomed of the Lord, The.
Ruined Cross, The.
Somewhere Or Other.
Song for the Least of All Saints, A.
Take No Thought for The Morrow.
Vigil of St. Peter.
Ye Are Come unto Mount Sion.
Rumi. Ground Cries Out, The.
Keep walking, though there's no place to get to.
You Sweep the Floor.
Schuyler, J. I Sit Down to Type.
Sexton. Small Wire.
Smith, S. Dream of Comparison, A.
God the Eater.
Stafford, W. Spirit of Place: Great Blue Heron.
Stock, R. Curriculum Vitae.
Stockton, A. On Hearing of the Out Powering
of the Divine Spirit in Nassau Hall.
Tennyson, A. On a Mourner.
Supposed Confessions of a Second-rate
Sensitive Mind.
Two Voices, The.
Thomas, D. Where Once the Waters of Your
Face.
Uhland. Boy's Death, The.
Very. Faith ("Hast thou but faith thou shalt the
mountain bid").

Faith in Time of War.
How Faith Comes.
Hymn: Nevertheless, when the Son of Man
cometh, shall he find faith on the earth? Luke
18:8.
Just Shall Live by Faith, The.
Justification by Faith.
Mustard Seed, The.
Nature ("Bubbling brook doth leap when I come
by, The").
Night.
Rock, The.
Sign, The.
Slowness of Belief in a Spiritual World, The.
Walcott. City's Death by Fire, A.
Warren, R. English Cocker: Old and Blind.
Lord Jesus, I Wonder.
Whittier. Adjustment.
Answer, The.
Eternal Goodness, The.
Hermit of the Thebaid, The.
In Quest.
Mantle of St. John de Matha, The.
My Dream.
Questions of Life.
Requirement.
"Rock" in El Ghor, The.
Sisters, The: A Picture by Barry, The.
Tauler.
Trust.
Watchers, The.
Well of Loch Maree, The.
Williams, C. K. Dream of Mind: The Gap, A.
They Warned Him Then They Threw Him
Away.
Williams, M. After the Revolution for Jesus a
Secular Man [*or* the Associate Professor]
Prepares His Final Remarks.
After You Die You Don't Give a Piddling
Damn.
And When in Scenes of Glory.
For Jordan With Love the Eighth Year of the
Slaughter.
He Speaks to His Arguing Friends and to
Himself.
In Your Own Words Without Lying Tell
Something of Your Background.
Lay of the Badde Wyf.
Some Lines Finished Just Before Dawn at the
Bedside of a Dying Student It has Snowed
All Night.
Why God Permits Evil.
Wordsworth, W. Forsaken, The.
In due observance of an ancient rite.
Wright, C. Journal of English Days, A.
Journal of Southern Rivers, A.
Journal of True Confessions, A.
Lost Bodies.
Wyatt, S. After great storms the calm returns.
Argument, Th'
Give place all ye that doth rejoice.
Live thou gladly if so thou may.
Steadfastness.
Thou hast no faith of him that hath none.
What should I say.
Ye know my heart, my lady dear.
Yeats. Tom the Lunatic.

Faith Healers
Larkin, P. Faith Healing.

Falcons
Bukowski. Sky Sign.
Dubie. Groom Falconer.
Duncan, R. My Mother Would Be a Falconress.
Elyas Yusof Nezami [*or* Nisami] Ganjavi].
While roses bloomed along the plain.
Graves, R. Falcon Woman, The.
Hopkins, G. Windhover, The.
Jeffers, R. New Year's Eve.
Merwin. Falcons, The.
Rossetti, C. Noble Sisters.
Sarton, M. Lady with a Falcon.

Fall
McHugh, H. Fall, The.
Rilke. Fall.

See also **Autumn**

Falling
Carrera Andrade. Notes of a Parachute Jumper.
Carver, R. Poem for Karl Wallenda, Aerialist
  Supreme.
Clifton, L. My Dream About Falling.
Creeley. Entre Nous.
  Look.
Place, The ("What is the form is the gro- /
  tesquerie—the accident").
Dickinson, E. It Dropped So Low in My
  Regard.
Ibn-i-Yamin [or Ibn Jemin or Amir Mahmud ibn
  Amir Yaminu'd-Din Tughra'i]. I read on the
  porch of a palace bold.
Komunyakaa. Falling-Down Song, The.
Lux. Falling Through the Leaves.
Meredith, W. Original Aversions.
Pagis. Footprints.
Raine, K. Falling Leaves.
Ramanujan. Fall, The.
  Fear No Fall.
  Snakes and Ladders.
Riley, J. Impromptu on Roller Skates, An.
Rilke. Saltimbanques.
Tomlinson, C. Elemental.
Williams, C. K. Vehicle: Conscience.

Fame
Ai. Paparazzi, The.
Armantrout. Our Nature.
Ashbery, J. He.
Auden. Iceland Revisited.
Baudelaire. These line I give to you in hopes
  my name.
Bierce. Contentment.
Blok. To My Friends.
Borges. Fame.
  To a Minor Poet of the Greek Anthology.
  Yellow Rose, A.
Bradstreet, A. In Honour of that High and
  Mighty Princess Queen Elizabeth.
Brontë, E. Old Stoic, The.
  Stanzas to———.
Browning, R. Popularity.
Bukowski. Best Way to Get Famous Is to Run
  Away, The.
Byron, G. Lines: "Dear Becher, you tell me to
  mix with mankind."
  Stanzas Written on the Road between Florence
  and Pisa.
  Thy Days Are Done.
Campion, T. Ad Carolum Fitz Geofridum.
  Ad Tho. Munsonium, equitem Auratum et
  Baronetum.
  In Cambrum.
  To. Campiani Epigramma de Instituto Authoris.
Cavafy. That's the Man.
Chuang Tzu. Turtle, The.
Coleridge, S. Epitaph: "Stop, Christian passer-
  by!—Stop, child of God."
Collins, B. Rival Poet, The.
Cowper, W. Another Version.
  Answer to Stanzas Addressed to Lady Hesketh.
  On Observing Some Names of Little Note
  Recorded in the "Biographia Britannica."
  To Dr. Austin.
  To Sir John Fenn.
  Translation of Verses to Lloyd.
Crane, H. Thou Canst Read Nothing..
Cummings, E. E. ?
  Hokku.
  Sonnet: "I dreamed I was among the
  conquerors."
Cunningham, J. Lector Aere Perennior.
  Memoir.
Dickinson, E. Above Oblivion's Tide there is a
  Pier.
  Aurora.
  Be Mine the Doom.
  Beggar at the Door for Fame, The.
  Fame is a bee.
  Fame is a fickle food.
  Fame is the one that does not stay.
  Fame is the tint that Scholars leave.
  Fame of Myself, to justify.
  Fame's Boys and Girls, who never die.
  First We knew of Him was Death, The.

I'm Nobody! Who are you?
  Publication—is the Auction.
Emerson, R. Fame.
  His instant thought the Poet spoke.
Frost, R. Provide, Provide.
Graves, R. Singleness in Love.
  Troublesome Fame.
Hacker, M. Elegy: "Crying from exile, I."
Hardy, T. Abbey Mason, The.
  To an Actress.
Herrick. Fame.
  Fame Makes Us Forward.
  Glorie.
  Glory.
  Pillar of Fame, The.
  To His Book[e].
  To the Most Accomplisht Gentleman Master
    Michael Oulsworth.
  To the Right Honourable Edward Earle of
    Dorset.
  Upon Himself.
  Wit Punisht, Prospers Most.
Hughes, L. Mellow.
Hughes, T. Famous Poet.
Jeffers, R. Giant's Ring, The.
  Let Them Alone.
Jonson, B. To Alphonso [or Alfonso]
  Ferrabosco, on His Book.
  To My Truly-Beloved Friend, Mr Browne: on
    His Pastorals.
  To Sir Henry Cary.
  To the Same [Alphonso Ferrabosco].
Keats. Addressed to Haydon.
  Great Spirits Now on Earth.
  This Mortal Body of a Thousand Days.
  To Kosciusko.
  When I Have Fears [That I May Cease to Be].
Kizer, C. Ashes, The.
  Second Time Around.
Lux. Frankly, I Don't Care.
Martial. 4.33: "You write, you tell me, for
  posterity."
Melville, H. On Sherman's Men.
Meredith, G. Chivalry.
  To Alex. Smith, the "Glasgow Poet," on His
    Sonnet to "Fame."
Merton. Elegy for Ernest Hemingway, An.
Milton. On Shakespear[e].
Nash, O. Parable for Sports Writers, Society
  Columnists, Bond Salesmen, and Poets, A.
Nemerov. Modern Poet, A.
Neruda. Another One.
Owen, W. To My Friend (With an Identity
  Disc).
Petrarch. That bravery, which came to flower in
  you.
Pope, A. To a Lady with the Temple of Fame.
Pound, E. White Stag, The.
Rich, A. Focus.
Riley, J. Dead in Sight of Fame.
  Humble Singer, A.
  Letter to a Friend, A.
Robinson, E. Old Trails.
  Three Quatrains.
Sandburg, C. Fame If Not Fortune.
  Soup.
  Vaudeville Dancer.
Shelley, P. Ozymandias.
Smith, S. Crown of Bays, The.
  Film Star, The.
Spender, S. Question of Identity, A.
Unknown. To My Dear Sister, the Author of
  these Poems.
Updike. At the End of the Rainbow.
  Little Poems.
  Newlyweds, The.
  Pop Smash, Out of Echo Chamber.
Villon. Ballade of the Ladies of Time Past.
Weiss, T. On Stuffing a Goose.
Whalen, P. International Date Line, Monday/
  Monday 27:XI:67.
Whitman, W. Fame's Vanity.
  When I Heard At The Close Of The Day.
Williams, M. Aging Actress Sees Herself a
  Starlet on the Late Show, The.
My Wife Reads the Paper at Breakfast on the

  Birthday of the Scottish Poet.
Wyatt, S. Stand Whoso List.
Yeats. While I, from that reed-throated
  whisperer.
See also **Greatness**

Family
Ai. Blue Suede Shoes.
Amichai [or Amikhai]. Beautiful Are the
  Families of Jerusalem.
  Family.
Armantrout. Crossing.
Auden. Household, A.
  Through the Looking-Glass.
Berry, W. My Great-Grandfather's Slaves.
Bishop, E. Poem: "About the size of an old-
  style dollar bill."
Brodsky, J. Ischia in October.
Broumas, O. Landscape with Next of Kin.
  Native.
Browning, R. Family, The.
Bukowski. Not To Worry.
  Some Picnic.
Carruth, H. Abandoned Ranch, Big Bend.
  Family Reunion.
Carver, R. Mail, The.
  Next Door.
  Schooldesk, The.
  To My Daughter.
  What I Can Do.
Ciardi, J. Bedlam Revisited.
  Call It a Day.
Cooper, J. Dream in Which the Routine Quality
  of My Imagination Is Fully Exposed.
  Hobby Lobby, The.
  In the House of the Dying.
Corbett, W. Family.
Creeley. Family, The.
  "For Some Weeks."
  Heaven ("I don't want").
  Home.
  I.
Dickey, J. Deborah as Scion.
Drummond de Andrade. Table, The.
  Travelling in the Family.
Dubie. Coyote Creek.
Eberhart, R. Orchard.
  Spite Fence.
Ferlinghetti, L. Home Home Home.
  I Genitori Perduti
Gallagher, T. Ballad of Ballymote, The.
  Cougar Meat.
  Woodcutting on Lost Mountain.
Ginsberg, A. White Shroud.
Glück, L. From the Japanese.
  Returning a Lost Child.
  Scraps.
  Still Life.
  Thanksgiving.
Graves, R. Brother.
  Great-Grandmother, The.
  Pride of Progeny.
Gunn, T. Hide and Seek.
  Slow Waker.
  Three.
Hacker, M. Callers, The.
  Elevens.
  For Elektra.
  Inheritances.
Hall, D. Family, The.
  Tomorrow.
Hardy, T. After the Burial.
  During Wind and Rain.
Hayden, R. Beginnings.
Heaney, S. Clearances.
Hopkins, G. Epithalamion: "Hark, hearer, hear
  what I do; lend a thought now, make believe."
Howe, S. Chanting at the Crystal Sea.
Hughes, T. Being Christlike.
  Walt.
Ignatow, D. And That Night.
Jackson, L. That Ancient Line.
Jeffers, R. At the Birth of an Age.
  Such Counsels You Gave to Me.
Kizer, C. Amusing Our Daughters.
  Month in Summer, A.
Koch, K. You Were Wearing.

Komunyakaa. Family Tree.
Korn. Generations.
Kumin, M. Family Reunion.
 Feeding Time.
 For My Great-Grandfather: A Message Long
  Overdue.
 Game of Monopoly in Chavannes.
 My Father's Neckties.
 Retrieval System, The.
 Sperm.
 Thirties Revisited, The.
Kunitz, S. Father and Son.
 Three Floors.
Larkin, P. Ambulances.
Laughlin, J. Easter in Pittsburgh.
 Family Council of the Yakovlevs, The.
 Family Portrait, The.
 Stranger in the House, The.
 Your Early Life.
Levertov. Arrival (North Wales, 1897), An.
Levine, P. I Was Born in Lucerne.
 Letters for the Dead.
 Sources.
Lindsay, N. Perfect Marriage, The.
Logan, J. Medicine Bow.
 Poem for My Brother.
 Returning Home.
 Transformation, The.
Lux. Autobiographical.
 Backyard Swingset.
MacLeish. Family Group.
MacNeice. Happy Families.
Mahon. Achill.
 Yaddo Letter, The.
Martial. 2.4: "Bert is beguiling with his
  mother."
Melville, H. Fragments of a Lost Gnostic Poem
  of the Twelfth [or 12th] Century.
Meredith, W. For His Father.
 Ten-Day Leave.
 Winter Verse for His Sister.
Merwin. Letter from Gussie, A.
Milosz, C. Family, A.
 My Grandfather Sigismund Kunat.
Nemerov. Midsummer's Day.
Niedecker. Paean to Place.
Oliver, M. Family, The.
Oppen. Niece.
Paley, G. Family.
 Suppertime.
Patchen. Easy Decision, An.
 Family Portrait.
 Kibali-Ituri.
Prunty. Family Portrait for Our Daughter, A.
 Lake House, The.
 Nineteenth Hole, The.
Ramanujan. August.
 Extended Family.
 In the Zoo.
 Love Poem for a Wife, 1.
 Small-scale Reflections on a Great House.
Ransom, J. First Travels of Max.
Rexroth, K. Family, The.
Riley, J. Spirits at Home.
Rimbaud, A. Memory.
 Remembrances of Senility.
Rossetti, C. Gone Before.
 Valentine, 1877, A.
Rukeyser, M. Absalom.
 Another Day. The Children Are All Eating.
 Double Ode.
 Four in a Family.
 Green Limits.
 Word of Mouth.
Sandburg, C. Home Fires.
Sarton, M. Child's Japan, A.
Schuyler, J. Over the Hills.
Sexton. All My Pretty Ones.
 Papa and Mama Dance, The.
Smith, S. Is It Happy?
 Tenuous and Precarious.
Spender, S. Elegy for Margaret.
Stafford, W. Catechism, A.
 Family Turn, A.
 How It Is with Family.
 One Home.

Reading with Little Sister: A Recollection.
 Writing It Down.
Stock, R. Scene From Life.
Szymborska, W. Family Album.
 In Praise of My Sister.
Tate, A. Farewell Rehearsed.
Tate, J. Land of Little Sticks, 1945.
 My Great Great Etc. Uncle Patrick Henry.
Tsang. Three Generations.
Updike. Due Respect.
Vroman. Our Family.
Walcott. Glory Trumpeter, The.
Walker, A. For Two Who Slipped Away Almost
  Entirely.
Warren, R. Ballad of Billie Potts, The.
 Old Love.
 Winter Wheat: Oklahoma.
Weiss, T. Heir Apparent, The.
 Youngest Son, The.
Whalen, P. Dream & Excursus, Arlington
  Massachusetts.
Williams, M. Going.
 Holiday Inn: Surrounded by Someone Else's
  Reunion He Comes to Terms.
Williams, T. Recuerdo.
Wordsworth, W. Fragment: "For let the
  impediment be what it may."
 Jewish Family (in a Small Valley Opposite St
  Goar, upon the Rhine), A.
Wright, C. Self-Portrait.
 Virginia Reel.
Wright, J. Cold Divinities, The.
 Family Reunion.
 Old Man Drunk.
 Willy Lyons.
Zukofsky, L. H.T.
 Men in the kitchens, The.
 My nephew / And my new.

Family Life
Armantrout. Fiction ("When the woman's face
  contorted and she clutched the railing for
  support, we knew she would die").
Byron, L. Blues, The.
Carver, R. Country Matters.
 From the East, Light.
 Next Year.
 On an Old Photograph of My Son.
 Summer in Sacramento, A.
 Suspenders.
 Tall Order, A.
Ciardi, J. Bedlam Revisited.
Clifton, L. If I Should.
Creeley. Boy, the.
 Gift of Great Value, A.
 Table, The.
Davie, D. Liverpool Epistle, A.
Dove, R. Daystar.
 Taking in Wash.
Drummond de Andrade. Family Portrait.
Dugan, A. Family Statements.
 Nomenclature.
 Poem: "Man with a box walked up to a woman
  with a boy, A."
Dunbar, P. At Candle-Lightin' Time.
 'Long To'ds Night.
Hayden, R. Those Winter Sundays.
Herrick. Upon Grubs.
Hughes, L. Piggy-back.
Jeffers, R. Cawdor.
 Tamar.
Lawrence, D. H. Red-Herring.
Logan, J. Whistling Wings or White Turtle in
  the Watertree.
Lowell, R. My Last Afternoon with Uncle
  Devereux Winslow.
McHugh, H. House, The.
 Mind.
Meredith, G. Orchard and the Heath, The.
Meredith, W. Look at Me! Look at Me!
Millay, E. Lament: "Listen, children: / Your
  father is dead."
Molière. Tartuffe.
Muldoon, P. Mixed Marriage, The.
Nash, O. Family Court.
Niedecker. Fancy Another Day Gone.
 Letter from Paul.

Ten o'clock.
O'Hara, F. Ave Maria.
Olson, C. All Pink from the Bath She Slept.
 Incunabula, 1958.
Orr, G. Excavation, The.
Paley, G. 20th Street Spring.
Prunty. Family Act, The.
 Wedding Stop, The.
Ramanujan. Routine Day Sonnet.
Rexroth, K. Organization Men in Affluent
  Society.
Rich, A. In the Wake of Home.
 Woman Mourned by Daughters, A.
Riley, J. George Mullen's Confession.
 King of Oo-Rinktum-Jing, The.
 Prior to Miss Belle's Appearance.
 Private Theatricals.
Roethke. Happy Three, The.
 My Papa's Waltz.
Rossetti, C. What Does the Bee Do?
Rukeyser, M. Victims, a Play for the Home,
  The.
Sandburg, C. Boy and Father.
 Population Drifts.
Sexton. Funnel.
 Mother and Jack and the Rain.
Smith, S. Emily Writes Such a Good Letter.
 House of Over-Dew, The.
 Mutchmore and Not-So.
 Sliding Mountain, The.
Stafford, W. Family Turn, A.
 Rescued Year, The.
Stein, G. Prudence Caution and Foresight: A
  Story of Avignon.
Stockton, A. To Miss Mary Stockton, an Epistle
  the 10th of Janu 78.
Updike. Home Movies.
 House Growing, The.
 Leaving Church Early.
 Living with a Wife.
 Relatives.
Van Duyn. Bedtime Stories.
 Folks built that barn, your great grandfather, and
  them, The.
 Growing Up Askew.
 Relationships.
Williams, C. K. Sanctity, The.
 Time: 1976.
 Time: 1978.
Williams, M. Potter, Vidalia.
 Shrinking Lonesome Sestina, The.
Wordsworth, W. Even as a dragon's eye that
  feels the stress.

Famine
Dubie. In the Time of False Messiahs.
Very. Potato Blight, The.
Walker, A. Few Sirens, A.
Wyatt, S. In doubtful breast whilst motherly
  Pity.

Fancy
Burns, R. Mary Morison.
Cowper, W. Anti-Thelyphthora.
See also **Imagination**

Fans
Bukowski. My Groupie.
 What to Do with Contributor's Copies?
Mallarmé. Another Fan; of Mademoiselle
  Mallarmé.
 Fan, A; of Madame Mallarmé.
 Fan, A; of Méry Laurent.
Montale. Fan, The.
Nash, O. Enthusiast Is a Devotee Is a Rooter,
  or, Mr. Hemingway, Meet Mr. Stengel, An.
Seifert. Fan, The.

Fantasies
Baudelaire. Exotic Scent.
 Voice, The.
Berrigan, T. Something Amazing Just
  Happened.
Borges. Note for a Fantastic Story.
Brodsky, J. Plato Elaborated.
Browning, E. Romance of the Swan's Nest,
  The.
Bukowski. Notations from a Muddled
  Indolence.

Seahorse.
Carver, R.   My Boat.
Ciardi, J.   Elaine.
Codrescu.   Winter in Istanbul.
Coleridge, S.   Frost at Midnight.
Lines Written at the King's Arms, Ross,
  Formerly the House of the "Man of Ross."
Crane, S.   Youth in apparel that glittered, A.
Creeley.   Flesh.
Cummings, E. E.   Boy and the Man, The.
Doll's boy's asleep / under a stile.
My sweet old etcetera.
Paper Palace, The.
Than(by yon sunset's wintry glow).
Will i ever forget that precarious moment?
De la Mare.   Fog.
Which?
Dove, R.   Adolescence—III.
Eberhart, R.   Commas in Wintertime.
Lament of a New England Mother, The.
Eliot, T. S.   Rhapsody on a Windy Night.
Ferlinghetti, L.   Imaginary Happening, London,
  An.
Wild Dreams of a New Beginning.
García Lorca.   Gypsy Nun, The.
"H. D."   At Baia.
Hardy, T.   Dream of the City Shopwoman.
Dream or No, A.
Imaginings.
Let Me Believe.
Herrick.   To the Maids to Walke Abroad.
Hughes, L.   As Befits a Man.
Flatted Fifths.
If-ing.
Our Land.
Ignatow, D.   Now.
You.
Jarrell, R.   Seele im Raum.
Kizer, C.   For Jan as the End Draws Near.
Laughlin, J.   So Slender.
Levine, P.   Roofs.
MacLeish.   Two Women Talking.
Pound, E.   Dance Figure.
Riley, J.   Fantasy, A.
Rossetti, C.   Echo.
In An Artist's Studio.
Rukeyser, M.   Along History.
Make and be eaten, the poet says.
Sarton, M.   Bears and Waterfalls.
Metaphysical Garden, The.
Nursery Rhyme.
Song: "No, I will never forget you and your
  great eyes."
These Were Her Nightly Journeys.
Spenser, E.   Muiopotmos: or The Fate of the
  Butterflie.
Stafford, W.   Old Prof.
Suckling, S.   Upon My Lady Carlisle's Walking
  in Hampton Court Garden.
Voznesensky [or Voznesenskii].   Antiworlds.
Walker, A.   She Said.
Wilbur, R.   Attention Makes Infinity.
Baroque Wall-Fountain in the Villa Sciarra, A.
Williams, C. K.   Don't.
Williams, M.   Affair, The.
Man Who Stays Up Late, The.
Williams, W.   Good Night.
Wilner, E.   Amelia.
Wyatt, S.   Answer, The.
Yeats.   He Tells of the Perfect Beauty.

Farewell
Amichai [or Amikhai].   Farewell: "Fare thee
  well, it was your face, and now the face of
  memory."
Ammons.   Some Months Ago.
Beckett, S.   Da Tagte Es.
Berryman.   Farewell to Miles.
Purgatory.
Bogan, L.   Fifteenth Farewell.
Bukowski.   Saying Goodbye to Love.
Byron, G.   Adieu, The.
Farewell Petition to J.C.H., Esq.
Farewell to the Muse.
From the French.
Napoleon's Farewell.
To Florence.

To Romance.
Carver, R.   Forever.
Late Night with Fog and Horses.
My Death.
Cavafy.   Come, O King of the Lacedaimonians.
God Forsakes Antony, The.
Ciardi, J.   Biography.
Vale.
Coleridge, S.   Sonnet on Quitting Christ's
  Hospital.
Corbett, W.   Bridgeport Station.
Crane, H.   With a Photograph to Zell, Now
  Bound for Spain.
Crane, S.   There came whisperings in the winds.
Davie, D.   Fare Thee Well.
Donne.   Expiration, The.
Fever, A.
Dryden, J.   To the Memory of Mr Oldham.
Dubie.   Double Sphere, Cloven Sphere.
Dugan, A.   On Leaving Town.
Summer Gale.
Dunbar, P.   My Love Irene.
Herrick.   His Tears to Thamesis [or Thamasis].
To Dianeme.
To His Booke.
To His Peculiar Friend Master Thomas Shapcott,
  Lawyer.
Housman.   Now hollow fires burn out to black.
Kipling, R.   King, The.
Lawrence, D. H.   Seven Seals.
Virgin Mother, The.
Logue, C.   Fragment.
MacLeish.   Cat in the Wood, The.
What Must.
Mandelstam [or Mandelshtam].   Tristia.
McHugh, H.   Point of Origin.
Merton.   Things and people goodbye / It is not
  that I prefer.
Merwin.   For Now.
Truth about Departures, The.
Pope, A.   Farewell to London in the Year 1715,
  A.
Ralegh, S.   Farewell to False Love, A.
Farewell to the Court.
Poem Put into My Lady Laiton's Pocket, A.
Ramanujan.   Instead of a Farewell.
Riley, J.   Good-by er Howdy-do.
Lost Love, A.
Song of Parting.
Rimbaud, A.   Departure.
Ritsos.   Moonlight Sonata.
Rossetti, C.   On the note you do not send me.
Till Tomorrow.
Sandburg, C.   Different Kinds of Good-by.
Epistle: "Jesus loved the sunsets on Galilee."
One Parting.
Spray.
Sidney, S.   Leave Me O Love.
Smith, S.   Farewell: "Farewell dear friends."
Stafford, W.   Friends, Farewell.
So Long.
Stockton, A.   Sweet Mariana gentle maid adieu.
Tears of Friendship, The. Elegy the 4th.
To a Friend Going to Sea.
Suckling, S.   Farewell to Love.
Song: "I prithee send me back my heart."
Swenson, M.   Goodbye, Goldeneye.
Tate, J.   Radical Departure, A.
Thoreau.   Farewell.
Loves Farewell.
Walcott.   Schooner Flight, The.
Walker, A.   Good Night, Willie Lee, I'll See
  You in the Morning.
Wheatley, P.   Elegy on Leaving, An.
Farewel[l] to America, A. To Mrs. S. W.
Williams, T.   Ave Atque Vale.
Valediction: "She went with morning on her
  lips."
Wordsworth, W.   Farewell, A: "Farewell thou
  little Nook of mountain-ground."
Wright, J.   To a Hostess Saying Goodnight.

Fargo, North Dakota
Wright, J.   Outside Fargo, North Dakota.

Farming and Farmers
Ai.   Hangman.
Tenant Farmer, The.

Young Farm Woman Alone.
Ammons.   Hardweed Path Going.
Silver.
Angelou.   Southeast Arkanasia.
Apollinaire.   Autumn.
Arendt.   Hands, The.
Atwood.   Planters, The.
Berry, W.   Contrariness of the Mad Farmer, The.
Current, The.
Enriching the Earth.
Farmer Among the Tombs, The.
Farmer and the Sea, The.
Farmer, Speaking of Monuments, The.
February 2, 1968.
Horses.
In This World.
Mad Farmer in the City, The.
Mad Farmer Revolution, The.
Man Born to Farming, The.
Planting Trees.
Rain.
River Bridged and Forgot, The.
Satisfactions of the Mad Farmer, The.
Seeds, The.
September 2, 1969.
Song in a Year of Catastrophe.
Sowing.
Standing Ground, A.
Wish to Be Generous, The.
Bishop, E.   Prodigal, The.
Bly, R.   Cornpicker Poem.
Snowfall in the Afternoon.
Burns, R.   Cotter's Saturday Night, The.
Campion, T.   Jack and Joan.
Carruth, H.   Baler, The.
Concerning Necessity.
Emergency Haying.
Green Mountain Idyl.
Lady.
Marshall Washer.
Ciardi, J.   In the Rich Farmer's Field.
Clampitt.   At Muker, Upper Swaledale.
Beethoven, Opus 111.
Black Buttercups.
On the Disadvantages of Central Heating.
Stacking the Straw.
Cowper, W.   Yearly Distress, The.
Creeley.   Counterpoint, A.
Cummings, E. E.   Nobody loses all the time.
Wee people / dwelling / between serene.
Davie, D.   Back of Affluence.
Dickey, J.   Farmers.
Dickinson, E.   Products of my Farm are these,
  The.
Dove, R.   Small Town.
Dubie.   Tomb Pond.
Dunbar, P.   Disappointed.
Eberhart, R.   Recollection of Childhood.
Sunday in October.
Van Black, an Old Farmer in His Dell.
Emerson, R.   Husband has the nearest acres,
  The.
King. If farmers make my land secure.
Musketaquid.
Frost, R.   Code, The.
Death of the Hired Man, The.
Girl's Garden, A.
Mowing.
Pasture, The.
Putting in the Seed.
Range-finding.
Strong Are Saying Nothing, The.
Gurney, I.   Hoe Scrapes Earth, The.
Turmut-Hoeing.
Hall, D.   Elegy for Wesley Wells.
Farm, The.
Henyard Round, The.
New Animals.
Ox Cart Man.
Han-shan.   Farmer with acres of mulberry
  groves, A.
I retired to the edge of a forest.
Hardy, T.   Calf, The.
Heaney, S.   Follower.
Harvest Bow, The.
Wife's Tale, The.

Herrick.　His Grange, or Private Wealth.
Hughes, T.　Bringing in New Couples.
　Crow Hill.
　Dehorning.
　February 17th.
　Tractor.
Jarrell, R.　Field and Forest.
Komunyakaa.　Banking Potatoes.
　Buried Light.
　Yellowjackets.
Kumin, M.　Family Reunion.
　Feeding Time.
　July, Against Hunger.
　Photograph, Maryland Agricultural College
　　Livestock Show, 1924.
Lawrence, D. H.　Love On the Farm.
Lindsay, N.　Cornfields, The.
Lux.　Commercial Leech Farming Today.
　Farmers.
　View From a Porch.
MacLeish.　Eleven.
Meredith, G.　Phoebus with Admetus.
Merwin.　Black Plateau, The.
　Dragonfly, The.
Millay, E.　From a Train Window.
Milosz, C.　1913.
Moraes, V.　Sonnet of Intimacy.
Muldoon, P.　Cauliflowers.
　Why Brownlee Left.
Nemerov.　Harvest Home, A.
Niedecker.　For sun and moon and radio.
　Government men said Don't plant wheat, The.
　Their apples fall down.
　To Paul too old enough to read.
Oliver, M.　Farm Country.
Olson, C.　Dry Ode, The.
Paley, G.　Dance in Jinotega, The.
Patchen.　Autumn Is the Crows' Time.
Plath.　Dispossessed, The.
　Memoirs of a Spinach-Picker.
Rich, A.　Roots.
Riley, J.　Boy Lives on Our Farm, The.
　How John Quit the Farm.
　Old Winters on the Farm.
　Raggedy Man, The.
　Thoughts fer the Discuraged Farmer.
　Us Farmers in the Country.
　What Smith Knew about Farming.
Ritsos.　Farmer.
　Interchanges.
Rossetti, C.　Margaret has a milking-pail, / And
　she rises early.
Sandburg, C.　Harvest Sunset.
　Illinois Farmer.
　Improved Farm Land.
　Laughing Corn.
　More Country People.
　Omaha.
　Onion Days.
　Plowboy.
　Prairie.
　Redhaw Rain.
　She Opens the Barn Door Every Morning.
　Smoke Blue.
　Village in Late Summer.
　Weeds.
Sarton, M.　Prothalamion.
Schuyler, J.　Under the Hanger.
Sexton.　Farmer's Wife, The.
Snyder, G.　Hay for the Horses.
Stafford, W.　Fiction.
　Light by the Barn, The.
Swenson, M.　My Farm.
Sze.　Brueghel.
Tennyson, A.　Northern Farmer: New Style.
Tomlinson, C.　At Holwell Farm.
　Farmer's Wife: at Fostons Ash, The.
　In December.
　Oxen: Ploughing at Fiesole.
Trakl.　Rats, The.
Unknown.　Another ["Take to thy bosom, gentle
　earth, a swain"].
Updike.　Hoeing.
　Pear like a Potato, A.
Van Duyn.　Folks built that barn, your great
　grandfather, and them, The.

Nap.
Old widow lady, and went out to do her chore,
　An.
Well, that old big fat man.
Very.　"Agriculture the Source of Individual and
　of National Prosperity."—Anne Pratt.
Warren, R.　Alf Burt, Tenant Farmer.
　Boy Wandering in Simms' Valley.
　Winter Wheat: Oklahoma.
Whitman, W.　Farm Picture, A.
Whittier.　Seed-Time and Harvest.
Wilbur, R.　Sonnet: "Winter deepening, the hay
　all in, The."
Williams, C. K.　Loss.
Williams, W.　Farmer, The.
Wordsworth, W.　Farmer of Tilsbury Vale, The.
　Solitary Reaper, The.
Wright, J.　From a Bus Window in Central Ohio,
　Just before a Thunder Shower.
　Milkweed.

Farmworkers
Carruth, H.　Marvin McCabe.
　Pa McCabe.
Hardy, T.　We Field-Women.
Kumin, M.　Photograph, Maryland Agricultural
　College Livestock Show, 1924.
Oliver, M.　Indonesia.
Prunty.　Haying.
Stafford, W.　Fiction.
Warren, R.　Orphanage Boy.
See also **Migrant Workers**

Fascism and Fascists
Bukowski.　22,000 Dollars in 3 Months.
Cullen, C.　Apostrophe to the Land.
Cummings, E. E.　Red-rag and pink-flag.
Dugan, A.　Untitled Poem: "I'm in the house
　because."
Hill, G.　Christmas Trees.
Hughes, L.　Broadcast on Ethiopia.
　Note to All Nazis Fascists and Klansmen.
　Song for Ourselves.
　Underground, The.
Montale.　Hitler Spring, The.
Williams, T.　Brain's Dissection, The.

Fashion
Collins, B.　Death of the Hat, The.
Dickinson, E.　Morns are meeker than they
　were, The.
Hughes, L.　What?
Jonson, B.　On English Monsieur.
Nash, O.　Allow Me, Madam, But It Won't
　Help.
　Don't Look Now.
　Man With Two New Suits, The.
　Thoughts Thought on an Avenue.
　What's the Use.
Nemerov.　History of a Literary Movement.
Niedecker.　Elegant office girl, The.
　Missus Dora.
Parker, D.　Satin Dress, The.
Pope, A.　Epistle [II,] to a Lady[: Of the
　Characters of Women].
Rexroth, K.　Revolt.
Rossetti, C.　Freaks of Fashion.
　If a pig wore a wig.
　Some ladies dress in muslin full and white.
Sandburg, C.　Proud and Beautiful.
　Style.
Stockton, A.　Satire on the Fashionable
　Pompoons Worn by the Ladies in the Year
　1753, A.
See also **Clothing**

Fasting
Broumas, O.　Fast.
Orr, G.　Fast, The.
Rumi.　Fasting.

Fate
Auden.　Like a Vocation.
　Walk After Dark, A.
Baudelaire.　Ever the Same.
Beckett, S.　Je suis ce cours de sable qui glisse.
　My way is in the sand flowing.
Berrigan, T.　Red Shift.
Bogan, L.　Cartography.
　Didactic Piece.

Borges.　Dream of Pedro Henríquez Ureña, The.
　Limit, The.
　Things That Might Have Been.
Bradstreet, A.　Here Follows Some Verses upon
　the Burning of Our House.
Brodsky, J.　North of Delphi.
Brontë, E.　Now trust a heart that trusts in you.
　Will the day be bright or cloudy?
Broumas, O.　Dactyls.
Browning, R.　Saint Martin's Summer.
Bukowski.　Blackbirds Are Rough Today, The.
　Love.
Burns, R.　Tam Glen.
　To a Mountain Daisy.
Byron, G.　To the Same.
Campion, T.　Elegie upon the Untimely Death of
　Prince *Henry*, An.
　In Obitum Hen. Mag. Brit. Principis.
Carew, T.　For a Picture Where a Queen
　Laments over the Tomb of a Slain Knight.
　To Celia, upon Love's Ubiquity.
　To His Mistress.
Carruth, H.　Lost.
Cavafy.　Trojans.
Chaucer.　Fortune.
Ciardi, J.　Minus One.
Collins, B.　Butterfly Effect, The.
Cowper, W.　Boadicea: An Ode.
　Fragment: "He came to him in the extasy of
　pray'r."
　How blest the youth whom Fate ordains.
　Mortals around your destin'd heads.
Creeley.　Curse.
　Kore.
　Oh No.
　Prejudice, The.
　Son: "What I took in my hand."
　Window, The.
Cuadra, P.　World Is a Round Earthenware Plate,
　The.
Cullen, C.　Judas Iscariot.
　Ultimatum.
De la Mare.　Captive, The.
　Even In The Grave.
　Iago.
　Round, The.
Dickinson, E.　Belshazzar had a Letter.
　Ended, ere it begun.
　He fumbles at your Soul.
　It Dropped So Low in My Regard.
　It is very wrong that you were ill.
　To earn it by disdaining it.
　Uncertain lease—develops lustre.
Donne.　Elegy upon the Untimely Death of the
　Incomparable Prince Henry.
Dugan, A.　In Memoriam: Aurelius Battaglia,
　and against His Tragic Sense of Life.
Dunbar, P.　Crisis, The.
　Robert Gould Shaw.
Duncan, R.　Poem Beginning with a Line by
　Pindar, A.
Eberhart, R.　American Hakluyt.
　Flux.
　Later or Sooner.
　Lorca.
　Lost, The.
　Necessity.
　Oedipus.
　Recognition.
Emerson, R.　All that thy virgin soul can ask be
　thine.
　Archangel Hope / Looks to the azure cope, The.
　Day's Ration, The.
　Divine Inviters! I accept.
　Fate.
　Guy.
　I must not borrow light.
　Is Jove immortal / So is Cerberus at his portal.
　Love / Asks nought his brother cannot give.
　Motto to "Fate."
　Nemesis.
　No fate, save by the victim's fault, is low.
　Perhaps thy lot in life is higher.
　Puff of air or dry or damp, A.
　Turtle in swamp.
Enzensberger, H.　Lachesis Lapponica.

Frost, R.   Design.
  Draft Horse, The.
  Gift Outright, The.
García Lorca.   Ballad of the Marked Man.
Ginsberg, A.   Wrote This Last Night.
Glück, L.   Liberation.
Graves, R.   Bank Account.
  Bweteen Hyssop and Axe.
  Meeting, The.
  Second-Fated, The.
Guillén, J.   Death, from a Distance.
Gurney, I.   Ballad of the Three Spectres.
  Generations.
  Old Dreams.
  What Evil Coil.
Hafiz [or Hafez].   Epitaph: "Bethink, poor heart,
  what bitter kind of jest."
HaNagid.   Flutter or Rest.
  War with Yadir, The.
Hardy, T.   Destined Pair, The.
  Hap.
  Last Love-Word.
  Man Was Drawing Near to Me, A.
  Mismet.
  Turnip-Hoer, The.
Herrick.   Change Common to All.
  Doomes-Day.
  End Decreed, An.
  Good Luck Not Lasting.
  Lots to Be Liked.
  Man's Dying-Place Uncertain.
  On Fortune.
  Parcæ, The; or, Three Dainty Destinies: The
    Armilet.
  Suffer Thou that Canst not Shift.
  Three Fatal[l] Sisters.
  To the Fever, Not To Trouble Julia.
Housman.   Along the field as we came by.
  As I gird on for fighting.
  Ask me no more, for fear I should reply.
  I promise nothing: friends will part.
  I to my perils.
  Now dreary dawns the eastern light.
  Young is the blood that yonder.
Hughes, L.   Bad Luck Card.
Jackson, L.   Fates and the Mothers, The.
Jarrell, R.   Widow's Song, The.
Johnson, S.   Vanity of Human Wishes, The.
Keats.   Endymion: A Poetic Romance.
Khayyám, O.   On two days it steads not to run
  from thy grave.
Kipling, R.   Answer, The.
  Gertrude's Prayer.
Komunyakaa.   Black String of Days.
Kunitz, S.   Approach to Thebes, The.
Lawrence, D. H.   Destiny.
Levine, P.   Salts and Oils.
MacNeice.   Birthright.
Maritain.   Glove, The.
Marvell.   Definition of Love, The.
McGrath, T.   Political Song for the Year's End.
Melville, H.   Apathy and Enthusiasm.
  Camoëns.
  Haglets, The.
  Immolated.
Meredith, G.   Karl Onyx.
  What makes it hard to understand.
  Will Whistle.
  World is full of different fates, The.
Meredith, W.   Consequences.
Merwin.   Fate.
Millay, E.   Buck in the Snow, The.
Milosz, C.   Aleksander Wat's Tie.
  Capri.
  Kazia.
Montale.   Above the scribbled wall.
  Flux.
  House by the Sea.
Moore, M.   Those Various Scalpels.
Nash, O.   Necessary Dirge, A.
Nemerov.   Sunderland.
Neruda.   Sitting Down.
Orr, G.   On the Lawn at Ira's.
Owen, W.   Fates, The.
  O World of Many Worlds.
  This is the Track.

Parker, D.   Temptress, The.
Patchen.   And He Had Wilder Moments.
  These Unreturning Destinies.
Poe.   To ———: "I heed not that my earthly
  lot."
Pound, E.   Arides.
Raine, K.   Fateless Ones, The.
  Lachesis.
Riley, J.   At Bay.
  Because.
Ritsos.   Orestes.
Robinson, E.   Eros Turannos.
Roethke.   Waking, The.
Rukeyser, M.   Beast in View.
  Game of Ball, A.
Sandburg, C.   Chamfort.
  Fate.
  Fight
  Mamie.
  On the Way.
  Scriptsmith.
  Sky Pieces.
  Three Fragments for Fishers of Destiny.
  Webs.
Sarton, M.   At Delphi.
Shapiro, K.   Auto Wreck.
Shelley, P.   Fragment: "And that I walk thus
  proudly crowned withal."
Shirley, J.   Love's Hue and Cry.
Simic.   Tomb of Stéphane Mallarmé, The.
Smith, S.   From the Greek.
Stafford, W.   Key of C— an interlude for
  Marvin.
Szymborska, W.   In Abundance.
Tomlinson, C.   Impalpabilities, The.
Weiss, T.   Another and Another and.
Wilbur, R.   Good Servant, The.
  Marginalia.
  Under Cygnus.
Williams, C. K.   Even If I Could.
Williams, M.   Believing in Symbols.
  Getting the Message.
Wyatt, S.   For shamefast harm of great and
  hateful need.
Yeats.   Leda and the Swan.
Zaturenska.   Siren Music.

See also **Chance; Fortune**

Fathers
Ai.   Cockfighter's Daughter, The.
Amichai [or Amikhai].   Anniversary of My
  Father's Death, The.
  Arab Shepherd Seeks a Kid on Mount Zion, A.
  Autobiography in the Year 1952.
  I am the figure of a Jewish father with a sack on
    his back, returning.
  I Guard the Children.
  Letter of Recommendation, A.
  My Father in a White Space Suit.
  My Father on Passover Eve.
  My Father's Death.
  My son, the softness of your face already
    shows.
  My son was born in Asuta hopital and since
    then.
  Song of Lies on Sabbath Eve, A.
  Yom Kippur.
  Your Life and Death, Father.
Ammons.   Father.
Angelou.   Amoebaean for Daddy.
Ashbery, J.   Boy, A.
Atwood.   Bedside.
Beckett, S.   Ainsi a-t-on beau.
Berry, W.   Elegy: "All day our eyes could find
  no resting place."
  Gathering, The.
Berryman.   Scholars at the Orchid Pavilion.
Bly, R.   Finding the Father.
  My Father's Wedding.
Borges.   Rain.
  To My Father.
Bradstreet, A.   To Her Father, with Some Verses.
  To Her Most Honored Father Thomas Dudley,
    Esquire, These Humbly Presented.
  To the Memory of My Dear and Ever Honored
    Father Thomas Dudley Esq.
Broumas, O.   Body.

  Easter.
  Host.
  On Earth.
  Périsprit.
Browning, E.   Romance of the Ganges, A.
  Romaunt of Margret, The.
Bukowski.   I Was Born to Hustle Roses Down
  the Avenues of the Dead.
  My Old Man.
Burns, R.   For the Author's Father.
Byron, G.   To My Son.
  What Matter the Pangs of a Husband and
    Father.
Carruth, H.   Little Fire in the Woods, The.
  My Father's Face.
  Of Brook and Stone.
Carver, R.   Bobber.
  Five O'Clock in the Morning.
  Kitchen, The.
  Meadow, The.
  My Dad's Wallet.
  Photograph of My Father in His Twenty-second
    Year.
  Trestle, The.
Chuang Tzu.   When a Hideous Man.
Ciardi, J.   Dear Sir.
  Elegy 2: "I dream awake in the uptown
    morning."
  Elegy 3, Cavalcante.
  Elegy: For You, Father.
  Elegy: "My father was born with a spade in his
    hand and traded it."
  Epithalamium at St. Michael's Cemetary.
  For Myra, John L., and Benn.
  It Took Four Flowerboats to Convoy My
    Father's Black.
  My Father Died Imperfect as a Man.
  My Father's Watch.
  Thursday.
  Tree Trimming.
Clampitt.   Beethoven, Opus 111.
Coleridge, S.   Exchange, The.
  Sonnet Composed on a Journey Homeward.
  Sonnet on Receiving a Letter Informing Me of
    the Birth of a Son.
  To the Rev. George Coleridge.
Collins, B.   Death of the Hat, The.
  Where I Live.
Cooper, J.   What the Seer Said.
Corbett, W.   Bridgeport Station.
  Quartet.
Creeley.   Fragment, A: "On the street I am met
  with constant hostility."
  Memory, 1930.
  Province, The.
  Variation, A.
Cullen, C.   Lines to My Father.
Cummings, E. E.   My Father Moved Through
  Dooms Of Love.
Davie, D.   Barnsley, 1966.
  Bella & Rosa.
  Father, the Cavalier.
  Fatherhood.
  My Father's Honour.
  Obiter Dicta.
  Our Father.
  Staffordshire.
Davitt.   Mirror, The.
Dickey, J.   Bee, The.
  Daughter.
  Fathers and Sons.
  Hospital Window, The.
Dickinson, E.   Home itself is far from home.
  I dream about father every night.
Dove, R.   Anti-Father.
  Father out Walking on the Lawn, A.
  Grape Sherbet.
  My Father's Telescope.
  Taking in Wash.
Drummond de Andrade.   Infancy.
  Table, The.
  Travelling in the Family.
Dubie.   About Infinity.
  Depth of Field, A.
  Night before Thanksgiving, The.
Dugan, A.   Coat of Arms.

Elegy: "I know but will not tell."
For Euthanasia and Pain-Killing Drugs.
On the Long Island Railroad System.
Portrait.
Dunbar, P.   Little Brown Baby.
Eberhart, R.   At Night.
Orchard.
Gallagher, T.   3 A.M. Kitchen: My Father
    Talking.
Black Money.
Boat Ride.
Even Now You Are Leaving.
Ginsberg, A.   Don't Grow Old.
Glück, L.   Departure.
Metamorphosis.
Mythic Fragment.
Gunn, T.   From an Asian Tent.
Hacker, M.   For Elektra.
Hall, D.   Day I Was Older, The.
Fathers and Sons.
Match.
Merle Bascom's .22.
White Apples.
Hamill, S.   Dead Letter.
Natural History.
HaNagid.   Did Your Father Leave You Glory.
Hardy, T.   After the Burial.
Forbidden Banns, The.
Her Father.
On the Doorstep.
To My Father's Violin.
Whipper-In, The.
Hayden, R.   Those Winter Sundays.
Heaney, S.   Digging.
Follower.
Man and Boy.
Seeing Things.
Strand, The.
Trial Runs.
Herrick.   To the Reverend Shade of His
    Religious Father.
Upon Dundrige.
Hopkins, G.   By Mrs. Hopley.
Hughes, L.   Cross.
Mama and Daughter.
Hughes, T.   Being Christlike.
Black Coat.
Dust As We Are.
Last of the 1st/5th Lancashire Fusiliers, The.
Out.
Ignatow, D.   1905.
Complex, The.
Envoi: "Strange judgment upon me."
Epitaph: "There were no hidden motives to his
    life."
Europe and America.
Father.
Father and Son.
For My Daughter.
Future, The.
His Name.
Lost Childhood.
Puzzle, The.
Requiem, A: "My father, listening to music,
    that's me."
Rightful One, The.
Stranger.
Jackson, L.   Lullaby, The.
Jacobsen, J.   Daughter to Archeologist.
Jonson, B.   Epigram on William, Lord
    Burl[eigh], An.
On My First Son[ne].
Kinnell.   Man in the Chair, The.
Kinsella, T.   Death Bed.
Messenger, The.
Kizer, C.   Antique Father.
My Good Father.
Thrall.
Komunyakaa.   Banking Potatoes.
Deck, The.
Moonshine.
My Father's Love Letters [or Loveletters].
Songs for My Father.
Whistle, The.
Kumin, M.   Appetite.
Hundred Nights, A.

Introducing the Fathers.
Life's Work.
My Father's Neckties.
Pawnbroker, The.
Kunitz, S.   Father and Son.
Journal for My Daughter.
Laughlin, J.   Asmodeus.
Ave Atque Vale.
Generations, The.
On learning that he was about.
Parable, A.
Step on His Head.
Lawrence, D. H.   Question.
Young Fathers.
Levertov.   Chill, The.
Split Mind, The.
Wings in the Pedlar's Pack.
Levine, P.   1933.
Face, The.
My Son and I.
Starlight.
Logan, J.   Ah, so our first load of honey heavy
    Christmas trees.
Coming of Age.
Day in the Sun, A.
Far off the road on the left on a slight rolling
    hill.
I did but taste a little of the honey with the.
If the half moon stamp of a sacred hoof showed
    Cadmus.
In my dream I know I see my father Saul a
    king.
Letter to a Young Father in Exile.
Letter to My Son.
Lines for His Son in Satin.
Lines to His Son on Reaching Adolescence.
Monologues of the Son of Saul.
My Daughter's Wedding.
Poem for My Son.
Logue, C.   For My Father.
Lorde.   Father Son and Holy Ghost.
Love Poem.
Lowell, R.   Commander Lowell.
Father.
Father in a Dream.
Father's Bedroom.
Home After Three Months Away.
Middle Age.
Terminal Days at Beverly Farms.
Lux.   For My Daughter When She Can Read.
Milkman and His Son, The.
Upon Seeing An Ultrasound Photo of an
    Unborn Child.
MacDiarmid, H.   At My Father's Grave.
MacNeice.   Strand, The.
Truisms, The.
Woods.
Mahon.   Yaddo Letter, The.
McGrath, T.   Afternoon of a McGrath.
Offering.
Poem: "My little son comes running with open
    arms!"
Meredith, G.   Doe: A Fragment, The.
Periander.
Meredith, W.   For His Father.
Merrill, J.   Scenes of Childhood.
Merwin.   Houses, The.
Oars, The.
Son.
Strawberries.
Sunset Water.
Waving of a Hand, The.
Who It Is.
Yesterday.
Michelangelo Buonarroti.   Already burdened
    with a heavy heart.
Milton.   To My Father.
Montale.   Mediterranean.
Voice That Came with the Coots.
Moore, M.   Silence.
Muldoon, P.   Cherish the Ladies.
Coney, The.
Immram.
Immrama.
Skeffington's Daughter.
Waking Father, The.

Wishbone, The.
Nash, O.   Ask Daddy, He Won't Know.
Good Parent's Garden of Vision, A.
In Which the Poet Is Ashamed but Pleased.
My Daddy.
My Trip Daorba.
Please Leave Father Alone.
Soliloquy in Circles.
Niedecker.   Death of my poor father, The.
He lived—childhood summers.
Museum man!, The.
My father said "I remember."
Your father to me in your eighth summer.
Olson, C.   Fathers, The.
Grandfather-Father Poem, The.
I saw, from under Him, the beginning.
Sit by the Window and Refuse.
Oppen.   Bronx Zoo.
From a Photograph.
Orr, G.   Excavation, The.
Fast, The.
Father's Song.
If There's a God.
Talk, The.
To My Father, Dying.
Paley, G.   Autumn.
My Father at 85.
My Father at 89.
My Father Said.
On Mother's Day.
One Day.
Patchen.   Autobiographical Note.
Worn on the.
Pinkerton, H.   Elegy at Beaverhead County,
    Montana.
Return, The.
Pinsky.   To My Father.
Plath.   Colossus, The.
Daddy.
Electra on Azalea Path.
Lament: "Sting of bees took away my father,
    The."
Little Fugue.
On the Decline of Oracles.
Prunty.   Covined Bird, The.
Hand-me-down, The.
Reading Before We Read, Horoscope and
    Weather.
Saying it Back.
Tent, The.
Raine, K.   My Father's Birthday.
Ramanujan.   Excerpts from a Father's Wisdom.
Obituary.
Self-Portrait.
Son to Father to Son.
Rexroth, K.   Mary and the Seasons.
Proust's Madeleine.
Rich, A.   After Dark.
Riley, J.   Michael Flynn and the Baby.
Pap's Old Sayin'
Them Old Cheery Words.
Rilke.   From Father to Son.
Ritsos.   Philoctetes; The Ultimate Mask.
Roethke.   Elegy for Jane.
My Papa's Waltz.
Premonition, The.
Reminder, The.
Rossetti, C.   Prodigal Son, A.
Rukeyser, M.   Ms. Lot.
Rumi.   Humble living does not diminish. It fills.
Sandburg, C.   Boy and Father.
Two Women and Their Fathers.
Sarton, M.   Celebration for George Sarton, A.
My Father's Death.
Sexton.   All My Pretty Ones.
And One for My Dame.
Boat, The.
"Daddy" Warbucks.
Death of the Fathers, The.
Divorce, Thy Name Is Woman.
How We Danced.
Moss of His Skin, The.
Oysters.
Santa.
Simic.   Closed House.
Inheritance.

Navigator.
Poem: "My father writes all day, all night."
Smith, S.   Correspondence between Mr.
  Harrison in Newcastle and Mr. Sholto Peach
  Harrison in Hull.
Father for a Fool, A.
Fuite d'Enfance.
Unser Vater.
Spender, S.   Public Son of a Public Man, The.
Stafford, W.   Circle of Breath.
Fall Journey.
Farewell, Age Ten, A.
Father and Son.
Father's Voice.
Listening.
My Father: October 1942.
Parentage.
Rescued Year, The.
Swerve, The.
Thanksgiving for My Father, A.
Troubleshooting.
Visit Home, A.
With Kit, Age 7, at the Beach.
Stevens, W.   Irish Cliffs of Moher, The.
Stock, R.   Mary on the Death of Joachim.
Stockton, A.   To Richard John Stockton Esqr.
Swenson, M.   Feel Me.
Tate, J.   Lost Pilot, The.
Thomas, D.   Do Not Go Gentle into That Good
  Night.
Do You Not Father Me.
My World Is Pyramid.
Tomlinson, C.   Poem for My Father.
Tu Fu.   My Home Town.
Updike.   How to Be Uncle Sam.
Van Duyn.   Letters from a Father.
Walcott.   Letter from Brooklyn, A.
Walker, A.   Forgive Me If My Praises.
Good Night, Willie Lee, I'll See You in the
  Morning.
Poem at Thirty-nine.
Warren, R.   Doubleness in Time.
Mortmain.
Night Walking.
Reading Late at Night, Thermometer Falling.
Ways of Day.
Weiss, T.   Death of Fathers, The.
Medium, The.
Whalen, P.   For My Father.
Whitman, W.   Dirge for Two Veterans.
Williams, C. K.   Child Psychology.
Easter.
Fifteen.
Instinct.
Sorrow, The.
Williams, T.   Cortege.
Williams, W.   Invitation.
To a Friend.
Wordsworth, W.   Anecdote for Fathers.
Childless Father, The.
Fragment: "For let the impediment be what it
  may."
Wright, J.   Evening.
Father.
First Principles.
Having Lost My Sons, I Confront the Wreckage
  of the Moon: Christmas, 1960.
Non-Birthday Poem for My Father, A.
Revelation, The.
Two Postures beside a Fire.
Youth.
Yeats.   Father and Child.
Zukofsky, L.   Head Lines.

Fathers-in-Law
Ciardi, J.   Censorship.
Corbett, W.   My Father-in-Law's Coat.

Fatigue
Amichai [or Amikhai].   Great Fatigue.
See also **Weariness**

Faults
Beckett, S.   Ce qu'a de pis.
Cavafy.   Death of a General.
Herrick.   In the Dark None Dainty.
No Fault in Women.
To the Generous Reader.
Larkin, P.   This Be The Verse.

Rossetti, C.   Sinner's own fault? So it was, The.
Williams, C. K.   Blame.

Fauns
Eberhart, R.   Reading Room, The New York
  Public Library.
Rimbaud, A.   Faun's Head.
Szymborska, W.   Thomas Mann.
Wilde, O.   In the Forest.

Faust
Ashbery, J.   Faust.
Crane, H.   For the Marriage of Faustus and
  Helen.
Gunn, T.   Faustus Triumphant.
Hill, G.   Doctor Faustus.
Jarrell, R.   Conversation with the Devil, A.
Sexton.   Faustus and I.
Shapiro, K.   Progress of Faust, The.

Fawkes, Guy
Crashaw.   On the Gunpowder-Treason.
Upon the Gunpowder Treason.
Jonson, B.   To William, Lord Mounteagle.
Milton.   On the Gunpowder Plot.

Fear
Amichai [or Amikhai].   Poem for Arbor Day.
Angelou.   Life Doesn't Frighten Me.
Armantrout.   Xenophobia.
Ashbery, J.   Young Son, The.
Atwood.   Highest Altitude.
Auden.   Leap Before You Look.
Never Stronger.
Baudelaire.   Lid, The.
Beckett, S.   En face.
Berry, W.   Creation Myth.
Fear of Love, The.
Berryman.   Conversation.
Defensio in Extremis.
Despair.
Letter to His Brother.
Song of the Bridegroom, The.
Bierce.   Judex Jocosus.
Bogan, L.   Frightened Man, The.
Borges.   Mirror, The.
Mirrors.
Browning, R.   Cardinal and the Dog, The.
Prospice.
Bukowski.   Guru.
Burns, R.   Cares o' love are sweeter far, The.
On the Seas and Far Away.
Prayer, in the Prospect of Death, A.
Song—(On Chloris Being Ill).
Stanzas on the Same Occasion [in the Prospect
  of Death].
To a Mouse; On Turning Her up in Her Nest.
Carver, R.   Conspirators.
Fear.
Not Far from Here.
River, The.
Sparrow Nights.
Threat.
Cavalcanti.   I fear from my misfortune.
My soul is wildly terrified.
Clampitt.   Nereids of Seriphos, The.
Codrescu.   Fear.
Coleridge, S.   Lines Suggested by the Last
  Words of Berengarius.
Corbett, W.   Nine Lives.
Crane, H.   Fear.
Crane, S.   Blustering god, / Stamping across the
  sky.
Man feared that he might find an assassin, A.
There was a great cathedral.
Creeley.   Box.
Dimensions.
For Fear.
Form of Women, A.
Hart Crane.
Hero, The.
I Am Held by My Fear of Death.
Knokke.
Sleep.
That day / in an oak tree—.
Tiger, The.
Window, The.
Cuadra, P.   World Is a Round Earthenware Plate,
  The.
Cummings, E. E.   Breathe with me this fear.

Even a pencil has fear to.
Right here the other night something.
This fear is no longer dear. You are not going to
  America and.
Who's most afraid of death? thou.
Davie, D.   Herefordshire.
His Themes.
De la Mare.   Fear.
I Sit Alone.
Reflections.
Tom's Angel.
Dickey, J.   Sheep Child, The.
Dickinson, E.   Danger is not at first.
Did you ever stand in a Cavern's Mouth.
Fear—like Dying, dilates trust.
I lived on Dread.
Peril as a Possession.
Snake, The.
There lurked a dread that you had gone.
While we were fearing it, it came.
Dove, R.   Motherhood.
Nightmare.
Dunbar, P.   Boogah Man, The.
Lullaby: "Kiver up yo' haid, my little lady,"
Eberhart, R.   Child, The.
New England Bachelor, A.
Scarf of June, The.
What Gives.
Emerson, R.   Bluebeard. Let the gentle wife
  prepare.
Leave me, Fear! thy throbs are base.
Teach me your mood, O patient stars!
When Jane was absent Edgar's eye.
Why fear to die.
Enzensberger, H.   Delete the Inapplicable.
Ferlinghetti, L.   Elegy on the Death of Kenneth
  Patchen, An.
Frost, R.   Assurance.
Fear of Man, The.
Fear, The.
Storm Fear.
Ginsberg, A.   Please Open the Window and Let
  Me In.
You Might Get in Trouble.
Glück, L.   12. 6. 71.
Garden, The.
Gretel in Darkness.
Graves, R.   Dreaming Children.
Frightened Men.
Straw, The.
Sun-Face and Moon-Face.
That Was the Night.
Tolling Bell.
Gunn, T.   Man With Night Sweats, The.
Memory Unsettled.
Secret Sharer, The.
Stealer, The.
Without a Counterpart.
"H. D."   I Said.
Hacker, M.   After the Revolution.
Gerda in the Aerie.
Hall, D.   "Scream, The."
Han-shan.   At sunset I went down the western
  slope.
HaNagid.   You Felt the Fear of Death.
Hardy, T.   January Night, A.
Plena Timoris.
To an Unborn Pauper Child.
Hayden, R.   Soledad.
Herrick.   Charm, A.
Empires.
Feare.
First Marrs or Makes, The.
Gods Mirth, Mans Mourning.
No Bashfulnesse in Begging.
No Danger to Men Desperate.
On Himselfe.
Reverence.
Ship-Wrack.
To His Muse, Another to the Same.
Upon Grubs.
Hughes, L.   Afraid.
Hughes, T.   Reckless Head.
Ignatow, D.   Going Down.
Jackson, L.   Earth.
Modern Superstition.

Jacobsen, J.   Arrival.
  Let Each Man Remember.
Jarrell, R.   Bird of Night, The.
  Fear.
  Prince, The.
Jeffers, R.   Nerves.
Jonson, B.   Of Death.
  To Fine Lady Would-Be.
Keats.   When I Have Fears [That I May Cease
  to Be].
Kipling, R.   That Day.
Komunyakaa.   Tour Guide.
  Venus's-flytraps.
Larkin, P.   Is It Now Or For Always.
Laughlin, J.   Deathfear.
  Frightened Bird, The.
Lawrence, D. H.   At the Front.
  Doe at Evening, A.
  Don't Look at Me.
  Humiliation.
  Kissing and Horrid Strife.
  Late at Night.
  People Who Care.
  Sickness.
  Snake.
  Song of a Man Who Has Come Through.
  Walk Warily.
  Why Does She Weep?
Levertov.   Age of Terror.
  Clouds.
  Sound of Fear, A.
  Talk in the Dark.
  Who Is at My Window.
Levi, P.   Crow's Song 2, The.
  There Were a Hundred.
Lorde.   Blackstudies.
  Generation II.
Lux.   At Least Let Me Explain.
  Cellar Stairs.
MacDiarmid, H.   Two Memories.
MacLeish.   What the Old Women Say.
MacNeice.   Heated Minutes, The.
  Intimations of Mortality.
Martial.   Out of Martiall.
McGrath, T.   Legendary Progress.
  Revisionist Poem: Machado.
Meredith, W.   Fear of Beasts, The.
  Freezing.
  Nausea.
  Original Aversions.
Merrill, J.   Days of 1941 and '44.
Merton.   Lament for Javier Heraud.
Merwin.   Apparition.
  Fear.
Michelangelo Buonarroti.   My soul without a
  friend, without a guide.
Millay, E.   Intense and terrible, I think, must be
  the loneliness.
Milosz, C.   Fear-Dream (1918).
Mistral, G.   Vigilant Woman, The.
Oliver, M.   Lightning.
Olson, C.   As though there were no flowing.
  Story of an Olson, and Bad Thing, The.
  Tanto e Amara.
  Translation, A.
Orr, G.   Hats, The.
  October.
Owen, W.   Next War, The.
  On My Songs.
  Storm.
Patchen.   Dazzling Burden, The.
  Poor Gorrel.
  Question Is, Who Is Afraid of What, The?
  Radiance in a Dark Wood, The.
  Rising a Little.
Petrarch.   Such is the fear those eyes strike into
  me.
Piercy.   Rape Poem.
Pinsky.   Woman, A.
Plath.   Pursuit.
Pope, A.   Epistle to Dr. Arbuthnot.
Ralegh, S.   On the Snuff of a Candle.
Ramanujan.   Entries for a Catalogue of Fears.
  Fear.
  Snakes.
Ransom, J.   Parting at Dawn.

Rexroth, K.   Motto on the Sundial, The.
Riley, J.   In the Night.
Ritsos.   Deadly Victory.
  Inevitably.
Robinson, E.   Avon's Harvest.
  Eros Turannos.
Roethke.   Against Disaster.
  Lull.
  Plaint.
Rossetti, C.   All beneath the sun hasteth, / All
  that hath begun wasteth.
  Care flieth, / Hope and fear together.
  Dead City, The.
  Earth Shall Tremble at the Look of Him, The.
  Everything that is born must die.
  Fisher-Wife, A.
  Goodbye in fear, goodbye in sorrow.
  Hope is the counterpoise of fear / While night
    enthrals us here.
  I Am Small and of No Reputation.
  Last Answer, The.
  Lord, I am here.—But, child, I look for thee.
  On the note you do not send me.
  Perfect Love Casteth Out Fear.
  Will These Hands Ne'er Be Clean?
  Ye Are Come unto Mount Sion.
Rukeyser, M.   Another Day (Child among his
  powers).
  Before Danger.
  His gay words, words of delight.
  Motive of All of It, The.
Rumi.   Craftsmanship and Emptiness.
  Don't let your throat tighten.
  Keep walking, though there's no place to get to.
Sandburg, C.   Chamfort.
Sexton.   Imitations of Drowning.
Shelley, P.   Fragment: Sufficient Unto the Day.
  Love, Hope, Desire and Fear.
  To ——: "I fear thy kisses, gentle maiden."
Simic.   Fear.
  Old Couple.
  Shortcut.
Smith, S.   Blood Flows Back, The.
  Voices about the Princess Anemone.
  Word, The.
Stafford, W.   In Fear and Valor.
  Parentage.
Stock, R.   Certain Pretexts.
  Lullaby for Now.
Tate, A.   Ode to Fear.
Updike.   Conversation.
Vallejo.   White Rose.
Walcott.   God Rest Ye Merry, Gentlemen.
Walker, A.   Old Warrior Terror, The.
  Threatened.
Warren, R.   Midnight Outcry.
  Variation: Ode to Fear.
Whittier.   Song of Slaves in the Desert.
Wilbur, R.   Peace of Cities, The.
Williams, C. K.   Bishop Tutu's Visit to the
  White House: 1984.
  Body, The.
  Dream, The.
  Patience Is When You Stop Waiting.
  Shells.
  Thirst.
  Vehicle: Conscience.
  Vehicle: Violence.
Williams, M.   Being Here.
  On the Way Home From Nowhere, New Year's
    Eve.
Williams, W.   Cure, The.
  Light Shall Not Enter.
  Misericordia.
Wordsworth, W.   Western clouds a deepening
  gloom display, The.
Wright, J.   Christmas Greeting, A.
  Fear Is What Quickens Me.
  I Was Afraid of Dying.
  In Terror of Hospital Bills.
  Lights in the Hallway, The.
Wyatt, S.   Driving to desire, adread also to dare.
  It may be good like it who list.
  Long love that in my thought doth harbo[u]r,
    The.
Yeats.   Presences.

  To His Heart, Bidding It Have No Fear.
  Who Goes with Fergus?
Feasts and Feasting
Browning, R.   Founder of the Feast, The.
  Gerousios Oinos.
Carew, T.   Upon a Mole in Celia's Bosom.
Carver, R.   Commerce.
Ciardi, J.   Barmecide Feast.
De la Mare.   Fool's Song, The.
Dunbar, P.   Back-Log Song, A.
Glück, L.   Thanksgiving.
Hall, D.   Eating the Pig.
Herrick.   Ceremonies for Christmas[se].
  Good Manners at Meat.
  Invitation, The.
MacGowran.   Description of an Irish Feast, The.
MacNeice.   This Is the Life.
Meredith, G.   Fusion.
  Tuck! Tuck! Once you would flatter me.
Muldoon, P.   Marriage of Strongbow and Aoife,
  The.
Nash, O.   Private Dining Room, The.
Rumi.   Breadmaking.
  Song about a Donkey, A.
Sheridan, T.   I Send This at Nine.
  Invitation, The.
  Invitation to Dinner, from Doctor Sheridan to
    Doctor Swift, An.
Swift, J.   Description of an Irish Feast, The.
Very.   Feast, The.
Whalen, P.   Raging Desire & c.
Wilbur, R.   Wedding Toast, A.
Williams, T.   Modus Vivendi.

February
Ammons.   February Beach.
Dickinson, E.   How luscious is the dripping.
  White as an Indian Pipe.
Gurney, I.   February Dawn.
Jacobsen, J.   February Midnight.
Kinsella, T.   Mirror in February.
Kumin, M.   February.
Levine, P.   Saturday Sweeping.
Paley, G.   In Montpelier, Vermont.
Sandburg, C.   Potomac Town in February.
Schuyler, J.   February.
  Thinness.
Simic.   February.

Federal Bureau of Investigation
Ai.   Hoover, Edgar J.

Feebleness
Herrick.   Crutches.
Olson, C.   This Man's Weakness Is Straw.
Rossetti, C.   Thy fainting spouse, yet still Thy
  spouse.

Feet
Ammons.   Foot-Washing, The.
Burns, R.   O Mally's Meek, Mally's Sweet.
Carver, R.   Toes, The.
Ciardi, J.   Washing Your Feet.
Dugan, A.   Barefoot Homiletics, after
  Wittgenstein and Boswell.
Herrick.   To Dianeme.
  Upon Her Feet.
  Upon Pimpe.
  Upon Smeaton.
Jacobsen, J.   Limbo Dancer, The.
Kumin, M.   Pawnbroker, The.
Logan, J.   Eight Poems on Portraits of the Foot.
Logue, C.   Middle-aged man is approaching an
  all-night lavatory, A.
Merwin.   Surf-Casting.
Pagis.   Real-Life Story.
Riley, J.   Charms.
Sexton.   Barefoot.
Stafford, W.   Freedom of Expression.
Warren, R.   Shoes In Rain Jungle.
Whittier.   Barefoot Boy, The.
Williams, W.   Overture to a Dance of
  Locomotives.
  Poem: "As the cat."
See also **Toes**
Fellowship
See **Brotherhood**

Feminism and Feminists
Armantrout. Birthmark: The Pretext.
Broumas, O. Banner.
  Cinderella.
  Circe.
Bukowski. Beginning, A.
  Some of My Readers.
Ciardi, J. On Meeting Miss B.
Clampitt. Seed.
Clifton, L. Wishes for Sons.
Gallagher, T. Conversation with a Fireman from
  Brooklyn.
Hacker, M. Ballad of Ladies Lost and Found.
  Graffiti from the Gare Saint-Manqué.
Kizer, C. Union of Women.
Lawrence, D. H. It's No Good!
Levertov. Hypocrite Women.
Meredith, G. Ballad of Fair Ladies in Revolt, A.
Millay, E. To Inez Milholland.
Nash, O. Don't Grin, or You'll Have to Bear It.
Oliver, M. Strawberry Moon.
Parker, D. Song of Perfect Propriety.
Rich, A. Final Notations.
  Natural Resources.
  Ninth Symphony of Beethoven Understood at
  Last as a Sexual Message, The.
  Snapshots of a Daughter-in-Law.
  Translations.
Rukeyser, M. Myth.
Swenson, M. Daffodildo.
Ward, N. Mercury shew'd Apollo, Bartas Book.

Fences
Blue Cloud. Old man's lazy, The.
Clampitt. Woodlot, The.
Dickey, J. Fence Wire.
Eberhart, R. Spite Fence.
Frost, R. Mending Wall.
Larkin, P. Wires.
Merwin. Road.
Sandburg, C. Fence, A.
Snyder, G. Fence Posts.
Tomlinson, C. Snow Fences, The.
See also **Walls**

Fencing and Fencers
Jonson, B. Epigram. To William, Earl of
  Newcastle, An.
Pound, E. For E. McC ("Gone while your tastes
  were keen to you").

Fenians
Meredith, G. Her trousers are red; she wears a
  coatee.

Ferns
Ammons. Lines.
Clampitt. Waterfall, The.
Eberhart, R. Velvet Rocks.
Hughes, T. Fern.
MacDiarmid, H. Bracken Hills in Autumn.
Milosz, C. Large finger-like leaves of an
  Hawaiian fern.
Schuyler, J. What Ails My Fern?
Whittier. Sweet Fern.
Wilbur, R. Fern-Beds in Hampshire County.

Ferry Boats
Davie, D. House-martin.
Housman. Crossing Alone the Nighted Ferry.
Lorde. Trip on the Staten Island Ferry, A.
Millay, E. Recuerdo.
Rossetti, C. Charon.
  Ferry Me across the Water.
Sexton. Letter Written on a Ferry While
  Crossing Long Island Sound.
Tomlinson, C. Crossing Brooklyn Ferry.
Whitman, W. Crossing Brooklyn Ferry.

Festivals
Cavafy. Sam el Nesim.
Faiz. Bangla Desh: 1.
Ginsberg, A. Kral Majales.
Hamill, S. Two Poems for Tanabata Matsuri.
Herrick. Quintell, The.
Merton. La Comparsa en Oriente.
Tomlinson, C. Harvest Festival: at Ozleworth.
  Matachines, The.
  Portobello Carnival 1973.

Feuds
García Lorca. Feud, The.
Hill, G. Florentines.
Kipling, R. Jubal and Tubal Cain.
Wordsworth, W. Brownie, The.

Fever
Burns, R. Scroggam.
Clampitt. Curfew, A.
Dickinson, E. These Fevered Days—to take
  them to the Forest.
Dubie. Fever.
  Old Woman's Vision, An.
Emerson, R. Things oft miscalling, as the hen-.
Gunn, T. Fever.
McHugh, H. Window: Thing as Participle.
Montale. Stanzas: "I'm searching vainly for the
  point the blood."
Plath. Fever 103°.
Ramanujan. In March.
Rukeyser, M. Girl at the Play.
Stafford, W. 1932.
Stock, R. Calentures.
Wright, J. How My Fever Left.

Fiddles and Fiddlers
Burns, R. Green Sleeves [and Tartan Ties]
  Macpherson's Farewell.
  Rattlin, Roarin Willie.
Dunbar, P. Itching Heels.
  My Sweet Brown Gal.
  Temptation.
Hardy, T. At the Aquatic Sports.
  At the Railway Station, Upway.
  Country Wedding, The.
Kinnell. First Song.
Sandburg, C. Hell on the Wabash.
Yeats. Fiddler of Dooney, The.
See also **Violins**

Fidelity
Auden. Legend.
  Lullaby: "Lay your sleeping head, my love."
Berry, W. Dance, The.
Brontë, E. Visionary, The.
Browning, E. Man's Requirements, A.
Browning, R. Bad Dreams I.
Burns, R. Bonie Bell.
  Godly Girzie.
  Jessie—A New Scots Song.
  Jockey Fou and Jenny Fain.
  Louis, What Reck I by Thee.
  My Collier Laddie.
  O Lay Thy Loof in Mine Lass.
  Open the Door to Me, Oh!
  Red, Red Rose, A.
  When wild War's deadly blast was blawn.
Campion, T. Now let her change and spare not.
  Shall I then hope when faith is fled?
  Thou Joy'st, Fond Boy.
  Why presumes thy pride on that, that must so
  private be.
Carver, R. Summer in Sacramento, A.
Char. Allegiance.
Chaucer. Complaint unto Pity, The.
  Womanly Noblesse.
Cooper, J. Faithful, The.
Cowper, W. Doves, The.
  Tale, A: "In Scotland's realm, where trees are
  few."
  To Delia.
Cullen, C. Street Called Crooked, The.
Cummings, E. E. My youthful lady will have
  other lovers.
  Nothing false and possible is love.
  This man's heart / is true to his.
  True lovers in each happening of their hearts.
Dickinson, E. Fidelity never flickers.
  Guest am I to have.
  He found my Being—set it up.
Donne. Anniversary [*or* Anniversarie], The.
  Indifferent, The.
  Legacy [*or* Legacie], The.
  Lovers' Infiniteness[e].
  Relic, The.
  Valediction, A: of My Name in the Window.

Graves, R. Arrow on the Vane.
  Broken Compact.
  Jus Primae Noctis.
  Poet's Curse, The.
  Song: Basket of Blossom.
  Song: Yesterday Only.
  That Other World.
  Unposted Letter.
Gunn, T. Monster, The.
Hardy, T. Catching Ballet of the Wedding
  Clothes, The.
  Faithful Swallow, The.
  Faithful Wilson.
  Harvest-Supper, The.
  Postponement.
Herrick. Bondman, The.
  Bracelet to Julia, The.
  His Protestation to Perilla.
  Love Me Little, Love Me Long.
  Parting Verse, Or Charge to His Supposed Wife
  When He Travelled, The.
  To Anthea, Who May Command Him Anything.
  To Julia.
Homer. Daughters of Pandarus, The.
  Gardens of Alcinous, The.
  Mindes of men are ever so affected, The.
  Muse, / tell me of this man of wit.
  Sun descending, the *Phæacian* train, The.
Housman. Shake hands, we shall never be
  friends, all's over.
Hughes, L. Faithful One.
Jackson, L. In Due Form.
Jonson, B. Epistle. To Katharine, Lady
  Aubigny.
Kipling, R. Old Song, An.
Kunitz, S. Promise Me.
Lawrence, D. H. Fidelity.
Meredith, G. Kiss, and a clasp, and an eye to
  eye, A.
  Preaching from a Spanish Ballad, A.
  Song: "Love within the lover's breast."
  Swallow came from over the sea, The.
  Think not, should your husband swear.
Millay, E. Modern Declaration.
  To the Not Impossible Him.
Milton. Sonnet 6: "Young, gentle, and candid
  lover that I am."
Parker, D. Somebody's Song.
  Song in a Minor Key.
  Ultimatum.
  War Song.
Petrarch. If I said it, may I be held to scorn.
Poe. Annabel Lee.
Riley, J. False and True.
  Man's Devotion.
Robinson, E. Luke Havergal.
Rossetti, C. Forget Me Not.
  Heart's Chill Between.
  Lisetta all' Amante.
  Meeting.
  That No Man Take Thy Crown.
"Shu Ting." Brother, I Am Here.
  To the Oak.
Spenser, E. Faerie Queene, The.
Van Duyn. Open Letter, Personal.
  Voyeur, The.
Whittier. King Volmer and Elsie.
Williams, M. Husband.
  Pity and Fear.
Wyatt, S. Deem as ye list. Upon good cause.
  Hate whom ye list for I care not.
  Long love that in my thought doth harbo[u]r,
  The.
  Mourning my heart doth sore oppress.
  Pain of all pain, the most grievous pain.
  Quondam was I in my lady's grace.
  Sometime I sigh, sometime I sing.
  Spite of their spite which they in vain.
  Steadfastness.
  What would ye more of me, your slave, require.
  Ye know my heart, my lady dear.
Yeats. Folly of Being Comforted, The.

Fields and Pastures

Ammons. Sap Is Gone Out of the Trees, The.
Berry, W. Stay Home.
Brodsky, J. Autumn in Norenskaia.
Broumas, O. Buenos Días.
Browning, R. Meeting at Night.
  Two in the Campagna.
Carver, R. Fields, The.
Clampitt. Woodlot, The.
Cowper, W. Poplar Field, The.
Crane, H. Alert Pillow, The.
Creeley. Juggler's Thought.
Davie, D. By the Road to Upper Midhope.
  Hill Field, The.
  January.
  March.
De la Mare. English Downs.
  Horse in a Field.
Dickey, J. Farmers.
Duncan, R. Often I Am Permitted to Return to
  a Meadow.
Emerson, R. Know he who tills this lonely
  field.
  Seyd planted where the deluge ploughed.
Frost, R. Cow in Apple Time, The.
  Pasture, The.
  Waiting.
Gunn, T. Aqueduct.
  For Signs.
Hall, D. Great Day in the Cows' House.
  High Pasture, The.
  Swan.
Hardy, T. Spot, A.
Heaney, S. Field Work.
  Land.
Herrick. To Meadows [or Meddowes].
Jarrell, R. Field and Forest.
Levertov. English Field in the Nuclear Age, An.
Marlowe. Passionate Shepherd To His Love,
  The.
Marvell. Mower's Song, The.
McHugh, H. Field, The.
Merwin. In the Night Fields.
  Watchers.
Millay, E. I Dreamed I Moved among the
  Elysian Fields.
Milton. Lycidas.
Olson, C. Dry Ode, The.
  Enniscorthy Suite.
  For a Man Gone to Stuttgart Who Left an
  Automobile Behind Him.
Orr, G. Moment, A.
Plath. In Midas' Country.
Prunty. Grown Men at Touch.
Riley, J. Green Fields and Running Brooks.
Roethke. All the Earth, All the Air.
  Meadow Mouse, The.
Rossetti, C. Green Cornfield, A.
Rukeyser, M. After Their Quarrel.
Sandburg, C. Bitter Summer Thoughts.
  Brown Gold.
  Corn Hut Talk.
  Cornucopia.
  Field People.
  Memoranda.
  You Shall Have Homes.
Sarton, M. Baroque Image.
Thomas, D. I, in My Intricate Image.
Thoreau. On fields oer which the reaper's hand
  has passed.
Wilbur, R. Exeunt.
  Grasshopper, A.
Williams, W. Desolate Field, The.
  Healall.
  Winter Quiet.
Wordsworth, W. Repentance; A Pastoral Ballad.
  Solitary Reaper, The.
Wright, J. I Was Afraid of Dying.
  Late November in a Field.
  To the Evening Star: Central Minnesota.

Fiesole, Italy

Hardy, T. In the Old Theatre, Fiesole.

Fig Trees and Figs

Dove, R. This Life.
Graves, R. Song: Fig Tree in Leaf.
Hall, D. Small Fig Tree, A.
Lawrence, D. H. Bare Fig-trees.
  Figs.
Merwin. Fig Tree, The.
Mistral, G. Fig, The.
Ritsos. Ascent.
Rumi. Empty Garlic, An.
Sarton, M. Fig, The.
Williams, W. Passaic, N.J.

Fights

Ausonius. Upon the Same.
Baudelaire. Mortal Combat.
Bishop, E. Argument.
Bourne, V. Cause Won, The.
Browning, R. Woman's Last Word, A.
Bukowski. 9 Rings.
  35 Seconds.
  225 Pounds.
  My Friend.
  Strange Moment, A.
  Thank God for Alleys.
  Who in the Hell is Tom Jones?
Burns, R. Gude Wallace.
Carver, R. Miracle.
  Suspenders.
Creeley. Broken Back Blues.
Cummings, E. E. Adhuc sub Judice Lis.
  I / (meet)t(touch).
  Spoke joe to jack.
De la Mare. Goliath.
Dugan, A. 2. Comment on "Business Jacob, the
  Angel Wrestler."
Dunbar, P. Rivals, The.
  Trouble in de Kitchen.
  Warrior's Prayer, The.
Eberhart, R. Airman Considers His Power, An.
Graves, R. Hero, The.
Gunn, T. Apartment Cats.
Hafiz [or Hafez]. To the Shah, from Hafiz.
Hardy, T. Fight on Durnover Moor, The.
Herrick. Satan.
Housman. As I gird on for fighting.
Kipling, R. Belts.
  Quest, The.
  Rhyme of the Three Sealers, The.
Kunitz, S. Gladiators, The.
Lawrence, D. H. Battle of Life.
  Repulsed.
  What Would You Fight For?
Lindsay, N. John L. Sullivan, the Strong Boy of
  Boston.
Meredith, W. Couple Overhead, The.
Merton. Ben's Last Fight.
Millay, E. Hearing Your Words, and Not a
  Word Among Them.
Parker, D. They Part.
Piercy. Night Letter.
Ransom, J. Captain Carpenter.
Rich, A. Blue Ghazals, The.
  Implosions.
  On Edges.
Riley, J. Way It Wuz, The.
Rossetti, C. I Have Fought a Good Fight.
Rumi. Ali in Battle.
Sandburg, C. Blue Maroons.
Sheridan, T. His Modest Apology for Knocking
  Out a News-Boy's Teeth.
Smith, S. Mistress Osmosis.
Trakl. Rats, The.
Van Duyn. Outlandish Agon.
Wilbur, R. Giaour and the Pacha, The.
Williams, C. K. Blades.
  I Am the Bitter Name.
  Peace.
  Toil.
Williams, M. Memphis, 2 P.M [or 2:00 P.M.].
Williams, W. Controversy, The.
  Fight, The.
Wright, J. Larry.

Fiji

Ginsberg, A. Bus Ride Ballad Road to Suva.

Filipinos
See **Philippines**
Film
See **Movies**
Financiers

Meredith, G. Capitalist, The.
See also **Banking and Bankers**

Finches

Berry, W. Finches, The.
Hamill, S. Dragon in the Clouds, A.
Oppen. Us.
Wordsworth, W. Green Linnet, The.

Fingers

Dugan, A. On Fingernails in Bloody Times.
Hall, D. Match.
Herrick. Upon the Losse of His Finger.
Ramanujan. Opposable Thumb, The.
Simic. Bestiary for the Fingers of My Right
  Hand.
Stock, R. Lines Upon Delia And to the
  Chevaliers of the Cordon Bleu.

Finland

Hacker, M. Rune of the Finland Woman.
Jacobsen, J. Reindeer and Engine.
Whittier. Conquest of Finland, The.

Fire and Fires

Ammons. Hope's Okay.
  When I Set Fire to the Reed Patch.
Atwood. Two Fires, The.
Berry, W. Autumn Burning, An.
  Supplanting, The.
Bishop, E. Armadillo, The.
  Casabianca.
  Night City.
Bogan, L. Feuer-Nacht.
Bradstreet, A. Here Follows Some Verses upon
  the Burning of Our House.
Byron, G. Darkness.
Carew, T. Song: To Her Again[e], She Burning
  in a Fe[a]ver.
  To My Mistress [or Mistris], I Burning in Love.
Carruth, H. Fat Lady, The.
  In Memoriam.
  My Hut.
Clampitt. Or Consider Prometheus.
Coleridge, S. Nose, The.
Cooper, J. Dream in Which the Routine Quality
  of My Imagination Is Fully Exposed.
Cowper, W. On the Burning of Lord
  Mansfield's Library.
  On the Same.
Creeley. Fire.
  Night Sky, A.
  Saturday Afternoon.
De la Mare. Invocation: "Burning fire shakes in
  the night, The."
  Making a fire.
  Moth, The.
  Vigil.
Dickey, J. Attempted Departure.
  Purgation.
  Walking the Fire Line.
Dickinson, E. Ashes denote that Fire was.
  Dare you see a Soul *at the White Heat?*
  Largest Fire ever known, The.
  You cannot put a Fire out.
Dubie. Baptismal.
  Wedding Party, The.
Dugan, A. Winter for an Untenable Situation.
Dunbar, P. Back-Log Song, A.
  Noddin' by de Fire.
Eberhart, R. Enigma, The.
  Extremity.
  Prometheus.
  Ship Burning and a Comet All in One Day, A.
  Wild Swans of Inverane, The.
Emerson, R. It takes a philosopher or fool.
  Sun is the sole inconsumable fire, The.
  That wandering fire to me appears.
Frost, R. Bonfire, The.
  Fire and Ice.
Gallagher, T. Crêpes Flambeau.
  Death of the Horses by Fire.
Graves, R. Dazzle of Darkness.
  Fire Walker.

Hearth, The.
Song: A Phoenix Flame.
Under the Pot.
Gunn, T.   Faustus Triumphant.
Gurney, I.   Quiet Fireshine.
Varennes.
"H. D."   Sea Violet.
Hall, D.   Coal Fire, The.
Swan.
Han-shan.   Children I implore you.
Fire and smoke raged within.
HaNagid.   What Are These.
Hardy, T.   Wood Fire, The.
Heaney, S.   Leavings.
Tinder.
Herrick.   Another to the Maids.
Hell Fire.
Scar[e]-Fire, The.
Upon Love.
Hughes, L.   Fire.
Fire-Caught.
Hughes, T.   Martyrdom of Bishop Farrar, The.
Notes for a Little Play.
Ignatow, D.   Of That Fire.
Jacobsen, J.   Fire Will Not Change.
Jeffers, R.   Fire.
Fire on the Hills.
Jonson, B.   Execration upon Vulçan, An.
Kinnell.   Another Night in the Ruins.
Olive Wood Fire, The.
Under the Maud Moon.
Kipling, R.   Fires, The.
Komunyakaa.   How I See Things.
You and I Are Disappearing.
Kumin, M.   Longing to Be Saved, The.
Laughlin, J.   At Our House.
Letter to Hitler, A.
Lawrence, D. H.   December Night.
Fire.
Four, The.
Levine, P.   Ashes.
Coming Home, Detroit, 1968.
Miracle, The.
Lindsay, N.   Here's to the Spirit of Fire.
Logan, J.   Pagan Saturday.
Two Poems for Women.
Lorde.   Day They Eulogized Mahalia, The.
Summer Oracle.
Lux.   Barn Fire.
MacNeice.   Brother Fire.
Major, C.   Montalban: Near the Ancient Fort.
McGrath, T.   Coal Fire in Winter, A.
McHugh, H.   Politics.
Meredith, G.   Fireside.
Merrill, J.   After the Fire.
Charles on Fire.
Log.
Mornings in a New House.
Merton.   Elegy for the Monastery Barn.
Merwin.   Burnt Child, The.
Flight, The.
Michelangelo Buonarroti.   Great beauty
scattering its brilliant flame.
If fire can melt down steel and shatter flint.
Only with fire can men at forge and flue.
So fond is fire of the frigid stone it waits.
What wonder that—seeing how, beside your
fire.
With heart of sulphur, flesh of tinder too.
Milosz, C.   On Parting with My Wife, Janina.
Mistral, G.   Christmas Star, The.
Montale.   Your Flight.
Moore, M.   To a Chameleon.
Nash, O.   There Are More Ways to Roast a Pig
than Burning the House Down.
Nemerov.   Flame of a Candle, The.
Marriage of Heaven and Earth, The.
Olson, C.   Here i am, naked.
Li Po.
What Had to Go.
Paley, G.   Woman invented fire and called it, A.
Patchen.   Green Fires, The.
Naked Land, The.
Petrarch.   Alas, I burn, and no one will believe
it.
That fire I liked to think had been extinguished.

There are some creatures in the world with eyes.
Piercy.   Few Ashes for Sunday Morning, A.
I Am A Light You Could Read By.
Noon of the Sunbather.
Shadows of the Burning.
Pinsky.   Shirt.
Plath.   Aftermath.
Burning the Letters.
Firesong.
Prunty.   Pyromaniac, The.
Raine, K.   It is in us they burn.
Six calices yellow gold.
Ramanujan.   Fire.
One More after Reading Homer.
Ransom, J.   Puncture.
Rexroth, K.   Andromeda Chained to Her Rock
the Great Nebula in Her Heart.
Rich, A.   Burning Oneself Out.
Riley, J.   Fire at Night.
Rilke.   Autumn Fire.
Fire's Reflection.
Ritsos.   After the Fire.
Rossetti, C.   Flint.
Love Is Strong as Death.
Stroke a flint, and there is nothing to admire.
Subject To Like Passions as We Are.
Rukeyser, M.   Burning Bush.
For Fun.
Waterlily Fire.
Rumi.   Bonfire at Midnight.
Center of the Fire, The.
Question, The.
Sandburg, C.   Anna Imroth.
Fire Pages.
Impossible Iambics.
Kin.
Seifert.   St George's Basilica.
Sexton.   Fire Thief, The.
Simic.   February.
Smith, S.   Humane Materialist at the Burning of
a Heretic, A.
Persian, The.
Snyder, G.   Burning the Small Dead.
Cool around the Fire, The.
Stafford, W.   Bridge Begins in the Trees, A.
Burning a Book.
Salvaged Parts.
Tillamook Burn, The.
Stock, R.   Again I'm Torched and Wonder What
We've Wrought.
Miracle of the Roses, The.
Swift, J.   On the Burning of Whitehall in 1698.
Sze.   Juniper Fires.
Tomlinson, C.   Fire in a Dark Landscape.
Flame.
Night-Piece: The Near and the Far.
Updike.   Burning Trash.
Song of the Open Fireplace.
Working Outdoors in Winter.
Van Duyn.   Along the Road.
Elementary Attitudes.
Walcott.   City's Death by Fire, A.
Warren, R.   Auto-da-fé.
Vision.
Weiss, T.   Fire at Alexandria, The.
House of Fire.
Into Summer.
Whitman, W.   By the Bivouac's Fitful Flame.
Whittier.   Burning Drift-Wood.
Chicago.
Legend of the Lake, A.
Wilbur, R.   Riddle, A.
Williams, C. K.   Bringing It Home.
Fire.
Hail goes / dancing, The.
It's over now. I watch.
Williams, M.   Newspaper Picture of Spectators
at a Hotel Fire, A.
Williams, T.   Part of a Hero.
Williams, W.   Crude Lament.
Wilner, E.   Zero at the Bone.
Zagajewski.   Fire.
Fire, Fire.
Flame, A.
Zukofsky, L.   Incident, An.

Fire-eaters
Carver, R.   Young Fire Eaters of Mexico City,
The.
Williams, M.   Firebreathers at the Café Deux
Magots, The.
Fire Engines
Wilbur, R.   Fire-Truck, A.
Williams, W.   Great Figure, The.
Firearms
See **Guns**
Firefighters
Gallagher, T.   Conversation with a Fireman from
Brooklyn.
Schuyler, J.   Witley Court.
Williams, C. K.   Fire.
Wright, J.   Red Jacket's Grave.
Fireflies
Dickinson, E.   Winged spark doth soar about, A.
Dubie.   Hour, The.
Frost, R.   Fireflies in the Garden.
Lawrence, D. H.   Fireflies in the Corn.
Levi, P.   Avigliana.
Marvell.   Mower to the Glowworms [*or* Glow-
Worms *or* Glo-Worms], The.
Michelangelo Buonarroti.   Night prevails where
Phoebus—that's our sun, The.
Tomlinson, C.   Fireflies.
On a May Night.
Very.   Fireflies, The.
Weiss, T.   Earthrise.
See also **Glowworms**
Fireworks
Nemerov.   Fourth of July, The.
Rich, A.   Celebration in the Plaza, The.
Sandburg, C.   Fourth of July Night.
Updike.   Fireworks.
First Church of The Millennium
See **Shakers (First Church of The Millennium)**
Fish
Bishop, E.   Fish, The.
Bly, R.   Dried Sturgeon, The.
Bukowski.   Goldfish.
Carruth, H.   When Howitzers Began.
Carver, R.   Current, The.
Eagles.
Sturgeon, The.
Chuang Tzu.   Joy of Fishes, The.
Man Is Born in Tao.
P'eng That Was a K'un, The.
Ciardi, J.   Aquarium.
Lung Fish, The.
Cowper, W.   On the High Price of Fish.
To the Immortal Memory of the Halibut.
Dickey, J.   Eagle's Mile, The.
Movement of Fish, The.
Dickey, W.   Post-Therapy Room.
Donne.   Bait[e], The.
Dove, R.   Fish in the Stone, The.
Dubie.   Fish, The.
Dugan, A.   Criticism of Bergson and Darwin.
Eberhart, R.   Ospreys in Cry.
Ferlinghetti, L.   Hilarious God.
Gray, T.   Ode on the Death of a Favourite [*or*
Favorite] Cat, Drowned in a Tub [*or* Bowl] of
Gold Fishes.
Hughes, T.   Pike.
Ignatow, D.   Fish That Lives at the Bottom, The.
Fisherwoman, The.
If We Could Be Brought.
Thinking.
Jacobsen, J.   Fish Tank Room, The.
Jeffers, R.   Birds and Fishes.
Purse-Seine, The.
Kumin, M.   Food Chain, The.
Kunitz, S.   King of the River.
Lawrence, D. H.   Fish.
Little Fish.
Levine, P.   To a Fish Head Found on the Beach
Near Málaga.
Lowell, R.   Fishnet.
Lux.   Pismire Rising.
MacDiarmid, H.   Dytiscus.
MacLeish.   Vicissitudes of the Creator.
McGrath, T.   Beyond Seattle.
Melville, H.   Maldive Shark, The.

Meredith, W. Fishvendor, The.
Moore, M. Egyptian Pulled Glass Bottle in the Shape of a Fish, An.
Fish, The.
Muldoon, P. Salmon of Knowledge, The.
Nash, O. Barmaids Are Diviner Than Mermaids.
Guppy, The.
Smelt, The.
Nemerov. Goose Fish, The.
Niedecker. City Talk.
Oliver, M. Fish, The.
Olson, C. Abstract #1, Yucatan.
Red Fish-of-Bones, The.
Pagis. Tidings.
Patchen. Plate of Steaming Fish, A.
Pinkerton, H. Pool, The.
Raine, K. In the Beck.
Ramanujan. Breaded Fish.
Rossetti, C. When fishes set umbrellas up.
Rumi. Three Fish, The.
Sandburg, C. Fish Crier.
Flying Fish.
Two Fish.
Sexton. Fish That Walked, The.
Smith, S. Fish, Fish.
Friends of the River Trent.
Look!
Snyder, G. Lines on a Carp.
Stafford, W. Fish Counter at Bonneville, The.
Sze. In Your Honor.
Szymborska, W. In Heraclitus' River.
Thoreau. Salmon Brook.
Whitman, W. Paumanok Picture, A.
Wilbur, R. Shad-Time.
Williams, M. Unto One of the Least of These.
Williams, W. Cod Head, The.
Fish.
Sea-Trout and Butterfish.
Wilner, E. Round Fish, The.
Wordsworth, W. Gold and Silver Fishes in a Vase.
Wright, C. Mondo Angelico.
Wright, J. Northern Pike.
Yeats. Fish, The.
Three Movements.

Fishing and Fishermen
Atwood. Fishing for Eel Totems.
Berry, W. Plan, The.
Bishop, E. At the Fishhouses.
Fish, The.
Carver, R. After Rainy Days.
Bobber.
Catch, The.
Debate, The.
Evening.
Its Course.
Kitchen, The.
Late Afternoon, April 8, 1984.
Near Klamath.
Net, The.
Night Dampness.
Out.
Oyntment to Alure Fish to the Bait.
Rest, The.
River, The.
What You Need to Know for Fishing.
White Field, The.
Windows of the Summer Vacation Houses, The.
Chung Yuan Liu. Birds have flown away from the mountains, The.
Ciardi, J. Benefits of an Education, The.
Figure Drawn in Wire, The.
Of Fish and Fishermen.
Clampitt. August Darks, The.
What the Light Was Like.
Collins, B. Fishing on the Susquehanna in July.
Crane, H. Bacardi Spreads the Eagle's Wing.
De la Mare. Old Angler, The.
Dickey, J. Shark's Parlor, The.
Donne. Bait[e], The.
Dubie. Not the Cuckold's Dream.
Dugan, A. Monologue of a Commercial Fisherman.
On Fishing Being a Chancy Life.
Touristic Note from the Gulf.

Dunbar, P. Fishing.
Lazy Day, A.
Till the Wind Gets Right.
Eberhart, R. Angels, The.
Deep Fishing.
Ferlinghetti, L. Baja Beatitudes.
Gallagher, T. Boat Ride.
Hall, D. Cold Water.
Han-shan. Where white clouds form high rugged crags.
Hayden, R. Smelt Fishing.
Heaney, S. Lough Neagh Sequence, A.
Spoonbait, The.
Heine, H. My Heart.
Hughes, L. Catch.
Hughes, T. Cormorant, A.
Earth-Numb.
Go Fishing.
Gulkana, The.
Milesian Encounter on the Sligachan.
Stealing Trout on a May Morning.
Ignatow, D. Fisherwoman, The.
Ivanov, G. Losing yourself in thought, daydreaming.
Jeffers, R. Drunken Charlie.
Purse-Seine, The.
Salmon Fishing.
Kumin, M. Food Chain, The.
Kunitz, S. Catch, The.
Logan, J. Whistling Wings or White Turtle in the Watertree.
Lowell, R. Drunken Fisherman, The.
Lux. At the Far End of a Long Wharf.
MacDiarmid, H. With the Herring Fishers.
MacLeish. Poet.
Major, C. Sand Flesh and Sky.
Meredith, W. Fishvendor, The.
Merrill, J. 16. ix. 65.
Parrot Fish, The.
Pier: Under Pisces, The.
Merwin. Finding a Teacher.
Fishing.
Some of the Masts.
Surf-Casting.
Milosz, C. Boy, A.
Muldoon, P. Paul Klee: *They're Biting*.
Waking Father, The.
Nash, O. Fish, The.
Nemerov. Casting.
Niedecker. Coopered at Fish Creek.
Dusk— / He's spearing from a boat.
Here it gives the laws for fishing thru the ice.
My man says the wind blows from the south.
River-marsh-drowse.
Olson, C. By Cure of—Sulfa.
is an archeology: eight fathom down, on Dogger Bank, the bones, The.
Oppen. Ballad: "Astrolabes and lexicons."
Pinkerton, H. Elegy at Beaverhead County, Montana.
Pool, The.
Plath. Net-Menders, The.
Rexroth, K. Survival of the Fittest.
Riley, J. At Broad Ripple.
Bin a-Fishin.'
Fishing Party, The.
Old-Timer, An.
Up and Down Old Brandywine.
Ritsos. Marine.
Roethke. Lady and the Bear, The.
Pike, The.
Rossetti, C. Fisher-Wife, A.
Smith, S. Fish, Fish.
Snyder, G. Shark Meat.
Stafford, W. Fish Counter at Bonneville, The.
Ice-Fishing.
In the Deep Channel.
Stevens, W. Thinking of a Relation between the Images of Metaphors.
Sze. Halibut, The.
Tate, A. Trout Map, The.
Tate, J. Reapers of the Water.
Thoreau. Salmon Brook.
Tomlinson, C. Mackinnon's Boat.
Night Fishers.
Updike. Crab Crack.

Very. To the Fishermen.
Walcott. Tarpon.
Weiss, T. Far Out, Far In.
Hook, The.
Whitman, W. Paumanok Picture, A.
Torch, The.
Whittier. Fishermen, The.
Skipper Ireson's Ride.
Wilbur, R. Trolling for Blues.
Williams, M. Trying to Remember.
Williams, W. Gentle Rejoinder, The.
Paul.
Ritualists, The.
Wilner, E. End of the Line, The.
Night Fishing in the Sound.
Off the Hook.
Wordsworth, W. Written upon a Blank Leaf in "The Compleat Angler."
Wright, J. Fishermen, The.
Lifting Illegal Nets by Flashlight.
Yeats. Fish, The.
Fisherman, The.
See also **Clams and Clamming; Crabs and Crabbing**

Fitzgerald, Edward
Browning, R. To Edward FitzGerald.
Tennyson, A. To E. Fitzgerald.

Fitzgerald, Ella
Komunyakaa. Nightbird.

Fitzgerald, F. Scott
Clampitt. Mulciber at West Egg.
Davie, D. Garden Party, The.

Flags
Amichai [*or* Amikhai]. How did a banner begin? Let's assume there was something whole.
Bierce. Confederate Flags, The.
Eberhart, R. Flag, The.
Hardy, T. Middle-Age Enthusiasms.
Hughes, L. Moscow.
Kipling, R. English Flag, The.
Kunitz, S. Eagle.
Merwin. Standards.
Montale. Near Capua.
Ritsos. Hues of a Cloud.
Spinelessly.
Rumi. No Flag.
Whitman, W. Ethiopia Saluting the Colors.
Whittier. Pine-Tree, The.

Flags, United States
Cummings, E. E. Our Flag.
Emerson, R. To the mizen, the main, & the fore.
Frost, R. Not of School Age.
Riley, J. Name of Old Glory, The.
Stafford, W. Old Glory.
Whitman, W. Bathed in War's Perfume.
Delicate Cluster.
Thick-Sprinkled Bunting.
World Take Good Notice.
Whittier. Barbara Frietchie.
Centennial Hymn.
Mantle of St. John de Matha, The.

Flamingos
MacLeish. Boy in the Roman Zoo.
Major, C. At the Zoo in Spain.
Swenson, M. One of the Strangest.

Flanders, Belgium
Hill, G. Canaan.
Owen, W. To a Comrade in Flanders.

Flapjacks
See **Pancakes**

Flappers
Parker, D. Ballade of a Not Insupportable Loss.

Flattery
Bukowski. Note to the Boys in the Back Room, A.
Burns, R. Brigs of Ayr, a Poem, The.
To Maria.
Byron, G. Answer to the Foregoing, Addressed to Miss——.
Written in "Letters to an Italian Nun and an English Gentleman: by J.J. Rousseau: Founded on Facts."
Clough. Because a Lady chose to say.

Cowper, W. In a Letter to the Same [C. P.].
Cunningham, J. I write you in my need. Please write.
Donne. To the Countess of Huntingdon ("Madam, / Man to God's image, Eve, to man's was made").
Emerson, R. In this sour world, o summerwind.
HaNagid. He Who Lingers at the Court of the King.
Herrick. Another Upon Her.
  Flatterie.
  To His Brother in Law Master John Wingfield.
  To His Honoured Friend, M. John Weare, Councellour.
  To His Honoured Friend, Sir John Mynts.
  To His Honoured Kinsman, Sir Richard Stone.
  To His Kinsman, Sir Tho. Soame.
  To His Kinswoman, Mrs. Penelope Wheeler.
  To His Worthy Kinsmen, Mr. Stephen Soame.
  To Oenone.
  To the Honoured, Master Endimion Porter.
  To the Right Honourable Edward Earle of Dorset.
Johnson, S. To Lyce, an Elderly Lady.
Jonson, B. To Robert, Earl of Salisbury ("What need hast thou of me, or of my muse").
Sheridan, T. Prologue Spoken before a Greek Play.
Smith, S. Rehearsal, The.
Unknown. On Flatterers.
Wordsworth, W. Written in the Strangers' Book at "The Station," Opposite Bowness.

Flaubert, Gustave
Creeley. Flaubert's Early Prose.
Warren, R. Flaubert in Egypt.

Fleas
Coleridge, S. On Donne's First Poem.
Donne. Flea, The.
Lindsay, N. Little Turtle, The.
Merwin. Flea's Carrying Words, A.
Riley, J. Jolly Miller, The.
Williams, C. K. Fleas, too, / have fled, The.

Fletcher, John
Herrick. Upon Master Fletchers Incomparable Playes.
Jonson, B. To the Worthy Author M[r] John Fletcher.

Flies
Amichai [or Amikhai]. Course of a Life, The.
Beckett, S. La Mouche.
Bukowski. Not All That Bad.
Carew, T. Fly That Flew into My Mistress'[s] Eye, A.
Cummings, E. E. Off a pane)the.
  Ohld song / you Know.
Dickinson, E. Butterfly in honored Dust, The.
  I heard a Fly buzz—when I died.
Eberhart, R. When Golden Flies Upon My Carcass Come.
Graves, R. Blue-Fly, The.
Hall, D. Flies.
Herrick. Amber Bead, The.
  Upon a Flie.
Hughes, T. Cranefly in September, A.
  Performance.
Ignatow, D. Buzz.
  I Killed a Fly.
Kinnell. Flies.
  Fly, The.
Komunyakaa. Observatory.
Levi, P. Fly, The.
Logue, C. Loyal to the King.
Lowell, R. Harriet.
MacLeish. Captivity of the Fly.
  La Foce.
MacNeice. Mayfly.
Major, C. Apple-Maggot Fly, The.
Merrill, J. House Fly, The.
Merwin. Flies.
Nash, O. Fly, The.
Nemerov. Between the Window and the Screen.
  Truth.
Olson, C. Big Fat Fly, A.
Prunty. Black Water.
  Four Winter Flies.
Ritsos. Bloodletting.

Tomlinson, C. Jam Trap, The.
Updike. Fly.
Weiss, T. Hostage, The.
  Sonata Pathétique.
Williams, C. K. My Fly.
Wordsworth, W. Written in Germany on One of the Coldest Days of the Century.
Yeats. Long-Legged Fly.

Flight
Ammons. Script.
  Windy Trees.
Berry, W. Star, The.
Bishop, E. Invitation to Miss Marianne Moore.
Blue Cloud. Crow's Flight.
Ciardi, J. Birds, like Thoughts.
De la Mare. Glimpse, The.
Dickey, J. Eagles.
  Eagle's Mile, The.
  Night Bird.
Dickinson, E. Bees.
Eberhart, R. Gulled.
  Incidence of Flight.
  Tree Swallows.
Frost, R. Kitty Hawk.
Gunn, T. Flying Above California.
  Small Plane in Kansas.
  Tamer and Hawk.
Hall, D. Idea of Flying, The.
  Old Pilot, The.
HaNagid. Soar, Don't Settle.
Hopkins, G. All as that moth call'd Underwing, alighted.
  Ecquis Binas.
Hughes, T. Swifts.
Ignatow, D. Question, The.
Kipling, R. Flight, The.
Kumin, M. Photograph, U.S. Army Flying School, College Park, Maryland, 1909.
Laughlin, J. Apsarases.
Levine, P. Poem of Flight, The.
Merwin. Flight, The.
Milosz, C. Fear-Dream (1918).
Nash, O. Bat, The.
  Caution to Everybody, A.
  It's Snug to Be Smug.
Oliver, M. Night Flight.
Piercy. Night Flight.
Rilke. "Victories," The.
  Winged Seed.
Rossetti, C. Fly Away, Fly Away.
  Paradise: in a Symbol.
Rukeyser, M. Flying Red Horse, The.
  Preamble.
  Theory of Flight.
Rukeyser, M. et al. Night Flight : New York.
Schuyler, J. In Wiry Winter.
Sexton. To a Friend Whose Work Has Come to Triumph.
Simic. Autumn Air.
Smith, S. I Wish.
  Look, Look.
  No Categories!
  No More People.
Spender, S. Icarus.
Stock, R. Incredible Activities in the Eyrie.
Swenson, M. Feel like a Bird.
Tomlinson, C. Encounter.
  Geese Going South.
  Sight and Flight.
Very. Birds of Passage, The.
Warren, R. Eagle Descending.
  Evening Hawk.
Wilbur, R. All These Birds.
Wright, J. Poem by Garnie Braxton, A.
  Presentation of Two Birds to My Son, A.

Flirtation
Amichai [or Amikhai]. Games.
Browning, E. Lady's "Yes," The.
Carver, R. Sinew.
Corbett, W. Earrings of Madame de, The.
Dove, R. Flirtation.
García Lorca. Street of the Mutes, The.
Gunn, T. Bally Power Play.
  Fever.
Han-shan. In spring women flaunt their looks.
Hardy, T. Watering-Place Lady Inventoried, A.

Herrick. Lips Tongueless[e].
  Sho[o]e Tying, The.
  Silken Snake, The.
  To His Mistress Objecting to Him Neither Toying or Talking.
Hopkins, G. Castara Victrix.
Laughlin, J. Hope Springs.
  If You Are Only Flirting.
Lawrence, D. H. Passing Visit to Helen.
  She Was a Good Little Wife.
Lindsay, N. For All Who Ever Sent Lace Valentines.
Logan, J. Picnic, The.
Meredith, G. Jolly Young Carpenter, The.
Rexroth, K. My Heart's as Gay as a Young Sunflower.
Rimbaud, A. Cunning.
Rumi. You've so distracted me.
Smith, S. Rencontres Funestes.
Tate, J. Mirror, The.
  To Fuzzy.
Updike. Flirt.
Williams, T. Little Horse.
Wyatt, S. Long love that in my thought doth harbo[u]r, The.
  Lover Showeth How He Is Forsaken of Such as He Sometime Enjoyed, The.

Flood, The
Merwin. Noah's Raven.
Riley, J. Song of the Cruise, A.

Floods
Atwood. After the Flood, We.
Berry, W. Wet Time, A.
Bishop, E. Flood, The.
Bly, R. Schoolcraft's Diary Written on the Missouri: 1830.
Brodsky, J. View with a Flood.
Chuang Tzu. Autumn Floods.
Davie, D. Siloam.
Dunbar, P. Right's Security.
Ferlinghetti, L. Wild Dreams of a New Beginning.
Frost, R. Flood, The.
Gjuzel. Flood at the International Writer's Workshop.
Gunn, T. Flooded Meadows.
Hayden, R. Burly Fading One, The.
Hughes, L. Mississippi Levee.
Kipling, R. Floods, The.
  Song of Seven Cities, The.
Lux. It's the Little Towns I Like.
MacDiarmid, H. Cheville.
MacNeice. River in Spate.
Marvell. Eyes and Tears.
Merwin. Deluge, The.
  High Water.
Orr, G. Spring Floods.
Pinsky. Uncreation, The.
Ramanujan. River, A.
Rimbaud, A. After the Flood.
Ritsos. Knocking.
Rukeyser, M. His Dream of Flood: And Eden.
  Tarpaper shack and the red rose bush, The.
  They dug up the grave, while a banjo and two guitars.
Tomlinson, C. Epilogue, The: "It was a dream delivered the epilogue."
  Flood, The.
Whitman, W. Voice from Death, A.
Wordsworth, W. When Severn's Sweeping Flood Had Overthrown.
Wright, J. To Flood Stage Again.

Florence, Italy
Akhmatova, A. Dante.
Blok. Florence.
Brodsky, J. December in Florence.
Browning, E. King Victor Emanuel Entering Florence, April, 1860.
Browning, R. Old Pictures in Florence.
Davie, D. Mr Sharp in Florence.
Hill, G. Florentines.
Lawrence, D. H. À La Maniere De D. H. Lawrence.
  Bat.
Lowell, R. Florence.
McGrath, T. Migration of Cities, The.

Michelangelo Buonarroti.   Your beauty an
   angel's, Lady, you were meant.
Montale.   Florentine Madrigals.
   Times at Bellosguardo.
Raine, K.   Daisies of Florence.
Rexroth, K.   Rosa Mundi.
Schuyler, J.   This Notebook.
Swenson, M.   Above the Arno.
Tomlinson, C.   Machiavelli in Exile.
Wilde, O.   By the Arno.
   San Miniato.
Wright, C.   With Simic and Marinetti at the
   Giubbe Rosse.

Florida (state)
Berryman.   Tampa Stomp.
Bishop, E.   Florida.
Carruth, H.   Études de Plusiers Paysages de
   l'Âme.
Ciardi, J.   Being Called.
Clampitt.   Discovery.
Cooper, J.   Being Southern.
Dunbar, P.   Florida Night, A.
   To the Miami.
Eberhart, R.   Angels, The.
   Opposition.
Emerson, R.   For fifteen winter days.
Glück, L.   To Florida.
Hughes, L.   Ballad of Harry Moore.
   Florida Road Workers.
McHugh, H.   Two St. Petersburgs.
Merton.   Dirge for the City of Miami.
Niedecker.   Florida.
Stevens, W.   Fabliau of Florida.
   Nomad Exquisite.
   O Florida, Venereal Soil.
Updike.   Miami.
Williams, W.   This Florida: 1924.

Florists
Koch, K.   Girl and Baby Florist Sidewalk Pram
   Nineteen Seventy Something.
Roethke.   Old Florist.

Flour
Mistral, G.   Flour.

Flowers
Amichai [or Amikhai].   Flowers in a Room.
Ammons.   Garden.
   Holly.
   Mirrorment.
Apollinaire.   Autumn Crocuses.
Ashbery, J.   Picture of Little J. A. in a Prospect
   of Flowers, The.
Bierce.   To Thee, My Darling.
Bly, R.   At the Time of Peony Blossoming.
Bogan, L.   Animal, Vegetable and Mineral.
Browning, E.   Deserted Garden, The.
   Flower in a Letter, A.
   Island, An.
   Man and Nature.
Browning, R.   Magical Nature.
   Spring Song.
Bukowski.   Pansies.
   Rose, Rose.
Burns, R.   Banks of the Devon, The.
   O Were My Love Yon Lilac[k] Fair.
   Posie, The.
Campion, T. et al.   And Would You See My
   Mistress' Face?
Cardozo.   Elegy for Maria Alves.
Carew, T.   Protestation [A Sonnet], The.
Carruth, H.   Almanach du Printemps Vivarois.
   Bouquet in Dog Time.
   Carnations.
   Chicory.
   Excursus of Reassurance in Begonia Time, An.
   Language of Flowers, Etc, The.
   Of Distress Being Humiliated by the Classical
      Chinese Poets.
   Song: So Why Does This Dead Carnation.
   Survival as Tao, Beginning at 5:00 A.M.
   This Decoration.
   This Song.
Cavafy.   Artificial Flowers.
   Bouquets.
   Elegy of the Flowers.
Celan.   Flower.
Ciardi, J.   Counting on Flowers.

Clampitt.   Cloudberry Summer.
   Field Pansy, The.
   High Culture.
   Horned Rampion, The.
   Lindenbloom.
   Smaller Orchid, The.
Coleridge, S.   Keepsake, The.
   On Observing a Blossom on the First of
      February 1796.
   Reproof and Reply, The.
   Snow-Drop, The.
Cooper, J.   Morning on the St. John's.
Cortes.   Flower of the Fruit, The.
Crane, H.   Moment Fugue.
   To Emily Dickinson.
Crane, S.   Trees in the garden rained flowers,
   The.
Creeley.   Flower, The.
   Late Comer, The.
   Rhyme, The.
   Snow, The.
   Such Flowers.
Cummings, E. E.   But the other / day i was
   passing a certain.
   I like / to think that on.
   If everything happens that can't be done.
   In time of daffodils(who know.
   Lily has a rose.
   One winter afternoon / (at the magical hour).
   Riverly is a flower.
   Rosetree,rosetree / —you're a song to
      see:whose.
   Should this fool die.
   Tumbling-hair / picker of buttercups.
"Dario."   Because of the Influence of Spring.
   In Autumn.
Davie, D.   Demi-Exile. Howth.
De la Mare.   April Moon.
   Bottle, The.
   Daisy, The.
   Hawthorn Hath a Deathly Smell, The.
   Imogen.
   Lucy.
   Miracle, The.
   Noon and Night Flower.
   Ophelia.
   Pot Of Musk, A.
   When the rose is faded.
Dickinson, E.   Apparently with no surprise.
   As Children bid the Guest "Good Night."
   Between My Country—and the Others.
   Bloom—is Result—to meet a Flower.
   Blossom perhaps is an introduction, A.
   Bulbs are in the sod, The.
   Career of flowers differs from ours, The.
   Clover's simple Flame, The.
   Come slowly—Eden!
   Daisy follows soft the Sun, The.
   Did the Harebell loose her girdle.
   Ferocious as a Bee without a wing.
   Flower keeps it's appointment.
   Flower must not blame the Bee, The.
   Flower will not trouble her, it has so small a
      Foot, A.
   Flowers—Well—if anybody.
   How many Flowers fail in Wood.
   I tend my flowers for thee.
   Immortality of Flowers, The.
   Intrusiveness of flowers.
   It would not know if it were spurned.
   "Lethe" in my flower.
   Lovely flowers embarrass me, The.
   My nosegays are for Captives.
   Nature's faithful Blossoms.
   Perhaps you'd like to buy a flower.
   South Winds jostle them.
   Stem of a departed Flower, The.
   There is a flower that Bees prefer.
   They ask but our Delight.
   We are snatching our jewels from the frost.
   When they come back—if Blossoms do.
   Whose are the little beds, I asked.
Dove, R.   In the Old Neighborhood.
   Then Came Flowers.
Dugan, A.   Argument to Love as a Person.
   On Flowers. On Negative Evolution.

To Paris: Fear of the Heights Reached.
Dunbar, P.   Seedling, The.
Eberhart, R.   Ceremony By the Sea, A.
   Forms of the Human.
   Gesture, The.
   Indian Pipe.
   Perception as a Guided Missile.
Eliot, T. S.   Easter: Sensations of April.
Emerson, R.   Dark Flower of Cheshire garden.
   Days pass over me, The.
   Go if thou wilt ambrosial Flower.
   Good Charles the springs adorer.
   He must have / Droll fancies sometimes cross
      his quiet thoughts.
   Humble-Bee, The.
   Know he who tills this lonely field.
   May.
   Rhodora, The [On Being Asked Whence Is the
      Flower].
   She walked in flowers around my field.
   What are all the flowers.
Frost, R.   Flower-Gathering.
   Leaves Compared with Flowers.
   Locked Out.
   Lodged.
   Passing Glimpse, A.
   Rose Pogonias.
   Subverted Flower, The.
   Tuft of Flowers, The.
   Wind and Window Flower.
Gallagher, T.   In Maceio.
   Rhododendrons.
Ginsberg, A.   In Back of the Real.
Glück, L.   Flowering Plum.
   Japonica.
   Mock Orange.
Graves, R.   Gardener.
   Song: Three Rings for Her.
   Troll's Nosegay, The.
Gunn, T.   Messenger, The.
   Moly.
"H. D."   At Baia.
   Evening.
   Garden.
   Sea Rose.
   Sea Violet.
   White World.
Hall, D.   Self-Portrait as a Bear.
Han-shan.   In Loyang so many girls.
Hardy, T.   Flower's Tragedy, The.
   Lodging-House Fuchsias, The.
   To Flowers from Italy in Winter.
Hayden, R.   Night-Blooming Cereus, The.
Herbert, G.   Flower, The.
   Life.
Herrick.   Dialogue Betwixt Himselfe and
      Mistresse Eliza, A.
   How Primroses Came Green.
   How the Wall-Flower Came First, and Why So
      Called.
   Meditation for His Mistress[e], A.
   Mrs. Eliz. Wheeler, Under the Name of the Lost
      Shepardesse.
   On Gelli-Flowers Begotten.
   Showre of Blossomes, The.
   To Anthea.
   To Blossoms.
   To Carnations.
   To Daffodils [or Daffadills].
   To Flowers.
   To Marygolds.
   To Violets.
   Upon Electra's Teares.
   Upon One Lillie, Who Marryed with a Maid
      Call'd Rose.
   Why Flowers Change Color.
Hill, G.   Sobieski's Shield.
Hopkins, G.   Basket broad of woven white rods,
   A.
   For a Picture of Saint Dorothea.
Housman.   I hoed and trenched and weeded.
   When green buds hang in the elm.
Hsüeh T'ao.   Spring-Gazing Songs.
Hughes, L.   Autumn Thought.
   Breath of a Rose.
   New Flowers.

Poppy Flower.
Troubled Woman.
Hughes, T. Honey Bee, The.
Rhododendrons.
Jackson, L. Nightmare, The.
Jacobsen, J. Next Summer.
Provider, The.
Khayyám, O. From Omar Chiam.
Kinnell. Flower Herding on Mount Monadnock.
Kipling, R. Flowers, The.
Kizer, C. Flower, The.
Lines to Accompany Flowers for Eve.
Komunyakaa. Venus's-flytraps.
Kunitz, S. As Flowers Are.
Laughlin, J. Bavarian Gentian, The.
Wild Anemone, The.
Lawrence, D. H. Andraitx—Pomegranate
Flowers.
Assuming the Burden.
Bavarian Gentians.
Flowers and Men.
Kiss, A.
Purple Anemones.
Revolutionary, The.
Levertov. Annuals.
Earliest Spring.
First Love.
Flowers of Sophia.
Intimation.
Métier of Blossoming, The.
Levine, P. New Season.
Lindsay, N. Fairy Bridal Hymn, The.
Logan, J. Return to the Island.
MacNeice. Flower Show.
Major, C. Flowers for My Date.
In the hidden garden.
Mallarmé. Flowers, The.
Marvell. Picture of Little T. C. in a Prospect of
Flowers, The.
Melville, H. American Aloe on Exhibition, The.
Meredith, G. Ballad of the Lady Eglantine, The.
Flower of the Ruins, The.
Glastonbury Thorn, The.
I saw young Spring leap over the hills.
Seed-Time.
Song: "Daisy now is out upon the green, The."
Wild Rose and the Snowdrop, The.
Yet what is this? the spring returns.
Merrill, J. In Nine Sleep Valley.
Milosz, C. Earth.
Mistral, G. Air Flower, The.
Nash, O. Max Schling, Max Schling, Lend Me
Your Green Thumb.
Solitude of Mr. Powers, The.
Nemerov. Flower Arrangements.
Niedecker. Something in the water.
Wintergreen Ridge.
Oliver, M. Moccasin Flowers.
Olson, C. Dogwood Comes Out Yellow, The.
Flower grows, The.
For a Man Gone to Stuttgart Who Left an
Automobile Behind Him.
Hymn to Proserpine.
Perfume / of flowers! A haw, The.
Perfume / of Flowers!, The.
Perfume!, The.
Po-sy, a Po-sy, A.
She Who Hits at Will.
Paley, G. False strawberry is.
No Love.
St. Johnswort! [or Saint-John's-wort!].
Parker, D. Vers Démodé.
Woodland Song.
Patchen. All the Flowery.
Day of Rabblement.
Delighted with Bluepink.
Flowers to the House.
Shadows and Spring Flowers.
Piercy. Daily Life of the Worker Bee, The.
Pinkerton, H. On Jan van Huysum's *Vase of
Flowers* (1722) in the J. Paul Getty Museum.
Pinsky. Flowers.
Plath. Among the Narcissi.
Fable of the Rhododendron Stealers.
I Am Vertical.
Leaving Early.

Pope, A. Garden, The.
Raine, K. Columbines.
Daisies of Florence.
Dream-flowers.
Flower, memory—.
Forest is multitude.
Kore.
Painting by Winifred Nicholson, A.
Rexroth, K. Blues.
Flower Sutra, The.
You did not know she was eternal? There.
Riley, J. Blossoms on the Trees, The.
Herr Weiser.
Lovely Child, The.
Pansies.
Them Flowers.
Rilke. Cemetary.
Pensive Flower.
Reading Flowers.
Three Carriers, The.
To Speak a Flower.
Rimbaud, A. Flowers.
What the Poet Is Told on the Subject of
Flowers.
Ritsos. Thief, The.
Roethke. Carnations.
Geranium, The.
Shape of the Fire, The.
Transplanting.
Rossetti, C. All Things Wait upon Thee.
Another Spring.
As Cold Water to a Thirsty Soul, So Is Good
News from a Far Country.
Balm in Gilead.
Blind from my birth, / Where flowers are
springing.
Buds and Babies.
Can I know it?—Nay.— / Shall I know it?—
Yea.
Comparisons.
Consider the Lilies of the Field.
Crown of Windflowers, A.
Dirge, A.
Flowers Appear on the Earth, The.
God's Acre.
Golden Glories.
Gone for Ever.
Heartsease in my garden bed, / With
sweetwilliam white and red.
Heavy heart, if ever heart was heavy, A.
Hope and Joy.
I dug and dug amongst the snow.
I Gave a Sweet Smell.
I Have a Message unto Thee.
If stars dropped out of heaven, / And if flowers
took their place.
In the meadow—what in the meadow?
Lily has a smooth stalk, / Will never hurt your
hand, The.
Lily has an air, / And the snowdrop a grace,
The.
Love hath a name of Death.
Mirrors of Life and Death.
October Garden, An.
Passing and Glassing.
Passion Flower hath sprung up tall, The.
Queen Rose.
Ring upon her finger, / Walks the bride, A.
Rivals.
Rose has thorns as well as honey, A.
Rose that blushes rosy red, The.
Roses blushing red and white, / For delight.
Sweet Death.
To My Fior-Di-Lisa.
To the End.
Who Hath Despised the Day of Small Things?
Why did baby die.
Within the Veil.
Rossetti, D. Woodspurge, The.
Rukeyser, M. Blue Flower, The.
Sandburg, C. Bitter Summer Thoughts—No.
XXII.
Bright Conversation with Saint-Ex.
Butter Colors.
Flowers Tell Months.
Follies.

Handfuls.
Harvest.
High Moments.
New Song for Indiana Ophelias.
Nightsong.
Out of the Rainbow End.
Spring Carries Surprises.
There Are Different Gardens.
Thou Art like a Flower.
Two.
Year, The.
Sarton, M. Flower-Arranging Summer, A.
Schuyler, J. Bluet, The.
Cornflowers.
Footnote.
In the Round.
Korean Mums.
Like Lorraine Ellison.
Roof Garden.
Three Gardens.
Yellow Flowers.
Seifert. Garland on the Wrist, A.
Sexton. Love Plant, The.
Shapiro, K. Cut Flower, A.
Spider Mums, The.
Shelley, P. On a Faded Violet.
Smith, S. I Love.
Stevens, W. Room on a Garden, A.
Woman Looking at a Vase of Flowers.
Stock, R. Calentures.
Swenson, M. Catbird in Redbud.
Look Closer.
Swinburne. Sundew, The.
Tennyson, A. Flower in the Cranied Wall.
Thoreau. I saw a delicate flower had grown up
two feet high.
Updike. Fleckings, The.
Natural Question.
Query.
Styles of Bloom.
Van Duyn. Annual and Perennial Problem, An.
Peony Stalks.
Very. Arethusa Meadow.
Autumn Flowers.
Autumn Flowers, The.
Bunch of Flowers, The.
Columbine, The.
Columbines and Anemones.
Crocus, The.
Fossil Flower, The.
Hepatica in Winter, The.
Houstonia, The.
Lament of the Flowers, The.
Life of the Flower, The.
On Seeing the Victoria Regia in Bloom, at the
Garden of J. Fisk Allen Esq. July 22d, 1853.
On Some Blue and Golden Columbines from
Pike's Peak, Colorado.
On Some Eternals from a Friend's Garden.
On the Wild Flowers of the Art Exhibition.
Painted Columbine, The.
Return of the Columbine, The.
Sensibility to the Beauty and Fragrance of
Flowers.
Snow Drop, The.
Solitary Gentian, The.
Spring and Summer Flowers.
Stock-Gilly Flowers, The.
Thanksgiving Flowers.
To the Misses Williams, on Seeing Their
Beautiful Paintings of Wild Flowers.
Torn Flower, The.
Violet, The.
Wind-Flower, The.
Woodwax, The.
Woodwax in Bloom, The.
Yellow Violets, The.
Walker, A. Enemy, The.
Whalen, P. Congress of Vienna, The.
Up in Michigan.
Whitman, W. Orange Buds by Mail from
Florida.
These I Singing in Spring.
Unseen Buds.
Whittier. First Flowers, The.
Flowers in Winter.

Hazel Blossoms.
Star of Bethlehem, The.
Trailing Arbutus, The.
Wilbur, R. In a Churchyard.
In the Field.
On Having Mis-identified a Wild Flower.
Wilde, O. Athanasia.
Williams, W. Ad Infinitum.
Asphodel, That Greeny Flower.
Aux Imagistes.
Blueflags.
Chicory and Daisies.
Daisy.
Flower, The.
Flowers Alone, The.
Flowers by the Sea.
Gayest of Bright Flowers, The.
It Is a Small Plant.
Ivy Crown, The.
La Flor.
Locust Tree in Flower, The.
Loving Dexterity, The.
Modest Achievement, The.
Paterson, Book 5: The River of Heaven.
Petunia, The.
Pink Locust, The.
Pot of Flowers, The.
Self-Portrait 2.
Song: "Russia! Russia! you might say."
Yellow Flower, The.
Wordsworth, W. Flower Garden at Coleorton
Hall, Leicestershire, A.
Foresight.
Love Lies Bleeding.
Poor Robin.
Primrose of the Rock, The.
So Fair, So Sweet, Withal So Sensitive.
To a Lady.
To a Snow-Drop.
Wright, C. Holy Ghost Asketh for Us with
Mourning and Weeping Unspeakable, The.
Zaturenska. Blue Flower, The.
Zukofsky, L. African Violet.
Aloe.
Alpine Rosy Bells.
Artemisia.
Aster.
Azalea.
Bayberry.
Bearded Iris.
Butter-and-Eggs.
Charlock per Winkle.
Chicory.
Chokecherry.
Chrysanthemum.
Cinquefoil.
Clover.
Cockle.
Coleus.
Crocus.
Dahlia.
Daisy.
Dandelion.
Deutzia.
Dogwood.
Dutch White Iris.
Forsythia.
Four-o'clock.
Grape-Hyacinth.
Grassflower.
Grecian Windflower.
Heart us invisbly thyme time.
Heart's Ease.
Honesty.
Honeysuckle.
Hyacinth.
Impatiens.
Jade.
Lavender Cotton.
Lilac.
Lilies.
Lily-of-the-Valley.
Lily-of-the-Valley Fortunei.
Liveforever.
Marigold.
Mountain Laurel.

Narcissus.
Oxalis.
Pachysandra.
Petunia.
Phlox.
Poppy Anemone.
Privet.
Pussy Willow.
Queen Anne's Lace.
Raspberry.
Rose-of-Sharon.
Roses.
Slipperwort.
Snow-Wreath.
Snowdrop.
Snowflake.
Spearmint.
Spider or Ribbon Plant.
Spirea.
Sprengeri.
Starglow.
Telephus Sedum.
Thyme.
Tulip.
Venus's Looking-glass.
Vines.
Violet.
Weeds.
White Begonia.
Wild Geranium.
Wild Honeysuckle.
Windflower.
"X."
Yarrow.
Yaupon.
Zebrina etc.
Zinnia.

Flutes
Browning, E. Musical Instrument, A.
Browning, R. Flute-Music, with an
Accompaniment.
Dryden, J. Song for St Cecilia's Day, 1687, A.
Eberhart, R. Kinaesthesia.
"H. D." Flute Song.
Jacobsen, J. April Asylum.
Lindsay, N. Flute of the Lonely, The.
Mahon. Andean Flute, The.
Muldoon, P. Lass of Aughrim, The.
Rexroth, K. Flute Overheard, A.
Ritsos. Flute-Player, The.
Rumi. Craftsman pulled a reed from the
reedbed, A.
Flute, The.
Flutes for Dancing.
Reed Flute's Song, The.
Seifert. Striking of the Tower Clock, The.
Sexton. To Lose the Earth.
Tomlinson, C. Flute Music.
Nine Variations in a Chinese Winter Setting.

Flying Dutchman (ship)
Robinson, E. Flying Dutchman, The.

Flying Saucers
Hayden, R. Unidentified Flying Object.

Foals
Cummings, E. E. Life / shuts &)opens the
world.
Hughes, T. New Foal.
Kumin, M. Rejoicing with Henry.
See also **Horses**

Fog
Ammons. Shore Fog.
Auden. Thank You, Fog.
Bierce. Study in Gray, A.
Carver, R. Summer Fog.
Clampitt. At Easterly.
Fog.
Gradual Clearing.
Cummings, E. E. Un / der fog / 's / touch.
De la Mare. Fog.
Dickey, J. Fog Envelops the Animals.
Dickinson, E. Sun and Fog Contested, The.
Eberhart, R. Flux.
Gunn, T. Night Piece, The.
Hayden, R. Traveling through Fog.
Hughes, L. Fog.

Jacobsen, J. Sea Fog, The.
Jarrell, R. Front, A.
Jeffers, R. Boats in a Fog.
Komunyakaa. Fog Galleon.
Levertov. Ground-Mist, The.
Logan, J. Girl in the Fog, The.
Millay, E. Impression: Fog Off the Coast of
Dorset.
Niedecker. Fog-thick morning.
Olson, C. Measure.
Mind's Notice, The.
Oppen. Forms of Love, The.
Orr, G. Overtaken by Fog while Climbing.
Patchen. Fog.
Fog over the Sea and the Sun Going Down.
Plath. Prospect.
Ramanujan. Fog.
Rexroth, K. Et pour Eux Seuls, les Paradis
Chantent Encore.
Privacy.
Rukeyser, M. Foghorn in Horror.
Sandburg, C. Baltic Fog Notes.
Far Rockaway Night till Morning.
Feather Lights.
Fog.
Fog Numbers.
Fog Portrait.
In the Shadow of the Palace.
Lost.
New Weather.
Pearl Fog.
Sea Slant.
Schuyler, J. Gray, Intermittently Blue, Eyed
Hero.
Thoreau. Fog.
Tomlinson, C. In December.
Voznesensky [*or* Voznesenskii]. Foggy Street.
Wordsworth, W. As when, upon the smooth
pacific deep.

Folly
Campion, T. Canto Quarto.
Jeffers, R. What Odd Expedients.
Kipling, R. City of Brass, The.
Suckling, S. Barley-Break , A.
Yeats. Down by the Šalley Gardens.

Food
Angelou. Health-Food Diner, The.
Atwood. Carrying Food Home in Winter.
Brodsky, J. Cabbage and Carrot.
Browning, R. Prologue: "Pray, Reader, have
you eaten ortolans."
Bukowski. Windy Night.
Burns, R. At Brownhill Inn.
To a Haggis.
Codrescu. At Home.
Jingling the Cookery.
Cowper, W. Lines after the Manner of Homer.
Dickinson, E. Am told that fasting gives to
food.
God gave a Loaf to every Bird.
Dunbar, P. Curiosity.
When de Co'n Pone's Hot.
Eberhart, R. Tree Swallows.
Winter Kill.
Ginsberg, A. C'mon Pigs of Western
Civilization Eat More Grease.
Gunn, T. Cafeteria in Boston.
Han-shan. Get your own clothes if you're cold.
Unfortunate human disorder, The.
Herrick. Custard, The.
Grace for Children, A.
Manna.
To God.
To His Book[e].
Upon Jack and Jill: Epigram.
Upon Ralph.
Hughes, L. Speaking of Food.
Jackson, L. Concerning Food.
Jacobsen, J. Food.
Jonson, B. Inviting a Friend to Supper.
Kipling, R. Big Steamers.
Such As in Ships.
Kumin, M. Feeding Time.
Lawrence, D. H. Bread upon the Waters.
Food of the North.
Living, A.

Levine, P.   Salts and Oils.
Lux.   Refrigerator, 1957.
  What Montezuma Fed Cortés and His Men.
Major, C.   Food for Thought; or, Death Is
  Physical.
Michelangelo Buonarroti.   Sweeter your face
  than grapes are, stewed to mush.
Moore, M.   To a Chameleon.
Nash, O.   Absentees, The.
  Are You a Snodgrass?
  Banquet, The.
  Caraway Seed, The.
  Clean Platter, The.
  Further Reflection on Parsley.
  I Can't Have a Martini, Dear, but You Take
    One, or, Are You Going to Sit There
    Guzzling All Night?
  Isn't That a Dainty Dish? No!
  Lines to Be Embroidered on a Bib, or, The
    Child Is Father of the Man, but Not for Quite
    a While.
  My Dear, How Ever Did You Think Up This
    Delicious Salad?
  Parsley for Vice-President!
  Parsnip, The.
  Private Dining Room, The.
  Table Talk.
  What, No Oysters?
Nemerov.   Grace to Be Said at the Supermarket.
  Lobsters.
Niedecker.   Consider at the outset.
Piercy.   Attack of the Squash People.
  Beauty I Would Suffer For.
  Consumer, The.
Ransom, J.   Survey of Literature.
Rexroth, K.   Observations in a Cornish Teashop.
Rossetti, C.   Three Plum Buns.
  Wee wee husband, / Give me some money.
Rumi.   Special Plates.
Schuyler, J.   Joint.
Sexton.   Food.
Smith, S.   Nourish Me on an Egg.
Snyder, G.   Song of the Taste.
Swenson, M.   Order of Diet.
Swift, J.   Epigram on Fasting.
Tate, J.   Sadness of My Neighbors, The.
Updike.   Food.
  On the Inclusion of Miniature Dinosaurs in
    Breakfast Cereal Boxes.
Van Duyn.   Reading of Rex Stout, A.
  Saleswomen in Bakery Shops.
Very.   My Meat and Drink.
Wilbur, R.   Rillons, Rillettes.
Williams, W.   Host, The.

See also **Cooking and Cooks; Eating; Gluttony
and Gluttons**

Fools
Baudelaire.   Cupid & Skull.
Bierce.   Two Types.
Blake, W.   Cromek Speaks.
  Great Men & Fools do often me Inspire.
  Lacedemonian Instruction.
  Madman I have been calld Fool they call thee.
  Sussex Men are Noted Fools, The.
  These are the Idiots chiefest arts.
Burns, R.   Holy Fair, The.
  Monody on Maria.
  On Capt. W——— R-dd-ck of C-rb—ton.
  On Commissary Goldie's Brains.
  On J-hn M-r-ne, Laird of L-gg-n.
  On W. R———, Esq.
  On William Graham [*or* W——— Gr-h-m],
    Esq., of Mossknowe [*or* M-sskn-w].
  Postscript [To W. S*****n, Ochiltree].
  To the Honble Mr. R. M———, of P-nm-re, on
    His High Phaeton.
Byron, G.   Verses Found in a Summer-House at
  Hales-Owen.
Clare, J.   Lout, The: "For Sunday's play he
  never makes excuse."
Collins, B.   Nightclub.
  Three Wishes, The.
Cowper, W.   Card, A.
  Lines with Two Cockscombs.
Creeley.   Counterpoint, A.
  Epigraph: "Lot's wife, / married to chance."

Cummings, E. E.   May my heart always be open
  to little.
  Out of the lie of no.
De la Mare.   Iago.
Donne.   Triple Fool, The.
Eberhart, R.   Man Who Was Blown Down by
  the Wind, A.
Emerson, R.   Bard or dunce is blest, but hard.
  It takes a philosopher or fool.
Han-shan.   I recall twenty years ago.
  I recently hiked to a temple in the clouds.
  There exists one kind of fool.
  Wise man isn't greedy, A.
HaNagid.   I'd Suck Bitter Poison from the
    Viper's Mouth.
  Wise Understand, The.
Herrick.   Foolishnesse.
Hughes, L.   Ballad of the Fool.
Jonson, B.   On Don Surly.
  On the Famous Voyage.
  On the Magnetic Lady.
  To a Friend, an Epigram of Him.
  To Courtling.
  To Fool or Knave.
  To Groom Idiot.
  To Inigo, Marquess Would Be, a Corollary.
  To Mime.
Kinsella, T.   Better is an handful with quietness.
Lindsay, N.   On the Road to Nowhere.
MacDiarmid, H.   Fool, The.
MacLeish.   Ship of Fools.
Melville, H.   Montaigne and His Kitten.
Meredith, G.   Camelus Saltat: Continued.
Merton.   Antipoem 1.
Olson, C.   Fool, The.
  Green Man, The.
Patchen.   Spirit of Noplace, The.
Pope, A.   Another [Epigram].
  Epigram from the French: "Sir, I admit your
    general [*or* gen'ral] Rule."
  Prologue to the *Three Hours after Marriage*.
  Verses to Be Placed under the Picture of
    England's Arch-Poet: Containing a Compleat
    Catalogue of His Works.
Pound, E.   Piere Vidal Old.
Ralegh, S.   Sir Walter Ra[u]le[i]gh to His
    Son[ne].
Sandburg, C.   Dreaming Fool.
Shih-te.   There exists one type of person.
Smith, S.   Father for a Fool, A.
Thoreau.   Any fool can make a rule.
Williams, W.   Hero.
  Naked.
Yeats.   Another Song of a Fool.
  Symbols.

See also **Jesters**

Football
Bukowski.   Gentleman and the Bastard, The.
Dickey, J.   Bee, The.
  For the Death of Vince Lombardi.
  In the Pocket.
Eberhart, R.   Harvard Stadium.
Jarrell, R.   Nursery Rhyme, A.
  Say Good-bye to Big Daddy.
Komunyakaa.   Phantasmagoria.
  Touch.
Nash, O.   One Man's Meed Is Another Man's
  Overemphasis.
Nemerov.   Watching Football on TV.
Prunty.   Grown Men at Touch.
Tomlinson, C.   Of the Winter Ball Game.
Wright, J.   Autumn Begins in Martins Ferry,
  Ohio.

See also **Soccer**

Forbidden Fruit
Carew, T.   Secrecy [*or* Secresie] Protested.
Cowper, W.   Bee and the Pine-Apple, The.
  Pine-Apple and the Bee, The.
Creeley.   Now Then.
Davie, D.   Dule of a Dewsbury Matron.
Milosz, C.   Adam and Eve.

Ford, Ed ("Whitey")
Pinsky.   Night Game, The.

Ford, Ford Madox
Cummings, E. E.   Possibly thrice we glimpsed.

Lowell, R.   Ford Madox Ford.
Williams, W.   To Ford Madox Ford in Heaven.

Forest Fires
Atwood.   Two Fires, The.
Dickey, J.   Walking the Fire Line.
Levine, P.   Late Answer, A.
Prunty.   Forest Fire.
Snyder, G.   Control Burn.
Wright, J.   Brush Fire.

Foresters
Stafford, W.   Peleg Lookout.
Whittier.   Ranger, The.

Forests
Atwood.   Paths and Thingscape.
Auden.   Reflections in a Forest.
Bishop, E.   Chemin de Fer.
Bly, R.   Solitude Late at Night in the Woods.
Browning, R.   Forest Thought, A.
Burns, R.   On a Bank of Flowers.
Collins, B.   Directions.
Cooper, J.   Olympic Rain Forest.
Cummings, E. E.   This / forest pool / A so.
Davie, D.   Sylvae.
  Tunstall Forest.
De la Mare.   Dwelling-Place, The.
  Mourn'st Thou Now?
  Sorcery.
Dickey, J.   Sleeping Out at Easter.
Dugan, A.   In the Forest.
Dunbar, P.   Forest Greeting, The.
Emerson, R.   I sat upon the ground.
  Waldeinsamkeit.
Frost, R.   Come In.
  Dream Pang, A.
  In winter in the woods alone.
  Into My Own.
  Stopping by Woods on a Snowy Evening.
Graves, R.   Gift of Sight.
"H. D."   Pursuit.
Hardy, T.   In a Wood.
  Yell'ham-Wood's Story.
Jarrell, R.   House in the Wood, The.
Kipling, R.   Way through the Woods, The.
Larkin, P.   Is It Now or for Always.
Levertov.   Life in the Forest.
  Marta (Brazil, 1928).
  Novices, The.
  Sound of the Axe.
Lindsay, N.   What the Forester Said.
Lux.   Green, The.
  His Job Is Honest and Simple.
MacNeice.   Woods.
Mahon.   Going Home.
McGrath, T.   Remembering the Children of
  Auschwitz.
Meredith, G.   South-West Wind in the
  Woodland.
Merwin.   Asians Dying, The.
Millay, E.   Through the Green Forest.
Milosz, C.   By a Stream.
Mistral, G.   Pine Forest.
Mörike [*or* Möricke].   Forest Murmurs.
Nemerov.   Deep Woods.
Oliver, M.   Rain.
  Sleeping in the Forest.
Olson, C.   Part of the Series on the Paths, A.
Paley, G.   For My Friend Who Planted a Tree
  for His Daughter Jane.
Ransom, J.   First Travels of Max.
Riley, J.   June at Woodruff.
Rimbaud, A.   Faun's Head.
Ritsos.   Deterioration.
Rukeyser, M.   All the way through the forest, a
  sound of birdsong.
  Child in the Great Wood.
  Gullies as deep as halls held these surveyors.
  Then I Saw What the Calling Was.
Sexton.   Expatriates, The.
Simic.   December Trees.
Smith, S.   I Rode with My Darling.
Swenson, M.   Forest.
Sze.   Juniper Fires.
Tomlinson, C.   In Arden.
  Operation, The.
Very.   Indian's Retort, The.
Walcott.   Air.

Forgery and Forgers

Warren, R.   Chain Saw at Dawn in Vermont in Time of Drouth.
Fear and Trembling.
Monologue at Midnight.
Whittier.   Ranger, The.
Wood Giant, The.
Wilbur, R.   Riddle, A.
Wilde, O.   In the Forest.
Williams, C. K.   Insult, The.
Wilner, E.   Abstraction.
Wordsworth, W.   Suggested by a View from an Eminence in Inglewood Forest.
Wright, J.   Fit against the Country, A.
On the Skeleton of a Hound.
Quail, The.
Zaturenska.   Forest of Arden.
Young Girl Singing, A.

Forgery and Forgers
Mahon.   Forger, The.
Nemerov.   To Clio, Muse of History.

Forges
Heaney, S.   Forge, The.
Ritsos.   Multidimensional.

Forgetfulness
Amichai [or Amikhai].   Elegy on the Lost Child.
Forgetting Someone.
How Much Time.
Sadness of Eyes and Descriptions of a Voyage.
Baudelaire.   Lethe.
Broumas, O.   Out of Mind.
Browning, R.   Memorabilia.
Carver, R.   Iowa Summer.
Spell.
Young Girls, The.
Chamfort.   Live and clean forget from day to day.
Chuang Tzu.   When the Shoe Fits.
Collins, B.   Forgetfulness.
Lines Lost among Trees.
Corbett, W.   Shower in June, A.
Cowper, W.   Epistle to Hill.
Crane, H.   Forgetfulness.
You Are That Frail.
Creeley.   Anywhere.
For the New Year.
It Is at Times.
Names.
Song: "What do you / want, love. To be."
There ("With all I know").
De la Mare.   Clear Eyes.
Dreamer, The.
Dickey, W.   Face-Paintings of the Caduveo Indians.
Dickinson, E.   If recollecting were forgetting.
Knows how to forget!
Sweet—You forgot—but I remembered.
To be forgot by thee.
Whether they have forgotten.
Dugan, A.   Untitled Poem in Two Parts.
Eberhart, R.   Formative Mastership.
Hardy, T.   Death of Regret, The.
Tess's Lament.
Hughes, T.   Egg-Head.
Lawrence, D. H.   Forget.
Levertov.   Woman Meets an Old Lover, A.
MacLeish.   1892–19—.
McGrath, T.   Memorial.
Meredith, G.   Dear, my friend & honour'd madam! of hard facts I'm not a hoarder.
Merwin.   Current, The.
Exercise.
Now and Again.
Millay, E.   Sonnet: "What lips my lips have kissed, and where, and why."
Montale.   Shears, don't cut away that face.
Nash, O.   Mr. Betts's Mind a Kingdom Is.
Parker, D.   Rosemary ("I wear your fragrant memory, like a spray of mignonette").
Testament.
Ramanujan.   On Memory.
Riley, J.   For You.
Rilke.   Lost Things.
No One Speaks of Them.
Rossetti, C.   Exceeding Bitter Cry, An.
Forget Me Not.
He and She.

Long Looked For.
Zara.
Rukeyser, M.   He starts awake in the city. Orion believing.
Tree of rivers seen and forgotten, The.
Wind arrow, wind rose, the wind currents in air.
Rumi.   Sometimes I Forget Completely.
Sandburg, C.   Forgotten Wars.
François Villon Forgotten.
Jan, the Son of Thomas.
Swinburne.   Interlude, An.
Szymborska, W.   End and the Beginning, The.
Warren, R.   Memory Forgotten.
Weiss, T.   Ten Little Rembrandts.
Williams, C. K.   Alzheimer's: The Wife.
Williams, M.   Documenting It.
Wilner, E.   Changing the Imperatives.
Wyatt, S.   Steadfastness.
Zukofsky, L.   Incident, An.

Forgiveness
Ammons.   Foot-Washing, The.
Berry, W.   Anger against Beasts.
Do Not Be Ashamed.
Browning, E.   That Day.
Browning, R.   Adam, Lilith, and Eve.
Byron, G.   On Revisiting Harrow.
To Anne.
Campion, T.   Wise men patience never want.
Carruth, H.   Reflexive.
Ciardi, J.   Darling.
Fast as You Can Count to Ten.
Coleridge, S.   Epitaph: "Stop, Christian passer-by!—Stop, child of God."
Corbett, W.   For the Old Year.
Creeley.   Flowers.
So Big.
Cunningham, J.   Not for Charity.
Davie, D.   Short Run to Camborne.
De la Mare.   Be angry now no more!
Clear Eyes.
Forgiveness.
How Blind!
Dickey, W.   At Maganosc / in the stone bedroom.
Here, in the summer city.
If forgiveness comes / it will be gradual.
In the Dreaming.
In the dreaming / we walk throug the streets of Oxford.
Thinking of me / think of what was.
We meet, eating, smoking.
Dickinson, E.   Of God we ask one favor.
"Remember me" implored the Thief!
'Tis true—They shut me in the Cold.
Donne.   Hymn[e] to God the Father, A.
Dunbar, P.   How Lucy Backslid.
Duncan, R.   Adoration of the Virgin, The.
Frost, R.   Forgive, O Lord, my little jokes on Thee.
Ginsberg, A.   Love Forgiven.
Graves, R.   Gold and Malachite.
Return.
Song: Reconciliation.
Three Words Only.
HaNagid.   Forgive the Man Who Sinned against You.
If You Don't Have the Power to Pay.
Hardy, T.   Burghers, The.
Husband's View, The.
Peace-Offering, The.
Tolerance.
Wife and Another, A.
Herbert, G.   Justice (2).
Love (3).
Herrick.   His Prayer for Absolution.
Hopkins, G.   Complaint, A.
Kipling, R.   Supplication of the Black Aberdeen.
Komunyakaa.   Please.
Kunitz, S.   Magic Curtain, The.
Lindsay, N.   Soul of a Butterfly, The.
Logue, C.   September Song.
Merton.   Ode to the Present Century.
Michelangelo Buonarroti.   Rid of a vexing and a heavy load.
O'Hara, F.   Poem: "Light clarity avocado salad in the morning."

Parker, D.   Prayer for a Prayer.
Raine, K.   Dear ones in the house of the dead.
Ritsos.   Bridge, The; An Uncalled-for Apology.
Robinson, E.   Partnership.
Unforgiven, The.
Rossetti, C.   Afterward He Repented, and Went.
Alas my Lord, / How should I wrestle all the livelong night.
Ash Wednesday.
Good Lord, today / I scarce find breath to say.
Hymn: "O the bitter shame and sorrow."
If thou be dead, forgive and thou shalt live.
Look on This Picture and on This.
O Lord, when Thou didst call me, didst Thou know.
Weigh all my faults and follies righteously.
Young Men Aye Were Fickle Found since Summer Trees Were Leafy.
Seidl.   Hans Euler.
Sexton.   My Friend, My Friend.
Smart, C.   Hymn to the Supreme Being.
Smith, S.   Forgive Me, Forgive Me.
when Walking.
Stafford, W.   November.
Whispered in Winter.
Stock, R.   This Book Is for Harriette.
Szymborska, W.   Under a Certain Little Star.
Very.   Forgiveness.
Villon.   Ballade of Forgiveness.
Whittier.   Forgiveness.
Requital.
Two Angels, The.
Two Rabbins, The.
Williams, C. K.   Penance.
Williams, W.   This Is Just to Say.
Yeats.   He Wishes His Beloved Were Dead.
Lover Asks Forgiveness because of His Many Moods.

Forks
Brodsky, J.   At the Helmet and Sword.
Simic.   Fork.

Fortitude
Kipling, R.   If—.
Moore, M.   Nevertheless.
See also **Endurance**

Fortune
Beckett, S.   À l'instant de s'entendre dire.
Burns, R.   Ill-fated Genius! Heaven-taught Fergusson.
Byron, G.   Love and Gold.
Campion, T.   In obitum Gual. Devoreux fratris clariss. Comitus Essexiae.
Carver, R.   Poems.
Cavalcanti.   Canzone: A Song of Fortune.
Char.   Septentrion.
Chaucer.   Fortune.
Chuang Tzu.   Good Fortune.
Cowper, W.   Verses Written at Bath on Finding the Heel of a Shoe.
Crashaw.   Epithalamium: "Come virgin Tapers of pure waxe."
Cummings, E. E.   That melancholy / fellow'll play / his handorgan.
Cunningham, J.   Epigram: "Good Fortune, when I hailed her recently."
De la Mare.   Dust to Dust.
Eberhart, R.   Fortune's Mist.
Emerson, R.   Divine Inviters! I accept.
Guy.
Van Buren.
Woods.
Gunn, T.   Wheel of Fortune, The.
Hardy, T.   Hap.
He Fears His Good Fortune.
Herrick.   Adversity.
All Things Run Well for the Righteous.
Change Common to All.
Discord Not Disadvantageous.
Felicitie Knowes No Fence.
Fortune.
Fortune Favours.
Good Luck Not Lasting.
No Paines, No Gaines.
Potentates.
Reverence to Riches.
Speake in Season.

Suffer Thou That Canst Not Shift.
Supreme Fortune Falls Soonest.
To Fortune.
To His Sister in Law, M. Susanna Herrick.
Housman. Lads in Their Hundreds, The.
Hughes, L. Elevator Boy.
Koch, K. Locks.
Laughlin, J. How Fortunate.
Meredith, G. My Theme.
Merton. Song: In the Shows of the Round Ox.
Merwin. Talk of Fortune.
Petrarch. Love, Fortune, and my mind (hardly aware).
Unless, through blind desire which breaks the heart.
Prudentius. Fortune and Hope! I've made my port.
Ralegh, S. From wisedome Fortune differs farre.
Riley, J. Be Our Fortunes as They May.
Rukeyser, M. Slow Death of the Dragon.
Sandburg, C. Fame if Not Fortune.
Joke Gold.
Unknown. I have come home. Fortune and Hope, goodbye!
Wyatt, S. Alas, Fortune, what aileth thee.
Fortune doth frown.
In faith I not [well] what to say.
Marvel No More.
Promise, A.

See also Chance; Fate; Luck

Fortunetelling and Fortunetellers
Auden. Model, The.
Broumas, O. Calypso.
Dactyls.
Soothsaying.
Carruth, H. Fat Lady, The.
Sonnet: "Well, she told me I had an aura. 'What?' I said."
Cavafy. On the March to Sinopi.
Graves, R. Man Does, Woman Is.
Hardy, T. Echo-Elf Answers, The.
Herrick. Upon Cupid.
Hughes, L. Bad Luck Card.
Ballad of the Fortune Teller.
Ballad of the Gypsy.
Fortune Teller Blues.
Madam and the Fortune Teller.
Lawrence, D. H. There Was a Gay Bird Named Christine.
Lindsay, N. I Know All This when Gipsy Fiddles Cry.
Marvell. Illustrissimo Viro Domino Lanceloto Josepho de Maniban Grammatomanti [To That Renowned Man Lord Lancelot Joseph de Maniban Graphologist].
Merrill, J. Last Mornings in California.
Milosz, C. Boy, A.
Nemerov. Fortune Teller, The.
Plath. Crystal Gazer.
Sandburg, C. Gypsy Mother.
Stock, R. Part of a Tarot Fortune.
Williams, T. Crepe de Chine.

Fossils
Ciardi, J. Goodnight.
Dove, R. Fish in the Stone, The.
Ferlinghetti, L. Cro-Magnons.
Nash, O. Next!
Pagis. Bestiary.
Very. Fossil Flower, The.
Williams, W. Smiling Dane, A.

Fountains
Baudelaire. Girandole, The.
Bogan, L. Roman Fountain.
Castiglione. On the Statue of Cleopatra, Made into a Fountain by Leo the Tenth.
Coleridge, S. Inscription for a Fountain on a Heath.
Ovidian Elegiac Metre, The.
Davie, D. Fountain, The.
Fountain of Arethusa, The.
Fountain of Cyanë, The.
Dubie. You.
Dugan, A. From Rome, for More Public Fountains in New York City.
Dunbar, P. Fount of Tears, The.

Eberhart, R. Garden God, The.
García Lorca. Ballad of the Little Square.
Guyon. Living Water.
Herrick. To Springs and Fountains.
To the Water Nymphs, Drinking at the Fountain.
Levertov. Fountain, The.
Mallarmé. Sigh.
Mistral, G. Prison Sentence, The.
Olson, C. Gate Is Prouti, The.
I Weep, Fountain of Jazer.
Story, A.
Prunty. Name, The.
Rilke. These Are the Days.
Rukeyser, M. Beast in View.
Swenson, M. Fountain Piece.
Foutains of Aix.
Tomlinson, C. Fountain.
Unknown. Pere Bouhours' Fountain Made Muddy by the Translator.
Whitticr. Fountain, The.
Wilbur, R. Ballade for the Duke of Orléans.
Baroque Wall-Fountain in the Villa Sciarra, A.
Williams, W. Spouts.
Wordsworth, W. Fountain, The.
Zaturenska. Cascades and Fountains.

Fourth of July
Berry, W. Independence Day.
Creeley. July: Fargo Street.
Hughes, L. Fourth of July Thought.
Komunyakaa. Happiness.
Insufficient Blue.
Lowell, R. Fourth of July in Maine.
McGrath, T. End of the Line, The.
Nemerov. Fourth of July, The.
Piercy. Rainy 4th.
Riley, J. McFeeters' Fourth.
Sandburg, C. Fourth of July Night.
Schuyler, J. At the Beach.
Quick, Henry, the Flit!
Very. Hymn: Sung at the Celebration of the Fourth of July, in Salem, 1854.
Wilbur, R. Fourth of July, The.
Williams, W. 4th of July.

Fox, Charles James
Wordsworth, W. Lines: "Loud is the Vale! the Voice is up."

Foxes
Burns, R. Fragment—on Glenriddel's Fox Breaking His Chain, A.
Clifton, L. Coming of Fox, The.
Dear Fox.
Dream of Foxes, A.
Fox.
Leaving Fox.
One Year Later.
Telling Our Stories.
Dickey, J. Dog Sleeping on My Feet, A.
Listening to Foxhounds.
Dubie. February: The Boy Breughel.
Dugan, A. On a Skunked Fox.
Eberhart, R. Wild Life and Tamed Life.
Emerson, R. No song so tuneful, quoth the fox.
Graves, R. To the Teumessian Vixen.
Hughes, T. Thought-Fox, The.
Kipling, R. Fox-Hunting.
Kumin, M. Homage to Binsey Poplars.
Levine, P. Fox, The.
Meredith, G. Young Reynard.
Muldoon, P. Fox, The.
Orr, G. Gray Fox, The.
Pagis. Freedom Machine, The.
Patchen. Fox, The.
Rich, A. Abnegation.
Sandburg, C. Early Moon.
Simic. Fable: "In my favorite one."
Stock, R. How They Hunt the Quick Red Fox.
Tomlinson, C. Fox, The.
Fox Gallery, The.
Foxes' Moon.
Very. Fox and the Bird, The.
Williams, T. Cried the Fox.
Wilner, E. Never Apologize for Poetry.
Wright, J. Blue Teal's Mother.

Foxgloves
Hughes, T. Sunstruck Foxglove.
Sandburg, C. Foxgloves.

France
Beckett, S. Dieppe.
Bierce. France.
Byron, G. Napoleon's Farewell.
Cowper, W. In Seditionem Horrendum.
Crane, H. I Rob My Breast.
Cullen, C. La Belle, La Douce, La Grande.
To France.
Cummings, E. E. Little ladies more / than dead exactly dance.
Davie, D. Brantôme.
Right Wing Sympathies.
Rodez.
Du Bellay. Heureux Qui, comme Ulysse, a Fait un Beau Voyage.
Sonnet from the Book of Regrets.
Eberhart, R. Mediterranean Song.
Ferlinghetti, L. Firenze, a Lifetime Later.
Late Impressionist Dream.
L'Occupation Obsédée.
Morlaix: Into the Future with Neil Young.
Gurney, I. Behind the Line.
Of Grandcourt.
Robecq Again.
Hacker, M. Graffiti from the Gare Saint-Manque.
Heaney, S. Night Drive.
Hill, G. Mystery of the Charity of Charles Péguy, The.
Hopkins, G. Duns Scotus's Oxford.
Jeffers, R. Dead to Clemenceau: November 1929, The.
Johnson, S. French Distichs.
Jonson, B. On English Monsieur.
Kipling, R. Curé, The.
France.
French Wars, The.
King's Pilgrimage, The.
Song of French Roads, A.
Song of Seventy Horses.
Major, C. Divine Law: A Blue Beach Sermon.
Home on Rue du Bourg-Tibourg.
In Absence of the Tree.
On the Old Roman Road.
Meredith, G. New Era the Army of the Future the Egg of an Army, The.
Three Eagles and the Sleepy Lion, The.
To P.A. Labouchère Esq.
To the Merry Men of France.
Meredith, W. Notre Dame de Chartres.
Millay, E. To the Maid of Orleans.
Milosz, C. From the Chronicles of the Town of Pornic.
Moore, M. Light Is Speech.
To the Peacock of France.
Niedecker. Laval, Pomeret, Pétain.
Tell me a story about the war.
Oppen. Dream, The.
Visit (1).
Paley, G. In Aix.
Parker, D. Song of Americans Resident in France.
Raine, K. Letter to Pierre Emmanuel.
Rexroth, K. Camargue.
La Vie en Rose.
Rimbaud, A. Bad Blood.
Blacksmith, The.
Dead of '92 and '93, The.
To Music.
Sarton, M. Evening Walk in France.
Smith, S. Bandol (Var).
Stafford, W. Merci Beaucoup.
Suckling, S. Cantilena Politica-Jocunda Facta Post Principis Discessum In Hispaniam.
Swenson, M. Alyscamps at Arles, The.
Swinburne. Les Noyades.
Tomlinson, C. Lacoste.
Updike. Farewell to the Shopping District of Antibes.
Some Frenchmen.
Very. Lessons of History Unlearned, The.
Whitman, W. France, the 18th Year of These States.
O Star of France (1870–71).
Whittier. Bartholdi Statue, The.
Thiers.

Wilde, O.   Louis Napoleon.
Wordsworth, W.   Calais, August 15, 1802.
   Great men have been among us; hands that
   penned.
   Near Dover, September 1802.
   October, 1803 ("One might believe that natural
   miseries").
Zagajewski.   Albi.
   Churches of France, The.
   Tarbes.
Zukofsky, L.   4 Other Countries.

Francesca, Piers delta
See **Piero della Francesca**

Francis of Assisi, Saint
Chesterton.   St. Francis of Assisi.
Dubie.   Chemin de Fer.
Kinnell.   Saint Francis and the Sow.
Lindsay, N.   Voice of St. Francis of Assisi, The.
Mistral, G.   Body, The.
   Lark, The.
Williams, W.   Mental Hospital Garden, The.

Franco, Francisco
Kizer, C.   Valley of the Fallen, The.
Wright, J.   Eisenhower's Visit to Franco, 1959.

Franco-Prussian War
Rimbaud, A.   Centre: the Emperor, apotheosis.
Rossetti, C.   German-French Campaign, 1870–
   1871, The.
Very.   Lessons of History Unlearned, The.
   Military surprises and the capture of capitals,
   are the events of a by-gone age. D'Israeli.
Whitman, W.   O Star of France (1870–71).
Whittier.   Thiers.

Frank, Anne
Meredith, W.   John and Anne.
Williams, C. K.   Day for Anne Frank, A.

Frankenstein
Atwood.   Speeches for Dr Frankenstein.

Frankfurt Book Fair
Celan.   Frankfurt, September.

Franklin, Benjamin
Sandburg, C.   Open Letter to the Poet Archibald
   MacLeish Who Has Forsaken His
   Massachusetts Farm to Make Propaganda for
   Freedom.
Stockton, A.   Lines on Hearing of the Death of
   Doctor Franklin.

Fraternity
See **Brotherhood**

Fratricide
Kipling, R.   Romulus and Remus.
Melville, H.   Battle of Stone River, Tennessee.
Very.   Thy Brother's Blood.
Whittier.   Fratricide, The.

Free Will
Atwood.   Torture.
Bierce.   Infralapsarian.
Cullen, C.   Ultimatum.
Frost, R.   Road Not Taken, The.
Herrick.   Another.
   Predestination.
Jarrell, R.   Conversation with the Devil, A.
Jonson, B.   Epode: "Not to know vice at all, and
   keep[e] true state."
Levertov.   Freedom.
Michelangelo Buonarroti.   O cruel star, or say
   instead, cruel will.
Orr, G.   On the Lawn at Ira's.
Pessoa.   Gods grant us this one, The.
Rumi.   Deliberation.
Szymborska, W.   One Version of Events.
Weiss, T.   Another and Another and.
Whittier.   Overruled.

Freedom
Amichai [*or* Amikhai].   Man with Knapsack.
Angelou.   Caged Bird.
   To a Freedom Fighter.
Atwood.   Lying here, everything in me.
Auden.   Watch Any Day.
Beckett, S.   Sitôt sorti de l'ermitage.
Berry, W.   Independence Day.
   Law That Marries All Things, The.
   Mad Farmer's Love Song, The.
Berryman.   Captain's Song, The.

Heaven.
Bierce.   False Prophecy, A.
   Saith the Czar.
   To the Bartholdi Statue.
Bishop, E.   Sonnet: "Caught—the bubble."
Blake, W.   How Sweet I Roamed [*or* Roam'd]
   from Field to Field.
Borges.   Spinoza.
Brontë, E.   To Imagination.
Broumas, O.   Body and Soul.
   Evensong.
Browning, E.   Calls on the Heart.
   Hiram Powers' "Greek Slave."
   King Victor Emanuel Entering Florence, April,
   1860.
   Runaway Slave at Pilgrim's Point, The.
   Sword of Castruccio Castracani, The.
Browning, R.   Why I Am a Liberal.
Bukowski.   Friendly Advice to a Lot of Young
   Men.
   Hello, Willie Shoemaker.
   Poem to a Most Affectionate Lady.
Burns, R.   Address of Beelzebub.
   Caledonia.
   Castle Gordon—*Intended to Be Sung to Morag.*
   De'il's [*or* Deil's] Awa wi' th' [*or* the]
   Exciseman, The.
   Fragment, A: "When *Guilford* good our Pilot
   stood."
   Fragment—on Glenriddel's Fox Breaking His
   Chain, A.
   I Hae a Wife o' My Ain.
   Ode [for General Washington's Birthday].
   On Johnson's Opinion of Hampden.
   Poetical Inscription, for an Altar to
   Independence at Kerrouchtry, the Seat of Mr.
   Heron, Written in Summer 1795.
   Scots Wha Hae.
   To the Beautiful Miss Eliza J————n, on Her
   Principles of Liberty and Equality.
   Tree of Liberty, The.
Byron, G.   Translation of the Famoue Greek
   War Song *Deute Paides Tov Ellenon.*
Campion, T.   Could my poore hart whole worlds
   of toungs employ.
Carew, T.   Song: The Willing Prisoner to His
   Mistress.
Carver, R.   Money.
Coleridge, S.   Foster-Mother's Tale, The.
Cowper, W.   Morning Dream, The.
   Negro's Complaint, The.
Creeley.   Ballad of the Despairing Husband.
   Places ("When I wake next").
Cullen, C.   Karenge Ya Marenge.
   Wind Bloweth Where It Listeth, The.
Cummings, E. E.   Am was. Are Leaves Few
   this. Is these a or.
   As freedom is a breakfastfood.
   Be of love(a little).
   F is for foetus(a).
   I say no world.
   If(touched by love's own secret)we,like homing.
   Let's,from some loud unworld's most rightful
   wrong.
   O to be in finland.
   There are possibly 2 1/2 or impossibly 3.
   Unlove's the heavenless hell and homeless
   home.
   What freedom's not some under's mere above.
   Why must itself up every of a park.
De la Mare.   Little Salamander, The.
Dickinson, E.   Could I but ride indefinite.
   No Prisoner be.
   No Rack can torture me.
   Power to fly is sweet, The.
   Sweet Land of Liberty.
   They shut me up in Prose.
Donne.   Canonization, The.
Dove, R.   Geometry.
   Pamela.
   Three Days of Forest, a River, Free.
   Transport or Slaves from Maryland to
   Mississippi, The.
Dunbar, P.   Ante-Bellum Sermon, An.
   Awakening, The.
   Emancipation.

   Sympathy.
Eberhart, R.   Critic with His Pained Eye, The.
   Humanist, The.
   Life as Visionary Spirit.
   Secret Heart, The.
   To the Mad Poets.
   Wedding, The.
Éluard, P.   Second Nature.
Emerson, R.   Ancient drop of feudal blood, An.
   Boston.
   Etienne de la Boéce.
   Few are free / All might be.
   Freedom.
   Give All to Love.
   Ode Sung in the Town Hall.
   Pilgrims, The.
   See how Romance adheres.
   Skeptic, The.
   Trimountain.
Enzensberger, H.   Historical Process.
Ferlinghetti, L.   Dog.
Ginsberg, A.   To the Punks of Dawlish.
Gjuzel.   On the Way Back.
Glück, L.   Legend.
   Undertaking, The.
Graves, R.   Freehold.
   Gooseflesh Abbey.
   Song: Come, Enjoy Your Sunday!
Gunn, T.   Tamer and Hawk.
Guyon.   Gratitude and Love to God.
"H. D."   Helmsman, The.
   In the Rain.
Hall, D.   Friend Revisited, A.
Han-shan.   Parrots live in western lands.
   Tientai Mountains are my home, The.
Hardy, T.   At the Railway Station, Upway.
   Orphaned Old Maid, The.
Hayden, R.   Frederick Douglass.
   Runagate Runagate.
Herrick.   His Answer to a Question.
   Liberty.
   More Potent, Lesse Peccant.
   To All Young Men That Love.
   To Love.
   Upon Love.
Hughes, L.   Ballad of the Seven Songs.
   Call of Ethiopia.
   Dream of Freedom.
   Explain It, Please.
   Freedom ("Freedom will not come").
   Freedom Seeker.
   Freedom Train.
   Freedom's Plow.
   Frosting.
   How About It, Dixie.
   Let America Be America Again.
   Refugee in America.
   Southern Negro Speaks.
   Uncle Tom ("Uncle Tom is a legend and a
   dream").
   What I Think.
Hughes, T.   Jaguar, The.
Ignatow, D.   On Freedom.
   Thinking.
Jarrell, R.   Emancipators, The.
   Lines, The.
   Port of Embarkation.
   Woman at the Washington Zoo, The.
Jeffers, R.   Coast-Road, The.
   Shine, Republic.
Keats.   Song: "I had a dove and the sweet dove
   died."
Kipling, R.   Benfactors, The.
   Ode to Liberty.
   Song of Travel, A.
Kizer, C.   Eleutheria.
Laughlin, J.   Floating Free.
Lawrence, D. H.   Free Will.
   Let Us Talk, Let Us Laugh.
   Liberty's Old Old Story.
Levi, P.   25 February 1944.
Levine, P.   Ashes.
   Children's Crusade, The.
Lindsay, N.   Old Horse in the City, The.
Longfellow, H.   Slave Singing at Midnight, The.
MacLeish.   Boy in the Roman Zoo.

Brave New World.
Good Man in a Bad Time, A.
Liberty.
MacNeice. Sunlight on the Garden, The.
Merton. All of the branches / None of the roots.
And the Children of Birmingham.
Elias—Variations on a Theme.
Freedom as Experience.
Millay, E. Not for a Nation.
Mistral, G. Chilean Earth.
Olson, C. Fool, The.
Pagis. Freedom Machine, The.
Parker, D. Song of the Conventions.
Patchen. And When Freedom Is Achieved.
Billion Freedoms, The.
Letter on Liberty, A.
Pessoa. I ask the gods only to forget me.
I only ask the gods to grant me.
Liberty.
Not just those who hate and those who envy us.
Piercy. Noon of the Sunbather.
Sabbath of Mutual Respect, The.
Sojourners.
Raine, K. Eudaimon.
Wind.
Ransom, J. Dog.
Rilke. Prisoners.
Rimbaud, A Comedy of Thirst.
Ritsos. After the Breakdown of the Treaty
between the Lacedaemonians and the
Athenians.
Fundamentals, The.
Need of Proof.
Ready.
Roethke. I Knew A Woman.
Rossetti, C. Linnet in a gilded cage,— / A
linnet on a bough, A.
Promises like Pie-Crust.
Song of the Star, The.
Rukeyser, M. Ann Burlak.
Game of Darts at the Chesterfield Arms, A.
In Our Time.
Juanita Tinsley.
Long Enough. Long Enough.
Secrets of American Civilization.
When the young man reaches his full height.
Sandburg, C. Cahokia.
Freedom Is a Habit.
Harbor, The.
Is There Any Easy Road to Freedom?
Limited.
Noon Hour.
Open Letter to the Poet Archibald MacLeish
Who Has Forsaken His Massachusetts Farm
to Make Propaganda for Freedom.
Shoes of Travel.
Sarton, M. Caged Bird, The.
On Being Given Time.
Phoenix, The.
Prisoner at a Desk.
Shelley, P. Cancelled Stanza.
Liberty.
Ode to Liberty.
Smith, S. Anger's Freeing Power.
Snyder, G. High Quality Information.
Off the Trail.
Once at Cold Mountain, troubles cease.
Stafford, W. For Our Party Last Night.
Freedom.
Message from the Wanderer, A.
Right to Die.
Swenson, M. Stripping and Putting On.
Tate, J. Consumed.
Thoreau. Independence.
Tollas, T. They've Blocked Every Window.
Vallejo. I am Freed.
Very. Freedom National, Slavery Sectional.
Hymn: Nature's Sympathy with Freedom.
"It is vain to say, that this is the country of the
'white man.' It is the country of man."
Charles Sumner.
Light of Freedom Necessary to National
Progress, The.
Walcott. Elegy: "Our hammock swung between
Americas."
Whalen, P. Bleakness, Farewell.

Wheatley, P. Liberty and Peace, a Poem.
To the Right Honourable William, Earl of
Dartmouth, His Majesty's Principal Secretary
of State for North America.
Voice of Freedom, The.
Whitman, W. Broadway Pageant, A.
Columbian's Song, The.
Commonplace, The.
Election Day, November, 1884.
France, The 18th Year of These States.
House of Friends, The.
Inca's Daughter, The.
Lo, Victress on the Peaks.
Old Age's Ship & Crafty Death's.
Old Salt Kossabone.
Poem of Remembrances for a Girl or a Boy of
These States.
Song of the Banner at Daybreak.
Spain, 1873–74.
Thoughts.
To Soar in Freedom and in Fullness of Power.
To the States.
Turn O Libertad.
Washington's Monument, February, 1885.
We Two, How Long We Were Fool'd.
Years of the Modern.
Whittier. After Election.
Arisen at Last.
Astræa at the Capitol.
At Port Royal.
Bartholdi Statue, The.
Brown Dwarf of Rügen, The.
Democracy.
Derne.
Eve of Election, The.
Exiles, The.
Expostulation.
Freed Islands, The.
Freedom in Brazil.
Garibaldi.
Greeting, A.
Hymn: "O Holy Father! just and true."
Hymn Sung at Christmas by the Scholars of St.
Helena's Island, S.C.
In the "Old South."
Jubilee Singers, The.
Kansas Emigrants, The.
King's Missive, The.
Kossuth.
Laus Deo!
Legend of St. Mark, The.
Letter, A.
Lexington.
Lines from a Letter to a Young Clerical Friend.
Lost Occasion, The.
Lost Statesman, The.
Massachusetts.
Mayflowers, The.
Moloch in State Street.
Moral Warfare, The.
New Hampshire.
New Year, The.
One of the Signers.
Pæan.
Pass of the Sierra, The.
Pennsylvania Hall.
Pennsylvania Pilgrim, The.
Pine-Tree, The.
Proclamation, The.
Proem: "I love the old melodious lays."
Rantoul.
Relic, The.
Rendition, The.
Ritner.
Song of the Vermonters, 1779, The.
Stanzas for the Times.
Summons, A.
Summons, The.
Sumner.
Thiers.
Thomas Starr King.
To Delaware.
To Faneuil Hall.
To Pennsylvania.
To the Memory of Charles B. Storrs.
To William H. Seward.

Toussaint L'Ouverture.
Vow of Washington, The.
What of the Day?
World's Convention, The.
Wilbur, R. On Freedom's Ground.
Regatta, The.
Still, Citizen Sparrow.
Wilde, O. Libertatis Sacra Fames.
Sonnet to Liberty.
Williams, M. Lay of the Badde Wyf.
Williams, W. In Chains.
Wordsworth, W. Composed at Cora Linn in
Sight of Wallace's Tower.
Eagle and the Dove, The.
Just Vengeance Claims Thy Soul for Rights
Invaded?
Ode to Lycoris.
Thought[s] of a Briton on the Subjugation of
Switzerland.
To a Skylark.
Wright, J. To a Fugitive.
Wednesday Night Prayer Meeting.
Wyatt, S. Ah, my heart, ah, what aileth thee.
If chance assigned [or assign'd].
Liberty.
Now must I le[a]rn[e] to live [or lyve] at rest.
Zagajewski, Fire.
Freedom Train
Hughes, L. Freedom Train.
Freemasonry
Burns, R. Farewell. To the Brethren of St.
James' Lodge, Tarbolton, The.
Sons of Old Killie, The.
Kipling, R. Mother-Lodge, The.
Freighters
Levertov. Don't You Hear that Whistle
Blowin'.
Frémont, John Charles
Whittier. Frémont Campaign Song, A.
Song, A: "Beneath thy skies, November!"
Song for the Time, A.
To John C. Frémont.
French (language)
Laughlin, J. Translation, A.
Stafford, W. Merci Beaucoup.
Weiss, T. Studying French.
French Revolution
Blake, W. Fayette beside King Lewis stood.
French Revolution, The.
Let the Brothels of Paris be opened.
When France got free Europe 'twixt Fools &
Knaves.
Chesterton. Danton.
Coleridge, S. Destruction of the Bastile.
Fears in Solitude [Written in April, 1798, during
the Alarm of an Invasion].
France: An Ode.
Ode on the Departing Year.
Recantation.
To a Young Lady.
Jarrell, R. 1789–1939.
Niedecker. Jefferson and Adams.
Rimbaud, A. Blacksmith, The.
Hands of Jeanne-Marie, The.
Paris War-Cry.
Parisian Orgy, or Paris Filling Up Again.
Stockton, A. Impromptu on Hearing that a Print
of the Guliteene with Our Beloved Presidents
Figure under It Was Executed in Mr Genets
Family—under His Sanction.
Tomlinson, C. Charlotte Corday.
For Danton.
Marat Dead.
Wordsworth, W. French Revolution as It
Appeared to Enthusiasts at Its Commencement.
Reprinted from "The Friend."
French, The
Davie, D. Killala.
Eberhart, R. Retrospective Forelook.
Gunn, T. Readings in French.
Hughes, L. Cubes.
Laughlin, J. French, The.
You Invited Me.
Nash, O. Chacun à Son Berlitz.
How Do You Say Ha-Ha in French.

If He Scholars, Let Him Go.
Strange Case of Mr. Palliser's Palate, The.
Try It Suns. and Hols.; It's Closed Then.
What Is Bibbidi-Bobbidi-Boo in Sanskrit?
O'Hara, F.   Ode: Salute to the French Negro
  Poets.
Schuyler, J.   Fauré Ballade, The.
Simone Signoret.

Freud, Sigmund
Auden.   In Memory of Sigmund Freud.
Celan.   Frankfurt, September.
Cunningham, J.   Oedipean Mom and Dad, An.
Dugan, A.   Nomenclature.
"H. D."   Master, The.
Hacker, M.   For Elektra.
MacLeish.   Dr. Sigmund Freud Discovers the
  Sea Shell.
Meredith, W.   Dying Away.
Paley, G.   One Day.
Parker, D.   Passionate Freudian to His Love,
  The.
Walker, A.   So We've Come at Last to Freud.

Friars
Cavalcanti.   Figure of my Lady, A.
Meredith, G.   Adieu, adieu, my Friar, he cried.
Orlandi, G.   If, my friend, you would have said
  of Mary so.
Ransom, J.   Necrological.

Friends, Society of
Clampitt.   At Muker, Upper Swaledale.
  War Memorial, The.
Whittier.   Abram Morrison.
  Anniversary Poem.
  Banished from Massachusetts.
  Barclay of Ury.
  Cassandra Southwick.
  Chalkley Hall.
  Cross, The.
  Daniel Wheeler.
  Exiles, The.
  Fair Quakeress, The.
  First-Day Thoughts.
  How the Women Went from Dover.
  King's Missive, The.
  Meeting, The.
  Pennsylvania Pilgrim, The.
  Quaker Alumni, The.
  Quaker of the Olden Time, The.
  Quakers Are Out, The.
  Revelation.
  Two Elizabeths, The.

Friendship
Amichai [or Amikhai].   Haydn, Opus 76,
  Number 5.
  My First Days in New York.
Ashbery, J.   Friends.
  Some Trees.
  Train Rising Out of the Sea.
Auden.   Thank You, Fog.
Austen.   To F.S., who accused the Author of
  partiality in writing verses for F C Fowle, &
  not for him.
Berrigan, T.   New Personal Poem.
  So Going around Cities.
Berry, W.   In Memory: Stuart Egnal.
  Kentucky River Junction.
  Marriage.
  Meeting, A.
  Plan, The.
  To Gary Snyder.
Berryman.   To Bhain Campbell.
  Winter-Piece to a Friend Away, A.
Bishop, E.   Letter to N.Y.
  Manuelzinho.
  Shampoo, The.
Blake, W.   If Men will act like a maid smiling
  over a Churn.
  [Look Flaxman & Stothard do] old acquaintance
  well.
  Mr Stothard to Mr Cromek.
  On Hayley.
  On H[ayle]ys Friendship.
  To H[ayley].
  To John Flaxman, 12 September 1800.
  Was I angry with Hayley who used me so ill.
Blue Cloud.   Old Friends.

Bly, R.   After Drinking All Night with a Friend,
  We Go Out in a Boat at Dawn to See Who Can
  Write the Best Poem.
Borges.   Epilogue: "Now that the number of
  steps you were given."
  Two Cathedrals, The.
  Unending Rose, The.
Brodsky, J.   Letters to a Roman Friend.
Brontë, E.   But the hearts that once adored me.
  Love and Friendship.
  Not many years but long enough to see.
  O hinder me by no delay.
Broumas, O.   Walk on the Water.
Browning, E.   Hugh Stuart Boyd [His
  Blindness].
  L.E.L.'s Last Question.
  Little Friend, The.
  Sea-side walk, A.
  Sleep, The.
  To Bettine.
  To Mary Russell Mitford.
Browning, R.   Clive.
  Fears and Scruples.
  Light Woman, A.
  Waring.
Bukowski.   Letter from the North.
  Reunion.
  What to Do with Contributor's Copies?
Burns, R.   Auld Lang Syne.
  Epistle to Captn Willm Logan at Park.
  Here's, a bottle and an honest friend.
  Interpolation.
  Reply to Robert Riddell.
  Second Epistle to Davie.
  Second Epistle to John Lapraik.
  Third Epistle to J. Lapraik.
  To Chloris.
  To James Smith.
  To Mr. John Kennedy.
  To Mrs. C———.
  To Renton of Lamerton.
  To Terraughty, on His Birth-Day.
Byron, G.   L'Amitié Est l'Amour sans Ailes.
  Lines Written on a Blank Leaf of the "Pleasures
  of Memory."
  On Revisiting Harrow.
  Pignus Amoris.
  To a Youthful Friend.
  To Edward Noel Long, Esq.
  To George, Earl Delawarr.
  To the Earl of Clare.
Campion, T.   Were My Heart as Some Men's
  Are.
Carew, T.   To My Worthy Friend, Master
  Davenant upon His Excellent Play, *The Just
  Italian*.
Carruth, H.   Pa McCabe.
Carver, R.   In the Year 2020.
  My Boat.
  Old Days, The.
Cavafy.   Stephanos Skilitsis.
Cavalcanti.   Each fresh and sweet source.
  Surely it wasn't your cultered mind.
Chuang Tzu.   Flight of Lin Hui, The.
  Three Friends.
Ciardi, J.   At O'Hare.
  Friends.
  Inscription for Richard Eberhard, An.
  Limits of Friendship, The.
Clough.   Mari Magno I.
  Sectantem levia nervi deficiunt.
Coleridge, S.   Duty Surviving Self-Love.
  Hexameters.
  Love and Friendship Opposite.
  To a Young Friend.
  To W. Wordsworth.
  To William Wordsworth.
Cooper, J.   Long, Disconsolate Lines.
  Mourning Picture.
  My Friend.
Cowper, W.   Catharina.
  Catharina, the Second Part.
  Epistle to Hill.
  Epistle to Lady Austen.
  Faithful Friend, The.
  Friendship.

On the Death of Russell.
This ev'ning, Delia, you and I.
To Hayley.
To Unwin.
Valediction, The: "Farewell, false hearts! whose
  best affections fail."
Winter Nosegay, The.
Crabbe, G.   On Receiving from a Lady a Present
  of a Ring.
Crane, H.   Postscript, A.
Crashaw.   Upon Two Greene Apricockes Sent to
  Cowley by Sir Crashaw.
  With a Picture Sent to a Friend.
Creeley.   Corn Close.
  Damon & Pythias.
  For a Friend.
  For Anybody.
  For Friendship.
  For Joel.
  For John Chamberlain.
  For John Duff.
  For Rainer Gerhardt.
  For Rene Ricard.
  For Tom.
  For Walter Chappell.
  Friend, The.
  Friends, The.
  Hart Crane.
  Last Mile, The.
  Lunch and After.
  Oh Max.
  Poem, A: "If the water forms."
  Saturday Afternoon.
  This wide, shallow bowl.
  Trees.
  Wishes.
Cullen, C.   Dear Friends and Gentle Hearts.
  Little Sonnet to Little Friends.
  Tableau.
Cummings, E. E.   "But / he" i / staring / into
  winter twi.
  W.H.W., Jr.
Cunningham, J.   I write you in my need. Please
  write.
da Bologna, B.   Inside that loving country girl.
Dante Alighieri.   Sonnet: He Imagines a
  Pleasant Voyage for Guido, Lapo Gianni, and
  Himself, with Their Three Ladies.
Davie, D.   Berkshire.
  Catullus on Friendship.
  Landfall among Friends.
  Recollection of George Oppen in a Letter to an
  English Friend.
  To C. T.
De la Mare.   Faithless.
Dickinson, E.   Are Friends Delight or Pain?
  Believing that we are to have no Face.
  By Chivalries as tiny.
  Friend is a / solemnity, A.
  Friends are nations in themselves.
  Gift of neither Heaven nor Earth, The.
  I am speechlessly grateful for a friend.
  I cannot depict a friend to my mind.
  I have the friend who loves me.
  I showed her Heights she never saw.
  I think it sad to have a friend.
  If Anybody's Friend be Dead.
  Is not an absent friend as mysterious.
  Must I lose the Friend that saved my Life.
  My friend must be a Bird.
  Shady friend—for Torrid days, A.
  Small weight is obnoxious, A.
  Sweet and soft as summer, Darlings.
  That you return to us alive.
  To which as to a Reservoir.
  Trudging to Eden, looking backward.
  Who loves you most.
  You asked me if I wrote now?
Donne.   To Mr C. B.
  To Mr I. L. ("Blessed [or Blesst] are your north
  parts, for all this long time").
  To Mr R. W. ("If, as mine is, thy life a slumber
  be").
  To Mr T. W. ("All hail, sweet poet, more full of
  more strong fire").
  To the Lady Bedford.

Dubie. Genesis Text for Larry Levis, Who Died Alone, A.
Dunbar, P. After the Quarrel.
Comrade.
Silence.
To a Dead Friend.
To Dr. James Newton Matthews, Mason, Ill.
Duncan, R. Among My Friends.
Eberhart, R. Wild Swans of Inverane, The.
Emerson, R. Always day & night.
For Genius made his cabin wide.
Friends to me are frozen wine.
Friendship.
From Frodmer's Drama "The Friends."
Hard is it to persuade the public mind of its plain duty & true interest.
I live among ideal men.
I must not borrow light.
Maiden Speech of the Æolian Harp.
Motto to "Considerations by the Way."
Rubies.
Faiz. Bangla Desh: 3.
Frost, R. Telephone, The.
Time to Talk, A.
Gallagher, T. Hug, The.
García Lorca. Fable and Round of the Three Friends.
Ginsberg, A. Elegy for Neal Cassady.
Glück, L. Triumph of Achilles, The.
Graves, R. At First Sight.
At the Well.
Song: Just Friends.
Gray, T. Epitaph on Sir William Williams.
Guillaume de Lorris et al. Romance [or Romaunt] of the Rose, The.
Gunn, T. J Car, The.
Reassurance, The.
Terminal.
To a Friend in Time of Trouble.
Gurney, I. Companion—North-East Dug-Out.
Hacker, M. Against Silence.
Chaplet for Judith Landry, A.
Country & Western II.
Dear Jool, I Miss You in Saint-Saturnin.
Elevens.
Gerda in the Aerie.
Late August Letter.
Letter from Goose Creek: April.
Little Robber Girl Gets On in the Wide World, The.
Nights of 1962: The River Merchant's Wife.
Nights of 1965: the Old Reliable.
Towards Autumn.
Hafiz [or Hafez]. Friendship.
Hall, D. Body Politic, The.
Cider 5¢ A Glass.
Friend Revisited, A.
Milkers Broken Up.
My Friend Felix.
Hamill, S. Cartographer's Wedding, The.
Friend.
Letter to Robert Hedin.
Han-shan. If others are worthy accept them.
HaNagid. Friends, The.
How Could You Loathe.
If You Leave a Long-Loved Friend.
Your Loved Ones Depress You.
Hayden, R. Letter.
Herbert, G. Unkindness.
Herrick. Deluge, The.
His Age, Dedicated to His Peculiar Friend, Master John Wickes, under the Name of Posthumus.
Hymne to Sir Clipseby Crew, A.
To His Friend, Master J. Jincks.
To His Friend to Avoid Contention of Words.
To His Honoured and Most Ingenious Friend Mr. Charles Cotton.
To M. Leonard Willan His Peculiar Friend.
True Friendship.
True Safety.
Housman. Friends.
Hughley Steeple.
Shake hands, we shall never be friends, all's over.
West, The.

When I would muse in boyhood.
Hughes, L. Death of Do Dirty: A Rounder's Song.
Poem: "I loved my friend."
Hughes, T. Six Young Men.
Ibn-i-Yamin [or Ibn Jemin or Amir Mahmud ibn Amir Yaminu'd-Din Tughra'i]. For two rewards, & nought beside.
Whilst I disdain the populace.
Ignatow, D. For All Friends.
Two Friends.
Jackson, L. Friendship on Visit.
Letter to Any Friend, A.
Jacobsen, J. Guide for Survivors.
Survivor's Ballad.
Variations on a theme.
Jami. Friend is he, who, hunted as a foe, A.
Jeffers, R. George Sterling.
No Resurrection.
Johnson, S. Ode on Friendship, An.
Jonson, B. Epigram. To a Friend and Son.
Epistle Answering to One That Asked to Be Sealed of the Tribe of Ben, An.
Epistle to a Friend, An ("Sir, I am thankful, first, to heaven, for you").
Epistle to Master Arth[ur] Squib, An.
Epistle to Master John Selden, An.
Poem Sent Me by Sir William Burlase, A.
To the Immortal[l] Memory [or Memorie] and Friendship of That Noble Pair[e], Sir Lucius Cary and Sir H. [or Henry] Morison.
To the Same [Benjamin Rudyerd] ("If I would wish, for truth, and not for show").
Keats. Bright Star.
To a Friend Who Sent Me Some Roses.
To Charles Cowden Clarke.
To George Felton Mathew.
Kipling, R. Follow Me 'Ome.
France.
Friends, The.
Thousandth Man, The.
Kizer, C. American Beauty, An.
Final Meeting.
For Jan, in Bar Maria.
Poem for Your Birthday.
To My Friend Who Rhymes with Peace.
Koch, K. Circus, The.
Departure from Hydra, The.
Fate.
Komunyakaa. Bennelong's Blues.
More Girl than Boy.
Kumin, M. Apostrophe to a Dead Friend.
Progress Report.
Laughlin, J. Leave-taking, A.
Tennesee.
Welcome, The.
Lawrence, D. H. Emotional Friend, The.
Henriette.
Lies about Love.
Refused Friendship.
To a Certain Friend.
Levertov. Crow Spring.
Letter.
Living for Two.
Levi, P. To My Friends.
Levine, P. Making It New.
Logan, J. Cambridge Revery.
Feast of Friends, A.
Lines for a Friend Who Left.
Lines for Michael in the Picture.
On the House of a Friend.
Poem for My Friend Peter at Pihana.
Poem: Tears, Spray, and Steam.
Rescue, The.
Three Moves.
Visit to Bill Merwin at His Hawaiian Home, A.
Logue, C. To My Fellow Artists.
Lorde. Dear Toni instead of a Letter of Congratulation.
Sister, Morning Is a Time for Miracles.
Lowell, R. Randall Jarrell 1. October 1965.
Randall Jarrell 2.
Randall Jarrell 3.
To Delmore Schwartz.
Lux. Elegy for Robert Winner.
MacDiarmid, H. To a Friend and Fellow Poet.

MacNeice. Casualty, The.
Mallarmé. Remembrance of Belgian Friends.
Meredith, G. Candid Friend who strikes because he loves, The.
I look'd for my poet—he came not!
It's many a penny you'll pay to go.
Madrigal: "Since Tuck is faithless found, no more."
To-morrow I am going.
Tuck, sweet charmer, tell me why.
Tuck! Tuck! Once you would flatter me.
Meredith, W. In the Middle of the Long Friendship.
Merrill, J. 16. ix. 65.
Black Mesa, The.
Clearing the Title.
Days of 1971.
Friend of the Fourth Decade, The.
Manos Karastefanís.
Strato in Plaster.
Words for Maria.
Merton. Message to Be Inscribed on Mark Van Doren's Hamilton Medal.
Merwin. James.
My Friends.
Michelangelo Buonarroti. Having, my friend, your letter here in hand.
Since I'm too obligated.
There's pleasure in great favors done, but hidden.
Milton. Damon's Epitaph.
Lycidas.
Montale. Visit to Fadin.
Muldoon, P. Soap-Pig, The.
Nash, O. Compliments of a Friend.
Crossing the Border.
Hush, Here They Come.
I Know You'll Like Them.
I'll Write Their Number Down When We Get Home.
Suppose I Darken Your Door.
Nemerov. Blue Suburban.
Day on the Big Branch, A.
Memory of My Friend, A.
Song: "Provide your friend with almanacs."
To a Friend.
Neruda. Oliverio Girondo.
Ní Dhomhnaill. Race, The.
Niedecker. You are my friend.
O'Hara, F. Aus Einem April.
Biotherm [for Bill Berkson].
John Button Birthday.
Poem Read at Joan Mitchell's.
Olson, C. Death of Europe, The.
Paley, G. For George (I).
Palmer, M. November Talks.
Parker, D. After a Spanish Proverb.
Fable: "Oh, there once was a lady, and so I've been told."
False Friends, The.
Leal, The.
Patchen. State of the Nation, The.
Piercy. Bumpity Road to Mutual Devotion, The.
Friend, The.
Morning Athletes.
Night Letter.
Pinkerton, H. Alike and Yet Unlike: General Richard Taylor Writes to Henry Adams.
Pinsky. Ice-Storm, The.
Pope, A. On Mr. Gay, in Westminster Abbey, 1732.
Presentation Verses to Nathaniel Pigott.
Pound, E. Amitites.
Prime, B. Poetical Correspondence between Palemon and Æmilia, A.
Ramanujan. To a Friend Far Away.
Rexroth, K. For Eli Jacobson.
Rich, A. Ghazal.
Riley, J. Back from Town.
Dan Paine.
Dave Field.
Erasmus Wilson.
George A. Carr.
Kneeling with Herrick.
Lines: "Thou little naked statuette."
My Friend.

My Old Friend.
Three Dead Friends.
To Edgar Wilson Nye.
To My Old Friend, William Leachman.
To the Judge.
Tom Van Arden.
Unknown Friends.
When We Three Meet.
Writin' Back to the Home Folks.
Rilke.　Departure.
Goodbyes, Still More Goodbyes.
Survival.
To M.
Ritsos.　Bridge, The; An Uncalled-for Apology.
Robinson, E.　How Annandale Went Out.
Long Race, The.
Old Story, An.
Sainte-Nitouche.
Roethke.　Chums, The.
Rossetti, C.　After Communion.
Along the highroad the way is too long.
Care flieth, / Hope and fear together.
Dumb Friend, A.
From Sunset to Star Rise.
Hail, noble face of noble friend!
I seek among the living & I seek.
Me you often meet / In London's crowded
　street.
Peal of Bells, A.
Promises like Pie-Crust.
River Thames (?).
To My Friend Elizabeth.
Zara.
Rukeyser, M.　Born in December.
Cats and a Cock.
Course.
Rumi.　Childhood Friends.
Force of Friendship, The.
Friend comes into my body, The.
Friend, our closeness is this.
Granary Floor, The.
I circle your nest tonight.
I'm Not Saying This Right.
Long String, The.
Mouse and a Frog, A.
Of Being Woven.
Phrasing Must Change, The.
Saladin's Begging Bowl.
Special Plates.
Talking through the Door.
Two Friends.
Water from Your Spring.
Waterwheel, The.
When you feel your lips becoming infinite.
Sadi [or Saadi or Sa'di].　Had I the world for
　my enemy.
Who loves his friend with his heart of hearts.
Schuyler, J.　Dear Joe.
June 30, 1974.
Poem: "I do not always understand what you
　say."
Sexton.　Big Heart, The.
Sheridan, T.　Humble Petition of Stella's
　Friends, The.
To the Same.
Smith, S.　Broken Friendship, The.
Dirge: "From a friend's friend I taste
　friendship."
Freddy.
Nor We of Her to Him.
Pleasures of Friendship, The.
Voice from the Tomb (4).
Spender, S.　Auden's Funeral.
Stafford, W.　Friends.
Key of C— an Interlude for Marvin.
That Year.
Stock, R.　Epistle to Simon Perchik.
Stockton, A.　Elegy in the Extreme Illness of a
　Friend Whose Disorder Was the Bursting of a
　Blood Vesel in His Breast, An.
Epistle to a Friend Who Urg'd to Have Some
　Poetry Sent Her in the Year 1759, in the
　Winter, An.
Lines on Seeing Mrs Elizabeth Witherspoon Put
　in the Grave.
Ode, to Amanda, An.

Ode to Doctor Smith on His Birth Day March
　the 16th, 1791, An.
Poetical Correspondence between Palemon and
　Æmilia, A.
Tears of Friendship. Elegy the Third.—To a
　Friend Just Married, and Who Had Promised
　to Write, on Parting, but Had Neglected It.
Tears of Friendship, The. Elegy the 4th.
To a Friend Going to Sea.
To a Friend Who Had Persuaded Emelia to
　Marry, an Ode.
To Doctor Smith on His Birth Day March 16th,
　92.
To Laura.
To Laura—a Card.
To Mrs Powel, an Ode.
To My Burrissa.
Swenson, M.　Zambesi and Ranee.
Swift, J.　Dean and the Duke, The.
In Sickness.
Part of a Summer, The.
To Stella, Visiting Me in My Sickness.
Twelve Articles.
Tate, J.　Epithalamion for Tyler.
How the Friends Met.
Tennyson, A.　In the Garden at Swainston.
To E. Fitzgerald.
Thomas, D.　To Others than You.
Thoreau.　Delay in Friendship.
Farewell.
Friends— / They cannot help.
Friendship ("I think awhile of Love, and while I
　think").
Great Friend.
Great God I ask thee for no meaner pelf.
I will obey the strictest law of love.
My friends, my noble friends, know ye.
Sympathy.
Wait not till I invite thee, but observe.
Tomlinson, C.　Backward Glance, A.
Tu Fu.　Thwarted.
Unknown.　On Flatterers.
Unknown, sometimes at. to Sir Walter Ralegh.
　To His Singular Friend, William Lithgow.
Van Duyn.　Open Letter, Personal.
Very.　Friendship.
Friendship: To J. M. S.
Walcott.　Sea Canes.
Village Life, A.
Walker, A.　These Days.
Warren, R.　Deep—Deeper Down.
Distance Between, The: Picnic of Old Friends.
For a Friend Who Thinks Himself Urbane.
For a Self-Possessed Friend.
To a Friend Parting.
Weiss, T.　Dance Called David, The.
Living Room, A.
Whalen, P.　20:vii:58, on Which I Renounce the
　Notion of Social Responsiblity.
Friendship Greetings.
How to Be Successful & Happy without
　Anybody Else Finding Out about It.
Wheatley, P.　On Friendship.
Whitman, W.　As Toilsome I Wander'd
　Virginia's Woods.
I Dream'd in a Dream.
I Saw in Louisiana a Live-Oak Growing.
In Paths Untrodden.
Not Heat Flames Up and Consumes.
Recorders Ages Hence.
Whittier.　Benedicite.
Ego.
Greeting.
Laurels, The.
Legacy, A.
My Namesake.
My Thanks.
Remembrance.
Response.
To Avis Keene.
To ———: "Fair Nature's priestesses! to
　whom."
To Fredrika Bremer.
Williams, C. K.　Signs.
Williams, M.　Friend, The.
Hello. I'll Bet You Don't Know Who This Is.

Jonathan Entertaining.
Sleeping with Friends.
Thinking about Bill, Dead of AIDS.
To One Who Went Too Far.
Williams, W.　Old Worshipper, The.
Wordsworth, W.　In the First Page of an Album
　by One Whose Handwriting Is Wretchedly
　Bad.
Tables Turned, The.
To a Child [Written in Her Album].
To I.F.
To the Lady E.B. and the Hon. Miss P.
Travelling.
Wright, C.　To Giacomo Leopardi in the Sky.
Yeats.　Friends.
Lover Pleads with His Friend for Old Friends,
　The.
Zagajewski.　Generation, The.
Islands and Towers.
Light of Lamps, The.
Zaturenska.　Elegy and Nocturne for Lora
　Baxter.
Friend's Song, A.
Image of a Friend.
Zukofsky, L.　On Valentine's Day to Friends.
To Friends, for Good Health.

Frietchie, Barbara
Whittier.　Barbara Frietchie.

Frog Prince, The
Smith, S.　Frog Prince, The.

Frogs
Blok.　Little Priest of the Fen, The.
Bly, R.　Night Frogs.
Bukowski.　It's Nothing to Laugh About.
Dickinson, E.　His Mansion in the Pool.
Long sigh of the Frog, The.
Eberhart, R.　On Returning to a Lake in Spring.
Graves, R.　Frog and the Golden Ball, The.
Heaney, S.　Death of a Naturalist.
Kinnell.　First Song.
Kumin, M.　Custodian.
MacLeish.　Peepers in Our Meadow, The.
Muldoon, P.　Frog, The.
Niedecker.　Frog noise / suddenly stops.
Ramanujan.　Dream in an Old Language.
Riley, J.　Frog, The.
Ritsos.　Wisdom.
Rossetti, C.　Frog's Fate, A.
Hopping frog, hop here and be seen.
Rumi.　Force of Friendship, The.
Long String, The.
Mouse and a Frog, A.
Sandburg, C.　Frog Songs.
Spring Cries.
Young Bullfrogs.
Sarton, M.　Frog, that Naked Creature, The.
Sexton.　Elegy in the Classroom.
Frog Prince, The.
Smith, S.　Frog Prince, The.
Tomlinson, C.　Poolville, N.Y.
Wright, J.　Small Frogs Killed on the Highway.

Frontiers
Heaney, S.　From the Frontier of Writing.
MacLeish.　Definition of the Frontiers.
Geography of this Time.
Orr, G.　Chateaubriand on the Niagara Frontier,
　1791.
Riley, J.　Child's Home—Long Ago, A.
Warren, R.　Inevitable Frontier.

Frontiersmen
Wang Ch'ang-ling.　Chant of the Frontiersman.
Williams, W.　Poem: "Daniel Boone, the father
　of Kentucky."

Frost
Beckett, S.　Vive morte ma seule saison.
Coleridge, S.　Frost at Midnight.
Dickinson, E.　Apparently with no surprise.
Frost was never seen, The.
Frost, R.　Peril of Hope.
Herrick.　Farewell Frost; or, Welcome the
　Spring.
Jacobsen, J.　Provider, The.
Meredith, G.　Carol of Jack Frost, A.
Niedecker.　Last night the trash barrel.
Raine, K.　Frost-rime edges blades of grass.

Riley, J.   After the Frost.
Sandburg, C.   Maroon with Silver Frost.
   Splinter.
Sze.   Frost.
Tomlinson, C.   Instance, The.
   Winter-Piece.
Updike.   Frost.
Very.   Frost, The.
Warren, R.   So Frost Astounds.
Whittier.   Frost Spirit, The.
Wilbur, R.   Two Quatrains for First Frost.

Frost, Robert
Berryman.   Lines to Mr Frost.
Brooks, G.   Of Robert Frost.
Eberhart, R.   Worldly Failure.
Kinnell.   For Robert Frost.
Lowell, R.   Robert Frost.
MacLeish.   In and Come In.
Meredith, W.   In Memory of Robert Frost.
Nemerov.   For Robert Frost, in the Autumn, in
   Vermont.
Rukeyser, M.   Double Dialogue: *Homage to
   Robert Frost.*

Fruit Trees and Fruit
Abu Nadhar 'Abdu'l 'Aziz.   Color, taste, and
   smell, smaragdus, sugar, and musk.
Cardozo   Elegy for Maria Alves.
Clampitt.   Cloudberry Summer.
   Gooseberry Fool.
Cortes.   Flower of the Fruit, The.
Cowper, W.   On Thurlow.
Dickinson, E.   We are snatching our jewels from
   the frost.
Hacker, M.   Late August.
Han-shan.   Aboard this boat of rotten wood.
Ignatow, D.   Their Mouths Full.
Keats.   To Autumn.
Kumin, M.   Appetite.
Lawrence, D. H.   Grapes.
Levertov.   O Taste and See.
MacLeish.   Ars Poetica.
McGrath, T.   Praises.
Merwin.   Questions to Tourists Stopped by a
   Pineapple Field.
Millay, E.   Never May the Fruit Be Plucked.
Mistral, G.   Fruit.
Moore, M.   Nevertheless.
   Nine Nectarines.
Muldoon, P.   De Secretis Mulierum.
Nash, O.   Cantaloupe, The.
Niedecker.   July, waxwings
Piercy.   September Afternoon at Four o'Clock.
Riley, J.   Fruit-Piece, A.
Rilke.   Growing Old.
   Three Carriers, The.
Roethke.   Pickle Belt.
Rossetti, C.   Currants on a bush, / And figs upon
   a stem.
   Goblin Market.
   Lily has a smooth stalk, / Will never hurt your
   hand, The.
   Oh fair to see / Bloom-laden cherry tree.
   Peach tree on the southern wall, The.
   Summer.
   What Is Pink?
Sarton, M.   Olive Grove, The.
Schuyler, J.   Jelly Jelly.
Stock, R.   Star-Apple.
   Storm.
Swenson, M.   One Morning in New Hampshire.
Thoreau.   Moon now rises to her absolute rule,
   The.
Whittier.   Fruit-Gift, The.
Williams, W.   Brief Lief.
   This Is Just to Say.
Zukofsky, L.   Pretty.
   Raspberry.

Frustration
Blok.   Artist, The.
   She Came in from the Frost.
Broumas, O.   Blockade.
Carver, R.   Our First House in Sacramento.
Creeley.   Jaws.
García Lorca.   Useless Song.
HaNagid.   Is There Any Frustration.
Parker, D.   Frustration.

Pessoa.   Sonnet: "Could I say what I think,
   could I express."
Prunty.   New Territory.
Ramanujan.   It.
   Not Knowing.
Riley, J.   Scrawl, A.
Stockton, A.   Caprice, a Fragment.
Whalen, P.   Native Speech.
Wilde, O.   Wasted Days.

Fry, Elizabeth
Whittier.   Two Elizabeths, The.

Fuchsia
Hardy, T.   Lodging-House Fuchsias, The.

Fujiyama
Wilner, E.   Mt. Fuji and the Martial Arts.

Fulfillment
Angelou.   Unmeasured Tempo.
Bly, R.   Love Poem in Twos and Threes.
   Man and a Woman Sit near Each Other.
Browning, E.   Lay of the Early Rose, A.
Browning, R.   At the "Mermaid."
   Now.
Bukowski.   Another Bed.
Chuang Tzu.   Man Is Born in Tao.
Clough.   In controversial foul impureness.
   O stream, descending to the sea.
Cullen, C.   From the Dark Tower.
Donne.   Good-Morrow, The.
Eberhart, R.   Transfer, The.
Graves, R.   Vow, The.
Hughes, L.   Fulfillment.
Keats.   Portrait, A.
Levertov.   Part, The.
Levine, P.   Words.
Meredith, G.   Line of eve o'er the moorland, A.
Oliver, M.   Stanley Kunitz.
Owen, W.   Music.
Parker, D.   Fulfillment.
Piercy.   Shadows of the Burning.
Riley, J.   When My Dreams Come True.
Rilke.   Two Poems.
   Water Lily.
Ritsos.   Fulfillment.
Robinson, E.   Three Quatrains.
Rossetti, C.   Buds and Babies.
Tomlinson, C.   Their Voices Rang.

Fuller, Margaret
Clampitt.   Margaret Fuller, 1847.
Dubie.   Shipwreck.
Hacker, M.   Ballad of Ladies Lost and Found.
Niedecker.   Margaret Fuller.

Fulton, Robert
Sandburg, C.   Trinity Place.

Fun
Cowper, W.   Impromptu ["So I have seen the
   maids in vain"].
Creeley.   Cheap Thrill.
   Sad Advice.
Eberhart, R.   Clerihew for Alan Gaylord, A.
Herrick.   Anacreontic.
   Frolic[k], A.
Merton.   Old.
See also **Play; Pleasure**

Funerals
Ai.   She Didn't Even Wave.
Amichai [*or* Amikhai].   As at Funerals.
Berry, W.   At a Country Funeral.
Brodsky, J.   On the Death of Zhukov.
Carruth, H.   None.
Cavafy.   Funeral of Sarpedon, The ("Heart of
   Zeus is filled with grief, The").
   Myris: Alexandria, 340 A.D.
Ciardi, J.   It Took Four Flowerboats to Convoy
   My Father's Black.
Clampitt.   Winter Burial, A.
Crane, S.   Grey and boiling street, A.
Cullen, C.   Brown Girl Dead, A.
Cummings, E. E.   After Seeing French Funeral.
   Old mr ly / fresh from a fu.
Dickinson, E.   Element of Elegy, The.
   I Felt a Funeral in My Brain.
   I heard a Fly buzz—when I died.
Donne.   Funeral[l], The.
Dove, R.   Tou Wan Speaks to Her Husband Liu
   Sheng.

Dubie.   Funeral, The.
   Ganges, The.
Emerson, R.   Bird was gone the ghastly trees,
   The.
Graves, R.   1805.
Hardy, T.   Choirmaster's Burial, The.
   Farmer Dunman's Funeral.
   Hatband, The.
   Leaving, A.
   Retty's Phases.
   She at His Funeral.
Heaney, S.   Funeral Rites.
Herrick.   Bucolick betwixt Two: Lacon and
   Thyrsis, A.
   Funeral[l] Rites of the Rose, The.
   His Embalming to Julia.
   To Flowers.
   To the Yew and Cypress to Grace His Funeral.
Housman.   Bredon Hill.
Hughes, L.   As Befits a Man.
   Ballad of the Man Who's Gone.
   Dead in There.
   Funeral.
   Night Funeral in Harlem.
Ignatow, D.   Off to the Cemetery.
Jackson, L.   Lying Spying.
Kinsella, T.   Dura Mater.
   Office of the Dead.
Komunyakaa.   April Fools' Day.
Laughlin, J.   Ave Atque Vale.
Lawrence, D. H.   Violets.
   Violets for the Dead.
Levine, P.   Goodbye.
Lindsay, N.   Drunkard's Funeral, The.
Logan, J.   Elegy for Dylan Thomas.
Longfellow, H.   Hawthorne.
Lowell, R.   Death of the Sheriff, The.
MacDiarmid, H.   Island Funeral.
Meleager.   Upon a Maid That Died [*or* Dyed]
   the Day She Was Married [*or* Marryed].
Meredith, W.   English Accounts.
Merrill, J.   Annie Hill's Grave.
Merwin.   Next, The.
Millay, E.   Dirge without Music.
Muldoon, P.   Grief.
Nash, O.   Maybe You Can't Take It with You,
   but Look What Happens When You Leave It
   Behind.
Nemerov.   One Moment in Eternity.
Niedecker.   Churchill's Death.
Olson, C.   Absolutely Vernal.
Oppen.   Laced gaiter, A.
Orr, G.   Driving Home after a Funeral.
Pagis.   Souvenir, The.
Parker, D.   Condolence.
Plath.   Bee Meeting, The.
Poe.   Lenore.
Prunty.   Funerals, The.
Ransom, J.   Bells for John Whiteside's
   Daughter.
   Emily Hardcastle, Spinster.
Riley, J.   Home-Voyage, The.
   Little White Hearse, The.
   Noblest Service, The.
   Oscar C. McCulloch.
   When the Hearse Comes Back.
Rilke.   Funeral.
Robinson, E.   Cortège.
   Whip, The.
Roethke.   On the Road to Woodlawn.
Rossetti, C.   "Ding a ding," / The sweet bells
   sing.
Rossetti, D.   Wellington's Funeral.
Sandburg, C.   And So Today.
   Pals.
   Repetitions.
   Waiting for the Chariot.
Schuyler, J.   Beautiful Funerals.
   Chapel, A.
Sexton.   Truth the Dead Know, The.
Smith, S.   King in Funeral Procession, A.
   Silence and Tears.
Stevens, W.   Cortège for Rosenbloom.
   Emperor of Ice-Cream, The.
Szymborska, W.   Funeral.
Tate, A.   Stranger.

Thomas, D.   After the Funeral.
Thoreau.   Funeral Bell, The.
Tomlinson, C.   Tax Inspector, The.
Very.   Funerals, The.
Walker, A.   Burial.
Warren, R.   Filling Night with the Name:
   Funeral as Local Color.
Whitman, W.   Interpolation Sounds.
Whittier.   Funeral Tree of the Sokokis.
Williams, M.   Beside an Open Grave the Mind
   of the Young Preacher Comes Almost to
   Terms.
   During a Funeral Service the Mind of the Young
      Preacher Wanders Again.
   Funeral.
   On the Death of a Middle-Aged Man.
   On the Symbolic Consideration of Hands and
      the Significance of Death.
   Remembering Walter.
   Wide Place in the Road.
   Widow, The.
Williams, T.   Cortege.
Williams, W.   Tract.
Wright, J.   Refusal, The.
Yeats.   Mountain Tomb, The.

Furnaces
McHugh, H.   Household.

Furniture
Borges.   Empty Drawing Room.
Carver, R.   Distress Sale.
Cowper, W.   Gratitude.
Creeley.   Table, The.
Eberhart, R.   Day-Bed, The.
Guillén, J.   Nature Alive.
Gunn, T.   Pierce Street.
Hardy, T.   Little Old Table, The.
Heaney, S.   Sofa in the Forties, A.
Lawrence, D. H.   Furniture.
McHugh, H.   What Could Hold Us.
Nash, O.   Have You Tried Staying Awake? or,
   They'll Find a Way to Stop That, Too.
Nemerov.   Singular Metamorphosis, A.
Rich, A.   Dreamwood.
Rimbaud, A.   Dresser, The.
Simic.   Furniture Mover.
Updike.   Furniture, The.
Williams, T.   Penates.

Fuseli, Henry
Blake, W.   To Hunt.
   William Cowper Esqre.
Browning, R.   Mary Wollstonecraft and Fuseli.

Future
Amichai [or Amikhai].   Hirbet Sayid.
Auden.   Gare du Midi.
Berry, W.   For the Future.
   To Tanya at Christmas.
   To What Listens.
Berryman.   Search, The.
Blue Cloud.   Tomorrow.
Bly, R.   Two Sounds When We Sit by the
   Ocean.
Borges.   1972.
Brodsky, J.   North of Delphi.
Broumas, O.   Song / for Sanna.
Carver, R.   Tomorrow.
Cavafy.   Bank of the Future, The.
Clough.   Mari Magno I.
   Nay draw not yet the cork, my friend.
Codrescu.   West Is the Best and the Future Is
   Near, The.
Coleridge, S.   Superstition.
Collins, B.   November.
   To a Stranger Born in Some Distant Country
      Hundreds of Years from Now.
Cooper, J.   Blue Anchor, The.
Corbett, W.   Painters, The.
Creeley.   Eye, The.
   Going to Bed.
   Massachusetts.
   Retrospect.
Cummings, E. E.   But being not
   amazing:without love.
   If(touched by love's own secret)we,like homing.
   In time's a noble mercy of proportion.
De la Mare.   Humanity.
Dickinson, E.   Future—never spoke, The.

If the future is mighty as the past.
   Oh Future! thou secreted peace.
Dunbar, P.   Beyond the Years.
   To Kelly Miller, Jr.
Eberhart, R.   May Evening.
Emerson, R.   Future, The.
   Shun passion, fold the hands of thrift.
   There is in all the sons of men.
   Valedictory Poem.
Enzensberger, H.   Poem about the Future.
   Research Council.
Frost, R.   Something for Hope.
Graves, R.   Non Cogunt Astra.
   Olive-Yard, The.
   Tomorrow's Envy of Today.
Gurney, I.   Time to Come.
Hardy, T.   1967.
   At a Fashionable Dinner.
   He Wonders about Himself.
   If You Had Known.
   Strange House, The.
Housman.   Lads in Their Hundreds, The.
Hughes, L.   Some Day.
   Youth.
Jarrell, R.   On the Railway Platform.
   Up in the sky the star is waiting.
   Winter's Tale, The.
Jeffers, R.   Granite and Cypress.
   Watch the Lights Fade.
Kipling, R.   Ballad of the *Clampherdown*, The.
   Before a Midnight Breaks in Storm.
   Storm Cone, The.
Larkin, P.   Arundel Tomb, An.
   Next, Please.
Laughlin, J.   Can I Catch Up with the Future?
   You Are My Future.
Lawrence, D. H.   Future States.
   Future War.
   Return of Returns.
   Signs of the Times.
   Wandering Cosmos, The.
   Wellsian Futures.
Lindsay, N.   Amaranth, The.
   Johnny Appleseed Speaks of Great Cities in the
      Future.
   On the Road to Nowhere.
Lux.   Early On, This Decade's Light Smelled.
   Triptych, Middle Panel Burning.
MacLeish.   Poetical Remains.
MacNeice.   Prospect.
Meredith, W.   For Two Lovers in the Year 2075
   in the Canadian Woods.
Merton.   Public Affairs.
Merwin.   It Is March.
   Way Ahead, The.
Milosz, C.   Boy, A.
Mistral, G.   Future, The.
Neruda.   Let's Wait.
O'Hara, F.   Poem: "Instant coffee with slightly
   sour cream."
Oppen.   West.
Pasternak, B.   Some Future Moon.
Patchen.   Soon It Will.
Piercy.   Seedlings in the Mail.
Rich, A.   Prospective Immigrants Please Note.
Rilke.   Future, The.
Robinson, E.   Ballade by the Fire.
Rossetti, C.   Cobwebs.
   Dost Thou Not Care?
   I sit a queen, and am no widow, and shall see no
      sorrow.
   Passing away the bliss, / The anguish passing
      away.
   Where love is, there comes sorrow / Today or
      else tomorrow.
   Where shall I find a white rose blowing?
Rukeyser, M.   King's Mountain.
   Victims, a Play for the Home, The.
Sandburg, C.   Answer, The.
   Between Worlds.
   Broken-Face Gargoyles.
   Haze.
   Wars.
Seifert.   When in the history books.
Shelley, P.   Lines: "Far, far away, O ye."
   To-Morrow.

Spender, S.   Pylons, The.
   Uncreating Chaos (Double Portrait in a Mirror),
      The.
Stafford, W.   In the White Sky.
Tate, J.   Dime Found in the Snow, A.
Walcott.   Prelude: "I, with legs crossed along the
   daylight, watch."
Whitman, W.   Apostroph.
   As in a Swoon.
   Full of Life Now.
   Going Somewhere.
   In the New Garden.
   Long, Long Hence.
   New Year's Day, 1848.
   One Song, America, before I Go.
   Our Future Lot.
   Poets to Come.
   Recorders Ages Hence.
   So Far, and So Far, and On toward the End.
   Thou Mother with Thy Equal Brood.
   Thoughts.
   To a Historian.
   To the Pending Year.
   Turn O Libertad.
   Years of the Modern.
Williams, C. K.   In the next life.
Williams, M.   After a Brubeck Concert.
   Geography of Time, The.
   Of History and Hope.
Wordsworth, W.   Presentiments.
   Sonnet: Composed while the Author Was
      Engaged in Writing a Tract Occasioned by
      the Convention of Cintra.
Wright, C.   Mount Caribou at Night.
Yeats.   Happy Townland, The.
Zagajewski.   There Will Be a Future.
Zaturenska.   Dark Year, The.
Zukofsky, L.   I Sent Thee Late.
   My nephew / And my new.

G

Gabriel
Browning, E.   Drama of Exile, A.
Dickinson, E.   Robin.
García Lorca.   St. Gabriel.
Hopkins, G.   Angelus Ad Virginem.
Rich, A.   Gabriel.
Rossetti, C.   Feast of the Annunciation.
Rumi.   Private Banquet, The.

Galatea
Brodsky, J.   Galatea Encore.

Galilee, Israel
Sandburg, C.   Epistle: "Jesus loved the sunsets
   on Galilee."

Galileo
Ciardi, J.   Galileo and the Laws.
Jarrell, R.   Emancipators, The.
Levi, P.   Sidereus Nuncius.
Smith, S.   Thought Is Superior.

Gallantry
Dickinson, E.   Your little mental gallantries.

Galley Slaves
Kipling, R.   Song of the Galley-Slaves.
Muldoon, P.   My Grandfather's Wake.

Gallows
Clampitt.   Palm Sunday.
Simic.   Gallows Etiquette.
See also **Hanging**

Galuppi, Baldassaro
Browning, R.   Toccata of Galuppi's, A.

Galway
See **County Galway, Ireland**

Gama, Vasco da
Mallarmé.   For the sake of voyaging—
   heedlessly.

Gambling and Gamblers
Auden.   Casino.
Baudelaire.   Games of Chance.
Bierce.   McAllister, of talents rich and rare.
Bukowski.   Day the Epileptic Spoke, The.
   Valentine Gift, A.
Carver, R.   Blood.

Cavafy. Days of 1908.
Codrescu. Secret Training.
Coleridge, S. To Fortune.
Cowper, W. Tale, Founded on a Fact, A.
Dickey, W. Gambling at Reno.
Dickinson, E. We lose—because we win.
Graves, R. Man Does, Woman Is.
Herrick. Upon Raspe.
Hughes, L. Crap Game.
  Madam and the Number Writer.
  Numbers.
  Saturday Night.
  Situation.
Jonson, B. Epistle to Mr Arthur Squib.
Lindsay, N. Gamblers, The.
  What the Ghost of the Gambler Said.
Muldoon, P. Immram.
Nash, O. How Long Has This Been Going On?
  Oh, Quite Long.
Olson, C. Friday, Good Friday, which.
  With what I got out.
Rumi. Gamble everything for love.
Sandburg, C. Cahoots.
  Crapshooters.
Tomlinson, C. Biography of the Author: A
  Cento, A.
Wright, J. Gambling in Stateline, Nevada.

Games
Amichai [or Amikhai]. Games.
Atwood. Game after Supper.
Berryman. At Chinese Checkers.
Blake, W. Blind-Man's Buff.
Borges. Truco.
Bukowski. It's the Way You Play the Game.
Burns, R. Johnie Blunt.
  Whistle. A Ballad, The.
Cummings, E. E. May I Feel Said He.
Eberhart, R. Ball Game.
  Time Passes.
  Vastness and Indifference of the World, The.
Gunn, T. Bally *Power Play*.
  Elegy: "I can almost see it."
  Hide and Seek.
  Inside-Outside Game, The.
  Seesaw.
Herrick. Beucolick, or Discourse of Neatherds,
  A.
  Cherry-Pit.
  Draw Gloves.
  Love's Play at Push-Pin.
  Stool-Ball.
  To the Maids to Walke Abroad.
  Upon Raspe.
Jacobsen, J. Dream of Games, A.
  Simon.
Kipling, R. Verses on Games.
Komunyakaa. Child's Play.
  Jumping Bad Blues.
  Mumble Peg.
Laughlin, J. Blowpipe Game, The.
  Step on His Head.
  Two Children.
MacNeice. Children's Games.
  Indoor Sports.
  Sports Page.
Merton. Song: In the Shows of the Round Ox.
Merwin. Quoit, The.
Nash, O. Queen Is in the Parlor, The.
  Your Lead, Partner, I Hope We've Read the
  Same Book.
Nemerov. Playing Skittles.
  Sonnet: "It seems to be the trouble, everyone."
Patchen. Mirru.
Ramanujan. Snakes and Ladders.
Rilke. Ball, The.
Rossetti, C. Hop-o'-my-thumb and little Jack
  Horner.
Rukeyser, M. Another Day. A Game of Toys.
  Paul, Telling the Game.
  Game of Darts at the Chesterfield Arms, A.
Stafford, W. Living Statues.
Stock, R. Go As Played in the Best Circles; Or
  Rotten Axe-Handle.
Swift, J. Ballad on the Game of Traffic, A.
Wilbur, R. Statues.
Williams, C. K. Baby, I don't want.

Game, The.
Williams, M. Catch with Reuben.
  Children's Games.
See also **Card Games; Sports**
Gandhi, Mohandas Karamchand
Cullen, C. Karenge Ya Marenge.
Hughes, L. Gandhi Is Fasting.
MacDiarmid, H. Why.
Ganges River, India
Dubie. Ganges, The.
Laughlin, J. At Benares.
Oppen. Tugs of Hull, The.
Gangs and Gangsters
Borges. Milonga of Albornoz.
Creeley. Gangster.
Cummings, E. E. Come from his gal's.
Gunn, T. Black Jackets.
Komunyakaa. Nothing to Do with Janice Drake.
  Rocks Push.
  Thorn Merchant's Right-Hand Man, The.
Muldoon, P. Immram.
  Sightseers, The.
  Weepies, The.
Gannets
Oliver, M. Gannets.
See also **Boobies**
Ganymede
Olson, C. Borne down by the inability to lift the
  heaviness.
Garages
Collins, B. Pinup.
Mahon. Garage in Co. Cork, A.
McGrath, T. Excursion: Or: O Columbus!, The.
Garbage and Garbage Men
Berry, W. Wild, The.
Corbett, W. 1991.
Dugan, A. On a Dispossess Precept. 1.
Ferlinghetti, L. Two Scavengers in a Truck,
  Two Beautiful People in a Mercedes.
Ginsberg, A. Rain-Wet Asphalt Heat, Garbage
  Curbed Cans Overflowing.
Ignatow, D. Refuse Man, The.
Jacobsen, J. Shrivers, The.
Nemerov. Town Dump, The.
Rich, A. Open-Air Museum.
Ritsos. Reverential Comparison.
Stafford, W. Gutters of Jackson: Cache Street
  North.
Tomlinson, C. From the Motorway.
Updike. Accumulation.
  Burning Trash.
Wilbur, R. After the Last Bulletins.
  Junk.
Williams, C. K. Men.
  Trash.
Zukofsky, L. Wire.
García Lorca, Federico
Clampitt. Sed de Correr.
Merton. In Memory of the Spanish Poet
  Federico Garcia Lorca.
Rexroth, K. Blood and Sand.
Seifert. Salute to the Madrid Barricades.
Wilner, E. Up against It.
Garda, Lake, Italy
Tennyson, A. Frater Ave Atque Vale.
Gardens and Gardening
Ai. Capture.
Amichai [or Amikhai]. Stroll in the Beautiful
  Gardens of the Valley of the Son of Hinnom,
  A.
Ammons. Circles.
  Equinox.
  Garden.
  Summer Session.
Atwood. Dream 1: the Bush Garden.
Auden. Their Lonely Betters.
Baudelaire. Enemy, The.
Berry, W. Planting Crocuses.
Bishop, E. Manuelzinho.
Bly, R. Glimpse of the Waterer.
Borges. Flow of Memories, The.
  Simplicity.
Broumas, O. Imaginary Sufi Garden.
  Sweeping the Garden.

Browning, E. Deserted Garden, The.
Burns, R. Gardener wi' His Paddle—or, The
  Gardener's March, The.
Campion, T. There is a garden in her face.
Campion, T. *et al.* And Would You See My
  Mistress' Face?
Carruth, H. "I've Never Seen Such a Real Hard
  Time Before": Three-Part Invention.
  Song of the Two Crows.
Carver, R. Garden, The.
Cavafy. House with a Garden.
Ciardi, J. Image of Man as a Gardener after
  Two World Wars.
  On the Patio.
  Suburban.
  Three Views of a Mother.
Clampitt. Palm Sunday.
  Townhouse Interior with Cat.
Collins, B. Picnic, Lightning.
Corbett, W. O, July 1992.
Cowper, W. Epigrams on His Garden Shed.
  Shrubbery, The.
Crane, H. Fernery, The.
  Garden Abstract.
  Postscript.
Crane, S. Trees in the garden rained flowers,
  The.
Creeley. Door, The.
  Nature.
Cummings, E. E. Sonnet IV.
Davie, D. For Doreen. A Voice from the
  Garden.
  Lily at Noon, A.
  Pietà.
De la Mare. In the Garden.
  Myself.
  Old Ben.
  Quiet Enemy, The.
  Sunken Garden, The.
Dickey, W. Lady of Shalott, Her Mirror Broken,
  The.
Dickinson, E. Little garden within, The.
  My Garden—like the Beach.
Donne. Twickenham [or Twicknam] Garden.
Dugan, A. Mirror Perilous, The.
Dunbar, P. In a English Garden.
Emerson, R. Dark Flower of Cheshire garden.
  Days.
  Go into the garden.
  I to my garden went.
  In My Garden.
Frost, R. Atmosphere.
  Girl's Garden, A.
  Late Walk, A.
  Winter Eden, A.
Ginsberg, A. Strange New Cottage in Berkeley,
  A.
Glück, L. Garden, The.
Graves, R. Ample Garden, The.
  Garden, The.
  Gardener.
  Hidden Garden, The.
Gunn, T. Garden of the Gods, The.
  Last Days at Teddington.
  Looking Glass.
Gurney, I. Garden, The.
  Hedger.
"H. D." Garden.
  Sheltered Garden.
Hall, D. Child's Garden, A.
  Digging.
Hamill, S. September Sowing.
  Tammuz in the Garden.
Hardy, T. Garden Seat, The.
Heaney, S. Call, A.
  Markings.
  Mint.
Herbert, G. Paradise.
Herrick. To a Bed of Tulips.
Jacobsen, J. Next Summer.
  Rock-Plant Wife, The.
Jarrell, R. In a Hospital Garden.
Jeffers, R. Carmel.
Kinsella, T. Secret Garden, The.
Kipling, R. Glory of the Garden, The.
Kizer, C. Shalimar Gardens.

Kumin, M. Beans.
  Mummies, The.
  Turning the Garden in Middle Age.
Kunitz, S. Snakes of September, The.
  Touch Me.
Laughlin, J. It Does Me Good.
Lawrence, D. H. Guelder Roses.
  Prophet in the Rose Garden, The.
  Snap-Dragon.
  Trees in the Garden.
Levertov. Annuals.
  Death in Mexico.
  Figure of Time, A.
  Living Alone (3).
  Quality of Genius, The.
Lindsay, N. On the Garden Wall.
  Song of the Garden-Toad, The.
Lowell, R. Public Garden, The.
Lux. Garden, The.
MacNeice. Sunlight on the Garden, The.
Major, C. In the hidden garden.
Marvell. Garden, The.
  Hortus.
  Mower against Gardens, The.
McGrath, T. Residencies.
Melville, H. Garden of Metrodorus, The.
  Ravaged Villa, The.
Meredith, G. Garden of Epicurus, The.
  Grace and Love.
Meredith, W. Rus in Urbe.
Merrill, J. Words for Maria.
Millay, E. Gardener in Haying-Time, The.
  Hardy Garden, The.
  Spring in the Garden.
  Steepletop.
Milosz, C. Gardener.
  Gates of the Arsenal, The.
Montale. Garden, The.
Muldoon, P. One Desire, The.
Nash, O. Correction: *Eve* Delved and *Adam*
  Span.
  He Digs, He Dug, He Has Dug.
Nemerov. In the Commercial Gardens.
  Salt Garden, The.
Niedecker. Swedenborg.
  When brown folk lived a distance.
Oppen. Poem about the Garden, A.
Orr, G. Weeds, The.
  Work Gloves.
Parker, D. Garden-Spot.
  Story of Mrs. W———.
Pasternak, B. God of Details, The.
Pessoa. Advice.
Piercy. Digging In.
  Love of Lettuce, The.
Pinsky. Garden, The.
Plath. Manor Garden, The.
Pope, A. Garden, The.
  To Mr. Gay, Congratulating Pope on Finishing
    His House and Gardens.
Pound, E. Garden, The.
Prunty. Dr. Williams' Garden.
  Vegetable Garden, The.
Raine, K. April's new apple buds on an old
    lichened tree.
  High Summer.
Ransom, J. Miriam Tazewell.
Rexroth, K. Such Was Our Garden.
  Unpeopled, Conventional Rose-Garden, The.
Rich, A. Design in Living Colors.
  For Memory.
Riley, J. Fruit-Piece, A.
Ritsos. Bridge, The; An Uncalled-for Apology.
  In the Old Garden.
  Renaissance.
  Striding Over.
Robinson, E. Garden, The.
  Tree in Pamela's Garden, The.
  Two Gardens in Linndale.
Roethke. Cuttings.
  Flower Dump.
  Frau Bauman, Frau Schmidt, and Frau
    Schwartze.
  Otto.
  Transplanting.
  Weed Puller.

Rossetti, C. Beloved, yeild thy time to God, for
    He / Will make eternity thy recompense.
  God's Acre.
  Heartsease in my garden bed, / With
    sweetwilliam white and red.
  In the meadow—what in the meadow?
  October Garden, An.
  On Keats, 18 January, 1948 (Eve of St Agnes).
  Shut Out.
Rukeyser, M. Fighting for Roses.
  In Hades, Orpheus.
  Mother Garden's Round.
Sandburg, C. Garden Wireless.
  Poppies.
Sarton, M. Garden of Childhood, The.
  Metaphysical Garden, The.
Schuyler, J. August First, 1974.
  Belated Birthday Poem, A.
  Blossoming Oakwood.
  For Bob Dash.
  Horse-Chestnut Trees and Roses.
  In the Round.
  Roof Garden.
  Three Gardens.
  We Walk.
  What Ails My Fern?
Seifert. Birds' Voices in the Tree Tops.
  Canal Gardens.
  Four Small Windows.
Snyder, G. Roots.
Stein, G. What Does She See When She Shuts
    Her Eyes.
Stevens, W. Cy Est Pourtraicte, Madame Ste
    Ursule, et Les Unze Mille Vierges.
  Room on a Garden, A.
Stock, R. Ballade to be Read in the Medici
    Gardens.
Stockton, A. Impromptu Written with a Pencil
    in a Chinese Temple in the Garden of Mr
    Elisha Boudinot.
  Lines to My Brother from a Pavillion in His
    Garden.
Suckling, S. Upon My Lady Carlisle's Walking
    in Hampton Court Garden.
Swenson, M. City Garden in April, A.
  Digging in the Garden of Age I Uncover a Live
    Root.
  Garden at St. John's, The.
Tate, J. Heatstroke.
Tennyson, A. Spirit Haunts the Year's Last
    Hours, A.
Tomlinson, C. Door in the Wall, The.
  Hawthorn in Trent Vale, The.
  In the Borghese Gardens.
  Juliet's Garden.
  Near and the Far, The.
  Under the Bridge.
Updike. Planting a Mailbox.
Van Duyn. Elementary Attitudes.
  Gardener to His God, The.
  Garland for Christopher Smart, A.
  Notes from a Suburban Heart.
  Oh well, they had such a big garden.
Very. My Garden.
Warren, R. Garden, The.
  Garden Waters.
Whalen, P. Hot Springs Infernal in the Human
    Beast.
Whittier. Chalkley Hall.
  Garden.
  Song of Harvest, A.
Wilbur, R. Caserta Garden.
  He Was.
Wilde, O. Garden of Eros, The.
  Le Jardin des Tuileries.
  Sen Artysty; or, The Artist's Dream.
Williams, W. At the Brink of the Winter.
  Every Day.
  Italian Garden, The.
  Quality of Heaven, The.
  Tulip Bed, The.
  Widow's Lament in Springtime, The.
Wilner, E. Atget's Gardens.
  Killing the Grubs.
  Secret Garden, The.
  What Was Going On.

  Winter Garden.
  Wright, J. Invention of a Garden, The.
  Yeats. Down by the Salley Gardens.
  Zaturenska. Garden at Cliveden, The.
Gardner, John
  Carver, R. Work.
Garfield, James Abram
  Whitman, W. Sobbing of the Bells, The.
Gargoyles
  Dugan, A. Gargoyle's Song for the Warming
    Trend.
  Sandburg, C. Broken-Face Gargoyles.
  Gargoyle.
Garibaldi, Giuseppe
  Browning, E. Garibaldi.
  King's Gift, The.
  Meredith, G. Centenary of Garibaldi, The.
  Whittier. Garibaldi.
Garlic
  Rumi. Empty Garlic, An.
  Stafford, W. Ode to Garlic.
Garrick, David
  Johnson, S. Prologue Spoken by Mr[.] Garrick
    at the Opening of the Theatre in Drury Lane,
    1747.
Garrison, William Lloyd
  Whittier. Garrison.
  To William Lloyd Garrison.
Gasoline Stations
  Bishop, E. Filling Station.
  Merwin. Service.
  Williams, M. Mecanic on Duty at All Times.
Gates
  Cavafy. Indian Image.
  Dickinson, E. Soul selects her own Society,
    The.
  Dunbar, P. Old Front Gate, The.
  Graves, R. Hidden Garden, The.
  Kunitz, S. Open the Gates.
  Patchen. It Was Being.
  Tomlinson, C. Gap, The.
  Gate, The.
Gauguin, Paul
  Hill, G. Terribilis Est Locus Iste; *Gaugin and
    the Pont-Aven School*.
  Logan, J. Spirit of the Dead Watching: after
    Gaugin.
  Yellow Christ, The; after Gaugin.
Gautier, Théophile
  Mallarmé. Funereal Toast.
Gawaine, Sir
  Cunningham, J. Your affair, my dear, need not
    be a mess.
  Meredith, G. Song of Courtesy, The.
  Robinson, E. Lancelot.
  Merlin.
Gazelles
  HaNagid. Gazelle, The.
  Where's that Coy Gazelle.
  Komunyakaa. Ode to a Drum.
  Lawrence, D. H. Gazelle Calf, The.
Geese
  Berry, W. To Gary Snyder.
  Wild Geese, The.
  Bierce. Political Economy.
  Bly, R. Snow Geese.
  Bukowski. I Cannot Stand Tears.
  Carruth, H. All Things.
  No Matter What, after All, and That Beautiful
    Word So.
  Carver, R. Limits.
  Cunningham, J. August Hail.
  Glück, L. Messengers.
  Herrick. Upon Gander.
  Kipling, R. Flight, The.
  Kumin, M. Homage to Binsey Poplars.
  Levertov. Life of Others, The.
  Mahon. Canadian Pacific.
  Nash, O. Gander, The.
  Oliver, M. Wild Geese.
  Olson, C. Landscape, without Color.
  Piercy. Postcard from the Garden.
  Plath. Rhyme.
  Sandburg, C. Bas-Relief.

Seven Eleven.
Stafford, W. Late at Night ("Falling separate into the dark").
Over the North Jetty.
Swenson, M. Snow Geese at Jamaica Bay, The.
Tomlinson, C. Geese Going South.
Prelude, A.
Weatherman.
Warren, R. Heart of Autumn.
Weiss, T. On Stuffing a Goose.

Gems
Byron, G. Cornelian, The.
Carew, T. Epitaph on the Lady S.: Wife of Sir W.S.
Carver, R. Afghanistan.
Cavafy. Indian Image.
Dickinson, E. Diamond on the Hand, A.
I held a Jewel in my fingers.
I'll clutch—and clutch.
'Tis little I— could care for Pearls.
Emerson, R. I wear no badge; no tinsel star.
Rubies.
Herrick. Amber Bead, The.
Rock of Rubies: and The Quarrie of Pearls, The.
To Julia.
To the Right Honourable Mildmay, Earl of Westmorland.
Jackson, L. Jewels and After.
Laughlin, J. On the Gift of a Sapphire to My Wife Ann.
Pagis. Twelve Faces of the Emerald.
Rossetti, C. Diamond or a coal? / A diamond, if you please, A.
Flint.
Rumi. Sunrise Ruby, The.
Schuyler, J. Fabergé.

Generals
Brodsky, J. On the Death of Zhukov.
Burns, R. Address to General Dumourier.
Cavafy. Death of a General.
Cummings, E. E. Neither awake / (there's your general).
Dubie. Confession.
Hughes, L. Battle Ground.
Hughes, T. Scapegoats and Rabies.
Kipling, R. Bobs.
General Joubert.
Lord Roberts.
Stellenbosch.
Li Po. Visitor, The.
Marvell, Upon Appleton House [To My Lord Fairfax].
Upon the Hill and Grove at Bilbrough.
Patchen. Attila.
Pope, A. Epitaph on General Henry Withers, in Westminster-Abbey, 1729.
Riley, J. General Lew Wallace.
Home-Voyage, The.
Smart, C. Ode to General Draper.
Wheatley, P. On the Capture of General Lee.
On the Death of General Wooster.

Generosity
Carruth, H. Pa McCabe.
Char. Convergence of the Many.
Creeley. Testament, A.
Dickinson, E. Seraphic shame generosity causes, The.
Gallagher, T. In Maceio.
Ginsberg, A. Do the Meditation Rock.
Hacker, M. She Bitches about Boys.
HaNagid. Cast Your Bread.
Hughes, L. Preference.
Jonson, B. Epigram. To K[ing] Charles for a[n] Hundred Pounds He Sent Me in My Sickness. 1629, An.
Kinnell. Cellist, The.
Levertov. Métier of Blossoming, The.
MacLeish. Rape of the Swan, The.
Merwin. Hosts, The.
Riley, J. Jim.
Rossetti, C. Will you be there? my yearning heart has cried.
Smart, C. Care and Generosity.
Munificence and Modesty.
Spender, S. Generous Days, The.
Stafford, W. Bess.

Genetics and Geneticists
Ciardi, J. Domestic Sonnet.
Creeley. Name, The.
See also **Evolution**

Geneva, Switzerland
Kumin, M. We Stood There Singing.
Laughlin, J. Trout, The.
Stevens, W. Doctor of Geneva, The.

Genghis Khan
Stock, R. Ashes Ashes All Fall Down.
Game of the Thunderbolt Goddesses, The.

Genitalia
Ai. Penis Envy.
Amichai [*or* Amikhai]. And I am always like this fleeing from hurt and pain.
Broumas, O. Tryst.
Codrescu. Architecture.
Near Sonnet.
Dugan, A. Esthetics of Circumcision, The.
Hard-on Death.
On a Fallen Statue Forbidden to the Women at Pompeii.
Perverse Explanation for Mutilated Statuary.
Eliot, T. S. Fragments: "There was a jolly tinker came across the sea."
Logan, J. Saturday Afternoon at the Movies.
McHugh, H. I Knew I'd Sing
Rexroth, K. Fact ("In the encyclopedia").
Rimbaud, A. Once, animals spewed sperm as they charged.

Genius
Blake, W. All Religions Are One.
Browning, E. To George Sand: A Recognition.
Clampitt. Local Genius, The.
Crane, H. Masters, The.
Davie, D. At the Cradle of Genius.
Dickinson, E. Genius is the ignition of affection.
Emerson, R. Atom displaces all atoms beside, The.
Graves, R. Casse-Noisette.
HaNagid. Rich Are Small, The.
Herrick. To the Genius of His House.
Hughes, L. Genius Child.
Jarrell, R. Boyg, Peer Gynt, the One Only One, The.
Kizer, C. Twelve o'Clock.
Mahon. Ovid in Tomis.
Meredith, G. To P.A. Labouchère Esq.
You ask me what is Genius? 'tis that.
Riley, J. Penalty of Genius, The.
Robinson, E. Ben Jonson Entertains a Man from Stratford.
Williams, W. Poem: "Plastic surgeon who has, The."

Genoa, Italy
Milosz, C. For My Eighty-eighth Birthday.
Wilde, O. Sonnet Written in Holy Week at Genoa.

Gentians
Dickinson, E. Fringed Gentian.
Gentian has a parched Corolla, The.
Lawrence, D. H. Bavarian Gentians.
Very. Solitary Gentian, The.
Whittier. Pressed Gentian, The.

Geography and Geographers
Cooper, J. For a Boy Born in Wartime.
Davie, D. Derbyshire Turf.
Donne. Hymn[e] to God My God, in My Sickness[e], A.
Hacker, M. Art of a Novel, The.
Koch, K. Geography.
Levi, P. First Atlas, The.
Major, C. Study for a Geographical Trail.
Rimbaud, A. Promontory.
Sandburg, C. Turn of the Wheel.
Whitman, W. Broadway Pageant, A.
Passage to India.

Geology and Geologists
Ammons. If Anything Will Level with You Water Will.
Undersea.
Carruth, H. Essay on Stone.
Ciardi, J. Goodnight.
Rexroth, K. Adonis in Summer.

Lesson in Geography, A.
Lyell's Hypothesis Again.
Prolegomenon to a Theodicy, A.
Snyder, G. What Happened Here Before.
Tomlinson, C. Gli Scafari.

Geometry
Amichai [*or* Amikhai]. Through Two Points Only One Straight Line Can Pass.
Ammons. Lines.
Cummings, E. E. Newly / cued / motif smites truly to beautifully.
Surely / Cued / motif smites truly to Beautifully, The.
Davie, D. Bolyai, the Geometer.
Dickinson, E. Best Witchcraft is Geometry.
Dove, R. Geometry.
Simic. Drawing the Triangle.
Zukofsky, L. "Further than."
See also **Euclid**

George I, King of England
Burns, R. German Lairdie, The.

George III, King of England
Cowper, W. Annus Memorabilis, 1789.
On His Majesty's Sea Bathing.
On the Queens's Visit to London.
Koch, K. You Were Wearing.
Wheatley, P. To the King's Most Excellent Majesty. 1768.
Wordsworth, W. November, 1813.
On the Death of His Majesty (George the Third).

George V, King of England
Kipling, R. King and the Sea, The.
King's Pilgrimage, The.

Georgia (state)
Angelou. Georgia Song, A.
Dickey, J. In the Marble Quarry.
Hughes, L. Georgia Dusk.
Governor Fires Dean.
Red Clay Blues.
Sun Song.
Vari-Colored Song.
Melville, H. March to the Sea, The.
Wright, C. Chickamauga.

Geraniums
Carruth, H. August First.
Eliot, T. S. Easter: Sensations of April.
Lawrence, D. H. Red Geranium and Godly Mignonette.
Olson, C. I was stretched out on the earth so that a wild geranium.
Rilke. Geranium.
Roethke. Geranium, The.
Swenson, M. Digging in the Garden of Age I Uncover a Live Root.
Wordsworth, W. Poor Robin.

German (language)
Borges. To the German Language.
Dickey, W. Die Älte Frau, Die Älte Marschallin.
Dugan, A. Untitled Poem: "Our German teacher used to say."
Enzensberger, H. Language of the Country.
Jarrell, R. Deutsch durch Freud.
Paley, G. Translation.

Germans, The
Dove, R. At the German Writers Conference in Munich.
Fenton, J. Doctor Gliedschirm, skin specialist, surgeries 14–16 hours or by appointment.
German Requiem, A.
Ferlinghetti, L. Expressionist History of German Expressionism.
Jarrell, R. Germans Are Lunatics, The.
Jeffers, R. Fourth Act.
Kipling, R. Justice.
Outlaws, The.
Laughlin, J. Hard to Translate.
In the Train.
Why Not?
Robinson, E. Rahel to Varnhagen.
Rukeyser, M. As he stood near the plane, they heard him say.
Smith, S. On the Death of a German Philosopher.

Williams, M.   Wiedersehen.
Williams, W.   Rare Gist, The.
Wordsworth, W.   Germans on the Heights of Hochheim, The.

Germany
Beckett, S.   Ne manquez pas à Stuttgart.
Bierce.   Strained Relations.
Bukowski.   Some of My Readers.
Carruth, H.   Spring Notes from Robin Hill.
Celan.   Deathfugue.
    Frankfurt, September.
    Tübingen, January.
Enzensberger, H.   Language of the Country.
Ginsberg, A.   Ruhr-Gebiet.
    Tübingen–Hamburg Schlafwagen.
Hardy, T.   England to Germany in 1914.
Hill, G.   De Jure Belli ac Pacis.
Jarrell, R.   Angels at Hamburg, The.
Jouve.   Kapuzinerberg (Salzburg).
Kipling, R.   Justice.
    Outlaws, The.
    Rowers, The.
Laughlin, J.   In Darmstadt.
    O Frères Humains.
    Song of the GIs & the MGs.
    Stuttgart: In a Nightclub (Illegal).
Lowell, R.   Exile's Return, The.
Meredith, G.   Emperor Frederick of Our Time, The.
    Pictures of the Rhine.
    Rhine-Land.
Merton.   Fable for a War.
Milosz, C.   Mittelbergheim.
    With Her.
Milton.   Elegy 4: To Thomas Young.
O'Hara, F.   Image of the Buddha Preaching.
Ramanujan.   Some Indian Uses of History on a Rainy Day.
Rukeyser, M.   Another Day (Day Lilies, Yellow Daisies).
Sandburg, C.   In the Shadow of the Palace.
Spender, S.   Helmut.
    Van der Lubbe.
Tomlinson, C.   Blaubeuren.
Whitman, W.   Dead Emperor, The.
Wordsworth, W.   Alas! what boots the long laborious quest.
    Prophecy February, 1807, A.
Zagajewski.   For Gabriela Münter.

Germs
Nash, O.   Germ, The.
Williams, M.   Euglena.
See also **Bacteria**

Gethsemane
Dickinson, E.   Gethsemene and Cana.
Kipling, R.   Gethsemane.
Very.   Christ's Capture in the Garden: A Paraphrase.

Gettysburg, Battle of (1863)
Whittier.   Hive at Gettysburg, The.

Ghana
Komunyakaa.   Under House Arrest.

Ghettos
Borges.   Spinoza.
Hughes, L.   Negro Ghetto.
Levertov.   Letter to Marek about a Photograph, A.
Levi, P.   Gedale's Song.
Lorde.   New York City 1970.
Piercy.   Community.
Williams, C. K.   Bread.

Ghosts
Auden.   Family Ghosts.
Brooks, G.   Mentors.
Byron, G.   Saul.
Cavafy.   That They Might Appear.
Ciardi, J.   I'm No Good for You.
Codrescu.   Ghouls of Candlemas, The.
Coleridge, S.   Phantom or Fact?
Crane, H.   To Conquer Variety.
Creeley.   Passage, The.
Cullen, C.   Ghosts.
    Two Who Crossed a Line (She Crosses).
Cummings, E. E.   Round face near the top of the stairs, A.

Davie, D.   Apparition, An.
    Departed, The.
    My Father's Honour.
    Sea of Tiberias.
    Thomas and Emma.
De la Mare.   Betrayal.
    Familiar, The.
    Ghost, The.
    Hospital.
    Imogen.
    Listeners, The.
    News.
    Revenant, The.
    Shadow.
    Solitude.
    Spectre, The.
    Thus Her Tale.
    Tryst, The.
    Twilight.
    Which Way?
    Who's that?
Dickey, J.   Craters.
Dickey, W.   At Maganosc / in the stone bedroom.
    Here, in the summer city.
    If forgiveness comes / it will be gradual.
    In the Dreaming.
    In the dreaming / we walk throug the streets of Oxford.
    Thinking of me / think of what was.
    We meet, eating, smoking.
Dickinson, E.   Distance that the dead have gone, The.
    I lift the lid to my box of Phantoms.
    My family of Apparitions.
    Only Ghost I ever saw, The.
Donne.   Apparition, The.
Dunbar, P.   Wraith, The.
Graves, R.   Ancestors.
    Coronation Murder, The.
    Country Mansion, A.
    No More Ghosts.
    Or to Perish before Day.
    Outlaws.
    Restless Ghost, A.
    Welsh Incident.
Gurney, I.   Ballad of the Three Spectres.
Hall, D.   Mount Kearsarge.
Hardy, T.   At Shag's Heath.
    At the Piano.
    Bird-Catcher's Boy, The.
    Dead Man Walking, The.
    Family Portraits.
    Garden Seat, The.
    Glimpse, The.
    Haunter, The.
    Head above the Fog, The.
    Her Haunting-Ground.
    I Have Lived with Shades.
    Monument-Maker, The.
    My Spirit Will Not Haunt the Mound.
    Noble Lady's Tale, The.
    Phantom Horsewoman, The.
    Re-Enactment, The.
    Second Night, The.
    Souls of the Slain, The.
    Spectres That Grieve.
    Spellbound Palace, A.
    Strange House, The.
    Vagg Hollow.
    Wistful Lady, The.
    Woman Driving, A.
    Woman I Met, The.
Heaney, S.   King of the Ditchbacks, The.
    Villanelle for an Anniversary.
Herrick.   Upon an Old Man a Residenciarie.
Housman.   In midnights of November.
    When I Watch the Living Meet.
Hughes, L.   Ghosts of 1619.
Jackson, L.   Biography of a Myth, The.
Jarrell, R.   Ghost, a Real Ghost, A.
Jeffers, R.   As the eye fails through age or disease.
    Ghost.
    Mara.
Kinsella, T.   Dream.

    Memory of W.H. Auden.
    Thinking of Mr D.
Kipling, R.   Looking Glass, The.
    Old Mother Laidinwool.
    Possibilities.
Kunitz, S.   Master and Mistress.
Laughlin, J.   Revenants, The.
Lawrence, D. H.   Erinnyes.
    Houseless Dead, The.
    Nostalgia.
    Spirits Summoned West.
    We Have Gone Too Far.
Levertov.   Spirits Appeased, The.
Levi, P.   Survivor, The.
    There Were a Hundred.
Lindsay, N.   Ghosts in Love.
Logan, J.   Spirit of the Dead Watching: after Gaugin.
Longfellow, H.   Cross of Snow, The.
McGrath, T.   All the Dead Soldiers.
McHugh, H.   Ghost, The.
Meredith, W.   Ghosts of the House, The.
Merwin.   Apparitions.
    Cat Ghosts.
    Is That What You Are.
    Meeting.
Millay, E.   Little Ghost, The.
    Wraith.
Mistral, G.   Useless Vigil, The.
Muldoon, P.   Longbones.
Oliver, M.   Aunt Elsie's Night Music.
Olson, C.   As the Dead Prey upon Us.
    At Yorktown.
Owen, W.   Kind Ghosts, The.
    Shadwell Stair.
Parker, D.   I Shall Come Back.
Plath.   Danse Macabre.
    Dialogue between Ghost and Priest.
Poe.   Conqueror Worm, The.
    Haunted Palace, The.
Pound, E.   Villonaud for This Yule.
Propertius.   Ghost, The.
Ramanujan.   Some People.
Ransom, J.   Spectral Lovers.
Rexroth, K.   Yugao.
Rich, A.   What Ghosts Can Say.
Riley, J.   Jolly Miller, The.
    Spirits at Home.
    To an Importunate Ghost.
Robinson, E.   Lingard and the Stars.
Rossetti, C.   Chilly Night, A.
    Coast-Nightmare, A.
    Ghost's Petition, The.
    Hour and the Ghost, The.
    Poor Ghost, The.
Sandburg, C.   Kisses, Can You Come Back Like Ghosts?
    Testimony Regarding a Ghost.
    Three Ghosts.
Seifert.   Struggle with the Angel.
Sexton.   Ghosts.
Shelley, P.   Fragment of a Ghost Story.
Simic.   Navigator.
Smith, S.   Ghost of Ware, The.
    King Hamlet's Ghost.
    Le Revenant.
    Longing for Death because of Feebleness.
    Old Ghosts.
    Parklands, The.
    Wanderer, The.
Spender, S.   Us.
Swenson, M.   Downward.
Thomas, D.   Do You Not Father Me.
Thoreau.   I have rolled near some other spirits path.
Tomlinson, C.   Apparition, The.
Van Duyn.   In the Old Country, then, two ladies and two boys.
    Just full of springs the world was in Illinois.
Walcott.   Verandah.
Whitman, W.   As if a Phantom Caress'd Me.
Whittier.   Garrison of Cape Ann, The.
    New Wife and the Old, The.
    Prayer-Seeker, The.
    Sisters, The.
Williams, C. K.   Giving It Up.

Williams, M.   Ghost of His Wife Comes to Tell Him How It Is, The.
Ghosts.
How We May By Chance Pronounce the Unsuspected Residence of a Ghost.
Story, The.
Woman in the Room, The.
Williams, T.   Dear Silent Ghost.
His Manner of Returning.
Wordsworth, W.   I find it written of SIMONIDES.
Lucy Gray; or, Solitude.
She was a Phantom of delight.
Wright, J.   Assignation, The.
Erinna to Sappho.
Ghost, The.
My Grandmother's Ghost.
Youth.
Yeats.   Apparitions, The.
Crazy Jane and Jack the Journeyman.
To a Shade.
Zaturenska.   Familiar, The.
Four Ghosts.
Mirrored Room, The.
Séance, The.
Strange Captivity.
Variation on a Polish Folk Song.
Voices in Air.

Giacometti, Alberto
Char.   Celebrating Giacometti.
Wilbur, R.   Giacometti.

Giants
Baudelaire.   Giantess, The.
Bly, R.   Near the Giant's House.
Cavafy.   Pelasgian Image.
Ciardi, J.   Colossus in Quicksand, The.
Hall, D.   Sleeping Giant, The.
Jeffers, R.   Giant's Ring, The.
Major, C.   Giant Red Woman.
Michelangelo Buonarroti.   Then there's this giant—tall! So tall he can't.
Millay, E.   Bean-Stalk, The.
Patchen.   Reason for Skylarks, The.
Plath.   Queen's Complaint, The.
Pope, A.   Lamentation of Glumdalclitch for the Loss of Grildrig, The.
To Quinbus Flestrin the Man-Mountain, a Lilliputian Ode.
Ralegh, S.   Giants did advance their wicked hand, The.
Riley, J.   Jack the Giant-Killer.
Truly Marvelous, The.
Very.   Giants, The.
Wilbur, R.   Giaour and the Pacha, The.
Wilner, E.   Generic Vision, 1991.

Gibbon, Edward
Hardy, T.   Lausanne: In Gibbon's Old Garden: 11–12 p.m.
Warren, R.   Wind and Gibbon.

Gibbs, Josiah Willard
Rukeyser, M.   Gibbs.

Gibraltar
Dickinson, E.   I have seen one Bird and part of another.

Gifts and Giving
Amichai [or Amikhai].   Gifts of Love.
Berrigan, T.   Something Amazing Just Happened.
Berry, W.   Gift of Gravity, The.
Brodsky, J.   December 24, 1971.
Browning, E.   Hugh Stuart Boyd [Legacies].
King's Gift, The.
Browning, R.   Lines for a Gift.
Burns, R.   Cardin o't, The.
Posie, The.
To a Young Lady, *Miss Jessy L———, Dumfries; with Books which the Bard Presented Her.*
To Miss L———.
To Mr. McMurdo, with a Pound of Lundiefoot Snuff.
Byron, G.   Chain I Gave, The.
Cornelian, The.
Carruth, H.   I Could Take.
Impossible Indispensability of the Ars Poetica, The.

Leaf from Mr. Dyer's Woods, A.
Cowper, W.   Lines with Two Cockscombs.
Thanks for a Gift of Pheasants.
To Anne Bodham.
To John Johnson.
To Mrs. King.
To Mrs. Newton.
To Mrs. Throckmorton.
Creeley.   Gift, The.
Gifts.
Kiki.
Later ("If I could get").
Cunningham, J.   With a Copy of Stevens' *Harmonium.*
Dickinson, E.   'Tis customary as we part.
We are snatching our jewels from the frost.
Your Gifts are from the Sky.
Dugan, A.   Gifts Accompaniment, A.
Dunbar, P.   She Gave Me a Rose.
Eberhart, R.   Mistaken Identity.
To Evan.
Emerson, R.   Give All to Love.
He whom God had thus preferred.
Motto to "Gifts."
Frost, R.   Gift Outright, The.
Gluck, L.   Swans.
Graves, R.   Love Gifts.
Name Day.
On Giving.
Song: Basket of Blossom.
Song: Beyond Giving.
Song: Come, Enjoy Your Sunday!
"H. D."   Acon.
At Croton.
Fragment 41: "Am I blind alas."
Gift, The.
Wine Bowl.
Hall, D.   Merle Bascom's .22.
Herrick.   Almes.
Carkanet, The.
Christs Part.
Gods Hands.
His Dream[e].
Jimmall Ring, or True-Love-Knot, The.
Larr's Portion, and the Poets Part.
New-Year's [or New-Yeares] Gift Sent to Sir Simeon Steward, A.
New-Yeeres Gift, The.
Pomander Bracelet, The.
Primrose, The.
Ring Presented to Julia, A.
Short Hymne to Larr, A.
Ternarie of Littles, upon a Pipkin of Jellie [or Jelly] Sent to a Lady, A.
To His Saviour, a Child; a Present, by a Child.
Hopkins, G.   Morning, Midday, and Evening Sacrifice.
Hughes, L.   Shepherd's Song at Christmas.
Ignatow, D.   Mystique.
Johnson, S.   To Miss —: On Her Giving the Author a Gold and Silk Net-work Purse.
Jonson, B.   To Mr John Burges.
Keats.   To a Friend Who Sent Me Some Roses.
To a Young Lady Who Sent Me a Laurel Crown.
Kizer, C.   Gift, The.
Komunyakaa.   Gift Horse.
Laughlin, J.   On the Gift of a Sapphire to My Wife Ann.
You Know How a Cat.
Lawrence, D. H.   New Year's Night.
Sick.
Logan, J.   Gift, The.
Present, The.
Lux.   Give It to the Wind.
MacLeish.   Revenant, The.
Meredith, G.   To R.H.H. with Daphne.
Merton.   Macarius the Younger.
Ointment, The.
Merwin.   Gift.
Mistral, G.   For Noel.
Nash, O.   I Remember Yule.
I'll Eat My Split-Level Turkey in the Breezeway.
I'm a Pleasure to Shop for.
Oliver, M.   Night Traveler, The.

Olson, C.   Friend, The.
On the equator east of my son I Orion bequeath to him my riches.
Orr, G.   Gift, The.
Parker, D.   Christmas, 1921.
Triolet: "It is never the cost of the gift."
With Best Wishes.
Pessoa.   I don't want the sincere gifts.
Pinkerton, H.   Gift, The.
Pope, A.   On Receiving from the Right Hon. the Lady Frances Shirley a Standish and Two Pens.
Raine, K.   Heirloom.
Rimbaud, A.   Orphans' New Year Gifts.
Roethke.   Her Reticence.
Rossetti, C.   Epiphany.
Lord, what have I that I may offer Thee?
Me and my gift: kind Lord, behold.
O Sailor, Come Ashore.
Ransomed of the Lord, The.
Rukeyser, M.   Gift.
Rumi.   Sheba's Gifts to Solomon.
Schuyler, J.   Stone Knife, A.
This Notebook.
Shelley, P.   To Emilia Viviani,
To———: "One word is too often profaned."
Smith, S.   Dear Karl.
Stafford, W.   At Fourth and Main in Liberal, Kansas, 1932.
Little Gift, A.
Mother's Day.
Stockton, A.   To Doctor Smith on His Birth Day March 16th, 92.
Swift, J.   Paper book is sent by Boyle, A.
Tate, J.   Grace.
Tomlinson, C.   Picture of J. T. in a Prospect of Stone, The.
Walker, A.   Gift.
Whittier.   To Avis Keene.
Wilbur, R.   Gifts, The.
Williams, W.   Gift, The.
Wordsworth, W.   Sonnet: To———.
With a Small Present.
Wright, J.   Birthday, The.
Wyatt, S.   Lady gave me a gift she had not, A.
To seek each where where man doth live.
Yeats.   Gift of Harun Al-Rashid, The.
He Gives His Beloved Certain Rhymes.
Never Give All the Heart.
To a Wealthy Man Who Promised a Second Subscription to the Dublin Municipal Gallery if It Were Proved the People Wanted Pictures.

Gilgamesh
Ammons.   Gilgamesh Was Very Lascivious.

Ginkgo Trees
Nemerov.   Ginkgoes in Fall.

Ginsberg, Allen
Berrigan, T.   Pandora's Box, an Ode.
Red Shift.
Carruth, H.   Thaw.
Creeley.   On Phrase from Ginsberg's *Kaddish.*
Please.
Talk ("Talking Ginsbergian").
Milosz, C.   To Allen Ginsberg.
Whalen, P.   For Allen, on His 60th Birthday.
Williams, W.   Cézanne.

Giraffes
Jacobsen, J.   Short Views in Africa.
Mistral, G.   Giraffe, The.
Moore, M.   To a Giraffe.
Stock, R.   Man-Giraffe.

Girdles
Sexton.   Woman with Girdle.

Girls
Alcman.   Astymelusa.
Amichai [or Amikhai].   Girl Goes Out in the Morning Like a Knight, A.
Modern Girl, A.
Two Girls Live in the Old House.
Ashbery, J.   Thoughts of a Young Girl.
Blue Cloud.   Girl Child.
Little Fawn.
Browning, R.   She was fifteen—had great eyes.
Bukowski.   Countryside.
Byron, G.   Here's to Her Who Long.

Campion, T.   Advice to a Girl.
There is a garden in her face.
Carruth, H.   Cappadocian Song.
Carver, R.   Young Girls, The.
Ciardi, J.   Thinking about Girls.
Clare, J.   Merry Maid.
Crane, S.   Once I saw thee idly rocking.
Cummings, E. E.   Jake hates / all the girls(the).
Newlys of silence.
Davie, D.   Grazia Deledda, Young.
De la Mare.   Mercutio.
Dickinson, E.   I'm Wife . . . .
Dugan, A.   Conversation with a Dirty-Minded
Little Girl.
Dunbar, P.   My Little March Girl.
Eberhart, R.   Gesture, The.
Eliot, T. S.   La Figlia Che Piange.
Frost, R.   Fear of Man, The.
García Lorca.   Two Girls.
Hacker, M.   Fourteen.
Gerda in the Aerie.
Hall, D.   Young Watch Us, The.
Han-shan.   Raise girls but not too many.
Hardy, T.   Maid of Keinton Mandeville, The.
Sitting on the Bridge.
West-of-Wessex Girl, The.
Heaney, S.   New Song, A.
Herrick.   Another to the Maids.
Hughes, L.   Girl.
Jazz Girl.
New Cabaret Girl, The.
Young Negro Girl.
Jacobsen, J.   You Can Take It with You.
Kinsella, T.   Girl on a Swing.
Koch, K.   Circus, The.
Laughlin, J.   Girls as Windmills.
Your Early Life.
Lawrence, D. H.   Jeune Fille, The.
Tarts.
Lindsay, N.   How a Little Girl Sang.
Logan, J.   Lament in Spring.
Spirit of the Dead Watching: after Gaugin.
MacDiarmid, H.   Love-sick Lass, The.
MacLeish.   Excavation of Troy.
Where the Hayfields Were.
Mahon.   Girls on the Bridge.
McHugh, H.   Two Holidays.
Merton.   Song for Our Lady of Cobre.
What Troubles I Have Seen in Birdlegged
Spring.
Milosz, C.   Portrait with a Cat, A.
Mistral, G.   Christmas Star, The.
Song of the Dead Girls.
Piercy.   Girl in White.
Morning Half-Life Blues, The.
Riley, J.   Extremes.
Little-Girl-Two-Little-Girls.
Little Girly-Girl.
Little Lady, The.
Rilke.   Child in Red.
Ritsos.   Absence.
Sacchetti.   On a Fine Day.
On a Wet Day.
Sandburg, C.   Red-Headed Resstaurant Cashier.
Sappho.   One Girl.
Seifert.   Song about Girls, A.
Simic.   Ballad: "What's that approaching like
dusk like poverty."
Old Mountain Road.
Smith, S.   La Speakerine de Putney.
What Is She Writing? Perhaps It Will Be Good.
Stockton, A.   To a Little Miss a Year Older than
the One to Whom the Glass Was Promised,
with a Toy Looking Glass.
To a Little Miss, with a Toy Lookingglass.
Szymborska, W.   Moment in Troy, A.
Whalen, P.   Vision of Delight, The.
Williams, M.   For a Girl I Know about to Be a
Woman.
Lost in Ladispoli.
Williams, T.   Winter Smoke Is Blue and Bitter.
Williams, W.   Girl, The.
His Daughter.
Lonely Street, The.
3 A.M. The Girl with the Honey Colored Hair.
3 Stances.

Yellow Tree Peony, The.
Wilner, E.   Of a Sun She Can Remember.
Wordsworth, W.   Solitary Reaper, The.
Westmoreland Girl, The.
Wright, J.   Girl in a Window, A.
Yeats.   Politics.
Zaturenska.   Four Ghosts.
Girl and Scarecrow.
See also **Adolescence; Childhood and Children;**
Youth

Giving
See **Gifts and Giving**
Glaciers
Ammons.   Late Romantic.
Blue Cloud.   Glacier Country.
Levi, P.   Glacier, The.
Meredith, G.   By the Rosanna.
Merwin.   Footprints on the Glacier.
Rexroth, K.   Ice Shall Cover Nineveh.
Tomlinson, C.   Glacier, The.
Very.   Glacial Marks on Our Hills, The.
Warren, R.   It Is Not Dead.
Glasgow, Scotland
Creeley.   Bruce & Linley's House.
Hall, D.   "O Flodden Field."
MacDiarmid, H.   Glasgow, 1960.
In the Slums of Glasgow.
Montale.   Argyll Tour.
Glass and Glassblowers
Clampitt.   Beach Glass.
Dugan, A.   Jewels of Indoor Glass.
Herrick.   Broken Christall, The.
Merrill, J.   Octopus, The.
Moore, M.   Egyptian Pulled Glass Bottle in the
Shape of a Fish, An.
Rukeyser, M.   Junk-Heap at Murano.
Tomlinson, C.   Glass Grain.
Prose Poem.
Glasses
McHugh, H.   Spectacles.
Weiss, T.   Views and Spectacles.
See also **Eyeglasses**
Glencoe, Scotland
Chesterton.   Glencoe.
Globes
Donne.   Valediction, A: of Weeping.
Ritsos.   Misunderstandings.
Glory
Ambrose.   Splendor Paternae Gloriae.
Amichai [*or* Amikhai].   And That Is Your Glory.
And This Is Your Glory.
Browning, E.   Night and the Merry Man.
Seraph and Poet, The.
Byron, G.   Last Words on Greece.
Ciardi, J.   Glory, The.
Dickey, J.   Olympian, The.
Dickinson, E.   For this—accepted Breath.
Glory is that bright tragic thing.
Her spirit rose to such a height.
I had the Glory—that will do.
Of Glory not a Beam is left.
Of this is Day composed.
'Twas my one Glory.
Eberhart, R.   Van Black, an Old Farmer in His
Dell.
Emerson, R.   Is Jove immortal / So is Cerberus
at his portal.
Graves, R.   Antorcha Y Corona, 1968.
Bird of Paradise.
Birth of Angels.
Torch and Crown, 1968.
Guyon.   Glory to God Alone.
HaNagid.   Did Your Father Leave You Glory.
Herrick.   Comforts in Crosses.
Credit of the Conquerer, The.
Glorie.
Glory.
Gods Prt.
Great Grief, Great Glory.
Ode, or Psalme, to God, An.
Posting to Printing.
Jeffers, R.   Moments of Glory.
Kipling, R.   Glories, The.
Komunyakaa.   Glory.
Melville, H.   On Sherman's Men.

Michelangelo Buonarroti.   When the occasioner
of my many a sigh.
Milton.   Paraphrase on Psalm 114, A.
Owen, W.   Fragment: "Not one corner of a
foreign field."
Storm.
To a Comrade in Flanders.
To My Friend (With an Identity Disc).
Patchen.   I suggest that this day be made holy.
In a Crumbling.
Petrarch.   I've never seen the sun rise in such
glory.
Lady much more radiant than the sun, A.
Ritsos.   Unanswered.
Rossetti, C.   As the Apple Tree among the Trees
of the Wood.
Chiefest among Ten Thousand, The.
Come cheer up, my lads, 'tis to glory we steer!
General Assembly and Church of the Firstborn,
The.
Heaviness May Endure for a Night, But Joy
Cometh in the Morning.
Hills are tipped with sunshine, while I walk / In
shadows dim and cold.
Hymn: "To the God Who reigns on high."
I Gave a Sweet Smell.
It Is Finished.
Let Everything That Hath Breath Praise the
Lord.
Love is all happiness, love is all beauty.
Minnie and Mattie.
O Lord, on Whom we gaze and dare not gaze, /
Increase our faith that gazing we may see.
Passiontide.
Praise of Love.
Sexagesima.
St. Michael and all Angels.
What do the stars do / Up in the sky.
Wouldst thou give me a heavy jewelled crown.
Rukeyser, M.   Trophies.
Swinburne.   Les Noyades.
Warren, R.   Have You Ever Eaten Stars?
Wilde, O.   Sen Artysty; or, The Artist's Dream.
Glossolalia
Hamill, S.   Gift of Tongues, The.
Tate, J.   Tabernacle, The.
Gloucester, Massachusetts
Olson, C.   By Cure of—Sulfa.
Librarian, The.
Gloves
Ciardi, J.   Manocalzata (Gloved Hand).
Logan, J.   On a Photograph by Aaron Siskind.
Maritain.   Glove, The.
Orr, G.   Work Gloves.
Pagis.   Devotion.
Petrarch.   I was so blest by sheer good luck and
Love.
O lovely hand, clutched tightly round my heart.
See also **Mittens**
Glowworms
Bourne, V.   Glow-worm, The.
Cowper, W.   Nightingale and Glow-Worm, The.
Lux.   Glow Worm.
Marvell.   Mower to the Glowworms [*or* Glow-
Worms *or* Glo-Worms], The.
Wordsworth, W.   Among all lovely things my
Love had been.
Pilgrim's Dream; or, The Star and the Glow-
Worm, The.
See also **Fireflies**
Gluttony and Gluttons
Carver, R.   Plus.
Éluard, P.   Confections.
Herrick.   Excesse.
Upon Chub.
Upon Magot a Frequenter of Ordinaries.
Upon Spokes.
Jonson, B.   On Gut.
Nash, O.   Nevertheless.
Quick, Hammacher, My Stomacher!
Piercy.   Consumer, The.
Plath.   Glutton, The.
Riley, J.   Billy Goodin'
Uncle Sidney's Rhymes.
Ritsos.   Silence.

Roethke. Goo Girl.
  Myrtle's Cousin.
  Verse with Allusions.
Rumi. Muhammad and the Huge Eater.
Very. Glutton, The.
Yeats. Chambermaid's First Song, The.

Gnats
Eberhart, R. Equivalence of Gnats and Mice.
  Gnat on My Paper.
  Gnats.
Graves, R. One Hard Look.
Hughes, T. Gnat-Psalm.
Lux. River Blindness (Onchocerciasis).
Rumi. Gnats inside the Wind.

Gnus
Ciardi, J. G, also inevitably, is for GNU.
Roethke. Gnu, The.

Goats
Ai. I Have Got to Stop Loving You. So I Have
  Killed My Black Goat.
Creeley. Disappointment, The.
Gallagher, T. Woman Who Raised Goats, The.
Hughes, T. Meeting.
Kipling, R. They killed a Child to please the
  Gods.
Lawrence, D. H. He-Goat.
  She-Goat.
Plath. Goatsucker.
Rumi. Lame Goat, The.
Simic. Old Mountain Road.
Williams, W. Goat, The.

Goblins
Herrick. Ceremony upon Candlemas Eve.
Plath. Princess and the Goblins, The.
Riley, J. Little Orphant Annie.
  Nine Little Goblins, The.
See also **Elves; Fairies; Ghosts**

God
Amichai [*or* Amikhai]. And That Is Your Glory.
  And This Is Your Glory.
  At the Seashore.
  Diameter of the Bomb, The.
  God Full of Mercy.
  God Has Pity on Kindergarten Children.
  God Takes Pity on Kindergarten Children.
  God's Hand in the World.
  Jews, The.
  Language School.
  My Father's Death.
  My First Days in New York.
Ammons. Hymn: "I know if I find you I will
  have to leave the earth."
Ashbery, J. Lament upon the Waters, The.
Atwood. Resurrection.
Auden. Friday's Child.
Baudelaire. Death to the Poor.
Beckett, S. Serena I.
Berryman. Amos.
  Apparition, The.
  Back.
  Certainty before Lunch.
  Compline.
  Eleven Addresses to the Lord.
  Facts & Issues, The.
  Form, The.
  Interstitial Office.
  Lauds.
  Matins.
  Nones.
  Opus Dei.
  Overseas Prayer.
  Pacifist's Song, The.
  Prayer After All, A.
  Prayer of the Middle-Aged Man, The.
  Prime.
  Sext.
  Somber Prayer.
  Terce.
  Unknowable? Perhaps Not Altogether.
  Usual Prayer, A.
  Vespers.
Bible, *O.T.* Psalms.
Bierce. Here Stanford lies, who thought it odd.
  Vision of Doom, A.
Blake, W. Book of Urizen [*or* First Book of

Urizen], The.
  I rose up at the dawn of day.
  There Is No Natural Religion.
  To Nobodaddy.
Bly, R. Waking from Sleep.
Borges. Alchemist, The.
  Benares.
  Chess.
  Emanuel Swedenborg.
  Everness.
  For a Version of *I Ching*.
  Golem, The.
  Poem of Quantity.
  Poem of the Gifts.
Bradstreet, A. Here Follows Some Verses upon
  the Burning of Our House [July 10th, 1666.
  Copied Out of a Loose Paper].
  My soul, rejoice thou in thy God.
  My thankful heart with glorying tongue.
  What God is like to him I serve?
Brontë, E. No Coward Soul Is Mine.
Brooks, G. God Works in a Mysterious Way.
Broumas, O. With God.
Browning, E. Child's Thought of God, A.
  Confessions.
  Heaven and Earth.
  Hugh Stuart Boyd [His Death, 1848].
  Human Life's Mystery.
  Island, An.
  Isobel's Child.
  Measure, The.
  Only a Curl.
  Seraphim, The.
  Since without Thee We Do No Good.
  Sleep, The.
  Soul's Travelling, The.
Browning, R. Boy and the Angel, The.
  Epilogue: "On the first of the Feast of Feasts."
  Johannes Agricola in Meditation.
  Porphyria's Lover.
  Prospice.
  Rephan.
  Reverie.
Burns, R. First Psalm, The.
  First Six Verses of the Ninetieth Psalm, The.
  Grace after Meat.
  Grace before Dinner, Extempore, A.
  Holy Willie's Prayer.
  Lying at a Reverend Friend's House One Night,
  the Author Left the Following *Verses* in the
  Room Where He Slept.
  Prayer, under the Pressure of Violent Anguish,
  A.
  Stanzas on the Same Occasion [in the Prospect
  of Death].
Byron, G. God Maddens Him Whom 'T Is His
  Will to Lose.
  Heaven and Earth.
  Prayer of Nature, The.
Campion, T. Author of light, revive my dying
  spright.
  Bravely deckt, come forth, bright day.
  Come Let Us Sound with Melodie.
  Heart's Music.
  Lift up to heav'n, sad wretch, thy heavy spright.
  O Come Quickly!
  Seek the Lord.
  Sing a song of joy.
  To Music Bent Is My Retired Mind.
Carruth, H. Ontological Episode of the Asylum.
Cavafy. Word and Silence.
Celan. Psalm: "No one kneads us again out of
  earth and clay."
  Tenebrae.
  Zurich, at the Stork.
Chaucer. Balade of Bon Conseill.
Chesterton. God of the Living, The.
  Holy of Holies, The.
Ciardi, J. Diary Entry.
  God.
  High Tension Lines across a Landscape.
  In Place of a Curse.
  Memo: Preliminary Draft of a Prayer to God the
  Father.
  Old Man Confesses, An.
  One Wet Iota.

Stations.
  Traffic Victim Sends a Sonnet of Confused
  Thanks to God as the Sovereign Host, A.
Clement of Alexandria. Logos Our Teacher,
  The.
  New Song, The.
Clifton, L. My Dream about God.
  Remembering the Birth of Lucifer.
Clough. Hymnos Aymnos.
  Irritability unnatural.
  Light words they were, and lightly, falsely said.
  Look you, my simple friend, 'tis one of those.
  What we, when face to face we see.
  When Israel Came out of Egypt.
  With Whom Is No Variableness, neither Shadow
  of Turning.
Coleridge, S. Philosophical Trinity, The.
  To Nature.
Cooper, J. After the Bomb Tests.
Cowper, W. Lines Written During a Period of
  Insanity.
  Lively Hope, and Gracious Fear.
  Lord Will Happiness Divine, The.
  My former hopes are fled.
  O Lord, my best desire fulfil
  Olney Hymns.
  True Pleasures.
Crane, H. Broken Tower, The.
Crane, S. All-feeling God, hear in the war-
  night.
  Blustering god, / Stamping across the sky.
  God fashioned the ship of the world carefully.
  In Heaven, / Some little blades of grass.
  Livid lightnings flashed in the clouds, The.
  When a people reach the top of a hill.
Crashaw. Song: "Lord, when the sense of Thy
  sweet grace."
Creeley. Awakening, The.
  From Pico & the Women: A Life.
  Song: "God give you pardon from gratitude."
Cullen, C. Dictum.
  Epitaph: "She leans across a golden table."
  For a Mouthy Woman.
  For an Atheist.
  Shroud of Color, The.
  Sonnet: "These are no wind-blown rumors, soft
  say-sos."
  To the Three for Whom the Book.
  Yet Do I Marvel.
Cummings, E. E. By little accurate saints
  thickly which tread.
  God.
  God,Thine the hand that doth extend.
  I am a little church(no great cathedral).
  I Thank You God.
  Jehovah buried,Satan dead.
  Maybe god / is a child.
  On souls robbed of their birth-right's better part.
  Round a so moon could dream(i sus).
  These from my mother's greatgrandmother's
  rosebush white.
  Vision.
  When any mortal(even the most odd).
  When god decided to invent.
  World is very big, and we, The.
"Dario." Golden tortoise walks across the
  carpet, The.
  Sum.
Davie, D. Being Angry with God.
  Cannibals.
  Curtains!
  If I Take the Wings of the Morning.
  Mandelstam's Hope for the Best.
  Meteorologist, September.
  Nosegay, The.
  On the Final Day.
  Ordinary God.
  Sing unto the Lord a New Song.
  Standings.
  Thou Art near at Hand, O Lord.
De la Mare. Hour-Glass, The.
  Last Chapter, The.
  Sunrise.
  Universe, The.
Dickey, J. Daughter.
Dickey, W. Ezekiel's Rabbit.

Dickinson, E.   All Circumstances are the Frame.
Alter! When the Hills do—.
Brain—is wider than the Sky, The.
Drowning is not so pitiful.
Expanse cannot be lost.
God is a distant—stately Lover.
God is indeed a jealous God.
God made no act without a cause.
God seems much more friendly.
He fumbles at your Soul.
"Heavenly Father"—take to thee.
How ruthless are the gentle.
I am afraid to own a Body.
I gave myself to Him—.
I got so I could take his name.
I had some things that I called mine.
I never felt at Home—Below.
I never saw a Moor.
Infinite a sudden Guest, The.
It was a quiet way—.
It was too late for Man.
It would have starved a Gnat.
Love Is That Later Thing.
Love of God may be taught, The.
My Life had stood—a Loaded Gun.
My Maker—let me be.
Nature and God—I neither knew.
Of God we ask one favor.
One who could repeat the Summer day, The.
Only God—detect the Sorrow.
Only News I know, The.
Publication—is the Auction.
Spring is the Period.
Struck, was I, not yet by Lightning.
Sun and Moon must make their haste, The.
There comes an hour when begging stops.
This was a Poet—It is That.
To know just how He suffered—would be dear.
Trees like Tassels—hit—and swung, The.
Truth—is as old as God.
"We thank thee Oh Father" for these strange Minds.
Who is it seeks my Pillow Nights.
Wild Nights—Wild Nights!
Donne.   Good Friday [or Goodfriday], 1613. Riding Westward.
Hymn[e] to Christ, at the Author's Last Going into Germany, A.
Hymn[e] to God My God, In My Sickness[e], A.
Drummond de Andrade.   Seven-Sided Poem.
Dubie.   Homage to Philip K. Dick.
True Story of God, A.
Dugan, A.   Against a Sickness: To the Female Double Principle God.
Against Veils on Exodus 33:23 and 34:33.
Crimes of Bernard, The.
Tourist Poem.
Dunbar, P.   Compensation.
Equipment.
Get Somebody Else.
God Reigns.
Hymn: "When storms arise."
Hymn, A: "Lead gently, Lord, and slow."
Night.
Not They Who Soar!
Plantation Melody, A.
Possession.
Resignation.
Spiritual, A.
To the Memory of Mary Young.
Duncan, R.   This Place Rumord to Have Been Sodom.
Eberhart, R.   Book of Nature, The.
Fury of Aerial Bombardment, The.
God and Man.
Harvard Stadium.
John Finley.
Meditation, A.
On a Squirrel Crossing the Road in Autumn, in New England.
Parker River, The.
Redemption.
Sometimes the Longing for Death.
Throwing the Apple.
Eliot, T. S.   Choruses from "The Rock."

Emerson, R.   And the best gift of God.
Be of good cheer, brave spirit; steadfastly.
Bohemian Hymn, The.
But God will keep his promise yet.
Dear Brother, Would You Know the Life.
Dull uncertain brain, A.
Γνωθι Σεαυτον.
Hard is it to persuade the public mind of its plain duty & true interest.
He walked the streets of great New York.
He whom God had thus preferred.
I am owner of the sphere.
I will not hesitate to speak the word.
I will not live out of me.
Is Jove immortal / So is Cerberus at his portal.
Leave me, Fear! thy throbs are base.
Lines on the Death of Miss M. B. Farnham.
Love / Asks nought his brother cannot give.
Mottoes to "History."
No. 13 Hymn Written in Concord Sept. 1814.
No fate, save by the victim's fault, is low.
On the Death of Mr. John Haskins.
Rules to men made evident, The.
Sun is the sole inconsumable fire, The.
There is in all the sons of men.
Threnody: "South-wind brings, The."
When success exalts thy lot.
Enzensberger, H.   Poison, The.
Farid-uddin Attar.   From "Bird Conversations."
Fenton, J.   God, a Poem.
Tauler.
Francis Xavier.   Translation of a Hymn of St. Francis Xavier.
Frost, R.   Bereft.
Concept Self-Conceived, A.
Fear of God, The.
Forgive, O Lord, my little jokes on Thee.
Masque of Reason, A.
García Lorca.   Prologue: "Here, my God, / is my heart."
Song for the Moon.
Ginsberg, A.   Holy Ghost on the Nod over the Body of Bliss.
Jaweh and Allah Battle.
Proclamation.
Psalm 4.
Psalm II: "Ah, still Lord, ah sweet Divinity."
Why Is God Love, Jack?
Glück, L.   Baskets.
Gift, The.
Lamentations.
Graves, R.   Knobs and Levers.
Gurney, I.   To God.
Guyon.   God Hides His People.
Repose in God.
see also Watching unto God in the Night-Season.
Soul That Loves God Finds Him Every Where, The.
"H. D."   Helen.
Magician [Master].
Orestes Theme.
Priest.
Two Poems for Christmas, 1937.
Hall, D.   Fathers and Sons.
Small Fig Tree, A.
HaNagid.   Earthquake, The.
He Whose Heart in His Heart.
On Fleeing His City.
On the Death of Isaac, His Brother.
Pass of Sand.
Two Eclipses.
War with Yadir, The.
When the Lord Is with You.
Hardy, T.   Agnosto Theo [To an Unknown God].
Bedridden Peasant, The.
Fragment: "At last I entered a long dark gallery."
God-Forgotten.
God's Education.
God's Funeral.
New Year's Eve.
Philosophical Fantasy, A.
Herbert, G.   Affliction (1).
Altar, The.
Antiphon (2): "Praised be the God of love."

Artillery [or Artillerie].
Bitter-Sweet.
Call, The.
Church-Floor[e], The.
Church-Lock and Key.
Clasping of Hands.
Collar, The.
Decay.
Dedication, The: "Lord, my first fruits present themselves to thee."
Denial[l].
Discipline.
Easter Wings.
Elixir [or Elixer], The.
Employment (1).
Evensong [or Even-Song].
Family [or Familie], The.
Forerunners, The.
Frailty.
Grace.
Home.
Hope.
Invitation, The.
Jordan (1).
Jordan (2).
Judgement.
Justice (1).
Knell, The.
L'Envoy.
Man.
Method, The.
Misery [or Miserie].
Obedience.
Odour, The. (2 Corinthians 2).
Offering, An.
Paradise.
Pearl, The. Matth. 13:45.
Perseverance.
Posy [or Posie], The.
Praise (2).
Praise (3).
Prayer (1): "Prayer the Church's banquet, Angels' age."
Prayer (2).
Providence.
Pulley, The.
Redemption.
Search, The.
Sepulchre.
Sion.
Sonnet: "Sure Lord, there is enough in thee to dry."
Thanksgiving, The.
To All Angels and Saints.
Twenty-third Psalm, The.
Unkindness.
Vanity [or Vanitie] (1).
Whitsunday.
Windows, The.
World, The.
Herrick.   Affliction.
Angells.
Another.
Another of God.
Another, to God.
Calling, and Correcting.
Charroll Presented to Dr. Williams Bp. of Lincolne as a Newyears Guift, A.
Clouds.
Confusion of Face.
Correction.
Evensong.
Free Welcome.
God.
God, and Lord.
God, and the King.
God Has a Twofold Part.
God Heares Us.
God Is One.
God Not to Be Comprehended.
God Sparing in Scourging.
God to Be First Served.
Gods Anger.
Gods Anger without Affection.
Gods Blessing.

Gods Descent.
Gods Dwelling.
Gods Grace.
Gods Hands.
Gods Keyes.
Gods Mercy.
Gods Mirth, Mans Mourning.
Gods Power.
Gods Presence.
Gods Time Must End Our Trouble.
Hardning of Hearts.
His Dream[e].
His Ejaculation to God.
His Petition.
His Power.
His Recantation.
JEHOVAH.
Judgment-Day, The.
Manna.
Neutrality Loathsome.
No Coming to God without Christ.
No Escaping the Scourging.
North and South.
Ode, or Psalme, to God, An.
Of all the good things whatsoe're we do.
Paine and Pleasure.
Pardon.
Position in the Hebrew Divinity, A.
Prayers Must Have Poise.
Prescience.
Reverence.
Riches and Poverty.
Right Hand, The.
Science in God.
Silence.
Staffe and Rod, The.
Teares.
This, and the Next World.
To Find[e] God.
To God.
To His Angrie God.
To His Ever-Loving God.
To His Saviour.
To Marygolds.
Upon God.
Upon Time.
Virgin Mary, The.
What God Is.
Whips.
Youth, and Age.
Hopkins, G.   As Kingfishers Catch Fire.
At the Wedding March.
Barnfloor and Winepress.
Carrion Comfort.
God's Grandeur.
Half-way House, The.
He hath abolished the old drouth.
In the Valley of the Elwy.
Let me be to Thee as the circling bird.
Nondum.
O Death, Death, He is come.
O Deus, Ego Amo Te.
Pied Beauty.
Spring and Fall.
Summa.
Thee, God, I come from, to thee go.
Thou Art Indeed Just, Lord.
Where art thou friend, whom I shall never see.
Housman.   Laws of God, the laws of man, The.
'Tis five years since, "An end," said I.
Hughes, L.   Acceptance.
Christian Country, A.
God.
Last Call.
Personal.
Who but the Lord?
Hughes, T.   Apple Tragedy.
Crow Blacker than Ever.
Crow's First Lesson.
God, The.
Gog.
Ignatow, D.   Complex, The.
I Wish a God Were Possible.
Jackson, L.   In the Beginning.
Then Follows.
Jacob, M.   Rainbow.

Jammes.   Prayer to Go to Paradise with the
Donkeys, A.
Jarrell, R.   Archangel's' Song, The.
Let's love each other for what we are.
Jeffers, R.   As the eye fails through age or
disease.
Birds and Fishes.
Birth-Dues.
Consciousness.
Excesses of God, The.
Fog.
Going to Horse Flats.
Intellectuals.
Noon.
Not Our Good Luck.
Patronymic.
Pearl Harbor.
Pleasures.
Point Pinos and Point Lobos.
Shine, Perishing Republic.
Silent Shepherds, The.
Soul's Desert, The.
Teheran.
There is no God but God; he is all that exists.
There is this infinite energy, the power of God
forever working.
Triad.
Johnson, S.   On Losing the Power of Speech.
Prayer: "Summe Deus, cui cæca patent
penetralia cordis."
Vanity of Human Wishes, The; The Tenth Satire
of Juvenal Imitated.
Jonson, B.   From The Touchstone of Truth.
Hymn[e] to God the Father, A.
Reverse on the Back Side, The.
Sinner's Sacrifice, The.
To Heaven.
To K[ing] Charles and Q[ueen] Mary, for the
Loss of Their First-Born. An Epigram
Consolatory. 1629.
Keats.   God of the Meridian.
Kipling, R.   Answer, The.
Carol, A: "Our Lord Who did the Ox
command."
Evarra and His Gods.
Natural Theology.
Necessitarian, The.
Non Nobis Domine!
Prayer of Miriam Cohen, The.
Rabbi's Song, The.
Recessional.
Song of the English, A.
Threshold, The.
Kizer, C.   Dixit Insipiens.
Kunitz, S.   Words of the Preacher, The.
Laughlin, J.   Old Dr God.
Lawrence, D. H.   Abysmal Immortality.
Ah, with His Blessing Bright on Thy Mouth and
Thy Brow.
At Midnight.
Bells.
Body of God, The.
Eloi, Eloi, Lama Sabachthani?
God.
God Is Born.
Hands of God, The.
Hymn to Nothingness.
Irreverent Thoughts.
Living Quetzalcoatl, The.
Lord of the Morning Star.
Lord's Prayer.
Man of Tyre, The.
Martyr à la Mode.
Mills of God, The.
Moth and Rust.
Only Man.
Pax.
Rainbow.
Religion.
Sight of God, The.
Silence.
Son of the Morning Star.
Song of Don Ramon, The.
Spanish Privilege.
Vengeance Is Mine.
When Wilt Thou Teach the People?

Why Does She Weep?
Work of Creation, The.
Levertov.   Flickering Mind.
Freedom.
In Whom We Live and Move and Have Our
Being.
Love of Morning, The.
Primary Wonder.
Suspended.
Levine, P.   On a Drawing by Flavio.
To My God in His Sickness.
Lindsay, N.   Heart of God.
Logan, J.   Spring of the Thief.
Lorde.   When the Saints Come Marching In.
Lowell, R.   Death and the Bridge.
Mr. Edwards and the Spider.
Watchmaker God.
Words.
Lux.   Irreconcilabilia.
Job's Problems.
Perfect God, The.
MacDiarmid, H.   Cheville.
Dying Earth, The.
Focherty.
Fool, The.
With the Herring Fishers.
MacLeish.   Creator.
Infinite Reason, The.
Learned Men, The.
Ship in the Tomb.
MacNeice.   Blasphemies, The.
Creditor, The.
Hands and Eyes.
Mahon.   Ecclesiastes.
Marvell.   Bermudas.
McHugh, H.   Big Ideas among Earthlings.
Breath.
For a Sad God.
Meaning Business.
Melville, H.   Camoëns.
Conflict of Convictions, The.
In the Desert.
Meredith, G.   As from the fall of candlelight.
Test of Manhood, The.
Meredith, W.   Notre Dame de Chartres.
Merton.   After the Night Office—Gethsemani
Abbey.
Candlemas Procession, The.
Elias—Variations on a Theme.
Freedom as Experience.
God Said "They Did Not Hear."
Hagia Sophia.
I Have Called You.
Landscape: Wheatfields.
Lord Is Good, The.
Natural History.
On a Day in August.
Psalm, A: "When psalms surprise me with their
music."
Reader, The.
Round and a Hope for Smithgirls, A.
Sincerity.
Sowing of Meanings, The.
Stranger.
Word—a Responsory, The.
Michelangelo Buonarroti.   If my rough hammer
shapes the obdurate stone.
If right desire takes wing.
Millay, E.   Blue-Flag in the Bog, The.
Milosz, C.   Alcoholic Enters the Gates of
Heaven, An.
Before Majesty.
Counsels.
Gardener.
Meditation.
Prayer: "Approaching ninety, and still with a
hope."
Thesis and Counter-Thesis.
To Mrs. Professor in Defense of My Cat's
Honor and Not Only.
Zdziechowski.
Milton.   Psalm 136.
To Cyriack Skinner.
Mistral, G.   Artist's Decalogue, The.
Montale.   In the Greenhouse.
Near Finistère.

Wind on the Crescent.
Nash, O.   Fly, The.
  Oh, Stop Being Thankful All over the Place.
Nemerov.   Death of God, The.
  God of This World, The.
  Primer of the Daily Round, A.
  View from Pisgah, The.
  Zander on God.
Neruda.   Gift, The.
Olson, C.   Go / Make a Bridge.
  I saw, from under Him, the beginning.
  This Year.
  To a Poet Who Read in Gloucester before the
    Cape Ann Historical Literary and Scientific
    Society.
  Winter Solstice.
Pagis.   Testimony.
Pasternak, B.   God of Details, The.
Patchen.   All the Roses of the World.
  At the Entrance to the Other World.
  Behold, One of Several Little Christs.
  Billion Freedoms, The.
  Breathe on the living.
  Builders, The.
  Christ! Christ! Christ! that the world.
  Deer and the Snake, The.
  Easy Rider.
  Expectant Shelters, The.
  How God Was Made.
  How silent are the things of heaven.
  In horror the God-thrown lie.
  Instructions for Angels.
  Lions of fire, The.
  Man Lives Here, A.
  Meben.
  Mohammed.
  Origin of Baseball, The.
  Overworld, The.
  Palms for a Catholic Child.
  Paxdominisit Sem Pervobiscum Etcumspiri
    Tutuo.
  Permanent Migrations, The.
  Poems which are written by the soul.
  Progress to a View of Life.
  Rites of Darkness, The.
  Snow is deep on the ground, The.
  Temple, A.
  There Is Nothing False in Thee.
  There Is One Who Watches.
  Unfulfilling Brightnesses, The.
  We Are Not Worthy, Lord.
Pessoa.   Beyond God.
Petrarch.   He Who reveals His providence and
    art.
Pinkerton, H.   Degrees of Shade.
  Sierra Nevada Hike.
Pinsky.   Hearts, The.
Plath.   Faun.
Pope, A.   Messiah [a Sacred Eclogue, in
    Imitation of Virgil's Pollio].
  Paraphrase on Thomas à Kempis, A.
  Universal Prayer [Deo Opt. Max.], The.
Pound, E.   Ballad for Gloom.
  Night Litany.
Raine, K.   It is in us they burn.
  Six calices yellow gold.
  Young or old / What was I but a story told.
Ralegh, S.   Authours Epitaph, Made by Himself,
    The.
  First of all is God, and the same last is he, The.
Rexroth, K.   Homestead Called Damascus, The.
Riley, J.   Enduring, The.
  God's Mercy.
  He Cometh in Sweet Sense.
  Legend Glorified, The.
Rilke.   He Can Find No Rest.
  Judgments.
  To Madame the Baronness Renée De Brimont.
  Two Poems.
Rimbaud, A.   Evil.
Robinson, E.   Octaves.
  Sonnet: "When we can all so excellently give."
Roethke.   Abyss, The.
  Decision, The.
  Elegy: "Should every creature be as I have
    been."

Marrow, The.
Rossetti, C.   Advent.
  After Communion.
  Afterthought, An.
  Afterward He Repented, and Went.
  Ah Lord, Lord, if my heart were right with
    Thine.
  Alas my Lord, / How should I wrestle all the
    livelong night.
  All Saints.
  "All Thy Works Praise Thee, O Lord": A
    Processional of Creation.
  Alone Lord God, in Whom our trust and peace.
  And Now Why Tarriest Thou?
  And There Was No More Sea.
  Annie.
  Answer, An.
  Antipas.
  Are They Not All Ministering Spirits?
  Are Ye Not Much Better than They?
  As a King, ...Unto the King.
  As froth on the face of the deep, / As foam on
    the crest of the sea.
  As the dove which found no rest / For the sole
    of her foot, flew back.
  As the Sparks Fly Upwards.
  As Thy Days, So Shall Thy Strength Be.
  Beautiful for Situation.
  Before the Beginning.
  Behold a Shaking.
  Behold, It Was Very Good.
  Books in the Running Brooks.
  By Way of Remembrance.
  Called to Be Saints.
  Chill blank world. Yet over the utmost sea, A.
  Christmas Carol, A: "In the bleak mid-winter."
  Consider.
  Cried Out with Tears.
  Darkness and light are both alike to Thee.
  Day Is at Hand, The.
  Dead Bride, The.
  Death Is Swallowed Up in Victory.
  Divine and Human Pleading.
  Do This, and He Doeth It.
  Dost Thou Not Care?
  Dying Man to His Betrothed, The.
  Earth Shall Tremble at the Look of Him, The.
  Easter Even.
  Easter Morning.
  Ellen Middleton.
  Escape to the Mountain.
  Eva.
  Experience bows a sweet contented face.
  Eye Hath Not Seen.
  Feast of the Presentation.
  For a Mercy Received.
  For Advent.
  For Thine Own Sake, O My God.
  From House to Home.
  Go in Peace.
  Gold of that Land Is Good, The.
  Grant us such grace that we may work Thy
    Will.
  Had Fortune parted us / Fortune is blind.
  Have I not striven, my God, and watched and
    prayed?
  He Cannot Deny Himself.
  Heart Knoweth Its Own Bitterness, The.
  Heaven.
  Her Seed; It Shall Bruise Thy Head.
  Holy City, New Jerusalem, The.
  Holy Innocents.
  Hymn: "O the bitter shame and sorrow."
  I Do Set My Bow in the Cloud.
  I followed Thee, my God, I followed Thee / To
    see the end.
  I Have Fought a Good Fight.
  I Look for the Lord.
  I, Lord, Thy foolish sinner low and small.
  I Will Arise.
  I Will Come and Heal Him.
  I Will Lift Up Mine Eyes unto the Hills.
  If not with hope of life, / Begin with fear of
    death.
  If Thou Sayest, Behold, We Knew It Not.
  Imitated from the Arpa Evangelica: Page 121.

In Patience.
Is It Well with The Child?
It is not death, O Christ, to die for Thee: / Nor
  is that silence of a silent land.
Joy of Saints, like incense turned to fire, The.
Let Everything That Hath Breath Praise the
  Lord.
Let Patience Have Her Perfect Work.
Life out of Death.
Life that was born today / Must make no stay.
Like As the Hart Desireth the Water Brooks.
Long Barren.
Lord, by what inconceivable dim road / Thou
  leadest man on footsore pilgrimage!
Lord, comest Thou to me?
Lord, give me love that I may love Thee much.
Lord, grant me grace to love Thee in my pain.
Lord, grant us eyes to see and ears to hear, /
  And souls to love and minds to understand.
Lord, grant us grace to rest upon Thy word.
Lord, hast Thou so loved us, and will not we.
Lord, I am feeble and of mean account.
Lord, I am here.—But, child, I look for thee.
Lord, make me one with Thine own faithful
  ones.
Lord, make me pure: / Only the pure shall see
  Thee as Thou art.
Lord, make us all love all: that when we meet /
  Even myriads of earth's myriads at Thy Bar.
Lord, Thou art fulness, I am emptiness.
Lord, we are rivers running to Thy sea.
Lord, what have I to offer? sickening fear.
Love builds a nest on earth and waits for rest.
Love Is Stronger than Death.
Love loveth Thee, and wisdom loveth Thee.
Love, to be love, must walk Thy way / And
  work Thy Will.
Lowest Place, The.
Martyr, A.
Martyr, The.
Martyrs' Song.
Master Is Come, and Calleth for Thee, The.
Maundy Thursday.
Me and my gift: kind Lord, behold.
Mid-Lent.
My God, wilt Thou accept, and will not we /
  Give aught to Thee?
O Death Where Is Thy Sting?
O Lord, I am ashamed to seek Thy Face / As
  tho' I loved Thee as Thy saints love Thee.
O Lord, I cannot plead my love of Thee.
O Lord, on Whom we gaze and dare not gaze, /
  Increase our faith that gazing we may see.
O Lord, when Thou didst call me, didst Thou
  know.
Offering of the New Law, the One Oblation
  Once Offered, The.
Our Widowed Queen.
Out of the Deep.
Palm Sunday.
Passiontide.
Patience of Hope.
Peace I Leave with You.
Perfect Love Casteth Out Fear.
Quinquagesima.
Rogationtide.
Rose Plant in Jericho, A.
Seven vials hold Thy wrath: but what can hold.
Shadows Today.
Shall not the Judge of all the earth do right?
Sinner's own fault? So it was, The.
Sit Down in the Lowest Room.
Slain in their high places: fallen on rest.
Song for the Least of All Saints, A.
Song: "We buried her among the flowers."
St. Elizabeth of Hungary.
St. Mark.
St. Michael and all Angels.
St. Peter.
Sursum Corda.
Sweetness of rest when Thou sheddest rest.
Take No Thought for the Morrow.
That Which Hath Been Is Named Already, and
  It Is Known that It Is Man.
Then They That Feared the Lord Spake Often
  One to Another.

There Remaineth Therefore a Rest.
There Remaineth Therefore a Rest to the People of God.
They lie at rest, our blessed dead.
They Shall Be as White as Snow.
They Toil Not, neither Do They Spin.
Three Nuns.
Thy fainting spouse, yet still Thy spouse.
Thy lilies drink the dew, / Thy lambs the rill, and I will drink them too.
Thy Servant Will Go and Fight with This Philistine.
Time of Waiting, The.
To Every Seed His Own Body.
To the End.
To What Purpose Is This Waste?
Tune Me, O Lord, into One Harmony.
Twice.
Two Pursuits.
Until the Day Break.
Vanity of Vanities.
Vigil of St. Bartholomew.
Vigil of the Presentation.
Was Thy Wrath against the Sea?
Watchers, The.
We are of those who tremble at Thy word.
Weary in Well-Doing.
What do the stars do / Up in the sky.
What Good Shall My Life Do Me?
What Hath God Wrought!
When I Was in Trouble I Called upon the Lord.
When My Heart Is Vexed, I Will Complain.
Where neither Rust nor Moth Doth Corrupt.
Whitsun Day.
Whitsun Eve.
Who Have a Form of Godliness.
Who sits with the King in His Throne? Not a slave but a Bride.
Who would wish back the Saints upon our rough.
Why?
Will of the Lord Be Done, The.
Wisdom.
Worship God.
Wouldst thou give me a heavy jewelled crown.
Ye Have Forgotten the Exhortation.
Young Death.
Zion Said.
Rukeyser, M.   Akiba.
Little Stone in the Middle of the Road, in Florida, A.
Mortal Girl.
Nuns in the Wind.
Place at Albert Bay, The.
Silence of Volcanoes.
Rumi.   Be Melting Snow.
Birdsong from Inside the Egg.
Bismillah.
Emptiness.
Fragile Vial, The.
Freshness, The.
Gamble everything for love.
In Between Stories.
Moses and the Shepherd.
Question, The.
Tending Two Shops.
Witness, the Darling, The.
Sandburg, C.   Ambassadors of Grief.
Brancusi.
Brass Keys.
Fire Dreams.
Four Brothers, The.
Glass House Canticle.
God Is No Gentleman.
Good Morning, America.
Manufactured Gods.
Many Hats.
Night's Nothings Again.
Our Prayer of Thanks.
Public Letter to Emily Dickinson.
Slabs of the Sunburnt West.
They Ask: Is God, Too, Lonely?
Wanting the Impossible.
Schuyler, J.   Six Something.
Seifert.   Sinful City.
Sexton.   Author of the Jesus Papers Speaks,

The.
Earth, The.
Faustus and I.
For Eleanor Boylan Talking with God.
God's Backside.
Is It True?
Keeping the City.
May 30th.
No So. Not So.
Praying to Big Jack.
Rowing Endeth, The.
Sickness unto Death, The.
Small Wire.
Wall, The.
Welcome Morning.
What the Bird with the Human Head Knew.
Smart, C.   Hail wond'rous being who in power supreme.
Hymn to the Supreme Being.
Jubilate Agno.
On the Eternity of the Supreme Being.
On the Goodness of the Supreme Being.
On the Immensity of the Supreme Being.
On the Omniscience of the Supreme Being.
On the Power of the Supreme Being.
Smith, S.   Away, Melancholy.
Breughel.
Conviction (i).
Dear Child of God.
Distractions and the Human Crowd.
Egocentric.
Fuite d'Enfance.
God and the Devil.
God Speaks.
God the Eater.
How Do You See?
I Was So Full.
Man Saul, The.
Mother, among the Dustbins.
Nature and Free Animals.
Never Again.
No Categories!
Oh Christianity, Christianity.
Passing Cloud, The.
Reason, The.
To Dean Inge Lecturing on Origen.
Stafford, W.   On a Church Lawn.
Ultimate Problems.
Why the Sun Comes Up.
Stampa.   With Deep Repentance for My Wasted Days.
Stevens, W.   Cy Est Pourtraicte, Madame Ste Ursule, et Les Unze Mille Vierges.
Stock, R.   God Victimized.
Hymn Directed Somewhere toward the Pantheon.
Pietà.
Stockton, A.   Fragment, Janu'ry 1786.
Hymn Written in the Year 1753, A.
On Exodus 30.18.
Swinburne.   Leper, The.
Tate, J.   Tabernacle, The.
Tennyson, A.   Flower in the Crannied Wall.
Supposed Confessions of a Second-rate Sensitive Mind.
Thomson, J.   Upon Happiness.
Thoreau.   Great God I ask thee for no meaner pelf.
Inspiration.
Unknown.   Prose in Advent Time.
Updike.   Trees Eat Sunshine.
Wind.
Vallejo.   Eternal Dice, The.
Van Duyn.   Gardener to His God, The.
Very.   Beginning and the End, The.
Change.
Comfort.
Complaint, The.
Cup, The.
Earth, The.
Eye and Ear, The.
Father, The.
First Atlantic Telegraph, The.
Flee to the Mountains.
Forgiveness.
Good Ground, The.

Hand and Foot, The [or Hand and the Foot, The].
Hast thou ever *heard* the voice of nature.
Hath the Rain a Father? Or Who Hath Begotten the Drops of Dew? Job 38:28.
Heavenly Rest, The.
Help.
Humble, The.
Hymn: "He loveth not! he knows not God!"
Hymn on the Logos: The Light Still Shining in the Darkness.
Interpreting God's Ways.
Kingdom of God Is within You, The.
Laborer, The.
Living God, The.
Lost, The ("Fairest day that ever yet has shone, The").
Man has forgot his Origin; in vain.
Mountain, The.
My Father's House.
My Meat and Drink.
My People are destroyed for lack of Knowledge.—Hosea 4:6.
My Sheep.
Night.
Not suffering for their sins in former state.
On an Ear of Wheat Brought, by My Brother, from the Field of Waterloo.
Origin of Man, The.
Plant, The.
Prayer, The ("Wilt Thou not visit me?").
Presence, The.
Promise, The ("I come the rushing wind that shook the place").
River, The.
Rock, The.
Salvation Is of the Lord: The Book of Jonah 2.9.
Silent, The.
Spheres, The.
Spirit, The.
Tree, The ("I too will wait with thee returning spring")
Voice of God, The.
Warrior, The.
Whither Shall I Go from Thy Spirit.
Word, The ("Word! it cannot fail; it ever speaks, The").
Yourself.
Villon.   Epitaph in Form of a Ballad, The.
Warren, R.   Function of Blizzard.
Interjection #6: What You Sometimes Feel on Your Face at Night.
Waiting.
Way to Love God, A.
When the Tooth Cracks—Zing!
Weiss, T.   House of Fire.
Wheatley, P.   Isaiah 63. 1–8.
On Being Brought from Africa to America.
Prayer: "Oh my Gracious Preserver!"
Thoughts on the Works of Providence.
Whitman, W.   Chanting the Square Deific.
Persian Lesson, A.
Prayer of Columbus.
While behind All, Firm and Erect.
Whittier.   All's Well.
Andrew Rykman's Prayer.
Benevolence.
Book, The.
Clear Vision, The.
Deity, The.
Divine Compassion.
Eternal Goodness, The.
Familist's Hymn, The.
Female Martyr, The.
Fragment, A: "Dreadful burden of our sins we feel, The."
Garden.
Grave by the Lake, The.
Hermit of the Thebaid, The.
Hymn for the House of Worship at Georgetown.
Hymn for the Opening of Plymouth Church.
Hymn for the Opening of Thomas Starr King's House of Worship.
Hymns from the French of Lamartine.
Hymns of the Brahmo Somaj.
Invocation: "Through Thy clear spaces, Lord, of

old."
Lakeside, The.
Last Walk in Autumn, The.
Lines on Leaving Appledore.
Mary Garvin.
Miriam.
My Dream.
My Psalm.
My Soul and I.
On a Prayer-Book.
Our River.
Over-Heart, The.
Overruled.
Palestine.
Palm-Tree, The.
Quaker Alumni, The.
Questions of Life.
Rabbi Ishmael.
Requirement.
Revelation.
River Path, The.
"Rock" in El Ghor, The.
Saint Gregory's Guest.
Song of Harvest, A.
Summer by the Lakeside.
Tauler.
Thy Will Be Done.
Vaudois Teacher, The.
What the Traveller Said at Sunset.
What the Voice Said.
Wife of Manoah to Her Husband, The.
Wish of To-day, The.
Word, The.
Wilbur, R. Dubious Night, A.
Proof, The.
Tywater.
Williams, C. K. Becoming Somebody Else.
Dominion: Depression.
Even if I Could.
For Children When They Grow Up.
For Gail, When I Was Five.
Innings.
Like Little Birds.
Little Shirt, The.
Loss.
Next to the Last Poem about God, The.
Poor Hope.
Race of the Flood, The.
Spit.
They Warned Him Then They Threw Him
 Away.
Williams, M. After the Revolution for Jesus a
 Secular Man [or the Associate Professor]
 Prepares His Final Remarks.
Entropy.
God.
If Every Person There Is but One.
In the Beginning.
Jonah on His Deathbed.
Jonathan Confronts the Question.
Out of a Clear Sky.
Why God Permits Evil: For Answers to This
 Question of Interest to Many Write Bible
 Answers, Dept. E-7.
Wilner, E. See-Saw.
Wordsworth, W. Fact, and an Imagination or,
 Canute and Alfred, on the Sea-Shore, A.
In My Mind's Eye a Temple, like a Cloud.
It is a beauteous evening, calm and free.
Matron of Jedborough and Her Husband, The.
On a High Part of the Coast in Cumberland.
Suggested at Tyndrum in a Storm.
Though Pulpits and the Desk May Fail.
Thoughts Suggested the Day Following, on the
 Banks of Nith, near the Poet's Residence.
Wright, J. Abstract of Knowledge, The / The
 First Test.
Eye of God, the Soul's First Vision, The.
Inscrutability.
Speak.
Wyatt, S. After great storms the calm returns.
Argument, Th'
Yeats. At Algeciras—a Meditation upon Death.
Black Tower, The.
Crazy Jane on God.
Dancer at Cruachan and Cro-Patrick, The.

Indian upon God, The [or An].
Paudeen.
Ribh Denounces Patrick.
Rose of the World, The.
Unappeasable Host, The.
Veronica's Napkin.
Zaturenska. Pilgrimage.
Zukofsky, L. For you I have emptied the
 meaning.
Gödel, Kurt
Enzensberger, H. Homage to Gödel.
Gods and Goddesses
Berry, W. Hidden Singer, The.
Observance.
Walking on the River Ice.
Berryman. Long Home, The.
Blake, W. If it is True What the Prophets write.
Blok. Intellect Cannot Measure the Divine, The.
Borges. Ragnarök.
Shinto.
Brodsky, J. Vertumnus.
Browning, E. Dead Pan, The.
Browning, R. Artemis Prologizes.
Carew, T. Cruel Mistress, A.
To the King, at His Entrance into Saxham: By
 Master John Crofts.
Cavafy. Ancient Tragedy.
Chaldaic Image.
Interruption.
Intervention of the Gods, The.
Ionian.
Memory.
One of Their Gods.
Chaucer. House of Fame, The.
Chuang Tzu. Autumn Floods.
Ciardi, J. Interruption, An.
Mystic River.
Clampitt. War Memorial, The.
Clement of Alexandria. Idol of Sarapis, The.
Priests of the Old Gods, The.
Zeus Is Dead.
Coleridge, S. Visit of the Gods, The.
Crane, S. God came to a man, A.
Man went before a strange god, A.
Crashaw. In the Glorious Epiphanie of Our
 Lord God.
Cummings, E. E. Epithalamion: "Thou aged
 unreluctant earth who dost."
No man,if men are gods;but if gods must.
De la Mare. Exile.
Mourn'st Thou Now?
Music.
Quarry, The.
Dickey, W. Coyote's Song.
Dugan, A. On a Summer Goddess Who Should
 Be Nameless.
Eberhart, R. Difficulty of Ideas, The.
Gods of Washington, D.C., The.
Skier and the Mountain, The.
Emerson, R. Around the man who seeks a
 noble end.
Culture.
For every god.
From high to higher forces.
Gods walk in the breath of the woods, The.
I have supped with the gods tonight.
If curses be the wage of love.
Think not the gods receive thy prayer.
Glück, L. Embrace, The.
Graves, R. Between Moon and Moon.
Friday Night.
In Her Praise.
Knobs and Levers.
Pandora.
Problems of Gender.
Return of the Goddess [Artemis].
Rhea.
Tousled Pillow.
Weather of Olympus, The.
White Goddess, The.
Gunn, T. Garden of the Gods, The.
Goddess, The.
Odysseus on Hermes.
Gurney, I. To Crickley.
"H. D." Ariadne.
At Croton.

At Eleusis.
Dodona.
Evadne.
God, The.
Helios.
Helios and Athene.
Hermonax.
Myrtle Bough.
Phaedra.
Psyche.
Pygmalion.
Sea Gods.
Sitalkas.
Thetis.
Tribute, The.
Hamill, S. Kali.
Heaney, S. Sheelagh na Gig.
Herrick. Devotion Makes the Deity.
Griefes.
Hymne to Juno, An.
Hymne, to the Lares, A.
Littlenesse No Cause of Leanesse.
Meane in Our Meanes, A.
Short Hymne to Venus, A.
To His Closet-Gods.
To His Household Gods.
To the Genius of His House.
Hill, G. Doctor Faustus.
Hölderlin. And you Diotima who walk humbly
 among the living.
Hughes, L. Gods.
Jonson, B. To His Lady, Then Mrs Cary.
Kinnell. Last Gods.
Kipling, R. Giffen's Debt.
Gods of the Copybook Headings, The.
Poseidon's Law.
Sacrifice of Er-Heb, The.
Song of the Men's Side.
Song of the Red War-Boat.
Kizer, C. Copulating Gods, The.
Dying Goddess, The.
Hera, Hung from the Sky.
Muse of Water, A.
Kunitz, S. Among the Gods.
Laughlin, J. Asmodeus.
Jealous Gods, The.
Nothing That's Lovely Can My Love Escape.
O Hermes Trismegistus.
Party on Olympus, The.
She Asks Me.
She Seemed to Know.
Lawrence, D. H. All Sorts of Gods.
Be It So.
Cabbage-Roses.
Cold Blood.
False Democracy and Real.
For a Moment.
Give Us Gods.
Glimpses.
Gods.
Gods, The.
Gods! The Gods!, The.
Goethe and Pose.
Huitzilopochtli Gives the Black Blade of Death.
Huitzilopochtli's Watch.
Like the Green Candles of Malintzi.
Lords of Life Are the Masters of Death, The.
Man Is More than *Homo Sapiens*.
Man of Tyre, The.
Maximus.
Men Like Gods.
Name the Gods!
Old Men.
Return of Returns.
Service.
Song of the Grey Dog, The.
Spiral Flame.
There Are No Gods.
Third Song of Huitzilopochtli.
Two Ways of Living and Dying.
What Are the Gods?
Worship.
Levertov. Death in Mexico.
Eros.
Postcards: A Triptych, The.
To the Reader.

Lindsay, N.   Queen of Bubbles, The.
Lorde.   Oya.
MacLeish.   Renovated Temple, The.
Mahon.   Banished Gods, The.
Marvell.   Mower against Gardens, The.
Melville, H.   Trophies of Peace.
Meredith, G.   Teaching of the Nude, The.
Merrill, J.   After Greece.
  Nike.
Merton.   Atlas and the Fatman.
  Songs of Experience; India, One.
Merwin.   Gods, The.
  Hosts, The.
  Lantern, The.
  Laughter.
Milosz, C.   Opposed to Each Other.
Milton.   On the Morning of Christ's Nativity.
Nemerov.   Companions, The.
  Distraction.
Olson, C.   Advantage, The.
  Applause.
  Distances, The.
  I Am So Small You Can Hardly See Me.
  In Cold Hell, in Thicket.
  In Wiro language.
  Lordly and Isolate Satyrs, The.
  She-Bear, The.
  Some partial cloudiness will flow locally,
    mostly.
  There Is No River Which Is Called Lethe.
  Unfinished (raw) hero -un-, The.
Patchen.   Outlaw of the Lowest Planet, The.
Pessoa.   Gods grant us this one, The.
  I ask the gods only to forget me.
  I only ask the gods to grant me.
  My gesture that destroys.
  No one, in the vast and virgin jungle.
  Not just those who hate and those who envy us.
  Note.
Petrarch.   Birds, singing and lamenting once
    again.
Pinsky.   Discretions of Alcibiades.
  Shiva and Parvati Hiding in the Rain.
  Uncreation, The.
Plath.   Full Fathom Five.
  Lorelei.
  Ouija.
Pound, E.   Return, The.
Ralegh, S.   From the Earth, and from thy bloud,
    O heaven, they came.
  Homage to Diana.
  Saturne to be the fatter is not knowne.
  Things thus agreed: Titan made Saturne sweare.
Ramanujan.   Devotee's Complaint, A.
  Prayers to Lord Murugan.
Riley, J.   To the Wine-God Merlus.
Rimbaud, A.   Genie.
Ritsos.   Known Consequences.
  Memorial Service at Poros.
  Models, The.
Robinson, E.   False Gods, The.
Rukeyser, M.   Game of Ball, A.
Sandburg, C.   Cheap Rent.
  Hammer, The.
Sarton, M.   Myth.
  Proteus.
  Return of Aphrodite, The.
Sexton.   Gods.
Smith, S.   God the Drinker.
  River God, The.
  Venus When Young Choosing Death.
Spender, S.   In Attica.
Stock, R.   Game of the Thunderbolt Goddesses,
    The.
  Rescuers, The.
Szymborska, W.   Palaeolithic Fertility Fetish, A.
Thomas, D.   Shall Gods Be Said to Thump the
    Clouds.
Thoreau.   Strange that so many fickle gods, as
    fickle as the weather.
  'Tis very fit the ambrosia of the gods.
Tomlinson, C.   For a Godchild.
  Mictlantecuhtli.
Updike.   Deities and Beasts.
  Milady Reflects.
Whalen, P.   Goddess.

  What About It?
Wilbur, R.   To Ishtar.
Wilde, O.   Charmides.
  Santa Decca.
  Sphinx, The.
Williams, T.   Stones Are Thrown.
Wilner, E.   See-Saw.
Yeats.   Conjunctions.
  Grey Rock, The.
Zagajewski.   Dark God, the Light God, The.

God's Protection
Angelou.   Just like Job.
Bierce.   Insectivora.
  Matter for Gratitude.
Browning, E.   Soul's Travelling, The.
Burns, R.   On the Birth of a Posthumous Child,
    Born in Peculiar Circumstances of Family
    Distress.
Cavafy.   Terror.
Clough.   That there are powers above us I
    admit.
Cummings, E. E.   Ballade of Soul.
De la Mare.   Imagination's Pride, The.
Emerson, R.   Nun's Aspiration.
  Worship.
HaNagid.   Dream, The.
  Friends, a Fence Surrounds Us.
  His Brother's Illness.
  Miracle at Sea, The.
  On Lifting the Siege.
  Send the Lord to the People.
  To Yehosef, His Son.
  Victory Over Seville, The.
Herbert, G.   Affliction (4).
  Affliction (5).
  Evensong [or Even-Song].
  Invitation, The.
  L'Envoy.
  Providence.
Herrick.   Goodnesse of His God, The.
  Rod, The.
  Way, The.
Kipling, R.   Ave Imperatrix!
  Covenant, The.
  Hymn before Action.
  Mulholland's Contract.
  What the People Said.
Kunitz, S.   Benediction.
Lindsay, N.   Invocation for "The Map of the
    Universe."
  Johnny Appleseed's Ship Comes In.
MacNeice.   Prayer before Birth.
Merton.   Be My Defender.
Mistral, G.   Heaven's Carriage.
Riley, J.   Out of Nazareth.
Rossetti, C.   Consider.
  I Will Arise.
  Lord, I am here.—But, child, I look for thee.
Smart, C.   On the Goodness of the Supreme
    Being.
Whittier.   Ein Feste Burg Ist Unser Gott.
  Familist's Hymn, The.
Wordsworth, W.   Jewish Family (in a Small
    Valley opposite St Goar, upon the Rhine), A.

Godwin, William
Coleridge, S.   To William Godwin.
Shelley, P.   Mighty Eagle.

Goebbels, Joseph
Lux.   Dr. Goebbels's Novels.

Goethe, Johann Wolfgang von
Arnold, M.   Memorial Verses.
Browning, E.   To Bettine.
Browning, R.   Burlesque for Palgrave on the
    Pronunciation of "Metamorphosis."
Emerson, R.   Solution.
  Written in a Volume of Goethe.
Lawrence, D. H.   Goethe and Pose.
Wright, J.   Three Stanzas from Goethe.

Gogh, Vincent van
Major, C.   Atelier Cézanne.
See also **Van Gogh, Vincent**

Gold
Blake, W.   I Saw a Chapel All of Gold.
Borges.   Alchemist, The.
Cino da Pistoia.   Madrigal: To His Lady

  Selvaggia Vergiolesi; Likening His Love to a
    Search for Gold.
Clampitt.   Brought from Beyond.
  Quarry, The.
Codrescu.   Goldrush, The.
Crane, H.   Key West.
De la Mare.   Gold.
Dickinson, E.   I never told the buried gold.
Dugan, A.   Poem: "Man applying gold leaf, A."
Dunbar, P.   Real Question, The.
Frost, R.   Nothing Gold Can Stay.
  Vindictives, The.
Gray, T.   Ode on the Death of a Favourite [or
    Favorite] Cat, Drowned in a Tub [or Bowl] of
    Gold Fishes.
Gunn, T.   Value of Gold, The.
"H. D."   Song: "You are as gold."
Hall, D.   Gold.
Herrick.   Gold and Frankincense.
Hopkins, G.   My Own Heart Let Me More Have
    Pity On.
Jonson, B.   Those that in blood such violent
    pleasure have.
Lorde.   Family Resemblance, A.
MacLeish.   Rainbow at Evening.
Merwin.   History of Alchemy.
Mistral, G.   In Praise of Gold.
Oppen.   Gold on Oak Leaves.
Riley, J.   Sutter's Claim.
Rossetti, C.   Golden Glories.
  Johnny.
Rumi.   Sheba's Gifts to Solomon.
Sandburg, C.   Crucible.
  Gold Mud.
  Joke Gold.
Stafford, W.   Looking for Gold.

Gold Mining and Gold Miners
Komunyakaa.   New Gold Mountain.
Lux.   Gold on Mule.
Merrill, J.   McKane's Falls.
Riley, J.   Sutter's Claim.
Robinson, E.   Klondike, The.
Williams, W.   Epigramme: "Hast ever seen a
    man."

Golden Age
Frost, R.   Lost Follower, The.
Whittier.   My Triumph.

Golden Mean
Ammons.   Golden Mean, The.
Eberhart, R.   Somewhere Else.
Sidney, S.   You better sure shall live, not
    evermore.
Unknown.   On Envy.

Golden Rule, The
Angelou.   Lord, in My Heart.
Herrick.   Like Pattern, Like People.
Riley, J.   Some Scattering Remarks of Bub's.

Goldenrod
Oliver, M.   Goldenrod.

Goldfinches
Cowper, W.   Faithful Friend, The.
  On a Goldfinch Starved to Death in His Cage.
Hardy, T.   Caged Goldfinch, The.
Oliver, M.   Goldfinches.
Wilbur, R.   Sketch, A.

Goldfish
Muldoon, P.   Thinking of the Goldfish.
Nemerov.   Goldfish.

Golem
Borges.   Golem, The.

Golf
Hamill, S.   Another Duffer.
Lowell, R.   Ford Madox Ford.
Nash, O.   Slow Down, Mr. Ganderdonk, You're
    Late.
  Strange Case of the Ambitious Caddy, The.
  Who Taught Caddies to Count? or A Burnt
    Golfer Fears the Child.
Prunty.   Nineteenth Hole, The.
Updike.   Golfers.

Goliath
De la Mare.   Goliath.
Duncan, R.   Helmet of Goliath, The.
Very.   Goliath.
Wheatley, P.   Goliath of Gath.

Good

Berry, W. Necessity of Faith, The.
Blake, W. Marriage of Heaven and Hell, The.
Browning, E. Futurity.
Bukowski. Strange Moment, A.
Burns, R. At Whigham's Inn, Sanquar.
First Psalm, The.
Written in Friar's Carse Hermitage on the Banks of Nith—June—1788.
Clough. To think that men of former days.
Dugan, A. Takeoff on Armageddon —For Ronald Reagan.
Wall, Cave, and Pillar Statements, after Asôka.
Dunbar, P. God Reigns.
Eberhart, R. Fantasy of a Small Idea.
Ineffable, The.
Meditation Two.
Emerson, R. Around the man who seeks a noble end.
I will not live out of me.
Frost, R. Quandary.
Hardy, T. Unkept Good Fridays.
Herrick. Almes.
His Confession.
Sin.
Hopkins, G. How all is one way wrought!
Hughes, L. Shall the Good Go Down?
Kipling, R. Curé, The.
Kunitz, S. Between the Acts.
Lindsay, N. Above the Battle's Front.
Milosz, C. One More Day.
Montale. Often I've encountered evil.
Parker, D. Biographies.
Veteran, The.
Pinkerton, H. Romantic Eros, The.
Pope, A. Version of the First Psalm, for the Use of a Young Lady, A.
Riley, J. As Created.
Just to Be Good.
Rossetti, C. At Last.
Watchers, The.
Who shall my wandering thoughts steady & fix.
Thoreau. Good how can we trust?, The.
Whitman, W. Roaming in Thought.
Young Grimes.
Whittier. Answer, The.
Eternal Goodness, The.
Lines Written in an Album.
Requirement.
Wordsworth, W. O'er the wide earth, on mountain and on plain.
Wright, J. Logbook of Judgments.
Trying to Pray.

Good Friday

Clampitt. Good Friday.
Davie, D. Rodez.
Donne. Good Friday [or Goodfriday], 1613. Riding Westward.
Hardy, T. Unkept Good Fridays.
Herbert, G. Good Friday.
Herrick. Good Friday: Rex Tragicus, or, Christ Going to His Cross[e].
Hill, G. Canticle for Good Friday.
Logan, J. Monologue for the Good Friday Christ.
Olson, C. Friday, Good Friday, which.
Pinkerton, H. Good Friday.
Rossetti, C. Bundle of Myrrh Is My Well-Beloved unto Me, A.
Good Friday.
Good Friday Evening.
Good Friday Morning.
Zagajewski. Good Friday in the Tunnels of the Métro.

Good Samaritan

Cummings, E. E. Man who had fallen among thieves, A.
Dickey, W. Coyote's Song.
Riley, J. Good Man, A.
Rossetti, C. Half Dead.
Very. Good Samaritan, The.

Goodman, Benny

Carruth, H. "Sure," Said Benny Goodman.

Gore-Booth, Eva

Yeats. In Memory of Eva Gore-Booth and Con Markievicz.

Gorse

Browning, E. Lessons from the Gorse.
Heaney, S. Whinlands.

Gospel Music

Collins, B. Sunday Morning with the Sensational Nightingales.
Dove, R. Gospel.
Hughes, L. Tambourines.

Gossip and Gossips

Auden. Love Feast, The.
Bukowski. Fleg.
I Have Shit Stains in My Underwear Too.
Clare, J. Scandal.
Davie, D. Against Confidences.
De la Mare. Juliet's Nurse.
Donne. Mercurius Gallo-Belgicus.
Dunbar, P. Circumstances Alter Cases.
Protest.
Emerson, R. Quoth Saadi, when I stood before.
Hardy, T. Victorian Rehearsal, A.
Herrick. On Himselfe.
Susption upon His Over-much Familiarity with a Gentlewoman, The.
Hopkins, G. Miss Story's character! too much you ask.
Jackson, L. Talking World, The.
Laughlin, J. Shameful Profession, The.
Nash, O. Don't Even Tell Your Wife, Particularly.
I Have It on Good Authority.
Never Mind the Overcoat, Button Up That Lip.
This Was Told Me in Confidence.
O'Hara, F. Personal Poem.
Parker, D. Any Porch.
Superfluous Advice.
Whistling Girl, The.
Riley, J. Trestle and the Buck-Saw, The.
Williams, C. K. Regulars, The.
Wordsworth, W. Personal Talk.

See also **Reputation; Rumor**

Government

Berry, W. Against the War in Vietnam.
Bierce. Statesmen, The.
Bly, R. Johnson's Cabinet Watched by Ants.
Brodsky, J. Once More by the Potomac.
Burns, R. Act Sederunt of the Session—A Scots Ballad.
Buy Braw Troggin. An Excellent New Song.
Election: A New Song, The.
Johnie B———'s Lament.
Wham will we send to London town.
Chuang Tzu. Cracking the Safe.
Cowper, W. Table Talk.
Emerson, R. Ode, Inscribed to W.H. Channing.
Politics.
Ginsberg, A. Capitol Air.
Gray, T. Alliance of Education and Government, The.
Han-shan. State relies on people, A.
Herrick. Another on the Same.
Gentlenesse.
Ill Government.
Obedience.
Obedience in Subjects.
Power in the People, The.
Present Government Grievous.
Rules for Our Reach.
Shame, No Statist.
Hill, G. Respublica.
Hughes, L. Un-American Investigators.
Ignatow, D. Simulacrum.
Kipling, R. Death-Bed, A.
MacDonough's Song.
Kunitz, S. System, The.
Lawrence, D. H. Change of Government.
Flapper Vote.
Lindsay, N. Preface to "Bob Taylor's Birthday."
Lorde. Revolution Is One Form of Social Change.
Marvell. First Anniversary of the Government under His Highness the Lord Protector, 1655, The.
Last Instructions to a Painter, The.
Music's Empire.
Merton. Note in Honor of Machiavelli, A.
Milosz, C. Higher Arguments in Favor of

Discipline Derived from the Speech before the Council of the Universal State in 2068.
Three Talks on Civilization.
Nemerov. Poverty Programs, The.
Rukeyser, M. Disease: After-Effects, The.
Sandburg, C. And They Obey.
Death Snips Proud Men.
Government.
Liars, The.
Mr. Longfellow and His Boy.
Snow.
Trinity Place.
Shelley, P. England in 1819.
Sze. Impressions of the New Mexico Legislature.
Tate, J. Smart and Final Iris.
Thoreau. Independence.
Unknown. Four Sambas.
Very. On the late Disgraceful Scene in Congress.
Williams, C. K. Another Dollar.
Bishop Tutu's Visit to the White House: 1984.
Poem for the Governments, A.
Wordsworth, W. 1801.
Yeats. Appointment, An.
Church and State.
Old Stone Cross, The.

Goya

Collins, B. Candle Hat.
Duncan, R. Poem Beginning with a Line by Pindar, A.
Ferlinghetti, L. Goya & the Sleep of Reason.
In Goya's greatest scenes we seem to see.
Pinkerton, H. On Goya's *Duel with Cudgels* (ca. 1820), a "Black Painting" in the Prado.
Van Duyn. Goya's "Two Old People Eating Soup."
Weiss, T. Clothes Maketh the Man.

Grace

Amichai [*or* Amikhai]. Hour of Grace, An.
Hour of Grace, The.
Armantrout. Grace.
Beckett, S. À elle l'acte calme.
Nuit qui fais tant.
Berry, W. Gift of Gravity, The.
Grace.
Browning, E. Work.
Campion, T. Author of light, revive my dying spright.
Loe, when backe mine eye.
View Mee, Lord.
Chaucer. ABC, An.
Cowper, W. Song of Mercy and Judgment, A.
Creeley. Birds, The.
Fire, The.
Le Fou.
Cullen, C. Atlantic City Waiter.
Cunningham, J. Predestined Space, The.
To My Daimon.
Dickinson, E. Anatomical dishabille.
Day that I was crowned, The.
Grace—Myself—might not obtain, The.
Her Grace is all she has.
How spacious must be the Heart.
I cross till I am weary.
Love a Life Can Show, The.
Oh what a Grace is this.
Sweetest Heresy received, The.
Eberhart, R. Incidence of Flight.
Words.
Emerson, R. Grace.
Ye have Grace.
Glück, L. Gift, The.
Guyon. Triumph of Heavenly Love Desired, The.
Herbert, G. Conscience.
Grace.
Love (3).
Temper (2), The.
Herrick. Affliction.
God.
Gods Dwelling.
Gods Grace.
Harding of Hearts.
Humility.
To God.

To the Handsome Mistresse Grace Potter.
Upon Gryll.
Hopkins, G.   Handsome Heart, The.
To What Serves Mortal Beauty?
Windhover, The.
Jackson, L.   Grace.
Jonson, B.   To Susan, Countess of Montgomery.
Kunitz, S.   Unwithered Garland, The.
Levertov.   Avowal, The.
Grace-Note, The.
Improbable Truth.
Logan, J.   Grace.
MacLeish.   Crossing.
Merton.   Grace's House.
Image of True Lovers' Death, The.
Snare, The.
Michelangelo Buonarroti.   For a reliable guide
   in my vocation.
Mistral, G.   Grace.
Nemerov.   Behavior.
Dancer's Reply, The.
Steps for a Dancer.
Patchen.   For whose adornment the mouths.
Pinkerton, H.   Gift, The.
Raine, K.   Returning from Church.
Ralegh, S.   Passionate Man[']s Pilgrimage, The.
Ramanujan.   Compensations.
Still Another View of Grace.
Rexroth, K.   Portrait of a Lady.
Robinson, E.   But for the Grace of God.
Rossetti, C.   Changing Chimes.
Do This, and He Doeth It.
Feast of the Presentation.
Grant us such grace that we may work Thy
   Will.
Helen Grey.
Lady Isabella.
Listening.
Lord, grant me grace to love Thee in my pain.
Lord, grant us grace to rest upon Thy word.
Lord, I am feeble and of mean account.
Lord, Thou art fulness, I am emptiness.
Night and Death.
O Lord, I am ashamed to seek Thy Face / As
   tho' I loved Thee as Thy saints love Thee.
Seven vials hold Thy wrath: but what can hold.
Sit Down in the Lowest Room.
St. Mark.
Valentines From C.G.R.
We know not when, we know not where.
What is it Jesus saith unto the soul?
Rukeyser, M.   Ninth Elegy. The Antagonists.
Rumi.   Pale sunlight.
Stafford, W.   Grace Abounding.
Tate, J.   Grace.
Tomlinson, C.   Given Grace, A.
Very.   Promise, The ("I come the rushing wind
   that shook the place").
Warren, R.   Amazing Grace in the Back
   Country.
Wilbur, R.   Grace.
Lament: "Nashe's old queens who bartered
   young and fair."
Wordsworth, W.   Composed During a Storm.
Yeats.   Countess Cathleen in Paradise, The.

Grackles
Ammons.   Windy Trees.
Nash, O.   Grackle, The.
Warren, R.   Grackles, Goodbye.

Graffiti
Dugan, A.   Thesis, Antithesis and Nostalgia.
Enzensberger, H.   Staircase, A.
Ginsberg, A.   Graffiti 12th Cubicle Men's Room
   Syracuse Airport.
Larkin, P.   Sunny Prestatyn.
Laughlin, J.   Blue Footprints, The.
Lux.   I Love You Sweatheart.
Rukeyser, M.   Backside of the Academy, The.

Graham, Martha
Laughlin, J.   Martha Graham.

Grammar
Ciardi, J.   English A.
Codrescu.   Grammar.
Creeley.   Not Again.
Sentence, The.
Cummings, E. E.   First president to be loved by

his, The.
Love's the i guess most only verb that lives.
Graves, R.   O.
Koch, K.   Permanently.
Kunitz, S.   Grammar Lesson.
Nash, O.   Oafishness Sells Good, like an
   Advertisement Should.
Pagis.   Opening to Satan, An.
Sheridan, T.   Of the Genders of Nouns.
Spender, S.   Subject, Object, Sentence.

Gramsci, Antonio
Pasolini.   Ashes of Gramsci, The.

Granada, Spain
García Lorca.   Ballad of the Three Rivers.
St. Michael.

Grand Canyon
Sandburg, C.   Many Hats.

Grandchildren
Bradstreet, A.   On My Dear Grandchild Simon
   Bradstreet.
Clifton, L.   Photograph.
Kumin, M.   Grandchild.
Logan, J.   My Rebel Grandmother.
Riley, J.   Schoolboy's Favorite, The.
Tennyson, A.   To Alfred Tennyson, My
   Grandson.
Williams, M.   Catch with Reuben.
For All Our Great-Grandchildren.
For Rebecca, for Whom Nothing Has Been
   Written Page after Page.
Manifold Usefulness of an Education, The.
Williams, W.   Paul.
Wordsworth, W.   Poet to His Grandchild; Sequel
   to "A Plea for Authors."
Sonnet: "Why should we weep or mourn,
   Angelic boy."

Granddaughters
Bradstreet, A.   In Memory of My Dear
   Grandchild Elizabeth Bradstreet.
Jeffers, R.   Granddaughter.
Kumin, M.   We Stood There Singing.
Laughlin, J.   My Granddaughter.
Parker, D.   For a Favorite Grand-Daughter.
Rossetti, C.   Lines to My Grandfather.
Williams, W.   3 Stances.
Suzy.

Grandfathers
Amichai [or Amikhai].   Luxury, A.
Berrigan, T.   Cranston near the City Line.
Bishop, E.   Manners.
Bukowski.   Gold Pocket Watch, A.
Clampitt.   Prairie, The.
Coleridge, S.   To the Rev. George Coleridge.
Cooper, J.   How Can I Speak for Her.
Crane, S.   Once I saw mountains angry.
Dove, R.   Roast Possum.
Sunday Night at Grandfather's.
Dubie.   Grandfather's Last Letter, A.
Safe Conduct.
Glück, L.   Legend.
Graves, R.   Age Gap.
Hacker, M.   Sword.
Hall, D.   Child's Garden, A.
Flies.
Maple Syrup.
Table, The.
Hamill, S.   Letter to Robert Hedin.
Heaney, S.   Digging.
Hughes, L.   Grandpa's Stories.
Komunyakaa.   Mismatched Shoes.
Kumin, M.   For My Great-Grandfather: A
   Message Long Overdue.
On Reading an Old Baedeker in Schloss
   Leopoldskron.
Sperm.
Levine, P.   Goodbye.
Nitrate.
Zaydee.
Logan, J.   Grandfather's Railroad.
Weeping, The.
Lowell, R.   Dunbarton.
Mahon.   Grandfather.
Milosz, C.   My Grandfather Sigismund Kunat.
Muldoon, P.   My Grandfather's Wake.
Niedecker.   Don't shoot the rail!

Grampa's got his old age pension.
Poet's Work.
Olson, C.   Grandfather-Father Poem, The.
Pagis.   Sugarduke.
Paley, G.   He Wanders.
Here.
Parker, D.   Grandfather Said It.
Riley, J.   Grampa's Choice.
Grandfather Squeers.
Waitin' fer the Cat to Die.
Rossetti, C.   Lines to My Grandfather.
Sexton.   Funnel.
Grandfather, Your Wound.
Warren, R.   Genealogy.
Minnesota Recollection.
Re-interment: Recollection of a Grandfather.

Grandmothers
Atwood.   Five Poems for Grandmothers.
Berry, W.   Grandmother, The.
Bishop, E.   Sestina: "September rain falls on the
   house."
Blue Cloud.   Grandma Marie Potts.
Ciardi, J.   Thinking about Girls.
Cooper, J.   Mary Coldwell.
Corbett, W.   Passed on.
Crane, H.   My Grandmother's Love Letters.
Creeley.   Provincetown.
Davie, D.   Housekeeping.
Dubie.   Grandmother.
Dunbar, P.   Opportunity.
Gallagher, T.   Coats, The.
Glück, L.   Grandmother in the Garden.
Graves, R.   Great-Grandmother, The.
Hall, D.   Flies.
Hughes, L.   Dime.
Kinsella, T.   Hand of Solo, A.
Tear.
Komunyakaa.   Little Man around the House.
Korn.   Generations.
Levine, P.   Grandmother in Heaven.
Logan, J.   Grandmother Dead in the Aeroplane.
My Rebel Grandmother.
Merwin.   Birdie.
Niedecker.   Just before she died.
Oliver, M.   Answers.
Oppen.   To the Muse.
Paley, G.   Here.
Patchen.   At Grandmother's Wake.
Piercy.   Snow in May.
Plath.   Point Shirley.
Ramanujan.   Lines to a Granny.
Rich, A.   Grandmothers.
Riley, J.   Granny.
Schoolboy's Favorite, The.
She "Displains" It.
Schuyler, J.   Quick, Henry, the Flit!
So Good.
Shapiro, K.   My Grandmother.
Snyder, G.   Old Dutch Woman, The.
Walker, A.   Medicine.
Williams, C. K.   What Did the Man Do with the
   Clouds?
Williams, W.   Last Words of My English
   Grandmother, The.
Last Words of My Grandmother.
Wright, J.   My Grandmother's Ghost.

Grandparents
Amichai [or Amikhai].   Parents Left the Child,
   The.
Hall, D.   Tomorrow.
Laughlin, J.   Upstate New York.
Lowell, R.   Grandparents.
Nash, O.   Come On in, the Senility Is Fine.
Olson, C.   To Gerhardt, There, among Europe's
   Things of Which He Has Written Us in His
   "Brief an Creely und Olson."
Paley, G.   Note to Grandparents.
Spender, S.   Grandparents.
Williams, M.   Story, A.

Granicus, Battle of (334 B.C.)
Dugan, A.   How We Heard the Name.

Grant, Ulysses Simpson
Bierce.   Contentment.
Death of Grant, The.
Riley, J.   Grant.
Sandburg, C.   Bronzes.

Cool Tombs.
Hammers Pounding.
Shapiro, K.   Grant's Tomb Revisited.
Whitman, W.   Death of General Grant.
What Best I See in Thee.
Wilbur, R.   Fourth of July, The.

Grapes
Amichai [*or* Amikhai].   Lots of Grapes.
Dickinson, E.   Grapes were big and fresh, The.
Emerson, R.   On a raisin stone.
Frost, R.   Wild Grapes.
Kumin, M.   Continuum: a Love Poem.
Lawrence, D. H.   Grapes.
Rexroth, K.   Song at the Winepresses, A.

Grass
Ammons.   Grass Miracles, The.
Berry, W.   On the Hill Late at Night.
Blue Cloud.   Sweetgrass.
Bly, R.   Grass from Two Years.
  Snowfall in the Afternoon.
Clampitt.   Grasses.
  Savannah.
Crane, S.   In Heaven, / Some little blades of
  grass.
Dickinson, E.   Grass, The.
  Snake, The.
Eberhart, R.   Cover Me Over.
Emerson, R.   For Lyra yet shall be the pole.
Gunn, T.   Grasses.
Hall, D.   Granite and Grass.
Heaney, S.   Fodder.
Hughes, T.   Stanbury Moor.
Larkin, P.   Cut Grass.
Lawrence, D. H.   Leaves of Grass, Flowers of
  Grass.
Merrill, J.   Grass.
Merton.   Bees love grass, The.
Merwin.   Grass Beginning July.
Pagis.   Art of Contraction, The.
Riley, J.   Green Grass of Old Ireland, The.
Rossetti, C.   Thou Knewest...Thou Oughtest
  Therefore.
Rumi.   Grasses, The.
Sandburg, C.   Grass.
  Grassroots.
  In Tall Grass.
  Man and Dog on an Early Winter Morning.
  Never Two Songs the Same.
  Spring Grass.
  Summer Grass.
Simic.   Evening.
Unknown.   Two Spring Charms.
Williams, T.   Heavenly Grass.
Williams, W.   Province, The.
Wordsworth, W.   This Lawn, a Carpet All Alive.
Zukofsky, L.   And so till we have died.

Grasshoppers
Clare, J.   Grasshoppers.
Cummings, E. E.   R-P-O-P-H-E-S-S-A-G-R.
Hughes, T.   In the Likeness of a Grasshopper.
Keats.   On the Grasshopper and [the] Cricket.
La Fontaine.   Grasshopper and the Ant, The.
Lindsay, N.   Explanation of the Grasshopper,
  An.
Milosz, C.   Thesis and Counter-Thesis.
Ramanujan.   Minor Sacrifice, A.
Tomlinson, C.   Desert Autumn.
Unknown.   On the Grasshopper.
Wilbur, R.   Grasshopper, A.

Gratitude
Bierce.   Matter for Gratitude.
Brodsky, J.   May 24, 1980.
Brontë, E.   My Comforter.
Burns, R.   To Mr. Graham of Fintry, on Being
  Appointed to My Excise Division.
Byron, G.   Stanzas to Augusta.
Campion, T.   To My Honourable Friend, Sr.
  Thomas Mounson, *Knight and Baronet.*
  To My Worthy Friend, Mr. John Mounson,
  Sonne and Heyre to Sir Thomas Mounson,
  Knight and Baronet.
  To the Right Honourable, Both in Birth and
  Vertue, Francis, Earle of Cumberland.
Carruth, H.   Dedication in These Days.
  When I Wrote a Little.
Carver, R.   Asia.

For Tess.
Gift, The.
Celan.   There stood / a splinter of fig on your
  lip.
Cowper, W.   Gratitude.
Creeley.   Song: "God give you pardon from
  gratitude."
  Thank You.
Dickinson, E.   Gratitude—is not the mention.
  Gratitude is the timid wealth.
Dunbar, P.   To an Ingrate.
Emerson, R.   Kind & holy were the words.
Frost, R.   Closed for Good.
  On Being Chosen Poet of Vermont.
Glück, L.   Gratitude.
Guyon.   Gratitude and Love to God.
Hacker, M.   Chaplet for Judith Landry, A.
Heaney, S.   Pillowed Head, A.
Herrick.   Primitiæ to Parents, The.
  To His Faithfull Friend, Master John Crofts,
  Cup-bearer to the King.
  To Sir Clipsebie Crew.
  To the Most Virtuous Mistress Pot, Who Many
  Times Entertained Him.
  Upon Flood, Or a Thankfull Man.
Hopkins, G.   In the staring darkness.
Jonson, B.   To Esmé, Lord Aubigny.
Koch, K.   Thank You.
Lawrence, D. H.   Wild Common, The.
Meredith, G.   Question Whither, The.
  To Plimmer, Verandah and Cello.
Michelangelo Buonarroti.   Since I'm too
  obligated.
Milton.   Manso.
Pasolini.   One of the Many Epilogs.
Petrarch.   Column of glory, strong stay and
  support.
  He Who reveals His providence and art.
Poe.   To M. L. S——.
Prunty.   Note of Thanks, A.
Riley, J.   Autographic.
Ritsos.   Thanksgiving.
Rossetti, C.   Christmas Carol, A: "Thank God,
  thank God, we do believe."
Smart, C.   Epistle to John Sherratt, Esq, An.
Snyder, G.   Prayer for the Great Family.
Stockton, A.   Birth Day Ode, A.
  Ode to Solitude Inscribed to Mrs Boudinot, An.
See also **Thankfulness**

Graves
Amichai [*or* Amikhai].   Luxury.
  Luxury, A.
Baudelaire.   Carefree Corpse, The.
Beckett, S.   Plus loin un autre commémore.
Bierce.   Cynic perforce from studying mankind.
  For those this mausoleum is erected.
  George Perry here is stiff and stark.
  Here lies the last of Deacon Fitch.
  Loring Pickering.
  McAllister, of talents rich and rare.
  Presentiment.
Broumas, O.   On Earth.
  Périsprit.
Browning, R.   Bad Dreams IV.
  Bishop Orders His Tomb at Saint Praxed's
  Church, The.
  Childe Roland to the Dark Tower Came.
  Spring Song.
Bukowski.   Beautiful Young Girl Walking Past
  the Graveyard—, The.
Byron, G.   Churchill's Grave.
Carver, R.   Walk, A.
Cavafy.   In the Month of Athyr.
Celan.   Profuse announcement.
Chesterton.   Elegy in a Country Churchyard.
  English Graves, The.
Ciardi, J.   Epithalamium at St. Michael's
  Cemetary.
  Leaving Longboat Key.
Cino da Pistoia.   Sonnet: Of the Grave of
  Selvaggia, on the Monte della Sambuca.
Clampitt.   Amherst.
  Paumanok.
Codrescu.   Epitaph (1): "Julio hernadez does not
  lie here."
  Epitaph (2): "He was a young guy with

  surrealist connections."
Coleridge, S.   Knight's Tomb, The.
Crashaw.   Epitaph upon Husband and Wife Who
  Died and Were Buried Together, An.
  Upon the Sepulchre of Our Lord.
Creeley.   For Leslie.
Davie, D.   No Epitaph.
De la Mare.   Beneath a motionless yew.
  England.
  Even in the Grave.
  Hawthorn Hath a Deathly Smell, The.
Dickey, J.   Escape, The.
Dickinson, E.   Ample make this Bed.
  Coffin—is a small Domain, A.
  Color of the Grave is Green, The.
  It was a Grave, yet bore no Stone.
  Mine—by the Right of the White Election!
  Not any higher stands the Grave.
  We do not play on Graves.
  Who could be motherless.
Donne.   Relic, The.
Eberhart, R.   Bones of Coleridge, The.
  Ceremony by the Sea, A.
  Concord Cats.
  Dead Skunk.
  Gesture, The.
  Grave Piece.
  I Walked Out to the Graveyard to See the Dead.
  I Walked over the Grave of Henry James.
  Ides of March, The.
  Suite in Prison.
  Ur Burial.
Emerson, R.   In Memoriam.
  Why fear to die.
Frost, R.   In a Disused Graveyard.
Goethe.   Anacreon's Grave.
Gray, T.   Elegy Written in a Country
  Churchyard.
Hall, D.   Maple Syrup.
  Sister on the Tracks, A.
Hamill, S.   At Rexroth's Grave.
Han-shan.   All the people I see.
  Buddhist monks don't keep their precepts.
  I spur my horse past ruins.
Hardy, T.   Ah, Are You Digging on My Grave?
  Before My Friend Arrived.
  By the Barrows.
  Evening Shadows.
  In the Evening.
  Marble Tablet, The.
  Nettles, The.
  Poet, A.
  Rain on a Grave.
  Roman Gravemounds, The.
  Sexton at Longpuddle, The.
Hayden, R.   Paul Laurence Dunbar.
Herrick.   Dirge upon the Death of the Right
  Valiant Lord, Bernard Stuart, A.
  Tapers.
  To Anthea.
  To Biancha.
  To Laurels.
  To Perenna.
  To Perenna, a Mistresse.
  To the Yew and Cypress to Grace His Funeral.
  Upon an Old Man a Residenciarie.
  Upon Ben Jo[h]nson.
  Upon His Departure Hence.
Housman.   Because I liked you better.
  Hughley Steeple.
  Rain, it streams on stone and hillock, The.
  Sigh that heaves the grasses, The.
  With Rue My Heart Is Laden.
Hughes, L.   Alabama Earth.
  Epitaph: "Within this grave lie."
Hughes, T.   Error, The.
  Soliloquy: "Whenever I am got under my
  gravestone."
Ignatow, D.   Pricing.
Jarrell, R.   Come to the Stone.
Jeffers, R.   Iona: the Graves of the Kings.
  My Burial Place.
  Shakespeare's Grave.
  Subjected Earth.
Larkin, P.   To Write One Song, I Said.
Lawrence, D. H.   All Souls.

Birthday.
Giorno dei Morti.
Levertov. At David's Grave.
Levine, P. Jewish Graveyards, Italy.
Lindsay, N. What the Sexton Said.
Logan, J. At Drumcliffe Churchyard, County Sligo.
On the Death of Keats; Lines for Those Who Drown Twice.
Longfellow, H. Jewish Cemetery at Newport, The.
Lorde. Father Son and Holy Ghost.
Lowell, R. At the Indian Killer's Grave.
Sailing Home from Rapallo.
Lux. Graveyard by the Sea.
MacNeice. Beni Hasan.
Introduction, The.
Mahon. Image from Beckett, An.
Mallarmé. Sonnet: "In the forgotten woods, when somber winter glowers."
Tomb.
Tomb of Charles Baudelaire, The.
Merwin. Wharf, The.
Millay, E. In the Grave No Flower.
Lines for a Grave-Stone.
Moore, M. Grave, A.
Muldoon, P. At Master McGrath's Grave
Milkweed and Monarch.
Oscar.
Niedecker. I Visit / the Graves.
Pagis. End of the Questionnaire.
Jason's Grave in Jerusalem.
Plath. November Graveyard.
Pope, A. Epitaph Intended for Mr. Rowe, in Westminster Abbey.
Raine, K. Rainbow, beautiful and clear light, A.
Riley, J. Decoration Day on the Place.
Silent Victors, The.
Rilke. Cemetary.
Cemetary in Flaach.
Graves.
Ritsos. Graves of Our Ancestors, The.
Perforation.
Robinson, E. Cortège.
Leonora.
Rossetti, C. Baby's cradle with no baby in it, A.
Flowers Appear on the Earth, The.
For Rosaline's Album.
Gone to his rest / Bright little Bouby!
One Sea-Side Grave.
Song: "When I am dead, my dearest."
There Remaineth Therefore a Rest.
Two Thoughts of Death.
Under Willows.
What to Do?
Year Afterwards, A.
Sandburg, C. Cool Tombs.
Graves.
Seifert. Dead of Lidice, The.
Grave of Signor Casanova, The.
Smith, S. Dream.
English Visitor, The.
Grave by a Holm-Oak.
Upon a Grave.
Stafford, W. At the Grave of My Brother.
Stevens, W. Dutch Graves in Bucks County.
Testamentum.
Stockton, A. Epitaph by a Young Lady, Design'd by Herself, An.
On an Enclosure of Roses in Which Is the Grave of Miss Mary Morgan.
Sze. Sliding Away.
Tate, J. Graveside.
Thomas, D. Tombstone Told when She Died, The.
Tomlinson, C. Arroyo Seco.
Death in the Desert, A.
Epitaph: "Enamoured by / Brevity in method."
Very. Ancient Burial Places in Peabody, The.
Whitman, W. As Toilsome I Wander'd Virginia's Woods.
Dirge for Two Veterans.
Whittier. Grave by the Lake, The.
Naples.
Rock-Tomb of Bradore, The.
Wilde, O. Grave of Shelley, The.

Requiescat.
Wordsworth, W. Gravestone upon the Floor in the Cloisters of Worcester Cathedral, A.
Wright, C. Jesuit Graves.
Wright, J. Albuquerque Graveyard, The.
Eclogue at Nash's Grove.
In a Viennese Cemetery.
Red Jacket's Grave.
Refusal, The.
Regeneration, The.
Way to Make a Living, A.
Zukofsky, L. For Zadkine.
I Sent Thee Late.
See also **Burial; Cemeteries; Mausoleums; Tombs**
Graves, Morris
Kizer, C. From an Artist's House.
Logan, J. Dream, The: A Reflection on Morris Graves's Paintings.
Three Poems on Morris Graves' Paintings.
Graves, Robert
Carver, R. In the Trenches with Robert Graves.
Graves, R. Face in the Mirror, The.
My Name and I.
Wright, C. After Rereading Robert Graves, I Go Outside to Get My Head Together.
Graveyards
Baudelaire. Lively Watering Hole, A.
Carver, R. Walk, A.
Han-shan. My path led through an old cemetery.
Hughes, L. Boarding House.
Grave Yard.
Young Gal's Blues.
Jackson, L. Lying Spying.
Kinnell. Cemetary Angels.
Sheffield Ghazal 5: Passing the Cemetary.
Levi, P. Epitaph: "Oh you, passing by this hill—one."
Logan, J. Pagan Saturday.
Returning Home.
Muldoon, P. Come into My Parlour.
Pinsky. Desecration of the Gravestone of Rose P.
Stafford, W. Paso por Aquí.
Stockton, A. Elegy on the Death of Miss Chandler, as if Written in Her Fathers Church Yard.
Swenson, M. Alyscamps at Arles, The.
Tomlinson, C. Churchyard Wall, The.
Zagajewski. Circus.
Zaturenska. Dream, The.
See also **Cemeteries**
Gravity
Ammons. Account, The.
Berry, W. Gift of Gravity, The.
Collins, B. Earthling.
Eberhart, R. Quanta.
Triptych.
Jacobsen, J. Limbo Dancer, The.
Major, C. Measure.
McHugh, H. Curve.
Ritsos. Earth's Attraction, The.
Simic. Gravity.
Wilbur, R. Juggler.
Lightness.
Gray, Thomas
Gray, T. Sketch of His Own Character.
Wilbur, R. In a Churchyard.
Great Britain
Clampitt. Elgin Marbles, The.
Davie, D. Monmouthshire.
Hughes, T. Milesian Encounter on the Sligachan.
Sunstruck.
Logue, C. I Shall Vote Labour.
See also **England; Northern Ireland; Scotland; Wales**
Great Depression
Dove, R. Hill of Beans, A.
Hall, D. 1934.
Hughes, L. Ballad of Roosevelt.
Madam's Past History.
Out of Work.
Relief.
Oppen. Blood from the Stone.

Williams, W. Portrait of the Times, A.
Great Lakes
Merton. Aubade: Lake Erie.
Niedecker. Lake Superior.
Sandburg, C. Lost.
Great Wall, China
Williams, W. World Contracted to a Recognizable Image, The.
Greatness
"Anvari." Shah Sandschar, whose lowest slave.
Cummings, E. E. All ignorance toboggans into know.
Dickinson, E. Go thy great way!
You said that I "was Great"—one Day.
Eberhart, R. John Ledyard.
Emerson, R. Γνωθι Σεαυτον.
Hughes, L. Shame on You.
Jeffers, R. Great Men.
Ocean.
Teheran.
Jonson, B. To the Memory of My Beloved, the Author Mr [or Master] William Shakespeare: And What He Hath Left Us.
Melville, H. On the Photograph of Corps Commander.
Nemerov. Chromium-Plated Hat. Inlaid with Scenes from Siegfried, A.
Piercy. Woman in the Ordinary, The.
Rumi. Slave, be aware that the Lord.
Spender, S. I Think Continually of Those Who Were Truly Great.
Suckling, S. Non Est Mortale Quod Opto.
Unknown. For pearls, plunge in the sea.
Whitman, W. Ambition.
By Blue Ontario's Shore.
Williams, M. Standing Close to Greatness.
Wordsworth, W. Great men have been among us; hands that penned.
See also **Fame**
Greece
Bierce. Eastern Question, The.
Broumas, O. Before the Elegy.
Body and Soul.
Lying In.
Massacre, The.
Namaste.
Native.
On Earth.
Sometimes, as a Child.
Browning, R. Cleon.
Byron, G. On This Day I Complete My Thirty-sixth Year.
Translation of the Famous Greek War Song *Deute Paides Tov Ellenon.*
Written after Swimming from Sestos to Abydos.
Carver, R. Rhodes.
Cavafy. Displeased Viewer, A.
In the Year 200 B.C.
Memory.
Tarantians Divert Themselves, The.
Clampitt. Ano Prinios.
Leaving Yannina.
Olive Groves of Thasos, The.
Remembering Greece.
Reservoirs of Mount Helicon, The.
Tempe in the Rain.
Thermopylae.
Cummings, E. E. One April dusk the.
Davie, D. Kavyria.
Middlesex.
Dove, R. Ants of Argos, The.
Nestor's Bathtub.
Pithos.
Dugan, A. On Herodotus.
Eberhart, R. Cousin Florence.
Love among the Ruins.
Young Greek, Killed in the Wars, A.
Emerson, R. Elizabeth Hoar.
Poem on Eloquence by R. W. Emerson.
Ferlinghetti, L. Sailing thru the straits of Demos.
Graves, R. Ouzo Unclouded.
Gray, T. Agrippina.
"H. D." In Our Town.
Islands, The.

Lais.
Nossis.
Hall, D.   At Delphi.
Mycenae.
Hamill, S.   Listen, Ianni.
Jacobsen, J.   Absence of Slaves, An.
Laughlin, J.   At Eleusis.
Two Letters on Samos.
Lawrence, D. H.   Argonauts, The.
Logan, J.   Two Poems of Greece.
Meredith, G.   Foresight and Patience.
Merrill, J.   After Greece.
Charioteer of Delphi, The.
Kostas Tympakianákis.
Piercy.   Cats of Greece, The.
Ritsos.   After the Breakdown of the Treaty
between the Lacedaemonians and the
Athenians.
After the Defeat.
Belfry.
Greek Cart-Drivers.
Immobilizing the Boundless.
Memorial Service at Poros.
Models, The.
One Word.
Our Land.
Our Old Men.
Peacocks of Perilampes, The.
Postponed Decision.
Romiosini.
Summer Noon at Karlovasi.
Rukeyser, M.   Canal.
His Head Is Full of Faces.
Rumi.   Chinese Art and Greek Art.
Sandburg, C.   Isle of Patmos.
Near Keokuk.
Sarton, M.   At Lindos.
Birthday on the Acropolis.
Mediterranean.
Myth.
Narcissus.
Thoreau.   Greece.
Updike.   Classical Optical.
Weiss, T.   Views and Spectacles.
Whittier.   Hero, The.
Wilde, O.   Impression de Voyage.
Theatre at Argos, The.

Greed
Berry, W.   We Who Prayed and Wept.
Berryman.   Desires of Men and Women.
Browning, E.   King's Gift, The.
Browning, R.   Gold Hair: A Story of Pornic.
Ponte dell' Angelo, Venice.
Burns, R.   Ken Ye What Meg o' the Mill Has
Gotten.
Ode, Sacred to the Memory of Mrs. ————.
Song: "O poortith cauld, and restless love."
Such a Parcel of Rogues in a Nation.
There's a youth in this city, it were a great pity.
Tibbie Fowler.
Byron, G.   Love and Gold.
Chaucer.   Proverbs: "What shul these clothes
thus manyfold."
Chuang Tzu.   Keng Sang Chu.
Clampitt.   Marginal Employment.
Crane, H.   Pillar and the Post, The.
You Are That Frail.
Cummings, E. E.   Greedy the people, The.
My(his from daughter's mother's zero mind).
You no / tice / nobod / y wants.
Cunningham, J.   Epigram: "You wonder why
Drab sells her love for gold?"
Dunbar, P.   For the Man Who Fails.
Eberhart, R.   Man's Greed and Envy Are So
Great.
Emerson, R.   Hamatreya.
Wealth.
Ferlinghetti, L.   Director of Alienation.
Frost, R.   Vindictives, The.
Ginsberg, A.   C'mon Pigs of Western
Civilization Eat More Grease.
Graves, R.   Accomplice, The.
Beggar Maid and King Cophetua, The.
Lack.
Han-shan.   Exhaust your mind for profit and
fame.

Greedy man who piles up wealth, A.
Wise man isn't greedy, A.
Hardy, T.   Vampirine Fair, The.
Herbert, G.   Avarice.
Size, The.
Herrick.   Again.
Any Way for Wealth.
Covetous Still Captives, The.
Upon Greedy.
Upon Much-More.
Upon Rush.
Jarrell, R.   Money.
Nollekens.
Wide Prospect, The.
Jonson, B.   On Bank the Usurer.
On Chuff, Banks the Usurer's Kinsman.
Those that in blood such violent pleasure have.
Kipling, R.   Rupaiyat of Omar Kal'vin, The.
Laughlin, J.   What the Animals Did.
Lawrence, D. H.   Modern Prayer.
What Is a Man to Do?
Young Are Not Greedy, The.
Lucilius.   Miser and the Mouse, The.
Menander.   From Menander.
Meredith, G.   Fusion.
Josepha.
Quake, quake, let us turn Quaker all!
Triad of British Evils, A.
Milton.   Fable of the Peasant and the Overlord,
The.
Nash, O.   Anybody for Money? or, Just Bring
Your Own Basket.
Niedecker.   What a woman!—hooks men like
rugs.
Olson, C.   *Scream* to the Editor, A.
War on the Mind in a Time of Love.
Pope, A.   Epistle III, to Allen Lord Bathurst.
Epistle IV, to Richard Boyle, Earl of Burlington.
On His Grotto at Twickenham.
Riley, J.   Squire Hawkins's Story.
Robinson, E.   Aaron Stark.
Rumi.   Cat and the Meat, The.
Dervish at the Door.
Sexton.   March 4th.
With Mercy for the Greedy.
Shapiro, K.   Waitress.
Smith, S.   Crown of Gold, The.
Death-Bed of a Financier.
Villains.
Tennyson, A.   Northern Farmer: New Style.
Unknown.   Another ["Art thou some individual
of a kind"].
Another ["Miser, traversing his house, A"].
Van Duyn.   Miser, The.
Whittier.   Haschish, The.
Valuation.
Wilbur, R.   Matthew VIII, 28 ff.
Williams, W.   Con Brio.
Question and Answer.
Wordsworth, W.   Andrew Jones.
At Furness Abbey.
October, 1803.
Proud Were Ye, Mountains, when, in Times of
Old.
Repentance; A Pastoral Ballad.
Star-Gazers.
To the Pennsylvanians.
Two Thieves, The; or, the Last Stage of Avarice.
Written in London, September, 1802.
Yeats.   Three Beggars, The.
Witch, The.
Green (color)
Berry, W.   Green and White.
Ciardi, J.   To W. T. Scott.
Clampitt.   Green.
Creeley.   Christmas: May 10, 1970.
Prospect.
Davie, D.   Wearing of the Green, The.
Dickey, J.   Poem: "For having left the birds that
left me."
García Lorca.   Somnambule Ballad.
Graves, R.   Variables of Green.
Heaney, S.   Fosterling.
Kunitz, S.   Green Ways.
Lawrence, D. H.   Green.
Logan, J.   Abstract Love Poem.

Logue, C.   Song of the Outsider, The.
Pagis.   Twelve Faces of the Emerald.
Rilke.   Moment between Masks.
Ritsos.   Idiot, The.
Schuyler, J.   I Think.
Stein, G.   Go in Green.
Stevens, W.   Candle a Saint, The.
Tomlinson, C.   Green Quinces.
Zukofsky, L.   Que J'ay Dit Devant.
Greenhouses
Cowper, W.   Winter Nosegay, The.
Hardy, T.   Frozen Greenhouse, The.
Pagis.   Tropical Greenhouse.
Roethke.   Big Wind.
Child on Top of a Greenhouse.
Forcing House.
Rossetti, C.   How many authors are my first!
Zagajewski.   Greenhouse, The.
Greenwich Village, New York City
Carruth, H.   Re-Acquaintance.
Clampitt.   Hedge of Rubber Trees. A.
Dugan, A.   His Hands Have Five Knives Each.
Gregory, Lady Augusta
Yeats.   Municipal Gallery Revisited, The.
Gregory, Robert
Yeats.   In Memory of Major Robert Gregory.
Grenada
Jacobsen, J.   Chosen, The.
Walcott.   Landfall, Grenada.
Greyhounds
Zaturenska.   Variation on a Polish Folk Song.
Grief
Ai.   Cuba, 1962.
Amichai [*or* Amikhai].   Death of Assia G., The.
My Father in a White Space Suit.
My Son, My Son, My Head, My Head.
Ammons.   Brooks & Other Notions.
Crippled Angel, A.
This Bright Day.
Berry, W.   Grief.
Poem for J.
Berryman.   Epilogue: "He died in December. He
must descend."
Parting as Descent.
Surviving Love.
Bierce.   Nanine.
Blok.   Autumn Day.
I Am Nailed to a Bar with Liquor.
Bogan, L.   Juan's Song.
Brontë, E.   Castle Wood.
Day Dream, A.
E.W. to A.G.A.
If grief for grief can touch thee.
Stanzas: "Often rebuked, yet always back
returning."
Broumas, O.   Mercy.
Browning, E.   Bereavement.
Claim, The.
Exaggeration.
Felicia Hemans.
Grief.
Sea-Mew, The.
Bukowski.   You Smoke a Cigarette.
Burns, R.   Elegy on Captain Matthew
Henderson [*or* Capt. M———— H————].
Fair Jenny.
Fragment, Which Was Meant for the Beginning
of an Elegy on the Late Miss Burnet, A.
Lament for James, Earl of Glencairn.
On Reading, in a Newspaper, the Death of J—
———— McL————, Esq.
Raving winds around her blowing.
Red, Red Rose, A.
Song: "Again rejoicing Nature sees."
Song.—In the Character of a Ruined Farmer.
Byron, G.   And Wilt Thou Weep when I Am
Low?
Away, Away, Ye Notes of Woe!
Ode to a Lady Whose Lover Was Killed by a
Ball, Which at the Same Time Shivered a
Portrait next His Heart.
Oh! Snatch'd Away in Beauty's Bloom.
Stanzas for Music.
Stanzas: "I heard thy fate without a tear."
To Florence.

Campion, T.   Could my heart more tongues imploy.
Elegie upon the Untimely Death of Prince *Henry*, An.
If any hath the heart to kill.
Illustrissimo, Potentissimoque Principi, *Frederico* Quinto, Rheni Comiti Palatino, Duci Bavariae, &c.
Since she, ev'n shee, for whom I liv'd.
To the Most Disconsolate Great Brittaine.
To the Most Sacred King James.
Carew, T.   Grief Engrossed.
To the Countess of Anglesey.
Upon the King's Sickness.
Carver, R.   Grief.
Cavalcanti.   If only Mercy befriended my desires.
Since I must bear a sorrowing heart.
Chiabrera.   O flower of all that springs from gentle blood.
O Lelius, beauteous flower of gentleness.
Ciardi, J.   Stone without Edges Has Not Been Mined, The.
Clampitt.   Camouflage.
Clifton, L.   Grief.
Coleridge, S.   Monody on the Death of Chatterton.
O Spirit blest! / Whether th' eternal Throne around.
On Receiving an Account that His Only Sister's Death Was Inevitable.
Cooper, J.   Holding Out.
Corbett, W.   Basil 1977-1993.
Crane, S.   Love forgive me if I wish you grief.
Creeley.   For Leslie.
Greendoon's Song.
De la Mare.   Argument, The.
Captive, The.
Clear Eyes.
Courage.
Disguise, The.
For All the Grief.
Music.
Oh, Why?
Reflections.
Riddlers, The.
Widow, The.
Dickinson, E.   Bereavement in their death to feel.
Bustle in a House, The.
Butterfly upon the Sky, The.
Grief is a Mouse.
Grief of wonder at her fate.
I Can Wade Grief.
I measure every Grief I meet.
If all the griefs I am to have.
Perhaps the dear, grieved Heart.
So glad we are—a Stranger'd deem.
Summers of bloom—and months of frost.
'Tis good—the looking back on Grief.
Donne.   Elegy on the L. C.
Triple Fool, The.
Valediction: Forbidding Mourning, A.
Dryden, J.   To the Memory of Mr Oldham.
Dunbar, P.   Change Has Come, The.
In the Tents of Akbar.
Love and Grief.
Love's Chastening.
Phyllis.
Sea speaks to me of you, The.
Yesterday and Tomorrow.
Eberhart, R.   Loss.
Trying to Hold It All Together.
Emerson, R.   I grieve that better souls than mine.
Frost, R.   Hill Wife, The.
Gallagher, T.   Rhododendrons.
Glück, L.   Triumph of Achilles, The.
Graves, R.   Brief Reunion.
Gentleman, The.
Hooded Flame.
Prison Walls.
Reproach.
Gray, T.   Amatory Lines.
Death of Hoel, The.
Epitaph on Mrs Jane Clarke.

Song: "Thyrsis, when we parted, swore."
Sonnet [on the Death of Mr. Richard West].
Gunn, T.   Blank, A.
Monster, The.
Hall, D.   Our Walk in Yorkshire.
Sister by the Pond, A.
Han-shan.   What makes a young man grieve.
HaNagid.   Among My Friends.
On the Death of Isaac, His Brother.
Why Should the Hearts of You Purists.
Hardy, T.   Bereft.
Confession to a Friend in Trouble, A.
He Prefers Her Earthly.
Heaney, S.   Mid-Term Break.
Herbert, G.   Affliction (1).
Affliction (3).
Confession.
Grief.
Herbert, Z.   Achilles. Penthesilea.
Herrick.   Anacreontike.
Bucolick betwixt Two: Lacon and Thyrsis, A.
Crosses.
Ease.
Faire after Foule.
Felicity, Quick of Flight.
Griefe.
Griefes.
Happinesse.
His Comfort.
His Weaknesse in Woes.
Observation.
To His Kinswoman, Mistresse Susanna Herrick.
To Primroses Filled with Morning Dew.
Upon the Bishop of Lincolne's Imprisonment.
Will Makes the Work, or Consent Makes the Cure, The.
Hopkins, G.   Felix Randal.
Nightingale, The.
No Worst, There Is None. Pitched Past Pitch of Grief.
Spring and Fall.
Housman.   Bredon Hill.
Land of Biscay, The.
Hughes, L.   Gal's Cry for a Dying Lover.
Grief.
Lament over Love.
Hughes, T.   Error, The.
God, The.
Jacobsen, J.   Country Drive-In.
Jonson, B.   On My First Son[ne].
Kinsella, T.   Cover Her Face.
Messenger, The.
Kipling, R.   Children, The.
London Stone.
Komunyakaa.   Man Who Carries the Desert Around inside Himself, The: For Wally.
Larkin, P.   Deep Analysis.
If Grief Could Burn Out.
Portrait.
Thaw.
Lawrence, D. H.   Another Ophelia.
Bereavement.
Brooding Grief.
Change of Life.
Going Back.
Grief.
Hymn to Priapus.
Sorrow.
Levertov.   During a Son's Dangerous Illness.
Dwellers at the Hermitage.
Grief.
Lamentation, A.
Photo Torn from The Times.
Talking to Grief.
Visitant.
Longfellow, H.   Cross of Snow, The.
Lorde.   Memorial I.
Suffer the Children.
MacDiarmid, H.   At My Father's Grave.
Marvell.   Mourning.
McHugh, H.   Form.
Melville, H.   Martyr, The.
Monody.
Meredith, G.   Chillianwallah.
Dost thou behold some woeful soul.
Flower of the Ruins, The.

If thou art sorrowful, hide thy face!
Lesson of Grief, The.
Two Blackbirds, The.
Merrill, J.   Willow.
Merwin.   Huckleberry Woman.
Next Moon, The.
Night Wind.
Presidents.
Michelangelo Buonarroti.   Already burdened with a heavy heart.
From one all loveliness and all allure.
It well may be, so vehement my sighing.
Man who's happy many a year, one hour, A.
Millay, E.   As to some lovely temple, tenantless.
Felicity of Grief!—even Death being kind.
Grief that is grief and properly so hight.
Interim.
Lament: "Listen, children: / Your father is dead."
Once more into my arid days like dew.
Song of a Second April.
Three Songs of Shattering.
Time does not bring relief; you all have lied.
To One Who Might Have Borne a Message.
When the tree-sparrows with no sound through the pearl-pale air.
Wood Road, The.
Milton.   On His Deceased Wife.
Mistral, G.   Bones of the Dead, The.
Muldoon, P.   Grief.
Nemerov.   Ahasuerus.
Anniversary.
Oliver, M.   Murderer's House, The.
Three Poems for James Wright.
Olson, C.   All You Can Do.
Orr, G.   His Grief.
Wedge, The.
Owen, W.   Happiness.
Hospital Barge at Cérisy.
Paley, G.   Luck.
Parker, D.   Little Words.
Midnight.
Pasolini.   Appendix to the "Religion': A Light.
Patchen.   'O Now the Drenched Land Wakes.'
Unanswering Correspondences, The.
Petrarch.   I weep all day; and in the night-time, when.
In doubtful state I weep, at times I sing.
She used to come and comfort me in sleep.
Sonnet: "If grief dismiss me not to them that rest."
Those eyes of which so warmly I would speak.
Time had come for me to establish peace, The.
What should I do? Love, what do you advise?
With no regret, not envying anyone.
Plath.   Departure.
Poe.   Annabel Lee.
For Annie.
Pope, A.   Weeping.
Prunty.   Husband.
Pugliesi.   Canzone: Of His Dead Lady.
Raine, K.   Spell against Sorrow.
Ralegh, S.   Farewell to the Court.
Rexroth, K.   Andrée Rexroth ("Years have gone, The. It is spring").
Maximian, Elegy 5.
Riley, J.   Harp of the Minstrel, The.
Little Woman, The.
Mad Lover, The.
Requiescat.
Since My Mother Died.
What They Said.
Ritsos.   Memorial Services.
Robinson, E.   Reuben Bright.
Roethke.   Apparition, The.
Sequel, The.
Rossetti, C.   All Flesh Is Grass.
Alleluia! or Alas! my heart is crying.
Better So.
By the Waters of Babylon.
Cried Out with Tears.
Death of a First-Born, A.
Death's Chill Between.
Despair.
Gone Before.
Heart Knoweth Its Own Bitterness, The.

Heart's Chill Between.
Hope in Grief.
If I Had Words.
Life Out of Death.
Love Defended.
Margery.
Novice, The.
On the Death of a Cat.
One of the Dead.
Passing away the bliss, / The anguish passing
    away.
Remember [Me].
Seeking Rest.
Song: "Stream moaneth as it floweth, The."
Sonnet from the Psalms.
Summer Is Ended, The.
Surely He Hath Borne Our Griefs.
Three Moments.
Undine.
Vanity of Vanities.
Yet a Little While.
Rossetti, D.   Woodspurge, The.
Rukeyser, M.   Christmas Eve.
Sandburg, C.   Right to Grief, The.
Sarton, M.   Of Grief.
Shelley, P.   Dirge, A: "Rough wind, that
    moanest loud."
    Fragment: "My head is wild with weeping for a
    grief."
    Sunset, The.
Smith, S.   And the Clouds Return after the Rain.
    Ceux Qui Luttent.
    English Visitor, The.
    Happiness.
    No Respect.
    So to Fatness Come.
    Spanish School.
    Story I Have Told, The.
Stevens, W.   Another Weeping Woman.
Stock, R.   Cushing.
    Grief.
Stockton, A.   Compos'd in a Dancing Room,
    December 69.
    Extemporal Ode in a Sleepless Night, An. By a
    Lady, (Mrs. S. of New-Jersey).
    Lyric Ode, A.—Feb. 28.
    Sudden Production of Mrs. Stockton's in One of
    Those Many Anxious Nights, A.
Suckling, S.   Upon the Black Spots Worn, by
    My Lady D.E.
Swenson, M.   In the Bodies of Words.
Swift, J.   Occasioned by Sir William Temple's
    Late Illness and Recovery.
Szymborska, W.   Parting with a View.
Tennyson, A.   Break, Break, Break.
Thomas, D.   Grief Ago, A.
    Grief Thief of Time.
    In My Craft or Sullen Art.
    Out of the Sighs.
Vallejo.   Down to the Dregs.
Very.   Grief.
Walker, A.   At First.
Warren, R.   Aged Man Surveys the Past.
    Apologia for Grief.
    Doubleness in Time.
Whitman, W.   Come Up from the Fields Father.
Whittier.   Funeral Tree of the Sokokis.
    Telling the Bees.
    To My Friend on the Death of His Sister.
    Vesta.
Wilde, O.   Requiescat.
Williams, W.   Widow's Lament in Springtime,
    The.
Wordsworth, W.   Force of Prayer, The; or, The
    Founding of Bolton Priory; A Tradition.
    Maternal Grief.
Wright, J.   Complaint.
    Listening to the Mourners.
    Poem Written under an Archway in a
    Discontinued Railroad Station, Fargo, North
    Dakota, A.
Wyatt, S.   Alas, the grief and deadly wo[e]ful
    smart[!].
    All heavy minds.
    At mo[o]st mischief.
    Blame Not My Lute.

Complaining, alas, without redress.
    Disdain.
    Duress of pains and grievous smart.
    Flaming sighs that boil within my breast, The.
    Lover's Appeal, The.
    Sighs are my food, drink are my tears.
Yeats.   Down by the Salley Gardens.
Zagajewski.   Elegy for the Living.

See also **Mourning and Mourners; Sorrow**

Grocers
Chesterton.   Song against Grocers, The.
Simic.   Grocery.
Williams, C. K.   Bread.
    Racists.

Groundhogs
Eberhart, R.   Groundhog, The.
    Groundhog Revisiting, The.
Frost, R.   Drumlin Woodchuck, A.
Kumin, M.   Woodchucks.
Plath.   Incommunicado.

Grouse
Montale.   Capercaillie, The.

Growth
Ashbery, J.   Boy, A.
    Grapevine, The.
    Spring Day.
    Young Son, The.
Berry, W.   Broken Ground, The.
    Familiar, The.
    Farmer among the Tombs, The.
    Seeds, The.
    Sycamore, The.
Browning, E.   Isobel's Child.
Clampitt.   Lindenbloom.
Cowper, W.   On a Plant of Virgin's Bower.
Cummings, E. E.   Am was. Are Leaves Few
    this. Is these a or.
    But also dying / (as well as).
    If everything happens that can't be done.
    Might these be thrushes climbing through
    almost(do they).
Dickinson, E.   Could you tell me how to grow.
    Growth of Man—like Growth of Nature.
    Her Sweet turn to leave the Homestead.
    I could not prove the Years had feet.
    Solemn thing within the Soul, A.
    We outgrow love like other things.
Dunbar, P.   Old Front Gate, The.
    Song: "My heart to thy heart."
Eberhart, R.   Cage, The.
    Forms of the Human.
    In after Time.
    Mind and Nature.
    Rumination.
    Stealth and Subtleties of Growth.
    Truncated Bird, The.
    What Gives.
Emerson, R.   Cloud upon cloud / The world is
    seeming.
    Coral worm beneath the sea, The.
    Go out into Nature and plant trees.
    Holidays.
    To Ellen, at the South.
    To every creature / Adam gave its name.
    What never was no, & still will be.
    Who saw the hid beginnings.
Gunn, T.   Aqueduct.
    Value of Gold, The.
Hall, D.   Exile.
Hardy, T.   Second Attempt, A.
Herbert, G.   Paradise.
Herrick.   To God.
Housman.   Loitering with a vacant eye.
Hughes, L.   For Russell and Rowena Jelliffe.
Jackson, L.   Growth.
Kipling, R.   'Eathen, The.
Levertov.   Her Lament.
    Scornful Reprieve.
Levine, P.   Pili's Wall.
    Winter Words.
Lorde.   Dear Toni instead of a Letter of
    Congratulation.
Lowell, R.   Growth (Harriet).
MacDiarmid, H.   To a Friend and Fellow Poet.
Major, C.   Giant Red Woman.

Meredith, W.   John and Anne.
    Roots.
Merwin.   Last One, The.
Montale.   Line of dancing children on the shore,
    The.
Nash, O.   Kitten, The.
Nemerov.   Mars.
O'Hara, F.   Cornkind.
    Poem: "There I could never be a boy."
Piercy.   Perpetual Migration, The.
Plath.   Mushrooms.
Raine, K.   Rose.
Rilke.   Child, The.
Roethke.   Cuttings.
Rukeyser, M.   He is breaking the nets in his
    wildness for the real.
    Hero Speech.
    Work in the loss of mass, The.
Sandburg, C.   Crabapple Blossoms.
    Follies.
    Laughing Corn.
    Loam.
    Out of the Rainbow End.
Tomlinson, C.   Witnesses, The.
Updike.   Planting Trees.
Whitman, W.   Return of the Heroes, The.
Wilbur, R.   Fern-Beds in Hampshire County.
    Seed Leaves.
    Wood, A.
Williams, C. K.   When / you were small, I.
Wordsworth, W.   Companion to the Foregoing
    [Love Lies Bleeding].
    My heart leaps up when I behold.
Wright, C.   Self-Portait.
Zukofsky, L.   Mountain Laurel.

Guadalajara, Mexico
Ashbery, J.   Instruction Manual, The.
Major, C.   Eighteen-Dollar Taxi Trip to Tizapan
    and Back to Chapala.
Williams, T.   Christus of Guadalajara, The.
Wright, J.   Homecoming.
    Morning: Leaving Calle Gigantes.

Guardia Civil
Arendt.   Hands, The.
García Lorca.   Ballad of the Spanish Civil
    Guard.
    Scene of the Lieutenant Colonel of the Civil
    Guard.
    Taking of Little Tony Camborio on the Seville
    Highway, The.

Guards
Amichai [*or* Amikhai].   I Guard the Children.
Borges.   Guardian of the Books, The.
Codrescu.   Partiti Sunt Vestimenta Mea Miserunt
    Sortem Contra Me ad Incarte Cla a Filii a
    Eniol Liebee Braya Braguesca et Belzebuth.
Jacobsen, J.   Night Watchman, The.
Logan, J.   Pathological Case in Pliny, A.
Lux.   Nazi at the Puppet Show, The.
Mistral, G.   Guardian Angel.
Stafford, W.   Star in the Hills, The.

Guatemala
Jacobsen, J.   Treaty.
Stevens, W.   Arrival at the Waldorf.
Williams, C. K.   Guatemala: 1964.

Guerrillas
Kipling, R.   Arithmetic on the Frontier.
    Ballad of Boh Da Thone, The.
    Grave of the Hundred Dead, The.
Wordsworth, W.   French and the Spanish
    Guerrillas, The.
    Spanish Guerillas 1811.

Guest, Edgar A
Nash, O.   Lines to a World-famous Poet Who
    Failed to Complete a World-famous Poem; or,
    Come Clean, Mr. Guest!

Guests
Berry, W.   Guest, The.
Berryman.   Mysteries, The.
Bishop, E.   House Guest.
Campion, T.   Ad Ge. Chapmannum.
De la Mare.   Feckless Dinner-Party, The.
Dickinson, E.   Infinite a sudden Guest, The.
Hall, D.   Wedding Party.
Jonson, B.   Inviting a Friend to Supper.

Logan, J. Concert Scene.
Nash, O. I Know Exactly Who Dropped the Overalls in Mrs. Murphy's Chowder.
Polterguest, My Polterguest.
There's Always an Ubblebub.
O'Hara, F. Poem: "Eager note on my door said 'Call me,' The."
Orr, G. After the Guest.
Patchen. Easy Decision, An.
Intimate Guest, The.
Riley, J. Law of the Perverse, The.
Parting Guest, A.
Proem to "Home-Folks."
Rumi. Guest House, The.
Sze. In Your Honor.
Yeats. Secret Rose, The.
Zaturenska. Uninvited Guest, The.
See also **Hospitality; Visiting and Visitors**
Guilt
Angelou. My Guilt.
Berry, W. Throwing away the Mail.
Bierce. Crime of 1903, The.
Brodsky, J. Bosnia Tune.
Burns, R. Penitential Thought, in the Hour of Remorse—Intended for a Tragedy, A.
Remorse.
Byron, G. Prayer of Nature, The.
Stanzas for Music.
Campion, T. *et al.* What harts content can he finde.
Carver, R. Company.
Lemonade.
Schooldesk, The.
Transformation.
Clampitt. Cormorant in Its Element, The.
Clough. In Stratis Viarum II.
Cooper, J. Messages.
Crashaw. To Pontius Washing His Hands.
Creeley. Teachings, The.
Cummings, E. E. Ballade: "Does something lie who'd rather stand."
Guilt is the cause of more disaulers.
It started when Bill's chip let on to.
Davie, D. Machineries of Shame.
Dickinson, E. These—saw Visions.
Dunbar, P. Debt, The.
Emerson, R. For that a man is a mark.
No fate, save by the victim's fault, is low.
Fenton, J. Vacant Possession, A.
Frost, R. Home Burial.
Gallagher, T. Small Garden Near a Field.
Ginsberg, A. Blame the Thought, Cling to the Bummer.
"Drive All Blames into One."
Graves, R. Blanket Charge.
Semi-Detached.
Trial of Innocence.
Gunn, T. High Fidelity.
Hall, D. By the Exeter River.
September Ode.
Hardy, T. Blow, The.
Brother, The.
Caricature, The.
Rake-hell Muses.
Vampirine Fair, The.
Herbert, G. Conscience.
Herrick. Blame.
Upon Paske a Draper.
Ignatow, D. Each of Us.
Jarrell, R. Bamberg.
Eighth Air Force.
Today is almost over.
Jeffers, R. Blood-Guilt, The.
Laughlin, J. In the Train.
Kind-, The.
Prisoner's Song, The.
Levertov. Visitant.
Levi, P. For Adolf Eichmann.
Survivor, The.
MacLeish. Carrion Crow, The.
Meredith, W. Effort at Speech.
Merrill, J. Renewal, A.
Merwin. Yesterday.
Milosz, C. Happenings Elsewhere.
Lessons.
Vipera Berus.

Nash, O. Down the Mousehole, and What Science Missed There.
Inter-Office Memorandum.
Strange Case of the Blackmailing Dove, The.
Neruda. Child of the Moon.
Danger, The.
Wars, The.
Oppen. Confession.
Orr, G. Gathering the Bones Together.
Pinkerton, H. Error Pursued.
Rich, A. Education of a Novelist.
Rape.
Upcountry.
Rossetti, C. Escape to the Mountain.
Surely there is an aching void within.
Weigh all my faults and follies righteously.
Rukeyser, M. Cannibal Bratuscha.
Song of Another Tribe, A.
Sandburg, C. Smoke.
Sarton, M. Tortured, The.
Who Wakes.
Sexton. Earth Falls Down, The.
Hex, The.
My Friend, My Friend.
Smith, S. Oh What Is the Thing He Done?
Spender, S. Double Shame, The.
Szymborska, W. Under a Certain Little Star.
Tate, J. Five Years Old.
I Take Back All My Kisses.
Very. Thy Brother's Blood.
Warren, R. Amazing Grace in the Back Country.
Crime.
Revelation.
Whitman, W. Of Many a Smutch'd Deed Reminiscent.
Wilbur, R. Peter.
Pity.
Williams, C. K. Another Dollar.
Blame.
Combat.
Image, The.
That night, / winter, / rain.
Williams, M. He Shuts His Eyes for the Layman's Long Prayer about Lust and the Mind of the Young Preacher Wanders Again.
Wright, C. California Spring.
Guitars
Brontë, E. Lady to Her Guitar, The.
Dickey, J. Rain Guitar, The.
Larkin, P. Two Guitar Pieces.
Riley, J. Her Light Guitar.
Old Guitar, The.
Stevens, W. Man with the Blue Guitar, The.
Gulls
Amichai [*or* Amikhai]. Sonnet from the Voyage.
Browning, E. Sea-Mew, The.
Ciardi, J. Gulls Land and Cease to Be.
Orders.
Coleridge, S. Looking Seaward.
Davie, D. Under St Paul's.
Eberhart, R. Gulled.
Hayden, R. Gulls.
Hughes, T. Tern.
Jeffers, R. Storm blowing up, rain and dark weather and the roaring wind, The.
MacLeish. Before March.
Mahon. Birdlife.
McGrath, T. Poem: "Through the fog / The gulls."
Meredith, W. Transport.
Nash, O. Sea-Gull, The.
Nemerov. Gulls, The.
Lives of Gulls and Children, The.
Niedecker. How white the gulls.
Olson, C. Pente cōst under the body of the gull flying directly over.
Sandburg, C. Harbor, The.
Sexton. Gull.
Smith, S. Numbers.
Tomlinson, C. Gull.
Updike. Seagulls.
Warren, R. Youth Stares at Minoan Sunset.
Wilbur, R. Two Songs in a Stanza of Beddoes'.
Williams, W. Gulls.

Song: "Black-winged gull, The."
Wright, J. Morality of Poetry, The.
Poem by Garnie Braxton, A.
Zukofsky, L. Gulls over a rotting hull.
Gum Trees
Frost, R. Gum-Gatherer, The.
Gunpowder Plot
See **Fawkes, Guy**
Guns
Ciardi, J. .22.
Two Songs for a Gunner.
Codrescu. First Icon with Gun, The.
License to Carry a Gun, The.
Cooper, J. Nightmare of the Suburbs, A.
Creeley. Two Times.
Cummings, E. E. Bigness of cannon, The.
Dickinson, E. My Life had stood—a Loaded Gun.
Dugan, A. Cop-Shooting: On a Newspaper Photograph.
Graves, R. Shot, The.
Hall, D. Merle Bascom's .22.
Hardy, T. Channel Firing.
Heaney, S. From the Frontier of Writing.
Housman. Shot? so quick, so clean an ending?
Kipling, R. Jacket, The.
Screw-Guns.
Snarleyow.
Komunyakaa. Le Xuan, Beautiful Spring.
Kunitz, S. Careless Love.
Lawrence, D. H. Murderous Weapons.
MacLeish. Hemingway.
Meredith, W. Battlewagon.
Merton. Guns of Fort Knox, The.
Merwin. Happens Every Day.
Milton. On the Inventor of Gunpowder.
Nemerov. September Shooting.
Niedecker. Shut up in woods.
Orr, G. Litany, A: "I remember him falling beside me."
Owen, W. Anthem for Doomed Youth.
Arms and the Boy.
Sonnet: "Be slowly lifted up, thou long black arm."
Pagis. Shot, The.
Ritsos. We Are Waiting.
Robinson, E. Richard Cory.
Sandburg, C. A. E. F.
Iron.
Long Guns.
Stafford, W. .38.
Warren, R. Orphanage Boy.
Weiss, T. Gunsight.
Whitman, W. Artilleryman's Vision, The.
Williams, C. K. Crime.
Wright, J. Echo for the Promise of Georg Trakl's Life.
Yeats. To a Squirrel at Kyle-Na-No.
Gustavus II (Gustavus Adolphus), King of Sweden
Carew, T. In Answer of an Elegiacal[l] Letter, Upon the Death of the King of Sweden.
Wordsworth, W. Call not the royal Swede unfortunate.
Guston, Phillip
Kunitz, S. Sea, That Has No Ending, The.
Guy Fawkes Day
See **Fawkes, Guy**
Guyana
Walcott. Guyana.
Gwyn, Nell
Williams, W. King!, The.
Gymnastics and Gymnasts
See **Acrobatics and Acrobats**
Gypsies
Baudelaire. Roving Gypsies.
Blok. Accordeon.
Broumas, O. Soothsaying.
Clare, J. Gipsies: "Gipsies seek wide sheltering woods again, The."
Emerson, R. Romany Girl, The.
García Lorca. Ballad of Black Pain.
Ballad of the Moon Moon.
Ballad of the Spanish Civil Guard.
Death of Little Tony Camborio, The.

Graphic of the Petenera.
Gypsy Nun, The.
Poem of the Gypsy *Siguiriya*.
Poem of the *Soleá*.
Preciosa and the Wind.
Scene of the Lieutenant Colonel of the Civil
   Guard.
Sleepwalking Ballad.
St. Gabriel.
Summer Madrigal.
Taking of Little Tony Camborio on the Seville
   Highway, The.
Unfaithful Wife, The.
Graves, R.   Batxóca.
Hughes, L.   Bad Luck Card.
  Ballad of the Gypsy.
  Gypsies.
Keats.   Meg Merrilies [*or* Merrilees].
Kipling, R.   Gipsy Trail, The.
Lawrence, D. H.   Gipsy.
Lenau.   Three Gipsies, The.
Lindsay, N.   I Know All This When Gipsy
  Fiddles Cry.
  Tramp's Refusal, The.
Mahon.   Gipsies.
Sandburg, C.   Fame If Not Fortune.
  Gypsy.
  Gypsy Mother.
Stafford, W.   Distractions.
Vogl.   Sweetheart of the Csikos, The.
  To an Old Gipsy.
Wordsworth, W.   Gypsies.
Wright, J.   Jason Visits His Gypsy.

H

"H. D." (Hilda Doolittle)
Davie, D.   H. D.
Habits
Atwood.   You take my hand and.
Beckett, S.   Vieil aller / vieux arrêts.
Clifton, L.   Dear Fox.
Creeley.   Mountains in the Desert, The.
  One Day.
  Operation, The.
Enzensberger, H.   Force of Habit, The.
Gallagher, T.   Sugar.
Graves, R.   Love Charms.
Herrick.   Upon Ralph.
  Upon Tubbs.
Merwin.   Habits.
Plath.   Love Letter.
Rumi.   My Worst Habit.
Hades
Baudelaire.   Don Juan in the Underworld.
Browning, E.   Psyche and Cerberus.
  Psyche and Proserpine.
Carruth, H.   None.
Cavafy.   Rest I Will Tell to Those below in
  Hades, The.
De la Mare.   Shade, The.
Herrick.   Orpheus and Pluto.
Jacobsen, J.   Pitch Lake.
Orr, G.   Entrance to the Underworld, The.
  Ghosts Listen to Orpheus Sing, The.
  When I was alive—only glimpses.
Raine, K.   Descent into Hades.
  These watery diamond spheres.
Rexroth, K.   Martial—12, 52.
Rukeyser, M.   In the Underworld.
Stock, R.   Aeneas Underground.
  Enigma of a Final Scene.
  Poet Mário Faustino Descends into Hades and
  Rises to the Empyrean.
Szymborska, W.   On the Banks of the Styx.
Unknown.   By Heraclides.
Williams, T.   Orpheus Descending.
Zagajewski.   Persephone.
Hafiz
Hafiz [*or* Hafez].   Friendship.
Haggis
Burns, R.   To a Haggis.
Haiku (form)
Collins, B.   Japan.

Kizer, C.   Month in Summer, A.
Milosz, C.   Reading the Japanese Poet Issa
  (1762–1826).
Wilbur, R.   Sleepless at Crown Point.
Hail
Cunningham, J.   August Hail.
Heaney, S.   Hailstones.
Hopkins, G.   Hailstorm in May.
Montale.   Is it salt that strafes or hail? It slays.
Williams, C. K.   Hail goes / dancing, The.
Zukofsky, L.   Rains, the rains, The.
Haile Selassie
Hughes, L.   Broadcast on Ethiopia.
  Emperor Haile Selassie.
Hair
Amichai [*or* Amikhai].   Ballad of the Washed
  Hair.
  Instead of Words.
  I've Grown Very Hairy.
  To My Love, Combing Her Hair.
Baudelaire.   Her Hair.
  Promise in a Pair of Eyes, The.
Bishop, E.   Shampoo, The.
Bly, R.   Conversation, A.
Bogan, L.   Medusa.
Broumas, O.   Body.
Bukowski.   Red Up and Down.
  Texan.
Burns, R.   Bonie Mary.
  Fragment: "Her flowing locks, the raven's
  wing."
Carver, R.   Haircut, A.
  Thermopylae.
Clifton, L.   Album.
Cowper, W.   Delia, th' unkindest girl on earth.
  To a Lady ["Star that beams on Anna's breast,
  The"].
Cummings, E. E.   Hair your a brook.
Dickey, W.   Pruned Roses, The.
Dickinson, E.   'Tis customary as we part.
Dove, R.   Nightmare.
Emerson, R.   And rival Coxcombs with
  enamored stare.
  Samson stark at Dagon's knee.
Enzensberger, H.   Fetish.
Gallagher, T.   Ever After.
Graves, R.   Snap-Comb Wilderness, The.
Gunn, T.   Skateboard.
HaNagid.   Black of My Hair, The.
Hardy, T.   Tresses, The.
Herrick.   Art above Nature, to Julia.
  Dew Sat on Julia's Hair.
  On Jone.
  Upon Blanch.
  Upon His Gray Haires.
  Upon Julia's Haire, Bundled up in a Golden
  Net.
Housman.   Oh who is that young sinner with the
  handcuffs on his wrists?
Ignatow, D.   Hair.
Laughlin, J.   Apsarases.
  Her Sweet Deceit.
  I Love the Way.
Lawrence, D. H.   So There!
Levertov.   Psalm Praising the Hair of Man's
  Body, A.
Lindsay, N.   To Lady Jane.
Lucilius.   On an Old Woman.
Mallarmé.   Flight of Flaming Hair, The.
McHugh, H.   Hag.
Montale.   Bangs, The.
Nash, O.   Electra Becomes Morbid.
  I'll Get One Tomorrow.
Nemerov.   History of Hair from World War II to
  the Present.
Niedecker.   Jim Poor's his name.
  There's a better shine.
Petrarch.   Gentle breeze that, through fresh
  greenery, The.
Piercy.   Hello Up There.
  Sign.
Pope, A.   Rape of the Lock, The; an Heroi-
  Comical Poem.
Rich, A.   Parting: II, The.
Riley, J.   Her Hair.
  Tress of Hair, A.

  When Mother Combed My Hair.
Rossetti, C.   Johnny.
Rukeyser, M.   Boy with His Hair Cut Short.
Sandburg, C.   Red-Headed Restaurant Cashier.
  Women Washing Their Hair.
Schuyler, J.   Suddenly.
Swinburne.   Kissing Her Hair.
Updike.   Klimt and Schiele Confront the Cunt.
Williams, T.   Sanctuary.
Williams, W.   Spring.
Yeats.   For Anne Gregory.
Haiti
Cullen, C.   Black Majesty.
Lux.   Haitian Cadavers.
Orr, G.   In Haiti [*or* Haitian Suite].
Whittier.   Toussaint L'Ouverture.
Halloween
Atwood.   Paper Bag, A.
Burns, R.   Halloween.
Clampitt.   Halloween Parade, The.
Cummings, E. E.   Hist whist / little ghostthings.
Dugan, A.   On Halloween.
Glück, L.   All Hallows.
Jacobsen, J.   Allhallows Party.
Komunyakaa.   Halloween, the Late Fifties.
Milosz, C.   All Hallows' Eve.
Piercy.   Hallow Eve with Spaces for Ghosts.
Prunty.   Wallace Stevens Remembers
  Halloween.
  Widow's Halloween, The.
Sandburg, C.   Theme in Yellow.
Hamilton, Alexander
Stockton, A.   Impromptu on Reading the Several
  Motions Made against Mr. Hamilton.
Hamlet
Bukowski.   Weather Report.
Cavafy.   King Claudius.
De la Mare.   Hamlet.
Dubie.   Elsinore in the Late Ancient Autumn.
Eberhart, R.   Broken Pen, The.
  Hamlet Father, The.
Lindsay, N.   Epitaphs for Two Players.
  Hamlet.
Nash, O.   Strange Case of the Lovelorn Letter
  Writer, The.
Nemerov.   Orphic Scenario.
Rimbaud, A.   Ophelia.
Sandburg, C.   They All Want to Play Hamlet.
Smith, S.   Easy.
Hammers and Hammering
Bogan, L.   Roman Fountain.
Creeley.   For Fear.
Dugan, A.   Repealer, The: "You're Too Wild."
Ignatow, D.   Now I Hear.
  Two.
Merwin.   Tool.
Michelangelo Buonarroti.   If my rough hammer
  shapes the obdurate stone.
Pinsky.   Ghost Hammer, The.
Rilke.   Autumn Hammer.
Warren, R.   Waking to Tap of Hammer.
Wilbur, R.   Folk Tune.
Hammocks
Davie, D.   Amazonian.
Riley, J.   In the Afternoon.
Handicaps and the Handicapped
Chuang Tzu.   Man with One Foot and the Marsh
  Pheasant, The.
Donne.   Lame Beggar, A.
Herrick.   Upon Truggin.
Kinsella, T.   Departure Platforms.
Levertov.   Too Much to Hope.
Owen, W.   Disabled.
Patchen.   Poor Child with the Hooked Hands,
  The.
Ramanujan.   Compensations.
Riley, J.   Little Lame Boy's Views, A.
Simic.   Great Infirmities.
Thomas, D.   Hunchback in the Park, The.
Williams, C. K.   Hooks.
Wordsworth, W.   Idiot Boy, The.
See also **Amputees; Birth Defects; Blindness;**
  Cripples; Deafness; Mental Retardation
Hands
Arendt.   Hands, The.

Atwood. You Begin.
Auden. Hands.
Berry, W. Current, The.
Bogan, L. Heard by a Girl.
Broumas, O. Dactyls.
Carver, R. For the Egyptian Coin Today, Arden, Thank You.
Jungle, The.
Letter.
Ciardi, J. Manocalzata (Gloved Hand).
Clifton, L. Wild Blessings.
Crane, H. Episode of Hands.
Creeley. Box, The.
Dimensions.
Figures, The.
For Friendship.
In an Act of Pity.
Medallion.
People, The.
Tally, A.
You ("Back and forth across").
Davie, D. Hot Hands.
Dickinson, E. Caterpillar.
Duncan, R. Upon Taking Hold.
Eberhart, R. Hand and the Shadow, The.
Hand, The.
Ferlinghetti, L. At the *Gare Bruxelles-Midi*.
Gallagher, T. Meeting, The.
Some with Wings, Some with Manes.
Gunn, T. Feel of Hands, The.
Man with Night Sweats, The.
Hall, D. Second Stanza, A.
Heaney, S. August Night, An.
Herrick. Hand and Tongue, The.
Right Hand, The.
Housman. As Through the Wild Green Hills of Wyre.
Ignatow, D. Mystique.
Jackson, L. Take Hands.
Jeffers, R. Hand.
Hands.
Johnson, S. Ballad: "I put my hat upon my head."
Keats. This Living Hand, Now Warm and Capable.
Laughlin, J. Hand Trick, The.
Holy Rivers, The.
Levine, P. Fist.
Lorde. Pirouette.
McGrath, T. Praises IV.
McHugh, H. Constructive.
Prothalamion.
Merwin. Apparitions.
Dead Hand.
Gardens of Zuñi, The.
Hands, The.
Span.
Surf-Casting.
Orr, G. Hand, The: "Brightness Falls from the Air."
Overtaken by Fog while Climbing.
Parker, D. Iseult of Brittany.
Patchen. There is the hand that has nothing attached to it, no arm no chest.
Petrarch. O lovely hand, clutched tightly round my heart.
Piercy. Friend, The.
Riley, J. At Madame Manicure's.
Dear Hands.
Her Beautiful Hands.
One Angel.
Reach Your Hand to Me.
Touch of Loving Hands, The.
With Her Face.
Rimbaud, A. Hands of Jeanne-Marie, The.
Ritsos. Danger Outstripped.
Hands.
Morning in Salerno 4.
Multidimensional.
One-Armed Man, The.
Rossetti, C. Twice.
Rumi. Birdwings.
Sandburg, C. White Hands.
Sexton. Maiden without Hands, The.
Touch, The.
Two Hands.

When the Glass of My Body Broke.
Shapiro, K. Love for a Hand.
Simic. Bestiary for the Fingers of My Right Hand.
Smith, S. Ceci est digne de gens sans dieu.
Snyder, G. After Work.
Stafford, W. My Hands.
Turn over Your Hand.
Witness.
Swenson, M. I Look at My Hand.
Sze. Black Lightning.
Thomas, D. Hand That Signed the Paper, The.
Tomlinson, C. Palm of the Hand.
Updike. Calder's Hands.
Wilbur, R. Good Servant, The.
Williams, C. K. Hooks.
Other Side, The.
Williams, M. On the Symbolic Consideration of Hands and the Significance of Death.
Wright, J. Red Jacket's Grave.
Yeats. Balloon of the Mind, The.
Zukofsky, L. Glad they were there.

Handwriting
Milosz, C. Sentences.
Nemerov. Writing.

Hanging
Ai. Hangman.
Ammons. Ritual for Eating the World.
Angelou. We Saw beyond Our Seeming.
Atwood. Marrying the Hangman.
Bishop, E. Hanging of the Mouse, The.
Burns, R. Macpherson's Farewell.
Cavafy. 27 June 1906, 2 P.M.
Eberhart, R. Snowy Owl.
Herrick. Upon Letcher: Epigram.
Housman. Carpenter's Son, The.
Culprit, The.
Eight o'Clock.
On moonlit heath and lonesome bank.
Kipling, R. Danny Deever.
Komunyakaa. Articulation & Class.
Chair Gallows.
Reflections.
Levine, P. L'Homme et La Bête.
Logan, J. Death of Southwell, The.
Logue, C. Lullaby.
MacLeish. Galán.
Melville, H. Portent, The.
Millay, E. Hangman's Oak.
Parker, D. Cherry White.
Résumé.
Plath. Hanging Man, The.
Rimbaud, A. Hanged Men Dance.
Ritsos. Question: "Man fades at the distant end of the street, A."
Undressing of the Hanged Man, The.
Sandburg, C. Hangman at Home, The.
Smith, S. Hostage, The.
Swift, J. Clever Tom Clinch Going to Be Hanged.
Unknown. Geordie [An Old Ballad].
Warren, R. Ballad of Mister Dutcher and the Last Lynching in Gupton.
Wilde, O. Ballad of Reading Gaol, The.
Williams, M. At Three Every Thursday Afternoon.
See also **Executions and Executioners; Lynching**

Hangovers
Burns, R. To William Stewart.
Wright, J. Two Hangovers.

Hansel and Gretel
Glück, L. Gretel in Darkness.
Jarrell, R. Quilt-Pattern, A.
McGrath, T. Remembering the Children of Auschwitz.
Sexton. Hansel and Gretel.

Hanukkah
Amichai [*or* Amikhai]. My Friend the Philosopher and Hanukah.

Happiness
Amichai [*or* Amikhai]. Hamadiya, Memory of Bliss.
I Sat in the Happiness.
Like the Streams in the Negev.
On the Wide Stairs—Lurking for Happiness.

Surplus of Flowers in the World.
Atwood. You Are Happy.
Auden. Detective Story.
Blok. Worlds Fly Past.
Borges. Happiness.
Remorse.
Brontë, E. How still, how happy! These [*or* Those] are words.
Broumas, O. Triple Muse.
Browning, R. At the "Mermaid."
Bukowski. Skaters, The.
Burns, R. First Psalm, The.
Guid Ale Keeps the Heart Aboon.
My Eppie.
Song: "My father was a farmer upon the Carrick border O."
Young Jockey was the blythest lad.
Byron, G. Well! Thou Art Happy.
Carew, T. Second Rapture, The.
To My Cousin (C.R.) Marrying My Lady (A.).
Carver, R. After Reading *Two Towns in Provence*.
Don't Run.
For Tess.
Happiness.
Happiness in Cornwall.
Highway 99E from Chico.
My Work.
Party, The.
Poem I Didn't Write, The.
Yesterday.
Chuang Tzu. Joy of Fishes, The.
Ciardi, J. Happiness.
Clare, J. Old Man, The.
Coleridge, S. Angel Visitant, An.
Happy Husband, The.
Homeless.
To Asra.
Cowper, W. Poet's New-Year's Gift, The.
Creeley. Air: "The Love of a Woman."
For Betsy and Tom.
For Joel.
For Pen ("Last day of year").
Heaven ("If life were easy").
If Happiness.
Indians.
Je Vois dans le Hasard Tous les Biens Que J'espere.
Lady Bird.
Later ("It feels things")
Reflections.
Soup ("Trembling / with delight").
Cullen, C. One Day We Played a Game.
Spring Reminiscence.
Cummings, E. E. I am so glad and very.
Out of more find than seeks.
You Shall above All Things Be Glad and Young.
Davie, D. Thomas and Emma.
Utterings.
De la Mare. I Sit Alone.
Self to self.
Dickinson, E. Accept my timid happiness.
By Chivalries as tiny.
Enough is so vast a sweetness.
Good times are always mutual.
"Happiness" without a cause, The.
I fear you have much happiness.
I had a daily Bliss.
She's happy, with a new Content.
Such is the Force of Happiness.
Dove, R. Pearls.
Du Bellay. Happy the Man.
Dunbar, P. Love Letter, A.
Eberhart, R. Adam Cast Forth.
Emerson, R. O sun! take off thy hood of clouds.
Ferlinghetti, L. 21.
Frost, R. Happiness Makes Up in Height for What It Lacks in Length.
Ginsberg, A. Scribble.
Today.
Glück, L. Happiness.
Letter from our Man in Blossomtime.
Graves, R. As When the Mystic.
Everywhere Is Here.

"H. D."   White World.
Hacker, M.   Late August Letter.
Hardy, T.   Occultation, The.
Hayden, R.   Islands, The.
Herrick.   Anacreontike.
  Felicitie Knowes No Fence.
  Felicity, Quick of Flight.
  Few Fortunate.
  Four[e] Things Make Us Happy Here.
  Happinesse.
  None Truly Happy Here.
Hughes, L.   Dream Boogie.
  Heaven.
Ivanov, G.   Affair was badly flawed, The.
  That pointless happiness, was it worth it?
Jackson, L.   Meanwhile.
Jacobsen, J.   Colloquy.
Jarrell, R.   Happy Cat, The.
Kinnell.   Running on Silk.
Kizer, C.   Afternoon Happiness.
Komunyakaa.   Happiness.
Larkin, P.   High Windows.
Lawrence, D. H.   Bat.
  Wedlock.
Levertov.   Joy.
  Libation.
  Of Being.
Levi, P.   Landing.
Levine, P.   Starlight.
Lindsay, N.   Sunshine.
Logue, C.   Epitaph: "I am old."
Lux.   Amiel's Leg.
MacDiarmid, H.   To Hell wi' Happiness!
Marlowe.   Passionate Shepherd to His Love,
  The.
Meredith, G.   J. C. M.
  Joy is Fleet.
Merton.   All of the branches / None of the roots.
Milosz, C.   Awakened.
  Gift.
  Hour, An.
Milton.   L'Allegro.
Montale.   Happiness achieved, for you.
Neruda.   Possessions.
Niedecker.   Why can't I be happy.
Oliver, M.   Goldfinches.
  Happiness.
  Hummingbird Pauses at the Trumpet Vine.
  Morning Poem.
  Poppies.
  Sunrise.
Oppen.   Theological Definition, A.
Owen, W.   Happiness.
Palmer, M.   Notes for Echo Lake 2.
Parker, D.   Comment.
  Lady's Reward, The.
  Song: "And shall we build a little nest."
Patchen.   What There Is.
Petrarch.   More happily than I no ship has ever.
Piercy.   Apologies.
Pinsky.   Sadness and Happiness.
Poe.   Dreams.
Pope, A.   Ode on Solitude.
  Version of the First Psalm, for the Use of a
    Young Lady, A.
Pound, E.   Salutation.
Raine, K.   Leaf, The.
  Oval Portrait: Jessie Wilkie, The.
Rexroth, K.   For Eli Jacobson.
Rich, A.   In the Woods.
Riley, J.   On Any Ordenary Man in a High State
  of Laughture and Delight.
  To a Boy Whistling.
Rilke.   Happy Men and Women.
  To Madame the Baronness Renée De Brimont.
Rimbaud, A.   O seasons, o châteaux.
  Sensation.
Ritsos.   Probabilities.
Robinson, E.   Cliff Klingenhagen.
Roethke.   Waking, The.
Rossetti, C.   Dancing on the hill-tops, / Singing
  in the valleys.
  I toiled on, but thou.
  In resurrection is it awfuller.
  Love is all happiness, love is all beauty.
  Trees' Counselling, The.

Will you be there? my yearning heart has cried.
  Young Death.
Rukeyser, M.   Chapultepec Park / I.
Rumi.   Sublime Generosity.
Sandburg, C.   Fellow Citizens.
  Happiness.
  Shag-Bark Hickory.
  Snatch of Sliphorn Jazz.
  Two Neighbors.
Shelley, P.   Past, The.
  Song: "Rarely, rarely, comest thou."
Smith, S.   And the Clouds Return after the Rain.
  Conviction IV.
  Happiness.
  Is It Happy?
  Mother.
  V.
Stafford, W.   Gift, The.
  Once in the 40s.
  Why I Am Happy.
Stockton, A.   Sweet Mariana gentle maid adieu.
  Wish to Miss Hannah Stockton, The.
Thomson, J.   Upon Happiness.
Tomlinson, C.   Jubilación.
Unknown.   Another of the Same Nature, Made
  Since.
  To Health.
Updike.   Pale Bliss.
Vallejo.   White Rose.
Walker, A.   Mississippi Winter II.
Warren, R.   Last Walk of Season.
  Unless.
  Weather Report.
Whalen, P.   How to Be Successful & Happy
  Without Anybody Else Finding Out about It.
  One of My Favorite Songs Is Stormy Weather.
Whitman, W.   Halcyon Days.
  Song of Joys, A.
  When I Heard at the Close of the Day.
Wilbur, R.   Wedding Toast, A.
Williams, M.   Jonathan Happy.
Williams, W.   Thinker, The.
Wordsworth, W.   These Chairs they have no
  words to utter.
Wright, J.   Blessing, A.
  Moon.
  Northern Pike.
  Today I Was So Happy, So I Made this Poem.
  Way to Make a Living, A.
Zukofsky, L.   Marriage Song for Florence and
  Harry, A.

See also **Contentment**

Harbors and Ports
  Amichai [*or* Amikhai].   So I Went Down to the
    Ancient Harbor.
  Cavafy.   In the Port.
  Dickinson, E.   To multiply the Harbors.
  Hardy, T.   Harbour Bridge, The.
    Marble-Streeted Town, The.
  Hughes, L.   Fog.
  Jarrell, R.   Metamorphoses, The.
  Merwin.   Port, The.
    Some of the Masts.
  Montale.   Dora Markus.
  O'Hara, F.   Blocks.
  Olson, C.   Intended Angle of Vision Is from My
    Kitchen, The.
  Oppen.   Belvedere.
    Men of Sheepshead, The.
  Plath.   Green Rock, Winthrop Bay.
  Ritsos.   Calm.
  Rukeyser, M.   Formosa.
    Wind arrow, wind rose, the wind currents in air.
  Sandburg, C.   Destroyers.
    Docks.
    Harbor, The.
  Tate, J.   Glassy Harbor, The.
  Tomlinson, C.   Arrival, The.
    Sconset.
  Walcott.   Harbour, The.
  Zukofsky, L.   Heights, The.
Hardin, John Wesley
  Carver, R.   Wes Hardin: From a Photograph.
Harding, Warren Gamaliel
  Ashbery, J.   Qualm.
  Cummings, E. E.   First president to be loved by

  his, The.
  O'Hara, F.   Poem: "That's not a cross look it's a
    sign of life."
  Wright, J.   Two Poems about President Harding.
Hardy, Thomas
  Cooper, J.   For Thomas Hardy.
  De la Mare.   Thomas Hardy.
  Dubie.   Thomas Hardy.
  Heaney, S.   Birthplace, The.
  Lawrence, D. H.   And Jude the Obscure and His
    Beloved.
  Tomlinson, C.   In Memoriam Thomas Hardy.
  Walcott.   Love in the Valley.
  Warren, R.   Literal Dream.
  Wright, J.   At Thomas Hardy's Birthplace, 1953.
Hares
  Burns, R.   On Seeing a Wounded Hare Limp by
    Me, Which a Fellow Had Just Shot At.
  Cowper, W.   Epitaph on a Hare.
    Epitaphium Alterum.
  De la Mare.   Hare, A.
  Enzensberger, H.   Hare in the Data Processing
    Centre, A.
  Hughes, T.   Hare, The.
  MacDiarmid, H.   Ross-shire Hills, The.
  Smart, C.   To the Rev. Mr. Powell.
  Unknown.   Names of the Hare, The.
  Yeats.   Two Songs of a Fool.
See also **Rabbits**
Harlem, New York City
  Angelou.   Harlem Hopscotch.
  Clampitt.   Sed de Correr.
  García Lorca.   King of Harlem, The.
  Hughes, L.   125th Street.
    Aesthete [*or* Esthete] in Harlem.
    Air Raid over Harlem.
    Ballad of Margie Polite, The.
    Broadcast to the West Indies.
    College Formal: Renaissance Casino.
    Death in Harlem.
    Dimout in Harlem.
    Disillusion.
    Dive.
    Harlem Dance Hall.
    Harlem ("Here on the edge of hell").
    Harlem Night.
    Harlem Night Club.
    Harlem Night Song.
    Harlem Sweeties.
    Heart of Harlem, The.
    Hope for Harlem.
    Jazzonia.
    Juke Box Love Song.
    Lenox Avenue Bar.
    Lenox Avenue: Midnight.
    Likewise.
    Movies.
    Negro Servant.
    Night Funeral in Harlem.
    Not a Movie.
    Passing.
    Prime.
    Projection.
    Reverie on the Harlem River.
    Stars.
    Summer Night.
    Theme for English B.
    Visitors to the Black Belt.
    Weary Blues, The.
    Young Prostitute.
    Young Singer.
  Merton.   Aubade—Harlem.
  Rukeyser, M.   Ballad of Orange and Grape.
  Schuyler, J.   Mood Indigo.
  Updike.   Eurydice.
Harper's Ferry, West Virginia
  Sandburg, C.   Landscape Including Three States
    of the Union.
Harps and Harpists
  Brontë, E.   Harp of wild and dream-like strain.
  Coleridge, S.   Ad Lyram.
    Snow-Drop, The.
  Dunbar, P.   Master-Player, The.
    To a Lady Playing the Harp.
  Eberhart, R.   Play, The.

Emerson, R.   He loved to watch & wake.
Lindsay, N.   Harps in Heaven.
Melville, H.   Aeolian Harp, The.
Merwin.   Old Boast, The.
Millay, E.   Ballad of the Harp-Weaver, The.
Orr, G.   Lament: "I thought of you."
Pinkerton, H.   On an Early Cycladic Harpist (2500 B.C.) in the Archaeological Museum in Athens.
On an Early Cycladic Harpist (2600-2500 B.C.) in the J. Paul Getty Museum.
Riley, J.   Bryant.
Harp of the Minstrel, The.
Harper, The.
Rumi.   Omar and the Old Poet.
Smart, C.   Inscriptions on an Aeolian Harp.
Williams, T.   Harp of Wales, The.
Wordsworth, W.   On Seeing a Needlecase in the Form of a Harp; the Work of E.M.S.

Harrison, Benjamin
Riley, J.   Benjamin Harrison.
Mrs. Benjamin Harrison.
Tribute of His Home, The.

Hartford, Connecticut
Stevens, W.   Of Hartford in a Purple Light.

Harvard University
Cummings, E. E.   Little joe gould has lost his teeth and doesn't know where.
Eberhart, R.   I Went to See Irving Babbitt.
Sanders Theater.
Heaney, S.   Villanelle for an Anniversary.
Moore, M.   In Lieu of the Lyre.
Nash, O.   Mind of Professor Primrose, The.
Updike.   Apologies to Harvard.
Widener Library, Reading Room.
Within a Quad.
Wheatley, P.   To the University of Cambridge, in New-England.
Wright, J.   W. E. B. DuBois at Harvard.

Harvest
Atwood.   November.
Auden.   As I Walked Out One Evening.
Blue Cloud.   Sweet Corn.
Bly, R.   Dawn in Threshing Time.
Carruth, H.   Emergency Haying.
Clampitt.   Olive Groves of Thasos, The.
Stacking the Straw.
De la Mare.   Scarecrow, The.
Glück, L.   All Hallows.
Heaney, S.   Blackberry-Picking.
Harvest Bow, The.
Wife's Tale, The.
Herrick.   Hock-Cart, or Harvest Home, The.
Upon Nodes.
Hopkins, G.   Hurrahing in Harvest.
Kumin, M.   After the Harvest.
July, against Hunger.
Lawrence, D. H.   Youth Mowing, A.
Longfellow, H.   Aftermath.
Melville, H.   Trophies of Peace.
Meredith, G.   Desired as Summer rain.
Song: "My chosen bride shall bless the plough."
Merwin.   Silence before Harvest, The.
Nash, O.   Not Even for Brunch.
Nemerov.   Harvest Home, A.
Pagis.   Harvests.
Pinkerton, H.   On Breughel the Elder's The Harvesters (1565) in the Metropolitan Museum.
Prunty.   Vegetable Garden, The.
Riley, J.   Autumn.
Full Harvest, A.
How John Quit the Farm.
Rossetti, C.   Amen.
For All.
For Each.
Rogationtide.
Seasons.
When My Heart Is Vexed I Will Complain.
Yea, I Have a Goodly Heritage.
Sandburg, C.   Corn Hut Talk.
Harvest.
You Shall Have Homes.
Sarton, M.   Prothalamion.
Swinburne.   August.
Sze.   Brueghel.

Thoreau.   Moon now rises to her absolute rule, The.
On fields oer which the reaper's hand has passed.
Tomlinson, C.   Harvest.
Harvest Festival: at Ozleworth.
Picking Mushrooms by Moonlight.
Very.   Forsaken Harvest Field, The.
Harvest, The ("Plant it springs it rears its drooping head, The").
Warren, R.   Alf Burt, Tenant Farmer.
August Revival: Crosby Junction.
Prairie Harvest.
Wild Oats.
Whittier.   Huskers, The.
Wilde, O.   Vita Nuova.
Wordsworth, W.   Solitary Reaper, The.
Wright, J.   In Fear of Harvests.

Hashish
Whittier.   Haschish, The.

Hasidism
Pagis.   Bridgehead Photograph.

Hate
Amichai [or Amikhai].   Half the People in the World.
Sort of an Apocalypse.
Ammons.   Making Waves.
Angelou.   Artful Pose.
Faces.
Auden.   There Will Be No Peace.
Baudelaire.   Cask of Hate, The.
Mortal Combat.
Berry, W.   Morning's News, The.
Blok.   To My Friends.
Blue Cloud.   Tomorrow.
Browning, R.   Halbert and Hob.
Soliloquy of the Spanish Cloister.
Bukowski.   Genius of the Crowd, The.
Chesterton.   World State, The.
Ciardi, J.   My Tribe.
Clifton, L.   Jasper Texas 1998.
Crashaw.   But Now They Have Seen, and Hated.
Creeley.   Crow, The.
Self-Portrait.
Cullen, C.   Apostrophe to the Land.
Black Christ, The.
Dickinson, E.   I had no time to Hate.
Dugan, A.   Nostalgia for a Language.
Dunbar, P.   To an Ingrate.
Eberhart, R.   Assassin, The.
Hatred of the Old River.
Frost, R.   Beyond Words.
Fire and Ice.
"H. D."   Epigrams.
Hopkins, G.   Love me as I love thee. O double sweet!
Housman.   In My Own Shire.
When I Watch the Living Meet.
Jackson, L.   Throe of Apocalypse.
Jeffers, R.   Bird with the Dark Plumes, The.
Jonson, B.   Little Shrub Growing By, A.
Kipling, R.   Beginnings, The.
Jubal and Tubal Cain.
Poison of Asps.
Lawrence, D. H.   Both Sides of the Medal.
Can't Be Borne.
Dead People.
Eloi, Eloi, Lama Sabachthani?
History.
Love.
Repulsed.
Lux.   People of the Other Village, The.
MacNeice.   Belfast.
McHugh, H.   Against a Dark Field.
Millay, E.   Blight.
Nash, O.   One Night in Oz.
O'Hara, F.   Poem: "Hate is only one of many responses."
Spleen.
Olson, C.   Fable for Slumber.
Hate.
Leader, The.
Poemless Rhymes for the Times.
Parker, D.   Actors; A Hate Song.
Actresses; A Hate Song.

Bohemians; A Hate Song.
Books; A Hymn of Hate.
Bores; A Hymn of Hate.
College Boys; A Hymn of Hate.
Drama, The; A Hymn of Hate.
Husbands; A Hymn of Hate.
Men; A Hate Song.
Movies; A Hymn of Hate.
Our Office; An Intimate Glimpse of Vanity Fair—En Famille a Hate Song.
Parties; A Hymn of Hate.
Relatives; A Hate Song.
Slackers; A Hymn of Hate.
Summer Resorts; A Hymn of Hate.
Wives; A Hymn of Hate.
Women; A Hate Song.
Younger Set, The; A Hymn of Hate.
Patchen.   Don't Wash Your Hair in the Streetcar, Nora Dear.
Piercy.   Letter to be Disguised as a Gas Bill.
Rape Poem.
Plath.   Daddy.
Robinson, E.   Avon's Harvest.
Roethke.   Lull.
Sandburg, C.   Hate.
Man, the Man-Hunter.
Sexton.   Children, The.
Shelley, P.   Hate-Song, A.
Lines to a Critic.
Smith, S.   I HATE THIS GIRL.
Suckling, S.   Barley-Break, A.
Love Turned to Hatred.
Szymborska, W.   Hatred.
Walker, A.   First, They Said.
January 10, 1973.
Williams, C. K.   Beyond.
In the Heart of the Beast.
Poor Hope.
Williams, W.   Love Poem, A: "Basic hatred / sometimes has a flower."
Mistrust of the Beloved.
Wright, J.   In the Face of Hatred.
Wyatt, S.   Such is the course that nature's kind hath wrought.
Varium et Mutabile.
Zukofsky, L.   Old.

Hats
Bishop, E.   Exchanging Hats.
Manuelzinho.
Burns, R.   Cock up Your Beaver.
To a Louse [On Seeing One on a Lady's Bonnet at Church].
Codrescu.   Casting.
Collins, B.   Candle Hat.
Death of the Hat, The.
Dove, R.   Headdress.
Dugan, A.   On Hat: On Vertical Mobility as a Concept.
Emerson, R.   Comfort with a purring cat.
Hall, D.   Second Stanza, A.
Hardy, T.   In the Days of Crinoline.
Herrick.   Upon Shift.
Johnson, S.   Ballad: "I put my hat upon my head."
Nash, O.   Drop of a Hat, The.
Nemerov.   Enthusiasm for Hats.
Orr, G.   Hats, The.
Sandburg, C.   Hats.
Quotations.
Sky Pieces.
Schuyler, J.   Hats.
Seifert.   Mr Krösing's Top Hat.
Smith, S.   Hat, The.
Magna Est Veritas.
My Hat.
Stafford, W.   Visit Home, A.
Tate, J.   List of Famous Hats, The.

Haunted Houses
De la Mare.   Feckless Dinner-Party, The.
Who's that?
Donne.   Apparition, The.
Frost, R.   Ghost House.
Graves, R.   Country Mansion, A.
Haunted House, The.
Hardy, T.   Strange House, The.
Hill, G.   Asmodai.

Havana, Cuba

Muldoon, P.   Big House, The.
Neruda.   Untenable Situation, An.
Parker, D.   I Know I Have Been Happiest.
Riley, J.   When de Folks Is Gone.

Havana, Cuba

Crane, H.   Eternity.
Ginsberg, A.   Havana 1953.
Hughes, L.   Havana Dreams.
   To the Little Fort of San Lazaro on the Ocean
   Front, Havana.
Stevens, W.   Academic Discourse at Havana.

Hawaii

Berryman.   Song of the Young Hawaiian, The.
Dickey, W.   Heroine, The.
Ginsberg, A.   Slack Key Guitar.
Logan, J.   Honolulu and Back.
   Middle-Aged Midwesterner at Waikiki Again.
   Poem for My Friend Peter at Pihana.
   Return to the Island.
   Visit to Bill Merwin at His Hawaiian Home, A.
Meredith, W.   Account of a Visit to Hawaii, An.
Merwin.   Questions to Tourists Stopped by a
   Pineapple Field.
   Sea Cliffs at Kailua in December, The.
Sze.   Keokea.
Updike.   Heading for Nandi.

Hawks

Ammons.   Anxiety.
Atwood.   Marsh, Hawk.
Brodsky, J.   Hawk's Cry in Autumn, The.
Ciardi, J.   Hawk.
"Dario."   Anagke.
Eberhart, R.   Forgotten Rock, The.
Gunn, T.   Tamer and Hawk.
Hopkins, G.   Windhover, The.
Hughes, T.   Hawk Roosting.
Jeffers, R.   Hurt Hawks.
   Old half blinded hawk—but how can he hunt
   with only one eye?—, The.
   Rock and Hawk.
Jonson, B.   To Sir Henry Goodyere.
MacLeish.   Poem for the Time of Change.
Oliver, M.   Hawk.
Oppen.   Technologies.
   Workman.
Pagis.   Harvests.
Pinkerton, H.   Red-Tailed Hawk.
Stafford, W.   Epitaph Ending in And, The.
Stock, R.   Errant Mole and the Loveliest of
   Hawks, The.
Thomas, D.   Over Sir John's Hill.
Thoreau.   To a Marsh Hawk in Spring.
Tomlinson, C.   Carrara Revisited.
   Hawks.
   How Still the Hawk.
Warren, R.   Evening Hawk.
   Mortal Limit.
   Problem in Spatial Composition, A.
   Red-Tail Hawk and Pyre of Youth.
Yeats.   Hawk, The.

Hawthorn (botany)

Heaney, S.   Haw Lantern, The.
Jarrell, R.   Trees in Spring, The.
Raine, K.   Frost-rime edges blades of grass.
Swift, J.   On Cutting Down the Old Thorn at
   Market Hill.
Tomlinson, C.   Hawthorn in Trent Vale, The.
   Providence.

Hawthorne, Nathaniel

Creeley.   Nathaniel Hawthorne.
Longfellow, H.   Hawthorne.
Lowell, R.   Hawthorne.
Melville, H.   Monody.
Thoreau.   But now "no war nor battle's sound."
Walcott.   Love in the Valley.

Hay and Haymaking

Clampitt.   Stacking the Straw.
Corbett, W.   Haying.
Dickinson, E.   I'm sorry for the Dead—Today.
Gunn, T.   At the Back of the North Wind.
Hall, D.   Table, The.
Heaney, S.   Fodder.
Kumin, M.   July, against Hunger.
MacLeish.   Where the Hayfields Were.
Meredith, G.   Windy Haymaking.

Muldoon, P.   Hay.
Prunty.   Haying.
Riley, J.   Old Haymow, The.
   That Other Maud Miller.
Stafford, W.   Haycutters.
Swenson, M.   Haymaking.
Tomlinson, C.   Harvest.
   Hay.
Wright, J.   Lament for My Brother on a
   Hayrake.

Haydn, Franz Joseph

Levertov.   Mystery of Deep Candor, The.

Haydon, Benjamin Robert

Browning, E.   On a Portrait of Wordsworth by
   B. R. Haydon.
Keats.   Great Spirits Now on Earth.
   To B.R. Haydon, with a Sonnet Written on
   Seeing the Elgin Marbles.
Wordsworth, W.   To B. R. Haydon.
   To B.R. Haydon, on Seeing His Picture of
   Napoleon Buonaparte.

Haymaking

See **Hay and Haymaking**

Haze

Enzensberger, H.   Shore.

See also **Fog**

Hazlitt, William

Coleridge, S.   W. H. *Eheu!*
Gurney, I.   Hazlitt.

Heads

Bradstreet, A.   Letter to Her Husband, Absent
   upon Public[k] Employment, A.
Bukowski.   12:18 A.M.
   Big Bastard with a Sword.
   Sword, The.
Eberhart, R.   Dream Journey of the Head and
   Heart.
Hall, D.   Second Stanza, A.
Herrick.   Head-Ake, The.
Hughes, T.   Reckless Head.
Jackson, L.   Pride of Head.
Johnson, S.   Ballad: "I put my hat upon my
   head."
Logan, J.   Dream, The: A Reflection on Morris
   Graves's Paintings.
Lux.   Men with Small Heads.
Major, C.   Balance and Beauty.
Meredith, W.   Thoughts on One's Head (In
   Plaster, with a Bronze Wash).
Pope, A.   Another [Epigram].
Sandburg, C.   Head.
Schuyler, J.   Head, A.

Healing

Amichai [*or* Amikhai].   Love Poem: "People use
   each other."
   NYU.
Ammons.   Yucca Moth, The.
Broumas, O.   Etymology.
Carver, R.   Where Water Comes Together with
   Other Water.
Ciardi, J.   Elegy 1: "I fell from the bouncing
   tailgate to roll in traffic."
   Stone without Edges Has Not Been Mined, The.
Faiz.   Bangla Desh: 2.
Jacobsen, J.   Chosen, The.
Komunyakaa.   Faith Healer.
   Safe Subjects.
   Surgery.
Logan, J.   Grace.
Lux.   Impingement Sydrome.
Meredith, W.   Grace.
Merwin.   Sickness at the Equinox, A.
Parker, D.   False Friends, The.
   Healed.
   Triolet: "Give back the heart that I gave."
Simic.   Healer, The.
Walker, A.   Remember?
Warren, R.   Lord Jesus, I Wonder.
Wheatley, P.   To a Gentleman on His Voyage to
   Great-Britain for the Recovery of His Health.

Health Clubs

Gunn, T.   To the Dead Owner of a Gym.

Heaney, Seamus

Davie, D.   Summer Lightning.

Heart Attacks

Dugan, A.   Heart Attack in Bad Air.

Hearts

Amichai [*or* Amikhai].   Heart Is a Corrupt Stage
   Director, The.
   In Those Days, in This Time.
   Poem without an End.
Angelou.   Greyday.
Atwood.   Heart Test with an Echo Chamber.
   Woman Makes Peace with Her Faulty Heart,
   The.
   Woman Who Could Not Live with Her Faulty
   Heart, The.
Baudelaire.   Confession.
Bishop, E.   Weed, The.
Bogan, L.   Song for the Last Act.
Browning, E.   Calls on the Heart.
   False Step, A.
   My Heart and I.
   To George Sand: A Recognition.
Browning, R.   Meeting at Night.
Burns, R.   My Heart's in the Highlands.
Byron, G.   On a Cornelian Heart Which Was
   Broken.
Carew, T.   Celia Bleeding, to the Surgeon.
   Mistake, The.
Carruth, H.   Apology for Using the Word
   "Heart" in Too Many Poems, An.
Chamfort.   How hollow heart and full.
Clough.   In Stratis Viarum IV.
Coleridge, S.   Exchange, The.
   Loss.
Collins, B.   My Heart.
   Night House, The.
Crane, H.   Hive, The.
Crane, S.   In the desert.
Crashaw.   Flaming Heart, The.
   To the Name above Every Name, the Name of
   Jesus, a Hymn.
Creeley.   Echo ("Broken heart, you / timeless
   wonder").
   Mind's Heart.
   Trap, The.
   Wanting You.
Cullen, C.   Foolish Heart, The.
   Proud Heart, The.
Cummings, E. E.   Dedication: "White rose my
   soul, The."
   I carry your heart with me(i carry it in).
   Lady you have written me a letter.
   Must being shall.
   These people socalled were not given hearts.
   Three wealthy sisters swore they'd never part.
Cunningham, J.   In the thirtieth year of life.
   To My Wife.
Davie, D.   Duplicity in Prayer.
   Heart Beats.
De la Mare.   Be angry now no more!
   Fleeting, The.
   Night.
Dickey, J.   Angina.
Dickinson, E.   Heart asks Pleasure—first, The.
   Heart has narrow Banks, The.
   Poor little Heart!
   This dirty—little—Heart.
Donne.   Blossom[e], The.
   Broken Heart, The.
   Legacy [*or* Legacie], The.
   Message, The.
Dugan, A.   Poem: "Tree was wet with the
   moon's, The."
Eberhart, R.   Anima.
   Dream Journey of the Head and Heart.
   Going.
   Secret Heart, The.
   Ways and Means.
Emerson, R.   Dost thou not hear me Ellen.
   I will not live out of me.
   If he go apart.
   Perhaps thy lot in life is higher.
   Roomy Eternity / Casts her schemes rarely.
   Though her eye seek other forms.
Frost, R.   Devotion.
   Dust of Snow.
Glück, L.   Portrait.
Gunn, T.   Sacred Heart.

Gurney, I.   Daily—Old Tale.
Hamill, S.   Journey, The.
HaNagid.   He Whose Heart in His Heart.
Heart holds hidden knowledge, The.
It's Heart That Discerns.
Multiple Troubles of Man, The.
Soul Opens inside You.
Why Should the Hearts of You Purists.
You Look through Open Eyes.
Hardy, T.   In a Cathedral City.
Herbert, G.   Altar, The.
Herrick.   Christs Part.
Frozen Heart, The.
Heart, The.
His Weaknesse in Woes.
Of Love. A Sonnet.
To Oenone.
Upon Lupes.
Wounded Heart, The.
Hopkins, G.   My Own Heart Let Me More Have
Pity On.
Hughes, L.   Heart.
Jacobsen, J.   Autopsy, The.
Kinsella, T.   Sacrifice.
Kizer, C.   Heart's Limbo.
Koch, K.   Simplicity of the Unknown Past, The.
Komunyakaa.   Brain to the Heart, The.
Kunitz, S.   Scourge, The.
Thing That Eats the Heart, The.
Larkin, P.   If Grief Could Burn Out.
If Hands Could Free You, Heart.
Laughlin, J.   Cardiac Autoscope, The.
Lawrence, D. H.   Heart of Man, The.
Know Deeply, Know Thyself More Deeply.
Metal for Resistance.
Logan, J.   Pathological Case in Pliny, A.
Lowell, R.   Colloquy in Black Rock.
Merton.   Sacred Heart 2.
Transformation: For the Sacred Heart, The.
Merwin.   Heart, The.
Montale.   English Horn.
Olson, C.   Heart is a clock, The.
Orr, G.   Heart.
Shaky Spectrum.
Pagis.   Sudden Heart.
Parker, D.   Autumn Valentine.
False Friends, The.
Homebody, The.
Threnody: "Lilacs blossom just as sweet."
Triolet: "Give back the heart that I gave."
Very Short Song, A.
Patchen.   Mechanical Heart, The.
Petrarch.   Weep now, my eyes; accompany my
heart.
Pinsky.   Dreamer, The.
Hearts, The.
Riley, J.   As Created.
Old Sweetheart of Mine, An.
Rilke.   Heart's Noise.
To Betsy Steiger.
Rimbaud, A.   Tortured Heart.
Rossetti, C.   As a King, ...Unto the King.
Because Thy Love hath sought me, / All mine is
Thine and Thine is mine.
Birthday, A.
From early dawn until the flush of noon.
Hope Carol, A.
If I should ever say "my heart is in my home."
Like As the Hart Desireth the Water Brooks.
Lord, comest Thou to me?
Sunday before Advent.
Twice.
When I Was in Trouble I Called upon the Lord.
Rumi.   This that is tormented and very tired.
Sandburg, C.   Beat, Old Heart.
Sarton, M.   Prothalamion.
Sexton.   Dead Heart, The.
Doctor of the Heart, The.
Old Dwarf Heart.
Shelley, P.   From the Arabic: An Imitation.
Lines: "When the lamp is shattered [or
shatter'd]."
Smith, S.   La Gretchen de Nos Jours (II).
Voice from the Tomb (3).
Stafford, W.   Size of a Fist, The.
Thomas, D.   When All My Five and Country

Senses See.
Walcott.   Fist, The.
Walker, A.   Never Offer Your Heart to Someone
Who Eats Hearts.
Warren, R.   What Was the Thought.
Williams, C. K.   Shells.
Williams, W.   Portrait of a Young Man with a
Bad Heart.
Wright, J.   At Thomas Hardy's Birthplace, 1953.
Jewel, The.
Wroth [or Wroath].   Love's Victorie.
Yeats.   Her Vision in the Wood.
Never Give All the Heart.
Owen Aherne and His Dancers.
Song, A: "I thought no more was needed."
Zukofsky, L.   Ashtray.
Finally a Valentine.
On Valentine's Day to Friends.
Sequence 1944-6.

Heat
Ammons.   Mid-August.
Bukowski.   Thermometer.
Cavafy.   Chandelier.
Ciardi, J.   Heatwave.
Coleridge, S.   Perspiration: A Travelling
Eclogue.
Davie, D.   Hardness of Light, The.
Dickey, J.   Basics.
Gila Bend.
Dunbar, P.   Summer Pastoral, A.
Eberhart, R.   Great Praises.
Nexus.
Graves, R.   Cool Web, The.
Gurney, I.   Cloud, The.
Hall, D.   Table, The.
Herrick.   Frozen Heart, The.
Health.
Hughes, T.   Sunstroke.
Jacobsen, J.   Linkwood Road.
Shade-Seller, The.
Kipling, R.   Pagett, M. P.
Koch, K.   Boiling Water, The.
McHugh, H.   Melted Money.
Merton.   Tropics.
Nash, O.   September Is Summer, Too.
Niedecker.   In Europe they grow a new bean
while here.
O'Hara, F.   My Heat.
Parker, D.   August.
Rich, A.   Burning Oneself In.
Riley, J.   At Ninety in the Shade.
August.
Stock, R.   Roseapples and Nudes.
Tate, J.   Heatstroke.
It's Not the Heat So Much as the Humidity.
Tomlinson, C.   Las Trampas U. S. A.
Walcott.   Midsummer, Tobago.
Warren, R.   Cycle.
Heat Wave Breaks.
Rattlesnake Country.
Small White House.
Zagajewski.   Summer.

Heather
Whittier.   Burns.

Heaven
Angelou.   Arrival.
"Anvari."   To the Shah, from Enweri.
Atwood.   Resurrection.
Bishop, E.   Seascape.
Blake, W.   Marriage of Heaven and Hell, The.
Borges.   Baltasar Gracián.
His End and His Beginning.
Of Heaven and Hell.
Bradstreet, A.   As Weary Pilgrim, Now at Rest.
Brontë, E.   Heaven's glory shone where he was
laid.
Lines: "Far away is the land of rest."
No Coward Soul Is Mine.
Stanzas: "Often rebuked, yet always back
returning."
Browning, E.   Heaven and Earth.
Isobel's Child.
Soul's Travelling, The.
Browning, R.   Reverie.
Byron, G.   Heaven and Earth.
Campion, T.   Most sweet and pleasing are thy

wayes, O God.
O Come Quickly!
Cavafy.   Hereafter, The.
Ciardi, J.   Starry Heavens, the Moral Law, The.
Clifton, L.   Heaven.
Clough.   O Heaven, and thou most loving
family.
Coleridge, S.   Faith, Hope, and Charity.
Kubla Khan: or, A Vision in a Dream.
Cowper, W.   Epitaph on Mrs. Higgins.
Crane, H.   And Bees of Paradise.
Crashaw.   I Am the Door [or Doore].
It Is Better to Go into Heaven with One Eye.
To the Infant Martyrs.
Upon the Infant Martyrs.
Creeley.   Drums, The.
Help Heaven.
Saints, The.
Sufi Sam Christian.
Cullen, C.   She of the Dancing Feet Sings.
Cummings, E. E.   If there are any heavens my
mother will (all by herself) have.
Davie, D.   Three Beyond.
De la Mare.   Night.
Sunrise.
Tryst, The.
Where Is Thy Victory?
Dickey, J.   Heaven of Animals, The.
Dickey, W.   Self Prepares for an Unwilling
Journey, The.
Dickinson, E.   "Arcturus" is his other name.
Cloud withdrew from the Sky, A.
Fact that Earth is Heaven, The.
Forever at His side to walk.
God's Residence.
Going to Heaven!
"Heaven" has different Signs—to me.
Heaven is but a little way.
Heaven is so far of the Mind.
"Heaven"—is what I cannot reach!
Heaven will not be as good as Earth.
How far is it to Heaven?
I am glad you are in the open Air.
I dwell in Possibility.
I never saw a Moor.
I reason, Earth is short.
I think just how my shape will rise.
I went to Heaven.
If roses had not faded.
Immortal is an ample word.
Immured in Heaven!
Is Heaven a Physician?
I've known a Heaven, like a Tent.
Lest this be Heaven indeed.
Like Flowers, that heard the news of Dews.
Meeting is well worth parting.
My life closed twice before its close.
My nosegays are for Captives.
Of Tolling Bell I ask the cause?
Pit—but Heaven over it, A.
She's happy, with a new Content.
Should you but fail at—Sea.
So much of Heaven has gone from Earth.
Surrender.
Take Your Heaven further on.
Thank God there is a world.
There is a Zone whose even Years.
'Tis so much joy! 'Tis so much joy!
To come from Heaven is casual.
To make even Heaven more heavenly.
We pray—to Heaven.
We shun it ere it comes.
What is—"Paradise."
What mystery pervades a well!
Where bells no more affright the morn.
Which is best? Heaven.
Why—do they shut Me out of Heaven?
You're right—"the way is narrow."
Donne.   Hymn to the Saints, and to Marquis
Hamilton, An.
To Mr Tilman after He Had Taken Orders.
Dryden, J.   Song for St Cecilia's Day, 1687, A.
Dunbar, P.   Path, The.
Theology.
W'en I Gits Home.
Dunbar, W.   Amendis [or Amends] to the

Telyouris [or Tailors] and Sowtaris.
Eberhart, R.   Birth and Death.
Blessed Are the Angels in Heaven.
Ideal and the Real, The.
Sestina: "I die, no matter what I do I die."
Emerson, R.   For Lucifer, that old athlete.
Go if thou wilt ambrosial Flower.
Hearst thou, sweet spirit, thou hast heard before.
Inscription on a Well in Memory of the Martyrs of the War.
O what is Heaven but the fellowship.
Shall the Muse sing for thousands & not sing.
Spiritual Laws.
Frost, R.   Trial by Existence, The.
Graves, R.   Green Castle, The.
Heaven.
True Joy.
Hacker, M.   Partial Analysis.
Hafiz [or Hafez].   Ghaselle.
Hall, D.   Sister on the Tracks, A.
Herbert, G.   Heaven.
Obedience.
Star[re], The.
Herrick.   Another.
Comfort to a Youth That Had Lost His Love.
God Heares Us.
Heaven.
His Creed.
Honours Are Hindrances.
Humility.
No Time in Eternity.
Ode, or Psalme, to God, An.
On Heaven.
Tapers.
Teares.
This, and the Next World.
To Heaven.
To His Ever-Loving God.
White Island.
Hopkins, G.   Ashboughs.
Earth and heaven, so little known, The.
Handsome Heart, The.
Heaven-Haven.
Hill / Heaven and every field, are still.
Il Mystico.
My prayers must meet a brazen heaven.
Not kind! to freeze me with forecast.
O Death, Death, He is come.
Housman.   Easter Hymn.
Hughes, L.   Heaven.
Judgment Day.
Hughes, T.   Crow Blacker than Ever.
River.
Jacopo da Lentino.   Sonnet: Of [or To] His Lady in Heaven.
Jammes.   Prayer to Go to Paradise with the Donkeys, A.
Johnson, S.   Vanity of Human Wishes, The; The Tenth Satire of Juvenal Imitated.
Jonson, B.   To Heaven.
Keats.   As from the Darkening Gloom a Silver Dove.
Ode: "Bards of passion and of mirth."
Kipling, R.   Dinah in Heaven.
Kumin, M.   Heaven as Anus.
Laughlin, J.   Dream Not of Other Worlds.
Lawrence, D. H.   Ah, with His Blessing Bright on Thy Mouth and Thy Brow.
Fallen Leaves.
Hymn to Nothingness.
Someone Will Enter between the Gates.
Levine, P.   Grandmother in Heaven.
Heaven.
Miracle, The.
Lindsay, N.   Celestial Circus, The.
General William Booth Enters into Heaven.
Harps in Heaven.
How Johnny Appleseed Walked Alone in the Jungles of Heaven.
In Memory of a Child.
Last Song of Lucifer, The.
Merton.   How Long We Wait.
Psalm 132: A Modern Monastic Revision.
Michelangelo Buonarroti.   Bracci, I, A. Alive because I'm dead.
If nature now deferred to death, dejected.

Just as you cannot not be lovely here.
Power of a beautiful face lifts me to heaven, The.
Millay, E.   Blue-Flag in the Bog, The.
Milosz, C.   How It Should Be in Heaven.
Milton.   On the Same ["Thus did you strive to vouchsafe James to Heaven"].
Paradise Lost.
Mistral, G.   Heaven's Carriage.
Nemerov.   Backward Look, The.
Morality, A.
Oliver, M.   Roses, Late Summer.
Patchen.   How silent are the things of heaven.
Naked Land, The.
Outlaw of the Lowest Planet, The.
What the Grecian Earns.
Petrarch.   Alas, that time has now passed over when.
Angels and the souls of the elect, The.
Go, my sad rhymes, until you reach the stone.
I fly on wings of fancy up to heaven.
I raised myself in thought to where I found.
I seem to hear that messenger once more.
If virtuous love can merit a reward.
Lady, who now with our Original.
My soul, who see, hear, read, think, speak, and write.
O time, O turning sky, speeding away.
Three days before, my soul reached such a place.
When little birds complaining, or green leaves.
Plath.   Sheep in Fog.
Pope, A.   Epigram: "Peter complains, that God has given."
Epitaph on the Monument of the Honourable Robert Digby, and of his Sister Mary.
Universal Prayer [Deo Opt. Max.], The.
Ralegh, S.   Passionate Man[']s Pilgrimage, The.
Riley, J.   Eternity.
Out of the Hitherwhere.
Ritsos.   It Exists.
Robinson, E.   Credo.
Supremacy.
Rossetti, C.   1878.
Afterthought, An.
Ah Lord, Lord, if my heart were right with Thine.
All heaven is blazing yet / With the meridian sun.
All Saints.
And Now Why Tarriest Thou?
Annie.
Antipas.
As Cold Water to a Thirsty Soul, So Is Good News from a Far Country.
As the Doves to Their Windows.
As the Sparks Fly Upwards.
As Thy Days, So Shall Thy Strength Be.
Awake, Thou That Sleepest.
Beautiful for Situation.
Before the Throne, and before the Lamb.
Behold a Shaking.
Behold, It Was Very Good.
Bride Song.
Burial Anthem.
Buried.
But Thy Commandment Is Exceeding Broad.
By Way of Remembrance.
Called to Be Saints.
Cast down but not destroyed, chastened not slain.
Christian and Jew. A Dialogue.
Convent Threshold, The.
Counsel, A.
Darkness and light are both alike to Thee.
Day Is at Hand, The.
De Profundis.
Death.
Death Is Swallowed Up in Victory.
Dirge, A.
Discovery, A.
Doeth Well...Doeth Better.
Earth and heaven.
Earth has clear call of daily bells, / A chancel-vault of gloom and star.
Earth Shall Tremble at the Look of Him, The.

Eleventh Hour, The.
Ellen Middleton.
Eva.
Eye Hath Not Seen.
Faint, yet Pursuing.
Flowers Appear on the Earth, The.
From House to Home.
General Assembly and Church of the Firstborn, The.
Goal in sight! Look up and sing, / Set faces full against the light, The.
Gold of that Land Is Good, The.
Gone Before.
Had Fortune parted us / Fortune is blind.
Hark! the Alleluias of the great salvation.
He Shall Go No More Out.
Heaven.
Heaven Is Heaven.
Heaven Is Not Far.
Heaven Overarches Earth and Sea.
Heaven's chimes are slow, but sure to strike at last.
Heaviness May Endure for a Night, but Joy Cometh in the Morning.
Heavy heart, if ever heart was heavy, A.
Her Seed; It Shall Bruise Thy Head.
His Banner over Me Was Love.
Holy City, New Jerusalem, The.
Holy Innocents.
How great is little man! / Sun, moon, and stars respond to him.
I Am Small and of No Reputation.
I Do Set My Bow in the Cloud.
I have done with hope.
I Look for the Lord.
I Will Lift Up Mine Eyes unto the Hills.
If stars dropped out of heaven, / And if flowers took their place.
Jerusalem of fire / And gold and pearl and gem.
Jesus alone:—if thus it were to me.
Joy of Saints, like incense turned to fire, The.
Lady Isabella.
Last Words of St. Telemachus, The.
Lay Up for Yourselves Treasures in Heaven.
Let Them Rejoice in Their Beds.
Life Hidden.
Life that was born today / Must make no stay.
Lift up thine eyes to seek the invisible.
Look on This Picture and on This.
Lord, by what inconceivable dim road / Thou leadest man on footsore pilgrimage!
Lord God of Hosts, most Holy and most High.
Lord, grant us eyes to see and ears to hear, / And souls to love and minds to understand.
Lord Jesus, who would think that I am Thine?
Lord, make me one with Thine own faithful ones.
Lord Thomas and Fair Margaret.
Lord, we are rivers running to Thy sea.
Love and Hope.
Man's life is but a working day / Whose tasks are set aright.
Martyr, The.
Marvel of Marvels.
Michael F. M. Rossetti.
Moonshine.
Mother and Child.
Mother Country.
Now They Desire.
O mine enemy / Rejoice not over me!
Only Believe.
Our heaven must be within ourselves / Our home and heaven the work of faith.
Paradise.
Paradise: in a Symbol.
Passion Flower hath sprung up tall, The.
Pause, A.
Resurrection Eve.
Rivals.
Rose Plant in Jericho, A.
Saints and Angels.
Shadows Today.
She Shall Be Brought unto the King.
Slain in their high places: fallen on rest.
Sleep, Sleep Happy Child; All Creation Slept and Smiled.

So Great a Cloud of Witnesses.
Son, Remember.
Song of the Star, The.
Song: "We buried her among the flowers."
St. Andrew's Church.
Strange voices sing among the planets which.
Sunday before Advent.
Sweetness of rest when Thou sheddest rest.
That Where I Am, There Ye May Be Also.
They lie at rest, our blessed dead.
This near-at-hand land breeds pain by measure.
Thou Knewest...Thou Oughtest Therefore.
Thy Name, O Christ, as incense streaming forth.
Till Tomorrow.
Time of Waiting, The.
To Every Seed His Own Body.
To the End.
To What Purpose Is This Waste?
Truly the Light Is Sweet.
Two Thoughts of Death.
Uphill.
Watchers, The.
We know not when, we know not where.
What are these lovely ones, yea, what are these?
What Good Shall My Life Do Me?
What Hath God Wrought!
What will it be, O my soul, what will it be.
Where Neither Rust nor Moth Doth Corrupt.
Where never tempest heaveth, / Nor sorrow
  grieveth.
Where shall I find a white rose blowing?
Whither the Tribes Go Up, Even the Tribes of
  the Lord.
Who cares for earthly bread tho' white?
Who sits with the King in His Throne? Not a
  slave but a Bride.
Who would wish back the Saints upon our
  rough.
Why?
Yawn, A.
Ye Are Come unto Mount Sion.
Ye Have Forgotten the Exhortation.
Ye That Fear Him, Both Small and Great.
Yet a Little While.
Rossetti, D.   Blessed Damozel, The.
Rumi   Soul, The.
Sandburg, C.   Hells and Heavens.
Sarton, M.   Annunciation.
Sexton.   Earth, The.
  Frenzy.
Shelley, P.   Daemon of the World, The; A
  Fragment.
  Ode to Heaven.
To———: "One word is too often profaned."
Smith, S.   Heavenly City, The.
  Noble and Ethereal.
Stevens, W.   Of Heaven Considered as a Tomb.
Stockton, A.   After a Night of Perplexing
  Dreams.
  Anniversary Elegy on the Death of Mr Stockton
  the 28th of Feb 1783.
Thoreau.   'T will soon appear if we but look.
Very.   Birds of Passage, The.
Walcott.   Orient and Immortal Wheat.
  Return to D'Ennery; Rain.
Wheatley, P.   Funeral Poem on the Death of C.
  E. an Infant of Twelve Months, A.
  To a Clergyman on the Death of His Lady.
  To Mr. and Mrs.—, on the Death of Their Infant
  Son.
Whittier.   Between the Gates.
  Mystery, A.
  Norembega.
  To My Friend on the Death of His Sister.
Wilbur, R.   Icarium Mare.
Wordsworth, W.   If thou indeed derive thy light
  from Heaven.
  Though narrow be that old Man's cares, and
  near.
Yeats.   He Thinks of His Past Greatness When a
  Part of the Constellations of Heaven.
  He Wishes for the Cloths of Heaven.
  Rose of Peace, The.
Zukofsky, L.   Pamphylian.

Hebe
Graves, R.   To Ogmian Hercules.

Hebrew
Amichai [or Amikhai].   National Thoughts.
Jacobsen, J.   Shibboleth.
Moore, M.   Past Is the Present, The.

Hebrides
Jeffers, R.   Now Returned Home.
MacLeish.   Hebrides.
  Thrush in the Gaelic Islands, The.
MacNeice.   Hebrides, The.

Hector
Browning, E.   Hector in the Garden.
Carruth, H.   Existence before Essence.
Cavafy.   Priam's Speeding Forth at Night.
Orr, G.   Tableau Vivant.

Hedgehogs
Clampitt.   Birdham.
Clare, J.   Hedgehog, The.
Cummings, E. E.   Porky & porkie.
Larkin, P.   Mower, The.
Muldoon, P.   Hedgehog.
Tomlinson, C.   Scream, The.

Hedonism
Archpoet.   Confession of Bishop Golias, The.
Cavafy.   Of the Jews (50 A.D.).
Cummings, E. E.   Since feeling is first.
Herrick.   Pleasures Pernicious.
Housman.   Think no more, lad; laugh, be jolly.
Lindsay, N.   Johnny Appleseed's Wife from the
  Palace of Eve.
Melville, H.   After the Pleasure Party.
Olson, C.   Laughing Ones, The.
Parker, D.   Flaw in Paganism, The.

Heine, Heinrich
Borges.   Paris, 1856.
Carruth, H.   Essay on Stone.
Heine, H.   From Heine.
Kizer, C.   Apostate, The.
  Old Gods, The.
  Tying One On in Vienna.
Logan, J.   Century Piece for Poor Heine, A.

Heisenberg, Werner
Kizer, C.   Twelve o'Clock.

Helen of Troy
Browning, R.   Helen's Tower.
Carruth, H.   Light in the Locust Tree.
Crane, H.   For the Marriage of Faustus and
  Helen.
Cummings, E. E.   Helen.
De la Mare.   Mirage.
Gunn, T.   Helen's Rape.
"H. D."   Helen.
Hamill, S.   Hellenic Triptych.
Jackson, L.   Helen's Burning.
  Helen's Faces.
Jeffers, R.   At the Fall of an Age.
  Tower beyond Tragedy, The.
Jonson, B.   Ode, An: "Helen, did Homer never
  see."
Poe.   To Helen.
Ritsos.   Helen.
Rossetti, D.   Troy Town.
Smith, S.   I Had a Dream.
Stock, R.   In Transformation of an Imago.
Valéry.   Helen.
Walcott.   Map of the New World.
Wilbur, R.   Voice from under the Table, A.
Wilde, O.   New Helen, The.
  Serenade: "Western wind is blowing fair, The."
Wilner, E.   Dinner Party.
Yeats.   Leda and the Swan.
  When Helen Lived.

Helicopters
Ciardi, J.   Image of Man as a Gardener after
  Two World Wars.

Heliogabalus
Meredith, W.   Revenant, The.

Hell
Auden.   Hell.
Beckett, S.   Jusque dans la caverne ciel et sol.
  Noire soeur.
Blake, W.   Marriage of Heaven and Hell, The.
Borges.   Of Heaven and Hell.
Brontë, E.   Stanzas: "Often rebuked, yet always
  back returning."
Broumas, O.   Maenad.

Browning, R.   Doctor———.
Buchanan, G.   Rome conquered earth with arms,
  the sea with ships.
Bukowski.   How Do They Get Your Number?
  Sad-Eyed Mules of Men.
Burns, R.   Kellyburnbraes.
Ciardi, J.   Sermon Notes.
Coleridge, S.   Alla Sua Amica.
Crashaw.   But Men Loved Darkness[e] Rather
  than [or then] Light.
De la Mare.   Making a fire.
  Outskirts, The.
Dickey, W.   Self Prepares for an Unwilling
  Journey, The.
Dickinson, E.   My life closed twice before its
  close.
  Pit—but Heaven over it, A.
  To attempt to speak of what has been.
  You're right—"the way is narrow."
Dubie.   Parallax Monograph for Rodin, The.
Dunbar, P.   Theology.
Dunbar, W.   Off Februar the fyiftene nycht.
Eberhart, R.   Blessed Are the Angels in Heaven.
  Enigma, The.
  Sestina: "I die, no matter what I do I die."
Glück, L.   Day without Night.
Graves, R.   Descent into Hell.
  Encounter, The.
  Hell.
  Instructions to the Orphic Adept.
  Sharp Ridge, The.
Gray, T.   Descent of Odin, The.
Gurney, I.   Hell's Prayer.
Hacker, M.   Partial Analysis.
Hafiz [or Hafez].   Ghaselle.
Heaney, S.   Afterwards, An.
Herrick.   Barley-Break; or, Last in Hell.
  Hell.
  Hell Fire.
  Sin and Strife.
Hill, G.   Ovid in the Third Reich.
Housman.   Hell Gate.
  Mill-stream, now that noises cease, The.
Hughes, L.   Enemy.
  Fire.
Hughes, T.   Once I said lightly.
Ignatow, D.   Who Could Have Believed It?
Jackson, L.   Need for Hell, A.
Jacob, M.   Hell Is Graduated.
Jeffers, R.   Wilson in Hell.
Keats.   On a Dream.
Kizer, C.   Damnation, The.
  In Hell with Virg and Dan.
Lawrence, D. H.   Someone Will Enter between
  the Gates.
Levi, P.   Another Monday.
Lindsay, N.   Last Song of Lucifer, The.
McGrath, T.   Passages.
McHugh, H.   What Hell Is.
Merton.   All the Way Down.
Millay, E.   Some Things Are Dark.
Milosz, C.   Garden of Earthly Delights, The:
  Hell.
  On the Other Side.
  Proof.
Milton.   Paradise Lost.
Olson, C.   Flower grows, The.
  I Believe in You.
  In Cold Hell, in Thicket.
  Loves of Anat, I, The.
Owen, W.   Strange Meeting.
Parker, D.   Coda: "There's little in taking or
  giving."
Rich, A.   Lucifer in the Train.
Rimbaud, A.   First Delirium. The Foolish
  Virgin. The Infernal Bridegroom.
  Night in Hell.
Robinson, E.   Supremacy.
Rossetti, C.   Sunday before Advent.
  Where Their Worm Dieth Not, and the Fire Is
  Not Quenched.
Sandburg, C.   Hells and Heavens.
  Our Hells.
Seifert.   Once only did I see / the sun so blood-
  red.
Smith, S.   Ambassador, The.

Thoughts about the Christian Doctrine of
   Eternal Hell.
Tate, A.   Cross, The.
Thoreau.   Have ye no work for a man to do.
Tomlinson, C.   Last Judgement.
Walcott.   Orient and Immortal Wheat.
Warren, R.   Golden Hills of Hell, The.
Williams, W.   Asphodel, That Greeny Flower.
   Paterson, Book 5: The River of Heaven.
Wright, J.   Ghost, The.
Yeats.   Rose of Peace, The.

Hellenism
Cavafy.   Coins.
   Epitaph of Antiochus, King of Kommagini.
   Greek from Ancient Times.
   Ionian.
   Philhellene.
   Poseidonians.
   Prince from Western Libya, A.
   Regiment of Pleasure, The.
   Return from Greece.

Hell's Angels
Ginsberg, A.   First Party at Ken Kesey's with
   Hell's Angels.
Gunn, T.   Black Jackets.

Heloise
See **Abelard and Heloise**

Help
Atwood.   I see you fugitive, stumbling across
   the prarie.
Berry, W.   Creation Myth.
Browning, E.   Sea-Mew, The.
Carew, T.   Lady, Rescued from Death by a
   Knight, Who in the Instant Leaves Her,
   Complains Thus, A.
Ciardi, J.   Being Called.
Dickinson, E.   These Strangers, in a Foreign
   World.
   To offer brave assistance.
Drummond de Andrade.   Song of Purification.
Faiz.   If I Were Certain.
Graves, R.   Grotesques.
Lindsay, N.   Flower of Mending, The.
Lorde.   To My Daughter the Junkie on a Train.
Merton.   Litany: "All holy souls / pray for us
   fellows."
Nash, O.   Everybody Wants to Get into the
   Baedeker.
Olson, C.   All You Can Do.
Riley, J.   Text, The.
Rossetti, C.   Out of the Deep.
Tate, J.   Up Here.

Hemingway, Ernest
Carver, R.   Poem for Hemingway & W. C.
   Williams.
Eberhart, R.   Key West.
Koch, K.   On Beauty.
Logan, J.   Papa's House, Son's Room.
MacLeish.   Hemingway.
Merton.   Elegy for Ernest Hemingway, An.
Nash, O.   Roll On, Thou Deep and Dark Blue
   Copy Writer—Roll!
Updike.   Meditation on a News Item.
Walcott.   Swamp, The.

Hemlocks
Dickinson, E.   I think the Hemlock likes to
   stand.
Millay, E.   Hedge of Hemlocks, The.

Hengist
Borges.   Hengist Wants Men (A.D. 449).

Henry I, King of England
Rossetti, D.   White Ship, The.

Henry V, King of England
Stock, R.   Shakespeare in Vietnam.

Henry VIII, King of England
Jacobsen, J.   Ballad of Henry, Bridegroom.
Wordsworth, W.   Recollection of the Portrait of
   King Henry Eighth, Trinity Lodge, Cambridge.
Zaturenska.   Lament of Catherine Howard, Fifth
   Queen of Henry VIII.

"Henry, O." (William Sydney Porter)
Lindsay, N.   Knight in Disguise, The.
Riley, J.   O. Henry.

Henry, Prince of England (the Young King)
Bertrans [*or* Bertran *or* Bertrand] de Born.
   Planh for the Young English King.

Hens
Bishop, E.   Trouvée.
Dubie.   City of the Olesha Fruit, The.
Emerson, R.   Things oft miscalling, as the hen-.
Hughes, T.   Hen, The.
Kinnell.   Hen Flower, The.
Ramanujan.   Black Hen, The.
Ransom, J.   Janet Waking.
Schuyler, J.   Wild Eggs.
Updike.   Wooden Darning Egg, A.
Wilbur, R.   Black November Turkey, A.
See also **Chickens**

Heraclitus
Atwood.   After Heraclitus.
Borges.   Maker, The.
   Museum.
   To Whoever Is Reading Me.
Dugan, A.   From Heraclitus.
Hopkins, G.   That Nature Is a Heraclitean Fire
   and of the Comfort of the Resurrection.
MacNeice.   Variation on Heraclitus.
Mahon.   Heraclitus on Rivers.
Merton.   Legacy of Herakleitos, The.
Milosz, C.   Heraclitus.
Orr, G.   A la Mystérieuse.
Szymborska, W.   In Heraclitus' River.
Zagajewski.   Fire, Fire.
   Lava.

Herbert, Zbigniew
Zagajewski.   Farewell for Zbigniew Herbert.

Herbs
Blue Cloud.   To-ta Ti-om.
Carruth, H.   Spring Notes from Robin Hill.
Emerson, R.   Blight.
   Where the fungus broad & red.
Gunn, T.   Fennel.
Kipling, R.   Our Fathers of Old.
Updike.   Sensualist, The.

Hercules
Dugan, A.   Marxist Analysis of the Fifth Labor
   of Hercules.
Emerson, R.   Turtle in swamp.
Graves, R.   Hercules at Nemea.
   To Ogmian Hercules.
Heaney, S.   Hercules and Antaeus.
Owen, W.   Antaeus: A Fragment.
Ritsos.   Apples of the Hesperides 1, The.
   Apples of the Hesperides 2, The.
   Golden Fleece, The.
Williams, C. K.   Hercules, Deianira, Nessus.
Wilner, E.   Recovery.

Herding
Whittier.   Drovers, The.
See also **Shepherds and Shepherdesses**

Heresy and Heretics
Baudelaire.   Examination of Conscience, The.
Codrescu.   Attempt to Spell, Incantate and
   Annoy.
Coleridge, S.   Foster-Mother's Tale, The.
Cowper, W.   Lines Written in the Monthly
   Review.
McHugh, H.   What He Thought.
Meredith, G.   John Lackland.

Heritage and Heredity
Amichai [*or* Amikhai].   National Thoughts.
   This Place.
   You're small and thin in the rain. A small target.
Carver, R.   Child, The.
Cavafy.   Poseidonians.
   Return from Greece.
Creeley.   Bruce & Linley's House.
   Theresa's Friends.
Davie, D.   So Make Them Melt as the
   Dishoused Snail.
Dugan, A.   On Breeding, from Plutarch.
Komunyakaa.   Mismatched Shoes.
Merwin.   Port, The.
   Sire.
Ramanujan.   Drafts.
   On the Very Possible Jaundice of an Unborn
   Daughter.
   Self-Portrait.

Rimbaud, A.   Bad Blood.

Hermit Crabs
Oliver, M.   Hermit Crab, The.

Hermits
Bishop, E.   Chemin de Fer.
Dubie.   To a Young Woman Dying at Weir.
Emerson, R.   Hermione.
Enzensberger, H.   Remote House.
Hall, D.   Oysters and Hermits.
Han-shan.   Hermit's heart is heavy, A.
   When hermits hide from society.
   You're not really hermits.
Jacobsen, J.   February Midnight.
Kinnell.   When One Has Lived a Long Time
   Alone.
Kumin, M.   After the Harvest.
   Hermit Meets the Skunk, The.
   Hermit Picks Berries, The.
   Hermit Prays, The.
   Hermit Wakes to Bird Sounds, The.
Logan, J.   Short Life of the Hermit, A.
Lowell, R.   Skunk Hour.
Mahon.   Mayo Tao, The.
Merwin.   Son.
Oliver, M.   Strawberry Moon.
Orr, G.   Story Sassetta Paints, A.
Petrarch.   I walk, alone and troubled, desert
   places.
Pinsky.   New Saddhus, The.
Plath.   Hermit at Outermost House, The.
Robinson, E.   Stafford's Cabin.
Stafford, W.   Looking across the River.
   Peleg Lookout.
Szymborska, W.   Hermitage.
Tate, J.   Aunt Edna.
   Radical Departure, A.
Van Duyn.   Hermit of Hudson Pond, The.
Walcott.   Winding Up.
Whalen, P.   Further Notice.
Williams, W.   Stylist, The.
Wordsworth, W.   Brownie, The.
   Brownie's Cell, The.
Yeats.   Three Hermits, The.

Hero and Leander
Byron, G.   Written after Swimming from Sestos
   to Abydos.
Campion, T.   Shall I come, if I swim? wide are
   the waves, you see.
Donne.   Hero and Leander.
Keats.   On a Leander Gem which Miss
   Reynolds, My Kind Friend, Gave Me.

Herod the Great
Cavafy.   Aristovoulos.

Herodotus
Dugan, A.   On Herodotus.

Heroes and Heroines
Atwood.   My beautiful wooden leader.
Auden.   O What Is That Sound [Which So
   Thrills the Ear].
Brooks, G.   "Negro" Hero.
Browning, E.   Fourfold Aspect, The.
   Sword of Castruccio Castracani, The.
Browning, R.   Hervé Riel.
Byron, G.   Elegiac Stanzas on the Death of Sir
   Peter Parker, Bart.
   Monody on the Death of the Right Hon. R. B.
   Sheridan.
   On the Star of "The Legion of Honour."
   Thy Days Are Done.
   Translation from Horace.
   Translation of the Epitaph on Virgil and
   Tibullus.
Carver, R.   Baker, The.
Cavafy.   Tyanan Sculptor.
Chesterton.   Refutation.
Clifton, L.   Final Note to Clark.
   Note, Passed to Superman.
Corbett, W.   Hero.
Creeley.   Heroes.
   Touchstone.
Cummings, E. E.   My Father Moved through
   Dooms of Love.
De la Mare.   Absalom.
   Peace.
Dickinson, E.   Gleam of an heroic Act, The.

To have been the missing Hero.
We never know how high we are.
Dugan, A.   Two Hatreds of Action.
Dunbar, P.   Lincoln.
Eberhart, R.   Protagonists.
Emerson, R.   Forerunners.
From high to higher forces.
Heroism.
Frost, R.   Trial by Existence, The.
Glück, L.   Parable, A.
Graves, R.   Miller's Man, The.
To Ogmian Hercules.
Gray, T.   Conan.
Gunn, T.   Byrnies, The.
Hall, D.   Persistence of 1937.
Hardy, T.   By the Barrows.
Herrick.   Ultimus Heroum: or, To the Most
Learned, and to the Right Honourable, Henry.
Jeffers, R.   Broadstone, The.
Epic Stars, The.
Jonson, B.   To William, Lord Mounteagle.
Keats.   To Kosciusko.
Kinsella, T.   Test Case.
Kipling, R.   Giffen's Debt.
Lawrence, D. H.   For the Heroes Are Dipped in
Scarlet.
Levine, P.   Francisco, I'll Bring You Red
Carnations.
Lindsay, N.   Galahad, Knight Who Perished.
Litany of the Heroes.
Longfellow, H.   Skeleton in Armor [or Armour],
The.
Lowell, R.   For the Union Dead.
Marvell.   Loyal Scot, The.
McGrath, T.   Heroes of Childhood, The.
Melville, H.   Commemorative of a Naval
Victory.
Meredith, G.   October 21, 1905.
Nemerov.   Hero Comes Home in His Hamper,
and Is Exhibited at the World's Fair, The.
Who Did Not Die in Vain.
Olson, C.   Unfinished (raw) hero—un-, The.
Parker, D.   Balto; The Lead Dog of the Team
that Brough Antitoxin to Nome.
Patchen.   Childhood of the Hero.
Plath.   Times Are Tidy, The.
Riley, J.   Nicholas Oberting.
William Brown.
Ritsos.   1972.
Rukeyser, M.   Hero Speech.
Trophies.
Smart, C.   Ode to Admiral Sir George Pocock.
Ode to General Draper.
Spender, S.   I Think Continually of Those Who
Were Truly Great.
Seascape.
Stafford, W.   Allegiances.
At the Grave of My Brother: Bomber Pilot.
Stock, R.   Certain Paralipomena to an Unbegun
Epic.
Szymborska, W.   Pietà.
Tomlinson, C.   Hero Sandwiches.
Whitman, W.   Return of the Heroes, The.
Wallabout Martyrs, The.
Whittier.   Derne.
Hero, The.
Wilbur, R.   Beowulf.
Williams, C. K.   Herakles.
Williams, T.   Part of a Hero.
Williams, W.   Childe Harold to the Round
Tower Came.
Hero.

Heroin
Ai.   Boys and Girls, Lenny Bruce, or Back from
the Dead.
Codrescu.   Junk Dawn, NYC.
Dubie.   Bus Stopped in Fields of Misdemeanor,
The.
See also **Drug Addiction**

Herons
Berry, W.   Heron, The.
Ciardi, J.   Snowy Heron.
Hamill, S.   Black Marsh Eclogue.
Jeffers, R.   People and a Heron.
Kizer, C.   Great Blue Heron, The.
Oliver, M.   Some Herons.

Roethke.   Heron, The.
Stafford, W.   Spirit of Place: Great Blue Heron.
Tomlinson, C.   To See the Heron.
Wright, J.   Old Age Compensation.
Small Blue Heron, The.

Herrick, Robert
Herrick.   On Himselfe.
Upon Himself.
Upon Himselfe.
Upon the Loss[e] of His Mistresses.

Herring
MacDiarmid, H.   With the Herring Fishers.

Hiawatha
Longfellow, H.   Hiawatha's Childhood.
Hiawatha's Fasting.

Hibiscus
Stevens, W.   Hibiscus on the Sleeping Shores.

Hiccups
MacNeice.   Messiah, The.

Highlands of Scotland
See **Scottish Highlands**

Highways
Carver, R.   Highway 99E from Chico.
Dugan, A.   Poem: "Whatever was living is
dead."
Laughlin, J.   Highway 66.
Levertov.   Merritt Parkway.
See also **Roads**

Hiking and Hikers
Carruth, H.   Lost.
Collins, B.   Directions.
Kinsella, T.   Route of the Táin, The.
Kumin, M.   You Are in Bear Country.
Merwin.   Hearing.
Muldoon, P.   Rucksack, The.
Pinkerton, H.   Sierra Nevada Hike.
Tomlinson, C.   Hill, The.
Warren, R.   Convergences.
Far West Once.
Last Walk of Season.

Hilary, Saint
Rossetti, D.   Pax Vobis.
World's Worth.

Hills and Mountains
Ammons.   Close-up.
Delaware Water Gap.
Ground Tide.
Height.
Mountain Talk.
Sorting.
Berry, W.   Song (2).
Bogan, L.   Last Hill in a Vista.
Brontë, E.   Stanzas: "Often rebuked, yet always
back returning."
What is that smoke that ever still.
Burns, R.   Written with a Pencil over the
Chimney-Piece, in the Parlour of the Inn.
Coleridge, S.   Stanger Minstrel, A.
To a Young Friend.
Crane, S.   On the horizon the peaks assembled.
Creeley.   Hill, The.
Cummings, E. E.   At dusk / just when.
Perished have safe small.
Sunset.
De la Mare.   Crazed.
Mountains, The.
Dickinson, E.   Alter! When the Hills do—.
Mountain sat upon the Plain, The.
Mountains grow—unnoticed, The.
Emerson, R.   Fable: "Mountain and the squirrel,
The."
Frost, R.   Meeting and Passing.
Mountain, The.
Gurney, I.   On Foscombe Hill.
Touchstone—Watching Malvern, The.
Hall, D.   Sleeping Giant, The.
Southwest of Buffalo.
Hardy, T.   Rome: On the Palatine.
Schreckhorn, The.
Under High-Stoy Hill.
Hopkins, G.   Hill / Heaven and every field, are
still.
Hughes, L.   Big Sur.
Hughes, T.   Bear, The.
Kinsella, T.   Liffey Hill, The.

Kipling, R.   Ballade of Burial, A.
Floods, The.
Sea and the Hills, The.
Kumin, M.   Halfway.
Larkin, P.   Hills in Their Recumbent Postures,
The.
Lawrence, D. H.   At the Cearne.
Hills, The.
MacDiarmid, H.   Ross-shire Hills, The.
MacLeish.   Pony Rock.
Merwin.   Calling under the Breath, The.
Dream Again, The.
Sleeping Mountain, The.
South.
Summits.
Palmer, M.   Idem 4.
Rexroth, K.   Toward an Organic Philosophy.
Your Birthday in the California Mountains.
Riley, J.   'Mongst the Hills o' Somerset.
Rilke.   Night Has Come.
Ritsos.   First Sensual Delight, The.
Hill, The.
Robinson, E.   Dark Hills, The.
Rossetti, C.   Uphill.
Rukeyser, M.   Alloy.
Sandburg, C.   Cornfield Ridge and Stream
Three Hills Look Different in the Moonshine.
Uplands in May.
Schuyler, J.   Awoke.
Snyder, G.   Mid-August at Sourdough Mountain
Lookout.
Sours of the Hills.
Spender, S.   Pylons, The.
Tomlinson, C.   Blaubeuren.
Hill, The.
Ute Mountain.
Warren, R.   Golden Hills of Hell, The.
Whittier.   Hill-Top, The.
Williams, W.   Stroller.
Wordsworth, W.   Trosachs, The.
Wansfell! This Household Has a Favoured Lot.
See also **Mountain Climbing**

Himalayas
Laughlin, J.   Mountain, The.
Szymborska, W.   Notes from a Nonexistent
Himalayan Expedition.

Hinduism and Hindus
Ginsberg, A.   On Illness.
Laughlin, J.   Apsarases.
At Benares.
Holy Rivers, The.
Layers.
Nothing That's Lovely Can My Love Escape.
MacNeice.   Mahabalipuram.
Merton.   Hrishikesa, destroyer of Titans, ogres
and canailles.
Pinsky.   Shiva and Parvati Hiding in the Rain.
Ramanujan.   Conventions of Despair.
Death and the Good Citizen.
Devotee's Complaint, A.
Difference, The.
HINDOO, THE: He Doesn't Hurt a Fly or a
Spider Either.
HINDOO, THE: He Reads His GITA and Is
Calm at All Events.
HINDOO, THE: The Only Risk.
One, Two, Maybe Three, Arguments against
Suicide.
Second Sight.
Snyder, G.   No Shoes No Shirt No Service.
Stock, R.   Again I'm Torched and Wonder What
We've Wrought.
Wilner, E.   Maya.
Nandin's Tail.
Yeats.   Indian upon God, The [or An].

Hippies
Angelou.   Take Time Out.
Dickey, J.   False Youth: Autumn: Clothes of the
Age.
Ferlinghetti, L.   John Lennon in the Porto Santo
Stefano.

Hippopotamuses
Eliot, T. S.   Hippopotamus, The.
Nash, O.   Hippopotamus, The.
Roethke.   Hippo, The.

Hips
Heaney, S.   Sheelagh na Gig.

Hiroshige, Ando
Szymborska, W.   People on the Bridge.
People on the Bridge, The.

Hiroshima, Japan
Levertov.   On the 32nd Anniversary of the
   Bombing of Hiroshima and Nagasaki.
Levine, P.   Horse, The.
Merton.   Original Child Bomb.
Stafford, W.   November.
Warren, R.   New Dawn.

History and Historians
Amichai [or Amikhai].   At the University of
   New Orleans.
Evidence.
False Interpretation.
History.
In a Foreign Country.
Late Marriage.
"Rustle of History's Wings," as They Used to
   Say Then, The.
Angelou.   Family Affairs.
Armantrout.   Natural History.
Ashbery, J.   Tapestry.
Atwood.   1837 War in Retrospect.
Comic Books vs. History.
Marrying the Hangman.
Auden.   Fall of Rome, The.
Homage to Clio.
Makers of History.
Beckett, S.   Ainsi a-t-on beau.
Berry, W.   Design of a House, The.
Dream, The.
Meditation in the Spring Rain.
Sowing.
Where.
Berryman.   Boston Common.
Borges.   Compass.
Gunnar Thorgilsson (1816-1879).
History of the Night.
Note for a Fantastic Story.
Page to Commemorate Colonel Suárez, Victor at
   Junín, A.
Brodsky, J.   Anno Domini.
Anti-Shenandoah: Two Skits and a Chorus.
Bust of Tiberius, The.
Cappadocia.
End of a Beautiful Era, The.
History of the Twentieth Century (A
   Roadshow).
Letters to a Roman Friend.
MCMXCIV.
Mexican Divertimento.
Photograph, A.
Twenty Sonnets to Mary Queen of Scots.
Bukowski.   It's Not Who Lived Here.
Burns, R.   Caledonia.
Epistle to Mr Tytler of Woodhouselee, Author
   of a Defence of Mary Queen of Scots.
Campion, T.   Ad Guil. Camdenum.
Carew, T.   To My Friend, Will. Davenant.
Carruth, H.   Sociology of Toyotas and Jade
   Chrysanthemums, The.
Sparrows.
Spring Notes from Robin Hill.
Carver, R.   Wake Up.
Cavafy.   Orophernis.
Celan.   Just Think.
Rogues' and Gonifs' Ditty, A.
Char.   At the Gates of Aerea.
Ciardi, J.   Back.
On Looking East to the Sea with a Sunset
   behind Me.
To a Young American the Day after the Fall of
   Barcelona.
Clampitt.   Dahlia Gardens, The.
Clifton, L.   Photograph, The: A Lynching.
Sorrow Song.
Why some people be mad at me sometimes.
Clough.   To think that men of former days.
Codrescu.   Brief (Remembered) *Histoire* of
   Rejection, A.
Comrade Past & Mister Present.
November 6, 1984.
Collins, B.   History of Weather, A.

History Teacher, The.
Lesson, The.
Tomes.
Cooper, J.   Past, The.
Cowper, W.   Ode on *Sir Charles Grandison*.
Cummings, E. E.   All nearness pauses, while a
   star can grow.
Puella Mea.
Remarked Robinson Jefferson.
Thou in whose swordgreat story shine the deeds.
Davie, D.   August, 1968.
Cowper's 'Yardley Oak': A Continuation.
Vancouver.
Vindication of Jovan Babič, The.
Wild Boar Clough.
Du Bellay.   Rome.
Dubie.   Reader of the Sentences, The.
Dugan, A.   On Herodotus.
Significance of Corn in American History, The.
Untitled Poem: "Once, one of my students read
   a book we had."
Eliot, T. S.   Defense of the Islands.
Emerson, R.   History & prophecy are alike.
I am owner of the sphere.
I must not borrow light.
Mottoes to "History."
Solution.
Thanks to those who go & come.
Enzensberger, H.   Historical Process.
Old Revolution.
Poem about the Future.
Summer Poem.
Thoughts on the Run 1.
Thoughts on the Run 3.
Ferlinghetti, L.   Cro-Magnons.
History of the World: a TV Docu-Drama.
Frost, R.   Never Naught Song, A.
Peaceful Shepherd, The.
Planners, The.
Gallagher, T.   Small Garden near a Field.
García Lorca.   St. Raphael.
Ginsberg, A.   Birdbrain!
Café in Warsaw.
Capitol Air.
Death to Van Gogh's Ear!
Either we blow ourselves up now and die, like
   the old tribe of man, arguing among neutrons.
Eroica.
Jaweh and Allah Battle.
Seabattle of Salamis Took Place off Perama.
Stotras to Kali Destroyer of Illusions.
Television Was a Baby Crawling toward That
   Deathchamber.
Glück, L.   Saturnalia.
Graves, R.   End of Play.
Gray, T.   Ode for Music.
Gunn, T.   Claus von Stauffenberg.
Hall, D.   Letter to an English Poet.
HaNagid.   I Quartered the Troops for the Night.
Hardy, T.   Aged Newspaper Soliloquizes, The.
Clasped Skeleton, The.
One We Knew.
Rome: Building a New Street in the Ancient
   Quarter.
Rome: On the Palatine.
Zermatt: To the Matterhorn.
Herbert, G.   Church Militant, The.
Hill, G.   History as Poetry.
Howe, S.   Cabbage Gardens.
Chanting at the Crystal Sea.
Hinge Picture.
Pythagorean Silence.
Secret History of the Dividing Line.
Some particular place fleeting.
Hughes, L.   Ballad of Negro History, A.
Ballad of the Seven Songs.
Freedom's Plow.
Goodbye Christ.
History.
Long View: Negro.
Negro Mother, The.
Negro Speaks of Rivers, The.
October 16: The Raid.
Prelude to Our Age.
Hughes, T.   Chinese History of Colden Water.
Jacobsen, J.   Rainy Night at the Writers'

Colony.
Jarrell, R.   Dead, The.
Memoirs of Glückel of Hameln, The.
Jeffers, R.   I Shall Laugh Purely.
Moon and Five Planets.
Ode to Hengist and Horsa.
Real and Half Real.
Jonson, B.   Mind of the Frontispiece to a Book,
   The.
To My Chosen Friend the Learnèd Translator of
   Lucan, Thomas May, Esquire.
To Sir Henry [or Henrie] Savile [upon His
   Translation of Tacitus].
Keats.   Lines Written in the Highlands after a
   Visit to Burns's Country.
Kipling, R.   Files, The.
France.
General Summary, A.
King's Task, The.
Land, The.
Philadelphia.
Pirates in England, The.
River's Tale, The.
Kizer, C.   Fin-de-Siècle Blues.
On a Line from Julian.
Kumin, M.   Festung, Salzburg, The.
History Lesson.
Photograph, U.S. Army Flying School, College
   Park, Maryland, 1909.
Kunitz, S.   Night Letter.
Larkin, P.   Arundel Tomb, An.
Plymouth.
Laughlin, J.   Like Him I Need the Past.
Lawrence, D. H.   Death of Our Era, The.
Under the Oak.
Levertov.   Desolate Light.
Shalom.
Winter Afternoons in the V & A, Pre-W.W. II.
Levi, P.   Pliny.
Levine, P.   Gift for a Believer.
New Season.
Sources.
Lindsay, N.   After Reading the Sad Story of the
   Fall of Babylon.
Litany of the Heroes.
Lowell, R.   History.
Lux.   Bodo.
History Books.
Mallarmé.   Hérodiade.
Marvell.   Upon Appleton House [To My Lord
   Fairfax].
McGrath, T.   Anniversaries.
In Praise of Necessity.
Political Song for the Year's End.
Theory, A.
Meredith, G.   I looked from the book of the
   story of men.
Il y a Cent Ans.
Karl Onyx.
Outside the Crowd.
Remember what a night of storm.
Merton.   King Solomon: my master and the
   imbeciles.
Tower of Babel.
Merwin.   For the Grave of Posterity.
Milosz, C.   1945.
Bypassing Rue Descartes.
Cabbies dozed under St. Mary's Tower.
Capri.
Child of Europe.
Earth.
Either-Or.
Family, A.
For Jan Lebenstein.
From the Chronicles of the Town of Pornic.
Hooks of a Corset, The.
I Do Not Understand.
In Warsaw.
Kazia.
La Belle Époque.
L'Accélération de l'Histoire.
Legend, A.
Ode for the Eightieth Birthday of Pope John
   Paul II.
On a Beach.
Preface: "First, plain speech in the mother

tongue."
Rivers ("'So lasting they are, the rivers!").
Six Lectures in Verse.
Spirit of the Laws, The.
Treatise on Poetry, A.
Under a linden tree, as before, daylight.
Undressing Justine.
Wanda.
Why.
Year 1900, The.
Muldoon, P. Madoc: A Mystery.
Nemerov. From a Record of Disappointment.
To Clio, Muse of History.
Truth of the Matter, The.
O'Hara, F. In Memory of My Feelings.
Olson, C. At Yorktown.
Ballad for Americans.
Bigmans II.
Buffalo Ode.
Collected Poems of, The.
He, Who, in His Abandnoned Infancy, Spoke of
 Jesus, Caesar, Those Who Beg, and Hell.
Kingfishers, The.
Mathematical Secret, and the Apron, The.
Praises, The.
To Gerhardt, There, among Europe's Things of
 Which He Has Written Us in His "Brief an
 Creely und Olson."
Oppen. Book of Job and a Draft of a Poem to
 Praise the Paths of the Living, The.
Eros.
Founder, The.
Language of New York, A.
Little Pin, The: Fragment.
Mayan Ground, The.
Pagis. Caveman Is Not about to Talk, The.
Pasolini. Ashes of Gramsci, The.
Desperate Vitality, A.
Plan of Future Works.
Poetry of the Tradition, The.
Religion of My Time, The.
Tears of the Excavator, The.
Patchen. History in a Minor Key.
History Is a Throne and a Gate.
Two for History.
Pessoa. Message.
Piercy. For Shoshana Rihn —Pat Swinton.
Pinsky. At Pleasure Bay.
Figured Wheel, The.
Ginza Samba.
Shirt.
Pope, A. Fragment of Brutus, an Epic.
Windsor-Forest [or Windsor Forest].
Prunty. Oh General, Oh Spy, Oh Bureaucrat!
Raine, K. Oracles.
Ralegh, S. Arcadians the earth inhabited, The.
Ramanujan. History.
If Eyes Can See.
Report, A.
Some Indian Uses of History on a Rainy Day.
Rexroth, K. Another Early Morning Exercise.
Dragon and the Unicorn, The.
From the Paris Commune to the Kronstadt
 Rebellion.
Harmodius and Aristogeiton.
New Objectives, New Cadres.
Past and Future Turn About.
Phoenix and the Tortoise, The.
Pliny—9, 36—Lampridius—29.
Rich, A. Culture and Anarchy.
Education of a Novelist.
Living Memory.
Mathilde in Normandy.
Readings of History.
Study of History.
Turning the Wheel.
Rimbaud, A. Dead of '92 and '93, The.
Rossetti, D. Burden of Nineveh, The.
Rukeyser, M. Book of the Dead, The.
Correspondences.
Sea Mercy.
Theory of Flight.
Sandburg, C. Accomplished Facts.
Bilbea.
Bronzes.
Coin, A.

Good Morning, America.
I Am the People, the Mob.
Many Hats.
Nigger.
Old Timers.
Santa Fe Sketches.
Savoir Faire.
Singing Nigger.
Statistics.
They Buy with an Eye to Looks.
Wars.
Windy City, The.
Schuyler, J. Eyes at the Window.
Fauré Ballade, The.
Seifert. At the Tomb of the Czech Kings.
Bombing of the Town of Kralupy, The.
Canal Gardens.
Head of the Virgin Mary, The.
Moscow.
Red-Hot Fruit.
When in the history books.
Year 1934, The.
Simic. East[ern] European Cooking.
History.
History Book.
Little Tear Gland That Says, The.
Soup, The.
Smith, S. How Cruel Is the Story of Eve.
Ride, The.
Snyder, G. Building.
What Happened Here Before.
Spender, S. Exiles, The.
Footnote, A.
Stafford, W. Being an American.
Entering History.
Ground Zero [June 1982].
History Display.
Something to Declare.
Stereopticon.
Stock, R. Henry Hudson.
Louis XI.
Triadic Node for Tim Reynold's Digestion.
Stockton, A. Thoughts on the Pythagorian
 System.
Sze. Axis, The.
Every Where and Every When.
Viewing Photographs of China.
Szymborska, W. Century's Decline, The.
Clochard.
Hatred.
Reality Demands.
Tale Begun, A.
Turn of the Century, The.
Tate, A. Historical Epitaphs.
Mediterranean, The.
Tomlinson, C. Assassin.
Compact, The: at Volterra.
History.
On the Tlacolula Bus.
Siena in Sixty-Eight.
Updike. Comp. Religion.
Klimt and Schiele Confront the Cunt.
Literary Dublin.
Sonnet to Man-Made Grandeur.
Very. Lessons of History Unlearned, The.
On the Neglect of the Study of History.
Reflections on the History of Nations.
Teaching of History Confirmed, The.
Villon. Ballade of the Ladies of Time Past.
Walcott. Sea Is History, The.
Warren, R. Empire.
Lesson in History.
Remark for Historians.
Shoes In Rain Jungle.
Two Studies in Idealism: Short Survey of
 American and Human History.
Wind and Gibbon.
Whalen, P. Occasional Dilemmas.
Whitman, W. Death of General Grant.
Few Drops Known, The.
On the Same Picture.
To a Historian.
To-day and Thee.
With Antecedents.
Whittier. Landmarks, The.
Sycamores, The.

Yorktown.
Wilbur, R. Looking into History.
Speech for the Repeal of the McCarran Act.
Waters, The.
Wilde, O. Humanitad.
Louis Napoleon.
Quantum Mutata.
Williams, C. K. This Is a Sin.
Williams, M. 10,000-Year-Old Tree Discovered
 Shades Two and Half Acres.
Architecture of the American Mind.
Of History and Hope.
Sir.
Tearing Down the Hotel.
Wilner, E. Amelia.
Wordsworth, W. Apology.
Artegal and Elidure.
Conclusion: "Why Sleeps the future, as a snake
 enrolled."
Ecclesiastical Sonnets.
Go Back to Antique Ages, if Thine Eyes.
In Allusion to Various Recent Histories and
 Notices of the French Revolution.
In Allusion to Various Recent Histories and
 Notices of the French Revolution, Concluded.
In Allusion to Various Recent Histories and
 Notices of the French Revolution, Continued.
In the Sound of Mull.
Massy Ways Carried across These Heights, The.
Mutability.
On the Same Occasion [on Seeing the
 Foundation Preparing for the Erection of
 Rydal Chapel].
Roman Antiquities.
Roman Antiquities Discovered at Bishopstone,
 Hereforshire.
To the Rev. Christopher Wordsworth, D.D.,
 Master of Harrow School.
Wright, C. Chickamauga.
Journal of the Year of the Ox, A.
Maple on the Hill.
Negatives 2.
To the Egyptian Mummy in the Etruscan
 Museum at Cortona.
Yeats. Lapis Lazuli.
Zagajewski. 1969.
Referendum.
Sails.
September Afternoon in the Abandoned
 Barracks.
Talk with Friedrich Nietzsche, A.
Thirties, The.
Zukofsky, L. Poem Beginning "The."

Hitchhiking and Hitchhikers

Ai. Hitchhiker, The.
Ciardi, J. Faces.
Laughlin, J. Hitchhiker, The.
Muldoon, P. Good Friday, 1971. Driving
 Westward.
Stafford, W. Once in the 40s.

Hitler, Adolf

Carruth, H. Adolf Eichmann.
Dugan, A. Memories of 1936–7.
Enzensberger, H. Portrait of a House Detective.
Gunn, T. Claus von Stauffenberg.
Hughes, L. Just an Ordinary Guy.
Total War.
Jeffers, R. Bowl of Blood, The.
Day Is a Poem, The.
Kunitz, S. Around Pastor Bonhoeffer.
Lowell, R. Attila, Hitler.
Montale. Hitler Spring, The.
Rukeyser, M. Another Day. A Game of Toys.
Paul, Telling the Game.
Another Day (You can't come).
Traditional Tune.
Szymborska, W. Hitler's First Photograph.
Updike. Munich.

Hitomaro (Kakinomoto no Hitomaro)

Hamill, S. Uta Mound, The.

Ho Chi Minh

Komunyakaa. Summer Night in Hanoi, A.

Hobbes, Thomas

Enzensberger, H. Cold Comfort.

Hoboes
Riley, J. Hobo Voluntary, A.
Lounger, A.
See also **Vagabonds**
Hoffa, Jimmy
Ai. Jimmy Hoffa's Odyssey.
Hogarth, William
Johnson, S. Epitaph on William Hogarth, An.
Hogg, James
Wordsworth, W. Extempore Effusion upon the
Death of James Hogg.
Hogue, La, Battle of (1692)
Cummings, E. E. No time ago / or else a life.
Hokusai, Katsushika
Hamill, S. Unforgiven.
Sandburg, C. His Own Face Hidden.
Hölderlin, Friedrich
Celan. Tübingen, January.
Holes
Laughlin, J. Holes.
Holiday, Billie
Carruth, H. Billie Holiday.
Hughes, L. Song for Billie Holiday.
O'Hara, F. Day Lady Died, The.
Holidays
Carver, R. Songs in the Distance.
Cavafy. Poseidonians.
Dickinson, E. Lest any doubt that we are glad
that they were born Today.
Gunn, T. At the Barriers.
Hardy, T. Yuletide in a Younger World.
Herrick. Ceremonies for Candlemas[se] Eve.
Lawrence, D. H. August Holidays.
MacNeice. Postcript to Iceland.
Merton. Old.
Nemerov. Home for the Holidays.
O'Hara, F. Ashes on a Saturday Afternoon.
Spender, S. Sign *Faehre nach Wilm*, The.
Williams, C. K. Holiday: / every / yard or, A.
Holland
Brodsky, J. Dutch Mistress.
Kizer, C. Postcards from Rotterdam.
See also **Netherlands**
Holly
Ammons. Holly.
Rossetti, C. Golden Holly.
Rose has thorns as well as honey, A.
Hollyhocks
Ammons. Clearing the Dark Symbiosis.
Hollywood, California
Jarrell, R. Lost World, The.
Thinking of the Lost World.
Laughlin, J. Cynthia in California.
Parker, D. Passionate Screen Writer to His
Love, The.
Song of Social Life in Hollywood.
Sandburg, C. Landscape.
Holmes, Oliver Wendell
Whittier. O. W. Holmes on His Eightieth
Birthday.
Our Autocrat.
To Oliver Wendell Holmes.
Holocaust
Amichai [*or* Amikhai]. Almost a Love Poem.
Hymn for Independence Day, A. So distant.
I Guard the Children.
Little Ruth.
Berry, W. Discipline, A.
Broumas, O. No Harm Shall Come.
Bukowski. When the Berry Bush Dies I'll
Swim Down the Green River with My Hair on
Fire.
Carruth, H. Adolf Eichmann.
Event Itself, The.
Celan. Aspen Tree.
Black Flakes.
Darkness.
Deathfugue.
In Prague.
It's all different from what you think, from what
I think.
Just Think.
Nearness of Graves.
Nocturne: "Sleep not. Be on your guard."

Shibboleth.
Sluice, The.
Tabernacle Window.
Tenebrae.
There stood / a splinter of fig on your lip.
Tübingen, January.
Winter.
Wolfsbean.
Clampitt. Burning Child, The.
Davie, D. Hawkshead and Dachau in a
Christmas Glass.
Fenton, J. Doctor Gliedschirm, skin specialist,
surgeries 14–16 hours or by appointment.
German Requiem, A.
Glück, L. Parable, A.
Hayden, R. From the Corpse Woodpiles, from
the Ashes.
Hill, G. I Had Hope When Violence Was
Ceas't.
Ovid in the Third Reich.
September Song.
Two Formal Elegies.
Jarrell, R. Camp in the Prussian Forest, A.
In the Camp There Was One Alive.
Protocols.
Levertov. During the Eichmann Trial.
When We Look Up.
Levi, P. 11 February 1946.
25 February 1944.
Buna.
Crow's Song 2, The.
For Adolf Eichmann.
Gedale's Song.
On Trial.
Reveille.
Shemà.
Singing.
Song of Those Who Died in Vain.
Sunset at Fossoli.
Survivor, The.
Waiting.
Lindsay, N. Scissors-Grinder, The.
Mahon. Disused Shed in Co. Wexford, A.
McGrath, T. Remembering the Children of
Auschwitz.
Merton. Epitaph for a Public Servant.
Milosz, C. Child of Europe.
Oliver, M. 1945—1985: Poem for the
Anniversary.
Olson, C. La Préface.
Pagis. Autobiography.
Draft of a Reparations Agreement.
Encounters.
Europe, Late.
Footprints.
Instructions for Crossing the Border.
Testimony.
Written in Pencil in the Sealed Railway-Car.
Paley, G. Translation.
Pinsky. Unseen, The.
Plath. Daddy.
Mary's Song.
Ramanujan. As Eichmann Said, My Brother
Said.
Schuyler, J. Let's All Hear It for Mildred
Bailey!
Seifert. Lost Paradise.
Sexton. After Auschwitz.
Uses.
Szymborska, W. Starvation Camp at Jasło.
Still.
Weiss, T. Late Train, The.
Pair of Shoes, A.
Williams, C. K. Spit.
Williams, M. Book, The.
Zagajewski. Generation, The.
Summer's Fullness.
Talk with Friedrich Nietzsche, A.
Three Kings, The.
Watching Shoah in a Hotel Room in America.
Zukofsky, L. Song for the Year's End, A.

Holy Baptism
See **Baptism**
Holy Communion
See **Eucharist**
Holy Family
Brodsky, J. Nativity.
Merton. Holy Child's Song, The.
Rossetti, D. Passover in the Holy Family, The.
Rukeyser, M. Holy Family.
Holy Ghost
Davie, D. Comforter, The.
Eberhart, R. Track.
Herbert, G. Whitsunday.
Lawrence, D. H. God and the Holy Ghost.
Rilke. Holy Ghost.
Rossetti, C. Whitsun Day.
Smith, S. How Do You See?
Holy Innocents
Rossetti, C. Holy Innocents.
Unspotted lambs to follow the one Lamb.
Holy Roman Empire
Lowell, R. Charles V by Titian.
Holy Spirit
Berry, W. To the Holy Spirit.
Davie, D. Cannibals.
Herrick. Gods Dwelling.
Milosz, C. Veni Creator.
Very. Help of the Spirit, The.
Hymn: Prayer for the Gift of the Holy Spirit.
Hymn: The Spirit Itself Maketh Intercession for
Us.
Lost, The ("Fairest day that ever yet has shone,
The").
So is every one who is born of the spirit.
Teachings of the Spirit, The.
Holy Thursday
Rossetti, C. Maundy Thursday.
Home
Amichai [*or* Amikhai]. Jews in the Land of
Israel.
Kibbutz Gevaram.
We Did What We Had To.
When a Man's Far Away from His Country.
Armantrout. Double.
Berry, W. Returning.
Stay Home.
Brodsky, J. Ischia in October.
October Tune.
Brooks, G. Ballad of Rudolph Reed, The.
Broumas, O. Native.
Burns, R. Banks of Nith, The.
My Heart's in the Highlands.
Song: "Their groves o' sweet myrtle let Foreign
Lands reckon."
Wren's Nest, The.
Byron, G. Wild Gazelle, The.
Cavafy. In the Same Space.
Ciardi, J. Talking Myself to Sleep at One More
Hilton.
Clampitt. John Donne in California.
Clough. Come Home, Come Home!
Coleridge, S. Happy Home, The.
Collins, B. Where I Live.
Creeley. Away.
Coming Home.
For the Graduation: Bolinas, 1972.
Mobile Homes.
Please.
Cummings, E. E. Home means that / when the
certainly.
De la Mare. Comfort.
Tryst, The.
Dickinson, E. Fairest Home I ever knew, The.
Home is the riddle of the wise.
Home itself is far from home.
I learned—at least—what Home could be.
Where Thou art—that—is Home.
You spoke of "Hope" surpassing "Home."
Donne. To Sir Henry Wotton ("Sir, more than
kisses, letters mingle souls").
Dove, R. Dusting.
Dunbar, P. Hope.
Possum Trot.
Eberhart, R. Examination of Psyche: Thoughts
of Home.

Eliot, T. S.   To the Indians Who Died in Africa.
Emerson, R.   Poet is at home, A.
  That each should in his house abide.
  Thou shalt make thy house.
  Una.
Frost, R.   Death of the Hired Man, The.
  Thatch, The.
Gallagher, T.   Coming Home.
  View from an Empty Chair.
Glück, L.   Adult Grief.
Gunn, T.   Thoughts on Unpacking.
Guyon.   Soul That Loves God Finds Him Every
  Where, The.
Hacker, M.   Two Cities.
Hamill, S.   Lover's Quarrel, A.
Han-shan.   Cold Mountain is a house.
Hardy, T.   Concerning His Old Home.
Herrick.   Thanksgiving to God for His House,
  A.
Housman.   Recruit, The.
Hughes, L.   Carolina Cabin.
  Kid in the Park.
Jeffers, R.   Salvage.
Kipling, R.   Coastwise Lights, The.
  Flowers, The.
  Lichtenberg.
  Native-Born, The.
  Recall, The.
  Roman Centurion's Song, The.
  Song of the Wise Children.
  Sussex.
  Virginity, The.
Larkin, P.   Home Is So Sad.
  Story.
Laughlin, J.   Die Heimat.
Lawrence, D. H.   End of Another Home
  Holiday.
Levertov.   Room.
Levi, P.   After R.M. Rilke.
Levine, P.   7 Years from Somewhere.
Lux.   He Has Lived in Many Houses.
MacLeish.   New England Weather.
  Sketch for a Portrait of Mme. G———M——.
  Where a Poet's From.
Mahon.   Afterlives.
  Ford Manor.
Major, C.   View from His Room.
Merrill, J.   Another August.
Merwin.   North Wind.
Millay, E.   On the Wide Heath.
Milosz, C.   In a City.
  My Grandfather Sigismund Kunat.
Mistral, G.   Request for Blanca, A.
Nemerov.   Home for the Holidays.
  Succession.
Parker, D.   Homebody, The.
Piercy.   Concerning the Mathematician.
  Homesick.
  Spring Offensive of the Snail, The.
Pinsky.   Street, The.
Prunty.   Intermittent Light, An.
  Lake House, The.
  Razed House, The.
Raine, K.   Message from Home.
  Spell to Bring Lost Creatures Home.
Rexroth, K.   Bread and Butter Letter, A.
Rich, A.   Strayed Village, The.
  Tourist and the Town, The.
  Wild Sky, The.
Riley, J.   His Love of Home.
  Home at Night.
  Home-Folks.
Rilke.   Dance on the Staircase, The.
Robinson, E.   House on the Hill, The.
Roethke.   Return, The.
Rossetti, C.   Discovery, A.
  End Is Not Yet, The.
  Hear what the mournful linnets say.
  How One Chose.
  Ruin.
Rukeyser, M.   Book of the Dead, The.
  Man in a plane looks at the surface of land, A.
  Song, from "Mr. Amazeen on the River."
  This House, This Country.
Sandburg, C.   Crimson Rambler.

Knucks.
Sarton, M.   Der Abschied.
Sexton.   January 19th.
Shelley, P.   Fragment: Home.
Sheridan, T.   To the Dean, when in England, in
  1726.
Snyder, G.   Not Leaving the House.
Stafford, W.   At Our House.
  Home State.
  Looking for You.
  One Home.
Szymborska, W.   Going Home.
Tomlinson, C.   Against Travel.
Updike.   House Growing, The.
Very.   Home of my youth! Where first my lot
  was cast.
  Home, The ("Love builds for us a bower").
Walcott.   Exile.
  Return to D'Ennery; Rain.
Walker, A.   On Being Asked to Leave a Place of
  Honor for One of Comfort.
Weiss, T.   Poem Recalled, A.
Whitman, W.   O Magnet-South.
Whittier.   Homestead, The.
Williams, M.   Shrinking Lonesome Sestina, The.
Wordsworth, W.   Admonition.
  Composed by the Sea-Shore.
  Composed when a Probability Existed of Our
    Being Obliged to Quit Rydal Mount.
  Farewell, A: "Farewell thou little Nook of
    mountain-ground."
  Ruined Cottage, The.
Wright, J.   Father.
Yeats.   Under Saturn.
Zaturenska.   Quiet House, The.

Homecoming
Amichai [or Amikhai].   Jerusalem, 1967.
Angelou.   Mothering Blackness, The.
Arnold, M.   Resignation.
Atwood.   Bus to Alliston, Ontario, The.
Beckett, S.   Sanies I.
Berry, W.   Homecoming, A.
Berryman.   Home Ballad, The.
Borges.   Odyssey, Book Twenty-three.
  To Manuel Mujica Lainez.
Burns, R.   When wild War's deadly blast was
  blawn.
Carew, T.   Upon Master Walter Montagu's
  Return from Travel.
Cavafy.   Ithaca.
Celan.   Homecoming.
Ciardi, J.   Homecoming—Massachusetts.
Corbett, W.   Late August.
Crane, S.   Behold, from the land of the farther
  suns.
Creeley.   Going Home.
Cummings, E. E.   Your homecoming will be my
  homecoming.
Dickey, J.   Coming Back to America.
Dove, R.   Son, The.
Dunbar, P.   Bein' Back Home.
  Goin' Back.
Eichendorff.   Moonlight Night.
Emerson, R.   Saadi loved the new & old.
Gay, J. et al.   Mary Gulliver to Capt. Lemuel
  Gulliver.
Graves, R.   Home-Coming, The.
Gurney, I.   After War.
Han-shan.   Last night I dreamt I went home.
Hardy, T.   Geographical Knowledge.
  His Visitor.
  Rover Come Home, The.
  Welcome Home.
Heaney, S.   Trial Runs.
Ho Ch'e Ch'ang.   Returning after I left my
  home in childhood.
Homer.   Daughters of Pandarus, The.
  Gardens of Alcinous, The.
  Mindes of men are ever so affected, The.
  Muse, / tell me of this man of wit.
  Sun descending, the Phæacian train, The.
Hughes, L.   Lover's Return.
Jarrell, R.   Transient Barracks.
Jeffers, R.   Northern Heather.
  Return.
Kinnell.   Road between Here and There, The.

Kipling, R.   Return, The.
  Troopin'
Kizer, C.   Ingathering.
Logan, J.   Returning Home.
MacLeish.   Journey Home.
Mahon.   Homecoming.
Meredith, G.   Periander.
  Richard Lionheart.
Meredith, W.   Ten-Day Leave.
Merrill, J.   Island in the Works.
Merton.   Poem in the Rain and the Sun.
Merwin.   Beginning of the Plains.
  Coming Back in the Spring.
  Home for Thanksgiving.
  Recognition.
  Way to the River, The.
Milosz, C.   And the City Stood in Its Brightness.
  City of My Youth.
  Lithuania, after Fifty-two Years.
Neruda.   Homecomings.
Olson, C.   How Things Change.
Owen, W.   Send-Off, The.
Pinkerton, H.   Return, The.
Raine, K.   On an Ancient Isle.
Rexroth, K.   Runaway.
Riley, J.   Back from Town.
  Home Again.
  Home Ag'in.
  How John Quit the Farm.
  Like His Mother Used to Make.
  Old Band, The
  Regardin' Terry Hut.
  We Must Get Home.
Rossetti, C.   Italia, Io Ti Saluto!
  Minnie bakes oaten cakes, / Minnie brews ale.
Rukeyser, M.   Fifth Elegy. A Turning Wind.
  Shortest Way Home, The.
  Welcome from War.
Sarton, M.   Return.
  To the North.
Schuyler, J.   Elizabethans Called It Dying, The.
  Up.
"Shu Ting."   Returning Home.
Stafford, W.   Homecoming.
  Looking for You.
Tu Fu.   My Home Town.
Unknown.   I have come home. Fortune and
  Hope, goodbye!
Vogl.   Recognition, The.
Walcott.   Homecoming: Anse La Raye.
Weiss, T.   Certain Village, A.
Whitman, W.   Twenty Years.
Wilner, E.   Coda, Overture.
Wordsworth, W.   Composed in the Valley near
  Dover, on the Day of Landing.
Wright, J.   Homecoming.
  Homecoming Singer, The.

Homeless, The
Ashbery, J.   Street Musicians.
Berryman.   Boston Common.
Bukowski.   Private First Class.
Clare, J.   Tramp, The.
Dickey, J.   Bums, on Waking.
Emerson, R.   There are beggars in Iran and
  Araby.
Ginsberg, A.   New Stanzas for Amazing Grace.
Gunn, T.   Improvisation.
  Old Meg.
  Outside the Diner.
Hughes, L.   Advertisement for the Waldorf-
  Astoria.
  Drama for Winter Night (Fifth Avenue).
  Grant Park.
  Park Bench.
Hughes, T.   November.
Komunyakaa.   "Everybody's Reading Li Po"
  Silkscreened on a Purple T-Shirt.
Laughlin, J.   He Lives in a Box.
  What Matters.
Lawrence, D. H.   Embankment at Night, before
  the War: Outcasts.
Merrill, J.   House, The.
Pessoa.   He came by, wanting to speak with me
  on a downtown street.
Ramanujan.   Poverty.
Rilke.   Dance on the Staircase, The.

Rimbaud, A. My Bohemia (Fantasy).
Sandburg, C. Old Woman.
Simic. Homeless, The.
Sze. Listening to a Broken Radio.
Thomas, D. Hunchback in the Park, The.
Williams, C. K. Harm.
  Park, The.
  Philadelphia: 1978.
  Thirst.
  Toil.
Williams, W. To a Poor Old Woman.

Homer
Atwood. Circe / Mud Poems.
Browning, R. Development.
Carruth, H. Light in the Locust Tree.
Carver, R. Wine.
Clampitt. Homer, A.D. 1982.
  Margate.
Cowper, W. Answer to Stanzas Addressed to
  Lady Hesketh.
  Inscription for a Bust of Homer.
  It is a maxim of much weight.
  On a Mistake in His Translation of Homer.
  To John Johnson.
Eberhart, R. Garden God, The.
Emerson, R. Solution.
Gurney, I. George Chapman—The Iliad.
Jeffers, R. Epic Stars, The.
Keats. On First Looking into Chapman's
  Homer.
  To Homer.
Kipling, R. When 'Omer Smote 'Is Bloomin'
  Lyre.
Oliver, M. Return, The.
Ramanujan. One More after Reading Homer.
Rexroth, K. Homer in Basic.
Ritsos. Conjunction "Or," The.
Tennyson, A. Lotus-Eaters, The.
Yeats. Woman Homer Sung, A.

Homer, Winslow
Pinkerton, H. On Winslow Homer's *Moonlight
  on Water* (1895).

Homesickness
Browning, R. Home-Thoughts, from Abroad.
Byron, G. Lachin y Gair.
Clampitt. Homeland.
Clough. Ye flags of Piccadilly, / Where I posted
  up and down.
Coleridge, S. Home-Sick.
  Lines Written in the Album at Elbingerode, in
  the Har[t]z Forest.
De la Mare. Homesick.
Du Bellay. Heureux Qui, comme Ulysse, a Fait
  un Beau Voyage.
  Sonnet from the Book of Regrets.
Dunbar, P. Home Longings.
  Letter, A.
  To the Eastern Shore.
García Lorca. Song of the Shop Boy.
Glück, L. Legend.
Homer. Daughters of Pandarus, The.
  Gardens of Alcinous, The.
  Mindes of men are ever so affected, The.
  Muse, / tell me of this man of wit.
  Sun descending, the *Phæacian* train, The.
Hughes, L. Homesick Blues.
Jarrell, R. Island, The.
Kipling, R. Broken Men, The.
  Fires, The.
  Moon of Other Days, The.
MacLeish. American Letter.
MacNeice. Nostalgia.
Petrarch. More I spread wings of desire to fly,
  The.
Ransom, J. Amphibious Crocodile.
Riley, J. Ringworm Frank.
Spender, S. Cornet Cornelius Rilke.
Wordsworth, W. Why, Minstrel, These
  Untuneful Murmurings.
Wright, J. Outside Fargo, North Dakota.

Homesteaders
Prunty. Covined Bird, The.
Whittier. Kansas Emigrants, The.

Homophobia
Broumas, O. Rumpelstiltskin.

Hughes, L. Café: 3 a.m.
Lorde. Poem for Women in Rage, A.
Williams, M. Coming Out.
Williams, T. I think the strange, the crazed, the
  queer.

Homosexuality and Homosexuals
Ai. Momento Mori.
Auden. Legend.
Berryman. Shirley & Auden.
Blake, W. Why was Cupid a Boy.
Broumas, O. Amazon Twins.
  Caritas.
  Innocence.
  Rumpelstiltskin.
  Snow White.
Byron, G. Cornelian, The.
  One Struggle More, and I Am Free.
  To Thyrza.
Cavafy. 25th Year of His Life, The.
  Days of 1896.
  Temethos, Antiochian; 400 A.D.
  Theater of Sidon (400 A.D.).
  Tobacco Shop Window, The.
  Two Young Men, 23 to 24 Years Old.
Crane, H. Modern Craft.
Creeley. All That Is Lovely in Men.
Cummings, E. E. In hammamet did camping
  queers et al).
Cunningham, J. Oedipean Mom and Dad, An.
Dickey, W. Alligators and Paris and North
  America.
  Rainbow Grocery, The.
Dickinson, E. You love me—you are sure.
García Lorca. Ode to Walt Whitman.
Ginsberg, A. Archetype Poem, The.
  Chances "R."
  Come All Ye Brave Boys.
  Everybody Sing.
  Howl.
  I Have Increased Power.
  Love Comes.
  Many Loves.
  Maybe Love.
  Please Master.
  Tethnakin D'oligo Pideuis Fainom Alaia.
  This Form of Life Needs Sex.
Gunn, T. At the Barriers.
  Blank, A.
  Bone.
  Differences, The.
  Menace, The.
  Miracle, The.
  Punch Rubicundus.
  San Francisco Streets.
  Sweet Things.
  Venetian Blind.
Hacker, M. Ballad of Ladies Lost and Found.
  Graffiti from the Gare Saint-Manqué.
  Partial Analysis.
Hughes, L. Café: 3 a.m.
Jonson, B. On Sir Voluptuous Beast.
Koch, K. Aus Einer Kindheit.
Lawrence, D. H. Ego-Bound Women.
  Modern Problems.
  Noble Englishman, The.
Lowell, R. Words for Hart Crane.
Meredith, W. Wholesome.
Michelangelo Buonarroti. You know, my Lord,
  that I too know you know.
Olson, C. Issues from the Hand of God.
Pasolini. Reality.
Plath. Lesbos.
Rimbaud, A. Deserts of Love, The.
  Idol, The. Arsehole Sonnet.
  Our buttocks aren't like theirs. Many times I've
  seen.
Schuyler, J. Morning of the Poem, The.
  Tom.
  Tom's Attempt to Seduce Big Brother Steve.
Sexton. Rapunzel.
Shapiro, K. Girls Fighting, Broadway.
Smith, S. Lord Barrenstock.
Stein, G. Men.
Van Duyn. Cities of the Plain, The.
Whitman, W. In Paths Untrodden.
  Not Heat Flames Up and Consumes.

Recorders Ages Hence.
  When I Heard at the Close Of The Day.
  Whoever You Are Holding Me Now in Hand.
Williams, M. Coming Out.
Williams, T. Blond Mediterraneans, The.
  Evening.
  I think the strange, the crazed, the queer.
  Pulse.
Wright, J. Sappho.

Honduras
Lorde. To the Girl Who Lives in a Tree.

Honesty
Atwood. We are hard on each other.
Burns, R. Epitaph on J-hn B-shby.
Campion, T. Dear if I with Guile.
  Faire if You Expect Admiring.
  Heart's Music.
  Maydes are simple, some men say.
  Some can flatter, some can faine.
  Were My Heart as Some Men's Are.
Cowper, W. Conversation.
  Friendship.
Creeley. Again.
  For Somebody's Marriage.
  Somebody Died.
Davie, D. Against Confidences.
Donne. Song: "Go and catch a falling star."
Dugan, A. Wall, Cave, and Pillar Statements,
  after Asôka.
Dunbar, P. My Sort o' Man.
Emerson, R. Hard is it to persuade the public
  mind of its plain duty & true interest.
  Papas Blondine / Grew tall & wise.
  Romany Girl, The.
Graves, R. Song: To Become Each Other.
Hall, D. Friend Revisited, A.
HaNagid. He'll Bring You Trouble.
Larkin, P. Talking in Bed.
Levertov. Mystery of Deep Candor, The.
Merwin. Walk-up.
Pessoa. Sonnet: "Could I say what I think,
  could I express."
Riley, J. Our Old Friend Neverfail.
  Somep'n Common-like.
Ritsos. Simple Honesty.
Rukeyser, M. Poem as Mask, The.
Rumi. Human Honesty.
Sandburg, C. Hogh Conspiratorial Persons.
  Implications.
  Tall Timber.
Shelley, P. Fragment: "What men gain fairly—
  that they should possess."
Van Duyn. What I Want to Say.
Whittier. Nauhaught, the Deacon.
Wyatt, S. Honesty.
Zukofsky, L. You three:—my wife.

Honey
Brooks, G. My Dreams, My Works Must Wait
  till after Hell.
Broumas, O. Sugar.
Dickinson, E. Within that little Hive.
Eberhart, R. Sunday in October.
Graves, R. Song: To a Rose.
"H. D." Fragment 113: "Not honey, / not the
  plunder of the bee."
Levertov. Second Didactic Poem.
Rossetti, C. Golden Glories.
  When the cows come home the milk is coming.
Sandburg, C. In Tall Grass.
Stafford, W. Looking for Gold.

Honey Eaters
Oliver, M. Happiness.

Honeymoons
Dubie. Buffalo Clouds over the Maestro Hoon.
Glück, L. Bridal Piece.
Hardy, T. Four Footprints.
Herrick. Epithalamy to Sir Thomas Southwell
  and His Lady, An.
Logan, J. New Poem.
Rexroth, K. It Is a German Honeymoon.
Rukeyser, M. Wedding Presents.
Seifert. Honeymoon.
Updike. Newlyweds, The.

Honeysuckle
Rossetti, C. O wind, where have you been.

Rossetti, D.   Honeysuckle, The.
Stafford, W.   Honeysuckle.
Zukofsky, L.   Wild Honeysuckle.

Hong Kong
Creeley.   Hong Kong Window.
Merton.   Picture of Lee Ying, A.

Honor
Berryman.   Scholars at the Orchid Pavilion.
Brontë, E.   M. Douglas to E.R. Gleneden.
Browning, R.   After.
   At the "Mermaid."
   Count Gismond.
Byron, G.   On Leaving Newstead Abbey.
Campion, T.   Ad Leam.
   O griefe, O spight, to see poore Vertue scorn'd.
Campion, T. *et al.*   Shall then a traiterous kis or
   a smile.
Carew, T.   To My Much Honoured Friend,
   Henry, Lord Carey of Leppington, Upon His
   Translation of Malvezzi.
Cavafy.   Anna Dalassini.
   Thermopylae.
   Those Who Fought for the Achaian Alliance.
Chaucer.   Lak of Stedfastnesse.
Chiabrera.   Pause, courteous Spirit!—Baldi
   supplicates.
Ciardi, J.   To One "Investigated" by the Last
   Senate Committee, or the Next.
Cowper, W.   To Dr. Darwin.
De la Mare.   Here Sleeps.
Dickinson, E.   All men for Honor hardest work.
   Judgment is justest.
   Sown in dishonor!
   There is nothing sweeter than Honor, but Love.
Donne.   To the Countess of Bedford ("Honour is
   so sublime perfection").
Dugan, A.   On Visiting a Veterans Hospital.
Emerson, R.   Quoth Saadi, when I stood before.
   Rex.
   Why honor the new men.
Graves, R.   Charm for Sound Sleeping, A.
   Song: Sword and Rose.
Herrick.   God to Be First Served.
   Studies to Be Supported.
   To His Learned Friend M. Jo. Harmar, Phisitian
   to Colledge of Westminster.
Hughes, L.   Crowns and Garlands.
Jeffers, R.   Tower beyond Tragedy, The.
Jonson, B.   Ode. To Sir William Sydney, on His
   Birthday.
   Song. To Celia ("Drink to me only with thine
   eyes").
   To Sir Edward Herbert.
   To Sir Henry Cary.
   To Sir Henry Nevil.
   To Thomas, Earl of Suffolk.
Kipling, R.   Dedication from "Barrack-Room
   Ballads."
   Pro-Consuls, The.
Levine, P.   Jewish Graveyards, Italy.
   My Poets.
   On the Murder of Lieutenant José Del Castillo
   by the Falangist Bravo Martinez.
   To Cipriano, in the Wind.
Lindsay, N.   Hearth Eternal, The.
   Honor among Scamps.
MacNeice.   Elegy for Minor Poets.
Melville, H.   College Colonel, The.
   On the Home Guards.
Meredith, G.   Preaching from a Spanish Ballad,
   A.
Olson, C.   Dramatis Personae.
Orlandi, G.   To the sound of trumpets rather
   than horns.
Owen, W.   S.I.W.
   To a Comrade in Flanders.
Petrarch.   Orso, upon your charger you may put.
   Victorious and triumphal laurel-tree.
Riley, J.   Noblest Service, The.
   Ours.
   To Edmund Clarence Stedman.
Roethke.   Reply to Censure.
Sandburg, C.   Bronzes.
   John Ericsson Day Memorial, 1918.
   Letters to Dead Imagists.
Suckling, S.   Loving and Beloved.

Sze.   In Your Honor.
Whitman, W.   To a Certain Cantatrice.
Wilbur, R.   Up, Jack.
Williams, M.   My Wife Reads the Paper at
   Breakfast on the Birthday of the Scottish Poet.
Wordsworth, W.   Say, what is Honour?—"'Tis
   the finest sense."
Wright, J.   Centenary Note: Inscribed to Little
   Crow, Leader of the Sioux Rebellion.
   In Memory of a Spanish Poet.
Wyatt, S.   Dido am I, the founder first of
   Carthage.

Hooch, Pieter de
Mahon.   Courtyards in Delft.

Hood, Thomas
Robinson, E.   Thomas Hood.

Hoopoes
Davie, D.   Depravity: Two Sermons.
Graves, R.   Hoopoe Tells Us How, The.
Montale.   Hoopoe, happy bird maligned.

Hoover, John Edgar
Ai.   Hoover, Edgar J.
   Hoover Trismegistus.

Hope
Amichai [*or* Amikhai].   Evening is lying at the
   horizon, donating blood, The.
   In this valley, where many waters.
   Oleander.
   Summer Evening in the Jerusalem Mountains.
   When I Was Young, the Whole Country Was
   Young.
Ammons.   Hope's Okay.
Angelou.   No No No No.
   Plagued Journey, A.
Arnold, M.   Self-Dependence.
Beckett, S.   Ce qu'ont les yeux.
Bly, R.   Poem in Three Parts.
Brontë, E.   And first an hour of mournful
   musing.
   Anticipation.
   Hope.
   Iernë's eyes were glazed and dim.
   What use is it to slumber here.
Broumas, O.   Betrothal / the Bride's Lament.
Browning, E.   Memory and Hope.
Browning, R.   Prologue: "O the old wall here!
   How I could pass."
Bukowski.   Crunch, The.
   One for the Shoeshine Man.
Burns, R.   Nithsdale's Welcome Hame.
   Song: "Anna, thy charms my bosom fire."
Byron, G.   Stanzas for Music.
Carruth, H.   Return to Love.
Carver, R.   Cutlery.
Chamfort.   Hope is a knave befools us
   evermore.
Clifton, L.   Hag Riding.
Coleridge, S.   Faith, Hope, and Charity.
   Fragment: "O'er the raised earth the gales of
   evening sigh."
   Hope and Tranquillity.
   Indifference of the Heavens, The.
   Lewti.
   Lines Suggested by the Last Words of
   Berengarius.
   Love, Hope, and Patience in Education.
   Love's Apparition and Evanishment.
   To Fortune.
   Visionary Hope, The.
   Work without Hope.
Cowper, W.   Hope.
   Hope, like the short-liv'd ray that gleams
   awhile.
Creeley.   Business, The.
   Carnival, The.
   For a Screaming Lady.
   Fragment, A: "On the street I am met with
   constant hostility."
   Mechanic, The.
   Myself.
   "Oh My Love."
   Wall, A.
   Walls.
Cullen, C.   Brown Boy to Brown Girl.
   From the Dark Tower.

Cummings, E. E.   Air, / be / comes / or.
   Chilly,murky night, A.
   !Hope / faith! / !life / love!
   So many selves(so many fiends and gods).
   Though your sorrows not.
   Thy face is a still white house of holy things.
   Unnoticed woman from whose kind large flesh.
Cunningham, J.   1 Corinthians 13: Commentary.
   "Dario."   Towers of God! Poets!
De la Mare.   Cage, The.
   Catechism, The.
   Euphrasy.
   Rachel.
   Virtue.
Dickinson, E.   Could Hope inspect her Basis.
   Faithful "I am sorry," A.
   Hope is a strange invention.
   Hope is a subtle Glutton
   "Hope" is the thing with feathers.
   I dwell in Possibility.
   I hope you may sometime be.
   Is this the Hope that opens and shuts.
   Promise is firmer than a Hope, A.
   Way Hope builds his House, The.
   You spoke of "Hope" surpassing "Home."
Donne.   To Mr T. W ("Pregnant again with th'
   old twins hope, and fear").
Dove, R.   Fiammetta Breaks Her Peace.
   First Kiss.
Dunbar, P.   Disappointed.
Eberhart, R.   Angels, The.
   Austere Poem.
   Breathless, The.
   Lost, The.
   Man Who Was Blown Down by the Wind, A.
   Poet, The.
Emerson, R.   And Ellen, when the greybeard
   years.
   Maiden Speech of the Æolian Harp.
Graves, R.   Desert Fringe.
   Home-Coming, The.
   Love without Hope.
   Lovers in Winter.
   Poor Others.
Gurney, I.   Wish, A.
Hall, D.   Sun, The.
Hardy, T.   Darkling Thrush, The.
   Song of Hope.
   To an Unborn Pauper Child.
Herbert, G.   Hope.
   Size, The.
Herrick.   Faith.
   His Hope or Sheet-Anchor.
   Hope Heartens.
   Hope Well and Have Well: or, Faire after Foule
   Weather.
   Impossibilities to His Friend.
   Sufferance.
   To God, on His Sickness[e].
   To Sapho.
Hopkins, G.   Leaden Echo and the Golden Echo,
   The.
Housman.   How clear, how lovely bright.
Jarrell, R.   Hope.
   Jews at Haifa.
   Lament of the Children of Israel in Rome.
   Utopian Journey, A.
Jeffers, R.   Hope Is Not for the Wise.
   Local Legend.
Johnson, S.   Vanity of Human Wishes, The; The
   Tenth Satire of Juvenal Imitated.
   Winter's Walk, The.
Keats.   To Hope.
Larkin, P.   Slight Relax of Air Where Cold Was,
   A.
Laughlin, J.   Hope Springs.
Levertov.   Beginners.
   For the New Year, 1981.
Levine, P.   Planting.
Lindsay, N.   Amaranth, The.
   Invocation for "The Map of the Universe."
   Town of American Visions, The.
Logan, J.   Only the Dreamer Can Change the
   Dream.
   Search, The.
MacLeish.   Pole Star for This Year.

Two Poems from the War.
MacNeice. Prospect.
Mahon. Everything Is Going to Be All Right.
Melville, H. Immolated.
Meredith, G. Friend, when the thundercloud is low.
Hilda's Morning and Evening Dose of Rhyme.
In all our daily war of words.
In the time of early love.
Linnet-Hawker, The.
Nature and Man.
New Year's Eve.
Promise in Disturbance, The.
Song: "Pass we to another land."
Sonnet: "Hateful are those false themes of speculation."
Soul, The.
Vittoria's *Italia* Song.
Meredith, W. My Mother's Life.
Merton. Round and a Hope for Smithgirls, A.
Merwin. Crossroads of the World Etc., The.
Island in the Harbor, An.
Wave, The.
Milosz, C. Appeal, An.
Montale. Little Testament.
Nash, O. Has Anybody Seen My Noumenon?
Song before Breakfast.
Nemerov. Hope.
Oliver, M. Aunt Elsie's Night Music.
Morning at Great Pond.
Olson, C. Distances, The.
Oppen. From Disaster.
Parker, D. Post-Graduate.
Pessoa. I don't want the sincere gifts. .
Petrarch. Closer that I come to that last day, The.
Good luck is slow to reach me, always late.
Her hard heart and her will to cruelty.
My heavy life is hanging on a thread.
My love for you has never wearied me.
Star of love was blazing in the east, The.
Poe. Dreams.
Prudentius. Fortune and Hope! I've made my port.
Raine, K. Polluted tide, / Desecrated earth destroyed.
Ramanujan. It Does Not Follow, but When in the Street.
Riley, J. Hope.
Rilke. To Jean-Louis Vandoyer.
Ritsos. Midnight Stroll.
Not Even.
Robinson, E. Old Trails.
Rossetti, C. All beneath the sun hasteth, / All that hath begun wasteth.
All heaven is blazing yet / With the meridian sun.
Alone Lord God, in Whom our trust and peace.
As froth on the face of the deep, / As foam on the crest of the sea.
Bury Hope out of sight, / No book for it and no bell.
But Thy Commandment Is Exceeding Broad.
Care flieth, / Hope and fear together.
Charity.
Come Unto Me.
Comparisons.
Dead Hope.
Doeth Well...Doeth Better.
End of Time, The.
Everything that is born must die.
Experience bows a sweet contented face.
Faith and Hope are wings to Love.
Greatest of These Is Charity, The.
Hope and Joy.
Hope Carol, A.
Hope in Grief.
Hope is the counterpoise of fear / While night enthralls us here.
I have done with hope.
I said "All's over"—& I made my.
If Only.
Last Answer, The.
Love and Hope.
Now They Desire a Better Country.
O Christ my God Who seest the unseen.

Of each sad word which is more sorrowful.
On the note you do not send me.
Our heaven must be within ourselves / Our home and heaven the work of faith.
Pause of Thought, A.
Redeeming the Time.
Serenade.
Song for the Least of All Saints, A.
Song: "Oh what comes over the sea."
Sorrow hath a double voice, / Sharp today but sweet tomorrow.
Sunshine.
Three Seasons.
Three Stages.
Toll, bell, toll. For hope is flying / Sighing from the earthbound soul.
We are of those who tremble at Thy word.
Where Their Worm Dieth Not, and the Fire Is Not Quenched.
Worship God.
Ye Are Come unto Mount Sion.
Yet A Little While.
Rossetti, D. Sunset Wings.
Rukeyser, M. Chapultepec Park / II.
Dreaming we were awake, we heard the rivers.
Juanita Tinsley.
Noguchi.
Who in One Lifetime.
Sandburg, C. Dream Girl.
It Is Much.
Passers-by.
Tangibles.
Sarton, M. Greeting.
March-Mad.
Sexton. Snow.
Shelley, P. England in 1819.
Lines: "Far, far away, O ye."
Lines Written among the Euganean Hills.
Love, Hope, Desire and Fear.
Smith, S. Friend, The.
La Gretchen de Nos Jours (II).
Reason, The.
Tomlinson, C. Ars Poetica.
Unknown. Circumstance.
Updike. Pooem.
Very. Hope.
Walker, A. Remember?
Warren, R. Aubade for Hope.
Hope.
Whittier. Star of Bethlehem, The.
Trust.
Williams, C. K. Dimensions.
In the Heart of the Beast.
Next to the Last Poem about God, The.
Poor Hope.
Williams, W. Min Schleppner.
To the Outer World.
Wordsworth, W. Composed near Calais, on the Road Leading to Ardres, August 7, 1802.
Evening Walk, An; Addressed to a Young Lady.
October, 1803.
Wishing-Gate, The.
Wright, C. Hawaii Dantesca.
Wright, J. Arrangements with Earth for Three Dead Friends.
Wyatt, S. I abide and abide and better abide.
Zaturenska. Another Snowstorm.
Zukofsky, L. Ah spring, when with a thaw of blue.
Glad they were there.
Green leaf that will outlast the winter.
Homage.
Honesty.
Valentine, A.
See also **Optimism**
Hopi, The
Tomlinson, C. Arizona Desert.
Death in the Desert, A.
Hopkins, Gerard Manley
Clampitt. Highgate Cemetery.
Eberhart, R. Killer, The.
Tomlinson, C. Response to Hopkins.
Hopper, Edward
Komunyakaa. South Carolina Morning.
Logan, J. Nighthawks: after Hopper's Painting.
Milosz, C. O! ("O what sadness unaware that

it's sadness!").
Horace
Auden. Horatians, The.
Cavafy. Horace in Athens.
Cowper, W. Reflection on the Foregoing Ode.
To Mrs. Throckmorton.
Davie, D. Wombwell on Strike.
Ignatow, D. With Horace.
Laughlin, J. I Know How Every Poet.
Lux. Horatian Notion, An.
MacNeice. Memoranda to Horace.
Robinson, E. Horace to Leuconoë.
Smart, C. On Taking a Batchelor's Degree.
Hornets
Ammons. Trouble Making Trouble.
Davie, D. Hornet.
Sexton. Hornet.
Horse Chestnut Trees and Horse Chestnuts
Gunn, T. Hampstead; the Horse Chestnut Trees.
Schuyler, J. Horse-Chestnut Trees and Roses.
Horse Racing
Bukowski. Bad Action.
Bravo.
Horsemeat.
Longshot.
Space Creatures.
Valentine Gift, A.
Hacker, M. Late August Letter.
Kipling, R. Mare's Nest, The.
Larkin, P. At Grass.
Montale. Palio.
Moore, M. Tom Fool at Jamaica.
Olson, C. There they were.
Sandburg, C. Alix.
Remorse.
Yeats. At Galway Races.
Horseback Riding
Browning, R. How They Brought the Good News from Ghent to Aix.
Last Ride Together, The.
Cummings, E. E. All in green went my love riding.
This(that / grey)white / (man)horse.
Davie, D. Father, the Cavalier.
Dickey, J. Sustainment.
García Lorca. Song of the Rider (1860).
Hardy, T. Circus-Rider to Ringmaster.
Jonson, B. Epigram. To William, Earl of Newcastle, An.
Kizer, C. Horseback.
Major, C. Riders.
Riley, J. Billy Could Ride.
Ritsos. Episode.
Roethke. Elegy for Jane.
Warren, R. Fierce Horsemen, The.
Wilbur, R. Ride, The.
Wright, J. Night Ride.
Horses
Ammons. Silver.
Beck, K. Hungarian Horse-Herd, The.
Berry, W. Horses.
Sorrel Filly, The.
Berryman. Whether There Is Sorrow in the Demons.
Bly, R. Watering the Horse.
Bourne, V. Cantab, The.
Browning, R. How They Brought the Good News from Ghent to Aix.
Burns, R. Auld Farmer's New-Year-Morning Salutation to His Auld Mare, Maggie.
Auld Man's Mare's Dead, The.
Elegy on Peg Nicholson.
Epistle to Hugh Parker.
Tam o' Shanter; A Tale.
To John Taylor.
Carruth, H. Sonnet: "'Whut do you spose thet thing is,' Oi said. 'Whut?'"
Cavafy. Horses of Achilles, The.
Ciardi, J. In the Rich Farmer's Field.
Crane, S. Fast rode the knight.
Creeley. Don't Sign Anything.
Folk Song, A: "Hitch up honey for the / market race all."
Gift of Great Value, A.
Rescue, The.

Cummings, E. E.   All in green went my love riding.
What a proud dreamhorse pulling(smoothloomingly)through.
Davie, D.   Equestrian Sestina.
De la Mare.   Assignation, The.
  Horse in a Field.
Dickey, J.   Dusk of Horses, The.
  Horses and Prisoners.
Dickinson, E.   I like to see it lap the Miles.
Dubie.   Danse Macabre.
  These Untitled Little Verses in Which, at Dawn, Two Obscure Dutch Peasants Struggled with an Auburn Horse.
Dugan, A.   Carla Is a Horse Lover.
  On an Old Advertisement and after a Photograph by Alfred Stieglitz.
  So-Called Wild Horses of the Water, The.
Dunbar, P.   Dat Ol' Mare o' Mine.
Emerson, R.   Like vaulters in the circus round.
Frost, R.   Draft Horse, The.
  Runaway, The.
Gallagher, T.   From Dread in the Eyes of Horses.
  His Shining Helmet; Its Horsehair Crest.
  Horse In the Drugstore, The.
  If Poetry Were Not a Morality.
García Lorca.   Song of the Rider (1860).
Glück, L.   Horse.
Graves, R.   Last Fistful, The.
Guillén, J.   Horses, The.
Hall, D.   Names of Horses.
  On a Horse Carved in Wood.
Hardy, T.   Horses Aboard.
Herrick.   Upon Spur.
Hopkins, G.   Felix Randal.
Hughes, T.   Bones.
  Horses, The.
  New Foal.
Jacobsen, J.   Hooves, The.
Jeffers, R.   Roan Stallion.
Jonson, B.   Epigram. To William, Earl of Newcastle, An.
Kipling, R.   Mare's Nest, The.
  Snarleyow.
  Undertaker's Horse, The.
  With Scindia to Delhi.
Komunyakaa.   Yellowjackets.
Kumin, M.   Agnostic Speaks to Her Horse's Hoof, The.
  Amanda Dreams She Has Died and Gone to the Elysian Fields.
  Amanda Is Shod.
  Eyes.
  Late Snow.
  Leaving My Daughter's House.
  Long Approach, The.
  Selling of the Slaves, The.
  Sleeping with Animals.
  Thinking of Death and Dogfood.
Larkin, P.   At Grass.
  Wedding-Wind.
Lawrence, D. H.   White Horse, The.
Lenau.   Postillion, The.
Levertov.   Ce bruit da la mer.
Levine, P.   Horse, The.
Lindsay, N.   Broncho That Would Not Be Broken, The.
  Old Horse in the City, The.
MacNeice.   River in Spate.
Major, C.   Three Views of Horse.
McGrath, T.   Dreams of Wild Horses, The.
  End of the Line, The.
  Used Up.
McHugh, H.   Hag.
Merrill, J.   Charioteer of Delphi, The.
Merwin.   Cart, The.
  Horse, The.
  Horses.
  Little Horse.
Moore, M.   Tom Fool at Jamaica.
Muldoon, P.   Dancers at the Moy.
  Horses.
Niedecker.   Horse, hello.
Ocampo.   Infinite Horses, The.
Oliver, M.   Bailing the Boat.

Spring.
Oppen.   Near the Beginning.
Orr, G.   Horses.
Patchen.   It Takes Few Kinds.
  Plow Horses.
Plath.   Whiteness I Remember.
Prunty.   Wild Horses, The.
Rexroth, K.   Living Pearl, A.
Riley, J.   Bedouin.
  Boy Lives on Our Farm, The.
  Cuored o' Skeerin.
  Hoss, The.
  Iron Horse, The.
Ritsos.   Episode.
Rossetti, C.   Horses of the Sea, The.
Rukeyser, M.   Flying Red Horse, The.
Sexton.   Horse.
  Pain for a Daughter.
Simic.   Travel[l]ing Slaughterhouse.
Smith, S.   Fugitive's Ride, The.
Snyder, G.   All through the Rains.
Stafford, W.   Few Snorts from a Wild One, A.
  Wild Horse Love.
Stevens, W.   Polo Ponies Practicing.
Stock, R.   Houynhnm's Holiday.
Swenson, M.   Centaur, The.
  Horse.
Thomas, D.   Because the Pleasure-Bird Whistles.
Tomlinson, C.   Poem: "Wakening with the window over fields."
  Saving the Appearances.
Very.   Arab Steed, The.
Vogl.   Sweetheart of the Csikos, The.
Walcott.   Polish Rider, The.
Warren, R.   Dead Horse in Field.
  Mission, The.
  When Life Begins.
Wilbur, R.   Ride, The.
Williams, C. K.   On Learning of a Friend's Illness.
  Work.
Williams, W.   Horse, The.
  When Structure Fails Rhyme Attempts to Come to the Rescue.
Wilner, E.   Facing into It.
Wordsworth, W.   Four Fiery Steed Impatient of the Rein.
  Horse, The.
Wright, J.   Blessing, A.
  Horse, The.
  Outside Fargo, North Dakota.
  Poems to a Brown Cricket.
  Sitting in a Small Screenhouse on a Summer Morning.
  Two Horses Playing in the Orchard.
Yeats.   Michael Robartes Bids His Beloved Be at Peace.
See also Colts; Foals; Horse Racing; Horseback Riding

Horseshoe Crabs
Ciardi, J.   Successful Species, A.

Horseshoes
Burns, R.   To John Taylor.
Hopkins, G.   Felix Randal.
Kumin, M.   Amanda Is Shod.

Hospitality
Burns, R.   At Whigham's Inn, Sanquar.
  Verse Composed and Repeated by *Burns*, to the Master of the House, on Taking Leave, A.
  Verses Written on a Window of the Inn at Carron.
Campion, T.   Ad Ge. Chapmannum.
De la Mare.   Hospital.
Dickinson, E.   Soul that hath a Guest, The.
Gurney, I.   La Gorgue.
Hardy, T.   At an Inn.
  Squire Hooper.
Herrick.   Happinesse to Hospitalitie, or a Hearty Wish to Good House-Keeping.
  To His Peculiar Friend M. Jo: Wicks.
  To the Most Virtuous Mistress Pot, Who Many Times Entertained Him.
  Upon Showbread [*or* Shewbread]: Epigram.
Jonson, B.   Inviting a Friend to Supper.
Kipling, R.   Ballad of East and West, The.

Logan, J.   Matinee.
Mahon.   Tolerable Wisdom, A.
Nash, O.   Just Keep Quiet and Nobody Will Notice.
  Polterguest, My Polterguest.
  Suppose I Darken Your Door.
  Visit from Dr. Fell, A.
Niedecker.   Come In.
Piercy.   Poet Dreams of a Nice Warm Motel, The.
Riley, J.   Parting Guest, A.
Robinson, E.   Cliff Klingenhagen.
Tomlinson, C.   Quarai.
Updike.   Neotony.
Whittier.   "I Was a Stranger and Ye Took Me in."
Williams, C. K.   Guatemala: 1964.
See also Guests

Hospitals
Berryman.   Hell Poem, The.
  I Know.
  Purgatory.
Brodsky, J.   Gorbunov and Gorchakov.
Broumas, O.   Moon of Mind against the Wooden Louver, The.
Bukowski.   Bedpans.
  Mexican Girls, The.
Ciardi, J.   Chelsea Naval Hospital.
Clampitt.   From a Clinic Waiting Room.
Clifton, L.   Dialysis.
Cooper, J.   Children's Ward, The.
  Infusion Room, The.
Creeley.   Heaven ("I don't want").
Cullen, C.   Lines for a Hospital.
Dickey, J.   Hospital Window, The.
  Poem: "For having left the birds that left me."
Dubie.   Inside the City Walls.
Dugan, A.   On Visiting a Veterans Hospital.
Graves, R.   Surgical Ward: Men.
Gunn, T.   Still Life.
Hall, D.   Tubes.
Hayden, R.   Broken Dark, The.
Hughes, T.   Waving goodbye, from your banked hospital bed.
Ignatow, D.   Harold.
  Sunday at the State Hospital.
  Walt Whitman in the Civil War Hospitals.
Jacobsen, J.   Mr. Mahoney.
Jarrell, R.   Christmas Roses, The.
  Field Hospital, A.
  In a Hospital Garden.
  Utopian Journey, A.
  X-Ray Waiting Room in the Hospital, The.
Kinsella, T.   Lady of Quality, A.
  Visiting Hour.
Kizer, C.   Medicine ("When the nurses, interns, doctors came running full tilt down the hall").
Larkin, P.   Building, The.
  Hospital Visits.
Levi, P.   Fly, The.
Levine, P.   Having Been Asked "What is a Man?" I Answer.
Lux.   Institute of Defectology.
MacDiarmid, H.   In the Children's Hospital.
Mahon.   Noon at St. Michael's.
Major, C.   Waiting in the Children's Hospital.
Mallarmé.   Windows, The.
Melville, H.   Camoëns.
Meredith, W.   Jain Bird Hospital in Delhi, The.
Merwin.   St. Vincent's.
Montale.   Ballad Written in a Hospital.
Muldoon, P.   Edward Kienholz: *The State Hospital*.
  Field Hospital, The.
Nash, O.   Visitors Laugh at Locksmiths or, Hospital Doors Haven't Got Locks Anyhow.
Oliver, M.   University Hospital, Boston.
Owen, W.   Conscious.
  Disabled.
  Hospital Barge at Cérisy.
  Mental Cases.
Paley, G.   For Jan.
Plath.   Face Lift.
  Morning in the Hospital Solarium.
  Poem for a Birthday.
  Surgeon at 2 A.M, The.

Tulips.
Prunty. Taking Down, The.
Ramanujan. Dancers in a Hospital.
Rukeyser, M. In Hades, Orpheus.
Sarton, M. Night Watch.
Schuyler, J. Arches.
Linen.
Pastime.
Sleep.
Sexton. August 17th.
Break, The.
Lullaby: "It is a summer evening."
Operation, The.
Unknown Girl in the Maternity Ward.
You, Doctor Martin.
Simic. Whispers.
Tomlinson, C. In the Ward.
Updike. Aerie.
Van Duyn. In the Hospital for Tests.
Recovery.
Whitman, W. Sight in Camp [in the Daybreak
Gray and Dim], A.
Williams, M. At the Children's Hospital in
Little Rock.
ICU: Space/Time in the Waiting Room.
Williams, W. Between Walls.
From a Window.
Spring and All.
Wright, J. She Hid in the Trees from the
Nurses.

Hotels
Amichai [or Amikhai]. Summer Night in the
King David Hotel.
Brodsky, J. Dutch Mistress.
Carver, R. In the Lobby of the Hotel del Mayo.
Gunn, T. 1975.
Corridor, The.
Hughes, L. Advertisement for the Waldorf-
Astoria.
Elevator Boy.
Larkin, P. Friday Night in the Royal Station.
Laughlin, J. Songbird, The.
Merrill, J. Hotel de l'Univers et Portugal.
Nash, O. Change Here for Wichita Falls, or,
Has Anybody Seen My Wanderlust?
Have a Seat behind the Potted Palm, Sir.
Mrs. Purvis Dreads Room Service.
Traveler's Rest.
Orr, G. Hotel St. Louis, New York City, Fall
1969.
Prunty. Name, The.
Wedding Stop, The.
Rossetti, C. Uphill.
Stein, G. Hotel François Ier.
Stevens, W. Arrival at the Waldorf.
Swenson, M. Wednesday at the Waldorf.
Tate, J. Up Here.
Warren, R. Nocturne: Traveling Salesman in
Hotel Bedroom.
Weiss, T. Charm against the Toothache, A.
Zagajewski. Watching Shoah in a Hotel Room
in America.
See also **Motels**

Hourglasses
Borges. Hourglass, The.
De la Mare. Hour-Glass, The.
Jonson, B. Hour-Glass [or Houre-Glasse], The.
McHugh, H. Dry Time.
Merrill, J. Hourglass.

House Painting
Schuyler, J. White.

Housekeeping
Bukowski. Fragile!
Carver, R. Tall Order, A.
Clifton, L. Study the Masters.
Davie, D. Sorting the Personae.
Dove, R. Dusting.
Pomade.
Frost, R. Housekeeper, The.
Merrill, J. Three Chores.
Nash, O. You Have More Freedom in a House.
Niedecker. Cleaned all surfaces.
Old Mother turns blue and from us.
Popcorn-can cover.
Ramanujan. Ruler, A.

Schuyler, J. Below the Stairs.
Song: "I'm about to go shopping."
Things to Do.
White.
Whalen, P. Rich Interior, after Thomas Mann.
See also **Housewives**

Houses
Amichai [or Amikhai]. Early in the morning,
you lean on the wall of an old house.
I Walked Past a House Where I Lived Once.
Open Internalized.
Poem about Repairs to My House.
Two Disappeared into a House.
Atwood. Small Cabin, The.
Baudelaire. I Haven't Forgotten.
Berry, W. Design of a House, The.
For the Rebuilding of a House.
New Roof, The.
Berryman. Long Home, The.
Bishop, E. End of March, The.
Jerónimo's House.
Blue Cloud. Dedication of a Roundhouse.
Borges. Adrogué.
Patio.
Bradstreet, A. Here Follows Some Verses upon
the Burning of Our House.
Brodsky, J. Residence, The.
Brooke, H. Quilca House to the Dean.
Browning, R. House.
Love in a Life.
Carew, T. To Saxham.
Carruth, H. Crow's Mark.
Meadow House.
My Hut.
New Hartford.
Carver, R. Locking Yourself Out, Then Trying
to Get Back In.
Our First House in Sacramento.
Cavafy. Before the House.
Ciardi, J. Divorced, Husband Demolishes
House.
I Remember the House That Was.
January 2, 1978.
Talking Myself to Sleep at One More Hilton.
Cooper, J. Builder of Houses, The.
These High White Walls.
Creeley. House, The ("Mas-Soñer / Restaurat—
Any").
Picture, A.
Some Place.
Davie, D. Among Artisans' Houses.
De la Mare. Alone.
Empty House, The.
Old Summerhouse, The.
Sleeper, The.
Dickey, J. Courtship, The.
Two Poems of Going Home.
Dickinson, E. Eden is that Old-Fashioned
House.
God's Residence.
I know some lonely Houses off the Road.
Props assist the House, The.
Dove, R. House on Bishop Street, The.
Dugan, A. Love Song: I and Thou.
On Being a Householder.
Dunbar, P. Old Homestead, The.
Eberhart, R. Key West.
Emerson, R. These trees like tho'ts that to
visions congeal.
What avails it me.
Frost, R. Black Cottage, The.
Cocoon, The.
Directive.
Four-room shack aspiring high.
In the Home Stretch.
Steeple on the House, A.
Gallagher, T. Death of the Horses by Fire.
Ginsberg, A. Strange New Cottage in Berkeley,
A.
Graves, R. Not at Home.
Gunn, T. Last Days at Teddington.
Nature of an Action, The.
Pierce Street.
Waking in a Newly Built House.
Hall, D. Alligator Bride, The.
Dump, The.

Flies.
In the Old House.
Old Houses.
Han-shan. Children I implore you.
Cold Mountain is a house.
Cold Mountain owns a house.
In this village is a house.
Pitiful hundred-year house, A.
Hardy, T. Architectural Masks.
Domicilium.
Fallow Deer at the Lonely House, The.
House with a History, A.
To a Well-Named Dwelling.
Two Houses, The.
Heaney, S. Summer Home.
Herbert, G. Redemption.
World, The.
Herrick. Observation.
Thanksgiving to God for His House, A.
Hopkins, G. In the Valley of the Elwy.
Hughes, L. Carolina Cabin.
Empty House.
House in the World.
Ibn-i-Yamin [or Ibn Jemin or Amir Mahmud ibn
Amir Yaminu'd-Din Tughra'i]. I read on the
porch of a palace bold.
Jacobsen, J. Gesture, The.
Laurentides.
Jarrell, R. Happy Cat, The.
Jeffers, R. To the House.
To the Rock that Will Be a Cornerstone of the
House.
Jonson, B. To Penshurst.
Kinnell. 52 Oswald Street.
Kizer, C. From an Artist's House.
Koch, K. Variations on a Theme by William
Carlos Williams.
Kumin, M. Henry Manley Blues, The.
Kunitz, S. In a Strange House.
Old Darned Man, The.
Larkin, P. Home Is So Sad.
Laughlin, J. House of Light, The.
People Boxes, The.
Lawrence, D. H. Parliament Hill in the
Evening.
Levertov. Letter to Marek about a Photograph,
A.
What My House Would Be Like if It Were a
Person.
Lindsay, N. Flying House, and the May Queen
Eternal, The.
Logan, J. On the House of a Friend.
Lorde. Rooming Houses are Old Women.
Lowell, R. For Sale.
Lux. Backyard Swingset.
He Has Lived in Many Houses.
MacLeish. Population Explosion.
MacNeice. Château Jackson.
House on a Cliff.
Order to View.
Selva Oscura.
McHugh, H. Household.
Patronage.
Who Made Her.
Meredith, G. Autumn Even-Song.
Meredith, W. American Living Room, The: A
Tract.
Ghosts of the House, The.
Merrill, J. House, The.
Merwin. House to the West, A.
Houses, The.
Red House, The.
Millay, E. Second Fig.
Montale. House of the Customs Men, The.
Where the tennis court once was.
Muldoon, P. Beaver.
Murray, P. Receipt to Frighten away the Dean,
A.
Nash, O. Little Feet.
Maybe You Can't Take It with You, but Look
What Happens When You Leave It Behind.
No Wonder Our Fathers Died.
Turtle, The.
You Have More Freedom in a House.
Neruda. Midday Construction.
Niedecker. He built four houses.

In Europe they grow a new bean while here.
New-sawed.
Property is poverty.
Sunday's motor-cars.
Terrible things coming up.
That woman!—eyeing houses.
You know, he said, they used to make.
Olson, C.   *Scream* to the Editor, A.
Oppen.   Birthplace: New Rochelle.
Paley, G.   House: Some Instructions.
Housing.
Sad Children's Song, The.
Palmer, M.   As a Real House.
Patchen.   If We Are to Know Where We Live.
May I Ask You a Question, Mr. Youngstown
Sheet & Tube?
Pinsky.   Round.
Plath.   Landowners.
Point Shirley.
Tour, The.
Prunty.   Breaking Child, The.
Razed House, The.
Rooms without Walls.
Stick Builder.
Stillness.
Raine, K.   For the Visitors' Book.
Ramanujan.   Small-scale Reflections on a Great
House.
Ransom, J.   Old Mansion.
What Ducks Require.
Rexroth, K.   Old Street.
Rich, A.   House at the Cascades, The.
Rilke.   Summer Day.
Ritsos.   Helen's House.
Need of Proof.
Perforation.
Perspective.
Robinson, E.   Fragment: "Faint white pillars that
seem to fade."
House on the Hill, The.
Roethke.   Sale.
Rukeyser, M.   Crayon House.
Sandburg, C.   Even Numbers.
Schuyler, J.   Buttered Greens.
Seifert.   Demolition Report.
Sexton.   February 11th.
Sheridan, T.   Description of Doctor Delany's
Villa, A.
To the Dean, when in England, in 1726.
Tom Punsibi's Letter to Dean Swift.
Smith, S.   Grange, The.
House of Over-Dew, The.
Spender, S.   Empty House.
Stafford, W.   Big House, The.
Stevens, W.   Gallant Chateau.
Swenson, M.   Question.
Swift, J.   On the Little House by the Churchyard
of Castleknock.
To Quilca.
True and Faithful Inventory of the Goods
Belonging to Dr. Swift, Vicar of Laracor.
Sze.   Opal, The.
Silence, The.
Szymborska, W.   Great Man's House, A.
Tate, J.   Failed Tribute to the Stonemason of Tor
House, Robinson Jeffers.
Paint 'Til You Faint.
Thoreau.   For though the eaves [*or* Caves] were
rabitted [*or* rabbeted *or* rabbited].
Tomlinson, C.   Faring, The.
Fox Gallery, The.
House in the Quarry, The.
On the Hall at Stowey.
Ruin, The.
Updike.   Hot Water.
Very.   Old Houses of Salem: Illustrated by
George M. White.
Walcott.   Ruins of a Great House.
Warren, R.   Praises for Mrs. Dodd.
Small White House.
Vision.
Weiss, T.   November Late.
Whalen, P.   America inside & outside Bill
Brown's House in Bolinas.
Wilbur, R.   Altitudes.
Wellfleet: The House.

Williams, M.   House in the Vacant Lot, The.
Williams, T.   Color of a House, The.
Williams, W.   Defective Record, The.
House, The.
Old House, The.
Wordsworth, W.   Highland Hut.
Inscription for the Moss-Hut at Dove Cottage.
Ruined Cottage, The.
Zagajewski.   House, The.
September.
Zaturenska.   Old House, The.
See also **Home**
Housewives
Dove, R.   Daystar.
Emerson, R.   Bluebeard. Let the gentle wife
prepare.
Graves, R.   Any Honest Housewife.
Jarrell, R.   Next Day.
Nash, O.   I Know Exactly Who Dropped the
Overalls in Mrs. Murphy's Chowder.
Parker, D.   Day-Dreams.
Sexton.   Housewife.
Risk, The.
Smith, S.   Wretched Woman.
Van Duyn.   Caring for Surfaces.
Williams, W.   Young Housewife, The.
See also **Housekeeping**
Housman, Alfred Edward
Auden.   A. E. Housman.
Huayna Capac
Levi, P.   Huayna Capac.
Hudson Bay, Canada
Frost, R.   Empty Threat, An.
Hudson, Henry
Stock, R.   Henry Hudson.
Hudson River, New York
Amichai [*or* Amikhai].   Poems along the
Hudson River.
Dugan, A.   Three as a Magic Number.
García Lorca.   Christmas on the Hudson.
Levertov.   From the Roof.
Lowell, R.   Mouth of the Hudson, The.
Oppen.   Night Scene.
Time of the Missile.
Rexroth, K.   It Rolls On.
Schuyler, J.   Dining Out with Doug and Frank.
Hudson Ferry.
Weiss, T.   Egyptian Passage, An.
Zaturenska.   May Morning: Hudson Pastoral.
Hughes, Langston
Brooks, G.   Langston Hughes.
Komunyakaa.   Langston Hughes.
Hughes, Ted
Plath.   Ode for Ted.
Hugo, Victor
Meredith, G.   Fall'n Is Lucifer.
Huguenots
Whittier.   St. John.
Human Folly
Atwood.   How to Tell One Country from
Another.
Beckett, S.   Ce qu'a de pis.
Fous qui disiez.
Bradstreet, A.   Contemplations.
Bukowski.   Playing It Out.
Chamfort.   How hollow heart and full.
Ciardi, J.   True or False.
Clough.   Because a Lady chose to say.
Coleridge, S.   Lines to Thomas Poole.
Ode to Tranquillity.
Cowper, W.   Bee and the Pine-Apple, The.
Human Frailty.
Pine-Apple and the Bee, The.
Cummings, E. E.   Humanity i love you.
Dickinson, E.   How Human Nature dotes.
Eberhart, R.   Big Rock.
Éluard, P.   Second Nature.
Enzensberger, H.   Cold Comfort.
Ferlinghetti, L.   25.
Endless Life.
History of the World: a TV Docu-Drama.
Morlaix: Into the Future with Neil Young.
Triumph of the Postmodern.
Uses of Poetry.

Graves, R.   Fools.
Oath, The.
Shot, The.
Song: The Sundial's Lament.
Guyon.   God neither Known nor Loved by the
World.
Hall, D.   Grace, A.
Herbert, G.   Dotage.
Justice (1).
Herrick.   Delay.
Out of Time, out of Tune.
Hughes, L.   Acceptance.
Jackson, L.   Seizure of the World.
Jeffers, R.   Advice to Pilgrims.
As the eye fails through age or disease.
Beautiful Captive, The.
Dawn.
De Rerum Virtute.
Faith.
Orca.
Original Sin.
Roan Stallion.
Salvage.
Soul's Desert, The.
Unformed volcanic earth, a female thing, The.
World's Wonders, The.
Laughlin, J.   Merry Madness Hall.
Logue, C.   Professor Tucholsky's Facts.
Singing Prayer, A.
Meredith, G.   Were men of such importance as
they deem.
Nash, O.   Grasshoppers Are Very Intelligent.
Little Miss Muffet Sat on a Prophet—and Quite
Right, Too!
Neruda.   This Is Simple.
Owen, W.   Arms and the Boy.
Sonnet: "Be slowly lifted up, thou long black
arm."
Patchen.   For Miriam.
Origin of Baseball, The.
Rich, A.   He Remembereth that We Are Dust.
Scott, S.   Spindle Song, The.
Shapiro, K.   Fly, The.
Stafford, W.   Mr. or Mrs. Nobody.
Van Duyn.   Causes.
Serious Case, A.
To Poets' Worksheets in the Air-Conditioned
Vault of a Library.
Williams, C. K.   That the world / is going.
Then the Brother of the Wind.
Williams, M.   Visitor's Guide to the Blue Planet,
The.
Wright, C.   Language Journal.
Last Journal.
Looking at Pictures.
May Journal.
New Year's Eve, 1979.
Vesper Journal.
Human Race
Cavafy.   Chaldaic Image.
Ciardi, J.   Dawn of the Space Age.
H is, reluctantly, for HUMAN, a word.
Starry Heavens, the Moral Law, The.
Creeley.   Human Song.
Davie, D.   Where Depths Are Surfaces.
Hughes, L.   Comment.
Some Day.
Jacobsen, J.   Birds, The.
Tears.
Levertov.   Her Judgement.
Logue, C.   Professor Tucholsky's Facts.
Lux.   Solo Native.
MacLeish.   Men.
Merwin.   Finding of Reasons, The.
Widow, The.
Milosz, C.   Human Fly, A.
Opposed to Each Other.
Rexroth, K.   Discrimination.
Stock, R.   Monkey's Address to Others of His
Kind, A.
Swenson, M.   Gods I Children.
Szymborska, W.   No End of Fun.
Note, A.
One Version of Events.
Word on Statistics, A.
Thoreau.   How little curious is man.

I knew a man by sight.
Man Man is the Devil.
Tell me ye wise ones if ye can.
Wilde, O.   Humanitad.
Williams, M.   Notes from the Agent on Earth:
  How to be Human.
People.
Visitor's Guide to the Blue Planet, The.
Williams, T.   Comforter and the Betrayer, The.
Zagajewski.   Three Angels.
See also **Mankind**

Humility
Berry, W.   Want of Peace, The.
We Who Prayed and Wept.
Browning, E.   Confessions.
Reed, A.
Carew, T.   On the Marriage of T. K. and C. C.:
  The Morning Stormy.
Coleridge, S.   Forbearance.
Humility the Mother of Charity.
Crane, S.   In Heaven, / Some little blades of
  grass.
Cullen, C.   Any Human to Another.
Davie, D.   Creon's Mouse.
De la Mare.   Imagination's Pride, The.
Dickinson, E.   Tiniest ones are the mightiest,
  The.
Dunbar, P.   Love's Humility.
Emerson, R.   And he like me is not too proud.
Experience.
I care not whither I may go.
Nature 1.
Frost, R.   Demiurge's Laugh, The.
Ginsberg, A.   Man's Glory.
Guyon.   God Hides His People.
Nativity, The.
Herbert, G.   Church-Lock and Key.
Discharge, The.
Humility.
Misery [or Miserie].
Posy [or Posie], The.
Praise (1).
Sighs and Groans [or Grones].
To the Right Hon. the Lord Chancellor (Bacon).
Herrick.   Humility.
Meane Things Overcome Mighty.
To Worthy Friend, M. Tho. Falconbirge.
Johnson, S.   Paraphrase.
Kipling, R.   If—.
Non Nobis Domine!
Recessional.
Laughlin, J.   It Does Me Good.
Lawrence, D. H.   Fireflies in the Corn.
Humility.
Humility Mongers.
Tender Reverence.
Lindsay, N.   In the Immaculate Conception
  Church.
Johnny Appleseed's Hymn to the Sun.
Meredith, G.   Believe me, I have studied men.
While Janet eyes the Lanthorn's Magic.
Merton.   Ode to the Present Century.
Michelangelo Buonarroti.   If obligated by so
  great a favor.
To be less unworthy, my exalted lady.
Mistral, G.   In Praise of Small Towns.
Nash, O.   Confession to Be Traced on a
  Birthday Cake.
Olson, C.   Concerning Exaggeration, or How,
  Properly, to Heap Up.
Petrarch.   Under the wrath of my dear enemy.
Ransom, J.   Amphibious Crocodile.
Riley, J.   Humble Singer, A.
Old John Henry.
Robinson, E.   Cliff Klingenhagen.
Rossetti, C.   I Will Come and Heal Him.
Lowest Place, The.
Sit Down in the Lowest Room.
Ye Are Come unto Mount Sion.
Rumi.   Humble living does not diminish. It fills.
Mouse and the Camel, The.
New Moon, Hilal.
Stockton, A.   To Laura.
Very.   Humility.
Wilbur, R.   Finished Man, A.
Williams, C. K.   Easter.

Men.
Wordsworth, W.   Fact, and an Imagination or,
  Canute and Alfred, on the Sea-Shore, A.
Narrow girdle of rough stones and crags, A.
When Haughty Expectations Prostrate Lie.
Wright, C.   Chinese Journal.
Night Journal.

Hummingbirds
Ciardi, J.   11:02 A.M. The Bird Disappeared.
Corbett, W.   Vermont Apollinaire.
Dickinson, E.   Hummingbird, A.
Within my Garden, rides a Bird.
Dubie.   Hummingbirds.
Eberhart, R.   Vision.
Komunyakaa.   Nothing Big.
Lawrence, D. H.   Humming-Bird.
Levertov.   Revivals.
Turn of the Head, A.
Oliver, M.   Hummingbird Pauses at the Trumpet
  Vine.
Very.   Humming Bird, The.
Humming-Bird, The.
Whalen, P.   Hot Springs Infernal in the Human
  Beast.

Hunchbacks
Byron, G.   Deformed Transformed, The.
Glück, L.   Cell, The.
McGrath, T.   Emblems of Exile.
Thomas, D.   Hunchback in the Park, The.
Yeats.   Saint and the Hunchback, The.

Hundred Years War
Cummings, E. E.   Thou in whose swordgreat
  story shine the deeds.

Hungary
Cummings, E. E.   Thanksgiving (1956).
Very.   Kossuth.
Whittier.   Kossuth.

Hunger
Angelou.   Starvation.
Atwood.   More and More.
Auden.   Healthy Spot, A.
Berry, W.   Sparrow.
Bierce.   Saith the Czar.
Ciardi, J.   Captain Nicholas Strong.
Collins, B.   Osso Buco.
Creeley.   Down Home.
Hunger.
Words.
Dickinson, E.   Great Hungers feed themselves.
I had been hungry, all the Years.
It would have starved a Gnat.
Dugan, A.   For an Obligate Parasite.
Funeral Oration for a Mouse.
Ferlinghetti, L.   Astonished Heart, The.
Hall, D.   Wolf Knife.
Han-shan.   Frequent guest of hunger and cold,
  A.
Herrick.   Hunger.
Hughes, L.   Evenin' Air Blues.
God to Hungry Child.
Park Benching.
Success.
Ignatow, D.   In Ancient Times.
Mystique.
Jackson, L.   Concerning Food.
Komunyakaa.   Banking Potatoes.
Lamp Carrier, The.
Laughlin, J.   Hard to Translate.
In Darmstadt.
In the Train.
Stuttgart: In a Nightclub (Illegal).
What the Animals Did.
Levertov.   O Taste and See.
Levine, P.   They Feed They Lion.
Lorde.   Woman Thing, The.
Lux.   Kwashiorkor; Marasmus.
Major, C.   In the Armpit of the Hill.
Lost in the Desert.
Merwin.   Bread.
One Way.
Niedecker.   Alliance.
Land of four o'clocks is here, The.
Van Gogh.
Orr, G.   Going Out.
Piercy.   What the Owl Sees.

Rimbaud, A.   Festivals of Hunger.
Rossetti, C.   Prodigal Son, A.
Rumi.   Food Sack, The.
Sandburg, C.   Galoots.
Horse Fiddle.
Hunger and Cold.
Schuyler, J.   Dog Wants His Dinner, The.
Sexton.   Food.
Shout, The.
Simic.   Autumn Air.
Smith, S.   Dream of Nourishment, A.
Szymborska, W.   Starvation Camp at Jasło.
Very.   They Who Hunger.
Walker, A.   Few Sirens, A.
Wilbur, R.   Potato.
Williams, C. K.   With Ignorance.
Wright, J.   Before a Cashier's Window in a
  Department Store.
To a Friendly Dun.

Hunt, Leigh
Keats.   On Receiving a Laurel Crown from
  Leigh Hunt.
To Leigh Hunt, Esq.
Written on the Day that Mr. Leigh Hunt Left
  Prison.

Hunting and Hunters
Ai.   One Man Down.
Atwood.   Dream 2: Brian the Still-Hunter.
Auden.   Decoys, The.
Hunting Season.
Berry, W.   For the Hog Killing.
Long Hunter, The.
Berryman.   Not to Live.
Bierce.   Californian Summer Pictures.
Blue Cloud.   Hunt, Its Chant, A.
Yellowjacket.
Browning, R.   Donald.
Burns, R.   Hunting Song.
On Seeing a Wounded Hare Limp by Me,
  Which a Fellow Had Just Shot At.
Carver, R.   Cougar, The.
Elk Camp.
Grant, The.
Hunter.
Limits.
Shooting.
Ciardi, J.   Hawk.
Clampitt.   Bertie Goes Hunting.
Clare, J.   Badger.
Marten.
Mole-Catcher, The.
Cowper, W.   Needless Alarm, The.
Crane, S.   Chatter of a death-demon from a tree-
  top, The.
Cummings, E. E.   All in green went my love
  riding.
Cunningham, J.   Chase, The.
"Dario."   In Summer.
De la Mare.   Hunter, The.
Quarry, The.
Dickey, J.   Fox Blood.
Springer Mountain.
Summons, The.
Dickinson, E.   Cat.
My Life had stood—a Loaded Gun.
Dobyns.   Connections.
Dubie.   Amen.
Dugan, A.   Untitled Poem: "I'm in the house
  because."
Dunbar, P.   Forest Greeting, The.
Hunting Song.
Eberhart, R.   Young Hunter, The.
Frost, R.   Rabbit Hunter, The.
Gallagher, T.   Cougar Meat.
Glück, L.   Liberation.
Gray, T.   Caradoc.
"H. D."   Huntress.
Hall, D.   High Pasture, The.
Han-shan.   I recall the days of my youth.
Hardy, T.   Puzzled Game-Birds, The.
Herbert, G.   Affliction (4).
Housman.   Atys.
R. L. S.
Hughes, L.   For an Indian Screen.
Hughes, T.   Hare, The.
Isidorus.   On a Fowler.

Jacobsen, J.   In the Crevice of Time.
   My Small Aunt.
Jarrell, R.   Bird of Night, The.
Jeffers, R.   Shooting Season.
   Wind-Struck Music, The.
Jonson, B.   To Sir Henry Goodyere.
Kinnell.   Bear, The.
   Perch, The.
Kipling, R.   Fox-Hunting.
Komunyakaa.   Ode to a Drum.
Kumin, M.   Food Chain, The.
   Woodchucks.
Laughlin, J.   Hunting Dog, The.
Lawrence, D. H.   Mountain Lion.
Levi, P.   Elephant, The.
Lincoln, A.   Bear Hunt, The.
Lorde.   Woman Thing, The.
Mahon.   Hunt by Night, The.
Marvell.   Nymph Complaining for the Death of
   Her Faun [or Fawn], The.
Meredith, G.   Gordon, Jim, / Life and Limb.
   Long was the conflict, but now 'tis done.
   No boats oar slow, no barges pass.
   Song: "I would be the bounding deer."
   With the Huntress.
   Young Reynard.
Merwin.   Avoiding News by the River.
Millay, E.   Huntsman, What Quarry?
   October—An Etching.
Milosz, C.   Idea.
Montale.   Punta del Mesco.
Nash, O.   Hunter, The.
O'Hara, F.   Poem: "I ran through the snow like
   a young Czarevitch!"
Oliver, M.   Hunter's Moon—Eating the Bear.
   Wolf Moon.
Orr, G.   Gathering the Bones Together.
   Pond, The.
Patchen.   Fox, The.
   Hunter, The.
Petrarch.   Under the very hills where at the first.
Prunty.   Covined Bird, The.
   Eyeing the World.
   Saying it Back.
Raine, K.   Silver Stag, The.
Riley, J.   Coon-Dog Wess.
   Hunter Boy, The.
   Three Jolly Hunters, The.
Ritsos.   Extinction.
   Hunters.
Rukeyser, M.   Beast in View.
   Shooting Gallery.
Sandburg, C.   Early Hours.
Scott, S.   Hunting Song.
Sexton.   Loving the Killer.
Smart, C.   Country Squire and the Mandrake,
   The.
Smith, S.   Es War Einmal.
   I Am a Girl Who Loves to Shoot.
   Shooting Incident, The.
Stafford, W.   At Lascaux.
   Many Things are Hidden by the Light.
   Our People.
   Survival.
Stock, R.   How They Hunt the Quick Red Fox.
   Translated from Silence.
Tomlinson, C.   At the Autumn Equinox.
Van Duyn.   Hermit of Hudson Pond, The.
Warren, R.   Deep—Deeper Down.
   Red-Tail Hawk and Pyre of Youth.
   Season Opens on Wild Boar in Chianti.
   Winter Dreams.
Wilbur, R.   Castles and Distances.
Williams, M.   How It's Born in Us to
   Understand that There Are Two Sides to Every
   Question.
Williams, T.   Cried the Fox.
Wilner, E.   American Sublime, The: Robert
   Penn Warren.
   Hunting Manual.
   Literal = The Abstract, The: A Demonstration.
Wordsworth, W.   Simon Lee, the Old Huntsman;
   with an incident in which he was concerned.
Wright, J.   Fear Is What Quickens Me.
Wyatt, S.   Whoso List to Hunt.
Yeats.   Ballad of the Foxhunter, The.
   Hound Voice.

Hurdy-Gurdies
Cummings, E. E.   At the head of this street a
   gasping organ is waving moth-eaten.

Hurricanes
Blue Cloud.   Hurricane Andrew.
Clampitt.   Edge of the Hurricane, The.
   Hurricane and Charlotte Mew, The.
Crane, H.   Hurricane, The.
Dugan, A.   Surviving the Hurricane.
MacLeish.   Hurricane.
McHugh, H.   Hurricane Can Cast, A.
   Meantime.
Millay, E.   Dream of Saba.
Simic.   Hurricane Season.
Swenson, M.   Hurricane at Sea, A.
Wheatley, P.   To a Lady on Her Remarkable
   Preservation in an Hurricane.
Williams, M.   Form and Theory of Poetry.
See also **Storms**

Husbands
Angelou.   To a Husband.
Berry, W.   Marriage.
Bradstreet, A.   For the Restoration of My Dear
   Husband from a Burning Ague.
   In My Solitary Hours in My Dear Husband His
   Absence.
   In Thankful Acknowledgement for the Letters I
   Received from My Husband out Of England.
   In Thankful[l] Remembrance for My Dear
   Husband[']s Safe Arrival[l].
   Letter to Her Husband, Absent upon Public[k]
   Employment, A.
   To My Dear and Loving Husband.
Browning, R.   Any Wife to Any Husband.
Byron, G.   What Matter the Pangs of a Husband
   and Father.
Campion, T.   In Crispinum.
Carver, R.   Sunbather, to Herself, The.
Clifton, L.   Death of Fred Clifton, The.
Coleridge, S.   Happy Husband, The.
Dove, R.   Recovery.
Gay, J. *et al.*   Mary Gulliver to Capt. Lemuel
   Gulliver.
Graves, R.   Slice of Wedding Cake, A.
Hardy, T.   Every Artemisia.
   Her Second Husband Hears Her Story.
Herrick.   Good Husband, A.
   Upon Blanch.
Ignatow, D.   Across the Room.
Jonson, B.   Epigram to My Muse, the Lady
   Digby, on Her Husband, Sir Kenelm Digby,
   An.
Lawrence, D. H.   Good Husbands Make
   Unhappy Wives.
   I Heard Her Say.
Lowell, R.   To Speak of Woe That Is in
   Marriage.
Nash, O.   How to Harry a Husband, or, Is That
   Accessory Really Necessary?
   Perfect Husband, The.
   Trouble with Women Is Men, The.
   Very Funny, Very Funny.
Parker, D.   Husbands; A Hymn of Hate.
   Social Note.
Prunty.   Husband.
Rossetti, C.   I have a little husband / And he is
   gone to sea.
   Wee wee husband, / Give me some money.
Sexton.   And One for My Dame.
   Now.
   Where It Was at Back Then.
   Your Face on the Dog's Neck.
Stockton, A.   By a Lady in America to Her
   Husband in England.
   Elegy Inscribed to Richard J Stockton Esqr
   [Feb. 28, 1787].
   Short Elegy to the Memory of Her Husband, A.
   Sudden Production of Mrs. Stockton's in One of
   Those Many Anxious Nights.
Williams, C. K.   Alzheimer's: The Husband.
Williams, M.   She Talks to Her Sister, Briefly
   By on the Way to West Memphis.

Hyacinths
Cooper, J.   Leaving Water Hyacinths.

Eliot, T. S.   Song for Simeon, A.
Glück, L.   Hyacinth.
"H. D."   Shepherd, The.
Millay, E.   Hyacinth.
Raine, K.   Hyacinth, The.
Sappho.   One Girl.
Zukofsky, L.   Hyacinth.

Hydrangeas
Sandburg, C.   Dragoons, I tell you the white
   hydrangeas turn rust and go soon.
Williams, W.   Lesson, The.

Hyenas
Hughes, T.   Crow's Elephant Totem Song.
Kipling, R.   Hyænas [or Hyenas], The.

Hymns
Bishop, E.   Hymn to the Virgin.
Browning, E.   Since without Thee We Do No
   Good.
Crashaw.   Apology [or Apologie] for the
   Foregoing Hymn[e], An.
   Hymn for New Year's Day.
   In the Glorious Epiphanie of Our Lord God.
   Vexilla Regis.
Dugan, A.   On a Hymn, Misprinted.
Emerson, R.   For every god.
Hardy, T.   Barthélémon at Vauxhall.
Mahon.   Songs of Praise.
Riley, J.   Hymn Exultant.
   Peace-Hymn of the Republic, A.

Hypnosis and Hypnotists
Browning, R.   Mesmerism.

Hypocrisy and Hypocrites
Berryman.   Farewell to Miles.
Blake, W.   On Hayley.
   On Sir Joshua Reynolds.
Bly, R.   Johnson's Cabinet Watched by Ants.
Brodsky, J.   Kolo.
Browning, E.   Man's Requirements, A.
Browning, R.   Bishop Blougram's Apology.
   Soliloquy of the Spanish Cloister.
Burns, R.   Address to the Unco Guid, or the
   Rigidly Righteous.
   Holy Willie's Prayer.
   To the Rev. John McMath, Inclosing a Copy of
   Holy Willie's Prayer.
Byron, G.   New Vicar of Bray, The.
Cavafy.   Hospitality of Lagides, The.
   Julian in Nicomedia.
Clampitt.   Palm Sunday.
Clough.   Latest Decalogue, The.
Cowper, W.   Love of the World Reproved, The.
Creeley.   Wait for Me.
Cummings, E. E.   Come, gaze with me upon this
   dome.
   Next to of Course God America I.
   Opening of the chambers close.
   Season 'tis, my lovely lambs, The.
Davie, D.   Church Militant.
Dickinson, E.   Mine—by the Right of the White
   Election!
Dunbar, P.   Religion.
Emerson, R.   I've found the dainty malice out.
Graves, R.   Sick Love.
Guyon.   God neither Known nor Loved by the
   World.
Han-shan.   You're not really hermits.
HaNagid.   House of Prayer, The.
Hughes, L.   Children's Rhymes ("By what
   sends").
   Dinner Guest: Me.
   Merry Christmas.
   To Certain "Brothers."
Jonson, B.   On Court-Parrot.
   On Don Surly.
   On the Town's Honest Man.
   To Sir Ra[l]ph Shelton.
Kipling, R.   Islanders, The.
   Rhyme of the Three Captains, The.
   Tommy.
   Waster, The.
Kizer, C.   Wars in Sweden, The.
Lawrence, D. H.   British Sincerity.
   Commandments.
   Humility Mongers.
   Keep It Up.

Retort to Jesus.
Retort to Whitman.
Levertov. Hypocrite Women.
Lindsay, N. At Mass.
Why I Voted the Socialist Ticket.
Lorde. Vietnam Addenda.
MacLeish. Hypocrite Auteur.
Meredith, G. Martin's Puzzle.
Milosz, C. In Black Despair.
Mid-Twentieth-Century Portrait.
Nation, A.
Nash, O. Nevertheless.
Olson, C. Jas Jargon.
Parker, D. Interview.
Piercy. Kneeling at the Pipes.
Peaceable Kingdom, The.
Pope, A. Epigram in a Maid of Honour's
Prayer-Book.
Ramanujan. Guru, The.
Rimbaud, A. First Communions.
Tartufe's Punishment.
Rukeyser, M. Movie.
Rumi. After the Meditation.
Human Honesty.
Shapiro, K. Drug Store.
Mongolian Idiot.
Tennyson, A. Character, A.
Unknown, sometimes at. to Sir Walter Ralegh.
Epitaph on the Earl of Salisbury.
Whittier. Christian Slave, The.
Clerical Oppressors.
Gallows, The.
Leggett's Monument.
Letter from a Missionary of the Methodist
Episcopal Church South, in Kansas.
Lines on the Portrait of a Celebrated Publisher.
Pastoral Letter, The.
To Englishmen.
Williams, W. Early Martyr, An.
Graph for Action.

I

Ibsen, Henrik
Dubie. Fox Who Watched for the Midnight
Sun, The.
Rich, A. Juvenilia.

Ibycus
Graves, R. Ibycus of Samos.

Icarus
Auden. Musée des Beaux Arts.
Baudelaire. Laments of an Icarus, The.
Rukeyser, M. Waiting for Icarus.
Sexton. To a Friend Whose Work Has Come to
Triumph.
Spender, S. Icarus.
Wilbur, R. Icarium Mare.

Ice
Ammons. King of Ice, The.
Creeley. Blue.
Dickey, J. Adam in Winter.
Dickey, W. Avalanche.
Frost, R. Fire and Ice.
Hayden, R. Ice Storm.
Mallarmé. Virginal, vibrant, and beautiful dawn,
The.
Meredith, W. Crossing Over.
Merwin. Glimpse of the Ice.
Muldoon, P. Twice.
Nemerov. Icehouse in Summer, The.
Olson, C. Here i am, naked.
Pagis. Early Winter, Long Island.
Prunty. Sneeze, The.
Ritsos. Unacceptable, The.
Rukeyser, M. Ice-gate over the land, a shock of
closure.
Sandburg, C. Metamorphosis.
Stafford, W. Ice-Fishing.
Swenson, M. Zero in the Cove.
Very. Sailing on Cakes of Ice in the North
River.
Wilbur, R. Glance from the Bridge, A.
Stop.

Ice Cream
Komunyakaa. Happiness.
Nash, O. Tableau at Twilight.
Tomlinson, C. Ice Cream at Blauenberg.
Van Duyn. In the Cold Kingdom.

Ice Floes
Sze. Whiteout.

Ice Hockey
Bly, R. Hockey Poem, The.
Bukowski. Hog.

Ice Skating and Ice Skaters
Corbett, W. Family.
Niedecker. Watching Dan- / cers on Skates.
Prunty. Falling through the Ice.
Zamboni's Law.
Stafford, W. One Evening.
Weiss, T. Gothic Tale, A.
See also **Skating and Skaters**

Icebergs
Bishop, E. Imaginary Iceberg, The.
Cowper, W. On the Ice Islands Seen Floating in
the German Ocean.
Dickey, J. Form.
Dickinson, E. Icebergs italicize the Sea.
Hardy, T. Convergence of the Twain, The.
MacNeice. Icebergs.
Melville, H. Berg, The.
Rukeyser, M. Outpost.

Iceland
Auden. Journey to Iceland.
Borges. Gunnar Thorgilsson (1816-1879).
Iceland.
Nostalgia for the Present.
Enzensberger, H. Reprieve, The.
MacNeice. Eclogue from Iceland.
Iceland.
Letter to Graham and Anna.

Icicles
Ammons. Lollapalooza: 22 February.
Frost, R. Beyond Words.
Pinsky. Icicles.
Wilbur, R. Courtyard Thaw, A.

Idaho (state)
Kizer, C. Running Away from Home.
Wright, J. Frontier, The.

Idealism and Idealists
Browning, E. Tale of Villafranca, A.
Cavafy. Artificial Flowers.
Creeley. Revelation, The.
Cunningham, J. Metaphysical Amorist, The.
This Tower of Sun.
Dickinson, E. Ideals are the Fairy Oil.
Taking up the fair Ideal.
Eberhart, R. Difficulty of Ideas, The.
Fantasy of a Small Idea.
Emerson, R. I live among ideal men.
Idealism.
Graves, R. Perfectionists.
What Is Love?
Herrick. No Loathsomnesse in Love.
Hughes, L. Let America Be America Again.
Teacher.
Kunitz, S. Summing-up, The.
Lawrence, D. H. For the Heroes Are Dipped in
Scarlet.
Mess of Love, The.
Lindsay, N. Johnny Appleseed's Wife from the
Palace of Eve.
Lux. Neighborhood of Make-Believe, The.
Milosz, C. Idea.
Milton. On the Platonic Idea as Aristotle
Understood It.
Neruda. Gift, The.
Olson, C. Heart is a clock, The.
Parker, D. Day-Dreams.
Idyl.
Plath. Letter to a Purist.
Ransom, J. Address to the Scholars of New
England.
Rich, A. Ideal Landscape.
Shelley, P. Prince Athanase; a Fragment.
Wyatt, S. *In aeternum* I was once determed.

Identity
Amichai [*or* Amikhai]. As for the World.
I Lost My Identity Card.

I've Already Been Weaned.
What Kind of Man.
You Can Rely on Him.
Ammons. Risks and Possibilities.
Armantrout. My Associates.
Borges. Beppo.
Borges and I.
I.
I Am.
Watcher, The.
Brodsky, J. Anti-Shenandoah: Two Skits and a
Chorus.
Clampitt. Anatomy of Migraine, An.
Clifton, L. My Dream about Being White.
Codrescu. Casting.
Talismanic Ceremony for Lucian, March 9,
1971, Intersection Church, San Francisco.
Creeley. Theresa's Friends.
Cunningham, J. Identity, that spectator.
Enzensberger, H. Identity Check.
Other, The.
Ginsberg, A. Marijuana Notation.
Hughes, L. Consider Me.
Me and the Mule.
New Cabaret Girl, The.
Theme for English B.
Ignatow, D. Say Pardon.
Jackson, L. Advertisement.
Care in Calling.
I Am.
One Self.
Postponement of Self.
Reasons of Each, The.
Signature, The.
Tiger, The.
Who.
Kunitz, S. Layers, The.
Laughlin, J. Layers.
Shard of History, A.
Levertov. Long Way Round, The.
Mallarmé. Clown Chastised, The.
Meredith, W. Where He's Staying Now.
Merwin. Sire.
Track, The.
Montale. There the Tritone surges.
Niedecker. My life is hung up.
Oppen. Myself I Sing.
Palmer, M. She says, Into the dark.
Song of the Round Man.
This Time.
To Robert E. Symmes 1933 for a gift of
resemblances.
Pessoa. Recalling who I was, I see somebody
else.
Pinsky. In Berkeley.
Pound, E. Portrait d'une Femme.
Ramanujan. Alien.
No Amnesiac King.
Rilke. Masks Offer Themselves.
Stafford, W. Identities.
RX Creative Writing: Identity.
Story That Could Be True, A.
Swenson, M. I Look at My Hand.
Szymborska, W. In Abundance.
Tate, J. Tell Them Was Here.
Warren, R. Antinomy: Time and Identity.
Covered Bridge.
Identity and Argument for Prayer.
Why Boy Came to Lonely Place.
Whalen, P. Sad Song.
Williams, M. Unknown Sailor, The.
Wright, C. As Our Bodies Rise, Our Names
Turn into Light.
Wright, J. Abstract of Knowledge, The / The
First Test.
Inscrutability.
Zagajewski. Circus.
Self, The.

Identity Crisis
Amichai [*or* Amikhai]. To Gather Something.
Arnold, M. Self-Dependence.
Atwood. Double Voice, The.
Two-Headed Poems.
Bukowski. Last Generation, The.
Ciardi, J. Apprehendee Then Exited Vee-hicle.
Landscapes of My Name.

Creeley. Thinking.
Dickinson, E. I'm Nobody! Who are you?
Dugan, A. Note of Quits.
What a Circus.
Eberhart, R. Mistaken Identity.
Hayden, R. Names.
Hughes, T. Wodwo.
Jarrell, R. Woman at the Washington Zoo, The.
Komunyakaa. Somewhere Else.
McHugh, H. Disappearee's Song.
Merton. Fall, The.
With the World in My Blood Stream.
Merwin. Glass.
Not These Hills.
Montale. Moiré.
Muldoon, P. Identities.
Olson, C. In Cold Hell, in Thicket.
Pavement, The.
Pessoa. I'm a Runaway.
Lisbon Revisited (1926).
Ramanujan. Lines: "Who's this out there."
Rumi. Who Makes These Changes?
Sarton, M. Ballad of Johnny, The.
Schuyler, J. Poem, A: "Tags of songs, like
salvaged buttons."
Shapiro, K. I Am an Atheist Who Says His
Prayers.
Spender, S. Question of Identity, A.
Stafford, W. First Grade.
Tranströmer. Name, The.
Van Duyn. Good Resolution, The.
Williams, T. Penates.

Idleness
Berryman. Young Woman's Song.
Ciardi, J. Morning in the Park.
Creeley. Summer.
De la Mare. Idleness.
Emerson, R. And do I waste my time.
Apology, The.
Herrick. Disswasions from Idlenesse.
Jackson, L. Cycle of Industry, The.
Keats. Ode on Indolence.
Kinsella, T. Chrysalides.
Lindsay, N. Beggar Speaks, The.
Mahon. Dejection [Ode].
Riley, J. He and I.
June.
Summer Afternoon, A.
Uninterpreted.
With the Current.
Ritsos. Bitter Knowledge.
Smith, S. Lament of a Slug-a-Bed's Wife.
Spender, S. Unemployed.
Tomlinson, C. Idyll: "Door: / PER
L'UNIVERSO / is what it says, A."
Warren, R. Platonic Lassitude.
Whalen, P. Chanson d'Outre Tombe.
See also **Sloth**

Idolatry
Ammons. Image.
Cavafy. Illness of Kleitos, The.
Cavalcanti. Figure of my Lady, A.
Dickinson, E. Save me from the idolatry.
Frost, R. On Being Idolized.
Herrick. Devotion Makes the Deity.
Kipling, R. Evarra and His Gods.
Lawrence, D. H. Film Passion.
Lindsay, N. My Lady in Her White Silk Shawl.
To a Golden-Haired Girl in a Louisiana Town.
MacNeice. Leaving Barra.
Merton. Captives—a Psalm, The.
Orlandi, G. If, my friend, you would have said
of Mary so.
Ralegh, S. Ah wretched they that worship
vanities.
Rilke. Migration of Powers, The.
Sandburg, C. Hammer, The.
Manufactured Gods.
Wilde, O. Charmides.

Ignorance
Angelou. Bump d'Bump.
Beckett, S. Gnome.
Campion, T. Ad Rusticum.
Cowper, W. Lines Written upon a Window-
Shutter at Weston.
On One Ignorant and Arrogant.

Creeley. For the Graduation.
Love Comes Quietly.
Wisdom.
Cummings, E. E. All ignorance toboggans into
know.
Lis / -ten / you know what i mean when.
Love's function is to fabricate unknownness.
Now dis "daughter" uv eve(who aint precisely
slim)sim.
Of Ever-Ever Land i speak.
Old age sticks / up Keep.
Frost, R. Dust in the Eyes.
Gjuzel. My Sister's Letter.
Gray, T. Hymn to Ignorance.
Hacker, M. Autumn 1980.
Han-shan. All I see are fools.
Fire and smoke raged within.
Three Worlds swarm with people, The.
We hear about the ministers of state.
Hardy, T. Saying Good-bye.
Xenophanes, the Monist of Colophon.
Hughes, L. Ballad of the Fool.
Hughes, T. Childish Prank, A.
Egg-Head.
Jackson, L. Cure of Ignorance.
Jarrell, R. What's the Riddle.
Komunyakaa. Confessing My Ignorance.
Salt.
Larkin, P. Ignorance.
Lawrence, D. H. Know-All.
Levertov. Speech: For Antidraft Rally, D.C.,
March 22, 1980, A.
Lorde. Sewerplant Grows in Harlem or I'm a
Stranger Here Myself.
MacLeish. Some Aspects of Immortality.
Merwin. Crossroads of the World Etc., The.
To the Rain.
Montale. Farewells, whistling in the dark,
waves, coughs.
I free your forehead of the ice.
What you knew of me.
Nash, O. Caesar Knifed Again, or, Culture Biz
Gets Hep, Boffs Profs.
Everybody Wants to Get into the Baedeker.
So I resigned from the Chu Chin Chowder and
Marching Club.
Who Did Which? or Who Indeed?
Olson, C. Asymptotes.
Pagis. Homily.
Ramanujan. Not Knowing.
Ransom, J. Man without Sense of Direction.
Ritsos. Courage or Ignorance.
Stages of Ignorance.
Rossetti, C. Sketch, A.
Rukeyser, M. Do you know what I play to be,
in bed at night?
Sandburg, C. Unknown War, The.
Sarton, M. Hard Death, A.
Sexton. Poet of Ignorance, The.
Shapiro, K. Solipsism.
Spender, S. Louis MacNeice.
Very. Flood, The.
Williams, C. K. Secrets.
Williams, W. Immortal.
Yeats. Dawn, The.

Illegitimacy
Burns, R. Duncan Gray ["Weary fa' you,
Duncan Gray"].
Poet's Welcome to His Love-Begotten Daughter,
A.
Rantin Laddie, The.
Rowin 't in Her Apron, The.
Written under the Picture of the Celebrated Miss
Burns.
Hardy, T. Dead Bastard, The.
Fight on Durnover Moor, The.
Hurried Meeting, A.
Husband's View, The.
Practical Woman, A.
Second Night, The.
Herrick. Bastards.
Upon Dundrige.
Hughes, L. Mulatto.
S-sss-ss-sh!
Nash, O. Birth Comes to the Archbishop.
Sexton. Unknown Girl in the Maternity Ward.
Smith, S. Infant.

Valuable.
Williams, C. K. Creams.
Wordsworth, W. Vaudracour and Julia.

Illinois (state)
Bly, R. Three Kinds of Pleasures.
Brooks, G. Lovers of the Poor, The.
Kinnell. First Song.
Lindsay, N. Angel and the Clown, The.
Sandburg, C. Crabapples.
Dialogue.
Illinois Farmer.
Letter S.
Young Bullfrogs.

Illiteracy
MacLeish. Le Seul Malheur Est que Je ne Sais
pas Lire.

Illness
Amichai [or Amikhai]. My Son, My Son, My
Head, My Head.
Now She's Breathing.
Atwood. Bedside.
Bierce. Literary Method, A.
Matter for Gratitude.
One Morning.
Bradstreet, A. Deliverance from a Fit of
Fainting.
For Deliverance from a Fever.
For the Restoration of My Dear Husband from a
Burning Ague.
From Another Sore Fit.
Upon a Fit of Sickness, Anno 1632.
Upon Some Distemper of Body.
Broumas, O. Moon of Mind against the
Wooden Louver, The.
Touched.
Browning, R. Confessions.
You are sick, that's sure—they say.
Burns, R. Duncan Gray.
Fragment: "Now health forsakes that angel
face."
Song—(On Chloris Being Ill).
Byron, G. Lines on Hearing that Lady Byron
Was Ill.
Carew, T. Upon the King's Sickness.
Upon the Sickness of E.S.
Carver, R. Medicine.
Migration.
What the Doctor Said.
Cavafy. Illness of Kleitos, The.
Chuang Tzu. Metamorphosis.
Ciardi, J. Mutterings.
To Dudley Fitts.
Clampitt. Cadenza, A.
Cure at Porlock, A.
Curfew, A.
Isle of Wight, The.
Clifton, L. Dialysis.
Donor.
Poem to My Uterus.
Clough. Bethesda: A Sequel.
Cooper, J. Children's Ward, The.
For My Mother in Her First Illness, from a
Window Overlooking Notre Dame.
Infusion Room, The.
Cowper, W. R.S.S. Written in a Fit of Illness.
To Mary.
Cummings, E. E. Glazed mind layed in a, A).
Harder perhaps than a newengland bed.
Davie, D. Screech-Owl.
Dickey, J. Angina.
Dickinson, E. Doctor calls it "revenge of the
nerves," The.
It is very wrong that you were ill.
Donne. Canonization, The.
Hymn[e] to God My God, In My Sickness[e],
A.
Dubie. Ghosts on the Northern Land of Ur.
Dugan, A. Against a Sickness: To the Female
Double Principle God.
Death's Chicken, Named Amelia.
Duncan, R. After a Long Illness.
Emerson, R. If thy body pine.
Written in Sickness.
Ginsberg, A. On Reading William Blake's "The
Sick Rose."
Glück, L. Descending Figure.

World: / Image on water, waves.
Rexroth, K.   Illusion.
Rossetti, C.   I dreamt I caught a little owl.
Rukeyser, M.   Palos Verdes Cliffs.
Rumi.   Question, The.
Shapiro, K.   I Am an Athetist Who Says His
   Prayers.
Shelley, P.   To ———: "Oh! there are spirits of
   the air."
Smith, S.   Conviction (iii).
Stevens, W.   Add This to Rhetoric.
   What We See Is What We Think.
Swift, J.   Occasioned by Sir William Temple's
   Late Illness and Recovery.
Tomlinson, C.   Mushrooms.
Whitman, W.   Apparitions.
   Are You the New Person Drawn toward Me?
   Eidolons.
   Mirages.
   Of the Terrible Doubt of Appearances.
Wilner, E.   Maya.
Wordsworth, W.   Oxford, May Thirtieth,
   Eighteen Twenty.
Wyatt, S.   Ye old mule, that thin[c]k your self so
   fair [or fayre].
Zukofsky, L.   Lines of this new song are
   nothing, The.

Imagination
Ammons.   He Held Radical Light.
   High Surreal.
   Image.
   Imagined Land, The.
   Laser.
   Play.
   Triphammer Bridge.
Baudelaire.   Landscape.
Beckett, S.   Fin fond du néant.
Bishop, E.   Little Exercise.
   Sleeping on the Ceiling.
Borges.   Benares.
Brontë, E.   Aye there it is! It wakes tonight.
   Gleneden's Dream.
   God of Visions.
   Little while, a little while, A.
   To Imagination.
Brooks, G.   Anniad, The.
   Lovers of the Poor, The.
Browning, R.   By the Fire-Side.
Bukowski.   Insomnia.
Carruth, H.   Existing Pool, The.
   To Know in Reverie the Only Phenomenology
   of the Absolute.
   Une Présence Absolue.
Carver, R.   Aspens.
   Wake Up.
Cavafy.   For the Shop.
   On Hearing of Love.
Clifton, L.   Imagining Bear.
Coleridge, S.   Fancy in Nubibus.
   Reason.
   Reason for Love's Blindness.
Crane, H.   Postscript.
Creeley.   Again.
   "Do You Think."
   Dying.
   Echo ("Yes but your sweetness").
   Ice Cream.
   Lion and the Dog, The.
   Los Guitaristas.
   Place, A.
   Sounds.
   "There."
   They.
   To the One in the Gray Coat.
   Up in the Air.
   Wicker Basket, A.
   Wife, The.
Cummings, E. E.   Dominic has / a doll wired.
   Eagle, The,
   If a cheerfulest Elephantangelchild should sit.
   In a middle of a room.
   It really must / be Nice,never to.
   No man,if men are gods;but if gods must.
   Nothing is more exactly terrible than.
   Open your heart: / i'll give you a treasure.
   River of Mist, The.

Sonnet entitled how to run the world).
   Thethe / the pink / Tartskids with.
   When rain whom fear.
   Whose are these(wraith a clinging with a
   wraith).
Cunningham, J.   Fancy.
Davie, D.   Dream Forest.
De la Mare.   Dreams.
   Imagination's Pride, The.
   Memory.
   O Childish Mind!
Dickinson, E.   I cannot dance upon my Toes.
   I never saw a Moor.
Donne.   Song: "Go and catch a falling star."
Dove, R.   Banneker.
   Geometry.
Dryden, J.   Prologue to the University of
   Oxford, 1674.
Dugan, A.   Untitled Poem: "Let them take to the
   air before."
Dunbar, P.   By the Stream.
Duncan, R.   Descriptions of Imaginary Poetries.
   Imagining in Writing.
   Often I Am Permitted to Return to a Meadow.
Eberhart, R.   Fables of the Moon.
   Fortune's Mist.
   Reading Room, the New York Public Library.
   Supreme Authority of the Imagination, The.
Eliot, T. S.   La Figlia Che Piange.
Frost, R.   Courage to Be New, The.
   Riders.
Ginsberg, A.   Green Automobile, The.
   Imaginary Rose in a Book, An.
   Psalm I.
   Sunset S.S. Azemour.
Graves, R.   Alice.
   Death Room, The.
   In Disguise.
   Secret Land, The.
   Troughs of Sea.
   Warning to Children.
Gunn, T.   Inside-Outside Game, The.
   Justin.
   Pierce Street.
Hacker, M.   Art of a Novel, The.
   Celles.
Hardy, T.   After a Romantic Day.
   Meditation on a Holiday.
   Sun on the Bookcase, The.
Heaney, S.   Pitchfork, The.
   Railway Children, The.
   Sofa in the Forties, A.
Herrick.   Upon Julia's Clothes.
Hill, G.   Imaginative Life, The.
Hughes, L.   After Many Springs.
Jarrell, R.   Carnegie Library, Juvenile Division,
   The.
   Children Selecting Books in a Library.
   Cinderella.
   Cow wandering in the bare field, The.
   Girl in a Library, A.
   Sick Child, A.
   Unicorn, The.
Keats.   Ode on a Grecian Urn.
   On Receiving a Curious Shell, and a Copy of
   Verses, from the Same Ladies.
   On "The Story of Rimini."
   To My Brother George.
Kinnell.   When One Has Lived a Long Time
   Alone.
Kipling, R.   Friends, The.
Koch, K.   In the Morning.
Kunitz, S.   Revolving Meditation.
Larkin, P.   Essential Beauty.
   Observation.
Laughlin, J.   Non-World, The.
Lawrence, D. H.   Amour.
Levertov.   For a Child.
   In Mind.
   Sequence, A.
Longfellow, H.   Children's Hour, The.
Lorde.   Summer Oracle.
Lux.   Neighborhood of Make-Believe, The.
MacDiarmid, H.   Harry Semen.
Merton.   In the Rain and the Sun.
   Moon smiles like a queen, The.

Merwin.   Animals from Mountains.
   Animals, The.
   Windows, The.
Millay, E.   Amorphous is the mind; its quality.
   From a Very Little Sphinx.
Muldoon, P.   Trance.
Nemerov.   Maia.
Oliver, M.   Aunt Leaf.
   Spring Azures.
   Swan, The.
Olson, C.   2nd Musical Form, for Dave Young,
   A.
   What's Wrong with Pindar.
   Writ, The.
Orr, G.   Solitary Confinement.
Owen, W.   Spells and Incantation (a Fragment).
Pagis.   Limits of Physics, The.
Palmer, M.   As a Real House.
   Yes in a circle.
Patchen.   He Was Alone (as in Reality) upon
   His Humble Bed.
Pessoa.   There are sicknesses worse than
   sicknesses.
   This.
Plath.   Letter to a Purist.
   November Graveyard.
   On the Difficulty of Conjuring Up a Dryad.
   On the Plethora of Dryads.
   Tale of a Tub.
Prunty.   Wild Horses, The.
Rexroth, K.   Value in Mountains.
Rich, A.   Poetry: III.
Riley, J.   Christine's Song.
Robinson, E.   Miniver Cheevy.
Rossetti, C.   Somewhere or Other.
Rukeyser, M.   Child wakes in the morning to
   enter a country, The.
   Risen Image Shines, The.
Sandburg, C.   Child Margaret.
   Hummingbird Woman.
Sarton, M.   Notes from India.
   These Images Remain.
Schuyler, J.   Greetings from the Chateau.
Sexton.   August 8th.
   February 3rd.
   Gold Key, The.
Shelley, P.   To ———: "Oh! there are spirits of
   the air."
Simic.   Prisoner, The.
Smart, C.   Reason and Imagination.
Smith, S.   Agnostic, An.
   Fairy Story.
   In Protocreation.
   My Hat.
   Our Bog Is Dood.
Snyder, G.   I can't stand these bird-songs.
Stafford, W.   Fiction.
Stevens, W.   Academic Discourse at Havana.
   High-Toned Old Christian Woman, A.
   Man with the Blue Guitar, The.
   Metaphor as Degeneration.
   Plain Sense of Things, The.
   Puella Parvula.
Stock, R.   Cushing.
Stockton, A.   Lyric Ode, A.—Feb. 28.
Suckling, S.   Upon My Lady Carlisle's Walking
   in Hampton Court Garden.
Swenson, M.   Centaur, The.
Szymborska, W.   Interview with a Child.
   Large Number, A.
   Pursuit.
   Thomas Mann.
Tomlinson, C.   Sense of Distance, A.
Updike.   Marching through a Novel.
Van Duyn.   Woman Waiting.
Wheatley, P.   On Imagination.
Whitman, W.   Ambition.
   Glimpse, A.
Whittier.   Tent on the Beach, The.
   To My Sister.
Wilbur, R.   Clearness.
   In the Elegy Season.
   La Rose des Vents.
   Sunlight Is Imagination.
   Walking to Sleep.
Williams, C. K.   Most excruciating / thing, The.

Near the Haunted Castle.
Williams, W.   Deep Religious Faith.
Wordsworth, W.   Her Only Pilot the Soft
  Breeze, the Boat.
In My Mind's Eye a Temple, like a Cloud.
Morning Exercise, A.
Pibroch's note, discountenanced or mute.
Weak is the will of Man, his judgement blind.
While Beams of Orient Light Shoot Wide and
  High.
Yarrow Visited [September, 1814].
Yes! Thou Art Fair, Yet Be Not Moved.
Yeats.   Those Images.
Zaturenska.   Song: "Life with her weary eyes."
Zukofsky, L.   Lines of this new song are
  nothing, the.
Some time has gone.

Immigration and Immigrants
Amichai [or Amikhai].   And the Migration of
  My Parents.
Name of the Place "Trieste," The.
Armantrout.   Visibility.
Atwood.   Disembarking at Quebec.
First Neighbours.
Further Arrivals.
Immigrants, The.
Cavafy.   In the Port.
Ciardi, J.   Letter to Mother.
Codrescu.   Ethnic Jammies.
School Daze.
Cummings, E. E.   Mary green / cheerful &
  generous.
Dugan, A.   On Being Out-Classed by Class.
Eberhart, R.   Statue of Liberty.
Fenton, J.   Chosun.
Ferlinghetti, L.   Poet's eye obscenely seeing,
  The.
Frost, R.   Immigrants.
García Lorca.   Song of the Shop Boy.
Glück, L.   Legend.
Hughes, L.   Second Generation: New York.
Hughes, T.   Descent.
Ignatow, D.   Europe and America.
Jarrell, R.   Night before the Night before
  Christmas, The.
To the New World.
Levertov.   Letter to Marek about a Photograph,
  A.
Settling.
MacLeish.   Burying Ground by the Ties.
MacNeice.   Last before America.
Refugees.
Mahon.   Canadian Pacific.
Chinese Restaurant in Portrush, The.
Meredith, G.   Patriot Engineer, The.
Merwin.   Émigré.
Fields, The.
Mistral, G.   Foreign Woman, The.
Paley, G.   Autumn.
Family.
Having Arrived by Bike at Battery Park.
Illegal Aliens.
Immigrant Story, The.
Letter.
Nature of This City, The.
Pinsky.   Window.
Prunty.   To be Sung on the Fourth of July.
Ramanujan.   Poor Man's Riches 1, A.
Rich, A.   Prospective Immigrants Please Note.
Riley, J.   Herr Weiser.
Shapiro, K.   My Grandmother.
Statue of Liberty.
Thoreau.   I am the little Irish boy.
Weiss, T.   Heir Apparent, The.
Pair of Shoes, A.
Whittier.   Pennsylvania Pilgrim, The.
Wilbur, R.   Speech for the Repeal of the
  McCarran Act.
Williams, W.   Sicilian Emigrant's Song.
Zagajewski.   Password.
Song of an Emigré.

Immortality
Angelou.   Wonder.
Arnold, M.   Shakespeare.
Ashbery, J.   How Much Longer Will I Be Able
  to Inhabit the Divine Sepulcher.

Atwood.   Bus along St Clair: December, A.
They Eat Out.
Berry, W.   Farmer, Speaking of Monuments,
  The.
Bierce.   Macrobian.
Blue Cloud.   Being Forever.
Bly, R.   Poem in Three Parts.
Bogan, L.   Homunculus.
Borges.   Poem Written in a Copy of *Beowulf*.
Browning, R.   Cleon.
  Earth's Immortalities.
Bukowski.   Upon First Reading the Immortal
  Literature of the World—.
Carruth, H.   Contra Mortem.
Cavafy.   Hereafter, The.
Memory.
Coleridge, S.   Human Life; on the Denial of
  Immortality.
Cuadra, P.   Meditation before an Ancient Poem.
Cummings, E. E.   But if a living dance upon
  dead minds.
Fame Speaks.
Helen.
Let us suspect,chérie,this not very big.
Mortals) / climbi / ng i / nto eachness begi.
So shy shy shy(and with a).
De la Mare.   Alexander.
Evening.
Not Only.
Dickey, J.   Immortals.
Dickinson, E.   Ambition cannot find him.
Because I could not stop for Death.
Extol thee—could I? Then I will.
Finite life, little sister, A.
Footlights cannot improve the grave.
Given in Marriage unto Thee.
If my Bark sink.
Immortality of Flowers, The.
Immortality she gave, The.
Is Immortality a bane.
It is an honorable Thought.
It may have been she came to show you.
It's thoughts—and just One Heart.
Letter always seemed to me, A.
My life closed twice before its close.
No heart that broke but further went.
Only News I know, The.
Reticent volcano keeps, The.
Risks of Immortality, The.
Soul's Superior instants, The.
Speculate with all our might.
Such are the inlets of the mind.
Take all away.
That Such have died enable Us.
Thirst.
Two—were immortal twice.
Unable are the Loved to die.
Vision of Immortal Life has been fulfilled, The.
Who abdicated Ambush.
Why should we hurry—why indeed?
With Pinions of Disdain.
Donne.   Good-Morrow, The.
Dugan, A.   Against the Text "Art Is Immortal."
Eberhart, R.   Hand, The.
R. G. E.
Ways and Means.
Emerson, R.   Brave Empedocles defying fools,
  The.
Eros.
Ferlinghetti, L.   I have not lain with beauty all
  my life.
Gallagher, T.   Instructions to the Double.
Ginsberg, A.   Poem Rocket.
Hall, D.   My Son, My Executioner.
Han-shan.   Hermit's heart is heavy, A.
I recently hiked to a temple in the clouds.
Hardy, T.   Her Immortality.
His Immortality.
Rome: At the Pyramid of Cestius near the
  Graves of Shelley and Keats.
Shelley's Skylark.
Herbert, G.   Death.
Virtue [or Vertue].
Herrick.   His Creed.
To His Peculiar Friend Master Thomas Shapcott,
  Lawyer.

Housman.   If truth in hearts that perish.
Hughes, L.   Scottsboro.
Jeffers, R.   Animula.
Post Mortem.
Keats.   Ode: "Bards of passion and of mirth."
Lawrence, D. H.   Resurrection.
Lindsay, N.   Beyond the Moon.
Lorde.   Maiden, The.
MacLeish.   Some Aspects of Immortality.
Merwin.   Distances, The.
Do Not Die.
Prayer of the Eyes, A.
Michelangelo Buonarroti.   Mere mortal once.
Divine, though, born to be.
My lady, how comes it about—what all can see.
Milosz, C.   After Enduring.
Milton.   On Shakespear[e].
Raine, K.   Kore.
Ralegh, S.   Because that stealing immortalitie.
Ramanujan.   Hindu to His Body, A.
Rexroth, K.   You did not know she was eternal?
There.
Robinson, E.   Dark House, The.
Man against the Sky, The.
Rossetti, C.   That No Man Take Thy Crown.
Rukeyser, M.   Mortal Girl.
Tate, J.   Immortals, The.
Tennyson, A.   Tithonus.
Very.   Cross, The ("I must go on, till in my
  tearful line").
New Birth, The.
This Mortal Shall put on Immortality.
Warren, R.   Immortality over the Dakotas.
Wheatley, P.   To a Gentleman and Lady on the
  Death of the Lady's Brother and Sister, and a
  Child of the Name Avis, Aged One Year.
Whitman, W.   Joy, Shipmate, Joy!
On the Beach at Night.
Woman Waits for Me, A.
Whittier.   Raphael.
Wilde, O.   Athanasia.
Williams, M.   Aging Actress Sees Herself a
  Starlet on the Late Show, The.
Wordsworth, W.   Ode: Intimations of
  Immortality from Recollections of Early
  Childhood.
Upon a Portrait.
Wright, C.   Laguna Dantesca.
Yeats.   Sailing to Byzantium.
Zagajewski.   Immortality.

Imperfections
Campion, T.   Vaile, love, mine eyes, O hide
  from me.
Coleridge, S.   Humility the Mother of Charity.
Creeley.   Cantos, The.
Immoral Proposition, The.
Cunningham, J.   Innocent to innocent.
Dickey, W.   Therefore.
Eberhart, R.   Meditation, A.
Éluard, P.   Out of Sight in the Direction of My
  Body.
Herrick.   No Loathsomnesse in Love.
To the Generous Reader.
Hughes, T.   I know well.
McHugh, H.   In Praise of Pain.
Pessoa.   Circle, The.
Stafford, W.   Sparkle Depends on Flaws in the
  Diamond, The.
Zagajewski.   Try to Praise the Mutilated World.
Zaturenska.   Imperfect, The.

Imperialism
Bierce.   Strained Relations.
Bly, R.   Hatred of Men with Black Hair.
Brodsky, J.   Anno Domini.
Carver, R.   Caucasus: A Romance, The.
News Carried to Macedonia, The.
Cavafy.   Before Antiochus Epiphanis.
In the Year 200 B.C.
Taken.
Clampitt.   Hispaniola.
"Dario."   What sign do you give, O Swan, with
  your curving neck.
Davie, D.   Bougainville.
From the New World.
Frontenac.
Letter to Curtis Bradford, A.

Dugan, A.   Decimation before Phraäta, The.
Eberhart, R.   Rape of the Cataract, The.
Frost, R.   Bad Island, The—Easter.
Hughes, L.   Broadcast on Ethiopia.
  Columbia.
  English, The.
  Gangsters.
  Lament for Dark Peoples.
  Letter from Spain.
  Merry Christmas.
  Roar China!
  What I Think.
Jeffers, R.   Bowl of Blood, The.
  Shine, Empire.
Kipling, R.   Kitchener's School.
  Recessional.
  Rowers, The.
  Song of the White Men, A.
  White Man's Burden, The.
Lawrence, D. H.   Combative Spirit, The.
  Triumph.
Lindsay, N.   Shantung[, or the Empire of China
  Is Crumbling Down].
Logue, C.   Song of the Imperial Carrion, The.
Lowell, R.   Cicero, the Sacrificial Killing.
  Marcus Cato 234–149 B.C.
McGrath, T.   Columbus.
  Fresco: Departure for an Imperialist War.
Meredith, G.   Chillianwallah.
  Gordon of Khartoum.
  Voyage of the "Ophir," The.
  Warning, The.
Merton.   Letter to Pablo Antonio Cuadra
  Concerning Giants, A.
Olson, C.   Bigmans II.
Ramanujan.   Image for Politics, An.
Szymborska, W.   Voices.
Thomas, D.   Incarnate Devil.
Updike.   B.W.I.
Wilde, O.   Ave Imperatrix.
Williams, M.   Green Mansions.

Impermanence
Ammons.   Put-Down Come On, The.
Browning, R.   James Lee's Wife.
Du Bellay.   Rome.
García Lorca.   Desire of a Statue.
Lux.   Irreconcilabilia.
Michelangelo Buonarroti.   Rancorous heart,
  cruel, pitiless, though showing.
Milosz, C.   1945.
  At Dawn.
  Hooks of a Corset, The.
  In Salem.
  Lastingness.
  No More.
  Should, Should Not.
  Whiteness.
Ramanujan.   Elements of Composition.
Seifert.   Red-Hot Fruit.
Sze.   Cloud Chamber, The.
  String Diamond, The.
Whalen, P.   Japanese Tea Garden Golden Gate
  Park in Spring.
Williams, T.   After a Visit.
  We Have Not Long to Love.
See also **Transience**

Impotence
Bukowski.   Sex and/or Love.
Carruth, H.   Sex.
Eberhart, R.   Meditation, A.
Eliot, T. S.   In the Department Store.
Graves, R.   Primrose Bed, The.
Herrick.   To His Mistress[es].
Laughlin, J.   Premula's Problem.
Rukeyser, M.   Portrait of a Man, with a
  Background of Holdings.
Rumi.   Sexual Urgency, What a Woman's
  Laughter Can Do, and the Nature of True
  Virility.
Williams, W.   Plea for Mercy, A.
Yeats.   Chambermaid's Second Song, The.

Impressionism and Impressionists
Ferlinghetti, L.   Late Impressionist Dream.
  Matisse at the Modern, Magritte at the Met.
  Returning to Paris with Pissarro.
McHugh, H.   Impressionist.

Weiss, T.   Views and Spectacles.
Wilde, O.   Impression du Matin.

Impulse
Creeley.   Dancing.
  Massachusetts.
  Post Cards.
Koch, K.   Departure from Hydra, The.
Zukofsky, L.   Drive, fast kisses.

Incantations
Carver, R.   Spell.
Cavafy.   Illness of Kleitos, The.
Riley, J.   Charms.
Swenson, M.   Incantation.

Incas
Levi, P.   Huayna Capac.
Mahon.   Andean Flute, The.

Incense
Blue Cloud.   Incense.
Ginsberg, A.   After Yeats.
Gurney, I.   Incense Bearers, The.

Incest
Ai.   False Witness.
Davie, D.   Dancing Measures.
García Lorca.   Thamar and Amnon.
Jeffers, R.   Such Counsels You Gave to Me.
  Tamar.

Incomprehensibility
Coleridge, S.   To Mr. Pye.
Creeley.   For Lewis, to Say It.
Meredith, W.   Chinese Banyan, The.
Nash, O.   It's about Time.
Wright, C.   December Journal.
  Journal of Three Questions, A.
  Saturday Morning Journal.

Inconstancy
Browning, E.   Change upon Change.
Bukowski.   Sexpot.
Burns, R.   Banks o' Doon, The ("Ye banks and
  braes o' bonie [or bonnie] Doon").
  Can You Leave Me Thus, My Katy.
  Eppie McNab.
  Scotish Ballad.
  Song: "Let not Woman e'er complain."
  Thou hast left me ever, Jamie.
Carruth, H.   R.M.D.
Chaucer.   Against Women Unconstant [or A
  Ballade against Woman Inconstant].
Cowper, W.   Friendship.
  Song, A: "On the green margin of the brook."
Eberhart, R.   Going to Maine.
Éluard, P.   Confections.
Graves, R.   Confess, Marpessa.
Hardy, T.   Inconsistent, The.
  Sun on the Letter, The.
Herbert, G.   Giddiness.
Herrick.   Upon Himself.
  Upon Trap.
Jonson, B.   Another. In Defense of Their
  Inconstancy [or Inconstancie]. A Song.
Kipling, R.   Ballade of Jakko Hill, A.
Parker, D.   Theory.
Pound, E.   In Epitaphium Eius.
Ralegh, S.   Advice, The.
Unknown.   On Female Inconstancy.

Indecision
Catullus.   85: "I hate and love her. If you ask
  me why."
Cavafy.   From the School of the Renowned
  Philosopher.
See also **Decisions**

Independence
Amichai [or Amikhai].   Hymn for Independence
  Day, A. So distant.
Arnold, M.   Self-Dependence.
Browning, E.   Calls on the Heart.
Burns, R.   I Hae a Wife o' My Ain.
  Poetical Inscription, for an Altar to
  Independence at Kerrouchtry.
  To Daunton Me.
Carver, R.   Margo.
Clampitt.   New Life, A.
Dunbar, P.   Easy-Goin' Feller, An.
Eberhart, R.   Concord Cats.
Eliot, T. S.   Cousin Nancy.
Emerson, R.   But Nature whistled with all her

  winds.
  Civil world will much forgive, The.
Frost, R.   Silken Tent, The.
Gallagher, T.   Beginning to Say No.
HaNagid.   He Who Depends on the Princes.
Jacobsen, J.   Sisters, The.
Jeffers, R.   My Dear Love.
  Thebaid.
Levertov.   Movement.
Merwin.   Place of Backs, The.
Parker, D.   Indian Summer.
Thoreau.   I'm not alone.
  Independence.
Whittier.   Hero, The.
Wilbur, R.   On Freedom's Ground.
Wordsworth, W.   Resolution and Independence.

India
Atwood.   Sunday Drive, A.
Baudelaire.   To a Girl in Malabar.
Carruth, H.   Godhulivela.
  Purana, Meaning Once upon a Time.
Cavafy.   Coins.
  Indian Image.
Cullen, C.   Karenge Ya Marenge.
Ginsberg, A.   Describe: The Rain on
  Dasaswamedh Ghat.
  Patna-Benares Express.
Hughes, L.   For an Indian Screen.
  Gandhi Is Fasting.
Kipling, R.   Army Headquarters.
  Cholera Camp.
  Christmas in India.
  Giffen's Debt.
  Grave of the Hundred Dead, The.
  Gunga Din.
  In Springtime.
  Lament of the Border Cattle Thief, The.
  Last Suttee, The.
  Legend of the Foreign Office, A.
  Man Who Could Write, The.
  Mandalay.
  Masque of Plenty, The.
  Moon of Other Days, The.
  Mother-Lodge, The.
  One Viceroy Resigns.
  Oonts.
  Open Door, The.
  Overland Mail, The.
Pagett, M. P.
  Plea of the Simla Dancers, The.
  Public Waste.
  Route Marchin'.
  Song for the Women, The.
  Song of the Wise Children.
  Study of an Elevation, in Indian Ink.
  Tale of Two Cities, A.
  To the City of Bombay.
  Truce of the Bear, The.
  Two Months.
  What Happened.
  With Scindia to Delhi.
Laughlin, J.   So Slender.
Lindsay, N.   I Know All This when Gipsy
  Fiddles Cry.
MacDiarmid, H.   Why.
MacNeice.   Letter from India.
Meredith, G.   Chillianwallah.
Meredith, W.   Jain Bird Hospital in Delhi, The.
Merton.   Darjeeling.
  Songs of Experience; India, One.
Nash, O.   How to Be Married without a Spouse,
  or, Mr. Kipling, What Have You Done with
  Mr. Hauksbee?
  Kipling's Vermont.
O'Hara, F.   Image of the Buddha Preaching.
Ramanujan.   Bulls.
  Compensations.
  In the Zoo.
  Last of the Princes, The.
  River, A.
  Small-scale Reflections on a Great House.
  Smalltown, South India.
  Some Indian Uses of History on a Rainy Day.
  Time and Time Again.
Rukeyser, M.   Ajanta.
Sarton, M.   Approach—Calcutta, The.

Nostalgia for India.
Notes from India.
Snyder, G.   On Our Way to Khajuraho.
Walcott.   Exile.
  Saddhu of Couva, The.
Weiss, T.   Place of Laughter, The.
Whitman, W.   Passage to India.

Indian Summer
Amichai [or Amikhai].   Indian Summer in
  Princeton.
Dickinson, E.   Indian Summer.
  These Indian-Summer Days.
Kunitz, S.   Indian Summer at Land's End.
Lindsay, N.   Indian Summer Day on the Prairie,
  An.
Orr, G.   Indian Summer.
Rexroth, K.   Heart Unbroken and the Courage
  Free, The.
Riley, J.   Autumnal Tonic, An.
Whittier.   St. Martin's Summer.
Williams, W.   Late for Summer Weather.
Wright, C.   Indian Summer 2.
  Peccatology.

Indiana (state)
Levine, P.   Helmet, The.
Riley, J.   From Delphi to Camden.
  His Love of Home.
  Hoosier Calendar, A.
  Hoosier Folk-Child, The.
  Hoosier in Exile, The.
  Hoosier Spring-Poetry.
  Indiana.
  Old Indiany.
  Regardin' Terry Hut.
  Right Here at Home.
Sandburg, C.   Mayor of Gary, The.
  New Song for Indiana Ophelias.
Updike.   Indianapolis.

Indians, American
Mistral, G.   Quechuan Song.
See also **Native Americans**

Indifference
Ammons.   Account, The.
Baudelaire.   In glistening shot-silk she seems to
  wind.
Beckett, S.   Bois seul.
Bukowski.   Beautiful Young Girl Walking Past
  the Graveyard—, The.
Byron, G.   To Caroline.
Cavafy.   Salome.
Cooper, J.   Gaza.
Creeley.   Crow, The.
  First Time, The.
  Song: "Were I myself more blithe."
Cummings, E. E.   Anyone Lived in a Pretty
  How Town.
Davie, D.   Rejoinder to a Critic.
Dickey, J.   Nameless.
Dickey, W.   More under Saturn.
Eliot, T. S.   Interlude in London.
Emerson, R.   I care not whither I may go.
Glück, L.   Return, The.
Han-shan.   Old Chung north of town.
Hardy, T.   At a Bridal.
Hughes, L.   Hard Daddy.
  Hurt.
  Kid Sleepy.
Lawrence, D. H.   Loggerheads.
  What Do I Care?
Levine, P.   Coming Home, *Detroit*, 1968.
Melville, H.   Pebbles.
Montale.   Often I've encountered evil.
Parker, D.   New Love, The.
Pessoa.   I heard it told that once when Persia.
  One after another, hard-pressed waves.
Ramanujan.   HINDOO, THE: The Only Risk.
Rossetti, C.   Love Attacked.
Smith, S.   Voice from the Tomb (3).
Williams, W.   She Who Turns Her Head.
Wright, C.   Landscape with Seated Figure and
  Olive Trees.
Wyatt, S.   Love whom ye list and spare not.

Indigestion
Bierce.   Trencher-Knight, A.
Herrick.   Upon Gut.

Individualism and Individualists
Arnold, M.   Self-Dependence.
Bukowski.   Last Generation, The.
Clough.   In the Great Metropolis.
Coleridge, S.   Phantom.
Crane, S.   "Think as I think," said a man.
Creeley.   Measure, The.
Cummings, E. E.   There are possibly 2 1/2 or
  impossibly 3.
Dickinson, E.   There seems a spectral power.
  To be singular under plural circumstances.
Dugan, A.   Untitled Poem: "Speciously
  individual."
Dunbar, P.   Bohemian, The.
  Path, The.
Emerson, R.   Easy to match what others do.
  Elizabeth Hoar.
  Etienne de la Boéce.
  I will not live out of me.
  Let not conceited sages laugh aloud.
  Ode, Inscribed to W.H. Channing.
  Simple people each with basket or tool, The.
Ferlinghetti, L.   Adieu À Charlot.
  Jack of Hearts, The.
Frost, R.   Road Not Taken, The.
Graves, R.   Portrait, The.
Jeffers, R.   Heavy and yellow with the clay
  wrack from the flooded valley.
Kipling, R.   Glories, The.
  Two Races.
Lawrence, D. H.   At Last.
  Be a Demon!
  Don'ts.
Levertov.   Melody Grundy.
MacNeice.   Individualist Speaks, The.
  Plurality.
Merton.   New Ribbon.
Nash, O.   Thoughts Thought on an Avenue.
O'Hara, F.   My Heart.
Olson, C.   Po-sy, a Po-sy, A.
Pagis.   Tropical Greenhouse.
Piercy.   I Will Not Be Your Sickness.
Riley, J.   Strange Young Man, The.
Sandburg, C.   Always the Mob.
  Personality.
  Style.
Stafford, W.   Over the North Jetty.
Swenson, M.   Manyone Flying.
Walker, A.   Be Nobody's Darling.
  Light Baggage.
  On Stripping Bark from Myself.
Whitman, W.   By Blue Ontario's Shore.
  One's-Self I Sing.
  Torch, The.
Williams, W.   On First Opening the Lyric Year.
Wyatt, S.   I am as I am and so will I be.
Yeats.   Coat, A.
Zukofsky, L.   Song for the Year's End, A.
See also **Egotism and Egotists**

Indonesia and Indonesians
Fenton, J.   Dead Soldiers.
Oliver, M.   Indonesia.
See also **Borneo**

Indulgences
Carver, R.   Grant, The.
Herrick.   Youth, and Age.
Meredith, G.   Certain People, A.
Riley, J.   Curly Locks.
  Spoiled Child, The.
Smith, S.   Mother's Hearse, A.

Indus River
Carver, R.   News Carried to Macedonia, The.

Industrial Revolution
Bishop, E.   Varick Street.

Industrial Workers of the World (IWW)
McGrath, T.   Heroes of Childhood, The.

Industrialization
Bukowski.   High-Rise of the New World, The.
Clampitt.   Dahlia Gardens, The.
Davie, D.   Cheshire.
Dunbar, P.   Ballade: "By Mystic's banks I held
  my dream."
Eberhart, R.   Hard Structure of the World, The.
Emerson, R.   New England Capitalist.
Frost, R.   Bursting Rapture.

Hall, D.   Foundations of American Industry,
  The.
Hopkins, G.   God's Grandeur.
Kinnell.   Tragedy of Bricks, The.
Koch, K.   Brassiere Factory, The.
Kumin, M.   Chain, The.
Kunitz, S.   War against the Trees, The.
Larkin, P.   Going, Going.
Lawrence, D. H.   Cross, The.
  Evening Land, The.
  Factory Cities, The.
  Gulf, The.
  New Houses, New Clothes.
  North Country, The.
  Oh Wonderful Machine!
  Robot Feelings.
  Side-Step, O Sons of Men!
  We Die Together.
  What Is a Man to Do?
  Why—?
Levertov.   For Floss.
Levine, P.   They Feed They Lion.
Merton.   Ohio River—Louisville, The.
Milosz, C.   Three Talks on Civilization.
Sandburg, C.   Five Towns on the B. and O.
  Prairie.
Sexton.   Mr. Mine.
Spender, S.   Landscape near an Aerodrome,
  The.
Tomlinson, C.   John Maydew or The Allotment.
Williams, W.   Sketch for a Portrait of Henry
  Ford.
Wright, C.   Lonesome Pine Special.

Ineptitude
Burns, R.   On Elphinston's Translation of
  Martial.
Emerson, R.   With the key of the secret he
  marches faster.
Kizer, C.   Election Day, 1984.
MacLeish.   Ship of Fools.
Nash, O.   He Digs, He Dug, He Has Dug.
Pope, A.   To Eustace Budgell, Esq., on His
  Translation of the Characters of Theophrastus.
  Translator, The.
  Verses to Be Placed under the Picture of
  England's Arch-Poet.

Infant Death
Ai.   Ice.
Crashaw.   To the Infant Martyrs.
  Upon the Infant Martyrs.
Dunbar, P.   Two Little Boots.
Jonson, B.   On My First Daughter.
  To K[ing] Charles and Q[ueen] Mary, for the
  Loss of Their First-Born.
Major, C.   Being and Becoming.
Marvell.   Picture of Little T. C. in a Prospect of
  Flowers, The.
Merwin.   To My Brother Hanson.
Williams, W.   Dead Baby, The.
See also **Death in Childhood**

Infanticide
Browning, E.   Runaway Slave at Pilgrim's Point,
  The.
Hall, D.   By the Exeter River.
Smith, S.   But Murderous.
Williams, M.   Ones that Are Thrown Out, The.
Wordsworth, W.   Thorn, The.

Infants
Laughlin, J.   Bit Different, A.
  Figlio Mio.
Pinkerton, H.   Celebration.
Sze.   Murmur, The.
See also **Babies**

Infatuation
Angelou.   Senses of Insecurity.
Baudelaire.   Lethe.
  Living Dead, The.
  Passing Glance, A.
  Song for an Afternoon.
  To a Madonna.
  Too Full of Life.
  Vampire, The.
Brooks, G.   Flags.
Browning, R.   Beatrice Signorini.
  Cristina.

Rudel to the Lady of Tripoli.
Sonnet: "Eyes, calm beside thee, (Lady couldst thou know!)."
Burns, R. Fragment, A: "When first I came to Stewart Kyle."
Carew, T. Mr. Carew to His Friend.
Cavafy. Epic in the Heart.
Coleridge, S. Lewti.
Dickinson, E. Her thot's tho' they are older.
I see thee better—in the Dark.
Emerson, R. Pair of crystal eyes will lead me, A.
When Jane was absent Edgar's eye.
Graves, R. Circus Ring.
Dream of Frances Speedwell, A.
Growing Pains.
Invitation to Bristol.
Poor Others.
Three Times in Love.
To Be in Love.
Traditionalist, The.
Herrick. Epitaph upon a Virgin, An.
Short Hymne to Venus, A.
To Oenone.
Upon a Black Twist, Rounding the Arm of the Countess of Carlisle.
Upon Love.
Writing.
Housman. Oh, when I Was In Love.
Kipling, R. Fall of Jock Gillespie, The.
Koch, K. In Love with You.
Spring.
To Marina.
To You.
Larkin, P. Spirit Wooed, The.
Milton. Sonnet 4: "Diodati, and I will say it to you with wonder."
Sonnet 5: "In truth your fair eyes, my lady."
Sonnet 6: "Young, gentle, and candid lover that I am."
Montale. If They've Compared You.
Ralegh, S. Poesie to Prove Affection Is Not Love, A.
Riley, J. Boy-Friend, The.
Sandburg, C. Dancer.
Old-Fashioned Requited Love.
Shirt.
Shelley, P. Fragments of an Unfinished Drama.
To Constantia, Singing.
Shirley, J. Love's Hue and Cry.
Smart, C. To Miss H—— with Some Music.
Smith, S. At School.
Stockton, A. Epistle—To Lucius.
Suckling, S. Upon My Lady Carlisle's Walking in Hampton Court Garden.
Williams, C. K. Game, The.
Williams, T. Lyric: "Her footsteps were a season's coming."
Wyatt, S. Avising the bright beams of these fair eyes.
It was my choice, it was no chance.
Love hath again.
O goodly hand.
Of purpose Love chose first for to be blind.
Pain of all pain, the most grievous pain.
What would ye more of me, your slave, require.

Infidelity
Angelou. Pickin Em Up and Layin Em Down.
Poor Girl.
They Went Home.
Auden. Lullaby: "Lay your sleeping head, my love."
Baudelaire. My Beatrice.
Bierce. T. A. H.
Brooks, G. My Little 'Bout-Town Gal Has Gone.
Browning, E. Bertha in the Lane.
Bianca among the Nightingales.
That Day.
Browning, R. Any Wife to Any Husband.
Forgiveness, A.
Worst of It, The.
Bukowski. Moaning and Groaning.
Burns, R. As I was a wand'ring ae midsummer e'enin.
Eppie McNab.

My Lady's Gown There's Gairs Upon't.
O an Ye Were Dead Gudeman.
Saw Ye My Phely (Quasi Dicat, Phillis).
She's fair and fause that causes my smart.
We'll Hide the Couper behint the Door.
Byron, G. On the Quotation "And My True Faith Can Alter Never, Though Thou Art Gone Perhaps Forever."
Remember Thee! Remember Thee!
To Woman.
When We Two Parted.
Campion, T. In Melleam.
Secret Love or Two I Must Confess[e], A.
Carew, T. Deposition from Love, A.
Carruth, H. Pray You Young Woman.
Chaucer. Anelida and Arcite.
Book of the Duchesse, The.
Troilus and Criseyde [or Criseide].
Coleridge, S. Alice Du Clos.
Collins, B. Jealousy.
Cowper, W. Love Abused.
Song, A: "On the green margin of the brook."
Cummings, E. E. It may not always be so; and i say.
Dickey, J. Adultery.
Dickey, W. And he lies dead—.
And I, who lay so warm and quiet there—.
Come, Doctor, we must fly somewhere where.
Doctor, I did not see that you were there.
For we have gone a curious way from there.
I did not know you when you came in there.
Part Song, with Concert of Recorders.
Who made you come and find the door to there?
Donne. Indifferent, The.
Love's Diet.
Message, The.
Song: "Go and catch a falling star."
Woman's Constancy.
Dove, R. Definition in the Face of Unnamed Fury.
García Lorca. Faithless Wife, The.
Unfaithful Wife, The.
Glück, L. Nurse's Song.
Graves, R. First Love.
Lament for Pasiphaë.
Never Such Love.
Should I Care.
Song: Though Once True Lovers.
Straw, The.
True Magic.
With Her Lips Only.
Hardy, T. Burghers, The.
Contretemps, The.
Dame of Athelhall, The.
Duel, The.
In the Days of Crinoline.
Military Appointment, A.
Moon Looks In, The.
Moth-Signal, The.
Newcomer's Wife, The.
Poor Man and a Lady, A.
Shiver, The.
Telegram, The.
Two Wives, The.
Wedding Morning, The.
Hayden, R. Burly Fading One, The.
Herrick. Chop-Cherry.
Eye, The.
To His False Mistris.
Upon Scobble [Epigram].
Housman. Along the field as we came by.
Spring Morning.
Hughes, L. Rent-Party Shout: For a Lady Dancer.
Hughes, T. Kreutzer Sonata.
Jeffers, R. Mara.
Steelhead, Wild Pig, the Fungus.
Thurso's Landing.
Keats. Gripus.
Song: "Hush, hush! tread softly! hush, hush my dear."
Kinnell. Running on Silk.
Kipling, R. Pink Dominoes.
Kizer, C. Summer near the River.
Koch, K. To Marina.
Komunyakaa. After Summer Fell Apart.

Combat Pay for Jody.
Fleshing-out the Season.
One More Loss to Count.
Thorn Merchant's Wife, The.
Laughlin, J. Bad Night on Third Avenue, A.
Lindsay, N. At Mass.
Lowell, R. Between the Porch and the Altar.
MacNeice. Prayer in Mid-Passage.
McHugh, H. Most, The.
Meredith, G. Waves are pressing up with force, The.
Millay, E. She Is Overheard Singing.
Thursday.
Mistral, G. God Wills It.
Moore, M. Injudicious Gardening.
Parker, D. Cassandra Drops into Verse.
Certain Lady, A.
Social Note.
Ralegh, S. Farewell to False Love, A.
Riley, J. Life Term, A.
Robinson, E. London Bridge.
Schuyler, J. This Dark Apartment.
Sexton. You All Know the Story of the Other Woman.
Stock, R. To the Discreet Reader: An Induction to Indiscretions.
Suckling, S. Guiltless Inconstant, The.
Swift, J. Satire on an Inconstant Lover, A.
Walker, A. My Husband Says.
Warren, R. Distance Between, The: Picnic of Old Friends.
Williams, C. K. Ethics.
Question, The.
Signs.
Williams, M. Man in the Bar Says He Has Something to Say, A.
Question of Time, A.
Williams, T. Changeling.
Williams, W. Exercise.
Wyatt, S. Accused though I be without desert.
Ah, Robin, / Jolly Robin.
Lover Showeth How He Is Forsaken of Such as He Sometime Enjoyed, The.
Spite hath no power to make me sad.
Unstable dream[e] [or dreme], according [or accordyng] to the place.
Whoso List to Hunt.
Yeats. Host of the Air, The.
See also **Adultery and Adulterers**

Infinity
Browning, E. Finite and Infinite.
Browning, R. Rephan.
Reverie.
Clough. As one who shoots an arrow overhead.
Coleridge, S. Traveller through Infinity, The.
Cummings, E. E. Life is more true than reason will deceive.
Structure,miraculous challenge,devout am.
Dickinson, E. Infinite a sudden Guest, The.
Show me Eternity, and I will show you Memory.
To the staunch Dust.
Dubie. About Infinity.
Dugan, A. Note: The Sea Grinds Things Up.
Eberhart, R. Seeing Is Deceiving.
Emerson, R. Bohemian Hymn, The.
Coil of space the cones of light, The.
Roomy Eternity / Casts her schemes rarely.
Enzensberger, H. Model towards a Theory of Cognition.
Ferlinghetti, L. Endless Life.
Herrick. God.
Ignatow, D. Forever.
Jackson, L. Scornful or Fond Infinity.
Nemerov. Two Sides to an Outside: Meditation from Empson.
Orr, G. Be–all.
Raine, K. Forest is multitude.
Rexroth, K. Late Half Moon.
Rukeyser, M. Place-Rituals.
Sandburg, C. Leather Leggings.
Szymborska, W. Pi.
Wilbur, R. All That Is.
Attention Makes Infinity.
Williams, C. K. Even if I Could.
Williams, T. Dark Arm, Hanging over the Edge

of Infinity.

Inflation

Emerson, R.   Since the devil hopping on.

Ingratitude

Brooke, H.   Quilca House to the Dean.

Carew, T.   In the Person of a Lady to Her
  Inconstant Servant.

Hayden, R.   Those Winter Sundays.

Herbert, G.   Unkindness.

Michelangelo Buonarroti.   If any of those old
  proverbs, lord, make sense.

Smith, S.   Will Man Ever Face Fact and Not
  Feel Flat?

Wordsworth, W.   Fragment: "For let the
  impediment be what it may."

Ingres, Jean Auguste Dominique

Rossetti, D.   For "Ruggiero and Angelica" by
  Ingres.

Inheritance

Angelou.   My Guilt.

Byron, G.   Werner; or, The Inheritance.

Chuang Tzu.   When a Hideous Man.

Ciardi, J.   Firsts.

Cowper, W.   Grief of an Heir, The.

De la Mare.   Isaac Meek.

Donne.   Disinherited.

Gunn, T.   Inherited Estate, The.

Hacker, M.   Inheritances.
  Sword.

Herrick.   Lyric[k] for Legacies.
  Upon Leech.

Johnson, S.   Short Song of Congratulation [or
  To a Young Heir], A.

Jonson, B.   On Chuff, Banks the Usurer's
  Kinsman.

Merwin.   Psalm: Our Fathers.

Niedecker.   Ash woods, willow, close to shore.

Prunty.   Breaking Child, The.

Ralegh, S.   Things thus agreed: Titan made
  Saturne sweare.

Rumi.   Night Air, The.

Simic.   Inheritance.

Tomlinson, C.   History.
  Jemez.

Whitman, W.   My Legacy.

Wordsworth, W.   Michael [A Pastoral Poem].

Injuries

Ammons.   Silver.

Blue Cloud.   Wolf.

Bly, R.   Winter Poem.

Carver, R.   Scratch, The.

Cavafy.   Bandaged Shoulder, The.

Crane, H.   Episode of Hands.

Creeley.   Man, The.

Dickey, J.   Scarred Girl, The.
  War Wound, The.

Dickinson, E.   Anatomical dishabille.

Dugan, A.   Fabrication of Ancestors.

Frost, R.   Not to Keep.

Graves, R.   Injuries.

Gunn, T.   Wound, The.

Heaney, S.   Damson.

Herrick.   Bleeding Hand: or, The Sprig of
  Eglantine Given to a Maid, The.

Jarrell, R.   X-Ray Waiting Room in the Hospital,
  The.

Kumin, M.   Henry Manley Looks Back.

Levertov.   Dragon of Revolutionary Love.

Mahon.   Noon at St. Michael's.

Muldoon, P.   Point, The.

Orr, G.   Father's Song.
  Parable, A.
  Singing the Pain Back into the Wound.

Plath.   Contusion.

Ransom, J.   Puncture.

Riley, J.   Ezra House.
  Thomas the Pretender.

Rossetti, C.   Hurt No Living Thing.

Rukeyser, M.   Another Day. For a Moment
  Slipping Back, Again the Unreal King.

Sandburg, C.   Brim.

Shelley, P.   Ode Written October, 1819, An.

Stafford, W.   Ceremony.

Swenson, M.   Bleeding.

Williams, C. K.   Crime.

Greed.

Men.

Scar.

Williams, W.   Injury, The.
  Interests of 1926.

Injustice

Berryman.   Interstitial Office.

Bierce.   Hesitating Veteran, The.

Blake, W.   Gwin, King of Norway.

Browning, R.   Heretic's Tragedy, The.

Cowper, W.   Sonnet Addressed to Mr. Phillips,
  A.

Cullen, C.   Scottsboro, Too, Is Worth Its Song.

Cummings, E. E.   Remarked Robinson
  Jefferson.
  Why must itself up every of a park.

Dugan, A.   Untitled Poem: "One tries to be
  sober and respectable."

Dunbar, P.   Haunted Oak, The.

Faiz.   Bangla Desh: 1.
  Bangla Desh: 2.

Ginsberg, A.   Death to Van Gogh's Ear!

Hall, D.   Small Fig Tree, A.

Herrick.   Bad Wages for Good Service.
  Bribes and Gifts Get All.
  Upon the Bishop of Lincolne's Imprisonment.

Housman.   Oh who is that young sinner with the
  handcuffs on his wrists?

Hughes, L.   Advertisement for the Waldorf-
  Astoria.
  August 19th.
  Ballad of the Landlord.
  Bitter River, The.
  Black Man Speaks, The.
  Mississippi.
  Shall the Good Go Down?
  Song after Lynching.
  Southern Negro Speaks.
  White Man.
  Who but the Lord?

Jonson, B.   On a Robbery.

Kipling, R.   Cleared.

Levertov.   In Memory of Muriel Rukeyser.

Levi, P.   Song of Those Who Died in Vain.

Lindsay, N.   Abraham Lincoln Walks at
  Midnight.
  Who Knows?

Lorde.   Revolution Is One Form of Social
  Change.
  Vietnam Addenda.

MacNeice.   Jericho.

Millay, E.   Justice Denied in Massachusetts.

Muldoon, P.   Ducking Stool, The.

Nash, O.   Bankers Are Just Like Anybody Else,
  Except Richer.

Owen, W.   Parable of the Old Men and the
  Young, The.

Patchen.   Hangman's Great Hands, The.
  Letter to a Policemen in Kansas City, A.

Rexroth, K.   Past and Future Turn About.

Rich, A.   For a Sister.

Sarton, M.   Prisoner at a Desk.

Tu Fu.   Testament.

Whittier.   Ein Feste Burg Ist Unser Gott.
  Expostulation.
  For Righteousness' Sake.
  Human Sacrifice, The.
  Hunters of Men, The.
  Massachusetts to Virginia.
  On a Prayer-Book.
  Prisoner for Debt, The.
  Sentence of John L. Brown, The.

Williams, C. K.   Rampage, The.

Williams, W.   Impromptu: The Suckers.

See also **Protest, Social**

Inkwells

Cavafy.   Inkwell, The.

Innisfree, Ireland

Yeats.   Lake-Isle of Innisfree, The.

Innocence

Angelou.   Martial Choreograph.

Ashbery, J.   Punishing the Myth.

Baudelaire.   Restless and Sad.

Berry, W.   Adze, The.

Boone.

Thief, The.

Berryman.   Curse, The.

Blok.   Do You Remember.

Bourne, V.   On the Picture of a Sleeping Child.

Brontë, E.   H.A. and A.S.
  Song to A.A.
  Tell me, tell me, smiling child.

Browning, E.   Child Asleep, A.
  Lost Bower, The.

Browning, R.   Pippa Passes.
  There goes a swallow to Venice—the stout
  seafarer!

Bukowski.   Notations from a Muddled
  Indolence.
  One for Old Snaggle-Tooth.

Burns, R.   Song: "O once I loved [or lov'd] a
  bonnie lass."

Campion, T.   Ad Amorem.

Carruth, H.   Cows at Night, The.
  President's Speech, The.
  Saving Way, The.

Ciardi, J.   Elegy for the Face at Your Elbow.
  To a Young American the Day after the Fall of
  Barcelona.

Coleridge, S.   Christabel.

Collins, B.   History Teacher, The.

Cooper, J.   Song: "Here I am yours, and here,
  and here."

Creeley.   Anywhere.
  Joke, The.
  Thinking of Yeats.

Cullen, C.   Dear Friends and Gentle Hearts.

Cummings, E. E.   Who were so dark of heart
  they might not speak.

Cunningham, J.   Innocent to innocent.

Davie, D.   Skelpick.

Eliot, T. S.   Hippopotamus, The.

Emerson, R.   God The Lord save Massachusetts.
  O sun! take off thy hood of clouds.

Fenton, J.   Nest of Vampires.

Ferlinghetti, L.   Deflowering.
  With bells for hooves in sounding streets.

García Lorca.   1910.
  Autumn Song.

Ginsberg, A.   Wild Orphan.

Graves, R.   Ages of Oath, The.
  Cliff Edge, The.
  Trial of Innocence.

Gunn, T.   Innocence.
  Sunlight.

Hall, D.   Child's Garden, A.
  September Ode.

Hardy, T.   Boys Then and Now.
  Child and the Sage, The.
  In a Waiting-Room.
  Leader of Fashion, A.
  Man with a Past, The.
  Sweet Hussy, The.

Herbert, G.   Holy Baptism (2).

Herrick.   To Julia.

Hill, G.   Holy Thursday.

Housman.   He, standing hushed, a pace or two
  apart.

Jacobsen, J.   Allhallows Party.
  Eyes of the Children at the Brink of the Sea's
  Grasp, The.
  For Those Who Have Not Eaten the Apple.
  Innocents, The.
  Planet, The.

Jarrell, R.   And did she dwell in innocence and
  joy.

Kunitz, S.   Testing-Tree, The.

Larkin, P.   Under a Splendid Chestnut Tree.

Lawrence, D. H.   Jeune Fille, The.

Levertov.   In Mind.
  May Our Right Hands Lose Their Cunning.
  Overland to the Islands.

Levi, P.   Song of Those Who Died in Vain.

Lindsay, N.   My Lady Is Compared to a Young
  Tree.

MacNeice.   Apple Blossom.
  Autobiography.
  When We Were Children.

Mahon.   Girls on the Bridge.
  Homecoming.

Melville, H.   On the Slain Collegians.

Meredith, G.   In the time of early love.
It is the young fresh rainy leaf.
Like a blind child is the loving heart.
Philosopher! 'tis said you wail.
What makes it hard to understand.
Milosz, C.   Inheritor.
Nash, O.   It's Snug to Be Smug.
Passionate Pagan and the Dispassionate Public, The.
Nemerov.   Remorse for Time, The.
Snow Globe, The.
Parker, D.   How Bold It Is.
Liebestod.
Plath.   Dream with Clam-Diggers.
Raine, K.   Eternal Child, The.
Ramanujan.   He Too Was a Light Sleeper Once.
Looking for a Cousin on a Swing.
Ransom, J.   Janet Waking.
Necrological.
Vaunting Oak.
Rich, A.   Amnesia.
Innocents, The.
Riley, J.   Just to Be Good.
To a Boy Whistling.
Uncle Sidney.
Rilke.   Ball, The.
Ritsos.   Final Hour.
Ultimate Innocence.
Robinson, E.   Souvenir.
Rossetti, C.   Once.
To Lalla, Reading My Verses Topsy-Turvy.
Word for the Dumb, A.
Rukeyser, M.   Do you know what I play to be, in bed at night?
Sandburg, C.   Brancusi.
Clean Curtains.
Clean Hands.
Crimson Changes People.
Sarton, M.   Giant in the Garden.
Shapiro, K.   Mongolian Idiot.
Shelley, P.   Fragment: "Gentle story of two lovers young, A."
Simic.   Little Tear Gland That Says, The.
Prodigy.
Smith, S.   Last Turn of the Screw, The.
My Heart Was Full.
Stafford, W.   Farewell, Age Ten, A.
Thomas, D.   Fern Hill.
Refusal to Mourn the Death, by Fire, of a Child in London, A.
Then Was My Neophyte.
Tomlinson, C.   Mélisande.
Warren, R.   Interjection #4: Bad Year, Bad War: A New Year's Card, 1969.
Little Boy and Lost Shoe.
Little Girl Wakes Early.
Picnic Remembered.
Ways of Day.
Whittier.   Changeling, The.
In School-Days.
Vanishers, The.
Wilde, O.   Madonna Mia.
Wasted Days.
Williams, C. K.   Acids.
Fifteen.
Gas Station, The.
Kingdom of Stinking Wishes, The.
Last Deaths, The.
Secrets.
Williams, M.   Rebecca at Play.
Williams, T.   My Little One.
Williams, W.   Woodpecker, The.
Wilner, E.   Ode to Innocence.
Wordsworth, W.   To the Highland Girl of Inversneyde.
Wright, J.   Morning: Leaving Calle Gigantes.
Yeats.   To a Child Dancing in the Wind.
Zukofsky, L.   It's hard to see but think of a sea.
So That Even a Lover.

Inns
Burns, R.   At Brownhill Inn.
At Roslin Inn.
At Whigham's Inn, Sanquar.
Epigram: "Whoe'er he be that sojourns here."
Verses Written on a Window of the Inn at Carron.

Creeley.   Inn / Kyoto.
Hardy, T.   At an Inn.
Laughlin, J.   Inn at Kirchstetten, The.
Rimbaud, A.   At the Green Inn, Five P.M.
Rossetti, C.   Uphill.
Warren, R.   Ballad of Billie Potts, The.
See also **Hotels; Motels**

Inquisition, The
Amichai [*or* Amikhai].   My Friend the Philosopher and Hanukah.
Browning, R.   Delivery to the Secular Arm, The: A Scene during the Existence of the Spanish Inquisition at Antwerp, 1570.

Insanity
Amichai [*or* Amikhai].   Suflah Spring in the Judean Mountains.
Ammons.   Discoverer.
Broumas, O.   Landscape with Leaves and Figure.
Dugan, A.   Jack-Off of the Graveyard Shift, The.
Gurney, I.   To God.
Kumin, M.   Halfway.
Orr, G.   Shelf Is a Ledge, A.
Ritsos.   Naked Face.
Rumi.   I have lived on the lip.
There is a light seed grain inside.
See also **Madness**

Insects
Auden.   Aliens, The.
Beckett, S.   Morte parmi.
Berryman.   They Have.
Bierce.   Insectivora.
Carver, R.   Earwigs.
Ciardi, J.   Small.
Clampitt.   Imago.
Corbett, W.   D-Day 1989.
Creeley.   Maria Speaks.
Davie, D.   Sonnet: "As massive and dispensable as sculpture."
De la Mare.   Round, The.
Dickinson, E.   Further in Summer than the Birds.
Eberhart, R.   Largess, The.
Emerson, R.   In Walden wood the chickadee.
Solar insect on the wing.
Hardy, T.   August Midnight, An.
Hughes, T.   To Paint a Water Lily.
Kinsella, T.   Leaf-eater.
Komunyakaa.   Dreambook Bestiary.
Kumin, M.   Creatures.
Kunitz, S.   By Lamplight.
Levertov.   Disclosure, The.
Lorde.   Brown Menace or Poem to the Survival of Roaches, The.
Lux.   Pismire Rising.
River Blindness (Onchocerciasis).
Meredith, G.   Garden Idyl, A.
O 'tis my delight / In the dead of the night.
Sweet o' the Year, The.
Nash, O.   Bugs.
Creeps and Crawls.
Glossina Morsitans, or, the Tsetse.
Strange Case of the Entomologist's Heart, The.
Oliver, M.   Buck Moon—From the Field Guide to Insects.
Orr, G.   Be–all.
Pagis.   Scarabs.
Plath.   Frog Autumn.
Ramanujan.   Striders, The.
Riley, J.   Home at Night.
Two Sonnets to the June-Bug.
Roethke.   Minimal, The.
Rossetti, C.   All Things Wait upon Thee.
Sandburg, C.   Bug Spots.
Purple Martins.
Small Homes.
Without Notice Beforehand.
Schuyler, J.   September.
Sexton.   June Bug.
Shapiro, K.   Fly, The.
Interlude, The.
Swift, J.   Wood, an Insect.
Tate, J.   Bug Sleep.
Thomas, D.   To-day, This Insect.

Updike.   Fritillary, The.
Wilbur, R.   Water Walker.
Wilner, E.   Killing the Grubs.
Wright, J.   Depressed by a Book of Bad Poetry, I Walk toward an Unused Pasture and Invite the Insects to Join Me.
I Was Afraid of Dying.
Invention of a Garden, The.
Zukofsky, L.   "Mantis."

Insomnia and Insomniacs
Angelou.   Insomniac.
Berry, W.   Awake at Night.
Berryman.   Henry by Night.
Borges.   Two Forms of Insomnia.
Bukowski.   Eaten by Butterflies.
Fragile!
Insomnia.
On a Night You Don't Sleep.
Burns, R.   Simmer's a Pleasant Time.
Campion, T.   Spyres Curten, The.
Carver, R.   Winter Insomnia.
Ciardi, J.   Three A.M. and Then Five.
Collins, B.   Insomnia.
Creeley.   Berlin: First Night & Early Morning.
"Dario."   Nocturne: "Silence of the night, a sorrowful silence."
Dubie.   Groom Falconer.
Dugan, A.   Night Song for a Boy.
García Lorca.   Ballad of One Doomed to Die.
Graves, R.   Not to Sleep.
Guyon.   Watching unto God in the Night-Season.
Hardy, T.   Lying Awake.
Hayden, R.   Broken Dark, The.
Ice Storm.
Hughes, L.   Summer Night.
Jacobsen, J.   Distance.
Insomniac's Bird.
Jarrell, R.   Prayer at Morning, A.
Kipling, R.   City of Sleep, The.
Kizer, C.   Night Sounds.
Larkin, P.   Bottle Is Drunk Out by One, The.
Laughlin, J.   Child, The.
Long Night, The.
Sleepless Night, A.
Lindsay, N.   Abraham Lincoln Walks at Midnight.
Lux.   If I Die before I Wake.
MacNeice.   Intimations of Mortality.
Meredith, W.   Grievances.
Millay, E.   Midnight Oil.
Nash, O.   Sedative Reflection.
Orr, G.   Trying to Sleep.
Petrarch.   Could I but take revenge upon that one.
Now earth and sky are still, winds blow no more.
Plath.   Insomniac.
Pope, A.   Of the Lady Who Could Not Sleep in a Stormy Night.
Prunty.   Insomnia.
Rexroth, K.   Lesson in Geography, A.
Rich, A.   Afterwake, The.
Insomniacs, The.
Night.
White Night.
Riley, J.   At Noon—and Midnight.
Time.
When I Do Mock.
Rilke.   Song: "You, to whom I don't confide."
Rossetti, D.   Insomnia.
Rumi.   When I am with you, we stay up all night.
Sappho.   Deduke Men A Selanna.
Sarton, M.   Who Wakes.
Schuyler, J.   O Sleepless Night.
Spender, S.   Sleepless.
Stockton, A.   Extemporal Ode in a Sleepless Night, An. By a Lady, (Mrs. S. of New-Jersey).
Soliliguy in a Sleepless Night.
Tate, J.   Recipe for Sleep.
Updike.   Insomnia the Gem of the Ocean.
Sleepless in Scarsdale.
Tossing and Turning.
Warren, R.   After Restless Night.

Better than Counting Sheep.
Midnight.
Whalen, P.   Metaphysical Insomnia Jazz.
  Mumonkan XXIX.
Wilbur, R.   Walking to Sleep.
Williams, W.   Song: "If I / could count the
  silence."
Zagajewski.   Lullaby.

Inspiration
Angelou.   Impeccable Conception.
Arnold, M.   Stanzas in Memory of the Author of
  "Obermann."
Baudelaire.   Hymn: "To Love and to the lovely
  eyes."
Bierce.   Geotheos.
  Possibility, A.
Blok.   Artist, The.
Bly, R.   Walking Swiftly.
Borges.   Hengist Wants Men (A.D. 449).
  Invocation to Joyce.
  Rubáïyát.
Bukowski.   Ah.
  On Going Back to the Street after Viewing an
    Art Show.
Burns, R.   Lovely Davies.
  O were I on Parnassus hill.
  To Miss Ferrier.
  Written with a Pencil over the Chimney-Piece,
    in the Parlour of the Inn at Kenmore.
Carew, T.   Celia Singing.
Carver, R.   His Bathrobe Pockets Stuffed with
    Notes.
  March into Russia, The.
  Radio Waves.
Cavafy.   Their Origin.
Codrescu.   Alice's Brilliance.
Creeley.   Door, The.
  Irish.
  Massachusetts.
  "Dario."   In Autumn.
  When the poor guy saw her pass.
  White Page, The.
Dunbar, P.   Inspiration.
Emerson, R.   Ah! not to me these dreams
    belong.
  Art.
  Fine presentiments controlled him.
  Honor bright o muse.
  I never knew but one.
  Inspired we must forget our books.
  O what are heroes prophets men.
  Pour the wine! pour the wine!
  S. R.
Ginsberg, A.   Blessed Be the Muses.
Graves, R.   At the Gate.
  Mid-Winter Waking.
Gurney, I.   Pleasance Window, The.
  Songs Come to the Mind.
  When from the Curve.
Hall, D.   Three Movements, The.
Herrick.   Departure of the Good Daemon, The.
  Draw, and Drinke.
  Not Every Day Fit for Verse.
  To Sir Clipsebie Crew.
  To Sir Clipseby Crew.
  To the Most Illustrious and Most Hopeful[l]
    Prince, Charles, Prince of Wales.
Hughes, T.   God, The.
Johnson, S.   Aurora Est Musis Amica.
Jonson, B.   And must I sing? What subject shall
    I choose?
Keats.   'How Many Bards Gild the Lapses of
    Time!'
  On Sitting Down to Read "King Lear" Once
    Again.
  Poet, The.
  To B.R. Haydon, with a Sonnet Written on
    Seeing the Elgin Marbles.
  Welcome Joy, and Welcome Sorrow.
Kinsella, T.   Brothers in the Craft.
Kizer, C.   Muse, A.
Koch, K.   Artist, The.
Laughlin, J.   My Muse.
  Tuesday at 87 Rue de Rome.
Levertov.   Cancion: "When I am the sky."
  Growth of a Poet.

In Memory of Muriel Rukeyser.
Lux.   Horatian Notion, An.
Mallarmé.   Fan, A; of Madame Mallarmé.
  Prose.
  Renewal.
  Weary of Bitter Sleep.
McHugh, H.   Excerpt from an Argument with
    Enthusiasts, Concerning Inspiration.
Meredith, G.   Later Alexandrian, A.
  Mentor and Pupils.
  On Combe Bottom: Surrey.
  Orson of the Muse, An.
  Star Sirius, The.
  To the Comic Spirit.
  You ask me what is Genius? 'tis that.
Meredith, W.   Illiterate, The.
  View of the Brooklyn Bridge, A.
Michelangelo Buonarroti.   If by its heaven-sent
    power the mind conceives.
Millay, E.   On Thought in Harness.
Milton.   Elegy 6: To Charles Deodati.
Parra, N.   Poetry Ends with Me.
Pessoa.   Salutation to Walt Whitman.
Riley, J.   Job Work.
Robinson, E.   Bokardo.
  Sonnet: "Oh for a poet—for a beacon bright."
Rossetti, C.   O ye, who are not dead and fit.
Rumi.   In your light I learn how to love.
Seifert.   Bach Concerto, A.
  To Be a Poet.
Stafford, W.   How the Real Bible Is Written.
  How These Words Happened.
Stock, R.   Synapse, The.
Stockton, A.   Caprice, a Fragment.
  Ode, An: "Yes tis an easy thing to view."
  Prospect, The. By a Lady in Princeton.
Swift, J.   To Mr. Congreve.
Tate, J.   Poem to Some of my Recent Poems.
Thoreau.   Inspiration.
Tomlinson, C.   Château de Muzot.
  Death of Will, The.
Very.   Promise, The ("I come the rushing wind
    that shook the place").
Warren, R.   To Certain Old Masters.
Whalen, P.   Complaint: To the Muse.
Wheatley, P.   To S. M., a Young African Painter,
    on Seeing His Works.
Wilbur, R.   Love Calls Us to the Things of This
    World.
Williams, M.   Muse, The.
Wordsworth, W.   Not Love, Not War, nor the
    Tumultuous Swell.
Zagajewski.   For You.
  Late Beethoven.
  That Force.
Zukofsky, L.   After Charles Sedley.
  Barely and *widely*.
  Some time has gone.
  You Who Were Made for This Music.

Instinct
Chuang Tzu.   Cutting up an Ox.
Cowper, W.   Beau's Reply.
Creeley.   Billfold.
  Mouths Nuzz.
  Way.
  Words.
  Young Woman.
Lawrence, D. H.   Immoral Man.
Oliver, M.   Being Country Bred.
  Lilies Break Open over the Dark Water, The.
  Turtle, The.
Roethke.   Manifestation, The.
Schuyler, J.   Running Footsteps.
Szymborska, W.   Returning Birds.
Thomas, D.   Before I Knocked.
  How Shall My Animal.
Updike.   Each Summer's Swallows.

Institutionalization
Atwood.   Visit to Toronto, with Companions.
Bogan, L.   Evening in the Sanitarium.
Carruth, H.   Asylum, The.
  Ontological Episode of the Asylum.
  That I Had Had Courage when Young.
Kipling, R.   Mother's Son, The.
Lowell, R.   Waking in the Blue.
Lux.   Institute of Defectology.

Muldoon, P.   Edward Kienholz: *The State
    Hospital.*
Plath.   Face Lift.
  Miss Drake Proceeds to Supper.
Sexton.   Double Image, The.
  Flee on Your Donkey.
  Lullaby: "It is a summer evening."
  Music Swims Back to Me.
  Ringing the Bells.
  You, Doctor Martin.
Thomas, D.   Love in the Asylum.

Insults
Bukowski.   Poem for Liz.
Burns, R.   Extempore—On Being Shown a
    Beautiful County Seat Belonging to the Same.
  [On] Maxwell of Cardoness.
Cowper, W.   Apology, An.
Cunningham, J.   Periphrastic Insult, Not a
    Banal, A.
Herrick.   Upon Jollies Wife.
  Upon Pearch.
Oliver, M.   Acid.
Riley, J.   Elmer Brown.
  Little Mock-Man, The.
Rochfort, G.   Answer.
Sheridan, T.   Another Picture of Dan.
  Answer.
  Cur Me Bespateras, Blaterans Furiosè Poeta.
  His Modest Apology for Knocking Out a News-
    Boy's Teeth, Who Told Him His Works
    Would Not Sell.
  On the Same.
  Sheridan to Dan Jackson.
Suckling, S.   Sir John Suckling's Answer.
Williams, C. K.   Allies: According to Herodotus.
  Insult, The.

Insurance
Hughes, L.   Madam and the Insurance Man.

Integrity
Ashbery, J.   Le Livre Est sur la Table.
Brontë, E.   All day I've toiled, but not with
    pain.
Byron, G.   Thou Art Not False, but Thou Art
    Fickle.
Ciardi, J.   Elegy for G. B. Shaw.
Creeley.   Like They Say.
Emerson, R.   But if thou do thy best.
  Heartily heartily sing.
Hopkins, G.   He might be slow and something
    feckless first.
Jeffers, R.   Answer, The.
Lowell, R.   Coleridge and Richard II.
  Marcus Cato 95–42 B.C.
Michelangelo Buonarroti.   All there's to say of
    him, no way of saying.
Pessoa.   To be great, be whole; exclude.
Rich, A.   Integrity.
Riley, J.   Erasmus Wilson.
  Good, Old-fashioned People, The.
  Our Kind of a Man.
  Our Old Friend Neverfail.
  Simple Recipe, A.
  William Pinkney Fishback.
Roethke.   Pure Fury, The.
Rukeyser, M.   Lilienthal said : I heard him
    saying words like these.

Intellect and Intellectuals
Cummings, E. E.   Ballad of an Intellectual.
  "Gay" is the captivating cognomen of a Young
    Woman of cambridge,mass.
  Mr youse needn't be so spry.
  My mind is.
  Since feeling is first.
  Trick of finding what you didn't lose, The.
Davie, D.   Brantôme.
Dickinson, E.   Brain—is wider than the Sky,
    The.
  Genius is the ignition of affection.
Eberhart, R.   Centennial for Whitman.
  Face, Ocean.
  In a Hard Intellectual Light.
  Man's Greed and Envy Are So Great.
  Poem as Trajectory, The.
  Sanders Theater.
Eliot, T. S.   Mr. Apollinax.
Emerson, R.   If he go apart.

Intellect.
Intellect / Gravely broods apart on joy.
Frost, R.   At Woodward's Gardens.
Han-shan.   Superior man's mind is terribly
   sharp, The.
Herrick.   His Desire.
Studies to Be Supported.
Wit Punisht, Prospers Most.
Hughes, L.   Ph.D.
Poem for an Intellectual on the Way Up to
   Submit to His Lady.
To Certain Intellectuals.
Laughlin, J.   Merry Madness Hall.
Lawrence, D. H.   Cerebral Emotions.
Chastity.
Climb Down, O Lordly Mind.
Little-Boy Brilliant.
Noli Me Tangere.
Touch.
What Matters.
Levertov.   Conversation in Moscow.
Vision, A.
MacDiarmid, H.   Glasgow, 1960.
Moore, M.   Mind, Intractable Thing, The.
Mind Is an Enchanting Thing, The.
Nash, O.   If He Scholars, Let Him Go.
Who Did Which? or Who Indeed?
Nemerov.   Blue Swallows, The.
Brainstorm.
Neruda.   Negative Hands.
Pasolini.   Plan of Future Works.
Rexroth, K.   Lucretius, 3, 1053–1076.
Pliny—9, 36—Lampridius—29.
Vitamins and Roughage.
Rumi.   Body Intelligence.
Shapiro, K.   Essay on Chess.
Intellectual, The.
Shelley, P.   Hymn to Intellectual Beauty.
Smith, S.   Oh, if Only.
Stockton, A.   Epigram Addressed to Two
   Clergymen, An.
Tate, A.   Intellectual Detachment.
Tomlinson, C.   Antecedents.
Something: a Direction.
Wilbur, R.   Mind.
Williams, M.   Mise-en-Scène.
Wright, J.   End of an Ethnic Dream, The.
Zagajewski.   R. Says.
See also **Mind; Rationalism and Rationalists;
   Reason**

Interment
See **Burial**

International Brigade
Hughes, L.   Hero—International Brigade.
Letter from Spain.
Postcard from Spain.
Kizer, C.   Valley of the Fallen, The.
See also **Civil War, Spain**

Internationalism
Clampitt.   Babel aboard the Hellas International
   Express.
See also **United Nations**

Internment
Ritsos.   After the Defeat.

Interracial Love and Marriage
Baudelaire.   To a Creole Lady.
Cullen, C.   Ballad of the Brown Girl, The.
Davie, D.   Black Hoyden.
Dule of a Dewsbury Matron.
Hacker, M.   Against Silence.
Hughes, L.   Cross.
Mellow.
Komunyakaa.   Fleshing-out the Season.
Rendezvous.
Maunick.   Seven Sides and Seven Syllables.
Walker, A.   Ballad of the Brown Girl.
Johann.
Williams, C. K.   Dog, The.

Intimacy
Amichai [or Amikhai].   Inside the Apple.
Instead of Words.
Jacob and the Angel.
Pity, A. We Were Such a Good Invention.
Threading.
To My Love, Combing Her Hair.

Ariosto.   Night and Day.
Armantrout.   Covers.
Byron, G.   To Thyrza.
Carver, R.   Adultery.
Afternoon, An.
Best Time of the Day, The.
Gift, The.
Haircut, A.
Nearly.
Slippers.
Ciardi, J.   Every Time You Are Sleeping and I.
In Pity as We Kiss and Lie.
Morning: I Know Perfectly How in a Minute
   You Will Stretch and Smile.
Stills and Rapids of Your Nakedness, The.
Three A.M. and Then Five.
To Judith Asleep.
Cooper, J.   Conversation by the Body's Light.
Creeley.   Beside Her to Lie.
Hamill, S.   Body of Summer, The.
Jackson, L.   Wishing More Dear.
Jacobsen, J.   Distance.
Margins of Choice.
Winter Castle.
Kinsella, T.   Madonna.
Remembering Old Wars.
We sat face to face at the kitchen table.
Kizer, C.   Light, The.
Komunyakaa.   Allegorical Seduction.
Woman, I Got the Blues.
Laughlin, J.   Can Language Be Taught with the
   Fingertips?
Can There Be a Female Bodhissatva?
Deep Pool, the.
Enlacement, The.
Escape, The.
Eyes Are the Guides of Love.
Hand Trick, The.
I Want to Breathe.
Maze, The.
Still Pond No More Moving.
Touching.
Two Spoons.
You've Set the Words.
Levertov.   What She Could Not Tell Him.
Logan, J.   Girl in the Fog, The.
Poem: Tears, Spray, and Steam.
Return to the Island.
Two Poems for Women.
Logue, C.   Middle-aged man is approaching an
   all-night lavatory, A.
Mahon.   First Love.
Major, C.   Birds.
McHugh, H.   Thought of Night.
Merwin.   Morning, The.
Mistral, G.   Paradise.
"Perse."   Blank of the Wall, The.
Rexroth, K.   Camargue.
Confusion of the Senses.
Gradualism.
Growing.
Lyell's Hypothesis Again.
No Word.
She Is Away [or Marthe Away (She Is Away)].
Still on Water.
Riley, J.   He and I.
In the Corridor.
Rumi.   In the Arc of Your Mallet.
They try to say what you are, spiritual or
   sexual?
Stafford, W.   In the Night Desert.
Stock, R.   Doctor Will Be Back Too Late, The.
Swenson, M.   I will be earth you be the flower.
Sze.   Morning Shutters.
Szymborska, W.   I am too close for him to
   dream about me.
Tate, J.   If You Would Disappear at Sea.
Warren, R.   Smile, The.
Williams, M.   Origami.
Williams, T.   Across the Space.
Death Is High.
We Have Not Long to Love.

Intolerance
Eberhart, R.   Scarf of June, The.
Hughes, T.   Martyrdom of Bishop Farrar, The.
Meredith, G.   Falling of Sally, The.

Wilde, O.   Quantum Mutata.
Williams, C. K.   End of Drought.
Hog Heaven.

Introspection
Amichai [or Amikhai].   Box, The.
Ammons.   Look for My White Self.
Russet Gold.
Angelou.   I Almost Remember.
Bly, R.   Chinese Tomb Guardians.
Four Ways of Knowledge.
Man Locked inside the Oak, The.
Meditation on Philosophy, A.
Brontë, E.   All hushed and still within the house.
Had there been falsehood in my breast.
I know not how it falls on me.
I'll come when thou art saddest.
My Comforter.
Self-Interrogation.
Bukowski.   As I Lay Dying.
Face while Shaving.
Goldfish.
Imbecile Night.
Reprieve and Admixture.
Cardenal.   Dog barks far out, A.
Every evening the L & N.
I do not know who is out in the snow.
I turned out the light to see the snow.
Like Empty Beer Cans.
Like the flights of ducks.
Long freight train / Wakes me in my cell, The.
Sound of passing cars, (if a car comes), The.
Spring has come with its smell of Nicaragua.
That auto horn sounds familiar.
When the first signs go on.
Zinc roofs in the moonlight, The.
Carruth, H.   Asylum, The.
Carver, R.   Company.
Poem on My Birthday, July 2.
Rain.
Scratch, The.
This Morning.
Ciardi, J.   Days.
Letter from a Metaphysical Countryside.
Creeley.   Hong Kong Window.
Later ("Later than any time").
Rain, The.
Reflections.
Song: "You look out and you see people."
Than I.
Walking.
Davie, D.   In the Stopping Train.
Northamptonshire.
Dickinson, E.   I often wish I was a grass.
It is solemn to remember.
Thousand questions rise to my lips, A.
Dunbar, P.   Ere Sleep Comes Down to Soothe
   the Weary Eyes.
Eliot, T. S.   Introspection.
Gallagher, T.   Amplitude.
Borrowed Ones, The.
Simple Sonatina.
García Lorca.   In Another Mode.
Gunn, T.   Plan of Self-Subjection, A.
Secret Sharer, The.
Herrick.   His Wish.
Hughes, T.   Go Fishing.
Kunitz, S.   Image-Maker, The.
Levertov.   Poem: "Some are too much at home
   in the role of wanderer."
Mahon.   Dawn at Saint Patrick's.
McGrath, T.   Seekers, The.
McHugh, H.   Inside.
Merton.   Stranger.
Milton.   Il Penseroso.
Montale.   My life, I ask of you no stable.
Nemerov.   From a Record of Disappointment.
Idea.
Loon's Cry, The.
Paraphrase from Notebooks.
Salt Garden, The.
Sanctuary, The.
Neruda.   Bell Tower of Authenay, The.
Homecomings.
One Comes Back.
Possessions.
Niedecker.   What bird would light.

Oliver, M.   Five A.M. in the Pinewoods.
Rexroth, K.   Dragon and the Unicorn, The.
Past and Future Turn About.
Reflecting Trees of Being and Not Being, The.
Signature of All Things, The.
Rich, A.   In the Woods.
Necessities of Life.
Storm Warnings.
Rumi.   Who Says Words with My Mouth.
Sarton, M.   Action of Therapy, The.
Fear of Angels, The.
Frog, that Naked Creature, The.
Work of Happiness, The.
Shapiro, K.   Tingling Back, The.
Smith, S.   After-Thought, The.
Swift, J.   Occasioned by Sir William Temple's
Late Illness and Recovery.
Van Duyn.   Advice to a God.
From Yellow Lake: An Interval.
Two Poems, with Birds.
Very.   Lost, The ("Fairest day that ever yet has
shone, The").
Walcott.   Hotel Normandie Pool, The.
Return to D'Ennery; Rain.
Walk, The.
Wilbur, R.   Aspen and the Stream, The.
Hole in the Floor, A.
Williams, C. K.   Bob.
On Learning of a Friend's Illness.
Trappers.
Wright, C.   Bicoastal Journal.
T'ang Notebook.
Zukofsky, L.   Not it was no dream of coming
death.

Invective
Jeffers, R.   Advice to Pilgrims.

Inventions and Inventors
Brodsky, J.   Daedalus in Sicily.
Eberhart, R.   Reading Room, the New York
Public Library.
Jeffers, R.   Edison.
Laughlin, J.   Patent Pending.
Lux.   Kalashnikov.
McGrath, T.   Portents.
Merwin.   Tool.
Nemerov.   Extract from Memoirs.
Neruda.   2 8 3 2 5 6 7 4 5 4 9.
Niedecker.   Hop press.
Rukeyser, M.   Parallel Invention.
Sandburg, C.   Solo for Saturday Night Guitar.
Spender, S.   Icarus.

Investment and Investors
Hughes, L.   Bonds for All.
Niedecker.   Hop press.
Stock, R.   Buried Talents, The.

Invocation
Ammons.   I Struck a Diminished Seventh.
With Ropes of Hemp.
Beckett, S.   Nuit qui fais tant.
De la Mare.   For All the Grief.
Herrick.   His Prayer to Ben Jonson.
Hughes, L.   Last Call.
MacNeice.   Invocation: "Dolphin plunge,
fountain play."
McHugh, H.   To God or Man.
Michelangelo Buonarroti.   I wish I'd want what
I don't want, Lord, at all.
Ramanujan.   Prayers to Lord Murugan.
Suckling, S.   Invocation, The: "Ye juster Powers
of Love and Fate."
Wheatley, P.   Ode to Neptune.

Io (mythology)
Broumas, O.   Io.

Iona, Scotland
Clampitt.   Westward.
Jeffers, R.   Iona: the Graves of the Kings.
Kipling, R.   Threshold, The.

Iowa (state)
Berrigan, T.   Poem: "Of morning, Iowa City,
blue."
Clampitt.   Black Buttercups.
Homeland.
Quarry, The.
Woodlot, The.
Davie, D.   Back of Affluence.

Or, Solitude.
Gallagher, T.   Boat Ride.
Sandburg, C.   Silver Point.
Updike.   Iowa.

Iphigenia
Merton.   Iphigenia: Politics.
Wilner, E.   Iphigenia, Setting the Record
Straight.

Iran and Iranians
Hughes, T.   Remembering Teheran.
See also **Persians**

Iraq and Iraqis
Armantrout.   Sets.

Ireland
Beckett, S.   Serena I.
Bierce.   Fair Division, A.
Byron, G.   Irish Avatar, The.
Clough.   O'Brien, most disconsolate of Men.
Davie, D.   Church of Ireland.
Demi-Exile. Howth.
Killala.
Townend, 1976.
Two from Ireland.
Donne.   H. W. in Hibernia Belligeranti.
Eberhart, R.   Inchiquin Lake, Penobscot Bay.
Graves, R.   Broken Girth, The.
Heaney, S.   Bogland.
Broagh.
In Memoriam Francis Ledwidge.
July.
New Song, A.
North.
Postscript.
Sheelagh na Gig.
Singer's House, The.
Singing School.
Stations of the West, The.
Strand at Lough Beg, The.
Jarrell, R.   Rhapsody on Irish Themes, A.
Jeffers, R.   In the Hill at Newgrange.
Irish Headland, An.
Northern Heather.
Ossian's Grave.
Kinsella, T.   In the Ringwood.
Irwin Street.
Route of the Táin, The.
Song of the Night.
Tao and Unfitness at Inistiogue on the River
Nore.
Kipling, R.   Ulster.
Larkin, P.   Importance of Elsewhere, The.
MacNeice.   Belfast.
Neutrality.
Valediction: "Their verdure dare not show . . .
their verdure dare not show."
Mahon.   Beyond Howth Head.
Homecoming.
Marvell.   Horatian Ode upon Cromwell's Return
from Ireland, An.
Meredith, G.   Ireland.
Moore, M.   Spenser's Ireland.
Muldoon, P.   Cauliflowers.
Christo's.
Duffy's Circus.
Earthquake, The.
Frog, The.
Good Friday, 1971. Driving Westward.
I Remember Sir Alfred.
Ireland.
Ma.
Sightseers, The.
Nash, O.   It's a Grand Parade It Will Be,
Modern Design.
Riley, J.   Green Grass of Old Ireland, The.
Town Karnteel, The.
Shelley, P.   To Ireland.
Sheridan, T.   To the Dean, when in England, in
1726.
Stevens, W.   Irish Cliffs of Moher, The.
Our Stars Come from Ireland.
Swift, J.   Ireland.
On the Irish Club.
On the Words "Brother Protestants and Fellow
Christians."
Thomas, D.   Fern Hill.

Whitman, W.   Old Ireland.
Whittier.   Exile's Departure, The.
Kathleen.
Yeats.   Alternative Song for the Severed Head in
"The King of the Great Clock Tower."
Dedication to a Book of Stories Selected from
the Irish Novelists.
Easter 1916.
Grey Rock, The.
Hosting of the Sidhe, The.
I Am of Ireland.
Into the Twilight.
Lake-Isle of Innisfree, The.
Municipal Gallery Revisited, The.
On a Political Prisoner.
O'Rahilly, The.
Parnell.
Parnell's Funeral.
Prayer for My Daughter, A.
Prologue to Responsibilities.
Red Hanrahan's Song about Ireland.
Rose Tree, The.
September 1913.
Three Songs to the One Burden.
To Ireland in the Coming Times.
See also **Northern Ireland**

Ireland, Northern
Heaney, S.   Toome.
See also **Northern Ireland**

Iris (flower)
Blok.   Florence.
Corbett, W.   Marie's irises / what with the
furnace.
"H. D."   Sea Iris.
Lawrence, D. H.   Scent of Irises.
Levine, P.   White Iris, The.
Mallarmé.   Prose.
Meredith, G.   To A.M.
Milosz, C.   O! ("O happiness! To see an iris").
Montale.   Iris.
Rukeyser, M.   Iris-Eaters, The.
Zukofsky, L.   Bearded Iris.

Irish, The
Creeley.   Theresa's Friends.
Cummings, E. E.   Mary green / cheerful &
generous.
Davie, D.   Belfast on a Sunday Afternoon.
Dublin Georgian.
Dugan, A.   Mockery against the Irish
Censorship.
Dunbar, P.   John Boyle O'Reilly.
Graves, R.   Single Fare.
Hardy, T.   Donaghadee.
Heaney, S.   Broagh.
Requiem for the Croppies.
Stations of the West, The.
Jarrell, R.   Rhapsody on Irish Themes, A.
Kipling, R.   Belts.
Irish Guards, The.
Lindsay, N.   Potatoes' Dance, The.
MacNeice.   Last before America.
Muldoon, P.   Anseo.
Armageddon, Armageddon.
Cows.
Cuba.
More a Man Has the More a Man Wants, The.
Quoof.
Whittier.   Abram Morrison.
Yeats.   O'Rahilly, The.
Remorse for Intemperate Speech.

Iron
Clifton, L.   Rust.
Cummings, E. E.   Chas sing does(who).
Dugan, A.   Importation of Landscapes.
Kipling, R.   Cold Iron.
Komunyakaa.   Believing in Iron.
Lawrence, D. H.   Things Made by Iron.
Rukeyser, M.   Simple Experiment, A.
Sandburg, C.   Iron.
Zagajewski.   Iron.

Irony
Borges.   Poem of the Gifts.
Bukowski.   86'd.
Beast, The.
Genius of the Crowd, The.

Trick to Dull Our Bleeding, A.
Creeley. Apology, The.
  Comfort.
  "Do You Think."
  Form of Adaptation, A.
  Gift of Great Value, A.
  Names, The.
  The ("Water / waiting far, The").
  What's for Dinner.
Davie, D. Ironist, The.
  Nosegay, The.
Gallagher, T. Survival of a Heart.
Graves, R. I'd Die for You.
  Under the Olives.
Hardy, T. After the War.
  Country Wedding, The.
  In a London Flat.
  Two Men, The.
  You Were the Sort that Men Forget.
Jeffers, R. Urchin, The.
Komunyakaa. Unnatural Deaths.
McGrath, T. Three Functions of Irony.
  War Resisters' Song.
Riley, J. Perversity.
  Sad Perversity.
Sandburg, C. Lavender Lilies.
Wilbur, R. Parable.
  Walgh-Vogel, The.
Williams, M. One of Those Rare Occurrences
  on a City Bus.
Zukofsky, L. Ashtray.
  Men in the kitchens, The.

Isaac
Amichai [or Amikhai]. Real Hero of the
  Sacrifice of Isaac, The.
  Real Hero, The.
Owen, W. Parable of the Old Men and the
  Young, The.
Wilner, E. Sarah's Choice.
  When Asked to Lie Down on the Altar.

Ishi
Komunyakaa. Quatrains for Ishi.
Stafford, W. Concealment, The: Ishi, the Last
  Wild Indian.

Ishmael
Duncan, R. Bring It Up from the Dark.

Ishtar
Levertov. Song for Ishtar.
Wilbur, R. To Ishtar.

Isis
Levertov. Her Prayer.
  Isis Speaks.
Shapiro, K. Interlude, The.

Islam
See **Muslims and Islam**

Islands
Auden. On This Island.
Bishop, E. Crusoe in England.
Bogan, L. Night.
Borges. Alexander Selkirk.
Brodsky, J. Ischia in October.
Browning, E. Island, An.
Browning, R. Isle's Enchantress, The.
Byron, G. Island, The.
Clampitt. Birdham.
  Hermit Thrush, A.
Cowper, W. Alexander Selkirk.
"Dario." Birds of the islands: in your gathering.
Davie, D. Emigrant, to the Receding Shore.
Dickey, W. Joy.
Dugan, A. Poem: "What was once an island
  with birds."
Eberhart, R. Moment of Equilibrium among the
  Islands.
Foscolo. Sonnet to Zante.
Hall, D. Stones.
Heaney, S. Disappearing Island, The.
Hughes, L. Island ("Wave of sorrow").
Jackson, L. Laura and Francisca.
Jarrell, R. Subway from New Britain to the
  Bronx, The.
Lawrence, D. H. Greeks Are Coming!, The.
Logan, J. Assateague.
MacDiarmid, H. Island Funeral.
MacNeice. No More Sea.

Mahon. Achill.
  Rathlin.
Mallarmé. Prose.
McHugh, H. North Island Songs.
  Syllables.
Melville, H. Archipelago, The.
  Enviable Isles, The.
Meredith, W. Chinese Banyan, The.
  Examples of Created Systems.
Merton. Poem: "Here is the man of the
  islands."
Merwin. Ferry Port.
  Island.
  Island City.
  Islands.
Millay, E. Ragged Island.
Milosz, C. Island.
Mistral, G. Caribbean Sea.
Oppen. Ballad: "Astrolabes and lexicons."
Pagis. Epilogue to Robinson Crusoe.
Pasternak, B. Portland.
Ramanujan. No Man Is an Island.
Rukeyser, M. Islands.
  Lover as Fox.
Shelley, P. Isle, The.
Stafford, W. Security.
Stock, R. To Tui: Not to Hie Herself off to
  Only God Knows How Dire & Pestilential a
  South Sea Island, but to Come with Us to
  Found Her Community in Brazil.
Sze. Edna Bay.
Tate, J. Stella Maris.
Walcott. As John to Patmos.
  Crusoe's Island.
  Islands.
Whittier. Brown Dwarf of Rügen, The.
Wilbur, R. Avowal, The.
  La Rose des Vents.
Williams, T. Island Is Memorable to Us, The.
  Separate Poem, A.
Wordsworth, W. Brownie's Cell, The.
Yeats. Lake-Isle of Innisfree, The.
Zaturenska. I Know an Island.
  Island, The.

Isolation
Borges. Alexander Selkirk.
Broumas, O. Cinderella.
Cavafy. Dünya Güzeli.
Creeley. Circles.
  Here Again ("No sadness").
  Place ("This is an empty landscape").
  Talking.
Cunningham, J. Towards Tucson.
Dugan, A. On Voyage.
  Philodendron.
Han-shan. Mountains are so cold, The.
Hughes, L. Crossing.
  Ruined Gal, A.
Ignatow, D. Finally.
  With Others.
Jacobsen, J. In Isolation.
  They Never Were Found.
Kunitz, S. Hermetic Poem.
Laughlin, J. Death Walkers, The.
  Stranger in the House, The.
McHugh, H. Postcard from Provincetown.
Merwin. Door, A ("What is dying all over the
  world").
  Herds, The.
  I Live Up Here.
  Lantern, The.
Oppen. Myself I Sing.
Parker, D. Portrait of the Artist.
  Sanctuary.
Pessoa. I'm beginning to know myself. I don't
  exist.
Pinsky. Poem about People.
Rexroth, K. Privacy.
Rich, A. I Am in Danger—Sir.
Riley, J. Quiet Lodger, The.
Tate, J. Late Harvest.
Zaturenska. Interpreter of Silence, The.
See also **Absence; Loneliness; Separation**

Isolde
Parker, D. Iseult of Brittany.
Pinsky. Jesus and Isolt.

See also **Tristram and Isolde**

Israel
Amichai [or Amikhai]. Akhziv.
  Almost a Love Poem.
  And as Far as Abu Ghosh.
  And in spite of all that, I must.
  Arab Shepherd Is Searching for His Goat on
    Mount Zion, An.
  Ashkelon.
  At the Monastery of Latroun.
  Beginning of Autumn in the Hills of Ephraim.
  Beit Guvrin.
  Blood that stands the member erect, The.
  City where I was born was destroyed by
    cannons, The.
  Dangerous Country.
  Deganya.
  End of Summer in the Judean Mountains.
  Even my loves are measured by the wars.
  From Jerusalem to the Sea and Back.
  Hadera.
  Hamadiya, Memory of Bliss.
  Hymn for Independence Day, A. So distant.
  I have nothing to say about the war.
  I left the Evening Land by the will of the night.
  In the summer, nations come to one another.
  Jews in the Land of Israel.
  Kibbutz Gevaram.
  Kibbutz Gvar-'Am.
  Land Knows, The.
  Late Marriage.
  Let Memory Mountain remember instead of me.
  Love of the Land.
  Man like That on a Bald Mountain in Jerusalem,
    A.
  Museum at Akhziv.
  My Children.
  My Mother Died on Shavuot.
  My Mother's Death and the Lost Battles for the
    Future of Her Children.
  Name of the Place "Trieste," The.
  National Thoughts.
  New homeland was built, The.
  North of Beer Sheba.
  North of San Francisco.
  On Mount Muhraka.
  On the lot that was a short-cut for lovers.
  Poems of Akhziv.
  Ramatayim.
  Shore of Ashkelon, The.
  Since Then.
  Sometimes I think of my fathers.
  Songs of Continuity.
  This Is the Life of Promises.
  Tourists.
  Travels of the Last Benjamin of Tudela.
  War broke out in autumn, in the no-man's land.
  We Did What We Had To.
  What a Complicated Mess.
  What Entanglement in This Small Country.
  What was the message of the burned man?
  When a man is away from his homeland for a
    long time.
  When a Man's Far Away from His Country.
  When I Was Young, the Whole Country Was
    Young.
  "Where was he wounded?" You don't know.
Bloch, C. We Did What We Had To.
Browning, R. First-Born of Egypt, The.
Byron, G. Oh! Weep for Those.
Carver, R. Contact, The.
  Transformation.
Celan. Just Think.
Clampitt. Letters from Jerusalem.
Clough. When Israel Came Out of Egypt.
Dove, R. Early Morning on the Tel Aviv-Haifa
  Freeway.
Emerson, R. To transmute crime to wisdom, &
  to stem.
Ginsberg, A. Galilee Shore.
Housman. When Israel out of Egypt came.
Jarrell, R. Jews at Haifa.
Kumin, M. In the Absence of Bliss.
  Itinerary of an Obsession.
Pagis. Siege.
  Twenty Years in the Valley.

Shapiro, K.   Israel.
Olive Tree, The.
Weiss, T.   Here and Now, The.

Issa (Kobayashi Issa)
Milosz, C.   Reading the Japanese Poet Issa (1762–1826).

Istanbul, Turkey
Codrescu.   Food.
Shop.
Winter in Istanbul.
Kizer, C.   Where I've Been All My Life.

Italians, The
Browning, R.   Italian in England, The.
Ciardi, J.   Feasts.
Clampitt.   Ringing Doorbells.
Davie, D.   Hyphens.
Ferlinghetti, L.   Old Italians Dying, The.
Logan, J.   Gallery Walk: Fifteen Italian Drawings 1780–1890.
Michelangelo Buonarroti.   I have your letter, thank you, as received.
Rossetti, C.   Enrica, 1865.
Schuyler, J.   Eyes.

Italy
Auden.   Good-Bye to the Mezzogiorno.
Bassani, G.   Looking Out from Ferrara.
Borges.   Ariosto and the Arabs.
Brodsky, J.   In Italy.
Ischia in October.
Vertumnus.
Browning, E.   First News from Villafranca.
Garibaldi.
Italy and the World.
King Victor Emanuel Entering Florence, April, 1860.
Napoleon III in Italy.
Nature's Remorses.
Sword of Castruccio Castracani, The.
Browning, R.   Englishman in Italy, The.
Fra Lippo Lippi.
Love among the Ruins.
Pippa Passes.
Sordello.
There goes a swallow to Venice—the stout seafarer!
Up at a Villa—Down in the City.
Carruth, H.   Two Romantic Pieces.
Cavafy.   Tarantians Divert Themselves, The.
Ciardi, J.   Back.
Fragments [or Poems] from Italy.
Clampitt.   From a Clinic Waiting Room.
In Umbria: A Snapshot.
Losing Track of Language.
Margaret Fuller, 1847.
Matrix (Villa Serbelloni, Lake Como).
Rain at Bellagio.
Trasimene.
Clough.   Amours de Voyage.
Peschiera.
Coleridge, S.   Garden of Boccaccio, The.
Collins, B.   Consolation.
Corbett, W.   Bowl of Progresso Minestrone.
Marga Barr.
Cummings, E. E.   Great Dante stands in Florence, looking down.
Memorabilia.
Davie, D.   Gemona-del-Friuli, 1961–1976.
Going to Italy.
Metals.
Tuscan Morning.
Via Portello.
Dickinson, E.   Our lives are Swiss.
Eberhart, R.   Cousin Florence.
Love among the Ruins.
Jarrell, R.   In Galleries.
Kizer, C.   For Jan, in Bar Maria.
Italian Kittens, The.
Laughlin, J.   Bit Different, A.
In Another Country.
Lawrence, D. H.   Cypresses.
Levi, P.   Crescenzago.
Levine, P.   Gift for a Believer.
I Was Born in Lucerne.
Logue, C.   Story of the Road, The.
Mahon.   Ghosts.
Major, C.   In Salute again.

We climbed the hill to the carriages.
McHugh, H.   What He Thought.
Meredith, G.   Centenary of Garibaldi, The.
Italy.
On Como.
Vittoria's *Italia* Song.
Meredith, W.   Journal Entry (April 1969, Villa Serbelloni).
Nausea.
Recollection of Bellagio.
Merrill, J.   Bronze.
Michelangelo Buonarroti.   I have your letter, thank you, as received.
Milosz, C.   In Milan.
Moore, M.   Web One Weaves of Italy, The.
Pasolini.   Ashes of Gramsci, The.
Desperate Vitality, A.
Plan of Future Works.
Reality.
Petrarch.   O Italy, my land, words cannot heal.
Pound, E.   Cino.
Quasimodo.   Agrigentum Road, The.
Rexroth, K.   Golden Section.
Vicenza.
Rich, A.   Recorders in Italy.
Rossetti, C.   Italia, Io Ti Saluto!
Schuyler, J.   Dorabella's Naples Watercolor.
Shelley, P.   Fragment: To Italy.
Lines Written among the Euganean Hills.
Sze.   Cornucopia, The.
Tennyson, A.   Daisy, The.
Frater Ave Atque Vale.
Tomlinson, C.   Above Carrara.
Retrospect, A: 1951–91.
Return, The.
Up at La Serra.
Updike.   South of the Alps.
Weiss, T.   Life of, The.
Whittier.   From Perugia.
Garibaldi.
Wilde, O.   Italia.
Sonnet on Approaching Italy.
Williams, T.   Brain's Dissection, The.
Wordsworth, W.   At Bologna, in Remembrance of the Late Insurrections, 1837.
At Bologna, in Remembrance of the Late Insurrections, 1837, Continued.
Memorials of a Tour in Italy, 1837.
Wright, C.   In the Valley of the Magra.
Italian Days.
Meditation on Song and Structure.
Remembering Spello, Sitting Outside in Prampolini's Garden.
Sprung Narratives.
To the Egyptian Mummy in the Etruscan Museum at Cortona.
Umbrian Dreams.
With Eddie and Nancy in Arezzo at the Caffè Grande.
Wright, J.   In Memory of Leopardi.
Zukofsky, L.   4 Other Countries.

Itching
Logan, J.   Poet Scratches His Head, The.
Nash, O.   Man Bites Dog-Days.
Requiem: "There was a young belle of old Natchez."
Taboo to Boot.

Ivy
Hardy, T.   Ivy-Wife, The.
Montale.   Fiesole Window.
Niedecker.   Oh ivy green.
Rossetti, C.   Under the ivy bush / One sits sighing.

J

Jack and the Beanstalk
Jarrell, R.   Jack.
Prunty.   Annals of Jack.
Riley, J.   Jack the Giant-Killer.

Jackals
Komunyakaa.   Eclogue at Twilight.

Jackdaws
Bourne, V.   Jackdaw, The.

Tomlinson, C.   At the Hill Fort.

Jackrabbits
Stevens, W.   Jack-Rabbit, The.

Jackson, Andrew
Lindsay, N.   Statue of Old Andrew Jackson, The.
Merwin.   Homeland.

Jackson, "Hurricane"
Dugan, A.   On Hurricane Jackson.

Jackson, Mahalia
Lorde.   Day They Eulogized Mahalia, The.

Jackson, Michael
Komunyakaa.   Never Land.

Jackson, Thomas Jonathan ("Stonewall")
Melville, H.   Stonewall Jackson.

Jacob (Bible)
Amichai [or Amikhai].   Jacob and the Angel.
Burns, R.   Patriarch, The.
Crane, H.   Dust Now Is.
Dickinson, E.   Audacity of Bliss, said Jacob to the Angel.
Little East of Jordan, A.
Dugan, A.   1. Business Jacob, the Angel Wrestler.
Herrick.   Beggars.
Levertov.   Jacob's Ladder, The.
Milton.   Paraphrase on Psalm 114, A.
Stock, R.   Jacob Agonistes.
Rachel and Leah.
Very.   Jacob Wrestling with the Angel.

Jacobites
Burns, R.   Battle of Sherra-Moor, The.
Killiecrankie.
Song: "Small birds rejoice in the green leaves returning, The."
There'll Never Be Peace till Jamie Comes Hame.
Up and Warn A' Willie.
Ye Jacobites by Name.

Jaguars
Cuadra, P.   Jaguar Myth, The.
Hughes, T.   Jaguar, The.
Second Glance at a Jaguar.

Jails
Clampitt.   Amaranth and Moly.
Codrescu.   I'm careful with my dreams of death.
Partiti Sunt Vestimenta Mea Miserunt Sortem Contra Me ad Incarte Cla a Filii a Eniol Liebee Braya Braguesca et Belzebuth.
Thing, A.
Logan, J.   Lines on Locks (or Jail and the Erie Canal).
Lux.   Autobiographical.
Mahon.   Jail Journal.
Wilde, O.   Ballad of Reading Gaol, The.
See also **Prisons and Prisoners**

Jam- and Jelly-making
Kumin, M.   Making the Jam without You.
Larkin, P.   April Sunday Brings the Snow, An.

Jamaica, West Indies
Williams, F.   Ode, An: "At length revolving fates th' expected year."
Williams, T.   Mendicant Order, A.

James, Frank
Niedecker.   Jesse James and his brother Frank.

James, Henry
Auden.   At the Grave of Henry James.
Davie, D.   Depravity: Two Sermons.
Gunn, T.   Jamesian.
Hall, D.   Beau of the Dead.
Laughlin, J.   Graceful Exit, A.
Ransom, J.   Old Mansion.
Schuyler, J.   This Notebook.

James I (1394–1437), King of Scotland
Rossetti, D.   King's Tragedy, The.

James I (1566–1625), King of England
Burns, R.   Lament of Mary Queen of Scots on the Approach of Spring.
Campion, T.   De Regis reditu e Scotia.
To the Most Sacred King James.
Jonson, B.   Dedication of the King's New Cellar. To Bacchus, The.
Panegyre, on the Happy Entrance of James, Our Sovereign, to His First High Session of

Parliament in This Kingdom.
To King James ("How, best of kings, dost thou a scepter bear[e]!").
Kipling, R.   James I.
Milton.   On the Gunpowder Plot.
On the Same ["James derided the Purgatorial fire of the soul"].
On the Same ["Thus did you strive to vouchsafe James to Heaven"].
On the Same ["Whom impious Rome had just marked out for her curses"].

James II (1633–1701), King of England
Jonson, B.   To the Ghost of Martial.

James, Jesse
Niedecker.   Jesse James and his brother Frank.

James, William
Niedecker.   Jesse James and his brother Frank.

Jamestown, Virginia
Hughes, L.   Ghosts of 1619.
Jarrell, R.   Jamestown.
Moore, M.   Enough.

January
Bishop, E.   Brazil, January 1, 1502.
Cavafy.   January 1904.
Eberhart, R.   Snow Cascades.
Rexroth, K.   January Night.
Sandburg, C.   Manitoba Childe Roland.
Schuyler, J.   In January.
Williams, W.   January.
Moon and Stars.
Zaturenska.   Snowstorm in January.

Janus
Borges.   Bust of Janus Speaks, A.
Carew, T.   To the New Year [For the Countess of Carlisle].
Eberhart, R.   Nexus.
Swift, J.   To Janus.

Japan
Borges.   Music Box.
Ciardi, J.   Massive Retaliation.
Creeley.   Later ("Drunks leaning on your arm").
Hamill, S.   Two Poems for Tanabata Matsuri.
Jarrell, R.   Rising Sun, The.
Siegfried.
Kipling, R.   Buddha at Kamakura.
Kumin, M.   How to Survive Nuclear War.
Mahon.   Snow Party, The.
Meredith, W.   Two Japanese Poems.
Milosz, C.   No More.
Reading the Japanese Poet Issa (1762–1826).
Sandburg, C.   Old Hokusai Print.
Sarton, M.   Child's Japan, A.
Japanese Prints.
Snyder, G.   Dullness in February: Japan.
Feathered Robe, The.
In the House of the Rising Sun.
Kai, Today.
Public Bath, The.
Rainbow Body.
Stafford, W.   Surrounded by Mountains.
Sze.   Flower Path, The.
Tomlinson, C.   Zipangu.
Wilner, E.   As Far as It Goes, and Back.
Green Connection, The.
Kazuko's Vision.
Mt. Fuji and the Martial Arts.
Winged Victory.

Japanese, The
Bukowski.   Japanese Wife, The.
Cummings, E. E.   YgUDuh / ydoan / yunnuhstan.
Dickey, J.   Performance, The.
Komunyakaa.   Corners of Night.
Nash, O.   Japanese, The.
Sarton, M.   Exchange of Gifts, An.
Whalen, P.   Birthday Poem.
Garden, The.
Success Is Failure.
Wilner, E.   Conversation with a Japanese Student.
Ume: *Plum.*

Jasmine
Amichai [or Amikhai].   Elecampane, Jasmine, Vine, and Oleander.
Jasmine.

HaNagid.   Jasmine.
Komunyakaa.   Jasmine.

Jason
Dickinson, E.   Finding is the first Act.
Pagis.   Jason's Grave in Jerusalem.
Swift, J.   Mr. Jason Hassard, a Woolen Draper in Dublin.

Jays
Ciardi, J.   Last Rites.
Dickinson, E.   I am studying music now with the jays.
I saw the Jays this Morning.
No Brigadier throughout the Year.
Prompt—executive Bird is the Jay, A.
Lawrence, D. H.   Blue Jay, The.
Major, C.   Textures of Space, The.
See also **Blue Jays**

Jazz
Brodsky, J.   In Memory of Clifford Brown.
Brooks, G.   We Real Cool.
Carruth, H.   For Papa.
Freedom and Discipline.
Homage to John Lyly and Frankie Newton.
How To.
Letter to Maxine Sullivan.
Little Old Funky Homeric Blues for Herm, A.
Meditation in the Presence of "Ostrich Walk."
Paragraphs.
"Sure," Said Benny Goodman.
What a Wonder among the Instruments Is the Walloping Tramboone!
Who Cares, Long as It's B-Flat.
Collins, B.   I Chop Some Parsley while Listening to Art Blakey's Version of "Three Blind Mice."
Man Listening to Disc.
Nightclub.
Cooper, J.   Wanda's Blues.
Corbett, W.   Thelonious Sphere Monk.
Creeley.   Broken Back Blues.
Cummings, E. E.   God pity me whom (god distinctly has).
Hayden, R.   Soledad.
Hughes, L.   Be-Bop Boys.
Cabaret.
Flatted Fifths.
Harlem Night Club.
Jam Session.
Jazz Band in a Parisian Cabaret.
Jazz Girl.
Jazzonia.
Neon Signs.
Nocturne for the Drums.
Song for Billie Holiday.
Young Singer.
Komunyakaa.   Changes; or, Reveries at a Window Overlooking a Country Road, with Two Women Talking Blues in the Kitchen.
Copacetic Mingus.
Dolphy's Aviary.
Elegy for Thelonious.
February in Sydney.
Gerry's Jazz.
Jasmine.
Nightbird.
Pepper.
Plea, The.
Testimony.
Larkin, P.   For Sidney Bechet.
Referred Back.
Levine, P.   On the Corner.
Logan, J.   Chicago Scene.
Major, C.   Cotton Club, The.
In Walked Bud with a Palette.
Round Midnight.
McGrath, T.   Guiffre's Nightmusic.
O'Hara, F.   Day Lady Died, The.
Rukeyser, M.   Bunk Johnson Blowing.
Homage to Literature.
Sandburg, C.   Honky Tonk in Cleveland, Ohio.
Jazz Fantasia.
Vaudeville Dancer.
Schuyler, J.   Let's All Hear It for Mildred Bailey!
Williams, M.   Death of Chet Baker, The.
Williams, T.   Tenor Sax Taking the Breaks.

Williams, W.   Shoot It Jimmy!
Wright, J.   End of an Ethnic Dream, The.

Jealousy
Ai.   Penis Envy.
Amichai [or Amikhai].   Dog after Love, A.
Auden.   Victor.
Austen.   To F.S., who accused the Author of partiality in writing verses for F C Fowle, & not for him.
Bly, R.   Danger of Loss, The.
Broumas, O.   Field.
Browning, R.   In a Balcony.
My Last Duchess.
Campion, T.   Ad Melleam.
Though your strangenesse frets my hart.
Turne all thy thoughts to eyes.
Carew, T.   To His Jealous Mistress.
To One That Desired to Know My Mistress [or Mistris].
Chaucer.   Complaint of Mars, The.
Complaint of Venus, The.
Chuang Tzu.   Great and Small.
Coleridge, S.   Not at Home.
Collins, B.   Jealousy.
Cooper, J.   Bedside Rune, A.
Crane, S.   Tell me why, behind thee.
Creeley.   Memory, The.
Cummings, E. E.   Spoke joe to jack.
"Dario."   My love, the night has come.
Dickinson, E.   God is indeed a jealous God.
You see we keep a jealous Heart.
Dugan, A.   Religious Question.
To a Colleague. From the Country.
Dunbar, P.   Jealous.
Eberhart, R.   Man's Greed and Envy Are So Great.
Glück, L.   Horse.
Graves, R.   Cat-Goddesses.
Dialogue on the Headland.
Dream of Hell, A.
I'd Die for You.
Jealous Man, A.
Lack.
Powers Unconfessed.
Prison Walls.
Prometheus.
To Beguile and Betray.
Tower of Love, The.
Gunn, T.   Road Map, The.
"H. D."   At Ithaca.
Red Roses for Bronze.
Hall, D.   Jealous Lovers, The.
Hardy, T.   Face at the Casement, The.
Love the Monopolist.
Rival, The.
To Carrey Clavel.
Heaney, S.   Dream of Jealousy, A.
Herrick.   How Marigolds Came Yellow.
Sonnet, A: "Ile dote noe more, nor shall mine eyes."
To Jealousie.
Upon a Wife That Dyed Mad with Jealousie.
Jackson, L.   And This Hard Jealousy.
Jeffers, R.   Give Your Heart to the Hawks.
Mara.
Jonson, B.   Against Jealousy [or Jealousie].
Keats.   Song: "Hush, hush! tread softly! hush, hush my dear."
Kipling, R.   Bill 'Awkins.
Koch, K.   Down at the Docks.
Larkin, P.   Dance, The.
I See a Girl Dragged by the Wrists.
Love Again.
Laughlin, J.   Bad Night on Third Avenue, A.
Jealous Gods, The.
Your Eyes.
Lawrence, D. H.   Jealousy.
Tease.
Meredith, G.   Desert vulture / jealousy, The.
Mistral, G.   Ballad: "He passed by with another woman."
God Wills It.
Nash, O.   Absence Makes the Heart Grow Heart Trouble.
Love Me but Leave My Dog Alone.
O'Hara, F.   For Grace, after a Party.

Hôtel Transylvanie.
Parker, D.   Mortal Enemy.
Petrarch.   Happy and sad, together and yet sole.
Plath.   Shrike, The.
Poe.   Annabel Lee.
Ralegh, S.   Excuse, The.
Ransom, J.   Vaunting Oak.
Riley, J.   Dearth.
Robinson, E.   Evangelist's Wife, An.
Rossetti, C.   Sister Maude.
Smith, S.   Mistress Osmosis.
Whitman, W.   Sometimes with One I Love.
Williams, C. K.   Cautionary, The.
 Image, The.
 Love: Youth.
 Silence, The.
 Soliliquies.
Wyatt, S.   Wandering gadling in the summer
  tide, The.
Yeats.   Anashuya and Vijaya.
Zukofsky, L.   Catullus viii.
See also **Envy**
Jeffers, Robinson
Davie, D.   Robinson Jeffers at Point Sur.
Milosz, C.   To Robinson Jeffers.
Rukeyser, M.   Citation for Horace Gregory.
Tate, J.   Failed Tribute to the Stonemason of Tor
  House, Robinson Jeffers.
Jefferson, Thomas
MacLeish.   Brave New World.
Niedecker.   Jefferson and Adams.
 Thomas Jefferson.
 Thomas Jefferson Inside.
 Three Americans.
Rukeyser, M.   Secrets of American Civilization.
Sandburg, C.   Open Letter to the Poet Archibald
  MacLeish Who Has Forsaken His
  Massachusetts Farm to Make Propaganda for
  Freedom.
Sarton, M.   Monticello.
Stafford, W.   New Letters from Thomas
  Jefferson.
Jehovah's Witnesses
Laughlin, J.   Bible Lady, The.
Jellyfish
Moore, M.   Jellyfish, A.
Nash, O.   Jellyfish, The.
Jeremiah (Bible)
Donne.   Lamentations of Jeremy, for the Most
  Part According to Tremeullius.
Jericho
Merton.   Rahab's House.
Jerome, Saint
Dubie.   Elegy for Wright & Hugo.
Jarrell, R.   Jerome.
Merton.   Two Desert Fathers.
Moore, M.   Leonardo Da Vinci's.
Jerusalem
Amichai [*or* Amikhai].   And in spite of all that,
  I must.
Beautiful Are the Families of Jerusalem.
Blood that stands the member erect, The.
City where I was born was destroyed by
  cannons, The.
Ecology of Jerusalem.
Even my loves are measured by the wars.
God's Hand in the World.
"He left two sons," they say.
Hymn to the Lovely Couple Varda and
  Schimmel.
I have nothing to say about the war.
I left the Evening Land by the will of the night.
In the Jerusalem Mountains.
In the Old City.
In the Room.
In the summer, nations come to one another.
Jerusalem.
Jerusalem 1967.
Jerusalem 1985.
Jerusalem Ecology.
Jerusalem Is Full of Used Jews.
Jerusalem the cradle city that rocks me.
Jerusalem's Suicide Attempts.
Land Knows, The.
Let Memory Mountain remember instead of me.

Love of Jerusalem.
Mayor, The.
New homeland was built, The.
North of Beersheba.
On the lot that was a short-cut for lovers.
On the Wide Stairs—Lurking for Happiness.
Poem about Repairs to My House.
Poems of continuity, mines and graves.
"Rustle of History's Wings," as They Used to
  Say Then, The.
Sleep in Jerusalem.
Sometimes I think of my fathers.
Sort of an Apocalypse.
Summer Evening in the Jerusalem Mountains.
Summer Night in the King David Hotel.
Tourists.
War broke out in autumn, in the no-man's land.
What was the message of the burned man?
"Where was he wounded?" You don't know.
Yehuda Ha-Levi.
You Must Not Show Weakness.
Blake, W.   I Give You the End of a Golden
  String.
 Jerusalem.
 Monk, The.
Byron, G.   On the Day of the Destruction of
  Jerusalem by Titus.
Cavafy.   To Jerusalem.
Celan.   Heat / counts us together, The.
 Song in the Wilderness, A.
 That shining, yes, the one that.
 There stood / a splinter of fig on your lip.
Clampitt.   Letters from Jerusalem.
Cullen, C.   At the Wailing Wall in Jerusalem.
Dickey, W.   Ezekiel's Rabbit.
Duncan, R.   Kingdom of Jerusalem, The.
Herrick.   To His Brother Nicolas Herrick.
MacNeice.   New Jerusalem.
Paley, G.   Warning, A.
Pasolini.   Southern Dawn.
Rich, A.   Jerusalem.
Rossetti, C.   All Saints.
 By the Waters of Babylon.
 Holy City, New Jerusalme, The.
 Jerusalem of fire / And gold and pearl and gem.
 Now They Desire.
 Whither the Tribes Go Up, Even the Tribes of
  the Lord.
Rukeyser, M.   Traditional Tune.
Weiss, T.   Here and Now, The.
 Making It.
See also **Zion**
Jesters
Broumas, O.   Innocence.
De la Mare.   Falstaff.
Hughes, L.   Jester, The.
Kipling, R.   Jester, The.
Nash, O.   If Fun Is Fun, Isn't That Enough?
Robinson, E.   Old King's New Jester, The.
Rumi.   Dalqak's Message.
Szymborska, W.   Warning.
Yeats.   Cap and Bells, The.
See also **Fools**
Jesuits
Davie, D.   Jesuits in North America, The.
Milosz, C.   Philology.
Wright, C.   Jesuit Graves.
Jesus Christ
Ammons.   Christmas Eve.
Auden.   Question, The: "All of us believe."
Baudelaire.   Saint Peter's Denial.
Berryman.   Disciple, The.
Bierce.   Christian.
Blake, W.   How Sweet I Roamed [*or* Roam'd]
  from Field to Field.
Bly, R.   Crazy Carlson's Meadow.
 Falling Asleep.
Borges.   Christ on the Cross.
 John I:14.
 Luke 23.
 Paradiso 31, 108.
Bradstreet, A.   Occasional Meditations: "By
  night, when others soundly slept."
Brodsky, J.   Nativity.
 Nunc Dimittis.

Star of the Nativity.
Brooks, G.   In Emanuel's Nightmare: Another
  Coming of Christ.
Browning, E.   Drama of Exile, A.
 Mediator, The.
 Past and Future.
 Seraphim, The.
 Thought for a Lonely Death-Bed, A.
 Virgin Mary to the Child Jesus, The.
Browning, R.   Death in the Desert, A.
 Epistle Containing the Strange Medical
  Experience of Karshish, An.
Carruth, H.   Sorrow Song, The.
Celan.   Mandorla.
Chesterton.   Calvary, The.
 Carpenter, The.
 Donkey, The.
Clement of Alexandria.   Logos Our Teacher,
  The.
Coleridge, S.   Epitaphium Testamentarium.
 My Baptismal Birthday [*or* Birth-Day].
 Religious Musings.
 Translation of a Passage in Ottfried's Metrical
  Paraphrase of the Gospel.
 Virgin's Cradle-Hymn, The.
Cowper, W.   Longing to Be with Christ.
Crane, H.   After Jonah.
 Lachrymae Christi.
Crashaw.   Authors Motto, The.
 But Now They Have Seen, and Hated.
 Christs Victory.
 Hymn in the Assumption.
 Hymne of the Nativity, Sung by the Shepheards,
  A.
 In Cicatrices Domini Jesu.
 In the Glorious Epiphanie of Our Lord God.
 In the Holy Nativity of Our Lord God.
 On the Bleeding Wounds of Our Crucified Lord.
 On the Still Surviving Markes of Our Saviours
  Wounds.
 On the Water of Our Lord's Baptism[e].
 On the Wounds of Our Crucified Lord.
 Our Lord in His Circumcision to His Father.
 Out of *Grotius* his Tragedy of *Christes*
  Sufferinges.
 Psalmus 1.
 To Our Blessed Lord upon the Choice of His
  Sepulchre.
 To Pontius Washing His Blood-Stained Hands.
 To Pontius Washing His Hands.
 To the Name above Every Name, the Name of
  Jesus, a Hymn.
 Upon the Asse That Bore Our Saviour.
 Upon the Sepulchre of our Lord.
Creeley.   Women, The.
Cullen, C.   Black Christ, The.
 Christus Natus Est.
 Judas Iscariot.
Cummings, E. E.   After-Glow.
 And i imagine.
 Jehovah buried,Satan dead.
 No time ago / or else a life.
 There are possibly 2 1/2 or impossibly 3.
 "Dario."   Spes.
Davie, D.   Miracle, The.
 Our Lady.
 Pilate.
 Sea of Tiberias.
De la Mare.   Break of Morning.
Dickey, J.   Magus, The.
Dickey, W.   Fred and the Holy Grail.
Dickinson, E.   At least—to pray—is left—is left.
 Dying! Dying in the night!
 God is a distant—stately Lover.
 He gave away his Life.
 I shall know why—when Time is over.
 Jesus! thy Crucifix.
 Just so—Jesus—raps.
 Life—is what we make it.
 Obtaining but our own Extent.
 One crown that no one seeks.
 Perhaps you think me stooping.
 Proud of my broken heart, since thou didst
  break it.
 Savior must have been, The.
 Savior's only signature, The.

So well that I can live without.
To be human is more than to be divine.
To have had such Daughters is sanctity.
"Unto me?" I do not know you.
Word made Flesh is seldom, A.
Donne.   Cross, The.
Resurrection, Imperfect.
Upon the Annunciation and Passion Falling
  upon One Day. 1608.
Dubie.   Looking up from Two Renaissance
  Paintings to the Massacre at Tiananmen
  Square.
Dugan, A.   Triptych.
Dunbar, W.   Ballat of the Passioun, Ane.
Done is a battell [or battle] on the dragon blak
  [or black].
Rorate, celi, desuper!
Duncan, R.   Adoration of the Virgin, The.
Eberhart, R.   Way Out, A.
Emerson, R.   No. 13 Hymn Written in Concord
  Sept. 1814.
Ferlinghetti, L.   Sometime during Eternity.
Gallagher, T.   Reading Aloud.
García Lorca.   Birth of Christ, The.
Ginsberg, A.   Epigram on a Painting of
  Golgotha.
Prayer Blues.
Glück, L.   Easter Season.
Nativity Poem.
Pietà.
Winter Morning.
Graves, R.   Descent into Hell.
In the Wilderness.
Gunn, T.   Jesus and His Mother.
Hacker, M.   Christmas Crown, A.
Hall, D.   Carol, A.
Small Fig Tree, A.
Hammon.   Evening Thought, An. Salvation by
  Christ with Penitential Cries.
Hardy, T.   Evening in Galilee, An.
Panthera.
Unkept Good Fridays.
Hayden, R.   Full Moon.
Herbert, G.   Aaron.
Affliction: "Kill me not every [or ev'ry] day."
Affliction (3).
Agony [or Agonie], The.
Bag, The.
Bunch of Grapes, The.
Business.
Church Militant, The.
Dawning, The.
Dialogue, A.
Dialogue-Anthem, A.
Dulness[e].
Easter Wings.
Good Friday.
Grieve Not the Holy Spirit, etc.
Holdfast, The.
Holy Baptism (1).
Holy Communion, The.
Jesu.
Justice (2).
Lent.
Longing.
Love.
Love (3).
Love-Joy.
Mary [or Marie] Magdalene.
Our Life Is Hid with Christ in God.
Redemption.
Reprisal[l], The.
Sacrifice, The.
Son[ne], The.
Sunday.
Thanksgiving, The.
Ungratefulness.
Herrick.   Another, to God.
Another, to His Saviour.
Christ.
Christs Action.
Christs Incarnation.
Christs Part.
Christs Sadnesse.
Christs Suffering.
Christs Words on the Crosse, My God, My God.

Coheires.
Coming to Christ.
Gods Descent.
Good Friday: Rex Tragicus, or, Christ Going to
  His Cross[e].
His Coming to the Sepulcher.
His Offering, with the Rest, at the Sepulcher.
His Saviour['.]s Words, Going to the Cross[e].
Martha, Martha.
New-Yeeres Gift, or Circumcisions Song, Sung
  to the King in the Presence, The.
No Coming to God without Christ.
To Christ.
To His Saviours Sepulcher: His Devotion.
Hopkins, G.   Angelus Ad Virginem.
As Kingfishers Catch Fire.
But what indeed is ask'd of me?
Easter.
Hope holds to Christ.
Jesu Dulcis Memoria.
Lantern Out of Doors, The.
Moonless darkness stands between.
Myself unholy, from myself unholy.
New Readings.
Oratio Patris Condren: O Jesu Vivens in Maria.
Soldier, The.
Spring.
Starlight Night, The.
Thee, God, I come from, to thee go.
Where art thou friend, whom I shall never see.
Windhover, The.
Housman.   Easter Hymn.
Hughes, L.   Ballad of Mary's Son.
Ballad of the Two Thieves.
Bible Belt.
Christ in Alabama.
Christmas Story, The.
Encounter.
Feet o' Jesus.
Goodbye Christ.
Judgment Day.
Ma Lord.
Pastoral: "Between the little clouds of heaven."
Shepherd's Song at Christmas.
Shout.
Hughes, T.   Being Christlike.
God, A.
Jeffers, R.   Dear Judas.
Meditation on Saviors.
Theory of Truth.
Jonson, B.   Hymn[e] on the Nativity [or
  Nativitie] of My Saviour, A.
Reverse on the Back Side, The.
Kipling, R.   Nativity, A.
Sons of Martha, The.
Kizer, C.   Oration, The.
Kumin, M.   Jesus Infection, The.
Kunitz, S.   He.
Laughlin, J.   Mountain Afterglow, The.
Patent Pending.
Lawrence, D. H.   Ballad of a Wilful Woman.
Coming of Quetzalcoatl, The.
Commandments.
Demiurge.
Jesus' Farewell.
Know Thyself.
Meeting among the Mountains.
My Name Is Jesus.
Quetzalcoatl Looks Down on Mexico.
Retort to Jesus.
Risen Lord, The.
Son of the Morning Star.
Song of Don Ramon, The.
Levertov.   Ikon: The Harrowing of Hell.
On a Theme from Julian's Chapter 20.
Salvator Mundi: Via Crucis.
Lindsay, N.   Daniel.
I Heard Immanuel Singing.
Johnny Appleseed's Hymn to the Sun.
Star of My Heart.
When Peter Jackson Preached in the Old
  Church.
Logan, J.   Monologue for the Good Friday
  Christ.
Month of Saints, A.
Spring of the Thief.

Yellow Christ, The; after Gaugin.
Lowell, R.   Drunken Fisherman, The.
MacDiarmid, H.   Harry Semen.
Innumerable Christ, The.
MacLeish.   Carrion Crow, The.
Seeing.
Marvell.   Clorinda and Damon.
Coronet, The.
Merton.   Argument: Of the Passion of Christ,
  An.
Betrayal, The.
Biography, The.
Cana.
Carol, A: "When Jesus got my broken back for
  Christmas, Juniors."
Early Mass.
Flight into Egypt, The.
Landfall, The.
Ointment, The.
Sacred Heart 2.
Senescente Mundo.
Song for the Blessed Sacrament.
Song of the Traveller, The.
Sponge Full of Vinegar, The.
Victory, The.
Vine, The.
Widow of Naim, The.
Michelangelo Buonarroti.   It leaves me plunged
  in gloom and pain—yet dear.
My eyes are saddened by so much they see.
One way remains to loose me yet, dear Lord.
Well-nigh the voyage now is overpast.
Millay, E.   Jesus to His Disciples.
Milosz, C.   Old Women.
Milton.   On the Morning of Christ's Nativity.
Passion, The.
Nemerov.   Ahasuerus.
Carol: "Now is the world withdrawn all."
Nicodemus.
Santa Claus.
Sonnet: "Form of Christ cut from dark wood,
  the pale, A."
Olson, C.   Easter.
Not a rat-hole, a cat-hole: the knife of time; on
  the ledge, overlooking.
Siena.
Owen, W.   At a Calvary near the Ancre.
Parker, D.   Maid-Servant at the Inn, The.
Petrarch.   Death has no power to make that
  sweet face bitter.
I am so weary and so heavy laden.
Pinkerton, H.   Error Pursued.
Good Friday.
Pinsky.   From the Childhood of Jesus.
Jesus and Isolt.
Pound, E.   Ballad of the Goodly Fere.
Raine, K.   Star of Bethlehem.
Ralegh, S.   On the Card[e]s, and Dice.
Ransom, J.   Armageddon.
Our Two Worthies.
Riley, J.   Child's Christmas Carol.
Christ, The.
Plantation Hymn.
Rilke.   Resurrected Christ, The.
Rimbaud, A.   Fragments According to the
  Gospel.
Ritsos.   Distinct Motion.
Robinson, E.   Calvary.
Rossetti, C.   Advent Sunday.
After This the Judgement.
As the Apple Tree among the Trees of the
  Wood.
Ascension Day.
Ascension Eve.
Ash Wednesday.
Because He First Loved Us.
Because Thy Love hath sought me, / All mine is
  Thine and Thine is mine.
Before the Paling of the Stars.
Before the Throne, and before the Lamb.
Behold the Man!
Better Resurrection, A.
Bruised Reed Shall He Not Break, A.
Candlemas Dialogue, A.
Changing Chimes.
Chiefest among Ten Thousand, The.

Christmas Day.
Christmas Eve.
Come unto Me.
Consider the Lilies of the Field.
Conversion of St. Paul.
Day and night the Accuser makes no pause.
Dear Angels and dear disembodied Saints.
Death of a First-Born, A.
Descent from the Cross, The.
Despised and Rejected.
Easter Monday.
Easter Tuesday.
Embertide.
Epiphany.
Epiphanytide.
Exceeding Bitter Cry, An.
For H.P.
God Is Our Hope and Strength.
God's Acre.
Good Friday Evening.
Good Friday Morning.
Good Shepherd, The.
Half Dead.
Heavy heart, if ever heart was heavy, A.
Her Seed; It Shall Bruise Thy Head.
Hymn for Christmas Day, A.
I Am Small and of No Reputation.
I Know You Not.
If I should ever say "my heart is in my home."
If Only.
It Is Finished.
Jesus alone:—if thus it were to me.
Judge Not According to the Appearance.
King of Kings and Lord of Lords.
Leaf from leaf Christ knows; / Himself the Lily and the Rose.
Let Them Rejoice in Their Beds.
Light of Light.
Long Barren.
Lord, carry me.—Nay, but I grant thee strength.
Lord, dost Thou look on me, and will not I.
Lord God of Hosts, most Holy and most High.
Lord, Grant Us Calm.
Lord Jesu, Thou art sweetness to my soul.
Lord Jesus, who would think that I am Thine?
Lord, what have I that I may offer Thee?
Love Is Strong as Death.
Love of Christ Which Passeth Knowledge, The.
Lowest Place, The.
Mary Magdalene and the Other Mary.
Name of Jesus, The.
New creatures; the Creator still the Same.
None other Lamb, none other Name.
None With Him.
Not Yours But You.
O Christ my God Who seest the unseen.
O Christ our All in each, our All in all!
O mine enemy / Rejoice not over me!
Of Him That Was Ready to Perish.
Offering of the New Law, the One Oblation Once Offered, The.
One of the Soldiers with a Spear Pierced His Side.
Our Church Palms are Budding Willow Twigs.
Our life is long. Not so, wise Angels say.
Passion Flower hath sprung up tall, The.
Purification of St. Mary the Virgin, The.
Ransomed of the Lord, The.
Rejoice with Me.
Sick Child's Meditation, A.
Slain from the Foundation of the World.
St. John, Apostle.
Surely He Hath Borne Our Griefs.
Take Care of Him.
That No Man Take Thy Crown.
That Where I Am, There Ye May Be Also.
This near-at-hand land breeds pain by measure.
Thou Art Fairer than the Children of Men.
Thou, God, Seest Me.
Three Enemies, The.
Thy Friend and Thy Father's Friend Forget Not.
Thy Name, O Christ, as incense streaming forth.
Tuesday in Holy Week.
Vigil of all Saints.
Vigil of St. Peter.
We know not when, we know not where.

Wednesday in Holy Week.
What is it Jesus saith unto the soul?
What Is That to Thee? Follow Thou Me.
When My Heart Is Vexed I Will Complain.
Whitsun Day.
Whitsun Eve.
Whitsun Tuesday.
Ye That Fear Him, Both Small and Great.
Yea, blessed and holy is he that hath part in the First / Resurrection!
Yea, if Thou wilt, Thou canst put up Thy sword.
Rossetti, D.   Virgin and Child, by Hans Memmeling, A; in the Academy of Bruges.
Rukeyser, M.   Holy Family.
Lynchings of Jesus, The.
Place-Rituals.
Traditional Tune.
Rumi.   Christ is the population of the world.
I called through your door.
Jesus on the Lean Donkey.
Spring Is Christ.
What Jesus Runs Away From.
Sandburg, C.   Child.
Early Lynching.
Epistle: "Jesus loved the sunsets on Galilee."
Loin Cloth.
Special Starlight.
Star Silver.
To a Contemporary Bunkshooter.
Sedulius.   Solis Ortus Cardine, A.
Sexton.   For God while Sleeping.
Is It True?
Jesus Asleep.
Jesus Awake.
Jesus Cooks.
Jesus Dies.
Jesus Raises Up the Harlot.
Jesus Suckles.
Jesus Summons Forth.
Jesus, the Actor, Plays the Holy Ghost.
Jesus Unborn.
Jesus Walking.
Protestant Easter.
Smith, S.   Ah, Will the Saviour...?
Airy Christ, The.
Christmas.
Conviction (i).
Conviction (ii).
Torquemada.
Was He Married?
Stafford, W.   Easter Morning.
Stock, R.   Pietà.
Stockton, A.   Hymn Written in the Year 1753, A.
Meditation on the 3d Verse of the 28th Chapter of Mathew.
Ode for Christmas Day, An.
Tate, J.   Goodtime Jesus.
Thomas, D.   This Bread I Break.
Thoreau.   In Adams fall.
Very.   Altar, The.
Apostle, The.
Ark, The.
Blessed Are They That Mourn.
Bread from Heaven, The.
Christ, The.
Christ Abiding Forever.
Christmas.
Christ's Capture in the Garden: A Paraphrase.
Christ's Compassion.
Christ's Final Victory.
Coming, The.
Compassion.
Cross, The ("I must go on, till in my tearful line").
Garden, The.
Great Facts of Christ's History, The.
Hallowed be thy Name.
How Faith Comes.
Hymn: "Thou who keepst us each together."
Hymn: Christ's Invitation in the Apocalypse.
Hymn: I Am the Way.
Hymn: Nevertheless, when the Son of Man cometh, shall he find faith on the earth? Luke 18:8.
Hymn: Waiting for Christ.

I Am the Bread of Life.
I Am the Light of the World.
I Am the Way.
Invitation, The ("There is no sound but thou dost hear my voice").
Laborer, The.
Message, The ("There is no voice but it is born of Me").
New Birth, The.
Praise.
Prayer, The ("Father! help them who walk in their own light").
Redeemed, The.
Return of the Savior, The.
Serpent, The.
Soldier of the Cross, The.
Son, The.
Son of Man, The.
Temptation, The.
Thou know'st not what thy Lord will say.
'Tis Finished.
Unto you is born a Saviour.
Weary and Heavy Laden, The.
Will, The.
Walcott.   Easter.
God Rest Ye Merry, Gentlemen.
Walker, A.   Abduction of Saints, The.
J, My Good Friend (Another Foolish Innocent).
Warren, R.   Lord Jesus, I Wonder.
Weiss, T.   Commonplace, A.
Wheatley, P.   Address to the Deist—1767, An.
Deism.
Whitman, W.   To Him That Was Crucified.
Whittier.   Chapel of the Hermits, The.
Child-Songs.
Crucifixion, The.
Dedication: "I would the gift I offer here."
Dole of Jarl Thorkell, The.
Easter Flower Gift, An.
Holy Land, The.
Meeting, The.
Our Master.
Over-Heart, The.
Palestine.
Woman, A.
Wilbur, R.   Matthew VIII, 28 ff.
Pelican, The.
Wilde, O.   Ave Maria Gratia Plena.
E Tenebris.
San Miniato.
Santa Decca.
Sonnet on the Massacre of the Christians in Bulgaria.
Williams, M.   It Came to Pass on a Planet Third from a Minor Sun in a Solar System.
One of the Crowd on the Shore Tells How It Was.
Think of Judas That He Did Love Jesus.
Vision and Prayer.
Williams, T.   Christus of Guadalajara, The.
Williams, W.   Gift, The.
Gothic Candor.
Wordsworth, W.   Fly, some kind Harbinger, to Grasmere-dale!
Inscription on a Rock at Rydal Mount.
Wright, J.   Saint Judas.
Yeats.   Conjunctions.
Stick of Incense, A.
Zagajewski.   Palm Sunday.

Jewelry

Baudelaire.   Jewels.
Browning, E.   King's Gift, The.
Bukowski.   Huge Ear Rings.
Carew, T.   Epitaph on the Lady S.: Wife of Sir W.S.
Cavafy.   For the Shop.
Cowper, W.   To a Lady ["Star that beams on Anna's breast, The"].
Dugan, A.   Gifts Accompaniment, A.
Graves, R.   Bracelet, A.
Song: Three Rings for Her.
With a Gift of Rings.
Herrick.   Bracelet of Pearle: To Silvia, The.
Carkanet, The.
Eare-rings.
Pomander Bracelet, The.

Seest thou those diamonds which she wears.
  To Julia.
Jacobsen, J. Things, The.
Komunyakaa. Woebegone.
Marvell. Bludius et Corona [Blood and the
  Crown].
Montale. Earrings, The.
  From the Train.
Sandburg, C. Thin Strips.
Schuyler, J. Fabergé.
See also **Rings**

Jigsaw Puzzles
Oppen. Solution.

Jitneys
Hughes, L. Jitney.

Joan of Arc
Glück, L. Jeanne d'Arc.
Jacobsen, J. Things, The.
Kumin, M. At a Private Showing in 1982.
MacNeice. Visit to Rouen.
Millay, E. To the Maid of Orleans.

Job (Bible)
Frost, R. Masque of Reason, A.
Lux. Job's Problems.
Pagis. Homily.
Robinson, E. Job the Rejected.
Weiss, T. House of Fire.
Wilner, E. Job's Wife, a Twentieth-Century
  Casting Script.

Jockeys
See **Horse Racing**

Jogging and Joggers
Stafford, W. Run before Dawn.
See also **Running and Runners**

Johannesburg, South Africa
Hughes, L. Johannesburg Mines.

"John Bull"
Byron, G. World Is a Bundle of Hay, The.

John of Austria
Chesterton. Lepanto.

John Paul II, Pope
Milosz, C. Ode for the Eightieth Birthday of
  Pope John Paul II.

John, Saint
Browning, R. Death in the Desert, A.
Emerson, R. Turtle in swamp.
Levertov. Woodcut, A.
Rexroth, K. Saint John.
Rossetti, C. "Beloved, let us love one another,"
  says St. John.
  St. John, Apostle.
Sandburg, C. Isle of Patmos.
Wilbur, R. John Chrysostom.
  Wedding Toast, A.

John the Baptist, Saint
Davie, D. Pacer in the Fresco, The. John the
  Baptist.
Logan, J. Homage to John the Baptist.
Mallarmé. Hérodiade.
Merrill, J. Salome.
Merton. Quickening of St. John the Baptist,
  The.
  St. John Baptist.
  St. John's Night.
Parker, D. Salome's Dancing-Lesson.
Paul the Deacon. Ut Queant.
Rossetti, C. Imitated From the Arpa Evangelica:
  Page 121.
Very. John.

"Johnny Appleseed"
See **Chapman, John ("Johnny Appleseed")**

Johnson, Lionel
Yeats. In Memory of Major Robert Gregory.

Johnson, Lyndon Baines
Paley, G. My Father at 85.
Stock, R. Shakespeare in Vietnam.
Wilbur, R. Miltonic Sonnet for Mr. Johnson on
  His Refusal of Peter Hurd's Official Portrait,
  A.

Johnson, Samuel
Cowper, W. Epitaph on Dr. Johnson.
Dunbar, P. Then and Now.
Laughlin, J. Temporary Poems.
Whalen, P. EAMD.

Wilbur, R. Epistemology.

Jokes
Broumas, O. Body and Soul.
Ciardi, J. Autobiography of a Comedian.
Laughlin, J. Hard to Translate.
Pinsky. Impossible to Tell.
Prunty. Baseball.
Riley, J. Dead Joke and the Funny Man, The.
  Thomas the Pretender.
  Thoughts on a Pore Joke.

Jonah (Bible)
Crane, H. After Jonah.
Jarrell, R. Jonah.
Nemerov. On a Text: Jonah IV, xi.
Pagis. Tidings.
Sexton. Making a Living.
Williams, M. Jonah on His Deathbed.
Wilner, E. Knowing the Enemy.

Jonathan (Bible)
Bradstreet, A. David's Lamentation for Saul
  and Jonathan.
Logan, J. Ah, so our first load of honey heavy
  Christmas trees.
  Far off the road on the left on a slight rolling
  hill.
  I did but taste a little of the honey with the.
  If the half moon stamp of a sacred hoof showed
  Cadmus.
  In my dream I know I see my father Saul a
  king.
  Monologues of the Son of Saul.

Jonson, Ben
Carew, T. To Ben Jonson.
Herrick. Another ["Thou had'st the wreath
  before, now take the Tree"].
  Bacchanalian Verse, A.
  His Prayer to Ben Jonson.
  Ode for Him [or Ben Jonson], An.
  Upon Ben Jo[h]nson.
  Upon M. Ben Jo[h]nson: Epigram.
Jonson, B. Humble Petition of Poor Ben to the
  Best of Monarchs, Masters, Men, King
  Charles, The.
Kizer, C. Not Writing Poems about Children.
Moore, M. No Better than a "Withered
  Daffodil."

Joplin, Janis
Hacker, M. Elegy: "Crying from exile, I."
Piercy. Burying Blues for Janis.
Schuyler, J. Janis Joplin's Dead: Long Live
  Pearl.
  Mike.

Joseph (Bible, *O.T.*)
Graves, R. Joseph and Mary.
Herbert, G. Joseph's Coat.
Nemerov. September, the First Day of School.
Pinkerton, H. On Rembrandt's Etching of
  Joseph Telling His Dream (1636).
Simic. Psalm: "Old ones to the side."

Joseph (Chief Joseph)
Warren, R. Chief Joseph of the Nez Perce.

Joseph, Saint
MacDiarmid, H. Harry Semen.

Journalism and Journalists
Ai. Interview with a Policeman.
  Journalist, The.
Donne. Mercurius Gallo-Belgicus.
Dubie. Confession.
Eliot, T. S. Airs of Palestine, No. 2.
  Ballade pour la grosse Lulu.
Heaney, S. I'm writing this just after an
  encounter.
  'Religion's never mentioned here,' of course.
  This morning from a dewy motorway.
Ignatow, D. Here I Am with Mike.
Jeffers, R. Be Angry at the Sun.
  Ordinary Newscaster, An.
Sandburg, C. Buttons.
  Press Is Peculiar, The.
Stafford, W. Holcomb, Kansas.
Williams, M. Journalist Buys a Pig Farm, The.
Williams, W. To a Dead Journalist.
Zukofsky, L. Michtam.
See also **Magazines; Newspapers**

Joy
Amichai [*or* Amikhai]. Eyn Gedi Preserve.
  Quiet Joy, A.
Beckett, S. Chaque jour envie.
Berryman. Heaven.
Bradstreet, A. As spring the winter doth
  succeed.
  On My Son's Return Out of England.
Brontë, E. Fair sinks the summer evening now.
  How golden bright from earth and heaven.
  How long will you remain? The midnight hour.
  Month after month, year after year.
  That wind, I used to hear it swelling.
  Through the hours of yesternight.
Browning, E. Christmas Gifts.
  Claim, The.
  Dance, The.
  Deserted Garden, The.
  Life.
  Love.
Browning, R. Now.
Burns, R. Seventh of November, The.
Byron, G. Spell Is Broke, the Charm Is Flown,
  The.
  Translation from Anacreon.
Campion, T. O what unhop't for sweet supply!
  So Tir'd Are All My Thoughts.
Campion, T. *et al.* If I hope, I pine, if I feare, I
  faint and die.
Carruth, H. Alive.
  November Jeans Song.
Cavafy. Addition.
  Good and Bad Weather.
  What Cannot Be.
Cavalcanti. Ballata: Concerning a Shepherd-
  maid.
Chuang Tzu. Perfect Joy.
Clough. In Stratis Viarum II.
Coleridge, S. Barberry-Tree, The.
Crashaw. Upon the birth of the Princesse
  Elizabeth.
Creeley. For W.C.W.
  Kids / Seoul.
Cummings, E. E. All stars are(and not one star
  only)love.
  Darling!because my blood can sing.
  Honour corruption villainy holiness.
  !Hope / faith! / !life / love!
  Humble one(gifted with / illimitable joy).
  If everything happens that can't be done.
  If(among / silent skies).
  Joyful your complete fearless and pure love.
  Love our so right.
  Might these be thrushes climbing through
  almost(do they).
  Open your heart: / i'll give you a treasure.
  Spring!may— / everywhere's here.
  Sweet spring is your.
  These(whom'etends / blue nothing).
  Though your sorrows not.
  Trees / were in(give).
  Until and i heard.
  When faces called flowers float out of the
  ground.
  Which is the very.
  You Shall Above All Things Be Glad and
  Young.
  Your homecoming will be my homecoming.
De la Mare. Disguise, The.
  Imp Within, The.
Dickey, J. In the Marble Quarry.
Dickinson, E. Bliss is the plaything of the child.
  Did life's penurious length.
  Did Our Best Moment last.
  Good times are always mutual.
  I Can Wade Grief.
  If all the griefs I am to have.
  In many and reportless places.
  Is Bliss then, such Abyss.
  Joy that has no stem nor core, The.
  Joy we most revere, The.
  No Rose, yet felt myself a'bloom.
  Oh, honey of an hour.
  One Joy of so much anguish.
  Rehearsal to Ourselves.
  So glad we are—a Stranger'd deem.

Sweet and soft as summer, Darlings.
There are Sweets of Pathos.
Thrill came slowly like a Boon for, The.
Who never wanted—maddest Joy.
With sorrow that the Joy is past.
Donne.　Ecstasy, The.
Dunbar, P.　Lesson, The.
Little Brown Baby.
Old Cabin, The.
To J. Q.
Duncan, R.　Years as Catches, The.
Eberhart, R.　Full of Joy Do Not Know; They
　Need Not, The.
Incidence of Flight.
My Brains Are Slipping in the Fields of Eros.
Oak, The.
Ode to Silence.
Poet, The.
Request.
To Kenya Tribesmen, the Turkana.
To the Mad Poets.
Emerson, R.　For joy & beauty planted it.
Intellect / Gravely broods apart on joy.
Oil & Wine, / Sparkling gems, & rich attire.
Water.
Written in Naples, March, 1833.
Ferlinghetti, L.　Voix Glauque.
Glück, L.　Nativity Poem.
Goethe.　Song: "Joyful / And woful."
Hafiz [or Hafez].　From the Persian of Hafiz.
Hardy, T.　First or Last.
Herrick.　Happinesse.
Pain[e] Ends in Pleasure.
Teares.
To Youth.
Upon Hanch a Schoolmaster.
Hopkins, G.　Hurrahing in Harvest.
Hughes, L.　Joy.
Jarrell, R.　Perfect Love Casteth Out Everything.
Jeffers, R.　Joy.
Jonson, B.　To Sir Henry Cary.
Keats.　Fancy.
Imitation of Spenser.
Song: "Spirit here that reignest!"
Welcome Joy, and Welcome Sorrow.
Kunitz, S.　First Love.
Larkin, P.　Many Famous Feet Have Trod.
Lawrence, D. H.　Autumn Sunshine.
Goodnight.
Kissing and Horrid Strife.
Many Mansions.
No Joy in Life.
Other Women Have Reared in Me.
She Looks Back.
Levertov.　Ache of Marriage, The.
Joy.
Matins.
Maritain.　Restoration of the Pictures, The.
McGrath, T.　Praises.
Meredith, G.　Beyond the meadow still where
　sweeps.
Dear Heaven! for this sweet pledge of life.
First-Born, The.
In the Woods.
She marries the knight she loves.
Sing aloud that she is mine.
Song: "Under boughs of breathing May."
Song in the Songless.
Sorrows and Joys.
Sweet o' the Year, The.
To a Skylark.
To Robin Redbreast.
When my little son leaps in my sight.
Years Had Worn Their Season's Belt, The.
Merwin.　Man with One Leaf in October Night.
Words.
Milosz, C.　Large finger-like leaves of an
　Hawaiian fern.
Meadow, A.
Milton.　L'Allegro.
To the Lord General Cromwell.
Mistral, G.　Lady Spring.
O'Hara, F.　Poem: "Khrushchev is coming on
　the right day!"
Oliver, M.　Blossom.
Humpbacks.

Olson, C.　All things stand out against the sky.
Day Song.
Only the Red Fox, Only the Crow.
Paley, G.　Middle-Age Poem.
Patchen.　Pathway, The.
Raine, K.　I could have told much by the way.
When I woke up to the snow.
Rilke.　Blank Joy.
Survival.
Roethke.　All the Earth, All the Air.
Moment, The.
Rossetti, C.　And There Was No More Sea.
Birthday, A.
De Profundis.
Easter Carol, An.
Easter Day.
Easter Even.
From early dawn until the flush of noon.
Hope and Joy.
Joy is but sorrow, / While we know.
Love and Hope.
Love Defended.
Methinks the ills of life I fain would shun.
Minnie bakes oaten cakes, / Minnie brews ale.
Praise of Love.
Present and Future.
Rose, The.
Seeking Rest.
Serenade.
Song: "We buried her among the flowers."
Sonnet: "Some say that love and joy are one:
　and so."
Then I Commended Mirth.
Unforgotten.
Valentine, 1877, A.
What will it be, O my soul, what will it be.
When My Heart Is Vexed I Will Complain.
Will you be there? my yearning heart has cried.
Rukeyser, M.　Ballad Theme, A.
Flying Red Horse, The.
Gift-Poem.
Make and be eaten, the poet says.
Reading Time : 1 Minute 26 Seconds.
Tenth Elegy. Elegy in Joy.
When the true things meet us at the place we
　reach, they are all.
Rumi.　I'm Not Saying This Right.
Joy at Sudden Disappointment.
We Three.
Sandburg, C.　Joy.
Sexton.　Welcome Morning.
Smith, S.　Word, The.
Spenser, E.　Epithalamion: "Ye learned sisters
　which have oftentimes."
Prothalamion.
Swift, J.　Satirical Elegy on the Death of a Late
　Famous General, A.
Sze.　Frost.
Updike.　Burning Trash.
Van Duyn.　Goya's "Two Old People Eating
　Soup."
Very.　Joy ("Joy Thou giv'st no man can take
　away, The").
Vogl.　Love of the Woods.
Warren, R.　Was It One of the Long Hunters of
　Kentucky Who Discovered Boone at Sunset?
Whitman, W.　I Saw in Louisiana a Live-Oak
　Growing.
Song of Joys, A.
Warble for Lilac-Time.
We Two, How Long We Were Fool'd.
Whittier.　Christmas Carmen, A.
June on the Merrimac.
Wilbur, R.　For Ellen.
Hamlen Brook.
Williams, C. K.　Acids.
Williams, W.　Martin and Katherine.
Wordsworth, W.　Along the mazes of this song I
　go.
I Wandered Lonely as a Cloud.
Wright, J.　Blessing, A.
Zagajewski.　Early Hours, The.
Zaturenska.　O like a Young Tree.
Spring Morning.
Zukofsky, L.　My nephew / And my new.
Perch Less.

Joyce, James
Borges.　Invocation to Joyce.
James Joyce.
Jacobsen, J.　Gentle Reader.
Kunitz, S.　Class Will Come to Order, The.
Logan, J.　Dublin Suite: Homage to James
　Joyce.
Walcott.　Volcano.
Judaism and Jews
Amichai [or Amikhai].　Aged Parents, The.
All the Generations before Me.
Almost a Love Poem.
And in spite of all that, I must.
Arab Shepherd Seeks a Kid on Mount Zion, A.
Beautiful Are the Families of Jerusalem.
Bedouin in Love.
Biblical Meditations.
Blood that stands the member erect, The.
Bull Returns, The.
City where I was born was destroyed by
　cannons, The.
Course of a Life, The.
End of Elul.
Eve of Rosh Hashanah, The.
Even my loves are measured by the wars.
Gods Come and Go, Prayers Remain Forever.
Hymn for Independence Day, A. So distant.
Hymn to a Masseuse.
Hymn to the Lovely Couple Varda and
　Schimmel.
I am the figure of a Jewish father with a sack on
　his back, returning.
I Feel Just Fine in My Pants.
I have nothing to say about the war.
I left the Evening Land by the will of the night.
Ibn Gabirol.
In the Old City.
In the summer, nations come to one another.
Indian Summer in Princeton.
Jerusalem, 1967.
Jerusalem Ecology.
Jerusalem Is Full of Used Jews.
Jerusalem's Suicide Attempts.
Jews, The.
Jews in the Land of Israel.
Karl Marx, cold mark that you are.
Kibbutz Gvar-'Am.
Let Memory Mountain remember instead of me.
Luxury.
Man crossing the field was a Chief Rabbi, The.
My Father on Passover Eve.
My First Days in New York.
My Mother Died on Shavuot.
My Mother's Death and the Lost Battles for the
　Future of Her Children.
National Thoughts.
New homeland was built, The.
North of Beersheba.
On the Day I Left.
On the lot that was a short-cut for lovers.
Place Where I Never Was, The.
Rabbi Nakhman of Bratslav.
Real Hero of the Sacrifice of Isaac, The.
Sharm A-Sheikh.
Sleep in Jerusalem.
Sometimes I think of my fathers.
Song of Lies on Sabbath Eve, A.
State of Affairs.
Straight from Prejudice.
Synagogue in Firenze, The.
There Are Candles That Remember.
To a Convert.
Tourist.
Travels of the Last Benjamin of Tudela.
War broke out in autumn, in the no-man's land.
What was the message of the burned man?
"Where was he wounded?" You don't know.
Yehuda Ha-Levi.
You Must Not Show Weakness.
Bachmann.　Maryam.
Browning, R.　Holy-Cross Day.
Cavafy.　Of the Jews (50 A.D.).
Celan.　Benedicta.
Black Flakes.
Deathfugue.
Frankfurt, September.

Heat / counts us together, The.
In Egypt.
In Prague.
It's all different from what you think, from what I think.
Just Think.
Mandorla.
Rogues' and Gonifs' Ditty, A.
Shibboleth.
Shofar place, The.
Sluice, The.
Song in the Wilderness, A.
Stretto.
Tabernacle Window.
There stood / a splinter of fig on your lip.
Voices, nicked into.
Zurich, at the Stork.
Chesterton. Before a Statue of Cromwell.
Clampitt. Letters from Jerusalem.
Seder Night.
Davie, D. Pilate.
De la Mare. Bitter Waters.
Owl, The.
Eliot, T. S. Burbank with a Baedeker: Bleistein with a Cigar.
Emerson, R. William Rufus and the Jew.
García Lorca. Jewish Cemetery.
Ginsberg, A. Jaweh and Allah Battle.
Yiddishe Kopf.
Glück, L. Parable, A.
Hacker, M. Days of 1944: Three Friends.
Graffiti from the Gare Saint-Manqué.
Inheritances.
Hayden, R. Rabbi, The.
Herbert, G. Jews, The.
Self-Condemnation.
Herrick. North and South.
Observation.
Hughes, L. America.
Likewise.
Jarrell, R. Jews at Haifa.
Lament of the Children of Israel in Rome.
Kinnell. Avenue Bearing the Initial of Christ into the New World, The.
Korn. Keep Hidden from Me.
Kumin, M. Chain, The.
In the Absence of Bliss.
Living Alone with Jesus.
Young Nun at Bread Loaf.
Levertov. Wings in the Pedlar's Pack.
Levi, P. Gedale's Song.
Ostjuden.
Passover.
Levine, P. Jewish Graveyards, Italy.
Longfellow, H. Jewish Cemetery at Newport, The.
Maritain. Chagall.
Montale. To Liuba, Leaving.
Nemerov. Debate with the Rabbi.
Memory of My Friend, A.
To the Babylonians.
Niedecker. New! / Reason explodes. Atomic split.
Oppen. Of Hours.
Semite.
To Find a Way.
Pagis. Bridgehead Photograph.
Paley, G. Letter.
Song Stanzas of Private Luck; To Be Added Sometimes and Sometimes to Be Subtracted.
Street Corner Dialogue.
Warning, A.
Patchen. To the Jewish People.
Pinsky. Avenue.
Ice-Storm, The.
Impossible to Tell.
In Berkeley.
Night Game, The.
Poem about People.
Poem with Refrains.
Rhyme of Reb Nachman, The.
Song of Reasons.
Visions of Daniel.
Plath. Daddy.
Rich, A. At the Jewish New Year.
Sources.

Yom Kippur 1984.
Riley, J. Wandering Jew, The.
Robinson, E. Wandering Jew, The.
Rossetti, C. Christian and Jew. A Dialogue.
Rukeyser, M. Akiba.
Christmas Eve.
Despisals.
Writer, The.
Seifert. Lost Paradise.
Sexton. My Friend, My Friend.
Uses.
Shapiro, K. Alphabet, The.
Israel.
Messias.
Olive Tree, The.
Synagogue, The.
Shelley, P. Wandering Jew's Soliloquy, The.
Smith, S. Jew Is Angry with His Friend Who Does Not Believe in Circumcision, A.
Songe d'Athalie.
Stock, R. Miracle of the Roses, The.
Szymborska, W. Still.
Tomlinson, C. Byzantium.
Williams, C. K. Spit.
Wilner, E. Miriam's Song.
On Ethnic Definitions.
When Asked to Lie Down on the Altar.
Wordsworth, W. Jewish Family (in a Small Valley Opposite St Goar, upon the Rhine), A.
Zagajewski. Good Friday in the Tunnels of the Métro.
Life Sentence.
Name Edmund, The.
Zukofsky, L. Song for the Year's End, A.

Judas Iscariot
Cullen, C. Judas Iscariot.
De la Mare. Ballad of Christmas, A.
Herrick. Beginnings and Endings.
Jeffers, R. Dear Judas.
Sandburg, C. Guaranteed Antique.
Sexton. Legend of the One-Eyed Man, The.
Swift, J. Judas.
Williams, M. Think of Judas That He Did Love Jesus.
Wright, J. Saint Judas.

Judges
Bierce. Error, An.
Growler, A.
Judex Judicatus.
To a Censor.
Davie, D. Pilate.
Dunbar, P. To Mary Church Terrell.
Hughes, L. Ballad of Gin Mary.
Judge William Hastie.
Jonson, B. Another to Him.
Epigram on Sir Edward Coke, when He Was Lord Chief Justice of England, An.
Epigram. To Thomas Lo[rd] Ellsmere, the Last Term He Sat Chancellor, An.
Kipling, R. Gallio's Song.
Gehazi.
Levi, P. On Trial.
Major, C. Dispute, The.
Merwin. Bread at Midnight.
Pinkerton, H. On the Southworth and Hawes Daguerreotype of Massachusetts Supreme Court Chief Justice Lemuel Shaw (1851).
Riley, J. Case in P'int, A.
To the Judge.
Rumi. Witness, the Darling, The.
Sandburg, C. Killers.
Simic. Summons, The.
Spender, S. Van der Lubbe.
Swift, J. Verses on the Upright Judge.
Updike. Mr. High-Mind.
Whittier. Prophecy of Samuel Sewall, The.
Williams, W. To a Friend.
Zagajewski. Trial, The.
Zukofsky, L. Judge and the Bird, The.

Judgment
Beckett, S. Somme toute / tout compte fait.
Berry, W. Do Not Be Ashamed.
Borges. Nightmare.
Byron, G. Queries to Casuists.
Carew, T. To the Reader of Master William Davenant's Play [*The Wits*].

Cavalcanti. Check out the humpback, Manny.
Chuang Tzu. Great Knowledge.
Clough. Thesis and Antithesis.
Cowper, W. Judgment of the Poets, The.
Lines Written during a Period of Insanity.
Crane, S. In Heaven, / Some little blades of grass.
Davie, D. Levity.
Saw I Never the Righteous Forsaken.
Three Beyond.
Witness.
Dickinson, E. Judgment is justest.
This Is My Letter to the World.
Emerson, R. For that a man is a mark.
Prudence.
Graves, R. Any Honest Housewife.
Myrrhina.
Han shan. As long as I stay in the village.
HaNagid. Assistants Come to Judgment In Groups.
If You Shame a Man.
If You're Finding the Good at Fault.
Is There Any Frustration.
It's Heart That Discerns.
Heaney, S. Haw Lantern, The.
Stone Verdict, The.
Herrick. To a Disdaynefull Fayre.
To Sir George Parrie, Doctor of the Civill Law.
Hill, G. Psalms of Assize.
Ritornelli.
Hughes, T. Flayed Crow in the Hall of Judgement, A.
Jackson, L. Judgment, The.
Jarrell, R. Variations.
Jonson, B. To the Worthy Author M[r] John Fletcher.
Kipling, R. Tomlinson.
Kizer, C. Long Line of Doctors, A.
Laughlin, J. Judges of the Secret Court, The.
Lawrence, D. H. Loggerheads.
Meredith, G. World's Advance, The.
Meredith, W. Vision of Good Secrets, A.
Merton. Dirge for the Proud World.
Reduced to This.
Milosz, C. Initiation.
Parker, D. Roundel: "She's passing fair; but so demure is she."
Petrarch. With my long-honoured, dear, and cruel lord.
Piercy. Thrifty Lover, The.
Ransom, J. Armageddon.
Hilda.
Moments of Minnie.
Rilke. Judgments.
Ritsos. Double Condemnation.
Unacceptable Man, The.
Rossetti, C. Sooner or later: yet at last / The Jordan must be past.
Rukeyser, M. Facing Sentencing.
Rumi. Solomon's Crooked Crown.
Simic. Cold, The.
Summons, The.
Smith, S. Death-Bed of a Financier.
Do Not!
Spender, S. Van der Lubbe.
Stafford, W. In the Book.
Judgments.
Tate, J. My Great Great Etc. Uncle Patrick Henry.
Walker, A. Judge Every One with Perfect Calm.
Whittier. By Their Works.
Williams, M. Serial Murderer Says Something to the Priest, The.
Wilner, E. Judgment.
Wright, J. At the Executed Murderer's Grave.
Logbook of Judgments.
Zaturenska. Listening Landscape, The.

Judgment Day
Baudelaire. Ransom, The.
Borges. Of Heaven and Hell.
Byron, G. Vision of Judgment, The.
Clough. What we, when face to face we see.
Coleridge, S. For a Market-Clock.
Cummings, E. E. Chérie / the very,picturesque,last Day.
Davie, D. On the Final Day.

De la Mare. Hawthorn Hath a Deathly Smell, The.
Dickey, W. Ezekiel's Rabbit.
Dickinson, E. Departed—to the Judgment.
Not what We did, shall be the test.
'Twas a long Parting—but the time.
Enzensberger, H. Keeping Cool.
HaNagid. Among My Friends.
Herbert, G. Death.
Doomsday.
Judgement.
Herrick. Comforts in Contentions.
Gods Providence.
Judgement Day, The.
Judgment-Day, The.
Upon Himselfe Being Buried.
Hill, G. Requiem for the Plantagenet Kings.
Hughes, L. Sunday Morning Prophecy.
Jarrell, R. Bamberg.
Sears Roebuck.
Kipling, R. Last Chantey, The.
MacDiarmid, H. Crowdieknowe.
Rumi. On Resurrection Day.
Simic. Psalm: "Old ones to the side."
Swift, J. Day of Judgement, The.
Thomas of Celano. Dies Irae.
Thoreau. Deeds of king and meanest hedger, The.
'T will soon appear if we but look.
Tomlinson, C. Last Judgement.
Unknown. Dies Irae (The Day of Wrath).
Very. Flood, The.
Repent for the kingdom of Heaven is at hand.
Whittier. Abraham Davenport.
Wilde, O. Sonnet on Hearing the *Dies Irae* Sung in the Sistine Chapel.
Yeats. Crazy Jane on the Day of Judgment.
Second Coming, The.
See also **Apocalypse; End of the World**
Judith (Apocrypha)
Ransom, J. Judith of Bethulia.
Juggling and Jugglers
Carver, R. Juggler at *Heaven's Gate,* The.
Ignatow, D. Juggler, The.
Major, C. Revelation at Cap Ferrat.
Meredith, G. Juggling Jerry.
Merwin. Initiate, The.
Wilbur, R. Juggler.
Williams, T. Dark Arm, Hanging over the Edge of Infinity.
Julian the Apostate
Cavafy. In the Districts Surrounding Antioch.
Julian and the Antiochians.
Julian at the Mysteries.
Julian in Nicomedia.
Julian, Seeing Contempt.
You Didn't Understand.
Julius Caesar
See **Caesar, Julius**
July
Bogan, L. July Dawn.
Eberhart, R. Coast of Maine.
Summer Landscape.
Swallows Return, The.
Tree Swallows.
Vision through Timothy.
Heaney, S. July.
Kumin, M. July, against Hunger.
Orr, G. Virginia Backyard: July.
Wilbur, R. My Father Paints the Summer.
Jumping
Carrera Andrade. Notes of a Parachute Jumper.
Creeley. Seventeenth Floor: Echoes of Singapore.
Jacobsen, J. You Can Take It with You.
Smith, S. Cousin, The.
Harold's Leap.
Tate, J. Leaping Woman.
June
Burns, R. Red, Red Rose, A.
Cowper, W. Judgment of the Poets, The.
Dickinson, E. I'm sorry for the Dead—Today.
Eberhart, R. Project, The.
Emerson, R. Low December vault in June be up-lifted high.

She walked in flowers around my field.
Glück, L. Solstice.
Gunn, T. June.
Kipling, R. Two Months.
Larkin, P. Cut Grass.
Lawrence, D. H. Andraitx—Pomegranate Flowers.
MacNeice. June Thunder.
Meredith, W. June: Dutch Harbor.
Nash, O. Here Usually Comes the Bride.
Niedecker. Hi, Hot-and-Humid.
Riley, J. In the Heart of June.
June.
Knee-deep in June.
When June Is Here.
Sandburg, C. Crabapple Blossoms.
Garden Wireless.
June.
Schuyler, J. I Think.
June.
Sexton. June Bug.
Sze. June Ghazal.
Tennyson, A. June Bracken and Heather.
Wilbur, R. June Light.
Wright, C. Reading Rorty and Paul Celan One Morning in Early June.
Jungles
Carrera Andrade. Cocoa Tree.
Eberhart, R. Recollection of Childhood.
Hughes, L. Poem: "All the tom-toms of the jungles beat in my blood."
Lindsay, N. Parvenu.
Nemerov. Two Poems.
Neruda. Some Beasts.
Oppen. Coastal Strip.
Rukeyser, M. Poem: "Green going through the jungle of those years."
Smith, S. Jungle Husband, The.
Williams, W. Jungle, The.
Juniper Trees
Heaney, S. Sloe Gin.
Stafford, W. Through the Junipers.
Sze. Juniper Fires.
Junk and Junkyards
Bukowski. Big John of Echo Park.
Carruth, H. Johnny Spain's White Heifer.
Clampitt. Salvage.
Dickey, J. Cherrylog Road.
Kunitz, S. Chariot.
Levine, P. Walk with Tom Jefferson, A.
Prunty. Crows, The.
Rukeyser, M. Junk-Heap at Murano.
Swenson, M. Scroppo's Dog.
Szymborska, W. Man's Household, A.
Tomlinson, C. Mirror in the Roadway, The.
Warren, R. Dream, Dump-Heap, and Civilization.
Wilbur, R. Junk.
Jupiter (god)
Emerson, R. When wrath & terror changed Jove's regal port.
Ralegh, S. Arcadians the earth inhabited, The.
Jupiter (planet)
Swenson, M. Seeing Jupiter.
Updike. Moons of Jupiter, The.
Very. Jupiter as the Evening Star.
Justice
Bierce. Law.
To a Bully.
Borges. Just, The.
Broumas, O. Stars in Your Name.
Browning, R. Instans Tyrannus.
Burns, R. Holy Willie's Prayer.
Campion, T. Ad Tho. Munsonium, equitem Auratum et Baronetum.
Carew, T. Upon My Lord Chief Justice's Election of My Lady Anne Wentworth [*or* A.W.] for His Mistress.
Cavafy. Athena's Vote.
Chuang Tzu. Advising the Prince.
Coleridge, S. Good Great Man, The.
Crane, S. Trees in the garden rained flowers, The.
Crashaw. Upon the Death of the Most Desired Mister Herrys.

Cummings, E. E. "Nothing" the unjust man complained.
De la Mare. In the Dock.
Dugan, A. Defendant.
Dunbar, P. Justice.
To Miss Mary Britton.
Eberhart, R. Vastness and Indifference of the World, The.
Emerson, R. Astraea.
Enzensberger, H. Cold Comfort.
Frost, R. Masque of Mercy, A.
Guyon. Divine Justice Amiable.
Hall, D. Small Fig Tree, A.
HaNagid. Truth Is Hard.
Herbert, G. Justice (2).
Herrick. God Sparing in Scourging.
Good, and Bad.
Like Pattern, Like People.
Mercy and Love.
Rapine Brings Ruine.
Smart.
To God.
Hill, G. Cowan Bridge; At the Site of 'Lowood School.'
Sobieski's Shield.
Song Contest.
Hughes, L. Justice.
Jeffers, R. Tower beyond Tragedy, The.
Jonson, B. On Lieutenant Shift.
Kinsella, T. Another September.
Kipling, R. Gallio's Song.
Gehazi.
Justice.
Lawrence, D. H. Deepest Sensuality, The.
Demon Justice.
Lies.
Vibration of Justice.
When Wilt Thou Teach the People?
Levertov. Beginners.
Levi, P. Shemà.
Lux. Tarantulas on the Lifebuoy.
MacDiarmid, H. Focherty.
Meredith, G. Blest is the sword that leaps from sheath.
Merton. Atlas and the Fatman.
Merwin. Bread at Midnight.
Moths, The.
Students of Justice, The.
Tool.
O'Hara, F. Ode: "Idea of justice may be precious, An."
Petrarch. Foul Babylon has overstepped the mark.
Plath. Dialogue between Ghost and Priest.
Ritsos. Unjust, The.
Sandburg, C. Implications.
Very. Just, The.
Warren, R. News Photo.
Whitman, W. Thought.
Whittier. Cities of the Plain, The.
Mithridates at Chios.
Slave-Ships, The.
To the Reformers of England.
Wilbur, R. Water Walker.
Williams, M. In Extremis in *Hardy, Arkansas.*
Williams, W. Early Martyr, An.
Impromptu: The Suckers.
Wilner, E. Judgment.
Wordsworth, W. Feelings of a French Royalist, on the Disinterment of the Remains of the Duke D'Enghien.
Humanity.
What if our numbers barely could defy.
See also **Injustice**
Justification
Bukowski. Darlings.
Emerson, R. Compensation.
Ferlinghetti, L. What could she say to the fantastic foolybear.
Laughlin, J. This One Rhymes.
Rich, A. Women.
Juvenile Delinquency
Brooks, G. We Real Cool.
Hughes, L. Delinquent.
McHugh, H. Amenities, The.
Riley, J. Preacher's Boy, The.

When Uncle Doc Was Young.

K

Kabbala
Borges.　Golem, The.
See also **Cabala**
Kabul, Afghanistan
Kipling, R.　Ford o' Kabul River.
Kafka, Franz
Carver, R.　Kafka's Watch.
　Moon, the Train, The.
Celan.　Frankfurt, September.
Clampitt.　Sed de Correr.
Dugan, A.　Tribute to Kafka for Someone
　Taken.
Laughlin, J.　Judges of the Secret Court, The.
Kahlo, Frida
Dubie.　Trolley from Xochimilco, The.
Kakinomoto no Hitomaro
See **Hitomaro (Kakinomoto no Hitomaro)**
Kalamazoo, Michigan
Lindsay, N.　Kalamazoo.
Sandburg, C.　Sins of Kalamazoo, The.
Kangaroos
Kumin, M.　Nurture.
Lawrence, D. H.　Kangaroo.
Nash, O.　Kangaroo, The.
Kansas City, Kansas and Missouri
Dickey, W.　Elegy before the Time.
Kansas (state)
Ai.　Hangman.
Clampitt.　Iola, Kansas.
Ferlinghetti, L.　Astonished Heart, The.
Ginsberg, A.　Kansas! Kansas! Shuddering at
　last!
　Wichita Vortex Sutra.
Gunn, T.　Small Plane in Kansas.
Lindsay, N.　Kansas.
　Santa-Fé Trail (A Humoresque), The.
Merwin.　Trail into Kansas, The.
Sandburg, C.　Flat Waters of the West in Kansas.
　Mockers Go to Kansas in Spring.
Stafford, W.　Across Kansas.
　At Fourth and Main in Liberal, Kansas, 1932.
　Ceremony.
　Holcomb, Kansas.
　Rescued Year, The.
　Stories from Kansas.
Warren, R.　Trips to California.
Whittier.　Burial of Barber.
　Kansas Emigrants, The.
　Le Marais du Cygne.
　Letter from a Missionary of the Methodist
　　Episcopal Church South, in Kansas, to a
　　Distiguished Politician.
Wilbur, R.　Piccola Commedia.
Karaoke
Sze.　Whiteout.
Katydids
Dunbar, P.　Whip-Poor-Will and Katy-Did.
Riley, J.　Katydids, The.
　Summer-Time and Winter-Time.
Wright, J.　Katy Did.
Kawabata, Yasunari
Ai.　Talking to His Reflection in a Shallow
　Pond.
Kayaks
Sze.　Kayaking at Night on Tomales Bay.
Keats, John
Byron, G.　Who Kill'd John Keats?
Ciardi, J.　Trenta-Sei of the Pleasure We Take in
　the Early Death of Keats, A.
Clampitt.　Chichester.
　Elgin Marbles, The.
　He Dreams of Being Warm.
　Isle of Wight, The.
　Margate.
　Teignmouth.
　Voyages.
　Winchester: The Autumn Equinox.
Cullen, C.　To John Keats, Poet, at Springtime.
Cummings, E. E.　Fame Speaks.

Davie, D.　Two Widows in Tashkent.
Gunn, T.　Keats at Highgate.
Hardy, T.　At a House in Hampstead.
　At Lulworth Cove a Century Back.
　Rome: At the Pyramid of Cestius near the
　　Graves of Shelley and Keats.
Keats.　Song about Myself, A.
Kinnell.　Oatmeal.
Levertov.　Memories of John Keats.
Logan, J.　On the Death of Keats; Lines for
　Those Who Drown Twice.
Lux.　"Mr John Keats Five Feet Tall" Sails
　Away.
Meredith, G.　Poetry of Keats, The.
Merton.　Philosophers, The.
Olson, C.　I'm with You.
Owen, W.　To My Friend (With an Identity
　Disc).
Rossetti, C.　On Keats, 18 January, 1948 (Eve of
　St Agnes).
Rukeyser, M.　From a Play: Publisher's Song.
　Homage to Literature.
Shelley, P.　Adonais; An Elegy on the Death of
　John Keats.
Wilde, O.　Grave of Keats, The.
　Sonnet on the Sale by Auction of Keats' Love
　Letters.
Keller, Helen
Cullen, C.　For Helen Keller.
Davie, D.　To Helen Keller.
Hughes, L.　Helen Keller.
Kennedy, John Fitzgerald
Ai.　Two Brothers.
Ammons.　Belief.
Berryman.　Formal Elegy.
Bly, R.　Kennedy's Inauguration.
Ferlinghetti, L.　Assassination Raga.
Frost, R.　For John F. Kennedy; His
　Inauguration.
Kinsella, T.　Good Fight, The.
Olson, C.　Hustings, The.
Oppen.　11/22/63.
　Armies of the Plain.
Kennedy, Robert Francis
Ai.　Two Brothers.
Ferlinghetti, L.　Assassination Raga.
Lowell, R.　For Robert Kennedy Nineteen
　Twenty-Five to Sixty-Eight.
Kennedy, Ted (Edward Moore Kennedy)
Ai.　Go.
Kent, England
Davie, D.　Kent.
Kentucky
Dunbar, P.　After a Visit.
Kumin, M.　Living Alone with Jesus.
Sandburg, C.　Knucks.
Sarton, M.　Night Watch.
Tate, A.　Swimmers, The.
Warren, R.　American Portrait: Old Style.
　Croesus in Autumn.
　Kentucky Mountain Farm.
　Old-Time Childhood in Kentucky.
　Was It One of the Long Hunters of Kentucky
　　Who Discovered Boone at Sunset?
Williams, W.　To Elsie.
Kerouac, Jack
Berrigan, T.　Pandora's Box, an Ode.
Ferlinghetti, L.　Canticle of Jack Kerouac, The.
　Late Impressionist Dream.
Ginsberg, A.　Memory Gardens.
　Sunflower Sutra.
　Sweet Levinsky.
Kesey, Ken
Ginsberg, A.　First Party at Ken Kesey's with
　Hell's Angels.
Kettles
Gurney, I.　Kettle Song.
Key West, Florida
Bishop, E.　Norther—Key West, A.
　Sunday at Key West.
Ciardi, J.　Christmas Alone in Key West.
　January 2, 1978.
Crane, H.　Key West.
Eberhart, R.　Key West.
Meredith, W.　Here and There.

Olson, C.　Key West.
Stevens, W.　Farewell to Florida.
　Idea of Order at Key West, The.
　Two Figures in Dense Violet Night.
Keys
Bishop, E.　One Art.
De la Mare.　Keys of Morning, The.
Merwin.　Apples.
　To the Hand.
Ritsos.　Esteem.
Kidnapping and Kidnappers
Dove, R.　Abduction, The.
Dubie.　On the Chinese Abduction of Tibet's
　Child Panchen Lama.
Mistral, G.　Song of the Dead Girls.
Ritsos.　Hues of a Cloud.
　Laugh, The.
　Real Hands.
Smith, S.　What Is the Time?; or, St. Hugh of
　Lincoln.
Kierkegaard, Søren
Dubie.　Elegies for the Ocher Deer on the Walls
　at Lascaux.
Zagajewski.　Kierkegaard on Hegel.
Kieslowski, Krzysztof
Zagajewski.　Morning in Vicenza, A.
Killing and Killers
Ai.　Jack Ruby on Ice.
Berry, W.　Bird Killer, The.
　For the Hog Killing.
Blue Cloud.　For a Dog-killed Doe.
　For Ace.
Borges.　Dagger, The.
Ciardi, J.　Baboon and the State, The.
Cowper, W.　On a Spaniel Called Beau Killing a
　Young Bird.
Crane, S.　Man feared that he might find an
　assassin, A.
　Youth in apparel that glittered, A.
Creeley.　Here ("Since I can't").
Eberhart, R.　Airman Considers His Power, An.
　Assassin, The.
　Fisher Cat, The.
　Killer, The.
　Vastness and Indifference of the World, The.
　Villanelle: "Christ is walking in your blood
　today."
　Winter Kill.
García Lorca.　Death of Little Tony Camborio,
　The.
　Feud, The.
Hall, D.　Body Politic, The.
　Kill, The.
Hayden, R.　Killing the Calves.
Heaney, S.　Triptych.
Hughes, L.　Ballad of the Killer Boy.
　Comment.
　Death in Yorkville.
Hughes, T.　Crow Tyrannosaurus.
　Esther's Tomcat.
　Hawk Roosting.
　Kreutzer Sonata.
　Tiger-Psalm.
Ignatow, D.　From the Beginning.
　Ritual One.
Jarrell, R.　Essay on the Human Will, An.
Jeffers, R.　To Kill in War Is Not Murder.
Kinnell.　Dead Shall Be Raised Incorruptible,
　The.
Kunitz, S.　Foreign Affairs.
　Gladiators, The.
Laughlin, J.　Busy Day.
MacNeice.　Grey Ones, The.
Mahon.　As It Should Be.
Merton.　Lament for Javier Heraud.
Milosz, C.　Ball, A.
Mistral, G.　Other, The.
Niedecker.　Du Bay.
Owen, W.　Strange Meeting.
Patchen.　Battle of Unameit, The.
　Destruction of Carthage, The.
　Have You Killed Your Man for Today?
　Meben.
　O Howling Cells.
　Quantity of Mercy, The.

Under the green ledge.
Ralegh, S.   Even they that have no murdrous will.
Ritsos.   Afternoon.
Sandburg, C.   Black Horizons.
   Hate.
   Hoodlums.
Seifert.   Sometimes we are tied down by memories.
Stafford, W.   Holcomb, Kansas.
   My Mother Was a Soldier.
Tomlinson, C.   Assassin.
Warren, R.   News Photo.
Williams, C. K.   How Humble We Were before This.
   Nut, The.
Williams, M.   Fred.
   Green Mansions.
   Missing Persons.
   Voice of America.

Kimonos
Merrill, J.   Kimono, The.
Wilner, E.   Private Space, A.

Kindness
Bourne, V.   Reciprocal Kindness the Primary Law of Nature.
Browning, E.   Island, An.
Chaucer.   Gentilesse.
Coleridge, S.   Charity in Thought.
   Pang More Sharp Than All, The.
Creeley.   Thank You.
Cullen, C.   Tribute.
Davie, D.   Master & Man.
Dickinson, E.   Had I a pleasure you had not.
   To do a magnanimous thing.
Dunbar, P.   My Sort o' Man.
   Plea, A.
Ginsberg, A.   Who Be Kind To.
Glück, L.   Gratitude.
Graves, R.   Apples and Water.
Han-shan.   If others are worthy accept them.
Hopkins, G.   Brothers.
Lawrence, D. H.   All I Ask.
   English Are So Nice!, The.
Levertov.   Kindness.
   Place of Kindness, A.
Meredith, G.   To Children.
Meredith, W.   Dalhousie Farm.
   Of Kindness.
Millay, E.   To Those without Pity.
Plath.   Kindness.
Riley, J.   Little Lame Boy's Views, A.
   What Redress.
Rossetti, C.   Behold, I stand at the door and knock.
   Night and Death.
   Rose, The.
Spender, S.   Acts Passed Beyond.
Stafford, W.   Aunt Mabel.
Thoreau.   True kindness is a pure divine affinity.
Very.   Kind Words.
Whittier.   Hill-Top, The.
Williams, W.   Raper from Passenack, The.
Wright, J.   Sappho.

King Kong
Cooper, J.   Seventeen Questions about KING KONG.

King Lear
Clampitt.   Margate.
Howe, S.   God's Spies.
   WHITE FOOLSCAP / Book of Cordelia.
Keats.   On Sitting Down to Read "King Lear" Once Again.
Laughlin, J.   Cordelia.
Williams, T.   Old Men Go Mad at Night.
Williams, W.   Lear.

King, Martin Luther, Jr
Lorde.   Rites of Passage.
Lowell, R.   Two Walls.
Merton.   April 4th 1968.
Rukeyser, M.   Martin Luther King, Malcolm X.
Sarton, M.   Easter, 1968.
Walker, A.   Abduction of Saints, The.
   Killers.

King, William, Archbishop of Dublin
Swift, J.   Excellent New Song upon His Grace Our Good Lord Archbishop of Dublin, An.

Kingfishers
Berry, W.   Before Dark.
Clampitt.   Kingfisher, The.
Fenton, J.   Kingfisher's Boxing Gloves, The.
Hopkins, G.   As Kingfishers Catch Fire.
Oliver, M.   Kookaburras, The.
Olson, C.   Kingfishers, The.

Kings
"Anvari."   Shah Sandschar, whose lowest slave.
   To the Shah, from Enweri.
Berryman.   Not to Live.
Bishop, E.   Twelfth Morning; or What You Will.
Blake, W.   Gwin, King of Norway.
   Prologue to King John.
Borges.   Alhambra.
   Milonga of Manuel Flores.
Bradstreet, A.   Four[e] Monarchies, The.
Brontë, E.   Song: "King Julius left the south country."
Browning, E.   King Victor Emanuel Entering Florence, April, 1860.
   Napoleon III in Italy.
   Sword of Castruccio Castracani, The.
Browning, R.   Solomon and Balkis.
   With Daniel Bartoli.
Burns, R.   Carl an the King Come.
   Dream, A.
Byron, G.   Harp the Monarch Minstrel Swept, The.
   On a Royal Visit to the Vaults.
   To Belshazzar.
   Very Mournful Ballad, A.
   Windsor Poetics.
Carew, T.   New Year's Gift. To the King, A.
   Upon the King's Sickness.
Cavafy.   Battle of Magnesia, The.
   Dareios.
   Epitaph of Antiochus, King of Kommagini.
   Eternity.
   Favor of Alexander Valas, The.
   Glory of the Ptolemies, The.
   Kaisarion.
   King Claudius.
   King Dimitrios.
   Of Dimitrios Sotir (162–150 B.C.).
   On the March to Sinopi.
   Orophernis.
Clough.   Sa Majestá Très Chrétienne.
Cowper, W.   Philosopher and the King, The.
Crashaw.   To the Queen's Majesty.
   Upon the Kings Coronation.
Cullen, C.   Black Majesty.
Davie, D.   Thyestes.
   Woe unto Thee!
De la Mare.   Maerchen.
   Never-to-Be.
Dickinson, E.   Belshazzar had a Letter.
   I met a King this afternoon!
Donne.   Anniversary [or Anniversarie], The.
Dubie.   Near the Bridge of Saint-Cloud.
Emerson, R.   Ancient lady who dwelt in Rome, An.
   King. If farmers make my land secure.
   William Rufus and the Jew.
Fenton, J.   Tauler.
Graves, R.   Beggar Maid and King Cophetua, The.
Gunn, T.   Court Revolt, The.
HaNagid.   Could Kings Right a People Gone Bad.
   King, The.
Hardy, T.   King's Soliloquy, A.
Herrick.   Bad Wages for Good Service.
   Blame.
   Blame the Reward of Princes.
   Caution in Councell.
   Clemency in Kings.
   Counsell.
   Cruelty.
   Dangers Wait on Kings.
   Difference betwixt King and Subjects, The.
   Distance Betters Dignities.
   Empires.

   Flatterie.
   God, and the King.
   Ill Government.
   King and No King, A.
   Kings.
   Kings and Tyrants.
   Love.
   Obedience.
   Obedience in Subjects.
   Patience in Princes.
   Power in the People, The.
   Strength to Support Soveraignty.
   To the King.
   To the King, to Cure the Evill.
   Twelfe Night, or King and Queene.
   Upon Kings.
   Warre.
Hill, G.   Requiem for the Plantagenet Kings.
Jeffers, R.   Ghosts in England.
Kipling, R.   Ballad of the King's Jest, The.
   Ballad of the King's Mercy, The.
   James I.
   King Henry VII. And the Shipwrights.
   King's Job, The.
   King's Task, The.
   My Father's Chair.
   Palace, The.
   Reeds of Runnymede, The.
   Song of Seven Cities, The.
Lawrence, D. H.   Snake.
Lindsay, N.   Curse for Kings, A.
   Doll's "Arabian Nights", A.
   King Arthur's Men Have Come Again.
   Who Knows?
Lowell, R.   Death of Alexander.
MacNeice.   Jehu.
   Rites of War.
Mahon.   Last of the Fire Kings, The.
Major, C.   Dispute, The.
Meredith, G.   Emperor Frederick of Our Time, The.
   Events in a Rustic Mirror.
   Head of Bran the Blest, The.
   John Lackland.
   Song of Drab, The.
Milosz, C.   King Popiel.
Olson, C.   King of the Wood / King of the Dead.
Parker, D.   Salome's Dancing-Lesson.
Ransom, J.   Two Gentlemen in Bonds.
Rich, A.   In the North.
Riley, J.   King, The.
   Romaunt of King Mordameer, The.
Rossetti, C.   After Communion.
   Maundy Thursday.
   Succession of Kings, The.
   What Hath God Wrought!
Rumi.   Ayaz and the King's Pearl.
   Imra'u 'l-Qays.
Sandburg, C.   Four Brothers, The.
   Hogh Conspiratorial Persons.
   Name Us a King.
   Savoir Faire.
Seifert.   At the Tomb of the Czech Kings.
Shelley, P.   England in 1819.
   Fragment: "I would not be a king—enough."
   Fragment: Pater Omnipotens.
   Ozymandias.
Smith, S.   King in Funeral Procession, A.
Stafford, W.   Moment Again.
   Story That Could Be True, A.
Suckling, S.   On New-Year's Day 1640, to the King.
Swift, J.   Ode to the King.
Tate, J.   Tragedy's Greatest Hits.
Walker, A.   In Uganda an Early King.
Wilbur, R.   Castles and Distances.
Wilde, O.   Louis Napoleon.
Williams, C. K.   Allies: According to Herodotus.
Wordsworth, W.   Emperors and Kings, How Oft Have Temples Rung.
   Fact, and an Imagination or, Canute and Alfred, on the Sea-Shore, A.
   Imitation of Juvenal — Satire VIII.
   King of Sweden, The.
Yeats.   Black Tower, The.

King and No King.
Madness of King Goll, The.
Model for the Laureate, A.
Two Kings, The.
Zagajewski.   King, A.

Kipling, Rudyard
Nash, O.   How to Be Married without a Spouse,
   or, Mr. Kipling, What Have You Done with
   Mr. Hauksbee?
Kipling's Vermont.
Riley, J.   To Rudyard Kipling.

Kisses
Berryman.   Venice, 182.
Blok.   Snow Wine.
Browning, E.   Romance of the Swan's Nest,
   The.
To George Sand: A Desire.
Burns, R.   And I'll kiss thee yet, yet.
Dusty Miller.
John Come Kiss Me Now.
Byron, G.   First Kiss of Love, The.
Campion, T.   Ad Caspiam.
Come, you pretty false-eyed wanton [or false-
   ey'd wanton].
In Lycium et Clytham.
In Melleam.
Kisses.
Thou Art Not Fair[e].
What Harvest Half So Sweet Is.
Carew, T.   Tooth-Ache Cured by a Kiss, The.
Catullus.   Let us live, my Lesbia, and let us love
   each other.
Ciardi, J.   In Pity as We Kiss and Lie.
Cummings, E. E.   B / et / wee / n no / w dis.
Being(just a little).
Come a little further—why be afraid.
Dirty colours of her kiss have just, The.
I have found what you are like.
Now that,more nearest even than your fate.
O my wholly unwise and definite.
Thing most new complete fragile intense, A.
Thy fingers make early flowers of.
Up into the silence the green.
Voices to voices, lip to lip.
What over and which under.
Cunningham, J.   Passion.
Donne.   Expiration, The.
Dove, R.   Adolescence—I.
Dugan, A.   Provincetown Totentanz.
Dunbar, P.   Breaking the Charm.
Come and Kiss Me Sweet and Twenty.
Her Thought and His.
Negro Love Song, A.
Phantom Kiss, The.
Emerson, R.   Pair of crystal eyes will lead me,
   A.
Ferlinghetti, L.   Short Story on a Painting of
   Gustav Klimt.
Gallagher, T.   Same Kiss after Many Years, The.
Graves, R.   Silent Visit.
Gunn, T.   Kiss at Bayreuth, The.
Hall, D.   "Kiss, The."
Hardy, T.   Kiss, A.
Last Time, The.
Mock Wife, The.
Sigh, The.
That Kiss in the Dark.
Thunderstorm in Town, A.
Two Lips.
Herrick.   Barley-Break; or, Last in Hell.
Chop-Cherry.
Draw Gloves.
Head-Ake, The.
His Embalming to Julia.
Hymne to Venus, and Cupid, A.
Kiss[e], A.
Kisse, The.
Kisses.
Kisses Loathesome.
Kissing and Bussing.
Kissing Usurie.
Leven.
Love Palpable.
Love Perfumes All Parts.
On Gelli-Flowers Begotten.
Teares.

Tithe [or Tythe]: To the Bride, The.
To Dianeme.
To Electra.
Upon a Free Maid, with a Foule Breath.
Upon a Virgin Kissing a Rose.
Upon Jack and Jill: Epigram.
Upon Lucia.
Jackson, L.   Eventual Love.
Take Hands.
Kinnell.   Kissing the Toad.
Kunitz, S.   Game, The.
Laughlin, J.   Da mi basia mille.
Kiss, The.
Kissing.
Les Amants.
Sweet Kiss, A.
Lawrence, D. H.   After School.
Appeal, The.
Assuming the Burden.
Decision, A.
Hyde Park at Night, before the War.
Kisses in the Train.
Lightning.
Mystery.
Seven Seals.
Lindsay, N.   By the Spring at Sunset.
Major, C.   Pupa.
Millay, E.   Sonnet: "What lips my lips have
   kissed, and where, and why."
Olson, C.   Real, The.
Treatment, The.
Paley, G.   Here.
Patchen.   Demonstration.
Petronius Arbiter.   Doing, a filthy pleasure is,
   and short.
Plath.   Never Try to Trick Me with a Kiss.
Rexroth, K.   Schatten Küsse, Schatten Liebe.
Riley, J.   For You.
Lost Thrill, The.
Rilke.   Poet, The.
Ritsos.   Interchanges.
Roethke.   Shy Man, The.
Rossetti, C.   Baby lies so fast asleep.
My baby has a mottled fist.
Our little baby fell asleep.
Rumi.   I saw you last night in the gathering.
I would love to kiss you.
Sandburg, C.   Counting.
Kisses, Can You Come Back like Ghosts?
Kisses Forgotten.
Seifert.   Dialogue.
In an Empty Room.
Sexton.   Kiss, The.
Knee Song.
Shelley, P.   Love's Philosophy.
Smith, S.   I HATE THIS GIRL.
Stock, R.   Lines upon Delia and to the
   Chevaliers of the Cordon Bleu.
Swinburne.   Kissing Her Hair.
Walker, A.   Kiss, The.
Whitman, W.   Behold This Swarthy Face.
Williams, C. K.   On the Other Hand.
Williams, T.   Not without Knowledge.
Wyatt, S.   Alas, madam[e], for stealing [or
   stelying] of a kiss [or kysse].
Lover Showeth How He Is Forsaken of Such as
   He Sometime Enjoyed, The.
Zukofsky, L.   Drive, fast kisses.

Kitchens
Brooks, G.   Mrs. Small.
Crane, H.   In a Court.
Dove, R.   Sunday Greens.
Dunbar, P.   Trouble in de Kitchen.
Hacker, M.   Shirland Road.
Ignatow, D.   Ontology, An.
Levertov.   Room.
Mahon.   Shapes and Shadows.
Roethke.   Last Words.

Kites (ornithology)
Blok.   Kite, The.

Kites (toys)
Ammons.   Up.
Davie, D.   Kites.
Dubie.   Diatribe of the Kite, The.
Heaney, S.   Kite for Michael and Christopher,
   A.

Prunty.   Kite, The.
Sexton.   Kite, The.
Stafford, W.   Father and Son.
Swenson, M.   Goodbye, Goldeneye.

Kittens
Eberhart, R.   Old Tom.
Jarrell, R.   Sign, The.
Lindsay, N.   Dirge for a Righteous Kitten, A.
Moore, M.   Reminiscent of a Wave at the Curl.
Nash, O.   Kitten, The.
Simic.   Cold Blue Tinge.
Smith, S.   Our Office Cat.
Stock, R.   J.
Williams, W.   Mujer.
Wordsworth, W.   Kitten and [the] Falling
   Leaves, The.

Klee, Paul
Dubie.   Sun and Moon Flowers: Paul Klee,
   1879–1940.
Muldoon, P.   Paul Klee: They're Biting.
Nemerov.   Painter Dreaming in the Scholar's
   House, The.
Stock, R.   Paul Klee.

Klimt, Gustav
Ferlinghetti, L.   Short Story on a Painting of
   Gustav Klimt.
Laughlin, J.   Kiss, The.
Milosz, C.   O! ("O lips half opened, eyes half
   closed, the rosy nipple of your unveiled
   nakedness, Judith!").

Knees
Sexton.   Knee Song.

Knife-Grinding and Knife-Grinders
Cummings, E. E.   Who sharpens every dull.
Lindsay, N.   Scissors-Grinder, The.
Whitman, W.   Sparkles from the Wheel.

Knighthood and Knights
Amichai [or Amikhai].   Girl Goes Out in the
   Morning like a Knight, A.
Borges.   Two Versions of "Knight, Death and
   the Devil."
Browning, E.   Romaunt of the Page, The.
Browning, R.   Childe Roland to the Dark Tower
   Came.
Heretic's Tragedy, The.
Coleridge, S.   Ballad of the Dark Ladié, The.
Crane, S.   Fast rode the knight.
Dunbar, P.   Knight, The.
Goethe.   Arabian Ballad.
Graves, R.   Absent Crusader.
Son Altesse.
Herrick.   To His Peculiar Friend Sir Edward
   Fish, Knight Baronet.
Jonson, B.   Speech Presented unto King James
   at a Tilting in the Behalf of the Two Noble
   Brothers S[ir] Robert and S[ir] Henry Rich, A.
To Sir Luckless Woo-All.
Keats.   Calidore. A Fragment.
King Stephen. A Fragment of a Tragedy.
La Belle Dame sans Merci [A Ballad].
Kipling, R.   Last Rhyme of True Thomas, The.
Lollius.
Quest, The.
Meredith, G.   Chivalry.
Song: "When on my faithful charger."
Song of Courtesy, The.
Poe.   Eldorado.
Rich, A.   Knight, The.
Robinson, E.   Lancelot.
Sandburg, C.   Horses and Men in the Rain.
Smith, S.   Behind the Knight.
Blue from Heaven, The.
Fafnir and the Knights.
Frozen Lake, The.
Tennyson, A.   Sir Galahad [or The Purple
   Heart].
Sir Launcelot and Queen Guinevere.
Whittier.   Knight of St. John, The.
Wordsworth, W.   Effusion in the Pleasure-
   Ground on the Banks of the Bran.
Fragments: Drafts, Mostly or All for a Poem on
   a Heroic Theme.

Knights of Pythias
Kipling, R.   New Knighthood, The.

Knitting and Knitters

Dickinson, E.   Autumn—overlooked my Knitting.
Levertov.   With Eyes at the Back of Our Heads.
Simic.   Gallows Etiquette.

Knives

Borges.   Milonga of Albornoz.
Brodsky, J.   At the Helmet and Sword.
Broumas, O.   Knife & the Bread, The.
Dugan, A.   On a Pocketknife. On Carrying.
Emerson, R.   I use the knife.
Hall, D.   Wolf Knife.
Komunyakaa.   Mumble Peg.
   Rocks Push.
Lorde.   Poem for Women in Rage, A.
McGrath, T.   Deprivation.
   Fatigue of Objects, The.
Schuyler, J.   Stone Knife, A.
Sexton.   Bayonet.
Simic.   Knife.
Swenson, M.   Bleeding.
Thomas, D.   Because the Pleasure-Bird Whistles.
Tomlinson, C.   Blade, The.

Knowledge

Amichai [or Amikhai].   I love these people in their tall house.
Ammons.   Crevice.
Atwood.   Procedures for Underground.
Berry, W.   At a Country Funeral.
   Creation Myth.
   Fall.
   Gathering, The.
   Horses.
   Recognition, The.
   To Know the Dark.
Berryman.   Spinning Heart, The.
Bishop, E.   At the Fishhouses.
Blake, W.   All Religions Are One.
Bogan, L.   Knowledge.
Bradstreet, A.   Of the Four Humors in Man's Constitution.
Browning, R.   Paracelsus.
   Reverie.
Carruth, H.   How Lewisburg, Pa., Escaped the Avenging Angel.
Celan.   Zurich, at the Stork.
Chuang Tzu.   Great Knowledge.
   Useless, The.
   When Knowledge Went North.
Ciardi, J.   Useless Knowledge.
Clifton, L.   What Did She Know, When Did She Know It.
   Wild Blessings.
Clough.   Questioning Spirit, The.
Cooper, J.   Knowledge that Comes through Experience, The.
Cowper, W.   Conversation.
   On Mrs. Montagu's Feather-Hangings.
Crane, S.   I met a seer.
Creeley.   End, The.
   Folk Song, A: "Hitch up honey for the / market race all."
   For Lewis, to Say It.
   On a Theme by Lawrence, Hearing Purcell.
   Somebody Died.
   Sunset.
   Wisdom.
Cummings, E. E.   Love's function is to fabricate unknownness.
   You Shall above All Things Be Glad and Young.
Cunningham, J.   Gnothi Seauton.
   Meditation on a Memoir.
   "Dario." Sum.
   What Gets You.
Davie, D.   Life Encompassed.
   Oak Openings.
Dickinson, E.   Inferential Knowledge, The.
   To know just how He suffered—would be dear.
   When overwhelmed to know.
Duncan, R.   Ballad of the Enamord Image, The.
   Circulations of the Song.
Eberhart, R.   Hardening into Print.
   Only in the Dream.
   Testimony.

Emerson, R.   I wear no badge; no tinsel star.
   Limits.
   Tell men what they knew before.
Enzensberger, H.   Model towards a Theory of Cognition.
Frost, R.   For Once, Then, Something.
   From Plane to Plane.
   Revelation.
Ginsberg, A.   Lysergic Acid.
   Psalm III: "To God: to illuminate all men. Beginning with Skid Road."
Gunn, T.   Merlin in the Cave: He Speculates without a Book.
Hacker, M.   Days of 1959.
HaNagid.   Heart holds hidden knowledge, The.
Hardy, T.   Fragment: "At last I entered a long dark gallery."
   If You Had Known.
   Known Had I.
   Masked Face, The.
   Not Known.
Herbert, G.   Pearl, The. Matth. 13:45.
Herrick.   Science in God.
   To Doctor Alabaster.
Howe, S.   Speeches at the Barriers.
Hughes, T.   Man Seeking Experience Enquires His Way of a Drop of Water, The.
Jeffers, R.   Science.
Keats.   Read Me a Lesson, Muse, and Speak It Loud.
Khayyám, O.   On earth's wide thoroughfares below.
Kipling, R.   Chartres Windows.
   Our Fathers of Old.
   Threshold, The.
Kizer, C.   Plaint of the Poet in an Ignorant Age.
Koch, K.   Taking a Walk with You.
Komunyakaa.   Confessing My Ignorance.
   Observatory.
   Raw Data for an Unfinished Questionnaire.
Korn.   Keep Hidden from Me.
Larkin, P.   Far Out.
Laughlin, J.   Knowledge.
Lawrence, D. H.   All-Knowing.
   Know-All.
   You.
Levertov.   Runes, The.
Levine, P.   Cemetery at Academy, California, The.
   On My Own.
   Silent in America.
MacLeish.   Autobiography.
   Land's End.
   Le Secret Humain.
   Learned Men, The.
McHugh, H.   Bear in English.
   Place Where Things Got.
Meredith, G.   From lamplight and an aged leaf.
Meredith, W.   In a Copy of Yeats' Poems.
Merton.   Wisdom.
Merwin.   Fate.
   Finding a Teacher.
Milosz, C.   Gardener.
   Six Lectures in Verse.
   Voyeur.
   Zone of Silence.
Moore, M.   To a Snail.
Muldoon, P.   Salmon of Knowledge, The.
Nash, O.   Ask Daddy, He Won't Know.
   Who Did Which? or Who Indeed?
Nemerov.   Boy with Book of Knowledge.
   Knowledge.
   To David, about His Education.
Niedecker.   Broad-leaved Arrow-head, The.
   Can knowledge be conveyed that isn't felt?
O'Hara, F.   Spleen.
Olson, C.   B Cs (2), A.
Oppen.   Image of the Engine.
   Knowledge not of sorrow, you were, The.
   Lighthouses, The.
   Narrative.
Parker, D.   Ballade at Thirty-Five.
Patchen.   Forms of Knowledge, The.
   Should Be Sufficient.
Pinsky.   Rhyme of Reb Nachman, The.
Poe.   Al Aaraaf.

Pound, E.   Tree, The.
Prunty.   Books, The.
Raine, K.   Chartres Annunciation, The.
   Dream-flowers.
   Message from Home.
   On a Shell-strewn Beach.
Ramanujan.   Not Knowing.
Rexroth, K.   Apple Garths of Avalon, The.
Rich, A.   From Morning-Glory to Petersburg.
   Merely to Know.
Riley, J.   If I Knew What Poets Know.
   Intellectual Limitations.
   Natural Perversities.
   No Boy Knows.
Rilke.   Lesson, The.
Ritsos.   Knowledge of the Ambiguous.
   Naked Face.
   Postponed Decision.
Roethke.   Marrow, The.
Rossetti, C.   Take No Thought for the Morrow.
   To Lalla, Reading My Verses Topsy-Turvy.
   We know not when, we know not where.
Rukeyser, M.   Afterwards.
   Knowledge my nakedness.
Rumi.   Sheikh Who Played with Children, The.
   Two Kinds of Intelligence.
Sandburg, C.   Leather Leggings.
   Pals.
   Peace between Wars.
   People with Proud Chins.
   Sea Hold, The.
   Unknown War, The.
Shapiro, K.   Solipsism.
Shelley, P.   Sonnet: Lift Not the Painted Veil.
Smart, C.   On the Omniscience of the Supreme Being.
Snyder, G.   Magpie's Song.
   My home was at Cold Mountain from the start.
Stafford, W.   Near.
   One Evening.
Stevens, W.   Conversation with Three Women of New England.
   No Possum, No Sop, No Taters.
   Presence of an External Master of Knowledge.
Stock, R.   Sir John Mandeville and I Sat Up Talking.
Sze.   Archipelago.
   Axis, The.
   Oolong.
   Redshifting Web, The.
   Silk Road, The.
Szymborska, W.   Opinion on the Question of Pornography, An.
   We're Extremely Fortunate.
Tennyson, A.   To —. With the Following Poem.
Thomas, D.   Was There a Time.
   Why East Wind Chills.
Thoreau.   Men say they know many things.
Very.   Eye and Ear, The.
Warren, R.   Not Quite like a Top.
   Problem of Knowledge.
Whalen, P.   For Brother Antoninus.
Whitman, W.   As in a Swoon.
   I Thought that Knowledge Alone Would Suffice.
   Savantism.
   That Music always Round Me.
Whittier.   Common Question, The.
   Questions of Life.
Wilbur, R.   In a Bird Sanctuary.
   Problem from Milton, A.
   Water Walker.
Williams, C. K.   I know / nothing anymore.
   Next to the Last Poem about God, The.
   Regulars, The.
Williams, M.   One of Those Rare Occurrences on a City Bus.
   Today Is Wednesday.
Wordsworth, W.   Composed on the Banks of a Rocky Stream.
Wright, C.   Miles Davis and Elizabeth Bishop Fake the Break.
   Negatives 2.
   Watching the Equinox Arrive in Charlottesville, September 1992.
Wright, J.   Abstract of Knowledge, The / The First Test.

Zagajewski. Don't Allow the Lucid Moment to Dissolve.
We Know Everything.

Kollwitz, Käthe
Rukeyser, M. Käthe Kollwitz.

Kopechne, Mary Jo
Ai. Go.

Koran
Davie, D. Articulacy. Hints from the Koran.
Merrill, J. Page from the Koran.
Merton. Night of Destiny, The.

Korean War
Carruth, H. On a Certain Engagement South of Seoul.
Jeffers, R. De Rerum Virtute.
McGrath, T. Ode for the American Dead in Korea.

Koreans
Creeley. Korean slang.
Seoul Sounds.

Koresh, David
Ai. Charisma.

Kosciusko, Thaddeus
Keats. To Kosciusko.

Kossuth, Louis (1802–94)
Very. Kossuth.

Krakow [or Cracow], Poland
Milosz, C. Return to Kraków in 1880.
Zagajewski. View of Krakow, A.

Ku Klux Klan
Hayden, R. Night, Death, Mississippi.
Hughes, L. Ballad of Sam Solomon.
Ku Klux.
Not a Movie.
Komunyakaa. Knights of the White Camellia & Deacons of Defense.

Kubla Khan
Coleridge, S. Kubla Khan: or, A Vision in a Dream.
Smith, S. Thoughts about the Person from Porlock.

Kyoto, Japan
Creeley. For Benny.
Inn / Kyoto.
Rexroth, K. Heart's Garden, the Garden's Heart, The.
Whalen, P. Sanjusangendo.
War Poem for Diane di Prima.
White River Ode.
Winter, The ("Why do I fear the true winter death to come").

L

La Hogue, Battle of
See Hogue, La, Battle of (1692)

Labor and Laborers
Ashbery, J. Bird's-Eye View of the Tool and Die Co.
Bukowski. Mexican Girls, The.
Sparks.
Winter Comes to a Lot of Places in August.
Coleridge, S. Work without Hope.
Crane, S. Man toiled on a burning road, A.
Many workmen / Built a huge ball of masonry.
Cummings, E. E. I say no world.
Dickey, W. Life Moving More Rapidly than Hands Can Manage.
Dickinson, E. Labor might fatigue.
Robin.
Dunbar, P. Equipment.
Not They Who Soar!
Eberhart, R. Maine Roustabout, A.
Emerson, R. Use will in man new grace reveal.
Enzensberger, H. Vanished Work.
Frost, R. Mowing.
"Out, Out—."
Tuft of Flowers, The.
Wood-Pile, The.
Gallagher, T. Black Money.
Gjuzel. On the Way Back.
Glück, L. School Children, The.
Hall, D. Foundations of American Industry,

The.
Hayden, R. Those Winter Sundays.
Herrick. End of His Work, The.
Gods Blessing.
Labour.
Recompence.
Rest.
Upon Trencherman.
Hill, G. Ovid in the Third Reich.
Hopkins, G. God's Grandeur.
Hughes, L. Chant for Tom Mooney.
Migrant.
Open Letter to the South.
Wait.
West Texas.
Ignatow, D. Errand Boy 1, The.
Jeffers, R. Bixby's Landing.
On Building with Stone.
Johnson, S. Paraphrase.
Kipling, R. Wage-Slaves, The.
Komunyakaa. Glory.
Whistle, The.
Work.
Larkin, P. Aubade: "I work all day, and get half-drunk at night."
Toads.
Toads Revisited.
Laughlin, J. In Darmstadt.
Lawrence, D. H. Morning Work.
Study.
Levine, P. Helmet, The.
You Can Have It.
Longfellow, H. Psalm of Life, A.
Village Blacksmith, The.
MacDiarmid, H. Seamless Garment, The.
MacLeish. Burying Ground by the Ties.
Millay, E. Men Working.
Nash, O. Grasshoppers Are Very Intelligent.
More about People.
Two Songs for a Boss Named Mr. Longwell.
Niedecker. In the great snowfall before the bomb.
Olson, C. O'Ryan.
Oppen. Men of Sheepshead, The.
Piercy. To Be of Use.
Pinsky. Shirt.
Riley, J. "Blue-Monday" at the Shoe Shop.
Raggedy Man, The.
Rukeyser, M. Absalom.
Alloy.
Bill, The.
Burnishing, Oakland.
Disease: After-Effects, The.
Doctors, The.
George Robinson: Blues.
Mearl Blankenship.
Power.
Praise of the Committee.
Statement: Philippa Allen.
Sandburg, C. Child of the Romans.
Dynamiter.
Horses and Men in the Rain.
Ice Handler.
Jack.
Masses.
Mayor of Gary, The.
Mill-Doors.
Muckers.
Old Flagman, The.
Onion Days.
Psalm of Those Who Go Forth before Daylight.
Three Ghosts.
To Certain Journeymen.
Work Gangs.
Working Girls.
Shelley, P. Song to the Men of England.
Smith, S. Alfred the Great.
Road Up.
Snyder, G. Hay for the Horses.
Late Snow & Lumber Strike of the Summer of Fifty-four, The.
Stockton, A. Impromptu Epitaph on the Grave Digger of Princeton—1769.
Swift, J. Description of the Morning, A.
Verses Spoken Extempore by Dean Swift on His Curate's Complaint of Hard Duty.

Sze. Edna Bay.
Moon Is a Diamond, The.
Tomlinson, C. Churchyard Wall, The.
Hand at Callow Hill Farm, The.
Lament for Doormen.
Steel.
Whitman, W. I Hear America Singing.
Whittier. Drovers, The.
Huskers, The.
Lumbermen, The.
Shoemakers, The.
Williams, M. Rock.
Wordsworth, W. Labourer's Noon-Day Hymn, The.
Yeats. Adam's Curse.

Labor Day
Glück, L. Labor Day.
Oliver, M. Stanley Kunitz.
Schuyler, J. Labor Day.

Labor Unions
Berryman. Thanksgiving: Detroit.
Hughes, L. Open Letter to the South.
Kizer, C. Union of Women.
Patchen. Joe Hill Listens to the Praying.
Sandburg, C. Ice Handler.
Teamster's Farewell, A.
See also **Strikes and Strikers**

Labrador, Canada
Crane, H. North Labrador.
Sandburg, C. Love in Labrador.
Williams, W. Labrador.

Labyrinths
Auden. Maze, The.
Borges. Labyrinth, The.
Palace, The.
Parable of the Palace.
Bourne, V. Maze, The.
Laughlin, J. Maze, The.
Orr, G. Investigation.
Ritsos. New Dance, The.
Rukeyser, M. Minotaur, The.
Tomlinson, C. Ariadne and the Minotaur.
Wilner, E. Labyrinth.

Lade, Sir John
Johnson, S. Short Song of Congratulation [*or* To a Young Heir], A.

Ladybirds
Eberhart, R. How It Is.
Rossetti, C. I caught a little ladybird.

Lafayette, Marie Joseph, Marquis de
Blake, W. Fayette beside King Lewis stood.
Emerson, R. Poem, Spoken before the ΦBK Society, August, 1834.
Very. Death of Lafayette.

Lake District, England
Arnold, M. Youth of Nature, The.
Wordsworth, W. Composed When a Probability Existed of Our Being Obliged to Quit Rydal Mount as a Residence.
Four Fiery Steed Impatient of the Rein.

Lakes and Ponds
Ai. Capture.
Atwood. Younger Sister, Going Swimming.
Brodsky, J. Swiss Blue.
Burns, R. On Scaring Some Waterfowl in Loch Turit, a Wild Scene among the Hills.
Byron, G. Sonnet to Lake Leman.
Carruth, H. Oldest Killed Lake in North America, The.
Underground the Darkness Is the Light.
Ciardi, J. Island Galaxy, An.
Clampitt. Trasimene.
Creeley. Thinking.
Way, The.
Cummings, E. E. This / forest pool / A so.
Davie, D. Corrib. An Emblem.
De la Mare. Visionary, The.
Dickey, J. Remnant Water.
Dunbar, P. Matter of Locality, A.
Eberhart, R. Loon Call, A.
On Returning to a Lake in Spring.
Emerson, R. He loved to watch & wake.
Miracle, The.
Frost, R. Spring Pools.
Glück, L. Pond, The.

Hall, D.   Day I Was Older, The.
  Sister by the Pond, A.
  Southwest of Buffalo.
Heaney, S.   Lough Neagh Sequence, A.
  Relic of Memory.
Hughes, T.   Lake, The.
  Widdop.
Kinsella, T.   Crab Orchard Sanctuary, Late
  October.
Kizer, C.   Two Poets by the Lake.
Komunyakaa.   Millpond, The.
Kunitz, S.   Goose Pond.
Logan, J.   Coming of Age.
Lux.   Snake Lake.
MacNeice.   Lake in the Park, The.
Major, C.   Swallow the Lake.
Maritain.   Lake, The.
McMichael.   Matins.
Meredith, G.   In the clear dark lake a lady
  dived.
Merwin.   Lake, The.
  Tidal Lagoon.
Millay, E.   Armenonville.
Milosz, C.   Lake.
Montale.   Lindau.
Muldoon, P.   Paul Klee: *They're Biting*.
Nemerov.   Pond, The.
Niedecker.   White / among the green pads.
O'Hara, F.   Mozart Chemisier.
Oliver, M.   At Blackwater Pond.
  Morning at Great Pond.
Plath.   Crossing the Water.
  Private Ground.
Poe.   Lake: To———, The.
Prunty.   Lake House, The.
Rexroth, K.   Bei Wannsee.
  Still on Water.
Riley, J.   Life at the Lake.
Rilke.   Sketch.
Ritsos.   Misunderstandings.
Rukeyser, M.   Sacred Lake.
Sandburg, C.   Dialogue.
  Flat Waters of the West in Kansas.
  Lake Michigan Morning.
  Night Stuff.
  Old Music for Quiet Hearts.
  Purple Martins.
Shelley, P.   Fragment: The Lake's Margin.
Smith, S.   Abominable Lake, The.
  Frozen Lake, The.
Stafford, W.   Lake Chelan.
Swenson, M.   Lake Scene, A.
Tate, J.   River's Story.
Tomlinson, C.   Gorge, The.
Whittier.   Grave by the Lake, The.
  Kenoza Lake.
  Lakeside, The.
  Storm on Lake Asquam.
  Summer by the Lakeside.
  Voyage of the Jettie.
  Well of Loch Maree, The.
Wilbur, R.   Marginalia.
Williams, W.   View of a Lake.
Wordsworth, W.   Passage from John Wilson's
  The Angler's Tent.
  Written in the Strangers' Book at "The Station,"
  Opposite Bowness.
Wright, J.   By a Lake in Minnesota.
  On Minding One's Own Business.

Lamb, Charles
Coleridge, S.   This Lime-Tree Bower My Prison.
  To a Friend [Charles Lamb] Who Had Declared
  His Intention of Writing No More Poetry.
Nash, O.   All, All Are Gone, the Old Familiar
  Quotations.
Wordsworth, W.   Farewell Lines.
  Written after the Death of Charles Lamb.

Lamb, Mary
Wordsworth, W.   Farewell Lines.

Lambs
Burns, R.   What Will I Do Gin My Hoggie Die.
Ciardi, J.   Lamb, The.
Dunbar, P.   Hymn: "O li'l lamb out in de col'."
Eberhart, R.   For a Lamb.
Hughes, T.   Bringing in New Couples.
  February 17th.

Ravens.
Sheep.
  What is it this time the dark barn again.
Kumin, M.   How It Goes On.
Larkin, P.   First Sight.
Lawrence, D. H.   St Mark.
Merrill, J.   Violent Pastoral.
Muldoon, P.   Behold the Lamb.
Roethke.   Lamb, The.
Rossetti, C.   Angels at the foot, / And Angels at
  the head.
  Frisky Lamb, A.
  Lambs at Play.
  Motherless soft lambkin / Alone upon a hill.
  Thy lilies drink the dew, / Thy lambs the rill,
  and I will drink them too.
Smith, S.   Death Bereaves Our Common Mother
  Nature Grieves for My Dead Brother.
Wordsworth, W.   Pet Lamb, The; A Pastoral.
  Westmoreland Girl, The.

Lament (form)
Burns, R.   Galloway Tam.
Song: "As I stood by yon roofless tower."
Carew, T.   Elegy upon the Death of the Dean of
  [St.] Paul's, Dr. John Donne, An.
Cortes.   Organ.
Cuadra, P.   Cup with a Jaguar for the Drinking
  of Health.
  Lament of a Maiden for the Warrior's Death.
De la Mare.   Fairy in Winter, The.
  News.
  Ophelia.
  Suicide, The.
  Sunk Lyonesse.
Eberhart, R.   Despair.
  Ode to Silence.
Emerson, R.   Hermione.
Herrick.   To Perenna.
Merton.   Dirge for the World Joyce Died In.
  Whitsun Canticle, A.
Wilbur, R.   Lament: "Nashe's old queens who
  bartered young and fair."
Wyatt, S.   'Resound my voice, ye woods.'

Lamplighting and Lamplighters
Emerson, R.   At Plymouth in the friendly crowd.
Kunitz, S.   Lamplighter: 1914.
Oliver, M.   Lamps, The.
Tomlinson, C.   Civilities of Lamplight.

Lampreys
See Eels

Lancashire, England
Carew, T.   To Saxham.
Davie, D.   Lancashire.

Lancelot du Lac
Ciardi, J.   Launcelot in Hell.
Creeley.   Bresson's Movies.
Robinson, E.   Lancelot.
Williams, W.   Con Brio.

Landlords and Landladies
Angelou.   Contemporary Announcement.
Atwood.   Landlady, The.
Berry, W.   Companions, The.
Bierce.   Fair Division, A.
Brodsky, J.   Blues.
Bukowski.   Breakout.
  Buffalo Bill.
  Nice Place, A.
Carver, R.   Autumn.
Dickinson, E.   Rat, The.
Herbert, G.   Redemption.
Hughes, L.   Ballad of the Landlord.
  Madam and the Rent Man.
Ritsos.   Corridor.

Landor, Walter Savage
Moore, M.   W. S. Landor.

Landscape
Amichai [*or* Amikhai].   Kibbutz Gevaram.
Atwood.   Place: Fragments, A.
Baudelaire.   Landscape.
Brodsky, J.   Ex Voto.
Broumas, O.   Landscape with Poets.
Browning, E.   Sea-Mew, The.
Burns, R.   Humble Petition of Bruar Water to
  the Noble Duke of Athole, The.
Cardenal.   Dog barks far out, A.

Every evening the L & N.
I do not know who is out in the snow.
I turned out the light to see the snow.
Like Empty Beer Cans.
Like the flights of ducks.
Long freight train / Wakes me in my cell, The.
Sound of passing cars, (if a car comes), The.
Spring has come with its smell of Nicaragua.
That auto horn sounds familiar.
When the first signs go on.
Zinc roofs in the moonlight, The.
Clampitt.   At Easterly.
Emerson, R.   Seemed, tho' the soft sheen all
  enchants.
Ferlinghetti, L.   Baja Revisited.
  Carrara, Looking Seaward.
Ginsberg, A.   Wales Visitation.
Gurney, I.   Coppice, The.
Hamill, S.   Pastoral.
Hardy, T.   Death-Day Recalled, A.
  In Front of the Landscape.
Heaney, S.   Field of Vision.
  Land.
Hughes, T.   Rain.
  Stanbury Moor.
Jacobsen, J.   Landscape Finally with Human
  Figure.
Jarrell, R.   Country Was, The.
Jonson, B.   To Sir Robert Wroth.
Kipling, R.   Run of the Downs, The.
Laughlin, J.   Here I Am.
Levertov.   From a Plane.
Logan, J.   Abstract Love Poem.
MacLeish.   Landscape as a Nude.
Major, C.   On the Nature of Perspective.
Marvell.   Upon Appleton House [To My Lord
  Fairfax].
  Upon the Hill and Grove at Bilbrough.
Melville, H.   Enviable Isles, The.
Meredith, W.   Kodiak Poem, A.
  Winter on the River.
Merwin.   Calling under the Breath, The.
  Calm in April, A.
Parker, D.   Landscape.
Patchen.   Continuation of the Landscape.
Raine, K.   Dream.
  Moon golden towards the full.
Rossetti, C.   Mirrors of Life and Death.
Rukeyser, M.   Breathing Landscape.
  Homage to Literature.
  Notes for a Poem.
Sandburg, C.   Back Yard.
  Flat Lands.
  Landscape.
  Nocturne in a Deserted Brickyard.
Schuyler, J.   Evening Wind.
  June.
  Just before Fall.
  View, A.
  White Boat, Blue Boat.
Swenson, M.   Sketch for a Landscape.
Tomlinson, C.   Appearance.
  At Stoke.
  Brilliant Silence.
  Casarola.
  Flight, The.
  Hedgerows.
  Hill Walk.
  In Winter Woods.
  Lines Written in the Euganean Hills.
  On a Landscape by Li Ch'eng.
  On the Mountain.
Van Duyn.   View, A.
Whittier.   Golden Wedding of Longwood, The.
  Pictures.
  Revisited.
Williams, M.   Waiting for the Paper to be
  Delivered.
Williams, W.   Storm, The.
Wordsworth, W.   Malham Cove.
  On the Sight of a Manse in the South of
  Scotland.
Wright, C.   Landscape with Seated Figure and
  Olive Trees.
Wright, J.   In Ohio.
  Quest, The.

Zagajewski. Tarbes.

Landscapes
Ashbery, J. Haunted Landscape.
  Purists Will Object.
Auden. In Praise of Limestone.
Broumas, O. Diagram of Abandoned Mosque.
Carver, R. In a Marine Light near Sequim,
  Washington.
Clampitt. Cove, The.
Creeley. 10:30 AM: Ralph Hotere's.
Davie, D. County Durham.
  Herefordshire.
  Low Lands.
  Winter Landscape near Ely, A.
Emerson, R. Inspired we must forget our books.
Graves, R. Lost Acres.
Gunn, T. Iron Landscapes (and the Statue of
  Liberty).
Heaney, S. Tollund.
Hopkins, G. Distance / Dappled with
  diminish'd trees.
Hughes, L. Our Land.
Levertov. Continent.
  From the Train, Eastward.
  Pig-song.
Lux. His Spine Curved Just Enough.
Melville, H. Enviable Isles, The.
  Pontoosuce.
Milosz, C. December 1.
  View, The.
Montale. Times at Bellosguardo.
  Where the tennis court once was.
Olson, C. Tenemency twilightish landscape.
Patchen. Saturday Night in the Parthenon.
Paz. Landscape.
Petrarch. I have been shown a myriad slopes
  and more.
Rexroth, K. High Provence.
  Song at the Winepresses, A.
Riley, J. From Delphi to Camden.
  Summer Sunrise, A.
Ritsos. Our Land.
Rukeyser, M. Landscape with Wave
  Approaching.
Sandburg, C. Localities.
  New Hampshire Again.
  Nocturn 4: "Claims of the sea, of the tide, move
  out, The."
Schuyler, J. Beaded Balustrade.
  Vermont Diary, A.
Stockton, A. Prospect, The. By a Lady in
  Princeton.
Tomlinson, C. Blaubeuren.
  Carrara Revisited.
  Saving the Appearances.
  Second Song.
  Zipangu.
Wilbur, R. Terrace, The.
Wilde, O. Burden of Itys, The.
Wordsworth, W. Lines Composed a Few Miles
  above Tintern Abbey on Revisiting the Banks
  of the Wye during a Tour, July 13, 1798.
  Written in Mrs Field's Album opposite a Pen-
  and-Ink Sketch in the Manner of a Rembrandt
  Etching Done by Edmund Field.
Wright, C. All Landscape Is Abstract, and
  Tends to Repeat Itself.
  Bad Memory Makes You a Metaphysician, a
  Good One Makes You a Saint, A.
  Disjecta Membra.
  Journal of the Year of the Ox, A.
  Landscape as Metaphor, Landscape as Fate and
  a Happy Life.
  Sitting at Dusk in the Back Yard after the
  Mondrian Retrospective.
  To the Egyptian Mummy in the Etruscan
  Museum at Cortona.
Zagajewski. Elegy: "It was a gray landscape,
  houses small."
Zaturenska. Island, The.

Landslides
Ammons. Clarity.
Dickey, J. Sustainment.

Language
Amichai [or Amikhai]. At the Beach.
  Eternal Mystery, The.

Language School.
Last Word Is the Captain, The.
When a man is away from his homeland for a
  long time.
When a Man's Far Away from His Country.
Ammons. Meteorology.
Armantrout. My Associates.
Ashbery, J. Paradoxes and Oxymorons.
  Soonest Mended.
Atwood. Fishing for Eel Totems.
  We hear nothing these days.
Auden. Natural Linguistics.
  Their Lonely Betters.
Beckett, S. Écoute-les / s'ajouter.
Bly, R. Words Rising.
Borges. Baltasar Gracián.
  Compass.
  Embarking on the Study of Anglo-Saxon
  Grammer.
  Poem Written in a Copy of *Beowulf*.
  Saxon (A.D. 449), A.
Brodsky, J. Ab Ovo.
  Infinitive.
Broumas, O. Artemis.
  If I Yes.
Campion, T. Think'st thou to seduce me then.
Carruth, H. Comparative Iconography.
  Fragment: "Who can know more deeply than I
  your loneliness there?"
  How Lewisburg, Pa., Escaped the Avenging
  Angel.
  Naming for Love.
  No Matter What, after All, and That Beautiful
  Word So.
  Of Distress Being Humiliated by the Classical
  Chinese Poets.
  Post-Impressionist Susurration for the First of
  November, 1983, A.
Cavafy. For Ammonis, Who at Died at 29, in
  610.
Celan. Speak You Too.
Ciardi, J. Poet's Words, The.
Clampitt. Losing Track of Language.
Clifton, L. Birth of Language, The.
  Here Yet Be Dragons.
Codrescu. Bi-lingual.
  Grammar.
  Poetry Paper.
  Sunday Sermon.
Collins, B. Idiomatic.
  Winter Syntax.
Crane, H. By Nilus Once I Knew.
Creeley. Arroyo.
  Echo ("Yes but your sweetness").
  Korean slang.
  Language, The.
  Love: "There are words voluptuous."
  Message, The.
  Method, A.
  Movie Run Backward, The.
  One.
  Pacing as with some consequent.
  Pay.
  To the One in the Gray Coat.
  Words.
Cummings, E. E. Here is little Effie's Head.
  Newly / cued / motif smites truly to beautifully.
  Oil tel duh woil doi sez.
  Surely / Cued / motif smites truly to Beautifully,
  The.
"Dario." Spaniard.
Davie, D. Hearing Russian Spoken.
  Northumberland.
  Warwickshire.
  Well-found Poem.
  With the Grain.
De la Mare. Incantation.
Dickinson, E. Could mortal lip divine.
Dugan, A. Nostalgia for a Language.
  Trial, A.
Duncan, R. For a Song of the Languagers.
  Poetry Disarranged.
  Source.
  Writing as Writing.
Eberhart, R. By the Stream.
  I Went to See Irving Babbitt.

Emerson, R. Brave Empedocles defying fools,
  The.
  Muse / Can at pleasure use, The.
  When thy soul / Is filled with a just image fear
  not thou.
Enzensberger, H. Further Reasons Why Poets
  Do Not Tell the Truth.
Ferlinghetti, L. Baja Beatitudes.
  General Song of Humanity, The.
  Sweet and various the woodlark.
Gallagher, T. Poem in Translation, A.
  Second Language.
Gjuzel. Flood at the International Writer's
  Workshop.
Glück, L. Illuminations.
Graves, R. Cool Web, The.
  Dance of Words.
  In Broken Images.
  In Time of Absence.
  O.
  Tilth.
Hacker, M. After the Revolution.
  For Jean Migrenne.
  Sestina: "For a week now our bodies have
  whispered."
Hall, D. Je Suis une Table.
Hamill, S. Gift of Tongues, The.
Hardy, T. History of an Hour, The.
  Liddell and Scott.
Heaney, S. Backward Look, The.
Herbert, G. Son[ne], The.
Howe, S. Cabbage Gardens.
  Hinge Picture.
  Pythagorean Silence.
  Secret History of the Dividing Line.
  Some particular place fleeting.
  Speeches at the Barriers.
  Tuning the Sky.
  We that were wood / when that a wide wood
  was.
Hughes, T. Shibboleth.
Jackson, L. Come, Words, Away.
  Of All the World.
  Signs of Knowledge, The.
  When Love Becomes Words.
  World and I, The.
Jacobsen, J. Language as an Escape from the
  Discrete.
  Language of Moss, The.
  Monosyllable, The.
  Painter at Xyochtl.
  Things, The.
Jonson, B. Fit of Rhyme [or Rime] against
  Rhyme [or Rime], A.
Kizer, C. Translation.
Koch, K. Permanently.
Laughlin, J. To My Lady in a Distant Land
  That She Forget Me Not.
Levertov. Caedmon.
  Craving.
  For the Blind.
  For X.
  O Taste and See.
Lorde. Coal.
Lux. Solo Native.
MacDiarmid, H. Caledonian Antisyzygy, The.
  Weapon, The.
Mahon. Tractatus.
Major, C. And as the memory of each.
  Words into Words Won't Go.
McGrath, T. Flint and Steel.
  Need for Dictionaries II, The.
McHugh, H. Bear in English.
  Inflation.
  Language Lesson 1976.
  Like.
  Place Where Things Got.
  Trouble with "In", The.
  Two-legged.
Meredith, W. Effort at Speech.
  Rhode Island.
Merrill, J. To My Greek.
Merwin. Last One, The.
  Mist.
Milosz, C. Appeal, An.
  Esse.

Riley, J.   Fool-Youngens.
Funny Little Fellow, The.
Laughing Song.
Laughter Holding Both His Sides.
Laughter of the Rain, The.
Liz-Town Humorist, A.
Old Chums.
Ritsos.   Moment.
Rumi.   Dying, Laughing.
Sandburg, C.   Bundles.
Laughing Blue Steel.
Thin Strips.
White Shoulders.
Smith, S.   Conventionalist, The.
Persian, The.
Updike.   Origin of Laughter, The.
Weiss, T.   Place of Laughter, The.
Williams, T.   Which Is My Little Boy.
Wyatt, S.   Caesar, when that the traitor of Egypt.
See also **Mirth**

Laundry and Laundering
Amichai [*or* Amikhai].   Laundry Cellar, The.
Ferlinghetti, L.   Away above a harborful.
Herrick.   Upon a Cheap Laundresse: Epigram.
Upon Sudds, a Laundress[e].
Housman.   From the wash the laundress sends.
Hughes, L.   Song to a Negro Wash-woman, A.
Jarrell, R.   Washing.
Kinsella, T.   Laundress, The.
Merrill, J.   Mad Scene, The.
Niedecker.   Clothesline post is set, The.
Laundromat.
Young girl to marry.
Sandburg, C.   Washerwoman.
Schuyler, J.   Closed Gentian Distances.
Steaming Ties.
Smith, S.   Small Lady, The.
Updike.   Bendix.
Wash.
Wilbur, R.   Love Calls Us to the Things of This World.
Williams, W.   Young Laundryman, The.

Laurels
Bogan, L.   Several Voices Out of a Cloud.
Dugan, A.   Apollo.
Herrick.   Mount of the Muses, The.
To Laurels.
To Mistress Katherine Bradshaw, the Lovely, That Crowned Him with Laurel.
Willow Garland, The.
Hughes, L.   Crowns and Garlands.
Keats.   To a Young Lady Who Sent Me a Laurel Crown.
Meredith, G.   Daphne.
Milton.   Lycidas.
Petrarch.   Apollo—if you nourish still desires.
I ran beneath the shade of shining leaves.
I saw a lady underneath green laurel.
If you, by showing signs of your unease.
Love with his right hand opened my left side.
My face and hair are changing; I grow old.
Noble tree, which I loved well and long, The.
Not the Ticino, Arno, Varo, Tiber.
On the left shore of the Tyrrhenian Sea.
One day when I was looking from my window.
Quickening Sun, that bough I love alone.
That which in colour and in scent outdid.
When the first tree was level with the ground.
Shelley, P.   Fragment: The False Laurel and the True.
Suckling, S.   Wits, The; A Session[s] of the Poets.

Lavender
Pagis.   April.

Law and Lawyers
Auden.   Law like Love.
Bierce.   Law.
To a Bully.
To an Insolent Attorney.
Unexpounded.
Browning, E.   Void in Law.
Browning, R.   Ponte dell' Angelo, Venice.
Carruth, H.   Lana.
Chuang Tzu.   Inner Law, The.
Ciardi, J.   Night Piece for My Twenty-seventh

Birthday.
Starry Heavens, the Moral Law, The.
Cowper, W.   Report of an Adjudged Case.
Trail of Admiral Keppel, The.
Davie, D.   Ecclesiastical Polity.
De la Mare.   In the Dock.
Polonius.
Dickinson, E.   It comforts the Criminal little to know.
Donne.   To Mr B. B.
Dugan, A.   Poem: "In the old days either the plaintiff or the defendant won or lost."
Dunbar, P.   Lawyers' Ways, The.
Frost, R.   Self-Seeker, The.
Graves, R.   Blanket Charge.
Gunn, T.   Legal Reform.
Herrick.   Lawes.
To His Honoured Friend, M. John Weare, Councellour.
Upon Case.
Housman.   Laws of God, the laws of man, The.
Hughes, L.   Mitchell Case, The.
Jacobsen, J.   There Is Good News.
Jonson, B.   Epigram to the Coucillor That Pleaded and Carried the Cause, An.
On Cheveril [*or* Cheverel].
On Cheveril [*or* Cheverel] the Lawyer.
Logue, C.   His case is typical.
Merton.   Plessy vs Ferguson: Theme and Variations.
Niedecker.   Du Bay.
Man of law, The.
Olson, C.   Law.
Pope, A.   Verbatim from Boileau.
Riley, J.   Down on Wriggle Crick.
Equity—?
Lawyer and Child.
Rukeyser, M.   Bill, The.
Disease: After-Effects, The.
Doctors, The.
Praise of the Committee.
Sandburg, C.   Lawyer.
Lawyers Know Too Much, The.
Swift, J.   Helter Skelter.
Updike.   Mr. High-Mind.
Williams, M.   In Extremis *in Hardy, Arkansas*.
Williams, W.   To a Friend.
Wilner, E.   Eleusis.
Zagajewski.   Trial, The.
Zukofsky, L.   Laws Can Say, The.

Lawes, Henry
Milton.   To Mr. H. Lawes on His Airs.

Lawn Mowers
Ciardi, J.   On the Orthodoxy and Creed of My Power Mower.
Saturday.
Hughes, T.   Sunstroke.
Ignatow, D.   Death of a Lawn Mower.
Niedecker.   Lawnmower's one of the babies I'd have, A.

Lawns
Ammons.   Space Travel.
Creeley.   For Helen.
Dickinson, E.   Presentiment—is that long Shadow—on the lawn.
Herrick.   Lawne, The.
Hughes, T.   Sunstroke.
Jacobsen, J.   Lawn Bowlers, The.
Spread of Mrs. Mobey's Lawn.
Logan, J.   Five Preludes for Buffalo's Own Forest Lawn.
Orr, G.   Virginia Backyard: July.
Warren, R.   Sitting on Farm Lawn on Sunday Afternoon.
Wordsworth, W.   This Lawn, a Carpet All Alive.
Zukofsky, L.   Guests, The.

Lawrence, D. H. (David Herbert)
Ferlinghetti, L.   Man Who Rode Away, The.
Lawrence, D. H.   No! Mr Lawrence!
O'Hara, F.   Poem: "I don't know as I get what D.H. Lawrence is driving at."
Williams, W.   Elegy for D.H. Lawrence, An.

Lawrence, Edward
Milton.   To Mr. Lawrence.

Lawrence, T. E. (Thomas Edward)
Niedecker.   T. E. Lawrence.

Lazarus (Bible)
Browning, R.   Epistle Containing the Strange Medical Experience of Karshish, the Arab Physician, An.
Clifton, L.   Lazarus ("I am not the same man").
Crashaw.   Upon Lazarus His Teares.
Dickey, J.   Lazarus to the Assembled.
Gunn, T.   Lazarus Not Raised.
Hill, G.   History as Poetry.
Robinson, E.   Lazarus.
Rossetti, C.   Son, Remember.
Sexton.   Jesus Summons Forth.
Stock, R.   Laying-Out of Lazarus.
Williams, M.   Adjusting to the Light.
Wright, J.   Come Forth.

Laziness
Burns, R.   Weary Pund o' Tow, The.
Campion, T.   Lighten, heavy hart, thy spright.
So Tir'd Are All My Thoughts.
Clough.   He sate, no stiller stands a rock.
Dunbar, P.   In the Morning.
Han-shan.   All my life too lazy to work.
Herrick.   Ass[e], The.
Long and Lazy [*or* Lazie].
Hughes, L.   Kid Sleepy.
Madam and the Army.
Lawrence, D. H.   Bathing Resort.
Nash, O.   Introspective Reflection.
Let's Not Climb the Washington Monument Tonight.
Where There's a Will, There's Velleity.
Who Called That Robin a Piccolo Player?
Neruda.   Ode to Laziness.
Riley, J.   Symptoms.
Roethke.   Poetaster.
Sloth, The.
Rumi.   Night Air, The.
Smith, S.   From the French (1).
Lament of a Slug-a-Bed's Wife.
Williams, W.   Portrait of a Woman in Bed.
Yeats.   Chambermaid's Second Song, The.

Leadership
Bierce.   Right.
Borges.   Milonga of Don Nicanor Paredes.
Byron, G.   Sonnet to the Prince Regent.
Cuadra, P.   Urn with a Political Profile.
Cummings, E. E.   To William F. Bradbury.
Eberhart, R.   Way Out, A.
Eliot, T. S.   Coriolan.
Emerson, R.   Go boldly forth, and feast on being's banquet.
Hardy, T.   Murmurs in the Gloom.
Herrick.   Examples, or Like Prince, Like People.
Like Pattern, Like People.
Society.
Hughes, T.   Guide, The.
Jonson, B.   To Sir Horace Vere.
To True Soldiers.
To William, Earl[e] of Pembroke.
Kipling, R.   Akbar's Bridge.
Bells and Queen Victoria, The.
Norman and Saxon.
One Viceroy Resigns.
Servant When He Reigneth, A.
Together.
Lindsay, N.   Abraham Lincoln Walks at Midnight.
Meredith, G.   Ambition.
Day is going, now 'tis noon, The.
Hawarden.
To J.M.
To Lord Palmerston.
Olson, C.   Leader, The.
Pagis.   Grand Duke of New York, The.
Ramanujan.   Ruler, A.
Ritsos.   Double Condemnation.
Robinson, E.   Master, The.
Rumi.   Lame Goat, The.
Sandburg, C.   Is There Any Easy Road to Freedom?
Whitman, W.   Not the Pilot.
Thought.
Wordsworth, W.   Emperors and Kings, How Oft Have Temples Rung.

Leander
Logan, J. Tale of a Later Leander.
See also **Hero and Leander**

Leap Year
Amichai [*or* Amikhai]. In a Leap Year.

Lear, Edward
Auden. Edward Lear.
Tennyson, A. To E.L., on His Travels in Greece.

Lear, King
See **King Lear**

Learning
Amichai [*or* Amikhai]. You Can Rely on Him.
Atwood. You Begin.
Beckett, S. Gnome.
Chuang Tzu. Duke Hwan and the Wheelwright.
Keng's Disciple.
Useless, The.
Coleridge, S. Lines to Thomas Poole.
Creeley. Learning.
Donne. Obscure Writer, An.
Glück, L. Illuminations.
Graves, R. Plea to Boys and Girls, A.
Han-shan. Child who doesn't have a teacher, A.
HaNagid. Stab Your Heart.
Herrick. Precepts.
Jarrell, R. Randall Jarrell, Office Hours 10-11.
Jonson, B. Epigram on Sir Edward Coke, when He Was Lord Chief Justice of England, An.
To the Same [Sir Henry Goodyere].
Koch, K. Some General Instructions.
Lorde. As I Grew Up Again.
Black Mother Woman.
Lux. You Go to School to Learn.
Meredith, G. My Theme: Continued.
Meredith, W. Fledglings.
Merwin. Piper, The.
Place of Backs, The.
Teachers.
Oliver, M. Learning about the Indians.
Starfish.
Olson, C. Of Lady, of Beauty, of Stream.
Rilke. Lesson, The.
Rossetti, C. 1 and 1 are 2— / That's for me and you.
Sandburg, C. Let Them Ask Your Pardon.
People with Proud Chins.
Shelley, P. To a Skylark.
Sheridan, T. Thus Cacus-like, His Calves He Backwards Pulls.
Snyder, G. Axe Handles.
For Example.
Stafford, W. Learning, Any Time.
Living on the Plains.
Things I Learned Last Week.
Tomlinson, C. Instead of an Essay.
Le Musée Imaginaire.
Whalen, P. Self-Portrait Sad, 22:ix:58.
Whitman, W. Lessons.
Whittier. Library, The.
Spiritual Manifestation, A.
Wilbur, R. Mechanist, The.
Williams, C. K. First Desires.
Spirit the Triumph, The.
Williams, M. Before.
Wordsworth, W. Oxford, May 30, 1820.
Yeats. Another Song of a Fool.

Leaves
Amichai [*or* Amikhai]. I am like a leaf that knows its limits.
Ammons. Event.
Phase.
Right On.
Shoreless Tide, The.
This Bright Day.
Berry, W. October 10.
Bishop, E. Quai d'Orléans.
Blue Cloud. Meditation of Leaves, A.
Carruth, H. I Could Take.
Leaf from Mr. Dyer's Woods, A.
Clampitt. Continental Drift.
Creeley. Fall.
Cummings, E. E. !blac / k / agains / t.
D-re-A-mi-N-gl-Y / leaves / (sEe).
L(a / le / af / fa / ll / s).

Dickey, J. Vessels.
Dickinson, E. I remember the leaves were falling.
Dunbar, P. Chase, The.
Frost, R. Gathering Leaves.
In Hardwood Groves.
Leaf-Treader, A.
Leaves Compared with Flowers.
Misgiving.
Graves, R. Everywhere Is Here.
Gurney, I. Between the Boughs.
Hall, D. Days, The.
Kicking the Leaves.
Stone Walls.
Hardy, T. June Leaves and Autumn.
Master and the Leaves, The.
Hopkins, G. Silver scarce-call-silver gloss, A.
Housman. When green buds hang in the elm.
Hughes, T. Leaves.
Ignatow, D. Autumn 2.
I Saw a Leaf.
I Shake My Fist at a Tree.
Information.
Leaf, A.
My Own House.
One Leaf.
Separate Dead, The.
Jackson, L. So Slight.
Jacobsen, J. Leaf with Berry.
Larkin, P. Trees, The.
Lawrence, D. H. Difference, The.
Fallen Leaves.
Leaves of Grass, Flowers of Grass.
Levertov. July 1968.
MacLeish. Old Men in the Leaf Smoke, The.
Mahon. Leaves.
McHugh, H. Fall, The.
Merwin. Man with One Leaf in October Night.
Sickness at the Equinox, A.
Writing on a Fallen Leaf, The.
Nemerov. Burning the Leaves.
Threshold.
Niedecker. Paul / when the leaves.
O'Hara, F. Les Étiquettes Jaunes.
Pastoral Dialogue, A.
Paley, G. For George (I).
Pessoa. Audible smile of the leaves.
Prunty. Box of Leaves, A.
Foliage Tour, The.
Late Fall, Late Light.
Raine, K. Falling Leaves.
Golden Leaf, The.
Leaf, The.
Rexroth, K. Falling Leaves and Early Snow.
Requiem: "Thousand leaves slant down across the rain, A."
Rilke. To Betsy Steiger.
Robinson, E. Pity of the Leaves, The.
Rossetti, C. Who Has Seen the Wind?
Sandburg, C. Auburn.
Bird Talk.
Cornucopia.
Little Sketch.
October Paint.
Sleep Impression.
Year, The.
Schuyler, J. 8/12/70.
Autumn Leaves.
Buttered Greens.
October.
We Are Leaves.
Sexton. Leaves That Talk.
Shelley, P. Ode to the West Wind.
Stevens, W. Course of a Particular, The.
Swenson, M. Look Closer.
Sze. Shapes of Leaves, The.
Tomlinson, C. Autumn Piece.
Elemental.
Very. Autumn Leaf, The.
Autumn Leaves.
Dying Leaf, The.
Falling Leaf, The.
Sumach Leaves, The.
Withered Leaf—Seen on a Poet's Table, A.
Warren, R. Aspen Leaf in Windless World.
Wilbur, R. Alatus.

March.
October Maples, Portland.
Then.
Two Quatrains for First Frost.
Under a Tree.
Williams, W. Avenue of Poplars, The.
Confidence, A.
Disputants, The.
Lines: "Leaves are greygreen."
Offering.
Quietness.
Soughing Wind, The.
To Be Closely Written on a Small Piece of Paper Which Folded into a Tight Lozenge Will Fit Any Girl's Locket.
Wilner, E. Mulch, The.
Wordsworth, W. Kitten and [the] Falling Leaves, The.
Whirl-blast from behind the hill, A.
Wright, J. To the August Fallen.
Zaturenska. Chorale for Autumn.
Zukofsky, L. Green leaf that will outlast the winter.
See also **Autumn**

Lebanon and Lebanese
Merton. Lubnan.

Leda
Bogan, L. Stanza: "No longer burn the hands that seized."
Broumas, O. Leda and Her Swan.
Clifton, L. Leda 1.
Leda 2.
Leda 3.
Cunningham, J. On Correggio's Leda.
"Dario." For just a moment, O Swan, I will link my longings.
Graves, R. Leda.
"H. D." Leda.
Lawrence, D. H. Leda.
Millay, E. I Dreamed I Moved among the Elysian Fields.
Van Duyn. Leda.
Leda Reconsidered.
Wilner, E. Leda's Handmaiden.
Yeats. Leda and the Swan.

Ledwidge, Francis
Heaney, S. In Memoriam Francis Ledwidge.

Lee, Robert Edward
Pinkerton, H. Crossing the Pedregal.
Sandburg, C. Hammers Pounding.

Legs
Cummings, E. E. My girl's tall with hard long eyes.
Graves, R. Legs, The.
Herrick. Her Legs.
To Dianeme.
Laughlin, J. Why.
Nash, O. Octopus, The.
Olson, C. Lalage!
Sexton. Barefoot.
Tate, J. Man with Wooden Leg Escape Prison.
Updike. Rockettes, The.
Whitman, W. Runner, The.
Williams, W. Cold Night, The.
Portrait of a Lady.

Leicester, Robert Dudley, Earl of
Ralegh, S. Epitaph on the Earl of Leicester [*or* Leceister].

Leisure
Carver, R. Loafing.
Dove, R. One Volume Missing.
Dunbar, P. Lazy Day, A.
Eliot, T. S. Interlude in London.
Hardy, T. Farmer Dunman's Funeral.
Hopkins, G. Penmaen Pool.
Riley, J. Knee-deep in June.
Rossetti, C. Pastime.
Pocket handkerchief to hem, A.
Reflection.
Song of Flight, A.
Swift and sure the swallow.
Snyder, G. Walk, A.
Wright, J. Lying in a Hammock at William Duffy's Farm in Pine Island, Minnesota.

Lemmings
Ciardi, J.   Down Narrow Stairs from a Thin Eye.
Lemons
Montale.   In the Greenhouse.
Lemons, The.
Rilke.   Lemon and Laburnum.
Ritsos.   Miniature.
Walcott.   Sunday Lemons.
Lenin, Vladimir Ilyich
Hughes, L.   Ballads of Lenin.
Lenin.
MacDiarmid, H.   Are my poems spoken in the factories and fields.
Skeleton of the Future, The.
MacLeish.   Background with Revolutionaries.
Rukeyser, M.   Motive of All of It, The.
Leningrad, Russia
See **Saint Petersburg** [*formerly* **Leningrad**], **Russia**
Lennon, John
Clampitt.   Dakota, The.
Codrescu.   Music.
Ferlinghetti, L.   John Lennon in the Porto Santo Stefano.
Lent
Broumas, O.   Lenten.
Herbert, G.   Lent.
Herrick.   Fast, or Lent, The.
To Keep a True Lent.
Upon Bungie.
Merton.   Lent.
Rossetti, C.   Mid-Lent.
Passiontide.
Schuyler, J.   Blossoming Oakwood.
Leonardo da Vinci
Ciardi, J.   Conversation with Leonardo, A.
Eberhart, R.   Cancer Cells, The.
Enzensberger, H.   Last Supper. Venetian, Sixteenth Century.
Moore, M.   Expedient, An—Leonardo da Vinci's—and a Query.
Leonardo Da Vinci's.
Rossetti, D.   For "Our Lady of the Rocks" by Leonardo da Vinci.
Shelley, P.   On the Medusa of Leonardo da Vinci in the Florentine Gallery.
Leopardi, Giacomo
Laughlin, J.   We Met in a Dream.
Zaturenska.   Luna and Leopardi.
Leopards
Dickinson, E.   Civilization—spurns—the Leopard!
With thee—in the Desert.
Jarrell, R.   Snow-Leopard, The.
Kumin, M.   Catchment.
Orr, G.   Visit to the Island of Lost Souls.
Leopold III, King of the Belgians
Berryman.   Moon and the Night and the Men, The.
Lepanto, Battle of (1571)
Chesterton.   Lepanto.
Lepidoptery and Lepidopterists
Laughlin, J.   Moths, The.
Leprechauns
Millay, E.   Singing-Woman from the Wood's Edge, The.
Leprosy and Lepers
Dubie.   Pennacesse Leper Colony for Women, Cape Cod, The: 1922.
Herrick.   To Women, to Hide Their Teeth, if They Be Rotten or Rusty.
Kipling, R.   Gehazi.
Komunyakaa.   Leper's Bell, The.
Merton.   Ointment, The.
Rites for the Extrusion of a Leper.
Rossetti, C.   Go in Peace.
Swinburne.   Leper, The.
Lesbians
Baudelaire.   Damned Women ("Half-hidden in the dying light's caress").
Begley, T.   Vowel Imprint.
Broumas, O.   Amazon Twins.
Backgammon.
Beauty and the Beast.

Bitterness.
Blues / for J.C.
Caritas.
Field.
Four Beginnings / for Kyra.
Leda and Her Swan.
Mornings Remembering Last Nights.
Namaste.
Ode: "Ask me no more."
Plunging into the Improbable.
Rapunzel.
Rumpelstiltskin.
Sleeping Beauty.
Snow White.
Vowel Imprint.
Logue, C.   Girls, The.
Lorde.   On a Night of the Full Moon.
See also **Homosexuality and Homosexuals**
Lesbos, Greece
Baudelaire.   Lesbos.
Millay, E.   Evening on Lesbos.
Lethargy
Dugan, A.   After a Poem by Carlos Drummond de Andrade Translated by Elizabeth Bishop as *Don't Kill Yourself.*
Duncan, R.   Dreamers, The.
Letter Carriers
See **Mail and Mailmen**
Letters
Amichai [*or* Amikhai].   Gifts of Love.
Letter, A.
Ashbery, J.   Thoughts of a Young Girl.
Atwood.   Postcard.
Auden.   Letter, The.
Berryman.   Winter-Piece to a Friend Away, A.
Bishop, E.   Letter to N.Y.
Bogan, L.   Packet of Letters.
Bradstreet, A.   Another.
In Thankful Acknowledgement for the Letters I Received from My Husband Out of England.
Browning, R.   To Miss Unger.
Bukowski.   Almost Made Up Poem, An.
Artists.
Love.
Note to the Boys in the Back Room, A.
Carew, T.   Elegy on the La: Pen: Sent to My Mistress Out of France, An.
My Mistress Commanding Me to Return Her Letters.
Carver, R.   Hummingbird.
Ciardi, J.   Letter Homeward.
Cooper, J.   95°.
Letters.
Little Vesper, A.
Cowper, W.   On a Letter of Miss Fanshawe.
Crane, H.   My Grandmother's Love Letters.
Creeley.   Interview, The.
Invoice, The.
Names.
Cummings, E. E.   "April" / this letter's dated.
Ecco a letter starting "dearest we."
Lady you have written me a letter.
Mr. smith / is reading / his letter.
Cunningham, J.   Letter, A.
On a Letter.
Dickinson, E.   Going—to—Her!
Going to Him! Happy letter!
In Ebon Box, when years have flown.
Interview is acres.
Letter always seemed to me, A.
Letter is a joy of Earth, A.
This is but a fragment.
Way I read a Letter's—this, The.
What a Hazard a Letter is!
Donne.   H. W. in Hibernia Belligeranti.
Letter Written by Sir H. G. and J. D. alternis vicibus, A.
To Mr T. W. ("Pregnant again with th' old twins hope, and fear").
To Mrs M. H.
To the Countess of Bedford ("To have written then, when you writ, seemed to me").
Dunbar, P.   Love Letter, A.
Emerson, R.   Letters.
Gallagher, T.   Under Stars.

Gjuzel.   My Sister's Letter.
Graves, R.   H.
Half-Finished Letter, The.
Love and Night.
Love Letter, The.
Not at Home.
Song: Of Course.
Strayed Message, The.
Gunn, T.   Invitation, An.
Hall, D.   Eleanor's Letters.
Hardy, T.   Letter's Triumph, The.
Love-Letters, The.
Read by Moonlight.
Sun on the Letter, The.
Thing Unplanned, The.
Torn Letter, The.
Wife in London, A.
Hayden, R.   Letter.
Hopkins, G.   Complaint, A.
Hughes, L.   Little Old Letter.
Personal.
Hughes, T.   Where I Sit Writing My Letter.
Ignatow, D.   Trough.
Jackson, L.   Letter to Any Friend, A.
Jarrell, R.   Burning the Letters.
Kinsella, T.   Artists' Letters.
Kizer, C.   Postcards from Rotterdam.
Koch, K.   Railway Stationery, The.
To Marina.
Kunitz, S.   Night Letter.
Larkin, P.   At Thirty-One, when Some Are Rich.
Laughlin, J.   Cultural Note.
Her Letters.
How Fortunate.
Two Letters on Samos.
Lawrence, D. H.   Correspondence in After Years.
No News.
Levertov.   Crosspurposes.
Postcard.
Sparks.
Writing to Aaron.
Levi, P.   After R.M. Rilke.
Lorde.   Martha.
Trip on the Staten Island Ferry, A.
McHugh, H.   A.
Meredith, G.   Dear, my friend & honour'd madam! of hard facts I'm not a hoarder.
Fair Bedfellow, The.
Grandfather Bridgeman.
She scarce has a word for Papa.
Thou pirate nested over Alde!
Meredith, W.   Mild-Spoken Citizen Finally Writes to the White House, A.
Merrill, J.   Friend of the Fourth Decade, The.
Merwin.   Letter.
Michelangelo Buonarroti.   Having, my friend, your letter here in hand.
Moore, M.   Bowls.
Muldoon, P.   Thrush.
Nash, O.   What's in a Name? Some Letter I Always Forget.
O'Hara, F.   Postcard from John Ashbery, A.
Oliver, M.   Letter from Home, A.
Owen, W.   Letter, The.
Paley, G.   Letter, A.
Palmer, M.   Dear M ("Sky today yes and no, The. I am writing a play about a man with a pebble").
Echo.
Parker, D.   Letter to Robert Benchley; Roughing It in the Country at the Birches, Maine.
Piercy.   Letter to be Disguised as a Gas Bill.
Plath.   Burning the Letters.
Pope, A.   Verses Occasioned by an & c. at the End of Mr. D'Urfy's Name in the Title.
Ransom, J.   Parting, without a Sequel.
Rich, A.   On Edges.
Postcard.
Your Letter.
Riley, J.   Writin' Back to the Home Folks.
Rossetti, C.   Lines to My Grandfather.
Otto ore suonano: / Picchia il postino!
Postman, The.
Sandburg, C.   Bilbea.
One Parting.

Sarah's Letter to Peter.
Schuyler, J.   Ilford Rose Book.
  Stone Knife, A.
  Voyage Autour de Mes Cartes Postales.
Seifert.   Fragment of a Letter.
Sexton.   Letter Written during a January
   Northeaster.
  Letter Written on a Ferry while Crossing Long
   Island Sound.
  Some Foreign Letters.
Smart, C.   Epistle to Dr. Nares.
Smith, S.   Emily Writes Such a Good Letter.
  Jungle Husband, The.
Stafford, W.   New Letters from Thomas
   Jefferson.
Sze.   Pentimento.
Szymborska, W.   Letters of the Dead, The.
Tomlinson, C.   Letter from Costa Brava.
  Letters from Amherst.
Van Duyn.   Letters from a Father.
  Relative and an Absolute, A.
Walcott.   Letter from Brooklyn, A.
Walker, A.   Suicide.
  What the Finger Writes.
Warren, R.   You Sort Old Letters.
Whalen, P.   Letter to Thomas Clark 22:VII:71
   from Bolinas Where He Sat beside Me, The.
Whitman, W.   Come Up from the Fields Father.
Wilbur, R.   Part of a Letter.
Wilde, O.   Sonnet on the Sale by Auction of
   Keats' Love Letters.
Williams, M.   La Ultima Carta: A Young Wife
   Writes to Her Husband in the Mountains.
Wordsworth, W.   Upon Perusing the "Epistle [To
   Sir George Howland Beaumont]."
Wright, J.   Idiotic and Politic.
Zagajewski.   Your Telephone Call.
Zaturenska.   Dream Message.
See also **Mail and Mailmen**

Lettuce
Piercy.   Love of Lettuce, The.

Levees
Hughes, L.   Mississippi Levee.

Leven River, Scotland
Burns, R.   Campbells Are Comin, The.

Levet, Robert
Johnson, S.   On the Death of Dr [*or* Mr] Robert
   Levet [a Practiser in Physic].

Leviathan
Levertov.   Ache of Marriage, The.

Lewis, Meriwether
Tate, J.   Lewis and Clark Overheard in
   Conversation.

Lexington and Concord, Battles of (1775)
Whittier.   Lexington.

Li Po
Komunyakaa.   "Everybody's Reading Li Po"
   Silkscreened on a Purple T-Shirt.
Levertov.   Poet Li Po Admiring a Waterfall,
   The.
MacLeish.   Poet's Laughter.
Rexroth, K.   To Another.
Sze.   Li Po.
Tu Fu.   To Li Po.
  Tu Fu to Li Po.
Wright, C.   Portrait of the Artist with Li Po.

Liars
Hughes, L.   Liars.
Jackson, L.   Rejoice, Liars.
See also **Lies and Lying**

Liberalism and Liberals
Angelou.   On Working White Liberals.
Browning, R.   Lost Leader, The.
  Why I Am a Liberal.
Hughes, L.   Northern Liberal.
Parker, D.   Slackers; A Hate Song.
Patchen.   Letter to the Liberals, A.
Tate, A.   Eclogue of the Liberal and the Poet.

Liberty
Bierce.   Invocation.
See also **Freedom**

Liberty Bell
Riley, J.   Voice of Peace, The.

Liberty, Statue of
Bierce.   To the Bartholdi Statue.
Cummings, E. E.   Woman / of bronze / unhappy,
   A.
Gunn, T.   Iron Landscapes (and the Statue of
   Liberty).
Whittier.   Bartholdi Statue, The.
Wilbur, R.   On Freedom's Ground.

Libraries and Librarians
Amichai [*or* Amikhai].   At the University of
   New Orleans.
Borges.   Alexandria, A.D. 641.
  For Leopoldo Lugones.
  Guardian of the Books, The.
  June, 1968.
  Poem of the Gifts.
  Readers.
Cavafy.   Tomb of the Grammarian Lysias.
Clampitt.   Balms.
Collins, B.   Books.
  Tomes.
Cowper, W.   On Mrs. Montagu's Feather-
   Hangings.
Davie, D.   Grace in the Fore Street.
Dugan, A.   In Favor of a Free Public Library
   System.
Eberhart, R.   Reading Room, the New York
   Public Library.
Ignatow, D.   Love Poem for the Forty-Second
   Street Library.
Jarrell, R.   Carnegie Library, Juvenile Division,
   The.
  Children Selecting Books in a Library.
  Girl in a Library, A.
Jonson, B.   Execration upon Vulcan, An.
Larkin, P.   New Eyes Each Year.
MacNeice.   British Museum Reading Room,
   The.
Milosz, C.   Beinecke Library.
  Book in the Ruins, A.
  Pierson College.
  Woe!
Milton.   To John Rouse.
Niedecker.   Broad-leaved Arrow-head, The.
Pinsky.   Library Scene.
Prunty.   Extravagant Love.
Rexroth, K.   Further Advantages of Learning.
  Under Soracte.
Stafford, W.   Afternoon in the Stacks, An.
Tomlinson, C.   Portrait of the Artist II.
Weiss, T.   Fire at Alexandria, The.
  Library Revisited, The.
Whittier.   Library, The.
Williams, C. K.   Critic, The.
Zaturenska.   Girl in a Library.

Lice
Burns, R.   To a Louse [On Seeing One on a
   Lady's Bonnet at Church].
Glück, L.   Chicago Train, The.
Niedecker.   Lights, lifts.
Williams, W.   Poor, The.

Lidice, Czech Republic [*formerly* Czechoslovakia]
Seifert.   Dead of Lidice, The.

Lies and Lying
Amichai [*or* Amikhai].   Song of Lies on
   Sabbath Eve, A.
  They Lied to Us.
Angelou.   How I Can Lie to You.
Atwood.   We are hard on each other.
Auden.   Their Lonely Betters.
Ausonius.   I am that Dido which thou here do'st
   see.
Berryman.   To Bhain Campbell.
Browning, E.   Garibaldi.
Browning, R.   Confessional, The.
Bukowski.   Old Gang, The.
Campion, T.   Faine would I my love disclose.
  In Barnum.
  Maid's Complaint, A.
Ciardi, J.   Knothole in Spent Time, A.
Coleridge, S.   Alice Du Clos.
Crane, S.   Yes, I have a thousand tongues.
Creeley.   Bed, The.
  Mind's Heart.
  Song: "Grit / of things, The."
Cullen, C.   To an Unknown Poet.

Cummings, E. E.   This evangelist / buttons with
   his big gollywog voice.
Donne.   Lame Beggar, A.
  Mercurius Gallo-Belgicus.
Dove, R.   Boast, The.
Dunbar, P.   We Wear the Mask.
Eberhart, R.   Critic with His Pained Eye, The.
  Hill Dream of Youth, Thirty Years Later.
Emerson, R.   This world is tedious.
Glück, L.   From the Japanese.
  Memo from the Cave.
Graves, R.   Iron Palace.
  Prepared Statement, The.
  Word, The.
Hall, D.   Grown-Ups, The.
Hardy, T.   Her Dilemma.
Herrick.   To Sapho.
  Upon Teage.
Hughes, L.   To Certain "Brothers."
Jackson, L.   Rejoice, Liars.
Jeffers, R.   Faith.
  Ink-Sack.
Kipling, R.   Pagett, M. P.
Lawrence, D. H.   Drawing-Room.
  Emotional Lies.
  I Am in a Novel.
  Laughter.
  Lies.
  Lies about Love.
  Poison.
MacLeish.   Ballad of the Corn-Cob and the Lie,
   The.
Merwin.   Owl, The.
Nash, O.   Golly, How Truth Will Out.
Parker, D.   Comment.
  Fable: "Oh, there once was a lady, and so I've
   been told."
  Social Note.
  Superfluous Advice.
  Unfortunate Coincidence.
Pope, A.   To the Earl of Burlington Asking Who
   Writ the Libels against Him.
Ralegh, S.   Lie, The.
Rich, A.   Cartographies of Silence.
  Our Whole Life.
Rilke.   Lies 1.
  Lies 2.
  Lies 3.
Robinson, E.   How Annandale Went Out.
  Lisette and Eileen.
  Uncle Ananias.
Rukeyser, M.   One Month.
  They rule out of our justice and our despair.
Rumi.   I honor those who try.
Sandburg, C.   Liars, The.
Schuyler, J.   On the Dresser.
Suckling, S.   Perjury Excused.
Tate, J.   Book of Lies, The.
Wilbur, R.   Lying.
Williams, M.   Jonathan's.
Wordsworth, W.   In Allusion to Various Recent
   Histories and Notices of the French
   Revolution.
  In Allusion to Various Recent Histories and
   Notices of the French Revolution, Concluded.

Life
Amichai [*or* Amikhai].   Course of a Life, The.
Ammons.   Cut the Grass.
Angelou.   Call Letters: Mrs. V.B.
  Lesson, The.
  Life Doesn't Frighten Me.
Armantrout.   Inside Out.
Ashbery, J.   Darlene's Hospital.
  Two Scenes.
Auden.   Precious Five.
Ausonius.   Out of Catullus.
Beckett, S.   D'où / la voix qui dit.
  Hors crâne seul dedans.
  My way is in the sand flowing.
  What would I do without this world faceless
   incurious.
Berrigan, T.   In the 51st State.
  Last Poem.
  Red Shift.
  Tambourine Life.
Berry, W.   Cold Pane, The.

Envoy: "Love, all day there has been at the edge of my mind."
Farmer among the Tombs, The.
For the Hog Killing.
Forty Years.
May Song.
Our Children, Coming of Age.
Poem of Thanks, A.
Praise.
Seeds, The.
Song (3).
Song (4).
Song Sparrow Singing in the Fall, A.
Sycamore, The.
To Think of the Life of a Man.
Berryman. Sympathy, a Welcome, A.
Bly, R. November Day at McClure's Beach.
Watcher, The.
Borges. Boast of Quietness.
My Whole Life.
Bradstreet, A. Of the Four Ages of Man.
Brodsky, J. Song of Welcome.
Browning, E. Felicia Hemans.
Human Life's Mystery.
Life.
Love.
Prospect, The.
Rhapsody of Life's Progress, A.
Sounds.
Browning, R. Master Hugues of Saxe-Gotha.
Pisgah-Sights. I.
Pisgah-Sights. II.
Rabbi Ben Ezra.
Reverie.
Bukowski. 86'd.
Love Poem, A.
One for the Shoeshine Man.
Overhead Mirrors.
Poem to a Most Affectionate Lady.
Windy Night.
Word on the Quick and Modern Poem-Makers, A.
Burns, R. Contented wi' Little.
Epistle to a Young Friend.
Here's, a bottle and an honest friend.
Lazy Mist, The.
Poem on Life.
Song: "My father was a farmer upon the Carrick border O."
Twa Dogs, The.
Byron, G. Egotism. A Letter to J.T. Becher.
If That High World.
Spell Is Broke, the Charm Is Flown, The.
Thoughts for a Speech of Lucifer, in the Tragedy of "Cain."
Cardenal. Dog barks far out, A.
Every evening the L & N.
I do not know who is out in the snow.
I turned out the light to see the snow.
Like Empty Beer Cans.
Like the flights of ducks.
Long freight train / Wakes me in my cell, The.
Sound of passing cars, (if a car comes), The.
Spring has come with its smell of Nicaragua.
That auto horn sounds familiar.
When the first signs go on.
Zinc roofs in the moonlight, The.
Carruth, H. Contra Mortem.
Wreck of the Circus Train, The.
Carver, R. Late Fragment.
Chamfort. Trouble with tragedy is the fuss it makes, The.
Chuang Tzu. Three Friends.
True Man, The.
Turtle, The.
Clough. Enough, small Room,—though all too true.
Here have I been these one and twenty years.
O stream, descending to the sea.
To spend unsolaced years of pain.
Coleridge, S. Epitaph: "Stop, Christian passer-by!—Stop, child of God."
Life.
On a Cataract.
Psyche.
Suicide's Argument, The.

What Is Life?
Wish, A.
Crashaw. Epithalamium: "Come virgin Tapers of pure waxe."
Creeley. Bresson's Movies.
Flowers.
On a Theme by Lawrence, Hearing Purcell.
People.
Sad Advice.
Cullen, C. I Have a Rendezvous with Life.
Life's Rendezvous.
More than a Fool's Song.
Protest.
Self Criticism.
Cummings, E. E. Anyone Lived in a Pretty How Town.
As freedom is a breakfastfood.
Ci-gît l Foetus(unborn to not die).
Conceive a man,should he have anything.
Death(having lost)put on his universe.
Denied night's face / have shadowless they?
Go(perpe)go / (tu)to(al).
Great advantage of being alive, The.
Honour corruption villainy holiness.
If everything happens that can't be done.
Into the strenuous briefness.
Life is more true than reason will deceive.
May my heart always be open to little.
Might these be thrushes climbing through almost(do they).
My Father Moved through Dooms of Love.
Out of midsummer's blazing most not night.
Plant Magic dust / expect hope doubt.
Precisely as unbig a why as i'm.
Rain or hail / sam done.
Sometimes i am alive because with.
Sonnet entitled how to run the world).
Suppose / Life is an old man carrying flowers on his head.
Will out of the kindness of their hearts a few philosophers tell me.
Cunningham, J. For a Woman with Child.
"Life flows to death as rivers to the sea."
"Dario." What Gets You.
De la Mare. Anatomy.
Argument, The.
Away.
Bright Life.
Courage.
Dreams.
Haunted.
Hunter, The.
Last Chapter, The.
Life.
Music Unheard.
Silence.
Snowflake, The.
Dickinson, E. Advance is Life's condition.
Between the form of Life and Life.
How sweet the "Life that now is."
I am alive—I guess.
Life is so strong a vision.
Life is the finest secret.
Life we have is very great, The.
Most of our Moments.
My Life had stood—a Loaded Gun.
Not all of life to live, is it.
Sweet is it as Life.
That it will never come again.
There is not so much Life as talk of Life.
This Is My Letter to the World.
To be alive—is Power.
Water, is taught by thirst.
We all have moments with the dust.
Word is dead, A.
Dove, R. Charm, The.
Fish in the Stone, The.
Ike.
This Life.
Dunbar, P. By Rugged Ways.
Common Things.
If.
Life.
Long Ago.
Passage, The.
Sum, The.

Duncan, R. After a Long Illness.
Eberhart, N. New Entrepreneurial Plan.
Eberhart, R. As if You Had Never Been.
Austere Poem.
Birth and Death.
Dead Skunk.
Evaluation under a Pine Tree, Lying on Pine Needles, An.
Examination of Psyche: Thoughts of Home.
Experience Evoked.
Extremity.
Flow of Thought.
Four Exposures.
Hard Structure of the World, The.
Hardening into Print.
Hardy Perennial.
Harvard Stadium.
Hill Dream of Youth, Thirty Years Later.
Human Being Is a Lonely Creature, The.
Ides of March, The.
In after Time.
John Ledyard.
Key West.
Lament of a New England Mother, The.
Later or Sooner.
Listing.
Long Swing, The.
Long Term Suffering.
Looking Head On.
Loss.
Lyric Absolute, The.
Meditation, A.
Meditation Two.
New Hampshire, February.
Oak, The.
Only in the Dream.
Quarrel with a Cloud.
Question Mark.
Return, The.
Rumination.
Suite in Prison.
To Kenya Tribesmen, the Turkana.
Usurper.
Ways and Means.
What Gives.
Worldly Failure.
You Think They Are Permanent but They Pass.
Young Greek, Killed in The Wars, A.
Emerson, R. Ah strange strange strange.
As the drop feeds its fated flower.
Blight.
But God will keep his promise yet.
Cloud upon cloud / The world is seeming.
Cup of life is not so shallow, The.
Days pass over me, The.
Day's Ration, The.
Far seen the river glides below.
Go boldly forth, and feast on being's banquet.
I use the knife.
Idealism.
Life.
Life is great / Men are small.
Nominalist and Realist.
O What have I to do.
On that night the poet went.
To J. W.
What never was no, & still will be.
Fenton, J. Skip, The.
Ferlinghetti, L. Autobiography.
Deep Chess.
Endless Life.
Heap of Broken Images, A.
Making Love in Poetry.
River Still to Be Found, A.
Sea Is Calm Tonight, The.
Sueño Real.
25.
Uses of Poetry.
Voix Glauque.
We squat upon the beach of love.
World is a beautiful place, The.
Frost, R. Master Speed, The.
On the Heart's Beginning to Cloud the Mind.
Question, A.
Road Not Taken, The.
Stopping by Woods on a Snowy Evening.

Gallagher, T.   Coats, The.
Ginsberg, A.   Four Haiku.
  Stool Pigeon Blues.
Graves, R.   To Evoke Posterity.
Gunn, T.   Confessions of the Life Artist.
  Incident on a Journey.
  Legal Reform.
  Rastignac at 45.
  Taylor Street.
"H. D."   White World.
Hacker, M.   Nights of 1962: The River
  Merchant's Wife.
Hall, D.   Carlotta's Confession.
Mr. Wakeville on Interstate 90.
Raisin, The.
HaNagid.   Lovers of Life.
Hardy, T.   Before Life and After.
  Chimes Play "Life's a Bumper!", The.
  Epitaph: "I never cared for Life: Life cared for
    me."
  Life Laughs Onward.
  Masked Face, The.
  Necessitarian's Epitaph, A.
  On One Who Lived and Died Where He Was
    Born.
  Placid Man's Epitaph, A.
  Thoughts from Sophocles.
  To Life.
  What's There to Tell?
Hayden, R.   Whipping, The.
Herbert, G.   Life.
  Water-Course, The.
Herrick.   Crosse and Pile.
  Four[e] Things Make Us Happy Here.
  Good Death, A.
  Life Is the Body's [or Bodies] Light.
  Readinesse.
  To His Closet-Gods.
  Upon Prickles.
Hill, G.   Scenes with Harlequins.
Hopkins, G.   Thou Art Indeed Just, Lord.
Housman.   Be still, my soul, be still; the arms
  you bear are brittle.
  Chestnut casts his flambeaux, and the flowers,
    The.
  First of May, The.
  From Far, from Eve and Morning.
  Immortal Part, The.
  Is my team plowing?
  Terence, This Is Stupid Stuff.
  Westward on the high-hilled plains.
Hughes, L.   Mother to Son.
Hughes, T.   October Salmon[, An].
  On the Reservations.
Jarrell, R.   Country Life, A.
  Rabbit hurries to the brim of its wood, The.
  Terms.
  Utopian Journey, A.
  Well Water.
  What's the Riddle.
Jeffers, R.   Animals.
  Ante Mortem.
  Praise Life.
  Purse-Seine, The.
  Treasure, The.
  Unformed volcanic earth, a female thing, The.
Jonson, B.   To William Roe ("When Nature bids
  us leave to live, 'tis late").
Keats.   Human Seasons, The.
  Ode to a Nightingale.
Kipling, R.   Envoi: "There's a whisper down the
  field where the year has shot her yield."
  Neighbours.
Larkin, P.   After-Dinner Remarks.
  Afternoons.
  And the Wave Sings because It Is Moving.
  Daily Things We Do, The.
  Days.
  Essential Beauty.
  Livings.
  Negative Indicative.
  Nothing to Be Said.
  Ultimatum.
  Under a Splendid Chestnut Tree.
Lawrence, D. H.   All That We Have Is Life.
  Battle of Life.

Being Alive.
Breath of Life, The.
Corot.
Doors.
Dreams Old and Nascent.
Fatality.
Full Life.
Kissing and Horrid Strife.
Life and the Human Consciousness.
Living, A.
Non-Existence.
On the Road.
Real Democracy.
Shades.
So Let Me Live.
Wandering Cosmos, The.
We Are Transmitters.
Levertov.   Journeyings.
  Living.
  O Taste and See.
  Web.
Levine, P.   Ashes.
  Ask the Roses.
  Blasting from Heaven.
  Clouds.
  Conductor of Nothing, The.
  Dog Poem.
  Genius.
  Gift for a Believer.
  Hold Me.
  How Much Earth.
  Let Me Begin Again.
  Lights I Have Seen Before.
  Look.
  Noon.
  On the Corner.
  Rain Downriver.
  Salami.
  Salts and Oils.
  Saturday Sweeping.
  Silent in America.
  Suit, The.
  Sweet Will.
  28.
  Walk with Tom Jefferson, A.
  Words.
Lindsay, N.   Being the Dedication of a Morning.
  I Want to Go Wandering.
Longfellow, H.   Psalm of Life, A.
  Village Blacksmith, The.
Lowell, R.   Bosworth Field.
Lux.   Triptych, Middle Panel Burning.
MacDiarmid, H.   Harry Semen.
  Water of Life.
  Wreck of the Swan, The.
MacLeish.   Rue Carpenter.
  Seafarer.
MacNeice.   Birthright.
  Habits, The.
  Half Truth from Cape Town.
  Now that the Shapes of Mist.
  Prayer before Birth.
Major, C.   Love against Death.
Melville, H.   Buddha.
Meredith, G.   Ballad of Past Meridian, A.
  Force and His Master.
  Gentleness of Death, The.
  Hear now the mission of good wine.
  Hymn to Colour.
  In the Dry.
  In the Woods.
  Riddle for Men, The.
  Sonnet: "Hateful are those false themes of
    speculation."
  Stave of Roving Tim, A.
Meredith, W.   Accidents of Birth.
Merrill, J.   Kostas Tympakianákis.
  Last Words.
  Peter.
Merton.   Early Legend, The.
  Vine, The.
Michelangelo Buonarroti.   Wo is me woe's me
  when I think.
Millay, E.   Thou famished grave, I will not fill
  thee yet.
Nash, O.   Any Millenniums Today, Lady?

What I Know about Life.
You and Me and P.B. Shelley.
Nemerov.   Life, A.
  Life Cycle of Common Man.
  Under the Bell Jar.
Neruda.   Possessions.
  Runaway Sun.
  Search.
  Today Isn't Everything.
O'Hara, F.   In Favor of One's Time.
  In Memory of My Feelings.
  Ode (To Joseph Lesueur) on the Arrow That
    Flieth by Day.
  Poem: "Instant coffeee with slightly sour
    cream."
  Steps.
Oliver, M.   Dogfish.
  Going to Walden.
  In Blackwater Woods.
  Magellan.
  One or Two Things.
  Ponds, The.
  Singapore.
  Summer Day, The.
  When Death Comes.
Olson, C.   A B Cs (3—for Rimbaud), A.
  Anniversary.
  Asymptotes.
  Binnacle, The.
  Chain of memory is resurrection I am a vain
    man, The.
  Conqueror.
  Distances, The.
  Drum World, The.
  He treads on edges of being where the drop.
  In one age or other, if not in this.
  K, The.
  Lamp, The.
  Peograms.
  Story of an Olson, and Bad Thing, The.
  Tomorrow.
  Will To, The.
Parker, D.   Coda: "There's little in taking or
  giving."
  Résumé.
Parra, N.   Piano Solo.
  What the Deceased Had to Say about Himself.
Patchen.   And I, Too, Am Something of a
  Stranger Here, My Friend.
  But of Life?
  Cloth of the Tempest, The.
  Continual Ministry of Thy Anger, The.
  Court of First Appeal.
  Cruelties of the Sportive Power.
  Examination into Life and Death, An.
  Fellow Soul, Sound Hunting to Thy
    Immeasurable Heart.
  Gautama in the Deer Park at Benares.
  Investigation of Certain Interesting Questions.
  It Is Big inside a Man.
  It Is for Us the Living.
  Meaning of Life, The.
  Message from the Assistant Chief of the Fly
    People, A.
  Old lean over the tombstones, the, The.
  Progress to a View of Life.
  Rites of Darkness, The.
  Roses of Life, The.
  There are no losses.
  Time to Believe!, A.
  Tribes of Rakala, The.
  Under the green ledge.
Piercy.   Right Thinking Man.
Plath.   Appearance, An.
  Channel Crossing.
  Life, A.
  Mystic.
Poe.   Dreams.
Pope, A.   Epistle I, to Sir Richard Temple, Lord
  Cobham.
Raine, K.   And that was all his life.
Ralegh, S.   What Is Our Life?
Rich, A.   Atlas of the Difficult World, An.
  Burning Oneself Out.
  Last Song.
  Living Memory.

Tattered Kaddish.
Transcendental Etude.
Rilke. Menace.
Nostalgia.
Robinson, E. Ballade by the Fire.
Llewellyn and the Tree.
Man against the Sky, The.
Octaves.
Roethke. Decision, The.
Judge Not.
Manifestation, The.
Orders for the Day.
Verse with Allusions.
Walk in Late Summer, A.
Rossetti, C. All Flesh Is Grass.
All heaven is blazing yet / With the meridian
sun.
Along the highroad the way is too long.
Annie.
Answer, An.
Autumn.
Awake, Thou That Sleepest.
Ballad of Boding, A.
Birthday, A.
Cobwebs.
Days of Vanity.
Dead Bride, The.
Dear Angels and dear disembodied Saints.
Eleventh Hour, The.
End Is Not Yet, The.
February 14. 1883.
From the Antique.
Goal in sihgt! Look up and sing, / Set faces full
against the light, The.
Half Dead.
Half Moon Shows a Face of Plaintive
Sweetness, The.
Have Patience.
Heaviness May Endure for a Night, But Joy
Cometh in the Morning.
I love you and you know it—this at least.
I said within myself: I am a fool.
I See that All Things Come to an End.
If love is not worth loving, then life is not worth
living.
If not with hope of life, / Begin with fear of
death.
"Immurata" Sister, An.
In resurrection is it awfuller.
Last *Complaint*, The.
Laughing Life cries at the feast.
Lent.
Life and Death.
Life that was born today / Must make no stay.
Life's Parallels, A.
Long Looked For.
Looking back along life's trodden way.
Man's life is but a working day / Whose tasks
are set aright.
Methinks the ills of life I fain would shun.
Mirrors of Life and Death.
My Old Friends.
Next of Kin.
Night and Death.
None with Him.
O foolish Soul! to make thy count / For languid
falls and much forgiven.
O thou who tell'st me that all hope is over.
O ye, who are not dead and fit.
Of My Life.
Our Church Palms are Budding Willow Twigs.
Our life is long. Not so, wise Angels say.
Pastime.
Pause of Thought, A.
Present and Future.
Redeeming the Time.
Saints and Angels.
Sappho.
Scarce tolerable life, which all life long.
So I began my walk of life; no stop.
Summer.
Then I Commended Mirth.
Then They That Feared the Lord Spake Often
One to Another.
Three Stages.
Time of Waiting, The.

To My First Love, My Mother.
Today's Burden.
Unforgotten.
Uphill.
Vanity of Vanities.
Water Spirit's Song, The.
Wednesday in Holy Week.
What Good Shall My Life Do Me?
What is the beginning? Love. What the course?
Love still.
World, The.
Wrens and robins in the hedge.
Yawn, A.
Yes, I too could face death and never shrink.
Yet a Little While.
You who looked on passed ages as a glass.
Rukeyser, M. All the Little Animals.
Six Canons, The.
Salinas, P. Not in Marble Palaces.
Sandburg, C. Almanac.
Always the Mob.
Anna Imroth.
Anywhere and Everywhere People.
Aprons of Silence.
Band Concert.
Bath.
Between Two Hills.
Between Worlds.
Blue Island Intersection.
Broken-Face Gargoyles.
Caboose Thoughts.
Chamfort.
Chillicothe.
Choices.
Clark Street Bridge.
Clean Hands.
Consolation Sonata.
Cripple.
Early Copper.
Eleventh Avenue Racket.
Flying Fish.
Gone.
Guaranteed Antique.
Hangman at Home, The.
Happiness.
Hazardous Occupations.
Heavy and Light.
Home Fires.
Hoodlums.
Humdrum.
Iglits and His Wife.
In a Breath.
In the Shadow of the Palace.
Jack.
Joke Gold.
Loam.
Long Guns.
Mag.
Many Hats.
Masses.
Mayor of Gary, The.
Methusaleh Saw Many Repeaters.
Mill-Doors.
Moon Riders.
Near Keokuk.
Night's Nothings Again.
Old Flagman, The.
Old Woman.
On the Way.
Onion Days.
Oomba.
Passers-by.
People of the Eaves, I Wish You Good Morning.
People Who Must.
Personalia.
Real Avenue News.
Red Son, The.
Right to Grief, The.
Shovel Man, The.
Silver Nails.
Sins of Kalamazoo, The.
Southern Pacific.
Still Life.
Teamster's Farewell, A.
Testament.
Themes in Contrast.

This Street Never Sleeps.
Three Ghosts.
Two Items.
Two Neighbors.
Variations on a Theme.
Whiffs of the Ohio River at Cinncinnati.
Without Notice Beforehand.
Working Girls.
Young Sea.
Schuyler, J. Few Days, A.
Hymn to Life.
Sky Eats Up the Trees, The.
Sexton. Courage.
End, Middle, Beginning.
Evil Eye, The.
Just Once.
Live.
Room of My Life, The.
Rowing.
Speaking Bitterness.
Shapiro, K. Interlude, The.
Shelley, P. Daemon of the World, The; A
Fragment.
Sonnet: Lift Not the Painted Veil: "Lift not the
painted veil which those who live."
Simic. Poem: "Every morning I forget how it
is."
Smith, S. All Things Pass.
Ceux Qui Luttent.
Come, Death (1).
Dream of Comparison, A.
God and the Devil.
Some Are Born.
Up and Down.
Snyder, G. Bed in the Sky, The.
Sinecure for P. Whalen, A.
Tiny Energies.
Stafford, W. Gift, The.
Journey, A.
Notes for the Program.
Quo Vadis.
Suckling, S. Ei Men Een Mathein.
Song: "I prithee spare me, gentle boy."
Swenson, M. Birthday.
Yes, the Mystery.
Swinburne. At Eleusis.
Szymborska, W. Allegro Ma Non Troppo.
Maybe All This.
Nothing's a Gift.
Tate, A. Meaning of Life, The.
Resurgam.
Tate, J. Prose Poem.
Thomas, D. All All and All the Dry Worlds
Lever.
Force That through the Green Fuse Drives the
Flower, The.
Foster the Light.
From Love's First Fever to Her Plague.
If I Were Tickled by the Rub of Love.
My World Is Pyramid.
This Bread I Break.
Twenty-four Years.
Thoreau. How little curious is man.
Ive searched my faculties around.
Life.
Life is a summer's day.
My friends, why should we live?
My life has been the poem I would have writ.
Sic Vita.
Tomlinson, C. Remembering Williams.
Updike. Furniture, The.
Hot Water.
Light Switches.
Sand Dollar.
Vallejo. Down to the Dregs.
Our Daily Bread.
Peace, the Wasp.
Van Duyn. Pot-au-feu.
Walcott. Prelude: "I, with legs crossed along the
daylight, watch."
Warren, R. Dragon-Tree.
Weiss, T. Barracks Apt. 14.
Whalen, P. Love Love Love Again.
Whitman, W. Beat! Beat! Drums!
Continuities.
Great Are the Myths.

Life.
Miracles.
My 71st Year.
Myself and Mine.
O Living Always, Always Dying.
To Be at All.
Two Rivulets.
Weave In, My Hardy Life.
When I Read the Book.
Whittier. At Eventide.
Wilbur, R. All That Is.
C Minor.
Driftwood.
In a Bird Sanctuary.
Leaving.
Ode to Pleasure.
Trolling for Blues.
"World without Objects Is a Sensible Emptiness, A."
Williams, C. K. Beyond.
Bread.
Cellophane.
Dimensions.
Faint Praise.
From Now On.
Hog Heaven.
Innings.
Like Little Birds.
Or.
Other Side, The.
Penance.
Race of the Flood, The.
Shade, The.
Sting, The.
This is what, / at last, it is.
Undead, The.
What Is and Is Not.
What Must I Do to Be Lost?
Williams, M. Liberal Imagination, The.
Living on the Surface.
People.
Waking from a Dream.
Williams, W. Butterandeggs.
History.
Horse Show, The.
Love Song: "Sweep the house clean."
Mind's Games, The.
Pastoral: "Little sparrows, The."
Pastoral 1: "Old man who goes about, The."
Some Simple Measures in the American Idiom and the Variable Foot.
Sunday.
Virtue.
You Have Pissed Your Life.
Wordsworth, W. Along the mazes of this song I go.
If This Great World of Joy and Pain.
Longest Day; Addressed to My Daughter, The.
Sweet was the walk along the narrow lane.
These Chairs they have no words to utter.
World is too much with us; late and soon, The.
Wright, C. Journal of the Year of the Ox, A.
Journal of True Confessions, A.
Laguna Blues.
Lost Souls.
Wright, J. American Twilights, 1957.
Angel, The.
Blue Teal's Mother.
Horse, The.
In Terror of Hospital Bills.
Inscription for the Tank.
Larry.
Life, The.
Many of Our Waters: Variations on a Poem by a Black Child.
Mutterings over the Crib of a Deaf Child.
Northern Pike.
Offense, The.
RIP.
River down Home, The.
Secret Gratitude, A.
To a Defeated Savior.
To a Friendly Dun.
To Harvey, Who Traced the Circulation.
Trying to Pray.
Undermining of the Defense Economy, The.

What the Earth Asked Me.
Yeats. Four Ages of Man, The.
Gyres, The.
Meru.
New Faces, The.
Scholars, The.
To Some I Have Talked with by the Fire.
What Magic Drum?
Wild Old Wicked Man, The.
Zagajewski. Elegy for the Living.
Fruit.
Zukofsky, L. Gamut.
Spook's Sabbath, Five Bowings.

Lifeguards
Amichai [or Amikhai]. Now the Lifeguards Have All Gone Home.
Dickey, J. Lifeguard, The.

Light
Amichai [or Amikhai]. Forgetting Someone.
People in the Dark Always See.
Ammons. City Limits, The.
I Broke a Sheaf of Light.
Two Motions.
Armantrout. Light.
Atwood. Eating Fire.
Berry, W. Breaking.
Returning.
Star, The.
Blake, W. To Morning.
Blue Cloud. First Light.
Bogan, L. Evening-Star.
Brontë, E. Not a vapour had stained the breezeless blue.
Still as she looked the iron clouds.
Browning, E. Best Thing in the World, The.
Romance of the Ganges, A.
Browning, R. Deaf and Dumb.
Byron, G. Darkness.
Campion, T. So sweet is thy discourse to me.
Carew, T. Beautiful Mistress, A.
Carver, R. Afterglow.
Cavafy. Chandelier.
Clampitt. Thinking Red.
Coleridge, S. Veil of Light, The.
Veil of Spirit, The.
Cooper, J. Morning on the St. John's.
Creeley. 10:30 AM: Ralph Hotere's.
Christmas: May 10, 1970.
Distance.
Kitchen.
Medallion.
Morning ("Light's bright glimmer").
Revelation, The.
Some Echoes.
To Say It.
Tunnel, The.
Two.
View, The.
World, The.
Cummings, E. E. Weazened Irrefutable unastonished.
Yes but even / 4 or(&).
Davie, D. Going to Italy.
Hardness of Light, The.
Sunburst.
De la Mare. Rose in Water, A.
Unforeseen.
Vigil.
Wanderers, The.
Dickey, J. Power and Light.
Spring-Shock.
Dickinson, E. Light exists in Spring, A.
Light is sufficient to itself.
Poets light but Lamps, The.
There's a certain Slant of light.
Donne. Nocturnal[l] upon Saint Lucy's [or S. Lucy's or S. Lucies] Day, Being the Shortest Day, A.
Dunbar, P. Light, The.
Light was on the golden sands, The.
Eberhart, R. Goal of Intellectual Man, The.
In after Time.
Incomparable Light, The.
Light from Above.
Light, Time, Dark.
Poetry and Games.

Return, The.
Emerson, R. And as the light divided the dark.
As the drop feeds its fated flower.
Coin the daydawn into lines.
On that night the poet went.
Enzensberger, H. Residual Light.
Ferlinghetti, L. Olbers' Paradox.
Gallagher, T. Bird-Window-Flying.
Gray Eyes.
Reading Aloud.
García Lorca. Little Mad Boy, The.
Graves, R. Children of Darkness.
Lament for Pasiphaë.
Sit Mihi Terra Levis.
Gunn, T. Lights among Redwood.
Map of the City, A.
Silver Age, The.
Sunlight.
Wrestling.
Gurney, I. Pleasance Window, The.
"H. D." Projector.
Projector II.
HaNagid. What Are These.
Hardy, T. Youth Who Carried a Light, The.
Heaney, S. Fireside.
Herrick. Life Is the Body's [or Bodies] Light.
Howe, F. Close Up.
Hughes, L. As I Grew Older.
Jackson, L. How Blind and Bright.
Jacobsen, J. Presences.
Kipling, R. Chartres Windows.
Coastwise Lights, The.
Kunitz, S. Round, The.
When the Light Falls.
Laughlin, J. House of Light, The.
What Is It Makes One Girl.
Lawrence, D. H. Let There Be Light!
Street Lamps.
Levertov. In Summer.
Levine, P. Belief.
Last Step, The.
Lights I Have Seen Before.
MacDiarmid, H. Milk-Wort and Bog Cotton.
Servant Girl's Bed.
MacLeish. No Lamp Has Ever Shown Us Where to Look.
Seeing.
MacNeice. Star-Gazer.
Mahon. Light Music.
Portrait of the Artist, A.
Marvell. Mower to the Glowworms [or Glow-Worms or Glo-Worms], The.
McHugh, H. Hag.
Shades.
Size of Spokane, The.
To See the Light.
McMichael. Inland Lighthouse, The.
Melville, H. In the Desert.
Merton. Candlemas Procession, The.
Millay, E. First Fig.
Milosz, C. Rays of Dazzling Light.
Montale. Don't escape into the shade.
Winter Light.
Nemerov. Advice from the Holy Tomb.
Madrigal: "She is the darkness where I wander."
Sunglasses, The.
Neruda. First Winter.
Inside.
Oliver, M. Buddha's Last Instruction, The.
Palmer, M. Maria's Gift.
Notes for Echo Lake 6.
Petrarch. I see, my noble lady.
There are some creatures in the world with eyes.
Piercy. Butt of Winter, The.
Pinkerton, H. Visible and Invisible.
Plath. Great Carbuncle, The.
Raine, K. Afternoon sunlight plays.
Images.
Oval the golden moon.
Path, The.
Rexroth, K. Mirror.
Monads.
Rich, A. Focus.
Insusceptibles, The.
Integrity.
Riley, J. Last Night—and This.

Ritsos. Provincial Spring.
Roethke. Light Listened.
Rossetti, C. Light of Light.
Shadows Today.
Truly the Light Is Sweet.
Whither the Tribes Go Up, Even the Tribes of the Lord.
Rukeyser, M. Risen Image Shines, The.
Sun-Artist, The.
Rumi. Light You Give Off, The.
Pale sunlight.
Shreds of Steam.
Zikr.
Sandburg, C. Butter Colors.
Evening Questions.
Feather Lights.
Haze Gold.
Light and Moonbells.
Little Candle.
Moonlight and Maggots.
Skyscraper Loves Night, The.
Smoke Shapes.
Star Silver.
Whitelight.
Winter Gold.
Sarton, M. Light Left On, A.
Schuyler, J. Light Within, The.
Shimmer.
Sun Cab, A.
This Soft October.
"Shu Ting." When You Come Past My Window.
Simic. Unknown One, The.
Smith, S. Light of Life, The.
Snyder, G. How Poetry Comes to Me.
Stafford, W. In Dear Detail, by Ideal Light.
Level Light.
Stevens, W. Of Hartford in a Purple Light.
Tattoo.
Swenson, M. April Light.
Thomas, D. Light Breaks Where No Sun Shines.
Tomlinson, C. Above the Rio Grande.
Bead, The.
Blade, The.
Brilliant Silence.
Carscape.
Civilities of Lamplight.
Cloud Change.
Couplet.
Down from Colonnata.
Frondes Agrestes.
Glass Grain.
In March.
In the Intensity of Final Light.
Night Ride.
Object in a Setting.
Of Beginning Light.
Sea is Open to the Light, The.
Urlicht.
Updike. Light Switches.
Very. Hymn on the Logos: The Light Still Shining in the Darkness.
Song: I Love the Light.
Walcott. Star.
Whittier. Light That Is Felt, The.
Wilbur, R. Five Women Bathing in Moonlight.
Williams, M. Gift of Prophecy Lost, The.
Light in the Eyes, The.
Williams, W. Seraph.
Wright, C. Appalachian Book of the Dead 3, The.
Cryopexy.
Meditation on Form and Measure.
Wright, J. Beginning.
Shadow and the Real, The.
To the Evening Star: Central Minnesota.
Yeats. He and She.
Zaturenska. Terraces of Light.
Zukofsky, L. Light.
Perch Less.

Lighthouses
Bishop, E. Seascape.
Clampitt. Baroque Sunburst, A.
Gunn, T. Round and Round.
Laughlin, J. Will We Ever Go to the

Lighthouse?
Oppen. Lighthouses, The.
Tomlinson, C. Lighthouse, The.
Very. Baker's Island Light, The.
Our Lighthouses.
Wilbur, R. Beacon, The.

Lightning
Ai. She Didn't Even Wave.
Dickey, J. Doorstep, Lightning, Waif-Dreaming.
Eagle's Mile, The.
Flash, The.
Dickinson, E. Lightning is a yellow Fork, The.
Lightning playeth—all the while, The.
Dubie. Bells in the Endtime of Gyurmey Tsultrim.
Emerson, R. At last the poet spoke.
Graves, R. Blackening Sky.
Hughes, T. Sometimes it comes, a gloomy flap of lightning.
Komunyakaa. Lightshow.
Kumin, M. Out in It.
Lawrence, D. H. Lightning.
Storm in the Black Forest.
MacDiarmid, H. Two Memories.
McHugh, H. Acts of God.
Montale. Green lizard, if it darts, The.
Nash, O. Watched Example Never Boils, A.
Oliver, M. Lightning.
Orr, G. Bolt from the Blue.
Paradise Lightning Dazzle.
Rexroth, K. It Turns Over.
Sandburg, C. Oak Arms.
Swenson, M. Lightning, The.
Updike. Old-Fashioned Lightning Rod.
Warren, R. Heat Lightning.
Twice Born.

Lightning Bugs
See **Fireflies**

Lilacs
Carruth, H. Ovid, Old Buddy, I Would Discourse with You a While.
Eberhart, R. Transformation.
MacLeish. Critics on the Lawn.
Schuyler, J. Lilacs.
Tate, J. Indian Undertaker, The.
Wilbur, R. Lilacs, The.
Zaturenska. Song of the Forsaken Lilac Tree.
Zukofsky, L. Lilac.

Lilies
Atwood. Squaw Lilies: Some Notes.
Berry, W. Lilies, The.
Cowper, W. Lily and the Rose, The.
Davie, D. Lily at Noon, A.
"H. D." Sea Lily.
Herrick. How Lillies Came White.
Upon One Lillie, Who Marryed with a Maid Call'd Rose.
Housman. Lent Lily, The.
Keats. La Belle Dame sans Merci [A Ballad].
Lawrence, D. H. Lilies in the Fire.
Montale. Red Lily, The.
Niedecker. Club 26.
Easter Greeting.
Oliver, M. Lilies.
Lilies Break Open over the Dark Water, The.
Ponds, The.
Rilke. White Lily.
Rimbaud, A. Lilies.
Rossetti, C. Consider the Lilies of the Field.
Lily has an air, / And the snowdrop a grace, The.
River Thames (?).
Rose that blushes rosy red, The.
Thy lilies drink the dew, / Thy lambs the rill, and I will drink them too.
Sandburg, C. Lavender Lilies.
Sexton. From the Garden.
Smart, C. On a Bed of Guernsey Lilies.
Very. Day Lily, The.
Nodding Meadow Lily, The.
Warren, R. Golden Hills of Hell, The.
Whalen, P. Message.
Williams, W. Lily, The.
Red Lily, The.
Zukofsky, L. Lilies.

Lilies of the Valley
Dunbar, P. Lily of the Valley, The.

Lilith
Levi, P. Lilith.
Rossetti, D. Eden Bower.
Wilner, E. What Was Going On.

Limbo
Auden. Limbo Culture.
Berrigan, T. After Peire Vidal, & Myself.
Coleridge, S. Limbo.
Creeley. For Cheryl.
Poe. Al Aaraaf.
Raine, K. Halt, The.

Limestone
Auden. In Praise of Limestone.
Jeffers, R. Bixby's Landing.

Lincoln, Abraham
Dunbar, P. Lincoln.
Eberhart, R. Fortune's Mist.
Hughes, L. Abe Lincoln.
Lincoln Monument: Washington.
Kunitz, S. Lincoln Relics, The.
Lindsay, N. Abraham Lincoln Walks at Midnight.
Babylon, Babylon, Babylon the Great.
Lowell, R. Abraham Lincoln.
MacLeish. At the Lincoln Memorial.
Melville, H. Martyr, The.
Riley, J. Lincoln.
Lincoln—The Boy.
Robinson, E. Master, The.
Sandburg, C. Cool Tombs.
Fire-Logs.
In a Back Alley.
Knucks.
Long Shadow of Lincoln: A Litany, The.
Potomac River Mist.
Sayings of Henry Stephens.
Tall Man, A.
Very. Finishing the Work.
Hymn: Sung at the Eulogy on Abraham Lincoln June 1st 1865.
Whitman, W. Abraham Lincoln, Born Feb. 12, 1809.
Memories of President Lincoln.
Whittier. Emancipation Group, The.
Quakers Are Out, The.

Lincolnshire, England
Davie, D. Lincolnshire.
Oriental Visitor, An.

Linden Trees
MacLeish. Linden Branch, The.
Linden Trees, The.
Zagajewski. Lindens.

Lindsay, Vachel
Ginsberg, A. To Lindsay.

Linen
Schuyler, J. Adverts.
Linen.
"Used Handkerchiefs 5¢."

Linnaeus, Carolus
Milosz, C. Linnaeus.

Linnets
Brontë, E. Song: "Linnet in the rocky dells, The."
De la Mare. Linnet, The.
Dubie. Elegy Asking that It Be the Last.
Meredith, G. Linnet-Hawker, The.
Rossetti, C. Hear what the mournful linnets say.
Linnet in a gilded cage,— / A linnet on a bough, A.
Wordsworth, W. Green Linnet, The.

Lions
Ammons. Lion::Mouse.
Turning.
Bourne, V. Reciprocal Kindness the Primary Law of Nature.
Bukowski. 10 Lions and the End of the World.
Carruth, H. Wreck of the Circus Train, The.
Creeley. Lion and the Dog, The.
Dubie. Buffalo Clouds over the Maestro Hoon.
Elegy for Wright & Hugo.
Dugan, A. Idyll of Ascension.
Duncan, R. In Waking.
Song of the Borderguard, The.

Lips
Eberhart, R.   Lions Copulating.
Ginsberg, A.   Lion for Real, The.
Graves, R.   Lion Lover.
  Song: Dream Warning.
  With the Gift of a Lion's Claw.
Herrick.   Upon Umber: Epigram.
Ignatow, D.   For Now.
Jacobsen, J.   Bush.
  Enemy of the Herds, the Lion, The.
  Lion under Maples.
  Man and the Lion.
  My Small Aunt.
Komunyakaa.   Eclogue at Twilight.
Lawrence, D. H.   St Mark.
Lindsay, N.   Lion, The.
MacLeish.   End of the World, The.
Merton.   Lion, The.
Nash, O.   Lion, The.
Patchen.   Lions of fire, The.
Meben.
  White lions are roaring on the water.
Riley, J.   This Man Jones.
Sarton, M.   Lion and the Rose, The.
Smith, S.   Reversionary.
  Roman Road, The.
  Sunt Leones.
  Zoo, The.
Stevens, W.   Lions in Sweden.
Swenson, M.   Zambesi and Ranee.
Lips
Broumas, O.   Still Life.
Carew, T.   Lips and Eyes.
Cummings, E. E.   Voices to voices, lip to lip.
Graves, R.   Touch My Shut Lips.
Herrick.   Captived Bee; or, The Little Filcher, The.
  Cherrie-Ripe.
  On Julias Lips.
  Rock of Rubies: and The Quarrie of Pearls, The.
  Upon His Julia.
  Upon Lucie.
  Weeping Cherry, The.
Lorde.   Pirouette.
Rumi.   When you feel your lips becoming infinite.
Lipscomb, Eugene
Jarrell, R.   Say Good-bye to Big Daddy.
Lisbon, Portugal
Brodsky, J.   Postcard from Lisbon.
Pessoa.   Lisbon Revisited (1923).
  Lisbon Revisited (1926).
Listening and Listeners
Amichai [or Amikhai].   In the Room.
Ammons.   Lollapalooza: 22 February.
Armantrout.   Overhearing.
Berrigan, T.   Paul Blackburn.
Berry, W.   To What Listens.
Carver, R.   Listening.
Codrescu.   It takes joy to listen and it is inspiring being listened to.
Corbett, W.   Listening for Jane.
Creeley.   Friends, The.
  Here ("Little earth, water").
  Mary's Fancy.
  Total Parts of a World, The.
Davie, D.   Having No Ear.
De la Mare.   Dove, The.
Dugan, A.   Northern Statement for St. Cecilia.
Emerson, R.   Dervish whined to *Said*, The.
Hall, D.   "Internal and External Forms."
Herrick.   Canticle to Apollo, A.
  Upon a Hoarse Singer.
Koch, K.   Hearing.
Laughlin, J.   Social Note.
Lawrence, D. H.   Listening.
Major, C.   Heartland Music.
McHugh, H.   Or Else.
Merwin.   Hearing.
  Hollow, A.
Nash, O.   Listen.
Palmer, M.   Musica Ficta.
Pessoa.   No, don't say a word!
Raine, K.   Triad.
  Who listens, when in the concert-hall.
Stafford, W.   Listening.
Tate, J.   Sensitive Ears.

Tomlinson, C.   Little Night Music, A.
  Word in Edgeways, A.
  Words for the Madrigalist.
Updike.   Mountain Impasse.
Williams, C. K.   In the middle / of a bite of.
Liszt, Franz
Carver, R.   Music.
Literature
Auden.   Dichtung und Wahrheit.
  Thanksgiving, A.
Berry, W.   Autumn Burning, An.
Berryman.   Crisis.
  Professor's Song, A.
  Tea.
Borges.   Parable of Cervantes and Don Quixote.
Byron, G.   No Infant Sotheby, Whose Dauntless Head.
Cummings, E. E.   Let's start a magazine.
Dickey, J.   Place of the Skull, The.
Donne.   To Mr R. W. ("Kindly I envy thy song's [or songs] perfection").
Eberhart, R.   Bones of Coleridge, The.
  Clerihew for Alan Gaylord, A.
  Nostalgia for Edith Sitwell.
Emerson, R.   Burn your literary verses.
Gunn, T.   Readings in French.
Hamill, S.   Arse Poetica.
Han-shan.   Four or five dumb upstarts.
Hill, G.   Bibliographers, The.
Laughlin, J.   Among the Roses.
  Graceful Exit, A.
  Like Him I Need the Past.
  Non-World, The.
Logan, J.   Protest after a Dream.
MacDiarmid, H.   Gairmscoile.
Moore, M.   Picking and Choosing.
Nash, O.   Literary Reflection.
Nemerov.   History of a Literary Movement.
Parker, D.   Figures in Popular Literature.
  Pig's-Eye View of Literature, A.
Ransom, J.   Survey of Literature.
Rexroth, K.   Lost Etc.
Riley, J.   At "The Literary."
Rilke.   To Miss Sophy Giauque.
Rukeyser, M.   Homage to Literature.
Smith, S.   Souvenir de Monsieur Poop.
Stafford, W.   Final Exam: American Renaissance.
Suckling, S.   To His Much Honoured the Lord Lepington upon His Translation of Malvezzi, His "Romulus" and "Tarquin."
Tomlinson, C.   Antecedents.
  Something: a Direction.
Walcott.   Love in the Valley.
Wilde, O.   Amor Intellectualis.
Williams, M.   Professor.
Williams, W.   Question and Answer.
Wordsworth, W.   Illustrated Books and Newspapers.
Zukofsky, L.   Poem Beginning "The."
See also **Authorship and Authors; Criticism and Critics**
Lithuania
Brodsky, J.   Lithuanian Divertissement.
  Lithuanian Nocturne.
Davie, D.   Forests of Lithuania, The.
Milosz, C.   City without a Name.
  I Do Not Understand.
  In Szetejnie.
  Lithuania, after Fifty-two Years.
  My Grandfather Sigismund Kunat.
  Philology.
  With Her.
Little Bighorn, Battle of (1876)
Whitman, W.   From Far Dakota's Cañons (June 25, 1876).
Little, Malcolm
See **Malcolm X (Malcolm Little)**
Little Red Riding Hood
Broumas, O.   Little Red Riding Hood.
Lizards
Blue Cloud.   Expedition.
Eberhart, R.   Let the Tight Lizard on the Wall.
García Lorca.   Lizard Is Crying, The.
  Old Lizard, The.

Hardy, T.   Lizard, The.
Lawrence, D. H.   Lizard.
MacLeish.   Old Man to the Lizard, The.
Montale.   Green lizard, if it darts, The.
Moore, M.   Plumet Basilisk, The.
Nash, O.   Skink, The.
Roethke.   Lizard, The.
  Wish for a Young Wife.
Rossetti, C.   When fishes set umbrellas up.
Stafford, W.   At the Bomb Testing Site.
Stock, R.   Logos.
Llamas
Nash, O.   Lama, The.
Lobsters
Ciardi, J.   Corpus Christi.
Clampitt.   What the Light Was Like.
Lowell, R.   Water.
Muldoon, P.   Something Else.
Nemerov.   Lobsters.
Oppen.   Ballad: "Astrolabes and lexicons."
Sexton.   Lobster.
Williams, W.   Rhymed Address: The Lobster.
Loch Ness
See **Ness, Loch, Scotland**
Locomotives
MacLeish.   Grazing Locomotives.
Riley, J.   Iron Horse, The.
Williams, W.   East Coocoo.
See also **Railroads; Trains**
Locusts
Berry, W.   Seventeen Years.
Carrera Andrade.   Radicals.
Nash, O.   Locust-Lovers, Attention!
Log Houses
Patchen.   Vanishing Institution, A.
Lombardi, Vince
Dickey, J.   For the Death of Vince Lombardi.
London, England
Beckett, S.   Serena I.
Berrigan, T.   Old-Fashioned Air.
Brodsky, J.   Thames at Chelsea, The.
Chesterton.   London.
  Old Song, The.
Ciardi, J.   Monday Morning: London.
Clampitt.   Fireweed.
  Hairline Fracture, A.
  London Inside and Outside.
  On the Disadvantages of Central Heating.
Creeley.   In London.
Davie, D.   To Londoners.
Donne.   To Mr E. G.
Eliot, T. S.   Airs of Palestine, No. 2.
  Interlude in London.
  Paysage Triste.
Ginsberg, A.   Studying the Signs.
Gjuzel.   On the Way Back.
Gunn, T.   Adolescence.
Gurney, I.   London.
Hardy, T.   East-End Curate, An.
  To a Tree in London.
Herrick.   His Return to London.
Hill, G.   Churchill's Funeral.
Housman.   Eight O'Clock.
  In My Own Shire.
Jarrell, R.   London.
Johnson, S.   London: A Poem.
Keats.   Lines on the Mermaid Tavern.
Kipling, R.   London Stone.
Lawrence, D. H.   Piccadilly Circus at Night.
  To Clarinda.
  Town in 1917.
MacNeice.   Goodbye to London.
  Homage to Wren.
  London Rain.
  Street Scene.
  Streets of Laredo, The.
  Whit Monday.
Mahon.   Kensington Notebook, A.
  October in Hyde Park.
Meredith, G.   London by Lamplight.
Owen, W.   Shadwell Stair.
Pope, A.   Farewell to London in the Year 1715, A.
Pound, E.   Portrait d'une Femme.
Raine, K.   London air dims.

Seifert. Umbrella from Piccadilly, An.
Shelley, P. On Leaving London for Wales.
Sheridan, T. To the Dean, when in England, in 1726.
Spender, S. Rejoice in the Abyss.
Suckling, S. Ballad[e] [upon a Wedding], A.
Thomas, D. Refusal to Mourn the Death, by Fire, of a Child in London, A.
Wilde, O. Impression du Matin.
  Symphony in Yellow.
Wordsworth, W. Composed upon Westminster Bridge, September 3, 1802.
  London 1802.

Londonderry, Northern Ireland
Mahon. Derry Morning.

Lone Ranger, The
Hall, D. Lone Ranger, The.

Loneliness
Ai. Young Farm Woman Alone.
Amichai [or Amikhai]. Hymn to Summer.
  I Have Dead People.
  In the Full Severity of Mercy.
  Poems of continuity, mines and graves.
  Threading.
  You Are So Small and Slight in the Rain.
Ammons. Late Romantic.
  Lonely Splendor.
  Three.
Angelou. Greyday.
  Traveler, The.
Apollinaire. Pretty Redhead, The.
Ashbery, J. Ivory Tower, The.
Auden. Alone.
  Loneliness.
  Pleasure Island.
  Witnesses, The.
Beckett, S. Lueurs lisières.
  Roundelay: "On all that strand."
Berryman. Handshake, the Entrance, The.
  He Resigns.
  Transit.
  World's Fair.
Bly, R. Man Writes to a Part of Himself, A.
  "Out of the Rolling Ocean, the Crowd . . ."
  Snowbanks North of the House.
Borges. Adam Is Your Ashes.
Bradstreet, A. In My Solitary Hours in My Dear Husband His Absence.
Brodsky, J. To Urania.
Brontë, E. And like myself lone, wholly lone.
  I paused on the threshold, I turned to the sky.
  If grief for grief can touch thee.
  Lonely at her window sitting.
  Sun Has Set, The.
Brooks, G. Empty Woman, The.
  Sunset of the City, A.
Bukowski. Alone with Everybody.
  Blue Cheese and Chili Peppers.
  Chicago.
  Christmas Eve, Alone.
  Crunch, The.
  Here I Am.
  Love Is a Dog from Hell.
  Me.
  Night I Fucked My Alarm Clock, The.
  Oh, Yes.
  Sword, The.
  Yellow Cab.
Burns, R. English Song.
  How lang and dreary is the night.
  Jockey's Ta'en the Parting Kiss.
  My Nannie's Awa'.
  Sae Far Awa.
  Wae Is My Heart.
Byron, G. I Would I Were a Careless Child.
  Stanzas: "Oh!—my lonely—lonely—lonely Pillow!"
Campion, T. My Life's Delight.
  Oft have I sigh'd for him that heares me not.
Carruth, H. Loneliness[: An Outburst of Hexasyllables].
Carver, R. Away.
  Medicine.
  Night Dampness.
  Still Looking Out for Number One.
  To Begin With.

Cavafy. January 1904.
Chumacero. Widower's Monologue.
Ciardi, J. Elaine.
Clampitt. High Noon.
Clare, J. Song: "I peeled bits of straw and I got switches too."
Clough. Enough, small Room,—though all too true.
Codrescu. Winter in Istanbul.
Coleridge, S. Blossoming of the Solitary Date-Tree, The.
  Hexameters.
  Homeless.
  Loss.
Cooper, J. 95°.
Crane, H. Legende.
  Moth That Made God Blind, The.
  Old Song.
Crane, S. I explain the silvered passing of a ship at night.
  I heard thee laugh.
Creeley. Door, The.
  End, The.
  Fire.
  For a Friend.
  For Somebody's Marriage.
  Moon, The.
  Not Now.
  Places ("When I wake next").
  She Is.
  There Is.
  Whip, The.
Cummings, E. E. I will cultivate within.
  L(a / le / af / fa / ll / s).
  Lily has a rose.
  Nothing is more exactly terrible than.
  Wind has blown the rain away and blown, A.
De la Mare. Alone.
  Old Men, The.
  Ophelia.
Dickinson, E. Could that sweet Darkness where they dwell.
  Door just opened on a street, A.
  Heart, not so heavy as mine.
  I hide myself within my flower.
  I thought to shun the Loneliness.
  I tried to think a lonelier Thing.
  I was with you in all the loneliness.
  I've none to tell me to but Thee.
  Loneliness One dare not sound, The.
  Shade upon the mind there passes, A.
  There is another Loneliness.
  We don't cry—Tim and I.
Dove, R. Catherine of Siena.
Dunbar, P. Lonesome.
  Memory of Martha, The.
  My Lady of Castle Grand.
Eberhart, R. Human Being Is a Lonely Creature, The.
Eliot, T. S. Le Directeur.
Emerson, R. Alone in Rome! Why Rome is lonely too.
  Good-bye.
  I cannot find a place so lonely.
  I grieve that better souls than mine.
  Thine Eyes Still Shined.
  What avails it me.
  Where art thou / Thou beautiful dream.
Frost, R. Acquainted with the Night.
  Bereft.
  Desert Places.
  Most of It, The.
García Lorca. Ballad of One Doomed to Die.
  Christmas on the Hudson.
  Rider's Song.
Ginsberg, A. 4 AM Blues.
  Asphodel, An.
  Desolation, A.
  Flash Back.
  Nov. 23, 1963: Alone.
Glück, L. 12. 6. 71.
  Return, The.
Graves, R. Crane, The.
  Love as Lovelessness.
  Raft, The.
"H. D." Chance.

Hacker, M. Elevens.
  Little Robber Girl Considers the Wide World, The.
Hall, D. Hut of the man alone, The.
  Toy Bone, The.
Hardy, T. Before Knowledge.
  Bereft.
  Fallow Deer at the Lonely House, The.
  Lonely Days.
  Nobody Comes.
  Orphaned Old Maid, The.
  Sailor's Mother, The.
  Song to an Old Burden.
  Son's Portrait, The.
  Voice of the Thorn, The.
Housman. Hughley Steeple.
  Rainy Pleiads wester, The.
  There pass the careless people.
  Weeping Pleiads wester, The.
  Winds out of the west land blow, The.
Hughes, L. Bound No'th Blues.
  Crossing.
  Desert.
  God.
  Hope ("Sometimes when I'm lonely").
  Late Corner.
  Little Song ("Lonely people").
  Lonely Nocturne.
  Lonesome Corner.
  Lonesome Place.
  Midnight Chippie's Lament.
  Miss Blues'es Child.
  One.
  Refugee.
Ignatow, D. Against the Evidence.
Jackson, L. Take Hands.
Jacobsen, J. Birds, The.
  Colloquy.
  Variations on a theme.
Jarrell, R. Eine Kleine Nachtmusik.
  Game at Salzburg, A.
  Ghost, a Real Ghost, A.
  Island, The.
  London.
  Lonely Man, The.
  See-er of Cities, The.
  Windows.
Kizer, C. Night Sounds.
Komunyakaa. Heart's Graveyard Shift, The.
  High on Sadness.
  Leper's Bell, The.
  Loneliness.
  Tenebrae.
  Thorn Merchant's Wife, The.
  When Loneliness Is a Man.
Kumin, M. July, against Hunger.
Laughlin, J. Prognosis.
  To Smile or Not to Smile.
Lawrence, D. H. Drunk.
  Elysium.
  Loneliness.
  Song of a Man Who Is Not Loved.
  Uprooted, The.
Levertov. Gone Away.
  In Abeyance.
  Letter.
  Wanderer, A.
Levi, P. Avigliana.
Levine, P. At the Fillmore.
  Planting.
  Poem Circling Hamtramck, Michigan, All Night in Search of You, The.
Lorde. Keyfoods.
MacLeish. Epitaph for John McCutcheon.
  Winter Is Another Country.
MacNeice. Autobiography.
  Eclogue between the Motherless.
  Heated Minutes, The.
  Lake in the Park, The.
  Nostalgia.
  Passage Steamer.
  Postscript to Iceland.
  Sand in the Air.
  Troll's Courtship.
Mahon. Achill.
  Jail Journal.

Major, C.   My Seasonal Body.
McGrath, T.   From a Long Way Out of Pah-Gatzin-Kay.
Little Odyssey of Jason Quint, of Science, Doctor, The.
Orphan, The.
Parable.
McHugh, H.   Syllables.
Meredith, G.   Black Richard.
Lesson of Grief, The.
Mortesto.
Meredith, W.   February 14.
Open Sea, The.
Merwin.   Departure's Girl-Friend.
Division.
Dogs.
On Each Journey.
Second Psalm: The Signals.
Millay, E.   On the Wide Heath.
Milosz, C.   Study of Loneliness.
Montale.   House of the Customs Men, The.
Nash, O.   Listen.
Solitude of Mr. Powers, The.
Very Unclubbable Man, The.
Neruda.   Bird.
Niedecker.   If only my friend.
No matter where you are.
Woman with Umbrella.
O'Hara, F.   On Looking at *La Grande Jatte,* the Czar Wept Anew.
Poem: "To be idiomatic in a vacuum."
Oliver, M.   Lilies.
Oppen.   Political Poem, A.
Pagis.   Runner Artist, The.
Parker, D.   —And Return.
Bric-à-Brac.
Excursion into Assonance.
Interior.
Light of Love.
Now at Liberty.
Patchen.   All the Day.
Each Is Alone, Each Is Everything.
Lonesome Boy Blues.
No one ever works alone.
Piercy.   Going In.
Prunty.   Crosswords.
Domestic of the Outer Banks.
Seasons.
Taking Down, The.
Raine, K.   Crossing the sound I summoned you in thought.
Lachesis.
Unloved, The.
Rexroth, K.   Advantages of Learning, The.
Andrée Rexroth ("Purple and green, blue and white").
Blue Sunday.
Gic to Har.
Inversely, as the Square of Their Distances Apart.
Loneliness.
On a Flyleaf of *Rime*—Gaspara Stampa.
Rich, A.   Song: "You're wondering if I'm lonely."
Riley, J.   Empty Song, The.
Folks at Lonesomeville.
From Below.
Her Lonesomeness.
Ritsos.   Assistance.
His Lamp.
Imitation of an Imitation.
Like a Prayer.
Lone Man's Night, A.
Maybe, Someday.
Unjust, The.
Robinson, E.   Mr Flood's Party.
Song at Shannon's, A.
Roethke.   His Foreboding.
Rossetti, C.   At Home.
Chilly Night, A.
Hoping against Hope.
Let Patience Have Her Perfect Work.
Lowest Room, The.
Repining.
Sappho.
Song: "Stream moaneth as it floweth, The."

Who Have a Form of Godliness.
Will These Hands Ne'er Be Clean?
Zara.
Sandburg, C.   Alone and Not Alone.
Canadians and Pottawatomies.
Love Is a Deep and a Dark and a Lonely.
M'Liss and Louie.
Stripes.
They Ask: Is God, Too, Lonely?
Sappho.   Deduke Men A Selanna.
Schuyler, J.   August Night.
Sexton.   January 24th.
Killing the Love.
Shelley, P.   Remembrance.
Sonnet: Political Greatness.
To Mary Shelley.
Simic.   Whispers in the Next Room.
Smith, S.   Deeply Morbid.
Orphan Reformed, The.
Unpopular, Lonely and Loving.
Voice from the Tomb (4).
Widowhood or The Home-Coming of Lady Ross.
Spender, S.   Not to You.
Room above the Square, The.
Stafford, W.   Assurance.
Bridge Begins in the Trees, A.
Widow.
Tate, J.   Epithalamion for Tyler.
Tennyson, A.   Mariana.
Mariana in the South.
Tomlinson, C.   Dream, The.
Trakl.   Helian.
Updike.   Grief of Cafeterias, The.
Vallejo.   Big People, The.
Testimony.
Van Duyn.   Open Letter from a Constant Reader.
Walker, A.   He Said.
Warren, R.   First Dawn Light.
John's Birches.
Mountain Mystery.
Place, The.
Why Boy Came to Lonely Place.
Winter Wheat: Oklahoma.
Weiss, T.   Rapture The.
Whitman, W.   As If a Phantom Caress'd Me.
I Saw in Louisiana a Live-Oak Growing.
This Moment Yearning and Thoughtful.
When I Peruse the Conquer'd Fame.
Whittier.   Autograph, An.
Missionary, The.
Williams, C. K.   Being Alone.
Fleas, too, / have fled, The.
Keep It.
Shame.
Williams, M.   Christmas Poem, A.
Jonathan Entertaining.
Williams, T.   Lament: "Too limpid streets have grown narrow, The."
Lonesome Man.
One and Two.
Rented Room, The.
Williams, W.   Ballet.
Man in a Room.
Wordsworth, W.   I Wandered Lonely as a Cloud.
Wright, J.   As I Step over a Puddle at the End of Winter, I Think of an Ancient Chinese Governor.
Assignation, The.
But Only Mine.
Elegy for the Poet Morgan Blum, An.
For the Marsh's Birthday.
Having Lost My Sons, I Confront the Wreckage of the Moon: Christmas, 1960.
I Am a Sioux Brave, He Said in Minneapolis.
Idea of the Good, The.
Inscription for the Tank.
Katy Did.
Many of Our Waters: Variations on a Poem by a Black Child.
Northern Pike.
Offense, The.
Poem about Breasts, A.
Poems to a Brown Cricket.
Revelation, The.

So She Said.
Speak.
To a Dead Drunk.
To a Friendly Dun.
To Harvey, Who Traced the Circulation.
Wyatt, S.   Lucks, my fair falcon, and your fellows all.
What Does This Mean?
Yeats.   Crazy Jane and Jack the Journeyman.
Two Songs Rewritten for the Tune's Sake.
Zagajewski.   Sad, Tired.
Zukofsky, L.   Homage.
Sequence 1944-6.
See also **Absence; Isolation; Separation**

Long Island, New York
Clampitt.   Paumanok.
Ferlinghetti, L.   Poem for Old Walt.
Glück, L.   Meridian.
Merton.   New Ribbon.
Pagis.   Early Winter, Long Island.
Schuyler, J.   Birds.
Whitman, W.   As I Ebb'd with the Ocean of Life.
Centenarian's Story, The.
From Montauk Point.
Ode: "O, God of Columbia! O, Shield of the Free!"
Paumanok.
Paumanok Picture, A.

Longfellow, Henry Wadsworth
Riley, J.   Longfellow.
Longfellow's Love for the Children.
Sandburg, C.   Mr. Longfellow and His Boy.
Schuyler, J.   Light from Canada.
Tomlinson, C.   In Longfellow's Library.
Whittier.   On a Fly-Leaf of Longfellow's Poems.
Poet and the Children, The.

Longing
Amichai [*or* Amikhai].   As for the World.
Flowers in a Room.
I Walked Past a House Where I Lived Once.
Instructions for Her Voyage.
Letter, A.
Memory of Love—Image.
My Mother Baked the Whole World for Me.
Smell of Gasoline Ascends in My Nose, The.
Suflah Spring in the Judean Mountains.
To Bake the Bread of Yearning.
Two Poets in Mexico.
White Negress.
Ashbery, J.   37 Haiku.
Business Personals.
Pursuit of Happiness, The.
Song: "Song tells us of our old way of living, The."
Baudelaire.   Exotic Scent.
Giantess, The.
Berrigan, T.   Heloise.
Berryman.   Fare Well.
Bierce.   One Morning.
Bly, R.   Cry Going Out over Pastures, The.
Dream of What Is Missing, A.
Finding the Father.
Bogan, L.   Girl's Song.
Brodsky, J.   Song, A: "I wish you were here, dear."
Törnfallet.
Brontë, E.   F. de Samara to A. G. A.
Shall Earth no more inspire thee.
Song By Julius Brenzaida To G.S.
Wind, sink to rest in the heather.
Brooks, G.   To Be in Love.
Broumas, O.   Bride.
Home Movies.
Namaste.
Song / for Sanna.
Soothsaying.
Browning, E.   Isobel's Child.
May's Love.
Romaunt of Margret, The.
Browning, R.   In Three Days.
Lovers' Quarrel, A.
Never the Time and the Place.
One Way of Love.
Pauline [*or* Pauline; A Fragment of a Confession].

Bukowski.   Dogs of Egypt, The.
Burns, R.   Answer to the Foregoing—
    Extempore [Clarinda].
Blue-Eyed Lassie, The.
Bonie Lad That's Far Awa, The.
Bonnie [or Bonny] Wee Thing, The.
Cauld Frosty Morning.
English Song.
Fragment: "Altho' my bed were in yon muir."
Here Awa' There Awa ["Here awa', there awa'
    wandering, Willie"].
Highland Harry Back Again.
Jockey's Ta'en the Parting Kiss.
Mary Morison.
Merry Hae I Been Teethin a Heckle.
My Heart's in the Highlands.
O Lay Thy Loof in Mine Lass.
On the Seas and Far Away.
Passion's Cry.
Revision for Clarinda.
Sae Far Awa.
Simmer's a Pleasant Time.
Somebody.
Song: "Again rejoicing Nature sees."
Sweet fa's the eve on Craigieburn.
Wilt thou be my Dearie.
Young Highland Rover, The.
Byron, G.   To Thyrza.
Campion, T.   Come away, arm'd with loves
    delights.
Carew, T.   Divine Mistress, A.
Lady, Rescued from Death by a Knight, Who in
    the Instant Leaves Her, Complains Thus, A.
Mr. Carew to His Friend.
To Her in Absence; a Ship.
To My Mistress[e] in My Absence.
Carver, R.   Torture.
Cavafy.   25th Year of His Life, The.
Days of 1903.
Half an Hour.
January 1904.
On the Stairs.
September 1903.
Young Man, a Writer—in His 24th Year, A.
Cavalcanti.   Ballata: Concerning a Shepherd-
    maid.
Because I expect never to return.
Eyes of that gentle country girl, The.
I fear from my misfortune.
I never used to think that my heart.
I pray you who speak of suffering.
I see it in my Lady's eyes.
I was deep in thoughts of Love when I found.
If I ask Pity not to be.
If it were mine, you'd see every value.
If only Mercy befriended my desires.
May I tell you the news of my eyes.
My foolish eyes, that first looked.
My latest cruel misfortune.
My soul is wildly terrified.
O my Lady, didn't you see him.
Pity came to lonely me.
Since I must bear a sorrowing heart.
We sad, despondent quills.
Why weren't my eyes blinded.
You could see when I met you.
You see me—one who goes crying.
Young Lady of Tolosa, A.
You've so filled my mind with pain.
Celan.   In Front of a Candle.
Clare, J.   I Am.
Coleridge, S.   Day-Dream, The.
If I Had but Two Little Wings.
Love.
Stanger Minstrel, A.
Collins, B.   Pavilion.
Cooper, J.   Letters.
Crane, H.   Carrier Letter.
Creeley.   Away.
Distance.
Flesh.
For Benny and Sabina.
In a Boat Shed.
Later ("If I could get").
Let something else be / the question—.
Loner.

Messengers, The.
Place ("Thinking of you asleep on a").
Pryaer, A.
Smoke.
Song: "Those rivers run from that land."
Cullen, C.   Lament: "Now let all lovely things
    embark."
To the Swimmer.
Cummings, E. E.   Always before your voice my
    soul.
Ballad of Love.
Before the fragile gradual throne of night.
Clown's smirk in the skull of a baboon, A.
Consider O / woman this / my body.
Ivory performing rose, The.
Lady / i pray to what is unimaginable.
Longing.
O Distinct / Lady of my unkempt adoration.
Spring has been exquisite and the, The.
Supposing i dreamed this).
Dante Alighieri.   Sestina: Of the Lady Pietra
    degli Scrovigni.
Sonnet: To the Lady Pietra degli Scrovigni.
"Dario."   Venus.
De la Mare.   Betrayal.
Eyes.
Monologue, The.
Thorn, The.
Vacant Day, The.
Dickey, W.   Kindness, A.
Dickinson, E.   Heart wants what it wants, The.
I envy seas—whereon He rides.
I many times thought Peace had come.
It's fragrant news, to know they pine.
Lady feeds her little Bird, The.
Longing is like the Seed.
Success is counted sweetest.
What shall I do now—it whimpers so.
Donne.   Fever, A.
Dove, R.   Boccaccio: The Plague Years.
Dugan, A.   Absent Good Girl, Life of My Mind.
Dunbar, P.   Longing.
Duncan, R.   Source.
Eberhart, R.   Sometimes the Longing for Death.
Eliot, T. S.   In the Department Store.
Love Song of J. Alfred Prufrock, Resumed, The.
Love Song of J. Alfred Prufrock, The.
Love Song of J. Alfred Prufrock, The (Prufrock
    among the Women).
Prufrock's Pervigilium.
Emerson, R.   To Rhea.
Ferlinghetti, L.   Astonished Heart, The.
Light, The.
Two Amsterdams.
Foscolo.   Sonnet to Zante.
Gallagher, T.   All Day the Light Is Clear.
Coming Home.
Under Stars.
García Lorca.   Autumn Song.
Ballad of Black Pain.
Death.
Desire.
Evening ("Rainy evening in exhausted gray").
Gacela of Desperate Love.
Gacela of the Morning Market.
Gacela of Unforeseen Love.
Gypsy Nun, The.
He Died at Dawn.
Madrigal: "I looked into your eyes."
New Heart.
Sleepwalking Ballad.
Somnambule Ballad.
Song of the Shop Boy.
Weathervane.
Your Childhood in Menton.
Ginsberg, A.   4 AM Blues.
Further Proposal, A.
Night-Apple, The.
Night Gleam.
Stanzas: Written at Night in Radio City.
Transcription of Organ Music.
Glück, L.   Brennende Liebe.
Fire, The.
Islander, The.
Graves, R.   As All Must End.
Crane, The.

Shift of Scene, A.
Song: Crown of Stars.
Guinicelli.   Canzone: Of the Gentle Heart.
Gunn, T.   Autobiography.
Gurney, I.   Billet.
First March.
Hacker, M.   Aube Provençale.
Home, and I've.
Han-shan.   In Loyang so many girls.
Yesterday was so long ago.
Hardy, T.   Conversation at Dawn, A.
Curtains Now Are Drawn, The.
From Her in the Country.
Last Leaf, The.
Musing Maiden, The.
Something Tapped.
Turnip-Hoer, The.
Voice, The.
Whitewashed Wall, The.
Hayden, R.   Ballad of Sue Ellen Westerfield,
    The.
Herbert, G.   Glimpse, The.
Longing.
Housman.   Because I liked you better.
Far in a western brookland.
He would not stay for me; and who can
    wonder?
Oh fair enough are sky and plain.
Spring Morning.
Wenlock Edge.
When the lad for longing sighs.
Hsüeh T'ao.   Spring-Gazing Songs.
Hughes, L.   As I Grew Older.
Black Gal.
Deferred.
Dressed Up.
Letter to Anne, A.
Miss Blues'es Child.
Our Land.
Red Clay Blues.
Six-Bits Blues.
Songs to the Dark Virgin.
Subway Face.
Summer Night.
Yesterday and Today.
Ignatow, D.   Longing.
Jeffers, R.   Maid's Thought, The.
Keats.   Day Is Gone and All Its Sweets Are
    Gone, The.
Endymion: A Poetic Romance.
Fill for Me a Brimming Bowl.
I Cry Your Mercy, Pity, Love—Ay, Love!
Isabella; or, The Pot of Basil.
To Fanny.
To ———: "Time's sea hath been five years at
    its slow ebb."
What Can I Do to Drive Away.
Kinnell.   Sheffield Ghazal 4: Driving West.
Kinsella, T.   Scylla and Charybdis.
Kipling, R.   Brookland Road.
Mother-Lodge, The.
Rebirth.
Recall, The.
Song of the Wise Children.
To the Unknown Goddess.
Virginity, The.
Komunyakaa.   Reminiscence.
Kumin, M.   Bangkok Gang, The.
Longing to Be Saved, The.
Seeing the Bones.
Kunitz, S.   Indian Summer at Land's End.
Sotto Voce.
Strange Calendar.
Laughlin, J.   Coming of Spring, The.
Da mi basia mille.
Delia Sequence, The.
Flavius to Postumia.
Il Pastor Fido.
In Hac Spe Vivo.
Near Zermatt: The Drahtseilbahn.
Properate Tempus.
This Is the Morte Saison.
To Smile or Not to Smile.
Visitor, The.
When I'm Missing You.
Why Do You Never Enter My Dreams.

Lawrence, D. H.   Coldness in Love.
Drunk.
North Country, The.
Search for Love.
Separated.
Levertov.   Cloak, A.
Fragment: "All one winter, in every crowded hall."
Unknown, The.
Levi, P.   Avigliana.
Li Po.   Solo.
Lindsay, N.   Alone in the Wind, on the Prairie.
Beggar's Valentine, The.
Gamblers, The.
In Praise of Songs That Die.
Logan, J.   Love Poem: "Last night you would not come."
Lorde.   Change of Season.
Memorial II.
Sowing.
To the Girl Who Lives in a Tree.
MacDiarmid, H.   Wheesht, Wheesht.
MacLeish.   Broken Promise.
Mahon.   Jail Journal.
Noon at St. Michael's.
Thinking of Inis Oírr in Cambridge, Mass.
Major, C.   Heartland Music.
Mallarmé.   Azure, The.
Futile Petition.
Sea Breeze.
Sigh.
McGrath, T.   Epitaph: "Again, traveller, you have come a long way led by that star."
Poem: "In the list of one thousand false addresses."
Repeated Journey, The.
McHugh, H.   Like.
McMichael.   She.
Meredith, G.   Blue Is the Sky.
Grace and Love.
I wish'd the world a blindness.
I would I were with Jean.
Line of eve o'er the moorland, A.
Love in the Valley.
Marian: "Clouds fly fast across the moon, The."
Mortesto.
My Lady has Diana's brows.
Night-Walk, The.
Night walks the earth with silver feet.
See the star yonder.
Shall I again have Lilac week?
She rides in the park on a prancing bay.
Shemselnihar.
Song: "Come to me in any shape!"
Three Maidens, The.
'Tis midnight in the skies, my dear.
We violets white and blue.
With the Persuader.
Young Usurper, The.
Youthful Quest, The.
Merrill, J.   Vision of the Garden, A.
Merwin.   Beyond You.
Calling under the Breath, The.
Meeting.
One Way.
Present, The.
Sadness, The.
Spring Equinox Full Moon.
Summer Doorway.
Michelangelo Buonarroti.   Although it's amply true your human face.
Although my heart had often been aflame.
As by subtracting, my lady, one creates.
As I've carried in my heart this many a year.
As, working in hard stone to make the face.
At times I project ahead.
Because there's half of me which, heaven-born.
Blissful spirit, thanks to whom new passion.
By a face of fiery cold, I'm set aflame.
Fear of death! Who'd shove, The.
From beneath two arching brows.
From grief I cherished to a rueful laugh.
From the first whimper to the expiring sigh.
From what these eyes, my lady, see of you.
Great beauty scattering its brilliant flame.
Great mercy, my lady, as likely as great pain.

Hating myself, the more I run away.
How much less torment to breathe out my soul.
I do believe, if you were made of stone.
I really believed, that first great day when, awed.
I was, for years and years now, wounded, killed.
I was happy, with fate favoring, to abide.
I weep, I burn—burn up!—my heart thereby.
I wouldn't if I could, Love, check the urge.
If a joyous heart makes beautiful the face.
If fire can melt down steel and shatter flint.
If I'm to believe my eyes now, your response.
If longings for the immortal, which exalt.
If sorrow makes one beautiful (it's said).
If, through our eyes, the heart's seen in the face.
If we constrain the eyes' easy response.
Impassioned as I am.
It's not enough, if it doesn't come from you.
Just when I'm lost in adoration of you.
Kindly to others, to itself unkind.
Life's quick and brief; the more my days fly by.
Looks thrown away on others.
Love long delayed comes kindly, by fortune's favor.
More it seems I agonize, the more, The.
My lady is so impetuous, devil-may-care.
Nature knows what it's doing: one cruel as you.
No doubt much peril lies.
No slightest chance on earth her heavenly eyes.
Not always so prized and cherished by us all.
Not even, in dreams sent soaring, can I imagine.
Please tell me, Love, if that lady had a soul.
Say the face I'm speaking of now, hers I mean.
So I can best endure.
So, Love, it hasn't healed, not even the least.
Such wealth of promise lies.
Supposing the passionate fire your eyes enkindle.
That whole way up to your brilliant diadem.
Though shouldered from the road I chose.
Through your fine eyes I see such mellow light.
Time now good-byes were said.
To see that your famous beauty still endures.
Uproot a plant—there's no way it can seal.
Whether or not the light I long for, sent.
Why ease the tension of this wild desire.
Why only at long last, why next to never.
With heart of sulphur, flesh of tinder too.
You revel in my torments, only you.
Your kindness to me, and the ways of fate.
Your lovely eyes, now bent.
Milosz, C.   Distance.
Mistral, F.   Obsession, The.
Mistral, G.   To See Him Again.
To the Clouds.
Montale.   Chrysalis.
Delta.
Flower that repeats, The.
For an Album.
From the Train.
In the Rain.
On an Unwritten Letter.
See the sign; it flares.
Mörike [or Möricke].   Beauty Rohtraut.
Muldoon, P.   Bran.
Neruda.   Cold.
Coming Back.
Runaway Sun.
Sick Man in the Sun.
Ni Dhomhnaill.   Orphan at the Door, An.
Olson, C.   As the Dead Prey upon Us.
Orr, G.   Self-Portrait at Twenty.
Owen, W.   My Shy Hand.
One Remains, The.
Parker, D.   Accursed, The.
Hearthside.
Song in a Minor Key.
Pasolini.   One of the Many Epilogs.
Pessoa.   Analysis.
Sensationist Poem, A.
Someone's about to enter the doorway . . . One feels the air smiling.
To be and not to be again! . . . Oh, lions born in cages!
Today the sky is heavy like the thought of never making port.

Your silence a ship, each sail taut in the wind.
Petrarch.   Air weighed down, and the oppressive cloud, The.
Alas her sweet expression, pleasure-filled.
Alas, I burn, and no one will believe it.
Alas, the last of days when I was glad.
Although another's fault takes from me what.
Because our life is short.
Because the road to mercy is shut off.
Breeze blowing those blond locks and curling them.
But—now her pleasant gentle modest mien.
By now there is no way I could break loose.
Clear, fresh, and pleasant water.
Clothing of green, deep crimson, black, or purple.
Could a more dreadful vision ever be?
Could I but pour out into powerful rhyme.
Could I but take revenge upon that one.
Cruel the star (if stars are powerful).
Each time I call to mind the hour, the place.
Father of heaven, for all the days now lost.
For every living creature on this earth.
Fresh, flowery hill, so full of shade, so green.
From Spain to the Hydaspes in the East.
From thought to thought, along each mountain top.
Full of that indescribable delight.
Full of that strong desire which sunders me.
Gentle breeze that, through fresh greenery, The.
Go, my warm sighs, and melt her frozen heart.
Gold and pearls, and blossoms, white and red, The.
Good luck is slow to reach me, always late.
Had but the light come just a little nearer.
Happy in sleep, content to lie around.
Happy season of my early prime, The.
He, who in Thessaly was all too keen.
He who is adamant to live his life.
Her hard heart and her will to cruelty.
Hills on which I left myself behind, The.
I cannot keep silent, and I fear my tongue.
I do not know, alas, where I should turn.
I feel the bitter rain of tears distilled.
I find no peace, yet have no war in hand.
I go on listening, but I cannot hear.
I have a thousand times, dear enemy.
I have by now my sixteenth year of sighs.
I really did believe I would go on.
I sang once: now I weep; and I take pleasure.
I saw a lady underneath green laurel.
I see, spread out and waving in the breeze.
I seem to hear that messenger once more.
I was so blest by sheer good luck and Love.
I weep all day; and in the night-time, when.
I wept, but now I sing: my living sun.
I wish to sing no more as once I did.
If an unfeigning heart, and amorous faith.
If but these thoughts that hurt.
If I could hope by dying to be rid.
If I said it, may I be held to scorn.
If, in this fourteenth year of all my sighs.
If the mountain by which this valley's closed.
If, when Simone laboured to depict.
I'm caught by Love within a harsh embrace.
In doubtful state I weep, at times I sing.
Julius Caesar, when false Ptolemy.
L'aura, my breeze, so often breathes upon.
L'aura, the gentle breeze that clears the hills.
Lightning-flashes of her lovely glance, The.
Little white-haired man moves off from where, The.
Long for the evening, loathe the coming dawn.
Long waiting has by now so worn me out.
Look at that hill, my sad heart, where we stood.
Looking upon the light of those clear eyes.
Lord Love, to whom all hearts and minds are known.
Lord Love, you see this lady full of scorn.
Love, I have sinned, and recognise my sin.
Love makes me go where I had rather not.
Love spurs and at the same time reins me in.
Lust goads, and Love goes with me as a guide.
Merely to look upon your sacred City.
My enemy, who often lets you gaze.
My eyes, that sun of ours is shut away.

My face and hair are changing; I grow old.
My heavy life is hanging on a thread.
My noble lord, all that I have in mind.
My vessel laden with oblivion.
Nine times Latona's son had turned his gaze.
Noble lineage with calm humility.
Not seldom, when her semblance has been kind.
Not the Ticino, Arno, Varo, Tiber.
Now earth and sky are still, winds blow no more.
Now if not love, what is it that I feel?
O dearest glances, O persuasive breath.
O lovely hand, clutched tightly round my heart.
O precious liberty, how you reveal.
O wasted steps, O wanderings in the mind.
O you, my one inestimable gem.
On the left shore of the Tyrrhenian Sea.
Once I had hopes (so fervent was my rhyme).
Out of a thousand ladies I saw one.
Over the course of time I think your smile.
Over the grasses Love had spread his net.
Place me where flowers and grass scorch in the sun.
Po, you are quick to take my outer shell.
Sea has not such creatures in its waves, The.
Seventeen years since first I felt the full.
Since through my destiny.
Since what I hope for's taking far too long.
So feeble is the thread that doth the burden stay.
Sparrow on house-top never was alone.
Star of love was blazing in the east, The.
Such is the fear those eyes strike into me.
Sweet anger, sweet disdain, sweet times of peace.
That fire I liked to think had been extinguished.
That window has my everlasting hate.
That window where one sun is visible.
There are some creatures in the world with eyes.
This creature with a bear's or tiger's heart.
Though I have tried to keep you from all blame.
Unless, through blind desire which breaks the heart.
Very instant he has loosed his shot, The.
Walking these woods and these unfriendly ways.
We are to be his victim after all.
What do you think, my soul? Will there be peace?
What fate of mine, what trickery, what force.
Whatever wonder is found.
When Lord Love makes her cast her glances down.
When the first tree was level with the ground.
When the sun sinks his golden chariot.
Whenever her white foot moves through the green.
Where did Love ever get the gold, to give.
Wherever I turn my eyes or let them rest.
While I still keep you turned, though tired, my eyes.
While my poor heart was being eaten still.
You were a haven once, my little room.
Poe.   To One in Paradise.
Pope, A.   Of the Lady Who Could Not Sleep in a Stormy Night.
Presenting a *Lark*.
Pound, E.   Marvoil.
O Atthis.
Speech for Psyche in the Golden Book of Apuleius.
Prunty.   Caligula in Blue.
Ralegh, S.   Like to a Hermit[e] Poor[e].
Ramanujan.   It.
LOVE 1: What She Said.
Rexroth, K.   Confusion.
Love Poems of Marichiko, The.
Pliny—9, 36—Lampridius—29.
Rich, A.   Continuum.
Demon Lover, The.
For the Conjunction of Two Planets.
Key, The.
Loser, The.
Paula Becker to Clara Westhoff.
Perennial Answer, The.
Riley, J.   Apart.
Blind Girl, The.
Cassander.

Curly Locks.
Fantasy, A.
For You.
Illileo.
Louella Wainie.
Mona Machree.
My Laddie wi' the Bashfu' Grace.
Old Guitar, The.
Only a Dream.
Orlie Wilde.
Passing of a Heart, The.
Ripest Peach, The.
Rose, The.
Say Something to Me.
Something.
Song: "O I would I had a lover!"
Suspense.
Unless.
Unspoken.
Rilke.   Ball, The.
Blank Joy.
To Pia Di Valmarana.
Ritsos.   Wreath, A.
Robinson, E.   Luke Havergal.
Rossetti, C.   Amore E Dovere.
Annie.
Confluents.
De Profundis.
Dream, A.
Dream, The.
Echo from Willowwood, An.
Fair World Tho' a Fallen, A.
Hope Carol, A.
Hoping against Hope.
Like as the Hart Desireth the Water Brooks.
Long Looked For.
Looking Forward.
Repining.
Song: "I have loved you for long long years Ellen."
Twilight Night.
Two Parted.
Wishes: Sonnet.
Rossetti, D.   Blessed Damozel, The.
Rukeyser, M.   Believing in Those Inexorable Laws.
Gift.
Song: Love in Whose Rich Honor.
Song: "World is full of loss; bring, wind, my love, The."
Young Girl of the Mississippi Valley, The.
Rumi.   Birdsong brings relief.
Blocked Road, The.
Dissolver of Sugar.
King and the Handmaiden and the Doctor, The.
Reed Flute's Song, The.
Three Brothers and the Chinese Princess, The.
You've so distracted me.
Sandburg, C.   Ambassadors of Grief.
Aztec.
Bricklayer Love.
Calls.
Circle of Doors.
Couple, A.
Home Thoughts.
M'Liss and Louie.
Old-Fashioned Requited Love.
Remembered Women.
River Moon.
Silver Wind.
Sappho.   He is, I should say, on a level.
Sarton, M.   Because What I Want Most Is Permanence.
Letter to James Stephens, A.
Schuyler, J.   August Night.
Await.
Day, The.
Evening.
O Sleepless Night.
Saturday Night.
Steaming Ties.
Sunday.
Table of Green Fields, A.
Seifert.   Apple Tree with Cobweb Strings.
Autobiography.
Bach Concerto, A.

Bombing of the Town of Kralupy, The.
Fan, The.
Hunt for the Kingfisher, The.
November Rain.
Silence Full of Sleighbells.
Struggle with the Angel.
Umbrella from Piccadilly, An.
Window on Birds' Wings.
Shelley, P.   Fragment: Igniculus Desiderii.
To ———: "Yet look on me—take not thine eyes away."
To Mary———.
To the Queen of My Heart.
"Shu Ting."   To ———.
Smith, S.   In the Night.
Lot's Wife.
Snyder, G.   Four Poems for Robin.
Seaman's Ditty.
Spender, S.   Not to You.
Stafford, W.   Something That Happens Right Now.
Stevens, W.   Bouquet of Belle Scavoir.
Stockton, A.   After a Night of Perplexing Dreams.
Almira to Celadon, Founded on a Story in a Magazine.
By a Lady in America to Her Husband in England.
Lavinia and Amanda, a Pastoral.
Ode—Written 1756, An.
Swift, J.   To Stella.
Szymborska, W.   Dream, A.
Tate, A.   Edges.
To a Prodigal Old Maid.
Tate, J.   Poem: "Silence that tunnels forever, A."
Tryst, The.
Wait for Me.
Updike.   Heading for Nandi.
Report of Health.
Van Duyn.   Goodbye, A.
Villon.   Ballade to End With, A.
Walker, A.   Will.
Weiss, T.   Caliban Remembers.
Whalen, P.   Irregular Ode, An.
Whitman, W.   I Heard You Solemn-Sweet Pipes of the Organ.
O You Whom I Often and Silently Come.
Out of the Cradle Endlessly Rocking.
Whittier.   Amy Wentworth.
At Last.
Summer Pilgrimage, A.
Wilbur, R.   Ballade for the Duke of Orléans.
Complaint.
Wilde, O.   Chanson.
Endymion.
La Bella Donna della Mia Mente.
Serenade: "Western wind is blowing fair, The."
Wasted Days.
Williams, C. K.   Acids.
Being Alone.
From Now On.
Gas Station, The.
Inches.
Long Bells, The.
Of What Is Past.
They Warned Him Then They Threw Him Away.
Time: 1978.
What Must I Do To Be Lost?
With Ignorance.
Williams, M.   La Ultima Carta: A Young Wife Writes to Her Husband in the Mountains.
Longing, The.
Manifold Usefulness of an Education, The.
My Wife Reads the Paper at Breakfast on the Birthday of the Scottish Poet.
Williams, T.   Lament: "Too limpid streets have grown narrow, The."
Letter to an Old Love.
Swimmer and Fish Group.
Williams, W.   Asphodel, That Greeny Flower.
Gentle Negress, The.
Paterson, Book 5: The River of Heaven.
Wordsworth, W.   Why, Minstrel, These Untuneful Murmurings.
With Ships the sea was sprinkled far and nigh.

Wright, C.   As Our Bodies Rise, Our Names
  Turn into Light.
  Bicoastal Journal.
  Composition in Grey and Pink.
  Disjecta Membra.
  Journal of True Confessions, A.
  May Journal.
  October.
  T'ang Notebook.
  To Giacomo Leopardi in the Sky.
Wright, J.   American Wedding.
  Birthday, The.
  Complaint.
  For the Marsh's Birthday.
  Idea of the Good, The.
  Poems to a Brown Cricket.
  Prayer in My Sickness, A.
  She Hid in the Trees from the Nurses.
  So She Said.
  Sun Tan at Dusk.
  To the Muse.
Wu of Han [or Wu Ti or Ou-ty or Liu Ch'e or
  Liu Ch'u].   Hiding Our Love.
Wyatt, S.   Absence! Absenting causeth me to
  complain.
  Answer, The.
  As power and wit will me assist.
  Ballad of Will, The.
  Comfort thyself, my wo[e]ful heart.
  Desire to sorrow doth me constrain.
  For want of [or I] will in woe I plain.
  Go, burning sighs, unto the frozen heart.
  Grudge on who list, this is my lot.
  Heart oppressed [or oppress'd] with desperate
    thought.
  If fancy [or fansy] would favour.
  It may be good like it who list.
  Knot which first my heart did strain, The.
  Madam, I you require.
  Might I as well within my song belay.
  My sweet, alas, forget me not.
  Promise, A.
  Such hap as I am happed in.
  Sufficed not, madame, that you did tear.
  There was never nothing more me pained [or
    payned].
  Though of the sort there be that feign.
  Though this the [or thy] port and I thy servant
    true.
  Was I never yet of your love grieved.
  What death is worse than this?
Zagajewski.   Summer.
Zaturenska.   Friend's Song, A.
  Siren Music.
Zukofsky, L.   Catullus viii.

Longshoremen
  Gallagher, T.   Black Money.

Lookout Mountain, Battle of (1863)
  Hayden, R.   On Lookout Mountain.

Loons
  Carruth, H.   Loon on Forrester's Pond, The.
  Eberhart, R.   Dream, A.
  Loon Call, A.

Lorelei
  Merrill, J.   Lorelei.
  Smith, S.   Die Lorelei.

Los Angeles, California
  Ai.   Riot Act, April 29, 1992.
  Dickey, J.   Exchanges.
  Ginsberg, A.   Overpopulation, overpopulation /
    Give me 3 acres of land.
  These States: into L.A.
  Jarrell, R.   Gleaning.
  Thinking of the Lost World.
  McGrath, T.   Return to Marsh Street.
  Merwin.   Late Wonders.
  Rukeyser, M.   Palos Verdes Cliffs.
  Updike.   L.A.
See also **Hollywood, California**

Loss
  Amichai [or Amikhai].   Elegy on the Lost Child,
    The.
  Farewell.
  Hamadiya.
  Lost Objects.

Place Where I Never Was, The.
Two Photographs.
Angelou.   No Loser, No Weeper.
Arnold, M.   Forsaken Merman, The.
Ashbery, J.   Leasing of September, The.
Atwood.   At first I was given centuries.
  Hesitations outside the Door.
  Precognition.
Berrigan, T.   Red Shift.
Berry, W.   Forty Years.
Berryman.   Ball Poem, The.
  Surviving Love.
Bierce.   Nanine.
Bishop, E.   One Art.
Blok.   Girl Was Singing, A.
Bly, R.   Visiting the Farallones.
Borges.   Paradiso 31, 108.
Brontë, E.   Alcona, in its changing mood.
  From our evening fireside now.
  Inspiring music's thrilling sound, The.
  O come again; what chains withhold.
  Old Hall of Elbë, ruined, lonely now.
  Was it with the fields of green.
Brooks, G.   Appendix to the Anniad.
Broumas, O.   Five Interior Landscapes.
Browning, E.   Lost Bower, The.
  Year's Spinning, A.
Browning, R.   Any Wife to Any Husband.
  In a Year.
  Lost Leader, The.
  Lost Mistress, The.
  Too Late.
  Waring.
  Youth and Art.
Bukowski.   I Made a Mistake.
  Longshot.
  Melancholia.
Burns, R.   Braes o' Ballochmyle, The.
  Fragment, Which Was Meant for the Beginning
    of an Elegy on the Late Miss Burnet, A.
  Highland Widow's Lament, The.
  Lass of Ecclefechan, The.
  Lines on Stirling.
  Lovely Lass o' Inverness, The.
  Man Was Made to Mourn, a Dirge.
  On the Death of the Late Lord President
    Dundas.
  Raving winds around her blowing.
  Song: "As I stood by yon roofless tower."
  Song.—In the Character of a Ruined Farmer.
  Sonnet on the Death of Robert Riddel, Esq. *of
    Glen Riddel, April* 1794.
  Strathallan's Lament.
  Thou Ling'ring Star.
  To Ruin.
  To William Creech.
  Winter It Is Past, The.
Byron, G.   Fragment Written Shortly after the
    Marriage of Miss Chaworth.
  Herod's Lament for Mariamne.
  On Finding a Fan.
  One Struggle More, and I Am Free.
  Remember Him Whom Passion's Power.
  There Was a Time, I Need Not Name.
  To a Lady.
  To the Countess of Blessington.
Campion, T.   Could my heart more tongues
    imploy.
  Peaceful Western Wind, The.
Campion, T. *et al.*   Let him that will be free and
    keep his h[e]art from care.
  Long have mine eies gaz'd with delight.
Carew, T.   Deposition from Love, A.
Carruth, H.   Lines Written in an Asylum.
Carver, R.   Cutlery.
  Hominy and Rain.
  Poem Not against Songbirds, A.
  Road, The.
Cavafy.   Craftsman of Winebowls.
  Days of 1903.
  Desperation.
  God Forsakes Antony, The.
  In the Wineshops.
Cavalcanti.   Ballata: He perceives that his
    highest Love is gone from him.
  Each day I come to you an infinity of times.

Celan.   Afternoon with Circus and Citadel.
  Assisi.
  Cologne, at the Station.
  Ice, Eden.
Ciardi, J.   True or False.
Clifton, L.   Oh where have you fallen to.
Clough.   Alteram Partem.
Codrescu.   Brief (Remembered) *Histoire* of
  Rejection, A.
  Three Types of Loss.
Coleridge, S.   Farewell to Love.
  On Seeing a Youth Affectionately Welcomed by
    a Sister.
Collins, B.   Lines Composed over Three
  Thousand Miles from Tintern Abbey.
Cooper, J.   Long, Disconsolate Lines.
Crane, H.   Her Eyes Had.
  Mermen, The.
  Sad Indian, The.
  Stark Major.
  Voyages.
Creeley.   Echoes ("Sudden / loss of hope, A").
  In an Act of Pity.
  Manila.
  On Phrase from Ginsberg's *Kaddish*.
  Sanine to Leda.
  To And.
Cullen, C.   Lament: "Now let all lovely things
    embark."
  Sonnet: "I know now how a man whose blood
    is hot."
  Therefore, Adieu.
  Threnody for a Brown Girl.
  Variations on a Theme.
  Wind Bloweth Where It Listeth, The.
Cummings, E. E.   "Could that"i marveled"be /
    you?"
  First Jock he / was kilt a handsome.
  In heavenly realms of hellas dwelt.
  Let it go—the.
  My little heart is so wonderfully sorry.
  Noster, The.
  O / the round / little man we.
  Of Ever-Ever Land i speak.
  Proud of his scientific attitude.
  W.H.W., Jr.
  When my sensational moments are no more.
  When what hugs stopping earth than silent is.
  Why did you go.
  Workingman with hand so hairy-sturdy.
  Worshipping same / they squirm and they
    spawn.
Davie, D.   Fatherhood.
  His Themes.
De la Mare.   Fare Well.
  Reserved.
Dickey, J.   Leap, The.
  To Be Done in Winter.
Dickinson, E.   Bereaved of all, I went abroad.
  Each Scar I'll keep for Him.
  Except the Heaven had come so near.
  Had I presumed to hope.
  Her sweet Weight on my Heart at Night.
  Home itself is far from home.
  How much of Source escapes with thee.
  How sweet that he rose in the morning.
  I cannot buy it—'tis not sold.
  I had a guinea golden.
  I lost a World—the other day!
  I never lost as much but twice.
  I trust you may have the dearest summer.
  If I'm lost—now.
  Loss of something ever felt I, A.
  Now I knew I lost her.
  Of so divine a Loss.
  Only Balmless Wound, The.
  Severer Service of myself.
  She went as quiet as the Dew.
  Stimulus of Loss, The.
  Things that never can come back, are several,
    The.
  To lose thee—sweeter than to gain.
  We miss a Kinsman more.
  Where I have lost, I softer tread.
  Who never lost, are unprepared.
  You love me—you are sure.

Donne. Broken Heart, The.
Computation, The.
To Mr I. L. ("Blessed [or Blesst] are your north parts, for all this long time").
Dove, R. Exeunt the Viols.
Dubie. Hours, The.
Dunbar, P. Golden Day, A.
Ione.
Jilted.
Wraith, The.
Yesterday and Tomorrow.
Eberhart, R. Broken Wing Theory.
Haystack, The.
Loss.
Eliot, T. S. Eyes That Last I Saw in Tears.
Hollow Men, The.
Journey of the Magi.
Emerson, R. Dost thou not hear me Ellen.
Give All to Love.
In Memoriam.
My days roll by me like a train of dreams.
Shall the Muse sing for thousands & not sing.
Threnody: "South-wind brings, The."
Where art thou / Thou beautiful dream.
Enzensberger, H. Notice of Loss.
Fenton, J. Skip, The.
Wind.
Ferlinghetti, L. Deflowering.
Gallagher, T. Calm, The.
Coming Home.
Even Now You Are Leaving.
I Save Your Coat, but You Lose It Later.
Ginsberg, A. Café in Warsaw.
Car Crash.
Elegy for Neal Cassady.
Garden State.
Over Denver Again.
Glück, L. Autumnal.
Dream of Mourning, The.
Egg, The.
Fire, The.
Here Are My Black Clothes.
Rosy.
Graves, R. As When the Mystic.
At the Gate.
Desert Fringe.
Lost Love.
Gray, T. Song: "Thyrsis, when we parted, swore."
Gunn, T. Autobiography.
Beautician, The.
Right Possessor, The.
Without a Counterpart.
"H. D." Calliope.
Chance Meeting.
Eros.
Fragment 40: "Keep love and he wings."
Hyacinth.
Loss.
Hacker, M. Against Silence.
Autumn 1980.
Geographer.
Sea Coming Indoors, The.
Hall, D. Elegy for Wesley Wells.
Red Branch, The.
Religious Articles.
Han-shan. What's this crying for.
Hardy, T. At a Seaside Town in 1869.
At Rushy-Pond.
Ballad of Love's Skeleton, The.
Boys Then and Now.
Change, The.
Evelyn G. of Christminster.
He Inadvertently Cures His Love-Pains.
I Said to Love.
Marble-Streeted Town, The.
Molly Gone.
On Martock Moor.
Re-Enactment, The.
Revulsion.
Signs and Tokens.
Song from Heine.
Song to an Old Burden.
Standing by the Mantlepiece.
That Moment.
They Would Not Come.

Under High-Stoy Hill.
Without Ceremony.
Hayden, R. Road in Kentucky, A.
Herrick. His Loss.
Losse from the Heat.
Plunder, The.
Upon a Comely, and Curious Maide.
Upon Skurffe.
Upon the Loss[e] of His Mistresses.
Vine, The.
Hopkins, G. Voice from the World, A.
Housman. Give me a land of boughs in leaf.
If truth in hearts that perish.
We'll to the woods no more.
Yon Far Country.
Howe, F. Conclusively.
Hughes, L. Bulwark.
Day.
Homecoming.
Monroe's Blues.
Young Gal's Blues.
Hughes, T. Snow.
Jackson, L. After So Much Loss.
Jarrell, R. Bad Music, The.
Che Farò Senza Euridice.
I loved you, too. There was no use. I had no time.
Leave.
Loss.
Lost Love, The.
Moving.
Northern Snows, The.
Second Air Force.
Street Has Changed, The.
Today is almost over.
Truth, The.
Jonson, B. Elegy, An: "Since you must go, and I must bid farewell."
Execration upon Vulcan, An.
To the World [A Farewell for a Gentlewoman, Virtuous and Noble].
Why I Write Not of Love.
Keats. In Drear-nighted December.
Kinnell. Lost Loves.
Kipling, R. Children, The.
Dove of Dacca, The.
Follow Me 'Ome.
For to Admire.
Gertrude's Prayer.
Lovers' Litany, The.
Mesopotamia.
Possibilities.
Recantation, A.
Russia to the Pacifists.
Soldier, Soldier.
Song in the Desert, A.
Widower, The.
With Scindia to Delhi.
Kizer, C. Anniversaries: Claremont Avenue, from 1945.
For Sappho/After Sappho.
Pearl.
Koch, K. To Marina.
Komunyakaa. Somewhere Else.
Kumin, M. How It Is.
Larkin, P. No Road.
So through that unripe day you bore your head.
Laughlin, J. Empty Room, The.
Smallest Blessing, The.
Lawrence, D. H. Another Ophelia.
Bereavement.
Bread upon the Waters.
Call into Death.
Drama, A.
Elegy: "Sun immense and rosy, The."
Grey Evening.
Humiliation.
Inheritance, The.
Kiss, A.
Last Words to Miriam.
Last Words to Muriel.
Love Message.
Love Song, A: "Reject me not if I should say to you."
On the Balcony.
Seekers.

Silence.
Submergence.
Witch II, The.
Levertov. News Items.
Passing Bell, The.
Levi, P. 11 February 1946.
Levine, P. Buying and Selling.
Lost and Found.
Li Yü. Silently I ascend the western pavilion.
Logan, J. Dawn and a Woman.
Longfellow, H. Cross of Snow, The.
Hawthorne.
Lorde. Sister, Morning Is a Time for Miracles.
MacLeish. Psyche with the Candle.
MacNeice. Sand in the Air.
Mallarmé. Beautiful suicide victoriously fled, The.
Marvell. Unfortunate Lover, The.
McGrath, T. Changeling, The.
End of the Line, The.
Meredith, G. C B M.
Dark on the ridge of the cold salt wave.
Hilda's Morning and Evening Dose of Rhyme.
Hungarian Air.
Love.
Song: "Should thy love die; / O bury it not under ice-blue eyes!"
Two Blackbirds, The.
Vittoria Concluding the Opera of "Camilla."
Meredith, W. Envoi: "Go, little book. If anybody asks."
Merton. Dirge for a Town in France.
Merwin. April.
Before That.
Huckleberry Woman.
Memory of the Loss of Wings.
Nails, The.
On the Silent Anniversary of a Reunion.
Port, The.
Spring.
Millay, E. If I should learn, in some quite casual way.
Sonnet: "What lips my lips have kissed, and where, and why."
Well, I have lost you; and I lost you fairly.
Milosz, C. Fall, The.
On Pilgrimage.
Rivers Grow Small.
Mistral, G. Hollow Walnut, The.
Things.
Montale. Eastbourne.
Eclogue: "It was good getting lost."
Flux.
You know: I'm going to lose you again.
Neruda. Ambassador, The.
Final.
O'Hara, F. Mayakovsky.
Oliver, M. Hattie Bloom.
In Blackwater Woods.
Olson, C. Pacific Lament.
Orr, G. Dream of Fifty, A.
What I'm Saying.
Pagis. Toward Home.
Palmer, M. November Talks.
Parker, D. Solace.
Pessoa. I don't want the sincere gifts.
Lightly, quickly, soft.
Petrarch. Column and the Laurel-tree are broken, The.
Death, you have left this world, without its sun.
If but that honoured branch which turns away.
If you want me again under your yoke.
In the best season of our earthly span.
Love was perhaps a happy thing onetime.
My soul, prophetic of your coming loss.
Noble tree, which I loved well and long, The.
O day, O hour, O instant at the last.
O happy spirit that so charmingly.
Sight of her, angelic and serene, The.
What should I do? Love, what do you advise?
Where is the forehead that with one slight shake.
Piercy. All Clear.
Never-Never.
Pinkerton, H. For an End.
Point Lobos, 1950.

Plath. Bucolics.
Denouement.
Poe. Dream, A.
Dream within a Dream, A.
Happiest Day, the Happiest Hour, The.
Sleeper, The.
To ———: "Bowers whereat, in dreams, I see,
The."
To One in Paradise.
Valley of Unrest, The.
Pope, A. Lamentation of Glumdalclitch for the
Loss of Grildrig, The.
Prunty. Cousins, Brothers, Sisters.
Times Between, The.
Raine, K. Her Room.
Ransom, J. Dead Boy.
Rashid, N. Izhab-O-Rasai (Expression and
Reach).
Rexroth, K. Cinque Terre.
Rich, A. Loser, The.
Stelae, The.
Riley, J. After the Frost.
Boys, The.
Our Little Girl.
What They Said.
Rilke. Holy Ghost.
Loss.
Lost Nights.
Lost Things.
Ritsos. Memorial Services.
Robinson, E. On the Night of a Friend's
Wedding.
Roethke. Apparition, The.
Beast, The.
Visitant, The.
Rossetti, C. Cousin Kate.
Despair.
Echo.
Grown and Flown.
Rukeyser, M. His father is lost and away.
Loan, The.
Of Money. And the Past.
Song: "World is full of loss; bring, wind, my
love, The."
Waiting for Icarus.
Sandburg, C. And This Will Be All?
Dreams in the Dusk.
Great Hunt, The.
Schuyler, J. August First, 1974.
Morning of the Poem, The.
Sexton. Ballad of the Lonely Masturbator, The.
December 2nd.
December 11th.
December 18th.
Eighteen Days without You.
Going Gone.
Inventory of Goodbyes, The.
Lost Ingredient, The.
Lost Lie, The.
Waking Alone.
Wedding Night, The.
Shapiro, K. Haircut.
Leg, The.
Shelley, P. Lines: "We meet not as we parted."
On a Faded Violet.
Sunset, The.
To Mary Shelley.
To William Shelley.
Smith, S. Arabella.
Broken Heart, The.
Gnädiges Fräulein.
House of Over-Dew, The.
Recluse, The.
Story I Have Told, The.
Spender, S. Double Shame, The.
Stafford, W. Farm on the Great Plains, The.
Homecoming.
Reaching out to Turn on a Light.
Saint Matthew and All.
Stock, R. Dance, The.
Sze. Before Completion.
String Diamond, The.
Tennyson, A. Œnone.
Thoreau. Brother where dost thou dwell?
Tomlinson, C. Death of the Infanta, The.
Elegy for Henry Street.

Tarquinia.
Updike. Lament, for Cocoa.
My Children at the Dump.
South of the Alps.
Walker, A. Walker.
Warren, R. Loss, of Perhaps Love, in Our
World of Contingency.
Wheatley, P. On the Death of Dr. Samuel
Marshall. 1771.
Whitman, W. Out of the Cradle Endlessly
Rocking.
Yonnondio.
Whittier. Farewell, The: "Gone, gone,—sold
and gone."
Fountain, The.
Inscription: "Eagle, stooping from yon snow-
blown peaks, The."
Rendition, The.
Singer, The.
Truce of Piscataqua, The.
Wilde, O. Canzonet.
From Spring Days to Winter.
Hélas!
Requiescat.
Williams, C. K. Call, The.
Covenant, The.
Downwards.
Le Petit Salvié.
Loss.
Vehicle: Absence.
Williams, M. To One Who Went Too Far.
Williams, T. Androgyne, Mon Amour.
Separate Poem, A.
Shadow Wood.
Williams, W. These.
Wordsworth, W. Complaint, A.
Composed when a Probability Existed of Our
Being Obliged to Quit Rydal Mount as a
Residence.
Elegiac Verses in Memory of My Brother, John
Wordsworth.
Grief, thou hast lost an ever ready friend.
Last of the Flock, The.
Peter Bell; a Tale.
Sonnet in the Pass of Killicranky.
Surprised by joy—impatient as the Wind.
Vaudracour and Julia.
Why, Minstrel, These Untuneful Murmurings.
Wishing-Gate Destroyed, The.
Written in London, September, 1802.
Wright, J. Gambling in Stateline, Nevada.
Having Lost My Sons, I Confront the Wreckage
of the Moon: Christmas, 1960.
Humming a Tune for an Old Lady in West
Virginia.
In Memory of the Horse David, Who Ate One
of My Poems.
Listening to the Mourners.
Quail, The.
Wroth [or Wroath]. Love's Victorie.
Wyatt, S. Help[e] me to seek [or seke] for I lost
it there.
I see the change from that that was.
Loss is small to lose such one, The.
My love took scorn my service to retain.
Where shall I have at mine own will.
Yeats. Crazy Jane Reproved.
King and No King.
Lover Mourns for the Loss of Love, The.
Never Give All the Heart.
Zukofsky, L. Marigold.

Lot (Bible)
Akhmatova, A. Lot's Wife.
Housman. Half-way, for one commandment
broken.
Kizer, C. Columns and Caryatids.
Nemerov. Lot Later.
Lot's Wife.
Rukeyser, M. Ms. Lot.
Stock, R. Taking Stock of Lot.

Lot's Wife (Bible)
Szymborska, W. Lot's Wife.

Lotus
Lawrence, D. H. Lotus and Frost.
Lindsay, N. Wedding of the Rose and the Lotus,
The.

Louis XIV, King of France
Marvell. Inscribenda Luparae [To Be Written
on the Louvre].

Louis XVI, King of France
Blake, W. French Revolution, The.
Rimbaud, A. Blacksmith, The.
Stockton, A. On the Celebration of the Birth of
the Dauphin of France.

Louis, Joe
Hughes, L. Joe Louis ("Joe Louis is a man").

Louis XI, King of France
Stock, R. Louis XI.

Louisiana (state)
Carruth, H. New Orleans.
Komunyakaa. Landscape for the Disappeared.
Sugar.
Laughlin, J. Ipse Dixit.
Whitman, W. I Saw in Louisiana a Live-Oak
Growing.

L'Ouverture, Toussaint
See **Toussaint L'Ouverture, François Dominique**

Love
Amichai [or Amikhai]. Good Time, A.
I Told You It Would Be So—And You Didn't
Believe.
Now to Break.
Baudelaire. Autumn Sonnet.
Fountain of Blood.
Hymn: "To Love and to the lovely eyes."
Ciardi, J. Credibility.
Creeley. If Happiness.
Oh Love ("My love is a boat").
Song: "Love has no other friends."
Cunningham, J. 1 Corinthians 13: Commentary.
Jonson, B. Song. To Celia ("Drink to me only
with thine eyes").
Levertov. Movement.
Prayer for Revolutionary Love.
Major, C. Young Woman.
McHugh, H. Ghost, The.
Merwin. She Who Was Gone.
Orr, G. Glukupikron.
Riley, J. Love's as Broad as Long.
Rumi. All Rivers at Once.
I Have Five Things to Say.
I'm Not Saying This Right.
Phrasing Must Change, The.
There's a strange frenzy in my head.
Way of love is not, The.
Shapiro, K. V-Letter.
Weiss, T. Dance Called David, The.
Whalen, P. Dear Mr President.
Love Love Love Again.
Williams, T. Mornings on Bourbon Street.
Yeats. Brown Penny.

See also **Affection; Companionship and
Companions; Courtship; Dating; Erotic Love**

Lovebirds
Eberhart, R. Bower, The.
Guillaume de Lorris et al. Romance [or
Romaunt] of the Rose, The.
Hall, D. Young Watch Us, The.
Hardy, T. Her Love-Birds.
Nash, O. Two and One Are a Problem.
Tomlinson, C. In the Borghese Gardens.
Wright, J. For the Marsh's Birthday.

Lovelace, Richard
Marvell. To His Noble Friend, Mr Richard
Lovelace, upon His Poems.

Lowell, Amy
Cullen, C. Epitaph: "She leans across a golden
table."
Cummings, E. E. Slightly before the middle of
Congressman Pudd.
Schuyler, J. Amy Lowell Thoughts.

Lowell, James Russell
Emerson, R. James Russell Lowell.
Whittier. Welcome to Lowell, A.

Lowell, Robert
Ai. Conversation.
Bishop, E. North Haven.
Brodsky, J. Elegy: For Robert Lowell.
Logan, J. Staying Awake.
Meredith, W. Last Things.

Remembering Robert Lowell.
Milosz, C.   To Robert Lowell.

Lowry, Malcolm
Mahon.   Homage to Malcolm Lowry.

Loyalty
Browning, E.   Rhyme of the Duchess May.
Browning, R.   Light Woman, A.
Burns, R.   Bannocks o' Bear-Meal.
Here's a Health to Them That's Awa'.
Highland Laddie.
My Collier Laddie.
O, for Ane-and-Twenty Tam.
O [or Oh] Wert Thou in the Cauld Blast.
Red, Red Rose, A.
Sutors o' Selkirk.
Toast, A.
Char.   Come Dance in Baronies.
Chaucer.   Balade of Complaint, A.
Cowper, W.   On Loyalty.
Creeley.   For Anybody.
She Went to Stay.
Eberhart, R.   Later or Sooner.
Emerson, R.   Quoth Saadi, when I stood before.
Glück, L.   Late Snow.
Hardy, T.   Broken Appointment, A.
In Weatherbury Stocks.
Housman.   As through the Wild Green Hills of Wyre.
Jeffers, R.   At the Birth of an Age.
House Dog's Grave, The.
Kipling, R.   Dinah in Heaven.
Gunga Din.
Ode: "So long as memory, valour, and faith endure."
Song of the Red War-Boat.
Ulster.
Lawrence, D. H.   Talk of Loyalty.
Logue, C.   Loyal to the King.
Melville, H.   Enthusiast, The.
Mistral, G.   Sonnets of Death 5.
Montale.   Many years, and one still harder.
Nash, O.   Father, Dear Father, Go Jump in the Lake, or You're Costlier than You Think.
Petrarch.   I used to take the blame, but now excuse.
Ralegh, S.   Advice, The.
"Shu Ting."   "?!"
Brother, I Am Here.
Unknown.   Ballade de Marguerite.
Whittier.   Answer, The.
Williams, C. K.   Being Alone.
Yeats.   Black Tower, The.
Zukofsky, L.   1959 Valentine.
Barely and *widely*.

Luck
Amichai [or Amikhai].   They Are All Dice.
Angelou.   On Aging.
Beckett, S.   À l'instant de s'entendre dire.
Broumas, O.   If I Yes.
Bukowski.   Luck.
Burns, R.   O raging Fortune's withering blast.
Carver, R.   Fishing Pole of the Drowned Man, The.
My Death.
Codrescu.   Secret Training.
Creeley.   Train Going By.
Cummings, E. E.   Lucky means finding / Holes where.
Dickinson, E.   Luck is not chance.
Dunbar, P.   Way T'ings Come, De.
Herrick.   Coming of Good Luck, The.
Crosse and Pile.
Good Luck Not Lasting.
Large Bounds Doe but Bury Us.
No Luck in Love.
Housman.   Now dreary dawns the eastern light.
Hughes, L.   Bad Luck Card.
Jackson, L.   Lullaby, The.
Levertov.   Libation.
McHugh, H.   Few Licks, A.
Merwin.   Talk of Fortune.
Nash, O.   How Long Has This Been Going On?
Oh, Quite Long.
Outcome of Mr. Buck's Superstition, The.
Prayer at the End of a Rope.
Turns in a Worm's Lane.

You Bet Travel Is Broadening.
Nemerov.   Sonnet: "It seems to be the trouble, everyone."
Paley, G.   Luck.
Parker, D.   Very Short Song, A.
Riley, J.   Scotty.
Rossetti, C.   Linnet in a gilded cage,— / A linnet on a bough, A.
Queen of Hearts, The.
Stafford, W.   Little Ways that Encourage Good Fortune, The.
Warren, R.   Old Love.
Wyatt, S.   Alas, Fortune, what aileth thee.
For shamefast harm of great and hateful need.
He is not de[a]d that sometime [or somtyme] hath a fall.
Zukofsky, L.   Honesty.

See also Chance; Fate; Fortune.

Lucknow, India
Whittier.   Pipes at Lucknow, The.

Lucretius
Whalen, P.   Homage to Lucretius.

Luddites
Byron, G.   Ode to the Framers of the Frame Bill, An.

Lullabies
Amichai [or Amikhai].   Mutual Lullaby, A.
Auden.   Lullaby: "Lay your sleeping head, my love."
Bishop, E.   Lullaby for the Cat.
Broumas, O.   Lullaby: "I see you, centered."
Browning, E.   Song against Singing, A.
Eberhart, R.   Line of Verse of Yeats, A.
Fenton, J.   Lullaby for a Summer Recess.
Herrick.   Upon a Child.
Hughes, L.   Lullaby (For a Black Mother).
Jacobsen, J.   Primer, The.
Keats.   'Tis the Witching Time [or Hour] of Night.
Mistral, G.   You Had Me.
Rossetti, C.   Holy Innocents.
Lie a-bed, / Sleepy head, / Shut up eyes, bo-peep.
Lullaby, oh lullaby! / Flowers are closed and lambs are sleeping.
Stock, R.   Lullaby for Now.
Wordsworth, D.   Cottager to Her Infant, (By My Sister), The.
Zaturenska.   Lullaby: "Ruin falls on blackening skies."

Lumbering and Lumbermen
Collins, B.   Splitting Wood.
Dickey, J.   Other, The.
Dugan, A.   Sawyer's Rage against Trees Noble as Horses, A.
Frost, R.   In winter in the woods alone.
Gurney, I.   Felling a Tree.
Han-shan.   Hundred-foot trees produced by Heaven.
Hardy, T.   Throwing a Tree.
Kizer, C.   Index, a Mountain.
Komunyakaa.   Poetics of Paperwood.
Meredith, G.   Woodman and Echo.
Snyder, G.   Ethnobotany.
Getting in the Wood.
Stock, R.   Solo for Four.
Tomlinson, C.   Operation, The.
Whitman, W.   Song of the Broad-Axe [or Broad-Ax].
Whittier.   Lumbermen, The.
Wilbur, R.   Folk Tune.
Williams, C. K.   Elms.

Lumumba, Patrice
Hughes, L.   Lumumba's Grave.

Lunch
Creeley.   Lunch and After.
Sopa.
Wishes.
Ginsberg, A.   Bricklayer's Lunch Hour, The.
Koch, K.   Lunch.
Nash, O.   Dance Unmacabre.
O'Hara, F.   Step Away from Them, A.
Patchen.   Lunch Wagon on Highway 57.
Ramanujan.   Still Life.
Tomlinson, C.   Hero Sandwiches.

Portrait of the Artist II.

Lungs
Piercy.   Bronchitis on the 14th Floor.
Rukeyser, M.   Disease, The.

Lust
Ai.   Priest's Confession, The.
Amichai [or Amikhai].   Bedouin Goes North, A.
Caffè Dante in New York—2.
First Rain, The.
My former student is in the traffic police.
Political Poem, A.
Stewardess.
Ammons.   Gilgamesh Was Very Lascivious.
Auden.   Love Feast, The.
Baudelaire.   Cat.
Dancing Serpent, The.
Giantess, The.
Ideal, The.
Jewels.
Martyr, A.
Still Unsatisfied.
Berryman.   Images of Elspeth.
Blake, W.   Visions of the Daughters of Albion.
Bukowski.   99 to One.
I Kneel.
Iron Mike.
My Groupie.
Burns, R.   Charlie He's My Darling.
Muirland Meg.
There's News Lasses News.
Trogger, The.
Cavafy.   At the Theater.
Chandelier.
He Swears.
In the Dull and Gloomy Village.
25th Year of His Life, The.
Ciardi, J.   Are We Through Talking, I Hope?
Collins, B.   Pinup.
Creeley.   American Love.
June 6, 1970.
Looking Out.
Cummings, E. E.   God pity me whom (god distinctly has).
My eyes are fond of the east side.
My girl's tall with hard long eyes.
On the Madam's best april the.
Poem her belly marched through me as, The.
Sh estiffl / ystrut sal.
Twentyseven bums give a prostitute the once.
What time is it i wonder never mind.
When i have thought of you somewhat too.
When thou hast taken thy last applause,and when.
Davie, D.   Toby to Aguecheek.
Dickinson, E.   Wild Nights—Wild Nights!
Dryden, J.   New Song, A: "Sylvia the fair, in the bloom of fifteen."
Dubie.   Obscure, The.
Dugan, A.   Absent Good Girl, Life of My Mind.
For a Lost Girl.
Untitled Poem: "I love the way the heel of my hand feels."
What the Hell, Rage, Give in to Natural Graces.
Duncan, R.   Albigenses, The.
Mirror, The.
Eberhart, R.   Enigma, The.
Mais l'Amour Infini Me Montera dans l'Ame.
Ginsberg, A.   Hardon Blues.
Sweet Boy, Gimme Yr Ass.
Graves, R.   Blue-Fly, The.
Down, Wanton, Down!
In Trance at a Distance.
Succubus, The.
Gunn, T.   Modes of Pleasure.
Herrick.   Julia's Petticoat.
Parting Verse, or Charge to His Supposed Wife when He Travelled, The.
Poet Loves a Mistress, but Not to Marry, The.
To Bacchus, a Canticle.
Vine, The.
Vision, The.
Housman.   When I Watch the Living Meet.
Jackson, L.   Be Grave, Woman.
Tale of Modernity.
Wishing More Dear.
Jarrell, R.   Sears Roebuck.

Jonson, B.   On Groin.
Kizer, C.   What the Bones Know.
Komunyakaa.   Captain Diable's Receptionist.
Le Xuan, Beautiful Spring.
Nocturne: "High-beam light swung, The."
Sorrow.
Thorn Merchant's Son, The.
Too Pretty for Serious Business.
When in Rome—Apologia.
Kunitz, S.   She Wept, She Railed.
Laughlin, J.   Girls as Windmills.
Lawrence, D. H.   Passing Visit to Helen.
Levertov.   Mutes, The.
MacNeice.   Libertine, The.
Major, C.   Ballroom Dark.
Melville, H.   After the Pleasure Party.
Michelangelo Buonarroti.   Not true that it's
   always grim with mortal sin.
Milosz, C.   Honest Description of Myself with a
   Glass of Whiskey at an Airport, Let Us Say, in
   Minneapolis, An.
Nemerov.   Don Juan to the Statue.
 Landscape with Figures.
 New Weapons in the Old War.
O'Hara, F.   Poem: "I don't know as I get what
   D.H. Lawrence is driving at."
Olson, C.   As the shield goddess, Mycenae.
 Hymn to the Word.
 Long Distance.
 Troilus.
 Woman's Nipples Is the Rose of the World, A.
Orr, G.   After Piero di Cosimo's *Venus, Mars,
   and Amor.*
Parker, D.   Little Old Lady in Lavender Silk,
   The.
Petronius Arbiter.   Doing, a filthy pleasure is,
   and short.
Plath.   Gigolo.
Ramanujan.   Pleasure.
Rexroth, K.   Advantages of Learning, The.
Rich, A.   Two Songs.
Rimbaud, A.   Deserts of Love, The.
 Tartufe's Punishment.
Robinson, E.   John Evereldown.
Rumi.   Nasuh.
 Sexual Urgency, What a Woman's Laughter Can
   Do, and the Nature of True Virility.
Suckling, S.   Upon My Lady Carlisle's Walking
   in Hampton Court Garden.
Swenson, M.   Blue.
Thomas, D.   Into Her Lying Down Head.
Updike.   Nuda Natens.
 Rockettes, The.
Van Duyn.   Billings and Cooings from "The
   Berkeley Barb."
Walker, A.   She Said.
Whitman, W.   I Am He That Aches with Love.
 Native Moments.
 Spontaneous Me.
Wilbur, R.   Loves of the Puppets.
Williams, M.   Affair, The.
 He Shuts His Eyes for the Layman's Long
   Prayer about Lust and the Mind of the Young
   Preacher Wanders Again.
 If Ever There Was One.
Williams, T.   Androgyne, Mon Amour.
Williams, W.   Canthara.
 From "The Birth of Venus," Song.
Wyatt, S.   For want of [*or* I] will in woe I plain.
 If thou wilt mighty be, flee from the rage.
 It burneth yet, alas, my heart's desire.
 So unwarely was never no man caught [*or*
   cawght].
 Such hap as I am happed in.
See also **Erotic Love; Sex**
Lutes
Campion, T.   When to Her Lute.
Dunbar, P.   Thou Art My Lute.
Herrick.   Upon Linnit.
 Upon Sapho, Sweetly Playing, and Sweetly
   Singing.
Meredith, W.   Orpheus.
Wyatt, S.   At mo[o]st mischief.
 Blame Not My Lute.
 My Lute, Awake!

Luther, Martin
Auden.   Luther.
Buchanan, G.   Pope from penance purgatorial,
   The.
Very.   Justification by Faith.
Luxemburg, Rosa
Codrescu.   Reverse.
Lying
Bierce.   To an Insolent Attorney.
Heaney, S.   Transgression, A.
Rilke.   Lying to a Child.
See also **Lies and Lying**
Lynching
Ai.   Hoover Trismegistus.
Carruth, H.   Song: The Famous Vision of
   America.
Clifton, L.   Photograph, The: A Lynching.
Dunbar, P.   Haunted Oak, The.
Hayden, R.   Night, Death, Mississippi.
Hughes, L.   Ballad of Walter White.
 Bitter River, The.
 Blue Bayou.
 Song after Lynching.
 Song for a Dark Girl.
Komunyakaa.   Summer Night in Hanoi, A.
Lorde.   Afterimages.
McGrath, T.   Deep South.
Patchen.   1935.
 Nice Day for a Lynching.
Rukeyser, M.   Lynchings of Jesus, The.
Tate, A.   Swimmers, The.
Warren, R.   Ballad of Mister Dutcher and the
   Last Lynching in Gupton.
Lynx
Sarton, M.   Godhead as Lynx, The.
Lyonnesse, Cornwall
De la Mare.   Sunk Lyonesse.
Hardy, T.   When I Set Out for Lyonnesse.
Plath.   Lyonnesse.
Lysergic Acid (LSD)
Ginsberg, A.   Lysergic Acid.
 Wales Visitation.
Gunn, T.   At the Centre.
 Fair in the Woods, The.
Ramanujan.   Looking for the Centre.
Whalen, P.   "I Told Myself": Bobbie
   Spontaneously.

M

Macbeth
Blok.   She Came in from the Frost.
De la Mare.   Macbeth.
Macedonia
Cavafy.   Battle of Magnesia, The.
Gjuzel.   Flood at the International Writer's
   Workshop.
Kizer, C.   Translation.
Machines
Ammons.   Needs.
Atwood.   Three Desk Objects.
Ciardi, J.   Machine.
Crane, H.   Supplication to the Muses on a
   Trying Day.
Eliot, T. S.   Engine, The.
Frost, R.   Egg and the Machine, The.
 Trial Run, A.
Ginsberg, A.   Manhattan Thirties Flash.
 Squeal.
Jonson, B.   On the New Motion.
Kipling, R.   McAndrew's Hymn.
 Secret of the Machines, The.
 Song of the Dynamo.
Komunyakaa.   Temples of Smoke.
Lawrence, D. H.   Departure.
 Evil World-Soul, The.
 Gulf, The.
 Hold Back!
 If You Are a Man.
 Man and Machine.
 Masses and Classes.
 Men Like Gods.
 Oh Wonderful Machine!

 On and On and On.
 Side-Step, O Sons of Men!
 Triumph of the Machine, The.
Logan, J.   Dialogue with La Mettrie, A.
Logue, C.   I've worked here all my life.
Merton.   Elegy for Five Old Ladies, An.
 Exploits of a Machine Age.
 Now the official nerve is analyzed.
 Tune for Festive Dances in the Nineteen Sixties,
   A.
Moore, M.   To a Steam Roller.
Nash, O.   Up from the Wheelbarrow.
 We Would Refer You to Our Service
   Department, if We Had One.
Nemerov.   Beautiful Lawn Sprinkler, The.
Oppen.   Image of the Engine.
Pagis.   Freedom Machine, The.
Rukeyser, M.   Power.
 Wedding Presents.
Snyder, G.   Removing the Plate of the Pump on
   the Hydraulic System of the Backhoe.
Tomlinson, C.   Crane, The.
Van Duyn.   Sentimental Delusion, A.
Williams, T.   Death Embrace, The.
Wordsworth, W.   Steamboats, Viaducts, and
   Railways.
Machismo
Davie, D.   Bowing the Head.
Komunyakaa.   Addendum.
MacLeish, Archibald
Rukeyser, M.   Citation for Horace Gregory.
Sandburg, C.   On a Flimmering Floom You
   Shall Ride.
MacNeice, Louis
MacNeice.   Autobiography.
Mahon.   In Carrowdore Churchyard.
Spender, S.   Louis MacNeice.
Macy's (department store)
Ferlinghetti, L.   Director of Alienation.
Paley, G.   34th Street Song.
Mad Song (genre)
Herrick.   Mad Maid's Song, The.
Madness
Arnold, M.   Summer Night, A.
Atwood.   Progressive Insanities of a Pioneer.
 Visit to Toronto, with Companions.
Berry, W.   Contrariness of the Mad Farmer, The.
 Mad Farmer Revolution, The.
 Meditation in the Spring Rain.
Berryman.   Mysteries, The.
 Song of the Demented Priest, The.
 Song of the Man Forsaken and Obsessed.
Bishop, E.   Visits to St. Elizabeths.
Blake, W.   Mad Song.
 Madman I have been calld Fool they call thee.
 To F[laxman].
 To Flaxman.
Bukowski.   Madness.
Campion, T.   Could my poore hart whole worlds
   of toungs employ.
Carruth, H.   Asylum, The.
 I Tell You for Several Years of My Madness I
   Heard the Voice of Lilith Singing in the Trees
   of Chicago.
 John Dryden.
 Lady.
 Lines Written in an Asylum.
 Ontological Episode of the Asylum.
 Re-Acquaintance.
 Simple.
 Unnatural Unselection.
Celan.   Tübingen, January.
Char.   Septentrion.
Chuang Tzu.   Confucius and the Madman.
Ciardi, J.   Bedlam Revisited.
 Incident.
Clare, J.   I Am.
Cummings, E. E.   Love is more thicker than
   forget.
 Tell me not how electricity or.
Davie, D.   Cambridgeshire.
De la Mare.   Banquo.
 Iago.
 Motley.
 Ophelia.

Dickey, W.   Alligators and Paris and North America.
Dickinson, E.   First Day's Night had come, The.
   I think I was enchanted.
   Much Madness is divinest Sense.
Dove, R.   Great Uncle Beefheart.
Dugan, A.   I Dreamed I Got a Letter from Ezra Pound.
Eberhart, R.   Birth of the Spirit, The.
   Killer, The.
   To the Mad Poets.
Emerson, R.   Skeptic, The.
Ferlinghetti, L.   Love Nut, The.
Ginsberg, A.   Crazy Spiritual, A.
   Howl.
   Vision 1948.
Glück, L.   Archipelago.
Graves, R.   Halls of Bedlam, The.
"H. D."   Gift, The.
Hardy, T.   Evening in Galilee, An.
   Forbidden Banns, The.
   Henley Regatta.
   Interloper, The.
   Mad Judy.
   Thoughts at Midnight.
Herrick.   Mad Maid's Song, The.
Hughes, T.   Egg-Head.
Ignatow, D.   Illusion, An.
Jarrell, R.   Germans Are Lunatics, The.
   Nursery Rhyme, A.
   Seele im Raum.
Jeffers, R.   Cassandra.
   To the Story-Tellers.
Kipling, R.   Kitchener's School.
Komunyakaa.   Cage Walker, The.
   Looking a Mad Dog Dead in the Eyes.
Kunitz, S.   Reflection by a Mailbox.
Laughlin, J.   Il Pastor Fido.
   Moment on Earth, A.
Lawrence, D. H.   At Last.
   Fear of Society Is the Root of All Evil.
   Money-Madness.
   Nemesis.
   Rallying-Point.
   Sane and Insane.
   Today.
   What's to Be Done.
Levine, P.   Lights I Have Seen Before.
   On the Edge.
Mahon.   As It Should Be.
Major, C.   Madman of the South Side.
Melville, H.   Berg, The.
Meredith, G.   But see what living glory floods the west.
   Events in a Rustic Mirror.
   John, John of Ottenhaw!
Millay, E.   Siege.
Milton.   To the Same ["Another Leonora captured the poet Torquato"].
Nash, O.   Literary Scene, The.
   Machinery Doesn't Answer, Either, but You Aren't Married to It.
   Miriam's Lucky Day.
Nemerov.   Poem of Margery Kempe, A.
Oliver, M.   Anne.
   Aunt Elsie's Night Music.
   Clam Man.
   Robert Schumann.
Owen, W.   Mental Cases.
Patchen.   He Thought of Mad Ellen's Ravings and of the Wretched Skeleton on the Rock.
   Let Us Have Madness Openly.
Plath.   Life, A.
   Miss Drake Proceeds to Supper.
Poe.   Conqueror Worm, The.
Pound, E.   Piere Vidal Old.
Raine, K.   Medea.
Riley, J.   Ere I Went Mad.
Roethke.   Heard in a Violent Ward.
   In a Dark Time.
   Lines upon Leaving a Sanitarium.
Rukeyser, M.   Minotaur, The.
Rumi.   Acts of Helplessness.
   Fragile Vial, The.
   Real value comes with madness.
Sandburg, C.   White Hands.

Schuyler, J.   Roxy.
   Walter Scott.
Sexton.   Anna Who Was Mad.
   Exorcists, The.
   Flee on Your Donkey.
   For the Year of the Insane.
   Iron Hans.
   Lullaby: "It is a summer evening."
   Noon Walk on the Asylum Lawn.
   Passion of the Mad Rabbit, The.
   Ringing the Bells.
Shapiro, K.   California Petrarchan.
Simic.   There They Stand Unaware of Their Wretchedness.
Smith, S.   Deserter, The.
   From the County Lunatic Asylum.
   Le Majeur Ydow.
Tate, A.   Madness.
Tomlinson, C.   Terminal Tramps.
Williams, C. K.   Cave, The.
   Flat.
Williams, M.   Little Poem, A.
Williams, T.   Beanstalk Country, The.
   Color of a House, The.
Williams, W.   To Elsie.
Wordsworth, W.   Her Eyes Are Wild.
   On the Death of His Majesty (George the Third).
Wright, J.   She Hid in the Trees from the Nurses.
Yeats.   Crazed Girl, A.
   Crazy Jane Talks with the Bishop.
   Tom the Lunatic.
See also **Mental Illness**

Madonnas
Baudelaire.   To a Madonna.
Clampitt.   Matrix (Villa Serbelloni, Lake Como).
Dickinson, E.   Only a Shrine, but Mine.
Montale.   Parades of 1949, The.
Muldoon, P.   Bearded Woman, by Ribera, The.
Rossetti, D.   For "Our Lady of the Rocks" by Leonardo da Vinci.

Madrid, Spain
Creeley.   Same.
Hughes, L.   Madrid [—1937].
McGrath, T.   Once We Meant It.
O'Hara, F.   Now That I Am in Madrid and Can Think.
Seifert.   Salute to the Madrid Barricades.
Van Duyn.   Madrid, 1974.
   Madrid, May, 1977.

Magazines
Hardy, T.   Hundred Years Since, A.
Whittier.   Farewell, A: "What shall I say, dear friends, to whom I owe."
   To Lucy Larcom.
Wilbur, R.   Playboy.
Wilner, E.   How to Get in the Best Magazines.
See also **Journalism and Journalists; Newspapers**
Maggots
Ammons.   Catalyst.
Dugan, A.   Rising in Fall.
Kipling, R.   Bees and the Flies, The.
Major, C.   Apple-Maggot Fly, The.
Williams, M.   Vision and Prayer.
Magi
Ciardi, J.   Magus, A.
Dickey, J.   Magus, The.
Eliot, T. S.   Journey of the Magi.
Glück, L.   Magi, The.
Herrick.   Gold and Frankincense.
Hughes, L.   Carol of the Brown King.
   On a Christmas Night.
   On a Pallet of Straw.
Kunitz, S.   He.
Pinkerton, H.   On G.B. Tiepolo's Etching *Adoration of the Magi* (1753).
Plath.   Magi.
Ralegh, S.   On the Card[e]s, and Dice.
Rossetti, C.   Epiphany.
   Epiphanytide.
Rumi.   We Three.
Williams, W.   Gift, The.
Yeats.   Magi, The.
Zagajewski.   Three Kings, The.

Magic
Bierce.   Abracadabra.
Bogan, L.   Sorcerer's Daughter, The.
Browning, R.   Natural Magic.
Cavafy.   Following the Formulas of Ancient Greco-Syrian Magicians.
Creeley.   New Moon.
Cuadra, P.   Eye Is a Dog Howling in the Distance, The.
Cummings, E. E.   "but why should" / the / greatest.
   Emperor / sleeps in a palace of porphyry, The.
   Now air is air and thing is thing:no bliss.
   Now all the fingers of this tree(darling)have.
   Now what were motionless move(exists no).
   Perished have safe small.
   That melancholy / fellow'll play / his handorgan.
   To stand(alone)in some.
Dante Alighieri.   Guido, I would like that you and Lapo and I.
De la Mare.   Sea-Magic.
Dickinson, E.   Ah, Necromancy Sweet!
   Best Witchcraft is Geometry.
   I think I was enchanted.
   It is of Realms unratified.
   Magic, as it electrifies.
   To see is perhaps never quite the sorcery.
Dugan, A.   Elegy for a Magician.
Eliot, T. S.   To Walter de la Mare.
Graves, R.   At Best, Poets.
   Casse-Noisette.
   Charm for Sound Sleeping, A.
   Gorgon Mask.
   St Antony of Padua.
   Unnamed Spell, The.
Han-shan.   Go ahead stockpile rhino horn.
Hardy, T.   Paphian Ball, The.
Keats.   La Belle Dame sans Merci [A Ballad].
Levi, P.   Witch, The.
Lorde.   Fantasy and Conversation.
   Neighbors.
   Summer Oracle.
Meredith, G.   Song of Courtesy, The.
Merton.   Macarius and the Pony.
   Seven Archaic Images.
Millay, E.   Ballad of the Harp-Weaver, The.
Olson, C.   Bagatto.
Patchen.   Magical Mouse, The.
Pinsky.   Rhyme of Reb Nachman, The.
Prunty.   Thaumatrope.
Ramanujan.   No Fifth Man.
Rilke.   Magician, The.
Ritsos.   Acrobatics.
   Almost a Conjuror.
Rukeyser, M.   Second Elegy. Age of Magicians.
Sandburg, C.   Impasse.
Swift, J.   Simile, A.
   Virtues of Sid Hamet the Magician's Rod, The.
Wordsworth, W.   Egyptian Maid; or, The Romance of the Water Lilly, The.
   Wishing-Gate, The.
Magnetism
Sze.   Magnetized.
Magnolias
Hughes, L.   Magnolia Flowers.
Ramanujan.   Ecology.
Sexton.   Wedding Night, The.
Magpies
Clampitt.   Brought from Beyond.
Milosz, C.   Magpiety.
Magritte, René
Ferlinghetti, L.   Matisse at the Modern, Magritte at the Met.
Laughlin, J.   Les Amants.
Tomlinson, C.   Ceci n'est pas une Pipe.
Mail and Mailmen
Auden.   Night Mail, The.
Berry, W.   Throwing away the Mail.
Bukowski.   Famous Writer, The.
   Transformation and Disfiguration.
Carver, R.   Mail, The.
   Mailman as Cancer Patient, The.
Codrescu.   Good Morning.
   Junk Mail.

Mail.
Corbett, W.   Crossing Borders.
Graves, R.   No Letter.
Ignatow, D.   Trough.
Jarrell, R.   Hope.
  Mail Call.
Kipling, R.   Overland Mail, The.
Kunitz, S.   Reflection by a Mailbox.
Laughlin, J.   God Bless America!
  Junk Mail.
Nash, O.   Ho, Varlet! My Two Cents' Worth of
  Penny Postcard!
  Please Keep on Forwarding.
  What's in a Name? Some Letter I Always
  Forget.
  Why the Postman Has to Ring Twice, or, Yellow
  Envelope, Where Have You Gone?
Prunty.   Since the Noon Mail Stopped.
Rossetti, C.   Postman, The.
Simic.   Rural Delivery.
Van Duyn.   Garland for Christopher Smart, A.
Whitman, W.   Orange Buds by Mail from
  Florida.
Whittier.   Summons, A.
Williams, W.   To Greet a Letter-Carrier.
See also **Letters**
Mail Order Catalogs
Collins, B.   Victoria's.
Laughlin, J.   She Is So Practical.
Prunty.   Retirement Catalogue, A.
Maine (state)
Clampitt.   Baroque Sunburst, A.
  Handed Down.
  What the Light Was Like.
Dubie.   Moths, The.
Eberhart, R.   Coast of Maine.
  Equivalence of Gnats and Mice.
  Going to Maine.
  Maine Roustabout, A.
  Spite Fence.
Kumin, M.   My Elusive Guest.
Lowell, R.   Fourth of July in Maine.
  Skunk Hour.
  Soft Wood.
  Water.
Millay, E.   Exiled.
Oppen.   Ballad: "Astrolabes and lexicons."
  Inlet.
  Mount Desert Island.
  Penobscot.
Schuyler, J.   Day, The.
  Penobscot.
Van Duyn.   Hermit of Hudson Pond, The.
  Moose in the Morning, Northern Maine.
Whittier.   Norembega.
Majorca (island), Spain
Jackson, L.   Laura and Francisca.
Malachy, Saint
Merton.   St. Malachy.
Malaga, Spain
García Lorca.   In Malaga.
Malaysia
Creeley.   Riding with Sal.
Hughes, L.   Last Prince of the East.
Malcolm X (Malcolm Little)
Hayden, R.   El-Hajj Malik El-Shabazz.
Rukeyser, M.   Martin Luther King, Malcolm X.
Walker, A.   Abduction of Saints, The.
  Malcolm.
Mallarmé, Stéphane
Laughlin, J.   Importance of Dictionaries, The.
  Tuesday at 87 Rue de Rome.
Simic.   Tomb of Stéphane Mallarmé, The.
Malls
See **Shopping Malls**
Malta
Byron, G.   Farewell to Malta.
Man in the Moon
Berry, W.   Winter Night Poem for Mary.
Collins, B.   Man in the Moon, The.
Man-of-War Birds
Whitman, W.   To the Man-of-War Bird.
Man, Primitive
Atwood.   Fishing for Eel Totems.

Cuadra, P.   Birth of the Sun, The.
De la Mare.   Owl, The.
Heaney, S.   Tollund Man, The.
Kipling, R.   River's Tale, The.
Merton.   Early Legend, The.
See also **Cavemen**
Manatees
Clampitt.   Discovery.
Kumin, M.   Thoughts on Saving the Manatee.
Mandalay, Burma
Kipling, R.   Mandalay.
Mandela, Nelson
Lorde.   Evening News, The.
Mandelstam, Osip
Celan.   Afternoon with Circus and Citadel.
  In One.
  It's all different from what you think, from what
  I think.
Clampitt.   Voyages.
Davie, D.   Mandelstam in the Crimea.
  Mandelstam, on Dante.
  Mandelstam's Hope for the Best.
Levertov.   Deaths.
Walcott.   Preparing for Exile.
Zagajewski.   In the Encyclopedias, No Room for
  Osip Mandelstam.
Mangoes
Crane, H.   Mango Tree, The.
Manhattan
Brodsky, J.   Blues.
Logan, J.   Manhattan Movements.
Orr, G.   Manhattan Island Poem.
See also **New York City**
Manitoba, Canada
Sandburg, C.   Manitoba Childe Roland.
Mankind
Arnold, M.   In Harmony with Nature.
Atwood.   Charivari.
Baudelaire.   Cupid & Skull.
Beckett, S.   D'abord / à plat sur du dur.
Berry, W.   Anger against Beasts.
  Discipline, A.
  Farmer, Speaking of Monuments, The.
  From the Distance.
  In This World.
  July, 1773.
  Morning's News, The.
  Slip, The.
  Walking on the River Ice.
  Wish to Be Generous, The.
Berryman.   Gislebertus' Eve.
  Spinning Heart, The.
  Traveller, The.
Bishop, E.   In the Waiting Room.
Brooks, G.   Riders to the Blood-Red Wrath.
Browning, E.   Human Life's Mystery.
Browning, R.   Parting at Morning.
Burns, R.   Epistle to a Young Friend.
  On Scaring Some Waterfowl in Loch Turit, a
  Wild Scene among the Hills of Oughtertyre.
  Sketch. Inscribed to the Rt. Hon. Ch. J. Fox
  Esq.
  To Robt. Graham of Fintry Esqr, with a Request
  for an Excise Division.
  Twa Dogs, The.
Byron, G.   Answer to a Beautiful Poem, Entitled
  "The Common Lot."
  World Is a Bundle of Hay, The.
Cortes.   Flower of the Fruit, The.
Crane, H.   I Have That Sure Enclitic.
Cummings, E. E.   Because you take life in your
  stride(instead.
  Humanity i love you.
  ,Mean- / hum / a)now / (nit.
  No man,if men are gods;but if gods must.
  Now does our world descend.
  oDE: "O / the sweet & aged people."
  Of all the blessings which to man.
  Pity This Busy Monster,Manunkind.
  POEM(or "the divine right of majorities, that
  illegitimate offspring of the divine right of
  kings" Homer Lea).
  Possibly thrice we glimpsed.
  This is the vase, Here.
  When serpents bargain for the right to squirm.

De la Mare.   All That's Past.
  Hour-Glass, The.
  Humanity.
Donne.   To Sir Edward Herbert, at Juliers [*or*
  Julyers].
  To the Countess of Salisbury.
Dunbar, P.   Slow through the Dark.
Duncan, R.   First Invention on the Theme of the
  Adam.
Emerson, R.   Life is great / Men are small.
  Turtle in swamp.
Frost, R.   I Will Sing You One-O.
  To an Ancient.
  Vantage Point, The.
Graves, R.   Mankind and Ocean.
Gray, T.   Ode on a Distant Prospect of Eton
  College.
Hardy, T.   By the Earth's Corpse.
  Caged Thrush Freed and Home Again, The.
  Heredity.
  His Country.
  I Said to Love.
  Thoughts at Midnight.
Herbert, G.   Justice (1).
  Man.
  Man's Medley.
  Pulley, The.
Herrick.   Angells.
  Upon Man.
Hopkins, G.   Epithalamion: "Hark, hearer, hear
  what I do; lend a thought now, make believe."
  How all is one way wrought!
  Lantern Out of Doors, The.
  Ribblesdale.
  Sea and the Skylark, The.
  Shepherd's Brow, The.
  To His Watch.
Housman.   'Tis five years since, "An end," said
  I.
Jarrell, R.   Islands, The.
  Place of Death, The.
  Tower, The.
Jeffers, R.   All night long the rush and trampling
  of water.
  Birth and Death.
  Broken Balance, The.
  Contrast.
  Dawn.
  End of the World.
  Extinct Vertebrate, An.
  Inquisitors, The.
  Passenger Pigeons.
  Prelude: "I drew solitude over me, on the lone
  shore."
  Science.
  To the Story-Tellers.
  Torch-Bearers' Race, The.
  Unformed volcanic earth, a female thing, The.
Johnson, S.   Vanity of Human Wishes, The; The
  Tenth Satire of Juvenal Imitated.
Jonson, B.   To William, Earl[e] of Pembroke.
Keats.   Human Seasons, The.
Kipling, R.   Divided Destinies.
  Four Angels, The.
  General Summary, A.
  If—.
  Legends of Evil, The.
  Mary's Son.
  Pilgrim's Way, A.
Lawrence, D. H.   Abysmal Immortality.
  But I Say unto You: Love One Another.
  Cowards.
  Deeper than Love.
  Democracy.
  Difference, The.
  Elemental.
  Elements, The.
  Factory Cities, The.
  False Democracy and Real.
  Flowers and Men.
  For the Heroes Are Dipped in Scarlet.
  Free Will.
  Gentleman, The.
  Gladness of Death.
  Glimpses.
  Gods! The Gods!, The.

Humanity Needs Pruning.
If You Are a Man.
Immoral Man.
Immorality.
Keep It Up.
Know-All.
Man, A.
Man and Machine.
Man Is More than *Homo Sapiens*.
Man's Image.
Men Are Not Bad.
Men Like Gods.
Michael Angelo.
Minorities in Danger.
Morality.
Multitudes.
My Way Is Not Thy Way.
Nemesis.
Obscenity.
Only Man.
Only the Best Matters.
People.
People, The.
Poison.
Retort to Whitman.
Risen Lord, The.
Sea, The.
Service.
Shades.
Side-Step, O Sons of Men!
Souls to Save.
Sun-Men.
There Are Too Many People.
There Is No Way Out.
Transformations.
Triumph of the Machine, The.
Two Ways of Living and Dying.
Universe Flows, The.
What Are the Wild Waves Saying?
What Have They Done to You?
Whatever Man Makes.
When Wilt Thou Teach the People?
Wild Things in Captivity.
Levertov. Beginners.
  During the Eichmann Trial.
  When We Look Up.
Levi, P. In the Beginning.
  Shemà.
Levine, P. Animals Are Passing from Our
    Lives.
  Conductor of Nothing, The.
  How Much Earth.
  Poem of Flight, The.
MacDiarmid, H. Glass of Pure Water, The.
  With the Herring Fishers.
McHugh, H. Just Man.
Mencius. Ox Mountain Parable, The.
Meredith, G. Alternation.
  Believe me, I have studied men.
  Brotherhood.
  Foresight and Patience.
  Men and Man.
  Test of Manhood, The.
Merton. Moment of Truth, The.
Merwin. For a Coming Extinction.
Millay, E. Apostrophe to Man.
  Epitaph for the Race of Man.
  He heard the coughing tiger in the night.
Neruda. Bomb (II).
  Gift, The.
  This Is Simple.
Oliver, M. Wild Geese.
Olson, C. 2 Propositions and 3 Proof.
  Adamo Me.
  Advantage, The.
  Anubis will stare.
  Applause.
  Babe, The.
  Bigmans II.
  Chain of memory is resurrection I am a vain
    man, The.
  Discrete Gloss, A.
  Double, double, root and branch.
  Every Man His Own Matador; or for That
    Matter Any Member of the Family.
  Fable for Slumber.

He / in the dark stall, no day now for him, to
    paw.
In Cold Hell, in Thicket.
K, The.
Kin.
Laughing Ones, The.
Lion upon the Floor, A.
Name-Day Night.
Not to permit himself to be.
Obit.
Ode on Nativity, An.
Only the Red Fox, Only the Crow.
Post Virginal, The.
Put him this way.
Said Adam.
Seven Songs, The.
Siena.
Thing Was Moving, The.
Whole World, The.
Writ, The.
Patchen. As in the green sky.
  Blind'd be the last of men.
  Elegy for the Silent Voices and the Joiners of
    Everything.
  "Gentle and Giving" and Other Sayings.
  I Got the Fat Poet into a Corner.
  If a Poem Can Be Headed into Its Proper
    Current.
  In shadings of an obscure punishment.
  Into another mission / Circling my exposed
    continent.
  It Is Big inside a Man.
  It Was a Bomby Evening.
  Lament for the Makers of Songs.
  Man Is to Man a Beast.
  Man Lives Here, A.
  O fiery river / Flow out over the land.
  Roses of Life, The.
  Second People, The.
  Shapes.
  So Near—And Yet.
  To Whom It May Concern.
  Way men live is a lie, The.
  Where Every Prospect.
  Wide, wide in the rose's side.
  You Must Have Some Idea Where They've
    Gone.
Pound, E. Meditatio.
Rich, A. For the Record.
Robinson, E. Octaves.
Rossetti, C. Day and night the Accuser makes
    no pause.
  He Shall Go No More Out.
  How great is little man! / Sun, moon, and stars
    respond to him.
  Let Patience Have Her Perfect Work.
  Lord, by what inconceivable dim road / Thou
    leadest man on footsore pilgrimage!
  Man's life is but a working day / Whose tasks
    are set aright.
  One Certainty, The.
  Rogationtide.
  That Which Hath Been Is Named Already, and
    It Is Known That It Is Man.
  Tuesday in Holy Week.
  Vanity of Vanities.
  Vigil of the Annunciation.
  Wednesday in Holy Week.
  What is this above thy head, / O Man?
Rukeyser, M. Myth.
Sandburg, C. Enemy Number One.
  God Is No Gentleman.
  Government.
  Jack.
  Man, the Man-Hunter.
  Masses.
  Pool.
  Psalm of the Bloodbank.
  Sayings of Henry Stephens.
  Skyscrapers Stand Proud.
  Solo for Saturday Night Guitar.
  They Ask: Is God, Too, Lonely?
  Walking Man of Rodin, The.
  Wilderness.
Sexton. After Auschwitz.
  Earth Falls Down, The.

Two Hands.
Smith, S. All Things Pass.
  Alone in the Woods.
  Away, Melancholy.
  Distractions and the Human Crowd.
  Do Not!
  From the Coptic.
  From the French (2).
  God and Man.
  God Speaks.
  Man Is a Spirit.
  New Age, The.
  So to Fatness Come.
  Touch and Go.
  Under Wrong Trees... or Freeing the Colonial
    Peoples.
  Will Man Ever Face Fact and Not Feel Flat?
Suckling, S. Ei Men Een Mathein.
Swift, J. Day of Judgement, The.
Tate, J. Guide to the Stone Age, The.
Vallejo. Eternal Dice, The.
Whitman, W. As I Ponder'd [or Pondered] in
    Silence.
  Going Somewhere.
  On the Same Picture.
  One's-Self I Sing.
  Our Future Lot.
  Thou Reader.
Wilbur, R. Ceremony.
Williams, C. K. Hounding Mercy.
  Innings.
  Nut, The.
  Race of the Flood, The.
  Ribbons.
  Spirit the Triumph, The.
  Then the Brother of the Wind.
  Three Seasons and a Gorilla.
Williams, W. Clouds, The.
Wordsworth, W. 1811.
  Character, A.
  Lines Written in Early Spring.
  O'er the wide earth, on mountain and on plain.
  Poet's Epitaph, A.
  There is a bondage worse, far worse, to bear.
  Those [or These] words were uttered as in [or in
    a] pensive mood.
  Weak is the will of Man, his judgement blind.
Wright, J. Goodbye to the Poetry of Calcium.
  In Shame and Humiliation.
  Secret Gratitude, A.
  Winter Day in Ohio, A.
Yeats. Four Ages of Man, The.
  Meditation in Time of War, A.
  Sorrow of Love, The.

Mannequins
  Bukowski. Trapped.
  Ginsberg, A. Spring Fashions.
  Jacobsen, J. 49th and 5th, December 13.
  Jarrell, R. Dummies.
  Nemerov. To the Mannequins.
  Sandburg, C. Caligari.
Manners
  Cooper, J. Bedside Rune, A.
  Riley, J. Company Manners.
  Land of Thus-and-So, The.
  Stafford, W. Style.
See also **Etiquette**
Mansfield, Katherine
  De la Mare. Horse in a Field.
Mantegna, Andrea
  Rossetti, D. For "An Allegorical Dance of
    Women" by Andrea Mantegna.
Mantis
See **Praying Mantis**
Mantua, Italy
  Laughlin, J. Endless Mirrors, The.
Mao Tse-tung
  Kizer, C. Cultural Evolution.
Maple Sugar and Maple Syrup
  Hall, D. Maple Syrup.
Maple Trees
  Ammons. Lonely Splendor.
  Pluralist.
  Carruth, H. Essay on Love.
  Leaf from Mr. Dyer's Woods, A.

Jacobsen, J. Lion under Maples.
Koch, K. Down at the Docks.
Laughlin, J. It's March.
MacLeish. Two Trees, The.
Paley, G. Leaves Apples.
  Walking in the Woods.
Rexroth, K. Red Maple Leaves.
Stafford, W. Something That Happens Right
  Now.
Trakl. Trumpets.
Updike. Maples in a Spruce Forest.
Wilbur, R. October Maples, Portland.
Williams, W. Non-Entity, The.
Wright, J. To a Troubled Friend.

Mapplethorpe, Robert
Dubie. Two Women on the Potomac Parkway.

Maps
Ashbery, J. Rivers and Mountains.
Atwood. Reincarnation of Captain Cook, The.
Auden. Half Way.
  Have a Good Time.
Bishop, E. Map, The.
Bogan, L. Cartography.
Borges. Museum.
Ciardi, J. Cartographer of Meadows, The.
Gunn, T. Map of the City, A.
Levi, P. First Atlas, The.
Meredith, W. Examples of Created Systems.
  Memoirs.
Nemerov. Mapmaker on His Art, The.
  Projection.
Paley, G. At the Battery.
Rilke. To Marie Laurencin.
Ritsos. Silent Agreement.
Stafford, W. Fiction.
Tate, A. Trout Map, The.

Marathon, Battle of (490 B.C.)
Browning, R. Echetlos.
Graves, R. Persian Version, The.

Marathon (race)
Dickey, J. For the Running of the New York
  City Marathon.
Wilbur, R. Running.

Marble
Crane, H. Island Quarry.
Dickey, J. In the Marble Quarry.
Eberhart, R. Cousin Florence.
Hall, D. Columns of the Parthenon, The.
Tomlinson, C. Above Carrara.

Marbles
Berryman. At Chinese Checkers.

March
Bishop, E. End of March, The.
Bogan, L. March Twilight.
Ciardi, J. March Morning.
Crane, H. March.
Dickinson, E. Dear March, Come in.
  In snow thou comest.
  March is the Month of Expectation.
  We like March.
  We like March—his shoes are Purple.
  Who could be ill in March.
Dunbar, P. My Little March Girl.
Eberhart, R. Ides of March, The.
Gurney, I. When March Blows.
Hall, D. Elegy for Wesley Wells.
Housman. March.
Jackson, L. March, 1937.
Laughlin, J. It's March.
Levine, P. White Iris, The.
MacLeish. March.
Niedecker. March.
Piccolo. Unstill Universe.
Prunty. March.
Raine, K. My Father's Birthday.
Riley, J. When Early March Seems Middle
  May.
Schuyler, J. March Here.
  Poem: "How about an oak leaf."
Stevens, W. Not Ideas about the Thing but the
  Thing Itself.
Tomlinson, C. In March.
Updike. March: A Birthday Poem.
Wilbur, R. March.
Williams, W. Celebration, A.

March.
March Is a Light.
Wordsworth, W. To My Sister.
  Written in March [While Resting on the Bridge
    at the Foot of Brother's Water].
Wright, J. March.
Zaturenska. O Lyric March.

Marching and Marches
Amichai [or Amikhai]. Children's Procession.
Beckett, S. Thither.
Dugan, A. Sixteen Lines on Marching.
Emerson, R. Days.
Gurney, I. First March.
Hopkins, G. At the Wedding March.
Hughes, L. Sister Johnson Marches.
Kipling, R. "Birds of Prey" March.
  Columns.
  Route Marchin'.
Larkin, P. March Past, The.
Lawrence, D. H. On the March.
Melville, H. Night-March, The.
Owen, W. Dulce et Decorum Est.
Riley, J. Dream-March.
Simic. Marching.
Stafford, W. Peace Walk.
Thoreau. Just Made Perfect, The.

See also **Parades**

Marcos, Ferdinand Edralin
Ai. Miracle in Manila.

Marcos, Imelda
Ai. Miracle in Manila.

Mariana
Rossetti, C. Mariana.
Tennyson, A. Mariana in the South.

Marigolds
Herrick. How Marigolds Came Yellow.
  To Marygolds.
Whalen, P. If You're So Smart, Why Ain't You
  Rich?
Williams, W. Negro Woman, A.
Zukofsky, L. Marigold.

Marijuana
Ginsberg, A. Consulting I Ching Smoking Pot
  Listening to the Fugs Sing Blake.
  Marijuana Notation.
Gunn, T. Smoking Pot on the Bus.
Hughes, L. Gauge.
Whalen, P. Public Opinions.
Williams, W. Wrong Door, The.

Marin County, California
Jeffers, R. Clouds of Evening.

Mariners
See **Sailing and Sailors**

Markets
De la Mare. Market-Place, The.
Emerson, R. Since the devil hopping on.
Glück, L. Baskets.
Hacker, M. Le Travail Rajeunit.
Hall, D. Ox Cart Man.
HaNagid. Commerce Has Markets.
  Market, The.
Hardy, T. No Buyers [or No Buyers: A Street
  Scene].
Hughes, L. Mexican Market Woman.
Jarrell, R. Indian Market in Mexico, An.
Komunyakaa. Hanoi Market, The.
Laughlin, J. Crystal Palace Market.
Levertov. Roast[ing] Potatoes.
Lorde. Keyfoods.
  Signs.
Nemerov. Market-Place, The.
Paley, G. Is There a Difference between Men
  and Women.
Ritsos. Morning in Salerno 4.
Sandburg, C. Unintentional Paint.
Wright, J. Prayer to Escape from the Market
  Place, A.

Markiewicz, Constance Georgine, Countess
Yeats. In Memory of Eva Gore-Booth and Con
  Markiewicz.

Marlborough, John Churchill, 1st Duke of
Swift, J. Satirical Elegy on the Death of a Late
  Famous General, A.

Marlowe, Christopher
Lowell, R. Marlowe.

Marpessa
Ritsos. Marpessa's Selection.

Marriage
Ai. Blood in the Water.
  Ravine, The.
  She Didn't Even Wave.
  Twenty-Year Marriage.
Amichai [or Amikhai]. Anniversaries of Love.
  Late Marriage.
  Way It Was, The.
Ashbery, J. Decoy.
Atwood. Habitation.
Berrigan, T. Red Shift.
Berry, W. Grandmother, The.
  In Rain.
  Marriage.
  Marriage, an Elegy, A.
  Seventeen Years.
Berryman. Canto Amor.
  Song of the Bridegroom, The.
Bly, R. Man and a Woman Sit near Each Other.
Bogan, L. Betrothed.
  For a Marriage.
Bradstreet, A. To My Dear and Loving
  Husband.
Brodsky, J. Six Years Later.
Brontë, E. Day Dream, A.
  From a Dungeon Wall in the Southern College.
Brooks, G. Bronzeville Mother Loiters in
  Mississippi, A. Meanwhile, a Mississippi
  Mother Burns Bacon.
  To Be in Love.
Browning, E. Aurora Leigh.
  Marriage of Psyche and Cupid.
  Poet's Vow, The.
  Romance of the Ganges, A.
  Sounds.
  Year's Spinning, A.
Browning, R. Any Wife to Any Husband.
  Doctor———.
  Flight of the Duchess, The.
  James Lee's Wife.
  Life in a Love.
  Love in a Life.
  Muckle-Mouth Meg.
  My Last Duchess.
  With Daniel Bartoli.
Bukowski. 103 Degrees.
  About Pain.
  Not To Worry.
Burns, R. Another [Epigram on Said Occasion].
  English Song.
  Epigram on Said Occasion.
  Epitaph on a Henpecked Country Squire.
  Henpeck'd Husband, The.
  John Anderson, My Jo.
  Kellyburnbraes.
  O Ay My Wife She Dang Me.
  O Lay Thy Loof in Mine Lass.
  O That I Had Ne'er Been Married.
  On Marriage.
  Tam Glen.
  To Alexander Cunnigham.
  Whistle o'er the Lave o't.
Byron, G. Blues, The.
  Sonnet on the Nuptials of the Marquis Antonio
    Cavalli with the Countess Clelia Rasponi.
Carew, T. Hymeneal[l] Dialogue, An.
  Married Woman, A.
  On the Marriage of T. K. and C. C.: The
    Morning Stormy.
Carruth, H. August First.
  Essay on Marriage.
Carver, R. Author of Her Misfortune, The.
  Hope.
  Late Night with Fog and Horses.
  Marriage.
  Memory 2.
  Miracle.
  My Wife.
  Offending Eel, The.
  Other Life, The.
  Out.
  Proposal.

Sunbather, to Herself, The.
To Begin With.
Cavafy. Che Fece . . . Il Gran Rifiuto.
Chaucer. Lenvoy de Chaucer a Bukton.
Ciardi, J. For Judith.
Men marry what they need. I marry you.
Morning: I Know Perfectly How in a Minute You Will Stretch and Smile.
N is for NANNYGOAT—the silly.
Three Eggs Up.
Clampitt. Highgate Cemetery.
Coleridge, S. Exchange, The.
Cooper, J. Eve.
In the Last Few Moments Came the Old German Cleaning Woman.
Nothing I Meant to Keep.
Urge to Tell the Truth, The.
Cowper, W. Anti-Thelyphthora.
Catharina, the Second Part.
Impromptu ["If John marries Mary, and Mary alone"].
Love Abused.
Mutual Forbearance.
Ode on the Marriage of a Friend.
Pairing Time Anticipated.
Crashaw. Epitaph upon Husband and Wife Who Died and Were Buried Together, An.
Epithalamium: "Come virgin Tapers of pure waxe."
On Marriage
Creeley. Ballad of the Despairing Husband.
Bed, The.
Crisis, The.
For Pen ("Last day of year").
Friend Says of Job.
Greeting Card.
Marriage, A.
Naughty Boy.
Rocks, The.
They Say.
Wait for Me.
Way, The.
Wife, The.
Cullen, C. Wind Bloweth Where It Listeth, The.
Cummings, E. E. If there are any heavens my mother will (all by herself) have.
Cunningham, J. Choice.
I married in my youth a wife.
Original Sin.
Prue loved her man: to clean, to mend.
Some twenty years of marital agreement.
Statistics.
To My Wife.
Davie, D. Autumn Imagined.
Christmas Syllabics for a Wife.
Vying.
Widower.
Dickey, W. Stella Dallas.
Dickinson, E. Her sweet Weight on my Heart at Night.
I am ashamed—I hide.
I'm Wife . . . .
Ourselves were wed one summer—dear.
Rearrange a "Wife's" affection!
She Rose to His Requirement—Dropt.
Title divine—is mine!
Wife—at Daybreak I shall be, A.
World—stands—solemner—to me, The.
Donne. Antiquary.
Epithalamion Made at Lincoln's Inn [or Lincolnes Inne].
Epithalamion, or Marriage Song on the Lady Elizabeth and Count Palatine Being Married on St. Valentine's Day, An.
Flea, The.
Dove, R. Beauty and the Beast.
Kadava Kumbis Devise a Way to Marry for Love, The.
Promises.
Refrain.
Taking in Wash.
Dubie. City of the Olesha Fruit, The.
Fever.
Dugan, A. Flower Grower in Aquarius.
General Prothalamion for Wartimes.
Love Song: I and Thou.

Monologue of a Commercial Fisherman.
On a Professional Couple in a Side-Show.
Poem: "It is no wonder that new lovers run."
Pretrial Hearing.
Prothalamion of Quantum Mechanics and Astrophysics against the Text "Philosophia Biou Kubernetes" (Philosophy the Guide of Life).
Summer Heaven, Angels, Heaven.
Untitled Poem: "I've promised that I will not care about things."
Dunbar, P. Bridal Measure, A.
Encouragement.
Eliot, T. S. Dedication to My Wife, A.
Emerson, R. She never comes to me.
Enzensberger, H. Divorce, The.
Old Couples.
Ferlinghetti, L. In Golden Gate Park that day.
Report on a Happening in Washington Square San Francisco, A.
Frost, R. Hill Wife, The.
Home Burial.
Love and a Question.
Place for a Third.
García Lorca. Lizard Is Crying, The.
Glück, L. Aphrodite.
Bridal Piece.
Edge, The.
Epithalamium: "There were others; their bodies."
Horse.
Morning.
Graves, R. Advice from a Mother.
Bower-Bird.
Call It a Good Marriage.
Court of Love, A.
For Ever.
Golden Anchor.
Henry and Mary.
Joan and Darby.
Lion-Gentle.
Ours is No Wedlock.
Semi-Detached.
Slice of Wedding Cake, A.
That Other World.
Through a Dark Wood.
When Love Is Not.
Gunn, T. Adultery.
His Rooms in College.
"H. D." Hymen.
Hacker, M. Country & Western II.
Hall, D. Dancers.
For an Exchange of Rings.
Han-shan. When an old man takes a young wife.
Hardy, T. Bride-Night Fire, The.
Catching Ballet of the Wedding Clothes, The.
Conformers, The.
Curate's Kindness, The.
Forbidden Banns, The.
Homecoming, The.
In the Night She Came.
News for Her Mother.
One Who Married above Him.
Pair He Saw Pass, The.
Poor Man and a Lady, A.
To a Bridegroom.
Heaney, S. Mother of the Groom.
Poem: "Love, I shall perfect for you the child."
Summer Home.
Underground, The.
Herrick. Caution, A.
Connubii Flores, or the Well-Wishes at Weddings.
Entertainment, or Porch-Verse, at the Marriage of Mr. Henry Northleigh [or Hen. Northly] and the Most Witty Mrs. Lettice Yard, The.
Epitaph on a Man Who Had a Scold to His Wife.
Epitaph upon a Sober Matron, An.
Epithalamy to Sir Thomas Southwell and His Lady, An.
His Answer to a Question.
His Comfort.
Hymne to Juno, An.
No Spouse but a Sister.

Nuptiall Song, or Epithalamie, on Sir Clipseby Crew and His Lady, A.
Nuptiall Verse to Mistresse Elizabeth Lee, Now Lady Tracie.
Poet Loves a Mistress, but Not to Marry, The.
Rosemarie Branch, The.
Single Life Most Secure.
To Rosemary and Baies.
To Silvia to Wed.
Upon Loach.
Hopkins, G. Epithalamion: "Hark, hearer, hear what I do; lend a thought now, make believe."
Queen's Crowning, The.
Housman. Epithalamium: "He is here, Urania's son."
Hughes, L. Ballad of Little Sallie.
Hughes, T. Her Husband.
Ibn-i-Yamin [or Ibn Jemin or Amir Mahmud ibn Amir Yaminu'd-Din Tughra'i]. From Ibn Jemin.
Ignatow, D. Consolation.
Notes for a Lecture.
Jacobsen, J. Ballad of Henry, Bridegroom.
Jarrell, R. Man Meets a Woman in the Street, A.
Jonson, B. Epithalamion: or, a Song.
On Giles and Joan.
Keats. Epithalamium.
Kinsella, T. Anniversaries.
Phoenix Park.
Kipling, R. Betrothed, The.
Fall of Jock Gillespie, The.
Mare's Nest, The.
Sergeant's Weddin', The.
Kizer, C. Afternoon Happiness.
Eleutheria.
Epithalamion: "You left me gasping on the shore."
Second Time Around.
Summer near the River.
Threatening Letter.
Komunyakaa. By Proxy.
Thorn Merchant's Wife, The.
Kunitz, S. Old Darned Man, The.
Route Six.
Touch Me.
Larkin, P. Long Roots Moor Summer to Our Side of Earth.
Maiden Name.
Marriages.
Self's the Man.
To My Wife.
Wedding-Wind.
Whitsun Weddings, The.
Laughlin, J. Family Council of the Yakovlevs, The.
On the Gift of a Sapphire to My Wife Ann.
Lawrence, D. H. Emotional Lies.
Gipsy.
Good Husbands Make Unhappy Wives.
Hands of the Betrothed, The.
She Looks Back.
Wedlock.
Young Wife, A.
Levertov. About Marriage.
Ache of Marriage, The.
Fellow Passengers.
Marriage, The.
Marriage 2, The.
Wedding-Ring.
Lindsay, N. Cold Sunbeams.
Epilogue to the Adventures while Preaching the Gospel of Beauty.
Ghosts in Love.
Perfect Marriage, The.
To Eve, Man's Dream of Wifehood as Described by Milton.
Logan, J. Bride's Song, The.
Bridgegroom's Song, The.
Complaint, The.
Epilogue.
Epilogue, Songs of the Spouses, Complaint of Love.
Honolulu and Back.
New Poem.
Tale of Courtship.

Lowell, R.   Flaw, The.
Man and Wife.
Our Twentieth Wedding Anniversary
(Elizabeth).
To Speak of Woe That Is in Marriage.
MacLeish.   Late Abed.
Old Gray Couple (1), The.
Old Gray Couple (2), The.
Poem in Prose.
Unfinished History.
MacNeice.   Eclogue between the Motherless.
Major, C.   Bernardston.
Birds.
McGrath, T.   Anniversaries.
Dream Range, The.
McHugh, H.   When the Future Is Black.
Whoosh.
Meredith, G.   Archduchess Anne.
Blue Is the Sky.
Earth and a Wedded Woman.
Friar uxorious!
Hymn to Colour.
Now dawns all waxen to your seal of life.
She marries the knight she loves.
Song: "Quick bird sings and pierces me, The."
Song: Autumn.
Think not, should your husband swear.
Meredith, W.   February 14.
Tree Marriage.
Millay, E.   Betrothal, The.
Return from Town, The.
Moore, M.   Marriage.
Muldoon, P.   Marriage of Strongbow and Aoife,
The.
Nash, O.   Advice outside a Church.
Anniversary, The.
Aside to Husbands.
Confession to Be Traced on a Birthday Cake.
Cuckoo, The.
Don't Wait, Hit Me Now!
Down the Mousehole, and What Science Missed
There.
I Do, I Will, I Have.
Lines to Be Mumbled at Ovington's.
Nymph and the Shepherd, or She Went That-a-
Way, The.
Outcome of Mr. Buck's Superstition, The.
Rapunzel, Rapunzel, Let's Let Down Our Hair.
Solitude of Mr. Powers, The.
Song to Be Sung by the Father of Infant Female
Children.
Strange Case of Mr. Donnybrooks's Boredom,
The.
Strange Case of the Blackmailing Dove, The.
There'll Always Be a War between the Sexes,
or, A Woman Can Be Sometimes Pleased, but
Never Satisfied.
They Won't Believe, on New Year's Eve, that
New Year's Day Will Come What May.
Tin Wedding Whistle.
Tune for an Ill-Tempered Clavichord.
Unselfish Husband, The.
What Almost Every Woman Knows Sooner or
Later.
Nemerov.   Common Wisdom, The.
Niedecker.   I married.
So you're married, young man.
Young girl to marry.
O'Hara, F.   Poem Read at Joan Mitchell's.
Olson, C.   Bride, The.
Paley, G.   Quarrel ("Bob and I / in different
rooms").
Parker, D.   Biographies.
Men I'm Not Married To.
Parra, N.   Imperfect Lover, The.
Piercy.   Breaking Camp.
Laocoön Is the Name of the Figure.
Married Walk in a Hot Place, A.
Pinkerton, H.   Crossing the Pedregal.
Plath.   Applicant, The.
Epitaph for Fire and Flower.
Wreath for a Bridal.
Zoo Keeper's Wife.
Prunty.   Actuarial Wife, The.
Sorrows of Lester Buster, The.
Wedding Stop, The.

Ramanujan.   Engagement.
Love Poem for a Wife, 1.
Love Poem for a Wife, 2.
Love Poem for a Wife and Her Trees.
Routine Day Sonnet.
Still Another for Mother.
Ransom, J.   Emily Hardcastle, Spinster.
Romance of a Youngest Daughter.
Rexroth, K.   Andrée Rexroth ("Now once more
gray mottled buckeye branches").
Dialogue of Watching, A.
Martial—12, 52.
Mocking Birds.
Reflecting Trees of Being and Not Being, The.
She Is Away [or Marthe Away (She Is Away)].
Rich, A.   Any Husband to Any Wife.
Autumn Equinox.
Blue Ghazals, The.
Marriage in the 'Sixties, A.
Marriage Portion, The.
Moving in Winter.
Novella.
Perennial Answer, The.
Snapshots of a Daughter-in-Law.
Riley, J.   Golden Wedding, A.
His Pa's Romance.
How It Happened.
In a Box.
Lost Love, A.
New Year's Time at Willards's, A.
On a Splendud Match.
Squire Hawkins's Story.
To a Poet on His Marriage.
Tradin' Joe.
When Lide Married *Him*.
Rimbaud, A.   First Delirium. The Foolish
Virgin. The Infernal Bridegroom.
Young Couple.
Ritsos.   Esteem.
Old House, The.
Separation.
Robinson, E.   Eros Turannos.
London Bridge.
Rahel to Varnhagen.
Woman and the Wife, The.
Rossetti, C.   Cousin Kate.
Hour and the Ghost, The.
Lowest Room, The.
Maude Clare.
Ring Posy, A.
True Story, A.
Wife to Husband.
Rukeyser, M.   Wedding Presents.
Rumi.   Cat and the Meat, The.
Man and a Woman Arguing, A.
Sheikh Kharraqani and His Wretched Wife.
Sandburg, C.   Blue Maroons.
Brim.
Couple, A.
Crimson Rambler.
Mag.
Maybe.
Put Off the Wedding Five Times and Nobody
Comes to It.
Soiled Dove.
Two Strangers Breakfast.
Sarton, M.   Death and the Lovers.
Sexton.   Doors, Doors, Doors.
February 17th.
For John, Who Begs Me Not to Enquire Further.
Interrogation of the Man of Many Hearts, The.
Maiden without Hands, The.
Man and Wife.
Twelve-Thousand-Day Honeymoon, The.
Wedlock, The.
White Snake, The.
Shapiro, K.   New Ring, The.
Simic.   Rough Outline.
Smith, S.   Castle, The.
Hat, The.
He Told His Life Story to Mrs. Courtly.
I Remember.
Lady "Rogue" Singleton.
Smile, The.
Starling, The.
Wedding Photograph, The.

Spender, S.   Polar Exploration.
Trance, The.
Spenser, E.   Epithalamion: "Ye learned sisters
which have oftentimes."
Prothalamion.
Stafford, W.   Once in the 40s.
Passing Remark.
Stein, G.   Brim Beauvais.
With a Wife.
Stock, R.   Again I'm Torched and Wonder What
We've Wrought.
Stockton, A.   Bridal Wish Adressed to Mr S.
Stockton and His Lady the Morning after Their
Maraige, The.
Epithalamium, The: "Ye woodland choirs come
consecrate the lay."
Poetical Epistle, Addressed by a Lady of New-
Jersey, to Her Niece, upon Her Marriage, in
This City, A.
Tears of Friendship. Elegy the Third.—To a
Friend Just Married, and Who Had Promised
to Write, on Parting, but Had Neglected It.
To a Friend Who Had Persuaded Emelia to
Marry, an Ode.
Suckling, S.   Lutea Allison.
Upon My Lord Brohall's Wedding.
Swift, J.   Phyllis [or Phillis] [or Progress of
Love, The].
Progress of Marriage, The.
Quiet Life and a Good Name, A.
Three Epigrams.
Tate, A.   Nuptials.
Tennyson, A.   Move Eastward, Happy Earth,
and Leave.
Northern Farmer: New Style.
Thomas, D.   On the Marriage of a Virgin.
Tomlinson, C.   Farmer's Wife: at Fostons Ash,
The.
Updike.   Marriage Counsel.
Newlyweds, The.
Van Duyn.   Fear of Flying, The.
In the Cold Kingdom.
Placet Experiri.
Time of Bees, A.
Toward a Definition of Marriage.
Winter's Tale, by a Wife, A.
Warren, R.   Midnight.
Williams, C. K.   Cautionary, The.
Experience.
Trash.
Williams, M.   And Then.
As You Both Shall Live.
Ballad of a Little Delta Town.
Clutter of Silence: Invention for Two Voices.
Despairing of Understanding We Fall Into
Decadence.
Divorce.
Fly Me to the Moon.
Fred.
Going.
Husband.
Love and How It Becomes Important in Our
Day to Day Lives.
Love Poem with Toast.
Man in the Bar Says He Has Something to Say,
A.
Picker.
Rodin: The Cathedral.
She Talks to Her Sister, Briefly by on the Way
to West Memphis.
Tenth Anniversary Photograph, 1952, A.
When I Am Dead, My Dearest.
You Wouldn't Say They Didn't Get Along
Exactly.
Williams, W.   Ballad: "To a man and his wife."
Invocation and Conclusion.
Marriage.
Marriage of Souls, The.
Marriage Ritual, A.
Wilner, E.   Job's Wife, a Twentieth-Century
Casting Script.
Wordsworth, W.   Composed on the Eve of the
Marriage of a Friend in the Vale of Grasmere,
1812.
Thorn, The.
Yeats.   Collarbone [or Collar-Bone] of a Hare,

The.
Zukofsky, L.   Marriage Song for Florence and Harry, A.

See also **Bigamy and Bigamists; Monogamy and Monogamists; Wedding Songs; Weddings**

Marriage, Arranged
Ai.   Ice.
Burns, R.   Altered from an Old English Song.
What can a young lassie, what shall a young lassie.

Mars (god)
Chaucer.   Complaint of Mars, The.
Herrick.   Vow to Mars, A.
Leonidas of Alexandria.   Upon Venus Putting on Mars His Armes.
Meredith, G.   Cageing of Ares, The.
Orr, G.   After Piero di Cosimo's *Venus, Mars, and Amor.*
Wyatt, S.   Venus, in sport, to please therewith her dear.

Mars (planet)
Berrigan, T.   Bean Spasms.
Chaucer.   Complaint of Mars, The.
Lowell, R.   March 1, The.

Marshall Plan
Hughes, L.   Relief.

Marshes
Ammons.   Celestial.
Sumerian.
Atwood,   Marsh, Hawk.
Ciardi, J.   Sea Marshes in Winter.
Clampitt.   Paumanok.
Dickey, J.   Salt Marsh, The.
Dove, R.   Delft.
Lawrence, D. H.   Doe at Evening, A.
Merwin.   Current, The.
Niedecker.   O late fall.
Paean to Place.
River-marsh-drowse.
Piercy.   Cod Summer.

Martens
Clare, J.   Marten.
Eberhart, R.   Fisher Cat, The.

Martha's Vineyard, Massachusetts
Nash, O.   Martha's Vineyard.

Martial Arts
Stafford, W.   Annals of *Tai Chi*: "Push Hands."
Wilner, E.   Mt. Fuji and the Martial Arts.

Martin, Saint
Gunn, T.   St. Martin and the Beggar.

Martins
Davie, D.   House-martin.
Komunyakaa.   Articulation & Class.

Martyrs
Borges.   John I:14.
Byron, G.   Spell Is Broke, the Charm Is Flown, The.
Thy Days Are Done.
Cavafy.   Simeon.
Chiabrera.   Destined to war from very infancy.
Crashaw.   To the Infant Martyrs.
Upon the Infant Martyrs.
Davie, D.   Oxfordshire.
Dickinson, E.   Martyr Poets—did not tell, The.
Through the strait pass of suffering.
Eliot, T. S.   Love Song of St. Sebastian, The.
Faiz.   Elegy for Hassan Nasir.
García Lorca.   Martyrdom of St. Eulalia.
Glück, L.   Jeanne d'Arc.
Guyon.   Joy in Martyrdom.
Herrick.   Christian Militant.
Dirge of Jephthah's Daughter, The.
Sufferance.
To Groves.
Hopkins, G.   Margaret Clitheroe.
Hughes, L.   Scottsboro.
Hughes, T.   Martyrdom of Bishop Farrar, The.
Kizer, C.   Race Relations.
Levi, P.   Singing.
Logan, J.   Death of Southwell, The.
Lowell, R.   Colloquy in Black Rock.
MacNeice.   Springboard, The.
Meredith, G.   Song of Theodolinda, The.
Merton.   From the Legend of St. Clement.

Invocation to St. Lucy, An.
St. Agnes: A Responsory.
Milosz, C.   Campo dei Fiori.
Oliver, M.   Sunrise.
Olson, C.   Leader, The.
Rexroth, K.   Again at Waldheim.
Rich, A.   Reliquary.
Rossetti, C.   All Saints: Martyrs.
Martyr, A.
Martyr, The.
Martyrs' Song.
Rukeyser, M.   Akiba.
Lynchings of Jesus, The.
Thoreau.   Rosa Sanguinea, The.
Villon.   Ballade to End With, A.
Walker, A.   They Who Feel Death.
Wheatley, P.   On the Death of Mr. Snider Murder'd by Richardson.
Whitman, W.   Wallabout Martyrs, The.
Whittier.   Barclay of Ury.
Cross, The.
Female Martyr, The.
How the Women Went from Dover.
Wordsworth, W.   Eagle and the Dove, The.

Marvell, Andrew
MacLeish.   You, Andrew Marvell.

Marx, Karl
Amichai [*or* Amikhai].   Karl Marx, cold mark that you are.
Codrescu.   Manifesto.
Dugan, A.   Marxist Analysis of the Fifth Labor of Hercules.
Triptych.
Enzensberger, H.   Karl Heinrich Marx.
Kizer, C.   Cultural Evolution.
Lorde.   Workers Rose on May Day or Postcript to Karl Marx, The.

Mary Magdalene
Crashaw.   Weeper, The.
Davie, D.   Magdalene.
Donne.   To Mrs Magdalen Herbert: of St. Mary Magdalen.
Duncan, R.   Adoration of the Virgin, The.
Herbert, G.   Mary [*or* Marie] Magdalene.
Jacobsen, J.   Ballad of the Four Saints.
Milosz, C.   Mary Magdalen and I.
Skull, A.
Pinkerton, H.   On the Two Marys in a Fresco of the Crucifixion.
Rossetti, C.   Mary Magdalene and the Other Mary.
Rossetti, D.   Mary Magdalene at the Door of Simon the Pharisee.
Simic.   Gospel Hour.
Stock, R.   Pietà.

Mary Queen of Scots
Brodsky, J.   Twenty Sonnets to Mary Queen of Scots.
Burns, R.   Campbells Are Comin, The.
Lament of Mary Queen of Scots on the Approach of Spring.
Lowell, R.   Mary Stuart.
Mahon.   Stanzas for Mary Stuart.
Wordsworth, W.   Captivity.—Mary Queen of Scots.
Lament of Mary Queen of Scots on the Eve of a New Year.

Mary, the Virgin
Angelou.   Avec Merci, Mother.
Berryman.   Prayer after All, A.
Bishop, E.   Hymn to the Virgin.
Brooks, G.   Penitent Considers Another Coming of Mary, A.
Browning, E.   Virgin Mary to the Child Jesus, The.
Carruth, H.   Chicory.
Chaucer.   ABC, An.
Clifton, L.   My Dream about the Second Coming.
Codrescu.   First Icon with Gun, The.
Coleridge, S.   Translation of a Passage in Ottfried's Metrical Paraphrase of the Gospel.
Virgin's Cradle-Hymn, The.
Crane, H.   Interludium.
To Liberty.

Crashaw.   O Gloriosa Domina.
On the Blessed Virgins Bashfulnesse.
Sancta Maria Dolorum.
Tear[e], The.
Davie, D.   Our Lady.
Dickey, J.   Magus, The.
Donne.   Upon the Annunciation and Passion Falling upon One Day. 1608.
García Lorca.   Ballad of Our Lady of the Boat.
Poet Prays to the Virgin for Help, The.
Glück, L.   Pietà.
Winter Morning.
Graves, R.   Birth of a Goddess.
Joseph and Mary.
Gunn, T.   Jesus and His Mother.
Hardy, T.   Evening in Galilee, An.
Herbert, G.   Anagram.
To All Angels and Saints.
Herrick.   Another.
Observation.
Upon Woman and Mary.
Virgin Mary, The.
Hopkins, G.   Blessed Virgin Compared to the Air We Breathe, The.
May Magnificat, The.
Rosa Mystica.
Jonson, B.   Garland [*or* Ghyrlond] of the Blessèd Virgin Mary [*or* Marie], The.
Reverse on the Back Side, The.
Kipling, R.   Our Lady of the Sackcloth.
Sons of Martha, The.
Lawrence, D. H.   Ballad of a Wilful Woman.
Jesus' Farewell.
Song to the Tune of *La Cucaracha.*
Levi, P.   Annunciation.
Logan, J.   Month of Saints, A.
Lowell, R.   Beyond the Alps.
MacDiarmid, H.   Harry Semen.
Meredith, W.   Notre Dame de Chartres.
Merton.   Blessed Virgin Mary Compared to a Window, The.
Canticle for the Blessed Virgin.
Evening of the Visitation, The.
La Salette.
To the Immaculate Virgin, on a Winter Night.
Orlandi, G.   If, my friend, you would have said of Mary so.
Parker, D.   Gentlest Lady, The.
Prayer for a New Mother.
Patchen.   I have lighted the candles, Mary.
Pinkerton, H.   On the Two Marys in a Fresco of the Crucifixion.
Poe.   Hymn: "At morn—at noon—at twilight dim."
Robinson, E.   Gift of God, The.
Rossetti, C.   Feast of the Annunciation.
Herself a Rose Who Bore the Rose.
Purification of St. Mary the Virgin, The.
Rossetti, D.   Ave.
Mary's Girlhood.
Sedulius.   Solis Ortus Cardine, A.
Sexton.   Angel Food Dogs, The.
For the Year of the Insane.
Jesus Suckles.
Jesus, the Actor, Plays the Holy Ghost.
Mary's Song.
Simic.   Psalm: "Old ones to the side."
Smith, S.   Dream of Comparison, A.
Stock, R.   Pietà.
Wilde, O.   San Miniato.
Williams, W.   For Eleanor and Bill Monahan.
Yeats.   Mother of God, The.

Masks
Atwood.   Paper Bag, A.
Baudelaire.   Mask, The.
Browning, E.   Mask, The.
Creeley.   Song, The: "It still makes sense."
De la Mare.   Veil, The.
Devecseri.   Women and Masks.
Dugan, A.   Speech to the Student Clowns at the Circus Clown School at Sarasota, Florida.
Dunbar, P.   We Wear the Mask.
Hayden, R.   Two Egyptian Portrait Masks.
Jackson, L.   Mask, The.
Komunyakaa.   Happy-Go-Lucky's Wolf Skull Dream Mask.

Untitled Blues; After a Photograph by Yevgeni Yevtushenko.
Kunitz, S.   Fitting of the Mask, The.
Major, C.   He gave the Fascisti salute.
Theme of Carnevale is a secret, The.
Meredith, W.   Two Masks Unearthed in Bulgaria.
Olson, C.   Yellow of the Mask, The.
Pagis.   How To.
Rilke.   Mask, The.
Masks Offer Themselves.
Migration of Powers, The.
Moment between Masks.
Ritsos.   Indications.
Philoctetes; The Ultimate Mask.
Rukeyser, M.   Poem as Mask, The.
Sandburg, C.   Aztec Mask.
Mask.
Thomas, D.   O Make Me a Mask.
Updike.   Modigliani's Death Mask.
Whitman, W.   Visor'd.
Yeats.   Mask, The.

Masochism
Ai.   One Man Down.
Codrescu.   Dear Masoch.
Dugan, A.   What It Really Means.
Ginsberg, A.   Please Master.
Graves, R.   Encounter, The.
Komunyakaa.   S & M.
Merton.   Psalm 132: A Modern Monastic Revision.
Nash, O.   Little Miss Muffet Sat on a Prophet—and Quite Right, Too!
Stafford, W.   Things That Hurt Me.

Mass Media
Ai.   Paparazzi, The.
Lux.   Frankly, I Don't Care.
Parker, D.   Figures in Popular Literature.

Massachusetts (state)
Bishop, E.   In the Waiting Room.
Ciardi, J.   Homecoming—Massachusetts.
Creeley.   Picnic, The.
Eberhart, R.   On a Squirrel Crossing the Road in Autumn, in New England.
Emerson, R.   Concord Hymn.
God The Lord save Massachusetts.
Lowell, R.   For the Union Dead.
Jonathan Edwards in Western Massachusetts.
Major, C.   Bernardston.
McHugh, H.   Postcard from Provincetown.
Nemerov.   To the Governor & Legislature of Massachusetts.
Plath.   Point Shirley.
Terry, L.   Bars Fight [August 28, 1746].
Thoreau.   Not unconcerned Wachusett rears his head.
Very.   Appeal.
Sunset in Haverhill, A.
Whalen, P.   Dream & Excursus, Arlington Massachusetts.
Whittier.   Album Verses.
Arisen at Last.
Bay of Seven Islands, The.
Cassandra Southwick.
Garrison of Cape Ann, The.
Haverhill.
John Underhill.
June on the Merrimac.
Kenoza Lake.
Letter to Lucy Larcom.
Massachusetts.
Massachusetts to Virginia.
Merrimac, The.
Norumbega Hall.
One of the Signers.
Our River.
Our State.
Pine-Tree, The.
Snow-Bound [or Snow-Bound; a Winter Idyl].
To Massachusetts.
Vale of the Merrimac, The.
Welcome to Lowell, A.
Witch of Wenham, The.
Wilbur, R.   Running.

Massacre of the Innocents
Lowell, R.   Holy Innocents, The.

Massacres
Ai.   Rwanda.
Ciardi, J.   Thought about Sheik Bedreddin, A.
Clampitt.   Odessa Steps, The.
Corbett, W.   D-Day 1989.
De la Mare.   Massacre, The.
Dubie.   Desert Deportation of 1915, The.
Indian Summer.
Looking up from Two Renaissance Paintings to the Massacre at Tiananmen Square.
Faiz.   Bangla Desh: 1.
Bangla Desh: 3.
Glück, L.   Slave Ship, The.
Jeffers, R.   Antrim.
Komunyakaa.   Jonestown: More eyes for Jadwiga's Dream.
Lowell, R.   At the Indian Killer's Grave.
Orr, G.   Nothing and the Incident in the Streets.
Rossetti, C.   In the Round Tower at Jhansi, June 8, 1857.
Scott, S.   On the Massacre of Glencoe, 1692.
Seifert.   Dead of Lidice, The.
Walcott.   Air.
Whittier.   Le Marais du Cygne.
Pentucket.
Wilde, O.   Sonnet on the Massacre of the Christians in Bulgaria.

Masts
Eberhart, R.   Broken Wing Theory.
Waiting to Lean to the Master's Command.
Olson, C.   Mast, The.

Maternity
Jeffers, R.   Haunted Country.
Levertov.   Her Task.
Robinson, E.   Aunt Imogen.

Mathematics and Mathematicians
Coleridge, S.   Mathematical Problem, A.
Cunningham, J.   Cantor's Theorem: In an Infinite Class the Whole Is No Greater than Some of Its Parts.
Davie, D.   Bolyai, the Geometer.
Dickey, J.   Math.
Dubie.   Clouds of Magellan (Aphorisms of Mr. Canon Aspirin), The.
Dugan, A.   On Zero.
Enzensberger, H.   Homage to Gödel.
Laughlin, J.   By the Numbers.
Millay, E.   "Euclid Alone Has Looked on Beauty Bare."
Olson, C.   Lie of 10, or the Concept of Zero, The.
Pagis.   Failure.
Ritsos.   For Greater Accuracy.
Rossetti, C.   1 and 1 are 2— / That's for me and you.
Sandburg, C.   Arithmetic.
Stockton, A.   Thoughts on the Pythagorian System.

See also Arithmetic

Mather, Cotton
Stevens, W.   Blue Buildings in the Summer Air, The.

Matisse, Henri
Ferlinghetti, L.   Matisse at the Modern, Magritte at the Met.

Matterhorn
Hardy, T.   Zermatt: To the Matterhorn.

Maturity
Amichai [or Amikhai].   My son, the softness of your face already shows.
Broumas, O.   Between Two Seas.
Clampitt.   Imago.
Clifton, L.   Album.
Creeley.   Peace ("You're looking at a chopper").
Cummings, E. E.   Boy and the Man, The.
Pretty a day, A.
Cunningham, J.   Arms and the man I sing, and sing for joy.
"Dario."   In Autumn ("I know that there are those who say, "Why don't you sing now'").
Dickey, J.   Little More, The.
Dickinson, E.   Maturity only enhances mystery.
Dove, R.   Obedience.
Dugan, A.   Poem: "Oh that was not a scrap of flying Daily News."

Ferlinghetti, L.   Firenze, a Lifetime Later.
Gallagher, T.   Breasts.
Graves, R.   To Come of Age.
Heaney, S.   Fosterling.
Hill, G.   Guardians, The.
Holy Thursday.
Jackson, L.   How Now We Talk.
Jacobsen, J.   Primer, The.
Jonson, B.   Ode. To Sir William Sydney, on His Birthday.
Kipling, R.   If—.
Larkin, P.   Maturity.
Lawrence, D. H.   I Heard Her Say.
Levine, P.   Last Step, The.
Meredith, G.   Atlas.
Merwin.   Birds on the Morning of Going, The.
Nash, O.   Lines to Be Scribbled on Somebody Else's Thirtieth Milestone.
Parker, D.   Fulfilment.
How Bold It Is.
Indian Summer.
Piercy.   Sign.
Prunty.   Yes.
Ransom, J.   Eclogue: "JANE SNEED BEGAN IT: My poor John, alas."
First Travels of Max.
Rexroth, K.   Letter to Wystan Hugh Auden, A.
Precession of the Equinoxes.
Rilke.   Child, The.
Rimbaud, A.   Impossible, The.
War.
Ritsos.   Invisible Glory.
Roethke.   Sententious Man, The.
Rossetti, C.   Once.
Within the Veil.
Rukeyser, M.   Boys of These Men Full Speed.
Smith, S.   To Carry the Child.
Stafford, W.   Farewell, Age Ten, A.
For My Young Friends Who Are Afraid.
Growing Up.
Whispered into the Ground.
Thoreau.   Manhood.
Warren, R.   Man Coming of Age.
Wordsworth, W.   My heart leaps up when I behold.
Zagajewski.   Speak Softly.
Zaturenska.   Girl Takes Her Place among the Mothers, The.

Mausoleums
Bierce.   Word to the Unwise, A.
MacDiarmid, H.   Skeleton of the Future, The.
Tomlinson, C.   Mausoleum, The.
Wordsworth, W.   Filial Piety.

See also Cemeteries; Graves; Monuments; Tombs

Maximilian (emperor of Mexico)
Wright, J.   Chapultepec Castle.

May
Auden.   May.
Berry, W.   May Song.
Bly, R.   In the Month of May.
Browning, R.   Home-Thoughts, from Abroad.
May and Death.
Burns, R.   Chloe.
Cowper, W.   Judgment of the Poets, The.
Davie, D.   Wearing of the Green, The.
De la Mare.   There Blooms No Bud in May.
Dickinson, E.   When they come back—if Blossoms do.
Dunbar, P.   Golden Day, A.
In May.
Eberhart, R.   May Evening.
Velvet Rocks.
Emerson, R.   May-Day.
Glück, L.   Brooding Likeness.
Graves, R.   Song: Olive Tree.
Gurney, I.   Incense Bearers, The.
Hardy, T.   Afterwards.
Herrick.   Corinna's Going a-Maying.
Hopkins, G.   Ad Mariam.
May Magnificat, The.
Housman.   First of May, The.
Jacobsen, J.   Hourglass.
Larkin, P.   Trees, The.
Levertov.   May Mornings, The.
MacLeish.   Spring in These Hills.
Meredith, G.   May Song.

Milton. Song: on [*or* of] May Morning.
Mir, M. Elegy: "In the May breeze."
Nash, O. Here We Go Quietly Nuts in May.
Nemerov. May Day Dancing, The.
Ritsos. Honesty.
Rossetti, C. May.
  May-Time.
Rossetti, D. Fin di Maggio.
Sandburg, C. Crossing the Ohio When Poppies
  Bloom in Ashtabula.
Dan.
Follies.
  Uplands in May.
Shelley, P. Fragment: May the Limner.
Spender, S. Remembering Cincinnatti, 1953.
Thoreau. May Morning.
Very. First of May, The.
  May Flower, The.
Whitman, W. Out of May's Shows Selected.
Williams, W. Bird Song.
  Locust Tree in Flower, The.
  Tulip Bed, The.
Wordsworth, W. Ode Composed on May
  Morning.
  To May.
Wyatt, S. May Time.
Zagajewski. In May.
May Day
Emerson, R. May.
  May-Day.
Herrick. May-Pole, The.
Hughes, L. Chant for May Day.
  First of May.
  Sister Johnson Marches.
Hughes, T. Mayday on Holderness.
Rexroth, K. Venice.
Rukeyser, M. Cats and a Cock.
Maya
Nemerov. Maia.
Oppen. Mayan Ground, The.
Mayflower (ship)
Plath. Mayflower.
Mayflowers
Thoreau. And once again.
Very. May Flower, The.
See also **Arbutus**
Mazepa, Ivan
Byron, G. Mazeppa.
McCarthy, Joseph
Ai. Blue Suede Shoes.
Dugan, A. On When McCarthy Was a Wolf
  among a Nation of Queer-Queers.
Hamill, S. Blue Monody.
Hughes, L. Un-American Investigators.
McKay, Eleanora Fagan
See **Holiday, Billie**
McKinley, William
Riley, J. William McKinley.
Mead
Millay, E. Oh, think not I am faithful to a vow!
Meadowlarks
Dunbar, P. Meadow Lark, The.
Eberhart, R. Now Is the Air Made of Chiming
  Balls.
Meadows
Ciardi, J. Cartographer of Meadows, The.
De la Mare. Crazed.
  Voices.
Duncan, R. Often I Am Permitted to Return to
  a Meadow.
Emerson, R. Patch of meadow & upland, A.
  Would you know what joy is hid.
Frost, R. Last Mowing, The.
  Rose Pogonias.
Gunn, T. Flooded Meadows.
Gurney, I. Dancers, The.
  Early Spring Dawn.
  Friendly Are Meadows.
  Two, The.
Hall, D. Our Walk in Yorkshire.
Herrick. To Meadows [*or* Meddowes].
Lawrence, D. H. Chief Mystery, The.
Milosz, C. Meadow, A.
Pagis. Art of Contraction, The.

Petrarch. Exhilarated flowers, and lucky
  grasses.
Roethke. Meadow Mouse, The.
Rossetti, C. In the meadow—what in the
  meadow?
  Mr. and Mrs. Scott, and I.
Rumi. Meadowsounds.
Sandburg, C. Meadow in Summer.
Simic. Pastoral: "I came to a meadow."
Thomas, D. I, in My Intricate Image.
Wilbur, R. Two Voices in a Meadow.
Wright, J. Eclogue at Nash's Grove.
Zagajewski. Blackened River, The.
See also **Fields and Pastures**
Meat
Angelou. Health-Food Diner, The.
Emerson, R. Stout Sparta shrined the god of
  Laughter.
Gunn, T. Meat.
Hardy, T. Bags of Meat.
Herrick. Grace for a Child.
  Great Boast, Small Rost.
  Upon Lungs.
  Upon Showbread [*or* Shewbread]: Epigram.
Komunyakaa. Smokehouse, The.
Levine, P. Salami.
Mølville, H. Maldive Shark, The.
Paley, G. Families.
Wilbur, R. Rillons, Rillettes.
Meath
See **County Meath, Ireland**
Mechanics
Collins, B. Pinup.
Levine, P. Detroit Grease Shop Poem.
McHugh, H. Impressionist.
Stafford, W. Fixers.
Williams, M. Mecanic on Duty at All Times.
Zukofsky, L. Pretty.
Medals
Merton. Message to Be Inscribed on Mark Van
  Doren's Hamilton Medal.
Ritsos. New Victory.
Sandburg, C. Medallion.
Medea
Byron, G. Translation from the Medea of
  Euripides.
Raine, K. Medea.
Medici, Lorenzo de'
Davie, D. Tuscan Brutus, The.
Medici, Piero de'
Dubie. Saints of Negativity, The.
Medicine
Blue Cloud. To-ta Ti-om.
Browning, R. Epistle Containing the Strange
  Medical Experience of Karshish, the Arab
  Physician, An.
Burns, R. Death and Doctor Hornbook [A True
  Story].
Cowper, W. To Dr. Austin.
Crashaw. Temperance or the Cheap Physitian
  upon the Translation of Lessius.
Graves, R. Apollo of the Physiologists.
Herrick. Great Maladies, Long Medicines.
  Head-Ake, The.
  Lenitie.
  Upon Leech.
Kipling, R. Our Fathers of Old.
Kizer, C. Medicine ("Practice of medicine,
  The").
Laughlin, J. Cardiac Autoscope, The.
Longfellow, H. Day Is Done, The.
Lux. Haitian Cadavers.
Meredith, G. Faith on Trial, A.
  Melampus.
Moore, M. Staff of Aesculapius, The.
Muldoon, P. Cure for Warts, The.
  Glanders.
Nash, O. Strange Case of the Lucrative
  Compromise, The.
Rich, A. 5:30 A.M.
Rossetti, C. Baby cry—/ Oh fie!
Rukeyser, M. Praise of the Committee.
Schuyler, J. Afterward.
  What.
Sheridan, T. I Like Your Collyrium.

Shih-te. I have millions of gathas.
Smith, S. Bottle of Aspirins, The.
Van Duyn. Death by Aesthetics.
  Remedies, Maladies, Reasons.
See also **Doctors; Hospitals; Illness; Nurses**
Mediocrity
Davie, D. To a Bad Poet.
Hughes, L. Communiqué.
Meditation
Ammons. Levitation.
Baudelaire. Meditation.
Berry, W. Meditation in the Spring Rain.
Blue Cloud. Meditation of Leaves, A.
Bly, R. Six Winter Privacy Poems.
Broumas, O. Home Movies.
  Jewel Lotus Harp.
  Landscape with Mantra.
Bukowski. T.M.
Carruth, H. Buddhist Painter Prepares to Paint,
  The.
Chuang Tzu. When Knowledge Went North.
Coleridge, S. Frost at Midnight.
Dubie. New Age at Airport Mesa.
Emerson, R. Apology, The.
Ginsberg, A. Cabin in the Rockies.
  Do the Meditation Rock.
  Mind Breaths.
  Thoughts on a Breath.
  Thoughts Sitting Breathing.
  Why I Meditate.
Graves, R. Ambience.
Guyon. Scenes Favourable to Meditation.
  Watching unto God in the Night-Season.
Herbert, G. Content.
Levertov. Sands of the Well.
  Three Meditations.
Meredith, G. Fireside Reverie.
  I seize in a central knot.
  Meditation under Stars.
Merton. Then from tomorrow.
Ramanujan. Meditation, A.
Rexroth, K. Empty Mirror.
Roethke. Meditation in Hydrotherapy.
Rumi. After the Meditation.
Stock, R. Koan for Two Minutes of Intensive
  Meditation.
Tate, J. First Lesson.
Very. Columbine, The.
Warren, R. Fear and Trembling.
Whalen, P. Bay Trees Were About to Bloom,
  The.
Williams, C. K. Listen carefully. / I'm
  meditating.
Wright, C. Driving to Passalacqua, 1960.
Mediterranean Sea
Brodsky, J. Venice: Lido.
Clampitt. Archaic Figure.
Cummings, E. E. Sunlight was over.
Eberhart, R. Mediterranean Song.
Hardy, T. Genoa and the Mediterranean.
Lawrence, D. H. Mediterranean in January.
  Middle of the World.
Montale. Mediterranean.
Tate, A. Mediterranean, The.
Tomlinson, C. Mediterranean, The.
Warren, R. Mediterranean Basin.
Medusa
Bierce. Tempora Mutantur.
Bogan, L. Medusa.
Clampitt. Athena.
  Medusa.
  Medusa at Broadstairs.
  Nereids of Seriphos, The.
Crane, H. Medusa.
Cullen, C. Medusa.
Dugan, A. Perverse Explanation for Mutilated
  Statuary.
Hayden, R. Perseus.
Petrarch. Heavenly breeze that breathes
  throughout the green, The.
Sarton, M. Muse as Medusa, The.
Shelley, P. On the Medusa of Leonardo da
  Vinci in the Florentine Gallery.
Stafford, W. In Fear and Valor.
Stock, R. Red Clay Speech.

Wilner, E.   Her Body Is Private.
Metamorphoses at a College for Women.
Zaturenska.   Head of Medusa.

Melampus
Meredith, G.   Melampus.

Melancholy
Baudelaire.   Ever the Same.
Brontë, E.   Wind, I hear it sighing, The.
Brooks, G.   Crazy Woman, The.
Bukowski.   Melancholia.
Carruth, H.   Chase in Spring, The.
Carver, R.   Vigil.
Cavafy.   Melancholy Hours.
Melancholy of Jason Kleander; Poet in
    Kommagini; 595 A.D.
Ciardi, J.   Memory of the Sad Chair, A.
Coleridge, S.   Dejection: An Ode.
Letter to Sara Hutchinson.
Nightingale, The.
This Lime-Tree Bower My Prison.
Corbett, W.   Melancholy.
Creeley.   Medallion.
Davie, D.   Winter Talent, A.
De la Mare.   Old Angler, The.
Son of Melancholy, The.
Dunbar, P.   Melancholia.
Emerson, R.   Teach me I am forgotten by the
    dead.
Written in Naples, March, 1833.
Ferlinghetti, L.   Thoughts to a Concerto of
    Telemann.
Ginsberg, A.   Moments Return, The.
Hughes, L.   Neighbor.
Weary Blues, The.
Keats.   Ode on Melancholy.
Kunitz, S.   Artist, The.
McGrath, T.   Woodcut.
Milton.   Il Penseroso.
Mistral, G.   Riches.
Nash, O.   So Penseroso.
Olson, C.   Your Eyes.
Parker, D.   Rondeau: "It isn't fair, to me, when
    you're away."
Rondeau Redoublé.
Plath.   Poppies in July.
Rexroth, K.   Unpeopled, Conventional Rose-
    Garden, The.
Riley, J.   Lines: "Portentous sound! mysteriously
    vast."
Robinson, E.   Charles Carville's Eyes.
Rossetti, C.   At Home.
If Only.
Schuyler, J.   February 13, 1975.
Heather and Calendulas.
Shelley, P.   Stanzas Written in Dejection, near
    Naples [or —December 1818, near Naples].
Smith, S.   Away, Melancholy.
Old Sweet Dove of Wiveton, The.
Swinburne.   Itylus.
Tate, J.   It's Not the Heat So Much as the
    Humidity.
Private Intrigue of Melancholy, The.
Warren, R.   Youthful Picnic Long Ago: Sad
    Ballad on Box.
Wordsworth, W.   I Wandered Lonely as a Cloud.
World is too much with us; late and soon, The.
Wyatt, S.   What rage is this? What furo[u]r of
    what kind [or kynd]?
Zukofsky, L.   Not it was no dream of coming
    death.

See also **Blues (mood); Dejection**

Meleager
Ciardi, J.   Carving the Turkey.

Melons
Plath.   Fiesta Melons.
Riley, J.   Liz-Town Humorist, A.
Rilke.   Melon.

Melville, Herman
Auden.   Herman Melville.
Borges.   Herman Melville.
Crane, H.   At Melville's Tomb.
Dubie.   Scrivener's Roses, The.
Koch, K.   You Were Wearing.
Logan, J.   Homage to Herman Melville.
Olson, C.   Letter for Melville 1951.

Pinkerton, H.   Lemuel Shaw's Meditation.
Melville's Letter to William Clark Russell.
Melvilliana.
Rukeyser, M.   After Melville.

Memento Mori
Graves, R.   Half-Finished Letter, The.

Memnon
Komunyakaa.   Doppelgängers.
Smart, C.   Inscriptions on an Aeolian Harp.

Memorial Day
Ciardi, J.   Memorial Day.
Dunbar, P.   Ode for Memorial Day.
McHugh, H.   Two Holidays.
Niedecker.   Memorial Day.
Olson, C.   Memorial Day.
Orr, G.   Memorial Day.
Prunty.   Memorial Day.
Williams, W.   Middle.

Memories
Ai.   Flashback.
Amichai [or Amikhai].   Anniversaries of War.
Autumn is Near and the Memory of My Parents.
Eyn Gedi Preserve.
Half-Sized Violin.
Huleikat—The Third Poem about Dicky.
In the Morning It Was Still Night.
Last Word Is Captain, The.
Little Ruth.
Lost Objects.
Memory of Love—Opening the Will.
Quiet Joy, A.
Ruhama.
Sadness of Eyes and Descriptions of a Voyage.
Signs and Evidence in the Orchard of Gan-
    Hayim.
To Hurl Haunting Memories.
Try to Remember Some Details.
When I was young, the country was young too.
    My father.
Baudelaire.   Black Bile ("No writing-desk
    crammed full of music, twine").
I Haven't Forgotten.
Perfume-flask, The.
Borges.   Adrogué.
Flow of Memories, The.
Parting.
Talismans.
Broumas, O.   After Lunch.
Carver, R.   Egress.
Harley's Swans.
Old Days, The.
Where They'd Lived.
Cavafy.   Afternoon Sun, The.
From the Ship.
Garments.
In the Evening.
Ciardi, J.   Reverie during Briefing.
Clampitt.   Black Buttercups.
Cadenza, A.
Manhattan.
On the Disadvantages of Central Heating.
Seder Night.
Whippoorwill in the Woods, A.
Clifton, L.   Memory.
Collins, B.   Forgetfulness.
Corbett, W.   Between sets.
Collarbone.
February 29, 1988.
Homefires.
Marga Barr.
Painters, The.
Youth.
Creeley.   Memory, 1930.
Memory ("Nancy finally").
Men.
Provincetown.
Cunningham, J.   In a few days now when two
    memories meet.
Dubie.   Lamentations.
Old Woman's Vision, An.
Widow Speaks to the Auroras of a December
    Night, A.
Enzensberger, H.   Camera Obscura.
García Lorca.   1910.
Gurney, I.   Battalion Is Now on Rest, The.
That Centre of Old.

Hardy, T.   Church Romance, A.
Heaney, S.   Strand, The.
Hughes, L.   Bells Toll Kindly, The.
Second Generation: New York.
Hughes, T.   Anniversary.
For the Duration.
Jackson, L.   Autobiography of the Present.
Jacobsen, J.   Loss of Sounds.
Kinnell.   Road between Here and There, The.
Kinsella, T.   In Memory.
Settings.
Thinking of Mr D.
Kizer, C.   For Jan as the End Draws Near.
Promising Author.
Komunyakaa.   Eye Witness.
Good Memory, A.
Reminiscence.
Kumin, M.   Apostrophe to a Dead Friend.
Appetite.
Deaths of the Uncles, The.
Game of Monopoly in Chavannes.
Grappling in the Central Blue.
Thirties Revisited, The.
Laughlin, J.   Remembrance.
Welcome, The.
When I'm Missing You.
Levertov.   Evening Train.
Room.
Logan, J.   First Prelude. Dream in Ohio: The
    Father.
Poem for My Son.
Poem in Progress.
Whatnot, The.
Major, C.   Matthew.
Unwanted Memory.
Merwin.   Banquet, The.
Numbered Apartment.
Remembering a Boatman.
Ship.
Ships Are Made Ready in Silence, The.
Sun and Rain.
Waters, The.
Web, The.
Milosz, C.   1913.
Mistral, G.   Things.
Orr, G.   Sunday School Picnic: What Endures.
Paley, G.   Sometimes.
Palmer, M.   This Time.
Parker, D.   Rosemary ("Ah, no, I dare not lose
    myself in dreams").
Second Love.
Petrarch.   Each time I call to mind the hour, the
    place.
I must direct these lines so full of sorrow.
My days have gone by swifter than a deer.
She comes to mind—no, is already there.
What fear is mine when I recall that day.
What is the matter? And why do you turn.
Pinkerton, H.   Return, The.
Prunty.   Stillness.
Ramanujan.   From Where?
Rexroth, K.   Flute Overheard, A.
Unpeopled, Conventional Rose-Garden, The.
Your Birthday in the California Mountains.
Riley, J.   Albumania.
Ancient Printerman, The.
As I Sit in the Silence.
Backward Look, A.
Enduring, The.
Honey Dripping from the Comb.
Little Girly-Girl.
Old Played-out Song, A.
Old Sweetheart of Mine, An.
Thinkin' Back.
To Annie.
Rilke.   Great Indulgent Heart.
In This Life of Neglect.
Lemon and Laburnum.
Rimbaud, A.   Memory.
Recollection.
Ritsos.   Helen.
Seifert.   At one of his readings a long time ago.
Autobiography.
Berthe Soucaret.
Demolition Report.
November Rain.

Sometimes we are tied down by memories.
Song of the Sweepings.
"Shu Ting." Brother, I Am Here.
Returning Home.
Simic. Closed House.
Stafford, W. Circle of Breath.
One Evening.
Our Way Those Days before These Days.
Wind from a Wing, A.
Sze. Apache Plume.
Red Octopus.
Tate, J. Manna.
Tomlinson, C. Letter to Uehata.
Return, The.
Warren, R. Ballad of Your Puzzlement.
Doubleness in Time.
If Ever.
John's Birches.
Millpond Lost.
Resolution.
Rumor at Twilight.
Safe in Shade.
Small Eternity.
Snowfall.
Weiss, T. Gunsight.
Living Room, A.
Slow Fuse, A.
Whalen, P. Past Ruin'd Ilion.
Wilde, O. Roses and Rue.
Williams, M. August Evening Outside of
Nashville, An
Hello. I'll Bet You Don't Know Who This Is.
How We May By Chance Pronounce the
Unsuspected Residence of a Ghost.
Remembering Walter.
Williams, T. Couple, The.
Williams, W. Asphodel, That Greeny Flower.
Paterson, Book 5: The River of Heaven.
Wright, C. Apologia Pro Vita Sua.
Yeats. Cold Heaven, The.
Zagajewski. For M.
Islands and Towers.
Lullaby.
Smoke.
Zaturenska. Invaders, The.
Snowy Woods, The.

Memory
Ai. Back in the World.
Amichai [or Amikhai]. 1924.
Early in the morning, you lean on the wall of an
old house.
Eternal Window, An.
Evidence.
I love these people in their tall house.
Last Word Is the Captain, The.
Ammons. Right On.
Angelou. I Almost Remember.
Memory, The.
Now Long Ago.
Remembering.
When You Come to Me.
Aragon. Lilacs and the Roses, The.
Armantrout. Postcards.
Ashbery, J. Hop o' My Thumb.
Houseboat Days.
Other Tradition, The.
Some Old Tires.
Atwood. Foundling, A.
Four Small Elegies.
Night Poem.
Nightshade on the Way to School.
Auden. On This Island.
Question, The.
Shock, A.
Since.
Talking to Myself.
Taller To-day.
Beckett, S. Ainsi a-t-on beau.
Pas davantage.
Son ombre une nuit.
Berrigan, T. Certain Slant of Sunlight, A.
Cranston near the City Line.
Last Poem.
Pandora's Box, an Ode.
Berry, W. At a Country Funeral.
Gathering, The.

In Memory: Stuart Egnal.
Meditation in the Spring Rain.
Praise, A.
Wild, The.
Berryman. Crisis.
Down & Back.
Heroes, The.
Images of Elspeth.
In & Out.
London.
Meditation.
Meeting.
Message.
My Special Fate.
Nowhere.
Recovery.
Two Organs.
Blake, W. Song: "Memory, hither come."
Blue Cloud. Incense.
Bogan, L. Memory.
Borges. Adam Cast Forth.
Blind Man, The.
Cambridge.
Instant, The.
Limits.
Maker, The ("He had never dwelled on the
pleasures of memory").
Rain.
Where Can They Have Gone?
Brodsky, J. Afterword.
Café Trieste: San Francisco.
Ex Voto.
I Sit by the Window.
In Italy.
Brontë, E. A.G.A. to A.S.
All hushed and still within the house.
Aye there it is! It wakes tonight.
Come hither, child—who gifted thee.
From a Dungeon Wall in the Southern College.
Harp of wild and dream-like strain.
I gazed upon the cloudless moon.
I.M. to I.G.
Lines by Claudia.
Lines: "Soft unclouded blue of air, The."
M.G. for the U.S.
Mild the mist upon the hill.
O Dream, where art thou now?
O mother, I am not regretting.
Remembrance.
Stanzas to———.
Starry night shall tidings bring, The.
Still beside that dreary water
That wind, I used to hear it swelling.
There let thy bleeding branch atone.
Warning and Reply.
What winter floods, what showers of spring.
When days of Beauty deck the earth.
Wind, I hear it sighing, The.
Brooks, G. Anniad, The.
Bean Eaters, The.
Broumas, O. Walk on the Water.
Browning, E. Dance, The.
Dead Rose, A.
L.E.L.'s Last Question.
Little Friend, The.
Memory and Hope.
Night and the Merry Man.
Browning, R. Appearances.
By the Fire-Side.
Confessions.
Dubiety.
Memorabilia.
Bukowski. Eulogy to a Hell of a Dame—.
Reunion.
Spain Sits like a Hidden Flower in My
Coffeepot.
Burns, R. O May Thy Morn.
Byron, G. And Thou Art Dead, as Young and
Fair.
Condolatory Address.
Egotism. A Letter to J.T. Becher.
If Sometimes in the Haunts of Men.
La Revanche.
Lines Written beneath a Picture.
Lines Written beneath an Elm in the Churchyard
of Harrow.

Lines Written in an Album, at Malta.
On a Distant View of the Village and School of
Harrow on the Hill.
Pignus Amoris.
Remember Thee! Remember Thee!
Remind Me Not, Remind Me Not.
Stanzas: "Chill and mirk is the nightly blast."
Stanzas for Music.
Stanzas to a Lady on Leaving England.
To a Lady.
To the Hon. Mrs. George Lamb.
Cardenal. Dog barks far out, A.
Every evening the L & N.
I do not know who is out in the snow.
I turned out the light to see the snow.
Like Empty Beer Cans.
Like the flights of ducks.
Long freight train / Wakes me in my cell, The.
Sound of passing cars, (if a car comes), The.
Spring has come with its smell of Nicaragua.
That auto horn sounds familiar.
When the first signs go on.
Zinc roofs in the moonlight, The.
Carew, T. To T. H., a Lady Resembling My
Mistress.
Carruth, H. Bearer, The.
Event Itself, The.
Carver, R. Hamid Ramouz (1818–1906).
Memory 1.
Shooting.
Spell.
White Field, The.
Cavafy. Before the House.
Far Off.
Gray.
Next Table, The.
Return.
Since Nine o'Clock.
When They Surge, Excited.
Cavalcanti. Canzone: He Laments the
Presumption and Incontinence of His Youth.
Celan. Mute autumn smells, The.
Sluice, The.
Stretto.
Voices, nicked into.
Chesterton. Donkey, The.
Ciardi, J. Call It a Day.
I Remember the House That Was.
Keeping.
On a Photo of Sgt. Ciardi a Year Later.
Overthrow, An.
Shaft, The.
Survival in Missouri.
Three Views of a Mother.
Tree Trimming.
Twice, Away from Jack, I Thought of Him.
What Was Her Name.
Cino da Pistoia. Canzone: His Lament for
Selvaggia.
Clampitt. Burning Child, The.
Clifton, L. Why some people be mad at me
sometimes.
Codrescu. Brief (Remembered) Histoire of
Rejection, A.
Coleridge, S. Lewti.
Collins, B. Lines Lost among Trees.
Cooper, J. Bloodroot.
For My Mother in Her First Illness, from a
Window Overlooking Notre Dame.
How Can I Speak for Her.
Snow in the City.
Corbett, W. Shower in June, A.
Crane, H. Emblems of Conduct.
Great Western Plains, The.
Havana Rose.
Legende.
Passage.
Postscript, A.
Repose of Rivers.
Crane, S. I have seen thy face aflame.
I wonder if sometimes in the dusk.
Creeley. Away.
Backwards.
Ball Game, The.
Drums, The.
Echo ("Faint, persistent").

Every Day.
Fire, The.
First Time, The.
For Leslie.
For My Mother: Genevieve Jules Creeley.
For the Graduation.
Guido, i' vorrei che tu e Lapo ed io.
Hole, The.
House, The ("Mas-Soñer / Restaurat—Any").
I.
In London.
Just Friends.
Memory ("Fresh, A").
Method of Actuality, The.
Movie Run Backward, The.
Oh, Love.
People, The.
Place, A.
Place, The ("Swoop of hawk").
Plan Is the Body, The.
Retrospect.
Something.
Souvenir, The.
Tally, A.
Teachings, The.
Two.
Variations.
Cullen, C.   At the Wailing Wall in Jerusalem.
To One Not There.
Youth Sings a Song of Rosebuds.
Cummings, E. E.   After five / times the poem.
Along the brittle treacherous bright streets.
An(fragrance)Of / (Begins) / millions.
Buncha hardboil guys frum duh A.C. fulla.
"But / he" i / staring / into winter twi.
Clown's smirk in the skull of a baboon, A.
Dedicated to Dear Nana Clarke.
Dick Mid's large bluish face without eyebrows.
GrEEn's d / an / cing on hollow was.
Grin without a / face(a look), A.
How this uncouth enchanted.
I remark that this beach has been used too.
    much Too. originally.
In spite of everything.
In time of daffodils(who know.
It is so long since my heart has been with yours.
Item:is / Clumsily with of.
Ivory performing rose, The.
Jack's white horse(up).
Joys faces friends / feet terrors fate.
Love is more thicker than forget.
Memory believes / fragrance of a town(whose).
Now two old ladies sit peacefully knitting.
Other guineahen, The.
Out of more find than seeks.
Silently little blue elephant shyly(he was terri),
    The.
We)under)over,the thing of floating Of.
What is strictly fiercely and wholly dies.
Y is a WELL KNOWN ATHLETE'S BRIDE.
Davie, D.   Boyhood Misremembered.
Eight Years After.
Sorting Old Papers.
Time Passing, Beloved.
De la Mare.   Cage, The.
Faithless.
Fare Well.
Juliet's Nurse.
Lucy.
Memory.
Miss Loo.
Mountains, The.
Music.
Old Ben.
Old Men, The.
Phantom, The.
Rachel.
Remembrance.
Rooks in October.
Sea-Magic.
Son of Melancholy, The.
To My Mother.
Treachery.
Unregarding.
Widow, The.
Winter.

Dickey, J.   To Be Done in Winter.
Dickey, W.   Anniversary, The.
At Your Old House.
Do they remember me?
Fretful and sick, you ask.
Fretful and sick, you long.
His Death from Cancer.
Memoranda.
Nevertheless, sleep / And as your eyes close.
No, the night has gone.
Things Kept.
Yes, they remember you.
Dickinson, E.   Blossoms will run away.
Flower keeps it's appointment.
Heart! We [or Heart, we] will forget him!
I remember your coming as serious sweetness.
If recollecting were forgetting.
In Ebon Box, when years have flown.
Like Some Old fashioned Miracle.
Memory is a strange Bell.
Memory is the Sherry Flower.
No Passenger was known to flee.
Pain Has an Element of Blank.
Pile of Years is not so high, The.
Remembrance has a Rear and Front.
Show me Eternity, and I will show you
    Memory.
Some Days retired from the rest.
That sacred Closet when you sweep.
This was in the White of the Year.
Through those old Grounds of memory.
To flee from memory.
Tropic, indeed, a memory.
When Memory is full.
You cannot make Remembrance grow.
You might not know I remembered you.
Dove, R.   Anniversary.
Charm, The.
Company.
Dusting.
Grape Sherbet.
In the Old Neighborhood.
Nothing Down.
Pomade.
Stroke, The.
Wingfoot Lake.
Drummond de Andrade.   In the Middle of the
    Road.
Dubie.   Depth of Field, A.
Dunbar, P.   At Sunset Time.
If I Could but Forget.
Little Lucy Landman.
Love-Song: "If Death should claim me for her
    own to-day."
Memory of Martha, The.
Old Homestead, The.
Old Story, The.
Parted.
Poor Withered Rose.
Retrospection.
Song, The: "My soul, lost in the music's mist."
To E. H. K.
To Pfrimmer.
When the Old Man Smokes.
Duncan, R.   After Reading H.D.'s *Hermetic
    Definitions*.
Eberhart, R.   Deep Fishing.
Formative Mastership.
In the Garden.
Loss.
Memory.
Whenever I See Beauty I See Death.
Eliot, T. S.   La Figlia Che Piange.
Rhapsody on a Windy Night.
Emerson, R.   Amulet, The.
Dear are the pleasant memories.
For Nature true & like in every place.
From Frodmer's Drama "The Friends."
Past, The.
Shall the Muse sing for thousands & not sing.
Thanks to those who go & come.
Thine Eyes Still Shined.
Where art thou / Thou beautiful dream.
Ferlinghetti, L.   And she "like a young year."
Firenze, a Lifetime Later.
In woods where many rivers run.

Photo of Emily, The.
26.
Foscolo.   Sonnet to Zante.
Frost, R.   Auspex.
Directive.
Gallagher, T.   As if It Happened.
Backdrop with Lovers, 1931.
Bonfire.
Corona.
Devotion: That It Flow; That There Be
    Concentration.
Open Fire near a Shed.
Woodcutting on Lost Mountain.
García Lorca.   Desire of a Statue.
New Heart.
Your Childhood in Menton.
Ginsberg, A.   Complaint of the Skeleton to
    Time.
Journal Night Thoughts.
Kaddish.
Memory Gardens.
On Neal's Ashes.
To Aunt Rose.
White Shroud.
Glück, L.   Lady in the Single, The.
Northwood Path.
Pond, The.
Scraps.
Tango.
Graves, R.   Plea to Boys and Girls, A.
Through Nightmare.
Gunn, T.   Autobiography.
Death's Door.
Memory Unsettled.
Gurney, I.   Memory.
To His Love.
"H. D."   At Eleusis.
Helen.
Lethe.
Hacker, M.   Geographer.
Hang-Glider's Daughter, The.
Letter from Goose Creek: April.
Hall, D.   1934.
Abroad Thoughts from Home.
Airstrip in Essex, 1960, An.
Beau of the Dead.
By the Exeter River.
Cider 5¢ a Glass.
Exile.
Farm, The.
Foundations of American Industry, The.
Kicking the Leaves.
Letter to an English Poet.
Love Is like Sounds.
Milkers Broken Up.
My Friend Felix.
"O Flodden Field."
Old Home Week.
Old Pilot, The.
Photographs of China.
September Ode.
Sleeping.
Three Movements, The.
Hardy, T.   After a Journey.
Afterwards.
Ah, Are You Digging on My Grave?
Ancient to Ancients, An.
Beyond the Last Lamp.
Burning the Holly.
Days to Recollect.
Gentleman's Second-Hand Suit, A.
Green Slates.
I Looked Back.
In the Mind's Eye.
Joys of Memory.
Last Journey, A.
Last Time, The.
Let Me Believe.
Little Old Table, The.
Louie.
Memory and I.
Molly Gone.
Mound, The.
Not Only I.
Old Gown, The.
One We Knew.

Outside the Casement.
Procession of Dead Days, A.
Rambler, The.
Reminiscences of a Dancing Man.
Revisitation, The.
She Revisits Alone the Church of Her Marriage.
Shut Out That Moon.
Silences.
Superseded, The.
That Kiss in the Dark.
Thoughts of Phena.
To Lizbie Browne.
Two Soldiers, The.
Unknowing.
Voice, The.
Where the Picnic Was.
Where Three Roads Joined.
Wife Comes Back, A.
Hayden, R.   Ballad of Sue Ellen Westerfield, The.
Burly Fading One, The.
Those Winter Sundays.
Whipping, The.
Heaney, S.   Anahorish.
Cloistered.
Relic of Memory.
Underground, The.
Herrick.   Upon His Sister-in-Law, Mistress Elizabeth Herrick.
Upon Parrat.
Hopkins, G.   Confirmed beauty will not bear a stress.
Hughes, L.   Blues at Dawn.
Drums.
Mean Old Yesterday.
Hughes, T.   Crow's Battle Fury.
Leaf Mould.
Memory.
Memory, A.
Ignatow, D.   I Shake My Fist at a Tree.
Journey, The.
Requiem, A: "My father, listening to music, that's me."
Sunlight, Piercing the Gloom of this House, The.
Jackson, L.   Forgiven Past, The.
Jarrell, R.   Burning the Letters.
Dead Wingman, The.
Elementary Scene, The.
Face, The.
In Those Days.
Perfectly Free Association, A.
Player Piano, The.
Venetian Blind, The.
When I Was Home Last Christmas.
Jeffers, R.   Ossian's Grave.
Johnson, S.   In Rivum a Mola Stoana Lichfeldiæ Diffluentem.
Jonson, B.   Mind of the Frontispiece to a Book, The.
Kinnell.   Frog Pond, The.
River That Is East, The.
Kipling, R.   Bells and Queen Victoria, The.
Files, The.
Fires, The.
Kizer, C.   Anniversaries: Claremont Avenue, from 1945.
Koch, K.   Circus, The.
Fate.
To Marina.
With Janice.
Komunyakaa.   Report from the Skull's Diorama.
When Loneliness Is a Man.
Kumin, M.   Envelope, The.
How It Is.
Kunitz, S.   Abduction, The.
Parting.
Larkin, P.   Daily Things We Do, The.
Heaviest of Flowers, the Head.
I Remember, I Remember.
Morning at Last: There in the Snow.
So through that unripe day you bore your head.
Story.
Whatever Happened?
Winter Palace, The.
Laughlin, J.   Bavarian Gentian, The.

Before I Die.
Deconstructed Man, The.
Eros as Archaeologist.
Interdiction, The.
It's Indelicate.
Lady Asks Me, A.
Leave-taking, A.
Parable, A.
Prisoner's Song, The.
Snow in May.
Summons, The.
When You Danced.
Lawrence, D. H.   After All Saints' Day.
After School.
Argonauts, The.
At the Cearne.
Dreams Old and Nascent.
Dreams Old and Nascent: Nascent.
Dreams Old and Nascent: Old.
Elegy: "Sun immense and rosy, The."
Forecast.
Hymn to Priapus.
Love Song, A: "Reject me not if I should say to you."
Piano.
Red-Herring.
Reminder.
Scent of Irises.
Southern Night.
Levertov.   Eyes and No-Eyes.
Note to Olga (1966), A.
Old People Dozing.
Time Past, A.
Travels.
Woman Meets an Old Lover, A.
Levine, P.   Genius.
Gift for a Believer.
Hold Me.
No One Remembers.
Winter Words.
Li Po.   Exile's Letter.
Lindsay, N.   Eagle That Is Forgotten, The.
Longfellow, H.   Fire of Drift-Wood, The.
My Lost Youth.
Lorde.   As I Grew Up Again.
Change of Season.
Hard Love Rock.
Martha.
Movement Song.
Spring People.
MacDiarmid, H.   Crystals like Blood.
Eemis-Stane, The.
MacLeish.   Baccalaureate.
Crossing.
De Votre Bonheur Il ne Reste Que Vos Photos.
Edwin Muir.
Ever Since.
Great Contemporary Discoveries.
Memory Green.
Return.
Sentiments for a Dedication.
Waking.
William Adams Delano.
MacNeice.   Carrick Revisited.
Casualty, The.
News-Reel, The.
Ravenna.
Soap Suds.
Mahon.   Thinking of Inis Oírr in Cambridge, Mass.
Major, C.   Guy I Know on 47th and Cottage, A.
Train Stop.
Mallarmé.   Remembrance of Belgian Friends.
Marvell.   Gallery, The.
McGrath, T.   In Praise of Necessity.
Memorial.
Remembering Loves and Deaths.
Residencies.
McHugh, H.   Curve.
Medici.   Beside a running brook my lady stands.
Melville, H.   Age of the Antonines, The.
Stonewall Jackson.
Meredith, R.   Change in Recurrence.
Epitaph on the Tombstone of James Christopher Wilson.
He where the great sun looks his last.

Youth in Memory.
Meredith, W.   In Memory of Donald A. Stauffer.
Merrill, J.   Amsterdam.
Another August.
Blue Grotto, The.
Broken Home, The.
Chimes for Yahya.
David's Night in Veliès.
Days of 1935.
Days of 1941 and '44.
Days of 1964.
Last Words.
Manos Karastefanís.
Mornings in a New House.
Scenes of Childhood.
Strato in Plaster.
Tenancy, A.
Up and Down.
Urban Convalescence, An.
Vision of the Garden, A.
Merton.   Early Legend, The.
Merwin.   Crossroads of the World Etc., The.
Mountain Town.
Poem, The: "Coming late, as always."
Recognition.
Talking.
To Be Sung while Still Looking.
Millay, E.   Cameo, The.
Mindful of you the sodden earth in spring.
Not only love plus awful grief.
Only until this cigarette is ended.
Sometimes, oh, often, indeed, in the midst of ugly adversity, beautiful.
Sonnet: "What lips my lips have kissed, and where, and why."
Time does not bring relief; you all have lied.
Milosz, C.   Capri.
Family, A.
I Do Not Understand.
In Salem.
Kazia.
Lastingness.
Mister Hanusevich.
Pierson College.
Polka-dot Dress, A.
Return.
Spirit of the Laws, The.
Yellow Bicycle.
Montale.   Delta.
From a Tower.
Muldoon, P.   History.
Soap-Pig, The.
Nash, O.   All, All Are Gone, the Old Familiar Quotations.
Ask Daddy, He Won't Know.
Mr. Betts's Mind a Kingdom Is.
Nemerov.   Amnesty.
Anniversary.
Blue Suburban.
For the Squadron.
For W———, Who Commanded Well.
Home for the Holidays.
Old Warplane, An.
Quarry, The.
Returning to Europe.
Snow Globe, The.
Sunderland.
To Clio, Muse of History.
Neruda.   Oliverio Girondo.
Today How Many Hours.
O'Hara, F.   Animals.
First Dances.
In Favor of One's Time.
In Memory of My Feelings.
Kitville.
Now That I Am in Madrid and Can Think.
Ode to Michael Goldberg ('s Birth and Other Births).
Poem: "That's not a cross look it's a sign of life."
Poem V (F) W.
Oliver, M.   Picking Blueberries, Austerlitz, New York, 1957.
Olson, C.   At Yorktown.
Chain of memory is resurrection I am a vain man, The.

February 10, One Year Too Late.
Incunabula, 1958.
She, Thus.
Spring Song for Cagli, A.
There Is No River Which Is Called Lethe.
Thing Was Moving, The.
Oppen. Dream, The.
Forms of Love, The.
Speech at Soli, The.
Owen, W. My Shy Hand.
Roads Also, The.
To My Friend (With an Identity Disc).
Unreturning, The.
Pagis. Final Examination.
Point of Departure.
Paley, G. People in My Family.
Palmer, M. November Talks.
Parker, D. But Not Forgotten.
Pasolini. Tears of the Excavator, The.
Patchen. Nervousness of Memory, The.
Pessoa. Recalling who I was, I see somebody else.
Whatever stops is death, and is our death.
Petrarch. So feeble is the thread that doth the burden stay.
Piercy. Valley Where I Don't Belong, A.
What the Owl Sees.
Pinsky. Pleasure Pier.
Questions, The.
Street of Furthest Memory, The.
Time of Year, the Time of Day, The.
Woman, A.
Plath. Green Rock, Winthrop Bay.
Thin People, The.
Poe. To F——.
Pound, E. Villonaud for This Yule.
Raine, K. After Fifty-five Years.
Ah, many, many are the dead.
Campanula.
Eider afloat in the bay.
Flower, memory—.
Images.
Petal of white rose.
Still skies, still seas.
Ramanujan. Breaded Fish.
Copper Vat, A.
On Memory.
Ransom, J. Antique Harvesters.
Equilibrists, The.
Rexroth, K. In the Memory of Andrée Rexroth.
Prolegomenon to a Theodicy, A.
Signature of All Things, The.
Singing Voice, A.
Rich, A. Dreamwood.
For L.G.: Unseen for Twenty Years.
For Memory.
From the Prison House.
Grandmothers.
Life and Letters.
Living Memory.
Mathilde in Normandy.
Pierrot Le Fou.
Stelae, The.
Riley, J. Old Man's Memory, An.
Ritsos. Plaster Model.
Remembrance.
Robinson, E. Alma Mater.
Calverly's.
Souvenir.
Roethke. Dream, The.
Memory.
Our Lady's Winter Words.
Praise to the End!
Premonition, The.
Reminder, The.
Sententious Man, The.
Rossetti, C. Echo.
From Sunset to Star Rise.
Have You Forgotten?
I said within myself: I am a fool.
I wish I were a little bird.
Last Look, The.
Listen, and I will tell you of a face.
Looking back along life's trodden way.
Love Lies Bleeding.
Memory.

One Sea-Side Grave.
Remember [Me].
Shall I Forget?
Song: "She sat and sang alway."
They Desire a Better Country.
Three Seasons.
Undine.
Zara.
Rossetti, D. Memory.
Portrait, The.
Rukeyser, M. Clouds, Airs, Carried Me Away.
For Memory.
Key, The.
Love and its Doors and Windows.
Sea has opened, the limit of his dream, The.
Seventh Elegy. Dream-Singing Elegy.
Sundays, They Sleep Late.
What Do I Give You?
Woman as Market.
Sandburg, C. Acquaintance with Death, Sir.
Aztec.
Bird Footprint.
Chords.
Consolation Sonata.
Drumnotes.
Dust.
Haunts.
Haze.
High Moments.
Home Thoughts.
Hungry and Laughing Men.
In a Back Alley.
Instructions.
Keepsake Boxes.
Kisses, Can You Come Back like Ghosts?
Medallion.
Medley.
Memoir of a Proud Boy.
Memoranda.
Metamorphosis.
New Hampshire Again.
Pearl Horizons.
Personalia.
Plaster.
River Moon.
Rose Bawn.
Scroll.
Shenandoah Journey.
Stars, Songs, Faces.
Swirl.
Tawny.
Throwbacks.
Timber Wings.
Troths.
Two.
Valley Song.
White Shoulders.
Sappho. Someone I tell you will remember us.
Sarton, M. Charleston Plantations.
Der Abschied.
Garden of Childhood, The.
Letter to James Stephens, A.
Schuyler, J. Autumn Leaves.
Hymn to Life.
Seifert. Bombing of the Town of Kralupy, The.
Fingerprints.
Merry-Go-Round with White Swan.
Sexton. Baby Picture.
Bells, The.
Cripples and Other Stories.
Divorce.
Exorcists, The.
February 4th.
For Johnny Pole on the Forgotten Beach.
Hex, The.
Hoarder, The.
House, The.
I Remember.
Inventory of Goodbyes, The.
January 1st.
Kind Sir: These Woods.
Kite, The.
Lost Lie, The.
Love Song: "I was / the girl of the chain letter."
Loving the Killer.
Mother and Jack and the Rain.

Old.
Speaking Bitterness.
Those Times.
Waking Alone.
Walking in Paris.
What's That.
Shapiro, K. Nigger.
Shelley, P. Fragment: The Sepulchre of Memory.
Letter to Maria Gisborne.
Lines: "Far, far away, O ye."
Ode Written October, 1819, An.
Past, The.
Remembrance.
To ——: "Music, when soft voices die."
"Shu Ting." Bits of Reminiscence.
Simic. Empire of Dreams.
Wall, A.
Smith, S. Northumberland House.
Portrait (I).
Ride, The.
Watchful.
Widowhood or The Home-Coming of Lady Ross.
Snyder, G. At White River Roadhouse in the Yukon.
For Lew Welch in a Snowfall.
For the Boy Who Was Dodger Point Lookout Fifteen Years Ago.
Four Poems for Robin.
Look Back.
Seaman's Ditty.
Working on the '58 Willys Pickup.
Spender, S. From My Diary.
Ice.
Photograph, The.
Sign *Faehre nach Wilm*, The.
Stafford, W. Fall Journey.
In the White Sky.
Remembering.
Troubleshooting.
Stevens, W. Anglais Mort à Florence.
Clear Day and No Memories, A.
Stockton, A. Elegy Inscribed to Richard J Stockton Esqr [Feb. 28, 1787].
Swinburne. Sundew, The.
Sze. Archipelago.
Before Completion.
Halibut, The.
Szymborska, W. May 16, 1973.
Séance.
Travel Elegy.
Tate, A. Bizarre.
Eye, The.
Mary McDonald.
Tennyson, A. In the Valley of Cauteretz.
Tomlinson, C. In Memoriam Thomas Hardy.
Movements.
Old Man at Valdez.
Poem for My Father.
Way of a World, The.
Unknown, sometimes at. to Sir Walter Ralegh.
Vertue the Best Monument.
Updike. Home Movies.
July.
Leaving Church Early.
Shillington.
Solitary Pond, The.
To a Dead Flame.
Van Duyn. Photographs.
Recovery.
Speak, Memory!
Stream, The.
Woman Waiting.
Very. Memory ("Soon the silver chord is broken").
To notice other days were pages given.
Walcott. Brise Marine.
Glory Trumpeter, The.
Letter from Brooklyn, A.
Parang.
Return to D'Ennery; Rain.
Village Life, A.
Warren, R. Far West Once.
I Am Dreaming of a White Christmas: The Natural History of a Vision.

Memory Forgotten.
Prophecy.
Small White House.
Upwardness.
Why You Climbed Up.
Weiss, T.   Poem Recalled, A.
Ten Little Rembrandts.
Whalen, P.   Slop Barrel, The.
Wheatley, P.   On Recollection.
Whitman, W.   As Toilsome I Wander'd
  Virginia's Woods.
Dying Veteran, The.
Glimpse, A.
Memories.
My Picture-Gallery.
Old Man's Thought of School, An.
Old War-Dreams.
Once I Pass'd through a Populous City.
Out of the Cradle Endlessly Rocking.
Whittier.   Abram Morrison.
Album Verses.
Autograph, An.
Burning Drift-Wood.
Countess, The.
Golden Wedding of Longwood, The.
Hampton Beach.
Hill-Top, The.
Homestead, The.
Kenoza Lake.
Last Walk in Autumn, The.
Lydia H. Sigourney.
Memories.
Remembrance.
Snow-Bound [or Snow-Bound; a Winter Idyl].
Sweet Fern.
Telling the Bees.
To My Old Schoolmaster.
Within the Gate.
Wilbur, R.   Finished Man, A.
He Was.
Mill, The.
Mind-Reader, The.
Pardon, The.
Piazza di Spagna, Early Morning.
Sirens, The.
Williams, C. K.   Ashes Ashes We All Fall
  Down.
Blades.
Clay out of Silence.
Combat.
I'd forgotten and / how could I ever.
Nostalgia.
Of What Is Past.
Repression.
Still Life.
This Is a Sin.
Time: 1976.
Williams, M.   Documenting It.
Memory.
Vanishing Point, The.
Williams, W.   Apparition, The.
Paterson, Book V: The River of Heaven.
Song: "You are forever April."
To a Dog Injured in the Street.
Wilner, E.   Changing the Imperatives.
Wordsworth, W.   Author's Voyage down the
  Rhine (Thirty Years Ago).
"Beloved Vale!" I said, "when I shall con."
Bothwell Castle.
Complaint, A.
Evening Walk, An; Addressed to a Young Lady.
Her Only Pilot the Soft Breeze, the Boat.
I Wandered Lonely as a Cloud.
Memory.
Remembrance of Collins, Composed upon the
  Thames near Richmond.
Sonnet (To an Octogenarian).
Surprised by joy—impatient as the Wind.
To Joanna.
Upon Perusing the "Epistle [To Sir George
  Howland Beaumont]" Thirty Years after Its
  Composition.
Wright, C.   All Landscape Is Abstract, and
  Tends to Repeat Itself.
Driving through Tennessee.
Gate City Breakdown.

Homage to Paul Cézanne.
In the Valley of the Magra.
Journal of the Year of the Ox, A.
Looking Again at What I Looked at for
  Seventeen Years.
Negatives 2.
Other Side of the River, The.
Self-Portrait.
Silent Generation, The.
Southern Cross, The.
Sprung Narratives.
Virginia Reel.
Waiting for Tu Fu.
Yard Journal.
Wright, J.   Albuquerque Graveyard, The.
Christmas Greeting, A.
In Memory of Leopardi.
Summer Memory in the Crowded City, A.
Sun Tan at Dusk.
Wyatt, S.   Lover Showeth How He Is Forsaken
  of Such as He Sometime Enjoyed, The.
My sweet, alas, forget me not.
Steadfastness.
When that I call unto my mind.
Yeats.   Broken Dreams.
Circus Animals' Desertion, The.
He Thinks of His Past Greatness When a Part of
  the Constellations of Heaven.
Image from a Past Life, An.
Old Memory.
People, The.
To a Young Girl.
Tower, The.
When You Are Old.
Zagajewski.   From Memory.
Fruit.
House, The.
Zaturenska.   Strange Captivity.
Zukofsky, L.   Record, The.
Strange / To reach that age.

Memphis, Tennessee
Clifton, L.   Memphis.
Hughes, L.   Beale Street.
Beale Street Love.

Men
Angelou.   Men.
To a Man.
Atwood.   Aging Female Poet Sits on the
  Balcony.
Eventual Proteus.
Werewolf Movies.
Berry, W.   To Think of the Life of a Man.
Berryman.   Huddle of Need, A.
Blake, W.   Woman scaly & a Man all Hairy, A.
Bly, R.   Fifty Males Sitting Together.
Bogan, L.   Men Loved Wholly beyond Wisdom.
Borges.   Hengist Wants Men (A.D. 449).
Brooks, G.   "Strong Men, Riding Horses."
Browning, E.   Island, An.
Man and Nature.
Bukowski.   Cows in Art Class.
Gypsies near Del Mar, The.
Burns, R.   Epitaph on a Henpecked Country
  Squire.
Green Grow[s] the Rashes.
On a Dog of Lord Eglinton's.
Song: "Let not Woman e'er complain."
To Daunton Me.
Carew, T.   Conquest by Flight.
Clifton, L.   Leda 3.
Codrescu.   "MAN" and "WOMAN," these are
  horrid words, they annoy me.
Creeley.   Circle, The.
Joke, The.
Men.
Sentence, The.
Cummings, E. E.   This young question mark
  man.
De la Mare.   Hare, A.
Speech.
Donne.   Manliness.
Dugan, A.   On a Myth. On a Conventional
  Wisdom.
Eberhart, R.   Bells of a Chinese Temple, The.
Death in the Mines.
Gnat on My Paper.

John Finley.
Man and Nature.
Man Who Was Blown Down by the Wind, A.
Marrakech.
Old Tree by the Penobscot.
Poet, The.
R. G. E.
Redemption.
Spring Mountain Climb.
To Kenya Tribesmen, the Turkana.
Vastness and Indifference of the World, The.
Waiting to Lean to the Master's Command.
Wild Life and Tamed Life.
Gallagher, T.   Black Silk.
Woman-Enough.
Glück, L.   Labor Day.
Palais des Arts.
Graves, R.   Dans un Seul Lit.
Frightened Men.
Gateway, The.
Iron Palace.
Sail and Oar.
With the Gift of a Lion's Claw.
Gunn, T.   Innocence.
"H. D."   Contest, The.
Dancer, The.
Master, The.
Hacker, M.   She Bitches about Boys.
Herrick.   Gods Mirth, Mans Mourning.
To the Ladyes.
Hughes, L.   Man into Men.
Ignatow, D.   Brief Cases.
Kipling, R.   Female of the Species, The.
If—.
Komunyakaa.   Unnatural State of the Unicorn.
Larkin, P.   Breadfruit.
Lawrence, D. H.   Fellow-Men.
Female Coercion.
How Beastly the Bourgeois Is.
I Dare Do All.
Let Us Be Men.
Men and Women.
Mournful Young Man.
She Said as Well to Me.
Sight of God, The.
Levertov.   Abel's Bride.
Mutes, The.
Levine, P.   Having Been Asked "What Is a
  Man?" I Answer.
Lorde.   Hard Love Rock II.
Seventh Sign, The.
MacDiarmid, H.   One of the Principal Causes of
  War.
McHugh, H.   Two Loves.
Melville, H.   On the Photograph of Corps
  Commander.
Meredith, G.   Ballad of Fair Ladies in Revolt, A.
Merton.   First Lesson about Man.
It would be wrong to let one man.
Man the Master.
Muldoon, P.   Why Brownlee Left.
Nash, O.   Hearts and Flowers or What I Know
  about Bolivar Black.
Just Wrap It Up, and I'll Throw It Away Later.
Oh, Shucks, Ma'am, I Mean Excuse Me.
Who Understands Who Anyhow?
Olson, C.   Bigmans.
Cause, the Cause, The.
Company of Men, The.
Gloss, A.
Help Me, Venus, You Who Led Me On.
Moebius Strip, The.
This Man's Weakness Is Straw.
Troilus.
Orr, G.   Like Any Other Man.
Who'd Want to Be a Man?
Paley, G.   Is There a Difference between Men
  and Women.
Parker, D.   Ballade of a Complete Flop.
Chant for Dark Hours.
De Profundis.
Experience.
Men.
Men; A Hate Song.
Men I'm Not Married To.
Second Oldest Story, The.

Song of One of the Girls.
Song of Perfect Propriety.
Plath. Gulliver.
  I Want, I Want.
Pope, A. To a Lady with the Temple of Fame.
Prime, B. Poetical Correspondence between
  Palemon and Æmilia, A.
Prunty. Grown Men at Touch.
Rich, A. For L.G.: Unseen for Twenty Years.
  From a Survivor.
  Likeness.
  Mother-Right.
  Natural Resources.
  Phenomenology of Anger, The.
  Re-forming the Crystal.
  Trying to Talk with a Man.
  Waking in the Dark.
Rimbaud, A. Once, animals spewed sperm as
  they charged.
Ritsos. Our Old Men.
Rossetti, C. Exultate Deo.
  Heaven Overarches Earth and Sea.
  Surely there is an aching void within.
  Two Rossettis (Brothers They), The.
Rukeyser, M. Light falling on that filled will
  drives.
Sandburg, C. Glimmer.
  Plaster.
  Three Shrines.
Schuyler, J. Royals.
Sexton. Assassin, The.
Smith, S. Beware the Man.
  Eng.
  Major Macroo.
  Man I Am, A.
Stafford, W. Men.
Stockton, A. Poetical Correspondence between
  Palemon and Æmilia, A.
  To Miss Mary Stockton, an Epistle upon Some
    Gentleman Refusing to Admit Ladies of Their
    Circle into the Parlour till Supper.
Swift, J. Dean Swift's Answer to the Reverend
  Dr. Sheridan.
Thomas, D. I, in My Intricate Image.
  I See the Boys of Summer.
  Seed-at-Zero, The.
Tomlinson, C. Word in Edgeways, A.
Van Duyn. Cities of the Plain, The.
Walker, A. Did This Happen to Your Mother?
  Did Your Sister Throw Up a Lot?
Ward, N. Mercury shew'd Apollo, Bartas Book.
Whitman, W. I Sing the Body Electric.
Williams, C. K. Dominion: Depression.
  It Is This Way with Men.
Williams, T. Everyman.
  Winter Smoke Is Blue and Bitter.
Williams, W. Atlantic City Convention, The.
  Gossips, The.
  Marriage.
  Men, The.
  Old Men, The.
Yeats. Man Young and Old, A.
  Men Improve with the Years.
Zukofsky, L. For you I have emptied the
  meaning.
  Green plant grows, The.
Menageries
See **Zoos**
Menopause
Clifton, L. To My Last Period.
Lawrence, D. H. Change of Life.
Menstruation
Clifton, L. Poem in Praise of Menstruation.
  Wishes for Sons.
Hacker, M. Peterborough.
Millay, E. Menses.
Rukeyser, M. Rite.
Sexton. Menstruation at Forty.
Mental Illness
Ammons. One More Time.
Berryman. Death Ballad.
  Hell Poem, The.
  I Know.
  Opus Dei.
  Purgatory.
Bishop, E. Faustina, or Rock Roses.

Bogan, L. Evening in the Sanitarium.
Brodsky, J. Gorbunov and Gorchakov.
Carver, R. Mother.
  Sensitive Girl, The.
Cowper, W. Shrubbery, The.
Davie, D. Garland for Ivor Gurney, A.
Dickey, J. Moon Flock.
Frost, R. Servant to Servants, A.
Ginsberg, A. Kaddish.
Gunn, T. Old Meg.
Hacker, M. Callers, The.
Hughes, T. Tender Place, The.
Jacobsen, J. April Asylum.
Kipling, R. Mother's Son, The.
Komunyakaa. Cops Call Him Charlie, The.
  John Says.
Larkin, P. Neurotics.
Lowell, R. Thanksgiving's Over.
  Waking in the Blue.
Lux. Institute of Defectology.
Mahon. Dawn at Saint Patrick's.
Millay, E. Visit to the Asylum, A.
Milosz, C. To Robert Lowell.
Muldoon, P. Edward Kienholz: *The State
  Hospital*.
Owen, W. Chances, The.
  Mental Cases.
Plath. Poem for a Birthday.
  Tulips.
Prunty. Distance into Place, The.
Schuyler, J. Pastime.
  Trip.
Sexton. Flee on Your Donkey.
  Music Swims Back to Me.
  Ringing the Bells.
  You, Doctor Martin.
Smith, S. Away, Melancholy.
  Deserter, The.
Tate, A. Madness.
Thomas, D. Love in the Asylum.
Van Duyn. Serious Case, A.
Williams, C. K. Cave, The.
Williams, M. At Three Every Thursday
  Afternoon.
Williams, W. Mental Hospital Garden, The.
Wordsworth, W. I Wandered Lonely as a Cloud.
  Oh What a Wreck! How Changed in Mien and
  Speech!
See also **Madness; Psychiatry and Psychiatrists**
Mental Retardation
Gunn, T. As Expected.
  Sweet Things.
Mephistopheles
See **Satan**
Mercenaries
Housman. Epitaph on an Army of Mercenaries.
Jonson, B. To Captain Hungry.
Li Po. Knight, The.
MacDiarmid, H. Another Epitaph on an Army
  of Mercenaries.
Petrarch. O Italy, my land, words cannot heal.
Merchants
Browning, R. Melon-Seller, The.
Cavafy. Alexandrian Merchant.
Dickinson, E. I asked no other thing.
HaNagid. Commerce Has Markets.
Herrick. Upon Rook: Epigram.
Jonson, B. To My Bookseller.
Kinsella, T. Scylla and Charybdis.
Meredith, G. Linnet-Hawker, The.
Meredith, W. Fishvendor, The.
Olson, C. Move Over.
Pagis. Sugarduke.
See also **Business and Businessmen; Clerks**
Mercury (god)
Browning, E. Mercury Carries Psyche to
  Olympus.
Carruth, H. Little Old Funky Homeric Blues for
  Herm, A.
Creeley. Prayer to Hermes.
Hamill, S. Hermes Rising.
Komunyakaa. Slam, Dunk, & Hook.
Lawrence, D. H. London Mercury.
  Maximus.
Ritsos. Messenger.

Unknown. On a Thief.
Williams, M. Getting the Message.
Mercy
Amichai [*or* Amikhai]. God Full of Mercy.
  God Has Pity on Kindergarten Children.
Angelou. On a Bright Day, Next Week.
Atwood. Not the Moon.
Beckett, S. Sanies II.
Berry, W. Poem of Thanks, A.
Bierce. Law.
Bishop, E. Fish, The.
Broumas, O. Mercy.
Browning, E. Cry of the Human, The.
Campion, T. Lift up to heav'n, sad wretch, thy
  heavy spright.
Cavalcanti. If only Mercy befriended my
  desires.
Chaucer. ABC, An.
Ciardi, J. Elegy 1: "I fell from the bouncing
  tailgate to roll in traffic."
  Plea, A.
Clough. In Stratis Viarum III.
Cooper, J. Infusion Room, The.
Emerson, R. Forbore the ant hill, shunned to
  tread.
Frost, R. Masque of Mercy, A.
Gunn, T. Clock, The.
Gurney, I. For Mercy of Death.
Hardy, T. Burghers, The.
  Often when Warring.
Herbert, G. Discipline.
Herrick. Calling, and Correcting.
  Clemency.
  Gods Mercy.
  Mercy.
  Mercy and Love.
  More Mighty, the More Merciful, The.
  Pittie, and Punishment.
  Song: "Burne, or drowne me, choose ye
  whether."
  To Heaven.
Hughes, L. Prayer ("Gather up / In the arms of
  your pity").
  Sinner.
Levertov. Many Mansions, The.
Levine, P. Angel Butcher.
Lindsay, N. Kind of Scorn, A.
Melville, H. Rebel Color-Bearers at Shiloh.
Meredith, G. At the Close.
  Main Regret, The.
Merton. Litany: "Sing miserere / For the men
  who must die."
Michelangelo Buonarroti. Great mercy, my
  lady, as likely as great pain.
  I'll surely be thought a dullard in talent, art.
  It seems, Love, out you've flung.
  Your kindness to me, and the ways of fate.
Milosz, C. Ballad of Levallois.
Patchen. Lasting Seasons, The.
  Quantity of Mercy, The.
Ralegh, S. Conjectural First Draft of the
  Petition to Queen Anne.
  Passionate Man[']s Pilgrimage, The.
Rich, A. Dien Bien Phu.
Riley, J. God's Mercy.
Rossetti, C. Alas my Lord, / How should I
  wrestle all the livelong night.
  Are Ye Not Much Better than They?
  Before the Beginning.
  Hymn: "O the bitter shame and sorrow."
  O Lord, I am ashamed to seek Thy Face / As
  tho' I loved Thee as Thy saints love Thee.
  One of the Soldiers with a Spear Pierced His
  Side.
  Out of the Deep.
  Seven vials hold Thy wrath: but what can hold.
  Sooner or later: yet at last / The Jordan must be
  past.
  Tuesday in Holy Week.
  Word for the Dumb, A.
Rumi. Cry Out in Your Weakness.
Sandburg, C. Rain Winds Blow Doors Open.
Sexton. Children, The.
Spender, S. Girl Who Has Drowned Herself
  Speaks, A.
Szymborska, W. Commemoration.

Villon. Epitaph in Form of a Ballad, The.
Wheatley, P. On Being Brought from Africa to America.
Whittier. Brother of Mercy, The.
  Captain's Well, The.
  Divine Compassion.
  Gift of Tritemius, The.
  Giving and Taking.
  How the Women Went from Dover.
  "I Was a Stranger and Ye Took Me in."
  King Solomon and the Ants.
  Rabbi Ishmael.
  Requital.
  Robin, The.
  Two Angels, The.
  Two Rabbins, The.
Williams, C. K. Cracks.
Wordsworth, W. Gravestone upon the Floor in the Cloisters of Worcester Cathedral, A.
Wright, J. Two Poems about President Harding.

Merlin
Emerson, R. Merlin.
  Merlin's Song.
Gunn, T. Merlin in the Cave: He Speculates without a Book.
Hill, G. Merlin.
Merton. Merlin and the Deer.
Robinson, E. Merlin.
Wilbur, R. Merlin Enthralled.
Wordsworth, W. Egyptian Maid; or, The Romance of the Water Lilly, The.

Mermaid Tavern, London
Keats. Lines on the Mermaid Tavern.

Mermaids and Mermen
De la Mare. Old Angler, The.
Hopkins, G. Vision of the Mermaids, A.
Hughes, L. Catch.
Jacobsen, J. Poet as Mute.
Lindsay, N. Queen Mab in the Village.
  Would-Be Merman, The.
Lowell, R. Mermaid Emerging.
MacLeish. Return.
Muldoon, P. Merman, The.
Nash, O. Mermaid, The.
Szymborska, W. Thomas Mann.
Wilner, E. Concerto.

Merrimac (ship)
See **Monitor (ship)**

Merriment
Burns, R. Epistle to J. R******, Enclosing Some Poems.
  Fête Champetre, The.
  Hey Ca' thro'.
  Hey Tuti Tatey.
  Night was still, and o'er the hill, The.
  Theniel Menzies' Bony Mary.
  To Clarinda.
Clare, J. Merry Maid.
Herrick. Ceremonies for Christmas[se].
  To Be Merry.
Rossetti, C. Dancing on the hill-tops, / Singing in the valleys.
  Summer.
  Then I Commended Mirth.

Merry-Go-Rounds
Carver, R. Brass Ring, The.
Hughes, L. Merry-Go-Round.
Seifert. Merry-Go-Round with White Swan.
Stock, R. Houynhnm's Holiday.

Merwin, W. S. (William Stanley)
Logan, J. Visit to Bill Merwin at His Hawaiian Home, A.

Mesopotamia
Cavafy. Chaldaic Image.

Messengers
Browning, R. How They Brought the Good News from Ghent to Aix.
Frost, R. Bearer of Evil Tidings, The.
Glück, L. Messengers.
Gunn, T. Messenger, The.
"H. D." Hermes of the Ways.
Herrick. Present: or, The Bag of the Bee, The.
Lawrence, D. H. Love Message.
  Maximus.
Maritain. Cloud, The.

Merton. Messenger from the Horizon, A.
Palmer, M. She says, into the dark.
Ritsos. Inertia.
  Messenger.
Rumi. Dalqak's Message.
Stock, R. Bellerophon and the Portable Universe.
Williams, M. Getting the Message.
Wilner, E. Messenger, The.

Messiah
Brooks, G. In Emanuel's Nightmare: Another Coming of Christ.
Celan. Heat / counts us together, The.
Hughes, T. Gog.
Kinnell. Supper after the Last, The.
Lindsay, N. Amaranth, The.
Merton. Messias.
Pope, A. Messiah [a Sacred Eclogue, in Imitation of Virgil's Pollio].
Rimbaud, A. Just Man, The.
Yeats. Second Coming, The.

Metals
Davie, D. Metals.

Metaphor
Burns, R. Calf, The.
Clampitt. John Donne in California.
Codrescu. Seeing out of the Sub.
Collins, B. Death of Allegory, The.
Creeley. Trees.
Davie, D. Poem as Abstract.
  With the Grain.
Dugan, A. Night Scene before Combat.
Hopkins, G. Yes for a time they held as well.
Jacobsen, J. At Night.
Levertov. Cat as Cat, The.
MacLeish. Hypocrite Auteur.
Major, C. Words into Words Won't Go.
Marvell. Definition of Love, The.
Nemerov. Sestina 1: "Thickness of paint or flesh cannot deface."
Olson, C. Concerning Exaggeration, or How, Properly, to Heap Up.
Plath. Metaphors.
  Sorcerer Bids Farewell to Seem, A.
Ramanujan. Anxiety.
  PAIN: Trying to Find a Metaphor.
Rumi. Awkward Comparison, An.
Stevens, W. Metaphor as Degeneration.
  Motive for Metaphor, The.
Thomas, D. If I Were Tickled by the Rub of Love.
Warren, R. Last Metaphor, The.
Williams, W. Sort of a Song, A.
See also **Symbols**

Metaphysics
Ciardi, J. Letter from a Metaphysical Countryside.
Graves, R. Synthetic Such.
Hamill, S. Sheep to Slaughter.
MacDiarmid, H. To My Friend the Late Beatrice Hastings.
MacNeice. London Rain.
Nemerov. Frozen City, The.
  Two Sides to an Outside: Meditation from Empson.
Pessoa. Beyond God.
Rich, A. Incipience.
Robinson, E. Burning Book [or the Contented Metaphysician], The.
Tomlinson, C. In Defence of Metaphysics.
Williams, T. Two Metaphysical Sonnets.
Wright, C. California Dreaming.
Zukofsky, L. Finally a Valentine.

Meteors and Meteorites
Ammons. Dominion.
Blok. Caught by the Blizzard.
Cooper, J. Meteors.
De la Mare. Spark, The.
Emerson, R. Wisp & meteor nightly falling.
Frost, R. Loose Mountain, A.
Jarrell, R. Meteorite, The.
Niedecker. In the transcendence.
Stafford, W. Star in the Hills, The.
Thoreau. Moon moves up her smooth and sheeny path, The.

Whitman, W. Year of Meteors (1859–60).

Methodism
Davie, D. Selina, Countess of Huntingdon.
  Short Run to Camborne.
Whittier. Letter from a Missionary of the Methodist Episcopal Church South, in Kansas, to a Distinguished Politician.

Metoposcopy
Laughlin, J. I am the Metoposcoper.

Mexican War
Whittier. Angels of Buena Vista, The.

Mexico
Ai. Pentecost.
Ashbery, J. Instruction Manual, The.
Borges. Mexico.
Brodsky, J. Mexican Divertimento.
Clampitt. Tepoztlán.
Corbière. Letter from Mexico (Vera Cruz, 10 February, 186–).
Crane, H. Purgatorio.
Dove, R. Night Watch.
Eberhart, R. Santa Claus in Oaxaca.
Ferlinghetti, L. Baja Beatitudes.
  Baja Revisited.
Ginsberg, A. Dream Record: June 8 1955.
  One could pass valuable months.
  Siesta in Xbalba.
  What solitude I've / finally inherited.
Graves, R. La Mejicana.
Hayden, R. Inference of Mexico, An.
Hughes, L. Mexican Market Woman.
Jacobsen, J. Painter at Xyochtl.
Jarrell, R. Indian Market in Mexico, An.
Lawrence, D. H. Beyond the Rockies.
  Coming of Quetzalcoatl, The.
  First Song of Huitzilopochtli.
  Jesus' Farewell.
  Living Quetzalcoatl, The.
  Quetzalcoatl Looks Down on Mexico.
  Second Song of Huitzilopochtli.
  Song of Don Ramon, The.
  Third Song of Huitzilopochtli.
  Welcome to Quetzalcoatl.
  What Quetzalcoatl Saw in Mexico.
Levertov. Five Poems from Mexico.
  Mystery (Oaxaca, Mexico), A.
Logan, J. Lines for a Young Wanderer in Mexico.
Lux. What Montezuma Fed Cortés and His Men.
Major, C. Rainy Season, The.
McGrath, T. Tourists at Ensenada.
Neruda. Heights of Macchu Picchu, III, The.
Oppen. Acapulco.
  Coastal Strip.
  Mayan Ground, The.
  Resort.
  To the Muse.
Paz. Hymn among the Ruins.
Rexroth, K. Gradualism.
  Oaxaca 1925.
Rukeyser, M. Gold Leaf.
Stevens, W. Sea Surface Full of Clouds.
Tomlinson, C. Bootblack, The.
  Constitution Day.
  Los Pobrecitos.
  Oaxaca Bus, The.
  On a Mexican Straw Christ.
  On the Tlacolula Bus.
  Plaza, The.
  Teotihuacán.
  Valle de Oaxaca.
  Well, The.
Van Duyn. Into Mexico.
Warren, R. Mexico Is a Foreign Country: Five Studies in Naturalism.
Williams, W. Desert Music, The.
Wright, J. Destination: Accomplished.
  Minneapolis Poem, The.

Mexico City
Dubie. Trolley from Xochimilco, The.
Wilner, E. Winged Victory.
Wright, J. Chapultepec Castle.
  Inside Chapultepec Castle.
  Meeting Her in Chapultepec.

Museums in Chapultepec, The.
Walking Chapultepec.

Mice
Ammons. Lion::Mouse.
Auden. Talking to Mice.
Bishop, E. Hanging of the Mouse, The.
Burns, R. To a Mouse; On Turning Her up in Her Nest, with the Plough, November, 1785.
Carruth, H. Mouse, The.
Celan. By Threes, By Fours.
Collins, B. I Chop Some Parsley while Listening to Art Blakey's Version of "Three Blind Mice."
Cummings, E. E. Four III.
Me Up at Does.
Mouse)Won / derfully is.
Dickinson, E. Papa above!
Dugan, A. Another Cat Poem. To a Cat Person.
Funeral Oration for a Mouse.
Eberhart, R. Emblem.
Equivalence of Gnats and Mice.
To the Field Mice.
Graves, R. One Hard Look.
Gunn, T. Last Days at Teddington.
Hughes, T. Cat and Mouse.
Memory.
Small Events.
Kunitz, S. Waltzer in the House, The.
Levi, P. Mouse, A.
Lindsay, N. Mouse That Gnawed the Oak-Tree Down, The.
What Grandpa Mouse Said.
Logue, C. Cats are full of death.
Lucilius. Miser and the Mouse, The.
Moore, M. Camellia Sabina.
Nash, O. Down the Mousehole, and What Science Missed There.
Pagis. Harvests.
Patchen. Magical Mouse, The.
Roethke. Meadow Mouse, The.
Rossetti, C. City Mouse and the Garden Mouse, The.
My Mouse.
Rumi. Force of Friendship, The.
Long String, The.
Mouse and a Frog, A.
Mouse and the Camel, The.
Smith, S. Cat Asks Mouse Out.
Stafford, W. By the Deschutes Shore.
Stevens, W. Dance of the Macabre Mice.
Unknown. Another ["Miser, traversing his house, A"].
Updike. Mouse Sex.
Williams, M. Inference.
Williams, W. Mujer.

Michael, Saint
García Lorca. St. Michael.
Ransom, J. First Travels of Max.
Rossetti, C. St. Michael and all Angels.

Michelangelo Buonarroti
Blake, W. Florentine Ingratitude.
Pitiful Case, A.
Sir Joshua Praises Michael Angelo.
Browning, R. "Moses" of Michael Angelo, The.
Dubie. Saints of Negativity, The.
Lawrence, D. H. Michael Angelo.
MacLeish. Ship in the Tomb.
Stock, R. Ballade to be Read in the Medici Gardens.

Michigan (state)
Ciardi, J. Was a Man.
Hall, D. Kicking the Leaves.
Letter to an English Poet.
Levine, P. Making It New.
Poem Circling Hamtramck, Michigan, All Night in Search of You, The.
Rain Downriver.
O'Hara, F. Ann Arbor Variations.
Riley, J. Artemus of Michigan, The.
Sandburg, C. Dialogue.
Lake Michigan Morning.
Whalen, P. Up in Michigan.

Microbes
Auden. New Year Greeting, A.
Williams, M. Euglena.

Microcosm
Ammons. Shoreless Tide, The.
Sphere.
World.
Ciardi, J. Island Galaxy, An.
Frost, R. Design.
McHugh, H. For a Good Man.

Microscopes
Dickinson, E. "Faith" is a fine invention.

Midas
Campion, T. To his sweet Lute *Apollo* sung the motions of the Spheares.
Kizer, C. Ungrateful Garden, The.
Swift, J. Fable of Midas, The.
Tomlinson, C. Legend.
Very. Midas.

Middle Age
Amichai [*or* Amikhai]. All the Generations before Me.
If Now in the Middle of My Life.
On My Birthday.
Auden. Walk after Dark, A.
Broumas, O. Between Two Seas.
Cunningham, J. In the thirtieth year of life.
Donne. Love's Usury.
Dugan, A. On When McCarthy Was a Wolf among a Nation of Queer-Queers.
Enzensberger, H. At Thirty-Three.
Glück, L. To Autumn.
Hall, D. To a Waterfowl.
Hardy, T. Middle-Age Enthusiasms.
Jarrell, R. Next Day.
Kumin, M. Introducing the Fathers.
Progress Report.
Turning the Garden in Middle Age.
Kunitz, S. End of Summer.
Lawrence, D. H. Change of Life.
So There!
Levertov. July 1968.
Logan, J. Middle-Aged Midwesterner at Waikiki Again.
Wooden Mirror, The.
Logue, C. Middle-aged man is approaching an all-night lavatory, A.
Longfellow, H. Mezzo Cammin.
Lowell, R. Middle Age.
MacLeish. "Dover Beach"—a Note to That Poem.
MacNeice. Libertine, The.
Nash, O. Crossing the Border.
Let's Not Climb the Washington Monument Tonight.
Middle, The.
Niedecker. Woman in middle life.
Parker, D. Ballade at Thirty-Five.
Ramanujan. Case History.
Middle Age.
Rexroth, K. Delia Rexroth ("Under your illkempt yellow roses").
Rich, A. Middle-Aged, The.
Rukeyser, M. Rondel: "Now that I am fifty-six."
Schuyler, J. Few Days, A.
Growing Dark.
Morning of the Poem, The.
Sexton. Menstruation at Forty.
Swift, J. Stella's Birthday; Written in the Year 1718[/9].
Walcott. Nearing Forty.
Williams, M. Fifty.
Wilner, E. Midway the Journey of This Life.

Middle Ages
Ammons. In Strasbourg in 1349.
Auden. Ode to the Medieval Poets.
Bly, R. Fire of Despair Has Been Our Savior, The.
Browning, R. Grammarian's Funeral, A.
Dubie. Annual of the Dark Physics, An.
Meister Eckhart.
Hill, G. Requiem for the Plantagenet Kings.
Jarrell, R. Clock in the Tower of the Church, The.
Kipling, R. Dawn Wind, The.
Stock, R. Louis XI.
Szymborska, W. Medieval Miniature, A.

Midgets
Levine, P. Midget, The.

Midnight
Ammons. Driving Through.
Creeley. La Noche.
Two Ways of Looking in a Mirror.
Donne. Nocturnal[l] upon Saint Lucy's [*or* S. Lucy's *or* S. Lucies] Day, Being the Shortest Day, A.
Gurney, I. Midnight.
Ignatow, D. Midnight.
Jacobsen, J. February Midnight.
Lawrence, D. H. At Midnight.
Major, C. Round Midnight.
Olson, C. At midnight, after hours of love, I ate.
Parker, D. Midnight.
Patchen. Midnight Special.
Riley, J. In the Dark.
Ritsos. Midnight.
Warren, R. Monologue at Midnight.
Whitman, W. Clear Midnight, A.
Zagajewski. At Midnight.

Midsummer
Davie, D. Midsummer's Eve.
Hardy, T. On a Midsummer Eve.
Riley, J. Old Friend, An.

Midwives
Enzensberger, H. Midwives, The.

Mignonettes
Lawrence, D. H. Red Geranium and Godly Mignonette.

Migraine
Clampitt. Anatomy of Migraine, An.
Ramanujan. Ecology.
Tomlinson, C. History of a Malady.

Migrant Workers
Hughes, L. Migrant.
Komunyakaa. Breaking Camp.
Merwin. Under the Migrants.
Orr, G. Migrant Camps, The.
Rukeyser, M. They pray. Security against oldness.
See also **Farmworkers**

Migration
Atwood. Migration: C.P.R.
Bukowski. Fall Out.
Carver, R. Migration.
Hughes, L. New Yorkers.
One-Way Ticket.
South, The.
Kumin, M. With the Caribou.
Longfellow, H. Evangeline, a Tale of Acadie.
Sandburg, C. Mockers Go to Kansas in Spring.
Tomlinson, C. Weatherman.
Wilbur, R. Event, An.

Milan, Italy
Levine, P. And the Trains Go On.

Militarism
Cummings, E. E. Neither awake / (there's your general).
Why must itself up every of a park.
Eliot, T. S. Coriolan.
Emerson, R. One hand washes the other.
Ginsberg, A. Chicago to Salt Lake by Air.
Pentagon Exorcism.
War Profit Litany.
Hardy, T. Channel Firing.
Merton. Original Child Bomb.
Milosz, C. Artificer.
Gates of the Arsenal, The.
Sandburg, C. Mohammed Bek Hadjetlache.
Tomlinson, C. Tarquinia.
Wright, J. Undermining of the Defense Economy, The.
Zukofsky, L. Motet.

Military Conscription
Cummings, E. E. Why must itself up every of a park.
Hughes, L. Draftees.
Levertov. Speech: For Antidraft Rally, D.C., March 22, 1980, A.
Logue, C. Song of the Dead Soldier, The.
MacNeice. Conscript, The.
Sexton. Papa and Mama Dance, The.

Military Justice
Kipling, R.   Cells.
Danny Deever.
Wheatley, P.   To the Hon.ble Commodore Hood on His Pardoning a Deserter.

Military Life
Clampitt.   Letters from Jerusalem.
Meredith, W.   June: Dutch Harbor.
Milosz, C.   Incarnated.

See also **Army Life**

Military Officers
Carver, R.   Caucasus: A Romance, The.
Ciardi, J.   Health of Captains, The.
Dubie.   On the Chinese Abduction of Tibet's Child Panchen Lama.
Dugan, A.   Riding Song for a Semi-Feudal Army, for Glubb Pasha, for Tortured Colonels.
García Lorca.   Scene of the Lieutenant Colonel of the Civil Guard.
Hughes, T.   Retired Colonel, The.
Milosz, C.   Incarnated.
Stockton, A.   To the Honourable Col. Peter Schuyler.
Wheatley, P.   To Captain H—D, of the 65th Regiment.
Williams, F.   Ode, An: "At length revolving fates th' expected year."

Milk and Milking
Broumas, O.   Stars in Your Name.
Frost, R.   Cow in Apple Time, The.
Hall, D.   Great Day in the Cows' House.
Heaney, S.   Churning Day.
Milk Factory, The.
Herrick.   Fresh Cheese and Cream.
Upon Sibilla.
Komunyakaa.   Wet Nurse.
Nash, O.   Cow, The.
Ramanujan.   Mythologies 1.
Rexroth, K.   Advent.
Rossetti, C.   Brownie, Brownie, let down your milk.
Rumi.   Held like this, to draw in milk.
Schuyler, J.   Milk.
Yeats.   Spilt Milk.

Milkmaids
Hardy, T.   Milkmaid, The.
Rossetti, C.   Milking-Maid, The.
Rosy maiden Winifred, / With a milkpail on her head.
Sandburg, C.   She Opens the Barn Door Every Morning.

Milkmen
Lux.   Milkman and His Son, The.
Riley, J.   Climatic Sorcery.

Milkweed
Blue Cloud.   Milkweed.
Reflections on Milkweed.
Frost, R.   From a Milkweed Pod.
Levine, P.   Milkweed.
Paley, G.   In Deepest Summer.
Wilbur, R.   Two Voices in a Meadow.
Wright, J.   Milkweed.

Milky Way, The
Frost, R.   Milky Way Is a Cowpath, The.

Millay, Edna St. Vincent
Ciardi, J.   Instances.
Williams, T.   I see them lying sheeted in their graves.

Millennium
Collins, B.   Dancing toward Bethlehem.
Eberhart, R.   Young and the Old, the.
Frost, R.   It Is Almost the Year Two Thousand.
Ginsberg, A.   Rising over Night-Blackened Detroit Streets.
Jarrell, R.   Clock in the Tower of the Church, The.
Nash, O.   Any Millenniums Today, Lady?
Whittier.   Astræa.
Yeats.   Second Coming, The.

Miller, Henry
Williams, W.   To the Dean.

Mills and Millers
Burns, R.   Dusty Miller.
Cowper, W.   Flatting Mill, The.

Davie, D.   Cheshire.
Hardy, T.   Second Visit, The.
Hughes, L.   Steel Mills.
Jarrell, R.   Miller, The.
Komunyakaa.   Gristmill.
Lawrence, D. H.   Dark Satanic Mills.
Give Us the Thebaïd.
Lowell, R.   Mills of the Kavanaughs, The.
Riley, J.   Jolly Miller, The.
Kingry's Mill.
Old Home by the Mill, The.
Robinson, E.   Mill, The.
Sandburg, C.   Hemlock and Cedar.
Whittier.   Birchbrook Mill.
Wilbur, R.   Mill, The.

Milton, John
Blake, W.   Milton.
Borges.   Rose and Milton, A.
Cowper, W.   Stanzas on Milton's Remains.
Creeley.   Milton Über Alles.
Dryden, J.   Milton.
Duncan, R.   Years as Catches, The.
Johnson, S.   New Prologue Spoken at the Representation of *Comus*, A.
Keats.   On Seeing a Lock of Milton's Hair.
Lindsay, N.   To Eve, Man's Dream of Wifehood as Described by Milton.
Marvell.   On Mr Milton's "Paradise Lost."
Meredith, G.   Milton.
Poetry of Milton, The.
Sandburg, C.   Our Hells.
To the Ghost of John Milton.
Shelley, P.   Fragment: Milton's Spirit.
Snyder, G.   Milton by Firelight.
Tate, A.   John Milton.
Tomlinson, C.   Giovanni Diodati.
Various authors.   Complimentary Pieces to Milton.
Warren, R.   Milton: A Sonnet.
Whittier.   Milton.
Wilde, O.   To Milton.
Wordsworth, W.   Fragment of an Intended Poem on Milton, Written in the Copy of *Paradise Lost* Which Belonged to Wordsworth at Cambridge.
London 1802.
Sonnet on Milton.

Mimes
Hughes, L.   For Dead Mimes.

Mind
Ammons.   Gain.
Landscape with Figures.
Limit, The.
Medicine for Tight Spots.
Plexus.
Prodigal.
Staking Claim.
Thaw.
Touching Down.
Blue Cloud.   First Light.
Carver, R.   Attic, The.
Collins, B.   Night House, The.
Corbett, W.   Recipe for Contemplation.
Creeley.   Learning.
Davie, D.   Jottings, not so Random.
Pelican.
Dugan, A.   Untitled Poem: "Let them take to the air before."
Eliot, T. S.   Introspection.
Enzensberger, H.   Limbic System.
Komunyakaa.   Two Cranial Murals.
Laughlin, J.   Junk Collector, The.
Levertov.   Human Being.
Milosz, C.   Philosopher's Home, A.
Oppen.   Cultural Triumph, A.
Orr, G.   Hotel St. Louis, New York City, Fall 1969.
Roethke.   In a Dark Time.
Stevens, W.   Credences of Summer.
Crude Foyer.
Dwarf, The.
Man and Bottle.
Mud Master.
Of Mere Being.
Snow Man, The.
Well Dressed Man with a Beard, The.

Stockton, A.   Ode, An: "Yes tis an easy thing to view."
Sze.   Network, The.
Zagajewski.   Kierkegaard on Hegel.

See also **Intellect and Intellectuals**

Minerals
Cavafy.   Bouquets.
Levertov.   What It Could Be.
MacDiarmid, H.   Crystals like Blood.
Rukeyser, M.   Disease: After-Effects, The.
Thomas, D.   I, in My Intricate Image.

See also **Metals; Mining and Miners**

Minerva
Byron, G.   Curse of Minerva, The.
Davie, D.   Owl Minerva, The.
Herrick.   Vow to Minerva, A.
Laughlin, J.   Owl of Minerva, The.

See also **Athena**

Mingus, Charles
Komunyakaa.   Copacetic Mingus.

Mining and Miners
Ammons.   Prospecting.
Dugan, A.   On an Architect.
Dunbar, P.   Gourd, The.
Heaney, S.   Singer's House, The.
Hughes, T.   Johannesburg Mines.
Larkin, P.   Explosion, The.
Levertov.   Nightingale Road.
Levine, P.   Nitrate.
Lindsay, N.   What the Miner in the Desert Said.
Merwin.   Pieces for Other Lives.
Montale.   Punta del Mesco.
Owen, W.   Miners.
Pinkerton, H.   Elegy at Beaverhead County, Montana.
Point Lobos, 1950.
Ralegh, S.   Calybes plough not their barren soile, The.
Rukeyser, M.   Tunnel, The.
Sandburg, C.   Pennsylvania.
Sayings of Henry Stephens.
Snyder, G.   Fire in the Hole.
Milton by Firelight.
Tomlinson, C.   Gladstone Street.
Shaft, The.
Wright, J.   Miners.

See also **Coal Mining and Coal Miners; Gold Mining and Gold Miners**

Ministers
Davie, D.   Three Pastors in Berlin.
Hughes, L.   Madam and the Minister.
Stockton, A.   Fragment on the Death of a Minester.
Wheatley, P.   Elegy, Sacred to the Memory of that Great Divine, the Reverend and Learned Dr. Samuel Cooper, An.
Elegy Sacred to the Memory of the Rev'd Samuel Cooper, D.D., An.
On the Death of the Rev. Dr. Sewell. 1769.
To the Rev. Dr. Thomas Amory on Reading His Sermons on Daily Devotion, in Which that Duty Is Recommended and Assisted.

See also **Clergy**

Mink
Muldoon, P.   Mink.

Minnesota (state)
Ai.   Ice.
Berryman.   Minnesota Thanksgiving.
Bly, R.   Driving toward the Lac Qui Parle River.
Eberhart, R.   United 555.
McGrath, T.   Afternoon of a McGrath.
Warren, R.   Minneapolis Story.
Minnesota Recollection.
Wright, J.   Blessing, A.
By a Lake in Minnesota.
Centenary Note: Inscribed to Little Crow, Leader of the Sioux Rebellion in Minnesota, 1862, A.
Larry.
Lying in a Hammock at William Duffy's Farm in Pine Island, Minnesota.
Minneapolis Poem, The.
River Down Home, The.

Minotaur
Merton.   From the Second Chapter of a Verse
  History of the World.
Nemerov.   On Getting Out of Vietnam.
Rukeyser, M.   Minotaur, The.
Tomlinson, C.   Ariadne and the Minotaur.
Wilner, E.   Labyrinth.

Minstrels
De la Mare.   Unheard Melodies.
Hughes, L.   Minstrel Man.
Montale.   Minstrels.
Riley, J.   Bryant.
  Harp of the Minstrel, The.
  Ole Bull.

Miracles
Bishop, E.   Miracle for Breakfast, A.
Bly, R.   Ants.
Bukowski.   Miracle Is the Shortest Time, The.
Clifton, L.   Lazarus.
Collins, B.   Walking across the Atlantic.
Crashaw.   On the Miracle of Loaves.
  On the Miracle of Multiplied [or Multiplyed]
    Loaves.
  To Our Lord, upon the Water Made Wine.
Creeley.   Kore.
Cummings, E. E.   From spiralling ecstatically
  this.
Dickey, J.   Lazarus to the Assembled.
Dickinson, E.   No Life can pompless pass away.
Donne.   Relic, The.
  Song: "Go and catch a falling star."
Dugan, A.   Holiday.
Ginsberg, A.   Galilee Shore.
Gunn, T.   Lazarus Not Raised.
Hardy, T.   Lost Pyx, The.
Herbert, G.   Whitsunday.
Herrick.   Widow's Tears [or Widdowes Teares]:
  or, Dirge of Dorcas, The.
Kipling, R.   Our Lady of the Sackcloth.
Levertov.   Poem Rising by Its Own Weight,
  The.
Levine, P.   Miracle, The.
Melville, H.   Margrave's Birthnight, The.
Meredith, G.   Glastonbury Thorn, The.
  Miracle, The.
Merton.   Cana.
Montale.   Maybe one morning, walking in dry,
  glassy air.
Plath.   Black Rook in Rainy Weather.
Prunty.   Thaumatrope.
Ritsos.   Common Miracles.
Simic.   Small Wonders.
Stafford, W.   In the Book.
Szymborska, W.   Miracle Fair.
Tate, J.   Manna.
Whitman, W.   Miracles.
Williams, M.   One of the Crowd on the Shore
  Tells How It Was.

Mirages
De la Mare.   Mirage.
Hayden, R.   Mirages, The.
Kinnell.   Supper after the Last, The.
Montale.   Correspondences.
Raine, K.   Path, The.
Shapiro, K.   Impact.
Whitman, W.   Mirages.
Whittier.   Norembega.

Mirrors
Amichai [or Amikhai].   Eternal Mystery, The.
Ammons.   Reflective.
Atwood.   Looking in a Mirror.
  Tricks with Mirrors.
Berrigan, T.   It's Important.
Bishop, E.   Gentleman of Shalott, The.
  To Be Written on the Mirror in Whitewash.
Bogan, L.   Cupola, The.
  Man Alone.
Borges.   Beppo.
  Blind Man, A.
  Iron Coin, The.
  Mirror, The.
  Mirrors.
  Moon, The.
  To a Cat.
Browning, R.   Love in a Life.
Burns, R.   Keekin' Glass, The.

Carew, T.   Looking-Glass, A.
Carrera Andrade.   Mirror's Mission, The.
Cavafy.   Mirror in the Vestibule, The.
Ciardi, J.   Clock in the Mirror, The.
  Dialogue.
Creeley.   Shot.
Cummings, E. E.   Clown's smirk in the skull of
  a baboon, A.
  Ohld song / you Know.
  Pieces(in darker / than small is dirtiest).
Dunbar, P.   Looking-Glass, The.
Emerson, R.   Such another peerless queen.
Graves, R.   Face in the Mirror, The.
  Foreboding, The.
  Pier-Glass, The.
  Spite of Mirrors.
Gunn, T.   Behind the Mirror.
  Looking Glass.
Hardy, T.   At the Dinner-Table.
  Cheval-Glass, The.
  Honeymoon Time at an Inn.
  Lament of the Looking-Glass, The.
  Moments of Vision.
Herrick.   Upon Sibb.
Housman.   Look not in my eyes, for fear.
Ignatow, D.   I Am.
  Image, The.
Ivanov, G.   Mirrors, reflecting each other.
Kipling, R.   Looking Glass, The.
Laughlin, J.   Endless Mirrors, The.
Levertov.   Looking-glass.
Lorde.   Good Mirrors are Not Cheap.
Lowell, R.   Fat Man in the Mirror, The.
MacNeice.   Reflections.
Mallarmé.   Her pure nails on high displaying
  their onyx.
McHugh, H.   In a World of Taking, the Mistake.
  Sebastian's Mirror.
Merrill, J.   In the Hall of Mirrors.
Merwin.   Glass.
Montale.   Earrings, The.
  Pool.
Nemerov.   Glass Dialectic.
  Mirror, The.
Oppen.   Old man, The.
Petrarch.   Gold and pearls, and blossoms, white
  and red, The.
  My enemy, who often lets you gaze.
Plath.   Mirror.
Rexroth, K.   Empty Mirror.
  Mirror in the Woods, The.
Rilke.   Child at the Mirror, The.
  Double in the Mirror, The.
  Telling You All.
  Woman at Her Mirror.
Ritsos.   Known Consequences.
  Morning.
  Strange Times.
Rossetti, C.   Passing and Glassing.
Rumi.   Childhood Friends.
  Polishing the Mirror.
  Shape of My Tongue, The.
Sandburg, C.   Chicago Poet.
Stafford, W.   Your Life.
Stockton, A.   To a Little Miss a Year Older than
  the One to Whom the Glass Was Promised,
  with a Toy Looking Glass.
  To a Little Miss, with a Toy Lookingglass.
Tate, J.   Mirror, The.
Tomlinson, C.   Mirror in the Roadway, The.
Updike.   Shaving Mirror.
Warren, R.   Mirror, The.
  Nature of a Mirror, The.
Whitman, W.   Eidolons.
  Hand-Mirror, A.
  This Day, O Soul.
Williams, W.   Mists over the River.
Zaturenska.   Golden Mirror, The.

Mirth
Ammons.   Dying in a Mirthful Place.
Herrick.   Best to Be Merry.
  Gods Mirth, Mans Mourning.
  His Lachrimae or Mirth, Turn'd to Mourning.
  Hock-Cart, or Harvest Home, The.
  Hymne, to the Lares, A.
  Lyric to Mirth, A.

  Meat without Mirth.
  Meddow Verse; or, Aniversary to Mistris
    Bridget Lowman, The.
  Mirth.
  To All Young Men That Love.
  To Live Merrily, and To Trust to Good Verses.
  Upon Bran.
Meredith, G.   To the Comic Spirit.
Milton.   To Cyriack Skinner.
Williams, W.   Hic Jacet.
See also **Laughter; Merriment**

Misanthropy
Bukowski.   Ginsberg?
  I'm Getting Back to Where I Was.
  Traffic Signals.
Jeffers, R.   Bird with the Dark Plumes, The.

Miscarriages
MacDiarmid, H.   Glen of Silence, The.
Plath.   Barren Woman.

Mischief
Byron, G.   Devil's Drive, The.
Clare, J.   Young Rabbits.
Cowper, W.   On a Mischievous Bull.
Graves, R.   Nobody.
Herrick.   Upon Pagget.
Lawrence, D. H.   Flapper.
Ralegh, S.   One fire than other burnes more
  forcibly.
Riley, J.   Hik-Tee-Dik.
  Naughty Claude.

Misfortune
Beckett, S.   Ooftish.
Browning, R.   Saint Martin's Summer.
Bukowski.   Something.
Burns, R.   Jeremiah 15th Ch. 10 V.
  Lament. Occasioned by the Unfortunate Issue of
    a Friend's Amour, The.
  Man Was Made to Mourn, a Dirge.
  O raging Fortune's withering blast.
  Song.—In the Character of a Ruined Farmer.
  Though fickle fortune has deceiv'd me.
  To a Mouse; On Turning Her up in Her Nest,
    with the Plough, November, 1785.
Carver, R.   Author of Her Misfortune, The.
  Fishing Pole of the Drowned Man, The.
Chuang Tzu.   Good Fortune.
Coleridge, S.   Addressed to a Young Man of
  Fortune.
Cowper, W.   Shrubbery, The.
Crashaw.   Upon the Faire Ethiopian Sent to a
  Gentlewoman.
Dickinson, E.   One need not be a Chamber—to
  be Haunted.
Donne.   Fall of a Wall.
Graves, R.   All Except Hannibal.
  Beggar Maid and King Cophetua, The.
  Pandora.
Gray, T.   Hymn to Adversity.
Han-shan.   I'm poor alas and I'm sick.
  Trifle poor in the past, a.
  We hear about the ministers of state.
Hughes, L.   Hard Luck.
Keats.   Isabella; or, The Pot of Basil.
  Otho the Great.
Kizer, C.   Silent Man, The.
Lenau.   Three Gipsies, The.
Meredith, G.   Song: "Thou tremblest O my love!
  thy hand in mine."
  Teaching of the Blows of Fortune, The.
Petrarch.   Ever mine [or myn] hap[pe] is slack
  and slo[w] in coming [or commyng].
Roethke.   Surly One, The.
Shelley, P.   Tale of Society as It Is, A: From
  Facts, 1811.
Simic.   Misfortune Is on the Way.
Swift, J.   Addenda Quaedam.
Updike.   Sleepless in Scarsdale.
Wordsworth, W.   Thorn, The.
Wyatt, S.   Being as none is, I do complain.
  Double, diverse, sullen, and strange.
  Hap happeth oft unlooked for.
  Lover Showeth How He Is Forsaken of Such as
    He Sometime Enjoyed, The.
  She that should most, perceiveth least.
  Since love is such that, as ye wot.

To my mishap, alas, I find.
Where shall I have at mine own will.
Yeats. Ballad of Moll Magee, The.

Mishima, Yukio
Ai. Nothing but Color.

Misogyny
Clare, J. Song: "I peeled bits of straw and I got switches too."
Lorde. Need: A Chorale for Black Woman Voices.
Rich, A. From an Old House in America.
Swift, J. Journal of a Modern Lady, The.
Williams, C. K. Madder.

Missionaries
Davie, D. Jesuits in North America, The.
Merton. Poet, to His Book, The.
Walcott. Koenig of the River.
Whittier. Missionary, The.
Vaudois Teacher, The.

Mississippi River
Carver, R. Tel Aviv and *Life on the Mississippi.*
Davie, D. Lasalle.
Dove, R. Someone's Blood.
Hayden, R. Night, Death, Mississippi.
Hughes, L. Mississippi Levee.
McGrath, T. Topography of History, The.
Ransom, J. Antique Harvesters.
Rexroth, K. Mississippi River.
Whitman, W. Mississippi at Midnight, The.

Mississippi (state)
Brooks, G. Bronzeville Mother Loiters in Mississippi, A. Meanwhile, a Mississippi Mother Burns Bacon.
Eberhart, R. La Crosse at Ninety Miles an Hour.
Hayden, R. Night, Death, Mississippi.
Hughes, L. Bitter River, The.
Bound No'th Blues.
Mississippi.
Jacobsen, J. Mississippi Anatomy.
Williams, T. Couple, The.

Missouri River
Whitman, W. Others May Praise What They Like.

Missouri (state)
Ciardi, J. Survival in Missouri.
Gallagher, T. 3 A.M. Kitchen: My Father Talking.
Ginsberg, A. Funky barn, black hills approaching Fulton.
Kansas City to Saint Louis.

Mist
Ammons. Early Morning in Early April.
Bishop, E. Cape Breton.
Brontë, E. Mild the mist upon the hill.
Burns, R. Lazy Mist, The.
Ciardi, J. Aspect of the Air, An.
Creeley. Out Window: Taylor's Mistake.
Cummings, E. E. Mi(dreamlike)st / makes / big each dim.
Mist.
De la Mare. Mist.
Dunbar, P. Misty Day, A.
Hughes, L. In the Mist of the Moon.
Keats. To Autumn.
Levertov. Ground-Mist, The.
Meredith, G. Pasture Alp is webbed with shade, The.
Merwin. Mist.
Paley, G. What is this whiteness on the field?
Rexroth, K. Et pour Eux Seuls, les Paradis Chantent Encore.
Sandburg, C. Changing Light Winds.
Last Answers.
Mist Forms.
Mist Marches across the Valley.
Mist, The.
Tomlinson, C. Gossamers, The.
Last of Night, The.
Mistlines.
Wilbur, R. Chronic Condition, A.
Williams, C. K. Dawn.
See also **Fog**

Mistletoe
Montale. Red Lily, The.

Mistresses
Ai. Blood in the Water.
Go.
Angelou. They Went Home.
Byron, G. To the Sighing Strephon.
Donne. Self[e] Accuser, A.
Eberhart, R. Mais l'Amour Infini Me Montera dans l'Ame.
Han-shan. Here's a poem for you young lords.
Herrick. Present: or, The Bag of the Bee, The.
To His Girles.
To His Mistresses.
Upon the Loss[e] of His Mistresses.
What Kind of Mistress[e] He Would Have.
Komunyakaa. Fleshing-out the Season.
Lawrence, D. H. Two Wives.
Lorde. Barren.
Marvell. To His Coy Mistress.
Meredith, G. Shemselnihar.
Smith, S. Infelice.
Suckling, S. Sonnet: "O[h]! for some honest lover's ghost."
Wright, J. Gesture by a Lady with an Assumed Name, A.

Misunderstanding
Amichai [*or* Amikhai]. What is it? An airplane at dawn. No.
Beckett, S. De pied ferme.
Cavafy. You Didn't Understand.
Ciardi, J. Sorrow of Obedience, The.
Week That Was, The.
Codrescu. On Translation.
Cowper, W. This ev'ning, Delia, you and I.
Creeley. Bird, The.
Gift, The.
Irishman's Lament on the Approaching Winter, An.
Song: "I woudn't / embarrass you."
Dickey, W. One Incident of Many.
Donne. Pyramus and Thisbe.
Emerson, R. Star seer Copernicus / Only could earn a curse.
Euripides. Chorus of Troizenian Women.
Chorus sing of escape, The.
Daemon initiate, spirit.
Lift my head, help me up.
Men you strike.
No more, O my spirit.
O Spirit, / spark by spark.
Ferlinghetti, L. Overpopulation.
Hardy, T. Her Confession.
Misconception.
Whaler's Wife, The.
Koch, K. Departure from Hydra, The.
Taking a Walk with You.
Lorde. Hard Love Rock II.
Sister, Morning Is a Time for Miracles.
Rich, A. Like This Together.
Pieces.
Trying to Talk with a Man.
When We Dead Awaken.
Ritsos. Misunderstandings.
Updike. Zulus Live in Land without a Square.
Williams, C. K. Cave, The.
Dirty Talker: D Line, Boston, The.
What Did the Man Do with the Clouds?

Mitchell, Arthur
Moore, M. Arthur Mitchell.

Mites
Frost, R. Considerable Speck, A.
Updike. Mites.

Mithridates the Great
Brodsky, J. Cappadocia.
Cavafy. Dareios.
Emerson, R. Mithridates.
Stock, R. Mithridates 5.
Whittier. Mithridates at Chios.

Mittens
Ritsos. Real Hands.
See also **Gloves**

Mobility
Kunitz, S. Summing-up, The.
Levi, P. Glacier, The.
Nash, O. What the Well-Read Patient Is Talking About, or, Look, Ma, What I Got!

Mockingbirds
Ammons. After Yesterday.
Making.
Ciardi, J. Yet Not to Listen to That Sung Nothing.
Gunn, T. Patch Work.
Hayden, R. Mourning Poem for the Queen of Sunday.
Jacobsen, J. Of Pairs.
Jarrell, R. Mockingbird, The.
Moore, M. Bird-witted.
Nash, O. Listen to the Linotype.
Prunty. Playing by Ear.
Rexroth, K. Mocking Birds.
Sandburg, C. Kansas Lessons.
Mockers Go to Kansas in Spring.
Stock, R. May Morning Admonition.
Warren, R. Patriotic Tour and Postulate of Joy.

Models
Browning, R. Lady and the Painter, The.
Dugan, A. To an Ex-Student.
Ferlinghetti, L. London / crossfigured / creeping with trams.
Hardy, T. Figure in the Scene, The.
Statue of Liberty, The.
Laughlin, J. Drawing Lesson, The.
Major, C. Dressed to Kill.
Riley, J. Discouraging Model, A.
Rossetti, C. In an Artist's Studio.
Seifert. Model, The.
Williams, M. Art Photographer Puts His Model at Ease, The.

Moderation
Cullen, C. Song in Spite of Myself.
Emerson, R. I know the appointed hour.
Herrick. Hony-Combe, The.
Love Is a Sirrup.
Meane, The.
Moderation.
Out of Time, Out of Tune.
Surfeits.
MacNeice. Ode: "To-night is so coarse with chocolate."
Oliver, M. Dream of Trees, A.
Rumi. Importance of Gourdcrafting, The.

Modern Man
Ai. Testimony of J. Robert Oppenheimer, The.
Amichai [*or* Amikhai]. Flock of Sheep near the Airport, A.
Modern Girl, A.
Aragon. Red Front, The.
Atwood. You want to go back.
Auden. Unknown Citizen, The.
Berry, W. Horses.
Purification, A.
Berryman. Have a Genuine American Horror-&-Mist on the Rocks.
Point of Age, A.
Rock-Study with Wanderer.
Trial, The.
Bierce. Macrobian.
Bishop, E. Varick Street.
Blue Cloud. Reflections on the St. Lawrence Seaway.
Brodsky, J. Vertumnus.
Clampitt. Berceuse.
Minor Tremor, A.
Seriphos Unvisited.
Clifton, L. Yeti Poet Returns to His Village to Tell His Story, The.
Codrescu. Comrade Past & Mister Present.
Poetry Paper.
Traffic.
Coleridge, S. Tombless Epitaph, A.
Crane, H. Supplication to the Muses on a Trying Day.
Creeley. Desultory Days.
Cummings, E. E. Blue woman with sticking out breasts hanging, A.
Boys i mean are not refined, The.
FULL SPEED ASTERN).
He does not have to feel because he thinks.
Jehovah buried,Satan dead.
Of Ever-Ever Land i speak.
Plato Told.
Proud of his scientific attitude.

Season 'tis, my lovely lambs, The.
Tell me not how electricity or.
These people socalled were not given hearts.
Will i ever forget that precarious moment?
Worshipping same / they squirm and they
   spawn.
Davie, D. Benedictus.
De la Mare. Owl, The.
  Reserved.
Eliot, T. S. Burbank with a Baedeker: Bleistein
  with a Cigar.
  Love Song of J. Alfred Prufrock, The.
  Love Song of J. Alfred Prufrock, The (Prufrock
  among the Women).
  Love Song of J. Alfred Prufrock, Resumed, The.
  Preludes.
  Prufrock's Pervigilium.
  Waste Land, The.
Enzensberger, H. Language of the Country.
Ferlinghetti, L. History of the World: a TV
  Docu-Drama.
  Home Home Home.
  In Goya's greatest scenes we seem to see.
  Living Theatre, The.
  Lost Parents.
  Sea and Ourselves at Cape Ann, The.
  Triumph of the Postmodern.
García Lorca. Dance of Death.
Ginsberg, A. Ballade of Poisons.
  Birdbrain!
  Change, The: *Kyoto-Tokyo Express*.
  C'mon Pigs of Western Civilization Eat More
  Grease.
  Either we blow ourselves up now and die, like
  the old tribe of man, arguing among neutrons.
  Grim Skeleton.
  Howl.
  Ruhr-Gebiet.
  Smoke Rolling Down Street.
  Sunflower Sutra.
  Television Was a Baby Crawling toward That
  Deathchamber.
  To the Body.
  Two Dreams.
  Who Be Kind To.
Gurney, I. Time to Come.
Hall, D. Tomorrow.
Hardy, T. I Said to Love.
  In St. Paul's a While Ago.
  Jingle on the Times, A.
  Misconception.
  Wet Night, A.
Jacobsen, J. Notes from a Lenten Bar.
Jarrell, R. Old and the New Masters, The.
Jeffers, R. Second-Best.
  Staggering Back toward Life.
  Time of Disturbance.
  Unnatural Powers.
Kinnell. First Day of the Future.
  Sheffield Ghazal 4: Driving West.
Kipling, R. New Knighthood, The.
Kumin, M. Photograph, U.S. Army Flying
  School, College Park, Maryland, 1909.
Kunitz, S. Night Letter.
Laughlin, J. Busy Day.
  Merry Madness Hall.
  Owl of Minerva, The.
Lawrence, D. H. Classes.
  Cross, The.
  Cry of the Masses.
  Death of Our Era, The.
  Dies Irae.
  Evil Is Homeless.
  Fear of Society Is the Root of All Evil.
  Give Us the Thebaïd.
  Hold Back!
  Impulse.
  Latent Desire, The.
  Latter-Day Sinners.
  Life and the Human Consciousness.
  Modern Prayer.
  Real Democracy.
  Religion.
  Robot-Democracy.
  Robot Feelings.
  Tale Told by an Idiot, A.

Today.
Wellsian Futures.
What Is a Man to Do?
What Then Is Evil?
What's Wrong.
Levi, P. Almanac.
Lowell, R. For the Union Dead.
Lux. Early On, This Decade's Light Smelled.
MacLeish. Observations of P. Ovidus Naso on
  the Incidence of Sex in the Contemporary
  Novel.
Mahon. Apotheosis of Tins, The.
  Gipsies.
  Glengormley.
McGrath, T. Citizen Dreaming, The.
Meredith, G. Age of petty tit-for-tat, An.
  Ah for that time when open daylight pours.
  London by Lamplight.
  Reason.
Merrill, J. Clearing the Title.
  Urban Convalescence, An.
Merton. Cables to the Ace.
  Captives—a Psalm, The.
  Exploits of a Machine Age.
  Letter to Pablo Antonio Cuadra Concerning
  Giants, A.
  Tune for Festive Dances in the Nineteen Sixties,
  A.
Merwin. Shore, The.
  What Is Modern.
Milosz, C. Preparation.
Nemerov. Life Cycle of Common Man.
  Make Love Not War.
Neruda. Century Dying, A.
  Pedro Is When.
  Wars, The.
Niedecker. Wintergreen Ridge.
O'Hara, F. Naphtha.
Olson, C. Connection, The.
  Conqueror.
  Dramatis Personae.
  I, Mencius, Pupil of the Master.
  In Cold Hell, in Thicket.
  It's Got to This.
  Morning News, The.
  Scream to the Editor, A.
  Stone and Flower Series.
  War on the Mind in a Time of Love.
Oppen. Blood from the Stone.
  Book of Job and a Draft of a Poem to Praise the
  Paths of the Living, The.
  Crowded Countries of the Bomb, The.
  Historic Pun.
  Language of New York, A.
  Philai Te Kou Philai.
  To the Poets: To Make Much of Life.
Parker, D. Oh Look—I Can Do It Too.
Pasolini. Ashes of Gramsci, The.
  Desperate Vitality, A.
  Poetry of the Tradition, The.
  Religion of My Time, The.
Patchen. For Miriam.
Ramanujan. Looking and Finding.
  On a Delhi Sundial.
  Report, A.
  Take Care.
Rich, A. Atlas of the Difficult World, An.
  Ghazal.
Rimbaud, A. City.
  What the Poet Is Told on the Subject of
  Flowers.
Robinson, E. Modernities.
Seifert. Dance of the Girls' Chemises.
  Dome of the Observatory, The.
  Plague Column, The.
Shapiro, K. Crucifix in the Filing Cabinet, The.
  Hospital.
  Humanities Building, The.
  Office Love.
  Pigeons, The.
Snyder, G. Spell against Demons.
  This Tokyo.
Spender, S. Man-Made World, A.
Stevens, W. Mozart, 1935.
  Of Modern Poetry.
Stock, R. National Anthem; Imitation of Carlos

  Drummond de Andrade's "*Hino Nacional*."
Sze. Great White Shark, The.
Thoreau. In the busy streets, domains of trade.
Updike. Dea ex Machina.
  On the Inclusion of Miniature Dinosaurs in
  Breakfast Cereal Boxes.
  Seven New Ways of Looking at the Moon.
  Superman.
Whalen, P. America!
Whitman, W. I Was Looking a Long While.
  One's-Self I Sing.
  Years of the Modern.
Williams, C. K. Cellophane.
  For Children When They Grow Up.
  In the Heart of the Beast.
  Inches.
  Last Deaths, The.
  Long Naked Walk of the Dead, The.
  Madder.
  Poor Hope.
  Race of the Flood, The.
  Spit.
Williams, M. Lesson on the Twentieth Century,
  A.
  On Seeing Projected Figures for War Dead in
  the Twentieth Century.
  Talking to Himself He Gets a Few Things
  Settled in His Mind.
Williams, W. Exercise, An.
Wordsworth, W. Men of the Western World! In
  Fate's Dark Book.
Wright, C. Monastery at Vršac, The.
Yeats. Second Coming, The.
Zaturenska. Émigrés, The.

Modesty
Berry, W. Want of Peace, The.
Bierce. Humility.
Burns, R. Jessie—A New Scots Song.
Byron, G. To a Vain Lady.
Cowper, W. Of Himself.
Davie, D. Under a Skylight.
Herrick. Laxare Fibulam.
  More Modest, More Manly.
  Upon Sneape.
Kipling, R. English Way, The.
Lawrence, D. H. Behaviour.
  Editorial Office.
  She Said as Well to Me.
Meredith, G. Violets.
Niedecker. See the girls in shorts on their
  bicycles.
Riley, J. Motto, A.
Rossetti, C. Listening.
Smart, C. Munificence and Modesty.
Wordsworth, W. Ode to Apollo.

Moles
Dubie. Grandfather's Last Letter, A.
Levi, P. Old Mole.
Merton. Bureaucrats: Diggers.
Plath. Blue Moles.
Rossetti, C. Handy Mole who plied no shovel,
  A.
Sexton. Star-Nosed Mole.
Stock, R. Errant Mole and the Loveliest of
  Hawks, The.

Mona Lisa
Nash, O. Political Reflection.

Monarchy
Bradstreet, A. Four[e] Monarchies, The.
Brontë, E. Woe for the day; Regina's pride.
Cavafy. Alexandros Iannaios, and Alexandra.
  Anna Komnina.
  Before Antiochus Epiphanis.
  Coins.
  Come, O King of the Lacedaimonians.
  Dimaratos.
  Displeasure of Selefkides, The.
Cowper, W. Heroism.
Hardy, T. Coronation, The.
Pessoa. Message.

Monasteries
Amichai [*or* Amikhai]. At the Monastery of
  Latroun.
Arnold, M. Stanzas from the Grande
  Chartreuse.

Byron, G. Elegy on Newstead Abbey.
"Dario." Charterhouse, The.
Hopkins, G. Escorial, The.
Merton. Chee$e.
  Clairvaux.
  Clairvaux Prison.
  Elegy for Ernest Hemingway, An.
  In the Rain and the Sun.
  Letter to My Friends, A.
  Reader, The.
  Three Postcards from the Monastery.
  Trappist Abbey: Matins, The.
  Trappist Cemetery—Gethsemani, The.
  Winter Afternoon.
Merwin. Fig Tree, The.
Nash, O. Away from It All.
Whalen, P. Conditions That Prevail, The.
Williams, M. Morning at the Zagorsk
  Monastery outside Moscow.
Williams, W. Semblables, The.
Wright, C. Monastery at Vršac, The.
See also **Monks**

Monday
Ammons. Monday.
Hughes, L. Blue Monday.
Nash, O. Every Day Is Monday.
Plath. Everlasting Monday, The.
Rossetti, C. Monday in Holy Week.

Mondrian, Piet
Wright, C. Sitting at Dusk in the Back Yard
  after the Mondrian Retrospective.
  Summer Storm.

Monet, Claude
Cummings, E. E. Water-Lilies.
Hayden, R. Monet's "Waterlilies."

Money
Ai. Greed.
Amichai [*or* Amikhai]. Box, The.
Ammons. Devising.
Berrigan, T. Red Shift.
Bierce. Montefiore.
Brodsky, J. Blues.
Browning, R. Very Original Poem, Written with
  Even a Greater Endeavour than Ordinary after
  Intelligibility.
Bukowski. $$$$$$.
Burns, R. Hey for a Lass wi' a Tocher.
  Ken Ye What Meg o' the Mill Has Gotten.
  Lines Written on a Bank-Note.
  Poem: "Friend o' the Poet, tired and leal."
  Sandy and Jockie.
  What can a young lassie, what shall a young
  lassie.
Byron, G. For Orford and for Waldegrave.
Carver, R. Money.
  What I Can Do.
Chaucer. Complaint of Chaucer to His Empty
  Purse, The.
Ciardi, J. Audit at Key West.
  Philosophical Poem.
  Song for an Allegorical Play.
Codrescu. Looks from Money.
Crane, S. Ah, haggard purse, why ope thy
  mouth.
  Impact of a dollar upon the heart, The.
  My cross! / Your cross?
Creeley. Money.
  Still Too Young.
Cummings, E. E. Impossibly / motivated by
  midnight.
  Why / don't / be / sil / ly.
Dugan, A. Love and Money.
Dunbar, P. Real Question, The.
Eberhart, R. Four Exposures.
Gallagher, T. Black Money.
Ginsberg, A. American Change.
Graves, R. £. S. D.
Han-shan. No matter how lofty your spirit.
Herrick. Expenses Exhaust.
  Lyric[k] for Legacies.
  Money Gets the Mastery [*or* Masterie].
  Money Makes the Mirth.
  No Man without Money.
  Once Poore, Still Penurious.
  Upon Bunce: Epigram.

Upon Flimsey: Epigram.
Upon Huncks: Epigram.
Upon Prig.
Upon Roots.
Housman. When first my way to fair I took.
Hughes, L. Ballad of the Miser.
  Buddy.
  Green Memory.
  Little Lyric (*Of Great Importance*).
  Numbers.
  Plaint.
  Prime.
  Wooing, A.
Ibn-i-Yamin [*or* Ibn Jemin *or* Amir Mahmud ibn
  Amir Yaminu'd-Din Tughra'i]. From Ibn
  Jemin.
Ignatow, D. About Money.
Jarrell, R. In Nature There Is Neither Right nor
  Left nor Wrong.
  Money.
  Nollekens.
Jonson, B. Elegy [*or* Elegie], An: "'Tis true,
  I'm broke! Vows, oaths, and all I had."
  Epistle to Mr Arthur Squib.
  On Bank the Usurer.
  On Lieutenant Shift.
  To Master John Burges.
  To Mr Jonson upon these Verses.
  To the Right Honourable, the Lord Treasurer of
  England. An Epigram.
Larkin, P. Money.
Laughlin, J. Getting Paid.
Lawrence, D. H. Altercation.
  Always This Paying.
  Kill Money.
  Money.
  Money-Madness.
  Wages.
  What Is Man without an Income.
  Why—?
Levine, P. Walk with Tom Jefferson, A.
Lowell, R. Skunk Hour.
Lux. Money.
  You Go to School to Learn.
Nash, O. Bankers Are Just Like Anybody Else,
  Except Richer.
  I Burn Money.
  Ms. Found under a Serviette in a Lovely Home.
  Second Month It's Not Itemized, The.
  There'll Always Be a War between the Sexes,
  or, A Woman Can Be Sometimes Pleased, but
  Never Satisfied.
Nemerov. Dialogue.
  Money.
  Route Two.
Niedecker. I spent my money.
Paley, G. Middle-Age Poem.
Parker, D. Song for the First of the Month.
Pope, A. Epistle III, to Allen Lord Bathurst.
  Epistle IV, to Richard Boyle, Earl of Burlington.
Riley, J. Idiot, An.
Roethke. Reckoning, The.
  Song for the Squeeze-Box.
Rossetti, C. Wee wee husband, / Give me some
  money.
  What will you give me for my pound?
Sandburg, C. Girl in a Cage.
  In the Shadow of the Palace.
  Money, Politics, Love, and Glory.
  Soiled Dove.
  Theorem.
  To a Contemporary Bunkshooter.
  Two Items.
Sexton. March 4th.
Shih-te. Drunk on delusion greed and anger.
Stock, R. Interpretation of High Finance.
Swift, J. Mrs. Harris's Petition.
Tate, J. Twilight Sustenance Hiatus.
Tennyson, A. Northern Farmer: New Style.
Tu Fu. Thwarted.
Van Duyn. Economics.
Whalen, P. Penny for the Old Guy, A.
Wilbur, R. Finished Man, A.
Williams, C. K. Matter, The.
Williams, M. Money.
Williams, W. How Bad It Is to Say.

Words, the Words, the Words, The.
Wright, J. To a Friendly Dun.
Yeats. Brown Penny.

Mongolia
Dubie. At the Death of a Mongolian Peasant.

Mongooses
Jacobsen, J. On My Island.
Moore, M. Snakes, Mongooses, Snake-
  Charmers, and the Like.

Monitor (ship)
Melville, H. In the Turret.
  Utilitarian View of the Monitor's Fight, A.

Monk, Thelonius
Collins, B. Snow.
Corbett, W. Between sets.
Komunyakaa. Elegy for Thelonious.
  Plea, The.
Major, C. In Walked Bud with a Palette.
  Round Midnight.

Monkeys
Ciardi, J. At Cocktails.
  Dawn of the Space Age.
Emerson, R. On the chamber, on the stairs.
Frost, R. At Woodward's Gardens.
Kipling, R. Divided Destinies.
  Legends of Evil, The.
Komunyakaa. Monkey House, The.
Kumin, M. Caring: A Dream.
Lorde. Monkeyman.
Moore, M. Monkey Puzzle, The.
  Monkeys, The.
Riley, J. Funniest Thing in the World, The.
Swenson, M. Motherhood.
Szymborska, W. Brueghel's Two Monkeys.
Warren, R. Cross, The.
Williams, T. Miss Puma, Miss Who?
Williams, W. Jungle, The.

Monks
Baudelaire. Bad Monk, The.
Browning, R. Grammarian's Funeral, A.
  Soliloquy of the Spanish Cloister.
Byron, G. Fragment from the "Monk of Athos."
Clampitt. Reservoirs of Mount Helicon, The.
Codrescu. Attempt to Spell, Incantate and
  Annoy.
  Dear Editors.
  Faith Relearned.
  History of the Growth of Heaven, The ("*Tout
  ce qui existe est situé*" said max jacob and
  one day my situation").
  Monk, The.
  Sin of Wanting a New Refrigerator, The.
  To the Virgin as She Now Stands to the Monk
  after a Beatles Movie.
Coleridge, S. Mad Monk, The.
Dunbar, P. Monk's Walk, The.
Hall, D. Stones.
Han-shan. Again I see those who leave home.
  Hey you people who leave home.
  Homeless people I know, The.
Kinsella, T. Monk, The.
Lawrence, D. H. Apostrophe to a Buddhist
  Monk.
Levertov. Conversion of Brother Lawrence.
Lindsay, N. Strength of the Lonely, The.
Meredith, G. Hernani.
Merton. After the Night Office—Gethsemani
  Abbey.
  Elegy for a Trappist.
  Elegy for the Monastery Barn.
  Evening: Zero Weather.
  Image of True Lovers' Death, The.
  Litany: "All holy souls / pray for us fellows."
  Macarius the Younger.
  Old monk is turned loose / And can travel!, The.
  Practical Program for Monks, A.
  Psalm 132: A Modern Monastic Revision.
  Quickening of St. John the Baptist, The.
  Solitary Life.
  Special continuations: the Gethsemani racetrack.
  St. Maedoc.
  There is a little ceremony to be performed.
  Three Postcards from the Monastery.
  Trappists, Working.
Nash, O. Away from It All.

Ramanujan. Pleasure.
Shih-te. By and large the monks I meet.
Smith, S. Weak Monk, The.
Whittier. Brother of Mercy, The.
Williams, W. Venus Over the Desert.
Wilner, E. Illuminator, The.
Zagajewski. Quick Poem, A.
See also **Clergy; Monasteries**

Monmouth, James Scott, Duke of
Dryden, J. Absalom and Achitophel.
Meredith, G. Monmouth.

Monogamy and Monogamists
Cowper, W. Impromptu ["If John marries Mary,
  and Mary alone"].
Donne. Confined Love.
Lawrence, D. H. Love.
Meredith, W. Five Accounts of a Monogamous
  Man.
Parker, D. Reuben's Children.

Monotony
Cavafy. Monotony.
Hacker, M. Companion, The.
  Villanelle: Late Summer.
Hughes, L. Monotony.
Levine, P. Lights I Have Seen Before.
MacNeice. Nature Morte.
Roethke. Monotony Song, The.
Sandburg, C. Harmonica Humdrums.
  Humdrum.
Smith, S. Childe Rolandine.
Williams, C. K. Winter, / damn, / again.

Monroe, Marilyn
Ai. She Didn't Even Wave.
Armantrout. Birthmark: The Pretext.
Komunyakaa. Hanoi Market, The.

Monsters
Auden. Chimaeras, The.
Brodsky, J. Centaurs 1.
Creeley. Saturday Afternoon.
Cullen, C. To the Three for Whom the Book.
De la Mare. Gloria Mundi.
Dickey, J. Sheep Child, The.
Dunbar, P. Boogah Man, The.
Graves, R. Dream Recalled on Waking.
Gunn, T. From the Highest Camp.
Kinsella, T. Dream.
Levertov. Son, A.
Nash, O. And How Keen Was the Vision of Sir
  Launfal?
  Dragons Are Too Seldom.
  Under the Floor.
  Wendigo, The.
Nemerov. Beyond the Pleasure Principle.
Rossetti, C. Ballad of Boding, A.
Tennyson, A. Kraken, The.
Whittier. Double-Headed Snake of Newbury,
  The.
Wyatt, S. Vulcan begat me. Minerva me taught.
See also **Demons**

Mont Blanc
Coleridge, S. Hymn before Sunrise, in the Vale
  of Chamouni.
Shelley, P. Mont Blanc.

Mont-Saint-Michel
Oppen. Monument.

Montale, Eugenio
Codrescu. Eugenio Montale in California.

Montana (state)
Carruth, H. Eternity Blues.
Cunningham, J. Montana Fifty Years Ago.
  Montana Pastoral.
Dubie. Elegy to the Sioux.
Kizer, C. Running Away from Home.
Stafford, W. Godiva County, Montana.
  Over in Montana.
Wright, C. Landscape as Metaphor, Landscape
  as Fate and a Happy Life.
  Looking outside the Cabin Window, I
    Remember a Line by Li Po.
  Mount Caribou at Night.

Montevideo, Uruguay
Laughlin, J. Your Early Life.

Montezuma
Lux. What Montezuma Fed Cortés and His

Men.

Montfort, Simon de
Chesterton. Simon de Montfort.

Montgomery, Richard
Stockton, A. On the Death of General
  Montgomery.

Months
Herrick. Four Sweet Months, The.
Kipling, R. Verses on Games.
Laughlin, J. James My Namesake.
Merwin. From a Series.
Pagis. Wall Calender.
Ramanujan. August.
Riley, J. Hoosier Calendar, A.
Rossetti, C. Months, The.
  Year's Windfalls, A.
Sexton. Sermon of the Twelve
  Acknowledgements, The.

Montreal, Quebec
Ammons. Nucleus.

Monuments
Bierce. Contentment.
Bishop, E. Monument, The.
Carrera Andrade. Man from Ecuador beneath
  the Eiffel Tower, A.
Carruth, H. French Hill.
Ciardi, J. Manocalzata (Gloved Hand).
Dugan, A. On an Architect.
  There He Was.
  Wall, Cave, and Pillar Statements, after Asôka.
Emerson, R. Concord Hymn.
Hardy, T. Her Temple.
  Inscription, The.
  Monument-Maker, The.
  Old Workman, The.
  Sacred to the Memory.
Hughes, L. Lincoln Monument: Washington.
  Wall, The.
Jeffers, R. Monument.
Kipling, R. Grave of the Hundred Dead, The.
  Ode: "So long as memory, valour, and faith
    endure."
  Rhodes Memorial, Table Mountain.
Komunyakaa. Facing It.
Kunitz, S. Mound Builders, The.
Lowell, R. For the Union Dead.
MacLeish. Verses for a Centennial.
Melville, H. Inscription: "To them who crossed
  the flood."
Milosz, C. Day of Generation.
Muldoon, P. Easter Island.
Oppen. Eros.
  Ozymandias.
Prunty. Monument, The.
Rexroth, K. Again at Waldheim.
Riley, J. Monument for the Soldiers, A.
  Soldier, The.
Rukeyser, M. City of Monuments.
Sandburg, C. Bronzes.
  Momus.
  Ready to Kill.
  Washington Monument by Night.
Seifert. Head of the Virgin Mary, The.
  Plague Column, The.
Spenser, E. Virgils Gnat.
Stafford, W. For the Unknown Enemy.
Stevens, W. Dance of the Macabre Mice.
Whitman, W. Red Jacket (from Aloft).
Whittier. Leggett's Monument.
Wordsworth, W. Cenotaph.
  Countess' Pillar.
  Filial Piety.
  Hart-Leap Well.
  Written with a Slate Pencil upon a Stone, the
    Largest of a Heap Lying near a Deserted
    Quarry, upon One of the Islands at Rydal.
Yeats. Three Monuments, The.

Moods
Ashbery, J. Crazy Weather.
Creeley. For Somebody's Marriage.
Donne. Letter to the Lady Carey, and Mistress
  Essex Rich, from Amiens, A.
Dunbar, P. Response.
Emerson, R. What is it to sail.
Frost, R. Mood Apart, A.

Graves, R. Song: Sullen Moods.
  Superstition.
Levertov. Face.
Nash, O. Don't Be Cross, Amanda.
Rossetti, C. Fluttered Wings.
  Key-Note, The.
  Rose has thorns as well as honey, A.
Schuyler, J. Evening.
Walker, A. Moody.
Yeats. Lover Asks Forgiveness because of His
  Many Moods.
  Moods, The.

Moon
Ammons. I Went Out to the Sun.
Armantrout. View.
Atwood. Not the Moon.
Auden. Moon Landing.
  This Lunar Beauty.
Baudelaire. Affronted Moon, The.
  Melancholy Moon, The.
Berry, W. Winter Night Poem for Mary.
Berryman. Moon and the Night and the Men,
  The.
Bishop, E. Insomnia.
  Man-Moth, The.
Blake, W. Ah said Sipsop, I only wish Jack
  [*Hunter*] Tearguts had.
  Crowned king, A.
  Hear then the pride & knowledge of a Sailor.
  I say this evening we'll [*or* we'd] all get drunk.
  In the moon as Phebus stood over his oriental
    Gardening.
  O I say you Joe.
  Phebe drest like beauties Queen.
  Then the Cynic sung.
  Upon a holy thursday their innocent faces clean.
Bly, R. Late Moon.
Bogan, L. July Dawn.
Borges. 1971.
  Limit, The.
  Moon, The.
  Tankas.
Brontë, E. There shines the moon, at noon of
  night.
Browning, E. Night and the Merry Man.
  Romaunt of Margret, The.
Browning, R. Pan and Luna.
Burns, R. Lament. Occasioned by the
  Unfortunate Issue of a Friend's Amour, The.
Byron, G. So We'll Go No More A-Roving.
  Sun of the Sleepless!
Carruth, H. Insomniac Sleeps Well for Once
  and, The.
  Joy and Agony of Improvisation, The.
Carver, R. Romanticism.
Ciardi, J. Improvisation for a Southern Night.
Clifton, L. Moonchild.
Coleridge, S. Absence.
  Lunar Entrancement.
  Moon and the Waves, The.
  Soliloquy on the Full Moon, She Being in a
    Mad Passion, A.
Crane, H. O Moon, Thou Cool.
  Supplication to the Muses on a Trying Day.
Creeley. Eye, The.
  Form of Women, A.
  Gesture, The.
  La Noche.
  Littleton, N.H.
  Moon, The.
  New Moon.
  New Year's.
  Two Ways of Looking in a Mirror.
Cummings, E. E. Come(all your mischief- /
  hatchers hatch).
  F / eeble a blu / r of cr.
  I go to this window.
  Moon falls through the autumn Behind prisons
    she grins, The.
  &-moon-He-be-hind-a-mills.
  Moon looked into my window, The.
  Moon over gai.
  MOOn Over tOwns mOOn.
  ! / o(rounD)moon,how.
  T,h;r:u;s,h;e:s / are / silent / now.
  Tonight the moon is round golden entire. It.

Who is this / dai / nty mademoiselle.
Who knows if the moon's.
Who / threw the silver dollar up into the tree?
Young m / oon:be kind to olde.
De la Mare. April Moon.
Moonlight.
Night.
Unforeseen.
Dickey, J. Moon Flock.
Dickey, W. Afternoon Evening and Night in the
  Courtyard of the Museum of Modern Art.
Dickinson, E. I make His Crescent fill or lack.
I watched the Moon around the House.
Moon is distant from the Sea, The.
Moon upon her fluent Route, The.
Moon was but a Chin of Gold, The.
Dubie. Amulet, The.
Dunbar, P. Lover and the Moon, The.
Eberhart, R. Off Spectacle Island.
Emerson, R. Atom from atom yawns as far.
Coin the daydawn into lines.
Earth, The.
Frost, R. Freedom of the Moon, The.
Moon Compasses.
Two Leading Lights.
García Lorca. Ballad of the Moon Moon.
Dance of the Moon in Santiago.
Half Moon.
Interrupted Concert, The.
Moon Rising, The.
Song for the Moon.
Ginsberg, A. In a Moonlit Hermit's Cabin.
Glück, L. Mock Orange.
Graves, R. Between Moon and Moon.
Colours of Night, The.
Full Moon.
Moon's Last Quarter, The.
Problems Of Gender.
Song: The Far Side of Your Moon.
Turn of the Moon.
What Will Be, Is.
Gunn, T. For Signs.
Silver Age, The.
Wrestling.
"H. D." Moonrise.
Hall, D. Moon Clock.
Moon, The.
Hamill, S. Reading Seferis.
Han-shan. Above Cold Mountain the moon
  shines alone.
Before the cliffs I sat alone.
Multitude of stars is the late night's light, The.
My mind is like the autumn moon.
HaNagid. Fawn, The.
Hardy, T. At Rushy-Pond.
Seeing the Moon Rise.
Shut Out That Moon.
To the Moon.
Hayden, R. Full Moon.
Hopkins, G. Fragment of Anything You Like,
  A.
Moonrise.
Housman. White in the moon the long road lies.
Hughes, L. Change.
In the Mist of the Moon.
March Moon.
New Moon.
Winter Moon.
Hughes, T. Full Moon and Little Frieda.
Harvest Moon, The.
New Moon in January.
Ignatow, D. Midnight 2.
Jacobsen, J. Planet, The.
Jarrell, R. Romance of Science, The.
Jeffers, R. At the near approach of a star...huge
  tides.
I walk on my cliff above the Pacific Ocean and
  feel the tides.
Moon and Five Planets.
Our eyes by day are good enough: only the
  birds.
Keats. Bright Star.
Kipling, R. Moon of Other Days, The.
Kizer, C. After Basho.
Kunitz, S. Flight of Apollo, The.
Larkin, P. Moon Is Full Tonight, The.

Lawrence, D. H. Aware.
Brother and Sister.
Dream-Confused.
Hostile Sun, The.
Invocation to the Moon.
Moon Memory.
Moon New-Risen.
Moonrise.
New Moon.
Old Song.
Pang of Reminiscence, A.
Prayer: "Give me the moon at my feet."
Rebuked.
Red Moon-Rise.
Sea, the Sea, The.
Southern Night.
Troth with the Dead.
White Blossom, A.
Levertov. Le Motif.
Song for Ishtar.
Tropic Ritual.
Levine, P. Late Moon.
Lindsay, N. Beggar Speaks, The.
Caught in a Net.
Censer-Moon, The.
Drying Their Wings.
Encyclopædia, The.
Moon Is a Painter, The.
Moon's the North Wind's Cooky, The.
On the Garden Wall.
Rose of Midnight, The.
Sense of Humor, A.
Strength of the Lonely, The.
What Semiramis Said.
What the Clown Said.
What the Coal-Heaver Said.
What the Forester Said.
What the Ghost of the Gambler Said.
What the Gray-Winged Fairy Said.
What the Hyena Said.
What the Miner in the Desert Said.
What the Rattlesnake Said.
What the Snow Man Said.
Written for a Musician.
Logan, J. Twilight Land.
Lorde. Gemini.
Maiden, The.
MacDiarmid, H. Au Clair de la Lune.
MacLeish. Nocturne: "Earth, still heavy and
  warm with afternoon, The."
Selene Afterwards.
Voyage to the Moon.
McGrath, T. Guiffre's Nightmusic.
Meredith, G. Song: "Moon is alone in the sky,
  The."
Song of Ruark to Bhanavar the Beautiful.
Meredith, W. Journal Entry (With the Udalls,
  June 1968).
Merwin. Full Moonlight in Spring.
Looking East at Night.
Next Moon, The.
Millay, E. Enormous moon, that rise behind
  these hills.
"Oh, sleep forever in the Latmian cave."
Mistral, G. Little New Moon, The.
Montale. Another Moon Effect.
Nemerov. Backward Look, The.
Goose Fish, The.
Olson, C. Common Place.
Disposition, The.
May 31, 1961.
Moon Is the Number 18, The.
Moonset, Gloucester, December 1, 1957, 1:58
  A.M.
Thoughts of the Time.
Pasternak, B. Some Future Moon.
Patchen. Moon "Continued."
Petrarch. Sea has not such creatures in its
  waves, The.
Piercy. Crescent Moon Like a Canoe.
Plath. Everlasting Monday, The.
Maudlin.
Metamorphoses of the Moon.
Moon and the Yew Tree, The.
Moonsong at Morning.
Rival, The.

Thalidomide.
Raine, K. I went out in the naked light.
Moon golden towards the full.
Oval the golden moon.
Rexroth, K. Confusion of the Senses.
Late Half Moon.
Singing Voice, A.
Riley, J. Man in the Moon, The.
Rilke. To the Moon.
Rossetti, C. Death-Watches.
Half Moon Shows a Face of Plaintive
  Sweetness, The.
If the moon came from heaven, / Talking all the
  way.
Is the Moon Tired?
Mirrors of Life and Death.
O Lady Moon.
Rossetti, D. Match with the Moon, A.
Rukeyser, M. In Her Burning.
Nevertheless the Moon.
Rumi. New Moon, Hilal.
Sandburg, C. Auctioneer.
Baby Face.
Back Yard.
Balloon Faces.
Blizzard Notes.
Child Moon.
Cornucopia.
Dogheads.
Early Moon.
Feather Lights.
Flux.
Great Proud Wagon Wheels Go On, The.
Half Moon in a High Wind.
Horse Fiddle.
I Sang.
Interior.
Light and Moonbells.
Milk-White Moon, Put the Cows to Sleep.
Moist Moon People.
Moon Hammock.
Moon Path.
Moon Rondeau.
Moonlight and Maggots.
Moonset.
Night Stuff.
Nocturn Cabbage.
Nocturne in a Deserted Brickyard.
Pearl Horizons.
River Moon.
River Moons.
This—For the Moon—Yes?
Three Hills Look Different in the Moonshine.
Timber Moon.
Two Moon Fantasies.
Was Ever a Dream a Drum?
Whitelight.
Schuyler, J. En Route to Southampton.
Moon.
Seifert. Lunar Ironmongery.
Sexton. Moon Song, Woman Song.
Shelley, P. Fragment: To the Moon.
To the Moon.
To the Moonbeam.
Waning Moon, The.
Sheridan, T. Thus Puppies that Adore the Dark.
Shih-te. Behold the glow of the moon.
Snyder, G. Once Only.
Stevens, W. Lunar Paraphrase.
Swenson, M. After the Flight of Ranger 7.
Day Moon, The.
Landing on the Moon.
Of Rounds.
Orbiter 5 Shows How Earth Looks from the
  Moon.
Sleeping Overnight on the Shore.
Thoreau. Moon, The.
Tomlinson, C. Death of Elizabeth Grieve, The.
Foxes' Moon.
Harvest.
Journey, The.
Picking Mushrooms by Moonlight.
Recompense, The.
Under the Moon's Reign.
Updike. Condo Moon.
Moons of Jupiter, The.

Seven New Ways of Looking at the Moon.
Vallejo. Divine Falling of Leaves, A.
Walcott. Morning Moon, The.
Warren, R. Dream of a Dream.
  Hope.
  Moonlight's Dream, The.
  On into the Night.
Weiss, T. Earthrise.
Whalen, P. To the Moon.
Whitman, W. Look Down Fair Moon.
Wilbur, R. Five Women Bathing in Moonlight.
Williams, W. Full Moon.
  La Lune, A.
  Moon, The.
  Rigamarole.
  Summer Song.
  Suzanne.
  To a Solitary Disciple.
  View.
Wilner, E. Moonsnails.
Wordsworth, W. Beauty and Moonlight.
  How Beautiful the Queen of Night, on High.
  Night Thought, A.
  Once I could hail (howe'er serene the sky).
  Shepherd, looking eastward softly said, The.
  Sweet was the walk along the narrow lane.
  To the Moon (Composed by the Seaside,—on the Coast of Cumberland).
  To the Moon (Rydal).
  Who but Is Pleased to Watch the Moon on High.
  Written in a Grotto.
Wright, C. After Reading Wang Wei, I Go Outside to the Full Moon.
  Appalachian Book of the Dead 3, The.
  Paesaggio Notturno.
Wright, J. Beginning.
  Fear Is What Quickens Me.
  Having Lost My Sons, I Confront the Wreckage of the Moon: Christmas, 1960.
  Message Hidden in an Empty Wine Bottle that I Threw into a Gully of Maple Trees One Night at an Indecent Hour, A.
  Moon.
  Morality of Poetry, The.
  Secret Gratitude, A.
  Today I Was So Happy, so I Made this Poem.
Yeats. Cat and the Moon, The.
  Crazed Moon, The.
  He and She.
  Phases of the Moon, The.
Zaturenska. Hymn to Artemis, the Destroyer.
  Luna and Leopardi.
  Lunar Tides, The.
  Song of the Forsaken Lilac Tree.

Mooney, Thomas J.
Hughes, L. Chant for Tom Mooney.

Moonshiners
Komunyakaa. Moonshine.
Muldoon, P. Kate Whiskey.
Nemerov. Moonshine.
Riley, J. Moonshiner's Serenade.
Williams, M. Rituals.

Moore, Henry
Hall, D. "Internal and External Forms."
  "King and Queen."
  Notes for Nobody.
  "Reclining Figure."

Moore, Marianne
Bishop, E. Invitation to Miss Marianne Moore.
Cummings, E. E. Marianne Moore.
Kumin, M. Marianne, My Mother, and Me.
Tomlinson, C. Over Brooklyn Bridge.
Williams, W. Marianne Moore.

Moore, Thomas
Byron, G. As the Liberty Lads o'er the Sea.
  To Thomas Moore.

Moors (geography)
Brontë, E. Blue bell is the sweetest flower, The.
Clampitt. Exmoor.
Dickinson, E. I never saw a Moor.
Emerson, R. She paints with white & red the moors.
Enzensberger, H. Lachesis Lapponica.
Hardy, T. Wet Night, A.

Hughes, T. Bringing in New Couples.
  Moors.
  Stanbury Moor.
  Telegraph Wires.
Plath. Two Views of Withens.

Moors (people)
Byron, G. Very Mournful Ballad, A.
Hughes, L. Letter from Spain.

Moose
Bishop, E. Moose, The.
Dubie. True Story of God, A.
Dugan, A. On the Elk, Unwitnessed.
Duncan, R. Poetry, a Natural Thing.
Hayden, R. Moose Wallow, The.
Kumin, M. My Elusive Guest.
Lux. Wife Hits Moose.
Sexton. Moose.
Van Duyn. Moose in the Morning, Northern Maine.

Morandi, Giorgio
Wright, C. Giorgio Morandi and the Talking Eternity Blues.
Zagajewski. Morandi.

More, Sir Thomas (Saint Thomas More)
Carver, R. Scale.
Cunningham, J. Friend, on This Scaffold Thomas More Lies Dead.
Lowell, R. Sir Thomas More.

Moreau, Gustave
Cavafy. Oedipus.

Morgues
Laughlin, J. Dylan.

Morison, Sir Henry
Jonson, B. To the Immortal[l] Memory [or Memorie] and Friendship of That Noble Pair[e], Sir Lucius Cary and Sir H. [or Henry] Morison.

Morley, Christopher
Parker, D. Chris-Cross; On Confusing Messrs. Morley and Robin.

Mormons
Bierce. Mormon Question, The.
Davie, D. Red Rock of Utah.
Laughlin, J. Cincinnatus in Utah.

Morning
Ambrose. Aeterne Rerum Conditor.
Ammons. Off.
Atwood. Morning, A.
Berrigan, T. Old-Fashioned Air.
Berry, W. April Woods: Morning.
  Architecture, An.
  Plan, The.
Bishop, E. Sunday, 4 A.M.
Blake, W. Morning.
  To Morning.
Bly, R. July Morning.
  Poem in Three Parts.
  Waking from Sleep.
Bogan, L. Italian Morning.
  Morning.
Brodsky, J. Reveille.
Brontë, E. Stars.
Broumas, O. Mornings Remembering Last Nights.
Bukowski. 4:30 A.M.
  6 A.M.
Burns, R. Cauld Frosty Morning.
  Lover's Morning Salute to His Mistress, The.
  Rosebud, The.
  Up in the Morning Early.
Carruth, H. Sometimes When Lovers Lie Quietly Together, Unexpectedly One of Them Will Feel the Other's Pulse.
Carver, R. At Least.
  Such Diamonds.
  This Morning.
Ciardi, J. At First Flower of the Easy Day.
  Come Morning.
  Goodmorning with Light.
  Morning.
Collins, B. Tuesday, June 4, 1991.
Crane, H. Annunciations.
Creeley. Morning (8:10 AM).
  Morning ("Light's bright glimmer").
  That's the way.

Cummings, E. E. At just 5 a / m i hear eng.
  Dawn / and now.begins / feeling.
  Inthe,exquisite; / morning sure lyHer eye s exactly sit,ata little roundtable.
  Lady of Silence.
  O It's Nice To Get Up In,the slipshod mucous kiss.
  O / nly this / darkness(in).
  O the sun comes up-up-up in the opening.
  Raise the shade.
  When you went away it was morning.
Davie, D. Morning.
De la Mare. Assignation, The.
  Imp Within, The.
  Keys of Morning, The.
  Martins: September.
Dickey, J. Morning, A.
Dickinson, E. And this of all my Hopes.
  Morning.
  "Morning"—means "Milking"—to the Farmer.
  Morning that comes but once.
  Morning without you is a dwindled Dawn.
  Safe in their Alabaster Chambers.
  Sleep is supposed to be.
  Sun—just touched the Morning, The.
  To Whom the Mornings stand for Nights.
Donne. Break[e] of Day.
  Sun Rising, The.
Dugan, A. Morning Song.
  This Morning Here.
Dunbar, P. Barrier, The.
  In the Morning.
  Morning.
  Morning Song of Love.
Eberhart, R. By the Stream.
Eliot, T. S. Morning at the Window.
Emerson, R. Written in Naples, March, 1833.
Ferlinghetti, L. Roman Morn.
Frost, R. Valley's Singing Day, The.
Ginsberg, A. We Rise on Sun Beams and Fall in the Night.
Graves, R. On Rising Early.
Guillén, J. Love Song to a Morning.
Gurney, I. Awakening, The.
Hacker, M. Aube Provençale.
Hall, D. Valley of Morning.
Hardy, T. On a Fine Morning.
Herbert, G. Mattens.
Herrick. Matins [or Mattens], or Morning Prayer.
  To His Sweet Saviour.
Housman. In the morning, in the morning.
  Reveille.
  Yonder see the morning blink.
Hughes, L. Blues at Dawn.
  Walkers with the Dawn.
Hughes, T. Horses, The.
  Stealing Trout on a May Morning.
Jacobsen, J. Let Each Man Remember.
Jarrell, R. Nestus Gurley.
Koch, K. In the Morning.
Kunitz, S. Round, The.
Larkin, P. Horns of the Morning, The.
  Morning at Last: There in the Snow.
  Morning Has Spread Again.
Laughlin, J. Alba.
  Song: "O lovely lovely so lovely."
Lawrence, D. H. Dawn Verse, The.
  First Morning.
  Married in June.
  Mid-Day Verse, The.
  Morning Work.
  Next Morning.
  Wedding Morn.
Levertov. Instant, The.
  Love of Morning, The.
  Matins.
  May Mornings, The.
Levine, P. Ordinary Morning, An.
  To My God in His Sickness.
  Wednesday.
Lowell, R. Waking Early Sunday Morning.
MacNeice. Morning Sun.
  Slow Movement.
  Sunday Morning.
Mahon. Everything Is Going to Be All Right.

McMichael. Matins.
Meredith, W. Poem about Morning.
Merton. Aubade: Lake Erie.
Merwin. In One of the Retreats of Morning.
  Morning, The.
Milosz, C. Happiness.
Mistral, G. Grace.
  Morning.
Muldoon, P. Avenue, The.
Nash, O. Song before Breakfast.
Nemerov. Morning Sun.
O'Hara, F. Getting Up ahead of Someone (Sun).
  Jane Awake.
  Joe's Jacket.
Oliver, M. Morning in a New Land.
  Morning Poem.
Olson, C. Clouds, The.
  Variations Done for Gerald Van De Wiele.
Orr, G. Morning Song.
Pasolini. Beautiful Banners, The.
Petrarch. Long for the evening, loathe the
  coming dawn.
Pinsky. First Early Mornings Together.
Plath. Sheep in Fog.
Ramanujan. Sometimes.
Rexroth, K. Open the Blind.
Riley, J. Morning.
  To Bliss Carman.
  Wait for the Morning.
Rilke. Morning Melancholy.
  Two Poems.
Rimbaud, A. Lovely Morning Thought.
Ritsos. Morning.
Roethke. Carnations.
Rossetti, C. Margaret has a milking-pail, / And
  she rises early.
Rukeyser, M. Song: "Voice flew out of the river
  as morning flew, A."
Sandburg, C. Bitter Summer Thoughts—No. 3.
  Early Hours.
  Far Rockaway Night till Morning.
  Halsted Street Car.
  Lake Michigan Morning.
  Margaret.
  Moon Riders.
  Pass, Friend.
Schuyler, J. Birds.
  Good Morning.
  In Earliest Morning.
  Morning, The.
Sexton. Welcome Morning.
Simic. Summer Morning.
Smith, S. Hendecasyllables.
Spender, S. Awaking.
Stafford, W. Five AM.
Swenson, M. Early Morning: Cape Cod.
  One Morning in New Hampshire.
  This Morning.
Swift, J. Description of the Morning, A.
Sze. Morning Shutters.
Thomas, D. When I woke.
Thoreau. Cock-crowing.
  Guido's Aurora.
  May Morning.
  Morning.
  Sluggish smoke curls up from some deep dell,
  The.
Tomlinson, C. Drive.
  Greeting, The.
Vallejo. Our Daily Bread.
Very. Clouded Morning, The ("Morning comes,
  and thickening clouds prevail, The").
  Fair Morning, The.
  Morning.
  Morning Watch, The.
  This Morn.
Weiss, T. Sultry Dawn.
  Sum of Destructions, A.
Whalen, P. Three Mornings.
Whittier. Waiting, The.
Wilbur, R. For Ellen.
  Late Aubade, A.
  Love Calls Us to the Things of This World.
  Summer Morning, A.
Wilde, O. Impression du Matin.
  Impression: Le Réveillon.

Williams, C. K. Mornings: Catherine.
Williams, T. Lyric: "Can it be again."
Williams, W. Morning.
  Summer Song.
Wordsworth, W. Composed upon Westminster
  Bridge, September 3, 1802.
Wright, C. California Spring.
Zagajewski. Creation of the World, The.
  Early Hours, The.
Zaturenska. Cold Morning Sky.

Morning Glories
Ammons. Clearing the Dark Symbiosis.
  Next Day, The.
  Quince Bush, The.
  Transfer.
Ciardi, J. Bees and Morning Glories.
Levertov. Concurrence.
Sandburg, C. Morning Glory Blue.
Wilner, E. Conversation with a Japanese
  Student.

Morocco
Eberhart, R. Marrakech.
Meredith, W. Grace.
  In the Rif Mountains.

Morris, William
Niedecker. His Carpets Flowered.
Sandburg, C. Salvage.

Mortality
Amichai [or Amikhai]. I Lost My Identity Card.
  If Now in the Middle of My Life.
  Man in His Life, A.
  Poems of Spring in the Appalachian Mountains.
  State of Affairs.
  Support for My Breathing.
  To Hurl Haunting Memories.
  What Kind of a Person.
Ammons. Joshua Tree.
  Sap Is Gone Out of the Trees, The.
  This Black Rich Country.
  Wind Coming Down From, The.
Ashbery, J. Absence of a Noble Presence, The.
Atwood. Aging Female Poet on Laundry Day.
  Book of Ancestors.
  Girl and Horse, 1928.
  No Name.
Auden. Lullaby: "Lay your sleeping head, my
  love."
Baudelaire. Carrion.
  Dancing Death.
  End of the Day, The.
Berrigan, T. Last Poem.
Bierce. Word to the Unwise, A.
Blake, W. Caverns of the Grave [I've Seen],
  The.
Blok. Song of the Wind, The.
Bly, R. Ant Mansion, The.
  August Rain.
  Conversation, A.
  Defeated.
  Digging Worms.
  Empty Place, An.
  Hawk, The.
  Hollow Tree, A.
  Home in Dark Grass, A.
  July Morning.
  Kneeling Down to Look [or Peer] into a
  Culvert.
  Night.
  November Day at McClure's Beach.
  On a Ferry across Chesapeake Bay.
  Sitting on Some Rocks in Shaw Cove.
  When the Dumb Speak.
Borges. Adam Is Your Ashes.
  Alchemist, The.
  Boast of Quietness.
  Enigmas, The.
  Mexico.
  Milonga of Manuel Flores.
  Museum.
  Palace, The.
  Things.
  To One No Longer Young.
  To Whoever Is Reading Me.
  Two Forms of Insomnia.
  Web, The.
Bradstreet, A. Before the Birth of One of Her

  Children.
Brodsky, J. Anthem: "Praised be the climate."
  So Forth.
  Song of Welcome.
Brontë, E. Self-Interrogation.
Browning, E. Stanzas: "I may sing; but
  minstrel's singing."
Burns, R. Song: "Sensibility how charming."
  To a Mountain Daisy [On Turning One Down,
  with the Plough, in April—1786].
Byron, G. Fragment, A: "When, to their airy
  hall, my fathers' voice."
  Manfred.
  To Caroline.
Campion, T. Come, Cheerful Day!
  Lamentation, A.
  To the Most Illustrious and Mighty Fredericke
  the Fifth, Count Palatine of the Rhein.
  What If a Day [or a Month or a Year].
  Where are all thy beauties now, all hearts
  enchaining? [or harts enchayning?].
Carew, T. Song[, A]: "Ask[e] me no more
  where Jove bestow[e]s."
Carruth, H. New Hartford.
  Sex.
Carver, R. Afterglow.
  Contact, The.
  Fields, The.
  In the Year 2020.
  Its Course.
  Lightning Speed of the Past, The.
  Meadow, The.
  Migration.
  Movement.
  Proposal.
  Through the Boughs.
Cavafy. Aimilianos Monai, Alexandrian, 628–
  655 A.D.
  Candles.
  Four Walls of My Room, The.
  Interruption.
  Manuel Komninos.
Celan. Afternoon with Circus and Citadel.
  Tankards, The.
Ciardi, J. At Least with Good Whiskey.
  For Myra, John L., and Benn.
  In the Audience.
  Last Rites.
Clifton, L. 1994.
  Rust.
Coleridge, S. Superstition.
Collins, B. Death of the Hat, The.
  My Number.
  Picnic, Lightning.
Cowper, W. Mortals around your destin'd
  heads.
  On a Similar Occasion for the Year 1788.
  On a Similar Occasion for the Year 1789.
  On a Similar Occasion for the Year 1790.
  On a Similar Occasion for the Year 1792.
  On a Similar Occasion for the Year 1793.
  Stanzas Subjoined to the Yearly Bill of
  Mortality of the Parish of All Saints,
  Northampton; for the Year 1787.
Creeley. Be of Good Cheer.
  Catching Cold.
  Cebu.
  Death.
  Desultory Days.
  Fact, The.
  Here again, / shifting days.
  Last Mile, The.
  Love: "Will you be dust."
  Outside.
  Question.
Cuadra, P. Meditation before an Ancient Poem.
Cullen, C. Epitaph: "She leans across a golden
  table."
  Nothing Endures.
  Sonnet: "These are no wind-blown rumors, soft
  say-sos."
Cunningham, J. All in Due Time.
  Consolatio Nova.
  Letter, A.
"Darío." Autumn Poem, The.
  Nocturne: "I want to express my anguish in

verses that tell."
Davie, D.   I Have Said, Ye Are Gods.
Immortal Longings. Before Surgery.
Put Not Your Trust in Princes.
Winter Landscapes.
De la Mare.   Corner Stone, The.
Queen Wasp, A.
Self to self.
Dickinson, E.   Because I could not stop for
   Death.
Exultation is the going.
"Heavenly Father"—take to thee.
I fear we think too lightly of.
My Life had stood—a Loaded Gun.
Parting is one of the exactions.
Somehow myself survived the Night.
'Tis not that Dying hurts us so.
To venerate the simple days.
Visitor in Marl, A.
We knew not that we were to live.
Wounded Deer Leaps Highest, A.
Donne.   Anniversary [or Anniversarie], The.
Farewell to Love.
Song: "Sweetest love, I do not go[e]."
Dugan, A.   Butcher!, Borges, What a Shock!,
   The.
Elegy for a Gifted Child.
Portrait.
Untitled Poem: "I've promised that I will not
   care about things."
Dunbar, P.   Mortality.
Dunbar, W.   Lament for the Makaris [or Makars
   or Makers].
Eberhart, R.   To Evan.
Eliot, T. S.   Whispers of Immortality.
Emerson, R.   Good-bye.
Hamatreya.
Seemed to me—never maid.
To J. W.
Enzensberger, H.   Keeping Cool.
Ferlinghetti, L.   Paris Transformations.
García Lorca.   Autumn Song.
Rider's Song.
Spring Song.
Ginsberg, A.   Autumn Leaves.
May Days 1988.
Glück, L.   Fortress, The.
Garden, The.
Triumph of Achilles, The.
Graves, R.   In Her Praise.
Gray, T.   Elegy Written in a Country
   Churchyard.
Gurney, I.   Moments.
Swift and Slow.
Guyon.   Happy Solitude—Unhappy Men.
Hall, D.   Black Faced Sheep, The.
For an Exchange of Rings.
Tubes.
Han-shan.   Emperor Wu of the Han they say.
Go ahead stockpile rhino horn.
HaNagid.   Among My Friends.
I Quartered the Troops for the Night.
Soul Opens inside You.
You Think There's No Hell That Will Hold You.
Hardy, T.   Dead and the Living One, The.
Doom and She.
Last Week in October.
Later Autumn, The.
Sine Prole.
Tenant-for-Life, The.
Heaney, S.   Dog Was Crying Tonight in
   Wicklow Also, A.
Herbert, G.   Church Monuments.
Employment: "He that is weary, let him sit."
Frailty.
Man's Medley.
Mortification.
Time.
Virtue [or Vertue].
Herrick.   Anacreontic.
Changes to Corinna, The.
Death Ends All Woe.
End Decreed, An.
Great Spirits Supervive.
His Charge to Julia at His Death.
His Own Epitaph.

Last Stroke Strike Sure, The.
Man's Dying-Place Uncertain.
Never Too Late to Dye.
None Free from Fault.
Paranæticall, or Advisive Verse, to His Friend,
   M. John Wicks.
Plunder, The.
Things Mortal Still Mutable.
To Enjoy the Time.
To His Kinswoman, Mistresse Susanna Herrick.
To His Sweet Saviour.
To the Reverend Shade of His Religious Father.
Upon a Young Mother of Many Children.
Upon His Departure Hence.
Upon the Troublesome Times.
Watch, The.
Hill, G.   Order of Service, An.
Hopkins, G.   Spring and Fall.
Housman.   Be still, my soul, be still; the arms
   you bear are brittle.
Chestnut casts his flambeaux, and the flowers,
   The.
Clunton and Clunbury.
I hoed and trenched and weeded.
I promise nothing: friends will part.
If truth in hearts that perish.
It is no gift I tender.
Oh turn not in from marching.
Rain, it streams on stone and hillock, The.
Sage to the Young Man, The.
With Rue My Heart Is Laden.
You smile upon your friend to-day.
Hughes, L.   Bells Toll Kindly, The.
Day.
Numbered.
Search.
Sport.
Hughes, T.   October Salmon[, An].
Walt.
Ignatow, D.   Here I Am.
Here I Am with Mike.
I Close My Eyes.
Knowledge.
Permanence.
Ivanov, G.   Mirrors, reflecting each other.
Jackson, L.   Benedictory.
Christmas.
Dilemmist, The.
It Is Not Sad.
Tree-Sense.
Jacobsen, J.   Gathering, The.
Presences.
Shrivers, The.
Spring, Says the Child.
Uninvited, The.
Jarrell, R.   Author to the Reader, The.
I loved you, too. There was no use. I had no
   time.
Kirilov on a Skyscraper.
Jeffers, R.   Age in Prospect.
To Death.
Wise Men in Their Bad Hours.
Johnson, S.   On a Lady's Presenting a Sprig of
   Myrtle to a Gentleman.
Soon fades the rose; once past the fragrant hour.
Keats.   Gif Ye Wol Stonden Hardie Wight.
Ode on a Grecian Urn.
Ode to a Nightingale.
Stanzas on Some Skulls in Beauly Abbey, near
   Inverness.
When I Have Fears [That I May Cease to Be].
Why Did I Laugh Tonight?
Written in Disgust of Vulgar Superstition.
Kinnell.   Fergus Falling.
Hen Flower, The.
Lastness.
Little Sleep's-Head Sprouting Hair in the
   Moonlight.
Kizer, C.   In the Night.
Kumin, M.   Envelope, The.
Our Ground Time Here Will Be Brief.
Thinking of Death and Dogfood.
We Are.
Kunitz, S.   Deciduous Branch.
Open the Gates.
Single Vision.

Words of the Preacher, The.
Larkin, P.   Aubade: "I work all day, and get
   half-drunk at night."
Laughlin, J.   Child, The.
Death Walkers, The.
Deathfear.
Junk Collector, The.
Occidit brevis lux.
Levertov.   Autumnal.
Earth Psalm.
Her Sadness.
In Question.
Levi, P.   Crow's Song 2, The.
Thieves.
Toward the Valley.
Unresolved Burdens.
Lindsay, N.   Being the Dedication of a Morning.
Logan, J.   Dead Man's Room, The.
Longfellow, H.   Mezzo Cammin.
Morituri Salutamus.
Nature.
Lowell, R.   Death from Cancer.
Lux.   Irreconcilabilia.
Moon-Annoyed, Cognac's Ashen Thrill.
MacLeish.   1892—19—.
Actfive.
Signature for Tempo.
MacNeice.   Plant and Phantom.
Sunlight on the Garden, The.
Mahon.   Heraclitus on Rivers.
Martial.   Out of Martiall.
Marvell.   Picture of Little T. C. in a Prospect of
   Flowers, The.
McGrath, T.   In Early Autumn.
McHugh, H.   After Rilke.
Denomination.
Melville, H.   Pontoosuce.
Tom Deadlight.
Meredith, G.   Dirge in Woods.
Faith on Trial, A.
Hymn to Colour.
Last Contention, The.
Question Whither, The.
Thrush in February, The.
Merwin.   Divinities.
For Saying That It Won't Matter.
For the Anniversary of My Death.
Last People.
October.
Resolution.
Wharf, The.
Michelangelo Buonarroti.   At times I project
   ahead.
Certain of death, though not yet of the hour.
From clutch of clock and calendar now fled.
From heaven my beauty, flawless and divine.
If, vulnerable from early youth, a heart.
I'm here to say you've given earth your all.
It seems, Love, out you've flung.
Life's quick and brief; the more my days fly by.
My soul without a friend, without a guide.
No differently the guilty wretch hangs back.
On earth, it's no unworthy soul that nurses.
Once born, death's our destination.
This face, says art, alone.
Through many a year and many a vain assay.
To one of taste both flawless and robust.
With much of time and life gone, all the more.
Millay, E.   At least, my dear.
Be sure my coming was a sharp offense.
First Fig.
How healthily their feet upon the floor.
Lament: "Listen, children: / Your father is
   dead."
Leaf and the Tree, The.
Mariposa.
Mortal Flesh, Is Not Your Place in the Ground?
Poet and His Book, The.
Pretty Love, I Must Outlive You.
Small Hands, Relinquish All.
What's this of death, from you who never will
   die?
When you, that at this moment are to me.
Milosz, C.   Christoper Robin.
Dawns.
Either-Or.

Encounter.
Human Fly, A.
I Do Not Understand.
Journey, The.
Lake.
Mistake, A.
New Province, A.
Photograph, A.
Poet at Seventy.
Portal, A.
Rays of Dazzling Light.
Song, The: "Earth flows away from the shore
    where I stand."
Table 1.
Table 2.
Those Corridors.
Voyeur.
When after a Long Life.
Winter.
Mistral, G.   Dusk.
Montale.   Don't escape into the shade.
Seacoasts, / a few blades of sword grass are
    enough.
Neruda.   Egoist.
Niedecker.   Death of my poor father, The.
Just before she died.
Tradition.
Oliver, M.   Beyond the Snow Belt.
Dream of Trees, A
In Blackwater Woods.
Lonely, White Fields.
October.
When Death Comes.
Olson, C.   This.
Oppen.   Image of the Engine.
Population.
West.
Orr, G.   Best.
What I'm Saying.
Owen, W.   A Terre.
Anthem for Doomed Youth.
Exposure.
Send-Off, The.
Pagis.   Already.
Brain.
Sominex.
Paley, G.   Drowning (II).
Fear.
Palmer, M.   Symmetrical Poem: They were
    afraid of death.
Parker, D.   Tombstones in the Starlight.
Pasolini.   Appendix to the "Religion": A Light.
Pessoa.   Lydia, when our Autumn comes.
Nothing comes of nothing. We are nothing.
Whatever stops is death, and is our death.
Petrarch.   As life eternal is the sight of God.
Closer that I come to that last day, The.
From lovely clear and polished living ice.
I cannot keep silent, and I fear my tongue.
I saw a lady underneath green laurel.
I think and think, and in my thoughts I feel.
Life flies from us, and does not pause one hour.
My faithful glass has very often told.
My heavy life is hanging on a thread.
Nightingale, that so harmoniously, The.
Once more Love sends to me that pleasing
    thought.
These kindly rhymes by which you have made
    known.
We are to be his victim after all.
What fate of mine, what trickery, what force.
Who wants to see what can be done by Nature.
Pinkerton, H.   Subjectivity.
Poe.   Eldorado.
Pound, E.   Song in the Manner of Housman.
Propertius.   When Thou Must Home.
Prunty.   Domestic of the Outer Banks.
Foliage Tour, The.
Four Winter Flies.
Towards a Relative Ending.
Raine, K.   Last night I seemed in your embrace.
Ramanujan.   Fizzle.
One More on a Deathless Theme.
Saturdays.
Some Monarchs and a Wish.
Ransom, J.   Piazza Piece.

Rexroth, K.   Lute Music.
Time Spirals.
Riley, J.   Dead Joke and the Funny Man, The.
O Life! O Beyond!
Singer, The.
Ritsos.   Fundamentals, The.
Marpessa's Selection.
More Sufficient, The.
Perhaps.
Robinson, E.   Pity of the Leaves, The.
Rossetti, C.   I See That All Things Come to an
    End.
Rossetti, D.   Ardour and Memory.
Autumn Idleness.
Barren Spring.
Beauty's Pageant.
Birth-Bond, The.
Body's Beauty.
Bridal Birth.
Broken Music.
Choice, The ("Eat thou and drink; to-morrow
    thou shalt die").
Choice, The ("Think thou and act; to-morrow
    thou shalt die").
Choice, The ("Watch thou and fear; to-morrow
    thou shalt die").
Cloud and Wind,
Dark Day, A.
Dark Glass, The.
Day of Love, A.
Death-in-Love.
Death's Songsters.
Equal Troth.
Farewell to the Glen.
From Dawn to Noon.
Genius in Beauty.
Gracious Moonlight.
He and I.
Heart of the Night, The.
Heart's Compass.
Heart's Haven.
Heart's Hope.
Her Gifts.
Hero's Lamp.
Hill Summit, The.
Hoarded Joy.
Hope Overtaken.
Inclusiveness.
Kiss, The.
Known in Vain.
Lamp's Shrine, The.
Landmark, The.
Last Fire.
Life-in-Love.
Life the Beloved.
Lost Days.
Lost on Both Sides.
Love and Hope.
Love Enthroned.
Love-Letter, The.
Love-Moon, The.
Love-Sweetness.
Lovers' Walk, The.
Love's Baubles.
Love's Fatality.
Love's Last Gift.
Love's Lovers.
Love's Testament.
Lovesight.
Memorial Thresholds.
Michelangelo's Kiss.
Mid-Rapture.
Monochord, The.
Moonstar, The.
Morrow's Message, The.
Newborn Death ("And thou, O Life, the lady of
    all bliss").
Newborn Death ("To-day Death seems to me an
    infant child").
Nuptial Sleep.
Old and New Art (Not as These).
Old and New Art (St Luke the Painter).
Old and New Art (The Husbandmen).
One Hope, The.
Parted Love.
Passion and Worship.

Portrait, The.
Pride of Youth.
Retro me, Sathana!
Secret Parting.
Severed Selves.
Silent Noon.
Sleepless Dreams.
Song-Throe, The.
Sonnet, A: "Sonnet is a moment's monument,
    A."
Soul-Light.
Soul's Beauty.
Soul's Sphere, The.
Stillborn Love.
Sun's Shame, The ("As some true chief of men,
    bowed down with stress").
Sun's Shame, The ("Beholding youth and hope
    in mockery caught").
Superscription, A.
Supreme Surrender.
Through Death to Love.
Transfigured Life.
Trees of the Garden, The.
True Woman (Her Heaven).
True Woman (Her Love).
True Woman (Herself).
Vain Virtues.
Vase of Life, The.
Venus Victrix.
Willowwood ("And now Love sang: but his was
    such a song").
Willowwood ("I sat with Love upon a woodside
    well").
Willowwood ("O ye, all ye that walk in
    Willowwood").
Willowwood ("So sang he: and as meeting rose
    and rose").
Winged Hours.
Without Her.
Youth's Antiphony.
Youth's Spring-Tribute.
Rukeyser, M.   Blue Flower, The.
Thousands of Days.
Seifert.   Cry of the Spectres, The.
Fragment of a Letter.
Funeral under My Window.
Shapiro, K.   Cut Flower, A.
Shelley, P.   Dialogue, A.
Smith, S.   Company.
Spender, S.   One More New Botched Beginning.
Sleepless.
Tom's a-Cold.
Stafford, W.   Last Class, The.
Stevens, W.   Clear Day and No Memories, A.
Peter Quince at the Clavier.
Stock, R.   May Morning Admonition.
Sitting for a Self-Portrait.
Stockton, A.   Birth Day Ode, A.
Elegy on the Death of Miss Chandler, as if
    Written in Her Fathers Church Yard.
Lines on a Young Gentleman Who Died of the
    Yellow Fever at Princeton a Day or Two after
    He Fled from the City for Fear of It.
Sze.   Before Completion.
Cloud Chamber, The.
Six Persimmons.
String Diamond, The.
Szymborska, W.   Nothing's a Gift.
Tate, A.   Anabasis, The.
Non Omnis Moriar.
Ode to the Confederate Dead.
Tennyson, A.   Tithonus.
Tomlinson, C.   After a Death.
Ungaretti.   Meditations on Death.
Unknown.   From the Persian (1).
Updike.   Bath after Sailing.
Granite.
Melancholy of Storm Windows, The.
Omega.
Sea Knell.
Van Duyn.   Challenger, The.
Villon.   Ballade in Old French.
Warren, R.   Acquaintance with Time in Early
    Autumn.
After the Dinner Party.
Identity and Argument for Prayer.

Morticians

Mirror, The.
Old Dog Dead.
Paradox of Time.
Sunset Walk in Thaw-Time in Vermont.
Variation: Ode to Fear.
Whalen, P. To the Memory Of.
Whitman, W. As at Thy Portals Also Death.
City Dead-House, The.
Quicksand Years.
This Compost.
Thought.
Whittier. Autograph, An.
Wilbur, R. Flumen Tenebrarum.
La Rose des Vents.
Lament: "Nashe's old queens who bartered young and fair."
Lilacs, The.
To His Skeleton.
Williams, M. I Can Only Stay for Fifteen Minutes.
Jonathan Confronts the Question.
Quantum Theory Made Simple.
Thanatopsis.
Williams, T. Daybreak Thought for Maria, A.
Intimations.
Modus Vivendi.
Sacre de Printemps.
Stonecutter's Angels, The.
Stones Are Thrown.
Why do I want to go away?
Wordsworth, W. Calm is the Fragrant air, and loth to lose.
Extempore Effusion upon the Death of James Hogg.
Most Alluring Clouds That Mount the Sky, The.
November, 1836.
'Tis He Whose Yester-Evening's High Disdain.
Trosachs, The.
Upon a Portrait.
Wright, C. Apologia Pro Vita Sua.
Disjecta Membra.
Lives of the Saints.
Meditation on Summer and Shapelessness.
Quotations.
With Eddie and Nancy in Arezzo at the Caffè Grande.
Wright, J. Eye of God, the Soul's First Vision, The.
Zagajewski. To.
To Myself, in an Album.
Zaturenska. Dream, The.
Flowing of the River, The.
Winter Rose, The.
See also **Death and the Dead**

Morticians

Dubie. Parish.
Dugan, A. On a Benign Bureaucratization of Death.
See also **Undertakers**

Moscow, Russia

Davie, D. Scythian Charioteers, The.
Hughes, L. Moscow.
Levertov. Conversation in Moscow.
Pasternak, B. Earth, The.
White Night.
Seifert. Moscow.
Voznesensky [*or* Voznesenskii]. Phone Booth.
Wordsworth, W. By Moscow Self-Devoted to a Blaze.

Moses

Amichai [*or* Amikhai]. Giving of the Torah, The.
Dickinson, E. It always felt to me—a wrong.
Glück, L. Day Without Night.
Hopkins, G. Soliloquy of One of the Spies Left in the Wilderness, A.
Nemerov. Moses.
Rumi. Moses and the Shepherd.
Stock, R. Moses on Pisgah.
Very. Moses as Leader of Israel.
Moses at the Bush.
Moses in Infancy.
Wilner, E. Epitaph: "Young then, / we were bored already."

Mosques

Broumas, O. Diagram of Abandoned Mosque.

Rumi. Far Mosque, The.

Mosquitoes

Dubie. New England, Autumn.
Lawrence, D. H. Mosquito Knows, The.
Mosquito, The.
Lindsay, N. Little Turtle, The.
Oppen. Amalgamated, The.
Updike. Mosquito.

Moss

Codrescu. Moss.
Jacobsen, J. Language of Moss.
Roethke. Moss-Gathering.
Wilner, E. Zero at the Bone.
Wordsworth, W. Thorn, The.

Motels

Creeley. Blue Skies Motel.
Jacobsen, J. Motel in Troy, New York, A.
McHugh, H. Two St. Petersburgs.
See also **Hotels**

Mother Goose

Jacobsen, J. Primer, The.
Riley, J. Mother Goose.

Mothers

Ai. She Didn't Even Wave.
Amichai [*or* Amikhai]. For My Mother.
My Mother Died on Shavuot.
My Mother Once Told Me.
My Mother's Death and the Lost Battles for the Future of Her Children.
My Son.
Now She's Breathing.
With My Mother.
Yom Kippur.
Angelou. Mothering Blackness, The.
Atwood. Christmas Carols.
Letter from Persephone.
Mothers.
Red Shirt, A.
Baudelaire. You were so jealous of our nursemaid's love.
Berrigan, T. Certain Slant of Sunlight, A.
Berry, W. Poem for J.
Bradstreet, A. Before the Birth of One of Her Children.
Epitaph on my Dear and Ever Honored Mother Mrs. Dorothy Dudley.
In Reference to Her Children, 23 June, 1659 [*or* 1659].
Upon My Son Samuel His Going For England.
Brodsky, J. In Memoriam.
Brooks, G. Jessie Mitchell's Mother.
Mrs. Small.
Womanhood, The.
Broumas, O. After Lunch.
Eye of Heart.
Little Red Riding Hood.
Lullaby: "I see you, centered."
No Harm Shall Come.
Périsprit.
Snow White.
Stars in Your Name.
Woman with Child.
Browning, E. Isobel's Child.
Mother and Poet.
Mourning Mother, The.
Bukowski. Imagination and Reality.
Mother and Son.
Burns, R. Waukrife Minnie, A.
Campion, T. Fain Would I Wed.
Carruth, H. Fragment: "Who can know more deeply than I your loneliness there?"
Mother.
Song: So Often, So Long I Have Thought.
Carver, R. Mother.
Son.
Where the Groceries Went.
Cavafy. 27 June 1906, 2 P.M.
Anna Dalassini.
In Sparta.
Celan. Aspen Tree.
Black Flakes.
In Front of a Candle.
Nearness of Graves.
Travel Companion, The.
Winter.

Wolfsbean.
Ciardi, J. Addio.
And Thy Mother.
Epithalamium at St. Michael's Cemetary.
God.
Late Peaches.
Letter to Mother.
M is for MOTHERS, who are, above all.
My Father Died Imperfect as a Man.
Shaft, The.
Three Views of a Mother.
Thursday.
Tragedy-Maker, The.
Clampitt. New Life, A.
Clifton, L. Death of Thelma Sayles.
Lot's Wife 1988.
Memory.
Message of Thelma Sayles, The.
What Did She Know, When Did She Know It.
Coleridge, S. Ode to Georgiana, Duchess of Devonshire.
Collins, B. Iron Bridge, The.
Tomes.
Cooper, J. For My Mother in Her First Illness, from a Window Overlooking Notre Dame.
My Mother in Three Acts.
My Young Mother.
Corbett, W. Dear Joe.
Last Words.
Poem for Me Mother.
Putting socks away.
Cowper, W. On the Receipt of My Mother's Picture out of Norfolk [the Gift of My Cousin Ann Bodham].
Creeley. For My Mother: Genevieve Jules Creeley.
Four Years Later.
Gesture, The.
Kid ("Kid left / out back waits, The").
Method of Actuality, The.
She Went to Stay.
Two.
Wind, The.
Cullen, C. Tribute.
Davie, D. Mother.
Nottinghamshire.
De la Mare. On the Esplanade.
Owl, The.
To My Mother.
Winter Dusk.
Dickey, J. Birth, A.
Buckdancer's Choice.
Deborah as Scion.
Voyage of the Needle, The.
Dickey, W. Elegy before the Time.
Stella Dallas.
Dickinson, E. Grief of wonder at her fate.
If Nature smiles—the Mother must.
Mama never forgets her birds.
"Mother," to me, is so sacred a Name.
Mother's dying almost stunned my spirit.
Upon the gallows hung a wretch.
Who could be motherless.
Dove, R. Bird Frau, The.
Motherhood.
Drummond de Andrade. Infancy.
Dugan, A. Address to a Bird on a Visit Home.
For an Obligate Parasite.
On a Benign Bureaucratization of Death.
On a Dispossess Precept. 2.
Dunbar, P. Appreciation.
Scamp.
Turning of the Babies in the Bed, The.
Duncan, R. My Mother Would Be a Falconress.
Eberhart, R. At Night.
Examination of Psyche: Thoughts of Home.
Orchard.
Soul Longs to Return Whence It Came, The.
Emerson, R. Philosophers are lined with eyes within.
Gallagher, T. Coming Home.
Croce e Delizia al Cor.
Each Bird Walking.
García Lorca. Elegy: "Like a censer filled with desire."
Silly Song.

Ginsberg, A.   Kaddish.
  White Shroud.
Glück, L.   For My Mother.
  Love Poem.
  Morning.
  My Cousin in April.
  Nurse's Song.
  Pomegranate.
  School Children, The.
Graves, R.   Advice from a Mother.
  Frosty Night, A.
  Sweet-Shop round the Corner, The.
Hacker, M.   1976.
  Autumn 1980.
  Callers, The.
  Fifteen to Eighteen.
  Fourteen.
  Iva's Birthday Poem.
  Iva's Pantoum.
  Mother.
  Mother II.
  Robber Woman, The.
  Towards Autumn.
Hall, D.   Sister by the Pond, A.
Hamill, S.   Egg, the.
Hardy, T.   In Childbed.
  Lacking Sense, The.
Hayden, R.   Whipping, The.
Heaney, S.   Mother of the Groom.
  Pillowed Head, A.
Herrick.   Upon a Lady That Dyed in Child-Bed,
  and Left a Daughter behind Her.
  Upon a Young Mother of Many Children.
  Upon the Lady Crew.
Hopkins, G.   Mothers are doubtless happier for
  their babes.
Howe, F.   Conclusively.
Hughes, L.   Buddy.
  Cross.
  Lullaby (For a Black Mother).
  Mama and Daughter.
  Mother in Wartime.
  Mother to Son.
  Negro Mother, The.
  S-sss-ss-sh!
Hughes, T.   Anniversary.
  Birth of Rainbow.
  Dogs Are Eating Your Mother, The.
  Memory.
  Revenge Fable.
Ignatow, D.   And Rest.
  Bothering Me at Last.
  Bread Itself, The.
  For My Mother Ill.
  Kaddish.
Jackson, L.   Back to the Mother Breast.
  Fates and the Mothers, The.
  In the Beginning.
Jarrell, R.   Bats.
  Death of the Ball Turret Gunner, The.
  Lost Children, The.
Jeffers, R.   Solstice.
Jonson, B.   Eptiaph on Katherine, Lady Ogle.
Kinnell.   My Mother's R & R.
Kinsella, T.   At the Head Table.
  Dura Mater.
  Our Mother.
  Visiting Hour.
Kipling, R.   Nativity, A.
Kizer, C.   Blessing, The.
  Columns and Caryatids.
  Intruder, The.
  Long Line of Doctors, A.
  Muse, A.
  Pearl.
Koch, K.   On Beauty.
Komunyakaa.   Boys in Dresses.
  My Father's Love Letters [or Loveletters].
Korn.   Generations.
Kumin, M.   Atlantic City 1939.
  Birthday Poem.
  Envelope, The.
  February.
  Grandchild.
  Life's Work.
  Marianne, My Mother, and Me.

Nurture.
  Seeing the Bones.
  Sunbathing on a Rooftop in Berkeley.
  We Stood There Singing.
Kunitz, S.   My Mother's Pears.
Laughlin, J.   Bit Different, A.
  Sweet Kiss, A.
  When Does the Play Begin?
Lawrence, D. H.   Everlasting Flowers.
  Grief.
  Lady Wife.
  Monologue of a Mother.
  She Looks Back.
  Virgin Mother, The.
Levertov.   90th Year, The.
  Chill, The.
  Daughter (1), A.
  Death in Mexico.
  Dragonfly-Mother, The.
  Instant, The.
  Soothsayer, The.
  Soul-Cake, A.
  Visitant.
Levine, P.   Late Moon.
  Look.
  On the Birth of Good & Evil during the Long
    Winter of '28.
Logan, J.   Avocado.
  Lines on His Birthday.
  Long Search, The.
  On the Death of the Poet's Mother Thirty-Three
    Years Later.
Lorde.   Black Mother Woman.
  Dear Toni Instead of a Letter of Congratulation.
  Now that I Am Forever with Child.
  To the Girl Who Lives in a Tree.
Lowell, R.   During Fever.
  Mother, 1972.
  Sailing Home from Rapallo.
  Soft Wood.
Lux.   Emily's Mom.
  Fourth Grade, The.
  It Must Be the Monk in Me.
MacDiarmid, H.   Two Parents, The.
MacLeish.   Burial, The.
  For the Anniversary of my Mother's Death.
Major, C.   First.
  Honey Dripper.
  Mother Junkie.
  String, The.
Meredith, G.   Little Foot-Page, The.
  M. M.
  Mother to Babe.
  Queen Zuleima.
Meredith, W.   My Mother's Life.
Merrill, J.   After the Fire.
Millay, E.   Ballad of the Harp-Weaver, The.
  Courage that my mother had, The.
Milosz, C.   Old Women.
  With Her.
  Yokimura.
Mistral, G.   Escape, The.
  My Mother.
  Rocking.
  Sad Mother, The.
Montale.   To My Mother.
Muldoon, P.   Brazil.
  Cheesecake.
  Ma.
  Oscar.
Nash, O.   Epilogue to Mother's Day, Which Is
  to Be Published on Any Day but Mother's
  Day.
Niedecker.   Oh ivy green.
  Old Mother turns blue and from us.
O'Hara, F.   Ave Maria.
  Poem: "There I could never be a boy."
Olson, C.   It isn't my word but my mother's.
  Just inside the Vigil of Christmas.
  La Chute III.
Oppen.   Mother and Child.
Orr, G.   City of Salt, The.
  Everything.
  Spring Floods.
  Weeds, The.
Paley, G.   Boy His Mother, The.

In San Salvador (I).
  In San Salvador (II).
  Letter, A.
  My Mother: 33 Years Later.
  On the Bank Street Pier.
Parker, D.   Fulfilment.
  Prayer for a New Mother.
Pasolini.   Appendix to the "Religion": A Light.
  Prayer to My Mother.
Patchen.   Career for a Child of Five.
  For the Mother of My Mother's Mother.
  Niobe.
Piercy.   Crescent Moon like a Canoe.
Pinsky.   History of My Heart.
  Poem with Refrains.
Plath.   Disquieting Muses, The.
  Heavy Women.
  Morning Song.
  Parliament Hill Fields.
Poe.   To My Mother.
Prunty.   Lake House, The.
Raine, K.   Binah.
  Columbines.
  Dear ones in the house of the dead.
  Dream.
  Heirloom.
  My Mother's Birthday.
Ramanujan.   Ecology.
  LOVE 3: What He Said, Remembering.
  Of Mothers.
  Still Another for Mother.
Rexroth, K.   Delia Rexroth ("California rolls
  into").
Rich, A.   Mother-Right.
  Night-Pieces: For a Child.
Riley, J.   Being His Mother.
  Boy's Mother, A.
  His Mother.
  His Mother's Way.
  I' Got to Face Mother To-Day!
  Mother.
  Mother-Song, A.
  Since My Mother Died.
  To the Mother.
  When Mother Combed My Hair.
Rilke.   Child at the Window Sill.
  Motherhood.
Rimbaud, A.   Orphans' New Year Gifts.
Ritsos.   Orestes.
  Philoctetes; The Ultimate Mask.
Rossetti, C.   1878.
  1879.
  1884.
  1885. St. Valentine's Day.
  1886, St. Valentine's Day.
  Ballad: "Soft white lamb in the daisy meadow."
  Brandons Both.
  Chilly Night, A.
  Crimson curtains round my mother's bed.
  Crying, my little one, footsore and weary?
  Death.
  For Rosaline's Album.
  Holy Innocents.
  Johnny.
  Lambs at Play.
  Life out of Death.
  Light Love.
  Lullaby: "Love me,—I love you / Love me, my
    baby."
  Mother and Child.
  Motherless baby and babyless mother.
  Our little baby fell asleep.
  Our Mothers, lovely women pitiful; / Our
    sisters, gracious in their life and death.
  There Is a Budding Morrow in Midnight.
  To My First Love, My Mother.
  To My Mother on Her Birthday.
  Valentine to My Mother, A.
  Versi.
  Wishes: Sonnet.
Rukeyser, M.   Birth, A.
  More Clues.
  Night Feeding.
  On the Death of Her Mother.
  Question, The.
  Speech of the Mother, from "The Middle of the

Air."
Trinity Churchyard.
Schuyler, J.   Name Day, A.
On the Dresser.
Seifert.   Autobiography.
Sexton.   Child Bearers, The.
Christmas Eve.
Dreaming the Breasts.
For the Year of the Insane.
Mothers.
Red Shoes, The.
Two Sons.
Simic.   Cold Blue Tinge.
Needle.
Sewing Machine.
Spoons with Realistic Dead Flies on Them.
Smith, S.   Human Affection.
I'll Have Your Heart.
Mother.
Mother, among the Dustbins.
Mother's Hearse, A.
N'est-ce pas assez de ne me point haïr?
Queen and the Young Princess, The.
Sad Mother, The.
She Said..
Virtuoso, The.
Snyder, G.   Gen.
Spender, S.   Furies, The.
Stafford, W.   Clash.
In Fear and Valor.
Memorial for My Mother, A.
My Mother Was a Soldier.
Our Kind.
Ruby Was Her Name.
Some Shadows.
Vacation Trip.
Stevens, W.   Woman That Had More Babies
than That, The.
Stock, R.   Mary on the Death of Joachim.
Trajectory of a Scream.
Stockton, A.   To Mrs Rush, on Her Birth Day.
Swenson, M.   Motherhood.
Nature.
Rusty Autumn.
Szymborska, W.   Born.
Pietà.
Tate, A.   Mother and Son.
Tate, J.   For Mother on Father's Day.
Thomas, D.   My World Is Pyramid.
Updike.   Fall.
Young Matrons Dancing.
Van Duyn.   Remedies, Maladies, Reasons.
Stream, The.
Very.   Hymn: The Efficacy of a Mother's
Prayer.
My Mother's Voice.
Our Dear Mother.
Vogl.   Recognition, The.
Warren, R.   Doubleness in Time.
Only Poem, The.
Revelation.
Tale of Time.
There's a Grandfather's Clock in the Hall.
Whalen, P.   Life and Death and a Letter to My
Mother beyond Them Both.
Whitman, W.   Mother and Babe.
Williams, C. K.   Good Mother: Out.
My Mother's Lips.
Williams, M.   Good Son, A.
On a Photograph of My Mother at Seventeen.
Showing Late Symptoms She First Tries to Fix
Herself in the Minds of Her Children.
Williams, T.   In Jack-O'-Lantern's Weather.
Speech from the Stairs.
Williams, W.   Crude Lament.
Dedication for a Plot of Ground.
Eternity, An.
Horse Show, The.
Painting, The.
Resemblance, The.
Two Pendants: For the Ears.
Young Woman at a Window.
Wilner, E.   As Soft and as Pink as a Nursery.
Made by Hand.
My Mother's Portrait.
Wordsworth, W.   Affliction of Margaret, The.

By a Blest Husband Guided, Mary Came.
Complaint of a Forsaken Indian Woman, The.
Emigrant Mother, The.
Her Eyes Are Wild.
Maternal Grief.
No spade for leagues had won a rood of earth.
Sailor's Mother, The.
Three Graves, The.
Wright, J.   Origins.
Yeats.   Song from "The Player Queen," A.
Song of the Old Mother, The.
Zagajewski.   Airport in Amsterdam.
Zukofsky, L.   Poem Beginning "The."

Mother's Day
Nash, O.   Epilogue to Mother's Day, Which Is
to Be Published on Any Day but Mother's
Day.
Please Leave Father Alone.
Paley, G.   On Mother's Day.
Stafford, W.   Mother's Day.

Mothers-in-Law
Ciardi, J.   Censorship.
Gunn, T.   First Meeting with a Possible Mother-
in-Law.
Rich, A.   Mother-in-Law.
Riley, J.   Speeding of the King's Spite, The.
Zagajewski.   Epicure from My Staircase, The.

Moths
Ammons.   Yucca Moth, The.
Carruth, H.   August First.
Clampitt.   Whippoorwill in the Woods, A.
Collins, B.   Japan.
Crane, H.   Moth That Made God Blind, The.
De la Mare.   Moth, The.
Dickinson, E.   Moth the hue of this, A.
Dubie.   Night before Thanksgiving, The.
Frost, R.   To a Moth Seen in Winter.
Hopkins, G.   All as that moth call'd Underwing,
alighted.
Hughes, L.   Fire-Caught.
Laughlin, J.   Moths, The.
Lux.   Green, The.
Merwin.   Peril.
Montale.   Old Lines.
Petrarch.   Just as a moth, enamoured of the
light.
Rumi.   Judge a Moth by the Beauty of Its
Candle.
Sandburg, C.   Goldwing Moth.
Sarton, M.   Moth in the Schoolroom.
Schuyler, J.   Day, The.
Stafford, W.   Not Very Loud.
Stevens, W.   Hibiscus on the Sleeping Shores.
Williams, T.   Lament for the Moths.
Williams, W.   Prelude to Winter.
Zagajewski.   Moths.

Motion
Ammons.   Cascadilla Falls.
Round.
Viable.
What This Mode of Motion Said.
Beckett, S.   Dread Nay.
Serena III.
Carver, R.   Movement.
Creeley.   To And.
Cummings, E. E.   Now what were motionless
move(exists no).
Emerson, R.   I sat upon the ground.
Gunn, T.   On the Move.
Koch, K.   On the Great Atlantic Rainway.
Levertov.   Improbable Truth.
MacNeice.   Hold-up.
Montale.   My life, I ask of you no stable.
Pessoa.   Whatever stops is death, and is our
death.
Plath.   Years.
Rimbaud, A.   Movement.
Rukeyser, M.   Eccentric Motion.
Rumi.   Secret turning in us, A.
Walk to the well.
You have said what you are.
Snyder, G.   Spring water in the green creek is
clear.
Zagajewski.   It Comes to a Standstill.

Motorcycles and Motorcycling
Carver, R.   Its Course.
Ferlinghetti, L.   Ladakh Buddhess Biker.
Gunn, T.   On the Move.
Unsettled Motorcyclist's Vision of His Death,
The.
Hughes, T.   Motorbike, A.
Olson, C.   Tenemeny twilightish landscape.
Stafford, W.   Fifteen.
Thirteenth and Pennsylvania.
Tate, J.   Motorcyclists, The.
Van Duyn.   What the Motorcycle Said.
Walker, A.   Kiss, The.

Mottoes
Byron, G.   Ich Dien.
Kipling, R.   Boy Scouts' Patrol Song, A.
Ubique.
Stein, G.   Brim Beauvais.
Yet Dish.
Swift, J.   Whitshed's Motto on His Coach.

Mount Vernon, Virginia
Meredith, W.   Firescreen at Mount Vernon, A.

Mountain Climbing
Amichai [or Amikhai].   Life.
Ammons.   One More Time.
Atwood.   Highest Altitude.
Eberhart, R.   Spring Mountain Climb.
Frost, R.   Time Out.
Hardy, T.   Zermatt: To the Matterhorn.
Kinnell.   Flower Herding on Mount Monadnock.
Laughlin, J.   Mountain, The.
Merwin.   Mountain Days.
Snowline.
Wine, The.
Muldoon, P.   Rucksack, The.
Petrarch.   From thought to thought, along each
mountain top.
Rexroth, K.   Climbing Milestone Mountain,
August 22, 1937.
Ice Shall Cover Nineveh.
Incarnation.
North Palisade, the End of September, 1939.
On What Planet.
Rich, A.   Phantasia for Elvira Shatayev.
Rossetti, C.   Resurgam.
Snyder, G.   Across Lamarck Col.
On Climbing the Sierra Matterhorn Again after
Thirty-One Years.
Stafford, W.   Research Team in the Mountains,
The.
Stock, R.   Just Another Apotheosis.
Van Duyn.   Colorado.
Warren, R.   Mountain Mystery.
Williams, T.   Descent.
Wordsworth, W.   To—, on Her First Ascent to
the Summit of Helvellyn.

Mountain Lions
Carver, R.   Cougar, The.
Lawrence, D. H.   Mountain Lion.
Warren, R.   Part of What Might Have Been a
Short Story, Almost Forgotten.

Mountain Men
Carruth, H.   John Dryden.
Han-shan.   Mountain man lives under thatch, A.
Levine, P.   7 Years from Somewhere.
Sandburg, C.   Proud of Their Rags.

Mountains
Amichai [or Amikhai].   End of Summer in the
Judean Mountains.
In the Jerusalem Mountains.
On Mount Muhraka.
Summer Evening in the Jerusalem Mountains.
Ammons.   Classic.
Close-up.
Eyesight.
Further On.
He Said.
High & Low.
Mountain Liar.
Mountain Talk.
Reversal.
Virtu.
Atwood.   Morning, A.
Blue Cloud.   For a Child.
Storm Mountain Face.

Brontë, E.   Farewell To Alexandria, A.
Burns, R.   My Heart's in the Highlands.
  Yon wild, mossy mountains sae lofty and wide.
Carruth, H.   Mountain Cabin, The.
Ciardi, J.   Peaks.
Crane, S.   Once I saw mountains angry.
Creeley.   Mountains in the Desert, The.
  Thinking.
Cummings, E. E.   Fire stop thief help murder
  save the world.
Dickey, W.   Avalanche.
Dickinson, E.   Bloom upon the Mountain—
  stated.
  Sweet Mountains—Ye tell Me no lie.
Eberhart, R.   Burden.
  Skier and the Mountain, The.
Emerson, R. · Earth, The.
  Score of airy miles will smooth, A.
Feng-kan.   I have been to Tientai.
Frost, R.   Fountain, a Bottle, a Donkey's Ears
  and Some Books, A.
Ginsberg, A.   Teton Village.
Gunn, T.   From the Highest Camp.
"H. D."   All Mountains.
Hall, D.   Mount Kearsarge.
  Scenic View.
  Stone Walls.
Han-shan.   Cold Cliff's remoteness is what I
  like.
  Cold Mountain is a leakproof cliff.
  Cold Mountain is nothing but clouds.
  I hiked yesterday to the summit.
  I love the joys of the mountains.
  I see Tientai summit.
  Mountain I live on, The.
  Mountains are so cold, The.
  On Cold Mountain Road.
  People who wander among clouds.
  Rising beyond the sky.
  Tientai Mountains are my home, The.
Hill, G.   God's Little Mountain.
Ignatow, D.   Content.
Jeffers, R.   Red Mountain.
  Treasure, The.
Kizer, C.   Index, a Mountain.
Laughlin, J.   Ein Kitzbuehler Tag (1947).
  Mountain Afterglow, The.
  Near Zermatt: The Drahtseilbahn.
  Sinking Stone, The.
Lawrence, D. H.   Meeting among the
  Mountains.
  Men in New Mexico.
Levertov.   Effacement.
  Elusive.
  Instant, The.
  Mountain's Daily Speech Is Silence, The.
  Open Secret.
  Pentimento.
  Presence.
  Witness.
Mahon.   Mt. Gabriel.
Marvell.   Epigramma in Duos Montes
  Amosclivium et Bilboreum: Farfacio [Epigram
  on Two Mountains, Almscliff and Bilbrough:
  To Fairfax].
McHugh, H.   Hard.
Meredith, G.   Swathed round in mist and
  crown'd with cloud.
Meredith, W.   In the Rif Mountains.
  Kodiak Poem, A.
Merwin.   Horses.
  Houses, The.
  In the Red Mountains.
  Visitation.
Mistral, G.   Escape, The.
  Summit.
Olson, C.   From *The Song of Ullikummi*.
  Obit.
Palmer, M.   False Portrait of Hanna H.
Petrarch.   If the mountain by which this valley's
  closed.
Plath.   Above the Oxbow.
Rexroth, K.   Fish Peddler and Cobbler.
  Heart's Garden, the Garden's Heart, The.
  Ice Shall Cover Nineveh.
  New Year, The.

Night below Zero.
Value in Mountains.
Wheel Revolves, The.
Robinson, E.   Monadnock through the Trees.
  Vickery's Mountain.
Rukeyser, M.   King's Mountain.
  Summer, the Sacramento.
Sandburg, C.   Blue Ridge.
  Lackawanna Twilight.
  March of the Hungry Mountains.
  Smoke Blue.
Shih-te.   I have millions of gathas.
Smith, S.   Sliding Mountain, The.
  Touch and Go.
Snyder, G.   I have lived at Cold Mountain.
  I settled at Cold Mountain long ago.
  In the mountains it's cold.
  Meeting the Mountains.
  Path to Han-shan's place is laughable, The.
  Poem Left in Sourdough Mountain Lookout.
  Spring water in the green creek is clear.
Stafford, W.   Over the Mountains.
  Research Team in the Mountains, The.
  Tillamook Burn, The.
Stevens, W.   Poem That Took the Place of a
  Mountain, The.
Swenson, M.   North Rim, The.
Sze.   Mushroom Hunting in the Jemez
  Mountains.
Thoreau.   Forever in my dream & in my
  morning thought.
  Mountains in the Horizon, The.
  Not unconcerned Wachusett rears his head.
  To the Mountains.
Tomlinson, C.   Above the Rio Grande.
  At a Glance.
  Gorge, The.
  On the Mountain.
Updike.   Mountain Impasse.
Very.   Lines on Mount Auburn.
  Mt. Shasta: A Painting, by H. O. Young.
  On Seeing the White Mountains from Cook's
  Hill, in West Peabody.
Warren, R.   Convergences.
  Globe of Gneiss.
  Have You Ever Eaten Stars?
  Language Barrier.
  Mountain Mystery.
  Myth of Mountain Sunrise.
  Vision under the October Mountain: A Love
  Poem.
Whalen, P.   For Albert Saijo.
  Sourdough Mountain Lookout.
Whitman, W.   Spirit That Form'd This Scene.
Whittier.   Mount Agiochook.
  Mountain Pictures.
Williams, C. K.   That night, / winter, / rain.
Williams, W.   Alighting from my horse to drink
  with you.
Wordsworth, W.   Even as a dragon's eye that
  feels the stress.
  Fairest, brightest, hues of ether fade, The.
  Farewell, A: "Farewell thou little Nook of
  mountain-ground."
  Forth from a Jutting Ridge, around Whose Base.
  Fragments from the Alfoxden Note-Book (III).
  November 1 [1815].
  Pelion and Ossa flourish side by side.
  To—, on Her First Ascent to the Summit of
  Helvellyn.
  View from the Top of Black Comb.
  Voice of the Derwent, The.
  Written with a Slate Pencil on a Stone, on the
  Side of the Mountain of Black Comb.
Zukofsky, L.   "Further than."

See also **Hills and Mountains**

Mountebanks
  Apollinaire.   Mountebanks.

Mourning and Mourners
  Amichai [*or* Amikhai].   Death of Assia G., The.
  From Man You Came and to Man You Shall
  Return.
  Itzhak's Last Kit Bag.
  Too Many.
  Try to Remember Some Details.
  Wonderful Baker, The.

Ammons.   Father.
  Nelly Myers.
Angelou.   Mourning Grace.
Atwood.   Precognition.
Baudelaire.   You were so jealous of our
  nursemaid's love.
Beckett, S.   Je voudrais que mon amour meure.
  Mort de A.D.
  Poem: "I would like my love to die."
Bierce.   J.F.B.
Bion.   Lament for Adonis.
Bradstreet, A.   David's Lamentation for Saul
  and Jonathan.
  Epitaph on my Dear and Ever Honored Mother
  Mrs. Dorothy Dudley.
  In Memory of My Dear Grandchild Anne
  Bradstreet Who Deceased June 20, 1669,
  Being Three Years and Seven Months Old.
  In Memory of My Dear Grandchild Elizabeth
  Bradstreet Who Deceased August, 1665,
  Being a Year and Half Old.
  On My Dear Grandchild Simon Bradstreet,
  [Who Died on 16th November, 1669, Being
  but A Month and One Day Old].
  To the Memory of My Dear and Ever Honored
  Father Thomas Dudley Esq. Who Deceased
  July 31, 1653, and of His Age 77.
  To the Memory of My Dear Daughter in Law,
  Mrs. Mercy Bradstreet.
Brodsky, J.   Funeral of Bobò, The.
Brontë, E.   To A.S., 1830.
  To a Wreath of Snow.
Browning, E.   Child's Grave at Florence, A.
  Court Lady, A.
  Died.
  Felicia Hemans.
  Grief.
  Mourning Mother, The.
  My Kate.
Bukowski.   Conversation in a Cheap Room.
  Japanese Wife, The.
Burns, R.   Elegy on Captain Matthew
  Henderson [*or* Capt. M——— H———] [A
  Gentleman Who Held the Patent for His
  Honours Immediately from Almighty God!].
  Epitaph. Here Lies Robert Fergusson, Poet.
  Man Was Made to Mourn, a Dirge.
  Thou Ling'ring Star.
Byron, G.   And Thou Art Dead, as Young and
  Fair.
  Bright Be the Place of Thy Soul!
  Elegiac Stanzas on the Death of Sir Peter
  Parker, Bart.
  Epitaph on a Friend.
  If Sometimes in the Haunts of Men.
  Monody on the Death of the Right Hon. R. B.
  Sheridan.
  Oh factious viper! whose envenom'd tooth.
  On the Death of a Young Lady.
  One Struggle More, and I Am Free.
Callimachus.   By Callimachus.
Campion, T.   Illustrissimo, Potentissimoque
  Principi, *Frederico* Quinto, Rheni Comiti
  Palatino, Duci Bavariae, &c.
  To the Most Disconsolate Great Brittaine.
  To the Most Illustrious and Mighty Fredericke
  the Fifth, Count Palantine of the Rhein.
  To the Most Sacred Queen Anne.
  What Then Is Love but Mourning?
Carew, T.   Another [Epitaph on the Lady Mary
  Villiers].
  Elegy upon the Death of the Dean of [St.]
  Paul's, Dr. John Donne, An.
  To the Countess of Anglesey.
Carver, R.   All Her Life.
  Cranes, The.
  Forever.
  Lightning Speed of the Past, The.
  Phone Booth, The.
  Summer Fog.
Cavafy.   27 June 1906, 2 P.M.
  Aristovoulos.
  Flowers White and Beautiful, as Were Most
  Becoming.
  Kimon, Son of Learchos, Age 22, Student of
  Greek Literature (in Kyrini).

Myris: Alexandria, 340 A.D.
Priam's Speeding Forth at Night.
Priest at the Serapeion.
Tomb of Lanis, The.
Celan. Black Flakes.
Epitaph for François.
Chaucer. Book of the Duchesse, The.
Chiabrera. Not without heavy grief of heart did
    He.
Weep not, belovèd Friends! nor let the air.
Chuang Tzu. Lao Tzu's Wake.
Three Friends.
Ciardi, J. Alec.
Elegy 2: "I dream awake in the uptown
    morning."
Elegy 3, Cavalcante.
Elegy for Sam.
Elegy: For You, Father.
Ugliness.
Clampitt. 'Eighty-Nine.
Matrix (Villa Serbelloni, Lake Como).
Clifton, L. Imagining Bear.
Coleridge, S. Israel's Lament.
Sonnet [to Charles Lloyd].
Cooper, J. Calling, The.
Faithful, The.
Iron.
Long, Disconsolate Lines.
Mourning Picture.
Corbett, W. Joe Brainard.
Poem: "French blue morning."
Cowper, W. Epitaph on Mr. Chester.
Grief of an Heir, The.
Crane, S. Behold, the grave of a wicked man.
Ocean said to me once, The.
Crashaw. Elegy upon the Death of Mr.
    Stanninow Fellow of Queenes Colledge.
Epitaph. Upon Doctor Brooke, An.
To Pontius Washing His Blood-Stained Hands.
Upon the Death of a Gentleman.
Upon the Death of Mister Herrys.
Creeley. Four Years Later.
Friend.
Oh Max.
Cuadra, P. Lament of a Maiden for the
    Warrior's Death.
Dante Alighieri. Sonnet: To Certain Ladies;
    when Beatrice Was Lamenting Her Father's
    Death.
Sonnet: To the Same Ladies; with Their Answer.
Davie, D. G. M. B.
Pietà.
Rutland.
Widowers.
De la Mare. Mourn'st Thou Now?
Dickinson, E. Bustle in a House, The.
Last Night that She Lived, The.
Of nearness to her sundered Things.
That bleeding beginning that every mourner
    knows.
Donne. Valediction: Forbidding Mourning, A.
Dugan, A. Elegy for a Gifted Child.
On a Benign Bureaucratization of Death.
Dunbar, P. Easter Ode, An.
Weltschmertz.
Emerson, R. My days roll by me like a train of
    dreams.
Faiz. Bangla Desh: 1.
Elegy for Hassan Nasir.
Frost, R. Home Burial.
García Lorca. Graphic of the Petenera.
Lament for Ignacio Sánchez Mejías.
Ginsberg, A. Kaddish.
Glück, L. Dream of Mourning, The.
Graves, R. Strangling in Merrion Square, The.
Gray, T. Elegy Written in a Country
    Churchyard.
Sonnet [on the Death of Mr. Richard West].
Gurney, I. To Crickley.
To His Love.
Han-shan. Old Chung north of town.
Hardy, T. After the Burial.
Caged Goldfinch, The.
Carrier, The.
Clock-Winder, The.
Colour, The.

Death-Day Recalled, A.
Dissemblers, The.
If You Had Known.
Last Words to a Dumb Friend.
Mother Mourns, The.
Regret Not Me.
Roman Gravemounds, The.
Harrison, M. Poem on the Death of Mrs. Smith,
    A.
Hayden, R. Approximations.
Mourning Poem for the Queen of Sunday.
Herrick. Comfort to a Lady upon the Death of
    Her Husband.
Dirge upon the Death of the Right Valiant Lord,
    Bernard Stuart, A.
False Mourning.
His Charge to Julia at His Death.
His Lachrimae or Mirth, Turn'd to Mourning.
Mad Maid's Song, The.
To Anthea.
To His Dying Brother, Master William Herrick.
To His Lovely Mistresses.
To Perenna, a Mistresse.
To the Lady Crew, upon the Death of her Child.
Upon a Maid.
Upon a Maid[e].
Upon an Old Man a Residenciarie.
Upon His Kinswoman Mrs. M. S.
Upon His Sister-in-Law, Mistress Elizabeth
    Herrick.
Upon the Much Lamented, Mr. J. Warr.
Hughes, L. As Befits a Man.
Bombings in Dixie.
Irish Wake.
Monroe's Blues.
Night Funeral in Harlem.
To a Dead Friend.
Wake.
Widow Woman.
Hughes, T. Day He Died, The.
Error, The.
Waving goodbye, from your banked hospital
    bed.
Ignatow, D. Bread Itself, The.
His Name.
Kaddish.
Semblance, A.
Jacobsen, J. Mourner Betrayed.
Rock-Plant Wife, The.
Jeffers, R. Hungerfield.
May-June, 1940.
Johnson, S. Stella in Mourning.
Jonson, B. On My First Son[ne].
To the Same [Sir John Roe].
Keats. Ah! Ken Ye What I Met the Day.
Faery Song.
Kinnell. Neverland.
Kinsella, T. Cover Her Face.
Vertical Man.
Kipling, R. Gift of the Sea, The.
Last Suttee, The.
London Stone.
Kizer, C. Trio.
Komunyakaa. Cenotaph.
Facing It.
Wokanmagulli.
Kumin, M. How It Is.
In Memoriam P. W. Jr. 1921–1980.
Progress Report.
Splitting Wood at Six Above.
Kunitz, S. Way Down, The.
Laughlin, J. Building 520, Bellevue.
Sorrow.
Lawrence, D. H. Sorrow.
Levertov. At David's Grave.
For Bet.
Olga Poems.
Logan, J. Grandmother Dead in the Aeroplane.
Lament for Misenus.
Logue, C. For My Father.
MacDiarmid, H. At the Cenotaph.
MacNeice. Tam Cari Capitis.
Major, C. Dismal Moment Passing.
Mallarmé. Sonnet: "In the forgotten woods,
    when somber winter glowers."
Martial. 1.33: "In private she mourns not the

    late-lamented."
Marvell. Mourning.
Meredith, G. C B M.
Meredith, W. In Memoriam Stratton
    Christensen.
Merwin. Mourner, The.
Thread, The.
Michelangelo Buonarroti. Already burdened
    with a heavy heart.
Among the memory of all lovely things.
Be sure, my eyes, you know.
His life gave yours rich reason for thanksgiving.
If, while I lived, a someone, eyes on me.
My fervent prayer, if any pity me.
Peace, life—he found them in my open eyes.
So it wouldn't need to retrieve the total sum.
To see that your famous beauty still endures.
Too early fallen asleep here, I'm alive.
What wonder that—seeing how, beside your
    fire.
Who grieve now at my grave, in vain they pray.
Millay, E. Interim.
Milosz, C. In Warsaw.
On Parting with My Wife, Janina.
With Her.
Milton. Elegy 2: On the Death of the Beadle of
    Cambridge University.
Elegy 3: On the Death of the Bishop of
    Winchester.
Lycidas.
Mir, M. Elegy: "In the May breeze."
Montale. Is it salt that strafes or hail? It slays.
Poems for Camillo Sbarbaro.
Muldoon, P. Big Foot.
Norton, J. Funeral Elegy upon that Pattern and
    Patron of Virtue, A.
Olson, C. Death of Europe, The.
Town, The.
Orr, G. After a Death.
Far below, plowed fields vibrated.
Gathering the Bones Together.
His Lament.
Lament: "I thought of you."
Song: Early Death of the Mother.
Wedge, The.
Parker, D. Of a Woman, Dead Young.
Prayer for a Prayer.
Testament.
Parra, N. Imperfect Lover, The.
Petrarch. Alas, that time has now passed over
    when.
Blazing knot which twenty-one whole years,
    The.
Blest soul, so often coming back to me.
Column and the Laurel-tree are broken, The.
Could a more dreadful vision ever be?
Death has no power to make that sweet face
    bitter.
Death has put out the sun which dazed my eyes.
Death, you have left this world, without its sun.
Descending from the sky I see Aurora.
Every day seems to me a thousand years.
From loveliest eyes, and from the visage which.
Go, my sad rhymes, until you reach the stone.
Had I believed those words would turn out dear.
How often do I come to this retreat.
I feel the ancient breeze, see with delight.
I go in mourning for those years of mine.
I know that never with a tranquil mind.
I thought my wings were fledged for such a
    flight.
I used to stray far from the fountainhead.
I used to take the blame, but now excuse.
If Love does not bring better thoughts to bear.
In the best season of our earthly span.
Is this the nest in which my phoenix put.
Kindly fortune that made me once so happy.
Leave me, unhappy thoughts, leave me in
    peace!
Life flies from us, and does not pause one hour.
Love, lend a hand to my afflicted mind.
Love was perhaps a happy thing onetime.
Love, who in good times kept me company.
My eyes, that sun of ours is shut away.
Nightingale, that so harmoniously, The.
No loving mother doting on her son.

Not stars that wander through the open sky.
Now could I but describe with what sweet breath.
Now that your soul is loosened from that knot.
Now Zephirus brings back the better weather.
O day, O hour, O instant at the last.
O happy spirit that so charmingly.
O you, my one inestimable gem.
One day when I was looking from my window.
Out of a thousand ladies I saw one.
Poor little bird, singing as you flit by.
Sennuccio, though you leave your friend alone.
She was alive in me upon a time.
Sight of her, angelic and serene, The.
That lovely lady who possessed your heart.
That other sun by whom the path was shown.
Thinking of what today adorns the sky.
Those eyes of which so warmly I would speak.
Through her I swapped the Arno for the Sorgue.
Valley re-echoing with woes of mine.
Weep, ladies; as you weep, let Love weep too.
What is the matter? And why do you turn.
What pitying messenger, what angel was.
What should I do? Love, what do you advise?
When hope was flourishing.
When little birds complaining, or green leaves.
Whenever my gentle faithful comforter.
Where is the forehead that with one slight shake.
With food in which Lord Love seems to abound.
With my deep sighs I fill the ambient air.
Yearning yet chaste eyes she held upon, The.
You've made the loveliest face, O Death, turn pale.
Pinkerton, H.   Autumn Drought.
Elegy at Beaverhead County, Montana.
For Edgar Bowers.
Pinsky.   Ice-Storm, The.
Impossible to Tell.
Poem with Refrains.
Prunty.   Hand-me-down, The.
Ramanujan.   Elegy: "Grown son's tears in a restaurant mix their salt, A."
Rexroth, K.   Andrée Rexroth ("Now once more gray mottled buckeye branches").
Rich, A.   Mourning Picture.
Valediction Forbidding Mourning, A.
Riley, J.   After the Frost.
Bride, A.
Dead in Sight of Fame.
Dead Wife, The.
Edgar Wilson Nye.
Even as a Child.
Josh Billings.
Leave-Taking, A.
Mrs. Benjamin Harrison.
Old Year and the New, The.
Ole Bull.
Serenade—To Nora.
Uncomforted.
What a Dead Man Said.
What They Said.
When Our Baby Died.
You May Not Remember.
Ritsos.   Memorial Services.
Robinson, E.   Book of Annandale, The.
Reuben Bright.
Roethke.   Elegy for Jane.
Rossetti, C.   After Death.
Death's Chill Between.
Remember [Me].
Song: "When I am dead, my dearest."
Why did baby die.
Rossetti, D.   Portrait, The.
Rukeyser, M.   Long Past Moncada.
One Month.
Scott, S.   Jock of Hazeldean.
Seifert.   November 1918.
Sexton.   Curse against Elegies, A.
Truth the Dead Know, The.
Shelley, P.   Adonais; An Elegy on the Death of John Keats.
Smith, S.   Arabella.
Spenser, E.   Teares of the Muses, The.
Stafford, W.   108 East 19th.
Ceremony, A: Doing the Needful.

Consolations.
Joe's Corner.
Letting You Go.
Memorial for My Mother, A.
That Year.
Stock, R.   Mary on the Death of Joachim.
Verses after Which the Mourning Statue Is Presumed to Speak.
Stockton, A.   Anniversary Elegy on the Death of Mr Stockton the 28th of Feb 1783.
Compos'd in a Dancing Room, December 69.
Elegiack Ode on the 28th Day of February 1782, An. The Anniversary of Mr. Stockton's Death.
Elegy: "For thee I drop the tender tear."
Elegy Inscribed to Richard J Stockton Esqr [Feb. 28, 1787].
Elegy on the Death of a Young Lady, An.
Elegy on the Death of Miss Chandler, as if Written in Her Fathers Church Yard.
Elegy on the Death of Mrs Dickinson. The Event Was Communicated at the Sea Shore.
Elegy on the Death of Mrs Wilson, April the 19, 1786, An.
Fragment on Hearing the Account of Mrs Ramseys Death.
Fragment on the Death of a Minester.
Lines on Hearing of the Death of Doctor Franklin.
Lines on the Death of Mrs Hill Suppos'd to Be Spoken by Her Sister Mrs Clymer.
Lines on the Death of Mrs Petit of Philadelphia.
Resignation, an Elegiac Ode, February the 28th, 1788.
Short Elegy to the Memory of Her Husband, A.
To Amanda—Who Was Obliging Enough to Delight Her Friend with Singing Every Evening Two Songs Which She Was Very Fond Off.
To Richard John Stockton Esqr, Inclosing the Preceding Elegy [Feb. 28, 1787].
Why wanders my friend in this grove?
Szymborska, W.   Parting with a View.
Thomas, D.   In the White Giant's Thigh.
Thoreau.   Funeral Bell, The.
Sympathy.
Tomlinson, C.   Ars Poetica.
Unknown.   Another ["Painter, this likeness is too strong"].
Ballade de Marguerite.
Unknown, sometimes at. to Sir Walter Ralegh.   Songe Made by Sir Walter Rawley, A.
Van Duyn.   Creation, The.
Stream, The.
Very.   Mourner, The.
Walker, A.   Natural Star.
Warren, R.   Admonition to Those Who Mourn.
Tale of Time.
Wheatley, P.   Elegy, Sacred to the Memory of that Great Divine, the Reverend and Learned Dr. Samuel Cooper, An.
Elegy Sacred to the Memory of the Rev'd Samuel Cooper, D.D., An.
Elegy, to Miss. Mary Moorhead, on the Death of Her Father, the Rev. Mr. John Moorhead, An.
On the Death of Dr. Samuel Marshall. 1771.
On the Death of the Rev. Dr. Sewell. 1769.
To a Lady and Her Children, on the Death of Her Son and Their Brother.
To His Honour the Lieutenant-Governor, on the Death of His Lady. March 24, 1773.
To the Honourable T. H. Esq; on the Death of His Daughter.
Whitman, W.   Sobbing of the Bells, The.
Vigil Strange I Kept on the Field One Night.
Whittier.   Lament, A: "Circle is broken, one seat is forsaken, The."
Lines on the Death of S. Oliver Torrey.
Wilbur, R.   To an American Poet Just Dead.
Wilde, O.   Lotus Leaves.
True Knowledge, The.
Williams, C. K.   Le Petit Salvié.
Vehicle: Absence.
Villanelle of the Suicide's Mother.
Williams, M.   Jonathan in Mourning.

June Twenty, Three Days After.
Williams, T.   Valediction: "She went with morning on her lips."
Wreath for Alexandra Molostvova, A.
Wordsworth, W.   Dirge Sung by a Minstrel.
Elegiac Stanzas (Addressed to Sir G.H.B. upon the Death of His Sister-in-Law).
Elegy Written in the Same Place upon the Same Occasion.
Epitaph in the Chapel Yard of Langdale, Westmoreland.
On the Death of an Unfortunate Lady.
Sonnet Written by Mr — Immediately after the Death of His Wife.
Surprised by joy—impatient as the Wind.
Wright, J.   Angel, The.
At the Slackening of the Tide.
Centenary Note: Inscribed to Little Crow, Leader of the Sioux Rebellion in Minnesota, 1862, A.
Gesture by a Lady with an Assumed Name, A.
Girl Walking into a Shadow, A.
Listening to the Mourners.
Paul.
Poem about George Doty in the Death House, A
Refusal, The.
Winter Day in Ohio, A.
Wyatt, S.   Mourning my heart doth sore oppress.
Yeats.   Crazy Jane Reproved.
John Kinsella's Lament for Mrs. Mary Moore.
Zagajewski.   Airport in Amsterdam.
Blackbird.
Night.

See also Funerals; Grief

Mouths
Codrescu.   Muffled by a Belt across the Mouth.
Creeley.   Language, The.
Mouths Nuzz.
Ferlinghetti, L.   Mouth of truth, The.
Rilke.   Divine Disgrace.

Movies
Ashbery, J.   Forties Flick.
Lonedale Operator, The.
Berryman.   Dispossessed, The.
Carver, R.   No Heroics, Please.
Clampitt.   Godfather Returns to Color TV, The.
Odessa Steps, The.
Codrescu.   Les Fleurs du Cinéma.
To the Virgin as She Now Stands to the Monk after a Beatles Movie.
Collins, B.   Movies, The.
Corbett, W.   Prayer.
Creeley.   Bresson's Movies.
Movie Run Backward, The.
Cummings, E. E.   Mind's(/ I never you never), The.
O pr / gress verily thou art m.
Davie, D.   Lincolnshire.
Tiger at the Movie-Show.
Dubie.   Grand Illusion.
Sanctuary.
Through a Glass Darkly.
Ginsberg, A.   Methedrine Vision in Hollywood, A.
Hayden, R.   Double Feature.
Hughes, L.   Madam and the Movies.
Movies.
Ignatow, D.   Folk Singer, The.
Jacobsen, J.   Country Drive-In.
Komunyakaa.   Summer Night in Hanoi, A.
Kumin, M.   At a Private Showing in 1982.
Casablanca.
Kunitz, S.   Magic Curtain, The.
Laughlin, J.   Kissing.
Nowadays.
Lawrence, D. H.   Film Passion.
When I Went to the Film.
Levertov.   Film, The.
Logan, J.   Saturday Afternoon at the Movies.
Major, C.   In Hollywood with the Zuni God of War.
McGrath, T.   Ars Poetica: Or: Who Lives in the Ivory Tower?
Merwin.   Late Wonders.
Muldoon, P.   Key, The.

Weepies, The.
Nash, O.   Screen with the Face with the Voice, The.
What's in a Name? Here's What's in a Name, or, I Wonder What Became of John and Mary.
O'Hara, F.   Ave Maria.
Image of Leda, An.
To the Film Industry in Crisis.
Pagis.   Silent Movie.
Parker, D.   Movies; A Hymn of Hate.
Passionate Screen Writer to His Love, The.
Pinsky.   Picture.
Rich, A.   Pierrot Le Fou.
Roethke.   Double Feature.
Rukeyser, M.   Song: Remembering Movies.
Schuyler, J.   Simone Signoret.
Smith, S.   Film Star, The.
Szymborska, W.   Leaving the Cinema.
Slapstick.
Tate, J.   Same Tits.
Updike.   Déjà, Indeed.
Home Movies.
In Memoriam.
Movie House.
Whalen, P.   Talking Picture, The.
That One.
Wilbur, R.   Prisoner of Zenda, The.
Williams, W.   Light Becomes Darkness.
Wilner, E.   Love of What Is Not, The.
Zagajewski.   Watching Shoah in a Hotel Room in America.

Moving and Movers
Berryman.   Narcissus Moving.
Dickey, W.   New Place, The.
Gunn, T.   Last Days at Teddington.
Thoughts on Unpacking.
Jarrell, R.   Moving.
Lorde.   Moving Out or the End of Cooperative Living.
Merrill, J.   Mornings in a New House.
Nemerov.   Going Away.
Pinsky.   Exile.
Rich, A.   Moving in Winter.
Passing On.
Schuyler, J.   Sorting, Wrapping, Packing, Stuffing.
Simic.   Furniture Mover.
Updike.   Note to the Previous Tenants.

Mowing and Mowers
Ammons.   Needs.
Ciardi, J.   On the Orthodoxy and Creed of My Power Mower.
Dickey, J.   Poem: "For having left the birds that left me."
Frost, R.   Last Mowing, The.
Mowing.
Tuft of Flowers, The.
Ignatow, D.   Death of a Lawn Mower.
Kumin, M.   Distance.
Territory.
Lawrence, D. H.   Mowers, The.
Youth Mowing, A.
Marvell.   Damon the Mower.
Mower against Gardens, The.
Mower to the Glowworms [or Glow-Worms or Glo-Worms], The.
Mower's Song, The.
Meredith, W.   Old Field Mowed for Appearances' Sake, An.
Merwin.   Watchers.
Muldoon, P.   Coney, The.
Prunty.   Memorial Day.

Mozart, Wolfgang Amadeus
MacLeish.   Men of My Century Loved Mozart.
Meredith, G.   I humm'd an air of sweet Mozart.
Orr, G.   Dinner, The.
Seifert.   Nocturnal Divertimento.
Stevens, W.   Mozart, 1935.
Zukofsky, L.   Record, The.

Mud
Ammons.   Upright.
Creeley.   House, The ("Mud put / upon mud").
Cummings, E. E.   In Just.
Heaney, S.   Bann Clay.
Mud Vision, The.

Ignatow, D.   I Dream.
Kumin, M.   Mud.
Lux.   Pismire Rising.
Williams, W.   K. McB.

Muffs
See Gloves; Mittens

Muhammad
Coleridge, S.   Mahomet.
Lowell, R.   Like Henry VIII, Mohammed got religion.
Rumi.   Basket of Fresh Bread, A.
Deliberation.
I Come before Dawn.
Joy at Sudden Disappointment.
Muhammad and the Huge Eater.
New Moon, Hilal.
One Who Wraps Himself.
Polishing the Mirror.
Private Banquet, The.
Witness, the Darling, The.
Whittier.   Requital.

Mulberry Trees
Plath.   Moonrise.
Riley, J.   Mulberry Tree, The.
Stevens, W.   Banjo Boomer.

Mules
Ammons.   Mule Song.
Silver.
Ciardi, J.   Mule.
Hughes, L.   Me and the Mule.
Lawrence, D. H.   Ass, The.
Logan, J.   Cycle for Mother Cabrini, A.
Lux.   Gold on Mule.
Muldoon, P.   Mules.
Nash, O.   Mules, The.
Patchen.   Mule of water, The.
Sandburg, C.   New Farm Tractor.
Williams, M.   Stopping to Look at a Crèche in a Jewelry Store Window.

Mulzac, Hugh Nathaniel
Hughes, L.   To Captain Mulzac.

Mummies
Eberhart, R.   On Seeing an Egyptian Mummy in Berlin, 1932.
Heaney, S.   Punishment.
Parra, N.   Mummies.
Sandburg, C.   Mummy.
Wilde, O.   Athanasia.
Wright, C.   To the Egyptian Mummy in the Etruscan Museum at Cortona.

Munch, Edvard
Hall, D.   "Between the Clock and the Bed."
"Kiss, The."
"Marat's Death."
"Scream, The."
Mahon.   Girls on the Bridge.

Münter, Gabriele
Zagajewski.   For Gabriela Münter.

Murder and Murderers
Ai.   Detective, The.
Good Shepherd, The: Atlanta, 1981.
Hitchhiker, The.
Kid, The.
Penis Envy.
Rapture.
Stalking Memory.
Atwood.   Robber Bridegroom, The.
Auden.   Victor.
Bandeira.   Brazilian Tragedy.
Baudelaire.   Murderer's Wine.
Berry, W.   Morning's News, The.
Blake, W.   Fair Elenor.
Brodsky, J.   Homage to Yalta.
Brontë, E.   Death Of A.G.A., The.
Brooks, G.   Bronzeville Mother Loiters in Mississippi, A. Meanwhile, a Mississippi Mother Burns Bacon.
Browning, R.   Forgiveness, A.
Laboratory, The (Ancien Régime).
Porphyria's Lover.
Byron, G.   Marino Faliero, Doge of Venice.
Carew, T.   Another [On the Duke of Buckingham].
Murdering Beauty.
On the Duke of Buckingham.

Cavafy.   King Claudius.
One of the dead woman's days, the ghost of a day.
Clampitt.   Seed.
Clifton, L.   Jasper Texas 1998.
Codrescu.   Music.
Coleridge, S.   Alice Du Clos.
Mad Monk, The.
Crashaw.   To Pontius Washing His Blood-Stained Hands.
Cummings, E. E.   So you're hunting for ann well i'm looking for will.
De la Mare.   Banquo.
Heresy.
Macbeth.
Dickey, W.   And he lies dead—.
And I, who lay so warm and quiet there—.
Come, Doctor, we must fly someotherwhere.
Doctor, I did not see that you were there.
For we have gone a curious way from there.
I did not know you when you came in there.
Part Song, with Concert of Recorders.
Who made you come and find the door to there?
Dunbar, P.   Murdered Lover, The.
Eberhart, R.   Am I My Neighbor's Keeper.
Snowy Owl.
Villanelle: "Christ is walking in your blood today."
García Lorca.   Death of Antonito el Camborio, The.
Death of Little Tony Camborio, The.
Murder.
Glück, L.   Murderess, The.
Graves, R.   Coronation Murder, The.
Dangerous Gift, The.
Nobody.
Strangling in Merrion Square, The.
Gunn, T.   Victim, The.
Hardy, T.   Fight on Durnover Moor, The.
Flirt's Tragedy, The.
Forbidden Banns, The.
Her Second Husband Hears Her Story.
Mock Wife, The.
Single Witness, The.
Sound in the Night, A.
Herbert, Z.   Achilles. Penthesilea.
Herrick.   Upon Faunus.
Upon Leech.
Housman.   Farewell to barn and stack and tree.
True Lover, The.
Hughes, L.   Death in Harlem.
Death of Do Dirty: A Rounder's Song.
Ignatow, D.   And That Night.
Murderer, The.
Play Again.
Jacobsen, J.   Painter at Xyochtl.
Jarrell, R.   Eighth Air Force.
La Belle au Bois Dormant.
Jeffers, R.   Give Your Heart to the Hawks.
Margrave.
Solstice.
Such Counsels You Gave to Me.
Kipling, R.   Ballad of Fisher's Boardinghouse, The.
Cain and Abel.
Cleared.
What Happened.
Komunyakaa.   Butterfly-toed Shoes.
By Proxy.
Epilogue to the Opera of Dead on Arrival.
Nothing to Do with Janice Drake.
Reconstructing a Crime.
Lawrence, D. H.   Late War, The.
Murder.
Murderous Weapons.
Lorde.   Need: A Chorale for Black Woman Voices.
Lowell, R.   Mary Stuart.
Lux.   Fourth Grade, The.
Meredith, G.   Josepha.
Merton.   Chant to Be Used in Processions around a Site with Furnaces.
Merwin.   Free, The.
Last One, The.
Nash, O.   Strange Case of the Dead Divorcee, The.

Warning to Wives, A.
Nemerov. August, 1945.
  Murder of William Remington, The.
  Place of Value, The.
Neruda. Danger, The.
  Wars, The.
Olson, C. Poemless Rhymes for the Times.
Patchen. From My High Love.
  If We Are to Know Where We Live.
  Murder of Two Men by a Young Kid Wearing
    Lemon-colored Gloves, The.
  Polly—An Almost-True Story.
Plath. Daddy.
Poe. Scenes from Politian.
Prunty. Sorrows of Lester Buster, The.
Ritsos. Nocturnal Episode.
  Strange Times.
Sexton. Assassin, The.
  Killing the Love.
Smith, S. Bag-Snatching in Dublin.
  But Murderous.
  From My Notes for a Series of Lectures on
    Murder.
  Murder.
  Murderer, The.
  One of Many.
  Who Killed Lawless Lean?
Stock, R. Instructions to Any Painter for a
  "Coronation of Inés de Castro."
Swinburne. Phaedra.
Sze. Knife at the Jugular.
Thomas, D. Ballad of the Long-legged Bait.
Walker, A. 1971.
  Family Of.
  Killers.
  Revolutionary Petunias.
Warren, R. Ballad of Billie Potts, The.
  Crime.
Whittier. Burial of Barber.
Wilde, O. Ballad of Reading Gaol, The.
Williams, C. K. In the Heart of the Beast.
Williams, M. Believing.
  Everything Is Fine Here. How Are You?
  Serial Murderer Says Something to the Priest,
    The.
Williams, T. Liturgy of Roses, A.
Wright, J. At the Executed Murderer's Grave.
  Life, The.
  Poem about George Doty in the Death House,
    A.
  Secret Gratitude, A.

Murfreesboro, Battle of (1862–1863)
Tate, A. Battle of Murfreesboro.

Muses
Ammons. Muse.
Baudelaire. In Praise of My Françoise.
  Mercenary Muse, The.
  Sick Muse, The.
Berryman. Images of Elspeth.
Blake, W. To the Muses.
Blok. Among the Admirers of Carmen.
  To the Muse.
Bradstreet, A. Prologue, The.
Brodsky, J. To Urania.
Broumas, O. Triple Muse.
Burns, R. To Robt. Graham of Fintry Esqr, with
  a Request for an Excise Division.
Byron, G. Farewell to the Muse.
Cavafy. Poet and the Muse, The.
Ciardi, J. Apology for Not Invoking the Muse,
  An.
Clough. If help there is not, but the Muse.
Cowper, W. In a Letter to C.P.
Crashaw. To the Morning. Satisfaction for
  Sleepe.
Creeley. Door, The.
Cullen, C. After a Visit.
"Dario." Ballad in Honor of the Muses of Flesh
  and Blood.
De la Mare. Child Asleep, A.
Donne. To Mr R. W. ("Zealously my Muse doth
  salute all thee").
Dugan, A. Mock Translation from the Greek.
Duncan, R. Festivals, The.
  For a Muse Meant.
Éluard, P. Lady Love.

Emerson, R. Best of life is presence of a muse,
  The.
  For deathless powers to verse belong.
  From Nature's beginning.
  Honor bright o muse.
  House, The.
  I spread my gorgeous sail.
  James Russell Lowell.
  Loss and Gain.
  Muse / Can at pleasure use, The.
  Saadi held the Muse in awe.
  Shall the Muse sing for thousands & not sing.
  Solution.
  Test, The.
Glück, L. Poem: "In the early evening, as now,
  a man is bending."
Graves, R. At the Gate.
  Beware, Madam!
  Darien.
  Her Beauty.
Gray, T. Ode on the Pleasure Arising from
  Vicissitude.
  Progress of Poesy, The.
"H. D." Thetis.
Hardy, T. Rome: The Vatican: Sala delle Muse.
Herrick. Departure of the Good Daemon, The.
  His Winding-Sheet.
  Hymne to the Muses, A.
  Mount of the Muses, The.
  On Himselfe.
  Pride Allowable in Poets.
  To His Muse.
  To His Muse, Another to the Same.
  To the High and Noble Prince, George, Duke,
    Marquesse, and Earle of Buckingham.
Ignatow, D. Melpomene in Manhattan.
Jacobsen, J. When the Five Prominent Poets.
Johnson, S. Aurora Est Musis Amica.
Jonson, B. And must I sing? What subject shall
  I choose?
  Elegy [or Elegie], An: "Let me be what I am, as
    Virgil cold."
  Epistle. To My Lady Covell.
  To Benjamin Rudyerd.
  To Lucy, Countess[e] of Bedford, with Mr.
    Donne's Satires [or Satyres].
  To My Muse.
Keats. Ode to Apollo.
  Sonnet: "Where didst thou find, young Bard, thy
    sounding lyre?"
  To George Felton Mathew.
Kizer, C. Muse, A.
Komunyakaa. Night Muse & Mortar Round.
Laughlin, J. Care and Feeding of a Poet, The.
  My Muse.
Levertov. Illustration [—a Footnote], The.
  To the Muse.
  Well, The.
Meredith, G. Two Masks, The.
Milton. Elegy 6: To Charles Deodati.
O'Hara, F. Muse Considered as a Demon
  Lover, The.
Olson, C. Atalanta.
  La Chute II.
  Muse / is the "fate" of the poem, The.
Orr, G. Muse of Midnight.
Petrarch. Now blessed be the day, the month,
  the year.
Plato. They said the Muses were but nine, and
  then.
Smith, S. Dear Muse.
  My Muse.
  Who Is This Who Howls and Mutters?
Spenser, E. Teares of the Muses, The.
Stafford, W. When I Met My Muse.
Stock, R. Double Ballade of Newfangled
  Ladies, A.
  Synapse, The.
Swift, J. To Mr. Congreve.
Tennyson, A. Parnassus.
Thoreau. Inspiration.
Tomlinson, C. Poem: "It falls onto my page like
  rain."
Walcott. Upstate.
Whalen, P. Complaint: To the Muse.
  To a Poet.

Wheatley, P. On Recollection.
  To Maecenas.
Wilbur, R. Advice from the Muse.
Williams, M. Muse of the Evening.
  Muse, The.
Wilner, E. Muse, The.
Woodbridge. Upon the Author. By a Known
  Friend.
Wordsworth, W. Her Only Pilot the Soft
  Breeze, the Boat.
  Not Love, Not War, nor the Tumultuous Swell.
  On Seeing a Needlecase in the Form of a Harp;
    the Work of E.M.S.
  To Melpomene.
Wright, J. To the Muse.
Yeats. Those Images.
Zaturenska. Bird and the Muse.
  Homage to Christina Rossetti.
Zukofsky, L. *Barely* and *widely*.

Museums
Amichai [or Amikhai]. At the Maritime
  Museum.
Auden. Our Bias.
Clampitt. Leaving Yannina.
Collins, B. Brooklyn Museum of Art, The.
Cunningham, J. I, Too, Have Been to the
  Huntington.
Dickey, W. Afternoon Evening and Night in the
  Courtyard of the Museum of Modern Art.
Dugan, A. Fragment on the British Museum.
Enzensberger, H. Old Revolution.
Gunn, T. Expression.
Hardy, T. Haunting Fingers.
  In a Museum.
Hughes, L. Metropolitan Museum.
Jarrell, R. In Galleries.
Kinsella, T. Museum.
Laughlin, J. In the Museum at Teheran.
  Logistics.
Levertov. Winter Afternoons in the V & A, Pre-
  W.W.II.
Logan, J. Believe It.
  March. The Museum. Buffalo. de Chirico.
MacNeice. Museums.
  National Gallery, The.
  Time for a Smoke.
Meredith, W. At the Natural History Museum.
  At the Prado.
  Nausea.
Milosz, C. Wall of a Museum, The.
Niedecker. Art Center.
Pagis. Moment at the Louvre, A.
Plath. Morning Song.
Ramanujan. Time to Stop.
Rich, A. Love in the Museum.
Ritsos. Vatican Museum.
Sandburg, C. Dinosaur Bones, The.
Schuyler, J. Back.
Sze. Los Alamos Museum, The.
Szymborska, W. Museum.
Updike. Roman Portrait Busts.
  Room 28.
Very. East India Marine Museum, The.
Wilbur, R. Museum Piece.
Williams, M. Curator, The.
Wright, C. To the Egyptian Mummy in the
  Etruscan Museum at Cortona.
Wright, J. Museums in Chapultepec, The.
Yeats. Municipal Gallery Revisited, The.
Zagajewski. Covenant.
  Senza Flash.

Mushrooms
Atwood. Mushrooms.
Dickey, W. Virginia Woolf Gathers Mushrooms.
Dickinson, E. Mushroom is the Elf of Plants,
  The.
Dugan, A. Rising in Fall.
Eberhart, R. Mistaken Identity.
Jacobsen, J. Chanterelles, The.
Mahon. Disused Shed in Co. Wexford, A.
Merwin. Looking for Mushrooms at Sunrise.
Muldoon, P. Gathering Mushrooms.
Oliver, M. Mushrooms.
Plath. Mushrooms.
Rossetti, C. Toadstool comes up in a night, A.
Sze. Mushroom Hunting in the Jemez

Mountains.
Tomlinson, C. Mushrooms.
Picking Mushrooms by Moonlight.
Warren, R. Have You Ever Eaten Stars?
Music and Musicians
Amichai [or Amikhai]. Changes, Mistakes, Loves.
Ammons. Composing.
One Composing.
Ashbery, J. Syringa.
Auden. Composer, The.
Music Is International.
Baudelaire. Music.
Beckett, S. Dortmunder.
Berry, W. Mad Farmer in the City, The.
Music, A.
Stones, The.
Bierce. To Thee, My Darling.
Bishop, E. Sonnet: "I am in need of music that would flow."
View of the Capitol from the Library of Congress.
Blue Cloud. Night Room Composition.
Bly, R. Listening to the Köln Concert.
Bogan, L. M., Singing.
Musician.
Song for a Slight Voice.
Sub Contra.
Borges. Music Box.
To Johannes Brahms.
Bourne, V. Strada's Nightingale.
Brontë, E. Come hither, child—who gifted thee.
Brooks, G. Piano after War.
Broumas, O. Family.
Browning, E. Heaven and Earth.
Island, An.
Musical Instrument, A.
Browning, R. Abt Vogler.
Flute-Music, with an Accompaniment.
Master Hugues of Saxe-Gotha.
Toccata of Galuppi's, A.
Transcendentalism: A Poem in Twelve Books.
What a pretty tale you told me.
Bukowski. Bee's 5th.
Sweet Music.
Trench Warfare.
Burns, R. Amang the trees, where humming bees.
Red, Red Rose, A.
Byron, G. My Soul Is Dark.
Stanzas for Music.
Campion, T. Ad Io. Dolundum.
Follow your saint, follow with accents sweet.
Of This Ensuing Discourse.
Peacefull westerne winde the wintrye stormes hath calmde, The.
To Campiani Epigramma de Instituto Authoris.
To his sweet Lute *Apollo* sung the motions of the Spheares.
To Music Bent Is My Retired Mind.
To the Worthy Author.
When to Her Lute.
Carew, T. Celia Singig.
Carruth, H. Æolian.
Backyard in California, A.
Cowshed Blues, The.
Expatiation on the Combining of Weathers at Thirty-Seventh and Indiana Where the Southern More or Less Crosses the Dog, An.
Freedom and Discipline.
Homage to John Lyly and Frankie Newton.
How To.
Letter to Maxine Sullivan.
Listen.
Living Alone.
Paragraphs.
What a Wonder among the Instruments Is the Walloping Tramboone!
Who Cares, Long as It's B-Flat.
Carver, R. Music.
Cavafy. Timolaos the Syracusan.
Chesterton. Strange Music, The.
Chuang Tzu. Breath of Nature, The.
Ciardi, J. Prayer to the Mountain, A.
Clampitt. High Culture.
Sunday Music.

Syrinx.
Codrescu. Music.
Coleridge, S. Ode on the Ottery and Tiverton Church Music.
To the Rev. W. J. Hort.
Tribute to Wordsworth.
Collins, B. Piano Lessons.
Serenade: "Let the other boys from the village."
Some Final Words.
Cooper, J. My Friend.
Wanda's Blues.
Corbett, W. Thelonious Sphere Monk.
Crane, H. Black Tambourine.
Broken Tower, The.
Carmen de Boheme.
Crashaw. Music[k]'s Duel[l].
Upon the Death of a Freind.
Creeley. Canzone: "As would any sound make."
Chasing the Bird.
Country Western.
Greendoon's Song.
Los Guitaristas.
They.
Water Music.
Cullen, C. Night Rain.
Singing in the Rain.
Cummings, E. E. God pity me whom (god distinctly has).
Music.
Nocturne: "When the lithe moonlight silently."
Of evident invisibles / exquisite the hovering.
Oil tel duh woil doi sez.
Davie, D. Garland for Ivor Gurney, A.
Heart Beats.
De la Mare. Bells, The.
Clavichord.
Faint Music.
Music.
Music Unheard.
Rose.
Sallie's Musical Box.
Dickey, J. From Time.
Dickey, W. Die Älte Frau, Die Älte Marschallin.
Dickinson, E. Better—than Music! For I—who heard it.
Dying at my music!
Fascinating chill that music leaves, The.
He fumbles at your Soul.
I would not paint—a picture.
I've heard an Organ talk, sometimes.
Put up my lute!
Trees like Tassels—hit—and swung, The.
Your relentless Music.
Dove, R. Definition in the Face of Unnamed Fury.
Event, The.
Jiving.
Left-Handed Cellist, The.
Robert Schumann, Or: Musical Genius Begins with Affliction.
Shakespeare Say.
Variation on Pain.
Dryden, J. Alexander's Feast; or, The Power of Music [or Musique].
Song for St Cecilia's Day, 1687, A.
Dubie. Pictures at an Exhibition.
Dugan, A. Lament for Cellists and Jacqueline DuPré.
Poem for Elliot Carter on His 90th Birthday.
Dunbar, P. Concert, The.
Corn-Stalk Fiddle, The.
Master-Player, The.
Musical, A.
Ol' Tunes, The.
Question, A.
Thou Art My Lute.
To a Lady Playing the Harp.
Valse, The.
Virginia Reel, A.
Voice of the Banjo, The.
When Malindy Sings.
Duncan, R. Bending the Bow.
Reaper, The.
Eberhart, R. Four Exposures.

Ives.
Kinaesthesia.
Rifkin Movement.
River Water Music.
Emerson, R. By art, by music, overthrilled.
From a far mountain creeping down.
I spread my gorgeous sail.
Music.
O what are heroes prophets men.
Saadi.
Ferlinghetti, L. Moscow in the Wilderness, Segovia in the Snow.
San Jose Symphony Reception.
Thoughts to a Concerto of Telemann.
Frost, R. Never Again Would Birds' Song Be the Same.
García Lorca. Flamenco Vignettes.
Graphic of the Petenera.
Poem of the Gypsy *Siguiriya*.
Poem of the *Soleá*.
Three Cities.
Ginsberg, A. Portland Coliseum.
Graves, R. Double Bass.
Grace Notes.
Gray, T. Ode for Music.
Stanzas to Mr. Bentley.
Gunn, T. Before the Carnival.
Elvis Presley.
Listening to Jefferson Airplane.
Outdoor Concert, The.
Victim, The.
Gurney, I. Hedger.
"H. D." Flute Song.
Hardy, T. Chapel-Organist, The.
Fiddler, The.
Haunting Fingers.
Music in a Snowy Street.
Musical Incident, A.
Selfsame Song, The.
Heaney, S. Given Note, The.
Herbert, G. Church-Music[k].
Herrick. Beucolick, or Discourse of Neatherds, A.
Canticle to Apollo, A.
Soft Musick.
To Apollo.
To His Worthy Friend M. John Hall, Student of Grayes-Inne.
To M. Henry Lawes, the Excellent Composer[,] of his Lyrics.
To Music.
To Music: A Song.
To Music, to Becalm a Sweet-sick Youth.
To Music, to Becalm His Fever.
Upon M. William Lawes, the Rare Musitian.
Upon Sapho, Sweetly Playing, and Sweetly Singing.
Voice and Violl, The.
Hopkins, G. When eyes that cast about the heights of heaven.
Hughes, L. Be-Bop Boys.
Blues on a Box.
Boogie: 1 a.m.
Cabaret.
Cat and the Saxophone (2 a.m.), The.
Communiqué.
Conservatory Student Struggles with Higher Instrumentation.
Daybreak in Alabama.
Dream Boogie: Variation.
Drums.
Easy Boogie.
Fantasy in Purple.
Harlem Dance Hall.
Hey-Hey Blues.
Jam Session.
Juice Joint: Northern City.
Juke Box Love Song.
Ma Man.
Negro Servant.
Neon Signs.
Nocturne for the Drums.
Note on Commercial Theatre.
Request for Requiems.
Sport.
Testimonial.

To Midnight Nan at Leroy's.
Trumpet Player.
Weary Blues, The.
Hughes, T. Cadenza.
Lines about Elias.
Opus 131.
Jeffers, R. Natural Music.
Johnson, S. Epitaph upon the Celebrated Claudy Phillips, Musician, Who Died Very Poor, An.
To Miss —: On Her Playing upon the Harpsichord.
To Miss Hickman Playing on the Spinet.
Keats. 'How Many Bards Gild the Lapses of Time!'
Of Late Two Dainties Were before Me Placed.
Kinnell. Cellist, The.
Kinsella, T. 1.
Harmonies.
Kipling, R. In the Neolithic Age.
Song of the Banjo, The.
Kizer, C. Muse of Water, A.
Koch, K. Hearing.
Komunyakaa. Copacetic Mingus.
Elegy for Thelonious.
February in Sydney.
Hanoi Hannah.
Music That Hurts, The.
Pepper.
Piccolo, The.
Villon/Leadbelly.
Kumin, M. Bangkok Gang, The.
Larkin, P. Two Guitar Pieces.
Laughlin, J. Asmodeus.
Why Shouldn't I.
Lawrence, D. H. Listen to the Band!
Piano.
Red.
Levertov. For Those Whom the Gods Love Less.
Music, A.
Six Variations.
Lindsay, N. Master of the Dance, The.
Logan, J. Concert Scene.
Matinee.
Piano Scholar, The.
Longfellow, H. Occultation of Orion, The.
MacDiarmid, H. Bagpipe Music.
MacLeish. Music and Drum.
Pablo Casals.
MacNeice. Bagpipe Music.
Mahon. Andean Flute, The.
Rock Music.
Major, C. Cotton Club, The.
Mallarmé. Saint.
Marvell. Music's Empire.
McGrath, T. Guiffre's Nightmusic.
Meredith, G. Flower of the Ruins, The.
I humm'd an air of sweet Mozart.
Phoebus with Admetus.
Song: "Might I lie where leans her lute."
Meredith, W. Music.
Quartet in F Major.
Merrill, J. Victor Dog, The.
Merwin. Memory of Spring.
Palace, The.
Millay, E. Concert, The.
On Hearing a Symphony of Beethoven.
Milosz, C. In Music.
Master, The.
Milton. At a Solemn Music[k].
To Mr. H. Lawes on His Airs.
Montale. English Horn.
Is it salt that strafes or hail? It slays.
Minstrels.
Your hand was trying the keyboard.
Moore, M. Melchior Vulpius.
Mind Is an Enchanting Thing, The.
Moschus. By Moschus.
Nemerov. Chromium-Plated Hat. Inlaid with Scenes from Siegfried, A.
Four Ages, The.
Lines & Circularities.
Playing the Inventions.
Sarabande.
Niedecker. Adirondack Summer.

Am I real way out in space.
Dear Paul: / the sheets of your father's book of poetry.
L. Z. ("Acre of music, An").
Slip of a girl-announcer, The.
Some have chimes.
To Aeneas who closed his piano.
Understand me, dead is nothing.
Violin Debut.
Your father to me in your eighth summer.
O'Hara, F. Day Lady Died, The.
Fantasy.
Radio.
Romanze, or the Music Students.
Oliver, M. Robert Schumann.
Olson, C. 2nd Musical Form, for Dave Young, A.
Her Dream, Half Remembered.
Igor Stravinsky.
Orr, G. I was moving down the bank.
Owen, W. Music.
Pagis. Europe, Late.
Palmer, M. Man undergoes pain sitting at a piano, A.
Pinsky. Ginza Samba.
Hearts, The.
History of My Heart.
Plath. Snakecharmer.
Poe. Israfel.
Pope, A. Ode for Music on St. Cecilia's Day.
Of a Lady Singing to Her Lute.
Pastorals.
Prunty. Player Piano, The.
Playing by Ear.
Raine, K. House of Music, A.
Rexroth, K. Ausonius, Epistle 7.
Ōkeanos and the Golden Sickle.
Rose Colored Glasses.
Un Bel di Vedremo.
Rich, A. At a Bach Concert.
Ninth Symphony of Beethoven Understood at Last as a Sexual Message, The.
Recorders in Italy.
Solfeggietto.
Transcendental Etude.
Riley, J. Her Light Guitar.
Kathleen Mavourneen.
Little Man in the Tin-Shop, The.
Ole Bull.
On Reading Dr. Henry van Dyke's Volume of Poems—Music.
Serenade, The: "Midnight is not more bewildering, The."
To the Serenader.
Your Violin.
Rilke. Cruel Song.
Fire's Reflection.
Gong.
Soloist.
Ritsos. Bitter Knowledge.
Flute-Player, The.
Robinson, E. L'Envoi.
Rochfort, G. With Music and Poetry Equally Blessed.
Rossetti, D. Carillon, The.
Rukeyser, M. Asleep and Awake.
Bunk Johnson Blowing.
Certain Music, A.
Iris-Eaters, The.
Ives.
Orpheus.
Spirals and Fugues.
Rumi. All day and night, music.
Constant Conversation.
Each Note.
Music Master.
Where Everything Is Music.
Sandburg, C. Bath.
Clefs.
Clinton South of Polk.
Consolation Sonata.
Jan Kubelik.
Jazz Fantasia.
Old Music for Quiet Hearts.
To Know Silence Perfectly.
Sarton, M. Clavichord, The.

Evening Music.
Girl with 'Cello.
Song: "Now let us honor with violin and flute."
Schuyler, J. Beautiful Funerals.
Fauré's Second Piano Quartet.
Grand Duo.
Greetings from the Chateau.
Let's All Hear It for Mildred Bailey!
Man in Blue, A.
Mood Indigo.
Rachmaninoff's Third.
Seifert. Bach Concerto, A.
Nocturnal Divertimento.
Striking of the Tower Clock, The.
Sexton. Music Swims Back to Me.
To Lose the Earth.
Wonderful Musician, The.
Shelley, P. Another Fragment to Music.
Fragment: Music and Sweet Poetry.
Fragment: To Music, A.
Hymn of Pan.
Music.
Ode to the West Wind.
To ———: "Music, when soft voices die,"
Smith, S. Virtuoso, The.
Spender, S. Beethoven's Death Mask.
Late Stravinsky Listening to Late Beethoven.
Stevens, W. Anglais Mort à Florence.
Mozart, 1935.
Peter Quince at the Clavier.
Sad Strains of a Gay Waltz.
Sick Man, The.
Sze. Dazzled.
New Wave.
Rehearsal, The.
To a Composer.
Szymborska, W. Classic, The.
Tate, J. Hostile Philharmonic Orchestra, The.
Initiation, The.
Read the Great Poets.
Thomas, D. Was There a Time.
Thoreau. Each more melodious note I hear.
Just Made Perfect, The.
Music.
Tomlinson, C. Before the Concert.
Chaconne for Unaccompanied Violin.
Consolations for Double Bass.
Da Capo.
Flute Music.
Little Night Music, A.
Melody.
Music's Trinity.
Ode to Arnold Schoenberg.
Programme Note.
Spring Symphony, The.
Words for the Madrigalist.
Updike. Player Piano.
Recital.
Vow.
Vogl. To an Old Gipsy.
Walcott. Piano Practice.
Walker, A. Hymn: "I well remember / A time when."
Weiss, T. Sonata Pathétique.
Whalen, P. Ode to Music, The.
Song for 2 Balalaikas on the Corner of 3rd & Market.
To a Poet.
Whitman, W. Italian Music in Dakota.
Mystic Trumpeter, The.
Proud Music of the Storm.
Wilbur, R. C Minor.
L'Etoile.
Wilde, O. From Spring Days to Winter.
Hélas!
Williams, C. K. First Desires.
Junior High School Concert: Salle Rossini.
Prodigy, The.
Williams, M. For Victor Jara.
Schumann Adds Trombones to His Second Symphony after Mendelssohn Conducts the First Performance.
Williams, T. Ice-Blue Wind, The.
Williams, W. Ballad: "To a man and his wife."
Dance, The.
Note to Music: Brahms 1st Piano Concerto.

Ol' Bunk's Band.
Orchestra, The.
Shoot It Jimmy!
Tapiola.
Two Deliberate Exercises.
Wordsworth, W.   I Heard (Alas! 'Twas Only in a Dream).
   Lyre! Though Such Power Do in Thy Magic Live.
   On the Power of Sound.
   Power of Music.
   Why, Minstrel, These Untuneful Murmurings.
Wright, J.   Poem for Kathleen Ferrier.
   Rhythm, Charts and Changes.
Yeats.   Crazed Girl, A.
   Fiddler of Dooney, The.
   Madness of King Goll, The.
   Spirit Medium, The.
Zagajewski.   Death of a Pianist.
   Electric Elegy.
   Late Beethoven.
   Opus Posthumous.
   Quick Poem, A.
Zaturenska.   Background with Harpsichord.
   Woman at the Piano.
Zukofsky, L.   Atque in Perpetuum A.W.
   Non Ti Fidar.
   Old Poet Moves to a New Apartment 14 Times, The.
   One lutenist played *look*; your through was *drink*.
   Record, The.
   Spook's Sabbath, Five Bowings.
   This Is after All Vacation.
   You Who Were Made for This Music.
See also **Blues (music); Gospel Music**

Music Halls
Levine, P.   At the Fillmore.
Niedecker.   Violin Debut.
Raine, K.   Who listens, when in the concert-hall.
Rukeyser, M.   Paper Anniversary.

Musk Oxen
Hall, D.   Long River, The.
Moore, M.   Arctic Ox, The.

Muslims and Islam
Campion, T.   To the World.
Cavafy.   Dünya Güzeli.
Coleridge, S.   Mahomet.
Creeley.   Riding with Sal.
Ginsberg, A.   Jaweh and Allah Battle.
Merton.   Moslems' Angel of Death, The.
   Night of Destiny, The.
   Readings from Ibn Abbad.
Pinsky.   In Berkeley.
Rumi.   Chinese Art and Greek Art.
   Granary Floor, The.
   Hallaj.
   Muhammad and the Huge Eater.
Whittier.   Palm-Tree, The.

Mussels
Oliver, M.   Mussels.
Plath.   Mussel Hunter at Rock Harbor.

Mussolini, Benito
Williams, T.   Brain's Dissection, The.

Mutability
Dunbar, W.   Of[f] Lentren in the first mornyng [or morning].
Wyatt, S.   Sonnet: 'Each man me telleth.'

Muteness
Ciardi, J.   Miss Olivia Branton.
García Lorca.   Little Mute Boy, The.
Hall, D.   Je Suis une Table.
Hill, G.   Song Contest.
Jacobsen, J.   Deaf-Mutes at the Ballgame.
   Poet as Mute.
Pessoa.   Sonnet: "Could I say what I think, could I express."
Sze.   Empty Words.

Mystery
Amichai [or Amikhai].   Eternal Mystery, The.
Angelou.   Phenomenal Woman.
Berry, W.   To the Unseeable Animal.
Borges.   Lines That Could Have Been Written and Lost round about 1922.
   To a Cat.

Brooks, G.   God Works in a Mysterious Way.
Carruth, H.   To Artemis.
Clifton, L.   Female.
Cortes.   Truth, The. ·
Cullen, C.   Yet Do I Marvel.
Cummings, E. E.   Kind) / YM&WC / (of sort of).
   Now that,more nearest even than your fate.
   Should far this from mankind's unmysteries.
   Silently if,out of not knowable.
Davie, D.   Christmas Week, 1948.
De la Mare.   Interlude, An.
   Snowdrop, The.
Devecseri.   Women and Masks.
Dickey, W.   Rainbow Grocery, The.
Dickinson, E.   Mysteries of human nature, The.
   Promise is firmer than a Hope, A.
   Some things that fly there be.
Duncan, R.   Maiden, The.
Eberhart, R.   Going.
   Height of Man, The.
   Humanist, The.
   Loon Call, A.
   Mystery of the Abstract.
   Only in the Dream.
   Sanders Theater.
   Wisdom of Insecurity, The.
Emerson, R.   Ah strange strange strange.
   But never yet the man was found.
   Know he who tills this lonely field.
Ferlinghetti, L.   Hidden Door.
"H. D."   Mysteries, The.
Hardy, T.   No Bell-Ringing.
   Third Kissing-Gate, The.
Koch, K.   To You.
Laughlin, J.   Vagrant, The.
Lawrence, D. H.   Terra Incognita.
Levertov.   Primary Wonder.
   What Harbinger?
   Window, A.
MacDiarmid, H.   Light and Shadow.
MacLeish.   Autobiography.
Melville, H.   Field Asters.
Meredith, G.   Forest History.
   'Twas in a glimmering starlight.
   Wind on the Lyre.
Montale.   Correspondences.
Moore, M.   By Disposition of Angels.
Muldoon, P.   Why Brownlee Left.
Nash, O.   Calling Spring VII-MMMC.
Nemerov.   There.
Neruda.   I Went.
Orr, G.   A la Mystérieuse.
Raine, K.   Dreams.
Rich, A.   Diving into the Wreck.
Riley, J.   Uninterpreted.
Rumi.   Flute, The.
   Inside water, a waterwheel turns.
   Mystery does not get clearer by repeating the question, The.
   Who sees inside from outside?
Sarton, M.   Approach—Calcutta, The.
   Light Left On, A.
   Metaphysical Garden, The.
Schuyler, J.   Eyes at the Window.
Shelley, P.   Sonnet: "Lift not the painted veil which those who live."
Stock, R.   Word with Norman Rosten.
Swenson, M.   Yes, the Mystery.
Sze.   Kaiseki.
Updike.   Agatha Christie and Beatrix Potter.
Williams, C. K.   Room.
Wright, C.   Chinese Journal.
   Night Journal II.
Yeats.   He Remembers Forgotten Beauty.
   Magi, The.

Mysticism
Blok.   I Sense Your Coming.
   Introduction to the Second Book of Poems.
   O What Is the Setting Sun's Radiance to Me.
Broumas, O.   Imaginary Sufi Garden.
Cavafy.   Singer.
Dubie.   Meister Eckhart.
   Trees of Madame Blavatsky, The.
Emerson, R.   S. R.
Guyon.   Joy in Martyrdom.

"H. D."   Dead Priestess Speaks, A.
Hayden, R.   O Daedalus, Fly Away Home.
Lawrence, D. H.   Mystic.
Levertov.   Of Being.
Merwin.   Words from a Totem Animal.
Nemerov.   Frozen City, The.
Pinsky.   Rhyme of Reb Nachman, The.
Rumi.   All Rivers at Once.
   Birdsong from Inside the Egg.
   Bismillah.
   Body Intelligence.
   Checkmate.
   Childhood Friends.
   Children's Game, A.
   Daylight, full of small dancing particles.
   Do you think I know what I'm doing?
   Dove in the Eaves, A.
   Drumsound rises on the air.
   Egypt That Doesn't Exist, An.
   Father Reason.
   Food Sack, The.
   Granary Floor, The.
   Green Ears.
   I am filled with you.
   If the beloved is everywhere.
   In a boat down a fast-running creek.
   In Between Stories.
   In the slaughterhouse of love, they kill.
   Joy at Sudden Disappointment.
   Like This.
   Meadowsounds.
   Milk of Millennia, The.
   Music, The.
   Music Master.
   Night Air, The.
   No better love than love with no object.
   Not a Day on Any Calendar.
   Omar and the Old Poet.
   Out beyond ideas of wrongdoing and rightdoing.
   Phrasing Must Change, The.
   Put This Design in Your Carpet.
   Quietness.
   Reed Flute's Song, The.
   Rough Metaphors.
   Say I Am You.
   Seed Market, The.
   Something opens our wings. Something.
   Sunrise Ruby, The.
   There's Nothing Ahead.
   These gifts from the Friend, a robe.
   This moment this love comes to rest in me.
   This We Have Now.
   Two Friends.
   Two Ways of Running.
   Visions of Daquqi, The.
   Wax.
   We have this way of talking, and we have another.
   Where Are We?
   Where Everything Is Music.
   You have said what you are.
   Zikr.
Simic.   Writings of the Mystics, The.
Tate, J.   Mystic Moment.
Whitman, W.   Persian Lesson, A.
   When I Heard the Learn'd Astronomer.
Whittier.   Mystic's Christmas, The.
   Vision of Echard, The.
Williams, C. K.   Cave, The.
   Halves.
   Last, The.
Wright, C.   Holy Thursday.
   Local Journal.
Zagajewski.   Mysticism for Beginners.

Mythology
Auden.   Atlantis.
Berry, W.   Mad Farmer Revolution, The.
Bierce.   Tempora Mutantur.
Bishop, E.   Thunder.
Blake, W.   Book of Urizen [or First Book of Urizen], The.
   Imitation of Spen[s]er, An.
Blue Cloud.   Gentle Earthquake, A.
   White Corn Sister.
Borges.   Maker, The ("He had never dwelled on the pleasures of memory").

Browning, E.   Ode to the Swallow.
Browning, R.   Artemis Prologizes.
Carew, T.   Divine Love, A.
Song[, A]: "Ask[e] me no more where Jove bestow[e]s."
Carruth, H.   Mythology of Dark and Light, The.
Purana, Meaning Once upon a Time.
Cavafy.   Ancient Tragedy.
Chaldaic Image.
Footsteps, The.
Footsteps of the Eumenides, The.
Indian Image.
Ithaca.
Tears of the Sisters of Phaeton, The.
Tyanan Sculptor.
Clampitt.   Athena.
Atlas Immobilized.
Dodona: Asked of the Oracle.
Hippocrene.
Nereids of Seriphos, The.
Perseus.
Remembering Greece.
Seriphos Unvisited.
Tempe in the Rain.
Clement of Alexandria.   New Song, The.
Coleridge, S.   Mighty Fountain, A.
Cuadra, P.   Jaguar Myth, The.
Cullen, C.   To the Three for Whom the Book.
Cummings, E. E.   Epithalamion: "Thou aged unreluctant earth who dost."
One nonsufficiently inunderstood.
"Dario."   Colloquy of the Centaurs.
Davie, D.   Fountain of Arethusa, The.
Fountain of Cyanë, The.
Garland for Ronsard, A.
On Sutton Strand.
Dugan, A.   From the Greek Anthology.
On a Myth. On a Conventional Wisdom.
Dunbar, P.   Black Samson of Brandywine.
Eberhart, R.   Kaire.
Wild Swans of Inverane, The.
Eliot, T. S.   Mr. Apollinax.
Sweeney among the Nightingales.
Emerson, R.   Hermione.
Glück, L.   Hyacinth.
Mythic Fragment.
Graves, R.   Conjunction.
Darien.
Good Night to the Old Gods.
Gorgon Mask.
Ibycus of Samos.
In Procession.
Instructions to the Orphic Adept.
Judgement of Paris.
Lyceia.
New Legends.
Penthesileia.
Sirocco at Deyá.
Song: A Phoenix Flame.
"H. D."   Charioteer.
Holy Satyr.
Lais.
Hardy, T.   By the Runic Stone.
Christmas in the Elgin Room.
Meditation on a Holiday.
Heaney, S.   Dog Was Crying Tonight in Wicklow Also, A.
Herbert, Z.   Achilles. Penthesilea.
Hill, G.   Orpheus and Eurydice.
Housman.   Atys.
Crossing Alone the Nighted Ferry.
Howe, S.   Pythagorean Silence.
Jackson, L.   Biography of a Myth, The.
Keats.   Fall of Hyperion, The; A Dream.
Hyperion.
In After-Time, a Sage of Mickle Lore.
On Visiting Staffa.
Kizer, C.   Fearful Women.
Hera, Hung from the Sky.
Kunitz, S.   Proteus.
Spark of Laurel, A.
Laughlin, J.   Apsarases.
Asmodeus.
Party on Olympus, The.
Persephone Wears Bluejeans.
Lawrence, D. H.   Argonauts, The.

Logan, J.   Ah, so our first load of honey heavy Christmas trees.
Far off the road on the left on a slight rolling hill.
I did but taste a little of the honey with the.
If the half moon stamp of a sacred hoof showed Cadmus.
In my dream I know I see my father Saul a king.
Monologues of the Son of Saul.
Two Poems of Greece.
Meredith, W.   Orpheus.
Poem: "Swans on the river, a great, The."
Starlight.
Merrill, J.   Banks of a Stream Where Creatures Bathe.
Merton.   Atlas and the Fatman.
Gloss on the Sin of Ixion.
Martin's Predicament or Atlas Watches Every Evening.
Merwin.   Judgment of Paris, The.
Woman from the River.
Milosz, C.   King Popiel.
Moore, M.   Charity Overcoming Envy.
Nemerov.   Beyond the Pleasure Principle.
Nerval.   Antéros.
Petrarch.   But—now her pleasant gentle modest mien.
When that tree moves from where it ought to be.
Piercy.   Icon.
Pinsky.   Discretions of Alcibiades.
Ramanujan.   Mythologies 1.
Mythologies 2.
One More after Reading Homer.
Rexroth, K.   Adonis in Winter.
After the Anthology.
Dragon and the Unicorn, The.
Rilke.   Poet, The.
Rimbaud, A.   Sun and Skin.
Ritsos.   Alcméne.
Imitation of an Imitation.
Other Precision, The.
Philomel.
Talos.
Robinson, E.   As a World Would Have It.
Rossetti, C.   Lotus-Eaters: Ulysses to Penelope, The.
Zara.
Rossetti, D.   For Spring, by Sandro Botticelli, in the Accademia of Florence.
Rukeyser, M.   Clouds, Airs, Carried Me Away.
In the Underworld.
Mortal Girl.
Sandburg, C.   Atlas, How Have You Been?
Sarton, M.   At Delphi.
At Lindos.
Binding the Dragon.
Birthday on the Acropolis.
Furies, The.
Narcissus.
Proteus.
Shelley, P.   Prometheus Unbound [A Lyrical Drama in Four Acts].
Sheridan, T.   Original of Punning, The.
Simic.   Childhood of Parmenides, The.
Spender, S.   In Attica.
Stock, R.   Bellerophon and the Portable Universe.
Double Ballade of Newfangled Ladies, A.
In Transformation of an Imago.
Silenus' Epitaph.
Swinburne.   Phaedra.
Szymborska, W.   Thomas Mann.
Tennyson, A.   Tithonus.
Unknown.   Punegyric upon Tom Pun-sibi's *Ars Pun-ica,* A.
Walcott.   Europa.
From This Far.
Wheatley, P.   Address to the Atheist, by P. Wheatley at the Age of 14 Years—1767, An.
Atheism.
Niobe in Distress for Her Children Slain by Apollo, from *Ovid's* Metamorphoses, Book 6. And from a View of the Painting of Mr. *Richard Wilson.*

Ocean.
To a Gentleman of the Navy.
Whittier.   Dole of Jarl Thorkell, The.
How the Robin Came.
Robin, The.
Vanishers, The.
Wilbur, R.   Lying.
Wilde, O.   Burden of Itys, The.
Canzonet.
Charmides.
Garden of Eros, The.
Santa Decca.
Sphinx, The.
Williams, C. K.   Hercules, Deianira, Nessus.
Williams, W.   Asphodel, That Greeny Flower.
Paterson, Book 5: The River of Heaven.
Wilner, E.   Those Who Come After.
Wordsworth, W.   Artegal and Elidure.
Laodamia.
Wyatt, S.   Iopas's Song.
Yeats.   Leda and the Swan.

N

Nabakov, Vladimir
Ferlinghetti, L.   Deep Chess.
Laughlin, J.   Moths, The.

Nagasaki, Japan
Levertov.   On the 32nd Anniversary of the Bombing of Hiroshima and Nagasaki.
Wilner, E.   Conversation with a Japanese Student.

Nakedness
Baudelaire.   I love the thought of Ages of Undress.
Browning, R.   Rhyme for a Child Viewing a Naked Venus in a Painting [of "The Judgement of Paris"].
Bukowski.   6 A.M.
Cavafy.   Days of 1908.
Ciardi, J.   Stills and Rapids of Your Nakedness, The.
Corbett, W.   Under Ideal Conditions.
Creeley.   Pool, The.
Seventeenth Floor: Echoes of Singapore.
Davie, D.   After the Match.
Dickey, W.   You White Cunning Devils.
Dubie.   Lamentations.
Emerson, R.   Painting and Sculpture.
García Lorca.   Casida of the Reclining Woman.
Gunn, T.   Three.
Hamill, S.   Gnostology.
Herrick.   Laxare Fibulam.
Lilly in a Christal, The.
Upon Electra.
Hughes, L.   March Moon.
Laughlin, J.   Fate of Actaeon, The.
Levertov.   Cloak, A.
Logan, J.   Cambridge Revery.
Nude Kneeling in Sand.
Spring of the Thief.
MacLeish.   My Naked Aunt.
Millay, E.   How Naked, How without a Wall.
Rimbaud, A.   First Night.
Our buttocks aren't like theirs. Many times I've seen.
Tartufe's Punishment.
Ritsos.   Beauty.
Maturity.
Provincial Spring.
Stripped Naked.
Succession.
Transposition.
Ultimate Innocence.
Rukeyser, M.   Knowledge my nakedness.
Swenson, M.   Truth Is Forced, The.
Unknown.   From the Persian (1).
Warren, R.   Birth of Love.
Wilner, E.   Her Body Is Private.
Wright, J.   Prayer to the Lord Ramakrishna, A.

Names
Angelou.   Calling of Names, The.
Atwood.   Squaw Lilies: Some Notes.
Borges.   Clouds ("High in the air these placid

mountains or").
Compass.
Golem, The.
Broumas, O.   Body and Soul.
Browning, E.   Pet-Name, The.
 To George Sand: A Recognition.
Browning, R.   Names, The.
Byron, G.   Lines Written in an Album, at Malta.
Carruth, H.   Marge.
 Names.
 Septic Tanck.
Chuang Tzu.   Tao.
Ciardi, J.   J is, splendidly, for JOHN, my.
 Landscapes of My Name.
Clampitt.   Botanical Nomenclature.
 Matoaka.
Coleridge, S.   Exile, An.
 Names.
Corbett, W.   Fred Astaire.
Crane, H.   Name for All, A.
Crashaw.   To the Name above Every Name, the
 Name of Jesus, a Hymn.
Creeley.   It Is at Times.
Davie, D.   Yorkshire.
Dickinson, E.   I'm ceded—I've stopped being
 Theirs.
Donne.   To Mrs Magdalen Herbert: of St. Mary
 Magdalen.
Dugan, A.   Nomenclature.
Eberhart, R.   Request.
Emerson, R.   And though he dearly prized the
 bards of fame.
 To every creature / Adam gave its name.
Enzensberger, H.   Historical Process.
Frost, R.   Maple.
Gallagher, T.   Meeting, The.
Graves, R.   My Name and I.
 Name.
Gunn, T.   Vox Humana.
Hamill, S.   Naming the Beast.
Hayden, R.   'Mystery Boy' Looks for Kin in
 Nashville.
 Names.
Hughes, L.   Madam and the Census Man.
 Poem for an Intellectual on the Way Up to
 Submit to His Lady.
Jackson, L.   Care in Calling.
Jeffers, R.   Patronymic.
Jonson, B.   To My Lord Ignorant.
Kizer, C.   What Was in a Name.
Komunyakaa.   Audacity of the Lower Gods.
 Mismatched Shoes.
Larkin, P.   Maiden Name.
Laughlin, J.   Among the Roses.
 Go West Young Man.
 Modest Proposal, A.
 Social Note.
Lawrence, D. H.   Name the Gods!
Levertov.   I Learned That Her Name Was
 Proverb.
Levine, P.   Making Light of It.
 Renaming the Kings.
 Wednesday.
Lux.   Boat in the Forest, A.
McGrath, T.   Need for Dictionaries II, The.
McHugh, H.   A.
 Spot in Space and Time.
Merton.   Fall, The.
Milosz, C.   Linnaeus.
Montale.   You've named a tree for me? It isn't
 nothing.
Nash, O.   Anybody Else Hate Nickynames?
 Everything's Haggis in Hoboken, or, Scots Wha
 Hae Hae.
 Guppy, The.
 Happy Ending of Mr. Train, The.
 I Happen to Know.
 Name Is Too Familiar, The.
 Not Even for Brunch.
 Sic Semper Mr. Sherman's Temper, or Kindly
 Place Your Order in English.
 Snark Was a Boojum Was a Prawn, The.
 What's in a Name? Here's What's in a Name,
 or, I Wonder What Became of John and
 Mary.
 What's in a Name? Some Letter I Always

 Forget.
Olson, C.   Tomorrow.
Oppen.   Myth of the Blaze.
Orr, G.   Fall.
Petrarch.   When I begin to send out sighs and
 call.
Pope, A.   Epigram on the Toasts of the Kit-Cat
 Club, Anno 1716.
 Verses Occasioned by an & c. at the End of Mr.
 D'Urfy's Name in the Title to One of His
 Plays.
Prunty.   Namesake, The.
Riley, J.   By Any Other Name.
 Goldie Goodwin.
 Name Us No Names No More.
Rilke.   Magician, The.
Robinson, E.   Theophilus.
Rossetti, C.   King of Kings and Lord of Lords.
Rumi.   Phrasing Must Change, The.
Sandburg, C.   Blacklisted.
 Corn and Beans.
 Man the Moon Shooter.
Seifert.   Lost Paradise.
Sexton.   Telephone.
Swenson, M.   If I Had Children.
Szymborska, W.   Still.
Tranströmer.   Name, The.
Updike.   Clan, The.
 Fritillary, The.
 I Missed His Book, but I Read His Name.
 Kenneths.
Van Duyn.   Garland for Christopher Smart, A.
 To My Godson, on His Christening.
Walcott.   Names.
Warren, R.   Small Eternity.
Whitman, W.   What Am I after All.
Whittier.   Kallundborg Church.
 My Namesake.
 Name, A.
Wilbur, R.   Melongène.
 On Having Mis-identified a Wild Flower.
 Rillons, Rillettes.
Williams, W.   And Thus with All Praise.
Wilner, E.   So Quietly the World.
Wright, C.   As Our Bodies Rise, Our Names
 Turn into Light.
 Writing Life, The.
Wright, J.   Minneapolis Poem, The.
Zagajewski.   Name Edmund, The.
Zukofsky, L.   Claims.

See also **Place Names**
Nantucket, Massachusetts
Brodsky, J.   At the City Dump in Nantucket.
Glück, L.   Phenomenal Survivals of Death in
 Nantucket.
Hamill, S.   End of the Road from Nantucket,
 The.
Lowell, R.   Quaker Graveyard in Nantucket,
 The.
Orr, G.   Nantucket Morning / This World.
Whittier.   Exiles, The.
Williams, W.   Nantucket.
Naples, Italy
Carruth, H.   Two Romantic Pieces.
Schuyler, J.   Dorabella's Naples Watercolor.
Shelley, P.   Ode to Naples.
Whittier.   Naples.
 Prisoners of Naples, The.
Napoleon I
Blake, W.   When France got free Europe 'twixt
 Fools & Knaves.
Browning, E.   Crowned and Buried.
Browning, R.   Incident of the French Camp.
Byron, G.   From the French.
 Napoleon's Farewell.
 Napoleon's Snuff-Box.
 Ode from the French.
 Ode to Napoleon Buonaparte.
 Once Fairly Set Out on His Party of Pleasure.
Coleridge, S.   Mighty Fountain, A.
De la Mare.   Napoleon.
Dubie.   Apocrypha of Jacques Derrida, The.
 Evening of the Pyramids, The.
Emerson, R.   Poem, Spoken Before the ΦBK
 Society, August, 1834.
Kipling, R.   St. Helena Lullaby, A.

Lowell, R.   Napoleon.
Meredith, W.   Memoirs.
Plath.   Swarm, The.
Rexroth, K.   Bonapartisme.
Robinson, E.   Island, An.
Sandburg, C.   Statistics.
Shelley, P.   Feelings of a Republican on the Fall
 of Bonaparte.
 Lines Written on Hearing the News of the Death
 of Napoleon.
Tate, J.   List of Famous Hats, The.
Wilde, O.   Louis Napoleon.
Wordsworth, W.   1801.
 Eagle and the Dove, The.
 Look now on that Adventurer who hath paid.
 October, 1803 ("When, looking on the present
 face of things").
 Ode: "Who rises on the banks of Seine."
 To B.R. Haydon, on Seeing His Picture of
 Napoleon Buonaparte on the Island of St
 Helena.
Napoleon III
Browning, E.   Napoleon III in Italy.
Meredith, G.   Ode to H.I.M. Napoleon 3d.
 'Tis I have seen the coming man.
Rimbaud, A.   Caesars' Rage.
 Centre: the Emperor, apotheosis.
 Child who picked up bullets, Pubescent Lad,
 The.
 Old Lady's Old Men!
 Recollection.
Napoleonic Wars
Browning, R.   Incident of the French Camp.
Hardy, T.   Alarm, The.
 Bridge of Lodi, The.
 Leipzig.
 Peasant's Confession, The.
Wordsworth, W.   1810.
 And is it among rude untutored Dales.
 Brave Schill! by death delivered, take thy flight.
 By Moscow Self-Devoted to a Blaze.
 Feelings of a Noble Biscayan at One of Those
 Funerals 1810.
 Feelings of the Tyrolese.
 French and the Spanish Guerrillas, The.
 French Army in Russia 1812–1813, The.
 Hail, Zaragoza! If with unwet eye.
 Hofer.
 Indignation of a High-Minded Spaniard 1810.
 Invocation to the Earth; February, 1816.
 Martial courage of a day is vain, The.
 November, 1806.
 Ode: 1814.
 Ode: 1815.
 Ode: The Morning of the Day Appointed for a
 General Thanksgiving. January 18, 1816.
 On the Final Submission of the Tyrolese.
 On the Same Occasion.
 Spanish Guerillas 1811.
 To the Men of Kent (October, 1803).
Narcissism and Narcissists
Dickey, W.   Narcissus Unbound.
Dugan, A.   Mirror Perilous, The.
Eberhart, R.   'If I Could Only Live at the Pitch
 That Is near Madness'
Ginsberg, A.   I made love to myself.
Housman.   Look not in my eyes, for fear.
Lawrence, D. H.   Noble Englishman, The.
Nash, O.   Swan, The.
Petrarch.   My enemy, who often lets you gaze.
Narcissus (botany)
García Lorca.   Narcissus.
Levertov.   Volupté.
Plath.   Among the Narcissi.
Zukofsky, L.   Narcissus.
Narcissus (mythology)
Calas.   Narcissus in the Desert.
Cunningham, J.   Reason and Nature.
Davie, D.   At the Café Parnasse.
Dickey, J.   Daybreak.
Dugan, A.   Narcissus 2.
Gunn, T.   Behind the Mirror.
Housman.   Look not in my eyes, for fear.
Lawrence, D. H.   Narcissus.
Logan, J.   Narcisses: Vision and Retrospect.

McHugh, H.   Nymph to Narcissus, The.
Nemerov.   Glass Dialectic.
Rilke.   Narcissus.
Sarton, M.   Narcissus.
Wilner, E.   Comment on the Relevance of Modern Science to the Everyday Lives of the Larger Animals, A.

Narcotics
Williams, T.   Soft City, The.
See also **Drug Addiction**

Nash, Ogden
Parker, D.   Letter to Ogden Nash.

Nasturtiums
Clampitt.   Balms.
Gunn, T.   Nasturtium.
Whalen, P.   Haiku for Mike.

Nationalism
Atwood.   Two-Headed Poems.
Brontë, E.   Song by Julius Angora.
Dickinson, E.   Is it Intellect that the Patriot means.
   My Country, 'tis of thee.
Du Bellay.   Heureux Qui, comme Ulysse, A Fait un Beau Voyage.
Dugan, A.   Nostalgia for a Language.
Herrick.   Lawes.
Lorde.   Seventh Sign, The.
Merton.   Why Some Look up to Planets and Heroes.
Nash, O.   Goody for Our Side and Your Side Too.
Patchen.   We Mutually Pledge to Each Other.
Raine, K.   Letter to Pierre Emmanuel.
Ritsos.   Those Years.
Sandburg, C.   Is There Any Easy Road to Freedom?
   Old Timers.
   Threes.
Shapiro, K.   Washington Cathedral.
Szymborska, W.   Psalm: "How leaky are the borders of man-made states!"

Native Americans
Ai.   Ice.
   Ravine, The.
Berry, W.   July, 1773.
Berryman.   Navajo Setting the Record Straight.
Blue Cloud.   Alcatraz.
   Crazy Horse Monument.
   Death Chant.
   Dedication of a Roundhouse.
   For Ace.
   White Corn Sister.
   Yellowjacket.
Bly, R.   Pilgrim Fish Heads.
   Schoolcraft's Diary Written on the Missouri: 1830.
Carruth, H.   Rimrock, Where It Is.
   Sorrow Song, The.
Ciardi, J.   Ritual for Singing Bat.
Clampitt.   Matoaka.
Crane, H.   Sad Indian, The.
   They Were There.
Cummings, E. E.   Moon-in-the-Trees, / The old canoe awaits you.
Davie, D.   Amazonian.
   Frontenac.
   Jesuits in North America, The.
   Pontiac.
   Sunday Morning.
Dove, R.   Taking in Wash.
Dugan, A.   Significance of Corn in American History, The.
Emerson, R.   For fifteen winter days.
Frost, R.   Vanishing Red, The.
Ginsberg, A.   Rolling Thunder Stones.
Hughes, L.   Lament for Dark Peoples.
Hughes, T.   On the Reservations.
Jeffers, R.   Inquisitors, The.
   New Mexican Mountain.
Kizer, C.   By the Riverside.
Koch, K.   Thanksgiving.
Komunyakaa.   Quatrains for Ishi.
Kunitz, S.   Mound Builders, The.
Lawrence, D. H.   Beyond the Rockies.
   Men in New Mexico.

Lindsay, N.   Ghosts of the Buffaloes, The.
Logan, J.   Five Preludes for Buffalo's Own Forest Lawn.
   Whistling Wings or White Turtle in the Watertree.
Lowell, R.   At the Indian Killer's Grave.
MacLeish.   Wildwest.
MacNeice.   Indian Village.
Major, C.   Gallup Swill-Hole, A; or, Cantina Blues.
   In Hollywood with the Zuni God of War.
   Lost in the Desert.
   Tewa Victories.
McGrath, T.   Buffalo Coat, The.
   You Can Start the Poetry Now, or: News from Crazy Horse.
Merwin.   February.
   Free, The.
   Homeland.
   Huckleberry Woman.
   Old Room, The.
   Presidents.
   Prints, The.
   Removal, The.
Muldoon, P.   Indians on Alcatraz, The.
   Madoc: A Mystery.
   My Father and I and Billy Two Rivers.
Niedecker.   Black Hawk held: In reason.
   War.
Oliver, M.   Learning about the Indians.
   Two Kinds of Deliverance.
Olson, C.   Buffalo Ode.
   Dance, of the Grizzly Bear, The.
   Morning News, The.
Paley, G.   Having Arrived by Bike at Battery Park.
Sandburg, C.   Alice Corbin Is Gone.
   Cahokia.
   Coin, A.
   Early Copper.
   Yes, the Dead Speak to Us.
Sendak.   Navajo Blanket, The.
Snyder, G.   Anasazi.
   Manzanita.
Stafford, W.   At the Klamath Berry Festival.
   Before It Burned Over: A Sioux Grass Chant.
   By a River in the Osage Country.
   Concealment, The: Ishi, the Last Wild Indian.
   In the Oregon Country.
   Indian Cave Jerry Ramsey Found, The.
   Paso por Aquí.
   Returned to Say.
   Sound from the Earth, A.
   Vacation.
Sze.   Do Not Speak Keresan to a Mescalero Apache.
   Tsankawi.
Terry, L.   Bars Fight [August 28, 1746].
Tomlinson, C.   Albuquerque.
   Chief Standing Water.
   Cochiti.
   Jemez.
   Old Man at Valdez.
   Quarai.
   Ute Mountain.
Very.   Indian Relics.
   Indian Remains.
   Indians' Belief in a Future State, The.
   Indian's Petition, The.
   Indian's Retort, The.
   King Philip.
Warren, R.   Chief Joseph of the Nez Perce.
Whitman, W.   Osceola.
   Red Jacket (from Aloft).
   Yonnondio.
Whittier.   Bridal of Pennacook, The.
   Fountain, The.
   Funeral Tree of the Sokokis.
   How the Robin Came.
   Inscription: "Eagle, stooping from yon snow-blown peaks, The."
   Metacom.
   Mogg Megone.
   Mount Agiochook.
   Nauhaught, the Deacon.
   On the Big Horn.

   Pentucket.
   Truce of Piscataqua, The.
   Vanishers, The.
Williams, C. K.   Guatemala: 1964.
Williams, W.   Graph.
Wilner, E.   Desert Parable.
Wordsworth, W.   Complaint of a Forsaken Indian Woman, The.

Nativity, The
Brodsky, J.   Nativity.
   Star of the Nativity.
Chesterton.   Joseph.
   Nativity by Botticelli, The.
Coleridge, S.   Christmas Carol, A: "Shepherds went their hasty way, The."
   Translation of a Passage in Ottfried's Metrical Paraphrase of the Gospel.
Crashaw.   Hymne of the Nativity, Sung by the Shepheards, A.
   In the Holy Nativity of Our Lord God.
Davie, D.   Christmas Week, 1948.
Dunbar, W.   Rorate, celi, desuper!
Glück, L.   Nativity Poem.
Guyon.   Nativity, The.
Hall, D.   Carol, A.
Hill, G.   Picture of a Nativity.
Hughes, L.   Carol of the Brown King.
   Christmas Story, The.
   On a Christmas Night.
   On a Pallet of Straw.
   Shepherd's Song at Christmas.
Lawrence, D. H.   Ballad of a Wilful Woman.
Milton.   On the Morning of Christ's Nativity.
Pinkerton, H.   On G.B. Tiepolo's Etching *Adoration of the Magi* (1753) in the Stanford Museum.
Stockton, A.   Impromptu Ode before Day on the 24th of Dec, Christmas Morning, An.
Swinburne.   Christmas Carol, A: "Three damsels in the queen's chamber."
See also **Christmas**

Naturalists
Heaney, S.   Death of a Naturalist.
Logan, J.   Homage to John Muir.
Merwin.   Other Travelers to the River.
Nash, O.   Mr. Burgess, Meet Mr. Barmecide.
Niedecker.   Thure Kumlien.
Rich, A.   Observer, The.
Riley, J.   Naturalist, The.
   Rest, The.

Nature
Abu Nadhar 'Abdu'l 'Aziz.   Color, taste, and smell, smaragdus, sugar, and musk.
Ammons.   Arc inside and out, The.
   Bees Stopped.
   Cut the Grass.
   Gravelly Run.
   Hymn: "I know if I find you I will have to leave the earth."
   Hymn 2: "So when the year had come full round."
   Hymn 4: "I hold you responsible for."
   Life in the Boondocks.
   Plunder.
   Schooling.
   Some Months Ago.
   Terrain.
   Three.
   Viable.
Arnold, M.   In Harmony with Nature.
   Quiet Work.
Ashbery, J.   Rivers and Mountains.
Atwood.   Boat, A.
   Landcrab II.
Auden.   Bucolics.
   Fall of Rome, The.
   Natural Linguistics.
   Ode to Gaea.
Baudelaire.   Correspondences.
   Giantess, The.
   Universal Analogies.
Berry, W.   Arrival, The.
   Broken Ground, The.
   Design of a House, The.
   Enriching the Earth.
   Familiar, The.

Gift of Gravity, The.
Green and White.
Hidden Singer, The.
In This World.
Independence Day.
July, 1773.
Man Born to Farming, The.
Man Walking and Singing, A.
Observance.
Peace of Wild Things, The.
Song in a Year of Catastrophe.
Song Sparrow Singing in the Fall, A.
Sowing.
Standing Ground, A.
To What Listens.
Where.
Wish to Be Generous, The.
Bierce. Science.
Bishop, E. Brazil, January 1, 1502.
Cold Spring, A.
North Haven.
Song for the Rainy Season.
Blue Cloud. Being Forever.
Camp.
Hobo Bird.
Quebec, rattling chains of Separatism.
Walking thru twisted hollow pathways.
Bly, R. After Drinking All Night with a Friend,
We Go Out in a Boat at Dawn to See Who Can
Write the Best Poem.
Fifty Males Sitting Together.
Hawk, The.
In the Month of May.
Out Picking up Corn.
Bogan, L. Night.
Brontë, E. How long will you remain? The
midnight hour.
I've been wandering in the greenwoods.
Only some spires of bright green grass.
Shall Earth no more inspire thee.
Stanzas: "Often rebuked, yet always back
returning."
Tell me, tell me, smiling child.
Was it with the fields of green.
Why do I hate that lone green dell?
Browning, E. Hugh Stuart Boyd [His Death,
1848].
Love.
Man and Nature.
Patience Taught by Nature.
Romaunt of Margret, The.
Sea-Mew, The.
Browning, R. Forest Thought, A.
Magical Nature.
Bukowski. Ants, The.
Sun Wields Mercy, The.
Burns, R. Allan Water.
Castle Gordon—*Intended to Be Sung to Morag.*
Dainty Davie.
Humble Petition of Bruar Water to the Noble
Duke of Athole, The.
Lament of Mary Queen of Scots on the
Approach of Spring.
Lassie wi' the Lintwhite Locks.
Lover's Morning Salute to His Mistress, The.
My Heart's in the Highlands.
Nature's Law.
Ode to Spring.
On Scaring Some Waterfowl in Loch Turit, a
Wild Scene among the Hills of Oughtertyre.
Phillis the Fair.
Rosebud, The.
Scotch Song.
Scotish Song.
Song: "Again rejoicing Nature sees."
Song. On Miss W. A.
To a Mouse; On Turning Her up in Her Nest,
with the Plough, November, 1785.
Written with a Pencil over the Chimney-Piece,
in the Parlour of the Inn at Kenmore,
Taymouth.
Yon wild, mossy mountains sae lofty and wide.
Byron, G. Cornelian, The.
Wild Gazelle, The.
Campion, T. I Care Not for These Ladies.
Sing a song of joy.

Carew, T. Divine Love, A.
Love's Force.
Protestation [A Sonnet], The.
Spring, The.
To My Friend G.N. from Wrest.
To My Worthy Friend Master George Sands [*or*
Sandys], on His Translation of the Psalms.
Carruth, H. All Things.
Existing Pool, The.
Homecoming.
I Know, I Remember, But How Can I Help You.
My Meadow.
President's Speech, The.
Ravine, The.
Silence.
Thaw.
Underground the Darkness Is the Light.
Carver, R. This Morning.
Vigil.
Cavafy. Melancholy Hours.
Chaucer. House of Fame, The.
Chuang Tzu. Breath of Nature, The.
Five Enemies, The.
Great and Small.
In My End Is My Beginning.
Inner Law, The.
Man Is Born in Tao.
Metamorphosis.
P'eng That Was a K'un, The.
Symphony for a Sea Bird.
Ciardi, J. At First Flower of the Easy Day.
Bees and Morning Glories.
Fragment: "To the laboratory then I went. What
little."
Gray Spring Morning, A.
Image of Man as a Gardener after Two World
Wars.
In the Audience.
One Wet Iota.
Thoughts on Looking into a Thicket.
Tommy's Pond.
Clampitt. Cloudberry Summer.
Clare, J. Evening.
Sonnet: "I love to see the summer beaming
forth."
Clifton, L. Earth Is a Living Thing, The.
Clough. Resignation—to Faustus.
Coleridge, S. Barberry-Tree, The.
Frost at Midnight.
Inscription for a Fountain on a Heath.
Nightingale, The.
Picture, The.
Reflections on Having Left a Place of
Retirement.
This Lime-Tree Bower My Prison.
To a Young Friend.
To Nature.
Unity with Nature.
Work without Hope.
Corbett, W. Driving Jazz.
Cowper, W. Retirement.
Song: "When all within is peace."
Task, The.
To the Rev. Mr. Newton.
Crane, H. Annunciations.
Creeley. As We Sit.
Here ("Little earth, water").
If Happiness.
In the Fall.
Innocence, The.
Intervals.
Kid, The.
Messengers, The.
Persons.
Picnic, The.
Picture, A.
Prospect.
Sign ("What you know of me").
Song: "Those rivers run from that land."
Temper, The.
Wish, A.
Cullen, C. Singing in the Rain.
Cummings, E. E. Beyond the stolid iron pond.
Epithalamion: "Thou aged unreluctant earth who
dost."
Here's s / omething round(& so).

I Thank You God.
If(you are i why certainly).
Let's,from some loud unworld's most rightful
wrong.
Moon-in-the-Trees, / The old canoe awaits you.
Night.
Nocturne: "When the lithe moonlight silently."
O Sweet Spontaneous.
Sonnet: "For that I have forgot the world these
days."
They have hung the sky with arrows.
When serpents bargain for the right to squirm.
Wherelings whenlings / (daughters of if but
offspring of hopefear).
Wind is a Lady with, The.
De la Mare. All That's Past.
April.
Awake!
Dreamer, The.
Phantom, The.
Reawakening, The.
Reserved.
Spark, The.
They Told Me.
Vacant Day, The.
Vain Questioning.
Dickey, J. For a Time and Place.
Springhouse, Menses, Held Apple, House and
Beyond.
Dickinson, E. Banish Air from Air.
Bring me the sunset in a cup.
Changelessness / is Nature's change.
Earth has many keys, The.
Further in Summer than the Birds.
Her sovereign People.
How strange that Nature does not knock.
However you stem Nature.
I had been hungry, all the Years.
I Taste a Liquor Never Brewed.
I write in the midst of Sweet-Peas.
If Nature smiles—the Mother must.
It bloomed and dropt, a Single Noon.
Moth the hue of this, A.
Nature affects to be sedate.
Nature and God—I neither knew.
Nature can do no more.
Nature is a Haunted House.
Nature is our eldest mother.
"Nature" is what we see.
Nature must be too young to feel.
Nature, seems it to myself.
Nature—sometimes sears a Sapling.
Nature—the Gentlest Mother is.
Of Nature I shall have enough.
Sky is low—the Clouds are mean, The.
Snake, The.
So valiant is the intimacy.
Their Barricade against the Sky.
These are the Signs to Nature's Inns.
This Is My Letter to the World.
To my quick ear the Leaves—conferred.
Touch lightly Nature's sweet Guitar.
Travel why to Nature.
Trees like Tassels—hit—and swung, The.
Twice had Summer her fair Verdure.
Veins of other Flowers, The.
We introduce ourselves.
Were nature mortal lady.
Worthlessness of Earthly things, The.
Dove, R. Fish in the Stone, The.
Dugan, A. On Naming a Baby Mimosa.
Dunbar, P. From the Porch at Runnymede.
Lapse, The.
Nature and Art.
Secret, The.
Eberhart, R. Angels, The.
Big Rock.
Book of Nature, The.
Burden.
Centennial for Whitman.
Child, The.
Coast of Maine.
Concord Cats.
Day-Bed, The.
Death in the Mines.
Gnats.

Go to the Shine That's on a Tree.
Groundhog Revisiting, The.
Hard Structure of the World, The.
Hop-Toad, The.
Illusion of Eternity, The.
Indian Pipe.
Largess, The.
Learning from Nature.
Man Who Was Blown Down by the Wind, A.
Mind and Nature.
News.
Oak, The.
Old Tom.
On a Squirrel Crossing the Road in Autumn, in New England.
On Returning to a Lake in Spring.
Opulence.
Parker River, The.
Prometheus.
Recollection of Childhood.
River Water Music.
Sea-Hawk.
Skier and the Mountain, The.
Snowfall, A.
Spider, The.
Spring Mountain Climb.
Standards, The.
Van Black, an Old Farmer in His Dell.
Where Are Those High and Haunting Skies.
Wild Life and Tamed Life.
Emerson, R.   Adirondacs, The.
Ah strange strange strange.
Awed I behold once more.
Berrying.
Blackbird's song the blackbird's song, The.
Blight.
But Nature whistled with all her winds.
But never yet the man was found.
But O to see his solar eyes.
Circles.
Dear Brother, Would You Know the Life.
Dirge: "Knows he who tills this lonely field."
Each and All.
Experience.
Fine presentiments controlled him.
For Nature true & like in every place.
From Nature's beginning.
From the stores of eldest Matter.
Go out into Nature and plant trees.
He lives not who can refuse me.
He must have / Droll fancies sometimes cross his quiet thoughts.
How drearily in College hall.
I leave the book, I leave the wine.
I left my dreamy page & sallied forth.
If wishes would carry me over the land.
In My Garden.
Is the pace of nature slow?
Know he who tills this lonely field.
Land was all electric, The.
Miracle, The.
Musketaquid.
My Garden.
Nature.
Nature 1.
Nature 2.
Nature [1836].
Nature [1844].
Nature saith / I am not infinite.
Nature says, / These craggy hills that front the dawn.
Nature will not lose.
Natures web star broidered.
Nun's Aspiration.
October woods, wherein.
Parks & ponds are good by day.
Problem, The.
Queen rejoices in her peers, A.
See how Romance adheres.
She had wealth of mornings in her year.
She paints with white & red the moors.
Shout to the Shepherds, A.
Softens the air so cold & rude.
Song of Nature.
Tell me maiden dost thou use.
These trees like tho'ts that to visions congeal.

Though her eye seek other forms.
To every creature / Adam gave its name.
Waldeinsamkeit.
What all the books of ages paint, I have.
What never was no, & still will be.
Where the fungus broad & red.
Who saw the hid beginnings.
Why fear to die.
Woodnotes I ("For this present, hard").
Woodnotes II ("As sunbeams stream through liberal space").
Would you know what joy is hid.
Xenophanes.
Fenton, J.   Killer Snails, The.
Kingfisher's Boxing Gloves, The.
Lollipops of the Pomeranian Baroque.
Ferlinghetti, L.   Overpopulation.
Upon Reflection.
Frost, R.   Design.
Directive.
Fountain, a Bottle, a Donkey's Ears and Some Books, A.
From Iron.
Lucretius versus the Lake Poets.
On Going Unnoticed.
Our Hold on the Planet.
Something for Hope.
Time Out.
Vantage Point, The.
Gallagher, T.   Croce e Delizia al Cor.
Refusing Silence.
García Lorca.   Morning.
Ginsberg, A.   Bixby Canyon.
Bixby Canyon Ocean Path Word Breeze.
Carmel Valley.
Easter Sunday.
Past Silver Durango over Mexic Sierra-Wrinkles.
Sonora Desert-Edge.
Wales Visitation.
Graves, R.   Ambience.
Ample Garden, The.
Around the Mountain.
Beds of Grainne and Diarmuid, The.
Climate of Thought, The.
Consortium of Stones.
Deliverance.
Endless Pavement.
Finding of Love, The.
Fragment: "Are you shaken, are you stirred."
Horizon.
Interruption.
Love in Barrenness.
Love Story, A.
Mankind and Ocean.
Meeting, The.
Nature's Lineaments.
Return of the Goddess [Artemis].
She Tells Her Love while Half Asleep.
Song: The Far Side of Your Moon.
To Juan at the Winter Solstice.
To Walk on Hills.
Turn of the Moon.
Wedding, The.
Guillén, J.   Love Song to a Morning.
Nature Alive.
Gunn, T.   Aqueduct.
Faustus Triumphant.
Rooftop, The.
Thomas Bewick.
To a Friend in Time of Trouble.
Gurney, I.   Sea-Marge.
"H. D."   Dancer, The.
Scribe.
Wash of cold river.
White World.
Hacker, M.   Crépusule Provençale.
Languedocienne.
Hall, D.   Cold Water.
Granite and Grass.
New Hampshire.
Stories.
Han-shan.   Clambering up the Cold Mountain path.
Hardy, T.   At a Bridal.
At Moonrise and Onwards.

Discouragement.
Ditty: "Beneath a knap where flown."
Five Students, The.
Genitrix Laesa.
Growth in May.
In a Wood.
Middle-Age Enthusiasms.
Nature's Questioning.
Pat of Butter, The.
Unkindly May, An.
We Field-Women.
Heaney, S.   Anahorish.
Herrick.   Art above Nature, to Julia.
Country Life: To His Brother, M. Tho: Herrick.
God, and Lord.
Painting Sometimes Permitted.
Putrefaction.
Sin.
To Find[e] God.
Upon Man.
Upon Time.
Hill, G.   Elegiac Stanzas: On a Visit to Dove Cottage.
Two Chorale-Preludes: On Melodies by Paul Celan,
Hopkins, G.   Earth and heaven, so little known, The.
Epithalamion: "Hark, hearer, hear what I do; lend a thought now, make believe."
God's Grandeur.
I must hunt down the prize.
Inversnaid.
O what a silence is this wilderness!
O where is it, the wilderness.
Or else their cooings came from bays of trees.
Pied Beauty.
That Nature Is a Heraclitean Fire and of the Comfort of the Resurrection.
What being in rank-old nature should earlier have that breath been.
When eyes that cast about the heights of heaven.
Windy Day in Summer, A.
Hughes, T.   Autumn Notes.
Earth-Numb.
Fern.
Gog.
Mayday on Holderness.
Moors.
Pibroch.
Roe-Deer.
Song: "O lady, when the tipped cup of the moon blessed you."
Thrushes.
Ignatow, D.   I Live Admiring the Sky.
I Want to Be Buried.
In No Way.
Jacobsen, J.   Hourglass.
Jarrell, R.   Field and Forest.
Rabbit hurries to the brim of its wood, The.
Jeffers, R.   All the Little Hoof-Prints.
Boats in a Fog.
Broken Balance, The.
Contrast.
Cycle, The.
Excesses of God, The.
Metamorphosis.
Natural Music.
Noon.
Not Our Good Luck.
Oh, Lovely Rock.
Place for No Story, The.
Point Joe.
Red Mountain.
Unnatural Powers.
Keats.   Hence Burgundy, Claret, and Port.
I Stood Tip-Toe upon a Little Hill.
Imitation of Spenser.
O! How I Love, on a Fair Summer's Eve.
On "The Story of Rimini."
Song of Four Faeries.
To Some Ladies.
To the Ladies Who Saw Me Crowned.
Kinnell.   Lastness.
Middle of the Way.
Kipling, R.   Charm, A.

Run of the Downs, The.
Larkin, P.   I Put My Mouth.
Long Roots Moor Summer to Our Side of Earth.
Laughlin, J.   Here I Am.
Lawrence, D. H.   Corot.
Elemental.
Elements, The.
Escape.
Glory.
Gods.
Last Hours.
Letter from Town: On a Grey Morning in
   March.
Many Mansions.
Morality.
Paltry-Looking People.
Poverty.
Proper Pride.
Reading a Letter.
Renascence.
Sane Universe, The.
Self-Protection.
Sinners.
Wild Common, The.
Wild Things in Captivity.
Levertov.   3 a.m., September 1, 1969.
Breathing, The.
Craving.
Listening to Distant Guns.
Living.
Night on Hatchet Cove.
Sojourns in the Parallel World.
Levi, P.   Almanac.
Li Po.   Poem by the Bridge at Ten-shin.
River Song, The.
Lindsay, N.   Being the Dedication of a Morning.
Genesis.
I Want to Go Wandering.
Path in the Sky, The.
Logan, J.   Homage to John Muir.
Longfellow, H.   Aftermath.
Snow-Flakes.
Lorde.   Echo.
Oaxaca.
October.
Return.
Lowell, R.   Das ewig Weibliche.
MacDiarmid, H.   Cheville.
Happy on Heimaey.
MacLeish.   Sunset Piece, The.
MacNeice.   Evening in Connecticut.
House on a Cliff.
Jungle Clearance Ceylon.
Old Masters Abroad.
Western Landscape.
Marlowe.   Passionate Shepherd to His Love,
   The.
Marvell.   Mower against Gardens, The.
McGrath, T.   Autumn Song.
Return, The.
Up the Dark Valley.
Melville, H.   Haglets, The.
Little Good Fellows, The.
Malvern Hill.
Pontoosuce.
Mencius.   Ox Mountain Parable, The.
Meredith, G.   Change in Recurrence.
Could we know how kin we are.
Dirge in Woods.
Earth and Man.
Earth's Preference.
Earth's.
Force and His Master.
Forest History.
Gentleness of Death, The.
Hard Weather.
Invitation to the Country.
Love in the Valley.
Melampus.
Nature and Life.
Ode to the Spirit of Earth in Autumn.
Orson of the Muse, An.
Poetry of Wordsworth, The.
South-West Wind in the Woodland.
Spirit of Shakespeare, The.
This love of nature, that allures to take.

Three Singers to Young Blood, The.
We need some rallying point round which.
Whimper of Sympathy.
Woodland Peace.
Meredith, W.   Three Sorts of Violence, The.
Merrill, J.   Channel 13.
In Nine Sleep Valley.
Syrinx.
Merton.   It would be wrong to let one man.
Natural History.
On a Day in August.
Song: Contemplation.
Merwin.   In the Red Mountains.
Now It Is Clear.
Millay, E.   Assault.
Doubt No More that Oberon.
God's World.
Journey.
Look how the bittersweet with lazy muscle
   moves aside.
Pastoral: "If it were only still!"
Milosz, C.   By a Stream.
Far West.
Gates of the Arsenal, The.
Linnaeus.
Slow River.
Song, The: "Earth flows away from the shore
   where I stand."
Those Corridors.
Three Talks on Civilization.
To Mrs. Professor in Defense of My Cat's
   Honor and Not Only.
Unde Malum.
Milton.   Nature Does Not Suffer Decay.
Montale.   Sit the noon out, pale and lost in
   thought.
Moraes, V.   Sonnet of Intimacy.
Muldoon, P.   Beaver.
Nash, O.   Bas Ben Adhem, A.
Little Miss Muffet Sat on a Prophet—and Quite
   Right, Too!
Mr. Burgess, Meet Mr. Barmecide.
Nine Miles to the Railroad.
Nothing but Nature.
Nemerov.   Companions, The.
Dependencies, The.
Elegy for a Nature Poet.
Figures of Thought.
Holding the Mirror Up to Nature.
Midsummer's Day.
Nature Morte.
Salt Garden, The.
Singular Metamorphosis, A.
Neruda.   Cold.
Coming Back.
Earth.
First Winter.
I Went.
Star.
This Is Simple.
To Puente Curvo on the Maldonado Spit in
   Uruguay.
Winter.
Niedecker.   Paean to Place.
War.
O'Hara, F.   Captain Bada.
Easter.
Oliver, M.   Family, The.
Ghosts.
In Blackwater Woods.
Landscape.
Lilies Break Open over the Dark Water, The.
Moths, The.
Nature.
On Winter's Margin.
Skunk Cabbage.
Snowshoe Hare, The.
Some Questions You Might Ask.
Turtle, The.
Wild Geese.
Olson, C.   Conqueror.
Cross-Legged, the Spider and the Web.
Day Song.
Dragon-Fly, The.
Drum World, The.
Epigon.

Every Man His Own Matador; or for That
   Matter Any Member of the Family.
Going from Battle to Battle.
Lower Field—Enniscorthy.
May 20, 1959.
On the Shore.
Other Than.
Post Virginal, The.
Praises, The.
Said Adam.
She Who Hits at Will.
Story of an Olson, and Bad Thing, The.
Turn now and rise.
What's Wrong with Pindar.
Will: termite mothers.
Writ, The.
Owen, W.   Elegy in April and September.
From My Diary, July 1914.
Pagis.   Cycle, The.
Paley, G.   Fear.
Patchen.   Country Excursion.
Deer and the Snake, The.
Like a Mourningless Child.
Manifold Fusions, The.
On My Side.
Pastoral: "Dove walks with sticky feet, The."
Unnatural History of Peru, The.
We Must Be Slow.
Pessoa.   And there are poets who are artists.
At night I suddenly waken.
Four songs that follow now, The.
From the highest window of my house.
I go indoors, and shut the window.
I never kept sheep.
I'd give anything if only my life were an oxcart.
If at times I say that flowers smile.
If I could take a bite of the whole earth.
If they want me to be a mystic, fine. I'm a
   mystic.
I'm a keeper of sheep.
Moonlight behind the tall branches, The.
My glance is clear like a sunflower.
On a terribly clear day.
Once at mid-day in late spring.
One way or another.
Only Nature is divine, and she's not divine.
Rather the flight of the bird passing and leaving
   no trace.
Rhymes mean nothing to me. Only rarely.
To think of God is to disobey God.
Today I read nearly two pages.
Petrarch.   I have been nowhere else where I
   could see.
Love, who in good times kept me company.
Valley re-echoing with woes of mine.
Piercy.   Cod Summer.
Intruding.
Postcard from the Garden.
Skimpy Day at the Solstice.
Plath.   Dark Wood, Dark Water.
Wreath for a Bridal.
Wuthering Heights.
Poe.   Stanzas: "How often we forget all time,
   when lone."
Valley of Unrest, The.
Pope, A.   Epistle I, to Sir Richard Temple, Lord
   Cobham.
Epitaph on Sir Godfrey Kneller, in Westminster-
   Abbey, 1723.
Intended for Sir Isaac Newton.
On His Grotto at Twickenham.
Pound, E.   Coitus.
Spring, The.
Raine, K.   Acacia Tree.
Amo Ergo Sum.
Angelus.
Canna's Basalt Crags.
Childhood.
Fateless Ones, The.
Harvest of learning I have reaped.
Heirloom.
Hyacinth, The.
I could have told much by the way.
If, into this evening as the grass receives the
   dew.
Into what pattern, into what music have the

spheres whirled us.
Marriage of Psyche, The.
Message from Home.
Moment, The.
Natura Naturans.
Night in Martindale.
On an Ancient Isle.
On Leaving Ullswater.
Poet Answers the Accuser, The.
Return, The.
Self.
Seventh Day.
Soliloquy Upon Love.
Spell of Sleep.
Today: / This leafy apple-tree, gray.
Traveller, The.
Triad.
Under these hills too high and bare.
What have I to regret.
Wilderness, The.
Winter Paradise.
Winter Solstice.
Word Made Flesh.
Your gift of life was idleness.
Ransom, J.   Morning.
Prometheus in Straits.
Rexroth, K.   Floating.
Hapax.
Hiking on the Coast Range.
On Flower Wreath Hill.
Prolegomenon to a Theodicy, A.
Silver Swan, The.
Rich, A.   In the Woods.
Upcountry.
Riley, J.   All-kind Mother, The.
Loveliness, The.
South Wind and the Sun, The.
Uninterpreted.
Vision of Summer, A.
Rimbaud, A.   Sensation.
Ritsos.   Accented Colors.
Robinson, E.   Monadnock through the Trees.
Torrent, The.
Roethke.   Bring the Day!
Field of Light, A.
Genesis.
Give Way, Ye Gates.
Her Time.
I Cry, Love! Love!
I Waited.
Light Poem.
Manifestation, The.
Minimal, The.
O Lull Me, Lull Me.
O, Thou Opening, O.
Otto.
Praise to the End!
Sequel, The.
Shape of the Fire, The.
Small, The.
Thing, The.
Unfold! Unfold!
Visitant, The.
Walk in Late Summer, A.
Words for the Wind.
Rossetti, C.   Are Ye Not Much Better than
   They?
Books in the Running Brooks.
Cobwebs.
Dead City, The.
Easter Morning.
Exultate Deo.
Fluttered Wings.
For Advent.
Frisky Lamb, A.
From early dawn until the flush of noon.
Green Cornfield, A.
Heartsease in my garden bed, / With
   sweetwilliam white and red.
Hills are tipped with sunshine, while I walk / In
   shadows dim and cold.
I Have a Message unto Thee.
I sit among the green shady valleys oft.
Immalee.
In the Lane.
Judge Not According to the Appearance.

May.
Minnie and Mattie.
Patience of Hope.
Rosy maiden Winifred, / With a milkpail on her
   head.
Seasons.
Sir Winter.
Song: "Two doves upon the selfsame branch."
Spring Fancies.
Spring Quiet.
Summer.
To What Purpose Is This Waste?
What Good Shall My Life Do Me?
What Is Pink?
Who Has Seen the Wind?
Wintry Sonnet, A.
World's Harmonies, The.
Wouldst thou give me a heavy jewelled crown.
Rukeyser, M.   Mountain. One from Bryant.
Rumi.   Meadowsounds.
Sandburg, C.   Just before April Came.
So to Speak.
Sumach and Birds.
Wind Horses.
Sarton, M.   Apple Tree in May.
Composition.
Easter Morning.
Fig, The.
Guest, A.
Invocation: "Come out of the dark earth."
Journey toward Poetry.
March-Mad.
Mud Season.
Of the Seasons.
These Images Remain.
Schuyler, J.   Beaded Balustrade.
Buttered Greens.
Closed Gentian Distances.
Gulls.
Poem: "Your enchantment / enchains me,
   stretched."
Sonnet: "August, tasting of ripe grapes and
   afternoon sleep."
Today.
Under the Hanger.
With Frank and George at Lexington.
Seidl.   Hans Euler.
To the High-Flyers.
Shapiro, K.   Travelogue for Exiles.
Shelley, P.   Fragment: "When soft winds and
   sunny skies."
Fragment: Rome and Nature.
Love's Philosophy.
Mont Blanc.
To a Skylark.
To Jane: The Invitation.
Smart, C.   On a Bed of Guernsey Lilies.
Smith, S.   Alone in the Woods.
Away, Melancholy.
Every Lovely Limb's a Desolation.
Lady "Rogue" Singleton.
Nature and Free Animals.
Pretty.
Touch and Go.
Will Man Ever Face Fact and Not Feel Flat?
Snyder, G.   Berry Feast, A.
Burning Island.
By Frazier Creek Falls.
For All.
Milton by Firelight.
Old Rotting Tree Trunk Down.
Old Woman Nature.
Path to Han-shan's place is laughable, The.
Piute Creek.
Ripples on the Surface.
Six Years.
Sours of the Hills.
Target Practice.
Wave.
We Make Our Vows Together with All Beings.
Stafford, W.   How to Regain Your Soul.
Oregon Message, An.
Something to Declare.
Stein, G.   Study Nature.
What Does She See When She Shuts Her Eyes.
Stevens, W.   Anecdote of the Jar.

Botanist on Alp (No. 1).
Room on a Garden, A.
Stock, R.   Space between Two Blades of Grass
   Meets an Intractable Ego, The.
Transfiguration: Natura Naturans.
Swenson, M.   Big-Hipped Nature.
Crossing, The.
Earth Your Dancing Place.
Green Red Brown and White.
Her Management.
Sze.   Apache Plume.
Archipelago.
Before Completion.
Cloud Chamber, The.
Great White Shark, The.
Kaiseki.
Mushroom Hunting in the Jemez Mountains.
Oolong.
Redshifting Web, The.
Silk Road, The.
Six Persimmons.
Streamers.
String Diamond, The.
Szymborska, W.   Birthday.
Conversation with a Stone.
Returning Birds.
Thomas Mann.
View with a Grain of Sand.
Tate, J.   Nature Poem: Demanding Stiff
   Sentences.
Tennyson, A.   Edwin Morris.
Flower in the Crannied Wall.
Thomas, D.   All All and All the Dry Worlds
   Lever.
Find Meat on Bones.
Foster the Light.
Process in the Weather of the Heart, A.
This Bread I Break.
Why East Wind Chills.
Thoreau.   "Book of Gems," The.
Cock-crowing.
Freshet, The.
Great Friend.
Inward Morning, The.
Mountains in the Horizon, The.
Nature.
Poet's Delay, The.
Rabbit leaps, The.
Respectable folks, The.
Strange that so many fickle gods, as fickle as the
   weather.
When breathless noon hath paused on hill and
   vale.
Within the circuit of this plodding life.
Tomlinson, C.   Discrepancies.
Four Kantian Lyrics.
Frondes Agrestes.
In Winter Woods.
John Maydew or the Allotment.
Nature Poem.
Reflections.
Response to Hopkins.
Unknown.   Another of the Same Nature, Made
   Since.
Song of Blodeuwedd, The.
Updike.   Lamplight.
Nature.
Penumbrae.
Solitary Pond, The.
Telephone Poles.
To a Box Turtle.
Van Duyn.   Along the Road.
Ballad of Blossom, The.
Dwarf in the Woods.
End of May.
From Yellow Lake: An Interval.
Gentle Snorer, The.
Good Man, The.
Postcards from Cape Split.
Quebec Suite.
View, A.
West Branch Ponds, Kokadjo, Maine.
Very.   Hast thou ever *heard* the voice of nature.
Hymn: Nature's Sympathy with Freedom.
Hymn: The Forms of Nature, and the Unity of
   Their Origin.

Interpreting Nature.
Nature ("Bubbling brook doth leap when I come by, The").
Nature a Living Teacher.
Nature Intelligible.
Nature Repeats Her Lessons.
Silent, The.
Song, The.
To the Pure All Things Are Pure.
Walk in the Pastures, A.
Weiss, T.   Local Matter, A.
Whalen, P.   For Brother Antoninus.
Violins in Chaos?
Wheatley, P.   Elegy on Leaving, An.
Whitman, W.   Give Me the Splendid Silent Sun.
Italian Music in Dakota.
Me Imperturbe.
Proud Music of the Storm.
Spontaneous Me.
To a President.
We Two, How Long We Were Fool'd.
When I Heard at the Close of The Day.
World below the Brine, The.
Whittier.   Birchbrook Mill.
Hive at Gettysburg, The.
Outdoor Reception, An.
Over-Heart, The.
Revisited.
River Path, The.
Summer Pilgrimage, A.
Tent on the Beach, The.
Worship of Nature, The.
Wilbur, R.   Ceremony.
Flumen Tenebrarum.
Hamlen Brook.
Mined Country.
Part of a Letter.
Problem from Milton, A.
Sunlight Is Imagination.
Wilde, O.   Humanitad.
Panthea.
Williams, C. K.   Clay out of Silence.
Downwards.
Hounding Mercy.
Just Right.
Sky, Water.
Williams, T.   Nature's Thanksgiving.
Williams, W.   Ballet.
Love Song: "Daisies are broken."
Martin and Katherine.
Pastoral: "If I say I have heard voices."
Pastoral 2: "If I talk to things."
Promenade.
Raleigh Was Right.
Three Sonnets.
Wilner, E.   Continuous Is Broken, and Resumes, The.
Ex Libris.
Wordsworth, W.   Airey-Force Valley.
By the Side of Rydal Mere.
Come ye that are disturbed, this steady voice.
Companion to the Foregoing [Love Lies Bleeding].
Composed at Neidpath Castle, the Property of Lord Queensberry,1803.
Composed by the Side of Grasmere Lake.
Composed on the Banks of a Rocky Stream.
Composed upon an Evening of Extraordinary Splendour and Beauty.
Composed while the Author Was Engaged in Writing a Tract, Occasioned by the Convention of Cintra.
Contrast; the Parrot and the Wren, The.
Descriptive Sketches Taken during a Pedestrian Tour among the Alps.
Evening Walk, An; Addressed to a Young Lady.
Expostulation and Reply.
Farewell, A: "Farewell thou little Nook of mountain-ground."
Filial Piety.
Fragment: "In vain did Time and Nature."
Fragment: Redundance.
Fragments from the Alfoxden Notebook (I).
Fragments from the "Christabel" Note-book.
Highland Hut.
I love upon a stormy night.

In These Fair Vales Hath Many a Tree.
Incipient Madness.
It was an April morning: fresh and clear.
Lines Composed a Few Miles above Tintern Abbey on Revisiting the Banks of the Wye during a Tour, July 13, 1798.
Lines Written in Early Spring.
LITTLE onward Lend Thy Guiding Hand, A.
Mark the concentrated hazels that enclose.
More May Not Be by Human Art Exprest.
Motto Intended for Poems on the Naming of Places.
Not in the Lucid Intervals of Life.
Ode: Intimations of Immortality from Recollections of Early Childhood.
Ode to Lycoris; May, 1817.
On the Projected Kendal and Windermere Railway.
Oxford, May 30, 1820.
Oxford, May Thirtieth, Eighteen Twenty.
Peter Bell; a Tale.
Proud Were Ye, Mountains, When, in Times of Old.
Retirement.
Rural Illusions.
So Fair, So Sweet, Withal So Sensitive.
Stars Are Mansions Built by Nature's Hand, The.
Stray Pleasures.
Suggested at Tyndrum in a Storm.
Suggested by a Picture of the Bird of Paradise.
Tables Turned, The.
There is a bondage worse, far worse, to bear.
There is an Eminence,—of these our hills.
Thorn, The.
Though the Bold Wings of Poesy Affect.
To a Young Lady Who Had Been Reproached for Taking Long Walks in the Country.
To M. H.
Trosachs, The.
Vale of Esthwaite, The.
View from the Top of Black Comb.
Western clouds a deepening gloom display, The.
When, to the attractions of the busy world.
World is too much with us; late and soon, The.
Written in London, September, 1802.
Written in March [While Resting on the Bridge at the Foot of Brother's Water].
Written in Very Early Youth.
Wright, C.   Bicoastal Journal.
California Spring.
Chinese Journal.
Dead Color.
December Journal.
George Trakl Journal.
Holy Thursday.
Journal of English Days, A.
Journal of One Significant Landscape, A.
Journal of Southern Rivers, A.
Laguna Dantesca.
Language Journal.
Last Journal.
Local Journal.
Lonesome Pine Special.
May Journal.
Mount Caribou at Night.
Night Journal.
Night Journal II.
Primitive Journal II.
Saturday Morning Journal.
Self-Portrait.
Silent Journal.
Spring Abstract.
Vesper Journal.
Yard Journal.
Wright, J.   Depressed by a Book of Bad Poetry, I Walk toward an Unused Pasture and Invite the Insects to Join Me.
Fit against the Country, A.
Goodbye to the Poetry of Calcium.
Horse, The.
Prayer to Escape from the Market Place, A.
Rhythm, Charts and Changes.
She Hid in the Trees from the Nurses.
Witches Waken the Natural World in Spring.
Wyatt, S.   'Resound my voice, ye woods.'

Yeats.   Coole Park, 1929.
Her Anxiety.
Indian to His Love, The.
Lake-Isle of Innisfree, The.
Sorrow of Love, The.
Zaturenska.   O Like a Young Tree.
Zukofsky, L.   Alba (1952).
Bird that cries like a baby, The.
Guests, The.
Mountain Laurel.
So sounds grass, and if it is sun or no sun.
Xenophanes.

Navaho, The
Carruth, H.   None.
Stafford, W.   In the All-Verbs Navaho World.
Tomlinson, C.   Before the Dance.
Williams, W.   Navajo.

Naval Battles
Cavafy.   31 B.C. in Alexandria.
Donne.   Burnt Ship, A.
Ginsberg, A.   Battleship Newsreel.
Keats.   See, the Ship in the Bay Is Riding.
Kipling, R.   Ballad of the *Clampherdown*, The.
Destroyers, The.
Verdicts, The.
Marvell.   Loyal Scot, The.
On the Victory Obtained by Blake over the Spaniards, in the Bay of Santa [or Sancta] Cruz, in the Island of Tenerife, 1657.
Melville, H.   At the Cannon's Mouth.
Commemorative of a Naval Victory.
In the Turret.
Temeraire, The.
Utilitarian View of the Monitor's Fight, A.

Navy, France
Browning, R.   Hervé Riel.

Navy, Great Britain
Davie, D.   1945.
Kipling, R.   Cruisers.
Destroyers, The.
Farewell and adieu to you, Harwich Ladies.
Lowestoft Boat, The.
Mine Sweepers.
North Sea Patrol, The.
Soldier an' Sailor Too.
Song in Storm, A.
Tin Fish.
Trade, The.
Verdicts, The.
When the Great Ark.
White Horses.
Rossetti, D.   Last Three from Trafalgar, The.
Smart, C.   Ode to Admiral Sir George Pocock.
Wheatley, P.   To a Gentleman of the Navy.

Navy Life
Burns, R.   Silver Tassie, The.
Prunty.   Baseball Team of Unknown Navy Pilots, Pacific Theater, 1944, A.
Stafford, W.   At Fort Worden: Calling Names.

Nazis
Dubie.   Widow of the Beast of Ingolstadt, The.
Dugan, A.   Memories of 1936–7.
Hill, G.   Canaan.
Christmas Trees.
Ovid in the Third Reich.
Hughes, L.   Underground, The.
Komunyakaa.   Nazi Doll, The.
Kumin, M.   On Reading an Old Baedeker in Schloss Leopoldskron.
Levi, P.   Proxy.
Lux.   Nazi at the Puppet Show, The.
Merton.   Chant to Be Used in Processions around a Site with Furnaces.
Epitaph for a Public Servant.
Niedecker.   Brown muskrat, noiseless, The.
European Travel / (Nazi New Order).
Oliver, M.   1945—1985: Poem for the Anniversary.
Plath.   Daddy.
Lady Lazarus.
Ramanujan.   As Eichmann Said, My Brother Said.
Sandburg, C.   Man with the Broken Fingers, The.
Spender, S.   Perhaps.

Wilbur, R.   On the Eyes of an SS Officer.
Williams, C. K.   Combat.
  Spit.
Wright, J.   Small Blue Heron, The.

Nebraska (state)
Sandburg, C.   Band Concert.
  Limited.
  Omaha.
  Sunset from Omaha Hotel Window.
Shapiro, K.   Nebraska.
  Tornado Warning.

Nebuchadnezzar
Donne.   Liar, The.
Keats.   Nebuchadnezzar's Dream.
Nemerov.   Nebuchadnezzar, Solus.
Pinsky.   Visions of Daniel.

Necrophilia
Dugan, A.   Untitled Poem: "Why feel guilty
  because the death of a lover causes lust?"
O'Hara, F.   Ode on Necrophilia.
See also **Corpses**

Need
Achterberg.   Statue.
Ai.   Stalking Memory.
Ammons.   Needs.
Armantrout.   Natural History.
Atwood.   I see you fugitive, stumbling across
  the prarie.
  You are the sun / in reverse, all energy.
Berry, W.   Wild Geese, The.
Bukowski.   Everything.
  Quiet Clean Girls in Gingham Dresses.
Burns, R.   Grace at Kirkudbright.
Cooper, J.   Suicide Note.
Creeley.   Dream, The.
  For W.C.W.
  Hello.
  Soup ("Trembling / with delight").
Cunningham, J.   I write you in my need. Please
  write.
"Dario."   Poet put in his verses, The.
Dickinson, E.   Had I not This, or This, I said.
  I meant to have but modest needs.
  Undue Significance a starving man attaches.
Emerson, R.   Do that which you can do.
HaNagid.   When You're Desperate.
Herrick.   No Want Where There's Little.
  Want.
Hughes, T.   Folktale.
Ignatow, D.   Of That Fire.
Jackson, L.   Need to Confide, The.
Jacobsen, J.   Birds, The.
  Rainy Night at the Writers' Colony.
Komunyakaa.   Blue Light Lounge Sutra for the
  Performance Poets at Harold Park Hotel.
Nemerov.   Song: "Provide your friend with
  almanacs."
Orr, G.   Caged Owl, The.
  Tristan and Iseult.
Pessoa.   I only ask the gods to grant me.
Pinsky.   Time of Year, the Time of Day, The.
Riley, J.   There Is a Need.
Rossetti, C.   Diamond or a coal? / A diamond, if
  you please, A.
  Motherless baby and babyless mother.
Rukeyser, M.   Ballad Theme, A.
Walker, A.   Did This Happen to Your Mother?
  Did Your Sister Throw Up a Lot?
  Threatened.
Whalen, P.   If You're So Smart, Why Ain't You
  Rich?
Whitman, W.   Not Heaving from My Ribb'd
  Breast Only.
See also **Poverty**

Needles
Dickey, J.   Voyage of the Needle, The.
Eberhart, R.   Evaluation under a Pine Tree,
  Lying on Pine Needles, An.
Rossetti, C.   Pin Has a Head, A.
Simic.   Needle.

Neglect
Berryman.   Drugs Alcohol Little Sister.
Dubie.   Trakl.
Mahon.   Disused Shed in Co. Wexford, A.
Rilke.   In This Life of Neglect.

Stockton, A.   Tears of Friendship. Elegy the
  Third.—To a Friend Just Married, and Who
  Had Promised to Write, on Parting, but Had
  Neglected It.
Wilbur, R.   Shame.

Negro Spirituals
Dunbar, P.   When Malindy Sings.
See also **Spirituals**

Neighborhoods
Hughes, L.   Little Song on Housing.
Lux.   Neighborhood of Make-Believe, The.

Neighbors
Amichai [*or* Amikhai].   Elizabeth Swados.
Ammons.   Winter Saint.
Atwood.   First Neighbours.
Bukowski.   3:30 A.M. Conversation.
  Experience.
  Fleg.
  High-Rise of the New World, The.
  New Place, The.
  Puzzle, The.
Carruth, H.   Line, The.
  Marshall Washer.
Carver, R.   Account, An.
Ciardi, J.   January 2, 1978.
Corbett, W.   Neighborhood.
Creeley.   Neighbors.
Cummings, E. E.   There are 6 doors.
De la Mare.   Peeping Tom.
Dove, R.   House on Bishop Street, The.
Dunbar, P.   Differences.
Frost, R.   Mending Wall.
Gunn, T.   All Do Not All Things Well.
  Girls Next Door, The.
Hacker, M.   Two Cities.
Hardy, T.   Old Neighbour and the New, The.
Heaney, S.   At the Wellhead.
  Other Side, The.
Herrick.   Upon Bran.
Hughes, T.   Green Wolf, The.
Ignatow, D.   East Side West.
  Neighbors.
  White Ceiling, The.
Kumin, M.   Hello, Hello Henry.
  Henry Manley Blues, The.
  Henry Manley Looks Back.
  Rejoicing with Henry.
Lawrence, D. H.   As Thyself!
  Commandments.
  Love Thy Neighbour.
Logue, C.   Urbanal.
Lorde.   Cables to Rage or I've Been Talking on
  This Street Corner.
  Moving Out or the End of Cooperative Living.
Meredith, W.   Couple Overhead, The.
Merwin.   Line of Trees.
Millay, E.   Portrait by a Neighbour.
Nash, O.   People upstairs, The.
Oppen.   Neighbors.
Orr, G.   Neighbors.
Piercy.   Neighbor, The.
Pinsky.   Street, The.
Prunty.   Downtown Bus, The.
  Memorial Day.
Riley, J.   Home-Folks.
Robinson, E.   Neighbors.
Sandburg, C.   Neighbors.
Stafford, W.   With Neighbors One Afternoon.
Stock, R.   Impromptu with a Breeze.
Tate, J.   Heatstroke.
  Neighbors.
Thoreau.   I knew a man by sight.
Wilbur, R.   He Was.
Williams, M.   Jonathan at Last.
  Missing Persons.
  Neighbor, The.
  Rock.
Williams, W.   Exercise No. 2.

Nelson, Horatio Nelson, Viscount
Davie, D.   Suffolk.
Graves, R.   1805.
Melville, H.   *Temeraire*, The.
Meredith, G.   October 21, 1905.
  Trafalgar Day.
Rossetti, D.   Last Three from Trafalgar, The.

Nepal
Kipling, R.   Sacrifice of Er-Heb, The.
Williams, M.   Remembering the Man.

Neptune (god)
Campion, T.   Hymn in Praise of Neptune, A.
Hall, D.   On a Horse Carved in Wood.
Herrick.   Another to Neptune.
Kipling, R.   Poseidon's Law.
Wheatley, P.   Ode to Neptune.

Nero
Cavafy.   Footsteps of the Eumenides, The.
  Footsteps, The.
  Nero's Term.
Dubie.   Simple Philo of Alexandria.
Gray, T.   Agrippina.
Herrick.   Cruelties.

Neruda, Pablo
Ferlinghetti, L.   General Song of Humanity, The.
  Hidden Door.
Kizer, C.   October 1973.
McGrath, T.   Lament for Pablo Neruda.
  Warrant for Pablo Neruda, A.
Rukeyser, M.   Neruda, the Wine.
Williams, W.   Tribute to Neruda the Poet
  Collector of Seashells.

Nerval, Gérard de
Muldoon, P.   Something Else.

Ness, Loch, Scotland
Burns, R.   Written with a Pencil, Standing by
  the Fall of Fyers, near Loch-Ness.

Nests
Ammons.   Configurations.
Ciardi, J.   Socializing with a Creature.
Muldoon, P.   Blowing Eggs.
Riley, J.   Empty Nest, An.
See also **Birds' Nests**

Netherlands
Clampitt.   Note from Leyden, A.
Coleridge, S.   Netherlands, The.
Cowper, W.   To Lady Austen.
Dubie.   *Principia Mathematica:* Einstein's Exile
  in an Old Dutch Winter.
Kizer, C.   Where I've Been All My Life.
Marvell.   Character of Holland, The.
  In Legationem Domini Oliveri St John ad
  Provincias Foederatas [On the Embassy of
  Lord Oliver St John to the United Provinces].

Nettles
Housman.   With seed the sowers scatter.

Nevada (state)
Carruth, H.   Too Tenuous.
Dickey, W.   Gambling at Reno.
Sandburg, C.   March of the Hungry Mountains.
Stafford, W.   Vacation.
Wright, J.   Gambling in Stateline, Nevada.

New England
Borges.   New England, 1967.
Carruth, H.   Crow's Mark.
  Essay on Love.
  Fourth.
  Marshall Washer.
Clampitt.   Low Tide at Schoodic.
Creeley.   For Anybody.
Cunningham, J.   Identity, that spectator.
Dickinson, E.   Field of Stubble, lying sere, A.
  Robin's my Criterion for Tune, The.
Dubie.   New England, Springtime.
Eberhart, R.   Explorer on Main Street, The.
  Going to Maine.
  Ides of March, The.
  River Water Music.
Eliot, T. S.   Cousin Nancy.
Emerson, R.   Monadnoc.
Frost, R.   Hundred Collars, A.
Ginsberg, A.   Autumn again, you wouldn't
  know in the city.
  Autumn Gold: New England Fall.
Hall, D.   Scenic View.
Lowell, R.   Fourth of July in Maine.
Merrill, J.   Summer People, The.
Nemerov.   For Robert Frost, in the Autumn, in
  Vermont.
Olson, C.   Move Over.
  New England March.
Oppen.   Product.

New Hampshire (state)

Rich, A.   Orion plunges like a drunken hunter.
  Spirit of Place, The.
Rukeyser, M.   Ives.
Schuyler, J.   Now and Then.
  Seeking.
Sexton.   Expatriates, The.
Thoreau.   On Ponkawtasset, since, we took our
  way.
  Such water do the gods distill.
Walcott.   Old New England.
Wheatley, P.   America.
  Farewel[l] to America, A. To Mrs. S. W.
Whittier.   Extract from "A New England
  Legend."
  Mogg Megone.
  Mountain Pictures.
  To G. G.
Williams, W.   New England.

New Hampshire (state)

Brodsky, J.   Exeter Revisited.
Eberhart, R.   River Water Music.
  Snowy Owl.
  Three Kids.
Emerson, R.   Monadnoc.
Frost, R.   Generations of Men, The.
  New Hampshire.
Hall, D.   Black Faced Sheep, The.
  Elegy for Wesley Wells.
  Granite and Grass.
  New Hampshire.
  Speeches.
  Twelve Seasons.
Kinnell.   Flower Herding on Mount Monadnock.
  Freedom, New Hampshire.
Robinson, E.   Monadnock through the Trees.
Sandburg, C.   New Hampshire Again.
Whittier.   Mount Agiochook.
  New Hampshire.

New Jersey (state)

Ammons.   Batsto.
  Corsons Inlet.
  North Jersey.
Brodsky, J.   Blues.
Ciardi, J.   Bicentennial.
Clampitt.   Reedbeds of the Hackensack, The.
Dubie.   World Isn't a Wedding of the Artists of
  Yesterday, The.
Ginsberg, A.   Bayonne Entering NYC.
  Garden State.
  Ode to the Setting Sun.
Komunyakaa.   NJ Transit.
Levertov.   For Floss.
Oppen.   *City of Keansburg*, The.
  Undertaking in New Jersey, The.
Pinsky.   At Pleasure Bay.
  Long Branch, New Jersey.
  Long Branch Song, A.
  Pleasure Pier.
Schuyler, J.   Over the Hills.
Tomlinson, C.   Ice Cream at Blauenberg.
Whitman, W.   Patrolling Barnegat.
Williams, W.   Better than flowers.
  Episode 17.
  I bought a new.
  Passaic, N.J.
  Paterson.
  Semblables, The.
  When I saw.

New Jerusalem, The

Very.   New Jerusalem, The ("I saw the city,
  'twas not built by hands").

New Mexico (state)

Ai.   Chance.
Carruth, H.   Coming Down to the Desert at
  Lordsburg, N.M.
  Shake, Well before Using.
Creeley.   For John Duff.
Jeffers, R.   New Mexican Mountain.
Komunyakaa.   Loneliness.
Lawrence, D. H.   Autumn at Taos.
  Eagle in New Mexico.
  Men in New Mexico.
Sandburg, C.   Joliet.
  Santa Fe Sketches.
Snyder, G.   I Went into the Maverick Bar.
Sze.   Do Not Speak Keresan to a Mescalero

  Apache.
  Impressions of the New Mexico Legislature.
  Listening to a Broken Radio.
  Mushroom Hunting in the Jemez Mountains.
  North to Taos.
  Three A.M., in Winter.
Tomlinson, C.   Albuquerque.
  Matachines, The.
Wright, J.   Non-Birthday Poem for My Father,
  A.

New Orleans, Louisiana

Carruth, H.   New Orleans.
Komunyakaa.   Untitled Blues; After a
  Photograph by Yevgeni Yevtushenko.
Larkin, P.   For Sidney Bechet.
Williams, T.   Mornings on Bourbon Street.

New Year

Berryman.   New Year's Eve.
Borges.   Year's End.
Burns, R.   Elegy on the Year 1788.
  Sketch. New Year's Day. To Mrs. Dunlop.
  To Miss L———.
Byron, G.   Here's a Happy New Year! But with
  Reason.
Carew, T.   New Year's Gift. To the King, A.
  New Year's Sacrifice: To Lucinda, A.
  To the New Year [For the Countess of Carlisle].
Ciardi, J.   January 1, 1973.
  New Year's Eve.
Crashaw.   Hymn for New Year's Day.
Cummings, E. E.   Passing of the Year, The.
Davie, D.   New Year Wishes for the English.
Donne.   To the Countess of Bedford at New
  Year's Tide.
Ginsberg, A.   December 31, 1978.
Graves, R.   Ancestors.
Gurney, I.   New Year's Eve.
Hardy, T.   At the Entering of the New Year.
  New Year's Eve.
  New Year's Eve in War Time, A.
Herrick.   New-Year's [or New-Yeares] Gift Sent
  to Sir Simeon Steward, A.
Jonson, B.   New Year's Gift Sung to King
  Charles. 1635, A.
  New years [or yeares], expect new gifts: sister,
  your harp[e].
Larkin, P.   New Year.
Meredith, G.   New Year's Eve.
  Time.
  Wassail for the New Year, A.
Merwin.   Early January.
Nash, O.   Good-By, Old Year, You Oaf or Why
  Don't They Pay the Bonus.
  Good Riddance, but Now What?
  Put Back Those Whiskers, I Know You.
Paz.   January First.
Rexroth, K.   New Year, The.
Rich, A.   At the Jewish New Year.
  New Year Morning.
Riley, J.   Good-by, Old Year.
  Larry Noolan's New Year.
  New Year's Nursery Jingle.
  New Year's Plaint, A.
  New Year's Time at Willards's, A.
  Old Year and the New, The.
  Old Year's Address, An.
  Song of the New Year.
Rimbaud, A.   Orphans' New Year Gifts.
Rossetti, C.   Hail, noble face of noble friend!
Sarton, M.   Greeting.
Schuyler, J.   Empathy and New Year.
Suckling, S.   On New-Year's Day 1640, to the
  King.
Swenson, M.   Last Day.
Swift, J.   New Year's Gift for Bec, A.
  To Janus.
Very.   New Year, The.
Warren, R.   Late Subterfuge.
Whitman, W.   New Year's Day, 1848.
Wilbur, R.   Year's End.
Wordsworth, W.   Lament of Mary Queen of
  Scots on the Eve of a New Year.
Wright, C.   Reading Lao Tzu Again in the New
  Year.
Zukofsky, L.   Celia's Birthday Poem.

New York City

Angelou.   Awaking in New York.
  Times-Square-Shoeshine-Composition.
Berrigan, T.   American Express.
  Bean Spasms.
  February Air.
  For You.
  I Heard Brew Moore Say, One Day.
  In the 51st State.
  Red Shift.
  Things to Do in New York (City).
  Whitman in Black.
Bishop, E.   Invitation to Miss Marianne Moore.
  Letter to N.Y.
  Trouvée.
Clampitt.   Amaranth and Moly.
  Halloween Parade, The.
  Hedge of Rubber Trees. A.
  Manhattan.
  Nothing Stays Put.
  Real Estate.
  Ringing Doorbells.
  Subway Singer, The.
  Times Square Water Music.
Codrescu.   1st Avenue Basics.
  Music.
  New York.
Cooper, J.   P.O.W.
Corbett, W.   Air and Light, The.
Crane, S.   There exists the eternal fact of
  conflict.
Creeley.   Days and Days.
  NYC—.
Cummings, E. E.   At the ferocious phenomenon
  of 5 o'clock i find myself gently decompos.
  By god i want above fourteenth.
  Fragrant sag of fruit distinctly grouped, A.
  Hanged / if n / y in a real hot spell.
  I was sitting in mcsoreley's. outside it was New
  York and beauti- / fully snowing.
  Noise.
  Woman / of bronze / unhappy, A.
Dickey, J.   Coming Back to America.
Dugan, A.   Boast.
  From Rome, for More Public Fountains in New
  York City.
  Monologue for a Sixth Avenue Screamer.
Eberhart, R.   Fragment of New York, 1929.
  Sailing to Buck's Harbor.
  Snowy Owl.
Emerson, R.   He walked the streets of great
  New York.
Ferlinghetti, L.   26.
  Retired Ballerinas, Central Park West.
García Lorca.   Christmas on the Hudson.
  Dance of Death.
  Dawn.
  Dawn, The.
  Jewish Cemetery.
  Landscape of a Pissing Multitude.
  Murder.
  New York.
  Ode to Walt Whitman.
  Sleepless City.
Ginsberg, A.   'Back on Times Square, Dreaming
  of Times Square.'
  Bayonne Entering NYC.
  Charnel Ground, The.
  Hospital Window.
  Manhattan May Day Midnight.
  Mugging.
  My Sad Self.
  New York Blues.
  345 W. 15th St.
  Tonite I walked out of my red apartment door
  on East tenth street's dusk.
  Two Sonnets.
  Uptown.
  Waking in New York.
  White Shroud.
Gunn, T.   Iron Landscapes (and the Statue of
  Liberty).
Hughes, L.   Advertisement for the Waldorf-
  Astoria.
  Christmas Eve: Nearing Midnight in New York.
  Death in Yorkville.

Drama for Winter Night (Fifth Avenue).
Grant Park.
New Yorkers.
Pennsylvania Station.
Projection.
Second Generation: New York.
Subway Face.
Ignatow, D. How Come?
Love Poem for the Forty-Second Street Library.
Melpomene in Manhattan.
Where Nothing Is Hidden.
Jacobsen, J. 49th and 5th, December 13.
Survivor's Ballad.
Kinnell. Avenue Bearing the Initial of Christ
into the New World, The.
River That Is East, The.
Kizer, C. Anniversaries: Claremont Avenue,
from 1945.
Streets of Pearl and Gold.
Koch, K. Thanksgiving.
Komunyakaa. Insufficient Blue.
Uncertainty in Blue.
Laughlin, J. Above the City.
Levertov. From the Roof.
Levine, P. Winter Words.
Logan, J. Manhattan Movements.
New York Scene: May 1958.
Lorde. Birthday Memorial to Seventh Street, A.
New York City 1970.
Lowell, R. Inauguration Day: January 1953.
Opposite House, The.
MacLeish. & Forty-Second Street.
McGrath, T. Drowned Man: Death between
Two Rivers, The.
Merrill, J. Urban Convalescence, An.
Merton. Holy Communion: the City.
Hymn of Not Much Praise for New York City.
Merwin. Coming Back in the Spring.
Numbered Apartment.
St. Vincent's.
Moore, M. New York.
Nash, O. Brief Guide to New York, A.
I Always Say There's No Place like New York
in the Summer, or, That Cottage Small by a
Waterfall Was Snapped Up Last February.
Strange Case of Mr. Niobob's
Transmogrification, The.
Nemerov. Frozen City, The.
Metropolitan Sunday.
Two Poems.
O'Hara, F. Adieu to Norman, Bon Jour to Joan
and Jean-Paul.
Commercial Variations.
Essay on Style.
F. (Missive & Walk) I. #53.
Poem: "Khrushchev is coming on the right
day!"
Rhapsody.
Saint.
Second Avenue.
Step Away from Them, A.
Steps.
"Unfinished," The.
You Are Gorgeous and I'm Coming.
Oppen. Antique.
Language of New York, A.
Tourist Eye.
Orr, G. Hotel St. Louis, New York City, Fall
1969.
Poem in New York.
Pagis. Grand Duke of New York, The.
Paley, G. 20th Street Spring.
34th Street Song.
Arboreal Mystery, An.
At the Battery.
Bob Visits Friends.
Having Arrived by Bike at Battery Park.
Housing.
Nature of This City, The.
On Mother's Day.
On the Bank Street Pier.
On the Fourth Floor.
Psalm: "Their shoes are stuccoed with sawdust
and blood."
Pasternak, B. New York in August.
Piercy. I Awoke with the Room Cold.

Skyscrapers of the Financial District Dance with
Gasman, The.
Pound, E. N. Y.
Rich, A. Upper Broadway.
Rukeyser, M. Leaving New York, I looked back
fourteen times.
Seventh Avenue.
Rukeyser, M. Night Flight : New York.
Sandburg, C. Eleventh Avenue Racket.
Neighbors.
Night Movement—New York.
This Street Never Sleeps.
Three Slants at New York.
Schuyler, J. Alice Faye at Ruby Foo's.
April and Its Forsythia.
Back.
December.
Dining Out with Doug and Frank.
East Window on Elizabeth Street, An.
Few Days, A.
Flashes.
Greenwich Avenue.
Hudson Ferry.
Let's All Hear It for Mildred Bailey!
Moon.
Morning of the Poem, The.
Sleep-Gummed Eyes,
Sun Cab, A.
This Dark Apartment.
Thursday.
Wonderful World.
Sexton. Riding the Elevator into the Sky.
Shapiro, K. Cathedral Bells, The.
Sze. Shuttle.
Tate, A. Aeneas at New York.
Tate, J. Contagion.
Tomlinson, C. Above Manhattan.
All Afternoon.
Arrival, The.
At the Trade Center.
Byzantium.
Landing, The.
On Eleventh Street.
On Madison.
Updike. Summer: West Side.
Walcott. Bleecker Street, Summer.
Blues
God Rest Ye Merry, Gentlemen.
Piano Practice.
Village Life, A.
Warren, R. I Am Dreaming of a White
Christmas: The Natural History of a Vision.
Internal Injuries.
Weiss, T. Building, A.
Whitman, W. City of Orgies.
City of Ships.
Crossing Brooklyn Ferry.
First O Songs for a Prelude.
Give Me the Splendid Silent Sun.
Mannahatta.
Whittier. To a Poetical Trio in the City of
Gotham.
Williams, W. Place (Any Place) to Transcend
All Places, A.
Wright, J. End of an Ethnic Dream, The.
Homecoming.
To the Poets in New York.
Zukofsky, L. Last cigarette / a companion, A.
See also **Broadway, New York City; Bronx, The,
New York City; Brooklyn, New York City;
Harlem, New York City; Queens, New York
City; Rockefeller Center, New York City**
New York (state)
Ferlinghetti, L. New York—Albany.
Hall, D. Southwest of Buffalo.
Laughlin, J. Upstate New York.
Lindsay, N. Niagara.
Merwin. Lackawanna.
Olson, C. Buffalo Ode.
Rich, A. Breakfast in a Bowling Alley in Utica,
New York.
Sandburg, C. Slants at Buffalo, New York.
Schuyler, J. Few Days, A.
Morning of the Poem, The.
Walcott. Upstate.
Wilbur, R. Sleepless at Crown Point.

Williams, W. Rapid Transit.
New Zealand
Creeley. Doggie Bags.
Maybe.
Summa wancha.
This wide, shallow bowl.
Meredith, G. Song of the New Zealander
among the Ruins of Old London.
Newfoundland, Canada
Crane, H. North Labrador.
Newgate Prison, London
Byron, G. Would You Go to the House by the
True Gate.
Newman, John Henry, Cardinal
Rossetti, C. Cardinal Newman.
News
Berry, W. Morning's News, The.
Bishop, E. 12 o'Clock News.
Burns, R. To a Gentleman Who Had Sent Him
a News-Paper, and Offered to Continue It Free
of Expense.
Clampitt. Anniversary, The.
Creeley. News of the World.
News, The.
Dickinson, E. Death obtains the Rose.
How News must feel when travelling.
I sued the News—yet feared—the News.
Myself can read the Telegrams.
Eberhart, R. News.
Ignatow, D. Here I Am with Mike.
Jackson, L. It Has Been Read by All.
Jarrell, R. News.
Mahon. Morning Radio.
McHugh, H. Lifelike.
Merton. Picture of Lee Ying, A.
Muldoon, P. Profumo.
Nash, O. Everybody Tells Me Everything.
Nemerov. Truth of the Matter, The.
Olson, C. Morning News, The.
Owen, W. Six o'clock in Princes Street.
Paley, G. Reading the Newspaper at the Village
Store.
Ramanujan. One Reads.
Ritsos. News Report.
Simic. History.
Stafford, W. New Every Day.
Time Capsule.
Thoreau. Evening Wind, The.
Warren, R. News Photo.
Whitman, W. Nay, Tell Me Not To-day the
Publish'd Shame.
Williams, M. Journalist Buys a Pig Farm, The.
Zagajewski. Electric Elegy.
Newspapers
Atwood. It Is Dangerous to Read Newspapers.
Berryman. World-Telegram.
Bierce. Something in the Papers.
Burns, R. To a Gentleman Who Had Sent Him
a News-Paper, and Offered to Continue It Free
of Expense.
Codrescu. New Gazette, The.
Crane, S. In a lonely place.
Newspaper is a collection of half-injustices, A.
Cummings, E. E. Insu nli gh t / o / verand.
Donne. Mercurius Gallo-Belgicus.
Eliot, T. S. Airs of Palestine, No. 2.
Ballade pour la grosse Lulu.
Boston Evening Transcript, The.
Hughes, L. Madam and the Newsboy.
Ignatow, D. Reading the Headlines.
Jarrell, R. Nestus Gurley.
Kipling, R. Delilah.
Files, The.
Man Who Could Write, The.
Press, The.
Lawrence, D. H. Great Newspaper Editor to His
Subordinate, The.
Logan, J. Paperboys, The.
Nash, O. I Am Full of Previous Experience.
Listen to the Linotype.
Political Reflection.
Nemerov. Daily Globe, The.
Keeping Informed in D.C.
Picture, A.
Truth of the Matter, The.

Niedecker. Cricket-song.
Owen, W. Smile, Smile, Smile.
Paley, G. Reading the Newspaper at the Village
  Store.
Patchen. Pick Up the Evening Paper.
Prunty. Reading before We Read, Horoscope
  and Weather.
Sandburg, C. Press Is Peculiar, The.
Schuyler, J. Ajaccio Violets.
  Picnic Cantata, A.
Smith, S. Magnificent Words.
Van Duyn. To Record One Must Be Unwary.
Very. Newspaper, The.
  To the Salem Gazette, on the Completion of Its
    First Century.
Whitman, W. Nay, Tell Me Not To-day the
  Publish'd Shame.
Wilbur, R. After the Last Bulletins.
Williams, C. K. Reading: Early Sorrow.
Williams, M. Newspaper Picture of Spectators
  at a Hotel Fire, A.
  Reading the Newspaper on Microfilm.
Zukofsky, L. Head Lines.
See also **Journalism and Journalists; Magazines**
Newton, Sir Isaac
  Blake, W. Mock On, Mock On, Voltaire,
    Rousseau.
  Eberhart, R. Quanta.
  Jarrell, R. Emancipators, The.
  Pope, A. Intended for Sir Isaac Newton.
  Wilbur, R. Worlds.
Newts
  Milosz, C. In a Jar.
  Williams, W. Ordeal, The.
Nez Percé
  Warren, R. Chief Joseph of the Nez Perce.
Niagara Falls
  Dugan, A. Poem: "It is no wonder that new
    lovers run."
  Lindsay, N. Niagara.
  Logan, J. Poem: Tears, Spray, and Steam.
  Very. On Viewing the Falls of Niagara, as
    Photographed by George Barker.
Nicaragua
  Paley, G. Dance in Jinotega, The.
  Sze. Axis, The.
  Walker, A. Songless.
Nietzsche, Friedrich
  Simic. There They Stand Unaware of Their
    Wretchedness.
  Weiss, T. Giant Yea, The.
  Zagajewski. Talk with Friedrich Nietzsche, A.
Nigeria and Nigerians
  Hughes, L. Azikiwe in Jail.
  Komunyakaa. Ogoni.
Night
  Amichai [*or* Amikhai]. Trap rises from the
    earth on a summer night, A.
  Ammons. River.
  Atwood. Night Poem.
  Auden. Nocturne: "Do squamous and
    squggling fish."
    Summer Night, A.
    Walk after Dark, A.
  Bassani, G. Idyll: "As a horn of the high moon
    veers in clear skies over Main Street."
  Baudelaire. Last Light.
    Last Rays of the Romantic Sun.
  Beckett, S. Dortmunder.
    La nuit venue où l'âme allait.
    Lueurs lisières.
    Nuit qui fais tant.
    Rentrer / À la nuit.
  Berrigan, T. February Air.
  Berry, W. Before Dark.
    On the Hill Late at Night.
    Thief, The.
    Winter Night Poem for Mary.
    Winter Nightfall.
  Berryman. Conversation.
    Curse, The.
    Night and the City.
    Possessed, The.
    Spinning Heart, The.
  Bishop, E. Late Air.

Man-Moth, The.
Blue Cloud. Night Room Composition.
Bly, R. Night.
  Solitude Late at Night in the Woods.
  Upward Moon and the Downward Moon, The.
Bogan, L. Night.
Borges. Cyclical Night, The.
  History of the Night.
  Street with a Pink Corner Store.
Brontë, E. Coldly, bleakly, drearily.
  Written in Aspin Castle.
Browning, E. Night and the Merry Man.
  Romance of the Ganges, A.
  Romaunt of Margret, The.
Browning, R. Meeting at Night.
Bukowski. 12:18 A.M.
Burns, R. Night was still, and o'er the hill, The.
  Song: "As I stood by yon roofless tower."
  Winter Night, A.
Byron, G. She Walks in Beauty.
  So We'll Go No More A-Roving.
  Song: "Breeze of the night in gentler sighs."
Campion, T. Now Winter Nights Enlarge.
Carruth, H. · Joy and Agony of Improvisation,
  The.
  Loneliness[: An Outburst of Hexasyllables].
  Moonset.
Carver, R. Best Time of the Day, The.
  Rest, The.
  Sparrow Nights.
Cavafy. Terror.
Celan. Nocturne: "Sleep not. Be on your
  guard."
Ciardi, J. Boy or Girl.
  Conversation with Leonardo, A.
  Night Freight, Michigan.
  Night Piece for My Twenty-seventh Birthday.
Clough. Darkness.
Crane, H. Fear.
  In Shadow.
  Persuasion, A.
Crane, S. I explain the silvered passing of a
  ship at night.
  Lad and a maid at a curve in the stream, A.
Creeley. Chasing the Bird.
  End of the Day, The.
  Hero, The.
  Night Time.
  Old Song.
  Roads.
  Somewhere.
  Son: "What I took in my hand."
Cullen, C. Night Rain.
Cummings, E. E. After all white horses are in
  bed.
  Chilly, murky night, A.
  Come(all your mischief- / hatchers hatch).
  Do you remember when the fluttering dusk.
  Helves surling out of eakspeasies
    per(reel)hapsingly.
  Here is the ocean, this is moonlight:say.
  Hokku.
  If learned darkness from our searched world.
  If night's mostness(and whom did merely day /
    close).
  If within tonight's erect.
  Impression.
  Is / it / because there struts a distinct silver lady.
  Kind) / YM&WC / (of sort of).
  Light Out), A.
  &-moon-He-be-hind-a-mills.
  Moon is hiding in, The.
  Night.
  Night shall eat these girls and boys.
  Nite) / thatthis / crou / ched.
  Nocturne: "When the lithe moonlight silently."
  One day a nigger.
  Out of night's almosT Floats a colour(in).
  Over us if(as what dusk becomes).
  Put off your faces, Death:for day is over.
  Silently if, out of not knowable.
  Summer Silence.
  T,h;r:u;s,h;e:s / are / silent / now.
  There is a / moon sole.
  Tonight the moon is round golden entire. It.
  Vision.

  What time is it i wonder never mind.
  When citied day with the sonorous homes.
  When parsing warmths of dusk construe.
  Windows go orange in the slowly.
  Young m / oon:be kind to olde.
Cunningham, J. Sonnet on a Still Night.
"Dario." My love, the night has come.
Davie, D. House-martin.
De la Mare. Banquo.
  Beware!
  Birthnight: To F, The.
  Fear.
  Fleeting, The.
  Forests.
  Little Salamander, The.
  Night.
  Noon and Night Flower.
  Peace.
  Snowing.
  Vigil.
Dickey, J. Jewel, The.
Dickinson, E. Aurora.
  First Day's Night had come, The.
  Good Morning—Midnight.
  Night is my favorite Day.
  Night—there lay the Days between, A.
  Night was wide, and furnished scant, The.
  Our share of night to bear.
  Some say goodnight—at night.
  To Whom the Mornings stand for Nights.
  When Night is almost done.
  Wild Nights—Wild Nights!
Dove, R. Nigger Song: An Odyssey.
  Night Watch.
  To Bed.
Dugan, A. Travel Advisory for a Night Shift.
  Untitled Poem: "I used to enjoy the night-time."
Dunbar, P. At Candle-Lightin' Time.
  Barrier, The.
  Evening.
  'Long To'ds Night.
  Night.
  Night, Dim Night.
  Night of Love.
  Summer Night, A.
  Twell de Night Is Pas'.
  With the Lark.
Eberhart, R. By the Stream.
  Commitment, A.
  Concord Cats.
  Cover Me Over.
  Hoot Owls.
  Looking at the Stars.
  Mystical Beast in the Shadows, The.
  Off Spectacle Island.
  Scouring, The.
Eichendorff. Moonlight Night.
Eliot, T. S. Rhapsody on a Windy Night.
Éluard, P. From the Outside.
Emerson, R. Always day & night.
  I left my dreamy page & sallied forth.
  Original—"Apropos."
  Parks & ponds are good by day.
Ferlinghetti, L. Olbers' Paradox.
  Plough of Time, The.
Frost, R. Acquainted with the Night.
  Evening in a Sugar Orchard.
  Now Close the Windows.
  Two Tramps in Mud Time.
Gallagher, T. With Stars.
García Lorca. Interrupted Concert, The.
  Schematic Nocturne.
  Sun Has Set, The.
Ginsberg, A. Last Night in Calcutta.
  Night Gleam.
Glück, L. Fortress, The.
  Night Piece.
  Pond, The.
Graves, R. Arrears of Moonlight.
  Between Moon and Moon.
  Colours of Night, The.
  Frosty Night, A.
  Horizon.
  Outlaws.
  Troughs of Sea.
  Visitation, The.

Gunn, T.   All Night, Legs Pointed East.
Night Piece, The.
Gurney, I.   Between the Boughs.
London.
Old Martinmas Eve.
On the Night.
Guyon.   Watching unto God in the Night-Season.
"H. D."   Evening.
Night.
Hall, D.   Passage to Worship.
HaNagid.   Gazing through the Night.
Hardy, T.   Midnight on Beechen, 187–.
Night in the Old Home.
On a Heath.
On the Esplanade.
Shut Out That Moon.
Winter Night in Woodland.
Hayden, R.   O Daedalus, Fly Away Home.
Heaney, S.   Fireside.
Herrick.   Dream[e]s.
Night-Piece, to Julia, The.
No Difference in the Dark [or i'th'dark].
Old Wives Prayer, The.
To Daisies, Not to Shut So Soon[e].
To His Sweet Saviour.
Hopkins, G.   Tom's Garland: Upon the Unemployed.
Housman.   Bells in tower at evening toll.
Hughes, L.   After Many Springs.
Harlem Night Song.
Moonlight Night: Carmel.
Night: Four Songs.
Night Song.
Stars.
Summer Night.
Hughes, T.   Thought-Fox, The.
Ignatow, D.   Midnight 2.
Night.
Ontology, An.
Jackson, L.   Previous Night, A.
Jacobsen, J.   At Night.
Country Bath.
"It's a Cold Night," Said Coney to Coney.
Lovers, The.
Night Watchman, The.
Jarrell, R.   Bird of Night, The.
Breath of Night, The.
City, City!
Eine Kleine Nachtmusik.
Miller, The.
November Ghosts, The.
Over the florid capitals.
Jeffers, R.   Hooded Night.
Night.
Night without Sleep.
October Week-End.
Watch the Lights Fade.
Keats.   In Drear-nighted December.
Kinnell.   How Many Nights.
Middle of the Way.
Poem of Night.
Kinsella, T.   Good Night.
Komunyakaa.   Nocturne: "High-beam light swung, The."
When Loneliness Is a Man.
Kumin, M.   Eyes.
Kunitz, S.   Image-Maker, The.
Nocturne.
What of the Night?
Larkin, P.   Bottle Is Drunk Out by One, The.
Coming at Last to Night's Most Thankful Springs.
Midsummer Night, 1940.
Night-Music.
Sad Steps.
Street Lamps.
When the Night Puts Twenty Veils.
Lawrence, D. H.   At the Window.
Attack, The.
Dolour of Autumn.
Elegy: "Sun immense and rosy, The."
Firelight and Nightfall.
Forecast.
Late at Night.
Liaison.

Little Town at Evening, The.
Moon New-Risen.
Night.
Night Songs.
Nonentity.
Old Song.
Our Day Is Over.
Piccadilly Circus at Night.
Rebuked.
Red Moon-Rise.
Ruination.
Shadow of Death, The.
Southern Night.
Street Lamps.
Third Song of Huitzilopochtli.
Train at Night, A.
Weeknight Service.
Yew-Tree on the Downs, The.
Lenau.   Postillion, The.
Levertov.   In Summer.
Night on Hatchet Cove.
Stems.
That Passeth All Understanding.
Tropic Ritual.
Levi, P.   Memorandum Book.
Nachtwache.
Li Po.   Spotting the moonlight at my bedside.
Lindsay, N.   Written for a Musician.
Longfellow, H.   Day Is Done, The.
Lorde.   Gemini.
Lowell, R.   Night Sweat.
Lux.   Night So Bright a Squirrel Reads, The.
MacDiarmid, H.   Dying Earth, The.
Eemis-Stane, The.
MacLeish.   Ancestral.
Bahamas.
Nocturne: "Earth, still heavy and warm with afternoon, The."
You, Andrew Marvell.
MacNeice.   Evening Indoors.
Intimations of Mortality.
Nocturne: "Dark blood of night-time, The."
Rest House, The.
Marvell.   Mower to the Glowworms [or Glow-Worms or Glo-Worms], The.
McGrath, T.   Dreams of Wild Horses, The.
Guiffre's Nightmusic.
Night Work.
Nocturne Militaire.
Such Simple Love.
McHugh, H.   Song Calls the Star Little, The.
Thought of Night.
Melville, H.   Night-March, The.
Meredith, G.   Carol of Jack Frost, A.
Child's Prayer, A.
I Chafe at Darkness.
In the Woods.
London by Lamplight.
Night of Frost in May.
Night-Walk, The.
Night walks the earth with silver feet.
O 'tis my delight / In the dead of the night.
Sleeping City, The.
Song: "Moon is alone in the sky, The."
'Tis midnight in the skies, my dear.
'Twas in a glimmering starlight.
Meredith, W.   Recollection of Bellagio.
Winter Verse for His Sister.
Merrill, J.   House, The.
Merton.   Fall of Night, The.
Nocturne: "Night has a sea which quenches the machine."
Song: "Come where the grieving rivers of the night."
Winter's Night, The.
Merwin.   December Night.
In the Night Fields.
Memory of the Loss of Wings.
Paw, The.
Summer Night on the Stone Barrens.
Under Black Leaves.
Vocations.
Michelangelo Buonarroti.   Every shut-in room or space, every covered one.
Night prevails where Phoebus—that's our sun, The.

O night, comforting night, dark though you are.
One Who made, and from utter nothing too, The.
Millay, E.   Night is my sister, and how deep in love.
Winter Night.
Milton.   Il Penseroso.
Mistral, G.   Night.
Nash, O.   Complaint to Four Angels.
Nemerov.   According to His Seasons.
Frozen City, The.
Stare of the Man from the Provinces, The.
Two Poems.
Neruda.   Some Creature.
Niedecker.   And what you liked.
Autumn Night.
Subliminal.
Oliver, M.   Morning at Great Pond.
White Night.
Olson, C.   Boat, The.
Dragon-Fly, The.
House, The.
Night, The.
Ode on Nativity, An.
Rosy, It Was
Seven Songs, The.
Oppen   Animula.
Parker, D.   Small Hours, The.
Pasternak, B.   White Night.
Patchen.   Fall of the Evening Star.
I Got the Fat Poet into a Corner.
'In the footsteps of the walking air.'
Moon came out full, you could see the white breathing of the.
Night Has Been as Beautiful as Virginia.
Petrarch.   For every living creature on this earth.
Sea has not such creatures in its waves, The.
Piercy.   Longest Night, The.
Pinsky.   Falling Asleep.
Plath.   By Candlelight.
Moonrise.
Poe.   Evening Star.
Pound, E.   Night Litany.
Prunty.   Flying at Night.
Raine, K.   Banked winter cloud.
Nocturn: "Night comes, an angel stands."
Rexroth, K.   Another Spring.
January Night.
Night below Zero.
Theory of Numbers.
Thin Edge of Your Pride, The.
Yugao.
Rich, A.   Night.
Riley, J.   Her Lonesomeness.
Home at Night.
In the Night.
Last Night—and This.
Moon-drowned.
My Night.
That Night.
Watches of the Night, The.
Rilke.   Evening Love Song.
Geranium.
Its Summer Night.
Lost Nights.
Nothing's Left.
Ritsos.   Always So.
Imponderous Night, The.
Midnight.
Midnight Stroll.
Nocturnal.
Unhidden, The.
Unjust, The.
Robinson, E.   John Evereldown.
Roethke.   Idyll: "Now as from maple to elm the flittermice skitter and twirl."
Rossetti, C.   Awake, Thou That Sleepest.
From Sunset to Star Rise.
Have You Forgotten?
If the moon came from heaven, / Talking all the way.
Is the Moon Tired?
Lord, grant us grace to rest upon Thy word.
O Lucifer, Son of the Morning!
O ye who love today, / Turn away / From Patience with her silver ray.

Oh knell of a passing time, / Will it never cease to chime?
Praying Always.
Serenade.
Smile and a Sigh, A.
Summer nights are short, / Where northern days are long, The.
Rukeyser, M.   Evening Plaza, San Miguel.
Eyes of Night-Time.
Formosa.
In a Dark House.
In the Night the Sound Woke Us.
Night-Music.
Overthrow of One o'Clock at Night, The.
Study in a Late Subway.
Rumi.   Be Melting Snow.
Inside water, a waterwheel turns.
Some nights stay up till dawn.
Sandburg, C.   Clark Street Bridge.
Far Rockaway Night till Morning.
Good Night.
High Moments.
Interior.
Moonset.
Night Bells.
Night Movement—New York.
Night Stuff.
Night's Nothings Again.
Nightsong.
Nocturne in a Deserted Brickyard.
Pass, Friend.
Pearl Horizons.
Picnic Boat.
Shag-Bark Hickory.
Skyscraper Loves Night, The.
Special Starlight.
Tall Timber.
Window.
Seifert.   Nocturnal Darkness.
Sexton.   In the Beach House.
Starry Night, The.
Shelley, P.   Lines: "Cold earth slept below, The."
Stanzas—April, 1814.
Summer Evening Churchyard, A.
To Jane: The keen stars were twinkling.
To Night.
"Shu Ting."   To ——.
Simic.   Trees at Night.
Smith, S.   Aubade: "My dove, my doe."
Goodnight.
Light of Life, The.
Up and Down.
Snyder, G.   Everybody Lying on Their Stomachs, Head toward the Candle, Reading, Sleeping, Drawing.
Kyoto: March.
Night.
Pine Tree Tops.
Stafford, W.   Bridge Begins in the Trees, A.
In the Night Desert.
Late at Night ("Falling separate into the dark").
One Night.
Stevens, W.   Candle a Saint, The.
Domination of Black.
Girl in a Nightgown.
Night-wind of August, The.
Reality Is an Activity of the Most August Imagination.
Two Figures in Dense Violet Night.
Valley Candle.
Stock, R.   Prometheus Passes the Toast.
Stockton, A.   Ode, to Amanda, An.
Swenson, M.   Goodnight.
November Night.
Sleeping Overnight on the Shore.
Woods at Night, The.
Tasso.   White moon, star-strewn sky.
Tate, A.   Ditty: "Moon will run all consciences to cover, The."
Tennyson, A.   Move Eastward, Happy Earth, and Leave.
Thomas, D.   In Country Sleep.
Thoreau.   Moon moves up her smooth and sheeny path, The.
Tomlinson, C.   Night Transfigured.
Trakl.   Rats, The.

Winter Night, A.
Updike.   3 A.M.
Van Geel.   Sleepwalking.
Very.   Influence of the Night on Faith and Imagination, The.
Morning Watch, The.
Night.
What of the Night?
Winter Night, The.
Walcott.   God Rest Ye Merry, Gentlemen.
Nights in the Gardens of Port of Spain.
Warren, R.   After Restless Night.
Antinomy: Time and Identity.
August Moon.
Birth of Love.
Death Mask of a Young Man.
Eidolon.
Last Night Train.
Midnight Outcry.
Moonlight's Dream, The.
Night Walking.
On into the Night.
Whitman, W.   After an Interval.
After the Dazzle of Day.
Night on the Prairies.
On the Beach at Night.
Whittier.   In Peace.
Wilbur, R.   After the Last Bulletins.
For Ellen.
Peace of Cities, The.
Sonnet: "Winter deepening, the hay all in, The."
Terrace, The.
Williams, W.   At Night.
Eternity.
Good Night.
Goodnight, A.
Night.
Night Rider, The.
Peace on Earth.
Rigamarole.
Wordsworth, W.   How Beautiful the Queen of Night, on High.
I watch, and long have watched, with calm regret.
Night-Piece, A.
Night Thought, A.
Western clouds a deepening gloom display, The.
Winter's Evening, A.
Wright, C.   Paesaggio Notturno.
Still Life with Stick and Word.
Wright, J.   Morning Hymn to a Dark Girl.
Yeats.   To Dorothy Wellesley.
Zagajewski.   Night.
She Wrote in Darkness.
Wind at Night.
Zaturenska.   Listening Landscape, The.
Metaphysics of the Night.
See also **Evening**

Night-blooming Cereus
Very.   Night Blooming Cereus, The.

Nightclubs
Berryman.   Enemies of the Angels, The.
Bukowski.   Very.
Cummings, E. E.   Between nose-red gross.
Helves surling out of eakspeasies per(reel)hapsingly.
In Healey's Palace I was sitting.
Infinite jukethrob smoke & swallow to dis.
Hughes, L.   Cabaret.
Cat and the Saxophone (2 a.m.), The.
College Formal: Renaissance Casino.
Death in Harlem.
Harlem Night Club.
Jazz Band in a Parisian Cabaret.
Jazz Girl.
Jazzonia.
Lady in Cabaret.
Midnight Dancer.
Minnie Sings Her Blues.
Negro Dancers.
Negro Servant.
Neon Signs.
New Cabaret Girl, The.
Nocturne for the Drums.
Puzzlement.
Saturday Night.

Sport.
To Midnight Nan at Leroy's.
Young Singer.
Komunyakaa.   Jasmine.
Laughlin, J.   Stuttgart: In a Nightclub (Illegal).
Nightgowns
Orr, G.   Girl with Eighteen Nightgowns, The.
Stevens, W.   Disillusionment of Ten o'Clock.
Nighthawks
Berry, W.   September 2, 1969.
Nightingales
Borges.   To the Nightingale.
Bourne, V.   Strada's Nightingale.
Browning, E.   Bianca among the Nightingales.
Poet and the Bird, The.
Coleridge, S.   Nightingale, The.
Cowper, W.   Nightingale and Glow-Worm, The.
To the Nightingale.
De la Mare.   Sotto Voce.
Eberhart, R.   Ultimate Song.
Elyas Yusof Nezami [*or* Nisami] Ganjavi].
While roses bloomed along the plain.
Heaney, S.   Serenades.
Herrick.   To the Nightingale, and Robin-Red-Brest.
Hopkins, G.   Nightingale, The.
Keats.   Ode to a Nightingale.
Lawrence, D. H.   Paltry-Looking People.
Lindsay, N.   Chinese Nightingale, The.
Marvell.   Mower to the Glowworms [*or* Glow-Worms *or* Glo-Worms], The.
Meredith, G.   Poetry of Keats, The.
Three Maidens, The.
To a Nightingale.
Milton.   Sonnet 1: "O Nightingale, that on yon bloomy Spray."
Muldoon, P.   Nightingales.
Paley, G.   In Aix.
Petrarch.   Nightingale, that so harmoniously, The.
Ransom, J.   Philomela.
Rilke.   Small Notebook.
Ritsos.   Philomel.
Rossetti, C.   Bird Raptures.
Rumi.   Bird delegation came to Solomon complaining, A.
Schuyler, J.   Three Gardens.
Seifert.   Song of the Nightingale, The.
Wilde, O.   By the Arno.
Wordsworth, W.   Cuckoo and the Nightingale, The.
O Nightingale! thou surely art.
Nightmares
Atwood.   No Name.
Borges.   Leaves of the Cypress, The.
Nightmare.
Brontë, E.   Sudden chasm of ghastly light, A.
Browning, R.   Bad Dreams I.
Bukowski.   Rat Rises, A.
Carver, R.   Trying to Sleep Late on a Saturday Morning in November.
Yesterday, Snow.
Coleridge, S.   Night-Mare Death in Life, The.
Creeley.   Dreams.
De la Mare.   Drugged.
Dickinson, E.   Night's capacity varies.
Dove, R.   Nightmare.
Dugan, A.   Moral Dream.
Fenton, J.   Lullaby for a Summer Recess.
Vuccerìa.
Glück, L.   Night Piece.
Graves, R.   Castle, The.
Dawn Bombardment.
Gratitude for a Nightmare.
Lost Jewel, A.
Nightmare of Senility.
Theme of Death, The.
Tolling Bell.
Hughes, L.   Nightmare Boogie.
Jackson, L.   Nightmare, The.
Jacobsen, J.   Hooves, The.
Jarrell, R.   Prince, The.
Quilt-Pattern, A.
Jeffers, R.   Apology for Bad Dreams.
Nightpiece.
Kumin, M.   Nightmare Factory, The.

Lawrence, D. H.   In the Dark.
Levertov.   Her Nightmare.
Lorde.   Conclusion.
MacNeice.   Bad Dream.
Major, C.   Descendant of Solomon and the
   Queen of Sheba.
Merton.   Saint Jason.
Nemerov.   Nightmare.
Oppen.   Primitive.
Pessoa.   Some mysterious phantom's sudden
   hand.
Raine, K.   Bad Dream, A.
Rossetti, C.   Coast-Nightmare, A.
   So I grew half delirious and quite sick.
Sarton, M.   Tortured, The.
Trakl.   Sleep.
Warren, R.   Midnight Outcry.
   Original Sin[: A Short Story].
Williams, C. K.   Dream, The.
See also **Dreams and Dreaming**

Nihilism
Beckett, S.   Flux cause.
Creeley.   Rhythm, The.
Lawrence, D. H.   December Night.
   Robot Feelings.
Lowell, R.   Nihilist as Hero, The.
Pessoa.   If you want to kill yourself, how come
   you don't want to kill yourself.
   Nothing comes of nothing. We are nothing.
   Tobacco Shop.
Wilde, O.   Libertatis Sacra Fames.
Williams, T.   One and Two.
Zukofsky, L.   Guillaume de Machault (1300-
   1377) Ballade: Plourès, dames.

Nijinsky, Vaslav
Wilbur, R.   Grace.

Nile, Battle of the (1798)
Moore, M.   New York.

Nile (river)
Keats.   To the Nile.
Lux.   Sudd as Metaphor, The.
Shelley, P.   To the Nile.

1960s
Angelou.   Riot: 60's.
Carruth, H.   Spring 1967.
Codrescu.   Toward the End of 1969.
Ginsberg, A.   And ninety-nine soldiers piled on
   the train at Amarillo.
   Beginning of a Poem of These States.
   Crossing Nation.
   Funky barn, black hills approaching Fulton.
   Hiway Poesy: L.A.–Albuquerque–Texas–
      Witchita.
   Iron Horse.
   Kansas City to Saint Louis.
   Kansas! Kansas! Shuddering at last!
   Northwest Passage.
   Overpopulation, overpopulation / Give me 3
      acres of land.
   Returning North of Vortex.
   These States: into L.A.
   Violence.
   Wichita Vortex Sutra.
Hacker, M.   Nights of 1965: the Old Reliable.
Komunyakaa.   How I See Things.
Lorde.   Equinox.
McGrath, T.   Note on the Late Elections, A.
Merton.   Fall '66.
   Tune for Festive Dances in the Nineteen Sixties,
      A.
Neruda.   Century Dying, A.
Piercy.   Learning Experience.
Schuyler, J.   Empathy and New Year.
Van Duyn.   Christmas Card, after the
   Assassinations, A.
   Eros to Howard Nemerov.
   What the Motorcycle Said.
Williams, C. K.   Flight.
Zagajewski.   1969.

1930s
Auden.   Bride in the 30's, A.
Kumin, M.   Thirties Revisited, The.
Prunty.   Depression, the War, and Gypsy Rose
   Lee, The.
Tomlinson, C.   Gladstone Street.

Nineveh (capital of ancient Assyria)
Pound, E.   And Thus in Nineveh.
Rossetti, D.   Burden of Nineveh, The.

Niobe
Donne.   Niobe.
Patchen.   Niobe.
Ritsos.   Niobe.
Rukeyser, M.   Niobe Now.
Unknown.   On Hermocratia.
   On Niobe.
Wheatley, P.   Niobe in Distress for Her Children
   Slain by Apollo, from *Ovid's* Metamorphoses,
   Book 6. And from a View of the Painting of
   Mr. *Richard Wilson.*

Nirvana
Rexroth, K.   It Is a German Honeymoon.

Nixon, Richard Milhous
Ai.   Knock, Knock.
Carruth, H.   Regarding Chainsaws.
Dugan, A.   On Being Asked How Do You Feel
   after an Operation with Inadequate Anesthesia.
   This Is How I Feel.
Levertov.   Poem at Christmas, 1972, during the
   Terror-Bombing of North Vietnam, A.
McGrath, T.   Note on the Late Elections, A.
Meredith, W.   Nixon's the One.
Paley, G.   My Father at 85.

Noah
Davie, D.   Dancing Measures.
Dickinson, E.   I am sure I feel as Noah did.
Graves, R.   After the Flood.
   Ark, The.
Herrick.   Fast, or Lent, The.
Kipling, R.   Legends of Evil, The.
Merwin.   Noah's Raven.
Rossetti, C.   As the dove which found no rest /
   For the sole of her foot, flew back.
Wilbur, R.   Still, Citizen Sparrow.
Wilner, E.   American Painting, with Rain.

Nobility
Brontë, E.   None of my kindred now can tell.
Burns, R.   Elegy on Captain Matthew
   Henderson [*or* Capt. M——— H———] [A
   Gentleman Who Held the Patent for His
   Honours Immediately from Almighty God!].
   O Kenmure's on and awa, Willie.
Campion, T.   To the Most Illustrious and Mighty
   Fredericke the Fifth, Count Palantine of the
   Rhein.
   What Fair[e] Pomp[e].
Carew, T.   To My Much Honoured Friend,
   Henry, Lord Carey of Leppington, upon His
   Translation of Malvezzi.
Cavafy.   In Sparta.
Coleridge, S.   Lines Written at the King's Arms,
   Ross, Formerly the House of the "Man of
   Ross."
Cummings, E. E.   For any ruffian of the sky.
Dickinson, E.   There is a Shame of Nobleness.
   Why is it Nobleness makes us ashamed.
Dugan, A.   On Breeding, from Plutarch.
Gray, T.   Impromptu.
Hall, D.   Revolution, The.
Han-shan.   When Master Tung was young.
Hardy, T.   Man, A.
Jeffers, R.   New Year's Eve.
   Salvage.
Jonson, B.   To the Most Noble, and above His
   Titles, Robert, Earl of Somerset.
Lawrence, D. H.   Death of the Baron, The.
   Noble.
Nash, O.   Ms. Found under a Serviette in a
   Lovely Home.
Rossetti, C.   Maggie a Lady.
Sheridan, T.   Letter of Advice to the Right Hon.
   John Earl of Orrery, A.
Unknown.   On Pedigree.
Whittier.   Countess, The.
   Isabella of Austria.
Wordsworth, W.   Song at the Feast of Brougham
   Castle upon the Restoration of Lord Clifford.
   To the Lady Fleming on Seeing the Foundation
   Preparing for the Erection of Rydal Chapel.

Noblesse Oblige
Emerson, R.   King. If farmers make my land

   secure.
Nash, O.   Ms. Found under a Serviette in a
   Lovely Home.

Noises
Bukowski.   Trench Warfare.
Ciardi, J.   Prayer to the Mountain, A.
Coleridge, S.   Thought, A.
Creeley.   Tiny Place, A.
Cummings, E. E.   After screamgroa / ning.ish:ly.
   Noise.
   O the sun comes up-up-up in the opening.
De la Mare.   Market-Place, The.
Dugan, A.   Empirical Scene.
Dunbar, P.   When Malindy Sings.
Emerson, R.   From a far mountain creeping
   down.
Graves, R.   Death by Drums.
Gunn, T.   Grasses.
Hughes, T.   Cock-Crows.
Koch, K.   Hearing.
McHugh, H.   Spilled.
Montale.   Day and Night.
Nash, O.   I Didn't Say a Word, or, Who Called
   That Piccolo Player a Father?
   Party Next Door, The.
   People upstairs, The.
   Under the Floor.
Niedecker.   Sunday's motor-cars.
Plath.   Night Shift.
Ramanujan.   Leaky Tap after a Sister's
   Wedding, A.
Ritsos.   Deadly Victory.
   There.
Rossetti, C.   What does the donkey bray about?
Sandburg, C.   Clinton South of Polk.
Smith, S.   Up and Down.
Tate, J.   Flight.
Tomlinson, C.   Shout, The.
Warren, R.   Little Black Heart of the Telephone.
   Loose Shutter, The.
Wordsworth, W.   Morning Exercise, A.
   On the Power of Sound.
Zukofsky, L.   When the crickets.

Noon
Clampitt.   Meridian.
Corbett, W.   Cold Lunch.
Davie, D.   Lily at Noon, A.
   Tuscan Morning.
De la Mare.   Noon and Night Flower.
   Sotto Voce.
Dickinson, E.   It's like the Light.
Dugan, A.   Noon's World.
Dunbar, P.   Noon.
Eberhart, R.   By the Stream.
Jeffers, R.   Noon.
Levine, P.   Noon.
Milosz, C.   At Noon.
Montale.   Sit the noon out, pale and lost in
   thought.
Nemerov.   Advice from the Holy Tomb.
Riley, J.   Noon Interval, A.
Ritsos.   Noon.
Stevens, W.   What We See Is What We Think.
Thoreau.   Noon.
Wordsworth, W.   Labourer's Noon-Day Hymn,
   The.

Norfolk, England
Davie, D.   Norfolk.
   Some Shires Revisited.
Mahon.   September in Gt. Yarmouth.

Normandy, Invasion of (1944)
Williams, M.   Normandy Beach.

North Carolina (state)
Glück, L.   Cottonmouth Country.
Lorde.   Poem for a Poet, A.
Mahon.   Globe in [North] Carolina, The.
Muldoon, P.   Promises, Promises.
Rukeyser, M.   Outer Banks, The.

North Dakota (state)
McGrath, T.   Beyond the Red River.
   Something Is Dying Here.
Tate, J.   Tragedy Comes to the Bad Lands.
Wright, J.   Outside Fargo, North Dakota.
   Poem Written under an Archway in a
   Discontinued Railroad Station, Fargo, North

Dakota, A.
To Flood Stage Again.

North Pole
Jarrell, R.   90 North.

North, The, United States
Carruth, H.   North Winter.
Hughes, L.   Northern Liberal.
Melville, H.   Fortitude of the North, The.
Riley, J.   North and South.
Whittier.   Album Verses.
What State Street Said to South Carolina, and
What South Carolina Said to State Street.

North Wind
Graves, R.   Love in Barrenness.
Lindsay, N.   Moon's the North Wind's Cooky,
The.
Merwin.   North Wind.
Montale.   News from Mount Amiata.

Northamptonshire, England
Davie, D.   Northamptonshire.

Northern Ireland
Heaney, S.   Anahorish.
Casualty.
England's Difficulty.
Funeral Rites.
I'm writing this just after an encounter.
July.
'Religion's never mentioned here,' of course.
Singing School.
Strand at Lough Beg, The.
This morning from a dewy motorway.
Trial Runs.
Kinsella, T.   Butcher's Dozen.
Kipling, R.   Ulster.
MacNeice.   Carrickfergus.
Mahon.   Camus in Ulster.
Ecclesiastes.
Glengormley.
Northern Star.
Muldoon, P.   Mink.
More a Man Has the More a Man Wants, The.

Northumberland, England
Davie, D.   Northumberland.
Smith, S.   Watchful.

Noses
Coleridge, S.   Nose, The.
Hall, D.   Nose.
Herrick.   Upon Center a Spectacle-Maker with a
Flat Nose.
Upon Coone.
Upon His Julia.
Upon Lulls.
Upon Megg.
Williams, W.   Smell.

Nostalgia
Angelou.   Just for a Time.
Berrigan, T.   Red Shift.
Bierce.   Golden Age, The.
Borges.   Nostalgia for the Present.
Byron, G.   Childish Recollections.
I Would I Were a Careless Child.
There Was a Time, I Need Not Name.
Campion, T.   Wise men patience never want.
Carruth, H.   Letter to Maxine Sullivan.
November: Indian Summer.
Carver, R.   Those Days.
Trestle, The.
Woolworth's, 1954.
Cavafy.   In the Same Space.
Ciardi, J.   Letter for Those Who Grew Up
Together.
Clampitt.   Homeland.
My Cousin Muriel.
Coleridge, S.   Lines Written in the Album at
Elbingerode, in the Har[t]z Forest.
Collins, B.   Nostalgia.
Creeley.   Hamilton Hotel.
Old Song.
Picnic, The.
So Big.
Still Dancers.
Cummings, E. E.   Boy and the Man, The.
Even if all desires things moments be.
That famous fatheads find that each.
Davie, D.   By the Road to Upper Midhope.

Dudwood.
Hampshire.
Remembering the 'Thirties.
Shropshire.
Stratford on Avon.
Dickey, J.   Shark's Parlor, The.
Two Poems of Going Home.
Drummond de Andrade.   Memories of the
Ancient World.
Dubie.   Skeleton for Mr. Paul in Paradise, A.
Dunbar, P.   Land o' Used to Be, The.
Old High School and the New, The.
Old Memory, An.
Eliot, T. S.   Marina.
Ferlinghetti, L.   Plan du Centre de Paris à Vol
D'Oiseau.
Returning to Paris with Pissarro.
Tunisian Nostalgia.
Frost, R.   Range-finding.
Ginsberg, A.   After Yeats.
Europe! Europe!
Flying Elegy.
I Have Increased Power.
Mad Gleam, A.
Gurney, I.   Old Thought.
Old Times.
When the Body Might Free.
Hall, D.   Maple Syrup.
Toy Bone, The.
Hardy, T.   After a Journey.
Bygone Occasion, A.
Christmas in the Elgin Room.
Jog-Trot Pair, A.
Last Signal, The.
Lines to a Movement in Mozart's E-Flat
Symphony.
Lost Love.
Old Excursions.
Old Furniture.
Old Likeness, An.
On a Discovered Curl of Hair.
Paths of Former Time.
Photograph, The.
Place on the Map, The.
Places.
She Would Welcome Old Tribulations.
Two-Years' Idyll, A.
Hughes, T.   Leaf Mould.
Jarrell, R.   In Those Days.
Lot is vacant still, The.
Player Piano, The.
Times Worsen, The.
Kipling, R.   King, The.
Lovers' Litany, The.
Moon of Other Days, The.
Three-Decker, The.
Virginity, The.
Kumin, M.   For My Great-Grandfather: A
Message Long Overdue.
Larkin, P.   Midsummer Night, 1940.
Lawrence, D. H.   Nostalgia.
Piano.
Twenty Years Ago.
Levertov.   Romance.
Wanderer, The.
Lindsay, N.   By the Spring at Sunset.
MacLeish.   Baccalaureate.
MacNeice.   Nostalgia.
Mahon.   Autobiographies.
Brighton Beach.
Nostalgias.
Old Snaps, The.
Rock Music.
McGrath, T.   In Praise of Necessity.
Remembering Loves and Deaths.
Repeated Journey, The.
Melville, H.   Aeolian Harp, The.
Age of the Antonines, The.
Archipelago, The.
Hearts-Of-Gold.
Temeraire, The.
Meredith, G.   Hungarian Air.
To a Skylark.
Youth in Memory.
Montale.   Shore of Versilia.
Muldoon, P.   Bran.

Ned Skinner.
Nash, O.   Middle, The.
Neruda.   Ambassador, The.
Final.
O'Hara, F.   Commercial Variations.
Orr, G.   Daffodil Poem.
Paley, G.   One day when I was a child long ago.
Parker, D.   Rosemary ("Ah, no, I dare not lose
myself in dreams").
Patchen.   Street Corner College.
Plath.   Eye-Mote, The.
Prunty.   Box of Leaves, A.
Name, The.
Rexroth, K.   Old Street.
Rich, A.   Living Memory.
Riley, J.   Babyhood.
Christmas Long Ago, The.
Days Gone By, The.
Dream of Long Ago, A.
Friday Afternoon.
'Mongst the Hills o' Somerset.
Mulberry Tree, The.
Muskingum Valley, The.
My White Bread.
Name Us No Names No More.
Old Days, The.
Old-fashioned Bible, The.
Old-Fashioned Roses.
Old Friend, An.
Old Man's Nursery Rhyme.
Old Times Were the Best, The.
Old Trundle-Bed, The.
Orchard Lands of Long Ago, The.
Our Boyhood Haunts.
Out to Old Aunt Mary's.
Romancin'.
Scraps.
Summer's Day, A.
Tale of the Airly Days, A.
Up and Down Old Brandywine.
When Mother Combed My Hair.
When We First Played "Show."
Where the Children Used to Play.
Rilke.   Nostalgia.
Rimbaud, A.   Dresser, The.
Robinson, E.   Miniver Cheevy.
Roethke.   Otto.
Rossetti, C.   Milking-Maid, The.
Schuyler, J.   Alice Faye at Ruby Foo's.
At Darragh's I.
Morning of the Poem, The.
Sexton.   45 Mercy Street.
Love Song for K. Owyne.
Smith, S.   Archie and Tina.
Snyder, G.   Soy Sauce.
Spender, S.   I Think Continually of Those Who
Were Truly Great.
Stafford, W.   Biography.
Farm on the Great Plains, The.
Stereopticon.
Stock, R.   Scene from Life.
Tennyson, A.   Break, Break, Break.
Tomlinson, C.   Etruria Vale.
Warren, R.   Youthful Picnic Long Ago: Sad
Ballad on Box.
Whitman, W.   Dying Veteran, The.
Old Man's Thought of School, An.
Williams, C. K.   Nostalgia.
Sanctity, The.
Sleeping Over.
Soon.
Still Life.
Williams, M.   Everything Is Fine Here. How
Are You?
In Your Own Words without Lying Tell
Something of Your Background.
Williams, W.   Raleigh Was Right.
Wright, C.   Arkansas Traveller.
Driving through Tennessee.
Homage to Claude Lorrain.
Italian Days.
Journal of the Year of the Ox, A.
Journal of True Confessions, A.
Lonesome Pine Special.
Lost Bodies.
Lost Souls.

Mantova.
Other Side of the River, The.
Roma I.
Roma II.
Yeats.   He Remembers Forgotten Beauty.
Meditation of the Old Fisherman, The.

Nothingness
Ammons.   Then One.
Tossup.
Baudelaire.   Abyss, The.
Curious Man's Dream, A.
Beckett, S.   Fin fond du néant.
Flux cause.
Ne manquez pas à Stuttgart.
Pas à pas.
Rentrer / À la nuit.
Rien nul / n'aura été.
Something There.
Borges.   I Am.
Suicide, The.
Bukowski.   Alone with Everybody.
Green.
Naked at 92 Degrees.
Carruth, H.   Words in a Certain Appropriate
Mode.
Celan.   Mandorla.
Psalm: "No one kneads us again out of earth
and clay."
Chuang Tzu.   Lost Pearl, The.
Man of Tao, The.
Starlight and Non-Being.
Tao.
Two Kings and No-Form.
When Knowledge Went North.
Where Is Tao?
Coleridge, S.   On an Insignificant.
Creeley.   Fancy.
I Am Held by My Fear of Death.
Message, The.
Moment.
Rhyme, The.
Some Afternoon.
Cummings, E. E.   Come nothing to my
comparable soul.
Don't get me wrong oblivion.
If within tonight's erect.
Now does our world descend.
Only as what(out of a flophouse)floats.
What Got him was Noth.
De la Mare.   Never-To-Be.
Dickinson, E.   By homely gift and hindered
Words.
Donne.   Negative Love.
Dugan, A.   On Zero.
"Space Is Not Merely a Background for Events,
But Possesses an Autonomous Structure." —
A. Einstein.
Eberhart, R.   As If You Had Never Been.
Mystery of the Abstract.
García Lorca.   Nocturne of Emptied Space.
Graves, R.   Gorge, The.
Nothing.
Gunn, T.   Annihilation of Nothing, The.
Herrick.   Gods Presence.
Hughes, L.   End.
Hughes, T.   Conjuring in Heaven.
Widdop.
Ivanov, G.   Thank god there is no Tsar.
Jackson, L.   All Nothing, Nothing.
Keats.   When I Have Fears [That I May Cease
to Be].
Laughlin, J.   Atman, The.
Lawrence, D. H.   After All the Tragedies Are
Over.
Blank.
Dies Irae.
Non-Existence.
Nullus.
Resurrection of the Flesh.
Worm Turns, The.
Levi, P.   Black Stars, The.
MacLeish.   End of the World, The.
Mallarmé.   Her pure nails on high displaying
their onyx.
Throw of the Dice, A.
When the shadow menaced with its fatal law.

Melville, H.   Buddha.
Milosz, C.   Meaning.
Montale.   In the Park at Caserta.
Neruda.   Search.
Niedecker.   What horror to awake at night.
Olson, C.   Lie of 10, or the Concept of Zero,
The.
Orr, G.   Nothing and the Incident in the Streets.
Two Poems about Nothing.
Pessoa.   Nothing comes of nothing. We are
nothing.
Some mysterious phantom's sudden hand.
Piercy.   Death of the Small Commune, The.
Hallow Eve with Spaces for Ghosts.
Morning Half-Life Blues, The.
Never-Never.
Right Thinking Man.
S. Dead.
Thrifty Lover, The.
Pinkerton, H.   Good Friday.
Raine, K.   World, The.
Ramanujan.   Salamanders.
Rilke.   Nothing's Left.
Ritsos.   Need to Express.
Robinson, E.   Man against the Sky, The.
Roethke.   Abyss, The,
Duet.
Rumi.   Fragile Vial, The.
Simic.   Invention of Nothing.
What the White Had to Say.
Smith, S.   Dream of Comparison, A.
Stevens, W.   Clear Day and No Memories, A.
Snow Man, The.
Szymborska, W.   Cave, The.
Nothing nothinged itself for me as well.
Poem in Honor Of, A.
Tate, J.   Saint John of the Cross in Prison.
Tomlinson, C.   Event.
Williams, W.   To Have Done Nothing.
Wright, C.   Composition in Grey and Pink.
Disjecta Membra.
Journal of Southern Rivers, A.
October.
Sitting outside at the End of Autumn.
Wright, J.   Goodbye to the Poetry of Calcium.
See also **Nihilism**

Notoriety
Bukowski.   Best Way to Get Famous Is to Run
Away, The.
Carver, R.   Music.
Cavafy.   Days of 1896.
Riley, J.   Johnson's Boy.

Notre Dame Cathedral
Cummings, E. E.   It is winter a moon in the
afternoon.
Rilke.   Notre Dame.

Nottingham, England
Davie, D.   Nottinghamshire.
Lawrence, D. H.   In Nottingham.
Nottingham's New University.

Nova Scotia, Canada
Bishop, E.   First Death in Nova Scotia.
Poem: "About the size of an old-style dollar
bill."

Novels
Bukowski.   2nd Novel, The.
Dear Friend.
Coleridge, S.   With Fielding's *Amelia*.
MacLeish.   Observations of P. Ovidus Naso on
the Incidence of Sex in the Contemporary
Novel.
Milosz, C.   Undressing Justine.
Nemerov.   Exasperations of a Novelist.
Novelists.
Reflexion of a Novelist.
Style.
To the Bleeding Hearts Association of American
Novelists.
Williams, M.   Learning to Read.

Novelty
Blok.   Do You Remember.
Browning, E.   Poet, The.
Dugan, A.   Advertising in Paris.
Herrick.   Nothing New.
Larkin, P.   When First We Faced, and Touching

Showed.
MacNeice.   Idle Talk.
Milton.   Sonnet 3: "As on a rugged mountain at
the darkening of evening."

November
Atwood.   November.
Brontë, E.   Redbreast, Early in the Morning.
Carruth, H.   Once and Again.
Crane, H.   This Way Where November.
Dickinson, E.   Day grew small, surrounded
tight, The.
November always seemed to me.
Dunbar, P.   Nutting Song.
Frost, R.   My November Guest.
Hardy, T.   At Day-Close in November.
Hughes, T.   November.
Jeffers, R.   November Surf.
Lawrence, D. H.   November by the Sea.
Levertov.   Air of November.
MacLeish.   April in November.
November.
McGrath, T.   News and the Weather, The.
Merwin.   New Moon in November.
Nemerov.   Elegy of Last Resort.
Patchen.   November in Ohio.
Rexroth, K.   November has hung the locust.
Riley, J.   Song—for November.
Sandburg, C.   Prairie Woodland.
Suburban Sicilian Sketches.
Without Notice Beforehand.
Schuyler, J.   November.
Vermont Diary, A.
Stafford, W.   November.
Swenson, M.   November Night.
Tomlinson, C.   Saving the Appearances.
Whittier.   Day, A.
St. Martin's Summer.
Williams, W.   Woodpecker, The.
Wright, J.   Late November in a Field.

Nuclear Accidents
Levertov.   English Field in the Nuclear Age, An.
Paley, G.   In Aix.
See also **Radiation and Radiation Sickness**

Nuclear Energy
Carruth, H.   Phone.
Ginsberg, A.   Plutonian Ode.
Komunyakaa.   1984.
Levertov.   Split Mind, The.
What It Could Be.
Williams, C. K.   Tar.

Nuclear Tests
Ai.   Chance.
Cooper, J.   After the Bomb Tests.
Stafford, W.   At the Bomb Testing Site.

Nuclear War
Broumas, O.   Eros.
Clampitt.   Berceuse.
Creeley.   Some Afternoon.
Frost, R.   Planners, The.
Ginsberg, A.   Everybody's Fantasy.
Nagasaki Days.
Hughes, T.   Woman Unconscious, A.
Jacobsen, J.   Fittest, The.
Jeffers, R.   Beautiful Captive, The.
Explosion.
Monument.
Kinnell.   Fundamental Project of Technology,
The.
Kizer, C.   Election Day, 1984.
Twelve o'Clock.
Komunyakaa.   For You, Sweetheart, I'll Sell
Plutonium Reactors.
Kumin, M.   After the Harvest.
How to Survive Nuclear War.
Laughlin, J.   Small Group, A.
Levertov.   Age of Terror.
English Field in the Nuclear Age, An.
Talk in the Dark.
Lowell, R.   Fall 1961.
McGrath, T.   Nuclear Winter.
War Resisters' Song.
Merton.   Chant to Be Used in Processions
around a Site with Furnaces.
Letter to Pablo Antonio Cuadra Concerning
Giants, A.

Original Child Bomb.
Niedecker. Could You Be Right.
Oppen. Crowded Countries of the Bomb, The.
Time of the Missile.
Rich, A. Ultimate Act, The.
Rukeyser, M. Surrounded, The.
Sandburg, C. Call the Next Witness.
Unknown War, The.
Walker, A. We Have a Map of the World.
See also **Atomic Bomb; Radiation and Radiation Sickness**

Nudity and Nudists
Creeley. Apology, The.
Cummings, E. E. Perhaps it was Myself sits down in this chair. There were two chairs,in fact.
Graves, R. Naked and the Nude, The.
Herrick. Upon Julia's Fall.
Lawrence, D. H. Elixir.
Give Me a Sponge.
Gross, Coarse, Hideous.
Innocent England.
Olson, C. Here i am, naked.
Stafford, W. Adults Only.
Swenson, M. Naked in Borneo.
Walker, A. Streaking (A Phenomenon Following the Sixties).
Wilbur, R. Playboy.
Williams, M. Art Photographer Puts His Model at Ease, The.

Numbers
Cavafy. Addition.
Creeley. Numbers.
Piece, A.
Donne. Primrose, The; Being at Montgomery Castle, upon the Hill, on Which It Is Situate.
Hughes, L. Problems.
Koch, K. Magic of Numbers, The.
Laughlin, J. By the Numbers.
Levi, P. 2000.
Nash, O. Calling Spring VII-MMMC.
Neruda. 2 8 3 2 5 6 7 4 5 4 9.
Olson, C. 2nd Musical Form, for Dave Young, A.
Lie of 10, or the Concept of Zero, The.
Ritsos. Probabilities.
Rossetti, C. 1 and 1 are 2— / That's for me and you.
Sandburg, C. Child Margaret.
City Number.
Crossed Numbers.
Number Man.
Simic. Figuring.
Szymborska, W. Pi.
Williams, M. Man Who Believes in Five, The.
Zukofsky, L. To My Valentines.

Nuns
García Lorca. Gypsy Nun, The.
Glück, L. Cell, The.
Graves, R. Gooseflesh Abbey.
Liadan and Curithir.
Han-shan. Again I see those who leave home.
Hey you people who leave home.
Homeless people I know, The.
Hopkins, G. Heaven-Haven.
Wreck of the Deutschland, The.
Kizer, C. Election Day, 1984.
Kumin, M. Halfway.
Young Nun at Bread Loaf.
Logan, J. Cycle for Mother Cabrini, A.
Lowell, R. Mother Marie Therese.
Merton. To a Severe Nun.
Milton. Sonnet 9: "Ladie [or Lady], that in the prime of earliest youth."
Rukeyser, M. Nuns in the Wind.
Williams, W. Nun's Song.

Nuremberg, Germany
Levi, P. On Trial.

Nursery Rhymes
Creeley. Names, The.
Frost, R. Lines Written in Dejection on the Eve of Great Success.
Lux. Criss Cross Apple Sauce.
Rexroth, K. Mother Goose.
Riley, J. Book of Joyous Children, The.

New Year's Nursery Jingle.
To Hattie—on Her Birthday.
To Joel Chandler Harris.
With a Child-Book.
Robinson, E. Old King Cole.
Simic. Nursery Rhyme.
Warren, R. Nursery Rhymes.

Nurses
Browning, E. Isobel's Child.
De la Mare. Juliet's Nurse.
Dugan, A. Oxymoronic Hospital Blues.
Glück, L. Nurse's Song.
Graves, R. Wild Cyclamen.
Hughes, L. Where Service Is Needed.
Ignatow, D. Nurse.
Jarrell, R. Well-to-Do Invalid, A.
Kipling, R. Dirge of Dead Sisters.
Komunyakaa. Sunset Threnody.
Milosz, C. Mister Hanusevich.
Poe. To M. L. S——.
Prunty. Taking Down, The.
Rich, A. Dien Bien Phu.
Whitman, W. Wound-Dresser, The.

Nursing Homes
Davie, D. Bella & Rosa.
Piercy. Proposal for Recycling Wastes, A.

Nurturing
Kumin, M. Nurture.
Mistral, G. Rocking.

Nymphs
Apollinaire. Rhenish Night.
Broumas, O. Thetis.
Carew, T. Good Counsel to a Young Maid.
Pastoral[l] Dialogue, A.
Cavafy. Interruption.
"H. D." Oread.
Heaney, S. Undine.
Herrick. To the Water Nymphs, Drinking at the Fountain.
Laughlin, J. Nereid, The.
MacLeish. How the River Ninfa Runs through the Ruined Town beneath the Lime Quarry.
Mallarmé. Afternoon of a Faun.
Afternoon of a Faun, The.
Marvell. Nymph Complaining for the Death of Her Faun [or Fawn], The.
Meredith, G. Rape of Aurora, The.
Piccolo. Veneris Venefica Agrestis.
Rossetti, C. Water Spirit's Song, The.
Swift, J. Lines from Cadenus to Vanessa.
Wilbur, R. Ceremony.
Under a Tree.
Wordsworth, W. Dog—An Idyllium, The.

O

Oafs
Nemerov. What Kind of a Guy Was He?

Oak Trees
Ammons. Locus.
With Ropes of Hemp.
Blue Cloud. Fallen Oak, A.
Byron, G. To an Oak at Newstead.
Cowper, W. Yardley Oak.
Creeley. Love ("Not enough. The question: what is").
Eberhart, R. Oak, The.
Emerson, R. By kinds I keep my kinds in check.
Hall, D. Acorns.
Heaney, S. Bog Oak.
Herrick. All Things Decay and Die.
Hughes, T. I see the oak's bride in the oak's grasp.
Your tree—your oak.
Lawrence, D. H. Under the Oak.
MacLeish. Survivor.
Millay, E. Here in a Rocky Cup.
Oak-Leaves, The.
Ransom, J. Parting, without a Sequel.
Rossetti, C. Toadstool comes up in a night, A.
Sandburg, C. Oak Arms.
October Paint.
"Shu Ting." To the Oak.

Very. Oak and the Poplar, The.
Warren, R. Bearded Oaks.
Mountain Plateau.
Trying to Tell You Something.
Whitman, W. I Saw in Louisiana a Live-Oak Growing.
Wilbur, R. Wood, A.
Wordsworth, W. Oak and the Broom, The; A Pastoral.
Oak of Guernica! Tree of holier power.

Oases
Ammons. Self-Portrait.
Dugan, A. Oasis.
See also **Deserts**

Obesity
Amichai [or Amikhai]. I Am Big and Fat.
Bukowski. Space Creatures.
Burns, R. Epigram on Capt. Francis Grose, the Celebrated Antiquary.
Ciardi, J. Washing Your Feet.
Creeley. Dear.
Davie, D. Toby to Aguecheek.
De la Mare. Fat Woman, The.
Rossetti, C. Ye Are Come unto Mount Sion.

Obituaries
Cavafy. Tomb of Evrion.
Ciardi, J. Obit.
Hall, D. Day I Was Older, The.
Laughlin, J. Reading the Obituary Page in *The Times*.
Lowell, R. Alfred Corning Clark.
Lux. Frankly, I Don't Care.
Ramanujan. Obituary.
Riley, J. Charles H. Philips.
Luther A. Todd.

Oblivion
Amichai [or Amikhai]. First Rain on a Burned Car, The.
Baudelaire. Desire for Oblivion.
Obsession.
Blok. Worlds Fly Past.
Borges. Clouds ("There cannot be a single thing which is").
Everness.
Ewigkeit.
I Am.
To a Minor Poet of the Greek Anthology.
Waking Up.
Bukowski. Dow Jones: Down.
Codrescu. Brief (Remembered) *Histoire* of Rejection, A.
Cowper, W. On Observing Some Names of Little Note Recorded in the "Biographia Britannica."
Creeley. Places ("When I wake next").
Cunningham, J. Convalescence.
"Dario." What Gets You.
Eberhart, R. On a Squirrel Crossing the Road in Autumn, in New England.
Hughes, L. Shame on You.
Jacobsen, J. For Those Who Have Not Eaten the Apple.
Kunitz, S. Prophecy on Lethe.
Lawrence, D. H. Change.
Forget.
Know-All.
Phoenix.
Shadows.
Tabernacle.
Temples.
Levi, P. Valley, A.
MacDiarmid, H. Eemis-Stane, The.
Mallarmé. Her pure nails on high displaying their onyx.
Milosz, C. Flight.
On a Beach.
Neruda. Search.
Oliver, M. Last Days.
Little Owl Who Lives in the Orchard.
Moccasin Flowers.
Pinkerton, H. Subjectivity.
Smith, S. Oblivion.
Szymborska, W. End and Beginning.
Nothing nothinged itself for me as well.
Williams, C. K. Clay out of Silence.

They Warned Him Then They Threw Him
Away.
What Must I Do to Be Lost?
Williams, M.   When I Am Dead, My Dearest.
Williams, T.   Speech from the Stairs.
Zukofsky, L.   Drive, fast kisses.

Obscenity
Bukowski.   Buffalo Bill.
Cavafy.   Theater of Sidon (400 A.D.).
Herrick.   Lasciviousnesse.
Jonson, B.   To Playwright.
Lawrence, D. H.   Broadcasting to the G.B.P.
Censors.
Give Me a Sponge.
Innocent England.
Nash, O.   King Leer.
See also **Pornography**

Obscurity
Donne.   Obscure Writer, An.
Dubie.   Parallax Monograph for Rodin, The.
Graves, R.   Mist.
Herrick.   To Cedars.
Kizer, C.   To an Unknown Poet.
Kunitz, S.   Words for the Unknown Makers.
Meredith, G.   Lied von Castelli.
Merwin.   For the Grave of Posterity.
Milton   Canzone: "Scoffing, amorous maidens
and young men."
Nash, O.   Name Is Too Familiar, The.
Rich, A.   Focus.
Rossetti, C.   Frog's Fate, A.
Sir Eustace Grey.
Sandburg, C.   Mist Marches across the Valley.
Pearl Fog.
Tu Fu.   Testament.
Wilbur, R.   All That Is.
Five Women Bathing in Moonlight.
Wright, J.   On Minding One's Own Business.

Observatories
Zagajewski.   Planetarium.
See also **Astronomy and Astronomers**

Obsessions
Ai.   Stalking Memory.
Baudelaire.   Obsession.
Poison.
Possessed.
Berryman.   Canto Amor.
Brontë, E.   Sleep Not, Dream Not.
Bukowski.   Mother and Son.
Burns, R.   Hue and Cry of John Lewars, The.
Byron, G.   Last Words on Greece.
Coleridge, S.   Presence of Love, The.
Recollections of Love.
Dickey, W.   Gambling at Reno.
Dunbar, P.   Disturber, The.
Eberhart, R.   Two Loves.
Emerson, R.   To Eva.
Enzensberger, H.   Fetish.
Graves, R.   Double Bass.
Hughes, T.   Lovesong: "He loved her and she
loved him."
Lawrence, D. H.   Bawdy Can Be Sane.
Release.
Mistral, F.   Obsession, The.
Montale.   In the Greenhouse.
Nash, O.   Curl Up and Diet.
Strange Case of the Entomologist's Heart, The.
Parker, D.   Thoughts.
Petrarch.   Be it, Sennuccio, clearly understood.
Now blessed be the day, the month, the year.
Orso, there never was a lake or river.
That fire I liked to think had been extinguished.
That lady whom I always have in mind.
When I have stared for some time fixedly.
Ramanujan.   LOVE 1: What She Said.
Sappho.   He is, I should say, on a level.
Stafford, W.   Things That Hurt Me.
Williams, C. K.   Resentment.
Williams, W.   Love Song: First Version, 1915,
A.
Wyatt, S.   Driven by desire to set affection.
I am ready and ever will be.
I might by no means surmise.
Longer to trow ye.
Process of time worketh such wonder.

Shall she never out of my mind.
Spite of their spite which they in vain.
To whom should I sue to ease my pain?
What would ye more of me, your slave, require.
Zaturenska.   White Dress, The.

Obsolescence
Ciardi, J.   Obsolescence.

Occult, The
Browning, R.   Mr Sludge, "The Medium."

Occupations
Cavafy.   From the School of the Renowned
Philosopher.
Chuang Tzu.   Active Life.
Ciardi, J.   Philosophical Poem.
Laughlin, J.   Hard to Translate.
Logistics.
Song of the GIs & the MGs.
Lux.   His Job Is Honest and Simple.
Parker, D.   Grandfather Said It.
Pour Prendre Congé.
Wordsworth, W.   Poet's Epitaph, A.

Ocean
Borges.   Elegy: "Three very ancient faces stay
with me."
Brodsky, J.   New Jules Verne, The.
Clampitt.   Marine Surface, Low Overcast.
Crane, S.   I explain the silvered passing of a
ship at night.
Ocean said to me once, The.
Creeley.   Sound, The.
Dugan, A.   Untitled Poem: "Once on the beach
at night I heard the waves."
Emerson, R.   Sea-Shore.
Frost, R.   West-Running Brook.
García Lorca.   Ocean.
Jeffers, R.   Evening Ebb.
Lawrence, D. H.   Spray.
Levertov.   For Nikolai, Many Thousand Miles
Away.
Major, C.   Rainy Season, The.
Marvell.   Bermudas.
Meredith, W.   Seasons' Difference, The.
Transport.
Waking Dream about a Lost Child.
Merwin.   Pause by the Water.
Milosz, C.   Ocean.
Oppen.   Confession.
Pinsky.   Volume, The.
Prunty.   Great Thoughts and Noble Feelings.
Ramanujan.   Traces.
Rumi.   Are you jealous of the ocean's
generosity.
Flutes for Dancing.
We are the night ocean filled.
Stevens, W.   Somnambulisma.
Swenson, M.   Ocean, Whale-Shaped.
Running on the Shore.
Very.   Sight of the Ocean, The.
Wheatley, P.   Ocean.
Wilner, E.   Changing the Imperatives.
See also **Sea**

O'Connor, Flannery
Stafford, W.   Song in the Manner of Flannery
O'Connor, A.

October
Angelou.   Late October.
Berry, W.   October 10.
Brodsky, J.   October Tune.
Carruth, H.   All Things.
Dunbar, P.   October.
Eberhart, R.   Prometheus.
Vision through Timothy.
Emerson, R.   October woods, wherein.
Frost, R.   October.
Hayden, R.   October.
Jeffers, R.   October Evening.
Kinsella, T.   Crab Orchard Sanctuary, Late
October.
Kumin, M.   Grappling in the Central Blue.
Levertov.   October.
Logan, J.   Cambridge Revery.
Mahon.   October in Hyde Park.
Merwin.   Love for October, The.
Millay, E.   October—An Etching.
Milosz, C.   All Hallows' Eve.

Nemerov.   Autumnal.
Late Butterflies.
Observation of October.
Niedecker.   Transition.
Oliver, M.   October.
Paley, G.   Arboreal Mystery, An.
When I Was Asked How I Could Leave
Vermont in the Middle of October.
Rich, A.   Break, The.
Riley, J.   Old October.
Rossetti, C.   Golden Holly.
October Garden, An.
Sandburg, C.   Crabapples.
Redhaw Rain.
Ripe Corn.
Schuyler, J.   Going.
October.
October 5, 1981.
Snyder, G.   Late October Camping in the
Sawtooths.
Swenson, M.   October.
Thomas, D.   Especially when the October Wind.
Poem in October.
Tomlinson, C.   In October.
October.
Very.   October.
Williams, T.   October Song.
Wright, C.   Appalachian Book of the Dead 2,
The.
October 2.

Octopuses
Brodsky, J.   New Jules Verne, The.
Laughlin, J.   Like the Octopus.
Levertov.   Art of the Octopus: Variations on a
Found Theme, The.
Merrill, J.   Octopus, The.
Montale.   Indian Serenade.
Moore, M.   Octopus, An.
Nash, O.   Octopus, The.
Stafford, W.   If I Could Be Like Wallace
Stevens.

Odysseus
Amichai [*or* Amikhai].   Takis Sinopolus, Greek
Poet.
Cavafy.   Ithaca.
Second Odyssey, A.
Cunningham, J.   Helmsman, The; an Ode.
Komunyakaa.   Surgery.
Rexroth, K.   Homer in Basic.
Ritsos.   At Nausicä's House.
Gradations.
Penelope's Despair.
Trivial Details.
Wilner, E.   Ambition.
World Is Not a Meditation, The.
Zaturenska.   Silence and the Wayfarer.
See also **Ulysses**

Oedipus
Borges.   Oedipus and the Enigma.
Cavafy.   Oedipus.
Cunningham, J.   Oedipean Mom and Dad, An.
Eberhart, R.   Oedipus.
Gallagher, T.   Sugar.
Ignatow, D.   Oedipus Reformed.
Jarrell, R.   Sphinx's Riddle to Oedipus, The.
Jeffers, R.   Meditation on Saviors.
Kunitz, S.   Approach to Thebes, The.
Ramanujan.   LOVE 3: What He Said,
Remembering.
Rukeyser, M.   Myth.
Shelley, P.   Oedipus Tyrannus; or, Swellfoot the
Tyrant.
Wilner, E.   Classical Proportions of the Heart.

Office Workers
Amichai [*or* Amikhai].   Early in the morning,
you lean on the wall of an old house.
Carver, R.   Kafka's Watch.
Ciardi, J.   Wafflebutt.
Dugan, A.   Poem: "Always prudent but
unprepared."
Winter's Onset from an Alienated Point of
View.
Gunn, T.   Waitress.
Kinsella, T.   Administrator.
String Puppets.

Laughlin, J.   Hope Springs.
Nash, O.   Dance Unmacabre.
Niedecker.   Elegant office girl, The.
  Keen and lovely man moved as in a dance.
  President of the Holding Company, The.
Parker, D.   Our Office; An Intimate Glimpse of
  Vanity Fair—En Famille a Hate Song.
Roethke.   Dolor.
Williams, M.   Office Party, The.
Williams, W.   Return to Work, The.
See also **Clerks; Secretaries**

Ogres
Auden.   August 1968.
Graves, R.   Ogres and Pygmies.
See also **Monsters; Trolls**

O'Hara, Frank
Berrigan, T.   Frank O'Hara.
  Red Shift.
Ciardi, J.   East Sixty-seventh Street.
Corbett, W.   Dear Joe.
  Lines Written after Reading Frank O'Hara's "A
  Step Away from Them."
Ginsberg, A.   City Midnight Junk Strains.
Koch, K.   Circus, The.
  Fate. ·
O'Hara, F.   Day Lady Died, The.
Palmer, M.   Notes for Echo Lake 3.
Schuyler, J.   Beautiful Funerals.
  Fauré Ballade, The.
  Four Poems.
  To Frank O'Hara.
Whalen, P.   Friendship Greetings.

Ohio River
Merton.   City after Noon, The.
  Ohio River—Louisville, The.
Ransom, J.   Antique Harvesters.
Sandburg, C.   Whiffs of the Ohio River at
  Cinncinnati.
Wright, J.   Three Sentences for a Dead Swan.

Ohio (state)
Clampitt.   At a Rest Stop in Ohio.
Crane, H.   Porphyro in Akron.
Ferlinghetti, L.   Ascending over Ohio.
Koch, K.   Artist, The.
Levine, P.   One for the Rose.
Oliver, M.   River Styx, Ohio, The.
Patchen.   November in Ohio.
Riley, J.   Old John Clevenger on Buckeyes.
Sandburg, C.   Crossing the Ohio when Poppies
  Bloom in Ashtabula.
Updike.   Ohio.
Wright, J.   At the Executed Murderer's Grave.
  Autumn Begins in Martins Ferry, Ohio.
  From a Bus Window in Central Ohio, Just
  before a Thunder Shower.
  In Ohio.
  In Response to a Rumor that the Oldest
  Whorehouse in Wheeling, West Virginia, Has
  Been Condemned.
  Katy Did.
  Many of Our Waters: Variations on a Poem by a
  Black Child.
  Miners.

Oil
Emerson, R.   There is no evil but can speak.
Ginsberg, A.   Who Runs America?
Nemerov.   Breaking of Rainbows, The.

Oil Industry
Ginsberg, A.   Who Runs America?
Komunyakaa.   Ogoni.
Stafford, W.   Boom Town.

Oisin
Yeats.   Wanderings of Oisin, The.

O'Keeffe, Georgia
Clampitt.   Fog.
Cooper, J.   *Evening Star* (Georgia O'Keeffe).
  Winter Road, The.
Kumin, M.   Calling, A.

Oklahoma City Bombing (1995)
Ai.   Antihero, The.

Oklahoma (state)
Gallagher, T.   Boat Ride.
Stevens, W.   Life Is Motion.
Updike.   Tulsa.

Zukofsky, L.   Belly Locks Shnooks Oakie.

Old Age
Amichai [*or* Amikhai].   Deir Ayub, a Heap of
  Watermelons and the Rest of My Life.
  Late in my life, I come to you.
  Like the Streams in the Negev.
  NYU.
Angelou.   Last Decision, The.
  On Aging.
Arnold, M.   Growing Old.
Atwood.   Daguerreotype Taken in Old Age.
  Wish: Metamorphosis to Heraldic Emblem.
Baudelaire.   Little Old Women, The.
  Seven Old Men, The.
Berry, W.   Boone.
  Companions, The.
Blake, W.   In a Myrtle [*or* Mirtle] Shade.
Blok.   Song of the Wind, The.
Blue Cloud.   At Bald Rock with Old John.
  Hunt, Its Chant, A.
Bogan, L.   Crows, The.
Borges.   In Praise of Darkness.
  To the German Language.
Brodsky, J.   Daedalus in Sicily.
Brontë, E.   From a Dungeon Wall in the
  Southern College.
  Love and Friendship.
Brooks, G.   Bean Eaters, The.
Browning, R.   Aeschylus' Soliloquy.
  Dîs Aliter Visum; or, Le Byron de Nos Jours.
  Rabbi Ben Ezra.
Bukowski.   2 Outside, as Bones Break in My
  Kitchen.
  Eating My Senior Citizen's Dinner at the
  Sizzler.
  Here I Am.
  Millionaire, The.
  Patriot of Life, A.
  Traffic Signals.
Burns, R.   Auld Man's Winter Thought, The.
  There'll Never Be Peace till Jamie Comes
  Hame.
  What can a young lassie, what shall a young
  lassie.
Byron, G.   Lament of Tasso, The.
Campion, T.   Ad nobiliss. virum Gul. Percium.
  Ad Rob. Caraeum Equitem Auratum
  Nobilissimum.
  In obitum Iacobi Huissii.
  Though You Are Young [*or* Yoong].
Carver, R.   In the Year 2020.
  Where the Groceries Went.
Cavafy.   Old Man, An.
  Old Men's Souls, The.
  Very Seldom.
Ciardi, J.   Aging Lovers, The.
  December 13, 1979.
  Love Poem, A: "I have labored for her love."
  Mr. & Mrs.
  Old Man.
  Old Man Confesses, An.
  Thinking about Girls.
  To Dudley Fitts.
Clampitt.   Hedge of Rubber Trees. A.
Clare, J.   Old Man, The.
Coleridge, S.   Love's Apparition and
  Evanishment.
  Old Man of the Alps, The.
  Sonnet [to Charles Lloyd].
  Youth and Age.
Cooper, J.   Bermuda.
  For a Very Old Man, on the Death of His Wife.
Corbett, W.   Passed on.
Crane, H.   Fernery, The.
Creeley.   Age ("He is thinking of everyone").
  Epic Expands, The.
  If.
  On Phrase from Ginsberg's *Kaddish*.
  Outside.
  Rachel Had Said.
  Self-Portrait.
Cullen, C.   To France.
Cummings, E. E.   Fearlessandbosomy / this /
  grand:gal.
  Noone" autumnal this great lady's gaze.
oDE: "O / the sweet & aged people."

Old age sticks / up Keep.
  Says ol man no body.
  Why / do the / fingers.
Cunningham, J.   On a Line from Bodenham's
  "Belvedere."
Davie, D.   Poet Redeemed & Dead.
  They, to Me.
De la Mare.   All That's Past.
  Alone.
  Beneath a motionless yew.
  Dust to Dust.
  Fat Woman, The.
  In a Library.
  Karma.
  Last Arrow, The.
  Last Chapter, The.
  Nod.
  Old Angler, The.
  Old Ben.
  Old Men, The.
  Old Susan.
  Waiting.
Dickey, W.   At Your Old House.
  Die Alte Frau, Die Alte Marschallin.
  Do they remember me?
  Fretful and sick, you ask.
  Fretful and sick, you long.
  Nevertheless, sleep / And as your eyes close.
  No, the night has gone.
  Yes, they remember you.
Donne.   Canonization, The.
Dugan, A.   Provincetown *Totentanz*.
  Soliloquy: Ghost Dance for a Cripple.
Dunbar, P.   Goin' Back.
  Growin' Gray.
  Old.
  Old Story, The.
  Parted.
  When the Old Man Smokes.
Eberhart, R.   White Pines, Felled 1984.
Eliot, T. S.   Gerontion.
  Lines for an Old Man.
Emerson, R.   Old Age.
  Terminus.
Enzensberger, H.   Old Couples.
Ferlinghetti, L.   Just as I used to say.
  Old Italians Dying, The.
  Old Sailors, The.
Frost, R.   Old Man's Winter Night, An.
  Provide, Provide.
Gallagher, T.   Each Bird Walking.
García Lorca.   Old Lizard, The.
Glück, L.   Grandmother in the Garden.
  To Florida.
Graves, R.   Advent of Summer.
  Age Gap.
  Broken Girth, The.
  Gentleman, The.
  Great-Grandmother, The.
  Grotesques.
  Imminent Seventies, The.
  Nightmare of Senility.
  Oldest Soldier, The.
  Septuagenarian, The.
  Serpent's Tail.
  Song: Seven Fresh Years.
  Title of Poet, The.
  Two Crucial Generations.
Gunn, T.   At an Intersection.
  Conversation of Old Men, The.
  Lines for My 55th Birthday.
  Old Woman, The.
  Sand Man, The.
  Well Dennis O'Grady.
Hall, D.   By the Exeter River.
  Dump, The.
  Old Home Week.
  On Reaching the Age of Two Hundred.
  Rocker, The.
Han-shan.   Cold Cliff's remoteness is what I
  like.
  I have heard on Mount Tientai.
  Mistress Tsou of Tiyen.
  Old and sick final years over a hundred.
  One day I left the mountains.
Hardy, T.   Aged Newspaper Soliloquizes, The.

Ancient to Ancients, An.
Faded Face, The.
He Never Expected Much.
I Look into My Glass.
Near Lanivet, 1872.
Old Workman, The.
Seventy-four and Twenty.
Singing Woman, The.
Superseded, The.
Tresses, The.
Two Rosalinds, The.
Harris, L. Father William.
Heaney, S. Follower.
  Man and Boy.
Herbert, G. Forerunners, The.
Herrick. Age Unfit for Love.
  His Age, Dedicated to His Peculiar Friend,
    Master John Wickes, under the Name of
    Posthumus.
  His Wish to God.
  Hymne to the Graces, A.
  Long Life.
  On Himself[e].
  On Himselfe.
  To a Gentlewoman Objecting to Him His Grey
    Hairs.
  To His Girles Who Would Have Him Sportfull.
  To His Maid Prew.
  To Perilla.
  Upon a Bleare-Ey'd Woman.
  Upon His Gray Haires.
  Upon One Who Said She Was Alwayes Young.
  Youth, and Age.
Hopkins, G. Leaden Echo and the Golden Echo,
  The.
Hughes, L. Mexican Market Woman.
  Old Age.
  Old Sailor.
  Parisian Beggar Woman.
  Young Gal's Blues.
Hughes, T. Retired Colonel, The.
Ignatow, D. And Rest.
  Father.
  Leaf, A.
  Pricing.
  Requiem, A: "My father, listening to music,
    that's me."
  Separate Rooms.
  Sunlight, Piercing the Gloom of this House,
    The.
  Wait.
  White-Haired, I Walk in on My Parents.
Jacobsen, J. Linkwood Road.
  Mr. Mahoney.
  Mr. Tantripp's Day.
  They Never Were Found.
Jarrell, R. Face, The.
  Faded.
  Women on a Bus.
Jeffers, R. Age in Prospect.
  Birthday (Autobiography).
  Deer Lay Down Their Bones, The.
  Fawn's Foster-Mother.
  Hand.
  I am seventy-four years old and suddenly all my
    strength.
  Old age hath clawed me with his scaly clutch.
  Old half blinded hawk—but how can he hunt
    with only one eye?—, The.
  Oysters.
  Pleasures.
  Salvage.
  Seventieth Birthday.
Kinsella, T. Tear.
Kipling, R. Old Men, The.
  Our Fathers Also.
  Our Lady of the Sackcloth.
Komunyakaa. Changes; or, Reveries at a
  Window Overlooking a Country Road, with
  Two Women Talking Blues in the Kitchen.
Kumin, M. Distance.
  Henry Manley Blues, The.
Kunitz, S. I Dreamed That I Was Old.
  Touch Me.
Larkin, P. Heads in the Women's Ward.
Laughlin, J. Junk Mail.

Occidit brevis lux.
Old Comedian, The.
  Prognosis.
Lawrence, D. H. Beautiful Old Age.
  Courage.
  Elderly Discontented Women.
  Failure, A.
  Grudge of the Old, The.
  Old Men.
  Old People.
  Young and Their Moral Guardians, The.
Levertov. 90th Year, The.
  Death Psalm: O Lord of Mysteries.
  Old Adam, The.
  Old People Dozing.
  Visit, A.
Logan, J. Matinee.
Logue, C. Epitaph: "I am old."
Lowell, R. Elizabeth.
  Grandparents.
  Mother and Father 1.
Lux. Old Man Shoveling Snow.
  So You Put the Dog to Sleep.
MacDiarmid, H. Old Wife in High Spirits.
  Wheesht, Wheesht.
MacLeish. Survivor.
  Wild Old Wicked Man, The.
MacNeice. When We Were Children.
Mahon. Greta.
  Refusal to Mourn, A.
Meredith, G. Infancy and Age.
  State of Age, The.
  Wisdom of Eld, The.
  Youth in Age.
Meredith, W. Homage to a Rake-Hell.
  On Falling Asleep to Birdsong.
Merwin. Age.
  Direction.
  Fountain, The.
  Kin.
  Prayer of the Eyes, A.
  Span.
Michelangelo Buonarroti. Alas! Alas! for the
  way I've been betrayed.
  Although time presses hard and prods us on.
  From beneath two arching brows.
  From where you triumphed in me, Love, right
    here.
  Had I, when young, been leery of the glow.
  If a god, Love, can't you do.
  If, vulnerable from early youth, a heart.
  If, when it caught my eye first, I'd been bolder.
  It leaves me plunged in gloom and pain—yet
    dear.
  Life's final hours: brought there by many a year.
  Love long delayed comes kindly, by fortune's
    favor.
  No differently the guilty wretch hangs back.
  No need at all for your angel loveliness.
  So, Love, it hasn't healed, not even the least.
  Such wealth of promise lies.
  Though bent with age, to me.
  Time now good-byes were said.
  Too late for Love to set my heart aflame.
  What file's incessant bite.
  What's to become of me? What's this you're
    doing.
  When with a clanking chain a master locks.
  Woman's beauty, new, A.
Milosz, C. For My Eighty-eighth Birthday.
  How Ugly.
  Late Ripeness.
  New Province, A.
  Old Women.
  Prayer: "Approaching ninety, and still with a
    hope."
  Retired.
  Return.
  Run, A.
  Submerged.
  Texas.
  Winter.
Nash, O. Come on in, the Senility Is Fine.
  Crossing the Border.
  I Didn't Say a Word, or, Who Called That
    Piccolo Player a Father?

I'll Eat My Split-Level Turkey in the
  Breezeway.
  Old Men.
  Peekaboo, I Almost See You.
  Portrait of the Artist as a Prematurely Old Man.
  Preface to the Past.
  Voluble Wheel Chair, The.
  You Can Be a Republican, I'm a Genocrat.
Nemerov. Brief Journey West, The.
  Landscape with Figures.
  Moonshine.
  Near the Old People's Home.
Niedecker. Dear Mona, Mary and all.
  In moonlight lies.
  Two old men.
Oliver, M. Ice.
Olson, C. Toss, for John Cage, A.
Oppen. Confession.
  Old man, The.
  Seated Man.
Orr, G. Excavation, The.
  To My Father, Dying.
Owen, W. Parable of the Old Men and the
  Young, The.
Pagis. For How Long.
  Moments of Old Age.
Paley, G. Age.
  Hand-Me-Downs.
  He Wanders.
  Here.
  My Father at 89.
  On the Deck.
  People in My Family.
  Question.
  Therefore.
  When this old body.
  Winter Afternoon.
Parker, D. Little Old Lady in Lavender Silk,
  The.
Patchen. Letter to the Old Men.
  Old Man.
Petrarch. Little white-haired man moves off
  from where, The.
  Love had revealed to me a tranquil harbour.
  Love kept me burning one-and-twenty years.
  My faithful glass has very often told.
  Till both my temples are completely white.
Piercy. Half Past Home.
  Proposal for Recycling Wastes, A.
Pinsky. Cold, The.
  Faeryland.
  Old Man, An.
  Old Woman.
Pope, A. Prologue Design'd for Mr. Durfy's
  Last Play.
  To Mr. Thomas Southern, on His Birth-Day,
    1742.
Prunty. Domestic of the Outer Banks.
  Effervescent Mrs. G, The.
  Elderly Lady Crossing on Green.
  Seasons.
Raine, K. I felt, under my old breasts, this April
  day.
  Long ago I thought you young, bright daimon.
  What have I to regret.
Ransom, J. Captain Carpenter.
  Old Man Playing with Children.
  Piazza Piece.
Rexroth, K. Neoclassicist, A.
  Red Maple Leaves.
Riley, J. Ancient Printerman, The.
  Art and Love.
  Exceeding All.
  Father William.
  In Days to Come.
  Jack-in-the-Box.
  Kathleen Mavourneen.
  Kind Old Man, The.
  Laughter.
  Little Woman, The.
  Mother.
  My Old Friend.
  Old Home by the Mill, The.
  Old Man, The.
  Old Man's Memory, An.
  Old Swimmin'-Hole, The.

Old-Timer, An.
Pen-Pictur' of a Cert'in Frivvolus Old Man, A.
Tired Out.
When Evening Shadows Fall.
Rimbaud, A. Seated.
Ritsos. Helen.
  Unjustly.
  Without a Mirror Now.
Robinson, E. Mr Flood's Party.
  Voice of Age, The.
Roethke. Infirmity.
Rossetti, C. Dear old woman in the lane, The.
  Have Patience.
  Helen Grey.
  My old admiration before I was twenty.
Seifert. Garland on the Wrist, A.
  Head of the Virgin Mary, The.
  Lines for the Painter Ota Janeček.
  Plague Column, The.
Sexton. Doors, Doors, Doors.
  Old.
  Two Sons.
  Waiting Head, The.
  Wallflower.
Shelley, P. Tale of Society as It Is, A: From
  Facts, 1811.
Simic. Northern Exposure.
  Old Couple.
Smith, S. Advice to Young Children.
  Bandol (Var).
  He Told His Life Story to Mrs. Courtly.
  Homage to John Cowper Powys.
  Lord Mope.
  What Is the Time?; or, St. Hugh of Lincoln.
  Widowhood or The Home-Coming of Lady
    Ross.
Stafford, W. Crossing Our Campground.
  Few Snorts from a Wild One, A.
  Size of a Fist, The.
  Trying to Tell It.
  Waiting in Line.
Stockton, A. On the Birth Day of the Revd
    Doctor Witherspoon, 1788.
Swenson, M. Captain Holm.
  How to Be Old.
  Rusty Autumn.
Swift, J. Satirical Elegy on the Death of a Late
    Famous General, A.
Sze. Moon Is a Diamond, The.
Tennyson, A. Tithonus.
  Ulysses.
Thomas, D. Do Not Go Gentle into That Good
    Night.
Tomlinson, C. In the Ward.
  Walks.
Updike. Elderly Sex.
Van Duyn. Goya's "Two Old People Eating
    Soup."
  Letters from a Father.
  Stream, The.
  Very. Old Age.
Walcott. Glory Trumpeter, The.
  Letter from Brooklyn, A.
  Parang.
  Saddhu of Couva, The.
Walker, A. Medicine.
Warren, R. Aged Man Surveys the Past.
  Ballad of Your Puzzlement.
  Distance Between, The: Picnic of Old Friends.
  English Cocker: Old and Blind.
  I Am Dreaming of a White Christmas: The
    Natural History of a Vision.
  Old Flame.
  Reading Late at Night, Thermometer Falling.
  Safe in Shade.
Weiss, T. Pair of Shoes, A.
  Slow Fuse, A.
Whalen, P. Garden, The.
Whitman, W. Centenarian's Story, The.
  Hours Continuing Long.
  I Thought That Knowledge Alone Would
    Suffice.
  In Former Songs.
  Old Age's Lambent Peaks.
  Old Age's Ship & Crafty Death's.
  Queries to My Seventieth Year.

Supplement Hours.
Thanks in Old Age.
To Get the Final Lilt of Songs.
To Old Age.
Youth, Day, Old Age and Night.
Wilbur, R. Next Door.
Williams, C. K. Rungs.
  When.
Williams, M. Going.
  Jonathan Aging.
  Morning at the Zagorsk Monastery Outside
    Moscow.
  On a Photograph of My Mother at Seventeen.
  Ruby Tells All.
  Summer Afternoon an Old Man Gives Some
    Thought to the Central Questions, A.
  Talking to Himself He Gets a Few Things
    Settled in His Mind.
Williams, T. Kitchen Door Blues.
  Lady with No One at All, The.
  Little Town, The.
  Old Men Are Fond.
  Old Men Go Mad at Night.
  Old Men with Sticks.
  Old Things.
  Rented Room, The.
  Shadow Boxes.
  Those Who Ignore the Appropriate Time of
    Their Going.
  Turning Out the Bedside Lamp.
  Wolf's Hour.
Williams, W. All the Fancy Things.
  Centenarian, The.
  Election Day.
  Fire Spirit.
  Greeting for Old Age.
  Last Words of My English Grandmother, The.
  Last Words of My Grandmother.
  Moral, The.
  Old Men, The.
  Pastoral 1: "Old man who goes about, The."
  To a Poor Old Woman.
  To an Old Jaundiced Woman.
  To Waken an Old Lady.
Wordsworth, W. Animal Tranquillity and
    Decay.
  Fountain, The.
  I know an aged Man constrained to dwell.
  Old Man Travelling [Animal Tranquillity and
    Decay, a Sketch].
  Simon Lee, the Old Huntsman; with an incident
    in which he was concerned.
  Sonnet (To an Octogenarian).
  Though narrow be that old Man's cares, and
    near.
  To —, in Her Seventieth Year.
  Two Thieves, The; or, the Last Stage of Avarice.
Wright, J. Poem Written under an Archway in a
    Discontinued Railroad Station, Fargo, North
    Dakota, A.
Yeats. Acre of Grass, An.
  Apparitions, The.
  Are You Content.
  Black Tower, The.
  Coming of Wisdom with Time, The.
  Girl's Song.
  Imitated from the Japanese.
  In Tara's Halls.
  Lamentation of the Old Pensioner, The.
  Meeting.
  Old Men Admiring Themselves in the Water,
    The.
  Prayer for Old Age, A.
  Quarrel in Old Age.
  Sailing to Byzantium.
  Scholars, The.
  Spur, The.
  Those Dancing Days Are Gone.
  Tower, The.
  Two Years Later.
  When You Are Old.
  Wild Old Wicked Man, The.
Zaturenska. Dialogue.
Zukofsky, L. Homage.

See also **Pensions and Pensioners; Retirement
  and Retirees; Old Age**

Oldham, John
Dryden, J. To the Memory of Mr Oldham.
Olive Trees and Olives
Clampitt. Olive Groves of Thasos, The.
Graves, R. Oleaster, The.
Herrick. Olive Branch, The.
Housman. Olive, The.
McGrath, T. Mediterranean.
Merrill, J. Olive Grove.
Quasimodo. Agrigentum Road, The.
Sze. Olive Grove, The.
Tomlinson, C. Valestrieri.
Wilbur, R. Grasse: The Olive Trees.
Williams, M. How the Elephant Got His Hump.
Olympics
Clampitt. Olympia.
Dickey, J. Olympian, The.
Eberhart, R. Noble Man, The.
Graves, R. Antorcha Y Corona, 1968.
  Torch and Crown, 1968.
Rukeyser, M. Voices.
Omens
Atwood. Four Auguries.
Burns, R. Tam Glen.
Ciardi, J. Magus, A.
Cowper, W. To a Young Friend.
Creeley. For the New Year.
De la Mare. Foreboding.
  Shadow.
Emerson, R. Motto to "Fate."
Graves, R. On Portents.
  Spoils.
Hardy, T. Premonitions.
  Prophetess, The.
Herrick. Bachanalian Verse, A.
  Olive Branch, The.
  Sonnet of Perilla, A.
Johnson, S. Comets and Princes.
Kipling, R. Undertaker's Horse, The.
Komunyakaa. Omen.
Kunitz, S. Day of Foreboding.
  Signs and Portents.
Melville, H. Portent, The.
Merton. What to Think when It Rains Blood.
Nash, O. Any Millenniums Today, Lady?
Poe. Raven, The.
Rossetti, C. Bird's-Eye View, A.
Shelley, P. Fragment: Omens.
Wordsworth, W. Presentiments.
  To a Snow-Drop.
Omnipotence
Browning, E. Soul's Travelling, The.
Dickinson, E. How can we thank each other.
Eberhart, R. Two Loves.
  Undercliff Evening.
Emerson, R. This shining hour is an edifice.
Farid-uddin Attar. From "Bird Conversations."
MacNeice. Creditor, The.
Pessoa. My gesture that destroys.
Ralegh, S. First of all is God, and the same last
    is he, The.
Smart, C. On the Power of the Supreme Being.
Williams, M. Why God Permits Evil: For
    Answers to This Question of Interest to Many
    Write Bible Answers, Dept. E-7.
O'Neill, Shane
Jeffers, R. Shane O'Neill's Cairn.
Onions
Pagis. For a Literary Survey.
Szymborska, W. Onion, The.
Wilbur, R. Shallot, A.
Williams, C. K. Poem for the Governments, A.
Williams, W. To Be Hungry Is to Be Great.
Ontario, Canada
Davie, D. Frontenac.
Muldoon, P. Ontario.
Opera
Ashbery, J. Faust.
Blok. Among the Admirers of Carmen.
  As the Ocean Changes Colour.
Cavafy. Lohengrin.
  Suspicion.
Eliot, T. S. Opera.
  Paysage Triste.
Ignatow, D. Requiem, A: "My father, listening

to music, that's me."
Jarrell, R.   Love for One Orange, The.
   Seductive Piece of Business, A.
Kinsella, T.   Overture.
Laughlin, J.   Large Opera Singer, The.
   Night at the Opera, A.
   Songbird, The.
Lawrence, D. H.   After the Opera.
Meredith, W.   About Opera.
Merrill, J.   Matinees.
Montale.   Keepsake.
Tomlinson, C.   Night at the Opera, A.
   Programme Note.

Ophelia
De la Mare.   Ophelia.
Hughes, T.   Ophelia.
Ivanov, G.   Sleeping he saw Ophelia in his
   dream.
Lawrence, D. H.   Ballad of Another Ophelia.
Nash, O.   Strange Case of the Lovelorn Letter
   Writer, The.
Raine, K.   Dream of Roses, A.
Rimbaud, A.   Ophelia.
Sandburg, C.   New Song for Indiana Ophelias.

Opium
Broumas, O.   Instruction.
Codrescu.   Manifesto.
   Opium for Archie Anderson.
   Opium for Britt Wilkie.
Coleridge, S   Kubla Khan: or, A Vision in a
   Dream.
De la Mare.   Bottle, The.
Mahon.   De Quincey in Later Life.
Pessoa.   Opium Eater.

Opossums
Dunbar, P.   Possum.

Oppen, George
Davie, D.   Recollection of George Oppen in a
   Letter to an English Friend.
Tomlinson, C.   In Memory of George Oppen.

Oppenheimer, J. Robert
Ai.   Testimony of J. Robert Oppenheimer, The.
Dubie.   Renunciation of the Desert Primrose, A.

Opportunity
Browning, R.   Dîs Aliter Visum; or, Le Byron
   de Nos Jours.
   Youth and Art.
Cooper, J.   Blue Anchor, The.
Cummings, E. E.   Will suddenly trees leap up
   from winter and will.
Emerson, R.   Heartily heartily sing.
Hardy, T.   Midnight on the Great Western.
   Musical Box, The.
   She Opened the Door.
   You on the Tower.
Kipling, R.   Penalty, The.
Lawrence, D. H.   All That We Have Is Life.
Lindsay, N.   Empty Boats, The.
Muldoon, P.   February.
Nash, O.   Brief Guide to New York, A.
   Doctor Fell? I Thought So.
Parker, D.   Now at Liberty.
Rukeyser, M.   What do you know of America? I
   asked a little Russian schoolgirl.
Shelley, P.   Allegory, An.

Opposites
Carruth, H.   Mythology of Dark and Light, The.
Emerson, R.   Brahma.
Graves, R.   Despite and Still.
   In Broken Images.
   Laugh, The.
   Pact, The.
   Song of Contrariety.
   Song: Wherever We May Be.
Herrick.   Light Lightly Pleased.
   Upon His Gray Haires.
Kipling, R.   Bonfires, The.
Koch, K.   Simplicity of the Unknown Past, The.
Melville, H.   Art.
Michelangelo Buonarroti.   Nature knows what
   it's doing: one cruel as you.
Petrarch.   Looking upon the light of those clear
   eyes.
Prunty.   Our Tree of Opposites.
Ramanujan.   Contraries.

Riley, J.   Natural Perversities.
Robinson, E.   Vain Gratuities.
Rukeyser, M.   If you look at your succession of
   desires.
Sze.   Axis, The.
Szymborska, W.   Negative.
Tomlinson, C.   Oppositions.
Whalen, P.   Mahayana.

Oppression
Angelou.   To a Freedom Fighter.
   We Saw beyond Our Seeming.
Blok.   Factory, The.
Bly, R.   Romans Angry about the Inner World.
Broumas, O.   Massacre, The.
Byron, G.   On Jordan's Banks.
Carruth, H.   I Tell You for Several Years of My
   Madness I Heard the Voice of Lilith Singing in
   the Trees of Chicago.
Clifton, L.   Libation.
   Study the Masters.
   What I Think When I Ride the Train.
   Why some people be mad at me sometimes.
Crane, H.   Black Tambourine.
Cummings, E. E.   O to be in finland.
   Thanksgiving (1956).
Dove, R.   Parsley.
Dugan, A.   Defendant.
Hughes, L.   As I Grew Older.
   Bitter River, The.
   Black Clown, The.
   Black Man Speaks, The.
   Black Seed.
   Brass Spittoons.
   Death in Yorkville.
   Dixie Man to Uncle Sam.
   Envoy to Africa.
   Explain It, Please.
   Freedom Train.
   Gandhi Is Fasting.
   How about It, Dixie.
   I, Too.
   In Explanation of Our Times.
   Kids Who Die.
   Lament for Dark Peoples.
   Let America Be America Again.
   Memo to Non-White Peoples.
   Merry Christmas.
   Militant.
   Negro Ghetto.
   Oppression.
   Question and Answer.
   Roar China!
   Shadows.
   Share-Croppers.
   Uncle Tom ("Within— / The beaten pride").
   Union.
   Wait.
   West Texas.
   What I Think.
   White Man.
Ignatow, D.   For Medgar Evers.
Lawrence, D. H.   Being Alive.
   City-Life.
   Cry of the Masses.
   Give Us the Thebaïd.
   Gulf, The.
   Hold Back!
   Kill Money.
   Listen to the Band!
   Love as an Escape.
   Mills of God, The.
   Money-Madness.
   North Country, The.
   Poor Young Things.
   Sex Won't Work.
   Wages.
   We Die Together.
   What Have They Done to You?
Mahon.   Disused Shed in Co. Wexford, A.
McGrath, T.   Incident in the Life of a Prophet,
   An.
   Poet of the Prison Isle: Ritsos against the
   Colonels, The.
Merrill, J.   Domino.
Merwin.   Homeland.
   Removal, The.

Olson, C.   Barley or rye / blue and white green.
   Cause, the Cause, The.
   Gonfalon Raised Tonight, The.
   Kingfishers, The.
   She-Bear, The.
   She-Bear (II), The.
   To the She-Bear: *The 1st Song*.
Paley, G.   In San Salvador (I).
   In San Salvador (II).
Pessoa.   Not just those who hate and those who
   envy us.
Piercy.   High Frequency.
   Unlearning to Not Speak.
Raine, K.   Eudaimon.
Rich, A.   Burning of Paper instead of Children,
   The.
   Culture and Anarchy.
   For Ethel Rosenberg.
   From an Old House in America.
   Heroines.
   Hunger.
   North American Time.
Rimbaud, A.   Paris War-Cry.
Ritsos.   Final Obol, The.
Rossetti, C.   Pastime.
Rukeyser, M.   Ann Burlak.
Shapiro, K.   University.
   Waitress.
Shelley, P.   Fragment: To the People of England.
   Ode Written October, 1819, An.
Stafford, W.   Objector.
Walker, A.   Ndebele.
Whittier.   Cassandra Southwick.
   St. John.
Williams, C. K.   Keep It.
   Poem for the Governments, A.
Yeats.   Fascination of What's Difficult, The.
Zagajewski.   Iron.
   Password.
See also **Dehumanization; Sexism; Slavery and**
Slaves; Tyranny

Optimism
Burns, R.   Occasional Address, Spoken by Miss
   Fontenell, on Her Benefit Night, Decr. 4th.
   1793.—Written by Mr Burns.
Campion, T. *et al.*   If I hope, I pine; if I feare, I
   faint and die.
Clough.   Say Not the Struggle Nought Availeth.
Creeley.   For a Screaming Lady.
   Hi There!
   Invitation, The.
   Traveller, The.
   Wish, A.
Dunbar, P.   Keep A-Pluggin' Away.
Emerson, R.   Papas Blondine / Grew tall &
   wise.
Graves, R.   Pact, The.
   Song: Olive Tree.
Hamill, S.   Letter to John Logan from La Push.
Herrick.   Hope Well and Have Well: or, Faire
   after Foule Weather.
Hughes, L.   Some Day.
Lawrence, D. H.   Optimist, The.
Lenau.   Three Gipsies, The.
Mahon.   Everything Is Going to Be All Right.
McGrath, T.   Against the False Magicians.
Meredith, G.   From labours through the night,
   outworn.
   In the Sap.
   New Year's Eve.
   Open horizons round.
   Song: "Daisy now is out upon the green, The."
   Sonnet: "Hateful are those false themes of
   speculation."
   This love of nature, that allures to take.
   Wilding little stubble flower, A.
   Will Whistle.
   World is young, the world is well, The.
Nash, O.   Look for the Silver Lining.
   Lucy Lake.
Neruda.   Cherries.
Parker, D.   Comment.
   De Profundis.
   Far-Sighted Muse, The.
   Poem in the American Manner.
Riley, J.   Snow in the Air.

Thoughts fer the Discuraged Farmer.
What Little Saul Got, Christmas.
Whatever the Weather May Be.
Ritsos. Method for Optimism.
Robinson, E. Caput Mortuum.
Smith, S. Away, Melancholy.
Warren, R. For a Friend Who Thinks Himself
   Urbane.
Wyatt, S. Venomous thorns that are so sharp
   and keen.

Oracles
Ammons. Strait, The.
Brodsky, J. North of Delphi.
Cavafy. In the Districts Surrounding Antioch.
Clampitt. Dodona: Asked of the Oracle.
Dugan, A. Last Statement for a Last Oracle.
Housman. Oracles, The.
Meredith, G. Wind on the Lyre.
Merton. Oracle, The.
Montale. On the Highest Column.
Raine, K. Oracles.
Updike. On the Way to Delphi.
Yeats. Delphic Oracle upon Plotinus, The.

Orange (color)
O'Hara, F. Why I Am Not a Painter.

Orange Trees and Oranges
Ammons. Communication.
Davie, D. Poem as Abstract.
Ramanujan. Poem on Particulars, A.
Walcott. In a Green Night.
Williams, W. Berket and the Stars.

Oratory
Brodsky, J. At a Lecture.
Byron, G. Parenthetical Address.
Cowper, W. Sonnet to Henry Cowper.
Kizer, C. Oration, The.
Larkin, P. Nothing Significant Was Really Said.
Riley, J. Jap Miller.
Ritsos. Memorial Service at Poros.
Updike. Miss Moore at Assembly.

Orchards
Amichai [or Amikhai]. Orchard.
Clampitt. Hickory Grove, The.
Crane, H. There Are the Local.
Eberhart, R. Recollection of Childhood.
Frost, R. Evening in a Sugar Orchard.
   Good-by and Keep Cold.
   Peril of Hope.
Graves, R. Language of the Seasons.
"H. D." Orchard.
Lawrence, D. H. Old Orchard, The.
Nemerov. To Lu Chi.
Paz. Grove, The.
Riley, J. Orchard Lands of Long Ago, The.
   Rambo-Tree, The.
Rilke. Orchard.
Rukeyser, M. Children's Orchard, The.
Rumi. Come to the orchard in Spring.
Sandburg, C. Wind Song.
Sze. Olive Grove, The.
Warren, R. Composition in Gold and Red-Gold.
Wilbur, R. He Was.
   Orchard Trees, January.
Williams, W. Wild Orchard.
Wright, J. Offering for Mr. Bluehart, An.
   Two Horses Playing in the Orchard.

Orchids
Clampitt. Smaller Orchid, The.
Dugan, A. On the Supposed Immorality of
   Orchids.
"H. D." At Baia.
Roethke. Orchids.
Williams, C. K. Orchid, The.

Order
Amichai [or Amikhai]. Precise Woman, A.
Ammons. Corsons Inlet.
   Hymn 5: "Assure us you side with order:
      throw."
   Identity.
   Looking over the Acreage.
   Misfit, The.
   Muse.
   Sharp Lookout.
   Village, Town, City—Highway, Road, Path.
Ashbery, J. Ivory Tower, The.

Borges. Causes, The.
Chuang Tzu. Two Kings and No-Form.
Crane, S. Once there came a man.
Creeley. Peace ("Waiting for a bus").
   Window, The.
Davie, D. Ezra Pound in Pisa.
   Method. For Ronald Gaskell.
Eberhart, R. Great Praises.
   Hard Structure of the World, The.
   Light from Above.
Emerson, R. But O to see his solar eyes.
   Who saw the hid beginnings.
Hall, D. Lone Ranger, The.
Heaney, S. Markings.
Herbert, G. Family [or Familie], The.
Ignatow, D. Discussion, A.
Mahon. Rage for Order.
Melville, H. Milan Cathedral.
Meredith, G. Lucifer in Starlight.
Raine, K. Vegetation.
Rexroth, K. They Say This Isn't a Poem.
Sandburg, C. Many Handles.
Stevens, W. Anecdote of the Jar.
   Bed of Old John Zeller, The.
   Connoisseur of Chaos.
   Idea of Order at Key West, The.
   Room on a Garden, A.
Tu Fu. Visit in Winter to the Temple of His
   Mystical Majesty, A.
Wilbur, R. In a Bird Sanctuary.
Williams, M. Politics.

Oregon (state)
Broumas, O. Oregon Landscape with Lost
   Lover.
Kinnell. Burn, The.
Kizer, C. Running Away from Home.

Orestes (mythology)
"H. D." Orestes Theme.
Jarrell, R. Orestes at Tauris.
Jeffers, R. Tower beyond Tragedy, The.
Ritsos. Orestes.

Organs and Organists
Cortes. Organ.
Dickinson, E. I've heard an Organ talk,
   sometimes.
Very. Old Organ of the East Society Salem,
   The.

Orient
Ginsberg, A. After Yeats.
Nash, O. So I resigned from the Chu Chin
   Chowder and Marching Club.
Rimbaud, A. Impossible, The.

Origami
Merton. Paper Cranes.
Sze. Red Octopus.

Original Sin
Dickinson, E. "Heavenly Father"—take to thee.
Glück, L. Murderess, The.
Herrick. Rose, The.
Milosz, C. Lessons.
Nash, O. Ha! Original Sin!
Thomas, D. Incarnate Devil.
Thoreau. In Adams fall.
Very. Garden, The.
Walcott. Orient and Immortal Wheat.
Warren, R. Original Sin[: A Short Story].

Orioles
Dickinson, E. One of the ones that Midas
   touched.
   To Hear an Oriole Sing.
Dunbar, P. Summer in the South.
Lowell, R. Fall 1961.
Mandelstam [or Mandelshtam]. Summer
   Solstice.

Orion (constellation)
Dickinson, E. Follow wise Orion.
Rexroth, K. It Turns Over.
Rich, A. Orion.

Orion (mythology)
"H. D." Orion Dead.

Orphans
Ai. Detective, The.
Davie, D. Dublin Georgian ("Thin brown
   orphan in his washed-out blue, A").
Hardy, T. To a Motherless Child.

Unrealized.
Herrick. To His Verses.
Levertov. Arrival (North Wales, 1897), An.
Levine, P. On My Own.
Meredith, G. Little Foot-Page, The.
Ni Dhomhnaill. Orphan at the Door, An.
Riley, J. Little Orphant Annie.
Rilke. Orphan Song.
   Orphan, The.
Rimbaud, A. Orphans' New Year Gifts.
Rossetti, C. Iniquity of the Fathers upon the
   Children, The.
   My baby has a father and a mother.
Smith, S. Orphan Reformed, The.
   Thank You.
Warren, R. Orphanage Boy.
Williams, C. K. Before This.

Orpheus
Atwood. Eurydice.
   Orpheus (1).
   Orpheus (2).
Auden. Orpheus.
Browning, R. Eurydice to Orpheus.
Campion, T. To Campiani Epigramma de
   Instituto Authoris.
   Umbra.
Cowper, W. Ode on the Marriage of a Friend.
Davie, D. Orpheus.
Dugan, A. On a Baroque Clock.
   Orpheus.
Herrick. Orpheus and Pluto.
Hill, G. Orpheus and Eurydice.
Kunitz, S. In the Dark House.
Levertov. Tree Telling of Orpheus, A.
Maritain. Eurydice.
Meredith, W. Orpheus.
Merrill, J. Orfeo.
Nemerov. Orphic Scenario.
Orr, G. Entrance to the Underworld, The.
   Far below, plowed fields vibrated.
   Ghosts Listen to Orpheus Sing, The.
   His Dream: The Black Tree / Thirst.
   His Grief.
   I was moving down the bank.
   In the cave mouth I stopped.
   In the shadows at the clearing's.
   My body was never married.
   Wedge, The.
   When Eurydice saw him.
   When I first saw her.
   When they said I must leave hell.
Rich, A. I Dream I'm the Death of Orpheus.
   Postcard.
Ritsos. Descent.
   To Orpheus.
Rukeyser, M. In Hades, Orpheus.
   Orpheus.
   Poem as Mask, The.
Shelley, P. Orpheus.
Spenser, E. Epithalamion: "Ye learned sisters
   which have oftentimes."
Williams, T. Orpheus Descending.

Orthodox Eastern Church
Cavafy. In Church.

Ospreys
Eberhart, R. Ospreys in Cry.

Ostriches
Moore, M. He "Digesteth Harde Yron."

Oswald, Lee Harvey
Ai. Jack Ruby on Ice.
   Oswald Incognito & Astral Travels.
Corbett, W. Collarbone.
Oppen. Armies of the Plain.

Otterburn, Battle of (1388)
Kipling, R. English Way, The.

Otters
Gunn, T. Life of the Otter, The.
Heaney, S. Otter, The.
Hughes, T. Otter, An.

Ouija Boards
Merrill, J. Voices from the Other World.

Outlaws
Ignatow, D. Outlaw, The.
Parker, D. Gunman and the Débutante, The.
See also **Crime and Criminals**

Ovenbirds
Frost, R.   Oven Bird, The.
Overpopulation
Brodsky, J.   Postcard, A.
Creeley.   Buildings.
   Davao Insular Hotel.
Ovibos
See **Musk Oxen**
Ovid (Publius Ovidius Naso)
Carruth, H.   Ovid, Old Buddy, I Would
   Discourse with You a While.
Codrescu.   School Daze.
Dubie.   Ibis.
Hill, G.   Ovid in the Third Reich.
Laughlin, J.   La Tristesse.
Mahon.   Ovid in Tomis.
Pinsky.   Creation According to Ovid.
Pope, A.   Sandys's Ghost, or a Proper New
   Ballad on the New Ovid's Metamorphosis.
Ransom, J.   Philomela.
Walcott.   Hotel Normandie Pool, The.
Owain Gwynedd, Prince of North Wales
Gray, T.   Triumphs of Owen, The.
Owen, Wilfred
Hughes, T.   Wilfred Owen's Photographs.
Jacobsen, J.   For Wilfred Owen.
Williams, M.   WWI.
Owls
Ammons.   Jungle Knot.
Baudelaire.   Owls.
Bishop, E.   Song for the Rainy Season.
Davie, D.   Screech-Owl.
De la Mare.   Evening.
  Owl, The.
Dickey, J.   Owl King, The.
Dickinson, E.   Judge is like the Owl, The.
Duncan, R.   Sentinels, The.
Eberhart, R.   Emblem.
  Hoot Owls.
Enzensberger, H.   End of Owls, The.
Frost, R.   Questioning Faces.
Graves, R.   Like Owls.
Hegedüs, J.   Owl, The.
Herrick.   Vow to Minerva, A.
Hughes, T.   Owl's Song.
Jarrell, R.   Bird of Night, The.
  Owl's Bedtime Story, The.
Laughlin, J.   Owl of Minerva, The.
Lindsay, N.   What Grandpa Mouse Said.
Major, C.   Great Horned Owl, The.
Merton.   Christina.
Merwin.   Owl, The.
Mistral, G.   Owl, An.
Niedecker.   Monster owl, A.
Oliver, M.   Little Owl Who Lives in the
   Orchard.
  Lonely, White Fields.
  Nature.
  This Morning Again It Was in the Dusty Pines.
  White Owl Flies into and out of the Field.
Orr, G.   Caged Owl, The.
Piercy.   What the Owl Sees.
Plath.   Owl.
Schuyler, J.   Korean Mums.
Shelley, P.   Aziola, The.
Simic.   Great Horned Owl, The.
Swenson, M.   Camping in Madera Canyon.
  Snowy, The.
  Woods at Night, The.
Sze.   Owl, The.
Van Duyn.   Ballad of Blossom, The.
Warren, R.   Owl, The.
Wordsworth, W.   Leaves That Rustled on This
   Oak-Crowned Hill, The.
Oxen
Ciardi, J.   O is for ox, by which word we.
"Dario."   Exploit in the Bullring.
Hardy, T.   Oxen, The.
Kipling, R.   Beasts Are Very Wise, The.
  Between the waving tufts of jungle-grass.
Tomlinson, C.   Oxen: Ploughing at Fiesole.
Whitman, W.   Ox-Tamer, The.
Oxford, England
Arnold, M.   Scholar Gypsy, The.
Auden.   Oxford.

Clampitt.   Alice.
  Having Lunch at Brasenose.
Cowper, W.   Epigram on the Refusal of the
   University of Oxford to Subscribe to His
   Translation of Homer.
Davie, D.   Oxfordshire.
Eberhart, R.   To Auden on His Fiftieth.
Hall, D.   Christ Church Meadows, [Oxford].
Hopkins, G.   Cheery Beggar.
  Duns Scotus's Oxford.
  Oxford Bells.
  To Oxford.
Keats.   On Oxford.
Kipling, R.   Clerks and the Bells, The.
Larkin, P.   Poem about Oxford.
Lawrence, D. H.   Oxford Voice, The.
MacNeice.   Relics.
Ransom, J.   Philomela.
Updike.   Oxford, Thirty Years After.
Wilde, O.   Burden of Itys, The.
Wordsworth, W.   Oxford, May 30, 1820.
Oysters
Cowper, W.   Poet, the Oyster, and Sensitive
   Plant, The.
  To Mrs. Newton.
Hall, D.   Oysters and Hermits.
Heaney, S.   Oysters.
Levi, P.   Pearl Oyster.
Nash, O.   Oyster, The.
  What, No Oysters?
See also **Clams and Clamming; Shells**
Ozark Mountains
Van Duyn.   In the Missouri Ozarks.

P

Pacific Ocean
Clampitt.   John Donne in California.
Davie, D.   Out of East Anglia.
Dickey, J.   Exchanges.
Frost, R.   Once by the Pacific.
Gunn, T.   Discovery of the Pacific, The.
Jeffers, R.   Coast-Road, The.
  Eye, The.
  Gray Weather.
  I walk on my cliff above the Pacific Ocean and
   feel the tides.
Levertov.   Heights, Depths, Silence, Unceasing
   Sound of the Surf.
Oppen.   California.
  Coastal Strip.
Stevens, W.   Doctor of Geneva, The.
  Sea Surface Full of Clouds.
Warren, R.   Pacific Gazer.
  Swimming in the Pacific.
Whitman, W.   Facing West from California's
   Shores.
Wright, C.   Looking West from Laguna Beach at
   Night.
Pacifism and Pacifists
Berryman.   Pacifist's Song, The.
Cummings, E. E.   I Sing of Olaf Glad and Big.
  I'm / asking / you dear to.
  When your honest redskin toma.
Housman.   Oh stay at home, my lad, and
   plough.
Jeffers, R.   Time of Disturbance.
Lowell, R.   After the Surprising Conversions.
  Memories of West Street and Lepke.
Millay, E.   Conscientious Objector.
Parker, D.   Slackers; A Hate Song.
Shapiro, K.   Conscientious Objector, The.
Stafford, W.   At the Un-National Monument
   along the Canadian Border.
  Dedication, A: "We stood by the library. It was
   an August night."
  Learning.
  Objector.
  Peace Walk.
Walker, A.   QPP, The.
Whittier.   Brown of Ossawatomie.
  Disarmament.
See also **Conscientious Objectors**

Paganini, Niccolò
Palmer, M.   False Portrait of D.B. as Niccolò
   Paganini.
Paganism and Pagans
Baudelaire.   Pagan's Prayer, The.
Cavafy.   Dangerous Remarks.
  Grand Procession of Priests and Laymen.
  If Actually Dead.
  In the Cemetery.
  In the Districts Surrounding Antioch.
  Julian at the Mysteries.
  Julian in Nicomedia.
  Julian, Seeing Contempt.
  Myris: Alexandria, 340 A.D.
  Of the Jews (50 A.D.).
  Priest at the Serapeion.
Cullen, C.   Pagan Prayer.
Eberhart, R.   Soul Longs to Return Whence It
   Came, The.
Emerson, R.   To transmute crime to wisdom, &
   to stem.
Herrick.   Upon Faunus.
Melville, H.   Age of the Antonines, The.
Mistral, G.   Bread.
Montale.   There the Tritone surges.
Parker, D.   Flaw in Paganism, The.
Wordsworth, W.   World is too much with us;
   late and soon, The.
Pain
Amichai [*or* Amikhai].   God's Hand in the
   World.
  Ibn Gabirol.
Angelou.   Kind of Love, Some Say, A.
Atwood.   Rest, The.
Berry, W.   To My Children, Fearing for Them.
  Way of Pain, The.
Berryman.   Venice, 182.
Bierce.   Mystery, A.
Bogan, L.   Chanson un Peu Naïve.
Brontë, E.   God of Visions.
  If grief for grief can touch thee.
Broumas, O.   Beauty and the Beast.
Browning, E.   Night and the Merry Man.
Bukowski.   About Pain.
  Condition, The.
Burns, R.   Address to the Tooth-Ache.
Carew, T.   Mistake, The.
  To Master W. Montague.
  To My Inconstant Mistress [*or* Mistris].
Carruth, H.   Poet, The.
Carver, R.   Projectile, The.
Cavalcanti.   Sonnet: Of His Pain from a New
   Love.
  You've so filled my mind with pain.
Ciardi, J.   Poet's Words, The.
Coleridge, S.   Dejection: An Ode.
  Two Founts, The.
Cooper, J.   Infusion Room, The.
Crane, H.   Hive, The.
Crane, S.   Love walked alone.
Creeley.   Chicago.
  Flower, The.
  For Fear.
  Goodbye.
  Letter, The.
  Phone.
  Pieces.
  Snow, The.
  Versions.
  Visit, The.
Cuadra, P.   Pain Is an Eagle Clinging to Your
   Name.
Cullen, C.   Protest.
  Saturday's Child.
  Song in Spite of Myself.
  Sonnet: "I know now how a man whose blood
   is hot."
Davie, D.   Hypochondriac Logic.
  Machineries of Shame.
Dickinson, E.   After great pain a formal feeling
   comes.
  Anguish sometimes gives a cause.
  Crisis is sweet and yet the Heart.
  Each Scar I'll keep for Him.
  Final Inch, The.
  Friend Anguish reveals is, The.

Hallowing of Pain, The.
I Can Wade Grief.
I never knew a broken Heart.
I shall not murmur if at last.
I watched her face to see which way.
If pain for peace prepares.
If the anguish of others helped one with one's own.
I'm Wife . . . .
It is Anguish I long conceal from you.
It is easier to look behind at a pain.
It is easy to work when the soul is at play.
Months have ends—the Years—a knot, The.
Morning after Woe, The.
Nearness to Tremendousness, A.
One Anguish—in a Crowd.
Pain—expands the Time.
Pain Has an Element of Blank.
Pain has but one Acquaintance.
Rehearsal to Ourselves.
There is a Languor of the Life.
There is a pain—so utter.
'Tis not that Dying hurts us so.
To all except anguish.
'Twas the old—road—through pain.
Vastest earthly Day, The.
Weight with Needles on the pounds, A.
Wounded Deer Leaps Highest, A.
Dove, R.   Variation on Pain.
Dunbar, P.   Itching Heels.
Eberhart, R.   Critic with His Pained Eye, The.
Full of Joy Do Not Know; They Need Not, The.
On Seeing an Egyptian Mummy in Berlin, 1932.
Truth, The.
Emerson, R.   Intellect / Gravely broods apart on joy.
Gallagher, T.   Harmless Streets.
García Lorca.   Ballad of Black Pain.
Glück, L.   Epithalamium: "There were others; their bodies."
Love Poem.
World Breaking Apart.
Graves, R.   Cure, The.
Fire Walker.
Growing Pains.
Stolen Jewel.
Gunn, T.   Her Pet.
Innocence.
Man with Night Sweats, The.
Painkillers.
Gurney, I.   For Mercy of Death.
Last of the Book, The.
Pain.
There Is a Man.
To Crickley.
"H. D." Halcyon.
Hacker, M.   Country & Western.
Hall, D.   Hole, The.
To the Loud Wind.
Hardy, T.   End of the Episode, The.
I Thought, My Heart.
Wish for Unconsciousness, A.
Wound, The.
Hayden, R.   Road in Kentucky, A.
Whipping, The.
Herrick.   Persecutions Profitable.
Hughes, T.   At the bottom of the Arctic sea, they say.
Crow's Battle Fury.
God, A.
Jackson, L.   And I.
Beyond.
Celebration of Failure.
Jacobsen, J.   Tree Angel.
Jarrell, R.   90 North.
Essay on the Human Will, An.
Field Hospital, A.
Jeffers, R.   Day Is a Poem, The.
Praise Life.
World's Wonders, The.
Keats.   Ode to a Nightingale.
Kipling, R.   Comforters, The.
Hymn to Physical Pain.
Power of the Dog, The.
Laughlin, J.   Crucifixion in the Desert.
Lawrence, D. H.   Assuming the Burden.

Kissing and Horrid Strife.
Levertov.   Ache of Marriage, The.
As It Happens.
Levine, P.   How Much Can It Hurt?
I Could Believe.
No One Remembers.
Lindsay, N.   Love and Law.
Lorde.   Hard Love Rock.
Lux.   Impingement Sydrome.
Merwin.   Beggars and Kings.
Different Stars, The.
From a Series.
Teachers.
Words.
Millay, E.   And must I then, indeed, Pain, live with you.
Not only love plus awful grief.
Who hurt you so.
Milosz, C.   Body.
Helene.
I Sleep a Lot.
Montale.   I know the moment when a raw grimace.
Nemerov.   Creation of Anguish.
To the Memory of John Wheelwright.
Virgin and Martyr.
Neruda.   Some Creature.
O'Hara, F.   Savoy.
Oliver, M.   Anne.
Olson, C.   Cry pain, & the dogs of yrself devour.
Orr, G.   Singing the Pain Back into the Wound.
Owen, W.   Greater Love.
Hospital Barge at Cérisy.
Winter Song.
Paley, G.   For George (II).
Palmer, M.   Man undergoes pain sitting at a piano, A.
Parker, D.   Ultimatum.
Piercy.   Root Canal, The.
Prunty.   Recovery.
Raine, K.   Descent into Hades.
I could have told much by the way.
If I choose remorse.
Ralegh, S.   No Pleasure, without Some Payne.
Ramanujan.   Pain.
PAIN: Trying to Find a Metaphor.
Pleasure.
Ransom, J.   Moments of Minnie.
Rexroth, K.   Phronesis.
Rich, A.   Dien Bien Phu.
Letters: March 1969.
Pieces.
Splittings.
Rossetti, C.   Acme.
Ah welladay and wherefore am I here?
Balm in Gilead.
Chilly Night, A.
Chruchyard Song of Patient Hope, A.
Dream, The.
Eva.
February 14. 1883.
Henry Hardiman.
Hope in Grief.
I said "All's over"—& I made my.
I Will Lift Up Mine Eyes unto the Hills.
Introspective.
Joy is but sorrow, / While we know.
Looking Forward.
Lord, grant me grace to love Thee in my pain.
Martyr, A.
Martyr, The.
Methinks the ills of life I fain would shun.
Monday in Holy Week.
None with Him.
O thou who tell'st me that all hope is over.
One Foot on Sea, and One on Shore.
Piteous my rhyme is / What while I muse of love and pain.
Sick Child's Meditation, A.
Sonnet: "Some say that love and joy are one: and so."
Spring is come again not as at first.
St. Bartholomew.
Vanity of Vanities.
What Sappho Would Have Said Had Her Leap

Cured Instead of Killing Her.
Whom the Lord Loveth He Chasteneth.
Zara.
Rukeyser, M.   Judith.
Man sits in the rocking bedroom, claws, The.
Slow Dialogue between Pain and Roosevelt.
To keep the weakness secret. To deny it and break through.
Wheels and galleries of the control of tears.
Sadi [or Saadi or Sa'di].   Pain of love's a better fate, The.
Sandburg, C.   At a Window.
Broken Hearted Soprano.
Kisses Forgotten.
Sarton, M.   Burial.
Humpty Dumpty.
Tortured, The.
Sexton.   Big Boots of Pain, The.
Grandfather, Your Wound.
Pain for a Daughter.
Shapiro, K.   Hospital.
Shelley, P.   Invocation to Misery.
To William Shelley.
Sidney, S.   Scourge of life, and death's extreme disgrace, The.
Thou Pain, the only guest of loathed constraint.
When Love, puffed up with rage of high disdain.
Smith, S.   Doctor, The.
Lads of the Village, The.
Seymour and Chantelle or Un Peu de Vice.
Spender, S.   Nocturne: "Their six-weeks-old daughter lies."
Stafford, W.   Things That Hurt Me.
Suckling, S.   Love's Offence.
Song: "I prithee spare me, gentle boy."
Thomas, D.   Lie Still, Sleep Becalmed.
Updike.   Pain.
Van Duyn.   Ringling Brothers, Barnum and Bailey.
Voznesensky [or Voznesenskii].   Arrow in the Wall, An.
Walcott.   Fist, The.
Walker, A.   Excuse.
Whitman, W.   I Sit and Look Out.
Wilbur, R.   Another Voice.
Williams, C. K.   Alzheimer's: The Wife.
I Am the Bitter Name.
Image, The.
Three Seasons and a Gorilla.
Williams, M.   Thinking about Bill, Dead of AIDS.
Williams, W.   Birth of Venus, The.
Comfort.
Wordsworth, W.   Complaint, A.
Wright, J.   Blue Teal's Mother.
Prayer to the Lord Ramakrishna, A.
Refusal, The.
Wyatt, S.   Alas, the grief and deadly wo[e]ful smart[!].
All heavy minds.
Being as none is, I do complain.
Complaining, alas, without redress.
Duress of pains and grievous smart.
Flaming sighs that boil within my breast, The.
I love, loved, and so doth she.
If I might have at mine own will.
If with complaint the pain might be expressed.
Might I as well within my song belay.
Sighs are my food, drink are my tears.
Thou sleepest fast and I with woeful heart.
Though I cannot your cruelty constrain.
Venomous thorns that are so sharp and keen.
What word is that that changeth not.
Within my breast I never thought it gain.
Yeats.   Lady's First Song, The.

Paine, Thomas
Cowper, W.   Sonnet Addressed to Mr. Phillips, A.

Painting and Painters
Ai.   Back in the World.
"Anvari."   Body and Soul.
Ashbery, J.   Painter, The.
Atwood.   Quattrocento.
Auden.   Musée des Beaux Arts.
Baudelaire.   'Lola de Valence' by Manet.

'Tasso in Prison' by Delacroix.
Bembo, P. On Raphael.
Bishop, E. Large Bad Picture.
Pleasure Seas.
Poem: "About the size of an old-style dollar bill."
Blake, W. Sir Joshua Reynolds.
Browning, R. Andrea del Sarto.
Beatrice Signorini.
Face, A.
Fra Lippo Lippi.
Guardian-Angel, The.
Lady and the Painter, The.
Of Pacchiarotto, and How He Worked in Distemper.
Old Pictures in Florence.
Pictor Ignotus.
Bukowski. Artist.
Cows in Art Class.
Greek, The.
Promise, The.
Carew, T. To the Painter.
Carver, R. Bonnard's Nudes.
Painter & the Fish, The.
What You Need for Painting.
Cavafy. Oedipus.
Painted.
Celan. Below a Painting
In-edger: Rembrandt.
Mandorla.
Chesterton. Nativity by Botticelli, The.
Ciardi, J. Cézanne.
Sleep (by Rousseau), A.
Codrescu. Lady Painter, The.
Why Paint?
Collins, B. Brooklyn Museum of Art, The.
Fishing on the Susquehanna in July.
Not Touching.
Cooper, J. Evening Star (Georgia O'Keeffe).
In a Room with Picassos.
S. Eliason 66: Double Portrait of Emily Dickinson and the Rev. Charles Wadsworth.
Scattered Words for Emily Dickinson.
Corbett, W. Air and Light, The.
Painters, The.
Cowper, W. To Sir Joshua Reynolds.
Crane, H. Sunday Morning Apples.
Crashaw. Flaming Heart, The.
Cummings, E. E. Of my / soul a street is.
Water-Lilies.
Davie, D. Death of a Painter.
Pacer in the Fresco, The. John the Baptist.
De la Mare. Breughel's Winter.
Dickinson, E. I would not paint—a picture.
Those fair—fictitious People.
Dove, R. Agosta the Winged Man and Rasha the Black Dove.
Dubie. Looking up from Two Renaissance Paintings to the Massacre at Tiananmen Square.
Trolley from Xochimilco, The.
Emerson, R. For Nature true & like in every place.
Painting and Sculpture.
Enzensberger, H. Apocalypse. Umbrian Master, about 1490.
Dream, A.
Gillis van Conninxloo, Landscape. Panel, 65 x 119 cm.
Last Supper. Venetian, Sixteenth Century.
Rest of the Flight, The. Flemish, 1521.
Visiting Ingres.
Ferlinghetti, L. Don't Let That Horse.
Expressionist History of German Expressionism.
Matisse at the Modern, Magritte at the Met.
Painter's Dream, The.
Sarolla's women in their picture hats.
García Lorca. Ode to Salvador Dalí.
Gunn, T. In Santa Maria del Popolo.
Hacker, M. Le Travail Rajeunit.
Hall, D. "Scream, The."
Han-shan. Seng-yao I hear was a talented man.
Hardy, T. Collector Cleans His Picture, The.
Herrick. Painting Sometimes Permitted.
To His Nephew, to Be Prosperous in His Art of Painting.

To the Painter, to Draw Him a Picture.
Upon Umber: Epigram.
Hughes, T. To Paint a Water Lily.
Jacobsen, J. Enemy of the Herds, the Lion, The.
In the Crevice of Time.
Painter at Xyochtl.
Jonson, B. Poem Sent Me by Sir William Burlase, A.
Kizer, C. Halation.
Komunyakaa. Cubism.
Olympia.
South Carolina Morning.
Trapper's Bride, The.
Kumin, M. Calling, A.
Kunitz, S. Artist, The.
Sea, That Has No Ending, The.
Laughlin, J. Kiss, The.
Les Amants.
Paintings in the Museums of Munich and Vienna.
Real Bones.
Reclining Position, The.
Lawrence, D. H. 13 Pictures.
Auto-Da-Fé.
Give Me a Sponge.
Innocent England.
Painter's Wife, The.
Levertov. For Those Whom the Gods Love Less.
Life of Art, The.
Salvator Mundi: Via Crucis.
Servant-Girl at Emmaus (A Painting by Velazquez), The.
Logan, J. Dream, The: A Reflection on Morris Graves's Paintings.
Gallery Walk: Fifteen Italian Drawings 1780–1890.
March. The Museum. Buffalo. de Chirico.
Nighthawks: after Hopper's Painting.
Spirit of the Dead Watching: after Gaugin.
Three Poems on Morris Graves' Paintings.
Yellow Christ, The; after Gaugin.
Lowell, R. Rembrandt.
Lux. Floating Baby Paintings.
MacDiarmid, H. Well Hung.
MacLeish. Oil Painting of the Artist as the Artist.
Mahon. Forger, The.
Portrait of the Artist, A.
Shapes and Shadows.
Major, C. Atelier Cézanne.
Clay Bison in a Cave.
Un Poco Loco.
Mallarmé. Homage: "Even a Dawn too numb."
Maritain. Chagall.
McHugh, H. Where.
Melville, H. Bench of Boors, The.
Meredith, W. At the Prado.
February 14.
Hazard's Optimism.
Look at Me! Look at Me!
Winter: He Shapes Up.
Michelangelo Buonarroti. Goiter it seems I got from this backward craning, A.
If a joyous heart makes beautiful the face.
If by its heaven-sent power the mind conceives.
Milosz, C. At Yale.
Biography of an Artist.
Mary Magdalen and I.
O! ("O lips half opened, eyes half closed, the rosy nipple of your unveiled nakedness, Judith!").
Pastels by Degas.
Portrait with a Cat, A.
Realism.
Montale. Fan, The.
Muldoon, P. Bearded Woman, by Ribera, The.
Nemerov. Conversing with Paradise.
Most Expensive Picture in the World, The.
Nature Morte.
Old Picture, An.
Painting a Mountain Stream.
Sestina 1: "Thickness of paint or flesh cannot deface."
Vermeer.
Niedecker. As I paint the street.

Audubon.
Bird singing.
In Leonardo's light.
To whom / can I leave.
O'Hara, F. Having a Coke with You.
Naphtha.
On Looking at La Grande Jatte, the Czar Wept Anew.
Why I Am Not a Painter.
Orr, G. After Botticelli's Birth of Venus.
After Piero di Cosimo's Venus, Mars, and Amor.
Story Sassetta Paints, A.
Paley, G. On the Ramblas a Tree a Girl.
Palmer, M. False Portrait of Hanna H.
Petrarch. If Polyclitus studied earnestly.
Pinkerton, H. On a Painting by Todd Price of the 16th Michigan Infantry on Little Round Top, July 2, 1863.
On Blakelock's Moonlit Landscape in the de Young Museum.
On Breughel the Elder's The Harvesters (1565) in the Metropolitan Museum.
On Erastus Salisbury Field's The Israelites Crossing the Red Sea (1863?).
On Fitz Hugh Lane's Approaching Storm, Owl's Head, 1860.
On Gari Melchers's Writing (1905) in the Los Angeles County Museum of Art.
On Jan van Huysum's Vase of Flowers (1722) in the J. Paul Getty Museum.
On Rembrandt's Self-Portrait (1658) in the Frick Museum.
On Vermeer's Young Woman with a Water Jug (1658) in the Metropolitan Museum.
On Watteau's Pilgrimage to Cythera (1717) in the Louvre.
Pinsky. Volume, The.
Plath. Midsummer Mobile.
Pope, A. Epistle to Mr. Jervas, with Dryden's Translation of Fresnoy's Art of Painting.
To Sir Godfrey Kneller, on His Painting for Me the Statues of Apollo, Venus and Hercules.
Pound, E. Of Jacopo del Sellaio.
Picture, The.
Raine, K. Old Paintings on Italian Walls.
Painting by Winifred Nicholson, A.
Ramanujan. Museum.
Riley, J. Discouraging Model, A.
Wife-Blessed, The.
Ritsos. Abstracted Painter.
Subject for an Oil Painting.
Vatican Museum.
Robinson, E. Her Eyes.
Rembrandt to Rembrandt.
Rossetti, C. In An Artist's Studio.
Rossetti, D. For "An Allegorical Dance of Women" by Andrea Mantegna.
For "Ruggiero and Angelica" by Ingres.
For Spring, by Sandro Botticelli, in the Accademia of Florence.
For 'The Wine of Circe' by Edward Burne Jones.
Marriage of St Katharine, by the same, A; in the Hospital of St John at Bruges.
Venetian Pastoral, by Giorgone, in the Louvre, A.
Virgin and Child, by Hans Memmeling, A; in the Academy of Bruges.
Rukeyser, M. Birth of Venus, The.
For a Mexican Painter.
· Painters.
Sandburg, C. Four Steichen Prints.
Old Hokusai Print.
People Who Must.
Unintentional Paint.
Sarton, M. Dutch Interior.
Seifert. Four Small Windows.
Lines for the Painter Ota Janeček.
Model, The.
Visit to the Painter Vladimír Komárek, A.
Sexton. Starry Night, The.
Shapiro, K. Dome of Sunday, The [or A].
Smith, S. Spanish School.
Stafford, W. At Lascaux.
Cave Painting.
Stevens, W. Prelude to Objects.

Stock, R.   Battle Scene.
Giorgione's *Tempest.*
Grate, The.
Instructions to Any Painter for a "Coronation of
   Inés de Castro."
Prose for the Children of Aborted Revolution.
Swenson, M.   Day Like Rousseau's *Dream*, A.
Picasso: "Dream." Oil 1932.
Sze.   Brueghel.
Pentimento.
Taoist Painter, The.
Szymborska, W.   Landscape.
People on the Bridge.
Rubens' Women.
Tate, J.   Paint 'til You Faint.
Tomlinson, C.   Cézanne at Aix.
Composition.
Farewell to Van Gogh.
Garland for Thomas Eakins, A.
Marat Dead.
Meditation on John Constable, A.
Miracle of the Bottle and the Fishes, The.
On a Landscape by Li Ch'eng.
Paring the Apple.
Self-Portrait: David, A.
Unknown.   Another ["Painter, this likeness is too
   strong"].
Updike.   Gradations of Black.
Painted Wives.
Very.   Sumach Leaves, The.
To the Misses Williams, on Seeing Their
   Beautiful Paintings of Wild Flowers.
Warren, R.   Aging Painter Sits Where the Great
   Tower Heaves Down Midnight.
Weiss, T.   Fresh Paint.
Wheatley, P.   To S. M., a Young African Painter,
   on Seeing His Works.
Whitman, W.   Death's Valley.
Whittier.   Raphael.
Wilbur, R.   Dutch Courtyard, A.
Giaour and the Pacha, The.
L'Etoile.
Museum Piece.
My Father Paints the Summer.
Objects.
Wilde, O.   Impression du Matin.
In the Gold Room: A Harmony.
Williams, T.   Dangerous Painters, The.
Williams, W.   Dance, The.
Parable of the Blind, The.
Pictures from Brueghel.
Raindrops on a Briar.
Tribute to the Painters.
Wilner, E.   American Painting, with Rain.
Instructions to Painters by Wang Wei, Eighth
   Century.
My Mother's Portrait.
Private Space, A.
Trümmerfrauen.
Wordsworth, W.   Anacreon.
Elegiac Stanzas Suggested by a Picture of Peele
   Castle, in a Storm, Painted by Sir George
   Beaumont.
Foregoing Subject Resumed, The.
Gleaner (Suggested by a Picture), The.
Picture of Daniel in the Lions' Den, at Hamilton
   Palace.
Sonnet to a Picture by Lucca Giordano in the
   Mureo Borbonico at Naples.
To a Painter.
To B. R. Haydon.
Upon a Portrait.
Upon seeing a Coloured Drawing of the Bird of
   Paradise in an Album.
Wright, C.   Looking at Pictures.
Wyatt, S.   In Spayn.
Zagajewski.   Canvas.
Degas: *The Milliner's Shop.*
Dutch Painters.
For Gabriela Münter.
Vermeer's Little Girl.
Zukofsky, L.   4 Other Countries.

Paleontology and Paleontologists
Ignatow, D.   Debate, The.
Rexroth, K.   Fact ("Chirotherium tracks occur").
See also **Dinosaurs; Evolution; Extinction; Fossils**

Palestine
Hardy, T.   Jezreel.
Milosz, C.   Caesarea.
Whittier.   Holy Land, The.
Palestine.
See also **Israel**

Palm Sunday
Chesterton.   Donkey, The.
Clampitt.   Palm Sunday.
Dugan, A.   Sailing to Jerusalem.
Muldoon, P.   Palm Sunday.
Rossetti, C.   Palm Sunday.
Zagajewski.   Palm Sunday.

Palm Trees
Campion, T.   Thus I Resolve.
Crane, H.   Royal Palm.
Graves, R.   Song: The Palm Tree.
Maritain.   Recipe.
Merwin.   Palm.
Mistral, G.   Coconut Palms, The.
Stevens, W.   Of Mere Being.
Whittier.   Palm-Tree, The.

Pan (god)
Browning, E.   Dead Pan, The.
Flush or Faunus.
Musical Instrument, A.
Psyche and Pan.
Browning, R.   Pan and Luna.
Byron, G.   Aristomenes.
Campion, T.   To his sweet Lute *Apollo* sung the
   motions of the Spheares.
Codrescu.   Hymn of Pan the Flower, The.
Cummings, E. E.   Of evident invisibles /
   exquisite the hovering.
"Dario."   Prayer for the Dead (To Verlaine).
De la Mare.   Sorcery.
They Told Me.
Emerson, R.   Patient Pan / Drunken with nectar,
   The.
Frost, R.   Pan with Us.
Gunn, T.   Rites of Passage.
Gurney, I.   What Was Dear.
Kipling, R.   Pan in Vermont.
Marvell.   Clorinda and Damon.
Riley, J.   Glimpse of Pan, A.
Great God Pan, The.
Pan.
Pipes of Pan, The.
Shelley, P.   Hymn of Pan.
Wilde, O.   Pan: Double Villanelle.

Panama
Bierce.   Crime of 1903, The.

Pancakes
Rossetti, C.   Mix a Pancake.

Pandora
Rossetti, D.   Pandora.
Zaturenska.   Casket of Pandora, The.

Pansies
Clampitt.   Field Pansy, The.
Dickinson, E.   That a pansy is transitive.
Herrick.   How Pansies or Hearts-Ease Came
   First.
To Pansies.
Riley, J.   Pansies.

Pantheism and Pantheists
Emerson, R.   You shall not love me for what
   daily spends.
Wilde, O.   Panthea.
Wordsworth, W.   It is a beauteous evening, calm
   and free.

Panthers
Muldoon, P.   Panther, The.
Nash, O.   Panther, The.
Patchen.   Black Panther and the Little Boy, The.

Papacy
Carver, R.   For the Record.
Ciardi, J.   Apartment with a View, An.
García Lorca.   Cry to Rome.
Komunyakaa.   Quality of Light, A.
Michelangelo Buonarroti.   Chalices hammered
   into sword and helmet!
Petrarch.   Foul Babylon has overstepped the
   mark.
Fountain of sorrow, dwelling-place of wrath.
May heaven's anger blaze down on your head!

Scott, S.   Gray Brother, The.
Whittier.   To Pius IX.
Wilde, O.   Easter Day.
Italia.
Rome Unvisited.
See also **Catholicism and Catholics**

Paperclips
Laughlin, J.   Her Reply.
I Love to See You.

Paperweights
Merrill, J.   Prism.

Parachuting and Parachutists
Ciardi, J.   Pilot in the Jungle, The.
Ramanujan.   Fall, The.
Wilner, E.   Bailing Out—A Poem for the 1970s.
Landing.
See also **Sky Diving and Sky Divers**

Parades
Clampitt.   Halloween Parade, The.
Ginsberg, A.   After the Big Parade.
Hughes, L.   Parade.
Lindsay, N.   Village Improvement Parade, The.
Montale.   Parades of 1949, The.
Nash, O.   It's a Grand Parade It Will Be,
   Modern Design.
Olson, C.   Memorial Day.
This Year.
Riley, J.   Circus-Day Parade, The.
Circus Parade, The.
Rimbaud, A.   Parade.
Ritsos.   Evening Procession.
Schuyler, J.   Scarlet Tanager.
Updike.   How to Be Uncle Sam.
Whitman, W.   Boston Ballad [1854], A.
Broadway Pageant, A.
See also **Marching and Marches**

Paradise
Atwood.   Galiano Coast: Four Entrances.
Berry, W.   Aristocracy, The.
Fall.
Browning, R.   Variation on Lines of Landor, A.
Byron, G.   Impromptu.
Cavafy.   Nichori.
Clifton, L.   Garden of Delight, The.
Report from the angel of eden.
De la Mare.   Dwelling-Place, The.
Three Strangers, The.
Dickinson, E.   I lift the lid to my box of
   Phantoms.
I never felt at Home—Below.
Of Paradise' existence.
Paradise is of the option.
Paradise is that old mansion.
Road to Paradise is plain, The.
Writing is brief and fleeting.
You are most illustrious.
Eberhart, R.   Adam Cast Forth.
Dream, The.
Emerson, R.   Dear Ellen, many a golden year.
Goethe.   Mignon's Song.
Graves, R.   Conjunction.
East Wind, An.
Gold Cloud.
Green Castle, The.
Hidden Garden, The.
Nothing Now Astonishes.
True Joy.
Herbert, G.   Paradise.
Herrick.   New Charon, The.
Paradise.
Hölderlin.   And you Diotima who walk humbly
   among the living.
Ignatow, D.   I've Wanted to Write My Way into
   Paradise.
Kipling, R.   L'Envoi.
Levertov.   City Psalm.
Kingdoms of Heaven.
Levi, P.   Another Monday.
Merton.   Psalm, A: "When psalms surprise me
   with their music."
What is beyond reproof / Is done in this
   building.
Mistral, G.   Paradise.
Orr, G.   Paradise Lightning Dazzle.
Parra, N.   Paradise of Squares.

Pound, E.   Rosa Sempiterna.
Rexroth, K.   Thin Edge of Your Pride, The.
Riley, J.   Dreamer, Say.
Rossetti, C.   Afterthought, An.
  As Cold Water to a Thirsty Soul, So Is Good
    News from a Far Country.
  Beautiful for Situation.
  Earth has clear call of daily bells, / A chancel-
    vault of gloom and star.
  Easter Tuesday.
  Eye Hath Not Seen.
  Flowers Appear on the Earth, The.
  I Will Lift Up Mine Eyes unto the Hills.
  Only Believe.
  Paradise: in a Symbol.
  Rivals.
  So Great a Cloud of Witnesses.
  That Eden of earth's sunrise cannot vie.
  When wickedness is broken as a tree / Paradise
    comes to light, ah holy land!
  Where never tempest heaveth, / Nor sorrow
    grieveth.
Sarton, M.   Mediterranean.
Seifert.   Once only did I see / the sun so blood-
  red.
Shapiro, K.   California Petrarchan.
Swenson, M.   Day Like Rousseau's *Dream*, A.
Very.   Nature ("Bubbling brook doth leap when
  I come by, The")
Whittier.   Lay of Old Time, A.
Wright, C.   May Journal.
Wright, J.   Father.
  Quest, The.
Yeats.   Running to Paradise.

See also **Heaven**

Paradise Lost
Marvell.   On Mr Milton's "Paradise Lost."
Sandburg, C.   To the Ghost of John Milton.

See also **Milton, John**

Paradoxes
Ashbery, J.   Paradoxes and Oxymorons.
Bukowski.   Genius of the Crowd, The.
Creeley.   A.
  But.
  Gemini.
  Here ("Here is").
  Look.
  No.
  Paradox, The.
  Sanine to Leda.
  Shame, The.
  Time ("Moment to / moment the").
  Xmas Poem: Bolinas.
Cullen, C.   More than a Fool's Song.
Eberhart, R.   Hardy Perennial.
  Poet, The.
  Santa Claus in Oaxaca.
Gallagher, T.   Not There.
Graves, R.   Logic.
Hardy, T.   Paradox.
Warren, R.   Paradox.
Zukofsky, L.   And Without.
  H.T.

Parakeets
MacNeice.   Budgie.
Stevens, W.   Bird with the Coppery, Keen
  Claws, The.

Paralysis
Carver, R.   Circulation.
Clampitt.   Hippocrene.
Creeley.   Tiger, The.
Dickinson, E.   I've dropped my Brain—My Soul
  is numb.
Hughes, T.   Green Wolf, The.
McGrath, T.   Something Is Dying Here.
Meredith, W.   Freezing.
Ramanujan.   Fog.
Shapiro, K.   Figurehead, The. .

Paranoia
Carver, R.   Caution.
  Cheers.
  Conspirators.
  Man Outside, The.
  Not Far from Here.
  Where the Groceries Went.

Creeley.   Dishonest Mailmen, The.
Dugan, A.   Untitled Poem: "Consternation in
  household!"
Laughlin, J.   Shard of History, A.
Nash, O.   Ms. Found in a Quagmire.
Sexton.   Noon Walk on the Asylum Lawn.
Williams, C. K.   Soliliquies.

Pardons and Pardoners
Browning, R.   Martin Relph.
Creeley.   Song: "God give you pardon from
  gratitude."
Herrick.   Gods Pardon.
  Pardon.
  Pardons.
Rossetti, C.   Dying Man to His Betrothed, The.
Vallejo.   Our Daily Bread.
Wheatley, P.   To the Hon.ble Commodore Hood
  on His Pardoning a Deserter.

Parenthood
Amichai [*or* Amikhai].   Family.
  I Was the Moon.
  My son was born in Asuta hopital and since
    then.
  On the Day My Daughter Was Born Not a
    Single Person Died.
Berry, W.   To My Children, Fearing for Them.
  Way of Pain, The.
Borges.   Things That Might Have Been.
Broumas, O.   Demeter.
Burns, R.   Poet's Welcome to His Love-
  Begotten Daughter [the First Instance that
  Entitled Him to the Venerable Appellation of
  Father], A.
Ciardi, J.   Boy.
  Craft.
  Echoes.
  Encounter.
  For My Son John.
  For Myra out of the Album.
  Lines for Myra to Grow To.
  Poem for Benn's Graduation from High School,
    A.
  Two Hours.
  Two Poems for Benn.
Coleridge, S.   Sonnet to a Friend Who Asked
  How I Felt When the Nurse First Presented My
  Infant to Me.
Corbett, W.   Marni's Birthday.
Creeley.   Human Song.
  If You're Going to Have One.
  Name, The.
  Time ("Out window roof's slope").
Davie, D.   Fatherhood.
  Seeing through Me.
Dove, R.   Daystar.
Eberhart, R.   To Evan.
Jonson, B.   On My First Daughter.
Kinnell.   After Making Love We Hear
  Footsteps.
  Olive Wood Fire, The.
  Under the Maud Moon.
Kizer, C.   Children.
  Parents' Pantoum.
Kumin, M.   Bangkok Gang, The.
  Changing the Children.
  Family Reunion.
  Grandchild.
Levertov.   During a Son's Dangerous Illness.
Lorde.   What My Child Learns of the Sea.
Mahon.   Yaddo Letter, The.
Meredith, G.   I have a hope that's like a star.
  To a Nightingale.
Meredith, W.   Parents.
Milton.   To My Father.
Nash, O.   Posies from a Second Childhood, or,
  Hark How Gaffer Do Chaffer.
  Preface to the Past.
Orr, G.   Father's Song.
  My Father's Voice.
  Voyages, The.
Plath.   Morning Song.
Prunty.   Good-bye.
Ramanujan.   This Pair.
Rich, A.   Afterwake, The.
  Night-Pieces: For a Child.
Riley, J.   At Last.

  Being His Mother.
  Lost Kiss, The.
Rilke.   Lesson, The.
Rossetti, C.   Lullaby: "Love me,—I love you /
  Love me, my baby."
  Three little children / On the wide wide earth.
Shelley, P.   To William Shelley.
Stafford, W.   Any Time.
  At Our House.
  For a Lost Child.
  Memorial: Son Bret, A.
Sze.   Murmur, The.
Warren, R.   Midnight Outcry.
Yeats.   Prayer for My Daughter, A.

Parents
Amichai [*or* Amikhai].   Aged Parents, The.
  And the Migration of My Parents.
  Autobiography, 1952.
  Autumn is Near and the Memory of My Parents.
  Parents Left the Child, The.
  Yom Kippur.
  You Can Rely on Him.
Auden.   Through the Looking-Glass.
Berryman.   Sympathy, a Welcome, A.
Bly, R.   For My Son Noah, Ten Years Old.
Broumas, O.   Offertory.
Bukowski   Dear Pa and Ma.
Burns, R.   Altered from an Old English Song.
Carver, R.   Balsa Wood.
  Energy.
Ciardi, J.   Bridal Photo, 1906.
Corbett, W.   First of September.
Creeley.   If You're Going to Have One.
Cullen, C.   Fruit of the Flower.
Cummings, E. E.   If there are any heavens my
  mother will (all by herself) have.
Davie, D.   Liverpool Epistle, A.
Dunbar, P.   Dilettante, The: A Modern Type.
Ferlinghetti, L.   Lost Parents.
Glück, L.   Adult Grief.
Hall, D.   My Son, My Executioner.
Herrick.   God to Be First Served.
  Primitiæ to Parents, The.
Housman.   Culprit, The.
Hughes, L.   Second Generation: New York.
Ignatow, D.   Prologue: "Mine was the life
  planned to go wrong."
  Sky.
  Wait.
  White Ceiling, The.
  White-Haired, I Walk in on My Parents.
Jacobsen, J.   Three Children, The.
Jarrell, R.   Player Piano, The.
  Quilt-Pattern, A.
Jeffers, R.   Birthday (Autobiography).
Komunyakaa.   My Father's Love Letters [*or*
  Loveletters].
Kunitz, S.   Tutored Child, The.
  Unquiet Ones, The.
Larkin, P.   This Be the Verse.
Laughlin, J.   Upstate New York.
Lowell, R.   Hard Way, The.
  Mother and Father 1.
  Mother and Father 2.
  Returning.
  To Daddy.
MacDiarmid, H.   Two Parents, The.
Meredith, G.   First-Born, The.
Merrill, J.   Broken Home, The.
  Childlessness.
Merwin.   Apparitions.
  Sun and Rain.
Muldoon, P.   Mixed Marriage, The.
  October 1950.
Nash, O.   Child's Guide to Parents, A.
  Father, Dear Father, Go Jump in the Lake, or,
    You're Costlier than You Think.
  Fragonard.
  Good Riddance, but Now What?
  Judgment Day.
  "My Child Is Phlegmatic..."—Anxious Parent.
  Parent, The.
  Some of My Best Friends Are Children.
Olson, C.   One Night Ma / Lay with Pa.
Oppen.   Sara in Her Father's Arms.
Prunty.   Breaking Child, The.

Depression, the War, and Gypsy Rose Lee, The.
Name, The.
Ramanujan. This Pair.
Riley, J. Her Poet-Brother.
Intellectual Limitations.
Parent Reprimanded, A.
Rilke. Orphan Song.
Rossetti, C. My baby has a father and a mother.
Why did baby die.
Your brother has a falcon.
Rukeyser, M. More Clues.
Oh, he *is* sweet. I do love him sometimes.
Sandburg, C. Curse of a Rich Polish Peasant on
His Sister Who Ran Away with a Wild Man.
Sexton. Cripples and Other Stories.
Doors, Doors, Doors.
Money Swing, The.
Shelley, P. To William Shelley.
Smith, S. Maximilian Esterhazy.
Spender, S. Nocturne: "Their six-weeks-old
daughter lies."
Stafford, W. 108 East 19th.
Biography.
Story That Could Be True, A.
Third Street.
Vocation.
Swenson, M. I Look at My Hand.
Van Duyn. Photographs.
Relationships.
Zukofsky, L. Air.

Paris, France
Apollinaire. Zone.
Aragon. Red Front, The.
Baudelaire. First Light.
Swan, The.
Beckett, S. Arènes de Lutèce.
Rue de Vaugirard.
Sanies II.
Bishop, E. Paris, 7 A.M.
Borges. Paris, 1856.
Brodsky, J. Twenty Sonnets to Mary Queen of
Scots.
Carrera Andrade. Man from Ecuador beneath
the Eiffel Tower, A.
Clampitt. Scaffold, A.
Cummings, E. E. Along the brittle treacherous
bright streets.
Inthe,exquisite; / morning sure lyHer eye s
exactly sit,ata little roundtable.
It is winter a moon in the afternoon.
Moon-lit snow is falling like strange candy into
the big eyes of the, The.
Paris,*,is April sunset completely utters.
Paris,thou art not.
Perhaps it was Myself sits down in this chair.
There were two chairs,in fact.
Rain Is a Handsome Animal, The.
Sometime,perhaps in Paris we will.
Through the tasteless minute efficient room.
Two X.
Workingman with hand so hairy-sturdy.
Dugan, A. Advertising in Paris.
To Paris: Fear of the Heights Reached.
Eliot, T. S. Fourth Caprice in Montparnasse.
Ferlinghetti, L. In Paris in a loud dark winter.
Paris Transformations.
Plan du Centre de Paris à Vol D'Oiseau.
Returning to Paris with Pissarro.
Hacker, M. Two Cities.
Hughes, L. Cubes.
Jazz Band in a Parisian Cabaret.
Montmartre.
Parisian Beggar Woman.
Komunyakaa. 1938.
Laughlin, J. Before I Die.
Unsatisfactory Dream, The.
Logan, J. Bridge of Change, The.
MacLeish. Years of the Dog.
McGrath, T. Migration of Cities, The.
Once We Meant It.
Merrill, J. Days of 1971.
Millay, E. Armenonville.
To S. V. B.—June 15, 1940.
Milosz, C. And the City Stood in Its Brightness.
Ballad of Levallois.
Bypassing Rue Descartes.

Esse.
Hooks of a Corset, The.
Lecture, A.
Muldoon, P. Paris.
Nash, O. Absence Makes the Heart Grow Heart
Trouble.
O'Hara, F. Petit Poème en Prose.
Oppen. Eros.
Historic Pun.
Pound, E. In a Station of the Metro.
Ransom, J. Amphibious Crocodile.
Rimbaud, A. Hands of Jeanne-Marie, The.
Paris War-Cry.
Parisian Orgy, or Paris Filling Up Again.
Rossetti, D. Place de la Bastille, Paris.
Seifert. November 1918.
Sexton. Walking in Paris.
Stock, R. Louis XI.
Szymborska, W. Clochard.
Tomlinson, C. Paris in Sixty-Nine.
Weiss, T. Ten Little Rembrandts.
Whitman, W. Bravo, Paris Exposition!
Wilbur, R. Place Pigalle.
Wilde, O. Le Jardin des Tuileries.
Williams, C. K. Le Petit Salvié.
Zagajewski. Good Friday in the Tunnels of the
Métro.
Holy Saturday in Paris.
Referendum.
Square D'Orléans.

Parker, Charlie
Creeley. Bird, the Bird, the Bird, The.
Chasing the Bird.
Dubie. Somebody'll Hav' to Shoot Ya Down.
Komunyakaa. Testimony.

Parks
Borges. Elegy for a Park.
Ciardi, J. Morning in the Park.
Creeley. Park ("Why did that man").
Cummings, E. E. Dim / i / nu / tiv / e this park
is e.
Gunn, T. Back to Life.
Hamill, S. From the Bunkers.
Hughes, L. Kid in the Park.
Park Benching.
Lawrence, D. H. Hyde Park at Night, before the
War.
Lowell, R. Public Garden, The.
MacNeice. Park, The.
Millay, E. Armenonville.
Montale. In the Park.
In the Park at Caserta.
Nemerov. Statues in the Public Gardens, The.
Niedecker. Park / "a Darling Walk / for the
Mind," The.
Rexroth, K. Adonis in Summer.
Rimbaud, A. Ruts.
Rukeyser, M. Chapultepec Park / I.
Smith, S. Cousin, The.
November.
Stevens, W. Vacancy in the Park.
Swenson, M. City Garden in April, A.
Thomas, D. Hunchback in the Park, The.
Tomlinson, C. In a Brooklyn Park.
In Verdi Square.
Square, The.
Tu Fu. Lo Yu Park.
Updike. Sunday in Boston.
Williams, C. K. Park, The.
Williams, W. Franklin Square.

Parliament, Great Britain
Byron, G. New Song to the Tune of "Whare
Hae Ye Been a' Day, My Boy Tammy O?
Courting O' a Young Thing, Just Come Frae
Her Mammie O?"
Would You Go to the House by the True Gate.
Coleridge, S. Parliamentary Oscillators.
Fenton, J. Lullaby for a Summer Recess.
Herrick. Parliament of Roses to Julia, The.
Upon Case.
Hughes, L. Crow Goes, Too.
Hughes, T. Wilfred Owen's Photographs.
Jonson, B. Panegyre, on the Happy Entrance of
James, Our Sovereign, to His First High
Session of Parliament in This Kingdom, the 19
of March, 1603, A.

To the Parliament.
To William, Lord Mounteagle.
Kipling, R. Declaration of London, The.
Lawrence, D. H. Daddy-Do-Nothing.
Sheridan, T. Joshua Battus's Spepeech to the
Paparliament.
Yeats. Ghost of Roger Casement, The.

Parmigianino
Ashbery, J. Self-Portrait in a Convex Mirror.

Parnell, Charles Stewart
Kipling, R. Cleared.
Yeats. Come Gather Round Me Parnellites.
Parnell.
Parnell's Funeral.

Parnell, Thomas
Pope, A. Epistle to Robert Earl of Oxford and
Earl Mortimer.

Parodies
Campion, T. In Barnum.
Cummings, E. E. Out of the pants which cover
me.
Koch, K. Variations on a Theme by William
Carlos Williams.
Meredith, G. It's many a penny you'll pay to
go.
Manfred.
Parody of Alfred Austin.
Yes, we'll pic-nic in the woods.

Parrots
Bourne, V. Parrot, The.
Dove, R. Parsley.
Han-shan. Parrots live in western lands.
Jacobsen, J. Wild Parrots of Blood Bay, The.
Laughlin, J. No Comparison.
Lux. Small Tin Parrot Pin, A.
Mistral, G. Parrot, The.
Rossetti, C. I have a Poll parrot, / And Poll is
my doll.
Sarton, M. Parrot, A.
Smith, S. Parrot.
Who Killed Lawless Lean?
Whittier. Common Question, The.
Wordsworth, W. Contrast; the Parrot and the
Wren, The.
Wright, J. For the Marsh's Birthday.

Parsifal
See **Arthurian Legend**

Parthenon
Hall, D. Columns of the Parthenon, The.
Jacobsen, J. Absence of Slaves, An.
Keats. On Seeing the Elgin Marbles.
Melville, H. Apparition, The.
Parthenon, The.
Patchen. Saturday Night in the Parthenon.

Parties
Auden. At the Party.
Love Feast, The.
Berrigan, T. Dinner at George & Katie
Schneeman's.
Berryman. Drunks.
Meeting.
Broumas, O. Five Interior Landscapes.
Bukowski. Good Time Girl.
Social.
Burns, R. Extempore Reply to an Invitation.
Fête Champetre, The.
To Captain G———, on Being Asked Why I
Was Not to Be of the Party with Him and His
Brother K-nm-rė at Syme's.
De la Mare. Feckless Dinner-Party, The.
Dickey, W. Stella Dallas.
Dugan, A. On a Party.
Provincetown *Totentanz*.
Dunbar, P. Party, The.
Eliot, T. S. Mr. Apollinax.
Ginsberg, A. First Party at Ken Kesey's with
Hell's Angels.
In Society.
Glück, L. Portrait of the Queen in Tears.
Gunn, T. Another All-Night Party.
Punch Rubicundus.
Hardy, T. At a Fashionable Dinner.
Harvest-Supper, The.
In the Marquee.
Lament: "How she would have loved."

Queen Caroline to Her Guests.
Hughes, L. Rent-Party Shout: For a Lady Dancer.
Jacobsen, J. Birthday Party, The.
Kizer, C. Arthur's Party.
Larkin, P. Dance, The.
Party Politics.
Laughlin, J. Party on Olympus, The.
Meng Hao Jan. After the Party.
Meredith, G. Friar uxorious!
Tuck, my treasure! Tuck, my pleasure!
Merwin. Fountain, The.
Muldoon, P. Bechbretha.
Nash, O. Banquet, The.
Children's Party.
Drusilla.
I Know You'll Like Them.
Life of the Party, The.
Mr. Peachey's Predicament or No Mot Parades.
Next!
One Night in Oz.
Party, The.
Party Next Door, The.
There's Always an Ubblebub.
What's in a Name? Here's What's in a Name, or, I Wonder What Became of John and Mary.
Niedecker. Now go to the party.
O'Hara, F. For Grace, after a Party.
Joe's Jacket.
Parker, D. Parties; A Hymn of Hate.
Plath. Yaddo: The Grand Manor.
Rukeyser, M. Charm for Cantinflas, A.
Three Sides of a Coin.
Sandburg, C. Picnic Boat.
Stafford, W. At the Chairman's Housewarming.
For Our Party Last Night.
Stock, R. Banquet, The.
Tu Fu. Lo Yu Park.
Updike. Party Knee.
Thoughts while Driving Home.
Warren, R. After the Dinner Party.
Cocktail Party.
Wilbur, R. Leaving.
Williams, C. K. Flight.
On the Other Hand.
Williams, M. Office Party, The.
Williams, W. Delicacies, The.
Wright, J. To a Hostess Saying Goodnight.
Yeats. Mountain Tomb, The.

Parting
Amichai [or Amikhai]. Balled in the Streets of Buenos Aires.
On the Day I Left.
Smell of Gasoline Ascends in My Nose, The.
Threading.
To Bake the Bread of Yearning.
Angelou. Gamut, The.
Lie, The.
Prelude to a Parting.
Atwood. Departure from the Bush.
Newsreel: Man and Firing Squad.
Auden. Witnesses, The.
Beckett, S. Da Tagte Es.
Berryman. Old Man Goes South Again Alone.
Parting as Descent.
Bierce. To Nanine.
Blok. Introduction to the Second Book of Poems.
Bogan, L. Fifteenth Farewell.
Borges. 1964.
Parting.
Bradstreet, A. Before the Birth of One of Her Children.
Brontë, E. F. de Samara to A. G. A.
Broumas, O. Song / for Sanna.
Browning, E. Night and the Merry Man.
Parting Lovers.
Valediction, A: "God be with thee, my beloved,—God be with thee!"
Browning, R. Parting at Morning.
Rosny.
Burns, R. Can You Leave Me Thus, My Katy.
Clarinda.
Farewell, The: "Farewell, old Scotia's bleak domains."

Gloomy December.
Highland Lassie O.
It Was A' for Our Rightfu' King.
Northern Lass, The.
On a Scotch Bard Gone to the West Indies.
Red, Red Rose, A.
Silver Tassie, The.
Song: "Behold the hour, the boat arrive."
Wrote on the Blank Leaf of a Copy of My First Edition, Which I Sent to an Old Sweetheart, Then Married.
Byron, G. Fare Thee Well.
Lines to Mr Hodgson.
Love's Last Adieu.
Maid of Athens, Ere We Part.
On Parting.
On the Quotation "And My True Faith Can Alter Never, Though Thou Art Gone Perhaps Forever."
Stanzas for Music.
Stanzas to a Lady on Leaving England.
Stanzas to Augusta.
To Caroline.
To Emma.
To Florence.
Well! Thou Art Happy.
When We Two Parted.
Campion, T. Kisses.
Tarry sweete love.
Campion, T. et al. Sweete, come againe.
Carew, T. Parting, Celia Weeps.
Pastoral[l] Dialogue, A.
To His Mistress.
To My Mistress[e] in My Absence.
Carver, R. Five o'Clock in the Morning.
No Need.
Cary, T. On His Mistress[e] Going to Sea.
Cassian. Tirade for the Next-to-Last Act.
Clough. That out of sight is out of mind.
Coleridge, S. Ode to the Rain, An.
On My Joyful Departure from the City of Cologne.
Cowper, W. On Her Endeavoring to Conceal Her Grief at Parting.
Creeley. Breaking Up Is Hard to Do.
Just Friends.
Cullen, C. At a Parting.
If You Should Go.
Two Who Crossed a Line.
Two Who Crossed a Line (She Crosses).
Cummings, E. E. Because / you go away i give roses who.
Goodby Betty, don't remember me.
T.A.M.
This fear is no longer dear. You are not going to America and.
Davie, D. Emigrant, to the Receding Shore.
Fare Thee Well.
Seeing Her Leave.
De la Mare. Adieu.
Good-bye.
Dickinson, E. Auctioneer of Parting, The.
Frigid and sweet Her parting Face.
I thought to shun the Loneliness.
Meeting is well worth parting.
My life closed twice before its close.
Parting is one of the exactions.
Parting with Thee reluctantly.
Some say goodnight—at night.
'Tis customary as we part.
Donne. Song: "Sweetest love, I do not go[e]."
Valediction: Forbidding Mourning, A.
Dove, R. Then Came Flowers.
Thomas at the Wheel.
Dunbar, P. Farewell Song.
My Love Irene.
Parted.
Premonition.
Emerson, R. Discontented Poet: A Masque, The.
Ferlinghetti, L. At the Gare Bruxelles-Midi.
New York—Albany.
Gallagher, T. All Day the Light Is Clear.
Calm, The.
Words Written near a Candle.
Ginsberg, A. Lover's Garden, A.

Glück, L. Aubade: "Today above the gull's call."
Departure.
Here Are My Black Clothes.
Letters, The.
Graves, R. As a Less than Robber.
Hills of May, The.
I Will Write.
In the Vestry.
Restless Ghost, A.
That Was the Night.
"H. D." Chance.
Orestes Theme.
Hacker, M. For K.J., Leaving and Coming Back.
Last Time, The.
Late August.
Living in the Moment.
Somewhere in a Turrent.
Han-shan. What's this crying for.
HaNagid. If You Leave a Long-Loved Friend.
On Fleeing His City.
Hardy, T. After Schiller.
At the Wicket-Gate.
Cross-Currents.
Days to Recollect.
Expostulation, An.
Going, The.
In the Vaulted Way.
Leaving, A.
Opportunity, The.
Parting-Scene, A.
Saying Good-bye.
We Say We Shall Not Meet.
Hayden, R. Ballad of Sue Ellen Westerfield, The.
Road in Kentucky, A.
Heaney, S. Good-night.
Herrick. Dialogue betwixt Himselfe and Mistresse Eliza: Wheeler, under the Name of Amarillis, A.
Farewell, The: "Sweetest Loue since wee must part."
His Parting from Mistress Dorothy Keneday.
Hymne to Sir Clipseby Crew, A.
Lovers How They Come and Part.
Parting Verse, or Charge to His Supposed Wife When He Travelled, The.
Parting Verse, the Feast There Ended, The.
Song upon Silvia, A.
To His Dying Brother, Master William Herrick.
To Larr [or Lar].
Upon Parting.
Housman. Shake hands, we shall never be friends, all's over.
White in the moon the long road lies.
Hughes, L. Farewell, A.
Jackson, L. To a Loveless Lover.
Jacobsen, J. It Is the Season.
Jarrell, R. Good-bye, Wendover; Good-bye, Mountain Home.
Moving.
Jonson, B. Elegy, An: "Since you must go, and I must bid farewell."
To William Roe ("Roe (and my joy to name) th'art now, to go").
Keats. On Leaving Some Friends at an Early Hour.
See, the Ship in the Bay Is Riding.
Think Not of It, Sweet One, So.
Kinsella, T. Rituals of Departure.
Kipling, R. Appeal, The.
Lovers' Litany, The.
Parting of the Columns, The.
Roman Centurion's Song, The.
Larkin, P. Love, We Must Part Now.
Lawrence, D. H. Butterfly.
Drama, A.
End, The.
Going Back.
Last Words to Muriel.
Mutilation.
Seven Seals.
Winter's Tale, A.
Levertov. September 1961.
She and the Muse.

Levi, P.   Leavetaking.
Li Po.   In the Wineshop of Chinling.
  Taking Leave of a Friend.
Logue, C.   Air for the Witness of a Departure.
Lorde.   Movement Song.
  To the Girl Who Lives in a Tree.
MacLeish.   Ever Since.
Marvell.   Daphnis and Chloe.
McGrath, T.   Fresco: Departure for an
  Imperialist War.
  Get Out of Town.
  When We Say Goodbye.
Meredith, G.   Jack & Harry.
  Kiss, and a clasp, and an eye to eye, A.
  Schubert's "Farewell."
  To-morrow I am going.
  We sat beneath the humming pines.
Merrill, J.   Renewal, A.
Merwin.   As by Water.
  Falcons, The.
  Going from the Green Window.
  Plane.
  Reunion.
  Truth about Departures, The.
Millay, E.   To a Friend Estranged from Me.
  To S. M.
Montale.   To Liuba, Leaving.
Muldoon, P.   Avenue, The.
  Holy Thursday.
  Something of a Departure.
Nash, O.   Lament on the Eve of Parting.
  Song for Pier Something or Other.
Nemerov.   Going Away.
Niedecker.   On a Row of Cabins / Next My
  Home.
O'Hara, F.   Now That I Am in Madrid and Can
  Think.
Oliver, M.   Journey, The.
Owen, W.   One Remains, The.
Pagis.   Ready for Parting.
Parker, D.   Finis.
  I Know I Have Been Happiest.
  Recurrence.
  Renunciation.
  Rondeau Redoublé.
  Surprise.
  They Part.
Petrarch.   Look at that hill, my sad heart, where
  we stood.
  She used to come and comfort me in sleep.
  So feeble is the thread that doth the burden stay.
Plath.   Departure.
Prunty.   Good-bye.
Ramanujan.   Instead of a Farewell.
  Still Another for Mother.
Rexroth, K.   Sharp in My Heart.
Rich, A.   Continuum.
  Parting: I, The.
  Parting: II, The.
  Platform, The.
  Stepping Backward.
  Valediction Forbidding Mourning, A.
Riley, J.   Apart.
  Being His Mother.
  End, An.
  Good-By, A.
  Lullaby: "Maple strews the embers of its leaves,
  The."
  Onward Trail, The.
  Song of Parting.
  Test, A.
Rilke.   Departure.
  Goodbyes, Still More Goodbyes.
Rimbaud, A.   Departure.
Robinson, E.   Afterthoughts.
  Clinging Vine, The.
  John Gorham.
  Unforgiven, The.
Rossetti, C.   Echo from Willowwood, An.
  I said "All's over"—& I made my.
  Light Love.
  Love Lies Bleeding.
  One Foot on Sea, and One on Shore.
  Twilight Night.
  Wife to Husband.
Rukeyser, M.   Lat. 10 Degrees North, Long. 45

Degrees West.
  Leaving New York, I looked back fourteen
  times.
Sadi [or Saadi or Sa'di].   I said, "I do not fear
  the."
Seifert.   Parting.
Shelley, P.   Buona Notte.
  Good-Night.
  Lines: "We meet not as we parted."
  On Fanny Godwin.
Sidney, S.   Oft Have I Mused.
Smith, S.   In My Dreams.
Snyder, G.   Saying Farewell at the Monastery
  after Hearing the Old Master Lecture on
  "Return to the Source."
Stevens, W.   Farewell to Florida.
Stockton, A.   Tears of Friendship, The. Elegy
  the 4th.
  To a Friend Going to Sea.
  To Mr Stockton on His Departure from America
  to England, 1769.
Suckling, S.   To My Lady E.C. at Her Going
  Out of England.
Swenson, M.   Feel Me.
Swinburne.   Before Parting.
  In the Orchard.
  Leave-taking, A.
  Triumph of Time, The.
Szymborska, W.   Parting with a View.
Tate, A.   Edges.
Thoreau.   Farewell.
Tomlinson, C.   Departure.
Tsvetayeva [or Tsvetaeva].   Seeing off the
  beloved ones, I.
Updike.   Farewell to the Shopping District of
  Antibes.
  Goodbye, Göteborg.
Van Duyn.   Advice to a God.
  Fear of Flying, The.
  Peony Stalks.
Walker, A.   Even as I Hold You.
  He Said.
  Instant of Our Parting, The.
  Mornings / of an impossible love.
Warren, R.   Departure.
  End of Season.
  Goodbye.
  To a Friend Parting.
Whitman, W.   After the Supper and Talk.
  Good-Bye My Fancy.
  Good-Bye, My Fancy!
  Now Finalè to the Shore.
  Now Lift Me Close.
  Once I Pass'd through a Populous City.
  Sail Out for Good, Eidólon Yacht!
  So Long!
  To the Reader at Parting.
  What Think You I Take My Pen in Hand?
Whittier.   Godspeed.
  Gone.
  Lament, A: "Circle is broken, one seat is
  forsaken, The."
  Lines on Leaving Appledore.
Wilbur, R.   Leaving.
Wilde, O.   Sweet I blame you not for mine the
  fault was, had I not been made of common
  clay.
Williams, M.   E-mail.
Williams, T.   Why do I want to go away?
Williams, W.   Translations from the Spanish.
Wordsworth, W.   Cantata, from Metastasio.
  Composed When a Probability Existed of Our
  Being Obliged to Quit Rydal Mount as a
  Residence.
  Departure from the Vale of Grasmere. August,
  1803.
  Extract from the Conclusion of a Poem,
  Composed in Anticipation of Leaving School.
  Farewell Lines.
Wright, C.   Three Poems of Departure.
Wright, J.   Preparing to Leave Home.
Wyatt, S.   Lover's Appeal, The.
  My heart I gave thee not to do it pain.
Yeats.   Falling of the Leaves, The.
  Parting.

Pascal, Blaise
  Baudelaire.   Abyss, The.
  Wright, C.   Blaise Pascal Lip-syncs the Void.
  Zagajewski.   Fire, Fire.
Passion
  Amichai [or Amikhai].   Herbal Tea.
  Precise Woman, A.
  When a man is away from his homeland for a
  long time.
  Apollinaire.   Pretty Redhead, The.
  Arnold, M.   Growing Old.
  Ashbery, J.   As We Know.
  Atwood.   Torture.
  Baudelaire.   Cats.
  Berryman.   Cadenza on Garnette.
  Venice, 182.
  Blok.   As the Ocean Changes Colour.
  Bly, R.   In the Month of May.
  Bogan, L.   Knowledge.
  Second Song.
  Brodsky, J.   Six Years Later.
  Brontë, E.   D.G.C. to J.A.
  I'm standing in the forest now.
  Shall Earth no more inspire thee.
  Song by J. Brenzaida To G.S.
  Song by Julius Brenzaida To G.S.
  To A.G.A.
  Brooks, G.   Flags.
  To Be in Love.
  Broumas, O.   Beauty and the Beast.
  Bitterness.
  Landscape with Leaves and Figure.
  Browning, E.   Vanities.
  Bukowski.   6 Foot Goddess, The.
  Burns, R.   Cares o' love are sweeter far, The.
  O were I on Parnassus hill.
  Song: "Mark yonder pomp of costly fashion."
  To Alexander Cunnignham.
  Byron, G.   Last Words on Greece.
  On Finding a Fan.
  Parisina.
  Remember Him Whom Passion's Power.
  Stanzas to Jessy.
  To a Lady.
  To ———: "But once I dared to lift my eyes."
  To the Sighing Strephon.
  When I Roved a Young Highlander.
  Campion, T.   Beauty, Since You So Much
  Desire.
  Fire, fire, fire, fire!
  I Care Not for These Ladies.
  Mistris [or Mistress] Since You So Much
  Desire.
  When the God of Merrie Love.
  Campion, T. et al.   Reprove not love, though
  fondly thou hast lost.
  Carew, T.   Mediocrity in Love Rejected.
  Prayer to the Wind, A.
  Rapture, A.
  Carruth, H.   Cross My Heart and Hope to Die, It
  Was the Very Same Song Exactly.
  Cavafy.   Before the House.
  Bouquets.
  Dangerous Remarks.
  In the Evening.
  In the House of the Soul.
  In the Street.
  Next Table, The.
  One Night.
  Passing Through.
  Salome.
  To Abide.
  Young Man, a Writer—in His 24th Year, A.
  Chaucer.   Queen Annelida and False Arcite.
  Chuang Tzu.   True Man, The.
  Ciardi, J.   Memoir of a One-Armed Harp
  Teacher.
  On Passion as a Literary Tradition.
  Cino da Pistoia.   Canzone: On the Death of
  Beatrice Portinari.
  Clough.   When panting sighs the bosom fill.
  Coleridge, S.   Alla Sua Amica.
  Improvisatore, The.
  Night-Scene, The.
  Cowper, W.   See Where the Thames, the Purest
  Stream.

Crane, H. Possessions.
Creeley. Circle.
Marriage, A.
Poem for Beginners.
Two Ways of Looking in a Mirror.
Way, The.
Cullen, C. Love's Way.
Nothing Endures.
One Day We Played a Game.
Pity the Deep in Love.
Song in Spite of Myself.
Sonnet: "I have not loved you in the noblest
way."
Cummings, E. E. Now air is air and thing is
thing:no bliss.
This mind made war.
Cunningham, J. Aged Lover Discourses in the
Flat Style, The.
Agnosco Veteris Vestigia Flammae.
Passion.
Ripeness Is All.
Davie, D. Bride of Reason, The.
Jacob's Ladder.
Dickinson, E. Heart is the only workman, The.
Mob within the heart, The.
Said Death to Passion.
Voraciousness of that only gaze, The.
Donne. Canonization, The.
Dunbar, P. Passion and Love.
Duncan, R. Among My Friends.
Beginning of Writing, The.
Circulations of the Song.
Dreamers, The.
I Am a Most Fleshly Man.
Eberhart, R. Emily Dickinson.
Hamlet Father, The.
Sanders Theater.
Somewhere Else.
Villanelle: "Christ is walking in your blood
today."
What Gives.
Emerson, R. I have found a nobler love.
Philosophers are lined with eyes within.
Shun passion, fold the hands of thrift.
Fazio degli Uberti. Canzone: His Portrait of His
Lady, Angiola of Verona.
Ferlinghetti, L. Café Notre Dame.
García Lorca. Elegy: "Like a censer filled with
desire."
Faithless Wife, The.
Minor Song.
Ginsberg, A. Green Automobile, The.
Glück, L. Abishag.
Graves, R. All I Tell You from My Heart.
Blackening Sky.
Deliverance.
Elsewhere.
Friday Night.
In Perspective.
Lion Lover.
Lure of Murder.
Measure of Casualness, A.
Metaphor, The.
Never Such Love.
None the Wiser.
Seldom Yet Now.
Song of Contrariety.
Succubus, The.
Theme of Death, The.
Three Times in Love.
True Evil.
When and Why.
Window Pane, The.
Guillén, J. Love Song to a Morning.
Gunn, T. JVC.
Guyon. Love Pure and Fervent.
"H. D." Fragment 113: "Not honey, / not the
plunder of the bee."
Hafiz [or Hafez]. They say, through patience,
chalk.
Herrick. Caution, A.
Passion.
To Electra.
Hopkins, G. Beginning of the End, The.
Hughes, L. Ma Man.
Minnie Sings Her Blues.

Nonette.
Soledad.
Jacobsen, J. Birds,The.
Jacopo da Lentino. Sonnet: Of His Lady's Face.
Jonson, B. Fair friend, 'tis true, your beauties
move.
Nymph's Passion, A.
Keats. Lines: "Unfelt, unheard, unseen."
Kizer, C. Season of Lovers and Assassins.
Kunitz, S. Lovers Relentlessly.
Laughlin, J. After Rochester (or somebody).
Lawrence, D. H. Birth Night.
Both Sides of the Medal.
Deeper than Love.
Excursion Train.
History.
Kisses in the Train.
Know Deeply, Know Thyself More Deeply.
Last Words to Miriam.
Lightning.
Love-Passage, A.
Love Storm.
Mystery.
No! Mr Lawrence!
Passing Visit to Helen.
Primal Passions, The.
Release.
Twofold.
Worm Turns, The.
Levine, P. At the Fillmore.
For Fran.
Lindsay, N. Caught in a Net.
Queen Mab in the Village.
MacDiarmid, H. As Lovers Do.
MacLeish. Selene Afterwards.
Wild Old Wicked Man, The.
Mallarmé. Afternoon of a Faun.
Negress, A.
Marlowe. Passionate Shepherd to His Love,
The.
McGrath, T. World; The Lovers; Falling Stars,
The.
Medici. Beside a running brook my lady stands.
Meredith, G. Mentor and Pupils.
Remember what a night of storm
Song: "Love within the lover's breast."
Merrill, J. Days of 1964.
Merwin. Bread and Butter.
Michelangelo Buonarroti. All rage, all misery,
all show of strength.
If I'm more alive because love burns and chars
me.
Only with fire can men at forge and flue.
Should the senses' rapturous burning override.
When with a clanking chain a master locks.
Why only at long last, why next to never.
Mistral, G. Bones of the Dead, The.
Montale. Spirit that dispenses, The.
Nemerov. Sunderland.
O'Hara, F. Blocks.
Hôtel Transylvanie.
My Heat.
Savoy.
Second Avenue.
Orlandi, G. ("Friend, I well know that you
know how to polish").
Parker, D. Fair Weather.
Interior.
Promise.
Whistling Girl, The.
Pasolini. Ashes of Gramsci, The.
Reality.
Religion of My Time, The.
Tears of the Excavator, The.
Pessoa. Maritime Ode.
Petrarch. I think and think, and in my thoughts
I feel.
Julius Caesar, when false Ptolemy.
O wasted steps, O wanderings in the mind.
When my passion—that with two glowing
spurs.
Poe. Eulalie—A Song.
Romance.
Tamerlane.
Pope, A. Epistle I, to Sir Richard Temple, Lord
Cobham.

Propertius. When Thou Must Home.
Ransom, J. Address to the Scholars of New
England.
Good Ships.
Spiel of [the] Three Mountebanks.
Rich, A. Paula Becker to Clara Westhoff.
Riley, J. Autumnal Extravaganza, An.
Blind.
Eros.
Her Choice.
Lost Thrill, The.
Song Discordant.
To the Serenader.
Rimbaud, A. What the Poet Is Told on the
Subject of Flowers.
Roethke. Her Words.
Rossetti, C. Bed of Forget-Me-Nots, A.
Subject To Like Passions as We Are.
Rukeyser, M. Flashing Cliff, A.
Rumi. Buoyancy.
Dying, Laughing.
Each Note.
Fragile Vial, The.
Granite and Wineglass.
I want to hold you close like a lute.
In Baghdad, Dreaming of Cairo: In Cairo,
Dreaming of Baghdad.
Someone Digging in the Ground.
Thirsty Fish, A.
We are the mirror as well as the face in it.
When I am with you, we stay up all night.
Salinas, P. Not in Marble Palaces.
Sandburg, C. Aztec Mask.
Evening Sunsets Witness and Pass On, The.
Face.
Fog Numbers.
Head.
High Moments.
Honey and Salt.
Hunger and Cold.
Love beyond Keeping.
Night's Nothings Again.
On the Breakwater.
Population Drifts.
Sarah's Letter to Peter.
Sea Chest.
They Met Young.
Three Shrines.
Under the Harvest Moon.
White Shoulders.
Sarton, M. Evening Music.
Scott, S. Spindle Song, The.
Sexton. Fierceness of Female, The.
Frenzy.
Shelley, P. Lines: "When the lamp is shattered
[or shatter'd]."
Love's Philosophy.
To Constantia.
To the Queen of My Heart.
To ———: "When passion's trance is overpast."
"Shu Ting." Singing Flower, The.
When You Come Past My Window.
Smith, S. Francesca in Winter.
I HATE THIS GIRL.
Spender, S. Ice.
Stampa. Portrait of Her Lover.
Stevens, W. Chaos in Motion and Not in
Motion.
Stockton, A. Lavinia and Amanda, a Pastoral.
Ode—Written 1756, An.
Suckling, S. Song: "Unjust decrees, that do at
once exact."
Swinburne. Anactoria.
Laus Veneris.
Sze. Chance, The.
Tate, J. Last Days of April, The.
Walcott. Return to D'Ennery; Rain.
Whitman, W. Native Moments.
Once I Pass'd through a Populous City.
Wilbur, R. Gifts, The.
Wilde, O. Charmides.
Hélas!
Silentium Amoris.
Williams, C. K. After That.
Wright, J. Idea of the Good, The.
Morning Hymn to a Dark Girl.

Paul.
Quail, The.
Quest, The.
To Harvey, Who Traced the Circulation.
To the Muse.
Wyatt, S.   Avising the bright beams of these fair
  eyes.
From thought to thought, from hill to hill love
  doth me lead.
Lo, what it is to love!
Lover Showeth How He Is Forsaken of Such as
  He Sometime Enjoyed, The.
Perdy [or Perdie or Perdye], I said[e] it [or yt]
  not.
Since love is such that, as ye wot.
Take heed betime, lest ye be spied.
Your looks so often cast.
Yeats.   Indian to His Love, The.

See also Desire; Erotic Love; Lust

Passivity
Berry, W.   Thief, The.
Creeley.   As We Sit.
Cullen, C.   Requiescam.
Glück, L.   Game, The.
Levertov.   Goodbye to Tolerance.
Meredith, G.   Woodland Peace.
Nash, O.   I Never Even Suggested It.
Wilbur, R.   Shame.

Passover
Amichai [or Amikhai].   My Father on Passover
  Eve.
Clampitt.   Seder Night.
Levi, P.   Passover.
Rossetti, D.   Passover in the Holy Family, The.

Past
Ai.   Twenty-Year Marriage.
Amichai [or Amikhai].   Evidence.
  Hirbet Sayid.
  How Much Time.
  I Walked Past a House Where I Lived Once.
  In Those Days, in This Time.
Angelou.   Reverses.
  Still I Rise.
Beckett, S.   D'où / la voix qui dit.
  Dread Nay.
  Pas davantage.
  Rien nul / n'aura été.
Berrigan, T.   Pandora's Box, an Ode.
Berryman.   Trial, The.
Bierce.   Golden Age, The.
Blok.   Red Glow in the Sky, A.
Blue Cloud.   Old Friends.
Borges.   Elegy for a Park.
  Empty Drawing Room.
  Iceland.
  To a Sword at York Minster.
  Yesterdays.
Browning, R.   Apparent Failure.
  Love among the Ruins.
Burns, R.   Wrote on the Blank Leaf of a Copy
  of My First Edition, Which I Sent to an Old
  Sweetheart, Then Married.
Carew, T.   Love's Force.
Carruth, H.   Burning Dawn.
Carver, R.   Garden, The.
Chaucer.   Former Age, The.
Collins, B.   November.
  Some Final Words.
Cooper, J.   Past, The.
Crane, H.   Enrich My Resignation.
  Modern Craft.
  My Grandmother's Love Letters.
  Tenderness and Resolution.
Creeley.   Backwards.
  Diction.
  Drums, The.
  Fall.
  For Fear.
  For Helen.
  Here ("What / has happened").
  Kitchen.
  Love Comes Quietly.
  Night in NYC.
  One Day.
  One Way.
  Place ("Long gone time").
  Puritan Ethos, The.

Teachings, The.
  Was.
Cullen, C.   Litany of the Dark People, The.
Cummings, E. E.   "April" / this letter's dated.
  Does yesterday's perfection seem not quite.
  Even if all desires things moments be.
  Workingman with hand so hairy-sturdy.
Cunningham, J.   Moral Poem, A.
Davie, D.   Bella & Rosa.
  Rodez.
  Sorting Old Papers.
  Twilight on the Waste Lands.
  Viper-Man.
De la Mare.   Humanity.
Dickey, J.   Buckdancer's Choice.
Dickinson, E.   After a hundred years.
  Glass was the Street—in tinsel Peril.
  Past is not a package, The.
  Past is such a curious Creature, The.
Drummond de Andrade.   Memories of the
  Ancient World.
Dugan, A.   This Morning Here.
  Winter for an Untenable Situation.
Dunbar, P.   Long Ago.
  Ol' Tunes, The.
  Passage, The.
Eberhart, R.   May Evening.
  Testament, A.
Emerson, R.   And Ellen, when the greybeard
  years.
  Dear are the pleasant memories.
  I rake no coffined clay, nor publish wide.
  Past, The.
Enzensberger, H.   Sightseeing Tour.
Ferlinghetti, L.   Hidden Door.
  Queens Cemetery, Setting Sun.
  Retired Ballerinas, Central Park West.
  Sailing thru the straits of Demos.
Frost, R.   Cliff Dwelling, A.
  Directive.
  Ghost House.
  To an Ancient.
Ginsberg, A.   Night Gleam.
  To Aunt Rose.
Glück, L.   Letters, The.
  Love Poem.
Graves, R.   No More Ghosts.
  Song: From Otherwhere or Nowhere.
  Song: The Queen of Time.
Gunn, T.   Drive to Los Alamos, A.
Gurney, I.   Yesterday Lost.
"H. D."   Helen.
Hall, D.   Beau of the Dead.
  Letter to an English Poet.
Hardy, T.   Ghost of the Past, The.
  Inscriptions for a Peal of Eight Bells.
  Jubilate.
  Missed Train, The.
  Spellbound Palace, A.
Hayden, R.   Locus.
  'Mystery Boy' Looks for Kin in Nashville.
  Return, The.
Herrick.   His Age, Dedicated to His Peculiar
  Friend, Master John Wickes, under the Name
  of Posthumus.
Housman.   Yon Far Country.
Hughes, L.   Metropolitan Museum.
  Negro Speaks of Rivers, The.
  Poem for Youth.
  Shame on You.
Jackson, L.   Forgiven Past, The.
Jarrell, R.   Augsburg Adoration, The.
  Farewell Symphony, The.
  I loved you, too. There was no use. I had no
    time.
  In Those Days.
  Lot is vacant still, The.
  Memoirs of Glückel of Hameln, The.
  Northern Snows, The.
  Summer Night, A.
  Times Worsen, The.
  When I Was Home Last Christmas.
Jeffers, R.   Haunted Country.
  To the Rock that Will Be a Cornerstone of the
    House.
Jonson, B.   Ode: "If men, and times were now."

Kinnell.   First Day of the Future.
Kipling, R.   Our Fathers of Old.
  Philadelphia.
  Three-Decker, The.
  Way through The Woods, The.
Kizer, C.   Anniversaries: Claremont Avenue,
    from 1945.
  Bitch.
Kumin, M.   Chain, The.
Larkin, P.   When First We Faced, and Touching
    Showed.
Laughlin, J.   Eros as Archaeologist.
  It's Indelicate.
  Your Early Life.
Lawrence, D. H.   Dreams Old and Nascent:
    Nascent.
  History.
  Humming-Bird.
  Nostalgia.
  Old Idea of Sacrifice, The.
  Things Men Have Made.
  Think—!
Levertov.   Travels.
Levine, P.   28.
  Winter Words.
Lindsay, N.   Chinese Nightingale, The.
Lowell, R.   Dames du Temps Jadis.
MacDiarmid, H.   First Love.
McHugh, H.   It Is 70 Degrees in Late
    November. Opening a Window, You Nearly
    Know.
Merrill, J.   Transfigured Bird.
Merwin.   Bridges, The.
  Talking.
Milosz, C.   And the City Stood in Its Brightness.
  At Dawn.
  At Noon.
  Book in the Ruins, A.
  Encounter.
  Farewell: "I speak to you, my son."
  In a City.
  In Warsaw.
  King Popiel.
  Legend, A.
  Mister Hanusevich.
  My Grandfather Sigismund Kunat.
  Polka-dot Dress, A.
  Readings.
  This Only.
  To a Hazel Tree.
  What Once Was Great.
  Year 1900, The.
Montale.   Local Train.
  Well's pulley creaks, The.
Nash, O.   Ho, Varlet! My Two Cents' Worth of
    Penny Postcard!
Nemerov.   Blue Suburban.
  Endegeeste.
  For the Squadron.
  Guide to the Ruins.
  Home for the Holidays.
  Midsummer's Day.
  Old Days, The.
  Old Soldiers' Home, The.
  Old Warplane, An.
  Photograph of a Girl, The.
  Returning to Europe.
  Snow Globe, The.
  Succession.
  Sunderland.
Neruda.   Possessions.
  Today How Many Hours.
  Today Isn't Everything.
Pagis.   Point of Departure.
Paley, G.   One of the Softer Sorrows of Age.
Parker, D.   Godspeed.
Pasolini.   Beautiful Banners, The.
  Tears of the Excavator, The.
Pessoa.   Recalling who I was, I see somebody
    else.
Pinsky.   At Pleasure Bay.
  Generation Before, The.
  Pleasure Pier.
  Questions, The.
Plath.   Ouija.
Raine, K.   All things new / But I: no shadow.

Journey, The.
On Leaving Ullswater.
Painting by Winifred Nicholson, A.
When I woke up to the snow.
With a Wave of Her Old Hand.
Ramanujan. Waterfalls in a Bank.
Rexroth, K. No!
Rich, A. Turning the Wheel.
Riley, J. Land of Used-to-Be, The.
Used-to-Be, The.
Rimbaud, A. Blackcurrant River.
Robinson, E. Long Race, The.
Miniver Cheevy.
Villanelle of Change.
Roethke. Slug.
Rossetti, C. Counterblast on Penny Trumpet.
Passing and Glassing.
Spring is come again not as at first.
Summer Is Ended.
Rossetti, D. Even So.
Rukeyser, M. Eighth Elegy. Children's Elegy.
Of Money. And the Past.
Portrait of a Man, with a Background of
Holdings.
Sandburg, C. Keepsake Boxes.
Schuyler, J. Ilford Rose Book.
Salute.
Seifert. Berthe Soucaret.
Grave of Signor Casanova, The.
Merry-Go-Round with White Swan.
Moscow.
Mr Krösing's Top Hat.
Nocturnal Divertimento.
Plague Column, The.
Prospect of Prague, A.
Silence Full of Sleighbells.
Sexton. Expatriates, The.
Funnel.
Lost Ingredient, The.
Some Foreign Letters.
What's That.
Shelley, P. Lines: "That time is dead for ever,
child!"
Past, The.
Smith, S. Days of Yore, The.
In Protocreation.
Past, The.
Spender, S. Barn, The.
Little Coat, The.
One More New Botched Beginning.
Tom's a-Cold.
Stafford, W. Some Shadows.
Stevens, W. Arcades of Philadelphia the Past.
Irish Cliffs of Moher, The.
Poesie Abrutie.
Stock, R. Singing, The.
Swenson, M. Downward.
Szymborska, W. Family Album.
No Title Required.
Thomas, D. Because the Pleasure-Bird
Whistles.
Do You Not Father Me.
Twenty-four Years.
Very. Past, The.
Villon. Ballad[e] of Dead Ladies, The.
Ballade of the Ladies of Time Past.
Warren, R. If Ever.
Loose Shutter, The.
Whalen, P. Past Ruin'd Ilion.
Whitman, W. Death of General Grant.
New Year's Day, 1848.
Now Precedent Songs, Farewell.
Old Chants.
Proud Music of the Storm.
To-day and Thee.
To Get the Final Lilt of Songs.
Unnamed Lands.
With Antecedents.
Whittier. Memories.
Norsemen, The.
Wilbur, R. Pardon, The.
Williams, C. K. Blades.
Cellophane.
Combat.
Floor.
Hood.

Nostalgia.
Of What Is Past.
Past, The.
Sorrow, The.
Williams, M. After a Brubeck Concert.
Geography of Time, The.
Ghosts.
House in the Vacant Lot, The.
Memory.
Wordsworth, W. June, 1820.
Wright, C. Apologia Pro Vita Sua.
Ars Poetica.
Bar Giamaica, 1959-60.
In the Kingdom of the Past, the Brown-Eyed
Man Is King.
Looking at Pictures.
Maple on the Hill.
Self-Portrait.
Southern Cross, The.
Two Stories.
Wyatt, S. When that I call unto my mind.
Yeats. Bronze Head, A.
Circus Animals' Desertion, The.
Ego Dominus Tuus.
Image from a Past Life, An.
Seven Sages, The.
Three Marching Songs.
Zagajewski. In the Past.
September.
Stary Sacz.
Thirties, The.
Zukofsky, L. Alba (1952).
As to How Much.
I Sent Thee Late.
My nephew / And my new.
See also **Memory**

Pasternak, Boris
Levertov. In Memory of Boris Pasternak.
Pasternak, B. Death of a Voice.
Walcott. Love in the Valley.
Weiss, T. Russian Lesson.

Pastoral Verse
Eberhart, R. Recollection of Childhood.
Summer Landscape.
Mallarmé. Afternoon of a Faun, The.
Marlowe. Passionate Shepherd to His Love,
The.
Milton. L'Allegro.
Lycidas.
Montale. Eclogue: "It was good getting lost."
Ralegh, S. Nymph's [*or* Nimphs] Reply to the
Shepherd [*or* Sheepheard], The.

Pastures
Laughlin, J. Out in the Pasture.
Merwin. Warm Pastures.
Rilke. Prose Poem.
See also **Fields and Pastures**

Paterson, New Jersey
Dubie. Physical Moon beyond Paterson, A.
Prunty. Dr. Williams' Garden.
Williams, W. Better than flowers.
Episode 17.
I bought a new.
Paterson.
When I saw.

Paths
Atwood. Paths and Thingscape.
Berry, W. In Rain.
Crane, S. Wayfarer / Perceiving the pathway to
truth, The.
Cummings, E. E. Seeker of truth / follow no
path.
Merwin. Route with No Number.
Riley, J. Country Pathway, A.
Lost Path, The.
Onward Trail, The.
Song of the Road, A.
Rossetti, C. Amor Mundi.
Simic. Shortcut.
Snyder, G. Elk Trails.
Off the Trail.
Path to Han-shan's place is laughable, The.
Riprap.
Stock, R. Curriculum Vitae.
Swenson, M. Green Red Brown and White.
Sze. Owl, The.

Whittier. River Path, The.
Wordsworth, W. Simplon Pass, The.
Patience
Bourne, V. Cantab, The.
Browning, E. Patience Taught by Nature.
Perplexed Music.
Bukowski. Object Lesson.
Carver, R. Waiting.
Ciardi, J. Damn Her.
Coleridge, S. Ballad of the Dark Ladié, The.
Love, Hope, and Patience in Education.
Cowper, W. Needless Alarm, The.
Rose, The.
Creeley. For No Clear Reason.
Indians.
Out of Sight.
Tiny Place, A.
Young Woman.
Cullen, C. Two Thoughts of Death.
Dickinson, E. Patience—has a quiet Outer.
Dunbar, P. Plantation Melody, A.
Emerson, R. Fine presentiments controlled him.
Forbearance.
Go if thou wilt ambrosial Flower.
Shun passion, fold the hands of thrift.
Ginsberg, A. Do the Meditation Rock.
Graves, R. Carol of Patience.
Not at Home.
Patience.
Time of Waiting, A.
Guyon. Love Increased by Suffering.
Hafiz [*or* Hafez]. They say, through patience,
chalk.
Hardy, T. Waiting Both.
Herbert, G. Size, The.
Herrick. Dream, The.
His Weaknesse in Woes.
Patience in Princes.
Patience, or Comforts in Crosses.
Persecutions Profitable.
Speake in Season.
To Fortune.
To God.
Upon Flood, Or a Thankfull Man.
Upon God.
Hopkins, G. My Own Heart Let Me More Have
Pity On.
Sonnet: "Patience, hard thing! the hard thing but
to pray."
Jacob, M. Patience of an Angel.
Jarrell, R. Tree, The.
Kinnell. Wait.
Lawrence, D. H. Be Still!
What's to Be Done.
Levertov. Balance, The.
Marta (Brazil, 1928).
Levi, P. 12 July 1980.
Nash, O. I'm Sure She Said Six-Thirty.
Slow Down, Mr. Ganderdonk, You're Late.
Paley, G. Learning from Barbara Deming.
Pope, A. For Sir W. Trumbull.
Riley, J. Who Bides His Time.
Rilke. Wait, The.
Rossetti, C. Are They Not All Ministering
Spirits?
As Thy Days, So Shall Thy Strength Be.
By Way of Remembrance.
Have Patience.
Let Patience Have Her Perfect Work.
Lord, It Is Good for Us to Be Here.
O ye who love today, / Turn away / From
Patience with her silver ray.
Patience must dwell with Love, for Love and
Sorrow.
Sorrow hath a double voice, / Sharp today but
sweet tomorrow.
Study (A Soul), A.
Sweetness of rest when Thou sheddest rest.
Thou Knewest...Thou Oughtest Therefore.
Trees' Counselling, The.
Will of the Lord Be Done, The.
Rumi. I have phrases and whole pages
memorized.
"Shu Ting." "?!"
Thoreau. Better wait.
Then spend an age in whetting thy desire.

Whittier. Angel of Patience, The.
Williams, C. K. In the middle / of a bite of.
  Patience Is When You Stop Waiting.
Wordsworth, W. Force of Prayer, The; or, The
  Founding of Bolton Priory; A Tradition.
Wyatt, S. Patience.
  Patience, for I have wrong.
  Patience for my device.
  Patience of all my smart.
Yeats. Down by the Salley Gardens.
Zukofsky, L. Sequence 1944-6.

Patients
Brodsky, J. Gorbunov and Gorchakov.
Carver, R. Mailman as Cancer Patient, The.
  Poem for Dr Pratt, a Lady Pathologist.
Cooper, J. Twins.
Davie, D. Artifex in Extremis.
Dugan, A. Untitled Poem: "Doctor and I have
  become intimate, The."
Jacobsen, J. April Asylum.
Merton. Rites for the Extrusion of a Leper.
Montale. Ballad Written in a Hospital.
Ramanujan. Pain.
Schuyler, J. Arches.
Williams, T. What's Next on the Agenda, Mr.
  Williams?
See also **Hospitals; Illness; Mental Illness**

Patriarchy
Olson, C. Barley or rye / blue and white green.
  Bigmans.
  Bigmans II.
  Fathers, The.
  She-Bear (II), The.
  So the Norse / were neurotic.
  To the She-Bear: *The 1st Song*.
Piercy. Barbie Doll.
Plath. I Want, I Want.
  Jailer, The.
  Lady Lazarus.
Rich, A. Cartographies of Silence.
  From a Survivor.
  Heroines.
  Hunger.
  Meditations for a Savage Child.
  Natural Resources.
  Paula Becker to Clara Westhoff.
Stein, G. Patriarchal Poetry.

Patrick, Saint
Davie, D. Comforter, The.
Parker, D. Paging Saint Patrick.
Whittier. Proclamation, The.

Patriotic Songs, Scotland
Burns, R. Highland Laddie.
  Sutors o' Selkirk.

Patriotism and Patriots
Atwood. Thoughts from Underground.
Bierce. Eastern Question, The.
  Here Salomon's body reposes.
  Invocation.
Browning, R. Patriot, The [An Old Story].
  Sordello.
Burns, R. Dumfires Volunteers, The.
  On the Death of Sir J. Hunter Blair.
Byron, G. Epigrams: "Oh, Castlereagh! thou art
  a patriot now."
Coleridge, S. British Stripling's War-Song, The.
Cowper, W. Address to the Mob, An.
  Modern Patriot, The.
Crane, S. There exists the eternal fact of
  conflict.
Cummings, E. E. Come,gaze with me upon this
  dome.
  I Sing of Olaf Glad and Big.
  Next to of Course God America I.
Dickinson, E. Is it Intellect that the Patriot
  means.
Emerson, R. Song: "Shout for those whose
  course is done."
Gurney, I. Servitude.
Hall, D. Body Politic, The.
Hopkins, G. What Shall I Do for the Land that
  Bred Me.
Housman. New Mistress, The.
Jeffers, R. So Many Blood-Lakes.
Jonson, B. To True Soldiers.

Keats. Happy Is England! I Could Be Content.
Kipling, R. Recessional.
Larkin, P. MCMXIV.
Lawrence, D. H. As for Me, I'm a Patriot.
  Canvassing for the Election.
Lindsay, N. Hail to the Sons of Roosevelt.
  Yankee Doodle.
MacDiarmid, H. Conception.
MacNeice. Western Landscape.
Meredith, G. Loyal Soldier, The.
  Patriot Engineer, The.
  Song: "Who says, she is in danger."
Owen, W. Dulce et Decorum Est.
Patchen. Letter to Those Who Are About to
  Die.
Pope, A. Epitaph on Sir William Trumbal.
Riley, J. Boy Patriot, The.
  Drum, The.
  McFeeters' Fourth.
  Morton.
  To the Boy with a Country.
  Youthful Patriot, The.
Rukeyser, M. Road, The.
Scott, S. On the Massacre of Glencoe, 1692.
  Pibroch of Donuil Dhu.
Stockton, A. Impromptu on Hearing that a Print
  of the Guliteene with Our Beloved Presidents
  Figure under It Was Executed in Mr Genets
  Family—under His Sanction.
  On the Return of Col Laurens from His
  Confinement in the Tower of London.
  To the Honourable Col. Peter Schuyler.
Updike. Minority Report.
Whitman, W. Beat! Beat! Drums!
  I Hear America Singing.
Whittier. Barbara Frietchie.
Wordsworth, W. Composed by the Sea-Side,
  near Calais, August, 1802.

Patrons
Burns, R. Brigs of Ayr, a Poem. Inscribed to J.
  B*********, Esq; Ayr, The.
  Dedication to G**** H******* Esq, A.
  Lament for James, Earl of Glencairn.
  Lines Sent to Sir John Whiteford, of Whiteford,
  Bart. with the Foregoing Poem.
  Sketch. Inscribed to the Rt. Hon. Ch. J. Fox
  Esq.
Campion, T. To the Right Honourable, Both in
  Birth and Vertue, Francis, Earle of
  Cumberland.
Dubie. Saints of Negativity, The.
Dugan, A. American Variation on How Rilke
  Loved a Princess and Got to Stay in Her
  Castle.
Herrick. To the Honoured, Master Endimion
  Porter.
  To the Most Learned, Wise, and Arch-
  Antiquary, M. John Selden.
  To the Patron of Poets, M. End: Porter.
  To the Right Honourable, Philip, Earle of
  Pembroke, and Montgomerie.
Hughes, L. Poet to Patron.
Jonson, B. Epigram. To the Household. 1630,
  An.
  Humble Petition of Poor Ben to the Best of
  Monarchs, Masters, Men, King Charles, The.
  To Lucy, Countess of Bedford.
  To Lucy, Countess[e] of Bedford, with Mr.
  Donne's Satires [*or* Satyres].
  To Master John Burges.
  To the Right Honourable, the Lord High
  Treasurer of England. An Epistle Mendicant.
  1631.
McHugh, H. Patronage.
Petrarch. Column of glory, strong stay and
  support.
Smart, C. On Gratitude.

Paul, Saint
Hardy, T. In St. Paul's a While Ago.
Herrick. Beginnings and Endings.
  Upon Paul.
Jacobsen, J. Ballad of the Four Saints.
Kipling, R. At His Execution.
  Gallio's Song.
Merton. St. Paul.
Orr, G. Shelf Is a Ledge, A.

Pinkerton, H. On Caravaggio's *Conversion of
  St. Paul* (1600) in Santa Maria del Popolo,
  Rome.
Ransom, J. Our Two Worthies.
Robinson, E. Three Taverns, The.
Rossetti, C. Conversion of St. Paul.
  In weariness and painfulness St. Paul.
  St. Barnanbas.

Pawnbrokers and Pawnshops
Hughes, L. Ballad of the Pawnbroker.
  Could Be.
Sandburg, C. Kreisler.
  Three Balls.

Pawnshops and Pawnbrokers
Sandburg, C. Street Window.

Paz, Octavio
Tomlinson, C. Paris in Sixty-Nine.

Peace
Amichai [*or* Amikhai]. Hour of Grace, An.
  Like the Streams in the Negev.
  My Child Wafts Peace.
  Orchard.
  Peace of Mind, Peace of Mind.
  Temporary Poem of My Time.
  U.N. Headquarters in the High Commissioner's
  House in Jerusalem, The.
  Wild Peace.
  Wildpeace.
Angelou. Georgia Song, A.
Auden. Taller To-day.
Beckett, S. Nuit qui fais tant.
Berry, W. Mad Farmer's Love Song, The.
  Marriage, an Elegy, A.
  Peace of Wild Things, The.
  Praise, A.
  To Think of the Life of a Man.
Berryman. Rock-Study with Wanderer.
Bierce. Year's "Casualties," A.
Bly, R. After Long Busyness.
  After Working.
  Asian Peace Offers Rejected without
  Publication.
Browning, E. First News from Villafranca.
Burns, R. When wild War's deadly blast was
  blawn.
  Ye Jacobites By Name.
Byron, G. She Walks In Beauty.
Campion, T. Elegeia I (1595).
  Most sweet and pleasing are thy wayes, O God.
Chuang Tzu. Advising the Prince.
Clement of Alexandria. Soldiers of Peace.
Clough. In controversial foul impureness.
Cowper, W. Heroism.
  Nightingale and Glow-Worm, The.
  Ode to Peace.
  Song on Peace.
  Song: "When all within is peace."
Crane, H. Enrich My Resignation.
  In a Court.
  Interior.
  Meditation.
Creeley. For No Clear Reason.
  Song: "How simply / for another."
  War & Peace.
Cullen, C. Apostrophe to the Land.
  Wise, The.
Cummings, E. E. All nearness pauses,while a
  star can grow.
  Denied night's face / have shadowless they?
  Enter no(silence is the blood whose flesh).
De la Mare. England.
  Ghost, The.
  Homesick.
  Interlude, An.
  Peace.
  Vain Questioning.
Dickinson, E. Chilly Peace infests the Grass, A.
  Peace is a fiction of our Faith.
  Port of Peace has many Coves, The.
Dugan, A. Brutalization under the Heart of
  Peace.
  Free Variation on a Translation from Greek.
Dunbar, P. At Loafing-Holt.
  Ere Sleep Comes Down to Soothe the Weary
  Eyes.
  From the Porch at Runnymede.

Eberhart, R. Airman Considers His Power, An.
On Seeing an Egyptian Mummy in Berlin, 1932.
Solace.
United 555.
Eliot, T. S. Song for Simeon, A.
Emerson, R. One hand washes the other.
Enzensberger, H. For the Grave of a Peace-Loving Man.
Towards Eternal Peace.
Ginsberg, A. Neruda's "Que dispierte el leñador."
Graves, R. Love Charms.
Solomon's Seal.
Gunn, T. Captain in Time of Peace.
Philemon and Baucis.
Gurney, I. After War.
Old Martinmas Eve.
Guyon. Entire Surrender, The.
"H. D." Trance.
Triplex.
Hamill, S. Conscientious Objection.
Hardy, T. According to the Mighty Working.
And There Was a Great Calm.
Christmas Ghost-Story, A.
Peace Peal, The.
Sick Battle-God, The.
Herbert, G. L'Envoy.
Peace.
Herrick. Farewell Frost; or, Welcome the Spring.
Hand and Tongue, The.
Pardons.
Peace not Permanent.
Power and Peace.
Rainbow, The.
Things of Choice, Long a Comming.
Hill, G. Pastoral, A: "Mobile, immaculate and austere."
Hopkins, G. Il Mystico.
Peace.
Housman. Soldier from the wars returning.
Hughes, L. Give Us Our Peace.
Hughes, T. Match, A.
Ignatow, D. Peace.
Peace for Awhile.
Rockets, The.
Jacobsen, J. Noon.
Keats. O! How I Love, on a Fair Summer's Eve.
On Peace.
Kipling, R. American Rebellion, The.
Benfactors, The.
Peace of Dives, The.
Settler, The.
Koch, K. Pleasures of Peace, The.
Larkin, P. Coming.
Lawrence, D. H. Attila.
Bei Hennef.
Choice.
Compari.
Dead People.
Pax.
Peace.
Peace and War.
Secret Waters, The.
Today.
Wealth.
What Would You Fight For?
Levertov. Making Peace.
Levine, P. Ask the Roses.
Conductor of Nothing, The.
Miracle, The.
Lindsay, N. Jingo and the Minstrel, The.
Sew the Flags Together.
Tale of the Tiger Tree, The.
To Jane Addams at the Hague.
With a Rose, to Brunhilde.
Longfellow, H. Arsenal at Springfield, The.
Occultation of Orion, The.
MacDiarmid, H. Skald's Death.
MacNeice. Apple Blossom.
Meredith, G. Britain.
Cageing of Ares, The.
Congress of Nations, The.
Progress.
Word from the Cannon's Mouth, A.

Meredith, W. On Falling Asleep by Firelight.
Merton. Earthquake.
Guns of Fort Knox, The.
Paper Cranes.
Michelangelo Buonarroti. And sweet it is to see in summer time.
Moore, M. In Distrust of Merits.
Muldoon, P. Truce.
Nemerov. Peace in Our Time.
Song of Degrees, A.
Olson, C. May 20, 1959.
Patchen. Here might have been the thinking of mountains.
How Old the World Is!
Pastoral: "Dove walks with sticky feet, The."
Peace in this green field.
Raine, K. My sight with the clouds'
Ransom, J. Spiel of [the] Three Mountebanks.
Riley, J. Peace-Hymn of the Republic, A.
Ritsos. Peace.
Robinson, E. Peace on Earth.
Roethke. No Bird.
Rossetti, C. Behold the Man!
Better So.
Counsel, A.
Discovery, A.
From the Antique.
I sit among the green shady valleys oft.
In a Certain Place.
In Patience.
Life Hidden.
Looking Forward.
Resurrection Eve.
Sir Eustace Grey.
Sleep, Sleep Happy Child; All Creation Slept and Smiled.
Song of the Star, The.
Song: "Stream moaneth as it floweth, The."
There Remaineth Therefore a Rest.
Who sits with the King in His Throne? Not a slave but a Bride.
Rukeyser, M. Breaking the nets of the world, in glimpses going.
Flying to Hanoi.
He is breaking the nets in his wildness for the real.
Hero Speech.
It Is There.
Palos Verdes Cliffs.
Peace the great meaning has not been defined.
Song, the Brain-Coral.
Statement by Willkie after Returning from England.
Time Hinder Not Me; His Arms Reach Here and There.
Sandburg, C. A. E. F.
For You.
Open Letter to the Poet Archibald MacLeish Who Has Forsaken His Massachusetts Farm to Make Propaganda for Freedom.
Peace Between Wars.
Sarton, M. Nativity.
Work of Happiness, The.
Schuyler, J. May, 1972.
Simic. My Weariness of Epic Proportions.
Smith, S. Dear Child of God.
In Canaan's Happy Land.
Stafford, W. At the Un-National Monument along the Canadian Border.
Epitaph Ending in And, The.
Just Thinking.
Stockton, A. Peace, a Pastoral Dialogue.—Part the Second.
Thoreau. When with pale cheek and sunken eye I sang.
Very. Finishing the Work.
Hymn: The Cause of Peace.
Man's Heart Prophesieth of Peace.
Wolf and the Lamb Shall Feed Together, The.
Walcott. Season of Phantasmal Peace, The.
Whitman, W. Base of All Metaphysics, The.
Halcyon Days.
O Sun of Real Peace.
Of Many a Smutch'd Deed Reminiscent.
Reconciliation.
Whittier. After Election.

Battle Autumn of 1862, The.
Disarmament.
Garrison.
Hive at Gettysburg, The.
In Peace.
Lost Occasion, The.
On the Big Horn.
Peace Autumn, The.
Peace Convention at Brussels, The.
Peace of Europe, The.
To the Thirty-Ninth Congress.
William Francis Bartlett.
Wilbur, R. Grasshopper, A.
Peace of Cities, The.
Wilde, O. E Tenebris.
Williams, C. K. Peace.
Yours.
Williams, M. War and Peace.
Williams, W. And Who Do You Think "They" Are?
Peace.
Solstice.
Wordsworth, W. Address to Silence.
Danish Boy; A Fragment, The.
Emperors and Kings, How Oft Have Temples Rung.
Fairest, brightest, hues of ether fade, The.
Forsaken, The.
Invocation to the Earth; February, 1816.
Not Love, not War, nor the Tumultuous Swell.
Ode: 1815.
Ode: The Morning of the Day Appointed for a General Thanksgiving. January 18, 1816.
Rest and Be Thankful!
These Chairs they have no words to utter.
Written in Very Early Youth.
Wright, C. T'ang Notebook.
Wright, J. Offering for Mr. Bluehart, An.
She Hid in the Trees from the Nurses.
Yeats. Against Unworthy Praise.
Michael Robartes Bids His Beloved Be at Peace.
Peace.
Rose of Peace, The.
Zaturenska. Question, The.
Quiet House, The.

Peach Trees and Peaches
Ammons. Hymn 2: "So when the year had come full round."
Atwood. Late August.
Blake, W. Angel, The.
Ciardi, J. Late Peaches.
Graves, R. Blue-Fly, The.
Lawrence, D. H. Peach.
Riley, J. Ripest Peach, The.
Rossetti, C. Peach tree on the southern wall, The.
Sandburg, C. Peach Blossoms.
Spanish.
Spring Carries Surprises.
Stevens, W. Dish of Peaches in Russia, A.

Peacocks
Bierce. Inauspiciously.
Dickey, W. Things Kept.
Dugan, A. From the Greek Anthology.
Hall, D. Apples.
Hopkins, G. Peacock's Eye, The.
Jacobsen, J. Mexican Peacock, The.
Lawrence, D. H. Peacock.
Merrill, J. Peacock, The.
Mistral, G. Peacock, The.
Moore, M. To the Peacock of France.
Ritsos. Peacocks of Perilampes, The.
Rossetti, C. Look on This Picture and on This.
Stevens, W. Domination of Black.

Pear Trees and Pears
Ciardi, J. Cézanne.
"H. D." Orchard.
Pear Tree.
Kunitz, S. My Mother's Pears.
Lawrence, D. H. Pear-Blossom.
Lux. View From a Porch.
Millay, E. Pear Tree, The.
Stevens, W. Study of Two Pears.
Tomlinson, C. Fruit, for sculpture.
Updike. Pear like a Potato, A.

Query.
Wilbur, R.   June Light.
Wright, J.   Autumnal.

Pearl Diving
Wilbur, R.   Conjuration.
Williams, T.   Diver.
   Swimmer and Fish Group.

Pearl Harbor
Jeffers, R.   Pearl Harbor.
Smith, S.   Little Daughters of America, The.

Pearls
Browning, R.   Pearl, a Girl, A.
Dickinson, E.   Her breast is fit for pearls.
   'Tis little I— could care for Pearls.
Dugan, A.   About the Pseudo St. Dionysius.
   Admonitor: A Pearl for Arrogance.
Dunbar, P.   Roses and Pearls.
Graves, R.   Pearl, The.
Herrick.   Rock of Rubies: and The Quarrie of
   Pearls, The.
Lindsay, N.   Pearl of Biloxi, The.
Lorde.   Bridge Through My Window.
Olson, C.   What's Wrong with Pindar.
   Without the Season of Structure, Modes Lie
      Like Gods Thrown Down, Helpless Before
      the Newness Upsets Genesis When the Young
      Men Pour In.
Rumi.   Ayaz and the King's Pearl.
Unknown.   For pearls, plunge in the sea.

Peas
Ammons.   Four Motions for the Pea Vines.
Clampitt.   Beach Pea, The.
Kumin, M.   In the Pea Patch.
Rumi.   Chickpea to Cook.
Sandburg, C.   Pods.

Peasants
Campion, T.   Ad Rusticum.
Dickinson, E.   So from the mould / Scarlet and
   Gold.
Dubie.   At the Death of a Mongolian Peasant.
   These Untitled Little Verses in Which, at Dawn,
      Two Obscure Dutch Peasants Struggled with
      an Auburn Horse.
Merwin.   Peasant.
Sexton.   Little Peasant, The.
Wilner, E.   Last Man, The.

Pedantry and Pedants
Byron, G.   On a Change of Masters at a Great
   Public School.
Davie, D.   To a Teacher of French.
Emerson, R.   Borrow Urania's subtle wings.
   Pedants all / They would be original.
Nash, O.   Purist, The.
Whitman, W.   When I Heard the Learn'd
   Astronomer.
See also **Scholarship and Scholars**

Peddling and Peddlers
Burns, R.   Trogger, The.
Cavafy.   31 B.C. in Alexandria.
Emerson, R.   King. If farmers make my land
   secure.
Levertov.   Mystery (Oaxaca, Mexico), A.
Ritsos.   Encounters.
   Etesian Winds.
Suckling, S.   Pedlar of Small-Wares, A.

Pedestrians
Collins, B.   Man Listening to Disc.
Levertov.   Rainwalkers, The.

Peeping Toms
Clifton, L.   Peeping Tom.
See also **Voyeurism and Voyeurs**

Pelicans
Eberhart, R.   Key West.
Jeffers, R.   Pelicans.
MacNeice.   Jungle Clearance Ceylon.
Milosz, C.   Pelicans.
Moore, M.   Frigate Pelican, The.
Wilbur, R.   Pelican, The.

Pembroke, Mary Sidney Herbert, Countess of
Donne.   Upon the Translation of the Psalms by
   Sir Philip Sidney, and the Countess of
   Pembroke His Sister.

Penelope (mythology)
Borges.   Odyssey, Book Twenty-three.

Cowper, W.   On Flaxman's Penelope.
Dubie.   Penelope.
"H. D."   At Ithaca.
Homer.   Daughters of Pandarus, The.
   Gardens of Alcinous, The.
   Mindes of men are ever so affected, The.
   Muse, / tell me of this man of wit.
   Sun descending, the *Phæacian* train, The.
Millay, E.   Ancient Gesture, An.
Oliver, M.   Return, The.
Parker, D.   Penelope.
Ritsos.   Penelope's Despair.
Stevens, W.   World as Meditation, The.
Wilner, E.   Ambition.
   World Is Not a Meditation, The.

Penguins
Kumin, M.   In Warm Rooms, Before a Blue
   Light.

Peninsular War (1808–14)
Wordsworth, W.   Epigram on an Event in Col.
   Evans's Redoubted Performances in Spain.
   Squib on Colonel Evans, A.

Pennsylvania (state)
Codrescu.   3/6/81, Amtrack.
Kinsella, T.   Wyncote, Pennsylvania: A Gloss.
Sandburg, C.   Pennsylvania.
Updike.   Returning Native.
Whitman, W.   Voice from Death, A.
Whittier.   Chalkley Hall.
   Golden Wedding of Longwood, The.
   New Year, The.
   Pennsylvania Pilgrim, The.
Ritner.
   To Pennsylvania.
Wordsworth, W.   To the Pennsylvanians.

Pens
Carver, R.   Pen, The.
Collins, B.   Budapest.
Pagis.   Writers.

Pensions and Pensioners
Riley, J.   Down to the Capital.
See also **Old Age; Retirement and Retirees**

Pentecost
Hill, G.   Bidden Guest, The.
Olson, C.   Pente côst under the body of the gull
   flying directly over.
Rossetti, C.   Whitsun Day.
   Whitsun Eve.
   Whitsun Monday.
   Whitsun Tuesday.

Penthesilea
Warren, R.   Fatal Interview: Penthesilea and
   Achilles.

Peonies
Levine, P.   Having Been Asked "What is a
   Man?" I Answer.
Oliver, M.   Peonies.

Pepper, Art
Komunyakaa.   Pepper.

Peppers
Ciardi, J.   Aunt Mary.
Ritsos.   Encounters.

Perception
Ammons.   Corsons Inlet.
   Definitions.
   Guide.
   Image.
   Locus.
   Loft.
   Object.
   Spiel.
   Woodsroad, The.
Beckett, S.   Ce qu'ont les yeux.
   Fin fond du néant.
   Hors crâne seul dedans.
   Something There.
Bogan, L.   Late.
Brontë, E.   I gazed upon the cloudless moon.
Brooks, G.   To Be in Love.
Campion, T. *et al.*   And would you faine the
   reason know.
Carruth, H.   To Know in Reverie the Only
   Phenomenology of the Absolute.
Cavafy.   Morning Sea.

Ciardi, J.   Differences.
   On a Photo of Sgt. Ciardi a Year Later.
   Selectivity.
   Three Views of a Mother.
Coleridge, S.   Apologia pro Vita Sua.
   Lunar Entrancement.
   Reason for Love's Blindness.
Collins, B.   Bonsai.
Creeley.   "Do You Think."
   Echo ("Yes but your sweetness").
   End, The.
   Enough.
   Family, The.
   For Love.
   Here ("No one / else in the room").
   Learning.
   Man, The.
Cullen, C.   For Helen Keller.
Cummings, E. E.   &(all during the / dropsin).
   But if i should say.
   For prodigal read generous.
   Hate blows a bubble of despair into.
   I shall imagine life.
   If up's the world a world grows greener.
   Love's absence is illusion,alias time.
   Mr youse needn't be so spry.
   One's not half two. It's two are halves of one.
   So shy shy shy(and with a).
   Somewhere i have never travelled, gladly
      beyond.
   This little bride & groom are.
   This mind made war.
   What freedom's not some under's mere above.
Cunningham, J.   L'Esprit de Géométrie et
   L'Esprit de Finesse.
Dickinson, E.   I heard a Fly buzz—when I died.
   Much Madness is divinest Sense.
   Perception of an object costs.
   Tint I cannot take—is best, The.
Dugan, A.   Empirical Scene.
   On Naming a Baby Mimosa.
Duncan, R.   First Invention on the Theme of the
   Adam.
Eliot, T. S.   Rhapsody on a Windy Night.
Emerson, R.   Astræa.
   Heartily heartily / Nothing be false.
   I live among ideal men.
   Illusions.
   No song so tuneful, quoth the fox.
   Seyd planted where the deluge ploughed.
Fenton, J.   This Octopus Exploits Women.
Ferlinghetti, L.   Poet as Fisherman.
Gallagher, T.   Accomplishment.
Ginsberg, A.   I learned a world from each.
   Land O'Lakes, Wisconsin: Vajrayana Seminary.
   Marijuana Notation.
   Terms in Which I Think of Reality, The.
   Who.
Graves, R.   In Perspective.
   Like Owls.
   Utter Rim, The.
Hardy, T.   Alike and Unlike.
   House of Silence, The.
   In Her Precincts.
   Prophetess, The.
   Protean Maiden, The.
   Seven Times, The.
   So Various.
   Week, A.
   Winsome Woman, A.
Jackson, L.   Prisms.
Jarrell, R.   Jamestown.
   Orient Express, The.
   Picture in the Paper, A.
   Seele im Raum.
   When you and I were all.
Kipling, R.   Conundrum of the Workshops, The.
   Looking Glass, The.
   Story of Ung, The.
Koch, K.   On Beauty.
Komunyakaa.   Passions.
Kunitz, S.   Organic Bloom.
Levertov.   Letter to William Kinter of
   Muhlenberg, A.
   Two Artists.
   Witness.

MacLeish. Seeing.
McGrath, T. Proverbs of the Middle World.
McHugh, H. From 20,000 Feet.
Merwin. Third Psalm: The September Vision.
  When the Horizon Is Gone.
Milosz, C. Watering Can.
Montale. Moiré.
  So be it. Blare of a cornet.
Nemerov. Companions, The.
Niedecker. From my bed I see.
  Scythe.
Olson, C. Cross-Legged, the Spider and the
  Web.
Paley, G. Life.
Palmer, M. Thee thou on looking out.
Patchen. Always Another Viewpoint.
Pessoa. Live, you say, in the present.
Piercy. In the Men's Room(s).
Raine, K. Angelus.
  Elementals, The.
  Message.
Ramanujan. Christmas.
  Time to Stop.
Ransom, J. Painted Head.
Rexroth, K. Apple Garths of Avalon, The.
  In the Memory of Andrée Rexroth.
Rossetti, D. Woodspurge, The.
Rukeyser, M. Phaneron.
  Seeming, The.
  Shooting Gallery.
Rumi. Elephant in the Dark.
  Food Sack, The.
  If you want what visible reality.
  Wean Yourself.
  Where Are We?
Schuyler, J. Freely Espousing.
  View, A.
Smith, S. Not Waving But Drowning.
Snyder, G. Men ask the way to Cold Mountain.
  Nooksack Valley.
  Through the Smoke Hole.
  When men see Han-Shan.
Stafford, W. Near.
Stevens, W. Add This to Rhetoric.
  Angel Surrounded by Paysans.
  Anglais Mort à Florence.
  Arcades of Philadelphia the Past.
  Bantams in Pine-Woods.
  Bouquet of Roses in Sunlight.
  Conversation with Three Women of New
    England.
  Course of a Particular, The.
  Credences of Summer.
  Idea of Order at Key West, The.
  Man Carrying Thing.
  Motive for Metaphor, The.
  On the Road Home.
  Poem Written at Morning.
  Poems of Our Climate, The.
  Reality Is an Activity of the Most August
    Imagination.
  Repetitions of a Young Captain.
  Sea Surface Full of Clouds.
  Snow Man, The.
  Study of Two Pears.
  Thinking of a Relation between the Images of
    Metaphors.
  Thirteen Ways of Looking at a Blackbird.
  What We See Is What We Think.
  Woman Looking at a Vase of Flowers.
Sze. Apache Plume.
  Archipelago.
  Before Completion.
  Black Lightning.
  Cloud Chamber, The.
  Cornucopia, The.
  Empty Words.
  Frost.
  Great White Shark, The.
  Halibut, The.
  Ice Floe.
  In Your Honor.
  Juniper Fires.
  Magnetized.
  Miracles.
  Network, The.

Oolong.
Parallax.
Pentimento.
Redshifting Web, The.
Silk Road, The.
Six Persimmons.
Sound Lag.
Streamers.
String Diamond, The.
Whiteout.
Szymborska, W. View with a Grain of Sand.
Thoreau. Only the slave knows of the slave.
Tomlinson, C. Appearance.
  Chance.
  Gap, The.
  Greeting, The.
  Reflections.
  Variant on a Scrap of Conversation.
Updike. Revelation.
Van Duyn. Spell of Conjunctivitis, A.
Walcott. Map of Europe, A.
Whitman, W. Of the Terrible Doubt of
  Appearances.
  Song of the Rolling Earth, A.
Whittier. Hill-Top, The.
  Star of Bethlehem, The.
Williams, C. K. It's over now. I watch.
Williams, M. Little Poem, A.
Williams, W. Flattery.
  Men, The.
  New Clouds, The.
  Shadows.
  Short Poem.
Wordsworth, W. Glad Sight Wherever New
  with Old.
  Hint from the Mountains for Certain Political
    Pretenders.
  Morning Exercise, A.
  Ode to Lycoris.
  To a Painter.
  To ———: "Let other bards of angels sing."
  Yarrow Visited [September, 1814].
Wright, C. Cryopexy.
  Dead Color.
  Yard Journal.
Yeats. Nativity, A.

Percy, Sir Henry
Kipling, R. English Way, The.

Perfection
Ammons. Come Prima.
Chuang Tzu. Apologies.
  Empty Boat, The.
  Perfect Joy.
Cowper, W. R.S.S.
Creeley. Sign ("What you know of me").
Cummings, E. E. I / never / guessed any /
  thing(even a).
Dickey, W. Androids.
Donne. Negative Love.
Eberhart, R. In a Hard Intellectual Light.
  Meditation, A.
  Memory.
  Noble Man, The.
Graves, R. Judges, The.
  Those Who Came Short.
Hamill, S. Getting It Wrong Again.
Heaney, S. Pitchfork, The.
Herrick. God.
  Gods Grace.
  His Request to Julia.
Hughes, T. Bride and Groom Lie Hidden for
  Three Days.
Lawrence, D. H. Only the Best Matters.
Lux. Perfect God, The.
Millay, E. Inert Perfection.
Oliver, M. Buck Moon—From the Field Guide
  to Insects.
  Ponds, The.
Olson, C. As the Dead Prey upon Us.
Raine, K. Statues.
Rossetti, C. Love and Hope.
  Thou Art Fairer Than the Children of Men.
Stevens, W. Asides on the Oboe.
Stock, R. Ultimate Poem, The.
Tomlinson, C. Images of Perfection.
  Parsnips.

Perfection, The.
Rhymes.
Walker, A. Perfection.
Yeats. Before the World Was Made.
  Old Tom Again.

Perfumes
Baudelaire. Perfume-flask, The.
Cowper, W. Lines after the Manner of Homer.
Dickinson, E. Essential oils—are wrung.
Herrick. Another on Her.
  Love Perfumes All Parts.
  On a Perfum'd Lady.
  Pomander Bracelet, The.
  To His Mistresses.
  Upon Julia's Unlacing Her Self.
Michelangelo Buonarroti. Though quite
  expensive, look, I've bought you this
Rilke. Some Perfume.

Perplexity
Creeley. Echo ("I'm almost / done, the hour").
  For No Clear Reason.
  Form of Adaptation, A.
  Lady in Black.
  Rain (2).
  Still
  Trees.
  Wanting You.
Gunn, T. Birthday Poem.

Persecution
Borges. Accomplice, The.
Celan. Rogues' and Gonifs' Ditty, A.
  Shibboleth.
Chesterton. Before a Statue of Cromwell.
Ciardi, J. To One "Investigated" by the Last
  Senate Committee, or the Next.
Hamill, S. Blue Monody.
Hayden, R. From the Corpse Woodpiles, from
  the Ashes.
Housman. Oh who is that young sinner with the
  handcuffs on his wrists?
Hughes, T. Descent.
Kumin, M. In the Absence of Bliss.
Longfellow, H. Jewish Cemetery at Newport,
  The.
MacNeice. Among These Turf-Stacks.
  Visit to Rouen.
Merwin. February.
  Free, The.
  Night of the Shirts, The.
  Old Room, The.
  Presidents.
  Prints, The.
  Removal, The.
Montale. To Liuba, Leaving.
Pagis. Last Ones, The.
Pasolini. Reality.
Szymborska, W. Some People.
Whittier. Banished from Massachusetts.
  Barclay of Ury.
  Exiles, The.
  How the Women Went from Dover.
  King's Missive, The.
  Witch of Wenham, The.
Wilde, O. Quantum Mutata.
Williams, M. Man Who Believes in Five, The.

Persephone
Atwood. Letter from Persephone.
Browning, E. Psyche and Proserpine.
Campion, T. Umbra.
Creeley. Kore.
Glück, L. Pomegranate.
Graves, R. Food of the Dead.
Laughlin, J. Persephone Wears Bluejeans.
Lawrence, D. H. Bavarian Gentians.
  Purple Anemones.
Merwin. Kore.
Orr, G. My body was never marred.
Rexroth, K. Adonis in Winter.
Smith, S. Persephone.
Williams, W. Misericordia.
Zagajewski. Persephone.

Perseus
Clampitt. Perseus.
  Perseus Airborne.
Hayden, R. Perseus.

MacNeice.　Perseus.
Plath.　Perseus.
Zaturenska.　Head of Medusa.

Perseverance
Atwood.　Beyond truth, / tenacity: of those.
　Orpheus (2).
Brodsky, J.　May 24, 1980.
Bukowski.　History of a Tough Motherfucker,
　The.
Burns, R.　I dream'd I lay where flowers were
　springing.
　O, for Ane-and-Twenty Tam.
　Though fickle fortune has deceiv'd me.
Calas.　Agony Among the Crowd, The.
Campion, T.　Turne all thy thoughts to eyes.
Carew, T.　Eternity of Love Protested.
Ciardi, J.　Lung Fish, The.
Clough.　Say Not the Struggle Nought Availeth.
Cooper, J.　Mission with the Night, A.
Creeley.　Circle.
　Gesture, The.
　Marriage, A.
　Oh No.
　You ("Back and forth across").
Cullen, C.　Thorn Forever in the Breast, A.
Dunbar, P.　Joggin' Erlong.
Emerson, R.　Cloud upon cloud / Clouds after
　rain.
　Skeptic, The.
　Suum Cuique.
Han-shan.　Who takes the Cold Mountain Road.
Hardy, T.　Why Do I?
Herbert, G.　Employment: "He that is weary, let
　him sit."
Herrick.　End, The.
　Perseverance.
　Purposes.
Hopkins, G.　Carrion Comfort.
　Il Mystico.
Hughes, L.　Mother to Son.
　Still Here.
Jarrell, R.　Knight, Death, and the Devil, The.
Kipling, R.　Old Men, The.
Kunitz, S.　Harsh Judgment, The.
Larkin, P.　Continuing to Live.
Lawrence, D. H.　To Let Go Or to Hold on—?
Lindsay, N.　Babylon, Babylon, Babylon the
　Great.
Longfellow, H.　Psalm of Life, A.
McGrath, T.　Woodcut.
Meredith, G.　Ah for that time when open
　daylight pours.
　From labours through the night, outworn.
　Hilda's Morning and Evening Dose of Rhyme.
　Lady C. M, The.
　Song: "Should thy love die; / O bury it not
　under ice-blue eyes!"
　Teaching of the Blows of Fortune, The.
　Wilding little stubble flower, A.
Moore, M.　Nevertheless.
Olson, C.　Adamo Me.
　Gloss, A.
　Return, The.
　Story of an Olson, and Bad Thing, The.
Piercy.　Phyllis Wounded.
　To Be of Use.
Rich, A.　For a Sister.
Riley, J.　Wait.
Sandburg, C.　Beat, Old Heart.
　Upstream.
Sexton.　Live.
Stafford, W.　My Mother Was a Soldier.
Swenson, M.　Fable for When There's No Way
　Out.
Tennyson, A.　Ulysses.
Thoreau.　Then spend an age in whetting thy
　desire.
Whitman, W.　Noiseless Patient Spider, A.
　To You.
Williams, C. K.　Resentment.
　War.
Williams, W.　Pink Locust, The.
　Problem, The.
Wordsworth, W.　When Haughty Expectations
　Prostrate Lie.
Zagajewski.　Sad, Tired.

View of Delft, A.

Persia
Borges.　Rubaíyát.
Cavafy.　Before Antiochus Epiphanis.
　Satrapy, The.
Hughes, T.　Remembering Teheran.
Meredith, W.　Miniature.
See also **Iran and Iranians**

Persian Gulf War
Ai.　Antihero, The.
Clampitt.　In Umbria: A Snapshot.
Corbett, W.　Desert Storm.
Ginsberg, A.　After the Big Parade.
Hamill, S.　Yellow Ribbons, Madness, Victory.
Kizer, C.　On a Line from Valéry.
Komunyakaa.　Dolphy's Aviary.
Laughlin, J.　Creatures of Prometheus, The.
　Crucifixion in the Desert.
Stafford, W.　Entering History.
Wilner, E.　Operations: Desert Shield, Desert
　Storm.

Persian Wars (500 B.C.–449 B.C.)
Carver, R.　Spring, 480 BC.
　Thermopylae.
Cavafy.　Dareios.
　Dimaratos.
　Naval Battle, The.
Graves, R.　Persian Version, The.

Persians
"Anvari."　Shah Sandschar, whose lowest slave.
Dickey, W.　Love among the Manichees.
Graves, R.　Persian Version, The.
Lindsay, N.　Rhyme for All Zionists, A.
Patchen.　Empire of Persia, The.
Williams, C. K.　Allies: According to Herodotus.

Persimmon Trees
Snyder, G.　Persimmons, The.

Peru
Patchen.　Unnatural History of Peru, The.

Pessimism
Carruth, H.　On Being Asked to Write a Poem
　Against the War in Vietnam.
Creeley.　Business, The.
　Changes, The.
　I Am Held by My Fear of Death.
　Turn, The.
　Wall, A.
Cullen, C.　For a Pessimist.
Dickinson, E.　His little Hearse like Figure.
Dunbar, P.　What's the Use.
Gallagher, T.　Boat Ride.
Hardy, T.　Epitaph on a Pessimist.
Lorde.　Conclusion.
Lowell, R.　Waking Early Sunday Morning.
MacNeice.　Aubade: "Having bitten on life like
　a sharp apple."
Meredith, G.　I Chafe at Darkness.
Nash, O.　No Woe Is Gossamer to Mr.
　Bessemer.
　When You Say That, Smile! or All Right Then,
　Don't Smile.
Parker, D.　Prophetic Soul.
　Symptom Recital.
Pessoa.　If you want to kill yourself, how come
　you don't want to kill yourself.
Pound, N.　Song in the Manner of Housman.
Rich, A.　Ghost of a Chance.
Ritsos.　Method for Optimism.
Smith, S.　Lot's Wife.
Zukofsky, L.　And Without.

Pesticides
Kumin, M.　Woodchucks.

Peter, Saint
Baudelaire.　Saint Peter's Denial.
Browning, E.　Look, The.
　Meaning of the Look, The.
　Two Sayings, The.
　View Across the Roman Campagna.
Crashaw.　On Saint Peter Cutting of Malchus
　His Eare.
　On St. *Peter* Casting Away His Nets at Our
　Saviours Call.
　St. Peter's Shadow.
Hardy, T.　In the Servants' Quarters.
Herrick.　Peter-penny, The.

Jacobsen, J.　Ballad of the Four Saints.
Levertov.　St. Peter and the Angel.
Merton.　House of Caiphas, The.
Rossetti, C.　I followed Thee, my God, I
　followed Thee / To see the end.
　St. Peter.
　Vigil of St. Peter.
Wilbur, R.　Peter.

Peterloo Massacre (1819)
Shelley, P.　Song to the Men of England.

Petra, Jordan
Whittier.　"Rock" in El Ghor, The.

Petrarch (Francesco Petrarca)
Orr, G.　Western Invention of Lyrical Nature,
　The.

Petrels
Very.　Petrels, The.
Whitman, W.　To the Man-of-War Bird.

Pets
Cavafy.　House with a Garden.
Ciardi, J.　Going to the Dogs.
Collins, B.　Dharma.
Cowper, W.　Epitaph on a Hare.
　Epitaphium Alterum.
　On the Lamented Death of Mrs. Throckmorton's
　Bullfinch.
　Retired Cat, The.
Creeley.　If You.
Dickey, W.　Chickens in San Francisco.
Gunn, T.　Her Pet.
Hardy, T.　Last Words To a Dumb Friend.
Herrick.　Upon His Spaniel[l] Tracie [*or* Tracy].
　Upon Mudge.
　Upon the Death of His Sparrow; an Elegie.
Hughes, T.　Lovepet, The.
Kumin, M.　Retrieval System, The.
Larkin, P.　Take One Home for the Kiddies.
Levertov.　Her Destiny.
　Her Lament.
　Her Sadness.
　Winterpig.
MacNeice.　Pet Shop.
McHugh, H.　My Shepherd.
Muldoon, P.　Thinking of the Goldfish.
Prunty.　Coach.
Ransom, J.　Janet Waking.
Riley, J.　Guiney-Pigs.
　Iry and Billy and Jo.
　Pet Coon, The.
　When Old Jack Died.
Roethke.　Meadow Mouse, The.
Rossetti, C.　Dog lies in his kennel, The.
　Word for the Dumb, A.
Smith, S.　Croft.
　Heber.
　Mrs. Blow and her Animals.
　Shooting Incident, The.
Snyder, G.　Nansen.
Spender, S.　Boy, Cat, Canary.
Tate, J.　Pet Deer, The.
　Riven Doggeries.
Updike.　Another Dog's Death.
Wilbur, R.　Marché aux Oiseaux.
Williams, C. K.　My Fly.
Williams, M.　Animals.
Yeats.　Two Songs of a Fool.

Pewees [*or* Pewits]
Niedecker.　On Hearing / the Wood Pewee.

Peyote
Carruth, H.　Sorrow Song, The.

Phaeton
Cavafy.　Tears of the Sisters of Phaeton, The.
Meredith, G.　Phaéthôn.
Thoreau.　That Phaeton of our day.

Phantoms
Baudelaire.　Fantastic Engraving, A.
Cavafy.　Since Nine O'Clock.
De la Mare.　Captive, The.
　Reverie.
　Which?
Graves, R.　Sea Horse, The.
Meredith, G.　Phantasy.
Merwin.　Apparition.
Pessoa.　Some mysterious phantom's sudden
　hand.

Pheasants
Cowper, W.   Thanks for a Gift of Pheasants.
Creeley.   Happy love, this.
Eberhart, R.   I Walked Out to the Graveyard to
   See the Dead.
Plath.   Pheasant.

Philadelphia, Pennsylvania
Kinsella, T.   Song of the Night.
Kipling, R.   Philadelphia.
Tomlinson, C.   Garland for Thomas Eakins, A.
Whittier.   Pennsylvania Hall.
  Relic, The.
Wilner, E.   On the Road to Larry Robin's
   Bookstore.

Philanthropy and Philanthropists
Meredith, G.   Angela Burdett-Coutts.
Whitman, W.   Outlines for a Tomb.
Williams, M.   For J William Fulbright on the
   Day of His Death.
See also **Charity**

Philippines
Ai.   Miracle in Manila.
Creeley.   Apocalypse Now.
  Cebu.
  Country Western.
  Davao Insular Hotel.
  Manila.
Kipling, R.   White Man's Burden, The.

Philistines
Pound, E.   Les Millwin.

Philomela
Herrick.   Charon and Phylomel, a Dialogue
   Sung.
Ransom, J.   Philomela.
Ritsos.   Philomel.

Philosophy and Philosophers
Amichai [*or* Amikhai].   My Friend the
   Philosopher and Hanukah.
  Yehuda Ha-Levi.
Ammons.   Hibernaculum.
  Uh, Philosophy.
Auden.   Voltaire at Ferney.
Blake, W.   Mock On, Mock On, Voltaire,
   Rousseau.
Bly, R.   Meditation on Philosophy, A.
Boethius.   Book III. Metre 6.
  Consolation of Philosophy, The ("De
   Consolacione Philosophie").
  Give me, O Father! to thy throne access.
  Happy he whose eyes have view'd.
  Man who pants for ample Sway, The.
  O thou, whose all-creating hands sustain.
  O thou whose pow'r o'er moving worlds
   presides.
  Prudent Hind intent on Gain, The.
  Though countless as the Grains of Sand.
  Through Gripus Grounds let rich Pactolus roll.
  Truth in platonic ornaments bedeck'd.
  Unless the soul, to vice a thrall.
  Vainly the Tyrian Purple bright.
  Wouldst thou to some stedfast Seat.
Borges.   Baltasar Gracián.
  Descartes.
  Things ("Fallen volume, hidden by the others,
   The").
Burns, R.   Letter to J———s T———t, Gl—
   nc———r.
Carruth, H.   Survival as Tao, Beginning at 5:00
   A.M.
Cavafy.   From the School of the Renowned
   Philosopher.
Cavalcanti.   Syllogism makes one from many,
   A.
Clement of Alexandria.   Logos Our Teacher,
   The.
Clough.   Away, haunt not thou me.
  Look you, my simple friend, 'tis one of those.
Coleridge, S.   Drinking versus Thinking.
  Philosophical Trinity, The.
Cowper, W.   Philosopher and the King, The.
Cummings, E. E.   Will out of the kindness of
   their hearts a few philosophers tell me.
Cunningham, J.   Metaphysical Amorist, The.
"Dario."   Cleopompus and Heliodemos.
Dubie.   Open Happens in the Midst of Beings,

  The.
  Simple Philo of Alexandria.
Dugan, A.   What It Really Means.
Eberhart, R.   Great Principles Are Thrown
   Down by Time.
Emerson, R.   Humble-Bee, The.
  It takes a philosopher or fool.
  Philosophers are lined with eyes within.
Enzensberger, H.   Dept. of Philosophy.
  Summer Poem.
Graves, R.   Nothing.
Hardy, T.   Drinking Song.
  Our Old Friend Dualism.
Howe, S.   Pythagorean Silence.
  Some particular place fleeting.
Jarrell, R.   Charles Dodgson's Song.
  Zeno.
Jeffers, R.   Great Men.
  What's the best life for a man?
Larkin, P.   Days.
Logan, J.   Dialogue with La Mettrie, A.
MacDiarmid, H.   To My Friend the Late
   Beatrice Hastings.
Mahon.   Consolations of Philosophy.
  Tractatus.
McHugh, H.   Scenes from a Death.
Melville, H.   Fragments of a Lost Gnostic Poem
   of the Twelfth [*or* 12th] Century.
Meredith, G.   Garden of Epicurus, The.
Merton.   Legacy of Herakleitos, The.
  Origen.
  Philosophers, The.
  Song for the Death of Averroës.
Milosz, C.   Heraclitus.
  Idea.
  Philosopher's Home, A.
  What I Learned from Jeanne Hersch.
  Zdziechowski.
Milton.   Philosopher on His Way to His Death,
   A.
Muldoon, P.   Madoc: A Mystery.
Nemerov.   Epitaph on a Philosopher.
  Philosophy.
  Two Views of a Philosopher.
Nerval.   Mute Phenomena, The.
Niedecker.   Horse, hello.
  Mourning Dove.
Parker, D.   Veteran, The.
Patchen.   Shapes and Intensities of This Man,
   This Confucius, The.
Rexroth, K.   Dragon and the Unicorn, The.
  Neatness Is All.
  Phoenix and the Tortoise, The.
  They Say This Isn't a Poem.
  Time Is an Inclusion Series Said McTaggart.
  Value Neuter.
  Vitamins and Roughage.
Riley, J.   My Philosofy.
Rimbaud, A.   Impossible, The.
Ritsos.   Biased Man, The.
Robinson, E.   Captain Craig.
Sandburg, C.   Lovable Babblers.
  Two Neighbors.
Schuyler, J.   Bleeding Gums.
  Unlike Joubert.
Sheridan, T.   Thus Did Great Socrates Improve
   the Mind.
Simic.   There They Stand Unaware of Their
   Wretchedness.
Smith, S.   Distractions and the Human Crowd.
  On the Death of a German Philosopher.
Stevens, W.   Homunculus et La Belle Etoile.
  To an Old Philosopher in Rome.
Stock, R.   Motives of a Two-Headed Turtle.
  Sigismundo Malatesta Brings His Favorite
   Philosopher's Bones to Italy.
Stockton, A.   On Reading Dr Beaties Hermit.
  Thoughts on the Pythagorian System.
Tomlinson, C.   In Defence of Metaphysics.
  Machiavelli in Exile.
Very.   Philosophy and Religion.
Warren, R.   Basic Syllogism.
Weiss, T.   Giant Yea, The.
Whitman, W.   Base of All Metaphysics, The.
  Roaming in Thought.
Whittier.   Follen.

To ———: "Maiden! with the fair brown
   tresses."
Williams, M.   Thinking Friday Night with a
   Gothic Storm Going About Final Causes and
   Logos and Mitzi Mayfair.
Wordsworth, W.   To the Utilitarians.
Wright, C.   Passing the Morning under the
   Serenissima.
Zagajewski.   Fire, Fire.
  Kierkegaard on Hegel.
  Lava.
  My Aunts.
  Name Edmund, The.
  Philosophers.
  Schopenhauer's Crying.
  Talk with Friedrich Nietzsche, A.

Phoebus Apollo
Cavafy.   Funeral of Sarpedon, The ("Heart of
   Zeus is filled with grief, The").
Michelangelo Buonarroti.   What a chance I had!
   I should have, while I could.
Petrarch.   When that tree moves from where it
   ought to be.
See also **Apollo**

Phoenix
Atwood.   Eating Fire.
Carew, T.   Song[, A]: "Ask[e] me no more
   where Jove bestow[e]s."
Carruth, H.   Fact of the Matter, The.
Chuang Tzu.   Owl and Phoenix.
Cullen, C.   That Bright Chimeric Beast.
Cunningham, J.   Phoenix, The.
Dickinson, E.   I knew a Bird that would sing as
   firm.
Jonson, B.   Phoenix Analysed, The.
Kinnell.   Another Night in the Ruins.
Lawrence, D. H.   Phoenix.
Merrill, J.   About the Phoenix.
Michelangelo Buonarroti.   If Braccio's beauty,
   phoenix-like, could be.
Nash, O.   Phenix, The.
Nemerov.   Phoenix, The.
Petrarch.   Is this the nest in which my phoenix
   put.
  One day when I was looking from my window.
  This phoenix, so extravagantly plumed.
Raine, K.   Traveller, The.
Sarton, M.   Phoenix, The.
Wilbur, R.   Cottage Street, 1953.

Photography and Photographers
Ai.   Paparazzi, The.
Amichai [*or* Amikhai].   I Know a Man.
  Two Photographs.
Atwood.   Daguerreotype Taken in Old Age.
  This Is a Photograph of Me.
Auden.   I Am Not a Camera.
Beckett, S.   Rue de Vaugirard.
Borges.   Empty Drawing Room.
Brodsky, J.   Photograph, A.
  Polar Explorer, A.
Broumas, O.   Before the Elegy.
Bukowski.   Photographs.
Carver, R.   Afterglow.
  On an Old Photograph of My Son.
  Photograph of My Father in His Twenty-second
   Year.
  Wes Hardin: From a Photograph.
Cavafy.   From the Drawer.
Ciardi, J.   Bridal Photo, 1906.
  On a Photo of Sgt. Ciardi a Year Later.
  Thanks to a Botanist, A.
Clampitt.   Exmoor.
Clifton, L.   Photograph.
  Photograph, The: A Lynching.
Codrescu.   About Photography.
  Old Photo.
Cooper, J.   Leaving Water Hyacinths.
  Olympic Rain Forest.
Creeley.   Chance, The.
Dickinson, E.   Picture of the pretty Home, The.
Dubie.   After Three Photographs of Brassaï.
  Elegy to the Pulley of Superior Oblique.
  Renunciation of the Desert Primrose, A.
Dunbar, P.   Photograph, The.
Ferlinghetti, L.   Photo of Emily, The.
Gallagher, T.   Time Lapse with Tulips.

Glück, L. Pictures of the People in the War.
Still Life.
Gunn, T. Song of a Camera.
Hall, D. Photographs of China.
Hamill, S. Photograph of Kavafis, A.
Heaney, S. Royal Prospect, A.
Walk, The.
Hughes, T. Black Coat.
Six Young Men.
Ignatow, D. And That Night.
Jackson, L. Second-Death.
Komunyakaa. Touch-up Man.
Untitled Blues; After a Photograph by Yevgeni
Yevtushenko.
Kumin, M. Photograph, Maryland Agricultural
College Livestock Show, 1924.
Larkin, P. Lines on a Young Lady's Photograph
Album.
Whatever Happened?
Laughlin, J. Her Reply.
I Love to See You.
Levertov. In Thai Binh (Peace) Province.
Letter to Marek about a Photograph, A.
Photo Torn from The Times.
Logan, J. Cape Elizabeth: A Photograph.
Day in the Sun, A.
Eight Poems on Portraits of the Foot.
Lines for Michael in the Picture.
On a Photograph by Aaron Siskind.
Suite of Six Pieces for Siskind, A.
Three Poems on Aaron Siskind's Photographs.
Transformation, The.
Whatnot, The.
Mahon. Old Snaps, The.
Major, C. Posing.
Melville, H. On the Photograph of Corps
Commander.
Meredith, W. Old Photograph of Strangers, An.
Merrill, J. David's Night in Veliès.
Merwin. Photograph.
Milosz, C. Anka.
Human Fly, A.
Photograph, A.
Muldoon, P. Cheesecake.
Twice.
Nemerov. Old Photograph, An.
Photograph of a Girl, The.
Picture, A.
Olson, C. There they were.
Oppen. Civil war photo.
From a Photograph.
Old man, The.
Pagis. Bridgehead Photograph.
Ein Leben.
Pages in an Album.
Paley, G. In San Salvador (I).
Palmer, M. I killed a bee on the Street of
Scissors.
Prunty. Depression, the War, and Gypsy Rose
Lee, The.
Ramanujan. Man and Woman in Camera and
Out.
Rich, A. Photograph of the Unmade Bed, The.
Schuyler, J. Shaker.
Simic. Baby Pictures of Famous Dictators.
Smith, S. Photograph, The.
Spender, S. Photograph, The.
Stafford, W. Archival Print, An.
When You Go Anywhere.
Stock, R. Scene From Life.
Sze. Viewing Photographs of China.
Szymborska, W. Family Album.
Frozen Motion.
Hitler's First Photograph.
Negative.
Tomlinson, C. Snapshot.
Updike. Camera.
Exposure.
Little Poems.
Snapshots.
Van Duyn. Photographs.
Very. On Viewing the Falls of Niagara, as
Photographed by George Barker.
Warren, R. News Photo.
Old Photograph of the Future.
Wilbur, R. Looking into History.

Williams, C. K. Floor.
Williams, M. Art Photographer Puts His Model
at Ease, The.
Newspaper Picture of Spectators at a Hotel Fire,
A.
On a Photograph of My Mother at Seventeen.
On Seeing a Photograph by Mathew Brady.
Story, The.
Tenth Anniversary Photograph, 1952, A.
Williams, W. View by Color Photography on a
Commercial Calendar.
Wilner, E. Atget's Gardens.
Tucson Gardens.
Wright, C. Looking at Pictures.
Zagajewski. Senza Flash.
To Myself, In an Album.
See also **Cameras**

Physical Handicaps
Michelangelo Buonarroti. Goiter it seems I got
from this backward craning, A.

Physicians
Armantrout. Visibility.
Ciardi, J. Credo ("I asked the doctor who had
pronounced me dead").
Dugan, A. Suffering Ophthalmologist, The.
Untitled Poem: "Doctor and I have become
intimate, The."
Stafford, W. Meditation in the Waiting Room.
Warren, R. Pursuit.
Williams, M. I Can Only Stay for Fifteen
Minutes.
See also **Doctors**

Physics and Physicists
Ammons. Miss.
Auden. After Reading a Child's Guide to
Modern Physics.
Dugan, A. Prothalamion of Quantum
Mechanics and Astrophysics against the Text
"Philosophia Biou Kubernetes" (Philosophy the
Guide of Life).
Eberhart, R. Quanta.
Lawrence, D. H. Relativity.
Pagis. Limits of Physics, The.
Visit to a Physicist.
Tomlinson, C. On the Principle of Blowclocks.
Updike. Cosmic Gall.
Mobile of Birds.
News from the Underworld.
Williams, M. Associate Professor (Mad
Scientist) to (His Love) His Student in Physics
100 Lab.
Quantum Theory Made Simple.
Waking from a Dream.

Pianos
Bukowski. Chopin Bukowski.
Codrescu. Piano & Everything Nice.
Collins, B. Piano Lessons.
Dickey, J. From Time.
Dubie. Several Measures for the Little Lost.
Dugan, A. Empirical Scene.
Frost, R. Investment, The.
Gurney, I. Hedger.
Hardy, T. Duettist to her Pianoforte, A.
Lawrence, D. H. Piano.
Piano, The.
Logan, J. Piano Scholar, The.
Nash, O. Piano Tuner, Untune Me That Tune.
Paley, G. In This Dream.
Palmer, M. Man undergoes pain sitting at a
piano, A.
Prunty. Player Piano, The.
Rukeyser, M. Gradus ad Parnassum.
Sandburg, C. Chords.
Stevens, W. Mozart, 1935.
Updike. Player Piano.
Zagajewski. Death of a Pianist.

Picasso, Pablo
Cooper, J. In a Room with Picassos.
Cummings, E. E. Picasso / you give us Things.
Hughes, L. Dove, The.
Swenson, M. Picasso: "Dream." Oil 1932.
Williams, W. Genius, The.

Pickup Trucks
Ai. Twenty-Year Marriage.

Picnics and Barbecues
Clampitt. Hermit Thrush, A.
Creeley. Souvenir, The.
Hardy, T. Where the Picnic Was.
Logan, J. Picnic, The.
Muldoon, P. Truce.
Orr, G. Sunday School Picnic: What Endures.
Plath. Whitsun.
Riley, J. In Fervent Praise of Picnics.
Roethke. Thing, The.
Rossetti, C. Mr. and Mrs. Scott, and I.
Schuyler, J. Picnic Cantata, A.
Tennyson, A. Audley Court.
Warren, R. Distance Between, The: Picnic of
Old Friends.
October Picnic Long Ago.
Picnic Remembered.
Youthful Picnic Long Ago: Sad Ballad on Box.
Wilbur, R. Terrace, The.
Williams, C. K. Holiday: / every / yard or, A.

Piero della Francesca
Sarton, M. Nativity.

Pierrot
Hughes, L. Black Pierrot, A.
Heart.
Pierrot.

Pies
Dunbar, P. Reluctance.
Niedecker. You know, he said, they used to
make.
Paley, G. Poet's Occasional Alternative, The.
Riley, J. Gustatory Achievement, A.

Piety
Amichai [or Amikhai]. At the Monastery of
Latroun.
Blok. I Enter the Dark Church Slowly.
Byron, G. Queries to Casuists.
Coleridge, S. Lines Suggested by the Last
Words of Berengarius.
Crashaw. Acts 21; I Am Ready Not Onely To
Be Bound but To Dye.
Epitaph upon Mr. Ashton, a Conformable
Citizen, An.
In Amorem Divinum.
It Is Better To Go into Heaven with One Eye.
On St. *Peter* Casting Away His Nets at Our
Saviours Call.
Recommendation, The.
Donne. Hymn[e] to Christ, at the Author's Last
Going into Germany, A.
Glück, L. Jeanne d'Arc.
Herrick. Another, to His Saviour.
Chewing [of] the Cud, The.
Gods Commands.
His Offering, with the Rest, at the Sepulcher.
To God, His Gift.
To Keep a True Lent.
Kumin, M. Sisyphus.
Laughlin, J. Piteous Sight, A.
Major, C. Divine Law: A Blue Beach Sermon.
Meredith, G. Certain People, A.
Petrarch. When I begin to send out sighs and
call.
Rossetti, C. St. Elizabeth of Hungary.
Rumi. When We Pray Alone.
Smith, S. Unpopular, Lonely and Loving.
Stock, R. Sixth Station, The.
Williams, M. Morning at the Zagorsk
Monastery Outside Moscow.
Old Man Leaves His Church for the Last Time,
An.

Pigeons
Bishop, E. Paris, 7 A.M.
Ciardi, J. Dead Pigeon on South Street.
Old Man.
Clampitt. Man Feeding Pigeons.
Progress at Building Site With (Fewer) Pigeons.
Vacant Lot with Tumbleweed and Pigeons.
Dugan, A. 851.
Eberhart, R. Incidence of Flight.
Jacobsen, J. Good Fortune of Pigeons, The.
Jeffers, R. Passenger Pigeons.
Kunitz, S. Reckoning, The.
Larkin, P. Pigeons.
Merwin. Fly.

Rossetti, C. 4th May Morning.
On the Wing.
Sandburg, C. Pigeon.
Timber Wings.
Understandings in Blue.
Swenson, M. Pigeon Woman.
Poplar's Shadow, The.
Very. Wounded Pigeon, The.
Zukofsky, L. Madrigal for 3 Voices, A.

Pigs
Berry, W. For the Hog Killing.
Dubie. Blue Hog, A.
Obscure, The.
Gunn, T. Moly.
Hall, D. Eating the Pig.
Han-shan. Pigs devour dead human flesh.
Herrick. Upon Spokes.
Hughes, T. View of a Pig.
Ignatow, D. Adonis.
Kinnell. Saint Francis and the Sow.
Sow Piglet's Escapes, The.
Kipling, R. Dark children of the mere and
marsh.
Lawrence, D. H. Food of the North.
Levertov. Bride, The.
Catpig, The.
Dogbrothers.
Her Delight.
Her Destiny.
Her Judgement.
Her Lament.
Her Nightmare.
Her Prayer.
Her Sadness.
Her Secret.
Her Sister.
Her Task.
Her Vision.
Isis Speaks.
Pig-song.
Winterpig.
Levine, P. Animals Are Passing from Our
Lives.
L'Homme et La Bête.
Nash, O. Pig, The.
Plath. Sow.
Rossetti, C. If a pig wore a wig.
Sexton. Hog.
Hutch.
Snyder, G. Mother of the Buddhas, Queen of
Heaven, Mother of the Sun; Marici, Goddess
of the Dawn.
Wilbur, R. Matthew VIII, 28 ff.
Williams, M. One of the Crowd on the Shore
Tells How It Was.
Williams, W. To a Mexican Pig-Bank.
Wilner, E. Working the Block.

Pike (fish)
Hughes, T. Pike.

Pike's Peak
Schuyler, J. Money Musk.

Pilgrim Fathers
Emerson, R. Boston Hymn.
Longfellow, H. Courtship of Miles Standish,
The.
Riley, J. Quest of the Fathers, The.
Very. Calling, The.
Farewell: "Farewell dear England, and thy
Church farewell!"
Whittier. Banished from Massachusetts.
John Underhill.
Mayflowers, The.

Pilgrimages and Pilgrims
Arnold, M. Resignation.
Berry, W. Springs, The.
Bradstreet, A. As Weary Pilgrim, Now at Rest.
Chaucer. Canterbury Tales, The.
Cummings, E. E. Chaucer.
De la Mare. Decoy, The.
Dubie. Hours, The.
Enzensberger, H. Thoughts on the Run 4.
García Lorca. Ballad of Our Lady of the Boat.
St. Michael.
Hall, D. Woolworth's.
Hardy, T. Hap.

Herrick. To His Brother Nicolas Herrick.
Kumin, M. Itinerary of an Obsession.
Levertov. Pilgrim Dreaming, A.
Merton. Pilgrims' Song.
Merwin. South.
Milosz, C. On Pilgrimage.
Orr, G. Beginning.
Pinkerton, H. On Watteau's *Pilgrimage to
Cythera* (1717) in the Louvre.
Rossetti, C. After This the Judgement.
Uphill.
Rumi. Sheikh Kharraqani and His Wretched
Wife.
Seifert. Place of Pilgrimage.
Spender, S. Marston.
Whittier. Summer Pilgrimage, A.
Yeats. Pilgrim, The.
Zaturenska. Pilgrimage.

Pilots
Apollinaire. Zone.
Ciardi, J. Death of a Bomber.
Morning: I Know Perfectly How in a Minute
You Will Stretch and Smile.
Pilot in the Jungle, The.
Dickey, J. Patience: In the Mill.
"H. D." R.A.F.
Hall, D. Man in the Dead Machine, The.
Jarrell, R. Pilot from the Carrier, A.
Kipling, R. Hymn of the Triumphant Airman.
Meredith, W. For Air Heroes.
Navy Field.
Notes for an Elegy.
Merton. Comedy Card for a Serious Case.
Prunty. Baseball Team of Unknown Navy
Pilots, Pacific Theater, 1944, A.
Old Cadets, The.
Robinson, E. Pilot, The.
Sandburg, C. To Beachey, 1912.
Stafford, W. At the Grave of My Brother:
Bomber Pilot.
Tate, J. Lost Pilot, The.
See also **Air Warfare**

Pimps
Hughes, L. Sliver of Sermon
What?

Pindar
Duncan, R. Poem Beginning with a Line by
Pindar, A.

Pine Island, Minnesota
Wright, J. Lying in a Hammock at William
Duffy's Farm in Pine Island, Minnesota.

Pine Trees
Amichai [*or* Amikhai]. On the Day My
Daughter Was Born No One Died.
Ammons. Interval.
Eberhart, R. Evaluation Under a Pine Tree,
Lying On Pine Needles, An.
Old Tree by the Penobscot.
White Pines, Felled 1984.
Emerson, R. I sat upon the ground.
"H. D." Oread.
McHugh, H. Some Kind of Pine.
Merwin. Line of Trees.
Mistral, G. Pine Forest.
Muldoon, P. Yggdrasill.
Pagis. Conversation.
Plath. Black Pine Tree in an Orange Light.
Smith, S. Now Pine-Needles.
Snyder, G. Foxtail Pine.
Kušiwoqqób.
Thoreau. Die and be buried who will.
Needles of the pine, The.
Warren, R. Return, The: An Elegy.

Pins
Lux. Small Tin Parrot Pin, A.

Pioneers
Atwood. Progressive Insanities of a Pioneer.
Clampitt. Field Pansy, The.
Imago.
Prairie, The.
Quarry, The.
Venice Revisited.
Westward.
Cooper, J. Mary Coldwell.
Eberhart, R. Statue of Liberty.

Emerson, R. Forerunners.
Kipling, R. Lost Legion, The.
Voortrekker, The.
Logan, J. Thirteen Preludes for Pioneer Square.
McGrath, T. Seekers, The.
Underground, The.
Merwin. Trail into Kansas, The.
Moore, M. New York.
Muldoon, P. Tract.
Niedecker. Pioneers.
Olson, C. Bigmans II.
Rich, A. Face to Face.
From an Old House in America.
Riley, J. Child's Home—Long Ago, A.
Van Duyn. That was in 1875, and we come
through.
Whitman, W. Pioneers! O Pioneers!
Whittier. Pass of the Sierra, The.
Williams, T. Inheritors.
Williams, W. Poem: "Daniel Boone, the father
of Kentucky."

Pipers
Browning, R. Pied Piper of Hamelin, The.
Ignatow, D. From the Beginning.
Mallarmé. Afternoon of a Faun, The.
Riley, J. Pipes of Pan, The.

Piracy and Pirates
Dugan, A. Portrait.
Frost, R. Discovery of the Madeiras, The.
Hughes, L. To the Little Fort of San Lazaro on
the Ocean Front, Havana.
Kipling, R. Rhyme of the Three Captains, The.
Parker, D. Song of Perfect Propriety.
Pessoa. Maritime Ode.
Plath. Bluebeard.

Pisa, Italy
Melville, H. Pisa's Leaning Tower.
Shelley, P. Evening: Ponte al Mare, Pisa.

Pitt, William
Burns, R. On Mr. Pitt's [*or* Pit's] Hair-Powder
Tax.
Davie, D. Somerset.

Pity
Amichai [*or* Amikhai]. God Takes Pity on
Kindergarten Children.
With All the Rigor of Pity.
Apollinaire. Pretty Redhead, The.
Blake, W. Terror in the house does roar.
Campion, T. Good men, shew, if you can tell.
Cavalcanti. Dante, a sighing messenger of the
heart.
I pray you who speak of suffering.
If I ask Pity not to be.
Love's amorous spiritual glance.
Pity came to lonely me.
Sonnet: He reports, in a feigned Vision, the
successful Issue of Lapo Gianni's Love.
Sonnet: To a Friend who does not pity his Love.
You see me—one who goes crying.
Chaucer. Complaint unto Pity, The.
Ciardi, J. In Pity as We Kiss and Lie.
Joe with a Wooden Leg.
Coleridge, S. Addressed to a Young Man of
Fortune.
Dungeon, The.
Love.
Collins, B. I Chop Some Parsley While
Listening to Art Blakey's Version of "Three
Blind Mice."
Cowper, W. Pity for Poor Africans.
Creeley. In an Act of Pity.
Variation, A.
De la Mare. Blind Boy, The.
Catechism, The.
Dickinson, E. I cried at Pity—not at Pain.
'Tis easier to pity those when dead.
Eberhart, R. When Doris Danced.
Graves, R. Man of Evil.
Pity.
Hall, D. September Ode.
Hardy, T. Her Dilemma.
Herrick. His Ejaculation to God.
Pitie to the Prostrate.
Hopkins, G. My Own Heart Let Me More Have
Pity On.

Pius IX, Pope

Keats.   I Cry Your Mercy, Pity, Love—Ay, Love!
Kinnell.   To a Child in Calcutta.
Kunitz, S.   Tutored Child, The.
Levi, P.   Give Us.
MacLeish.   Pity's Sake.
McHugh, H.   For a Sad God.
Millay, E.   Pity me not because the light of day.
Petrarch.   Glancing by chance at my unusual pallor.
  He, who in Thessaly was all too keen.
  I wept, but now I sing: my living sun.
  My love for you has never wearied me.
  O you, my one inestimable gem.
  That powerful lord from whom we cannot hide.
  What pitying messenger, what angel was.
Prunty.   Elderly Lady Crossing on Green.
Riley, J.   My Foe.
Rossetti, C.   After Death.
  Good Lord, today / I scarce find breath to say.
  Plague, The.
  Vanity of Vanities.
Schuyler, J.   Self-Pity Is a Kind of Lying, Too.
Shelley, P.   To Harriet.
Smith, S.   In the Park.
Spender, S.   Coward, The.
Stock, R.   Form of Pity, A.
Tate, J.   Pity Ascending with the Fog.
Unknown.   On Envy.
Wilbur, R.   Pity.
  Undead, The.
Williams, C. K.   Beginning of April, The.
  Scar.
  Ten Below.
Wright, J.   American Twilights, 1957.
  At the Executed Murderer's Grave.
  Inscription for the Tank.
  What the Earth Asked Me.
Yeats.   Pity of Love, The.
Zaturenska.   Virgin, the Doe, and the Leper, The.

Pius IX, Pope

Whittier.   Dream of Pio Nono, The.
  From Perugia.
  To Pius IX.
Wilde, O.   Sonnet on Approaching Italy.

Pius XII, Pope

Whittier.   Prisoners of Naples, The.

Pixies

Riley, J.   Pixy People, The.

See also **Fairies**

Place Names

Hopkins, G.   Bellisle! that is a fabling name, but we.
Major, C.   Study for a Geographical Trail.
Milosz, C.   Rivers ("So lasting they are, the rivers!" Only think. Sources somewhere in the mountains").
Sandburg, C.   Localities.

Plague

Ammons.   In Strasbourg in 1349.
Dove, R.   Fiammetta Breaks Her Peace.
Melville, H.   In the Desert.
Rossetti, C.   Plague, The.
Seifert.   Plague Column, The.
Very.   Plagues of Egypt, The.

Plains

Carver, R.   On the Pampas Tonight.
Merwin.   Beginning of the Plains.
Stafford, W.   Living on the Plains ("Carefully, sending leaves always toward the sun").
  Slow News from Our Place.

See also **Prairies**

Planets

Bogan, L.   At a Party.
Collins, B.   Earthling.
Frost, R.   A-Wishing Well.
Jacobsen, J.   Planet, The.
Jeffers, R.   Moon and Five Planets.
MacDiarmid, H.   Bonnie Broukit Bairn, The.
Petrarch.   This noble soul, starting to move away.
Rexroth, K.   On What Planet.
Sandburg, C.   Bright Conversation with Saint-Ex.

Plants

Amichai [*or* Amikhai].   Elecampane, Jasmine, Vine, and Oleander.
  Oleander.
Berry, W.   April Woods: Morning.
  Broken Ground, The.
Burns, R.   On Chloris Requesting Me to Give Her a Spray of a Sloe-Thorn in Full Blossom.
Clampitt.   Alders.
  Beach Pea, The.
  Fireweed.
  Kudzu Dormant.
  Spruce Has No Taproot, The.
  Sun Underfoot Among the Sundews, The.
Cowper, W.   On a Plant of Virgin's Bower.
  Poet, the Oyster, and Sensitive Plant, The.
De la Mare.   Miracle, The.
Dickinson, E.   Plants went into camp last night, The.
Dugan, A.   On Naming a Baby Mimosa.
  Philodendron.
  Spring Song for *Symplocarpus Fœtida* and Me.
Eberhart, R.   Forms of the Human.
Emerson, R.   Spices in the plants that run.
Glück, L.   Tree House, The.
Gunn, T.   Mandrakes.
  Rooftop, The.
  Yellow Pitcher Plant.
Gurney, I.   Of Cruelty.
Hardy, T.   At the Royal Academy.
Heaney, S.   Mint.
  Whinlands.
Hill, G.   Sorrel.
Hopkins, G.   From any hedgerow, any copse.
Jacobsen, J.   Rock-Plant Wife, The.
Johnson, S.   On a Lady's Presenting a Sprig of Myrtle to a Gentleman.
Jonson, B.   Garland [*or* Ghyrlond] of the Blessèd Virgin Mary [*or* Marie], The.
Levertov.   For Floss.
  Quality of Genius, The.
Levi, P.   Agave.
Levine, P.   Later Still.
MacDiarmid, H.   Bracken Hills in Autumn.
  Happy on Heimaey.
McHugh, H.   Labor.
Meredith, G.   Song in the Songless.
Millay, E.   Hawkweed, The.
Milton.   Sonnet 3: "As on a rugged mountain at the darkening of evening."
Montale.   Agave on the Reef, The.
Moore, M.   Nevertheless.
Muldoon, P.   Thrush.
Niedecker.   Broad-leaved Arrow-head, The.
  Consider.
Piercy.   High Frequency.
Raine, K.   Vegetation.
Rich, A.   Corpse-Plant, The.
Rilke.   Lemon and Laburnum.
Roethke.   Cuttings.
  Moss-Gathering.
  Root Cellar.
  Transplanting.
Rossetti, C.   Summer.
Schuyler, J.   Blossoming Oakwood.
  Three Gardens.
  What Ails My Fern?
Sexton.   Love Plant, The.
Smart, C.   Country Squire and the Mandrake, The.
Smith, S.   Stroke, The.
Stock, R.   Plant Called Yarrow, The.
  Saxifrage.
Swinburne.   Sundew, The.
Szymborska, W.   Silence of Plants, The.
Walker, A.   Woman Is Not a Potted Plant, A.
Wilbur, R.   Children of Darkness.
  Fern-Beds in Hampshire County.
  Seed Leaves.
Williams, W.   It Is a Small Plant.

Plath, Sylvia

Ciardi, J.   Trying to Feel Something.
Kumin, M.   Apostrophe to a Dead Friend.
Sexton.   Sylvia's Death.
Updike.   Upon Looking into Sylvia Plath's *Letters Home.*
Wilbur, R.   Cottage Street, 1953.

Plato

Auden.   No, Plato, No.
Clough.   Uranus.
Eberhart, R.   Commitment, A.
  Great Principles Are Thrown Down by Time.
Lawrence, D. H.   For the Heroes Are Dipped in Scarlet.
Milton.   On the Platonic Idea as Aristotle Understood It.
Orr, G.   Available Now: Archaic Torsos of Both Sexes.
Raine, K.   Afternoon sunlight plays.
Stock, R.   Hostage, The.
  Wherein the Maker's Right Hand Moralizes the Way to a Familiar but Rare Felicity, Whatwhile the Left Hand Seemingly Knoweth Not Its Brother's Ambages and So Falleth in the Way of an Undiscerning Subtraction.
Unknown.   Spirit of Plato.
Yeats.   His Bargain.
  Statistics.
  What Then?

Platonic Love

"Dario."   I love the faces pallid.
Donne.   Air[e] and Angels.
  Ecstasy, The.
Eberhart, R.   Hand, The.
Logan, J.   Paperboys, The.
Michelangelo Buonarroti.   For a wound from the searing arrows Love lets fly.
  From heaven it ventured forth, there must return.
  He who beguiles both time and death together.
  If right desire takes wing.
  My gaze saw no mere mortal on the day.
  Not true that it's always grim with mortal sin.
  Pray tell me, Love, if what my eyes can see.
  Where my love lives is nowhere in my heart.
Pessoa.   Interval.
  Sensationist Poem, A.
Petrarch.   I used to take the blame, but now excuse.
  My soul, who see, hear, read, think, speak, and write.
  O time, O turning sky, speeding away.
  Pleasant obduracy, and calm rejection.
Riley, J.   My Laddie wi' the Bashfu' Grace.
Sandburg, C.   Little Word, Little White Bird.
Schuyler, J.   Dear Joe.
  Looking Forward to See Jane Real Soon.
  Night, The.
  Sky Eats Up the Trees, The.
  Tomorrow.

Play

Angelou.   Harlem Hopscotch.
Ashbery, J.   Paradoxes and Oxymorons.
Borges.   Note for a Fantastic Story.
Carew, T.   To the Reader of Master William Davenant's Play [*The Wits*].
Collins, B.   Some Days.
Cowper, W.   Impromptu ["So I have seen the maids in vain"].
Dickinson, E.   God is indeed a jealous God.
  It is easy to work when the soul is at play.
Eberhart, R.   Wild Life and Tamed Life.
Ginsberg, A.   Bop Lyrics.
Gunn, T.   Hide and Seek.
  Menace, The.
  Seesaw.
Gurney, I.   Hedges.
Hughes, L.   Piggy-back.
Komunyakaa.   Playthings.
Kunitz, S.   Testing-Tree, The.
Lawrence, D. H.   Disagreeable Advice.
  Man at Play on the River, A.
Levi, P.   Chess.
  Chess 2.
Logan, J.   Pagan Saturday.
Lux.   Princess Summer Fall Winter Spring.
Meredith, G.   Alternation.
  And tho' my friar's mandate is severe.

I say, that but for black Foakes'-day.
Millay, E. From a Very Little Sphinx.
Nemerov. Warning: Children at Play.
Orr, G. Ditch, The.
Palmer, M. As a Real House.
Prunty. Grown Men at Touch.
Ransom, J. Old Man Playing with Children.
Riley, J. Company Manners.
  When Baby Played.
  When We First Played "Show."
  Where the Children Used to Play.
Rossetti, C. Clever little Willie wee, / Bright
  eyed, blue eyed little fellow.
  Frisky Lamb, A.
  I caught a little ladybird.
  Playing at bob cherry / Tom and Nell and Hugh.
Rumi. Sheikh Who Played with Children, The.
Sandburg, C. Props.
Simic. Game, The.
Smith, S. I Like to Play with Him.
Snyder, G. Hop, Skip, and Jump.
Stafford, W. At the Playground.
Swenson, M. Centaur, The.
Wordsworth, W. Intent on Gathering Wool from
  Hedge and Brake.
Zagajewski. Just Children.

Playhouses
Swenson, M. Playhouse, The.
See also **Theater and Theaters**

Playmates
Gunn, T. Seesaw.
Kipling, R. Playmate, The.
Riley, J. Boys, The.
  George A. Carr.
  Hik-Tee-Dik.
  Little Fat Doctor, The.
  Me and Mary.
  Old Haymow, The.
Rossetti, C. Clever little Willie wee, / Bright
  eyed, blue eyed little fellow.
  Lambs at Play.
  Playing at bob cherry / Tom and Nell and Hugh.
Stafford, W. First Grade.
Williams, C. K. Gift, The.
Yeats. To a Squirrel at Kyle-Na-No.

Pleasure
Baudelaire. L'Invitation au Voyage.
  Pagan's Prayer, The.
Berrigan, T. Many Happy Returns.
  Peace.
Borges. Just, The.
Broumas, O. Buenos Días.
  Choir, The.
  Days of Argument and Blossom.
  Tryst.
Browning, E. Best Thing in the World, The.
Burns, R. Down the Burn Davie.
  Here's, a bottle and an honest friend.
  My Love She's But a Lassie Yet.
  Sandy and Jockie.
Byron, G. Translation from Anacreon.
Carver, R. Afghanistan.
  Grant, The.
Cavafy. I Went.
  Imenos.
  In the Street.
  Julian and the Antiochians.
  Pleasure in the Flesh.
  Regiment of Pleasure, The.
  Their Origin.
Coleridge, S. Kubla Khan: or, A Vision in a
  Dream.
Corbett, W. Under Ideal Conditions.
Cowper, W. Progress of Error, The.
Creeley. For Arthur Okamura.
  For Martin.
  Was.
  Woman, The.
Cummings, E. E. I'm very fond of.
  Out of a supermetamathical subpreincestures.
Dickinson, E. Expectation—is Contentment.
  Heart asks Pleasure—first, The.
  I Taste a Liquor Never Brewed.
  Stagnant pleasure like a Pool, A.
  There is an arid Pleasure.
Dugan, A. Untitled Poem: "I never saw any

point."
Eberhart, R. Thrush Song at Dawn.
Emerson, R. Mask thy wisdom with delight.
  See how Romance adheres.
Gray, T. Ode on the Pleasure Arising from
  Vicissitude.
Gunn, T. Modes of Pleasure.
  Sweet Things.
Gurney, I. March.
  What Was Dear.
Hacker, M. Canzone: "Consider the three
  functions of the tongue."
Hall, D. Digging.
  Set of Seasons, A.
Hamill, S. Scrutability.
Hardy, T. Before and after Summer.
  Child and the Sage, The.
  Great Things.
  You on the Tower.
Herrick. On Himself.
  On Himself[e].
  On Himselfe.
  To the Maids to Walke Abroad.
Ignatow, D. Orgasm.
  Without Recrimination.
Jeffers, R. Pleasures.
Johnson, S. Short Song of Congratulation [*or*
  To a Young Heir], A.
Levertov. On the Way.
  Pleasures.
Lorde. Sacrifice.
MacLeish. Starved Lovers.
Marvell. Dialogue Between The Resolved Soul
  and Created Pleasure, A.
Melville, H. Montaigne and His Kitten.
Merton. Song: Sensation Time at the Home, A.
Merwin. Reunion.
Millay, E. Portrait.
Milosz, C. Confession, A.
Milton. L'Allegro.
Olson, C. Whole World, The.
Orr, G. Paradise Lightning Dazzle.
Patchen. Pleasures of This Gentle Day.
Pessoa. Lightly, quickly, soft.
Pound, E. Immorality, An.
Ralegh, S. No Pleasure, Without Some Payne.
Ramanujan. Pleasure.
Rilke. Bitter Pleasure.
Rossetti, C. Candlemas Dialogue, A.
  Do This, and He Doeth It.
  Goblin Market.
  Lay Up for Yourselves Treasures in Heaven.
  Mariana.
  Memento Mori.
  Passing away the bliss, / The anguish passing
  away.
  River Thames (?).
  Sorrow hath a double voice, / Sharp today but
  sweet tomorrow.
  What?
  Where love is, there comes sorrow / Today or
  else tomorrow.
  Yea, I Have a Goodly Heritage.
Seifert. Bach Concerto, A.
Shelley, P. Birth of Pleasure, The.
  Love, Hope, Desire and Fear.
Snyder, G. Under the Skin of It.
Very. Pleasure ("Goddess of pleasure, where
  thy golden car?").
Warren, R. Interjection #8: Or, Sometimes,
  Night.
Weiss, T. Pleasure, Pleasure.
Wilbur, R. Ode to Pleasure.
  Simile for Her Smile, A.
  Statues.
Yeats. Chambermaid's First Song, The.

Pleiades
Muldoon, P. Three Deer, Mount Rose, August
  1995.
Schuyler, J. Just before Fall.
Thoreau. Atlantides, The.
Whitman, W. On the Beach at Night.

Plowing and Plowmen
Burns, R. Ploughman, The.
Dubie. These Untitled Little Verses in Which, at
  Dawn, Two Obscure Dutch Peasants Struggled

with an Auburn Horse.
Frost, R. Plowmen.
Heaney, S. Follower.
Hopkins, G. Harry Ploughman.
Housman. When smoke stood up from Ludlow.
Sandburg, C. Plowboy.
Stevens, W. Silver Plough-Boy, The.
Tomlinson, C. Lines.
Whitman, W. As I Watch'd the Ploughman
  Ploughing.

Plum Trees and Plums
Atwood. Late August.
Carruth, H. Bears at Raspberry Time.
Glück, L. Flowering Plum.
Millay, E. Plum Gatherer, The.
Rexroth, K. Bread and Butter Letter, A.
Snyder, G. Aged Tamba Temple Plum Tree
  Song.
Whalen, P. Dharmakaya.
  Plums, Metaphysics, an Investigation, a Visit,
  and a Short Funeral Ode.
Williams, W. This Is Just to Say.
  To a Poor Old Woman.
Wilner, E. Ume: *Plum*.
Wright, C. Lives of the Artists.

Plumbing and Plumbers
Dugan, A. On Plumbing after an Air Raid.
Merwin. Plumbing, The.
Nash, O. Pipe Dreams.
Niedecker. Nursery Rhyme.
  To My Pres- / sure Pump.
Ritsos. Message.

Plunder and Plundering
Cavafy. On an Italian Shore.
Fenton, J. Nest of Vampires.
Herrick. Rapine Brings Ruine.

Plutonium
Ginsberg, A. Plutonian Ode.

Plymouth, England
Davie, D. Among Artisans' Houses.
Hardy, T. Marble-Streeted Town, The.
Spender, S. Air Raid Across the Bay at
  Plymouth.

Poaching and Poachers
Ciardi, J. Feasts.
Kipling, R. Ballad of Minepit Shaw, The.
  Rhyme of the Three Sealers, The.
Wright, J. Lifting Illegal Nets by Flashlight.

Pocahontas
Clampitt. Matoaka.
Lindsay, N. Our Mother Pocahontas.
Nash, O. Captain John Smith.
Sandburg, C. Cool Tombs.

Poe, Edgar Allan
Carruth, H. Mild Winter.
Dubie. Jeremiad.
Ginsberg, A. Haunting Poe's Baltimore.
  To Poe: Over the Planet, Air Albany–Baltimore.
Gunn, T. Readings in French.
Koch, K. You Were Wearing.
Levine, P. On the Edge.
Lindsay, N. Wizard in the Street, The.
Lux. Edgar Allan Poe Meets Sarah Hale
  (Author of "Mary Had a Little Lamb").
Mallarmé. Tomb of Edgar Poe, The.
Smith, S. After-Thought, The.
Very. Forevermore.

Poetic Meter
Eberhart, R. Why.
Koch, K. Art of Poetry, The.
Meredith, W. About Poetry.
Sheridan, T. Of Figures Peculiar to Prosody.
Tennyson, A. Hendecasyllabics.
Williams, W. Asphodel, That Greeny Flower.
  Paterson, Book 5: The River of Heaven.

Poetry and Poets
Amichai [*or* Amikhai]. Beit Guvrin.
  Dennis Was Very Sick.
  Ibn Gabirol.
  North of Beersheba.
  On the Day My Daughter Was Born No One
  Died.
  On the Day My Daughter Was Born Not a
  Single Person Died.
  Summer Evening in the Jerusalem Mountains.

Takis Sinopolus, Greek Poet.
Two Poets in Mexico.
Yehuda Ha-Levi.
Ammons. Alternatives.
Conserving the Magnitude of Uselessness.
Essay on Poetics.
Extremes and Moderations.
Garden.
Hibernaculum.
Hippie Hop.
Medium.
Motion.
Muse.
Plunder.
Poetics.
Positions.
Put-Down Come On, The.
Reassessing.
Summer Session.
Swan Ritual, The.
Archpoet. Confession of Bishop Golias, The.
Armantrout. Birthmark: The Pretext.
Inside Out.
Manufacturing.
Ashbery, J. Paradoxes and Oxymorons.
What Is Poetry.
Atwood. Aging Female Poet Sits on the
Balcony.
Auden. Dichtung und Wahrheit.
Bandeira. My Last Poem.
Baudelaire. Albatross, The.
Benediction.
Mercenary Muse, The.
My Beatrice.
Sun, The.
'Tasso in Prison' by Delacroix.
To Theodore de Banville.
Wine of the Solitary Man, The.
Begley, T. Photovoltaic.
Sappho's Gymnasium.
Bierce. Bride, The.
Humility.
Literary Method, A.
Possibility, A.
To a Dejected Poet.
Vision of Doom, A.
Blok. Among the Admirers of Carmen.
Borges. Accomplice, The.
Ariosto and the Arabs.
Ars Poetica.
Browning Resolves to Be a Poet.
Camden, 1892.
Matthew 25:30.
Moon, The.
Other Tiger, The.
Parable of the Palace.
Paris, 1856.
Poet of the Thirteenth Century, A.
South, The.
That Man.
To a Minor Poet of 1899.
To a Minor Poet of the Greek Anthology.
To a Saxon Poet.
To Manuel Mujica Lainez.
Two Cathedrals, The.
Bradstreet, A. In Honour of that High and
Mighty Princess Queen Elizabeth of Happy
Memory.
Prologue, The.
Brodsky, J. Elegy: For Robert Lowell.
Brooke, H. Quilca House to the Dean.
Broumas, O. Artemis.
Demeter.
Five Interior Landscapes.
Photovoltaic.
Sappho's Gymnasium.
Browning, E. Earth and Her Praisers.
Browning, R. How It Strikes a Contemporary.
One Word More.
Prologue: "Poet's age is sad: for why?, The."
Bukowski. Beauti-ful.
Byron, G. E Nihilo Nihil.
To Lord Thurlow.
Campion, T. Ad Librum.
Carew, T. Elegy upon the Death of the Dean of
[St.] Paul's, Dr. John Donne, An.

Carruth, H. Birth of Venus, The.
Godhulivela.
Impossible Indispensability of the Ars Poetica,
The.
Master, Grieved with Age, The.
Meadow House.
Tabula Rasa.
Carver, R. Account, An.
Cougar, The.
Grant, The.
March into Russia, The.
My Crow.
One More.
Pen, The.
Pipe, The.
Poems.
Radio Waves.
Reaching.
Some Prose on *Poetry*.
Sunday Night.
Cavafy. And I Reclined and Lay on Their Beds.
Byzantine Gentleman, in Exile, Composing
Verses, A.
Correspondence According to Baudelaire.
First Step, The.
For Ammons, Who Died at 29, in 610.
Inkwell, The.
I've Gazed So Long, So Much.
Melancholy of Jason Kleander; Poet in
Kommagini; 595 A.D.
Mimiambi of Herodas, The.
Nous N'osons Plus Chanter les Roses.
Poet and the Muse, The.
Ships, The.
Simeon.
Temethos, Antiochian; 400 A.D.
That's the Man.
Theater of Sidon (400 A.D.).
Understanding.
Very Seldom.
When They Surge, Excited.
Cavalcanti. Each day I come to you an infinity
of times.
Sonnet: He interprets Dante's Dream, related in
the first Sonnet of the Vita Nuova.
Sonnet: He rebukes Dante for his way of Life,
after the death of Beatrice.
Syllogism makes one from many, A.
Wanting I send you certain poems.
Celan. Afternoon with Circus and Citadel.
Argumentum e Silentio.
By Threes, By Fours.
In Memoriam Paul Éluard.
It's all different from what you think, from what
I think.
Tübingen, January.
Vinegrowers dig up.
Wolfsbean.
Ciardi, J. At Least with Good Whiskey.
For Miller Williams.
Guide to Poetry, A.
Instances.
Interruption, An.
It Is for the Waking Man to Tell His Dreams.
Letter from a Metaphysical Countryside.
No White Birds Sings.
Nothing Is Really Hard but to Be Real.
On Meeting Miss B.
On Passion as a Literary Tradition.
On the Poet as a Damned Poor Thing.
Poetry.
Poet's Words, The.
Praise of Good Poets in a Bad Age, A.
Some Figures for Who Must Speak.
To W. T. Scott.
Was a Man.
Cino da Pistoia. Sonnet: He answers the
foregoing Sonnet, and prays Dante, in the
name of Beatrice, to continue his great Poem.
Sonnet: He conceives of some Compensation in
Death.
Sonnet: He impugns the verdicts of Dante's
Commedia.
Sonnet: He interprets Dante's Dream, related in
the first Sonnet of the Vita Nuova.
Sonnet: He owes nothing to Guido as a Poet.

Clampitt. Chichester.
Coleorton.
Cure at Porlock, A.
Elgin Marbles, The.
He Dreams of Being Warm.
Hurricane and Charlotte Mew, The.
Imago.
Isle of Wight, The.
Margate.
Teignmouth.
Voyages.
Winchester: The Autumn Equinox.
Clifton, L. Here Yet Be Dragons.
My Dream About the Poet.
Study the Masters.
Telling Our Stories.
Clough. About what sort of thing.
Veni.
Codrescu. De Natura Rerum.
Eugenio Montale in California.
My Next Book.
Paper on Humor.
Poem: "Supreme test of one's poem, The."
Poetry.
Poetry Paper.
Coleridge, S. Homeric Hexameter, The.
Metrical Feet.
Ovidian Elegiac Metre, The.
Collins, B. American Sonnet.
Flight of the Reader, The.
Introduction to Poetry.
Japan.
Lines Composed over Three Thousand Miles
from Tintern Abbey.
Madmen.
Paradelle for Susan.
Plight of the Troubadour.
Purity.
Reading an Anthology of Chinese Poems of the
Sung Dynasty, I Pause to Admire the Length
and Clarity of Their Titles.
Rival Poet, The.
Sonnet: "All we need is fourteen lines, well,
thirteen now."
Taking Off Emily Dickinson's Clothes.
Workshop.
Cooper, J. Calling, The.
Green Notebook, The.
Long View from the Suburbs.
Ordinary Detail.
Poem with Capital Letters, A.
Praise.
Corbett, W. In out of this shower.
Of Small Delights in Idleness.
"Poetry," John Wieners.
Putting socks away.
Reading C. K. Williams's "The Critic."
This Morning After.
To Kate Bluestein.
Tu Fu in English.
When I Read John Wieners's Selected Poems.
Cowper, W. Ode: Secundum Artem, An.
Table Talk.
Crane, S. Tell me not in joyous numbers.
Creeley. The ("A's").
Corn Close.
Dishonest Mailmen, The.
Early Reading.
End.
Epic Expands, The.
For Rene Ricard.
Method, A.
Talk ("Talking Ginsbergian").
Thanks.
There ("With all I know").
Theresa's Friends.
Touchstone.
Cullen, C. After a Visit.
Poet, The.
Sonnet: "What I am saying now was said
before."
That Bright Chimeric Beast.
To an Unknown Poet.
Yet Do I Marvel.
Cummings, E. E. Four III.
If I Have Made, My Lady.

Little joe gould has lost his teeth and doesn't know where.
My Prayer.
No man,if men are gods;but if gods must.
Out of the pants which cover me.
Phonograph may(if it likes)be prophe, The.
Since feeling is first.
Sonnet entitled how to run the world).
To start,to hesitateø stop.
Cunningham, J. Fancy.
For My Contemporaries.
Lector Aere Perennior.
Obsequies for a Poetess.
Symposium, The.
With a Copy of Stevens' *Harmonium*.
Dante Alighieri. Sonnet: Written in Exile.
"Dario." Exploit in the Bullring.
In Autumn ("I know that there are those who say, "Why don't you sing now'").
Poet put in his verses, The.
Salvador Díaz Mirón.
Towers of God! Poets!
When the poor guy saw her pass.
Davie, D. Bent, The.
Berryman.
Bits and Pieces.
Elders and Betters.
Garland for Ivor Gurney, A.
Having No Ear.
Heart Beats.
Hypochondriac Logic.
In the Stopping Train.
Leicestershire.
Lost Bride, The.
Love-Poems: for Mairi MacInnes.
Mandelstam in the Crimea.
North & South.
Oak Openings.
Or, Solitude.
Pastor Errante.
Poem as Abstract.
Poet Redeemed & Dead.
Poet-Scholar, The.
Replying to Reviewers.
Six Epistles to Eva Hesse.
Somerset.
Summer Lightning.
Thomas and Emma.
To a Bad Poet.
To C. T.
To Certain English Poets.
Zip!
De la Mare. Happy Encounter, The.
Delany, P. From My Much Honored Friend at Heldelville.
Upon the Author.
Dickinson, E. All the letters I can write.
I dwell in Possibility.
I reckon—when I count at all.
They shut me up in Prose.
To learn the Transport by the Pain.
To see the Summer Sky.
Drummond de Andrade. Irritated Office, The.
Dubie. Clouds of Magellan (Aphorisms of Mr. Canon Aspirin), The.
For Milarepa, In Ruse, on Rice Paper.
Friary at Blossom, Prologue & Instructions, The.
Ode to the Spectral Thief, Alpha.
Dugan, A. After a Poem by Carlos Drummond de Andrade Translated by Elizabeth Bishop as *Don't Kill Yourself*.
American Variation on How Rilke Loved a Princess and Got to Stay in Her Castle.
Another Cat Poem. To a Cat Person.
Branches of Water or Desire, The.
February Twelfth Birthday Statement.
In Favor of a Free Public Library System.
In Memoriam. Unfinished. For Robert Barlow. 1950.
Poem: "After your first poetry reading."
Speech for Auden.
Dunbar, P. To E. H. K.
Dunbar, W. Lament for the Makaris [*or* Makars *or* Makers].
Duncan, R. Poetry, a Natural Thing.
Eberhart, R. 21st Century Man.

At the End of the War.
Deep Fishing.
Emerson's Concord.
Killer, The.
Life and Death.
Long Term Suffering.
Meaningless Poem.
Moment of Vision, The.
News.
Place, The.
Poem as Trajectory, The.
Poetry and Games.
Refrains.
Sacrifice, The.
To William Carlos Williams.
Undercliff Evening.
Winter Kill.
Worldly Failure.
Eliot, T. S. Note on War Poetry, A.
Triumph of Bullshit, The.
Emerson, R. I grieve that better souls than mine.
Merlin.
Motto to "The Poet."
Seyd planted where the deluge ploughed
Test, The.
William does thy frigid soul.
Enzensberger, H. Further Reasons Why Poets Do Not Tell the Truth.
Faiz. If I Were Certain.
Fenton, J. Letter to John Fuller.
Frost, R. In a Poem.
Gallagher, T. Instructions to the Double.
Redwing.
Refusing Silence.
García Lorca. Crossroad.
Lullaby in Death for Rosalía de Castro.
New Songs.
Ginsberg, A. City Midnight Junk Strains.
Contest of Bards.
G.S. Reading Poesy at Princeton.
Grim Skeleton.
I attempted to concentrate.
Last Night in Calcutta.
Psalm 4.
Reading French Poetry.
Returning to the Country for a Brief Visit.
To an Old Poet in Peru.
Written in My Dream by W. C. Williams.
Youth the color of the hills laughed delighted at his Vanity, The.
Gjuzel. When I Came Back.
Goethe. Confession.
Graves, R. De Arte Poetica.
Poem: A Reminder.
Gurney, I. Compensations.
First Poem.
Garden, The.
Last of the Book, The.
Poet, The.
Soft Rain.
There Have Been Anguishes.
Two, The.
War Poet.
We Who Praise Poets.
"H. D." Heliodora.
Hacker, M. Feeling and Form.
Rhetoric.
Riposte.
Untoward Occurance at Embassy Poetry Reading.
Hamill, S. Another Duffer.
Blue Monody.
Letter to Robert Hedin.
October Frost.
Old Bones.
Organic Form.
Reading Seferis.
True Illumination Is Habitude.
Han-shan. Disappointed impoverished scholars.
My five-word poems number five hundred.
People laugh about my poems.
When stupid people read my poems.
Whoever has Cold Mountain's poems.
HaNagid. Critique, The.
He'll Bring You Trouble.

Heaney, S. Fosterling.
Poet's Chair.
Singing School.
Whitby-sur-Moyola.
Helsham, R. Prologue to *Hippolytus*, Spoken by a Boy of Six Years Old.
Herbert, G. Jordan (1).
Jordan (2).
Quidditie [*or* Quiddity], The.
Sonnet: "My God, where is that ancient heat towards Thee."
Herrick. His Prayer for Absolution.
Ode for Him [*or* Ben Jonson], An.
To Live Merrily, and To Trust to Good Verses.
Verses.
Hill, G. Four Poems Regarding the Endurance of Poets.
History as Poetry.
Hughes, L. Anne Spencer's Table.
Formula.
Metropolitan Museum.
My Beloved.
Poet to Patron.
Hughes, T. Chaucer.
Earthenware Head, The.
Famous Poet.
Poets.
Ignatow, D. Hello.
I'm a Depressed Poem.
In a Dream 1.
With My Back.
Ivanov, G. Mirrors, reflecting each other.
Jackson, L. Dilemmist, The.
March, 1937.
Poem Only.
Poet: A Lying Word.
Then Follows.
Jacobsen, J. Birdsong of the Lesser Poet.
Gentle Reader.
Lines to a Poet.
Minor Poet, The.
Poet as Mute.
There Is Good News.
When the Five Prominent Poets.
Jonson, B. Elegy [*or* Elegie], An: "Let me be what I am, as Virgil cold."
Epistle Answering to One That Asked to Be Sealed of the Tribe of Ben, An.
Fit of Rhyme [*or* Rime] against Rhyme [*or* Rime], A.
Proludium.
Sonnet to the Noble Lady, the Lady Mary Wroth, A.
To John Donne ("Who shall doubt, Donne, where [*or* whe'er] I a poet be[e]").
To the Memory of My Beloved, the Author Mr [*or* Master] William Shakespeare: And What He Hath Left Us.
Kinnell. For Robert Frost.
Oatmeal.
Kinsella, T. Brothers in the Craft.
I wonder whether one expects.
Magnanimity.
Open Court.
Stranger, The.
Kizer, C. Afternoon Happiness.
Ashes, The.
Days of 1986.
Eleutheria.
Fin-de-Siècle Blues.
Final Meeting.
For Sappho/After Sappho.
In the First Stanza.
Ingathering.
Linked Verses.
Marriage Song: "We begin with the osprey who cries, "Clang, clang!"."
Muse, A.
Not Writing Poems about Children.
Plaint of the Poet in an Ignorant Age.
Poem, Small and Delible.
Poet's Household, A.
Reading Your Poems in Your House While You Are Away.
Silent Man, The.
Singing Aloud.

To a Visiting Poet in a College Dormitory.
To an Unknown Poet.
Translation.
Two Poets by the Lake.
Way We Write Letters, The.
Koch, K.   Art of Poetry, The.
Pleasures of Peace, The.
Komunyakaa.   1938.
  Blue Light Lounge Sutra for the Performance
    Poets at Harold Park Hotel.
  Borinken Blues.
  De Síntoma Profundo.
  Death Threat Note.
  House of Snow, A.
  Insufficient Blue.
  Letter to Bob Kaufman.
  Recital of Water over Stones.
  Returning the Borrowed Road.
  Under House Arrest.
  What Counts.
Kumin, M.   Calling, A.
  Marianne, My Mother, and Me.
Kunitz, S.   Class Will Come to Order, The.
  Spark of Laurel, A.
  Three Small Parables for My Poet Friends.
Laughlin, J.   After Martial.
  Among the Roses.
  Antiphilus.
  Beautiful Morning.
  Blowpipe Game, The.
  Care and Feeding of a Poet, The.
  Deconstructed Man, The.
  Dylan.
  Folk Wisdom.
  Getting Paid.
  Happy Poets, The.
  I Hate Love.
  I Know How Every Poet.
  I Take a Certain Pride.
  If a Poet.
  Importance of Dictionaries, The.
  Ingenium Nobis Ipsa Puella Facit.
  Inner Life of the Septic Tank, The.
  Job Description, A.
  La Tristesse.
  Lady Asks Me, A.
  Leave-taking, A.
  Like the Octopus.
  Metropolitan Bard.
  Moment on Earth, A.
  My Instructions.
  My Muse.
  No Comparison.
  O Hermes Trismegistus.
  Person, The.
  Poem Factory, The.
  Poem Seen as a Shell Game, The.
  Poets.
  Power of Poesy, The.
  Preguntas sin respuestas for Nicanor Parra.
  Reclining Position, The.
  Shameful Profession, The.
  So Much Depends.
  Some Memories of E. P. (Drafts & Fragments).
  Some of Us Come to Live.
  Some People Think.
  Technical Notes.
  Temporary Poems.
  Then and Now.
  Tuesday at 87 Rue de Rome.
  We Met in a Dream.
  Why.
  Why Shouldn't I.
  You Know How a Cat.
Levertov.   Artist to Intellectual (Poet to
    Explainer).
  Cancion: "When I am the sky."
  Cloak, A.
  Conversation in Moscow.
  For X.
  Goodbye to Tolerance.
  Grey Sparrow Addresses the Mind's Ear.
  Growth of a Poet.
  Illustrious Ancestors.
  Kingdoms of Heaven.
  Making Peace.

Memories of John Keats.
Poem Rising by Its Own Weight, The.
Poet and Person.
Poet Li Po Admiring a Waterfall, The.
Prayer, The.
To Antonio Machado.
Too Easy: to Write of Miracles.
Williams: An Essay.
Writing in the Dark.
Levi, P.   Leavetaking.
  Memorandum Book.
Li Po.   Present for Tu Fu from Li Po, A.
Logan, J.   Century Piece for Poor Heine, A.
  Death of Southwell, The.
  Elegy for Dylan Thomas.
  Elegy for the Rev. Mr. James B. Hodgson
    (1892–1963).
  Feast of Friends, A.
  Homage to Christina Rossetti.
  Homage to Rainer Maria Rilke.
  Lines Against A Loved American Poet After
    Hearing An Irish One's Nickman.
  Lives of the Poet, The.
  On the Death of Keats; Lines for Those Who
    Drown Twice.
  Poem, Slow to Come, On the Death of
    Cummings (1894-1962).
  Poem: Tears, Spray, and Steam.
  Poet Scratches His Head, The.
  Search, The.
  Staying Awake.
  To a Young Poet Who Fled.
  Visit to Bill Merwin at His Hawaiian Home, A.
Logue, C.   Fragment.
  To My Fellow Artists.
Lowell, R.   Randall Jarrell 1. October 1965.
Lux.   At the Far End of a Long Wharf.
  Edgar Allan Poe Meets Sarah Hale (Author of
    "Mary Had a Little Lamb").
  Elegy for Robert Winner.
  "Mr John Keats Five Feet Tall" Sails Away.
  Walt Whitman's Brain Dropped on Laboratory
    Floor.
MacLeish.   Ars Poetica.
  Theory of Poetry.
Mahon.   Drawing Board, The.
  Rage for Order.
Mallarmé.   Album Leaf.
  Azure, The.
  Bell-Ringer, The.
  Entire soul evoked, The.
  Fan, A; of Madame Mallarmé.
  Flowers, The.
  Funereal Toast.
  Her pure nails on high displaying their onyx.
  Little Air (Martial).
  Prose.
  Salutation.
  Tomb.
  Tomb of Charles Baudelaire, The.
  Tomb of Edgar Poe, The.
  Weary of Bitter Sleep.
  When the shadow menaced with its fatal law.
Marvell.   On Mr Milton's "Paradise Lost."
McGrath, T.   Against the False Magicians.
  Flint and Steel.
  You Can Start the Poetry Now, Or: News from
    Crazy Horse.
McHugh, H.   Blue Streak.
  What He Thought.
  What Poems Are For.
Meredith, G.   Empty Purse: A Sermon to our
    Later Prodigal Son, The.
  To R.H.H. with Daphne.
  Tuck, Demitroïa, / Ariadne, and Froyja.
Meredith, W.   About Poetry.
  American Living Room, The: A Tract.
  Cheer, The.
  Envoi: "Go, little book. If anybody asks."
  For Guillaume Apollinaire.
  Grace.
  Ideogram.
  In a Copy of Yeats' Poems.
  In Loving Memory of the Late Author of *Dream
    Songs*.

In Memory of Robert Frost.
Orpheus.
Poem: "Swans on the river, a great, The."
Remembering Robert Lowell.
Talking Back (To W. H. Auden).
Merwin.   Berryman.
  Envoy from d'Aubigné.
  Third Psalm: The September Vision.
  We Continue.
Millay, E.   I will put Chaos into fourteen lines.
Milosz, C.   1945.
  Against the Poetry of Philip Larkin.
  Aleksander Wat's Tie.
  Cabbies dozed under St. Mary's Tower.
  Dedication: "You whom I could not save."
  In Black Despair.
  In Milan.
  In Szetejnie.
  Lecture, A.
  Magic Mountain, A.
  New Province, A.
  No More.
  On Poetry, upon the Occasion of Many
    Telephone Calls after Zbigniew Herbert's
    Death.
  On the Death of a Poet.
  Poet at Seventy.
  Poetic State, A.
  Preface: "First, plain speech in the mother
    tongue."
  Prescription.
  Reading the Japanese Poet Issa (1762–1826).
  Reading the Notebook of Anna Kamienska.
  Reconciliation.
  Report.
  Rozewicz.
  Secretaries.
  Selecting Iwaszkiewicz's Poems for an Evening
    of His Poetry at the National Theater in
    Warsaw.
  Texas.
  This.
  Thistle, the Nettle, The.
  To Allen Ginsberg.
  To find my home in one sentence, concise, as if
    hammered in metal.
  To Robinson Jeffers.
  Translating Anna Swir on an Island of the
    Caribbean.
  Treatise on Poetry, A.
  Under a linden tree, as before, daylight.
  Winter.
  You Who Wronged.
Milton.   To Mr. H. Lawes On His Airs.
Montale.   For an "Homage to Rimbaud."
  Syria.
  Winter Light.
Moore, M.   Past Is the Present, The.
  Poetry: "I, too, dislike it: there are things that
    are important beyond all this fiddle."
Muldoon, P.   Green Gown.
  Key, The.
Nash, O.   Brief Guide to Rhyming, or, How Be
    the Little Busy Doth?, A.
Niedecker.   Ballad of Basil, The.
  Cricket-song.
  Dear Paul: / the sheets of your father's book of
    poetry.
  If I Were a Bird.
  In the great snowfall before the bomb.
  I've been away from poetry.
  Letter from Ian.
  LZ ("He walked—loped—the bridge").
  LZ's.
  Man of law, The.
  Mourning Dove.
  Now in one year.
  Oh ivy green.
  Otherwise.
  Santayana's.
  They live a cool distance.
  To a Maryland Editor, 1943.
  Your father to me in your eighth summer.
O'Hara, F.   To Gottfried Benn.
Olson, C.   Muse / is the "fate" of the poem,
    The.

You know, verse.
Oppen. Any Way But Back.
Boy's Room.
Cultural Triumph, A.
Five Poems about Poetry.
Gold on Oak Leaves.
If It All Went Up in Smoke.
In Memoriam Charles Reznikoff.
Latitude, Longitude.
Lighthouses, The.
Little Pin, The: Fragment.
Phonemes, The.
Poem, The ("How shall I light").
Semite.
Song, The.
Song, the Winds of Downhill.
To the Poets: To Make Much of Life.
Two Romance Poems.
O'Rahilly. Poet Egan O'Rahilly, Homesick in Old Age, The.
Orlandi, G. Prolonged Sonnet: He finds fault with the Conceits of the foregoing Sonnet.
Orr, G. Elegy: "Not only doesn't the Ohio."
Journey, The.
Lucky.
Poem in New York.
Some Part of the Lyric.
There.
Visit to the Island of Lost Souls.
Wild Heart.
Owens, S. Poem, A: "Ye Sons of Levi, Church Divines."
Pagis. Deceased Writer, The: Photograph in the Rain.
Memorial Evening.
Out of Line.
Small Poetics, A.
Paley, G. Letter, A.
Poet's Occasional Alternative, The.
Responsibility.
Palmer, M. Called Poem of the End.
Lies of the Poem.
Mei-mei, here is the table.
Notes for Echo Lake 3.
Thee thou on looking out.
Parker, D. Bric-à-Brac.
Daylight Savings.
Far-Sighted Muse, The.
Fighting Words.
For a Lady Who Must Write Verse.
From a Letter from Lesbia.
Lines on Reading Too Many Poets.
Oh Look—I Can Do It Too.
Pig's-Eye View of Literature, A.
Pour Prendre Congé.
Song in the Worst Possible Taste.
Verses in the Night.
Pasolini. Desperate Vitality, A.
Plan of Future Works.
Poetry of the Tradition, The.
Pasternak, B. Oh had we known it turns out so.
To Anna Akhmátova.
Patchen. Often Was It.
Poem Written after Reading Certain Poets Sired by the English School and Bitched by the C.P.
Poems which are written by the soul.
Pavlovski, R. Climate and Lyre.
Pessoa. And there are poets who are artists.
At night I suddenly waken.
Autopsychography.
Four songs that follow now, The.
From the highest window of my house.
I go indoors, and shut the window.
I have a terrible cold.
I never kept sheep.
I'd give anything if only my life were an oxcart.
If at times I say that flowers smile.
If I could take a bite of the whole earth.
If they want me to be a mystic, fine. I'm a mystic.
I'm a keeper of sheep.
Moonlight between the tall branches, The.
My glance is clear like a sunflower.
On a terribly clear day.
Once at mid-day in late spring.

One way or another.
Only Nature is divine, and she's not divine.
Rather the flight of the bird passing and leaving no trace.
Rhymes mean nothing to me. Only rarely.
Startling reality of things, The.
To think of God is to disobey God.
Today I read nearly two pages.
Petrarch. Alexander, before the sepulchre.
Breath, the fragrance, and the cooling shade, The.
Gluttony, sleep, swans-down of idleness.
Had I believed those words would turn out dear.
I knew—so much heaven opened up my eyes.
I know that never with a tranquil mind.
I see, my noble lady.
I wish to sing no more as once I did.
I would write poems of love of such a kind.
If but that honoured branch which turns away.
If but these thoughts that hurt.
If I had lingered longer in the cave.
If Virgil and Homer had but seen that sun.
It makes me weary when I realise.
Kindly fortune that made me once so happy.
Love, lend a hand to my afflicted mind.
My wish has always been to live alone
Now blessed be the day, the month, the year.
Once I had hopes (so fervent was my rhyme).
Sennuccio, though you leave your friend alone.
Since through my destiny.
Sometimes I am ashamed that I have never.
That bravery, which came to flower in you.
That miracle—which in these days of ours.
These kindly rhymes by which you have made known.
Through her I swapped the Arno for the Sorgue.
To some it may well seem I pitch my style.
Towards the dawn, when *l'aura* (the mild breeze).
Weep, ladies; as you weep, let Love weep too.
When I hear you attractively speak out.
While my poor heart was being eaten still.
With my long-honoured, dear, and cruel lord.
Pinkerton, H. Autumn Drought.
For Edgar Bowers.
Pinsky. If You Could Write One Great Poem, What Would You Want It to Be About?
Impossible to Tell.
Poe. Enigma, An.
Pound, E. And Thus in Nineveh.
Cino.
Coda: "O My songs."
Epilogue: "I bring you the spoils, my nation."
Ité.
L'Art.
Leviora.
Marvoil.
Salvationists.
Swinburne: A Critique.
To E. B. B.
To Guido Cavalcanti.
Prunty. Dr. Williams' Garden.
Letter for the End.
Ramanujan. Any Cow's Horn Can Do It.
Black Hen, The.
No Fifth Man.
On the Death of a Poem.
Poetry and Our City.
River, A.
Rashid, N. Izhab-O-Rasai (Expression and Reach).
Rexroth, K. 140 Syllables.
Bonapartisme.
Codicil.
Hanged Man, The.
Harmodius and Aristogeiton.
Letter to Yvor Winters, A.
Stone and Flower.
Sufficient The.
To Another.
Untitled: "I am fifty-two years old."
Very Early Morning Exercise, A.
Rich, A. I Am in Danger—Sir.
Poetry: I.
Riley, J. Art and Poetry.
Christmas Season.

Ginoine Ar-tickle, The.
If I Knew What Poets Know.
Job Work.
Lisping in Numbers.
Little Dead Man, The.
Little Old Poem That Nobody Reads, The.
Meredith Nicholson.
Nessmuk.
On a Fly-Leaf.
On Reading Dr. Henry van Dyke's Volume of Poems—Music.
Poems Here at Home, The.
Poet of the Future, The.
Prose or Verse?
Rhymes of Ironquill, The.
Songs of a Life-Time.
To Bliss Carman.
To Edmund Clarence Stedman.
To My Good Master.
Wash Lowry's Reminiscence.
When We Three Meet.
Wholly Unscholastic Opinion, A.
Why.
Worn-out Pencil, A.
Written in Bunner's "Airs from Arcady."
Your Height Is Ours.
Rilke. Poet, The.
Stubborn Man.
To Madame Jeanne-Renée Dubost.
To Monique and Blaise Briod.
Rimbaud, A. Drunken Boat.
Second Delirium. Alchemy of the Word.
Seven-year-old Poets.
What the Poet is Told on the Subject of Flowers.
Ritsos. Descent.
Extinction.
Farmer.
Final Hour.
Hints.
His Lamp.
His Lamp toward Daybreak.
Honesty.
Last Will and Testament.
Meaning of Art, The.
Meaning of Simplicity, The.
Moonlight Sonata.
Necessary Explanation.
New Pretexts.
Not Even.
Poet's Space, The.
Reverential Comparison.
Revival.
Trivial Details.
Twilight.
Unaccomplished.
Rochfort, G. With Music and Poetry Equally Blessed.
Rossetti, C. Charades.
New Enigmas.
Roundel seems to fit a round of days, A.
Rossetti, D. On Burns.
Rukeyser, M. Poem White Page White Page Poem.
Sixth Night: Waking, The.
Rumi. Listen to presences inside poems.
Music, The.
No Flag.
Sanai.
Sandburg, C. Cups of Coffee.
Impossible Iambics.
Letters to Dead Imagists.
Now They Bury Her Again.
Sketch of a Poet.
Tentative (First Model) Definitions of Poetry.
Schuyler, J. What.
Seifert. And Now Goodbye.
At one of his readings a long time ago.
Bach Concerto, A.
Chaplet of Sage, A.
Hunt for the Kingfisher, The.
If you call poetry a song.
Lunar Ironmongery.
Prologue: "To be a poet is no easy task."
Red-Hot Fruit.
Relay Tower, The.
Reluctant whispers of kissed lips.

Salute to the Madrid Barricades.
Smoke of Marijuana, The.
Song from an Intermezzo.
To Be a Poet.
Sexton.   Obsessive Combination of Ontological
   Inscape, Trickery and Love, An.
Sheridan, T.   Cur Me Bespateras, Blaterans
   Furiosè Poeta.
Figures of Speech.
His Modest Apology for Knocking Out a News-
   Boy's Teeth, Who Told Him His Works
   Would Not Sell.
I Can't but Wonder, Mr. Dean.
I'll Write While I Have Half an Eye in My
   Head.
Last Speech and Dying Words of Daniel
   Jackson, The.
Letter from a Cobbler in Patrick's Street to Jet
   Black, A.
My Pedagogue Dear, I Read with Surprise.
Now to Lampoon Myself for My Presumption.
Of Epigram.
Of Figures Peculiar to Prosody.
Of Quantity Which Depends upon the Authority
   of the Poets.
Palinodia.
Pedagogue's Answer, The.
Perlegi Versus Versos, Jonathan Bone, Tersos.
Sheridan to Dan Jackson.
To Dean Swift.
To George Nim-Dan-Dean, Esq. upon His
   Incomparable Verses, &c. of August 2d,
   1721.
To the Author of "Tom Pun-Sibi
   Metamorphosed."
To the Dean.
To the Dean of St. Patrick's ("Dear Sir, since
   you in humble wise").
To the Rev. Doctor Swift, Dean of St. Patrick's.
   A Birthday Poem. Nov. 30, 1736.
To the Same.
You Made Me in Your Last a Goose.
Shih-te.   I have millions of gathas.
My poems are poems alright.
Smart, C.   Epistle to John Sherratt, Esq, An.
Snyder, G.   As for Poets.
Axe Handles.
How Poetry Comes to Me.
What You Should Know to Be a Poet.
Stafford, W.   Are you Mr. William Stafford?
Final Exam: American Renaissance.
How These Words Happened.
Introduction to Some Poems, An.
Notice What This Poem Is Not Doing.
Poetry.
Report from a Far Place.
Slow News from Our Place.
Why I Am a Poet.
Stevens, W.   Arrival at the Waldorf.
As You Leave the Room.
High-Toned Old Christian Woman, A.
Of Modern Poetry.
Planet on the Table, The.
Poem That Took the Place of a Mountain, The.
Poetry Is a Destructive Force.
Stock, R.   Anacreontic for a Chinese Scholar.
Epistle to Simon Perchik.
Epistle to Suzanne Joslyn Fosberg.
First Last Will & Testament.
Great High Feasts on the Birthdays of Little
   Men.
Hand.
Imitation of Horace; Carmina 1.6.
Impromptu with a Breeze.
Lock, The.
Nightmare Song.
Poem Written on the Typewriter.
Poet Mário Faustino Descends Into Hades and
   Rises to the Empyrean.
Poet's Bestiary.
Poet's Prescription of Shamelessness, The.
Selected Poems of Mañuel Bandeira, The.
Signing the Poem.
Synapse, The.
That the Sestina is What it is Despite What it is
   Not.

Ultimate Poem, The.
Stockton, A.   Epistle to a Friend Who Urg'd to
   Have Some Poetry Sent Her in the Year 1759,
   in the Winter, An.
On Reading Dr Beaties Hermit.
Thoughts on the Pythagorian System.
To Aspasio.
To Doctor Smith on His Birth Day March 16th,
   92.
To Miss Mary Stockton, an Epistle the 10th of
   Janu 78.
Suckling, S.   To My Friend Will. Davenant,
   upon His Poem of "Madagascar."
Swenson, M.   Daffodildo.
In the Bodies of Words.
Truth is Forced, The.
Swift, J.   To Thomas Sheridan.
Sze.   Li Po.
Wang Wei.
Szymborska, W.   Evaluation of an Unwritten
   Poem.
In Broad Daylight.
In Praise of My Sister.
Poetry Reading.
Some Like Poetry.
Stage Fright.
Tate, J.   Interruptions.
Nature Poem: Demanding Stiff Sentences.
Poem to Some of my Recent Poems.
Thomas, D.   In My Craft or Sullen Art.
Thoreau.   My life has been the poem I would
   have writ.
Poet's Delay, The.
Tisdall, W.   Tom Pun-Sibi Metamorphosed: Or,
   The Giber Gibed.
Tomlinson, C.   Backward Glance, A.
Chances of Rhyme, The.
Doggerel for My Seventieth Birthday, A.
In Memory of George Oppen.
Orion over Farne.
Retrospect, A: 1951-91.
To Ivor Gurney.
Tu Fu.   Thwarted.
Tu Fu to Li Po.
Unknown.   Answer, The [By the Gentleman of
   the Navy].
Ballata: Of True and False Singing.
Elegy on the Deplorable Death of Mr. Thomas
   Sheridan, Author of *Alexander's Overthrow,
   or, The Downfall of Babylon*, Who Departed
   This Mortal Life on Thursday the 8th of
   March, 1721/22, An.
Letter to Tom Punsibi, Occasioned by Reading
   His Excellent Farce, Called *Alexander's
   Overthrow, or, The Downfall of Babylon*, A.
Myself and Pangur.
New Jingle on Tom Dingle, A.
Poem on Tom Pun——bi on Occasion of His
   Late Death, and in Vindication of Some
   Verses Written, Entitled "Sheridan's
   Resurrection," A.
Punegyric upon Tom Pun-sibi's *Ars Pun-ica*, A.
Rivals, The.
To My Worthy Friend T S——, D. D. On His
   Incomparable Translation of and Notes on
   Persius.
Tom Pun-Sibi's Resurrection Disproved.
Tom Punsibi's Farewell to the Muses.
Vallejo.   Testimony.
Very.   Poet, The.
Poet's Plea, The.
Sonnet, To the Rev. James Flint, D. D., On
   reading his Collection of Poems.
Warren, R.   Corner of the Eye, The.
Only Poem, The.
To Certain Old Masters.
Weiss, T.   Before the Night.
Library Revisited, The.
Living Room, A.
Preface.
"Yes, But . . ."
Whalen, P.   Dear Mr President.
International Date Line, Monday/Monday
   27:XI:67.
Life of Literature, The.
Literary Life in the Golden West.

Plums, Metaphysics, an Investigation, a Visit,
   and a Short Funeral Ode.
Prose Take-Out, Portland, 13:ix:58.
Since You Ask Me.
Success Is Failure.
Take, 25:iii:59.
To a Poet.
True Confessions.
What About It?
Winter, The ("Why do I fear the true winter
   death to come").
Wheatley, P.   Philis's Reply to the Answer in
   Our Last by the Gentleman in the Navy.
To Maecenas.
Whitman, W.   Out of the Cradle Endlessly
   Rocking.
Wilbur, R.   Event, An.
Wilde, O.   Garden of Eros, The.
Sweet I blame you not for mine the fault was,
   had I not been made of common clay.
Theoretikos.
To My Wife: With a Copy of My Poems.
With a Copy of 'A House of Pomegranates'
Williams, C. K.   Yours.
Williams, M.   And Then I Headed on Back
   Home.
Excuse Me.
For Rebecca, for Whom Nothing Has Been
   Written Page after Page.
Form and Theory of Poetry.
Let Me Tell You.
On Hearing About the Death of Mitzi Mayfair.
Style.
Things.
To a Friend, an Unhappy Poet.
Williams, T.   As I stood in my room tonight,
   drinking a solitary toast.
Challenge to Poets, A.
I see them lying sheeted in their graves.
New Poet, The.
Song: "Girls that have loved me."
Under the April Rain.
Williams, W.   Come On!
Coronal, A.
Defense.
Dish of Fruit, The.
Entity, The.
Phoenix and the Tortoise, The.
Poet and His Poems, The.
Riposte.
Uses of Poetry, The.
Wilner, E.   Ars Poetica.
Filling in the Blanks.
How to Get in the Best Magazines.
Lament: "All morning I have been reading
   poems."
Never Apologize for Poetry.
Poem of Exile, A.
Postscript.
Salute to Donald Davie.
What Was Left Over.
Wordsworth, W.   Scorn not the Sonnet; Critic,
   you have frowned.
To the Poet, John Dyer.
Valedictory Sonnet.
Wright, C.   After Rereading Robert Graves, I Go
   Outside to Get My Head Together.
Cicada Blue.
Lives of the Artists.
Miles Davis and Elizabeth Bishop Fake the
   Break.
Poem Half in the Manner of Li Ho.
Reply to Wang Wei.
Thinking About the Night Sky, I Remember a
   Poem by Tu Fu.
Waiting for Tu Fu.
With Simic and Marinetti at the Giubbe Rosse.
Yard Work.
Wright, J.   Many of Our Waters: Variaitons on a
   Poem by a Black Child.
Non-Birthday Poem for My Father, A.
Yeats.   Adam's Curse.
He Gives His Beloved Certain Rhymes.
Spirit Medium, The.
When You Are Old.
Zagajewski.   Chinese Poem.

Farewell for Zbigniew Herbert.
For You.
Houston, 6 P.M.
Immortality.
Long Afternoons.
Lullaby.
New World.
Poems on Poland.
Russia Comes Into Poland.
Self-Portrait.
Separation.
September.
Speak Softly.
That Force.
To.
Transformation.
World's Prose, The.
Zaturenska. Homage to Christina Rossetti.
Zukofsky, L. Her face the Book of—Love
  Delights in—Praises.
Lines of this new song are nothing, The.
"Mantis," An Interpretation.
Old Poet Moves to a New Aprtment 14 Times,
  The.
Peri Poietikes.
See also **Writing and Writers**
Poetry: Study and Teaching
Williams, W. Asphodel, That Greeny Flower.
Paterson, Book 5: The River of Heaven.
Pogroms
See **Massacres**
Poison
Baudelaire. Poison.
Burns, R. Lord Ronald My Son.
Cavafy. Bouquets.
Donne. To Sir Edward Herbert, at Juliers [*or*
  Julyers].
Emerson, R. At last the poet spoke.
Enzensberger, H. Poison, The.
Graves, R. Poisoned Day.
Herrick. Upon Love.
Kizer, C. On a Line from Valéry.
Nemerov. And Is Silent.
Pagis. In the Laboratory.
Pinsky. Heartmoss, The.
Ritsos. Wells and People.
Sandburg, C. Anecdote of Hemlock for Two
  Athenians.
Stock, R. Banquet, The.
Williams, M. How the Elephant Got His Hump.
Poison Oak
Pinkerton, H. Nature Note: The California
  Poison Oak.
Poker
Dugan, A. Portrait of a Local Politician.
Nemerov. Day on the Big Branch, A.
Myth & Ritual.
Pinsky. Ice-Storm, The.
Sexton. Rowing Endeth, The.
Poland
Berryman. 1 September 1939.
Brodsky, J. Martial Law Carol, A.
Clampitt. Anniversary, The.
Davie, D. In Chopin's Garden.
Dubie. In the Time of False Messiahs.
Lamentations.
Milosz, C. Dedication: "You whom I could not
  save."
Hooks of a Corset, The.
King Popiel.
My Faithful Mother Tongue.
Nation, A.
Selecting Iwaszkiewicz's Poems for an Evening
  of His Poetry at the National Theater in
  Warsaw.
Undressing Justine.
With Her.
Szymborska, W. In Broad Daylight.
Vocabulary.
Weiss, T. But suppose / you could, like a
  painter, nail down.
By this eye, north of its frowning.
Envoy: "So, to complete the spectrum."
O, no, except for newsreels, books.
Over the phone a good friend asks.
Painting, finished, A.

Polish Question, The.
Stacks of illustrations.
Suppose your powers such.
Theory of Repetition, The.
Thick smoke coils up, the shriveled.
We talked the last of the mild.
Words, words, such deeds words, come.
Zagajewski. Fever.
Poems on Poland.
Polish Biographical Dictionary in a Library in
  Houston, The.
Russia Comes Into Poland.
Stary Sacz.
To Go to Lvov.
Watching Shoah in a Hotel Room in America.
Police and Police Stations
Ai. Antihero, The.
Interview with a Policeman.
Brooks, G. "Negro" Hero.
Chesterton. Christmas Carol, A: "God rest you
  merry gentlemen."
Codrescu. Police, The.
Cummings, E. E. Two X.
Dugan, A. Cop-Shooting: On a Newspaper
  Photograph.
Ginsberg, A. Kral Majales.
Hughes, L. Ballad of Ozie Powell.
Black Maria.
Café: 3 a.m.
Third Degree.
Who but the Lord?
Jacobsen, J. For Any Member of the Security
  Police.
Komunyakaa. Cage Walker, The.
Lawrence, D. H. Gross, Coarse, Hideous.
Man in the Street, The.
Levertov. Grace-Note, The.
Lowell, R. Opposite House, The.
MacNeice. Mahavveray.
Niedecker. Working man appeared in the street,
  A.
Orr, G. On a Highway East of Selma, Alabama.
Patchen. Letter to a Policemen in Kansas City,
  A.
Rich, A. Frame.
Rumi. Drunks fear the police.
Sandburg, C. Stripes.
Van Duyn. That was my grandfather, nearly
  went to prison.
Williams, C. K. Crime.
Police States
Brodsky, J. Martial Law Carol, A.
Ritsos. Real Hands.
Simic. Shaving at Night.
Zagajewski. Iron.
Politics and Politicians
Ai. Blood in the Water.
Blue Suede Shoes.
Go.
Hoover Trismegistus.
Miracle in Manila.
Amichai [*or* Amikhai]. Let the Coin Decide.
Mayor.
Poems of Resigning.
Political Poem, A.
What a Complicated Mess.
Armantrout. Sets.
Atwood. Torture.
Auden. Partition.
Bierce. France.
Statesmen, The.
Blake, W. Blind-Man's Buff.
Blue Cloud. Quebec, rattling chains of
  Separatism.
Brodsky, J. Anno Domini.
Kolo.
Once More by the Potomac.
To the President-elect.
Broumas, O. Artemis.
Browning, E. August Voice, An.
Italy and the World.
Summing Up in Italy.
Tale of Villafranca, A.
Burns, R. Act Sederunt of the Session—A Scots
  Ballad.
Author's Earnest Cry and Prayer, to the Right

Honorable and Honorable, the Scotch
  Representatives in the House of Commons,
  The.
Awa Whigs Awa.
Ballad, A: "While Prose-work and rhymes."
Buy Braw Troggin. An Excellent New Song.
Election: A New Song, The.
Epistle to Robt. Graham Esq: of Fintry on the
  Election for the Dumfries String of Boroughs,
  Anno 1790.
Extempore [on the *Loyal Natives'* Verses].
Fête Champetre, The.
Five Carlins—A Ballad—Tune, Chevy Chase,
  The.
Johnie B———'s Lament.
Ode to the Departed Regency-Bill—1789.
On the Death of the Late Lord President
  Dundas.
Solemn League and Covenant, The.
Song: "O, Logan, sweetly didst thou glide."
Wham will we send to London town.
Cavafy. Death of the Emperor Tacitus, The.
Chesterton. Elegy in a Country Churchyard.
Chuang Tzu. Man with One Foot and the Marsh
  Pheasant, The.
Ciardi, J. Week That Was, The.
Clampitt. Dahlia Gardens, The.
Coleridge, S. Character, A.
Verses Addressed to J. Horne Tooke and the
  Company Who Met on 28 June 1796 to
  Celebrate His Poll at the Westminster
  Election.
Cowper, W. On Thurlow.
Creeley. Menu, The.
News of the World.
Cummings, E. E. Ballad of an Intellectual.
F is for foetus(a).
Next to of Course God America I.
Nobody could / in superhuman flights.
Opening of the chambers close.
Politician, A.
Red-rag and pink-flag.
Salesman, A.
This evangelist / buttons with his big gollywog
  voice.
Way to hump a cow is not, The.
When muckers pimps and tratesmen.
Davie, D. After a Change of Régime.
Barnsley and District.
Chernobyl. A Disaster.
Elect, The.
Heroine of the Academy, A.
Right Wing Sympathies.
T. S. Eliot (1928).
Dryden, J. To My Honoured [*or* Honour'd]
  Kinsman, John Driden [of Chesterton in the
  County of Huntingdon, Esquire].
Dubie. Nine Black Poppies for Chac.
Two Women on the Potomac Parkway.
Dugan, A. Love and Money.
On When McCarthy Was a Wolf among a
  Nation of Queer-Queers.
Portrait of a Local Politician.
Dunbar, P. Speakin' at de Cou't-House.
Eberhart, R. Rape of the Cataract, The.
Eliot, T. S. Coriolan.
Emerson, R. Van Buren.
Fenton, J. Lullaby for a Summer Recess.
Ferlinghetti, L. Sandinista Avioncitos.
Frost, R. Build Soil.
No Holy Wars for Them.
To a Thinker.
García Lorca. Cry to Rome.
Ginsberg, A. America.
Ballad of the Skeletons, The.
Birdbrain!
Capitol Air.
Kral Majales.
Overpopulation, overpopulation / Give me 3
  acres of land.
These States: into L.A.
These States: to Miami Presidential Convention.
Thoughts on a Breath.
Glück, L. Exile.
Gurney, I. Portraits.
Hacker, M. Untoward Occurance at Embassy

Poetry Reading.
HaNagid.   Could Kings Right a People Gone
  Bad.
Herrick.   To His Kinsman, Sir Tho. Soame.
  To Sir John Berkeley, Governour of Exeter.
  True Safety.
Hughes, L.   Ballad of Roosevelt.
  Corner Meeting.
  Final Call.
  Governor Fires Dean.
  Mitchell Case, The.
  NAACP.
  To Certain Negro Leaders.
  Un-American Investigators.
Ignatow, D.   Simulacrum.
Jarrell, R.   English Garden in Austria, An.
  State, The.
Jeffers, R.   Greater Grandeur.
  Ink-Sack.
  Sinverguenza.
  Stars Go Over the Lonely Ocean, The.
Johnson, S.   Translation of the Latin Epitaph on
  Sir Thomas Hanmer, Written by Doctor Freind,
  A.
Jonson, B.   New Cry, The.
  To Robert, Earl of Salisbury ("Who can
    consider thy right courses run").
  To the Parliament.
  To the Same [Robert, Earl of Salisbury] [Upon
    the Accension of the Treasurership to Him].
  To Thomas, Lord Chancellor.
Keats.   Otho the Great.
Kipling, R.   Declaration of London, The.
  Things and the Man.
Kizer, C.   Death of a Public Servant, The.
  Valley of the Fallen, The.
Komunyakaa.   Good Joe.
Kunitz, S.   Daughters of the Horseleech, The.
  System, The.
Laughlin, J.   Ipse Dixit.
Lawrence, D. H.   Hard-Boiled Conservatives.
  Hibiscus and Salvia Flowers.
Levertov.   Split Mind, The.
Lindsay, N.   Bryan, Bryan, Bryan, Bryan.
  What the Moon Saw.
  Why I Voted the Socialist Ticket.
Logue, C.   I Shall Vote Labour.
Lowell, R.   Words.
McGrath, T.   Note on the Late Elections, A.
Meredith, W.   Mild-Spoken Citizen Finally
    Writes to the White House, A.
  Nixon's the One.
  On Jenkins' Hill.
  Politics.
Merrill, J.   Roger Clay's Proposal.
Merton.   Note in Honor of Machiavelli, A.
  Original Child Bomb.
  Public Affairs.
Merwin.   Caesar.
Milosz, C.   Higher Arguments in Favor of
    Discipline Derived from the Speech Before the
    Council of the Universal State in 2068.
  In Milan.
  Mid-Twentieth-Century Portrait.
  Nation, A.
  You Who Wronged.
Nash, O.   Election Day Is a Holiday.
Nemerov.   To the Rulers.
Olson, C.   Issue, Mood.
  Memory, Mind, and Will.
  Rufus Woodpecker visited the President.
Oppen.   From Up-State.
Paley, G.   Leaflet.
  My Father at 85.
  What If (This Week).
Pasolini.   Ashes of Gramsci, The.
  Plan of Future Works.
  Poetry of the Tradition, The.
Patchen.   I Don't Want to Startle You but They
    Are Going to Kill Most of Us.
Piercy.   Curse of the Earth Magician on a Metal
    Land.
Pinsky.   Discretions of Alcibiades.
Pope, A.   Epitaph on James Craggs, Esq., in
    Westminster Abbey.
  Epitaph on Sir William Trumbal.

Ramanujan.   Image for Politics, An.
  Lac into Seal.
  Ruler, A.
Rexroth, K.   New Objectives, New Cadres.
Rich, A.   Atlas of the Difficult World, An.
Riley, J.   Jap Miller.
  John McKeen.
  Local Politician from Away Back, A.
Robinson, E.   On the Way.
Rukeyser, M.   Until I stand on the January
    platform.
Sandburg, C.   Money, Politics, Love, and Glory.
  Under the Capitol Dome.
Shelley, P.   Similes for Two Political Characters
    of 1819.
Sheridan, T.   Joshua Battus's Spepeech to the
    Paparliament.
Simonides.   On a Military Graveyard.
Smith, S.   Hast Du Dich Verirrt?
Spender, S.   Helmut.
Stevens, W.   Sketch of the Ultimate Politician.
Stockton, A.   Impromptu on Hearing that a Print
    of the Guliteene with Our Beloved Presidents
    Figure under It Was Executed in Mr Genets
    Family—under His Sanction.
  Impromptu on Reading the Several Motions
    Made against Mr. Hamilton.
Swift, J.   Dog and the Thief, The.
  Simile, A.
Sze.   Axis, The.
  Impressions of the New Mexico Legislature.
Szymborska, W.   Children of Our Age.
  Children of Our Era.
  Smiles.
Tomlinson, C.   Machiavelli in Exile.
  Siena in Sixty-Eight.
Updike.   Sin City, D.C.
  Washington: Tourist View.
Very.   On the late Disgraceful Scene in
    Congress.
  Political Ambition.
Warren, R.   Patriotic Tour and Postulate of Joy.
  Terror.
Whitman, W.   Song for Certain Congressmen.
  Thought.
  Thoughts.
  To a President.
Whittier.   King Solomon and the Ants.
  Lost Statesman, The.
  One of the Signers.
  Samuel J. Tilden.
  Thiers.
  To a Poetical Trio in the City of Gotham.
  To a Southern Statesman.
  To William H. Seward.
  Wilson.
Wilbur, R.   Miltonic Sonnet for Mr. Johnson on
    His Refusal of Peter Hurd's Official Portrait,
    A.
Wilde, O.   To Milton.
Williams, C. K.   Interrogation II.
  Politics.
Williams, F.   Ode, An: "At length revolving
    fates th' expected year."
Williams, M.   Politics.
  Senator Explains a Vote, The.
Wordsworth, W.   Blest Statesman He, Whose
    Mind's Unselfish Will.
  Composed after Reading a Newspaper of the
    Day.
  Help for the Memory of the Grand Independent;
    A New Song, A.
  Hint from the Mountains for Certain Political
    Pretenders.
  Placard for a Poll Bearing an Old Shirt.
  Prelude, Prefixed to the Volume Entitled "Poems
    Chiefly of Early and Late Years."
  Protest against the Ballot.
  Sonnets upon the Punishment of Death.
  Squib on Colonel Evans, A.
  To the Utilitarians.
Wright, J.   Eisenhower's Visit to Franco, 1959.
Yeats.   Politics.
Zagajewski.   Referendum.

Pollution
Ammons.   North Jersey.

Working Still.
Auden.   Curse, A.
Davie, D.   Conditioned Air, A.
Dugan, A.   Hope against Pollution, A.
  Untitled Poem: "One used to be able to say."
Ginsberg, A.   Ballade of Poisons.
  Homework.
  Swirls of Black Dust on Avenue D.
Graves, R.   Poisoned Day.
Kizer, C.   On a Line from Valéry.
Komunyakaa.   Fog Galleon.
Laughlin, J.   End of It All, The.
Lawrence, D. H.   Obscenity.
Meredith, W.   Country Stars.
Merwin.   Lackawanna.
Milosz, C.   Rivers ("'So lasting they are, the
    rivers!' Only think. Sources somewhere in the
    mountains").
Neruda.   Bomb (II).
Olson, C.   Every Man His Own Matador; or for
    That Matter Any Member of the Family.
Raine, K.   Polluted tide, / Desecrated earth
    destroyed.
  What message from imagined Paradise.
Sexton.   As It Was Written.
Smith, S.   Friends of the River Trent.
Snyder, G.   Bomb Test.
Williams, T.   Demon Smoke.
See also **Conservation; Ecology and Ecologists**
Polo
Stevens, W.   Polo Ponies Practicing.
Polo, Marco
Clampitt.   Brought from Beyond.
Pomegranates
Glück, L.   Pomegranate.
Lawrence, D. H.   Andraitx—Pomegranate
    Flowers.
  Pomegranate.
Mistral, G.   Mother Pomegranate.
Pomp
Meredith, G.   Cool you proceed at speed.
Pompeii, Italy
Ciardi, J.   Back Home in Pompeii.
Dickey, J.   In the Lupanar at Pompeii.
Dugan, A.   On a Fallen Statue Forbidden to the
    Women at Pompeii.
Levi, P.   Girl-Child of Pompei, The.
Shelley, P.   Ode to Naples.
Updike.   Pompeii.
Very.   Pompeii.
Walcott.   Early Pompeian.
Ponds
Kinnell.   Fergus Falling.
  Frog Pond, The.
  Vapor Trail Reflected in the Frog Pond.
Kumin, M.   We Are.
McHugh, H.   Ozone.
Orr, G.   Pond, The.
Stafford, W.   Connections.
Swenson, M.   Water Picture.
Warren, R.   Millpond Lost.
See also **Lakes and Ponds**
Ponies
Ciardi, J.   Tommy's Pond.
Moore, M.   Blue Bug.
Sandburg, C.   Half Way.
Wright, J.   Blessing, A.
Pontius Pilate
Davie, D.   Pilate.
Merwin.   Pilate.
Pinkerton, H.   On Dürer's Etching of Pilate
    Washing His Hands (1512).
Pony Express
Emerson, R.   Too late the anxious fire came.
Muldoon, P.   Radio Horse, The.
Pool (game)
Brooks, G.   We Real Cool.
Carruth, H.   Capper Kaplinski at the North Side
    Cue Club.
Muldoon, P.   Green Gown.
Poorhouses
Hardy, T.   Curate's Kindness, The.
Hughes, L.   Young Gal's Blues.

Pope, Alexander
Johnson, S.   To Eliza Plucking Laurel in Mr
  Pope's Gardens.
Lux.   Mr. Pope.
Pope, A.   Dialogue, A.
Swift, J.   Dr. Swift to Mr. Pope.
Tate, A.   Mr. Pope.

Poplar Trees
Cowper, W.   Poplar Field, The.
García Lorca.   In Memoriam.
"H. D."   Mid-day.
Hopkins, G.   Binsey Poplars (Felled 1879).
Mistral, G.   Poplar Trees, The.
Sandburg, C.   Follies.
  Moonset.
  Poplar and Elm.
Smart, C.   To My Worthy Friend, Mr. T.B. One
  of the People Called Quakers.
Swenson, M.   Poplar's Shadow, The.
Very.   Oak and the Poplar, The.
Wilbur, R.   Poplar, Sycamore.
See also **Aspen Trees**

Poppies
"H. D."   Choros Sequence.
  Sea Poppies.
Levine, P.   Holding On.
Merwin.   White Summer Flower.
Mistral, G.   California Poppy.
Oliver, M.   Poppies.
Plath.   Poppies in July.
  Poppies in October.
Sandburg, C.   Crossing the Ohio When Poppies
  Bloom in Ashtabula.
  Poppies.

Porcupines
Atwood.   Porcupine Meditation.
  Porcupine Tree.
Kinnell.   Porcupine, The.
Nash, O.   Porcupine, The.
Parker, D.   Parable for a Certain Virgin.
Sexton.   Porcupine.

Pornography
Cavafy.   So.
Ciardi, J.   Blue Movie.
Creeley.   Erotica.
Dubie.   Two Women on the Potomac Parkway.
Hacker, M.   Pornographic Poem.
Komunyakaa.   Seeing in the Dark.
Logan, J.   Saturday Afternoon at the Movies.
Muldoon, P.   Cheesecake.
Shapiro, K.   Adult Bookstore.
Szymborska, W.   Opinion on the Question of
  Pornography, An.
Tate, J.   Same Tits.
Updike.   In Memoriam Felis Felis.
Williams, C. K.   Floor.
Williams, W.   Drugstore Library.
  Picture of a Nude in a Machine Shop.
See also **Obscenity**

Porters
Hughes, L.   Porter.

Portland, Maine
Glück, L.   Portland, 1968.
Longfellow, H.   My Lost Youth.

Portraits
Ashbery, J.   Self-Portrait in a Convex Mirror.
Baudelaire.   On a Portrait of Honoré Daumier.
Bourne, V.   Denner's Old Woman.
  Tears of a Painter, The.
Browning, E.   On a Portrait of Wordsworth by
  B. R. Haydon.
  Portrait, A.
  Two Sketches.
Browning, R.   Likeness, A.
  My Last Duchess.
Byron, G.   To Mary on Receiving Her Picture.
Cavafy.   From the Ship.
  Picture of a Young Man, Twenty-three, Done by
    His Friend of the Same Age, an Amateur.
  Tomb of Lanis, The.
Coleridge, S.   Lines on a Portrait of a Lady.
  Melancholy.
  To the Young Artist.
Collins, B.   Candle Hat.
Cowper, W.   On Hayley's Portrait.

On His Portrait.
On Receiving Hayley's Picture.
On the Engraver of His Pourtrait.
On the Receipt of My Mother's Picture out of
  Norfolk [the Gift of My Cousin Ann
  Bodham].
De la Mare.   Portrait, A.
  Son of Melancholy, The.
Dickinson, E.   Brow is that of Deity, The.
  Portraits are to daily faces.
Donne.   Phryne.
Drummond de Andrade.   Family Portrait.
Ferlinghetti, L.   It was a face which darkness
  could kill.
  Jack of Hearts, The.
  Ladakh Buddhess Biker.
  Love Nut, The.
  Mouth of truth, The.
  That fellow on the boattrain who insisted.
Graves, R.   Face in the Mirror, The.
Gurney, I.   Portraits.
Hardy, T.   Enemy's Portrait, The.
  Family Portraits.
  On the Portrait of a Woman About to Be
    Hanged.
Herrick.   On Julia's Picture.
  Upon a Painted Gentlewoman.
Hopkins, G.   On the Portrait of Two Beautiful
  Young People.
Jonson, B.   Poem Sent Me by Sir William
  Burlase, A.
  To the Reader ("This figure, that thou here seest
    put").
Laughlin, J.   Family Portrait, The.
  Reclining Position, The.
Lawrence, D. H.   Portraits.
Lindsay, N.   Moon Is a Painter, The.
Lowell, R.   Charles Vby Titian.
MacLeish.   Contemporary Portrait.
Melville, H.   Formerly a Slave.
Meredith, G.   Fireside Reverie.
Michelangelo Buonarroti.   One of the Bracci, I.
  Now, as you see.
Pagis.   Portrait, The.
Petrarch.   If Polyclitus studied earnestly
  If, when Simone laboured to depict.
Pope, A.   On Lady Mary Wortley Montagu's
  Portrait.
Raine, K.   Oval Portrait: Jessie Wilkie, The.
Ramanujan.   Self-Portrait.
Rexroth, K.   Portrait of a Lady.
Riley, J.   On a Youthful Portrait of Stevenson.
  Uncle William's Picture.
Rochfort, G.   Answer.
Rossetti, C.   In An Artist's Studio.
Rossetti, D.   Portrait, The.
Sandburg, C.   Cartoon.
  Even Numbers.
  Fog Portrait.
  His Own Face Hidden.
  Paula.
  Portrait.
  Sins of Kalamazoo, The.
  Slants at Buffalo, New York.
  Under a Telephone Pole.
  Winter Milk.
Sarton, M.   Portrait by Holbein.
Sexton.   Portrait of an Old Woman on the
  College Tavern Wall.
Sheridan, T.   Another Picture of Dan.
  Answer.
  On the Same.
Stock, R.   Sitting for a Self-Portrait.
Tomlinson, C.   Against Portraits.
Very.   On Seeing the Portrait of Helen Ruthven
  Waterston.
  Portrait, The.
Wilbur, R.   Miltonic Sonnet for Mr. Johnson on
  His Refusal of Peter Hurd's Official Portrait,
  A.
Wordsworth, W.   Effusion in the Pleasure-
  Ground on the Banks of the Bran, Near
  Dunkeld.
  Lines Suggested By a Portrait from the Pencil of
    F. Stone.
  On a Portrait of the Duke of Wellington upon

the Field of Waterloo, by Haydon.
  Recollection of the Portrait of King Henry
    Eighth, Trinity Lodge, Cambridge.
  Sonnet to a Picture by Lucca Giordano in the
    Mureo Borbonico at Naples.
  To a Painter.
  To B.R. Haydon, On Seeing His Picture of
    Napoleon Buonaparte on the Island of St
    Helena.
  To the Author's Portrait.
  Upon a Portrait.
  Upon the Sight of the Portrait of a Female
    Friend.
Zagajewski.   Self-Portrait.
See also **Painting and Painters; Photography and
  Photographers**

Ports
Amichai [*or* Amikhai].   Closing the Jaffa Port.
  Then I went down to the ancient port: human
    actions.
See also **Harbors and Ports**

Portugal and the Portuguese
Borges.   Borges, The.
Pessoa.   Message.
Wyatt, S.   In Spayn.

Possums
See **Opossums**

Posterity
Blok.   To My Friends.
Brodsky, J.   After Us.
Burns, R.   Nature's Law.
Byron, G.   Last Words on Greece.
Cavafy.   Enemies, The.
Eberhart, R.   R. G. E.
Emerson, R.   Cup of life is not so shallow, The.
  Future, The.
  Limits.
  Nature says, / These craggy hills that front the
    dawn.
  Nature will not lose.
  Thank the gods thy governors.
Hardy, T.   John and Jane.
  Life Laughs Onward.
  Sine Prole.
Herrick.   On Himselfe.
  To His Verses.
  To His Worthy Friend, M. Arthur Bartly.
  To the Earle of Westmerland.
  Upon His Verses.
Jonson, B.   Epigram on the Prince's Birth. 1630,
  An.
  Epistle to Elizabeth, Countess of Rutland.
Kipling, R.   Disciple, The.
  England's Answer.
  Heritage, The.
Laughlin, J.   My Ambition.
MacLeish.   Epistle to be Left in the Earth.
  Sentiments for a Dedication.
Merwin.   For the Grave of Posterity.
  Sire.
  To My Brother Hanson.
Milosz, C.   Beinecke Library.
  Inheritor.
  Thistle, the Nettle, The.
  Those Corridors.
Montale.   Where the tennis court once was.
Sandburg, C.   Call the Next Witness.
  Enemy Number One.
Shapiro, K.   Manhole Covers.
Snyder, G.   For the Children.
  Surrounded by Wild Turkeys.
Whitman, W.   From My Last Years.
  Full of Life Now.
  L. of G.'s Purport.
  My Legacy.
  No Labor-Saving Machine.
  Poem of Remembrances for a Girl or a Boy of
    These States.
Whittier.   Autograph, An.
  Name, A.
Wordsworth, W.   Poet to His Grandchild; Sequel
  to "A Plea for Authors."

Postmen
Rexroth, K.   On the Post Office.
See also **Mail and Mailmen**

Potatoes
Heaney, S. Digging.
Komunyakaa. Banking Potatoes.
Levertov. Roast[ing] Potatoes.
Lindsay, N. Potatoes' Dance, The.
Plath. Poems, Potatoes.
Simic. Amazing Potato Peeler, The.
Swenson, M. Deciding.
Very. Potato Blight, The.
Wilbur, R. Potato.

Potomac River
Sandburg, C. Potomac River Mist.
Potomac Town in February.
Smoke Rose Gold.
Whitman, W. By Broad Potomac's Shore.

Pottery and Potters
Ammons. Utensil.
Cavafy. Craftsman of Winebowls.
Clampitt. Sacred Hearth Fire, The.
Dugan, A. On Finding the Meaning of
"Radiance."
Homer. Epigram of Homer, An.
Hughes, L. Dove, The.
Komunyakaa. Back Then.
Ritsos. Potter, The.
Sandburg, C. Jug.
Schuyler, J. Andrew Lord Poems.
Snyder, G. Firing, The.
Whalen, P. Morning Walk, A.
Williams, W. Stone Crock, The.

Pound, Ezra
Berryman. Heroes, The.
Davie, D. England, for Ezra Pound.
Ezra Pound in Pisa.
On a Proposed Celebration of Ezra Pound.
Six Epistles to Eva Hesse.
Ferlinghetti, L. Pound at Spoleto.
Hall, D. Sestina: "Hang it all, Ezra Pound, there
is only the one sestina."
Koch, K. Art of Poetry, The.
Laughlin, J. And Ole Ez said that the.
Beautiful Morning.
La Tristesse.
Like Him I Need the Past.
Reclining Position, The.
Some Memories of E. P. (Drafts & Fragments).
Some of Us Come to Live.
Levertov. September 1961.
MacLeish. Ezry.
Mahon. Kensington Notebook, A.
Olson, C. Lustrum for You, E.P, A.
Oppen. Of Hours.
Rexroth, K. Lost Etc.
Snyder, G. Axe Handles.
Williams, W. To My Friend Ezra Pound.
Wright, C. Landscape with Seated Figure and
Olive Trees.

Poverty
Angelou. Bump d'Bump.
Ashbery, J. Street Musicians.
Baudelaire. Death of the Poor, The.
Death to the Poor.
Mercenary Muse, The.
Seven Old Men, The.
Beckett, S. Sanies II.
Bierce. Judex Judicatus.
Bishop, E. Miracle for Breakfast, A.
Pink Dog.
Bly, R. Man Writes to a Part of Himself, A.
Brodsky, J. MCMXCIV.
Brooks, G. Bean Eaters, The.
Lovers of the Poor, The.
Browning, E. Song for the Ragged Schools of
London, A.
Bukowski. Meek Have Inherited, The.
Trench Warfare.
Burns, R. Address of Beelzebub.
Auld Rob Morris.
Country Lassie.
Jeremiah 15th Ch. 10 V.
Lines Written on a Bank-Note.
New Psalm for the Chapel of Kilmarnock, on
the Thanksgiving-Day for His Majesty's
Recovery, A.
O Mally's Meek, Mally's Sweet.
O That I Had Ne'er Been Married.

Penitential Thought, in the Hour of Remorse—
Intended for a Tragedy, A.
Poem on Life.
Ronalds of the Bennals, The.
Song: "Mark yonder pomp of costly fashion."
Sonnet—On Hearing a Thrush Sing on a
Morning Walk in January.
Why Should Na Poor Folk Mowe.
Campion, T. In Crispinum.
In Nervam.
Carruth, H. If It Were Not for You.
John Dryden.
Song of the Two Crows.
Cavafy. Days of 1909, '10 and '11.
Flowers White and Beautiful, as Were Most
Becoming.
One Who Has Failed.
Cavalcanti. Canzone: A Song against Poverty.
Sonnet: To a newly enriched Man; reminding
him of the Wants of the Poor.
Chaucer. Complaint of Chaucer to His Empty
Purse, The.
Clare, J. Impromptu on Winter.
My Mary.
Tramp, The.
Crane, S. Ah, haggard purse, why ope thy
mouth.
My cross! / Your cross?
Creeley. News of the World.
Poor.
Cullen, C. Saturday's Child.
Cummings, E. E. Unnoticed woman from
whose kind large flesh.
Davie, D. Back of Affluence.
Right Lads, The.
De la Mare. Slum Child, The.
Dickinson, E. I play at Riches—to appease.
None can experience stint.
Dubie. Oration: Half-Moon in Vermont.
Dugan, A. Credo.
To a Red-Headed Do-Good Waitress.
Dunbar, P. Common Things.
Companion's Progress, A.
Precedent.
Éluard, P. Confections.
Emerson, R. Chartist's Complaint, The.
Have ye seen the caterpillar.
New England Capitalist.
Frost, R. Equalizer, An.
Glück, L. Bridal Piece.
Letter from Provence.
Gunn, T. Tenderloin.
Gurney, I. It Is Winter.
Hall, D. Wreckage, The.
Han-shan. Don't stay poor my friend.
Frequent guest of hunger and cold, A.
I was so poor in the past.
I'm poor alas and I'm sick.
Man with a good head and belly, A.
Old lady who lives to the east, An.
They laugh at me hey farm boy.
HaNagid. People Welcome the Rich.
Tyrant Who Rules the Homeless and Poor, The.
Hardy, T. Reminder, The.
Herrick. Plunder, The.
Poore Mans Part, The.
Poores Portion, The.
Poverty and Riches.
Poverty the Greatest Pack.
To God, His Good Will.
To His Deere God.
Upon Adam Peapes.
Upon Boreman. Epig.
Upon Flood, Or a Thankfull Man.
Upon Grubs.
Upon Her Almes.
Upon Tubbs.
Housman. When first my way to fair I took.
Hughes, L. Advertisement for the Waldorf-
Astoria.
Ballad of Roosevelt.
Ballad of the Man Who's Gone.
Barefoot Blues.
Broke.
Crowns and Garlands.
Dime.

Down and Out.
Ennui.
Grant Park.
If-ing.
Madam and the Rent Man.
Necessity.
Park Bench.
Poor Girl's Ruination.
Prayer for a Winter Night.
Success.
Visitors to the Black Belt.
Jeffers, R. Blind Horses.
Jonson, B. Elegy [*or* Elegie], An: "'Tis true,
I'm broke! Vows, oaths, and all I had."
To Alchemists.
To the Right Honourable, the Lord High
Treasurer of England. An Epistle Mendicant.
1631.
Kinnell. To a Child in Calcutta.
Kipling, R. Last of the Light Brigade, The.
Masque of Plenty, The.
Kizer, C. Suppressing the Evidence.
To an Unknown Poet.
Komunyakaa. Breaking Camp.
Kumin, M. Pawnbroker, The.
Laughlin, J. People Boxes, The.
Lawrence, D. H. Altercation.
Poverty.
Young Fathers.
Levertov. For Chile, 1977.
Mystery (Oaxaca, Mexico), A.
Wealth of the Destitute, The.
Lindsay, N. Beggar's Valentine, The.
Honor Among Scamps.
Prologue to "Rhymes to be Traded for Bread."
Logan, J. Dublin Suite: Homage to James
Joyce.
Lux. Empty Pitchforks.
Kwashiorkor; Marasmus.
MacDiarmid, H. Glass of Pure Water, The.
Hokum.
In the Slums of Glasgow.
MacNeice. Slum Song.
McGrath, T. Long Way Outside Yellowstone,
A.
Tourists at Ensenada.
Trouble with the Times, The.
Meredith, W. Korean Woman Seated by a Wall,
A.
Merton. Letter to America, A.
Merwin. Ballade of Sayings.
Millay, E. Ballad of the Harp-Weaver, The.
Nash, O. Lines Indited with All the Depravity
of Poverty.
Nemerov. Poverty Programs, The.
Niedecker. Country's economics sick, A.
Nothing nourishing.
Property is poverty.
Seven years a charming woman wore.
Oppen. Song, the Winds of Downhill.
Street.
Orr, G. Hotel St. Louis, New York City, Fall
1969.
Patchen. Down in Ol' Dontcaradama.
I Can't Understand! I Can't Understand!
It's a Smallworld.
Piercy. Half Past Home.
Pound, E. Garret, The.
Ralegh, S. Have speciall care, that valiant
povertie.
Ramanujan. If Eyes Can See.
Poor Man's Riches 1, A.
Poverty.
Rexroth, K. Bad Old Days, The.
Lucretius, 3, 1053–1076.
Riley, J. "Blue-Monday" at the Shoe Shop.
Folks at Lonesomeville.
Little Mandy's Christmas Tree.
New Year's Plaint, A.
Poor Man's Wealth, A.
Poor Student, The.
Prospective Glimpse, A.
Rimbaud, A. Festivals of Hunger.
Poor People in Church.
Wide-eyed.
Ritsos. Final Obol, The.

Moment.
Same as Always.
Robinson, E.   Poor Relation, The.
Rossetti, C.   Who Have a Form of Godliness.
Rukeyser, M.   Chapultepec Park / II.
Silence of Volcanoes.
Rumi.   I Have Such a Teacher.
Man and a Woman Arguing, A.
Scott, S.   Palmer, The.
Seifert.   Mr Krösing's Top Hat.
Simic.   Austerities.
Black Days.
Smith, S.   Alfred the Great.
Spender, S.   Elementary School Classroom in a
Slum, An.
Hamburg, 1929.
In Railway Halls.
Stafford, W.   Dedication, A: "We stood by the
library. It was an August night."
Swift, J.   Phyllis [or Phillis] [or Progress of
Love, The].
Sze.   Cornucopia, The.
Thoreau.   Poverty.
Tu Fu.   Testament.
Updike.   Eurydice.
Vallejo.   Anger.
Van Duyn.   Ja, we had it hard.
Walcott.   Laventille.
Walker, A.   Facing the Way.
Talking to My Grandmother Who Died Poor.
Whittier.   Poor Voter on Election Day, The.
Williams, T.   Couple, The.
Williams, W.   Pastoral: "When I was younger."
Poor, The.
Proletarian Portrait.
To a Poor Old Woman.
Wilner, E.   Oldest Desire, The.
Wordsworth, W.   Alice Fell; or, Poverty.
Fragment: The Baker's Cart.
Goody Blake and Harry Gill.
I know an aged Man constrained to dwell.
No spade for leagues had won a rood of earth.
Placard for a Poll Bearing an Old Shirt.
Prelude, Prefixed to the Volume Entitled "Poems
Chiefly of Early and Late Years."
Wright, J.   Before a Cashier's Window in a
Department Store.
In Terror of Hospital Bills.
Poor Washed Up by Chicago Winter, The.
Yeats.   Ballad of Moll Magee, The.
Zaturenska.   Future in Miniature.
Song: "Life with her weary eyes."
See also **Need**

Power
Ai.   Hoover, Edgar J.
Atwood.   I am sitting on the / edge of the
impartial.
I see you fugitive, stumbling across the prarie.
Procedures for Underground.
Torture.
We hear nothing these days.
Women's Issue, A.
You did it / it was you who started the
countdown.
Auden.   Epitaph on a Tyrant.
Managers, The.
Berry, W.   Dark with power.
To Think of the Life of a Man.
Browning, R.   Reverie.
Cavafy.   Theodotos.
Chuang Tzu.   Active Life.
Advising the Prince.
Cracking the Safe.
Inner Law, The.
Kingly Man, The.
Need to Win, The.
Owl and Phoenix.
Codrescu.   & Power.
Power.
Dickey, J.   Power and Light.
Dickinson, E.   I Can Wade Grief.
One crown that no one seeks.
Power is a familiar growth.
Dugan, A.   Memories of a Boss in an Ad
Agency.
Remembering an Account Executive.

Eberhart, R.   Birth of the Spirit, The.
Death in the Mines.
Man's Greed and Envy Are So Great.
Request for Offering.
Sea-Hawk.
Sea-Ruck.
Snowfall, A.
Transfer, The.
Waiting To Lean to the Master's Command.
Words.
Emerson, R.   From high to higher forces.
Motto to "Power."
Vain against him were hostile blows.
Ginsberg, A.   Please Master.
Graves, R.   Powers Unconfessed.
Gunn, T.   Legal Reform.
Loot.
Gurney, I.   When From the Curve.
"H. D."   Pygmalion.
Hacker, M.   Rune of the Finland Woman.
Hayden, R.   Wheel, The.
Herrick.   Bad Princes Pill Their People.
Credit of the Conquerer, The.
Cruelty Base in Commanders.
Factions.
Gods Power.
His Power.
More Mighty, the More Merciful, The.
On Himselfe.
Power and Peace.
Shame, No Statist.
Strength to Support Soveraignty.
Hughes, T.   Ghost Crabs.
Jeffers, R.   Be Angry at the Sun.
Blind Horses.
Machine, The.
Unnatural Powers.
What Odd Expedients.
Kizer, C.   Hera, Hung from the Sky.
Lawrence, D. H.   Escape.
Lord's Prayer.
Revolutionary, The.
Levertov.   Action.
Great Wave, The.
Lindsay, N.   Queen of Bubbles, The.
Meredith, G.   Capitalist, The.
Milosz, C.   Counsels.
Nemerov.   To Clio, Muse of History.
Olson, C.   Lion upon the Floor, A.
Oppen.   Power, the Enchanted World.
Patchen.   Poem in the Form of a Letter: to Lauro
de Bosis.
Ransom, J.   Judith of Bethulia.
Robinson, E.   Old King's New Jester, The.
Richard Cory.
Sunken Crown, The.
Rossetti, C.   O glorious sea that in each
climbing wave.
What Hath God Wrought!
Yea, if Thou wilt, Thou canst put up Thy sword.
Rukeyser, M.   Not leaves, not lightning, not the
greatness of rivers.
Structure is rising. It takes on shape, it takes on
meaning, A.
To follow the hard sunlight on the northern
harbor.
Tree of rivers flowing through our lives, A.
Sandburg, C.   Fireborn Are at Home in Fire,
The.
Sarton, M.   Binding the Dragon.
Sexton.   Admonitions to a Special Person.
Shapiro, K.   Essay on Chess.
Office Love.
Shelley, P.   Cancelled Stanza.
Daemon of the World, The; A Fragment.
Fragment: "I would not be a king—enough."
Smart, C.   On the Power of the Supreme Being.
Spender, S.   War God, The.
Thomas, D.   Hand That Signed the Paper, The.
Whalen, P.   Vision of Delight, The.
What Are You Studying, These Days?
Wilbur, R.   She.
Williams, C. K.   Beginning of April, The.
Wordsworth, W.   Calais, August, 1802.
What if our numbers barely could defy.
Wyatt, S.   Of Carthage he, that worthy warrior.

Yeats.   Poet Pleads with the Elemental Powers,
The.
Zagajewski.   Apes.
Zukofsky, L.   You Who Were Made for This
Music.
**Prague, Czech Republic [formerly
Czechoslovakia]**
Celan.   In Prague.
Ginsberg, A.   Kral Majales.
Kizer, C.   Silent Man, The.
Seifert.   Canal Gardens.
Fingerprints.
Four Small Windows.
Head of the Virgin Mary, The.
Lost Paradise.
Lunar Ironmongery.
Merry-Go-Round with White Swan.
Mr Krösing's Top Hat.
Nocturnal Divertimento.
Opening Poem.
Plague Column, The.
Prague.
Prospect of Prague, A.
Relay Tower, The.
Royal Pavilion, The.
Silence Full of Sleighbells.
Sinful City.
Sometimes we are tied down by memories.
Song about Girls, A.
Striking of the Tower Clock, The.
To Prague.
Verses from an Old Tapestry.
View from Charles Bridge.
Wet Picture.
Zagajewski.   September.
Prairies
Carruth, H.   Song: The Famous Vision of
America.
Clampitt.   Prairie, The.
Dickinson, E.   To make a prairie it takes a
clover and one bee.
Kipling, R.   Prairie, The.
Lindsay, N.   Prairie Battlements, The.
Roethke.   In Praise of Prairie.
Sandburg, C.   Haze.
Interior.
Prairie.
Prairie Waters by Night.
Prairie Woodland.
Rusty Crimson.
Two Nocturns.
Stafford, W.   Prairie Town.
Stories from Kansas.
Warren, R.   Prairie Harvest.
Whitman, W.   Night on the Prairies.
Prairie-Grass Dividing, The.
Prairie States, The.
Praxiteles
Ferlinghetti, L.   In hintertime Praxiteles.
Prayer
Amichai [or Amikhai].   Gods Come and Go,
Prayers Remain Forever.
Psalm: "Psalm on the day, A."
Angelou.   Thank You, Lord.
Ashbery, J.   Painter, The.
Atwood.   Three Praises.
Baudelaire.   Reversibility.
Beckett, S.   Sanies II.
Berry, W.   Prayer after Eating.
Purification, A.
Berryman.   Night and the City.
Blok.   Little Priest of the Fen, The.
Bradstreet, A.   Deliverance from a Fit of
Fainting.
For the Restoration of My Dear Husband from a
Burning Ague.
From Another Sore Fit.
Here Follows Some Verses upon the Burning of
Our House [July 10th, 1666. Copied Out of a
Loose Paper].
In My Solitary Hours in My Dear Husband His
Absence.
In Thankful Acknowledgement for the Letters I
Received from My Husband Out Of England.
In Thankful[l] Remembrance for My Dear
Husband['ls Safe Arrival[l].

My thankful heart with glorying tongue.
Upon My Daughter Hannah Wiggin her Recovery from a Dangerous Fever.
Upon My Dear and Loving Husband His Going into England.
Upon My Son Samuel His Going For England.
What God is like to him I serve?
Brontë, E.   Old Stoic, The.
Browning, E.   Earth and Her Praisers.
Isobel's Child.
Browning, R.   Guardian-Angel, The.
Burns, R.   Holy Willie's Prayer.
Lying at a Reverend Friend's House One Night, the Author Left the Following *Verses* in the Room Where He Slept.
Campion, T.   Out of My Soul's Depth.
Cavafy.   Prayer: "To her depths the sea has taken a sailor."
Ciardi, J.   Statement.
Clampitt.   Antiphonal.
Clifton, L.   Slaveship[s].
Clough.   O Qui Me—!
Qui Laborat, Orat.
Cortes.   Great Prayer.
Cowper, W.   Fragment: "He came to him in the extasy of pray'r."
Crashaw.   Authors Motto, The.
C[h]aritas Nimia; or, The Dear[e] Bargain.
Christs Victory.
Compline.
Evensong.
For the Hour of Prime.
Howres for the Hours of Matines, The.
Lauda Sion Salvatorem.
O Gloriosa Domina.
Ode on a Prayer-Book.
On Mr. G. Herberts Booke, The Temple.
Out of Euphormio.
Out of *Grotius* his Tragedy of *Christes* Sufferinges.
Prayer, A.
Song: "Lord, when the sense of Thy sweet grace."
To the Name above Every Name, the Name of Jesus, a Hymn.
Two Went Up into the Temple To Pray.
Vexilla Regis.
Creeley.   Prayer to Hermes.
Cullen, C.   Pagan Prayer.
Cummings, E. E.   Ballade of Soul.
Noster, The.
Cunningham, J.   Wandering Scholar's Prayer to St. Catherine of Egypt, The.
D'Arezzo.   Sonnet: To the Blessed Virgin Mary.
"Dario."   Om.
Davie, D.   Benedictus.
Bowing the Head.
Thirty-ninth Psalm, Adapted, The.
De la Mare.   Motley.
Prayer, A.
Dickey, J.   Approaching Prayer.
Dickinson, E.   At least—to pray—is left—is left.
My period had come for Prayer.
Of Course—I prayed.
Prayer is the little implement.
We pray—to Heaven.
Donne.   Hymn[e] to God the Father, A.
Litany, A.
Dubie.   Coyote Creek.
Fish, The.
Dugan, A.   Grace for Thursday.
Dunbar, P.   Crisis, The.
Eliot, T. S.   Song for Simeon, A.
Emerson, R.   Dervish whined to *Said*, The.
I am alone. Sad is my solitude.
Think not the gods receive thy prayer.
When success exalts thy lot.
García Lorca.   Poet Prays to the Virgin for Help, The.
Ginsberg, A.   Father Guru.
Prayer Blues.
Glück, L.   Cell, The.
Graves, R.   Awakening, The.
Grace Notes.
Gunn, T.   Well Dennis O'Grady.
"H. D."   If You Will Let Me Sing.

Prayer: "White, O white face."
Triplex.
Hall, D.   Grace, A.
HaNagid.   Pain, The.
Hayden, R.   Incense of the Lucky Virgin.
Herbert, G.   Antiphon (2): "Praised be the God of love."
Antiphon: "Let all the world in ev'ry corner sing / *My God and King*."
Bag, The.
Denial[l].
Evensong.
Gratefulness.
Home.
Mattens.
Obedience.
Offering, An.
Praise (2).
Praise (3).
Prayer (1): "Prayer the Church's banquet, Angels' age."
Prayer (2).
Temper (1), The.
Wreath, A.
Herrick.   Another.
Confusion of Face.
Devotion Makes the Deity.
Evensong.
Gods Gifts Not Soon[e] Granted.
Gods Part.
Grace for a Child.
Heart, The.
His Prayer for Absolution.
His Wish.
Hymne to the Muses, An.
Matins [*or* Mattens], or Morning Prayer.
Old Wives Prayer, The.
Pray and Prosper.
Prayer.
Prayers Must Have Poise.
Psalme or Hymne to the Graces, A.
Thanksgiving to God for His House, A.
To Anthea.
To Apollo.
To God.
To God: an Anthem, Sung in the Chapel at White-Hall, Before the King.
To God, in Time of Plundering.
To His Sweet Saviour.
To Julia.
To Julia in the Temple.
To Silvia.
Upon Spenke.
Vow to Minerva, A.
Hill, G.   Cycle.
Hymns to Our Lady of Chartres.
Hopkins, G.   My prayers must meet a brazen heaven.
Hughes, L.   Prayer Meeting.
Sinner.
Hughes, T.   Cat and Mouse.
Ignatow, D.   Semblance, A.
Jacobsen, J.   We Pray Most Earnestly.
Johnson, S.   On Losing the Power of Speech.
Prayer: "Summe Deus, cui cæca patent penetralia cordis."
Jonson, B.   To Heaven.
Keats.   Fragment of an Ode to Maia Written on May Day, 1818.
God of the Meridian.
Kinnell.   Prayer.
Kipling, R.   Rabbi's Song, The.
Recessional.
Kumin, M.   Hermit Prays, The.
Larkin, P.   Come Then to Prayers.
Compline.
Faith Healing.
Lawrence, D. H.   Ah, Muriel!
Hands of God, The.
Lord's Prayer.
No Joy in Life.
Prophet in the Rose Garden, The.
Levertov.   Prayer, The.
Levine, P.   Jewish Graveyards, Italy.
To Cipriano, in the Wind.
Lindsay, N.   Invocation for "The Map of the

Universe."
Look You, I'll Go Pray.
Logan, J.   Monologue for the Good Friday Christ.
Narcisses: Vision and Retrospect.
Lorde.   October.
Release Time.
Lux.   If I Die Before I Wake.
MacNeice.   Prayer Before Birth.
Prayer in Mid-Passage.
McGrath, T.   Restless Night, The.
Meredith, G.   Child's Prayer, A.
Merrill, J.   Santo.
Merton.   Christina.
Evening Prayer.
Fugitive.
Litany: "All holy souls / pray for us fellows."
Reader, The.
Theory of Prayer.
To the Immaculate Virgin, on a Winter Night.
Two States of Prayer.
Whitsun Canticle, A.
Millay, E.   Poem and Prayer for an Invading Army.
Milosz, C.   On Angels.
On Prayer.
Mistral, G.   Drops of Gall.
Olson, C.   Hear my prayer my father.
Parker, D.   Prayer for a New Mother.
Prayer for a Prayer.
Pasolini.   Prayer to My Mother.
Petrarch.   Alas how unprepared I was at first.
Poe.   Hymn: "At morn—at noon—at twilight dim."
Pope, A.   Universal Prayer [Deo Opt. Max.], The.
Pound, E.   Sandalphon.
Raine, K.   Spell of Sleep.
Ralegh, S.   Authours Epitaph, Made by Himself, The.
Ramanujan.   Mythologies 2.
Prayers to Lord Murugan.
Riley, J.   Anselmo.
Ike Walton's Prayer.
Mortul Prayer, A.
Prayer Perfect, The.
Ritsos.   Like a Prayer.
Moment of Contrition.
Rossetti, C.   Alas my Lord, / How should I wrestle all the livelong night.
Ash Wednesday.
Changing Chimes.
Christmas Carol, A: "Thank God, thank God, we do believe."
Eleventh Hour, The.
End Is Not Yet, The.
Exceeding Bitter Cry, An.
Exultate Deo.
For H.P.
I Do Set My Bow in the Cloud.
Imitated From the Arpa Evangelica: Page 121.
Last Answer, The.
O Lord, I cannot plead my love of Thee.
Palm Sunday.
Praying Always.
Sinner's own fault? So it was, The.
St. Andrew's Church.
Take No Thought for The Morrow.
That Which Hath Been Is Named Already, and It Is Known That It Is Man.
Then Shall Ye Shout.
There Remaineth Therefore a Rest to the People of God.
They Toil Not, Neither Do They Spin.
Thou, God, Seest Me.
Thro' burden and heat of the day.
Way of the World, The.
What Is That to Thee? Follow Thou Me.
When My Heart Is Vexed I Will Complain.
World's Harmonies, The.
Rukeyser, M.   Place-Rituals.
Rumi.   Checkmate.
Love Dogs.
Moses and the Shepherd.
Servant Who Loved His Prayers, The.
When We Pray Alone.

Sandburg, C.   Fire Dreams.
Our Prayer of Thanks.
Prayer after World War.
Sappho.   Bright-throned, undying Aphrodite.
Sarton, M.   Prayer before Work.
Schuyler, J.   Our Father.
Seifert.   Our Lady of Žižkov.
Sexton.   Cigarettes and Whiskey and Wild, Wild
Women.
Praying on a 707.
Praying to Big Jack.
Smart, C.   Jubilate Agno.
Smith, S.   In the Park.
Why Are the Clergy...?
Spender, S.   Rejoice in the Abyss.
Thomas, D.   Conversation of Prayer, The.
Vision and Prayer.
Thomas of Celano.   Dies Irae.
Thomson, J.   Complaint on the Miseries of Life,
A.
Tomlinson, C.   Weeper in Jalisco.
Van Duyn.   Gardener to His God, The.
Very.   Hymn: The Efficacy of a Mother's
Prayer.
My Meat and Drink.
Prayer for Rain.
Prayer of Jabez, The.
Prayer, The ("Father! help them who walk in
their own light").
Warren, R.   Answer to Prayer.
Identity and Argument for Prayer.
Whitman, W.   Prayer of Columbus.
Whittier.   Andrew Rykman's Prayer.
Dedication: "I would the gift I offer here."
Garrison of Cape Ann, The.
Prayer of Agassiz, The.
Prayer-Seeker, The.
Swan Song of Parson Avery, The.
Truce of Piscataqua, The.
Wish of To-day, The.
Wilde, O.   E Tenebris.
Williams, M.   Note to God Concerning a Point
from an Earlier Communication, A.
Vision and Prayer.
Wordsworth, W.   Devotional Incitements.
Force of Prayer, The; or, The Founding of
Bolton Priory; A Tradition.
On a High Part of the Coast in Cumberland.
Upon the Late General Fast. March, 1832.
Wright, J.   Confession to J. Edgar Hoover.
Elegy for the Poet Morgan Blum, An.
Prayer in My Sickness, A.
Prayer to the Lord Ramakrishna, A.
Trying to Pray.
Yeats.   Blessed, The.
Mohini Chatterjee.
Prayer for My Daughter, A.
Prayer for My Son, A.
Zagajewski.   Flame, A.
Praying Mantis
Komunyakaa.   Two.
Zukofsky, L.   "Mantis."
"Mantis," An Interpretation.
Preaching and Preachers
Cummings, E. E.   Skinny voice / of the
leatherfaced, The.
This evangelist / buttons with his big gollywog
voice.
Dickinson, E.   He fumbles at your Soul.
Herrick.   Upon Parson Beanes.
Hughes, L.   Sunday Morning Prophecy.
Kipling, R.   At His Execution.
Mulholland's Contract.
Komunyakaa.   Cooling Board, The.
Laughlin, J.   Easter in Pittsburgh.
Riley, J.   Brudder Sims.
Roethke.   Judge Not.
Smith, S.   Where Are You Going?
Tate, J.   Reapers of the Water.
Tomlinson, C.   For Miriam.
Very.   Preacher, The.
Warren, R.   Amazing Grace in the Back
Country.
Easter Morning: Crosby Junction.
Whitman, W.   Child's Amaze, A.
Whittier.   Daniel Wheeler.

Preacher, The.
To J. P.
Williams, M.   At the Christening of an Infant
the Mind of the Young Preacher Wanders
Again.
Beside an Open Grave the Mind of the Young
Preacher Comes Almost to Terms.
During a Funeral Service the Mind of the Young
Preacher Wanders Again.
During the Hymn Before the Christmas Sermon
the Mind of the Young Preacher Wanders
Again.
Groom Kisses the Bride and the Mind of the
Young Preacher Wanders Again, The.
He Shuts His Eyes for the Layman's Long
Prayer about Lust and the Mind of the Young
Preacher Wanders Again.
If Ever There Was One.
She Prays for Her Husband, the Good Pastor,
Lying on His Deathbed at Last.
Unto One of the Least of These.
See also **Clergy**
Predators
Clampitt.   Good Friday.
Clifton, L.   Fox.
Dugan, A.   Another Cat Poem: A Cat Is Not a
Dancer but a Hunter.
Another Cat Poem. To a Cat Person.
Idyll of Ascension.
Eberhart, R.   Ospreys in Cry.
Swallows Return, The.
Fenton, J.   Killer Snails, The.
Kinsella, T.   Clearing, The.
Komunyakaa.   April's Anarchy.
Kumin, M.   Catchment.
Food Chain, The.
Laughlin, J.   Failure of Communication in the
Animal Kingdom, A.
Lindsay, N.   Spider and the Ghost of the Fly,
The.
What Grandpa Mouse Said.
Melville, H.   Maldive Shark, The.
Merrill, J.   Violent Pastoral.
Mistral, G.   Rat, The.
Montale.   From a Swiss Lake.
Niedecker.   Some float off on chocolate bars.
Owen, W.   Arms and the Boy.
Rossetti, C.   Handy Mole who plied no shovel,
A.
Rumi.   Think that you're gliding out from the
face of a cliff.
Shelley, P.   Bigotry's Victim.
Stock, R.   Errant Mole and the Loveliest of
Hawks, The.
Tomlinson, C.   How Still the Hawk.
Warren, R.   What Was the Throught.
Williams, M.   How It's Born in Us to
Understand That There Are Two Sides to
Every Question.
Predestination
Carver, R.   Foreboding.
Eberhart, R.   Sacrifice, The.
Hardy, T.   Subalterns, The.
Herrick.   Another.
Predestination.
Lindsay, N.   North Star Whispers to the
Blacksmith's Son, The.
Nemerov.   Western Approaches, The.
Pregnancy
Berry, W.   Poem for J.
Berryman.   Damned.
Brodsky, J.   On Love.
Burns, R.   To the Weaver's Gin Ye Go.
Wha'll M-w Me Now.
Codrescu.   Souls Looking for Bodies.
Crane, H.   Stark Major.
Creeley.   "For Some Weeks."
Cunningham, J.   For a Woman with Child.
Dickey, J.   At the Home for Unwed Mothers.
Dove, R.   Weathering Out.
Graves, R.   Name.
Hacker, M.   1973.
Heaney, S.   Act of Union.
Hughes, L.   What? So Soon!
Jeffers, R.   Loving Shepherdess, The.
Kumin, M.   Sleeping with Animals.

Lawrence, D. H.   Youth Mowing, A.
Lorde.   Now That I Am Forever with Child.
Lux.   Upon Seeing An Ultrasound Photo of an
Unborn Child.
Mahon.   Ford Manor.
Unborn Child, An.
Merwin.   Forbears, The.
Molodovsky [or Molodowsky].   There Are Such
Springlike Nights.
Muldoon, P.   Birth, The.
Cuckoo Corn.
Footling.
Sonogram, The.
Upriver Incident, The.
Orr, G.   Fifth Month, The.
Voyages, The.
Piercy.   Provocation of the Dream, The.
Plath.   Heavy Women.
Metaphors.
Ramanujan.   When It Happens.
Rilke.   To the Moon.
Rukeyser, M.   All the Little Animals.
Tunnel, The.
Unborn Song.
Sandburg, C.   Poppies.
Seifert.   Our Lady of Žižkov.
Snyder, G.   Berry Feast, A.
Spender, S.   Dream, The.
One.
Stock, R.   Man Who Was Pregnant with Envy,
The.
Swenson, M.   Motherhood.
Updike.   March: A Birthday Poem.
Origin of Laughter, The.
Williams, M.   Rubaiyat for Sue Ella Tucker.
Williams, W.   Raper from Passenack, The.
Wright, J.   Trouble.
Prehistoric Man
Ignatow, D.   In Ancient Times.
See also **Cavemen; Man, Primitive**
Prejudice
Amichai [or Amikhai].   Straight from Prejudice.
Ciardi, J.   My Tribe.
Dugan, A.   Nostalgia for a Language.
Dunbar, P.   To Miss Mary Britton.
Hacker, M.   For Jean Migrenne.
Kipling, R.   Jobson's Amen.
Stranger, The.
Tommy.
Komunyakaa.   Rocks Push.
Meredith, W.   Do Not Embrace Your Mind's
New Negro Friend.
Moore, M.   Labors of Hercules, The.
Ralegh, S.   If a Phoenincian born I am, what
then?
Rexroth, K.   Discrimination.
Rukeyser, M.   What Do We See?
Sandburg, C.   Man, the Man-Hunter.
Shelley, P.   Bigotry's Victim.
See also **Racial Prejudice; Racism and Racists;
Sexism**
Presbyterianism and Presbyterians
Logan, J.   Long Search, The.
Presence
Achterberg.   City.
Borges.   Instant, The.
Nostalgia for the Present.
Coleridge, S.   Angel Visitant, An.
Creeley.   As real as thinking.
Fire, The.
Here ("No one / else in the room").
Like They Say.
Photo.
Smell of gum wrappers as of Saturday afternoon
at movies.
Two Times.
Woman, The.
Davie, D.   Thou Art Near at Hand, O Lord.
Dugan, A.   Apology (to the Muse).
Eliot, T. S.   Mélange Adultère de Tout.
Gallagher, T.   Hands of the Blindman, The.
Hafiz [or Hafez].   Dearest, where thy shadow
falls.
Hamill, S.   Gnostology.
HaNagid.   Be Glad, She Said.

Everything Hidden.
Herrick.   Gods Presence.
Presence and Absence.
Jacobsen, J.   Presences.
Kumin, M.   Presence, The.
Levertov.   Once Only.
Presence, The.
Thread, The.
Wings, The.
Parker, D.   Thin Edge, The.
Rumi.   This We Have Now.
Szymborska, W.   No Title Required.
Warren, R.   Another Dimension.
Whalen, P.   Haiku, for Gary Snyder.
Treading More Water.
Williams, M.   Thought as It Turns, A.
Walking After Supper.
Zagajewski.   Moment.
Presence.
Zukofsky, L.   Air.
You three:—my wife.

Presents
Riley, J.   Lines: "Thou little naked statuette."
See also **Gifts and Giving**

Presidency, The, United States
Bierce.   Right.
Brodsky, J.   To the President-elect.
Hall, D.   Presidentiad, The.
Jeffers, R.   Woodrow Wilson.
Laughlin, J.   Bless You, Mr President.
Lindsay, N.   Bryan, Bryan, Bryan, Bryan.
Roosevelt.
MacLeish.   State Funeral: March 31, 1969.
Meredith, W.   Mild-Spoken Citizen Finally
Writes to the White House, A.
Merwin.   Presidents.
Olson, C.   Hustings, The.
Rufus Woodpecker visited the President.
Riley, J.   Tribute of His Home, The.
What Title?
Stockton, A.   To the President of the United
States.
Whalen, P.   Dear Mr President.
Whitman, W.   Sobbing of the Bells, The.
To the States, To Identify the 16th, 17th, or 18th
Presidentiad.
Whittier.   Song, A: "Beneath thy skies,
November!"
Williams, M.   Of History and Hope.

Presley, Elvis
Gunn, T.   Elvis Presley.
Painkillers.
Sandburg, C.   Graceland.

Presumption
Baudelaire.   Debut of the Dancer, A. B., The.
Cummings, E. E.   But granted that it's nothing
paradoxically enough beyond mere personal.
Space being(don't forget to remember)Curved.
Dickinson, E.   Presumption has it's Affliction.
Graves, R.   Cliff Edge, The.
Kipling, R.   Lollius.
Neruda.   This Is Simple.
Williams, C. K.   Next to the Last Poem about
God, The.
Shame.
Wright, C.   March Journal.

Pretension
Burns, R.   Epitaph Extempore, on a Person
Nicknamed the Marquis, Who Desired Burns
to Write One on Him.
Monody on Maria.
Toadeater, The.
Campion, T.   Heart's Music.
Clare, J.   Braggart.
Clough.   Go foolish thoughts, and join the
throng.
Eberhart, R.   Laocoön.
Eliot, T. S.   Conversation Galante.
Portrait of a Lady.
Emerson, R.   Park, The.
Romany Girl, The.
Herbert, G.   Jordan (2).
Jonson, B.   On English Monsieur.
To Sir Annual Tilter.
Lawrence, D. H.   Gentleman, The.

Natural Complexion.
To Be Superior.
Tolerance.
Nash, O.   Reflections on the Vernacular.
There Were Giants in Those Days or Maybe
There Weren't.
What's in a Name? Here's What's in a Name,
or, I Wonder What Became of John and
Mary.
Olson, C.   Issues from the Hand of God.
Pope, A.   To Eustace Budgell, Esq., on His
Translation of the Characters of Theophrastus.
Pound, E.   Portrait d'une Femme.
Shapiro, K.   University.
Spender, S.   Art Student.
Tomlinson, C.   To Vasko Popa In Rome.

Pride
Ammons.   Increment.
Angelou.   Phenomenal Woman.
Ausonius.   On Nanus Mounted on an Ant.
Baudelaire.   Punishment of Pride.
Bukowski.   Poem for Liz.
Burns, R.   Ronalds of the Bennals, The.
Song: "As I cam down by yon castle wa'."
Toadeater, The.
Cavafy.   One Who Has Failed.
Ciardi, J.   Poetry.
Cowper, W.   Truth.
Creeley.   "For Some Weeks."
Gangster.
Cullen, C.   Advice to a Beauty.
To an Unknown Poet.
Cunningham, J.   In a few days now when two
memories meet.
"Dario."   Spaniard.
Dickey, W.   For Every Last Batch When the
Next One Comes Along.
Dickinson, E.   Poor little Heart!
Dove, R.   Sunday Greens.
Emerson, R.   Bended to fops who bent to him.
Bluebeard. Let the gentle wife prepare.
Good-bye.
Frost, R.   Haec Fabula Docet.
Graves, R.   Child with Veteran.
My Ghost.
Pride of Love.
Progress, The.
Questions in a Wood.
Unicorn and the White Doe.
Hacker, M.   Iva's Birthday Poem.
Hamill, S.   Arse Poetica.
Han-shan.   Man descended from Pride, A.
HaNagid.   I'd Suck Bitter Poison From The
Viper's Mouth.
If You Don't Have The Power To Pay.
Hardy, T.   Dear, The.
Whaler's Wife, The.
Herbert, G.   Church Monuments.
Flower, The.
Vanity [*or* Vanitie] (1).
Herrick.   Pride Allowable in Poets.
Sobriety in Search.
To Dianeme.
To His Honour'd Friend, Sir Thomas Heale.
Upon Tubbs.
Hughes, L.   Color.
Emperor Haile Selassie.
Jackson, L.   Pride of Head.
Jeffers, R.   Rock and Hawk.
Kipling, R.   English Flag, The.
Islanders, The.
Legend of Mirth, The.
Lawrence, D. H.   Conceit.
Finding Your Level.
Fireflies in the Corn.
Humiliation.
Proper Pride.
Levine, P.   Animals Are Passing from Our
Lives.
Lindsay, N.   Kind of Scorn, A.
Meredith, G.   Believe me, I have studied men.
Bellerophon.
Creed.
Lucifer in Starlight.
Reason.
Were men of such importance as they deem.

Meredith, W.   Illiterate, The.
Nash, O.   Platitudinous Reflection.
Neruda.   This Is Simple.
O'Hara, F.   Savoy.
Owen, W.   Parable of the Old Men and the
Young, The.
Parker, D.   Fighting Words.
Light of Love.
Ralegh, S.   Have speciall care, that valiant
povertie.
Riley, J.   Poor Man's Wealth, A.
Rimbaud, A.   Once, animals spewed sperm as
they charged.
Rossetti, C.   Dead City, The.
Helen Grey.
Standing Afar Off for the Fear of Her Torment.
Surely there is an aching void within.
Young Men Aye Were Fickle Found Since
Summer Trees Were Leafy.
Rukeyser, M.   Bubble of Air.
Rumi.   Dog in the Doorway, The.
Sandburg, C.   Acquaintance with Death, Sir.
Primer Lesson.
Proud and Beautiful.
Proud of Their Rags.
Proud Torsos.
Skyscrapers Stand Proud.
Swell People.
Sarton, M.   Exchange of Gifts, An.
Franz, a Goose.
Hard Death, A.
Memory of Swans.
Sexton.   Civil War, The.
Shelley, P.   Ozymandias.
Smith, S.   My Cats.
Stafford, W.   Our Kind.
Trakl.   Winter Night, A.
Unknown.   Do Not, Oh, Do Not Prize.
Updike.   Commencement, Pingree School.
Whitman, W.   Inca's Daughter, The.
Punishment of Pride, The.
Woman Waits for Me, A.
Whittier.   Cities of the Plain, The.
Forgiveness.
Judith at the Tent of Holofernes.
Maids of Attitash, The.
Yankee Girl, The.
Williams, C. K.   Spirit the Triumph, The.
Williams, M.   Mise-en-Scène.
Williams, T.   Events Proceed.
Wordsworth, W.   Lines: "Nay, Traveller."
Pilgrim's Dream; or, The Star and the Glow-
Worm, The.
Wright, J.   In Shame and Humiliation.
Yeats.   Peacock, The.

Priests
Ai.   Life Story.
Priest's Confession, The.
Blok.   Little Priest of the Fen, The.
Dubie.   Village Priest, A.
Hughes, T.   Tree.
Jacobsen, J.   Pondicherry Blues.
Kinsella, T.   Social Work.
Laughlin, J.   Piteous Sight, A.
Logan, J.   Death of Southwell, The.
Rimbaud, A.   I was sitting in a Third-Class
carriage; an old priest.
Tate, J.   Stella Maris.
Very.   Priest, The.
See also **Clergy**

Primitive Man
Lux.   Bodo.
Stafford, W.   Cro-Magnon.
See also **Man, Primitive**

Primroses
Burns, R.   Primrose, The.
Donne.   Primrose, The; Being at Montgomery
Castle, upon the hill, on which it is situate.
Hardy, T.   Unplanted Primrose, The.
Herrick.   Primrose, The.
Jackson, L.   After So Much Loss.
Parker, D.   Evening Primrose, The.
Wordsworth, W.   Primrose of the Rock, The.
Tuft of Primroses, The.

Princes and Princesses
"Anvari." Shah Sandschar, whose lowest slave.
Bierce. France.
Byron, G. Fragment of an Epistle to Thomas
 Moore.
 Sonnet to the Prince Regent.
Campion, T. To the Most High and Mighty
 Prince Charles.
Cavafy. Prince from Western Libya, A.
Coleridge, S. On a Late Connubial Rupture in
 High Life.
Crashaw. Upon the birth of the Princesse
 Elizabeth.
"Dario." Sonatina.
Davie, D. Put Not Your Trust in Princes.
De la Mare. Heresy.
 Mourn'st Thou Now?
Dubie. Elegy Asking that It Be the Last.
Graves, R. Frog and the Golden Ball, The.
Herrick. Bad Princes Pill Their People.
 Gentlenesse.
 Pollicie in Princes.
 Prevision, or Provision.
 To the Right Gratious Prince, Lodwick, Duke of
 Richmond and Lenox.
Hughes, L. Last Prince of the East.
Komunyakaa. Exchange Student Awaits the
 Arrival of an African Princess, An.
Lux. Princess Summer Fall Winter Spring.
MacLeish. Acknowledgement.
Mörike [or Möricke]. Beauty Rohtraut.
Patchen. Legend for a Little Child.
Plath. Princess and the Goblins, The.
Ramanujan. Last of the Princes, The.
Riley, J. Dream of the Little Princess, The.
Rimbaud, A. Tale.
Rossetti, C. Royal Princess, A.
Rumi. Judge a Moth by the Beauty of Its
 Candle.
 Three Brothers and the Chinese Princess, The.
Sexton. Frog Prince, The.
 Twelve Dancing Princesses, The.
Smith, S. Days of Yore, The.
 Forlorn Sea, The.
 Voices about the Princess Anemone.
Stockton, A. On the Celebration of the Birth of
 the Dauphin of France.
Tate, J. Pet Deer, The.
Unknown. Dole of the King's Daughter, The.
Wilbur, R. Up, Jack.

Princeton, New Jersey
Kumin, M. In April, in Princeton.
Stockton, A. Prospect, The. By a Lady in
 Princeton.

Princeton University
Eberhart, R. Half-bent Man.

Printing and Printers
Hughes, L. Madam's Calling Cards.
Kipling, R. Press, The.
Pope, A. Translator, The.
 Verses Occasioned by an & c. at the End of Mr.
 D'Urfy's Name in the Title to One of His
 Plays.
 Verses to be Prefix'd before Bernard Lintot's
 New Miscellany.
Riley, J. Ancient Printerman, The.
Updike. Tune, in American Type.
Very. To Charles W. Felt Esq. On His New
 Type-Setting Machine.
Whitman, W. Font of Type, A.

Prisoners of War
Brontë, E. Gleneden's Dream.
 Organ swells, the trumpets sound, The.
Cooper, J. P.O.W.
Davie, D. Huntingdonshire.
Dickey, J. Performance, The.
Fenton, J. Prison Island.
 Vucceria.
Heaney, S. Visitant.
Jarrell, R. Stalag Luft.
Komunyakaa. Eyeball Television.
 One-legged Stool, The.
Levertov. Pilots, The.
Patchen. What Happened in the Camps.
Rukeyser, M. Breaking Open.
Wheatley, P. On the Capture of General Lee.

Williams, M. Wiedersehen.

Prisons and Prisoners
Ai. Penis Envy.
 Prisoner, The.
Angelou. Prisoner.
Baudelaire. 'Tasso in Prison' by Delacroix.
Blake, W. Crystal Cabinet, The.
 How Sweet I Roamed [or Roam'd] from Field
 to Field.
Blue Cloud. Alcatraz.
 When's the Last Boat to Alcatraz?
Brodsky, J. Martial Law Carol, A.
Brontë, E. Ierné's eyes were glazed and dim.
 M.A. Written on the Dungeon Wall.
 Written in the Gaaldine Prison Caves to A.G.A.
 Written on Returning to the P. of I. on the 10th
 of January, 1827.
Broumas, O. Family.
Browning, E. Prisoner, The.
Burns, R. Fragment—Epistle from Esopus to
 Maria.
 Lament of Mary Queen of Scots on the
 Approach of Spring.
Byron, G. Oh You, Who in All Names Can
 Tickle the Town.
Campion, T. To My Honourable Friend, Sr
 Thomas Mounson, *Knight and Baronet.*
Carruth, H. Lana.
Coleridge, S. Dungeon, The.
Cooper, J. Threads: Rosa Luxemburg from
 Prison.
Cortes. Aegeus in Prison.
Creeley. Blues.
Cullen, C. Thoughts in a Zoo.
Cummings, E. E. But if a living dance upon
 dead minds.
 Mind is its own beautiful prisoner, The.
 Moon falls through the autumn Behind prisons
 she grins, The.
De la Mare. In the Dock.
 Monologue, The.
 One in the Public Gallery.
Dickey, J. When.
Dickinson, E. How soft this Prison is.
 I never hear the word "escape."
 Mine—by the Right of the White Election!
 Of Paul and Silas it is said.
 Prison gets to be a friend, A.
Dubie. Arkhangel'sk.
 Friary at Blossom, Prologue & Instructions, The.
Dugan, A. Portrait.
Dunbar, P. Garret, The.
 Sympathy.
Eberhart, R. In Prisons of Established Craze.
Enzensberger, H. Security Considerations.
Fenton, J. Prison Island.
Frost, R. Line-Gang, The.
Ginsberg, A. Meaningless Institution, A.
 Sometime Jailhouse Blues.
Graves, R. Certain Mercies.
 Love Without Hope.
 Philosopher, The.
 Reduced Sentence, A.
Gunn, T. In the Tank.
 La Prisonnière.
 Tamer and Hawk.
Gurney, I. To God.
"H. D." Prisoners.
Hamill, S. Between You and Me.
 Lifer.
HaNagid. Earth to Man.
Hayden, R. Prisoners, The.
Housman. Oh who is that young sinner with the
 handcuffs on his wrists?
Hughes, L. Azikiwe in Jail.
 Chant for Tom Mooney.
 Freedom Seeker.
Hughes, T. Jaguar, The.
Jacobsen, J. Interrogation.
Jarrell, R. O My Name It Is Sam Hall.
 Officers' Prison Camp Seen from a Troop-Train,
 An.
 Prisoners.
 Wild Birds, The.
Keats. Written on the Day That Mr. Leigh Hunt
 Left Prison.

Kipling, R. Captive, The.
 Cells.
 Half-Ballad of Waterval.
 We now, held in captivity.
Laughlin, J. Prisoner's Song, The.
Levine, P. Heaven.
Lindsay, N. Gamblers, The.
Lowell, R. After the Surprising Conversions.
 In the Cage.
 Memories of West Street and Lepke.
Meredith, W. Examples of Created Systems.
Merrill, J. To a Butterfly.
Merton. Tropics.
Merwin. Island in the Harbor, An.
Montale. Prisoner's Dream, The.
Orr, G. Solitary Confinement.
 Trick, The.
Paley, G. Women's Prison, The: El Salvador /
 The Ballad of Visiting Day.
Pasolini. One of the Many Epilogs.
Patchen. He Is Guarded by Crowds and
 Shackled with Formalities.
 How Jimsey O'Roon and Peter Stack, Coal
 Miners, Came to Be Put in the Ferbettville
 (Pa.) Jail Early One Saturday Night.
 Theory of Nato-geography as Advanced by the
 Tiaphidian Man, With a Comment on the
 Character of His Penal System, A.
Petrarch. Love, who can promise so
 beguilingly.
Plath. Jailer, The.
Pope, A. Epistle to Robert Earl of Oxford and
 Earl Mortimer.
Ralegh, S. My Body in the Walls Captived.
Rich, A. From the Prison House.
 Prisoners, The.
Riley, J. Back from a Two-Years' Sentence.
 Life Term, A.
Rilke. Prisoners.
Ritsos. Contradictions.
 Invention of the Center.
 Normal Occurence.
 Prison Tree and the Women, The.
Rossetti, C. Epitaph: "Slave yet wearing on my
 head a crown, A."
 Tasso and Leonora.
Sandburg, C. Bars.
 Teamster's Farewell, A.
Shelley, P. Fragment: To a Friend Released
 from Prison.
Simic. Drawn to Perspective.
 Prison.
 Prisoner, The.
 Rough Outline.
 Shaving at Night.
Smith, S. Commuted Sentence, The.
Spender, S. Prisoners, The.
Stafford, W. Grace Abounding.
 Messae from the Wanderer, A.
Stockton, A. On the Return of Col Laurens
 from His Confinement in the Tower of London.
Sze. Ansel Adams Card, The.
 Knife at the Jugular.
 Written the Day I Was to Begin a Residency at
 the State Penitentiary.
Tate, J. Man with Wooden Leg Escape Prison.
 Saint John of the Cross in Prison.
Tollas, T. Prison Poem.
 They've Blocked Every Window.
Walcott. Forest of Europe.
Warren, R. Penological Study: Southern
 Exposure.
Weiss, T. Hostage, The.
Whitman, W. Singer in the Prison, The.
Whittier. Prisoner for Debt, The.
Wilde, O. Ballad of Reading Gaol, The.
Williams, C. K. Saturday.
Williams, M. Prison.
Wordsworth, W. Captivity.—Mary Queen of
 Scots.
 Convict, The.
 I know an aged Man constrained to dwell.
 Sonnet: "Nuns fret not at their convent's narrow
 room."
 When Philoctetes in the Lemnian Isle.
Wright, J. American Twilights, 1957.

Privacy
  Davie, D. Against Confidences.
  Dickinson, E. I'm Nobody! Who are you?
    To my quick ear the Leaves—conferred.
  Graves, R. Secrecy.
  Herrick. His Wish to Privacie.
  Moore, M. Injudicious Gardening.
  Nash, O. I Spy, or, The Depravity of Privacy.
    Mrs. Purvis Dreads Room Service.
    My Daddy.
  Niedecker. What bird would light.
  Pessoa. Advice.
  Piercy. Somehow.
  Plath. Eavesdropper.
  Rexroth, K. Privacy.
  Ritsos. Private Place.
  Wilner, E. Her Body Is Private.
See also **Solitude**
Privateers
  Kipling, R. When the Great Ark.
Procrastination
  Ammons. Grass Miracles, The.
  Collins, B. Victoria's.
  Dugan, A. Resolution of Hesitancies.
  Dunbar, P. Lapse, The.
  Jackson, L. Postponement of Self.
  Levertov. Action.
  Merwin. Something I've Not Done.
  Milosz, C. Preparation.
  Nash, O. I'll Get One Tomorrow.
    Procrastination Is All of the Time.
  Riley, J. We Defer Things.
  Thoreau. Poet's Delay, The.
Prodigal Son
  Bishop, E. Prodigal, The.
  Rossetti, C. Prodigal Son, A.
Prodigality
  Meredith, G. Empty Purse, The.
  Riley, J. Philiper Flash.
  Very. Prodigal, The.
Profumo, John Dennis
  Muldoon, P. Profumo.
Progress
  Atwood. Alternate Thoughts from
    Underground.
  Is/Not / Not.
  Auden. Moon Landing.
  Berry, W. Against the War in Vietnam.
    Horses.
    Manifesto: the Mad Farmer Liberation Front.
    Want of Peace, The.
  Bierce. Macrobian.
  Browning, E. Rhapsody of Life's Progress, A.
  Cavafy. Builders.
  Ciardi, J. Cartographer of Meadows, The.
  Clampitt. On the Disadvantages of Central
    Heating.
    Seriphos Unvisited.
  Clifton, L. Yeti Poet Returns to His Village to
    Tell His Story, The.
  Clough. To think that men of former days.
  Cummings, E. E. Jehovah buried,Satan dead.
    O pr / gress verily thou art m.
    Of all the blessings which to man.
    Pity This Busy Monster,Manunkind.
  Davie, D. Mustered into the Avant-Garde.
  Eberhart, R. On Shooting Particles beyond the
    World.
    Parker River, The.
    United 555.
  Emerson, R. Once the priest / Lived in an age.
  Enzensberger, H. Poison, The.
    Research Council.
    Residual Light.
    Thoughts on the Run 3.
  Fenton, J. Kingfisher's Boxing Gloves, The.
  Frost, R. Some Science Fiction.
  Graves, R. Personal Packaging, Inc.
  Gunn, T. Considering the Snail.
  Gurney, I. Wish, A.
  Hall, D. Elegy for Wesley Wells.
    Red Branch, The.
  Hardy, T. Christmas: 1924.
    Discouragement.
    Hundred Years Since, A.

  Inscriptions for a Peal of Eight Bells.
  Heaney, S. From the Canton of Expectation.
    Mud Vision, The.
  Hughes, T. Do Not Pick Up the Telephone.
  Jackson, L. Seizure of the World.
  Jeffers, R. Broken Balance, The.
    Cycle, The.
    Decaying Lambskins.
    Dog in the Sky, The.
    Torch-Bearers' Race, The.
    What is Worthless?
  Kipling, R. Benfactors, The.
    Secret of the Machines, The.
  Kumin, M. Photograph, U.S. Army Flying
    School, College Park, Maryland, 1909.
  Levine, P. 7 Years from Somewhere.
  Lindsay, N. Rhyme About an Electrical
    Advertising Sign, A.
  Mahon. Apotheosis of Tins, The.
    Banished Gods, The.
    Glengormley.
  McGrath, T. Legendary Progress.
    Portents.
  Meredith, G. Congress of Nations, The.
    Labourer, The.
    Progress.
    Progression.
    World's Advance, The.
  Merton. Old monk is turned loose / And can
    travel!, The.
  Millay, E. We have gone too far; we do not
    know how to stop: impetus.
  Nash, O. Caesar Knifed Again, or, Culture Biz
    Gets Hep, Boffs Profs.
    Look What You Did, Christopher!
    No Wonder Our Fathers Died.
    Up from the Wheelbarrow.
    What, No Sheep?
  Nemerov. Great Society, Mark X, The.
    Wheel King, The.
  Oppen. Bicycles and the Apex, The.
    Building of the Skyscraper, The.
    Technologies.
  Pagis. Information.
  Paley, G. Bob Visits Friends.
  Rexroth, K. Gas or Novocain.
    Organization Men in Affluent Society.
  Rich, A. Amnesia.
  Rimbaud, A. Lightning.
    Progress, big baby, wore shoes by Humanity.
  Robinson, E. Modernities.
    Town Down the River, The.
  Rukeyser, M. Book of the Dead, The.
    Breaking the nets of the world, in glimpses
    going.
    Trophies.
  Sandburg, C. Bitter Summer Thoughts.
    Four Preludes on Playthings of the Wind.
    Prairie.
    Smoke Blue.
  Snyder, G. L M F B R.
  Stafford, W. Cro-Magnon.
  Swenson, M. Landing on the Moon.
  Szymborska, W. Century's Decline, The.
  Tomlinson, C. Gladstone Street.
    On the Hall at Stowey.
    Quarry, The.
    Return to Hinton.
  Very. Light of Freedom Necessary to National
    Progress, The.
  Whitman, W. Going Somewhere.
  Williams, C. K. Spirit the Triumph, The.
  Williams, M. Main Street.
    Talking to Himself He Gets a Few Things
    Settled in His Mind.
Proletariat
  Dugan, A. Morning at Speed Products.
  Hughes, L. Always the Same.
    Chant for May Day.
    Good Morning Revolution.
    Open Letter to the South.
    Wait.
  Ritsos. Proletarian Speaker, A.
  Seifert. Opening Poem.
  Williams, T. Death Embrace, The.
See also **Bourgeoisie**

Prometheus
  Aeschylus. But Fortune governed all their
    works[,] till when.
    Prometheus Bound.
  Byron, G. Prometheus.
  Clampitt. Or Consider Prometheus.
  Dunbar, P. Prometheus.
  Graves, R. Prometheus.
  Hughes, T. Now I know I never shall.
    Prometheus On His Crag.
  Laughlin, J. Creatures of Prometheus, The.
  Milton. On the Inventor of Gunpowder.
  Rich, A. Always the Same.
  Shelley, P. Prometheus Unbound [A Lyrical
    Drama in Four Acts].
  Swift, J. Prometheus.
  Tomlinson, C. Prometheus.
Promiscuity
  Amichai [*or* Amikhai]. You're small and thin in
    the rain. A small target.
  Cunningham, J. Epigram: "You ask me how
    Contempt who claims to sleep."
    Lights of Love, The.
    Reader, it's time reality was faced.
  Hughes, L. Ballad of the Girl Whose Name Is
    Mud.
  Laughlin, J. Amo Amas Amat.
    Apotropaic Decision, An.
    Bad Night on Third Avenue, A.
    Cynthia in California.
    Trout, The.
  Parker, D. Little Old Lady in Lavender Silk,
    The.
  Stock, R. Enigma of a Final Scene.
  Williams, T. Changeling.
    Tuesday's Child.
Promises
  Amichai [*or* Amikhai]. This Is the Life of
    Promises.
  Burns, R. Thou hast left me ever, Jamie.
  Byron, G. Endorsement to the Deed of
    Separation, in the April of 1816.
  Creeley. Hotel Merlin.
  Dickinson, E. Promise is firmer than a Hope, A.
  Emerson, R. But God will keep his promise yet.
    She never comes to me.
  Graves, R. As All Must End.
    Court of Love, A.
    Earlier Lovers.
    Elsewhere.
    Falcon Woman, The.
    Impossible, The.
    Lion-Gentle.
    Oath, The.
    Purification.
    Rose, The.
    Scared Child, The.
    Song: Basket of Blossom.
    Song: The Promise.
    To Tell and Be Told.
    Until We Both.
    Vow, The.
  Gurney, I. Song: "O were there anything by
    half."
  Herrick. Gods Time Must End Our Trouble.
    Rainbow; or Curious Covenant, The.
    To God.
    To His Conscience.
    To His Mistress[e].
  Homer. Epigram of Homer, An.
  Housman. Westward on the high-hilled plains.
  Larkin, P. Is It Now Or For Always.
  MacLeish. America Was Promises.
    Broken Promise.
  Meredith, G. Hernani.
    Song: "Thou steppest from thy splendour."
  Parker, D. Mood.
    Promise.
    Somebody's Song.
  Robinson, E. Vickery's Mountain.
  Rossetti, C. Moonshine.
    Promises like Pie-Crust.
  Rukeyser, M. Loan, The.
    Risen Image Shines, The.
  Smart, C. To the Rev. Mr. Powell.
  Swift, J. Twelve Articles.

Swinburne. Old Saying, An.
Whittier. Curse of the Charter-Breakers, The.
Williams, T. Covenant.
Wright, J. Assignation, The.
Devotions.
Wyatt, S. Thy promise was to love me best.
What should I say.
Yeats. Deep-sworn Vow, A.
Under Saturn.

Pronunciation
Nash, O. Brief Guide to Rhyming, or, How Be
the Little Busy Doth?, A.
Strange Case of the Renegade Lyric Writer, The.
Tomlinson, C. Class.
Zukofsky, L. Claims.

Propaganda
Komunyakaa. Hanoi Hannah.
Meredith, G. On the Danger of War.

Propertius, Sextus
Propertius. Ghost, The.

Property
Burns, R. Extempore—On Being Shown a
Beautiful County Seat Belonging to the Same
[Maxwell of Cardoness].
Inventory, The.
Chuang Tzu. Cracking the Safe.
Creeley Still Too Young.
Dickinson, E. I am afraid to own a Body.
Dugan, A. On a Dispossess Precept. 1.
On the Death of Norman Dukes.
Untitled Poem: "I've promised that I will not
care about things."
Frost, R. Trespass.
Lawrence, D. H. Lord Tennyson and Lord
Melchett.
Property and No-Property.
Property Question, The.
Solomon's Baby.
St George and the Dragon.
Way Out, The.
Merwin. Things.
Muldoon, P. Beaver.
Niedecker. Don't tell me property is sacred!
Foreclosure.
Property is poverty.
Sheridan, T. Description of Doctor Delany's
Villa, A.
Swift, J. True and Faithful Inventory of the
Goods Belonging to Dr. Swift, Vicar of
Laracor; upon Lending His House to the
Bishop of Meath, until His Own Was Built [or
till His Palace Was Rebuilt], A.
Whitman, W. Thoughts.
Wilbur, R. Dutch Courtyard, A.
Williams, M. Closing the House.

Prophecy and Prophets
Amichai [or Amikhai]. I Am a Poor Prophet.
Poems of continuity, mines and graves.
With Her in an Apple.
Bierce. Inauspiciously.
Oneiromancy.
Vision of Doom, A.
Blake, W. Merlins Prophecy.
Bukowski. Day the Epileptic Spoke, The.
Byron, G. Saul.
Cavafy. Unfaithfulness.
Chuang Tzu. Good Fortune.
Ciardi, J. Annals.
Cooper, J. What the Seer Said.
Crane, S. When the prophet, a complacent fat
man.
Dickey, W. Ezekiel's Rabbit.
Dubie. Diamond Persona, The.
Dugan, A. Admonitor: A Pearl for Arrogance.
Emerson, R. Gods walk in the breath of the
woods, The.
History & prophecy are alike.
Enzensberger, H. Keeping Cool.
Research Council.
Ginsberg, A. Prophecy, A.
Graves, R. Christmas Robin, The.
Young Sibyl, The.
Herrick. Prognostick, A.
Hopkins, G. Not kind! to freeze me with
forecast.

Jackson, L. Decline of Prophecy.
Jeffers, R. Blood-Guilt, The.
Meditation on Saviors.
Kipling, R. Disciple, The.
Kunitz, S. Proteus.
Lawrence, D. H. Anaxagoras.
Prophet.
Prophet in the Rose Garden, The.
Lindsay, N. Scissors-Grinder, The.
Lorde. Equinox.
MacLeish. Seeing.
McGrath, T. End of the World, The.
Incident in the Life of a Prophet, An.
Meredith, G. Creation and the Prophet.
Song of the New Zealander among the Ruins of
Old London.
Merton. Advice to a Young Prophet.
Elias—Variations on a Theme.
La Salette.
Prophet.
Montale. Ezekiel Saw the Wheel.
Patchen. 'In the footsteps of the walking air'
Pinsky. Hearts, The.
Visions of Daniel.
Rukeyser, M. Second Elegy. Age of Magicians.
Simic. Ax.
Spender, S. Pylons, The.
Stock, R. Prophets, The.
Silenus' Epitaph.
Swift, J. Windsor Prophecy, The.
Szymborska, W. Soliloquy for Cassandra.
Tennyson, A. Dead Prophet, The.
Tomlinson, C. Lesson, The.
Portrait of the Artist I.
Providence.
Vallejo. Black Stone on Top of a White Stone.
Very. Prophet, The.
Whalen, P. Inside Stuff.
Whittier. Cobbler Keezar's Vision.
Prophecy of Samuel Sewall, The.
What of the Day?
Wilbur, R. Advice to a Prophet.
Williams, W. Portent.
Wordsworth, W. Picture of Daniel in the Lions'
Den, at Hamilton Palace.
Sonnet: Composed While the Author Was
Engaged in Writing a Tract Occasioned by
the Convention of Cintra.

See also **Oracles**

Prose
Armantrout. Anti-Short Story.
Bishop, E. Rainy Season; Sub-Tropics.
Riley, J. Prose or Verse?
Zagajewski. World's Prose, The.

Proserpina [or Proserpine]
Rossetti, D. Proserpina.

See also **Persephone**

Prospero
Hughes, T. Prospero and Sycorax.

Prostitution and Prostitutes
Ai. Everything: Eloy, Arizona, 1956.
Sweet, The.
Ammons. One Composing.
Bandeira. Brazilian Tragedy.
Baudelaire. Fountain of Blood.
Metamorphoses of the Vampire.
One night I had some ghastly jewish whore.
Still Unsatisfied.
To a Girl in Malabar.
When boredom gnaws your soul.
Broumas, O. Etymology.
Bukowski. Artist.
Fear.
Pacific Telephone.
Prayer in Bad Weather.
Price, The.
Quiet Clean Girls in Gingham Dresses.
Cavafy. Days of 1909, '10 and '11.
Sophist Departing from Syria.
Clare, J. Scandal.
Cullen, C. Black Magdalens.
For Daughters of Magdalen.
Cummings, E. E. Between the breasts / of
bestial.
Curtains part) / the peacockappareled.

Dick Mid's large bluish face without eyebrows.
First she like a piece of ill-oiled.
Five Americans.
In making Marjorie god hurried.
"Kitty". sixteen,5'1",white,prostitute.
Little ladies more / than dead exactly dance.
Twentyseven bums give a prostitute the once.
Waddling / madam star, The.
Wanta / spendsix / dollars Kid.
When you rang at Dick Mid's Place.
Davie, D. Knave of Hearts, The.
Dickey, J. Mercy.
Dickey, W. Confidence.
Donne. Klockius.
Self[e] Accuser, A.
Dubie. After Three Photographs of Brassaï.
Dugan, A. Memories of the Bowery.
Eliot, T. S. Sweeney Erect.
Éluard, P. Scene.
Gjuzel. Prostitution.
Hardy, T. Chapel-Organist, The.
Julie-Jane.
Reluctant Confession.
Ruined Maid, The.
Herrick Upon Doll.
Upon Luggs.
Upon Slouch.
Upon Snare, an Usurer.
Hughes, L. Chippy.
Midnight Chippie's Lament.
Natcha.
Port Town.
Ruby Brown.
Sliver of Sermon.
To the Dark Mercedes of "El Palacio de Amor."
Young Prostitute.
Jonson, B. Epigram on the Court Pucell, An.
On Bawds and Usurers.
On Cashiered Capt[ain] Surly.
On Gypsy.
On the New Hot-House.
To Hornet.
Komunyakaa. Edge, The.
Saigon Bar Girls, 1975.
Tu Do Street.
Lindsay, N. Trap, The.
Mallarmé. Anguish.
Milosz, C. No More.
Olson, C. Bigmans.
Plath. Strumpet Song.
Rimbaud, A. Fête Galante.
Sandburg, C. Harrison Street Court.
It Is Much.
Trafficker.
Woman with a Past.
Sexton. Buying the Whore.
Jesus Raises Up the Harlot.
Stock, R. Miracle of the Roses, The.
Swift, J. Beautiful Young Nymph Going to Bed,
A.
Whitman, W. City Dead-House, The.
To a Common Prostitute.
Wilbur, R. Place Pigalle.
Wilde, O. Harlot's House, The.
Impression du Matin.
Williams, C. K. Gas Station, The.
Medusa.
Williams, T. Androgyne, Mon Amour.
Blond Mediterraneans, The.
Cinder Hill.
Counsel.
Interior of the Pocket, The.
Young Men Waking at Daybreak.
Williams, W. King!, The.
Wright, J. Gesture by a Lady with an Assumed
Name, A.
In Response to a Rumor that the Oldest
Whorehouse in Wheeling, West Virginia, Has
Been Condemned.
Morning Hymn to a Dark Girl.

Protest, Social
Ai. Journalist, The.
Angelou. Take Time Out.
Atwood. Notes towards a Poem That Can
Never Be Written.
Bly, R. At a March against the Vietnam War.

Brooks, G. Lovers of the Poor, The.
Browning, E. Song for the Ragged Schools of London, A.
Chesterton. Secret People, The.
Clough. Latest Decalogue, The.
Corbett, W. D-Day 1989.
Fall 1970.
Shoe, The.
Cullen, C. Scottsboro, Too, Is Worth Its Song.
Cummings, E. E. Season 'tis,my lovely lambs, The.
Two X.
Davie, D. Barnsley and District.
Thanks to Industrial Essex.
Dugan, A. Confession of Heresy.
Portrait of a Lady.
Dunbar, W. To the Merchant[i]s of Edinburgh.
Emerson, R. Ode, Inscribed to W.H. Channing.
Enzensberger, H. Song for Those Who Know.
García Lorca. Cry to Rome.
Ode to Walt Whitman.
Ginsberg, A. America.
Anti-Vietnam War Peace Mobilization.
Capitol Air.
Death to Van Gogh's Ear!
Either we blow ourselves up now and die, like the old tribe of man, arguing among neutrons.
Everybody's Fantasy.
Going to Chicago.
Grant Park: August 28, 1968.
Howl.
Kansas! Kansas! Shuddering at last!
Nagasaki Days.
Paterson.
Television Was a Baby Crawling toward That Deathchamber.
Verses Written for Student Antidraft Registration Rally 1980.
Wichita Vortex Sutra.
Gurney, I. Strange Hells.
Hughes, L. Advertisement for the Waldorf-Astoria.
Air Raid over Harlem.
Always the Same.
August 19th.
Backlash Blues, The.
Ballad of Harry Moore.
Ballad of Sam Solomon.
Beaumont to Detroit: 1943.
Birmingham Sunday.
Black Clown, The.
Black Man Speaks, The.
Black Panther.
Black Seed.
Broadcast to the West Indies.
Brotherly Love.
Call to Creation.
Chant for Tom Mooney.
Crow Goes, Too.
Dear Mr. President.
Demonstration.
Dixie Man to Uncle Sam.
Dream of Freedom.
Final Call.
Freedom ("Freedom will not come").
Freedom Train.
Gandhi Is Fasting.
Get Up Off That Old Jive.
Ghosts of 1619.
Give Us Our Peace.
Good Morning Revolution.
Goodbye Christ.
How About It, Dixie.
I, Too.
In Explanation of Our Times.
Jim Crow's Last Stand.
Judge William Hastie.
Kids Who Die.
Labor Storm.
Let America Be America Again.
Memo to Non-White Peoples.
Message to the President.
Militant.
Mitchell Case, The.
NAACP.
New Song, A.

Open Letter to the South.
Poem to Uncle Sam.
Question and Answer.
Roland Hayes Beaten (Georgia: 1942).
Scottsboro.
Shall the Good Go Down?
Sister Johnson Marches.
To Captain Mulzac.
Undertow.
Union.
Wait.
White Man.
Will V-Day Be Me-Day Too?
Ignatow, D. All Quiet.
Kizer, C. First of June Again, The.
Poem, Small and Delible.
Race Relations.
Wars in Sweden, The.
Komunyakaa. 2527th Birthday of the Buddha.
How I See Things.
Keeper of the Vigil.
Knights of the White Camellia & Deacons of Defense.
Kunitz, S. This Day This World.
Lawrence, D. H. How Beastly the Bourgeois Is.
Stand Up!
Levertov. About Political Action in Which Each Individual Acts from the Heart.
Distance, The.
Psalm: People Power at the Die-in.
Speech: For Antidraft Rally, D.C., March 22, 1980, A.
What It Could Be.
Writing in the Dark.
Logue, C. Story of the Road, The.
Lorde. Revolution Is One Form of Social Change.
Workers Rose on May Day or Postcript to Karl Marx, The.
Lowell, R. After the Surprising Conversions.
Memories of West Street and Lepke.
McGrath, T. Blues for the Old Revolutionary Woman.
Meredith, G. Old Chartist, The.
Millay, E. Apostrophe to Man.
Milosz, C. Undressing Justine.
Oppen. Book of Job and a Draft of a Poem to Praise the Paths of the Living, The.
Return.
Orr, G. Demonstration, The.
Nothing and the Incident in the Streets.
On a Highway East of Selma, Alabama.
Paley, G. Responsibility.
Street Corner Dialogue.
Rexroth, K. Bad Old Days, The.
Rich, A. Burning of Paper instead of Children, The.
Education of a Novelist.
For a Russian Poet.
For a Sister.
From the Prison House.
Leaflets.
Tear Gas.
To Frantz Fanon.
Rimbaud, A. Blacksmith, The.
Ritsos. Compromises.
Rukeyser, M. Boys in the Branches.
For Kay Boyle.
How We Did It.
Wherever.
Shelley, P. Song to the Men of England.
Stafford, W. Peace Walk.
Walker, A. Chic Freedom's Reflection.
Whittier. Astræa.
Calef in Boston.
Human Sacrifice, The.
Men of Old, The.
Panorama, The.
Problem, The.
Quaker of the Olden Time, The.
Reformer, The.
To the Reformers of England.
Voices, The.
Wilbur, R. For the Student Strikers.
Williams, C. K. In the Heart of the Beast.
Keep It.

Wordsworth, W. On the Projected Kendal and Windermere Railway.
Placard for a Poll Bearing an Old Shirt.
Protest against the Ballot.
See also **Civil Rights Movement**

Protestantism and Protestants
Crashaw. Upon the Ensuing Treatises [of Mr. Shelford].
Davie, D. Bedfordshire.
North Dublin.
Herbert, G. British Church, The.
see also To the Lady Elizabeth Queen of Bohemia.
To the Lady Elizabeth Queen of Bohemia.
Hill, G. Christmas Trees.
Lawrence, D. H. Protestant Churches, The.
Sexton. Protestant Easter.
Swift, J. On the Words "Brother Protestants and Fellow Christians."

Proust, Marcel
Dubie. Duchesse's Red Shoes, The.
Ferlinghetti, L. Late Impressionist Dream.
Gunn, T. Readings in French.
Jarrell, R. Man Meets a Woman in the Street, A.
Merrill, J. For Proust.
Schuyler, J. Stun.

Provence, France
Browning, R. Count Gismond.
Collins, B. Plight of the Troubadour.
Glück, L. Letter from Provence.
Koch, K. Ma Provence.
MacLeish. Voyage en Provence.
Millay, E. Cap D'Antibes.
Memory of Cassis.
Pound, E. Piere Vidal Old.
Rexroth, K. Aix-en-Provence.
High Provence.
Leaving L'Atelier—Aix-en-Provence.
Tomlinson, C. Hill Walk.
Wilbur, R. Grasse: The Olive Trees.
Williams, W. To Ford Madox Ford in Heaven.
Zagajewski. Sénanque.
Sunrise Over Cassis.

Providence
Cowper, W. Epistle to Lady Austen.
Expostulation.
Fable, A: "Raven, while with glossy breast, A."
Emerson, R. Motto to "New England Reformers."
Herrick. Gods Providence.
Gods Time Must End Our Trouble.
Parker, D. Temptress, The.
Tomlinson, C. Providence.
Wheatley, P. Thoughts on the Works of Providence.

Providence, Rhode Island
Berrigan, T. Things To Do in Providence.

Prudes
Cummings, E. E. "Gay" is the captivating cognomen of a Young Woman of cambridge,mass.
Lawrence, D. H. Young and Their Moral Guardians, The.
Nash, O. First Limick.
Pope, A. Answer to the Following Question of Mrs. Howe.

Psyche (mythology)
Browning, E. Marriage of Psyche and Cupid.
Mercury Carries Psyche to Olympus.
Psyche and Cerberus.
Psyche and Pan.
Psyche and Proserpine.
Psyche and Venus.
Psyche Gazing on Cupid.
Psyche Propitiating Ceres.
Psyche Wafted by Zephyrus.
Pyche and the Eagle.
"Dario." Divine Psyche, sweet invisible Butterfly.
Duncan, R. Poem Beginning with a Line by Pindar, A.
Keats. Ode to Psyche.
MacLeish. Psyche with the Candle.
Merrill, J. From the Cupola.

Pound, E.   Speech for Psyche in the Golden Book of Apuleius.
Swift, J.   On Psyche.

Psychiatry and Psychiatrists
Carruth, H.   Ekstase, Alptraum, Schlaf in einem Nest von Flammen.
Olson, C.   True Numbers.
Pinsky.   Essay on Psychiatrists.
Sarton, M.   Christmas Letter to a Psychiatrist.
Sexton.   I called him *Comfort*.
  I'm dreaming the My Lai soldier again.
  It's music you've never heard.
  Letters to Dr. Y.
  What has it come to, Dr. Y.
Walker, A.   After the Shrink.
Wilner, E.   Eleusis.

See also **Mental Illness**

Psychoanalysis and Psychoanalysts
Cummings, E. E.   Listen my children and you.
Cunningham, J.   True Religion, The.
"H. D."   Master, The.
McHugh, H.   To See the Light.
O'Hara, F.   To a Poet.
Parker, D.   Passionate Freudian to His Love, The.
Sexton.   Cripples and Other Stories.
  Hoarder, The.
  Letters to Dr. Y.
  Said the Poet to the Analyst.
Van Duyn.   Birthday Card for a Psychiatrist.
Williams, C. K.   Child Psychology.
Wilner, E.   Muse, The.

Psychological Testing
Ciardi, J.   Letter to Virginia Johnson.

Ptolemaic Dynasty
Cavafy.   Alexandrian Kings.
  Displeasure of Selefkides, The.
  Envoys from Alexandria.
  Glory of the Ptolemies, The.
  Hospitality of Lagides, The.
  Kaisarion.

Puberty
Lorde.   Generation II.
Rimbaud, A.   Remembrances of Senility.
Rukeyser, M.   Rite.
Sexton.   Young.
Warren, R.   Platonic Drowse.

Publicity Stunts
Milosz, C.   Human Fly, A.

Publishing and Publishers
Byron, G.   For Orford and for Waldegrave.
  To Mr. Murray.
  You Ask for a "Volume of Nonsense."
Ciardi, J.   Guide to Poetry, A.
Corbett, W.   Putting socks away.
Herrick.   To the Right Honourable Mildmay, Earl of Westmorland.
Koch, K.   Thank You.
Lawrence, D. H.   To Pino.
Niedecker.   Now in one year.
Riley, J.   Youthful Press, The.
Roethke.   Reply to a Lady Editor.
Smith, S.   To an American Publisher.
Updike.   Rack of Paperbacks, A.
Whittier.   Lines on the Portrait of a Celebrated Publisher.

Puccini, Giacomo
Clampitt.   Cadenza, A.

Puddles
Frost, R.   Spring Pools.
Sandburg, C.   Lumber Yard Pools at Sunset.
Schuyler, J.   Sparks.

Puerto Ricans
Kinnell.   Avenue Bearing the Initial of Christ into the New World, The.
Komunyakaa.   Borinken Blues.

Puerto Rico
Ginsberg, A.   Vomit Express.
Mistral, G.   Caribbean Sea.
Palés Matos.   Prelude in Boricua.
Paley, G.   Bridges.

Pumas
Carver, R.   Cougar, The.
Williams, T.   Miss Puma, Miss Who?

Pumpkins
Prunty.   Widow's Halloween, The.
Sandburg, C.   Theme in Yellow.
Whittier.   Pumpkin, The.

Punctuality
Frost, R.   Lone Striker, A.
Nash, O.   There's Always an Ubblebub.
Updike.   Time's Fool.

Punctuation
Lux.   Virgule.
Tomlinson, C.   Hyphens.
Wilbur, R.   &.
  Games One.

Punishment
Arnold, M.   Sick King in Bokhara, The.
Beckett, S.   Noire soeur.
Burns, R.   Holy Willie's Prayer.
  Ode, Sacred to the Memory of Mrs. ——— of ———.
Ciardi, J.   Boy.
  Poem for Benn's Graduation from High School, A.
Crane, S.   Chant you loud of punishments.
Cummings, E. E.   Poets yeggs and thirsties.
Dugan, A.   Decimation before Phraäta, The.
Emerson, R.   Merlin's Song.
  Nemesis.
  Traitors tho' plumed & steel equipped.
Glück, L.   Game, The.
Graves, R.   Wreath, The.
HaNagid.   Tyrant Who Rules the Homeless and Poor, The.
Hardy, T.   In Weatherbury Stocks.
Hayden, R.   Whipping, The.
Heaney, S.   Punishment.
Herrick.   Gods Providence.
  Hell Fire.
  No Escaping the Scourging.
  Patience in Princes.
  Persecutions Purifie.
  Pittie, and Punishment.
  Rewards and Punishments.
  Sin Severely Punisht.
  Sinners.
  Smart.
  Sufferings.
  To God.
  Whips.
  Will the Cause of Woe, The.
Jonson, B.   On Reformed Gamester.
Kipling, R.   Ballad of the King's Jest, The.
  Ballad of the King's Mercy, The.
  Lament of the Border Cattle Thief, The.
Laughlin, J.   Fate of Actaeon, The.
  Jealous Gods, The.
  Judges of the Secret Court, The.
  Sweet Kiss, A.
Lawrence, D. H.   Punisher, The.
Lindsay, N.   City That Will Not Repent, The.
Mallarmé.   Clown Chastised, The.
Milosz, C.   Happenings Elsewhere.
Milton.   On the Gunpowder Plot.
Patchen.   Lions of fire, The.
Ralegh, S.   Nine furlongs strecht lies Tityus, who for his wicked deedes.
Ransom, J.   Man without Sense of Direction.
Rossetti, C.   Brother Bruin.
  By the Waters of Babylon. B.C. 570.
Rukeyser, M.   Chapman.
Sheridan, T.   If These Can't Keep Your Ladies Quiet.
Whittier.   Branded Hand, The.
  Wife of Manoah to Her Husband, The.
Wilde, O.   Ballad of Reading Gaol, The.
Williams, C. K.   Man Who Owns Sleep, The.
Wordsworth, W.   When Philoctetes in the Lemnian Isle.
Wright, J.   Song for the Middle of the Night, A.

Punks
Ginsberg, A.   Punk Rock Your My Big Crybaby.
Sze.   New Wave.

Puns
Bierce.   Pun, The.
Campion, T.   Verba volant; verum: quid enim velocius illis?

Crashaw.   Upon Ford's Two Tragedies, "Loves Sacrifice" and "The Broken Heart."
Jonson, B.   On the New Hot-House.
Ralegh, S.   From the Diary of John Manningham of the Middle Temple.
Ramanujan.   On the Death of a Poem.
Sheridan, T.   Original of Punning, The.
Tomlinson, C.   Misprint.
Unknown.   Punegyric upon Tom Pun-sibi's *Ars Pun-ica*, A.
Zukofsky, L.   All of December Toward New Year's.
  Hyacinth.
  I's (Pronounced *Eyes*).
  "One oak fool box";—the pun.

Puppets and Puppeteers
Cummings, E. E.   A(ncient)a / weigh / tless.
Eliot, T. S.   Convictions (Curtain Raiser).
  Humouresque.
Lux.   Man Takes His Daughter, Age Five, To a Public Execution by Guillotine, Paris, 1857, A.
  Nazi at the Puppet Show, The.
  Princess Summer Fall Winter Spring.
Sheridan, T.   Prologue to the Farce of *Punch Turned Schoolmaster*.
Wilde, O.   Harlot's House, The.

Puppies
Dickey, W.   Anniversary, The.
Kipling, R.   His Apologies.
Ramanujan.   Epitaph on a Street Dog.
Sheridan, T.   Thus Puppies that Adore the Dark.
Stafford, W.   How It Began.
Williams, W.   Stormy.

Purcell, Henry
Hopkins, G.   Henry Purcell.

Purgatory
Kumin, M.   Purgatory.
Merwin.   Purgatory, A.
Milosz, C.   If.
Milton.   On the Same ["James derided the Purgatorial fire of the soul"].

Puritanism and Puritans
Bly, R.   Pilgrim Fish Heads.
Donne.   Cross, The.
Dugan, A.   Significance of Corn in American History, The.
Eberhart, R.   Opposition.
Jonson, B.   On Lip[pe] the Teacher.
Lowell, R.   After the Surprising Conversions.
Meredith, G.   Certain People, A.
Very.   Influence of Puritanism.
Wilbur, R.   Puritans, The.

Purity
Baudelaire.   Allegory.
Brontë, E.   Not a vapour had stained the breezeless blue.
Browning, E.   Prospect, The.
Burns, R.   Scotish Song.
Carew, T.   To the Painter.
Ciardi, J.   Evil Eye, The.
  Two Egrets.
Clough.   From the contamination / Of laudation.
Creeley.   Love ("Thing comes, The").
Dickinson, E.   Candor—my tepid friend.
Eberhart, R.   Supreme Authority of the Imagination, The.
Emerson, R.   Papas Blondine / Grew tall & wise.
Graves, R.   Purification.
Guyon.   Love Pure and Fervent.
  Swallow, The.
HaNagid.   Why Should the Hearts of You Purists.
Herbert, G.   Superliminare.
Herrick.   Another New-Yeeres Gift, or Song for the Circumcision.
  Julia's Churching, or Purification.
  North and South.
  Parasceve, or Preparation, The.
  Persecutions Purifie.
  To God.
  To Julia.
  To Perenna.
  To Silvia.
  Upon Jone and Jane.

Kunitz, S.   Vita Nuova.
Laughlin, J.   Inviolable Maiden, The.
Levine, P.   Genius.
Lindsay, N.   General William Booth Enters into
   Heaven.
MacNeice.   Individualist Speaks, The.
Meredith, G.   Margaret's Bridal-Eve.
Merton.   Night-Flowering Cactus.
Millay, E.   "Love is not all: it is not meat nor
   drink."
Mistral, G.   In Praise of Salt.
Nash, O.   Reflection On a Wicked World.
Nemerov.   Earthquake in the West, The.
Parker, D.   Interview.
Patchen.   Ecstasy of the Pure.
Rossetti, C.   Isidora.
   Lord, make me pure: / Only the pure shall see
      Thee as Thou art.
   Purification of St. Mary the Virgin, The.
   They Shall Be as White as Snow.
   Thou Art Fairer Than the Children of Men.
   Thy lilies drink the dew, / Thy lambs the rill,
      and I will drink them too.
   Whitsun Monday.
Sandburg, C.   White Ash.
   White Hands.
Shapiro, K.   Back, The.
Snyder, G.   To Fire.
Williams, C. K.   Acids.
   Kingdom of Stinking Wishes, The.
Wright, J.   All the Beautiful are Blameless.
   Eclogue at Nash's Grove.

Pursuit
Chuang Tzu.   Tower of the Spirit, The.
Clough.   To spend unsolaced years of pain.
Cowper, W.   Song on Peace.
Crane, S.   I saw a man pursuing the horizon.
Eberhart, R.   1934.
Frost, R.   Escapist—Never.
"H. D."   Pursuit.
Hall, D.   Cops and Robbers.
Ignatow, D.   Bagel, The.
Komunyakaa.   False Leads.
   Vigilante.
Laughlin, J.   Ever So.
MacNeice.   Explorations.
Meredith, G.   Song: "When on my faithful
   charger."
   With the Huntress.
   Youthful Quest, The.
Merwin.   Animals, The.
   Diggers, The.
Nash, O.   Emancipation of Mr. Poplin, or, Skoal
   to the Skimmerless.
Oppen.   Leviathan.
Plath.   Pursuit.
Robinson, E.   Dear Friends.
Tate, J.   Rape in the Engineering Building.
Zukofsky, L.   Sequence 1944-6.

Pushers
Angelou.   Pusher, The.
Gunn, T.   Street Song.
See also **Drug Addiction**

Pushkin, Aleksandr Sergeyevich
Davie, D.   Dream Forest.
   Pushkin. A Didactic Poem.

Puvis de Chavannes, Pierre
Mallarmé.   Homage: "Even a Dawn too numb."

Pygmalion
Ovid.   Galatea.
Petrarch.   If, when Simone laboured to depict.
Williams, T.   Sonnet for Pygmalion.
Wordsworth, W.   Lady Whom You here Behold,
   The.
   Prithee, Gentle Lady, List.

Pygmies
Graves, R.   Ogres and Pygmies.
Weiss, T.   Letter from the Pygmies, A.

Pyramids
Ammons.   Miss.
Dubie.   Evening of the Pyramids, The.

Pyramus and Thisbe
Donne.   Pyramus and Thisbe.

Pythagoras
Borges.   Cyclical Night, The.

"Dario."   In the Constellations.
Stockton, A.   Thoughts on the Pythagorian
   System.

Q

Quail
Carver, R.   Away.
Stafford, W.   Inheriting the Earth: Quail.
   Survival.
Wright, J.   Quail, The.

Quakers
Clampitt.   Dahlia Gardens, The.
Very.   Solitary Worshipper, The.

See also **Friends, Society of**

Quarrels
Burns, R.   Holy Tulzie, The.
Byron, G.   Brave Champions! Go On with the
   Farce.
Carver, R.   From the East, Light.
   Little Room, The.
   Tall Order, A.
Cowper, W.   Lily and the Rose, The.
   On Madan's Answer to Newton.
   Written in a Quarrel.
Creeley.   One Way.
Davie, D.   Admiral to His Lady, The.
Dunbar, P.   After the Quarrel.
Frost, R.   From Plane to Plane.
"H. D."   Halcyon.
Hamill, S.   With the Gift of a Nootka Rose.
Herrick.   Epitaph on a Man who Had a Scold to
   His Wife.
   Upon Jolly and Jilly.
Hughes, L.   Early Evening Quarrel.
Lawrence, D. H.   Henriette.
Major, C.   Kitchen Chair Poem #4.
McGrath, T.   News and the Weather, The.
Muldoon, P.   Sushi.
Nash, O.   Birdies, Don't Make Me Laugh.
   Don't Wait, Hit Me Now!
   Frailty, Thy Name Is a Misnomer.
   I Do, I Will, I Have.
   I Never Even Suggested It.
   Nothing but Nature.
   They Won't Believe, on New Year's Eve, that
      New Year's Day Will Come What May.
Olson, C.   Common Place.
Paley, G.   Quarrel ("Bob and I / in different
   rooms").
Plath.   Snowman on the Moor, The.
Pope, A.   Epigram: "My Lord complains, that
   Pope, stark mad with gardens."
Rich, A.   Novella.
Riley, J.   Quarrel, The.
Rukeyser, M.   After Their Quarrel.
Schuyler, J.   Was It.
Williams, C. K.   Color of Time, The.
   Peace.
   Toil.

See also **Anger**

Quarries
Clampitt.   Quarry, The.
Hardy, T.   Green Slates.
Jeffers, R.   Bixby's Landing.
Kumin, M.   Quarry, Pigeon Cove.
Montale.   Autumn Quarries.
Rukeyser, M.   Sand-Quarry with Moving
   Figures.
Tomlinson, C.   Above Carrara.
   Carrara Revisited.
   Down From Colonnata.
   House in the Quarry, The.
   Quarry, The.
Wordsworth, W.   Written with a Slate Pencil
   upon a Stone, the Largest of a Heap Lying near
   a Deserted Quarry, upon One of the Islands at
   Rydal.

Quebec City, Canada
Atwood.   Disembarking at Quebec.
Eberhart, R.   Sainte Anne De Beaupré.

Quebec (province), Canada
Atwood.   1837 War in Retrospect.
Blue Cloud.   Quebec, rattling chains of

   Separatism.
Van Duyn.   Quebec Suite.
Wheatley, P.   Answer to the *Rebus*, by the
   Author of These Poems, An.

Queen Anne's Lace
Stock, R.   Queen Anne's Lace.
Williams, W.   Queen-Anne's-Lace.

Queens
Broumas, O.   Innocence.
Browning, E.   Crowned and Wedded.
   Nature's Remorses.
Campion, T.   To the Most Sacred Queen Anne.
Ciardi, J.   Q may as well be for QUEEN.
Crashaw.   To the Queen, an Apologie for the
   Length of the Following Panegyricke.
De la Mare.   Gold.
   Queen Djenira.
Emerson, R.   Queen rejoices in her peers, A.
   Such another peerless queen.
Hall, D.   Pictures of Philippa.
Herrick.   To the Queene.
   Twelfe Night, or King and Queene.
Housman.   1887.
Jonson, B.   Epigram to the Queen, Then Lying
   In. 1630, An.
   Ode, or Song, by All the Muses, An.
Kipling, R.   Bells and Queen Victoria, The.
Marvell.   In Eandem Reginae Sueciae
   Transmissam [To Christina, Queen of Sweden].
   Letter to Doctor Ingelo, A.
Meredith, G.   Queen Zuleima.
Plath.   Queen's Complaint, The.
Ralegh, S.   Conjectural First Draft of the
   Petition to Queen Anne.
   If Cynthia Be a Queen.
   Sir Walter Ralegh to the Queen.
   Sir Walter Ralegh's [*or* S.W. Raghlies] Petition
      to the Queene 1618.
Rimbaud, A.   Royalty.
Rossetti, C.   I sit a queen, and am no widow,
   and shall see no sorrow.
   She Came from The Uttermost Part of the Earth.
   Succession of Kings, The.
Szymborska, W.   Beheading.
Wilbur, R.   Lament: "Nashe's old queens who
   bartered young and fair."
Wilde, O.   Queen Henrietta Maria.
Yeats.   Old Age of Queen Maeve, The.
Zaturenska.   Lament of Catherine Howard, Fifth
   Queen of Henry VIII.

Queens, New York City
Ferlinghetti, L.   Queens Cemetery, Setting Sun.
Oppen.   Sunnyside Child.

Questions
Amichai [*or* Amikhai].   Great Tranquillity:
   Questions and Answers, A.
Auden.   Question, The.
Beckett, S.   Que ferais-je sans ce monde sans
   visage sans questions.
   What would I do without this world faceless
      incurious.
Bishop, E.   Mountain, The.
Borges.   Web, The.
Browning, E.   Question and Answer.
Cary, T.   Methodus Amandi.
Creeley.   Ballad, A: "We have a song for the
   death in her body."
   Down Home.
   Fire.
   Lover, The.
   Pedigree, The.
   Riddle, The.
Cummings, E. E.   Will out of the kindness of
   their hearts a few philosophers tell me.
   Will you teach a.
De la Mare.   Last Chapter, The.
   Vain Questioning.
   Which Way?
Dunbar, P.   Mystery, The.
Duncan, R.   Among My Friends.
Eberhart, R.   Configuration.
   Old Question.
   Question Mark.
Emerson, R.   Sphinx, The.
Graves, R.   Possibly.
   What is Love?

When and Why.
HaNagid.   You Who'd Be Wise.
Herrick.   Upon Love, by Way of Question and
  Answer.
Ignatow, D.   For My Daughter in Reply to a
  Question.
Jackson, L.   As Many Questions As Answers.
Jacobsen, J.   Interrogation.
Laughlin, J.   Preguntas sin respuestas for
  Nicanor Parra.
  Problem Struck Me, The.
Levine, P.   How Much Can It Hurt?
  Late Answer, A.
Neruda.   And why is the sun such a poor friend.
  Are the salt and the sugar at work.
  At whom is the rice grinning.
  Can't you think death lives.
  Do you hear yellow detonations.
  Don't you also feel danger.
  How long would a rhinoceros last.
  If all rivers are sweet.
  If I'm dead and don't know it.
  Is 4 always 4 for everybody?
  Is all peace a dove's peace?
  Is it true that amber contains.
  Is there anything crazier in this life.
  Spelling book, can you love me.
  Tell me, is the rose really naked.
  That solemn Senator / who claimed I had
    castles.
  To whom does the raggedy condor.
  What are you hiding under your hump?
  What can it mean to endure.
  What forced labor / for Hitler in Hell?
  What will the Poles think of my hat.
  When does the butterfly read.
  Where is the child that I was.
  Who can persuade the sea.
  Whom can I ask / what I meant to achieve in
    this world?
  Won't our life be a tunnel?
Owen, W.   Asleep.
  Maundy Thursday.
Paley, G.   What If (This Week).
Patchen.   Investigation of Certain Interesting
  Questions.
  Naked Land, The.
Robinson, E.   Two Men.
Rossetti, C.   Grown Cold.
  Maiden May.
  Of Him That Was Ready to Perish.
  Until the Day Break.
Rukeyser, M.   Private Life of the Sphinx.
Sandburg, C.   Brass Keys.
  Haze.
  Honey and Salt.
  How Much?
  Little Word, Little White Bird.
  Money, Politics, Love, and Glory.
  Oomba.
  Out of White Lips.
  Questionnaire.
  Sphinx, A.
Tomlinson, C.   Question, The.
Warren, R.   Question and Answer.
  Questions You Must Learn to Live Past.
Whitman, W.   To the States.
Williams, C. K.   Question, The.
Williams, M.   For Robert, Son of Man.
  Old Detective Begins His Last Interrogation
    Looking for the Truth as Always, The.
Wright, J.   What the Earth Asked Me.
Yeats.   At Algeciras—a Meditation upon Death.
Zaturenska.   Question, The.
Quests
Ashbery, J.   And I'd Love You to Be in It.
Browning, R.   Childe Roland to the Dark Tower
  Came.
Carruth, H.   Journey to a Known Place.
Cooper, J.   Mission with the Night, A.
Cowper, W.   Four Ages, The.
De la Mare.   Mistress Fell.
Dickinson, E.   Each Life Converges to some
  Centre.
Eliot, T. S.   Waste Land, The.
Emerson, R.   Beauty.

García Lorca.   Gacela of the Flight.
Graves, R.   White Goddess, The.
Herrick.   Sobriety in Search.
Hopkins, G.   I must hunt down the prize.
Hughes, L.   Search.
Kunitz, S.   Pivot, The.
Lindsay, N.   I Went Down into the Desert to
  Meet Elijah.
  Mouse That Gnawed the Oak-Tree Down, The.
Logan, J.   Search, The.
MacNeice.   Good Dream.
  This Way Out.
Merwin.   Search, The.
  Spring.
Milosz, C.   This Only.
Montale.   Wind on the Crescent.
Poe.   Eldorado.
Ramanujan.   Looking and Finding.
  Looking for the Centre.
Riley, J.   At Sea.
  Quest, The.
  Wandering Jew, The.
Ritsos.   Forbidden Ground.
Robinson, E.   Sage, The.
  Siege Perilous.
Rossetti, C.   Confluents.
  Darkness and light are both alike to Thee.
  Discovery, A.
  How One Chose.
  I Do Not Look for Love That Is a Dream.
  My Old Friends.
  Of Him That Was Ready to Perish.
  Resurgam.
  What is the beginning? Love. What the course?
    Love still.
  Yet A Little While.
Rukeyser, M.   Brilliant, the full-bodied, the real
  of the world in their powers, The.
  Searching / Not Searching.
Rumi.   There's Nothing Ahead.
Sandburg, C.   Circle of Doors.
Sexton.   God-Monger, The.
  Gods.
Tate, J.   My Girl.
Thoreau.   I am bound, I am bound, for a distant
  shore.
Warren, R.   Pursuit.
  Why Have I Wandered the Asphalt of
    Midnight?
Whitman, W.   Song of Myself.
Whittier.   In Quest.
Williams, W.   Wanderer, The: A Rococo Study.
Wordsworth, W.   Alas! what boots the long
  laborious quest.
Wright, J.   Abstract of Knowledge, The / The
  First Test.
  Quest, The.
Zagajewski.   Three Kings, The.
Quilts and Quilting
Clifton, L.   Quilting.
Cowper, W.   To Mrs. King.
Dunbar, P.   Quilting, The.
Piercy.   Looking at Quilts.
Rich, A.   Aunt Jennifer's Tigers.
Quince Trees and Quinces
Ciardi, J.   Flowering Quince.
Merwin.   Quince.
Quinces
Tomlinson, C.   Green Quinces.
Quotidian
Hall, D.   Coffee Cup, The.
  Widows, The.
Heaney, S.   Night Drive.
Herrick.   Upon Mudge.
Nash, O.   I Must Tell You about My Novel.
Schuyler, J.   Few Days, A.
  Red Brick and Brown Stone.
Simic.   Small Wonders.
Stafford, W.   Allegiances.
Williams, M.   Love Poem: "Six o'clock and /
  the sun rises."

Rabbis
Amichai [or Amikhai].   Man crossing the field
  was a Chief Rabbi, The.
  Rabbi Nakhman of Bratslav.
Borges.   Golem, The.
Dubie.   In the Time of False Messiahs.
Hayden, R.   Rabbi, The.
Kumin, M.   In the Absence of Bliss.
Nemerov.   Debate with the Rabbi.
Whittier.   Rabbi Ishmael.
Rabbits
Bukowski.   Look, The.
Clare, J.   Young Rabbits.
Cunningham, J.   Chase, The.
De la Mare.   Dry August Burned.
Dunbar, P.   Winter's Approach.
Larkin, P.   Myxomatosis.
Lawrence, D. H.   Rabbit Snared in the Night.
Lux.   Ditto.
Millay, E.   Rabbit, The.
Milosz, C.   Encounter.
Muldoon, P.   Coney, The.
Nash, O.   Rabbits, The.
Piercy.   Sojourners.
Plath.   Rabbit Catcher, The.
Riley, J.   Rabbit.
  Rabbit in the Cross-Ties.
Rossetti, C.   When the cows come home the
  milk is coming.
Sexton.   Passion of the Mad Rabbit, The.
Stafford, W.   Farewell, Age Ten, A.
See also **Hares; Jackrabbits**
Raccoons
Ammons.   April.
  Coon Song.
Jacobsen, J.   Cul de Sac.
Kunitz, S.   Raccoon Journal.
Rexroth, K.   Doubled Mirrors.
Riley, J.   Pet Coon, The.
Sexton.   Raccoon.
Snyder, G.   True Night.
Stafford, W.   Connections.
Rachel (Bible)
Amichai [or Amikhai].   Man crossing the field
  was a Chief Rabbi, The.
Burns, R.   Patriarch, The.
Stock, R.   Rachel and Leah.
Very.   Rachel.
Rachmaninov, Sergei
Carruth, H.   Freedom and Discipline.
O'Hara, F.   On Rachmaninoff's Birthday.
Schuyler, J.   Rachmaninoff's Third.
Racial Prejudice
Angelou.   Bump d'Bump.
  No No No No.
Bly, R.   Hatred of Men with Black Hair.
Brooks, G.   Ballad of Rudolph Reed, The.
  Bronzeville Woman in a Red Hat.
Broumas, O.   Massacre, The.
Browning, E.   Runaway Slave at Pilgrim's Point,
  The.
Cooper, J.   Clementene.
Cullen, C.   Colors.
  Incident.
  Tableau.
  Uncle Jim.
Eberhart, R.   Request for Offering.
Hacker, M.   1973.
Hughes, L.   Backlash Blues, The.
  Beaumont to Detroit: 1943.
  Bitter River, The.
  Black Man Speaks, The.
  Brass Spittoons.
  Children's Rhymes ("By what sends").
  Colored Soldier, The.
  Cross.
  Crow Goes, Too.
  Dear Mr. President.
  Death in Yorkville.
  Dinner Guest: Me.
  Dream Boogie.
  How About It, Dixie.

I, Too.
Jim Crow's Last Stand.
Judge William Hastie.
Southern Negro Speaks.
This Puzzles Me.
To Captain Mulzac.
Visitors to the Black Belt.
Will V-Day Be Me-Day Too?
Kizer, C.   Race Relations.
Komunyakaa.   Jasmine.
Sex, Magnolias, & Speed.
Story, A.
Summer Night in Hanoi, A.
Lorde.   Poem for Women in Rage, A.
Revolution Is One Form of Social Change.
MacDiarmid, H.   With the Herring Fishers.
Major, C.   Coon Showman.
Slave Trade, The: View from the Middle
Passage.
Merton.   Plessy vs Ferguson: Theme and
Variations.
Patchen.   Nice Day for a Lynching.
Walcott.   Blues.
Gulf, The.
Walker, A.   First, They Said.
January 10, 1973.
Once.
Right to Life, The: What Can the White Man
Say to the Black Woman?
South: The Name of Home.
Whittier.   On a Prayer-Book.
Williams, C. K.   Racists.
See also **Racism and Racists**
Racing and Racers
Cavafy.   Favor of Alexander Valas, The.
Dubie.   Death of the Race Car Driver, The.
Montale.   Buffalo.
Pagis.   Tortoise, The.
See also **Horse Racing; Track Athletics**
Racism and Racists
Ai.   Hoover Trismegistus.
Passing Through.
Angelou.   Miss Scarlet, Mr. Rhett and other
Latter-Day Saints.
No No No No.
Blok.   Scythians, The.
Brooks, G.   Ballad of Rudolph Reed, The.
Bronzeville Mother Loiters in Mississippi, A.
Meanwhile, a Mississippi Mother Burns
Bacon.
Bronzeville Woman in a Red Hat.
Chicago *Defender* Sends a Man to Little Rock,
The.
Gay Chaps at the Bar.
"Negro" Hero.
White Troops Had Their Orders but the Negroes
Looked Like Men.
Broumas, O.   Pealing, The.
Clifton, L.   Jasper Texas 1998.
Memory.
My Dream About Being White.
What I Think When I Ride the Train.
Cooper, J.   Being Southern.
Clementine.
Cullen, C.   Ballad of the Brown Girl, The.
Black Christ, The.
Incident.
Uncle Jim.
Cummings, E. E.   YgUDuh / ydoan /
yunnuhstan.
Dubie.   Pennacesse Leper Colony for Women,
Cape Cod, The: 1922.
Dunbar, P.   Harriet Beecher Stowe.
Hayden, R.   [American Journal].
Frederick Douglass.
From the Corpse Woodpiles, from the Ashes.
Monet's "Waterlilies."
'Mystery Boy' Looks for Kin in Nashville.
Hughes, L.   Argument ("White is right, / Yellow
mellow").
Ballad of Harry Moore.
Ballad of Margie Polite, The.
Ballad of Ozie Powell.
Ballad of Sam Solomon.
Ballad of the Landlord.
Ballad of Walter White.

Bible Belt.
Black Clown, The.
Black Seed.
Blue Bayou.
Brass Spittoons.
Brotherly Love.
Children's Rhymes ("When I was a chile we
used to play").
Colored Soldier, The.
Dixie Man to Uncle Sam.
Do You Reckon?
Envoy to Africa.
Explain It, Please.
Freedom Train.
Governor Fires Dean.
Harlem ("Here on the edge of hell").
House in the World.
Imagine.
In Explanation of Our Times.
Jim Crow Car.
Jim Crow's Last Stand.
Ku Klux.
Lament for Dark Peoples.
Little Song on Housing.
Mellow.
Memo to Non-White Peoples.
Merry-Go-Round.
Message to the President.
Mississippi.
Mitchell Case, The.
Movies.
Mulatto.
NAACP.
Not a Movie.
Note on Commercial Theatre.
Note to All Nazis Fascists and Klansmen.
One-Way Ticket.
Poem to Uncle Sam.
Poet to Bigot.
Question ("When the old junk man Death").
Red Cross.
Restrictive Covenants.
Ruby Brown.
Song after Lynching.
Song of Adoration.
Southern Mammy Sings.
Tell Me.
This Puzzles Me.
Total War.
Uncle Tom ("Within—/ The beaten pride").
Vari-Colored Song.
Where Service Is Needed.
Where? When? Which?
White Man.
White Ones, The.
Worriation.
Ignatow, D.   Harold.
Jacobsen, J.   Spread of Mrs. Mobey's Lawn.
Kizer, C.   Race Relations.
Komunyakaa.   History Lessons.
Jumping Bad Blues.
New Gold Mountain.
Newport Beach, 1979.
One-legged Stool, The.
Salt.
Tu Do Street.
Tuesday Night at the Savoy Ballroom.
Untitled Blues; After a Photograph by Yevgeni
Yevtushenko.
Whistle, The.
Kumin, M.   Long Approach, The.
Photograph, Maryland Agricultural College
Livestock Show, 1924.
Levertov.   Long Way Round, The.
Lorde.   Afterimages.
Suffer the Children.
Who Said It Was Simple.
Major, C.   And who must remain.
Coon Showman.
Descendant of Solomon and the Queen of
Sheba.
In Hollywood with the Zuni God of War.
McGrath, T.   Deep South.
Merton.   Picture of a Black Child with a White
Doll.
Plessy vs Ferguson: Theme and Variations.

Niedecker.   When brown folk lived a distance.
Orr, G.   On a Highway East of Selma, Alabama.
Rexroth, K.   Discrimination.
Rich, A.   Frame.
Sandburg, C.   Sayings of Henry Stephens.
Stafford, W.   Serving with Gideon.
Walcott.   Blues.
Glory Trumpeter, The.
Walker, A.   Thing Itself, The.
Warren, R.   Ballad of Mister Dutcher and the
Last Lynching in Gupton.
News Photo.
Pondy Woods.
Williams, W.   Impromptu: The Suckers.
See also **Racial Prejudice**
Radiation and Radiation Sickness
Ammons.   Involved.
Piercy.   Long Death, The.
See also **Nuclear Accidents; Nuclear War**
Radio
Carver, R.   Listening.
Radio Waves.
Creeley.   Mary's Fancy.
Dugan, A.   "Space Is Not Merely a Background
for Events, But Possesses an Autonomous
Structure." —A. Einstein.
Enzensberger, H.   Remote House.
Hall, D.   Tomorrow.
Komunyakaa.   Hanoi Hannah.
Mahon.   Morning Radio.
Muldoon, P.   Radio Horse, The.
O'Hara, F.   Radio.
Rexroth, K.   Rose Colored Glasses.
Un Bel di Vedremo.
Zagajewski.   Electric Elegy.
Rahab
Merton.   Rahab's House.
Railroad Wrecks
Carruth, H.   Wreck of the Circus Train, The.
Whittier.   Conductor Bradley.
Railroads
Cooper, J.   Wanda's Blues.
Davie, D.   Northern Metres.
Dickey, J.   Folk Singer of the Thirties, A.
Dickinson, E.   I like to see it lap the Miles.
Dugan, A.   On the Long Island Railroad System.
Frost, R.   On the Heart's Beginning to Cloud the
Mind.
Ginsberg, A.   In Back of the Real.
Sunflower Sutra.
Glück, L.   Departure.
Hall, D.   Sister on the Tracks, A.
Hughes, L.   Homesick Blues.
Mitchell Case, The.
Kipling, R.   Public Waste.
Koch, K.   Railway Stationery, The.
Laughlin, J.   In Darmstadt.
O Frères Humains.
Levine, P.   Conductor of Nothing, The.
MacLeish.   Burying Ground by the Ties.
Grazing Locomotives.
Merwin.   Wheels of the Trains, The.
Nash, O.   Riding on a Railroad Train.
Niedecker.   Get a load.
Roethke.   Night Journey.
Rukeyser, M.   Campaign.
There is a knotless line westward, past terraces.
Up past the burnt hills. Distance and the crowd.
Young Men, The.
Sandburg, C.   Caboose Thoughts.
Child of the Romans.
Five Towns on the B. and O.
Jack.
Old Flagman, The.
Pods.
Slow Program.
Southern Pacific.
Still Life.
Work Gangs.
Tate, J.   Pride's Crossing.
Thoreau.   What's the railroad to me?
Very.   Rail Road, The.
Whitman, W.   To a Locomotive in Winter.
Wilbur, R.   In the Smoking-Car.
Stop.

Williams, W.   Period Piece: 1834.
Wordsworth, W.   At Furness Abbey.
On the Projected Kendal and Windermere
 Railway.
Proud Were Ye, Mountains, When, in Times of
 Old.
Wright, J.   Outside Fargo, North Dakota.
Poem Written under an Archway in a
 Discontinued Railroad Station, Fargo, North
 Dakota, A.
See also **Locomotives; Trains**

Railway Stations
Eberhart, R.   Analogue of Unity in Multeity.
Graves, R.   Between Trains.
Hughes, L.   Pennsylvania Station.
Jarrell, R.   La Belle au Bois Dormant.
Traveler, The.
Komunyakaa.   NJ Transit.
Major, C.   Train Stop.
Riley, J.   Christmas along the Wires.
Ritsos.   On Form.
Seifert.   Struggle with the Angel.
Szymborska, W.   Railroad Station, The.
Wilbur, R.   For the New Railway Station in
 Rome.
Stop.
Wright, J.   Poem Written under an Archway in a
 Discontinued Railroad Station, Fargo, North
 Dakota, A.
Zagajewski.   Stary Sacz.
Wanderer, A.

Railway Travel
Amichai [*or* Amikhai].   Travel by Train.
Berryman.   On the London Train.
Clampitt.   Babel Aboard the Hellas International
 Express.
Codrescu.   3/6/81, Amtrack.
Davie, D.   In the Stopping Train.
Wiltshire.
De la Mare.   Railway Junction, The.
Ginsberg, A.   Sunset.
Hardy, T.   Faintheart in a Railway Train.
Jarrell, R.   Orient Express, The.
Lawrence, D. H.   Excursion Train.
Train at Night, A.
Levertov.   From the Train, Eastward.
Merton.   Kandy Express.
Night Train, The.
Montale.   Local Train.
Nash, O.   Riding on a Railroad Train.
Oppen.   Any Way But Back.
Prunty.   Old Declaratives.
Ramanujan.   Poona Train Window.
Riley, J.   Another Ride from Ghent to Aix.
Train-Misser, The.
Rukeyser, M.   Street corner to corner he will
 talk all day.
Sandburg, C.   Slabs of the Sunburnt West.
Schuyler, J.   En Route to Southampton.
Seifert.   Honeymoon.
Stafford, W.   Vacation.
Tate, J.   Mystic Moment.
Updike.   English Train Compartment.
Wilbur, R.   In the Smoking-Car.
Williams, T.   Jockeys at Hialeah, The.
Man in the Dining Car, The.
Road, The.
Zagajewski.   At Daybreak.
Opus Posthumous.

Rain
Amichai [*or* Amikhai].   And After All That—
 the Rain.
Autumn Rain in Tel Aviv.
First Rain on a Burned Car.
First Rain, The.
You Are So Small and Slight in the Rain.
Ammons.   After Yesterday.
Clearing.
Fall Creek.
Halfway.
Ithaca, N.Y.
Mediation.
Off.
Russet Gold.
Tight.
Translating.

Baudelaire.   Black Bile ("Pluvius, venting spleen
 on all enclaves").
Berry, W.   Falling Asleep.
In Rain.
Rain.
Winter Rain, The.
Bishop, E.   Imber Nocturnus.
Sestina: "September rain falls on the house."
Blue Cloud.   Sweetgrass.
Bly, R.   August Rain.
Reading in Fall Rain.
Borges.   Rain.
Brodsky, J.   August Rain.
Brontë, E.   'Tis evening now, the sun descends.
Bukowski.   Star, The.
Carruth, H.   Far-removed Mountain Men, The.
Missing the Bo in the Henhouse.
Carver, R.   Rain.
Sudden Rain.
Cavafy.   Rain.
Ciardi, J.   Thursday.
Two Dry Poems.
Clampitt.   At Easterly.
At Muker, Upper Swaledale.
Continental Drift.
Note from Leyden, A.
Rain at Bellagio.
Clare, J.   Clown, The.
Coleridge, S.   Ode to the Rain, An.
Cooper, J.   Morning on the St. John's.
Corbett, W.   Fall 1970.
Cowper, W.   To Lady Austen.
Creeley.   Falling.
First Rain.
Funny.
Midnight.
Out.
Place, A.
Rain.
Rain (2).
Rain, The.
Rose, The.
Cullen, C.   Night Rain.
Singing in the Rain.
Cummings, E. E.   But the other / day i was
 passing a certain.
Dim / i / nu / tiv / e this park is e.
Early Summer Sketch.
I have found what you are like.
Now comes the good rain farmers pray for(and).
N(o)w / the / how / dis(appeared cleverly)world.
O / nly this / darkness(in).
Sky a silver, The.
Sonnet: "Rain-drop on the eyelids of the earth,
 A."
Take for example this.
When rain whom fear.
You asked me to come:it was raining a little.
Davie, D.   Rain on South-East England.
Dickey, J.   Six, The.
Dickinson, E.   Drop fell on the Apple Tree, A.
Like Rain it sounded till it curved.
Dubie.   Old Night and Sleep.
Dunbar, P.   Drizzle.
Rain-Songs.
Time to Tinker 'Roun'!
Éluard, P.   From the Inside.
Emerson, R.   He lives not who can refuse me.
More sweet than my refrain.
Frost, R.   In Time of Cloudburst.
Gallagher, T.   Ever After.
Hands of the Blindman, The.
Message for the Sinecurist.
Open Fire Near a Shed.
Second Language.
Sudden Journey.
Women's Tug of War at Lough Arrow.
García Lorca.   Madrigal to the City of Santiago.
Graves, R.   Around the Mountain.
Turn of the Moon.
Gurney, I.   Soaking, The.
Soft Rain.
Hall, D.   Sun, The.
Hamill, S.   Classical Tragedy.
Cloistered.
Hardy, T.   Autumn Rain-Scene, An.

Expectation and Experience.
On the Doorstep.
Rain on a Grave.
Sundial on a Wet Day, The.
Thunderstorm in Town, A.
We Sat at the Window.
Weathers [*or* Weather].
Wet August, A.
Heaney, S.   Gifts of Rain.
Rain Stick, The.
Hughes, L.   April Rain Song.
In Time of Silver Rain.
Hughes, T.   Heptonstall.
Rain.
Rain-charm for the Duchy.
Jacobsen, J.   Arrival of Rain.
Jeffers, R.   Distant Rainfall.
Koch, K.   On the Great Atlantic Rainway.
Kumin, M.   Continuum: a Love Poem.
First Rain of Spring, The.
Larkin, P.   Card-Players, The.
Whitsun Weddings, The.
Laughlin, J.   Then and Now.
Lawrence, D. H.   Autumn Rain.
Malade.
There Is Rain in Me.
Levertov.   Antiphon, The: "And then once
 more."
Rain Spirit Passing.
Scornful Reprieve.
Levine, P.   Jewish Graveyards, Italy.
Making It New.
Rain Downriver.
White Iris, The.
Lindsay, N.   Song of the Sturdy Snails, The.
Logan, J.   Abstract Love Poem.
New York Scene: May 1958.
Lorde.   My Fifth Trip to Washington Ended in
 Northeast Delaware.
MacDiarmid, H.   Dying Earth, The.
MacLeish.   De Votre Bonheur Il ne Reste Que
 Vos Photos.
MacNeice.   Glass Falling.
June Thunder.
London Rain.
Wiper, The.
Mahon.   Kinsale.
Major, C.   Pencil Sketch.
Meredith, G.   Desired as Summer rain.
Earth and a Wedded Woman.
Song: "I would I were the drop of rain."
Merrill, J.   Childlessness.
Merton.   Song: "When rain, (sings light) rain
 has devoured my house."
Spring Storm.
Merwin.   After the Harvests.
June Rain.
Sun and Rain.
Sunset after Rain.
To the Rain.
Millay, E.   If it should rain—(the sneezy moon).
Mistral, G.   Slow Rain, The.
Montale.   In the Rain.
Muldoon, P.   Boundary Commission, The.
Plovers.
Nash, O.   Tomorrow, Partly Cloudy.
Nemerov.   Ending, An.
Neruda.   I Went.
Niedecker.   Look, the woods, the sky, our home.
O'Hara, F.   Poem: "Now the violets are all gone,
 the rhinoceroses, the cymbals."
Oliver, M.   Marengo.
Rain in Ohio.
Parker, D.   Rainy Night.
Patchen.   Biography of Southern Rain.
Pessoa.   It's raining. There is silence, since the
 rain itself.
Piercy.   Rainy 4th.
Pinsky.   Round.
Street of Furthest Memory, The.
Prunty.   This.
Raine, K.   These watery diamond spheres.
Rexroth, K.   Fragrance of the teapot, The.
Rich, A.   Rain of Blood, The.
Riley, J.   Ballade of the Coming Rain, The.
Laughter of the Rain, The.

Rainy Morning, The.
Sun and Rain.
We to Sigh Instead of Sing.
Wet-Weather Talk.
When It Rains.
Ritsos.   In the Rain.
Misconstructions.
Roethke.   Cycle, The.
Interlude.
Rossetti, C.   And is this August weather? nay
not so.
If all were rain and never sun.
O wind, why do you never rest.
Winter Rain.
Sandburg, C.   Lumber Yard Pools at Sunset.
Monotone.
New Weather.
Rain Winds Blow Doors Open.
Redhaw Rain.
Santa Fe Sketches.
Summer Grass.
Three Balls.
Without Notice Beforehand.
Sarton, M.   Japanese Prints.
Schuyler, J.   Fauré's Second Piano Quartet.
Poem: "I got my hair cut."
Rain.
Running Footsteps.
Standing and Watching.
Suddenly.
Sexton.   Mother and Jack and the Rain.
Shapiro, K.   And Now, the Weather..
Shelley, P.   Cloud, The.
Fragment: Rain.
Smith, S.   Suburb.
Stafford, W.   Glass Face in the Rain, A.
Ground Zero [June 1982].
Stock, R.   Small Rain, The.
Swenson, M.   Rain at Wildwood.
What I Did on a Rainy Day.
Swift, J.   Description of a City Shower, A.
Sze.   Wang Wei.
Tomlinson, C.   During Rain.
Updike.   Code, The.
Raining in Magens Bay.
Sunday Rain.
Wash.
Vallejo.   Down to the Dregs.
Testimony.
Very.   Blessing of Rain, The.
Hath the Rain a Father? Or Who Hath Begotten
the Drops of Dew? Job 38:28.
Latter Rain, The ("Latter rain, it falls in anxious
haste, The").
Prayer for Rain.
Rain Clouds.
Rain, The ("Rain descends; each drop some
drooping flowers, The").
Winter Rain, The.
Walcott.   Dark August.
Return to D'Ennery; Rain.
Warren, R.   Sonnets of Two Summers.
Tires on Wet Asphalt at Night.
Vermont Ballad: Change of Season.
Weiss, T.   Blithewood.
Whalen, P.   April Showers Bring Rain?
Prose Take-Out, Portland, 13:ix:58.
Whitman, W.   Lingering Last Drops.
Voice of the Rain, The.
Wilbur, R.   My Father Paints the Summer.
Williams, C. K.   It Is Teeming.
Souls.
That night, / winter, / rain.
Williams, M.   Everyone Dies in a Light Rain.
Williams, W.   Advent of Today.
Contemporania.
Dark Day, The.
Hermaphroditic Telephones, The.
Idyl: "Wine of the grey sky."
Rain.
Red Wheelbarrow, The.
Self-Portrait 2.
Wilner, E.   American Painting, with Rain.
Wordsworth, W.   Rains at length have ceased,
the winds are stilled, The.
Written in March [While Resting on the Bridge

at the Foot of Brother's Water].
Wright, C.   Freezing Rain.
Thinking about the Poet Larry Levis One
Afternoon in Late May.
Wright, J.   Living by the Red River.
Rain.
Zagajewski.   Anecdote of Rain.
Chinese Poem.
Zukofsky, L.   Rains, the rains, The.

Rain-in-the-Face
Whittier.   On the Big Horn.

Rainbows
Dickinson, E.   Delight is as the flight.
Dunbar, P.   Place Where the Rainbow Ends,
The.
Emerson, R.   Sun athwart the cloud thought it
no sin, The.
What are all the flowers.
Frost, R.   Iris by Night.
Graves, R.   Nothing Now Astonishes.
Herrick.   Rainbow; or Curious Covenant, The.
Rainbow, The.
Hopkins, G.   Rainbow, The.
Lawrence, D. H.   Rainbow.
Rainbow, The.
MacDiarmid, H.   Watergaw, The.
MacLeish.   Rainbow at Evening.
Melville, H.   Canticle, A.
Mistral, G.   Round of the Rainbow.
Nemerov.   Breaking of Rainbows, The.
Raine, K.   Rainbow, beautiful and clear light, A.
Rossetti, C.   If all were rain and never sun.
Rainbow, The.
Sandburg, C.   Bubbles.
Fins.
Gold Mud.
Out of the Rainbow End.
Tomlinson, C.   Double Rainbow, The.
Wordsworth, W.   My heart leaps up when I
behold.

Ralegh, Sir Walter
Spenser, E.   Colin Clouts Come Home Againe.

Rameses II, King of Egypt
Shelley, P.   Ozymandias.

Rams
Amichai [or Amikhai].   Real Hero of the
Sacrifice of Isaac, The.
Real Hero, The.
See also **Sheep**

Ranches
Laughlin, J.   Cincinnatus in Utah.

Rape
Ai.   Sleeping Beauty.
Amichai [or Amikhai].   End of the
Archaeological Season in Eyn Gedi.
Atwood.   Women's Issue, A.
Bukowski.   99 to One.
Campion, T.   Umbra.
Clampitt.   Seed.
Davie, D.   Fountain of Cyanë, The.
Donne.   Apparition, The.
Dugan, A.   On Rape Unattempted.
Eberhart, R.   Snowy Owl.
García Lorca.   Thamar and Amnon.
Gunn, T.   Helen's Rape.
Hacker, M.   Why We Are Going Back to
Paradise Island.
Ignatow, D.   Play Again.
Komunyakaa.   Re-creating the Scene.
Larkin, P.   Deceptions.
Lindsay, N.   Trap, The.
MacLeish.   Rape of the Swan, The.
Meredith, G.   Falling of Sally, The.
Rape of Aurora, The.
Olson, C.   Hymn to Proserpine.
O'Ryan.
Piercy.   Rape Poem.
Rich, A.   Rape.
Swift, J.   Excellent New Ballad, An.
Tate, J.   Rape in the Engineering Building.
Walker, A.   Thing Itself, The.
Williams, W.   Raper from Passenack, The.
Yeats.   Leda and the Swan.

Raphael, Saint
Blake, W.   Pretty Epigram for [Those] the

Entertainment of Those Who [Pay] Have Paid
Great Sums in the Venetian & Flemish Ooze,
A.
Rafael Sublime Majestic Graceful Wise.
García Lorca.   St. Raphael.
Hardy, T.   Cardinal Bembo's Epitaph on
Raphael.
Jacobsen, J.   Reading on the Beach.
Whittier.   Raphael.

Rationalism and Rationalists
Blake, W.   Mock On, Mock On, Voltaire,
Rousseau.
Eberhart, R.   Blessed Are the Angels in Heaven.
Recapitulation, The.
Oppen.   Rationality.
Poe.   Sonnet—To Science.
See also **Intellect and Intellectuals; Reason**

Rats
Browning, R.   Pied Piper of Hamelin, The.
Ciardi, J.   R is for RAT, the noise in man's wall.
Dickinson, E.   Rat surrendered here, A.
Rat, The.
Dugan, A.   On a Dispossess Precept. 2.
Emerson, R.   Van Buren.
Hall, D.   Poem With One Fact.
Hughes, T.   Song of a Rat.
Logue, C.   Rat, O Rat.
Merwin.   New Season, The.
Mistral, G.   Rat, The.
Olson, C.   Will: the rat.
Sandburg, C.   Rat Riddles.
Simic.   Note.
Smith, S.   Pretty.
To a Dead Vole.
Stock, R.   Elemental Trust.
Trakl.   Rats, The.
Updike.   Rats.
Williams, W.   Rat, The.
Wright, J.   Eclogue at Nash's Grove.

Rattlesnakes
Atwood.   Eating Snake.
Carver, R.   Wenas Ridge.
Ciardi, J.   Stations.
Dickey, J.   Blowgun and Rattlesnake.
Dugan, A.   Why There Is No Class Solidarity in
America I Read It In *The Times*. Aug. 2, 1987.
Lindsay, N.   What the Rattlesnake Said.
Tomlinson, C.   Abiquiu.
Warren, R.   Rattlesnake Country.

Ravenna, Italy
Blok.   Ravenna.
MacNeice.   Ravenna.
Montale.   Dora Markus.
Wilde, O.   Ravenna.

Ravens
Bukowski.   All I Know.
Carruth, H.   Mild Winter.
Coleridge, S.   Raven, The.
Cowper, W.   Fable, A: "Raven, while with
glossy breast, A."
De la Mare.   Omen, The.
Hughes, T.   Ravens.
Kinsella, T.   We sat face to face at the kitchen
table.
Merwin.   Noah's Raven.
Poe.   Raven, The.
Rich, A.   Raven, The.
Rossetti, C.   Bird's-Eye View, A.

Reading and Readers
Ashbery, J.   Sonnet: "Each servant stamps the
reader with a look."
Baudelaire.   Epigraph for a Condemned Book.
To the Reader.
Voice, The.
Berrigan, T.   Things To Do in Providence.
Berryman.   Olympus.
Bierce.   Reminded.
Bly, R.   Reading in Fall Rain.
Borges.   Readers.
To Manuel Mujica Lainez.
To the German Language.
To Whoever Is Reading Me.
Bukowski.   As I Lay Dying.
Hustle, The.
Little Girls, The.

Professors, The.
Byron, G.   Answer to Some Elegant Verses.
I Read the "Christabel."
To Harriet.
To Hook the Reader, You, John Murray.
To the Author of a Sonnet Beginning " 'Sad Is
   My Verse,' You Say, 'And Yet No Tear' ."
Campion, T.   Ad ampliss. totius Angliae
   Cancellarium, Fr. Ba.
Ad Ed. Mychelburnum.
Ad Guil. Camdenum.
Ad Io. Davisium.
In Honour of the Author by *Tho: Campion
   Doctor in Physicke. To the Reader.*
To the Reader.
Carruth, H.   Dedication in These Days.
In Memoriam.
Ray.
Carver, R.   After Reading *Two Towns in
   Provence.*
Reading.
Reading Something in the Restaurant.
Cavafy.   He Came to Read.
Ciardi, J.   Man and a Woman Might at This
   Moment, A.
Codrescu.   Books.
Collins, B.   First Reader.
Flight of the Reader, The.
Marginalia.
Reading an Anthology of Chinese Poems of the
   Sung Dynasty, I Pause to Admire the Length
   and Clarity of Their Titles.
Corbett, W.   August.
For Joe Pernice.
Reading.
When I Read John Wieners's Selected Poems.
Creeley.   Early Reading.
For Pen ("Reading, in the chair").
Irish.
The ("Water / waiting far, The").
Cummings, E. E.   For prodigal read generous.
Cunningham, J.   Bookplate.
Coffee.
On Doctor Drink.
To the Reader.
With a Copy of Stevens' *Harmonium.*
De la Mare.   Old Susan.
Omen, The.
Vigil.
Winter Dusk.
Dickinson, E.   It is still as distinct as Paradise.
There is no Frigate like a Book.
Dove, R.   Reading Hölderlin on the Patio with
   the Aid of a Dictionary.
Dubie.   Clouds of Magellan (Aphorisms of Mr.
   Canon Aspirin), The.
Of Politics, & Art.
Parallax Monograph for Rodin, The.
Dugan, A.   After a Poem by Carlos Drummond
   de Andrade Translated by Elizabeth Bishop as
   Don't Kill Yourself.
Dunbar, P.   End of the Chapter, The.
Duncan, R.   Human Communion. Traces, The.
Emerson, R.   He must have / Droll fancies
   sometimes cross his quiet thoughts.
I grieve that better souls than mine.
What all the books of ages paint, I have.
Gallagher, T.   His Shining Helmet; Its Horsehair
   Crest.
Reading Aloud.
Graves, R.   Colophon.
Gunn, T.   His Rooms in College.
Gurney, I.   Snow.
Hamill, S.   Classical Tragedy.
Herrick.   Glorie.
His Wish to God.
Ode to Sir Clipsebie Crew, An.
To His Book[e].
To His Booke.
To Momus.
To My Ill Reader.
To the Sour[e] Reader.
To Vulcan.
Hughes, L.   To You.
Ignatow, D.   Against the Evidence.
Reading at Night.

Jackson, L.   Courtesies of Authorship, The.
Readers, The.
Troubles of a Book, The.
Unread Pages.
Jacobsen, J.   Gentle Reader.
Reading Aloud at Dusk.
Reading on the Beach.
Jarrell, R.   Reader, The.
Jonson, B.   To Groom Idiot.
To the Reader ("Pray thee, take care, that tak'st
   my book[e] in hand").
Keats.   On First Looking into Chapman's
   Homer.
On Receiving a Curious Shell, and a Copy of
   Verses, from the Same Ladies.
On Sitting Down to Read "King Lear" Once
   Again.
Written on a Blank Space at the End of
   Chaucer's Tale of "The Floure and the Lefe."
Kinsella, T.   Drowsing over *The Arabian Nights.*
Larkin, P.   Fiction and the Reading Public.
Study of Reading Habits, A.
Laughlin, J.   Can Language Be Taught with the
   Fingertips?
Graceful Exit, A.
Inn at Kirchstetten, The.
Knowledge.
Lady Asks Me, A.
Poem Seen as a Shell Game, The.
Prognosis.
Welcome, The.
Lawrence, D. H.   Reading a Letter.
Reading in the Evening.
Levertov.   Hunting the Phoenix.
To the Reader.
Logan, J.   On Reading Camus In Early March.
Longfellow, H.   Day Is Done, The.
Lux.   Voice You Hear When You Read Silently,
   The.
McGrath, T.   Ars Poetica: Or: Who Lives in the
   Ivory Tower?
Praises IV.
Use of Books, The.
You Can Start the Poetry Now, Or: News from
   Crazy Horse.
Meredith, G.   Hail, Common Sense! most rare
   of all!
Rosalind.
Thou pirate nested over Alde!
Merton.   Reading Translated Poets, Feb. 1.
Milosz, C.   Adam and Eve.
Readings.
Moore, M.   Poetry: "I, too, dislike it: there are
   things that are important beyond all this
   fiddle."
Niedecker.   Ten o'clock.
To Paul now old enough to read.
Olson, C.   I'm With You.
Orr, G.   Reading Late in the Cottage.
Pagis.   Story, The.
Palmer, M.   Notes for Echo Lake 5.
Secret remains in the book, The.
Symmetrical Poem.
Parker, D.   Lines on Reading Too Many Poets.
Pinsky.   Library Scene.
Prunty.   Tent, The.
Rexroth, K.   Giant Weapon, The.
Homer in Basic.
To Another.
Rich, A.   Diving into the Wreck.
Riley, J.   Close the Book.
Go Read Your Book!
To Almon Keefer.
Rilke.   To Mimi Romanelli.
To Monique and Blaise Briod.
Tuck a Child.
Ritsos.   Myopic Child, A.
Sexton.   Sweeney.
Smith, S.   To an American Publisher.
Stafford, W.   Afternoon in the Stacks, An.
Magic Mountain, The.
Trouble with Reading, The.
Stevens, W.   House Was Quiet and the World
   Was Calm, The.
Large Red Man Reading.
Phosphor Reading by His Own Light.

Reader, The.
Tate, J.   Dear Reader.
Thoughts While Reading *The Sand Reckoner.*
Thoreau.   In days of yore, tis said, the
   swimming alder.
Tomlinson, C.   Double Rainbow, The.
Dream, A.
Hyphens.
Walcott.   Volcano.
Warren, R.   Literal Dream.
Wind and Gibbon.
Weiss, T.   Egyptian Passage, An.
Whalen, P.   Preface, The: "Continous fabric
   (nerve movie?) exactly as wide as these lines,
   A."
That One.
Whitman, W.   For Us Two, Reader Dear.
Thou Reader.
To the Reader at Parting.
Who Is Now Reading This?
Whoever You Are Holding Me Now in Hand.
Whittier.   Lines on a Fly-Leaf.
Williams, M.   Excuse Me.
To a Friend, an Unhappy Poet.
Wordsworth, W   Illustrated Books and
   Newspapers.
Lines Written on a Blank Leaf in a Copy of the
   Author's Poem "The Excursion", upon
   Hearing of the Death of the Late Vicar of
   Kendal.
Yeats.   Ribh at the Tomb of Baile and Aillinn.
When You Are Old.
Zagajewski.   Letter from a Reader.
Reading Books.
Zaturenska.   Once in an Ancient Book.
Zukofsky, L.   After reading.
Reading and Talking.

Reagan, Ronald W.
Codrescu.   November 6, 1984.
Dugan, A.   Takeoff on Armageddon —For
   Ronald Reagan.
Kizer, C.   Election Day, 1984.
Williams, C. K.   Bishop Tutu's Visit to the
   White House: 1984.

Real Estate
Clampitt.   Real Estate.
Sandburg, C.   Real Avenue News.

Reality
Ammons.   Corsons Inlet.
Atwood.   Comic Books vs. History.
Double Voice, The.
How To Tell One Country from Another.
Borges.   Break of Day.
Clouds ("There cannot be a single thing which
   is").
Descartes.
His End and His Beginning.
Other Tiger, The.
Yellow Rose, A.
Brodsky, J.   Afterword.
Browning, R.   Statue and the Bust, The.
Bukowski.   Nice Try.
Nothing Subtle.
Trick to Dull Our Bleeding, A.
Burns, R.   Fragment: "Why, why tell thy lover."
Carruth, H.   Une Présence Absolue.
Chuang Tzu.   Where Is Tao?
Ciardi, J.   Differences.
Dragons.
Fragment of a Bas Relief.
Knothole in Spent Time, A.
On a Photo of Sgt. Ciardi a Year Later.
On the Patio.
One Jay at a Time.
Reality and Willie Yeats.
To a Lovely Lady Gone to Theory.
Codrescu.   Les Fleurs du Cinéma.
Coleridge, S.   Phantom or Fact?
Cortes.   Truth, The.
Creeley.   As real as thinking.
City, The.
"Do You Think."
Echo ("Broken heart, you / timeless wonder").
Numbers.

Province, The.
Surgeons.
"There."
Token, A.
Cummings, E. E.   &(all during the / dropsin).
As freedom is a breakfastfood.
But observe‚though / once is never the beginning
of.
Dive for dreams / or a slogan may topple you.
Dominic has / a doll wired.
Great advantage of being alive, The.
Hate blows a bubble of despair into.
I shall imagine life.
If.
In a middle of a room.
Love is a place.
Lucky means finding / Holes where.
My darling since / you and.
My sweet old etcetera.
Now air is air and thing is thing:no bliss.
Of Ever-Ever Land i speak.
Out of the lie of no.
There is a here and.
This little bride & groom are.
This mind made war.
When serpents bargain for the right to squirm.
Cunningham, J.   Illusion and delusion are that
real.
De la Mare.   I Sit Alone.
Looking Glass, The.
Dove, R.   Anti-Father.
Dugan, A.   On an Architect.
Duncan, R.   Imagining in Writing.
Writing as Writing.
Eberhart, R.   Ceremonial.
Commas in Wintertime.
Kaire.
Looking Head On.
Mystery of the Abstract.
On the Subtle Man.
Poem as Trajectory, The.
Stopping a Kaleidoscope.
Vision through Timothy.
Way Out, A.
Emerson, R.   But as this fugitive sunlight.
Proteus.
Enzensberger, H.   Appearances.
Fenton, J.   Skip, The.
Ferlinghetti, L.   Sarolla's women in their picture
hats.
Sueño Real.
Sweet and various the woodlark.
Gallagher, T.   Candle, Lamp & Firefly.
Ginsberg, A.   Change, The: *Kyoto-Tokyo
Express.*
Imaginary Universes.
Metaphysics.
Hardy, T.   At Waking.
Beauty, The.
History of an Hour, The.
Just the Same.
There Seemed a Strangeness.
To Sincerity.
Tragedian to Tragedienne.
Howe, S.   Pythagorean Silence.
Some particular place fleeting.
Ignatow, D.   Get the Gasworks.
Jarrell, R.   Jamestown.
Märchen, The.
Picture in the Paper, A.
Jeffers, R.   Boats in a Fog.
Real and Half Real.
Jonson, B.   Epigram. To William, Earl of
Newcastle, An.
Keats.   And What Is Love? It Is a Doll Dressed
Up.
Komunyakaa.   Out There There Be Dragons.
Laughlin, J.   Dream Not of Other Worlds.
Non-World, The.
Tuesday at 87 Rue de Rome.
Lawrence, D. H.   Demiurge.
Red Geranium and Godly Mignonette.
Ultimate Reality.
Levertov.   Emblem (2).
Ground-Mist, The.
MacLeish.   Einstein.

MacNeice.   News-Reel, The.
Plain Speaking.
Under the Mountain.
Mahon.   Tractatus.
Mallarmé.   Bell-Ringer, The.
Little Air 1.
Throw of the Dice, A.
Windows, The.
Merwin.   To the Hand.
Widow, The.
Millay, E.   "Love is not all: it is not meat nor
drink."
Milosz, C.   Appeal, An.
Powers.
Return.
What I Learned from Jeanne Hersch.
Montale.   Maybe one morning, walking in dry,
glassy air.
Nemerov.   Maia.
Neruda.   Child of the Moon.
O'Hara, F.   Poem: "Now the violets are all gone,
the rhinoceroses, the cymbals."
Olson, C.   Applause.
B Cs (3—for Rimbaud), A.
Concerning Exaggeration, or How, Properly, to
Heap Up.
Discrete Gloss, A.
He treads on edges of being where the drop.
Moon Is the Number 18, The.
Put him this way.
Signs.
There Are Sounds.
Oppen.   From a Phrase of Simone Weil's and
Some Words of Hegel's.
Leviathan.
Technologies.
Who Shall Doubt.
Pessoa.   Live, you say, in the present.
Psyche-type (Psychotype).
Piercy.   Erasure.
Pinsky.   Hearts, The.
Raine, K.   Bad Dream, A.
World: / Image on water, waves.
Ransom, J.   Somewhere Is Such a Kingdom.
Rexroth, K.   Suchness.
Time Is an Inclusion Series Said McTaggart.
Rossetti, C.   Hopeless Case, A.
Rossetti, D.   Sea-Limits, The.
Rukeyser, M.   When the true things meet us at
the place we reach, they are all.
Rumi.   Dream That Must Be Interpreted, The.
Grasses, The.
Sandburg, C.   Moonlight and Maggots.
Schuyler, J.   Letter to a Friend: Who Is Nancy
Daum?
Sexton.   Self in 1958.
Simic.   Midpoint.
Snyder, G.   Milton by Firelight.
Nanao Knows.
Truth Like the Belly of a Woman Turning, The.
Stevens, W.   Add This to Rhetoric.
Angel Surrounded by Paysans.
As You Leave the Room.
Bed of Old John Zeller, The.
Bouquet of Roses in Sunlight.
Conversation with Three Women of New
England.
Course of a Particular, The.
Credences of Summer.
Man Carrying Thing.
Man on the Dump, The.
Motive for Metaphor, The.
Not Ideas about the Thing but the Thing Itself.
Of Mere Being.
Plain Sense of Things, The.
Poems of Our Climate, The.
Repetitions of a Young Captain.
So-and-So Reclining on Her Couch.
Sunday Morning.
Woman That Had More Babies than That, The.
Sze.   Apache Plume.
Archipelago.
Axis, The.
Before Completion.
Dazzled.
Kaiseki.

Magnetized.
Network, The.
Noah's / Dove.
Oolong.
Redshifting Web, The.
Silk Road, The.
Six Persimmons.
Sound Lag.
Streamers.
String Diamond, The.
Szymborska, W.   Interview with a Child.
No Title Required.
Palaeolithic Fertility Fetish, A.
View with a Grain of Sand.
We're Extremely Fortunate.
Tomlinson, C.   Aesthetic.
Descartes and the Stove.
Observation of Facts.
Song: "To enter the real."
Updike.   Reel.
Van Duyn.   Causes.
Voznesensky [*or* Voznesenskii].   Antiworlds.
Warren, R.   Interjection #2: Caveat.
Rather Like a Dream.
Whatever You Now Are.
Whitman, W.   Ambition.
That Shadow My Likeness.
Wilbur, R.   Hole in the Floor, A.
Thyme Flowering among Rocks.
Williams, C. K.   Beginning of April, The.
Harm.
Williams, M.   He Speaks to His Arguing Friends
and to Himself. ·
If Every Person There Is But One.
Learning to Read.
Thinking Friday Night with a Gothic Storm
Going About Final Causes and Logos and
Mitzi Mayfair.
Waking from a Dream. ·
Williams, T.   Tonight I stay at the Summit
Temple.
Williams, W.   Paterson.
Wordsworth, W.   Hint from the Mountains for
Certain Political Pretenders.
Oxford, May Thirtieth, Eighteen Twenty.
To the Utilitarians.
Yarrow Visited [September, 1814].
Wright, C.   Apologia Pro Vita Sua.
Appalachian Book of the Dead, The.
Basic Dialogue.
Blaise Pascal Lip-syncs the Void.
East of the Blue Ridge, Our Tombs Are in the
Dove's Throat.
Easter 1989.
Giorgio Morandi and the Talking Eternity Blues.
Last Journal.
Lives of the Saints.
Local Journal.
Meditation on Form and Measure.
October 2.
Reading Lao Tzu Again in the New Year.
Sprung Narratives.
Still Life with Stick and Word.
Under the Nine Trees in January.
Waiting for Tu Fu.
Watching the Equinox Arrive in Charlottesville,
September 1992.
With Eddie and Nancy in Arezzo at the Caffè
Grande.
Writing Life, The.
Yeats.   Meru.
Realists, The.
Zagajewski.   Lava.
Reaping and Reapers
Berry, W.   Mad Farmer Revolution, The.
Davie, D.   Midsummer's Eve.
Wilde, O.   Wasted Days.
Wordsworth, W.   Solitary Reaper, The.
Reason
Ammons.   Countering.
Discoverer.
Blake, W.   Mock On, Mock On, Voltaire,
Rousseau.
Bogan, L.   Sonnet: "Since you would claim the
sources of my thought."
Borges.   Causes, The.

Brontë, E. God of Visions.
Campion, T. *et al.* And would you faine the reason know.
Carew, T. Lover, upon an Accident Necessitating His Departure, Consults with Reason, A.
Love's Force.
Chaucer. Lak of Stedfastnesse.
Ciardi, J. Are We Through Talking, I Hope?
Credibility.
Logician's Nocturne, The.
Clough. When panting sighs the bosom fill.
Coleridge, S. Reason.
Cowper, W. Report of an Adjudged Case.
Creeley. Poem for Beginners.
Stone.
Cunningham, J. Fancy.
Davie, D. Bride of Reason, The.
Dickinson, E. I reason, Earth is short.
Dove, R. Geometry.
Dugan, A. On Being Unhappily in Love with Reason.
Working World's Bloody Flux, The.
Eberhart, R. Fables of the Moon.
Recapitulation, The.
Somewhere Else.
Emerson, R. And Ellen, when the greybeard years.
Brave Empedocles defying fools, The.
Hard is it to persuade the public mind of its plain duty & true interest.
Frost, R. Masque of Reason, A.
Graves, R. Ageless Reason.
Synthetic Such.
Within Reason.
Hardy, T. Philosophical Fantasy, A.
Jeffers, R. Contemplation of the Sword.
Komunyakaa. Brain to the Heart, The.
Lux. At Least Let Me Explain.
Mallarmé. Prose.
McGrath, T. Little Odyssey of Jason Quint, of Science, Doctor, The.
Melville, H. Reasonable Constitution, A.
Meredith, G. To the Comic Spirit.
Milosz, C. Incantation.
What I Learned from Jeanne Hersch.
Nash, O. Passionate Pagan and the Dispassionate Public, The.
Philemon. By Philemon.
Plath. Death of Myth-making, The.
Pope, A. Epistle I, to Sir Richard Temple, Lord Cobham.
On a Certain Lady at Court.
Rossetti, C. In the Willow Shade.
Rumi. Father Reason.
Smart, C. Reason and Imagination.
Suckling, S. Barley-Break , A.
Tate, A. Intellectual Detachment.
Whitman, W. When I Heard the Learn'd Astronomer.
Williams, C. K. Love: Wrath.
Vehicle: Violence.
Wordsworth, W. Alas! what boots the long laborious quest.
Zukofsky, L. Can a mote of sunlight defeat its purpose.
To My Valentines.
See also **Intellect and Intellectuals; Rationalism and Rationalists**

Rebellions and Rebels
Atwood. 1837 War in Retrospect.
Baudelaire. Rebel, The.
Berry, W. Manifesto: the Mad Farmer Liberation Front.
Browning, R. Italian in England, The.
Through the Metidja to Abd-el-Kadr.
Bukowski. This.
Burns, R. Birth-Day Ode. December 31st 1787, A.
Johnie Cope.
Strathallan's Lament.
Campion, T. Bravely deckt, come forth, bright day.
Carruth, H. Smallish Son, The.
Carver, R. Caucasus: A Romance, The.
Celan. For Eric.

Ciardi, J. Encounter.
Coleridge, S. Foster-Mother's Tale, The.
Cowper, W. Modern Patriot, The.
Crashaw. Upon the Powder Day.
Cummings, E. E. Boys i mean are not refined, The.
Crazy jay blue) / demon laughshriek.
If i / or anybody don't.
Timeless / ly this / (merely and whose).
Dunbar, P. Conquerors, The.
Eberhart, R. Throwing the Apple.
Emerson, R. Uriel.
Frost, R. Not Quite Social.
Ginsberg, A. Elegy Che Guevara.
Hardy, T. At Shag's Heath.
Heaney, S. Requiem for the Croppies.
Kipling, R. Ballad of Boh Da Thone, The.
Ballad of the Red Earl, The.
Ulster.
Kunitz, S. This Day This World.
Lawrence, D. H. Don'ts.
Lindsay, N. Factory Windows Are Always Broken.
Lorde. Relevant Is Different Points on the Circle.
McGrath, T. Restless Night, The.
Meredith, G. Monmouth.
Nash, O. Child Is Father to the Man, But with More Authority, The.
O'Hara, F. On Seeing Larry Rivers' *Washington Crossing the Delaware* at the Museum of Modern Art.
Olson, C. Put him this way.
Paley, G. Women's Prison, The: El Salvador / The Ballad of Visiting Day.
Pasolini. Poetry of the Tradition, The.
Plath. Bull of Bendylaw, The.
Pope, A. Epistle to Dr. Arbuthnot.
Rexroth, K. From the Paris Commune to the Kronstadt Rebellion.
Rich, A. North American Time.
Phenomenology of Anger, The.
Tear Gas.
Rimbaud, A. Just Man, The.
Seven-year-old Poets.
Rukeyser, M. For Kayle Boyle.
Stafford, W. Objector.
Thomas, D. Find Meat on Bones.
Walker, A. Be Nobody's Darling.
Rage.
Whitman, W. We Two Boys Together Clinging.
Whittier. Bolivar.
Dream of Pio Nono, The.
From Perugia.
Garibaldi.
Italy.
Kossuth.
Slaves of Martinique, The.
Song of the Vermonters, 1779, The.
Toussaint L'Ouverture.
Williams, W. In San Marco, Venezia.
Poem for Norman Macleod, A.
Wordsworth, W. At Bologna, in Remembrance of the Late Insurrections, 1837.
At Bologna, in Remembrance of the Late Insurrections, 1837, Continued: "As leaves are to the tree wheron they grow."
Eagle and the Dove, The.
Just Vengeance Claims Thy Soul for Rights Invaded?
Wright, J. Centenary Note: Inscribed to Little Crow, Leader of the Sioux Rebellion in Minnesota, 1862, A.
Yeats. Upon a House Shaken by the Land Agitation.
See also **Revolution and Revolutionaries**

Rebirth
Ai. Boys and Girls, Lenny Bruce, or Back from the Dead.
More.
Berry, W. Autumn Burning, An.
Envoy: "Love, all day there has been at the edge of my mind."
Song in a Year of Catastrophe.
Bly, R. Home in Dark Grass, A.
Brodsky, J. Elegy: "About a year has passed.

I've returned to the place of battle."
Cummings, E. E. I Thank You God.
Now does our world descend.
When God Lets My Body Be.
Who before dying demands not rebirth.
Dickey, J. For a Time and Place.
Eberhart, R. Return of Odysseus, The.
Ferlinghetti, L. Wild Dreams of a New Beginning.
Frost, R. Onset, The.
Glück, L. Cottonmouth Country.
Graves, R. Ages of Oath, The.
Song: The Palm Tree.
Survivor, The.
"H. D." In the Rain.
Han-shan. Among the sages of the past.
For an image of life and death
If you were too dumb the life before.
One bottle is cast in gold.
Suffering of the Wheel is relentless, The.
There is no limit to changes.
Three-spoked Wheel is relentless, The.
When will the treadmill of life and death stop.
Hardy, T. For Life I Had Never Cared Greatly.
Hughes, L. In Time of Silver Rain.
Kinnell. Saint Francis and the Sow.
Kunitz, S. Poem: "O Heart: this is a dream I had, or not a dream."
Vita Nuova.
Way Down, The.
Levine, P. Belief.
Let Me Begin Again.
Told.
Waking an Angel.
MacNeice. April Manifesto, An.
McGrath, T. Drowned Man: Death Between Two Rivers, The.
Passages.
Merton. On the Anniversary of My Baptism.
Michelangelo Buonarroti. If it could be, to revive my life once more.
If the soul, in truth, from body once set free.
Millay, E. Renascence.
Oliver, M. Alligator Poem.
Meeting, A.
Orléans, C. Rondeau: "Year has cast its cloak away, The."
Piercy. Butt of Winter, The.
Inside Chance, The.
Raine, K. Journey, The.
Rossetti, C. Shut Out.
Sandburg, C. Falltime.
October Paint.
Uplands in May.
Thomas, D. I Dreamed My Genesis.
I Have Longed to Move Away.
Saint About to Fall, A.
Whittier. April.
First Flowers, The.
Wilbur, R. Alatus.
April 5, 1974.
Black Birch in Winter, A.
Children of Darkness.
Flumen Tenebrarum.
Lilacs, The.
Orchard Trees, January.
Shad-Time.
Then.
To Ishtar.
Wilde, O. Vita Nuova.
Williams, W. Spring and All.
Wordsworth, W. Peter Bell; a Tale.
Wright, J. Come Forth.
Mary Bly.
Moon.
On the Skeleton of a Hound.
See also **Regeneration; Renewal**

Rebuilding
Ammons. Eternal City, The.
Laughlin, J. In Darmstadt.
O Frères Humains.
People Boxes, The.
Szymborska, W. End and the Beginning, The.

Recognition
Amichai [*or* Amikhai]. Season of Recognition.
Berry, W. Recognition, The.

Browning, R. Popularity.
Bukowski. On Being Recognized.
  Some of My Readers.
Cooper, J. Conversation by the Body's Light.
Creeley. Smell of gum wrappers as of Saturday
  afternoon at movies.
Dickinson, E. Like Eyes that looked on Wastes.
  You'll know Her—by Her Foot.
Ferlinghetti, L. One of These Days.
Hardy, T. He Did Not Know Me.
  Poet's Thoughts, A.
Herrick. To his Faithfull Friend, Master John
  Crofts, Cup-bearer to the King.
Housman. Look not in my eyes, for fear.
Laughlin, J. Limper, The.
Lindsay, N. Prayer to All the Dead Among
  Mine Own People, A.
MacLeish. Speech to the Detractors.
MacNeice. Elegy for Minor Poets.
Meredith, W. Walter Jenks' Bath.
Merwin. Recognition.
Patchen. I always return to this place.
Piercy. If They Come in the Night.
Ransom, J. Jack's Letter.
Ritsos. Recognition.
Rumi. Slave, be aware that the Lord.
Tomlinson, C. Insistence of Things, The.
Voznesensky [or Voznesenskii]. Foggy Street.
Whitman, W. Death and Burial of McDonald
  Clarke, a Parody, The.
  Last Droplets.
  Long, Long Hence.
Williams, C. K. Philadelphia: 1978.

Reconciliation
Bly, R. Conversation with a Holy Woman Not
  Seen for Many Years.
Carruth, H. Gods.
Cowper, W. Alexander Selkirk.
Creeley. Operation, The.
De la Mare. Reconciliation.
Faiz. Bangla Desh: 2.
  Bangla Desh: 3.
Frost, R. Dream Pang, A.
Graves, R. Song: Reconciliation.
Hardy, T. At the Word "Farewell."
Herrick. To the Rose; a Song.
Kinsella, T. At the Head Table.
Logan, J. Poem for My Brother.
Melville, H. America.
Meredith, G. War.
Nash, O. Nothing but Nature.
Oliver, M. Visitor, A.
Petrarch. How oft have I, my dear [or dere] and
  cruel[l] foe.
Piercy. Night Letter.
Ransom, J. Armageddon.
  Parting at Dawn.
Riley, J. George Mullen's Confession.
Robinson, E. Partnership.
  Story of the Ashes and the Flame, The.
Schuyler, J. Was It.
Shelley, P. Cancelled Stanza.
Whitman, W. While Not the Past Forgetting.
Wyatt, S. Alas, dear heart! what hap [or hope]
  had I.
Yeats. Reconciliation.

Reconstruction, United States
Dunbar, P. To the South.
Piercy. Community.
Very. Ends for Which a Nation Exists, The.
  National Unity ("Unity complete, assured, and
  high, A").
  Nation's Life of Slow Growth, A.
  Political Ambition.
Whittier. Howard at Atlanta.
  To the Thirty-Ninth Congress.

Record Players
Creeley. Love ("Tracking through this").
Cummings, E. E. Phonograph may(if it likes)be
  prophe, The.
Meredith, W. Music.
Merwin. Still Afternoon Light.

Recordings
Seifert. Song of the Nightingale, The.

Red (color)
Atwood. Red Shirt, A.
Clampitt. Thinking Red.
Dugan, A. One Waking in a Northern Fall.
Eberhart, R. Vermont Idyll.
Hughes, L. When Sue Wears Red.
Parker, D. Red Dress, The.
Raine, K. Quenching the Red.
Rilke. Child in Red.
Ritsos. Marine.
Rukeyser, M. Salamander.

Red Cross
Hughes, L. Red Cross.

Red Jacket (Seneca Chief)
Whitman, W. Red Jacket (from Aloft).

Red Riding Hood
Riley, J. Red Riding-Hood.

Red Sea
Pinkerton, H. On Erastus Salisbury Field's *The
  Israelites Crossing the Red Sea* (1863?).

Redemption
Amichai [or Amikhai]. Aching bones of lovers,
  The.
  How goodly are your tents, Jacob. Even when
  there are no.
Baudelaire. Irreparable, The.
  Ransom, The.
  Restless and Sad.
  Spiritual Dawn.
Brontë, E. Lines: "Soft unclouded blue of air,
  The."
Campion, T. Author of light, revive my dying
  spright.
  Come Let Us Sound With Melodie.
  Seek the Lord.
  View Mee, Lord.
Celan. Vinegrowers dig up.
Cowper, W. Longing To Be with Christ.
  Song of Mercy and Judgment, A.
"Dario." Spes.
Davie, D. Livingshayes.
De la Mare. I Sit Alone.
Dickinson, E. Danger is not at first.
  Summer day on which you came, The.
  To congratulate the Redeemed is perhaps
  superfluous.
  Work is a bleak redeemer.
Donne. Good Friday [or Goodfriday], 1613.
  Riding Westward.
Eberhart, R. Redemption.
Graves, R. Gold and Malachite.
  Point of No Return.
Han-shan. I have six brothers.
Herbert, G. Faith.
  Holy Baptism (1).
  Jews, The.
  Love (2).
  Nature.
  Parody [or Parodie], A.
  Pulley, The.
  Redemption.
  Repentance.
  Sion.
  Vanity (2).
  World, The.
Herrick. Christs Incarnation.
  To Julia, the Flaminica Dialis, or Queen-Priest.
Hopkins, G. God's Grandeur.
  To him who ever thought with love of me.
Jacobsen, J. Dishwasher as Absolution.
Jeffers, R. Redeemer, A.
Lindsay, N. Look You, I'll Go Pray.
MacLeish. Infinite Reason, The.
MacNeice. Return, The.
Mahon. Globe in [North] Carolina, The.
Merton. Biography, The.
  Cana.
  Holy Communion: the City.
  I Have Called You.
  Rahab's House.
Moore, M. To a Giraffe.
Nemerov. Carol: "Now is the world withdrawn
  all."
Oppen. Any Way But Back.
Paul the Deacon. Ut Queant.

Ralegh, S. Passionate Man[']s Pilgrimage, The.
Ramanujan. Fear No Fall.
Robinson, E. Dark House, The.
Rossetti, C. God Is Our Hope and Strength.
  Heart Knoweth Its Own Bitterness, The.
  Rejoice with Me.
Smart, C. Hymn to the Supreme Being.
Thomas, D. There Was a Saviour.
Thoreau. Sic Vita.
Very. I Was Sick and in Prison.
Whalen, P. Confession and Penance.
Wilbur, R. Proof, The.
Wilde, O. E Tenebris.

Redwood Trees
Ammons. Kind.
Kizer, C. First of June Again, The.
See also **Sequoia Trees**

Reeds
Ammons. When I Set Fire to the Reed Patch.
Browning, E. Reed, A.
Clampitt. Reedbeds of the Hackensack, The.
Herrick. Poet Hath Lost His Pipe, The.
Rumi. Constant Conversation.
  Reed Flute's Song, The.
Tomlinson, C. Reeds.
Unknown. On the Reed.

Refinement
Cavafy. Apollonios of Tyana in Rhodes.
Laughlin, J. Take Off Your Socks!!
Riley, J. Youthful Press, The.
Sarton, M. Lady with a Falcon.
Stockton, A. Impromptu on Seeing a Very
  Agreeable Gentleman and Lady, Particular
  Friends Conversing Together.
  Some Traits of the Character of Mrs. Powel as a
  Model for a Young Lady Who Said She
  Admired Her More than Any Other Woman.
  Wise nature here has done her kindest part.

Reflections
Ai. Talking to His Reflection in a Shallow
  Pond.
Atwood. Tricks With Mirrors.
Berry, W. Porch over the River, The.
Bishop, E. Gentleman of Shalott, The.
  To Be Written on the Mirror in Whitewash.
Borges. Beppo.
  I Am.
  Watcher, The.
Bukowski. 10 Lions and the End of the World.
  Anthony.
  Face While Shaving.
  Layover.
  One Night Stand.
  Sleep.
Burns, R. Of A' the Airts [the Wind Can Blow].
Carew, T. To T. H., a Lady Resembling My
  Mistress.
Carruth, H. Point, The.
Creeley. Awakening, The.
  Eye, The.
  For Joel.
  It Is at Times.
  Kind of Act Of, The.
Cuadra, P. Faces of Girls Looking at
  Themselves in the River.
Cunningham, J. Reason and Nature.
De la Mare. Looking Glass, The.
  Reflections.
Dickey, W. His Death from Cancer.
Emerson, R. Sea reflects the rosy sky, The.
Ferlinghetti, L. 21.
Frost, R. For Once, Then, Something.
Gallagher, T. My Mother Remembers That She
  Was Beautiful.
Graves, R. Foreboding, The.
  Spite of Mirrors.
Ignatow, D. Image, The.
Jacobsen, J. Animal Inside the Animal, The.
Jarrell, R. Game at Salzburg, A.
Komunyakaa. Facing It.
  Reflections.
Laughlin, J. Endless Mirrors, The.
  Il Pastor Fido.
Levertov. Eyes and No-Eyes.
  On the Way.

Logan, J. Wooden Mirror, The.
Lorde. Birthday Memorial to Seventh Street, A.
MacNeice. Corner Seat.
Perdita.
To Hedli.
Maritain. Lake, The.
Martial. Some good, some middling, and some bad.
McGrath, T. Proverbs of the Middle World.
World of the Perfect Tear, The.
McHugh, H. Ozone.
Merrill, J. In the Hall of Mirrors.
Merwin. Sadness, The.
Tidal Lagoon.
Michelangelo Buonarroti. Your lovely eyes, now bent.
Montale. Metropolitan Christmas, A.
Pool.
Nemerov. Mirror, The.
Palmer, M. False Portrait.
This Time.
Prunty. Black Water.
Raine, K. Golden Leaf, The.
Message.
Peace of Mind.
Rexroth, K. Doubled Mirrors.
Fish Peddler and Cobbler.
Homestead Called Damascus, The.
Signature of All Things, The.
Rilke. Double in the Mirror, The.
Fire's Reflection.
Telling You All.
Woman at Her Mirror.
Rukeyser, M. Asylum Song.
Sandburg, C. Chicago Poet.
Hungry and Laughing Men.
Old Music for Quiet Hearts.
Pool of Bethesda.
Sarton, M. Charleston Plantations.
Myself to Me.
Nostalgia for India.
Schuyler, J. Sparks.
Stock, R. Wind in the Mirror.
Stockton, A. To a Little Miss, with a Toy Lookingglass.
Swenson, M. Water Picture.
Sze. Sound Lag.
Tomlinson, C. Below Tintern.
Canal.
Given Grace, A.
Reflections.
Well, The.
Windshield, The.
Warren, R. Blessèd Accident.
Mirror, The.
Whalen, P. Homage to Hart Crane.
Wilbur, R. Aspen and the Stream, The.

Refrigerators
Codrescu. Sin of Wanting a New Refrigerator, The.
Us.
Lux. Refrigerator, 1957.

Refugees
Amichai [or Amikhai]. Czech Refugee in London, A.
Smell of Gasoline in My Nose, The.
Browning, R. Italian in England, The.
Clampitt. Sed de Correr.
Cummings, E. E. Belgium.
Dickinson, E. These Strangers, In a Foreign World.
Duncan, R. Bring It Up from the Dark.
Enzensberger, H. Thoughts on the Run 1.
Thoughts on the Run 2.
Thoughts on the Run 4.
Ginsberg, A. September on Jessore Road.
Hacker, M. Days of 1944: Three Friends.
Hardy, T. Appeal to America on Behalf of the Belgian Destitute, An.
Cry of the Homeless.
On the Belgian Expatriation.
Hughes, L. Song of the Refugee Road.
Jarrell, R. Refugees, The.
To the New World.
Komunyakaa. Boat People.
Longfellow, H. Evangeline, a Tale of Acadie.

MacNeice. Refugees.
Merton. Picture of Lee Ying, A.
Milosz, C. Fear-Dream (1918).
Rukeyser, M. Another Day (Day Lilies, Yellow Daisies).
Another Day (You can't come).
Fourth Elegy. The Refugees.
Story, A.
Zagajewski. Refugees.

Regeneration
Berry, W. Slip, The.
Sycamore, The.
Bukowski. Numb Your Ass and Your Brain and Your Heart—.
García Lorca. Spring Song.
Hall, D. Day I Was Older, The.
Herrick. Sonnet of Perilla, A.
To Anthea.
Upon Trigg.
Hopkins, G. God's Grandeur.
Ignatow, D. Invocation: "Dirt and stone, if I may know you as you know yourselves."
Montale. Eel, The.
Niedecker. When do we live again Ann.
Oliver, M. Rabbit, The.
Three Poems for James Wright.
Orr, G. Celestial Desolations.
Paley, G. In Deepest Summer.
Pound, E. Return, The.
Shapiro, K. Leg, The.
Stock, R. Poem on Holy Saturday.
Wilner, E. Natural History.
Wright, C. Mount Caribou at Night.
Wright, J. Beginning Again.
See also **Rebirth; Renewal**

Regret
Angelou. Refusal.
Berrigan, T. Paul Blackburn.
Brontë, E. Why ask to know what date, what clime?
Bukowski. Oh, Yes.
Burns, R. Remorse.
To a Mouse; On Turning Her up in Her Nest, with the Plough, November, 1785.
Byron, G. Herod's Lament for Mariamne.
Lament of Tasso, The.
To the Sighing Strephon.
Carruth, H. In Tobey Woods.
Carver, R. Wine.
Cavafy. Old Man, An.
Understanding.
Clifton, L. One Year Later.
Clough. Oh, I have done those things that my Soul fears.
Coleridge, S. Elegy Imitated from One of Akenside's Blank-Verse Inscriptions.
Mad Monk, The.
Corbett, W. Dear Joe.
Crane, H. Meditation.
Pastorale.
Creeley. Eye, The.
Oh Mabel.
Prejudice, The.
Teachings, The.
"You've Tried the World, Try Jesus."
Cullen, C. Song of Sour Grapes, A.
Cummings, E. E. As Joe Gould says in.
It really must / be Nice,never to.
Cunningham, J. Moral Poem, A.
"Dario." First, a look.
Dickinson, E. No matter—now—Sweet.
Within my reach!
Dunbar, P. Debt, The.
Life's Tragedy.
Old Memory, An.
Eliot, T. S. Love Song of J. Alfred Prufrock, Resumed, The.
Love Song of J. Alfred Prufrock, The.
Love Song of J. Alfred Prufrock, The (Prufrock among the Women).
Prufrock's Pervigilium.
Enzensberger, H. Short History of the Bourgeoisie.
Fenton, J. Skip, The.
Gallagher, T. Love Poem to Be Read to an Illiterate Friend.

Same Kiss After Many Years, The.
Tableau Vivant.
García Lorca. New Heart.
Weathervane.
Ginsberg, A. Sickness Blues.
Gunn, T. Incident on a Journey.
Gurney, I. Regrets After Death.
Hacker, M. 1976.
Hall, D. Tubes.
Hardy, T. Beauty's Soliloquy during Her Honeymoon, A.
Dead Bastard, The.
Fetching Her.
Lady of Forebodings, The.
Month's Calendar, The.
Question of Marriage, A.
Song to Aurore.
Watcher's Regret, A.
Hayden, R. Ballad of Sue Ellen Westerfield, The.
Hopkins, G. But what indeed is ask'd of me?
Housman. How clear, how lovely bright.
Westward on the high-hilled plains.
When the bells justle in the tower.
Hughes, L. Mean Old Yesterday.
Po' Boy Blues.
Reverie on the Harlem River.
Hughes, T. Crow Tyrannosaurus.
Ignatow, D. Signal, The.
Kipling, R. Follow Me 'Ome.
Penalty, The.
Koch, K. To Marina.
Kunitz, S. Illumination, The.
Reckoning, The.
Lawrence, D. H. Ah, Muriel!
End, The.
Everlasting Flowers.
Last Words to Muriel.
Married in June.
Mutilation.
Pear-Blossom.
Sick.
Sigh No More.
Levertov. Daughter (2), A.
Levi, P. Unfinished Business.
Levine, P. Uncle.
MacNeice. Slow Starter, The.
Mahon. After the Titanic.
Day Trip to Donegal.
Meredith, G. Main Regret, The.
Merrill, J. Renewal, A.
Merton. Regret, The.
Merwin. Home for Thanksgiving.
Indigestion of the Vampire, The.
Purgatory, A.
Michelangelo Buonarroti. Had I, when young, been leery of the glow.
Life's final hours: brought there by many a year.
Though shouldered from the road I chose.
Millay, E. At least, my dear.
Nash, O. Raven, Don't Stay Away from My Door—A Chant for April First.
Olson, C. All things stand out against the sky.
February 10, One Year Too Late.
Orr, G. Talk, The.
Owen, W. A Terre.
Strange Meeting.
Parker, D. For a Sad Lady.
Petrarch. I was so blest by sheer good luck and Love.
What fear is mine when I recall that day.
Piercy. Never-Never.
Visiting a Dead Man on a Summer Day.
Pinsky. Old Man, An.
Poe. Bridal Ballad.
Pound, E. Villanelle: The Psychological Hour.
Raine, K. Columbines.
Ramanujan. I Could Have Rested.
Ransom, J. Hilda.
Parting, without a Sequel.
Riley, J. Me and Mary.
Perversity.
Rilke. Dead, The.
Robinson, E. Miniver Cheevy.
Rossetti, C. Soeur Louise De La Miséricorde.
Rossetti, D. Even So.

Sandburg, C.   Choices.
  Wistful.
Schuyler, J.   Salute.
Seifert.   Garland on the Wrist, A.
Sexton.   Anna Who Was Mad.
  Lament: "Someone is dead."
Shelley, P.   Time Long Past.
Sheridan, T.   Palinodia.
Smith, S.   La Gretchen de Nos Jours (I).
  Piggy to Joey.
  Warden, The.
Stafford, W.   Afterwards.
  It's heavy to drag, this big sack of what.
Swift, J.   Apology to the Lady Carteret, An.
Tate, J.   Coda: "Love is not worth so much."
Thoreau.   Sympathy.
Tibullus.   Sulpicia to Cerinthus.
Unknown.   Another ["At three-score winters'
  end I died"].
Updike.   Academy.
  Report of Health.
Walcott.   Parang.
Warren, R.   Aged Man Surveys the Past.
  Doubleness in Time.
  Reading Late at Night, Thermometer Falling.
  What is the Voice that Speaks?
Whittier.   Maud Muller.
Wilbur, R.   Sirens, The.
Wilde, O.   Roses and Rue.
Williams, C. K.   Time: 1976.
Williams, M.   Tenth Anniversary Photograph,
  1952, A.
Williams, T.   Can I forget.
Wilner, E.   Without Regret.
Wordsworth, W.   Repentance; A Pastoral Ballad.
Wyatt, S.   Had I wist that now I wot.
Yeats.   Down by the Salley Gardens.
  Imitated from the Japanese.
  Men Improve with the Years.
  People, The.
Zaturenska.   Dark Year, The.

Reich, Wilhelm
Paley, G.   Desert Wasn't Loved Enough said
  Reich, The.

Reincarnation
Atwood.   Metempsychosis.
Clifton, L.   Lives.
Collins, B.   Pavilion.
"Dario."   Metempsychosis.
  Reincarnations.
Donne.   Progress of the Soul, The.
Glück, L.   Easter Season.
Graves, R.   Serpent's Tail.
Hardy, T.   Transformations.
Jackson, L.   Incarnations.
Jeffers, R.   Resurrection.
Kumin, M.   Reviewing the Summer and Winter
  Calender of the Next Life.
Levine, P.   Fox, The.
  Let Me Be.
Mahon.   Lives.
Merwin.   Cow, The.
Neruda.   Today Isn't Everything.
Pinsky.   At Pleasure Bay.
Ramanujan.   HINDOO, THE: He Doesn't Hurt a
  Fly or a Spider Either.
  HINDOO, THE: He Reads His GITA and Is
  Calm at All Events.
  Second Sight.
Rexroth, K.   Metempsychosis.
Rumi.   Unmarked Boxes.
Snyder, G.   For/From Lew.
Stockton, A.   Thoughts on the Pythagorian
  System.

Reindeer
Jacobsen, J.   Reindeer and Engine.
Moore, M.   Rigorists.
Warren, R.   Caribou.

Rejection
Angelou.   Refusal.
Baudelaire.   One night I had some ghastly
  jewish whore.
Beckett, S.   Cascando.
Browning, E.   Amy's Cruelty.
  Denial, A.
  False Step, A.

Bukowski.   Beds, Toilets, You and Me—.
Change of Habit, A.
Chicago.
Defeat.
Eat Your Heart Out.
For Al—.
I Made a Mistake.
Love Is a Dog from Hell.
Numb Your Ass and Your Brain and Your
  Heart—.
One to the Breastplate.
Retreat, The.
Turnabout.
Waving and Waving Goodbye.
Burns, R.   Auld Rob Morris.
Craigieburn-Wood—A Song.
Eppie McNab.
Fair Eliza.
Gloomy December.
Here's to Thy Health My Bonie Lass.
Jeremiah 15th Ch. 10 V.
Let Me in This Ae Night.
Lord Gregory.
Open the Door to Me, Oh!
Song: "Again rejoicing Nature sees."
To Captain G———, on Being Asked Why I
  Was Not to Be of the Party with Him and His
  Brother K-nm-re at Syme's.
Campion, T.   Dolus.
Faire If You Expect Admiring.
Fire that must flame is with apt fuell fed.
Good men, shew, if you can tell.
If any hath the heart to kill.
Leave prolonging thy distresse.
Now let her change and spare not.
Shall I Come, Sweet Love.
Shall I then hope when faith is fled?
So Quicke, So Hot, So Mad is Thy Fond Sute.
Where shall I refuge seeke, if you refuse mee?
Campion, T. *et al.*   Aye me, that love should
  natures workes accuse!
If I urge my kinde desires.
If she forsake me, I must die.
Carew, T.   My Mistress Commanding Me to
  Return Her Letters.
Spring, The.
To My Inconstant Mistress [*or* Mistris].
Chaucer.   Complaint unto His Lady, A.
Complaynt d'Amours.
To Rosamounde.
Codrescu.   Brief (Remembered) *Histoire* of
  Rejection, A.
Coleridge, S.   Ad Vilmum Axiologum.
Alla Sua Amica.
Elegy Imitated from One of Akenside's Blank-
  Verse Inscriptions.
Love and Friendship Opposite.
Lover's Complaint to His Mistress, A.
Cooper, J.   Long View from the Suburbs.
Cowper, W.   Symptoms of Love, The.
Creeley.   In an Act of Pity.
Invoice, The.
Cummings, E. E.   I spoke to thee.
Nobody loved this.
Dante Alighieri.   Sonnet: To the Lady Pietra
  degli Scrovigni.
Dickey, W.   Here There Are Three of Us
  Driving South in This Expensive Car.
Læestrygonians, The.
Stella Dreams.
Dickinson, E.   Could I—then—shut the door.
Poor little Heart!
Donne.   Damp[e], The.
Love's Deity [*or* Deitie].
Dove, R.   Aircraft.
Dunbar, P.   Jilted.
Euripides.   Chorus of Troizenian Women.
Chorus sing of escape, The.
Daemon initiate, spirit.
Lift my head, help me up.
Men you strike.
No more, O my spirit.
O Spirit, / spark by spark.
Ginsberg, A.   Lack Love.
Glück, L.   12. 6. 71.
Fire, The.

Game, The.
Hesitate to Call.
My Life Before Dawn.
Graves, R.   As All Must End.
Confess, Marpessa.
Discarded Love Poem, The.
Love as Lovelessness.
Song: How Can I Care?
Song: Though Once True Lovers.
Wall, The.
Gray, T.   Amatory Lines.
Gunn, T.   Carnal Knowledge.
Monster, The.
Hardy, T.   Daughter Returns, A.
Love-Letters, The.
One Who Married above Him.
She Did Not Turn.
They Would Not Come.
Torn Letter, The.
Two Serenades.
Herbert, G.   Denial[l].
Herrick.   Cruell Maid, The.
His Covenant or Protestation to Julia.
To Myrrha Hard-Hearted.
To Pansies.
Housman.   He would not stay for me; and who
  can wonder?
Hughes, L.   Black Pierrot, A.
Late Last Night.
Jonson, B.   Song. To Celia ("Drink to me only
  with thine eyes").
Keats.   Stanzas: "You say you love; but with a
  voice."
Kizer, C.   Bitch.
Kunitz, S.   How Long Is the Night?
Larkin, P.   Since the Majority of Me.
Laughlin, J.   Apotropaic Decision, An.
Folk Wisdom.
Visitor, The.
Lawrence, D. H.   Lilies in the Fire.
Reminder.
Repulsed.
Turned Down.
Levertov.   Crosspurposes.
Passing Bell, The.
Lorde.   Dozens, The.
MacDiarmid, H.   First Love.
Meredith, G.   My Lady has Diana's brows.
Roar through the Tall Twin Elm-Trees, A.
Schubert's "Farewell."
Michelangelo Buonarroti.   Now that I'm banned
  and routed from the fire.
Millay, E.   Love me no more, now let the god
  depart.
Milosz, C.   Farewell: "I speak to you, my son."
Muldoon, P.   Grass Widow.
O'Hara, F.   Mayakovsky.
Meditations in an Emergency.
Paley, G.   I Gave Away That Kid.
Parker, D.   After a Spanish Proverb.
Folk Song.
Landscape.
Pattern.
Song: "When summer used to linger."
Trifler, The.
Triolets: "Herewith I send you my heart."
Two-Volume Novel.
Plath.   Jilted.
To a Jilted Lover.
Ralegh, S.   Fayne Would I But I Dare Not.
Nymph's [*or* Nimphs] Reply to the Shepherd
  [*or* Sheepheard], The.
Poem Put into My Lady Laiton's Pocket, A.
Shall I, Like an Hermit, Dwell.
Ransom, J.   Romance of a Youngest Daughter.
Riley, J.   To a Jilted Swain.
Rimbaud, A.   Sisters of Charity.
Robinson, E.   Job the Rejected.
Rossetti, C.   Amore E Dispetto.
Corydon's Lament and Resolution.
Despised and Rejected.
Jessie Cameron.
No, Thank You, John.
Schuyler, J.   Sleep.
Shelley, P.   To———: "One word is too often
  profaned."

Smith, S.　Lady "Rogue" Singleton.
　Pad, Pad.
　Sorrowful Girl, The.
Suckling, S.　Proffered Love Rejected.
Swinburne.　Leave-taking, A.
Tate, J.　Deaf Girl Playing.
Tennyson, A.　Locksley Hall.
Thomas, D.　Not from This Anger.
Unknown.　Art Thou That She.
Whitman, W.　Sometimes with One I Love.
Whittier.　Isabel.
Williams, W.　Birds and Flowers.
Wordsworth, W.　Ellen Irwin; or, The Braes of Kirtle.
Wyatt, S.　All in thy sight my life doth whole depend.
　Disdain me not without desert.
　Like as the swan towards her death.
　Lively sparks that issue from those eyes, The.
　My heart I gave thee not to do it pain.
　Pass forth, my wonted cries.
　That time that mirth did steer my ship.
　When first mine eyes did view and mark.

Relatives
Berryman.　Poem for Bhain, A.
Bukowski.　What to Do with Contributor's Copies?
Eberhart, R.　To Harriet Monroe.
Herrick.　To His Kinsman, Master Thomas Herrick, Who Desired to Be in His Book.
　To His Sister in Law, M. Susanna Herrick.
Kumin, M.　Caring: A Dream.
　For My Great-Grandfather: A Message Long Overdue.
Lorde.　And What About the Children.
Nash, O.　I Must Tell You about My Novel.
Parker, D.　Relatives; A Hate Song.
Robinson, E.　Poor Relation, The.
Sandburg, C.　Destroyers.

Relativity
Amichai [*or* Amikhai].　Relativity.
Ammons.　Center.
　Extremes and Moderations.
　Spiel.
Auden.　Law like Love.
Carew, T.　To the Reader of Master William Davenant's Play [*The Wits*].
Ciardi, J.　Clock in the Mirror, The.
Collins, B.　Bar Time.
Cullen, C.　Sonnet: "Some for a little while do love, and some for long."
Cummings, E. E.　Space being(don't forget to remember)Curved.
Dunbar, P.　Comparison.
Hardy, T.　King's Experiment, The.
Kunitz, S.　Change.
Lawrence, D. H.　Relativity.
MacNeice.　Perspectives.
　What is truth? says Pilate.
McHugh, H.　For a Good Man.
　Inside.
Merwin.　At the Same Time.
　Lantern, The.
　Room, The.
　Signs.
　When the Horizon Is Gone.
Michelangelo Buonarroti.　If two hours' dying steals a hundred years.
Montale.　At first light, when.
Olson, C.　Discrete Gloss, A.
Pessoa.　And there are poets who are artists.
　At night I suddenly waken.
　Audible smile of the leaves.
　Four songs that follow now, The.
　From the highest window of my house.
　I go indoors, and shut the window.
　I never kept sheep.
　I'd give anything if only my life were an oxcart.
　If at times I say that flowers smile.
　If I could take a bite of the whole earth.
　If they want me to be a mystic, fine. I'm a mystic.
　I'm a keeper of sheep.
　Live, you say, in the present.
　Moonlight behind the tall branches, The.
　My glance is clear like a sunflower.

　On a terribly clear day.
　Once at mid-day in late spring.
　One way or another.
　Only Nature is divine, and she's not divine.
　Rather the flight of the bird passing and leaving no trace.
　Rhymes mean nothing to me. Only rarely.
　To think of God is to disobey God.
　Today I read nearly two pages.
Rexroth, K.　Death, Judgment, Heaven, Hell.
Szymborska, W.　Dream of the Old Tortoise, The.
　Interview with a Child.
　Surplus.
　View with a Grain of Sand.

Relief
Cowper, W.　R.S.S. Written in a Fit of Illness.
Creeley.　For Anybody.
　Jack's Blues.
Dickinson, E.　Summer day on which you came, The.
Emerson, R.　Sunshine was he.
Herrick.　Griefes.
　Sauce for Sorrowes.
Kunitz, S.　Long Boat, The.
Lindsay, N.　Johnny Appleseed Speaks of the Appleblossom Amaranth That Will Come to This City.
　What the Miner in the Desert Said.
Michelangelo Buonarroti.　If, to rejoice, you crave our tears and woe.
Nash, O.　Middle of the Month, The.
Petrarch.　That cheek of yours that has been tired with weeping.
Rich, A.　Break, The.
Riley, J.　Someday.
Rossetti, C.　Lord, comest Thou to me?
Smith, S.　Bottle of Aspirins, The.
Wordsworth, W.　On the Death of His Majesty (George the Third).

Religion
Amichai [*or* Amikhai].　Course of a Life, The.
　Dangerous Country.
　Great Calm: Questions and Answers.
　Great Tranquillity; Questions and Answers, A.
Beckett, S.　Home Olga.
　Whoroscope.
Berry, W.　Desolation.
　Meditation in the Spring Rain.
　Song (1).
Berryman.　Handshake, the Entrance, The.
Bishop, E.　Hymn to the Virgin.
Blake, W.　All Religions Are One.
　Lacedemonian Instruction.
　Mock On, Mock On, Voltaire, Rousseau.
　There Is No Natural Religion.
Boethius.　Book III. Metre 6.
　Consolation of Philosophy, The ("De Consolacione Philosophie").
　Give me, O Father! to thy throne access.
　Happy he whose eyes have view'd.
　Man who pants for ample Sway, The.
　O thou, whose all-creating hands sustain.
　O thou whose pow'r o'er moving worlds presides.
　Prudent Hind intent on Gain, The.
　Though countless as the Grains of Sand.
　Through Gripus Grounds let rich Pactolus roll.
　Truth in platonic ornaments bedeck'd.
　Unless the soul, to vice a thrall.
　Vainly the Tyrian Purple bright.
　Wouldst thou to some stedfast Seat.
Borges.　Shinto.
Broumas, O.　Eros.
Browning, E.　Sabbath Morning at Sea, A.
Browning, R.　Confessional, The.
　Easter-Day.
　Holy-Cross Day.
Buchanan, G.　Pope from penance purgatorial, The.
Burns, R.　Ballad, A: "While Prose-work and rhymes."
　Epistle to a Young Friend.
　Epistle to John Goldie in Kilmarnock, Author of, the Gospel Recovered.
　Holy Fair, The.

　Holy Tulzie, The.
　Kirk's Alarm, The.
　Letter to J———s T———t, Gl—nc———r.
　Ordination, The.
　Postscript [To W. S*****n, Ochiltree].
　To the Rev. John McMath, Inclosing a Copy of *Holy Willie's Prayer*, Which He Had Requested.
Byron, G.　Spirit Pass'd Before Me, A.
　Were My Bosom As False As Thou Deem'st It to Be.
Campion, T.　To the Right, Noble, and Vertuous, Henry Lord Clifford, Sonne and Heyre to the Right Honourable, Francis, Earle of Cumberland.
Cavafy.　Julian and the Antiochians.
　Julian, Seeing Contempt.
Chaucer.　Canterbury Tales, The.
　January and May, or the Merchant's Tale.
　Manciple's Tale—A Modernization, The.
　Prioress' Tale—A Modernization, The.
　Wife of Bath, The.
Ciardi, J.　Echoes.
　Palaver's No Prayer.
Codrescu.　Indecent Assumption, the Slaughter Songs, The.
　Sunday Sermon.
　Talismanic Ceremony for Lucian, March 9, 1971, Intersection Church, San Francisco.
Coleridge, S.　Catullian Hendecasyllables.
Cooper, J.　After the Bomb Tests.
Cowper, W.　Table Talk.
Crane, S.　I have heard the sunset song of the birches.
　When a people reach the top of a hill.
Crashaw.　On the Frontispiece of Isaacsons Chronologie Explained.
　Upon the Ensuing Treatises [of Mr. Shelford].
Creeley.　After Lorca.
Cummings, E. E.　Candles and / Here Comes a glass box.
　Like most godhouses this particular house.
　This evangelist / buttons with his big gollywog voice.
Cunningham, J.　True Religion, The.
"Dario."　Om.
Davie, D.　North Sea, The.
Dickey, J.　Circuit.
　Eagle's Mile, The.
　Tapestry and Sail.
Dickey, W.　Fred and the Holy Grail.
　Love among the Manichees.
　You White Cunning Devils.
Dickinson, E.　I'm ceded—I've stopped being Theirs.
　Some keep the Sabbath going to Church.
　There's a certain Slant of light.
　'Tis little I— could care for Pearls.
Donne.　Canonization, The.
　To the Countess of Bedford ("Honour is so sublime perfection").
Dove, R.　Receiving the Stigmata.
Dugan, A.　Religious Question.
Dunbar, P.　Faith.
　How Lucy Backslid.
　Possession.
　Spiritual, A.
　Temptation.
Eliot, T. S.　Choruses from "The Rock."
　Hippopotamus, The.
　Mr. Eliot's Sunday Morning Service.
　Song for Simeon, A.
Emerson, R.　Dervish whined to *Said*, The.
　Problem, The.
Frost, R.　Innate Helium.
Gallagher, T.　If Blood Were Not as Powerful as It Is.
　Linoleum.
Ginsberg, A.　Jaweh and Allah Battle.
Glück, L.　Winter Morning.
Graves, R.　Awakening, The.
　Good Night to the Old Gods.
Gunn, T.　Vigil of Corpus Christi, The.
"H. D."　Priest.
Hall, D.　Religious Articles.
Hardy, T.　Christmas: 1924.

Dream Question, A.
Graveyard of Dead Creeds, The.
Quid Hic Agis?
Respectable Burgher, The.
Whispered at the Church-Opening.
Hayden, R.   Those Winter Sundays.
Herrick.   Slavery.
Hopkins, G.   But what indeed is ask'd of me?
    On the Portrait of Two Beautiful Young People.
    Wreck of the Deutschland, The.
Housman.   New Year's Eve.
Howe, S.   Hinge Picture.
Hughes, L.   Gods.
    Goodbye Christ.
    Madam and the Minister.
    Mystery.
Jacob, M.   Patience of an Angel.
Jeffers, R.   Great Men.
    Theory of Truth.
Kinnell.   Avenue Bearing the Initial of Christ
    into the New World, The.
    Sheffield Ghazal 5: Passing the Cemetary.
Kipling, R.   Buddha at Kamakura.
    Disciple, The.
    MacDonough's Song.
Kizer, C.   By the Riverside.
    Dixit Insipiens.
Kumin, M.   In the Park.
    Jesus Infection, The.
    Living Alone with Jesus.
Larkin, P.   Church Going.
    High Windows.
    Water.
Laughlin, J.   Bible Lady, The.
    Old Dr God.
    Patent Pending.
    Piteous Sight, A.
    Saeta.
Lawrence, D. H.   Bells.
    Future Religion.
    Quetzalcoatl Looks Down on Mexico.
    Religion.
    Resurrection of the Flesh.
    Spiral Flame.
Levertov.   Flickering Mind.
Lindsay, N.   I Went Down into the Desert to
    Meet Elijah.
    Incense.
    Soul of the City Receives the Gift of the Holy
        Spirit, The.
    Sun Says His Prayers, The.
Lorde.   Release Time.
    When the Saints Come Marching In.
    Winds of Orisha, The.
Lowell, R.   Like Henry VIII, Mohammed got
    religion.
    Tenth Muse.
Lux.   Traveling Exhibit of Torture Instruments.
MacDiarmid, H.   Covenanters, The.
    Credo.
    To My Friend the Late Beatrice Hastings.
    Two Memories.
MacLeish.   Two Priests, The.
MacNeice.   Carol: "To end all carols, darling."
Melville, H.   Fragments of a Lost Gnostic Poem
    of the Twelfth [or 12th] Century.
Meredith, G.   Martin's Puzzle.
Merton.   Baroque Gravure, A.
    There Is a Way.
Milosz, C.   1945.
    After Enduring.
    Either-Or.
    Helene's Religion.
    How It Was.
    Master, The.
    Mid-Twentieth-Century Portrait.
    Why.
    Zdziechowski.
Muldoon, P.   Madoc: A Mystery.
    Our Lady of Ardboe.
Nash, O.   Birth Comes to the Archbishop.
    Seven Spiritual Ages of Mrs. Marmaduke
        Moore, The.
Nemerov.   Boom!
Nimatullah [or Ni'matu'llah].   Song of Seyd [or
    Seid] Nimetollah of Kuhistan.

Olson, C.   Applause.
    Concerning Exaggeration, or How, Properly, to
        Heap Up.
Pasolini.   Religion of My Time, The.
Patchen.   Mohammed.
Pinsky.   Avenue.
    Pilgrimage.
Ralegh, S.   Ah wretched they that worship
    vanities.
    I sacrifice to God the Beefe, which you adore.
Ramanujan.   Guru, The.
Rexroth, K.   Dragon and the Unicorn, The.
Rich, A.   Air without Incense.
Rossetti, C.   Dream, A.
    Lord, dost Thou look on me, and will not I.
    Ruined Cross, The.
    Sonnet: "Some say that love and joy are one:
        and so."
    Three Nuns.
Rukeyser, M.   Gates, The.
Rumi.   I Come Before Dawn.
    I Have Five Things to Say.
    Man and a Woman Arguing, A.
    Moses and the Shepherd.
    Only Breath.
    Spring Is Christ.
Sandburg, C.   Broken Tabernacles.
    To a Contemporary Bunkshooter.
Schuyler, J.   I Sit Down to Type.
Scott, S.   Gray Brother, The.
Sexton.   My Friend, My Friend.
    With Mercy for the Greedy.
Shelley, P.   Prometheus Unbound [A Lyrical
    Drama in Four Acts].
Sidney, S.   Leave Me O Love.
Smith, S.   From the County Lunatic Asylum.
    Religious Man, A.
Spender, S.   Landscape near an Aerodrome,
    The.
Stafford, W.   Religion Back Home.
    Ultimate Problems.
Stevens, W.   Blue Buildings in the Summer Air,
    The.
    Botanist on Alp (No. 2).
    Gray Stones and Gray Pigeons.
    High-Toned Old Christian Woman, A.
    Sunday Morning.
    Winter Bells.
Stockton, A.   Fragment on the Death of a
    Minester.
    To Doctor Rush Enclosing the Foregoing Ode of
        1782.
Updike.   Comp. Religion.
    Earthworm.
Very.   Philosophy and Religion.
    Religion.
Whalen, P.   Dying Tooth Song.
Wheatley, P.   Atheism.
Whittier.   Cassandra Southwick.
    Hymn for the Opening of Plymouth Church.
    In the "Old South."
    Mary Garvin.
    Miriam.
    Pennsylvania Pilgrim, The.
    Preacher, The.
    Worship.
Wilbur, R.   Matthew VIII, 28 ff.
    Pelican, The.
Williams, M.   And When in Scenes of Glory.
Williams, W.   Choral: The Pink Church.
    Host, The.
    Semblables, The.
Wordsworth, W.   Conclusion: "Why Sleeps the
    future, as a snake enrolled."
    Ecclesiastical Sonnets.
    Lines Written as a School Exercise at
        Hawkshead, Anno Aetatis 14.
    Mutability.
Wright, C.   Lives of the Saints.
    Looking at Pictures.
Wright, J.   Sketch for an Aesthetic Project.
    Wednesday Night Prayer Meeting.
Yeats.   Church and State.
    Wisdom.
Zukofsky, L.   Poem Beginning "The."
See also **Faith**

Religious Life
Achterberg.   Eben Haëzer.
Arnold, M.   Dover Beach.
Berryman.   Terce.
Brooks, G.   Firstly Inclined to Take What It Is
    Told.
Byron, G.   Fragment from the "Monk of Athos."
Cowper, W.   Lively Hope, and Gracious Fear.
    Lord Will Happiness Divine, The.
    My former hopes are fled.
    O Lord, my best desire fulfil.
    Olney Hymns.
    True Pleasures.
Crane, H.   Emblems of Conduct.
Crashaw.   Description of a Religious House and
    Condition of Life.
    On Mr. G. Herberts Booke, The Temple.
    To a Young Gentle-Woman, Councel
        Concerning Her Choice.
Cunningham, J.   Elders at their services begin,
    The.
Dickinson, E.   I prayed, at first, a little Girl.
    I've heard an Organ talk, sometimes.
    Ourselves we do inter with sweet derision.
    This is a Blossom of the Brain.
    Who were "the Father and the Son."
    You love the Lord—you cannot see.
Donne.   To the Countess of Bedford at New
    Year's Tide.
Fenton, J.   Kingfisher's Boxing Gloves, The.
García Lorca.   Poem of the *Saeta*.
Herbert, G.   Affliction (1).
    Content.
    Dulness[e].
    H[oly] Communion, The.
    Invitation, The.
    Perirrhanterium.
Herrick.   Thanksgiving to God for His House,
    A.
Hopkins, G.   Barnfloor and Winepress.
    Glimmer'd along the square-cut steep.
    Half-way House, The.
    I Wake and Feel the Fell of Dark, Not Day.
    Il Mystico.
    In Honour of St. Alphonsus Rodriguez.
    Let me be to Thee as the circling bird.
    Lines for a Picture of St. Dorothea.
    Margaret Clitheroe.
    Morning, Midday, and Evening Sacrifice.
    On St. Winefred.
    St. Dorothea.
    Summa.
    Times are nightfall, look, their light grows less,
        The.
    To Seem the Stranger.
    Voice from the World, A.
Jonson, B.   To Heaven.
Lindsay, N.   Where Is the Real Non-Resistant?
Logan, J.   Cycle for Mother Cabrini, A.
Meredith, G.   Angelic Love.
    Creed.
    Jump-to-Glory Jane.
    St. Thérèse.
    Story of Sir Arnulph, The.
    To Cardinal Manning.
    Twilight Music.
Merton.   Elegy for a Trappist.
    La Comparsa en Oriente.
    Moment of Truth, The.
    Practical Program for Monks, A.
    Quickening of St. John the Baptist, The.
    Solitary Life.
    Three Postcards from the Monastery.
    When in the Soul of the Serene Disciple.
Nemerov.   Boom!
    Common Saw, A.
Pinsky.   New Saddhus, The.
Ransom, J.   Prometheus in Straits.
Roethke.   Abyss, The.
    Right Thing, The.
Rossetti, C.   Portrait, A.
    Quinquagesima.
Snyder, G.   Tōji.
Tate, A.   True Believer.
Very.   Presence, The.
Whittier.   Adjustment.

Brother of Mercy, The.
Chapel of the Hermits, The.
Ezekiel.
Hermit of the Thebaid, The.
Hymn of the Dunkers.
Hymns of the Brahmo Somaj.
Knight of St. John, The.
My Soul and I.
Reward, The.
Shadow and the Light, The.
Two Elizabeths, The.
Wordsworth, W.   Decay of Piety.
For the Spot Where the Hermitage Stood on St Herbert's Island, Derwent-Water.

See also **Clergy; Convents; Monasteries; Monks; Nuns; Rabbis**

Religious Wars
Coleridge, S.   Sancti Dominici Pallium.
Crashaw.   On the Gunpowder-Treason.
Upon the Gunpowder Treason.
Jonson, B.   Epistle to a Friend, to Persuade [*or* Perswade] Him to the Wars [*or* Warres], An.
Lindsay, N.   Foreign Missions in Battle Array.
King Arthur's Men Have Come Again.

Rembrandt, Harmenszoon van Rijn
Blake, W.   Florentine Ingratitude.
Celan.   In-edger; Rembrandt.
Lowell, R.   Rembrandt.
Pinkerton, H.   On Rembrandt's Etching of Joseph Telling His Dream (1636).
On Rembrandt's Self-Portrait (1658) in the Frick Museum.
Robinson, E.   Rembrandt to Rembrandt.
Walcott.   Polish Rider, The.
Zagajewski.   Dutch Painters.

Remorse
Baudelaire.   Irreparable, The.
Posthumous Remorse.
Bly, R.   Getting Up Late.
Borges.   Remorse.
Brontë, E.   A.G.A. to A.S.
Come, walk with me.
If grief for grief can touch thee.
Lady, in your Palace Hall.
O Dream, where art thou now?
Starry night shall tidings bring, The.
Still beside that dreary water.
There let thy bleeding branch atone.
When days of Beauty deck the earth.
Where were ye all? and where wert thou?
Browning, E.   Nature's Remorses.
Burns, R.   Penitential Thought, in the Hour of Remorse—Intended for a Tragedy, A.
Prayer, in the Prospect of Death, A.
Remorse.
Carver, R.   Harley's Swans.
Locking Yourself Out, Then Trying to Get Back In.
Trestle, The.
Cavalcanti.   Canzone: He laments the Presumption and Incontinence of his Youth.
Cino da Pistoia.   Canzone: His Lament for Selvaggia.
Davie, D.   Berkshire.
De la Mare.   Thus Her Tale.
Dickinson, E.   Remorse—is Memory—awake.
Donne.   Hymn[e] to God the Father, A.
Emerson, R.   Amulet, The.
Gallagher, T.   Same Kiss After Many Years, The.
Tableau Vivant.
Hardy, T.   His Heart.
Herrick.   Mora Sponsi, the Stay of the Bridegroome.
Penitencie.
Housman.   Rain, it streams on stone and hillock, The.
Lawrence, D. H.   Piano.
Lorde.   Separation.
Mallarmé.   Anguish.
Michelangelo Buonarroti.   Alas! Alas! for the way I've been betrayed.
What a chance I had! I should have, while I could.
Nash, O.   Clean Conscience Never Relaxes, A.
Hearts of Gold.

Nemerov.   Remorse for Time, The.
Petrarch.   I go in mourning for those years of mine.
You who can hear in scattered rhymes the sound.
Raine, K.   If I choose remorse.
Riley, J.   At Noon—and Midnight.
Lost Kiss, The.
Song of the New Year.
Ritsos.   Putting out the Lamp.
Remorse.
Under Oblivion.
Sandburg, C.   Remorse.
Very.   Torn Flower, The.
Wilde, O.   New Remorse, The.
Williams, C. K.   Beginning of April, The.
Conscience.
With Ignorance.

Renaissance
Borges.   Ariosto and the Arabs.
Browning, R.   Fra Lippo Lippi.
Collins, B.   Death of Allegory, The.
Dubie.   Saints of Negativity, The.
Hill, G.   Humanist, The.
Pre-Raphaelite Notebook, A.
Kipling, R.   Dawn Wind, The.
Stock, R.   Louis XI.

Renewal
Amichai [*or* Amikhai].   And After All That—the Rain.
Eve of Rosh Hashanah, The.
Hamadiya, Memory of Bliss.
Angelou.   Recovery.
Request.
Atwood.   Departure from the Bush.
Head against White.
Last Day.
Berry, W.   Anniversary, An.
Rain.
Setting Out.
Berryman.   Caravan.
Brodsky, J.   New Life.
Brontë, E.   Here, with my knee upon thy stone.
Burns, R.   John Barleycorn [a Ballad].
Campion, T.   Peacefull westerne winde the wintrye stormes hath calmde, The.
Carruth, H.   Coming Down to the Desert at Lordsburg, N.M.
Return to Love.
Celan.   It's all different from what you think, from what I think.
Crane, H.   Interludium.
Creeley.   House, The ("Mas-Soñer / Restaurat—Any").
Old Saying.
Rose, The.
There ("Miles back").
Cummings, E. E.   Love is the every only god.
Mist.
Now that fierce few.
N(o)w / the / how / dis(appeared cleverly)world.
Paris,*ₓₓ*is April sunset completely utters.
Semi-Spring.
Sonnet: "Rain-drop on the eyelids of the earth, A."
Spring is like a perhaps hand.
When faces called flowers float out of the ground.
"Dario."   Because of the Influence of Spring.
De la Mare.   Fleeting, The.
Oh, Why?
Dickinson, E.   Then will I not repine.
Donne.   Cales and Guiana.
To Mr R. W ("Kindly I envy thy song's [*or* songs] perfection").
Eberhart, R.   Parker River, The.
Ginsberg, A.   Eastern Ballad, An.
Gurney, I.   Near Spring.
Hamill, S.   Saprophyte.
Hardy, T.   Something that Saved Him, The.
Hill, G.   Veni Coronaberis.
Hölderlin.   Too long we lived for work and wages, we.
Hughes, L.   Black Maria.
Girl.
To You.

Jackson, L.   After So Much Loss.
Jeffers, R.   Point Pinos and Point Lobos.
Practical People.
Shiva.
Kipling, R.   Pan in Vermont.
Rector's Memory, A.
Song of Seven Cities, The.
Kumin, M.   On Being Asked to Write a Poem in Memory of Anne Sexton.
Turning the Garden in Middle Age.
Kunitz, S.   Round, The.
Laughlin, J.   At Eleusis.
O Frères Humains.
You Are My Future.
Lawrence, D. H.   Climbing Down.
First Morning.
Flowers.
Love Comes Late.
New Heaven and Earth.
New Word, The.
Phoenix.
Real Democracy.
Sleep and Waking.
Sun in Me.
Welcome to Quetzalcoatl.
Levertov.   Seedtime.
Levine, P.   Let Me Begin Again.
Told.
Melville, H.   American Aloe on Exhibition, The.
Merrill, J.   Renewal, A.
Variations: The Air Is Sweetest That a Thistle Guards.
Merton.   Earthquake.
Litany: "It yawns at me the cavernous gulf."
Responsory, A.
Michelangelo Buonarroti.   Though bent with age, to me.
Who rides by night on horseback, come the day.
Milosz, C.   After Enduring.
This World.
Mistral, G.   Morning.
Sea, The.
Montale.   Syria.
Winter Light.
Niedecker.   Scuttle up the workshop.
Oliver, M.   Marengo.
Morning in a New Land.
Roses.
Olson, C.   Chain of memory is resurrection I am a vain man, The.
Going from Battle to Battle.
La Torre.
Orléans, C.   Rondeau: "Year has cast its cloak away, The."
Orr, G.   Leaving the Asylum.
Pagis.   Cycle, The.
Paley, G.   In the Bus.
Pasolini.   Tears of the Excavator, The.
Pasternak, B.   Orford.
Petrarch.   If you want me again under your yoke.
Piercy.   Ache's End.
Rilke.   Springtime.
To Betsy Steiger.
Roethke.   Renewal, The.
Vernal Sentiment.
Rossetti, C.   Easter Carol, An.
First Spring Day, The.
Go In Peace.
Greatest of These Is Charity, The.
Seasons.
Vigil of all Saints.
Wintry Sonnet, A.
Sandburg, C.   Bath.
Seifert.   Song: "We wave a handkerchief."
Shelley, P.   Zucca, The.
Smith, S.   New Age, The.
Stafford, W.   Animal That Drank up Sound, The.
Stock, R.   Poet Mário Faustino Descends Into Hades and Rises to the Empyrean.
Stockton, A.   On the Suns Setting Clear after a Three Days Storm.
Szymborska, W.   End and Beginning.
End and the Beginning, The.
Reality Demands.
Thoreau.   Music.

Walcott. City's Death by Fire, A.
Walker, A. These Mornings of Rain.
Whitman, W. Soon Shall the Winter's Foil Be Here.
Whittier. Chicago.
Cypress-Tree of Ceylon, The.
Dream of Summer, A.
Easter Flower Gift, An.
My Psalm.
Wilbur, R. Then.
Williams, C. K. Bread.
Williams, W. Paterson: The Falls.
Rewaking, The.
Wordsworth, W. From the Dark Chambers of Dejection Freed.
I watch, and long have watched, with calm regret.
Ode Composed on May Morning.
To May.
Wright, J. Eye of God, the Soul's First Vision, The.
Zagajewski. I Walked Through the Medieval Town.
Zaturenska. Cascades and Fountains.
Young Dancers, The.
Zukofsky, L. Chrysanthemum.
I Walk in the Old Street.

See also **Rebirth; Regeneration**

Repentance
Bierce. Incurable.
Burns, R. To Mr. S. McKenzie.
Campion, T. Awake, Awake! [Thou Heavy Sprite].
Lift up to heav'n, sad wretch, thy heavy spright.
Loe, when backe mine eye.
Cowper, W. Tale, Founded on a Fact, A.
Dickinson, E. Renunciation—is a piercing Virtue.
Herbert, G. Business.
Cross[e], The.
Discipline.
Mary [*or* Marie] Magdalene.
Parody [*or* Parodie], A.
Reprisal[l], The.
Rose, The.
Sighs and Groans [*or* Grones].
Sinner, The.
Sin's Round.
Storm, The.
Trinity Sunday.
Herrick. Bad May Be Better.
Calling, and Correcting.
Cunctation in Correction.
Penitence.
Penitencie.
Position in the Hebrew Divinity, A.
Sin.
Sinners.
To God.
Jeffers, R. At the Birth of an Age.
Jonson, B. Hymn[e] to God the Father, A.
Kipling, R. Supplication of the Black Aberdeen.
Lindsay, N. When Peter Jackson Preached in the Old Church.
Lowell, R. Death of Alexander.
Meredith, G. He where the great sun looks his last.
Merton. Epitaph for a Public Servant.
Millay, E. Penitent, The.
Nash, O. Reminiscent Reflection.
Petrarch. Love kept me burning one-and-twenty years.
Pope, A. Epigram in a Maid of Honour's Prayer-Book.
Ritsos. Succession.
Rossetti, C. Ash Wednesday.
Convent Threshold, The.
Cried Out with Tears.
Divine and Human Pleading.
O Lord, I am ashamed to seek Thy Face / As tho' I loved Thee as Thy saints love Thee.
Rumi. Nasuh.
Smith, S. Repentance of Lady T, The.
Stampa. With Deep Repentance for My Wasted Days.
Williams, C. K. Penance.

Williams, M. To One Who Went Too Far.
Wordsworth, W. Upon the Late General Fast. March, 1832.

Repression
Bishop, E. Sonnet: "Caught—the bubble."
Bly, R. Executive's Death, The.
Cavafy. Hidden Things.
Codrescu. *Petite Histoire* of Red Fascism, A.
Coleridge, S. Two Founts, The.
Cummings, E. E. Red-rag and pink-flag.
Frost, R. Home Burial.
Ginsberg, A. Kral Majales.
Hughes, L. Dream Boogie.
Lawrence, D. H. Hands of the Betrothed, The.
Virgin Youth.
McGrath, T. Warrant for Pablo Neruda, A.
Milosz, C. Higher Arguments in Favor of Discipline Derived from the Speech Before the Council of the Universal State in 2068.
Shapiro, K. Buick.
Wilde, O. Wasted Days.
Williams, C. K. Repression.
Williams, M. Well-Ordered Life, The.
Williams, T. Photograph and Pearls.
Williams, W. Slow Movement.

Reproach
Atwood. You did it / it was you who started the countdown.
Bly, R. Executive's Death, The.
Carver, R. One More.
Chaucer. Chaucer's Wordes unto Adam, his Owne Scriveyn.
Lenvoy de Chaucer a Scogan.
Creeley. Mirror, The.
Cullen, C. For an Atheist.
Dugan, A. Monologue for a Sixth Avenue Screamer.
Graves, R. Dialogue on the Headland.
Reproach.
Hardy, T. Her Reproach.
Jonson, B. Epigram on the Court Pucell, An.
Epistle to a Friend, An ("Censure not sharply then, but me advise").
Li Po. Jewel Stairs' Grievance, The.
MacLeish. You Also, Gaius Valerius Catullus.
Merton. What is beyond reproof / Is done in this building.
Riley, J. Parent Reprimanded, A.
Stockton, A. Impromptu on Hearing that a Print of the Guliteene with Our Beloved Presidents Figure under It Was Executed in Mr Genets Family—under His Sanction.
Sarcasm against the Ladies in a Newspaper, A; An Impromptu Answer.
Satire on the Fashionable Pompoons Worn by the Ladies in the Year 1753. by a Gentleman, A; Answered by a Young Lady of Sixteen.

Reputation
Amichai [*or* Amikhai]. You Can Rely on Him.
Borges. Where Can They Have Gone?
Byron, G. Lines Written in the Travellers' Book at Orchomenus.
Campion, T. Ad Leam.
Respect my faith, regard my service past.
Donne. Epitaph on Himself.
Graves, R. 1805.
Deed of Gift.
Herrick. Care a Good Keeper.
Honours Are Hindrances.
Poetry Perpetuates the Poet.
To His Honoured Kinsman Sir William Soame.
Upon Pievish.
Hughes, L. Ballad of the Girl Whose Name Is Mud.
Poor Girl's Ruination.
Snob.
Jeffers, R. Old Wolf My Father, The.
Jonson, B. To Sir Edward Herbert.
To the Memory of My Beloved, the Author Mr [*or* Master] William Shakespeare: And What He Hath Left Us.
Kizer, C. Days of 1986.
MacLeish. Poetical Remains.
Nash, O. Lines to Be Embroidered on a Bib, or, The Child Is Father of the Man, but Not for Quite a While.

Pope, A. To a Lady with the Temple of Fame.
Robinson, E. Flammonde.
Sheridan, T. Letter of Advice to the Right Hon. John Earl of Orrery, A.
Williams, M. Jonathan at Last.
Williams, T. Goths, The.
Yeats. Father and Child.

Rescues
Atwood. My beautiful wooden leader.
Borges. Alexander Selkirk.
Carew, T. Lady, Rescued from Death by a Knight, Who in the Instant Leaves Her, Complains Thus, A.
Carver, R. Account, An.
Celan. There stood / a splinter of fig on your lip.
Ciardi, J. Captain Nicholas Strong.
Clifton, L. If I Should.
Dugan, A. Attempted Rescue, The.
Kumin, M. Caring: A Dream.
Longing to Be Saved, The.
Levertov. Re-Rooting.
Logan, J. Rescue, The.
MacNeice. Burnt Bridge, The.
Pinsky. Spelunker.
Ransom, J. Lady Lost.
Riley, J. Nicholas Oberting.
Stock, R. Rescuers, The.
Tate, J. Rescue.

Resilience
Stockton, A. On a Little Boy Going to Play on a Place from Whence He Had Just Fallen.

Resistance
Atwood. Roominghouse, Winter.
Campion, T. Sweet, exclude me[e] not, nor be divided.
Carew, T. Boldness[e] in Love.
Protestation [A Sonnet], The.
Celan. Just Think.
Creeley. Sea, The.
Cullen, C. In Spite of Death.
Emerson, R. O what is Heaven but the fellowship.
Ferlinghetti, L. Short Story on a Painting of Gustav Klimt.
Frost, R. One Step Taken Backward.
Herrick. To Virgins.
Will To Be Working, A.
Hill, G. De Jure Belli ac Pacis.
Hughes, L. Ballad of Sam Solomon.
Note to All Nazis Fascists and Klansmen.
Underground, The.
Lawrence, D. H. Metal for Resistance.
Merton. For the Spanish Poet Miguel Hernandez.
Oliver, M. Rain.
Plath. Resolve.
Ritsos. Simple Honesty.
Rukeyser, M. Don Baty, the Draft Resister.
Williams, C. K. Drought.
Peace.
Wyatt, S. No! Indeed.

Respectability
Bukowski. Soul.
Cunningham, J. Helmsman, The; an Ode.
Davie, D. Grudging Respect.
Eberhart, R. Hop-Toad, The.
New England Bachelor, A.
Emerson, R. O Boston city lecture-hearing.
Frost, R. Considerable Speck, A.
HaNagid. Respect and Discretion.
Jackson, L. Respect for the Dead.
Lindsay, N. Hearth Eternal, The.
Riley, J. Armazindy.
Dead, My Lords.
Jim.
Sandburg, C. 'Boes.
Memoir.
Silver Nails.
Stafford, W. Thanksgiving for My Father, A.
Stockton, A. Some Traits of the Character of Mrs. Powel as a Model for a Young Lady Who Said She Admired Her More than Any Other Woman.
Thoreau. Respectable folks, The.

Responsibility
Amichai [or Amikhai]. Eve of Rosh Hashanah, The.
  Ibn Gabirol.
  We Did What We Had To.
Angelou. On Working White Liberals.
Bierce. To a Dejected Poet.
Bloch, C. We Did What We Had To.
Borges. Matthew 25:30.
Burns, R. Libel Summons.
Carver, R. Debate, The.
  Mother.
  One More.
  Summer in Sacramento, A.
  White Field, The.
Clifton, L. Times, The.
Creeley. Easter.
Cuadra, P. Written Next to a Blue Flower.
Dugan, A. Stability before Departure.
Kipling, R. Natural Theology.
  Question, The.
  Reformers, The.
Levertov. Part, The.
  Split Mind, The.
MacNeice. Yours Next.
Meredith, G. Atlas.
Merton. What is beyond reproof / Is done in this building.
Merwin. To My Brother Hanson.
  Yesterday.
Paley, G. Responsibility.
Parker, D. Song of the Conventions.
Rich, A. For the Record.
Riley, J. Armazindy.
Rimbaud, A. Comedy of Thirst.
Rukeyser, M. Despisals.
Simic. Man, The.
Stafford, W. With Kit, Age 7, at the Beach.
Whalen, P. 20:vii:58, On Which I Renounce the Notion of Social Responsiblity.
Williams, C. K. Alzheimer's: The Husband.
  Another Dollar.
Williams, M. After You Die You Don't Give a Piddling Damn.
  Good Son, A.
Wright, C. Self-Portrait.

Rest
Amichai [or Amikhai]. Poem: "As at the beginning of birth."
Berry, W. Requiem: "We will see no more."
  Song (2).
  Winter Nightfall.
Bukowski. Pace is the Essence.
Chuang Tzu. Hat Salesman and a Capable Ruler, A.
Corbett, W. August.
Cowper, W. Inscription for a Bust of Homer.
  Inscription for a Moss-House.
  Inscription for an Hermitage.
Cummings, E. E. Rain or hail / sam done.
  When the proficient poison of pure sleep.
Cunningham, J. Summer Idyll.
Davie, D. Felicity's Fourth Order.
De la Mare. Last Coachload, The.
Dugan, A. On Hibernation in the Country.
Dunbar, P. Noddin' by de Fire.
Eberhart, R. Bells of a Chinese Temple, The.
  Cover Me Over.
Frost, R. Acceptance.
Gurney, I. Brimscombe.
  Signallers.
Guyon. Repose in God.
  Testimony of Divine Adoption, The.
Hardy, T. A.H., 1855–1912.
  Drizzling Easter Morning, A.
  Epeisodia.
Herbert, G. Pulley, The.
Herrick. End of His Work, The.
  Rest.
  Rest Refreshes.
Keats. To One Who Has Been Long in City Pent.
Lawrence, D. H. Last Hours.
Levi, P. Landing.
Levine, P. Holding On.
  Sleepless Night, A.

MacNeice. Sunday in the Park.
Mahon. No Rest for the Wicked.
Meredith, W. Ghosts of the House, The.
Oliver, M. Creeks.
Poe. For Annie.
Riley, J. How Did You Rest, Last Night?
  Passing Hail, A.
Rilke. He Can Find No Rest.
Rossetti, C. Better So.
  Burial Anthem.
  Cardinal Newman.
  Counsel, A.
  Death Is Swallowed Up in Victory.
  I toiled on, but thou.
  Let Them Rejoice in Their Beds.
  Lotus-Eaters: Ulysses to Penelope, The.
  Love loveth Thee, and wisdom loveth Thee.
  Martyr, A.
  My Old Friends.
  Rest.
  Sir Eustace Grey.
  Sleeping at Last.
  Sonnet from the Psalms.
  Sweetness of rest when Thou sheddest rest.
  Then I Commended Mirth.
  There Remaineth Therefore a Rest to the People of God.
  Three Nuns.
  Thro' burden and heat of the day.
  Today's Burden.
  Uphill.
  What will it be, O my soul, what will it be.
Simic. History.
Smith, S. Road Up.
Spender, S. Dusk.
Swenson, M. Subconscious Sea.
Tomlinson, C. Against Travel.
Whitman, W. Ended Day, An.
  Evening Lull, An.
  We All Shall Rest at Last.
Whittier. Autumn Thoughts.
Wilbur, R. Sonnet: "Winter deepening, the hay all in, The."
Wordsworth, W. Inscription for a Seat by a Roadside, Half Way up a Steep Hill, Facing the South.
  Inscription for a Seat by the Pathway Side Ascending to Windy Brow.
  Labourer's Noon-Day Hymn, The.
  Rest and Be Thankful!
  Water Fowl.
  Written with a Slate Pencil on a Stone, on the Side of the Mountain of Black Comb.
Yeats. Lover's Song, The.
  Michael Robartes Bids His Beloved Be at Peace.

Restaurants
Armantrout. Counter.
Bukowski. Eating My Senior Citizen's Dinner at the Sizzler.
  Krutz.
  Plate Glass Window, A.
Carver, R. Reading Something in the Restaurant.
Codrescu. 3/6/81, Amtrack.
Collins, B. Waitress, The.
Cummings, E. E. Item.
  One April dusk the.
Dugan, A. Closing Time at the Second Avenue Deli.
  On Work.
  What Happened? What Do You Expect?
Hughes, T. In the M5 Restaurant.
Keats. Lines on the Mermaid Tavern.
Komunyakaa. Rendezvous.
Laughlin, J. Waiters' Ballet, The.
Mahon. Chinese Restaurant in Portrush, The.
McHugh, H. Most, The.
Muldoon, P. Holy Thursday.
  Paris.
Nash, O. Try It Suns. and Hols.; It's Closed Then.
Riley, J. Like His Mother Used to Make.
Schuyler, J. Dining Out with Doug and Frank.
Simic. Partial Explanation, The.
Tomlinson, C. Hero Sandwiches.

Updike. To an Usherette.
Williams, W. Brilliant Sad Sun.

Restlessness
Borges. Street with a Pink Corner Store.
Creeley. Midnight.
  On Vacation.
  Surf: An Elegy, The.
De la Mare. Out Of Bounds.
Dugan, A. On Cabin Fever, On Boredom in the Countryside.
Gunn, T. All Night, Legs Pointed East.
Longfellow, H. Seaweed.
Oliver, M. Whelks.
Parker, D. White Lady, The.
Pessoa. At the wheel of the Chevrolet on the road to Sintra.
Riley, J. Ringworm Frank.
Updike. Poisoned in Nassau.
Wordsworth, D. Cottager to Her Infant, (By My Sister), The.

Restraint
Bukowski. Hey, Ezra, Listen to This.
Carruth, H. They Accuse Me of Not Talking.
De la Mare. Imagination's Pride, The.
Glück, L. Palais des Arts.
Graves, R. Fetter, The.
"H. D." She Contrasts with Herself Hippolyta.
Kizer, C. Bitch.
Lawrence, D. H. Passing Visit to Helen.
Merwin. Bread and Butter.
Petrarch. When my passion—that with two glowing spurs.
Piercy. Work of Artifice, A.
Rich, A. Unsaid Word, An.
Rilke. Divine Disgrace.
Wyatt, S. Though I myself be bridled of my mind.
Zagajewski. Sad, Tired.

Resurrection, The
Crashaw. Easter Day.
Davie, D. Attar of Roses.
Dickey, J. Gila Bend.
Dickinson, E. And with what body do they come?
  Business enough indeed.
  I lift the lid to my box of Phantoms.
  No Crowd that has occurred.
  Safe in their Alabaster Chambers.
Donne. Resurrection, Imperfect.
  Upon the Annunciation and Passion Falling upon One Day. 1608.
Dunbar, W. Done is a battell [or battle] on the dragon blak [or black].
Graves, R. To Bring the Dead to Life.
Herbert, G. Dawning, The.
  Easter.
Herrick. God Has a Twofold Part.
  Resurrection, Possible, and Probable, The.
  Resurrection, The.
Hopkins, G. That Nature Is a Heraclitean Fire and of the Comfort of the Resurrection.
Kinnell. Supper after the Last, The.
Lawrence, D. H. Resurrection.
Levertov. Ikon: The Harrowing of Hell.
Merton. Trappist Cemetery—Gethsemani, The.
Riley, J. Hymn Exultant.
Rilke. Resurrected Christ, The.
Rossetti, C. Better Resurrection, A.
  Easter Even.
  In resurrection is it awfuller.
  Resurrection Eve.
Sexton. Protestant Easter.
Updike. Seven Stanzas at Easter.
Very. Christmas.
  Christ's Final Victory.
  Faith in the Resurrection Confirmed.
  Resurrection, The.
Wordsworth, W. Composed in One of the Valleys of Westmoreland, on Easter Sunday.

Retirement and Retirees
Cowper, W. Retirement.
Cunningham, J. To Whom It May Concern.
Dove, R. Satisfaction Coal Company, The.
Herrick. Mr. Robert Hericke His Farwell unto Poetrie.
Hughes, T. Retired Colonel, The.

Jacobsen, J.   Hourglass.
Lowell, R.   Charles Vby Titian.
   Terminal Days at Beverly Farms.
Marvell.   Garden, The.
   Upon the Hill and Grove at Bilbrough.
Prunty.   New Territory.
   Retirement Catalogue, A.
Riley, J.   Old Retired Sea-Captain, The.
Smith, S.   Bandol (Var).
Stafford, W.   Last Class, The.
   Retirement.
   Toward the End.
Stockton, A.   To Mr Lewis Pintard on His
   Retirement at New Rochelle.
Tomlinson, C.   Jubilación.
Williams, C. K.   Alzheimer's: The Husband.
   Rungs.
Williams, M.   Journalist Buys a Pig Farm, The.
See also **Old Age**
Retribution
Bukowski.   Trying to Get Even.
   Turnabout.
Cowper, W.   Expostulation.
Eberhart, R.   Fury of Aerial Bombardment, The.
Faiz.   Bangla Desh: 1.
Herrick.   To Myrrha Hard-Hearted.
Jeffers, R.   Home.
Kipling, R.   Justice.
Scott, S.   Gray Brother, The.
Reunions
Amichai [*or* Amikhai].   1978 Reunion of
   Palmach Veterans at Ma-ayan Harod.
   Late in my life, I come to you.
Beckett, S.   Alba.
   Arènes de Lutèce.
Berry, W.   Kentucky River Junction.
   Meeting, A.
Berryman.   Hello.
Bradstreet, A.   On My Son's Return Out of
   England.
Browning, E.   Exile's Return, The.
Burns, R.   Auld Lang Syne.
   Banks of Cree.
   Lassie Lie near Me.
Carew, T.   Upon Master Walter Montagu's
   Return from Travel.
Carruth, H.   Family Reunion.
Cavafy.   Following the Formulas of Ancient
   Greco-Syrian Magicians.
Cowper, W.   On the Queens's Visit to London.
Creeley.   Versions.
Cullen, C.   Two Who Crossed a Line.
Donne.   Valediction: Forbidding Mourning, A.
Eberhart, R.   Inchiquin Lake, Penobscot Bay.
   Return, The.
Glück, L.   My Life Before Dawn.
Graves, R.   Brief Reunion.
Hacker, M.   For K.J., Leaving and Coming
   Back.
   Somewhere in a Turrent.
Hardy, T.   Minute before Meeting, The.
   Revisitation, The.
   Song of the Soldiers' Wives and Sweethearts.
   Two Soldiers, The.
   Woman Who Went East, The.
Hughes, L.   Lover's Return.
Kipling, R.   Friends, The.
   Widower, The.
Kizer, C.   Semele Recycled.
Koch, K.   Fate.
Kumin, M.   Family Reunion.
Lawrence, D. H.   Chief Mystery, The.
   Reach Over.
   Return.
Levertov.   Woman Meets an Old Lover, A.
Logan, J.   First Prelude. Dream in Ohio: The
   Father.
   Poem in Progress.
MacLeish.   Hotel Breakfast.
MacNeice.   Bluebells.
   Happy Families.
McGrath, T.   Celebration.
   Once We Meant It.
   Poem: "How could I have come so far?"
Merwin.   Reunion.
   Tale.

Owen, W.   Unreturning, The.
Petrarch.   Lady, who now with our Original.
   Love used to weep, and sometimes I did too.
Plath.   Family Reunion.
Rich, A.   Face to Face.
Riley, J.   Back from a Two-Years' Sentence.
   Ballad, A: "Crowd about me, little children."
   When She Comes Home.
   When We Three Meet.
Rossetti, C.   Birthday, A.
   Last Words of St. Telemachus, The.
   Lord Thomas and Fair Margaret.
Rukeyser, M.   More of a Corpse Than a
   Woman.
Rumi.   Bonfire at Midnight.
Schuyler, J.   Reunion, A.
Stafford, W.   Together Again.
Tu Fu.   Visit.
Updike.   Oxford, Thirty Years After.
Whittier.   Reunion, The.
   To a Friend.
Williams, M.   Holiday Inn: Surrounded by
   Someone Else's Reunion He Comes to Terms.
Revelation (Bible)
Blake, W.   Mental Traveller, The.
Herrick.   To God.
Sarton, M.   Storm of Angels, A.
Revelry
Brontë, E.   Through the hours of yesternight.
Herrick.   Tinkers Song, The.
   Twelfe Night, or King and Queene.
Keats.   Song: "Spirit here that reignest!"
Riley, J.   Chairley Burke's in Town.
Revenge
Baudelaire.   Cask of Hate, The.
Browning, R.   Forgiveness, A.
Burns, R.   Bonie Laddie, Highland Laddie.
   Where Helen Lies.
Byron, G.   And Dost Thou Ask the Reason of
   My Sadness?
Carew, T.   In the Person of a Lady To Her
   Inconstant Servant.
   To My Inconstant Mistress [*or* Mistris].
Cavafy.   Footsteps of the Eumenides, The.
   Footsteps, The.
Creeley.   Lady Bird.
Davie, D.   Revenge for Love.
Dickinson, E.   Mine Enemy is growing old.
Donne.   Apparition, The.
Emerson, R.   When devils bite.
García Lorca.   Death of Little Tony Camborio,
   The.
Graves, R.   Return.
   Wreath, The.
HaNagid.   If You Don't Have The Power To
   Pay.
   They Stole My Sleep.
Hardy, T.   Brother, The.
   Sacrilege, The.
Herbert, G.   Reprisal[l], The.
Herrick.   Bubble; a Song, The.
   Revenge.
Hughes, T.   Kreutzer Sonata.
   Revenge Fable.
Jeffers, R.   At the Birth of an Age.
   At the Fall of an Age.
   Medea.
Kipling, R.   Pagett, M. P.
Kizer, C.   Threatening Letter.
Komunyakaa.   Fragging.
Lawrence, D. H.   Vengeance Is Mine.
   Welcome Death.
Melville, H.   Martyr, The.
Meredith, G.   King Harald's Trance.
Merwin.   Last One, The.
Millay, E.   Oh, Oh, you will be sorry for that
   word!
Parker, D.   Frustration.
Plath.   Lady Lazarus.
   Shrike, The.
Ritsos.   Orestes.
Sandburg, C.   Mascots.
Smith, S.   King Hamlet's Ghost.
Stock, R.   Hand.
Williams, M.   Rubaiyat for Sue Ella Tucker.
Wilner, E.   Eleusis.

Revivalism and Revivalists
Dunbar, P.   *with music.*
Rich, A.   Revivalist in Boston, A.
Riley, J.   Sister Jones's Confession.
Warren, R.   Amazing Grace in the Back
   Country.
See also **Evangelism and Evangelists; Religion**
Revolution and Revolutionaries
Ai.   Pentecost.
Aragon.   Red Front, The.
Borges.   Conjectural Poem.
   Page to Commemorate Colonel Suárez, Victor at
   Junín, A.
Browning, E.   Italy and the World.
Burns, R.   Scots Wha Hae.
Cavafy.   In a Large Greek Colony, 200 B.C.
Celan.   In One.
Clampitt.   Margaret Fuller, 1847.
Codrescu.   Reverse.
   Sunday Sermon.
Cooper, J.   Poetry as Continuity.
Davie, D.   Chrysanthemums.
Dickinson, E.   Revolution is the Pod.
Dubie.   Nine Black Poppies for Chac.
Dugan, A.   Against France: On the Algerian
   Pleasures of Entity.
   Confession of Heresy.
   Marxist Analysis of the Fifth Labor of Hercules.
   Portrait of a Lady.
   Untitled Poem: "I'm in the house because."
Emerson, R.   Boston.
Enzensberger, H.   Old Revolution.
Ferlinghetti, L.   Sandinista Avioncitos.
Frost, R.   Semi-Revolution, A.
Gallagher, T.   That Kind of Thing.
Ginsberg, A.   Neruda's "Que dispierte el
   leñador."
   Vow, A.
Glück, L.   Exile.
Gunn, T.   Court Revolt, The.
Hall, D.   Revolution, The.
Hardy, T.   Sergeant's Song, The.
Herrick.   Warre.
Hughes, L.   Always the Same.
   Ballads of Lenin.
   Chant for Tom Mooney.
   Final Call.
   Good Morning Revolution.
   In Explanation of Our Times.
   Kids Who Die.
   Last Prince of the East.
   Letter to the Academy.
   New Song, A.
   One More "S" in the U.S.A.
   Revolution.
   Roar China!
   Song of the Revolution.
   Wait.
Kizer, C.   October 1973.
Lawrence, D. H.   Fight! O My Young Men.
   It's Either You Fight or You Die.
   Minorities in Danger.
   O! Start a Revolution.
   Revolutions as Such!
   Sane Revolution, A.
   Softly, Then, Softly.
Levertov.   For Chile, 1977.
Lorde.   NOW.
MacLeish.   Background with Revolutionaries.
   Revolution of the Children.
Maunick.   Seven Sides and Seven Syllables.
McGrath, T.   Blues for the Old Revolutionary
   Woman.
   Incident in the Life of a Prophet, An.
   Lament for Pablo Neruda.
   Praises IV.
   Underground, The.
   Vision of Three Angels Viewing the Progress of
   Socialism.
   Warrant for Pablo Neruda, A.
Merton.   Letters to Che: Canto Bilingue.
   Never Call a Babysitter in a Thunderstorm.
Muldoon, P.   Lunch with Pancho Villa.
Niedecker.   Bonpland.
   Country's economics sick, A.
Patchen.   Ladder, The.

O What a Revolution!
Small but Brilliant Fire Blazed in the Grate, A.
To Whom It May Concern.
Pope, A.   Epistle to Dr. Arbuthnot.
Rexroth, K.   Another Early Morning Exercise.
From the Paris Commune to the Kronstadt
   Rebellion.
Lost Etc.
New Objectives, New Cadres.
Noretorp-Noretsyh.
Rich, A.   To Frantz Fanon.
Uncle Speaks in the Drawing Room, The.
Rimbaud, A.   Dead of '92 and '93, The.
Democracy.
Hands of Jeanne-Marie, The.
Paris War-Cry.
What do they mean to us, my heart, the sheets
   of blood.
Rossetti, C.   Royal Princess, A.
Rukeyser, M.   Child and Mother.
Sandburg, C.   Dynamiter.
Sarton, M.   Ballad of the Sixties.
We'll to the Woods No More, the Laurels Are
   Cut Down.
Snyder, G.   Revolution in the Revolution in the
   Revolution.
Tomlinson, C.   Revolution Piazza Di Spagna.
Walcott.   Elegy: "Our hammock swung between
   Americas."
Walker, A.   Facing the Way.
Lost My Voice? Of Course.
Well.
Whalen, P.   Bleakness, Farewell.
Whitman, W.   To a Foil'd European
   Revolutionaire.
Transpositions.
Wilde, O.   Libertatis Sacra Fames.
Sonnet to Liberty.
Williams, T.   Dangerous Painters, The.
Yeats.   Great Day, The.
See also **Rebellions and Rebels**

Revolutionary War, American
Wheatley, P.   Liberty and Peace, a Poem.
On the Capture of General Lee.
On the Death of General Wooster.
See also **American Revolution**

Rewards
Chuang Tzu.   Keng Sang Chu.
Coleridge, S.   Good Great Man, The.
Herrick.   Gods Gifts Not Soon[e] Granted.
Nothing Free-Cost.
Recompence.
Rewards.
Rewards and Punishments.
Jonson, B.   To Mr Ben Jonson in His Journey,
   by Mr Craven.
Lindsay, N.   Dancing for a Prize.

Rexroth, Kenneth
Hamill, S.   At Rexroth's Grave.

Reynolds, Sir Joshua
Blake, W.   Cripple every step Drudges &
   labours, The.
Florentine Ingratitude.
Pitiful Case, A.
Sir Jo[s]hua praised Rubens with a Smile.
Sir Joshua Reynolds.
To the Royal Academy.
Cowper, W.   To Sir Joshua Reynolds.
Wordsworth, W.   Anacreon.

Reznikoff, Charles
Oppen.   In Memoriam Charles Reznikoff.

Rhine (river), Germany
Apollinaire.   Rhenish Night.
Coleridge, S.   Cologne.
Wordsworth, W.   Author's Voyage down the
   Rhine (Thirty Years Ago).
Germans on the Heights of Hochheim, The.

Rhinoceroses
Ciardi, J.   Bird in Whatever Name, The.
Nash, O.   Rhinoceros, The.

Rhode Island (state)
Meredith, W.   Rhode Island.
Whittier.   Spiritual Manifestation, A.

Rhône Valley, France
Zagajewski.   Simone Weil Watches the Rhône

Valley.

Rhythm
Amichai [*or* Amikhai].   All These Make a
   Dance Rhythm.
Carruth, H.   Sometimes When Lovers Lie
   Quietly Together, Unexpectedly One of Them
   Will Feel the Other's Pulse.
Creeley.   Rhythm, The.
"Dario."   Love your rhythm and give rhythm to
   your actions.
Duncan, R.   Book of Resemblances, A.
Eberhart, R.   Long Swing, The.
Jeffers, R.   Rearmament.
Komunyakaa.   Rhythm Method.
Levertov.   Elusive.
Rukeyser, M.   To Enter That Rhythm Where the
   Self Is Lost.
Stock, R.   Epistle to Suzanne Joslyn Fosberg.

Ribbons
Carew, T.   Upon a Ribbon [*or* Ribband].
Herrick.   Bracelet to Julia, The.
Upon a Black Twist, Rounding the Arm of the
   Countess of Carlisle.
Upon Julia's Ribband.

Rice
Bly, R.   Dawn in Threshing Time.
Komunyakaa.   Buried Light.
Oliver, M.   Rice.

**Richard I (Richard Coeur de Lion), King of
England**
Chaucer.   Lak of Stedfastnesse.
Meredith, G.   Richard Lionheart.

Richard II, King of England
Lowell, R.   Coleridge and Richard II.

Richard III, King of England
Lowell, R.   Bosworth Field.

Richardson, Samuel
Cowper, W.   Ode on *Sir Charles Grandison.*

Riches
See **Wealth**

Riddles
Beckett, S.   Tailpiece.
Bourne, V.   Ænigma, An.
   Manual, A.
Bowdoin, J.   Rebus, by *I. B.*, A.
Cowper, W.   Riddle: "I am just two and two, I
   am warm, I am cold."
De la Mare.   Riddle, A.
Riddlers, The.
Dickinson, E.   Riddle we can guess, The.
Snake, The.
Hayden, R.   Sphinx.
Heaney, S.   Riddle, The.
Jarrell, R.   What's the Riddle.
Lindsay, N.   Two Old Crows.
MacLeish.   What Riddle Asked the Sphinx.
MacNeice.   Riddle, The.
Meredith, G.   Riddle for Men, The.
Muldoon, P.   Rune.
Nash, O.   Unanswered by Request.
Poe.   Valentine, A.
Riley, J.   Home-made Riddles.
Robinson, E.   How Annandale Went Out.
Rossetti, C.   Charades.
New Enigmas.
Peacock has a score of eyes, The.
Pin Has a Head, A.
Riddle, A: "There is one that has a head without
   an eye."
Sandburg, C.   Riddles and Whims.
Sheridan, T.   Riddle, A: "Because I am by
   nature blind."
To Dean Swift.
To the Dean.
Simic.   Solving the Riddle.
Swift, J.   Answer to Delany's Riddle, The.
Probatur Aliter.
Riddling Letter, A.
Wheatley, P.   Answer to the *Rebus*, by the
   Author of These Poems, An.
Wilbur, R.   Eight Riddles from Symphosius.
Riddle, A.
Some Riddles from Symphosius.
Two Riddles from Aldhelm.

Rifles
Ciardi, J.   .22.
Hall, D.   Merle Bascom's .22.
Kipling, R.   Brown Bess.
Lux.   Kalashnikov.
Orr, G.   Moment, A.
Sandburg, C.   A. E. F.

Righteousness
Ciardi, J.   Thought about Sheik Bedreddin, A.
Cummings, E. E.   World is very big, and we,
   The.
Davie, D.   Saw I Never the Righteous Forsaken.
Their Rectitude Their Beauty.
Woe unto Thee!
Lindsay, N.   Galahad, Knight Who Perished.
Statue of Old Andrew Jackson, The.
Meredith, G.   Blest is the sword that leaps from
   sheath.
Pope, A.   Version of the First Psalm, for the Use
   of a Young Lady, A.
Ralegh, S.   Lie, The.
Rossetti, C.   Escape to the Mountain.
I have done with hope.

Riley, James Whitcomb
Bierce.   Literary Method, A.
Dunbar, P.   James Whitcomb Riley.
Kipling, R.   To James Whitcomb Riley.

Rilke, Rainer Maria
Dugan, A.   Answer to the Rilke Question.
Eberhart, R.   Portrait of Rilke.
Levertov.   To Rilke.
Levi, P.   After R.M. Rilke.
Logan, J.   Homage to Rainer Maria Rilke.
Lux.   Rilke and Lou.
MacDiarmid, H.   Seamless Garment, The.
MacLeish.   Infinite Reason, The.
Merton.   Rilke's Epitaph.
Nemerov.   On Reading "The Love and Death of
   Cornet Christopher Rilke."
O'Hara, F.   Poem: "To be idiomatic in a
   vacuum."
Rich, A.   After a Sentence in "Malte Laurids
   Brigge."
Paula Becker to Clara Westhoff.

Rimbaud, Arthur
Auden.   Rimbaud.
Ferlinghetti, L.   Sweet and various the woodlark.
Logan, J.   Lines to Catherine.
Lives of the Poet, The.
MacLeish.   Aeterna Poetae Memoria.
Against Illuminations.
Montale.   For an "Homage to Rimbaud."
Olson, C.   Put him this way.
Schuyler, J.   Fauré Ballade, The.

Rings
Amichai [*or* Amikhai].   Now She's Breathing.
Crabbe, G.   On Receiving from a Lady a Present
   of a Ring.
Cummings, E. E.   Girl's Ring, A.
Donne.   Jet Ring Sent, A.
Eberhart, R.   Oak, The.
García Lorca.   Lizard Is Crying, The.
Graves, R.   Golden Anchor.
Song: Three Rings for Her.
St Antony of Padua.
With a Gift of Rings.
Herrick.   Jimmall Ring, or True-Love-Knot,
   The.
Ring Presented to Julia, A.
Levertov.   Wedding-Ring.
Rossetti, C.   Ring upon her finger, / Walks the
   bride, A.
Sexton.   Wedding Ring Dance, The.
Shapiro, K.   New Ring, The.

Riots and Rioters
Ai.   Riot Act, April 29, 1992.
Angelou.   Riot: 60's.
Cowper, W.   Address to the Mob, An.
On the Burning of Lord Mansfield's Library.
On the Same.
Creeley.   Barcelona: February 13, 1977.
Hughes, L.   Ballad of Margie Polite, The.
Beaumont to Detroit: 1943.
Melville, H.   House-Top, The.
Piercy.   Curse of the Earth Magician on a Metal

Land.
Rexroth, K.   Again at Waldheim.
Very.   Destruction of Public Property by Mobs, The.
Williams, M.   Aesthetic Distance.

Risorgimento
Whittier.   Dream of Pio Nono, The.
From Perugia.
Italy.
Prisoners of Naples, The.
To Pius IX.

Rituals
Atwood.   Some Objects of Wood and Stone.
Carew, T.   New Year's Sacrifice: To Lucinda, A.
To the King, at His Entrance into Saxham: By Master John Crofts.
Ciardi, J.   Glory, The.
Codrescu.   Talismanic Ceremony for Lucian, March 9, 1971, Intersection Church, San Francisco.
Crane, S.   On the desert.
Davie, D.   Energies.
Dickey, W.   Pruned Roses, The.
Dugan, A.   On Being Easy in the Ritual of Separation.
Eberhart, R.   Lorca.
Hall, D.   Eating the Pig.
Herrick.   Another New-Yeeres Gift, or Song for the Circumcision.
Frankincense, The.
New-Yeeres Gift, or Circumcisions Song, Sung to the King in the Presence at White Hall, The.
Perfume, The.
Spell, The.
Steam in Sacrifice.
Sweetnesse in Sacrifice.
To Julia.
To Julia, the Flaminica Dialis, or Queen-Priest.
To the Reverend Shade of His Religious Father.
Ignatow, D.   Ritual One.
Komunyakaa.   Memory Cave.
Laughlin, J.   At Eleusis.
Saeta.
Lawrence, D. H.   Bells.
McGrath, T.   Reading the Names of the Vietnam War Dead.
Merton.   Seven Archaic Images.
There is a little ceremony to be performed.
Milosz, C.   Plato's Dialogues.
Olson, C.   Morning News, The.
Pinsky.   Pilgrimage.
Ransom, J.   First Travels of Max.
Ritsos.   Liturgical.
Night Ritual.
Rukeyser, M.   Three Black Women.
Snyder, G.   Uluru Wild Fig Song.
Stafford, W.   Ceremony, A: Doing the Needful.
Sze.   Great White Shark, The.
Tsankawi.
Tomlinson, C.   Cochiti.
Harvest Festival: at Ozleworth.
On a Mexican Straw Christ.
Very.   My Meat and Drink.
Whittier.   Dead Feast of the Kol-Folk, The.
Funeral Tree of the Sokokis.
Williams, M.   Glass Darkly, A.
Rituals.
Yeats.   Collarbone [or Collar-Bone] of a Hare, The.

Rivalry
Bukowski.   Who in the Hell is Tom Jones?
Burns, R.   Auld Rob Morris.
Dean of Faculty—a New Ballad, The.
Epistle to Robt. Graham Esq: of Fintry on the Election for the Dumfries String of Boroughs, Anno 1790.
Carew, T.   Fly That Flew into My Mistress'[s] Eye, A.
To My Rival.
Truce in Love Intreated.
Collins, B.   Rival Poet, The.
Creeley.   Carnival, The.
Emerson, R.   By the unacknowledged tie.
Jackson, L.   And I.
Kipling, R.   Cain and Abel.

Melville, H.   Battle of Stone River, Tennessee.
Meredith, G.   Archduchess Anne.
Internal Harmony.
Nemerov.   Deposition, The.
Petrarch.   I saw a lady; on each side a lover.
Pound, E.   Marvoil.
Stock, R.   Man-Giraffe.
Sigismundo Malatesta Brings His Favorite Philosopher's Bones to Italy.
Suckling, S.   My dearest rival, lest [or least] our love.
To His Rival.
Upon Two Sisters.
Unknown.   Rivals, The.
Williams, C. K.   Hood.
See also **Competition**

Rivera, Diego
Dubie.   Trolley from Xochimilco, The.

Rivers
Ammons.   River.
Auden.   River Profile.
Beckett, S.   Fleuves et océans.
Berry, W.   Heron, The.
March 22, 1968.
March Snow.
Observance.
Porch over the River, The.
River Bridged and Forgot, The.
Slip, The.
Bishop, E.   One Art.
Santarém.
Bly, R.   Schoolcraft's Diary Written on the Missouri: 1830.
Borges.   Ars Poetica.
Broumas, O.   Absence of Noise Presence of Sound.
Oregon Landscape with Lost Lover.
Roadside.
Browning, E.   Romance of the Ganges, A.
Sounds.
Bukowski.   I Was Born to Hustle Roses Down the Avenues of the Dead.
Burns, R.   Banks of Nith, The.
Banks of the Devon, The.
Flow Gently, Sweet Afton.
Fragment, A: "One night as I did wander."
Jessie—A New Scots Song.
Written with a Pencil, Standing by the Fall of Fyers, near Loch-Ness.
Byron, L.   Stanzas to the Po.
Campion, T.   Fire, fire, fire, fire!
Carew, T.   To My Mistress Sitting by a River's Side; an Eddy.
Carruth, H.   In Russia.
Carver, R.   Downstream.
Night Dampness.
River, The.
Where Water Comes Together with Other Water.
Woman Bathing.
Ciardi, J.   Mystic River.
Clifton, L.   Poem in Praise of Menstruation.
Clough.   From thy far sources 'mid mountains airily climbing.
Coleridge, S.   Sonnet to the River Otter.
Cooper, J.   Morning on the St. John's.
River in All Lights, from an Upstairs Window, The.
Cowper, W.   Comparison, A.
Crane, H.   Repose of Rivers.
Creeley.   Memory, The.
Davie, D.   Evening on the Boyne.
Green River.
Late Anniversary, A.
Ox-bow.
De la Mare.   Voices.
Dickinson, E.   I like to see it lap the Miles.
Dove, R.   Event, The.
In the Bulrush.
Dugan, A.   Advertising in Paris.
Dunbar, P.   On the River.
Duncan, R.   Source.
Eberhart, R.   Hatred of the Old River.
La Crosse at Ninety Miles an Hour.
Lost Children, The.
Parker River, The.
Emerson, R.   Far seen the river glides below.

Musketaquid.
Two Rivers.
Ferlinghetti, L.   Hilarious God.
Reading Apollinaire by the Rogue River.
River Still To Be Found, A.
Frost, R.   Too Anxious for Rivers.
Gallagher, T.   Reading Aloud.
García Lorca.   Ballad of the Three Rivers.
Death of Antonito el Camborio, The.
Nocturne of the Drowned Youth.
Saint Raphael (Córdoba).
Gurney, I.   Water Colours.
"H. D."   Pursuit.
Wash of cold river.
Hacker, M.   Going Back to the River.
Hall, D.   Long River, The.
Photographs of China.
Hardy, T.   On Sturminster Foot-Bridge.
Heaney, S.   Broagh.
New Song, A.
Toome.
Undine.
Herrick.   Another upon Her Weeping.
Proof to No Purpose.
To Dean-bourn, a Rude River in Devon, by Which Sometimes He Lived.
Hughes, L.   Bitter River, The.
Negro Speaks of Rivers, The.
Reverie on the Harlem River.
Suicide's Note.
Wide River.
Hughes, T.   Cormorant, A.
Eel, An.
Gulkana, The.
Japanese River Tales.
Low Water.
Match, A.
Milesian Encounter on the Sligachan.
Performance.
River.
River in March, The.
Salmon Eggs.
Stealing Trout on a May Morning.
Jeffers, R.   Heavy and yellow with the clay wrack from the flooded valley.
Johnson, S.   In Rivum a Mola Stoana Lichfeldiæ Diffluentem.
Translation of the Beginning of *Rio Verde.*
Kinnell.   River That Is East, The.
Kinsella, T.   Tao and Unfitness at Inistiogue on the River Nore.
Kipling, R.   Ford o' Kabul River.
Kizer, C.   By the Riverside.
Komunyakaa.   Confluence.
Kunitz, S.   King of the River.
Larkin, P.   Thaw.
Laughlin, J.   Holy Rivers, The.
Lawrence, D. H.   Kiss, A.
Man at Play on the River, A.
River Roses.
Levertov.   Eros at Temple Stream.
Music, A.
Levine, P.   Noon.
Renaming the Kings.
Lux.   River Between the Train and the Highway, The.
River That Scolds at All the Other Rivers, The.
Winter River.
MacLeish.   What Any Lover Learns.
McGrath, T.   Beyond the Red River.
Edge of the River, The.
History.
Return to Marsh Street.
Melville, H.   Muster, The.
Meredith, G.   By the Passeyr.
Pictures of the Rhine.
Rhine-Land.
Song: "I would I were the drop of rain."
There is for me no sweeter holiday.
Meredith, W.   At the Confluence of the Colorado and the Little Colorado.
Ideogram.
Winter on the River.
Merrill, J.   Current, The.
River Poem.
Merwin.   High Water.

Inscription for a Burned Bridge.
Lackawanna.
Oars, The.
Sound of Rapids of Laramie River in Late
  August.
Way to the River, The.
Milosz, C. Rivers ("So lasting they are, the
  rivers!" Only think. Sources somewhere in the
  mountains").
Mistral, G. Argentine Round.
Montale. Bibe a Ponte all'Asse.
Boats on the Marne.
Near Capua.
You've named a tree for me? It isn't nothing.
Muldoon, P. Clonfeacle.
Nemerov. Dead River.
Niedecker. Along the river / wild sunflowers.
In moonlight lies.
River-marsh-drowse.
Oliver, M. Snowshoe Hare, The.
Olson, C. There Is No River Which Is Called
  Lethe.
Oppen. Coastal Strip.
Travelogue.
Orr, G. Elegy: "Not only doesn't the Ohio."
River, The.
Paley, G. On the Bank Street Pier.
Patchen. Anna Karenina and the Love-sick
  River.
Petrarch. Not the Ticino, Arno, Varo, Tiber.
Po, you are quick to take my outer shell.
Rushing river, forcing your rapid way.
Piercy. Let Us Gather at the River.
Plath. Lorelei.
Poe. To the River ——.
Pope, A. River, The.
Prunty. Letter.
Poem, The: "Gnarled avenues the years have
  mapped."
Rio.
Ramanujan. River, A.
Rexroth, K. Okeanos and the Golden Sickle.
Rich, A. Concord River.
Riley, J. Down around the River.
With the Current.
Rimbaud, A. Blackcurrant River.
Tear.
Roethke. Long Alley, The.
River Incident.
Rossetti, C. River Thames (?).
Rose, The.
Whitsun Monday.
Rukeyser, M. Dam, The.
Gullies as deep as halls held these surveyors.
Rock Flow, River Mix.
Rumi. Gift of Water, The.
Sandburg, C. Chromo.
Cornfield Ridge and Stream.
Letter S.
On a Railroad Right of Way.
Prairie Woodland.
River Moons.
River Roads.
They Ask Each Other Where They Came From.
Smith, S. Friends of the River Trent.
River Deben, The.
River God, The.
River Humber, The.
Snyder, G. River in the Valley.
Stafford, W. Ask Me.
At Cove on the Crooked River.
By a River in the Osage Country.
Ceremony.
Climbing along the River.
Cottonwood.
In Hurricane Canyon.
In the Deep Channel.
Looking across the River.
People of the South Wind.
Prairie Town.
Stevens, W. Metaphor as Degeneration.
River of Rivers in Connecticut, The.
This Solitude of Cataracts.
Swenson, M. Above the Arno.
Little Rapids, The.
Szymborska, W. In Heraclitus' River.

Tate, J. River's Story.
Thoreau. Assabet, The.
Far oer The bow.
Freshet, The.
I was born upon thy bank, river.
Voyagers Song.
Tomlinson, C. Below Tintern.
Hacienda.
Race, The.
Severnside.
Tu Fu. Déjeuner sur l'herbe.
Very. Naumkeck River.
North River.
River, The.
South River at Sunset, The.
Whitman, W. As Consequent, Etc.
Crossing Brooklyn Ferry.
Whittier. June on the Merrimac.
Merrimac, The.
Mystery, A.
Our River.
R. S. S., at Deer Island on the Merrimac.
Red River Voyageur, The.
River Path, The.
To G. G.
Vale of the Merrimac, The.
Wilbur, R. Aspen and the Stream, The.
Glance from the Bridge, A.
Problem from Milton, A.
Puritans, The.
Shad-Time.
Williams, C. K. Sky, Water.
Williams, W. Flowing River, A.
Mind Hesitant, The.
Mists Over the River.
River Rhyme.
River Rhyme II.
Sluggishly.
Wilner, E. Middle-Class Vantage.
Wordsworth, W. Avon, The.
Composed upon Westminster Bridge, September
  3, 1802.
Dear native brooks, your ways I have pursued.
Wright, C. Appalachian Book of the Dead 4,
  The,
Looking Outside the Cabin Window, I
  Remember a Line by Li Po.
Wright, J. Living by the Red River.
Morning Hymn to a Dark Girl.
RIP.
To the Poets in New York.
Zagajewski. Blackened River, The.
On Swimming.
River, A.
Zaturenska. Flowing of the River, The.
Zukofsky, L. World autumn, The.

See also **Brooks and Streams**

Roaches
Merwin. Standing Nowhere.

See also **Cockroaches**

Roads
Blue Cloud. Road 37C.
Bly, R. Three Kinds of Pleasures.
Broumas, O. Blockade.
Roadside.
Burns, R. Epigram on Rough Roads.
Cavafy. Ode and Elegy of the Roads.
Chesterton. Rolling English Road, The.
Creeley. Poem for Bob Leed.
Traveller, The.
Dickey, J. Craters.
Dickinson, E. Little Road—not made of Man,
  A.
Dove, R. Corduroy Road.
Early Morning on the Tel Aviv-Haifa Freeway.
Drummond de Andrade. In the Middle of the
  Road.
Dugan, A. Memory of Old Forms under Hell's
  Angels.
Dunbar, P. On the Road.
Riding to Town.
Roadway, A.
To the Road.
Frost, R. Middleness of the Road, The.
Road Not Taken, The.
García Lorca. Road, The.

Han-shan. Cold Mountain Road is strange, The.
Who takes the Cold Mountain Road.
Hardy, T. By Henstridge Cross at the Year's
  End.
Roman Road, The.
Weary Walker, The.
Hughes, L. Bound No'th Blues.
Florida Road Workers.
Kinnell. Road Between Here and There, The.
Kipling, R. Fox-Hunting.
Song of French Roads, A.
Way Through The Woods, The.
Larkin, P. No Road.
Laughlin, J. Danger / Road under Repair.
Lawrence, D. H. On the Road.
Levertov. Merritt Parkway.
Lux. Black Road Over Which Green Trees
  Grow.
MacLeish. Companions.
McGrath, T. Winter Roads.
Merwin. Road.
Nash, O. I'll Take the High Road Commission.
Song of the Open Road.
Patchen. Appian Way, The.
Rilke. Fugitives, The
Rimbaud, A. Ruts.
Stock, R. Unmapped Road.
Thoreau. Old Marlborough Road, The.
Tomlinson, C. Arizona Highway.
Bridges.
Question, The.
Williams, C. K. I know / nothing anymore.
Williams, W. Autumn.
Wordsworth, W. Massy Ways Carried across
  These Heights, The.
Road extended o'er a heath, The.
Wright, C. Lonesome Pine Special.

See also **Streets**

"Rob Roy" (Robert MacGregor, Scottish hero)
Wordsworth, W. Rob Roy's Grave.

Robbers
Ai. Interview with a Policeman.

See also **Crime and Criminals**

Robert I [*or* Robert the Bruce], King of Scotland
Burns, R. Scots Wha Hae.

Robeson, Paul
Hayden, R. Homage to Paul Robeson.

Robespierre, Maximilien Marie Isidore
Lowell, R. Robespierre and Mozart as Stage.

Robin Hood
Davie, D. Nottinghamshire.
Keats. Robin Hood.

Robins
Bourne, V. Invitation to the Redbreast.
Ciardi, J. This Moving Meaninglessness.
Cowper, W. Epitaph on a Free but Tame
  Redbreast.
Cummings, E. E. Christ but they're few.
Sentinel robins two / guard me and you.
De la Mare. Robin, A.
Dickinson, E. Come show thy Durham Breast.
I knew a Bird that would sing as firm.
I raise only robins on my farm.
Quite empty, quite at rest.
Robin.
Robin for the Crumb, The.
Robin is the One, The.
"Robins?" They are writing now, The.
Hardy, T. Robin, The.
Herrick. To Robin Redbreast.
To the Nightingale, and Robin-Red-Brest.
Upon Mistress Elizabeth Wheeler under the
  Name of Amarillis.
Hughes, T. Robin Song.
Keats. Song: "Stay, ruby-breasted warbler,
  stay."
Kunitz, S. Robin Redbreast.
Melville, H. Little Good Fellows, The.
Meredith, G. To Robin Redbreast.
Merwin. Robin.
Nash, O. Who Called That Robin a Piccolo
  Player?
Niedecker. Easter.
Riley, J. Robins' Other Name, The.
Rossetti, C. Bread and Milk for Breakfast.

I am a King, / Or an Emperor rather.
Key-Note, The.
Wrens and robins in the hedge.
Very. Invitation to the Robin.
Robin, The.
Robin's Song, The.
Whittier. How the Robin Came.
Robin, The.
Wordsworth, W. I know an aged Man
  constrained to dwell.
Redbreast Chasing the Butterfly, The.
Redbreast, The [Suggested in a Westmoreland
  Cottage].

Robinson Crusoe
Bishop, E. Crusoe in England.
Borges. Alexander Selkirk.
Brodsky, J. Robinsonade.
Drummond de Andrade. Infancy.
Jarrell, R. Island, The.
Pagis. Epilogue to Robinson Crusoe.
Walcott. Crusoe's Island.

Robots
Dickey, W. Androids.
Jonson, B. On the New Motion.

Rochester, John Wilmot, 2d Earl of
Pope, A. Verses Left by Mr. Pope, on His Lying
  in the Same Bed which Wilmot, the Celebrated
  Earl of Rochester, Slept in, at Adderbury, then
  Belonging to the Duke of Argyle, July 9th,
  1739.

Rock and Roll
Ginsberg, A. Punk Rock Your My Big Crybaby.
Meredith, W. Music.
Muldoon, P. Sleeve Notes.

Rockefeller Center, New York City
Schuyler, J. December.

Rockefeller, John Davison
Bierce. Compliance.

Rockets
Clampitt. Discovery.
Dubie. Simple Philo of Alexandria.
Ignatow, D. Rockets, The.
Niedecker. Beautiful girl.
Stafford, W. Our City Is Guarded by Automatic
  Rockets.
See also **Space and Space Travel**

Rocking Chairs
Bishop, E. Sunday at Key West.
Hall, D. Rocker, The.

Rocks
Kinsella, T. St Paul's Rocks: 16 February 1832.
Kunitz, S. Between Me and the Rock.
McHugh, H. Fast.
Tomlinson, C. Above the Rio Grande.
Warren, R. Globe of Gneiss.
See also **Stones and Rocks**

Rocky Mountains
Lawrence, D. H. Beyond the Rockies.

Rodin, Auguste
Dubie. Parallax Monograph for Rodin, The.
Hall, D. Notes For Nobody.
Whalen, P. Homage to Rodin.
Williams, M. Rodin: The Cathedral.

Roethke, Theodore
Ciardi, J. Was a Man.
Cooper, J. Starting with a Line from Roethke.
Davie, D. July, 1964.

Roland
Lowell, R. Death of Count Roland.
MacLeish. Too-Late Born, The.

Roller-Coasters
Kinnell. Fire in Luna Park.

Roller Skating and Roller Skaters
Riley, J. Impromptu on Roller Skates, An.
See also **Skunks**

Roman Catholicism
Rimbaud, A. Sealed Lips. Seen in Rome.
See also **Catholicism and Catholics**

Romania
Codrescu. School Daze.

Romanticism and Romantics
Bogan, L. Romantic, The.
Browning, E. Romaunt of Margret, The.

Bukowski. Spain Sits Like a Hidden Flower in
  My Coffeepot.
Carruth, H. Two Romantic Pieces.
Carver, R. Romanticism.
  Squall, A.
Cummings, E. E. Let's live suddenly without
  thinking.
Davie, D. Derbyshire.
De la Mare. Mercutio.
Jarrell, R. English Garden in Austria, An.
MacNeice. All Over Again.
Ramanujan. Elegy: "Grown son's tears in a
  restaurant mix their salt, A."
Robinson, E. Miniver Cheevy.
Tate, A. To a Romantic.
To a Romantic Novelist.
To the Romantic Traditionists.

Rome, Italy
Alberti. From empty windows / Voice of dead
  eyes.
Nights belong to / What hurts.
Other night I saw... / Who did I see?, The.
Take, O take the key of Rome.
You did not come to Rome to dream.
Amichai [*or* Amikhai]. Three Times I Came to
  Rome.
Bierce. Inauspiciously.
Brodsky, J. Bust of Tiberius, The.
Letters to a Roman Friend.
Porta San Pancrazio.
Roman Elegies.
Via Funari.
Browning, E. View Across the Roman
  Campagna.
Browning, R. Protus.
Two in the Campagna.
Buchanan, G. Rome conquered earth with arms,
  the sea with ships.
Bukowski. Anthony.
Carruth, H. Eternal City.
Castiglione. On the Statue of *Cleopatra*, Made
  into a Fountain by *Leo* the Tenth.
Cavafy. Displeased Viewer, A.
  Waiting for the Barbarians.
Ciardi, J. Apartment with a View, An.
  Roman Diary: 1951.
  S.P.Q.R. A Letter from Rome.
Clough. Amours de Voyage.
Cooper, J. Roman Dream.
Cowper, W. Boadicea: An Ode.
Cummings, E. E. I met a man under the moon.
Du Bellay. Rome.
  Ruins of Rome.
Emerson, R. Alone in Rome! Why Rome is
  lonely too.
  Ancient lady who dwelt in Rome, An.
  Poem on Eloquence by R. W. Emerson.
Ferlinghetti, L. Roman Morn.
García Lorca. Cry to Rome.
Graves, R. Cuirassiers of the Frontier, The.
Gunn, T. Silver Age, The.
Gurney, I. Bare Line of the Hill, The.
Hardy, T. Rome: At the Pyramid of Cestius near
  the Graves of Shelley and Keats.
Rome: Building a New Street in the Ancient
  Quarter.
Rome: On the Palatine.
Jarrell, R. Lament of the Children of Israel in
  Rome.
Jonson, B. To My Chosen Friend the Learnèd
  Translator of Lucan, Thomas May, Esquire.
To Sir Henry [*or* Henrie] Savile [upon His
  Translation of Tacitus].
To the Same; on the Same.
Kinsella, T. O Rome.
Kipling, R. Roman Centurion's Song, The.
  Romulus and Remus.
Kunitz, S. Thief, The.
Laughlin, J. Rome: In the Café.
Lowell, R. Cicero, the Sacrificial Killing.
  Marcus Cato 95–42 B.C.
  Marcus Cato 234–149 B.C.
Mahon. Roman Script.
Marvell. Flecknoe, an English Priest at Rome.
Milosz, C. Caffé Greco.
  Campo dei Fiori.

"Panormitanus." Rome.
Pasolini. Ashes of Gramsci, The.
  Religion of My Time, The.
  Tears of the Excavator, The.
Patchen. Appian Way, The.
Petrarch. Merely to look upon your sacred City.
  Noble spirit, the ruler of that body.
  Seed of Charlemagne, his noble head, The.
Piercy. Track of the Master Builder, The.
Ritsos. Vatican Museum.
Rossetti, C. True Story, A.
Rukeyser, M. Lost Romans, The.
Shapiro, K. Room in Rome, A.
Shelley, P. Fragment: A Roman's Chamber.
  Fragment: Rome and Nature.
Sisson. Carmen Saeculare.
Spenser, E. Ruines of Time, The.
Stevens, W. To an Old Philosopher in Rome.
Tomlinson, C. Down From Colonnata.
  In the Borghese Gardens.
  To Vasko Popa In Rome.
Wilbur, R. Baroque Wall-Fountain in the Villa
  Sciarra, A.
  For the New Railway Station in Rome.
  Piazza di Spagna, Early Morning.
Wilde, O. Rome Unvisited.
  Urbs Sacra Æterna.
Williams, M. 10,000-Year-Old Tree Discovered
  Shades Two and Half Acres.
  Aesthetic Distance.
  Evening: A Studio in Rome.
  Lost in Ladispoli.
Wordsworth, W. Eagle and the Dove, The.
  Roman Antiquities.
  Roman Antiquities Discovered at Bishopstone,
  Hereforshire.
  Sonnet: "Why should we weep or mourn,
  Angelic boy."
Wright, C. Roma I.
  Roma II.

Romeo and Juliet
Davie, D. Bride of Reason, The.
Hughes, L. Juliet.
Kumin, M. Purgatory.
Laughlin, J. Cultural Note.

Ronsard, Pierre de
Davie, D. Garland for Ronsard, A.

Roofing and Roofers
Berry, W. New Roof, The.
Bukowski. 2 Outside, As Bones Break in My
  Kitchen.
Heaney, S. Thatcher.
Levine, P. Roofs.
Rich, A. Roofwalker, The.
Roethke. Ceiling, The.
Williams, C. K. Tar.
Williams, W. Fine Work with Pitch and Copper.

Rooks
Mahon. Birdlife.
Plath. Black Rook in Rainy Weather.
  Prospect.

Rooming Houses
Cavafy. One Night.
See also **Boarding Houses**

Roosevelt, Franklin Delano
Hughes, L. Ballad of Roosevelt.
  Dear Mr. President.
  Message to the President.
Jeffers, R. Wilson in Hell.
Kizer, C. Anniversaries: Claremont Avenue,
  from 1945.
Laughlin, J. Confidential Report.
Rukeyser, M. Slow Dialogue between Pain and
  Roosevelt.
Sandburg, C. When Death Came April Twelve
  1945.
Williams, W. Death by Radio.

Roosevelt, Theodore
Bierce. After Portsmouth.
"Dario." To Roosevelt.
Dunbar, P. For Theodore Roosevelt.
Hall, D. President and Poet.
Kipling, R. Great-Heart.
Lindsay, N. In Which Roosevelt Is Compared to
  Saul.

Roosevelt.
Robinson, E.   Revealer, The.

Roosters

Bishop, E.   Roosters.
Burns, R.   To Alexander Findlater.
Ciardi, J.   Come Morning.
Dickey, J.   Gamecock.
Graves, R.   Cock in Pullet's Feathers.
Hall, D.   Henyard Round, The.
Herrick.   Cock-Crow.
Hughes, T.   Cock-Crows.
Meredith, G.   Prestige.
Nash, O.   Rooster, The.
Piercy.   Valley Where I Don't Belong, A.
Rossetti, C.   "Kookoorookoo! kookoorookoo!" /
   Crows the cock before the morn.
Smart, C.   Story of a Cock and a Bull, A.
Smith, S.   Cock-a-Doo.
Stafford, W.   At the Old Place.
Stevens, W.   Bantams in Pine-Woods.
Tate, J.   Rooster.
See also **Chickens**

Rope

Komunyakaa.   How I See Things.
Longfellow, H.   Ropewalk, The.
Nemerov.   Rope's End, The.

Rosa, Salvator

Milosz, C.   O! ("O the quiet of water under the
   rocks, and the yellow silence of the
   afternoon").

Rosary

Browning, E.   Lay of the Brown Rosary, The.
Smith, S.   Violent Hand, The.

Rosenberg, Julius and Ethel

Dubie.   Amen.

Roses

Amichai [*or* Amikhai].   Rosebush Hangs over
   the Wall, A.
Apollinaire.   Annie.
Ashbery, J.   White Roses.
Bishop, E.   Faustina, or Rock Roses.
Bly, R.   Bouquet of Ten Roses, A.
Borges.   Rose and Milton, A.
   Yellow Rose, A.
Brontë, E.   Love and Friendship.
Browning, E.   Dead Rose, A.
   Lay of the Early Rose, A.
Browning, R.   Women and Roses.
Bukowski.   Destroying Beauty.
Burns, R.   Banks o' Doon, The ("Ye banks and
   braes o' bonie [*or* bonnie] Doon").
   Red, Red Rose, A.
   Rosebud, The.
Byron, G.   Translation from Anacreon.
Carew, T.   On a Damask[e] Rose, Sticking upon
   a Lady's Breast.
   Red and White Roses.
Carver, R.   Cherish.
Celan.   Psalm: "No one kneads us again out of
   earth and clay."
Ciardi, J.   On the Patio.
Clampitt.   Antiphonal.
Cowper, W.   Lily and the Rose, The.
   Rose, The.
   To Gravina.
Creeley.   Question, The.
   Rose, The.
   Sanine to Leda.
Cummings, E. E.   &(all during the / dropsin).
   Dedication: "White rose my soul, The."
   Every one of the red roses opened.
   Rose / is dying the, The.
   These from my mother's greatgrandmother's
     rosebush white.
   Un(bee)mo / vi / n(in)g.
De la Mare.   Epitaph, An: "Last, Stone, a little
   yet."
   Rose in Candlelight, A.
   Rose in Water, A.
Dickey, J.   Deborah as Scion.
Dickinson, E.   Bird must sing to earn the
   Crumb, The.
   Essential oils—are wrung.
   Full fed Rose on meals of Tint, A.
   Go not too near a House of Rose.

If I should cease to bring a Rose.
Many can boast a hollyhock.
Nobody knows this little Rose.
Where Roses would not dare to go.
Dugan, A.   Poem: "Flowering balls!"
Dunbar, P.   Fulfilment.
   Poor Withered Rose.
   Promise.
   Roses.
   Roses and Pearls.
   She Gave Me a Rose.
   Summer in the South.
Eliot, T. S.   Dedication to My Wife, A.
Emerson, R.   By kinds I keep my kinds in
   check.
   God only knew how Saadi dined.
Frost, R.   Rose Family, The.
Glück, L.   Brennende Liebe.
Graves, R.   Florist Rose, The.
   Rose, The.
   Song: Sword and Rose.
   Song: To a Rose.
"H. D."   Garden.
   Sea Rose.
   White Rose.
Hall, D.   Old Roses.
Hamill, S.   With the Gift of a Nootka Rose.
Hardy, T.   Fading Rose, The.
   If You Had Known.
   Spell of the Rose, The.
Herbert, G.   Rose, The.
Herrick.   Funeral[l] Rites of the Rose, The.
   How Roses Came Red.
   Meditation for His Mistress[e], A.
   Parliament of Roses to Julia, The.
   Rosarie, The.
   Showre of Roses, The.
   To Roses in Julia's Bosome.
   Upon a Virgin Kissing a Rose.
   Upon Her Blush.
   Upon One Lillie, Who Marryed with a Maid
     Call'd Rose.
   Upon Roses.
   Upon the Roses in Julias Bosome.
   Vow to Venus, A.
Hopkins, G.   All as that moth call'd Underwing,
   alighted.
Hughes, L.   Breath of a Rose.
Keats.   To a Friend Who Sent Me Some Roses.
Kipling, R.   Answer, The.
Laughlin, J.   Among the Roses.
Lawrence, D. H.   All of Roses.
   Cabbage-Roses.
   Gloire de Dijon.
   Grapes.
   Guelder Roses.
   I Am like a Rose.
   Love Storm.
   Married in June.
   Prophet in the Rose Garden, The.
   River Roses.
   Rose Is Not a Cabbage, A.
   Rose of All the World.
   Rose of England, The.
   Roses.
   Roses on the Breakfast Table.
   Song-Day in Autumn.
Levine, P.   One for the Rose.
Lindsay, N.   Rose of Midnight, The.
   Wedding of the Rose and the Lotus, The.
   With a Rose, to Brunhilde.
MacDiarmid, H.   Little White Rose, The.
Mallarmé.   Fan, A; of Méry Laurent.
McHugh, H.   After Rilke.
   White Mind and Roses.
Melville, H.   Rosary Beads.
Meredith, G.   Wild Rose, The.
   Young Usurper, The.
Merton.   Rilke's Epitaph.
Millay, E.   Hardy Garden, The.
Mistral, G.   Prison Sentence, The.
   Rose, The.
Neruda.   Herbalist's Rose, The.
Oliver, M.   Roses.
Paley, G.   Bee! / drowning in, A.
Parker, D.   One Perfect Rose.

Rondeau: "Give me a rose, cool-petaled, virgin
   white."
Patchen.   As Frothing Wounds of Roses.
   Roses of Life, The.
   Who Walks There?
Pessoa.   I the roses love in the gardens of
   Adonis.
Petrarch.   Two blushing roses, gathered recently.
Pound, E.   Rosa Sempiterna.
Raine, K.   Dream of Roses, A.
   Petal of white rose.
   Rose.
Riley, J.   Old-Fashioned Roses.
   Rose, The.
   Rose-Lady, The.
   Sermon of the Rose, The.
Rilke.   Rose.
   Rose on Sunday.
Robinson, E.   Garden, The.
Rossetti, C.   Brandons Both.
   Comparisons.
   Floral Teaching.
   I have but one rose in the world.
   Lily has a smooth stalk, / Will never hurt your
     hand, The.
   Lily has an air, / And the snowdrop a grace,
     The.
   Maiden May.
   October Garden, An.
   Queen Rose.
   Rose Plant in Jericho, A.
   Rose that blushes rosy red, The.
   Rose, The.
   Rose with such a bonny blush, The.
   Solitary Rose, The.
   Summer Is Ended.
   Summer Wish, A.
   Where shall I find a white rose blowing?
Rukeyser, M.   Among Grass.
   Fighting for Roses.
Sandburg, C.   Dust.
   Great Hunt, The.
   Little Word, Little White Bird.
   Poems Done on a Late Night Car.
   Public Letter to Emily Dickinson.
   Red and White.
   Rose Bawn.
   Throw Roses.
   Whirls.
Sappho.   Song of the Rose.
Sarton, M.   Lion and the Rose, The.
Schuyler, J.   Horse-Chestnut Trees and Roses.
   Princess Di.
   Rose of Marion, The.
Smith, S.   Broken Heart, The.
   Saint Anthony and the Rose of Life.
Stevens, W.   Bouquet of Roses in Sunlight.
Stock, R.   Rose in Ice.
Stockton, A.   On an Enclosure of Roses in
   Which Is the Grave of Miss Mary Morgan a
   Young Lady of 13 Years of Age Daughter of
   Col Morgan.
Swenson, M.   Couple, A.
Tennyson, A.   Roses on the Terrace, The.
Thoreau.   Rosa Sanguinea, The.
Tomlinson, C.   Fireflies.
   Rose for Janet, A.
   Rose-hips.
Very.   On the Beautiful Roses, in front of the
   Mansion of John Hodges, Esq.
   Rose, The.
   Wild Rose of Plymouth, The.
Whittier.   Winter Roses.
Wilbur, R.   Beautiful Changes, The.
Williams, T.   Liturgy of Roses, A.
   Of Roses.
Williams, W.   Act, The.
   Crimson Cyclamen, The.
   Poem: "Rose fades, The."
   Rewaking, The.
   Rose, The.
   Rosebush in an Unlikely Garden, A.
   To Flossie.
Wordsworth, W.   Waterfall and the Eglantine,
   The.

Yeats.   Lover Tells of the Rose in His Heart,

The.
Secret Rose, The.
To the Rose upon the Rood of Time.
Zaturenska. Winter Rose, The.
Zukofsky, L. Roses.
Starglow.

Rosh Hashanah
Amichai [or Amikhai]. Eve of Rosh Hashanah, The.

Rossetti, Christina Georgina
Logan, J. Homage to Christina Rossetti.
Zaturenska. Homage to Christina Rossetti.

Rothko, Mark
Kunitz, S. Artist, The.

Rousseau, Henri
Ciardi, J. Sleep (by Rousseau), A.
Dubie. Near the Bridge of Saint-Cloud.
Plath. Yadwigha, on a Red Couch, among Lilies.
Swenson, M. Day Like Rousseau's *Dream*, A.

Rousseau, Jean Jacques
Blake, W. Mock On, Mock On, Voltaire, Rousseau.
Davie, D. Rousseau in His Day.
Whittier. Chapel of the Hermits, The.

Rowing and Rowers
Bly, R. After Drinking All Night with a Friend, We Go Out in a Boat at Dawn to See Who Can Write the Best Poem.
Coleridge, S. Water Ballad.
Eberhart, R. Loon Call, A.
Kipling, R. Akbar's Bridge.
Galley-Slave, The.
Lowell, R. Mills of the Kavanaughs, The.
Niedecker. Voyageurs / sang, rowed.
Oppen. Preface, A: "If he goes rowing in the park tho he may row so well that."
Sexton. Rowing.
Rowing Endeth, The.
Smith, S. River Deben, The.
Tomlinson, C. Rower.
Wright, J. On Minding One's Own Business.

Royalty
Angelou. Let's Majeste.
Bierce. Right.
Browning, E. August Voice, An.
Browning, R. Cristina.
Burns, R. Birth-Day Ode. December 31st 1787, A.
Lines on Stirling.
O'er the Water to Charlie.
Scots Ballad.
Carew, T. For a Picture Where a Queen Laments over the Tomb of a Slain Knight.
Cavafy. Alexandrian Kings.
Anna Dalassini.
In Sparta.
Orophernis.
De la Mare. Maerchen.
Dickey, W. Stella Dallas.
Dickinson, E. Mine—by the Right of the White Election!
One dignity delays for all.
Frost, R. How Hard It Is to Keep from Being King When It's in You and in the Situation.
Graves, R. Coronation Murder, The.
Henry and Mary.
Gunn, T. Julian the Apostate.
Han-shan. When Master Tung was young.
Herrick. Dialogue Betwixt Himselfe and Mistresse Eliza: Wheeler, Under the Name of Amarillis, A.
Princes and Favourites.
Ultimus Heroum: or, To the Most Learned, and to the Right Honourable, Henry, Marquesse of Dorchester.
Hopkins, G. Queen's Crowning, The.
Jacobsen, J. Ballad of Henry, Bridegroom.
Keats. Cap and Bells; or, The Jealousies, The.
Otho the Great.
Laughlin, J. Ein Kitzbuehler Tag (1947).
Major, C. We climbed the hill to the carriages.
Meredith, G. 'Tis I have seen the coming man.
Petrarch. Royal nature, and a most refined, A.
Ramanujan. Chess under Trees.

Last of the Princes, The.
Rimbaud, A. Royalty.
Rossetti, C. I am a King, / Or an Emperor rather.
If I Were a Queen.
Royal Princess, A.
Succession of Kings, The.
Rumi. Sexual Urgency, What a Woman's Laughter Can Do, and the Nature of True Virility.
Smith, S. Lord Barrenstock.
Spenser, E. Prosopopoia: or Mother Hubberds Tale.
Updike. Visions of Mackenzie King, The.
Wilde, O. Louis Napoleon.
Wilner, E. Epitaph: "Young then, / we were bored already."
Wordsworth, W. Calais, August, 1802.
Wroth [or Wroath]. Urania.
Yeats. Fallen Majesty.

See also **Kings; Princes and Princesses; Queens**

Rozewicz, Tadeusz
Milosz, C. Rozewicz.
Unde Malum.

Rubens, Peter Paul
Blake, W. I Rubens am a Statesman & a Saint.
Pretty Epigram for [Those] the Entertainment of Those Who [Pay] Have Paid Great Sums in the Venetian & Flemish Ooze, A.
Rafael Sublime Majestic Graceful Wise.
Swelld limbs with no outline that you can descry.
To English Connoisseurs.
Szymborska, W. Rubens' Women.

Ruby, Jack
Ai. Jack Ruby on Ice.
Oppen. Armies of the Plain.

Rugs and Carpets
Merrill, J. Carpet Not Bought, A.
Ritsos. Forged Passport.

Ruins
Ammons. Dropping Eyelids Among the Aerial Ash.
Berry, W. Supplanting, The.
Brodsky, J. Elegy: "About a year has passed. I've returned to the place of battle."
Brontë, E. Old Hall of Elbë, ruined, lonely now.
Browning, R. Love among the Ruins.
Burns, R. Lines on Stirling.
Byron, G. Newstead Abbey.
Carruth, H. Rimrock, Where It Is.
Cummings, E. E. Earth like a tipsy.
Ponder, darling, these busted statues.
Cunningham, J. There is a ghost town of abandoned love.
De la Mare. Corner Stone, The.
Not Only.
Dove, R. Ants of Argos, The.
Nestor's Bathtub.
Sightseeing.
Dubie. Chemin de Fer.
Eberhart, R. Dry Rot, The.
Emerson, R. For fifteen winter days.
Hall, D. Traffic.
Han-shan. I spur my horse past ruins.
HaNagid. Come Up and See the Court.
Jacobsen, J. Interrupted, The.
Kinnell. Ruins under the Stars.
Kipling, R. City of Brass, The.
Levertov. Fragrance of Life, Odor of Death.
MacLeish. Sheep in the Ruins, The.
Major, C. See that stern castle?
McGrath, T. Need for Stoicism in the Stoa of Attalus, The.
Melville, H. Off Cape Colona.
Ravaged Villa, The.
Merton. Dry Places.
Merwin. Chase, The.
Church, The.
Crossroads of the World Etc., The.
Milosz, C. Book in the Ruins, A.
Farewell: "I speak to you, my son."
Nemerov. Guide to the Ruins.
Quarry, The.
Pagis. Scarabs.

Paz. Hymn Among the Ruins.
Pope, A. Epistle V, to Mr. Addison.
Ramanujan. Time and Time Again.
Rexroth, K. Letter to Wystan Hugh Auden, A.
Mirror in the Woods, The.
Travelers in Erewhon.
Rich, A. Villa Adriana.
Rilke. To Natalie Clifford Barney.
Ritsos. Forbidden Ground.
Indiscriminately.
Robinson, E. Garden, The.
House on the Hill, The.
Rossetti, C. Ruin.
Shelley, P. Fragment: The Vine-Shroud.
Lines Written During the Castlereagh Administration.
Ozymandias.
Stock, R. Farewell to Baedeker.
Tomlinson, C. Idrigill.
Ruin, The.
Walcott. Ruins of a Great House.
Warren, R. Boy Wandering in Simms' Valley.
Whittier. Homestead, The.
Wilbur, R. For the New Railway Station in Rome.
Wilde, O. Theatre at Argos, The.
Williams, M. House in the Vacant Lot, The.
Wilner, E. Trümmerfrauen.
Wordsworth, W. At Furness Abbey.
Brownie, The.
Brownie's Cell, The.
Composed among the Ruins of a Castle in North Wales.
Earl of Breadalbane's Ruined Mansion, and Family Burial-Place, near Killin, The.
Massy Ways Carried across These Heights, The.
Yarrow Visited [September, 1814].
Zukofsky, L. 4 Other Countries.

Rukeyser, Muriel
Cooper, J. Calling, The.
Hotel de Dream.
Levertov. In Memory of Muriel Rukeyser.

Rumor
Burns, R. Verses: "I am a keeper of the law."
Byron, G. What News, What News? Queen Orraca.
Creeley. Photo.
Emerson, R. South Wind.
Herrick. Lips Tongueless[e].
Suspision upon His Over-much Familiarity with a Gentlewoman, The.
Jeffers, R. Old Wolf My Father, The.
Kipling, R. Ballad of the King's Jest, The.
Runners, The.
Tomlinson, C. Rumour.
Warren, R. Rumor Verified.
Wright, C. Virginia Reel.

See also **Fame; Gossip and Gossips; Reputation**

Running and Runners
Armantrout. Anti-Short Story.
Davie, D. Pacer in the Fresco, The. John the Baptist.
Dickey, J. Sprinter at Forty, The.
Eberhart, R. Track.
Herrick. Upon Patrick a Footman.
Housman. To an Athlete Dying Young.
Laughlin, J. Long-Distance Runner, The.
Milosz, C. Run, A.
Nash, O. Birthday on the Beach.
Pagis. Runner Artist, The.
Piercy. Morning Athletes.
Ritsos. Until Daybreak.
Stafford, W. Run before Dawn.
Swenson, M. Running on the Shore.
Warren, R. Paradox.
Whitman, W. Runner, The.
Wilbur, R. Running.
Williams, C. K. Or.

Ruskin, John
Niedecker. Wild strawberries.
Tomlinson, C. Frondes Agrestes.

Russell, Lucy, Countess of Bedford
Jonson, B. Author ad Librum.
On Lucy, Countess[e] of Bedford.
To Lucy, Countess[e] of Bedford, with Mr.

Donne's Satires [or Satyres].

Russia
Bierce.   Saith the Czar.
Blok.   Autumn Freedom.
Intellect Cannot Measure the Divine, The.
Kite, The.
O What is the Setting Sun's Radiance to Me.
On the Field of Kulikovo.
Russia ("Again, as in the golden age").
Russia and I.
Scythians, The.
Shamelessly, Endlessly Sinning.
Those Born in the Years of Stagnation.
Bly, R.   Aban Kavost and Ivar Oakeson.
Brodsky, J.   Autumn in Norenskaia.
Classical ballet, let's say, is beauty's keep, The.
Homage to Chekhov.
Kellomäki.
To Urania.
Carruth, H.   In Russia.
Carver, R.   Caucasus: A Romance, The.
Celan.   Afternoon with Circus and Citadel.
Chesterton.   Before a Statue of Cromwell.
Codrescu.   In Praise of the New Russian
Writers.
Creeley.   She Went to Stay.
Ferlinghetti, L.   Moscow in the Wilderness,
Segovia in the Snow.
Ignatow, D.   1905.
Jarrell, R.   Love for One Orange, The.
Jeffers, R.   Teheran.
Larkin, P.   When the Russian Tanks Roll
Westward.
Laughlin, J.   Shard of History, A.
Lawrence, D. H.   Now It's Happened.
Meredith, G.   Crisis, The.
Three Eagles and the Sleepy Lion, The.
Moore, M.   Combat Cultural.
O'Hara, F.   On Looking at La Grande Jatte, the
Czar Wept Anew.
Paley, G.   Song Stanzas of Private Luck; To Be
Added Sometimes and Sometimes to Be
Subtracted from as Events Prove One More
Wrong than Right.
Rossetti, D.   Czar Alexander the Second.
Rukeyser, M.   Willkie: Words from Russia.
Stevens, W.   Dish of Peaches in Russia, A.
Updike.   Poem for a Far Land.
Postcards from Soviet Cities.
Very.   Abolition of Serfdom in Russia, The.
Williams, M.   Learning Russian.
Morning at the Zagorsk Monastery Outside
Moscow.
Williams, W.   Russia.
Wordsworth, W.   French Army in Russia 1812–
1813, The.
On the Same Occasion.
Russian Fugitive, The.
Zagajewski.   Russia Comes Into Poland.

Russian Revolution
Aragon.   Red Front, The.
Blok.   Twelve, The.
Clampitt.   Odessa Steps, The.
Cooper, J.   Poetry as Continuity.
Kipling, R.   Russia to the Pacifists.
Milosz, C.   Mister Hanusevich.
Tomlinson, C.   At Trotsky's House.
Dream, A.

Russians, The
Berryman.   Communist.
Byron, G.   Fragment of an Epistle to Thomas
Moore.
Davie, D.   Hearing Russian Spoken.
Dubie.   Seagull, The.
Niedecker.   Brown muskrat, noiseless, The.
Rukeyser, M.   What do you know of America? I
asked a little Russian schoolgirl.
Weiss, T.   Slow Fuse, A.
Williams, W.   Foreign.
When Fresh, It Was Sweet.

Ruth, George Herman ("Babe")
Bukowski.   End, The.

Rwanda
Ai.   Rwanda.

Rydal Water, England
Wordsworth, W.   By the Side of Rydal Mere.
Ryder, Albert Pinkham
Rukeyser, M.   Ryder.

S

Sabbath
Auden.   Sabbath, The.
Browning, E.   Sabbath Morning at Sea, A.
Coleridge, S.   Reproof and Reply, The.
Dickinson, E.   Some keep the Sabbath going to
Church.
Herbert, G.   Sunday.
Herrick.   Sabbaths.
Jacobsen, J.   Non Sum Dignus.
MacNeice.   Sunday in the Park.
Sunday Morning.
Very.   Sabbath, The ("Thy rest has come thy
long expected rest").
Walcott.   Sabbaths, W.I.
See also **Sunday**
Sacco-Vanzetti Case
Cullen, C.   Not Sacco and Vanzetti.
Millay, E.   As men have loved their lovers in
times past.
Justice Denied in Massachusetts.
Where can the heart be hidden in the ground.
Rexroth, K.   Climbing Milestone Mountain,
August 22, 1937.
Williams, W.   Impromptu: The Suckers.
Sacher-Masoch, Leopold von
Codrescu.   Dear Masoch.
Sachs, Nelly
Celan.   Zurich, at the Stork.
Zagajewski.   She Wrote in Darkness.
Sacraments
See **Baptism; Eucharist; Extreme Unction;
Marriage**
Sacrifice
Ai.   I Have Got to Stop Loving You. So I Have
Killed My Black Goat.
Amichai [or Amikhai].   Real Hero of the
Sacrifice of Isaac, The.
Ammons.   Libation.
Bukowski.   Minor Impulse to Complain, A.
Byron, G.   Jephtha's Daughter.
Carew, T.   Cruel Mistress, A.
Carruth, H.   No Supervening Thought of Grace.
Ciardi, J.   Lamb, The.
Coleridge, S.   To Nature.
Crane, H.   Possessions.
Emerson, R.   And when I am entombed in my
place.
Beauty.
Give All to Love.
Love / Asks nought his brother cannot give.
To Rhea.
Ginsberg, A.   Voice of Rock, The.
Glück, L.   Late Snow.
Winter Morning.
Guyon.   Gratitude and Love to God.
Perfect Sacrifice, The.
Self-Diffidence.
Truth and Divine Love Rejected by the World.
Hardy, T.   Aristodemus the Messenian.
Herbert, G.   Obedience.
Herrick.   Ass[e], The.
Cheerfulnesse in Charitie: or, The Sweet
Sacrifice.
Good Friday: Rex Tragicus, or, Christ Going to
His Cross[e].
Hymne to Love, An.
Lip Labour.
Perfume, The.
Sacrifice, by Way of Discourse betwixt Himselfe
and Julia, The.
Scar[e]-Fire, The.
Smell of the Sacrifice, The.
Steam in Sacrifice.
Sweetnesse in Sacrifice.
To God, His Good Will.
Vow to Mars, A.
Vow to Minerva, A.

Housman.   If it chance your eye offend you.
Hughes, T.   Contender, The.
God, A.
Ignatow, D.   In Ancient Times.
Jeffers, R.   But I Am Growing Old and Indolent.
Kinsella, T.   Sacrifice.
Kipling, R.   Heritage, The.
Sacrifice of Er-Heb, The.
They killed a Child to please the Gods.
Lawrence, D. H.   Old Idea of Sacrifice, The.
Self-Sacrifice.
Shedding of Blood.
Levi, P.   Witch, The.
Lindsay, N.   Doll's "Arabian Nights," A.
Johnny Appleseed's Hymn to the Sun.
Where Is the Real Non-Resistant?
McGrath, T.   Offering.
Melville, H.   At the Cannon's Mouth.
Meredith, G.   Angelic Love.
Antigone.
Shipwreck of Idomeneus, The.
Merton.   Seven Archaic Images.
Mistral, G.   Air Flower, The.
Olson, C.   Dura.
Owen, W.   To Eros.
Piercy.   Market Economy, The.
Rich, A.   Leaflets.
Rossetti, C.   Johnny.
Lord God of Hosts, most Holy and most High.
My God, wilt Thou accept, and will not we /
Give aught to Thee?
Slain from the Foundation of the World.
Take Care Of Him.
"Shu Ting."   "?!"
Stevens, W.   Cy Est Pourtraicte, Madame Ste
Ursule, et Les Unze Mille Vierges.
Tennyson, A.   Charge of the Light Brigade, The.
Warren, R.   Ransom.
Whittier.   Two Loves, The.
Williams, M.   Note to God Concerning a Point
from an Earlier Communication, A.
Wilner, E.   Sarah's Choice.
What Was Left Over.
Working the Block.
Sacrilege
Han-shan.   They don't walk the Noble Path.
Lindsay, N.   City That Will Not Repent, The.
Whittier.   Official Piety.
Sabbath Scene, A.
Sade, Donatien Alphonse François, Marquis de
Graves, R.   Encounter, The.
Nash, O.   Literary Scene, The.
Sadism and Sadists
Ai.   One Man Down.
Baudelaire.   To a Madonna.
Bukowski.   Beast, The.
On the Failure of a Poet.
Regard Me.
Dugan, A.   What It Really Means.
Komunyakaa.   S & M.
Merton.   Psalm 132: A Modern Monastic
Revision.
Riley, J.   Dream, A.
Sadness
Amichai [or Amikhai].   Eyn Gedi Preserve.
I Am Big and Fat.
Open Closets Are Sad.
Sadness of Eyes and Descriptions of a Voyage.
Ammons.   Grace Abounding.
Auden.   Lady[,] Weeping at the Crossroads.
Baudelaire.   Merciless Madrigal.
Bogan, L.   Didactic Piece.
Solitary Observation Brought Back from a
Sojourn in Hell.
Borges.   1964.
Brontë, E.   Had there been falsehood in my
breast.
Inspiring music's thrilling sound, The.
Old church tower and garden wall, The.
Bukowski.   All the Casualties.
Melancholia.
Burns, R.   Address to the Woodlark.
My Nannie's Awa'
Scotch Song.
Carruth, H.   Cows at Night, The.
Cross My Heart and Hope to Die, It Was the

Very Same Song Exactly.
Cavalcanti. Ballata: He perceives that his highest Love is gone from him.
Ciardi, J. At Least with Good Whiskey.
Trenta-Sei of the Pleasure We Take in the Early Death of Keats, A.
Creeley. Air: "The Love of a Woman."
Disappointment, The.
Illness, An.
Love ("Tracking through this").
Oh Mabel.
Passage, The.
Total Parts of a World, The.
"Dario." Nocturne: "Silence of the night, a sorrowful silence."
Sonatina.
Dickey, W. New Place, The.
Dickinson, E. How happy I was if I could forget.
I should not dare to be so sad.
Donne. Song: "Sweetest love, I do not go[e]."
Eberhart, R. Despair.
Emerson, R. I am alone. Sad is my solitude.
Frost, R. Hannibal.
Gallagher, T. Dim House, Bright Face.
García Lorca. Evening ("Rainy evening in exhausted gray").
Ginsberg, A. My Sad Self.
HaNagid. Sad Friend.
Hardy, T. Christmastide.
Place on the Map, The.
Woman in the Rye, The.
Herbert, G. Storm, The.
Herrick. Christs Sadnesse.
Wounded Heart, The.
Housman. In My Own Shire.
Hughes, L. Dressed Up.
Late Last Night.
Miss Blues'es Child.
Jackson, L. It Is Not Sad.
Sad Boy, The.
Jarrell, R. Three Bills.
Kipling, R. Roman Centurion's Song, The.
Larkin, P. Femmes Damnees.
Home Is So Sad.
Laughlin, J. La Tristesse.
Revenants, The.
Levertov. Blue Rim of Memory, The.
Dwellers at the Hermitage.
Her Sadness.
Talking to Grief.
Levi, P. Monday.
Levine, P. Buying and Selling.
Midget, The.
Longfellow, H. Day Is Done, The.
MacDiarmid, H. Love-sick Lass, The.
Mahon. Dejection [Ode].
Mallarmé. Summer Sadness.
Meredith, G. Ask, is Love divine.
Dark on the ridge of the cold salt wave.
Fair Bedfellow, The.
Merwin. Sadness, The.
Millay, E. Anguish, The.
Ashes of Life.
Macdougal Street.
Spring and the Fall, The.
To a Young Girl.
To the Wife of a Sick Friend.
Milton. Il Penseroso.
Montale. Encounter.
Nash, O. So Penseroso.
Nemerov. View from an Attic Window, The.
Owen, W. Happiness.
Pagis. Fragments of an Elegy.
Palmer, M. Song of the Round Man.
Parker, D. Paths.
Small Hours, The.
Solace.
Patchen. Great Sadnesses, The.
Two Ghosts Together.
Pessoa. At the wheel of the Chevrolet on the road to Sintra.
Pinsky. Sadness and Happiness.
Rich, A. Mirror in Which Two Are Seen as One, The.
Roethke. Dolor.

Elegy: "Should every creature be as I have been."
Rossetti, C. At Home.
Corydon's Lament and Resolution.
Faithless Shepherdess, The.
Golden Silences.
Hear what the mournful linnets say.
I have but one rose in the world.
In resurrection is it awfuller.
Trees' Counselling, The.
Unforgotten.
Why did baby die.
Zara.
Sandburg, C. And This Will Be All?
Swell People.
Schuyler, J. So Good.
Shelley, P. Cancelled Passage.
Invocation to Misery.
On a Faded Violet.
Stanzas—April, 1814.
To Mary Shelley.
To Mary, Who Died in This Opinion.
To William Shelley.
Suckling, S. Invocation, The: "Ye juster Powers of Love and Fate."
Trakl. De Profundis.
Very. Grief.
Walker, A. S M.
Warren, R. Goodbye.
Williams, M. Dust.
Williams, W. Sadness of the Sea, The.
Twelve Line Poem.
Wordsworth, W. Sonnet on Seeing Miss Helen Maria Williams Weep at a Tale of Distress.
Wright, J. American Wedding.
Breath of Air, A.
Yeats. He Reproves the Curlew.
To the Rose upon the Rood of Time.
Zagajewski. Sad, Tired.
Zukofsky, L. As to How Much.
H.T.

Sailing and Sailors
Amichai [or Amikhai]. At the Maritime Museum.
Ammons. Raft.
Angelou. Martial Choreograph.
Auden. Fleet Visit.
Berryman. Conversation.
Bishop, E. Imaginary Iceberg, The.
Santarém.
Unbeliever, The.
Bogan, L. Putting to Sea.
Browning, R. Hervé Riel.
Burns, R. On the Seas and Far Away.
Byron, G. Farewell Petition to J.C.H., Esq.
Island, The.
Julian [A Fragment].
Lines to Mr Hodgson.
Oh How I Wish That an Embargo.
Stanzas: "Through cloudless skies, in silvery sheen."
Cardenal. Drake in the Southern Sea.
Carver, R. Asia.
Cavafy. Prayer: "To her depths the sea has taken a sailor."
Chiabrera. There never breathed a man who, when his life.
Clough. Come Home, Come Home!
Qua Cursum Ventus.
Ye flags of Piccadilly, / Where I posted up and down.
Coleridge, S. Catullian Hendecasyllables.
Rime of the Ancient Mariner, The.
Cooper, J. Meteors.
Corbière. Letter from Mexico (Vera Cruz, 10 February, 186–).
Crane, H. Phantom Bark, The.
Traveller Born, A.
Crane, S. I explain the silvered passing of a ship at night.
Cummings, E. E. So standing.our eyes filled with the wind,and the.
Davie, D. Admiral to His Lady, The.
After the Calamitous Convoy (July 1942).
Bougainville.
Commodore Barry.

Lady Cochrane.
Norfolk.
Trevenen.
Vancouver.
De la Mare. Never More, Sailor.
Dickey, J. Expanses.
Tapestry and Sail.
Dickinson, E. Adrift! A little boat adrift!
Eternity.
Exultation is the going.
It tossed—and tossed.
Once more, my now bewildered Dove.
Sailor cannot see the North, The.
'Twas such a little little boat.
Where Ships of Purple—gently toss.
Whether my bark went down at sea.
Wild Nights—Wild Nights!
Donne. Calm[e], The.
Hymn[e] to Christ, at the Author's Last Going into Germany, A.
Storm[e], The.
Dugan, A. Landfall.
Life and Death of the Cantata System, The.
Sailing to Jerusalem.
Untitled Poem: "Once on the beach at night I heard the waves."
Dunbar, P. Sailor's Song, A.
Eberhart, R. American Hakluyt.
Going Backward Going Forward.
Sailing to Buck's Harbor.
Sea Burial from the Cruiser *Reve*.
Voyage, The.
Waiting To Lean to the Master's Command.
Emerson, R. For fifteen winter days.
I love thy music, mellow bell.
I spread my gorgeous sail.
What is it to sail.
Frost, R. Flower Boat, The.
García Lorca. Christmas on the Hudson.
Two Sailors on the Beach.
Ginsberg, A. Dakar Doldrums.
Glück, L. Archipelago.
Goll, I. Jean Sans Terre at the Final Port.
Graves, R. Furious Voyage, The.
Gurney, I. Advice.
Dream, The.
"H. D." In Our Town.
Look-out, The.
Sea Heroes.
Shrine, The.
Hardy, T. Sea Fight, The.
Heaney, S. Lough Neagh Sequence, A.
Herrick. Ship-Wrack.
Hill, G. Guardians, The.
Homer. Daughters of Pandarus, The.
Gardens of Alcinous, The.
Mindes of men are ever so affected, The.
Muse, / tell me of this man of wit.
Sun descending, the *Phæacian* train, The.
Housman. Land of Biscay, The.
Oh were he and I together.
R. L. S.
Hughes, L. Fog.
Old Sailor.
Port Town.
Sailing Date.
Sailor.
Seascape.
To Captain Mulzac.
Young Sailor.
Jarrell, R. O weary mariners, here shaded, fed.
Kipling, R. Anchor Song.
Ballad of Fisher's Boardinghouse, The.
Ballad of the "Bolivar", The.
Coastwise Lights, The.
Coiner, The.
Exiles' Line, The.
First Chantey, The.
Frankie's Trade.
French Wars, The.
In the Matter of One Compass.
Last Chantey, The.
McAndrew's Hymn.
Merchántmen, The.
Mulholland's Contract.
Poseidon's Law.

Rhyme of the Three Sealers, The.
Sea-Wife, The.
Second Voyage, The.
Song of Diego Valdez, The.
Song of the Dead, The.
Song of the Red War-Boat.
Truthful Song, The.
Wet Litany, The.
When the Great Ark.
With Drake in the Tropics.
Kizer, C. Voyager.
Koch, K. Poem: "Thing / To do / Is organize / The sea, The."
Levertov. Heights, Depths, Silence, Unceasing Sound of the Surf.
Leaving Forever.
Levine, P. Let Me Begin Again.
Lindsay, N. Song in July, A.
Longfellow, H. Wreck of the *Hesperus*, The.
MacDiarmid, H. Wreck of the *Swan*, The.
MacLeish. Lines for a Prologue.
Seafarer.
Ship's Log.
Yacht for Sale.
MacNeice. Passage Steamer.
Major, C. Sailing.
Mallarmé. Salutation.
Sea Breeze.
Marvell. Bermudas.
McGrath, T. Excursion: Or: O Columbus!, The.
Melville, H. Commemorative of a Naval Victory.
Haglets, The.
In the Turret.
Jack Roy.
Tom Deadlight.
Meredith, G. Camelus Saltat: Continued.
Last Contention, The.
Olive Branch, The.
Periander.
Shipwreck of Idomeneus, The.
Merwin. Estuary, The.
Helmsmen, The.
Ships Are Made Ready in Silence, The.
Shore.
Milosz, C. Caesarea.
Montale. Another Moon Effect.
Nash, O. Columbus.
O'Hara, F. To the Harbormaster.
Oliver, M. Magellan.
Olson, C. Mast, The.
Morning News, The.
Rosy, It Was.
Shut in kept off.
Six Inch Chapter—in Verse, A.
Oppen. Mast / Inaudibly soars; bole-like, tapering, The.
Three wide / Funnels raked aft, and the masts slanted, The.
Tugs of Hull, The.
Parker, D. Chantey.
Patchen. Plate of Steaming Fish, A.
Petrarch. He who is adamant to live his life.
I saw twelve ladies sailing at their ease.
Love makes me go where I had rather not.
My vessel laden with oblivion.
Pinsky. Volume, The.
Plath. Channel Crossing.
Riley, J. Old Retired Sea-Captain, The.
Sea-Song from the Shore, A.
Where Shall We Land?
While the Musician Played.
Whitheraways, The.
Ritsos. Moment.
Robinson, E. Lost Anchors.
Pasa Thalassa Thalassa.
Pilot, The.
Return of Morgan and Fingal, The.
Wise Brothers, The.
Rossetti, C. Ballad of Boding, A.
I have a little husband / And he is gone to sea.
O Sailor, Come Ashore.
Rossetti, D. Last Three from Trafalgar, The.
Rukeyser, M. Suite for Lord Timothy Dexter.
Sandburg, C. All Day Long.
Baltic Fog Notes.

Deep Sea Wandering.
From the Shore.
Lief the Lucky.
Old Deep Sing-Song.
Sea Slant.
Waiting.
Way of the World, The.
Young Sea.
Sexton. Love Song for K. Owyne.
Smith, S. Die Lorelei.
Look!
Snyder, G. 7.IV.64.
Engine Room, S.S. Sappa Creek, The.
Longitude 170° West, Latitude 35° North.
Twelve Hours Out of New York After Twenty-Five Days at Sea.
Stevens, W. Sailing after Lunch.
Swenson, M. Captain Holm.
Overboard.
Sze. Network, The.
Tate, A. Mediterranean, The.
Tennyson, A. Crossing the Bar.
Thoreau. Friend, The.
Unknown. Battle of Brunanburh.
Seafarer, The.
Updike. Bath after Sailing.
Sails on All Saints' Day.
Very. Barque Aurelia of Boston, The.
Coasters, The.
East India Marine Museum, The.
Moon was shining on the deck, The.
Walcott. Sea-Chantey, A.
Wheatley, P. On Messrs Hussey and Coffin.
To a Gentleman of the Navy.
Whitman, W. In Cabin'd Ships at Sea.
Old Age's Ship & Crafty Death's.
Old Salt Kossabone.
Sail Out for Good, Eidólon Yacht!
Ship Ahoy!
Ship Starting, The.
Song for All Seas, All Ships.
Twenty Years.
Whittier. Bay of Seven Islands, The.
Branded Hand, The.
Slave-Ships, The.
Wilbur, R. Regatta, The.
Superiorities.
Williams, M. Unknown Sailor, The.
Williams, T. No Shaken Seas.
Williams, W. Seafarer.
Yachts, The.
Wordsworth, W. As when, upon the smooth pacific deep.
Composed by the Sea-Shore.
Sailor's Mother, The.
Yeats. Colonel Martin.
Shadowy Waters, The.
Zagajewski. That's Sicily.

Saint Peter's Church, Rome
Clough. From far and near / He drew the scattered ciphers.
Petrarch. Little white-haired man moves off from where, The.
Wilde, O. Easter Day.

Saint Petersburg [*formerly* Leningrad], Russia
Brodsky, J. Gorbunov and Gorchakov.
Jacobsen, J. How We Learn.
McHugh, H. Two St. Petersburgs.
Niedecker. Gen. Rodimstev's Story / (Stalingrad).
Palmer, M. (Overheard at the) Maykovsky Station.
Rilke. Night Drive.

Saints
Berry, W. Springs, The.
Brontë, E. Heaven's glory shone where he was laid.
Cavafy. Simeon.
Codrescu. My Next Book.
Crashaw. Flaming Heart, The.
Cummings, E. E. Candles and / Here Comes a glass box.
"Dario." It was a gentle air, with leisurely turns.
Dickinson, E. I Taste a Liquor Never Brewed.
No matter where the Saints abide.
Donne. Canonization, The.

Relic, The.
Dove, R. Catherine of Alexandria.
Dugan, A. On a Travel Story from Wormwood Valley.
Graves, R. St Antony of Padua.
Gunn, T. Here Come the Saints.
Heaney, S. St Kevin and the Blackbird.
Herbert, G. To All Angels and Saints.
Herrick. Teares.
Temptations.
To Groves.
To Julia.
Upon a Maide.
Hill, G. In Piam Memoriam.
Hopkins, G. For a Picture of Saint Dorothea.
In Honour of St. Alphonsus Rodriguez.
Lines for a Picture of St. Dorothea.
On St. Winefred.
St. Dorothea.
St. Thecla.
Jacobsen, J. Ballad of the Four Saints.
Jeffers, R. Delusion of Saints.
Lawrence, D. H. St John.
St Luke.
St Mark.
St Matthew.
Logan, J. Cycle for Mother Cabrini, A.
Lines to Catherine.
Month of Saints, A.
Recollection on the Day of a First Book.
Revisit to the Room of a Saint.
Short Life of the Hermit, A.
MacLeish. What Riddle Asked the Sphinx.
MacNeice. Stylite.
Major, C. You set out on a morning bright.
Mallarmé. Saint.
Merton. Clairvaux.
Invocation to St. Lucy, An.
Listen, Saints.
Macarius and the Pony.
Rievaulx: St. Ailred.
St. Agnes: A Responsory.
St. Alberic.
Two Desert Fathers.
Merwin. Saint of the Uplands, The.
St. Vincent's.
Muldoon, P. Lives of the Saints.
Nemerov. Situation Does Not Change, The.
Orr, G. Story Sassetta Paints, A.
Ramanujan. Fear No Fall.
Rich, A. Reliquary.
Rossetti, C. Alas, alas! for the self-destroyed / Vanish as images from a glass.
All Flesh Is Grass.
All Saints.
All Saints: Martyrs.
As dying, and behold we live!
Before the Throne, and Before the Lamb.
Cast down but not destroyed, chastened not slain.
Dear Angels and dear disembodied Saints.
Embertide.
Every One That Is Perfect Shall Be as His Master.
Eye Hath Not Seen.
General Assembly and Church of the Firstborn, The.
Hark! the Alleluias of the great salvation.
I Gave a Sweet Smell.
Jerusalem of fire / And gold and pearl and gem.
Joy of Saints, like incense turned to fire, The.
Let Them Rejoice in Their Beds.
Lift up thine eyes to seek the invisible.
Our life is long. Not so, wise Angels say.
So Great a Cloud of Witnesses.
St. Barnabas.
St. Bartholomew.
St. Elizabeth of Hungary.
St. Mark.
Thy Servant Will Go and Fight with This Philistine.
To Every Seed His Own Body.
Vigil of all Saints.
Vigil of St. Bartholomew.
Vigil of the Annunciation.
What are these lovely ones, yea, what are these?

What is this above thy head, / O Man?
Who would wish back the Saints upon our rough.
Rossetti, D.   Marriage of St Katharine, by the same, A; in the Hospital of St John at Bruges.
Sexton.   Saints Come Marching In, The.
Stock, R.   At an Abandoned Shrine of Saint Mary Aegyptian.
Tate, J.   Saint John of the Cross in Prison.
Tennyson, A.   St. Simeon Stylites.
Thomas, D.   Saint About to Fall, A.
Tomlinson, C.   Santa Maria delle Nevi.
Weeper in Jalisco.
Walker, A.   Abduction of Saints, The.
Whittier.   Legend of St. Mark, The.
Two Elizabeths, The.
Wordsworth, W.   St Catherine of Ledbury.
Wright, C.   Holy Ghost Asketh for Us with Mourning and Weeping Unspeakable, The.

Salads
Cowper, W.   Salad, The.
Lux.   Endive.

Salamanders
Ramanujan.   Salamanders.
Zaturenska.   World of the Salamanders, The.

Salamis, Battle of (480 B.C.)
Cavafy.   Naval Battle, The.

Salem, Massachusetts
Eberhart, R.   Salem.
Very.   Old Houses of Salem: Illustrated by George M. White.
Salem ("Boast not, my native spot, thy sons were first").
Sliding Rock, The.

Sales Clerks
See **Clerks**

Salesmen
Carver, R.   World Book Salesman, The.
Cummings, E. E.   Salesman, A.
Levine, P.   Buying and Selling.
Sandburg, C.   Fish Crier.
Simic.   Amazing Potato Peeler, The.
Smith, S.   In Canaan's Happy Land.
Warren, R.   Nocturne: Traveling Salesman in Hotel Bedroom.
Williams, T.   Road, The.

Salisbury, England
Hardy, T.   In a Cathedral City.

Salmon
Carver, R.   At Night the Salmon Move.
Ciardi, J.   On Being Sure and of What.
Hughes, T.   Milesian Encounter on the Sligachan.
October Salmon[, An].
Salmon Eggs.
That Morning.
Muldoon, P.   Chinook.
Salmon of Knowledge, The.
Rexroth, K.   Time Spirals.

Salome
Cavafy.   Aristovoulos.
Salome.
Hughes, L.   For Salome.
Mallarmé.   Hérodiade.
Parker, D.   Salome's Dancing-Lesson.

Salt
Collins, B.   Design.
Dove, R.   Nightmare.
Lawrence, D. H.   Boundary Stone, The.
Salt.
Spilling the Salt.
Levine, P.   Nitrate.
Mistral, G.   In Praise of Salt.

Salt Lake City, Utah
Ginsberg, A.   Chicago to Salt Lake by Air.

Salvation
Blok.   I Seek Salvation.
Borges.   Just, The.
Bradstreet, A.   As spring the winter doth succeed.
As Weary Pilgrim, Now at Rest.
From Another Sore Fit.
My soul, rejoice thou in thy God.
Occasional Meditations: "By night, when others soundly slept."
What God is like to him I serve?
Cavalcanti.   I see it in my Lady's eyes.
Clement of Alexandria.   Soldiers of Peace.
Crane, H.   Recitative.
Cullen, C.   Shroud of Color, The.
Dickinson, E.   Province of the Saved, The.
Summer day on which you came, The.
Eberhart, R.   Suite in Prison.
Eliot, T. S.   Hippopotamus, The.
Song for Simeon, A.
Emerson, R.   God The Lord save Massachusetts.
Fergusson, E.   Poem on the Death of Richard Stockton, A.
Graves, R.   Song: Lift-Boy.
Hammon.   Evening Thought, An. Salvation by Christ with Penetential Cries.
Poem for Children with Thoughts on Death, A.
Han-shan.   Children I implore you.
Herbert, G.   Bunch of Grapes, The.
Business.
Call, The.
Clasping of Hands.
Conscience.
Dialogue, A.
Divinity.
Easter Wings.
Giddiness.
Grieve Not the Holy Spirit, etc.
Holdfast, The.
Holy Baptism (1).
Love Unknown.
Man's Medley.
Peace.
Perseverance.
Redemption.
Water-Course, The.
Herrick.   All Things Run Well for the Righteous.
Charroll Presented to Dr. Williams Bp. of Lincolne as a Newyears Guift, A.
Cloaths for Continuance.
Purgatory.
To Christ.
To His Saviour.
Hopkins, G.   Myself unholy, from myself unholy.
Hughes, L.   Madam and the Minister.
Sunday Morning Prophecy.
Hughes, T.   Lines about Elias.
Sometimes it comes, a gloomy flap of lightning.
Jarrell, R.   Song: Not There.
Jonson, B.   Hymn[e] on the Nativity [or Nativitie] of My Saviour, A.
Kipling, R.   Mulholland's Contract.
Lawrence, D. H.   Huitzilopochtli Gives the Black Blade of Death.
Nothing to Save.
Salvation.
Levine, P.   Hear Me.
Lindsay, N.   Daniel.
Galahad, Knight Who Perished.
General William Booth Enters into Heaven.
Look You, I'll Go Pray.
Merciful Hand, The.
Merton.   Biography, The.
Peril, The.
Michelangelo Buonarroti.   It leaves me plunged in gloom and pain—yet dear.
One way remains to loose me yet, dear Lord.
Who rides by night on horseback, come the day.
Milosz, C.   Dedication: "You whom I could not save."
Montale.   Anniversary.
Nemerov.   Morality, A.
Oliver, M.   In Blackwater Woods.
Petrarch.   How strangely this world wags! Now what distressed.
I am so weary and so heavy laden.
I go in mourning for those years of mine.
Most glorious Virgin, you are clothed in glory.
Pleasant obduracy, and calm rejection.
Three days before, my soul reached such a place.
Piercy.   Let Us Gather at the River.
Ralegh, S.   Authours Epitaph, Made by Himself, The.
Ransom, J.   Rose, The.
Riley, J.   Highest Good, The.
Plantation Hymn.
Someday.
Rimbaud, A.   Just Man, The.
Rossetti, C.   Chill blank world. Yet over the utmost sea, A.
Christian and Jew. A Dialogue.
I lift mine eyes to see: earth vanisheth.
I, Lord, Thy foolish sinner low and small.
Isidora.
Lord, hast Thou so loved us, and will not we.
Lord, I am here.—But, child, I look for thee.
Lord Jesu, Thou art sweetness to my soul.
Lord, Save Us, We Perish.
None other Lamb, none other Name.
O foolish Soul! to make thy count / For languid falls and much forgiven.
O mine enemy / Rejoice not over me!
Peace I Leave wth You.
Thy Friend and Thy Father's Friend Forget Not.
Smith, S.   Ah, Will the Saviour...?
Breughel.
Conviction (i).
Man I Am, A.
Stafford, W.   Easter Morning.
Stockton, A.   How blest the soul to whom indulgent heaven.
Meditation on the 3d Verse of the 28th Chapter of Mathew.
Tate, A.   Cross, The.
Unknown.   Prose in Advent Time.
Very.   Forevermore.
Garden, The.
Wheatley, P.   Isaiah 63. 1–8.
Whittier.   Crucifixion, The.
Cry of a Lost Soul, The.
Over-Heart, The.
Williams, C. K.   Yours.
Wordsworth, W.   Composed During a Storm.
Wright, C.   Bad Memory Makes You a Metaphysician, a Good One Makes You a Saint, A.

Salzburg, Austria
Kumin, M.   Festung, Salzburg, The.

Samson
Amichai [*or* Amikhai].   Shore of Ashkelon, The.
Cooper, J.   Gaza.
Crashaw.   Samson to His Delilah.
Emerson, R.   Samson stark at Dagon's knee.
Graves, R.   Angry Samson.
Levi, P.   Delilah.
Samson.
Lindsay, N.   How Samson Bore Away the Gates of Gaza.
Longfellow, H.   Warning, The.
Meredith, G.   Dalila.
Stock, R.   Shield Against the Trampling Foe, A.
Tomlinson, C.   Bone.

San Francisco, California
Amichai [*or* Amikhai].   North of San Francisco.
Brodsky, J.   Café Trieste: San Francisco.
Codrescu.   Late Night, San Francisco.
San Francisco for Whomever.
Ferlinghetti, L.   Report on a Happening in Washington Square San Francisco, A.
They were putting up the statue.
Ginsberg, A.   Continuation of a Long Poem of These States.
Sunflower Sutra.
Gunn, T.   Invitation, An.
San Francisco Streets.
Sand Man, The.
Hughes, L.   City.
Trip: San Francisco.
Lindsay, N.   City That Will Not Repent, The.
Logan, J.   San Francisco Poem.
Saturday Afternoon at the Movies.
Milosz, C.   I Sleep a Lot.
Olson, C.   Who slays the Spanish sun.
Oppen.   Niece.
Some San Francisco Poems.
To the Muse.
Rexroth, K.   Another Early Morning Exercise.
Hiking on the Coast Range.

Leda Hidden.
Noretorp-Noretsyh.
Rukeyser, M.   Bunk Johnson Blowing.
Sandburg, C.   Portrait of a Child Settling Down
   for an Afternoon Nap.
Schuyler, J.   Blossoming Oakwood.
   Shadowy Room.
Snyder, G.   Night Herons.
   North Beach Alba.
Tomlinson, C.   Idyll: "Door: / PER
   L'UNIVERSO / is what it says, A."
Updike.   Scenic.
Whalen, P.   Historical Disquisitions.
Zukofsky, L.   Head Lines.

Sancho Panza
Borges.   Soldier of Urbina, A.

Sanctuaries
Ammons.   Ocean City.
   Triphammer Bridge.
Cooper, J.   All These Dreams.
Creeley   Coming Home.
Eberhart, R.   Bower, The.
Han-shan.   Cold Mountain is a leakproof cliff.
   Looking for refuge.
   On Cold Mountain Road.
Hughes, L.   House in the World.
Kizer, C.   Shalimar Gardens.
Parker, D.   Sanctuary.
Pessoa.   Lydia, we know nothing. We are
   strangers.
Petrarch.   How often do I come to this retreat.
   Love, who in good times kept me company.
   Such is the fear those eyes strike into me.
Riley, J.   His Room.
   Light of Love, The.
Sandburg, C.   Palladiums.
Stafford, W.   Our Cave.
Williams, T.   I walk the path that.
   Sanctuary.
Wordsworth, W.   By the Side of Rydal Mere.

Sand
Ammons.   Dunes.
   Interference.
Blue Cloud.   Sandhills That None May Visit.
Clampitt.   Outer Bar, The.
Codrescu.   Mail.
Creeley.   All That Is Lovely in Men.
De la Mare.   Mermaids, The.
Eberhart, R.   Ceremony By the Sea, A.
Emerson, R.   Asmodaean feat be mine, The.
   Chladni strewed on glass the sand.
Frost, R.   Neither Out Far Nor In Deep.
Gunn, T.   Sand Man, The.
Levertov.   Sands of the Well.
Logan, J.   Nude Kneeling in Sand.
McHugh, H.   Dry Time.
Merwin.   Looking Back.
Millay, E.   Second Fig.
Pagis.   Snake.
Rossetti, C.   I dug and dug amongst the snow.
Sandburg, C.   Flux.
Thomas, D.   We Lying by Seasand.
Tomlinson, C.   Writing on Sand.

"Sand, George" (Amandine Aurore Lucie Dupin, Baronne Dudevant)
Browning, E.   To George Sand: A Desire.
   To George Sand: A Recognition.

Sandpipers
Bishop, E.   Sandpiper.
Carruth, H.   Summer's Early End at Hudson's
   Bay.
Nemerov.   Sandpipers.
Sandburg, C.   Sand Scribblings.
   Sandpipers.

Sanitary Engineering and Sanitary Engineers
See **Garbage and Garbage Men; Sewers**

Santa Barbara, California
Rexroth, K.   Song at the Winepresses, A.

Santa Claus
Eberhart, R.   Santa Claus in Oaxaca.
Jacobsen, J.   49th and 5th, December 13.
Mistral, G.   For Noel.
Moore, M.   Saint Nicholas.
Nemerov.   Santa Claus.
Riley, J.   Christmas Afterthought.

Das Krist Kindel.
Defective Santa Claus, A.
To Santa Claus.
What "Old Santa" Overheard.
Who Santy Claus Wuz.

Santa Fe Trail
Sandburg, C.   Slabs of the Sunburnt West.

Santayana, George
Lowell, R.   For George Santayana.
Niedecker.   Santayana's.
Stevens, W.   To an Old Philosopher in Rome.

Santiago de Compostela, Spain
García Lorca.   Dance of the Moon in Santiago.
Madrigal for the City of Santiago.

Sappho
Baudelaire.   Lesbos.
Begley, T.   Sappho's Gymnasium.
Broumas, O.   Sappho's Gymnasium.
Herrick.   Apron of Flowers, The.
   To Sapho.
   Upon Sapho.
Kizer, C.   For Sappho/After Sappho.
Millay, E.   Of what importance, O my lovely
   girls, my dancers, O my lovely boys.
   Sappho Crosses the Dark River into Hades.
Olson, C.   For Sappho, Back.
Orr, G.   Glukupikron.
Plato.   They said the Muses were but nine, and
   then.
Pope, A.   Sappho to Phaon.
Riley, J.   Out-worn Sappho, An.
Rossetti, C.   Sappho.
Sexton.   Red Dance, The.
Swinburne.   Sapphics.
Williams, W.   Sappho, Be Comforted.
   To a Lovely Old Bitch.
Wordsworth, W.   Alcaeus to Sappho.
Wright, J.   Erinna to Sappho.
   Sappho.

Sarah (Bible)
Nemerov.   Nicodemus.
Van Duyn.   Cities of the Plain, The.
Wilner, E.   Sarah's Choice.

Sarajevo, Yugoslavia
Milosz, C.   Sarajevo.
Nemerov.   Sarajevo.

Sarto, Andrea del
Browning, R.   Andrea del Sarto.

Sashimi and Sushi
Muldoon, P.   Sushi.
Sze.   In Your Honor.

Satan
Auden.   Et in Arcadia Ego.
Baudelaire.   Litanies to Satan.
   Total Harmony.
Berryman.   Whether There Is Sorrow in the
   Demons.
Bierce.   Binnacle, The.
Blake, W.   Book of Urizen [or First Book of
   Urizen], The.
   I rose up at the dawn of day.
Browning, R.   Doctor———.
   Ponte dell' Angelo, Venice.
Burns, R.   Address to the Deil.
   Epigram on Capt. Francis Grose, the Celebrated
   Antiquary.
   On J-hn M-r-ne, Laird of L-gg-n.
   Poem on Life.
   To an Artist.
Byron, G.   Devil's Drive, The.
   On Sam Rogers.
Chesterton.   Aristocrat, The.
Clampitt.   Mulciber at West Egg.
Coleridge, S.   Devil's Thoughts, The.
Cullen, C.   Dictum.
   For a Mouthy Woman.
Cummings, E. E.   Devil crept in eden wood.
   In Just.
Davie, D.   Ironist, The.
Dickinson, E.   Devil, had he fidelity, The.
   Snake, The.
   We read in a tremendous Book.
Eberhart, R.   Assassin, The.
Emerson, R.   For Lucifer, that old athlete.
Herrick.   Another.

Satan.
To Julia.
Upon Pink an Ill-Fac'd Painter.
Hill, G.   Bibliographers, The.
Hopkins, G.   Dark-out Lucifer detesting this,
   The.
Jacob, M.   Rainbow.
Kipling, R.   Conundrum of the Workshops, The.
Lawrence, D. H.   Lucifer.
   Old Archangels.
   Root of Our Evil, The.
   When Satan Fell.
Meredith, G.   Lucifer in Starlight.
Nemerov.   Poem of Margery Kempe, A.
Olson, C.   He is the Devil. He whores Nature.
   Love is a word in his Mouth. He has no
   Mouth.
Pagis.   Homily.
   Opening to Satan, An.
Pinkerton, H.   Error Pursued.
Plath.   Sonnet to Satan.
Rich, A.   Lucifer in the Train.
Rimbaud, A.   Hanged Men Dance.
Rossetti, C.   O Lucifer, Son of the Morning!
   Three Enemies, The.
Shelley, P.   Devil's Walk, The.
   Fragment: Satan Broken Loose.
Smith, S.   Fallen, Fallen.
   God and the Devil.
   I Was So Full.
Snyder, G.   Milton by Firelight.
Thomas, D.   Incarnate Devil.
Very.   Serpent, The.
Whitman, W.   Punishment of Pride, The.

Satie, Erik
Merrill, J.   Angel.

Satire and Satirists
Bierce.   Substance or Shadow.
Campion, T.   Verba volant; verum: quid enim
   velocius illis?
Cavafy.   Mimiambi of Herodas, The.
De la Mare.   Satire, The.
Graves, R.   Research and Development:
   Classified.
Hacker, M.   Pornographic Poem.
Herrick.   On Poet Prat.
MacNeice.   Satirist, The.
Nerval.   Mute Phenomena, The.
Shelley, P.   Fragment of a Satire on Satire.
Spenser, E.   Prosopopoia: or Mother Hubberds
   Tale.

Satiric Verse
Meredith, G.   Empedocles.
   Jump-to-Glory Jane.
Swift, J.   On Reading Dr. Young's Satires.
See also **Satire and Satirists**

Saturday
Beckett, S.   Samedi répit.
Ramanujan.   Saturdays.
See also **Sabbath**

Saul (Bible)
Bradstreet, A.   David's Lamentation for Saul
   and Jonathan.
Browning, R.   Saul.
Byron, G.   Song of Saul before His Last Battle.
Lindsay, N.   Hail to the Sons of Roosevelt.
   In Which Roosevelt Is Compared to Saul.
Logan, J.   Ah, so our first load of honey heavy
   Christmas trees.
   Far off the road on the left on a slight rolling
   hill.
   I did but taste a little of the honey with the.
   If the half moon stamp of a sacred hoof showed
   Cadmus.
   In my dream I know I see my father Saul a
   king.
   Monologues of the Son of Saul.
Merton.   St. Paul.
Smith, S.   Man Saul, The.
Wilbur, R.   Water Walker.

Saunas
Milosz, C.   Plato's Dialogues.
See also **Baths and Bathing**

Savannah, Georgia
Davie, D.   Savannah.

Savonarola, Girolamo
  Merwin.   Savonarola.
Sawmills and Sawyers
  Carruth, H.   Regarding Chainsaws.
  Dugan, A.   Sawyer's Rage against Trees Noble
    as Horses, A.
Scandinavia and Scandinavians
  Dubie.   Everlastings, The.
Scarecrows
  De la Mare.   Scarecrow, The.
  Dubie.   Tomb Pond.
  Lindsay, N.   What the Scarecrow Said.
  Mahon.   Going Home.
  Murray, P.   Receipt to Frighten away the Dean,
    A.
  Nemerov.   Sonnet at Easter.
  Wilbur, R.   Sonnet: "Winter deepening, the hay
    all in, The."
  Wright, J.   Dog in a Cornfield.
  Zaturenska.   Girl and Scarecrow.
Scarlatti, Domenico
  Zaturenska.   Background with Harpsichord.
Schiele, Egon
  Laughlin, J.   Doppelgaengers, The.
Schoenberg, Arnold
  Tomlinson, C.   Ode to Arnold Schoenberg.
Scholarship and Scholars
  Arnold, M.   Scholar Gypsy, The.
  Baudelaire.   Cats.
  Browning, R.   Development.
    Grammarian's Funeral, A.
  Carver, R.   Possible, The.
  Cavafy.   Tomb of the Grammarian Lysias.
  Cowper, W.   Retaliation.
  Cummings, E. E.   Ballad of the Scholar's
    Lament.
    Voices to voices, lip to lip.
  Cunningham, J.   To a Friend, on Her
    Examination for the Doctorate in English.
  Davie, D.   Poet-Scholar, The.
  Diogenes Laertius.   Be gone ye blockheads,
    Heraclitus cries.
  Donne.   To Mr S. B.
  Eberhart, R.   Lucubration.
  Eliot, T. S.   Mr. Apollinax.
  Emerson, R.   Scholar is a ball thats spent.
  Frost, R.   Lesson for Today, The.
  Graves, R.   Complaint and Reply.
  Han-shan.   I met a brilliant scholar once.
    There's a brilliant man somewhere.
  HaNagid.   House of Prayer, The.
  Hughes, L.   Ph.D.
  Kizer, C.   Marriage Song: "We begin with the
    osprey who cries, "Clang, clang!"."
  Laughlin, J.   Among the Roses.
    Maledictus In Plebe Sit.
    My Ambition.
    O Hermes Trismegistus.
  Merton.   Origen.
  Milosz, C.   Philology.
  Nemerov.   To a Scholar in the Stacks.
  Niedecker.   Your erudition.
  Pasolini.   Plan of Future Works.
  Pinsky.   Rhyme of Reb Nachman, The.
  Riley, J.   Man of Many Parts, A.
    Monsieur le Secretaire.
    Ye Scholar.
  Sheridan, T.   You That Would Read the Bible.
  Shih-te.   I sigh when I see learned men.
  Stevens, W.   On [*or* Of] the Manner of
    Addressing Clouds.
  Stock, R.   Anacreontic for a Chinese Scholar.
  Yeats.   Gratitude to the Unknown Instructors.
    Scholars, The.
  Zagajewski.   Apartment for Scholars.
See also **Pedantry and Pedants; Students;
  Teaching and Teachers**
School and Schools
  Atwood.   Comic Books vs. History.
  Auden.   Schoolchildren.
  Brooks, G.   We Real Cool.
  Browning, E.   Song for the Ragged Schools of
    London, A.
  Browning, R.   Epigram on School Days.

  Burns, R.   Tale, A.
  Ciardi, J.   Knothole in Spent Time, A.
    Miss Olivia Branton.
    Ode for School Convocation.
    Poem for Benn's Graduation from High School,
    A.
  Clough.   Effusions of a School-Patriarch, The.
  Coleridge, S.   Sonnet on Quitting Christ's
    Hospital.
  Collins, B.   Schoolsville.
  Cooper, J.   Wanda's Blues.
  Davie, D.   Sorting the Personae.
  Dickey, J.   Mangham.
  Dickinson, E.   From all the Jails the Boys and
    Girls.
  Dubie.   Of Politics, & Art.
  Dugan, A.   Teacher's Lament.
  Dunbar, P.   Old High School and the New, The.
    Wadin' in de Crick.
  Eberhart, R.   Long Term Suffering.
  Emerson, R.   How drearily in College hall.
    It takes a philosopher or fool.
  Frost, R.   Not of School Age.
    To the Right Person.
  Glück, L.   School Children, The.
  Gunn, T.   Drive to Los Alamos, A.
  Hardy, T.   He Revisits His First School.
    High-School Lawn, The.
  Heaney, S.   Transgression, A.
  Helsham, R.   Prologue to *Hippolytus*, Spoken by
    a Boy of Six Years Old.
  Hill, G.   Cowan Bridge; At the Site of 'Lowood
    School.'
  Hughes, L.   Graduation.
    Kids in School with Me, The.
  Jacobsen, J.   Class, The.
  Kipling, R.   Kitchener's School.
    School Song, A.
    Waster, The.
  Larkin, P.   Administration.
    By Day, a Lifted Study-Storehouse.
    School in August, The.
  Laughlin, J.   Love Is a School.
  Lawrence, D. H.   Best of School, The.
    Children Singing in School.
    How can I teach you when your blue.
    Last Lesson of the Afternoon.
    School on the Outskirts.
    Schoolmaster [A], The.
    Snowy Day at School, A.
    Snowy Day in School, A.
  Levine, P.   On My Own.
  Lorde.   Bees, The.
    Release Time.
  Lux.   You Go To School To Learn.
  McHugh, H.   Five Threes (Fast Bike).
  Merton.   News from the School at Chartres.
  Moore, M.   Student, The.
  Muldoon, P.   Anseo.
    Geography Lesson, The.
    How to Play Championship Tennis.
  Niedecker.   Young ones go away to school, The.
  Oliver, M.   Spring in the Classroom.
  Paley, G.   For Danny.
    Tenth Grade.
  Piercy.   Learning Experience.
  Riley, J.   Friday Afternoon.
  Ritsos.   School Holidays.
  Rukeyser, M.   Backside of the Academy, The.
  Sexton.   Elegy in the Classroom.
  Sheridan, T.   Epilogue to *Julius Caesar*, The.
    Mr. Sheridan's Prologue to the Greek Play of
    Phaedra and Hippolytus.
    Prologue Spoken at Mr. Sheridan's School.
    Prologue Spoken before a Greek Play, at the
    Reverend Dr. Sheridan's School.
  Simic.   School for Dark Thoughts.
  Smith, S.   At School.
    Parents.
    Si Peu Séduisante.
    To School!
  Spender, S.   Elementary School Classroom in a
    Slum, An.
  Stafford, W.   At Liberty School.

  Dropout.
    School Days.
  Swift, J.   Description of the Morning, A.
  Very.   Common School, The.
    Hacker School House, The.
  Whitman, W.   Old Man's Thought of School,
    An.
  Whittier.   At School-Close.
    In School-Days.
    To My Old Schoolmaster.
    Vanishers, The.
  Williams, C. K.   Hood.
    Soon.
  Wright, J.   Little Girl on Her Way to School, A.
  Yeats.   Among School Children.
  Zagajewski.   Planetarium.
See also **Colleges and Universities**
Schoolmasters
  Helsham, R.   Prologue to *Hippolytus*, Spoken by
    a Boy of Six Years Old.
  Sheridan, T.   Epilogue to *Julius Caesar*, The.
    Prologue Designed for the Play of *Oedipus*,
    Written in Greek, A.
    Prologue Spoken at Mr. Sheridan's School.
    To His Excellency Our Lord Carteret, Lord
    Lieutenant of Ireland.
  Thoreau.   Pens to mend, and hands to guide.
See also **Teaching and Teachers**
Schopenhauer, Arthur
  Carruth, H.   World as Will and Representation,
    The.
  Lawrence, D. H.   Schoolmaster [B], The.
  Zagajewski.   Schopenhauer's Crying.
Schubert, Franz
  Schuyler, J.   Grand Duo.
  Zagajewski.   Franz Schubert: A Press
    Conference.
    Opus Posthumous.
    Seventeen.
Schwartz, Delmore
  Dubie.   World Isn't a Wedding of the Artists of
    Yesterday, The.
  Koch, K.   Pleasures of Peace, The.
  Laughlin, J.   He Did It to Please His Mother.
    Sleepless Night, A.
  Lowell, R.   To Delmore Schwartz.
Science and Scientists
  Ai.   Testimony of J. Robert Oppenheimer, The.
  Amichai [*or* Amikhai].   On the Day My
    Daughter Was Born No One Died.
    On the Day My Daughter Was Born Not a
    Single Person Died.
  Ammons.   Exotic.
  Auden.   Ode to Terminus.
  Bierce.   Science.
  Ciardi, J.   Fragment: "To the laboratory then I
    went. What little."
  Cooper, J.   After the Bomb Tests.
  Cummings, E. E.   Beware beware beware /
    because because because.
    But granted that it's nothing paradoxically
    enough beyond mere personal.
    Kind) / YM&WC / (of sort of).
    Of Ever-Ever Land i speak.
    Pity This Busy Monster,Manunkind.
    Proud of his scientific attitude.
    Space being(don't forget to remember)Curved.
    Who before dying demands not rebirth.
  De la Mare.   Happy Encounter, The.
  Dickinson, E.   Science will not trust us.
  Dubie.   American Scene, An.
  Dugan, A.   Criticism of Bergson and Darwin.
  Enzensberger, H.   Research Council.
    Thoughts on the Run 3.
  Fenton, J.   Kingfisher's Boxing Gloves, The.
  Frost, R.   Any Size We Please.
    Reflex, A.
    Why Wait for Science.
  Graves, R.   Research and Development:
    Classified.
  Herrick.   Science in God.
  Jarrell, R.   Charles Dodgson's Song.
    Emancipators, The.

Romance of Science, The.
Jeffers, R.   Curb Science?
Mathematicians and physics men, The.
Science.
Staggering Back Toward Life.
Kizer, C.   Twelve O'Clock.
Koch, K.   Poem: "Thing / To do / Is organize /
    The sea, The."
Kumin, M.   Heaven as Anus.
Larkin, P.   Ape Experiment Room.
Laughlin, J.   Bless You, Mr President.
Lawrence, D. H.   Anaxagoras.
    Scientific Doctor, The.
    Self-Protection.
MacDiarmid, H.   Poetry and Science.
MacLeish.   Dr. Sigmund Freud Discovers the
    Sea Shell.
McGrath, T.   Little Odyssey of Jason Quint, of
    Science, Doctor, The.
Milosz, C.   After Enduring.
    Linnaeus.
Nash, O.   Purist, The.
Niedecker.   Swedenborg.
Patchen.   It Depends on Whose Science.
Poe.   Sonnet—To Science.
Pope, A.   Intended for Sir Isaac Newton.
Rich, A.   Meditations for a Savage Child.
Rukeyser, M.   Gyroscope, The.
Tate, J.   Teaching the Ape to Write Poems.
Updike.   Bitter Life, A.
    In Praise of $(C_{10}H_9O_5)x$.
V. B. Nimble, V. B. Quick.
Very.   Man of Science, The.
Wordsworth, W.   Lines Written as a School
    Exercise at Hawkshead, Anno Aetatis 14.

Science Fiction
Collins, B.   Man in Space.

Scopes Trial
See **Evolution**

Scorn
Blok.   Earth's Heart Is Growing Cold Again.
Carew, T.   Looking-Glass, A.
    To My Mistress Sitting by a River's Side, an
    Eddy.
De la Mare.   Iago.
Donne.   Apparition, The.
Emerson, R.   Quoth Saadi, when I stood before.
Glück, L.   Horse.
Kunitz, S.   Ambergris.
Lorde.   Poem for Women in Rage, A.
Michelangelo Buonarroti.   As, working in hard
    stone to make the face.
    By light more brilliant of a star more bright.
    Fear of death! Who'd shove, The.
    From the first whimper to the expiring sigh.
    From what these eyes, my lady, see of you.
    I wouldn't if I could, Love, check the urge.
    If I'm to believe my eyes now, your response.
    If she rejoices in my tears, and you.
    Impassioned as I am.
    Please tell me, Love, if that lady had a soul.
    Say the face I'm speaking of now, hers I mean.
    She's made her mind up, the.
    You revel in my torments, only you.
Petrarch.   If you, by showing signs of your
    unease.
Ransom, J.   Moments of Minnie.
Robinson, E.   Miniver Cheevy.
Wyatt, S.   I see my plaint with open ears.

Scorpions
Dugan, A.   Barefoot for a Scorpion.
Han-shan.   Two turtles aboard an ox cart.
Komunyakaa.   Praising Dark Places.
Pagis.   In the Laboratory.
Ramanujan.   Death in Search of a Comfortable
    Metaphor.
    Minor Sacrifice, A.
Smith, S.   Scorpion.

Scotland
Auden.   Night Mail, The.
Berryman.   Scots Poem.
Brodsky, J.   Twenty Sonnets to Mary Queen of
    Scots.
Burns, R.   Act Sederunt of the Session—A Scots
    Ballad.

Address of Beelzebub.
Address to Edinburgh.
Amang the trees, where humming bees.
Author's Earnest Cry and Prayer, to the Right
    Honorable and Honorable, the Scotch
    Representatives in the House of Commons,
    The.
Awa Whigs Awa.
Banks of Nith, The.
Banks of the Devon, The.
Battle of Sherra-Moor, The.
Birks of Aberfeldy, The [Composed on the
    Spot].
Birth-Day Ode. December 31st 1787, A.
Bonie Laddie, Highland Laddie.
Buy Braw Troggin. An Excellent New Song.
Ca' the Ewes [*or* Yowes] [to the Knowes].
Caledonia.
Campbells Are Comin, The.
Castle Gordon—*Intended to Be Sung to Morag.*
Cotter's Saturday Night [nscribed to Robert
    Aiken [*or* R. A****], Esq.], The.
Dainty Davie.
Dumfires Volunteers, The.
Election: A New Song, The.
Epistle to Mr Tytler of Woodhouselee, Author
    of a Defence of Mary Queen of Scots
Epistle to Robt. Graham Esq: of Fintry on the
    Election for the Dumfries String of Boroughs,
    Anno 1790.
Epitaph. Here Lies Robert Fergusson, Poet.
Extempore [on the *Loyal Natives'* Verses].
Five Carlins—A Ballad—Tune, Chevy Chase,
    The.
Frae the friends and Land I love.
Halloween.
Here's a Health to Them That's Awa'
Highland Balou, The.
Highland Laddie.
It Was A' for Our Rightfu' King.
Jessie—A New Scots Song.
John Barleycorn [a Ballad].
Johnie B———'s Lament.
Kirk's Alarm, The.
Lines on Stirling.
Lines Written on a Bank-Note.
Nithsdale's Welcome Hame.
O Kenmure's on and awa, Willie.
Ode [for General Washington's Birthday].
On the Death of Sir J. Hunter Blair.
On the Death of the Late Lord President
    Dundas.
On the Late Captain Grose's Peregrinations
    thro' Scotland, Collecting the Antiquities of
    That King.
Prologue: "When by a generous Public's kind
    acclaim."
Scotch Drink.
Scots Ballad.
Scots Prologue, *For Mrs. Sutherland's Benefit
    Night,* Spoken at the Theatre Dumfries.
Scots Wha Hae.
Second Epistle to John Lapraik.
Song: "As I stood by yon roofless tower."
Song. On Miss W. A.
Such a Parcel of Rogues in a Nation.
Sutors o' Selkirk.
Tam o' Shanter; A Tale.
There'll Never Be Peace Till Jamie Comes
    Hame.
To a Haggis.
To William Simpson, Ochiltree.
Toast, A.
Up and Warn A' Willie.
Wham will we send to London town.
White Cockade, The.
Written with a Pencil over the Chimney-Piece,
    in the Parlour of the Inn at Kenmore,
    Taymouth.
Yon wild, mossy mountains sae lofty and wide.
Clampitt.   Westward.
Davie, D.   Strathnaver.
Jonson, B.   On the Union.
Keats.   Lines Written in the Highlands after a
    Visit to Burns's Country.

MacDiarmid, H.   Conception.
    Dìreadh III.
    Gairmscoile.
    John Maclean (1879-1923).
    Little White Rose, The.
    Scotland.
    Scotland Small?
    Vision of Scotland, A.
MacNeice.   Bagpipe Music.
Raine, K.   For the Visitors' Book.
Scott, S.   Hellvellyn.
    On the Massacre of Glencoe, 1692.
    Pibroch of Donuil Dhu.
Tomlinson, C.   Mr. Brodsky.
    Of Lady Grange.
Unknown.   Geordie [An Old Ballad].
    Tam Lin.
Whittier.   Burns.
    Memory, A.
Wordsworth, W.   Bothwell Castle.
    Brownie's Cell, The.
    Composed at Cora Linn in Sight of Wallace's
    Tower.
    Composed in the Glen of Loch Etive.
    Effusion in the Pleasure-Ground on the Banks of
    the Bran, Near Dunkeld.
    Help for the Memory of the Grand Independent;
    A New Song, A.
    Highland Broach, The.
    Highland Hut.
    On the Sight of a Manse in the South of
    Scotland.
    Suggested by a View from an Eminence in
    Inglewood Forest.

Scots, The
Burns, R.   Address to Edinburgh.
    Author's Earnest Cry and Prayer, to the Right
    Honorable and Honorable, the Scotch
    Representatives in the House of Commons,
    The.
    Battle of Sherra-Moor, The.
    Birth-Day Ode. December 31st 1787, A.
    Buy Braw Troggin. An Excellent New Song.
    Cock up Your Beaver.
    Cotter's Saturday Night [nscribed to Robert
    Aiken [*or* R. A****], Esq.], The.
    Election: A New Song, The.
    Five Carlins—A Ballad—Tune, Chevy Chase,
    The.
    Gude Wallace.
    Here's a Health to Them That's Awa'
    Highland Laddie.
    Johnie B———'s Lament.
    Johnie Cope.
    O Kenmure's on and awa, Willie.
    Ode [for General Washington's Birthday].
    On Miss J. Scott, of Ayr.
    Scotch Drink.
    Scots Wha Hae.
    Such a Parcel of Rogues in a Nation.
    To a Haggis.
    Toast, A.
    Verses Intended to Be Written below a Noble
    Earl's Picture.
    Wham will we send to London town.
    Whistle. A Ballad, The.
Byron, G.   Address Intended to be Recited at the
    Caledonian Meeting.
Graves, R.   Single Fare.
Kipling, R.   Fall of Jock Gillespie, The.
    McAndrew's Hymn.
MacDiarmid, H.   Hokum.
    Weapon, The.
Nash, O.   Everything's Haggis in HOboken, or,
    Scots Wha Hae Hae.
    Genealogical Reflection.

Scott, Sir Walter
Schuyler, J.   Eyes at the Window.
    Walter Scott.
Wordsworth, W.   On the Departure of Sir Walter
    Scott from Abbotsford, for Naples.
    Yarrow Revisited.

Scottish Highlands
Burns, R.   Bannocks o' Bear-Meal.
    Highland Widow's Lament, The.

Killiecrankie.
My Heart's in the Highlands.
Verse Composed and Repeated by *Burns*, to the Master of the House, on Taking Leave at a Place in the Highlands, Where He Had Been Hospitably Entertained, A.
Byron, G.   Address Intended to be Recited at the Caledonian Meeting.
When I Roved a Young Highlander.

Scottsboro Case
Cullen, C.   Scottsboro, Too, Is Worth Its Song.
Hughes, L.   August 19th.
Ballad of Ozie Powell.
Scottsboro.
Town of Scottsboro, The.

Screams
Amichai [*or* Amikhai].   False Interpretation.
Creeley.   Turn, The.
Hall, D.   "Scream, The."
Hughes, T.   Scream, The.
Kinnell.   Fire in Luna Park.
Laughlin, J.   Ever So.
Orr, G.   Screaming Out Loud.
Riley, J.   Want to Be Whur Mother Is.
Stock, R.   Trajectory of a Scream.
Tomlinson, C.   Scream, The.

Scribes
Chaucer.   Chaucer's Wordes unto Adam, his Owne Scriveyn.
See also **Secretaries**

Sculpture and Sculptors
Berryman.   Ecce Homo.
Borges.   Bust of Janus Speaks, A.
Broumas, O.   Aphrodite.
Browning, E.   Hiram Powers' "Greek Slave."
Byron, G.   On the Bust of Helen by Canova.
Carew, T.   Carver. To His Mistress, The.
Cavafy.   Tyanan Sculptor.
Char.   Celebrating Giacometti.
Ciardi, J.   Fragment of a Bas Relief.
Codrescu.   Near Sonnet.
Creeley.   Two Kids.
Davie, D.   Ars Poetica.
Sculptures in Hungary.
Sonnet: "As massive and dispensable as sculpture."
De la Mare.   Image, The.
Dubie.   Saints of Negativity, The.
Dugan, A.   Fragment on the British Museum.
Eberhart, R.   Cousin Florence.
Laocoön.
Looking Head On.
Emerson, R.   Painting and Sculpture.
Ferlinghetti, L.   Goya & the Sleep of Reason.
In hintertime Praxiteles.
García Lorca.   In Malaga.
"H. D."   Gift.
Hall, D.   Notes For Nobody.
"Reclining Figure."
Hardy, T.   Children and Sir Nameless, The.
Question of Marriage, A.
Hughes, T.   Earthenware Head, The.
Jacobsen, J.   Interrupted, The.
Jarrell, R.   Bronze David of Donatello, The.
Keats.   On Seeing the Elgin Marbles.
Komunyakaa.   Lost Wax.
Lawrence, D. H.   London Mercury.
Levertov.   Hidden Monsters at the Mount Auburn Cemetery. A Found Poem.
Logan, J.   On a Prize Crucifix by a Student Sculptor.
Meredith, W.   Thoughts on One's Head (In Plaster, with a Bronze Wash).
Merrill, J.   Dream (Escape from the Sculpture Museum) and Waking.
Michelangelo Buonarroti.   As by subtracting, my lady, one creates.
As, working in hard stone to make the face.
His beautiful eyes! I hardly saw them, only.
How can it be, as long experience shows.
If by its heaven-sent power the mind conceives.
If my rough hammer shapes the obdurate stone.
My lady, how comes it about—what all can see.
Sonnet of Michel Angelo Buonaroti.
This face, says art, alone.

Through many a year and many a vain assay.
To one of taste both flawless and robust.
Moore, M.   No Swan So Fine.
Pagis.   Moment at the Louvre, A.
Piercy.   For Jeriann's Hands.
Plath.   Sculptor.
Riley, J.   Conqueror, The.
Rilke.   Mask, The.
Ritsos.   Craftsman, The.
Sandburg, C.   Face.
Head.
Mask.
Shapiro, K.   Calder, A.
Stock, R.   Invisible Golden Sections.
Rococo Birdbath with Figurine of Daphne as Warning to Virgins.
Tomlinson, C.   Maillol.
Portrait in Stone.
Updike.   Roman Portrait Busts.
Weiss, T.   Hook, The.
Wilbur, R.   Giacometti.
Williams, T.   Stonecutter's Angels, The.
Testa Dell' Effebo.
Williams, W.   Gothic Candor.
Wilner, E.   Fourth David, The.
Winged Victory.
Yeats.   Bronze Head, A.
Statues, The.
Zukofsky, L.   1892-1941.

Sea
Amichai [*or* Amikhai].   So I Went Down to the Ancient Harbor.
Then I went down to the ancient port: human actions.
Ammons.   Expressions of Sea Level.
So I Said I Am Ezra.
Undersea.
Arnold, M.   Dover Beach.
Ashbery, J.   Painter, The.
Auden.   On This Island.
Baudelaire.   Man and Sea.
Beckett, S.   Dieppe.
Fleuves et océans.
La Mouche.
Berry, W.   Farmer and the Sea, The.
Berryman.   Ceremony and Vision.
Bishop, E.   At the Fishhouses.
Cootchie.
Large Bad Picture.
Map, The.
Pleasure Seas.
Quai d'Orléans.
Riverman, The.
Seascape.
Song: "Summer is over upon the sea."
Twelfth Morning; or What You Will.
Wave, The.
Blue Cloud.   Reflections on the St. Lawrence Seaway.
Bly, R.   Calm Day at Drake's Bay.
On a Ferry across Chesapeake Bay.
Sitting on Some Rocks in Shaw Cove.
Two Sounds When We Sit by the Ocean.
Borges.   Herman Melville.
Sea, The.
Broumas, O.   Bride.
Sea Change.
Thetis.
Browning, E.   Earth and Her Praisers.
Man and Nature.
Sea-Mew, The.
Sea-side walk, A.
Sounds.
Browning, R.   Amphibian.
Meeting at Night.
Parting at Morning.
Bukowski.   Beach Trip.
Gypsies Near Del Mar, The.
Monday Beach, Cold Day.
Shit Time.
Burns, R.   Song: "As I stood by yon roofless tower."
Carruth, H.   Far-removed Mountain Men, The.
Cary, T.   On His Mistress[e] Going to Sea.
Cavafy.   Morning Sea.
Voice from the Sea.

Chuang Tzu.   Autumn Floods.
Ciardi, J.   On Looking East to the Sea with a Sunset behind Me.
Saipan.
Sea-Birds.
Sea Burial.
Sea Shines, The.
Clampitt.   Beach Glass.
Cowper, W.   To Mr. Newton [on His Return from Ramsgate].
Crane, H.   And Bees of Paradise.
At Melville's Tomb.
Mermen, The.
Sea Raised Up, The.
Voyages.
Crane, S.   Man adrift on a slim spar, A.
To the maiden.
Creeley.   As You Come.
Memory ("Fresh, A").
Place ("Faded mind, / fading colors").
Sea ("Ever / to sleep").
Cullen, C.   For Joseph Conrad.
Cummings, E. E.   As is the sea marvelous.
Because i love you)last night.
Beyond the brittle towns asleep.
God gloats upon Her stunning flesh. Upon.
Here is the ocean,this is moonlight:say.
How many moments must(amazing each).
I remark that this beach has been used too. much Too. originally.
Maggie and Milly and Molly and May.
What is / a / voyage / ?
Davie, D.   North Sea, in a Snowstorm, The.
North Sea, The.
Our Lady.
Where Depths Are Surfaces.
De la Mare.   Flotsam.
Good Company.
Mermaids, The.
Never-To-Be.
Sea-Magic.
Thule.
Dickey, J.   Daybreak.
Expanses.
Immortals.
Lakes of Värmland.
Dickinson, E.   By the Sea.
Drop, that wrestles in the Sea, The.
Escaping backward to perceive.
How slow the Wind.
My River runs to thee.
We send the Wave to find the Wave.
Wild Nights—Wild Nights!
Dove, R.   Fish in the Stone, The.
Dugan, A.   Note: The Sea Grinds Things Up.
Plague of Dead Sharks.
Sailing to Jerusalem.
Dunbar, P.   Fisher Child's Lullaby, The.
Mystic Sea, The.
On the Sea Wall.
Sea speaks to me of you, The.
Wind and the Sea, The.
Duncan, R.   Achilles' Song.
Eberhart, R.   Deep Fishing.
Froth.
Going Backward Going Forward.
Man and Nature.
Moment of Equilibrium among the Islands.
Off Spectacle Island.
Old Tree by the Penobscot.
Ospreys in Cry.
Recognition.
Sea-Ruck.
Sea Storm.
Ship Burning and a Comet All in One Day, A.
Tree Swallows.
Verbalist of Summer, The.
Voyage, The.
Emerson, R.   At Sea, September 1833.
For fifteen winter days.
Heavy blue chain, The.
Nahant.
Sea reflects the rosy sky, The.
Sea-Shore.
Trimountain.
What is it to sail.

Fenton, J.   This Octopus Exploits Women.
Ferlinghetti, L.   Grottamare.
  Old Sailors, The.
  Sea and Ourselves at Cape Ann, The.
Frost, R.   Does No One at All Ever Feel This
    Way in the Least?
  Neither Out Far Nor In Deep.
  Once by the Pacific.
García Lorca.   Ballad of the Water of the Sea.
Glück, L.   Inlet, The.
  Meridian.
  Phenomenal Survivals of Death in Nantucket.
  Portland, 1968.
  Swans.
Graves, R.   Beach, The.
  Door, The.
  Mankind and Ocean.
Gunn, T.   Lerici.
"H. D."   Hermes of the Ways.
  Hermonax.
  Oread.
  Other Sea-Cities.
  Sea Gods.
  Sea Heroes.
  Sea Lily.
  Thetis.
Hall, D.   Blue Wing, The.
  On a Horse Carved in Wood.
  Sea, The.
Hamill, S.   Word for Spring, A.
Hardy, T.   Beeny Cliff.
  Once at Swanage.
Herrick.   Faire Shewes Deceive.
  Gods Mercy.
  Proof to No Purpose.
Hill, G.   Wreaths.
Hopkins, G.   Sea Took Pity, The.
Hughes, L.   Sea Calm.
  Sea Charm.
Hughes, T.   Black Coat.
  Crow on the Beach.
  Mayday on Holderness.
  Relic.
  Still Life.
  Violet at Lough Aughresberg, A.
Jacob, M.   Rainbow.
Jacobsen, J.   Eyes of the Children at the Brink
    of the Sea's Grasp, The.
Jarrell, R.   Birth of Venus, The.
  Iceberg, The.
Jeffers, R.   All night long the rush and trampling
    of water.
  Beach, The.
  Evening Ebb.
  Eye, The.
  July Fourth by the Ocean.
  Morro Bay.
  November Surf.
  Ocean.
  Ocean's Tribute, The.
  Place for No Story, The.
  Their Beauty Has More Meaning.
  Watch the Lights Fade.
  Winged Rock.
Keats.   On the Sea.
Kinnell.   Spindrift.
Kipling, R.   Anchor Song.
  Bell Buoy, The.
  Deep-Sea Cables, The.
  Dykes, The.
  First Chantey, The.
  Gift of the Sea, The.
  In the Matter of One Compass.
  Last Chantey, The.
  Merchantmen, The.
  North Sea Patrol, The.
  Poseidon's Law.
  Sea and the Hills, The.
  Sea-Wife, The.
  Song of the Dead, The.
  Song of the Red War-Boat.
  Wet Litany, The.
Kizer, C.   Epithalamion: "You left me gasping
    on the shore."
Koch, K.   Poem: "Thing / To do / Is organize /
    The sea, The."

Kumin, M.   Night Launch.
Kunitz, S.   Mulch, The.
  Sea, That Has No Ending, The.
Larkin, P.   Absences.
  To the Sea.
Lawrence, D. H.   Butterfly.
  Desire Goes Down into the Sea.
  Forte Dei Marmi.
  Mana of the Sea.
  November by the Sea.
  Sea, The.
  Sea, the Sea, The.
  Spray.
  They Say the Sea Is Loveless.
Lindsay, N.   Queen Mab in the Village.
  Song in July, A.
  Would-Be Merman, The.
Longfellow, H.   Seaweed.
Lorde.   Maiden, The.
  What My Child Learns of the Sea.
Lowell, R.   Near the Ocean.
  Water.
Lux.   Graveyard by the Sea.
MacDiarmid, H.   On the Ocean Floor.
  Water of Life.
MacLeish.   Boatmen of Santorin, The.
  For the Anniversary of my Mother's Death.
  Hurricane.
  Land's Fnd.
  Lost Speakers, The.
  Men of My Century Loved Mozart.
  Out of Sleep Awakened.
  Return.
MacNeice.   Atlantic Tunnel, The.
  Leaving Barra.
  North Sea, The.
  Round the Corner.
  Sailing Orders.
  Thalassa.
  Upon This Beach.
Mahon.   Birdlife.
  Sea in Winter, The.
Major, C.   At Pointe de Rompe Talon.
Mallarmé.   Sea Breeze.
Marvell.   Bermudas.
McGrath, T.   Encounter.
  Poem: "Through the fog / The gulls."
Melville, H.   Far Off-Shore.
  Maldive Shark, The.
  March to the Sea, The.
  Pebbles.
Meredith, G.   Dark on the ridge of the cold salt
    wave.
  Olive Branch, The.
  Wind & sea are as playmates.
Meredith, W.   In Memoriam Stratton
    Christensen.
  Open Sea, The.
Merrill, J.   Island in the Works.
  Remora.
Merton.   Song: "Bottom of the sea has come,
    The."
Merwin.   Sea Cliffs at Kailua in December, The.
Millay, E.   Above These Cares.
  Exiled.
  Hearing Your Words, and Not a Word Among
    Them.
  Inland.
  Mist in the Valley.
  Ragged Island.
Milosz, C.   On a Beach.
Mistral, G.   Sea, The.
Montale.   Agave on the Reef, The.
  Dead, The.
  End of Childhood.
Moore, M.   Fish, The.
  Grave, A.
  Jellyfish, A.
Muldoon, P.   Briefcase, The.
Nash, O.   Beginner's Guide to the Ocean, A.
Nemerov.   Salt Garden, The.
Neruda.   Another One.
  Bomb (II).
  Different Ship, A.
  Search.
Oliver, M.   Sea, The.

Olson, C.   Adamo Me.
  Disposition, The.
  Easter.
  Flower grows, The.
  is an archeology: eight fathom down, on Dogger
    Bank, the bones, The.
  Shut in kept off.
  Thy Gleeman Who Flattered Thee.
Oppen.   Animula.
  Bahamas.
  Gold on Oak Leaves.
  Party on Shipboard.
Parker, D.   Chantey.
  Sea, The.
Patchen.   Fog Over the Sea and the Sun Going
    Down.
Pessoa.   Message.
Plath.   Aquatic Nocturne.
  Blackberrying.
  Full Fathom Five.
  Man in Black.
  Point Shirley.
  Winter Ship, A.
Poe.   Annabel Lec.
  City in the Sea, The.
  To Helen.
  To One in Paradise.
Raine, K.   All that is: / The unbroken surface of
    the sea.
  I went out in the naked light.
  Moment, The.
  My feet in the ever-moving sea.
  Petal of white rose.
  There Shall Be No More Sea.
  Turner's Seas.
Rexroth, K.   Camargue.
Rich, A.   Insusceptibles, The.
Rimbaud, A.   Drunken Boat.
  Seascape.
Ritsos.   Immobilizing the Boundless.
  Knocking.
  Moment.
  Stripped Naked.
Roethke.   On the Quay.
Rossetti, C.   By the Sea.
  Heaven Overarches Earth and Sea.
  His Banner over Me Was Love.
  Horses of the Sea, The.
  O glorious sea that in each climbing wave.
  Roses on a brier, / Pearls from out the bitter sea.
  Song: "Oh what comes over the sea."
  Was Thy Wrath against the Sea?
  Water Spirit's Song, The.
  What Are Heavy?
  Wind Has Such a Rainy Sound, The.
Rossetti, D.   From the Cliffs: Noon.
  Sea-Limits, The.
Rukeyser, M.   After Melville.
  Believing in Those Inexorable Laws.
  Child and Mother.
  Green Limits.
  In the Night the Sound Woke Us.
  Landscpe with Wave Approaching.
  Network that emerges. At the ocean, A.
  Outer Banks, The.
  Running of the Grunion, The.
  Sea Mercy.
  Suite for Lord Timothy Dexter.
  Summer, the Sacramento.
Sandburg, C.   Adelaide Crapsey.
  Alone and Not Alone.
  Baltic Fog Notes.
  Be Ready.
  Bones.
  Changing Light Winds.
  Chasers.
  Deep Sea Wandering.
  Docks.
  Evening Sea Wind.
  Fins.
  Fog Portrait.
  Have Me.
  How Yesterday Looked.
  Kin.
  Nocturn 4: "Claims of the sea, of the tide, move
    out, The."

North Atlantic.
On the Breakwater.
Sand Scribblings.
Sea Chest.
Sea Hold, The.
Sea Slant.
Sea-Wash.
Sea Wisdom.
Sketch.
Spray.
Thimble Islands.
Throw Roses.
Two Nocturns.
Two Women.
Under.
Way of the World, The.
Sarton, M.   Sun Boat.
Schuyler, J.   Amy Lowell Thoughts.
  Crystal Lithium, The.
Sexton.   Consecrating Mother, The.
  In Excelsis.
  There You Were.
Shelley, P.   Time.
Smith, S.   Death's Ostracism.
  Engine Drain, The.
  Forlorn Sea, The.
  Will Ever?
Snyder, G.   Rainbow Body.
  Real Work, The.
Spender, S.   Seascape.
Stevens, W.   Farewell to Florida.
  Idea of Order at Key West, The.
  Paltry Nude Starts on a Spring Voyage, The.
  Sea Surface Full of Clouds.
  Woman That Had More Babies than That, The.
Swenson, M.   At Truro.
  Even Sea, The.
  From Sea Cliff, March.
  Hurricane at Sea, A.
  Out of the Sea, Early.
  Overboard.
  Sea, The.
  Staring at the Sea on the Day of the Death of
    Another.
  Tide at Long Point, The.
  Waking from a Nap on the Beach.
  Wave and the Dune, The.
Sze.   Noah's / Dove.
Tennyson, A.   Break, Break, Break.
  Crossing the Bar.
  Kraken, The.
Thoreau.   Fisher's Son, The.
Tomlinson, C.   Aesthetic.
  Last of Night, The.
  Marine.
  Mediterranean, The.
  Sea Change.
  Sea is Open to the Light, The.
  Sea Poem.
Unknown.   Battle of Brunanburh.
  Song of Blodeuwedd, The.
Updike.   Bitter Life, A.
  Sand Dollar.
  Sea Knell.
  Shipbored.
  Winter Ocean.
Vallejo.   I am Freed.
Van Geel.   Homecoming.
Very.   Moon was shining on the deck, The.
Walcott.   Missing the Sea.
  Sea is History, The.
Warren, R.   End of Season.
  Mr. Dodd's Son.
  Question at Cliff-Thrust.
  Sea Hates the Land, The.
  True Nature of Time, The.
Weiss, T.   Far Out, Far In.
Whitman, W.   After the Sea-Ship.
  As I Ebb'd with the Ocean of Life.
  Facing West from California's Shores.
  From Montauk Point.
  In Cabin'd Ships at Sea.
  Out of the Cradle Endlessly Rocking.
  Out of the Rolling Ocean the Crowd.
  Patrolling Barnegat.
  Ship Starting, The.

Song for All Seas, All Ships.
To the Man-of-War Bird.
With Husky-Haughty Lips, O Sea!
World below the Brine, The.
Whittier.   Cable Hymn, The.
  Hampton Beach.
  Ocean.
  Palatine, The.
Wilbur, R.   Beacon, The.
  Conjuration.
  From the Lookout Rock.
  Games One.
  Waters, The.
  Wellfleet: The House.
Wilde, O.   Vita Nuova.
Williams, W.   Cod Head, The.
  Flowers by the Sea.
  In Harbor.
  Sadness of the Sea, The.
  Sea, The.
  Yachts, The.
Wordsworth, W.   Address to the Ocean.
  At the Isle of Wight. 1793.
  Beauty and Moonlight.
  By the Sea-Side.
  Composed by the Sea-Shore.
  Fact, and an Imagination or, Canute and Alfred,
    on the Sea-Shore, A.
  It is a beauteous evening, calm and free.
  Lines Written While Sailing in a Boat at
    Evening.
  To Melpomene.
Wright, J.   American Wedding.
  Cold Divinities, The.
  Fishermen, The.
  Morality of Poetry, The.
  Old Age Compensation.
  Snowstorms in the Midwest.
  Way to Make a Living, A.
Yeats.   White Birds, The.
Zukofsky, L.   It's hard to see but think of a sea.
  World autumn, The.

See also **Sailing and Sailors**
Sea Battles
Cavafy.   In a Township of Asia Minor.
  Naval Battle, The.
HaNagid.   Miracle at Sea, The.
Meredith, W.   Carrier.

See also **Naval Battles**
Sea Chanteys
Lindsay, N.   Sea Serpent Chantey, The.
Sea Creatures
Brodsky, J.   New Jules Verne, The.
De la Mare.   Sunk Lyonesse.
Emerson, R.   Lobster-car, boat, or fishbasket.
Fenton, J.   This Octopus Exploits Women.
Graves, R.   Sea Horse, The.
HaNagid.   Miracle at Sea, The.
Moore, M.   Fish, The.
  Sea Unicorns and Land Unicorns.
Nash, O.   Snark Was a Boojum Was a Prawn,
    The.
Olson, C.   His house / in the branches of.
Rexroth, K.   Fundamental Disagreement with
    Two Contemporaries.
Riley, J.   Craqueodoom.
Tennyson, A.   Kraken, The.
Williams, W.   Sea-Elephant, The.

Sea Gulls
Brodsky, J.   At the City Dump in Nantucket.
Dugan, A.   Dyng Seagull and the Great Whore
    of the World, The.
Levi, P.   Gulls of Settimo, The.

See also **Gulls**
Sea Hawks
Eberhart, R.   Ospreys in Cry.
  Sea-Hawk.
Sea Monsters and Sea Serpents
Lindsay, N.   Sea Serpent Chantey, The.
Tennyson, A.   Kraken, The.
Sea Shells
Ignatow, D.   Lightly.
Pagis.   Seashell.

See also **Shells**

Sea Voyages
Amichai [*or* Amikhai].   Sonnet from the
    Voyage.
Borges.   To a Coin.
Brodsky, J.   New Jules Verne, The.
Cavafy.   Alexandrian Merchant.
Clampitt.   Handed Down.
Crane, S.   God fashioned the ship of the world
    carefully.
Hughes, L.   Long Trip.
Kizer, C.   Voyager.
Levertov.   Voyage.
Levi, P.   Pliny.
Lux.   "Mr John Keats Five Feet Tall" Sails
    Away.
Mallarmé.   For the sake of voyaging—
    heedlessly.
  Salutation.
Pessoa.   Opium Eater.
Sze.   Network, The.
Wheatley, P.   Ode to Neptune.
  To a Gentleman on His Voyage to *Great-Britain*
    for the Recovery of His Health.
Wilde, O.   Impression de Voyage.

See also **Voyages**
Seacoasts
Ammons.   Corsons Inlet.
Atwood.   Galiano Coast: Four Entrances.
Berryman.   Ceremony and Vision.
Bishop, E.   Little Exercise.
Browning, E.   Soul's Travelling, The.
Carruth, H.   Études de Plusiers Paysages de
    l'Âme.
Clampitt.   Cove, The.
  High Noon.
  Midsummer in the Blueberry Barrens.
Crane, H.   To Liberty.
De la Mare.   Flotsam.
Emerson, R.   Lobster-car, boat, or fishbasket.
  Seashore.
Graves, R.   Sea Side.
"H. D."   Shrine, The.
  When I Am a Cup.
Hopkins, G.   Sea and the Skylark, The.
Hughes, L.   Moonlight Night: Carmel.
  Seascape.
Jeffers, R.   Point Pinos and Point Lobos.
Keats.   To Ailsa Rock.
Larkin, P.   I Dreamed of an Out-Thrust Arm of
    Land.
Mahon.   Chinese Restaurant in Portrush, The.
  Day Trip to Donegal.
Merrill, J.   Summer People, The.
Mistral, G.   Talcahuano.
Montale.   Seacoasts, / a few blades of sword
    grass are enough.
Nemerov.   Still Life I.
Oliver, M.   Winter.
Olson, C.   By Cure of—Sulfa.
  Compleynt Blossoms April to July.
  On the Shore.
  Purgatory Blind.
Oppen.   Book of Job and a Draft of a Poem to
    Praise the Paths of the Living, The.
  California.
  Coastal Strip.
  Inlet.
  Lighthouses, The.
  Little Pin, The: Fragment.
  Monument.
  Primitive.
  Theological Definition, A.
  West.
Pinsky.   Woman, A.
Plath.   Finisterre.
  Two Lovers and a Beachcomber by the Real
    Sea.
  Whitsun.
Roethke.   Her Time.
  Shy Man, The.
Rossetti, D.   Even So.
Schuyler, J.   Crystal Lithium, The.
Sexton.   In the Beach House.
Smith, S.   Engine Drain, The.
  Numbers.
Stevens, W.   Doctor of Geneva, The.

Fabliau of Florida.
Hibiscus on the Sleeping Shores.
Somnambulisma.
Stock, R.   Grunion Run.
Thomas, D.   Author's Prologue.
Tomlinson, C.   Cronkhite Beach.
  Fiascherino.
  Icos.
  Two Poems on titles proposed by Octavio and
    Marie José Paz.
Warren, R.   Star-Fall.
Williams, W.   Cod Head, The.
  Metric Figure.
Wordsworth, W.   At the Isle of Wight. 1793.
  Narrow girdle of rough stones and crags, A.

See also **Beaches; Shores**

Seafaring and Seafarers
Cavafy.   Second Odyssey, A.
"H. D."   Shrine, The.
Howe, S.   Cabbage Gardens.
Hughes, L.   Death of an Old Seaman.
  Return to Sea.
  Water-Front Streets.
Jackson, L.   There Is No Land Yet.
Logue, C.   Isles of Jessamy, The.
Longfellow, H.   Wreck of the Hesperus, The.
Meredith, W.   Wreck of the Thresher, The (Lost
  at Sea, April 10, 1963).
Mistral, G.   Sea, The.
Oppen.   Memory of Oars.
Pessoa.   Maritime Ode.
  Message.
Poe.   To Helen.
Rimbaud, A.   Drunken Boat.
Unknown.   Seafarer, The.

See also **Sailing and Sailors**

Seals
Bly, R.   Dead Seal [near McClure's Beach], The.
Eberhart, R.   Off Spectacle Island.
  Seals, Terns, Time.
Kipling, R.   Rhyme of the Three Sealers, The.
Lowell, R.   Soft Wood.
McHugh, H.   Seal.
Sexton.   Seal.
Smith, S.   Hymn to the Seal.
Updike.   Seal in Nature.

Seamstresses
Bishop, E.   House Guest.

Séances
Zaturenska.   Séance, The.

Seashores
Amichai [or Amikhai].   At the Seashore.
  Now the Lifeguards Have All Gone Home.
  Sea and the Shore, The.
Ammons.   Wagons.
Bierce.   Basilica.
Creeley.   Question.
  There Is Water.
Logan, J.   Cape Elizabeth: A Photograph.
Montale.   Mediterranean.
  Shore of Versilia.
Tomlinson, C.   Headland, The.
Warren, R.   Pacific Gazer.
Wilde, O.   Vita Nuova.

See also **Beaches; Shores**

Seasickness
Meredith, G.   *Irene* ducks and runs amuck, The.

Seasons
Ammons.   Further On.
Auden.   In Due Season.
Baudelaire.   Mist and Rain.
Berry, W.   Familiar, The.
  Finches, The.
  Song (4).
Bishop, E.   Song for the Rainy Season.
Bogan, L.   Zone.
Bradstreet, A.   Four Seasons of the Year, The.
Brontë, E.   M.G. For The U.S.
  Song.
Browning, R.   Lovers' Quarrel, A.
Burns, R.   Address, to the Shade of Thomson,
  on Crowning His Bust, at *Ednam, Roxburgh-
  shire,* with Bays.
  Bonie Bell.
Clampitt.   Nondescript.

Clough.   In Stratis Viarum IV.
  July's Farewell.
Cooper, J.   March.
Cowper, W.   Winter Nosegay, The.
Cummings, E. E.   All ignorance toboggans into
  know.
  Autumn is:that between there and here.
  Coming of May, The.
  Goo-dmore-ning(en / ter)nize-aday(most).
  In time of daffodils(who know.
  Metamorphosis.
  Open green those / (dear).
  Skating.
  Song: "But we've the may / (for you are in
    love)."
  Summer is over / —it's no use demanding.
  Yes is a pleasant country.
  You are like the snow only.
"Dario."   Autumn Verses.
Davie, D.   Meteorologist, September.
De la Mare.   Children of Stare, The.
  Episodes.
  Futility.
  In Vain.
  Memory.
  Willow, The.
Dickinson, E.   As imperceptibly as grief.
  I remember the leaves were falling.
  It was a quiet way—.
  Now the Grass is Glass.
  Summer begins to have the look.
  'Twas later when the summer went.
  Twice had Summer her fair Verdure.
Donne.   Love's Growth.
  Nocturnal[l] upon Saint Lucy's [*or* S. Lucy's *or*
    S. Lucies] Day, Being the Shortest Day, A.
Dugan, A.   Winter's Onset from an Alienated
  Point of View.
Dunbar, P.   Foolin' wid de Seasons.
  Love's Seasons.
  Roses.
Eberhart, R.   Hornets by the Sill.
  Seasons, The.
  Spider, The.
Emerson, R.   In My Garden.
  Softens the air so cold & rude.
  Thermometer.
  To Ellen, at the South.
Frost, R.   Oven Bird, The.
Graves, R.   Language of the Seasons.
  Mid-Winter Waking.
Gurney, I.   Autumn.
  Change, The.
Hall, D.   September Ode.
  Set of Seasons, A.
  Sister by the Pond, A.
  Twelve Seasons.
Han-shan.   Seasonal round never stops, The.
Hardy, T.   Before and after Summer.
  June Leaves and Autumn.
  Master and the Leaves, The.
  Seasons of Her Year, The.
  We Field-Women.
Herrick.   After Autumne, Winter.
Housman.   Winter.
Hughes, L.   Poem: "When young spring comes."
  Year Round.
Hughes, T.   October Dawn.
  Two Tortoiseshell Butterflies.
Ignatow, D.   Seasons, The.
Jacobsen, J.   Gesture, The.
  Time Exposure.
Keats.   Human Seasons, The.
  To Autumn.
Kipling, R.   Two Months.
Larkin, P.   All Catches Alight.
  We See the Spring Breaking across Rough
    Stone.
Levine, P.   Later Still.
  New Season.
  Voice, The.
  Walk with Tom Jefferson, A.
  Winter Words.
Lindsay, N.   Lame Boy and the Fairy, The.
  Sweethearts of the Year.
Lorde.   Change of Season.

Father, the Year Has Fallen.
  Return.
  What My Child Learns of the Sea.
MacNeice.   April Manifesto, An.
  August.
  Spring Voices.
Melville, H.   Little Good Fellows, The.
  Pontoosuce.
Meredith, G.   Appeasement of Demeter, The.
  Wild Rose and the Snowdrop, The.
Meredith, W.   Seasons' Difference, The.
  Winter: He Shapes Up.
  Winter Song.
Merrill, J.   Under Libra: Weights and Measures.
Merton.   Vine, The.
Millay, E.   Hardy Garden, The.
Montale.   Autumn Quarries.
Nash, O.   It's Never Fair Weather.
  One Third of a Calendar.
Nemerov.   Anniversary.
  Fall Song.
  First Snow.
  Late Summer.
  Madrigal: "She is the darkness where I wander."
  Old Days, The,
Niedecker.   I lost you to water, summer.
O'Hara, F.   Ann Arbor Variations.
  July Is Over and There's Very Little Trace.
  Poem: "So many echoes in my head."
Owen, W.   Winter Song.
Parker, D.   Apple Tree, The.
  Transition.
Patchen.   Nocturne for the Heirs of Light.
Pessoa.   Lydia, when our Autumn comes.
Petrarch.   I ran beneath the shade of shining
  leaves.
Piercy.   Snow, Snow.
  Wind is the Wall of the Year.
Pinsky.   Time of Year, the Time of Day, The.
Plath.   Couriers, The.
Pope, A.   Garden, The.
Prunty.   March.
Ramanujan.   Towards Simplicity.
Ransom, J.   Vaunting Oak.
Rexroth, K.   Hojoki.
  Toward an Organic Philosophy.
  We Come Back.
Riley, J.   Climatic Sorcery.
Rilke.   Autumn Hammer.
  Moment Between Masks.
Rimbaud, A.   O seasons, o châteaux.
Ritsos.   Conformity.
Rossetti, C.   Autumn.
  Autumn Violets.
  Cor Mio.
  Daughter of Eve, A.
  Diamond or a coal? / A diamond, if you please,
    A.
  Fly Away, Fly Away.
  Gone for Ever.
  Grown and Flown.
  If Only.
  Key-Note, The.
  Mirrors of Life and Death.
  Months: A Pageant, The.
  Months, The.
  Mr. and Mrs. Scott, and I.
  O wind, where have you been.
  Once for All. (Margaret).
  Seasons.
  Tempus Fugit.
  Under Willows.
  Year's Windfalls, A.
Rukeyser, M.   After Their Quarrel.
Sandburg, C.   Autumn Movement.
  Brown Gold.
  Bug Spots.
  Cheap Blue.
  Corn Hut Talk.
  Cornfield Ridge and Stream.
  First Sonata for Karlen Paula.
  Lesson.
  Never Two Songs the Same.
  Prairie.
  Year, The.
Sarton, M.   Apple Tree in May.

First Autumn, The.
March-Mad.
Mud Season.
Of the Seasons.
Schuyler, J.　Almanac, An.
Bluet, The.
Hymn to Life.
Looking Forward to See Jane Real Soon.
Poem: "Wind tears up the sun, The."
Thursday.
Seifert.　Window on Birds' Wings.
Shelley, P.　Ode to the West Wind.
Stanza: "If I walk in Autumn's even."
Smith, S.　Saffron.
Stevens, W.　Dwarf, The.
Stockton, A.　Epistle to a Friend Who Urg'd to
Have Some Poetry Sent Her in the Year 1759,
in the Winter, An.
Tate, A.　Seasons of the Soul.
These Deathy Leaves.
Thomas, D.　Here in This Spring.
Thoreau.　Pray to what earth does this sweet
cold belong.
Tomlinson, C.　Northern Spring.
Prelude, A.
Weathercocks, The.
Updike.　Calendar.
Melancholy of Storm Windows, The.
Snowdrops 1987.
Van Duyn.　Fall.
Very.　Change in the Seasons.
Seasons, The.
Walcott.　In a Green Night.
Warren, R.　Cycle.
Glimpses of Seasons.
Paradigm of Seasons.
Seasons.
Vermont Ballad: Change of Season.
Was It One of the Long Hunters of Kentucky
who Discovered Boone at Sunset?
Wilbur, R.　April 5, 1974.
Courtyard Thaw, A.
Fall in Corrales.
In the Elegy Season.
Storm in April, A.
Then.
Two Quatrains for First Frost.
Two Songs in a Stanza of Beddoes'
Winter Spring.
Williams, T.　Sacre de Printemps.
Williams, W.　Another Year.
Wordsworth, W.　Lines Composed a Few Miles
above Tintern Abbey on Revisiting the Banks
of the Wye During a Tour, July 13, 1798.
Ode to Lycoris; May, 1817.
September, 1819.
Thoughts on the Seasons.
Wright, C.　Disjecta Membra.
Journal of English Days, A.
Journal of One Significant Landscape, A.
Wright, J.　Fit against the Country, A.
Mary Bly.
Seasonless, The.
Three Steps to the Graveyard.
To a Troubled Friend.
To the August Fallen.
Yeats.　Wheel, The.
Zaturenska.　Chorale for the Seasons.
Song for a Season.

Seattle, Washington
Ginsberg, A.　Afternoon Seattle.
Logan, J.　Thirteen Preludes for Pioneer Square.
Updike.　Seattle Uplift.

Seaweed
Lawrence, D. H.　Sea-Weed.
Longfellow, H.　Seaweed.
Melville, H.　Tuft of Kelp, The.

Sebastian, Saint
Eliot, T. S.　Love Song of St. Sebastian, The.
Williams, T.　San Sebastiano de Sodoma.

Seclusion
Auden.　Thank You, Fog.
Browning, R.　Dubiety.
Prologue: "O the old wall here! How I could
pass."
Hamill, S.　Cloistered.

Han-shan.　I usually live in seclusion.
Hayden, R.　Soledad.
Levertov.　Closed World, The.
Night on Hatchet Cove.
Mahon.　Craigvara House.
Woods, The.
Melville, H.　Garden of Metrodorus, The.
Pessoa.　Lisbon Revisited (1923).
Ralegh, S.　Like to a Hermit[e] Poor[e].
Rich, A.　Holding Out.
I Am in Danger—Sir.
Letter from the Land of Sinners.
Shapiro, K.　Intellectual, The.
Shelley, P.　Fragment: "Follow to the deep
wood's weeds."
Stafford, W.　Oregon Message, An.
Walcott.　As John to Patmos.

Second Coming
Clifton, L.　My Dream About the Second
Coming.
Jarrell, R.　Clock in the Tower of the Church,
The.
Merton.　Peril, The.
Very.　Coming, The.
Hymn: Nevertheless, when the Son of Man
cometh, shall he find faith on the earth? Luke
18:8.
Hymn: Waiting for Christ.
Return of the Savior, The.
Yeats.　Second Coming, The.
See also **Millennium**

Secrecy and Secrets
Ammons.　Hosts.
Angelou.　In a Time.
Auden.　Household, A.
Secrets.
Berrigan, T.　Scorpio.
Berryman.　Cadenza on Garnette.
Blake, W.　Love's.
Brontë, E.　My Comforter.
Browning, E.　Deserted Garden, The.
Browning, R.　Meeting at Night.
Burns, R.　I Love My Love in Secret.
Whistle, and I'll Come to You, My Lad.
Byron, G.　When We Two Parted.
Carew, T.　Secrecy [*or* Secresie] Protested.
Cavafy.　Hidden Things.
Cowper, W.　Apology, An.
On Her Endeavoring to Conceal Her Grief at
Parting.
Creeley.　Ear, The.
Innocence, The.
De la Mare.　Empty House, The.
Image, The.
Portrait, A.
Voice, The.
Dickey, W.　History of the Moon, The.
Dickinson, E.　Life is the finest secret.
Murmur in the Trees—to note, A.
Secret told, A.
"Secrets" is a daily word.
Donne.　Undertaking, The.
Dove, R.　Adolescence—I.
Dunbar, P.　We Wear the Mask.
Emerson, R.　Dull uncertain brain, A.
On a raisin stone.
Secret that should not be blown, The.
Sphinx, The.
Frost, R.　Secret Sits, The.
Graves, R.　Love and Night.
Secrecy.
Secret Theatre.
Song: Just Friends.
Strayed Message, The.
Three Years Waiting.
Ugly Secret, The.
Unposted Letter.
Gunn, T.　Outdoor Concert, The.
Hacker, M.　After the Revolution.
Sestina: "For a week now our bodies have
whispered."
Hall, D.　Mr. Wakeville on Interstate 90.
HaNagid.　See the Fraud Flow By.
Hardy, T.　Her Secret.
Hill, G.　Turtle Dove, The.
Jacobsen, J.　Distance.

Jonson, B.　Nymph's Passion, A.
To One that Desired Me Not to Name Him.
To Person Guilty ("Guilty, be wise; and though
thou know'st the crimes").
Kipling, R.　Delilah.
Kizer, C.　Antique Father.
Laughlin, J.　Eyes Are the Guides of Love.
Shameful Profession, The.
Lawrence, D. H.　Liaison.
Tease.
Levertov.　Her Secret.
Secret, The.
MacLeish.　Le Secret Humain.
Night Dream, The.
McGrath, T.　Poem: "You out there, so secret."
Meredith, G.　She had a secret—bonny Bess!
Meredith, W.　Vision of Good Secrets, A.
Merwin.　Plaster, The.
Milosz, C.　Lessons.
My Secrets.
Muldoon, P.　Hedgehog.
Nash, O.　Mr. Barcalow's Breakdown.
Parker, D.　Plea.
Patchen.　Strange, Moving Lights of People
Handle Holinesses Unknown, The.
Pessoa.　Interval.
Plath.　Secret, A.
Rich, A.　When We Dead Awaken.
Rossetti, C.　Brandons Both.
Seeking Rest.
Winter: My Secret.
Rukeyser, M.　Private Life of the Sphinx.
Rumi.　All our lives we've looked.
Sandburg, C.　Has-Been, The.
Shelley, P.　Fragment: A Roman's Chamber.
"Shu Ting."　To ———.
Simic.　Suitcase Strapped with a Rope, A.
Smith, S.　Portrait (I).
Stafford, W.　Trying to Tell It.
Stock, R.　Anonymous Secrets.
To The Discreet Reader: An Induction to
Indiscretions.
Warren, R.　Ballad of Mister Dutcher and the
Last Lynching in Gupton.
Whitman, W.　Riddle Song, A.
To You.
Williams, C. K.　Secrets.
Trash.
Wilner, E.　Secret Garden, The.
Wordsworth, W.　Protest against the Ballot.
Said Secrecy to Cowardice and Fraud.
Wyatt, S.　Lover Showeth How He Is Forsaken
of Such as He Sometime Enjoyed, The.
Yeats.　Secret Rose, The.

Secretaries
Dugan, A.　Poem: "Person who can do, The."
Laughlin, J.　Secretary's Story, The.
Piercy.　Secretary Chant, The.
See also **Scribes**

Sectarianism
Davie, D.　Belfast on a Sunday Afternoon.
Cold Spring in Essex.
Two from Ireland.
Dugan, A.　Mockery Against the Irish
Censorship.
Ferlinghetti, L.　Buddha in the Woodpile, A.
Heaney, S.　Casualty.
England's Difficulty.
I'm writing this just after an encounter.
'Religion's never mentioned here,' of course.
Singing School.
This morning from a dewy motorway.
Herbert, G.　Church-Rents and Schisms.
Kinsella, T.　Butcher's Dozen.
Meredith, G.　Jump-to-Glory Jane.
Riley, J.　God's Mercy.

Security
Amichai [*or* Amikhai].　I Was Waiting for My
Girl and Her Steps Were Absent.
Bukowski.　Pace is the Essence.
Promenade.
Sad Poem, A.
Chuang Tzu.　Wholeness.
Collins, B.　Movies, The.
Creeley.　Places ("When I wake next").
Cullen, C.　For a Poet.

Cummings, E. E.   Of Ever-Ever Land i speak.
Dickey, W.   New Place, The.
Dugan, A.   2. Comment on "Business Jacob, the Angel Wrestler."
Dunbar, P.   Farm Child's Lullaby, The.
Eberhart, R.   Wisdom of Insecurity, The.
Frost, R.   Provide, Provide.
Gunn, T.   Hug, The.
  La Prisonnière.
  Reassurance, The.
Hacker, M.   Robber Woman, The.
Herrick.   Bellman, The.
  No Shipwrack of Vertue. To a Friend.
  Old Wives Prayer, The.
  Suspicion Makes Secure.
  True Safety.
Jacobsen, J.   For Any Member of the Security Police.
Koch, K.   Locks.
Lawrence, D. H.   Song of a Man Who Is Loved.
Levi, P.   Shemà.
McGrath, T.   Poem: "When I carry my little son in the cold."
Meredith, G.   Song: "My darling's love shall close me up."
Roethke.   Reckoning, The.
Rossetti, C.   Safe where I cannot lie yet, / Safe where I hope to lie too.
Rukeyser, M.   Another Day. In a Field of Peace the Child, Playing. The Child Preparing for Daytime Sleep.
Sarton, M.   Because What I Want Most Is Permanence.
Stafford, W.   Security.
Voznesensky [or Voznesenskii].   Dead Still.

Seduction
Beckett, S.   Serena II.
Blok.   Accordeon.
Broumas, O.   Backgammon.
Bukowski.   3:30 A.M. Conversation.
  Escape, The.
Burns, R.   As I Went Out Ae May Morning.
  Had I the Wyte She Bade Me.
  Jumpin John.
  Taylor, The.
  Wha Is That at My Bower-Door?
Campion, T.   Be Wise, and Fly Not.
  Blame Not My Cheekes.
  Faire If You Expect Admiring.
  Follow your saint, follow with accents sweet.
  If thou longst so much to learne (sweet boy) what 'tis to love.
  It Fell on a Summer's [or Sommers] Day [or Daie].
  Maid's Complaint, A.
  O Love, where are thy Shafts, thy Quiver, and thy Bow?
  Sweet, exclude me[e] not, nor be divided.
  Think'st thou to seduce me then.
  Thrice Toss[e] These Oaken Ashes in the Air [or Ayre].
  Turn Back, You Wanton Flyer.
  Where She Her Sacred Bower Adorns.
  Your Fair[e] Look[e]s Inflame [My Desire].
Campion, T. et al.   Unlesse there were consent twixt hell and heaven.
Carruth, H.   Green Mountain Idyl.
Carver, R.   For Semra, with Martial Vigor.
Clifton, L.   Eve's version.
Coleridge, S.   Wills of the Wisp, The.
De la Mare.   Decoy, The.
Donne.   Flea, The.
Graves, R.   Scared Child, The.
  Song: The Sigil.
Gunn, T.   Odysseus on Hermes.
  To a Dead Graduate Student.
Hall, D.   Conduct and Work.
Hardy, T.   Dark-Eyed Gentleman, The.
Herrick.   Art above Nature, to Julia.
  Delight in Disorder.
  Upon Julia's Clothes.
Hughes, T.   Speech Out of Shadow.
Laughlin, J.   Arachne.
  If a Poet.
  Like the Octopus.
Levi, P.   Delilah.

Lorde.   On a Night of the Full Moon.
Marvell.   Fair Singer, The.
Meredith, G.   Daphne.
  Penetration and Trust.
  Teaching of the Nude, The.
Parker, D.   Song: "Clarabelle has golden hair."
Ramanujan.   LOVE 2: What He Said, Groping.
Ransom, J.   April Treason.
  Judith of Bethulia.
Riley, J.   Dolores.
  Werewife, The.
Rimbaud, A.   First Night.
  Nina Answers Back.
  To Music.
  Winter Dream.
Rukeyser, M.   Mrs. Walpurga.
Schuyler, J.   Tom's Attempt to Seduce Big Brother Steve.
Seifert.   Smoke of Marijuana, The.
Stock, R.   Man-Giraffe.
  Poet's Prescription of Shamelessness, The.
  Study of a House with Garden Attached.
Williams, C. K.   Medusa.
Williams, M.   Jonathan Seduced.
  Stripper, The.
Williams, T.   To Anna Jean.
Wyatt, S.   Lover Showeth How He Is Forsaken of Such as He Sometime Enjoyed, The.

Seeds
Berry, W.   Seeds, The.
Blue Cloud.   Sculpture in Soil.
Carver, R.   Seeds.
Clampitt.   Seed.
Dunbar, P.   Seedling, The.
Housman.   I hoed and trenched and weeded.
Jacobsen, J.   Next Summer.
Meredith, G.   Seed-Time.
Muldoon, P.   Cuckoo Corn.
Nash, O.   Caraway Seed, The.
Nemerov.   Cabinet of Seeds Displayed, A.
Piercy.   Seedlings in the Mail.
Ramanujan.   Foundlings in the Yukon.
Rilke.   Winged Seed.
Rumi.   Seed Market, The.
  Wished-For Song, A.
Stafford, W.   B C.
  Whispered into the Ground.
Thomas, D.   After the Funeral.
  Seed-at-Zero, The.
Very.   Elm Seed, The.
Warren, R.   Wild Oats.
Whittier.   Utterance.
Wilbur, R.   Seed Leaves.

Seine (river), France
Apollinaire.   Mirabeau Bridge.
Logan, J.   Bridge of Change, The.
Major, C.   Seine Split.
Wordsworth, W.   Ode: "Who rises on the banks of Seine."

Self
Amichai [or Amikhai].   Autobiography, 1952.
Ammons.   Chasm.
  Schooling.
  So I Said I Am Ezra.
Angelou.   Reverses.
Ashbery, J.   Paradoxes and Oxymorons.
Atwood.   Looking in a Mirror.
  More and More.
  Solipsism While Dying.
  You refuse to own / yourself, you permit.
Auden.   Alone.
  Contrast, A.
  Lullaby: "Din of work is subdued, The."
  Prologue at Sixty.
  Talking to Myself.
Baudelaire.   Enemy, The.
Berrigan, T.   Last Poem.
Berryman.   Defensio in Extremis.
  Matins.
  Sext.
  Views of Myself.
Bly, R.   Chinese Tomb Guardians.
  Man Locked Inside the Oak, The.
Bogan, L.   Man Alone.
Borges.   Borges and I.
  Exile (1977), The.

I.
I Am.
  You Are Not the Others.
Brodsky, J.   At a Lecture.
  I Sit by the Window.
Brontë, E.   Stanzas: "Often rebuked, yet always back returning."
Brooks, G.   My Dreams, My Works Must Wait Till after Hell.
  Sundays of Satin-Legs Smith, The.
Browning, E.   Isobel's Child.
Browning, R.   At the "Mermaid."
  House.
  Reverie.
Cavafy.   Confusion.
  Morning Sea.
Chuang Tzu.   Inner Law, The.
  Lao Tzu's Wake.
  Man of Tao, The.
Ciardi, J.   Dogmatism.
  Figure Drawn in Wire, The.
Coleridge, S.   Phantom.
  What Is Life?
Crane, S.   In the desert.
Creeley.   Answer, The.
  Billfold.
  But You.
  "Do You Think.."
  Edge, The ("Long over whatever edge").
  Evening.
  For a Friend.
  Form of Women, A.
  Hamilton Hotel.
  Hong Kong Window.
  Intervals.
  Mirror, The.
  Mountains in the Desert, The.
  Myself.
  Not Again.
  Now.
  Pattern, The.
  Person.
  Poem for D. H. Lawrence.
  Pool, The.
  Puritan Ethos, The.
  Self-Portrait.
  Skeleton, The.
  Some Place.
  Song: "You look out and you see people."
  Than I.
  Walls.
  Wife, The.
  Window.
  You ("You will remember little of yourself").
Cullen, C.   For Myself.
Cummings, E. E.   Dive for dreams / or a slogan may topple you.
  Doveglion.
  Ecco a letter starting "dearest we."
  God,Thine the hand that doth extend.
  How generous is that himself the sun.
  How this uncouth enchanted.
  I am a beggar always.
  I am a little church(no great cathedral).
  I go to this window.
  It's / so damn sweet when Anybody.
  Maggie and Milly and Molly and May.
  Nobody wears a yellow.
  Noone and a star stand,am to am.
  One day a nigger.
  These from my mother's greatgrandmother's rosebush white.
  Total stranger one black day, A.
  When / (day's amazing murder with).
Cunningham, J.   Noon.
  Who am I? I have pondered with my peers.
De la Mare.   How Blind!
  Moment, The.
  Queen Wasp, A.
Dickinson, E.   Aurora.
  I am alive—I guess.
  I could not weigh myself, Myself.
  I heard, as if I had no Ear.
  I often wish I was a grass.
  Me from Myself—to banish.
  Perhaps you smile at me.

Soto! Explore thyself!
Those that die seem near me.
We meet no Stranger.
We must be less than Death.
Donne. Self Love.
Drummond de Andrade. Seven-Sided Poem.
Dunbar, P. Advice.
  Vagrants.
Duncan, R. Roots and Branches.
Eberhart, R. 1934.
  Birth and Death.
  Gnat on My Paper.
  I Walked Out to the Graveyard to See the Dead.
  In the Garden.
  Laocoön.
  Mistaken Identity.
  Soul.
  Throwing Yourself Away.
  Vision through Timothy.
Enzensberger, H. Other, The.
Ferlinghetti, L. Mock Confessional.
  Plan du Centre de Paris à Vol D'Oiseau.
  True Confessional.
Frost, R. Any Size We Please.
  Iota Subscript.
Gallagher, T. Black Silk.
  Sudden Journey.
Ginsberg, A. Autumn again, you wouldn't
    know in the city.
  Autumn Gold: New England Fall.
Graves, R. From the Embassy.
  Our Self.
  Second-Fated, The.
Gunn, T. Legal Reform.
  Plan of Self-Subjection, A.
Guyon. Divine Love Endures No Rival.
  Necessity of Self-Abasement.
  Self-Diffidence.
  Self-Love and Truth Incompatible.
"H. D." Pygmalion.
Hamill, S. Lover's Quarrel, A.
Hayden, R. Names.
Herbert, G. Jordan (2).
Herrick. On Himselfe.
Hopkins, G. Candle Indoors, The.
  —I am like a slip of comet.
  I Wake and Feel the Fell of Dark, Not Day.
  My Own Heart Let Me More Have Pity On.
  Times are nightfall, look, their light grows less,
    The.
Housman. Oh, When I Was In Love.
Hughes, L. Final Curve.
Hughes, T. I know well.
  Man Seeking Experience Enquires His Way of a
    Drop of Water, The.
  Swallow—rebuilding, The.
  Trees.
Jackson, L. Growth.
  One Self.
  Postponement of Self.
  Reasons of Each, The.
Jarrell, R. Children Selecting Books in a
    Library.
  Face, The.
  Let's love each other for what we are.
  Story, A.
  Venetian Blind, The.
  Woman at the Washington Zoo, The.
Jeffers, R. Fog.
Keats. Ode on Indolence.
Kipling, R. Mother's Son, The.
Koch, K. Alive for an Instant.
  Girl and Baby Florist Sidewalk Pram Nineteen
    Seventy Something.
Kumin, M. After Love.
Kunitz, S. Fitting of the Mask, The.
Larkin, P. Conscript.
  Counting.
  Self's the Man.
Lawrence, D. H. At a Loose End.
  Eloi, Eloi, Lama Sabachthani?
  Escape.
  I Am in a Novel.
  Nonentity.
  Rose of All the World.
  Self-Sacrifice.

There Is Rain in Me.
  Underneath.
  Unhappy Souls.
  Wild Common, The.
Levertov. In Mind.
  Looking-glass.
Levi, P. Autobiography.
Levine, P. Baby Villon.
Lorde. Good Mirrors are Not Cheap.
Lowell, R. Fat Man in the Mirror, The.
MacDiarmid, H. Wind-bags, The.
MacNeice. Carrick Revisited.
Major, C. Coon Showman.
  Revelation at Cap Ferrat.
  Seine Split.
  Unwanted Memory.
McHugh, H. ID.
Merrill, J. Dreams About Clothes.
  Remora.
  Syrinx.
Merwin. Child, The.
Milosz, C. Thesis and Counter-Thesis.
  This Only.
Mistral, G. Other, The.
Nemerov. Angel and Stone.
  Companions, The.
  Earthquake in the West, The.
  Flame of a Candle, The.
  Glass Dialectic.
  Knowledge.
  Mirror, The.
  Returning to Europe.
  Salt Garden, The.
  Sanctuary, The.
Neruda. Dying.
  Egoist.
  One Comes Back.
  Successions.
O'Hara, F. Mayakovsky.
  To the Harbormaster.
Oliver, M. Journey, The.
Olson, C. As the Dead Prey upon Us.
  Dogwood Comes Out Yellow, The.
  Key West.
  Love.
  Motion, The.
  My belly / sounds like an owl.
  My poor dumb body.
  Of the United States.
  Pavement, The.
Oppen. From a Phrase of Simone Weil's and
    Some Words of Hegel's.
Orr, G. Domestic Life.
  (Trauma) Storm.
Pagis. Snake.
Paley, G. Tenth Grade.
Palmer, M. Word is coming up on the screen,
    give me a moment, A.
Pessoa. Advice.
Piercy. Unlearning to Not Speak.
Plath. I Am Vertical.
  In Plaster.
  Nick and the Candlestick.
  Ravaged Face, The.
Raine, K. All things new / But I: no shadow.
  Amo Ergo Sum.
  Blue butterflies' eyed wings.
  Harvest of learning I have reaped.
  Night Sky.
  Night Thought.
  Poet Answers the Accuser, The.
  Self.
  This little house / No smaller than the world.
  Today as I / Looked up at the sky's great face.
  Two Invocations of Death.
  What have I to regret.
Ramanujan. Elements of Composition.
  Self-Portrait.
Rich, A. Delta.
  Double Monologue.
  Integrity.
  Moth Hour.
  Our Whole Life.
  Trying to Talk with a Man.
  Upper Broadway.
  When We Dead Awaken.

Rimbaud, A. Bad Blood.
  Fête Galante.
  Second Delirium. Alchemy of the Word.
  What do they mean to us, my heart, the sheets
    of blood.
Roethke. Prayer before Study.
  Renewal, The.
  Sensibility! O La!
Rossetti, C. Hymn: "O the bitter shame and
    sorrow."
  Our heaven must be within ourselves / Our
    home and heaven the work of faith.
  Thread of Life, The.
Rukeyser, M. Easter Eve 1945.
  Light falling on that filled will drives.
  Not to Be Printed, Not to Be Said, Not to Be
    Thought.
  Red bridge fastening this city to the forest, A.
  Song from Puck Fair.
  Then I Saw What the Calling Was.
  To Enter That Rhythm Where the Self Is Lost.
Rumi. I stand up, and this one of me.
  Late, by myself, in the boat of myself.
  Servant Who Loved His Prayers, The.
  Two Friends.
Sandburg, C. Chicago Poet.
Sexton. Ballad of the Lonely Masturbator, The.
  Bat.
  Civil War, The.
  For John, Who Begs Me Not to Enquire Further.
  Going Gone.
  House, The.
  Old Dwarf Heart.
  Other, The.
  Self in 1958.
Shelley, P. Fragment: "Methought I was a
    billow in the crowd."
  Fragment: Wedded Souls.
  Sonnet: Political Greatness.
Simic. Charles Simic.
  Further Adventures of Charles Simic.
  Inner Man, The.
  My Shoes.
  Quiet Talk with Oneself, A.
Smith, S. Portrait (II).
Spender, S. Solipsist.
Stafford, W. What's in My Journal.
Stevens, W. Anglais Mort à Florence.
  Dwarf, The.
  Idiom of the Hero.
  Man on the Dump, The.
  Poems of Our Climate, The.
  Well Dressed Man with a Beard, The.
Stock, R. And You, Too, Brutus.
Swenson, M. Beast.
  Stripping and Putting On.
Sze. Chance, The.
Szymborska, W. In Abundance.
Tate, A. Meaning of Life, The.
Tate, J. Interruptions.
  Shadowboxing.
Thomas, D. How Shall My Animal.
  I, in My Intricate Image.
  Out of the Sighs.
Thoreau. Great God I ask thee for no meaner
    pelf.
  I was made erect and lone.
Updike. Amoeba.
Van Duyn. Pot-au-feu.
Walcott. Hotel Normandie Pool, The.
  Love after Love.
  Prelude: "I, with legs crossed along the daylight,
    watch."
Warren, R. Interjection #1: The Need For Re-
    evaluation.
  Place, The.
  Prairie Harvest.
  Whatever You Now Are.
Whalen, P. Old Age Echoes.
  Something Nice About Myself.
Whitman, W. Ah Poverties, Wincings, and
    Sulky Retreats.
  Are You the New Person Drawn toward Me?
  As I Lay with My Head in Your Lap Camerado.
  Hand-Mirror, A.
  Here the Frailest Leaves of Me.

I Saw in Louisiana a Live-Oak Growing.
One's-Self I Sing.
Small the Theme of My Chant.
Song of Myself.
That Shadow My Likeness.
Woman Waits for Me, A.
Wilbur, R.　Leaving.
Williams, C. K.　Bad Mouth.
One of the Muses.
Or.
Resentment.
Shade, The.
Thinking Thought.
Twice More.
Williams, T.　Siege, The.
Williams, W.　Danse Russe.
Self-Portrait 1.
Self, The.
Wright, C.　In the Kingdom of the Past, the
Brown-Eyed Man is King.
Not everyone can see the truth, but he can be it.
Self-Portrait.
Watching the Equinox Arrive in Charlottesville,
September 1992.
Wyatt, S.　Promise, A.
Yeats.　Dialogue of Self and Soul, A.
Zagajewski.　Self, The.
Zukofsky, I.　Not it was no dream of coming
death.

Self-Deceit

Berrigan, T.　New Personal Poem.
Crane, S.　I saw a man pursuing the horizon.
Creeley.　One Way.
Gallagher, T.　Ever After.
Ginsberg, A.　Ode: My 24th Year.
Hardy, T.　Collector Cleans His Picture, The.
Dissemblers, The.
Jeffers, R.　Self-Criticism in February.
Laughlin, J.　Les Amants.
Lawrence, D. H.　Men Like Gods.
MacNeice.　Alcohol.
Mixer, The.
Merton.　To a Severe Nun.
Merwin.　Owl, The.
Nash, O.　Happy Ending of Mr. Train, The.
Pessoa.　Poem in a Straight Line.
Plath.　Fearful, The.
Other Two, The.
Ransom, J.　Parting at Dawn.
Rexroth, K.　Illusion.
Rich, A.　Power.
Riley, J.　Plain Sermons.
Shih-te.　Drunk on delusion greed and anger.
Smith, S.　Infelice.
No Respect.
Swinburne.　Ballad of Life, A.
Whittier.　Changeling, The.
Haschish, The.
Williams, W.　Love Charm, The.
Wright, C.　May Journal.

Self-Doubt

Berryman.　Huddle of Need, A.
Somber Prayer.
Bukowski.　35 Seconds.
Byron, G.　Soliloquy of a Bard in the Country.
Creeley.　Chicago.
Song, The: "It still makes sense."
Cullen, C.　Self Criticism.
Davie, D.　Humanly Speaking.
On Not Deserving.
Gallagher, T.　Rhododendrons.
Ginsberg, A.　Fragment 1956.
Graves, R.　My Ghost.
"H. D."　Centaur Song.
Herbert, G.　Love (3).
Ignatow, D.　Stability.
Jeffers, R.　Love the Wild Swan.
Koch, K.　Days and Nights.
MacLeish.　Tyrant of Syracuse.
Milosz, C.　Temptation.
Neruda.　One Comes Back.
Olson, C.　Day Song, the Day After.
Purgatory Blind.
Orr, G.　Visit to the Island of Lost Souls.
Rich, A.　Dialogue.
Letters: March 1969.

Roofwalker, The.
Sexton.　Lessons in Hunger.
Stafford, W.　Meditation in the Waiting Room.
Swift, J.　On Burning a Dull Poem.
Updike.　Thoughts While Driving Home.
Walcott.　Codicil.
Walk, The.
Williams, C. K.　Body, The.
Cautionary, The.
Solid, The.
Williams, M.　Origami.
Wright, C.　Laguna Blues.
Yeats.　Stream and Sun at Glendalough.
Zukofsky, L.　You three:—my wife.

Self-Knowledge

Amichai [or Amikhai].　Here.
What Kind of a Person.
What Kind of Man.
When I Have a Stomachache.
Ammons.　Chasm.
Concerning the Exclusions of the Object.
High & Low.
Reflective.
So I Said I Am Ezra.
Up.
Angelou.　When I Think about Myself.
Arnold, M.　Self-Dependence.
Ashbery, J.　And Others, Vaguer Presences.
Atwood.　You refuse to own / yourself, you
permit.
Berrigan, T.　Around the Fire.
It's Important.
Borges.　Fame.
Maker, The.
Yesterdays.
Browning, R.　Reverie.
Carruth, H.　Lost.
Chuang Tzu.　Keng's Disciple.
Ciardi, J.　Birthday.
Dialogue.
Dialogue with Outer Space.
Knowing Bitches.
Coleridge, S.　Self-Knowledge.
Cooper, J.　Knowledge that Comes through
Experience, The.
Corbett, W.　Above the cold.
Creeley.　Awakening, The.
Loop, A.
Reason, A.
Return.
Cummings, E. E.　Maggie and Milly and Molly
and May.
Total stranger one black day, A.
Cunningham, J.　Gnothi Seauton.
Somnium Narrare, Vigilantis Est.
To My Daimon.
"Dario."　Eheu!
I am the one who just yesterday spoke.
In the Constellations.
Love your rhythm and give rhythm to your
actions.
De la Mare.　Memory.
Self to self.
Dickinson, E.　Though we are each unknown to
ourself.
Duncan, R.　After a Long Illness.
Eliot, T. S.　Do I know how I feel? Do I know
what I think?
Enzensberger, H.　Homage to Gödel.
Identity Check.
Gallagher, T.　Into the Known.
Story of a Citizen, The.
Ginsberg, A.　And ninety-nine soldiers piled on
the train at Amarillo.
Iron Horse.
Sather Gate Illumination.
Shrouded Stranger, The.
Glück, L.　Gemini.
Graves, R.　Spite of Mirrors.
Hacker, M.　Rhetoric.
Hall, D.　Abroad Thoughts from Home.
Han-shan.　How many ancient sages.
I recall twenty years ago.
Is there a self or not.
I've always loved friends of the Way.
Hardy, T.　Beauty, The.

Surview [or Surview: Cogitavi Vias Meas].
Hughes, L.　Theme for English B.
Hughes, T.　Wodwo.
Jackson, L.　Advertisement.
No More Than Is.
Originally.
Jeffers, R.　Self-Criticism in February.
Kipling, R.　Glories, The.
Kunitz, S.　Between Me and the Rock.
King of the River.
Larkin, P.　If My Darling.
Reasons for Attendance.
Lawrence, D. H.　After All the Tragedies Are
Over.
Know Deeply, Know Thyself More Deeply.
Know Thyself.
Know Thyself, and That Thou Art Mortal.
Levertov.　Long Way Round, The.
Three Meditations.
Logue, C.　Song of Autobiography, The.
Lorde.　For Each of You.
MacNeice.　Aubade for Infants.
McGrath, T.　Seekers, The.
You Taught Me.
McHugh, H.　ID.
Round Time.
Untitled.
Merwin.　Finally.
Piper, The.
Milosz, C.　Confession, A.
Father Ch., Many Years Later.
Montale.　What you knew of me.
Nash, O.　Sage of Darien, The.
Nemerov.　Glass Dialectic.
Neruda.　Cold.
Conditions.
Heavy Surf, A.
Pardon Me.
Star.
Olson, C.　Cross-Legged, the Spider and the
Web.
In Cold Hell, in Thicket.
Lamp, The.
Moonset, Gloucester, December 1, 1957, 1:58
A.M.
Newly Discovered "Homeric" Hymn, A.
Sit by the Window and Refuse.
Oppen.　Confession.
Of Hours.
Semite.
What Will Happen.
Orr, G.　Hand, The: "Brightness Falls from the
Air."
Owen, W.　Show, The.
Parker, D.　Fairly Sad Tale, A.
Pasolini.　Reality.
Pessoa.　I'm beginning to know myself. I don't
exist.
Raine, K.　Bad Dream, A.
Ransom, J.　Amphibious Crocodile.
Rexroth, K.　Codicil.
Reflecting Trees of Being and Not Being, The.
Rich, A.　Afterward.
August.
Essential Resources.
Letter from the Land of Sinners.
Stranger, The.
Rimbaud, A.　Second Delirium. Alchemy of the
Word.
Roethke.　Lines upon Leaving a Sanitarium.
O, Thou Opening, O.
Open House.
Rumi.　Shape of My Tongue, The.
Unfold Your Own Myth.
Sandburg, C.　Questionnaire.
Sarton, M.　Myself to Me.
Sexton.　Kind Sir: These Woods.
Simic.　Quiet Talk with Oneself, A.
Smith, S.　Do Not!
Stafford, W.　Story That Could Be True, A.
Turn Over Your Hand.
Your Life.
Stevens, W.　Prelude to Objects.
Stock, R.　Sitting for a Self-Portrait.
Tate, A.　Homily.
Meaning of Life, The.

Thoreau. Great God I ask thee for no meaner pelf.
Sic Vita.
Van Duyn. Essay on Criticism, An.
Three Valentines to the Wide World.
Very. Lost, The ("Fairest day that ever yet has shone, The").
Walcott. Harbour, The.
Warren, R. Ballad of Your Puzzlement.
Covered Bridge.
Dreaming in Daylight.
Man Coming of Age.
Problem of Autobiography / Vague Recollection or Dream?
Sunset.
Weiss, T. Another and Another and.
Autobiographia Illiteraria.
Whalen, P. Self-Portrait Sad, 22:ix:58.
Whitman, W. Out from Behind This Mask.
Perfections.
Wilbur, R. Driftwood.
Williams, C. K. Bad Mouth.
Becoming Somebody Else.
Beyond.
Did I write this.
Failure.
Jetsam.
What we are / given.
Williams, M. Rebecca at Play.
Williams, W. Sale, The.
Slow Movement.
Wordsworth, W. Ode to Lycoris.
Wright, C. California Dreaming.
Chinese Journal.
Disjecta Membra.
Gate City Breakdown.
Mid-winter Snowfall in the Piazza Dante.
Self-Portrait.
Waiting for Tu Fu.
Wright, J. Three Stanzas From Goethe.
Yeats. Two Trees, The.
Zagajewski. Self-Portrait.
Zaturenska. Golden Mirror, The.

Self-Pity
Amichai [or Amikhai]. If My Belly Aches.
Bukowski. About My Very Tortured Friend, Peter.
Empire of Coins, An.
Reprieve and Admixture.
Carver, R. Schooldesk, The.
Coleridge, S. Addressed to a Young Man of Fortune.
Creeley. Love ("Tracking through this").
Cunningham, J. Aged Lover Discourses in the Flat Style, The.
Dubie. New Age at Airport Mesa.
Kipling, R. Natural Theology.
Lawrence, D. H. Self-Pity.
Tragedy.
Major, C. No Time for Self-Pity.
Michelangelo Buonarroti. Although time presses hard and prods us on.
Neruda. Conditions.
Pessoa. He came by, wanting to speak with me on a downtown street.
I have a terrible cold.
Tobacco Shop.
Schuyler, J. Self-Pity Is a Kind of Lying, Too.
Sexton. Killing the Spring.
Smith, S. Analysand.
Sad Heart, The.
Tate, J. Success Comes to Cow Creek.
Warren, R. Interjection #5: Solipsism and Theology.
Williams, C. K. Fat.
Thinking Thought.
Yeats. Sad Shepherd, The.
Zukofsky, L. Guillaume de Machault (1300-1377) Ballade: Plourès, dames.
In the midst of things.

Self-Reliance
Amichai [or Amikhai]. Do Not Accept.
You Must Not Show Weakness.
Arnold, M. Self-Dependence.
Brontë, E. Stanzas: "Often rebuked, yet always back returning."

Strong I stand, though I have borne.
Weaned from life and torn away.
Browning, R. At the "Mermaid."
Creeley. Xmas Poem: Bolinas.
Cunningham, J. In the thirtieth year of life.
Dugan, A. Philodendron.
Emerson, R. Poet is at home, A.
Simple people each with basket or tool, The.
Frost, R. Figure in the Doorway, The.
Hughes, L. Madam's Past History.
Ignatow, D. My Place.
Lawrence, D. H. Deeper Than Love.
Levi, P. Dromedary, The.
Melville, H. In a Garret.
Nash, O. Compliments of a Friend.
Neruda. Bird.
Oppen. Myself I Sing.
Parker, D. Neither Blood Nor Bowed.
Rich, A. Song: "You're wondering if I'm lonely."
Rilke. Judgments.
Rossetti, C. I seek among the living & I seek.
Smith, S. Company.
Stafford, W. Wanderer Awaiting Preferment, The.
Tate, J. Twilight Sustenance Hiatus.
Whalen, P. Further Notice.
Williams, T. One and Two.
Wright, J. Sense of Comedy, The: 1.
Zukofsky, L. Catullus viii.
Peri Poietikes.

Self-Restraint
Brontë, E. All day I've toiled, but not with pain.
Crane, S. God came to a man, A.
Davie, D. At the Café Parnasse.
Eberhart, R. Throwing Yourself Away.
Glück, L. Reproach, The.
Housman. Because I liked you better.
Jeffers, R. Nightpiece.
Kunitz, S. Green Ways.
Williams, C. K. Thinking Thought.
Williams, M. Self-Control.
Williams, W. Defiance to Cupid.
Zukofsky, L. Catullus viii.

Self-Righteousness
Amichai [or Amikhai]. Place Where We Are Right, The.
Baudelaire. Concerning a Jackass.
Burns, R. Holy Willie's Prayer.
Dubie. Poem for My Friend, Clare. Or, With White Stupas We Remember Buddha.
Eliot, T. S. Ballade pour la grosse Lulu.
Gallagher, T. That Kind of Thing.
Hughes, L. Naughty Child, The.
Northern Liberal.
Kizer, C. Wars in Sweden, The.
Lawrence, D. H. Censors.
Lindsay, N. Drunkards in the Street, The.
Kind of Scorn, A.
O'Hara, F. Spleen.
Williams, M. Promotion, The.
Zagajewski. Lightning.

Selfishness
Bierce. Something in the Papers.
Burns, R. There's a youth in this city, it were a great pity.
Cowper, W. Against Interested Love.
Retired Cat, The.
Davie, D. At the Cradle of Genius.
Dickinson, E. Mine—by the Right of the White Election!
Dunbar, P. Career, A.
Han-shan. I see people everywhere.
Rich have so many cares, The.
Rich men met in an elegant hall.
This year's grain being still unripe.
Those days when I had money.
Unfortunate human disorder, The.
Hughes, L. Preference.
Larkin, P. Love.
None of the Books Have Time.
Lawrence, D. H. All I Ask.
Chimaera.
Conceit.
Furniture.

Immorality.
Intimates.
Painter's Wife, The.
Sphinx.
To a Certain Friend.
True Love at Last.
Ultimate Reality.
Vengeance Is Mine.
Woe.
Lindsay, N. Curse for Kings, A.
Meredith, G. Quake, quake, let us turn Quaker all!
Society.
Michelangelo Buonarroti. You give me only what you're glutted with.
Nash, O. Doctor Fell? I Thought So.
Olson, C. Cinos.
Rich, A. Boundary.
Roethke. Poetaster.
Shapiro, K. Intellectual, The.
Smith, S. Analysand.
Egocentric.
Major Macroo.
Snyder, G. Spel Against Demons.
Swift, J. To Stella.
Tennyson, A. Character, A.
Williams, C. K. Like Little Birds.
Williams, M. Promotion, The.

Semele
Graves, R. Ambrosia of Dionysus and Semele, The.
Kizer, C. Semele Recycled.

Seneca
Merton. Seneca.

Senegal
Hughes, L. Cubes.

Senility
Davie, D. Alzheimer's Disease.
Graves, R. Nightmare of Senility.
Hall, D. By the Exeter River.
Levertov. Old Adam, The.
Paley, G. He Wanders.
My Father at 89.
Prunty. Seasons.
Tomlinson, C. Last Days of the Miser.
Williams, C. K. Tails.
Williams, T. Lady with No One at All, The.
Williams, W. Another Old Woman.
Two Pendants: For the Ears.

Sennacherib, King of Assyria
Byron, G. Destruction of Sennacherib, The.

Senses
Abu Nadhar 'Abdu'l 'Aziz. Color, taste, and smell, smaragdus, sugar, and musk.
Angelou. Senses of Insecurity.
Atwood. Fortification, A.
Nothing.
Bogan, L. Spirit's Song.
Browning, R. Transcendentalism: A Poem in Twelve Books.
Creeley. For Helen.
Penitent, The.
Pryaer, A.
Two.
Variations.
Way.
Davie, D. Seur, near Blois.
Dickinson, E. I heard a Fly buzz—when I died.
Light exists in Spring, A.
Dugan, A. Poem: "Pythagorean Silences, The."
Emerson, R. Go into the garden.
I call her beautiful;—she says.
Herrick. Eyes before the Eares, The.
Komunyakaa. Passions.
Lawrence, D. H. Cabbage-Roses.
Deepest Sensuality, The.
Renascence.
Satisfaction.
Sense of Truth.
Mallarmé. Fan, A; of Méry Laurent.
Merrill, J. Amsterdam.
Merton. Holy Sacrament of the Altar, The.
Niedecker. To My Small / Electric Pump.
Olson, C. Red Mallows.
Orr, G. Paradise Lightning Dazzle.

Raine, K. Hieros Gamos.
Ramanujan. Blind Spots.
Eyes, Ears, Noses, and a Thing about Touch.
Roethke. Prayer: "If I must of my Senses lose."
Sandburg, C. Slabs of the Sunburnt West.
Schuyler, J. Freely Espousing.
Spender, S. Never Being.
Stevens, W. Arcades of Philadelphia the Past.
Poem Written at Morning.
Thinking of a Relation between the Images of
   Metaphors.
Szymborska, W. View with a Grain of Sand.
Thomas, D. When All My Five and Country
   Senses See.
Very. Eye and Ear, The.
Wilbur, R. Lamarck Elaborated.
Zukofsky, L. All Wise.
When the crickets.

Sensitivity
Burns, R. Rusticity's ungainly form.
Creeley. Pryaer, A.
Cuadra, P. Written Next to a Blue Flower.
Gunn, T. Saturnalia.
Herrick. Vertue Is Sensible of Suffering.
Laughlin, J. Sorrows of Smindyrides, The.
Levertov. O Taste and See.
Lindsay, N. Song for Elizabeth, A.
Meredith, G. Triad of British Evils, A.
Nash, O. That's Funny, Wasn't It? No, It Won't
   Be.
Nemerov. View from an Attic Window, The.
Owen, W. Insensibility.
Rossetti, C. "Immurata" Sister, An.
Smith, S. Rencontres Funestes.
Van Duyn. Death By Aesthetics.

Sensuality
Amichai [or Amikhai]. Now That the Water
   Presses Hard.
Atwood. Nothing.
Baudelaire. Cat, The.
Pagan's Prayer, The.
Promise in a Pair of Eyes, The.
Broumas, O. Amazon Twins.
Caritas.
Days of Argument and Blossom.
Leda and Her Swan.
Oregon Landscape with Lost Lover.
Perennial.
Plunging into the Improbable.
Sometimes, as a Child.
Carver, R. Two Worlds.
Cavafy. In an Old Book
Picture of a Young Man, Twenty-three, Done by
   His Friend of the Same Age, an Amateur.
Pleasure in the Flesh.
Return.
Ciardi, J. Stills and Rapids of Your Nakedness,
   The.
Creeley. Flesh.
Flower, The.
Love: "There are words voluptuous."
P—.
Cummings, E. E. After your poppied hair
   inaugurates.
Emperor / sleeps in a palace of porphyry, The.
Moon is hiding in, The.
My lady is an ivory garden.
My love / thy hair is one kingdom.
Nearer:breath of my breath:take not thy tingling.
Of evident invisibles / exquisite the hovering.
Since feeling is first.
Sometimes i am alive because with.
(Swooning)a pillar of youngly.
Through the tasteless minute efficient room.
What is thy mouth to me?
You said Is / there anything which.
Yours is the music for no instrument.
Dubie. Lord Myth.
Eberhart, R. Giantess, The.
Ferlinghetti, L. Away above a harborful.
Gallagher, T. Backdrop With Lovers, 1931.
García Lorca. Variations.
Hacker, M. Canzone: "Consider the three
   functions of the tongue."
Han-shan. In Loyang so many girls.
Moth-browed girl in town, A.

Hopkins, G. Epithalamion: "Hark, hearer, hear
   what I do; lend a thought now, make believe."
Hughes, T. Bride and Groom Lie Hidden for
   Three Days.
Lovesong: "He loved her and she loved him."
Low Water.
Sunstruck Foxglove.
Jacobsen, J. Lovers, The.
Kinnell. Cellist, The.
Kizer, C. Complex Autumnal.
Komunyakaa. Passions.
Levertov. Eros at Temple Stream.
Volupté.
Logan, J. Nude Kneeling in Sand.
Lux. Say Yes.
McHugh, H. Fix.
Merwin. Spring Equinox Full Moon.
Milosz, C. Anka.
Confession, A
In Milan.
Montale. On the Greve.
O'Hara, F. Poem: "Twin spheres full of fur and
   noise."
Orr, G. Leaving the Asylum.
Owen, W. Purple.
Pound, E. Alba.
Encounter, The.
Immorality, An.
Ransom, J. Rose, The.
Rexroth, K. Among the Cypresses at the End of
   the Way of the Cross.
Confusion of the Senses.
Floating.
Incarnation.
Incense.
Runaway.
Still on Water.
Riley, J. In the Heart of June.
Judith.
My Night.
That Night.
Rimbaud, A. First Night.
Sun and Skin.
Ritsos. First Sensual Delight, The.
Rukeyser, M. Child in the Great Wood.
Song: Lying in Daylight.
Sappho. Sappho.
Simic. My Beloved.
Snyder, G. Running Water Music II.
Stein, G. Sonatina Followed by Another, A.
Stevens, W. Dish of Peaches in Russia, A.
Stock, R. Revelation According to the Beloved.
Swenson, M. Sketch for a Landscape.
Unknown. From the Persian (1).
Van Duyn. Annual and Perennial Problem, An.
Death By Aesthetics.
With Warm Regards to Miss Moore and Mr.
   Ransom.
Whitman, W. From Pent-up Aching Rivers.
To the Garden the World.
Wilde, O. In the Gold Room: A Harmony.
Williams, T. Evening.
Williams, W. Crystal Maze, A.
Translation.
Yeats. Chosen.

Seoul, Korea
Creeley. Seoul Sounds.

Separation
Ai. Back in the World.
Amichai [or Amikhai]. Farewell.
In the Morning It Was Still Night.
Memory of Love—Image.
Parents Left the Child, The.
Pity, A. We Were Such a Good Invention.
Ammons. Spinejacking.
Angelou. My Life Has Turned to Blue.
Arnold, M. Forsaken Merman, The.
Ashbery, J. Recent Past, The.
Rivers and Mountains.
Atwood. Postcard.
Beckett, S. Cascando.
Berry, W. Except.
Kentucky River Junction.
Berryman. He Resigns.
Bishop, E. Argument.
Blue Cloud. Old man's lazy, The.

Bly, R. Man Writes to a Part of Himself, A.
Bradstreet, A. Another.
Brodsky, J. On Love.
Second Christmas by the shore, A.
Song to No Music, A.
Via Funari.
Brontë, E. A. G. A. to A. E.
Alcona, in its changing mood.
Companions, all day long we've stood.
I gazed within thine earnest eyes.
I see around me tombstones grey.
It is too late to call thee now.
O mother, I am not regretting.
Song By J. Brenzaida To G.S.
Song: "O between distress and pleasure."
There shines the moon, at noon of night.
Thousand sounds of happiness, A.
'Tis moonlight, summer moonlight.
Where were ye all? and where wert thou?
Wind was rough which tore, The.
Written on Returning to the P. of I. on the 10th
   of January, 1827.
Yes, holy be thy resting place.
Browning, E. Catarina to Camoens.
Browning, R. In a Gondola.
In Three Days.
Last Ride Together, The.
Lovers' Quarrel, A.
Too Late.
Waring.
Bukowski. All the Casualties..
Communion.
Day I Kicked Away a Bankroll, The.
Burns, R. Bonie Lad That's Far Awa, The.
English Song.
Frae the friends and Land I love.
Here Awa' There Awa ["Here awa', there awa'
   wandering, Willie"].
Highland Balou, The.
Highland Harry Back Again.
Highland Mary.
How lang and dreary is the night.
I Look to the North.
Jockey's Ta'en the Parting Kiss,
Musing on the roaring ocean.
My Nannie's Awa'
Northern Lass, The.
On the Seas and Far Away.
Red, Red Rose, A.
Sae Far Awa.
Shepherd's Wife, The.
Silver Tassie, The.
Somebody.
Song: "Behold the hour, the boat arrive."
There Was a Bonie Lass.
To William Creech.
Winter It Is Past, The.
Young Highland Rover, The.
Byron, G. Epistle to Augusta.
Fare Thee Well.
On Parting.
When We Two Parted.
Carew, T. Elegy on the La: Pen: Sent to My
   Mistress Out of France, An.
To Her in Absence; a Ship.
To Mistress Katherine Neville, on Her Green
   Sickness.
Carver, R. Deschutes River.
Forge, and a Scythe, A.
Hope.
Memory 2.
My Wife.
Offending Eel, The.
Still Looking Out for Number One.
To Begin With.
Cary, T. On His Mistress[e] Going to Sea.
Cavafy. Before Time Could Change Them.
Ciardi, J. Expendability.
Letter from an Empty House.
Letter from an Island.
Poem for a Soldier's Girl.
Poem for My Twenty-ninth Birthday.
Clough. Were I with you or you with me.
Coleridge, S. If I Had but Two Little Wings.
On a Late Connubial Rupture in High Life.
Separation from Asra.

Wedded Love.
Cooper, J. In the Last Few Moments Came the Old German Cleaning Woman.
Letters.
Cowper, W. Bid adieu, my sad heart, bid adieu to thy peace.
Hope, like the short-liv'd ray that gleams awhile.
Written after Leaving Her at New Burns.
Crashaw. Alexias.
Creeley. America.
Ballad of the Despairing Husband.
Enough.
Envoi: "Particulars they want."
For Pen ("Thinking out / of the heart").
For Rainer Gerhardt.
Irishman's Lament on the Approaching Winter, An.
Kid ("Kid left / out back waits, The").
Knokke.
She Is.
Sight, A.
Soup ("I know what you'd say").
Cullen, C. Dictum.
Therefore, Adieu.
To One Not There.
Cummings, E. E. Ballad of Love.
Clown's smirk in the skull of a baboon, A.
It is so long since my heart has been with yours.
Or who and who.
S.F.D.
T.A.M.
Up into the silence the green.
We miss you,jack—tactfully you(with one cocked).
When my sensational moments are no more.
When thou art dead,dead,and far from the splendid sin.
You being in love.
Cunningham, J. Jack and Jill.
Dickinson, E. Air is soft as Italy, The.
Busy missing you.
Crumbling elms and evergreens, The.
Morning without you is a dwindled Dawn.
Today or this noon.
We miss Her, not because We see.
Donne. Computation, The.
Legacy [or Legacie], The.
Valediction: Forbidding Mourning, A.
Dove, R. Someone's Blood.
Dubie. Double Sphere, Cloven Sphere.
Dunbar, P. Comrade.
Lyric, A: "My lady love lives far away."
Duncan, R. Passage Over Water.
Eliot, T. S. Portrait of a Lady.
Emerson, E. Last Farewell, The.
Emerson, R. Ah strange strange strange.
Atom from atom yawns as far.
To Eva.
Unity.
Ferlinghetti, L. In Golden Gate Park that day.
Third World Calling.
Two Amsterdams.
Two Scavengers in a Truck, Two Beautiful People in a Mercedes.
Wild Life Cameo, Early Morn.
Frost, R. Flower-Gathering.
Gallagher, T. Bird-Window-Flying.
Kidnap[p]er.
With Stars.
García Lorca. Nocturne of Emptied Space.
Ginsberg, A. Message.
Gjuzel. My Sister's Letter.
Glück, L. From the Japanese.
Hesitate to Call.
Horse.
Return, The.
Rosy.
World Breaking Apart.
Graves, R. Fortunate Child.
Full Moon.
Her Brief Withdrawal.
I Will Write.
In the Vestry.
Sentence, The.
Snapped Thread, The.

Song: Of Course.
Song: The Clocks of Time.
Tower of Love, The.
True Magic.
Gunn, T. During an Absence.
June.
Separation, The.
"H. D." Toward the Piraeus.
Hacker, M. Companion, The.
Crépusule Provençale.
Going Back to the River.
Home, and I've.
Letter from Goose Creek: April.
Living in the Moment.
Separate Lives.
Somewhere in a Turrent.
Villanelle: "Every day our bodies separate."
Hamill, S. First Snow.
Han-shan. Last night I dreamt I went home.
Willows grow dark like mist, The.
Yesterday was so long ago.
Hardy, T. After the Visit.
Amabel.
At Castle Boterel.
Difference, The.
Going of the Battery, The.
Her Song.
I Say, "I'll Seek Her."
In a Cathedral City.
In Death Divided.
In Vision I Roamed.
My Cicely.
Old Gown, The.
On the Departure Platform.
Tarrying Bridegroom, The.
They Would Not Come.
To Louisa in the Lane.
Walk, The.
When Wearily We Shrink Away.
Heaney, S. Westering.
Herrick. His Sailing from Julia.
Pastorall Sung to the King: Montano, Silvio, and Mirtillo, Shepards, A.
Presence and Absence.
Housman. As Through the Wild Green Hills of Wyre.
Because I liked you better.
He would not stay for me; and who can wonder?
Now hollow fires burn out to black.
Oh were he and I together.
White in the moon the long road lies.
Winds out of the west land blow, The.
Hughes, L. Bulwark.
Letter to Anne, A.
Poem: "I loved my friend."
So Long.
Wide River.
Yesterday and Today.
Hughes, T. Opus 131.
Sheep.
What is it this time the dark barn again.
Jarrell, R. Story, A.
Street Has Changed, The.
Keats. Endymion: A Poetic Romance.
Kipling, R. Song in the Desert, A.
Widower, The.
Kizer, C. Postcards from Rotterdam.
Race Relations.
Semele Recycled.
Komunyakaa. My Father's Love Letters [or Loveletters].
Kumin, M. Seeing the Bones.
Kunitz, S. Parting.
Larkin, P. As a War in Years of Peace.
Within the Dream You Said.
Laughlin, J. Death Walkers, The.
Delia Sequence, The.
In the Museum at Teheran.
In the Salzkammergut.
La Tristesse.
Mysterious Disappearance, The.
Lawrence, D. H. Mutilation.
Reach Over.
Separated.
Walk Warily.

Levertov. Crosspurposes.
Divorcing.
For Nikolai, Many Thousand Miles Away.
Holiday.
Writing to Aaron.
Li Po. Letter, A.
Long Banister Lane.
Logan, J. Lines for a Friend Who Left.
Lorde. Memorial III—from a Phone Booth on Broadway.
MacNeice. Bluebells.
Letter from India.
This Way Out.
Mahon. Globe in [North] Carolina, The.
Mandelstam [or Mandelshtam]. Tristia.
Marvell. Definition of Love, The.
Merwin. As by Water.
Come Back.
Different Stars, The.
Division.
From a Series.
In the Gorge.
In the Night Fields.
Nails, The.
Separation.
Ships Are Made Ready in Silence, The.
This Day of This Month of This Year of This.
When You Go Away.
Michelangelo Buonarroti. How could I, since it's so.
I'm dearer dead than ever I was, before.
My lover stole my heart, just over there.
Milosz, C. Distance.
On Parting with My Wife, Janina.
Mistral, G. Vigilant Woman, The.
Montale. Flower that repeats, The.
Gerti's Carnival.
Gondola that glides, The.
Hope of even seeing you again, The.
In the Rain.
Metropolitan Christmas, A.
Personae Separatae.
Reed that softly, The.
You know: I'm going to lose you again.
Muldoon, P. Grass Widow.
Nash, O. Tin Wedding Whistle.
Nemerov. De Anima.
Niedecker. If only my friend.
Olson, C. Newly Discovered "Homeric" Hymn, A.
Orr, G. Once the two of us.
Pagis. Fragments of an Elegy.
Parker, D. Dramatists, The.
Rondeau: "It isn't fair, to me, when you're away."
Pasternak, B. Breakup, The.
Pinkerton, H. Coast Hillside.
Plath. Monologue at 3 A.M.
Parliament Hill Fields.
Rival, The.
Pope, A. Epistle to Miss [or Miss Teresa] Blount, on Her Leaving the Town after the Coronation.
Pugliesi. Canzone: Of his Dead Lady.
Raine, K. Crossing the sound I summoned you in thought.
I went out in the naked light.
Poet is of those, The.
Ramanujan. To a Friend Far Away.
Ransom, J. Jack's Letter.
Spectral Lovers.
Two in August.
Rich, A. Boundary.
Natural Resources.
Pieces.
Prisoners, The.
Splittings.
Riley, J. Christmas Memory, A.
George Mullen's Confession.
Last Words.
Leonainie.
My Father's Halls.
Their Sweet Sorrow.
When She Comes Home.
Whitheraways, The.
Ritsos. Hour of Song.

Separation.
Suddenly.
Rossetti, C.   Cor Mio.
Dream, A.
Dream, The.
Echo from Willowwood, An.
Goodbye in fear, goodbye in sorrow.
Had Fortune parted us / Fortune is blind.
Hoping Against Hope.
Husband and Wife.
I have a little husband / And he is gone to sea.
I said "All's over"—& I made my.
In July / No goodbye.
Isidora.
Last Words of St. Telemachus, The.
May.
Meeting.
Next of Kin.
One Foot on Sea, and One on Shore.
Parting after parting, / Sore loss and gnawing
   pain.
Remember [Me].
Rosalind.
Two Parted.
Rossetti, D.   Blessed Damozel, The.
Insomnia.
Rukeyser, M.   Meeting, The.
Story, A.
Young Girl of the Mississippi Valley, The.
Sexton.   December 2nd.
December 11th.
December 18th.
Eighteen Days without You.
Keeping the City.
Shapiro, K.   Glass Poem.
Haircut.
Homewreck.
V-Letter.
Snyder, G.   Fear Not.
Spender, S.   Absence.
Double Shame, The.
Not to You.
Room above the Square, The.
Song: "Stranger, you who hide my love."
Stockton, A.   Almira to Celadon, Founded on a
   Story in a Magazine.
By a Lady in America to Her Husband in
   England.
Szymborska, W.   I am too close for him to
   dream about me.
Tennyson, A.   Fatima.
Updike.   Report of Health.
Walker, A.   Walker.
Warren, R.   To a Friend Parting.
Whitman, W.   Good-Bye, My Fancy!
Hours Continuing Long.
Out of the Rolling Ocean the Crowd.
Whittier.   Amy Wentworth.
Memories.
Williams, M.   La Ultima Carta: A Young Wife
   Writes to Her Husband in the Mountains.
On the Sacrifice of a Siamese Twin at Birth.
Williams, W.   I Will Sing a Joyous Song.
Wordsworth, W.   Complaint, A.
To ———: "O dearer far than light and life are
   dear."
Tradition of Oker Hill in Darley Dale,
   Derbyshire, A.
Wright, C.   Dead Color.
March Journal.
Wright, J.   Morning Hymn to a Dark Girl.
Wu of Han [or Wu Ti or Ou-ty or Liu Ch'e or
   Liu Ch'u].   Hiding Our Love.
Wyatt, S.   If it be so that I forsake thee.
Zagajewski.   Your Telephone Call.
Zaturenska.   Friend's Song, A.
Image of a Friend.
Voices in Air.
Zukofsky, L.   Catullus viii.
Finally a Valentine.
See also Absence; Isolation; Loneliness

Sepoy Rebellion
Kipling, R.   Veterans, The.
Rossetti, C.   In the Round Tower at Jhansi, June
   8, 1857.

September
Ammons.   September Drift.
Carruth, H.   Essay on Love.
This Song.
Carver, R.   September.
Dickinson, E.   September's Baccalaureate.
Eberhart, R.   In the Garden.
Graves, R.   September Landscape.
Hall, D.   September Ode.
Hamill, S.   September Sowing.
Housman.   Tell Me Not Here [It Needs Not
   Saying].
Kinnell.   Blackberry Eating.
Kinsella, T.   Another September.
Kipling, R.   Two Months.
Lawrence, D. H.   Bavarian Gentians.
Mahon.   September in Gt. Yarmouth.
Merwin.   September.
Nemerov.   Crossing, The.
Roethke.   Carnations.
Sandburg, C.   Dragoons, I tell you the white
   hydrangeas turn rust and go soon.
Home Fires.
Proud Torsos.
Tate, J.   Tryst, The.
Wordsworth, W.   September, 1815.
Zagajewski.   Close of Summer, The.
Sequoia Trees
Gunn, T.   Lights among Redwood.
Jeffers, R.   Summit Redwood, The.
Stafford, W.   B.C.
Whalen, P.   Giant Sequoias.
Serenity
Brontë, E.   Awaking morning laughs from
   heaven.
Chuang Tzu.   True Man, The.
Clough.   Sweet streamlet bason! at thy side.
Coleridge, S.   Hope and Tranquillity.
Ode to Tranquillity.
Creeley.   Picture, A.
Eberhart, R.   Parker River, The.
Glück, L.   Porcelain Bowl.
Guillén, J.   Horses, The.
Han-shan.   Give me a hidden eddy.
Hayden, R.   Monet's "Waterlilies."
Hopkins, G.   She Schools the Flighty Pupils of
   Her Eyes.
Kipling, R.   If—.
Kunitz, S.   Long Boat, The.
Melville, H.   Off Cape Colona.
Merwin.   Pause by the Water.
Sandburg, C.   Flanders.
Peace, Night, Sleep.
Three Pieces on the Smoke of Autumn.
Simic.   Summer Morning.
Snyder, G.   Once at Cold Mountain, troubles
   cease.
Stafford, W.   Just Thinking.
Wilbur, R.   From the Lookout Rock.
Zukofsky, L.   So sounds grass, and if it is sun or
   no sun.
Serfs
Bierce.   Saith the Czar.
Rossetti, D.   Czar Alexander the Second.
Very.   Abolition of Serfdom in Russia, The.
See also Slavery and Slaves
Sermons
Browning, R.   Impromptu on Hearing a Sermon
   by the Rev. T. R—Pronounced "Heavy."
Dickey, J.   May Day Sermon to the Women of
   Gilmer County, Georgia, by a Woman Preacher
   Leaving the Baptist Church.
Wheatley, P.   To the Rev. Dr. Thomas Amory on
   Reading His Sermons on Daily Devotion, in
   Which that Duty Is Recommended and
   Assisted.
Servants
Ammons.   Nelly Myers.
Angelou.   When I Think about Myself.
Baudelaire.   You were so jealous of our
   nursemaid's love.
Bishop, E.   Cootchie.
Borges.   Matthew 25:30.
Brooks, G.   Bronzeville Woman in a Red Hat.
Clare, J.   My Mary.

Dubie.   Ibis.
Eliot, T. S.   Aunt Helen.
Emerson, R.   Be of good cheer, brave spirit;
   steadfastly.
Frost, R.   Blueberries.
Glück, L.   Abishag.
Hall, D.   Revolution, The.
Heaney, S.   Servant Boy.
Herrick.   To His Maid Prew.
Upon Prue [or Prew], His Maid.
Hughes, L.   Madam and Her Madam.
Negro Servant.
Jonson, B.   On Mill, My Lady's Woman.
Kipling, R.   Servant When He Reigneth, A.
Kizer, C.   Gerda.
Kunitz, S.   Magic Curtain, The.
Lawrence, D. H.   Young Soldier with Bloody
   Spurs, The.
Levertov.   Servant-Girl at Emmaus (A Painting
   by Velazquez), The.
Lindsay, N.   Aladdin and the Jinn.
Logue, C.   Ass's Song, The.
Mistral, G.   Air Flower, The.
Muldoon, P.   Big House, The.
Murray, P.   Receipt to Frighten away the Dean,
   A.
Riley, J.   Our Hired Girl.
Rossetti, C.   Prodigal Son, A.
Rumi.   Servant Who Loved His Prayers, The.
Simic.   Devotions.
Stock, R.   Study of a House with Garden
   Attached.
Swift, J.   Mary the Cook-Maid's Letter to Dr.
   Sheridan.
Mrs. Harris's Petition.
Unknown.   Ballade de Marguerite.
Wilbur, R.   Complaint.
Good Servant, The.
Summer Morning, A.
Wilner, E.   Leda's Handmaiden.
Wyatt, S.   Heart and service to you proffered,
   The.
Service (botany)
Davie, D.   Life of Service, The.
Service Stations
See **Gasoline Stations**
Sestina (form)
Bishop, E.   Miracle for Breakfast, A.
Sestina: "September rain falls on the house."
Cooper, J.   Morning on the St. John's.
Hall, D.   Sestina: "Hang it all, Ezra Pound, there
   is only the one sestina."
Seurat, Georges
Bishop, E.   Pleasure Seas.
O'Hara, F.   On Looking at *La Grande Jatte*, the
   Czar Wept Anew.
Zagajewski.   Georges Seurat: Factory.
Seven Deadly Sins
De la Mare.   Quiet.
Dunbar, W.   Off Februar the fyiftene nycht.
Severn River, England
Gurney, I.   Musers Afar Will Say.
Wordsworth, W.   When Severn's Sweeping
   Flood Had Overthrown.
Seville, Spain
García Lorca.   Ballad of the Three Rivers.
Poem of the *Saeta*.
St. Gabriel.
Laughlin, J.   Saeta.
Sewall, Samuel
Whittier.   Samuel E. Sewall.
Sewers
Dugan, A.   Gargoyle's Song for the Warming
   Trend.
Kipling, R.   Municipal.
Laughlin, J.   Inner Life of the Septic Tank, The.
Sewing
Bishop, E.   House Guest.
Clampitt.   Sunday Music.
Dickinson, E.   Don't put up my Thread and
   Needle.
Dunbar, P.   Quilting, The.
Hall, D.   Sew.
Niedecker.   Hand Crocheted Rug.
Pagis.   Recognition.

Simic. Sewing Machine.
Wilner, E. Made by Hand.
Wordsworth, W. On Seeing a Needlecase in the
  Form of a Harp; the Work of E.M.S.
See also **Seamstresses; Tailoring and Tailors**
Sex
Ai. Blood in the Water.
 Capture.
 One Man Down.
 Reunions with a Ghost.
 Twenty-Year Marriage.
 Why Can't I Leave You?
Amichai [*or* Amikhai]. Herbal Tea.
 I Know a Man.
 Poems to a Girl on the Seashore.
 Shifra and Batya promised.
 Voyeur, The.
 We Did It.
 What a man on a bald mountain in Jerusalem!
 You Carry the Weight of Heavy Buttocks.
Ammons. Bearing Mercy.
 Open.
Angelou. Remembrance.
 Zorro Man, A.
Ariosto. Night and Day.
Atwood. Aging Female Poet Sits on the
  Balcony.
 Pre-Amphibian.
Baudelaire. Metamorphoses of the Vampire.
 Rara Avis.
Beckett, S. À elle l'acte calme.
 Dread Nay.
 Être là sans mâchoires sans dents.
 Serena III.
Berrigan, T. Dinner at George & Katie
  Schneeman's.
Berryman. Damned.
 Freshman Blues.
 Huddle of Need, A.
Bishop, E. Exchanging Hats.
Blake, W. Long John Brown & Little Mary
  Bell.
 Visions of the Daughters of Albion.
Broumas, O. Amberose Triste.
 Attitude.
 Backgammon.
 Blues / for J.C.
 Caritas.
 Choir, The.
 Days of Argument and Blossom.
 Eros.
 Eye of Heart.
 For Every Heart.
 Four Beginnings / for Kyra.
 Innocence.
 Love Lines.
 Mornings Remembering Last Nights.
 P.S.
 Pastoral Jazz.
 Plunging into the Improbable.
 Rumpelstiltskin.
 She Loves.
 Tryst.
Bukowski. 6 Foot Goddess, The.
 99 to One.
 225 Pounds.
 Alone with Everybody.
 Another Bed.
 Ashes.
 Ass But No Class.
 Cold Plums.
 Conversation on Morality, Eternity and
  Copulation, A.
 Dead Now.
 End of a Short Affair, The.
 Fuck.
 Good Life, The.
 How Come You're Not Unlisted?
 I Fall into It Without Trying.
 Layover.
 Like a Flower in the Rain.
 Love Poem, A.
 Making It.
 Mercy, Wherever You Are, Come Running in to
  Me and Grab Me in Your Good Arms—.
 Moaning and Groaning.

Night I Fucked My Alarm Clock, The.
 One of the Hottest.
 Place Didn't Look Bad, The.
 Prayer in Bad Weather.
 Problems About the Other Woman.
 Red Up and Down.
 Scarlet.
 Sweaty Day in August, A.
 T.M.
 This Then—.
 Trying to Get Even.
 Waving and Waving Goodbye.
Burns, R. Adam A———'s Prayer.
 As I Cam[e] O'er [the] Cairney Mount.
 As I Went Out Ae May Morning.
 Ballad, A: "While Prose-work and rhymes."
 Bob o' Dumblane, The.
 Bonie Mary.
 Can Ye Labor Lea.
 Captain's Lady, The.
 Deuks Dang o'er My Daddie, The.
 Duncan Gray ["Weary fa' you, Duncan Gray"].
 Fornicator. A New Song, The.
 Gie the Lass her Fairin'
 Godly Girzie.
 Here's His Health in Water.
 I'm Owre [*or* O'er] Young to Marry Yet.
 Jolly Gauger, The.
 Lea-Rig, The.
 Libel Summons.
 Muirland Meg.
 Nine Inch Will Please a Lady.
 O Saw Ye My Maggie.
 Ode to Spring.
 On a Bank of Flowers.
 Patriarch, The.
 Ploughman, The.
 Robert Burns' Answer [to Epistle from a
  Taylor].
 Scroggam.
 Shepherd's Wife, The.
 Song: "I'll tell you a tale of a Wife."
 Taylor fell thro' the bed, thimble an' a', The.
 There's News Lasses News.
 Trogger, The.
 Waukrife Minnie, A.
 Wha Is That at My Bower-Door?
 Wha'll M-w Me Now.
 Why Should Na Poor Folk Mowe.
Campion, T. In se.
Carew, T. On the Marriage of T. K. and C. C.:
  The Morning Stormy.
 Rapture, A.
Carruth, H. Alive.
 August.
 Capper Kaplinski at the North Side Cue Club.
 Pray You Young Woman.
 Sex.
 Three Songs.
 Valentine.
Carver, R. Woolworth's, 1954.
 Yesterday.
Cavafy. Next Table, The.
 Nous N'osons Plus Chanter les Roses.
 One Night.
 Passing Through.
 Their Origin.
 To Abide.
Cavalcanti. I found a shepherdess in a grove.
Ciardi, J. Blue Movie.
 Censorship.
 Donne Ch'avete Intellètto d'Amore.
 In Pity as We Kiss and Lie.
 Overthrow, An.
 Sometimes the Foundering Fury.
 Two Hours.
Clifton, L. Leaving Fox.
Codrescu. For Marg So She Could Fuck Again.
 It takes joy to listen and it is inspiring being
  listened to.
 New York.
 Partiti Sunt Vestimenta Mea Miserunt Sortem
  Contra Me ad Incarte Cla a Filii a Eniol
  Liebee Braya Braguesca et Belzebuth.
 To the Virgin as She Now Stands to the Monk
  after a Beatles Movie.

War & Peace.
Collins, B. Purity.
Cooper, J. Acceptances.
 Circle, a Square, a Triangle and a Ripple of
  Water, A.
 Obligations.
Creeley. Alba.
 Curse.
 Let something else be / the question—.
 Way, The.
 Woman, The.
Cummings, E. E. Amiable putrescence
  carpenters, An.
 Bed is not very big, The.
 Between the breasts / of bestial.
 Devil crept in eden wood.
 Dirty colours of her kiss have just, The.
 Don't cries to please my.
 First she like a piece of ill-oiled.
 Five Americans.
 Her careful distinct sex whose sharp lips comb.
 Her / flesh / Came / at.
 I like my body when it is with your.
 I will be / M o ving in the Street of her.
 In making Marjorie god hurried.
 Innerly / UningstrolL / (stamens & pistil).
 Irreproachable ladies firmly lewd.
 Light cursed falling in a singular block.
 Light Out), A.
 Luminous tendril of celestial wish.
 May I Feel Said He.
 Moan / (is) / ing / the she of the.
 &-moon-He-be-hind-a-mills.
 My deathly body's deadly lady.
 My strength becoming wistful in a glib.
 Noise.
 O by the by / has anybody seen.
 O It's Nice To Get Up In,the slipshod mucous
  kiss.
 Poor But TerFLY / went(flesh is grass).
 Raise the shade.
 She being Brand.
 She had that softness which is falsity.
 She,straddling my lap.
 So you're hunting for ann well i'm looking for
  will.
 Sunlight was over.
 When the spent day begins to frail.
 When you went away it was morning.
 Whereas by dark really released,the modern.
 Who's most afraid of death?thou.
Cunningham, J. Original Sin.
 Statistics.
Davie, D. Autumn Imagined.
 By the Road to Upper Midhope.
 Christening, A.
 Jacob's Ladder.
 Under a Skylight.
Dickey, J. Form.
 Sheep Child, The.
Dickey, W. Androids.
 Making Love.
Dove, R. Adolescence—II.
Dubie. After Spring Snow, What They Saw.
 American Scene, An.
Dugan, A. For Masturbation.
 General Prothalamion for Wartimes.
 General Prothalamion in Populous Times.
 On a Myth. On a Conventional Wisdom.
 On an Old Advertisement and After a
  Photograph by Alfred Stieglitz.
 Summer Heaven, Angels, Heaven.
Dunbar, P. Confirmation.
Duncan, R. I Am a Most Fleshly Man.
 Mirror, The.
Eberhart, R. Request for Offering.
Eliot, T. S. Fragments: "There was a jolly tinker
  came across the sea."
Ferlinghetti, L. Imaginary Happening, London,
  An.
 Love Nut, The.
 See / it was like this when.
 What could she say to the fantastic foolybear.
García Lorca. Faithless Wife, The.
 Unfaithful Wife, The.
Ginsberg, A. After Thoughts.

Archetype Poem, The.
Change, The: *Kyoto-Tokyo Express*.
C'mon Jack.
Fie My Fum.
Howl.
Love Comes.
Love Poem on Theme by Whitman.
Many Loves.
Maybe Love.
On Neal's Ashes.
Please Master.
Pull My Daisy.
Pussy Blues.
Sphincter.
Tethnakin D'oligo Pideuis Fainom Alaia.
This Form of Life Needs Sex.
Glück, L. Edge, The.
Labor Day.
Memo from the Cave.
Mock Orange.
Murderess, The.
My Life Before Dawn.
Portrait of the Queen in Tears.
Return, The.
Wound, The.
Graves, R. Dans un Seul Lit.
Death Grapple, The.
Deed of Gift.
Ecstasy of Chaos.
Encounter, The.
Fact of the Act.
In Time of Absence.
Measure of Casualness, A.
Metaphor, The.
Quiet Glades of Eden, The.
Starred Coverlet, The.
Thieves, The.
Visitation, The.
What Did You Say?
Woman of Greece.
Gunn, T. Adultery.
Amorous Debate, An.
At the Barriers.
Barren Leaves.
Carnal Knowledge.
Loot.
Menace, The.
Miracle, The.
Modes of Pleasure.
New York.
Saturnalia.
Tenderloin.
Hall, D. Material.
Hamill, S. Mountains and Rivers without End.
Heaney, S. Act of Union.
Herrick. Delaying Bride, The.
Epithalamy to Sir Thomas Southwell and His
    Lady, An.
Good-Night, or Blessing, The.
On Himselfe.
Poet Loves a Mistress, but Not to Marry, The.
To a Maid.
To Anthea.
To Electra.
Upon a Lady Faire, but Fruitlesse.
Upon Doll.
Upon Groynes.
Upon Jolly and Jilly.
Vision to Electra, The.
Hughes, T. Bride and Groom Lie Hidden for
    Three Days.
Eclipse.
Fragment of an Ancient Tablet.
Sunstruck Foxglove.
Ignatow, D. Coupling.
Despite the Plainness of the Day.
I Dream I Hurl a Spear.
Knowledge.
Opening Paths.
See.
Jacobsen, J. Lovers, The.
Jarrell, R. In Nature There Is Neither Right nor
    Left nor Wrong.
Jeffers, R. Tamar.
Jonson, B. To Pertinax Cob.
Keats. O Blush Not So! O Blush Not So!

Kinnell. After Making Love We Hear
    Footsteps.
Conception.
Last Gods.
Rapture.
Waking, The.
Kizer, C. Copulating Gods, The.
Komunyakaa. Glass Ark, The.
No Love in This House.
Nude Interrogation.
Reconstructing a Crime.
Rhythm Method.
Sunday Afternoons.
Woman, I Got the Blues.
Kumin, M. After Love.
Laughlin, J. Advice to Aurelius.
After Rochester (or somebody).
First Night, The.
French, The.
I Like You.
I Love the Way.
It Was the First Time.
Lines after Cummings.
Love Is Cumulative.
Nowadays.
O Best of All Nights, Return and Return Again.
Why.
Your Eyes.
Lawrence, D. H. After Many Days.
At the Cearne.
Bawdy Can Be Sane.
Cross, The.
Jeune Fille, The.
Leave Sex Alone.
London Mercury.
Love as an Escape.
Love On the Farm.
Men and Women.
Noble Englishman, The.
Puss-Puss!
Red Moon-Rise.
Rose of All the World.
Scent of Irises.
Sex and Trust.
Sex Isn't Sin.
Sex Won't Work.
These Clever Women.
Wild Things in Captivity.
Young Want to Be Just, The.
Levertov. Ache of Marriage, The.
Bride, The.
To the Snake.
Logan, J. Bride's Song, The.
Bridegroom's Song, The.
Complaint, The.
Epilogue.
Epilogue, Songs of the Spouses, Complaint of
    Love.
Lines for an Unknown Lover.
Tale of Courtship.
Logue, C. When I was serving my country.
Lowell, R. Like Henry VIII, Mohammed got
    religion.
Lux. Sex in History.
MacLeish. German Girls! The German Girls!,
    The.
Hearts' and Flowers'
Observations of P. Ovidus Naso on the
    Incidence of Sex in the Contemporary Novel.
Wild Old Wicked Man, The.
You Also, Gaius Valerius Catullus.
Major, C. Beyond impasse.
Frenzy.
Little Rock.
Stillness and Vertigo.
McGrath, T. Love in a Bus.
Rediscovery.
McHugh, H. Coming.
Meantime.
Not a Sin.
Numberless.
Stall.
Millay, E. I, Being Born A Woman.
Muldoon, P. Bang.
Blewits.
Green Gown.

History.
Little Black Book, The.
October 1950.
Sky-Woman.
Whim.
Nash, O. Nevertheless.
Neruda. Physics.
O'Hara, F. Ave Maria.
Captain Bada.
Cornkind.
Easter.
Mary Desti's Ass.
Ode to Michael Goldberg ('s Birth and Other
    Births).
Poem: "Twin spheres full of fur and noise."
Olson, C. As the shield goddess, Mycenae.
From *The Song of Ullikummi*
Hymn to the Word.
Long Distance.
One Night Ma / Lay with Pa.
Picture, The.
Under every green tree, sex.
Patchen. Figure Motioned with Its Mangled
    Hand Toward the Wall Behind It, The.
Heaven and Earth.
New Being, The.
On the South West Coast of Erehwemos Stands
    a Romantic Little Village.
Queer Client and the Forest-Inn, The.
Waking into Sleep.
Petronius Arbiter. Doing, a filthy pleasure is,
    and short.
Piercy. Cats Like Angels.
Crabs.
Greater Grand Rapids Lover, The.
Lansing Bad Penny Come Again Blues, The.
Some Collisions Bring Luck.
You Ask Why Sometimes I Say Stop.
Plath. Gigolo.
Ramanujan. LOVE 5.
Poor Man's Riches 2, A.
Rexroth, K. Cinque Terre.
Floating.
Gradualism.
Inversely, as the Square of Their Distances
    Apart.
Love Poems of Marichiko, The.
Mocking Birds.
Sottoportico San Zaccaria.
Travelers in Erewhon.
Under Soracte.
Rich, A. Demon Lover, The.
For L.G.: Unseen for Twenty Years.
Two Songs.
Waking in the Dark.
Rimbaud, A. Fête Galante.
First Night.
Idol, The. Arsehole Sonnet.
Ritsos. Fulfillment.
Small Dialogue.
Roethke. Four for Sir John Davies.
Moment, The.
Sensualists, The.
Rukeyser, M. Anemone.
Double Ode.
Drunken Girl.
Loan, The.
Mortal Girl.
Orgy.
Rondel: "Now that I am fifty-six."
Transgress, The.
Tunnel, The.
Watchers, The.
Wedding Presents.
Welcome from War.
What I See.
Rumi. Breadmaking.
Sexual Urgency, What a Woman's Laughter Can
    Do, and the Nature of True Virility.
Two Ways of Running.
Sexton. Ballad of the Lonely Masturbator, The.
Barefoot.
Farmer's Wife, The.
From the Garden.
Jesus Awake.
Old Dwarf Heart.

Song for a Lady.
Us.
When Man Enters Woman.
Shapiro, K. First Time, The.
Simic. Breasts.
Smith, S. Conviction IV.
Snyder, G. Song of the Slip.
Song of the Tangle.
Stein, G. Lifting Belly.
Stock, R. Haiku: "You are the bright bird."
Small Rain, The.
To Peg.
Swenson, M. Laocoön Dream Recorded in Diary Dated 1943.
Sze. Morning Shutters.
Tate, J. Chaste Stranger, The.
Coming Down Cleveland Avenue.
Hostile Philharmonic Orchestra, The.
Up Here.
Thomas, D. Into Her Lying Down Head.
My World Is Pyramid.
Updike. Cunts.
Elderly Sex.
Fellatio.
In Memoriam Felis Felis.
Mouse Sex.
Squirrels Mating.
Van Duyn. Billings and Cooings from "The Berkeley Barb."
Walker, A. She Said.
Warren, R. You Sort Old Letters.
Whalen, P. Confession and Penance.
Whitman, W. Ages and Ages Returning at Intervals.
Dalliance of the Eagles, The.
From Pent-up Aching Rivers.
Woman Waits for Me, A.
Wilbur, R. Late Aubade, A.
Under a Tree.
Williams, C. K. Cautionary, The.
Combat.
Crawl.
Madder.
Nut, The.
Portions of Manslayer.
Saint Sex.
Soliliquies.
Williams, M. Affair, The.
Original Sin.
Rubaiyat for Sue Ella Tucker.
Sleeping With Friends.
Williams, T. Iron is the Winter.
Life Story.
Liturgy of Roses, A.
Wolf's Hour.
Williams, W. April is the Saddest Month.
Wright, J. Moral Poem Freely Accepted from Sappho, A.
See also **Erotic Love; Homosexuality and Homosexuals; Lust; Sexuality**

Sexism
Browning, E. Lord Walter's Wife.
Collins, B. Man in Space.
Davie, D. Heroine of the Academy, A.
Dickinson, E. Over the fence.
Dugan, A. Pretrial Hearing.
Sexist Lament: Ruin by Monitor.
What the Hell, Rage, Give in to Natural Graces.
Gallagher, T. Conversation with a Fireman from Brooklyn.
Han-shan. Raise girls but not too many.
Jackson, L. Divestment of Beauty.
Kizer, C. Fearful Women.
Koch, K. Sleeping with Women.
Lorde. Revolution Is One Form of Social Change.
Who Said It Was Simple.
Millay, E. I, Being Born A Woman.
Piercy. Barbie Doll.
Ramanujan. On Not Learning from Animals.
Rich, A. Snapshots of a Daughter-in-Law.
Stockton, A. To Miss Mary Stockton, an Epistle upon Some Gentleman Refusing to Admit Ladies of Their Circle into the Parlour till Supper Where They Met for Conversation and Business Once a Week.

To the Visitant, from a Circle of Ladies, on Reading His Paper. No. 3, in the Pennsylvania Chronicle.
Yeats. Nativity, A.
Sexton, Anne
Ciardi, J. Trying to Feel Something.
Dugan, A. Drunken Memories of Anne Sexton.
Kumin, M. On Being Asked to Write a Poem in Memory of Anne Sexton.
Sexton. Ambition Bird, The.
Angel Food Dogs, The.
Baby Picture.
Cigarettes and Whiskey and Wild, Wild Women.
Gods.
Hurry Up Please It's Time.
Is It True?
January 1st.
Letters to Dr. Y.
Speaking Bitterness.
Sweeney.
Talking to Sheep.
Williams, C. K. Suicide: Anne.
Sexual Abuse
Ai. False Witness.
Life Story.
Clifton, L. Shapeshifter Poems.
Frost, R. Subverted Flower, The.
Komunyakaa. Nude Tango.
Stafford, W. Not in the Headlines.
Williams, M. Everything Is Fine Here. How Are You?
Late Show.
Wilner, E. Eleusis.
Sexual Exploitation
Bukowski. Frozen Food Section.
Girl on the Bus Stop Bench, The.
Girls Coming Home.
Girls in Pantyhose.
Hughes, L. Mulatto.
Komunyakaa. Cinderella at Big Sur.
Kunitz, S. She Wept, She Railed.
Laughlin, J. Why Not?
Sexuality
Ai. Hoover Trismegistus.
Broumas, O. Backgammon.
Dactyls.
Heart Believes with Blows.
Little Red Riding Hood.
Perennial.
Rapunzel.
Rumpelstiltskin.
Snow White.
Bukowski. Girls at the Green Hotel, The.
Making It.
Sex.
Sexpot.
You.
Burns, R. Green Grow[s] the Rashes.
Cavafy. And I Reclined and Lay on Their Beds.
Days of 1896.
I Went.
In a Town of Osroini.
In an Old Book.
Passing Through.
Picture of a Young Man, Twenty-three, Done by His Friend of the Same Age, an Amateur.
Celan. In Egypt.
Clifton, L. Peeping Tom.
Codrescu. Dear Masoch.
Operations of Desire, The.
Traffic.
Creeley. Dear Dorothy.
Hands, The.
Hole, The.
Cummings, E. E. "Gay" is the captivating cognomen of a Young Woman of cambridge,mass.
Dickey, W. Performances.
You White Cunning Devils.
Dickinson, E. Wild Nights—Wild Nights!
Dubie. Monologue of Two Moons, Nudes with Crests. 1938.
Eliot, T. S. Whispers of Immortality.
Ferlinghetti, L. Dark Portrait, A.
García Lorca. Elegy: "Like a censer filled with desire."

Preciosa and the Wind.
Summer Madrigal.
Thamar and Amnon.
Ginsberg, A. Green Automobile, The.
This Form of Life Needs Sex.
Typical Affair, A.
Graves, R. Cry Faugh!
Gunn, T. Courage, a Tale.
Hacker, M. Adult Entertainment.
Days of 1959.
Hughes, L. Desire.
Jazzonia.
Listen Here Blues.
Mellow.
Red Silk Stockings.
To Midnight Nan at Leroy's.
Komunyakaa. Thorn Merchant's Mistress, The.
Kumin, M. Atlantic City 1939.
Larkin, P. Annus Mirabilis.
Two Portraits of Sex.
Laughlin, J. Cynthia in California.
Herodotus Reports.
Maze, The.
Real Bones.
Stuttgart: In a Nightclub (Illegal).
Trout, The.
Levertov. Mutes, The.
Logue, C. Girls, The.
Major, C. Sexual Conduct.
Mallarmé. Anguish.
Beautiful suicide victoriously fled, The.
Negress, A.
Melville, H. After the Pleasure Party.
Milosz, C. Father Ch., Many Years Later.
Voyeur.
Muldoon, P. Kissing and Telling.
Unicorn Defends Himself, The.
Olson, C. Assuming the Soul Is a Bitch.
Cause, the Cause, The.
Help Me, Venus, You Who Led Me On.
Mazdaism / has overcome.
White Horse.
Woman's Nipples Is the Rose of the World, A.
Orr, G. Adolescence.
Walking Home after the First Encounter.
Pasolini. Civil Song.
Lines from the Testament.
Southern Dawn.
Piercy. Cats Like Angels.
You Ask Why Sometimes I Say Stop.
Pinsky. History of My Heart.
Rich, A. Dialogue.
Rimbaud, A. Deserts of Love, The.
Once, animals spewed sperm as they charged.
Remembrances of Senility.
Rukeyser, M. Along History.
Schuyler, J. Tom.
Sexton. When the Glass of My Body Broke.
Stock, R. Poem on Holy Saturday.
Van Duyn. Billings and Cooings from "The Berkeley Barb."
Whitman, W. As Adam Early in the Morning.
Behold This Swarthy Face.
From Pent-up Aching Rivers.
Spontaneous Me.
To the Garden the World.
Wilbur, R. Catch, The.
Williams, C. K. Love: Beginnnings.
Saint Sex.
Williams, W. Transitional.
Yeats. Her Triumph.
Whence Had They Come?
Shadbush
See **Service (botany)**
Shadows
Amichai [*or* Amikhai]. In Those Days, in This Time.
Ammons. Recovery.
Angelou. Life Doesn't Frighten Me.
Atwood. Night Poem.
Beckett, S. Son ombre une nuit.
Bishop, E. Imber Nocturnus.
Bogan, L. Division.
Mark, The.
Browning, E. Romaunt of Margret, The.
Campion, T. Follow Thy Fair Sun[ne]

[Unhappy Shadow].
Shadowes before the shining sunne do vanish.
Carrera Andrade.   Mirror's Mission, The.
Celan.   Speak You Too.
Crane, H.   At Melville's Tomb.
  Garden Abstract.
Cummings, E. E.   Mrs / and mr across the way
  are kind of.
De la Mare.   Death-Dream, The.
  Fear.
  Music Unheard.
  Phantom, The.
  Shade, The.
  Shadow.
  Tired Cupid, The.
  Where?
  Where Is Thy Victory?
Dickey, W.   History of the Moon, The.
  Silver Creek Falls.
Dickinson, E.   Like Men and Women Shadows
  walk.
Donne.   Lecture upon the Shadow, A.
Eberhart, R.   Hand and the Shadow, The.
Enzensberger, H.   Shadow Realm.
Gallagher, T.   Into the Known.
García Lorca.   Song of the Barren Orange Tree.
Glück, L.   Hawk's Shadow.
Hardy, T.   In the Garden.
Hayden, R.   Broken Dark, The.
Heaney, S.   Good-night.
Hill, G.   Of Coming-into-Being and Passing-
  Away.
Hughes, L.   Shadows.
Jacobsen, J.   Animal Inside the Animal, The.
  Shade-Seller, The.
Jonson, B.   Song, A: "Come, let us here enjoy
  the shade."
Laughlin, J.   Step on His Head.
Lawrence, D. H.   Shades.
  Sympathy.
Lindsay, N.   Caught in a Net.
Logan, J.   Lines for Michael in the Picture.
Mahon.   Katie at the Pool.
McGrath, T.   When We Say Goodbye.
Merwin   By Day and by Night.
  Last One, The.
  Sickness at the Equinox, A.
Mistral, G.   Body, The.
Montale.   Other Lines.
  Voice That Came with the Coots.
Orr, G.   Some Notes on Shadows.
Pinkerton, H.   Degrees of Shade.
Prunty.   Intermittent Light, An.
Raine, K.   Afternoon sunlight plays.
Ramanujan.   Shadows.
Riley, J.   When Evening Shadows Fall.
Rilke.   Butterfly.
  Shade.
Rossetti, C.   In the Willow Shade.
Rumi.   Enough Words?
Sandburg, C.   Evening Questions.
  Losses.
  Out of the Rainbow End.
  Shadows Fall Blue on the Mountains.
  Sketch.
  Smoke Shapes.
  Wall Shadows.
Schuyler, J.   Light Within, The.
Simic.   Position without a Magnitude.
Smith, S.   Conviction (iii).
Stock, R.   Just Another Apotheosis.
Tate, J.   Shadowboxing.
Tomlinson, C.   All Afternoon.
  Blade, The.
  Shadow, The.
  White Van, The.
Updike.   Long Shadow.
Walcott.   Season of Phantasmal° Peace, The.
Wilbur, R.   Gnomons.
  Sunlight Is Imagination.
Wilde, O.   Harlot's House, The.
Williams, C. K.   It's over now. I watch.
Williams, M.   Friend, The.
Williams, W.   Halfworld, The.
Wilner, E.   Never Apologize for Poetry.
Wright, J.   Girl Walking into a Shadow, A.

RIP.
  Shadow and the Real, The.
Yeats.   New Faces, The.
Zukofsky, L.   All of December Toward New
  Year's.
  Can a mote of sunlight defeat its purpose.
Shaftesbury, Anthony Ashley Cooper, 1st Earl of
Dryden, J.   Absalom and Achitophel.
Shakers (First Church of The Millennium)
Hall, D.   Religious Articles.
Schuyler, J.   Shaker.
Shakespeare, William
Arnold, M.   Shakespeare.
Bogan, L.   To an Artist, to Take Heart.
Borges.   Everything and Nothing.
Browning, R.   Names, The.
Bukowski.   Kings Are Gone, The.
Crane, H.   To Shakespeare.
Cullen, C.   Cor Cordium.
Dickinson, E.   He has had his Future.
Dubie.   Elsinore in the Late Ancient Autumn.
Eberhart, R.   Broken Pen, The.
  Hamlet Father, The.
Emerson, R.   Turtle in swamp.
Gray, T.   William Shakespeare to Mrs Anne,
  Regular Servant to the Rev. Mr Precentor of
  York.
Gurney, I.   Hazlitt.
Hardy, T.   To Shakespeare.
Hopkins, G.   Shakspere.
Hughes, T.   Prospero and Sycorax.
Jackson, L.   Tale of Modernity.
Jeffers, R.   Shakespeare's Grave.
Jonson, B.   To the Memory of My Beloved, the
  Author Mr [or Master] William Shakespeare:
  And What He Hath Left Us.
  To the Reader ("This figure, that thou here seest
  put").
Keats.   On Sitting Down to Read "King Lear"
  Once Again.
Kipling, R.   Coiner, The.
  Craftsman, The.
Lawrence, D. H.   When I Read Shakespeare.
MacLeish.   Verses for a Centennial.
Major, C.   And who must remain.
Melville, H.   Coming Storm, The.
Meredith, G.   Poetry of Shakespeare, The.
  Rosalind.
  Spirit of Shakespeare: Continued, The.
  Spirit of Shakespeare, The.
Milton.   On Shakespear[e].
Niedecker.   Brought the enemy down.
  Ten o'clock.
Rimbaud, A.   Ophelia.
Robinson, E.   Ben Jonson Entertains a Man
  from Stratford.
Stock, R.   Prose Parables.
  Shakespeare in Vietnam.
Suckling, S.   Supplement of an Imperfect Copy
  of Verses of Mr. William Shakespeare's, By the
  Author, A.
Van Duyn.   Birthday Card for a Psychiatrist.
Very.   On the Three Hundredth Anniversary of
  Shakespeare's Birthday.
Whitman, W.   Shakspeare-Bacon's Cipher.
Wilbur, R.   Up, Jack.
Zaturenska.   Shakespearean Cycle, A.
Zukofsky, L.   Stratford-on-Avon.
Shamans
Milosz, C.   I Sleep a Lot.
Muldoon, P.   Glanders.
Shame
Ai.   Antihero, The.
Amichai [or Amikhai].   Aged Parents, The.
Angelou.   Memory, The.
Berry, W.   Do Not Be Ashamed.
Brontë, E.   Sleep Not, Dream Not.
Burns, R.   Rantin Laddie, The.
  Wha'll M-w me Now.
Byron, G.   When We Two Parted.
Cavalcanti.   Sonnet: Guido answers the
  foregoing Sonnet, speaking with shame of his
  changed face.
Creeley.   Shame, The.
  Song: "I wouldn't / embarrass you."

Davie, D.   Berkshire.
  Machineries of Shame.
Dickinson, E.   Embarrassment of one another.
  His Cheek is his Biographer.
  Seraphic shame generosity causes, The.
  Shame is the shawl of Pink.
  There is a Shame of Nobleness.
Donne.   Flea, The.
  Triple Fool, The.
Emerson, R.   If curses be the wage of love.
Hacker, M.   Mother II.
Hardy, T.   Spectres That Grieve.
Herrick.   Another.
  Shame, No Statist.
  Sins Loathed, and Yet Loved.
  Upon Peason.
Jackson, L.   I Remember.
  Plighted to Shame.
Lawrence, D. H.   Rallying-Point.
Logan, J.   Lines for a Young Man Who Talked.
MacLeish.   Conversation in a Belfry.
Meredith, G.   Falling of Sally, The.
Merwin.   Avoiding News by the River.
Milosz, C.   Distance.
  Prayer: "Approaching ninety, and still with a
  hope."
Nemerov.   Fall Again, The.
Oliver, M.   Strawberry Moon.
Olson, C.   Translation, A.
Petrarch.   I think and think, and in my thoughts
  I feel.
  Love, I have sinned, and recognise my sin.
Rimbaud, A.   Shame.
Rossetti, C.   Behold the Man!
Sarton, M.   Who Wakes.
Stock, R.   Poet's Prescription of Shamelessness,
  The.
Wilbur, R.   Shame.
Williams, C. K.   Shame.
Wright, J.   In Shame and Humiliation.
  In Terror of Hospital Bills.
Shaped Poetry
Cummings, E. E.   R-P-O-P-H-E-S-S-A-G-R.
Herbert, G.   Our Life Is Hid with Christ in God.
Herrick.   Pillar of Fame, The.
Sharecroppers
Hughes, L.   Share-Croppers.
Komunyakaa.   Birthday Song.
Niedecker.   I'm a sharecropper.
Sharks
Dickey, J.   Shark's Parlor, The.
Dugan, A.   Plague of Dead Sharks.
Melville, H.   Maldive Shark, The.
Nash, O.   Shark, The.
Pinsky.   Volume, The.
  Want Bone, The.
Stock, R.   One of the Old Ones.
Sze.   Great White Shark, The.
Shaving
Jarrell, R.   Transient Barracks.
Laughlin, J.   Ars Gratia Artis.
Nash, O.   And Three Hundred and Sixty-Six in
  Leap Year.
Simic.   Shaving at Night.
Updike.   Upon Shaving Off One's Beard.
Shaw, George Bernard
Ciardi, J.   Elegy for G. B. Shaw.
Eberhart, R.   Explorer on Main Street, The.
Kumin, M.   Accolade of the Animals, The.
Williams, W.   For G.B.S., Old.
Shaw, Robert Gould
Dunbar, P.   Robert Gould Shaw.
Lowell, R.   For the Union Dead.
Sheba, Queen of (Bible)
Amichai [or Amikhai].   Visit of the Queen of
  Sheba, The.
Rumi.   Sheba's Gifts to Solomon.
  Sheba's Hesitation.
  Sheba's Throne.
  Solomon to Sheba.
Sheep
Amichai [or Amikhai].   Sheepskin Coat.
Atwood.   November.
Berry, W.   Birth (Near Port William), The.

Blake, W.   Answer to the Parson, An.
Browning, E.   Sounds.
Burns, R.   Death and Dying Words of Poor
  Mailie, the Author's Only Pet Yowe, an Unco
  Mournfu' Tale, The.
  Poor Mailie's Elegy.
Cowper, W.   Needless Alarm, The.
Cummings, E. E.   After-Glow.
Davie, D.   Skelpick.
Hall, D.   Black Faced Sheep, The.
  Kill, The.
  Our Walk in Yorkshire.
Hamill, S.   Sheep to Slaughter.
Hardy, T.   Sheep Fair, A.
Hopkins, G.   Io.
Hughes, L.   Shearing Time.
Hughes, T.   Sheep.
  What is it this time the dark barn again.
Jarrell, R.   Country Was, The.
Larkin, P.   To a Very Slow Air.
Laughlin, J.   Out in the Pasture.
MacLeish.   Mark's Sheep.
Muldoon, P.   Behold the Lamb.
Paley, G.   Families.
Ramanujan.   Turning Around.
Rossetti, C.   Lambs of Grasmere, 1860, The.
Sandburg, C.   Sheep.
  Suburban Sicilian Sketches.
Sexton.   Sheep.
  Talking to Sheep.
Simic.   Strictly Bucolic.
Wilbur, R.   Grace.
See also **Lambs**

Sheepshearing and Sheepshearers
Hughes, L.   Shearing Time.
Hughes, T.   Memory, A.

Sheets
Gurney, I.   Traffic in Sheets.
Stevens, W.   Silver Plough-Boy, The.

Shelley, Mary Wollstonecraft
Niedecker.   Who was Mary Shelley?

Shelley, Percy Bysshe
Browning, R.   Memorabilia.
Carver, R.   Squall, A.
Cullen, C.   Cor Cordium.
Gunn, T.   Lerici.
Hardy, T.   Rome: At the Pyramid of Cestius near
  the Graves of Shelley and Keats.
  Shelley's Skylark.
Logan, J.   Byron at Shelley's Burning.
Meredith, G.   Poetry of Shelley, The.
Meredith, W.   English Accounts.
Millay, E.   To a Poet that Died Young.
Nash, O.   You and Me and P.B. Shelley.
Rukeyser, M.   From a Play: Publisher's Song.
Wilde, O.   Grave of Shelley, The.

Shells
Blue Cloud.   Abalone.
Codrescu.   Near Sonnet.
Dugan, A.   Natural Enemies of the Conch, The.
Graves, R.   Judges, The.
MacLeish.   Dr. Sigmund Freud Discovers the
  Sea Shell.
  Triumph of the Shell, The.
Moore, M.   Paper Nautilus, The.
Nemerov.   Shells.
Oliver, M.   Whelks.
Raine, K.   On a Shell-strewn Beach.
  Shells.
Tomlinson, C.   Shell, The.
Williams, W.   Tribute to Neruda the Poet
  Collector of Seashells.
Wilner, E.   Two Pairs of Eyes.
See also **Clams and Clamming; Oysters; Snails**

Shellshock
Owen, W.   Chances, The.
  Conscious.
  Dead-Beat, The.
  Dulce et Decorum Est.
  Mental Cases.

Shenandoah River and Shenandoah Valley
Melville, H.   Portent, The.
Sandburg, C.   Shenandoah.
  Shenandoah Journey.

Shepherds and Shepherdesses
Amichai [*or* Amikhai].   Arab Shepherd Is
  Searching for His Goat on Mount Zion, An.
  Arab Shepherd Seeks a Kid on Mount Zion, A.
Carew, T.   Pastoral[l] Dialogue, A.
Cavalcanti.   Ballata: Concerning a Shepherd-
  maid.
  I found a shepherdess in a grove.
Crashaw.   Hymne of the Nativity, Sung by the
  Shepheards, A.
  In the Holy Nativity of Our Lord God.
Cummings, E. E.   After-Glow.
De la Mare.   Nod.
Emerson, R.   Shout to the Sheperds, A.
"H. D."   Shepherd, The.
Hall, D.   Black Faced Sheep, The.
Hardy, T.   Sheep-Boy, The.
  Unkindly May, An.
Herbert, G.   Twenty-third Psalm, The.
Herrick.   Pastorall Sung to the King: Montano,
  Silvio, and Mirtillo, Shepards, A.
Hopkins, G.   Richard.
  Shepherd's Brow, The.
Hughes, L.   Shepherd's Song at Christmas.
Jeffers, R.   Loving Shepherdess, The.
  Silent Shepherds, The.
Lawrence, D. H.   St Mark.
MacNeice.   Eclogue by a Five-Barred Gate.
  Nuts in May.
Marlowe.   Passionate Shepherd To His Love,
  The.
Marvell.   Clorinda and Damon.
Merrill, J.   Violent Pastoral.
Merton.   Fall of Night, The.
Merwin.   My Brothers the Silent.
  Visitation.
Pope, A.   Pastorals.
Ralegh, S.   Nymph's [*or* Nimphs] Reply to the
  Shepherd [*or* Sheepheard], The.
Ramanujan.   Turning Around.
Rilke.   Song: "Let's pretend we are shepherds."
Rossetti, C.   Faithless Shepherdess, The.
  Good Shepherd, The.
  Hymn for Christmas Day, A.
  Lambs of Grasmere, 1860, The.
Simic.   Strictly Bucolic.
Spenser, E.   Colin Clouts Come Home Againe.
Stockton, A.   Lavinia and Amanda, a Pastoral.
  Lucinda and Aminta, a Pastoral.
  Peace, a Pastoral Dialogue.—Part the Second.
Unknown.   Another of the Same Nature, Made
  Since.
  Maid, The.
Wilner, E.   Classical Proportions of the Heart.
Wordsworth, W.   Idle Shepherd-Boys, The; or,
  Dungeon-Ghyll Force. A Pastoral.
  Last of the Flock, The.
  Michael [A Pastoral Poem].
  Norman Boy, The.
  Shepherd, looking eastward softly said, The.
  Song at the Feast of Brougham Castle.
Yeats.   Shepherd and Goatherd.
  Song of the Happy Shepherd, The.

Sheridan, Philip Henry
Melville, H.   Sheridan at Cedar Creek.
Whitman, W.   Interpolation Sounds.

Sheridan, Thomas
Brooke, H.   Quilca House to the Dean.
Delany, P.   From My Much Honored Friend at
  Heldelville.
  Upon the Author.
Murray, P.   Receipt to Frighten away the Dean,
  A.
Owens, S.   Poem, A: "Ye Sons of Levi, Church
  Divines."
Swift, J.   Ad Amicum Eruditum Thomam
  Sheridan [To My Learned Friend, Thomas
  Sheridan].
  To Thomas Sheridan.
Tisdall, W.   Tom Pun-Sibi Metamorphosed: Or,
  The Giber Gibed.
Unknown.   Elegy on the Deplorable Death of
  Mr. Thomas Sheridan.
  Imitation of Anacreon's Grasshopper, An.
  New Jingle on Tom Dingle, A.
  Poem on Tom Pun——bi on Occasion of His

Late Death, A.
  Punegyric upon Tom Pun-sibi's *Ars Pun-ica*, A.
  Rivals, The.
  To My Worthy Friend T S——, D. D. On His
  Incomparable Translation of and Notes on
  Persius.
  Tom Pun-Sibi's Resurrection Disproved.
  Tom Punsibi's Farewell to the Muses.
  Upon Mr. Sheridan's Turning Author, 1716.

Sherman, William Tecumseh, Union general
Ferlinghetti, L.   Sherman's March Reglitterized.
Melville, H.   March to the Sea, The.
Whitman, W.   Ethiopia Saluting the Colors.
Whittier.   Howard at Atlanta.

Shields
Dugan, A.   On Shields. Against World War 3.
Sarton, M.   Baroque Image.

Shiloh, Battle of (1862)
Melville, H.   Rebel Color-Bearers at Shiloh.
  Shiloh [A Requiem].

Ships and Shipbuilding
Ammons.   Ship.
Bishop, E.   Casabianca.
  Large Bad Picture.
  Song: "Summer is over upon the sea."
Brodsky, J.   Venice: Lido.
Byron, G.   Oh How I Wish That an Embargo.
Carew, T.   To Her in Absence; a Ship.
Carver, R.   Asia.
  At Least.
Cavafy.   Ships, The.
Ciardi, J.   Benefits of an Education, The.
Clifton, L.   Slaveship[s].
Clough.   Qua Cursum Ventus.
Corbière.   Old Roscoff.
Crane, S.   God fashioned the ship of the world
  carefully.
  I explain the silvered passing of a ship at night.
Davie, D.   Reminded of Bougainville.
De la Mare.   Sea-Magic.
Dickinson, E.   There is no Frigate like a Book.
Dunbar, P.   Ships That Pass in the Night.
Eliot, T. S.   Engine, The.
Emerson, R.   Letters.
Gallagher, T.   Still Moment at Dun Laoghaire.
Glück, L.   Slave Ship, The.
Graves, R.   Former Attachment, A.
  Shot, The.
Han-shan.   All of you are priceless gems.
Herrick.   No Shipwrack of Vertue. To a Friend.
Hughes, L.   "Jesus, The."
  Seascape.
  To Captain Mulzac.
Ignatow, D.   Ship, The.
Jacobsen, J.   Sea Fog, The.
Kinsella, T.   Navigators.
Kipling, R.   Ballad of the "Bolivar", The.
  Big Steamers.
  Cruisers.
  Derelict, The.
  Destroyers, The.
  King Henry VII. And the Shipwrights.
  King, The.
  Liner She's a Lady, The.
  Mary Gloster, The.
  Such As in Ships.
  Truthful Song, The.
Larkin, P.   North Ship, The.
Laughlin, J.   Confidential Report.
  Ship, The.
  Two Ships.
Lawrence, D. H.   Argonauts, The.
  Greeks Are Coming!, The.
  Ship of Death, The.
  Ships in Bottles.
Levi, P.   Laid Up.
Lindsay, N.   Johnny Appleseed's Ship Comes
  In.
MacLeish.   Ship of Fools.
MacNeice.   Atlantic Tunnel, The.
  Death of an Old Lady.
  North Sea, The.
  Passage Steamer.
Melville, H.   Berg, The.
  Temeraire, The.
Meredith, G.   *Irene* ducks and runs amuck, The.

Olive Branch, The.
Meredith, W. Battlewagon.
Carrier.
Transport.
Wreck of the Thresher, The (Lost at Sea, April 10, 1963).
Merwin. Ship.
Mistral, G. Talcahuano.
Montale. Haul your paper ships on the seared.
Neruda. Different Ship, A.
Niedecker. Allied Convoy / Reaches Russia.
Consider.
Oppen. Bolt / In the frame.
Carpenter's Boat.
City of Keansburg, The.
Confession.
Palmer, M. Idem 1.
Plath. On Deck.
Winter Ship, A.
Ransom, J. Good Ships.
Rossetti, C. Rainbow, The.
Rukeyser, M. Cruise, The.
Sandburg, C. Sketch.
Snyder, G. Goofing Again.
Oil.
Sappa Creek, The.
Stevens, W. Farewell to Florida.
Tomlinson, C. Barque Nornen.
Faring, The.
Ship's Waiters.
Updike. Azores.
Shipbored.
Whitman, W. Aboard at a Ship's Helm.
After the Sea-Ship.
Beauty of the Ship, The.
Dismantled Ship, The.
Patrolling Barnegat.
Ship Starting, The.
Song for All Seas, All Ships.
Whittier. Ship-Builders, The.
To a Cape Ann Schooner.
Williams, W. In Harbor.
Wordsworth, W. Where lies the Land to which yon Ship must go?
With Ships the sea was sprinkled far and nigh.
Zukofsky, L. Hill.
See also **Boats and Boating; Freighters; Tugboats; Yachts**

Shipwrecks
Ammons. Whaleboat Sturck,The.
Brodsky, J. New Jules Verne, The.
Byron, G. Julian [A Fragment].
Ciardi, J. Letter from a Rubber Raft.
Coleridge, S. To a Lady.
Corbière. Old Roscoff.
Cowper, W. Castaway, The.
On the Loss of the *Royal George*.
De la Mare. Wreck, The.
Dickinson, E. Glee—The great storm is over.
Dubie. November 23, 1989.
Shipwreck.
Graves, R. Furious Voyage, The.
Hardy, T. Convergence of the Twain, The.
Herrick. Safety on the Shore.
Ship-Wrack.
Hopkins, G. Loss of the Eurydice, The.
Nightingale, The.
Sea Took Pity, The.
Wreck of the Deutschland, The.
Longfellow, H. Wreck of the *Hesperus*, The.
MacDiarmid, H. Wreck of the *Swan*, The.
Mallarmé. Throw of the Dice, A.
Marvell. Unfortunate Lover, The.
McGrath, T. Offering.
Melville, H. Aeolian Harp, The.
Berg, The.
Far Off-Shore.
Haglets, The.
Off Cape Colona.
Meredith, W. English Accounts.
Merwin. Hulk, The.
Oppen. Squall.
Petrarch. He who is adamant to live his life.
Raine, K. Turner's Seas.
Rich, A. Diving into the Wreck.
Rossetti, C. Bird's-Eye View, A.

Rossetti, D. White Ship, The.
Tomlinson, C. Barque Nornen.
Very. "Tuesday night, the schooner Weaver, of Glen Creek, N.J., went to pieces near Sandy Hook, and her entire crew were lost."
Walcott. Castaway, The.
Whitman, W. To the Man-of-War Bird.
Whittier. Dead Ship of Harpswell, The.
Palatine, The.
Skipper Ireson's Ride.
Swan Song of Parson Avery, The.
Three Bells, The.
Wreck of Rivermouth, The.
Wilner, E. Minor Epic.
Wordsworth, W. I find it written of SIMONIDES.

Shirts
Housman. From the wash the laundress sends.
Merwin. Night of the Shirts, The.
Pinsky. Shirt.
Sandburg, C. Summer Shirt Sale.
Simic. Shirt.

Shiva
Jeffers, R. Shiva.
Ramanujan. Devotee's Complaint, A.
Mythologies 3.
Wilner, E. Nandin's Tail.

Shoemakers
Dunbar, W. Amendis [*or* Amends] to the Telyouris [*or* Tailors] and Sowtaris [*or* Soutaris *or* Soutars *or* Shoemakers].
Riley, J. "Blue-Monday" at the Shoe Shop.
Shoemaker, The.

Shoes
Ai. Miracle in Manila.
Riot Act, April 29, 1992.
Amichai [*or* Amikhai]. False Interpretation.
Sandals.
Corbett, W. Shoe, The.
Cowper, W. Let Banister now lend his aid.
Verses Written at Bath on Finding the Heel of a Shoe.
Dubie. Last Poem, Snow Tree.
Enzensberger, H. Dream, A.
Hardy, T. Satin Shoes, The.
Herrick. Gain and Gettings.
Sho[o]e Tying, The.
Upon Cob.
Upon Pimpe.
Upon Prigg.
Upon Rush.
Upon Smeaton.
Hughes, L. Barefoot Blues.
Komunyakaa. Butterfly-toed Shoes.
Levertov. Broken Sandal.
Merwin. Ascent.
Shoe Repairs.
Pagis. Real-Life Story.
Patchen. Daft Little Shoe Clerk Decided It Would Be Fun to Go Up and See What Things Are Like above the Sky, The.
Old Pair of Shoes, An.
Ritsos. Secret Pain of the Decor, The.
Sexton. Red Shoes, The.
Simic. My Shoes.
Thoreau. My Boots.
Warren, R. Little Boy and Lost Shoe.
Shoes In Rain Jungle.
Weiss, T. Pair of Shoes, A.
Whittier. Shoemakers, The.
Williams, C. K. Time: 1978.
Williams, W. Nightingales, The.
Thinker, The.

Shopping and Shops
Browning, R. Shop.
Bukowski. Lovely Couple, A.
Enzensberger, H. Ironmonger's Shop, The.
Gunn, T. Wind in the Street.
Hacker, M. Fourteen.
Hall, D. Green Shelf, The.
Han-shan. Whose wine shop is this aglow.
Kumin, M. Shopping in Ferney with Voltaire.
Larkin, P. Scratch on the Scratch Pad.
Laughlin, J. God Bless America!
MacNeice. Christmas Shopping.
McGrath, T. Trouble with the Times, The.

Nash, O. Friendly Touch, The.
I Remember Yule.
Just Wrap It Up, and I'll Throw It Away Later.
Nemerov. Night before Christmas, The.
Olson, C. In an Automotive Store.
Rumi. Tending Two Shops.
Simic. Grocery.

Shopping Malls
Ginsberg, A. Spring Fashions.

Shores
Amichai [*or* Amikhai]. At the Seashore.
North of San Francisco.
Poems to a Girl on the Seashore.
Ammons. Admission.
Bourn.
So I Said I Am Ezra.
Bishop, E. Little Exercise.
Browning, R. Meeting at Night.
Ciardi, J. On Looking East to the Sea with a Sunset behind Me.
Sea Marshes in Winter.
Sea Shines, The.
Shore Piece.
Clampitt. August Darks, The.
Tidewater Winter.
Coleridge, S. On Revisiting the Sea-Shore, after Long Absence.
Davie, D. Emigrant, to the Receding Shore.
On Sutton Strand.
Robinson Jeffers at Point Sur.
Emerson, R. Sea-Shore.
Enzensberger, H. Shore.
Frost, R. Once by the Pacific.
Hardy, T. On the Esplanade.
Heaney, S. Postscript.
Jacobsen, J. Noon.
Kinnell. Spindrift.
Kinsella, T. Navigators.
Song of the Night.
Larkin, P. To the Sea.
Levertov. Memories of John Keats.
Logan, J. Big Sur: Partington Cove.
Carmel: Point Lobos.
Shore Scene.
Lorde. Bridge Through My Window.
MacNeice. Littoral.
Lugubrious, Salubrious Seaside, The.
Meredith, G. Orchard and the Heath, The.
Merwin. Inscription Facing Western Sea.
Shore.
Millay, E. I shall go back.
Montale. House by the Sea.
Oppen. Edge of the ocean, The.
Patchen. Turner.
Pinkerton, H. Coast Hillside.
Rimbaud, A. Promontory.
Seascape.
Roethke. Young Girl, The.
Snyder, G. Wild Edge, The.
Swenson, M. November Night.
Running on the Shore.
Sleeping Overnight on the Shore.
Subject of the Waves, A.
Zero in the Cove.
Thomas, D. We Lying by Seasand.
Thoreau. Friend, The.
Tomlinson, C. Response to Hopkins.
Warren, R. Sea Hates the Land, The.
Weiss, T. Far Out, Far In.
Whitman, W. As I Ebb'd with the Ocean of Life.
From Montauk Point.
Patrolling Barnegat.
Paumanok.
Whittier. Burning Drift-Wood.
See also **Beaches**

Show Business
See **Acting and Actors; Movies; Theater and Theaters**

Shrews
Burns, R. Extempore Pinned to a Lady's Coach.
Kellyburnbraes.
Hardy, T. She Charged Me.
Nash, O. Introduction, The.

Shrines
Berry, W. Springs, The.
Clampitt. Dakota, The.
  Tempe in the Rain.
Komunyakaa. Shrines.
Laughlin, J. At Eleusis.
Logan, J. Revisit to the Room of a Saint.
Sandburg, C. Three Shrines.
Stock, R. At an Abandoned Shrine of Saint
  Mary Aegyptian.
See also **Mausoleums; Monuments**

Shropshire, England
Davie, D. Shropshire.
Housman. On Wenlock Edge.

Shrouds
Cavafy. La Jeunesse Blanche.
De la Mare. Snow.
Donne. Funeral[l], The.

Sibyl
Eberhart, R. Difficulty of Ideas, The.
Frost, R. Our Doom to Bloom.
Graves, R. Young Sibyl, The.
Hopkins, G. Spelt from Sibyl's Leaves.
Merwin. Sibyl.

Sicily
Eberhart, R. Mediterranean Song.
Lawrence, D. H. Almond Blossom.
  Bare Almond-Trees.
  Hibiscus and Salvia Flowers.
Sandburg, C. Suburban Sicilian Sketches.
Zagajewski. That's Sicily.

Sickness
Amichai [*or* Amikhai]. Dennis Was Very Sick.
  My Mother's Death and the Lost Battles for the
  Future of Her Children.
Ammons. Monday.
  Run-Through, The.
Codrescu. Ode to Laryngitis.
García Lorca. Little Stanton.
Ginsberg, A. Sickness Blues.
  What You Up To?
Hughes, L. Lover's Return.
  Sick Room.
Ignatow, D. Sunday at the State Hospital.
Jacobsen, J. Chosen, The.
McHugh, H. Literal.
Merwin. Cow, The.
  Sickness at the Equinox, A.
Montale. Frost on the windowpanes; the sick.
Petrarch. Soon as *madonna* comes into my
  heart.
Riley, J. Evagene Baker.
  Them Flowers.
Ritsos. Invalid's Day, An.
  Slight Ailment.
  Therapy.
  Unacceptable, The.
Stafford, W. 1932.
Very. Sick, The.
  Sickness.
See also **Illness**

Sideshows
Dugan, A. On a Professional Couple in a Side-
  Show.
Williams, M. Firebreathers at the Café Deux
  Magots, The.

Sidmouth, Henry Addington, Viscount
Shelley, P. Similes for Two Political Characters
  of 1819.

Sidney, Sir Philip
Bradstreet, A. Elegy Upon that Honorable and
  Reknowned Knight Sir Philip Sydney, An.
Campion, T. De obitu Phil. Sydnaei equitis
  aurati generosissimi.
Donne. Upon the Translation of the Psalms by
  Sir Philip Sidney, and the Countess of
  Pembroke His Sister.
Jonson, B. To Elizabeth, Countess of Rutland.
  To Mary, Lady Wroth ("How well, fair crown of
  your fair sex, might he").
  To Mrs Phillip Sidney.
  To Penshurst.
Ralegh, S. Epitaph on Sir Philip Sidney.

Siegfried
Dugan, A. On Shields. Against World War 3.

Siena, Italy
Montale. Near Siena.
  Palio.
Tomlinson, C. Siena in Sixty-Eight.

Sierra Nevada Mountains
Jeffers, R. Ascent to the Sierras.
Levine, P. Wednesday.
Rexroth, K. Blues.
  Strength through Joy.
  Toward an Organic Philosophy.
Whittier. Pass of the Sierra, The.

Siestas
Mistral, G. Mayten, The.

Sight
Auden. Heard and Seen.
Borges. Blind Man, A.
  History of the Night.
  In Praise of Darkness.
Cavalcanti. Sonnet: Of his Pain from a new
  Love.
Ciardi, J. Aquarium.
Crane, H. Visible the Untrue, The.
Creeley. For Allen.
  Ice Cream.
  Night Sky, A.
  Statue, The.
  Window, The.
De la Mare. Window, The.
Delany, P. To Thomas Sheridan.
Enzensberger, H. Appearances.
Frost, R. Wish to Comply, A.
Gallagher, T. Reading Aloud.
Graves, R. Gift of Sight.
Gurney, I. What Evil Coil.
Herrick. Upon His Eye-Sight Failing Him.
  Upon One-Ey'd Broomsted.
Hughes, L. Blind.
Koch, K. On Beauty.
Laughlin, J. Your Eyes.
Lowell, R. Eye and Tooth.
  Myopia: a Night.
McHugh, H. Untitled.
Michelangelo Buonarroti. My lady, these eyes
  see vividly—far, near.
Milosz, C. Esse.
  Honest Description of Myself with a Glass of
  Whiskey at an Airport, Let Us Say, in
  Minneapolis, An.
Montale. Near Finistère.
Olson, C. Well.
Pessoa. Analysis.
  If, after I die, they want to write my biography.
Petrarch. Orso, there never was a lake or river.
Ramanujan. Eyes, Ears, Noses, and a Thing
  about Touch.
  LOVE 6: Winter.
  Second Sight.
Ritsos. Maybe, Someday.
Rumi. I am so small I can barely be seen.
  Who sees inside from outside?
Sheridan, T. I Like Your Collyrium.
Stevens, W. Poem Written at Morning.
  Tattoo.
Stock, R. Anonymous Secrets.
Swift, J. To Thomas Sheridan.
Tomlinson, C. Sight and Flight.
Weiss, T. Before the Night.
Whalen, P. Look Look Look.
  Many Pages Must Be Thrown Away.
Williams, T. Eyes, The.
Williams, W. Eyeglasses, The.
Wilner, E. Freed from Another Context.
Zagajewski. Moses.
  To See.

Sign Language
Major, C. Sign Language.
Pinsky. If You Could Write One Great Poem,
  What Would You Want It to Be About?
Sze. Empty Words.

Silence
Amichai [*or* Amikhai]. In the Room.
Ammons. Rack.
  Unsaid.
Angelou. On Aging.
Auden. Homage to Clio.

Beckett, S. Bon bon il est un pays.
  Musique de l'indifférence.
  Silence tel que ce qui fut.
Berry, W. Elegy: "All day our eyes could find
  no resting place."
  Except.
  Silence, The.
  Sorrel Filly, The.
  To Gary Snyder.
  Where.
Bogan, L. Poem in Prose.
  Train Tune.
Brontë, E. How still, how happy! These [*or*
  Those] are words.
Broumas, O. Prayer with Martial Stance.
Browning, E. Hugh Stuart Boyd [Legacies].
  Substitution.
Byron, G. When We Two Parted.
Carruth, H. Line, The.
  Silence.
  To Artemis.
Cavafy. Word and Silence.
Chuang Tzu. Action and Non-Action.
Ciardi, J. Biography.
Clampitt. Silence, A.
Codrescu. Silence.
Coleridge, S. Eros aei lalethros hetairos.
  Silent City, A.
Creeley. After Mallarmé.
  Apple Uppfle.
  Eye, The.
  Going to Bed.
  Kitchen.
  Return.
  Song, A: "I had wanted a quiet testament."
  Sound.
  Waiting ("He pushes behind the words").
  Words.
Cummings, E. E. Because / an obstreperous
  grin minutely floats.
  Do you remember when the fluttering dusk.
  Enter no(silence is the blood whose flesh).
  Hush) / noones / are coming.
  Silence / .is / a / looking.
  Summer Silence.
  & sun & / sil / e / nce.
  These children singing in stone a.
Cunningham, J. Monday Morning.
Davie, D. Expecting Silence.
  Nashville Mornings.
  Reticence.
De la Mare. Autumn.
  Bells, The.
  Dark Château, The.
  Echo.
  Faint Music.
  Fear.
  Listeners, The.
  Market-Place, The.
  Myself.
  Quiet.
  Silence.
  Snowflake, The.
  Stranger, The.
  Swallows Flown.
  Taciturn, The.
  Time Passes.
  Where?
Dickinson, E. Cherishing that is speechless,
  The.
  Death's Waylaying not the sharpest.
  I fear a Man of frugal Speech.
  Night is my favorite Day.
  Silence is all we dread.
  Silence' oblation to the Ear.
  Still—Volcano—Life, A.
  There is no Silence in the Earth—so silent.
  To those who can estimate silence.
  Words the happy say, The.
Dugan, A. Northern Statement for St. Cecilia.
Dunbar, P. Silence.
Duncan, R. Sentinels, The.
Eberhart, R. Bower, The.
  Emblem.
  Grave Piece.
  Hatred of the Old River.

Parker River, The.
Snow Cascades.
Velvet Rocks.
Why.
Elyas Yusof Nezami [or Nisami] Ganjavi].
  While roses bloomed along the plain.
Emerson, R. As I walked in the woods.
Dangerous gift & grace is mine, A.
Future, The.
Merops.
Pedants all / They would be original.
Silence.
Enzensberger, H. Remote House.
Ferlinghetti, L. He with the Beating Wings.
García Lorca. Elegy: To Silence.
Interrupted Concert, The.
Pause of the Clock.
Ginsberg, A. Funny Death.
Glück, L. Exile.
Horse.
Graves, R. Black Goddess, The.
Nobody.
Touch My Shut Lips.
Yet Unsayable, The.
Gurney, I. Old Martinmas Eve.
Hacker, M. Against Silence.
Hall, D. Je Suis une Table.
Hamill, S. Gnostology.
Hardy, T. Duettist to her Pianoforte, A.
He Resolves to Say No More.
I Look in Her Face.
Silences.
Herrick. Silence.
Hughes, L. Silence.
Jacobsen, J. Language as an Escape from the
  Discrete.
Jeffers, R. Northern Heather.
Kinnell. That Silent Evening.
Kizer, C. Antique Father.
Silent Man, The.
Komunyakaa. In the Background of Silence.
Legacy.
Larkin, P. If Grief Could Burn Out.
Myxomatosis.
Talking In Bed.
Lawrence, D. H. Listening.
Poor Bit of a Wench!
Sickness.
Silence.
Winter-Lull.
Levertov. Living Alone (2).
Mountain's Daily Speech is Silence, The.
What Were They Like?
Levi, P. Voices.
Levine, P. Face, The.
Last Step, The.
Silent in America.
Winter Words.
Lorde. Suspension.
MacDiarmid, H. Glen of Silence, The.
MacLeish. Epitaph for John McCutcheon.
Lost Speakers, The.
Wood Dove at Sandy Spring, The.
Meredith, G. Meeting.
Nature and Life.
Night-Walk, The.
We stood in the garden alone.
Merton. In Silence.
Love Winter When the Plant Says Nothing.
O Sweet Irrational Worship.
Song: If You Seek.
St. Alberic.
Merwin. Horses.
Kin.
On Each Journey.
She Who Was Gone.
Silence before Harvest, The.
Millay, E. Ode to Silence.
Milosz, C. Thistle, the Nettle, The.
Zone of Silence.
Montale. I know the moment when a raw
  grimace.
Moore, M. Silence.
Nash, O. That Reminds Me.
Patchen. Limpidity of Silences.
Pessoa. No, don't say a word!

Sensationist Poem, A.
Snow threw a silent towel over everything, The.
Petrarch. Not seldom, when her semblance has
  been kind.
Piercy. At the Core.
Plath. Courage of Shutting-Up, The.
Munich Mannequins, The.
Poe. Sonnet—Silence.
Pope, A. On Silence.
Prunty. Tent, The.
Raine, K. Once I heard your voice.
Rexroth, K. Speak not, let no word break.
Rich, A. Cartographies of Silence.
Riley, J. As I Sit in the Silence.
Best of All.
Nothin' to Say.
Quiet Lodger, The.
Silence.
Rilke. Silent Whole, The.
Telling You All.
To Monique and Blaise Briod.
Ritsos. Departures 2.
Distant, The.
Hearing.
Memorial Service at Poros.
Places of Refuge.
Stripped Naked.
Suddenly.
Summer at Dhiminio.
They.
Unacceptable Man, The.
Unaccomplished.
Rossetti, C. Golden Silences.
I See That All Things Come to an End.
I seek among the living & I seek.
I sit among the green shady valleys oft.
Introspective.
Sonnet from the Psalms.
Then Shall Ye Shout.
Way of the World, The.
Rukeyser, M. Breathing Landscape.
Rumi. Enough Words?
Quietness.
There is a way between voice and presence.
Sandburg, C. Alone and Not Alone.
Answer, The.
Aprons of Silence.
At the Gates of Tombs.
First Sonata for Karlen Paula.
Gong of Time, The.
Gypsy.
Honey and Salt.
Is There Any Easy Road to Freedom?
Sandhill People.
Speech.
To Know Silence Perfectly.
Year, The.
Schuyler, J. "From the next."
Sometimes.
Sexton. Silence, The.
Shelley, P. Fragment: Apostrophe to Silence.
Summer Evening Churchyard, A.
Simic. Dismantling the Silence.
Smith, S. King Hamlet's Ghost.
Nor We of Her to Him.
Snyder, G. Without.
Stock, R. One of the Old Ones.
Translated from Silence.
Szymborska, W. Silence of Plants, The.
Thoreau. Cliffs.
Tomlinson, C. Awakening, The.
Hand at Callow Hill Farm, The.
Headland, The.
Very. Silent, The.
Walcott. Oddjob, a Bull Terrier.
Warren, R. No Bird Does Call.
On Into the Night.
Star-Fall.
Whitman, W. After the Dazzle of Day.
When I Heard the Learn'd Astronomer.
Wilbur, R. Games Two.
Wilde, O. Silentium Amoris.
Williams, C. K. One of the Muses.
Patience Is When You Stop Waiting.
Williams, W. Silence.
Stillness.

Wordsworth, W. Address to Silence.
Wright, C. George Trakl Journal.
Night Journal II.
Silent Journal.
Wright, J. Arriving in the Country Again.
Baptism in the Lead Avenue Ditch.
Echo for the Promise of Georg Trakl's Life.
In the Face of Hatred.
Snowstorms in the Midwest.
Sparrows in a Hillside Drift.
Yeats. After Long Silence.
Long-Legged Fly.
Maid Quiet.
Zagajewski. It Comes to a Standstill.
Zaturenska. Interpreter of Silence, The.
Zukofsky, L. Or a Valentine.

Silk
Herrick. Upon Franck.
Upon Julia's Clothes.
Lux. Say Yes.
Pound, E. Garden, The.
Schuyler, J. Steaming Ties.

Silkworms
Bourne, V. Silk Worm, The.
Very. Worm, The.

Silver
Dunbar, P. Real Question, The.
Emerson, R. At Plymouth in the friendly crowd.
Swift, J. Simile, A.

Simeon (Bible)
Brodsky, J. Nunc Dimittis.

Similes
Sheridan, T. New Simile for the Ladies, A.
Szymborska, W. Note, A.
See also **Metaphor**

Simon of Cyrene
Cullen, C. Simon the Cyrenian Speaks.

Simplicity
Amichai [or Amikhai]. My Mother Comes
  From the Days.
Berry, W. Throwing away the Mail.
Borges. Simplicity.
Broumas, O. Buenos Días.
Browning, E. Mountaineer and Poet.
Burns, R. Song: "Adown winding Nith I did
  wander."
Campion, T. Jack and Joan.
Carver, R. Simple.
Chuang Tzu. Five Enemies, The.
Importance of Being Toothless, The.
Turtle, The.
When the Shoe Fits.
Cowper, W. Retirement.
Creeley. "Bolinas and Me."
Pryaer, A.
Song: "How simply / for another."
Wall, A.
Cunningham, J. Predestined Space, The.
Davie, D. Love-Poems: for Mairi MacInnes.
Dickinson, E. My life has been too simple and
  stern.
Du Bellay. Happy the Man.
Emerson, R. For what need I of book or priest.
I live among ideal men.
Gunn, T. Corridor, The.
Hall, D. Clown, The.
Herbert, G. Wreath, A.
Herrick. Covetous Still Captives, The.
Expenses Exhaust.
No Want Where There's Little.
Hopkins, G. Shepherd's Brow, The.
Isidorus. On a Fowler.
Jeffers, R. Wind-Struck Music, The.
Kinsella, T. I have known the hissing
  assemblies.
Larkin, P. Modesties.
Laughlin, J. Some People Think.
Lux. Amiel's Leg.
MacDiarmid, H. Covenanters, The.
Mahon. Mayo Tao, The.
McHugh, H. Preferences.
Merwin. To Where We Are.
Vocations.
Michelangelo Buonarroti. New and more
  commendable delight, A.

Mistral, G.   In Praise of Small Towns.
Nash, O.   I Will Arise and Go Now.
  "My Child Is Phlegmatic..."—Anxious Parent.
  Reflection on Ingenuity.
Olson, C.   It's Got to This.
Pessoa.   And there are poets who are artists.
  At night I suddenly waken.
  Cat, you tumble down the street.
  Four songs that follow now, The.
  From the highest window of my house.
  I go indoors, and shut the window.
  I never kept sheep.
  I'd give anything if only my life were an oxcart.
  If at times I say that flowers smile.
  If I could take a bite of the whole earth.
  If they want me to be a mystic, fine. I'm a
    mystic.
  I'm a keeper of sheep.
  Liberty.
  Moonlight behind the tall branches, The.
  My glance is clear like a sunflower.
  On a terribly clear day.
  Once at mid-day in late spring.
  One way or another.
  Only Nature is divine, and she's not divine.
  Rather the flight of the bird passing and leaving
    no trace.
  Rhymes mean nothing to me. Only rarely.
  Startling reality of things, The.
  To think of God is to disobey God.
  Today I read nearly two pages.
Ransom, J.   Captain Carpenter.
Riley, J.   Somep'n Common-like.
Rilke.   From Father to Son.
Ritsos.   Meaning of Simplicity, The.
Rossetti, C.   Milking-Maid, The.
Sandburg, C.   Fellow Citizens.
  Oomba.
Simic.   Evening.
Stafford, W.   Thinking about Being Called
  Simple by a Critic.
Thoreau.   Conscience is instinct bred in the
  house.
Whittier.   To James T. Fields.
Wilbur, R.   Baroque Wall-Fountain in the Villa
  Sciarra, A.
Wordsworth, W.   Farmer of Tilsbury Vale, The.
Zukofsky, L.   You three:—my wife.

Simpson, O. J. (Orenthal James Simpson)
Ai.   Rapture.

Sin
Ai.   Priest's Confession, The.
Archpoet.   Confession of Bishop Golias, The.
Baudelaire.   Out of the Blue.
Beckett, S.   Dortmunder.
Berry, W.   Purification, A.
Berryman.   Curse, The.
  Gislebertus' Eve.
Blake, W.   Washer Womans Song, The.
Blok.   Shamelessly, Endlessly Sinning.
Borges.   Luke 23.
  Remorse.
Bradstreet, A.   Flesh and the Spirit, The.
Brontë, E.   Sleep Not, Dream Not.
  There let thy bleeding branch atone.
Browning, E.   Lay of the Brown Rosary, The.
  Weeping Saviour, The.
Browning, R.   Adam, Lilith, and Eve.
Burns, R.   Song: "I'll tell you a tale of a Wife."
Byron, G.   Prayer of Nature, The.
Campion, T.   View Mee, Lord.
Cavalcanti.   Gianni, Guido greets.
Codrescu.   Sin of Wanting a New Refrigerator,
  The.
Cowper, W.   Epistle to a Protestant Lady in
  France, An.
Crane, H.   This Way Where November..
Crane, S.   Black riders came from the sea.
  There was One I met upon the road.
Crashaw.   But Men loved Darkness[e] Rather
  Than [or Then] Light.
  On Saint Peter Cutting of Malchus His Eare.
Creeley.   Kind of Act Of, The.
Cullen, C.   For Daughters of Magdalen.
Cummings, E. E.   Now dis "daughter" uv
  eve(who aint precisely slim)sim.

Cunningham, J.   To My Daimon.
"Dario."   Charterhouse, The.
Davie, D.   Dancing Measures.
  Levity.
  Morning.
  Witness.
Donne.   Flea, The.
  Licentious Person, A.
Dugan, A.   Elegy for a Puritan Conscience.
Dunbar, P.   Distinction.
  How Lucy Backslid.
Eberhart, R.   Adam Cast Forth.
Emerson, R.   Puff of air or dry or damp, A.
  Sun athwart the cloud thought it no sin, The.
Glück, L.   Murderess, The.
Guyon.   Testimony of Divine Adoption, The.
Hall, D.   Conduct and Work.
HaNagid.   In Fact I Love That Fawn.
  Why Repeat the Sins.
  Your Loved Ones Depress You.
Herbert, G.   Agony [or Agonie], The.
  Church-Lock and Key.
  Confession.
  Foil, The.
  Good Friday.
  Judgement.
  Love (3).
  Sin (1).
  Sin (2): "O that I could a sin once see!"
  Sinner, The.
  Sin's Round.
  Storm, The.
Herrick.   Another.
  Bad May Be Better.
  Baptisme.
  Bell-Man, The.
  Christs Incarnation.
  Cock-Crow.
  Eucharist, The.
  Evill.
  Eye, The.
  God Has a Twofold Part.
  Gods Pardon.
  Good, and Bad.
  Loading and Unloading.
  Long Life.
  Mirth.
  More Potent, Lesse Peccant.
  None Free from Fault.
  Our Owne Sinnes Unseen.
  Pain[e] Ends in Pleasure.
  Pardon.
  Penitencie.
  Position in the Hebrew Divinity, A.
  Prescience.
  Sin.
  Sin and Strife.
  Sin Seen.
  Sin Severely Punisht.
  Sins Loathed, and Yet Loved.
  Soule, The.
  Three Fatal[l] Sisters.
  To God: an Anthem, Sung in the Chapel at
    White-Hall, Before the King.
  To His Conscience.
  Upon Groynes.
  Will To Be Working, A.
Hopkins, G.   Glimmer'd along the square-cut
  steep.
  Myself unholy, from myself unholy.
Housman.   Epitaph, An: "Stay, if you list, O
  passer by the way."
  Stars, I have seen them fall.
Hughes, L.   Ballad of the Sinner.
  Fire.
  It Gives Me Pause.
  Madam and the Minister.
  Sinner.
Jacobsen, J.   Reading Aloud at Dusk.
Jeffers, R.   Give Your Heart to the Hawks.
  Original Sin.
Jonson, B.   Epode: "Not to know vice at all, and
  keep[e] true state."
  Hymn[e] to God the Father, A.
  Of Life and Death.
  Sinner's Sacrifice, The.

Larkin, P.   High Windows.
Laughlin, J.   Voices, The.
Lawrence, D. H.   Demon Justice.
  En Masse.
  Eve.
  God and the Holy Ghost.
  Humility.
  In a Spanish Tram-Car.
  Irreverent Thoughts.
  Latter-Day Sinners.
  Little Wowser, The.
  Sex Isn't Sin.
  Sinners.
  Spanish Privilege.
Lindsay, N.   Unpardonable Sin, The.
Lowell, R.   Worst Sinner, Jonathan Edwards'
  God, The.
Lux.   Sex in History.
MacNeice.   Blasphemies, The.
Marvell.   Coronet, The.
  Mower Against Gardens, The.
Merton.   Biography, The.
  On the Anniversary of My Baptism.
  Sponge Full of Vinegar, The.
Michelangelo Buonarroti.   I live for sinning, for
  the self that dies.
  Maybe, so I'd look kindly on souls in need.
  Rid of a vexing and a heavy load.
Mistral, G.   Confession.
Moore, M.   To a Giraffe.
Nash, O.   Ha! Original Sin!
  Inter-Office Memorandum.
  Nevertheless.
  Portrait of the Artist as a Prematurely Old Man.
Nemerov.   Poem of Margery Kempe, A.
Olson, C.   Sin is inferiority. The mother's
  cooperation in the birth of her daughter.
Orlandi, G.   If, my friend, you would have said
  of Mary so.
Patchen.   Wide, wide in the rose's side.
Petrarch.   Love, I have sinned, and recognise my
  sin.
Pinkerton, H.   Error Pursued.
  Original Sin.
Raine, K.   It is in us they burn.
Ralegh, S.   Diseases, famine, enemies, in us no
  change have wrought.
Rimbaud, A.   Once, if I remember well, my life
  was a banquet where all hearts opened.
  Remembrances of Senility.
  Tartufe's Punishment.
Robinson, E.   Tavern, The.
Rossetti, C.   Afterward He Repented, and Went.
  Amor Mundi.
  Ash Wednesday.
  Behold, I stand at the door and knock.
  Cannot Sweeten.
  For Thine Own Sake, O My God.
  He Shall Go No More Out.
  If thou be dead, forgive and thou shalt live.
  Lord, what have I to offer? sickening fear.
  O Christ my God Who seest the unseen.
  O Lord, when Thou didst call me, didst Thou
    know.
  Sinner's own fault? So it was, The.
  Standing Afar Off for the Fear of Her Torment.
  Surely there is an aching void within.
  Weigh all my faults and follies righteously.
  Who shall my wandering thoughts steady & fix.
  World, The.
Rukeyser, M.   Sun on the faces. On the knotted
  rocks.
Sandburg, C.   Quotations.
  Washerwoman.
Scott, S.   Gray Brother, The.
Seifert.   Sinful City.
Smith, S.   Man I Am, A.
  Oh What Is the Thing He Done?
  Recognition Not Enough.
Stock, R.   Miracle of the Roses, The.
Swinburne.   Phaedra.
Tennyson, A.   St. Simeon Stylites.
  Vision of Sin, The.
Thomas, D.   Incarnate Devil.
  It Is the Sinner's Dust-Tongued Bell.
Very.   Flood, The.

Forgive Me My Trespasses.
Serpent, The.
Walcott. Crusoe's Island.
Walker, A. Compulsory Chapel.
  Mississippi Winter II.
Warren, R. Original Sin[: A Short Story].
Whittier. Two Rabbins, The.
Wilbur, R. Pelican, The.
Wilde, O. E Tenebris.
  Tædium Vitæ.
Williams, M. Original Sin.
Williams, W. From "The Birth of Venus," Song.
Wright, C. Peccatology.

See also **Original Sin; Seven Deadly Sins**

Singing and Singers
Angelou. Shaker, Why Don't You Sing?
  Singer Will Not Sing, The.
Auden. As I Walked Out One Evening.
Berry, W. Architecture, An.
  Law That Marries All Things, The.
  Man Walking and Singing, A.
  Song Sparrow Singing in the Fall, A.
  To Go By Singing.
Blok. Girl Was Singing, A.
Blue Cloud. Little Fawn.
Bogan, L. M., Singing.
Browning, E. King's Gift, The.
  Seraph and Poet, The.
Browning, R. On Singers.
Burns, R. Of A' the Airts [the Wind Can Blow].
Campion, T. When to Her Lute.
Carew, T. Celia Singig.
  Celia Singing.
Carver, R. Songs in the Distance.
Cavafy. Singer.
Chesterton. Christmas Carol, A: "God rest you
  merry gentlemen."
Ciardi, J. No White Birds Sings.
Clampitt. Subway Singer, The.
Coleridge, S. On a Volunteer Singer.
Collins, B. Sunday Morning with the
  Sensational Nightingales.
Cowper, W. Catharina.
Crane, S. There was a man with tongue of
  wood.
Creeley. Air: "The Love of a Woman."
  Poem for Bob Leed.
  Xmas.
Cullen, C. Colored Blues Singer.
Cummings, E. E. All which isn't singing is
  mere talking.
  Now(more near ourselves than we).
  These children singing in stone a.
  Until and i heard.
  Voices to voices, lip to lip.
  You shall sing my songs, O earth.
"Dario." Singer goes all over the world, The.
De la Mare. In Vain.
  Rachel.
Dickey, J. Buckdancer's Choice.
  Folk Singer of the Thirties, A.
Dickinson, E. "Hope" is the thing with feathers.
  I shall keep singing!
  To Hear an Oriole Sing.
Dubie. Audabe of the Singer and Saboteur,
  Marie Triste.
Dugan, A. Life and Death of the Cantata
  System, The.
Dunbar, P. Banjo Song, A.
  Deacon Jones' Grievance.
  Lesson, The.
  Question, A.
  Sympathy.
  When Malindy Sings.
  When Sam'l Sings.
  With the Lark.
Emerson, R. Saadi.
Faiz. If I Were Certain.
Ferlinghetti, L. Carrara, Looking Seaward.
Frost, R. Aim Was Song, The.
  Hill Wife, The.
  Our Singing Strength.
  Oven Bird, The.
  Valley's Singing Day, The.
García Lorca. Flamenco Vignettes.
Graves, R. Bards, The.

Love Without Hope.
Gurney, I. Songs I Had, The.
Hacker, M. Elegy: "Crying from exile, I."
Hall, D. Blue Wing, The.
Han-shan. Oriole on a flowering branch, An.
  This maid is from Hantan.
  Where white clouds form high rugged crags.
Hardy, T. He Inadvertently Cures His Love-
  Pains.
  To a Lady Playing and Singing in the Morning.
Heaney, S. At the Wellhead.
  Serenades.
  Singer's House, The.
Herrick. Againe.
  Another.
  His Lachrimae or Mirth, Turn'd to Mourning.
  Poet Hath Lost His Pipe, The.
  Upon a Gentlewoman with a Sweet Voice.
  Upon a Hoarse Singer.
  Upon Comely a Good Speaker but an Ill Singer.
  Upon Her Voice.
  Upon Julia's Voice.
  Upon Linnit.
  Upon Sapho, Sweetly Playing, and Sweetly
    Singing.
  Voice and Violl, The.
Hughes, L. Oppression.
  Song for Billie Holiday.
  Songs.
  Spirituals.
  To Dorothy Maynor.
  To Midnight Nan at Leroy's.
  Weary Blues, The.
  Young Singer.
Hughes, T. Owl's Song.
Ignatow, D. Folk Singer, The.
  His Name.
Jonson, B. And must I sing? What subject shall
  I choose?
  Musical Strife, The; in a Pastoral Dialogue.
Keats. Ode to a Nightingale.
Kipling, R. Army Headquarters.
  In the Neolithic Age.
  Last Rhyme of True Thomas, The.
  Recantation, A.
Komunyakaa. Chair Gallows.
  Nightbird.
Laughlin, J. Dropkick Me Jesus.
  Large Opera Singer, The.
  Saeta.
  Songbird, The.
  You Invited Me.
Lawrence, D. H. Piano.
Levertov. Nightingale Road.
Levi, P. Singing.
Lindsay, N. How a Little Girl Sang.
Logan, J. Concert Scene.
Lorde. Day They Eulogized Mahalia, The.
  For My Singing Sister.
Lux. Criss Cross Apple Sauce.
MacDiarmid, H. Empty Vessel.
MacNeice. Death of an Actress.
Mahon. Aran.
Marvell. Fair Singer, The.
McHugh, H. Act, The.
Melville, H. Jack Roy.
Meredith, W. Here and There.
Merwin. Singer, The.
Milosz, C. Lastingness.
Milton. To Leonora Singing in Rome.
  To the Same ["Another Leonora captured the
    poet Torquato"].
  To the Same ["Why, credulous Naples, do you
    vaunt your clear-voiced Siren"].
Nash, O. It's Snug to Be Smug.
  Screen with the Face with the Voice, The.
  Strange Case of the Renegade Lyric Writer, The.
Niedecker. Not all that's heard is music. We
  leave.
O'Hara, F. Day Lady Died, The.
Olson, C. Green Man, The.
Orr, G. Ghosts Listen to Orpheus Sing, The.
Patchen. Irate Songster, The.
Pinkerton, H. On an Attic Red-Figured
  Amphora (490 B.C.) by the "Berlin Painter" in
  the Metropolitan Museum.

Pinsky. At Pleasure Bay.
  Uncreation, The.
Pope, A. Pastorals.
Rexroth, K. Rose Colored Glasses.
  Singing Voice, A.
Riley, J. Boys of the Old Glee Club, The.
  Humble Singer, A.
  One with a Song.
  Silent Singer, The.
  Singer, The.
  Song of Singing, A.
  Songs of a Life-Time.
  Southern Singer, A.
  Summer-Time, The.
  To Benj. S. Parker.
  To Hear Her Sing.
Rilke. Fugitives, The.
  Prisoners.
Ritsos. Hour of Song.
Rossetti, C. All Saints.
  Before the Throne, and Before the Lamb.
  Birthday, A.
  Easter Day.
  Eleanor.
  Joy of Saints, like incense turned to fire, The.
  Lullaby: "Love me,—I love you / Love me, my
    baby."
  Sing me a song— / What shall I sing?
  Songs in a Cornfield.
  Then Shall Ye Shout.
Rukeyser, M. Seventh Elegy. Dream-Singing
  Elegy.
Rumi. Let your throat-song.
Sandburg, C. I Sang.
  Splinter.
Schuyler, J. Beautiful Funerals.
  Janis Joplin's Dead: Long Live Pearl.
  Let's All Hear It for Mildred Bailey!
Seifert. If you call poetry a song.
Shelley, P. Fragment: To One Singing.
  To Jane: The keen stars were twinkling.
Smith, S. Singing Cat, The.
  Songster, The.
Stevens, W. Country Words.
  Idea of Order at Key West, The.
Stock, R. Patio.
  Singing, The.
Stockton, A. To Amanda—Who Was Obliging
  Enough to Delight Her Friend with Singing.
Thomas, D. In My Craft or Sullen Art.
Tomlinson, C. At Wells: Polyphony.
Unknown. Ballata: Of True and False Singing.
Very. Congregational Singing.
  Evening Choir, The.
  Song, The.
Whitman, W. Chanting the Square Deific.
  Dead Tenor, The.
  I Hear America Singing.
  Singer in the Prison, The.
  To a Certain Cantatrice.
Whittier. Singer, The.
Williams, C. K. Mornings: Catherine.
Williams, W. Late Singer, The.
Wordsworth, W. Solitary Reaper, The.
Wright, J. Homecoming Singer, The.
Wyatt, S. Marvel No More.
  My Lute, Awake!
Zagajewski. In May.
  Where the Breath Is.
Zaturenska. Young Girl Singing, A.

See also **Tenors**

Sioux, The
Dubie. Elegy to the Sioux.
Oliver, M. Ghosts.
Stafford, W. Before It Burned over: A Sioux
  Grass Chant.
Wright, J. Centenary Note: Inscribed to Little
  Crow, Leader of the Sioux Rebellion in
  Minnesota, 1862, A.

Sirens (mythology)
De la Mare. Alexander.
  Not that way.
Mallarmé. Salutation.
Milton. At a Solemn Music[k].
  To the Same ["Why, credulous Naples, do you
    vaunt your clear-voiced Siren"].

Rossetti, D.   Sea-Spell, A.
Wilbur, R.   Merlin Enthralled.
Sirens, The.
Zaturenska.   Silence and the Wayfarer.
Siren Music.

Sirens (warning devices)
Wilbur, R.   Fire-Truck, A.

Siskind, Aaron
Logan, J.   On a Photograph by Aaron Siskind.
Suite of Six Pieces for Siskind, A.
Three Poems on Aaron Siskind's Photographs.

Sisters
Bogan, L.   Sleeping Fury, The.
Broumas, O.   No Harm Shall Come.
Browning, E.   Bertha in the Lane.
Byron, G.   Epistle to Augusta.
Campion, T.   To the Most Princely and Vertuous the Lady Elizabeth.
Clifton, L.   Amazons.
Coleridge, S.   On Receiving an Account That His Only Sister's Death Was Inevitable.
On Seeing a Youth Affectionately Welcomed by a Sister.
To Two Sisters.
De la Mare.   Brother and Sister.
Reflections.
Rose.
Dickey, J.   Veer-Voices: Two Sisters under Crows.
Dickinson, E.   One Sister have I in our house.
Emerson, R.   Elizabeth Hoar.
Hearst thou, sweet spirit, thou hast heard before.
Kind & holy were the words.
Enzensberger, H.   Ironmonger's Shop, The.
Gallagher, T.   Still Moment at Dun Laoghaire.
Gjuzel.   My Sister's Letter.
Glück, L.   Descending Figure.
Silverpoint.
Tango.
Gunn, T.   Girls Next Door, The.
Hardy, T.   Logs on the Hearth.
Herrick.   To My Dearest Sister M. Mercie Herrick.
Jacobsen, J.   Sisters, The.
Keats.   Acrostic.
Kinnell.   Neverland.
Kumin, M.   In Memoriam P. W. Jr. 1921–1980.
Kunitz, S.   My Sisters.
Levertov.   Her Sister.
Lorde.   Family Resemblance, A.
Lux.   Oxymoron Sisters, The.
Merwin.   Voice.
Millay, E.   Night is my sister, and how deep in love.
Mistral, G.   Request for Blanca, A.
Oppen.   Niece.
Plath.   Babysitters, The.
Prunty.   Sisters.
Ramanujan.   Leaky Tap after a Sister's Wedding, A.
Rich, A.   Sisters.
Transit.
Women.
Riley, J.   Prior to Miss Belle's Appearance.
Roethke.   To My Sister.
Rossetti, C.   Lowest Room, The.
Maiden-Song.
Noble Sisters.
Our Mothers, lovely women pitiful; / Our sisters, gracious in their life and death.
Sister Maude.
Summer Is Ended, The.
Rukeyser, M.   Two Years.
Sexton.   One-Eye, Two-Eyes, Three-Eyes.
Smith, S.   Barlow.
Stockton, A.   Lines on the Death of Mrs Hill Suppos'd to Be Spoken by Her Sister Mrs Clymer.
Suckling, S.   Upon Two Sisters.
Szymborska, W.   In Praise of My Sister.
Tate, J.   Five Years Old.
Walker, A.   For My Sister Molly Who in the Fifties.
Telling.
Whittier.   Singer, The.
Sisters, The.

To My Friend on the Death of His Sister.
To My Sister.
Williams, C. K.   Kin.
Wilner, E.   Admonition.
Epitaph: "Young then, / we were bored already."
Wordsworth, W.   Forth from a Jutting Ridge, Around Whose Base.
Fragment: "Witness thou / The dear companion of my lonely walk."
Seven Sisters; or, the Solitude of Binnorie, The.
Wright, J.   Death of an Unfamiliar Sister, The.
Family Reunion.
Zagajewski.   Twenty-Five Years.

Sistine Chapel
Rimbaud, A.   Sealed Lips. Seen in Rome.

Sisyphus
Glück, L.   Mountain, The.
Kumin, M.   Sisyphus.
Stock, R.   Prose Parables.
Williams, M.   Rock.

Size
Ciardi, J.   Small.
Collins, B.   Bonsai.
Jackson, L.   Life-Size Is Too Large.
McHugh, H.   Big Ideas among Earthlings.
Riley, J.   Very Tall Boy, A.

Skateboarding and Skateboarders
Gunn, T.   Skateboard.
See also **Roller Skating and Roller Skaters**

Skating and Skaters
Atwood.   Woman Skating.
Bukowski.   Skaters, The.
Cummings, E. E.   Skating.
Johnson, S.   Translations of Roy's Verses on Skaters.
Riley, J.   Hoodoo, The.
Rukeyser, M.   Boys of These Men Full Speed.
See also **Roller Skating and Roller Skaters; Skateboarding and Skateboarders**

Skeletons
Dubie.   Skeleton for Mr. Paul in Paradise, A.
Jacobsen, J.   Pitch Lake.
Longfellow, H.   Skeleton in Armor [*or* Armour], The.
Stevens, W.   As You Leave the Room.
Wilbur, R.   To His Skeleton.
Wright, J.   On the Skeleton of a Hound.
See also **Bones**

Skepticism
Very.   Scepticism with Regard to the Gospels.
See also **Doubt**

Skiing and Skiers
Cummings, E. E.   Skies may be blue;yes.
Eberhart, R.   Skier and the Mountain, The.
Jarrell, R.   January 1938.
Laughlin, J.   Ein Kitzbuehler Tag (1947).
Skiing without Skis.
Logan, J.   White Pass Ski Patrol.
Merrill, J.   Up and Down.
Rexroth, K.   Night below Zero.
Rich, A.   Transit.
Updike.   Tsokadze O Altitudo.

Skin
Angelou.   Passing Time.
Creeley.   Skeleton, The.
Dugan, A.   Prison Song.
Herrick.   Lawne, The.
To Electra.
Upon Blinks.
Larkin, P.   Skin.
Olson, C.   Her skin / covered me, illuminated.
Pagis.   Exposure.
Ritsos.   Therapy.
Williams, C. K.   Scar.
Williams, M.   Book, The.

Skulls
Beckett, S.   Hors crâne seul dedans.
Eberhart, R.   Meditation, A.
Keats.   Stanzas on Some Skulls in Beauly Abbey, Near Inverness.
MacDiarmid, H.   Perfect.
Milosz, C.   Skull, A.
Nemerov.   Decorated Skull in a University Museum.

Pagis.   Caveman Is Not about to Talk, The.
Riley, J.   To a Skull.
Ritsos.   Tricks.
Rumi.   I circle your nest tonight.
Tomlinson, C.   Skullshapes.
Tiger Skull.

Skunks
Dugan, A.   On a Skunked Fox.
Eberhart, R.   Dead Skunk.
Heaney, S.   Skunk, The.
Jeffers, R.   Skunks.
Kumin, M.   Hermit Meets the Skunk, The.
Lowell, R.   Skunk Hour.
Oliver, M.   Certain Sharpness in the Morning Air, A.

Sky
Ammons.   This Bright Day.
Ashbery, J.   Variant.
Auden.   Summer Night, A.
Baudelaire.   Uncertain Skies.
Byron, G.   She Walks In Beauty.
Carruth, H.   I Know, I Remember, But How Can I Help You.
Coleridge, S.   Indifference of the Heavens, The.
Crane, H.   To the Cloud Juggler.
Creeley.   From Pico & the Women: A Life.
Traveller, The.
Water.
Cummings, E. E.   If up's the wordd a world grows greener.
Like a little bear twilight.
Luminous tendril of celestial wish.
The / sky / was / can dy lu.
These(whom'etends / blue nothing).
They have hung the sky with arrows.
Vision.
Davie, D.   If I Take the Wings of the Morning.
On Sutton Strand.
De la Mare.   Bright Life.
Mermaids, The.
Dickinson, E.   Aurora.
Brain—is wider than the Sky, The.
Competitions of the sky, The.
It troubled me as once I was.
Lightly stepped a yellow star.
Not what the stars have done.
Of Yellow was the outer Sky.
Slash of Blue, A.
Sun retired to a cloud, The.
Wild Blue sky abreast of Winds, A.
Dove, R.   Teach Us to Number Our Days.
Dubie.   After Sky X.
Eberhart, R.   Child, The.
Light From Above.
Looking At The Stars.
Looking at the Stars.
Standards, The.
Emerson, R.   But O to see his solar eyes.
Low December vault in June be up-lifted high.
Sea reflects the rosy sky, The.
That wandering fire to me appears.
Ferlinghetti, L.   Poet as Fisherman.
Figueredo.   Naked.
Frost, R.   A-Wishing Well.
Astrometaphysical.
Han-shan.   Multitude of stars is the late night's light, The.
Ignatow, D.   Blue.
I Dream.
Jacobsen, J.   Landscape Finally with Human Figure.
Jeffers, R.   Their Beauty Has More Meaning.
Kinnell.   Daybreak.
Kinsella, T.   Ancient Ballet, An.
Kizer, C.   On a Line from Valéry.
Levertov.   Clouds.
Mallarmé.   Azure, The.
Meredith, G.   Blue Is the Sky.
South-Wester, The.
Winter Heavens.
Merwin.   School on the Roof, The.
Nemerov.   Above.
Olson, C.   Rosy, It Was.
Signs.
Thoughts of the Time.
Palmer, M.   Dear M ("Sky today yes and no,

The. I am writing a play about a man with a pebble").
Pessoa. Poem: "Sky, the blueness of quiet light."
Raine, K. Night Sky.
Today as I / Looked up at the sky's great face.
Rexroth, K. Untitled, 6 September 1969.
Ritsos. Month of Cleansing.
Rossetti, C. Fluttered Wings.
Mirrors of Life and Death.
Rukeyser, M. Haying Before Storm.
Preamble.
Sandburg, C. Be Ready.
Broken Sky.
Love in Labrador.
Schuyler, J. Blue.
Smith, S. Coeur Simple.
Snyder, G. Blue Sky, The.
Stafford, W. Sky.
Swenson, M. Cloud-Mobile, The.
Cumuli.
Szymborska, W. Sky.
Tomlinson, C. Images of Perfection.
Sky Writing.
Vallejo. Divine Falling of Leaves, A.
Warren, R. Another Dimension.
Nature of a Mirror, The.
Sky.
Timeless, Twinned.
Whitman, W. After an Interval.
On the Beach at Night.
On the Beach at Night Alone.
Year of Meteors (1859–60).
Williams, W. At Night.
Conquest.
Desolate Field, The.
Peace on Earth.
Tree and Sky.
Wordsworth, W. Volant Tribe of Bards on Earth Are Found, A.
See also **Constellations; Stars**

Sky Diving and Sky Divers
Meredith, W. Hazard's Optimism.
See also **Parachuting and Parachutists**

Skye, Isle of, Scotland
Johnson, S. Ode, De Skia Insula.
Skia, An Ode on the Isle of Skye.

Skylarks
Hughes, T. Skylarks.
See also **Larks**

Skyscrapers
Creeley. Buildings.
Park ("Like in the Brownie Books").
Laughlin, J. Above the City.
Oppen. Building of the Skyscraper, The.
Piercy. Gasman Invites the Skyscrapers to Dance.
Skyscrapers of the Financial District Dance with Gasman, The.
Sandburg, C. Good Morning, America.
Prayers of Steel.
Skyscraper.
Skyscraper Loves Night, The.
Skyscrapers Stand Proud.
Tomlinson, C. All Afternoon.

Slander
Byron, G. Epitaph for Joseph Blacket.
Clare, J. Scandal.
Coleridge, S. Lines on a Friend.
Cowper, W. To Warren Hastings.
Trail of Admiral Keppel, The.
Herrick. Accusation.
No Despight to the Dead.
MacLeish. Black Day, The.
Pope, A. To the Earl of Burlington Asking Who Writ the Libels against Him.
Yeats. Against Unworthy Praise.
He Thinks of Those Who Have Spoken Evil of His Beloved.

Slaughter of the Innocents
See **Massacre of the Innocents**

Slaughterhouses
Dugan, A. On a Hymn, Misprinted.
Kumin, M. Vealers, The.
Nash, O. Calf, The.

Oliver, M. Farm Country.
Orr, G. Friday Lunchbreak.
Rumi. In the slaughterhouse of love, they kill.

Slavery and Slaves
Angelou. My Guilt.
One More Round.
Slave Coffle.
Song for the Old Ones.
Southeast Arkansia.
Berry, W. My Great-Grandfather's Slaves.
Bierce. False Prophecy, A.
Hesitating Veteran, The.
Browning, E. Hiram Powers' "Greek Slave."
Runaway Slave at Pilgrim's Point, The.
Burns, R. Slave's Lament, The.
Clifton, L. Libation.
Slaveship[s].
Cowper, W. Charity.
Epigram: "To purify their wine some people bleed."
Morning Dream, The.
Negro's Complaint, The.
Pity for Poor Africans.
Sweet Meat Has Sour Sauce.
To William Wilberforce, Esq.
Cullen, C. Negro Mother's Lullaby, A.
De la Mare. Gloria Mundi.
Dickey, J. Slave Quarters.
Dove, R. Abduction, The.
Adolescence—I.
Belinda's Petition.
House Slave, The.
Kentucky, 1833.
Pamela.
Slave's Critique of Practical Reason, The.
Transport or Slaves From Maryland to Mississippi, The.
Dubie. Her Monologue of Dark Crepe with Edges of Light.
Dunbar, P. Ante-Bellum Sermon, An.
Corn-Song, A.
Deserted Plantation, The.
News, The.
Old Cabin, The.
Parted.
Sympathy.
To the South.
Emerson, R. Boston Hymn.
God The Lord save Massachusetts.
I am not black in my mind.
Pilgrims, The.
Glück, L. Slave Ship, The.
Hacker, M. Inheritances.
Part of a True Story.
Sword.
Hayden, R. Ballad of Nat Turner, The.
Frederick Douglass.
Middle Passage.
Runagate Runagate.
Hughes, L. American Heartbreak.
Aunt Sue's Stories.
Ballad of the Seven Songs.
Drums.
Ghosts of 1619.
"Jesus, The."
Slave.
Slave Song.
Uncle Tom ("Uncle Tom is a legend and a dream").
Jacobsen, J. Absence of Slaves, An.
Kipling, R. Galley-Slave, The.
Song of the Galley-Slaves.
Komunyakaa. Back Then.
Family Tree.
Lost Wax.
Lawrence, D. H. Liberty's Old Old Story.
Moth and Rust.
Longfellow, H. Slave Singing at Midnight, The.
Warning, The.
Lux. All the Slaves.
Major, C. Slave Trade, The: View from the Middle Passage.
Martial. 2.68: "That I now call you by your name."
Maunick. Seven Sides and Seven Syllables.
Melville, H. Formerly a Slave.

Misgivings.
Paley, G. Is There a Difference between Men and Women.
Pinkerton, H. Lemuel Shaw's Meditation.
Riley, J. Gladness.
Plantation Hymn.
Ponchus Pilut.
Robinson, E. Sonnet: "Master and the slave go hand in hand, The."
Rossetti, C. Epitaph: "Slave yet wearing on my head a crown, A."
Rukeyser, M. Secrets of American Civilization.
Sandburg, C. Mammy Hums.
Nigger.
Osawatomie.
Smith, S. Was It Not Curious?
Thoreau. Wait not till slaves pronounce the word.
Unknown, fr. Sumerian cuneiform. Slave, Come to My Service!
Very. Freedmen of the Mississippi Valley, The.
Freedom National, Slavery Sectional.
Fugitive Slaves, The.
Lines, Written on Reading Stuart's Account of the Treatment of Slaves in Charleston.
On the Nebraska Bill.
Slave, The.
Slavery.
Walker, A. Early Losses: a Requiem.
Right to Life, The: What Can the White Man Say to the Black Woman?
Wheatley, P. On Being Brought from Africa to America.
To the Right Honourable William, Earl of Dartmouth.
Whitman, W. Blood-Money.
Song for Certain Congressmen.
Whittier. Astræa at the Capitol.
At Washington.
Branded Hand, The.
Christian Slave, The.
Clerical Oppressors.
Crisis, The.
Expostulation.
Farewell, The: "Gone, gone,—sold and gone."
For Righteousness' Sake.
Haschish, The.
Hunters of Men, The.
Hymn: "O Thou, whose presence went before."
Ichabod[!].
Kathleen.
Legend of St. Mark, The.
Letter, A.
Letter from a Missionary of the Methodist Episcopal Church South.
Lines on the Portrait of a Celebrated Publisher.
Massachusetts to Virginia.
Mithridates at Chios.
Moral Warfare, The.
New Exodus, The.
Official Piety.
Panorama, The.
Pastoral Letter, The.
Ritner.
Sabbath Scene, A.
Sentence of John L. Brown, The.
Slave-Ships, The.
Slaves of Martinique, The.
Song for the Time, A.
Song of Slaves in the Desert.
Sumner.
Texas.
To a Southern Statesman.
To Delaware.
To George B. Cheever.
To Massachusetts.
To the Memory of Thomas Shipley.
To William Lloyd Garrison.
Yankee Girl, The.
Yorktown.
Wordsworth, W. To Thomas Clarkson, on the Final Passing of the Bill for the Abolition of the Slave Trade. March, 1807.
Wright, J. Sketch for an Aesthetic Project.

Sleds
Levertov. Winterpig.

Riley, J. His Christmas Sled.
Stafford, W. Sayings from the Northern Ice.
Wilner, E. Water Lace and White Eyes.
See also **Sleighs**

Sleep
Amichai [*or* Amikhai]. Lullaby 1957.
  Mutual Lullaby, A.
  My Sleep.
Ammons. Watch, The.
Armantrout. Plot, The.
Atwood. Pre-Amphibian.
  Variation on the Word *Sleep*.
Auden. Lullaby: "Din of work is subdued,
  The."
Berrigan, T. Things To Do in Providence.
Berry, W. Birth (Near Port William), The.
  Design of a House, The.
  Poem of Thanks, A.
  Sleep.
  Winter Nightfall.
Berryman. Henry by Night.
Bishop, E. Insomnia.
  Lullaby for the Cat.
  Sleeping on the Ceiling.
  Sleeping Standing Up.
  Unbeliever, The.
Blok. Russia.
Bly, R. Falling Asleep.
  Waking from Sleep.
Bogan, L. Tears in Sleep.
Borges. Anticipation of Love.
  Poem: "You were asleep. I wake you."
Bourne, V. On the Picture of a Sleeping Child.
Brontë, E. Sleep brings no joy to me.
  Song: "Linnet in the rocky dells, The."
Broumas, O. Landscape with Angels.
  Sleeping Beauty.
Browning, E. Child Asleep, A.
  Isobel's Child.
  Sleep, The.
  Sleeping and Watching.
Browning, R. Bad Dreams I.
Burns, R. Flow Gently, Sweet Afton.
  On a Bank of Flowers.
  Simmer's a Pleasant Time.
Byron, G. Song: "Breeze of the night in gentler
  sighs."
Campion, T. As on a day Sabina fell asleepe.
  Awake, thou spring of speaking grace, mute rest
    becomes not thee.
  Come, Cheerful Day!
  In eosdem.
  In Lycium et Clytham.
  It Fell on a Summer's [*or* Sommers] Day [*or*
    Daie].
  Sleep, Angry Beauty.
Carruth, H. Insomniac Sleeps Well for Once
  and, The.
Carver, R. Quiet Nights.
  Sleeping.
  Two Worlds.
Chamfort. Sleep till death.
Ciardi, J. 4:00 A.M. on the Terrace.
  After Sunday Dinner We Uncles Snooze.
  Deaths about You when You Stir in Sleep, The.
  Every Time You Are Sleeping and I.
  It Is for the Waking Man to Tell His Dreams.
  To Judith Asleep.
Codrescu. Work.
Coleridge, S. If I Had but Two Little Wings.
  Ode to Sleep.
  Pains of Sleep, The.
  Virgin's Cradle-Hymn, The.
  Wish for Dreamful Sleep, A.
Crabbe, G. World of Dreams, The.
Crashaw. To the Morning. Satisfaction for
  Sleepe.
Creeley. Don't Sign Anything.
  Je Vois dans le Hasard Tous les Biens Que
    J'espere.
  Plan, The.
  Sing Song.
  Sleep.
  Thinking.
Cullen, C. Night Rain.
Cummings, E. E. As any(men's hells having

wrestled with).
Fl / a / tt / ene / d d.
If you and i awakening.
If you can't eat you got to.
Light Out), A.
Love was—entire excellently steep.
Now winging selves sing sweetly, while
  ghosts(there).
Un(bee)mo / vi / n(in)g.
Us if therefore must forget ourselves.
When you are silent,shining host by guest.
White guardians of the universe of sleep.
Why why / How many winds make wonderful.
You are tired, / (I think).
Cunningham, J. Night-piece.
  On Correggio's Leda.
De la Mare. Awake!
  Forests.
  Galliass, The.
  Homesick.
  Nocturne: "'Tis not my voice now speaks; but
    as a bird."
  Nod.
  Queen Djenira.
  Sleep.
  Sleeper, The.
  Tailor, The.
  Thule.
  Visionary, The.
  Where Is Thy Victory?
Dickey, J. Heads.
Dickinson, E. I had no Cause to be awake.
  On that specific Pillow.
  Sleep is supposed to be.
Donne. Song: "Sweetest love, I do not go[e]."
Dove, R. Lines Muttered in Sleep.
Dugan, A. 1. Business Jacob, the Angel
    Wrestler.
  Landfall.
  Noon's World.
  Romance of the Escaped Children.
Dunbar, P. At Night.
  Ere Sleep Comes Down to Soothe the Weary
    Eyes.
  Farm Child's Lullaby, The.
  Fisher Child's Lullaby, The.
  Good-Night.
  Johnny Speaks.
  Lullaby: "Bedtime's come fu' little boys."
  Sand-Man, The.
Duncan, R. Banners, The.
  Four Songs the Night Nurse Sang.
  In Waking.
Eberhart, R. Caravan of Silence.
  Secret Heart, The.
  Ur Burial.
Enzensberger, H. Sleeping Pill.
Fayzi [*or* Faydi *or* Feisi *or* Feizi]. Eternal
    Watcher, who doth wake, The.
Frost, R. Stopping by Woods on a Snowy
    Evening.
Gallagher, T. Under Stars.
  Willingly.
Graves, R. Charm for Sound Sleeping, A.
  Coronet of Moonlight.
  Death Grapple, The.
  Friday Night.
  Rose, The.
  She Tells Her Love While Half Asleep.
  Song: Once More.
  Through Nightmare.
  Twin of Sleep, The.
Guillén, J. I Want to Sleep.
Gunn, T. Conversation, The.
  Differences, The.
  For Signs.
  Hug, The.
  Incident on a Journey.
  Night Piece, The.
  Phaedra in the Farm House.
  Sacred Heart.
  Touch.
Hall, D. Moon Clock.
  Passage to Worship.
  Six Naps in One Day.
  Sleeping.

HaNagid. They Stole My Sleep.
Herrick. Bellman, The.
  Epitaph upon a Virgin, An.
  To Daisies, Not to Shut So Soon[e].
  Upon a child.
  Upon His Kinswoman Mistris Elizabeth Herrick.
  Upon Mistress Elizabeth Wheeler under the
    Name of Amarillis.
Housman. I lay me down and slumber.
Hughes, L. Fired.
  Morning After.
  Sleep.
Hughes, T. Bear, The.
Ignatow, D. I Sleep.
Jackson, L. Sleep Contravened.
Jacobsen, J. Distance.
  Insomniac's Bird.
Jarrell, R. Afterwards.
  Dreams.
  Prayer at Morning, A.
  Variation on "To Say to Go to Sleep," A.
Keats. To Sleep.
Kinnell. 52 Oswald Street.
Kinsella, T. Before Sleep.
  Endymion.
  Night Songs.
Kipling, R. City of Sleep, The.
Koch, K. Sleeping with Women.
Kumin, M. Sleeping with Animals.
Kunitz, S. Night-Piece.
  Particular Lullaby.
  Science of the Night, The.
Kuo Mo-jo. Phoenix Undying, *sel.*
Larkin, P. How to Sleep.
  Midwinter Waking.
Laughlin, J. Atman of Sleep, The.
  Enlacement, The.
  Ever So.
  In Half Darkness.
  Two Spoons.
  You Were Asleep.
Lawrence, D. H. Baby Asleep after Pain, A.
  In the Dark.
  Martyr à la Mode.
  Sleep.
  Song of the Grey Dog, The.
  To Toss the Troubled Night Long.
Levertov. Tide, The.
Levine, P. Making Light of It.
Lorde. Dreams Bite.
Lowell, R. Sleepless.
Lux. If I Die Before I Wake.
  Man Asleep in a Child's Bed.
MacLeish. Ancestral.
  Waking.
  Way-Station.
  Words in Time.
MacNeice. Cradle Song: "Clock's untiring
    fingers wind the wool of darkness, The."
  Rest House, The.
Major, C. Bricks and Sleep.
Mallarmé. Rondel: "Nothing you have when
    you awake."
McGrath, T. In Sickness Like Sleep.
  Such Simple Love.
McHugh, H. Debtor's Prison Road.
  Double Agent.
Melville, H. Bench of Boors, The.
Meredith, G. Song: "Flower unfolds its
    dawning cup, The."
Meredith, W. On Falling Asleep by Firelight.
  REM Sleep.
Merrill, J. About the Phoenix.
  Dream (Escape from the Sculpture Museum)
    and Waking.
Merwin. Sleeping Mountain, The.
Michelangelo Buonarroti. Grateful is Sleep, my
    life in stone bound fast.
  O night, comforting night, dark though you are.
  To sleep, even more be made of stone: how
    these.
Milosz, C. Window.
Milton. Elegiac Verses.
  Slothful Sleep.
Mistral, G. Sad Mother, The.
Montale. In Sleep.

Moore, M.   Peter.
Muldoon, P.   Vespers.
Nash, O.   Cat Naps Are Too Good for Cats.
  Complaint to Four Angels.
  Pappy Wants a Poppy.
  Plea for a League of Sleep, A.
  What, No Sheep?
Nemerov.   To the Memory of John
  Wheelwright.
Niedecker.   As praiseworthy / The power of
  breathing.
  Subliminal.
O'Hara, F.   Jane Awake.
  Sleeping on the Wing.
Oliver, M.   Sleeping in the Forest.
  White Flowers.
  White Night.
Orr, G.   Sleeping Alone in a Small Room.
Owen, W.   Asleep.
  Sleeping Beauty, The.
Pagis.   Silent Movie.
Palmer, M.   Idem 4.
  Night Sky, The.
Parker, D.   Lullaby: "Sleep, pretty lady, the
  night is enfolding you."
  Threat to a Fickle Lady.
Patchen.   Naked Land, The.
Pessoa.   I sleep. If I dream, I do not know on
  waking.
  Sleep that comes over me, The.
Pinsky.   Falling Asleep.
Plath.   Ghost's Leavetaking, The.
  Sleepers, The.
Raine, K.   Behind the lids of sleep.
  From vague regions of sleep I come again.
  Spell of Sleep.
Ramanujan.   He Too Was a Light Sleeper Once.
Ransom, J.   Janet Waking.
Rexroth, K.   Camargue.
  She Is Away [or Marthe Away (She Is Away)].
Rich, A.   Night.
Riley, J.   By Her White Bed.
  Dream of Inspiration, A.
  Dream Unfinished, A.
  How Did You Rest, Last Night?
  Invocation, An.
  No Boy Knows.
  Romaunt of King Mordameer, The.
  Serenade—To Nora.
  Sleep.
  Slumber-Song.
  Through Sleepy-Land.
  When Baby Slept.
Rilke.   Night Has Come.
  Sleep.
Ritsos.   Wonder.
Roethke.   Root Cellar.
  Waking, The.
Rossetti, C.   Angels at the foot, / And Angels at
  the head.
  Chill, A.
  Crying, my little one, footsore and weary?
  Daughter of Eve, A.
  Holy Innocents.
  Hopeless Case, A.
  Lie a-bed, / Sleepy head, / Shut up eyes, bo-
  peep.
  Lullaby, oh lullaby! / Flowers are closed and
  lambs are sleeping.
  O Death Where Is Thy Sting?
  Our little baby fell asleep.
  So I grew half delirious and quite sick.
  Song of Flight, A.
  Sound Sleep.
  There Remaineth Therefore a Rest for the
  People of God.
Rukeyser, M.   Another Day. In a Field of Peace
  the Child, Playing.
  He starts awake in the city. Orion believing.
  Watchers, The.
  Water Night.
Rumi.   Breeze at dawn has secrets to tell you,
  The.
  Vigil, The.
Sandburg, C.   Atlas, How Have You Been?
  Bringers.

Drowsy.
  Peace, Night, Sleep.
  Portrait of a Child Settling Down for an
  Afternoon Nap.
  Sheep.
  Sleep Song.
  Sleepyheads.
  Smoke Shapes.
  Wind Song.
  Work Gangs.
Schuyler, J.   Watching You.
Sexton.   Three Green Windows.
Shelley, P.   Fragment: The Deserts of Dim
  Sleep.
  To ———: "When passion's trance is overpast."
Sheridan, T.   Upon Stealing a Crown when the
  Dean Was Asleep.
Simic.   Pillow, The.
  Sleep.
Smith, S.   Goodnight.
  Siesta.
Spender, S.   One.
Stafford, W.   One Night.
  Waking at 3 A.M.
Stock, R.   Doctor Will Be Back Too Late, The.
Swenson, M.   Love Sleeping.
  Waking from a Nap on the Beach.
Tate, J.   Bug Sleep.
  Recipe for Sleep.
Thomas, D.   I Fellowed Sleep.
  In Country Sleep.
  Lie Still, Sleep Becalmed.
Tomlinson, C.   Arizona Highway.
Trakl.   Sleep.
  Winter Night, A.
Updike.   Pillow.
  Stunt Flier, The.
  To a Waterbed.
Van Geel.   Sleepwalking.
Very.   Call, The ("Why art thou not awake my
  son?").
  Morning Watch, The.
Voznesensky [or Voznesenskii].   Dead Still.
Warren, R.   Better Than Counting Sheep.
  To One Awake.
  Twice Born.
Warton, T.   Come, gentle sleep, death's image
  though thou art.
Wilbur, R.   After the Last Bulletins.
  Beasts.
  In Limbo.
  In the Smoking-Car.
  Walking to Sleep.
Williams, C. K.   Man Who Owns Sleep, The.
  Waking Jed.
Williams, M.   Man Who Stays Up Late, The.
Williams, T.   Dark Arm, Hanging over the Edge
  of Infinity.
  Her Head on the Pillow.
  Turning Out the Bedside Lamp.
Williams, W.   Death the Barber.
  Goodnight, A.
Wordsworth, D.   Cottager to Her Infant, (By My
  Sister), The.
Wordsworth, W.   To Sleep.
Wright, C.   Homage to Cesare Pavese.
Wright, J.   American Wedding.
  In the Cold House.
  March.
Yeats.   Lullaby: "Beloved, may your sleep be
  sound."
Zagajewski.   Europe Goes to Sleep.
  Lullaby.
  Separation.
Zaturenska.   Lullaby: "Ruin falls on blackening
  skies."
Zukofsky, L.   Alba (1952).
  Atque in Perpetuum A.W.
  When the crickets.

Sleeping Beauty
Angelou.   Let's Majeste.
Carruth, H.   Sleeping Beauty, The.
Clifton, L.   Sleeping Beauty.
Nemerov.   Sleeping Beauty.
Sexton.   Briar Rose (Sleeping Beauty).

Sleepwalking and Sleepwalkers
Jacobsen, J.   Terrible Naïve, The.
Sleet
Tate, J.   Dear Reader.
Sleighs
Cummings, E. E.   So many selves(so many
  fiends and gods).
Seifert.   Silence Full of Sleighbells.
Very.   Sleigh Ride.
Slides
Prunty.   Water Slide Along the Beach.
Sligo
See **County Sligo, Ireland**
Sloth
Campion, T.   Lighten, heavy hart, thy spright.
Nash, O.   Procrastination Is All of the Time.
  Where There's a Will, There's Velleity.
Roethke.   Sloth, The.
Sandburg, C.   Galoots.
Smith, S.   Lament of a Slug-a-Bed's Wife.
Sloths
Roethke.   Sloth, The.
Slugs
Roethke.   Slug.
See also **Snails**
Slums
Brooks, G.   Lovers of the Poor, The.
De la Mare.   Slum Child, The.
Dove, R.   Teach Us to Number Our Days.
Glück, L.   Letter from Provence.
Hayden, R.   Summertime and the Living.
Ignatow, D.   Get the Gasworks.
MacNeice.   Slum Song.
Merton.   Aubade—Harlem.
Oppen.   Bicycles and the Apex, The.
  Source, The.
Pasolini.   Southern Dawn.
Patchen.   Slums, The.
Spender, S.   Elementary School Classroom in a
  Slum, An.
Walcott.   Laventille.
Smallpox
Jonson, B.   Epigram. To the Small-Pox, An.
Muldoon, P.   Meeting the British.
Smart, Christopher
Browning, R.   With Christopher Smart.
Van Duyn.   Garland for Christopher Smart, A.
Smells
Amichai [or Amikhai].   Ballad of the Washed
  Hair.
Auden.   Smelt and Tasted.
Baudelaire.   Exotic Scent.
Bishop, E.   Prodigal, The.
Cavafy.   Correspondence According to
  Baudelaire.
Clampitt.   Ringing Doorbells.
Clare, J.   Bean Field, The.
Coleridge, S.   Cologne.
  On My Joyful Departure from the City of
  Cologne.
Creeley.   Echo ("Faint, persistent").
Cummings, E. E.   Whereas by dark really
  released,the modern.
Davie, D.   Kingship.
De la Mare.   Pot Of Musk, A.
Dickinson, E.   Essential oils—are wrung.
Gunn, T.   At the Back of the North Wind.
  Fennel.
  Grasses.
Gurney, I.   Incense Bearers, The.
Hall, D.   Repeated Shapes, The.
Heaney, S.   Mint.
Herbert, G.   Odour, The. (2 Corinthians 2).
Herrick.   Another on Her.
  Frankincense, The.
  On a Perfum'd Lady.
  On Julia's Breath.
  Perfume, The.
  To Cherry-Blossomes.
  To the Most Fair and Lovely Mistress Anne
  Soame, Now Lady Abdie.
  Upon a Sowre-Breath Lady.
  Upon Burr.
  Upon Coone.

Upon Gorgonius.
Upon His Kinswoman Mistresse Bridget
  Herrick.
Upon Julia's Sweat.
Upon Julia's Unlacing Her Self.
Upon Skoles.
Jonson, B. On Sir Cod the Perfumed.
 To Sir Cod.
 To the Same Sir Cod.
Kipling, R. Lichtenberg.
Levertov. Laying the Dust.
Lux. After a Few Whiffs of Another World.
 History Books.
MacDiarmid, H. Happy on Heimaey.
Major, C. Downwind.
McGrath, T. Praises IV.
Meredith, G. Tuck, thou graceless sinner!—.
Mistral, G. Round of Aromas.
Olson, C. Of Mathilde.
 Perfume / of Flowers!, The.
 Perfume!, The.
Ramanujan. Eyes, Ears, Noses, and a Thing
  about Touch.
Rexroth, K. Fragrance of the teapot, The.
Ritsos. Remembrance.
Sandburg, C. Blossom Themes.
Sheridan, T. Upon William Tisdall, D. D.
Swift, J. Lady's Dressing Room, The.
Tomlinson, C. Hay.
Whittier. Sweet Fern.
Williams, C. K. Hog Heaven.
Williams, W. Smell.
 Sonnet in Search of an Author.

Smiles
Angelou. I Almost Remember.
Auden. In Schrafft's.
Blake, W. Smile, The.
Burns, R. Song: "Full well thou knowest I love
  thee dear."
Byron, G. I Saw Thee Weep.
Creeley. Happy Man, The.
 Oh No.
Cummings, E. E. Chas sing does(who).
 "Kitty". sixteen,5'1",white,prostitute.
 You which could grin three smiles into a dead.
Dickinson, E. Her smile was shaped like other
  smiles.
 They might not need me—yet they might.
Dunbar, P. Made to Order Smile, The.
 Philosophy.
 Response.
 We Wear the Mask.
Graves, R. One Hard Look.
Hardy, T. Neutral Tones.
Hughes, T. Smile, The.
Jackson, L. After Smiling.
Laughlin, J. What Are You Smiling About.
Levertov. Cabdriver's Smile, The.
Montale. I think back on your smile, and for me
  it's a clear pool.
Riley, J. Her Smile of Cheer and Voice of Song.
 We Are Not Always Glad When We Smile.
Ritsos. Laugh, The.
Smith, S. Smile, The.
Szymborska, W. Smiles.
Warren, R. Smile, The.
Wilbur, R. Simile for Her Smile, A.
Wilner, E. All the Wide Grin of Him.
Wordsworth, W. What Heavenly Smiles! O
  Lady Mine.

Smith, Adam
Dugan, A. Triptych.

Smith, Bessie
Hayden, R. Homage to the Empress of the
  Blues.

Smith, John (1580–1631)
Clampitt. Matoaka.
Nash, O. Captain John Smith.

Smoke
Amichai [or Amikhai]. My God, the soul you
  gave me.
Brontë, E. What is that smoke that ever still.
Carruth, H. Woodsmoke at 70.
Creeley. Smoke.
Hill, G. September Song.

Komunyakaa. Smokehouse, The.
Niedecker. Last night the trash barrel.
Palmer, M. Notes for Echo Lake 2.
Ritsos. Incense.
Rukeyser, M. This is going to be about smoke.
Sandburg, C. Smoke.
 Smoke Shapes.
Stafford, W. Smoke.
Thoreau. Sluggish smoke curls up from some
  deep dell, The.
Tomlinson, C. Night-Piece: The Near and the
  Far.
Williams, T. Demon Smoke.
Williams, W. Classic Scene.
Zagajewski. Smoke.

Smoking and Smokers
Angelou. Health-Food Diner, The.
Baudelaire. Pipe.
Broumas, O. Instruction.
Carver, R. Ashtray, The.
Collins, B. Best Cigarette, The.
Creeley. Sound.
Cunningham, J. Night-piece.
Dunbar, P. Companion's Progress, A.
 My Corn-Cob Pipe.
 When the Old Man Smokes.
Ginsberg, A. Put Down Your Cigarette Rag
  (Dont Smoke).
Montale. New Stanzas.
Riley, J. I Smoke My Pipe.
Sandburg, C. Crimson.
Snyder, G. Makings.
Williams, M. How to Stop Smoking.
Williams, T. Life Story.
Williams, W. M.B.

Smuggling and Smugglers
Kipling, R. Poor Honest Men.
Logan, J. Big Sur: Partington Cove.

Snails
Bourne, V. Snail, The.
Carver, R. Forever.
Fenton, J. Killer Snails, The.
Gunn, T. Considering the Snail.
Hughes, L. Snail.
Levi, P. Snail, The.
Lindsay, N. Haughty Snail-King, The.
 Song of the Sturdy Snails, The.
 Visit to Mab, The.
MacLeish. Out of Sleep Awakened.
Moore, M. To a Snail.
Orr, G. Snail, The.
Piercy. Spring Offensive of the Snail, The.
Sarton, M. Eine Kleine Snailmusik.
Sexton. Snail.
Wilner, E. Moonsnails.
See also Shells; Slugs

Snakebites
Dickey, J. Snakebite.
 Venom.

Snakes
Ammons. I Came Upon a Plateau.
 Jungle Knot.
Armantrout. Falling: 1.
Atwood. After Heraclitus.
 Bad Mouth.
 Psalm to Snake.
 Quattrocento.
 She.
 Snake Woman.
Berry, W. Snake, The.
Blake, W. I Saw a Chapel All of Gold.
Carruth, H. Mix the Ingredients.
Clifton, L. Lucifer Speaks in His Own Voice.
Cowper, W. Colubriad, The.
Crane, S. On the desert.
De la Mare. Dream, A.
Dickey, J. Blowgun and Rattlesnake.
 Goodbye to Serpents.
 Poisoned Man, The.
 Venom.
Dickinson, E. In Winter in my Room.
 Snake, A.
 Snake, The.
Dugan, A. On a Snake.
Duncan, R. Albigenses, The.

Eberhart, R. Ode to the Chinese Paper Snake.
Frost, R. Hill Wife, The.
"H. D." Helios and Athene.
Herrick. Silken Snake, The.
Hopkins, G. Cold whip-adder unespied, The.
Hughes, L. Snake.
Hughes, T. Apple Tragedy.
 Cleopatra to the Asp.
 Horrible Religious Error, A.
Kipling, R. Poison of Asps.
Komunyakaa. Eclogue at Daybreak.
 Omen.
Kunitz, S. Snakes of September, The.
Lawrence, D. H. Snake.
Levertov. Closed World, The.
 To the Snake.
Lowell, R. Serpent, The.
 Snake.
Lux. Snake Lake.
Marvell. Coronet, The.
Millay, E. To a Snake.
Milosz, C. Vipera Berus.
Moore, M. Snakes, Mongooses, Snake-
  Charmers, and the Like.
Nash, O. Asp, The.
 Cobra, The.
O'Hara, F. In Memory of My Feelings.
Oliver, M. Water Snake.
Pagis. Information.
 Snake.
Patchen. Deer and the Snake, The.
 Who Walks There?
Plath. Medallion.
 Snakecharmer.
Ramanujan. Moulting.
 Old Indian Belief.
 Snakes.
Roethke. Serpent, The.
 Snake.
Rumi. Jesus on the Lean Donkey.
 Snake-Catcher and the Frozen Snake, The.
Sacchetti. On a Wet Day.
Sexton. Snake.
Shelley, P. Fragment: "Wake the serpent not—
  lest he."
Stafford, W. Boom Town.
Sze. Sliding Away.
Thomas, D. Incarnate Devil.
Warren, R. Unless.
Whittier. Double-Headed Snake of Newbury,
  The.
Wilbur, R. Fable, A.
Williams, C. K. Tails.
Williams, W. Sort of a Song, A.
Zaturenska. Death Is the Serpent.

Snapdragons
Ammons. Rectitude.
 Timing.
Lawrence, D. H. Snap-Dragon.
Zukofsky, L. Butter-and-Eggs.

Sneezing
Prunty. Sneeze, The.

Snipes
Heaney, S. Backward Look, The.

Snobbery and Snobs
Bukowski. O, We Are the Outcasts.
 Parts of an Opera, Parts of a Guitar, Part of
  Nowhere.
Burns, R. Epigram: "Whoe'er he be that
  sojourns here."
 Song: "Tibby I hae seen the day."
Dickey, W. Being Asked To Define Bourgeois
  Individuality.
Dunbar, P. Jealous.
Glück, L. My Neighbor in the Mirror.
Hughes, L. Low to High.
 Snob.
 To Certain Intellectuals.
Meredith, G. Fusion.
 Miss Millicent Maxse was fond of her Ma.
Moore, M. Labors of Hercules, The.
Nash, O. Ms. Found under a Serviette in a
  Lovely Home.
 Now Tell Me About Yourself.
Sandburg, C. Balloon Faces.
Smith, S. Parents.

See also **Social Class**

Snoring
Hughes, L.   Morning After.
Nash, O.   Arthur.

Snow
Ammons.   Lollapalooza: 22 February.
  Snow Log.
  Snow Whirl.
Berrigan, T.   For You.
Berry, W.   March 22, 1968.
  March Snow.
Blake, W.   Soft Snow.
Bly, R.   Dream on the Night of First Snow, A.
  Night of First Snow.
  Six Winter Privacy Poems.
  Snowfall in the Afternoon.
Brontë, E.   Farewell To Alexandria, A
  It was night, and on the mountains.
Broumas, O.   Blockade.
Carew, T.   To My Mistress [or Mistris], I
  Burning in Love.
Carruth, H.   Continuo.
  Essay on Marriage.
  Sound of Snow, The.
Carver, R.   Such Diamonds.
  Yesterday, Snow.
Celan.   Homecoming.
  Winter.
Ciardi, J.   Hometown after a War.
  January 2, 1978.
  March Morning.
  Storm.
Clampitt.   Resumption, Or Possibly a
  Remission, A.
  White.
Coleridge, S.   Two Round Spaces on the
  Tombstone, The.
Collins, B.   Shoveling Snow with Buddha.
  Snow.
  Snow Day.
Cooper, J.   Snow in the City.
Creeley.   As Now It Would Be Snow.
  Snow, The.
  To And.
  Xmas Poem: Bolinas.
Cummings, E. E.   Ballade: "White night roared
  with a huge north-wind, The."
  Beautiful / is the / unmea.
  Blossoming are people / nimbler than Really.
  Comedian stands on a corner,the sky is, The.
  I was sitting in mcsoreley's. outside it was New
    York and beauti- / fully snowing.
  Infinite jukethrob smoke & swallow to dis.
  One / t / hi / s / snowflake.
  SNO / a white idea(Listen).
  Snow means that / life is a black cannonadin.
  Snow)says!Says / over un / graves.
  This man's heart / is true to his.
Cunningham, J.   Monday Morning.
De la Mare.   Snow.
  Snowdrop, The.
  Snowflake, The.
  Snowing.
  There Blooms No Bud in May.
  Winter.
Dickey, J.   Snow on a Southern State.
  Snow Thickets.
  To Be Done in Winter.
Dickey, W.   Avalanche.
Dickinson, E.   I remember the leaves were
  falling.
  Safe in their Alabaster Chambers.
  Snow beneath whose chilly softness.
  Snow that never drifts, The.
  Snow, The.
  Verily it snows.
Dubie.   Last Poem, Snow Tree.
  Safe Conduct.
Dugan, A.   Imperial Song for Warmth.
  Untitled Poem: "Our German teacher used to
    say."
Dunbar, P.   Grievance, A.
  Snowin'
Eberhart, R.   Homage to the North.
  Skier and the Mountain, The.
  Snow Cascades.

Snowfall, A.
Emerson, R.   All the great & good.
  Snow-Storm [or Snowstorm], The.
Enzensberger, H.   Towards Eternal Peace.
Frost, R.   Afterflakes.
  Desert Places.
  Dust of Snow.
  Onset, The.
  Patch of Old Snow, A.
  Snow.
  Stopping by Woods on a Snowy Evening.
  Storm Fear.
Gallagher, T.   My Mother Remembers That She
  Was Beautiful.
  Snowheart.
Glück, L.   Late Snow.
Graves, R.   Like Snow.
  She Tells Her Love While Half Asleep.
Gurney, I.   Snow.
Hall, D.   Love Is Like Sounds.
  Snow, The.
Hamill, S.   First Snow.
Hardy, T.   Light Snow-Fall after Frost, A.
  Snow in the Suburbs.
Hayden, R.   Snow.
Housman.   Eight O'Clock.
  Loveliest of Trees, the Cherry Now.
Hughes, L.   Angels Wings.
Hughes, T.   Bringing in New Couples.
  Snow.
Ignatow, D.   Inside Me Is the Peace of an Egg.
Jacobsen, J.   Escape in Ice.
Jarrell, R.   Winter's Tale, The.
Kinsella, T.   Liffey Hill, The.
Kumin, M.   Getting Through.
  Late Snow.
  Presence, The.
Laughlin, J.   In the Snow.
  It's March.
  Sinking Stone, The.
Lawrence, D. H.   Snowy Day at School, A.
Levine, P.   Snow.
Lindsay, N.   What the Snow Man Said.
Logan, J.   On Reading Camus In Early March.
Longfellow, H.   Cross of Snow, The.
  Snow-Flakes.
Lorde.   Woman Thing, The.
Lux.   Ditto.
  Old Man Shoveling Snow.
MacDiarmid, H.   Lourd on My Hert.
MacLeish.   Snow Fall, The.
  Snowflake Which Is Now and Hence Forever,
    The.
MacNeice.   Snow.
Mahon.   Snow Party, The.
Mallarmé.   Virginal, vibrant, and beautiful dawn,
  The.
McGrath, T.   Afternoon of a McGrath.
  Everything in Order.
Merwin.   Late Snow.
  Snowfall.
  Snowline.
Millay, E.   Buck in the Snow, The.
  Snow Storm, The.
Muldoon, P.   Apple Slump.
Nash, O.   Jangle Bells.
Nemerov.   First Snow.
  From a Record of Disappointment.
  Winter Lightning, The.
Niedecker.   March.
O'Hara, F.   Second Avenue.
Oliver, M.   First Snow.
Olson, C.   Li Po.
  She Who Hits at Will.
  Snow, The.
Pagis.   For How Long.
Paley, G.   Tenth Grade.
  Weather.
Pasternak, B.   Inside the Storm.
Patchen.   Snow is deep on the ground, The.
Pessoa.   Snow threw a silent towel over
  everything, The.
Piercy.   Snow in May.
  Snow, Snow.
Prunty.   Cold.
  Two Kinds of Cause.

Raine, K.   What does this day bestow?
Rexroth, K.   Falling Leaves and Early Snow.
  Gradualism.
  Leda Hidden.
Rich, A.   Snow.
Rossetti, C.   I dug and dug amongst the snow.
  O wind, why do you never rest.
  Seasons.
  There's Snow on the Fields.
Rukeyser, M.   Another Day. For a Moment
  Slipping Back, Again the Unreal King.
  Face of the Dam: Vivian Jones.
Sandburg, C.   Red and White.
Sarton, M.   First Snow.
  Girl with 'Cello.
  Snow Light, The.
Schuyler, J.   Afterward.
  April and Its Forsythia.
  Blizzard.
  Empathy and New Year.
  February 13, 1975.
  Snow, The.
  White City, A.
Sexton.   Letter Written During a January
  Northeaster.
  Oh.
  Snow.
Smith, S.   Angel Face.
Spender, S.   Driving through Snow.
Stafford, W.   Near.
  Whispered in Winter.
Stevens, W.   Annual Gaiety.
  Snow Man, The.
Stock, R.   Barrier Snow.
Swenson, M.   Fluffy Stuff, The.
  Thickening Mat, The.
  This Morning.
Tate, J.   Coming Down Cleveland Avenue.
  Dear Reader.
  Storm.
Tomlinson, C.   Santa Maria delle Nevi.
  Second Song.
  Shadow, The.
  Snow Fences, The.
  Snow Signs.
  Tree, The.
Trakl.   Winter Night, A.
Updike.   Dream and Reality.
  Flurry.
  Snowdrops 1987.
Very.   April Snow, The.
  On the Sudden Snow.
Warren, R.   Function of Blizzard.
  Minneapolis Story.
  Minnesota Recollection.
  Mountain Plateau.
  Passers-By on Snowy Night.
  Preternaturally Early Snowfall in Mating
    Season.
  Snowfall.
  Snowshoeing Back to Camp in Gloaming.
  Time as Hypnosis.
Weiss, T.   Camel in the Snow.
Wilbur, R.   First Snow in Alsace.
  Storm in April, A.
Williams, C. K.   Snow: I.
  Snow: II.
Williams, M.   Listen.
  Waiting for the Paper to be Delivered.
Williams, W.   Naked.
  Polar Bear, The.
  Snow Begins, The.
Wilner, E.   Kazuko's Vision.
  Now I Can Go On and On.
Wright, J.   Blue Teal's Mother.
  In Fear of Harvests.
  Seasonless, The.
  Snowstorms in the Midwest.
  Sparrows in a Hillside Drift.
  To the August Fallen.
Zagajewski.   World's Prose, The.
Zaturenska.   Another Snowstorm.
  Snowstorm in January.
  Snowy Woods, The.
Zukofsky, L.   After reading.
  As to How Much.

(Ryokan's scroll).
See also **Snowflakes; Snowmen**
Snow White
  Jarrell, R.   Ways and the Peoples, The.
  Sexton.   Snow White and the Seven Dwarfs.
Snowdrops
  Hughes, T.   Snowdrop.
  Meredith, G.   When stormy day is cold & gray.
  Rossetti, C.   Baby lies so fast asleep.
  Schuyler, J.   Snowdrop, The.
  Very.   Snow Drop, The.
  Wordsworth, W.   To a Snow-Drop.
Snowflakes
  Bly, R.   Watering the Horse.
  Cummings, E. E.   S(/ these out of in).
  Dickinson, E.   Snow flakes / I counted till they
    danced so.
  Nemerov.   Snowflakes.
  Stafford, W.   November.
  Swenson, M.   Fluffy Stuff, The.
See also **Snow**
Snowmen
  Lindsay, N.   What the Snow Man Said.
  MacNeice.   Snow Man, The.
  Nemerov.   Journey of the Snowmen.
  Pagis.   End of Winter, The.
  Plath.   Snowman on the Moor, The.
  Wilbur, R.   Boy at the Window.
Soap
  Ignatow, D.   How Come?
  MacNeice.   Soap Suds.
  Muldoon, P.   Soap-Pig, The.
  Rilke.   Soap Bubbles.
Sobriety
  Carver, R.   Gravy.
  Hope.
  Possible, The.
  Cowper, W.   Truth.
  Eberhart, R.   Old Dichotomy: Choosing Sides.
  Herrick.   Abstinence.
  Excesse.
  Sobriety in Search.
  Keats.   Portrait, A.
  Whittier.   Brewing of Soma, The.
  Drunkard to His Bottle, The.
  Yeats.   Drunken Man's Praise of Sobriety, A.
Soccer
  Beckett, S.   Ascension.
  Broumas, O.   Body and Soul.
  Heaney, S.   Markings.
  Hughes, T.   Football at Slack.
Social Class
  Angelou.   Bump d'Bump.
  Sepia Fashion Show.
  Bierce.   Fair Division, A.
  Brodsky, J.   Residence, The.
  Bukowski.   Darlings.
  Private First Class.
  Sparks.
  Burns, R.   Toadeater, The.
  When She Cam Ben She Bobbed.
  Byron, G.   To E——.
  Carver, R.   Marriage.
  Cavafy.   Beizades to His Beloved.
  Clare, J.   My Mary.
  Codrescu.   Circle Jerk.
  Seeing out of the Sub.
  Cooper, J.   Class.
  Cummings, E. E.   Come,gaze with me upon this
    dome.
  Little joe gould has lost his teeth and doesn't
    know where.
  Davie, D.   Right Lads, The.
  Dugan, A.   Love Song: Class Analysis.
  On Being Out-Classed by Class.
  Untitled Poem: "I love the way the heel of my
    hand feels."
  Why There Is No Class Solidarity in America I
    Read It In *The Times*. Aug. 2, 1987.
  Eberhart, R.   Blessed Are the Angels in Heaven.
  Gnats.
  Hop-Toad, The.
  Lament of a New England Mother, The.
  Maine Roustabout, A.
  Nostalgia for Edith Sitwell.

Eliot, T. S.   Afternoon.
  Paysage Triste.
Emerson, R.   And man of wit & mark.
Enzensberger, H.   Middle Class Blues.
  Short History of the Bourgeoisie.
Fenton, J.   This Octopus Exploits Women.
Han-shan.   I have a coat.
  Mistress Tsou of Tiyen.
  We hear about the ministers of state.
Hardy, T.   Lady Vi.
  Question of Marriage, A.
Hughes, L.   Graduation.
  High to Low.
  Low to High.
  Park Bench.
  Puzzlement.
  Question ("When the old junk man Death").
  Undertow.
Hughes, T.   Rhododendrons.
Jacobsen, J.   Travelers, The.
Keats.   Pensive They Sit, and Roll Their
  Languid Eyes.
Laughlin, J.   Gracious Living.
  Take Off Your Socks!!
Lawrence, D. H.   Amo Sacrum Vulgus.
  Are You Pining?
  Be a Demon!
  Classes.
  Climbing Up.
  Have Done With It.
  Masses and Classes.
  Middle-Class Children.
  Middle Classes, The.
  O! Start a Revolution.
  Rise in the World, A.
  Saddest Day, The.
  Softly, Then, Softly.
  True Democracy.
  Up He Goes!
  What Is He?
  Working Man, The.
Lindsay, N.   Drunkards in the Street, The.
Lux.   Swimming Pool, The.
Major, C.   Young Woman.
Moore, M.   People's Surroundings.
Niedecker.   We know him—Law and Order
  League.
Oppen.   Guest Room.
Piercy.   Market Economy, The.
Pound, E.   Garden, The.
  Portrait d'une Femme.
Riley, J.   That Other Maud Miller.
Rukeyser, M.   Gradus ad Parnassum.
Smith, S.   Parents.
Stein, G.   Little Novel, A.
Stockton, A.   Impromptu Epitaph on the Grave
  Digger of Princeton—1769.
Thoreau.   Deeds of king and meanest hedger,
  The.
Van Duyn.   That was my grandfather, nearly
  went to prison.
Whitman, W.   Song for Occupations, A.
Whittier.   Maud Muller.
  Our Country.
  Problem, The.
Williams, M.   Affair, The.
  Potter, Vidalia.
  Wide Place in the Road.
Wordsworth, W.   Composed after Reading a
  Newspaper of the Day.
Zagajewski.   Fire.
Social Protest
  Clampitt.   Dahlia Gardens, The.
See also **Protest, Social**
Social Service
  Hughes, L.   For Russell and Rowena Jelliffe.
Social Work and Social Workers
  Kinsella, T.   Social Work.
  Williams, M.   Potter, Vidalia.
Socialism
  Carrera Andrade.   Radicals.
  Carruth, H.   My Father's Face.
  Frost, R.   Build Soil.
  Hughes, L.   Always the Same.
  Good Morning Revolution.

One More "S" in the U.S.A.
  Jarrell, R.   Night before the Night before
    Christmas, The.
  Lawrence, D. H.   Hibiscus and Salvia Flowers.
  Lindsay, N.   Net to Snare the Moonlight, A.
  Why I Voted the Socialist Ticket.
  McGrath, T.   Vision of Three Angels Viewing
    the Progress of Socialism.
  Sandburg, C.   Dynamiter.
  Tomlinson, C.   Rich, The.
Socrates
  Carruth, H.   Anent Socrates, or Somebody.
  Heaney, S.   Poet's Chair.
  Jackson, L.   Many Gentlemen.
  McHugh, H.   Scenes from a Death.
  Rexroth, K.   Flute Overheard, A.
  Sheridan, T.   Thus Did Great Socrates Improve
    the Mind.
Sodom
  Akhmatova, A.   Lot's Wife.
  Duncan, R.   This Place Rumord to Have Been
    Sodom.
  Kizer, C.   Columns and Caryatids.
  Nemerov.   Lot Later.
  Van Duyn.   Cities of the Plain, The.
  Whittier.   Cities of the Plain, The.
Solace
  Browning, E.   Isobel's Child.
  Carver, R.   Window, The.
  De la Mare.   Sunday, A.
  Hardy, T.   On a Fine Morning.
  Herrick.   Comfort to a Lady Upon the Death of
    Her Husband.
  Mirth.
  Miseries.
  Ode to Master Endymion Porter, upon His
    Brother's Death, An.
  To the Lady Crew, Upon the Death of her Child.
  To the Willow-Tree.
  Hopkins, G.   No Worst, There Is None. Pitched
    Past Pitch of Grief.
  Nash, O.   I Can Hardly Wait for the Sandman.
  Neruda.   I Come Back from a Journey.
  Petrarch.   Whenever Love makes his assaults on
    me.
  Ransom, J.   Winter Remembered.
  Sandburg, C.   Old Music for Quiet Hearts.
  Sarton, M.   Return.
  Stockton, A.   Anniversary Elegy on the Death of
    Mr Stockton the 28th of Feb 1783.
  Ode—Written 1756, An.
  Resignation, an Elegiac Ode, February the 28th,
    1788.
  To Doctor Rush Enclosing the Foregoing Ode of
    1782.
  Wilbur, R.   Avowal, The.
Soldiers
  Ai.   Flashback.
  Albizzi.   Prolonged Sonnet: When the Troops
    were Returning from Milan.
  Amichai [*or* Amikhai].   And I am always like
    this fleeing from hurt and pain.
  Since Then.
  Soldiers in the grave say: you, up there, The.
  Atwood.   Machine. Gun. Nest.
  Projected Slide of an Unknown Soldier.
  Auden.   O What Is That Sound [Which So
    Thrills the Ear].
  Ode: "Though aware of our rank and alert to
    obey orders."
  Taller To-day.
  Berryman.   Captain's Song, The.
  White Feather.
  Bly, R.   As the Asian War Begins.
  Teeth Mother Naked at Last, The.
  Borges.   Sepulchral Inscription.
  Soldier of Urbina, A.
  Brecht, B.   Legend of the Dead Soldier, The.
  Brooks, G.   Gay Chaps at the Bar.
  Looking.
  Broumas, O.   Easter.
  Browning, E.   Forced Recruit, The.
  Parting Lovers.
  Bukowski.   Troops, The.
  Burns, R.   Bonie Dundee.
  Charlie He's My Darling.

Extempore.
Highland Laddie.
I'll Mak You Be Fain to Follow Me.
It Was A' for Our Rightfu' King.
There Was a Bonie Lass.
When wild War's deadly blast was blawn.
Byron, G.　As the Liberty Lads o'er the Sea.
Campion, T.　In Barnum.
Carver, R.　Eve of Battle, The.
Cavafy.　Those Who Fought for the Achaian
　Alliance.
Chesterton.　Last Hero, The.
Ciardi, J.　Goodmorning with Light.
On Sending Home My Civilian Clothes.
Poem for a Soldier's Girl.
Port of Aerial Embarkation.
Ritual for Singing Bat.
Two Songs for a Gunner.
Corbière.　Letter from Mexico (Vera Cruz, 10
　February, 186–).
Cowper, W.　Epitaph, An: "Here lies one, who
　never drew."
Crane, S.　Do not weep, maiden, for war is kind.
Soldier, young in years, young in ambitions, A.
Dickey, J.　Drinking from a Helmet.
Enclosure, The.
Dickinson, E.　Bless God, he went as soldiers.
Donne.　Canonization, The.
Dugan, A.　Decimation before Phraäta, The.
General Prothalamion in Populous Times.
Imperial Song for Warmth.
Memories of Verdun.
Night Scene before Combat.
Notes Toward a Spring Offensive.
On the Civil War on the East Coast of the
　United States of North America 1860–64.
Portrait from the Infantry.
Self-Exhortation on Military Themes.
Sixteen Lines on Marching.
Stentor and Mourning.
Two Hatreds of Action.
Dunbar, P.　Black Samson of Brandywine.
Colored Soldiers, The.
Dirge for a Soldier.
Our Martyred Soldiers.
Veteran, The.
When Dey 'Listed Colored Soldiers.
Emerson, R.　Voluntaries.
Frost, R.　Not to Keep.
Soldier, A.
Graves, R.　Oldest Soldier, The.
Gunn, T.　As Expected.
Captain in Time of Peace.
Corporal, The.
Incident on a Journey.
Innocence.
Market at Turk.
Gurney, I.　Bach and the Sentry.
Billet.
Bohemians, The.
Canadians.
First Time In.
La Gorgue.
Mangel-Bury, The.
Servitude.
Signallers.
Song: "I had a girl's fancies."
Varennes.
HaNagid.　I Quartered the Troops for the Night.
Hardy, T.　Casterbridge Captains, The.
Colonel's Soliloquy, The.
Dance at the Phoenix, The.
Departure.
Dolls, The.
Drummer Hodge.
Man He Killed, The.
Men Who March Away.
Military Appointment, A.
Often When Warring.
Panthera.
Parting-Scene, A.
Sitting on the Bridge.
Subalterns, The.
Hayden, R.　Dream, The.
Heaney, S.　Toome Road, The.
Trial Runs.

Visitant.
Herrick.　To the Right Gratious Prince, Lodwick,
　Duke of Richmond and Lenox.
Hopkins, G.　Soldier, The.
Housman.　Day of Battle, The.
Deserter, The.
Epitaph.
Epitaph on an Army of Mercenaries.
Farewell to a name and a number.
Grenadier.
I did not lose my heart in summer's even.
In valleys green and still.
Lancer.
New Mistress, The.
Oh stay at home, my lad, and plough.
Recruit, The.
Soldier from the wars returning.
Street sounds to the soldiers' tread, The.
Hughes, L.　Battle Ground.
Casualty.
Colored Soldier, The.
Dear Mr. President.
Expendable.
Madam and the Army.
Poem to a Dead Soldier.
When the Armies Passed.
Will V-Day Be Me-Day Too?
Without Benefit of Declaration.
Hughes, T.　Bayonet Charge.
Scapegoats and Rabies.
Six Young Men.
Warriors of the North, The.
Jarrell, R.　Absent with Official Leave.
Description of Some Confederate Soldiers, A.
Eighth Air Force.
Good-bye, Wendover; Good-bye, Mountain
　Home.
Gunner.
Learners, The.
Lines, The.
Lullaby, A: "For wars his life and half a world
　away."
Mail Call.
New Georgia.
O My Name It Is Sam Hall.
Port of Embarkation.
Prisoners.
Sick Nought, The.
Soldier [T. P.].
Soldier Walks under the Trees of the University,
　The.
Jonson, B.　On Sir John Roe ("What two brave
　perils of the private sword").
To Sir Horace Vere.
To Sir John Radcliffe.
To the Same; on the Same.
To True Soldiers.
Kinnell.　Vapor Trail Reflected in the Frog Pond.
Kipling, R.　Absent-Minded Beggar, The.
Arithmetic on the Frontier.
Back to the Army Again.
Ballad of East and West, The.
Belts.
"Birds of Prey" March.
Bobs.
Boots.
Bridge-Guard in the Karroo.
Brown Bess.
Cells.
Chant-Pagan.
Cholera Camp.
Columns.
Danny Deever.
Dedication from "Barrack-Room Ballads."
'Eathen, The.
Expert, The.
Follow Me 'Ome.
For All We Have and Are [1914].
Fuzzy-Wuzzy.
Gentlemen-Rankers.
Gunga Din.
Instructor, The.
Irish Guards, The.
Jacket, The.
Lichtenberg.
Loot.

M. I.
Married Man, The.
Men That Fought at Minden, The.
Oonts.
Parting of the Columns, The.
Pharaoh and the Sergeant.
Piet.
Pro-Consuls, The.
Recessional.
Return, The.
Roman Centurion's Song, The.
Route Marchin.'
Sappers.
Screw-Guns.
Service Man, The.
Shillin' a Day.
Shut-Eye Sentry, The.
Snarleyow.
Soldier an' Sailor Too.
Soldier, Soldier.
Song of the Old Guard, The.
Stellenbosch.
That Day.
To Thomas Atkins.
Tommy.
Troopin.'
Ubique.
Widow at Windsor, The.
Widow's Party, The.
Wilful-Missing.
Young British Soldier, The.
Komunyakaa.　Communiqué.
For the Walking Dead.
Short-timer's Calendar.
Kunitz, S.　Careless Love.
Customs Collector's Report, The.
Larkin, P.　Homage to a Government.
MCMXIV.
Laughlin, J.　Song of the GIs & the MGs.
Lawrence, D. H.　Guards.
Obsequial Ode.
Tommies in the Train.
Levine, P.　Planting.
To P.L., 1916–1937.
Lindsay, N.　Yankee Doodle.
Logue, C.　Song of the Imperial Carrion, The.
When I was serving my country.
MacDiarmid, H.　Another Epitaph on an Army
　of Mercenaries.
MacLeish.　Lines for an Interment.
Memorial Rain.
MacNeice.　Bottleneck.
Mallarmé.　Little Air (Martial).
McGrath, T.　All the Dead Soldiers.
Blues for Warren.
Go Ask the Dead.
In the Sleep of Reason.
Nocturne Militaire.
Ode for the American Dead in Korea.
Melville, H.　Ball's Bluff.
March into Virginia, The.
On the Grave.
Meredith, G.　Atkins.
Grandfather Bridgeman.
Merrill, J.　Peter.
Merwin.　When the War Is Over.
Milton.　When the Assault Was Intended to the
　City.
Muldoon, P.　Crossing the Line.
Narrow Road to the Deep North, The.
Truce.
Nemerov.　Fable of the War, A.
For the Squadron.
Grand Central, with Soldiers, in Early Morning.
Old Soldiers' Home, The.
Soldier Who Lived through the War, The.
Olson, C.　King's Mountain.
This Year.
Owen, W.　A Terre.
Anthem for Doomed Youth.
Apologia Pro Poemate Meo.
Arms and the Boy.
At a Calvary near the Ancre.
Disabled.
Dulce et Decorum Est.
Exposure.

Fragment: "Not one corner of a foreign field."
Futility.
Insensibility.
Mental Cases.
Send-Off, The.
Show, The.
Soldier's Dream.
Spring Offensive.
Strange Meeting.
To a Comrade in Flanders.
Training.
Paley, G.   I Gave Away That Kid.
Parker, D.   War Song.
Patchen.   Being so hideous that the air weeps blood.
Body Beside the Ties, The.
Class of 1934.
Constant Bridegrooms, The.
Known Soldier, The.
Letter to the Young Men, A.
This Man Was Your Brother.
Pope, A.   Epitaph on General Henry Withers, in Westminster-Abbey, 1729.
Rexroth, K.   Giant Weapon, The.
Riley, J.   Boy Patriot, The.
Conqueror, The.
Decoration Day on the Place.
Ezra House.
Monument for the Soldiers, A.
Old Man and Jim, The.
Silent Victors, The.
Soldier, The.
Rimbaud, A.   Centre: the Emperor, apotheosis.
Ritsos.   New Victory.
Philoctetes; The Ultimate Mask.
Ready.
Return of a Deserter.
Women.
Robinson, E.   Field of Glory, The.
Rossetti, C.   Come cheer up, my lads, 'tis to glory we steer!
Rukeyser, M.   One Soldier.
Sandburg, C.   Among the Red Guns.
And They Obey.
Buttons.
Dunes.
Fight.
House.
John Ericsson Day Memorial, 1918.
Killers.
Medallion.
Old Timers.
Places.
Remembered Women.
Simonides.   On a Military Graveyard.
Smith, S.   Private Means Is Dead.
Soldier Dear to Us, A.
Spender, S.   Stopwatch and an Ordnance Map, A.
Stafford, W.   How It Is.
My Mother Was a Soldier.
Stevens, W.   Death of a Soldier, The.
Dutch Graves in Bucks County.
Gigantomachia.
Repetitions of a Young Captain.
Suckling, S.   Soldier, A.
Tate, J.   Bluebird Houses.
Tennyson, A.   Charge of the Light Brigade, The.
Thoreau.   At midnight's hour I raised my head.
Unknown.   On Miltiades.
Verlaine.   Asleep in the Valley.
Very.   Soldier of the Cross, The.
Weiss, T.   Gunsight.
Whalen, P.   Homage to William Seward Burroughs.
Whitman, W.   Adieu to a Soldier.
Army Corps on the March, An.
Artilleryman's Vision, The.
As Toilsome I Wander'd Virginia's Woods.
Ashes of Soldiers.
Ashes of Soldiers: Epigraph.
Bravest Soldiers, The.
By the Bivouac's Fitful Flame.
Camps of Green.
Cavalry Crossing a Ford.
Centenarian's Story, The.

How Solemn as One by One.
I Saw Old General at Bay.
March in the Ranks Hard-Prest, and the Road Unknown, A.
O Tan-Faced Prairie-Boy.
Race of Veterans.
Sight in Camp [in the Daybreak Gray and Dim], A.
Spirit Whose Work Is Done.
Vigil Strange I Kept on the Field One Night.
Wound-Dresser, The.
Whittier.   Lost Occasion, The.
Wilbur, R.   Place Pigalle.
Williams, C. K.   Creams.
Williams, M.   For Jordan with Love the Eighth Year of the Slaughter: A Minuet for Army Boots and Orchestra.
Voice of America.
Williams, T.   Reveille.
Wordsworth, W.   Character of the Happy Warrior.
Epigram on an Event in Col. Evans's Redoubted Performances in Spain.
Pelayo.
Squib on Colonel Evans, A.
Wright, J.   Confession to J. Edgar Hoover.
Speak.
Yeats.   Irish Airman Foresees His Death, An.
Zagajewski.   River, A.
September Afternoon in the Abandoned Barracks.
Twenty-Year-Old Soldiers.
See also **War**

Solidarity
Celan.   Afternoon with Circus and Citadel.
In One.
Shibboleth.
Hughes, L.   Always the Same.
Broadcast to the West Indies.
Chant for May Day.
Open Letter to the South.
Union.
We, Too.
Kizer, C.   Union of Women.

Solipsism
Atwood.   Solipsism While Dying.
Brontë, E.   It's over now; I've known it all.
Creeley.   La Noche.
Not Again.
Cunningham, J.   Solipsist, The.
Housman.   I Counsel You Beware.
Oppen.   Speech at Soli, The.
Plath.   Soliloquy of the Solipsist.
Warren, R.   Interjection #5: Solipsism and Theology.

Solitude
Amichai [*or* Amikhai].   Flock of Sheep near the Airport, A.
My Mother Once Told Me.
Travels of the Last Benjamin of Tudela.
Apollinaire.   Mirabeau Bridge.
Atwood.   Georgia Beach.
Auden.   Alone.
Two Climbs.
Baudelaire.   Melancholy Moon, The.
Wine of the Solitary Man, The.
Beckett, S.   Bois seul.
Bon bon il est un pays.
Lueurs lisières.
Berry, W.   Cold, The.
Except.
Stay Home.
Berryman.   Meditation.
Song of the Man Forsaken and Obsessed.
Blue Cloud.   Tsier.
Bly, R.   After Long Busyness.
Falling Asleep.
"Out of the Rolling Ocean, the Crowd . . ."
Six Winter Privacy Poems.
Solitude Late at Night in the Woods.
Borges.   Saturday, A.
Someone.
Stranger, The.
Streets, The.
Susana Bombal.
Brontë, E.   And like myself lone, wholly lone.

Away, away, resign me now.
Blue bell is the sweetest flower, The.
I am the only being whose doom.
Little while, a little while, A.
Redbreast, Early in the morning.
That wind, I used to hear it swelling.
There are two trees in a lonely field.
To Imagination.
Written in Aspin Castle.
Broumas, O.   Memory Piece / for Baby Jane.
Browning, R.   Aeschylus' Soliloquy.
Amphibian.
Prologue: "O the old wall here! How I could pass."
Bukowski.   2nd Novel, The.
Chopin Bukowski.
Defeat.
Hangover and Sick Leave.
Patriot of Life, A.
Somebody Always Breaking My Dainty Solitude.
Burns, R.   Song: "Had I a cave on some wild, distant shore."
Strathallan's Lament.
Byron, G.   Lines: "Dear Becher, you tell me to mix with mankind."
Carruth, H.   Alive.
Living Alone.
Simple.
Carver, R.   Company.
Rest, The.
Chuang Tzu.   Tower of the Spirit, The.
Clare, J.   I Am.
Love and Solitude.
Song: "I peeled bits of straw and I got switches too."
Cooper, J.   Builder of Houses, The.
Earthquake, The.
Cowper, W.   Alexander Selkirk.
Inscription for a Bust of Homer.
Inscription for a Moss-House.
To the Nightingale.
Creeley.   Flower, The.
Loner.
One.
Cummings, E. E.   Among / these / red pieces of.
BrIght / bRight s??? big / (soft).
Dim / i / nu / tiv / e this park is e.
I will cultivate within.
Nothing is more exactly terrible than.
Davie, D.   Or, Solitude.
Pietà.
De la Mare.   April Moon.
Captive, The.
Epitaph, An: "Last, Stone, a little yet."
Estranged.
Haunted.
I Sit Alone.
Solitude.
Dickey, J.   Gila Bend.
Heads.
One, The.
Three, The.
Dickinson, E.   Society for me my misery.
There is a solitude of space.
This Is My Letter to the World.
Dove, R.   Daystar.
Weathering Out.
Dugan, A.   American against Solitude.
Conspiracy of Two against the World.
Untitled Poem: "City is empty, like a dangerous area, The."
Dunbar, P.   Career, A.
Lost Dream, A.
Duncan, R.   Passage over Water.
Eberhart, R.   Ode to Silence.
Éluard, P.   Universe-Solitude.
Emerson, R.   As I walked in the woods.
Civil world will much forgive, The.
Comrade of the snow & wind.
I am alone. Sad is my solitude.
I have no brothers & no peers.
Lover's Petition.
Manners.
O What have I to do.
Pale Genius roves alone.

Enzensberger, H.   Camera Obscura.
Ironmonger's Shop, The.
Fenton, J.   Chosun.
Vacant Possession, A.
Frost, R.   Acquainted with the Night.
Desert Places.
Good Hours.
Most of It, The.
Gallagher, T.   Amplitude.
On Your Own.
García Lorca.   Ballad of Black Pain.
Ballad of the Marked Man.
Solitude.
Glück, L.   12. 6. 71.
Graves, R.   Singleness in Love.
Song: Crown of Stars.
Unicorn and the White Doe.
Gunn, T.   L'Epreuve.
Gurney, I.   Walking Song.
Guyon.   Child of God Longing to See Him
   Beloved, A.
God Neither Known nor Loved by the World.
Happy Solitude—Unhappy Men.
Love Faithful in the Absence of the Beloved.
Love Increased by Suffering.
Scenes Favourable to Meditation.
Secrets of Divine Love Are to Be Kept, The.
Self-Love and Truth Incompatible.
Watching unto God in the Night-Season.
Hacker, M.   Dear Jool, I Miss You in Saint-
   Saturnin.
Going Back to the River.
Home, and I've.
Han-shan.   Beneath high cliffs I live alone.
Clambering up the Cold Mountain path.
Cold Cliff's remoteness is what I like.
Cold Mountain is nothing but clouds.
Give me a hidden eddy.
Mountain I live on, The.
Where clouds and mountains are piled to the
   sky.
Hardy, T.   Midnight on Beechen, 187–.
Hayden, R.   Road in Kentucky, A.
Herrick.   His Wish to Privacie.
Meat without Mirth.
Not to Love.
To Julia.
Upon the Loss[e] of His Mistresses.
Hopkins, G.   Heaven-Haven.
Hughes, L.   Reverie on the Harlem River.
Soledad.
Hughes, T.   Thought-Fox, The.
Jacobsen, J.   Country Bath.
They Never Were Found.
Jarrell, R.   90 North.
Ghost, a Real Ghost, A.
Le Poète Contumace.
Jeffers, R.   Fog.
Pleasures.
Keats.   Bright Star.
O Solitude! If I Must with Thee Dwell.
Kinnell.   When One Has Lived a Long Time
   Alone.
Kipling, R.   For to Admire.
Larkin, P.   Best Society.
Kick Up the Fire, and Let the Flames Break
   Loose.
Reasons for Attendance.
Ugly Sister.
Wants.
Lawrence, D. H.   Deeper than Love.
Delight of Being Alone.
Desire.
Effort of Love, The.
Image-Making Love.
Lonely, Lonesome, Loney—O!
Man Reaches a Point.
People.
Song of a Man Who Is Not Loved.
Tarantella.
Uprooted, The.
Levertov.   Life in the Forest.
Living Alone (1).
Living Alone (2).
Living Alone (3).
Losing Track.

Poem: "Some are too much at home in the role
   of wanderer."
Shalom.
Strange Song.
Way It Is, The.
Woman Alone, A.
Levi, P.   Monday.
MacLeish.   Definition of the Frontiers.
MacNeice.   Lake in the Park, The.
Postcript to Iceland.
Solitary Travel.
Marvell.   Garden, The.
McGrath, T.   Emblems of Exile.
From a Long Way Out of Pah-Gatzin-Kay.
Letter for Marian, A.
Near Pah-Gotzin-Kay.
Night Work.
Ordonnance.
Perpetual Motion.
Poem: "You out there, so secret."
Progress of the Soul, The.
Return, The.
Topography of History, The.
Meredith, G.   If thou art sorrowful, hide thy
   face!
Sleeping City, The.
Merrill, J.   Hourglass.
Merton.   Song for Nobody.
Song: If You Seek.
Song: "When rain, (sings light) rain has
   devoured my house."
Things and people goodbye / It is not that I
   prefer.
Merwin.   Pause by the Water.
Milton.   Il Penseroso.
Mistral, G.   Useless Vigil, The.
Nemerov.   Loon's Cry, The.
Observation of October.
Paraphrase from Notebooks.
Small Moon.
These Words Also.
Winter Exercise.
Neruda.   Another.
Egoist.
Some Creature.
Niedecker.   Alone / a still state hard.
Shut up in woods.
T. E. Lawrence.
O'Hara, F.   1951.
Autobiographia Literaria.
Essay on Style.
Poem: "Eager note on my door said "Call me,"
   The."
Rant, A.
Parker, D.   Sanctuary.
Pasolini.   Beautiful Banners, The.
Lines from the Testament.
Petrarch.   My wish has always been to live
   alone.
You were a haven once, my little room.
Piercy.   All Clear.
Death of the Small Commune, The.
Going In.
Pinkerton, H.   On Vermeer's *Young Woman with
   a Water Jug* (1658) in the Metropolitan
   Museum.
Plath.   Wuthering Heights.
Pope, A.   Ode on Solitude.
Prunty.   Kite, The.
Ralegh, S.   Like to a Hermit[e] Poor[e].
Rexroth, K.   On Flower Wreath Hill.
Still on Water.
Rich, A.   Night in the Kitchen.
Roadway, The.
Riley, J.   Country Pathway, A.
Rilke.   Solitude.
Rimbaud, A.   Tear.
Ritsos.   After the Breakdown of the Treaty
   between the Lacedaemonians and the
   Athenians.
Robinson, E.   Aaron Stark.
Tree in Pamela's Garden, The.
Roethke.   Pure Fury, The.
Rossetti, C.   Autumn.
Hopeless Case, A.
L. E. L.

Novice, The.
Scarce tolerable life, which all life long.
Solitary Rose, The.
Rukeyser, M.   Key, The.
Pouring Milk Away.
Speech for the Assistant, from Houdini.
Rumi.   Which is worth more, a crowd of
   thousands.
Sandburg, C.   Have Me.
Sarton, M.   Gestalt at Sixty.
Glass of Water, A.
House in Winter, The.
Sexton.   For John, Who Begs Me Not to
   Enquire Further.
Shelley, P.   Fragment: Thoughts Come and Go
   in Solitude.
Solitary, The.
Sonnet: Political Greatness.
Stanzas—April, 1814.
Simic.   Chairs.
Immortal Prankster.
Solitude.
Smith, S.   Failed Spirit, The.
Forgive Me, Forgive Me.
Forgot!
Lot's Wife.
Recluse, The.
Snyder, G.   In a tangle of cliffs I chose a place.
I've lived at Cold Mountain—how many
   autumns.
Mid-August at Sourdough Mountain Lookout.
Stafford, W.   Peleg Lookout.
So Long.
We Interrupt to Bring You.
Stevens, W.   No Possum, No Sop, No Taters.
Stock, R.   Patio.
Solo for Four.
Stockton, A.   Ode to Solitude Inscribed to Mrs
   Boudinot, An.
Tate, A.   Light.
Tate, J.   Pride's Crossing.
Tennyson, A.   Palace of Art, The.
Thomas, D.   Ears in the Turrets Hear.
Hunchback in the Park, The.
Tollas, T.   Prison Poem.
Tomlinson, C.   Chaconne for Unaccompanied
   Violin.
Farmer's Wife: at Fostons Ash, The.
Updike.   Oddly Lovely Day Alone, An.
Pillow.
Solitary Pond, The.
Van Geel.   Sleepwalking.
Very.   I Was Sick and in Prison.
Walcott.   Letter from Brooklyn, A.
Winding Up.
Walker, A.   Be Nobody's Darling.
These Mornings of Rain.
Warren, R.   Better Than Counting Sheep.
No Bird Does Call.
Whitman, W.   I Saw in Louisiana a Live-Oak
   Growing.
Wilbur, R.   Clearness.
Williams, C. K.   On the Roof.
Solid, The.
Trappers.
Williams, M.   Prison.
Williams, T.   Lady with No One at All, The.
Williams, W.   Danse Russe.
Wordsworth, W.   Cento Made by Wordsworth,
   A.
For the Spot Where the Hermitage Stood on St
   Herbert's Island, Derwent-Water.
Solitary Reaper, The.
There is an Eminence,—of these our hills.
These Chairs they have no words to utter.
Written in Very Early Youth.
Wright, C.   Reply to Wang Wei.
Wright, J.   Echo for the Promise of Georg
   Trakl's Life.
Prayer to Escape from the Market Place, A.
Two Postures beside a Fire.
Yeats.   Apparitions, The.
Lake-Isle of Innisfree, The.
Zagajewski.   History of Solitude, A.
In the Beauty Created by Others.
Zukofsky, L.   Even if love convey.

Judge and the Bird, The.
Solomon (Bible)
Amichai [or Amikhai].　Visit of the Queen of
　Sheba, The.
Browning, R.　Solomon and Balkis.
Graves, R.　Solomon's Seal.
Herbert, G.　Sion.
Hill, G.　Solomon's Mines.
Major, C.　Dispute, The.
Merton.　King Solomon: my master and the
　imbeciles.
Moore, M.　O to Be A Dragon.
Nemerov.　False Solomon's Seal.
Rossetti, C.　Consider the Lilies of the Field.
Rumi.　Bird delegation came to Solomon
　complaining, A.
Far Mosque, The.
Gnats inside the Wind.
Sheba's Gifts to Solomon.
Sheba's Hesitation.
Sheba's Throne.
Solomon to Sheba.
Solomon's Crooked Crown.
Whittier.　King Solomon and the Ants.
Yeats.　On Woman.
Solomon and the Witch.
Solomon to Sheba.
Somerset, England
Clampitt.　Exmoor.
Coleridge, S.　This Lime-Tree Bower My Prison.
Davie, D.　Somerset.
Songs
Apollinaire.　Rhenish Night.
Berry, W.　Bird Killer, The.
Silence, The.
Song (3).
Song Sparrow Singing in the Fall, A.
Bishop, E.　Songs for a Colored Singer.
Sonnet: "I am in need of music that would
　flow."
Blue Cloud.　Girl Child.
Browning, E.　Deserted Garden, The.
Last Translation, The.
Byron, G.　Here's to Her Who Long.
In the Valley of Waters.
To the Hon. Mrs. George Lamb.
Campion, T.　Peacefull westerne winde the
　wintrye stormes hath calmde, The.
Cavafy.　Voice from the Sea.
Coleridge, S.　Tribute to Wordsworth.
Crane, H.　Song for Happy Feast Days, A.
Crane, S.　Once, I knew a fine song.
Creeley.　Fragments: "Decorous, and forbearing
　further correction."
Here ("Little earth, water").
Mary's Fancy.
Song, A: "I had wanted a quiet testament."
Davie, D.　Cypress Avenue, The.
De la Mare.　Fool's Song, The.
Interlude, An.
Linnet, The.
Nocturne: "'Tis not my voice now speaks; but
　as a bird."
Rooks in October.
Sotto Voce.
Dickey, J.　Buckdancer's Choice.
Donne.　Triple Fool, The.
Dunbar, P.　Compensation.
Corn-Song, A.
Joggin' Erlong.
Just Whistle a Bit.
Keep a Song Up on de Way.
Ol' Tunes, The.
Poet and his Song, The.
Prometheus.
Remembered.
Songs.
Duncan, R.　Reaper, The.
Eberhart, R.　Evening Bird Song.
Later or Sooner.
Sacrifice, The.
Thrush Song at Dawn.
To William Carlos Williams.
Ultimate Song.
Emerson, R.　Blackbird's song the blackbird's
　song, The.

Dull uncertain brain, A.
If bright the sun, he tarries.
Merlin's Song.
Music.
To Ellen, at the South.
Fenton, J.　Killer Snails, The.
Nothing.
Song That Sounds like This, The.
Ferlinghetti, L.　Dove sta amore / Where lies
　love.
Gallagher, T.　If Poetry Were Not a Morality.
García Lorca.　Ballad of the Little Square.
Graves, R.　Grace Notes.
Haunted House, The.
Gurney, I.　Had I a Song.
Songs Come to the Mind.
"H. D."　If You Will Let Me Sing.
Hall, D.　Whip-Poor-Will.
Hardy, T.　Any Little Old Song.
Bridge of Lodi, The.
Donaghadee.
On the Tune Called the Old-Hundred-and-
　Fourth.
Sitting on the Bridge.
Hughes, L.　Cat and the Saxophone (2 a.m.),
　The.
Gypsy Melodies.
Songs.
Sun Song.
Keats.　On the Grasshopper and [the] Cricket.
Song: "Stay, ruby-breasted warbler, stay."
Larkin, P.　Love Songs in Age.
Lawrence, D. H.　Children Singing in School.
Song of Death.
Lindsay, N.　In Praise of Songs That Die.
Last Song of Lucifer, The.
Longfellow, H.　Day Is Done, The.
MacLeish.　Linden Branch, The.
Lost Speakers, The.
MacNeice.　Off the Peg.
McGrath, T.　Little Song about Charity, A.
Meredith, G.　Lark Ascending, The.
Rhine-Land.
Olson, C.　Name-Day Night.
Song, The: "More than the sennet of the solstice
　pipe."
Pinsky.　Song of Reasons.
Riley, J.　Nonsense Rhyme, A.
Old Played-out Song, A.
Order for A Song, An.
Scraps.
Roethke.　Light Listened.
Reply, The.
Song, The: "I met a ragged man."
Voice, The.
Rossetti, C.　Blind from my birth, / Where
　flowers are springing.
Heaven Is Heaven.
In the Day of His Espousals.
Key-Note, The.
Lord, give me love that I may love Thee much.
Lord, grant us grace to rest upon Thy word.
Paradise: in a Symbol.
Summer nights are short, / Where northern days
　are long, The.
Way of the World, The.
World's Harmonies, The.
Rukeyser, M.　Another Day (I will now sing).
Another Day (Miss Lorence).
Segre Song.
This Place in the Ways.
Rumi.　Wished-For Song, A.
Sandburg, C.　Bee Song.
Evening Waterfall.
Far Rockaway Night till Morning.
Frog Songs.
Horse Fiddle.
Kansas Lessons.
Mammy Hums.
Man and Dog on an Early Winter Morning.
Potato Blossom Songs and Jigs.
Singing Nigger.
Three Violins.
Work Gangs.
Sarton, M.　Song: "Now let us honor with violin
　and flute."

Scott, S.　Hunting Song.
Sexton.　Little Uncomplicated Hymn, A.
Shelley, P.　To a Skylark.
Stafford, W.　Vocatus atque Non Vocatus.
Stock, R.　Poem to Be Printed on a Very White
　Page.
Suckling, S.　Ballad[e] [upon a Wedding], A.
Tennyson, A.　Dying Swan, The.
Very.　Childhood's Songs.
Whitman, W.　Chanting the Square Deific.
My Canary Bird.
Out of the Cradle Endlessly Rocking.
Unexpress'd, The.
Wilbur, R.　Cicadas.
Plain Song for Comadre, A.
Song, A: "As at the bottom of a seething well."
Williams, W.　Botticellian Trees, The.
I Will Sing a Joyous Song.
Rendezvous.
Sicilian Emigrant's Song.
Wordsworth, W.　Reverie of Poor Susan, The.
Wright, J.　Cold Divinities, The.
Humming a Tune for an Old Lady in West
　Virginia.
Morality of Poetry, The.
Poem for Kathleen Ferrier.
Written in a Copy of Swift's Poems, for Wayne
　Burns.
Yeats.　Coat, A.
Lover Speaks to the Hearers of His Songs in
　Coming Days, The.
Three Marching Songs.
Zukofsky, L.　Letter of Poor Birds, The.
What are these songs.
Sonnets
Bogan, L.　Single Sonnet.
Brodsky, J.　Twenty Sonnets to Mary Queen of
　Scots.
Burns, R.　Sonnet upon Sonnets, A.
Collins, B.　American Sonnet.
Sonnet: "All we need is fourteen lines, well,
　thirteen now."
Creeley.　Apology, The.
Donne.　Canonization, The.
Drummond de Andrade.　Irritated Office, The.
Dunbar, P.　Poet and the Baby, The.
Keats.　If by Dull Rhymes Our English Must Be
　Chained.
Poe.　Enigma, An.
Riley, J.　To James Newton Matthews.
Rossetti, C.　To My First Love, My Mother.
Stafford, W.　Putting the Sonnet to Work.
Wordsworth, W.　Scorn not the Sonnet; Critic,
　you have frowned.
Sonnet: "Nuns fret not at their convent's narrow
　room."
Sonora Desert
Hamill, S.　George Seferis in Sonora.
Sons
Amichai [or Amikhai].　Aged Parents, The.
Arab Shepherd Is Searching for His Goat on
　Mount Zion, An.
My Son.
My Son, My Son, My Head, My Head.
My son, the softness of your face already
　shows.
My son was born in Asuta hotital and since
　then.
To Bake the Bread of Yearning.
Your Life and Death, Father.
Armantrout.　Fiction ("When the woman's face
　contorted and she clutched the railing for
　support, we knew she would die").
Berry, W.　Gathering, The.
Poem for J.
Berryman.　Sympathy, a Welcome, A.
Bly, R.　Prodigal Son, The.
Borges.　To the Son.
Bradstreet, A.　On My Son's Return Out of
　England.
Upon My Son Samuel His Going For England.
Brodsky, J.　Odysseus to Telemachus.
Byron, G.　To My Son.
Campion, T.　To the Most Sacred Queen Anne.
Carruth, H.　Little Fire in the Woods, The.
Missing the Bo in the Henhouse.

Of Brook and Stone.
Smallish Son, The.
Song: The Young Man with the Guitar, Testing.
Carver, R. Child, The.
Mother.
On an Old Photograph of My Son.
Photograph of My Father in His Twenty-second Year.
Son.
Celan. Flower.
For Eric.
Ciardi, J. Dear Sir.
For My Son John.
One Morning.
Poem for Benn's Graduation from High School, A.
Prayer to the Mountain, A.
Two Poems for Benn.
Clifton, L. Donor.
Wishes for Sons.
Codrescu. Talismanic Ceremony for Lucian, March 9, 1971, Intersection Church, San Francisco.
Coleridge, S. Sonnet on Receiving a Letter Informing Me of the Birth of a Son.
To the Rev. George Coleridge.
Corbett, W. Bridgeport Station.
Creeley. Variation, A.
Cunningham, J. Dear child whom I begot.
"Dario." To Phocas the Peasant.
De la Mare. Virtue.
Dickey, J. Bee, The.
Birth, A.
Fathers and Sons.
Drummond de Andrade. Travelling in the Family.
Dugan, A. Portrait.
Duncan, R. My Mother Would Be a Falconress.
Eberhart, R. Examination of Psyche: Thoughts of Home.
Emerson, R. What from this barren being do we reap.
Gallagher, T. Each Bird Walking.
García Lorca. Silly Song.
Glück, L. Seconds.
Hall, D. Fathers and Sons.
My Son, My Executioner.
HaNagid. To Yehosef, His Son.
Hardy, T. Geographical Knowledge.
Whitewashed Wall, The.
Heaney, S. Errand, The.
Mother of the Groom.
Herrick. Correction.
Hughes, L. Mother to Son.
Mulatto.
Hughes, T. Revenge Fable.
Ignatow, D. Bread Itself, The.
Envoi: "Strange judgment upon me."
Father and Son.
Requiem, A: "My father, listening to music, that's me."
Rightful One, The.
Stranger.
Jonson, B. On My First Son[ne].
To My L[ord] the King, on the Christening His Second Son James.
Kinnell. After Making Love We Hear Footsteps.
Kipling, R. My Boy Jack.
Recantation, A.
Sons of Martha, The.
Komunyakaa. Bui Doi, Dust of Life.
Moonshine.
Kunitz, S. Father and Son.
Laughlin, J. Building 520, Bellevue.
Experience of Blood.
Generations, The.
Sorrow.
Levertov. Son, A.
Son, The.
Levine, P. Face, The.
Look.
Starlight.
Logan, J. Ah, so our first load of honey heavy Christmas trees.
Coming of Age.

Day in the Sun, A.
Far off the road on the left on a slight rolling hill.
I did but taste a little of the honey with the.
If the half moon stamp of a sacred hoof showed Cadmus.
In my dream I know I see my father Saul a king.
Lament for Misenus.
Letter to My Son.
Lines for His Son in Satin.
Monologues of the Son of Saul.
Papa's House, Son's Room.
Poem for My Son.
McGrath, T. Enemy, The.
Poem: "My little son comes running with open arms!"
Meredith, G. Ah! little Angel, child of bliss!
And tho' my friar's mandate is severe.
Dear Heaven! for this sweet pledge of life.
Dear, my friend & honour'd madam! of hard facts I'm not a hoarder.
Of Robin Redbreast's babes I told.
Periander.
Shipwreck of Idomeneus, The.
When my little son leaps in my sight.
Yet what is this? the spring returns.
Merwin. Houses, The.
Son.
Yesterday.
Milton. To My Father.
Olson, C. In an Automotive Store.
On the equator east of my son I Orion bequeath to him my riches.
Orr, G. Fast, The.
Talk, The.
Paley, G. Boy His Mother, The.
Pasolini. Appendix to the "Religion": A Light.
Plath. For a Fatherless Son.
Prunty. Saying it Back.
Ramanujan. Moulting.
Son to Father to Son.
Rich, A. Jerusalem.
Riley, J. His Mother.
Mother.
Rilke. From Father to Son.
Robinson, E. Old King Cole.
Rossetti, C. Johnny.
Sexton. Hangman, The.
Two Sons.
Simic. Spoons with Realistic Dead Flies on Them.
Smith, S. Correspondence between Mr. Harrison in Newcastle and Mr. Sholto Peach Harrison in Hull.
Upon a Grave.
Stafford, W. Crossing Our Campground.
Father and Son.
Memorial: Son Bret, A.
Stockton, A. Impromptu on the Morning of my Sons Weding Day Which Was Ushered in by a Fall of Snow and Soon after Cleared by a Very Bright Sun.
To Richard John Stockton Esqr, Inclosing the Preceding Elegy [Feb. 28, 1787].
Tate, A. Mother and Son.
Tate, J. For Mother on Father's Day.
Warren, R. Mr. Dodd's Son.
Night Walking.
Only Poem, The.
Ways of Day.
Weiss, T. Youngest Son, The.
Whalen, P. For My Father.
Whitman, W. Dirge for Two Veterans.
Vigil Strange I Kept on the Field One Night.
Williams, C. K. Easter.
Instinct.
Williams, M. For Robert, Son of Man.
Good Son, A.
Williams, W. Genesis.
Wordsworth, W. Affliction of Margaret, The.
Wright, J. Father.
First Principles.
Having Lost My Sons, I Confront the Wreckage of the Moon: Christmas, 1960.
Non-Birthday Poem for My Father, A.

Revelation, The.
Two Postures beside a Fire.
Youth.
Yeats. Prayer for My Son, A.
Zukofsky, L. Record, The.
So That Even a Lover.

Sophism and Sophists
Cavafy. Enemies, The.
Herodis Attikos.
Hospitality of Lagides, The.
Salome.
Stockton, A. Epigram Addressed to Two Clergymen Who Had Been Trying in Jest to Put Some Constructions on the Conversation That Was Not Meant, An.

Sophocles
Arnold, M. Dover Beach.
To a Friend.
Wilde, O. Vision, A.

Sorcery and Sorcerers
Graves, R. At Best, Poets.
Lindsay, N. Sorceress!, The.

Sorrow
Amichai [or Amikhai]. Psalm: "Psalm on the day, A."
Rosebush Hangs over the Wall, A.
Such as Sorrow.
Ammons. Convergence.
Dark Song.
Ashbery, J. Variant.
Baudelaire. Black Bile ("When heavy, threatening skies weigh like a lid").
Beckett, S. Enueg II.
Poem: "I would like my love to die."
Samedi répit.
Berryman. Fare Well.
Bogan, L. If We Take All Gold.
Borges. Shinto.
Bourne, V. No Sorrow Peculiar to the Sufferer.
Bradstreet, A. For the Restoration of My Dear Husband from a Burning Ague.
Brodsky, J. To Urania.
Brontë, E. From our evening fireside now.
Geraldine.
Harp of wild and dream-like strain.
I am the only being whose doom.
Inspiring music's thrilling sound, The.
Lady to Her Guitar, The.
May flowers are opening.
O God of heaven! the dream of horror.
Redbreast, Early in the morning.
She dried her tears, and they did smile.
Spellbound.
Browning, E. Court Lady, A.
Cry of the Children, The.
Dead Rose, A.
Last Translation, The.
Mask, The.
My Heart and I.
My Kate.
Psyche Wafted by Zephyrus.
Year's Spinning, A.
Bukowski. All I Know.
Burns, R. Banks o' Doon, The ("Ye banks and braes o' bonie [or bonnie] Doon").
Cares o' love are sweeter far, The.
Craigieburn-Wood—A Song.
Despondency, an Ode.
Fair Eliza.
Fair Jenny.
Gloomy December.
Man Was Made to Mourn, a Dirge.
Musing on the roaring ocean.
Red, Red Rose, A.
Saw Ye My Phely (Quasi Dicat, Phillis).
Song: "Farewell, thou stream that winding flows."
Sonnet on the Death of Robert Riddel, Esq. of Glen Riddel, April 1794.
Wae Is My Heart.
Where Helen Lies.
Byron, G. And Dost Thou Ask the Reason of My Sadness?
By the Rivers of Babylon We Sat Down and Wept.
Impromptu, in Reply to a Friend.

My Soul Is Dark.
Oh! Weep for Those.
Campion, T. Beauty Is but a Painted Hell.
Campion, T. *et al.* Let him that will be free and keep his h[e]art from care.
No grave for woe, yet earth my watrie teares devoures.
Carew, T. Conquest by Flight.
Epitaph on the Lady Mary Villiers.
Lover, upon an Accident Necessitating His Departure, Consults with Reason, A.
Parting, Celia Weeps.
To Celia, upon Love's Ubiquity.
Upon the Sickness of E.S.
Carruth, H. Essay.
For Papa.
Marshall Washer.
Reflexive.
Cavafy. Good and Bad Weather.
Timolaos the Syracusan.
Cavalcanti. Ballata: In Exile at Sarzana.
Ballata: Of his Lady among other Ladies.
If I ask Pity not to be.
Since I must bear a sorrowing heart.
We sad, despondent quills.
You see me—one who goes crying.
Chaucer. Anelida and Arcite.
Balade of Complaint, A.
Book of the Duchesse, The.
Complaint unto His Lady, A.
Complaynt d'Amours.
Clifton, L. Sorrow Song.
Coleridge, S. Anthem for the Children of Christ's Hospital.
Cowper, W. Bid adieu, my sad heart, bid adieu to thy peace.
Shrubbery, The.
Crane, S. Intrigue.
Crashaw. Alexias.
To Pontius Washing His Blood-Stained Hands.
Creeley. Late Comer, The.
Cullen, C. Any Human to Another.
Lament: "Now let all lovely things embark."
Love Tree, The.
Pagan Prayer.
Saturday's Child.
Two Who Crossed a Line (She Crosses).
Variations on a Theme.
Cummings, E. E. Always before your voice my soul.
But being not amazing:without love.
My little heart is so wonderfully sorry.
Though your sorrows not.
Dante Alighieri. Sonnet: On the 9th of June 1290.
"Dario." To Phocas the Peasant.
Davie, D. Skelpick.
De la Mare. At Ease.
Dove, The.
Forgiveness.
Ghost, The.
Hamlet.
Old Summerhouse, The.
Stratagem, The.
Dickinson, E. Faithful "I am sorry," A.
I wish I might say one liquid word.
Love's stricken "why."
One need not be a Chamber—to be Haunted.
Sorrow almost resents love.
Sorrow, benighted with Fathoms.
That Sorrow dare to touch the Loved.
There are Sweets of Pathos.
To divulge itself is Sorrow's Right.
We read the words but know them not.
Donne. Lamentations of Jeremy, for the Most Part According to Tremeullius.
Dunbar, P. Song, The: "My soul, lost in the music's mist."
We Wear the Mask.
Duncan, R. Among My Friends.
Kingdom of Jerusalem, The.
Éluard, P. Scarcely Disfigured.
Emerson, R. Bended to fops who bent to him.
I am an exile from my home; heavily.
Where art thou / Thou beautiful dream.
Yet sometimes to the sorrow stricken.

Ferlinghetti, L. Elegy to Dispel Gloom, An.
Frost, R. Love and a Question.
My November Guest.
Gallagher, T. Four Dancers at an Irish Wedding.
Stepping Outside.
García Lorca. Autumn Song.
Casida of the Golden Girl.
Crossroad.
Elegy: "Like a censer filled with desire."
Minor Song.
Narcissus.
Glück, L. Elms.
Portland, 1968.
Return, The.
Seated Figure.
Graves, R. Dream of Hell, A.
Hooded Flame.
Lost Love.
Love as Lovelessness.
Primrose Bed, The.
Song: Though Once True Lovers.
Song: Victims of Calumny.
Wand, The.
Guyon. Joy of the Cross, The.
Testimony of Divine Adoption, The.
Hacker, M. Separate Lives.
Hamill, S. What the Water Knows.
Hardy, T. Going, The.
I Rose and Went to Rou'tor Town.
Penance.
Sunday Morning Tragedy, A.
Heaney, S. Wanderer, The.
Herbert, G. Joseph's Coat.
Herrick. Bad Season Makes the Poet Sad, The.
Griefe.
Miseries.
On Himselfe.
Roaring.
Sauce for Sorrowes.
Sin and Strife.
Sorrowes.
Sorrows Succeed.
To Dianeme.
To His Angrie God.
To the Willow-Tree.
Upon Her Weeping.
Hill, G. Sorrel.
Housman. They say my verse is sad: no wonder.
When first my way to fair I took.
Hsüeh T'ao. Weaving Love-Knots.
Hughes, L. Island ("Wave of sorrow").
Night: Four Songs.
Song for Billie Holiday.
Troubled Woman.
Jeffers, R. Distant Rainfall.
Steelhead, Wild Pig, the Fungus.
Keats. O Thou Whose Face Hath Felt the Winter's Wind.
Ode to a Nightingale.
Think Not of It, Sweet One, So.
Welcome Joy, and Welcome Sorrow.
Kipling, R. Power of the Dog, The.
Song in the Desert, A.
Komunyakaa. When Loneliness Is a Man.
Larkin, P. Many Famous Feet Have Trod.
Lawrence, D. H. Goodnight.
Grey Evening.
Human Face, The.
Loss.
Sympathy.
Levertov. Blue Rim of Memory, The.
To Speak.
Levi, P. Crow's Song, The.
Levine, P. Red Dust.
Li Yü. Bella Donna Iu.
MacLeish. Before March.
Meredith, G. Joy Is Fleet.
Sorrows and Joys.
We sat beneath the humming pines.
Merrill, J. Black Swan, The.
Merwin. Economy.
Michelangelo Buonarroti. If sorrow makes one beautiful (it's said).
Millay, E. Kin to Sorrow.
Sorrow.

Milton. Lycidas.
Neruda. Oliverio Girondo.
Niedecker. Sorrow moves in wide waves.
Why can't I be happy.
O'Hara, F. Aus Einem April.
Owen, W. Roads Also, The.
Winter Song.
Parker, D. Anecdote.
Autumn Valentine.
Ballade of a Great Weariness.
Fulfilment.
Light of Love.
Post-Graduate.
Rainy Night.
Temps Perdu.
There Was One.
Pessoa. Lightly, listlessly, my thoughts.
Petrarch. Air weighed down, and the oppressive cloud, The.
Clear, fresh, and pleasant water.
I have by now my sixteenth year of sighs.
Unless, through blind desire which breaks the heart.
Poe. Bridal Ballad.
Haunted Palace, The.
To ———: "I heed not that my earthly lot."
Valley of Unrest, The.
Pound, E. Song of the Bowmen of Shu.
Raine, K. Spell against Sorrow.
Two Invocations of Death.
Ralegh, S. Like to a Hermit[e] Poor[e].
Rexroth, K. Delia Rexroth ("Under your illkempt yellow roses").
Riley, J. Ballad from April, A.
Their Sweet Sorrow.
We Are Not Always Glad When We Smile.
We to Sigh Instead of Sing.
Rossetti, C. Acme.
Ah welladay and wherefore am I here?
Chruchyard Song of Patient Hope, A.
Daughter of Eve, A.
Dost Thou Not Care?
Good Friday.
Goodbye in fear, goodbye in sorrow.
I Gave a Sweet Smell.
I sit a queen, and am no widow, and shall see no sorrow.
Lord, give me love that I may love Thee much.
Luscious and Sorrowful.
Memento Mori.
Of each sad word which is more sorrowful.
One woe is past. Come what come will.
Our Mothers, lovely women pitiful; / Our sisters, gracious in their life and death.
Patience must dwell with Love, for Love and Sorrow.
Present and Future.
Remember [Me].
Shut Out.
Sorrow hath a double voice, / Sharp today but sweet tomorrow.
Under the ivy bush / One sits sighing.
Where love is, there comes sorrow / Today or else tomorrow.
Where shall I find a white rose blowing?
Whom the Lord Loveth He Chasteneth.
Rukeyser, M. Foghorn in Horror.
Sandburg, C. Fellow Citizens.
Poems Done on a Late Night Car.
Sarton, M. Gestalt at Sixty.
Winter Carol.
Scott, S. Spindle Song, The.
Shelley, P. To Mary Shelley.
To ———: "One word is too often profaned."
Smith, S. I Do Not Speak.
Satin-Clad.
Sorrowful Girl, The.
Stockton, A. Elegy on the Death of Mrs Dickinson. The Event Was Communicated at the Sea Shore.
Ill Penserosa, an Ode.
Lyric Ode, A.—Feb. 28.
On Hearing the Cooing of a Dove, a Song.
To Doctor Rush Enclosing the Foregoing Ode of 1782.
Swinburne. Anactoria.

In the Orchard.
Tasso. White moon, star-strewn sky.
Thoreau. Brother where dost thou dwell?
  Greater is the depth of sadness.
Trakl. Trumpets.
Villon. Complaint of the Fair Armoress [or
  Armoures], The.
Walcott. Oddjob, a Bull Terrier.
  Return to D'Ennery; Rain.
Warren, R. Filling Night with the Name:
  Funeral as Local Color.
  Mountain Plateau.
Whitman, W. Hours Continuing Long.
  I Sit and Look Out.
Wilbur, R. Song, A: "As at the bottom of a
  seething well."
Williams, C. K. After That.
  When.
Williams, T. Harp of Wales, The.
  In Jack-O'-Lantern's Weather.
Williams, W. Waiting.
  Widow's Lament in Springtime, The.
Wordsworth, W. Elegiac Verses in Memory of
  My Brother, John Wordsworth.
Wyatt, S. All ye that know of care and
  heaviness.
  Divers[e] [or Dyvers] doth[e] use, as I have
    heard and kno[w].
  I know not where my heavy sighs to hide.
  Joy so short alas, the pain so near, The.
Yeats. Cloak, the Boat, and the Shoes, The.
  Sad Shepherd, The.
Zaturenska. Affliction of William Cowper, The.
See also **Funerals; Grief; Mourning and**
Mourners

Soul
Amichai [or Amikhai]. Human Bodies.
  Man's Soul, A.
  My God, the soul you gave me.
Ammons. Terrain.
Angelou. Willie.
Atwood. Soul, Geologically, A.
Beckett, S. La nuit venue où l'âme allait.
Berryman. Defensio in Extremis.
Borges. Recoleta Cemetary.
Brontë, E. My Comforter.
  No Coward Soul Is Mine.
Broumas, O. Sweeping the Garden.
Browning, E. Felicia Hemans.
  Finite and Infinite.
  Hugh Stuart Boyd [His Death, 1848].
  Insufficiency.
  Prospect, The.
  Soul's Expression, The.
Browning, R. You are sick, that's sure—they
  say.
Burns, R. [On] Maxwell of Cardoness.
Campion, T. Are you what your faire lookes
  expresse?
Cavafy. Confusion.
  In the House of the Soul.
  Old Men's Souls, The.
  Stephanos Skilitsis.
Ciardi, J. Tenzone.
Clough. Nay draw not yet the cork, my friend.
  These vulgar ways that round me be.
Codrescu. Souls Looking for Bodies.
Coleridge, S. Body Imaging Soul.
  Psyche.
  To a Lady.
Collins, B. Night House, The.
Cortes. Dirty Souls.
Crane, H. Bridge of Estador, The.
Cullen, C. For an Evolutionist and His
  Opponent.
  Sonnet Dialogue.
Cummings, E. E. Cambridge ladies who live in
  furnished souls, The.
  Dedication: "White rose my soul, The."
  If being mortised with a dream.
  Into a truly / curving form.
  Of my / soul a street is.
  On souls robbed of their birth-right's better part.
  Out of the mountain of his soul comes.
  These people socalled were not given hearts.
  This is a rubbish of human rind.

Three wealthy sisters swore they'd never part.
"Dario." Divine Psyche, sweet invisible
  Butterfly.
I am the one who just yesterday spoke.
Davie, D. Attar of Roses.
De la Mare. Reconciliation.
  Where?
Dickey, W. Self Prepares for an Unwilling
  Journey, The.
Dickinson, E. Choice.
  Dare you see a Soul *at the White Heat?*
  Death is a Dialogue between.
  Difference between Despair, The.
  Faith—is the Pierless Bridge.
  Go slow, my soul, to feed thyself.
  He fumbles at your Soul.
  "Hope" is the thing with feathers.
  How lonesome to be an Article!
  I cannot see my soul but know 'tis there.
  Its Hour with itself.
  No Rack can torture me.
  Of nearness to her sundered Things.
  Props assist the House, The.
  Single Screw of Flesh, A.
  Soul has Bandaged moments, The.
  Soul selects her own Society, The.
  Soul should always stand ajar, The.
  Soul that hath a Guest, The.
  Soul unto itself, The.
  Soul's distinct connection, The.
  Spirit is the Conscious Ear, The.
  Spirit lasts, but in what mode, The.
  To try to speak, and miss the way.
  Too little way the House must lie.
  You cannot take itself.
Donne. Air[e] and Angels.
  Ecstasy, The.
  Funeral[l], The.
  Progress of the Soul, The.
  Resurrection, Imperfect.
  To Sir Henry Goodyer.
  To the Countess of Bedford ("Honour is so
    sublime perfection").
  To the Countess of Salisbury.
  Valediction: Forbidding Mourning, A.
Dugan, A. On Gaining a Soul.
  Poem: "Tree was wet with the moon's, The."
Dunbar, P. Ere Sleep Comes Down to Soothe
  the Weary Eyes.
  Light was on the golden sands, The.
  Vagrants.
Eberhart, R. Anima.
  Configuration.
  Emily Dickinson.
  Lucubration.
  Mistaken Identity.
  My Bones Flew Apart.
  Nothing But Change.
  Refrains.
  Rifkin Movement.
  Soul.
  Truncated Bird, The.
  Truth, The.
  Wisdom of Insecurity, The.
  Worldly Failure.
Eliot, T. S. Animula.
Emerson, R. And the best gift of God.
  Atom displaces all atoms beside, The.
  Crowning hour when bodies vie with souls, The.
  Dost thou not hear me Ellen.
  Few are free / All might be.
  Γνωθι Σεαυτον.
  I call her beautiful;—she says.
  Pale Genius roves alone.
  S. R.
  Though her eye seek other forms.
  When thy soul / Is filled with a just image fear
    not thou.
  World-Soul, The.
Glück, L. Day without Night.
  Gemini.
Graves, R. Sun-Face and Moon-Face.
  Virgin Mirror.
Guillén, J. I Want to Sleep.
Guyon. Aspirations of the Soul after God.
Hall, D. Sister by the Pond, A.

HaNagid. Know of the Limbs.
  Soul Opens inside You.
Heaney, S. Spoonbait, The.
Herbert, G. Our Life Is Hid with Christ in God.
  Virtue [or Vertue].
Herrick. Another.
  Great Spirits Supervive.
  How His Soule Came Ensnared.
  Love Palpable.
  Need.
  On Himselfe.
  Paradise.
  Soul Is the Salt, The.
  Tapers.
Hopkins, G. Caged Skylark, The.
Housman. Be still, my soul, be still; the arms
  you bear are brittle.
Jacobsen, J. Animal inside the Animal, The.
Jeffers, R. Animula.
  Cruel Falcon, The.
Kipling, R. Tomlinson.
Kumin, M. Body and Soul: A Meditation.
Larkin, P. Spirit Wooed, The.
Laughlin, J. Atman, The.
Lawrence, D. H. At a Loose End.
  At Midnight.
  Behaviour.
  End, the Beginning, The.
  Fatigue.
  Glory of Darkness.
  Healing.
  Mid-Day Verse, The.
  Moon Memory.
  Shadows.
  Souls to Save.
  Tarantella.
  There Is Rain in Me.
  Underneath.
  Unhappy Souls.
Levertov. Slowly.
  Weeping Woman.
Lindsay, N. Prayer to All the Dead Among
  Mine Own People, A.
Longfellow, H. Psalm of Life, A.
MacDiarmid, H. O Ease My Spirit.
MacLeish. Midsummer Dawn.
Marvell. Dialogue between the Resolved Soul
  and Created Pleasure, A.
  Dialogue between the Soul and [the] Body, A.
  Gallery, The.
  On a Drop of Dew.
  Ros.
McGrath, T. Revisionist Poem—Octavio Paz.
McHugh, H. Animal Song.
Meredith, G. Soul, The.
Merton. Some Bloody Mutiny.
Merwin. Animula.
  Lemuel's Blessing.
Michelangelo Buonarroti. As by subtracting,
  my lady, one creates.
  Because there's half of me which, heaven-born.
  Cecchino here has laid his body low.
  From heaven it ventured forth, there must
    return.
  Here I'm thought dead. Alive, I comforted.
  If nature now deferred to death, dejected.
  If the soul returns, that last.
  If true (and it is) that with body's final breath.
  Inside, his soul could not be outside too.
  Man within a woman—no, I'd say, A.
  My lady, you raise me so.
  No mortal object did these eyes behold.
  On earth, it's no unworthy soul that nurses.
  Soul lives on, I know it, lying here, The.
  Souls rise alive from the body's sad last bed.
  Whenever remembrance of the one I love.
Millay, E. Above These Cares.
Milosz, C. I Sleep a Lot.
Moore, M. What Are Years?
Nemerov. Flame of a Candle, The.
  Speculation.
  Spy, The.
  Tale.
  There.
Neruda. Heavy Surf, A.
  Heights of Macchu Picchu, III, The.

Niedecker. Swedenborg.
Oliver, M. Maybe.
Some Questions You Might Ask.
Olson, C. As though there were no flowing.
Assuming the Soul Is a Bitch.
Chain of memory is resurrection I am a vain man, The.
Dogwood Comes Out Yellow, The.
Love.
Of the United States.
Proper Soul / in the Proper Body, The.
Quail.
To a Poet Who Read in Gloucester before the Cape Ann Historical Literary and Scientific Society.
Oppen. Animula.
Owen, W. Fragment: "As bronze may be much beautified."
O World of Many Worlds.
Show, The.
This is the Track.
Patchen. To Be Holy, Be Wholly Your Own.
Pessoa. Note.
Petrarch. Three days before, my soul reached such a place.
Poe. Sonnet—Silence.
To One in Paradise.
Ulalume [or Ulalume—a Ballad].
Raine, K. Dead, The.
High Summer.
Night Thought.
Nocturn: "Night comes, an angel stands."
Ralegh, S. Lie, The.
Roethke. Her Reticence.
In a Dark Time.
Light Breather, A.
Motion, The.
Renewal, The.
Restored, The.
Song: "This fair parcel of summer's."
Tranced, The.
Rossetti, C. As the dove which found no rest / For the sole of her foot, flew back.
Baby's cradle with no baby in it, A.
Castle-Builder's World, A.
Confluents.
From early dawn until the flush of noon.
I Will Lift Up Mine Eyes unto the Hills.
Introspective.
O foolish Soul! to make thy count / For languid falls and much forgiven.
Of My Life.
Pause, A.
Soul rudderless, unbraced.
Study (A Soul), A.
To the End.
What is it Jesus saith unto the soul?
Ye Have Forgotten the Exhortation.
Rumi. Birdsong brings relief.
Bowl, A.
Daylight, full of small dancing particles.
Soul, The.
Talking in the Night.
Salinas, P. Not in Marble Palaces.
Sandburg, C. Under a Hat Rim.
Sarton, M. All Souls.
Sexton. Civil War, The.
God-Monger, The.
Shelley, P. Fragment: Wedded Souls.
Simic. Body and Soul.
Evening with the Master, An.
Smith, S. Animula, Vagula, Blandula.
Childe Rolandine.
Lord Barrenstock.
Man Is a Spirit.
My Soul.
Scorpion.
Spender, S. Conscript, The.
Man-Made World, A.
Spiritual Explorations.
Stevens, W. Lions in Sweden.
Swinburne. Ballad of Life, A.
Walcott. Saddhu of Couva, The.
Wheatley, P. On Being Brought from Africa to America.
Whitman, W. Come, Said My Soul.

Last Invocation, The.
Noiseless Patient Spider, A.
Whittier. My Soul and I.
Wilbur, R. Love Calls Us to the Things of This World.
Wilde, O. Hélas!
Williams, C. K. Interrogation II.
Williams, W. Man to a Woman, A.
Virtuous Agent, The.
Wordsworth, W. It is no spirit who from heaven hath flown.
Yeats. Dialogue of Self and Soul, A.
Lady's Second Song, The.
Lady's Third Song, The.
Zagajewski. Soul, The.
Zaturenska. Question, The.

Sound
Ammons. Breaks.
Viable.
Angelou. Sounds like Pearls.
Auden. Heard and Seen.
Beckett, S. Roundelay: "On all that strand."
Berrigan, T. Crystal.
Browning, E. Sounds.
Ciardi, J. Selectivity.
Size of Song, The.
Clampitt. Syrinx.
Creeley. As You Come.
Hart Crane 2.
Herd, The.
Here ("Sounds like ball").
Place ("Faded mind, / fading colors").
Sound.
Sounds.
Dickey, J. Sleepers.
Dickinson, E. Spirit is the Conscious Ear, The.
Wind, The.
Eberhart, R. Sea-Ruck.
Emerson, R. Chladni strewed on glass the sand.
From a far mountain creeping down.
Gurney, I. Midnight.
Heaney, S. Rain Stick, The.
Hughes, T. Howling of Wolves, The.
Jackson, L. Footfalling.
Jacobsen, J. Loss of Sounds.
Koch, K. Hearing.
Kumin, M. Bangkok Gang, The.
Hermit Wakes to Bird Sounds, The.
Levertov. Magic.
Overheard.
Lux. Onomatopoeia.
MacNeice. Ear, The.
Niedecker. Not all harsh sounds displease.
Olson, C. There Are Sounds.
Owen, W. All Sounds Have Been as Music.
Palmer, M. Maria's Gift.
Poem.
Raine, K. House of Music, A.
Who listens, when in the concert-hall.
Rilke. Gong.
Heart's Noise.
Ritsos. Audible and the Inaudible, The.
Rossetti, C. Wind Has Such a Rainy Sound, The.
Sandburg, C. So to Speak.
Young Bullfrogs.
Schuyler, J. "From the next."
Seifert. Song of the Nightingale, The.
Stafford, W. Animal That Drank Up Sound, The.
Sze. Sound Lag.
Tate, J. Sensitive Ears.
Thoreau. They who prepare my evening meal below.
Tomlinson, C. In the Studio.
Sea Poem.
Whip, The.
Whitman, W. Proud Music of the Storm.
That Music Always Round Me.
Wordsworth, W. Morning Exercise, A.
On the Power of Sound.
To the Cuckoo.
Unremitting Voice of Nightly Streams, The.
Wright, J. Depressed by a Book of Bad Poetry, I Walk toward an Unused Pasture and Invite the Insects to Join Me.

Poem for Kathleen Ferrier.
Soup
Angelou. This Winter Day.
Carver, R. At Noon.
Corbett, W. Bowl of Progresso Minestrone.
Creeley. Soup ("I know what you'd say").
Sandburg, C. Soup ("I know what you'd say").
Simic. Soup, The.
Tate, J. Soup of Venus, The.
Van Duyn. Goya's "Two Old People Eating Soup."
South Africa
Hughes, L. Dixie South Africa.
Kipling, R. Chant-Pagan.
English Flag, The.
Parting of the Columns, The.
Settler, The.
South Africa.
Two Kopjes.
Kizer, C. Race Relations.
Komunyakaa. Blasphemy.
Lorde. Evening News, The.
Williams, C. K. Bishop Tutu's Visit to the White House: 1984.
South African War
See **Boer War**
South America
"Dario." To Roosevelt.
What sign do you give, O Swan, with your curving neck.
Dubie. La Pampa.
Muldoon, P. Brazil.
Niedecker. Bonpland.
South Carolina (state)
Whittier. At Port Royal.
Hymn Sung at Christmas by the Scholars of St. Helena's Island, S.C.
South Dakota (state)
Niedecker. Badlands, The.
Wright, J. Having Lost My Sons, I Confront the Wreckage of the Moon: Christmas, 1960.
Sitting in a Small Screenhouse on a Summer Morning.
South, The, United States
Angelou. Georgia Song, A.
Miss Scarlet, Mr. Rhett and other Latter-Day Saints.
Southeast Arkanasia.
Clampitt. Savannah.
Clifton, L. Memphis.
Cooper, J. Being Southern.
Clementene.
How Can I Speak for Her.
Davie, D. Siloam.
Dickey, J. Spring-Shock.
Dove, R. Nothing Down.
Dugan, A. On the Civil War on the East Coast of the United States of North America 1860–64.
Dunbar, P. Chrismus on the Plantation.
Plantation Child's Lullaby, The.
Hayden, R. Runagate Runagate.
Tour 5.
Hughes, L. Bitter River, The.
Blue Bayou.
Brotherly Love.
Christ in Alabama.
Dixie Man to Uncle Sam.
Merry-Go-Round.
Mulatto.
Not a Movie.
One-Way Ticket.
Open Letter to the South.
Po' Boy Blues.
Song for a Dark Girl.
South, The.
Southern Mammy Sings.
Sunset in Dixie.
Total War.
Komunyakaa. Gristmill.
History Lessons.
Jumping Bad Blues.
One-legged Stool, The.
Kumin, M. Chain, The.
Lorde. Afterimages.

McGrath, T.　Deep South.
Nash, O.　First Families Move Over!
Orr, G.　On a Highway East of Selma, Alabama.
Riley, J.　North and South.
Rukeyser, M.　Lynchings of Jesus, The.
Schuyler, J.　Procession.
Walker, A.　Hymn: "I well remember / A time when."
　Once.
　South: The Name of Home.
Whitman, W.　O Magnet-South.
Whittier.　To a Southern Statesman.
　What State Street Said to South Carolina, and What South Carolina Said to State Street.
Williams, T.　Couple, The.
　Impressions through a Pennsy Window.
Wright, C.　Poem Almost Wholly in My Own Manner.
Wright, J.　Invitation to Madison County, An.

South Wind
Emerson, R.　South Wind.
Lindsay, N.　Moon's the North Wind's Cooky, The.
Riley, J.　South Wind and the Sun, The.
Sandburg, C.　South Wind Says So, The.

Southey, Robert
Coleridge, S.　To Robert Southey.
Muldoon, P.　Madoc: A Mystery.

Soviet Union
Brodsky, J.　End of a Beautiful Era, The.
　Fifth Anniversary, The.
　Gorbunov and Gorchakov.
　Homage to Yalta.
　On the Death of Zhukov.
　Photograph, A.
Hughes, L.　Good Morning, Stalingrad.
　Moscow.
　Salute to Soviet Armies.
　When the Armies Passed.
See also **Russia**

Soy Sauce
Snyder, G.　Soy Sauce.

Space and Space Travel
Ammons.　Spaceship.
Auden.　Moon Landing.
Borges.　1971.
Carver, R.　Trying to Sleep Late on a Saturday Morning in November.
Ciardi, J.　Dawn of the Space Age.
Clampitt.　Discovery.
Dickey, J.　Apollo.
Eberhart, R.　Dam Neck, Virginia.
　On Shooting Particles beyond the World.
Emerson, R.　Coil of space the cones of light, The.
Frost, R.　But outer Space.
Ginsberg, A.　In a Moonlit Hermit's Cabin.
Jeffers, R.　Dog in the Sky, The.
Kumin, M.　Night Launch.
Kunitz, S.　Flight of Apollo, The.
Larkin, P.　Time and Space Were Only Their Disguises.
Lawrence, D. H.　Space.
Merton.　Why Some Look up to Planets and Heroes.
Pagis.　Spaceship.
Seifert.　Dome of the Observatory, The.
Sexton.　Venus and the Ark.
Swenson, M.　After the Flight of Ranger 7.
　Landing on the Moon.
　Orbiter 5 Shows How Earth Looks from the Moon.
Szymborska, W.　Warning.
Tomlinson, C.　Ararat.
Updike.　Exposé.
　Moons of Jupiter, The.
　Open Letter to Voyager II, An.
　Skyey Developments.
Williams, M.　Sitting Alone at Sunrise: Problems in the Space-Time Continuum.
Williams, W.　Gossips, The.
　Heel & Toe to the End.
　World Contracted to a Recognizable Image, The.
Wilner, E.　Recovery.

Spain
Arendt.　Hands, The.
Browning, R.　Cristina.
Byron, G.　Girl of Cadiz, The.
Crane, H.　Imperator Victus.
Creeley.　Spring in San Feliu.
　Waiting for a Bus "en Frente de la Iglesia."
"Dario."　Concerning the Cid.
　Spaniard.
Emerson, R.　For fifteen winter days.
Ferlinghetti, L.　Goya & the Sleep of Reason.
García Lorca.　Lullaby in Death for Rosalía de Castro.
　Madrigal to the City of Santiago.
　Saint Raphael (Córdoba).
　Scene of the Lieutenant Colonel of the Civil Guard.
　Song of the Shop Boy.
Hamill, S.　Historical Romance.
Hughes, L.　Song of Spain.
Hughes, T.　You Hated Spain.
Jeffers, R.　Sinverguenza.
Kipling, R.　When the Great Ark.
Kizer, C.　Valley of the Fallen, The.
Laughlin, J.　When You Danced.
Lawrence, D. H.　At the Bank in Spain.
　Spanish Privilege.
　Spanish Wife, The.
Levine, P.　Face, The.
　Holding On.
　Let Me Begin Again.
　Midget, The.
　On the Murder of Lieutenant José Del Castillo by the Falangist Bravo Martinez, July 12, 1936.
　Salami.
MacLeish.　Spanish Lie, The.
Marvell.　On the Victory Obtained by Blake over the Spaniards, in the Bay of Santa [or Sancta] Cruz, in the Island of Tenerife, 1657.
Millay, E.　Say that We Saw Spain Die.
Mistral, G.　Catalonian Woman.
Plath.　Alicante Lullaby.
Rexroth, K.　Requiem for the Spanish Dead.
Rukeyser, M.　Word of Mouth.
Seifert.　Spanish Vineyards.
Shelley, P.　Ode Written October, 1819, An.
Smith, S.　Spanish School.
Spender, S.　Port Bou.
Van Duyn.　Madrid, 1974.
　Madrid, May, 1977.
Whitman, W.　Spain, 1873–74.
　Spanish Lady, The.
Wordsworth, W.　And is it among rude untutored Dales.
　Avaunt all specious pliancy of mind.
　Composed while the Author Was Engaged in Writing a Tract, Occasioned by the Convention of Cintra.
　1810.
　Hail, Zaragoza! If with unwet eye.
　Pelayo.
　Spanish Guerillas 1811.
Wright, J.　Eisenhower's Visit to Franco, 1959.
　In Memory of a Spanish Poet.

Spanish-American War
Crane, S.　There exists the eternal fact of conflict.
Kipling, R.　White Man's Burden, The.

Spanish Armada
Campion, T.　Ad Thamesin.
Kipling, R.　Together.

Spanish Civil War
Celan.　Shibboleth.
See also **Civil War, Spain**

Spankings
Dunbar, P.　When a Feller's Itchin' to be Spanked.
Hayden, R.　Whipping, The.
Herrick.　Upon Pagget.

Sparrows
Ammons.　Glass.
Berry, W.　Sparrow.
Bourne, V.　Sparrows Self-Domesticated.
Bukowski.　Farewell Thing while Breathing, A.

Carruth, H.　Snow, The.
　Sparrows.
Ciardi, J.　Minus One.
Creeley.　Sparrows.
Cummings, E. E.　N / ot eth / eold almos.
Dickinson, E.　Sparrow took a Slice of Twig, A.
Dunbar, P.　Sparrow, The.
Emerson, R.　Sparrow is rich in her nest, THe.
Herrick.　Upon the Death of His Sparrow; an Elegie.
Jarrell, R.　Augsburg Adoration, The.
Levine, P.　Goodbye.
Lux.　Green, The.
Millay, E.　English Sparrows.
Niedecker.　Nothing to speak of.
Oppen.　She Steals Birds.
　Stranger's Child.
Rossetti, C.　Wisdom.
Smith, S.　When the Sparrow Flies.
Very.　Our Native Sparrows.
　Sparrows and the Crop of Weeds, The.
Williams, W.　Breakfast.
　Pastoral: "Little sparrows, The."
　Pastoral 1: "Old man who goes about, The."
　Sleeping Brute, The.
　Sparrow, The.
　Sparrows among Dry Leaves.
　To a Sparrow.
Wordsworth, W.　Sparrow's Nest, The.
Wright, J.　Elegy in a Firelit Room.
　Sparrows in a Hillside Drift.
Zagajewski.　Dead Sparrow.

Sparta, Greece
Browning, R.　Pheidippides.
Cavafy.　Come, O King of the Lacedaimonians.
　In Sparta.
Dugan, A.　On Breeding, from Plutarch.
　Self-Exhortation on Military Themes.
Julian.　From Julianus.
Palladas [or Pallades].　By Palladas.

Spas
Merton.　Song: Sensation Time at the Home, A.
Sheridan, T.　Ballyspellin.

Speech
Ammons.　Breaks.
Berry, W.　Silence, The.
Bogan, L.　Henceforth, from the Mind.
Carruth, H.　Sonnet: "Well, she told me I had an aura. "What?" I said."
Cavafy.　Word and Silence.
Celan.　Speak You Too.
Clough.　Light words they were, and lightly, falsely said.
Codrescu.　Muffled by a Belt across the Mouth.
　Ode to Laryngitis.
Corbett, W.　Dear Joe.
Creeley.　Charm, The.
　Pattern, The.
　Shame, The.
　Speech.
　Words.
Davie, D.　Articulacy. Hints from the Koran.
　Mamertinus on Rhetoric, A.D. 291.
De la Mare.　Speech.
Dickinson, E.　How precious Thought and Speech are!
Emerson, R.　Merops.
　Poem on Eloquence by R. W. Emerson.
　There is no evil but can speak.
Enzensberger, H.　Delete the Inapplicable.
Gallagher, T.　Gray Eyes.
Graves, R.　Cool Web, The.
Hamill, S.　Io no piangeva.
HaNagid.　Delay Your Speech.
　You're Trapped, My Tongue.
Herrick.　Teares are Tongues.
　Upon Julia's Fall.
Hughes, T.　Chaucer.
Ignatow, D.　My Place.
Jackson, L.　O Vocables of Love.
Kizer, C.　Antique Father.
Laughlin, J.　My Granddaughter.
Levertov.　Sequence, A.
Lux.　Shaving the Graveyard.
MacLeish.　Speech to a Crowd.
Merwin.　Invocation: "Day hanging by its feet

with a hole, The."

Montale. Don't ask us for the word to frame.

Oppen. Neighbors.

Paley, G. In France.

Palmer, M. No Page (Unturned).
Said the Speaker.

Prunty. Baseball.

Rashid, N. Izhab-O-Rasai (Expression and Reach).

Rich, A. Apology.

Riley, J. Lisper, The.
Smitten Purist, The.

Rilke. Divine Disgrace.
To Speak a Flower.

Ritsos. Places of Refuge.
Proletarian Speaker, A.
Relation of the Unrelated, The.

Rukeyser, M. Effort at Speech between Two People.
In Our Time.

Sandburg, C. Basket.
Languages.
Speech.

Stevens, W. On [*or* Of] the Manner of Addressing Clouds.
Two Figures in Dense Violet Night.

Thoreau. Cliffs.

Warren, R. What Is the Voice that Speaks?

Whittier. Summons, A.

Williams, C. K. Don't.
My Mother's Lips.

Williams, T. Tangier: The Speechless Summer.

Wright, C. May Journal.
Primitive Journal II.

Zagajewski. Speak Softly.

Zukofsky, L. 1959 Valentine.

See also **Screams; Talk**

Speed

Browning, E. Soul's Travelling, The.

Codrescu. &.

Emerson, R. Is the pace of nature slow?

Frost, R. Master Speed, The.

Herrick. Haste Hurtfull.

Levertov. Traveler, A.

Nash, O. Ho, Varlet! My Two Cents' Worth of Penny Postcard!
It Would Have Been Quicker to Walk, or, Don't Tell Me We're There Already.
Mrs. Purvis Dreads Room Service.
Slow Down, Mr. Ganderdonk, You're Late.
We Don't Need to Leave Yet, Do We? Or, Yes We Do.

Rossetti, C. Swift and sure the swallow.

Rukeyser, M. Lover as Fox.
Speed, We Say.
Study in a Late Subway.
Target Practice.

Swenson, M. Speed.

Spelling

Nash, O. What's in a Name? Some Letter I Always Forget.

Spelling Bees

Dunbar, P. Spellin'-Bee, The.

Spender, Stephen

Eberhart, R. Face, Ocean.

Spenser, Edmund ("Colin Clout")

Campion, T. Ad Ed. Spencerum.

Davie, D. On Edmund Spenser's House in Ireland.

Keats. Specimen of an Induction to a Poem.
Spenser! A Jealous Honourer of Thine.

Koch, K. Art of Poetry, The.

Meredith, G. Poetry of Spenser, The.

Wordsworth, W. White Doe of Rylstone, The; or, The Fate of the Nortons.

Sphinx

Borges. Oedipus and the Enigma.

Cavafy. Oedipus.

Duncan, R. Huon of Bordeaux.

Eberhart, R. Sphinx.

Emerson, R. Sphinx, The.

Hayden, R. Sphinx.

MacLeish. What Riddle Asked the Sphinx.

Riley, J. Sphinx, The.

Rukeyser, M. Myth.

Private Life of the Sphinx.

Sandburg, C. Sphinx, A.

Stock, R. Singing, The.

Wilde, O. Sphinx, The.

Spider Webs

Ammons. Identity.

Bukowski. Escape, The.

Carver, R. Cobweb, The.

Eberhart, R. Spider, The.

Hayden, R. Web, The.

Laughlin, J. Arachne.

Levertov. Web.

Lux. Spiders Wanting.

Meredith, G. Garden Idyl, A.

Merwin. Encampment at Morning, An.
Web, The.

Nemerov. End of Summer School, The.

Rich, A. Knot, The.

Sandburg, C. Sun Dancer.
Webs.

Whalen, P. Duerden's Garage, Stinson Beach.

Whitman, W. Noiseless Patient Spider, A.

Williams, C. K. Spider Psyche.

Spiders

Ammons. Identity.
Spiel.

Armantrout. Dusk.

Beckett, S. Morte parmi.

Blue Cloud. Brief History (June–December 1994).

Bukowski. Death Wants More Death.
Escape, The.
Spider, The.

Ciardi, J. Thoughts on Looking into a Thicket.

Dickinson, E. Alone and in a Circumstance.
Spider as an Artist, The.
Spider holds a Silver Ball, The.
Spider sewed at Night, A.

Dubie. Thomas Merton and the Winter Marsh.

Eberhart, R. Spider, The.

Frost, R. Design.

Graves, R. Philosopher, The.

Hall, D. Some Oddities.

Hughes, T. Eclipse.

Jackson, L. Elegy in a Spider's Web.

Lawrence, D. H. Malade.

Levi, P. Arachne.

Lindsay, N. Spider and the Ghost of the Fly, The.

Lowell, R. Mr. Edwards and the Spider.

Lux. Spiders Wanting.
Streak of Blood That Once Was a Tiny Red Spider, A.

Meredith, G. Garden Idyl, A.
Outer and Inner.

Merwin. Encampment at Morning, An.

Milosz, C. Spider.

Plath. Spider.

Ramanujan. HINDOO, THE: He Doesn't Hurt a Fly or a Spider Either.

Rexroth, K. Doubled Mirrors.

Rich, A. Knot, The.

Riley, J. Dream, A.

Sandburg, C. Drowsy.
Sun Dancer.

Smith, S. On Walking Slowly after an Accident.

Tollas, T. Prison Poem.

Whitman, W. Noiseless Patient Spider, A.

Williams, C. K. Spider Psyche.

Williams, T. Wolf's Hour.

Spies

See **Spying and Spies**

Spinning and Spinners

Burns, R. Bess[y] and Her Spinning-Wheel.
Weary Pund o' Tow, The.

Warren, R. Not Quite Like a Top.

Wordsworth, W. Grief, thou hast lost an ever ready friend.
Song for the Spinning Wheel (Founded upon a Belief Prevalent among the Pastoral Vales of Westmoreland).
Through Cumbrian wilds, in many a mountain cove.

Spinoza, Baruch

Borges. Baruch Spinoza.

Spinoza.

Muldoon, P. Ontario.

Spinsters

Auden. Miss Gee.

Byron, G. Epigram on an Old Lady Who Had Some Curious Notions Respecting the Soul.

Campion, T. In Laurentiam.

García Lorca. Spinster at Mass, The.

Hardy, T. Retty's Phases.

Herrick. To the Little Spinners.
Upon Himself.

McHugh, H. Hag.

Plath. Ella Mason and Her Eleven Cats.
Spinster.

Smith, S. Gnädiges Fräulein.
Mrs Simpkins.

Spiritualism and Spiritualists

Brontë, E. I'm happiest when most away.
O wander not so far away!
Strong I stand, though I have borne.

Browning, E. Sleep, The.

Duncan, R. Circulations of the Song.

Eberhart, R. Recapitulation, The.

Emerson, R. Be of good cheer, brave spirit; steadfastly.
Leave me, Fear! thy throbs are base.

Kipling, R. En-Dor.

Levine, P. Holding On.
Voice, The.

Lorde. October.
Oya.
Signs.
Winds of Orisha, The.

O'Hara, F. Ode to Tanaquil Leclercq: "Smiling through my own memories of painful excitement your wide eyes."

Patchen. Cloth of the Tempest, The.
'In the footsteps of the walking air.'
Temple, A.

Sarton, M. Action of Therapy, The.
Annunciation.
Behind What Little Mirror.
Olive Grove, The.
Storm of Angels, A.
These Pure Arches.

Smith, S. From the County Lunatic Asylum.
Mrs Simpkins.

Wright, C. To Giacomo Leopardi in the Sky.

Wright, J. On the Skeleton of a Hound.

Spirituals

Hughes, L. Spirituals.

Sarton, M. At Muzot.
Prayer before Work.

Spittoons

Cummings, E. E. As that named Fred.

Dugan, A. Untitled Poem: "Speciously individual."

Hughes, L. Brass Spittoons.

Spoons

Simic. Spoon.

Sports

Beckett, S. Ascension.

Clampitt. Olympia.

Housman. Twice a week the winter thorough.

Hughes, T. Football at Slack.
Sunstruck.

Jonson, B. Epigram to My Jovial Good Friend Mr Robert Dover, on His Great Instauration of His Hunting and Dancing at Cotswold, An.
To Sir Henry Goodyere.

Kipling, R. Verses on Games.

Kumin, M. 400-Meter Freestyle.

Pinsky. Tennis.

Updike. Sometime Sportsman Greets the Spring, The.

Wright, J. Mad Fight Song for William S. Carpenter, 1966, A.

See also **Athletics and Athletes; Games**

Spring

Albinovanus Pedo. Plants and trees made poore and old, The.

Amichai [*or* Amikhai]. Now That the Water Presses Hard.
Poem of Spring.
Somber Spring.

Ammons. March Song.
  Spring Coming.
  Spring Song.
  Thaw.
Ashbery, J. Spring Day.
Atwood. Spring again, can I stand it.
Berry, W. Another Descent.
  March 22, 1968.
  Purification, A.
  Returning.
Berryman. Caravan.
Bishop, E. Cold Spring, A.
Blake, W. To Spring.
Blok. O Spring without End.
Blue Cloud. Crow.
  Sculpture in Soil.
Bly, R. Early Spring between Madison and
  Bellingham.
Bradstreet, A. As spring the winter doth
  succeed.
Brontë, E. May flowers are opening.
Browning, R. Home-Thoughts, from Abroad.
  Spring Song.
Burns, R. Auld Man's Winter Thought, The.
  Chloe.
  Gardener wi' His Paddle or, The Gardener's
    March, The.
  Lament of Mary Queen of Scots on the
    Approach of Spring.
  O Were My Love Yon Lilac[k] Fair.
  Ode to Spring.
  Scotch Song.
Byron, G. Stanzas: "Could Love for ever."
Campion, T. Elegia I (1619).
  Peaceful Western Wind, The.
Carew, T. Spring, The.
Carruth, H. Chase in Spring, The.
  Incident of May.
  Spring Notes from Robin Hill.
Ciardi, J. March Morning.
  Saturday, March 6.
  Spring in Statue Square.
  Spring Song ("Do you remember by morning
    when the sun").
Clampitt. High Culture.
  Nothing Stays Put.
Clare, J. Dying Child, The.
Coleridge, S. Answer to a Child's Question.
  Lines to a Beautiful Spring in a Village.
Cowper, W. To the Rev. Mr. Newton.
Crane, H. Lachrymae Christi.
Creeley. Spring.
Cullen, C. Spring Reminiscence.
  To John Keats, Poet, at Springtime.
Cummings, E. E. And this day it was
    Spring....us.
  Ardensteil-henarub-izabeth) / this noN.
  Because it's / Spring / thingS.
  But the other / day i was passing a certain.
  "but why should" / the / greatest.
  Darling!because my blood can sing.
  Greedy the people, The.
  Here's to opening and upward,to leaf and to sap.
  If(among / silent skies).
  In Just.
  In / Spring comes(no- / one).
  Let us lie here in the disturbing grass.
  (Listen) / this a dog barks and.
  Metamorphosis.
  Never could anyone / who simply lives to die.
  Nouns to nouns / wan / wan.
  Now i lay(with everywhere around).
  O Sweet Spontaneous.
  Rain Is a Handsome Animal, The.
  Semi-Spring.
  Skies may be blue;yes.
  Sometimes / in)Spring a someone will
    lie(glued).
  Sonnet: "Long since, the flicker brushed with
    shameless wing."
  Spring is like a perhaps hand.
  Spring!may— / everywhere's here.
  Spring omnipotent goddess thou dost.
  Spring(side / walks are)is.
  Sweet spring is your.
  There are so many tictoc.

Tonight the moon is round golden entire. It.
  Trees / were in(give).
  Weazened Irrefutable unastonished.
  When faces called flowers float out of the
    ground.
  When / from a sidewalk.
  Yes is a pleasant country.
  You asked me to come:it was raining a little.
"Dario." Because of the Influence of Spring.
  In Spring.
Davie, D. March.
  Oriental Visitor, An.
  Spring Song, A.
De la Mare. Reawakening, The.
  Riddle, A.
  Spectre, The.
Dickinson, E. Before you thought of Spring.
  Dear March, Come in.
  I cannot meet the Spring unmoved.
  I dreaded that first Robin, so.
  I have a Bird in spring.
  Inundation of the Spring, The.
  Letter to Bee.
  Light exists in Spring, A.
  Little Madness in the Spring, A.
  Notice that is called the Spring, The.
  Ones that disappeared are back, The.
  Spring comes on the World.
  Spring is a happiness so beautiful.
  Spring is the Period.
  Spring's first conviction is a wealth.
  That sweet Physician, an approaching spring.
  Trusting the happy flower.
  Violets are by my side, The.
  When they come back—if Blossoms do.
Donne. Love's Growth.
Dugan, A. Notes toward a Spring Offensive.
  Sixteen Lines on Marching.
  Spring Song for *Symplocarpus Fœtida* and Me.
Dunbar, P. Come and Kiss Me Sweet and
    Twenty.
  Little Lucy Landman.
  Song: "Bee hit sip some honey f'om de
    matermony vine, De."
  Spring Fever.
  Spring Song.
  Spring Wooing, A.
  When Winter Darkening All Around.
Eberhart, R. Apple Buds.
  Day-Bed, The.
  On Returning to a Lake in Spring.
  Scarf of June, The.
  This Fevers Me.
  Three Kids.
  Where Are Those High and Haunting Skies.
Eliot, T. S. Easter: Sensations of April.
Emerson, R. April.
  For Genius made his cabin wide.
  Gentle Spring has charmed the earth.
  Good Charles the springs adorer.
  May.
  May-Day.
  Musketaquid.
Frost, R. Cloud Shadow, A.
  Prayer in Spring, A.
  Spring Pools.
García Lorca. Spring Song.
Ginsberg, A. Easter Sunday.
Glück, L. Easter Season.
  Flowering Plum.
  For Jane Myers.
  Letter from our Man in Blossomtime.
  My Cousin in April.
  Shad-Blow Tree, The.
Graves, R. Primrose Bed, The.
  Song: Fig Tree in Leaf.
  Spring 1974.
Gray, T. Ode on the Spring.
Gurney, I. Compensations.
  Early Spring Dawn.
  Near Spring.
"H. D." Late Spring.
Hall, D. Love Is Like Sounds.
Hamill, S. Word for Spring, A.
Han-shan. New year ends a year of sorrow,
  The.

Hardy, T. Backward Spring, A.
  Growth in May.
  If It's Ever Spring Again.
  Joys of Memory.
  Spring Call, The.
  Year's Awakening, The.
Herrick. Apron of Flowers, The.
  Farewell Frost; or, Welcome the Spring.
  Four Sweet Months, The.
  Meddow Verse; or, Aniversary to Mistris
    Bridget Lowman, The.
Hill, G. Cycle.
Hopkins, G. Ad Mariam.
  Furl of fresh-leaved dogrose down, The.
  May Magnificat, The.
  See how Spring opens with disabling cold.
  Spring.
  Spring and Death.
  Spring and Fall.
Housman. Loveliest of Trees, the Cherry Now.
  Oh see how thick the goldcup flowers.
  Spring Morning.
Hughes, L. Earth Song.
  In Time of Silver Rain.
  Poem: "When young spring comes."
  Red Roses.
  Signs of Spring.
Hughes, T. Swifts.
  Two Tortoiseshell Butterflies.
Jackson, L. After So Much Loss.
Jacobsen, J. Blue-Eyed Exterminator, The.
  First Woman.
  Good Fortune of Pigeons, The.
  Hourglass.
  Time Exposure.
Jarrell, R. Trees in Spring, The.
Keats. After Dark Vapours Have Oppressed Our
    Plains.
  Extracts from an Opera.
  I Stood Tip-Toe upon a Little Hill.
Kinsella, T. Fifth Sunday after Easter.
Kipling, R. Cuckoo Song.
  In Springtime.
  Pan in Vermont.
Koch, K. Desire for Spring.
Kumin, M. Custodian.
  First Rain of Spring, The.
  Late Snow.
  Relearning the Language of April.
Larkin, P. Coming.
  First Sight.
  Fragment from May.
  May Weather.
  Spring.
  Spring Warning.
Laughlin, J. Coming of Spring, The.
  Persephone Wears Bluejeans.
Lawrence, D. H. Campions.
  Come Spring, Come Sorrow.
  Craving for Spring.
  Disagreeable Advice.
  Drained Cup, The.
  Enkindled Spring, The.
  Spring Morning.
Lenau. Postillion, The.
Levertov. Another Spring.
  April in Ohio.
  Earliest Spring.
  Talking to Oneself.
Levi, P. Thaw, The.
Levine, P. Nitrate.
  Sleepless Night, A.
  To Cipriano, in the Wind.
  Waking an Angel.
Li Po. Spring Song.
Logan, J. February Awakening.
  Lament in Spring.
  Song on the Dread of a Chill Spring.
  Spring Revelations.
MacLeish. March.
MacNeice. Another Cold May.
  April Manifesto, An.
  Pale Panther, The.
  Spring Cleaning.
  Spring Voices.
Mallarmé. Renewal.

McGrath, T.   Black Train, The.
  What We Think We Know.
  Winter Roads.
McHugh, H.   Fix.
Meng Hao Jan.   In spring you sleep and never
  know when the morn comes.
Meredith, G.   Death of Winter, The.
  Fresh Spring has come with flower and leaf to
  warn.
  Fullness of love sleeps in us like a sea.
  I saw young Spring leap over the hills.
  Invitation to the Country.
  May Song.
  Song: "Daisy now is out upon the green, The."
  Song: Spring.
  Song: The Wren.
  Sweet o' the Year, The.
  Tardy Spring.
  When stormy day is cold & gray.
Meredith, W.   Perhaps the Best Time.
  Squire Hazard Walks.
Merton.   April.
  City's Spring, The.
  Sowing of Meanings, The.
  Spring: Monastery Farm.
  What Troubles I Have Seen in Birdlegged
    Spring.
Merwin.   Spring.
  Spring Equinox Full Moon.
Millay, E.   New England Spring, 1942.
  Spring.
  Spring and the Fall, The.
  Spring in the Garden.
  Spring Song.
Milosz, C.   Farewell: "I speak to you, my son."
  Journey, The.
  Slow River.
Milton.   Elegy 5: On the Coming of Spring.
Mistral, G.   Lady Spring.
  What Do You Feel Underground?
Molodovsky [or Molodowsky].   There Are Such
  Springlike Nights.
Nash, O.   Eternal Vernal, or, In All My Dreams
  My Fair Face Beams, The.
  Individualist, The.
  Passionate Pagan and the Dispassionate Public,
    The.
  Spring Song.
Nemerov.   Zalmoxis.
Neruda.   Same Story.
Niedecker.   How white the gulls.
  I sit in my own house.
  Spring / stood there.
  Springtime's wide.
  Swept snow, Li Po.
O'Hara, F.   Captain Bada.
  Easter.
  Poem: "Ivy is trembling in the hammock, The."
Oliver, M.   Spring.
  Two Kinds of Deliverance.
Olson, C.   Day Song.
  Day Song, the Day After.
  It's SPRing AgAIN!
  Variations Done for Gerald Van De Wiele.
Orléans, C.   Rondeau: "Year has cast its cloak
  away, The."
Owen, W.   Spring Offensive.
Parker, D.   Somewhat Delayed Spring Song.
  Spring Song.
Pasternak, B.   Earth, The.
  Orford.
Patchen.   Shadows and Spring Flowers.
Petrarch.   Now Zephirus brings back the better
  weather.
  When that planet which divides the hours.
Piercy.   Inside Chance, The.
  Snow, Snow.
Plath.   April Aubade.
  Prologue to Spring.
Raine, K.   April's new apple buds on an old
  lichened tree.
  Flower, memory—.
  I felt, under my old breasts, this April day.
  Winter Solstice.
Rexroth, K.   Yin and Yang.
Riley, J.   First Bluebird, The.

Hint of Spring, A.
Hoosier Spring-Poetry.
Spring Song and a Later, A.
When Early March Seems Middle May.
When the Green Gits Back in the Trees.
Rilke.   Loss.
  Memories of Muzot.
  Some Perfume.
  Spring.
  Springtime.
Ritsos.   Provincial Spring.
Roethke.   Bring the Day!
  Light Comes Brighter, The.
  Vernal Sentiment.
Rossetti, C.   Amen.
  Another Spring.
  Bride Song, A.
  Child's Talk in April.
  Cor Mio.
  Days are clear, / Day after day, The.
  Death-Watches.
  Easter Carol, An.
  First Spring Day, The.
  L. E. L.
  May.
  One Swallow Does Not Make a Summer.
  Spring.
  Spring Fancies.
  Spring is come again not as at first.
  Spring Quiet.
  St. Valentine's Day 1881.
  There Is a Budding Morrow in Midnight.
  To Mary Rossetti.
  What Sappho Would Have Said Had Her Leap
    Cured Instead of Killing Her.
  What's in a Name?
  Who Hath Despised the Day of Small Things?
  Winter: My Secret.
  Wintry Sonnet, A.
Rossetti, D.   For Spring, by Sandro Botticelli, in
  the Accademia of Florence.
Rukeyser, M.   Fighting for Roses.
  Gift-Poem.
  Wooden Spring.
Rumi.   Spring.
  Spring Is Christ.
Sandburg, C.   Blossom Themes.
  Child Face.
  Crisscross.
  Elm Buds.
  Frog Songs.
  Lines Written for Gene Kelly to Dance To.
  New Song for Indiana Ophelias.
  Population Drifts.
  Spring Carries Surprises.
  Spring Cries.
  Spring Grass.
  Spring Wind.
  Three Spring Notations on Bipeds.
  Understandings in Blue.
  Wind Sings Welcome in Early Spring, The.
Sarton, M.   Metamorphosis.
Schuyler, J.   Industrial Archaeology.
  May 24th or So.
  Spring.
  Thinness.
  3/23/66.
Seifert.   Garland on the Wrist, A.
Sexton.   It is a Spring Afternooon.
  Killing the Spring.
Shelley, P.   Cloud, The.
  Fragment: May the Limner.
  Question, The.
Smart, C.   On a Bed of Guernsey Lilies.
Snyder, G.   Migration of Birds.
  Sixth-Month Song in the Foothills.
  What Have I Learned.
Stafford, W.   Animal That Drank up Sound, The.
  As Pippa Lilted.
Stevens, W.   Depression before Spring.
Swenson, M.   Another Spring Uncovered.
  April Light.
  City Garden in April, A.
  Spring by Robert Lowell / (Photograph by Trudi
  Fuller).
  Spring Uncovered.

Tree in Spring, A.
Swinburne.   Interlude, An.
Szymborska, W.   Parting with a View.
Tate, A.   Seasons of the Soul.
Tate, J.   Spring Was Begging to Be Born.
Tennyson, A.   To Mary Boyle.
Thomas, D.   From Love's First Fever to Her
  Plague.
  Here in This Spring.
  Holy Spring.
  I, in My Intricate Image.
Thoreau.   Thaw, The.
Tomlinson, C.   Hesitation, The.
  Northern Spring.
  Order of Saying, The.
Tu Fu.   Lo Yu Park.
Unknown.   Two Spring Charms.
Updike.   Melting.
  Query.
  Sometime Sportsman Greets the Spring, The.
  Spring Song.
  Styles of Bloom.
  Touch of Spring.
Van Duyn.   Notes from a Suburban Heart.
Very.   Crocus, The.
  Heralds of the Spring, The.
  Longing for the Spring, A.
  May Flower, The.
  Song of the Early Spring.
  Spirit, The.
  Spring ("I have not lived the flesh has hedged
    me in").
  Spring in the Soul.
  What more delightful than to wander forth.
  Winter Rain, The.
Weiss, T.   Last Day and the First, The.
Whalen, P.   Spring Musick.
Whitman, W.   First Dandelion, The.
  Out of May's Shows Selected.
  Soon Shall the Winter's Foil Be Here.
Whittier.   April.
  First Flowers, The.
  Mayflowers, The.
  My Psalm.
  Pageant, The.
  Wind of March, The.
Wilbur, R.   April 5, 1974.
  Avowal, The.
  Cicadas.
  Next Door.
  Seed Leaves.
  To Ishtar.
  Winter Spring.
Wilde, O.   From Spring Days to Winter.
Williams, C. K.   Spring: another / joke. / This
  run-down.
Williams, T.   Sacre de Printemps.
  Sonnets for the Spring (A Sequence).
Williams, W.   April.
  Bird Song.
  Bitter World of Spring, The.
  Della Primavera Transportata al Morale.
  Hermaphroditic Telephones, The.
  Late Singer, The.
  March.
  May 1st Tomorrow.
  Memory of April.
  Shadow, The.
  She Who Turns Her Head.
  Spring and All.
  Spring Is Here Again, Sir.
  Spring Strains.
  Two Aspects of April.
Wilner, E.   Green Connection, The.
  Mulch, The.
Wordsworth, W.   In Part from Moschus's
  Lament for Bion.
  Lines Written in Early Spring.
  Ode Composed on May Morning.
  Ode to Lycoris; May, 1817.
  Poor Robin.
  Stray Pleasures.
  Thoughts on the Seasons.
  To a Snow-Drop.
  To Lady Beaumont.
  To May.

To My Sister.
To S.H.
To the Cuckoo.
Vernal Ode.
Written in March [While Resting on the Bridge at the Foot of Brother's Water].
Wright, C.   Basic Dialogue.
  Easter 1989.
  Still Life with Spring and Time to Burn.
Wright, J.   March.
  Spring Images.
  Witches Waken the Natural World in Spring.
Zagajewski.   Fever.
  Lindens.
Zukofsky, L.   Ah spring, when with a thaw of blue.
  And Without.
  Chrysanthemum.
  I Walk in the Old Street.
  Last cigarette / a companion, A.

Springfield, Illinois
Lindsay, N.   Soul of the City Receives the Gift of the Holy Spirit, The.

Springs
Amichai [or Amikhai].   Suflah Spring in the Judean Mountains.
Berry, W.   Springs, The.
Herrick.   How Springs Came First.
Levertov.   To Antonio Machado.
Rumi.   Water from Your Spring.
Sheridan, T.   Ballyspellin.
Snyder, G.   Spring, The.
Stafford, W.   Well Rising, The.
Very.   Cold Spring in North Salem, The.
Wordsworth, W.   Suggested by Mr W. Westall's Views of the Caves, etc., in Yorkshire.

Spruce Trees
Rukeyser, M.   Blue Spruce.
Schuyler, J.   Buried at Springs.
  Light from Canada.
Tomlinson, C.   Stair, The.

Spying and Spies
Auden.   Secret Agent, The.
Bukowski.   Breakout.
Codrescu.   Ode to Curiosity.
De la Mare.   Peeping Tom.
Jonson, B.   On Spies.
Kipling, R.   Spies' March, The.
Lawrence, D. H.   Police Spies.
Wilbur, R.   Agent, The.

Squash (botany)
Wilbur, R.   Melongène.

Squirrels
Ciardi, J.   December 13, 1979.
Creeley.   Love ("Thing comes, The").
Dickinson, E.   Saucer holds a Cup, A.
Eberhart, R.   On a Squirrel Crossing the Road in Autumn, in New England.
Emerson, R.   Fable: "Mountain and the squirrel, The."
McGrath, T.   What We Think We Know.
Nash, O.   Squirrel, The.
O'Hara, F.   Pastoral Dialogue, A.
Oppen.   Squirrel's Stance, The.
Schuyler, J.   Deep Winter.
Tomlinson, C.   Stair, The.
Updike.   Squirrels Mating.
Williams, M.   71 South.
Wilner, E.   Bridge Passage: Variations on Two Scales.
Wright, J.   Today I Was So Happy, so I Made this Poem.
Yeats.   Appointment, An.
  To a Squirrel at Kyle-Na-No.

Sri Lanka
Merton.   Kandy Express.

St. Agnes' Eve
Keats.   Eve of St Agnes, The.
Merton.   Prelude: For the Feast of St. Agnes, A.

St. Cecilia's Day
Swift, J.   Dean to Himself on St. Cecilia's Day, The.

St. Louis, Missouri
Ginsberg, A.   Funky barn, black hills approaching Fulton.

Kansas City to Saint Louis.
Lorde.   St. Louis out of Time.

St. Mark's Eve
Keats.   Eve of St. Mark, The.

St. Patrick's Day
Nash, O.   It's a Grand Parade It Will Be, Modern Design.

St. Paul's Cathedral
Davie, D.   Under St Paul's.
Hardy, T.   In St. Paul's a While Ago.
MacNeice.   Homage to Wren.
Wordsworth, W.   St Paul's.

St. Valentine's Day
See **Valentine's Day**

Stables
Gunn, T.   Phaedra in the Farm House.
Hall, D.   Carol, A.
Herrick.   Another Charme for Stables.
Kinsella, T.   Stable, The.

Stained Glass
Hardy, T.   Young Glass-Stainer, The.
Kipling, R.   Chartres Windows.

Stairs
Ammons.   Choice.
Hughes, T.   Mother to Son.
Ignatow, D.   From a Dream.
Levertov.   Jacob's Ladder, The.
Lindsay, N.   Sweet Briars of the Stairways.
Lux.   Cellar Stairs.
Ritsos.   Stairs, The.
Tomlinson, C.   Revolution Piazza Di Spagna.
  Stair, The.
Wilner, E.   Beyond the Second Landing.
Zagajewski.   Esprit D'Escalier.

Stalin, Joseph
Dubie.   Arkhangel'sk.
Lowell, R.   Stalin.

Stalingrad, Battle of (1942–1943)
Hughes, L.   Good Morning, Stalingrad.
  Stalingrad: 1942.
Jacobsen, J.   How We Learn.

Stalking and Stalkers
Ai.   Stalking Memory.

Stampa, Gaspara
Rexroth, K.   On a Flyleaf of *Rime*—Gaspara Stampa.

Standish, Miles
Longfellow, H.   Courtship of Miles Standish, The.

Stanford, Frank
Lux.   Elegy for Frank Stanford.

Starfish
Bly, R.   Starfish, The.
Jacobsen, J.   Starfish, The.
Kinnell.   Daybreak.
Oliver, M.   Starfish.

Starlings
Ciardi, J.   Days.
Hardy, T.   Starlings on the Roof.
Hayden, R.   Plague of Starlings, A.
Hughes, T.   Where I Sit Writing My Letter.
Prunty.   New Territory.
Schuyler, J.   So Good.
Smith, S.   British Song, A.
Wilbur, R.   Writer, The.
Williams, W.   Against the Sky.
  Maneuver [or Manoeuvre], The.

Stars
Ammons.   Body Politic.
"Anvari."   To the Shah, from Enweri.
Auden.   More Loving One, The.
Baudelaire.   Living Torch, The.
Berry, W.   Star, The.
Blake, W.   How Sweet I Roamed [or Roam'd] from Field to Field.
  To the Evening Star.
Borges.   South, The.
Brontë, E.   Stars.
Browning, E.   Heaven and Earth.
  Romance of the Ganges, A.
  Romaunt of Margret, The.
Browning, R.   My Star.
Byron, G.   On the Star of "The Legion of Honour."

She Walks in Beauty.
Char.   Fighters.
Clough.   Uranus.
Codrescu.   Star Book.
Creeley.   Colors.
Cuadra, P.   Secret of the Burning Stars, The.
Cullen, C.   To Endymion.
Cummings, E. E.   All stars are(and not one star only)love.
  I was considering how.
  Over us if(as what dusk becomes).
De la Mare.   Birthnight: To F, The.
  Flight, The.
  Night.
  O Childish Mind!
Dickinson, E.   Moon upon her fluent Route, The.
  My best Acquaintances are those.
  Not what the stars have done.
  Outer—from the Inner, The.
Dugan, A.   To a Kid Who Believes in Astrology.
Dunbar, P.   Love Is a Star.
  Starry Night, A.
Eberhart, R.   Looking at the Stars.
  Looking at the Stars.
Emerson, R.   Atom from atom yawns as far.
  Earth, The.
  I have supped with the gods tonight.
  If he go apart.
  On that night the poet went.
  Teach me your mood, O patient stars!
  Wisp & meteor nightly falling.
Ferlinghetti, L.   Plough of Time, The.
  Rebels, The.
Frost, R.   Canis Major.
  Choose Something like a Star.
  Come In.
  Literate Farmer and the Planet Venus, The.
  Skeptic.
  Star in a Stoneboat, A.
  Stars.
Gallagher, T.   Rijl.
  With Stars.
Glück, L.   Under Taurus.
Graves, R.   Everywhere Is Here.
Gunn, T.   Blackie, the Electric Rembrandt.
  My Sad Captains.
Gurney, I.   Between the Boughs.
  Stars Sliding.
"H. D."   Two Poems for Christmas, 1937.
Hamill, S.   Two Poems for Tanabata Matsuri.
Han-shan.   Multitude of stars is the late night's light, The.
Hardy, T.   Waiting Both.
Hayden, R.   Stars.
Herbert, G.   Artillery [or Artillerie].
  Star[re], The.
Hopkins, G.   Lover's Stars, The.
  Starlight Night, The.
  Stars were packed so close that night, The.
Housman.   Stars, I have seen them fall.
Hughes, L.   Slave Song.
  Stars.
Hughes, T.   Fire-Eater.
  That Star.
Ignatow, D.   For My Daughter.
Jacobsen, J.   Distance.
Jarrell, R.   Evening Star, The.
  Lament: "All is far."
Jeffers, R.   At the near approach of a star...huge tides.
  Epic Stars, The.
  My Dear Love.
  Nova.
  October Week-End.
  Polar ice-caps are melting, the mountain glaciers, The.
Keats.   Bright Star.
Kinnell.   Daybreak.
Kinsella, T.   Ancient Ballet, An.
Kipling, R.   Astrologer's Song, An.
  Penalty, The.
Komunyakaa.   Black String of Days.
Larkin, P.   Far Out.
Lawrence, D. H.   In a Boat.

Like the Green Candles of Malintzi.
Lord of the Morning Star.
Son of the Morning Star.
Levertov.   For Nikolai, Many Thousand Miles
  Away.
Look at the Night (Temple, Early '60's), A.
Lindsay, N.   Star of My Heart.
Logan, J.   Twilight Land.
Longfellow, H.   Occultation of Orion, The.
Lorde.   Separation.
MacLeish.   Epistle to Be Left in the Earth.
Pole Star for This Year.
Signal, The.
MacNeice.   Star-Gazer.
Maritain.   Glass Orchard.
Meredith, G.   Lucifer in Starlight.
Meditation under Stars.
Star Sirius, The.
Union in Disseverance.
Winter Heavens.
Meredith, W.   Country Stars.
Examples of Created Systems.
Starlight.
Merton.   Tonight There Is a Showing of
  Champion Lights.
Merwin.   Under Black Leaves.
Mistral, G.   Christmas Star, The.
Heaven's Carriage.
Muldoon, P.   Ontario.
Nemerov.   Speculation.
Parker, D.   Star Light, Star Bright.
Patchen.   Stars go to sleep so peacefully, The.
Petrarch.   I saw twelve ladies sailing at their
  ease.
Plath.   Stars over the Dordogne.
Poe.   Evening Star.
Raine, K.   Banked winter cloud.
Star of Bethlehem.
Ramanujan.   Traces.
Rexroth, K.   Andromeda Chained to Her Rock
  the Great Nebula in Her Heart.
Family, The.
Lights in the Sky are Stars, The.
Phaedo.
Theory of Numbers.
Rich, A.   Planetarium.
Rilke.   Funeral.
Ritsos.   Afternoon.
Contradictions.
Nocturne.
Same Star, The.
Robinson, E.   Credo.
Rossetti, C.   If stars dropped out of heaven, /
  And if flowers took their place.
Song of the Star, The.
What do the stars do / Up in the sky.
Where Innocent Bright-Eyed Daisies Are.
Rukeyser, M.   Cats and a Cock.
Darkness Music.
Song: The Star in the Nets of Heaven.
Rumi.   Inside water, a waterwheel turns.
Sandburg, C.   Baby Toes.
Bright Conversation with Saint-Ex.
Broken Hearted Soprano.
Cadenza.
Monkey of Stars.
Offering and Rebuff.
Silver Point.
Special Starlight.
Star Silver.
Stars.
Summer Stars.
There Are Different Gardens.
We Have Gone through Great Rooms Together.
Yellow Evening Star.
Shelley, P.   To a Star.
Stevens, W.   Homunculus et La Belle Etoile.
Nuances of a Theme by Williams.
Swenson, M.   As Long Ago as Far Away.
Szymborska, W.   Surplus.
Thoreau.   On Ponkawtasset, since, we took our
  way.
Updike.   Skyey Developments.
White Dwarf.
Very.   Spheres, The.
Star, The.

Stars, The.
Walcott.   Star.
Warren, R.   Star-Fall.
Whitman, W.   On the Beach at Night.
On the Beach at Night Alone.
When I Heard the Learn'd Astronomer.
Wilbur, R.   Games One.
In the Field.
Under Cygnus.
Williams, W.   At Night.
El Hombre.
Flight to the City.
Wordsworth, W.   Composed by the Side of
  Grasmere Lake.
I watch, and long have watched, with calm
  regret.
It is no spirit who from heaven hath flown.
Pilgrim's Dream; or, The Star and the Glow-
  Worm, The.
Stars Are Mansions Built by Nature's Hand,
  The.
To the Evening Star over Grasmere Water.
Wright, C.   Meditation on Form and Measure.
Star Turn.
Star Turn 2.
Wright, J.   To the Evening Star: Central
  Minnesota.
Zagajewski.   Planetarium.
See also **Astronomy and Astronomers**

Statistics
Cunningham, J.   Meditation on Statistical
  Method.

Statue of Liberty
Dugan, A.   Untitled Poem: "Who can abide
  whom or what? That's."
See also **Liberty, Statue of**

Statues
Atwood.   My beautiful wooden leader.
Baudelaire.   Mask, The.
Berryman.   Boston Common.
Statue, The.
Bogan, L.   Statue and Birds.
Brodsky, J.   Bust of Tiberius, The.
Galatea Encore.
Torso.
Browning, R.   Protus.
Statue and the Bust, The.
Bukowski.   Experience.
Castiglione.   On the Statue of *Cleopatra*, Made
  into a Fountain by *Leo* the Tenth.
Cavafy.   Before the Statue of Endymion.
Clampitt.   Archaic Figure.
Crane, H.   To the Empress Josephine's Statue.
Creeley.   Figures, The.
Statue, The.
Cummings, E. E.   Great Dante stands in
  Florence, looking down.
Dugan, A.   Autobiographical Libation to Erato
  Muse of Lyric Poetry.
On a Fallen Statue Forbidden to the Women at
  Pompeii.
Perverse Explanation for Mutilated Statuary.
There He Was.
Eberhart, R.   Angels, The.
Anxiety I Felt in Guanajuato, The.
Statue of Liberty.
García Lorca.   Saint Raphael (Córdoba).
Hardy, T.   Statue of Liberty, The.
Heaney, S.   Sheelagh na Gig.
Herrick.   To His Honoured Kinsman, Sir
  Richard Stone.
Laughlin, J.   In the Museum at Teheran.
Lindsay, N.   Statue of Old Andrew Jackson,
  The.
Lorde.   Sacrifice.
MacNeice.   Stylite.
McHugh, H.   Two St. Petersburgs.
Merrill, J.   Bronze.
Santo.
Milosz, C.   Statue of a Couple.
Nemerov.   Don Juan to the Statue.
Statues in the Public Gardens, The.
Oppen.   Giovanni's *Rape of the Sabine Women*
  at Wildenstein's.
Orr, G.   Available Now: Archaic Torsos of Both

Sexes.
Ovid.   Galatea.
Petrarch.   That bravery, which came to flower in
  you.
Pinkerton, H.   On the Jamb-Statues of the
  Portail Royal (1150) on Chartres Cathedral.
Plath.   Colossus, The.
Touch-and-Go.
Raine, K.   Statues.
Riley, J.   Lines: "Thou little naked statuette."
Ritsos.   After Death.
Charioteer 1970.
Conformity.
Eyes of the Statue, The.
Face or Mask?
Generalization of Distrust.
Imitation of an Imitation.
Immobilizing the Boundless.
Known Consequences.
Meaning of Art, The.
Niobe.
Nocturnal Episode.
Old House, The.
One Word.
Perspective.
Plaster Model.
Presence.
Return.
Shelters.
Signals.
Statue in the Cafe, The.
Statues, The.
Statues in the Cemeteries, The.
Unacceptable, The.
Until Daybreak.
Wax Dummies.
Why the Question?
Witnesses Everywhere.
Rossetti, C.   Study (A Soul), A.
Rossetti, D.   Burden of Nineveh, The.
Sandburg, C.   Cheap Rent.
Has-Been, The.
Seifert.   Cry of the Spectres, The.
Fingerprints.
Head of the Virgin Mary, The.
Shapiro, K.   Statue of Liberty.
Shelley, P.   Ozymandias.
Spender, S.   Cyril Connolly.
Stafford, W.   Living Statues.
Stevens, W.   Dance of the Macabre Mice.
Stock, R.   Red Clay Speech.
Verses after Which the Mourning Statue is
  Presumed to Speak.
Szymborska, W.   Palaeolithic Fertility Fetish, A.
Tomlinson, C.   In Verdi Square.
Thunder in Tuscany.
Wilbur, R.   Statues.
Wordsworth, W.   Lady Whom You Here Behold,
  The.
Prithee, Gentle Lady, List.
Yeats.   Statues, The.

Steak
Creeley.   Naughty Boy.

Steam Baths
Rumi.   Steambath, The.
See also **Baths and Bathing**

Steam Rollers and Steam Rolling
Moore, M.   To a Steam Roller.

Steamers
Kipling, R.   McAndrew's Hymn.
MacLeish.   Steamboat Whistle, The.
Nash, O.   Song for Pier Something or Other.
See also **Ships and Shipbuilding**

Steel
Ammons.   North Jersey.
Hughes, L.   Steel Mills.
Ignatow, D.   Two.
Sandburg, C.   Laughing Blue Steel.
Prayers of Steel.
Smoke and Steel.
Tomlinson, C.   Etruria Vale.
Steel.
Williams, C. K.   Hooks.
See also **Iron**

Steeples
Frost, R.   Steeple on the House, A.
Williams, W.   To a Solitary Disciple.

Steers
See **Oxen**

Stein, Gertrude
Muldoon, P.   More a Man Has the More a Man
   Wants, The.
Stock, R.   Portrait of Gertrude Stein.

Stella (Hester Johnson)
Howe, S.   Fragments of a Liquidation.
   God's Spies.
   THEIR / Book of Stella.
Sheridan, T.   Humble Petition of Stella's
   Friends, The.
   Invitation to Dinner, from Doctor Sheridan to
   Doctor Swift, An.

Stendhal (Marie Henri Beyle)
Laughlin, J.   Somewhere in France.

Stenographers
See **Scribes; Secretaries**

Stepfathers and Stepmothers
Smith, S.   Papa Love Baby.
Whittier.   Kathleen.

Stepmothers
Komunyakaa.   Stepmother: A Boy's Song.
Riley, J.   Stepmother, The.
See also **Stepfathers and Stepmothers**

Sterility
Mallarmé.   Anguish.
   Renewal.
   Weary of Bitter Sleep.
Montale.   Feeble sistrum in the wind.

Sterne, Laurence
Muldoon, P.   Yggdrasill.

Stevedores
See **Longshoremen**

Stevens, Wallace
Ciardi, J.   Praise of Good Poets in a Bad Age,
   A.
Clampitt.   Voyages.
Cunningham, J.   With a Copy of Stevens'
   Harmonium.
Eberhart, R.   At the Canoe Club.
Meredith, W.   Here and There.
Prunty.   Wallace Stevens Remembers
   Halloween.
Roethke.   Rouse for Stevens, A.
Schuyler, J.   Fauré Ballade, The.
Stafford, W.   If I Could Be Like Wallace
   Stevens.

Stevenson, Robert Louis
Riley, J.   On a Youthful Portrait of Stevenson.
   To Robert Louis Stevenson.

Stewards and Stewardesses
Amichai [*or* Amikhai].   Stewardess.

Still Lifes
Atwood.   Against Still Life.
Levertov.   Engraved.
Ramanujan.   Still Life.
Sandburg, C.   Still Life.
Tomlinson, C.   Fruit, for sculpture.
   Montage.
   Paring the Apple.
   View, The.
Wilbur, R.   Objects.
Zukofsky, L.   Che Di Lor Suona Su Nella Tua
   Vita.

Stockholm, Sweden
Kizer, C.   Wars in Sweden, The.
Sandburg, C.   Mohammed Bek Hadjetlache.
   Savoir Faire.
   Two Items.

Stoicism
Brontë, E.   Old Stoic, The.
Dickinson, E.   It might be lonelier.
Riley, J.   T. C. Philips.
Rossetti, C.   Study (A Soul), A.

Stonecutting and Stonecutters
Davie, D.   'Sculpture' of Rhyme, The.
   To a Brother in the Mystery.
Jeffers, R.   Old Stone-Mason, The.
   To the Stone-Cutters.
Levertov.   Stonecarver's Poem, The.

Merwin.   Dry Stone Mason, The.
Wright, J.   In a Viennese Cemetery.

Stonehenge, England
Muldoon, P.   Easter Island.

Stones and Rocks
Amichai [*or* Amikhai].   Temporary Poem of My
   Time.
Ammons.   Apologia pro Vita Sua.
   Eolith.
   If Anything Will Level with You Water Will.
   Impulse.
   Upland.
Atwood.   Some Objects of Wood and Stone.
Berry, W.   Dance, A.
   Stones, The.
Bierce.   On Stone.
Blue Cloud.   Gift of Stone.
Broumas, O.   Aphrodite.
Carruth, H.   Almanach du Printemps Vivarois.
   Essay on Stone.
   Naming for Love.
   On Canann Mountain Meadow.
   Song of the Two Crows.
Cooper, J.   Rock Climbing.
Creeley.   After Mallarmé.
   Divisions.
   "I Keep to Myself Such Measures."
   Poem, A: "If the water forms."
   Stone.
Davie, D.   Orpheus.
   Twilight on the Waste Lands.
De la Mare.   Epitaph, An: "Last, Stone, a little
   yet."
   Taciturn, The.
Dickey, J.   Six, The.
Dickinson, E.   How happy is the little Stone.
   Soul selects her own Society, The.
   Too cold is this.
Dove, R.   Fish in the Stone, The.
Drummond de Andrade.   In the Middle of the
   Road.
Eberhart, R.   Big Rock.
   La Crosse at Ninety Miles an Hour.
   Sphinx.
Emerson, R.   Rubies.
   Upon a rock yet uncreate.
Enzensberger, H.   Consistency.
Frost, R.   Of the Stones of the Place.
Graves, R.   Consortium of Stones.
Hall, D.   Granite and Grass.
   Waters.
Heaney, S.   Sandstone Keepsake.
Hughes, T.   Still Life.
   Stone, The.
   Water.
Ignatow, D.   And Step.
   Debate, The.
   Each Stone.
   Invocation: "Dirt and stone, if I may know you
   as you know yourselves."
   Metamorphosis, The.
   Need, The.
Jacobsen, J.   Greek Wind, The.
   Laurentides.
Jeffers, R.   Rock and Hawk.
   To the Stone-Cutters.
Kumin, M.   Stones.
Laughlin, J.   Sinking Stone, The.
Levine, P.   Breath.
   Renaming the Kings.
MacDiarmid, H.   Crystals like Blood.
McGrath, T.   Passages.
Merwin.   Eyes of Summer.
   Prayer of the Eyes, A.
Millay, E.   Second Fig.
Mistral, G.   In Praise of Stones.
Olson, C.   Other Than.
   Stone and Flower Series.
Orr, G.   Field in New England, A.
   Large White Rock Called "The Sleeping
   Angel," A.
Paz.   Landscape.
Plath.   Child's Park Stones.
Raine, K.   Rock.
Rexroth, K.   Lesson in Geography, A.
Ritsos.   Moderation.

   Ready.
   Stones.
   With These Stones.
Roethke.   Harsh Country, The.
Sandburg, C.   Chasers.
   Slabs of the Sunburnt West.
Simic.   Stone.
Szymborska, W.   Conversation with a Rock.
   Conversation with a Stone.
Tomlinson, C.   Head Hewn with an Axe.
   In Defence of Metaphysics.
   Picture of J. T. in a Prospect of Stone, The.
   Stone Speech.
Updike.   Phenomena.
Very.   Sliding Rock, The.
Walcott.   Ruins of a Great House.
Warren, R.   Interjection #2: Caveat.
   It Is Not Dead.
Wilbur, R.   From the Lookout Rock.
   Giacometti.
   On the Marginal Way.
   Thyme Flowering among Rocks.
   Two Voices in a Meadow.
Williams, M.   Rock.
Williams, W.   Rock-Old Dogma, The.
Wordsworth, W.   Inscription on a Rock at Rydal
   Mount.
   Mark the concentrated hazels that enclose.
   To Joanna.
   Who fancied what a pretty sight.
Zukofsky, L.   For Zadkine.

Storms
Ammons.   Heat.
   Monday.
   Rectitude.
   Storm.
   Translating.
Auden.   First Things First.
Bishop, E.   Electrical Storm.
   Little Exercise.
   Norther—Key West, A.
Brontë, E.   'High waving heather.'
   How loud the storm sounds round the Hall!
Broumas, O.   Elegy: "Somebody left the world
   last night, I felt it."
Browning, R.   Adam, Lilith, and Eve.
Burns, R.   Strathallan's Lament.
   Tam o' Shanter; A Tale.
   Winter Night, A.
Byron, G.   Julian [A Fragment].
   Stanzas: "Chill and mirk is the nightly blast."
Carruth, H.   Listen.
   Mountain Cabin, The.
Carver, R.   Downstream.
   Squall, A.
   Window, The.
Clampitt.   Edge of the Hurricane, The.
   Meridian.
Codrescu.   Reverse.
Cowper, W.   Thunder Storm, A.
Crane, H.   Echoes.
   Eternity.
Creeley.   Eye o' the Storm.
Cummings, E. E.   N(o)w / the / how /
   dis(appeared cleverly)world.
Davie, D.   Admiral to His Lady, The.
   Meteorologist, September.
   North Sea, in a Snowstorm, The.
   Sing unto the Lord a New Song.
De la Mare.   Macbeth.
Dickinson, E.   Awful Tempest mashed the air,
   An.
   Cap of Lead across the sky, A.
   Clouds their Backs together laid, The.
   Glee—The great storm is over.
   It struck me—every Day.
   Storm.
   Symptom of the Gale, The.
   There is a tall—pale snow storm.
   These are the Nights that Beetles love.
   Wind begun to knead the Grass, The.
   Wind drew off, The.
   Wind took up the Northern Things, The.
Donne.   Storm[e], The.
Dubie.   Parish.
Dugan, A.   Poem: "What was once an island

with birds."
Summer Gale.
Winter Gale.
Dunbar, P.   Changing Time.
Right's Security.
Rising of the Storm, The.
Eberhart, R.   Scouring, The.
Sea Storm.
Emerson, R.   Seemed, tho' the soft sheen all
    enchants.
Snow-Storm [or Snowstorm], The.
Frost, R.   Line-Storm Song, A.
Lodged.
Once by the Pacific.
Our Singing Strength.
Snow.
Storm Fear.
Graves, R.   Apple Island.
Rhea.
Sirocco at Deyá.
Window Pane, The.
"H. D."   Storm.
Hall, D.   Granite and Grass.
Hamill, S.   Listen, Ianni.
Hardy, T.   Night-Time in Mid-Fall.
She Hears the Storm.
Thunderstorm in Town, A.
Hayden, R.   Electrical Storm.
Herbert, G.   Storm, The.
Herrick.   His Hope or Sheet-Anchor.
Hopkins, G.   Hailstorm in May.
Why if it be so, for the dismal morn.
Hughes, T.   Wind.
Jacobsen, J.   Escape in Ice.
Jarrell, R.   Night before the Night before
    Christmas, The.
November Ghosts, The.
Jeffers, R.   Gale in April.
Storm blowing up, rain and dark weather and
    the roaring wind, The.
Kipling, R.   Before a Midnight Breaks in Storm.
Egg-Shell, The.
Song of the Red War-Boat.
Storm Cone, The.
Kizer, C.   Season of Lovers and Assassins.
Komunyakaa.   After the Fall [of Saigon].
Monoon Season.
Kumin, M.   Out in It.
Lawrence, D. H.   Lightning.
Love Storm.
Passing-Bell, A.
Storm in the Black Forest.
Lindsay, N.   Storm-Flower, The.
Lorde.   Oaxaca.
Suspension.
MacDiarmid, H.   Dying Earth, The.
Wind-bags, The.
MacLeish.   April in November.
November.
McGrath, T.   History.
McHugh, H.   Hurricane Can Cast, A.
Melville, H.   Enviable Isles, The.
Misgivings.
Meredith, G.   Hard Weather.
Roar through the Tall Twin Elm-Trees, A.
Shipwreck of Idomeneus, The.
There fell a sudden rain.
When stormy day is cold & gray.
Merton.   Spring Storm.
Storm at Night, The.
Merwin.   After a Storm.
Millay, E.   Hearing Your Words, and Not a
    Word among Them.
Montale.   Ark, The.
Arsenio.
Storm, The.
Nash, O.   Watched Example Never Boils, A.
Nemerov.   Brainstorm.
Lightning Storm on Fuji.
Storm Windows.
Sunday at the End of Summer.
Oliver, M.   Lightning.
Oppen.   Squall.
Paley, G.   For Jan.
Palmer, M.   No Page (Unturned).
Poem.

Pasternak, B.   Inside the Storm.
Pinkerton, H.   On Fitz Hugh Lane's
    Approaching Storm, Owl's Head, 1860.
Pinsky.   Round.
Plath.   Insolent Storm Strikes at the Skull.
Prunty.   Great Thoughts and Noble Feelings.
Ransom, J.   Miriam Tazewell.
Rexroth, K.   Sottoportico San Zaccaria.
Rich, A.   Attention.
Eastport to Block Island.
Storm Warnings.
Riley, J.   Plantation Hymn.
Shower, The.
Sudden Shower, A.
Ritsos.   Method of Salvation.
Roethke.   Storm, The.
Rossetti, C.   His Banner over Me Was Love.
Love and Death.
Rukeyser, M.   Jetty. Dover, The.
Ringling.
Sandburg, C.   Blizzard Notes.
Storms Begin Far Back.
Way of the World, The.
Sarton, M.   Snow Light, The.
Schuyler, J.   Crocus Night.
Running Footsteps.
Sexton.   Letter Written during a January
    Northeaster.
Shelley, P.   Vision of the Sea, A.
Snyder, G.   It.
Stafford, W.   Found in a Storm.
People Who Went By in Winter.
Storm Warnings.
Stock, R.   Storm.
Stockton, A.   Lyric Ode, A.—Feb. 28.
On the Suns Setting Clear after a Three Days
    Storm.
Swenson, M.   Beginning to Squall.
Swift, J.   Description of a City Shower, A.
Storm, The.
Tate, J.   Storm.
Thomas, D.   Shall Gods Be Said to Thump The
    Clouds.
Tomlinson, C.   After the Storm.
Awakening, The.
Thunder in Tuscany.
Walcott.   Dark August.
Warren, R.   Ah, Anima!
Fierce Horsemen, The.
Heat Wave Breaks.
Sonnets of Two Summers.
Twice Born.
Weiss, T.   Summer Thunderstorm, A.
Wheatley, P.   On Messrs Hussey and Coffin.
Whitman, W.   Patrolling Barnegat.
Proud Music of the Storm.
Whittier.   Palatine, The.
Sisters, The.
Storm on Lake Asquam.
Wilbur, R.   March.
Storm in April, A.
Williams, C. K.   Baby, I don't want.
Snow: I.
Storm, The.
Williams, M.   Thinking Friday Night with a
    Gothic Storm Going about Final Causes and
    Logos and Mitzi Mayfair.
Williams, W.   Dark Day, The.
Lady speaks, The.
Spring Storm.
Storm, The.
Wordsworth, W.   Composed During a Storm.
Fragment of a "Gothic" Tale.
I love upon a stormy night.
Whirl-blast from behind the hill, A.
Wright, C.   Spring Storm.
Wright, J.   At Thomas Hardy's Birthplace, 1953.
From a Bus Window in Central Ohio, Just
    before a Thunder Shower.
Snowstorms in the Midwest.
Yeats.   Mad as the Mist and Snow.
Pity of Love, The.
Zagajewski.   Over America.
See also **Blizzards; Hurricanes; Tornadoes**
Storytelling and Storytellers
Angelou.   When I Think about Myself.

Armantrout.   Plot, The.
Atwood.   True Stories.
Blue Cloud.   Old Tom would tell us.
White Corn Sister.
Clifton, L.   Telling Our Stories.
Coleridge, S.   Love.
Creeley.   Bresson's Movies.
Childish.
Epic.
Hero.
Story, The.
Tell Story.
Than I.
They Say.
Think.
Davie, D.   Remembering the 'Thirties.
De la Mare.   Martha.
Dickinson, E.   Ended, ere it begun.
Dove, R.   Roast Possum.
Dunbar, P.   Cabin Tale, A.
Harriet Beecher Stowe.
Frost, R.   Girl's Garden, A.
Gallagher, T.   Boat Ride.
Graves, R.   Devil's Advice to Story-Tellers, The.
To Juan at the Winter Solstice.
Hall, D.   Stories.
Hamill, S.   Arse Poetica.
Hughes, L.   Aunt Sue's Stories.
Hughes, T.   Crow's Account of the Battle.
Kipling, R.   Captive, The.
Coiner, The.
To James Whitcomb Riley.
Komunyakaa.   Moonshine.
Story, A.
Laughlin, J.   Hitchhiker, The.
Levertov.   Marta (Brazil, 1928).
Lorde.   Teacher.
Lux.   Wife Hits Moose.
Major, C.   Tewa Victories.
Merrill, J.   Kostas Tympakianákis.
Merwin.   Old Flag.
Muldoon, P.   Frog, The.
Seanchas.
Nash, O.   Fee Fi Ho Hum, No Wonder Baby
    Sucks Her Thumb.
There Were Giants in Those Days or Maybe
    There Weren't.
Olson, C.   As I went in and out I heard pieces.
Pagis.   Epilogue to Robinson Crusoe.
Paley, G.   How to Tell a Story (My Method)
    (Most of the Time).
Poem about Storytelling, A.
Parker, D.   Song for an April Dusk.
Pessoa.   Nothing comes of nothing. We are
    nothing.
Ramanujan.   Lines to a Granny.
Riley, J.   Evensong.
Little Orphant Annie.
Robinson, E.   Captain Craig.
Lost Anchors.
Stafford's Cabin.
Rossetti, C.   If the sun could tell us half / That
    he hears and sees.
Sing me a song— / What shall I sing?
Rumi.   Humble living does not diminish. It fills.
In between Stories.
Minute I heard my first love story, The.
Story Water.
Sandburg, C.   Fire Pages.
Iglits and His Wife.
Legends.
Sexton.   Cinderella.
Gold Key, The.
Rowing.
Story for Rose on the Midnight Flight to
    Boston, A.
Wallflower.
Simic.   Bedtime Story.
Fable: "In my favorite one."
Point, The.
Stafford, W.   Story Time.
Tomlinson, C.   Dialectic.
Walcott.   Man Who Loved Islands, The.
Warren, R.   How to Tell a Love Story.
Whalen, P.   Murals Not Yet Dreamed.
Whittier.   Tent on the Beach, The.

Wilbur, R.   Fable, A.
 Folk Tune.
Williams, C. K.   Bob.
 Herakles.
 Near the Haunted Castle.
Williams, T.   Life Story.
Wilner, E.   As Soft and as Pink as a Nursery.
 Renegade.
Wordsworth, W.   Motto Intended for Poems on
 the Naming of Places.
Yeats.   Grey Rock, The.
 Under the Moon.

Stowe, Harriet Beecher
Dunbar, P.   Harriet Beecher Stowe.
Schuyler, J.   Reunion, A.
Whittier.   Greeting, A.

Strangers
Ai.   Capture.
Borges.   Stranger, The.
Brontë, E.   And now the house-dog stretched
 once more.
Carver, R.   Reading Something in the
 Restaurant.
Celan.   In Egypt.
Cummings, E. E.   Once like a spark.
De la Mare.   Exile.
 Galliass, The.
 Mistress Fell.
 Peeping Tom.
 Stranger, The.
 Three Strangers, The.
 Who?
Ferlinghetti, L.   Ladakh Buddhess Biker.
Frost, R.   Love and a Question.
Gallagher, T.   Hug, The.
Graves, R.   Fortunate Child.
Gunn, T.   First Meeting with a Possible Mother-
 in-Law.
Herrick.   Once Seen, and No More.
Hughes, L.   Madam and the Wrong Visitor.
 Subway Face.
Ignatow, D.   Each of Us.
Kinsella, T.   Stranger, The.
Kipling, R.   Stranger, The.
Larkin, P.   Strangers.
Laughlin, J.   Stranger in the House, The.
 That Other World.
Logan, J.   Lines for an Unknown Lover.
 Paperboys, The.
MacNeice.   Restaurant Car.
Meredith, W.   Old Photograph of Strangers, An.
Merwin.   Who It Is.
Patchen.   Stranger, The.
Riley, J.   Man by the Name of Bolus, A.
Rilke.   Unknown Woman's Afternoon.
Ritsos.   Doubtful Encounters.
Robinson, E.   Flammonde.
 Fleming Helphenstine.
Sandburg, C.   Two Strangers Breakfast.
Sarton, M.   Strangers.
Very.   Strangers, The.
 Yourself.
Warren, R.   Instant on Crowded Street.
 Passers-By on Snowy Night.
 Somewhere.
 To a Face in the Crowd.
Whitman, W.   This Moment Yearning and
 Thoughtful.
 To a Stranger.
 To You.
Wilbur, R.   Caserta Garden.
 Transit.
Williams, C. K.   On the Other Hand.

Strawberries
Logue, C.   Good Taste.
Merwin.   Strawberries.
Millay, E.   Strawberry Shrub, The.
Mistral, G.   Wild Strawberry, The.
Paley, G.   False strawberry is.
 When the wild strawberry leaves turn.
Plath.   Bitter Strawberries.
Wordsworth, W.   Foresight.

Streams
Stock, R.   Several Large Rocks in a Swiftly
 Rushing Stream.

See also **Brooks and Streams**

Street People
Ignatow, D.   Illusion, An.
 Say Pardon.

See also **Homeless, The**

Street Performers
Ashbery, J.   Street Musicians.
Clampitt.   Subway Singer, The.
Cummings, E. E.   At the head of this street a
 gasping organ is waving moth-eaten.
 It is winter a moon in the afternoon.
Simic.   Amazing Potato Peeler, The.

Streetcars
Levine, P.   On the Birth of Good & Evil during
 the Long Winter of '28.
Merwin.   Cart, The.
Sandburg, C.   Halsted Street Car.

Streetlights
Hughes, L.   Late Corner.

Streets
Ammons.   Street Song.
Angelou.   Letter to an Aspiring Junkie.
Borges.   Street with a Pink Corner Store.
 Streets, The.
 Unknown Street.
Crane, H.   Euclid Avenue.
Crane, S.   Grey and boiling street, A.
Creeley.   Colors.
 Place, A.
 Return.
Cummings, E. E.   As usual i did not find him in
 cafes,the more dissolute atmosphere.
 At the head of this street a gasping organ is
 waving moth-eaten.
Eberhart, R.   Fragment of New York, 1929.
Gunn, T.   Release, The.
 San Francisco Streets.
Hardy, T.   In a Cathedral City.
Hughes, L.   Railroad Avenue.
Kinsella, T.   Irwin Street.
Larkin, P.   Street Lamps.
Lawrence, D. H.   Street Lamps.
Levertov.   Whisper, The.
Levi, P.   Via Cigna.
Levine, P.   On the Corner.
 These Streets.
MacNeice.   Street Scene.
Nemerov.   Frozen City, The.
O'Hara, F.   Step Away from Them, A.
Olson, C.   Stone and Flower Series.
Owen, W.   Six o'clock in Princes Street.
Paz.   Along Galeana Street.
Pinsky.   Street of Furthest Memory, The.
 Street, The.
Riley, J.   Lockerbie Street.
Sandburg, C.   Streets Too Old.
Schuyler, J.   Back.
Shapiro, K.   Manhole Covers.
Tomlinson, C.   Mirror in the Roadway, The.
Warren, R.   Insant on Crowded Street.
Williams, W.   Attic Which Is Desire, The.
 Term, The.
Zagajewski.   From Memory.

See also **Roads**

Strength
Amichai [*or* Amikhai].   You Must Not Show
 Weakness.
 You Mustn't Show Weakness.
Arnold, M.   Growing Old.
Blue Cloud.   First Brother.
Bly, R.   Indigo Bunting, The.
Bogan, L.   Single Sonnet.
Brooks, G.   "Strong Men, Riding Horses."
Browning, E.   Weakest Thing, The.
Bukowski.   John Dillinger Marches On.
Burns, R.   Prayer, under the Pressure of Violent
 Anguish, A.
Clifton, L.   Female.
Coleridge, S.   Eagle and the Tortoise, The.
Crane, S.   Chant you loud of punishments.
Creeley.   Song, The: "It still makes sense."
Cullen, C.   Minutely Hurt.
 To the Swimmer.
Dickinson, E.   Banish Air from Air.
 I hope you may sometime be.

Not to discover weakness is.
Dunbar, P.   Warrior's Prayer, The.
Eberhart, R.   Birth of the Spirit, The.
Emerson, R.   Compensation.
 I leave the book, I leave the wine.
 Samson stark at Dagon's knee.
 Vain against him were hostile blows.
 With the key of the secret he marches faster.
Graves, R.   Lion Lover.
 Superstition.
Gunn, T.   Diagrams.
 Exercise, The.
HaNagid.   Soar, Don't Settle.
Heaney, S.   Antaeus.
Herbert, G.   Constancy.
Herrick.   By Use Comes Easinesse.
 Christian Militant.
 Upon Julias Recovery.
Hughes, T.   Contender, The.
 Sketching a Thatcher.
Jeffers, R.   Contemplation of the Sword.
 Give Your Heart to the Hawks.
 Rock and Hawk.
Lawrence, D. H.   Hills, The.
Levi, P.   Glacier, The.
Meredith, G.   Angel, be ye ne'er in doubt, An.
 Burden of Strength, The.
 Lady C. M., The.
Moore, M.   Peter.
Olson, C.   Double, double, root and branch.
Patchen.   Sturdy Legs, That.
Piercy.   For Strong Women.
 Icon.
 Woman in the Ordinary, The.
Plath.   Mushrooms.
Ransom, J.   Spiel of [the] Three Mountebanks.
Rich, A.   Phantasia for Elvira Shatayev.
 Power.
Rossetti, C.   And Now Why Tarriest Thou?
 Helpmeet For Him, A.
 If I Had Words.
 Martyr, A.
 O glorious sea that in each climbing wave.
 Our Widowed Queen.
 Resurgam.
 Study (A Soul), A.
Rukeyser, M.   When the young man reaches his
 full height.
Sandburg, C.   Love beyond Keeping.
 Telegram.
 Upstream.
Smith, S.   I Do Not Speak.
Tennyson, A.   Will.
Very.   Mountain, The.
Whittier.   Help.
 Our State.
Wordsworth, W.   Translation of a Celebrated
 Greek Song.
Yeats.   Wild Old Wicked Man, The.

Strikebreakers
Hughes, L.   Labor Storm.

Strikes and Strikers
Berryman.   Thanksgiving: Detroit.
Dugan, A.   Love and Money.
Frost, R.   Lone Striker, A.
McGrath, T.   Triumphal March.
Niedecker.   We know him—Law and Order
 League.
Rexroth, K.   Hiking on the Coast Range.
Rukeyser, M.   Time of finks and nobles, A.

String
Major, C.   String, The.
Rumi.   Long String, The.

See also **Rope**

Striptease
Baudelaire.   Dancing Serpent, The.
 'Lola de Valence' by Manet.
Beckett, S.   Serena III.
Cummings, E. E.   Sh estiffl / ystrut sal.
Cunningham, J.   It Was in Vegas. Celibate and
 able.
 New York: 5 March 1957.
Dubie.   Genesis Text for Larry Levis, Who Died
 Alone, A.
McHugh, H.   Gig at Big Al's.

Muldoon, P. Big Liz.
Olson, C. As the shield goddess, Mycenae.
Prunty. Depression, the War, and Gypsy Rose
  Lee, The.
Ramanujan. Highway Stripper.
Rukeyser, M. Burlesque.
Sandburg, C. Three Slants at New York.
Stafford, W. Adults Only.
Williams, M. Stripper, The.

Strokes
Dove, R. Recovery.
  Stroke, The.
Dubie. Physical Moon beyond Paterson, A.
Hall, D. Green Shelf, The.
McHugh, H. Stroke.
Plath. Paralytic.
Rukeyser, M. Resurrection of the Right Side.

Struwwelpeter
Kumin, M. Fräulein Reads Instructive Rhymes.

Stuart, Charles Edward (The Young Pretender)
Burns, R. O'er the Water to Charlie.

**Stuart, James Francis Edward (The Old
  Pretender)**
Burns, R. There'll Never Be Peace till Jamie
  Comes Hame.
  Up and Warn A' Willie.

Students
Amichai [or Amikhai]. Giving of the Torah,
  The.
Angelou. Communication II.
Ashbery, J. And You Know.
Browning, E. Student, The.
Ciardi, J. Emeritus Addresses the School, An.
  Generation Gap.
  Memoir of a One-Armed Harp Teacher.
  On Flunking a Nice Boy out of School.
  To My Students.
Codrescu. School Daze.
Collins, B. Marginalia.
  Monday Morning.
  Schoolsville.
Davie, D. Sorting the Personae.
Gunn, T. To a Dead Graduate Student.
HaNagid. Good Students Tend, The.
Heaney, S. Alphabets.
  Cloistered.
  Singing School.
Hughes, L. Conservatory Student Struggles with
  Higher Instrumentation.
  Theme for English B.
Ignatow, D. Notes for a Lecture.
Jarrell, R. Randall Jarrell, Office Hours 10-11.
Lawrence, D. H. Study.
Logan, J. Assessment, The.
  Lines for a Young Man Who Talked.
  On a Prize Crucifix by a Student Sculptor.
  Papa's House, Son's Room.
  Staying Awake.
Lorde. Workers Rose on May Day or Postcript
  to Karl Marx, The.
Meredith, W. Fledglings.
  His Students.
Milosz, C. Lecture, A.
Milton. Elegy 1: To Charles Diodati.
Moore, M. Student, The.
Nemerov. September, the First Day of School.
O'Hara, F. Romanze, or the Music Students.
Oppen. Students Gather, The.
Owen, W. Bold Horatius.
Riley, J. My Henry.
  Penalty of Genius, The.
  Poor Student, The.
Sheridan, T. Epilogue to *Julius Caesar*, The.
  Prologue Designed for the Play of *Oedipus*,
    Written in Greek, and Performed by Mr.
    Sheridan's Scholars, A.
  Prologue Spoken at Mr. Sheridan's School.
  Prologue Spoken before a Greek Play, at the
    Reverend Dr. Sheridan's School, at the
    Breaking-Up of His Scholars for Christmas.
  Thus Cacus-like, His Calves He Backwards
    Pulls.
  To His Excellency Our Lord Carteret, Lord
    Lieutenant of Ireland: The Humble Petition of
    Lord Viscount Mont-Cashel, and the Rest of

His School-Fellows.
Stafford, W. Address to the Senior Class.
  At This Point on the Page.
Stockton, A. Addressed to a Student of
  Divinity.
Very. Scholar Dreaming, The.
Warren, R. To Certain Old Masters.
Wheatley, P. To the University of Cambridge, in
  New-England.
Whitman, W. To a Western Boy.
Wilbur, R. For the Student Strikers.
Williams, M. For J. William Fulbright on the
  Day of His Death.
  Young Instructor Talks to Himself Winding Up
    the Semester, The.

Stupidity
Cummings, E. E. Ballad of an Intellectual.
  "Economic secu / rity" is a cu.
  That famous fatheads find that each.
  Yonder deadfromtheneckup graduate of a.
De la Mare. Pollie.
Dryden, J. Mac Flecknoe [or, A Satire upon the
  True-Blue Protestant Poet T. S.].
Han-shan. Four or five dumb upstarts.
  Superior man's mind is terribly sharp, The.
Hughes, L. Prize Fighter.
Lawrence, D. H. Life and the Human
  Consciousness.
MacDiarmid, H. Lourd on My Hert.
Milosz, C. Account.
Nash, O. It Would Have Been Quicker to Walk,
  or, Don't Tell Me We're There Already.
  Rapunzel, Rapunzel, Let's Let Down Our Hair.
Parker, D. Sonnet: "Sweeter your laugh than
  trill of lark at dawn."
Williams, W. Education a Failure.
  For a Low Voice.
  Hey Red!
  These Purists.
Wright, J. Presentation of Two Birds to My
  Son, A.

Stuttering and Stutterers
Dugan, A. Stutterer.
Sheridan, T. Joshua Battus's Sepeech to the
  Paparliament.

Sublimity
Mahon. Antarctica.

Submarines
Codrescu. Seeing out of the Sub.
Kipling, R. Farewell and adieu to you, Harwich
  Ladies.
  Tin Fish.
Stafford, W. At Fort Worden: Calling Names.

Submission
Angelou. Song for the Old Ones.
Auden. Legend.
Byron, G. Last Words on Greece.
Cowper, W. Attempt at the Manner of Waller,
  An.
  Dog and the Water-Lily, The.
Dickey, J. Leap, The.
Frost, R. Reluctance.
Gunn, T. In Santa Maria del Popolo.
Guyon. Divine Justice Amiable.
Herbert, G. Submission.
Herrick. Obedience in Subjects.
  To Anthea, Who May Command Him Anything.
Kizer, C. Bitch.
Kunitz, S. Master and Mistress.
Laughlin, J. It's Warm under Your Thumb.
Meredith, G. Ireland.
  To A.M.
Montale. House by the Sea.
Nash, O. Tweedledee and Tweedledoom.
Neruda. Star.
Piercy. Friend, The.
  Unclench Yourself.
Rossetti, C. Lord, what have I that I may offer
  Thee?
Rukeyser, M. Long Enough. Long Enough.
Sidney, S. Since, shunning pain, I ease can
  never find.
Tomlinson, C. Oxen: Ploughing at Fiesole.
Whittier. Common Question, The.

Suburbs and Suburban Life
Angelou. Through the Inner City to the
  Suburbs.
Atwood. City Planners, The.
  Letter from Persephone.
Bishop, E. Flood, The.
Borges. Northern Suburb.
Ciardi, J. Boy or Girl.
  Suburban.
  Suburban Homecoming.
Clampitt. New Life, A.
Cooper, J. Nightmare of the Suburbs, A.
Cummings, E. E. E / cco the uglies / t.
Cunningham, J. Statistics.
Davie, D. Hertfordshire.
Dugan, A. Love Song: Class Analysis.
Hall, D. Poem with One Fact.
Hardy, T. Snow in the Suburbs.
Ignatow, D. Peace for Awhile.
Jacobsen, J. Cul de Sac.
Jeffers, R. Carmel Point.
Kizer, C. Suburbans, The.
Lawrence, D. H. Flat Suburbs, S.W., in the
  Morning.
  Suburbs on a Hazy Day.
Levertov. Ways of Conquest.
McGrath, T. Excursion: Or: O Columbus!, The.
Nemerov. Suburban Prophecy.
Oppen. Nation.
Prunty. Downtown Bus, The.
Riley, J. Town and Country.
Rimbaud, A. To Music.
Roethke. Idyll: "Now as from maple to elm the
  flittermice skitter and twirl."
Sandburg, C. Suburban Sicilian Sketches.
Schuyler, J. Man in Blue, A.
  Sky Eats Up the Trees, The.
Smith, S. Suburb.
  Suburban Classes, The.
Tomlinson, C. Gladstone Street.
Updike. Short Days, The.
  Sleepless in Scarsdale.
  Suburban Madrigal.
Van Duyn. Evening Stroll in the Suburbs.
  Walking the Dog: A Diatribe.
Warren, R. Commuter's Entry in a Connecticut
  Diary.
Wilbur, R. To an American Poet Just Dead.
Williams, M. Love Poem: "Six o'clock and /
  the sun rises."
  Main Street.

Subways
Clampitt. Amaranth and Moly.
  Subway Singer, The.
  Times Square Water Music.
Ferlinghetti, L. 26.
Glück, L. Cripple in the Subway, The.
Hughes, L. Midnight Raffle.
  Subway Face.
  Subway Rush Hour.
Ignatow, D. Subway.
Laughlin, J. Before I Die.
Logan, J. Brothers: Two Saltimbanques, The.
Merrill, J. After the ball.
Milosz, C. Esse.
Oppen. Vulcan.
Pound, E. In a Station of the Metro.
Rukeyser, M. Study in a Late Subway.
Sandburg, C. Subway.
Simic. Punch Minus Judy.
Tate, A. Subway, The.
Walcott. Village Life, A.

Success
Auden. Managers, The.
Carver, R. Commerce.
Cavafy. Procession of Dionysus.
Ciardi, J. Freshman Sonnet: Success.
Crane, S. Successful man has thrust himself,
  The.
Creeley. Money.
Dickinson, E. Success is counted sweetest.
  Success is dust, but an aim.
  We grow accustomed to the Dark.
Emerson, R. Cloud upon cloud / Clouds after
  rain.
  Fate.

When success exalts thy lot.
Graves, R.   Fragment of a Lost Poem.
HaNagid.   Pass of Sand.
Respect and Discretion.
Hardy, T.   Ruined Maid, The.
Herrick.   Merits Make the Man.
Poets Good Wishes for the Most Hopefull and
Handsome Prince, the Duke of Yorke, The.
Pray and Prosper.
Regression Spoiles Resolution.
To His Nephew, to Be Prosperous in His Art of
Painting.
To Worthy Friend, M. Tho. Falconbirge.
Wassaile, The.
Hughes, L.   Success.
Jacobsen, J.   Minor Poet, The.
Jonson, B.   Elegy, An: "Can beauty that did
prompt me first to write."
Kipling, R.   If—.
Larkin, P.   Success Story.
Lawrence, D. H.   Are You Pining?
Played-Out Game, A.
Meredith, G.   Aimée.
Nash, O.   Kindly Unhitch That Star, Buddy.
Rexroth, K.   Untitled: "I am fifty-two years
old."
Riley, J.   Claude Matthews.
Griggsby's Station.
John McKeen.
Lines to Perfesser John Clark Ridpath.
Robinson, E.   Old Trails.
Rukeyser, M.   Everything here is real and of our
joy.
Spender, S.   Public Son of a Public Man, The.
Whitman, W.   When I Heard at the Close of The
Day.
Whittier.   Seeking of the Waterfall, The.
Williams, C. K.   Spirit the Triumph, The.
Yeats.   To a Friend Whose Work Has Come to
Nothing.

Sudan
Kipling, R.   Fuzzy-Wuzzy.
Kitchener's School.
Lux.   Sudd as Metaphor, The.

Suez Canal
Nemerov.   Reflexions on the Seizure of the
Suez, and on a Proposal to Line the Banks of
That Canal with Billboard Advertisements.

Suffering
Amichai [or Amikhai].   Do Not Accept.
I Have Dead People.
If My Belly Aches.
Love Poem: "People use each other."
Atwood.   You did it / it was you who started the
countdown.
Auden.   Musée des Beaux Arts.
Baudelaire.   Meditation.
Reversibility.
Berryman.   On the London Train.
Bierce.   Mystery, A.
Borges.   Christ on the Cross.
Bradstreet, A.   Upon Some Distemper of Body.
Brontë, E.   Far, far away is mirth withdrawn.
Stars.
That dreary lake, that midnight sky.
Brooks, G.   My Dreams, My Works Must Wait
Till after Hell.
Bukowski.   462-0614.
Crunch, The.
Burns, R.   Prayer, under the Pressure of Violent
Anguish, A.
Byron, G.   Epistle to a Friend.
What Matter the Pangs of a Husband and
Father.
Carruth, H.   Saving Way, The.
Cavafy.   Love, A.
Cavalcanti.   Because I expect never to return.
Eyes of that gentle country girl, The.
I pray you who speak of suffering.
I saw Love in eyes.
My latest cruel misfortune.
Oh you, whose eyes carry.
Why weren't my eyes blinded.
You could see when I met you.
Celan.   Tenebrae.
Ciardi, J.   Lines while Walking Home from a

Party on Charles Street.
Tragedy-Maker, The.
Clifton, L.   Leda 1.
Creeley.   Fact, The.
On a Theme by Lawrence, Hearing Purcell.
Revelation, The.
Versions.
Cullen, C.   Harsh World That Lashest Me.
Magnets.
Shroud of Color, The.
Thorn Forever in the Breast, A.
Cunningham, J.   Hymn in Adversity.
"Dario."   Nocturne: "I want to express my
anguish in verses that tell."
Spes.
Davie, D.   Across the Bay.
Heart Beats.
Dickinson, E.   After great pain a formal feeling
comes.
For each ecstatic instant.
For the comprehension of Suffering.
I wish one could be sure the suffering.
It is a Suffering, to have a sea.
Through the strait pass of suffering.
Time does go on.
To know just how He suffered—would be dear.
Unto a broken heart.
Dubie.   Elegy to the Pulley of Superior Oblique.
Dugan, A.   On a Desolation of the Animals at
Night.
Suffering Ophthalmologist, The.
Teacher's Vacation Lament in the Country.
Untitled Poem: "I never saw any point."
Dunbar, P.   Prayer, A: "O Lord, the hard-won
miles."
We Wear the Mask.
Eberhart, R.   Edgar Lee Masters.
Emerson, R.   Heroism.
Enzensberger, H.   Employee, The.
Faiz.   If I Were Certain.
García Lorca.   Elegy: "Like a censer filled with
desire."
It Is True.
Prologue: "Here, my God, / is my heart."
Your Childhood in Menton.
Ginsberg, A.   Change, The: *Kyoto-Tokyo
Express.*
September on Jessore Road.
Under the World There's a Lot of Ass, a Lot of
Cunt.
Glück, L.   Autumnal.
Elms.
Pictures of the People in the War.
Poem: "In the early evening, as now, a man is
bending."
Seated Figure.
Graves, R.   Records.
Stolen Jewel.
Gurney, I.   Drachms and Scruples.
For Mercy of Death.
Last of the Book, The.
What Evil Coil.
Hafiz [or Hafez].   From the Persian of Hafiz.
HaNagid.   Luxuries Ease.
Multiple Troubles of Man, The.
Suffer the World.
Hardy, T.   Hap.
Hayden, R.   Soledad.
Herbert, G.   Dialogue, A.
Love Unknown.
Repentance.
Herrick.   Christs Suffering.
Comforts in Contentions.
Great Grief, Great Glory.
His Saviour[']s Words, Going to the Cross[e].
Patience, or Comforts in Crosses.
Satisfaction for Sufferings.
Suffer Thou that Canst not Shift.
Sufferance.
Sufferings.
To God.
Hughes, L.   Cora.
How Thin a Blanket.
Hurt.
Minstrel Man.
Nonette.

Soledad.
Strange Hurt.
Hughes, T.   Emily Brontë.
God, A.
Sacrifice.
Ivanov, G.   Sleeping he saw Ophelia in his
dream.
Jackson, L.   Wind Suffers [of Blowing], The.
Jeffers, R.   Calm and Full the Ocean.
King of Beasts, The.
We Are Those People.
Kinnell.   Burn, The.
Kinsella, T.   Better is an handful with quietness.
Kizer, C.   Suppressing the Evidence.
Kunitz, S.   Welcome the Wrath.
Laughlin, J.   Now Love Speaks.
Rome: In the Café.
Lawrence, D. H.   Bei Hennef.
End, The.
Levertov.   Of Being.
Lindsay, N.   Who Knows?
Mallarmé.   Anguish.
Jinx, The.
Melville, H.   Armies of the Wilderness, The.
Pebbles
Meredith, G.   Martin's Puzzle.
Riddle for Men, The.
War.
Year's Sheddings, The.
Meredith, W.   Korean Woman Seated by a Wall,
A.
Merwin.   Chaff, The.
Michelangelo Buonarroti.   Fear of death! Who'd
shove, The.
Humbly I bow my shoulders, bear the yoke.
I weep, I burn—burn up!—my heart thereby.
If fire, so quick to char.
If I'm more alive because love burns and chars
me.
If she rejoices in my tears, and you.
Love in your eyes? No; life and death are there.
More it seems I agonize, the more, The.
My death is what I live on; seems to me.
My reason, out of sorts with me, deplores.
O blessed souls, who high in heaven delight.
So I can best endure.
What's to become of me? What's this you're
doing.
You revel in my torments, only you.
Your merciful, sweet care.
Millay, E.   Ancient Gesture, An.
Fatal Interview.
Felicity of Grief!—even Death being kind.
Here is a wound that never will heal, I know.
Pity me not because the light of day.
That Love at length should find me out and
bring.
Milosz, C.   Alcoholic Enters the Gates of
Heaven, An.
Counsels.
Helene.
Prescription.
Story, A.
Theodicy.
Why.
Mistral, G.   Summit.
Montale.   Reed that softly, The.
Nash, O.   What the Well-Read Patient Is Talking
About, or, Look, Ma, What I Got!
Nemerov.   Virgin and Martyr.
Olson, C.   All You Can Do.
Ode on Nativity, An.
Orr, G.   Screaming Out Loud.
Some Part of the Lyric.
Parker, D.   For a Lady Who Must Write Verse.
Incurable.
Portrait, A.
Pour Prendre Congé.
Second Oldest Story, The.
Temptress, The.
To a Much Too Unfortunate Lady.
Patchen.   I Can't Understand! I Can't
Understand!
Pessoa.   Autopsychography.
Opium Eater.
Petrarch.   After I fled the place where many

years.
Clothing of green, deep crimson, black, or
  purple.
Good luck is slow to reach me, always late.
Happy in sleep, content to lie around.
I feel the bitter rain of tears distilled.
I go on listening, but I cannot hear.
I really did believe I would go on.
If an unfeigning heart, and amorous faith.
If I could hope by dying to be rid.
If, in this fourteenth year of all my sighs.
Love was perhaps a happy thing onetime.
Sea has not such creatures in its waves, The.
Since what I hope for's taking far too long.
Sparrow on house-top never was alone.
Sweet anger, sweet disdain, sweet times of
  peace.
That time of day the rapid sky inclines.
That window has my everlasting hate.
Very instant he has loosed his shot, The.
Whatever wonder is found.
When I look back and see how the swift years.
When the sun sinks his golden chariot.
You were a haven once, my little room.
Piercy. Burying Blues for Janis.
Ransom, J. Lady Lost.
  Necrological.
Riley, J. O Life! O Beyond!
  Our Queer Old World.
  Unless.
Rilke. Happy Men and Women.
Rimbaud, A. Tortured Heart.
Ritsos. Roots of the World, The.
Robinson, E. As a World Would Have It.
Rossetti, C. Endure Hardness.
  Love Attacked.
  Sappho.
  Sick Child's Meditation, A.
  There's Snow on the Fields.
  What is it Jesus saith unto the soul?
  Yes, I too could face death and never shrink.
Seifert. Opening Poem.
  When in the history books.
  Year 1934, The.
Spender, S. Epilogue to a Human Drama.
Stockton, A. On Hearing the Cooing of a Dove,
  a Song.
  Soliliguy in a Sleepless Night.
  Sudden Production of Mrs. Stockton's in One of
    Those Many Anxious Nights in Which She
    Watched with Mr. Stockton in His Last
    Illness, A.
Sze. Moenkopi.
Tate, J. Success Comes to Cow Creek.
Very. My People are destroyed for lack of
  Knowledge.—Hosea 4:6.
Walker, A. At First.
  Diamonds on Liz's Bosom, The.
Warren, R. Internal Injuries.
  Ransom.
Whittier. Christian Slave, The.
  Watchers, The.
Williams, C. K. Dog, The.
  On the Roof.
  This Is a Sin.
Williams, T. Little Town, The.
Williams, W. Complaint.
Wright, J. In Memory of Leopardi.
  Three Stanzas From Goethe.
Wyatt, S. All ye that know of care and
  heaviness.
  Alone musing, / Remembering.
  At last withdraw your cruelty.
  Complaining, alas, without redress.
  Farewell, all my welfare.
  Fortune, what aileth thee.
  His Reward.
  I love, loved, and so doth she.
  I see my plaint with open ears.
  Might I as well within my song belay.
  My love is like unto th'eternal fire.
  Now must I learn to feign.
  O miserable sorrow withouten cure!
  Suffering in sorrow, in hope to attain.
  To make an end of all this strife.
  To whom should I sue to ease my pain?

When that I call unto my mind.
Ye know my heart, my lady dear.
Yeats. Fascination of What's Difficult, The.
Zagajewski. Life Sentence.
See also **Pain**
Suffolk, England
  Davie, D. Suffolk.
  Tomlinson, C. Hedgerows.
  Poem for My Father.
Suffrage
  Orr, G. Demonstration, The.
See also **Voting and Voters**
Sugar
  Clampitt. Hispaniola.
  Gallagher, T. Sugar.
  Komunyakaa. Sugar.
  Merrill, J. Domino.
  Pagis. Sugarduke.
  Rumi. Dissolver of Sugar.
Sugar Cane
  Ai. Cuba, 1962.
  Clampitt. Hispaniola.
  Fayzi [*or* Faydi *or* Feisi *or* Feizi]. Wilt thou
    life's best elixir drain?
  Komunyakaa. Sugar.
Suicide
  Ai. Antihero, The.
    Nothing but Color.
    Star Vehicle (My Senior Year in High School).
    Talking to His Reflection in a Shallow Pond.
  Amichai [*or* Amikhai]. Jerusalem's Suicide
    Attempts.
  Ammons. Ritual for Eating the World.
  Angelou. Chicken-Licken.
  Ashbery, J. Illustration.
  Berryman. Death Ballad.
    Of Suicide.
  Borges. Suicide, The.
  Brontë, E. F. de Samara to A. G. A.
    O hinder me by no delay.
  Broumas, O. Landscape with Poets.
  Bukowski. Almost Made Up Poem, An.
    Green.
    Suicide.
  Carruth, H. Re-Acquaintance.
  Ciardi, J. Mutterings.
    Tragedy-Maker, The.
    Trying to Feel Something.
  Clampitt. Dahlia Gardens, The.
  Coleridge, S. Suicide's Argument, The.
  Cooper, J. For the Recorder of Suicides.
    Messages.
    Suicide Note.
  Creeley. Hart Crane.
    Two Times.
    Up Here.
    What's for Dinner.
  Cullen, C. Ballad of the Brown Girl, The.
    Mood.
  Cummings, E. E. In a middle of a room.
    Will i ever forget that precarious moment?
  Davie, D. Mens Sana in Corpore Sano.
  De la Mare. Suicide, The.
  Dickey, J. Leap, The.
  Dickinson, E. He scanned it—staggered.
  Drummond de Andrade. Don't Kill Yourself.
  Dubie. *Anima Poeta:* A Christmas Entry for the
    Suicide, Mayakovsky.
  Dugan, A. In Memoriam: Donald Mark Fall.
  Dunbar, P. Right to Die, The.
  Eberhart, R. Flow of Thought.
    Hardy Perennial.
    How It Is.
    On Returning to a Lake in Spring.
    Parker River, The.
    Suicide Note.
  Euripides. Chorus of Troizenian Women.
    Chorus sing of escape, The.
    Daemon initiate, spirit.
    Lift my head, help me up.
    Men you strike.
    No more, O my spirit.
    O Spirit, / spark by spark.
  Fenton, J. Letter to John Fuller.
  Ferlinghetti, L. And she "like a young year."

Gallagher, T. Their Heads Bent toward Each
    Other Like Flowers.
  Ginsberg, A. To Lindsay.
  Graves, R. Call It a Good Marriage.
    Song: Lift-Boy.
    Suicide in The Copse, The.
  Gunn, T. Elegy: "I can almost see it."
  Gurney, I. Appeal for Death, An.
  Hall, D. Carlotta's Confession.
  Hardy, T. Newcomer's Wife, The.
    Plena Timoris.
    Second Night, The.
    War-Wife of Catknoll, The.
  Housman. I Counsel You Beware.
    It nods and curtseys and recovers.
    Shot? so quick, so clean an ending?
    Sinner's Rue.
  Hughes, L. Exits.
    Suicide.
    Suicide's Note.
    Ways.
  Hughes, T. Dogs Are Eating Your Mother, The.
    Locket, The.
    Sacrifice.
  Ignatow, D. For John Berryman.
    Prose Poem in Six Parts.
  Jeffers, R. Give Your Heart to the Hawks.
    Mara.
  Kizer, C. Death of a Public Servant, The.
  Komunyakaa. 2527th Birthday of the Buddha.
    Chair Gallows.
  Kumin, M. How It Is.
    Progress Report.
  Kunitz, S. Artist, The.
    Portrait, The.
  Laughlin, J. Building 520, Bellevue.
    Experience of Blood.
    Moment on Earth, A.
    Sorrow.
  Levi, P. Unresolved Burdens.
  Lowell, R. After the Surprising Conversions.
    Marcus Cato 95–42 B.C.
  Lux. Elegy for Frank Stanford.
  MacNeice. Springboard, The.
    Suicide, The.
  Mahon. Antarctica.
  Major, C. Unwanted Memory.
  Meredith, W. Dreams of Suicide.
    In Loving Memory of the Late Author of *Dream
      Songs.*
  Merrill, J. Roger Clay's Proposal.
  Merton. Songs.
  Michelangelo Buonarroti. Were one allowed to
    kill himself right here.
  Millay, E. Pond, The.
    Suicide, The.
  Muldoon, P. Cuckoo Corn.
    Lives of the Saints.
    Upriver Incident, The.
  Nash, O. Asp, The.
  Nemerov. To D———, Dead by Her Own
    Hand.
  Niedecker. So you're married, young man.
  Olson, C. Diaries of Death.
    Here i am, naked.
    You, Hart Crane.
  Orr, G. Bridge, The.
    Screaming Out Loud.
    Teachers, The.
  Owen, W. S.I.W.
  Pagis. Deceased Writer, The: Photograph in the
    Rain.
    Shot, The.
  Paley, G. This Life.
  Parker, D. Cherry White.
    Résumé.
    Rhyme against Living.
  Pessoa. If you want to kill yourself, how come
    you don't want to kill yourself.
  Pinsky. At Pleasure Bay.
  Plath. Ariel.
    Edge.
    Lady Lazarus.
    Lesbos.
    Suicide off Egg Rock.
  Poe. Scenes from Politian.

Ramanujan. One, Two, Maybe Three, Arguments against Suicide.
Rich, A. From a Survivor.
  Tattered Kaddish.
Rimbaud, A. Lightning.
Robinson, E. Bokardo.
  Growth of "Lorraine," The.
  Mill, The.
  Richard Cory.
Roethke. Kitty-Cat Bird, The.
Rossetti, C. In the Round Tower at Jhansi, June 8, 1857.
  Jessie Cameron.
Rukeyser, M. Double Dialogue: *Homage to Robert Frost.*
  Exile of Music.
  F.O.M.
  Gates, The.
  Power of Suicide, The.
  Suicide Blues.
  Victims, a Play for the Home, The.
Schuyler, J. Night, The.
  Trip.
  Virginia Woolf.
Sexton. Double Image, The.
  Red Dance, The.
  Risk, The.
  Suicide Note.
  Wanting to Die.
Smith, S. Death Came to Me.
  Death in the Rose Garden.
  Dido's Farewell to Aeneas.
  Doctor, The.
  Does No Love Last?
  Exeat.
  Father for a Fool, A.
  I Am.
  Starling, The.
  Suicide's Epitaph.
Spender, S. Girl Who Has Drowned Herself Speaks, A.
Szymborska, W. Suicide's Room, The.
Tate, A. Suicide.
Tennyson, A. Two Voices, The.
Van Duyn. Hermit of Hudson Pond, The.
Walker, A. Suicide.
Warren, R. Day Dr. Knox Did It, The.
  You Sort Old Letters.
Weiss, T. Last Letters, The.
Whalen, P. To the Memory Of.
Whitman, W. Inca's Daughter, The.
Williams, C. K. Suicide: Anne.
Williams, M. Ballad of a Little Delta Town.
  Her, Though.
  Rituals.
Williams, T. Les Etoiles d'un Cirque.
Williams, W. Death of See, The.
Wordsworth, W. Argument for Suicide.
  'Tis said that some have died for love.
Wright, J. Minneapolis Poem, The.
Wyatt, S. Absence! Absenting causeth me to complain.
  Horrible of hue, hideous to behold.
Zukofsky, L. Send regards to Ida the bitch.

Sumac
Sandburg, C. Sumach and Birds.
Schuyler, J. 8/12/70.
Very. Sumach Leaves, The.

Summer
Amichai [*or* Amikhai]. End of Elul.
  End of Summer in the Judean Mountains.
  Hymn to Summer.
  Summer Begins.
  Summer or Its End, A.
Ammons. Summer Session.
  Winter Saint.
Ashbery, J. Summer.
Bishop, E. Late Air.
  Song: "Summer is over upon the sea."
  Summer's Dream, A.
Blake, W. How Sweet I Roamed [*or* Roam'd] from Field to Field.
  To Summer.
Bogan, L. Dark Summer.
  Roman Fountain.
  Song for a Lyre.

Summer Wish.
Brodsky, J. Eclogue 5: Summer.
Brontë, E. 'Twas one of those dark, cloudy days.
Burns, R. Birks of Aberfeldy, The [Composed on the Spot].
  On a Bank of Flowers.
  Simmer's a Pleasant Time.
  Winter It Is Past, The.
Carruth, H. Ravine, The.
  Song: "Summer burns on the edges of day."
  Speaking for Them.
Carver, R. Best Time of the Day, The.
Ciardi, J. Catalpa, The.
Clampitt. Cloudberry Summer.
  High Noon.
  Meridian.
  Midsummer in the Blueberry Barrens.
  What the Light Was Like.
Clare, J. Sonnet: "I love to see the summer beaming forth."
Cooper, J. 95°.
Creeley. Morning ("Light's bright glimmer").
  Summer.
Cummings, E. E. Do you remember when the fluttering dusk.
  Early Summer Sketch.
  O It's Nice To Get Up In,the slipshod mucous kiss.
  O purple finch / please tell me why.
  Out of midsummer's blazing most not night.
  Summer Silence.
  Summer Song.
  Sunset.
Cunningham, J. August Hail.
  Summer Idyll.
"Dario." In Summer.
Davie, D. Hardness of Light, The.
  Viper-Man.
De la Mare. Vacant Day, The.
Dickey, W. Kindness, A.
Dickinson, E. Acts of Light which beautified, The.
  As imperceptibly as grief.
  As Summer into Autumn slips.
  Bee is not afraid of me, The.
  Consulting summer's clock.
  Further in Summer than the Birds.
  How near this suffering Summer.
  I know a place where Summer strives.
  I trust you may have the dearest summer.
  Indian Summer.
  It will be Summer—eventually.
  Last of Summer is Delight, The.
  Midsummer, was it, when They died.
  Renunciation.
  Revolution is the Pod.
  Slips of the last rose of summer, The.
  So much Summer.
  Soft Sea washed around the House, A.
  Some one prepared this mighty show.
  Something in a summer's Day, A.
  Summer for thee, grant I may be.
  Summer has been wide and deep, The.
  Summer has two Beginnings.
  Summer laid her simple Hat.
  Summer that we did not prize, The.
  Summer—we all have seen.
  There is a June when Corn is cut.
  To see the Summer Sky.
  'Twas here my summer paused.
  We wear our sober Dresses when we die.
  What shall I do when the Summer troubles.
  When Roses cease to bloom, Sir.
  Your coming is a symptom of Summer.
Dunbar, P. Boy's Summer Song, A.
  In Summer.
  In Summer Time.
  Lover's Lane.
  Song, A: "On a summer's day as I sat by a stream."
  Song of Summer.
  Summer in the South.
  Summer Night, A.
  Summer Pastoral, A.
  Summer's Night, A.

  Two Songs.
Eberhart, R. Great Praises.
  Project, The.
  Summer Landscape.
  To the Field Mice.
  Van Black, an Old Farmer in His Dell.
  Verbalist of Summer, The.
Emerson, R. In this sour world, o summerwind.
Glück, L. Letter from Provence.
  Solstice.
Graves, R. Advent of Summer.
  Blue-Fly, The.
  Midsummer Duet.
Hall, D. Whip-Poor-Will.
Hardy, T. Before and after Summer.
  Best She Could, The.
  It Never Looks Like Summer.
  On the Esplanade.
  Summer Schemes.
  This Summer and Last.
  We Sat at the Window.
  When Oats Were Reaped.
Hayden, R. Summertime and the Living.
Heaney, S. Summer Home.
Herrick Four Sweet Months, The.
Hopkins, G. Epithalamion: "Hark, hearer, hear what I do, lend a thought now, make believe."
  Summer Malison, The.
  Windy Day in Summer, A.
Hughes, L. Poem: "When young spring comes."
Jackson, L. Midsummer Duet.
Jacobsen, J. Chanterelles, The.
  Gesture, The.
  It Is the Season.
Jarrell, R. All or None.
Jonson, B. Epithalamion: or, a Song.
Kinsella, T. Chrysalides.
  Midsummer.
  Moment's Peace, A.
Kipling, R. Two Months.
Kizer, C. Month in Summer, A.
Koch, K. Summery Weather.
Kunitz, S. Touch Me.
Larkin, P. Mother, Summer, I.
  Summer Nocturne.
Levine, P. Making Light of It.
Lowell, R. Long Summer.
  Wildrose.
Lux. Beneath the Apple Branches Bent Dumbly.
  There Were Some Summers.
MacLeish. Danger in the Air, The.
  Long Hot Summer.
MacNeice. Solstice.
Mallarmé. Summer Sadness.
Mandelstam [*or* Mandelshtam]. Summer Solstice.
McGrath, T. Black Train, The.
  Poem: "Long wound of the summer—, The."
McHugh, H. Whoosh.
Meredith, G. July.
  Longest Day, The.
  Song: "Two wedded lovers watched the rising moon."
  Song: The Wren.
  To a Nightingale.
Meredith, W. Pastoral: "Girl lies down on the hill, The."
Merrill, J. Another August.
  Summer People, The.
  To a Butterfly.
Merwin. Early One Summer.
  End of Summer.
  Eyes of Summer.
  Middle of the Summer, The.
  Now and Again.
  Sheep Clouds.
  Summer Doorway.
  Summer Night on the Stone Barrens.
Millay, E. Three Songs from "The Lamp and the Bell."
Nash, O. Fahrenheit *Gesundheit.*
  I Always Say There's No Place Like New York in the Summer, or, That Cottage Small by a Waterfall Was Snapped Up Last February.
  Man Bites Dog-Days.

September Is Summer, Too.
Summer Serenade.
Summergreen for President.
Nemerov.   End of Summer School, The.
Late Summer.
Summer's Elegy.
Niedecker.   Hi, Hot-and-Humid.
O'Hara, F.   Summer Breezes.
Oppen.   As I lift the glass to drink.
Owen, W.   From My Diary, July 1914.
Paley, G.   Connections: Vermont Vietnam (I).
St. Johnswort! [or Saint-John's-wort!].
Parker, D.   Apple Tree, The.
August.
Song: "When summer used to linger."
Patchen.   Latesummer Blues.
This Summer Day.
This summer earth.
Piercy.   Cod Summer.
Pinsky.   Ralegh's Prizes.
Plath.   Frog Autumn.
Rexroth, K.   Adonis in Summer.
Rich, A.   6/21.
Holiday.
Riley, J.   Go, Winter!
Summer Sunrise, A.
Summer-Time, The.
Vision of Summer, A.
Wraith of Summer-Time, A.
Rilke.   Great Indulgent Heart.
Its Summer Night.
Summer Day.
Rimbaud, A.   At the Green Inn, Five P.M.
On summer nights, under the shopfront's
piercing eyes.
Sensation.
Ritsos.   Summer.
Summer in the City.
Summer Noon at Karlovasi.
Roethke.   Song: "This fair parcel of summer's."
Rossetti, C.   Bitter for Sweet.
Cor Mio.
Fly Away, Fly Away.
Have You Forgotten?
Heaven Is Heaven.
In the Lane.
October Garden, An.
Seasons.
Summer.
Summer Is Ended.
Summer Wish, A.
Rukeyser, M.   Children's Orchard, The.
Letter, Unposted.
Summer, the Sacramento.
Sandburg, C.   Bird Talk.
Bitter Summer Thoughts.
Bitter Summer Thoughts—No. 3.
Cricket Match.
Crisscross.
Foxgloves.
Mask.
Meadow in Summer.
Potato Blossom Songs and Jigs.
Silver Wind.
Small Homes.
Summer Grass.
Summer Shirt Sale.
Summer Stars.
Timber Wings.
Under the Harvest Moon.
Village in Late Summer.
Sarton, M.   Flower-Arranging Summer, A.
We Sat Smoking at a Table.
Schuyler, J.   Buried at Springs.
Haze.
I Think.
Jelly Jelly.
Overcast, Hot.
Shimmer.
Sexton.   I Remember.
In the Beach House.
Loving the Killer.
Shelley, P.   Summer and Winter.
Summer Evening Churchyard, A.
Smith, S.   I Love.
Spender, S.   Lost Days.

Stafford, W.   Cottonwood.
Stevens, W.   Credences of Summer.
Night-wind of August, The.
Swenson, M.   Flag of Summer.
Summer's Bounty.
Swift, J.   Part of a Summer, The.
Tate, A.   Idyl: "In a valley late bees with
whining gold."
Seasons of the Soul.
Tate, J.   It's Not the Heat So Much as the
Humidity.
Thoreau.   Each summer sound.
Tomlinson, C.   Conspiracy, The.
Lesson, The.
Witnesses, The.
Updike.   Island Sun.
July.
Summer: West Side.
Van Duyn.   End of May.
Walcott.   Bleecker Street, Summer.
Lesson for This Sunday, A.
Midsummer, Tobago.
Warren, R.   Aging Man at Noon in Timeless
Noon of Summer.
Autumnal Equinox on Mediterranean Beach.
Cycle.
Fear and Trembling.
First Moment of Autumn Recognized.
Sonnets of Two Summers.
Summer Afternoon and Hypnosis.
Weiss, T.   Into Summer.
Rapture The.
Whittier.   At School-Close.
Dream of Summer, A.
June on the Merrimac.
Summer by the Lakeside.
Summer Pilgrimage, A.
Wilbur, R.   Exeunt.
June Light.
My Father Paints the Summer.
Praise in Summer.
Song, A: "As at the bottom of a seething well."
Two Songs in a Stanza of Beddoes.'
Williams, C. K.   Shade, The.
Williams, W.   At the Faucet of June.
Botticellian Trees, The.
Ivy Crown, The.
Primrose.
Summer Song.
Wordsworth, W.   Longest Day; Addressed to My
Daughter, The.
Wright, R.   After Rereading Robert Graves, I Go
outside to Get My Head Together.
American Twilight.
China Mail.
Meditation on Summer and Shapelessness.
Wright, J.   Eleutheria.
Zagajewski.   Close of Summer, The.
How High the Moon.
Summer.
Summer's Fullness.
Zukofsky, L.   Anew, sun, to fire summer.
Sumner, Charles
Dickinson, E.   When Continents expire.
Very.   "It is vain to say, that this is the country
of the 'white man.' It is the country of man."
Charles Sumner.
Whittier.   Sumner.
To Charles Sumner.
Sun
Ammons.   I Went Out to the Sun.
Photosynthesis.
Transducer.
Baudelaire.   Sun, The.
Berry, W.   April Woods: Morning.
Bierce.   My Day of Life.
Brontë, E.   How golden bright from earth and
heaven.
It will not shine again.
Will the day be bright or cloudy?
Browning, E.   Man and Nature.
Browning, R.   Parting at Morning.
Byron, G.   On the Eyes of Miss A——— H—.
Ossian's Address to the Sun in "Carthon."
Version of Ossian's Address to the Sun, A.
Campion, T.   Follow Thy Fair Sun[ne]

[Unhappy Shadow].
Shadowes before the shining sunne do vanish.
Carruth, H.   Saving Way, The.
Carver, R.   Sunbather, to Herself, The.
Ciardi, J.   Improvisation for a Southern Night.
In the Year of Many Conversions and the
Private Soul.
Clampitt.   Sun Underfoot among the Sundews,
The.
Crashaw.   On a Foule Morning, Being Then to
Take a Journey.
Creeley.   Anger.
Flowers.
Gesture, The.
To the One in the Gray Coat.
Cuadra, P.   Birth of the Sun, The.
Cummings, E. E.   How generous is that himself
the sun.
Davie, D.   Sunburst.
De la Mare.   Mist.
Twice Lovely.
Dickey, J.   Sun.
Dickinson, E.   After the Sun comes out.
Alter! When the Hills do—.
Blazing in Gold and quenching in Purple.
Daisy follows soft the Sun, The.
Had I not seen the Sun.
How good his Lava Bed.
My God—He sees thee.
Pattern of the sun, The.
Sun and Fog Contested, The.
Sun is one—and on the Tare, The.
Sun—just touched the Morning, The.
Sun kept stooping—stooping—low!, The.
Sun retired to a cloud, The.
Thank her dear power for having come.
To interrupt His Yellow Plan.
We can but follow to the Sun.
We would'nt mind the sun, dear.
When I have seen the Sun emerge.
Yellow Man, Purple Man.
Dickinson, G.   Sun is gay or stark, The.
Donne.   Resurrection, Imperfect.
Sun Rising, The.
Eberhart, R.   Autumnal.
I Will Not Dare to Ask One Question.
Key West.
Let the Tight Lizard on the Wall.
Opulence.
Perception as a Guided Missile.
Emerson, R.   But as this fugitive sunlight.
He lives not who can refuse me.
Sun is the sole inconsumable fire, The.
Ferlinghetti, L.   Man Who Rode Away, The.
Frost, R.   Two Leading Lights.
Gallagher, T.   Corona.
Zero.
Glück, L.   Silverpoint.
Graves, R.   Blessed Sun.
Chink, The.
Lament for Pasiphaë.
Near Eclipse, The.
Problems Of Gender.
Song: The Far Side of Your Moon.
What Will Be, Is.
Gunn, T.   Sunlight.
Value of Gold, The.
Wrestling.
"H. D."   Helios.
Hall, D.   Sun, The.
Hardy, T.   Coming Up Oxford Street: Evening.
Sun's Last Look on the Country Girl, The.
Herbert, G.   Son[ne], The.
Hill, G.   Of Coming-into-Being and Passing-
Away.
Hopkins, G.   I am like a slip of comet.
Housman.   Revolution.
Hughes, L.   Sun Song.
Hughes, T.   Crow's Last Stand.
Sometimes it comes, a gloomy flap of lightning.
Ignatow, D.   In the Garden.
Jackson, L.   All Things.
Jarrell, R.   Archangel's' Song, The.
Jeffers, R.   Nova.
Kipling, R.   Hymn of the Triumphant Airman.
Komunyakaa.   (E)Motion.

Larkin, P.   Solar.
Lawrence, D. H.   Aristocracy of the Sun.
Democracy.
Elements, The.
Forte Dei Marmi.
Hostile Sun, The.
Immorality.
Mid-Day Verse, The.
Space.
Sun in Me.
Sun-Men.
Sun-Women.
Tropic.
Levertov.   Postcard.
Lindsay, N.   Indian Summer Day on the Prairie, An.
Sun Says His Prayers, The.
Sunshine.
What the Rattlesnake Said.
MacDiarmid, H.   My Love Is to the Light of Lights.
MacLeish.   Autumn.
Men of My Century Loved Mozart.
No Lamp Has Ever Shown Us Where to Look.
Old Man to the Lizard, The.
Salute.
You, Andrew Marvell.
MacNeice.   Morning Sun.
Spring Sunshine.
Sunlight on the Garden, The.
Major, C.   Lost in the Desert.
Marvell.   On a Drop of Dew.
McHugh, H.   Fix.
Meredith, G.   Phaéthôn.
Sunrise.
Merrill, J.   Little Fanfare for Felix Magowan.
Merton.   Poem: "Watching, among the rifled branches, for the sun, our hero."
Merwin.   By Day and by Night.
Sun and Rain.
Water of the Suns, The.
Michelangelo Buonarroti.   One Who made, and from utter nothing too, The.
Montale.   Glory of expanded noon.
Moore, M.   Sun.
Nemerov.   Blue Swallows, The.
Sunglasses, The.
Neruda.   First Winter.
Niedecker.   My friend tree.
O'Hara, F.   True Account of Talking to the Sun at Fire Island, A.
Oliver, M.   Sun, The.
Olson, C.   Advantage, The.
Maya Against Itzas.
Right in My Eye.
Oppen.   Light of Day.
Owen, W.   Futility.
Paley, G.   One Day I Decided.
Woman invented fire and called it, A.
Patchen.   Blood of the Sun.
Colony of the Sun, The.
World Whose Sun Retreats before the Brave, A.
Petrarch.   I saw a lady; on each side a lover.
Piercy.   Noon of the Sunbather.
Raine, K.   Childhood Memory.
Holy Isles, The.
To the Sun.
What message from imagined Paradise.
Rexroth, K.   After the Anthology.
Riley, J.   On the Sunny Side.
South Wind and the Sun, The.
Sun and Rain.
Rimbaud, A.   Sun and Skin.
Ritsos.   Center, The.
Doxology.
Etesian Winds.
Small Invitation, A.
Succession.
Rossetti, C.   Death-Watches.
If all were rain and never sun.
If the sun could tell us half / That he hears and sees.
Let Everything That Hath Breath Praise the Lord.
Mirrors of Life and Death.
O ye who love today, / Turn away / From

Patience with her silver ray.
Rose with such a bonny blush, The.
Song of Flight, A.
Sunshine.
Rukeyser, M.   In Her Burning.
Panacea.
Sun-Artist, The.
Rumi.   Sun is love, The. The lover.
Sandburg, C.   Cahokia.
Haze Gold.
Monotone.
Women Washing Their Hair.
Schuyler, J.   We Walk.
Seifert.   Once only did I see / the sun so blood-red.
Sexton.   Sun, The.
Yellow.
Shelley, P.   Fragment: "Unrisen splendour of the brightest sun."
Stafford, W.   Are you Mr. William Stafford?
People of the South Wind.
Stevens, W.   Brave Man, The.
Not Ideas about the Thing but the Thing Itself.
Swenson, M.   Of Rounds.
Sleeping Overnight on the Shore.
Solar Corona.
Sze.   June Ghazal.
Thomas, D.   How Soon the Servant Sun.
Thoreau.   On the Sun Coming Out in the Afternoon.
Stanzas: "Nature doth have her dawn each day."
That Phaeton of our day.
Tomlinson, C.   De Sole.
Door in the Wall, The.
Head Hewn with an Axe.
Very.   Spheres, The.
Sun, The.
Whitman, W.   Give Me the Splendid Silent Sun.
Thou Orb Aloft Full-Dazzling.
Wilbur, R.   Black November Turkey, A.
Courtyard Thaw, A.
For Ellen.
Grasse: The Olive Trees.
Poplar, Sycamore.
Sun and Air.
Sunlight Is Imagination.
Wellfleet: The House.
Williams, W.   Conquest.
Daisy.
Hula-Hula
Light Hearted William.
Metric Figure.
Sun Bathers, The.
Sun, The.
Wilner, E.   Of a Sun She Can Remember.
Wordsworth, W.   What is it that tells my soul the Sun is setting?
Wright, J.   Shadow and the Real, The.
Zukofsky, L.   Can a mote of sunlight defeat its purpose.

Sunday
Berrigan, T.   Sandy's Sunday Best.
Bishop, E.   Sunday, 4 A.M.
Sunday at Key West.
Brooks, G.   Sundays of Satin-Legs Smith, The.
Clough.   O Qui Me—!
Cowper, W.   Tale, Founded on a Fact, A.
Creeley.   Midnight.
De la Mare.   Sunday, A.
Dickinson, E.   Organ is moaning, The.
Dove, R.   Kentucky, 1833.
Hardy, T.   Farmer Dunman's Funeral.
Hayden, R.   Mourning Poem for the Queen of Sunday.
Those Winter Sundays.
Hughes, L.   Sunday by the Combination.
Jackson, L.   Sunday.
MacNeice.   Sunday Morning.
Merwin.   Their Week.
Nemerov.   Metropolitan Sunday.
Sunday.
Sunday at the End of Summer.
Olson, C.   Proensa.
Rexroth, K.   Blue Sunday.
Rich, A.   Mother-in-Law.
Schuyler, J.   June 30, 1974.

Picnic Cantata, A.
Sunday.
Updike.   Leaving Church Early.
Sunday.
Walcott.   Lesson for This Sunday, A.
Sabbaths, W.I.
Williams, W.   Sunday.
See also **Sabbath**

Sundews
Clampitt.   Sun Underfoot among the Sundews, The.
Swinburne.   Sundew, The.

Sundials
Graves, R.   *Song*: The Sundial's Lament.
Hardy, T.   Sundial on a Wet Day, The.
McHugh, H.   Mox Note.
Ramanujan.   On a Delhi Sundial.
Rexroth, K.   Fragrance of the teapot, The.
Motto on the Sundial, The.
Stock, R.   Four Inscriptions for the Sundial of a Lost Race of Polyphemus.
Wilbur, R.   Gnomons.

Sunflowers
Amichai [or Amikhai]   Fields of Sunflowers.
Ginsberg, A.   Sunflower Sutra.
Levertov.   For Floss.
Montale.   Bring me the sunflower, let me plant it.
Oliver, M.   Sunflowers, The.
Ritsos.   Sunflowers.
Sandburg, C.   Cripple.
Updike.   Sunflower.
Williams, W.   Sunflowers.
Wilner, E.   Sunflowers, Repossessed.

Sunrise
Angelou.   Plagued Journey, A.
Berryman.   Prime.
Blue Cloud.   Walking thru twisted hollow pathways.
Bogan, L.   July Dawn.
Carver, R.   Poem I Didn't Write, The.
Collins, B.   Center.
Cowper, W.   Sunset and Sunrise.
Creeley.   Morning (8:10 AM).
De la Mare.   Sunrise.
Dickey, J.   Morning, A.
Dickinson, E.   I had no Cause to be awake.
I'd rather recollect a setting.
I'll tell you how the Sun rose.
Sun went down—no Man looked on, The.
Sunrise runs for Both, The.
Donne.   Sun Rising, The.
HaNagid.   Rise Early.
Hardy, T.   Life and Death at Sunrise.
Herrick.   Maiden-Blush, The.
Housman.   Reveille.
Hughes, L.   Black Maria.
Hey! Hey!
Meredith, W.   Sunrise with Crows.
Merrill, J.   Radiometer.
Oliver, M.   Buddha's Last Instruction, The.
Sun, The.
Sunrise.
Plath.   Southern Sunrise.
Riley, J.   Summer Sunrise, A.
Ritsos.   Always So.
Roethke.   Unextinguished, The.
Rumi.   Sunrise Ruby, The.
Stafford, W.   Why the Sun Comes Up.
Swenson, M.   Out of the Sea, Early.
Wheatley, P.   Hymn to the Morning, An.
Whittier.   Waiting, The.
Zagajewski.   Sunrise over Cassis.
Zaturenska.   Cold Morning Sky.

Sunset
Amichai [or Amikhai].   Eternal Mystery, The.
Ammons.   Left.
Orientale.
Atwood.   Sunset II.
Baudelaire.   Balcony,The.
Evening Harmony.
Last Rays of the Romantic Sun.
Bly, R.   Evening When the Full Moon Rose as the Sun Set, An.
Bogan, L.   March Twilight.

Borges. Sunset over Villa Ortúzar.
Brontë, E. Evening Sun, The.
  Fair sinks the summer evening now.
  'Tis evening now, the sun descends.
Ciardi, J. On Looking East to the Sea with a
  Sunset behind Me.
Clampitt. Baroque Sunburst, A.
Coleridge, S. Sunset, A.
Cortes. Sundown.
Cowper, W. Sunset and Sunrise.
Creeley. For Pen ("Thinking out / of the
  heart").
Cummings, E. E. Beyond the brittle towns
  asleep.
  E / cco the uglies / t.
  Finis.
  Of this sunset(which is so).
  Paris%is April sunset completely utters.
  Sunset.
  This(let's remember)day died again and.
  Who are you,little i.
  Writhe and / gape of tortured.
Dickinson, E. Crickets sang, The.
  Fairer through Fading—as the Day.
  How the old Mountains drip with Sunset.
  I send Two Sunsets.
  I'd rather recollect a setting.
  Ignorance a Sunset, An.
  I'll tell you how the Sun rose.
  Presentiment—is that long Shadow—on the
  lawn.
  Sun in reining to the West, The.
  Sun went down—no Man looked on, The.
  Sunset at Night—is natural.
  Sunset stopped on Cottages, The.
  Sunset that screens, reveals.
Dunbar, P. Sunset.
Eberhart, R. Sea-Ruck.
Frost, R. Acceptance.
Graves, R. Allie.
  Land of Whipperginny, The.
Hughes, L. Blue Bayou.
  Caribbean Sunset.
  Hey!
  Sunset—Coney Island.
  Sunset in Dixie.
Jeffers, R. Ocean's Tribute, The.
Kinnell. Daybreak.
Laughlin, J. Mountain Afterglow, The.
Lawrence, D. H. Fall of Day, The.
  In Trouble and Shame.
  Love On the Farm.
  Our Day Is Over.
  Ruination.
  Sunset.
  Sunset Verse, The.
Levertov. Chant: Sunset, Somerville, Late Fall
  '75.
  Coming Fall, The.
Levi, P. Sunset at Fossoli.
MacLeish. Cummings.
Mahon. Globe in [North] Carolina, The.
Mallarmé. Beautiful suicide victoriously fled,
  The.
  Little Air 1.
McHugh, H. Message at Sunset for Bishop
  Berkeley.
Meredith, G. Union in Disseverance.
Merton. Sundown.
Merwin. Memory of Summer Facing West.
  Sunset after Rain.
  Sunset Water.
Oliver, M. Sun, The.
Petrarch. Quickening Sun, that bough I love
  alone.
  That time of day the rapid sky inclines.
Rich, A. Colophon.
Ritsos. Absence.
Robinson, E. Dark Hills, The.
Rossetti, D. Sunset Wings.
Sandburg, C. Aloof.
  Evening Sunsets Witness and Pass On, The.
  Flash Crimson.
  Flat Waters of the West in Kansas.
  Flux.
  Harvest Sunset.

Hits and Runs.
Hoof Dusk.
Letter S.
Little Sketch.
Lumber Yard Pools at Sunset.
Maroon with Silver Frost.
Mist Forms.
Plowboy.
Runaway Colors.
Rusty Crimson.
Slabs of the Sunburnt West.
Slow Program.
Smoke Rose Gold.
Sunset from Omaha Hotel Window.
Sunsets.
Thimble Islands.
Three Slants at New York.
Valley Song.
Yellow Evening Star.
Schuyler, J. Poem: "This beauty that I see."
  Sunset.
Smart, C. Sweets of Evening, The.
Stockton, A. On the Suns Setting Clear after a
  Three Days Storm.
Swenson, M. Day Is Laid By, A.
Tate, A. Dusk.
Tennyson, A. Crossing the Bar.
  Move Eastward, Happy Earth, and Leave.
Tomlinson, C. In the Intensity of Final Light.
  Landing, The.
  Perfection, The.
  Suggestions for the Improvement of a Sunset.
Very. Evening Walk, An.
  South River at Sunset, The.
  Sunset, The.
  Sunset after a Clouded Day in April.
  Sunset in Derby's Woods.
  Sunset in Haverhill, A.
Warren, R. Basic Syllogism.
  Sunset.
  Sunset Scrupulously Observed.
  Winter Wheat: Oklahoma.
  Youth Stares at Minoan Sunset.
Whitman, W. Prairie Sunset, A.
  Song at Sunset.
Whittier. Sunset on the Bearcamp.
  What the Traveller Said at Sunset.
Williams, M. Sunset: The Canary Islands.
Williams, W. Winter Sunset.
Wright, C. Dog Day Vespers.
  East of the Blue Ridge, Our Tombs Are in the
  Dove's Throat.
Zaturenska. Death Is the Serpent.

Superiority
Emerson, R. Such another peerless queen.
Lawrence, D. H. Amo Sacrum Vulgus.
  Are You Pining?
  Conceit.
  Finding Your Level.
  Have Done with It.
  Prestige.
  Saddest Day, The.
  To Be Superior.
Owen, W. Bold Horatius.
Rich, A. Artificial Intelligence.
Wilbur, R. Superiorities.
Williams, C. K. Ribbons.

Superman
Clifton, L. Final Note to Clark.
  Further Note to Clark.
  If I Should.
  Note, Passed to Superman.

Supermarkets
Bukowski. Frozen Food Section.
Codrescu. In the Supermarket.
Enzensberger, H. Portrait of a House Detective.
Ginsberg, A. Supermarket in California, A.
Merwin. Line.
Nemerov. Grace to Be Said at the Supermarket.

Supernatural
Burns, R. Tam o' Shanter; A Tale.
Coleridge, S. Rime of the Ancient Mariner,
  The.
Eberhart, R. Undercliff Evening.
Graves, R. Watch, The.
Hardy, T. She Saw Him, She Said.

Herrick. Upon God.
Keats. La Belle Dame sans Merci [A Ballad].
Longfellow, H. Skeleton in Armor [or Armour],
  The.
Milosz, C. Powers.
Poe. City in the Sea, The.
  Raven, The.
  Ulalume [or Ulalume—a Ballad].
Unknown. Tam Lin.
Warren, R. Eidolon.
Williams, M. Gift of Prophecy Lost, The.
Yeats. Leda and the Swan.

Superstition
Burns, R. Epistle to John Goldie in Kilmarnock,
  Author of, the Gospel Recovered.
  Halloween.
  Holy Fair, The.
Ciardi, J. Daemons.
  Evil Eye, The.
Coleridge, S. Superstition.
Dove, R. Cholera.
Graves, R. Superstition.
Hardy, T. Honeymoon Time at an Inn.
  In the Garden.
  Signs and Tokens.
Herrick. Charme, or an Allay for Love, A.
  Observation.
Jackson, L. Modern Superstition.
Keats. Gif Ye Wol Stonden Hardie Wight.
Kipling, R. Bees and the Flies, The.
  Our Fathers of Old.
Melville, H. American Aloe on Exhibition, The.
Milosz, C. On Angels.
  Should, Should Not.
Nash, O. Outcome of Mr. Buck's Superstition,
  The.
Oppen. Any Way But Back.
Rich, A. For the Conjunction of Two Planets.
Smith, S. From the Italian.
Williams, M. Believing.
  Believing in Symbols.

Supper
Dugan, A. Grace for Thursday.
Nash, O. Out Is Out.
Paley, G. Suppertime.
Riley, J. Law of the Perverse, The.
Roethke. Supper with Lindsay.

Supplication
Achterberg. Statue.
Browning, E. Supplication for Love, A.
Herrick. Another, to God.
  To His Ever-Loving God.
Levertov. Her Prayer.
Michelangelo Buonarroti. My eyes are
  saddened by so much they see.
Petrarch. Father of heaven, for all the days now
  lost.
  Most glorious Virgin, you are clothed in glory.
Riley, J. Mortul Prayer, A.
Stockton, A. Elegy in the Extreme Illness of a
  Friend Whose Disorder Was the Bursting of a
  Blood Vesel in His Breast, An.
  Fragment, Janu'ry 1786.
  On Exodus 30.18.
Wheatley, P. Prayer: "Oh my Gracious
  Preserver!"

Surfing and Surfers
Gunn, T. From the Wave.
Tomlinson, C. Moment, The.

See also **Swimming and Swimmers**

Surgery
Clifton, L. Donor.
  Lumpectomy Eve.
  Poem to My Uterus.
Codrescu. Dream (1).
Dugan, A. On Being Asked How Do You Feel
  after an Operation with Inadequate Anesthesia.
  This Is How I Feel.
  On Going up to Surgery in the Morning and in
  Favor of Pain-Killing Drugs.
Graves, R. Surgical Ward: Men.
Jacobsen, J. Autopsy, The.
Lux. Commercial Leech Farming Today.
Meredith, W. Grace.
Plath. Surgeon at 2 A.M, The.

Sexton. Operation, The.
Weiss, T. Gunsight.
See also **Doctors; Hospitals; Medicine**

Surprise
Berry, W. Aristocracy, The.
Ciardi, J. Saturday, March 6.
Creeley. Hello.
Lady in Black.
People, The.
Something.
Swinging Down Central.
Warning, The.
Water (2).
Window, The.
Dickinson, E. As if some little Arctic flower.
Facts by our side are never sudden.
Incredible never surprises us, The.
Surprise is like a thrilling—pungent.
Graves, R. At First Sight.
Grotesques.
Hardy, T. Collector Cleans His Picture, The.
Discovery, The.
Experience, An.
Laughlin, J. Her Sweet Deceit.
Lawrence, D. H. Love Comes Late.
MacLeish. Revenant, The.
Melville, H. Lone Founts.
Olson, C. Fish Is the Flower of Water, A.
Pound, E. Pagani's, November 8.
Rilke. Child at the Mirror, The.
Rossetti, C. Her Seed; It Shall Bruise Thy Head.
Simic. Note.
Whittier. Hazel Blossoms.
Williams, C. K. Easter.
Zukofsky, L. Strange / To reach that age.

Surrealism and Surrealists
Ammons. High Surreal.
Carver, R. Artaud.
Codrescu. Epitaph (2): "He was a young guy with surrealist connections."
Creeley. "You've Tried the World, Try Jesus."
Éluard, P. Lady Love.
Ferlinghetti, L. Matisse at the Modern, Magritte at the Met.
Rexroth, K. Fundamental Disagreement with Two Contemporaries.
Van Duyn. Dwarf in the Woods.

Survival
Ai. Reunions with a Ghost.
Amichai [*or* Amikhai]. Half the People of the World.
Of a Vanished Kingdom.
Ammons. Viable.
Angelou. Alone.
Song for the Old Ones.
Ashbery, J. Untilted.
Atwood. Place: Fragments, A.
Roominghouse, Winter.
They Are Hostile Nations.
Berry, W. Poem: "Willing to die, / you give up."
Berryman. Surviving Love.
Brodsky, J. Admonition, An.
Byron, G. Julian [A Fragment].
Carruth, H. Smallish Son, The.
Carver, R. Soda Crackers.
Char. Faction du Muet.
Ciardi, J. Fable of Survival, A.
Gift, The.
Letter from a Rubber Raft.
Clare, J. Marten.
Cooper, J. Blue Anchor, The.
Creeley. Door, The.
Swinging Down Central.
You ("Back and forth across").
Cullen, C. Harsh World That Lashest Me.
Only the Polished Skeleton.
Donne. Prohibition, The.
Dove, R. Zeppelin Factory, The.
Dugan, A. Qualifications of Survivors.
Weeds as Partial Survivors.
Eberhart, R. Fisher Cat, The.
Let the Tight Lizard on the Wall.
Man's Type.
To the Field Mice.

Emerson, R. With the key of the secret he marches faster.
Enzensberger, H. Remote House.
Reprieve, The.
Fenton, J. Children in Exile.
Glück, L. Inlet, The.
Phenomenal Survivals of Death in Nantucket.
Graves, R. Survivor, The.
Uncalendared Love.
Gunn, T. Rastignac at 45.
Han-shan. Cold Mountain is so cold.
I see hundreds of dogs.
Hardy, T. Heredity.
Hughes, T. How Water Began to Play.
Notes for a Little Play.
Jacobsen, J. Fittest, The.
Food.
Guide for Survivors.
Survivor's Ballad.
Kinnell. Bear, The.
Kinsella, T. Survivor.
Kipling, R. England's Answer.
Kumin, M. After the Harvest.
How to Survive Nuclear War.
Survival Poem, The.
Thoughts on Saving the Manatee.
Kunitz, S. Old Cracked Tune, An.
Three Small Parables for My Poet Friends.
Levi, P. Agave.
Autobiography.
Survivor, The.
Logue, C. Good Taste.
Lorde. Brown Menace or Poem to the Survival of Roaches, The.
MacLeish. Geography of this Time.
Mahon. After the Titanic.
Major, C. No Single Thing by Itself.
McGrath, T. Nuclear Winter.
Revisionist Poem: Machado.
Three Functions of Irony.
World of the Perfect Tear, The.
Meredith, G. Whimper of Sympathy.
Meredith, W. Freezing.
Merwin. Number, A.
Passage.
Second Time, The.
Sheridan.
Michelangelo Buonarroti. For a safe haven, for escape at last.
Milosz, C. Aleksander Wat's Tie.
Anka.
Capri.
Mistral, G. Caribbean Sea.
Montale. Your Flight.
Nemerov. Soldier Who Lived through the War, The.
To My Least Favorite Reviewer.
Who Did Not Die in Vain.
Oliver, M. Rabbit, The.
Swimming Lesson, The.
Oppen. Myth of the Blaze.
Orr, G. Beggar's Song.
Bolt from the Blue.
Cage, The.
Hotel St. Louis, New York City, Fall 1969.
Tin Cup.
(Trauma) Storm.
Pagis. Encounters.
Parker, D. Now at Liberty.
Petrarch. I sensed my spirits flagging day by day.
Piercy. Best Defense Is Offensive, The.
Rilke. Survival.
What Survives.
Rukeyser, M. His father is lost and away.
Stafford, W. My Mother Was a Soldier.
People Who Went By in Winter.
Swenson, M. Dream after Nanook.
Sze. Moenkopi.
Thoreau. I saw a delicate flower had grown up two feet high.
Whitman, W. True Conquerors.
Williams, C. K. Faint Praise.
Williams, M. Survivor, The.
Wyatt, S. Alas! my dear, the word thou spakest.
Zaturenska. Song: "Life with her weary eyes."

Susanna (Bible)
Stevens, W. Peter Quince at the Clavier.

Sussex, England
Davie, D. Sussex.
Kipling, R. Run of the Downs, The.
Sussex.
Very Many People.

Suttee
Kipling, R. Last Suttee, The.

Sutter, John
Riley, J. Sutter's Claim.

Swallows
Browning, E. Ode to the Swallow.
Cooper, J. Little Vesper, A.
Corbett, W. Poem: "Chalky swallow shit."
De la Mare. Swallows Flown.
Eberhart, R. Summer Landscape.
Swallows Return, The.
Tree Swallows.
Euenus. To the Swallow.
Guyon. Swallow, The.
Hopkins, G. Earth and heaven, so little known, The.
Meredith, G. Swallow came from over the sea, The.
Nemerov. Blue Swallows, The.
Ritsos. Interchanges.
Small Song for Éri.
Rossetti, C. Fly Away, Fly Away.
Snyder, G. Sixth-Month Song in the Foothills.
Stafford, W. Well Rising, The.
Stock, R. Patio.
Swinburne. Itylus.
Szymborska, W. Commemoration.
Williams, M. Evening: A Studio in Rome.
Yeats. Coole Park, 1929.

Swamps
Ammons. Precursors.
Frost, R. Wood-Pile, The.
Heaney, S. Bogland.
Komunyakaa. Landscape for the Disappeared.
Lux. Pismire Rising.
Sudd as Metaphor, The.
Moore, M. I May, I Might, I Must.
Oliver, M. Crossing the Swamp.
Rain.
Orr, G. Ditch, The.
Swamp Songs.
Swenson, M. Shu Swamp, Spring.
Very. Azalea Swamp.
Walcott. Swamp, The.
Whittier. Le Marais du Cygne.

Swans
Bogan, L. Winter Swan.
Browning, E. Romance of the Swan's Nest, The.
Carruth, H. Burning Dawn.
Wild Swans at Norfolk, The.
Clifton, L. Leda 3.
Coleridge, S. On a Volunteer Singer.
"Dario." For just a moment, O Swan, I will link my longings.
What sign do you give, O Swan, with your curving neck.
Davie, D. Winter Landscapes.
Dubie. Jeremiad.
Duncan, R. Four Songs the Night Nurse Sang.
Eberhart, R. Wild Swans of Inverane, The.
Glück, L. Palais des Arts.
Swans.
Graves, R. Leda.
"H. D." Leda.
Herrick. To Apollo.
Jacobsen, J. Motel in Troy, New York, A.
Jarrell, R. Black Swan, The.
Jeffers, R. Flight of Swans.
It was good of my father, whom I hated at times.
Love the Wild Swan.
Kumin, M. Bringing Back the Trumpeter Swan.
Lawrence, D. H. Give Us Gods.
Swan.
Won't It Be Strange—?
Logan, J. February Awakening.
Lux. Farmers.

Pecked to Death by Swans.
MacDiarmid, H.   Two Memories.
MacLeish.   Rape of the Swan, The.
Mallarmé.   Virginal, vibrant, and beautiful dawn, The.
Meredith, W.   Poem: "Swans on the river, a great, The."
Merrill, J.   Black Swan, The.
Millay, E.   Wild Swans.
Moore, M.   Critics and Connoisseurs.
No Swan So Fine.
Nash, O.   Swan, The.
Oliver, M.   Swans on the River Ayr.
Patchen.   Cruelkind Swans, The.
Lives of the Swan.
Rexroth, K.   Bei Wannsee.
Leda Hidden.
Ritsos.   Gradually Stripped Bare.
Roethke.   Swan, The.
Sarton, M.   Memory of Swans.
Swans, The.
Smith, S.   Bereaved Swan, The.
Tennyson, A.   Dying Swan, The.
Tomlinson, C.   Canal.
Van Duyn.   Leda.
Leda Reconsidered.
Wilner, E.   You, Failed Pronoun.
Wright, J.   Three Sentences for a Dead Swan.
Yeats.   Among School Children.
Leda and the Swan.
Wild Swans at Coole, The.

Sweat Lodges
Blue Cloud.   Sweat Lodge—The Afterwards.

Sweatshops
Pinsky.   Shirt.

Sweden
Dickey, J.   Lakes of Värmland.
Marvell.   Letter to Doctor Ingelo, A.
Milton.   To Christina.
Moore, M.   Carriage from Sweden, A.
Stevens, W.   Lions in Sweden.
Wordsworth, W.   Call not the royal Swede unfortunate.

Swift, Jonathan
Berryman.   Cloud and Flame.
Bogan, L.   Hypocrite Swift.
Brooke, H.   Quilca House to the Dean.
Howe, S.   Fragments of a Liquidation.
God's Spies.
THEIR / Book of Stella.
Jarrell, R.   Boyg, Peer Gynt, the One Only One, The.
Mahon.   Dawn at Saint Patrick's.
Murray, P.   Receipt to Frighten away the Dean, A.
Pope, A.   Happy Life of a Country Parson, The.
Lines on a Drawing of a Monument to Swift's Grandfather.
Sheridan, T.   Birthday Poem on the Anniversary of the Birth of the Rev. Dr. Swift, D. S. P. D. Nov. 30, 1737, A.
I Can't but Wonder, Mr. Dean.
Invitation to Dinner, from Doctor Sheridan to Doctor Swift, An.
Joshua Battus's Spepeech to the Paparliament.
New Year's Gift for the Dean of St. Patrick's Given Him at Quilca, 1723/24, A.
Perlegi Versus Versos, Jonathan Bone, Tersos.
Poem Delivered to the Reverend Doctor Swift, Dean of St. Patrick's, Dublin, by a Young Nobleman, November 30, 1725, Being the Dean's Birthday, A.
To Dean Swift.
To the Dean.
To the Dean of St. Patrick's ("Dear Sir, since you in humble wise").
To the Dean, when in England, in 1726.
To the Rev. Doctor Swift, Dean of St. Patrick's. A Birthday Poem. Nov. 30, 1736.
To the Same.
Tom Punsibi's Letter to Dean Swift.
Upon Stealing a Crown when the Dean Was Asleep.
Swift, J.   Author upon Himself, The.
Author's Manner of Living, The.
Life and Genuine Character of Dr Swift, The.

True and Faithful Inventory of the Goods Belonging to Dr. Swift, Vicar of Laracor; upon Lending His House to the Bishop of Meath, until His Own Was Built [or till His Palace Was Rebuilt], A.
Verses on the Death of Dr. Swift, D.S.P.D.
Tisdall, W.   Tom Pun-Sibi Metamorphosed: Or, The Giber Gibed.
Unknown.   New Jingle on Tom Dingle, A.
Rivals, The.
Unknown, sometimes at. to Thomas Sheridan.
On the Revd. Dr. Swift, D. S. P. D. Leaving His Fortune to Build an Hospital for Idiots and Lunatics.
On the Same.
Wright, J.   Written in a Copy of Swift's Poems, for Wayne Burns.
Yeats.   Swift's Epitaph.

Swifts
Very.   Swift, The.

Swimming and Swimmers
Amichai [or Amikhai].   Now the Lifeguards Have All Gone Home.
Atwood.   Younger Sister, Going Swimming.
Browning, R.   Amphibian.
Byron, G.   Written After Swimming from Sestos to Abydos.
Codrescu.   Alberta.
Opium for Britt Wilkie.
Cullen, C.   To the Swimmer.
Dickey, J.   Awaiting the Swimmer.
Lifeguard, The.
Night Pool, The.
Olympian, The.
Dickinson, E.   Water is deeper than the land, The.
Dubie.   Ars Poetica.
Glück, L.   Swimmer, The.
Hopkins, G.   Epithalamion: "Hark, hearer, hear what I do; lend a thought now, make believe."
Kumin, M.   400-Meter Freestyle.
Morning Swim.
To Swim, to Believe.
Laughlin, J.   Deep Pool, The.
In Another Country.
Levertov.   Avowal, The.
Her Nightmare.
Levine, P.   Belle Isle, 1949.
Logan, J.   Tale of a Later Leander.
Lux.   Snake Lake.
Swimming Pool, The.
Mahon.   Swim in Co. Wicklow, A.
Merrill, J.   Swimming by Night.
Merwin.   Sunset Water.
Millay, E.   Above These Cares.
Oliver, M.   Swimming Lesson, The.
Olson, C.   All Havens Astern.
Pagis.   Sport.
Riley, J.   In Swimming-Time.
Old Swimmin'-Hole, The.
Saba, U.   Siren, A.
Sexton.   Nude Swim, The.
Smith, S.   Come On, Come Back.
Swenson, M.   Swimmers.
Tomlinson, C.   Swimming Chenango Lake.
Updike.   You Who Swim.
Warren, R.   Swimming in the Pacific.
Weiss, T.   Far out, Far In.
Zagajewski.   On Swimming.
See also **Surfing and Surfers**

Swinburne, Algernon Charles
Hardy, T.   Refusal, A.
Singer Asleep, A.
Meredith, G.   There was a young poet of Chelsea.
Pound, E.   Swinburne: A Critique.

Swings
Eberhart, R.   Long Swing, The.
Heaney, S.   Swing, The.
Kinsella, T.   Girl on a Swing.
Lux.   Backyard Swingset.
Ramanujan.   Looking for a Cousin on a Swing.
Riley, J.   Waitin' fer the Cat to Die.
Stafford, W.   At the Playground.

Switzerland
Brodsky, J.   Swiss Blue.
Carver, R.   In Switzerland.
Dickinson, E.   Our lives are Swiss.
Hardy, T.   Lausanne: In Gibbon's Old Garden: 11–12 p.m.
Jeffers, R.   After Lake Leman.
It was good of my father, whom I hated at times.
Laughlin, J.   Near Zermatt: The Drahtseilbahn.
Skiing without Skis.
Merrill, J.   Country of a Thousand Years of Peace, The.
Shelley, P.   Mont Blanc.
Updike.   Switzerland.
Williams, W.   View by Color Photography on a Commercial Calendar.
Wordsworth, W.   Descriptive Sketches Taken during a Pedestrian Tour among the Alps.
Feelings of the Tyrolese.
Hofer.
Thought[s] of a Briton on the Subjugation of Switzerland.

Swordfish
Dickey, J.   Undersea Fragment in Colons.

Swords
Borges.   Blade in the Northside, A.
Tankas.
To a Sword at York Minster.
Coleridge, S.   Song: "Though veiled in spires of myrtle wreath."
Crane, S.   Supposing that I should have the courage.
De la Mare.   Massacre, The.
Emerson, R.   And as the light divided the dark.
Herrick.   Upon Pagget.
Muldoon, P.   Point, The.
Seifert.   At the Tomb of the Czech Kings.
Smith, S.   Frozen Lake, The.
Stock, R.   With a Machet across My Knees.

Sydney, Australia
Creeley.   Yah.

Symbiosis
Ammons.   Clearing the Dark Symbiosis.
Carruth, H.   I Could Take.
Meredith, G.   Woodman and Echo.
Niedecker.   Alliance.
Oliver, M.   Fish, The.
Hunter's Moon—Eating the Bear.

Symbols
Berry, W.   Below.
Burns, R.   Posie, The.
Primrose, The.
Byron, G.   Ich Dien.
Carruth, H.   Sonnet: "'Whut do you spose thet thing is,' Oi said. 'Whut?'"
"Dario."   Golden tortoise walks across the carpet, The.
De la Mare.   Assignation, The.
Rose in Candlelight, A.
Dove, R.   Five Elephants.
Eberhart, R.   Flag, The.
"H. D."   Sheltered Garden.
Hardy, T.   Sign-Seeker, A.
Herbert, G.   Church-Floor[e], The.
Herrick.   Primrose, The.
Jackson, L.   Signs of Knowledge, The.
Kipling, R.   English Flag, The.
Levertov.   Whisper, The.
MacNeice.   In Lieu.
Merrill, J.   To a Butterfly.
Merwin.   Standards.
Milosz, C.   Sentences.
Olson, C.   2nd Musical Form, for Dave Young, A.
B Cs (2), A.
B Cs (3—for Rimbaud), A.
Lie of 10, or the Concept of Zero, The.
Troilus.
Pessoa.   Circle, The.
Psyche-type (Psychotype).
Rexroth, K.   Human, Avian, Vegetable, Blood.
Rich, A.   Design in Living Colors.
Ritsos.   Unfamiliar Instrument.
Rossetti, C.   Rose, The.

Roses blushing red and white, / For delight.
Sandburg, C.   Shirt.
Stevens, W.   Thirteen Ways of Looking at a
Blackbird.
Tate, J.   Smart and Final Iris.
Warren, R.   Aspen Leaf in Windless World.
Whalen, P.   M.
Williams, M.   Believing in Symbols.
Williams, W.   Formal Design, A.
Rose, The.
Still Lifes.
See also **Metaphor**

Sympathy
Ammons.   Eolith.
Angelou.   Poor Girl.
To a Freedom Fighter.
Atwood.   Rest, The.
Brontë, E.   Sympathy.
Cowper, W.   Mutual Forbearance.
Poet, the Oyster, and Sensitive Plant, The.
To Miss Macartney.
Creeley.   Friend.
Friend, The.
Phone.
Cullen, C.   Magnets.
Cummings, E. E.   Our touching hearts slenderly
comprehend.
Davie, D.   Condolence.
Rejoinder to a Critic.
Dove, R.   Variation on Gaining a Son.
Dunbar, P.   Passion and Love.
Sympathy.
Hardy, T.   Often When Warring.
Herrick.   Sadness of Things for Sappho's
Sickness, The.
Kipling, R.   Recantation, A.
Lawrence, D. H.   Retort to Whitman.
Levine, P.   Angel Butcher.
Mahon.   Gipsies.
Michelangelo Buonarroti.   I'd feel the more
secure.
Montale.   Your hand was trying the keyboard.
Petrarch.   How fortunate that instant when there
came.
Now should my life endure to this extent.
Pinsky.   Questions, The.
Rich, A.   For a Sister.
For the Dead.
Roots.
White Night.
Riley, J.   He Cometh in Sweet Sense.
Let Something Good Be Said.
Rumi.   Saladin's Begging Bowl.
Sandburg, C.   Choose.
Stockton, A.   Fragment on Hearing the Account
of Mrs Ramseys Death.
Wilbur, R.   Another Voice.
Next Door.
Williams, C. K.   Bringing It Home.
Color of Time, The.
Saturday.
Williams, M.   How It's Born in Us to
Understand That There Are Two Sides to
Every Question.
Wordsworth, W.   Feel for the Wrongs of
Universal Ken.
Fragments from the Alfoxden Notebook (I).
Yeats.   Words.

Synagogues
Amichai [*or* Amikhai].   Poem without an End.
Synagogue in Firenze, The.
Schuyler, J.   Sometimes.
Tomlinson, C.   On Eleventh Street.

Synge, John Millington
Yeats.   Coole Park, 1929.
In Memory of Major Robert Gregory.
Municipal Gallery Revisited, The.

Syphilis
Wilbur, R.   Pangloss's Song: A Comic-Opera
Lyric.
See also **Venereal Disease**

Syria
Cavafy.   Of Dimitrios Sotir (162–150 B.C.).
Simeon.

Syrinx
See **Pan (god)**

T

Tagus River, Spain and Portugal
Wyatt, S.   In Spayn.

Tahiti
Eberhart, R.   Sailing to Buck's Harbor.

Tailoring and Tailors
Burns, R.   Taylor, The.
De la Mare.   Tailor, The.
Dunbar, W.   Amendis [*or* Amends] to the
Telyouris [*or* Tailors] and Sowtaris [*or* Soutaris
or Soutars *or* Shoemakers].
Heaney, S.   At Banagher.
Nash, O.   Consider the Lapel, Sir.
Paley, G.   In Hanoi 1969.

Taj Mahal
Whalen, P.   Imagination of the Taj Mahal.

Talk
Angelou.   Thirteens (Black), The.
Thirteens (White), The.
Beckett, S.   Écoute-les / s'ajouter.
Silence tel que ce qui fut.
Coleridge, S.   Eros aei lalethros hetairos.
Creeley.   Talk ("One thing, strikes in").
Talking.
Cummings, E. E.   All which isn't singing is
mere talking.
De la Mare.   On the Esplanade.
Dugan, A.   In Memoriam: Aurelius Battaglia,
and against His Tragic Sense of Life.
Emerson, R.   Burn your literary verses.
Graves, R.   She to Him.
Yet Unsayable, The.
Hall, D.   "Internal and External Forms."
Jackson, L.   How Now We Talk.
Talking World, The.
Kipling, R.   Puzzler, The.
Lawrence, D. H.   Effort of Love, The.
Let Us Talk, Let Us Laugh.
Levertov.   Marriage 2, The.
McHugh, H.   Spilled.
Merwin.   Talking.
Nash, O.   Let's Not Play Lotto, Let's Just Talk.
Parker, D.   Any Porch.
Lady in Back, The.
Rexroth, K.   Education.
Riley, J.   Say Something to Me.
Rilke.   Telling You All.
Ritsos.   Honest Confrontation.
Roethke.   Boy and the Bush, The.
Rumi.   Send the Chaperones Away.
There is a way between voice and presence.
Stafford, W.   At the Chairman's Housewarming.
Szymborska, W.   Tower of Babel, The.
Wilner, E.   Women Talking.
See also **Speech**

Talmud, The
HaNagid.   House of Prayer, The.

Tamerlane
Poe.   Tamerlane.

Tammuz
Hamill, S.   Tammuz in the Garden.

Tanagers
Eberhart, R.   Truncated Bird, The.
Schuyler, J.   Scarlet Tanager.

Tangier, Morocco
Beckett, S.   Ne manquez pas à Tanger.
Williams, T.   Tangier: The Speechless Summer.

Tannhäuser
Swinburne.   Laus Veneris.

Taoism and Taoists
Han-shan.   Buddhist monks don't keep their
precepts.
I recently hiked to a temple in the clouds.
Looking for refuge.
Mahon.   Mayo Tao, The.
Orr, G.   King of the Earthworms, The.
Ramanujan.   Butcher's Tao.
Sze.   Taoist Painter, The.
Williams, T.   Tonight I stay at the Summit

Temple.
Wright, C.   Reading Lao Tzu Again in the New
Year.
Zagajewski.   Treatise on Emptiness.

Taos, New Mexico
Hughes, L.   House in Taos, A.
Jeffers, R.   New Mexican Mountain.

Tapestries
Hughes, L.   For an Indian Screen.
Tapestry.
Moore, M.   Charity Overcoming Envy.
Muldoon, P.   Unicorn Defends Himself, The.
Nemerov.   Tapestry, The.
Pagis.   Recognition.
Rich, A.   Aunt Jennifer's Tigers.
Design in Living Colors.
Rumi.   Least Figure, The.
Simic.   Tapestry.
Swenson, M.   Red Bird Tapestry, The.
Wilner, E.   Unstrung.

Tarantulas
Dugan, A.   American Tourist to a Guatemalan
Tarantula.
Lux.   Tarantulas on the Lifebuoy.

Taste
Auden.   Smelt and Tasted.
Browning, R.   De Gustibus.
Hacker, M.   Canzone: "Consider the three
functions of the tongue."
Lawrence, D. H.   My Naughty Book.
Levertov.   O Taste and See.
Niedecker.   Consider at the outset.
Riley, J.   Little Tiny Kickshaw, The.
Stafford, W.   Ode to Garlic.

Tattoos
Gunn, T.   Blackie, the Electric Rembrandt.
Hayden, R.   Tattooed Man, The.
Hughes, L.   Sailor.
Komunyakaa.   Messages.
O'Hara, F.   Easter.
Ramanujan.   Rickshaw-Wallah, The.
Rumi.   Tattooing in Qazwin.

Taverns
Baudelaire.   Lively Watering Hole, A.
Burns, R.   At Whigham's Inn, Sanquar.
Versicles on Sign-Posts.
De la Mare.   Falstaff.
Good Company.
Dunbar, P.   At the Tavern.
Jonson, B.   Over the Door at the Entrance into
the Apollo.
Keats.   Lines on the Mermaid Tavern.
MacDiarmid, H.   Old Wife in High Spirits.
Milosz, C.   Table 1.
Table 2.
Robinson, E.   Tavern, The.
Rumi.   Who Says Words with My Mouth.
Sexton.   Portrait of an Old Woman on the
College Tavern Wall.

Taxes
Bierce.   To the Bartholdi Statue.
Burns, R.   De'il's [*or* Deil's] Awa wi' th' [*or*
the] Exciseman, The.
Inventory, The.
Jolly Gauger, The.
Lines *Written on a Window, at the King's Arms
Tavern, Dumfries.*
On Mr. Pitt's [*or* Pit's] Hair-Powder Tax.
To Alexander Findlater.
Cowper, W.   Yearly Distress, The.
Rimbaud, A.   Customs Men, The.
Swenson, M.   On the Edge.

Taxidermy
Warren, R.   Red-Tail Hawk and Pyre of Youth.

Taxis
Creeley.   NYC—.
Davie, D.   Mother.
Dickey, J.   Spring-Shock.
Gallagher, T.   Open Fire near a Shed.
Gunn, T.   Night Taxi.
Levertov.   Cabdriver's Smile, The.
MacNeice.   Taxis, The.
Major, C.   Eighteen-Dollar Taxi Trip to Tizapan
and Back to Chapala.
Nash, O.   It Would Have Been Quicker to Walk,

or, Don't Tell Me We're There Already.
Strange Case of the Pleasing Taxi-Driver, The.
Sandburg, C.   Madison and 42nd.
Schuyler, J.   Sun Cab, A.
Williams, C. K.   Travelers.

Taylor, Bayard
Whittier.   Bayard Taylor.

Tea
Amichai [*or* Amikhai].   Herbal Tea.
Browning, R.   Classicality Applied to Tea-Dealing: A Fancy Inspired by Westbourne Grove.
Chesterton.   Song of Right and Wrong, The.
Clampitt.   Sacred Hearth Fire, The.
Dickinson, E.   Little package of Ceylon, The.
Gurney, I.   Kettle Song.
Johnson, S.   Ballad: "I therefore pray thee, Renny dear."
MacNeice.   Poussin.
Meredith, G.   Bumble Bee—the Bumble Bee, The.
Muldoon, P.   Tea.
Rexroth, K.   Fragrance of the teapot, The.
Riley, J.   Cup of Tea, A.
Ritsos.   Departures 3.
Stafford, W.   With Neighbors One Afternoon.
Warren, R.   After Teacups.
See also **Teahouses**

Teaching and Teachers
Amichai [*or* Amikhai].   Oh, my old, venerable teacher, life.
Ammons.   Summer Session.
Angelou.   Communication II.
Berryman.   Professor's Song, A.
Brodsky, J.   At a Lecture.
Burns, R.   Epitaph on a Schoolmaster.
Carruth, H.   How To.
Ciardi, J.   Generation Gap.
  Memoir of a One-Armed Harp Teacher.
  Miss Olivia Branton.
  On Flunking a Nice Boy out of School.
  To My Students.
Collins, B.   History Teacher, The.
  Piano Lessons.
  Schoolsville.
Corbett, W.   Shoe, The.
  Way to Go, The.
  Youth.
Cummings, E. E.   To William F. Bradbury.
Davie, D.   To a Teacher of French.
Dubie.   Of Politics, & Art.
  Several Measures for the Little Lost.
Dugan, A.   Teacher's Vacation Lament in the Country.
  Untitled Poem: "Our German teacher used to say."
Eberhart, R.   I Went to See Irving Babbitt.
  Mysticism Has Not the Patience to Wait for God's Revelation.
Emerson, R.   S. R.
Glück, L.   Mountain, The.
Gunn, T.   Autumn Chapter in a Novel.
  His Rooms in College.
Hall, D.   Brief Lives.
Han-shan.   Child who doesn't have a teacher, A.
Herrick.   Eare-rings.
  Upon Fone a School-master. Epigram.
Hughes, L.   Teacher.
Hughes, T.   Crow's First Lesson.
Ignatow, D.   Now.
Jonson, B.   To William Camden.
Kinsella, T.   Death and the Professor.
  Land of Loss, The.
Larkin, P.   Schoolmaster.
Laughlin, J.   Lament of Professor Turbojet, The.
  Love Is a School.
  My Instructions.
  Premula's Problem.
  Some Memories of E. P. (Drafts & Fragments).
Lawrence, D. H.   Best of School, The.
  Discipline.
  How can I teach you when your blue.
  Schoolmaster [A], The.
  Schoolmaster [B], The.
  Snowy Day in School, A.
Lindsay, N.   Master of the Dance, The.

Logan, J.   Assessment, The.
Elegy for the Rev. Mr. James B. Hodgson (1892–1963).
Lines for a Young Man Who Talked.
Piano Scholar, The.
To a Young Poet Who Fled.
Lorde.   Teacher.
Major, C.   Measure.
McGrath, T.   You Taught Me.
Meredith, W.   Fledglings.
  His Students.
  In Memory of Donald A. Stauffer.
Merrill, J.   Three Chores.
Merwin.   Direction.
Millay, E.   Cairn, The.
Moschus.   By Moschus.
Nash, O.   Caesar Knifed Again, or, Culture Biz Gets Hep, Boffs Profs.
  Purist, The.
Oliver, M.   Spring in the Classroom.
Pagis.   Modest Sum, A.
Paley, G.   For Danny.
  Learning from Barbara Deming.
  One day when I was a child long ago.
Pinkerton, H.   Autumn Drought.
Prunty.   Miss Lucy.
Riley, J.   Lines to Perfesser John Clark Ridpath.
  My Henry.
  To My Good Master.
Rossetti, C.   Hollow-Sounding and Mysterious.
  O Christ our All in each, our All in all!
  Quinquagesima.
Rukeyser, M.   Another Day (You sit there).
Rumi.   Basket of Fresh Bread, A.
  Hallaj.
  I Have Such a Teacher.
  Sublime Generosity.
  These gifts from the Friend, a robe.
Sandburg, C.   Mr. Attila.
  Scripture.
Sheridan, T.   Epilogue to *Julius Caesar*, The.
Simic.   Evening with the Master, An.
Snyder, G.   Axe Handles.
Stafford, W.   At This Point on the Page.
  Last Class, The.
  Lit Instructor.
  Old Prof.
  On Quitting a Little College.
Swift, J.   Ad Amicum Eruditum Thomam Sheridan [To My Learned Friend, Thomas Sheridan].
Tomlinson, C.   High Summer.
  Instead of an Essay.
Unknown.   Teach your child to earn his meal.
Updike.   Humanities Course.
Very.   Oliver C. Felton, Esq., of Brookfield.
Weiss, T.   Off to Patagonia.
Whittier.   At School-Close.
  Memorial, A.
  To My Old Schoolmaster.
Williams, M.   Associate Professor Delivers an Exhortation to His Failing Students, The.
  Associate Professor (Mad Scientist) to (His Love) His Student in Physics 100 Lab.
  Paying Some Slight Attention to His Birthday the Associate Professor Goes about His Business Considering What He Sees.
  Professor.
  Young Instructor Talks to Himself Winding Up the Semester, The.
Williams, W.   Ballad: "To a man and his wife."
Wilner, E.   Metamorphoses at a College for Women.
Wordsworth, W.   Address to the Scholars of the Village School of—1798.
Zagajewski.   My Masters.
See also **Scholarship and Scholars**

Teahouses
Rexroth, K.   Observations in a Cornish Teashop.
See also **Tea**

Team Spirit
Kipling, R.   Song in Storm, A.

Teamsters
Ai.   Jimmy Hoffa's Odyssey.
See also **Trucks and Truckers**

Tears
Amichai [*or* Amikhai].   Among the Stars You May Be right.
  Time Has Come to Collect Evidence, The.
Angelou.   Tears.
Beckett, S.   Samedi répit.
Bishop, E.   Reprimand, The.
Bogan, L.   Solitary Observation Brought Back from a Sojourn in Hell.
  Tears in Sleep.
Brontë, E.   If grief for grief can touch thee.
  She dried her tears, and they did smile.
Browning, E.   Cry of the Children, The.
  Flush or Faunus.
  Tears.
Byron, G.   I Saw Thee Weep.
  Lines to a Lady Weeping.
  Tear, The.
  When We Two Parted.
Carew, T.   Conquest by Flight.
  Elegy on the La: Pen: Sent to My Mistress Out of France, An.
Cavafy.   Tears of the Sisters of Phaeton, The.
Cavalcanti.   Ballata: Of His Lady among Other Ladies.
Crane, H.   To Emily Dickinson.
Crashaw.   Tear[e], The.
  Weeper, The.
Creeley.   Sea, The.
"Dario."   When the poor guy saw her pass.
De la Mare.   Forgiveness.
  Irrevocable, The.
  TO E. T.: 1917.
Dickinson, E.   Each Scar I'll keep for Him.
  Honest Tear, An.
  Life's Trades.
Donne.   Twickenham [*or* Twicknam] Garden.
  Valediction, A: of Weeping.
Dunbar, P.   Fount of Tears, The.
Ginsberg, A.   Tears.
Graves, R.   Love as Lovelessness.
  Scared Child, The.
  Three Words Only.
Hardy, T.   Had You Wept.
Herbert, G.   Grief.
Herrick.   Another upon Her Weeping.
  Deluge, The.
  His Parting from Mistress Dorothy Keneday.
  Seest thou those diamonds which she wears.
  Teare Sent to Her from Stanes, The.
  Teares.
  Teares, and Laughter.
  Teares are Tongues.
  To Primroses Filled with Morning Dew.
  Upon Electra's Teares.
  Upon Her Weeping.
  Upon Shopter.
  Upon Teares.
Jacobsen, J.   Tears.
Jarrell, R.   On the Railway Platform.
Kipling, R.   Recall, The.
  To James Whitcomb Riley.
Lawrence, D. H.   Punisher, The.
Levertov.   Weeping Woman.
Levine, P.   Told.
Logan, J.   Weeping, The.
Marvell.   Eyes and Tears.
McGrath, T.   World of the Perfect Tear, The.
McHugh, H.   Hard.
Merwin.   Cry, The.
Michelangelo Buonarroti.   It well may be, so vehement my sighing.
Pope, A.   Weeping.
Rich, A.   Peeling Onions.
Riley, J.   When It Rains.
Rilke.   Our Tears.
Rossetti, C.   Heart Knoweth Its Own Bitterness, The.
  Sonnet from the Psalms.
  Three Moments.
Sandburg, C.   Bundles.
Smith, S.   Death Sentence, The.
  Satin-Clad.
Suckling, S.   Upon L.M. Weeping.
Thomas, D.   Hand That Signed the Paper, The.
Walker, A.   S M.

Whitman, W. Tears.
Williams, C. K. Dirty Talker: D Line, Boston,
  The.
  Good Mother: Out.
  Rampage, The.
  Villanelle of the Suicide's Mother.
Wordsworth, W. Away, away, it is the air.
  Sonnet on Seeing Miss Helen Maria Williams
    Weep at a Tale of Distress.
Yeats. He Reproves the Curlew.

Technology and Technologists
Armantrout. Manufacturing.
Carruth, H. "I've Never Seen Such a Real Hard
  Time Before": Three-Part Invention.
Cummings, E. E. In heavenly realms of hellas
  dwelt.
Cunningham, J. I grow old, but I know that
  Science some.
Emerson, R. Adirondacs, The.
Ferlinghetti, L. Overpopulation.
Hughes, T. Do Not Pick Up the Telephone.
Jarrell, R. Machine-Gun, The.
  Winter's Tale, The.
Kinnell. Fundamental Project of Technology,
  The.
  Sheffield Ghazal 4: Driving West.
Kipling, R. After Horace, Book 5, Ode 3.
Kumin, M. Photograph, U.S. Army Flying
  School, College Park, Maryland, 1909.
Lawrence, D. H. Dies Irae.
Lux. Early On, This Decade's Light Smelled.
McHugh, H. Blue Streak.
Tomlinson, C. Hacienda.
Updike. Telephone Poles.
Williams, C. K. Work.
Williams, M. Lesson on the Twentieth Century,
  A.
Williams, T. Death Embrace, The.

Tecumseh (Shawnee Chief)
Oliver, M. Tecumseh.

Teddy Bears
Enzensberger, H. Strange Attractor.
Williams, C. K. Souls.

Teenagers
Ai. Star Vehicle (My Senior Year in High
  School).
Brooks, G. We Real Cool.
Ciardi, J. Craft.
  Poem for Benn's Graduation from High School,
    A.
  Prayer to the Mountain, A.
Dove, R. Adolescence—I.
  Adolescence—II.
  Adolescence—III.
Hall, D. Material.
Komunyakaa. Different Story, A.
  Thorn Merchant's Son, The.
Lux. Swimming Pool, The.
Stafford, W. Sure You Do.
Sze. New Wave.
Updike. Due Respect.
Williams, W. No Good Too.

Teeth
Ammons. Renovating.
Hardy, T. Gap in the White, The.
Herrick. Candor of Julias Teeth, The.
  Rock of Rubies: and The Quarrie of Pearls, The.
  To Women, to Hide Their Teeth, if They Be
    Rotten or Rusty.
  Upon Bridget.
  Upon Franck.
  Upon Horne.
  Upon Lucie.
  Upon One Who Said She Was Alwayes Young.
  Upon Ursley.
Lux. Little Tooth, A.
Melville, H. Maldive Shark, The.
Piercy. Root Canal, The.
Rukeyser, M. Back Tooth.
Updike. Orthodontia.
Warren, R. When the Tooth Cracks—Zing!
Whalen, P. Dying Tooth Song.

See also **Dentistry and Dentists; Toothaches**

Tel Aviv, Israel
Amichai [*or* Amikhai]. Autumn Rain in Tel
  Aviv.
  Closing the Jaffa Port.
Carver, R. Mosque in Jaffa, The.

Telegrams
Codrescu. Good Morning.
Davie, D. Nineteen-Seventeen.
Kipling, R. Mare's Nest, The.
Sandburg, C. Telegram.

Telegraph
Hughes, T. Telegraph Wires.
Kipling, R. Deep-Sea Cables, The.
Nash, O. Why the Postman Has to Ring Twice,
  or, Yellow Envelope, Where Have You Gone?
  Woman Pulls the Wires.
Very. First Atlantic Telegraph, The.
  First Telegraphic Message, The.
  On the Completion of the Pacific Telegraph.
Whittier. Cable Hymn, The.

Telemachus
Brodsky, J. Odysseus to Telemachus.

Telephones and Telephoning
Angelou. Telephone, The.
Bukowski. 9 Rings.
  462-0614.
  Good One, A.
  How Come You're Not Unlisted?
  Macho Man.
  Pacific Telephone.
  Wrong Number.
Carruth, H. Phone.
Carver, R. Old Days, The.
  Phone Booth, The.
Cummings, E. E. Your little voice / Over the
  wires came leaping.
Dugan, A. Introduction to the Telephone.
Ginsberg, A. I Am a Victim of Telephone.
Heaney, S. Call, A.
Hughes, L. Madam and the Phone Bill.
  We're All in the Telephone Book.
Hughes, T. Do Not Pick Up the Telephone.
  Telegraph Wires.
Jacobsen, J. Calling Collect.
Kizer, C. By the Riverside.
Kumin, M. Hello, Hello Henry.
Laughlin, J. My Muse.
Lorde. Memorial III—from a Phone Booth on
  Broadway.
Merrill, J. Doodler, The.
Nemerov. Dial Tone, The.
  Primer of the Daily Round, A.
Piercy. Hand Games.
Plath. Words Heard, by Accident, over the
  Phone.
Sandburg, C. Manual System.
  Pick-Offs.
  Under a Telephone Pole.
Stafford, W. Farm on the Great Plains, The.
  Long Distance.
Updike. Why the Telephone Wires Dip and the
  Poles Are Cracked and Crooked.
Very. Telephone, The.
Voznesensky [*or* Voznesenskii]. Phone Booth.
Warren, R. Little Black Heart of the Telephone.
Whalen, P. Palimpsest.
Williams, C. K. Call, The.
Williams, M. Late Show.
Williams, W. Thing, The.
Zagajewski. Your Telephone Call.

Television
Bukowski. Numb Your Ass and Your Brain and
  Your Heart—.
Clampitt. Godfather Returns to Color TV, The.
Codrescu. Telyric.
Dubie. Looking up from Two Renaissance
  Paintings to the Massacre at Tiananmen
  Square.
  Radio Sky.
Eberhart, R. How It Is.
Ferlinghetti, L. History of the World: a TV
  Docu-Drama.
Ginsberg, A. Either we blow ourselves up now
  and die, like the old tribe of man, arguing
  among neutrons.
  Television Was a Baby Crawling toward That
  Deathchamber.

Gunn, T. Death's Door.
Hughes, T. TV Off.
Ignatow, D. First on TV, A.
Kumin, M. In Warm Rooms, before a Blue
  Light.
Laughlin, J. Full Life, The.
McHugh, H. Lifelike.
  Two Holidays.
Merrill, J. Channel 13.
Nemerov. Late Late Show.
  Mousemeal.
  Singular Metamorphosis, A.
  TV.
  Way of Life, A.
O'Hara, F. Poem: "O solo mio, hot diggety, nix
  'I wather think I can.'"
Stafford, W. Atwater Kent.
  We Interrupt to Bring You.
Williams, M. Late Show.
  Weatherman.

Tell, William
Coleridge, S. Ode to Georgiana, Duchess of
  Devonshire.
  Tell's Birth-Place.
Stafford, W. My Name Is William Tell.

Temperance
Cavafy. Old Man, An.
Lindsay, N. On Reading Omar Khayyam.
Riley, J. Tom Johnson's Quit.
Whittier. Brewing of Soma, The.
  Disenthralled, The.
  Drunkard to His Bottle, The.
  Khan's Devil, The.

Temptation
Baudelaire. Ruin.
Burns, R. Poem on Life.
Byron, G. To a Lady Who Presented to the
  Author a Lock of Hair Braided with His Own,
  and Appointed a Night in December to Meet
  Him in the Garden.
Carew, T. Song: The Willing Prisoner to His
  Mistress.
  To a Lady, Not Yet Enjoyed by Her Husband.
  To His Jealous Mistress.
Carver, R. Debate, The.
  No Heroics, Please.
Cavafy. Dangerous Remarks.
  He Swears.
Ciardi, J. Temptation.
Cullen, C. Street Called Crooked, The.
De la Mare. Outskirts, The.
  Stratagem, The.
Dickey, W. You White Cunning Devils.
Dickinson, E. I often wonder how.
Dunbar, P. After Many Days.
  Reluctance.
  Temptation.
Emerson, R. Go into the garden.
Gunn, T. In Time of Plague.
"H. D." Why Have You Sought?
Hall, D. Small Fig Tree, A.
Herbert, G. Quip, The.
  Self-Condemnation.
  Sin (1).
Herrick. Parting Verse, or Charge to His
  Supposed Wife When He Travelled, The.
  Sin.
  Temptations.
Hughes, T. Theology.
Jarrell, R. Conversation with the Devil, A.
Komunyakaa. Work.
Lorde. Generation.
  Monkeyman.
  To a Girl Who Knew What Side Her Bread Was
    Buttered On.
Marvell. Dialogue between the Resolved Soul
  and Created Pleasure, A.
Meredith, G. She had a secret—bonny Bess!
  Will o' the Wisp.
Nash, O. Never Mind the Overcoat, Button Up
  That Lip.
Petrarch. Since you and I so many times have
  seen.
Ransom, J. Tall Girl, The.
Rossetti, C. Goblin Market.
  O Lord, when Thou didst call me, didst Thou

know.
  Prince's Progress, The.
  World, The.
Swinburne. Ballad of Death, A.
Tennyson, A. Œnone.
Very. Temptation, The.
Warren, R. Athenian Death.
Williams, C. K. Medusa.
Williams, T. Legend, The.
Yeats. All Things Can Tempt Me.

Ten Commandments
Clough. Latest Decalogue, The.
Coleridge, S. Reproof and Reply, The.
Lawrence, D. H. Know Thyself.

Tennessee (state)
Davie, D. Nashville Mornings.
  Through Bifocals.
Lindsay, N. Preface to "Bob Taylor's Birthday."
Melville, H. Shiloh [A Requiem].
Nash, O. Fourth Limick.
Stevens, W. Anecdote of the Jar.
Wright, J. Homecoming Singer, The.

Tennis
Jarrell, R. Northern Snows, The.
Kinnell. On the Tennis Court at Night.
Kumin, M. Prothalamion.
Pinsky. Tennis.

Tennyson, Alfred Tennyson, 1st Baron
Davie, D. Seeing through Me.
Lawrence, D. H. Lord Tennyson and Lord
  Melchett.
Riley, J. Tennyson.

Tenors
Whitman, W. Dead Tenor, The.

Tents
Frost, R. Silken Tent, The.
Prunty. Tent, The.
Ritsos. Ready.
Rumi. Tent, The.

Termites
Nash, O. Termite, The.

Terns
Eberhart, R. Seals, Terns, Time.
Piercy. Gracious Goodness.
Snyder, G. Straits of Malacca 24 Oct 1957.

Terror
Amichai [or Amikhai]. Beautiful Are the
  Families of Jerusalem.
Ammons. Fall, The.
Bierce. Judex Jocosus.
Blake, W. Terror in the house does roar.
Bukowski. There Once Was a Woman Who Put
  Her Head into an Oven.
Carver, R. In the Lobby of the Hotel del Mayo.
  Man Outside, The.
Cavafy. Terror.
  Theodotos.
Cooper, J. Messages.
De la Mare. Gloria Mundi.
Dickey, W. Performances.
Eberhart, R. Transfer, The.
  World War.
Gunn, T. Old Woman, The.
Hughes, L. Mississippi.
Hughes, T. Bayonet Charge.
Kinnell. How Many Nights.
Laughlin, J. Child, The.
Levertov. Candles in Babylon.
  Concurrence.
  English Field in the Nuclear Age, An.
  Grey August.
Lowell, R. Fall 1961.
Orr, G. On a Highway East of Selma, Alabama.
  Vase, The.
Ramanujan. Mythologies 1.
Rexroth, K. Memorandum.
Seifert. Our Lady of Žižkov.
Swenson, M. Laocoön Dream Recorded in
  Diary Dated 1943.
Warren, R. Terror.
Yeats. Mother of God, The.

Terrorism and Terrorists
Ai. Antihero, The.
Amichai [or Amikhai]. Diameter of the Bomb,
  The.

  Good Time, A.
  Jerusalem the cradle city that rocks me.
Carruth, H. Essay on Death.
Corbett, W. Lockerbie.
Davie, D. Two from Ireland.
Dugan, A. Portrait of a Lady.
Heaney, S. Two Lorries.
Kinsella, T. Butcher's Dozen.
Mahon. Afterlives.
Szymborska, W. Terrorist, He's Watching, The.

Texas (state)
Ai. Greed.
Apollinaire. Annie.
Borges. Texas.
Clampitt. Dallas–Fort Worth: Redbud and
  Mistletoe.
Creeley. For John Chamberlain.
Ferlinghetti, L. Buddha in the Woodpile, A.
Gallagher, T. Crêpes Flambeau.
Ginsberg, A. Guru Om.
Hughes, L. West Texas.
Milosz, C. Texas.
Rukeyser, M. I used to press tools in the Texas
  oil fields.
Whittier. Texas.
Williams, W. Desert Music, The.
Zagajewski. Vaporetto.

Thames (river), England
Brodsky, J. Thames at Chelsea, The.
Campion, T. Ad Thamesin.
Cowper, W. See Where the Thames, the Purest
  Stream.
Davie, D. Surrey.
De la Mare. Old Summerhouse, The.
Gunn, T. Conversation of Old Men, The.
Herrick. His Tears to Thamesis [or Thamasis].
Kipling, R. River's Tale, The.
Wilde, O. Symphony in Yellow.
Wordsworth, W. Remembrance of Collins,
  Composed upon the Thames near Richmond.

Thankfulness
Berry, W. Poem of Thanks, A.
  Sorrel Filly, The.
Bierce. Matter for Gratitude.
Bradstreet, A. My thankful heart with glorying
  tongue.
  On My Son's Return out of England.
  Upon My Daughter Hannah Wiggin her
  Recovery from a Dangerous Fever.
Burns, R. Grace at Kirkudbright.
Carver, R. Late Fragment.
Ciardi, J. Memo: Preliminary Draft of a Prayer
  to God the Father.
Dickinson, E. I know not how to thank you.
  "Thank you" ebbs between us.
  Thank you in my heart obstructs, The.
Gunn, T. Lines for a Book.
HaNagid. Be Glad, She Said.
  Lovers of Life.
Herbert, G. Antiphon: "Let all the world in
  ev'ry corner sing / My God and King."
Herrick. Gods Bounty.
Logue, C. September Song.
Lux. Give It to the Wind.
  Poem in Thanks.
Marvell. Bermudas.
Mistral, G. My Mother.
  Refreshment.
Nash, O. Oh, Stop Being Thankful All over the
  Place.
Rexroth, K. Bei Wannsee.
Riley, J. Thanksgiving.
Sandburg, C. Our Prayer of Thanks.
Zagajewski. Three Angels.
  Try to Praise the Mutilated World.

See also **Gratitude**

Thanksgiving
Angelou. Thank You, Lord.
Berryman. Thanksgiving: Detroit.
Bradstreet, A. In Thankful[l] Remembrance for
  My Dear Husband[']s Safe Arrival[l].
Burns, R. Grace before Dinner, Extempore, A.
Cummings, E. E. I Thank You God.
Dunbar, P. Thanksgiving Poem, A.
Emerson, R. Grace.

Glück, L. Thanksgiving.
Herrick. Grace for a Child.
  Thanksgiving.
  Thanksgiving to God for His House, A.
  To God, in Time of Plundering.
Koch, K. Thanksgiving.
Merton. Prayer of Thanksgiving Written for
  Victor Hammer, A.
Millay, E. Thanksgiving Dinner.
Riley, J. America's Thanksgiving.
  Gustatory Achievement, A.
  Thanksgiving.
Sandburg, C. Fire Dreams.
Snyder, G. Prayer for the Great Family.
Whittier. Pumpkin, The.
Williams, T. Nature's Thanksgiving.

Thanksgiving Day
Berryman. Minnesota Thanksgiving.
Carruth, H. Family Reunion.
Ciardi, J. Carving the Turkey.
Cummings, E. E. Thanksgiving (1956).
Dickinson, E. One Day is there of the Series.
Dunbar, P. Signs of the Times.
Hughes, L. Thanksgiving Time.
Very. National Thanksgiving, The.
  Thanksgiving Flowers.

Theater and Theaters
Amichai [or Amikhai]. Heart Is a Corrupt Stage
  Director, The.
Burns, R. Prologue: "When by a generous
  Public's kind acclaim."
  Scots Prologue, *For Mrs. Sutherland's Benefit
  Night*, Spoken at the Theatre Dumfries.
Byron, G. Address.
  Elegy: "Behold the blessings of a lucky lot!"
  Good Plays Are Scarce.
  Occasional Prologue Delivered Previous to the
  Performance of "The Wheel of Fortune" at a
  Private Theatre, An.
Carver, R. Artaud.
Cavafy. Ancient Tragedy.
  Displeased Viewer, A.
  Young Men of Sidon (400 A.D.).
Ciardi, J. Oedipus Tyrannus.
Dryden, J. Mac Flecknoe [or, A Satire upon the
  True-Blue Protestant Poet T. S.].
Dugan, A. From the Theater Lobby.
Dunbar, P. Curtain.
Ferlinghetti, L. Living Theatre, The.
Frost, R. It Bids Pretty Fair.
Graves, R. Secret Theatre.
Helsham, R. Prologue to *Hippolytus*, Spoken by
  a Boy of Six Years Old.
Hughes, L. Lincoln Theatre.
  Note on Commercial Theatre.
Ignatow, D. Ritual One.
Jacobsen, J. Variations on Variety.
Johnson, S. Prologue Spoken by Mr[.] Garrick
  at the Opening of the Theatre in Drury Lane,
  1747.
Jonson, B. Ode to Himself, An.
  Ode to Himself[e].
  To My Dear Son, and Right-Learnèd Friend,
  Master Joseph Rutter.
  To the Memory of My Beloved, the Author Mr
  [or Master] William Shakespeare: And What
  He Hath Left Us.
Kumin, M. Purgatory.
Laughlin, J. When Does the Play Begin?
MacLeish. Brooks Atkinson.
Mallarmé. Homage: "Silence already funereal
  spreads a pall, The."
Meredith, G. Motley.
  There was a fair footman at Torrington Square.
  Two Masks, The.
Nash, O. Boop-Boop-Adieup, Little Group!
  Do, Do, Do What You Done, Done, Done
  Before, Before, Before.
  How to Harry a Husband, or, Is That Accessory
  Really Necessary?
  Theatrical Reflection.
  Wednesday Matinee.
O'Hara, F. Ave Maria.
  Mexican Guitar, A.
Palmer, M. Idem 1.
Parker, D. Drama, The; A Hymn of Hate.

Marilyn Marilyn.
To Marjorie Rambeau; In "Daddy's Gone A-Hunting."
Pope, A. On a Lady Who P-ssed [*or* P———st] at the Tragedy of Cato.
Prologue Design'd for Mr. Durfy's Last Play.
Prologue to a Play for Mr. Dennis's Benefit, in 1733, when He Was Old, Blind, and in Great Distress, a Little before His Death, A.
Riley, J. Little Man in the Tin-Shop, The.
Private Theatricals.
Rimbaud, A. Scenes.
Ritsos. Ancient Amphitheater.
Fate of the Observer, The.
Rukeyser, M. Girl at the Play.
Sandburg, C. In a Breath.
Props.
Sheridan, T. Epilogue, The: "Now all is done, learned spectators, tell."
Mr. Sheridan's Prologue to the Greek Play of Phaedra and Hippolytus; Designed to Have Been Spoke by a Boy of Six Years Old.
Pedagogue's Answer, The.
Prologue Designed for the Play of *Oedipus*, Written in Greek, and Performed by Mr. Sheridan's Scholars, at the King's Inn Hall, on Tuesday the 10th of December, 1723, A.
Prologue Spoken by Mr. Elrington at the Theatre-Royal on Saturday the First of April, A.
Prologue Spoken at Mr. Sheridan's School.
Prologue Spoken before a Greek Play, at the Reverend Dr. Sheridan's School, at the Breaking-Up of His Scholars for Christmas, 1728.
Prologue to a Play Performed at Mr. Sheridan's School Spoke by One of His Scholars, A.
Prologue to *Julius Caesar*, as It Was Acted at Madam Violante's Booth, Dec. the 15th, 1732, by Some of the Young Gentlemen in Dr. Sheridan's School, A.
Prologue to the Farce of *Punch Turned Schoolmaster*.
Simic. Note.
Position without a Magnitude.
Snyder, G. Feathered Robe, The.
Stafford, W. School Play.
Stevens, W. Of Modern Poetry.
Repetitions of a Young Captain.
Szymborska, W. Theatre Impressions.
Updike. Mimc.
Movie House.
Wilde, O. Camma.
Fabien dei Franchi.
Theatre at Argos, The.
Williams, T. Events Proceed.
Mummer's Rhyme.
Williams, W. Writer's Prologue to a Play in Verse.
Yeats. Fascination of What's Difficult, The.

Theft
Jacobsen, J. Thief, The.
Merwin. Happens Every Day.
Parker, D. Gunman and the Débutante, The.
Moral Tales for the Young ("Little Gormley stole a purse").
Riley, J. Piper's Son, The.
Very. Thieves, The.
Williams, M. Romance.
See also **Crime and Criminals; Thieves**

Theocritus
Wilde, O. Theocritus: A Villanelle.

Theology
Baudelaire. Punishment of Pride.
Bierce. Infralapsarian.
Borges. Emanuel Swedenborg.
Jonathan Edwards.
Collins, B. Questions about Angels.
Dickinson, E. He preached upon "Breadth" till it argued him narrow.
Dubie. Meister Eckhart.
Dugan, A. Crimes of Bernard, The.
Eliot, T. S. Mr. Eliot's Sunday Morning Service.
Hardy, T. Respectable Burgher, The.
Merton. Duns Scotus.
Hagia Sophia.
Hymn for the Feast of Duns Scotus.

Origen.
Milosz, C. Theodicy.
Sheridan, T. You That Would Read the Bible.
Stockton, A. Addressed to a Student of Divinity.
Very. Justification by Faith.
Williams, M. God.
Wordsworth, W. World is too much with us; late and soon, The.

Theresa, Saint, of Avila
Ciardi, J. Notes.
Codrescu. Life on Film of St. Theresa, The.
Crashaw. Flaming Heart, The.
Hymn to the Name and Hono[u]r of the Admirable Saint[e] Teresa, A.
Meredith, G. St. Thérèse.
Wilbur, R. Teresa.

Thermopylae, Battle of (480 B.C.)
Cavafy. Thermopylae.

Theseus
Euripides. Chorus of Troizenian Women.
Chorus sing of escape, The.
Daemon initiate, spirit.
Lift my head, help me up.
Men you strike.
No more, O my spirit.
O Spirit, / spark by spark.
Graves, R. Theseus and Ariadne.
Nemerov. On Getting Out of Vietnam.
Ritsos. New Dance, The.
See also **Minotaur**

Thetis (mythology)
Broumas, O. Thetis.

Thieves
Berry, W. Thief, The.
Bierce. Inauspiciously.
Borges. Luke 23.
Bukowski. Promise, The.
Stolen.
Walls, The.
Burns, R. Hughie Graham.
Chuang Tzu. Cracking the Safe.
Coleridge, S. Reproof and Reply, The.
Cowper, W. To a Young Lady Who Stole a Pen.
Dickey, J. Spring-Shock.
Dickinson, E. He that is robbed and smiles.
Sweets of Pillage, can be known, The.
Dugan, A. Significance of Corn in American History, The.
Graves, R. Thief.
Thieves, The.
Gunn, T. Idea of Trust, The.
Hacker, M. Little Robber Girl Gets On in the Wide World, The.
Robber Woman, The.
Herrick. Christmasse-Eve, Another Ceremonie.
Upon Letcher: Epigram.
Upon Prigg.
Upon Shark.
Jacobsen, J. Thief, The.
Kipling, R. Ballad of Fisher's Boardinghouse, The.
General Summary, A.
Lament of the Border Cattle Thief, The.
Loot.
Komunyakaa. Somewhere.
Kunitz, S. Thief, The.
Lawrence, D. H. Thief in the Night.
Levi, P. Thieves.
Logan, J. Spring of the Thief.
Meredith, G. Au voleur, au voleur, au voleur!—.
Milton. To John Rouse.
Nash, O. Strange Case of the Irksome Prude, The.
Plath. Fable of the Rhododendron Stealers.
Prunty. Note of Thanks, A.
Riley, J. Out of Nazareth.
Treasure of the Wise Man, The.
Ritsos. Thief, The.
Rumi. Checkmate.
Sandburg, C. Rakeoff and the Getaway, The.
Smith, S. Bag-Snatching in Dublin.
Swift, J. Mrs. Harris's Petition.
Unknown. On a Thief.
Very. Indian's Retort, The.

Warren, R. Convergences.
Williams, M. Romance.
Williams, W. Berket and the Stars.
Childe Harold to the Round Tower Came.
Wright, J. Gesture by a Lady with an Assumed Name, A.
Offering for Mr. Bluehart, An.
See also **Crime and Criminals**

Thinness
Codrescu. Remembrance of My Forgotten Skinniness.
Laughlin, J. Real Bones.
Lorde. Song for a Thin Sister.
Nash, O. Curl Up and Diet.
Orr, G. Trying to Sleep.
Plath. Frog Autumn.

Thirst
Clifton, L. Libation.
Dickey, J. Diabetes.
Dickinson, E. I could not drink it, Sweet.
Let me not thirst with this Hock at my Lip.
Levertov. Freeing of the Dust, The.
Levi, P. Flight.
Lux. Thirst of Turtles, The.
Meredith, W. Of Kindness.
Merwin. Meeting.
Mistral, G. Refreshment.
Rimbaud, A. Comedy of Thirst.
Wilbur, R. Ballade for the Duke of Orléans.
See also **Hunger**

Thistles
Hughes, T. Thistles.
Merrill, J. Variations: The Air Is Sweetest That a Thistle Guards.
Williams, C. K. Drought.
Williams, W. Thistle.

Thomas Aquinas, Saint
Herrick. Sin.
Hopkins, G. S. Thomae Aquinatis Rhythmus ad SS. Sacramentum.
Merton. St. Thomas Aquinas.

Thomas, Clarence
Ai. Penis Envy.

Thomas, Dylan
Berryman. In Memoriam (1914–1953).
Ciardi, J. Thousandth Poem for Dylan Thomas, A.
Ferlinghetti, L. Belated Palinode for Dylan Thomas.
Laughlin, J. Dylan.
Logan, J. Elegy for Dylan Thomas.
Olson, C. Dylan Thomas, and Now Matthew Mead—as He Himself, "To Edward Thomas."
Rexroth, K. Thou Shalt Not Kill.

Thomas, Edward ("Edward Eastaway")
Walcott. Homage to Edward Thomas.

Thomas More, Saint
See **More, Sir Thomas (Saint Thomas More)**

Thomas, Saint
Crashaw. Adoro Te. The Hymn of Saint Thomas in Adoration of the Blessed Sacrament.
Hill, G. Canticle for Good Friday.
Orr, G. Three Songs.

Thoreau, Henry David
Carruth, H. Concerning Necessity.
Dubie. True Story of God, A.
Kumin, M. Beans.
My Elusive Guest.
Oliver, M. Going to Walden.
Olson, C. Fish Is the Flower of Water, A.
Rich, A. Walden 1950.
Weiss, T. Working Day, A.

Thought
Amichai [*or* Amikhai]. Look: Thoughts and Dreams.
Ammons. Corsons Inlet.
Symmetry of Thought, A.
Armantrout. Purpose.
Berry, W. Awake at Night.
Breaking.
Clear Days, The.
Thought of Something Else, The.
Where.

Berryman. Possessed, The.
Bishop, E. Wit, The.
Bogan, L. Henceforth, from the Mind.
  Sonnet: "Since you would claim the sources of
    my thought."
Brontë, E. Philosopher, The.
Browning, E. Pain in Pleasure.
Browning, R. Transcendentalism: A Poem in
  Twelve Books.
Byron, G. If Sometimes in the Haunts of Men.
Chamfort. Ask of all-healing, all consoling
  thought.
Ciardi, J. Birds, like Thoughts.
Clough. O happy they whose hearts receive.
Coleridge, S. Constancy to an Ideal Object.
  Her Thoughts.
  Life.
  Love's Sanctuary.
Collins, B. Winter Syntax.
Creeley. After Mallarmé.
  Change.
  Circle, The.
  Dimensions.
  Echo ("Yes but your sweetness").
  Edge, The ("Place it, / make the space").
  Enough.
  Fancy.
  For a Bus on Its Side and the Man Inside It.
  "I Keep to Myself Such Measures."
  Juggler's Thought.
  Lion and the Dog, The.
  Measure, The.
  NYC—.
  On Acid.
  Place, The ("Swoop of hawk").
  Plan Is the Body, The.
  Rocks, The.
  Some Echo.
  Some Place.
  Time ("What happened to her").
  "To Work Is to Contradict Contradications, to
    Do Violence to Natural Violence."
  Up Here.
  Young Woman.
Davie, D. Fountain, The.
  Gardens No Emblems.
De la Mare. Idleness.
  Mist.
  Young Girl, A.
Dickinson, E. How precious Thought and
  Speech are!
  I felt a Cleaving in my Mind.
  If wrecked upon the Shoal of Thought.
  It is solemn to remember.
  One need not be a Chamber—to be Haunted.
  There seems a spectral power.
  We cannot believe for each other.
Dunbar, P. Unexpressed.
Duncan, R. Illustrative Lines.
Eberhart, R. Broken Pen, The.
Emerson, R. Ask not treasures from his store.
  But as this fugitive sunlight.
  Coil of space the cones of light, The.
  Comrade or the book is good, The.
  Ever the Rock of Ages melts.
  I wear no badge; no tinsel star.
  Idealism.
  Intellect.
  Love and Thought.
  My Thoughts.
  Oil & Wine, / Sparkling gems, & rich attire.
  Pale Genius roves alone.
  Terminus.
  What avails it me.
  When thou sittest moping.
Enzensberger, H. Model towards a Theory of
  Cognition.
Frost, R. All Revelation.
  Bond and Free.
  Etherealizing.
  Never Naught Song, A.
Graves, R. Climate of Thought, The.
  Thieves, The.
  To Sleep.
  Utter Rim, The.
Gray, T. Ode on the Pleasure Arising from

  Vicissitude.
Gunn, T. At the Centre.
  Confessions of the Life Artist.
  L'Epreuve.
  Lines for a Book.
  Merlin in the Cave: He Speculates without a
    Book.
Gurney, I. There Is a Man.
Hall, D. Poem, The: "It discovers by night."
Hardy, T. Aerolite, The.
  Freed the Fret of Thinking.
Hughes, L. Blues at Dawn.
Hughes, T. Reckless Head.
  Thought-Fox, The.
Ignatow, D. Lightly.
  Thinking.
Jackson, L. Footfalling.
  Opening of Eyes.
Keats. O! How I Love, on a Fair Summer's
  Eve.
Kipling, R. Seven Watchmen.
Laughlin, J. Our Meetings.
  Problem Struck Me, The.
Lawrence, D. H. Cerebral Emotions.
  Climb Down, O Lordly Mind.
  Demiurge.
  Prophet.
  Red Geranium and Godly Mignonette.
  Sex Isn't Sin.
  Thought.
Levertov. Old People Dozing.
Lux. It Must Be the Monk in Me.
MacDiarmid, H. At My Father's Grave.
  Light and Shadow.
  To Hell wi' Happiness!
MacNeice. Among These Turf-Stacks.
Major, C. At Pointe de Rompe Talon.
Meredith, G. When Will was at home in his
  palace of zinc.
Meredith, W. Here and There.
  Recollection of Bellagio.
  Thoughts on One's Head (In Plaster, with a
    Bronze Wash).
Merrill, J. Dedication: "Hans, there are
  moments when the whole mind."
  From the Cupola.
  River Poem.
Moore, M. Mind Is an Enchanting Thing, The.
Muldoon, P. Something Else.
Nemerov. Figures of Thought.
  Idea.
  Knowledge.
  One Way.
  Thought.
  Two Sides to an Outside: Meditation from
    Empson.
Niedecker. Energy glows at the lips.
  From my bed I see.
O'Hara, F. Colloque Sentimental.
  Day and Night in 1952.
  Heroic Sculpture.
  Poem: "And tomorrow morning at 8 o'clock in
    Springfield, Massachusetts."
Olson, C. At midnight, after hours of love, I
  ate.
  Moon Is the Number 18, The.
  My belly / sounds like an owl.
  My poor dumb body.
  Night, The.
  Shenandoah.
  Under every green tree, sex.
  Writ, The.
Owen, W. Spells and Incantation (a Fragment).
Pagis. Brain.
Palmer, M. Voice and Address.
Parker, D. Thoughts.
Pessoa. I'm so full of feeling.
  Psyche-type (Psychotype).
  Snow threw a silent towel over everything, The.
  Startling reality of things, The.
Plath. Apprehensions.
  Natural History.
Pope, A. Epistle I, to Sir Richard Temple, Lord
  Cobham.
Rich, A. Ghost of a Chance.
Robinson, E. Garden, The.

Roethke. Genesis.
  Give Way, Ye Gates.
  Prayer before Study.
Rukeyser, M. Notes for a Poem.
  Rang and rang, rang in a small boy's head.
Sandburg, C. Aprons of Silence.
  Back Yard.
  Bundles.
  Caboose Thoughts.
  Chillicothe.
  Crimson.
  Dialogue.
  Home Thoughts.
  Many Hats.
  Murmurings in a Field Hospital.
  Offering and Rebuff.
  Pool of Bethesda.
  Potato Blossom Songs and Jigs.
  Sandhill People.
  Santa Fe Sketches.
  Sixteen Months.
Schuyler, J. Evening Wind.
  Unlike Joubert.
Sexton. February 3rd.
  January 24th.
Shelley, P. Fragment: Thoughts Come and Go
  in Solitude.
Smith, S. After-Thought, The.
  Blood Flows Back, The.
  Lord Say-and-Seal.
  Night Thoughts.
  Thought Is Superior.
  White Thought, The.
Stafford, W. Inscribed on a Prayer Wheel and
  Spun.
Stevens, W. Bed of Old John Zeller, The.
  Crude Foyer.
  Homunculus et La Belle Etoile.
  Man Carrying Thing.
  Of Mere Being.
  Well Dressed Man with a Beard, The.
  What We See Is What We Think.
Szymborska, W. Opinion on the Question of
  Pornography, An.
Thoreau. I do not fear my thoughts will die.
Tomlinson, C. Flame.
  Movements.
Trakl. Helian.
Van Duyn. Insight.
  Two Poems, with Birds.
Warren, R. What Was the Throught.
Whalen, P. Metaphysical Insomnia Jazz.
  Mumonkan XXIX.
Whitman, W. Aboard at a Ship's Helm.
  By the Bivouac's Fitful Flame.
Wilbur, R. Event, An.
  Fire-Truck, A.
  Mind.
  Praise in Summer.
Williams, C. K. That night, / winter, / rain.
Williams, M. Jonathan in Awe.
  Walking after Supper.
Williams, W. Fruit, The.
  Gentle Man, The.
  Ogre, The.
  To the Shade of Po Chü-I.
Wordsworth, W. Character, A.
  On the Banks of a Rocky Stream.
  Those [or These] words were uttered as in [or in
    a] pensive mood.
  Travelling.
Wright, J. Breath of Air, A.
Yeats. Meru.
  Results of Thought, The.
Zukofsky, L. Claims.
  It's hard to see but think of a sea.
  Judge and the Bird, The.
  Sequence 1944-6.

See also **Intellect and Intellectuals; Reason**

Three Kings
See **Magi**

Three Mile Island, Pennsylvania
  Williams, C. K. Tar.

Three Wisemen
See **Magi**
Thrushes
Browning, E. Deserted Garden, The.
Burns, R. Sonnet—On Hearing a Thrush Sing on a Morning Walk in January.
Clampitt. Hermit Thrush, A.
Cummings, E. E. Might these be thrushes climbing through almost(do they).
Music.
Eberhart, R. Ultimate Song.
Frost, R. Come In.
Ginsberg, A. Voznesensky's "Silent Tingling."
Hardy, T. Caged Thrush Freed and Home Again, The.
Darkling Thrush, The.
Proud Songsters.
Reminder, The.
Hughes, T. Evening Thrush.
Thrushes.
MacLeish. Thrush in the Gaelic Islands, The.
Meredith, G. Thrush in February, The.
Millay, E. This / Is mine, and I can hold it.
Parker, D. Ornithology for Beginners.
Rossetti, C. Last Rites.
Wilbur, R. On Having Mis-identified a Wild Flower.
Williams, W. Woodthrush, The.
Wordsworth, W. Hark! 'Tis the Thrush, Undaunted, Undeprest.

Thumbs
Ramanujan. Opposable Thumb, The.
Sandburg, C. Personality.

Thunder
Bishop, E. Thunder.
Cowper, W. Thunder Storm, A.
Dickinson, E. Farthest Thunder that I heard, The.
Emerson, R. When wrath & terror changed Jove's regal port.
Lawrence, D. H. Trees in the Garden.
Lorde. Oaxaca.
MacNeice. June Thunder.
Montale. Why wait? The squirrel beats his torch-tail.
Nash, O. Watched Example Never Boils, A.
Sandburg, C. Blizzard Notes.
Tennyson, A. Kraken, The.
Tomlinson, C. Whip, The.

Thyme
Wilbur, R. Thyme Flowering among Rocks.
Zukofsky, L. Thyme.

Tibet
Ciardi, J. Peaks.
Dubie. On the Chinese Abduction of Tibet's Child Panchen Lama.

Tides
Ammons. Expressions of Sea Level.
Beckett, S. Fleuves et océans.
Bly, R. Calm Day at Drake's Bay.
Broumas, O. Thetis.
Clampitt. Beach Glass.
Low Tide at Schoodic.
Coleridge, S. Moon and the Waves, The.
Hall, D. Stones.
Hill, G. Wreaths.
Jeffers, R. At the near approach of a star...huge tides.
Kinsella, T. Ballydavid Pier.
Levertov. Tide, The.
Montale. Eastbourne.
Low Tide.
Nash, O. Beginner's Guide to the Ocean, A.
Parker, D. Fair Weather.
Piercy. Smalley Bar.
Sandburg, C. From the Shore.
Sketch.
Under.
Swenson, M. Tide at Long Point, The.
Tomlinson, C. Chance.
In the Estuary.
Promise, The.
Very. Tide, The.
Wilbur, R. Conjuration.
Zukofsky, L. Strange / To reach that age.

Tigers
Borges. Dreamtigers.
Gold of the Tigers, The.
My Last Tiger.
Other Tiger, The.
Tankas.
Ciardi, J. Dream, A.
Creeley. Tiger, The.
"Dario." In Summer.
Dickinson, E. Dying Tiger—moaned for Drink, A.
Hughes, L. For an Indian Screen.
Hughes, T. Calves harshly parted from their mamas.
Tiger-Psalm.
Jackson, L. Tiger, The.
Lindsay, N. Tale of the Tiger Tree, The.
Meredith, W. Fear of Beasts, The.
Moore, M. Tippoo's Tiger.
O'Hara, F. Chez Jane.
Olson, C. Afternoon.
Oppen. Myth of the Blaze.
Ramanujan. No Fifth Man.
Rich, A. Aunt Jennifer's Tigers.
Smith, S. Little Boy Sick.
Swenson, M. Zambesi and Ranee.
Tomlinson, C. Tiger Skull.
Walker, A. There are no tigers.

Tightropes and Tightrope Walkers
Dubie. Buffalo Clouds over the Maestro Hoon.
Pagis. Sudden Heart.
Rilke. Saltimbanques.
Ritsos. Dangers.
Tightrope Walker, The.
Stock, R. Tight-Rope Construction Surrounded by a Thousand Sonnets.
Williams, C. K. Vehicle: Conscience.
See also **Acrobatics and Acrobats**

Till, Emmett
Brooks, G. Last Quatrain of the Ballad of Emmett Till, The.
Hughes, L. Mississippi.
Lorde. Afterimages.

Time
Amichai [*or* Amikhai] Don't Prepare for Tomorrow.
In Those Days, in This Time.
Man in His Life, A.
On this evening, I think again.
People with No Future Love.
Ammons. Eyesight.
Passage.
Ship.
Timing.
Angelou. In a Time.
Apollinaire. Mirabeau Bridge.
Ashbery, J. As You Came from the Holy Land.
Ivory Tower, The.
Saying It to Keep It from Happening.
Soonest Mended.
Atwood. Four Small Elegies.
There Is Only One of Everything.
Auden. As I Walked Out One Evening.
Clocks cannot tell our time of day.
Homage to Clio.
If I Could Tell You.
Baudelaire. Clock, The.
Beckett, S. Home Olga.
My way is in the sand flowing.
Somme toute / tout compte fait.
Berry, W. Anger against Beasts.
Anniversary, An.
Dance, The.
Design of a House, The.
Discipline, A.
For the Rebuilding of a House.
From the Distance.
Meadow, The.
Seventeen Years.
Wheel, The.
Berryman. Statue, The.
Bishop, E. Anaphora.
Paris, 7 A.M.
Blake, W. From Cratetos.
Bogan, L. Come, Break with Time.
Mark, The.

Borges. Afternoon, The.
Elegy for a Park.
Hourglass, The.
In Praise of Darkness.
Instant, The.
Manuscript Found in a Book of Joseph Conrad.
Of Heaven and Hell.
Paris, 1856.
Someone.
To Whoever Is Reading Me.
Year's End.
Yesterdays.
You Are Not the Others.
Bradstreet, A. Contemplations.
Brontë, E. O evening, why is thy light so sad?
Self-Interrogation.
Tell me, tell me, smiling child.
There shines the moon, at noon of night.
Brooks, G. Old Mary.
Browning, E. Hugh Stuart Boyd [Legacies].
Browning, R. Prologue: "Poet's age is sad: for why?, The."
Speculative.
Burns, R. Bonie Bell.
Lazy Mist, The.
Prologue: "No song nor dance I bring from yon great city."
Sketch. New Year's Day. To Mrs. Dunlop.
Byron, G. Answer to a Beautiful Poem, Entitled "The Common Lot."
So We'll Go No More A-Roving.
Stanzas: "Could Love for ever."
Stanzas for Music.
To a Youthful Friend.
To an Oak at Newstead.
To Time.
Campion, T. De horologio portabili.
To the Right, Noble, and Vertuous, Henry Lord Clifford, Sonne and Heyre to the Right Honourable, Francis, Earle of Cumberland.
Carew, T. Persuasions to Enjoy.
Carruth, H. Horologikos.
Carver, R. Woman Bathing.
Cavafy. Vulnerant Omnes, Ultima Necat.
Celan. Corona.
Love Crown.
Tankards, The.
Char. At the Gates of Aerea.
Ciardi, J. Clock in the Mirror, The.
Letter from a Pander.
Possibilities.
S.P.Q.R. A Letter from Rome.
Thanks to a Botanist, A.
Time Is the Late Train into Albany.
Clough. He sate, no stiller stands a rock.
Coleridge, S. Bitter Reflection, A.
Hope and Time.
Time, Real and Imaginary.
Collins, B. Bar Time.
Days.
Nostalgia.
Cortes. Space Song.
Cowper, W. Comparison, A.
Crane, H. My Grandmother's Love Letters.
Sonnet: "Ere elfish Night shall sift another day."
Tenderness and Resolution.
Time Cannot Be Worn.
Crashaw. On the Frontispiece of Isaacsons Chronologie Explained.
Creeley. Again.
Clock.
"Do You Think."
Echo ("I'm almost / done, the hour").
For the Graduation.
For the Graduation: Bolinas, 1972.
Kitchen.
Love ("Not enough. The question: what is").
Master of All.
Measure, The.
Moment.
New Year's.
Of Years.
Re C—.
Rescue, The.
Sea ("Salt and water").
Sitting Here.

So There.
Still.
Then ("Put yourself where you'll be").
They.
Time ("Can't live / mindless").
Time, The.
Tunnel, The.
Up in the Air.
Which Is to Say.
Cummings, E. E.   All ignorance toboggans into
   know.
Anyone Lived in a Pretty How Town.
As is the sea marvelous.
Chérie / the very,picturesque,last Day.
Faithfully tinying at twilight voice.
Fire stop thief help murder save the world.
How many moments must(amazing each).
I say no world.
If everything happens that can't be done.
If(touched by love's own secret)we,like homing.
Impression.
In time's a noble mercy of proportion.
Love is a guess / that deepens.
Love's absence is illusion,alias time.
Much i cannot) / tear up the world:& toss.
Night shall eat these girls and boys.
Not time's how(anchored in what mountaining
   roots).
Now is a ship / which captain am.
Once White & Gold / daisy in the dust.
Out of more find than seeks.
Out of the mountain of his soul comes.
Ponder, darling, these busted statues.
Skies may be blue;yes.
Sonnet IV.
Stand with your lover on the ending earth.
Summer is over / —it's no use demanding.
There are so many tictoc.
Time,be kind;herself and i.
True lovers in each happening of their hearts.
What time is it?it is by every star.
Whatever's merely wilful, / and not miraculous.
When hair falls off and eyes blur And.
When the proficient poison of pure sleep.
When unto nights of autumn do complain.
Wherelings whenlings / (daughters of if but
   offspring of hopefear).
Where's Madge then / Madge and her men?
Which is the very.
Workingman with hand so hairy-sturdy.
Cunningham, J.   Coffee.
Consolatio Nova.
Davie, D.   And Our Eternal Home.
Curtains!
Preoccupation's Gift.
Time Passing, Beloved.
De la Mare.   Beneath a motionless yew.
Clear Eyes.
Decoy, The.
Flight, The.
Foreboding.
Memory.
Moment, The.
Music.
Not Only.
Of a Son.
Polonius.
Quiet Enemy, The.
Thule.
Time Passes.
Dickey, J.   Daughter.
From Time.
Dickinson, E.   Clock strikes one that just struck
   two, The.
Forever—is composed of Nows.
Great Streets of silence led away.
Hour is a Sea, An.
Is it a joyous expanse of Year.
Look back on Time, with kindly eyes.
Sic transit gloria mundi.
Some time is longer than the rest.
There comes a warning like a spy.
They Say That Time Assuages.
Things that never can come back, are several,
   The.

Time does go on.
Time feels so vast that were it not.
Time is short and full.
Time's wily Chargers will not wait.
Too happy Time dissolves itself.
We talked with each other about each other.
Donne.   Anniversary [or Anniversarie], The.
Computation, The.
Dove, R.   Hill Has Something to Say, The.
Du Bellay.   Rome.
Dugan, A.   On Trading Time for Life by Work.
Dunbar, P.   King Is Dead, The.
Love Despoiled.
Time to Tinker 'Roun'!
Eberhart, R.   Formative Mastership.
Garden God, The.
Human Being Is a Lonely Creature, The.
Illusion of Eternity, The.
Light from Above.
Light, Time, Dark.
Man and Nature.
My Bones Flew Apart.
Nothing But Change.
Poem as Trajectory, The.
Return, The.
Sanders Theater.
Soldier Rejects His Times Addressing His
   Contemporaries, A.
Standards, The.
Time Passes.
Usurper.
What Gives.
You Think They Are Permanent But They Pass.
Emerson, R.   Brother, no decrepitude.
Compensation.
Crowning hour when bodies vie with souls, The.
Dangerous gift & grace is mine, A.
Days.
Ever the Rock of Ages melts.
How drearily in College hall.
I know the appointed hour.
Nahant.
Nun's Aspiration.
On bravely through the sunshine & the showers.
Past, The.
Patient Pan / Drunken with nectar, The.
Poet of poets / Is Time, the distiller.
Pour the wine! pour the wine!
Seashore.
Test, The.
This shining hour is an edifice.
To every creature / Adam gave its name.
To the Clock.
Two Rivers.
Valedictory Poem.
Woods.
Ferlinghetti, L.   Hilarious God.
Frost, R.   I Could Give All to Time.
Nothing Gold Can Stay.
García Lorca.   Pause of the Clock.
Ginsberg, A.   In Death, Cannot Reach What Is
   Most Near.
Glück, L.   For My Mother.
Inlet, The.
Magi, The.
Saturnalia.
Shad-Blow Tree, The.
Graves, R.   Broken Neck.
Counting the Beats.
Flowering Aloe, The.
Gold Cloud.
In Time.
Joan and Darby.
Lost World, A.
Love Story, A.
Song: From Otherwhere or Nowhere.
Song: The Clocks of Time.
Song: The Queen of Time.
Song: The Sundial's Lament.
Spring 1974.
Time.
Uncalendared Love.
Guillén, J.   Death, from a Distance.
Gunn, T.   Inherited Estate, The.
Hall, D.   At Delphi.
"Between the Clock and the Bed."

Columns of the Parthenon, The.
Day I Was Older, The.
Exile.
Sea, The.
Shudder[, The].
Han-shan.   I close my overgrown door in vain.
HaNagid.   On Their Couches Stretched Out at
   the Treasury.
See the Fraud Flow By.
Time Defies and Betrays the Patricians.
Hardy, T.   Absolute Explains, The.
Anniversary, An.
Best Times.
Clasped Skeleton, The.
Clock of the Years, The.
Clock-Winder, The.
Commonplace Day, A.
Copying Architecture in an Old Minster.
During Wind and Rain.
Her Initials.
Hundred Years Since, A.
In a Eweleaze near Weatherbury.
In a Former Resort after Many Years.
Inquiry, An.
Long Plighted.
Man Who Forgot, The.
New Dawn's Business, The.
Old Furniture.
Places.
Second Attempt, A.
Second Visit, The.
Self-Unconscious.
She, to Him.
Sheep Fair, A.
So, Time.
Sunshade, The.
Ten Years Since.
Tenant-for-Life, The.
They Are Great Trees.
This Summer and Last.
Week, A.
When Wearily We Shrink Away.
Where They Lived.
Woman Who Went East, The.
Herbert, G.   Life.
Time.
Herrick.   Death Ends All Woe.
His Poetry His Pillar.
No Time in Eternity.
Present Time But Pleaseth, The.
Sabbaths.
To a Friend.
To the Virgins, to Make Much of Time.
Upon Time.
Watch, The.
Hopkins, G.   To His Watch.
Housman.   On Wenlock Edge.
Howe, S.   Pythagorean Silence.
Hughes, L.   Lady in Cabaret.
New Year.
Ignatow, D.   Premonitions.
White-Haired, I Walk in on My Parents.
Jackson, L.   And a Day.
Autobiography of the Present.
From Later to Earlier.
Jacobsen, J.   Clock, The.
In the Crevice of Time.
Lovers, The.
Notes toward Time.
Jarrell, R.   Bad Music, The.
Kirilov on a Skyscraper.
Lament: "All is far."
Man with the axe stands profound and termless,
   The.
Old orchard in the middle of the forest, The.
Picture in the Paper, A.
When you and I were all.
Jeffers, R.   All night long the rush and trampling
   of water.
Carmel Point.
Diagram.
Gray Weather.
It flows out of mystery into mystery: there is no
   beginning—.
Little Scraping, A.
Old Stone-Mason, The.

Polar ice-caps are melting, the mountain glaciers, The.
Soliloquy.
Stone Axe, The.
Johnson, S. In Rivum a Mola Stoana Lichfeldiæ Diffluentem.
Jonson, B. Hour-Glass [or Houre-Glasse], The.
Keats. To Ailsa Rock.
To James Rice.
Khayyám, O. From Omar Chiam.
Kinnell. Tragedy of Bricks, The.
Wait.
Kipling, R. Run of the Downs, The.
Song of Travel, A.
Truthful Song, The.
Kizer, C. Glass, The.
On a Line from Sophocles.
Kunitz, S. Change.
In a Strange House.
Old Clothes Man, The.
Strange Calendar.
Larkin, P. Days.
Disintegration.
This Is the First Thing.
Time and Space Were Only Their Disguises.
Laughlin, J. Bird of Endless Time, The.
Elusive Time.
Hour Glass, The.
Properate Tempus.
Tragedy of Time, The.
Lawrence, D. H. Corot.
Humming-Bird.
Song of a Man Who Has Come Through.
Levertov. Autumnal.
English Field in the Nuclear Age, An.
First Love.
Journeyings.
Seth Thomas: A Love Poem.
Talking to Oneself.
Winter Afternoons in the V & A, Pre-W.W.II.
Levi, P. Mouse, A.
Thieves.
Levine, P. Ask the Roses.
My Son and I.
New Day, A.
Ordinary Morning, An.
Sweet Will.
These Streets.
Winter Words.
Lindsay, N. After Reading the Sad Story of the Fall of Babylon.
Springfield of the Far Future, The.
Lowell, R. Between the Porch and the Altar.
Lux. Time.
MacDiarmid, H. First Love.
Last Song, A.
MacLeish. Farm, The.
Geography of this Time.
Grazing Locomotives.
Journey Home.
La Foce.
November.
Seeing.
Signature for Tempo.
Snow Fall, The.
Snowflake Which Is Now and Hence Forever, The.
Why the Face of a Clock Is not Truly a Circle.
Words in Time.
You, Andrew Marvell.
MacNeice. Another Cold May.
August.
Birthright.
Brandy Glass, The.
Cradle Song: "Clock's untiring fingers wind the wool of darkness, The."
Glacier, The.
Mayfly.
Meeting Point.
Perdita.
Slow Starter, The.
Star-Gazer.
Sunday Morning.
Train to Dublin.
Mahon. Heraclitus on Rivers.
Malherbe. Stanzas: "At length, my soul! thy

fruitless hopes give o'er."
Mallarmé. For the sake of voyaging— heedlessly.
Marvell. To His Coy Mistress.
McGrath, T. Blues for Jimmy.
Trinc: Praises II.
McHugh, H. To the Quick.
Melville, H. Enthusiast, The.
Meredith, G. Time.
Meredith, W. Last Things.
Merrill, J. Hourglass.
Merwin. After the Solstice.
Another Year Come.
From a Series.
Present, The.
Resolution.
Scale in May, A.
Second Sight.
This Day of This Month of This Year of This.
Vocations.
Michelangelo Buonarroti. Alas, Alas, that I am betrayed.
Wo is me woe's me when I think.
Millay, E. Sonnet: "Time, that renews the tissues of this frame."
Time does not bring relief; you all have lied.
Milosz, C. Book in the Ruins, A.
Day of Generation.
Mistake, A.
Rivers ("'So lasting they are, the rivers!" Only think. Sources somewhere in the mountains").
Milton. On Time.
To Mr. Lawrence.
Moore, M. Four Quartz Crystal Clocks.
Muldoon, P. February.
Nash, O. I Had No Idea It Was So Late.
Lady Thinks She Is Thirty, A.
Locust-Lovers, Attention!
Mr. Artesian's Conscientiousness.
Preface to the Past.
Reflection on the Passage of Time, Its Inevitability and Its Quirks.
They Won't Believe, on New Year's Eve, that New Year's Day Will Come What May.
Thoughts Thought While Waiting for a Pronouncement from a Doctor, an Editor, a Big Executive, the Department of Internal Revenue or Any Other Momentous Pronouncer.
Time Marches On.
Nemerov. First Leaf, The.
Guide to the Ruins.
Moment.
Old Photograph, An.
On Reading "The Love and Death of Cornet Christopher Rilke."
Paraphrase from Notebooks.
Photograph of a Girl, The.
Remorse for Time, The.
Sestina 1: "Thickness of paint or flesh cannot deface."
Situation Does Not Change, The.
Somewhere.
Sunderland.
Neruda. Bell-Ringer, The.
Initial.
Same Story.
Today How Many Hours.
O'Hara, F. Poetry.
Oliver, M. Hummingbird Pauses at the Trumpet Vine.
Olson, C. Kingfishers, The.
R².
Owen, W. Promisers, The.
Pagis. Visit to a Physicist.
Wall Calender.
Parker, D. Daylight Savings.
Patchen. History Is a Throne and a Gate.
Loyalty Is the Life You Are.
Night Has Been as Beautiful as Virginia.
Note for a Diary.
State of the Nation, The.
Paz. January First.
Penn, R.E. Dream.
Pessoa. Live, you say, in the present.
One after another, hard-pressed waves.

Petrarch. O time, O turning sky, speeding away.
Sonnet: "If grief dismiss me not to them that rest."
That window where one sun is visible.
Piercy. For Shoshana Rihn—Pat Swinton.
Plath. Sonnet: To Time.
Temper of Time.
Times Are Tidy, The.
To Eva Descending the Stair.
Poe. Coliseum, The.
Prunty. Towards a Relative Ending.
Quasimodo. Agrigentum Road, The.
Raine, K. Moment, The.
Oracles.
Return, The.
Ralegh, S. Authours Epitaph, Made by Himself, The.
Nymph's [or Nimphs] Reply to the Shepherd [or Sheepheard], The.
Poem of Sir Walter Rawleighs, A.
Ramanujan. At Zero.
Fog.
On a Delhi Sundial.
Sonnet: "Time moves in and out of me."
Rexroth, K. Another Spring.
Songs for Marie's Lutebook.
Time Is an Inclusion Series Said McTaggart.
Time Is the Mercy of Eternity.
Took.
Wheel Revolves, The.
Riley, J. Just as of Old.
Time.
Rilke. Future, The.
Ritsos. Miniature.
Robinson, E. Clerks, The.
Fragment: "Faint white pillars that seem to fade."
Three Quatrains.
Rossetti, C. Amen.
As the Doves to Their Windows.
Birchington Churchyard.
Death-Watches.
Earth Shall Tremble at the Look of Him, The.
End of Time, The.
For All.
Half Moon Shows a Face of Plaintive Sweetness, The.
Heaven's chimes are slow, but sure to strike at last.
How Many Seconds in a Minute?
Let Patience Have Her Perfect Work.
Life's Parallels, A.
Months, The.
Next of Kin.
Oh knell of a passing time, / Will it never cease to chime?
One Certainty, The.
Our little baby fell asleep.
Piteous my rhyme is / What while I muse of love and pain.
Redeeming the Time.
Resurgam.
Ruin.
Short is time, and only time is bleak.
Summer nights are short, / Where northern days are long, The.
Tempus Fugit.
Time lengthening, in the lengthening seemeth long.
Time passeth away with its pleasure and pain.
Time seems not short: / If so I call to mind.
Touching "Never."
Unforgotten.
You who looked on passed ages as a glass.
Rossetti, D. Ardour and Memory.
Autumn Idleness.
Barren Spring.
Beauty's Pageant.
Birth-Bond, The.
Body's Beauty.
Bridal Birth.
Broken Music.
Choice, The ("Eat thou and drink; to-morrow thou shalt die").
Choice, The ("Think thou and act; to-morrow thou shalt die").

Choice, The ("Watch thou and fear; to-morrow thou shalt die").
Cloud and Wind.
Dark Day, A.
Dark Glass, The.
Day of Love, A.
Death-in-Love.
Death's Songsters.
Equal Troth.
Farewell to the Glen.
From Dawn to Noon.
From the Cliffs: Noon.
Genius in Beauty.
Gracious Moonlight.
He and I.
Heart of the Night, The.
Heart's Compass.
Heart's Haven.
Heart's Hope.
Her Gifts.
Hero's Lamp.
Hill Summit, The.
Hoarded Joy.
Hope Overtaken.
Inclusiveness.
Kiss, The.
Known in Vain.
Lamp's Shrine, The.
Landmark, The.
Last Fire.
Life-in-Love.
Life the Beloved.
Lost Days.
Lost on Both Sides.
Love and Hope.
Love Enthroned.
Love-Letter, The.
Love-Moon, The.
Love-Sweetness.
Lovers' Walk, The.
Love's Baubles.
Love's Fatality.
Love's Last Gift.
Love's Lovers.
Love's Testament.
Lovesight.
Memorial Thresholds.
Michelangelo's Kiss.
Mid-Rapture.
Monochord, The.
Moonstar, The.
Morrow's Message, The.
Newborn Death ("And thou, O Life, the lady of all bliss").
Newborn Death ("To-day Death seems to me an infant child").
Nuptial Sleep.
Old and New Art (Not as These).
Old and New Art (St Luke the Painter).
Old and New Art (The Husbandmen).
One Hope, The.
Parted Love.
Passion and Worship.
Portrait, The.
Pride of Youth.
Retro me, Sathana!
Sea-Limits, The.
Secret Parting.
Severed Selves.
Silent Noon.
Sleepless Dreams.
Song-Throe, The.
Sonnet, A: "Sonnet is a moment's monument, A."
Soul-Light.
Soul's Beauty.
Soul's Sphere, The.
Stillborn Love.
Sun's Shame, The ("As some true chief of men, bowed down with stress").
Sun's Shame, The ("Beholding youth and hope in mockery caught").
Superscription, A.
Supreme Surrender.
Through Death to Love.
Transfigured Life.

Trees of the Garden, The.
True Woman (Her Heaven).
True Woman (Her Love).
True Woman (Herself).
Vain Virtues.
Vase of Life, The.
Venus Victrix.
Willowwood ("And now Love sang: but his was such a song").
Willowwood ("I sat with Love upon a woodside well").
Willowwood ("O ye, all ye that walk in Willowwood").
Willowwood ("So sang he: and as meeting rose and rose").
Winged Hours.
Without Her.
Youth's Antiphony.
Youth's Spring-Tribute.
Rukeyser, M.   Clouds, Airs, Carried Me Away.
Eel.
Overthrow of One o'Clock at Night, The.
Poem: "Green going through the jungle of those years."
Speech of the Mother, from "The Middle of the Air."
Sundays, They Sleep Late.
Thousands of Days.
Three Sides of a Coin.
Time Hinder Not Me; His Arms Reach Here and There.
Rukeyser, M. *et al.*   Night Flight : New York.
Sandburg, C.   Altgeld.
Bitter Summer Thoughts.
Blue Ridge.
Bronzes.
Counting.
Cumulatives.
Eleventh Avenue Racket.
Flowers Tell Months.
Four Preludes on Playthings of the Wind.
Gong of Time, The.
Harmonica Humdrums.
Has-Been, The.
Junk Man, The.
Keepsake Boxes.
Kin.
Languages.
Let Love Go On.
Limited.
Losses.
Man the Moon Shooter.
Mist, The.
Moon Hammock.
North Atlantic.
Santa Fe Sketches.
Solo for Saturday Night Guitar.
Stars, Songs, Faces.
Streets Too Old.
Striped Cats, Old Men and Proud Stockings.
Sunset from Omaha Hotel Window.
Turn of the Wheel.
Under.
Variations on a Theme.
Wind on the Way, The.
Sarton, M.   Now I Become Myself.
On Being Given Time.
These Images Remain.
Schuyler, J.   Hymn to Life.
Seifert.   Funeral under My Window.
Philosophy.
Sexton.   For Mr. Death Who Stands with His Door Open.
Road Back, The.
Shapiro, K.   Drug Store.
Shelley, P.   Fragment: Love the Universe To-day.
Lament, A: "O world! O life! O time!"
Ozymandias.
Time.
Smith, S.   All Things Pass.
Grange, The.
How Slowly Time Lengthens.
Intimation of Immortality.
Out of Time.
What Is the Time?; or, St. Hugh of Lincoln.

Snyder, G.   Four Poems for Robin.
I settled at Cold Mountain long ago.
Milton by Firelight.
One Year.
Years, The.
Spender, S.   In 1929.
In Railway Halls.
Spenser, E.   Ruines of Time, The.
Stafford, W.   Fall Wind.
Gift, The.
Inscribed on a Prayer Wheel and Spun.
Stevens, W.   Martial Cadenza.
This Solitude of Cataracts.
Suckling, S.   Love's Clock.
Swenson, M.   Loaf of Time, A.
Poplar's Shadow, The.
Skopus.
Swift, J.   Power of Time, The.
To Janus.
Swinburne.   Triumph of Time, The.
Szymborska, W.   Nothing Twice.
People on the Bridge.
Tate, J.   Time X.
Tennyson, A.   Break, Break, Break.
Thomas, D.   Force That through the Green Fuse Drives the Flower, The.
Hold Hard, These Ancient Minutes in the Cuckoo's Month.
Then Was My Neophyte.
When, like a Running Grave.
Thoreau.   Behold these flowers.
On shoulders whirled in some eccentric orbit.
Tomlinson, C.   During Rain.
End, The.
In the Fullness of Time.
Maintenant.
One World.
Sound of Time, The.
Wind.
Van Duyn.   Homework.
Very.   Clock, The.
Lost, The ("Fairest day that ever yet has shone, The").
Time.
Time's House.
Villon.   Ballade in Old French.
Voltaire.   To Madame du Châtelet.
Walcott.   In a Green Night.
Prelude: "I, with legs crossed along the daylight, watch."
Warren, R.   Acquaintance with Time in Early Autumn.
Aging Man at Noon in Timeless Noon of Summer.
Bearded Oaks.
Calendar.
Dream of a Dream.
Forever o'Clock.
Globe of Gneiss.
Interjection #1: The Need For Re-evaluation.
Monologue at Midnight.
Mortmain.
Nature of a Mirror, The.
Paradox of Time.
Resolution.
Summer Afternoon and Hypnosis.
There's a Grandfather's Clock in the Hall.
True Nature of Time, The.
Weiss, T.   After Five Years.
Whalen, P.   Morning Walk, A.
Whitman, W.   As Consequent, Etc.
For Him I Sing.
From My Last Years.
Hours Continuing Long.
Life and Death.
Or, from That Sea of Time.
Quicksand Years.
To Think of Time.
Who Learns My Lesson Complete.
Whittier.   Autograph, An.
Greeting.
Hampton Beach.
Homestead, The.
Past and Coming Year, The.
Reunion, The.
Winter Roses.

Wilbur, R.   Gnomons.
Mill, The.
On the Marginal Way.
Shad-Time.
Wellfleet: The House.
Year's End.
Williams, C. K.   When / you were small, I.
Williams, M.   Geography of Time, The.
House in the Vacant Lot, The.
Old Detective Begins His Last Interrogation
   Looking for the Truth as Always, The.
Sir.
Sitting Alone at Sunrise: Problems in the Space-
   Time Continuum.
Thought as It Turns, A.
Williams, T.   Events Proceed.
Morgenlied.
October Song.
Williams, W.   A, B & C of It, The.
Clock of the Years, The.
Counter, The.
Prelude, A: "I know only the bare rocks of
   today."
Tailpiece.
Time the Hangman.
To a Woman Seen Once.
Wordsworth, W.   At Furness Abbey.
"Beloved Vale!" I said, "when I shall con."
Calm is the Fragrant air, and loth to lose.
Composed among the Ruins of a Castle in North
   Wales.
Cuckoo-Clock, The.
Fragment: "In vain did Time and Nature.."
Go Back to Antique Ages, if Thine Eyes.
Longest Day; Addressed to My Daughter, The.
Massy Ways Carried across These Heights, The.
September, 1819.
Sequel to *Beggars* Composed Many Years After.
'Tis He Whose Yester-Evening's High Disdain.
To ———: "Look at the fate of summer
   flowers."
To a Painter.
Wright, C.   Apologia Pro Vita Sua.
Cicada.
Journal of English Days, A.
Light Journal.
Lost Souls.
March Journal.
Monastery at Vršac, The.
Portrait of the Artist with Hart Crane.
Southern Cross, The.
Still Life with Spring and Time to Burn.
Yard Journal.
Wright, J.   Devotions.
Fishermen, The.
RIP.
Sitting in a Small Screenhouse on a Summer
   Morning.
Three Steps to the Graveyard.
To the August Fallen.
Today I Was So Happy, so I Made this Poem.
Yeats.   Brown Penny.
Folly of Being Comforted, The.
Gyres, The.
His Bargain.
Lamentation of the Old Pensioner, The.
Moods, The.
Peace.
Tom at Cruachan.
Zaturenska.   Child in the Crystal.
Chorale for the Seasons.
Flowing of the River, The.
Metaphysics of the Night.
Reflections On a Centaur.
Zukofsky, L.   For Selma Gubin's Umbrellas.
Has the sum.
I Sent Thee Late.

Tinkers
Herrick.   Tinkers Song, The.
Plath.   Tinker Jack and the Tidy Wives.
Wordsworth, W.   Tinker, The.

Tinter Abbey
Wordsworth, W.   Lines Composed a Few Miles
   above Tintern Abbey on Revisiting the Banks
   of the Wye during a Tour, July 13, 1798.

Tiresias
Dugan, A.   On a Myth. On a Conventional
   Wisdom.
Gunn, T.   Book of the Dead, The.
Stock, R.   Inquest.

Tisdall, William
Owens, S.   Poem, A: "Ye Sons of Levi, Church
   Divines."
Sheridan, T.   Letter from a Cobbler in Patrick's
   Street to Jet Black, A.
Scribbler from the Northern Bear, A.
To the Author of "Tom Pun-Sibi
   Metamorphosed."
Upon William Tisdall, D. D.
Unknown.   Rivals, The.

Titanic (ship)
Ciardi, J.   Poetry.
Hardy, T.   Convergence of the Twain, The.
Mahon.   After the Titanic.

Tithonus
Tennyson, A.   Tithonus.

Titian (Tiziano Vecellio)
Lowell, R.   Charles Vby Titian.

Titmice
De la Mare.   Titmouse.
Rilke.   Small Notebook.
See also **Chickadees**

Titus (Roman emperor)
Chiabrera.   Perhaps some needful service of the
   State.

Toads
Eberhart, R.   Hop-Toad, The.
Kinnell.   Kissing the Toad.
Kinsella, T.   Folk Wisdom.
Kumin, M.   Territory.
Niedecker.   My mother saw the green tree toad.
Riley, J.   Mister Hop-Toad.
Rossetti, C.   Hopping frog, hop here and be
   seen.
Sexton.   March 7th.
Tomlinson, C.   John Maydew or The Allotment.
Wilbur, R.   Death of a Toad, The.

Toadstools
See **Mushrooms**

Tobacco
Baudelaire.   Pipe.
Byron, G.   Napoleon's Snuff-Box.
Cowper, W.   To Mr. Newton.
To the Rev. William Bull.
Eberhart, R.   Tobacconist of Eighth Street, The.
Kipling, R.   Poor Honest Men.
Melville, H.   Herba Santa.

Tobago
See **Trinidad and Tobago**

Toes
Carver, R.   Toes, The.
Logan, J.   Eight Poems on Portraits of the Foot.
Ritsos.   Separation.
Updike.   In Extremis.
See also **Feet**

Tokyo, Japan
Creeley.   Things to Do in Tokyo.

Toledo, Spain
Williams, W.   High Bridge above the Tagus
   River at Toledo, The.

Tolerance
Browning, E.   Adequacy.
Dunbar, P.   Accountability.
Fenton, J.   Chosun.
Heaney, S.   Weighing In.
Hughes, L.   Live and Let Live.
Lawrence, D. H.   Tolerance.
Nash, O.   Nevertheless.
Yes and No.
Plath.   Companionable Ills, The.
Williams, T.   I think the strange, the crazed, the
   queer.

Toller, Ernst
Auden.   In Memory of Ernst Toller.

Tollund Man
Heaney, S.   Tollund Man, The.

Tomatoes
Levertov.   Libation.

Tombs
Ashbery, J.   How Much Longer Will I Be Able
   to Inhabit the Divine Sepulcher.
Berry, W.   Farmer among the Tombs, The.
Blok.   Ravenna.
Borges.   Inscription on Any Tomb.
Brontë, E.   Darkness was overtraced on every
   face.
Start not! upon the minister wall.
Wide cathedral aisles are lone, The.
Carew, T.   Epitaph on the Lady Mary Villiers,
   An.
Cavafy.   In the Month of Athyr.
Tomb of Evrion.
Tomb of Iasis, The.
Tomb of Ignatios, The.
Tomb of the Grammarian Lysias.
Ciardi, J.   Notes.
Coleridge, S.   Love's Burial-Place.
Two Round Spaces on the Tombstone, The.
Cowper, W.   Another.
Stanzas on Milton's Remains.
"Dario."   Prayer for the Dead (To Verlaine).
Davie, D.   Under St Paul's.
De la Mare.   Stranger, The.
Dickey, J.   Tomb Stone.
Dickinson, E.   Admirations—and Contempts—
   of time, The.
Dimple in the Tomb, A.
It was a Grave, yet bore no Stone.
Sweet hours have perished here.
Donne.   Fall of a Wall.
Niobe.
Dubie.   Tomb Pond.
Eberhart, R.   I Will Not Dare to Ask One
   Question.
Emerson, R.   And when I am entombed in my
   place.
Hall, D.   Southwest of Buffalo.
Hardy, T.   Obliterate Tomb, The.
Herbert, G.   Church Monuments.
Herrick.   His Winding-Sheet.
To Robin Redbreast.
Upon a Flie.
Upon the Lady Crew.
Jackson, L.   Time Beneath, The.
Jacobsen, J.   Enemy of the Herds, the Lion, The.
Jeffers, R.   Broadstone, The.
Low Sky, The.
Jonson, B.   Little Shrub Growing By, A.
Keats.   This Living Hand, Now Warm and
   Capable.
Larkin, P.   Arundel Tomb, An.
Lindsay, N.   Trial of the Dead Cleopatra in Her
   Beautiful and Wonderful Tomb, The.
Michelangelo Buonarroti.   Ashes to ashes, spirit
   to the sky.
Braccio lies here. No less a tomb could show.
Cold stone, none knows but you, my gaol
   forever.
My lady, how comes it about—what all can see.
Within this tomb our handsome Braccio's laid.
Montale.   Sarcophagi.
Nash, O.   Funebrial Reflection.
Lather as You Go.
Orr, G.   Field in New England, A.
Patchen.   Old lean over the tombstones, the,
   The.
Poe.   Annabel Lee.
Pope, A.   Epitaph Intended for Mr. Rowe, in
   Westminster Abbey.
Epitaph on the Monument of the Honourable
   Robert Digby, and of his Sister Mary, Erected
   by their Father the Lord Digby.
Pound, E.   Tomb at [or of] Akr Çaar, The.
Rossetti, C.   Last Rites.
Sandburg, C.   Cool Tombs.
Seifert.   At the Tomb of the Czech Kings.
Stevens, W.   Worms at Heaven's Gate, The.
Stockton, A.   On an Enclosure of Roses in
   Which Is the Grave of Miss Mary Morgan a
   Young Lady of 13 Years of Age Daughter of
   Col Morgan.
Tomlinson, C.   Catacomb.
Unknown.   Another ["Take to thy bosom, gentle
   earth, a swain"].

Spirit of Plato.
Tomb Cover of Imam Riza.
Very.   Sepulchre of the Books, The.
Whalen, P.   Dream & Excursus, Arlington
    Massachusetts.
Wordsworth, W.   Surprised by joy—impatient as
    the Wind.
Zaturenska.   Dialogue.
See also **Cemeteries; Graves; Mausoleums;**
    Monuments

Tongues
Creeley.   Charm, The.
Dove, R.   Adolescence—II.
Hacker, M.   Canzone: "Consider the three
    functions of the tongue."
HaNagid.   You're Trapped, My Tongue.
Herrick.   Hand and Tongue, The.
Komunyakaa.   Tongue Is, The.
Rumi.   Shape of My Tongue, The.
Zagajewski.   Tongue.
Zukofsky, L.   Michtam.

Tools
Ammons.   Tooling Up.
Berry, W.   Adze, The.
Ciardi, J.   Measurements.
Eberhart, R.   Broken Pen, The.
Heaney, S.   Pitchfork, The.
Merwin.   Tool.
Sandburg, C.   Laughing Blue Steel.
Wordsworth, W.   To the Spade of a Friend (An
    Agriculturist).

Toothaches
Burns, R.   Address to the Tooth-Ache.
Carew, T.   Tooth-Ache Cured by a Kiss, The.
Herrick.   Upon Gorgonius.
Piercy.   Root Canal, The.
Weiss, T.   Charm against the Toothache, A.
See also **Teeth**

Torah, The
Amichai [*or* Amikhai].   Giving of the Torah,
    The.

Tornadoes
Clampitt.   Nereids of Seriphos, The.
McHugh, H.   Acts of God.
Riley, J.   Cyclone, The.
Shapiro, K.   Tornado Warning.
Very.   On the Late Tornado, at Wallingford,
    Conn.

Toronto, Ontario
Atwood.   Visit to Toronto, with Companions.

Tortoises
Atwood.   Elegy for the Giant Tortoises.
Carruth, H.   Cross My Heart and Hope to Die, It
    Was the Very Same Song Exactly.
Coleridge, S.   Eagle and the Tortoise, The.
"Dario."   Golden tortoise walks across the
    carpet, The.
Lawrence, D. H.   Baby Tortoise.
Lui et Elle.
Tortoise Family Connections.
Tortoise Gallantry.
Tortoise-Shell.
Tortoise Shout.
Nash, O.   Tortoise, The.
Pagis.   Tortoise, The.
Szymborska, W.   Dream of the Old Tortoise,
    The.

Torture
Ai.   Prisoner, The.
Arendt.   Hands, The.
Atwood.   Torture.
Baudelaire.   Voyage to Cythera, A.
Beckett, S.   Noire soeur.
Berryman.   Song of the Tortured Girl, The.
Bly, R.   Romans Angry about the Inner World.
Carew, T.   Murdering Beauty.
Carver, R.   Torture.
    Wake Up.
Dickey, W.   Post-Therapy Room.
Dubie.   La Pampa.
Dugan, A.   Against France: On the Algerian
    Pleasures of Entity.
    On Fingernails in Bloody Times.
Faiz.   Elegy for Hassan Nasir.
Fenton, J.   Vuccerìa.

García Lorca.   Martyrdom of St. Eulalia.
Hughes, T.   Tender Place, The.
Ignatow, D.   First on TV, A.
Jeffers, R.   Memoir.
Kumin, M.   At a Private Showing in 1982.
Levertov.   Modes of Being.
    On a Theme from Julian's Chapter 20.
Lindsay, N.   Dangerous Little Boy Fairies, The.
Lorde.   Barren.
Lux.   Traveling Exhibit of Torture Instruments.
Meredith, W.   Revenant, The.
Orr, G.   Solitary Confinement.
Paley, G.   In San Salvador (II).
Plath.   Hanging Man, The.
Rilke.   Saint Catherine.
Sandburg, C.   Man with the Broken Fingers,
    The.
Simic.   Rough Outline.
Smith, S.   My Cats.
Szymborska, W.   Torture.
    Tortures.
Walker, A.   Torture.
Williams, C. K.   Another Dollar.
    Interrogation II.

Touch
Atwood.   Axiom.
Borges.   Saturday, A.
Broumas, O.   Io.
    Moon Conjunct Ace of Cups.
    Touched.
Davie, D.   Condolence.
Graves, R.   Touch My Shut Lips.
Gunn, T.   Touch.
Hall, D.   Fête.
Kinnell.   Poem of Night.
Kumin, M.   We Are.
Laughlin, J.   Her Reply.
    Touching.
Lawrence, D. H.   Initiation Degrees.
    Night.
    Touch.
    Touch Comes.
Ramanujan.   Eyes, Ears, Noses, and a Thing
    about Touch.
    Rather Foolish Sentiment, A.
Riley, J.   Dear Hands.
    Passing of a Heart, The.
    Reach Your Hand to Me.
    Touch of Loving Hands, The.
Rossetti, C.   De Profundis.
Sexton.   Touch, The.
Swenson, M.   Feel Me.
Warren, R.   Rather like a Dream.
Williams, C. K.   Medusa.
Wilner, E.   Natural History.

Tourism and Tourists
Amichai [*or* Amikhai].   Love of Jerusalem.
    Tourist.
    Tourists.
Atwood.   At the Tourist Centre in Boston.
Bishop, E.   Arrival at Santos.
Carruth, H.   Baler, The.
Clampitt.   Midsummer in the Blueberry Barrens.
    Reservoirs of Mount Helicon, The.
    Sacred Hearth Fire, The.
    Thermopylae.
Clough.   Resignation—to Faustus.
Collins, B.   Consolation.
Creeley.   Davao Insular Hotel.
    Hotel Lobby.
    Spring in San Feliu.
    Waiting for a Bus "en Frente de la Iglesia."
Cummings, E. E.   Memorabilia.
Davie, D.   Kavyria.
    Nashville Mornings.
    Poreč.
Dove, R.   Sightseeing.
Dugan, A.   Memorial Service for the Invasion
    Beach Where the Vacation in the Flesh Is
    Over.
Eliot, T. S.   Burbank with a Baedeker: Bleistein
    with a Cigar.
Enzensberger, H.   Sightseeing Tour.
Ferlinghetti, L.   Baja Revisited.
Frost, R.   Importer, An.
Hall, D.   Christ Church Meadows, [Oxford].

Jacobsen, J.   Short Views in Africa.
    Waking.
Kumin, M.   Festung, Salzburg, The.
    On Reading an Old Baedeker in Schloss
    Leopoldskron.
Kunitz, S.   Thief, The.
Lawrence, D. H.   Tourists.
Mahon.   Roman Script.
Major, C.   Alone, I went into that special.
    And the single reality.
    Brief Visit to Venice.
    September Mendocino.
Merwin.   Questions to Tourists Stopped by a
    Pineapple Field.
Prunty.   Foliage Tour, The.
    Monument, The.
Rich, A.   Tourist and the Town, The.
Stock, R.   Farewell to Baedeker.
Tomlinson, C.   Ice Cream at Blauenberg.
    Teotihuacán.
Whittier.   Christian Tourists, The.
Wordsworth, W.   On Seeing Some Tourists of
    the Lakes Pass by Reading; a Practice Very
    Common.
Zagajewski.   Sénanque.
Zukofsky, L.   4 Other Countries.
    Stratford-on-Avon.

Tournaments
Dunbar, W.   Off Februar the fyiftene nycht.

Toussaint L'Ouverture, François Dominique
Whittier.   Toussaint L'Ouverture.
Wordsworth, W.   To Toussaint L'Ouverture.

Towns
Auden.   Who Will Endure.
Brodsky, J.   Kellomäki.
Browning, R.   Up at a Villa—Down in the City.
Collins, B.   Schoolsville.
Cummings, E. E.   Anyone Lived in a Pretty
    How Town.
Davie, D.   Townend, 1976.
    West Virginia's Auburn.
Dove, R.   Small Town.
Dunbar, P.   Possum Trot.
Eberhart, R.   Retrospective Forelook.
Frost, R.   Serious Step Taken Lightly, A.
Ginsberg, A.   Reflections in Sleepy Eye.
Gurney, I.   Robecq Again.
Hall, D.   Town of Hill, The.
Kinsella, T.   Tao and Unfitness at Inistiogue on
    the River Nore.
Larkin, P.   Here.
Laughlin, J.   Shameful Profession, The.
Lawrence, D. H.   End of Another Home
    Holiday.
    Inheritance, The.
    Little Town at Evening, The.
    Transformations.
    Whether or Not.
Lindsay, N.   Springfield of the Far Future, The.
Lux.   Grim Town in a Steep Valley.
    It's the Little Towns I Like.
    Somebody's Aunt Out Swabbing Her Birdbath.
Merrill, J.   Summer People, The.
Merwin.   Mountain Town.
Mistral, G.   In Praise of Small Towns.
Olson, C.   Gonfalon Raised Tonight, The.
    Town, The.
Oppen.   Undertaking in New Jersey, The.
Pagis.   Souvenir, The.
Patchen.   It's My Town!
    Just outside Tombstone.
    Knowledge of Old Towns, The.
Pinsky.   December Blues.
Prunty.   Old Declaratives.
Riley, J.   Little Town o' Tailholt, The.
    Town Karnteel, The.
Rukeyser, M.   Gauley Bridge.
Sandburg, C.   Between Two Hills.
    Chromo.
    Five Towns on the B. and O.
    Gone.
    Joliet.
    Potomac Town in February.
Schuyler, J.   Elizabethans Called It Dying, The.
Smith, S.   Avondale.
Snyder, G.   Arts Council Meets in Eureka, The.

Stafford, W. Boom Town.
It Still Happens Now.
Prairie Town.
Suckling, S. Summons to Town, A.
Tomlinson, C. Sconset.
Two Views of Two Ghost Towns.
Updike. Upon Learning That a Town Exists in
Virginia Called Upperville.
Van Duyn. In the Missouri Ozarks.
Whittier. Haverhill.
Williams, M. Main Street.
Williams, T. Towns Become Jewels.
Williams, W. Invitation.
Yeats. Happy Townland, The.
Zagajewski. I Walked through the Medieval
Town.
Stary Sacz.
See also **Cities; Villages**

Toys
Bishop, E. Cirque d'Hiver.
Bukowski. Look, The.
Dubie. Descent into the Hours of the Peregrine.
Ginsberg, A. Ghost May Come, A.
Hardy, T. New Toy, The.
Kinsella, T. Soft Toy.
Komunyakaa. Playthings.
Larkin, P. Toys.
Nemerov. Instructions for Use of This Toy.
Snow Globe, The.
Patchen. Orange Bears, The.
Ramanujan. Wobbly Top, A.
Riley, J. Jack-in-the-Box.
Squirt-Gun Uncle Maked Me, The.
Toy-Balloon, The.
Toy Penny-Dog, The.
Rilke. Toys.
Sandburg, C. Upstairs.
Simic. Toy Factory.
Williams, W. Chinese Toy, A.

Track Athletics
Whitman, W. Runner, The.

Tractors
Hughes, T. Tractor.
Sandburg, C. New Farm Tractor.
Tomlinson, C. Lines.

Tradition
Dugan, A. On Being Out-Classed by Class.
Graves, R. Traditionalist, The.
Hall, D. Family, The.
Herrick. Fast, or Lent, The.
Kipling, R. Irish Guards, The.
Land, The.
Lorde. Generation.
Mahon. Last of the Fire Kings, The.
Milosz, C. Undressing Justine.
Nash, O. Epstein, Spare That Yule Log!
Neruda. XIX, The.
Pasolini. Poetry of the Tradition, The.
Patchen. Letter to the Inventors of a Tradition,
A.
Ramanujan. Conventions of Despair.
Rich, A. At the Jewish New Year.
Cartographies of Silence.
Study of History.
Tear Gas.
Shapiro, K. Humanities Building, The.
Necropolis.
Wordsworth, W. Fancy and Tradition.
Highland Broach, The.
Young England—What Is Then Become of Old.

Trafalgar, Battle of (1805)
Meredith, G. October 21, 1905.
Trafalgar Day.
Rossetti, D. Last Three from Trafalgar, The.

Traffic
Amichai [*or* Amikhai]. My former student is in
the traffic police.
Beckett, S. Lueurs lisières.
Clifton, L. Signs.
Codrescu. Traffic.
Hall, D. Traffic.
Levi, P. Via Cigna.
Nash, O. It Would Have Been Quicker to Walk,
or, Don't Tell Me We're There Already.
Poor Mr. Strawbridge.

Strange Case of Mr. Niobob's
Transmogrification, The.
O'Hara, F. Walking to Work.
Sandburg, C. Blue Island Intersection.
Swenson, M. Bison Crossing Near Mt.
Rushmore.
Tate, J. In the Realm of the Ignition.
Wilbur, R. Simile for Her Smile, A.

Traffic Accidents
Carver, R. Cadillacs and Poetry.
Hughes, T. Motorbike, A.
See also **Automobile Accidents**

Traherne, Thomas
Wilbur, R. "World without Objects Is a Sensible
Emptiness, A."

Trains
Berryman. Traveller, The.
Bogan, L. Train Tune.
Carver, R. Moon, the Train, The.
Ciardi, J. Night Freight, Michigan.
Time Is the Late Train into Albany.
Clampitt. Babel aboard the Hellas International
Express.
Tidewater Winter.
Westward.
Clifton, L. Birthday 1999.
What I Think when I Ride the Train.
Codrescu. 3/6/81, Amtrack.
Trains.
Creeley. Train Going By.
Cummings, E. E. One Fine Day.
Will i ever forget that precarious moment?
Cunningham, J. Wandering Scholar's Prayer to
St. Catherine of Egypt, The.
Davie, D. Buckinghamshire.
Dickey, J. Folk Singer of the Thirties, A.
Dickinson, E. I like to see it lap the Miles.
Train went through a burial gate, A.
Dubie. Accident.
Train, The.
Dunbar, P. Ballade: "By Mystic's banks I held
my dream."
Eberhart, R. Analogue of Unity in Multeity.
Frost, R. On the Heart's Beginning to Cloud the
Mind.
Gallagher, T. Devotion: That It Flow; That
There Be Concentration.
Not There.
Glück, L. Chicago Train, The.
Hall, D. Sister on the Tracks, A.
Transcontinent.
Hardy, T. Faintheart in a Railway Train.
Midnight on the Great Western.
Hayden, R. Runagate Runagate.
Hughes, L. Freedom Train.
Jim Crow Car.
Six-Bits Blues.
Jacobsen, J. Reindeer and Engine.
Jarrell, R. On the Railway Platform.
Orient Express, The.
Larkin, P. Like the Train's Beat.
Laughlin, J. In the Train.
Lawrence, D. H. À la Maniere de D. H.
Lawrence.
Excursion Train.
Red Moon-Rise.
Tommies in the Train.
Train, The.
Levertov. Don't You Hear that Whistle Blowin'
Levi, P. Monday.
Levine, P. And the Trains Go On.
Lux. River between the Train and the Highway,
The.
MacLeish. Arrival and Departure.
Burying Ground by the Ties.
Empire Builders.
Grazing Locomotives.
Way-Station.
MacNeice. Contact, A.
Figure of Eight.
Hold-up.
Restaurant Car.
Slow Movement.
Train to Dublin.
Trains in the Distance.
McGrath, T. Black Train, The.

End of the Line, The.
Repeated Journey, The.
Something Is Dying Here.
Merwin. Trestle, The.
Wheels of the Trains, The.
Millay, E. From a Train Window.
Travel.
Montale. Local Train.
Muldoon, P. Train, The.
Nash, O. Dr. Fell and Points West.
Now You See It, Now I Don't.
September Morn.
Unwinged Ones, The.
Nemerov. Clock with No Hands, A.
Home for the Holidays.
Junction, on a Warm Afternoon, The.
Olson, C. Landscape, without Color.
Morning News, The.
Paley, G. Translation.
Patchen. Little Black Train, The.
Pinsky. Waiting.
Plath. Getting There.
Rich, A. Lucifer in the Train.
Sunday Evening.
Riley, J. Iron Horse, The.
Rimbaud, A. I was sitting in a Third-Class
carriage; an old priest.
Ritsos. Abstracted Painter.
Roethke. Night Journey.
Rukeyser, M. Campaign.
Grand Central Station.
Sandburg, C. Limited.
Southern Pacific.
Window.
Work Gangs.
Seifert. Fragment of a Letter.
November Rain.
Spender, S. Express, The.
Sign *Faehre nach Wilm*, The.
Stock, R. Cushing.
Lifeline Train to Puerto Limón.
Tate, J. Manna.
Success Comes to Cow Creek.
Thoreau. What's the railroad to me?
Tomlinson, C. Night-Train, The.
Warren, R. Ballad: Between the Boxcars
[1923].
Last Night Train.
Recollection in Upper Ontario, from Long
Before.
Whistle of the 3 A.M.
Weiss, T. Late Train, The.
Whitman, W. To a Locomotive in Winter.
Wilbur, R. In the Smoking-Car.
Williams, W. Overture to a Dance of
Locomotives.
Wilner, E. As Far as It Goes, and Back.
Wright, J. Baptism in the Lead Avenue Ditch.
Outside Fargo, North Dakota.
Zagajewski. At Daybreak.
Opus Posthumous.
See also **Locomotives; Railroads**

Traitors
Davie, D. Balancing Acts.
Stock, R. And You, Too, Brutus.
See also **Treason and Traitors**

Trakl, Georg
Berry, W. Sowing.
Bly, R. Getting Up Late.
Carew, T. My Mistress Commanding Me to
Return Her Letters.
To a Lady, Not Yet Enjoyed by Her Husband.
Dubie. Trakl.
Hamill, S. Homage to Trakl.
Herrick. Neglect.
Lorde. And Don't Think I Won't Be Waiting.
Need: A Chorale for Black Woman Voices.
St. Louis out of Time.
Orr, G. There.
Sarton, M. Hard Death, A.
Wilbur, R. Shame.
Williams, C. K. Neglect.
Souls.

Tramps
Gurney, I. Companions, The.

Riley, J. Old Tramp, The.
Rimbaud, A. Tramps.
Szymborska, W. Clochard.
See also **Vagabonds; Hoboes; Homeless, The**

Transcendence
Ai. Testimony of J. Robert Oppenheimer, The.
Ammons. Admission.
  Bourn.
  Having Been Interstellar.
  He Held Radical Light.
  Offset.
Baudelaire. Transcendence.
Celan. Flower.
  Ice, Eden.
  It's all different from what you think, from what
    I think.
Codrescu. Alice's Brilliance.
  Les Fleurs du Cinéma.
Crane, S. God came to a man, A.
Dickinson, E. After great pain a formal feeling
  comes.
  There's a certain Slant of light.
Dugan, A. Argument to Love as a Person.
García Lorca. Morning.
Ginsberg, A. Kral Majales.
  Magic Psalm.
Hughes, L. Dream Variation[s].
  Poem: "Ah, / My black one."
  Search.
Ignatow, D. I Live with My Contradictions.
  In This Dream I Do Not Exist.
  Question, The.
Laughlin, J. At Eleusis.
  By the Numbers.
  Escape, The.
  Floating Free.
Mallarmé. Azure, The.
  Bell-Ringer, The.
  Clown Chastised, The.
  Hérodiade.
  Jinx, The.
  Sea Breeze.
  Summer Sadness.
  Throw of the Dice, A.
  Virginal, vibrant, and beautiful dawn, The.
  Windows, The.
Merwin. Now It Is Clear.
Michelangelo Buonarroti. What in your
  handsome face I see, my lord.
Milosz, C. Appeal, An.
  Ball, A.
  Hall, A.
  How It Was.
  If.
  Philosopher's Home, A.
Montale. House by the Sea.
  Incantation.
  On the Threshhold.
Pessoa. It's raining. There is silence, since the
  rain itself.
Rimbaud, A. Second Delirium. Alchemy of the
  Word.
Rossetti, D. Ardour and Memory.
  Autumn Idleness.
  Barren Spring.
  Beauty's Pageant.
  Birth-Bond, The.
  Body's Beauty.
  Bridal Birth.
  Broken Music.
  Choice, The ("Eat thou and drink; to-morrow
    thou shalt die").
  Choice, The ("Think thou and act; to-morrow
    thou shalt die").
  Choice, The ("Watch thou and fear; to-morrow
    thou shalt die").
  Cloud and Wind.
  Dark Day, A.
  Dark Glass, The.
  Day of Love, A.
  Death-in-Love.
  Death's Songsters.
  Equal Troth.
  Farewell to the Glen.
  From Dawn to Noon.
  Genius in Beauty.

Gracious Moonlight.
He and I.
Heart of the Night, The.
Heart's Compass.
Heart's Haven.
Heart's Hope.
Her Gifts.
Hero's Lamp.
Hill Summit, The.
Hoarded Joy.
Hope Overtaken.
Inclusiveness.
Kiss, The.
Known in Vain.
Lamp's Shrine, The.
Landmark, The.
Last Fire.
Life-in-Love.
Life the Beloved.
Lost Days.
Lost on Both Sides.
Love and Hope.
Love Enthroned.
Love-Letter, The.
Love-Moon, The.
Love-Sweetness.
Lovers' Walk, The.
Love's Baubles.
Love's Fatality.
Love's Last Gift.
Love's Lovers.
Love's Testament.
Lovesight.
Memorial Thresholds.
Michelangelo's Kiss.
Mid-Rapture.
Monochord, The.
Moonstar, The.
Morrow's Message, The.
Newborn Death ("And thou, O Life, the lady of
  all bliss").
Newborn Death ("To-day Death seems to me an
  infant child").
Nuptial Sleep.
Old and New Art (Not as These).
Old and New Art (St Luke the Painter).
Old and New Art (The Husbandmen).
One Hope, The.
Parted Love.
Passion and Worship.
Portrait, The.
Pride of Youth.
Retro me, Sathana!
Secret Parting.
Severed Selves.
Silent Noon.
Sleepless Dreams.
Song-Throe, The.
Sonnet, A: "Sonnet is a moment's monument,
  A."
Soul-Light.
Soul's Beauty.
Soul's Sphere, The.
Stillborn Love.
Sun's Shame, The ("As some true chief of men,
  bowed down with stress").
Sun's Shame, The ("Beholding youth and hope
  in mockery caught").
Superscription, A.
Supreme Surrender.
Through Death to Love.
Transfigured Life.
Trees of the Garden, The.
True Woman (Her Heaven).
True Woman (Her Love).
True Woman (Herself).
Vain Virtues.
Vase of Life, The.
Venus Victrix.
Willowwood ("And now Love sang: but his was
  such a song").
Willowwood ("I sat with Love upon a woodside
  well").
Willowwood ("O ye, all ye that walk in
  Willowwood").
Willowwood ("So sang he: and as meeting rose

and rose").
Winged Hours.
Without Her.
Youth's Antiphony.
Youth's Spring-Tribute.
Rumi. Children's Game, A.
  Mystery does not get clearer by repeating the
    question, The.
  Omar and the Old Poet.
  Three Brothers and the Chinese Princess, The.
  Wax.
Seifert. Prologue: "To be a poet is no easy
  task."
Stevens, W. Sunday Morning.
Sze. Streamers.
  Three A.M., in Winter.
Wilde, O. Hélas!
  Humanitad.
Williams, T. Morgenlied.
Wright, C. Basic Dialogue.
  Disjecta Membra.
  Early Saturday Afternoon, Early Evening.
  East of the Blue Ridge, Our Tombs Are in the
    Dove's Throat.
  Indian Summer 2.
  It's Turtles All the Way Down.
  Lives of the Artists.
  Lives of the Saints.
  Looking across Laguna Canyon at Dusk, West-
    by-Northwest.
  Watching the Equinox Arrive in Charlottesville,
    September 1992.

Transformation
Ammons. Lion::Mouse.
  Song: "Merging into place against a slope of
    trees."
Atwood. Carrying Food Home in Winter.
  Songs of the Transformed.
Baudelaire. Metamorphoses of the Vampire.
Brontë, E. H.A. and A.S.
Browning, R. Rephan.
Carver, R. Two Carriages.
Chuang Tzu. Keng's Disciple.
Creeley. Song: "Grit / of things, The."
  Statue, The.
Cullen, C. Protest.
  That Bright Chimeric Beast.
Dickinson, E. He touched me, so I live to
  know.
Dugan, A. Transformation.
Duncan, R. Banners, The.
Emerson, R. Character.
  He could condense cerulean ether.
  Life is great / Men are small.
Ferlinghetti, L. Paris Transformations.
Gallagher, T. Present.
  Willingly.
García Lorca. Death.
Glück, L. Undertaking, The.
Hacker, M. Sea Coming Indoors, The.
Hall, D. Digging.
  Je Suis une Table.
  "King and Queen."
Hardy, T. Transformations.
Ignatow, D. Behind His Eyes.
  Cloud Creates, A.
  Metamorphosis, The.
Kipling, R. 'Eathen, The.
Kunitz, S. Layers, The.
Levertov. Acolyte, The.
  Unknown, The.
McGrath, T. Revisionist Poem—Octavio Paz.
Meredith, W. Roots.
Merrill, J. Transfigured Bird.
Merton. Macarius and the Pony.
  Transformation: For the Sacred Heart, The.
Muldoon, P. Centaurs, The.
Nemerov. Singular Metamorphosis, A.
Oliver, M. Spring Azures.
Pessoa. Master, my dear master!
Petrarch. Had but the light come just a little
  nearer.
  Happy season of my early prime, The.
Piercy. Woman in the Ordinary, The.
Plath. Love Letter.
Raine, K. Childhood.

I felt, under my old breasts, this April day.
If, into this evening as the grass receives the dew.
Ramanujan. Meditation, A.
Moulting.
Ritsos. Silent Agreement.
Rukeyser, M. Child of the root, among your apples and forests.
Rumi. Chickpea to Cook.
I reach for a piece of wood. It turns into a lute.
New Rule, The.
Sublime Generosity.
Think that you're gliding out from the face of a cliff.
Worm's Waking, The.
Sarton, M. In Time like Air.
Seifert. Transformations.
Shapiro, K. Haircut.
I Am an Athetist Who Says His Prayers.
Smith, S. Friskers, or, Gods and Men.
Frog Prince, The.
Stock, R. Reverse Metamorphosis.
Transfiguration: Natura Naturans.
Sze. Fern, Coal, Diamond.
Kaiseki.
Tomlinson, C. Door, The.
Metamorphosis, The.
Palm of the Hand.
Prometheus.
Under the Moon's Reign.
Van Duyn. Leda Reconsidered.
Wilbur, R. Beautiful Changes, The.
Wright, C. October.
Zagajewski. Transformation.
Zukofsky, L. After reading.
Daruma.
Marriage Song for Florence and Harry, A.
Rains, the rains, The.

Transience

Albinovanus Pedo. Plants and trees made poore and old, The.
Auden. As I Walked Out One Evening.
Berrigan, T. Ann Arbor Song.
Bierce. My Day of Life.
Browning, E. Change upon Change.
Browning, R. Prologue: "Poet's age is sad: for why?, The."
Rephan.
Speculative.
Burns, R. Epitaph: "Lo worms enjoy the seat of bliss."
Hey for a Lass wi' a Tocher.
Song: "Sensibility how charming."
Campion, T. Loe, when backe mine eye.
To Music Bent Is My Retired Mind.
What if a Day [or a Month or a Year].
Where are all thy beauties now, all hearts enchaining? [or harts enchayning?].
Carew, T. Song[, A]: "Ask[e] me no more where Jove bestow[e]s."
Carruth, H. Point, The.
Song: The Old, Old Man.
Two Romantic Pieces.
Woodsmoke at 70.
Carver, R. Prosser.
Crane, H. Passage.
Creeley. Faces, The.
Here again, / shifting days.
Step, A.
Time, The.
Cummings, E. E. Christ but they're few.
Cruelly,love / walk the autumn long.
Touching you i say(it being Spring).
Without the mercy of / your eyes your.
Dobyns. Connections.
Donne. Anniversary [or Anniversarie], The.
Eberhart, R. Groundhog, The.
Eliot, T. S. Mélange Adultère de Tout.
Emerson, R. Yet sometimes to the sorrow stricken.
Frost, R. Nothing Gold Can Stay.
Hardy, T. Obliterate Tomb, The.
Plaint to Man, A.
Roman Gravemounds, The.
Self-Unconscious.
St. Launce's Revisited.

Sunshade, The.
Thought in Two Moods, A.
Hayden, R. Theme and Variation.
Heaney, S. Blackberry-Picking.
Herbert, G. Virtue [or Vertue].
Herrick. Best to Be Merry.
Corinna's Going a-Maying.
Putrefaction.
To a Bed of Tulips.
To Blossoms.
To Daffodils [or Daffadills].
To Dianeme.
To Enjoy the Time.
To Live Freely.
Upon Craw.
Housman. Along the field as we came by.
Hughes, L. Breath of a Rose.
Jeffers, R. To the Stone-Cutters.
Kumin, M. Agnostic Speaks to Her Horse's Hoof, The.
Laughlin, J. Vagrant, The.
Levertov. Living.
May Mornings, The.
Levine, P. Sweet Will.
Lindsay, N. Wizard Wind, The.
Longfellow, H. Morituri Salutamus.
MacNeice. Sunlight on the Garden, The.
Malherbe. Stanzas: "At length, my soul! thy fruitless hopes give o'er."
McGrath, T. Return, The.
Melville, H. Malvern Hill.
Meredith, G. Creed.
Foresight and Patience.
From lamplight and an aged leaf.
In the Dry.
Song: "O the wind, the wind, the wind doth blow."
Stave of Roving Tim, A.
Time.
Unknown Fair Faces.
Merwin. Early One Summer.
Letter.
Now It Is Clear.
October.
Milosz, C. Annalena.
Gathering Apricots.
In a Buggy at Dusk.
Lastingness.
Return to Kraków in 1880.
Nemerov. Autumnal.
Dandelions.
Equations of a Villanelle.
Paraphrase from Notebooks.
Situation Does Not Change, The.
Olson, C. La Chute.
Pasolini. Lines from the Testament.
Pessoa. Lightly, quickly, soft.
No one, in the vast and virgin jungle.
Petrarch. Who wants to see what can be done by Nature.
Ralegh, S. Nymph's [or Nimphs] Reply to the Shepherd [or Sheepheard], The.
Poem of Sir Walter Rawleighs, A.
Ransom, J. Blue Girls.
Eclogue: "JANE SNEED BEGAN IT: My poor John, alas."
Robinson, E. Man against the Sky, The.
Rossetti, C. Bed of Forget-Me-Nots, A.
Days are clear, / Day after day, The.
Dead Bride, The.
Death Is Swallowed Up in Victory.
Earth and Heaven.
End of Time, The.
Have Patience.
I Have a Message unto Thee.
I said within myself: I am a fool.
Joy is but sorrow, / While we know.
Love Attacked.
Love Ephemeral.
Love hath a name of Death.
May.
Memento Mori.
Patience of Hope.
Present and Future.
Seasons.
Tempus Fugit.

Time of Waiting, The.
Sandburg, C. At the Gates of Tombs.
Autumn Movement.
Caboose Thoughts.
Flash Crimson.
Jabberers.
Languages.
Mist, The.
Out of the Rainbow End.
Runaway Colors.
Seifert. Wet Picture.
Sexton. Just Once.
Shapiro, K. Premises.
Shelley, P. Fragment: "When a lover clasps his fairest."
Hymn to Intellectual Beauty.
Ozymandias.
To ———: "When passion's trance is overpast."
Sidney, S. Leave Me O Love.
Stafford, W. Big House, The.
Swenson, M. On the Edge.
Sze. June Ghazal.
Tennyson, A. Break, Break, Break.
Unknown, sometimes at. to Sir Walter Ralegh.
As You Came from the Holy Land [of Walsingham].
Villon. Ballade in Old French.
Ballade of the Ladies of Time Past.
Gone Ladies.
Voltaire. To Madame du Châtelet.
Warren, R. Basic Syllogism.
Paradox of Time.
Whitman, W. As if a Phantom Caress'd Me.
Wilbur, R. La Rose des Vents.
Looking into History.
To the Etruscan Poets.
Transit.
Two Voices in a Meadow.
Wellfleet: The House.
Williams, M. After the Revolution for Jesus a Secular Man [or the Associate Professor] Prepares His Final Remarks.
Quantum Theory Made Simple.
Thought as It Turns, A.
Williams, T. Apparition.
Lyric: "Can it be again."
Sacre de Printemps.
This Cryptic Bone.
Wordsworth, W. Most Alluring Clouds That Mount the Sky, The.
Wright, C. Last Journal.
March Journal.
Portrait of the Artist with Hart Crane.
Wright, J. Eleutheria.
To a Troubled Friend.
Wyatt, S. I see the change from that that was.
Sonnet: 'Each man me telleth.'
Varium et Mutabile.

See also **Change**

Translation and Translators

Burns, R. On Elphinston's Translation of Martial.
Carew, T. To My Much Honoured Friend, Henry, Lord Carey of Leppington, upon His Translation of Malvezzi.
Ciardi, J. Letter to Dante.
Sorrow of Obedience, The.
Codrescu. On Translation.
Davie, D. Balancing Acts.
Mandelstam, on Dante.
Mandelstam's Hope for the Best.
Donne. Upon the Translation of the Psalms by Sir Philip Sidney, and the Countess of Pembroke His Sister.
Fenton, J. Lines for Translation into Any Language.
Gallagher, T. Poem in Translation, A.
Gurney, I. George Chapman—The Iliad.
Hacker, M. For Jean Migrenne.
Herbert, G. To the Right Hon. the Lord Chancellor (Bacon).
Jonson, B. On the Author, Work, and Translator.
To Clement Edmonds, on His *Caesar's Commentaries* Observed, and Translated.
To Mr Joshua Sylvester.

To My Chosen Friend the Learnèd Translator of Lucan, Thomas May, Esquire.

To My Worthy and Honoured Friend, Mr George Chapman, on His Translation of Hesiod's *Works and Days*.

To Sir Henry [or Henrie] Savile [upon His Translation of Tacitus].

To the Same; on the Same.

Keats. On First Looking into Chapman's Homer.

Kizer, C. Lost in Translation.
Translation.

Laughlin, J. Can Language Be Taught with the Fingertips?
Translation, A.

Marvell. To His Worthy Friend Doctor Witty upon His Translation of the "Popular Errors."

Merton. Reading Translated Poets, Feb. 1.
When class was in the garden at Greylands.

Milosz, C. Translating Anna Swir on an Island of the Caribbean.

Nash, O. What Is Bibbidi-Bobbidi-Boo in Sanskrit?

Nemerov. Translation.

Paley, G. Translation.

Patchen. And in Another Place Uses the Same Phrase.

Pope, A. Sandys's Ghost, or a Proper New Ballad on the New Ovid's Metamorphosis as it Was Intended to Be.

To Eustace Budgell, Esq., on His Translation of the Characters of Theophrastus.
Translator, The.

Ralegh, S. To the Translator of Lucan [or Lucan's Pharsalia, 1614].

Rich, A. Translations.

Stafford, W. Walking the Borders.

Suckling, S. To His Much Honoured the Lord Lepington upon His Translation of Malvezzi, His "Romulus" and "Tarquin."

Szymborska, W. Vocabulary.

Tomlinson, C. Las Trampas U. S. A.

Unknown. To My Worthy Friend T S——, D. D. On His Incomparable Translation of and Notes on Persius.

Weiss, T. Russian Lesson.

Transportation, Penal
Komunyakaa. Tally, The.

Transvestites
Ai. Hoover Trismegistus.
Major, C. Jake Flower, The.

Trapezes and Trapeze Artists
Koch, K. Circus, The.
Plath. Aerialist.
Prunty. Family Act, The.
Szymborska, W. Acrobat, The.
Williams, T. Les Etoiles d'un Cirque.

Trapping and Trappers
Hamill, S. Man in the Landscape.
Hughes, T. In the Likeness of a Grasshopper.
Komunyakaa. Trapper's Bride, The.
Larkin, P. Myxomatosis.
Moore, M. New York.
Muldoon, P. Mist-Net, The.
Simic. Day Marked with a Small White Stone, A.
Snyder, G. "One Should Not Talk to a Skilled Hunter about What Is Forbidden by the Buddha."

Trash
Clampitt. Salvage.
Vacant Lot with Tumbleweed and Pigeons.
Cunningham, J. My name is Ebenezer Brown.
Niedecker. Boy tossed the news, The.
Stevens, W. Man on the Dump, The.
See also **Garbage and Garbage Men**

Traveling and Travelers
Amichai [or Amikhai]. Elizabeth Swados.
From Jerusalem to the Sea and Back.
Instructions for Her Voyage.
People with No Future Love.
Poems from Buenos Aires.
Poems of Spring in the Appalachian Mountains.
Three Times I Came to Rome.
Travel by Train.

Travels of the Last Benjamin of Tudela.
Ammons. Back Country.
Angelou. Traveler, The.
Apollinaire. Zone.
Arnold, M. Scholar Gypsy, The.
Ashbery, J. Lament upon the Waters, The.
Atwood. Bus to Alliston, Ontario, The.
Journey to the Interior.
Auden. Legend.
On the Circuit.
Baudelaire. Invitation to a Voyage.
L'Invitation au Voyage.
Travellers.
Berry, W. Air and Fire.
Traveling at Home.
Berryman. Away.
Friendless.
London.
Point of Age, A.
Recovery.
Traveller, The.
Travelling South.
Bishop, E. Arrival at Santos.
Moose, The.
Over 2000 Illustrations and a Complete Concordance.
Questions of Travel.
Santarém.
Blok. Autumn Freedom.
Bly, R. Driving toward the Lac Qui Parle River.
Bradstreet, A. Upon My Son Samuel His Going For England.
Brodsky, J. Admonition, An.
Anti-Shenandoah: Two Skits and a Chorus.
Lagoon.
Broumas, O. Banner.
Field.
Browning, R. Home-Thoughts, from the Sea.
Bukowski. On the Continent.
Winter Comes to a Lot of Places in August.
Burns, R. Epigram on Rough Roads.
Highland Balou, The.
Ken ye ought o' Captain Grose?
Lass That Made the Bed for Me, The.
Byron, G. Lines to Mr Hodgson.
Once Fairly Set Out on His Party of Pleasure.
To a Lady.
Carew, T. Upon Master Walter Montagu's Return from Travel.
Carruth, H. In Russia.
Journey to a Known Place.
Chaucer. Canterbury Tales, The.
January and May, or the Merchant's Tale.
Manciple's Tale—A Modernization, The.
Prioress' Tale—A Modernization, The.
Troilus and Criseyde [or Criseide].
Wife of Bath, The.
Clampitt. Ano Prinios.
At a Rest Stop in Ohio.
Elgin Marbles, The.
Exmoor.
In Umbria: A Snapshot.
Iola, Kansas.
Losing Track of Language.
Procession at Candlemas, A.
Seriphos Unvisited.
Spruce Has No Taproot, The.
Tepoztlán.
Westward.
Witness.
Clifton, L. Further Note to Clark.
Clough. O Theos Meta Sou.
Coleridge, S. Delinquent Travellers, The.
Perspiration: A Travelling Eclogue.
Collins, B. Winter Syntax.
Cowper, W. Distressed Travellers, The.
Crane, H. Traveller Born, A.
Creeley. Berlin: First Night & Early Morning.
Breaking Up Is Hard to Do.
Catching Cold.
Doggie Bags.
Evening.
For Benny.
For Cheryl.
Hong Kong—Last Words.
Hotel Lobby.

Inn / Kyoto.
It's the scale.
Later ("It feels things").
Maybe.
Place ("Long gone time").
Places ("All but / for me and Paul").
Poem for Beginners.
River wandering down.
Say Something.
Soup ("I know what you'd say").
Table, The.
Then ("Don't go / to the mountains").
Things to Do in Tokyo.
Up Here.
Yah.
Cunningham, J. Traveller, the highway my guide, A.
Dante Alighieri. Sonnet: He imagines a pleasant Voyage for Guido, Lapo Gianni, and himself, with their three Ladies.
"Dario." Singer goes all over the world, The.
Davie, D. Epistle. To Enrique Caracciolo Trejo.
Mr Sharp in Florence.
Spring Song, A.
De la Mare. Last Coachload, The.
Listeners, The.
Railway Junction, The.
Three Strangers, The.
Dickey, J. Baggage King, The.
Dickey, W. Fred and the Holy Grail.
Dickinson, E. Caterpillar.
Go traveling with us!
I like to see it lap the Miles.
I watched the Moon around the House.
Road was lit with Moon and star, The.
Donne. Song: "Sweetest love, I do not go[e]."
Dove, R. Sahara Bus Trip, The.
Drummond de Andrade. Travelling in the Family.
Du Bellay. Happy the Man.
Heureux Qui, comme Ulysse, A Fait un Beau Voyage.
Sonnet from the Book of Regrets.
Dubie. Poem: "Mule kicked out in the trees, A. An Early."
Dugan, A. Memory of Old Forms under Hell's Angels.
Passing through the Banford Tolls.
Dunbar, P. Keep a Song Up on de Way.
Eliot, T. S. Journey of the Magi.
Emerson, E. Last Farewell, The.
Emerson, R. At Sea, September 1833.
I care not whither I may go.
If wishes would carry me over the land.
Saadi loved the new & old.
Una.
Enzensberger, H. Thoughts on the Run 4.
Feng-kan. I have been to Tientai.
Frost, R. Rogers Group, A.
Gallagher, T. Devotion: That It Flow; That There Be Concentration.
García Lorca. Dialogue of Amargo.
Rider's Song.
Gay, J. *et al.* Mary Gulliver to Capt. Lemuel Gulliver.
Ginsberg, A. And ninety-nine soldiers piled on the train at Amarillo.
Auto Poesy: On the Lam from Bloomington.
Beginning of a Long Poem of These States.
Bus Ride Ballad Road to Suva.
Continuation of a Long Poem of These States.
Defending the Faith.
Funky barn, black hills approaching Fulton.
Hiway Poesy: L.A.–Albuquerque–Texas– Witchita.
Iron Horse.
Kansas City to Saint Louis.
Message II.
One could pass valuable months.
Siesta in Xbalba.
Vomit Express.
What solitude I've / finally inherited.
Gjuzel. When I Came Back.
Glück, L. Magi, The.
To Florida.
Graves, R. Advocates.

Around the Mountain.
Cloak, The.
Furious Voyage, The.
Legs, The.
Next Time, The.
Gunn, T.   Discovery of the Pacific, The.
Gurney, I.   Song: "Only the wanderer."
Walking Song.
Hacker, M.   Country & Western.
Hall, D.   Abroad Thoughts from Home.
Han-shan.   I longed to visit the eastern cliff.
I recall the places I've been.
Man with a good head and belly, A.
Seasonal round never stops, The.
HaNagid.   Curse, A.
Hardy, T.   How She Went to Ireland.
Meditation on a Holiday.
Hayden, R.   Tour 5.
Heaney, S.   Stations of the West, The.
Herrick.   Salutation.
To His Brother Nicolas Herrick.
Hughes, L.   Bound No'th Blues.
I Thought It Was Tangiers I Wanted.
Jacobsen, J.   Explorer.
Foreign Lands, The.
Treaty.
Jarrell, R.   On the Railway Platform.
See-er of Cities, The.
Jonson, B.   On the Famous Voyage.
To the London Reader, on the Odcombian
Writer, Polytopian Thomas the Traveller.
To the Right Noble Tom, Tell-Troth of His
Travels, the Coriat of Odcombe, and His
Book Now Going to Travel.
Keats.   Keen, Fitful Gusts Are Whispering Here
and There.
Sweet, Sweet Is the Greeting of Eyes.
Kipling, R.   As the Bell Clinks.
Friends, The.
Gipsy Trail, The.
Sestina of the Tramp-Royal.
Song of Seventy Horses.
Song of Travel, A.
Kizer, C.   Where I've Been All My Life.
Koch, K.   Departure from Hydra, The.
Lunch.
Kumin, M.   Itinerary of an Obsession.
Long Approach, The.
Longing to Be Saved, The.
Larkin, P.   Arrivals, Departures.
Autobiography at an Air-Station.
Local Snivels through the Field, The.
Nursery Tale.
Laughlin, J.   Deconstructed Man, The.
Hard to Translate.
Highway 66.
That Other World.
Lawrence, D. H.   On the Road.
Travel Is Over.
Levertov.   Fellow Passengers.
Pilgrim Dreaming, A.
Traveler, A.
Travels.
Voyage.
Wanderer's Daysong.
Young Man Travelling, A.
Logan, J.   First Prelude. Dream in Ohio: The
Father.
Honolulu and Back.
Lines for a Young Wanderer in Mexico.
Poem in Progress.
Traveling.
Trip to Four or Five Towns, A.
Two Poems of Greece.
Lorde.   My Fifth Trip to Washington Ended in
Northeast Delaware.
Lux.   Towards.
MacLeish.   Arrival and Departure.
Cinema of a Man.
Ever Since.
Immortal Helix.
Old Man's Journey.
Tourist Death.
Voyage.
Why the Face of a Clock Is Not Truly a Circle.
MacNeice.   Ravenna.

Solitary Travel.
Major, C.   Bernardston.
Wyoming.
Martial.   2.5: "Believe me, sir, I'd like to spend
whole days."
McGrath, T.   Driving toward Boston I Run
across One of Robert Bly's Old Poems.
Edge of the River, The.
Epitaph: "Again, traveller, you have come a
long way led by that star."
Long Way outside Yellowstone, A.
Love in a Bus.
Poem: "How could I have come so far?"
Poem—Unfinished Poem.
Repeated Journey, The.
Tourists at Ensenada.
Meredith, G.   Familiar Things.
Meeting, The.
Pictures of the Rhine.
Will o' the Wisp.
Merrill, J.   Bronze.
Clearing the Title.
Days of 1971.
Flèche d'Or.
Friend of the Fourth Decade, The.
Last Mornings in California.
Santorini: Stopping the Leak.
Summer People, The.
Thousand and Second Night, The.
Merton.   Ash Wednesday.
Landfall, The.
Old monk is turned loose / And can travel!, The.
Prophet.
Song of the Traveller, The.
Welcome.
Merwin.   Banquet, The.
Going.
On Each Journey.
Road.
Traveling.
Wheels of the Trains, The.
Millay, E.   Travel.
Unexplorer, The.
Milosz, C.   1913.
Mittelbergheim.
Road-side Dog.
Milton.   Elegy 4: To Thomas Young.
Mistral, G.   Concepción.
Molodovsky [or Molodowsky].   White Night.
Montale.   Near Vienna.
Muldoon, P.   Brazil.
Identities.
Making the Move.
Nash, O.   Buses Headed for Scranton, The.
Change Here for Wichita Falls, or, Has
Anybody Seen My Wanderlust?
Everybody Eats Too Much Anyhow.
Have a Seat behind the Potted Palm, Sir.
Hi-Ho the Ambulance-O.
My Trip Daorba.
Traveler's Rest.
Unwinged Ones, The.
You Bet Travel Is Broadening.
Nemerov.   Home for the Holidays.
Sestina 2: "No waste is trackless: all terrain the
lost."
Sightseers.
Song of Degrees, A.
Neruda.   I Come Back from a Journey.
O'Hara, F.   Biotherm [for Bill Berkson].
Mary Desti's Ass.
Terrestrial Cuckoo, A.
You Are Gorgeous and I'm Coming.
Oliver, M.   Dreams.
Olson, C.   De Los Cantares.
Encounter, The.
Landscape, without Color.
Oppen.   Travelogue.
Visit (1).
Paley, G.   In Hanoi 1969.
Parker, D.   Hearthside.
Wanderlust.
Patchen.   Evidence? What Evidence...?
Pessoa.   To travel! Leave countries behind!
Written in a Book Abandoned on the Trip.
Plath.   Getting There.

Pound, E.   Cino.
Ramanujan.   In March.
Rexroth, K.   Travelers in Erewhon.
Rich, A.   Itinerary.
Riley, J.   Curse of the Wandering Foot, The.
Guide, The.
Little Dog-Woggy, The.
Traveling Man, The.
Rilke.   Departure.
Rimbaud, A.   Departure.
I was sitting in a Third-Class carriage; an old
priest.
Winter Dream.
Robinson, E.   John Evereldown.
Roethke.   Harsh Country, The.
Night Journey.
Rossetti, C.   Lord, by what inconceivable dim
road / Thou leadest man on footsore
pilgrimage!
Old-World Thicket, An.
Uphill.
Rukeyser, M.   Ajanta.
During the journey there come moments of
waking.
Grand Central Station.
Man in a plane looks at the surface of land, A.
Otherworld.
Road, The.
Willkie in the *Gulliver*.
Sandburg, C.   Red Son, The.
Road and the End, The.
Schuyler, J.   New Yorker, A.
Rose of Marion, The.
Voyage Autour de Mes Cartes Postales.
Seifert.   Honeymoon.
Place of Pilgrimage.
Shelley, P.   Ozymandias.
World's Wanderers, The.
Sheridan, T.   To the Dean, when in England, in
1726.
Simic.   Midpoint.
Pillow, The.
Travel[l]ing.
Smith, S.   Louise.
Where Are You Going?
Snyder, G.   In my first thirty years of life.
One Year.
Stafford, W.   In Fur.
Journey, A.
Looking for Someone.
Putting the Sonnet to Work.
Trip, The.
Wanderer Awaiting Preferment, The.
When You Go Anywhere.
Stein, G.   Marry Nettie.
Painted Lace.
Sonatina Followed by Another, A.
Stevens, W.   Arrival at the Waldorf.
Stock, R.   Dance, The.
Epistle to Prescott S. Liddell.
Sir John Mandeville and I Sat Up Talking.
Unmapped Road.
Voyager Takes Pause, A.
Swenson, M.   Speed.
Szymborska, W.   Travel Elegy.
Thoreau.   Departure, The.
For though the eaves [or Caves] were rabitted
[or rabbeted orrabbited].
I sailed up a river with a pleasant wind.
I seek the Present Time.
Old Marlborough Road, The.
Travelling.
Tomlinson, C.   Against Travel.
Or Traveller's Joy.
Return, The.
Unknown, sometimes at. to Sir Walter Ralegh.
To his Singular Friend, William Lithgow.
Updike.   Accumulation.
Airport.
Back from Vacation.
Capacity.
Goodbye, Göteborg.
Postcards from Soviet Cities.
Somewhere.
Van Duyn.   Into Mexico.
Small Excursion, A.

Very. Journey, The.
Traveller at the Depot, The.
Walcott. Fortunate Traveller, The.
Warren, R. Going West.
Nocturne: Traveling Salesman in Hotel Bedroom.
Passers-By on Snowy Night.
Trips to California.
Whitman, W. On Journeys through the States.
Promise to California, A.
Whittier. To a Cape Ann Schooner.
To a Friend.
Williams, C. K. Travelers.
Williams, M. For J. William Fulbright on the Day of His Death.
Wordsworth, W. Brugès ("Brugès I saw attired with golden light").
Descriptive Sketches Taken during a Pedestrian Tour among the Alps.
Incident at Brugès.
Memorials of a Tour in Italy, 1837.
Memorials of a Tour of the Continent; 1820.
No spade for leagues had won a rood of earth.
Poems Composed or Suggested during a Tour, in the Summer of 1833.
Road extended o'er a heath, The.
Stepping Westward.
Travelling.
Waggoner, The.
Wright, C. Self-Portait.
Wright, J. Destination: Accomplished.
Sitting in a Small Screenhouse on a Summer Morning.
Sketch for an Aesthetic Project.
Stages on a Journey Westward.
Zagajewski. In Strange Cities.
Opus Posthumous.
To Go to Lvov.
To See.
Traveler.
Vaporetto.
Wanderer, A.
Zukofsky, L. Jaunt.

Treason and Traitors
Brontë, E. M. Douglas to E.R. Gleneden.
Burns, R. Such a Parcel of Rogues in a Nation.
Crashaw. On the Gunpowder-Treason.
Upon the Gunpowder Treason.
Cullen, C. La Belle, La Douce, La Grande.
De la Mare. Ballad of Christmas, A.
Dickinson, E. Treason of an Accent, The.
Treason of an accent, The.
When the Astronomer stops seeking.
Hall, D. Body Politic, The.
Herrick. Treason.
Jeffers, R. War-Guilt Trials.
Kipling, R. Ballad of the Red Earl, The.
MacLeish. Treason Crime, The.
Rich, A. For Ethel Rosenberg.
Scott, S. On the Massacre of Glencoe, 1692.

Treasures
Dickinson, E. Where the Treasure is.
Emerson, R. Ask not treasures from his store.
Han-shan. I was so poor in the past.
HaNagid. On Their Couches Stretched Out at the Treasury.
Rossetti, C. Lay Up for Yourselves Treasures in Heaven.
Rumi. In Baghdad, Dreaming of Cairo: In Cairo, Dreaming of Baghdad.
Pickaxe, The.

Treaties
Ammons. Treaties.
Pagis. Draft of a Reparations Agreement.
Ritsos. After the Breakdown of the Treaty between the Lacedaemonians and the Athenians.
Thomas, D. Hand That Signed the Paper, The.
Whittier. Crisis, The.

Tree of Life
Dugan, A. On Finding the Tree of Life.
Milosz, C. Into the Tree.
Oppen. Biblical Tree, The.
Rukeyser, M. Speaking Tree, The.
Wilner, E. Having Eaten of the Tree of Knowledge.

Tree Surgeons
Hall, D. Stump.
Williams, C. K. Elms.

Tree Toads
Rexroth, K. Mocking Birds.
Riley, J. Tree-Toad, The.
See also **Toads**

Trees
Amichai [*or* Amikhai]. Here.
Poem for Arbor Day.
Ammons. Fall, The.
Jersey Cedars.
Mediation.
Money.
Sap Is Gone Out of the Trees, The.
Snow Log.
Song: "Merging into place against a slope of trees."
Storm.
Ashbery, J. Some Trees.
Atwood. Porcupine Tree.
Auden. Reflections in a Forest.
Berry, W. For the Future.
Planting Trees.
Porch over the River, The.
Sycamore, The.
Woods.
Bishop, E. To a Tree.
Blake, W. In a Myrtle [*or* Mirtle] Shade.
Blue Cloud. Dogwood Blossoms.
Brontë, E. There are two trees in a lonely field.
Woods, you need not frown on me.
Browning, E. Where's Agnes?
Burns, R. Amang the trees, where humming bees.
Tree of Liberty, The.
Carrera Andrade. Cocoa Tree.
Carruth, H. Anxious View of a Tree.
August.
Block.
"I've Never Seen Such a Real Hard Time Before": Three-Part Invention.
My Meadow.
Shake, Well before Using.
Way of the Conventicle of the Trees, The.
Chuang Tzu. Useless Tree, The.
Ciardi, J. Tree, The.
Tree Trimming.
Clampitt. Alders.
Waterfall, The.
Coleridge, S. Barberry-Tree, The.
Tree of Mystery, The.
Cooper, J. Urge to Tell the Truth, The.
Crane, H. Mango Tree, The.
Creeley. Air: "Cat Bird Singing."
For Helen.
Hunger.
In the Fall.
Kid, The.
To Bobbie.
Trees.
Turn, The.
Cullen, C. Love Tree, The.
Cummings, E. E. I am going to utter a tree,Noboby.
Into the smiting / sky tense.
Now all the fingers of this tree(darling)have.
Rosetree,rosetree / —you're a song to see:whose.
Timeless / ly this / (merely and whose).
Trees / were in(give).
Davie, D. Democrats.
Intervals in a Busy Life.
Pietà.
De la Mare. Foreboding.
Three Cherry Trees, The.
Dickey, J. Autumn.
One, The.
Seeking the Chosen.
Trees and Cattle.
Dickinson, E. Antiquated Tree, An.
Still as the Profile of a Tree.
Tree in Winter.
Dove, R. Dusting.
Dubie. About Infinity.
Last Poem, Snow Tree.

Dugan, A. On Looking for Models.
On Trees.
Sawyer's Rage against Trees Noble as Horses, A.
Dunbar, P. Haunted Oak, The.
Duncan, R. Four Songs the Night Nurse Sang.
Eberhart, R. Burden.
Christmas Tree.
Go to the Shine That's on a Tree.
There Is an Evil in the Air.
Emerson, R. Go out into Nature and plant trees.
See yonder leafless trees against the sky.
Where is Skrymir? Giant Skrymir?
Where the fungus broad & red.
Frost, R. Axe-Helve, The.
Birches.
Encounter, An.
On a Tree Fallen across the Road.
Sound of Trees, The.
Spring Pools.
Sycamore.
Tree at My Window.
Wild Grapes.
Gallagher, T. Clearing.
Some with Wings, Some with Manes.
Woodcutting on Lost Mountain.
García Lorca. Casida of the Branches.
Song of the Barren Orange Tree.
Trees.
Ginsberg, A. Those Two.
Trembling of the Veil, The.
Glück, L. Flowering Plum.
Shad-Blow Tree, The.
Tree House, The.
Graves, R. Advocates.
Woman and Tree.
Gunn, T. Exercise, The.
Hampstead; the Horse Chestnut Trees.
Kind of Ethics, A.
Philemon and Baucis.
Waking in a Newly Built House.
Gurney, I. Compensations.
Dark Tree, The.
Felling a Tree.
O Tree of Pride.
Possessions.
Quiet Talk.
Hall, D. Tree and the Cloud, The.
Hamill, S. Unforgiven.
Han-shan. Hundred-foot trees produced by Heaven.
I hiked yesterday to the summit.
I saw some trees by the river.
Tree grew here before the grove, A.
Hardy, T. At Day-Close in November.
Everything Comes.
They Are Great Trees.
Throwing a Tree.
To a Tree in London.
Tree, The.
Tree and the Lady, The.
Without Ceremony.
Heaney, S. Wishing Tree, The.
Herrick. All Things Decay and Die.
Another.
To Blossoms.
To Groves.
To Sycamores.
Upon the Losse of His Finger.
Hopkins, G. Binsey Poplars (Felled 1879).
Distance / Dappled with diminish'd trees.
Hughes, L. Little Green Tree.
Poème d'Automne.
Hughes, T. Autumn Notes.
Sometimes it comes, a gloomy flap of lightning.
Tree.
Trees.
Ignatow, D. Behind His Eyes.
Epilogue: "Trees are tall gods, The."
Hope, The.
I Shake My Fist at a Tree.
Information.
Life They Lead, The.
Talking to Myself.
To Stay Alive.
Jackson, L. Tree-Sense.

Jacobsen, J. Tree Angel.
Keats. In Drear-nighted December.
Kinnell. Perch, The.
Kumin, M. In April, in Princeton.
Kunitz, S. Deciduous Branch.
 Very Tree.
 War against the Trees, The.
Larkin, P. Trees, The.
Lawrence, D. H. Erotic.
 Reality of Peace, 1916.
 Trees in the Garden.
 Winter in the Boulevard.
Levertov. Ancient Tree, An.
 Life around Us, The.
 Message.
 Novices, The.
 Re-Rooting.
 Romance.
 Stems.
 Tree Telling of Orpheus, A.
Levi, P. Valley, A.
 Wooden Heart.
Levine, P. Sleepless Night, A.
Lindsay, N. Spice-Tree, The.
Logue, C. Urbanal.
Lorde. Ballad from Childhood.
 Song: "Wild trees have bought me "
Lux. River between the Train and the Highway,
 The.
MacLeish. Farm, The.
 Man's Work, A.
 March.
 Words to be Spoken.
MacNeice. Tree of Guilt, The.
 Tree Party.
Mahon. Going Home.
Major, C. And the single reality.
 They cut down the last tree.
McGrath, T. Long Goodbye.
McHugh, H. Ozone.
Meredith, W. Chinese Banyan, The.
 Couple of Trees, A.
 Dalhousie Farm.
 Roots.
 Tree Marriage.
Merrill, J. Trees Listening to Bach.
Merton. Silver bird is E backward in cool pond
 water, The.
Merwin. Horse, The.
 Trees.
Millay, E. City Trees.
 Counting-out Rhyme.
 Grow not too high, grow not too far from home.
 Leaf and the Tree, The.
Milosz, C. Into the Tree.
 To a Hazel Tree.
Mistral, G. Mayten, The.
 Pine Forest.
Montale. Chrysalis.
 In the Park.
 You've named a tree for me? It isn't nothing.
Moore, M. Sycamore, The.
Muldoon, P. Early Warning.
 Palm Sunday.
 Wind and Tree.
Nash, O. Song of the Open Road.
Nemerov. Learning by Doing.
 Learning the Trees.
 Thought of Trees, The.
 Trees.
Niedecker. My friend tree.
 They've lost their leaves.
Oliver, M. Black Walnut Tree, The.
Olson, C. 2 Propositions and 3 Proof.
 Merce of Egypt.
Oppen. Biblical Tree, The.
 Building of the Skyscraper, The.
 Return.
Orr, G. Elegy: "Not only doesn't the Ohio."
Paley, G. Arboreal Mystery, An.
Palmer, M. Notes for Echo Lake 6.
Patchen. Under a Tree.
Plath. I Am Vertical.
 On the Plethora of Dryads.
 Polly's Tree.
 Winter Trees.

 Words.
Pound, E. Tree, The.
Prunty. Letter.
Raine, K. Acacia Tree.
 Forest is multitude.
Ramanujan. Love Poem for a Wife and Her
 Trees.
 Meditation, A.
 That Tree.
Ransom, J. Dead Boy.
Rich, A. For the Felling of an Elm in the
 Harvard Yard.
 Tree, The.
 Trees, The.
Ritsos. Doxology.
 Harvest of the Void.
 Prison Tree and the Women, The.
 Tree, A.
Robinson, E. Archibald's Example.
Rossetti, C. Autumn.
 Dumb Friend, A.
 Mirrors of Life and Death.
 Trees' Counselling, The.
 Who Has Seen the Wind?
Rukeyser, M. Boys in the Branches.
Sandburg, C. Branches.
 Hemlock and Cedar.
 Lesson.
 Little Sketch.
 Never Two Songs the Same.
 Prairie Woodland.
 Proud Torsos.
 Shag-Bark Hickory.
 Tall Timber.
 Without Notice Beforehand.
Schuyler, J. Amy Lowell Thoughts.
 Autumn Leaves.
 Noon Office.
Shapiro, K. Calder, A.
Simic. December Trees.
 Peaceful Trees.
 Trees at Night.
Stafford, W. Cottonwood.
Stock, R. Antaeus.
Stockton, A. Elegy on the Destruction of the
 Trees by the Isicles Sunday and Monday of
 Feb, the 17th and 18th, 1788.
Swenson, M. All That Time.
 Tree in Spring, A.
Sze. Taoist Painter, The.
Tomlinson, C. Letter to Uehata.
 Operation, The.
 Poem: "Upended, it crouches on broken limbs."
 Scar, The.
 Tree.
 Tree, The.
 Witnesses, The.
Updike. Planting Trees.
Van Duyn. To Record One Must Be Unwary.
Very. Evergreen, The.
 To an Ancient Locust-Tree, opposite
 Carltonville.
 Tree, The ("I love thee when thy swelling buds
 appear").
Warren, R. Last Metaphor, The.
Whalen, P. Bay Trees Were About to Bloom,
 The.
 Homage to St. Patrick, García Lorca, & the
 Itinerant Grocer.
 Mask.
Whitman, W. I Saw in Louisiana a Live-Oak
 Growing.
Whittier. Sycamores, The.
 Wood Giant, The.
Wilbur, R. Alatus.
 Black Birch in Winter, A.
 Chronic Condition, A.
 Courtyard Thaw, A.
 Fern-Beds in Hampshire County.
 Orchard Trees, January.
 Poplar, Sycamore.
 Under a Tree.
 Wood, A.
Williams, M. 10,000-Year-Old Tree Discovered
 Shades Two and Half Acres.
Williams, W. Approach of Winter.

 Flowers Alone, The.
 Hunter, The.
 Hurricane, The.
 Locust Tree in Flower, The.
 To Waken an Old Lady.
 Tree.
 Tree and Sky.
 Trees.
 Trees, The.
 Winter Trees.
 Yellow Tree Peony, The.
 Young Sycamore.
Wilner, E. Bird in the Laurel's Song, The.
 Natural History.
Wordsworth, W. Desponding Father! Mark This
 Altered Bough.
 Hart's-Horn Tree, near Penrith.
 Laodamia.
 Nutting.
 Tradition of Oker Hill in Darley Dale,
 Derbyshire, A.
 Yew-Trees.
Wright, J. Seasonless, The.
Yeats. Ragged Wood, The.
Zagajewski. In the Trees
Zaturenska. Daphne.
 Twisted Tree, The.
Zukofsky, L. As to How Much.
 Gamut.
 George Washington.
 Pretty.

Trelawny, Edward John
 Meredith, W. English Accounts.

Trench Warfare
 Carver, R. In the Trenches with Robert Graves.
 Owen, W. Anthem for Doomed Youth.
 Exposure.

Tricksters
 Blue Cloud. Alcatraz.
 HaNagid. Foolish Enemy's Face Tells All, The.
 Williams, M. Caution.

Trinidad and Tobago
 Berryman. Old Man Goes South Again Alone.
 Walcott. Egypt, Tobago.
 Midsummer, Tobago.
 Spoiler's Return, The.

Trinity, The
 Herbert, G. Trinity Sunday.
 Ungratefulness.
 Herrick. Number of Two, The.
 To God.
 Jonson, B. Reverse on the Back Side, The.
 Sinner's Sacrifice, The.
 Merton. Freedom as Experience.
 Hymn for the Feast of Duns Scotus.
 Rossetti, C. All Saints: Martyrs.
 Trinity Sunday.
 Whittier. Trust.
 Yeats. Ribh Denounces Patrick.

Triolet (form)
 Hardy, T. How Great My Grief.

Tristram and Isolde
 Arnold, M. Iseult of Brittany.
 Orr, G. Tristan and Iseult.

Triviality
 Cavafy. As Long as You Can.
 Nash, O. What to Do until the Doctor Goes or
 It's Tomorrow than You Think.
 Sandburg, C. Aprons of Silence.
 Villon. Ballade of Forgiveness.
 Wilbur, R. Lightness.
 Williams, C. K. Regulars, The.

Troilus and Cressida
 Dryden, J. Can Life Be a Blessing.
 Wordsworth, W. Troilus and Cresida.

Trojan War
 Cavafy. Funeral of Sarpedon, The ("Heart of
 Zeus is filled with grief, The").
 Horses of Achilles, The.
 Priam's Speeding Forth at Night.
 Trojans.
 Chaucer. Troilus and Criseyde [or Criseide].
 Davie, D. Protesilaus and Laodamia.
 Dugan, A. Stentor and Mourning.
 "H. D." After Troy.

Heaney, S.   Mycenae Lookout.
Homer.   Daughters of Pandarus, The.
  Gardens of Alcinous, The.
  Mindes of men are ever so affected, The.
  Muse, / tell me of this man of wit.
  Sun descending, the *Phæacian* train, The.
Logan, J.   Achilles and the King: A Verse Re-
  telling.
Merton.   Greek Women, The.
Ritsos.   Agamemnon.
  Helen.
  Philoctetes; The Ultimate Mask.
Simic.   My Weariness of Epic Proportions.
Stock, R.   In Transformation of an Imago.
Valéry.   Helen.
Warren, R.   Fatal Interview: Penthesilea and
  Achilles.
Wilner, E.   Dinner Party.
  Iphigenia, Setting the Record Straight.
Yeats.   Leda and the Swan.

Trolleys
See **Streetcars**

Trolls
Smith, S.   Her-zie.
Whittier.   Brown Dwarf of Rügen, The.
  Kallundborg Church.

Trossachs, The, Scotland
Wordsworth, W.   Trosachs, The.

Trotsky, Leon
Ai.   Killing Floor.
Tomlinson, C.   Assassin.

Troubadours
Browning, R.   Rudel to the Lady of Tripoli.
  Sordello.
Collins, B.   Plight of the Troubadour.
Hardy, T.   Dead Man Walking, The.
Laughlin, J.   Lady Asks Me, A.
Pound, E.   In Epitaphium Eius.
  Marvoil.
  Na Audiart.

Trout
Dickey, J.   Winter Trout.
Hughes, T.   Night Arrival of Sea-Trout.
  Stealing Trout on a May Morning.
  Strangers.
Montale.   Black Trout, The.
Wilbur, R.   Hamlen Brook.

Troy
Cavafy.   Priam's Speeding Forth at Night.
Gunn, T.   Wound, The.
Hamill, S.   George Seferis in Sonora.
MacLeish.   Excavation of Troy.
Merton.   Like Ilium.
Nash, O.   First Limick.
Nemerov.   Home for the Holidays.
Walcott.   Map of the New World.
See also **Trojan War**

Truancy
Graves, R.   Death Room, The.

Trucks and Truckers
Bukowski.   Jack-Knife.
Dugan, A.   Night Scene before Combat.
Gunn, T.   Trucker, A.
Heaney, S.   Two Lorries.
Snyder, G.   Why Log Truck Drivers Rise Earlier
  Than Students of Zen.
Tomlinson, C.   At Barstow.

Trujillo Molina, Rafael Leonidas
Dove, R.   Parsley.

Trumpets
Dryden, J.   Song for St Cecilia's Day, 1687, A.
Larkin, P.   Reasons for Attendance.
Rilke.   Trumpets.
Tomlinson, C.   Valle de Oaxaca.
Trakl.   Trumpets.
Whitman, W.   Mystic Trumpeter, The.
Wordsworth, W.   Horn of Egremont Castle, The.

Trust
Angelou.   Sounds like Pearls.
Bogan, L.   Heard by a Girl.
Brontë, E.   Now trust a heart that trusts in you.
Char.   Come Dance in Baronies.
Creeley.   For Friendship.
  Form of Adaptation, A.

Cummings, E. E.   Nothing false and possible is
  love.
"Dario."   Dream's blue bird, The.
Graves, R.   Beware, Madam!
  Broken Compact.
  Loving True, Flying Blind.
  Oath, The.
  Through a Dark Wood.
  What is Love?
Gunn, T.   Idea of Trust, The.
Guyon.   Simple Trust.
HaNagid.   In Business Don't Get Involved.
Hardy, T.   Woman's Trust, A.
Herrick.   Eyes before the Eares, The.
  Multitude.
Kinsella, T.   Tête à Tête.
Larkin, P.   Out in the Lane I Pause.
Lawrence, D. H.   Being Alive.
  Emotional Friend, The.
  Sex and Trust.
  Trust.
MacLeish.   Treason Crime, The.
Michelangelo Buonarroti.   If pure devotion,
  passion without stain.
Piercy.   It Breaks.
Ritsos.   Proletarian Speaker, A.
Rossetti, C.   In Patience.
  Judge Nothing before the Time.
  Leaf from leaf Christ knows; / Himself the Lily
    and the Rose.
  Palm Sunday.
Thomas, D.   Ears in the Turrets Hear.
Williams, M.   Husband.
Zukofsky, L.   Peri Poietikes.

Truth
Angelou.   Accident.
Atwood.   True Stories.
Auden.   Dichtung und Wahrheit.
  History of Truth, The.
Bachmann.   What Is True.
Berry, W.   Song (1).
Borges.   Mirror, The.
Bradstreet, A.   Of the Four Humors in Man's
  Constitution.
Brontë, E.   Stanzas: "Often rebuked, yet always
  back returning."
  There was a time when my cheek burned.
Broumas, O.   Heart Believes with Blows.
Browning, E.   Best Thing in the World, The.
Browning, R.   Pippa Passes.
  Reverie.
  Summum Bonum.
  There goes a swallow to Venice—the stout
    seafarer!
Bukowski.   Funny.
  It's Not Who Lived Here.
Byron, G.   To Romance.
Campion, T.   Vain Men, Whose Follies.
Carew, T.   Disdain Returned.
Celan.   Rumbling: it is, A.
Chaucer.   Balade of Bon Conseill.
  Lak of Stedfastnesse.
Ciardi, J.   True or False.
Clough.   Look you, my simple friend, 'tis one of
  those.
  Old things need not be therefore true.
  Truth is a golden thread seen here and there.
  With Whom Is No Variableness, Neither
    Shadow of Turning.
Cooper, J.   Urge to Tell the Truth, The.
Cortes.   Truth, The.
Cowper, W.   Moralizer Corrected, The.
  Truth.
Crane, H.   Visible the Untrue, The.
Crane, S.   "Truth," said a traveller.
  Wayfarer / Perceiving the pathway to truth, The.
Creeley.   Bed, The.
  Echo ("Broken heart, you / timeless wonder").
  Fancy.
  Mind's Heart.
  My Love.
  Stone.
  Wisdom.
Cullen, C.   To Certain Critics.
Cummings, E. E.   As freedom is a
  breakfastfood.

If a cheerfulest Elephantangelchild should sit.
  Life is more true than reason will deceive.
  My darling since / you and.
  Out of the lie of no.
  Seeker of truth / follow no path.
  What freedom's not some under's mere above.
  When / (day's amazing murder with).
Davie, D.   Standings.
De la Mare.   Catechism, The.
Dickinson, E.   Counterfeit—a Plated Person, A.
  I died for Beauty—but was scarce.
  Opinion is a flitting thing.
  Quicker deceit dies, The.
  Tell all the Truth but tell it slant.
  That it is true, Master.
  Things of which we want the proof, The.
  Truth—is as old as God.
  Truth—is stirless, The.
Eberhart, R.   Airman Considers His Power, An.
  Anima.
  Austere Poem.
  Ceremonial.
  Flow of Thought.
  Four Exposures.
  Froth.
  Full of Joy Do Not Know; They Need Not, The.
  Humanist, The.
  I Walked Out to the Graveyard to See the Dead.
  Incomparable Light, The.
  Kaire.
  Mystery of the Abstract.
  R. G. E.
  Soul.
  Time Passes.
  Truth, The.
  Way Out, A.
Eliot, T. S.   Hippopotamus, The.
Emerson, R.   Dull uncertain brain, A.
  Easy to match what others do.
  Hard is it to persuade the public mind of its
    plain duty & true interest.
  Harp, The.
  Heartily heartily / Nothing be false.
  I live among ideal men.
  Panoply of Paradise is mine.
  Papas Blondine / Grew tall & wise.
  Shun passion, fold the hands of thrift.
  There is in all the sons of men.
  Uriel.
Enzensberger, H.   Further Reasons Why Poets
  Do Not Tell the Truth.
Ferlinghetti, L.   Elegy on the Death of Kenneth
  Patchen, An.
  Mouth of truth, The.
Glück, L.   Day without Night.
Graves, R.   Arrow Shots.
  Broken Compact.
  Chink, The.
  Compact.
  Dilemma, The.
  End of Play.
  Expect Nothing.
  Love Charms.
  Pier-Glass, The.
  Poet's Curse, The.
  Prepared Statement, The.
  Seven Years.
  Terraced Valley, The.
  To Put It Simply.
  Whole Love.
Gurney, I.   Song: "O were there anything by
  half."
Han-shan.   There's a brilliant man somewhere.
HaNagid.   Truth Is Hard.
Hardy, T.   To a Lady.
Herbert, G.   Jordan (1).
Herrick.   Truth.
  Truth and Error.
  Truth and Falsehood.
Hopkins, G.   Summa.
Hughes, L.   Comment on War.
  Theme for English B.
Jackson, L.   Helen's Burning.
  Regret of War Ways.
  Rejoice, Liars.
  Respect for the Dead.

Jeffers, R.   Advice to Pilgrims.
Cassandra.
Curb Science?
Faith.
Mathematicians and physics men, The.
Silent Shepherds, The.
Theory of Truth.
To the Story-Tellers.
What's the best life for a man?
Jonson, B.   From *The Touchstone of Truth*.
Keats.   Ode on a Grecian Urn.
Kinsella, T.   Another September.
Kipling, R.   Fabulists, The.
Poseidon's Law.
Larkin, P.   Send No Money.
Lawrence, D. H.   Elemental.
Satisfaction.
Search for Truth.
Sense of Truth.
Levertov.   Ground-Mist, The.
Illustration[—a Footnote], The.
Levine, P.   I Was Born in Lucerne.
Jewish Graveyards, Italy.
Poem of Flight, The.
Roofs.
Suit, The.
Lindsay, N.   Beyond the Moon.
MacNeice.   What is truth? says Pilate.
Melville, H.   Enthusiast, The.
Meredith, G.   Song: "Thou steppest from thy
splendour."
To Cardinal Manning.
Merton.   Philosophers, The.
Merwin.   Initiate, The.
Singer, The.
Millay, E.   Anguish, The.
Milosz, C.   What I Learned from Jeanne Hersch.
When the Moon.
Zone of Silence.
Moore, M.   Enough.
Nemerov.   Earthquake in the West, The.
Old Photograph, An.
Questions.
Seeing Things.
Sestina 1: "Thickness of paint or flesh cannot
deface."
To Clio, Muse of History.
Two Pair.
Neruda.   Little Devils.
Pedro Is When.
Olson, C.   Kingfishers, The.
Orlandi, G.   ("Friend, I well know that you
know how to polish").
Orr, G.   Poem: "Truth's in myth not fact, The."
Paley, G.   It's True.
Patchen.   Shapes and Intensities of This Man,
This Confucius, The.
Sure There Is Food.
Pessoa.   I'm so full of feeling.
Petrarch.   If I said it, may I be held to scorn.
Raine, K.   Halt, The.
Ralegh, S.   Conjectural First Draft of the
Petition to Queen Anne.
Lie, The.
Rich, A.   5:30 A.M.
Double Monologue.
Frame.
Riley, J.   Lawyer and Child.
Robinson, E.   Sainte-Nitouche.
Roethke.   Adamant, The.
Open House.
Rossetti, C.   All night I dream you love me well.
Hark! the Alleluias of the great salvation.
My Dream.
So I began my walk of life; no stop.
That Which Hath Been Is Named Already, and
It Is Known That It Is Man.
Rukeyser, M.   All the Little Animals.
Ballad of Orange and Grape.
Believing in Those Inexorable Laws.
Poem as Mask, The.
Say it depends on the interpretation.
Sandburg, C.   Accomplished Facts.
Do You Want Affidavits?
Good Morning, America.
On the Way.

Troths.
Who Am I?
Sexton.   Just Once.
Truth the Dead Know, The.
Shelley, P.   Sonnet: "Lift not the painted veil
which those who live."
Sonnet: To a Balloon Laden with Knowledge.
Smith, S.   Magna Est Veritas.
Stevens, W.   On the Road Home.
Swenson, M.   Truth Is Forced, The.
Tate, J.   Deaf Girl Playing.
Updike.   Fever.
Very.   On Finding the Truth.
Walker, A.   Confession.
Warren, R.   Cocktail Party.
Delusion?—No!
Lesson in History.
Remark for Historians.
Truth.
Unless.
Vision.
Whitman, W.   All Is Truth.
Whittier.   Brown of Ossawatomie.
Calef in Boston.
Friend's Burial, The.
Miriam.
Preacher, The.
Quaker Alumni, The.
Ritner.
To ———: "Maiden! with the fair brown
tresses."
To George B. Cheever.
Utterance.
Wilbur, R.   Clearness.
Epistemology.
Lying.
Williams, C. K.   Near the Haunted Castle.
Refuge, Serpent-Riders.
Williams, M.   Jonathan's.
Journalist Buys a Pig Farm, The.
Truth and Truthfulness.
Williams, W.   Fool's Song, The.
Hard Listener, The.
Wordsworth, W.   In Allusion to Various Recent
Histories and Notices of the French
Revolution, Continued.
Lines Written as a School Exercise at
Hawkshead, Anno Aetatis 14.
To ———: "Let other bards of angels sing."
Where Lies the Truth? Has Man in Wisdom's
Creed.
Wright, C.   Language Journal.
Reading Rorty and Paul Celan One Morning in
Early June.
Wright, J.   Accusation, The.
Logbook of Judgments.
Wyatt, S.   Mistrustful minds be moved.
Take heed betime, lest ye be spied.
To cause accord or to ag[g]re[e].
What should I say.
Within my breast I never thought it gain.
Yeats.   Leaders of the Crowd, The.
Song of the Happy Shepherd, The.
Zagajewski.   Don't Allow the Lucid Moment to
Dissolve.
How Does the Man Look Who's Right.
Truth.

Tu Fu
Corbett, W.   Tu Fu in English.
Hamill, S.   Scrutability.
September Sowing.
Rexroth, K.   For the Chinese Actress, Gardenia
Chang.
Wright, C.   China Mail.
Thinking About the Night Sky, I Remember a
Poem by Tu Fu.
Waiting for Tu Fu.

Tuberculosis
Dubie.   Immoralist, The.
Hughes, L.   Consumptive, The.
Levertov.   Nightingale Road.

Tubman, Harriet
Hacker, M.   Part of a True Story.
Hayden, R.   Runagate Runagate.

Tugboats
Oppen.   On the water, solid.

Tug against the river.
Tugs of Hull, The.

Tulips
"Anvari."   O'er the garden water goes the wind
alone.
Gallagher, T.   Time Lapse with Tulips.
Herrick.   Meditation for His Mistress[e], A.
To a Bed of Tulips.
Levertov.   Tulips, The.
MacNeice.   Another Cold May.
Plath.   Tulips.
Rexroth, K.   Confusion.
Sandburg, C.   Garden Wireless.
Schuyler, J.   February.
Williams, W.   Tulip Bed, The.
Zukofsky, L.   Tulip.

Tumbleweeds
Carruth, H.   Shake, Well before Using.

Turkey
Ammons.   At Dawn in 1098.
Bierce.   Eastern Question, The.
Byron, G.   Stanzas: "Chill and mirk is the
nightly blast."
Meredith, G.   Wassail for the New Year, A.
Merrill, J.   Thousand and Second Night, The.
Yánnina.

Turkeys
Ciardi, J.   Carving the Turkey.
Clare, J.   Turkeys.
Dunbar, P.   Soliloquy of a Turkey.
Lawrence, D. H.   Turkey-Cock.
Nash, O.   Turkey, The.
Wilbur, R.   Black November Turkey, A.

Turner, Joseph Mallord William
Carruth, H.   Excursus of Reassurance in
Begonia Time, An.
Raine, K.   Turner's Seas.

Turner, Nat
Hayden, R.   Ballad of Nat Turner, The.

Turtle Doves
Cowper, W.   Doves, The.
Montale.   From the Train.
See also **Doves**

Turtles
Ciardi, J.   T, the TURTLE, has been a long time
coming.
Han-shan.   Two turtles aboard an ox cart.
Jacobsen, J.   Death and the Turtle.
Lindsay, N.   Little Turtle, The.
Logan, J.   Whistling Wings or White Turtle in
the Watertree.
Lowell, R.   Bringing a Turtle Home.
Neo-Classical Urn, The.
Returning Turtle.
Lux.   Thirst of Turtles, The.
Nash, O.   Turtle, The.
Nemerov.   Mud Turtle, The.
Oliver, M.   Turtle, The.
Orr, G.   Ditch, The.
Pond, The.
Roethke.   Myrtle.
Stock, R.   Motives of a Two-Headed Turtle.
Swenson, M.   Living Tenderly.
Updike.   To a Box Turtle.
Williams, C. K.   In the middle / of a bite of.
Shells.
Williams, W.   Turtle, The.
See also **Tortoises**

Tuscany
Rexroth, K.   Among the Cypresses at the End of
the Way of the Cross.
Tomlinson, C.   Thunder in Tuscany.

Tuskegee Institute
Dunbar, P.   Tuskegee Song.

"Twain, Mark" (Samuel Langhorne Clemens)
Carver, R.   Tel Aviv and *Life on the Mississippi*.
Lindsay, N.   Three Poems about Mark Twain.
Stein, G.   Mark Twain Centenary.
Warren, R.   Last Laugh.

Twelfth Night
Hardy, T.   Burning the Holly.
Herrick.   Twelfe Night, or King and Queene.

Twickenham, England
Donne.   Twickenham [or Twicknam] Garden.

Twilight
Beckett, S.   Roundelay: "On all that strand."
Berry, W.   Before Dark.
Bogan, L.   Short Summary.
Carruth, H.   Anima.
  Eternal City.
  Twilight Comes.
Crane, H.   Interior.
Creeley.   End of the Day, The.
Cummings, E. E.   A- / float on some.
  If in beginning twilight of winter will stand.
  Like a little bear twilight.
  Nine birds(rising / through a gold
   moment)climb.
  Somebody knew Lincoln somebody Xerxes.
  Sonnet: "No sunset, but a grey, great, struggling
   sky."
  Sunset)edges become swiftly.
  This out of within itself moo.
  This(let's remember)day died again and.
  Twi- / is -Light bird.
  Utterly and amusingly I am pash.
  When parsing warmths of dusk construe.
De la Mare.   Evening.
  Market-Place, The.
  Reverie.
  Voices.
Dickey, J.   Dusk of Horses, The.
Dunbar, P.   Twilight.
Eberhart, R.   Four Lakes' Days.
  Solace.
Gunn, T.   Back to Life.
Herrick.   To Anthea Lying in Bed.
  Twilight.
Lawrence, D. H.   Bei Hennef.
  Dawn Verse, The.
  Sunset.
  Sunset Verse, The.
  Twilight.
Logan, J.   Twilight Land.
Longfellow, H.   Children's Hour, The.
McGrath, T.   Up the Dark Valley.
Meredith, G.   Ballad of Past Meridian, A.
  Longest Day, The.
  There fell a sudden rain.
  Twilight Music.
Merwin.   Twilight.
Montale.   Two in Twilight.
Owen, W.   Anthem for Doomed Youth.
Rexroth, K.   Among the Cypresses at the End of
  the Way of the Cross.
Riley, J.   Twilight Stories.
Ritsos.   Twilight.
Robinson, E.   Dark Hills, The.
  Twilight Song.
Rossetti, C.   Twilight Calm.
Sandburg, C.   Bringers.
  Dreams in the Dusk.
  Hoof Dusk.
  Lackawanna Twilight.
  Smoke Shapes.
Sarton, M.   Evening Walk in France.
Schiller.   Evening, after a Picture.
Schuyler, J.   Song: "Light lies layered in the
  leaves, The."
Shelley, P.   Summer Evening Churchyard, A.
Smart, C.   Sweets of Evening, The.
Spender, S.   Dusk.
Swenson, M.   Day Is Laid By, A.
Tomlinson, C.   Tramontana at Lerici.
  Under the Moon's Reign.
Warren, R.   Autumn Twilight Piece.
  Rumor at Twilight.
  Sky.
  What Voice at Moth-Hour.
Whitman, W.   Hours Continuing Long.
  Twilight.
Wilde, O.   By the Arno.
Wordsworth, W.   Hail, Twilight, sovereign of
  one peaceful hour!
  When slow from pensive twilight's latest
   gleams.
Wright, C.   American Twilight.
Wright, J.   By a Lake in Minnesota.
  Cold Divinities, The.
  Sun Tan at Dusk.

Twilights.
See also **Evening; Sunset**
Twins
Broumas, O.   Landscape with Next of Kin.
Graves, R.   Twins.
Muldoon, P.   Lag.
Riley, J.   Twins, The.
Rukeyser, M.   Destruction of Grief.
Shapiro, K.   Twins, The.
Van Duyn.   Twins, The.
Wilbur, R.   Gemini.
Williams, M.   On the Sacrifice of a Siamese
  Twin at Birth.

Typewriters
McHugh, H.   Typewriter's the Kind, The.
Pagis.   Point of Departure.
  Writers.
Paley, G.   In This Dream.
Stock, R.   Poem Written on the Typewriter.

Typing and Typists
Cummings, E. E.   Pound pound pound / on thy
  cold grey corona oh P.
Sexton.   That Day.
Stock, R.   Poem Written on the Typewriter.

Tyranny
Auden.   Epitaph on a Tyrant.
Blake, W.   Grey Monk, The.
Browning, R.   Instans Tyrannus.
Burns, R.   Altered from an Old English Song.
  Fragment—on Glenriddel's Fox Breaking His
   Chain, A.
  Ode [for General Washington's Birthday].
Byron, G.   On a Royal Visit to the Vaults.
  On Jordan's Banks.
  Windsor Poetics.
Cardenal.   Shots were heard last night / Out by
  the burial ground.
  Suddenly in the night the sirens.
  We wake up with guns going off.
Cummings, E. E.   F is for foetus(a).
Davie, D.   Creon's Mouse.
  Tuscan Brutus, The.
Fenton, J.   Chosun.
Gray, T.   Tophet.
HaNagid.   Tyrant Who Rules the Homeless and
  Poor, The.
Herrick.   Duty to Tyrants.
  Empires.
  Kings and Tyrants.
  Lawes.
  Love.
Jarrell, R.   English Garden in Austria, An.
  State, The.
Jeffers, R.   Ave Caesar.
Kinsella, T.   Tyrant Dying.
Kipling, R.   Benefactors, The.
  Ode to Liberty.
  Old Issue, The.
Lowell, R.   Bosworth Field.
MacLeish.   Tyrant of Syracuse.
Melville, H.   Timoleon.
Meredith, G.   Despots of Manchester, Oligarchs!
  Solon.
Milosz, C.   Higher Arguments in Favor of
  Discipline Derived from the Speech before the
  Council of the Universal State in 2068.
  You Who Wronged.
Poe.   Tamerlane.
Rukeyser, M.   Third Elegy. The Fear of Form.
Shelley, P.   Song to the Men of England.
Smith, S.   Christmas.
  Leader, The.
Thomas, D.   Hand That Signed the Paper, The.
Wordsworth, W.   1811.
  Imitation of Juvenal — Satire VIII.
  Is there a power that can sustain and cheer.
  Ode: "Who rises on the banks of Seine."

U

Uccello, Paolo
Stock, R.   Battle Scene.

UFOs
See **Flying Saucers**
Uganda
Walker, A.   In Uganda an Early King.
Ugliness
Brontë, E.   And now the house-dog stretched
  once more.
Burns, R.   I do confess thou art sae fair.
  Keekin' Glass, The.
  Sic a Wife as Willie Had.
Byron, G.   If for Silver, or for Gold.
  On Sam Rogers.
Chuang Tzu.   When a Hideous Man.
Creeley.   For Martin.
Cummings, E. E.   Dress was a suspicious
  madder,importing the cruelty of roses, The.
  N / Umb a / stree / t's wintr.
  Of an it ignoblest he, The.
Herrick.   Upon Blanch.
  Upon Deb.
  Upon Jollies Wife.
  Upon Madam Ursly.
  Upon Ursley.
Hughes, L.   Magnolia Flowers.
Hughes, T.   Rhododendrons.
Jackson, L.   Mask, The.
Jeffers, R.   Carmel Point.
Levi, P.   Agave.
Michelangelo Buonarroti.   Suppose a lady has
  no other graces.
Millay, E.   Still will I harvest beauty where it
  grows.
  Who hurt you so.
Milosz, C.   How Ugly.
Mistral, G.   Parrot, The.
Rimbaud, A.   My Little Lovebirds.
  Venus Emerging.
Robinson, E.   Rat, The.
Rossetti, C.   What is this above thy head, / O
  Man?
Suckling, S.   Deformed Mistress, The.
Swift, J.   Progress of Beauty, The.
Unknown.   On an Ugly Fellow.
  To Demosthenis.
Williams, C. K.   Becoming Somebody Else.
  Portions of Manslayer.
Williams, W.   In Sisterly Fashion.
Wyatt, S.   Ye old mule, that thin[c]k your self so
  fair [*or* fayre].
Ukraine
Celan.   Black Flakes.
  Winter.
Zagajewski.   Referendum.
Ultima Thule
Lux.   Ultima Thule.
Ulysses
Borges.   Exile (1977), The.
  Odyssey, Book Twenty-three.
Brodsky, J.   Odysseus to Telemachus.
Cavafy.   Second Odyssey, A.
Cowper, W.   On Flaxman's Penelope.
Dubie.   Penelope.
Graves, R.   Ulysses.
Gunn, T.   Book of the Dead, The.
  Odysseus on Hermes.
"H. D."   At Ithaca.
  Calypso.
Homer.   Daughters of Pandarus, The.
  Gardens of Alcinous, The.
  Mindes of men are ever so affected, The.
  Muse, / tell me of this man of wit.
  Sun descending, the *Phæacian* train, The.
Levi, P.   Ostjuden.
MacLeish.   Eplenor.
  Old Man's Journey.
Muldoon, P.   Making the Move.
Parker, D.   Penelope.
Pope, A.   Argus.
Rossetti, C.   Lotus-Eaters: Ulysses to Penelope,
  The.
Spenser, E.   Virgils Gnat.
Stevens, W.   Presence of an External Master of
  Knowledge.
  World as Meditation, The.
Tennyson, A.   Lotus-Eaters, The.

To Ulysses.
Ulysses.

Umbrellas
Dickinson, E. Bat, The.
Parasol is the umbrella's daughter, The.
Hall, D. Umbrella, The.
Ritsos. Misconstructions.
Rossetti, C. When fishes set umbrellas up.
Seifert. Umbrella from Piccadilly, An.
Zukofsky, L. For Selma Gubin's Umbrellas.

Uncertainty
Ammons. Way to Go.
Ashbery, J. Gazing Grain, The.
Beckett, S. Enueg II.
Browning, R. Dubiety.
Bukowski. Guru.
Saying Goodbye to Love.
Carver, R. Morning, Thinking of Empire.
Coleridge, S. Superstition.
Uncertainty in Love.
Creeley. Two.
Dickey, W. One Incident of Many.
Dickinson, E. If you were coming in the Fall.
Wonder—is not precisely Knowing.
Gallagher, T. Message for the Sinecurist.
Graves, R. In No Direction.
When and Why.
Why of the Weather, The.
"H. D." Fragment 36 [or Thirty-Six]: "I know
not what to do."
Hacker, M. Lines Declining a Transatlantic
Dinner Invitation.
Han-shan. Man lives less than a hundred years,
A.
Hardy, T. Come Not; Yet Come!
Hayden, R. Traveling through Fog.
Herrick. Things Mortal Still Mutable.
Komunyakaa. Uncertainty in Blue.
Levertov. In Question.
Knowing the Unknown.
MacNeice. Entirely.
Melville, H. Pisa's Leaning Tower.
Meredith, G. Chambers of my heart are many,
dear, The.
Merrill, J. About the Phoenix.
Neruda. Let's Wait.
O'Hara, F. Cornkind.
Meditations in an Emergency.
Olson, C. Fish Is the Flower of Water, A.
Parra, N. Soda Fountains.
Raine, K. Sphere, The.
Ritsos. Uncertain Obligations.
Smith, S. Reason, The.
Thomas, D. Should Lanterns Shine.
Tomlinson, C. Barometer, The.
Warren, R. Place, The.
Uncertain Season in High Country.
Whitman, W. As I Lay with My Head in Your
Lap Camerado.
Whittier. Song of Slaves in the Desert.
Williams, M. La Ultima Carta: A Young Wife
Writes to Her Husband in the Mountains.

Uncle Tom
Hughes, L. Epitaph: "Uncle Tom, / When he
was alive."
Uncle Tom ("Uncle Tom is a legend and a
dream").

Uncles
Ciardi, J. After Sunday Dinner We Uncles
Snooze.
Alec.
Elegy: "This is the body of my good gray
practical dead."
Cullen, C. Uncle Jim.
Cummings, E. E. My uncle / Daniel fought in
the civil.
Nobody loses all the time.
Dove, R. Great Uncle Beefheart.
Ferlinghetti, L. Old Sailors, The.
Hayden, R. Burly Fading One, The.
Jacobsen, J. My Uncle a Child.
Kumin, M. Deaths of the Uncles, The.
Levine, P. Uncle.
Patchen. Wouldn't You Be after a Jaunt of
964,000,000,000,000 Million Miles?
Piercy. Landed Fish.

Pinsky. Memorial.
Plath. Stopped Dead.
Rexroth, K. Parity.
Riley, J. As My Uncle Ust to Say.
Doodle-Bug's Charm, The.
To "Uncle Remus."
Tate, J. Uncle.
Unknown. On the Astrologers.
Wright, J. Willy Lyons.

Underground Railroad
Hayden, R. Runagate Runagate.
Logan, J. Grandfather's Railroad.

Underhill, John
Whittier. John Underhill.

Undertakers
Herrick. Upon Luske.
Kipling, R. Undertaker's Horse, The.
Nash, O. Tweedledee and Tweedledoom.
Sandburg, C. To Certain Journeymen.
Tate, J. Indian Undertaker, The.

Underwear
Carver, R. Woolworth's, 1954.
Collins, B. Victoria's.
Ferlinghetti, L. Underwear.
Herrick. Upon Skoles.

Unemployment
Angelou. Contemporary Announcement.
Bukowski. Fall Out.
Hello, Willie Shoemaker.
Carver, R. Looking for Work 1.
Looking for Work 2.
Shiftless.
Dugan, A. Memories of the Bowery.
Morning of the Dying Gigolo, The.
On Not Working and Then Working on Working
and Then Not Working.
Prayer: "God, I need a job because I need
money."
Saint Monday.
Hall, D. Waiting on the Corners.
Hopkins, G. Tom's Garland: Upon the
Unemployed.
Hughes, L. Broke.
Out of Work.
Park Benching.
Lawrence, D. H. British Workman and the
Government, The.
Milosz, C. Ballad of Levallois.
Niedecker. Let's play a game.
Sandburg, C. Muckers.
Spender, S. Unemployed.
Williams, C. K. Fast Food.

Unicorns
Cullen, C. That Bright Chimeric Beast.
Duncan, R. Banners, The.
Festivals, The.
Ferlinghetti, L. With bells for hooves in
sounding streets.
García Lorca. Fable: "Unicorns and cyclopses."
Graves, R. Unicorn and the White Doe.
Hall, D. Some Oddities.
Jarrell, R. Unicorn, The.
Moore, M. Sea Unicorns and Land Unicorns.
Muldoon, P. Unicorn Defends Himself, The.
Rilke. Unicorn, The.
Sarton, M. Lady and the Unicorn, The.
Stock, R. Shield against the Trampling Foe, A.
Wilner, E. Hunting Manual.

Unidentified Flying Objects
See **Flying Saucers**

Union of Soviet Socialist Republics
See **Soviet Union**

Unions
See **Labor Unions**

United Nations
Amichai [*or* Amikhai]. U.N. Headquarters in
the High Commissioner's House in Jerusalem,
The.
See also **Internationalism**

United States
Angelou. Request.
Berryman. American Lights, Seen from Off
Abroad.
Burns, R. Slave's Lament, The.

Ciardi, J. Box Comes Home, A.
Creeley. America.
Cummings, E. E. Next to of Course God
America I.
Opening of the chambers close.
Poem, or Beauty Hurts Mr. Vinal.
Season 'tis,my lovely lambs, The.
"Dario." To Roosevelt.
Davie, D. From the New World.
Dickey, J. Coming Back to America.
Dickinson, E. Sweet Land of Liberty.
Union.
Dubie. Indian Summer.
Dugan, A. Love and Money.
Eberhart, R. Yonder.
Emerson, R. Ode Sung in the Town Hall.
Frost, R. Gift Outright, The.
Record Stride, A.
Serious Step Taken Lightly, A.
Ginsberg, A. America.
Vow, A.
Who Runs America?
Hardy, T. On an Invitation to the United States.
Hughes, L. Columbia.
One More "S" in the U.S.A.
Jeffers, R. Eagle Valor, Chicken Mind.
Historical Choice.
Invasion.
Shine, Perishing Republic.
Kipling, R. American, An.
American Rebellion, The.
Choice, The.
Deep-Sea Cables, The.
Question, The.
White Man's Burden, The.
Lawrence, D. H. American Eagle, The.
Evening Land, The.
O! Americans.
Levertov. Continent.
MacLeish. American Letter.
Colloquy for the States.
Empire Builders.
Men.
Muldoon, P. Immram.
Olson, C. Hustings, The.
Of the United States.
Rufus Woodpecker visited the President.
Paley, G. Leaflet.
Patchen. Letter to Those Who Are about to Die.
Roethke. Night Journey.
Tate, A. Aeneas at Washington.
Historical Epitaphs.
Ode to the Confederate Dead.
Thoreau. Our Country.
Updike. Air Show.
Minority Report.
Very. Finishing the Work.
"It is vain to say, that this is the country of the
'white man.' It is the country of man."
Charles Sumner.
Light of Freedom Necessary to National
Progress, The.
National Unity ("Nobler unity, than that which
came, A").
State Rights.
What of Our Country?
Whitman, W. America.
For You O Democracy.
From Paumanok Starting I Fly like a Bird.
I Hear America Singing.
Passage to India.
Poem of Remembrances for a Girl or a Boy of
These States.
Starting from Paumanok.
States!
Thou Mother with Thy Equal Brood.
To the Leaven'd Soil They Trod.
To the States, to Identify the 16th, 17th, or 18th
Presidentiad.
Virginia—the West.
Wandering at Morn.
Whittier. On Receiving an Eagle's Quill from
Lake Superior.
Vow of Washington, The.

United States Army
Hughes, L. Dear Mr. President.

Madam and the Army.
Jeffers, R.   Eagle Valor, Chicken Mind.

Unity
Ammons.   Guide.
One:Many.
Unifying Principle, The.
Berry, W.   Falling Asleep.
Hidden Singer, The.
Law That Marries All Things, The.
Man Born to Farming, The.
On the Hill Late at Night.
Silence, The.
Wheel, The.
Bradstreet, A.   Another.
Letter to Her Husband, Absent upon Public[k]
Employment, A.
To My Dear and Loving Husband.
Carruth, H.   Contra Mortem.
Cowper, W.   Song, A: "Sparkling eye, the
mantling cheek, The."
Dickinson, E.   Love Thou Art High.
Donne.   Ecstasy, The.
Flea, The.
Eberhart, R.   Parker River, The.
Éluard, P.   Universe-Solitude.
Emerson, R.   All that thy virgin soul can ask be
thine.
Dear Ellen, many a golden year.
Each and All.
I cannot find a place so lonely.
Love and Thought.
Music.
Nature [1844].
None spares another yet it pleases me.
Poet of poets / Is Time, the distiller.
Rex.
Though her eye seek other forms.
Unity.
Xenophanes.
Glück, L.   Hawk's Shadow.
Pond, The.
Graves, R.   Cliff and Wave.
Fast Bound Together.
Song: Twinned Heart.
Three Locked Hoops.
To Tell and Be Told.
Toast to Death, A.
Gunn, T.   Saturnalia.
Herbert, G.   Clasping of Hands.
Herrick.   God is One.
JEHOVAH.
Power and Peace.
Jonson, B.   On the Union.
Komunyakaa.   "Everybody's Reading Li Po"
Silkscreened on a Purple T-Shirt.
Levertov.   Ache of Marriage, The.
In Whom We Live and Move and Have Our
Being.
On a Theme from Julian's Chapter 20.
Part, The.
Lindsay, N.   In Memory of My Friend, Joyce
Kilmer, Poet and Soldier.
Incense.
Sew the Flags Together.
Traveller-Heart, The.
What the Forester Said.
Lorde.   Hard Love Rock II.
MacDiarmid, H.   O Ease My Spirit.
With the Herring Fishers.
Melville, H.   Art.
Greek Masonry.
Little Good Fellows, The.
Meredith, G.   Earth and Man.
Progression.
Michelangelo Buonarroti.   If pure devotion,
passion without stain.
Moraes, V.   Sonnet of Intimacy.
Neruda.   Coming Back.
Earth.
Olson, C.   Heart is a clock, The.
Lamp, The.
Piercy.   Digging In.
Raine, K.   I breathe the air you have breathed.
I went out in the naked light.
My feet in the ever-moving sea.
This little house / No smaller than the world.

Ransom, J.   Two in August.
Rich, A.   Diving into the Wreck.
Hunger.
Phantasia for Elvira Shatayev.
Wave, The.
Rossetti, C.   St. Barnanbas.
To Every Seed His Own Body.
Rukeyser, M.   Conjugation of the Paramecium,
The.
Poem as Mask, The.
Return, The.
Rumi.   Awkward Comparison, An.
Cat and the Meat, The.
Flute, The.
Say I Am You.
This moment this love comes to rest in me.
Stafford, W.   How to Regain Your Soul.
Very.   National Unity ("Nobler unity, than that
which came, A").
Warren, R.   Brotherhood in Pain.
Whitman, W.   Crossing Brooklyn Ferry.
Germs.
One's-Self I Sing.
Over the Carnage Rose Prophetic a Voice.
To the Leaven'd Soil They Trod.
While Not the Past Forgetting.
World Take Good Notice.
Whittier.   Cable Hymn, The.
Greeting, A.
Word for the Hour, A.
Wilde, O.   Panthea.
Williams, C. K.   Just Right.
Williams, W.   Mists over the River.
Wright, C.   Composition in Grey and Pink.
Holy Thursday.
Journal of Southern Rivers, A.
Self-Portrait.

Universe
Ammons.   Constant, The.
Borges.   Everness.
Lines That Could Have Been Written and Lost
Round about 1922.
Poem of Quantity.
Poem Written in a Copy of *Beowulf*.
Browning, R.   Pisgah-Sights. I.
Pisgah-Sights. II.
Ciardi, J.   Tommy's Pond.
Crane, S.   Man said to the universe, A.
Cummings, E. E.   But if a living dance upon
dead minds.
Maybe god / is a child.
Over us if(as what dusk becomes).
De la Mare.   Flower, The.
Futility.
Humanity.
Universe, The.
Dickinson, E.   Bees.
Dugan, A.   On Inter-Relatedness in the
Universe.
Emerson, R.   All things rehearse.
Chladni strewed on glass the sand.
I call her beautiful;—she says.
I will not hesitate to speak the word.
Frost, R.   Skeptic.
Ginsberg, A.   Laughing Gas.
Hardy, T.   Philosophical Fantasy, A.
Housman.   Here are the skies, the planets seven.
Ignatow, D.   In No Way.
Stability.
Jarrell, R.   Archangel's' Song, The.
Jeffers, R.   Great Explosion, The.
It flows out of mystery into mystery: there is no
beginning—.
Silent Shepherds, The.
Lawrence, D. H.   Universe Flows, The.
Wandering Cosmos, The.
Lindsay, N.   Comet of Prophecy, The.
Meredith, G.   Meditation under Stars.
Merton.   Tonight There Is a Showing of
Champion Lights.
Nemerov.   Angel and Stone.
Celestial Globe.
First Day, The.
Questions.
Two Pair.
Two Sides to an Outside: Meditation from

Empson.
Olson, C.   Across Space and Time.
Liturgical / eighth day, The.
Patchen.   Strange, Moving Lights of People
Handle Holinesses Unknown, The.
Raine, K.   Scala Coeli.
Sphere, The.
Rexroth, K.   Hapax.
Rukeyser, M.   Spirals and Fugues.
Rumi.   Father Reason.
Stafford, W.   Big Bang.
Whitman, W.   Kosmos.
Who Learns My Lesson Complete.
Year of Meteors (1859–60).
Williams, M.   He Glimpses a Nobler Vision.
He Speaks to His Arguing Friends and to
Himself.
One of Those Rare Occurrences on a City Bus.
Wright, C.   China Journal.

Universities
See **Colleges and Universities**

Unknown Soldier
Cummings, E. E.   Opening of the chambers
close.
Sandburg, C.   And So Today.

Urania
Emerson, R.   Borrow Urania's subtile wings.
Wroth [*or* Wroath].   Urania.

Urban Life
Clampitt.   Man Feeding Pigeons.
Manhattan.
Real Estate.
Salvage.
Vacant Lot with Pokeweed.
Dugan, A.   On Leaving Town.
To a Colleague. From the Country.
Untitled Poem: "City is empty, like a dangerous
area, The."
Eliot, T. S.   Easter: Sensations of April.
First Caprice in North Cambridge.
Fourth Caprice in Montparnasse.
Preludes.
Second Caprice in North Cambridge.
Silence.
Ginsberg, A.   Charnel Ground, The.
Manhattan May Day Midnight.
Mugging.
Tonite I walked out of my red apartment door
on East tenth street's dusk.
Ignatow, D.   East Bronx.
Komunyakaa.   Doppelgängers.
Langston Hughes.
Urban Renewal.
Logan, J.   Thirteen Preludes for Pioneer Square.
Lux.   Crows of Boston and New York, The.
Major, C.   Kitchen Chair Poem #5.
Meredith, W.   Rus in Urbe.
Michelangelo Buonarroti.   New and more
commendable delight, A.
Niedecker.   City Talk.
Not all that's heard is music. We leave.
To see the man who took care of our stock.
Pinsky.   City Dark, The.
City Elegies.
Ramanujan.   Take Care.
Rexroth, K.   There shall come faint light.
Riley, J.   Town and Country.
Rimbaud, A.   Cities ("Official acropolis
surpasses the most colossal conceptions of
modern barbarity, The").
City.
Metropolitan.
Ritsos.   Summer in the City.
Simic.   Punch Minus Judy.
Stafford, W.   Universe Is One Place.
Wilner, E.   Love of What Is Not, The.
Zagajewski.   World's Prose, The.

Urbino, Italy
Stock, R.   Sigismundo Malatesta Brings His
Favorite Philosopher's Bones to Italy.

Uriel
Emerson, R.   Uriel.

Urns
Cuadra, P.   Urn with a Political Profile.
Cullen, C.   Uncle Jim.

Hughes, L. Metropolitan Museum.
Lowell, R. Neo-Classical Urn, The.

Ursa Major
McHugh, H. Night in a World, A.

Ursula, Saint
Stevens, W. Cy Est Pourtraicte, Madame Ste
Ursule, et Les Unze Mille Vierges.

U.S.S.R.
See **Soviet Union**

Usurpation
Burns, R. Birth-Day Ode. December 31st 1787,
A.
Scots Ballad.

Usury
Herrick. Upon Snare, an Usurer.
Jonson, B. On Bank the Usurer.
On Bawds and Usurers.
Williams, W. Usurers of Heaven, The.

Utah (state)
Davie, D. Red Rock of Utah.
Frost, R. On the Heart's Beginning to Cloud the
Mind.
Laughlin, J. Cincinnatus in Utah.
Sandburg, C. March of the Hungry Mountains.

Ute, The
Tomlinson, C. Ute Mountain.

Utopia
Coleridge, S. Kubla Khan: or, A Vision in a
Dream.
On the Prospect of Establishing a Pantisocracy
in America.
Pantisocracy.
Davie, D. Red Rock of Utah.
Lindsay, N. Celestial Circus, The.
Melville, H. Reasonable Constitution, A.
Ransom, J. Somewhere Is Such a Kingdom.
Riley, J. Where-Away.

V

Vacation
Carver, R. In Switzerland.
Rogue River Jet-Boat Trip, Gold Beach,
Oregon, July 4, 1977.
Clampitt. Rain at Bellagio.
Creeley. On Vacation.
Eberhart, R. Four Lakes' Days.
Enzensberger, H. Holiday, The.
Hopkins, G. Penmaen Pool.
Levertov. Postcard.
Logan, J. Whistling Wings or White Turtle in
the Watertree.
Merrill, J. Santorini: Stopping the Leak.
Up and Down.
Merwin. Ferry Port.
Nash, O. I Always Say There's No Place like
New York in the Summer, or, That Cottage
Small by a Waterfall Was Snapped Up Last
February.
Tomorrow, Partly Cloudy.
Nemerov. Sightseers.
O'Hara, F. Summer Breezes.
Parker, D. Letter to Robert Benchley; Roughing
It in the Country at the Birches, Maine.
Summer Resorts; A Hymn of Hate.
Schuyler, J. New Yorker, A.
You're.
Sheridan, T. To His Excellency Our Lord
Carteret, Lord Lieutenant of Ireland: The
Humble Petition of Lord Viscount Mont-
Cashel, and the Rest of His School-Fellows.
Stafford, W. Any Time.
Vacation.
Vacation Trip.
Szymborska, W. In Broad Daylight.
Updike. Antigua.
Back from Vacation.
Island Sun.
Poisoned in Nassau.
Van Duyn. Postcards from Cape Split.
Williams, W. On a Proposed Trip South.
Zagajewski. How High the Moon.
Vacation.

Vacuum Cleaners and Vacuum Cleaning
Nemerov. Vacuum, The.

Vagabonds
Bukowski. Insane Always Loved Me, The.
Swans Walk My Brain in April It Rains, The.
Clare, J. Lout, The: "No sort of learning ever
hurts his head."
Frost, R. Old Barn at the Bottom of the Fogs,
The.
Two Tramps in Mud Time.
Unstamped Letter in Our Rural Letter Box, An.
Hardy, T. Trampwoman's Tragedy, A.
Vagrant's Song.
Hayden, R. Rag Man, The.
Hughes, L. Vagabonds.
Hughes, T. November.
Kipling, R. Sestina of the Tramp-Royal.
Lawrence, D. H. Embankment at Night, before
the War: Outcasts.
Levine, P. And the Trains Go On.
McGrath, T. Long Way Outside Yellowstone,
A.
Riley, J. Mr. What's-His-Name.
Raggedy Man, The.
Rimbaud, A. Tramps.
Sandburg, C. 'Boes.
Tate, A. Traveller, The.
Tate, J. Vagabond, A.
Tomlinson, C. Terminal Tramps.
Thief's Journal, The.
Williams, C. K. Harm.
Williams, W. R R Bums, The.

Valentine's Day
Carruth, H. Valentine.
Chaucer. Parlement of Foules, The.
Dickinson, E. Valentine, A.
Donne. Epithalamion, or Marriage Song on the
Lady Elizabeth and Count Palatine Being
Married on St. Valentine's Day, An.
Herrick. To His Deare Valentine, Mistresse
Margaret Falconbrige.
To His Valentine, on S. Valentines Day.
Meredith, W. February 14.
Moore, M. For February 14th.
St. Valentine.
Nash, O. Strange Case of Mr. Ballantine's
Valentine, The.
Poe. Valentine, A.
Riley, J. Her Valentine.
Rossetti, C. 1878.
1879.
1884.
1885. St. Valentine's Day.
1886, St. Valentine's Day.
February 14. 1883.
St. Valentine's Day 1881.
Valentine to My Mother, A.
Valentines from C.G.R.
Valentines to My Mother, 1880.
Schuyler, J. February 13, 1975.
Sleep.
Williams, W. On St. Valentine's Day.
Zukofsky, L. 1959 Valentine.
On Valentine's Day to Friends.
This year / that Valentine is / late.

Valentino, Rudolph
Lawrence, D. H. Film Passion.

Valéry, Paul
Milosz, C. Lecture, A.
Nemerov. Master at a Mediterranean Port, The.

Valkyries
Gray, T. Fatal Sisters, The.
Wilner, E. Lament of the Valkyrie, The.

Vallejo, César
Komunyakaa. 1938.

Valleys
Amichai [*or* Amikhai]. In this valley, where
many waters.
These words, like heaps of feathers.
Ammons. Delaware Water Gap.
Possibility along a Line of Difference.
Browning, R. Man and Nature.
Byron, G. Lachin y Gair.
Clampitt. Tempe in the Rain.
Davie, D. Lancashire.

Dickey, J. Mexican Valley.
Hughes, T. Chinese History of Colden Water.
Lawrence, D. H. Misery.
Levi, P. Valley, A.
Lux. Grim Town in a Steep Valley.
McGrath, T. Up the Dark Valley.
Meredith, G. Pasture Alp is webbed with shade,
The.
Olson, C. Afica.
Patchen. Down in the Lone Valley.
Plath. Above the Oxbow.
Riley, J. Muskingum Valley, The.
Sandburg, C. Lackawanna Twilight.
Mist Forms.
Mist Marches across the Valley.
Moist Moon People.
Santa Fe Sketches.
They Ask Each Other Where They Came From.
Valley Song.
Wordsworth, W. Airey-Force Valley.
Yeats. He Tells a Valley Full of Lovers.

Value
Burns, R. On Being Asked Why God Had
Made Miss D——— So Little and Mrs A———
— So Big.
Sweetest May.
Chuang Tzu. Useless Tree, The.
Cowper, W. To Sir John Fenn.
Dickinson, E. How precious Thought and
Speech are!
I took one Draught of Life.
Nothing inclusive of a human Heart.
Gallagher, T. Refusing Silence.
Hacker, M. Riposte.
Herrick. Merits Make the Man.
Larkin, P. To Put One Brick upon Another.
McHugh, H. At a Loss.
Moore, M. Values in Use.
Nemerov. Place of Value, The.
Niedecker. I am sick with the Time's buying
sickness.
Oliver, M. Buddha's Last Instruction, The.
Sun, The.
Raine, K. I've read all the books but one.
Rexroth, K. Phoenix and the Tortoise, The.
Value in Mountains.
Value Neuter.
Valuta.
Rich, A. At Hertford House.
Rimbaud, A. Sales.
Sandburg, C. Again?
Buyers and Sellers.
How Much?
Very Very Important.
Shelley, P. Fragment: "What men gain fairly—
that they should possess."
Smith, S. Valuable.
Walker, A. We Alone.

Vampires
Baudelaire. Vampire, The.
Hughes, T. Vampire.
Kipling, R. Vampire, The.
Merrill, J. Narrow Escape, A.
Merwin. Indigestion of the Vampire, The.
Sandburg, C. Baby Vamps.
Testimony Regarding a Ghost.
Smith, S. Great Unaffected Vampires and the
Moon.
Wilbur, R. Undead, The.
Yeats. Oil and Blood.

Van Doren, Mark
Hayden, R. Ballad of Remembrance, A.
MacLeish. Danger in the Air, The.
Mark Van Doren and the Brook.
Merton. Message to Be Inscribed on Mark Van
Doren's Hamilton Medal.

Van Gogh, Vincent
Celan. Below a Painting.
Niedecker. Van Gogh.
Van Gogh could see.
Tomlinson, C. Farewell to Van Gogh.
Van Gogh.
Walker, A. If There Was Any Justice.
Wilner, E. Sunflowers, Repossessed.
Zagajewski. Van Gogh's Face.

Vanbrugh, Sir John
Swift, J.   Vanbrug's House.

Vandalism
Collins, B.   Madmen.
Dugan, A.   They Call It "Grumus Merdae."
Komunyakaa.   Initials on Aspens.
Pinsky.   Desecration of the Gravestone of Rose P.

Vane, Sir Henry
Milton.   To Sir Henry Vane the Younger.

Vanity
Berry, W.   Praise.
Berryman.   Vespers.
Borges.   Alhambra.
Bradstreet, A.   Flesh and the Spirit, The.
   Here Follows Some Verses upon the Burning of Our House [July 10th, 1666. Copied Out of a Loose Paper].
   Vanity of All Worldly Things, The.
Browning, E.   Vanities.
Bukowski.   Beach Trip.
Burns, R.   Song: "As I cam down by yon castle wa'."
   There's a youth in this city, it were a great pity.
Byron, G.   'All Is Vanity, Saith the Preacher.'
To ———: "Oh! well I know your subtle Sex."
   To a Vain Lady.
Campion, T.   Ad Chloen.
   Ev'ry Dame affects good fame, what ere her doings be.
Carew, T.   Ingrateful[l] Beauty Threatened.
Clough.   Go foolish thoughts, and join the throng.
Crane, S.   Upon the road of my life.
Creeley.   Apple Uppfie.
Cummings, E. E.   Cambridge ladies who live in furnished souls, The.
De la Mare.   Reflections.
Dickinson, E.   Ribbons of the Year.
Ginsberg, A.   Very Dove, A.
Graves, R.   Vain and Careless.
   Vanity.
Gunn, T.   Lines for a Book.
Guyon.   Glory to God Alone.
   Necessity of Self-Abasement.
   Self-Love and Truth Incompatible.
   Truth and Divine Love Rejected by the World.
Han-shan.   All I see are fools.
   Exhaust your mind for profit and fame.
   I see people everywhere.
   Three Worlds swarm with people, The.
   We hear about the ministers of state.
Hardy, T.   Lady Vi.
Herbert, G.   Vanity [or Vanitie] (1).
   Vanity (2).
Herrick.   Upon Rook: Epigram.
Hopkins, G.   Hope holds to Christ.
Hughes, T.   Crow's Vanity.
Jacobsen, J.   Minor Poet, The.
Johnson, S.   Vanity of Human Wishes, The; The Tenth Satire of Juvenal Imitated.
Keats.   When They Were Come unto the Faery's Court.
Kizer, C.   Through a Glass Eye, Lightly.
Lawrence, D. H.   Intimates.
   Narcissus.
   Natural Complexion.
   Snake.
   Tragedy.
   True Love at Last.
   Ultimate Reality.
Lux.   Great Advances in Vanity.
Melville, H.   Camoëns.
   Fortitude of the North, The.
Meredith, G.   Song: "Fair and false! No dawn will greet."
Merrill, J.   Peacock, The.
Nash, O.   Evening Out, The.
   Theatrical Reflection.
Oppen.   Ozymandias.
Parker, D.   Epitaph for a Darling Lady.
Petrarch.   Gold and pearls, and blossoms, white and red, The.
Piercy.   Barbie Doll.
Rossetti, C.   Beauty Is Vain.
   If love is not worth loving, then life is not worth

living.
   One Certainty, The.
   Soeur Louise De La Miséricorde.
   St. Andrew's Church.
   Testimony, A.
   Then Whose Shall Those Things Be?
   Vain Shadow, A.
   Vanity of Vanities.
Rukeyser, M.   Letter, Unposted.
Rumi.   Song about a Donkey, A.
   Think that you're gliding out from the face of a cliff.
Sarton, M.   Narcissus.
Sexton.   Snow White and the Seven Dwarfs.
Shelley, P.   Ozymandias.
Shih-te.   World has its know-it-alls, The.
Smith, S.   Adelaide Abner.
   Devil-My-Wife, The.
   Face, The.
   Hat, The.
Swift, J.   Lady's Dressing Room, The.
   Progress of Beauty, The.
Tate, J.   Teaching the Ape to Write Poems.
Tennyson, A.   Character, A.
Whitman, W.   Fame's Vanity.
Whittier.   Common Question, The.
Williams, C. K.   Mirror, The.
Wordsworth, W.   Emperors and Kings, How Oft Have Temples Rung.
   Soft as a Cloud Is Yon Blue Ridge.
   Wild Duck's Nest, The.
Yeats.   Two Trees, The.

See also **Pride**

Variety
Ammons.   One:Many.
Chuang Tzu.   Great and Small.
Emerson, R.   Three Dimensions, The.
MacNeice.   Plurality.
Riley, J.   Variation, A.

Vaudeville
Jacobsen, J.   Variations on Variety.
Major, C.   Coon Showman.

Vaughan, Henry
Davie, D.   Monmouthshire.

Vegetables
Dickey, W.   More under Saturn.
Dove, R.   Sunday Greens.
Jarrell, R.   My aunt kept turnips in a flock.
Kumin, M.   In the Root Cellar.
   Mummies, The.
Lux.   Endive.
McGrath, T.   Praises.
McMichael.   Vegetables, The.
Nash, O.   Parsnip, The.
Prunty.   Vegetable Garden, The.
Rossetti, C.   Lily has a smooth stalk, / Will never hurt your hand, The.
Schuyler, J.   Under the Hanger.
Whalen, P.   True Confessions.
Wilbur, R.   Melongène.
Williams, C. K.   Modern, The.
Williams, W.   Child and Vegetables.

Vegetarians
Chesterton.   Logical Vegetarian, The.
Dove, R.   Why I Turned Vegetarian.
Eberhart, R.   Explorer on Main Street, The.
Kumin, M.   Accolade of the Animals, The.

Velázquez, Diego Rodríguez de Silva y
Stock, R.   Prose for the Children of Aborted Revolution.

Venereal Disease
Crane, H.   Moment Fugue.

Vengeance
Brontë, E.   Gleneden's Dream.
Browning, R.   First-Born of Egypt, The.
Cavafy.   Dimaratos.
Clough.   Alcaics.
Codrescu.   Indecent Assumption, the Slaughter Songs, The.
Cowper, W.   Cock-Fighters Garland.
Davie, D.   Vengeance Is Mine, Saith the Lord.
De la Mare.   Thus Her Tale.
Dunbar, P.   Vengeance Is Sweet.
Eberhart, R.   Request for Offering.
Graves, R.   Return.

Herrick.   Abels Bloud.
   To the Fever, Not to Trouble Julia.
MacDiarmid, H.   Focherty.
Ransom, J.   On the Road to Wockensutter.
Riley, J.   What Redress.
Rossetti, C.   Will These Hands Ne'er Be Clean?
   Zara.
Seidl.   Hans Euler.
Whittier.   Cities of the Plain, The.
   Sicilian Vespers, The.
Wright, J.   Devotions.

Venice, Italy
Brodsky, J.   Homage to Girolamo Marcello.
   In Front of Casa Marcello.
   Lagoon.
   San Pietro.
   Venetian Stanzas 1.
   Venetian Stanzas 2.
   Venice: Lido.
Browning, R.   Goldoni.
   In a Gondola.
   Toccata of Galuppi's, A.
Byron, G.   Ode on Venice.
   Venice.
Carver, R.   Venice.
Clampitt.   Venice Revisited.
Eliot, T. S.   Burbank with a Baedeker: Bleistein with a Cigar.
Housman.   Far known to sea and shore.
Levertov.   Young Man Travelling, A.
Lowell, R.   Old snapshot from Venice 1952.
Major, C.   Alone, I went into that special.
   And who must remain.
   Brief Visit to Venice.
   He gave the Fascisti salute.
   In Salute again.
   Little places. / Corte stella.
   Santa Maria Dei Frari.
   Theme of Carnevale is a secret, The.
   There he was, a boy, looking over.
   They cut down the last tree.
   Venice dream of the mainland, A.
   You set out on a morning bright.
Melville, H.   In a Bye-Canal.
   Venice.
Milosz, C.   1913.
   No More.
Pound, E.   Night Litany.
   Partenza di Venezia.
Rexroth, K.   On a Flyleaf of *Rime*—Gaspara Stampa.
   Sottoportico San Zaccaria.
   Untitled, 6 September 1969.
   Venice.
Rilke.   To Pia Di Valmarana.
Tomlinson, C.   Death in Venice.
   Venice.
Wordsworth, W.   On the Extinction of the Venetian Republic.
Wright, C.   Passing the Morning under the Serenissima.
   Venetian Dog.
   Venexia 1.
   Venexia 2.
Zagajewski.   Vaporetto.

Venus (goddess)
Auden.   Venus Will Now Say a Few Words.
Ausonius.   Upon the Same.
Browning, E.   Psyche and Venus.
Carew, T.   Carver. To His Mistress, The.
   On Sight of a Gentlewoman's Face in the Water.
Carruth, H.   Birth of Venus, The.
Chaucer.   Complaint of Mars, The.
   Parlement of Foules, The.
Crashaw.   Out of Euphormio.
De la Mare.   Blind Boy, The.
   Encounter, The.
   Mercutio.
Eberhart, R.   Giantess, The.
Glück, L.   Letter from our Man in Blossomtime.
Guillaume de Lorris.   Romance [or Romaunt] of the Rose, The.
Hardy, T.   Well-Beloved, The.
Herrick.   Bag of the Bee, The.
   Cloud, The.
   How Lillies Came White.

How Violets Came Blue.
Hymne to Venus, and Cupid, A.
Short Hymne to Venus, A.
Vow to Venus, A.
Wounded Cupid, The.
Jarrell, R. Birth of Venus, The.
Lawrence, D. H. What Does She Want?
Leonidas of Alexandria. Upon Venus Putting on
  Mars His Armes.
Olson, C. Ring of, The.
Orr, G. After Botticelli's *Birth of Venus.*
  After Piero di Cosimo's *Venus, Mars, and Amor.*
Ovid. Galatea.
Rimbaud, A. Lovely Morning Thought.
  Sun and Skin.
  Venus Emerging.
Rossetti, C. Venus's Looking-Glass.
Rukeyser, M. Birth of Venus, The.
Smith, S. Votaries of Both Sexes Cry First to
  Venus.
Spenser, E. Epithalamion: "Ye learned sisters
  which have oftentimes."
Swinburne. Laus Veneris.
Wyatt, S. Venus, in sport, to please therewith
  her dear.
See also **Aphrodite**

Venus (planet)
Bogan, L. Evening-Star.
Brontë, E. Morning Star, The.
Chaucer. Complaint of Mars, The.
"Dario." Venus.
Frost, R. Literate Farmer and the Planet Venus,
  The.
Hamill, S. Cold Fire, A.
Millay, E. Truce for a Moment.
Olson, C. Objects, The.
Sexton. Venus and the Ark.
Simic. Venus.
Updike. Milady Reflects.
Wordsworth, W. To the Planet Venus.
  To the Planet Venus, an Evening Star.

Veracruz, Mexico
Stock, R. Farewell to Baedeker.

Verdi, Giuseppe
Tomlinson, C. In Verdi Square.

Verdun, Battle of (1916)
Dugan, A. Memories of Verdun.
Lowell, R. Verdun.
Merwin. Edouard.

Vergil
See **Virgil** [*or* **Vergil**]

Verlaine, Paul
"Dario." Prayer for the Dead (To Verlaine).
Logan, J. Lives of the Poet, The.
Mallarmé. Tomb.
Robinson, E. Verlaine.

Vermeer, Johannes
Pinkerton, H. On Vermeer's *Young Woman with
  a Water Jug* (1658) in the Metropolitan
  Museum.
Zagajewski. Vermeer's Little Girl.

Vermont (state)
Carruth, H. My Meadow.
  This Song.
  Vermont.
Corbett, W. Vermont Apollinaire.
Eberhart, R. Play, The.
  River Water Music.
Frost, R. "Out, Out—."
Kinnell. Frog Pond, The.
Kipling, R. Pan in Vermont.
Nash, O. Kipling's Vermont.
Paley, G. Connections: Vermont Vietnam (I).
  Connections: Vermont Vietnam (II).
  In Montpelier, Vermont.
  When I Was Asked How I Could Leave
  Vermont in the Middle of October.
Rich, A. Living Memory.
Schuyler, J. Afterward.
  Evenings in Vermont.
  Now and Then.
  Vermont Diary, A.
Updike. Vermont.
Warren, R. Fall Comes in Back-Country
  Vermont.

Sunset Walk in Thaw-Time in Vermont.
Vermont Ballad: Change of Season.
Whittier. Song of the Vermonters, 1779, The.

Verona, Italy
Laughlin, J. Cultural Note.
Milosz, C. Farewell: "I speak to you, my son."
Wilde, O. At Verona.
Wright, C. Homage to Claude Lorrain.
  Mid-winter Snowfall in the Piazza Dante.

Versailles, France
Moore, M. No Swan So Fine.
Patchen. Grand Palace of Versailles, The.
Rich, A. Versailles.

Veterans
Ai. Back in the World.
  Detective, The.
  Elegy: "Hundreds of flies."
  Flashback.
  I Can't Get Started.
Amichai [*or* Amikhai]. 1978 Reunion of
  Palmach Veterans at Ma-ayan Harod.
Bierce. At a "National Encampment."
  Hesitating Veteran, The.
Davie, D. 1945.
Dugan, A. Hard-on Death.
  On Visiting a Veterans Hospital.
  Portrait from the Infantry.
Dunbar, P. Veteran, The.
Fenton, J. Children in Exile.
  Vucceria.
Graves, R. Child with Veteran.
Hall, D. Man in the Dead Machine, The.
Hardy, T. San Sebastian.
Hughes, T. Dust As We Are.
  For the Duration.
  Walt.
Kipling, R. All the world over, nursing their
  scars.
  Chant-Pagan.
  Clerks and the Bells, The.
  Expert, The.
  Last of the Light Brigade, The.
  Scholars, The.
  Troopin'.
  Veterans, The.
Komunyakaa. Fever.
  Ghost Video.
  Legacy.
  Losses.
  Nude Interrogation.
  Phantasmagoria.
  Poplars, The.
  Report from the Skull's Diorama.
  Returning (1975).
  Steel Plate, The.
  Surgery.
Oppen. Seated Man.
Orr, G. Memorial Day.
Parker, D. Veteran, The.
Riley, J. Scotty.
Sandburg, C. And So Today.
  Graves.
Schuyler, J. Scarlet Tanager.
Whitman, W. Dying Veteran, The.
Williams, C. K. From My Window.
Wilner, E. Lament: "All morning I have been
  reading poems."
See also **Soldiers**

Veterans Day
See **Armistice**

Vice
Baudelaire. To the Reader.
Beckett, S. Ce qu'a de pis.
Bierce. Incurable.
Éluard, P. Out of Sight in the Direction of My
  Body.
Emerson, R. Γνωθι Σεαυτον.
  This world is tedious.
  To transmute crime to wisdom, & to stem.
Han-shan. Three Worlds swarm with people,
  The.
Herrick. Nothing New.
  Of Love.
  Two Things Odious.
Jeffers, R. Vices.

Lawrence, D. H. Bawdy Can Be Sane.
Mallarmé. Anguish.
Michelangelo Buonarroti. New and more
  commendable delight, A.
Nash, O. So That's Who I Remind Me Of.
Niedecker. Museum man!, The.
O'Hara, F. Poem V (F) W.
Parker, D. Biographies.
  Observation.
Petrarch. Gluttony, sleep, swans-down of
  idleness.
Whalen, P. Failing.
See also **Sin**

Vicenza, Italy
Zagajewski. Morning in Vicenza, A.

Victoria, Queen of England
Browning, E. Crowned and Wedded.
  Victoria's Tears.
  Young Queen, The.
Hardy, T. V.R. 1819–1901.
Housman. 1887.
Kipling, R. Ave Imperatrix!
  Bells and Queen Victoria, The.
  What the People Said.
  Widow at Windsor, The.
  Widow's Party, The.
Lawrence, D. H. Deadly Victorians, The.
Meredith, G. At the Funeral.
Nash, O. Don't Look Now.
Parker, D. Victoria.
Tennyson, A. To the Queen.
Whitman, W. For Queen Victoria's Birthday.
Wordsworth, W. Lines Inscribed in a Copy of
  His Poems Sent to the Queen for the Royal
  Library at Windsor.
  Ode on the Installation of His Royal Highness
  Prince Albert as Chancellor of the University
  of Cambridge, July, 1847.

Victory
Cavafy. In a Township of Asia Minor.
Ciardi, J. Memory of the Sad Chair, A.
  V-J Day.
Coleridge, S. Verses Addressed to J. Horne
  Tooke and the Company Who Met on 28 June
  1796 to Celebrate His Poll at the Westminster
  Election.
Creeley. Winner, The.
Dickinson, E. Neither fearing Extinction.
  Success is counted sweetest.
  Triumph—may be of several kinds.
  Victory comes late.
Emerson, R. Archangel Hope / Looks to the
  azure cope, The.
Gurney, D. Possessions.
HaNagid. On Lifting the Siege.
  War with Yadir, The.
Hardy, T. Men Who March Away.
  Young Churchwarden, The.
Herrick. Care a Good Keeper.
  Credit of the Conquerer, The.
  End, The.
  Last Stroke Strike Sure, The.
  To the King, upon His Taking of Leicester.
  To the Lord Hopton, on His Fight in Cornwall.
Jackson, L. Victory, The.
Jarrell, R. Terms.
Jeffers, R. Moments of Glory.
Kipling, R. Hymn of the Triumphant Airman.
Lawrence, D. H. Triumph.
Marvell. Fair Singer, The.
  Horatian Ode upon Cromwell's Return from
  Ireland, An.
Melville, H. Canticle, A.
  Dupont's Round Fight.
Petrarch. Hannibal won indeed, yet failed to
  take.
Ralegh, S. If Croesus over Halys goe.
Ransom, J. Judith of Bethulia.
Rilke. Victory Asleep.
Ritsos. After the Fire.
  Deadly Victory.
Roethke. Favorite, The.
Stockton, A. On Hearing of the News of the
  Capture of Lord Cornwallis and the British
  Army, by Gen. Washington.
Swift, J. Ode to the King.

Vienna, Austria
Whitman, W.   Old Salt Kossabone.
   Over the Carnage Rose Prophetic a Voice.
   True Conquerors.
   Turn O Libertad.
Whittier.   Emancipation Group, The.
Wordsworth, W.   Anticipation. October, 1803.
   By Moscow Self-Devoted to a Blaze.
   Germans on the Heights of Hochheim, The.
   Occasioned by the Battle of Waterloo February,
      1816.
   Occasioned by the Battle of Waterloo (the Last
      Six Lines Intended for an Inscription)
      February, 1816.
   Ode: 1814.
   Ode: 1815.
   On the Same Occasion.
   Siege of Vienna Raised by John Sobieski
      February, 1816.

Vienna, Austria
García Lorca.   Little Viennese Waltz.
Montale.   Near Vienna.
Seifert.   Nocturnal Divertimento.
Williams, W.   Lustspiel.

Vienna, Siege of (1683)
Wordsworth, W.   Siege of Vienna Raised by
   John Sobieski February, 1816.

Vietnam
Berry, W.   Against the War in Vietnam.
   Dark with power.
Bly, R.   Asian Peace Offers Rejected without
   Publication.
   At a March against the Vietnam War.
   Counting Small-Boned Bodies.
   Driving through Minnesota during the Hanoi
      Bombings.
   Teeth Mother Naked at Last, The.
Bukowski.   Simplicity of Everything in Viet
   Nam, The.
Carruth, H.   Birds of Vietnam, The.
Ginsberg, A.   Vow, A.
Komunyakaa.   Buried Light.
   Frontispiece.
   Ghost Video.
   Hanoi Market, The.
   Reed Boat, A.
   Shrines.
Levertov.   Advent 1966.
   Altars in the Street, The.
   Fragrance of Life, Odor of Death.
   Greeting to the Vietnamese Delegates to the
      U.N.
   In Thai Binh (Peace) Province.
   Tenebrae.
   Weeping Woman.
   What Were They Like?
MacLeish.   National Security.
McGrath, T.   Reading the Names of the Vietnam
   War Dead.
Merton.   Twenty Three Point Prospectus for
   Small College in the Badlands.
Nemerov.   On Getting Out of Vietnam.
Paley, G.   Connections: Vermont Vietnam (I).
   Connections: Vermont Vietnam (II).
   In Hanoi 1969.
   My Father at 85.
Rich, A.   Dien Bien Phu.
Rukeyser, M.   Flying to Hanoi.
Schuyler, J.   May, 1972.
Shapiro, K.   Vietnam Memorial.
Tomlinson, C.   Tarquinia.
Williams, C. K.   From My Window.
   In the Heart of the Beast.
Wilner, E.   Lament: "All morning I have been
   reading poems."

Vietnam War
Ai.   Detective, The.
   Flashback.
   Journalist, The.
Codrescu.   All Wars Are Holy.
Corbett, W.   Fall 1970.
Dugan, A.   Adultery.
Ginsberg, A.   And ninety-nine soldiers piled on
   the train at Amarillo.
   Funky barn, black hills approaching Fulton.
   Iron Horse.
   Kansas City to Saint Louis.

Kansas! Kansas! Shuddering at last!
   Wichita Vortex Sutra.
Ignatow, D.   All Quiet.
Kinnell.   Vapor Trail Reflected in the Frog Pond.
Kizer, C.   First of June Again, The.
Komunyakaa.   2527th Birthday of the Buddha.
   After the Fall [of Saigon].
   Ambush.
   Between Days.
   Boat People.
   Break from the Bush, A.
   Bui Doi, Dust of Life.
   Camouflaging the Chimera.
   Combat Pay for Jody.
   Communiqué.
   Dead at Quang Tri, The.
   Donut Dollies.
   Edge, The.
   Eyeball Television.
   Facing It.
   Fever.
   Fragging.
   Greenness Taller than Gods, A.
   Hanoi Hannah.
   Ia Drang Valley.
   Jungle Surrender.
   Le Xuan, Beautiful Spring.
   Losses.
   Missing in Action.
   Monoon Season.
   Night Muse & Mortar Round.
   Nothing Big.
   Nude Pictures.
   One-legged Stool, The.
   One More Loss to Count.
   Phantasmagoria.
   Phantom Limbs.
   Prisoners.
   Re-creating the Scene.
   Red Pagoda.
   Report from the Skull's Diorama.
   Returning (1975).
   Roll Call.
   Saigon Bar Girls, 1975.
   Sappers.
   Seeing in the Dark.
   Short-timer's Calendar.
   Somewhere Near Phu Bai.
   Starlight Scope Myopia.
   Sunset Threnody.
   Thanks.
   To Have Danced with Death.
   Toys in a Field.
   Tu Do Street.
   Tunnels.
   Water Buffalo.
   We Never Know.
   You and I Are Disappearing.
Laughlin, J.   Kind-, The.
Levertov.   Distance, The.
   Dragon of Revolutionary Love.
   Modes of Being.
   Poem at Christmas, 1972, during the Terror-
      Bombing of North Vietnam, A.
   Weeping Woman.
Major, C.   Waiter in a California Vietnamese
   Restaurant.
Merwin.   Asians Dying, The.
Paley, G.   Bridges.
   Two Villages.
Palmer, M.   Sun.
Prunty.   Nineteenth Hole, The.
Stock, R.   Imitation of Horace; Carmina 1.6.
   Shakespeare in Vietnam.
Warren, R.   Interjection #4: Bad Year, Bad War:
   A New Year's Card, 1969.
Whalen, P.   War Poem for Diane di Prima.
Wilner, E.   Closing Ceremonies for the
   Bicentennial.
See also **Vietnam; War**

Vigilantes
Komunyakaa.   Vigilante.

Vikings
Heaney, S.   Viking Dublin: Trial Pieces.
Kipling, R.   Dane-Geld.
   Song of the Red War-Boat.

Longfellow, H.   Skeleton in Armor [*or* Armour],
   The.
MacNeice.   North Sea, The.
Whittier.   Dole of Jarl Thorkell, The.
   Norsemen, The.

Vileness
Hughes, L.   Bad Man.
Pessoa.   Poem in a Straight Line.

Village Idiots
Graves, R.   Villagers and Death, The.
Ritsos.   Idiot, The.

Villages
Amichai [*or* Amikhai].   Elegy on an Abandoned
   Village.
Apollinaire.   Mountebanks.
Bierce.   Perverted Village, The.
Brodsky, J.   Autumn in Norenskaia.
   Elegy: "Sweetheart, losing your looks, go to live
      in a village."
Cavafy.   Nichori.
Dove, R.   Sightseeing.
Hall, D.   Village in East Anglia, A.
Levine, P.   Pili's Wall.
Longfellow, H.   Ropewalk, The.
   Village Blacksmith, The.
Lux.   People of the Other Village, The.
MacDiarmid, H.   Island Funeral.
McGrath, T.   Ah... to the Villages!
Milosz, C.   In Music.
Montale.   Valmorbia, flowering clouds of plants.
Oppen.   Founder, The.
Patchen.   Authority of Krajova, The.
   Kibali-Ituri.
   On the South-West Coast of Erehwemos Stands
      a Romantic Little Village.
   Village Tudda, The.
Robinson, E.   Dead Village, The.
Sandburg, C.   Pods.
   Weeds.
Smith, S.   Brickenden, Hertfordshire.
Tate, J.   Village 104.
Weiss, T.   Certain Village, A.
Williams, W.   Wind of the Village.
Zaturenska.   Fulfillment.
See also **Cities; Towns**

Villanelle (form)
Bishop, E.   One Art.

Villon, François
Komunyakaa.   Villon/Leadbelly.
Sandburg, C.   François Villon Forgotten.

Vinci, Leonardo da
See **Leonardo da Vinci**

Vines
Amichai [*or* Amikhai].   Elecampane, Jasmine,
   Vine, and Oleander.
Ammons.   Four Motions for the Pea Vines.
   Lines.
Clampitt.   Kudzu Dormant.
Dickey, J.   Kudzu.
Eberhart, R.   Stealth and Subtleties of Growth.
Lawrence, D. H.   Erotic.
MacLeish.   Population Explosion.
Merton.   Vine, The.
Patchen.   Vines with Their.
Rilke.   Das Kleine Weinjahr.
   Grisaille.
Rossetti, C.   Passion Flower hath sprung up tall,
   The.
Tomlinson, C.   Old Man's Beard.
Zukofsky, L.   Vines.

Vineyards
Merwin.   Vineyard, The.
Seifert.   Spanish Vineyards.

Violence
Ai.   Kid, The.
   Mother's Tale, The.
Ammons.   Spindle.
Beckett, S.   Dread Nay.
Berryman.   Letter to His Brother.
Blue Cloud.   Brief History (June–December
   1994).
Bukowski.   I Don't Need a Bedsheet with Slits
   for Eyes to Kill You In.
Carruth, H.   Mountain, The.
Crane, S.   Black riders came from the sea.

Creeley. Answer, The.
Names.
Reason, A.
Cummings, E. E. Come from his gal's.
Dugan, A. On a Myth. On a Conventional
Wisdom.
Eberhart, R. Dream, A.
My Golden and My Fierce Assays.
García Lorca. Ballad of the Spanish Civil
Guard.
Ginsberg, A. Violence.
Glück, L. Edge, The.
Egg, The.
Seconds.
Gunn, T. Mirror for Poets, A.
Hacker, M. 1976.
Why We Are Going Back to Paradise Island.
Hardy, T. On the Doorstep.
Hayden, R. [American Journal].
Locus.
Heaney, S. I'm writing this just after an
encounter.
'Religion's never mentioned here,' of course.
This morning from a dewy motorway.
Hughes, L. Beale Street Love.
Merry Christmas.
Not a Movie.
Southern Mammy Sings.
Third Degree.
Ignatow, D. I Dream I Hurl a Spear.
Jeffers, R. Bloody Sire, The.
Explosion.
Komunyakaa. Eye Witness.
My Father's Love Letters [or Loveletters].
Lawrence, D. H. Love-Passage, A.
Shedding of Blood.
Levertov. May Our Right Hands Lose Their
Cunning.
Levine, P. Letters for the Dead.
MacLeish. Black Humor.
Meredith, G. Candid Friend who strikes
because he loves, The.
Meredith, W. Three Sorts of Violence, The.
Merton. Hopeless and Felons.
Merwin. Happens Every Day.
Milosz, C. Gates of the Arsenal, The.
Nash, O. It Figures.
Nemerov. Trial and Death, a Double Feature.
Oliver, M. Murderer's House, The.
Olson, C. Anecdotes of the Late War.
Laughing Ones, The.
Trinacria.
Paley, G. Leaflet.
What If (This Week).
Pasolini. Southern Dawn.
Pound, E. Sestina: Altaforte.
Rich, A. 5:30 A.M.
Perennial Answer, The.
Violence.
Ritsos. Encounters.
Rukeyser, M. Second Elegy. Age of Magicians.
This is going to be about smoke.
This Morning.
Sexton. Wifebeater, The.
Shapiro, K. California Petrarchan.
Fly, The.
Girls Fighting, Broadway.
Shelley, P. Cancelled Stanza.
Smith, S. Violent Hand, The.
Spenser, E. Faerie Queene, The.
Terry, L. Bars Fight [August 28, 1746].
Walcott. Blues.
Whalen, P. International Date Line, Monday/
Monday 27:XI:67.
Wilbur, R. Tywater.
Williams, C. K. Crime, The.
Hounding Mercy.
How Humble We Were before This.
In the Heart of the Beast.
Innings.
Nut, The.
Poor Hope.
Rabbit Fights for His Life the Leopard Eats
Lunch, The.
Williams, W. Birth of Venus, The.
Drunk and the Sailor, The.

Mezzo Forte.
To All Gentleness.
Wordsworth, W. In the Sound of Mull.
Wyatt, S. Vulcan begat me. Minerva me taught.
Violets
Clampitt. Field Pansy, The.
Dunbar, P. To a Violet Found on All Saints'
Day.
"H. D." Sea Violet.
Herrick. How Violets Came Blue.
Meditation for His Mistress[e], A.
To Violets.
Hughes, T. Violet at Lough Aughresberg, A.
Kunitz, S. Approach of Autumn.
Lawrence, D. H. Violets for the Dead.
Levertov. Eyes and No-Eyes.
Meredith, G. Dearest Dimpling, we believe.
Violets.
We violets white and blue.
Parker, D. Sweet Violets.
Rossetti, C. Autumn Violets.
O wind, where have you been.
Who Hath Despised the Day of Small Things?
Shelley, P. On a Faded Violet.
Very. Violet, The.
Yellow Violets, The.
Zukofsky, L. Violet.
Violins
Amichai [or Amikhai]. Half-Sized Violin.
Creeley. Canzone: "As would any sound
make."
Dryden, J. Song for St Cecilia's Day, 1687, A.
Gallagher, T. Bonfire.
Hardy, T. To My Father's Violin.
Palmer, M. I am an architect in Vienna.
Riley, J. Your Violin.
Sandburg, C. Clefs.
Kreisler.
Three Violins.
Virgil [or Vergil]
Auden. Secondary Epic.
Cowper, W. On Receiving Heyne's Virgil.
On the Author of Letters on Literature.
Creeley. Heroes.
Kizer, C. In Hell with Virg and Dan.
Tennyson, A. To Virgil [or Vergil].
Virgin Islands
Williams, W. Calypsos.
Virgin Mary
D'Arezzo. Sonnet: To the Blessed Virgin Mary.
Dubie. Mercy Seat, The.
Jacobsen, J. Laurentides.
Levertov. Annunciation.
Petrarch. Most glorious Virgin, you are clothed
in glory.
Pinkerton, H. On Dieric Bouts's *Virgin and
Child* (1460) in the California Palace of the
Legion of Honor.
On the Virgin and Child Carved in Oak
(Auvergne, 1150-1200) in the Metropolitan
Museum.
Rossetti, D. Virgin and Child, by Hans
Memmeling, A; in the Academy of Bruges.
Seifert. Head of the Virgin Mary, The.
Our Lady of Žižkov.
Wilner, E. Trümmerfrauen.
See also **Mary, the Virgin**
Virginia (state)
Brodsky, J. Near Alexandria.
Burns, R. Slave's Lament, The.
Clampitt. Matoaka.
Notes on the State of Virginia.
Frost, R. Gift Outright, The.
Jarrell, R. Jamestown.
Moore, M. Virginia Britannia.
Nash, O. First Families Move Over!
Sarton, M. Monticello.
Whitman, W. As Toilsome I Wander'd
Virginia's Woods.
Virginia—the West.
Whittier. Farewell, The: "Gone, gone,—sold
and gone."
Randolph of Roanoke.
Wright, C. American Twilight.
Appalachian Book of the Dead, The.

Appalachian Book of the Dead 2, The.
Appalachian Book of the Dead 4, The.
China Mail.
Christmas East of the Blue Ridge.
Disjecta Membra.
East of the Blue Ridge, Our Tombs Are in the
Dove's Throat.
Meditation on Summer and Shapelessness.
Umbrian Dreams.
Virginia Reel.
Watching the Equinox Arrive in Charlottesville,
September 1992.
Virginity and Virgins
Blake, W. Merlins Prophecy.
On the Virginity of the Virgin Mary & Johanna
Southcott.
Visions of the Daughters of Albion.
Burns, R. Lass That Made the Bed for Me, The.
Campion, T. Her rosie cheekes, her ever
smiling eyes.
Carew, T. Maria Wentworth.
Obsequies to the Lady Anne Hay.
Cavafy. Days of 1901.
Codrescu. To the Virgin as She Now Stands to
the Monk after a Beatles Movie.
Cummings, E. E. She being Brand.
Donne. Flea, The.
Dryden, J. New Song, A: "Sylvia the fair, in the
bloom of fifteen."
Dugan, A. Conversation with a Dirty-Minded
Little Girl.
Ferlinghetti, L. Deflowering.
They were putting up the statue.
With bells for hooves in sounding streets.
Graves, R. Purification.
Virgin Mirror.
Hardy, T. Bad Example, The.
Herrick. Charmes.
Dirge of Jephthah's Daughter, The.
How Primroses Came Green.
To a Bed of Tulips.
To Anthea.
To the Virgins, to Make Much of Time.
To Violets.
To Virgins.
Upon a Crooked Maid.
Upon a Virgin.
Upon Doll.
Upon His Kinswoman Mrs. M. S.
Why Flowers Change Color.
Hopkins, G. St. Thecla.
Jackson, L. Virgin, The.
Jonson, B. Epigram on the Court Pucell, An.
Laughlin, J. Inviolable Maiden, The.
Lawrence, D. H. Virgin Youth.
Logan, J. New Poem.
Merton. Five Virgins, The.
Parker, D. Parable for a Certain Virgin.
Plath. Virgin in a Tree.
Ransom, J. Her Eyes.
Rilke. Wise and Foolish Virgins, The.
Rukeyser, M. Unborn Song.
Shapiro, K. First Time, The.
Stock, R. Shield against the Trampling Foe, A.
Thomas, D. On the Marriage of a Virgin.
Williams, W. From a Book.
Zaturenska. Virgin with a Lamp.
Virtue
Burns, R. Dedication to G**** H******* Esq,
A.
Extempore Verses on Dining with Lord Daer.
For G. H. Esq.
For the Author's Father.
Lines Addressed to Mr. John Ranken.
O Kenmure's on and awa, Willie.
On Mr. James Gracie.
To a Lady.
To Miss Graham of Fintray.
Byron, G. Lines to a Lady Weeping.
Sketch from Private Life, A.
Stanzas to Augusta.
Campion, T. Man of Life Upright, The.
O griefe, O spight, to see poore Vertue scorn'd.
Some can flatter, some can faine.
Thou Joy'st, Fond Boy.
To My Worthy Friend, Mr. John Mounson,

Sonne and Heyre to Sir Thomas Mounson, Knight and Baronet.

Why presumes thy pride on that, that must so private be.

Carew, T.   Complement, The.

Divine Mistress, A.

Epitaph on the Lady S.: Wife of Sir W.S.

In Praise of His Mistress.

Ingrateful[l] Beauty Threatened.

Married Woman, A.

Obsequies to the Lady Anne Hay.

Pastoral[l] Dialogue, A.

To A.D., Unreasonable, Distrustful of Her Own Beauty.

To My Rival.

To the Painter.

Cavafy.   Becoming Stronger.

In the House of the Soul.

Cavalcanti.   Beautiful Lady where Love shows himself, The.

Chaucer.   Complaint unto Pity, The.

Lak of Stedfastnesse.

Chuang Tzu.   Confucius and the Madman.

Keng Sang Chu.

Man of Tao, The.

Cowper, W.   Another Version.

Charity.

In Memory of John Thorton.

Ode on *Sir Charles Grandison*.

Progress of Error, The.

R.S.S.

To Miss Macartney.

Translation of Verses to Lloyd.

Crane, S.   Supposing that I should have the courage.

Crashaw.   Upon the Death of Mister Herrys.

Cullen, C.   Tribute.

"Dario."   I am the one who just yesterday spoke.

Davie, D.   Mamertinus on Rhetoric, A.D. 291.

Three Moral Discoveries.

De la Mare.   Virtue.

Donne.   Elegy on the Lady Markham.

Elegy upon the Death of Mistress Boulstred, An.

Letter to the Lady Carey, and Mistress Essex Rich, from Amiens, A.

Obsequies to the Lord Harrington, Brother to the Lady Lucy, Countess of Bedford.

To the Countess of Bedford ("Madam, / You have refined me, and to worthiest things").

Undertaking, The.

Emerson, R.   Alone in Rome! Why Rome is lonely too.

Cloud upon cloud / Clouds after rain.

Γνωθι Σεαυτον.

In the deep heart of man a poet dwells.

Leave me, Fear! thy throbs are base.

Loss and Gain.

Graves, A.   In the Name of Virtue.

Graves, R.   Golden Anchor.

Young Cordwainer, The.

Herbert, G.   Charms and Knots.

Constancy.

Foil, The.

Virtue [*or* Vertue].

Herrick.   Abstinence.

Choose for the Best.

Excesse.

Feare.

Gold, before Goodnesse.

Just Man, A.

King and No King, A.

Leprosie in Cloathes.

No Shipwrack of Vertue. To a Friend.

On Himself.

Parcell-gil't-Poetry.

Pleasures Pernicious.

Purposes.

To His Honoured Kinsman Sir William Soame.

To His Peculiar Friend Sir Edward Fish, Knight Baronet.

To the Most Accomplisht Gentleman Master Michael Oulsworth.

Vertue.

Vertue Best United.

Vertue Is Sensible of Suffering.

Jackson, L.   Need For Hell, A.

Jonson, B.   Elegy, An: "Though beauty be the mark of praise."

Epigram on Sir Edward Coke, when He Was Lord Chief Justice of England, An.

Epigram. To the Honoured————, Countess of————, An.

Epitaph on Elizabeth, L. H.

Epode: "Not to know vice at all, and keep[e] true state."

Ode. To Sir William Sydney, on His Birthday.

To Sir Henry Cary.

To Sir William Uvedale.

MacLeish.   Good Man in a Bad Time, A.

Speech to the Detractors.

Michelangelo Buonarroti.   Just as a flame, by wind and weather flailed.

Moore, M.   Blessed Is the Man.

To a Snail.

Nash, O.   Hand Me Down My Old School Sliding Pads, or, There's a Hint of Strawberry Leaves in the Air.

Stitch Too Late Is My Fate, A.

Parker, D.   Biographies.

Observation.

Patchen.   Virtue.

Petrarch.   Death, you have left this world, without its sun.

How strangely this world wags! Now what distressed.

Lady much more radiant than the sun, A.

My thoughts talked with each other pleasantly.

She, much more beautiful than others are.

Pope, A.   Epitaph on John Knight, Who Died Oct. 2, 1733.

Epitaph on Mrs. Corbet, Who Died of a Cancer in Her Breast.

Version of the First Psalm, for the Use of a Young Lady, A.

Riley, J.   Rosamond C. Bailey.

Shirley, J.   Would you know what's soft? I dare.

Smart, C.   To Mrs. Dacosta.

Smith, S.   Exeat.

Last Turn of the Screw, The.

Stockton, A.   Acrostic for Abby Stockton.

Impromptu Epitaph on the Grave Digger of Princeton—1769.

Wise nature here has done her kindest part.

Thoreau.   Conscience is instinct bred in the house.

Ep on a Good Man.

Rumors from an Aeolian Harp.

Sympathy.

Unknown.   On a Good Man.

Unknown, sometimes at. to Sir Walter Ralegh.

Vertue the Best Monument.

Wheatley, P.   On Virtue.

Williams, M.   Six Moral Virtues, The: Grace, Style, Class, Kindness, and Wisdom.

Wordsworth, W.   Inscription for a Seat by the Pathway Side Ascending to Windy Brow.

October, 1803.

Wright, J.   Moral Poem Freely Accepted from Sappho, A.

Viruses

Graves, R.   Virus, The.

Vishnu

Cavafy.   Eternity.

Ramanujan.   Difference, The.

Mythologies 2.

Vision

Amichai [*or* Amikhai].   Near the Wall of a House.

Ammons.   Image.

Off.

Offset.

Path.

Beckett, S.   Son ombre une nuit.

Berryman.   Apparition, The.

Browning, E.   Isobel's Child.

Poet, The.

Prospect, The.

Browning, R.   Cardinal and the Dog, The.

Carew, T.   On Sight of a Gentlewoman's Face in the Water.

Carver, R.   Phenomenon, The.

Cavalcanti.   Sonnet: He Reports, in a Feigned Vision, the Successful Issue of Lapo Gianni's Love.

Celan.   Flower.

Ice, Eden.

Mandorla.

Vinegrowers dig up.

Clough.   Upon the water in the boat.

Crane, H.   Hieroglyphic.

I Rob My Breast.

Wine Menagerie, The.

Crane, S.   I met a seer.

Creeley.   People.

Cummings, E. E.   All worlds have halfsight,seeing either with.

Davie, D.   Hill Field, The.

De la Mare.   Visionary, The.

What?

Dickinson, E.   Mine—by the Right of the White Election!

My family of Apparitions.

Eberhart, R.   Birth of the Spirit, The.

Dream, The.

Goal of Intellectual Man, The.

Going.

Great Principles Are Thrown Down by Time.

In a Hard Intellectual Light.

In after Time.

Life as Visionary Spirit.

Lucubration.

May Evening.

Memory.

Moment of Vision, The.

Mystical Beast in the Shadows, The.

Quarrel with a Cloud.

Stopping a Kaleidoscope.

Testimony.

Virgin, The.

Vision.

Vision through Timothy.

Emerson, R.   I live among ideal men.

In dreamy woods, what forms abound.

Why should I live.

Frost, R.   Neither out Far nor in Deep.

Gallagher, T.   Devotion: That It Flow; That There Be Concentration.

Ginsberg, A.   Psalm 4.

Graves, R.   Like Owls.

Gunn, T.   Unsettled Motorcyclist's Vision of His Death, The.

Hall, D.   Apples.

Hardy, T.   At a Seaside Town in 1869.

In Vision I Roamed.

She Who Saw Not.

Heaney, S.   Field of Vision.

Housman.   Look not in my eyes, for fear.

Hughes, L.   Blind.

Jarrell, R.   Orient Express, The.

Kipling, R.   Chartres Windows.

Laughlin, J.   At Eleusis.

With My Third Eye.

Lawrence, D. H.   Know Deeply, Know Thyself More Deeply.

Levertov.   Depths, The.

Eyes and No-Eyes.

Kingdoms of Heaven.

Puñal.

Sequence, A.

Two Artists.

Lindsay, N.   Town of American Visions, The.

Mallarmé.   Little Air 1.

McGrath, T.   Incident in the Life of a Prophet, An.

McHugh, H.   Message at Sunset for Bishop Berkeley.

To See the Light.

Meredith, W.   Seasons' Difference, The.

Merrill, J.   Blue Eye, The.

Octopus, The.

Remora.

Merton.   Macarius and the Pony.

Merwin.   In the Life of Dust.

Vision.

Milosz, C.   December 1.

Philosopher's Home, A.

Nash, O.   And How Keen Was the Vision of Sir

Launfal?
Nemerov. Frozen City, The.
I Only Am Escaped Alone to Tell Thee.
Maia.
Seeing Things.
Two Girls.
Niedecker. Art Center.
O'Hara, F. Day and Night in 1952.
Raine, K. Poet is of those, The.
Ramanujan. Eyes, Ears, Noses, and a Thing about Touch.
Rossetti, C. Blind from my birth, / Where flowers are springing.
Who Has Seen the Wind?
Rumi. Visions of Daquqi, The.
Seifert. Prologue: "To be a poet is no easy task."
Shapiro, K. Dome of Sunday, The [or A].
Glass Poem.
Swift, J. Occasioned by Sir William Temple's Late Illness and Recovery.
Tomlinson, C. Appearance.
At a Glance.
At the Edge.
Face and Image.
Mistlines.
Poem: "Muscles which move the eyeballs, The."
Ponte Veneziano.
Skullshapes.
Through Binoculars.
Through Closed Eyes.
Tout Entouré de Mon Regard.
Van Duyn. Vision Test, The.
Walcott. Hotel Normandie Pool, The.
Warren, R. Vision.
Weiss, T. Views and Spectacles.
Wilbur, R. Beacon, The.
Eye, The.
Poplar, Sycamore.
Sketch, A.

Visiting and Visitors
Ammons. Visit.
Bishop, E. Faustina, or Rock Roses.
Broumas, O. Lenten.
Byron, G. Oh You, Who in All Names Can Tickle the Town.
Cowper, W. Letter in Verse.
On His Approaching Visit to Hayley.
To My Dearest Cousin, on Her Removal of us from Silver End, to Weston.
To the Rev. Mr. Newton.
Dickinson, E. Infinite a sudden Guest, The.
Little poem we will write unto our Cousin John, A.
Dunbar, P. Opportunity.
Visitor, The.
Enzensberger, H. Staircase, A.
Frost, R. Time to Talk, A.
Graves, R. Silent Visit.
Herrick. Night-Piece, to Julia, The.
Ode to Sir Clipsebie Crew, An.
Panegyric to Sir Lewis Pemberton, A.
Hughes, L. Madam and the Wrong Visitor.
Jackson, L. Friendship on Visit.
Jacobsen, J. Arrival.
Guide for Survivors.
Levertov. Poet and Person.
Presence, The.
She and the Muse.
Lindsay, N. Visit to Mab, The.
Logan, J. Manhattan Movements.
Staying Awake.
MacLeish. Danger in the Air, The.
MacNeice. Return to Lahore.
Martial. 2.5: "Believe me, sir, I'd like to spend whole days."
Meredith, W. Journal Entry (April 1969, Villa Serbelloni).
Merwin. Visitation.
Mistral, G. Request for Blanca, A.
Nash, O. Grin and Bear Left.
On Waking to the Third Rainy Morning of a Long Week End.
Visit from Dr. Fell, A.
Visit, The.
Ni Dhomhnaill. Orphan at the Door, An.

O'Hara, F. Poem: "Eager note on my door said 'Call me,' The."
Paley, G. Bob Visits Friends.
Riley, J. Little Cousin Jasper.
Rossetti, C. Echo.
Enrica, 1865.
Schuyler, J. After Joe Was at the Island.
Sheridan, T. Tom Punsibi's Letter to Dean Swift.
Stein, G. Little Novel, A.
Stock, R. Night Crawlers.
Thoreau. Wait not till I invite thee, but observe.
Van Duyn. Gentle Snorer, The.
Williams, C. K. Bishop Tutu's Visit to the White House: 1984.
End of Drought.
Sleeping Over.
Williams, T. After a Visit.

Vitality
Baudelaire. Too Full of Life.
Blok. I Want to Live.
Cullen, C. Counter Mood.
Epilogue: "Lily, being white not red, The."
I Have a Rendezvous with Life.
Life's Rendezvous.
Emerson, R. Nature 2.
Hughes, L. Demand.
Koch, K. Departure from Hydra, The.
Lawrence, D. H. Vitality.
What's Wrong.
Williams, T. Madrigal: "Today, I am dull, I am dull!"

Vocations
See **Occupations**

Vodka
Ciardi, J. Vodka.

Vogler, Georg Joseph
Browning, R. Abt Vogler.

Voices
Amichai [or Amikhai]. Summer Evening in the Jerusalem Mountains.
Summer Rest and Words.
Sweet Voice from the Kibbutz, The.
You Will Speak.
Ammons. Rack.
Beckett, S. D'où / la voix qui dit.
Berry, W. Song in a Year of Catastrophe.
Bogan, L. Song for the Last Act.
Browning, R. Meeting at Night.
Cavafy. Sweet Voices.
Voice from the Sea.
Voices.
Celan. Voices, nicked into.
Crane, S. There came whisperings in the winds.
Creeley. Air: "Cat Bird Singing."
Bobbie ("Her voice").
Messengers, The.
There ("Place so, A").
Cummings, E. E. Voices to voices, lip to lip.
De la Mare. Voice, The.
Dickey, J. Sleepers.
Dunbar, P. Musical, A.
Eberhart, R. Transformation.
Emerson, R. In dreamy woods, what forms abound.
Hall, D. Friend Revisited, A.
White Apples.
Herrick. Againe.
Poet Hath Lost His Pipe, The.
Upon a Gentlewoman with a Sweet Voice.
Upon Her Voice.
Upon Julia's Voice.
Upon Sapho, Sweetly Playing, and Sweetly Singing.
Voice and Violl, The.
Laughlin, J. Voices, The.
Levertov. Grief.
Levi, P. Voices.
Levine, P. Voice, The.
Lux. Voice You Hear When You Read Silently, The.
MacNeice. Schizophrene.
Merwin. Invocation: "Day hanging by its feet with a hole, The."
Not These Hills.

Voice.
Montale. Spirit that dispenses, The.
Nash, O. I Didn't Say a Word, or, Who Called That Piccolo Player a Father?
Petrarch. When Lord Love makes her cast her glances down.
Raine, K. Once I heard your voice.
Triad.
Winds.
Riley, J. Voices, The.
Ritsos. Final Agreement.
Rolfe, E. Eyes of a Blind Man.
Rossetti, C. If I Had Words.
What does the donkey bray about?
Rukeyser, M. Song: "Voice flew out of the river as morning flew, A."
Rumi. You that come to birth and bring the mysteries.
Shelley, P. To ———: "Music, when soft voices die."
Smith, S. Singing Cat, The.
Stafford, W. Long Distance.
Tate, J. Uncle.
Tennyson, A. Break, Break, Break.
Tomlinson, C. At Wells: Polyphony.
Shout, The.
Their Voices Rang.
Warren, R. What Is the Voice that Speaks?
What Voice at Moth-Hour.
Williams, W. Pastoral: "If I say I have heard voices."
Wordsworth, W. Thought[s] of a Briton on the Subjugation of Switzerland.
Voice of the Derwent, The.
Wright, C. Absence inside an Absence.
Wright, J. For the Marsh's Birthday.
Speak.
To the Poets in New York.
Yeats. Everlasting Voices, The.
Zagajewski. Gothic, The.
Out Walking.
Three Voices.
See also **Screams; Speech; Talk**

Volcanoes
Bishop, E. Crusoe in England.
Cowper, W. Heroism.
Dickey, W. Heroine, The.
Dickinson, E. I have never seen "Volcanoes."
On my volcano grows the Grass.
Still—Volcano—Life, A.
Volcanoes be in Sicily.
When Etna basks and purrs.
Enzensberger, H. Reprieve, The.
Keats. Upon My Life, Sir Nevis, I Am Piqued.
Lawrence, D. H. Peace.
Logan, J. Poem for My Friend Peter at Pihana.
Snyder, G. Burning Island.
Walcott. Volcano.
Williams, W. Catastrophic Birth.

Voltaire, François Marie Arouet de
Auden. Voltaire at Ferney.
Blake, W. Mock On, Mock On, Voltaire, Rousseau.
Gallagher, T. Survival of a Heart.
Jackson, L. Vain Life of Voltaire, The.
Kizer, C. Long Line of Doctors, A.
Kumin, M. Shopping in Ferney with Voltaire.

Voting and Voters
Ciardi, J. Rite, The.
Dickinson, E. Mine—by the Right of the White Election!
Graves, R. Whole Love.
Hughes, L. Ballad of Sam Solomon.
Kizer, C. Election Day, 1984.
Lawrence, D. H. Flapper Vote.
Lindsay, N. Bryan, Bryan, Bryan, Bryan.
Why I Voted the Socialist Ticket.
Nash, O. Election Day Is a Holiday.
Olson, C. Hustings, The.
Swift, J. Dog and the Thief, The.
Very. Voting in the Old North Church.
Whittier. After Election.
Eve of Election, The.
Poor Voter on Election Day, The.
Quakers Are Out, The.
Wordsworth, W. Help for the Memory of the

Grand Independent; A New Song, A.
Protest against the Ballot.
Said Secrecy to Cowardice and Fraud.
See also **Campaigns, Political; Woman Suffrage**
Vowels
Burns, R.   Tale, A.
Rimbaud, A.   Vowels.
Sheridan, T.   Of Quantity Which Depends upon
    the Authority of the Poets.
Voyages
Berryman.   First Night at Sea.
Crane, H.   Voyages.
Cummings, E. E.   What is / a / voyage / ?
De la Mare.   Galliass, The.
Dickey, W.   Læestrygonians, The.
Eberhart, R.   Moment of Equilibrium among the
    Islands.
    Perception as a Guided Missile.
    Voyage, The.
Emerson, R.   Thine Eyes Still Shined.
Guyon.   Figurative Description of the Procedure
    of Divine Love, A.
Herrick.   His Sailing from Julia.
    Plaudite, or End of Life, The.
Howe, S.   Chanting at the Crystal Sea.
    Secret History of the Dividing Line.
Kizer, C.   Voyager.
Larkin, P.   North Ship, The.
Nash, O.   I Want a Drink of Water, but Not from
    the Thermos.
Oppen.   Preface, A: "If he goes rowing in the
    park tho he may row so well that."
Rossetti, C.   Today's Burden.
Sexton.   Crossing the Atlantic.
Simic.   Navigator.
Spender, S.   Cornet Cornelius Rilke.
    Marston.
Stock, R.   Voyager Takes Pause, A.
Walcott.   As John to Patmos.
    Harbour, The.
    Schooner Flight, The.
Whittier.   Godspeed.
Wilner, E.   Emigration.
Zaturenska.   Voyage.
Voyageurs
De la Mare.   Mirage.
Oliver, M.   No Voyage.
Voyeurism and Voyeurs
Amichai [*or* Amikhai].   Voyeur, The.
Bukowski.   Girl on the Bus Stop Bench, The.
    Girls Coming Home.
    Girls in Pantyhose.
    New Place, The.
Codrescu.   Ode to Curiosity.
Coleridge, S.   Picture, The.
Dickey, J.   Fiend, The.
Dove, R.   Small Town.
Gunn, T.   Corridor, The.
    Release, The.
    Taylor Street.
    Venetian Blind.
Hardy, T.   Seen by the Waits.
Komunyakaa.   Thorn Merchant's Son, The.
Lawrence, D. H.   Gloire de Dijon.
Meredith, G.   Teaching of the Nude, The.
Milosz, C.   Voyeur.
Ritsos.   Calculated Behavior.
Shapiro, K.   Dome of Sunday, The [*or* A].
Van Duyn.   Voyeur, The.
Wilbur, R.   Eye, The.
Williams, M.   Late Show.
Wright, J.   Girl in a Window, A.
Vuillard, Edouard
Rich, A.   Pictures by Vuillard.
Vulcan
Auden.   Shield of Achilles, The.
Bierce.   Oneiromancy.
Herrick.   To Vulcan.
Jonson, B.   Execration upon Vulcan, An.
Vulnerability
Amichai [*or* Amikhai].   You Must Not Show
    Weakness.
Ammons.   Autumn Song.
    Mark, The.
Beckett, S.   Thither.

Bly, R.   Fifty Males Sitting Together.
Bukowski.   Iron Mike.
Cavafy.   Aimilianos Monai, Alexandrian, 628–
    655 A.D.
Creeley.   Not Now.
    Pieces.
    Something.
Dickey, J.   Attempted Departure.
Ferlinghetti, L.   It was a face which darkness
    could kill.
Graves, R.   Injuries.
Gunn, T.   Odysseus on Hermes.
Jeffers, R.   To a Young Artist.
Laughlin, J.   If You Are Only Flirting.
McHugh, H.   Solitary's Solace in the Natural
    Sciences.
Michelangelo Buonarroti.   Nothing the best of
    artists can conceive.
Petrarch.   If that attractive look of hers can kill.
Piercy.   Rape Poem.
    You Ask Why Sometimes I Say Stop.
Ransom, J.   Winter Remembered.
Rich, A.   Antinoüs: The Diaries.
    Storm Warnings.
Shapiro, K.   First Time, The.
Tate, J.   Wait for Me.
Vulpius, Melchior
Moore, M.   Melchior Vulpius.
Vultures
Atwood.   Vultures.
Blok.   Kite, The.
Blue Cloud.   Gift of Stone.
Jeffers, R.   Vulture.
Oliver, M.   Field near Linden, Alabama.
    Vultures.
Piercy.   Best Defense Is Offensive, The.
Wilbur, R.   Still, Citizen Sparrow.
See also **Buzzards**

W

Wagner, Richard
Browning, R.   Impromptu on Richard Wagner.
Kinsella, T.   Overture.
Mallarmé.   Homage: "Silence already funereal
    spreads a pall, The."
Wagon Trains
Merwin.   Trail into Kansas, The.
Sandburg, C.   Great Proud Wagon Wheels Go
    On, The.
Wagtails
Roethke.   Wagtail, The.
Wailing Wall, The
Amichai [*or* Amikhai].   Jerusalem 1985.
    Jerusalem, 1985.
Cullen, C.   At the Wailing Wall in Jerusalem.
Waiters and Waitresses
Amichai [*or* Amikhai].   Caffè Dante in New
    York—1.
    Caffè Dante in New York—2.
Armantrout.   Counter.
Bukowski.   Krutz.
Collins, B.   Waitress, The.
Cullen, C.   Atlantic City Waiter.
Dugan, A.   To a Red-Headed Do-Good Waitress.
Gallagher, T.   Crêpes Flambeau.
Gunn, T.   Waitress.
Jacobsen, J.   Instances of Communication.
Komunyakaa.   Ghost Video.
Laughlin, J.   Waiters' Ballet, The.
Major, C.   Waiter in a California Vietnamese
    Restaurant.
Muldoon, P.   Holy Thursday.
Nash, O.   Banquet, The.
    Coffee with the Meal.
    Suppose He Threw It in Your Face.
    Try It Suns. and Hols.; It's Closed Then.
Piercy.   What You Waited For.
Simic.   East[ern] European Cooking.
Tomlinson, C.   Ship's Waiters.
Williams, M.   How We May By Chance
    Pronounce the Unsuspected Residence of a
    Ghost.
Ruby Tells All.

Williams, W.   Atlantic City Convention, The.
Waiting Rooms
Bishop, E.   In the Waiting Room.
Clampitt.   From a Clinic Waiting Room.
Creeley.   Illness, An.
Dugan, A.   Cooled Heels Lament against
    Frivolity, the Mask of Despair.
    Untitled Poem: "Patients in the waiting room,
    The."
Hardy, T.   In a Waiting-Room.
Nash, O.   Thoughts Thought while Waiting for a
    Pronouncement from a Doctor, an Editor, a Big
    Executive, the Department of Internal Revenue
    or Any Other Momentous Pronouncer.
Nemerov.   Waiting Rooms.
Warren, R.   Waiting.
Williams, M.   ICU: Space/Time in the Waiting
    Room.
Zagajewski.   There Will Be a Future.
    Wanderer, A.
Wakes
Chuang Tzu.   Lao Tzu's Wake.
Herrick.   Wake, The.
Rexroth, K.   Requiem for the Spanish Dead.
Tate, J.   Initiation, The.
Waking
Ammons.   Watch, The.
Angelou.   Awaking in New York.
Atwood.   Fortification, A.
    Pre-Amphibian.
Baudelaire.   Parisian Dream.
Bishop, E.   Love Lies Sleeping.
Bly, R.   Awakening.
    Poem in Three Parts.
    Waking from Sleep.
Borges.   Poem: "You were asleep. I wake you."
    Waking Up.
Broumas, O.   Aubade: "She wakes having
    flown."
Burns, R.   Lover's Morning Salute to His
    Mistress, The.
Carver, R.   At Least.
    Poem Not against Songbirds, A.
Ciardi, J.   Morning: I Know Perfectly How in a
    Minute You Will Stretch and Smile.
    Spring Song ("Wake early to the early robin").
    Stills and Rapids of Your Nakedness, The.
Coleridge, S.   If I Had but Two Little Wings.
Collins, B.   Center.
Crane, H.   Paraphrase.
Creeley.   Morning ("Dam's broke").
Cummings, E. E.   Raise the shade.
De la Mare.   Awake!
    Break of Morning.
    Imp Within, The.
    Queen Djenira.
    Sleeper, The.
Donne.   Good-Morrow, The.
Dugan, A.   Landfall.
    Morning Song.
    Noon's World.
    One Waking in a Northern Fall.
    Untitled Poem in Two Parts.
Duncan, R.   In Waking.
    Song of the Borderguard, The.
Fayzi [*or* Faydi *or* Feisi *or* Feizi].   Eternal
    Watcher, who doth wake, The.
Ginsberg, A.   Morning.
Gunn, T.   Apartment Cats.
    Waking in a Newly Built House.
Hall, D.   Exile.
HaNagid.   Rise Early.
Hardy, T.   Four in the Morning.
Jacobsen, J.   Let Each Man Remember.
    Waking.
Jarrell, R.   Venetian Blind, The.
Keats.   Bright Star.
Kinnell.   Rapture.
Kizer, C.   On Rising from the Dead.
Kunitz, S.   Grammar Lesson.
Laughlin, J.   Alba.
Lawrence, D. H.   Chief Mystery, The.
    Coming Awake.
    Quite Forsaken.
Levertov.   Dream Inscape.
Lowell, R.   Waking Early Sunday Morning.

MacLeish. Waking.
Mahon. Dawn Chorus, The.
Meredith, W. Poem about Morning.
Merwin. Widow, The.
Milton. Elegiac Verses.
Nash, O. Nature Knows Best.
Pappy Wants a Poppy.
Nemerov. Zalmoxis.
O'Hara, F. Getting Up ahead of Someone (Sun).
Jane Awake.
Sonnet for Jane Freilicher, A.
Orr, G. Sleeping Alone in a Small Room.
Pessoa. I sleep. If I dream, I do not know on waking.
Pinsky. First Early Mornings Together.
Waking Up.
Raine, K. Campanula.
From vague regions of sleep I come again.
Riley, J. Way the Baby Woke, The.
When Baby Woke.
Roethke. Waking, The.
Rossetti, C. Our little baby fell asleep.
Song of Flight, A.
Rukeyser, M. Child wakes in the morning to enter a country, The.
Rumi. Today, like every other day, we wake up empty.
Schuyler, J. Sleep-Gummed Eyes.
Simic. Poem: "Every morning I forget how it is."
Smith, S. Hendecasyllables.
Stafford, W. Waking at 3 A.M.
Stock, R. Revelation According to the Beloved.
Sze. Alba.
Thomas, D. When I woke.
Very. Call, The ("Why art thou not awake my son?").
Warren, R. Little Girl Wakes Early.
Waking to Tap of Hammer.
Whalen, P. Defective Circles.
Wilbur, R. Love Calls Us to the Things of This World.
Williams, C. K. Waking Jed.
Williams, W. Spring and All.
Wright, J. Sun Tan at Dusk.
Wyatt, T. Lover Showeth How He Is Forsaken of Such as He Sometime Enjoyed, The.

Walden Pond, Massachusetts
Emerson, R. In My Garden.
In Walden wood the chickadee.
Komunyakaa. Frontispiece.
Oliver, M. Going to Walden.
Thoreau. It is a real place.
Walden.

Waldenses
Wilde, O. Quantum Mutata.

Wales
Clough. Pont-Y-Wern.
Ferlinghetti, L. Spirit of the Crusades.
Ginsberg, A. Wales Visitation.
Graves, R. Welsh Incident.
Logue, C. To a Friend in Search of Rural Seclusion.
Shelley, P. On Leaving London for Wales.
Thomas, D. Author's Prologue.
Fern Hill.
Walcott. Wales.
Williams, T. Harp of Wales, The.
See also **Welsh, The**

Walking and Walkers
Ammons. Corsons Inlet.
Auden. As I Walked Out One Evening.
Walks.
Beckett, S. Arènes de Lutèce.
Enueg I.
Berry, W. Man Walking and Singing, A.
Bishop, E. Night City.
Bly, R. Out Picking up Corn.
Browning, E. Sea-side walk, A.
Bukowski. Promenade.
Burns, R. Dainty Davie.
Byron, G. She Walks In Beauty.
Carver, R. After Rainy Days.
Walk, A.
Clampitt. Hermit Thrush, A.

Outer Bar, The.
Codrescu. Traffic.
Collins, B. Man Listening to Disc.
Walking across the Atlantic.
Corbett, W. Lake Road.
Cowper, W. Away goes Sussex William with his pack.
Crane, H. In Shadow.
Creeley. "Bolinas and Me."
But.
For Betsy and Tom.
Oh Mabel.
Out.
Place ("There was a path").
Somebody Died.
Song: "Grit / of things, The."
Walking.
Davie, D. Measured Tread, A.
De la Mare. On the Esplanade.
Dunbar, P. Spring Wooing, A.
Eberhart, R. Track.
Frost, R. Acquainted with the Night.
Encounter, An.
Good Hours.
Late Walk, A.
Meeting and Passing.
Graves, R. Legs, The.
To Walk on Hills.
Gurney, I. Cotswold Ways.
Old Times.
Song of Autumn.
Walking Song.
Hacker, M. April Interval.
Hall, D. Our Walk in Yorkshire.
Second Stanza, A.
Hardy, T. Walk, The.
Weary Walker, The.
Heaney, S. Walk, The.
Hughes, L. Crossing.
Walkers with the Dawn.
Ignatow, D. Walk There.
Jackson, L. Footfalling.
Jacobsen, J. Softly.
Koch, K. Spring.
Laughlin, J. Die Heimat.
Levertov. Traveler, A.
Lux. Dawn Walk and Prayer.
Pedestrian.
Meredith, G. Night-Walk, The.
Meredith, W. Crossing Over.
Squire Hazard Walks.
Merwin. Air: "Naturally it is night."
Muldoon, P. Cider.
Niedecker. I walked / from Chicago to Big Bull Falls (Wausau).
O'Hara, F. F. (Missive & Walk) I. #53.
Petit Poème en Prose.
Poem: "Let's take a walk, you."
Walking to Work.
Olson, C. Pavement, The.
Plath. Hardcastle Crags.
Letter in November.
Song for a Summer's Day.
Prunty. New Territory.
Riley, J. Country Pathway, A.
Song of the Road, A.
Roethke. I Waited.
Rossetti, C. Once for All. (Margaret).
Rumi. Keep walking, though there's no place to get to.
Sarton, M. Prothalamion.
Schuyler, J. Walk, The.
Sexton. Noon Walk on the Asylum Lawn.
Smith, S. Bag-Snatching in Dublin.
November.
On Walking Slowly after an Accident.
Stafford, W. So Long.
Walk in the Country, A.
Walking West.
Thoreau. Tall Ambrosia.
Tomlinson, C. Comedy.
Hill Walk.
Paris in Sixty-Nine.
Walks.
Warren, R. August Moon.
Moonlight's Dream, The.

Night Walking.
Passers-By on Snowy Night.
Sunset Walk in Thaw-Time in Vermont.
Whalen, P. Distraction Fit, A.
Morning Walk, A.
Walking.
Whitman, W. Dalliance of the Eagles, The.
Whittier. Forgiveness.
Williams, M. Walking After Supper.
Williams, T. Heavenly Grass.
Old Men with Sticks.
Williams, W. Love Song: "Daisies are broken."
Poem: "As the cat."
Wordsworth, W. Evening Walk, An; Addressed to a Young Lady.
I Wandered Lonely As a Cloud.
Stepping Westward.
To a Young Lady Who Had Been Reproached for Taking Long Walks in the Country.
Zagajewski. I Walked Through the Medieval Town.
Out Walking.
Zukofsky, L. I Walk in the Old Street.

Wall Street, New York City
Piercy. Skyscrapers of the Financial District.
Dance with Gasman, The.
Rukeyser, M. Paper Anniversary.

Wallace, Sir William
Burns, R. Gude Wallace.
Ode [for General Washington's Birthday].
Scots Wha Hae.
Gunn, T. Adolescence.
Wordsworth, W. Composed at Cora Linn in Sight of Wallace's Tower.

Walls
Amichai [or Amikhai]. Like the Inner Wall of a House.
Near the Wall of a House.
Ammons. Terminus.
Tossup.
Bukowski. Walls, The.
Cavafy. Four Walls of My Room, The.
Walls.
Creeley. Walls.
De la Mare. Daisy, The.
Dickey, J. Wall and Cloud.
Donne. Fall of a Wall.
Eberhart, R. In Prisons of Established Craze.
Frost, R. Atmosphere.
Mending Wall.
Triple Bronze.
Hall, D. Stone Walls.
Hughes, L. As I Grew Older.
Kipling, R. Romulus and Remus.
Komunyakaa. Wall, The.
Merwin. Instructions to Four Walls.
Mistral, G. Wall.
O'Hara, F. Variations on Pasternak's "Mein Liebchen, Was Willst Du Noch Mehr?"
Palmer, M. Notes for Echo Lake 2.
Plath. Apprehensions.
Ralegh, S. My Body in the Walls Captived.
Sandburg, C. Wall Shadows.
Schuyler, J. Blue.
Sexton. Wall, The.
Simic. Wall, A.
Stafford, W. In a Corner.
Tennyson, A. Flower in the Crannied Wall.
Tomlinson, C. Churchyard Wall, The.
Rubh An' Dunain.
Stone Walls: at Chew Magna.
Wilbur, R. Caserta Garden.
Williams, W. On Gay Wallpaper.
See also **Fences**

Walnut Trees and Walnuts
Ammons. Devising.
Guillén, J. Nature Alive.
Oliver, M. Black Walnut Tree, The.
Rilke. Walnut Tree.

Walnuts
Mistral, G. Hollow Walnut, The.

Walpole, Robert, 1st Earl of Orford
Swift, J. Character of Sir Robert Walpole, The.

Walruses
Wilbur, R. Castles and Distances.

Walton, Izaak
Riley, J.   Ike Walton's Prayer.
Waltzes and Waltzing
García Lorca.   Little Viennese Waltz.
Roethke.   My Papa's Waltz.
Stevens, W.   Sad Strains of a Gay Waltz.
Wilde, O.   Harlot's House, The.
Wanderlust
Auden.   Wanderer, The.
Byron, G.   To a Lady.
De la Mare.   Journey, The.
Frost, R.   Encounter, An.
  Into My Own.
Ginsberg, A.   Ready to Roll.
Hall, D.   Abroad Thoughts from Home.
Hardy, T.   Vagrant's Song.
  Wanderer, The.
Hughes, L.   Farewell, A.
  Six-Bits Blues.
Kipling, R.   Anchor Song.
  Explorer, The.
  Feet of the Young Men, The.
  Sestina of the Tramp-Royal.
  Song of Travel, A.
Larkin, P.   House on the Edge of the Serious
  Wood, The.
  One Man Walking a Deserted Platform.
  Poetry of Departures.
  So You Have Been, Despite Parental Ban.
Lawrence, D. H.   Restlessness.
Nash, O.   Nymph and the Shepherd, or She
  Went That-a-Way, The.
Roethke.   My Papa's Waltz.
Shelley, P.   Fragment: A Wanderer.
Smith, S.   Lightly Bound.
  Wanderer, The.
Tennyson, A.   Ulysses.
Williams, W.   Wanderer, The: A Rococo Study.
Wordsworth, W.   Song for the Wandering Jew.
Yeats.   Madness of King Goll, The.
Wang Wei
Berryman.   Note to Wang Wei.
Meng Hao Jan.   To Wang Wei.
Wilner, E.   Instructions to Painters by Wang
  Wei, Eighth Century.
War
Ai.   Elegy: "Hundreds of flies."
Amichai [or Amikhai].   Aching bones of lovers,
  The.
  Among the Stars You May Be right.
  And in spite of all that, I must.
  Anniversaries of War.
  As It Was.
  Blood that stands the member erect, The.
  City where I was born was destroyed by
  cannons, The.
  Even my loves are measured by the wars.
  Evening is lying at the horizon, donating blood,
  The.
  "History's Wings Beating," They Used to Say.
  How did a banner begin? Let's assume there
  was something whole.
  I Dreamed.
  I have nothing to say about the war.
  I left the Evening Land by the will of the night.
  I Want to Die in My Own Bed.
  I Was Waiting for My Girl and Her Steps Were
  Absent.
  In the summer, nations come to one another.
  Let Memory Mountain remember instead of me.
  Look: Thoughts and Dreams.
  New homeland was built, The.
  On the lot that was a short-cut for lovers.
  Smell of Gasoline Ascends in My Nose, The.
  Sometimes I think of my fathers.
  War broke out in autumn, in the no-man's land.
  Way It Was, The.
  What is it? An airplane at dawn. No.
  What was the message of the burned man?
  When I Returned They Told Me There's No.
  "Where was he wounded?" You don't know.
  Wild Peace.
Ammons.   Dropping Eyelids Among the Aerial
  Ash.
Aragon.   Richard Coeur-de-Lion.
  Unoccupied Zone, The.

Arnold, M.   Dover Beach.
Ashbery, J.   Rivers and Mountains.
Atwood.   1837 War in Retrospect.
Auden.   Danse Macabre.
  Missing.
  Taller To-day.
Berry, W.   Against the War in Vietnam.
Berryman.   Moon and the Night and the Men,
  The.
  River Rouge, 1932.
Bierce.   After Portsmouth.
Bishop, E.   Wading at Wellfleet.
Blake, W.   Gwin, King of Norway.
  Prologue to King John.
  War Song [to Englishmen], A.
Blok.   Kite, The.
  On the Field of Kulikovo.
  Those Born in the Years of Stagnation.
Bly, R.   As the Asian War Begins.
  At a March against the Vietnam War.
  Counting Small-Boned Bodies.
  Driving through Minnesota during the Hanoi
  Bombings.
  Teeth Mother Naked at Last, The.
  War and Silence.
Brodsky, J.   Elegy: "About a year has passed.
  I've returned to the place of battle."
  Kolo.
Brontë, E.   Douglas's Ride.
  Far, far away is mirth withdrawn.
  Loud without the wind was roaring.
  On the Fall of Zalona.
  Rodric Lesley. 1830.
  Song by Julius Angora.
  Sudden chasm of ghastly light, A.
Brooks, G.   Looking.
  Progress, The.
  White Troops Had Their Orders but the Negroes
  Looked Like Men.
Broumas, O.   Family.
  Knife & the Bread, The.
Browning, E.   Dance, The.
  First News from Villafranca.
  Garibaldi.
  Italy and the World.
  Parting Lovers.
Browning, R.   Arcades Ambo.
  Pheidippides.
  Rosny.
  Sordello.
Bukowski.   22,000 Dollars in 3 Months.
  Conversation on Morality, Eternity and
  Copulation, A.
  Night They Took Whitey, The.
  Soirée.
Burns, R.   Battle of Sherra-Moor, The.
  Killiecrankie.
  Scots Wha Hae.
  Silver Tassie, The.
  Song: "O, Logan, sweetly didst thou glide."
  There Was a Bonie Lass.
  Up and Warn A' Willie.
  When wild War's deadly blast was blawn.
Byron, G.   By the Rivers of Babylon We Sat
  Down and Wept.
  Siege of Corinth, The.
  Song of Saul before His Last Battle.
  Song to the Suliotes.
  Translation of the Famous Greek War Song
  Deute Paides Tov Ellenon.
  Very Mournful Ballad, A.
Carew, T.   On Mistress N.
Carruth, H.   Algeria.
  Birds of Vietnam, The.
  Cappadocian Song.
  On Being Asked to Write a Poem Against the
  War in Vietnam.
  President's Speech, The.
  When Howitzers Began.
Cavafy.   Battle of Magnesia, The.
  Before Antiochus Epiphanis.
Chuang Tzu.   Advising the Prince.
Chumacero.   Wanderings of the Tribe, The.
Ciardi, J.   Baboon and the State, The.
  Bashing the Babies.
  Captain Nicholas Strong.

Chelsea Naval Hospital.
  Death of a Bomber.
  Expendability.
  Health of Captains, The.
  Hometown after a War.
  Letter from an Island.
  Monday Morning: London.
  Poem for My Twenty-ninth Birthday.
  Reply to S. K.
  Ritual for Singing Bat.
  Saipan.
  Spring Song ("Do you remember by morning
  when the sun").
  Thought about Sheik Bedreddin, A.
  Three Eggs Up.
  To Lucasta, about That War.
  Wafflebutt.
Clampitt.   Amherst.
  Anniversary, The.
  War Memorial, The.
Clough.   Alteram Partem.
Codrescu.   All Wars Are Holy.
Coleridge, S.   British Stripling's War-Song, The.
  Fire, Famine, and Slaughter.
Cooper, J.   For a Boy Born in Wartime.
  Meteors.
Corbett, W.   Desert Storm.
Crane, S.   All-feeling God, hear in the war-
  night.
  Do not weep, maiden, for war is kind.
  Fast rode the knight.
  Once there came a man.
  Soldier, young in years, young in ambitions, A.
  Tell brave deeds of war.
  There was crimson clash of war.
Creeley.   One World.
  War & Peace.
Cummings, E. E.   Along the justexisting road to
  Roupy.
  Hello is what a mirror says.
  I Sing of Olaf Glad and Big.
  I'm / asking / you dear to.
  My sweet old etcetera.
  Next to of Course God America I.
  Where's Jack Was / General Was.
Davie, D.   To a Staffordshireman, from a Devon
  Villa.
  War Criminal.
  Women and War.
De la Mare.   Marionettes, The.
  Motley.
  Truce.
Dickey, J.   Between Two Prisoners.
  Drinking from a Helmet.
  Lakes of Värmland.
Dickey, W.   Virginia Woolf Gathers Mushrooms.
Dickinson, E.   Their Barricade against the Sky.
  There's the Battle of Burgoyne.
Dubie.   Grand Illusion.
Dugan, A.   Brutalization under the Heart of
  Peace.
  General Prothalamion for Wartimes.
  General Prothalamion in Populous Times.
  On an East Wind from the Wars.
  On Shields. Against World War 3.
  Stentor and Mourning.
  War Duty.
Eberhart, R.   Airman Considers His Power, An.
  At the End of the War.
  Fury of Aerial Bombardment, The.
  Protagonists.
  World War.
Eliot, T. S.   Note on War Poetry, A.
Emerson, R.   Land was all electric, The.
Enzensberger, H.   Thoughts on the Run 1.
Fenton, J.   Cambodia.
  Children in Exile.
  Chosun.
  Dead Soldiers.
  In a Notebook.
  Nest of Vampires.
  Prison Island.
  Staffordshire Murderer, A.
  Wind.
Gallagher, T.   Harmless Streets.
Ginsberg, A.   Under the World There's a Lot of

Ass, a Lot of Cunt.
Glück, L.   Pictures of the People in the War.
Graves, R.   All Except Hannibal.
Apples and Water.
Armistice Day, 1918.
Field-Postcard, The.
Spoils.
Gray, T.   Death of Hoel, The.
Triumphs of Owen, The.
Grillparzer.   Field-Marshal Radetzky.
Gunn, T.   Adolescence.
Gurney, I.   First Time In.
Mangel-Bury, The.
Soft Rain.
Strange Hells.
War Poet.
"H. D."   Telesila.
Hacker, M.   Before the War.
Hall, D.   Body Politic, The.
Sister on the Tracks, A.
HaNagid.   First War.
Hardy, T.   Channel Firing.
In Time of "The Breaking of Nations."
Man He Killed, The.
Often When Warring.
Sick Battle-God, The.
Hayden, R.   Monet's "Waterlilies."
Heliodorus.   Beginning of Heliodorus, The.
Herrick.   Blame.
Clemency.
Eyes, The.
Hand and Tongue, The.
Hope Heartens.
Multitude.
Pardons.
Possesions.
Rainbow, The.
Things of Choice, Long a Comming.
To the Lord Hopton, on His Fight in Cornwall.
Vow to Mars, A.
Warre.
Housman.   Day of Battle, The.
Deserter, The.
Jar of Nations, The.
Recruit, The.
Howe, S.   Chanting at the Crystal Sea.
Pythagorean Silence.
Secret History of the Dividing Line.
Hughes, L.   Battle Ground.
Comment on War.
Mother in Wartime.
Some Day.
War.
Wisdom and War.
Without Benefit of Declaration.
Hughes, T.   Bayonet Charge.
For the Duration.
Last of the 1st/5th Lancashire Fusiliers, The.
Out.
Retired Colonel, The.
Scapegoats and Rabies.
Warriors of the North, The.
Woman Unconscious, A.
Ignatow, D.   Statement for the Times.
Jackson, L.   Regret of War Ways.
Victory, The.
Jacobsen, J.   For Wilfred Owen.
Jarrell, R.   Automaton, The.
Come to the Stone.
Dream of Waking, The.
Eighth Air Force.
Fat, aging, the child clinging to her hand.
Germans Are Lunatics, The.
Lullaby, A: "For wars his life and half a world
away."
Machine-Gun, The.
Nursery Rhyme, A.
Pilot from the Carrier, A.
Rising Sun, The.
Sick Nought, The.
Soldier, The.
War, A.
When Achilles fought and fell.
Wide Prospect, The.
Jeffers, R.   Air-Raid Rehearsals.
Antrim.

At the Birth of an Age.
Bloody Sire, The.
Bowl of Blood, The.
Calm and Full the Ocean.
Carmel.
Dead to Clemenceau: November 1929, The.
Eagle Valor, Chicken Mind.
Eye, The.
Fantasy.
Fire.
Historical Choice.
I saw a regiment of soldiers shuffling and
stumbling.
King of Beasts, The.
Moments of Glory.
Moon and Five Planets.
Neutrals, The.
Orca.
Real and Half Real.
Rearmament.
Skunks.
So Many Blood-Lakes.
Staggering Back Toward Life.
That Noble Flower.
To Kill in War Is Not Murder.
Urchin, The.
We Are Those People.
What Odd Expedients.
What of It?
Wilson in Hell.
Jonson, B.   Epigram. To William, Earl of
Newcastle, An.
Speech According to Horace, A.
Keats.   See, the Ship in the Bay Is Riding.
Kinnell.   Dead Shall Be Raised Incorruptible,
The.
Kinsella, T.   Remembering Old Wars.
Kipling, R.   Anvil, The.
Benfactors, The.
Boots.
Cold Iron.
Dane-Geld.
Dutch in the Medway, The.
Edgehill Fight.
For All We Have and Are [1914].
Ford o' Kabul River.
French Wars, The.
Fuzzy-Wuzzy.
Grave of the Hundred Dead, The.
Gunga Din.
Hymn before Action.
Storm Cone, The.
That Day.
Together.
Widow's Party, The.
With Scindia to Delhi.
Kizer, C.   On a Line from Valéry.
Wars in Sweden, The.
Komunyakaa.   At the Screen Door.
Kumin, M.   History Lesson.
Kunitz, S.   Foreign Affairs.
Hemorrhage, The.
Last Picnic, The.
Reflection by a Mailbox.
Signal from the House, The.
Larkin, P.   Homage to a Government.
MCMXIV.
Laughlin, J.   This One Rhymes.
Lawrence, D. H.   At the Front.
Attack, The.
Attila.
Bombardment.
Combative Spirit, The.
Future War.
Going Back.
Late War, The.
Noise of Battle.
On the March.
Peace and War.
Rondeau of a Conscientious Objector.
Song of a Man Who Has Come Through.
War-Baby.
Winter-Lull.
Levertov.   Advent 1966.
Grey August.
In Thai Binh (Peace) Province.

Life at War.
Listening to Distant Guns.
May Our Right Hands Lose Their Cunning.
Pilots, The.
Speech: For Antidraft Rally, D.C., March 22,
1980, A.
Tenebrae.
Levi, P.   Partisan.
Levine, P.   And the Trains Go On.
Baby Villon.
Heaven.
How Much Can It Hurt?
Planting.
To Cipriano, in the Wind.
Li Po.   Lament of the Frontier Guard.
Lindsay, N.   Curse for Kings, A.
King Arthur's Men Have Come Again.
Scissors-Grinder, The.
Unpardonable Sin, The.
Voice of St. Francis of Assisi, The.
Yankee Doodle.
Logan, J.   Letter to a Young Father in Exile.
Logue, C.   Loyal to the King.
Longfellow, H.   Arsenal at Springfield, The.
MacLeish.   German Girls!, The. The German
Girls!
Invocation to the Social Muse.
National Security.
Spanish Lie, The.
Too-Late Born, The.
Two Poems from the War.
What the Old Women Say.
MacNeice.   Aftermath.
Carrickfergus.
Death of an Actress.
Mixer, The.
Rites of War.
Swing-Song.
Mahon.   Afterlives.
One of These Nights.
Mallarmé.   Little Air (Martial).
Marvell.   Horatian Ode upon Cromwell's Return
from Ireland, An.
McGrath, T.   Encounter.
Fresco: Departure for an Imperialist War.
Nocturne Militaire.
Ordonnance.
Theory, A.
Melville, H.   Apathy and Enthusiasm.
Conflict of Convictions, The.
Utilitarian View of the Monitor's Fight, A.
Meredith, G.   Alternation.
At the Close.
Call, The.
England before the Storm.
Friend, when the thundercloud is low.
Grandfather Bridgeman.
Hatton's "God of War."
Lord of old has dealt in blood, The.
New Era the Army of the Future the Egg of an
Army, The.
On the Danger of War.
Song: "Twelve arrows, and a bow, and spear."
Three Eagles and the Sleepy Lion, The.
To Colonel Charles.
To the Merry Men of France.
War.
Ye noble Lords who bravely fight.
Meredith, W.   Battlewagon.
For Air Heroes.
Navy Field.
Merrill, J.   Nike.
Merton.   Fable for a War.
Great Men of Former Times, The.
Lent in a Year of War.
Long Enough.
Night Train, The.
Poem: 1939.
Merwin.   Ash.
War, The.
When the War Is Over.
Millay, E.   Apostrophe to Man.
Come home, victorious wounded!—let the dead.
Invocation to the Muses.
Memory of England.
Poem and Prayer for an Invading Army.

Read history: so learn your place in Time.
To the Maid of Orleans.
Milosz, C.   Book in the Ruins, A.
Earth.
Flight.
Legend, A.
Mister Hanusevich.
Preparation.
Sarajevo.
Song on Porcelain.
Spirit of the Laws, The.
Montale.   Anniversary.
Day and Night.
Distant, I was with you when your father.
Fan, The.
Frost on the windowpanes; the sick.
In Sleep.
Valmorbia, flowering clouds of plants.
Your Flight.
Moore, M.   In Distrust of Merits.
To Military Progress.
Muldoon, P.   Brock.
Meeting the British.
Nemerov.   Armistice.
Bacterial War, The.
Fable of the War, A.
For the Squadron.
For W———, Who Commanded Well.
Memory of the War, A.
Old Soldiers' Home, The.
Old Warplane, An.
On Getting Out Of Vietnam.
Peace in Our Time.
Redeployment.
Returning to Europe.
September Shooting.
Soldier Who Lived Through the War, The.
To Clio, Muse of History.
Trial and Death, a Double Feature.
Niedecker.   1937.
I fear this war.
Tell me a story about the war.
They came at a pace.
To war they kept.
War.
Olson, C.   Encounter, The.
Trinacria.
Oppen.   Survival: Infantry.
Owen, W.   A Terre.
Apologia Pro Poemate Meo.
Arms and the Boy.
At a Calvary near the Ancre.
Calls, The.
Chances, The.
Conscious.
Disabled.
Dulce et Decorum Est.
Exposure.
Fragment: "Cramped in that funnelled hole, they
watched the dawn."
Futility.
Insensibility.
Inspection.
Last Laugh, The.
Le Christianisme.
Letter, The.
Mental Cases.
Next War, The.
Parable of the Old Men and the Young, The.
S.I.W.
Send-Off, The.
Sentry, The.
Show, The.
Six o'clock in Princes Street.
Smile, Smile, Smile.
Soldier's Dream.
Sonnet: "Be slowly lifted up, thou long black
arm."
Spring Offensive.
Strange Meeting.
Pagis.   Beginning, The.
Twenty Years in the Valley.
Paley, G.   Connections: Vermont Vietnam (II).
People in My Family.
What If (This Week).
Parker, D.   Slackers; A Hate Song.

Patchen.   Among Ourselves and with All
Nations.
And He Had Wilder Moments.
And When Freedom Is Achieved.
Attila.
Avarice and Ambition Only Were the First
Builders of Towns and Founders of Empire.
Battle of Unameit, The.
Behold, One of Several Little Christs.
Being so hideous that the air weeps blood.
Billion Freedoms, The.
Boxers Hit Harder When Women Are Around.
But the Images of His Former Dreams Still
Haunted Him.
Can the Harp Shoot Through Its Propellers?
Class of 1934.
Climate of War, The.
Encounter at Nightfall.
Eve of St. Agony, or the Middle Class Was
Sitting on Its Fat.
Executions in Moscow, The.
Fields of Earth.
Firing, The.
First Crusades, The!
Heine, Too, Lived in Germany.
Hymn to a Trench Gun.
Known Soldier, The.
Last Full Measure of Devotion, The.
Leaflet (One).
Leaflet (Two).
Letter to the Young Men, A.
Letter to Those Who Are About to Die.
Loyalty Is the Life You Are.
O Howling Cells.
Old Lean Over the Tombstones, The.
Peter's Diary in Goodentown.
Poem: "Feeling chilled in that cold country."
Poem in the Form of a Letter: to Lauro de
Bosis.
Soldier and the Star, The.
Stars go to sleep so peacefully, The.
Strange thing I said to Sam is the way they die,
The.
There are no losses.
These Have Gone with Silent Hands, Seeking.
These Unreturning Destinies.
This Early Day.
This Man Was Your Brother.
Though I Had Much More To Say.
Thus Far So Nobly Advanced.
We Mutually Pledge to Each Other.
What Happened in the Camps.
What I'd like to know is.
When in the Course of Human Events.
You May All Go Home Now.
Petrarch.   Hannibal won indeed, yet failed to
take.
O Italy, my land, words cannot heal.
Piercy.   Peaceable Kingdom, The.
Plath.   Thin People, The.
Pound, E.   Sestina: Altaforte.
Ralegh, S.   Giants did advance their wicked
hand, The.
Ramanujan.   Bosnia.
Engagement.
Rexroth, K.   Light on the Pewter Dish, The.
Me Again.
Phoenix and the Tortoise, The.
Requiem for the Spanish Dead.
Stone and Flower.
Strength through Joy.
Riley, J.   Morton.
Rimbaud, A.   Evil.
War.
Ritsos.   News Report.
Robinson, E.   Field of Glory, The.
Rossetti, C.   For One Sake.
Massacre of Perugia, The.
Rukeyser, M.   All Souls.
Another Day. Paul in the Mountains of Fantasy.
Paul Tells His Adventure.
Chapultepec Park / II.
Correspondences.
Cruise, The.
Deep in the Century of Opposites.
Don Baty, the Draft Resister.

Eighth Elegy. Children's Elegy.
Facing Sentencing.
Father dreams that he was hid in a tree, The.
His Head is Full of Faces.
How We Did It.
It Is There.
Käthe Kollwitz.
Lat. 10 Degrees North, Long. 45 Degrees West.
Letter to the Front.
Long Past Moncada.
Looking.
M-Day's Child is Fair of Face.
Mendings.
My toes feel like nothing they are so cold.
Noguchi.
Not Yet.
Now he plays with the other children.
One Soldier.
Otherworld.
Poem: "I lived in the first century of world
wars."
Poem Out of Childhood.
Power of war leads to a plan of lives, The.
Sixth Elegy. River Elegy.
Sundays, They Sleep Late.
Tenth Elegy. Elegy in Joy.
This is going to be about smoke.
Welcome from War.
What Have You Brought Home from the Wars?
When he began to witness, it was not to a
journey.
Who in One Lifetime.
Sandburg, C.   Among the Red Guns.
And They Obey.
Bas-Relief.
Black Horizons.
Buttons.
Choices.
Crimson Changes People.
Dunes.
Fight.
Forgotten Wars.
Graves.
House.
Iron.
Jan, the Son of Thomas.
John Ericsson Day Memorial, 1918.
Killers.
Long Guns.
Memoir.
Memoir of a Proud Boy.
Mr. Longfellow and His Boy.
Murmurings in a Field Hospital.
New Feet.
Old Osawatomie.
Out of White Lips.
Peace Between Wars.
Places.
Prayer after World War.
Ready to Kill.
Remembered Women.
Salvage.
Smoke.
Statistics.
Three Pieces on the Smoke of Autumn.
Threes.
Unknown War, The.
Wars.
Sarton, M.   We'll to the Woods No More, the
Laurels Are Cut Down.
Schuyler, J.   May, 1972.
Scott, S.   On the Massacre of Glencoe, 1692.
Seifert.   At the Tomb of the Czech Kings.
Sexton.   Papa and Mama Dance, The.
Shapiro, K.   Conscientious Objector, The.
Scyros.
Shelley, P.   Ode Written October, 1819, An.
Simic.   Black Days.
Empire of Dreams.
Place, The.
Prodigy.
Smith, S.   Bye Baby Bother.
Come On, Come Back.
Poets Are Silent, The.
Who Shot Eugenie?
Spender, S.   Conscript, The.

Cornet Cornelius Rilke.
Epilogue to a Human Drama.
Hamburg, 1929.
In 1929.
Shadow of War.
Stafford, W. 1940.
Dedication, A: "We stood by the library. It was
an August night."
Entering History.
Epitaph Ending in And, The.
For the Unknown Enemy.
How It Is.
It Still Happens Now.
Learning.
Men.
Old Glory.
Some Remarks When Richard Hugo Came.
Something to Declare.
Time Capsule.
Wind from a Wing, A.
Stevens, W. Dry Loaf.
Gigantomachia.
Man and Bottle.
Repetitions of a Young Captain.
Stock, R. Pantoum on Some Lines From
Camões.
Trajectory of a Scream.
Swinburne. May Janet.
Szymborska, W. End and Beginning.
Reality Demands.
Some People.
We knew the world backwards and forwards.
Tate, A. Ode to Our Young Pro-consuls of the
Air.
Thomas, D. Hand That Signed the Paper, The.
Thoreau. When with pale cheek and sunken eye
I sang.
Unknown. Battle of Brunanburh.
Very. Faith in Time of War.
War, The.
Walcott. Beachhead.
Walker, A. Enemy, The.
Warren, R. Crusade.
Interjection #4: Bad Year, Bad War: A New
Year's Card, 1969.
Shoes In Rain Jungle.
Whalen, P. War Poem for Diane di Prima.
Whitman, W. As I Ponder'd [or Pondered] in
Silence.
Beat! Beat! Drums!
Columbian's Song, The.
Mystic Trumpeter, The.
Old War-Dreams.
Respondez!
To Thee Old Cause.
Whittier. Judith at the Tent of Holofernes.
Wilbur, R. Agent, The.
Another Voice.
First Snow in Alsace.
Fourth of July, The.
Looking into History.
Mined Country.
On Freedom's Ground.
Peace of Cities, The.
Place Pigalle.
Williams, C. K. Creams.
Dream, The.
How Humble We Were before This.
I Am the Bitter Name.
In the Heart of the Beast.
Last Deaths, The.
Little Shirt, The.
War.
Williams, M. La Ultima Carta: A Young Wife
Writes to Her Husband in the Mountains.
On Seeing a Photograph by Mathew Brady.
Williams, W. Illegitimate Things.
These.
Threnody: "Christian coin, The."
War, the Destroyer.
Wilner, E. Coda, Overture.
Conversation with a Japanese Student.
Wordsworth, W. 1811.
Anticipation. October, 1803.
Germans on the Heights of Hochheim, The.
Is there a power that can sustain and cheer.

Lines on the Expected Invasion 1803.
Ode: 1814.
Say, what is Honour?—"Tis the finest sense."
Sonnet in the Pass of Killicranky.
Wright, J. Mad Fight Song for William S.
Carpenter, 1966, A.
Yeats. Ancestral Houses.
I See Phantoms of Hatred and of the Heart's
Fullness and of the Coming Emptiness.
Irish Airman Foresees His Death, An.
Meditations in Time of Civil War.
My Descendants.
My House.
My Table.
On Being Asked for a War Poem.
Road at My Door, The.
Rose of Battle, The.
Stare's Nest by My Window, The.
Valley of the Black Pig, The.
What Was Lost.
Zagajewski. Death of a Pianist.
New World.
September Afternoon in the Abandoned
Barracks.
Twenty-Year-Old Soldiers.
Zukofsky, L. "One oak fool box";—the pun.
See also **Soldiers; War Casualties; War Dead**
War Casualties
Amichai [or Amikhai]. Huleikat—The Third
Poem about Dicky.
In the long nights our room was closed off and.
Lips of dead men whisper where they lie, The.
My father spent four years inside their war.
Preface first: the two of them, the brittle, A.
They Lied to Us.
Bierce. Year's "Casualties", A.
Bly, R. Driving through Minnesota during the
Hanoi Bombings.
Brodsky, J. Kolo.
Bukowski. On Seeing an Old Civil War
Painting with My Love.
Simplicity of Everything in Viet Nam, The.
Carruth, H. Song: So Often, So Long I Have
Thought.
Ciardi, J. Captain Nicholas Strong.
Ritual for Singing Bat.
Cummings, E. E. It's jolly / odd what pops into.
Dove, R. Bird Frau, The.
Eberhart, R. Protagonists.
World War.
Emerson, R. Inscription on a Well in Memory
of the Martyrs of the War.
Fenton, J. Children in Exile.
Dead Soldiers.
Prison Island.
Staffordshire Murderer, A.
Vacant Possession, A.
Ferlinghetti, L. Third World Calling.
Gurney, I. Mangel-Bury, The.
"H. D." R.A.F.
Hacker, M. Before the War.
Hardy, T. At the War Office, London.
Hughes, L. Casualty.
Jarrell, R. Field Hospital, A.
Sick Nought, The.
Terms.
Ward in the States, A.
Kinnell. Dead Shall Be Raised Incorruptible,
The.
Meredith, W. Carrier.
Muldoon, P. Field Hospital, The.
Owen, W. A Terre.
Chances, The.
Conscious.
Dead-Beat, The.
Disabled.
Dulce et Decorum Est.
Futility.
Letter, The.
Mental Cases.
Sentry, The.
Patchen. This Man Was Your Brother.
Rukeyser, M. Bringing.
Leg in a Plaster Cast, A.
Thomas, D. Among Those Killed in the Dawn
Raid Was a Man Aged a Hundred.

War of the G

Ceremony By the
Eliot, T. S. To th
Emerson, R. Co
Graves, R. Devi
Gray, T. Death o
Gurney, I. To Hi
Hamill, S. Dres
Hardy, T. At the
Casterbridge Ca
Drummer Hodg
I Looked Up fr
Man He Killed,
Sea Fight, The.
Son's Portrait,
Souls of the Sl
Wife in London
Heaney, S. In
Hill, G. Funera
Housman. Ast
Day of Battle,
Defeated, The.
Epitaph.
Epitaph on an
Farewell to a
On the idle hil
Recruit, The.
Hughes, T. Si
Jarrell, R. 19
Burning the
Come to the
Dead in Mela
Dead Wingm
Death of the
For the Mad
Gunner.
Losses.
New Georgi
Protocols.
Second Air
Subway fro
Jeffers, R.
Resurrectio
Kipling, R.
Children, T
Death-Bed,
Dirge of D
Epitaphs o
General Jo
Gethseman
Hyænas [
King's Pil
London S
Lord Rob
Memories
Mesopota
My Boy
Ode: "So
endure
Recantati
Rimmon
Soldier,
Komunya
Facing
For the
Nude In
Please.
To Hav
We Ne
Kumin,
Kunitz,
Larkin,
Leverto
Logan,
Lowell,
Holy
MacDi
of M
At the
MacL
Lines
Mem
Youn
McGr
Ode
Read
Melvi

Sea, A.
Indians Who Died in Africa.
ord Hymn.
s Advice to Story-Tellers, The.
Hoel, The.
Love.
en Cattle.
War Office, London.
tains, The.

m My Writing.
The.

he.
in, The.
, A.
Memoriam Francis Ledwidge.
l Music.
onomy.
The.

Army of Mercenaries.
name and a number.
l of summer.

x Young Men.
45: The Death of the Gods.
Letters.
Stone.
nesia, The.
an, The.
Ball Turret Gunner, The.
id Road.

.

Force.
n New Britain to the Bronx, The.
Drunken Charlie.
n.
American Rebellion, The.
he.
A.
ead Sisters.
the War [1914–1918].
ubert.
e.
r Hyenas], The.
rimage, The.
one.
rts.

mia.
ack.
long as memory, valour, and faith
"
on, A.

oldier.
aa. Between Days.
.
Walking Dead.
errogation.

Danced with Death.
er Know.
M. Casablanca.
. Customs Collector's Report, The.
P. MCMXIV.
. Two Variations.
. Lament for Misenus.
R. For the Union Dead.
nnocents, The.
rmid, H. Another Epitaph on an Army
ercenaries.
Cenotaph.
sh. Family Group.
for an Interment.
orial Rain.
g Dead Soldiers, The.
th, T. All the Dead Soldiers.
for the American Dead in Korea.
ing the Names of the Vietnam War Dead.
le, H. Inscription: "To them who crossed

the flood."
Meredith, G. Blest is the sword that leaps from
   sheath.
Merton. Bombarded City, The.
For My Brother: Reported Missing In Action,
   1943.
Long Enough.
Two British Airmen.
Nemerov. For W————, Who Commanded
   Well.
Neruda. Wars, The.
Owen, W. Anthem for Doomed Youth.
Asleep.
Dulce et Decorum Est.
Fragment: "As bronze may be much beautified."
Futility.
Greater Love.
Has Your Soul Sipped?
Inspection.
Last Laugh, The.
Miners.
Next War, The.
Send-Off, The.
Strange Meeting.
Paley, G. I Gave Away That Kid.
Ransom, J. Necrological.
Rexroth, K. At Lake Desolation.
Riley, J. Decoration Day on the Place.
Home-Voyage, The.
Last Words.
Monument for the Soldiers, A.
Old Man and Jim, The.
Sandburg, C. Grass.
Simonides. On a Military Graveyard.
Stevens, W. Dutch Graves in Bucks County.
Tate, A. Ode to the Confederate Dead.
Tate, J. Lost Pilot, The.
Tennyson, A. Charge of the Light Brigade, The.
Uhland. Good Comrade, The.
Warren, R. Two Studies in Idealism: Short
   Survey of American and Human History.
Whitman, W. As Toilsome I Wander'd
   Virginia's Woods.
Ashes of Soldiers.
Ashes of Soldiers: Epigraph.
Bravest Soldiers, The.
Camps of Green.
Come Up from the Fields Father.
Dirge for Two Veterans.
Look Down Fair Moon.
Pensive on Her Dead Gazing.
Reconciliation.
Sight in Camp [in the Daybreak Gray and Dim],
   A.
Vigil Strange I Kept on the Field One Night.
Williams, T. Reveille.
With Military Honors.
Yeats. Irish Airman Foresees His Death, An.
See also **Soldiers**
War of the Grand Alliance
Browning, R. Hervé Riel.
Warblers
Ciardi, J. In Some Doubt but Willingly.
Warren, R. Weather Report.
Warning
Baudelaire. Epigraph for a Condemned Book.
Berry, W. Warning to My Readers, A.
Bukowski. I Don't Need a Bedsheet with Slits
   for Eyes to Kill You In.
Carew, T. Deposition from Love, A.
Chaucer. Lenvoy de Chaucer a Bukton.
De la Mare. Beware!
Not that way.
Outskirts, The.
Dove, R. Primer for the Nuclear Age.
Dugan, A. Admonitor: A Pearl for Arrogance.
Eberhart, R. Going Backward Going Forward.
Graves, R. Gorgon Mask.
Herrick. Bellman, The.
Upon Luggs.
Housman. I wake from dreams and turning.
Hughes, L. Listen Here Blues.
Kipling, R. Bell Buoy, The.
Kizer, C. Threatening Letter.
Levertov. Candles in Babylon.
Her Judgement.

Lorde. For Each of You.
MacNeice. To a Communist.
Michelangelo Buonarroti. Flee from this Love,
   you lovers; flee the flame!
Piercy. Girl in White.
Plath. Admonitions.
Ralegh, S. Sir Walter Ra[u]le[i]gh to His
   Son[ne].
Sexton. Admonitions to a Special Person.
Smith, S. Advice to Young Children.
Beware the Man.
Songe d'Athalie.
Stafford, W. Storm Warnings.
Warren, R. Pondy Woods.
Yeats. Never Give All the Heart.
Warren, Joseph
Stockton, A. On Hearing that General Warren
   Was Killed on Bunker-Hill.
Warren, Robert Penn
Tate, A. To a Romantic.
Wilner, E. American Sublime, The: Robert
   Penn Warren.
Warsaw, Poland
Davie, D. Meeting of Cultures, A.
Milosz, C. Aleksander Wat's Tie.
Campo dei Fiori.
In Warsaw.
Mid-Twentieth-Century Portrait.
Songs of Adrian Zieliński.
Wanda.
Warts
Muldoon, P. Cure for Warts, The.
Warwickshire, England
Davie, D. Warwickshire.
Washing
Amichai [or Amikhai]. Ballad of the Washed
   Hair.
Bishop, E. Under the Window: Ouro Prêto.
Gallagher, T. Ritual of Memories, The.
Gurney, I. When March Blows.
Herrick. Another.
Sincerity.
Jacobsen, J. Dishwasher as Absolution.
Sandburg, C. Brainwashing.
Williams, C. K. They wash you / when.
See also **Baths and Bathing**
Washing Machines
See **Laundry and Laundering**
Washington, Booker Taliaferro
Dunbar, P. Booker T. Washington.
To Booker T. Washington.
Hughes, L. Alabama Earth.
Ballad of Booker T.
Washington, D.C.
Bishop, E. View of the Capitol from the Library
   of Congress.
Brodsky, J. Lines for the Winter Recess.
Once More by the Potomac.
View from the Hill.
Clampitt. Dahlia Gardens, The.
Dove, R. Banneker.
Eberhart, R. Gods of Washington, D.C, The.
Emerson, R. One night he dreamed of a palace
   fair.
Logan, J. Monument and the Shrine, The.
Lowell, R. July in Washington.
March 1, The.
Meredith, W. Homage to Paul Mellon, I. M.
   Pei, Their Gallery, and Washington City.
On Jenkins' Hill.
Milosz, C. Journey, The.
Piercy. Gift of Light, A.
Rich, A. Capital, The.
Riley, J. Down to the Capital.
Rukeyser, M. City of Monuments.
Sandburg, C. And So Today.
Smoke Rose Gold.
Tangibles.
Schuyler, J. Hymn to Life.
Shapiro, K. Washington Cathedral.
Snyder, G. It Pleases.
Travelling to the Capital.
Tate, A. Aeneas at Washington.

Updike. Sin City, D.C.
  Washington.
  Washington: Tourist View.
Whitman, W. How Solemn as One by One.
Whittier. Astræa at the Capitol.
  At Washington.

Washington, George
Berryman. Washington in Love.
Burns, R. Ode [for General Washington's
  Birthday].
Emerson, R. Hard is it to persuade the public
  mind of its plain duty & true interest.
Nash, O. Watchman, What of the First First
  Lady?
O'Hara, F. On Seeing Larry Rivers' *Washington
  Crossing the Delaware* at the Museum of
  Modern Art.
Stockton, A. Addressed to General Washington,
  in the Year 1777.
  Epistle to General Washington [May 26, 1787].
  Impromptu on Hearing that a Print of the
  Guliteene with Our Beloved Presidents.
  Lucinda and Aminta, a Pastoral.
  Ode on the Birth Day of the Illustrious George
  Washington, An.
  On Hearing of the News of the Capture of Lord
  Cornwallis and the British Army.
  Peace, a Pastoral Dialogue.—Part the Second.
  To General Washington, An Epistle.
  To General Washington [Aug. 26, 1783].
  To the President of the United States.
  Vision, The.
Tomlinson, C. Ice Cream at Blauenberg.
Updike. February 22.
Very. Washington.
Wheatley, P. To His Excellency General
  Washington.
Whitman, W. Washington's Monument,
  February, 1885.
Whittier. Vow of Washington, The.
Zukofsky, L. George Washington.

Washington Monument
Logan, J. Monument and the Shrine, The.
Sandburg, C. Washington Monument by Night.
Whitman, W. Washington's Monument,
  February, 1885.

Washington Square, New York City
Dugan, A. Variation on "Winter's Onset from
  an Alienated Point of View."

Washington (state)
Carver, R. Bobber.
  In a Marine Light near Sequim, Washington.
Hamill, S. From the Bunkers.
Kizer, C. Running Away from Home.
McGrath, T. Beyond Seattle.
Snyder, G. Mid-August at Sourdough Mountain
  Lookout.

Wasps
Cunningham, J. Dogdays.
De la Mare. Queen Wasp, A.
Dickey, J. Springhouse, Menses, Held Apple,
  House and Beyond.
Eberhart, R. New Hampshire, February.
Jacobsen, J. Language as an Escape from the
  Discrete.
Komunyakaa. Yellowjackets.
Nash, O. Wasp, The.
Prunty. Haying.

Wat, Aleksander
Milosz, C. Aleksander Wat's Tie.

Watches
Amichai [or Amikhai]. As It Was.
Bukowski. Gold Pocket Watch, A.
Carver, R. Kafka's Watch.
Ciardi, J. My Father's Watch.
  Obsolescence.
Gallagher, T. Kidnap[p]er.
Herrick. Watch, The.
Hughes, L. Could Be.
Nash, O. I Had No Idea It Was So Late.
Ritsos. Wonder.
Simic. Watch Repair.
Updike. Omega.
See also **Clocks**

Water
Ammons. Classic.
  Contingency.
  If Anything Will Level with You Water Will.
Auden. In Praise of Limestone.
Beckett, S. Fleuves et océans.
Berry, W. Wet Time, A.
  Winter Rain, The.
Bishop, E. Under the Window: Ouro Prêto.
Bly, R. Awakening.
Bogan, L. To Be Sung on the Water.
Borges. Poem of the Fourth Element.
  Sea, The.
Broumas, O. Away from Water.
  Bride.
Cardozo. Elegy for Maria Alves.
Carew, T. To My Mistress Sitting by a River's
  Side; an Eddy.
Carruth, H. Existing Pool, The.
  Far-removed Mountain Men, The.
Carver, R. Where Water Comes Together with
  Other Water.
Ciardi, J. Watching a Kettle Boil.
Clampitt. Marine Surface, Low Overcast.
  Or Consider Prometheus.
  Times Square Water Music.
Clifton, L. Further Note to Clark.
Coleridge, S. Netherlands, The.
Crashaw. To Our Lord, upon the Water Made
  Wine.
Creeley. 1971.
  Act of Love, The.
  Birds, The.
  Birthday, A.
  Divisions.
  Down Home.
  Falling.
  Flowers.
  For an Anniversary.
  For Benny.
  For Lewis, to Say It.
  For Marisol.
  For You.
  Funny.
  Just Friends.
  Poem, A: "If the water forms."
  Pool, The.
  Rocks, The.
  Sea ("Salt and water").
  Shot.
  Sign ("What you know of me").
  Spring.
  Stomping with Catullus.
  There Is Water.
  Total Parts of a World, The.
  Water.
  Water (2).
  The ("Water / waiting far, The").
  Wish, A.
Davie, D. Waterfall at Powerscourt, The.
Dickey, J. Circuit.
  Eagle's Mile, The.
  Rain Guitar, The.
  Remnant Water.
Dickinson, E. I think that the Root of the Wind
  is Water.
Dubie. You.
Dunbar, P. Gourd, The.
  Pool, The.
Eberhart, R. Froth.
  Garden God, The.
  Ichetucknee.
  Loon Call, A.
  Sea-Ruck.
  Standards, The.
Emerson, R. As the drop feeds its fated flower.
  Water.
  You shall not love me for what daily spends.
Frost, R. West-Running Brook.
Gallagher, T. Corona.
  If Blood Were Not as Powerful as It Is.
  Reading Aloud.
  Ritual of Memories, The.
  Women's Tug of War at Lough Arrow.
García Lorca. Ballad of the Water of the Sea.
  Morning.

  Variations.
Gunn, T. Geysers, The.
Gurney, I. On Foscombe Hill.
  Water Colours.
"H. D." Pool, The.
Hacker, M. Pantoum.
Hall, D. Child, The.
  Waters.
Hamill, S. What the Water Knows.
Heaney, S. Drink of Water, A.
  Grotus and Coventina.
Herrick. Another.
  Dew Sat on Julia's Hair.
  Proof to No Purpose.
  To the Water Nymphs, Drinking at the Fountain.
Hopkins, G. I hear a noise of waters drawn
  away.
Hughes, T. How Water Began to Play.
  Man Seeking Experience Enquires His Way of a
  Drop of Water, The.
  Water.
Jarrell, R. Well Water.
Keats. Bright Star.
Kizer, C. In the First Stanza.
  Muse of Water, A.
Koch, K. Boiling Water, The.
Komunyakaa. Water.
Kumin, M. Watering Trough.
Larkin, P. Water.
Lawrence, D. H. Four, The.
  Hark in the Dusk!
  Secret Waters, The.
  Snake.
  Third Thing, The.
  Wild Common, The.
Levertov. Earthwoman and the Waterwoman,
  The.
  Fountain, The.
  Laying the Dust.
  Ripple, The.
  Well, The.
Levi, P. Flight.
Levine, P. Belief.
  Gift for a Believer.
Lowell, R. Water.
MacDiarmid, H. Glass of Pure Water, The.
  Water of Life.
MacLeish. What Any Lover Learns.
MacNeice. Genesis.
  Our Sister Water.
  Rest House, The.
Mahon. Katie at the Pool.
McHugh, H. Well.
Meredith, W. Of Kindness.
Merwin. Waters, The.
Mistral, G. Refreshment.
Niedecker. My Life by Water.
  Something in the water.
Oliver, M. At Blackwater Pond.
Olson, C. Carrying water to the Youth in Honor
  of Sappho Jane Harrison & Miss Duncan if
  She Had.
  His house / in the branches of.
  I Weep, Fountain of Jazer.
  Other Than.
  Small Birds, to Agree with the Leaves, Come in
  the Fall.
  Snow, The.
  Stone and Flower Series.
  Story, A.
Palmer, M. Notes for Echo Lake 6.
Patchen. All Is Safe.
Piercy. Unclench Yourself.
Prunty. Black Water.
  Water.
Raine, K. Bright cloud, / Bringer of rain to far
  fields.
  Monessie Gorge.
  Night in Martindale.
  Peace of Mind.
  There Shall Be No More Sea.
  Water.
Ransom, J. Persistent Explorer.
Rilke. Orphan Wind.
  Three Carriers, The.
Ritsos. Lyric Poem.

Roethke.   Cycle, The.
Long Alley, The.
Rossetti, C.   Echo from Willowwood, An.
Lord, we are rivers running to Thy sea.
Mirrors of Life and Death.
Water Spirit's Song, The.
Rukeyser, M.   Asylum Song.
Boys in the Branches.
Delta Poems.
Divining Water.
Mrs. Walpurga.
Song, from "Mr. Amazeen on the River."
Wind arrow, wind rose, the wind currents in air.
Rumi.   Inside water, a waterwheel turns.
My Worst Habit.
Question, The.
Story Water.
Sandburg, C.   Landscape.
Metamorphosis.
Pool of Bethesda.
Prairie Waters by Night.
Sarton, M.   Glass of Water, A.
In Time Like Air.
Italian Garden.
Sexton.   Lost Ingredient, The.
Water.
Smith, S.   Abominable Lake, The.
Suckling, S.   Upon Sir John Lawrence's
Bringing Water over the Hills [to My L.
Middlesex His House at Witten].
Swenson, M.   Fountains of Aix.
Szymborska, W.   Water.
Thoreau.   Such water do the gods distill.
Tomlinson, C.   Hacienda.
Logic.
On Water.
Van Duyn.   Elementary Attitudes.
Whittier.   Captain's Well, The.
Wilbur, R.   Water Walker.
Wordsworth, W.   Suggested by Mr W. Westall's
Views of the Caves, etc., in Yorkshire.
Unremitting Voice of Nightly Streams, The.
Wright, J.   All the Beautiful are Blameless.
Humming a Tune for an Old Lady in West
Virginia.
To Flood Stage Again.
Zagajewski.   River, A.
Zaturenska.   Cascades and Fountains.
Zukofsky, L.   Ways, The
When the crickets.
Xenophanes.

Water Lilies
Cummings, E. E.   Water-Lilies.
Hughes, T.   To Paint a Water Lily.
Rilke.   Water Lily.
Wordsworth, W.   Egyptian Maid; or, The
Romance of the Water Lilly, The.
Zaturenska.   Water Lilies: A Nocturne.

Waterbeds
Updike.   Insomnia the Gem of the Ocean.
To a Waterbed.

Watercolors
Cavafy.   In an Old Book.
Plath.   Watercolor of Grantchester Meadows.

Waterfalls
Burns, R.   Humble Petition of Bruar Water to
the Noble Duke of Athole, The.
Written with a Pencil, Standing by the Fall of
Fyers, near Loch-Ness.
Clampitt.   Waterfall, The.
Coleridge, S.   Thought, A.
Davie, D.   Waterfall at Powerscourt, The.
Dickey, J.   Twin Falls, The.
Dickey, W.   Silver Creek Falls.
Dubie.   Buffalo Clouds over the Maestro Hoon.
Dugan, A.   So-Called Wild Horses of the Water,
The.
Hardy, T.   Under the Waterfall.
Hopkins, G.   At a Welsh Waterfall.
Noise of falls I am possessèd by, A.
Levertov.   Poet Li Po Admiring a Waterfall,
The.
MacDiarmid, H.   Of My First Love.
Meredith, G.   By the Passeyr.
Merrill, J.   McKane's Falls.
Merwin.   Hearing.

Oliver, M.   Waterfall, The.
Ramanujan.   Waterfalls in a Bank.
Snyder, G.   By Frazier Creek Falls.
Swenson, M.   Little Rapids, The.
Tomlinson, C.   Death of Elizabeth Grieve, The.
Race, The.
Warren, R.   Part of What Might Have Been a
Short Story, Almost Forgotten.
Whalen, P.   What's New?
Whittier.   Seeking of the Waterfall, The.
Williams, W.   Paterson: The Falls.
Wordsworth, W.   Louisa [After Accompanying
Her on a Mountain Excursion].
To the Torrent at the Devil's Bridge, North
Wales, 1824.
Waterfall and the Eglantine, The.

Waterfowl
Burns, R.   On Scaring Some Waterfowl in Loch
Turit, a Wild Scene among the Hills of
Oughtertyre.
Swenson, M.   Pair, A.
Willets, The.
Wordsworth, W.   Water Fowl.

Watergate
See **Nixon, Richard Milhous**

Waterloo, Battle of (1815)
Hardy, T.   Peasant's Confession, The.
Lowell, R.   Waterloo.
Very.   On an Ear of Wheat Brought, By My
Brother, from the Field of Waterloo.
Wordsworth, W.   Occasioned by the Battle of
Waterloo February, 1816.
Occasioned by the Battle of Waterloo (the Last
Six Lines Intended for an Inscription)
February, 1816.
Ode: 1815.
Ode: The Morning of the Day Appointed for a
General Thanksgiving. January 18, 1816.

Watermelons
Riley, J.   Wortermelon Time.
Simic.   Watermelons.

Watertowers
Auden.   Watertowers, The.
Clampitt.   Cooling Tower, The.

Waterwheels
Rumi.   Waterwheel, The.

Watteau, Jean-Antoine
Pinkerton, H.   On Watteau's *Pilgrimage to
Cythera* (1717) in the Louvre.

Waves
Ammons.   Making Waves.
Bishop, E.   Wave, The.
Browning, E.   Sea-Mew, The.
Clampitt.   Marine Surface, Low Overcast.
De la Mare.   Miracle, The.
Dickey, J.   Daybreak.
Emerson, R.   Nahant.
Gunn, T.   From the Wave.
Hall, D.   Sea, The.
Hamill, S.   Watching the Waves.
Herrick.   Just Man, A.
Hughes, L.   Moonlight Night: Carmel.
Hughes, T.   Tern.
Larkin, P.   And the Wave Sings Because It Is
Moving.
Lawrence, D. H.   What Are the Wild Waves
Saying?
Levertov.   Great Wave, The.
MacLeish.   "Dover Beach"—a Note to That
Poem.
Merwin.   Inscription Facing Western Sea.
Wave, The.
Oliver, M.   Winter.
Oppen.   Party on Shipboard.
Pessoa.   One after another, hard-pressed waves.
Rich, A.   Wave, The.
Rukeyser, M.   Poem White Page White Page
Poem.
Sandburg, C.   All Day Long.
Fins.
From the Shore.
Swenson, M.   At First, at Last.
At Truro.
How Everything Happens (Based on a Study of
the Wave).

Subject of the Waves, A.
Wave and the Dune, The.
Tomlinson, C.   Headland, The.
Wilbur, R.   Beacon, The.
Waters, The.
Williams, W.   Sound of Waves, The.
Yeats.   Nineteenth Century and After, The.
Zukofsky, L.   I Sent Thee Late.

Wealth
Brontë, E.   Old Stoic, The.
Burns, R.   Auld Rob Morris.
Epistle to Captn Willm Logan at Park.
My Lady's Gown There's Gairs upon't.
Ode, Sacred to the Memory of Mrs. ——— of
———.
Ronalds of the Bennals, The.
Song: "Mark yonder pomp of costly fashion."
Twa Dogs, The.
Cavalcanti.   Sonnet: To a newly enriched Man;
reminding him of the Wants of the Poor.
Chesterton.   Good Rich Man, The.
Ciardi, J.   Bashing the Babies.
In the Rich Farmer's Field.
Clampitt.   Marginal Employment.
Nothing Stays Put.
Coleridge, S.   Lines Written at the King's Arms,
Ross, Formerly the House of the "Man of
Ross."
Cowper, W.   R.S.S.
Crane, H.   All This..
Cummings, E. E.   Ci-gît l Foetus(unborn to not
die).
IKEY(GOLDBERG)'S WORTH I'M.
It's just like a coffin's.
Lord John Unalive(having a fortune of
fifteengrand).
Davie, D.   Garden Party, The.
Reticence.
Delany, P.   Elegy on the Much Lamented Death
of Mr. Demar, the Famous Rich Usurer [or
Man], An.
Dickey, J.   Folk Singer of the Thirties, A.
Dickinson, E.   Because 'twas Riches I could
own.
I made slow Riches but my Gain.
Your Riches—taught me—Poverty.
Dugan, A.   American Variation on How Rilke
Loved a Princess and Got to Stay in Her
Castle.
Remembering an Account Executive.
Untitled Poem: "I love the way the heel of my
hand feels."
Dunbar, P.   Common Things.
Place Where the Rainbow Ends, The.
Precedent.
Emerson, R.   Chartist's Complaint, The.
Compensation.
Have ye seen the caterpillar.
Oil & Wine, / Sparkling gems, & rich attire.
Ferlinghetti, L.   Two Scavengers in a Truck,
Two Beautiful People in a Mercedes.
Frost, R.   Equalizer, An.
Lovely Shall Be Choosers, The.
Han-shan.   All I see are fools.
Greedy man who piles up wealth, A.
Here's a poem for you young lords.
Old lady who lives to the east, An.
Rich have so many cares, The.
HaNagid.   Luxuries Ease.
People Welcome the Rich.
Rich Are Small, The.
Hardy, T.   Ruined Maid, The.
Herrick.   Adversity.
Amber Bead, The.
Any Way for Wealth
Gold, before Goodnesse.
His Grange, or Private Wealth.
Poverty and Riches.
Reverence to Riches.
To His Deere God.
Upon Croot.
Hill, G.   To the (Supposed) Patron.
Hughes, L.   Advertisement for the Waldorf-
Astoria.
God to Hungry Child.
Jacobsen, J.   Pondicherry Blues.

Jarrell, R.   Three Bills.
Johnson, E.   Elegy on the Much Lamented Death of Mr. Demar, the Famous Rich Usurer [or Man], An.
Johnson, S.   Short Song of Congratulation [or To a Young Heir], A.
Vanity of Wealth, The.
Kipling, R.   Lollius.
Kizer, C.   Suppressing the Evidence.
Laughlin, J.   Gracious Living.
Lawrence, D. H.   Bathing Resort.
Choice.
Poverty.
Riches.
MacNeice.   Godfather.
Melville, H.   In a Garret.
Merton.   Songs of Experience; India, One.
Mistral, G.   Riches.
Nash, O.   Eheu! Fugaces, or, What a Difference a Lot of Days Make.
I Yield to My Learned Brother or Is There a Candlestick Maker in the House?
Lines Indited with All the Depravity of Poverty.
Pride Goeth Before a Raise or Ah, There, Mrs. Cadwallader-Smith.
Reflection of the Fallibility of Nemesis.
Terrible People, The.
O'Hara, F.   Commercial Variations.
Olson, C.   Allegory of Wealth, The.
Friend, The.
Oppen.   Guest Room.
Parker, D.   And Oblige.
Choice, The.
Fulfillment.
Rhyme of an Involuntary Violet.
To Myrtilla, On Easter Day.
Pope, A.   Epistle III, to Allen Lord Bathurst.
Epistle IV, to Richard Boyle, Earl of Burlington.
On His Grotto at Twickenham.
Rexroth, K.   Untitled: "I am fifty-two years old."
Valuta.
Rich, A.   Uncle Speaks in the Drawing Room, The.
Riley, J.   Down to the Capital.
Griggsby's Station.
Robinson, E.   Bewick Finzer.
Richard Cory.
Rossetti, C.   Light of Light.
She Came from The Uttermost Part of the Earth.
There's Snow on the Fields.
Rukeyser, M.   Gradus ad Parnassum.
Rumi.   Sheba's Hesitation.
Sandburg, C.   Child of the Romans.
Graceland.
Schuyler, J.   New Yorker, A.
Sexton.   "Daddy" Warbucks.
Money Swing, The.
Sheridan, T.   Elegy on the Much Lamented Death of Mr. Demar, An.
Smith, S.   Satin-Clad.
Villains.
Swift, J.   Elegy on the Much Lamented Death of Mr. Demar, An.
Tate, J.   Sadness of My Neighbors, The.
Tomlinson, C.   Rich, The.
Unknown.   On a True Friend.
On Late-acquired Wealth or Riches.
Updike.   Handkerchiefs of Khaibar Khan, The.
Whalen, P.   To the Memory Of.
Whitman, W.   Thought.
Whittier.   Maids of Attitash, The.
Problem, The.
Wilbur, R.   Summer Morning, A.
Williams, C. K.   Allies: According to Herodotus.
Williams, W.   Look, there goes the young lady across the street.
Wordsworth, W.   Vale of Esthwaite, The.
Yeats.   Witch, The.

Weapons
Borges.   Blade in the Northside, A.
Cummings, E. E.   It's jolly / odd what pops into. Look at this) / a 75 done.
Dickey, J.   Lakes of Värmland.
Dickinson, E.   My Life had stood—a Loaded Gun.

Emerson, R.   Vain against him were hostile blows.
Hayden, R.   Zeus over Redeye.
Ignatow, D.   I Dream I Hurl a Spear.
Kipling, R.   Benfactors, The.
Song of the Men's Side.
Levertov.   May Our Right Hands Lose Their Cunning.
Muldoon, P.   Point, The.
Niedecker.   Beautiful girl.
Owen, W.   Arms and the Boy.
Soldier's Dream.
Tomlinson, C.   Bone.
Wilbur, R.   Giaour and the Pacha, The.

Weariness
Amichai [or Amikhai].   I've Grown Very Hairy.
Jerusalem Is Full of Used Jews.
Poems of Lies and Beauty.
Poems of Resigning.
Ammons.   Correction.
Beckett, S.   Enueg I.
Enueg II.
Berry, W.   Sleep.
Blok.   Introduction to the Second Book of Poems.
Song of the Wind, The.
Bradstreet, A.   As Weary Pilgrim, Now at Rest.
Brontë, E.   Lines: "Far away is the land of rest."
Browning, E.   My Heart and I.
Burns, R.   Lord Ronald My Son.
Byron, G.   So We'll Go No More A-Roving.
Carruth, H.   August First.
Carver, R.   Autopsy Room, The.
Sensitive Girl, The.
Tomorrow.
Codrescu.   Work.
Creeley.   Eros.
Cullen, C.   Mood.
Davie, D.   Inditing a Good Matter.
Dunbar, P.   Goin' Home.
Glück, L.   Islander, The.
Gurney, I.   Brimscombe.
Herrick.   To Sycamores.
Hughes, L.   Lonesome Place.
Po' Boy Blues.
So Tired Blues.
Weary Blues, The.
Komunyakaa.   (E)Motion.
Lawrence, D. H.   Fatigue.
Nonentity.
Merwin.   Late Night in Autumn.
Michelangelo Buonarroti.   No differently the guilty wretch hangs back.
So, Love, it hasn't healed, not even the least.
To sleep, even more be made of stone: how these.
Too late for Love to set my heart aflame.
What file's incessant bite.
Whenever my past unrolls before these eyes.
Molodovsky [or Molodowsky].   White Night.
Nash, O.   Every Day Is Monday.
Olson, C.   Knowing All Ways, Including the Transposition of Continents.
Parker, D.   Ballade of a Great Weariness.
Pessoa.   Sleep that comes over me, The.
Written in a Book Abandoned on the Trip.
Petrarch.   At every step, I find I must look back.
Death has put out the sun which dazed my eyes.
Had but the light come just a little nearer.
Happy in sleep, content to lie around.
I have by now my sixteenth year of sighs.
I must direct these lines so full of sorrow.
If but these thoughts that hurt.
It makes me weary when I realise.
Long waiting has by now so worn me out.
This creature with a bear's or tiger's heart.
Riley, J.   Dead Selves.
Out-worn Sappho, An.
Tired Out.
Wandering Jew, The.
Ritsos.   Encounter.
His Lamp.
Rossetti, C.   Along the highroad the way is too long.
Annie.
Dost Thou Not Care?

Ellen Middleton.
For Thine Own Sake, O My God.
From the Antique.
Have Patience.
Hills are tipped with sunshine, while I walk / In shadows dim and cold.
How One Chose.
I love you and you know it—this at least.
I sit among the green shady valleys oft.
I toiled on, but thou.
I Will Arise.
In Progress.
Is the Moon Tired?
Looking Forward.
Lord, by what inconceivable dim road / Thou leadest man on footsore pilgrimage!
Mid-Lent.
Of My Life.
Out of the Deep.
Sleeping at Last.
There Remaineth Therefore a Rest for the People of God.
Three Nuns.
Thro' burden and heat of the day.
Vigil of the Presentation.
Weary in Well-Doing.
What to Do?
Who Have a Form of Godliness.
Whole Head Is Sick, and the Whole Heart Faint, The.
Yawn, A.
Yes, I too could face death and never shrink.
Zion Said.
Shelley, P.   Fragment: Death in Life.
Spender, S.   Driving through Snow.
Wilde, O.   Tædium Vitæ.
Williams, T.   Madrigal: "Today, I am dull, I am dull!"
Wright, C.   Primitive Journal.

Weasels
Hughes, T.   Strawberry Hill.
Moore, M.   Wood Weasel, The.
Wright, J.   Blue Teal's Mother.

Weather
Amichai [or Amikhai].   Forecast.
Ammons.   Clearing.
Ashbery, J.   Crazy Weather.
Bassani, G.   Looking Out from Ferrara.
Berry, W.   Dance, A.
Elegy: "All day our eyes could find no resting place."
Bogan, L.   Fiend's Weather.
Brodsky, J.   After Us.
Anthem: "Praised be the climate."
Brontë, E.   Will the day be bright or cloudy?
Cavafy.   Good and Bad Weather.
Collins, B.   History of Weather, A.
Cooper, J.   Bermuda.
Weather of Six Mornings, The.
Crashaw.   On a Foule Morning, Being Then to Take a Journey.
Creeley.   Business, The.
Eye o' the Storm.
To Bobbie.
Cummings, E. E.   Painted wind has sprung, A.
De la Mare.   April.
Scarecrow, The.
Dickinson, E.   Sun and Fog Contested, The.
Dugan, A.   Poem: "Always prudent but unprepared."
Travel Advisory for a Night Shift.
Eberhart, R.   Flux.
Emerson, R.   Thermometer.
Frost, R.   Voice Ways.
Graves, R.   Language of the Seasons.
Love Story, A.
Weather of Olympus, The.
Why of the Weather, The.
Gurney, I.   April—Dull Afternoon.
Friendly Are Meadows.
Hardy, T.   Division, The.
Weathers [or Weather].
Herrick.   Fair[e] Days; or, Dawn[e]s Deceitful[l].
Hope Well and Have Well: or, Faire after Foule Weather.

Hughes, L. Strange Hurt.
There's Always Weather.
Ignatow, D. Cloud Creates, A.
Jackson, L. Meanwhile.
Jacobsen, J. Escape in Ice.
MacLeish. New England Weather.
Major, C. Rainy Season, The.
Nash, O. It's Never Fair Weather.
Nemerov. Observation of October.
To Lu Chi.
Walking Down Westgate in the Fall.
Weather of the World, The.
Niedecker. I hear the weather.
Olson, C. Some partial cloudiness will flow
locally, mostly.
Paley, G. Weather.
Petrarch. Air weighed down, and the oppressive
cloud, The.
Riley, J. At Ninety in the Shade.
Whatever the Weather May Be.
Rilke. Morning Melancholy.
Roethke. Dinky.
Sandburg, C. Broken Sonnet.
New Weather.
Schuyler, J. 3/23/66.
Advent.
April and Its Forsythia.
Flashes.
October 5, 1981.
Overcast, Hot.
So Good.
Stafford, W. Weather Report.
Where We Are.
Swenson, M. Weather.
Tate, J. Pity Ascending with the Fog.
Tomlinson, C. Barometer, The.
Discrepancies.
In the Balance.
Windshield, The.
Updike. Code, The.
Very. Meteorologists, The.
Voznesensky [or Voznesenskii]. Foggy Street.
Walcott. Oddjob, a Bull Terrier.
Warren, R. Weather Report.
Whitman, W. New Year's Day, 1848.
Wilbur, R. Chronic Condition, A.
Williams, C. K. Storm, The.
Williams, M. Weatherman.
Zukofsky, L. Rains, the rains, The.

Weathervanes
Carrera Andrade. Weathercock on the Cathedral
of Quito, The.
García Lorca. Fallen Weathervane, The.
Graves, R. Arrow on the Vane.
Tomlinson, C. Weathercocks, The.

Weaving and Weavers
Blue Cloud. Pomo Basketmaker.
Burns, R. Cardin o't, The.
Gallant Weaver, The.
To the Weaver's Gin Ye Go.
Emerson, R. Natures web star broidered.
"H. D." Archer.
At Ithaca.
Herrick. To the Little Spinners.
Levertov. Soothsayer, The.
MacDiarmid, H. Seamless Garment, The.
Merwin. Shuttles, The.
Sendak. Navajo Blanket, The.
Sheridan, T. Prologue Spoke by Mr. Elrington
at the Theatre-Royal, A.
Stevens, W. Dwarf, The.
Sze. Shuttle.
Wilner, E. Without Regret.
Yeats. Fragments: "Locke sank into a swoon."

Webster, Daniel
Emerson, R. On thee has God conferred.
Poem, Spoken Before the ΦΒΚ Society, August,
1834.
Webster.
Whittier. Ichabod[!].

Wedding Songs
Herrick. Nuptiall Song, or Epithalamie, on Sir
Clipseby Crew and His Lady, A.
Hopkins, G. At the Wedding March.
Housman. Epithalamium: "He is here, Urania's
son."

Meleager. Upon a Maid That Died [or Dyed]
the Day She Was Married [or Marryed].
Shelley, P. Another Version of the Same.
Bridal Song, A: "Golden gates of Sleep unbar,
The."
Epithalamium: "Night, with all thine eyes look
down!"

Weddings
Amichai [or Amikhai]. Hymn to the Lovely
Couple Varda and Schimmel.
Bly, R. My Father's Wedding.
Burns, R. Mauchline Wedding, The.
Song: "Mark yonder pomp of costly fashion."
Campion, T. Illustrissimo, Potentissimoque
Principi, *Frederico* Quinto, Rheni Comiti
Palatino, Duci Bavariae, &c.
Carew, T. Hymeneal Song, on the Nuptials of
the Lady Ann Wentworth and the Lord
Lovelace, An.
Ciardi, J. Bridal Photo, 1906.
Cummings, E. E. Logeorge / lo / wellifitisn't
eddy how's the boy.
This little bride & groom are.
Davie, D. Energies.
De la Mare. Episodes.
Donne. Epithalamion at the Marriage of the
Earl of Somerset.
Dove, R. In the Old Neighborhood.
Variation on Gaining a Son.
Dubie. Wedding Party, The.
Dunbar, P. To Dan.
Eberhart, R. Groundhog Revisiting, The.
Wedding on Cape Rosier, A.
Gallagher, T. Four Dancers at an Irish Wedding.
Glück, L. Morning.
Graves, R. Wedding, The.
Hall, D. Wedding Party.
Hamill, S. Cartographer's Wedding, The.
Hardy, T. At a Hasty Wedding.
Church and the Wedding, The.
Country Wedding, The.
Wedding Morning, The.
Heaney, S. Mother of the Groom.
Wedding Day.
Herrick. Bride-Cake, The.
Connubii Flores, or the Well-Wishes at
Weddings.
Delaying Bride, The.
Hopkins, G. At the Wedding March.
Jonson, B. Epithalamion: or, a Song.
Kinsella, T. Wedding Morning.
Larkin, P. Wedding-Wind.
Whitsun Weddings, The.
Lawrence, D. H. Wedding Morn.
Logan, J. My Daughter's Wedding.
McHugh, H. Trouble with "In," The.
Merton. Five Virgins, The.
Milosz, C. In Music.
Mistral, G. Rat, The.
Nash, O. Here Usually Comes the Bride.
Niedecker. I rose from marsh mud.
Patchen. Letter on the Use of Machine Guns at
Weddings, A.
Temple, A.
Plath. Wreath for a Bridal.
Poe. To ———: "I saw thee on thy bridal day."
Ramanujan. Leaky Tap after a Sister's
Wedding, A.
Riley, J. On a Splendud Match.
When Maimie Married.
Robinson, E. On the Night of a Friend's
Wedding.
Rossetti, C. Boy Johnny.
"Ding a ding," / The sweet bells sing.
Love from The North.
Ring upon her finger, / Walks the bride, A.
Sandburg, C. Thin Strips.
Wedding Postponed.
Sarton, M. Lady and the Unicorn, The.
Sexton. Wedding Ring Dance, The.
Spenser, E. Epithalamion: "Ye learned sisters
which have oftentimes."
Prothalamion.
Stock, R. Slaughtering the Cow.
Stockton, A. Epithalamium, The: "Ye woodland
choirs come consecrate the lay."

Impromptu on the Morning of my Sons Weding
Day.
Wish on a Wedding Day Morning, The.
Suckling, S. Ballad[e] [upon a Wedding], A.
Sze. Tsankawi.
Tate, J. Wedding, A.
Whittier. Bridal of Pennacook, The.
Wilbur, R. Wedding Toast, A.
Williams, M. Groom Kisses the Bride and the
Mind of the Young Preacher Wanders Again,
The.
Wright, J. American Wedding.
Zukofsky, L. My nephew / And my new.
See also **Marriage**

Weeds
Ammons. Butterflyweed.
Reflective.
Berry, W. May Song.
Bishop, E. Weed, The.
Clampitt. Fireweed.
Vacant Lot with Pokeweed.
De la Mare. Bindweed, The.
Twice Lovely.
Dickey, J. Weeds.
Dugan, A. Weeds as Partial Survivors.
Eberhart, R. Stealth and Subtleties of Growth.
García Lorca. Omega.
Hughes, T. Thistles.
Lindsay, N. Dandelion, The.
Millay, E. Weeds.
Milosz, C. Thistle, the Nettle, The.
Niedecker. They've lost their leaves.
Orr, G. Weeds, The.
Patchen. There Are Two.
Roethke. Long Live the Weeds.
Weed Puller.
Sandburg, C. Bright Conversation with Saint-
Ex.
Weeds.
Thoreau. 'Tis very fit the ambrosia of the gods.
Updike. Bindweed.
Very. Sparrows and the Crop of Weeds, The.
Weiss, T. Into Summer.
Preface.
Zukofsky, L. Weeds.

Weekends
Angelou. Weekend Glory.
Dugan, A. On a Seven-Day Diary.
Gunn, T. Hotblood on Friday.
Hughes, T. Sunstruck.

Weeping
Creeley. Mommy.
On Board.
García Lorca. Casida of the Lament.
Gacela of the Morning Market.
Hughes, L. Late Last Night.
Hughes, T. Crow Tyrannosaurus.
Jacobsen, J. Tears.
Martial. 1.33: "In private she mourns not the
late-lamented."
Michelangelo Buonarroti. Flooded, the soul
pours out.
Mistral, G. Slow Rain, The.
Parker, D. Pattern.
Trusting Heart, The.
Petrarch. I saw angelic qualities on earth.
I weep all day; and in the night-time, when.
I wept, but now I sing: my living sun.
That always bitter, always honoured day.
That cheek of yours that has been tired with
weeping.
Weep, ladies; as you weep, let Love weep too.
Rexroth, K. No!
Riley, J. Almost beyond Endurance.
Old School-Chum, The.
Rainy Morning, The.
Rilke. To M.
Simic. Terms, The.
Williams, T. Which Is My Little Boy.
Zagajewski. Schopenhauer's Crying.
See also **Tears**

Weight Lifting
Ignatow, D. Gentle Weight Lifter, The.

Weil, Simone
Zagajewski. Simone Weil Watches the Rhône

Valley.

Welcome
Angelou. Arrival.
Berry, W. Long Hunter, The.
Eberhart, R. Statue of Liberty.
Herrick. Free Welcome.
To His Kinsman, Master Thomas Herrick, Who Desired to Be in His Book.
To the King, upon His Welcome to Hampton-Court.
Keats. Sweet, Sweet Is the Greeting of Eyes.
Laughlin, J. Welcome, The.
Logan, J. On the House of a Friend.
Merwin. Finally.
Riley, J. To the Quiet Observer.
Stockton, A. To the Honourable Col. Peter Schuyler.
Wheatley, P. To a Lady on Her Coming to North-America with Her Son.
Whittier. Welcome to Lowell, A.

Welfare
Angelou. Momma Welfare Roll.
Levertov. News Items.

Wellington, Arthur Wellesley, 1st Duke of
Rossetti, D. Wellington's Funeral.
Wordsworth, W. On a Portrait of the Duke of Wellington upon the Field of Waterloo, by Haydon.

Wellington, New Zealand
Creeley. It's the scale.
Night ("Born and bred / in Wellington").
That's the way.

Wells
Ammons. Turning a Moment to Say So Long.
Dickey, J. Underground Stream, The.
Dickinson, E. I know where Wells grow—Droughtless Wells.
Well upon the Brook, The.
What mystery pervades a well!
Frost, R. For Once, Then, Something.
García Lorca. Little Girl Drowned in the Well.
Hall, D. Wells.
Heaney, S. Personal Helicon.
Jarrell, R. Well Water.
Levertov. Sands of the Well.
Merwin. Well, The.
Montale. Well's pulley creaks, The.
Pagis. Toward Home.
Rich, A. Well, The.
Ritsos. Wells and People.
Sexton. What the Bird with the Human Head Knew.
Stafford, W. Well Rising, The.
Tomlinson, C. Well, The.
Wordsworth, W. Hart-Leap Well.

Welsh, The
Davie, D. Monmouthshire.
Gurney, I. First Time In.
Housman. Welsh Marches, The.

See also **Wales**

Werewolves
Atwood. Wereman, The.
Werewolf Movies.
Riley, J. Werewife, The.
Wilbur, R. Beasts.

Wessex, England
Hardy, T. Milestone by the Rabbit-Burrow, The.
Spring Call, The.
Wessex Heights.
MacNeice. Wessex Guidebook.

West Indies
Clampitt. Hispaniola.
Crane, H. O Carib Isle!
Creeley. Problem, The.
Hughes, L. Broadcast to the West Indies.
Lorde. Za Ki Tan Ke Parlay Lot.
MacLeish. St. Philip's Church in Antigua.
Walcott. Tales of the Islands.

West, Richard
Gray, T. Sonnet [on the Death of Mr. Richard West].

West, The, United States
Ammons. Wagons.
Atwood. Backdrop Addresses Cowboy.

Berry, W. July, 1773.
Brooks, G. "Strong Men, Riding Horses."
Ciardi, J. To Westward.
Crane, H. Great Western Plains, The.
Cunningham, J. I drive Westward. Tumble and loco weed.
Davie, D. Sunday Morning.
Dunbar, P. Welcome Address.
Eberhart, R. Rape of the Cataract, The.
Ginsberg, A. Green Automobile, The.
Hacker, M. Country & Western.
Hall, D. Lone Ranger, The.
Komunyakaa. They Say in Yellow Jacket.
Laughlin, J. Go West Young Man.
Highway 66.
Levertov. Settling.
MacLeish. Landscape as a Nude.
Wildwest.
MacNeice. Western Landscape.
McGrath, T. Buffalo Coat, The.
Something Is Dying Here.
Merrill, J. McKane's Falls.
Merwin. Homeland.
Western Country.
Milosz, C. Far West.
Oliver, M. Dreams.
Ransom, J. On the Road to Wockensutter.
Rukeyser, M. Sun on the faces. On the knotted rocks.
There is a knotless line westward, past terraces.
Schuyler, J. Money Musk.
Snyder, G. Milton by Firelight.
Stafford, W. Is This Feeling about the West Real?
Walking West.
Warren, R. Far West Once.
Going West.
Whitman, W. Pioneers! O Pioneers!
Promise to California, A
Wright, J. Stages on a Journey Westward.

West Virginia (state)
Davie, D. West Virginia's Auburn.
Rukeyser, M. West Virginia.
Wright, J. Mad Fight Song for William S. Carpenter, 1966, A.

West Wind
Burns, R. Of A' the Airts [the Wind Can Blow].
Herrick. To the Western Wind.
Koch, K. West Wind.
Shelley, P. Ode to the West Wind.
Sze. Singer with Eyes of Sand, A.
Warren, R. Blow, West Wind.

Westminster Abbey
Hardy, T. Refusal, A.

Weston, Edward
Dubie. Elegy to the Pulley of Superior Oblique.

Whales and Whaling
Borges. Herman Melville.
Clampitt. Or Consider Prometheus.
Dugan, A. Two Hatreds of Action.
Hamill, S. End of the Road from Nantucket, The.
Hughes, T. Little Whale Song.
Jeffers, R. Ocean.
Ocean's Tribute, The.
Kumin, M. Repent.
Kunitz, S. Ambergris.
Wellfleet Whale, The.
Merwin. For a Coming Extinction.
Shore, The.
Oliver, M. Humpbacks.
Piercy. Why the Soup Tastes Like the *Daily News.*
Raine, K. Whales.
Rexroth, K. Park in the Public's or in the Public, Parks.
Roethke. Whale, The.
Sarton, M. Jonah.
Sexton. Whale.
Swenson, M. Wednesday at the Waldorf.
Tomlinson, C. Littleton Whale, The.
Wilner, R. Knowing the Enemy.
Salute to Donald Davie.

Wharves
Bishop, E. Bight, The.

Summer's Dream, A.
Ciardi, J. Benefits of an Education, The.

Wheat
Auden. As I Walked Out One Evening.
Carver, R. Prosser.
De la Mare. Gold.
Heaney, S. Harvest Bow, The.
Herrick. Larr's Portion, and the Poets Part.
Merton. Landscape: Wheatfields.
Merwin. Chaff, The.
Niedecker. Government men said Don't plant wheat, The.
Rossetti, C. Amen.
Sandburg, C. Buckwheat.
Very. On an Ear of Wheat Brought, By My Brother, from the Field of Waterloo.
Warren, R. August Revival: Crosby Junction.

Wheatley, Phillis
Hayden, R. Letter from Phillis Wheatley, A.

Wheelbarrows
Whalen, P. Winter, The ("Wheelbarrow's tire is flat, muddy ground now sets").
Williams, W. Red Wheelbarrow, The.

Wheelchairs
Lux. Elegy for Robert Winner.
Owen, W. Disabled.

Wheeling, West Virginia
Wright, J. In Response to a Rumor that the Oldest Whorehouse in Wheeling, West Virginia, Has Been Condemned.

Wheels
Bishop, E. Wading at Wellfleet.
Crane, S. Rumbling, buzzing, turning, whirling Wheels.
Emerson, R. There is no evil but can speak.
Gunn, T. Wheel of Fortune, The.
Heaney, S. Wheels within Wheels.
Komunyakaa. (E)Motion.
Montale. Ezekiel Saw the Wheel.
Nemerov. Extract from Memoirs.
Piercy. Twelve-Spoked Wheel Flashing, The.
Pinsky. Figured Wheel, The.
Prunty. Ferris Wheel, The.
Simic. Ballad of the Wheel, The.
Stock, R. Extra-Terrestrial Function of Spokes.
Wilbur, R.

Whippoorwills
Clampitt. Whippoorwill in the Woods, A.
Cummings, E. E. Whippoorwill this / moonday into.
Dickinson, E. Feather from the Whippoorwill, A.
Dunbar, P. Whip-Poor-Will and Katy-Did.
Frost, R. Nature Note, A.
Hall, D. Whip-Poor-Will.
Warren, R. Filling Night with the Name: Funeral as Local Color.

Whiskey
Burns, R. Author's Earnest Cry and Prayer, The.
John Barleycorn [a Ballad].
Scotch Drink.
Third Epistle to J. Lapraik.
Willie Brew'd [*or* Brewed] a Peck o' Maut.
Dugan, A. Teacher's Vacation Lament in the Country.
Untitled Poem: "Two shots down and I'm exalted."
Hughes, L. Bar.
Muldoon, P. Kate Whiskey.
Nemerov. Moonshine.
Williams, W. Centenarian, The.

Whistler, James Abbott McNeill
Mallarmé. Note to Whistler.
Wilde, O. Impression du Matin.
In the Gold Room: A Harmony.
Williams, W. Period Piece: 1834.

Whistling and Whistlers
Berry, W. First, The.
Bishop, E. Behind Stowe.
Dunbar, P. Breaking the Charm.
Just Whistle a Bit.
with music.
Komunyakaa. Whistle, The.
Riley, J. Stanzas for a New Song.

Tate, J.   Indian Undertaker, The.

White (color)
Berry, W.   Green and White.
Carew, T.   Red and White Roses.
Cavafy.   La Jeunesse Blanche.
Clampitt.   White.
Creeley.   Blue.
  Gift, The.
Dickey, J.   Expanses.
Eberhart, R.   Emblem.
Herrick.   To Electra.
Hughes, L.   Angels Wings.
Levertov.   Wings, The.
Milosz, C.   Whiteness.
Pasternak, B.   White Night.
Rilke.   White Lily.
Ritsos.   Experiences.
  Whitewash.
Rossetti, C.   Ballad: "Soft white lamb in the daisy meadow."
  They Shall Be as White as Snow.
  Whitsun Eve.
Sandburg, C.   Clean Curtains.
  March of the Hungry Mountains.
Schuyler, J.   White.
Simic.   What the White Had to Say.
Walcott.   Goats and Monkeys.
Williams, C. K.   Fast Food.

Whitefield, George
Davie, D.   Homage to George Whitefield.
Wheatley, P.   On the Death of the Rev. Mr. George Whitefield [1770].
Whittier.   Preacher, The.

Whiteouts
Sze.   Whiteout.

Whitman, Walt
Berrigan, T.   Whitman in Black.
Borges.   Camden, 1892.
  Lines That Could Have Been Written and Lost Round About 1922.
Bukowski.   When the Berry Bush Dies I'll Swim Down the Green River with My Hair on Fire.
Ciardi, J.   Instances.
Clampitt.   Seed.
"Dario."   Walt Whitman.
Eberhart, R.   Emerson's Concord.
Ferlinghetti, L.   Poem for Old Walt.
Gallagher, T.   Simple Sonatina.
García Lorca.   Ode to Walt Whitman.
Ginsberg, A.   Supermarket in California, A.
Gurney, I.   As They Draw to a Close.
Hughes, L.   Old Walt.
Ignatow, D.   I Write.
  Walt Whitman in the Civil War Hospitals.
Komunyakaa.   Kosmos.
Lux.   Walt Whitman's Brain Dropped on Laboratory Floor.
MacLeish.   In and Come In.
Major, C.   September Mendocino.
Meredith, G.   Orson of the Muse, An.
Pessoa.   Salutation to Walt Whitman.
Pound, E.   Pact, A.
Smith, S.   Dear Karl.
Tomlinson, C.   Crossing Brooklyn Ferry.
Whitman, W.   Now Precedent Songs, Farewell.
Williams, W.   End of the Rope, The.

Whitsunday
See Pentecost

Whittier, John Greenleaf
Dunbar, P.   Whittier.
Koch, K.   You Were Wearing.
Riley, J.   Whittier—at Newburyport.
Whitman, W.   As the Greek's Signal Flame.

Widows and Widowers
Ai.   Ice.
  Ravine, The.
Atwood.   At first I was given centuries.
Brodsky, J.   Törnfallet.
Burns, R.   Highland Widow's Lament, The.
Carew, T.   To the Countess of Anglesey.
Carver, R.   Grief.
  Happiness in Cornwall.
  Lightning Speed of the Past, The.
Cavafy.   Anna Komnina.

Clampitt.   High Noon.
Cooper, J.   For a Very Old Man, on the Death of His Wife.
Crashaw.   Widow[e]'s Mites, The.
Davie, D.   Two Widows in Tashkent.
  Widowers.
De la Mare.   Juliet's Nurse.
  Widow, The.
Dubie.   Inside the City Walls.
  New Age at Airport Mesa.
  Widow of the Beast of Ingolstadt, The.
  Widow Speaks to the Auroras of a December Night, A.
Glück, L.   Racer's Widow, The.
Hall, D.   Widows, The.
Hardy, T.   In a London Flat.
  Memorial Brass, The: 186–.
  Rash Bride, The.
  Widow Betrothed, The.
Herrick.   Upon an Old Woman.
  Upon Hanch a Schoolmaster.
  Widow's Tears [*or* Widdowes Teares]: or, Dirge of Dorcas, The.
Hughes, L.   Widow Woman.
Jarrell, R.   Burning the Letters.
  Widow's Song, The.
Jonson, B.   Epigram. To the Honoured————, Countess of————, An.
Kipling, R.   Akbar's Bridge.
  Widower, The.
Kizer, C.   Widow in Wintertime, A.
Komunyakaa.   Way the Cards Fall, The.
Lowell, R.   For Sale.
Merton.   Widow of Naim, The.
Merwin.   After the Harvests.
Milton.   On His Deceased Wife.
Plath.   Widow.
Poe.   Annabel Lee.
Prunty.   Crosswords.
  Husband.
  Seasons.
  Widow's Halloween, The.
Riley, J.   Dead Wife, The.
  Man's Devotion.
  Mother.
  My First Womern.
  Nothin' to Say.
  One Angel.
  Young Old Man, The
Robinson, E.   Book of Annandale, The.
Roethke.   Ballad of the Clairvoyant Widow.
Rossetti, C.   Our Widowed Queen.
Simic.   Whispers in the Next Room.
Smith, S.   He Told His Life Story to Mrs. Courtly.
  Silence and Tears.
  Widowhood or The Home-Coming of Lady Ross.
Stafford, W.   Widow.
Stock, R.   Invisible Golden Sections.
Stockton, A.   Anniversary Elegy on the Death of Mr Stockton the 28th of Feb 1783.
  Elegiack Ode on the 28th Day of February 1782, An. The Anniversary of Mr. Stockton's Death.
  Elegy Inscribed to Richard J Stockton Esqr [Feb. 28, 1787].
  Resignation, an Elegiac Ode, February the 28th, 1788.
  Why wanders my friend in this grove?
Swift, J.   Fable of the Widow and Her Cat, A.
Sze.   Moon Is a Diamond, The.
Very.   Widow, The.
Wheatley, P.   To a Clergyman on the Death of His Lady.
  To a Lady on the Death of Her Husband.
  To His Honour the Lieutenant-Governor, on the Death of His Lady. *March* 24, 1773.
Williams, M.   And Then.
  Widow, The.
Williams, W.   Widow's Lament in Springtime, The.
Wordsworth, W.   Ruined Cottage, The.
  To a Sexton.
  Widow on Windmere Side, The.

Wieners, John
Corbett, W.   "Poetry," John Wieners.
  When I Read John Wieners's Selected Poems.

Wigs
Lucilius.   On an Old Woman.
Rossetti, C.   If a pig wore a wig.

Wilberforce, William
Cowper, W.   To William Wilberforce, Esq.

Wilde, Oscar
Crane, H.   C33.

Wildebeests
See Gnus

Wilderness
Ammons.   Ocean City.
Atwood.   Further Arrivals.
  Journey to the Interior.
Berry, W.   Homecoming, A.
  Peace of Wild Things, The.
  Setting Out.
Carruth, H.   Loon on Forrester's Pond, The.
Carver, R.   Beginnings.
Eberhart, R.   Fisher Cat, The.
  Old Dichotomy: Choosing Sides.
  Wild Life and Tamed Life.
Emerson, R.   Comrade of the snow & wind.
  I to my garden went.
Graves, R.   In the Wilderness.
  Rocky Acres.
Guillén, J.   Nature Alive.
Hopkins, G.   Inversnaid.
Hughes, T.   Fourth of July.
  Stealing Trout on a May Morning.
Jacobsen, J.   Bush.
Jeffers, R.   Last Conservative, The.
  Morro Bay.
Kumin, M.   You Are in Bear Country.
Lorde.   Song: "Wild trees have bought me."
Nemerov.   Two Poems.
Parker, D.   Song of the Wildnerness.
Patchen.   Sovereign of the wilderness!
Rexroth, K.   Living Pearl, A.
Robinson, E.   Wilderness, The.
Sandburg, C.   Wilderness.
  Yes, the Dead Speak to Us.
Snyder, G.   Above Pate Valley.
  Arktos.
  At Tower Peak.
  Elk Trails.
  Message from Outside.
  Straight-Creek— Great Burn.
Stafford, W.   In Fur.
  Representing Far Places.
Stevens, W.   Anecdote of the Jar.
Whitman, W.   Italian Music in Dakota.
  Spirit That Form'd This Scene.
Wilbur, R.   Castles and Distances.
Williams, W.   Song: "I'd rather read an account."

Wildflowers
Ammons.   Kind.
Blake, W.   Wild Flower's Song, The.
Clampitt.   Botanical Nomenclature.
Melville, H.   Field Asters.
Meredith, W.   Assent to Wildflowers, An.
Rossetti, D.   Woodspurge, The.
Sandburg, C.   Windflower Leaf.
Tomlinson, C.   Under the Bridge.
Williams, W.   Queen-Anne's-Lace.
  Wildflower, The.

William III, King of England (William of Orange)
Byron, G.   Conquest, The.

Williams, Tennessee (Thomas Lanier Williams)
Jacobsen, J.   Moon Will Restore the Virginity of My Sister, The.
Laughlin, J.   Tennessee.
Williams, T.   Tangier: The Speechless Summer.
  What's Next on the Agenda, Mr. Williams?

Williams, William Carlos
Ammons.   WCW.
Carruth, H.   Fourth.
Carver, R.   Poem for Hemingway & W. C. Williams.
Ciardi, J.   Bicentennial.
  Credo ("Today / Dr. William Carlos Williams").

Creeley. For W.C.W.
Dubie. Physical Moon beyond Paterson, A.
Eberhart, R. Mystery of the Abstract.
  To William Carlos Williams.
Ginsberg, A. Death News.
Kinnell. For William Carlos Williams.
Koch, K. Variations on a Theme by William
  Carlos Williams.
Laughlin, J. So Much Depends.
  We Met in a Dream.
Levertov. September 1961.
  Williams: An Essay.
Logan, J. Trip to Four or Five Towns, A.
Lowell, R. William Carlos Williams.
Oppen. Bill before his death.
Prunty. Dr. Williams' Garden.
Weiss, T. "Yes, But . . ."
Whalen, P. Plums, Metaphysics, an
  Investigation, a Visit, and a Short Funeral Ode.

Willow Herbs
Davie, D. Nottinghamshire.
Herrick. Willow Garland, The.

Willow Trees
Ammons. Bourn.
  I Went Out to the Sun.
  March Song.
  Saying.
Bly, R. Hunting Pheasants in a Cornfield.
Crane, H. Repose of Rivers.
De la Mare. Willow, The.
Han-shan. Willows grow dark like mist, The.
Herrick. To the Willow-Tree.
Levertov. Braiding, The.
  Willows of Massachusetts, The.
MacDiarmid, H. Sauchs in the Reuch Heuch
  Hauch, The.
Merrill, J. Willow.
Parker, D. Willow, The.
Rossetti, C. In the Willow Shade.
  Under the ivy bush / One sits sighing.
  Under Willows.
Sandburg, C. Prairie Waters by Night.
Williams, W. Epitaph: "Old willow with hollow
  branches, An."
  Willow Poem.
Wright, J. Elegy in a Firelit Room.

Wills
Amichai [or Amikhai]. Memory of Love—
  Opening the Will.
Clough. Like one that in a dream would fain
  arise.
Coleridge, S. Epitaphium Testamentarium.
Dickinson, E. To fulfill the will of a powerless
  friend.
Donne. Disinherited.
  Will, The.
Kipling, R. Mary Gloster, The.
Larkin, P. Last Will and Testament.
Merrill, J. Will, The.
Niedecker. To whom / can I leave.
Ritsos. Last Will and Testament.
Rossetti, C. Bruised Reed Shall He Not Break,
  A.
Schuyler, J. Earth's Holocaust.
Stock, R. First Last Will & Testament.
Williams, M. For Lucinda, Robert, and Karyn.

Wilmot, John, 2d Earl of Rochester
See Rochester, John Wilmot, 2d Earl of

Wilson, Woodrow
Jeffers, R. Wilson in Hell.
  Woodrow Wilson.

Wiltshire, England
Davie, D. Wiltshire.

Winchester, England
Milton. Elegy 3: On the Death of the Bishop of
  Winchester.

Wind
Amichai [or Amikhai]. Poems of the Hot Wind.
Ammons. Brooks & Other Notions.
  Grassy Sound.
  Guide.
  In the Wind My Rescue Is.
  Joshua Tree.
  Mansion.
  Mission.

Phase.
Pluralist.
Project.
Small Song.
Virtu.
Wide Land, The.
Wind Coming Down From, The.
"Anvari." O'er the garden water goes the wind
  alone.
Beckett, S. Enueg I.
Berry, W. Birth (Near Port William), The.
Blake, W. Crystal Cabinet, The.
Blok. Song of the Wind, The.
Bogan, L. Zone.
Brontë, E. Loud without the wind was roaring.
  Night Wind, The.
  Sun Has Set, The.
  Wind, I hear it sighing, The.
Broumas, O. Paper Flute.
Browning, R. Englishman in Italy, The.
Burns, R. O [or Oh] Wert Thou in the Cauld
  Blast.
  Of A' the Airts [the Wind Can Blaw].
Campion, T. Peaceful Western Wind, The.
Carew, T. Prayer to the Wind, A.
Carruth, H. Continuo.
Carver, R. In a Greek Orthodox Church near
  Daphne.
  Poem for Karl Wallenda, Aerialist Supreme.
  Wind.
Clampitt. Woodlot, The.
Coleridge, S. Death Wish, A.
  Homeric Hexameter, The.
Cooper, J. Jittoku, Buddhist Mystic—15th
  Century.
Crane, H. Persuasion, A.
Creeley. Hart Crane 2.
  Hélas.
  Memory ("Fresh, A").
  Still Life Or.
  Wind, The.
Cummings, E. E. Painted wind has sprung, A.
  What If a Much of a Which of a Wind.
  Wind has blown the rain away and blown, A.
  Wind is a Lady with, The.
Davie, D. Aubade: "I wish for you that when
  you wake."
  Conditioned Air, A.
  Wind at Penistone, The.
De la Mare. Echo.
Dickinson, E. Duties of the Wind are few, The.
  How lonesome the Wind must feel Nights.
  How slow the Wind.
  I saw the wind within her.
  I think that the Root of the Wind is Water.
  South Wind—has a pathos, A.
  Spry Arms of the Wind, The.
  There came a Wind like a Bugle.
  Wild Nights—Wild Nights!
  Wind begun to knead the Grass, The.
  Wind that rose, A.
  Wind took up the Northern Things, The.
  Wind's Visit, The.
Dugan, A. 1. Enigma: Calm: Addressed to the
  Air.
  2. Comment on 1.
  On an East Wind from the Wars.
  Summer Gale.
  Winter Gale.
Dunbar, P. Chase, The.
  Plantation Child's Lullaby, The.
  Till the Wind Gets Right.
  Wind and the Sea, The.
Eberhart, R. Listing.
Eliot, T. S. Wind Sprang Up at Four o'Clock,
  The.
Emerson, R. Bird was gone the ghastly trees,
  The.
  God only knew how Saadi dined.
  Heartily heartily / Nothing be false.
  I sat upon the ground.
  In this sour world, o summerwind.
  Snow-Storm [or Snowstorm], The.
  Winds are cold, the days are dark, The.
Frost, R. Aim Was Song, The.
  Bereft.

Brown's Descent; or, The Willy-Nilly.
To the Thawing Wind.
Wind and Window Flower.
García Lorca. Preciosa and the Wind.
  Weathervane.
Graves, R. Arrow on the Vane.
  East Wind, An.
  Falcon Woman, The.
  Sirocco at Deyá.
  Weather of Olympus, The.
Gunn, T. At the Back of the North Wind.
  Cat and the Wind, The.
  Conversation of Old Men, The.
  Exercise, The.
  Sketch of the Great Dejection, A.
Gurney, I. April Gale.
  Possessions.
  When March Blows.
"H. D." Sea Rose.
  Wind Sleepers, The.
Hacker, M. Languedocienne.
Hall, D. To the Loud Wind.
Hamill, S. What the Water Knows.
Hardy, T. Wind's Prophecy, The.
Housman. Winds out of the west land blow,
  The.
Howe, F. Veteran.
Hughes, T. Guide, The.
  Wind.
Ignatow, D. To Stay Alive.
  Violence, The.
Jackson, L. Why of the Wind, The.
  Wind Suffers [of Blowing], The.
  Wind, the Clock, the We, The.
Jacobsen, J. Greek Wind, The.
  Wind in the Sunporch, The.
Jeffers, R. Gale in April.
Kipling, R. Dawn Wind, The.
  Fires, The.
Koch, K. West Wind.
Larkin, P. Climbing the Hill within the
  Deafening Wind.
  Portrait.
  Wedding-Wind.
  Who Whistled for the Wind, That It Should
  Break.
Lawrence, D. H. At the Window.
  Birdcage Walk.
  Butterfly.
  Suspense.
  Wind, the Rascal, The.
Levertov. Autumnal.
  In Whom We Live and Move and Have Our
  Being.
Levine, P. Voice, The.
Lindsay, N. Moon's the North Wind's Cooky,
  The.
  Wizard Wind, The.
Lorde. Blackstudies.
  Bloodbirth.
Lowell, R. These Winds.
Lux. Enemy the Wind, The.
  Give It to the Wind.
MacDiarmid, H. Moment in Eternity, A.
MacLeish. Cook County.
  Linden Trees, The.
  Mistral Over the Graves.
MacNeice. Nocturne: "Dark blood of night-
  time, The."
  Sleeping Winds.
Mahon. North Wind: Portrush.
Meredith, G. Song: "O the wind, the wind, the
  wind doth blow."
  South-West Wind in the Woodland.
  Stave of Roving Tim, A.
  Wind & sea are as playmates.
Merrill, J. House, The.
Merton. Lent in a Year of War.
Merwin. Continuo, The.
  Night Wind.
  On the Mountain.
Millay, E. I woke in the night and heard the
  wind, and it blowing half a gale.
Montale. Agave on the Reef, The.
  English Horn.
  On the Threshhold.

Other Lines.
Muldoon, P.   Wind and Tree.
Nash, O.   Word on Wind, A.
Neruda.   Heavy Surf, A.
O'Hara, F.   To Hell with It.
Oppen.   Little Pin, The: Fragment.
Pagis.   Wind From Variable Directions.
Pessoa.   No one, in the vast and virgin jungle.
Petrarch.   Towards the dawn, when *l'aura* (the mild breeze).
Prunty.   This.
Quasimodo.   Agrigentum Road, The.
Raine, K.   Lifelong ago such days.
Wind.
Winds.
Riley, J.   Edge of the Wind, The.
What the Wind Said.
Windy Day, A.
Rilke.   Orphan Wind.
Wind, The.
Ritsos.   Postponed Decision.
Wind's Body, The.
Wonder.
Roethke.   Big Wind.
Child on Top of a Greenhouse.
Mid-Country Blow.
Song: "From whence cometh song?"
Words for the Wind.
Rossetti, C.   Hollow-Sounding and Mysterious.
Mirrors of Life and Death.
O wind, where have you been.
O wind, why do you never rest.
Playing at bob cherry / Tom and Nell and Hugh.
Song of Flight, A.
Who Has Seen the Wind?
Wind Has Such a Rainy Sound, The.
Rumi.   Gnats inside the Wind.
Grasses, The.
Morning wind spreads its fresh smell, The.
Sun is love, The. The lover.
Sandburg, C.   Baby Song of the Four Winds.
Bitter Summer Thoughts—No. 3.
Blossom Themes.
Changing Light Winds.
Corn Prattlings.
Dan.
Evening Sea Wind.
Field People.
Four Preludes on Playthings of the Wind.
Head.
How Yesterday Looked.
Landscape.
Man and Dog on an Early Winter Morning.
Meadow in Summer.
Never Two Songs the Same.
North Atlantic.
Rain Winds Blow Doors Open.
Ripe Corn.
Sand Scribblings.
Sleep Impression.
Spring Wind.
Whirls.
Wind on the Way, The.
Wind Song.
Windflower Leaf.
Windy City, The.
Schuyler, J.   Day, The.
Evening Wind.
Seifert.   Funeral under My Window.
Shelley, P.   Dirge, A: "Rough wind, that moanest loud."
Smith, S.   When the Wind.
Stafford, W.   Note.
Storm Warnings.
Why I Am a Poet.
Wind World.
Stevens, W.   Chaos in Motion and Not in Motion.
Night-wind of August, The.
Valley Candle.
Wind Shifts, The.
Stock, R.   Impromptu with a Breeze.
Wind in the Mirror.
Swenson, M.   Goodnight.
Hearing the Wind at Night.
Tomlinson, C.   At the Hill Fort.

Embassy.
Wind.
Unknown.   Two Spring Charms.
Updike.   Wind.
Very.   Homeless Wind, The.
Warren, R.   Ah, Anima!
Blow, West Wind.
Eagle Descending.
Last Metaphor, The.
Wind and Gibbon.
Weiss, T.   November Late.
Wheatley, P.   On Messrs Hussey and Coffin.
Whitman, W.   To the Sun-set Breeze.
Wilbur, R.   After the Last Bulletins.
From the Lookout Rock.
Poplar, Sycamore.
Regatta, The.
Sleepless at Crown Point.
Williams, C. K.   Listen carefully. / I'm meditating.
Williams, T.   Ice-Blue Wind, The.
Williams, W.   Black Winds, The.
January.
Porous.
Wind Increases, The.
Wordsworth, W.   Flower Garden at Coleorton Hall, Leicestershire, A.
September, 1815.
There was a spot.
Wright, J.   Autumnal.
Listening to the Mourners.
Spring Images.
Zagajewski.   December Wind.
Wind at Night.
Zukofsky, L.   Wire.

See also **North Wind; Tornadoes; West Wind**

Windflowers
See **Anemones**

Windhovers
See **Falcons**

Windmills
Hall, D.   Swan.
Laughlin, J.   Girls as Windmills.

Window Shades
Lux.   Torn Shades.

Window Washing and Window Washers
Hayden, R.   Performers, The.
Prunty.   Window Washer, The.
Simic.   Window Washer.

Windows
Amichai [*or* Amikhai].   Eternal Window, An.
Beckett, S.   Rentrer / À la nuit.
Berry, W.   Cold Pane, The.
Brodsky, J.   I Sit by the Window.
Bukowski.   Liberty.
Cavafy.   By an Open Window.
Windows, The.
Cowper, W.   Lines Written upon a Window-Shutter at Weston.
Creeley.   Box, The.
Echoes ("Eight panes").
Goodbye.
Hong Kong Window.
Poem for D. H. Lawrence.
Window.
Cummings, E. E.   Spring is like a perhaps hand.
You / in win / ter who sit.
Dickinson, E.   I had been hungry, all the Years.
Donne.   Valediction, A: of My Name in the Window.
Gunn, T.   Monster, The.
Gurney, I.   Pleasance Window, The.
Hardy, T.   Love Watches a Window.
Herbert, G.   Windows, The.
Jackson, L.   Prisms.
Koch, K.   Simplicity of the Unknown Past, The.
Larkin, P.   Aubade: "I work all day, and get half-drunk at night."
Levertov.   Crack, The.
Lindsay, N.   Factory Windows Are Always Broken.
Longfellow, H.   Ropewalk, The.
MacDiarmid, H.   Gin but the oor 'ud chop and set me free.
Here in the hauf licht hoo I've grown!

Here in the hauf licht waitin' till the clock.
I'm weary o' the shapes mere chance can thraw.
That's the condition o't or near.
Mallarmé.   Windows, The.
McHugh, H.   Window: Thing as Participle.
Merwin.   Going from the Green Window.
Millay, E.   From a Train Window.
Nemerov.   Storm Windows.
Orr, G.   Reverie.
Patchen.   Opening the Window.
Ramanujan.   Christmas.
Rilke.   Child at the Window Sill.
Ritsos.   Silent Agreement.
Rossetti, C.   Reflection.
Sandburg, C.   Clean Curtains.
Foolish About Windows.
Panels.
Schuyler, J.   In Wiry Winter.
Seifert.   Four Small Windows.
"Shu Ting."   When You Come Past My Window.
Tollas, T.   They've Blocked Every Window.
Tomlinson, C.   Poem: "Space / window / that looks into itself."
View, The.
Warren, R.   Loose Shutter, The.
Problem in Spatial Composition, A.
Williams, M.   Evening: A Studio in Rome.
Williams, W.   Young Woman at a Window.
Zagajewski.   Moths.

Windsor Forest, England
Pope, A.   Windsor-Forest [*or* Windsor Forest].

Wine
Amichai [*or* Amikhai].   Itzhak's Last Kit Bag.
Baudelaire.   Lover's Wine.
Murderer's Wine.
Ragpickers' Wine.
Spirit of the Wine, The.
Wine of the Solitary Man, The.
Berrigan, T.   Certain Slant of Sunlight, A.
Bierce.   Bride, The.
Grape.
Blok.   Snow Wine.
Stranger, The.
Bogan, L.   To Wine.
Browning, E.   Wine of Cyprus.
Cavafy.   I Went.
Corbett, W.   Recipe for Contemplation.
Crashaw.   To Our Lord, upon the Water Made Wine.
Dickinson, E.   Let me not thirst with this Hock at my Lip.
Dove, R.   Champagne.
Emerson, R.   Bacchus.
Borrow Urania's subtle wings.
By art, by music, overthrilled.
Friends to me are frozen wine.
On a raisin stone.
Pour the wine! pour the wine!
She had wealth of mornings in her year.
"H. D."   Wine Bowl.
Hafiz [*or* Hafez].   From the Persian of Hafiz.
Han-shan.   Whose wine shop is this aglow.
HaNagid.   How I Helped the Wise.
Rouge In Appearance.
Sad Friend.
Take the Crystal.
Your Years Are Sleep.
Herrick.   Anacreontic[k] Verse.
Bachanalian Verse, A.
His Farewell [*or* Fare-well] to Sack.
How He Would Drinke His Wine.
Ode to Sir Clipsebie Crew, An.
To Live Merrily, and To Trust to Good Verses.
To Youth.
Upon Vinegar.
Welcome to Sack, The.
Hopkins, G.   Barnfloor and Winepress.
Hughes, L.   Midnight Dancer.
Jonson, B.   Dedication of the King's New Cellar. To Bacchus, The.
Epigram. To the Household. 1630, An.
Lindsay, N.   On Reading Omar Khayyam.
What Semiramis Said.
Martial.   4.69: "You serve the best wines always, my dear sir."

Merwin.   Wine, The.
Millay, E.   Wine from These Grapes.
Milton.   Elegy 6: To Charles Deodati.
Moore, M.   Camellia Sabina.
Piercy.   Gift of Light, A.
Ralegh, S.   I have no wine of Gaza, nor Falerna wine.
Rilke.   Das Kleine Weinjahr.
Rukeyser, M.   Neruda, the Wine.
Rumi.   Burnt Kabob.
   Flutes for Dancing.
   Gone, inner and outer.
   Many Wines, The.
   Send the Chaperones Away.
   We have a huge barrel of wine, but no cups.
   We Three.
   Why Wine Is Forbidden.
   Wine we really drink is our own blood, The.
Schuyler, J.   This Soft October.
Shelley, P.   Fragment: Wine of the Fairies.
Stock, R.   Banquet, The.
Szymborska, W.   Drinking Wine.
Tate, A.   Progress of Œnia, The.
Tate, J.   Lewis and Clark Overheard in Conversation.
Thomas, D.   This Bread I Break.
Updike.   Pale Bliss.
Wilbur, R.   Wedding Toast, A.
Williams, M.   Something to Believe In.
Yeats.   Drinking Song, A.
Zukofsky, L.   To My Baby Paul.

Wings
Ciardi, J.   Foolish Wing, The.
Dickey, J.   Moon Flock.
Dickinson, E.   Bat, The.
   Hours have Wings.
Dove, R.   Wingfoot Lake.
Herbert, G.   Easter Wings.
Hopkins, G.   Ecquis Binas.
   God's Grandeur.
Hughes, L.   Angels Wings.
   Freedom Seeker.
Levertov.   Wings, The.
Merwin.   Foreword.
Rossetti, C.   On the Wing.
Rumi.   Birdwings.
Sexton   To a Friend Whose Work Has Come to Triumph.
Warren, R.   Evening Hawk.
Wright, J.   To the August Fallen.
Yeats.   Mother of God, The.

Winnie-the-Pooh
Milosz, C.   Christopher Robin.

Winter
Ammons.   Doubling the Nerve.
   Jersey Cedars.
   Thaw.
   Winter Saint.
   Winter Scene.
Angelou.   This Winter Day.
Atwood.   Midwinter, Presolstice.
Baudelaire.   Cracked Bell, The.
Beckett, S.   Vive morte ma seule saison.
Berry, W.   Boone.
   Cold, The.
   Companions, The.
   Dance, A.
   Elegy: "All day our eyes could find no resting place."
   February 2, 1968.
   Finches, The.
   Winter Nightfall.
Berryman.   Winter-Piece to a Friend Away, A.
Bishop, E.   Colder the Air, The.
   Paris, 7 A.M.
Blake, W.   Song 3rd By an Old Shepherd.
   To Winter.
Bly, R.   Six Winter Privacy Poems.
   Three Kinds of Pleasures.
Borges.   Cambridge.
Bourne, V.   Silk Worm, The.
Brodsky, J.   Eclogue 4: Winter.
   Tsushima Screen.
   View from the Hill.
Brontë, E.   Castle Wood.
   I.M. to I.G.

Upon her soothing breast.
Burns, R.   Auld Man's Winter Thought, The.
   Cauld Is the E'enin Blast.
   Gloomy December.
   Impomptu, on Mrs. W. Riddell's Birthday, 4th Novr. 1793.
   Song: "On Cessnock banks a lassie dwells."
   Up in the Morning Early.
   Winter, a Dirge.
   Winter Night, A.
Campion, T.   Ad nobiliss. virum Gul. Percium.
   Now Winter Nights Enlarge.
Carruth, H.   Mild Winter.
   North Winter.
   Snow, The.
   To Artemis.
   Twilight Comes.
Celan.   Black Flakes.
   Winter.
Ciardi, J.   Hometown after a War.
   Winter Music.
Clampitt.   Runes, Blurs, Sap Rising.
   Teignmouth.
   Tidewater Winter.
   Winter Burial, A.
Clare, J.   Impromptu on Winter.
   Winter Evening.
Codrescu.   Winter in Istanbul.
Corbett, W.   February 29th.
Crane, H.   This Way Where November.
Creeley.   Interview, The.
   Irishman's Lament on the Approaching Winter, An.
   Winter.
Cummings, E. E.   Ballade: "White night roared with a huge north-wind, The."
   "But / he" i / staring / into winter twi.
   Enter no(silence is the blood whose flesh).
   Glory is fallen out of, The.
   I was sitting in mcsoreley's. outside it was New York and beauti- / fully snowing.
   Infinite jukethrob smoke & swallow to dis.
   Moon-lit snow is falling like strange candy into the big eyes of the, The.
   N / Umb a / stree / t's wintr.
   Nor woman / (just as it be).
   Numb(and / that was).
   Skating.
   Will suddenly trees leap up from winter and will.
   You / in win / ter who sit.
Davie, D.   January.
   Westmorland.
   Winter Landscapes.
   Winter Talent, A.
   Winter's Talents.
De la Mare.   Alone.
   Fairy in Winter, The.
   Tryst, The.
   Winter.
Dickey, J.   To Be Done in Winter.
Dickey, W.   More Under Saturn.
Dickinson, E.   Conjecturing a Climate.
   How luscious is the dripping.
   I remember the leaves were falling.
   I think the Hemlock likes to stand.
   Jay his Castanet has struck, The.
   No event of Wind or Bird.
   There's a certain Slant of light.
   These are the days that Reindeer love.
   This is a stern Winter.
   Tree in Winter.
   'Twas here my summer paused.
   Winter is good—his Hoar Delights.
   Winter under cultivation.
   Winters are so short, The.
Donne.   Nocturnal[l] upon Saint Lucy's [or S. Lucy's or S. Lucies] Day, A.
Dove, R.   November for Beginners.
   Snow King, The.
Dugan, A.   Glad at the Cold (1955).
   Sixteen Lines on Marching.
   Variation on "Winter's Onset from an Alienated Point of View."
Dunbar, P.   Jack Frost at Bedtime.
   Plantation Child's Lullaby, The.

Warm Day in Winter, A.
When Winter Darkening All Around.
Winter-Song.
Winter's Approach.
Winter's Day, A.
Eberhart, R.   Christmas Tree.
   Commas in Wintertime.
   Emblem.
   Homage to the North.
   Snow Cascades.
   Spider, The.
Eliot, T. S.   Journey of the Magi.
Emerson, R.   Seemed, tho' the soft sheen all enchants.
   Titmouse, The.
Frost, R.   Birches.
   Good Hours.
   Hillside Thaw, A.
   My Butterfly.
   Old Man's Winter Night, An.
   Onset, The.
   Reluctance.
   Stopping by Woods on a Snowy Evening.
   To a Moth Seen in Winter.
   Winter Eden, A.
Glück, L.   Early December in Croton-on-Hudson.
   Illuminations.
   Saturnalia.
Graves, R.   Frosty Night, A.
   Mid-Winter Waking.
Gunn, T.   At the Back of the North Wind.
Gurney, I.   Here, If Forlorn.
   It Is Winter.
Hacker, M.   Christmas Crown, A.
Hall, D.   Stump.
Han-shan.   Cold Mountain is so cold.
Hardy, T.   At Middle-Field Gate in February.
   Birds at Winter Nightfall.
   Faithful Swallow, The.
   Farm-Woman's Winter, The.
   Frozen Greenhouse, The.
   I Need Not Go.
   Ice on the Highway.
   Music in a Snowy Street.
   Neutral Tones.
   Prospect, The.
   Robin, The.
   Spellbound Palace, A.
   Unrealized.
   Winter in Durnover Field.
   Winter Night in Woodland.
Hayden, R.   Those Winter Sundays.
Hopkins, G.   Winter with the Gulf Stream.
Housman.   In midnights of November.
   Winter.
Hughes, L.   Midwinter Blues.
   Prayer for a Winter Night.
Hughes, T.   Roe-Deer.
   Snowdrop.
Jacobsen, J.   Winter Castle.
Jarrell, R.   Northern Snows, The.
   Windows.
   Winter's Tale, The.
Johnson, S.   Winter's Walk, The.
Jonson, B.   Elegy, An: "Since you must go, and I must bid farewell."
Keats.   In Drear-nighted December.
Larkin, P.   And Now the Leaves Sudddenly Lose Strength.
   Gathering Wood.
   Slight Relax of Air Where Cold Was, A.
   Winter.
   Winter Nocturne.
Laughlin, J.   Cold, The.
   Tanka: "Winter has come."
Lawrence, D. H.   Drained Cup, The.
   Parliament Hill in the Evening.
   To Clarinda.
   Winter in the Boulevard.
   Winter-Lull.
Levertov.   Crack, The.
Levi, P.   Thaw, The.
Levine, P.   On the Birth of Good & Evil During the Long Winter of '28.
   Walk with Tom Jefferson, A.

Logan, J.   Song on the Dread of a Chill Spring.
Logue, C.   Woke up this morning.
Longfellow, H.   Snow-Flakes.
Lorde.   Cables To Rage Or I've Been Talking
 On This Street Corner.
 Father, the Year Has Fallen.
 Teacher.
 Woman Thing, The.
Lowell, R.   Inauguration Day: January 1953.
Lux.   Ditto.
 Winter River.
MacDiarmid, H.   Lourd on My Hert.
Mahon.   Sea in Winter, The.
Mallarmé.   Fan, A; of Méry Laurent.
 Virginal, vibrant, and beautiful dawn, The.
McGrath, T.   Black Train, The.
 Don't Think You Know My Name!
 Face of the Precipice is Black with Lovers, The.
McHugh, H.   Message at Sunset for Bishop
 Berkeley.
Melville, H.   Apathy and Enthusiasm.
Meredith, G.   Death of Winter, The.
 Or the single path— / Which the cool moon
 sheds.
 Parody of Alfred Austin.
 Time.
Meredith, W.   Of Possessions, in Winter.
 Winter on the River.
 Winter Song.
Merton.   Early Blizzard.
 Evening: Zero Weather.
 Love Winter When the Plant Says Nothing.
 Messenger, The.
 Regret, The.
 Winter Afternoon.
 Winter's Night, The.
Merwin.   Banishment in Winter.
 Cold before the Moonrise, The.
 December among the Vanished.
 December Night.
 Dusk in Winter.
 Snow, The.
 Writing on a Fallen Leaf, The.
Millay, E.   Spring in the Garden.
 Winter Night.
Milosz, C.   It Was Winter.
Montale.   Bagni di Lucca.
Nash, O.   Summergreen for President.
 Word about Winter, A.
Nemerov.   Central Park.
 First Snow.
 From a Record of Disappointment.
 Rent in the Screen, The.
 Spell before Winter, A.
 Winter Exercise.
Neruda.   Winter.
Niedecker.   February almost March bites the
 cold.
 I sit in my own house.
 People, people.
 Summer's away, I traded my chicks for trees.
 Swept snow, Li Po.
O'Hara, F.   Music.
 Poem: "I watched an armory combing its bronze
 bricks."
 Poem In January.
Oliver, M.   Winter in the Country.
 Wolf Moon.
Olson, C.   Personality and dourness of winter,
 The.
 Song, The: "More than the sennet of the solstice
 pipe."
 Winter After, The.
 Winter Solstice.
Oppen.   From a Photograph.
Owen, W.   Exposure.
Pagis.   Early Winter, Long Island.
 End of Winter, The.
Paley, G.   Winter Afternoon.
Parker, D.   Small Hours, The.
 Song of a Contented Heart.
Pasternak, B.   Inside the Storm.
Patchen.   Winter at the Inn.
 Winter Poem.
 Wolf of winter, The.
Piercy.   Breaking Camp.

Butt of Winter, The.
Longest Night, The.
Skimpy Day at the Solstice.
Pinsky.   Cold, The.
 Icicles.
Plath.   By Candlelight.
 Magnolia Shoals.
 Private Ground.
 Wintering.
Pound, E.   Villonaud for This Yule.
Prunty.   Four Winter Flies.
Raine, K.   Winter Paradise.
 Winter Solstice.
Rich, A.   Purely Local.
Riley, J.   Brave Refrain, A.
 Go, Winter!
 Old Man's Nursery Rhyme.
 Old Winters on the Farm.
 Snow in the Air.
Rilke.   Winter.
Ritsos.   Snowy Weather.
Roethke.   Coming of the Cold, The.
Rossetti, C.   1885. St. Valentine's Day.
 1886, St. Valentine's Day.
 Amen.
 Autumn.
 Bread and Milk for Breakfast.
 Christmas Carol, A: "In the bleak mid-winter."
 Crying, my little one, footsore and weary?
 Endure Hardness.
 Grown and Flown.
 I dug and dug amongst the snow.
 One Swallow Does Not Make a Summer.
 Sir Winter.
 Song: "Stream moaneth as it floweth, The."
 St. Valentine's Day 1881.
 Summer.
 Tempus Fugit.
 There Is a Budding Morrow in Midnight.
 There's Snow on the Fields.
 Where shall I find a white rose blowing?
 Winter: My Secret.
 Wintry Sonnet, A.
Rukeyser, M.   Certain Music, A.
 Flashing Cliff, A.
Sandburg, C.   Aloof.
 Blossom Themes.
 Haze Gold.
 Hemlock and Cedar.
 Man and Dog on an Early Winter Morning.
 Winter Gold.
 Winter Weather.
Sarton, M.   First Snow.
 House in Winter, The.
 On a Winter Night.
 Snow Light, The.
 Winter Carol.
Schuyler, J.   Deep Winter.
 Empathy and New Year.
 In January.
Seifert.   Silence Full of Sleighbells.
Sexton.   Landscape Winter.
Shelley, P.   Dirge for the Year.
 Summer and Winter.
Simic.   December Trees.
 February.
 Winter Night.
Snyder, G.   Thin Ice.
Spender, S.   Ice.
Stafford, W.   Over in Montana.
 People Who Went By in Winter.
 Representing Far Places.
 Sayings from the Northern Ice.
 Whispered in Winter.
Stevens, W.   Annual Gaiety.
 Course of a Particular, The.
 Dwarf, The.
 No Possum, No Sop, No Taters.
 Poesie Abrutie.
 Snow Man, The.
Stockton, A.   Elegy on the Destruction of the
 Trees by the Isicles.
 Epistle to a Friend Who Urg'd to Have Some
 Poetry Sent Her, An.
 To Miss Mary Stockton, an Epistle the 10th of
 Janu 78.

Swenson, M.   Zero in the Cove.
Tate, A.   Seasons of the Soul.
Tennyson, A.   Spirit Haunts the Year's Last
 Hours, A.
Thomas, D.   Hold Hard, These Ancient Minutes
 in the Cuckoo's Month.
 Winter's Tale, A.
Thoreau.   Fair Haven ("When Winter fringes
 every bough").
 Pray to what earth does this sweet cold belong.
 Until at length the north winds blow.
 Within the circuit of this plodding life.
Tomlinson, C.   Fox, The.
 In Winter Woods.
 Maine Winter.
 Nine Variations in a Chinese Winter Setting.
 Snow Fences, The.
 Winter.
 Winter Encounters.
 Winter-Piece.
Trakl.   Winter Night, A.
Tu Fu.   Visit in Winter to the Temple of His
 Mystical Majesty, A.
Updike.   Late January.
 Winter Ocean.
 Working Outdoors in Winter.
Vallejo.   Our Daily Bread.
Van Duyn.   Two Poems for Sub-Zero Times.
Very.   Frost, The.
 Hepatica in Winter, The.
 Man's First Experience of Winter.
 On the Late Mild Winter.
 Spirit, The.
 Winter Bird, The.
 Winter Night, The.
 Winter ("Perils of the ocean safely o'er, The").
 Winter Rain, The.
Walcott.   Love in the Valley.
 Village Life, A.
Warren, R.   Answer to Prayer.
 Mission, The.
 Time as Hypnosis.
 Winter Dreams.
Weiss, T.   World to Do, A.
Whalen, P.   Winter, The ("Wheelbarrow's tire is
 flat, muddy ground now sets").
Whitman, W.   Sounds of the Winter.
 To a Locomotive in Winter.
Whittier.   Flowers in Winter.
 Frost Spirit, The.
 Letter to Lucy Larcom.
 Pressed Gentian, The.
 Red Riding-Hood.
 Snow-Bound [or Snow-Bound; a Winter Idyl].
 To E. C. S.
 Winter Roses.
Wilbur, R.   April 5, 1974.
 Courtyard Thaw, A.
 Orchard Trees, January.
 Sonnet: "Winter deepening, the hay all in, The."
 Storm in April, A.
 Two Songs in a Stanza of Beddoes'
 Winter Spring.
 Year's End.
Wilde, O.   From Spring Days to Winter.
 Le Jardin des Tuileries.
Williams, C. K.   Reading: Winter.
 That night, / winter, / rain.
 Winter, / damn, / again.
Williams, M.   Waiting for the Paper to be
 Delivered.
Williams, T.   Ice-Blue Wind, The.
 Iron is the Winter.
Williams, W.   Approach of Winter.
 Arrival.
 Bare Tree, The.
 Birds and Flowers.
 Cold Night, The.
 Decenber.
 Descent of Winter, The.
 Jersey Lyric.
 Midwinter.
 Soughing Wind, The.
 These.
 This Is Pioneer Weather.
 To a Woodpecker.

Winter.
Winter Quiet.
Winter Trees.
Woodthrush, The.
Wilner, E. It's Not Cold Here.
Water Lace and White Eyes.
Wordsworth, W. Composed near Calais, on the
 Road Leading to Ardres, August 7, 1802.
French Army in Russia 1812–1813, The.
On the Same Occasion.
Wright, C. After Reading Wang Wei, I Go
 Outside to the Full Moon.
As Our Bodies Rise, Our Names Turn into
 Light.
Christmas East of the Blue Ridge.
Half February.
Lives of the Saints.
Negatives 2.
Not everyone can see the truth, but he can be it.
Silent Generation, The.
Thinking of David Summers at the Beginning of
 Winter.
Under the Nine Trees in January.
Winter-Worship.
Wright, J. Elegy in a Firelit Room.
Frontier, The.
Late November in a Field.
Poor Washed Up by Chicago Winter, The.
Seasonless, The.
Sparrows in a Hillside Drift.
Yeats. Withering of the Boughs, The.
Zagajewski. December.
Europe in Winter.
For Gabriela Münter.
Iron.

Winters, Yvor
Gunn, T. To Yvor Winters, 1955.
Pinkerton, H. Autumn Drought.
Rexroth, K. Giant Weapon, The.
Letter to Yvor Winters, A.

Wisconsin (state)
Bly, R. Three Kinds of Pleasures.
Clampitt. Witness.
Eberhart, R. La Crosse at Ninety Miles an
 Hour.

Wisdom
Ammons. Golden Mean, The.
Whose Timeless Reach.
Arnold, M. Shakespeare.
Atwood. Procedures for Underground.
Bierce. Lacking Factor, A.
Bogan, L. Men Loved Wholly Beyond Wisdom.
Borges. Guardian of the Books, The.
Browning, E. Wisdom Unapplied.
Bukowski. Counsel.
Kings Are Gone, The.
Burns, R. Occasional Address, Spoken by Miss
 Fontenell.
Byron, G. R. C. Dallas.
Campion, T. Canto Quarto.
Cavafy. Becoming Stronger.
Wise Sense Imminent Events, The.
Chamfort. Better on your arse than on your
 feet.
Chuang Tzu. Action and Non-Action.
Importance of Being Toothless, The.
Wholeness.
Cowper, W. When little more than boy in age.
Crane, H. Praise for an Urn.
Crane, S. I met a seer.
In a lonely place.
Creeley. Wisdom.
Cullen, C. Threnody for a Brown Girl.
Wisdom Cometh with the Years.
Wise, The.
Cummings, E. E. If up's the word;and a world
 grows greener.
May my heart always be open to little.
Sitting in a tree-.
There is a here and.
Who were so dark of heart they might not
 speak.
You Shall Above All Things Be Glad and
 Young.
Cunningham, J. Helmsman, The; an Ode.
Who lives by wisdom and to others gives.

Davie, D. Measured Tread, A.
Obiter Dicta.
De la Mare. Catechism, The.
In a Library.
Moonlight.
Dickinson, E. I worked for chaff and earning
 Wheat.
If the foolish, call them "flowers."
We learned the Whole of Love.
"Why do I love" You, Sir?
Dunbar, P. At Cheshire Cheese.
Eberhart, R. My Golden and My Fierce Assays.
Mysticism Has Not the Patience To Wait for
 God's Revelation.
Sagacity.
Emerson, R. He walked the streets of great
 New York.
Limits.
Mask thy wisdom with delight.
O What have I to do.
Prudence.
To transmute crime to wisdom, & to stem.
Whoso alas is young.
Frost, R. Boeotian.
Graves, R. Myrrhina.
Within Reason.
Hacker, M. Rune of the Finland Woman.
Han-shan. There's a naked bug at Cold
 Mountain.
HaNagid. How I Helped the Wise.
Man's Wisdom Is In What He Writes.
Wise Understand, The.
You Who'd Be Wise.
Hardy, T. Child and the Sage, The.
Herbert, G. Elixir [or Elixer], The.
Hughes, L. Acceptance.
Wisdom.
Wise Men.
Ibn-i-Yamin [or Ibn Jemin or Amir Mahmud ibn
 Amir Yaminu'd-Din Tughra'i]. Whilst I
 disdain the populace.
Jarrell, R. Head of Wisdom, The.
Jeffers, R. Come Little Birds.
Prescription of Painful Ends.
Wise Men in Their Bad Hours.
Jonson, B. Lord Bacon's Birthday.
Ode, An: "High-spirited friend."
Kipling, R. King's Job, The.
Playmate, The.
Kunitz, S. Class Will Come to Order, The.
Lesson, The.
Laughlin, J. Owl of Minerva, The.
Lawrence, D. H. Fresh Water.
Race and Battle.
Salt of the Earth.
Logue, C. Singing Prayer, A.
MacLeish. With Age Wisdom.
Melville, H. Lone Founts.
Meredith, G. Discipline of Wisdom, The.
Earth and Man.
Earth's.
I seize in a central knot.
In the Sap.
My Theme: Continued.
Reason.
Three Singers to Young Blood, The.
We need some rallying point round which.
Wisdom of Eld, The.
Merrill, J. World and the Child, The.
Yánnina.
Merton. Hagia Sophia.
St. Alberic.
Wisdom.
Merwin. Different Stars, The.
Finding a Teacher.
Milosz, C. Woe!
Nash, O. If Fun Is Fun, Isn't That Enough?
Sage of Darien, The.
Nemerov. Interview, An.
Olson, C. Christmas.
Dance, of the Grizzly Bear, The.
He, Who, in His Abandnoned Infancy, Spoke of
 Jesus, Caesar, Those Who Beg, and Hell.
In the Hills South of Capernaum, Port.
Owen, G. Prudent Simplicity.
Parker, D. For an Unknown Lady.

Wisdom.
Patchen. Lao Tsze.
Petrarch. Two blushing roses, gathered recently.
Pope, A. Epistle I, to Sir Richard Temple, Lord
 Cobham.
Ralegh, S. From wisedome Fortune differs
 farre.
Ramanujan. Excerpts from a Father's Wisdom.
Guru, The.
Ransom, J. Address to the Scholars of New
 England.
Tall Girl, The.
Rexroth, K. Homer in Basic.
Riley, J. Treasure of the Wise Man, The.
Uncle Sidney's Views.
Ritsos. Wisdom.
Robinson, E. Master, The.
Sage, The.
Rossetti, C. Answer, An.
Counterblast on Penny Trumpet.
Let Everything That Hath Breath Praise the
 Lord.
Love loveth Thee, and wisdom loveth Thee.
Passing and Glassing.
She Came from The Uttermost Part of the Earth.
To Lalla, Reading My Verses Topsy-Turvy.
Was Thy Wrath against the Sea?
Wisdom.
Rumi. Gift of Water, The.
This piece of food cannot be eaten.
Three Fish, The.
Two Kinds of Intelligence.
Sandburg, C. Brass Keys.
Crossing the Paces.
Gypsy.
Has-Been, The.
Is Wisdom a Lot of Language?
Jabberers.
Let Them Ask Your Pardon.
Three Fragments for Fishers of Destiny.
Shih-te. Wine of wisdom is so cold, The.
Smith, S. Everything Is Swimming.
Homage to John Cowper Powys.
Is It Wise?
Portrait (II).
To Dean Inge Lecturing on Origen.
Snyder, G. Path to Han-shan's place is
 laughable, The.
Spender, S. Auden at Milwaukee.
Stafford, W. Little Ways that Encourage Good
 Fortune, The.
Swift, J. On Wisdom's Defeat in a Learned
 Debate.
Stella's Birthday ([March 13,] 1727).
Swinburne. At Eleusis.
Old Saying, An.
Thomas, D. Should Lanterns Shine.
Thoreau. Good how can we trust?, The.
He knows no change who knows the true.
Updike. Mountain Impasse.
Whitman, W. Song of Prudence.
When I Heard the Learn'd Astronomer.
Williams, M. Ruby Tells All.
Williams, W. Invitation.
Wordsworth, W. Lines: "Nay, Traveller."
Resolution and Independence.
Though narrow be that old Man's cares, and
 near.
Yeats. Another Song of a Fool.
Brown Penny.
Coming of Wisdom with Time, The.
Seven Sages, The.
Zagajewski. Shell.
Speak Softly.

See also **Reason**

Wisemen
Bierce. Abracadabra.
Montefiore.
Cunningham, J. Gnothi Seauton.
Levertov. Spirits Appeased, The.
Rumi. Jesus on the Lean Donkey.

See also **Magi**

Wishes
Berry, W. Wish to Be Generous, The.
Carew, T. New Year's Gift. To the King, A.
Ciardi, J. Emeritus Addresses the School, An.

Collins, B.   Three Wishes, The.
Cowper, W.   Poet's New-Year's Gift, The.
Creeley.   Apple Uppfle.
For Rainer Gerhardt.
Fragments: "Decorous, and forbearing further
    correction."
Friend, The.
Going.
In London.
Picnic, The.
Song: "Were I myself more blithe."
Wish, A.
Cummings, E. E.   Come a little further—why be
    afraid.
Luminous tendril of celestial wish.
O by the by / has anybody seen.
One day a nigger.
So many selves(so many fiends and gods).
Davie, D.   Aubade: "I wish for you that when
    you wake."
New Year Wishes for the English.
Eberhart, R.   Despair.
To Auden on His Fiftieth.
Verbalist of Summer, The.
Emerson, R.   If wishes would carry me over the
    land.
Enzensberger, H.   Concert of Wishes.
García Lorca.   Silly Song.
Ginsberg, A.   What I'd Like to Do.
Graves, R.   Richard Roe and John Doe.
Hardy, T.   Could I but Will.
Heaney, S.   Wishing Tree, The.
Herrick.   His Wish.
Poets Good Wishes for the Most Hopefull and
    Handsome Prince, the Duke of Yorke, The.
Upon Batt.
Upon Gubbs.
Housman.   If truth in hearts that perish.
Jarrell, R.   Man in Majesty.
Man Meets a Woman in the Street, A.
Johnson, S.   Vanity of Human Wishes, The; The
    Tenth Satire of Juvenal Imitated.
Larkin, P.   Born Yesterday.
I Am Washed upon a Rock.
Lawrence, D. H.   Labour Battalion.
Lindsay, N.   Aladdin and the Jinn.
Merwin.   Wish.
Orr, G.   Story Sassetta Paints, A.
Parker, D.   Star Light, Star Bright.
Patchen.   I Never Had Any Other Desire So
    Strong.
Riley, J.   Old, Old Wish, The.
Rossetti, C.   I planted a hand / And there came
    up a palm.
I wish I were a little bird.
Wishes: Sonnet.
Rukeyser, M.   Course.
Sandburg, C.   Ambassadors of Grief.
Do You Want Affidavits?
Good Night.
Mag.
Old Hokusai Print.
Poems Done on a Late Night Car.
Wanting the Impossible.
Wistful.
Stockton, A.   Wish to Miss Hannah Stockton,
    The.
Whittier.   Wishing Bridge, The.
Wordsworth, W.   Wishing-Gate, The.
Wright, J.   Moon.
Non-Birthday Poem for My Father, A.
Yeats.   He Wishes for the Cloths of Heaven.
Zukofsky, L.   Letter of Poor Birds, The.

Wisteria
Ciardi, J.   Everywhere That Universe.

Wit
Bishop, E.   Wit, The.
Campion, T.   De Epigrammate.
Chamfort.   Long after Chamfort.
Emerson, R.   And man of wit & mark.
From Nature's beginning.
Hadrian.   My little soul, my vagrant charmer.
Herrick.   His Losse.
To His Honoured Friend, Sir John Mynts.
To Perenna.
Hopkins, G.   Denis, / Whose motionable, alert,

most vaulting wit.
Meredith, G.   Glee.
Pope, A.   Impromptu to Lady Winchelsea.
Ralegh, S.   In the Grace of Wit, of Tongue and
    Face.
Suckling, S.   Prologue of the Author's to a
    Masque at Witten, A.

Witchcraft and Witches
Bishop, E.   Riverman, The.
Burns, R.   Tam o' Shanter; A Tale.
Cummings, E. E.   Hist whist / little ghostthings.
De la Mare.   Journey, The.
Dickey, W.   Dolls Play at Hansel and Gretel,
    The.
Dickinson, E.   Best Witchcraft is Geometry.
Witchcraft has not a Pedigree.
Witchcraft was hung, in History.
Dugan, A.   Suburban Exorcism.
Working World's Bloody Flux, The.
Eberhart, R.   Salem.
Frost, R.   Two Witches.
Graves, R.   Against Witchcraft.
Hag-Ridden.
Two Witches, The.
Gray, T.   Fatal Sisters, The.
Gurney, I.   I Would Not Rest.
Herrick.   Hag, The.
Upon an Old Woman.
Housman.   Her Strong Enchantments Failing.
Hughes, T.   Witches.
Kipling, R.   Egg-Shell, The.
Levi, P.   Witch, The.
Lindsay, N.   Sorceress!, The.
Lorde.   Neighbors.
Meredith, G.   Hectate.
Muldoon, P.   Ducking Stool, The.
Plath.   Vanity Fair.
Rich, A.   November 1968.
Sarton, M.   Intruder, An.
Sexton.   Her Kind.
Witch's Life, The.
Smith, S.   Little Boy Lost.
Small Lady, The.
Van Duyn.   Such things there are, we don't
    know.
Whittier.   Changeling, The.
Mabel Martin.
Witch of Wenham, The.
Wright, J.   Witches Waken the Natural World in
    Spring.
Yeats.   Song Of Wandering Aengus, The.

Wittgenstein, Ludwig Josef Johann
Mahon.   Tractatus.

Wives
Ai.   Mother's Tale, The.
Berry, W.   Marriage.
Browning, R.   Any Wife to Any Husband.
Burns, R.   Broom Besoms ["I maun hae a wife,
    whatsoe'er she be"].
English Song.
Henpeck'd Husband, The.
Kellyburnbraes.
My Wife's a Wanton Wee Thing.
My Wife's a Winsome Wee Thing.
Sic a Wife as Willie Had.
Weary Pund o' Tow, The.
Campion, T.   What is it that all men possesse,
    among themselves conversing?
Carver, R.   Bonnard's Nudes.
Cherish.
Coleridge, S.   Happy Husband, The.
Life in Death.
Cowper, W.   To Mary.
Creeley.   Obscene Poem, An.
Sing Song.
Cummings, E. E.   S.T.
Cunningham, J.   Epigram: "Here lies my wife.
    Eternal peace."
Prue loved her man: to clean, to mend.
Davie, D.   Christmas Syllabics for a Wife.
Lady Cochrane.
Dickinson, E.   Many an angel, with its needle.
Dove, R.   Daystar.
Dunbar, P.   To a Poet and a Lady.
To Alice Dunbar.
Eliot, T. S.   Dedication to My Wife, A.

Emerson, R.   All the great & good.
Dust unto dust! and shall no more be said.
Hearst thou, sweet spirit, thou hast heard before.
I am alone. Sad is my solitude.
She never comes to me.
Where art thou / Thou beautiful dream.
Written in Naples, March, 1833.
Frost, R.   Paul's Wife.
Hall, D.   Mr. and Mrs. Billings.
Hardy, T.   Every Artemisia.
I Sometimes Think.
Two Wives, The.
Wife Comes Back, A.
Wives in the Sere.
Woman's Fancy, A.
Heaney, S.   Afterwards, An.
Wife's Tale, The.
Ignatow, D.   Across the Room.
Shapely.
That's the Sum of It.
Jacobsen, J.   Ballad of Henry, Bridegroom.
Rock-Plant Wife, The.
Jarrell, R.   Next Day.
Well-to-Do Invalid, A.
Jonson, B.   Epistle. To Katharine, Lady
    Aubigny.
Kizer, C.   Columns and Caryatids.
Komunyakaa.   Fleshing-out the Season.
Laughlin, J.   Care and Feeding of a Poet, The.
Lawrence, D. H.   Good Husbands Make
    Unhappy Wives.
Lady Wife.
Painter's Wife, The.
She Was a Good Little Wife.
Spanish Wife, The.
Two Wives.
Levine, P.   For Fran.
Lindsay, N.   To Eve, Man's Dream of Wifehood
    as Described by Milton.
Logan, J.   Two Poems for Women.
Lorde.   Evening News, The.
Lowell, R.   Old Flame, The.
Lux.   Night So Bright A Squirrel Reads, The.
Wife Hits Moose.
MacLeish.   Late Abed.
Poem in Prose.
Meredith, G.   M. M.
Millay, E.   Witch-Wife.
Milosz, C.   On Parting with My Wife, Janina.
Milton.   On His Deceased Wife.
Nash, O.   Always Marry an April Girl.
How to Harry a Husband, or, Is That Accessory
    Really Necessary?
Machinery Doesn't Answer, Either, but You
    Aren't Married to It.
Very Funny, Very Funny.
Warning to Wives, A.
Watchman, What of the First First Lady?
Nemerov.   Lot's Wife.
Parker, D.   Wives; A Hymn of Hate.
Pope, A.   Version of the First Psalm, for the Use
    of a Young Lady, A.
Prunty.   Actuarial Wife, The.
Ramanujan.   Love Poem for a Wife, 2.
Love Poem for a Wife and Her Trees.
Rexroth, K.   Andrée Rexroth ("Now once more
    gray mottled buckeye branches").
Riley, J.   Gudewife, The.
My First Womern.
Mylo Jones's Wife.
Wife-Blessed, The.
Robinson, E.   Evangelist's Wife, An.
Roethke.   Wish for a Young Wife.
Rossetti, C.   Helpmeet For Him, A.
Husband and Wife.
I caught a little ladybird.
I have a little husband / And he is gone to sea.
Rosalind.
Wee wee husband, / Give me some money.
Sexton.   For My Lover, Returning to His Wife.
Interrogation of the Man of Many Hearts, The.
Simic.   Thus.
Smart, C.   Apollo and Daphne.
Smith, S.   Be Off!
Devil-My-Wife, The.
Major Macroo.

Swift, J. Portrait from the Life, A.
Tate, J. Prose Poem.
Tennyson, A. June Bracken and Heather.
Tomlinson, C. Farmer's Wife: at Fostons Ash, The.
Portrait of Mrs. Spaxton.
Updike. Living with a Wife.
Painted Wives.
Walker, A. In Uganda an Early King.
Whittier. New Wife and the Old, The.
Williams, C. K. Alzheimer's: The Wife.
Signs.
Williams, M. Ghost of His Wife Comes to Tell Him How It Is, The.
Lay of the Badde Wyf.
Man in the Bar Says He Has Something to Say, A.
Williams, W. Mezzo Forte.
Thinker, The.
Young Housewife, The.
Wilner, E. Job's Wife, a Twentieth-Century Casting Script.
Wordsworth, W. Fragment: A Somersetshire Tragedy.
Wright, J. Complaint.
Paul.
Zukofsky, L. Record, The.
See also **Marriage**

Wollstonecraft, Mary
Browning, R. Mary Wollstonecraft and Fuseli.

Wolverines
Dickey, J. For the Last Wolverine.

Wolves
Blue Cloud. Wolf.
Broumas, O. Landscape Without Touch.
Codrescu. Dream Dogs.
Éluard, P. Wolf, A.
Graves, R. Lyceia.
Gunn, T. Allegory of the Wolf Boy, The.
Hall, D. Wolf Knife.
Hughes, T. February.
Howling of Wolves, The.
Ignatow, D. Modern Fable, A.
Jacobsen, J. Night Patrol.
Kipling, R. Only Son, The.
Kumin, M. Territory.
Lawrence, D. H. Red Wolf, The.
MacNeice. Wolves.
Merwin. Hollow, A.
Lemuel's Blessing.
Nemerov. Wolves in the Zoo.
Rilke. Song: "Let's pretend we are shepherds."
Tate, A. Wolves, The.
Wilner, E. Being as I Was, How Could I Help.

Woman Suffrage
Hardy, T. Woman I Met, The.
See also **Voting and Voters**

Wombats
Nash, O. Wombat, The.

Women
Amichai [*or* Amikhai]. Advice for Good Love.
Outing with a Woman.
Angelou. Family Affairs.
Lady Luncheon Club.
Momma Welfare Roll.
Phenomenal Woman.
Woman Me.
Woman Work.
Apollinaire. Annie.
Armantrout. Getting Warm.
Atwood. Aging Female Poet Sits on the Balcony.
At first I was given centuries.
Christmas Carols.
Marrying the Hangman.
Torture.
Women's Issue, A.
Baudelaire. Cat, The.
Damned Women ("Like ruminating cattle on the sand").
Giantess, The.
Little Old Women, The.
Promise in a Pair of Eyes, The.
Sisina.
Beckett, S. À elle l'acte calme.

Elles viennent.
Serena II.
They come.
Berry, W. Earth and Fire.
Mad Farmer in the City, The.
Marriage.
Berryman. To a Woman.
Young Woman's Song.
Blake, W. Pair of Stays to mend the Shape, A.
Woman scaly & a Man all Hairy, A.
Bogan, L. Changed Woman, The.
Evening in the Sanitarium.
Portrait.
Women.
Bradstreet, A. In Honour of that High and Mighty Princess Queen Elizabeth.
Prologue, The.
Brooks, G. Mrs. Small.
Sunset of the City, A.
Womanhood, The.
Broumas, O. Calypso.
Cinderella.
Knife & the Bread, The.
Maenad.
Memory Piece / for Baby Jane.
Rapunzel.
Snow White.
Thetis.
Triple Muse.
Browning, E. Isobel's Child.
Lord Walter's Wife.
To George Sand: A Desire.
To George Sand: A Recognition.
Browning, R. Lady and the Painter, The.
Pearl, a Girl, A.
Bukowski. Beginning, A.
Cows in Art Class.
Girls From Nowhere.
Love Poem, A.
Me.
Sandra.
Tonight.
Burns, R. Answer, The [To the Guidwife of Wauchope-House].
Beware o' Bonie Ann.
Bonnie Lesley.
Bonnie Peg.
Chloe.
Epitaph on a Henpecked Country Squire.
Fragment: "Altho' my bed were in yon muir."
Green Grow[s] the Rashes.
Grim Grizzle.
Hue and Cry of John Lewars, The.
Ken Ye What Meg o' the Mill Has Gotten.
Lassie wi' the Lintwhite Locks.
Muirland Meg.
My Peggy's Face.
O leave novels, ye Mauchline belles.
O Mally's Meek, Mally's Sweet.
On Being Asked Why God Had Made Miss D—— So Little and Mrs A——— So Big.
On Miss J. Scott, of Ayr.
Rights of Woman—Spoken by Miss Fontenelle on Her Benefit Night, The.
She's fair and fause that causes my smart.
Song: "I'll tell you a tale of a Wife."
Song. On Miss P——— K———, A.
Song. On Miss W. A.
Tarbolton Lasses, The.
Theniel Menzies' Bony Mary.
There was twa wives, and twa witty wives.
There's News Lasses News.
Tibbie Fowler.
To Chloris.
To Maria.
To the Beautiful Miss Eliza J———n, on Her Principles of Liberty and Equality.
Yon wild, mossy mountains sae lofty and wide.
Byron, G. Egotism. A Letter to J.T. Becher.
Girl of Cadiz, The.
She Walks In Beauty.
To Eliza.
To Harriet.
To ———: "Oh! well I know your subtle Sex."
Campion, T. Ev'ry Dame affects good fame, what ere her doings be.

I Care Not for These Ladies.
If Love loves truth, then women do[e] not love.
In Sannium.
In se.
See Where She Flies.
So many loves have I neglected.
Vain Men, Whose Follies.
What is it that all men possesse, among themselves conversing?
Why presumes thy pride on that, that must so private be.
Young and Simple though I Am.
Carew, T. Conquest by Flight.
Rapture, A.
Song[, A]: "Ask[e] me no more where Jove bestow[e]s."
To My Mistress Sitting by a River's Side; an Eddy.
Carruth, H. Anima.
Assignment.
Cross My Heart and Hope to Die, It Was the Very Same Song Exactly.
I Tell You For Several Years of My Madness I Heard the Voice of Lilith Singing in the Trees of Chicago
Chaucer. Against Women Unconstant [*or* A Ballade against Woman Inconstant].
Legend of Good Women, The.
Ciardi, J. Rhetoric for Danny Keough to Recite at the Bar, A.
Clampitt. Dodona: Asked of the Oracle.
Field Pansy, The.
Written in Water.
Clifton, L. Dream of Foxes, A.
Female.
Poem in Praise of Menstruation.
Song at Midnight.
Women You Are Accustomed To, The.
Codrescu. "MAN" and "WOMAN," these are horrid words, they annoy me.
Coleridge, S. Love's Burial-Place.
To a Lady.
Collins, B. Man in Space.
Cooper, J. Eve.
Creeley. Air: "The Love of a Woman."
All That Is Lovely in Men.
Circle, The.
Dream, The.
Finger, The.
For Irving.
Form of Adaptation, A.
Hands, The.
Irish.
Letter, The.
Memory, The.
Name, The.
Paradox, The.
Person.
Photo.
Prejudice, The.
Sentence, The.
Son: "What I took in my hand."
Story, The.
Three Ladies, The.
Whip, The.
Woman, The.
Women.
Young Woman.
Cummings, E. E. 2 shes / both not quite / young perfectly.
Any man is wonderful.
As Joe Gould says in.
Ballade: "White night roared with a huge north-wind, The."
Between the breasts / of bestial.
By little accurate saints thickly which tread.
Cleopatra built / like a smooth arrow or.
Dress was a suspicious madder, importing the cruelty of roses, The.
Ev erythingex Cept: / that / 's what she's.
Fabulous against ,a,fathoming jelly.
Fearlessandbosomy / this / grand:gal.
Five Americans.
"Gay" is the captivating cognomen of a Young Woman of cambridge,mass.
Hips lOOsest OOping shoulders blonde&

pastoral hair,strong.
I have seen her a stealthily frail.
If I Have Made, My Lady.
Impossibly / motivated by midnight.
In making Marjorie god hurried.
Inthe,exquisite; / morning sure lyHer eye s
    exactly sit,ata little roundtable.
Irreproachable ladies firmly lewd.
Is there a flower(whom).
Like a / grey / rock wanderin, A.
Little ladies more / than dead exactly dance.
My girl's tall with hard long eyes.
My lady is an ivory garden.
My smallheaded pearshaped.
Perhaps it is to feel strike.
Pretty a day, A.
Puella Mea.
She sits dropping on a caret of clenched arms.
Which is the very.
Who(at / her nons- / elf).
You are like the snow only.
Cunningham, J.   Lights of Love, The.
Dante Alighieri.   Sestina: "I have reached, alas,
    the long shadow."
Sonnet: He imagines a pleasant Voyage for
    Guido, Lapo Gianni, and himself.
"Dario."   Ballad in Honor of the Muses of Flesh
    and Blood.
Flesh, a woman's heavenly flesh. Clay.
Davie, D.   Women and War.
De la Mare.   Here Sleeps.
Devecseri.   Women and Masks.
Dickey, J.   Enclosure, The.
Two Women.
Weeds.
Dickinson, E.   Her breast is fit for pearls.
Title divine—is mine!
What Soft—Cherubic Creatures.
Donne.   Community.
Indifferent, The.
Love's Alchemy [or Alchemie].
Manliness.
Primrose, The; Being at Montgomery Castle,
    upon the hill, on which it is situate.
Song: "Go and catch a falling star."
To the Countess of Huntingdon ("Madam, / Man
    to God's image, Eve, to man's was made").
Twickenham [or Twicknam] Garden.
Woman's Constancy.
Dove, R.   For Kazuko.
Spy.
Taking in Wash.
Dunbar, P.   Made to Order Smile, The.
On the Dedication of Dorothy Hall.
Turning of the Babies in the Bed, The.
Duncan, R.   Bending the Bow.
Maiden, The.
Eberhart, R.   Apple Buds.
Bells of a Chinese Temple, The.
Lament of a New England Mother, The.
Legend of Viable Women, A.
Marrakech.
Redemption.
Ruby Daggett.
Spring Mountain Climb.
To Harriet Monroe.
To Kenya Tribesmen, the Turkana.
Vastness and Indifference of the World, The.
Eliot, T. S.   Cousin Nancy.
Éluard, P.   Scene.
Universe-Solitude.
Emerson, R.   All that thy virgin soul can ask be
    thine.
Romany Girl, The.
Seemed to me—never maid.
Gallagher, T.   Breasts.
Conversation with a Fireman from Brooklyn.
From Dread in the Eyes of Horses.
Instructions to the Double.
On Your Own.
Story of a Citizen, The.
Woman Who Raised Goats, The.
Glück, L.   Aphrodite.
Autumnal.
Palais des Arts.
Porcelain Bowl.

Graves, R.   Above the Edge of Doom.
Antorcha Y Corona, 1968.
At Best, Poets.
Batxóca.
Dans un Seul Lit.
Gateway, The.
Hung Wu Vase, The.
In Her Praise.
Iron Palace.
La Mejicana.
Lyceia.
Portrait, The.
Robbers' Den.
Ruby and Amethyst.
Sail and Oar.
Secret Land, The.
She Is No Liar.
Snap-Comb Wilderness, The.
Song: Crown of Stars.
Song: Dew-Drop and Diamond.
Three-Faced, The.
To Beguile and Betray.
Torch and Crown, 1968.
Traditionalist, The.
Undead, The.
What Can We Not Ask?
White Goddess, The.
With the Gift of a Lion's Claw.
"H. D."   Dancer, The.
Huntress.
Master, The.
Hacker, M.   Azure striation swirls beyond the
    stones.
Ballad of Ladies Lost and Found.
Country & Western.
Elegy: "Crying from exile, I."
Mother II.
Pantoum.
Peterborough.
Prayer for my Daughter.
Rune of the Finland Woman.
Shirland Road.
Sisterhood.
Towards Autumn.
Hall, D.   Blue Wing, The.
Hardy, T.   Ballet, The.
Chosen, The.
Conjecture.
Coquette, and After, The.
Countenance, A.
Donaghadee.
Dream or No, A.
Elopement, The.
Epitaph on a Pessimist.
Her Definition.
I Knew a Lady.
Ice on the Highway.
On Stinsford Hill at Midnight.
One Ralph Blossom Soliloquizes.
Protean Maiden, The.
Rejected Member's Wife, The.
Rival, The.
So Various.
We Field-Women.
Winsome Woman, A.
Without, Not within Her.
Hayden, R.   Sphinx.
Herrick.   Defence for Women, A.
Deniall in Women No Disheartning to Men.
Descripcion; of a Woman, The.
I Call and I Call.
In Praise of Women.
Little and Loud.
No Fault in Women.
On Himselfe.
Request to the Graces, An.
Saint Distaffs Day, or the Morrow after Twelfth
    Day.
Short and Long Both Likes.
To His Girles.
To Meadows [or Meddowes].
To the Ladyes.
Upon Jone and Jane.
Upon Some Women.
Upon the Loss[e] of His Mistresses.
Women Uselesse.

Howe, F.   Nursery, The.
Hughes, L.   Harlem Sweeties.
Preference.
Hughes, T.   Fallgrief's Girlfriends.
Low Water.
Ignatow, D.   Brief Cases.
Jackson, L.   Helen's Faces.
Tiger, The.
Jacobsen, J.   First Woman.
Jarrell, R.   In Nature There Is Neither Right nor
    Left nor Wrong.
Next Day.
Jonson, B.   Another. In Defense of Their
    Inconstancy [or Inconstancie]. A Song.
In the Person of Womankind [A Song
    Apologetic].
Phoenix Analysed, The.
Satirical Shrub, A.
Song. That Women Are But Men's Shadows.
Keats.   Woman! When I Behold Thee Flippant,
    Vain.
Kinnell.   Cat, The.
Kinsella, T.   Ancestor.
Kipling, R.   Female of the Species, The.
Ladies, The.
Mary, Pity Women!
Song of the Lathes, The.
Vampire, The.
Kizer, C.   American Beauty, An.
Fearful Women.
Koch, K.   Sleeping with Women.
Kumin, M.   We Stood There Singing.
Larkin, P.   Deep Analysis.
Femmes Damnees.
In TImes When Nothing Stood.
Large Cool Store, The.
Letter to a Friend about Girls.
Mythological Introduction.
Laughlin, J.   Deconstructed Man, The.
Lawrence, D. H.   Dominant Woman.
Don't Look at Me.
Ego-Bound Women.
Energetic Women.
Female Coercion.
Flapper.
Frost Flowers.
I Wish I Knew a Woman.
In a Spanish Tram-Car.
It's No Good!
Men and Women.
Mournful Young Man.
One Woman to All Women.
Other Women Have Reared in Me.
Peacock.
Spirits Summoned West.
To Women, as Far as I'm Concerned.
Valentine's Night.
Volcanic Venus.
What Ails Thee?
Women Want Fighters for Their Lovers.
Wonderful Spiritual Women.
Levertov.   Abel's Bride.
Cancion: "When I am the sky."
Hypocrite Women.
In Mind.
Mutes, The.
Stepping Westward.
Woman Alone, A.
Woman, The.
Logan, J.   Dawn and a Woman.
Lorde.   For My Singing Sister.
Hard Love Rock II.
Keyfoods.
Need: A Chorale for Black Woman Voices.
NOW.
Poem for Women in Rage, A.
Seventh Sign, The.
Woman Thing, The.
MacDiarmid, H.   One of the Principal Causes of
    War.
Two Parents, The.
Vision of Scotland, A.
MacLeish.   Contemporary Portrait.
Steamboat Whistle, The.
Mahon.   Greta.
Major, C.   And who must remain.

Balance and Beauty.
Divine Law: A Blue Beach Sermon.
Dressed to Kill.
Giant Red Woman.
McGrath, T.   Behold the Woman.
Excursion: Or: O Columbus!, The.
McHugh, H.   Fable.
Two Loves.
Melville, H.   Marchioness of Brinvilliers, The.
Meredith, G.   Ballad of Fair Ladies in Revolt, A.
Marian: "She can be as wise as we."
Squireless Kate.
Meredith, W.   Korean Woman Seated by a Wall, A.
Merton.   Greek Women, The.
There Has to Be a Jail for Ladies.
Millay, E.   I, Being Born A Woman.
Oh, Oh, you will be sorry for that word!
Mistral, G.   Catalonian Woman.
Moore, M.   Sojourn in the Whale.
Nash, O.   Allow Me, Madam, But It Won't Help.
Cousin Euphemia Knows Best, or, Physician, Heal Somebody Else.
Frailty, Thy Name Is a Misnomer.
I Never Even Suggested It
It's about Time.
Just Wrap It Up, and I'll Throw It Away Later.
Lines to a Three-Name Lady.
Oh, Please Don't Get Up!
Oh, Shucks, Ma'am, I Mean Excuse Me.
That Reminds Me.
Thoughts Thought after a Bridge Party.
Wednesday Matinee.
What's the Use.
Who Understands Who Anyhow?
Woman Pulls the Wires.
Nemerov.   Lore.
Young Woman.
Niedecker.   She grew where every spring.
Woman in middle life.
Oliver, M.   Strawberry Moon.
Olson, C.   Anubis will stare.
As the shield goddess, Mycenae.
Barley or rye / blue and white green.
Cause, the Cause, The.
Conversation Galante.
Easter.
Ferrini—I.
For a Lady of Whom I Speak.
For Sappho, Back.
Help Me, Venus, You Who Led Me On.
I Believe in You.
Mazdaism / has overcome.
Moebius Strip, The.
Of Lady, of Beauty, of Stream.
O'Ryan.
Proensa.
She.
She-Bear, The.
She-Bear (II), The.
She, Thus.
So the Norse / were neurotic.
Soul, The.
To the She-Bear: *The 1st Song*.
Translation, A.
Troilus.
Woman's Nipples Is the Rose of the World, A.
Oppen.   Kind of Garden, A: A Poem for My Sister.
People, the People, The.
Source, The.
To the Muse.
Paley, G.   Is There a Difference between Men and Women.
My Father Said.
On the Fourth Floor.
On the Ramblas A Tree A Girl.
Song Stanzas of Private Luck; To Be Added Sometimes and Sometimes to Be Subtracted.
Woman invented fire and called it, A.
Parker, D.   Ballade of Unfortunate Mammals.
Gunman and the Débutante, The.
Lady in Back, The.
Lady's Reward, The.
On Being a Woman.

Second Oldest Story, The.
Song: "Clarabelle has golden hair."
Song of One of the Girls
Song of Perfect Propriety.
To a Lady.
Women; A Hate Song.
Patchen.   Letter on the Use of Machine Guns at Weddings, A.
Petrarch.   If that attractive look of hers can kill.
Piercy.   Burying Blues for Janis.
For Strong Women.
Juan's Twilight Dance.
Looking at Quilts.
Phyllis Wounded.
Right to Life.
Sabbath of Mutual Respect, The.
Unlearning to Not Speak.
What's That Smell in the Kitchen?
Window of the Woman Burning, The.
Woman in the Ordinary, The.
Plath.   Ariel.
Childless Woman.
Edge.
Female Author.
Old Ladies' Home.
Two Sisters of Persephone.
Vanity Fair.
Poe.   To Helen.
Valentine, A.
Pope, A.   Epistle [II,] to a Lady[: Of the Characters of Women].
Impromptu to Lady Winchelsea.
On a Certain Lady at Court.
On the Countess of Burlington Cutting Paper.
To a Lady with the Temple of Fame.
Version of the First Psalm, for the Use of a Young Lady, A.
Pound, E.   Tame Cat.
Prime, B.   Poetical Correspondence between Palemon and Æmilia, A.
Ramanujan.   Any Cow's Horn Can Do It.
Ransom, J.   Lady Lost.
Rich, A.   After Twenty Years.
Blood-Sister.
Cartographies of Silence.
Culture and Anarchy.
Education of a Novelist.
Essential Resources.
For Julia in Nebraska.
For L.G.: Unseen for Twenty Years.
From a Survivor.
From an Old House in America.
Heroines.
Hunger.
Meditations for a Savage Child.
Mirror in Which Two Are Seen as One, The.
Natural Resources.
Paula Becker to Clara Westhoff.
Phantasia for Elvira Shatayev.
Phenomenology of Anger, The.
Planetarium.
Re-forming the Crystal.
Roots.
Snapshots of a Daughter-in-Law.
To Judith, Taking Leave.
Transit.
Translations.
Upcountry.
Waking in the Dark.
When/Then.
White Night.
Woman Dead in Her Forties, A.
Women.
Rilke.   Unknown Woman's Afternoon.
Rimbaud, A.   First Communions.
Ritsos.   Prison Tree and the Women, The.
Same Star, The.
Women.
Roethke.   I Knew A Woman.
She.
Rossetti, C.   From the Antique.
Goblin Market.
Helpmeet For Him, A.
"Immurata" Sister, An.
Lady Isabella.
Listen, and I will tell you of a face.

Passing and Glassing.
Rukeyser, M.   Burning Bush.
Cries From Chiapas.
Judith.
Käthe Kollwitz.
Letter to the Front.
More of a Corpse Than a Woman.
Mrs. Walpurga.
Myth.
Painters.
Rite.
Searching / Not Searching.
Song from *Puck Fair*.
Waterlily Fire.
Wreath of Women.
Sandburg, C.   Adelaide Crapsey.
Bitter Summer Thoughts—No. XXII.
Cadenza.
Cartoon.
Glimmer.
Lief the Lucky.
Night Stuff.
Pigeon.
Remembered Women.
Shag-Bark Hickory.
Three Shrines.
Two Women.
Two Women and Their Fathers.
Working Girls.
Sarton, M.   My Sisters, O My Sisters.
Schuyler, J.   Velvet Roses.
Seifert.   Fan, The.
Lost Paradise.
Philosophy.
Sexton.   Breast, The.
Consorting with Angels.
Fierceness of Female, The.
Her Kind.
Hurry Up Please It's Time.
In Celebration of My Uterus.
Rapunzel.
To Like, to Love.
Shapiro, K.   Back, The.
Buick.
Dome of Sunday, The [or A].
Girls Fighting, Broadway.
Waitress.
Sheridan, T.   New Simile for the Ladies, A.
To Dean Swift.
To the Dean.
Smith, S.   Celts, The.
Dear Female Heart.
Feminine Charm.
Fool, The.
Girls!
House of Mercy, A.
Lady of the Well-Spring, The.
Wretched Woman.
Snyder, G.   Alabaster.
Could She See the Whole Real World with Her Ghost Breast Eyes Shut under a Blouse Lid?
Love.
Spenser, E.   Epithalamion: "Ye learned sisters which have oftentimes."
Stock, R.   Double Ballade of Newfangled Ladies, A.
Stockton, A.   On Seeing Mrs Macauly Graham.
Poetical Correspondence between Palemon and Æmilia, A.
Sarcasm against the Ladies in a Newspaper, A; An Impromptu Answer.
Satire on the Fashionable Pompoons Worn by the Ladies in the Year 1753. by a Gentleman, A; Answered by a Young Lady of Sixteen.
To Miss Mary Stockton, an Epistle upon Some Gentleman Refusing to Admit Ladies of Their Circle into the Parlour.
To the Visitant, from a Circle of Ladies, on Reading His Paper.
Suckling, S.   Verses: "I am confirm'd a woman can."
Woman's Constancy.
Swift, J.   Answer to a Scandalous Poem, An.
Cassinus and Peter.
Dean Swift's Answer to the Reverend Dr. Sheridan.

Death and Daphne.
Furniture of a Woman's Mind, The.
Hardship Put upon Ladies, The.
Journal of a Modern Lady, The.
Lady's Dressing Room, The.
Szymborska, W.　Rubens' Women.
Tennyson, A.　Dream of Fair Women, A.
Thomas, D.　In the White Giant's Thigh.
Tomlinson, C.　Black Nude.
Rhenish Winter.
Tu Fu.　Profile of a Lady.
Updike.　Cunts.
Klimt and Schiele Confront the Cunt.
Vallejo.　Down to the Dregs.
Van Duyn.　Cities of the Plain, The.
Villon.　Gone Ladies.
Vogl.　Sweetheart of the Csikos, The.
Walker, A.　Pagan.
Well.
Woman Is Not a Potted Plant, A.
Ward, N.　Mercury shew'd Apollo, Bartas Book.
Warren, R.　Portraits of Three Ladies.
Whitman, W.　I Sing the Body Electric.
Unfolded Out of the Folds.
Woman Waits for Me, A.
Whittier.　To a Friend.
Wilbur, R.　Catch, The.
She.
Williams, C. K.　Dominion: Depression.
Williams, T.　Winter Smoke Is Blue and Bitter.
Williams, W.　And Thus with All Praise.
Atlantic City Convention, The.
Classic Picture.
Cold Night, The.
Conventional Ballad.
Crystal Maze, A.
Fertile.
Girl, The.
In the 'Sconset Bus.
Mama.
Marriage.
Mounted as an Amazon.
Portrait of a Lady.
Portrait of a Woman in Bed.
Proletarian Portrait.
Queen-Anne's-Lace.
Three Sonnets.
To a Chinese Woman.
To a Friend Concerning Several Ladies.
To an Old Jaundiced Woman.
To Daphne and Virginia.
Woman Walking.
Wilner, E.　Maya.
Wordsworth, W.　Epitaph in Grasmere Church.
Lines Written in the Album of the Countess of
Lonsdale.
Lo! Where She Stands Fixed in a Saint-like
Trance.
She was a Phantom of delight.
Solitary Reaper, The.
To —, in Her Seventieth Year.
To the Lady E.B. and the Hon. Miss P.
Wright, J.　So She Said.
Witches Waken the Natural World in Spring.
Wyatt, S.　Divers[e] [or Dyvers] doth[e] use, as
I have heard and kno[w].
Lover Showeth How He Is Forsaken of Such as
He Sometime Enjoyed, The.
Yeats.　Crazy Jane Talks with the Bishop.
First Confession, A.
Friends.
He Tells a Valley Full of Lovers.
Heart of the Woman, The.
Lady's First Song, The.
Lady's Second Song, The.
Lapis Lazuli.
Michael Robartes and the Dancer.
No Second Troy.
On Woman.
Prayer for My Daughter, A.
Presences.
Thought from Propertius, A.
To an Isle in the Water.
Woman Homer Sung, A.
Zaturenska.　Girl Takes Her Place Among the
Mothers, The.

Zukofsky, L.　After Charles Sedley.
One lutenist played *look*; your through was
drink.

Wood
Bly, R.　Old Boards.
Carruth, H.　Block.
Collins, B.　Splitting Wood.
Dunbar, P.　To Pfrimmer.
Eberhart, R.　Dry Rot, The.
Frost, R.　Wood-Pile, The.
García Lorca.　Song of the Barren Orange Tree.
Gurney, I.　Felling a Tree.
Hardy, T.　Workbox, The.
Howe, S.　We that were wood / when that a
wide wood was.
Koch, K.　Down at the Docks.
Kumin, M.　Splitting Wood at Six Above.
Kunitz, S.　Knot, The.
Larkin, P.　Gathering Wood.
Lawrence, D. H.　Bowls.
Lowell, R.　Soft Wood.
MacLeish.　Cat in the Wood, The.
Merwin.　One Time.
Nash, O.　Termite, The.
Niedecker.　New-sawed.
Sze.　Wood Whittler, The.
Woodpeckers
Creeley.　Like They Say.
Williams, W.　To a Woodpecker.
Woodpecker, The.
Woods
Ammons.　Kind.
Love Song: "Rings of birch bark."
Woodsroad, The.
Berry, W.　Bird Killer, The.
Grace.
Independence Day.
Satisfactions of the Mad Farmer, The.
Stay Home.
Winter Night Poem for Mary.
Woods.
Carruth, H.　Bearer, The.
Existence Before Essence.
Far-removed Mountain Men, The.
Line, The.
Little Fire in the Woods, The.
No Supervening Thought of Grace.
Once More.
Poet, The.
Clampitt.　Green.
Hickory Grove, The.
Clare, J.　Gipsies: "Gipsies seek wide sheltering
woods again, The."
De la Mare.　Last Coachload, The.
Tom's Angel.
Tryst, The.
Emerson, R.　As I walked in the woods.
I to my garden went.
In dreamy woods, what forms abound.
Miracle, The.
October woods, wherein.
These trees like tho'ts that to visions congeal.
Titmouse, The.
Woods.
Frost, R.　Come In.
Glück, L.　Early December in Croton-on-
Hudson.
Graves, R.　Green Woods of Unrest, The.
Gunn, T.　Fair in the Woods, The.
Here Come the Saints.
Gurney, I.　Brimscombe.
Heaney, S.　Plantation, The.
Hopkins, G.　Woods in Spring.
Housman.　We'll to the woods no more.
Hughes, T.　Trees.
Ignatow, D.　Hope, The.
In the Woods.
Walk There.
Jacobsen, J.　Woods, The.
Kinnell.　Fergus Falling.
That Silent Evening.
Kinsella, T.　In the Ringwood.
Komunyakaa.　Poetics of Paperwood.
Kumin, M.　My Elusive Guest.
Kunitz, S.　River Road.
Levertov.　Breathing, The.

Vron Woods (North Wales), The.
Lux.　Night So Bright A Squirrel Reads, The.
Meredith, G.　Daphne.
In the Woods.
On Combe Bottom: Surrey.
Will o' the Wisp.
Youthful Quest, The.
Meredith, W.　For Two Lovers in the Year 2075
in the Canadian Woods.
Merwin.　Wood, A.
Muldoon, P.　Wood, The.
Nemerov.　Deep Woods.
Paley, G.　Then.
Walking in the Woods.
Patchen.　Beyond the Dark Cedars.
Petrarch.　Three days before, my soul reached
such a place.
Walking these woods and these unfriendly ways.
Rimbaud, A.　Fairy.
Roethke.　Light Poem.
Praise to the End!
Rossetti, D.　Young Fir-Wood, A.
Rukeyser, M.　Then I Saw What the Calling
Was.
Sacchetti.　On a Wet Day.
Schuyler, J.　Just before Fall.
Simic.　Forest Birds.
Smith, S.　Brickenden, Hertfordshire.
I Rode With My Darling.
Little Boy Lost.
Swenson, M.　Woods at Night, The.
Tomlinson, C.　At the Edge.
Vogl.　Love of the Woods.
Warren, R.　No Bird Does Call.
Rather Like a Dream.
Wilbur, R.　Children of Darkness.
Fern-Beds in Hampshire County.
Williams, W.　Source, The.
To a Wood Thrush.
Wordsworth, W.　Fragments from the
"Christabel" Note-book.
How sweet it is, when mother Fancy rocks.
Nutting.
Yeats.　Ragged Wood, The.
Zukofsky, L.　Guests, The.
See also **Forests**
Wool
Nash, O.　Shinking Song.
Woolf, Virginia
Clampitt.　Hippocrene.
Corbett, W.　Desert Storm.
Schuyler, J.　Virginia Woolf.
Woolworth Building, New York City
Sandburg, C.　Again?
Worcestershire, England
Davie, D.　Worcestershire.
Words
Amichai [*or* Amikhai].　Beit Guvrin.
Sea and the Shore, The.
Summer Rest and Words.
Ammons.　Motion.
Triphammer Bridge.
Armantrout.　Words.
Auden.　Words.
Beckett, S.　Mots survivants.
Tailpiece.
Berry, W.　Autumn Burning, An.
Meditation in the Spring Rain.
Bierce.　Abracadabra.
Borges.　Compass.
To a Minor Poet of 1899.
Brodsky, J.　Ab Ovo.
Broumas, O.　Etymology.
Bukowski.　Hey, Ezra, Listen to This.
Itch, Come and Gone.
Chuang Tzu.　Duke Hwan and the Wheelwright.
Clampitt.　Ano Prinios.
Clough.　Go foolish thoughts, and join the
throng.
Codrescu.　"MAN" and "WOMAN," these are
horrid words, they annoy me.
Muffled by a Belt across the Mouth.
Sunday Sermon.
Creeley.　Diction.
Epic Expands, The.

Gemini.
Language, The.
Numbers.
Oh, Love.
Phone.
Sign ("'SIEMENS" not").
Thinking.
To Say It.
Token, A.
Trees.
Waiting ("He pushes behind the words").
Water Music.
Words.
Cullen, C. Incident.
Karenge Ya Marenge.
Cummings, E. E. Here is little Effie's Head.
Little joe gould has lost his teeth and doesn't
know where.
Dickey, J. Basics.
Dickinson, E. Amazing human [or Human]
heart [or Heart].
Could mortal lip divine.
How vast is the chastisement of Beauty.
I hesitate which word to take.
Man may make a Remark, A.
To tell the Beauty would decrease.
Word is dead, A.
Dove, R. Ö.
Duncan, R. For a Muse Meant.
Poem in Stretching, A.
Upon Taking Hold.
Eberhart, R. Ideal and the Real, The.
Words.
Emerson, R. And as the light divided the dark.
I will not hesitate to speak the word.
On thee has God conferred.
S. R.
Frost, R. Beyond Words.
Ends.
Gallagher, T. Love Poem to Be Read to an
Illiterate Friend.
When You Speak to Me.
Graves, R. Dance of Words.
Forbidden Words.
Never Such Love.
Tilth.
Word, The.
Gunn, T. For a Birthday.
Words.
Hacker, M. Forage Sestina.
Hamill, S. Gift of Tongues, The.
Hughes, L. Songs.
Hughes, T. Poets.
Jackson, L. Come, Words, Away.
Hospitality to Words.
When Love Becomes Words.
World and I, The.
Jacobsen, J. Shibboleth.
Spring, Says the Child.
There Is Good News.
Jarrell, R. Islands, The.
Kizer, C. Arthur's Party.
Koch, K. Permanently.
Larkin, P. Talking In Bed.
Laughlin, J. Importance of Dictionaries, The.
You've Set the Words.
Lawrence, D. H. Conundrums.
Levi, P. Voices.
Levine, P. Words.
Longfellow, H. Day Is Done, The.
Lorde. Coal.
Lux. Kwashiorkor; Marasmus.
Onomatopoeia.
MacLeish. Reproach to Dead Poets.
They Come No More, Those Words, Those
Finches.
MacNeice. Idle Talk.
Plain Speaking.
Mahon. Glengormley.
Major, C. Swallow the Lake.
McHugh, H. I Knew I'd Sing.
To Have To.
Merrill, J. Dedication: "Hans, there are
moments when the whole mind."
Nightgown.
Merton. Tower of Babel.

Merwin. Unwritten, The.
Words.
Millay, E. It is the fashion now to wave aside.
Milosz, C. Philology.
Moore, M. Avec Ardeur.
Muldoon, P. Quoof.
Nash, O. Do You Plan to Speak Bantu? or
Abbreviation is the Thief of Sanity.
Literary Scene, The.
Reflections on the Vernacular.
Nemerov. One Way.
Neruda. Pedro Is When.
Olson, C. Abstract #1, Yucatan.
B Cs (3—for Rimbaud), A.
B Cs, A.
New Poem.
Orr, G. Glukupikron.
Tree, The.
Pagis. Lament for a Master of Style.
Paley, G. NOW.
Word Thrum, The.
Palmer, M. All those words we once used for
things but have now discarded in order to
come to know things.
Maria's Gift.
Notes for Echo Lake 3.
Sun.
Voice and Address.
Words say, mispell and mispell your name.
Parker, D. Little Words.
Patchen. To Be Charmed.
Piercy. At the Core.
Athena in the Front Lines.
Meetings Like Hungry Beaks.
Plath. Conversation among the Ruins.
Munich Mannequins, The.
Poems, Potatoes.
Sorcerer Bids Farewell to Seem, A.
Words.
Poe. Valentine, A.
Pope, A. Verses Occasioned by an & c. at the
End of Mr. D'Urfy's Name.
Raine, K. Night in Martindale.
Word Made Flesh.
Ritsos. Moderation.
Need to Express.
Same Meaning, The.
Rossetti, C. City plum is not a plum, A.
If I Had Words.
Rukeyser, M. Ballad of Orange and Grape.
Forerunners.
Rune.
Sandburg, C. Basket.
Crossing the Paces.
Different Kinds of Good-by.
Is Wisdom a Lot of Language?
Languages.
Little Girl, Be Careful What You Say.
Monosyllabic.
Precious Moments.
Seventeen Months.
Speech.
Threes.
Schuyler, J. Freely Espousing.
Sexton. Words.
Shelley, P. To———: "One word is too often
profaned."
Smith, S. La Speakerine de Putney.
Lord Say-and-Seal.
Pretty.
Snyder, G. Riprap.
Spender, S. Word.
Stafford, W. Putting the Sonnet to Work.
Report from a Far Place.
That Year.
Stein, G. More Grammar for a Sentence.
New.
Practice of Oratory.
Stock, R. Epistle to Simon Perchik.
"I'd Understand Yer Poemes Better," Writes the
Lady Editor from San Francisco, "If I
Knowed What the Words Mean."
Thomas, D. Especially When the October
Wind.
Once It Was the Colour of Saying.
Tomlinson, C. Double Rainbow, The.

Ritornello.
Walks.
Whitman, W. Font of Type, A.
Song of the Answerer.
Wilbur, R. Games Two.
Williams, M. Little Poem, A.
Logos.
Williams, W. Fragment: "As for him who."
Offering.
Sort of a Song, A.
Wright, C. Still Life with Stick and Word.
Wright, J. In Shame and Humiliation.
Morality of Poetry, The.
Yeats. Old Memory.
Song of the Happy Shepherd, The.
Words.
Zukofsky, L. Non Ti Fidar.
Peri Poietikes.
(Ryokan's scroll).
Translation, The.
You three:—my wife.
See also **Language**

Wordsworth, Dorothy
Clampitt. Coleorton.
Easedale Tarn.
Grasmere.
Rydal Mount.
Stock, R. On a Gift of Leaves From Dove
Cottage Close, Grasmere.
Zaturenska. Leaves from the Book of Dorothy
Wordsworth.

Wordsworth, William
Arnold, M. Memorial Verses.
Youth of Nature, The.
Browning, E. On a Portrait of Wordsworth by
B. R. Haydon.
Browning, R. Lost Leader, The.
Byron, G. Braziers, It Seems, Are Preparing to
Pass, The.
Epilogue: "There's something in a stupid ass."
Clampitt. Coleorton.
Easedale Tarn.
Grasmere.
Rydal Mount.
Coleridge, S. Hexameters.
To W. Wordsworth.
To William Wordsworth.
Tribute to Wordsworth.
Collins, B. Lines Composed over Three
Thousand Miles from Tintern Abbey.
Davie, D. Hawkshead and Dachau in a
Christmas Glass.
Meredith, G. Poetry of Wordsworth, The.
Shelley, P. To Wordsworth.
Stock, R. On a Gift of Leaves From Dove
Cottage Close, Grasmere.
Whittier. Wordsworth.
Wordsworth, W. 1811.
Zaturenska. Leaves from the Book of Dorothy
Wordsworth.

Work and Workers
Amichai [or Amikhai]. Beginning of Autumn in
the Hills of Ephraim.
Angelou. One More Round.
Woman Work.
Auden. Taller To-day.
Baudelaire. Posthumous Work.
Ransom, The.
Berry, W. Adze, The.
From the Distance.
Satisfactions of the Mad Farmer, The.
Berryman. Animal Trainer, The.
Blok. Factory, The.
Brodsky, J. Autumn in Norenskaia.
Broumas, O. Field.
Sweeping the Garden.
Browning, E. Work.
Work and Contemplation.
Bukowski. Fragile!
Green.
How I Got Started.
Sparks.
Transformation and Disfiguration.
Burns, R. Extemporaneous Effusion on Being
Appointed to the Excise, An.
Merry Hae I Been Teethin a Heckle.

Carver, R. Egress.
Kafka's Watch.
Mailman as Cancer Patient, The.
Work.
Ciardi, J. Elegy: "My father was born with a spade in his hand and traded it."
Clampitt. Marginal Employment.
Clifton, L. What I Think When I Ride the Train.
Codrescu. Old Photo.
Work.
Coleridge, S. Work without Hope.
Crane, S. Many workmen / Built a huge ball of masonry.
Creeley. On Vacation.
"To Work Is to Contradict Contradications, to Do Violence to Natural Violence."
Cummings, E. E. At the ferocious phenomenon of 5 o'clock i find myself gently decompos.
Davie, D. Felicity's Fourth Order.
Dickinson, E. It is easy to work when the soul is at play.
Some—Work for Immortality.
Work is a bleak redeemer.
Dove, R. Satisfaction Coal Company, The.
Zeppelin Factory, The.
Dugan, A. Credo.
Jack-Off of the Graveyard Shift, The.
Memories of a Boss in an Ad Agency.
Morning at Speed Products.
On a Seven-Day Diary.
On Work.
Prayer: "God, I need a job because I need money."
Swing Shift Blues.
Untitled Poem: "Two shots down and I'm exalted."
Dunbar, P. Get Somebody Else.
Not They Who Soar!
Eberhart, R. Clam Diggers and Diggers of Sea Worms, The.
Emerson, R. Comrade or the book is good, The.
On bravely through the sunshine & the showers.
When thou sittest moping.
Enzensberger, H. Employee, The.
Frost, R. "Out, Out—."
Gallagher, T. Black Money.
Ginsberg, A. Bricklayer's Lunch Hour, The.
Graves, R. Work-Room.
Gunn, T. To a Friend in Time of Trouble.
Gurney, I. I Would Not Rest.
Lock Keeper, The.
Servitude.
Hall, D. 1934.
Foundations of American Industry, The.
Stump.
Valley of Morning.
HaNagid. Stab Your Heart.
Hardy, T. At the Aquatic Sports.
Four in the Morning.
Unkindly May, An.
You on the Tower.
Heaney, S. Bann Clay.
Servant Boy.
Herrick. Beginning, Difficult.
First Work, and Then Wages.
Heaven.
No Paines, No Gaines.
Nothing Free-Cost.
To His Nephew, to Be Prosperous in His Art of Painting.
Upon Cuffe. Epig.
Upon Strut.
Housman. When smoke stood up from Ludlow.
Hughes, L. Always the Same.
Black Workers.
Brass Spittoons.
Buddy.
Chant for May Day.
Chant for Tom Mooney.
Elevator Boy.
Fired.
Florida Road Workers.
Good Morning Revolution.
Labor Storm.
Madam and Her Madam.

Man into Men.
Mississippi Levee.
Necessity.
Negro Servant.
Office Building: Evening.
One More "S" in the U.S.A.
Share-Croppers.
Song to a Negro Wash-woman, A.
Wait.
Hughes, T. Sketching a Thatcher.
Ignatow, D. Notes for a Lecture.
Jacobsen, J. Absence of Slaves, An.
Johnson, S. Gnothi Seauton (Post Lexicon Anglicanum Auctum et Emendatum).
Kinsella, T. Worker in Mirror, at his Bench.
Kipling, R. Imperial Rescript, An.
Jubal and Tubal Cain.
King's Job, The.
Mary's Son.
Sons of Martha, The.
Koch, K. Thank You.
Larkin, P. Dedicated, The.
Laughlin, J. Getting Paid.
Job Description, A.
Problem Struck Me, The.
Secretary's Story, The.
Lawrence, D. H. But I Say unto You: Love One Another.
City-Life.
Labour Battalion.
Moon Memory.
People, The.
Sex Won't Work.
Wages.
What Is He?
What Is Man Without an Income.
Why—?
Work.
Levertov. Visit, A.
Levi, P. Profession, A.
Proxy.
Work, The.
Levine, P. Look.
Sweet Will.
You Can Have It.
Lindsay, N. Sweet Briars of the Stairways.
Logue, C. I've worked here all my life.
Story of the Road, The.
Longfellow, H. Village Blacksmith, The.
Lux. Deadhouse at the Workhouse, The.
His Job is Honest and Simple.
Horatian Notion, An.
Old Man Shoveling Snow.
What I See When I Drive to Work.
McGrath, T. Little Song about Charity, A.
Proletarian in Abstract Light.
Meredith, G. I say, that but for black Foakes'-day.
Merrill, J. Three Chores.
Merton. Trappists, Working.
Merwin. Walking into Autumn.
Milosz, C. Ballad of Levallois.
Nash, O. Introspective Reflection.
Will Consider Situation.
Nemerov. Sunday at the End of Summer.
Neruda. Child of the Moon.
Negative Hands.
Niedecker. Can knowledge be conveyed that isn't felt?
No retiring summer stroke.
Working man appeared in the street, A.
Olson, C. Praises, The.
Oppen. Amalgamated, The.
Antique.
Debt.
It brightens up into the branches.
Men of Sheepshead, The.
Rationality.
Patchen. In Order to.
No one ever works alone.
Pessoa. Story of Salomon Waste, The.
Pinsky. Cold, The.
To My Father.
Rexroth, K. Working Day, The.
Riley, J. Toil.
Rilke. Rose on Sunday.

Rimbaud, A. Lightning.
Lovely Morning Thought.
Workers.
Ritsos. Models, The.
Roethke. Gentle, The.
Rossetti, C. 4th May Morning.
Can I know it?—Nay.— / Shall I know it?—Yea.
Candlemas Dialogue, A.
Crying, my little one, footsore and weary?
I fancy the good fairies dressed in white.
I toiled on, but thou.
I Will Arise.
In Patience.
In weariness and painfulness St. Paul.
Margaret has a milking-pail, / And she rises early.
Our life is long. Not so, wise Angels say.
Pastime.
Pocket handkerchief to hem, A.
Septuagesima.
There Remaineth Therefore a Rest to the People of God.
Today's Burden.
Until the Day Break.
Weary in Well-Doing.
Where Neither Rust Nor Moth Doth Corrupt.
Would that I were a turnip white.
Yet A Little While.
Rukeyser, M. Face of the Dam: Vivian Jones.
Statement: Philippa Allen.
Sandburg, C. Blue Island Intersection.
Hazardous Occupations.
Moon Riders.
Noon Hour.
Smoke and Steel.
Stripes.
Two Women and Their Fathers.
Simic. Man, The.
Thus.
Smith, S. Childe Rolandine.
Snyder, G. Painting the North San Juan School.
Yase: September.
Spender, S. Unemployed.
Stafford, W. Life Work.
Stein, G. Tillie.
Sze. Moon Is a Diamond, The.
Thoreau. Have ye no work for a man to do.
I arose before light.
Warren, R. August Revival: Crosby Junction.
Whitman, W. Song for Occupations, A.
Whittier. Dedication: "I would the gift I offer here."
Mrs. Choate's House-Warming.
Seed-Time and Harvest.
Wilbur, R. Plain Song for Comadre, A.
Summer Morning, A.
Williams, C. K. Fast Food.
Sanctity, The.
Work.
Williams, T. Death Embrace, The.
Williams, W. Rogation Sunday.
Well Disciplined Bargeman, The.
Wordsworth, W. At Furness Abbey.
Labourer's Noon-Day Hymn, The.
Wright, C. Yard Work.
Wright, J. Youth.
Yeats. Spirit Medium, The.
Zagajewski. Georges Seurat: Factory.
Philosophers.
Room I Work In, The.

See also **Labor and Laborers**

World
Creeley. This World.
Enzensberger, H. Purgatorio.
Mahon. Tractatus.
Pagis. Lesson in Observation, A.
Stafford, W. Assurance.
Message from Space, A.
Swenson, M. Survey of the Whole.

See also **Earth**

World Federation
See **United Nations**

World War I
Chesterton. Elegy in a Country Churchyard.

Ciardi, J. Image of Man as a Gardener after Two World Wars.
Cooper, J. Threads: Rosa Luxemburg from Prison.
Cummings, E. E. Belgium.
Bigness of cannon, The.
Come,gaze with me upon this dome.
Earth like a tipsy.
It's jolly / odd what pops into.
Lis / -ten / you know what i mean when.
Look at this) / a 75 done.
My sweet old etcetera.
Opening of the chambers close.
Davie, D. Sculptures in Hungary.
Dubie. Desert Deportation of 1915, The.
Dugan, A. Memories of Verdun.
García Lorca. Abandoned Church.
Graves, R. Armistice Day, 1918.
Field Postcard, The.
Gurney, D. Possessions.
Riez Bailleul ("Riez Bailleul in blue tea-time").
Gurney, I. After War.
Ballad of the Three Spectres.
Behind the Line.
Butchers and Tombs.
Canadians.
First Time In.
Laventie.
New Year's Eve.
Of Grandcourt.
On Somme.
Riez Bailleul ("Behind the line there mending reserve posts, looking").
That Centre of Old.
Touchstone—Watching Malvern, The.
While I Write.
Ypres—Minsterworth.
Hall, D. Six Naps in One Day.
Hardy, T. And There Was a Great Calm.
Appeal to America on Behalf of the Belgian Destitute, An.
Before Marching and After.
Call to National Service, A.
Channel Firing.
Cry of the Homeless.
England to Germany in 1914.
I Met a Man.
In Time of "The Breaking of Nations."
In Time of Wars and Tumults.
Jezreel.
Men Who March Away.
New Year's Eve in War Time, A.
Often When Warring.
On the Belgian Expatriation.
Peace Peal, The.
Pity of It, The.
Sea Fight, The.
Then and Now.
War-Wife of Catknoll, The.
Heaney, S. In Memoriam Francis Ledwidge.
Hill, G. Mystery of the Charity of Charles Péguy, The.
To the Nieuport Scout.
Housman. Epitaph.
Hughes, L. Colored Soldier, The.
Hughes, T. Walt.
Jacobsen, J. For Wilfred Owen.
Jarrell, R. 1914.
Kipling, R. Beginnings, The.
Children, The.
Choice, The.
Clerks and the Bells, The.
Covenant, The.
Death-Bed, A.
Epitaphs of the War [1914–1918].
Farewell and adieu to you, Harwich Ladies.
For All We Have and Are [1914].
Gethsemane.
Justice.
King's Pilgrimage, The.
London Stone.
Lord Roberts.
Lowestoft Boat, The.
Memories.
Mesopotamia.
Mine Sweepers.

My Boy Jack.
North Sea Patrol, The.
Ode: "So long as memory, valour, and faith endure."
Outlaws, The.
Question, The.
Recantation, A.
Scholars, The.
Song at Cock-Crow, A.
Song in Storm, A.
Song of French Roads, A.
Song of the Lathes, The.
Tin Fish.
Trade, The.
Verdicts, The.
Kunitz, S. Lamplighter: 1914.
Larkin, P. MCMXIV.
Lawrence, D. H. Reality of Peace, 1916.
Song of a Man Who Has Come Through.
Tommies in the Train.
Town in 1917.
Milosz, C. Fear-Dream (1918).
Nemerov. Sarajevo.
Owen, W. 1914.
A Terre.
Anthem for Doomed Youth.
Apologia Pro Poemate Meo.
Calls, The.
Chances, The.
Conscious.
Disabled.
Dulce et Decorum Est.
Exposure.
Futility.
Greater Love.
Inspection.
Last Laugh, The.
Letter, The.
Next War, The.
Parable of the Old Men and the Young, The.
S.I.W.
Send-Off, The.
Show, The.
Smile, Smile, Smile.
Spring Offensive.
Strange Meeting.
To a Comrade in Flanders.
Pound, E. Coming of War, The; Actaeon.
Sandburg, C. Four Brothers, The.
Jaws.
Liars, The.
Million Young Workmen, 1915, A.
Seifert. November 1918.
Spender, S. In 1929.
Stafford, W. 1940.
Tomlinson, C. Poem for My Father.
Williams, M. Wiedersehen.
WWI.
Yeats. On Being Asked for a War Poem.
Zaturenska. Unsepulchred, 1914–1918, The.

World War II
Aragon. Lilacs and the Roses, The.
Berryman. 1 September 1939.
Dangerous Year, The.
Moon and the Night and the Men, The.
Nineteen Thirty-Eight.
Rock-Study with Wanderer.
White Feather.
Brooks, G. Gay Chaps at the Bar.
Bukowski. Troops, The.
Carruth, H. Mountain, The.
Ciardi, J. Elegy Just in Case.
Formalities, The.
Image of Man as a Gardener after Two World Wars.
Massive Retaliation.
Memory of the Sad Chair, A.
V-J Day.
Clampitt. Anniversary, The.
Cullen, C. La Belle, La Douce, La Grande.
Cummings, E. E. Why must itself up every of a park.
YgUDuh / ydoan / yunnuhstan.
Davie, D. 1945.
Eight Years After.
Elect, The.

In Chopin's Garden.
Kent.
Reminded of Bougainville.
Well-found Poem.
Dickey, J. Firebombing, The.
Two Poems of the Military.
Dove, R. Aircraft.
Aurora Borealis.
Sightseeing.
Dubie. Nineteen Forty.
Reader of the Sentences, The.
Sun and Moon Flowers: Paul Klee, 1879–1940.
Dugan, A. Memorial Service for the Invasion Beach Where the Vacation in the Flesh Is Over.
On the Civil War on the East Coast of the United States of North America 1860–64.
Eliot, T. S. Defense of the Islands.
To the Indians Who Died in Africa.
Ferlinghetti, L. L'Occupation Obsédée.
Gunn, T. Berlin in Ruins.
"H. D." Ancient Wisdom Speaks.
Body and Soul.
Christmas 1944.
Ecce Sponsus.
May 1943.
Hacker, M. Days of 1944: Three Friends.
Heaney, S. England's Difficulty.
Trial Runs.
Visitant.
Hill, G. Canaan.
De Jure Belli ac Pacis.
Howe, S. Pearl Harbor.
Hughes, L. Beaumont to Detroit: 1943.
Bonds for All.
Bonds: In Memoriam.
Crow Goes, Too.
Fourth of July Thought.
Give Us Our Peace.
Good Morning, Stalingrad.
Green Memory.
Jim Crow's Last Stand.
Joe Louis ("Joe Louis is a man").
Just an Ordinary Guy.
Message to the President.
Poem to Uncle Sam.
Relief.
Salute to Soviet Armies.
Southern Negro Speaks.
Speaking of Food.
Stalingrad: 1942.
Total War.
Underground, The.
When the Armies Passed.
Will V-Day Be Me-Day Too?
World War II.
Hughes, T. Motorbike, A.
Jarrell, R. 1945: The Death of the Gods.
Absent with Official Leave.
Angels at Hamburg, The.
Burning the Letters.
Camp in the Prussian Forest, A.
Dead in Melanesia, The.
Dead Wingman, The.
Death of the Ball Turret Gunner, The.
Eighth Air Force.
Field Hospital, A.
Front, A.
Germans Are Lunatics, The.
Good-bye, Wendover; Good-bye, Mountain Home.
Leave.
Losses.
Lullaby, A: "For wars his life and half a world away."
Machine-Gun, The.
Metamorphoses, The.
New Georgia.
Pilot from the Carrier, A.
Pilots, Man Your Planes.
Port of Embarkation.
Range in the Desert, The.
Rising Sun, The.
Second Air Force.
Sick Nought, The.
Siegfried.

Soldier, The.
Stalag Luft.
Subway from New Britain to the Bronx, The.
To the New World.
Transient Barracks.
Truth, The.
Ward in the States, A.
Jeffers, R.   Fourth Act.
Greater Grandeur.
Invasion.
May-June, 1940.
Miching Mallecho.
Nerves.
Ordinary Newscaster, An.
Pearl Harbor.
Shine, Empire.
War-Guilt Trials.
Kizer, C.   Twelve O'Clock.
Kumin, M.   Atlantic City 1939.
Kunitz, S.   Around Pastor Bonhoeffer.
Last Picnic, The.
Levertov.   On the 32nd Anniversary of the
   Bombing of Hiroshima and Nagasaki.
Levi, P.   Girl-Child of Pompei, The.
Logue, C.   Song of Autobiography, The.
Lowell, R.   Exile's Return, The.
Holy Innocents, The.
Mad Negro Soldier Confined at Munich, A.
MacNeice.   Neutrality.
Streets of Laredo, The.
Mahon.   One of These Nights.
McGrath, T.   Blues for Warren.
Merton.   Fable for a War.
For My Brother: Reported Missing In Action,
   1943.
Poem: "Light plays like a radio in the iron tree."
Milosz, C.   1945.
Book in the Ruins, A.
Campo dei Fiori.
Child of Europe.
Dedication: "You whom I could not save."
Farewell: "I speak to you, my son."
Flight.
In Warsaw.
Mid-Twentieth-Century Portrait.
Nation, A.
Six Lectures in Verse.
Songs of Adrian Zieliński.
Wanda.
With Her.
Montale.   Ballad Written in a Hospital.
Florentine Madrigals.
Hitler Spring, The.
Magnolia's Shadow, The.
Prisoner's Dream, The.
Moore, M.   In Distrust of Merits.
Keeping Their World Large.
Nemerov.   August, 1945.
Memory of the War, A.
Niedecker.   Allied Convoy / Reaches Russia.
European Travel / (Nazi New Order).
Look close.
Number of Britons killed, The.
Oliver, M.   1945—1985: Poem for the
   Anniversary.
Olson, C.   Town, The.
Oppen.   Blood from the Stone.
Myth of the Blaze.
Of Hours.
Patchen.   I Don't Want to Startle You but They
   Are Going to Kill Most of Us.
Rexroth, K.   Ausonius, Epistle 7.
Falling Leaves and Early Snow.
North Palisade, the End of September, 1939.
Past and Future Turn About.
Un Bel di Vedremo.
Rukeyser, M.   Breaking Open.
Do you know Hitler? Does he like you?
His gay words, words of delight.
Willkie: Words from Russia.
Sandburg, C.   Man with the Broken Fingers,
   The.
Schuyler, J.   Let's All Hear It for Mildred
   Bailey!
Seifert.   Bombing of the Town of Kralupy, The.
Dead of Lidice, The.

To Prague.
When in the history books.
Shapiro, K.   Progress of Faust, The.
Simic.   Begotten of the Spleen.
Smith, S.   I Remember.
Voices against England in the Night.
Spender, S.   War God, The.
Stafford, W.   Explaining the Big One.
Stevens, W.   Martial Cadenza.
Szymborska, W.   In Broad Daylight.
Tate, A.   Ode to Our Young Pro-consuls of the
   Air.
Tate, J.   Lost Pilot, The.
Tomlinson, C.   On the Tlacolula Bus.
Updike.   Munich.
Warren, R.   New Dawn.
Wilbur, R.   On the Eyes of an SS Officer.
Williams, M.   Curator, The.
Williams, W.   Sleeping Brute, The.
Wilner, E.   Trümmerfrauen.

Worldliness
Brooks, G.   Mrs. Small.
Clough.   From the contamination / Of laudation.
These vulgar ways that round me be.
Eberhart, R.   To Harriet Monroe.
Herrick.   Temporall Goods.
Petrarch.   At every step, I find I must look back.
Gluttony, sleep, swans-down of idleness.
Thoreau.   'T will soon appear if we but look.
Warren, R.   For a Friend Who Thinks Himself
   Urbane.
Wordsworth, W.   World is too much with us;
   late and soon, The.
Zukofsky, L.   Song for the Year's End, A.

World's Fair (1939)
Hall, D.   Tomorrow.

Worms
Ammons.   Autumn Song.
Clampitt.   Sea Mouse.
Dickinson, E.   Our little Kinsmen—after Rain.
Dugan, A.   Butcher!, Borges, What a Shock!,
   The.
Kizer, C.   Worms, The.
Lawrence, D. H.   Worm Either Way.
Levertov.   Earth Worm, The.
Lindsay, N.   Song of the Garden-Toad, The.
Lux.   Commercial Leech Farming Today.
MacDiarmid, H.   Ex Vermibus.
MacLeish.   Triumph of the Shell, The.
Marvell.   Mower to the Glowworms [or Glow-
   Worms or Glo-Worms], The.
Orr, G.   King of the Earthworms, The.
Parker, D.   Thought for a Sunshiny Morning.
Rossetti, C.   Handy Mole who plied no shovel,
   A.
Rumi.   Worm's Waking, The.
Sandburg, C.   Worms and the Wind.
Sexton.   Earthworm.
Simic.   Interlude.
Smith, S.   Reversionary.
Stevens, W.   Worms at Heaven's Gate, The.
Updike.   Earthworm.

Wormwood
Thoreau.   Tall Ambrosia.

Worry
Berry, W.   To My Children, Fearing for Them.
Chuang Tzu.   Need to Win, The.
Creeley.   Worry.
Davie, D.   On Not Deserving.
Frost, R.   Armful, The.
Hall, D.   Jealous Lovers, The.
Han-shan.   Man lives less than a hundred years,
   A.
Herrick.   His Change.
Jackson, L.   Ageless Brow, An.
Levertov.   Marta (Brazil, 1928).
Who Is at My Window.
Nash, O.   Tin Wedding Whistle.
Patchen.   Catfish River Lullaby.
Riley, J.   At Last.
Passing Hail, A.
Sandburg, C.   Curse of a Rich Polish Peasant on
   His Sister Who Ran Away with a Wild Man.
Schuyler, J.   Letter to a Friend: Who Is Nancy
   Daum?

Shadowy Room.
Simic.   Spoons with Realistic Dead Flies on
   Them.
Whalen, P.   I wrote 2 letters & a postcard.
Williams, C. K.   Experience.
Williams, M.   He Glimpses a Nobler Vision.
Wordsworth, W.   Affliction of Margaret, The.
Zaturenska.   All Is Well with the Child.
Worship and Worshipers
Baudelaire.   Litanies to Satan.
Blok.   Girl Was Singing, A.
Browning, R.   Boy and the Angel, The.
Numpholeptos.
Byron, G.   On the Day of the Destruction of
   Jerusalem by Titus.
Carew, T.   New Years Gift. To the Queen, A.
New Year's Sacrifice: To Lucinda, A.
Cavafy.   Before the Statue of Endymion.
Cavalcanti.   Figure of my Lady, A.
If you've forgotten me forever, Mercy.
Clampitt.   Matrix (Villa Serbelloni, Lake Como).
Coleridge, S.   Love's Sanctuary.
Cummings, E. E.   Lady / i pray to what is
   unimaginable.
Lean candles hunger in.
Unto thee i / burn incense.
Cunningham, J.   Timor Dei.
Davie, D.   If I Take the Wings of the Morning.
Just You Wait!
Dickinson, E.   Because the Bee may blameless
   hum.
Some keep the Sabbath going to Church.
We shun because we prize her Face.
Emerson, R.   Sursum Corda.
García Lorca.   Spinster at Mass, The.
"H. D."   Hippolytus Temporizes.
Magician [Master].
Hall, D.   Passage to Worship.
Hardy, T.   Afternoon Service at Mellstock.
Herbert, G.   Altar, The.
Antiphon (2): "Praised be the God of love."
Christmas.
Gratefulness.
Holy Scriptures (1), The.
Love (2).
Misery [or Miserie].
Praise (2).
Prayer (1): "Prayer the Church's banquet,
   Angels' age."
Sunday.
Temper (1), The.
Temper (2), The.
Hopkins, G.   Pied Beauty.
Housman.   New Year's Eve.
Hughes, L.   Testimonial.
Keats.   Fragment of an Ode to Maia Written on
   May Day, 1818.
Kipling, R.   L'Envoi; Departmental Ditties.
Lawrence, D. H.   Absolute Reverence.
Worship.
Lindsay, N.   At Mass.
Beyond the Moon.
Johnny Appleseed's Hymn to the Sun.
Merton.   After the Night Office—Gethsemani
   Abbey.
Evening: Zero Weather.
In the Rain and the Sun.
O Sweet Irrational Worship.
Song for Our Lady of Cobre.
Trappists, Working.
Word—a Responsory, The.
Milosz, C.   Why.
Olson, C.   Winter Solstice.
Orlandi, G.   If, my friend, you would have said
   of Mary so.
Petrarch.   I ran beneath the shade of shining
   leaves.
My ills oppress me, and I fear the worst.
Ramanujan.   Devotee's Complaint, A.
Mythologies 3.
Rexroth, K.   Wednesday of Holy Week, 1940.
Rilke.   To Natalie Clifford Barney.
Rimbaud, A.   Genie.
Rossetti, C.   All Saints: Martyrs.
Antipas.
Ash Wednesday.

Charity Never Faileth.
Christmas Day.
Christmastide.
Epiphany.
Epiphanytide.
Eva.
I love you and you know it—this at least.
Imitated From the Arpa Evangelica: Page 121.
Jesus alone:—if thus it were to me.
Lift up thine eyes to seek the invisible.
Not Yours But You.
O Lord, on Whom we gaze and dare not gaze, /
    Increase our faith that gazing we may see.
Sursum Corda.
Valentines From C.G.R.
Vigil of the Presentation.
Worship God.
Sandburg, C.   Cahokia.
Tate, J.   Tabernacle, The.
Whittier.   First-Day Thoughts.
Hymns from the French of Lamartine.
Meeting, The.
Worship.
Wordsworth, W.   Fragment: Redundance.

See also **Churches; Prayer; Religion**

Wreaths
MacDiarmid, H.   Last Song, A.
One of the Principal Causes of War.
Ritsos.   Wreath, A.
Whitman, W.   Pallid Wreath, The.
Whittier.   Birthday Wreath, The.

Wrecks
Hall, D.   Blue Wing, The.
Stump.
Wreckage, The.

Wren, Sir Christopher
MacNeice.   Homage to Wren.

Wrens
De la Mare.   Jenny Wren.
Meredith, G.   Song: The Wren.
Prunty.   Our Tree of Opposites.
Rossetti, C.   Wrens and robins in the hedge.
Sandburg, C.   People of the Eaves, I Wish You
    Good Morning.
Sze.   Alba.
Wordsworth, W.   Contrast; the Parrot and the
    Wren, The.
Wren's Nest, A.

Wrestling and Wrestlers
Gunn, T.   Wrestling.
Heaney, S.   Antaeus.
Muldoon, P.   My Father and I and Billy Two
    Rivers.
Owen, W.   Antaeus: A Fragment.
Ramanujan.   At Forty.
Stock, R.   Jacob Agonistes.
Wrestling with Angels.
Tomlinson, C.   Wrestlers on the Vase, The.
Van Duyn.   Outlandish Agon.
Warren, R.   Wrestling Match, The.

Wright, James
Ai.   More.
Cooper, J.   Hotel de Dream.
Corbett, W.   February 29th.
Kizer, C.   Eleutheria.
Final Meeting.
Oliver, M.   Three Poems for James Wright.
Orr, G.   Elegy: "Not only doesn't the Ohio."

Writing and Writers
Amichai [*or* Amikhai].   Ibn Gabirol.
Ammons.   Swan Ritual, The.
Angelou.   Artful Pose.
Conceit, A.
Impeccable Conception.
Armantrout.   Ongoing.
Our Nature.
Writing.
Arnold, M.   Memorial Verses.
Ashbery, J.   And "Ut Pictura Poesis" Is Her
    Name.
Or in My Throat.
Sonnet: "Each servant stamps the reader with a
    look."
Atwood.   Aging Female Poet Reads Little
    Magazines.

Words Continue Their Journey, The.
Auden.   Dichtung und Wahrheit.
In Memory of W. B. Yeats.
Novelist, The.
Baudelaire.   Posthumous Work.
Berrigan, T.   Ann Arbor Song.
In Anselm Hollo's Poems.
Poem: "Of morning, Iowa City, blue."
Tambourine Life.
Words for Love.
Berry, W.   Warning to My Readers, A.
Berryman.   Antitheses.
Damn You, Jim D., You Woke Me Up.
Friendless.
Her & It.
Heroes, The.
Home Ballad, The.
Message.
Monkhood.
Of Suicide.
Relations.
Two Organs.
Bierce.   Loring Pickering.
Blake, W.   Blakes apology for His Catalogue.
When Klopstock England Defied.
Blok.   To My Friends.
Bly, R.   After Drinking All Night with a Friend,
    We Go Out in a Boat at Dawn to See Who Can
    Write the Best Poem.
Words Rising.
Bogan, L.   Poem in Prose.
Borges.   1972.
Borges and I.
Browning Resolves to Be a Poet.
Herman Melville.
Invocation to Joyce.
Maker, The.
Matthew 25:30.
Moon, The.
Parable of Cervantes and Don Quixote.
Poet of the Thirteenth Century, A.
Rubaíyát.
Saturday, A.
Susana Bombal.
To a Minor Poet of 1899.
To Manuel Mujica Lainez.
You Are Not the Others.
Bradstreet, A.   Elegy Upon that Honorable and
    Reknowned Knight Sir Philip Sydney, An.
In Honor of Du Bartas, 1641.
Prologue, The.
To Her Most Honored Father Thomas Dudley,
    Esquire, These Humbly Presented.
Brodsky, J.   Infinitive.
Brontë, E.   Alone I sat; the summer day.
Aye there it is! It wakes tonight.
God of Visions.
How long will you remain? The midnight hour.
Night Wind, The.
Browning, E.   Aurora Leigh.
Felicia Hemans.
Insufficiency.
North and the South, The.
Poet and the Bird, The.
To George Sand: A Desire.
To George Sand: A Recognition.
Vision of Poets, A.
Browning, R.   At the "Mermaid."
Thus I wrote in London, musing on my betters.
Bukowski.   2nd Novel, The.
462-0614.
About My Very Tortured Friend, Peter.
After the Reading.
Ah.
As Crazy As I Ever Was.
Beauti-ful.
Clean Old Man.
Dear Friend.
Famous Writer, The.
Farewell, Foolish Objects.
Gloomy Lady.
Horse on Fire.
How Come You're Not Unlisted?
How to Be a Great Writer.
Hustle, The.
I Am Visited by an Editor and a Poet.

I Have Lived in England.
Interviewed by a Guggenheim Recipient.
Lady Poet, The.
Last Generation, The.
Letter from the North.
Literary Life, The.
Little Girls, The.
My Comrades.
Note to the Boys in the Back Room, A.
O, We Are the Outcasts.
Old Buddy, An.
Old Gang, The.
Old Man, Dead in a Room.
On and Off the Road.
On Being Recognized.
Result.
Sad-Eyed Mules of Men.
Sad Poem, A.
Sickness, The.
Suggestion for an Arrangement.
Suicide.
This Poet.
Tonight.
Unkind Poem, An.
Very.
Word on the Quick and Modern Poem-Makers,
    A.
Writing Is a State of Trance.
Burns, R.   Address, to the Shade of Thomson,
    on Crowning His Bust.
Answer, The [To the Guidwife of Wauchope-
    House].
Bard's Epitaph, A.
Elegy on the Death of Robert Ruisseaux.
Epistle to Davie, a Brother Poet.
Epistle to John Lapraik.
Epitaph. Here Lies Robert Fergusson, Poet.
Extempore—on Some Commemorations of
    Thomson.
Extempore—To Mr. Gavin Hamilton.
Fragment—Epistle from Esopus to Maria.
Ill-fated Genius! Heaven-taught Fergusson.
O were I on Parnassus hill.
On a Scotch Bard Gone to the West Indies.
On Elphinston's Translation of Martial.
On Fergusson.
Robert Burns' Answer [to Epistle from a
    Taylor].
Second Epistle to Davie.
Second Epistle to John Lapraik.
Sketch.
To Captain Riddell.
To Peter Stuart.
To R***** G***** of F*****, Esq.
Byron, G.   Another Simple Ballat.
Answer to Some Elegant Verses.
Ballad: "Of all the twice ten thousand bards."
Dear Doctor, I Have Read Your Play.
E Nihilo Nihil.
Epitaph for Joseph Blacket.
From the French.
Good Plays Are Scarce.
My Dear Mr. Murray.
No Infant Sotheby, Whose Dauntless Head.
To a Knot of Ungenerous Critics.
To Harriet.
To Hook the Reader, You, John Murray.
To the Countess of Blessington.
When Thurlow This Damn'd Nonsense Sent.
Campion, T.   Ad Carolum Fitz Geofridum.
Ad Ed. Mychelburnum.
Ad Io. Davisium.
Ad Librum.
Ad Nashum.
De Catullo et Martiale.
De obitu Phil. Sydnaei equitis aurati
    generosissimi.
Eiusdem ad Authorem.
Incipit Thomas Campianus Medicinae Doctor. In
    Peragrantissimi, Itinerosissimi,
    *Montiscandentissimique Peditis, Thomae
    Coryati,* viginti-hebdomadarium *Diarium, sex
    pedibus gradiens,* partim vero claudicans,
    Encomiasticon.
Campion, T. *et al.*   Long have mine eies gaz'd
    with delight.

Carew, T.   Fancy, A.
To Ben Jonson.
To My Honoured Friend, Master Thomas May,
   Upon His Comedy *The Heir*.
To My Worthy Friend, Master Davenant Upon
   His Excellent Play, *The Just Italian*.
Carruth, H.   Apology for Using the Word
   "Heart" in Too Many Poems, An.
Assignment.
Cowshed Blues, The.
Dedication in These Days.
Essay on Marriage.
Fourth.
Freedom and Discipline.
Master, Grieved with Age, The.
Notes from Robin Hill Cottage.
On Being Asked to Write a Poem Against the
   War in Vietnam.
Poet, The.
Post-Impressionist Susurration for the First of
   November, 1983, A.
Stepping Backward.
When I Wrote a Little.
Carver, R.   Aspens.
Blue Stones, The.
His Bathrobe Pockets Stuffed with Notes.
Letter.
Pen, The.
Poem I Didn't Write, The.
Projectile, The.
Spell.
Sunday Night.
This Room.
Work.
Cavafy.   Ships, The.
Cavalcanti.   Of foul matters I must speak.
We sad, despondent quills.
Celan.   Frankfurt, September.
Chaucer.   Chaucer's Wordes unto Adam, his
   Owne Scriveyn.
Chiabrera.   Torquato Tasso rests within this
   tomb.
Ciardi, J.   Advertisement for a Reader.
Annals.
Apology for Not Invoking the Muse, An.
Bicentennial.
Gift, The.
I is, naturally enough, any author.
Love Sonnet: Believing Part of Almost All I
   Say.
One Easter Not on the Calendar I Woke.
Thousandth Poem for Dylan Thomas, A.
Trying to Feel Something.
Why Don't You Write for Me?
Clampitt.   Local Genius, The.
Sed de Correr.
Clifton, L.   Message of Thelma Sayles, The.
Clough.   If to write, rewrite, and write again.
Codrescu.   Attempt to Spell, Incantate and
   Annoy.
Comrade Past & Mister Present.
Dear Masoch.
In Praise of the New Russian Writers.
Late Night, San Francisco.
Why Write.
Coleridge, S.   Character, A.
Lines to a Comic Author, on an Abusive
   Review.
On Donne's Poetry.
To a Friend [Charles Lamb] Who Had Declared
   His Intention of Writing No More Poetry.
Collins, B.   Advice to Writers.
Best Cigarette, The.
Budapest.
Lines Lost among Trees.
Tuesday, June 4, 1991.
Cooper, J.   Long View from the Suburbs.
Poem with Capital Letters, A.
Corbett, W.   February 29th.
Found in a Notebook.
Cortes.   Three Sisters, The.
Cowper, W.   Ah brother Poet! send me of your
   shade.
Epistle to Robert Lloyd, Esq, An.
In Memory of John Thorton.
My pens are all spilt, and my ink-glass is dry.

Ode to Apollo.
On the Author of Letters on Literature.
To Dr. Darwin.
To Gravina.
To Mary Unwin.
To William Hayley, Esq.: In Reply to His
   Solicitation to Write with Him in a Literary
   Work.
Crane, H.   Passage.
Porphyro in Akron.
Crane, S.   Many red devils ran from my heart.
Crashaw.   On Mr. G. Herberts Booke, The
   Temple.
Upon Ford's Two Tragedies, "Loves Sacrifice"
   and "The Broken Heart."
Creeley.   After.
Apology, The.
Cheap Thrill.
Citizen.
End.
Flaubert's Early Prose.
Re C—.
Sound.
Trees.
Waiting ("He pushes behind the words").
Cullen, C.   To Certain Critics.
Yet Do I Marvel.
Cummings, E. E.   Chaucer.
Fame Speaks.
It was a goodly co.
Pound pound pound / on thy cold grey corona
   oh P.
To start,to hesitate;to stop.
We miss you,jack—tactfully you(with one
   cocked).
Cunningham, J.   Another novel, and the
   prostitute.
L'Esprit de Géométrie et L'Esprit de Finesse.
On Doctor Drink.
Reader, it's time reality was faced.
"Dario."   I pursue a form that my style does not
   find.
White Page, The.
Davie, D.   Alzheimer's Disease.
Cambridgeshire.
Chernobyl. A Disaster.
Church of Ireland.
Epistle. To Enrique Caracciolo Trejo.
His Themes.
July, 1964.
Knave of Hearts, The.
Method. For Ronald Gaskell.
Mustered into the Avant-Garde.
On Edmund Spenser's House in Ireland.
Preoccupation's Gift.
Pushkin. A Didactic Poem.
Rejoinder to a Critic.
Resolutions.
Revulsion.
'Sculpture' of Rhyme, The.
Surrey.
Sylvae.
Though Dry, Not Dry.
To an American Classicist.
To Thom Gunn in Los Altos, California.
Wild Boar Clough.
Winter's Talents.
De la Mare.   Scribe, The.
Delany, P.   From My Much Honored Friend at
   Heldelville.
Dickey, J.   False Youth: Autumn: Clothes of the
   Age.
For Robert Bhain Campbell.
To Landrum Guy, Beginning to Write at Sixty.
Dickey, W.   Virginia Woolf Gathers Mushrooms.
Dickinson, E.   All the letters I can write.
Going—to—Her!
Going to Him! Happy letter!
I reckon—when I count at all.
If it had no pencil.
Missing All—prevented Me, The.
Publication—is the Auction.
Tell all the Truth but tell it slant.
This Is My Letter to the World.
This was a Poet—It is That.
Word dropped careless on a Page, A.

Writing is brief and fleeting.
Your thoughts don't have words every day.
Donne.   Canonization, The.
To E. of D. with Six Holy Sonnets.
To Mr E. G.
To Mr R. W ("Kindly I envy thy song's [or
   songs] perfection").
To Mr S. B.
To Mr T. W ("All hail, sweet poet, more full of
   more strong fire").
Triple Fool, The.
Valediction, A: of the Book.
Dove, R.   At the German Writers Conference in
   Munich.
Nexus.
Dryden, J.   Mac Flecknoe [or, A Satire upon the
   True-Blue Protestant Poet T. S.].
Prologue to the University of Oxford, 1674.
Dubie.   City of the Olesha Fruit, The.
Clouds of Magellan (Aphorisms of Mr. Canon
   Aspirin), The.
For Randall Jarrell, 1914–1965.
Dugan, A.   On Herodotus.
On Work.
Dunbar, P.   Choice, A.
Confirmation.
Crumb, a Crumb, and a Little Seed, A.
Inspiration.
Lapse, The.
Misapprehension.
Poet and His Song, The.
Poet and the Baby, The.
Poet, The.
Prometheus.
Then and Now.
To a Poet and a Lady.
Duncan, R.   After Reading H.D.'s *Hermetic
   Definitions*.
Back to the figure.
Ballad of the Enamord Image, The.
Banners, The.
Beginning of Writing, The.
Bending the Bow.
Best of ways. That there be a law the Earth
   gives and the Mountain.
Book of Resemblances, A.
Circulations of the Song.
Descriptions of Imaginary Poetries.
Erecting beyond the boundaries of all
   government.
Festivals, The.
Helmet of Goliath, The.
I ask the unyielding Sentence that shows Itself
   forth in the language.
Illustrative Lines.
Imagining in Writing.
Kingdom of Jerusalem, The.
Master of Rime told me, You must learn to lose
   heart, The.
O Outrider! / when you come to the threshold of
   the stars.
Old women came from their caves to close the
   too many doors, The.
Poem in Stretching, A.
Poetry, a Natural Thing.
Poetry Disarranged.
Source.
There are memories everywhere then.
   Rememberd, we go out, as in.
This potion is love's portion. This herb.
What of the structure of Rime? I said.
Eberhart, R.   1934.
Broken Pen, The.
Face, Ocean.
Flow of Thought.
Ideal and the Real, The.
Long Term Suffering.
Man and Nature.
Question Mark.
Request.
Testament, A.
Yonder.
Emerson, R.   And he like me is not too proud.
By the unacknowledged tie.
God only knew how Saadi dined.
Gods walk in the breath of the woods, The.

His instant thought the Poet spoke.
Husband has the nearest acres, The.
Letters.
Poet is at home, A.
Poets are colorpots.
Saadi held the Muse in awe.
Saadi loved the new & old.
William does thy frigid soul.
Enzensberger, H. Blank Sheet, The.
Ferlinghetti, L. 21.
Adieu À Charlot.
Constantly Risking Absurdity.
Elegy on the Death of Kenneth Patchen, An.
In Paris in a loud dark winter.
Jack of Hearts, The.
L'Occupation Obsédée.
Mock Confessional.
Poem for Old Walt.
Poet as Fisherman.
Populist Manifesto.
Sea and Ourselves at Cape Ann, The.
Triste Corbiére.
Uses of Poetry.
Frost, R. It takes all sorts of in- and outdoor
schooling.
Lost Follower, The.
On Being Chosen Poet of Vermont.
Ginsberg, A. After All, What Else Is There to
Say?
Fyodor.
Howl.
On Burroughs, Work.
Poem Rocket.
Gjuzel. Flood at the International Writer's
Workshop.
Glück, L. Exile.
Mountain, The.
Poem: "In the early evening, as now, a man is
bending."
Goethe. Confession.
Graves, R. At the Gate.
Crucibles of Love.
Field-Postcard, The.
Last Poem, A.
Laureate, The.
Plea to Boys and Girls, A.
Poem: A Reminder.
Reader over My Shoulder, The.
Singleness in Love.
Something to Say.
Three Years Waiting.
Title of Poet, The.
To Be Poets.
Unpenned Poem, The.
Wall, The.
Work Drafts.
Work-Room.
Gray, T. Long Story, A.
Progress of Poesy, The.
Stanzas to Mr. Bentley.
Gunn, T. Drive to Los Alamos, A.
Expression.
J Car, The.
JVC.
Mirror for Poets, A.
Plan of Self-Subjection, A.
Gurney, I. Coppice, The.
Going Out at Dawn.
Hell's Prayer.
In the Old Time.
Midnight.
Song of Autumn.
Song: "Past my window dawn and down."
While I Write.
"H. D." Fragment 36 [or Thirty-Six]: "I know
not what to do."
Heliodora.
Poet, The.
Hacker, M. Art of a Novel, The.
Feeling and Form.
Late August Letter.
Riposte.
Rooms in Bloomsbury.
Untoward Occurance at Embassy Poetry
Reading.
Why We Are Going Back to Paradise Island.

Hall, D. To a Waterfowl.
HaNagid. Man's Wisdom Is In What He Writes.
Your Manuscript Shines.
Hardy, T. Epitaph for George Moore.
George Meredith (1828-1909).
I Looked Up from My Writing.
Hayden, R. Paul Laurence Dunbar.
Heaney, S. Afterwards, An.
Digging.
From the Frontier of Writing.
North.
Wolfe Tone.
Herbert, G. Jordan (2).
Posy [or Posie], The.
Sonnet: "My God, where is that ancient heat
towards Thee."
Herrick. Argument of His Book, The.
Departure of the Good Daemon, The.
Glorie.
His Desire.
His Poetry His Pillar.
His Prayer to Ben Jonson.
His Request to Julia.
Most Words, Lesse Workes.
Mr. Robert Hericke His Farwell unto Poetrie.
Not Every Day Fit for Verse.
On Himselfe.
Poets.
Pride Allowable in Poets.
To Cedars.
To God.
To His Book.
To His Booke.
To His Honour'd Friend, Sir Thomas Heale.
To His Muse.
To His Verses.
To M. Denham, on His Prospective Poem.
To the Generous Reader.
To the Reverend Shade of His Religious Father.
Upon His Verses.
Upon Master Fletchers Incomparable Playes.
Upon Nis.
When He Would Have His Verses Read.
Writing.
Housman. Terence, This Is Stupid Stuff.
They say my verse is sad: no wonder.
Howe, F. Goodbye, Post Office Square.
Howe, S. Speeches at the Barriers.
Hughes, L. Anne Spencer's Table.
Letter to the Academy.
Theme for English B.
Hughes, T. Famous Poet.
God, The.
Thought-Fox, The.
Ignatow, D. Epilogue: "Trees are tall gods,
The."
Finally.
I Write.
I've Wanted to Write My Way into Paradise.
Now I Hear.
Jackson, L. As to a Frontispiece.
Courtesies of Authorship, The.
Troubles of a Book, The.
Jacob, M. Rainbow.
Jacobsen, J. Rainy Night at the Writers'
Colony.
Variations on a theme.
Jarrell, R. Author to the Reader, The.
Le Poète Contumace.
Jeffers, R. But I Am Growing Old and Indolent.
Eagle and hawk with their great claws and
hooked heads.
George Sterling.
Goethe, they say, was a great poet, Pindar,
perhaps, was a great poet.
Hand.
Let Them Alone.
Love the Wild Swan.
Mathematicians and physics men, The.
On an Anthology of Chinese Poems.
On Building with Stone.
Second-Best.
Johnson, S. Prologue Spoken by Mr[.] Garrick
at the Opening of the Theatre in Drury Lane,
1747.
Prologue to Garrick's Lethe.

Prologue to Goldsmith's The Good Natur'd
Man.
Jonson, B. Here Follow Certain Other Verses,
as Charms to Unlock the Mystery of the
Crudities.
In Authorem.
Ode Allegoric.
Ode to Himself[e].
On Playwright ("Playwright convict of public
wrongs to men").
On Poet-Ape.
On the Honoured Poems of His Honoured
Friend, Sir John Beaumont, Baronet.
Sonnet to the Noble Lady, the Lady Mary
Wroth, A.
To Alphonso [or Alfonso] Ferrabosco, on His
Book.
To Francis Beaumont.
To His Friend the Author upon His Richard.
To Mrs Alice Sutcliffe, on Her Divine
Meditations.
To My Dear Son, and Right-Learnèd Friend,
Master Joseph Rutter.
To My Old Faithful Servant: And (by His
Continued Virtue) My Loving Friend.
To My Truly-Beloved Friend, Mr Browne: on
His Pastorals.
To My Worthy Friend, Master Edward Filmer,
on His Work Published.
To the Author.
To the London Reader, on the Odcombian
Writer, Polytopian Thomas the Traveller.
To the Right Noble Tom, Tell-Troth of His
Travels, the Coriat of Odcombe.
To the Same [Benjamin Rudyerd] ("Writing
thyself, or judging others' writ").
To Thomas Palmer [on His Book "The Sprite of
Trees and Herbs"].
Vision of Ben Jonson, on the Muses of His
Friend M. Drayton, The.
Keats. House of Mourning Written by Mr Scott,
The.
Ode: "Bards of passion and of mirth."
Ode to Apollo.
On Leaving Some Friends at an Early Hour.
On Receiving a Laurel Crown from Leigh Hunt.
On Seeing a Lock of Milton's Hair.
Poet, The.
Sleep and Poetry.
To J. H. Reynolds, Esq.
To My Brother George.
Where's the Poet? Show Him! Show Him.
Kinnell. Flies.
For William Carlos Williams.
Kinsella, T. Brothers in the Craft.
In Memory.
Kipling, R. Coiner, The.
Craftsman, The.
Dedication, A: "And they were stronger hands
than mine."
Prelude to "Departmental Ditties."
Samuel Pepys.
When 'Omer Smote 'Is Bloomin' Lyre.
Kizer, C. Fin-de-Siècle Blues.
Good Author, The.
Lost in Translation.
Promising Author.
Threatening Letter.
Way We Write Letters, The.
Koch, K. Art of Poetry, The.
Circus, The.
Days and Nights.
Fresh Air.
Pleasures of Peace, The.
Komunyakaa. Keeper of the Vigil.
My Father's Love Letters [or Loveletters].
Kumin, M. On Being Asked to Write a Poem
for the Centenary of the Civil War.
Young Nun at Bread Loaf.
Kunitz, S. Lesson, The.
Round, The.
Larkin, P. Good for You, Gavin.
Literary World, The.
Waiting for Breakfast, While She Brushed Her
Hair.
Writer, A.

Laughlin, J. 'As in Music / A Reprise / Across Time.
  At Our House.
  He Did It to Please His Mother.
  Merry Madness Hall.
  O Hermes Trismegistus.
  Questions, The.
  Scribe, The.
  Somewhere in France.
  Temporary Poems.
  What the Pencil Writes.
Lawrence, D. H. Correspondence in After Years.
  Fate and the Younger Generation.
  I Am in a Novel.
  My Naughty Book.
Levertov. Caedmon.
  Chekhov on the West Heath.
  Common Ground, A.
  Growth of a Poet.
  Hunting the Phoenix.
  Novel, The.
  Prayer, The.
  Quality of Genius, The.
  Secret, The.
  She and the Muse.
  Too Easy: to Write of Miracles.
  Voyage.
  Walk through the Notebooks, A.
  Writing in the Dark.
  Writing to Aaron.
Levi, P. Profession, A.
  Unfinished Business.
  Work, The.
Levine, P. My Poets.
  On the Edge.
  Theory of Prosody, A.
Lindsay, N. Apology for the Bottle Volcanic, An.
  Dream of All the Springfield Writers, The.
Logan, J. Homage to Rainer Maria Rilke.
  Letter to My Son.
  Recollection on the Day of a First Book.
  To a Young Poet Who Fled.
Lowell, R. Ford Madox Ford.
  Marlowe.
  Reading Myself.
Lux. Painfully Banal.
  Postcard to Baudelaire.
  This Space Available.
MacDiarmid, H. Ah, sweetheart, what a pool!
  Broad, deep, strong, silent, and sedate!
  And a poetry in which as in a film.
  And thus a poetry which fully understands.
  Caledonian Antisyzygy, The.
  Direadh III.
  Gairmscoile.
  Greatest poets undergo a kind of crisis in their art, The.
  Hokum.
  I dream of poems like the bread-knife.
  Poetry and Science.
  Poetry full of cynghanedd, and hair-trigger relationships, A.
  Poetry in which all connections will constantly render such services, A.
  Poetry like a lance at rest, A.
  Poetry like the barrel of a gun, A.
  Poetry like the character of Indian culture, A.
  Poetry like the hope of achieving ere very long.
  Poetry of such an integration as cannot be effected.
  Poetry that goes all the way, A.
  Poetry that never for a moment forgets, A.
  Poetry the quality of which, A.
  To a Friend and Fellow Poet.
MacFadden, E. In Pity First to Human Kind.
MacLeish. Ars Poetica.
  Cummings.
  Edwin Muir.
  Epistle to Léon-Paul Fargue.
  Great Contemporary Discoveries.
  Poet.
  Reasons for Music.
  Reproach to Dead Poets.
  Where a Poet's From.

MacNeice. Autolycus.
  Elegy for Minor Poets.
  Epitaph for Liberal Poets.
  To Hedli.
  To Posterity.
  To the Public.
Mahon. Attic, The.
  Craigvara House.
  De Quincey in Later Life.
  Roman Script.
  Sea in Winter, The.
  Yaddo Letter, The.
Martial. 4.33: "You write, you tell me, for posterity."
Marvell. Illustrissimo Viro Domino Lanceloto Josepho de Maniban Grammatomanti [To That Renowned Man Lord Lancelot Joseph de Maniban Graphologist].
  On Mr Milton's "Paradise Lost."
McGrath, T. Ars Poetica: Or: Who Lives in the Ivory Tower?
  For a Critic Who Tries to Write Poems.
  Ordonnance.
  Poet of the Prison Isle: Ritsos Against the Colonels, The.
  Uses of the Lost Poets.
McHugh, H. Meaning Business.
  Stroke.
Melville, H. Camoëns.
Meredith, G. As often in a bun.
  Au voleur, au voleur, au voleur!—.
  But see what living glory floods the west.
  Camelus Saltat.
  Empty Purse: A Sermon to our Later Prodigal Son, The.
  Hail, Common Sense! most rare of all!
  Later Alexandrian, A.
  Milton.
  My Theme.
  Poetry of Chaucer, The.
  Poetry of Coleridge, The.
  Poetry of Keats, The.
  Poetry of Milton, The.
  Poetry of Shakespeare, The.
  Poetry of Shelley, The.
  Poetry of Southey, The.
  Poetry of Spenser, The.
  Poetry of Wordsworth, The.
  Spirit of Shakespeare: Continued, The.
  There stood in her street a poor exile of Queen Je'n.
  There was a young poet of Chelsea.
  To Alex. Smith, the "Glasgow Poet," on His Sonnet to "Fame."
  To Carlyle.
  To R.H.H. with Daphne.
  Tuck, Demitroïa, / Ariadne, and Froyja.
  While Janet eyes the Lanthorn's Magic.
Meredith, W. Dreams of Suicide.
  Grievances.
  Housed (A Report on a Visiting Dog).
  What I Remember the Writers Telling Me When I Was Young.
Merrill, J. Angel.
  Clearing the Title.
  From a Notebook.
  From the Cupola.
  Marsyas.
  Prism.
Merton. Ceremony for Edward Dahlberg.
  In the Rain and the Sun.
  Message to Be Inscribed on Mark Van Doren's Hamilton Medal.
  Nombril Walketh on the Loam.
  Poet, to His Book, The.
  Prologo.
  Strife between the Poet and Ambition, The.
Merwin. Envoy from d'Aubigné.
  Man Who Writes Ants, The.
  My Friends.
  Pens, The.
  Plaster, The.
  Sibyl.
  Unwritten, The.
Milosz, C. Ars Poetica?
  In a Buggy at Dusk.

Preparation.
  Undressing Justine.
Milton. On Shakespear[e].
Montale. Poems for Camillo Sbarbaro.
Moore, M. Baseball and Writing.
  Novices.
  Poetry: "I, too, dislike it: there are things that are important beyond all this fiddle."
Muldoon, P. 7, Middagh Street.
  Armageddon, Armageddon.
  Briefcase, The.
  Lunch with Pancho Villa.
  Madoc: A Mystery.
Nemerov. Epitaph: "Of the Great World he knew not much."
  Exasperations of a Novelist.
  In the Glass of Fashion.
  Make Big Money at Home! Write Poems in Spare Time!
  Novelists.
  On the Platform.
  Praising the Poets of That Country.
  Reflexion of a Novelist.
  Style.
  To Lu Chi.
  To the Bleeding Hearts Association of American Novelists.
  Winter Lightning, The.
Neruda. Cherries.
  Child of the Moon.
  Conditions.
  Herbalist's Rose, The.
  Little Devils.
  Negative Hands.
  Pardon Me.
  Sitting Down.
  XIX, The.
Niedecker. I said to my head, Write somethng.
  To Paul now old enough to read.
  Who was Mary Shelley?
O'Hara, F. Adieu to Norman, Bon Jour to Joan and Jean-Paul.
  Answer to Voznesensky and Evtushenko.
  Ashes on a Saturday Afternoon.
  Avenue A.
  Critic, The.
  Day Lady Died, The.
  Getting Up Ahead of Someone (Sun).
  Les Luths.
  Memorial Day 1950.
  My Heart.
  Ode on Causality.
  Ode: Salute to the French Negro Poets.
  Personal Poem.
  Pleasant Thought from Whitehead, A.
  Poem: "I ran through the snow like a young Czarevitch!"
  Poetry.
  Post the Lake Poets Ballad.
  Spirit Ink, The.
  To a Poet.
  To Gottfried Benn.
  To Hell with It.
  Today.
  "Unfinished," The.
  Why I Am Not a Painter.
  Young Poet, A.
Oliver, M. Morning.
  Some Herons.
  Stanley Kunitz.
Olson, C. Black Mt. College Has a Few Words for a Visitor.
  Collected Poems of, The.
  Dylan Thomas, and Now Matthew Mead—as He Himself, "To Edward Thomas."
  New Poem.
  Peograms.
  To a Poet Who Read in Gloucester Before the Cape Ann Historical Literary and Scientific Society.
Owen, W. On My Songs.
Pagis. For a Literary Survey.
  Lament for a Master of Style.
  Small Poetics, A.
  Writers.
Paley, G. In France.

In This Dream.
On the Ramblas A Tree A Girl.
Traveler.
Palmer, M.   At the table we say.
Dear Lexicon, I died in you.
Dear M ("Sky today yes and no, The. I am writing a play about a man with a pebble").
Fifth Prose.
Idem 1.
Notes for Echo Lake 5.
Sun.
Word is coming up on the screen, give me a moment, A.
Parker, D.   After Dawn.
Chris-Cross; On Confusing Messrs. Morley and Robin.
Danger of Writing Defiant Verse, The.
Fighting Words.
Grandfather Said It.
Letter to Ogden Nash.
Our Own Home Talent.
Passionate Screen Writer to His Love, The.
Pig's-Eye View of Literature, A.
Verse Reporting Late Arrival at a Conclusion.
When We Were Very Sore; Lines on Discovering that You Have Been Advertised as America's A.A. Milne.
Parra, N.   Poetry Ends with Me.
Pasolini.   Plan of Future Works.
Pasternak, B.   God of Details, The.
Patchen.   And in Another Place Uses the Same Phrase.
I Got the Fat Poet into a Corner.
Pessoa.   Salutation to Walt Whitman.
This.
Petrarch.   How many times already Love has said.
If neither Love nor Death blights this endeavour.
Pinkerton, H.   On Gari Melchers's *Writing* (1905) in the Los Angeles County Museum of Art.
Plath.   Female Author.
Notes to a Neophyte.
On the Difficulty of Conjuring Up a Dryad.
Stillborn.
Pope, A.   Epigram from the French: "Sir, I admit your general [or gen'ral] Rule."
Epistle to Dr. Arbuthnot.
Epitaph for One Who Would Not Be Buried in Westminster Abbey.
Epitaph on Charles Earl of Dorset.
Epitaph on Mr. Elijah Fenton, at Easthamstead in Berks, 1730.
Impromptu to Lady Winchelsea.
On Lady Mary Wortley Montagu's Portrait.
On Mr. Gay, in Westminster Abbey, 1732.
Presentation Verses to Nathaniel Pigott.
Prologue Design'd for Mr. Durfy's Last Play.
Prologue to a Play for Mr. Dennis's Benefit, in 1733, when He Was Old, Blind, and in Great Distress, a Little before His Death, A.
Prologue to the *Three Hours after Marriage*.
Sandys's Ghost, or a Proper New Ballad on the New Ovid's Metamorphosis.
Three Gentle Shepherds, The.
To Belinda on the Rape of the Lock.
To Eustace Budgell, Esq., on His Translation of the Characters of Theophrastus.
To Mr. Thomas Southern, on His Birth-Day, 1742.
Translator, The.
Umbra.
Verses to Be Placed under the Picture of England's Arch-Poet.
Pound, E.   Epitaphs: "Fu I loved the high cloud and the hill."
Prunty.   Extravagant Love.
Raine, K.   My day's plan to write.
Poet Answers the Accuser, The.
Poet is of those, The.
Testimony.
Ralegh, S.   Epitaph on Sir Philip Sidney.
If Cynthia Be a Queen.
In Commendation of George Gascoigne's Steel Glass.

To the Translator of Lucan [or Lucan's Pharsalia, 1614].
Ramanujan, Bosnia.
Difficulty.
Ransom, J.   Survey of Literature.
Rexroth, K.   Horny Dilemma.
Last Visit to the Swimming Pool Soviets.
Light on the Pewter Dish, The.
Me Again.
Precession of the Equinoxes.
Thou Shalt Not Kill.
Rich, A.   Focus.
I Am in Danger—Sir.
Juvenilia.
North American Time.
Upper Broadway.
Riley, J.   To—"The J. W. R. Literary Club."
Ritsos.   Moderation.
Robinson, E.   Dark House, The.
Momus.
Shadrach O'Leary.
Sonnet: "Master and the slave go hand in hand, The."
Roethke.   Reply to a Lady Editor.
Supper with Lindsay.
Rossetti, C.   How many authors are my first!
L. E. L.
Rondel seems to fit a round of days, A.
Would that I were a turnip white.
You who looked on passed ages as a glass.
Rukeyser, M.   Artifact.
Louis Sonnet, A.
Song: Love in Whose Rich Honor.
Work, for the Day Is Coming.
Writer, The.
Rumi.   Thirsty Fish, A.
Sandburg, C.   Enemy Number One.
Jack London and O. Henry.
Many Handles.
One Modern Poet.
Pencils.
Sketch of a Poet.
Tentative (First Model) Definitions of Poetry.
Sarton, M.   My Sisters, O My Sisters.
Schuyler, J.   Dec. 28, 1974.
Dining Out with Doug and Frank.
Fauré Ballade, The.
Money Musk.
Morning of the Poem, The.
O Sleepless Night.
Perhaps.
To Frank O'Hara.
Virginia Woolf.
Wystan Auden.
Seifert.   At one of his readings a long time ago.
Sexton.   Ambition Bird, The.
Black Art, The.
Errand, The.
Fallen Angels, The.
February 20th.
Frenzy.
Obsessive Combination of Ontological Inscape, Trickery and Love, An.
Portrait of an Old Woman on the College Tavern Wall.
Shelley, P.   Adonais; An Elegy on the Death of John Keats.
Sheridan, T.   Pedagogue's Answer, The.
Scribbler from the Northern Bear, A.
To the Dean of St. Patrick's ("Since your poetic prancer is turned into Cancer").
You That Would Read the Bible.
Simic.   Description.
Evening with the Master, An.
Further Adventures of Charles Simic.
Poem: "My father writes all day, all night."
Smart, C.   To Ethelinda.
Smith, S.   Full Well I Know.
How Far Can You Press a Poet?
Lads of the Village, The.
Mrs. Arbuthnot.
My Muse.
Old Ghosts.
Pearl.
Poet!
Poet Hin, The.

Poets Are Silent, The.
Souvenir de Monsieur Poop.
To an American Publisher.
To School!
Voice from the Tomb (1).
What Is She Writing? Perhaps It Will Be Good.
Snyder, G.   As for Poets.
Axe Handles.
How Poetry Comes to Me.
Riprap.
Stafford, W.   At This Point on the Page.
Course in Creative Writing, A.
Final Exam: American Renaissance.
In the Book.
Influential Writers.
Keeping a Journal.
Way I Write, The.
Writing It Down.
Stein, G.   Comedy like That, A.
Subject-Cases: The Background of a Detective Story.
Stevens, W.   Prelude to Objects.
Stock, R.   That the Sestina is What it is Despite What it is Not.
Stockton, A.   On Seeing Mrs Macauly Graham.
Suckling, S.   To My Friend Will. Davenant, on His Other Poems.
To My Friend Will. Davenant, upon His Poem of "Madagascar."
Upon T.C. Having the Pox.
Wits, The; A Session[s] of the Poets.
Swift, J.   To Thomas Sheridan.
Szymborska, W.   Joy of Writing, The.
Stage Fright.
Thomas Mann.
Tate, A.   Non Omnis Moriar.
To a Romantic Novelist.
Tate, J.   Dear Reader.
Read the Great Poets.
Teaching the 'Ape to Write Poems.
Tennyson, A.   Prefatory Poem to My Brother's Sonnets.
Thomas, D.   Author's Prologue.
Especially When the October Wind.
In My Craft or Sullen Art.
My Hero Bares His Nerves.
On No Work of Words.
Tisdall, W.   Tom Pun-Sibi Metamorphosed: Or, The Giber Gibed.
Tomlinson, C.   Antecedents.
Art of Poetry, The.
Biography of the Author: A Cento, A.
Jubilación.
Macduff.
Nature Poem.
Oppositions.
Paris in Sixty-Nine.
Parsnips.
Poem: "It falls onto my page like rain."
Portrait of the Artist I.
Portrait of the Artist II.
Rose for Janet, A.
Something: a Direction.
To Vasko Popa In Rome.
Unknown.   Another to Mrs. Anne Bradstreet, Author of this Poem.
I cannot wonder at Apollo now.
In Praise of the Author, Mistress Anne Bradstreet, Virtue's True and Lively Pattern.
Rivals, The.
To My Dear Sister, the Author of these Poems.
To My Worthy Friend T S——, D. D. On His Incomparable Translation of and Notes on Persius.
Upon Mr. Sheridan's Turning Author, 1716.
Upon the Author.
Updike.   Angels, The.
At the End of the Rainbow.
Kenneths.
Literary Dublin.
Marching through a Novel.
Miss Moore at Assembly.
Ode, An: "I'm going to write a novel, hey."
Van Duyn.   Day in Late October, A.
Eros to Howard Nemerov.
Essay on Criticism, An.

Lives of the Poets.
Moose in the Morning, Northern Maine.
Quiet Afternoon at Home, A.
To Poets' Worksheets in the Air-Conditioned
   Vault of a Library.
Vision Test, The.
Walcott. Codicil.
Hotel Normandie Pool, The.
Islands.
Man Who Loved Islands, The.
Volcano.
Warren, R. Flaubert in Egypt.
Homage to Theodore Dreiser.
Milton: A Sonnet.
Weiss, T. Living Room, A.
This Gray Age.
Whalen, P. Homage to St. Patrick, García
   Lorca, & the Itinerant Grocer.
Inside Stuff.
Public Opinions.
Walking beside the Kamogawa, Remembering
   Nansen and Fudo and Gary's Poem.
What? Writing in the Dining Room?
Wheatley, P. To Maecenas.
Whitman, W. Ages and Ages Returning at
   Intervals.
As I Lay with My Head in Your Lap Camerado.
As I Sit Writing Here.
Death and Burial of McDonald Clarke, a
   Parody, The.
Excelsior.
Font of Type, A.
For Us Two, Reader Dear.
Here the Frailest Leaves of Me.
Last Droplets.
Not Youth Pertains to Me.
Now Precedent Songs, Farewell.
Old Chants.
Shakspeare-Bacon's Cipher.
So Far, and So Far, and On toward the End.
Thou Reader.
Thoughts—6: "Of What I Write."
To a Certain Civilian.
To Get the Final Lilt of Songs.
To Soar in Freedom and in Fullness of Power.
Unexpress'd, The.
You Lingering Sparse Leaves of Me.
Whittier. Fitz-Greene Halleck.
Greeting, A.
Mulford.
Proem: "I love the old melodious lays."
To a Poetical Trio in the City of Gotham.
To Lydia Maria Child.
Wilbur, R. Advice from the Muse.
Beasts.
Cottage Street, 1953.
To an American Poet Just Dead.
To the Etruscan Poets.
Writer, The.
Williams, C. K. Critic, The.
Did I write this.
One of the Muses.
Yours.
Williams, M. Before.
Learning to Read.
Let Me Tell You.
Muse of the Evening.
Muse, The.
On Not Writing a Love Poem.
Williams, W. Apology.
Cure, The.
Flower, The.
La Flor.
Lines on Receiving *The Dial's* Award: 1927.
Our (American) Ragcademicians.
Rhymed Address: The Lobster.
Sort of a Song, A.
To an Elder Poet.
Tolstoy.
Transitional.
Uses of Poetry, The.
Wind Increases, The.
Wilner, E. Elegy for a Writer.
Muse, The.
Woodbridge. Upon the Author. By a Known
   Friend.

Wordsworth, W. Distressful gift! this Book
   receives.
Her Only Pilot the Soft Breeze, the Boat.
In the First Page of an Album by One Whose
   Handwriting Is Wretchedly Bad.
Let More Ambitious Poets Take the Heart.
London 1802.
Ode to Apollo.
Orchard Pathway, The.
Poet and the Caged Turtledove, The.
Poet!—He Hath Put His Heart to School, A.
Poet's Epitaph, A.
Scorn not the Sonnet; Critic, you have frowned.
Sonnet: To———.
Stanzas Written in My Pocket-Copy of
   Thomson's "Castle of Indolence."
There Is a Pleasure in Poetic Pains.
Though Pulpits and the Desk May Fail.
Though the Bold Wings of Poesy Affect.
To ———: "If these brief Records, by the
   Muses' art."
Wright, C. Ars Poetica.
Black Zodiac.
California Dreaming.
Childhood's Body.
Cicada Blue.
Dog Day Vespers.
Journal of English Days, A.
Journal of the Year of the Ox, A.
Light Journal.
October 2.
Passing the Morning under the Serenissima.
Portrait of the Artist with Hart Crane.
Quotations.
Roma II.
Spring Abstract.
Tennessee Line.
Wright, J. To a Dead Drunk.
To the Poets in New York.
Wyatt, S. My Pen.
Yeats. Coole Park, 1929.
Ego Dominus Tuus.
Model for the Laureate, A.
On Being Asked for a War Poem.
Prologue to Responsibilities.
To a Poet, Who Would Have Me Praise Certain
   Bad Poets, Imitators of His and Mine.
Under Saturn.
Zagajewski. Early Hours, The.
Letter from a Reader.
R. Says.
Reading Books.
Room I Work In, The.
She Wrote in Darkness.
Talk with Friedrich Nietzsche, A.
Zaturenska. Leaves from the Book of Dorothy
   Wordsworth.
Shakespearean Cycle, A.
Zukofsky, L. *Barely* and *widely*.
"Mantis," An Interpretation.
***See also* Handwriting; Poetry and Poets**
Wyatt, Sir Thomas
Dubie. Friary at Blossom, Prologue &
   Instructions, The.
Wyeth, Andrew
Muldoon, P. My Grandfather's Wake.
Wilbur, R. Wyeth's Mild Cans.
Wyoming (state)
Major, C. Wyoming.
Stafford, W. Accountability.

X

X-Rays
Graves, R. Broken Neck.
Sze. Murmur, The.
Xenophanes
Emerson, R. Xenophanes.
Hardy, T. Xenophanes, the Monist of Colophon.

Y

Yachts
Eberhart, R. Sailing to Buck's Harbor.
Williams, W. Yachts, The.
***See also* Boats and Boating; Sailing and Sailors**
Yaks
Roethke. Yak, The.
Yale University
Milosz, C. At Yale.
Beinecke Library.
Pierson College.
Nash, O. Eight O'Clock Peril, The.
Yalta, Ukraine
Brodsky, J. Homage to Yalta.
Dubie. Seagull, The.
Yankees (New York baseball team)
Moore, M. Baseball and Writing.
Updike. Tao in the Yankee Stadium Bleachers.
Yarrow [*or* Yarrow Water], Scotland
Wordsworth, W. Yarrow Revisited.
Yarrow Unvisited [1803].
Yarrow Visited [September, 1814].
Years
Borges. Year's End.
Burns, R. Elegy on the Year 1788.
Corbett, W. 1991.
Dunbar, P. King is Dead, The.
Eberhart, R. Parker River, The.
Placation of Reality.
White Pines, Felled 1984.
Young and the Old, the.
Hardy, T. End of the Year 1912.
Hughes, L. New Year.
Komunyakaa. 1984.
Merwin. Early January.
Moore, M. What Are Years?
Olson, C. Year Is a Great Circle or the Year Is a
   Great Mistake, The.
Parker, D. Paths.
Rexroth, K. Advent.
Riley, J. Old Year's Address, An.
Shelley, P. Time.
Weiss, T. After Five Years.
Zaturenska. Dark Year, The.
Yeats, John Butler
Ferlinghetti, L. 26.
Yeats, William Butler
Auden. In Memory of W. B. Yeats.
Berryman. Away.
Ciardi, J. Reality and Willie Yeats.
Creeley. Thinking of Yeats.
Davie, D. Church of Ireland.
Eberhart, R. Young and the Old, the.
Ferlinghetti, L. 26.
Ginsberg, A. After Yeats.
Logan, J. At Drumcliffe Churchyard, County
   Sligo.
Meredith, W. In a Copy of Yeats' Poems.
Poem: "Swans on the river, a great, The."
Roethke. Dying Man, The.
Stock, R. With a Machet Across My Knees.
Tate, A. Winter Mask.
Yellow (color)
Creeley. Edge, The ("Place it, / make the
   space").
Yellow.
Dickinson, E. Nature rarer uses Yellow.
Eberhart, R. Vermont Idyll.
Herrick. How Marigolds Came Yellow.
Jacobsen, J. Yellow.
Olson, C. Yellow of the Mask, The.
Ramanujan. On the Very Possible Jaundice of
   an Unborn Daughter.
Sandburg, C. Crucible.
Stafford, W. Yellow Cars.
Wilde, O. Symphony in Yellow.
Williams, W. Primrose.
Zukofsky, L. Judge and the Bird, The.
Yew Trees
Herrick. To the Yew and Cypress to Grace His
   Funeral.
Lawrence, D. H. Yew-Tree on the Downs, The.
Muldoon, P. Palm Sunday.

Plath. Little Fugue.
Moon and the Yew Tree, The.
Wordsworth, W. Yew-Trees.

Yiddish
Sandburg, C. Home Fires.

Yoga and Yogis
Kumin, M. In April, in Princeton.
Wilner, E. Maya.

Yom Kippur
Amichai [or Amikhai]. Yom Kippur.

York, England
Davie, D. At Knaresborough.
Tomlinson, C. Near York.

Yorkshire, England
Clampitt. At Muker, Upper Swaledale.
Davie, D. Barnsley, 1966.
Northern Metres.
Yorkshire.
Hughes, T. Heptonstall.
Merton. Rievaulx: St. Ailred.
Wordsworth, W. Composed after a Journey
across the Hambleton [or Hamilton] Hills,
Yorkshire.

Yoruba
Lorde. Oya
Winds of Orisha, The.

Yosemite Valley, California
Logan, J. Homage to John Muir.

Youth
Albinovanus Pedo. Plants and trees made poore
and old, The.
Amichai [or Amikhai]. NYU.
When I was young, the country was young too.
My father.
Ashbery, J. Other Tradition, The.
Our Youth.
Beckett, S. Ascension.
Gnome.
Berryman. Down & Back.
Drunks.
Heroes, The.
In & Out.
My Special Fate.
Nowhere.
Olympus.
Song of the Young Hawaiian, The.
Two Organs.
Blok. Impulses of Youth, The.
Bly, R. For My Son Noah, Ten Years Old.
Bogan, L. Tale, A.
Brontë, E. There was a time when my cheek
burned.
Brooks, G. We Real Cool.
Broumas, O. Way a Child Might Believe, The.
Browning, R. Evelyn Hope.
Rabbi Ben Ezra.
She was fifteen—had great eyes.
Youth and Art.
Bukowski. Too Late.
Burns, R. I'm Owre [or O'er] Young to Marry
Yet.
Lovely Polly Stewart.
My Bonie Laddie's Young but He's Growin Yet.
Prologue: "No song nor dance I bring from yon
great city."
Byron, G. 'All Is Vanity, Saith the Preacher'
Childish Recollections.
Stanzas to a Lady on Leaving England.
Stanzas Written on the Road between Florence
and Pisa.
To a Youthful Friend.
To Edward Noel Long, Esq.
To George, Earl Delawarr.
When I Roved a Young Highlander.
Campion, T. First Love.
There is a garden in her face.
Though You Are Young [or Yoong].
What Fair[e] Pomp[e].
Carew, T. To My Cousin (C.R.) Marrying My
Lady (A.).
Carruth, H. That I Had Had Courage When
Young.
Cavafy. La Jeunesse Blanche.
Since Nine O'Clock.
Understanding.

Very Seldom.
Cavalcanti. Canzone: He laments the
Presumption and Incontinence of his Youth.
Ciardi, J. Childe Horvald to the Dark Tower
Came.
December 13, 1979.
Freshman Sonnet: Success.
Clampitt. 'Eighty-Nine.
Elgin Marbles, The.
Having Lunch at Brasenose.
Clifton, L. Moonchild.
Clough. Dance on, dance on, we see, we see.
Thesis and Antithesis.
Coleridge, S. Foster-Mother's Tale, The.
On a Cataract.
Sonnet [to Charles Lloyd].
Sonnet to William Linley.
Youth and Age.
Corbett, W. Youth.
Corkine. My Dearest Mistress.
Cowper, W. Inscription for the Tomb of
Hamilton.
Upon a Venerable Rival.
Crane, H. Legend.
Creeley. Ball Game, The.
For the Graduation.
Prejudice, The.
Cullen, C. Uncle Jim.
Wisdom Cometh with the Years.
Youth Sings a Song of Rosebuds.
Cummings, E. E. Boy and the Man, The.
I have seen her a stealthily frail.
Noone" autumnal this great lady's gaze.
Old age sticks / up Keep.
One Fine Day.
You Shall Above All Things Be Glad and
Young.
Young / man sitting, The.
Cunningham, J. I married in my youth a wife.
"Dario." Nocturne: "I want to express my
anguish in verses that tell."
Song of Autumn in Springtime.
Davie, D. Garden Party, The.
Middlesex.
Zion.
De la Mare. Age.
Dreams.
Foreboding.
Karma.
Keep Innocency.
Dickey, J. Leap, The.
Dickinson, E. Youth, like Indian Summer.
Donne. Love's Usury.
Obsequies to the Lord Harrington, Brother to
the Lady Lucy, Countess of Bedford.
Dugan, A. Summer Heaven, Angels, Heaven.
Teacher's Lament.
Dunbar, P. At Cheshire Cheese.
Ione.
Old Homestead, The.
Old Story, The.
Retrospection.
Eberhart, R. Haystack, The.
Portrait of Rilke.
Emerson, R. Dear are the pleasant memories.
Fame.
He must have / Droll fancies sometimes cross
his quiet thoughts.
I rake no coffined clay, nor publish wide.
Merlin's Song.
Stout Sparta shrined the god of Laughter.
Valedictory Poem.
Whoso alas is young.
Why honor the new men.
Written in Sickness.
Ferlinghetti, L. In hintertime Praxiteles.
John Lennon in the Porto Santo Stefano.
Morlaix: Into the Future with Neil Young.
Pennycandystore beyond the El, The.
Frost, R. Birches.
In a Vale.
What Fifty Said.
Gallagher, T. Backdrop With Lovers, 1931.
García Lorca. Madrigal: "I looked into your
eyes."
Two Girls.

Glück, L. Morning.
Graves, R. Song: Seven Fresh Years.
Tousled Pillow.
Gray, T. Ode on a Distant Prospect of Eton
College.
Hacker, M. Days of 1959.
Hafiz [or Hafez]. On prince or bride no
diamond stone.
Hall, D. Friend Revisited, A.
Han-shan. Moth-browed girl in town, A.
One day I left the mountains.
HaNagid. You Mock Me Now in Your Youth.
Youth Brings Us.
Hardy, T. Memory and I.
Passer-By, The.
Rival, The.
Seventy-four and Twenty.
Superseded, The.
Young Man's Exhortation, A.
Harris, L. Father William.
Hayden, R. Paul Laurence Dunbar.
Heaney, S. Guttural Muse, The.
Wanderer, The.
Herbert, G. Answer, The.
Herrick. Advice to a Maid.
Meane, The.
Song, A: "Loose no time nor youth but be."
To Be Merry.
To the Virgins, to Make Much of Time.
To Youth.
Upon a Lady Faire, but Fruitlesse.
Youth, and Age.
Hopkins, G. On the Portrait of Two Beautiful
Young People.
Housman. Epitaph.
Lads in Their Hundreds, The.
Loitering with a vacant eye.
On forelands high in heaven.
Sage to the Young Man, The.
Think no more, lad; laugh, be jolly.
West, The.
Westward on the high-hilled plains.
When I Was One-and-Twenty.
Hughes, L. Dark Youth of the U.S.A.
Kids Who Die.
Old Youth.
Poem for Youth.
Young Gal's Blues.
Youth.
Hughes, T. Leaf Mould.
Ignatow, D. White-Haired, I Walk in on My
Parents.
Jacobsen, J. Blue-Eyed Exterminator, The.
Jarrell, R. Face, The.
Jeffers, R. After Lake Leman.
Age in Prospect.
Miching Mallecho.
Oysters.
Johnson, S. Short Song of Congratulation [or
To a Young Heir], A.
Kinsella, T. Chrysalides.
Kipling, R. My Rival.
Komunyakaa. Child's Play.
Delicate Conspiracy, A.
Sex, Magnolias, & Speed.
Kumin, M. Life's Work.
Sisyphus.
Kunitz, S. Summing-up, The.
Larkin, P. Having Grown Up in Shade of
Church and State.
How Distant.
Pour Away That Youth.
Sad Steps.
Wild Oats.
Laughlin, J. In Another Country.
Lawrence, D. H. Beware, O My Dear Young
Men.
Dreams Old and Nascent.
Fight! O My Young Men.
Grudge of the Old, The.
It's Either You Fight or You Die.
Latter-Day Sinners.
Maybe.
Mournful Young Man.
Old People.
Poor Young Things.

Signs of the Times.
So There!
Stop It.
Tarts.
Vitality.
White Horse, The.
Young and Their Moral Guardians, The.
Young Are Not Mean in Material Things, The.
Young Want to Be Just, The.
Youth Mowing, A.
Levine, P. Last Step, The.
You Can Have It.
Lindsay, N. Leaden-eyed, The.
My Lady Is Compared to a Young Tree.
Logan, J. Assateague.
Lines for a Young Wanderer in Mexico.
New Poem.
Logue, C. Nell's Circular Poem.
Longfellow, H. My Lost Youth.
Lorde. Generation.
Mentor.
Spring People.
MacDiarmid, H. Of My First Love.
MacLeish. Yacht for Sale.
Years of the Dog.
MacNeice. Cyclist, The.
Sailing Orders.
Taken for Granted.
When We Were Children.
Mahon. Autobiographies.
Major, C. My Seasonal Body.
Young Woman.
Marvell. Horatian Ode upon Cromwell's Return
from Ireland, An.
Melville, H. Lone Founts.
On the Slain Collegians.
Meredith, G. Earth's Preference.
Time and Sentiment.
Years Had Worn Their Season's Belt, The.
Youth in Memory.
Meredith, W. Birthday Exercise, A.
His Students.
Myself, Rousseau, a Few Others.
Pastoral: "Girl lies down on the hill, The."
Merrill, J. Tenancy, A.
Merton. When class was in the garden at
Greylands.
Michelangelo Buonarroti. Bracci born, A. From
birth, born wailing, I'd.
Death didn't wish to lay Cecchino low.
I'm death's forever, who, that one forlorn.
So tell me, Death, why not possess some face.
Millay, E. Being Young and Green.
Milosz, C. For Jan Lebenstein.
Inheritor.
Youth.
Milton. I with foolish mind and heedless zeal
formerly.
L'Allegro.
Montale. Falsetto.
Nash, O. There's Nothing Like Instinct,
Fortunately.
You Can Be a Republican, I'm a Genocrat.
Nemerov. Blue Suburban.
Boy with Book of Knowledge.
Interview, An.
Young Woman.
Neruda. Ambassador, The.
Niedecker. How bright you'll find young
people.
My mother saw the green tree toad.
So this was I.
O'Hara, F. Animals.
Blocks.
Ode to Michael Goldberg ('s Birth and Other
Births).
Young Poet, A.
Olson, C. All things stand out against the sky.
Gloss, A.
Toss, for John Cage, A.
Oppen. New People, The.
Orr, G. Gray Fox, The.
Nothing and the Incident in the Streets.
Self-Portrait at Twenty.
Two Poems about Nothing.
Owen, W. Anthem for Doomed Youth.

Parable of the Old Men and the Young, The.
Sonnet, to a Child.
Paley, G. Question.
Parker, D. Braggart.
College Boys; A Hymn of Hate.
Moral Tales for the Young ("Little Gormley
stole a purse").
Of a Woman, Dead Young.
Veteran, The.
Younger Set, The; A Hymn of Hate.
Pasolini. Civil Song.
Poetry of the Tradition, The.
Religion of My Time, The.
Patchen. Street Corner College.
Petrarch. You who can hear in scattered rhymes
the sound.
Pinsky. History of My Heart.
Plath. Tinker Jack and the Tidy Wives.
Words for a Nursery.
Poe. Happiest Day, the Happiest Hour, The.
Lake: To———, The.
Raine, K. Long ago I thought you young, bright
daimon.
Oval Portrait: Jessie Wilkie, The.
Ralegh, S. Poem of Sir Walter Rawleighs, A.
Ramanujan. LOVE 4: What He Said, to His
Daughter.
Ransom, J. Piazza Piece.
Vision by Sweetwater.
Rexroth, K. For Eli Jacobson.
Portrait of the Author as a Young Anarchist.
Thou Shalt Not Kill.
Rich, A. At Majority.
Middle-Aged, The.
Recorders in Italy.
Riley, J. Best Times, The.
Exceeding All.
Father William.
His Heart of Constant Youth.
Kind Old Man, The.
Lines to an Onsettled Young Man.
Morning.
My Boy.
Thoughts of Youth, The.
Waitin' fer the Cat to Die.
Youth and Age.
Rimbaud, A. Romance.
Sisters of Charity.
Youth.
Ritsos. Adolescent.
After the Ceremony.
Ancient Amphitheater.
Bodies.
Charioteer 1970.
Misconstructions.
Moonlight Sonata.
Summer.
Robinson, E. Bon Voyage.
Roethke. Feud.
Her Words.
Sententious Man, The.
Wish for a Young Wife.
Rossetti, C. Dream-Love.
I Have a Message unto Thee.
Maiden May.
My old admiration before I was twenty.
Till Tomorrow.
Versi.
Whole Head Is Sick, and the Whole Heart Faint,
The.
Young Death.
Rukeyser, M. Bringing.
Delta Poems.
Down from Chicago Bryan came.
Drowning Young Man, The.
Eel.
Poem Out of Childhood.
Sappho. I loved you, Leslie, long ago.
Seifert. At one of his readings a long time ago.
Hunt for the Kingfisher, The.
Merry-Go-Round with White Swan.
Our Lady of Žižkov.
Plague Column, The.
Relay Tower, The.
Sexton. Mother and Daughter.
Young.

"Shu Ting." Returning Home.
Smith, S. Eng.
From the French (1).
Lord Mope.
Snyder, G. Go Round.
Spender, S. Art Student.
Generous Days, The.
Uncreating Chaos (Double Portrait in a Mirror),
The.
Us.
Stafford, W. For My Young Friends Who Are
Afraid.
Honeysuckle.
Young.
Stock, R. Cenotaph for Two Butterflies.
Stockton, A. Acrostic for Abby Stockton.
Wise nature here has done her kindest part.
Suckling, S. Against Fruition.
Swenson, M. How to Be Old.
Swift, J. Receipt to Restore Stella's Youth, A.
Swinburne. Les Noyades.
Thomas, D. I See the Boys of Summer.
Once below a Time.
Process in the Weather of the Heart, A.
Updike. Youth's Progress.
Van Duyn. What the Motorcycle Said.
Very. Haunts of my youth farewell! A while I
leave.
Home of my youth! Where first my lot was cast.
Voltaire. To Madame du Châtelet.
Walcott. Glory Trumpeter, The.
Orient and Immortal Wheat.
Parang.
Prelude: "I, with legs crossed along the daylight,
watch."
Warren, R. Apologia for Grief.
Blessèd Accident.
Folly on Royal Street before the Raw Face of
God.
John's Birches.
Millpond Lost.
Red-Tail Hawk and Pyre of Youth.
Snowshoeing Back to Camp in Gloaming.
So You Agree with What I Say? Well, What Did
I Say?
Whistle of the 3 A.M.
Youth Stares at Minoan Sunset.
Youthful Picnic Long Ago: Sad Ballad on Box.
Youthful Truth-Seeker, Half-Naked, at Night,
Running down Beach South of San Francisco.
Whitman, W. We Two Boys Together Clinging.
Youth, Day, Old Age and Night.
Whittier. Fountain, The.
June on the Merrimac.
Williams, C. K. Love: Beginnnings.
Prodigy, The.
World's Greatest Tricycle-Rider, The.
Williams, T. Can I forget.
Tenor Sax Taking the Breaks.
Williams, W. Deceptrices, The.
Invocation and Conclusion.
Sea, The.
To Wish Myself Courage.
Wanderer, The: A Rococo Study.
Young Woman at a Window.
Wordsworth, W. Author's Voyage down the
Rhine (Thirty Years Ago).
Evening Walk, An; Addressed to a Young Lady.
Inscription for a Seat by a Roadside, Half Way
up a Steep Hill, Facing the South.
Wright, C. Mid-winter Snowfall in the Piazza
Dante.
Sprung Narratives.
Wright, J. Trouble.
Wyatt, S. Lament my loss[e], my labo[u]r, and
my pain [or payne].
Since love is such that, as ye wot.
There was never file half so well filed.
Yeats. Brown Penny.
Crazy Jane Grown Old Looks at the Dancers.
Down by the Salley Gardens.
Girl's Song.
His Phoenix.
Image from a Past Life, An.
Man Young and Old, A.
Meditation of the Old Fisherman, The.

Old Memory.
Owen Aherne and His Dancers.
Politics.
To a Young Girl.
Two Years Later.
Whence Had They Come?
Who Goes with Fergus?
Young Man's Song.
Youth and Age.
Zagajewski. Epicure From My Staircase, The.
From Memory.
Lightning.
Planetarium.
Twenty-Year-Old Soldiers.
We Know Everything.
Zaturenska. Girl in a Library.
O Like a Young Tree.
Spring Morning.
Young Dancers, The.
Young Girl Singing, A.
Zukofsky, L. Homage.
Strange / To reach that age.

Yucatán, Mexico
Dubie. Gently Bent to Ease Us.
Dugan, A. Touristic Note from the Gulf.

Yugoslavia
Brodsky, J. Bosnia Tune.
Davie, D. Balancing Acts.
Poreč.
Vindication of Jovan Babič, The.
Ginsberg, A. Defending the Faith.

Yukio Mishima
See **Mishima, Yukio**

Yukon Territory
Ramanujan. Foundlings in the Yukon.
Robinson, E. Klondike, The.

Z

Zapata, Emiliano
Ai. Pentecost.

Zebras
Ignatow, D. For Now.
I Sink Back Upon the Ground, Expecting to
Die.
Stock, R. Lock, The.

Zen Buddhism
Dubie. Fifteenth-Century Zen Master, A.
Hamill, S. Kannon.
Logue, C. Good Taste.
Ramanujan. Chicago Zen.
Rexroth, K. Heart's Garden, the Garden's Heart,
The.
Snyder, G. On Vulture Peak.
Stock, R. Koan for Two Minutes of Intensive
Meditation.
Whalen, P. Conditions That Prevail, The.
Song to Begin *Rohatsu*.
See also **Buddha and Buddhism**

Zeppelins
See **Dirigibles**

Zeus
Borges. Labyrinth, The.
Olson, C. Borne down by the inability to lift the
heaviness.
Yeats. Leda and the Swan.

Zhukov, Georgy Konstantinovich
Brodsky, J. On the Death of Zhukov.

Zinnias
Ciardi, J. It Is the Same Place Always Once
Again.
Hayden, R. Zinnias.
Zukofsky, L. Zinnia.

Zion
Byron, G. In the Valley of Waters.
Davie, D. Except the Lord Build the House.
Zion.
Hughes, T. Mount Zion.
Merton. Sundown.

Zipcodes
Updike. Hymn to These Newly Abbreviated
States.

Zodiac
Davie, D. Zodiac, The.
Dickey, W. Sagittarius, Scorpio Rising.
Lawrence, D. H. Astronomical Changes.
Merrill, J. Under Libra: Weights and Measures.
Merwin. Lost Month.
O'Hara, F. Poem: "Now it is the 27th."
Olson, C. Year Is a Great Circle or the Year Is a
Great Mistake, The.
Yeats. Chosen.

Zola, Émile
Robinson, E. Zola.

Zoos
Ammons. Rome Zoo.
Bukowski. Rain or Shine.
Cullen, C. Thoughts in a Zoo.
Dickey, J. Encounter in the Cage Country.
Dugan, A. On the Liquidation of Zoology.
On Visiting Central Park Zoo.
Hughes, T. Jaguar, The.
Ignatow, D. I Sink Back Upon the Ground,
Expecting to Die.
Jacobsen, J. April Asylum.
Jarrell, R. Woman at the Washington Zoo, The.
Komunyakaa. Monkey House, The.
Logan, J. Zoo, The.
MacLeish. Boy in the Roman Zoo.
Major, C. At the Zoo in Spain.
Oppen. Bronx Zoo.
Orr, G. Teachers, The.
Prunty. Gnostic at the Zoo, The.
Ramanujan. In the Zoo.
Zoo Gardens Revisited.
Sandburg, C. Elephants Are Different to
Different People.
Sarton, M. Ballad of Johnny, The.
Stafford, W. Coyote in the Zoo, The.
Stock, R. Monkey's Address to Others of His
Kind, A
Swenson, M. Zambesi and Ranee.
Updike. Menagerie at Versailles in 1775, The.
Zoo Bats.
Van Duyn. Marriage, with Beasts.

Zukofsky, Louis
Niedecker. Cricket-song.
Dear Paul: / the sheets of your father's book of
poetry.
L. Z ("Acre of music, An").
LZ ("He walked—loped—the bridge").
They live a cool distance.
Your father to me in your eighth summer.
Palmer, M. Notes for Echo Lake 3.

Zulus
Lawrence, D. H. Immoral Man.
Oppen. Zulu Girl, The.
Updike. Zulus Live in Land without a Square.

Zuni
Major, C. Lost in the Desert.
Merwin. Gardens of Zuñi, The.

Zurich, Switzerland
Celan. Zurich, at the Stork.